CHILTON'S IMPORT CAR MANUAL 1981-1988

Editorial Director	Alan F. Turner
Editor-In-Chief	Kerry A. Freeman, S.A.E.
Managing Editor	Dean F. Morgantini, S.A.E.
Managing Editor	John H. Weise, A.S.E., S.A.E.
Assistant Managing Editor	David H. Lee, A.S.E., S.A.E.
Senior Editor	Richard J. Rivele, S.A.E.
Project Coordinator	W. Calvin Settle Jr., S.A.E.
Project Coordinator	Tony Molla, S.A.E.
Editorial Staff	John M. Baxter, S.A.E.
	Lawrence C. Braun, S.A.E., A.S.C.
	Dennis Carroll
	Nick D'Andrea,
	Carl Denny, A.S.E.
	Wayne Eiffes, A.S.E., S.A.E.
	Martin J. Gunther
	Robert McAnally
	Michael A. Newsome
	Richard T. Smith
	Ron Webb
Production Manager	John J. Cantwell
Art & Production Coordinator	Robin S. Miller
Supervisor Mechanical Paste-up	Margaret A. Stoner
Mechanical Artists	Cynthia Fiore
	William Gaskins

OFFICERS

President	Lawrence A. Fornasieri
Vice President & General Manager	John P. Kushnerick

CHILTON BOOK COMPANY
Chilton Way Radnor, Pa. 19089

Manufactured in USA
© 1987 Chilton Book Company
ISBN 0-8019-7758-7
ISSN No. 0271-3608
Library of Congress Card Catalog No.80-68280

1 2 3 4 5 6 7 8 9 0   8 9 0 1 2 3 4 5 6 7

ACKNOWLEDGEMENTS

AB Volvo, Göteborg, Sweden
American Honda Motor Company, Moorestown, New Jersey
American Isuzu Motors, Inc., Whittier, California
BMW of North America, Inc., Montvale, New Jersey
Branick Industries, Fargo, North Dakota
Chicago Rawhide Mfg. Company (Fuel/Water Separators), Elgin, Illinois
Chrysler Motors Corporation, Detroit, Michigan
Hyundai Motor America, Garden Grove, California
Mazda Motors of America, Inc., Compton, California
Mercedes-Benz of North America, Inc., Montvale, New Jersey
Mitsubishi Motor Sales, Inc. Fountain Valley, California
Nissan Motor Corporation of USA, Carson, California
Porsche Cars North America, Reno, Nevada
Racor Industries (Fuel/Water Separators), Modesto, California
Renault, Inc., Detroit, Michigan
Robert Bosch Corporation, Long Island City, New York
SAAB-Scania, New Haven, Connecticut
Subaru of America, Inc., Cherry Hill, New Jersey
Tokico America, Inc., Torrance, California
Toyo Kogyo, Ltd., Hiroshima, Japan
Toyota Motor Sales, USA, Inc., Torrance, California
Volkswagen of America, Inc., Troy, Michigan
Volvo, Inc., Rockleigh, New Jersey
Yugo America, Inc., Montvale, New Jersey

CONTENTS

Car Section

Unit Repair Section

INDEX

	Acura/Sterling	Audi	BMW	Chrysler Corp.	Honda	Hyundai	Isuzu	Mazda	Mercedes-Benz	Merkur
	1	2	3	4	5	6	7	8	9	10
DRIVE AXLE	33	55	59	40	44	22	43	61	60	22
Halfshaft	33	55	59	40	44	22	43	61	—	22
Driveshaft & U-Joints	—	56	59	42	44	—	43	62	60	23
Rear Axle Shaft	—	57	61	42	44	—	44	62	61	23
FWD Hub, Knuckle & Brg.	34	58	—	44	46	24	44	63	—	—
FRONT SUSPENSION	36	58	62	46	49	25	45	63	62	23
Shock Absorbers	36	—	—	—	49	—	46	—	62	—
MacPherson Strut	36	58	62	46	50	25	46	63	62	23
Springs	—	—	—	—	—	—	46	—	63	—
Torsion Bars	36	—	—	—	51	—	47	—	—	—
Ball Joints	37	60	—	48	51	25	47	64	64	—
Upper Control Arms	—	—	63	—	—	—	—	—	65	—
Lower Control Arms	37	60	—	48	52	26	47	63	65	24
Front Wheel Bearings	—	60	64	49	—	—	45	65	66	24
Front Wheel Alignment	38	61	66	50	52	26	48	65	67	25
REAR SUSPENSION	38	61	66	50	52	26	49	66	68	25
Shock Absorber	38	61	—	52	—	26	49	66	68	25
MacPherson Strut	38	61	66	52	53	—	—	66	—	—
Springs	39	—	66	50	54	26	49	67	69	25
Rear Control Arms	—	63	66	53	54	—	49	67	—	—
Rear Wheel Bearings	39	—	67	53	54	27	49	67	—	—
STEERING	40	64	67	54	56	27	50	67	71	26
Steering Wheel	40	64	67	54	56	27	50	67	71	26
Turn Signal Switch	—	—	67	54	—	—	—	—	—	27
Combination Switch	40	—	—	—	56	28	50	68	74	—
Ignition Lock/Switch	40	64	68	54	56	28	50	68	74	27
Manual Steering Gear	—	65	70	55	57	28	51	68	—	—
Power Steering Gear	40	65	71	—	58	29	51	69	71	27
Power Steering Pump	41	66	71	56	58	29	52	69	71	—
Tie Rod Ends	42	66	72	—	58	30	52	68	71	—
BRAKES	42	66	73	57	59	30	53	69	72	28
Master Cylinder	42	66	73	57	59	30	53	69	72	28
Proportioning Valve	—	66	73	—	—	30	—	—	—	28
Power Brake Booster	42	67	74	57	59	30	53	69	—	28
Wheel Cylinder	—	67	75	57	59	30	54	70	—	28
Parking Brake Cable	43	68	75	57	59	30	54	70	72	28
CHASSIS ELECTRICAL	43	68	77	58	60	31	54	70	73	29
Heater Blower	43	68	77	58	60	31	54	70	73	29
Heater Core	44	69	78	59	60	31	54	70	—	29
Radio	44	69	79	61	61	31	56	71	—	29
Wiper Switch	45	69	79	61	61	31	56	71	—	29
Wiper Motor	45	69	79	61	61	32	57	71	76	—
Instrument Cluster	45	70	—	62	61	32	58	71	73	30
Headlight Switch	45	70	—	—	62	32	—	—	—	30
Stoplight Switch	—	70	—	—	62	32	—	72	—	30
Fuses & Circuit Breakers	46	70	—	62	62	32	58	72	76	30

INDEX

HOW TO USE THIS MANUAL

This manual is arranged in two sections:

Car Section

Car sections are grouped by manufacturer (Audi, BMW, etc.) and arranged in alphabetical order. The text and illustrations that comprise the service procedures in each Car Section are arranged in the following order of systems and components:
Tune-Up, Engine Electrical, Engine Mechanical, Engine Lubrication, Engine Cooling, Emission Controls, Fuel System, Manual Transmission, Clutch, Automatic Transmission, Transaxle, Drive Axle, Rear Suspension, Front Suspension, Steering, Brakes, Heater, Radio, Windshield Wiper, Instrument Panel and Fuse Box.
Specification charts are always located at the front of each section. All illustrations are located as close as possible to the pertinent text. Procedures are for all models in the particular section unless specifically noted otherwise.

Unit Repair Section

The Unit Repair Section contains troubleshooting and overhaul procedures for the major components and systems of your car. This portion of the book is intended to be used in conjunction with the Car Sections.
For example: If your car's engine is misfiring and you do not know the cause, use the "Troubleshooting" portion of the Unit Repair Section to find the cause and its remedy. If the cause should prove to be defective piston rings which are allowing oil to foul the spark plugs, the remedy is to overhaul the engine. Then turn to the proper Car Section to find the procedure for removing the engine from the car. After you have removed the engine, turn to the "Engine Rebuilding" chapter in the Unit Repair Section and follow the steps listed there to overhaul the engine.
Every major Unit Repair Section contains an Identification or Application chart to correlate the information contained in that section. The sections are usually arranged by brands, manufacturers or types of components rather than models of cars.
All overhaul procedures in the Unit Repair Section begin with the component removed from the car. The reason for this division of material is an economic one. The steps involved in overhauling an engine are virtually the same for all engines. However, the operation of removing the engine from the car varies greatly from model to model. By combining where possible, and separating where necessary, we are able to publish the maximum amount of information.

Locating Information

The Table of Contents, at the front of the book, lists the beginning of each Car and Unit Repair Section in the manual.
The Index, also at the front of the book, is a comprehensive listing of all major mechanical sections and systems for every section in the book. The Index contains listings for Car Sections as well as for corresponding Unit Repair Sections.

To find where a particular Car Section is located in the book, you need only look in the Table of Contents. Once you have found the proper section, you may wish to find where specific procedures are located in that section. Turn to the Index and read across the top of the page until you reach the appropriate Car Section. When the proper manufacturer's column has been found, read down the side column to the procedure or system for which you are looking. The intersection of the two columns will provide the page number(s) where the procedure is located.

Safety Notice

Proper service and repair procedures are vital to the safe, reliable operation of all motor vehicles, as well as the personal safety of those performing repairs. This manual outlines procedures for servicing and repairing vehicles using safe effective methods. The procedures contain many NOTES, CAUTIONS and WARNINGS which should be followed along with standard safety procedures to eliminate the possibility of personal injury or improper service which could damage the vehicle or compromise its safety.

It is important to note that repair procedures and techniques, tools and parts for servicing motor vehicles, as well as the skill and experience of the individual performing the work vary widely. It is not possible to anticipate all of the conceivable ways or conditions under which vehicles may be serviced, or to provide cautions as to all of the possible hazards that may result. Standard and accepted safety precautions and equipment should be used when handling toxic or flammable fluids, and safety goggles or other protection should be used during cutting, grinding, chiseling, prying, or any other process that can cause material removal or projectiles.

Some procedures require the use of tools specially designed for a specific purpose. Before substituting another tool or procedure, you must be completely satisfied that neither your personal safety, nor the performance of the vehicle will be endangered.

Part Numbers

Part numbers listed in this book are not recommendations by Chilton for any product by brand name. They are references that can be used with interchange manuals and aftermarket supplier catalogs to locate each brand supplier's discrete part number.

Although information in this manual is based on industry sources and is as complete as possible at the time of publication, the possibility exists that some car manufacturers made later changes which could not be included here. Information on very late models may not be available in some circumstances. While striving for total accuracy, Chilton Book Company cannot assume responsibility for any errors, changes, or omissions that may occur in the compilation of this data.

Copyright Notice

Acura/Sterling 1

Integra, Legend/825S

SERIAL NUMBER IDENTIFICATION

Vehicle Identification (Chassis) Number

Accura/Sterling vehicle identification numbers are mounted on the top edge of the instrument panel and are visible from the outside. In addition, there is a Vehicle/Engine Identification plate under the hood, on the cowl.

Engine Serial Number

The engine serial number is stamped

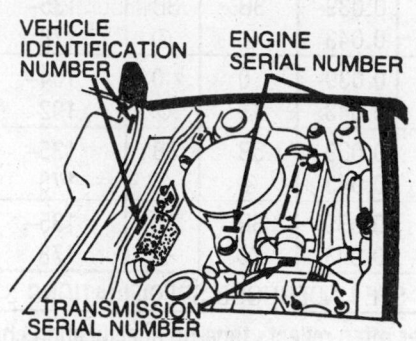

Accura/Sterling Identification numbers

into the clutch casing. The first five digits indicate engine model identification. The remaining numbers refer to production sequence.

Transaxle Serial Number

The transaxle serial number is stamped on the top of the transaxle/clutch case.

ENGINE IDENTIFICATION

Year	Model	Engine Displacement cu. in. (cc/liter)	Engine Series Identification	No. of Cylinders	Engine Type
1986	Integra	97 (1590/1.6)	D16AI	4	DOHC 16V
	Legend	152 (2494/2.5)	C25AI	6	OHC V6
1987-88	Integra	97 (1590/1.6)	D16AI	4	DOHC 16V
	Legend	152 (2494/2.5)	C25AI	6	OHC V6
	825	152 (2494/2.5)	C25AI	6	OHC V6

DOHC 16V Double Overhead Camshaft, 16 valve head
OHC Overhead Camshaft

GENERAL ENGINE SPECIFICATIONS

Year	Model	Engine Displacement cu. in. (cc)	Fuel System Type	Net Horsepower @ rpm	Net Torque @ rpm (ft. lbs.)	Bore × Stroke (in.)	Compression Ratio	Oil Pressure @ rpm
1986	Integra	97 (1590)	PGM-FI	113 @ 6250	99 @ 5500	2.95 × 3.54	9.3:1	43 @ 5000
	Legend	152 (249)	PGM-FI	151 @ 5800	154 @ 4500	3.31 × 2.95	9.0:1	71 @ 6500
1987-88	Integra	97 (1590)	PGM-FI	113 @ 6250	99 @ 5500	2.95 × 3.54	9.3:1	43 @ 5000
	Legend	152 (249)	PGM-FI	151 @ 5800	154 @ 4500	3.31 × 2.95	9.0:1	71 @ 6500
	825	152 (249)	PGM-FI	151 @ 5800	154 @ 4500	3.31 × 2.95	9.0:1	71 @ 6500

PGM-FI Electronic Fuel Injection

GASOLINE ENGINE TUNE-UP SPECIFICATIONS

Year	Model	Engine Displacement cu. in. (cc)	Spark Plugs Type	Spark Plugs Gap (in.)	Ignition Timing (deg.) MT	Ignition Timing (deg.) AT	Compression Pressure (psi)	Fuel Pump (psi)	Idle Speed (rpm) MT	Idle Speed (rpm) AT	Valve Clearance In.	Valve Clearance Ex.
1986	Integra	97 (1590)	①	0.039–0.043	0 ③	0 ③	164–192	36	750–850	750–850	.0051–.0067	.0059–.0075
	Legend	152 (2494)	②	0.039–0.043	3B ④	3B ④	135–178	36	670–770	670–770	Hyd.	Hyd.
1987	Integra	97 (1590)	①	0.039–0.043	0 ③	0 ③	164–192	36	750–850	750–850	.0051–.0067	.0059–.0075
	Legend	152 (2494)	②	0.039–0.043	3B ④	3B ④	135–178	36	670–770	670–770	Hyd.	Hyd.
	825	152 (2494)	②	0.039–0.043	3B ④	3B ④	135–178	36	670–770	670–770	Hyd.	Hyd.
1988					SEE UNDERHOOD SPECIFICATIONS STICKER							

NOTE: The Underhood Specifications sticker often reflects tune-up specification changes made in production. Sticker figures must be used if they disagree with those in this chart.

MT—Manual transmission
AT—Automatic transmission
NA—Not adjustable
A—After Top Dead Center
B—Before Top Dead Center
Hyd. —Hydraulic valve lash adjusters
① BCPR6EY-11
   BCPR6EY-N11
   Q20PR-U11

② BCPR6E-11
   Q20PR-U11
③ Vacuum advance hoses disconnected. White mark on crankshaft pulley
④ Vacuum advance hoses disconnected. Yellow mark on crankshaft pulley

FIRING ORDER

NOTE: To avoid confusion, always replace spark plug wires one at a time.

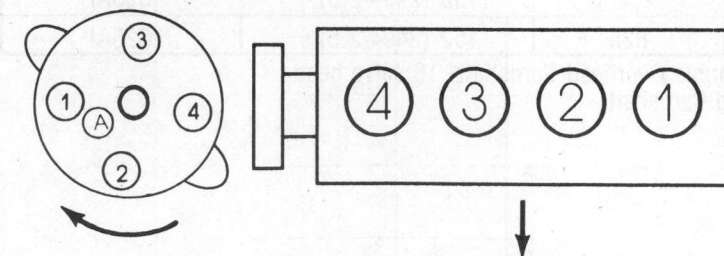

Integra
Firing order: 1-3-4-2
Rotation: clockwise

FRONT

FIRING ORDER

NOTE: To avoid confusion, always replace spark plug wires one at a time.

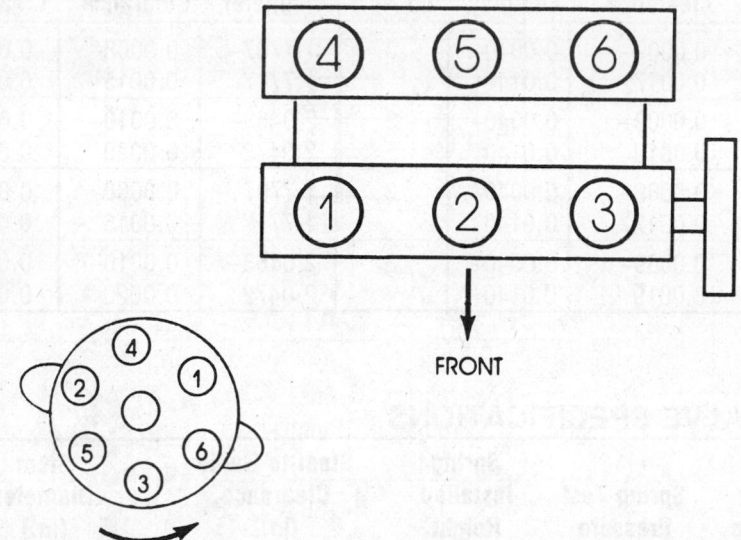

Legend/825S
Firing order: 1-4-2-5-3-6
Rotation: counterclockwise

FRONT

CAPACITIES

Year	Model	Engine Displacement cu. in. (cc)	Engine Crankcase with Filter	Engine Crankcase without Filter	Transmission (pts.) 4-Spd	Transmission (pts.) 5-Spd	Transmission (pts.) Auto.	Drive Axle (pts.)	Fuel Tank (gal.)	Cooling System (qts.)
1986	Integra	97.0 (1590)	3.7	3.2	—	4.8	5.0	—	13.2	6.0
	Legend	152.0 (2494)	4.8	4.2	—	4.6	6.8	—	18.0	9.2
1987-88	Integra	97.0 (1590)	3.7	3.2	—	4.8	5.0	—	13.2	6.0
	Legend	152.0 (2494)	4.8	4.2	—	4.6	6.8	—	18.0	9.2
	825	152.0 (2494)	4.8	4.2	—	4.6	6.8	—	18.0	9.2

CAMSHAFT SPECIFICATIONS

All measurements given in inches.

Year	Engine Displacement cu. in. (cc)	Journal Diameter 1	Journal Diameter 2	Journal Diameter 3	Journal Diameter 4	Journal Diameter 5	Lobe Lift In.	Lobe Lift Ex.	Bearing Clearance	Camshaft End Play
1986	97.0 (1590)	—	—	—	—	—	1.2822	1.2733	0.0020–0.0040	0.0020–0.0060
	152.0 (2494)	—	—	—	—	—	1.5578	1.5561	0.0018–0.0032	0.0020–0.0060
1987-88	97.0 (1590)	—	—	—	—	—	1.2822	1.2733	0.0020–0.0040	0.0020–0.0060
	152.0 (2494)	—	—	—	—	—	1.5578	1.5561	0.0018–0.0032	0.0020–0.0060

CRANKSHAFT AND CONNECTING ROD SPECIFICATIONS
All measurements are given in inches.

| Year | Engine Displacement cu. in. (cc) | Crankshaft | | | | Connecting Rod | | |
		Main Brg. Journal Dia.	Main Brg. Oil Clearance	Shaft End-play	Thrust on No.	Journal Diameter	Oil Clearance	Side Clearance
1986	97.0 (1590)	2.1644–2.1654	0.0009–0.0017	0.0040–0.0140	3	1.7707–1.7717	0.0008–0.0015	0.0060–0.0120
	152.0 (2494)	2.5187–2.5197	0.0009–0.0019	0.0040–0.0140	3	2.0463–2.0472	0.0010–0.0020	0.0060–0.0120
1987	97.0 (1590)	2.1644–2.1654	0.0009–0.0017	0.0040–0.0140	3	1.7707–1.7717	0.0008–0.0015	0.0060–0.0120
	152.0 (2494)	2.5187–2.5197	0.0009–0.0019	0.0040–0.0140	3	2.0463–2.0472	0.0010–0.0020	0.0060–0.0120

VALVE SPECIFICATIONS

| Year | Engine Displacement cu. in. (cc) | Seat Angle (deg.) | Face Angle (deg.) | Spring Test Pressure (lbs.) | Spring Installed Height (in.) | Stem-to-Guide Clearance (in.) | | Stem Diameter (in.) | |
						Intake	Exhaust	Intake	Exhaust
1986	97.0 (1590)	45	45	—	—	0.0010–0.0020	0.0020–0.0030	0.2591–0.2594	0.2579–0.2583
	152.0 (2494)	45	45	—	—	0.0010–0.0020	0.0020–0.0030	0.2591–0.2594	0.2579–0.2583
1987-88	97.0 (1590)	45	45	—	—	0.0010–0.0020	0.0020–0.0030	0.2591–0.2594	0.2579–0.2583
	152.0 (2494)	45	45	—	—	0.0010–0.0020	0.0020–0.0030	0.2591–0.2594	0.2579–0.2583

TORQUE SPECIFICATIONS
All readings in ft. lbs.

Year	Engine Displacement cu. in. (cc)	Cylinder Head Bolts	Main Bearing Bolts	Rod Bearing Bolts	Crankshaft Pulley Bolts	Flywheel Bolts	Manifold Intake	Manifold Exhaust	Spark Plugs
1986	97.0 (1590)	①	40	23	83	②	16	23	13
	152.0 (2494)	③	④	32	83	⑤	16	⑥	13
1987-88	97.0 (1590)	①	40	23	83	②	16	23	13
	152.0 (2494)	③	④	32	83	⑤	16	⑥	13

① 1st step—22 ft. lbs.; 2nd step—47 ft. lbs.
② MT—87 ft. lbs.; AT—54 ft. lbs.
③ 1st step—29 ft. lbs.; 2nd step—29 ft. lbs.
④ Cap bolt (9mm)—29 ft. lbs.
　Cap bridge bolt (11mm)—49 ft. lbs.
　Side bolt (10mm)—36 ft. lbs.
⑤ MT—76 ft. lbs.; AT—54 ft. lbs.
⑥ 8mm nuts—22 ft. lbs.; 10mm nuts—40 ft. lbs.

PISTON AND RING SPECIFICATIONS
All measurments are given in inches.

Year	Engine Displacement cu. in. (cc)	Piston Clearance	Ring Gap Top Compression	Ring Gap Bottom Compression	Ring Gap Oil Control	Ring Side Clearance Top Compression	Ring Side Clearance Bottom Compression	Ring Side Clearance Oil Control
1986	97.0 (1590)	0.0004–0.0024	0.0060–0.0140	0.0060–0.0140	0.0080–0.0280	0.0012–0.0024	0.0012–0.0022	—
	152.0 (2494)	0.0002–0.0013	0.0080–0.0140	0.0080–0.0140	0.0080–0.0280	0.0008–0.0018	0.0008–0.0018	—
1987-88	97.0 (1590)	0.0004–0.0024	0.0060–0.0140	0.0060–0.0140	0.0080–0.0280	0.0012–0.0024	0.0012–0.0022	—
	152.0 (2494)	0.0002–0.0013	0.0080–0.0140	0.0080–0.0140	0.0080–0.0280	0.0008–0.0018	0.0008–0.0018	—

BRAKE SPECIFICATIONS
All measurements in inches unless noted

Year	Model	Lug Nut Torque (ft. lbs.)	Master Cylinder Bore	Brake Disc Minimum Thickness	Brake Disc Maximum Runout	Standard Brake Drum Diameter	Minimum Lining Thickness Front	Minimum Lining Thickness Rear
1986	Integra	80	—	①	②	—	0.12	0.06
	Legend	80		③	④	—	0.12	0.06
1987-88	Integra	80		①	②	—	0.12	0.06
	Legend	80		③	④	—	0.12	0.06
	825	80		③	④	—	0.12	0.06

① Front—0.67
  Rear—0.31
② Front—0.004
  Rear—0.006
③ Front—0.75
  Rear—0.31
④ Front—0.004
  Rear—0.004

WHEEL ALIGNMENT

Year	Model		Caster Range (deg.)	Caster Preferred Setting (deg.)	Camber Range (deg.)	Camber Preferred Setting (deg.)	Toe-in (in.)	Steering Axis Inclination (deg.)
1986	Integra	(F)	$1^3/_{16}$P–$3^3/_{16}$P	$2^3/_{16}$P	$1^1/_2$N–$^1/_2$P	$^1/_2$N	$^1/_{32}$N	NA
		(R)	—	—	1N–$^1/_2$N	$^3/_4$N	$^1/_{16}$P	—
	Legend	(F)	$^{11}/_{16}$P–$2^1/_{16}$P	$1^{11}/_{16}$P	1N–1P	0	0	NA
		(R)	—	—	1N–1P	0	0	—
1987-88	Integra	(F)	$1^3/_{16}$P–$3^3/_{16}$P	$2^3/_{16}$P	$1^1/_2$N–$^1/_2$P	$^1/_2$N	$^1/_{32}$N	NA
		(R)	—	—	1N–$^1/_2$N	$^3/_4$N	$^1/_{16}$P	—
	Legend	(F)	$^{11}/_{16}$P–$2^1/_{16}$P	$1^{11}/_{16}$P	1N–1P	0	0	NA
		(R)	—	—	1N–1P	0	0	—
	825	(F)	$^{11}/_{16}$P–$2^1/_{16}$P	$1^{11}/_{16}$P	1N–1P	0	0	NA
		(R)	—	—	1N–1P	0	0	—

(F) Front
(R) Rear
NA Not Available
N Negative
P Positive

TUNE-UP PROCEDURES

Ignition Timing

Accura/Sterling recommends that the ignition timing be checked at 48 months, or 60,000 mile intervals. On both the 1590cc and the 2494cc engines, the timing marks are located on the crankshaft pulley, with a pointer on the timing belt cover; the 1590cc engine marks are visible from the driver's side of the engine compartment and the 2494cc timing marks are visible from the passengers side of the engine compartment.

In all cases, the timing is checked with the engine warmed to operating temperature (after the cooling fan comes on once), with the engine idling in Neutral.

ADJUSTMENT

Integra

1. Stop the engine, and hook up a tachometer according to the manufacturer's instructions.

NOTE: On some models you will have to pull back the rubber ignition coil cover to reveal the terminals.

2. Hook up a timing light to the engine according to the manufacturer's instructions.

3. Make sure that all wires are clear of the cooling fan and hot exhaust manifolds. Start the engine. Point the timing light at the timing mark pointer and the crankshaft pulley.

4. Disconnect and plug the No.2 and No.5 vacuum hoses from the vacuum advance diaphragm. The pointer should be on the "white mark" (0 degrees ±2 degrees) on the crankshaft pulley.

5. If necessary, adjust the timing by loosening the distributor adjusting bolts and slowly rotate the distributor in the required direction while observing the timing marks.

— CAUTION —

Do not grasp the top of the distributor cap while the engine is running as you might get a nasty shock. Instead, grab the distributor housing to rotate.

After making the necessary adjustment, tighten the holddown bolts, taking care not to disturb the adjustment and reinstall the cap on the upper adjusting bolt.

6. Unplug the No.2 vacuum hose and check for 20 in. Hg (500mmHg) of vacuum. If the vacuum is not to specification check the hose and its port on the throttle body.

7. Connect the No.2 vacuum hose to the advance diaphragm. The timing should advance 6 ±2 degrees, half way between the "white" and "red" marks. If the timing does not advance check the advance diaphragm.

8. Unplug the No.5 vacuum hose and check for vacuum. If the hose has no vacuum, check the ignition control solenoid valve. Rapidly open and release the throttle. The vacuum should momentarily go to 0. If the vacuum does not drop to 0, check the ignition control solenoid valve.

9. Connect the No.5 vacuum hose to the advance diaphragm. The timing should advance to 12 ±2 degrees (on the "red" mark). If the timing does not advance check the advance diaphragm.

Legend/825S

1. Disconnect the vacuum hoses from the vacuum advance diaphragm and, while the engine idles, check each hose for vacuum. The No.4 and No.11 hoses should both have vacuum. If the No.11 hose has no vacuum, check the solenoid valve "A". If the No.4 hose has no vacuum, check the solenoid valve "B" vacuum hoses disconnected, plug the end of the hoses.

2. Stop the engine, and hook up a tachometer according to the manufacturer's instructions.

NOTE: On some models you will have to pull back the rubber ignition coil cover to reveal the terminals.

3. Hook up a timing light to the engine according to the manufacturer's instructions.

4. Make sure that all wires are clear of the cooling fan and hot exhaust manifolds. Start the engine. Point the timing light at the timing mark pointer and the crankshaft pulley.

5. Adjust the initial timing, if necessary to the following specification. The pointer should be on the "yellow mark" on the crankshaft pulley (3 degrees BTDC) at 720 ±50 rpm.

6. If necessary, adjust the timing by loosening the distributor adjusting bolt and slowly rotate the distributor in the required direction while observing the timing marks.

— CAUTION —

Do not grasp the top of the distributor cap while the engine is running as you might get a nasty shock. Instead, grab the distributor housing to rotate.

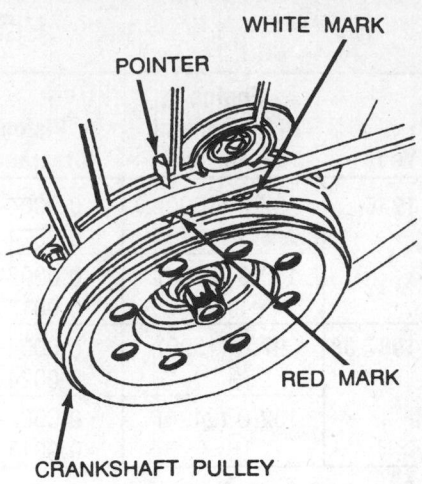

Ignition timing marks—1590cc engine

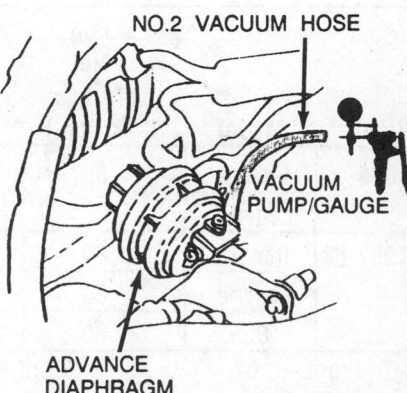

Number 2 vacuum hose location

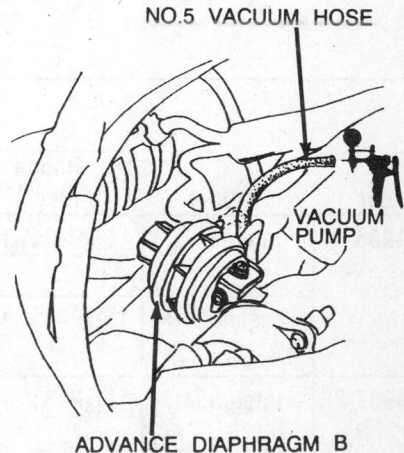

Number 5 vacuum hose location

After making the necessary adjustment, tighten the holddown bolts, taking care not to disturb the adjustment and reinstall the cap on the upper adjusting bolt.

6. Connect the No.4 and No.11 vacuum hoses to the vacuum advance and inspect the ignition timing at idle. The ignition timing should be:

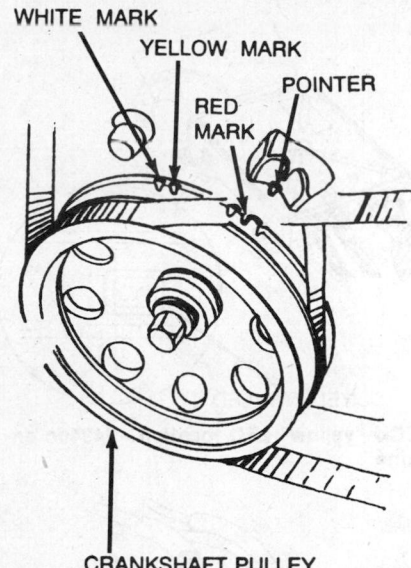

WHITE MARK
YELLOW MARK
POINTER
RED MARK
CRANKSHAFT PULLEY

Ignition timing marks—2494cc engine

Manual transaxle—23 ±2 degrees ("red" mark) at idle, Automatic transaxle—18 ±2 degrees ("red" mark) at idle. If the advance is not to specification, check the advance diaphragm and the distributor advance mechanism.

Valve Lash

Accura recommends that the valve clearance on the 1590cc Integra engine be checked at 15,000 mile intervals. The Accura Legend and the Sterling 825S 2494cc engine uses hydraulic lash adjusters and does not require periodic adjustment.

ADJUSTMENT

Integra

NOTE: While all valve adjustments must be as accurate as possible, it is better to have that valve adjustment slightly loose than slightly tight, as burned valves may result from overly tight adjustments.

1. Make sure that the engine is cold (cylinder head temperature below 100°F).
2. Remove the valve cover.
3. Set the No. 1 cylinder (cylinder closest to the camshaft sprockets) to top dead center TDC. The word "UP" should appear at the top, and the TDC grooves on the back side of the pulley should align with the cylinder head surface. You can double check this by checking the position of the distributor rotor. Take some chalk or a pencil and mark where the No. 1 spark plug wire goes into the distributor cap on

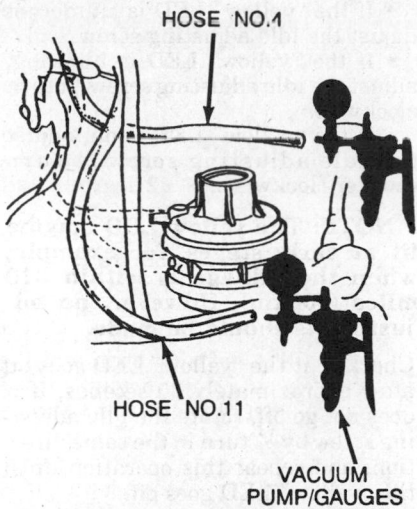

HOSE NO.1
HOSE NO.11
VACUUM PUMP/GAUGES

Vacuum hose locations

the distributor body. Then, remove the cap and check that the rotor points toward that mark.

4. With the No. 1 cylinder at TDC adjust the valves on the No. 1 cylinder.

Make the valve adjustments as follows:

a. Check the valve clearance with a flat feeler gauge between the tip of the rocker arm and the top of the valve. There should be a slight drag on the feeler gauge.

b. If there is no drag or if the gauge cannot be inserted, loosen the valve adjusting the screw locknut.

c. Turn the adjusting screw with a screwdriver to obtain the proper clearance.

d. Hold the adjusting screw and tighten the locknut.

e. Recheck the clearance.

5. Turn the crankshaft 180 degrees counterclockwise (the cam pulley will turn 90 degrees). With the No. 3 cylinder at TDC (the distributor rotor should be pointing to the No. 3 plug wire), and the "UP" marks should be

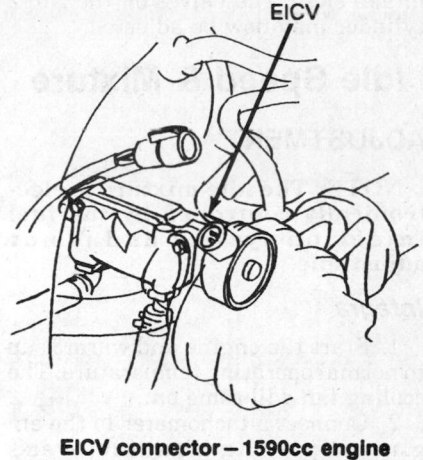

EICV

EICV connector—1590cc engine

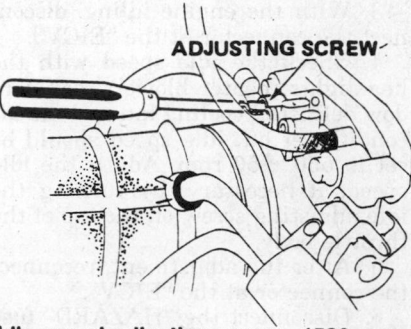

ADJUSTING SCREW

Idle speed adjusting screw—1590cc engine

at the exhaust side, adjust the valves on the No. 3 cylinder.

6. Turn the crankshaft 180 degrees counterclockwise (the cam pulley will turn 90 degrees). With the No. 4 cylinder at TDC (both "UP" marks should now be at the bottom and the distributor rotor now pointing to the No. 4 plug wire) adjust the valves on the No. 4 cylinder.

7. Turn the crankshaft 180 degrees counterclockwise once again. The No. 2 cylinder will now be on TDC (this can be confirmed by the distributor rotor pointing to the No. 2 plug wire and the "UP" marks should be at the

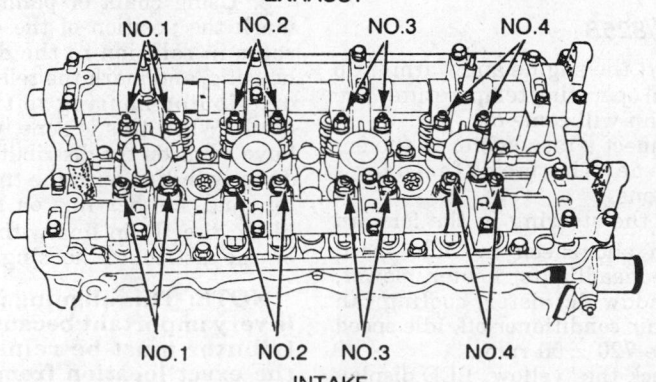

EXHAUST
NO.1   NO.2   NO.3   NO.4

NO.1   NO.2   NO.3   NO.4
INTAKE

Valve locations—1590cc engine

intake side). The valves on the No. 2 cylinder may now be adjusted.

Idle Speed & Mixture

ADJUSTMENT

NOTE: The idle mixture is electronically controlled by the fuel injection system and is not adjustable.

Integra

1. Start the engine and warm it up to normal operating temperature. The cooling fan will come on.

2. Connect a tachometer to the engine as per the manufacturer's instructions.

3. With the engine idling, disconnect the connector at the "EICV".

4. Check the idle speed with the headlights, heater blower, rear window defroster, cooling fan and the air conditioner off. Idle speed should be set to 550 ±50 rpm. Adjust the idle speed, if necessary, by turning the idle adjusting screw on the top of the throttle body.

5. After the adjustment, reconnect the connector at the "EICV".

6. Disconnect the "HAZARD" fuse at the battery terminal for at least 10 seconds to reset the ECU memory.

7. Start the engine and warm it up to normal operating temperature. The cooling fan will come on.

8. Check the idle speed with the headlights, heater blower, rear window defroster, cooling fan and the air conditioner off. Idle speed should be 800 ±50 rpm.

9. Check the idle speed under the following conditions:
• With headlights and rear window defogger ON
• With the air conditioner compressor ON
• On Auto. transaxle models, when shifted in gear (except "P" or "N")
The idle should remain stable at 800 ±50 rpm.

Legend/825S

1. Start the engine and warm it up to normal operating temperature. The cooling fan will come on.

2. Connect a tachometer to the engine as per the manufacturer's instructions.

3. Set the steering in the forward condition and check the idle speed with the headlights, heater blower, rear window defroster, cooling fan and the air conditioner off. Idle speed should be 720 ±50 rpm.

4. Check the "yellow" LED display at the ECU under the passenger's seat and perform the following:

• If the "yellow" LED is off, do not adjust the idle adjusting screw.
• If the "yellow" LED is blinking, adjust the idle adjusting screw ¼ turn clockwise.
• If the "yellow" LED is on, adjust the idle adjusting screw ¼ turn counter clockwise.

NOTE: The yellow LED may be lit at early stages, for example, when the millage is within 310 miles (500km). However, no adjustments should be made.

Check that the "yellow" LED goes off after approximately 30 seconds. If it does not go off, rotate the idle adjusting screw by ¼ turn in the same direction, and repeat this operation until the "yellow" LED goes off.

5. Check the idle speed under the following conditions:
• With headlights and rear window defogger ON
• With the steering wheel turning
• With the air conditioner compressor ON
• On Auto. transaxle models, when shifted in gear (except "P" or "N")
The idle should remain stable at 720 ±50 rpm.

ENGINE ELECTRICAL

Distributor

REMOVAL & INSTALLATION

1. Disconnect the high tension and primary lead wires, and the radio noise condenser wire that runs from the distributor to the coil.

2. Remove the two distributor cap holddown screws, and remove the distributor cap. Position it out of the way.

3. Using chalk or paint, carefully mark the position of the distributor rotor in relation to the distributor housing, and mark the relation of the distributor housing to the engine block. When this is done, you should have a line on the distributor housing directly in line with the tip of the rotor, and another line on the engine block directly in line with the mark on the distributor housing.

NOTE: This aligning procedure is very important because the distributor must be reinstalled in the exact location from which it was removed, if correct ignition timing is to be maintained.

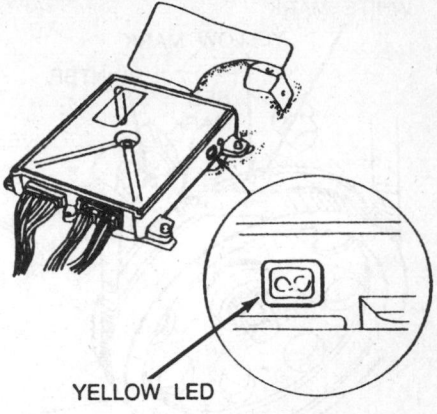

YELLOW LED

ECU "yellow" LED location—2494cc engine

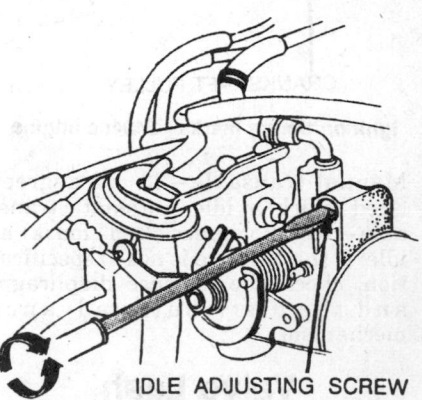

IDLE ADJUSTING SCREW

Idle speed adjusting screw—2494cc engine

4. Note the position of the vacuum lines on the vacuum diaphragm with masking tape and then disconnect the lines from the vacuum unit.

5. Remove the distributor holddown bolts then remove the distributor from the cylinder head.

——— **CAUTION** ———
Do not disturb the engine while the distributor is removed. If you attempt to start the engine with the distributor removed, you will have to retime the engine.

6. To install, place the rotor on the distributor shaft and align the tip of the rotor with the line that you made on the distributor housing.

7. With the rotor and housing aligned, insert the distributor into the engine while aligning the mark on the housing with the mark on the block, cylinder head or extension housing.

NOTE: The distributor is equipped with a coupling that connects them to the camshaft. The lugs at the end of the coupling and its mating grooves in the end of the camshaft are offset to prevent installing the distributor 180 degrees out of time.

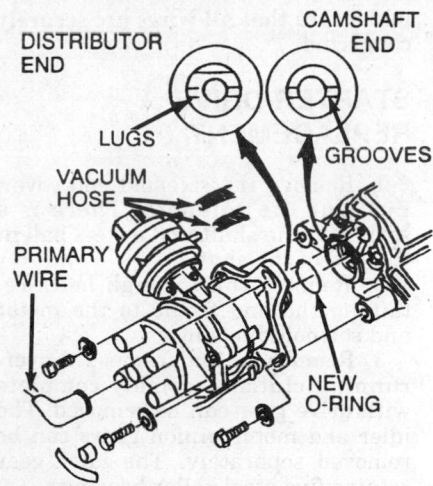

Distributor lug positioning—1590cc engine

8. When the distributor is fully seated in the engine, install and tighten the distributor retaining bolts.

9. Align and install the distributor cap, then install the two holddown screws.

10. Install the high tension and primary wires and the radio noise condenser wire onto the coil.

11. Check the ignition timing.

Alternator

PRECAUTIONS

• Observe the proper polarity of the battery connections by making sure that the positive (+) and negative (–) terminal connections are not reversed. Misconnection will allow current to flow in the reverse direction, resulting in damaged diodes and an overheated wire harness.

• Never ground or short out any alternator or alternator regulator terminals.

Never operate the alternator with any of its or the battery's leads disconnected.

• Always remove the battery or disconnect its output lead while charging it.

• Always disconnect the ground cable when replacing any electrical components.

• Never subject the alternator to excessive heat or dampness if the engine is being steam cleaned.

• Never use arc welding equipment with the alternator connected.

REMOVAL & INSTALLATION

1. Disconnect the negative (–) battery terminal.

2. Label and unplug the wires from the plugs on the rear of the alternator.

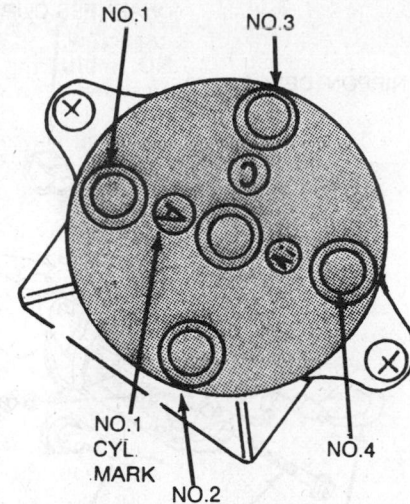

Distributor cap wire locations—1590cc engine

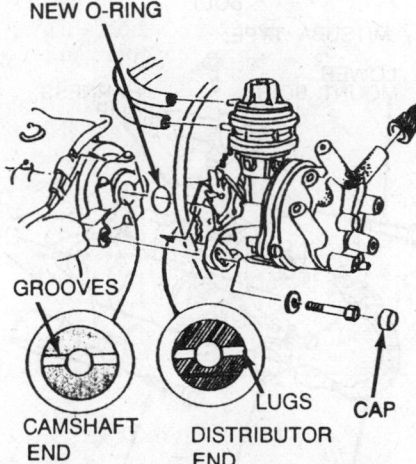

Distributor lug positioning—2494cc engine

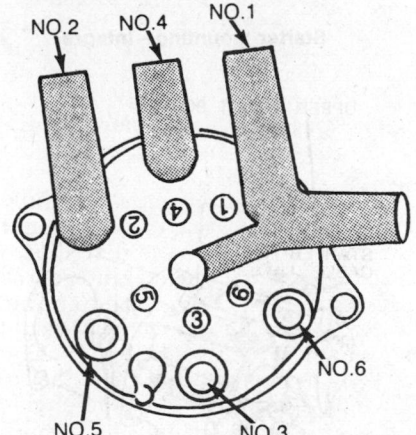

Distributor cap wire locations—2494cc engine

3. Loosen and remove the alternator mounting bolts and remove the V-belt and alternator assembly.

4. To install, reverse the removal

procedure. Adjust the alternator belt tension according to the Belt Tension Adjustment section below.

BELT TENSION ADJUSTMENT

The initial inspection and adjustment to the alternator drive belt should be performed after the first 3,000 miles or if the alternator has been moved for any reason. Afterward, you should inspect the belt tension every 30,000 miles. Before adjusting, inspect the belt to see that it is not cracked or worn. Be sure that its surfaces are free of grease and oil.

1. Push down on the belt halfway between pulleys with a force of about 22 lbs. The belt should deflect 0.25–0.38 in. (7–10mm) on the 1590cc engine or 0.71–0.87 in. (18–22mm) on the 2494cc engine.

2. If the belt tension requires adjustment, loosen the adjusting link bolt and move the alternator with a pry bar positioned against the front of the alternator housing.

NOTE: Do not apply pressure to any other part of the alternator.

3. After obtaining the proper tension, tighten the adjusting link bolt.

NOTE: Do not overtighten the belt. Damage to the alternator bearings could result.

Voltage Regulator

REMOVAL & INSTALLATION

The voltage regulator is mounted inside the alternator and requires disassembly of the alternator for removal.

1. Remove the alternator following the procedures listed above.

2. Remove the retaining nuts and remove the alternator (rear) end cover.

3. Remove the screws retaining the regulator to the rear housing assembly and remove the regulator.

4. Reverse the disassembly procedure to install.

Starter

REMOVAL & INSTALLATION

Integra

1. Disconnect the ground cable at the battery negative (–) terminal, and the starter motor cable at the positive terminal.

2. Remove the engine compartment sub wire harness from the harness clip on the starter motor.

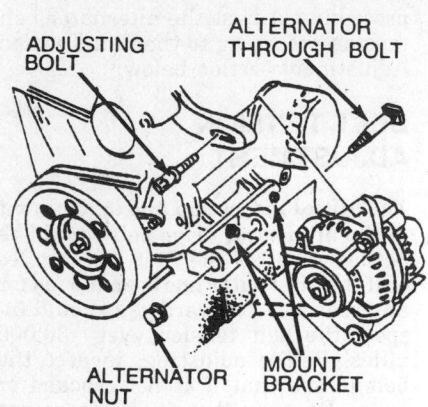

Alternator mounting – 1590cc engine

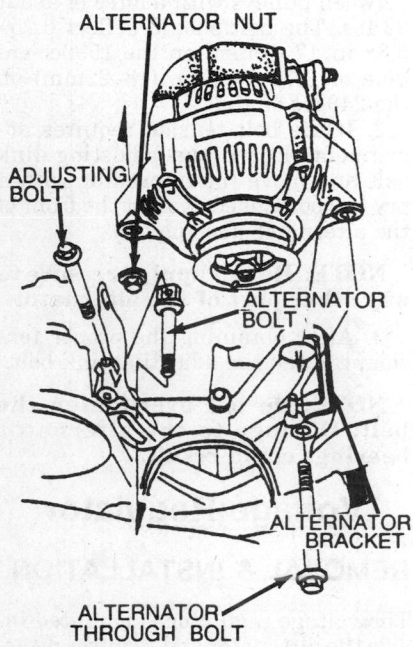

Alternator mounting – 2494cc engine

3. Disconnect the wire from the "S" terminal on the starter solenoid.

4. Remove the two attaching bolts and remove the starter.

5. Reverse the removal procedure to install the motor. Be sure to tighten the attaching bolts to 32 ft. lbs. and make sure that all wires are securely connected.

Legend/825S

1. Disconnect the ground cable at the battery negative (–) terminal, and the starter motor cable at the positive terminal.

2. Disconnect the wire from the "S" terminal on the starter solenoid.

3. Remove the two attaching bolts and remove the starter.

4. Reverse the removal procedure to install the motor. Be sure to tighten the attaching bolts to 32 ft. lbs. and

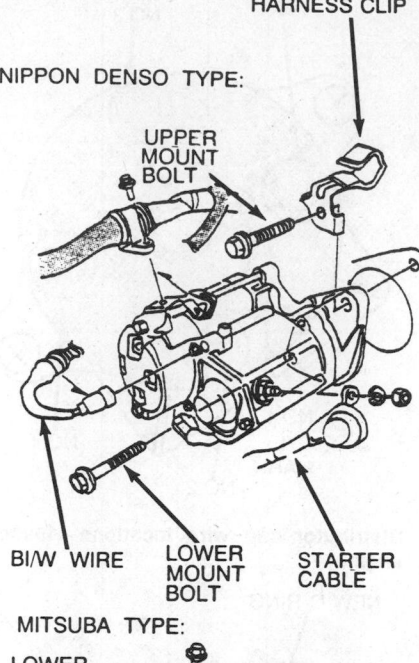

NIPPON DENSO TYPE:

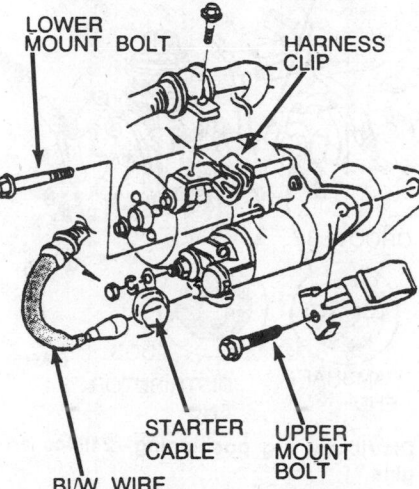

MITSUBA TYPE:

Starter mounting – Integra

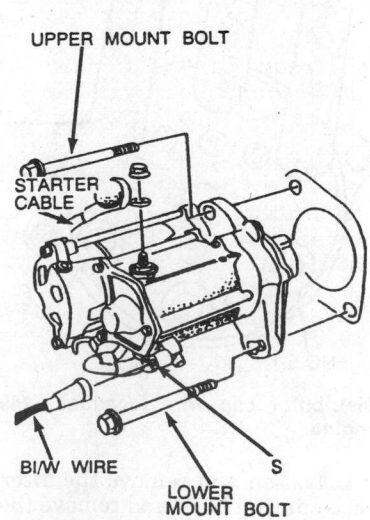

Starter mounting – Legend/825S

make sure that all wires are securely connected.

STARTER DRIVE REPLACEMENT

1. Remove the solenoid end cover. Pull out the solenoid. There is a spring on the shaft and a steel ball at the end of the shaft.

2. Remove the through bolts retaining the end frame to the motor and solenoid housing.

3. Remove the end frame. The overrunning clutch assembly complete with drive gear can be removed. The idler and motor pinion gears can be removed separately. The idler gear retains five steel roller bearings.

4. The clutch assembly is held together by a circlip. Push down on the gear against the spring inside the clutch assembly and remove the circlip with a circlip expander. Slide the stopper ring, gear, spring, and washer out of the clutch assembly.

5. Assembly is the reverse of disassembly. The stopper ring is installed with the smaller end lip toward the clutch. Be sure that the steel ball is in place at the end of the solenoid shaft. Grease all sliding surfaces of the solenoid before reassembly.

ENGINE MECHANICAL

Engine

REMOVAL & INSTALLATION

— CAUTION —

If any repair of operations requires the removal of a component of the air conditioning system (on which vehicles so equipped), only a person trained in such procedures should attempt these repairs. The air conditioning system contains freon under pressure. This gas can be very dangerous. Therefore, under no circumstances should an untrained person attempt to disconnect the air conditioner refrigerant lines.

Integra

1. Apply the parking brake and place blocks behind the rear wheels. Raise the front of the car and support it on jackstands. Remove the engine and wheelwell splash shields.

2. Disconnect the battery cables from the battery. Remove the battery, and then remove the battery tray from the engine compartment.

3. Scribe a line where the hood brackets meet the inside of the hood. This will help realign the hood during the installation. Disconnect and remove the washer fluid tube, then, unbolt and remove the hood.

4. Drain the oil from the engine, the coolant from the radiator, and the transaxle oil/fluid from the transaxle.

NOTE: Removal of the filler plug or cap will speed the draining process.

5. Remove the following:
   a. The intake duct and the front air intake duct.
   b. The throttle control cable or clutch cable.
   c. The coil wire and ignition primary leads.
   d. The cruise control cable.
6. Relieve the fuel pressure by slowly loosening the service bolt on the top of the fuel filter about one turn.

NOTE: Place a rag under the filter during this procedure to prevent fuel from spilling onto the engine.

7. Disconnect the fuel hose from the fuel filter. Remove the special nut and then remove the fuel hose.
8. Disconnect the following:
   a. The engine compartment sub-harness connector.
   b. The engine secondary cable.
   c. Remove the AUX fuse holder connector.
   d. The brake booster vacuum hose.
9. Disconnect the control box connector(s). Remove the control box(s) from the bracket(s), and let it hang next to the engine.
10. Loosen the throttle cable locknut and adjusting nut, then slip the cable end out of the throttle bracket, removing the cable.
11. Remove the mounting bolts and V-belt from the power steering pump, then without disconnecting the hose, pull the pump away from its mounting bracket.
12. Remove the center console from the inside of the car.
13. Put the shift lever in reverse and remove the lock pin from the end of the shift cable.
14. Remove the radiator and heater hoses from the engine.

NOTE: Label the heater hoses so they will be reinstalled in their original locations.

15. Remove the oil cooler hoses at the transaxle, let the fluid drain from the hoses then prop the hoses up out of the way near the radiator.
16. Remove the speedometer cable

ENGINE MOUNT TORQUE SEQUENCE

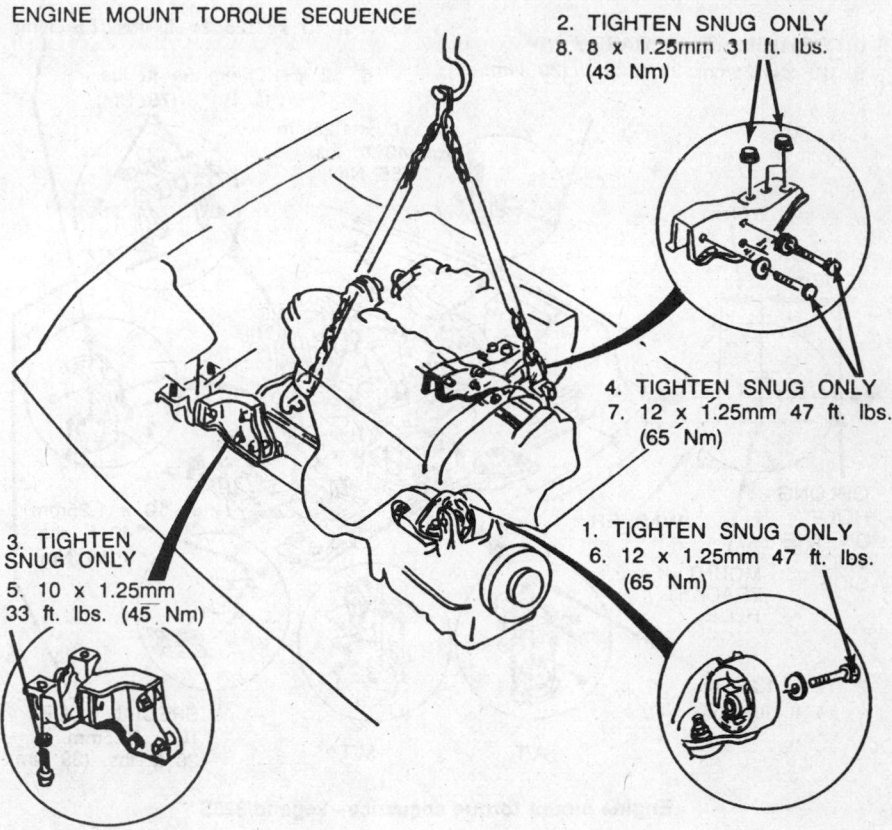

2. TIGHTEN SNUG ONLY
8. 8 x 1.25mm 31 ft. lbs. (43 Nm)

4. TIGHTEN SNUG ONLY
7. 12 x 1.25mm 47 ft. lbs. (65 Nm)

1. TIGHTEN SNUG ONLY
6. 12 x 1.25mm 47 ft. lbs. (65 Nm)

3. TIGHTEN SNUG ONLY
5. 10 x 1.25mm 33 ft. lbs. (45 Nm)

Engine mount torque sequence—Integra

clip, then pull the cable out of the holder.

NOTE: Do not remove the holder from the transaxle as it may cause the speedometer gear to fall into the transaxle.

17. On A/C equipped cars:
   a. Loosen the belt adjusting bolts and remove the belt.
   b. Remove the mounting bolts to the A/C compressor, then wire it up out of the way on the front beam.

NOTE: DO NOT disconnect the A/C freon lines. The compressor can be moved without discharging the system.

   c. Remove the lower compressor mounting bracket.
18. Disconnect the alternator wiring harness connectors. Remove the alternator belt. Remove the alternator mounting bolts and remove the alternator.
19. Squirt penetrating oil on the nuts holding the exhaust header pipe in place. Loosen and remove the nuts and pipe.
20. Remove the halfshaft as follows:
   a. Remove the jackstands and lower the car. Loosen the spindle nuts with a socket. Raise the car and support on jackstands.

   b. Remove the front wheel, and the spindle nut.
   c. Place a floor jack under the lower control arm, then remove the ball joint cotter pin and nut.

NOTE: Be certain the lower control arm is positioned securely on top of the floor jack so that it doesn't suddenly jump or spring off when the ball joint remover is used.

   d. Using a ball joint puller, separate the ball joint from the front hub.
   e. Slowly, lower the floor jack to lower the control arm. Pull the hub outward and off the halfshaft.
   f. Using a small pry bar, pry out the inboard CV-joint approximately 13mm on order to release the spring clip from the groove in the differential.
   g. Pull the halfshaft out of the transaxle case.
21. Attach a lifting sling to the engine block and raise the hoist to remove the slack from the chain.
22. Remove the rear transaxle mount, and remove the bolts from the front transaxle mount and the engine side mount.
23. Check that the engine and trans-

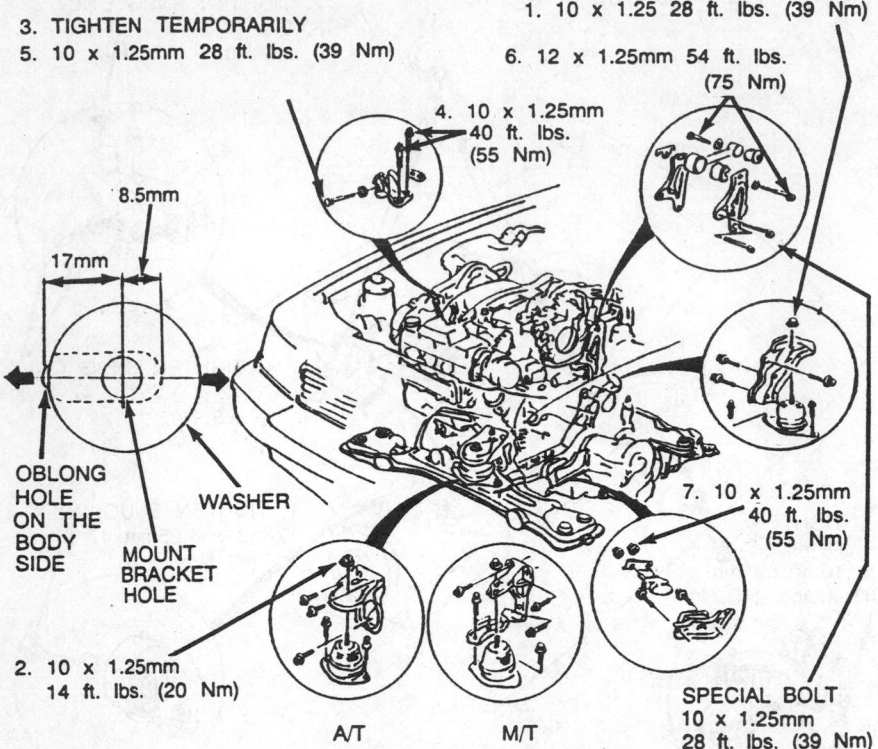

3. TIGHTEN TEMPORARILY
5. 10 x 1.25mm 28 ft. lbs. (39 Nm)

1. 10 x 1.25 28 ft. lbs. (39 Nm)

6. 12 x 1.25mm 54 ft. lbs. (75 Nm)

4. 10 x 1.25mm 40 ft. lbs. (55 Nm)

8.5mm

17mm

OBLONG HOLE ON THE BODY SIDE

WASHER

MOUNT BRACKET HOLE

2. 10 x 1.25mm 14 ft. lbs. (20 Nm)

A/T   M/T

7. 10 x 1.25mm 40 ft. lbs. (55 Nm)

SPECIAL BOLT 10 x 1.25mm 28 ft. lbs. (39 Nm)

Engine mount torque sequence—Legend/825S

axle are free from any hoses or electrical connectors.

24. Slowly raise the engine up and out of the car.

25. To install, reverse the removal procedures. Pay special attention to the following:

a. Torque the engine mounting bolts in the proper sequence.

b. Be sure that the spring clip on the end of each halfshaft clicks into the differential.

NOTE: Always use new spring clips on installation.

c. Bleed the air from the cooling system.

d. Adjust the belt(s) tension, and the throttle cable tension.

e. Check the clutch pedal free play.

Legend/825S

1. Apply the parking brake and place blocks behind the rear wheels. Raise the front of the car and support it on jackstands.

2. Disconnect both battery cables from the battery. Remove the battery, and then remove the battery tray from the engine compartment.

3. Position the hood in the vertical position by removing the open stay mounting bolt on the hood side and fitting it to the mounting hole near the hinge.

4. Remove the air intake tube, air cleaner and resonator tube as an assembly.

5. Remove the splash guard from under the engine.

6. Remove the oil filler cap and drain the engine oil.

NOTE: When replacing the drain plug be sure to use a new washer.

7. Remove the radiator cap, then open the radiator drain petcock and drain the coolant from the radiator.

8. Remove the transaxle filler plug, then remove the drain plug and drain the transaxle.

9. Disconnect the pressure switch wire from the oil filter case.

10. Disconnect the two water hoses from the engine oil cooler.

11. Remove the drain bolt from the oil filter case to drain the oil.

12. Remove the oil filter case from the engine block.

13. Disconnect the upper and lower radiator hoses from the radiator.

14. Disconnect the automatic transaxle cooler hose from the bottom of the radiator (auto. transaxle only).

15. Disconnect the following engine sub-harness connectors from the body side:

a. Four right-side connectors and clamp

b. Two left-side main fuse connectors

c. Coil wire and primary lead connectors, and the condenser connector

d. Two ground cables from the cylinder head and the transaxle.

16. Disconnect the connector from the power steering pump, then disconnect the two hoses.

17. Disconnect the hose from the cruise control actuator.

18. Disconnect the hose from the power brake booster.

19. Using the following procedures relieve the fuel system pressure. Place a shop rag over the fuel filter to absorb any gasoline which may be sprayed on the engine while relieving the pressure. Slowly loosen the service bolt approximately one full turn. This will relieve any pressure in the system. Using a new sealing washer, tighten the service bolt.

20. Disconnect the fuel return hose from the pressure regulator. Remove the banjo nut and then remove the fuel hose.

21. Disconnect the throttle cable from the throttle body.

22. Disconnect the rubber tube from the control box from the connection stay.

23. Remove the speed sensor from the transaxle.

24. Remove the air conditioning compressor as follows:

a. Remove the compressor clutch lead wire.

b. Loosen the belt adjusting bolt.

NOTE: DO NOT remove the air conditioner hoses. The air conditioner compressor can be moved without discharging the air conditioner system.

c. Remove the compressor mounting bolts, then lift the compressor out of the bracket with the hoses attached, and hang it to the front bulkhead with a piece of wire.

25. Remove the exhaust pipe from the front and rear manifolds.

26. Disconnect the control wire from the selector side of the transaxle (automatic transaxle only).

27. Remove the gear change rod and gear change extension (manual transaxle only).

28. Remove the clutch slave cylinder (manual transaxle only).

29. Remove the halfshaft as follows:

a. Remove the jackstands and lower the car. Loosen the 32mm spindle nuts with a socket. Raise the car and support on jackstands.

b. Remove the front wheel, and the spindle nut.

c. Remove the damper fork and

the damper pinch bolts. Remove the damper fork.

d. Remove the ball joint bolt and separate the ball joint from lower control arm control.

e. Disconnect the tie rods from the steering knuckles.

f. Remove the sway bar bolts (Accord only).

g. Pull the front hub outward and off the halfshaft.

h. Using a small pry bar, pry out the inboard CV-joint approximately 13mm in order to release the spring clip from the differential, then pull the halfshaft out of the transaxle case.

NOTE: When installing the halfshaft, insert the shaft until the spring clip clicks into the groove. Always use a new spring clip when installing the halfshaft.

30. Attach a chain hoist to the engine and raise it just enough to remove the slack.

31. Remove the engine side mount bracket bolts.

32. Remove the front engine mount nut, then remove the rear engine mount nut.

33. Loosen and remove the alternator belt. Disconnect the alternator wire harness and remove the alternator.

34. Remove the bolt from the rear torque rod at the engine, then loosen the bolt in the frame mount and swing the rod up and out of the way.

35. Raise the engine carefully from the car checking that all wires and hoses have been removed from the engine/transaxle. Raise the engine all the way up and remove it from the car.

36. Install the engine in the reverse order of removal, making the following checks:

a. Torque the engine mounting bolts in the proper sequence.

b. Bleed the air from the cooling system.

c. Adjust the clutch pedal free play.

d. Adjust the throttle cable tension.

e. Make sure the transaxle shifts properly.

Cylinder Head

REMOVAL & INSTALLATION

Integra

———— CAUTION ————
Cylinder head temperature must be below 100°F.

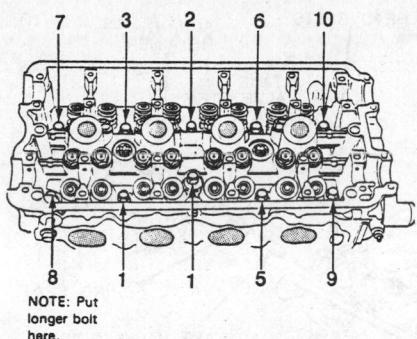

NOTE: Put longer bolt here.

Cylinder head torque sequence—1590cc engine

Before removing the cylinder head check the following:

• Inspect the timing belt.
• Turn the flywheel so that the No.1 cylinder is at TDC.
• Mark all emission hoses before disconnecting them.

1. Disconnect the negative battery cable.

2. Drain the radiator.

3. Remove the air cleaner:

a. Remove the air cleaner cover and filter.

b. Disconnect the hot and cold air intake ducts, and remove the air chamber hose.

c. Remove the air cleaner.

4. Relieve the fuel pressure using the following procedure:

a. Slowly loosen the service bolt on the top of the fuel filter about one turn.

NOTE: Place a rag under the filter during this procedure to prevent fuel from spilling onto the engine.

b. Disconnect the fuel return hose from the pressure regulator. Remove the special nut and then remove the fuel hose.

5. Remove the brake booster vacuum tube from the intake manifold.

6. Remove the engine ground wire from the valve cover.

7. Disconnect the spark plug wires from the spark plugs, then remove the distributor assembly.

8. Disconnect the hoses from the charcoal canister, and from the No. 1 control box at the tubing manifold.

9. Disconnect the idle control solenoid hoses (w/air conditioning only).

10. Disconnect the upper radiator heater and bypass hoses.

11. Disconnect the engine sub harness connectors and the following couplers from the head and the intake manifold:

The four injector couplers
The TA sensor connector
The ground connector

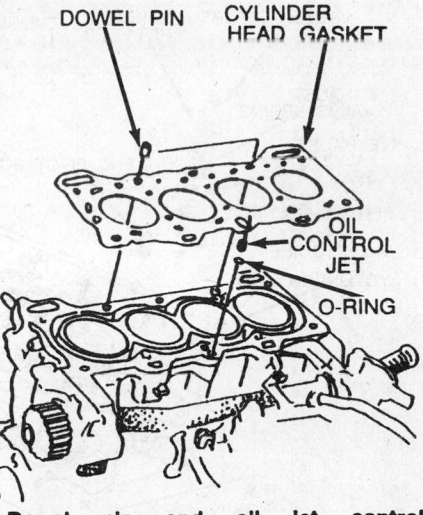

Dowel pin and oil jet control locations—1590cc engine

The TW sensor connector
The throttle sensor connector
The crankshaft angle sensor coupler

12. Remove the thermostat housing-to-intake manifold hose.

13. Disconnect the oxygen sensor coupler.

14. Remove the exhaust manifold bracket and manifold bolts, then remove the manifold.

15. Remove the bolts from the intake manifold and bracket.

16. Disconnect the hose from the breather chamber to the intake manifold.

17. Remove the valve and timing belt covers.

18. Loosen the timing belt tensioner adjustment bolt, then remove the belt.

19. Remove the camshaft holder bolts, then remove the camshaft holders, the camshafts, and the rocker arms.

20. Remove the cylinder head bolts in the reverse order given in the head bolt torque sequence.

NOTE: Unscrew the bolts ⅓ of a turn each time and repeat the sequence to prevent cylinder head warpage.

21. Carefully remove the cylinder head from the engine.

22. To install, reverse the removal procedure, being sure to pay attention to the following points:

a. Always use a new head gasket and make sure the head, engine block, and gasket are clean.

b. Be sure the No. 1 cylinder is at top dead center and the camshaft pulleys "UP" mark is on the top before positioning the head in place.

c. The cylinder head dowel pins

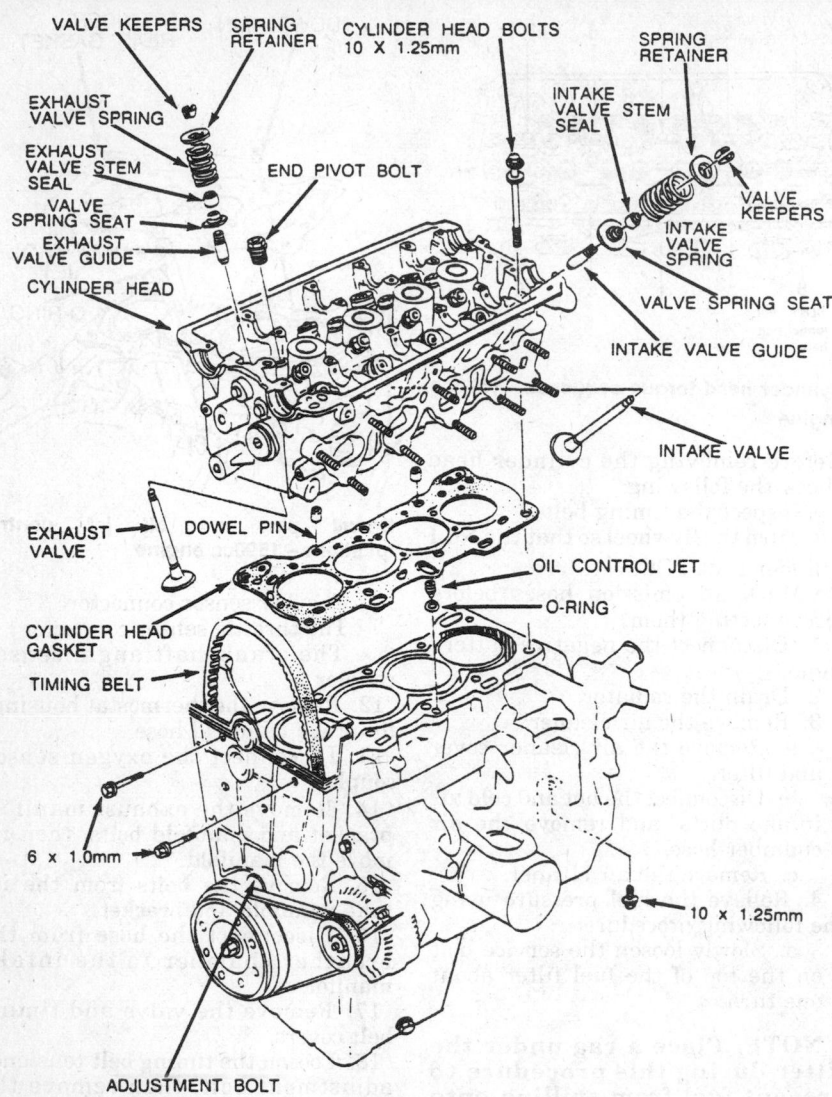

Cylinder head and related components—1590cc engine

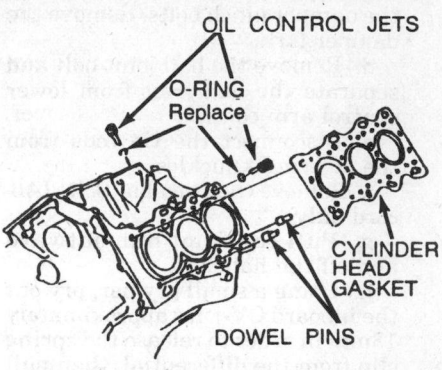

Dowel pin and oil jet control locations—2494cc engine

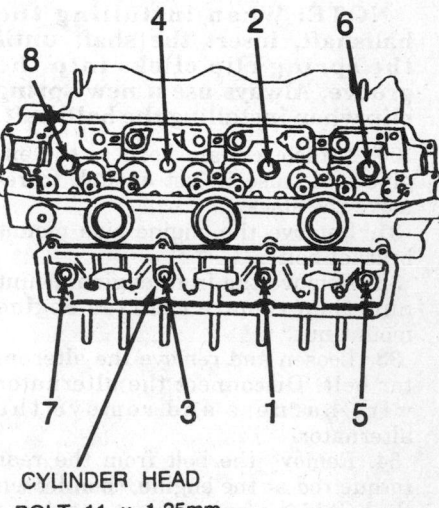

Cylinder head torque sequence—2494cc engine

and oil control jet must be aligned.

d. Tighten the cylinder head bolts in two progressive steps as shown in the torque sequence diagram. First to 22 ft. lbs. (30 Nm) in sequence, then to 47 ft. lbs. (65 Nm) in the same sequence.

e. Use the longer bolt in the No. 8 position.

f. After installation, check to see that all hoses and wires are installed correctly.

Legend/825S

─── **CAUTION** ───

Cylinder head temperature must be below 100°F.

Before removing the cylinder head check the following:
• Inspect the timing belt.
• Turn the flywheel so that the No.1 cylinder is at TDC.

• Mark all emission hoses before disconnecting them.

1. Disconnect the battery ground cable.

2. Drain the cooling system.

3. Remove the vacuum hose from the brake booster.

4. Remove the secondary ground cable from the cylinder head and the transaxle housing.

5. Disconnect the radio noise condenser connector, ignition coil wire and the ignition primary connector.

6. Remove the air cleaner cover.

7. Relieve the fuel pressure using the following procedure:

a. Slowly loosen the service bolt on the top of the fuel filter about one turn.

NOTE: Place a rag under the filter during this procedure to prevent fuel from spilling onto the engine.

b. Disconnect the fuel return hose from the pressure regulator. Remove the special nut and then remove the fuel hose.

8. Disconnect the throttle cable and at the throttle valve.

9. Disconnect the charcoal canister hose at the throttle valve.

10. Disconnect the engine sub harness connectors and the following couplers from the head and the intake manifold:
The six injector couplers
The TA sensor connector
The temperature unit connector
The ground connector
The TW sensor connector
The throttle sensor connector
The crankshaft angle sensor coupler
The EGR valve connector
The four wire harness clamps

11. Disconnect the oxygen sensor coupler.

12. Disconnect the cooling system hoses at the cylinder head.

13. Disconnect the spark plug wires

from the spark plugs, then remove the distributor assembly.

14. Remove the intake manifold cover from the intake manifold.

15. Remove the wire harness cover.

16. Remove the alternator pulley cover.

17. Remove the alternator and belt.

18. Remove the power steering pump and disconnect the pump hoses. Also, remove the hose clamp bolt on the body.

19. On models with air conditioning, disconnect the idle boost solenoid hoses.

20. Remove the cruise control actuator.

21. Remove the exhaust header pipe and pull it clear of the exhaust manifold.

22. Remove the air cleaner base mount bolts and disconnect the hose from the intake manifold to the breather chamber.

23. Remove the air cleaner base from the intake manifold.

24. Remove the EGR tube nuts from the cylinder hear.

25. Remove the exhaust manifold cover nuts.

26. Remove the air suction tube nuts from the exhaust manifold and air suction valve.

27. Remove the intake manifold assembly from the cylinder head.

28. Remove the water passage assembly from the front and rear of the cylinder head.

29. Remove the timing belt upper covers.

30. Loosen the tensioner adjustment bolt, then remove the timing belt.

NOTE: Advance the crankshaft by about 15 degrees before removing the timing belt to prevent interference between the piston and the valve.

31. Remove the front and rear camshaft pulleys using the following procedure:

a. Before removing the rear pulley, adjust the cam position so that no valve is fully open.

b. Remove the pulley mounting bolts with a universal holder and a double-end wrench. For the rear pulley, first remove the top two bolts and then the remaining bolt.

32. Remove the upper cover back plates.

33. Remove the valve covers and the head side covers.

34. Remove the bearing cap pipes and the bearing caps, then remove the camshaft.

35. Remove the intake and exhaust inside rocker arms and pushrods.

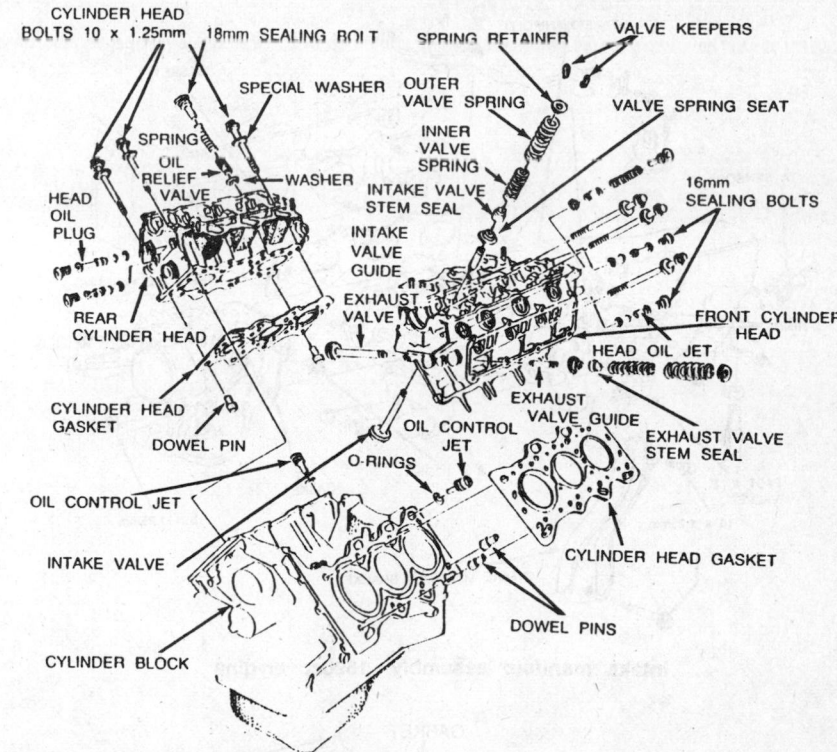

Cylinder head and related components—2494cc engine

NOTE: Label all valve train components to ensure reinstallation in their proper locations.

36. Remove the cylinder head bolts and remove the head.

NOTE: Unscrew the cylinder head bolts 1/3 of a turn in the reverse order of the torque sequence each turn until loose to prevent warpage to the cylinder head.

37. Installation is the reverse of the removal procedure, taking note of the following items:

a. Make sure the cylinder head gasket surfaces are clean.

b. Make sure the "UP" mark on the timing belt pulley is at the top.

c. Turn the crankshaft so the NO.1 piston is at TDC.

d. The cylinder head dowel pins and oil control jet must be aligned.

e. Adjust the valve timing.

f. Torque the cylinder head bolts in two steps. Torque all bolts in sequence to 29 ft. lbs. (40 Nm), then to 56 ft. lbs. (78 Nm) in the final step.

Intake Manifold

REMOVAL & INSTALLATION

1. Drain the coolant from the radiator.

2. Remove the air duct from the throttle body.

3. Remove the intake manifold bracket, fast idle valve, the air suction valve and the EGR tube on the V6 engines.

4. Label and remove any wires running to the intake manifold.

5. Remove the intake manifold attaching nut in a crisscross pattern, beginning from the center and moving out to both ends. Then remove the manifold.

6. Clean all the old gasket material from the manifold and the cylinder head.

7. If the intake manifold is to be replaced, transfer all the necessary components to the new manifold.

8. To install, reverse the removal procedures, being sure to observe the following points:

a. Always use a new gasket.

b. Tighten the nuts in a crisscross patter in 2–3 steps, starting with the inner nuts.

c. Be sure all hoses and wires are correctly connected.

Exhaust Manifold

REMOVAL & INSTALLATION

——— CAUTION ———

Do not perform this operation on a warm or hot engine.

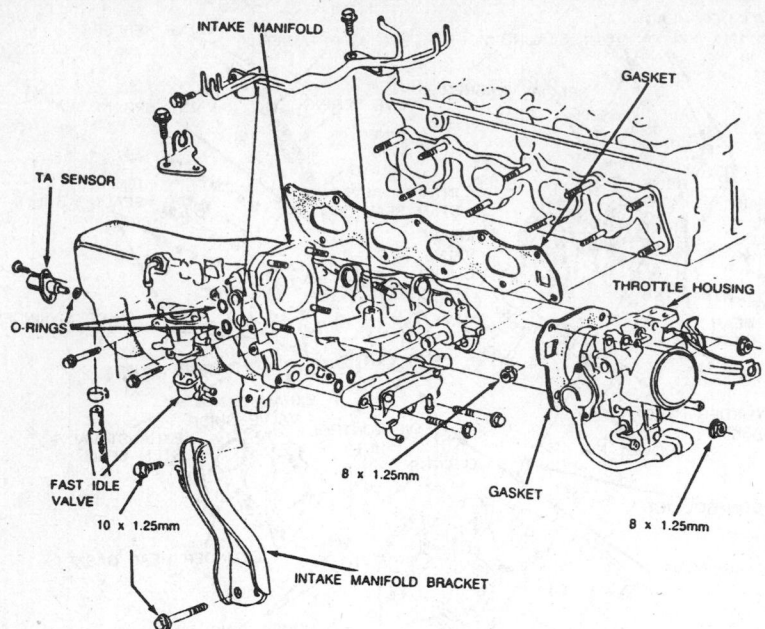

Intake manifold assembly—1590cc engine

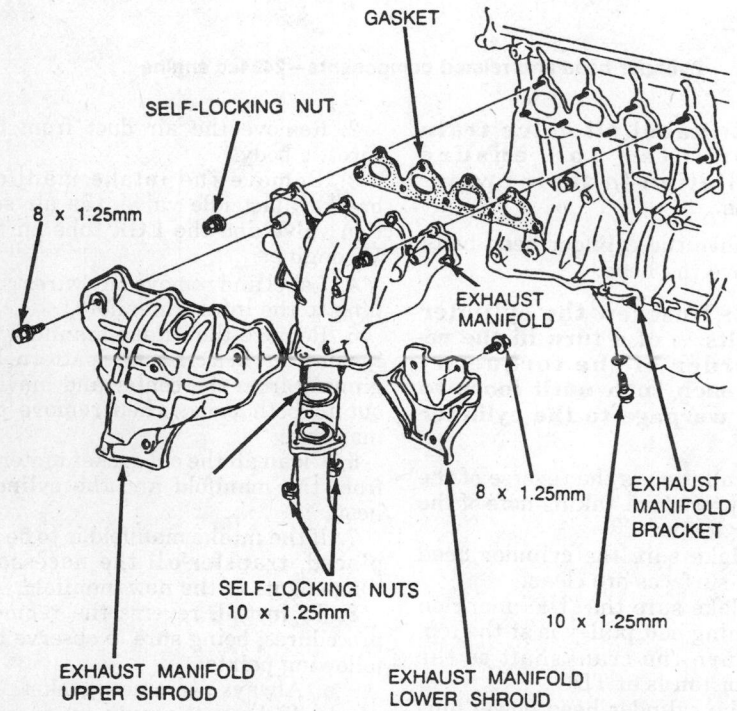

Exhaust manifold assembly—1590cc engine

1. Remove the header pipe or catalytic converter-to-exhaust manifold attaching bolts.
2. Remove the oxygen sensor (if so equipped).
3. Remove the EGR and the air suction tubes (if so equipped).
4. Remove the exhaust manifold shroud.

5. Remove the exhaust manifold bracket bolts.
6. Remove the exhaust attaching nuts in a crisscross pattern starting from the center, and remove the manifold.
7. To install, reverse the removal procedure. Use new gaskets and tighten the manifold bolts in a crisscross pattern starting from the center.

Timing Belt Cover

REMOVAL & INSTALLATION

1. Align the crankshaft pulley, or flywheel pointer, at Top Dead Center (TDC).
2. Remove the bolt(s) which hold the timing belt upper cover and remove the cover.
3. Loosen the alternator and remove the pulley belt(s).
4. Remove the crankshaft pulley attaching bolt. Use a two-jawed puller to remove the crankshaft pulley.
5. Remove the lower timing belt cover retaining bolts and the timing belt cover.
6. To install, reverse the removal procedure. Make sure that the timing belt and the front oil seal are properly installed on the crankshaft and before replacing the cover.

Timing Belt

ADJUSTMENT

Integra

NOTE: Always adjust the timing belt tension with the engine cold. The tensioner is spring-loaded to apply the proper tension to the belt automatically after making the following adjustments.

1. Turn the crankshaft pulley until No.1 is at Top Dead Center of the compression stroke. This can be determined by observing the valves (all closed) or by feeling for pressure in the spark plug hole (with your thumb or a compression gauge) as the engine is turned.
2. Loosen the adjusting bolt on the tensioner pulley.
3. Rotate the crankshaft counterclockwise 3-teeth on the camshaft pulley to create tension on the timing belt.
4. Tighten the adjusting bolt on the tensioner pulley to 33 ft. lbs. (45 Nm).
5. If the crankshaft pulley broke loose while turning the crank, torque it to 83 ft. lbs. (115 Nm).

NOTE: Put the transaxle in gear and set the parking brake before torquing the pulley bolt.

Legend/825S

NOTE: Always adjust the timing belt tension with the engine cold. The tensioner is spring-loaded to apply the proper tension to the belt automatically after making the following adjustments.

1. Turn the crankshaft pulley until

No.1 is at Top Dead Center of the compression stroke. This can be determined by observing the valves (all closed) or by feeling for pressure in the spark plug hole (with your thumb or a compression gauge) as the engine is turned.

2. Rotate the crankshaft clockwise (as viewed from the pulley side of the engine) 9-teeth on the camshaft pulley, (The blue mark on the camshaft pulley should match the pointer on the lower cover).

3. Loosen the adjusting bolt to create tension on the timing belt.

4. Tighten the adjusting bolt to 31 ft. lbs. (43 Nm).

REMOVAL & INSTALLATION

Integra

1. Turn the crankshaft pulley until No.1 is at Top Dead Center of the compression stroke. This can be determined by observing the valves (all closed) or by feeling for pressure in the spark plug hole (with your thumb or a compression gauge) as the engine is turned.

2. Remove the alternator belt, crankshaft pulley, and timing gear cover. Mark the direction of timing belt rotation.

3. Loosen, but do not remove, the tensioner adjusting bolt.

4. Slide the timing belt off the camshaft sprocket, crankshaft sprocket and the water pump sprocket, then remove it from the engine.

5. To remove the camshaft timing sprocket, first remove the center bolt and then remove the sprocket with a pulley remover or a brass hammer. This can be accomplished by simply removing the timing belt upper cover, loosening the tensioner bolts, and sliding the timing belt off to expose the sprocket for removal.

NOTE: If you remove the timing sprocket with the timing belt cover in place, be sure not to let the woodruff key fall inside the timing cover when removing the sprocket from the camshaft.

Inspect the timing belt. Replace it if it is oil soaked (find source of oil leak also), or if it appears worn on the leading edges of the belt teeth.

6. To install, reverse the removal procedure. Be sure to position the crankshaft and camshaft timing sprockets in the top dead center position.

When installing the timing belt, do not allow oil to come in contact with the belt. Oil will cause the rubber to swell. Be careful not to bend or twist the belt unnecessarily, since it is

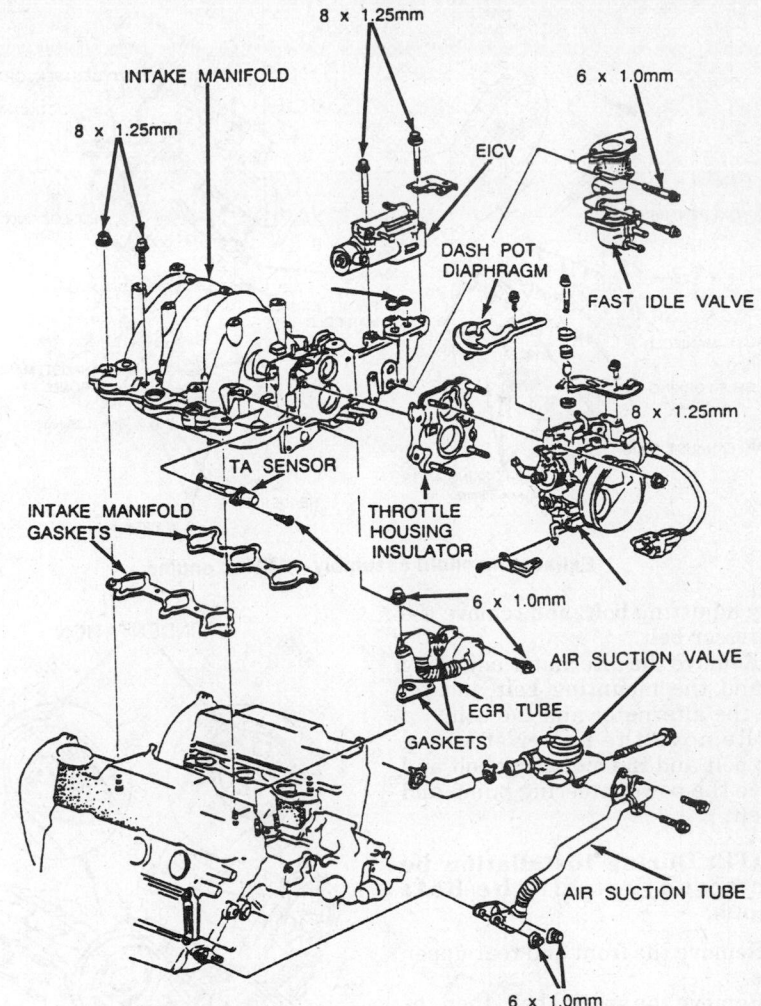

Intake manifold assembly—2494cc engine

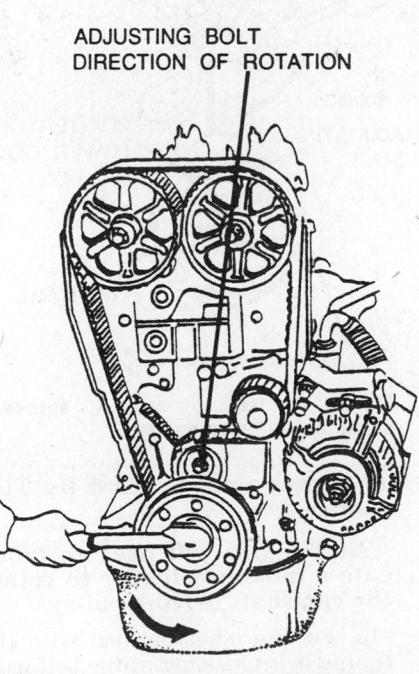

Timing belt adjustment—1590cc engine

made of fiberglass. Nor should you use tools having sharp edges when installing or removing the belt. Be sure to install the belt with the arrow facing in the same direction it was facing during removal.

After installing the timing belt, adjust the belt tension.

Legend/825S

1. Remove the pulley cover and the harness cover from above the timing belt upper cover.

2. Remove the engine sub-harness clamp.

3. Remove the engine support bolts, loosen the side mount rubber, and raise the side mount bracket.

NOTE: An engine crane or chain hoist should be used here to raise and support the engine.

4. Remove the 12 bolts and two screws, and remove the lower splash guard.

5. Loosen the air conditioning idle

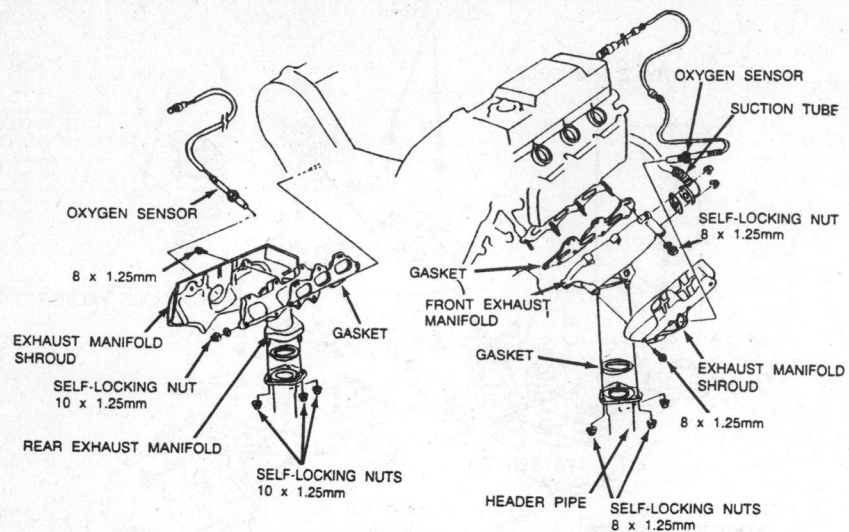

Exhaust manifold assembly—2494cc engine

pulley adjusting bolt, and remove the compressor belt.

6. Remove the alternator adjusting bolt and the mounting bolt and remove the alternator and the belt.

7. Remove the power steering pump bolt and the mounting bolt and remove the power steering pump and the belt.

NOTE: During installation be sure to adjust all the belt tensions.

8. Remove the front and rear upper covers.

9. Remove the special bolt, then remove the crankshaft pulley.

10. Remove the lower cover.

11. Loosen the adjusting bolt then remove the timing belt. Inspect the timing belt. Replace it if it is oil soaked (find source of oil leak also), or if it appears worn on the leading edges of the belt teeth.

12. To install, reverse the removal procedure. Be sure to follow the key steps mentioned below.

When installing the timing belt, do not allow oil to come in contact with the belt. Oil will cause the rubber to swell. Be careful not to bend or twist the belt unnecessarily, since it is made of fiberglass. Nor should you use tools having sharp edges when installing or removing the belt. Be sure to install the belt with the arrow facing in the same direction it was facing during removal.

13. Remove all the spark plugs from the engine.

14. Advance the crankshaft by about 15 degrees from the No. 1 cylinder compression TDC. After adjusting the front and rear camshaft pulleys to the No. 1 cylinder compression TDC, return the crankshaft pulley by about

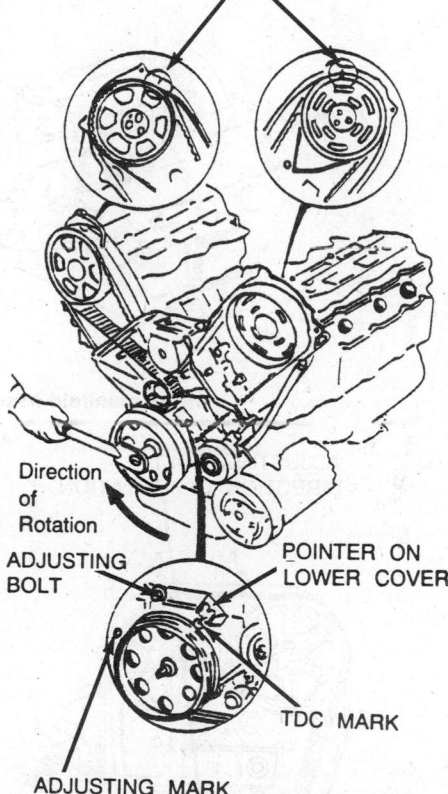

Timing belt and sprocket assembly—1590cc engine

15 degrees again to adjust the TDC position.

NOTE: You will need to fabricate a universal holder to rotate the camshaft driving pulley.

15. Fix the adjusting bolt with the timing belt tensioner at the belt loosening position as follows;

a. Push the tensioner bracket with a flat blade screwdriver to loosen the belt tension.

b. DO NOT push on the timing belt.

16. Install the timing belt as follows;

a. Install the timing belt in the following sequence; crankshaft pulley, front crankshaft pulley, water pump pulley, tensioner and rear camshaft pulley.

b. For ease of installation, advance the rear camshaft pulley by about a half tooth from the TDC position.

17. Loosen the adjusting bolt, and retighten it after tensioning the belt.

18. Rotate the crankshaft about 5 or 6 turns clockwise so that the belt may fit in position on the pulleys.

19. Follow the procedures listed under "Timing Belt adjustment" given above.

Camshaft

REMOVAL & INSTALLATION

Integra

NOTE: To facilitate installation, make sure that No. 1 piston is at Top Dead Center before removal of the camshafts.

1. Follow the Cylinder Head removal procedure before attempting to remove the camshaft.

2. Loosen and remove the camshaft holder bolts, then remove the camshaft holders and the camshafts and the rocker arms.

3. Lift out the camshaft(s), wipe them clean, then inspect the lift ramps. Replace the camshaft(s) if the lobes are pitted, scored, or excessively worn.

To Install:

4. Check the following before installing the camshafts;

a. Be certain the keyways on the camshafts are facing UP (No. 1 cylinder at TDC).

b. The valve locknuts should be loosened and the adjusting screws backed off before installation.

c. Replace the rocker arms in there original positions.

5. Place the rocker arms on the pivot bolts and the valve stems.

6. Install the camshafts and the camshaft seals with the open side (spring) facing in and observe the following;

a. The marks "Ï" or "E" are stamped on the camshaft holders.

b. Do not apply oil to the holder mating surface of the camshaft seals.

7. Apply liquid gasket to the head

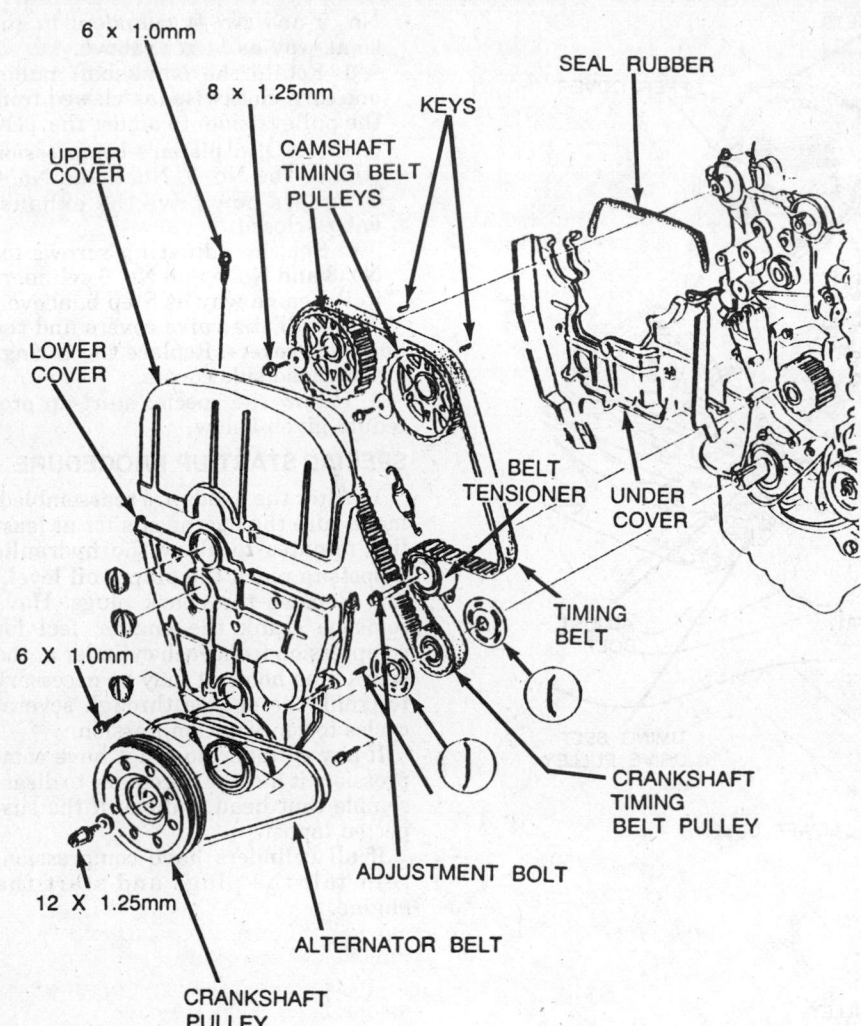

6 x 1.0mm

8 x 1.25mm

KEYS

SEAL RUBBER

UPPER COVER

CAMSHAFT TIMING BELT PULLEYS

LOWER COVER

BELT TENSIONER

UNDER COVER

6 X 1.0mm

TIMING BELT

CRANKSHAFT TIMING BELT PULLEY

ADJUSTMENT BOLT

12 X 1.25mm

ALTERNATOR BELT

CRANKSHAFT PULLEY

mating surfaces of the No. 1 and No. 6 camshaft holders then install them along with the No. 2, 3, 4, and 5.

8. Temporarily tighten the camshaft holders while making sure that the rocker arms are positioned on the valve stems.

9. Using an oil seal driver, special tool No. 07947–SB00100 or equivalent, press new oil seals into the No. 1 camshaft holders.

10. Tighten each bolt two turns at a time while checking that the rockers do not bind on the valves.

11. Install the camshaft pulley keys onto the grooves in the camshafts.

12. Push the camshaft pulleys onto the camshafts, then tight the retaining bolts to 27 ft. lbs. (38 Nm).

13. Adjust the valve timing, then check that all tubes, hoses and connectors have been installed correctly.

Legend/825S

NOTE: To facilitate installa-tion, make sure that No. 1 piston is at **Top Dead Center** before removal of the camshafts.

1. Follow the Cylinder Head removal procedure before attempting to remove the camshaft.

2. Loosen and remove the camshaft holder bolts, then remove the camshaft holders and the camshafts and the rocker arms.

3. Lift out the camshaft(s), wipe them clean, then inspect the lift ramps. Replace the camshaft(s) if the lobes are pitted, scored, or excessively worn.

To Install:

4. Pour engine oil into the cylinder head hydraulic tappet mounting hole, up to the level of the oil path.

5. Install the hydraulic tappets into the cylinder head while observing the following;

a. Do not rotate the hydraulic tappet while inserting it.

b. Carefully follow the special start-up procedure given below af-

ter the head is reassembled to allow the lifters to fill with oil

6. Pour engine oil into the oil fillers on the cylinder head.

7. Install the push rod and rocker arms while observing the following;

a. Install each part in its original position.

b. Loosen the rocker arm adjusting screws and locknuts before installation.

8. Install the camshafts and the camshaft oil seals as follows;

NOTE: The front camshaft has a groove in front driving the distributor.

a. Make sure that the camshaft is mounted parallel with the rocker arm slipper surface.

b. Advance the camshaft by 15 degrees from the No. 1 cylinder TDC of the compression stroke to prevent interference between the piston and the valve.

c. Place the rear camshaft on the cylinder head at the position where the cam is not pushing the valve.

d. Preset the oil seal, with its spring side facing inward.

e. Install the rear camshaft sealing rubber.

f. Do not apply oil to the cam holder side of the oil seal.

9. Apply liquid gasket sealer to the camshaft oil seal mounting surface and on the head contact surface. Temporarily tighten the bearing caps as shown in the illustration.

10. Carefully fit the camshaft oil seal until it contacts the bearing cap.

11. Tighten the bearing caps diagonally from the center of the head while observing the following;

a. Tighten the 6mm bolts last.

b. Make sure the oil seal is properly positioned.

c. Tighten the 8mm bolts to 20 ft. lbs. (28 Nm).

d. Tighten the 6mm bolts to 9 ft. lbs. (12 Nm).

12. Install the upper timing belt cover plate.

13. Install the camshaft pulley.

14. Install the timing belt.

15. Adjust the timing belt tension and the valve timing.

16. Adjust the exhaust rocker arm screws as follows;

a. Adjust the front and rear camshafts at No. 1 TDC of the compression stroke. The No. 1, No. 2 and No. 4 cylinders now have the exhaust valves closed.

b. Tighten the adjusting screw from the No. 1 cylinder. (When you feel the screw contact the valve, tighten the screw 1½ turns). Tighten the locknut firmly.

c. Set the adjusting screws for

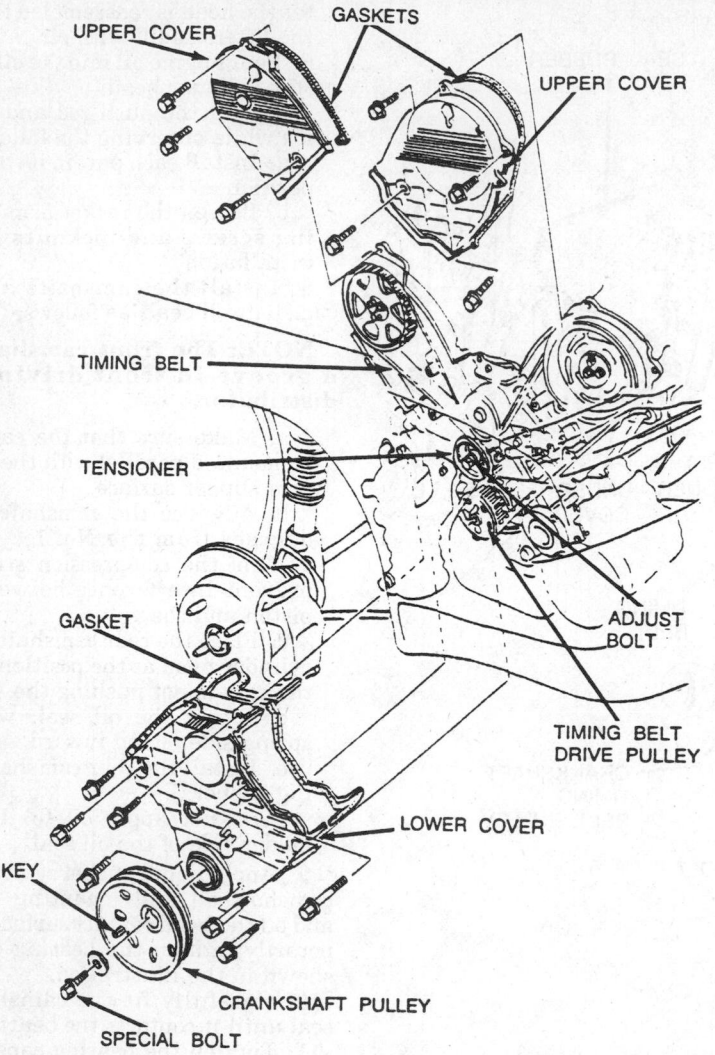

Timing belt and sprocket assembly—2494cc engine

No. 2 and No. 4 cylinders in the same way as Step b. above.

d. Rotate the crankshaft pulley one turn clockwise (as viewed from the pulleys side) to adjust the TDC of the NO. 5 piston's compression stroke. The No. 3, No. 5 and No. 6 cylinders now have the exhaust valves closed.

c. Set the adjusting screws for No. 3 and No. 5 and No. 6 cylinders in the same way as Step b. above.

17. Install the valve covers and the head side covers. Replace the O-rings for the head side covers.

18. Follow the special start-up procedure given below.

SPECIAL START-UP PROCEDURE

1. After the heads are reassembled, make sure the engine sits for at least five minutes to allow the hydraulic tappets to reach the proper oil level.

2. Remove the spark plugs. Have someone crank the engine; feel for compression from each cylinder at the spark plug holes. It may be necessary to crank the engine through several cycles to confirm compression.

If any cylinder does not have compression, it may be necessary to disassemble that head and check the suspected tappet.

If all cylinders have compression, reinstall the plugs and start the engine.

Pistons and Connecting Rods

POSITIONING

For all piston and connecting rod overhaul procedures, please refer to "Engine Rebuilding" in the Unit Repair section.

For correct piston and rod positioning refer to the illustrations below.

Integra

The arrow must face the timing belt side of the engine and the connecting rod oil hole must face the intake manifold.

Legend/825S

The arrow must face the timing belt side of the engine and the connecting rod oil hole must face the rear side of the engine.

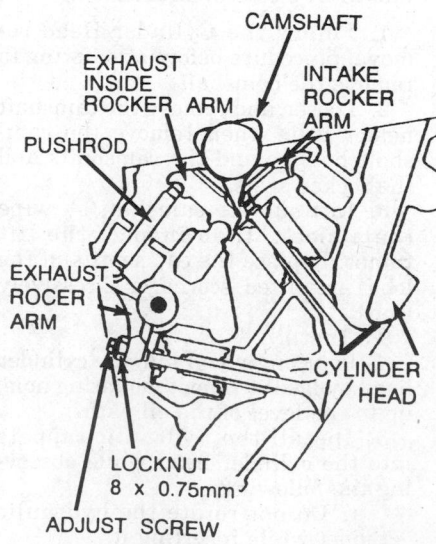

Camshaft tightening sequence—2494cc engine

Rocker arm adjustment—2494cc engine

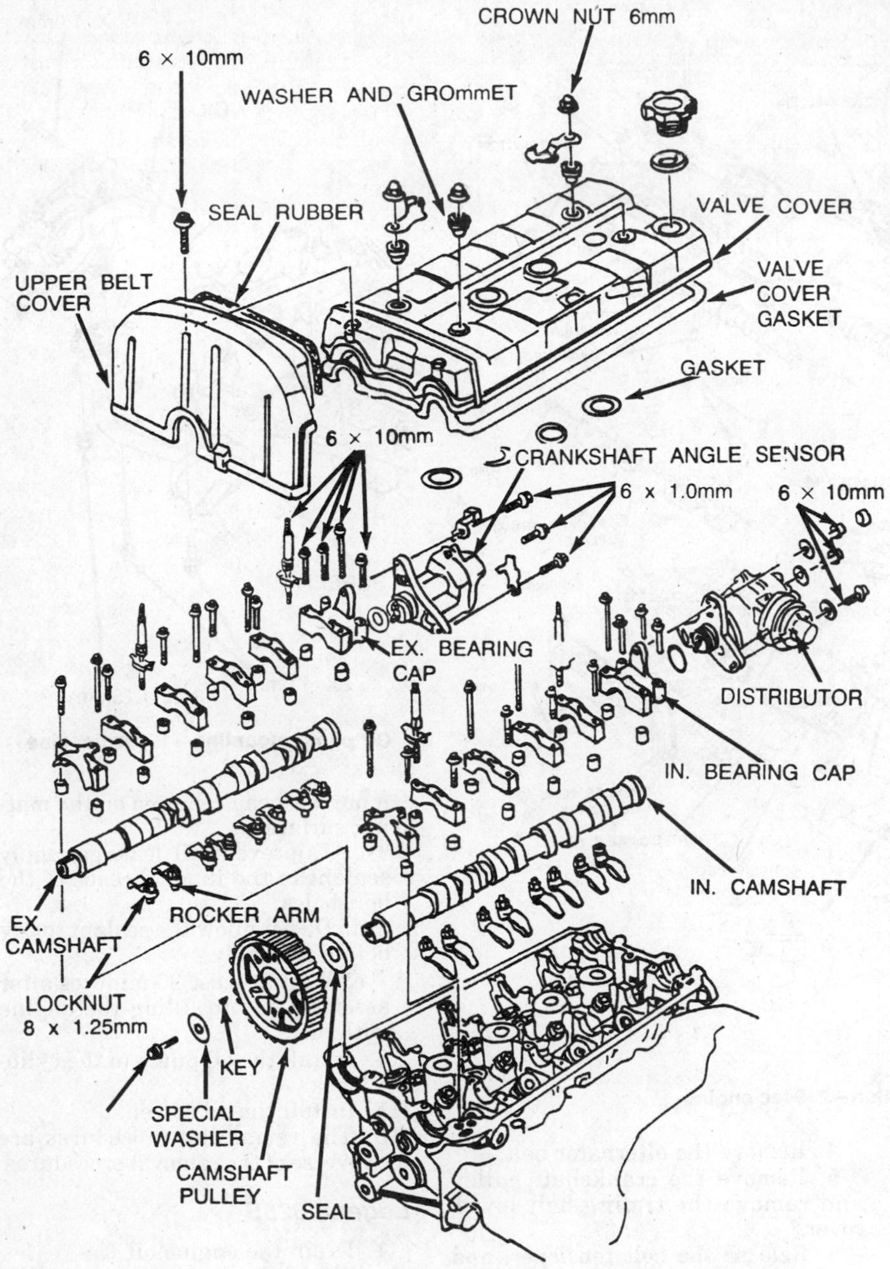

CROWN NUT 6mm

6 × 10mm

WASHER AND GROmmET

SEAL RUBBER

UPPER BELT COVER

VALVE COVER

VALVE COVER GASKET

GASKET

6 × 10mm

CRANKSHAFT ANGLE SENSOR

6 × 1.0mm   6 × 10mm

EX. BEARING CAP

DISTRIBUTOR

IN. BEARING CAP

IN. CAMSHAFT

EX. CAMSHAFT

ROCKER ARM

LOCKNUT 8 x 1.25mm

KEY

SPECIAL WASHER

CAMSHAFT PULLEY

SEAL

Camshaft Installation—1590cc engine

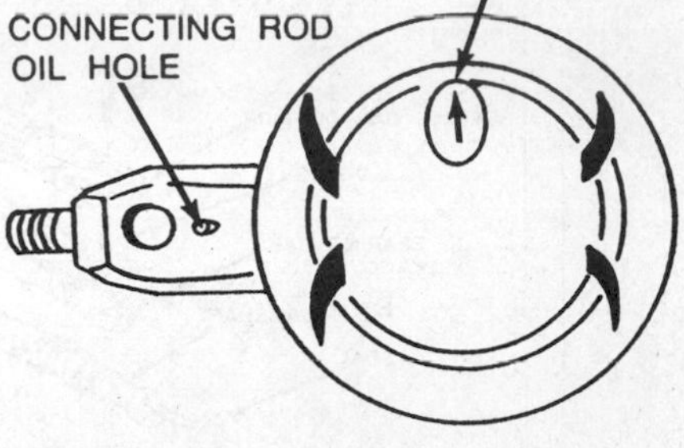

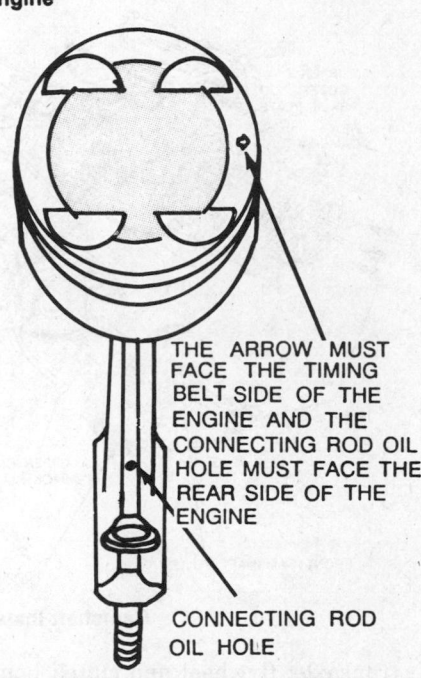

THE ARROW MUST FACE THE TIMING BELT SIDE OF THE ENGINE AND THE CONNECTING ROD OIL HOLE MUST FACE THE INTAKE MANI-FOLD.

CONNECTING ROD OIL HOLE

Piston and rod positioning—1590cc engine

THE ARROW MUST FACE THE TIMING BELT SIDE OF THE ENGINE AND THE CONNECTING ROD OIL HOLE MUST FACE THE REAR SIDE OF THE ENGINE

CONNECTING ROD OIL HOLE

Piston and rod positioning—2494cc engine

ENGINE LUBRICATION

Oil Pan

REMOVAL & INSTALLATION

1. Drain the engine oil.
2. Raise the front of the car and support it with jackstands. Remove the lower splash pan (if so equipped).
3. Attach a chain to the bracket on the transaxle case and raise just enough to take the load off the center mount.

NOTE: Do not remove the left engine mount.

4. Remove the center beam and engine lower mount.
5. Loosen the oil bolts and remove the oil pan flywheel dust shield.

NOTE: Loosen the bolts in a criss-cross pattern beginning with the outside bolt. To remove the oil pan, lightly tap the corners of the oil pan with a mallet. It is not necessary to remove the gasket unless it is damaged.

6. To install, reverse the removal procedure. Apply a coat of sealant to the entire mating surface of the cylinder block, except the crankshaft oil seal, before fitting the oil pan. Tighten the bolts in a circular sequence, beginning in the center and working out toward the ends.

Rear Main Oil Seal

REPLACEMENT

The rear oil seal is installed in the rear main bearing cap. Replacement of the seal requires the removal of the

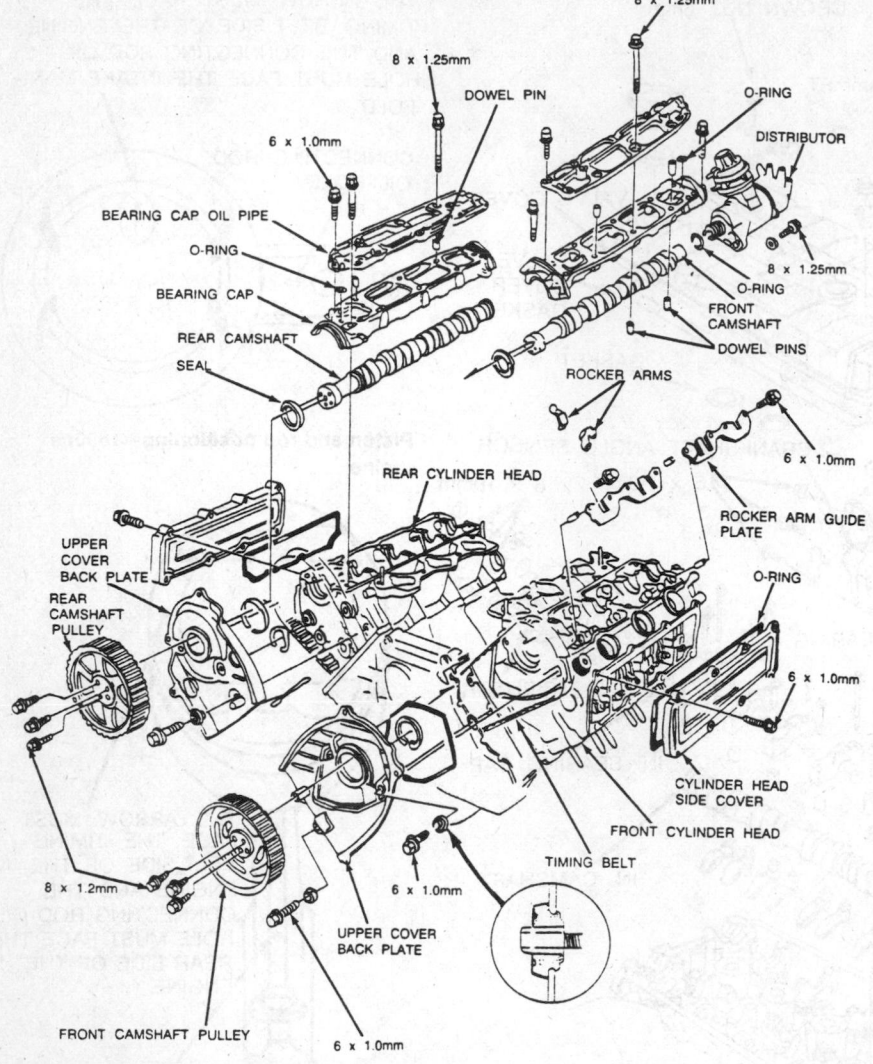

Camshaft Installation—2494cc engine

Labels: 8 x 1.25mm, 6 x 1.0mm, DOWEL PIN, O-RING, DISTRIBUTOR, BEARING CAP OIL PIPE, O-RING, BEARING CAP, 8 x 1.25mm, O-RING, REAR CAMSHAFT, FRONT CAMSHAFT, SEAL, DOWEL PINS, ROCKER ARMS, REAR CYLINDER HEAD, 6 x 1.0mm, ROCKER ARM GUIDE PLATE, UPPER COVER BACK PLATE, O-RING, REAR CAMSHAFT PULLEY, 6 x 1.0mm, CYLINDER HEAD SIDE COVER, FRONT CYLINDER HEAD, 8 x 1.2mm, 6 x 1.0mm, TIMING BELT, UPPER COVER BACK PLATE, FRONT CAMSHAFT PULLEY, 6 x 1.0mm

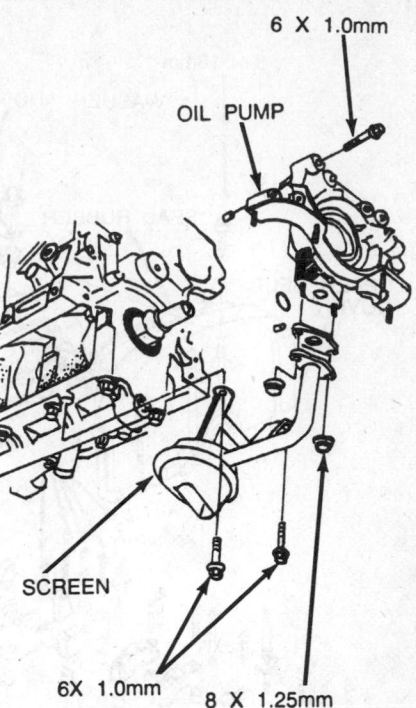

Oil pump mounting—1590cc engine

Labels: 6 X 1.0mm, OIL PUMP, SCREEN, 6X 1.0mm, 8 X 1.25mm

transaxle, flywheel and clutch housing, as well as the oil pan. Refer to the appropriate sections for the removal and installation of the above components. Both the front and rear main seal are installed after the crankshaft bearing caps have been torqued, if the crankshaft has been removed. Special drivers must be used.

Oil Pump

REMOVAL & INSTALLATION

Integra

1. Drain the engine oil.
2. Turn the crankshaft pulley and align the "T" mark on the crankshaft pulley with the index mark on the cover.
3. Remove the cylinder head cover and the timing belt upper cover.

4. Remove the alternator belt.
5. Remove the crankshaft pulley and remove the timing belt lower cover.
6. Release the belt tensioner, and remove the timing belt and the driven pulley.
7. Remove the oil pan.
8. Remove the oil screen.
9. Remove the mounting bolts and the oil pump assembly.

To install:
10. Check that the oil pump turns freely.
11. Apply a light coat of oil to the seal lip.
12. Install the two dowel pins and a new O-ring on the cylinder block.
13. Apply liquid gasket sealer to the cylinder block mating surface of the oil pump and observe the following:
  a. Check the mating surfaces are clean and dry before applying the liquid gasket.
  b. Apply liquid gasket evenly in

a narrow bead centered on the mating surface.
  c. To prevent oil leakage, apply sealant to the inner threads of the bolt holes.
  d. Do not allow the sealant to dry before assembly.
  e. Wait at least 30 minutes after assembly before filling the engine with oil.
14. Install the oil pump to the cylinder block.
15. Install the oil screen.
16. The remaining procedures are the reverse of the removal procedures.

Legend/825S

1. Drain the engine oil.
2. Turn the crankshaft pulley and align the "TDC" mark on the crankshaft pulley with the index mark on the cover.
3. Remove the timing belt upper cover.
4. Remove the alternator belt, power steering belt and the air compressor belt.
5. Remove the splash guard.
6. Remove the crankshaft pulley and remove the timing belt lower cover.
7. Release the belt tensioner, and remove the timing belt and the driven pulley.
8. Remove the oil filter assembly.
9. Remove the oil pan.
10. Remove the oil screen.
11. Remove the baffle plate.

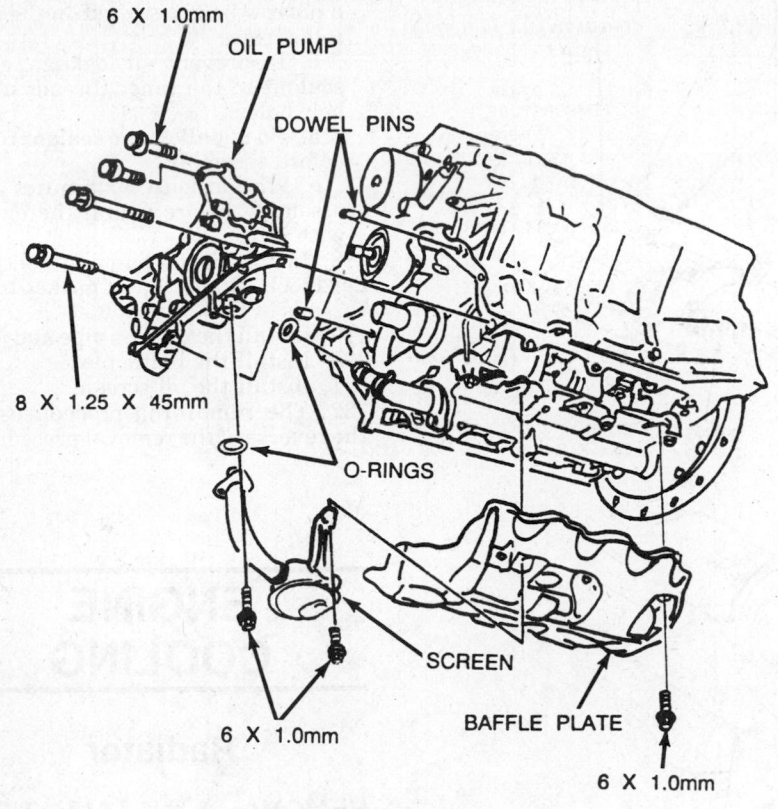

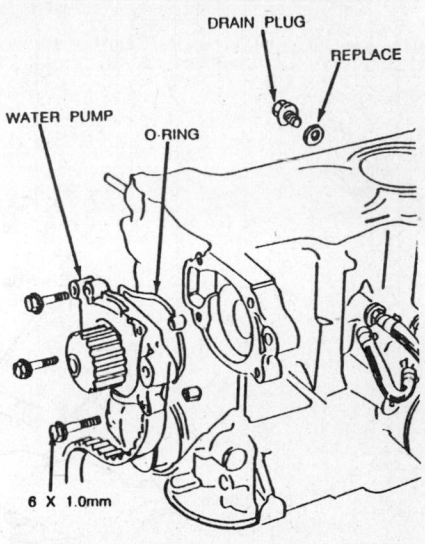

Water pump mounting—1590cc engine

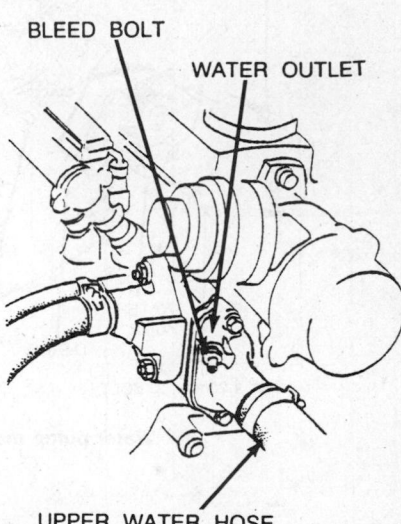

Cooling system bleed bolt—1590cc engine

Oil pump mounting—2494cc engine

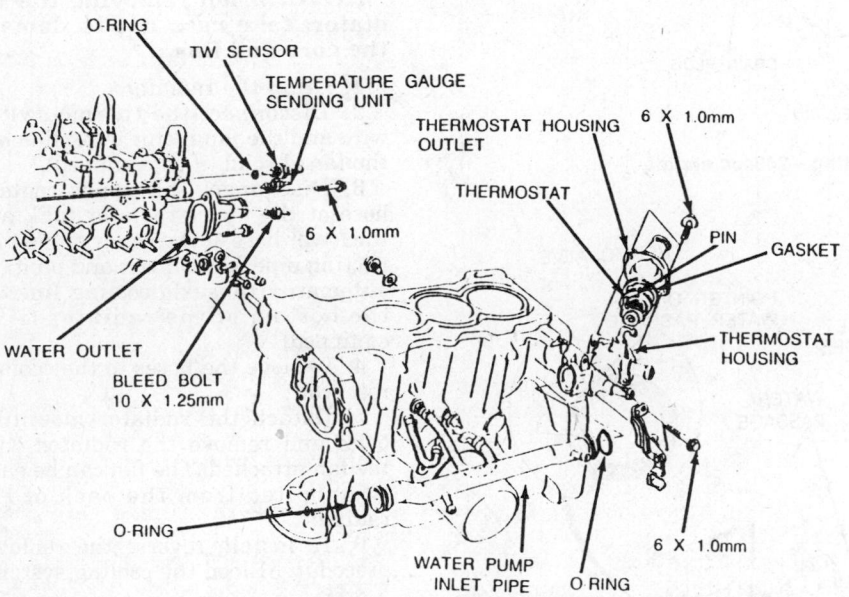

Thermostat location—1590cc engine

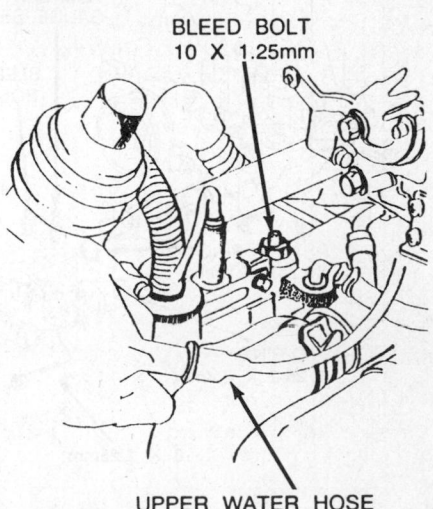

Cooling system bleed bolt—2494cc engine

12. Remove the oil pass pipe and joint.

13. Remove the mounting bolts and the oil pump assembly.

To install:

14. Check that the oil pump turns freely.

15. Apply a light coat of oil to the seal lip.

16. Install the two dowel pins and a new O-ring on the cylinder block.

17. Apply liquid gasket sealer to the cylinder block mating surface of the oil pump and observe the following:

a. Check the mating surfaces are clean and dry before applying the liquid gasket.

b. Apply liquid gasket evenly in

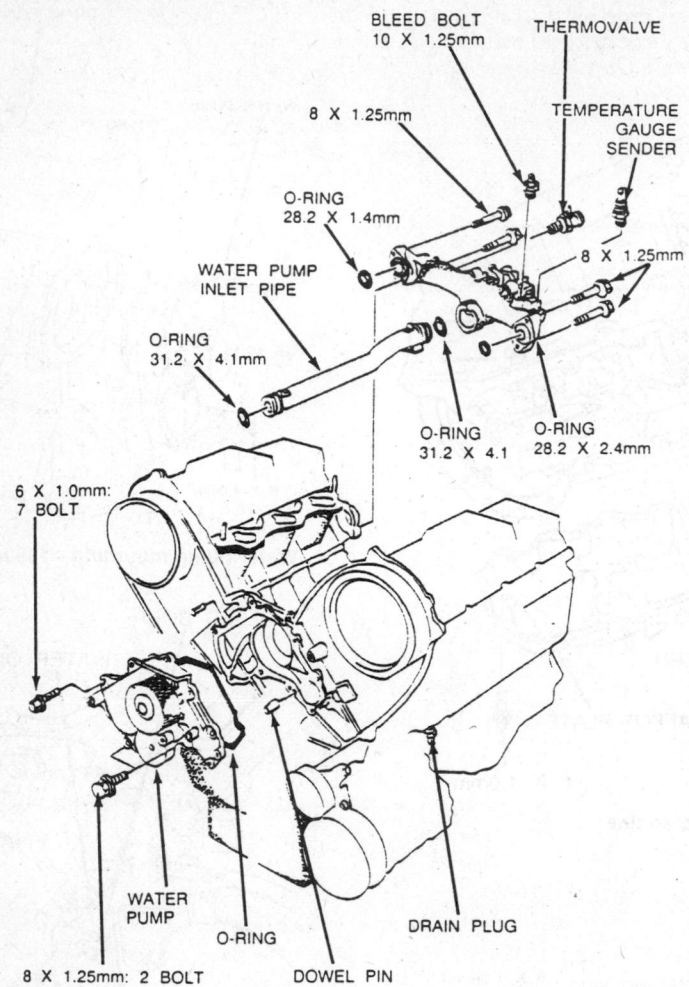

BLEED BOLT 10 X 1.25mm
THERMOVALVE
8 X 1.25mm
TEMPERATURE GAUGE SENDER
O-RING 28.2 X 1.4mm
WATER PUMP INLET PIPE
8 X 1.25mm
O-RING 31.2 X 4.1mm
O-RING 31.2 X 4.1
O-RING 28.2 X 2.4mm
6 X 1.0mm: 7 BOLT
WATER PUMP
O-RING
DRAIN PLUG
8 X 1.25mm: 2 BOLT
DOWEL PIN

Water pump mounting—2494cc engine

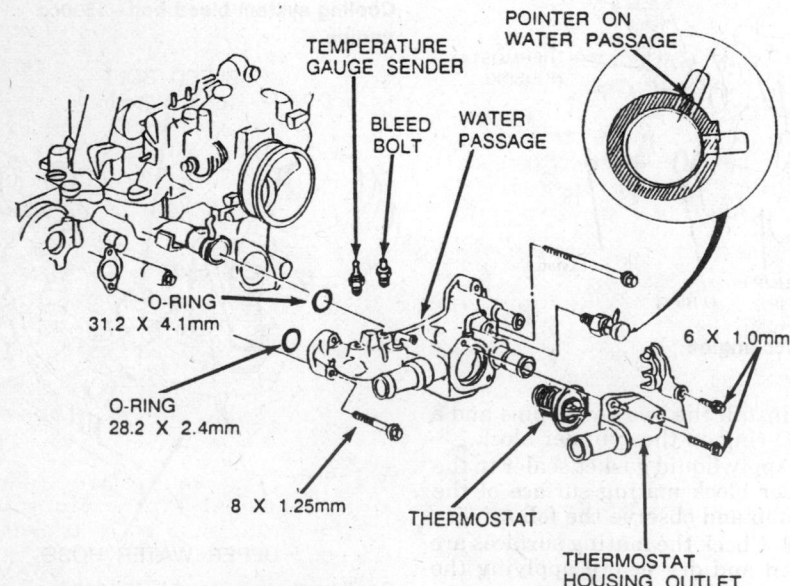

THERMOVALVE
POINTER ON WATER PASSAGE
TEMPERATURE GAUGE SENDER
BLEED BOLT
WATER PASSAGE
O-RING 31.2 X 4.1mm
O-RING 28.2 X 2.4mm
8 X 1.25mm
6 X 1.0mm
THERMOSTAT
THERMOSTAT HOUSING OUTLET

Thermostat location—2494cc engine

a narrow bead centered on the mating surface.

c. To prevent oil leakage, apply sealant to the inner threads of the bolt holes.

d. Do not allow the sealant to dry before assembly.

e. Wait at least 30 minutes after assembly before filling the engine with oil.

18. Install the oil pump to the cylinder block. Apply liquid gasket to the threads of the 8mm bolt.

19. Install the oil pass pipe and joint.

20. Install the baffle plate.

21. Install the oil screen.

22. The remaining procedures are the reverse of the removal procedures.

ENGINE COOLING

Radiator

REMOVAL & INSTALLATION

NOTE: When removing the radiator, take care not to damage the core and fins.

1. Drain the radiator.

2. Disconnect the thermo-switch wire and the fan motor wire. Remove the fan shroud (if so equipped).

3. Disconnect the upper coolant hose at the upper radiator tank and the lower hose at the water pump connecting pipe. Disconnect and plug the automatic transaxle cooling lines at the bottom of the radiator (if so equipped).

4. Remove the hoses to the coolant reservoir.

5. Detach the radiator mounting bolts and remove the radiator with the fan attached. The fan can be easily unbolted from the back of the radiator.

6. To install, reverse the removal procedure. Bleed the cooling system.

Water Pump

REMOVAL & INSTALLATION

1. Drain the radiator.

2. Following the procedures shown under Timing belt and Tensioner, remove the timing belt from the water pump drive sprocket.

3. Loosen the water pump mounting bolts and remove together with

the drive sprocket.

4. To install, reverse the removal procedure using a new O-ring. Bleed the cooling system.

Thermostat

REMOVAL & INSTALLATION

1. The thermostat housing is located at the end of the water pump inlet tube on the 1590cc engine, and beneath the throttle body on the 2494cc engine.

2. Unbolt and remove the thermostat cover and pull the thermostat from the housing.

3. To install, reverse the removal procedure. Always install the spring end of the thermostat toward the engine. Tighten the two cover bolts to 9 ft. lbs (12 Nm). Always use a new gasket. Bleed the cooling system.

COOLING SYSTEM BLEEDING

1. Loosen the air bleed bolt in the water outlet, and then fill the radiator to the bottom of the filler neck with antifreeze/coolant. Tighten the bleed bolt as soon as the coolant starts to run out in a steady stream without any air bubbles in it.

2. With the radiator cap off, start the engine and allow it to warm up (the cooling fan should go on at least twice). Then if necessary add more antifreeze/coolant to bring the level back up to the bottom of the filler neck.

3. Put the radiator cap on, restart the engine and check for any leaks.

EMISSION CONTROLS

Please refer to "Emission Control" in the Unit Repair section for system maintenance procedures. Due to the complex nature of modern electronic engine control system, comprehensive diagnosis and testing procedures fall outside the confines of this repair manual. For complete information on diagnosis, testing and repair procedures concerning all

modern engine and emission control systems, please refer to "Chilton's Guide to Electronic Engine Controls".

FUEL SYSTEM

Both Accura and Sterling use Honda's Programmed Fuel Injection system. This system is a multiport electronic fuel injection system that uses manifold absolute information and a RPM sensor. The PGM-FI system is based on sequential port injection by which each injector is timed to provide the proper amount of fuel to each cylinder based on the engine speed and the load condition.

Fuel Filter

REPLACEMENT

Fuel Injected Engine

The fuel filter on the fuel injected models is located on the firewall in the engine compartment. It should be replaced every 60,000 miles, or whenever the fuel pressure drops below 36–41 psi (250–279 kPa) with the vacuum pressure hose disconnected, and after checking the fuel pump and pressure regulator for proper operation.

1. Disconnect the negative battery cable from the battery.

2. Relieve the fuel pressure by slowly loosening the service bolt on the top of the fuel filter about one turn.

NOTE: Always place rag under the filter during this procedure to prevent fuel from spilling onto the engine. Always replace the washer between the service bolt and the banjo bolt, whenever the service bolt has been loosened.

3. Remove the 12mm sealing bolts from the fuel filter.

4. Remove the fuel filter clamp and the fuel filter.

5. To assemble, reverse the removal procedures. Always use new washers on assembly.

Electrical Fuel Pump

REMOVAL & INSTALLATION

Integra

1. Disconnect the negative battery cable from the battery.

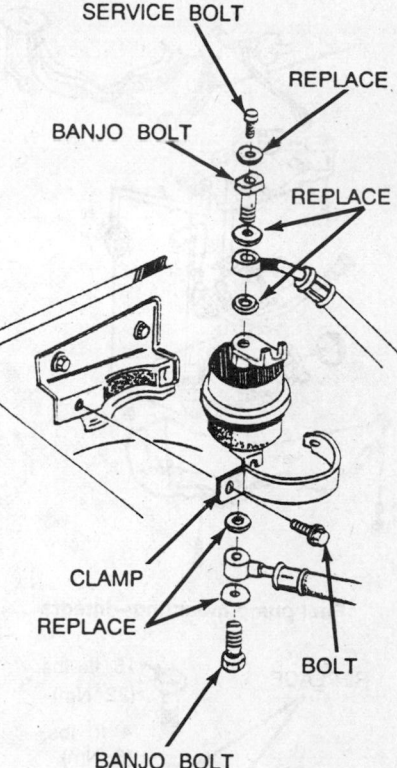

Fuel filter assembly—Integra

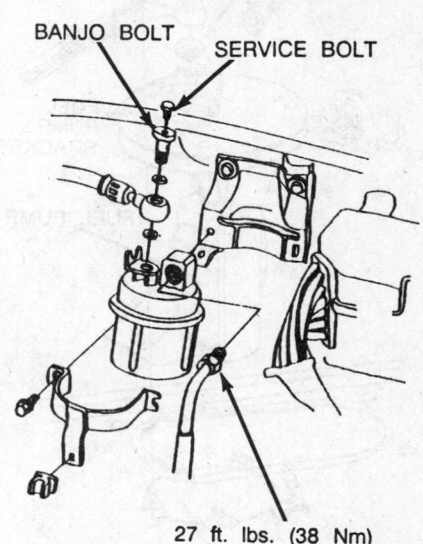

27 ft. lbs. (38 Nm)

Fuel filter assembly—Legend/825S

2. Relieve the fuel pressure by slowly loosening the service bolt on the top of the fuel filter about one turn.

NOTE: Place a rag under the filter during this procedure to prevent fuel from spilling onto the engine. Always replace the washer between the service bolt and the banjo bolt, whenever the service bolt has been loosened.

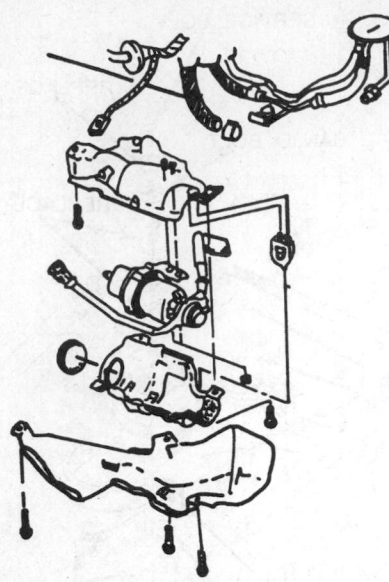

Fuel pump mounting – Integra

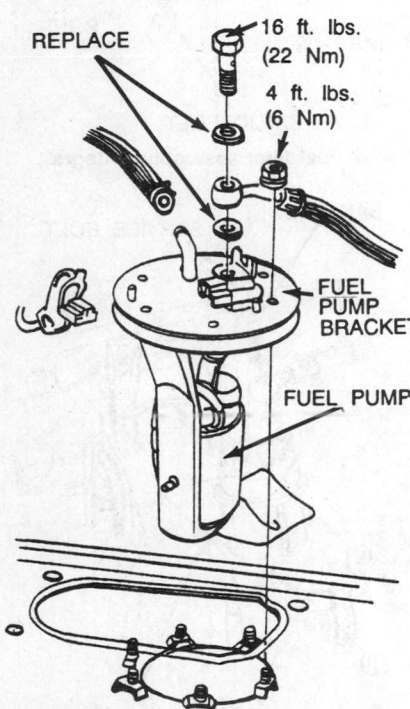

REPLACE

16 ft. lbs. (22 Nm)

4 ft. lbs. (6 Nm)

FUEL PUMP BRACKET

FUEL PUMP

Fuel pump mounting – Legend/825S

3. Raise the car and support on jackstands.

4. Remove the left rear wheel.

5. Remove the fuel pump cover bolts, then remove the cover.

6. Remove the mounting bolts from the fuel pump mount, then remove the fuel pump with its mount.

7. Disconnect the fuel lines and the electrical connectors.

8. Remove the clamp and remove the fuel pump from the mounting bracket.

9. Remove the fuel line and silencer from the pump.

10. To install, reverse the removal procedures. Turn on the ignition switch and check for fuel leaks.

Legend/825S

1. Disconnect the negative battery cable from the battery.

2. Relieve the fuel pressure by slowly loosening the service bolt on the top of the fuel filter about one turn.

NOTE: Place a rag under the filter during this procedure to prevent fuel from spilling onto the engine. Always replace the washer between the service bolt and the banjo bolt, whenever the service bolt has been loosened.

3. Remove the maintenance access cover in the luggage area.

4. Disconnect the fuel lines and the electrical connectors.

5. Remove the fuel pump from the fuel tank.

6. To install, reverse the removal procedures. Turn on the ignition switch and check for fuel leaks.

Fuel Injection

Due to the complex nature of modern fuel injection systems, comprehensive diagnosis and testing procedures fall outside the confines of this repair manual. For complete information on fuel injection diagnosis, testing and repair procedures please refer to *Chilton's Guide to Fuel Injection And Feedback Carburetors.*

MANUAL TRANSAXLE

REMOVAL & INSTALLATION

Integra

1. Disconnect the battery ground cable at the battery and the transaxle.

2. Unlock the steering and place the transaxle in neutral.

3. Disconnect the following wires in the engine compartment:

   a. Battery positive cable from the starter.

   b. Black/white wire from the solenoid.

   c. Green/black and yellow wires from the back-up light.

4. Unclip and remove the speedometer cable at the transaxle. Do not disassemble the speedometer gear holder!

5. Disconnect the clutch cable at the release arm.

6. Remove the side and top starter mounting bolts. Loosen the front wheel lug nuts. Remove the front wheels.

7. Raise and support the car.

8. Drain the transaxle.

9. Remove the splash shields from the underside.

10. Remove the stabilizer bar.

11. Disconnect the left and right lower ball joints and tie end rods, using a ball joint remover.

CAUTION

Use caution when removing the ball joints. Place a floor jack under the lower control arm securely at the ball joint. Otherwise, the lower control arm may jump suddenly away from the steering knuckle as the ball joint is removed.

12. Turn the right steering knuckle out as far as it will go. Place a prybar against the inboard CV-joint, pry the right axle out of the transaxle about 13mm. This will force the spring clip out of the groove inside the differential gear splines. Pull it out the rest of the way. Repeat this procedure on the other side.

13. Screw a 10mm bolt at the engine block and attach a hoist and chain to the bolt; attach the other end of the chain on the opposite side, to the engine hanger plate, then lift the engine slightly to take the weight off the mounts.

14. Disconnect the header pipe at the exhaust manifold.

15. Disconnect the shift lever torque rod from the clutch housing.

16. Remove the bolt from the shift rod clevis.

17. Raise the transmission jack securely against the transaxle to take up the weight.

18. Remove the bolts from the front transaxle mount at the front engine stiffener.

19. Remove the intake manifold bracket and the rear engine mount bracket.

20. Remove the transaxle housing bolts from the engine torque bracket.

21. Remove the remaining starter mounting bolts and take out the starter.

22. Remove the remaining transaxle mounting bolts.

23. Pull the transaxle away from the engine until it clears the 14mm dowel pins, then lower on the transmission jack.

24. Separate the mainshaft from the clutch pressure plate and remove the transaxle by lowering the jack.

To install:

25. Install the transaxle on a transmission jack. Clean and lubricate the

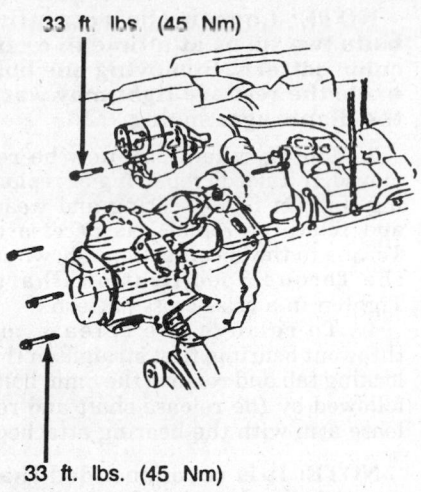

33 ft. lbs. (45 Nm)

33 ft. lbs. (45 Nm)

Transaxle removal—Integra

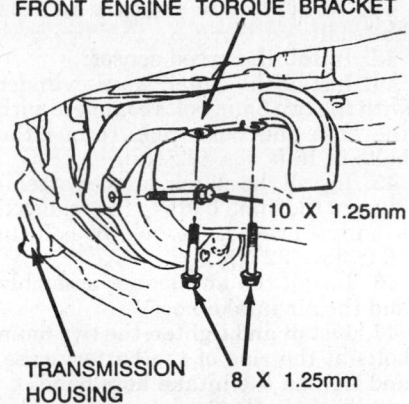

FRONT ENGINE TORQUE BRACKET

10 X 1.25mm

TRANSMISSION HOUSING

8 X 1.25mm

Front transaxle mount tightening sequence

clutch release bearing surfaces.

26. Check that the two 14mm dowel pins are installed in the clutch housing.

27. Raise the transaxle high enough to align the dowel pins with the matching holes in the block.

28. Roll the transaxle toward the engine and fit the mainshaft into the clutch disc splines. If the driver's side suspension was left in place , install new spring clips on both axles, then carefully insert the left axle into the differential as you install the transaxle.

NOTE: Install new 26mm spring clips on both axles. Make sure that the axles fully bottom out. Slide the axle in until you feel the spring clip engage the differential.

29. Push and wiggle the transaxle until it fits flush with the flange.

30. Bolt the transaxle to the engine with the mounting bolts from the engine side. Torque the bolts to 50 ft. lbs. (68 Nm).

31. Install the rear mount bracket on the transaxle housing. Torque its mounting bolts to 47 ft. lbs. (65 Nm).

32. Install the engine torque bracket on the transaxle housing. Torque its mounting bolts to 33 ft. lbs. (45 Nm).

33. Loosely install the bolts for the front of the transaxle mount, then torque them in the sequence shown in the illustration.

34. Install the starter mounting bolts and tighten them to 33 ft. lbs. (45 Nm).

35. Install the intermediate shaft and, the right and left halfshaft.

36. Turn the right steering knuckle/axle assembly outward far enough to insert the free end of the

axle into the transaxle. Repeat this procedure on the other side.

NOTE: Make sure that the axles fully bottom out. Slide the axle in until you feel the spring clip engage the differential.

37. Reconnect the shift rod and the shift lever torque rod.

38. Reconnect the lower arm to the ball joints and torque them to 33 ft. lbs. (45 Nm).

39. Reconnect the tie rod end ball joints and torque them to 33 ft. lbs. (45 Nm).

40. Install the engine and wheelwell splash shields.

41. Reconnect the exhaust header pipe.

42. Install the front wheels, lower the car to the ground and tighten the lug nuts.

43. Remove the chain hoist from the 10mm bolt on the cylinder head and the engine hanger plate.

44. Install the speedometer cable.

45. Install the transaxle housing bolts and torque them to 33 ft. lbs. (45 Nm).

46. Connect the clutch cable to the release arm, then attach the cable housing end to the transaxle bracket.

47. Connect the engine compartment wiring:

   a. Battery positive cable from the starter.

   b. Black/white wire from the solenoid.

   c. Green/black and yellow wires from the back-up light.

48. With the ignition key turned OFF, connect the ground cable to the battery and the transaxle.

49. Refill the transaxle with SAE 30, 10W–30, 10W–40, or 20W–40, and adjust the clutch free play.

50. Check the transaxle for smooth operation.

Legend/825S

1. Disconnect the positive and negative battery cables from the battery.

2. Disconnect the starter and ground cables.

3. Disconnect the back-up light wires from the engine harness.

4. Loosen the 6mm bolt attaching the harness holder at the side of the transaxle hanger, and the release harness from the transaxle.

5. Loosen the 6mm bolts at the side of the battery base and the intake hose band.

6. Remove the air cleaner case assembly along with the intake hose.

7. Remove the 8mm bolts and the clutch slave cylinder with the clutch hose and the push rod.

NOTE: Do not operate the clutch pedal once the slave cylinder has been removed.

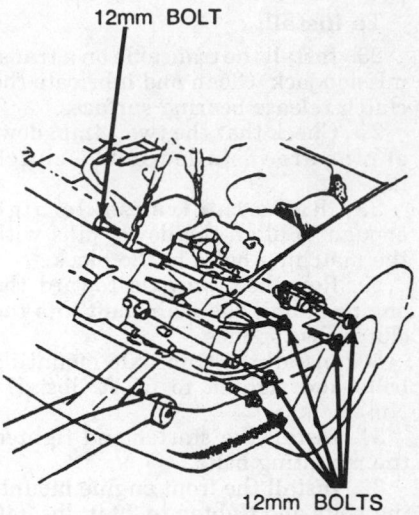

12mm BOLT

12mm BOLTS

Transaxle removal—Legend/825S

8. Remove the 8mm bolts and clutch damper assembly from the transaxle hanger bracket.

9. Remove the power steering speed sensor with the sensor hose intact.

10. Drain the oil from the transaxle.

11. Remove the halfshaft from the vehicle, refer to "Halfshaft Removal and Installation" for those procedures.

12. Remove the 3 bolts securing the intermediate shaft and remove the shaft.

13. Remove the shift rod and the shift extension.

14. Remove the 2 bolts attaching the torque rod bracket to the clutch case.

NOTE: Replace the torque rod bolts whenever loosened or removed.

15. Place a transmission jack securely beneath the transaxle.

16. Remove the sub frame center beam.

17. Attach a engine support chain with two 10mm bolts to the engine block, one on each bank.

18. Then lift the engine slightly to take the weight off the mounts.

19. Remove the center stop bracket from the transaxle.

20. Remove the clutch cover.

21. Remove the two rear engine mounting bolts from the transaxle.

22. Remove the two front engine mounting bolts from the transaxle housing.

23. Remove the starter mounting bolts and the starter assembly.

24. Remove the remaining transaxle mounting bolts.

25. Pull the transaxle away from the engine until it clears the 14mm dowel pins, then lower on the transmission jack.

To install:

26. Install the transaxle on a transmission jack. Clean and lubricate the clutch release bearing surfaces.

27. Check that the two 14mm dowel pins are installed in the clutch housing.

28. Raise the transaxle high enough to align the dowel pins with the matching holes in the block.

29. Roll the transaxle toward the engine and fit the mainshaft into the clutch disc splines.

30. Install the transaxle mounting bolts and tighten to 55 ft. lbs. (75 Nm).

31. Install the starter and tighten the mounting bolts.

32. Install the front engine mounting bolts and tighten to 29 ft. lbs. (40 Nm).

33. Install the rear engine mounting bolts and tighten to 29 ft. lbs. (40 Nm).

34. Install the center stopper bracket bolts and tighten to 29 ft. lbs. (40 Nm).

35. Install the clutch cover.

36. Install the center beam.

37. Remove the transmission jack.

38. Install and tighten the new torque rod bracket bolts to 29 ft. lbs. (40 Nm).

NOTE: Replace the torque rod bolts whenever loosened or removed.

39. Remove the engine support chain by removing the two 10mm bolts.

40. Install the shift rod and shift extension.

41. Install the intermediate shaft with the three 8mm bolts. Tighten the bolts to 29 ft. lbs. (40 Nm).

42. Install the right and left halfshaft.

43. Install the speed sensor.

44. Install the clutch slave cylinder with the two 8mm bolts complete with the hose and push rod. Torque the bolts to 16 ft. lbs. (22 Nm).

45. Install the clutch damper assembly and the 8mm bolts to the transaxle hanger bracket. Torque the bolts to 16 ft. lbs. (22 Nm).

46. Install the air cleaner assembly and the air intake hose.

47. Install and tighten the two 6mm bolts at the side of the battery case, and tighten the intake hose band.

48. Tighten the 6mm harness holder bolt at the side of the transaxle hanger.

49. Connect the back-up light switch wire to the engine harness.

50. Connect the starter and ground cables.

51. Connect the battery cables.

52. Refill the transaxle with SAE 10W-30 or 10W-40.

53. Check the transaxle for smooth operation.

SHIFT LINKAGE ADJUSTMENT

The Accura/Sterling shift linkage is non-adjustable. However, if the linkage is binding, or if there is excessive play, check the linkage bushings and pivot points. Lubricate with light oil, or replace worn bushings as necessary.

OVERHAUL

For all manual transaxle overhaul procedures, please refer to "Manual Transaxle" in the Unit Repair section.

CLUTCH

All models use a single dry disc with a diaphragm spring type pressure plate. On the Integra model the clutch is cable operated. However, on the Legend and the 825S models, a hydraulic master and slave cylinder system is used.

REMOVAL & INSTALLATION

1. Follow the transaxle removal procedure, previously given. Match mark the flywheel and clutch for easy reassembly.

2. Hold the flywheel ring gear with a tool made for the purpose, remove the retaining bolts and remove the pressure plate and clutch disc.

NOTE: Loosen the retaining bolts two turns at a time in a circular pattern. Removing one bolt while the rest are tight may warp the diaphragm spring.

3. The flywheel can now be removed, if it needs repairing or replacing. Inspect it for scoring and wear, and reface or replace as necessary. Torque to the specifications shown in the Torque Specification Chart. Tighten in a criss-cross pattern.

4. To remove the release, or throwout bearing, first straighten the locking tab and remove the 8mm bolt, followed by the release shaft and release arm with the bearing attached.

NOTE: It is recommended that the release bearing be removed after the release arm has been removed from the casing. Trying to remove or install the bearing with the release arm in the case will damage the retaining clip.

5. To assemble and install the clutch, reverse the removal procedure. Be sure to pay attention to the following points:

   a. Make sure that the flywheel and the end of the crankshaft are clean before assembly.

   b. When installing the pressure plate, align the mark on the outer edge of the flywheel with the alignment mark on the pressure plate. Failure to align these marks will result in imbalance.

   c. When tightening the pressure plate bolts, use a pilot shaft to center the friction disc. The pilot shaft can be bought at any large auto supply store or fabricated from a wooden dowel. After centering the disc, tighten the bolts two turns at a time, in a criss-cross pattern to avoid warping the diaphragm springs; tighten to 19 ft. lbs. (26 Nm).

   d. When installing the release shaft and arm, place a lock tab washer under the retaining bolt.

   e. When installing the transaxle, make sure that the mainshaft is properly aligned with the disc spline and the aligning pins are in place, before tightening the case bolts.

FREE PLAY ADJUSTMENT

Integra

1. Adjust the clutch free play at the release lever by turning the adjusting nut.

2. Make sure there is $5/32$–$13/64$ in. (4.0–5.0mm) of free play at the tip of the release arm after the adjustment.

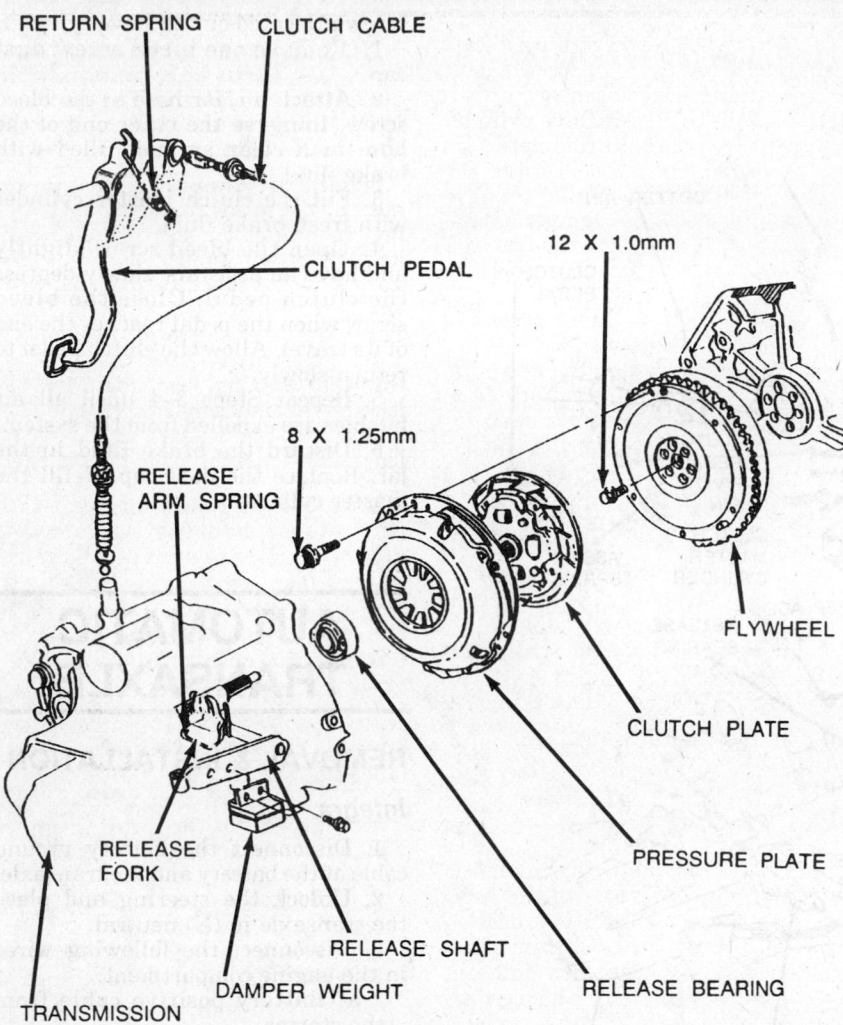

Clutch assembly—Integra

Clutch Master Cylinder

REMOVAL & INSTALLATION

Legend/825S

The clutch master cylinder is located on the firewall in the engine compartment next to the brake master cylinder.

1. Remove the cotter pin which retains the pivot pin in the yoke of the pushrod (under the instrument panel at the clutch pedal).
2. Remove the two nuts retaining the master cylinder to the firewall. Remove the master cylinder from the engine compartment.
3. Remove the banjo bolt and hose from the master cylinder.
4. Disconnect the reservoir hose from the master cylinder by removing the clip.
5. Installation is the reverse of removal. Bleed the system after installation.

Clutch Slave Cylinder

REMOVAL & INSTALLATION

Legend/825S

1. The slave cylinder is retained by two bolts. Disconnect and plug the hydraulic line at the slave cylinder.
2. Remove the two mounting bolts, then the slave cylinder from the clutch case.
3. Installation is the reverse of removal. Bleed the system after installation.

CLUTCH HYDRAULIC SYSTEM BLEEDING

Legend/825S

The hydraulic system must be bled whenever the system has been leaking or has been dismantled. The bleed

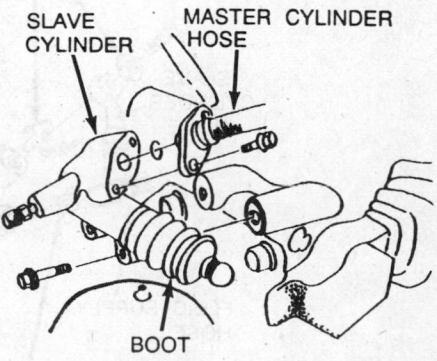

Clutch slave cylinder mounting— Legend/825S

---

3. On cruise control equipped cars, turn the adjuster (above the clutch pedal) until the clutch pedal stroke is 5.31–5.51 in. (135–140mm), then tighten the locknut securely.

Legend/825S

Total clutch free play is 0.35–0.59 in. (9–15mm).

1. Loosen the lock nut on the clutch pedal switch.
2. Loosen the lock nut on the clutch master cylinder push rod. Turn the push rod in or out to obtain the correct stroke and height at the clutch pedal.
   Stroke at pedal: 5.7–5.9 in. (145–150mm)
   Clutch pedal height: 7.0 in. (179mm) (to floor carpet)
3. Tighten the lock nut on the clutch master cylinder push rod.
4. Screw the clutch pedal switch until it contacts the pedal.

5. Turn the switch another ¼–½ turn. Tighten the lock nut.

Clutch Cable

REMOVAL & INSTALLATION

Integra

1. Loosen the clutch cable adjusting nut on the transaxle near the release shaft arm.
2. Remove the cable from the release shaft arm by sliding the cable end retainer through the elongated hole in the release shaft arm.
3. From the interior of the car release the cable from the top of the clutch cable assembly.
4. Pull the cable out of the firewall and remove from the car.
5. To install reverse the removal procedure and adjust the clutch free play.

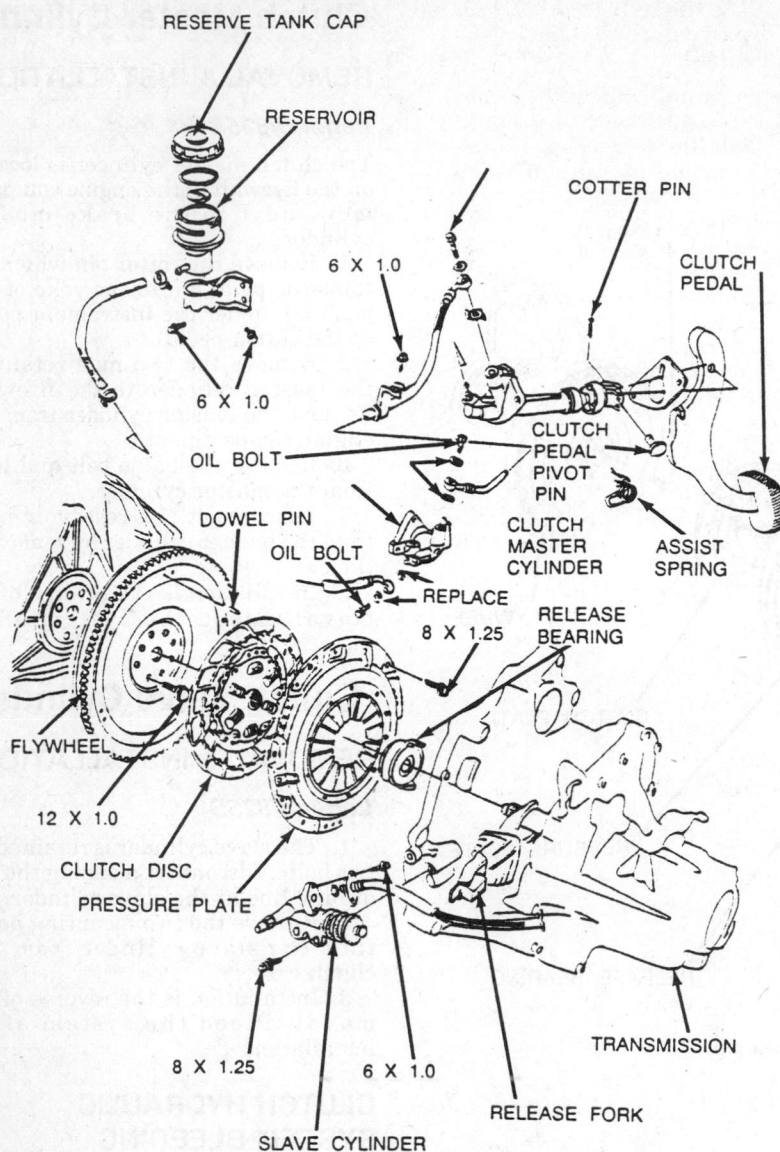

Clutch assembly—Legend/825S

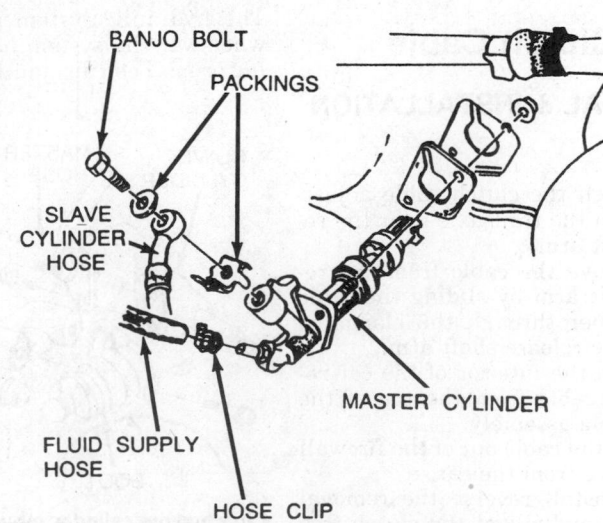

Clutch master cylinder mounting—Legend/825S

screw is located on the slave cylinder.

1. Remove the bleed screw dust cap.

2. Attach a clear hose to the bleed screw. Immerse the other end of the hose in a clear jar half filled with brake fluid.

3. Fill the clutch master cylinder with fresh brake fluid.

4. Open the bleed screw slightly and have an assistant slowly depress the clutch pedal. Close the bleed screw when the pedal reaches the end of its travel. Allow the clutch pedal to return slowly.

5. Repeat Steps 3–4 until all air bubbles are expelled from the system.

6. Discard the brake fluid in the jar. Replace the dust cap. Refill the master cylinder.

AUTOMATIC TRANSAXLE

REMOVAL & INSTALLATION

Integra

1. Disconnect the battery ground cable at the battery and the transaxle.

2. Unlock the steering and place the transaxle in (N) neutral.

3. Disconnect the following wires in the engine compartment:

    a. Battery positive cable from the starter.

    b. Black/white wire from the solenoid.

    c. transaxle ground cable.

4. Drain the transaxle.

5. Disconnect the speedometer cable.

6. Disconnect the transaxle cooler hoses, and wire them up next to the radiator so the ATF won't drain out.

7. Remove the center console, then disconnect the shift cable by removing the adjusting pin.

8. Unscrew the cable guide bolt, then pull out the throttle cable.

9. Remove the right and left halfshaft and intermediate shaft.

10. Screw a 10mm bolt at the cylinder head and attach a hoist and chain to the bolt; attach the other end of the chain to the engine hanger plate, then lift the engine slightly to take the weight off the mounts.

11. Remove the engine splash shields.

12. Disconnect the header pipe at the exhaust manifold.

13. Place a transmission jack under the transaxle and raise the transaxle just enough to take the weight off the mounts.

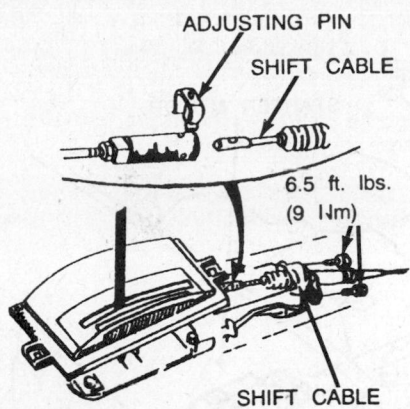

Shift cable adjusting pin—Integra

14. Remove the bolts from the front transaxle mount at the front engine bracket.

15. Remove the rear transaxle mount bracket by removing the mounting bolts.

16. Remove the transaxle housing bolts from the front transaxle mount bracket.

17. Remove the torque converter cover.

18. Remove the drive plate tightening bolts by turning the engine crankshaft pulley.

NOTE: The crankshaft pulley bolt is a right hand thread, and may be loosened when the pulley is turned counterclockwise. After removing the drive plate, check that the pulley bolt is torqued properly.

19. Remove the starter mounting bolts and take out the starter.

20. Remove the remaining transaxle mounting bolts.

21. Pull the transaxle away from the engine until it clears the 14mm dowel pins, then lower on the transmission jack.

To install:

22. Install the transaxle on a transmission jack.

23. Check that the two 14mm dowel pins are installed in the torque converter housing.

24. Raise the transaxle high enough to align the dowel pins with the matching holes in the block. Align the torque converter bolt heads with holes in the drive plate.

25. If the driver's side suspension was left in place, install new spring clips on both axles, then carefully insert the left axle into the differential as you roll the transaxle up to the engine.

NOTE: Install new 26mm spring clips on both axles. Make sure that the axles fully bottom

out. Slide the axle in until you feel the spring clip engage the differential.

26. Push and wiggle the transaxle until it fits flush with the flange.

27. Bolt the transaxle to the engine with the mounting bolts from the engine side. Torque the bolts to 50 ft. lbs. (68 Nm).

28. Attach the torque converter to the drive plate with eight 12mm bolts, and tighten to 9 ft lbs. (12 Nm). Rotate the crank as necessary to tighten the bolts to ½ torque, then final torque in a criss-cross pattern. Check for free rotation after tightening the last bolt.

29. Install the shift cable.

30. Remove the transmission jack.

31. Install the torque converter cover plate.

32. Install the rear mount bracket on the transaxle housing. Torque its mounting bolts to 48 ft. lbs. (65 Nm).

33. Install the front transaxle mount bracket. Torque its mounting bolts to 33 ft. lbs. (45 Nm).

34. Loosely install the bolts for the front of the transaxle mount, then torque them in the sequence shown in the illustration.

Front transaxle mount tightening sequence

35. Install the starter mounting bolts and tighten them to 33 ft. lbs. (45 Nm).

36. Install the intermediate shaft and, the right and left halfshaft.

37. Turn the right steering knuckle/axle assembly outward far enough to insert the free end of the axle into the transaxle. Repeat this procedure on the other side.

NOTE: Make sure that the axles fully bottom out. Slide the axle in until you feel the spring clip engage the differential.

38. Reconnect the lower arm to the ball joints and torque them to 33 ft. lbs. (45 Nm).

39. Reconnect the tie rod end ball joints and torque them to 33 ft. lbs. (45 Nm).

40. Install the engine splash shields.

41. Reconnect the exhaust header pipe.

42. Install the front wheels, lower the car to the ground and tighten the lug nuts.

43. Remove the chain hoist from the 10mm bolt on the cylinder head and the engine hanger plate.

44. Install the speedometer cable.

45. Install the three top transaxle mounting bolts and torque them to 48 ft. lbs. (65 Nm).

46. Connect the cooler hoses, then torque the banjo bolts to 21 ft. lbs. (29 Nm).

47. Attach the shift control cable to the shaft lever with the pin and clip, if removed. Check the adjustment.

48. Reinstall the center console.

49. Connect the engine compartment wiring:

    a. Battery positive cable from the starter.

    b. Black/white wire from the solenoid.

    c. transaxle ground cable.

50. With the ignition key turned OFF, connect the ground cable to the battery and the transaxle.

51. Unscrew the dipstick from the top of the transaxle housing and add 2.5 quarts of Dexron® ATF through the hole. Reinstall the dipstick.

NOTE: If the torque converter was replaced, the transaxle fill quantity is 5.7 quarts.

52. Start the engine, set the parking brake, then shift the transaxle through all gears three times. Check for proper control cable adjustment.

53. Let the engine reach operating temperature with the transaxle in Neutral or Park, then turn it off and check the fluid level.

54. Install and adjust the throttle control cable.

Legend/825S

1. Disconnect the negative and positive battery cables from the battery.

2. Disconnect the starter motor and ground cables.

3. Drain the transmission fluid from the transaxle.

4. Remove the two 6mm bolts located at the side of the battery base, and

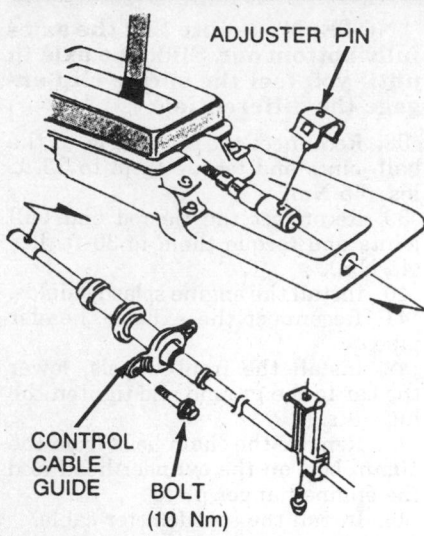

Control cable removal—Legend/825S

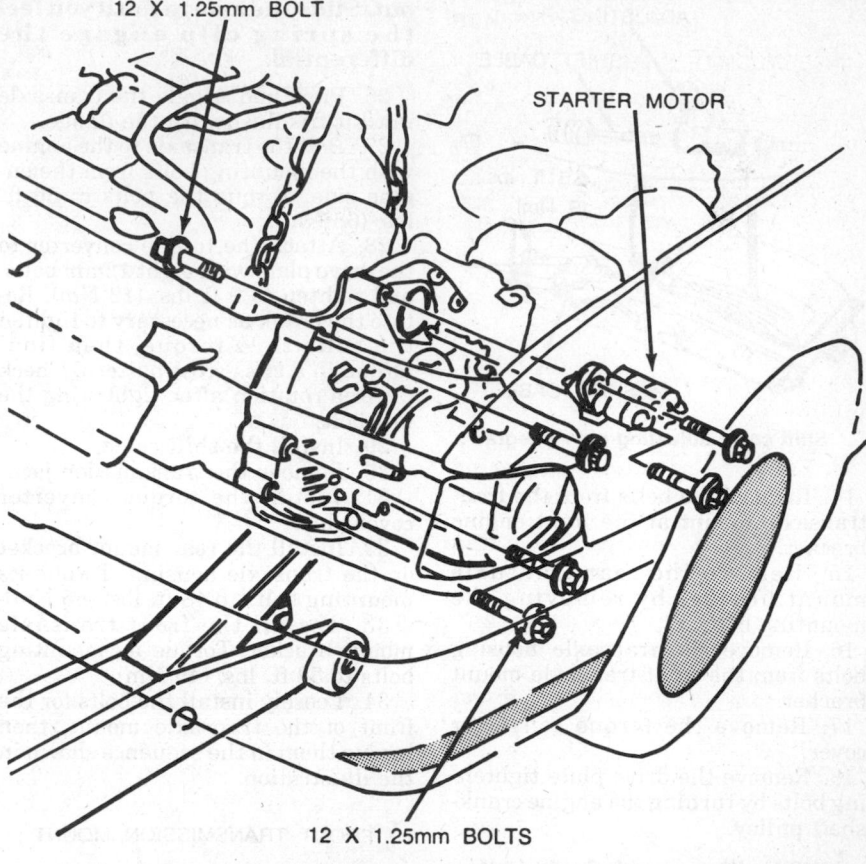

Automatic transaxle removal—Legend/825S

the intake hose band at the throttle body.

5. Remove the air cleaner assembly along with the intake hose.

6. Remove the speedometer gearbox complete with the power steering speed sensor hose.

7. Disconnect the control cable at the throttle body.

8. Disconnect the transaxle cooler hoses at the joint pipes. Turn the ends up to prevent the transmission fluid from flowing out.

9. Disconnect the lockup control solenoid valve wire connector (located near the oil cooler pipe bracket).

10. Remove the center console, pry off the adjuster pin, then disconnect the control cable.

11. Remove the control cable guide bolts, then pull out the cable assembly.

12. Remove the right and left axles, then remove the intermediate shaft.

13. Remove the torque converter case mounting bolts from the torque rod bracket.

14. Attach a chain hoist with two bolts, then raise the engine slightly to unload the mounts.

15. Remove the two front engine mount bolts from the transaxle housing.

16. While holding the locknut, turn off the radius rod.

17. Remove the center beam.

18. Remove the center stopper bracket from the transaxle.

19. Remove the torque converter cover.

20. Place a jack under the transaxle and raise the transaxle just enough to take the weight off the mounts.

21. Remove the two rear engine mount bolts from the transaxle.

22. Remove the plug, then remove

the drive plate bolts one at a time while rotating the crankshaft pulley.

23. Remove the starter mounting bolts and remove the starter.

24. Remove the remaining bolts attaching the transaxle housing to the engine.

25. Pull the transaxle away from the engine, then lower on the transmission jack.

To install:

26. Install the transaxle on a transmission jack and raise to engine level.

27. Secure the transaxle to the engine with the mounting bolts.

28. Install the starter motor.

29. Attach the torque converter to the drive plate with mounting bolts, and torque to 8 ft. lbs. (10 Nm). Rotate the crank as necessary to tighten the bolts to ½ torque, the to the final torque, in a criss-cross pattern. Check for free rotation after torquing the last bolt.

30. Install the transaxle to the rear engine mount bracket with two bolts.

31. Install the torque converter cover.

32. Install the center stopper bracket to the transaxle.

33. Install the center beam.

34. Connect the radius rod.

35. Install the front engine mount bolts an tighten to 29 ft. lbs. (40 Nm).

36. Remove the chain hoist from the engine.

37. Install the torque rod bracket and torque the bolts to 29 ft. lbs. (40 Nm).

NOTE: Always replace the torque rod bolts with new ones whenever they have been loosened or removed.

38. Remove the transmission jack.

39. Connect the intermediate shaft, then install the right and left axles.

40. Route the control cables to the center console through the cable guide and secure with the bolt.

41. Connect the control cable with the adjuster pin, then reinstall the center console.

42. Connect the lockup control solenoid valve wire connector.

43. Connect the cooler hoses to the joint pipes.

44. Connect the control cable on the throttle body side.

45. Install the speedometer gearbox.

46. Install the air cleaner assembly and the air intake hose.

47. Install the two 6mm bolts located at the side of the batter base, and tighten the intake hose band on the throttle body.

48. Refill the transaxle with ATF.

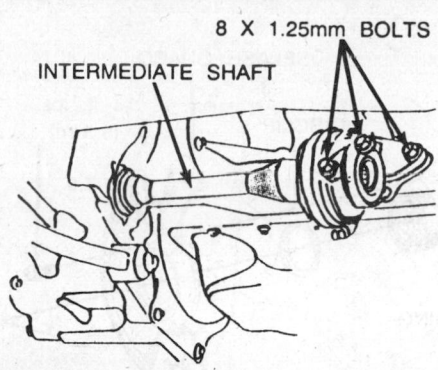

Intermediate shaft installation – Legend/825S

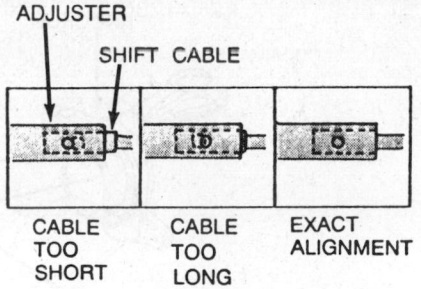

Shift cable adjustment

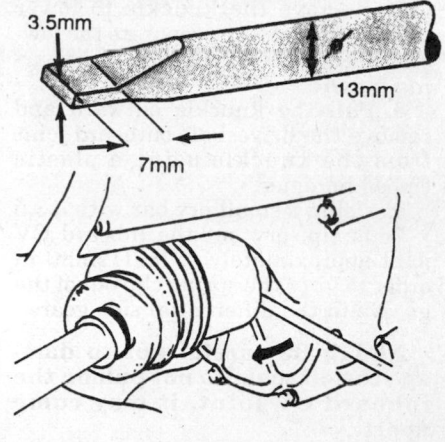

49. Connect the starter and ground cables.
50. Connect the battery cables.
51. Start the engine, set the parking brake, then shift the transaxle through all gears three times. Check for proper control cable adjustment.
52. Let the engine reach operating temperature with the transaxle in Neutral or Park, then turn it off and check the fluid level.

Shift Lever

ADJUSTMENT

1. Start the engine. Shift the transaxle to reverse to see if the reverse gear engages. If not, other problems are suspect.
2. Stop the engine. Remove the center console retaining screws, and pull away the console to expose the shift control cable and the adjuster.
3. Shift the transaxle to; "Reverse"—Integra, "Drive"—Legend/825S, then remove the lock pin from the cable adjuster.
4. Check that the hole in the adjuster is perfectly aligned with the hole in the shift cable.

NOTE: There are two holes in the end of the shift cable. They are positioned 90 degrees apart to allow cable adjustments in ¼ turn increments.

5. If they are not perfectly aligned, loosen the locknut on the shift cable and adjust as required.
6. Tighten the locknut, then install the lock pin on the adjuster.

NOTE: If you feel the lock pin binding as you reinstall it, the cable is still out of adjustment and must be readjusted.

7. Install the center console. Start the engine and check the shift lever in all gears.

DRIVE AXLE

Halfshaft

REMOVAL & INSTALLATION

The front halfshaft assembly consists of a sub-axle shaft and a halfshaft with two universal joints.

A constant velocity ball joint is used for both universal joints, which are factory packed with special grease and enclosed in sealed rubber boots. The outer joint cannot be disassembled except for removal of the boot.

Integra

1. Loosen, but do not remove, the front wheel spindle nut with a 32mm socket wrench.
2. Raise the front of the car and support it with jackstands.
3. Drain the transaxle.
4. Remove the wheel lug nuts and then the wheel.
5. Remove the spindle nut.
6. Using a floor jack to support the lower control arm, remove the lower arm ball joint cotter pin and nut.

——— CAUTION ———
Make sure that a floor jack is positioned securely under the lower control arm, at the ball joint. Otherwise, the lower control arm may jump suddenly away from the steering knuckle as the ball joint is removed.

7. Separate the ball joint from the front hub with a ball joint puller.
8. Slowly lower the floor jack to lower the control arm.
9. Using a small pry bar with a 3.5 x 7mm tip, pry out the inboard CV joint approximately ½ in. (12mm) in order to force the spring clip out of the groove in the differential side gears.

NOTE: Be careful not to damage the oil seal. Do not pull on the inboard CV joint, it may come apart.

10. Pull the halfshaft out of the differential or the intermediate shaft.

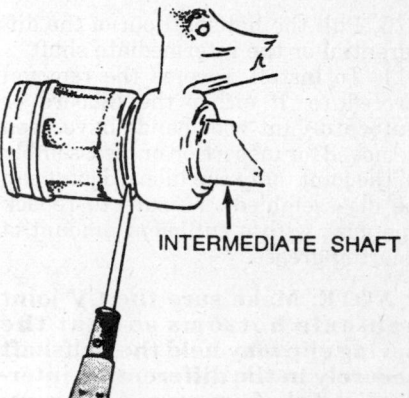

Halfshaft removal – Integra

11. To install, reverse the removal procedure. If either the inboard or outboard joint boot bands have been removed for inspection or disassembly of the joint (only the inboard joint can be disassembled), be sure to repack the joint with a sufficient amount of bearing grease.

NOTE: Make sure the CV joint sub-axle bottoms so that the spring clip may hold the halfshaft securely in the differential/ intermediate shaft groove. Always replace the spring clip with a new one!

Legend/825S

1. Loosen the front wheel lug nuts.
2. Raise the front of the car and support it with jackstands.
3. Drain the transaxle.

NOTE: It is not necessary to drain the transaxle when the right halfshaft is removed.

4. Remove the wheel lug nuts and then the wheel.
5. Raise the locking tab on the spindle nut and remove it with a 36mm socket wrench.
6. Remove the damper fork bolt and the damper pinch bolt. Remove the damper fork.

7. Remove the knuckle to lower arm castle nut, then separate the lower arm from the knuckle using a bearing puller.

8. Pull the knuckle outward and remove the driveshaft outboard joint from the knuckle using a plastic tipped hammer.

9. Using a small pry bar with a 3.5 x 7mm tip, pry out the inboard CV joint approximately ½ in. (12mm) in order to force the spring clip out of the groove in the differential side gears.

NOTE: Be careful not to damage the oil seal. Do not pull on the inboard CV joint, it may come apart.

10. Pull the halfshaft out of the differential or the intermediate shaft.

11. To install, reverse the removal procedure. If either the inboard or outboard joint boot bands have been removed for inspection or disassembly of the joint (only the inboard joint can be disassembled), be sure to repack the joint with a sufficient amount of bearing grease.

NOTE: Make sure the CV joint sub-axle bottoms so that the spring clip may hold the halfshaft securely in the differential/ intermediate shaft groove. Always replace the spring clip with a new one!

Intermediate Shaft

REMOVAL & INSTALLATION

1. Drain the oil from the transaxle.
2. Remove the three 10mm bolts (Integra), three 8mm and one 10mm bolt (Legend/825S).
3. Lower the bearing support close to the steering gearbox and remove the intermediate shaft from the differential.

NOTE: To avoid damage to the differential oil seal, hold the intermediate shaft horizontal until it clears the differential.

4. To install, reverse the removal procedure.

CV-JOINT OVERHAUL

For all overhaul procedures, please refer to "CV-Joint Overhaul" in the Unit Repair Section.

Front Axle Hub and Bearings

REMOVAL & INSTALLATION

NOTE: The following proce-

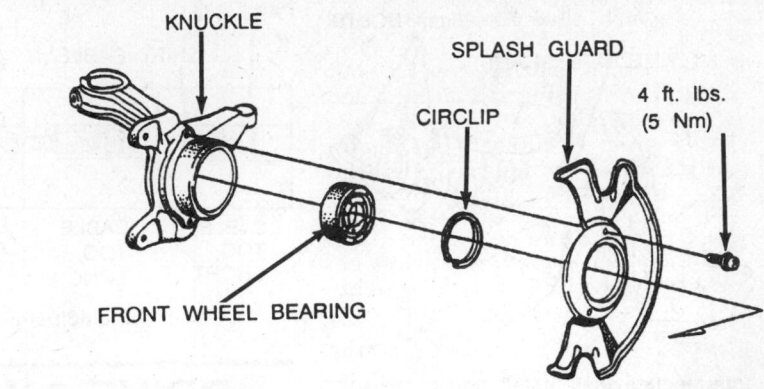

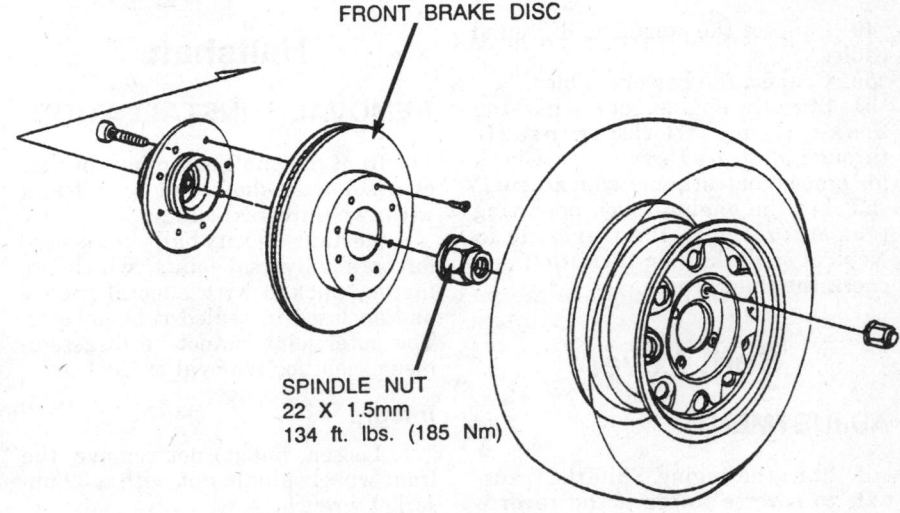

Front steering knuckle, hub and bearing—Integra

dures for hub and wheel bearing removal and installation necessitate the use of many special tools and a hydraulic press. **Do not attempt this procedure without these special tools.**

Integra

1. Pry the lock tab away from the spindle, then loosen the nut. Slightly loosen the lug nuts.
2. Raise the front of the car and support it with jackstands. Remove the front wheel and spindle nut.
3. Remove the bolts retaining the brake caliper and remove the caliper from the knuckle. Do not let the caliper hang by the brake hose, support it with a length of wire.
4. Remove the disc brake rotor retaining screws (if so equipped). Screw two 8 x 1.25 x 12mm bolts into the disc brake removal holes, and turn the bolts to push the rotor away from the hub.

NOTE: Only turn each bolt two turns at a time to prevent cocking the disc excessively.

5. Remove the tie rod from the knuckle using a tie rod end removal tool. Use care not to damage the ball joint seals.
6. Use a floor jack to support the lower control arm, then remove the cotter pin from the lower arm ball joint and remove the castle nut.

— CAUTION —
Be sure to place the jack securely beneath the lower control arm at the ball joint. Otherwise, the tension from the torsion bar may cause the arm to suddenly jump away from the steering knuckle as the ball joint is removed.

7. Remove the lower arm from the knuckle using the ball joint remover.
8. Loosen the pinch bolt which retains the shock in the knuckle. Tap the top of the knuckle with a hammer and slide it off the shock.
9. Remove the knuckle and hub, if still attached, by sliding the assembly off of the halfshaft.
10. Remove the hub from the knuckle using special tools and a hydraulic press.
Bearing Removal:

11. Remove the splash guard and the snapring.

12. Press the bearing outer race out of the knuckle using special tools and a hydraulic press.

13. Remove the outboard bearing inner race from the hub using special tools and a bearing puller.

NOTE: Whenever the wheel bearings are removed, always replace them with a new set of bearings and an outer dust seal.

14. Clean all old grease from the halfshaft and spindles on the car.

15. Remove the old grease from the hub and knuckle and thoroughly dry and wipe clean all components.

16. To install the bearings, press the bearing outer race into the knuckle using the special tools as used above, plus the installing base tool.

17. Install the snapring, then install the splash guard.

18. Place the hub in the special tool fixture, then set the knuckle in position on the press and apply downward pressure.

19. The remaining step are the reverse of the removal procedure. Use a new spindle nut, and stake after torquing.

Legend/825S

1. Pry the lock tab away from the spindle, then loosen the 36mm nut. Slightly loosen the lug nuts.

2. Raise the front of the car and support it with jackstands. Remove the front wheel and spindle nut.

3. Remove the bolts retaining the brake caliper and remove the caliper from the knuckle. Do not let the caliper hang by the brake hose, support it with a length of wire.

4. Remove the disc brake rotor retaining screws (if so equipped). Screw two 8 x 1.25 x 12mm bolts into the disc brake removal holes, and turn the bolts to push the rotor away from the hub.

NOTE: Only turn each bolt two turns at a time to prevent cocking the disc excessively.

5. Remove the tie rod from the knuckle using a tie rod end removal tool. Use care not to damage the ball joint seals.

6. Remove the cotter pin from the lower arm ball joint and remove the castle nut.

7. Remove the lower arm from the knuckle using the ball joint remover.

8. Remove the cotter pin from the upper arm ball joint and remove the castle nut.

9. Remove the upper arm from the knuckle using the ball joint remover.

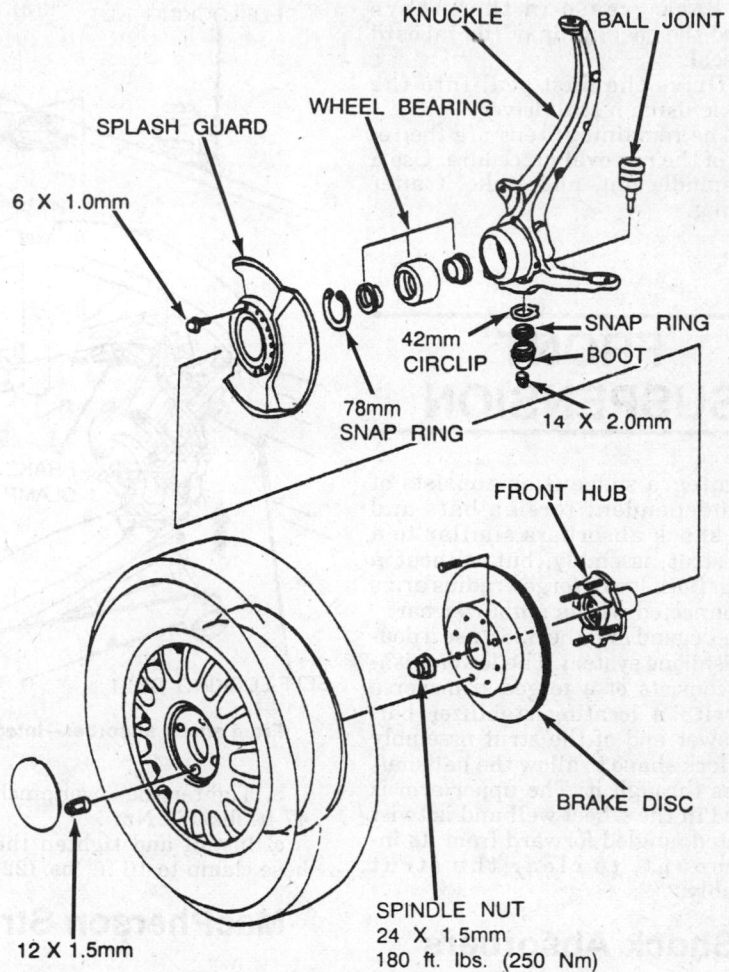

Front steering knuckle, hub and bearing—Legend/825S

10. Remove the knuckle and hub by sliding the assembly off of the halfshaft.

11. Remove the two back splash guard screws from the knuckle.

12. Remove the hub from the knuckle using special tools and a hydraulic press.

Bearing Removal:

13. Remove the splash guard, dust seal and the snapring, then remove the outer bearing race.

14. Turn the knuckle over and remove the inboard dust seal, bearing and inner race and bearing.

15. Press the bearing outer race out of the knuckle using special tools and a hydraulic press.

16. Remove the outboard bearing inner race from the hub using special tools and a bearing puller.

17. Remove the outboard dust seal from the hub.

NOTE: Whenever the wheel bearings are removed, always replace with a new set of bearings and outer dust seal.

18. Clean all old grease from the halfshaft spindles on the car.

19. Remove all old grease from the hub and knuckle and thoroughly dry and wipe clean all components.

20. To install the bearings, press the bearing outer race into the knuckle using the special tools used as above, plus the installing base tool.

21. Install the outboard ball bearing and its inner race in the knuckle.

22. Install the snapring. Pack grease in the groove around the sealing lip of the outboard grease dust seal.

23. Drive the outboard grease seal into the knuckle, using a seal driver and hammer, until it is flush with the knuckle surface.

24. Install the splash guard, then turn the knuckle upside down and install the inboard ball bearing and its inner race.

25. Place the hub in the special tool fixture, then set the knuckle in position on the press and apply downward pressure.

26. Pack grease in the groove around the sealing lip of the inboard dust seal.

27. Drive the dust seal into the knuckle using a seal driver.

28. The remaining steps are the reverse of the removal procedure. Use a new spindle nut, and stake it after torquing.

FRONT SUSPENSION

The Integra suspension consists of two independent torsion bars and front shock absorbers similar to a front strut assembly, but without a spring. Both lower forged radius arms are connected with a stabilizer bar.

The Legend and the 825S use a double wishbone system. The lower wishbone consists of a forged transverse link with a locating stabilizer bar. The lower end of the strut assembly has a fork shape to allow the halfshaft to pass through it. The upper arm is located in the wheel well and is twist mounted, angled forward from its inner mount, to clear the strut assembly.

Shock Absorbers

REMOVAL & INSTALLATION

Integra

1. Raise the front of the car and support it on jackstands. Remove the front wheels.
2. Remove the brake hose clamp bolt.
3. Place a floor jack beneath the lower control arm to support it.
4. Remove the lower shock retaining bolt from the steering knuckle, then slowly lower the jack.

— CAUTION —

Be sure the jack is positioned securely beneath the lower control arm at the ball joint. Otherwise, the tension from the torsion bar may cause the lower control arm to suddenly jump away from the shock absorber as the pinch bolt is removed.

5. Compress the shock absorber by hand, then remove the two upper lock nuts and remove from the car.
6. Installation is the reverse of the removal procedure, taking note of the following:

    a. Use new self locking nuts on the top of the shock assembly and torque to 28 ft. lbs. (39 Nm).

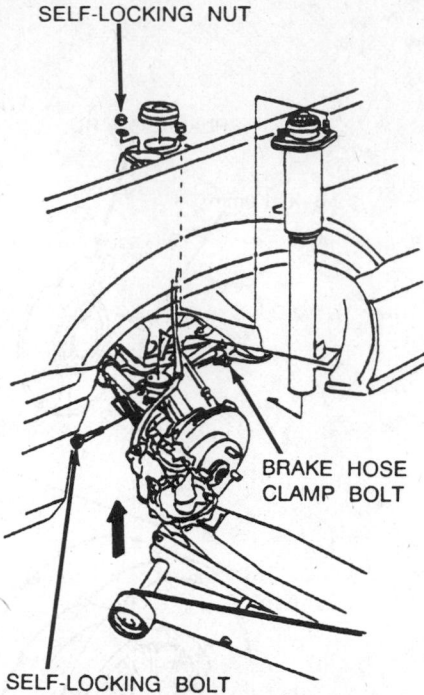

SELF-LOCKING NUT

BRAKE HOSE CLAMP BOLT

SELF-LOCKING BOLT

Front shock absorber—Integra

    b. Tighten the lower pinch bolt to 47 ft. lbs. (65 Nm).

    c. Install and tighten the brake hose clamp to 16 ft. lbs. (22 Nm).

MacPherson Strut

INSPECTION

1. Check for wear or damage to the bushings and needle bearings.
2. Check for oil leaks from the struts.
3. Check all rubber parts for wear or damage.
4. Bounce the car to check shock absorber effectiveness. The car should continue to bounce for no more than two cycles.

REMOVAL & INSTALLATION

Legend/825S

1. Raise the front of the car and support it on jackstands. Remove the front wheels.
2. Remove the shock absorber locking bolt.
3. Remove the shock fork bolt and remove the shock fork.
4. Remove the shock absorber assembly.
5. Installation is the reverse of the removal procedure, taking note of the following:

    a. Align the shock absorber aligning tab with the slot in the shock absorber fork.

    b. The mounting base bolt should be tightened with the weight of the car placed on the shock.

    c. Torque the upper mounting bolts to 29 ft. lbs. (39 Nm), the shock locking bolt to 32 ft. lbs. (44 Nm), and the shock fork bolt to 47 ft. lbs. (65 Nm).

OVERHAUL

For all spring and shock absorber removal and installation procedures, and all strut overhaul procedures, please refer to "Strut Overhaul" in the Unit Repair section.

Torsion Bar Assembly

REMOVAL & INSTALLATION

Integra

1. Raise the front of the car and support it on jackstands.
2. Remove the height adjusting nut and the torque tube holder.
3. Remove the 30mm circlip.
4. Remove the torsion bar cap, then remove the torsion bar clip by tapping the bar out of the torque tube.

NOTE: The torsion bar will slide easier if you move the lower arm up and down.

5. Tap the torsion bar backward, out of the torque tube and remove the torque tube.
6. Install a new seal onto the torque tube. Coat the torque tube seal and torque with grease, then install them on the rear beam.
7. Grease the ends of the torsion bar and insert into the torque tube from the back.
8. Align the projection on the torque tube splines with the cutout in the torsion bar splines and insert the torsion bar approximately 0.394 in. (10mm).

NOTE: The torsion bar will slide easier if the lower arm is moved up and down.

9. Install the torsion bar clip and cap, then install the 30mm circlip and the torque tube cap.

NOTE: Push the torsion bar to the front so there is no clearance between the torque tube and the 30mm circlip.

10. Coat the cap bushing with grease and install it on the torque tube. Install the torque tube holder.
11. Temporarily tighten the height adjusting nut.

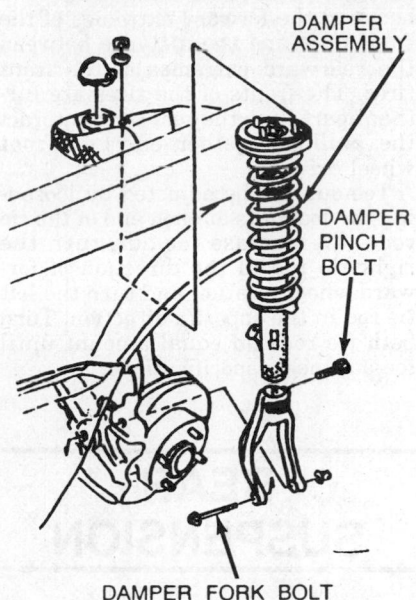

Front shock absorber—Legend/825S

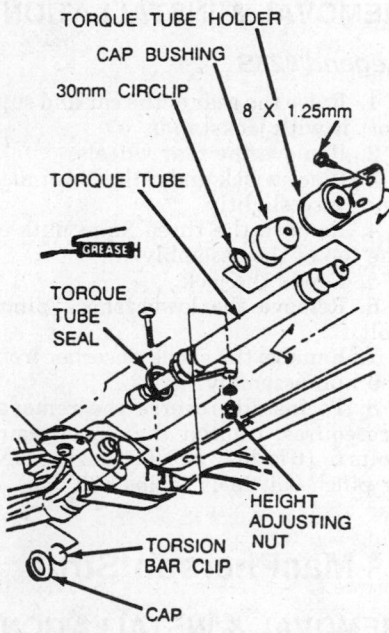

Torsion bar assembly—Integra

12. Remove the jackstands and lower the car to the ground. Adjust the torsion bar spring height.

TORSION BAR ADJUSTMENT

1. Measure the torsion bar spring height between the ground and the highest point of the wheel arch. The measurement should be 25.7 in. (653mm).
2. If the spring height does not meet the specification above, make the following adjustment.
    a. Raise the front wheels off the ground.

Torsion bar adjustment—Integra

b. Adjust the spring height by turning the height adjusting nut. Tightening the nut raises the height, and loosening the nut lowers the height.

NOTE: The height varies 5mm per turn of the adjusting nut.

c. Lower the front wheels to the ground, then bounce the car up and down several times and recheck the spring height to see if it is within specification.

Lower Ball Joints

INSPECTION

Check ball joint play as follows:
    a. Raise the front of the car and support it with jackstands.
    b. Clamp a dial indicator onto the lower control arm and place the indicator tip on the knuckle, near the ball joint.
    c. Place a pry bar between the lower control arm and the knuckle. Replace the lower control arm if the play exceeds 0.5mm.

REMOVAL & INSTALLATION

Integra

If the ball joint play exceeds 0.05mm the ball joint and lower radius arm must be replaced as an assembly.

Legend/825S

NOTE: This procedure is performed after the removal of the steering knuckle and requires the use of the following special tools or their equivalent: A Accura part no. 07GAF–SD40330 Ball Joint Removal Base, 07GAF–SD40320 Ball Joint Installation Base, and 07GAG–SD40700 Clip Guide Tool.

1. Pry the snapring off and remove the boot.
2. Pry the snapring out of the groove in the ball joint.

3. Install the ball joint removal tool with the large end facing out and tighten the ball joint nut.
4. Position the ball joint removal tool base on the ball joint and set the assembly in a large vise. Press the ball joint out of the steering knuckle.
5. Position the new ball joint into the hole of the steering knuckle.
6. Install the ball joint installer tool with the small end facing out.
7. Position the ball joint installation base tool on the ball joint and set the assembly in a large vise. Press the ball joint into the steering knuckle.
8. Seat the snapring in the groove of the ball joint.
9. Install the boot and snapring using the clip guide tool.

Radius Arm

REMOVAL & INSTALLATION

Integra

1. Raise the front of the car off the ground and support it on jackstands. Remove the front wheels.
2. Place a floor jack beneath the lower control arm, then remove the ball joint cotter pin and nut.

— **CAUTION** —
Be sure to place the jack securely beneath the lower control arm at the ball joint. Otherwise, the tension from the torsion bar may cause the arm to suddenly jump away from the steering knuckle as the ball joint is removed.

3. Using a ball joint remover, remove then ball joint from the steering knuckle.
4. Remove the radius arm locking nuts and the stabilizer locking nut, then separate the radius arm from the stabilizer bar.
5. Remove the lower arm bolts and remove the radius arm by pulling it down and then forward.
6. Installation is the reverse of the removal procedure. Tighten all the rubber bushings and dampered parts only after the car is placed back on the ground.

Lower Control Arm

REMOVAL & INSTALLATION

Legend

1. Raise the front of the car and support it with jackstands. Remove the front wheels.
2. Disconnect the lower arm ball joint. Be careful not to damage the seal.
3. Remove the stabilizer bar re-

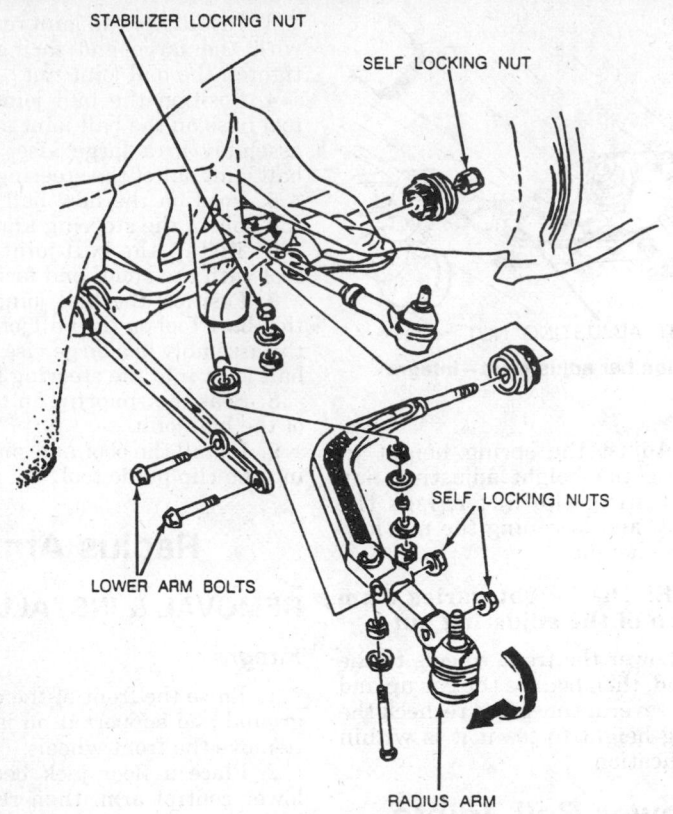

STABILIZER LOCKING NUT

SELF LOCKING NUT

SELF LOCKING NUTS

LOWER ARM BOLTS

RADIUS ARM

Radius arm assembly—Integra

taining brackets, starting with the center brackets.

4. Remove the lower arm pivot bolt.

5. Disconnect the radius rod and remove the lower arm.

6. To install, reverse the removal procedure. Be sure to tighten the components to their proper torque.

Front End Alignment

CASTER & CAMBER ADJUSTMENT

Integra

Caster and camber cannot be adjusted on the Integra. If caster, camber or kingpin angle is incorrect or front end parts are damaged or worn, they must be replaced.

Legend

NOTE: Wheel alignment adjustments must be performed in the following order: camber, caster and then toe-in.

The camber adjustment can be made by loosening the two nuts on the upper control arm and sliding the ball joint until the camber meets specifications. The caster adjustment can be made by loosening the 16mm nuts on

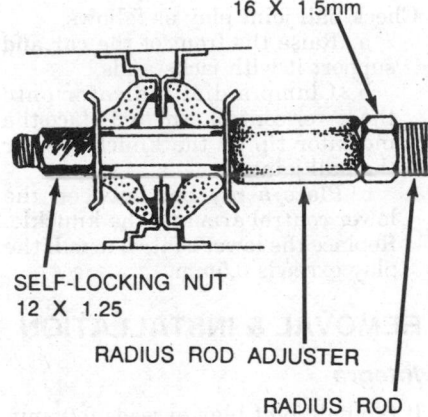

16 X 1.5mm

SELF-LOCKING NUT
12 X 1.25

RADIUS ROD ADJUSTER

RADIUS ROD

Caster adjustment—Legend/825S

the front beam radius rods and then turning the locknut to make the adjustment. Turning the nut clockwise decreases the caster and turning it counterclockwise increases the caster. After adjusting it to specifications, hold the nylon locknut and lightly tighten the adjuster. Tighten the 16mm nut to 58 ft. lbs. (80 Nm), then tighten the locknut to 32 ft. lbs. (44 Nm) while holding the 16mm nut.

TOE-OUT ADJUSTMENT

Toe is the difference of the distance between the forward extremes of the front tires and the distance between the rearward extremes of the front tires. The fronts of the tires are further apart than the rear to counteract the pulling together effect of front wheel drive.

Toe-out can be adjusted by loosening the locknuts at each end of the tie rods. To increase toe-out, turn the right tie rod in the direction of forward wheel rotation and turn the left tie rod in the opposite direction. Turn both tie rods an equal amount until toe-out meets specifications.

REAR SUSPENSION

Shock Absorber

REMOVAL & INSTALLATION

Legend/825S

1. Raise the rear of the car and support it with jackstands.
2. Remove the rear wheels.
3. Place a jack under the lower arm and raise slightly.
4. Remove the three 8mm nuts at the top of the assembly.
5. Lower the jack.
6. Remove the lower shock pinch bolt.
7. Remove the shock absorber from the hub assembly.
8. To install, reverse the removal procedures, tighten the upper 8mm bolts to 16 ft. lbs. (22 Nm) and the lower pinch bolt to 47 ft. lbs. (65 Nm).

MacPherson Strut

REMOVAL & INSTALLATION

Integra

1. Raise the rear of the car and support it with jackstands.
2. Remove the rear wheels.
3. Place a jack under the rear axle beam.
4. Remove the shock maintenance lid and the self locking nut.
5. Lower the jack gradually and remove the self-locking bolt, rear spring, and spring seat.

To install:

6. Fit the upper spring seat into the frame.
7. Install the shock protector on the shock absorber assembly, and install the dust cover, shock mounting collar,

and rear spring, then temporarily tighten the shock at the axle beam.

8. Fit the inner shock mount rubber into the frame.

9. Jack up the axle beam so that the damper shaft fits into the hole in the frame.

10. Install the outer shock mount rubber and washer and then tighten the self-locking nut.

11. Install the shock maintenance lid.

12. Tighten the shock on the rear axle beam with the weight of the vehicle placed on the ground.

Springs

REMOVAL & INSTALLATION

Legend/825S

1. Raise the rear of the car and support it with jackstands.

2. Place a floor jack under the lower arm.

3. Pull out the hub carrier lower bolt.

4. Loosen the lower arm outside bolt.

5. Pull out the lower arm inside bolt.

6. Lower the jack gradually and remove the rear spring.

7. To install, reverse the removal procedures. Install the rear spring with the lower end of the spring outside. Tighten the nuts and bolts with the weight of the vehicle on the ground.

Rear Wheel Hub Bearings

REMOVAL & INSTALLATION

Legend

1. Slightly loosen the rear lug nuts. Raise the car and support safely on jackstands.

2. Release the parking brake. Remove the rear wheels and the brake calipers.

3. Remove the brake disc.

4. Remove the rear bearing hub cap and nut.

5. Pull the hub unit off of the spindle.

6. Installation is the reverse order of removal. Tighten the new spindle nut to 134 ft. lbs. (185 Nm), then stake the nut.

Legend/825S

1. Slightly loosen the rear lug nuts. Raise the car and support it safely on jackstands.

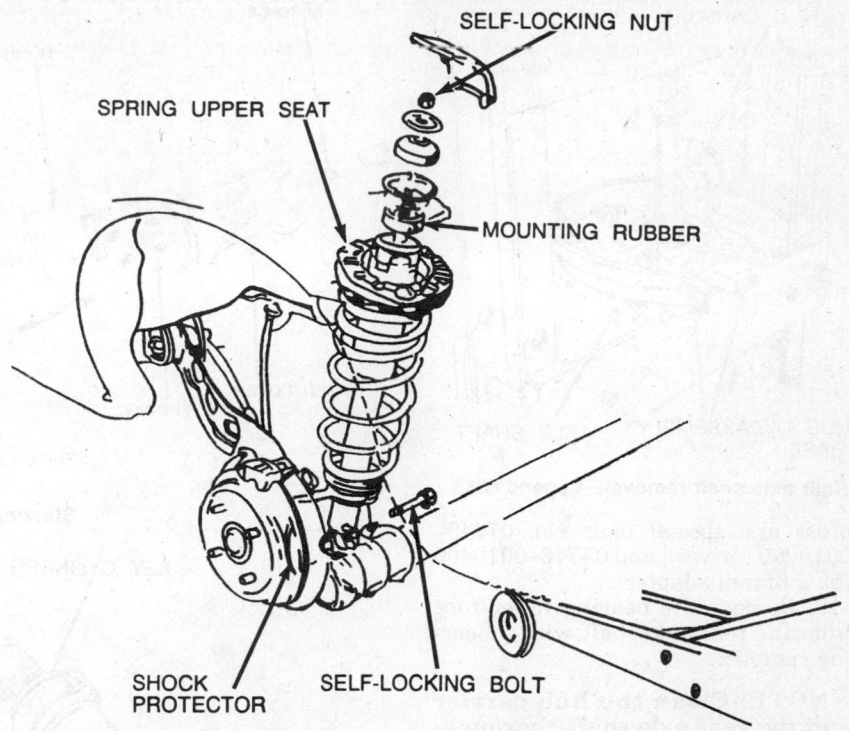

Rear strut assembly-Integra

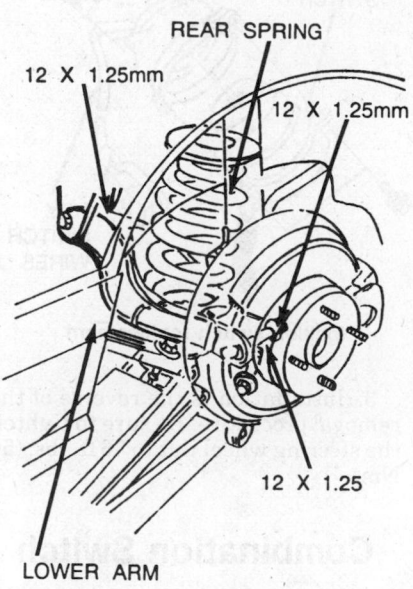

Spring removal—Legend/825S

2. Release the parking brake. Remove the rear wheels.

3. Remove the bolts retaining the brake caliper and remove the caliper from the knuckle. Do not let the caliper hang by the brake hose; support it with a length of wire.

4. Remove the rear bearing hub cap.

5. Pry the spindle nut lock tab away from the axle shaft.

6. Remove the spindle nut using a 36mm socket.

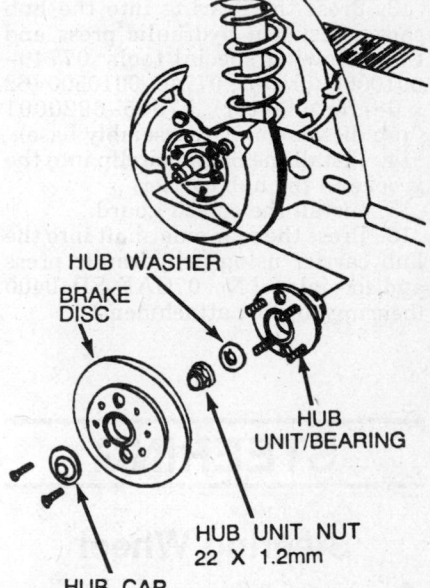

Rear hub/bearing assembly—Integra

7. Remove the splash guard bolts from the hub carrier.

8. Separate the rear axle shaft from the hub carrier using a hydraulic press and special tool No. 07GAF–SD40700 (hub disassembly/ reassembly base)

9. Remove the splash guard.

10. Remove the 68mm circlip.

11. Remove the bearing from the rear hub carrier with a hydraulic

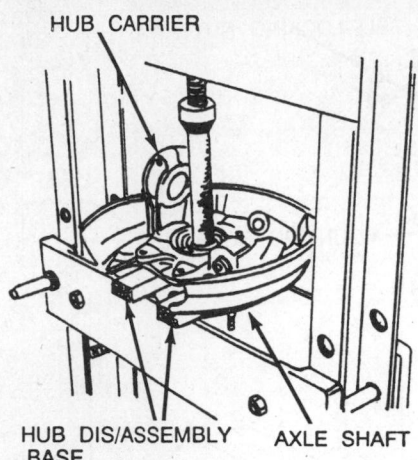

Rear axle shaft removal—Legend/825S

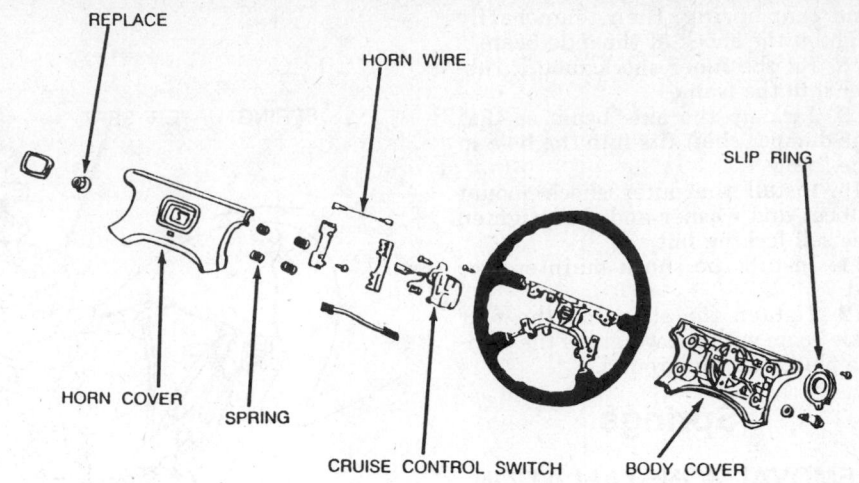

Steering wheel—typical

press and special tools No. 07749–0010000 (driver), and 07746–0010400 (52 x 55mm adapter).

12. Remove the bearing inner race from the rear axle shaft with a bearing remover.

NOTE: Clean the hub carrier and the rear axle shaft thoroughly before reassembly. Always replace the bearing with a new one after removal.

13. Press the bearing into the hub carrier using a hydraulic press and the following special tools; 07749–0010000 (driver), 07746–0010500 (62 x 68mm adapter), 07965–6920001 (hub dissassembly/reassembly base).

14. Install the 68mm circlip into the groove in the hub carrier.

15. Install the splash guard.

16. Press the rear axle shaft into the hub carrier using a hydraulic press and special tool No. 07GAF–SD40400 (bearing support attachment)

STEERING

Steering Wheel

REMOVAL & INSTALLATION

1. Remove the steering wheel pad by lifting it off.

2. Remove the steering wheel retaining nut. Gently hit the backside of each of the steering wheel spokes with equal force from the palms of your hands.

——— **CAUTION** ———
Avoid hitting the wheel or the shaft with excessive force. Damage to the shaft could result.

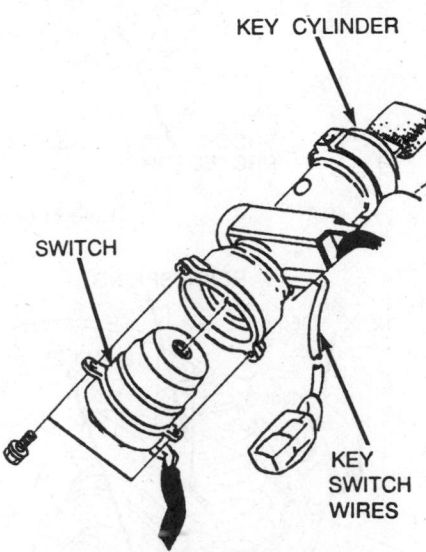

Ignition switch replacement

3. Installation is the reverse of the removal procedure. Be sure to tighten the steering wheel nut to 36 ft. lbs. (50 Nm).

Combination Switch

REMOVAL & INSTALLATION

1. Remove the steering wheel.

2. Disconnect the column wiring harness and coupler.

——— **CAUTION** ———
Be careful not to damage the steering column or shaft.

3. Remove the upper and lower column covers.

4. On models so equipped, remove the cruise control slip ring.

5. Remove the turn signal cancelling sleeve.

6. Remove the switch retaining screws, then remove the switch.

7. To assemble and install, reverse the above procedure.

Ignition Lock/Switch

REMOVAL & INSTALLATION

Lock Assembly

1. Remove the steering column housing lower cover.

2. Disconnect the ignition switch wiring at the couplers.

3. The ignition switch assembly is held onto the column by two shear bolts. Remove these bolts, using a drill, to separate and remove the ignition switch.

4. To install, reverse the removal procedure. You will have to replace the shear bolts with new ones.

Switch assembly

1. Remove the steering column lower cover.

2. Disconnect the electrical connector at the switch.

3. Insert the key and turn it to the "0" position.

4. Remove the two switch retaining screws, then remove the switch (base) from the rest of the switch.

Power Steering Gear

REMOVAL & INSTALLATION

Integra

1. Remove the steering joint cover, remove the bolts in the steering shaft connector, then pull the connector up off the pinion shaft seal.

2. Raise the front of the car and support it safely on jackstands.

3. Remove the front wheels.

4. Remove the cotter pins, and unscrew the tie rod end ball joint nuts halfway.

5. Break the tie rod ball joint nuts loose using a tie rod end removal tool.

6. Remove the nuts and lift the tie rod ends out of the steering knuckles.

7. On manual transaxle models;

a. Remove the shift extension from the transaxle case.

b. Slide the pin retainer out of the way, then drive out the spring pin with a punch and disconnect the shift control rod.

8. On automatic transaxle models;

a. Remove the shift cable guide from the floor and pull the shift cable down by hand.

9. Drain the power steering fluid.

10. Remove the front exhaust pipe. Clean the gasket areas thoroughly.

11. Disconnect the three fluid lines from the valve body.

12. Remove the gearbox mounting bolts.

13. Drop the gearbox far enough so that the end of the pinion shaft comes out of its hole in the frame channel, then rotate it forward until the shaft is pointing to the rear. Slide the gearbox to the right until the tie rod clears the rear beam, then drop it down and out of the car to the left.

14. To install reverse the removal procedures. Fill the reservoir with new power steering fluid. Start the engine and let it run at fast idle, then turn the steering wheel from lock-to-lock several times to bleed the air out. Check the fluid again and add if necessary. Check the system for leaks.

Legend/825S

1. Remove the steering joint cover, and disconnect the steering shaft from the gearbox.

2. Drain the power steering fluid.

3. Remove the gearbox shield.

4. Using cleaning solvent and a brush, clean the control unit, its lines, and the end of the gearbox. Blow dry with compressed air if possible.

5. Raise the front of the car and support it safely on jackstands.

6. Remove the front wheels.

7. Remove the cotter pins, and unscrew the tie rod end ball joint nuts halfway.

8. Break the tie rod ball joint nuts loose using a tie rod end removal tool.

9. Remove the nuts and lift the tie rod ends out of the steering knuckles.

10. On manual transaxle models;

a. Remove the shift extension from the transaxle case.

b. Disconnect the gearshift rod from the transaxle case by removing the 8mm spring pin.

11. On automatic transaxle models;

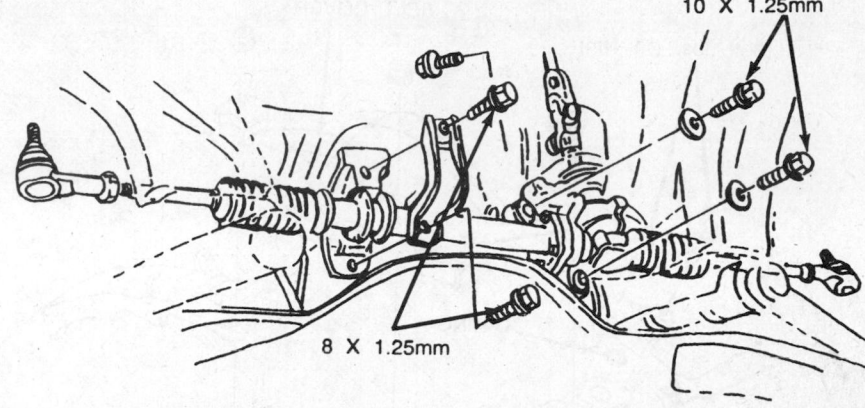

Gearbox mounting—Integra

a. Remove the shift control cable from the clamp.

12. Remove the center beam bolts and the center beam.

NOTE: Replace the self-locking nuts retaining the center beam if worn.

13. Disconnect the exhaust header pipe at the manifold. Replace the exhaust gasket and the self-locking nuts when you reinstall the pipe.

14. Remove the header pipe joint nuts and remove the header pipe.

15. Disconnect the four lines from the control unit.

16. Slide the tie rod all the way to the right side.

17. Slide the gear box right so that the left tie rod clears the bottom of the rear beam, then remove the gearbox.

18. To install reverse the removal procedures. Fill the reservoir with new power steering fluid. Start the engine and let it run at fast idle, then turn the steering wheel from lock-to-lock several times to bled the air out. Check the fluid again and add if necessary. Check the system for leaks.

ADJUSTMENT

Integra

1. Loosen the locknut on the rack guide screw with special tool No. 07916–SA50001 or equivalent.

2. Tighten the guide screw until it compresses the spring against the guide; then loosen it, and tighten it to about 3 ft. lbs. (4 Nm) and back it off about 25 degrees.

3. Tighten the locknut to about 18 ft. lbs. (25 Nm) while preventing the guide screw from moving.

Legend/825S

1. Loosen the locknut on the rack guide screw with special tool No. 07916–SA50001 or equivalent.

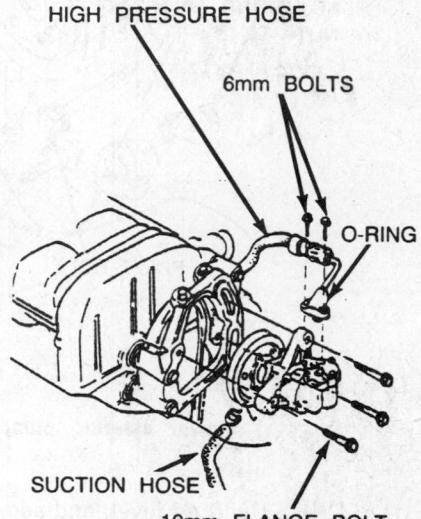

Power steering pump mounting—Integra

2. Tighten the guide screw until it compresses the spring against the guide; then loosen it, and retighten it to about 2 ft. lbs. (3 Nm) and back it off about 20 degrees.

3. Tighten the locknut to about 18 ft. lbs. (25 Nm) while preventing the guide screw from moving.

Power Steering Pump

REMOVAL & INSTALLATION

Integra

1. Disconnect the hoses from the reservoir.

2. Remove the three 10mm flange bolts, remove the belt from the pulley, then remove the pump assembly.

3. To install reverse the removal procedures. Be sure to observe the following:

a. Connect the hoses tightly.

b. Adjust the belt tension.

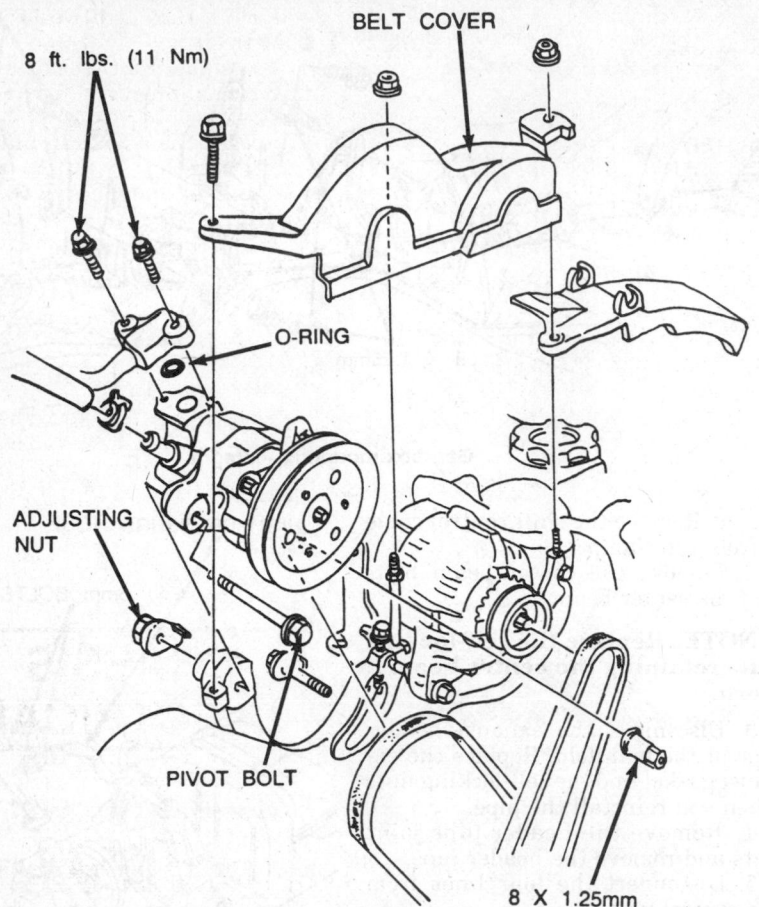

8 ft. lbs. (11 Nm)

BELT COVER

O-RING

ADJUSTING NUT

PIVOT BOLT

8 X 1.25mm

Power steering pump mounting—Legend/825S

c. Check the fluid level, and add if necessary.
d. Bleed the air from the system.

Legend/825S

1. Remove the belt cover.
2. Drain the fluid from the system.
3. Disconnect the inlet and outlet hoses from the pump and plug them.
4. Remove the belt by loosening the pump pivot bolt and adjusting nut.
5. Remove the bolt and nut, then remove the pump assembly.
6. To install reverse the removal procedures. Be sure to observe the following:
   a. Fill the reservoir with new fluid to the "Upper Level" on the reservoir.
   b. Connect the hoses tightly.
   c. Adjust the belt tension.
   d. Bleed the air from the system.
   e. Check the fluid level, and add if necessary.

BELT ADJUSTMENT

1. Loosen the bolt on the adjuster arm.
2. Move the pump toward or away from the engine, until the belt can be depressed approximately $3/4-15/16$ in. (19–24mm) at the midpoint between the two pulleys under moderate thumb pressure. If the tension adjustment is being made on a new belt, the deflection should only be about 11mm, to allow for the initial stretching of the belt.
3. Tighten the bolt and recheck the adjustment.

Tie Rod Ends

REMOVAL & INSTALLATION

1. Raise the front of the car and support it with jackstands. Remove the front wheels.
2. Use a ball joint remover to remove the tie rod from the knuckle.
3. Disconnect the air tube at the dust seal joint. Remove the tie rod dust seal bellows clamps and move the rubber bellows on the tie rod rack joints.
4. Straighten the tie rod lockwasher tabs at the tie rod-to-rack joint and remove the tie rod by turning it with a wrench.

5. To install, reverse the removal procedure. Always use a new tie rod lockwasher during reassembly. Fit the locating lugs into the slots on the rack and bend the outer edge of the washer over the flat part of the rod, after the tie rod nut has been properly tightened.

BRAKES

For all brake system repair and service procedures not detailed below, please refer to "Brakes" in the Unit Repair section.

Master Cylinder

REMOVAL & INSTALLATION

— CAUTION —

Before removing the master cylinder, cover the body surfaces with fender covers and rags to prevent damage to painted surfaces by brake fluid.

1. Disconnect and plug the brake lines at the master cylinder.
2. Remove the master cylinder-to-vacuum booster attaching bolts and remove the master cylinder from the car.
3. To install, reverse the removal procedure. Before operating the car, you must bleed the brake system.

Power Brake Booster

INSPECTION

A preliminary check of the vacuum booster can be made as follows:
   a. Depress the brake pedal several times using normal pressure. Make sure that the pedal height does not vary.
   b. Hold the pedal in the depressed position and start the engine. The pedal should drop slightly.
   c. Hold the pedal in the above position and stop the engine. The pedal should stay in the depressed position for approximately 30 seconds.
   d. If the pedal does not drop when the engine is started or rises after the engine is stopped, the booster is not functioning properly.

REMOVAL & INSTALLATION

1. Disconnect the vacuum hose at the booster.

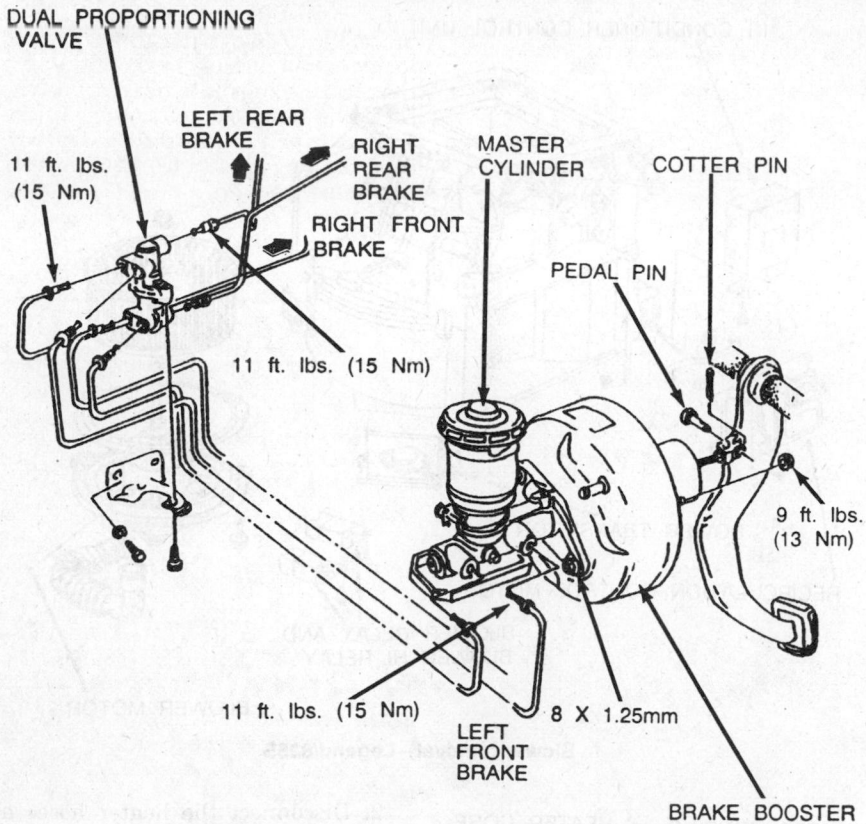

Master cylinder and booster assembly—typical

d. Check the rear brake adjustment.

1. Block the front wheels and jack up the rear of the car. Support the car on jackstands.

2. Loosen the adjusting nut, located in the console. Check that the caliper lever is in contact with the pin at both the right and left rear calipers.

3. Pull the parking brake lever up one notch.

4. Tighten the adjusting nut until the rear brakes drag slightly.

5. Release the brake lever and check that the rear brakes do not drag.

6. The rear brakes should be locked when the hand brake lever is pulled; (4–8 notches Integra), (7–11 notches Legend/825S).

CHASSIS ELECTRICAL

Heater Blower

REMOVAL & INSTALLATION

Integra

WITHOUT AIR CONDITIONING

1. Remove the glove box.
2. Remove the frame to the glove box.
3. Remove the blower duct.
4. Disconnect the wire connections from the blower.
5. Remove the blower assembly.
6. Installation is the reverse of removal. Check that there are no air leaks in the blower case.

WITH AIR CONDITIONING

1. Remove the glove box.
2. Remove the frame to the glove box and the side frame.
3. Remove the two bolts and the retractor control unit with the bracket.
4. Unbolt the dashboard lower bracket "A" from bracket "B" and insert a small prybar to pry a 12–15mm clearance, to ease in the removal of the evaporator. Loosen the sealing band toward the right side.
6. Disconnect the wire connections from the blower.
7. Remove the three bolts retaining the blower and remove the blower assembly.
8. Installation is the reverse of removal. Check that there are no air leaks in the blower case.

2. Disconnect and plug the brake lines at the master cylinder.

3. Remove the brake pedal-to-booster link pin and the four nuts retaining the booster. The pushrod and nuts are located inside the car under the instrument panel.

4. Remove the booster with the master cylinder attached.

5. To install, reverse the removal procedure. Check the vacuum booster pushrod-to-master cylinder piston clearance as outlined in the master cylinder removal procedure. Don't forget to bleed the brake system before operating the car.

Parking Brake Cable

REMOVAL & INSTALLATION

1. Remove the adjusting nut from the equalizer mounted on the console on and separate the cable from the equalizer.

2. Set the parking brake lever to a fully released position and remove the cotter pin at the rear caliper assembly.

3. After removing the cotter pin, pull out the pin which connects the cable and the lever.

4. Detach the cable from the guides at the calipers and remove the cable.

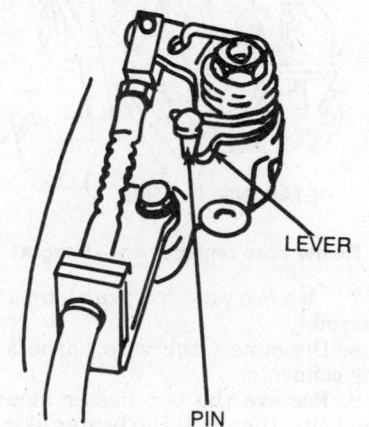

Rear brake cable lever—Integra, Legend/825S similar

5. To install, reverse the removal procedure, making sure that grease is applied to the cable and the guides.

ADJUSTMENT

Inspect the following items:
    a. Check the ratchet for wear.
    b. Check the cables for wear or damage and the cable guide and equalizer for looseness.
    c. Check the equalizer cable where it contracts the equalizer and apply grease if necessary.

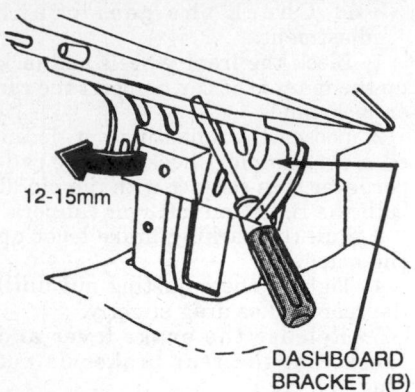

Lower heater bracket "B" — Integra

12-15mm

DASHBOARD BRACKET (B)

Legend/825S

─────── **CAUTION** ───────

This procedure requires discharging the air conditioning system. This should only be performed by people experienced with air conditioning recharging procedures.

1. Disconnect the negative battery cable.
2. Remove the three screws and remove the glove box lower cover.
3. Remove the two screws and remove the glove box.
4. Remove the retaining screws, then remove the glove box frame, the clips and the heater duct.
5. Discharge the refrigerant from the air conditioning system.
6. Remove the evaporator.
7. Disconnect the wire connectors from the blower.
8. Remove the three mounting bolts from the blower and remove the blower assembly.
9. Installation is the reverse of removal. Check that there are no air leaks in the blower case. Recharge the air conditioning system.

Heater Core

REMOVAL & INSTALLATION

Integra

1. Drain the cooling system.
2. Disconnect the heater hoses at the firewall.

NOTE: Coolant will run out of the heater hoses when disconnected, place a drain pan under them to catch the coolant.

3. Disconnect the heater valve cable from the heater valve..
4. Remove the heater assembly lower mounting nut.
5. Remove the console.
6. Disconnect the air mix cable from the heater.

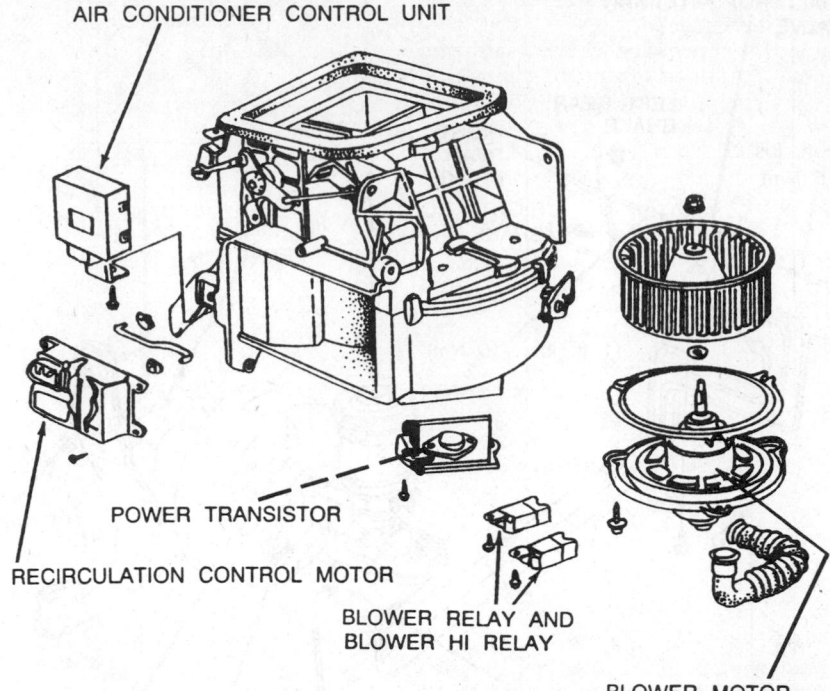

AIR CONDITIONER CONTROL UNIT

POWER TRANSISTOR

RECIRCULATION CONTROL MOTOR

BLOWER RELAY AND BLOWER HI RELAY

BLOWER MOTOR

Blower removal — Legend/825S

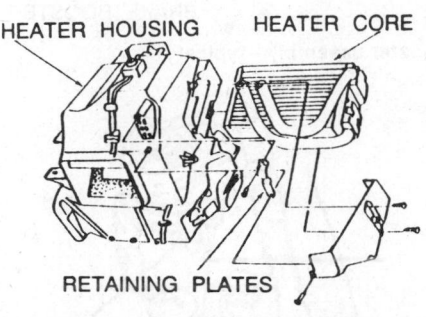

HEATER HOUSING   HEATER CORE

RETAINING PLATES

Heater core replacement — Integra

7. Remove the dashboard assembly.
8. Disconnect the wire harness at the connector.
9. Remove the two heater mounting bolts, then pull the heater assembly away from the body.
10. Remove the self tapping screws and the retaining plate.
11. Pull the heater core out of heater housing.
12. Installation is the reverse of the removal procedures, observe the following:
   a. Apply sealant to the grommets.
   b. Do not interchange the inlet and outlet hoses.
   c. Bleed the cooling system.
   d. Connect all cable and adjust them properly.

Legend/825S

1. Drain the cooling system.

2. Disconnect the heater hoses at the firewall.

NOTE: Coolant will run out of the heater hoses when disconnected, place a drain pan under them to catch the coolant.

3. Remove the dashboard.
4. Disconnect the wire harness and the vacuum hoses.
5. Remove the two heater mounting bolts, then pull the heater assembly away from the body.
6. Remove the self tapping screws and the retaining plate.
7. Pull the heater core out of the heater housing.
8. Installation is the reverse of the removal procedures, observe the following:
   a. Apply sealant to the grommets.
   b. Do not interchange the inlet and outlet hoses.
   c. Bleed the cooling system.
   d. Connect all cable and adjust them properly.

Radio

REMOVAL & INSTALLATION

Integra

1. Disconnect the negative battery cable at the battery.
2. Remove the ashtray, then remove the three screw and the ashtray holder assembly.

3. Remove the two screws from the rear radio bracket.

4. Disconnect the wire harness and the antenna lead from the radio.

5. Slide out and remove the radio.

6. Installation is the reverse of removal.

Legend/825S

1. Disconnect the negative battery cable at the battery.

2. Remove the front console and the radio trim panel.

3. Remove the screws from the front of the radio panel.

4. Disconnect the wire harness and the antenna lead from the radio.

5. Slide out and remove the radio.

6. Installation is the reverse of removal.

Windshield Wiper Switch

REMOVAL & INSTALLATION

Integra

1. Remove the steering wheel.

2. Disconnect the column wiring harness and coupler.

— **CAUTION** —

Be careful not to damage the steering column or shaft.

3. Remove the upper and lower column covers.

4. On models so equipped, remove the cruise control slip ring.

5. Remove the turn signal cancelling sleeve.

6. Remove the switch retaining screws, then remove the switch.

7. To assemble and install, reverse the above procedure.

Legend/825S

1. Remove the negative (–) cable from the battery.

2. Remove the dashboard lower panel and disconnect the 6-pin and 8-pin connectors from the wiper control unit on the lower panel.

3. Disconnect the 10-pin connector from the wiper/washer switch.

4. Remove the steering wheel, then remove the steering column lower cover and disconnect the 6-pin connector from the winter position switch.

5. Remove the upper cover from the steering column.

6. Remove the two screws and slide the wiper/washer switch out of the housing.

7. Installation is the reverse of removal.

Windshield Wiper

Motor

REMOVAL & INSTALLATION

1. Remove the negative (–) cable from the battery.

2. Remove the wiper arm retaining nuts and remove the wiper arms.

3. Remove the front air scoop and hood seal located over the wiper linkage at the bottom of the windshield.

4. Disconnect the linkage from the wiper motor.

5. Remove the wiper motor water seal cover clamp, and remove the cover.

6. Disconnect the wiper motor electrical connector, remove the motor mounting bolts and remove the motor.

7. Installation is the reverse of the removal procedure. Coat the linkage joints with grease and make sure the linkage moves smoothly.

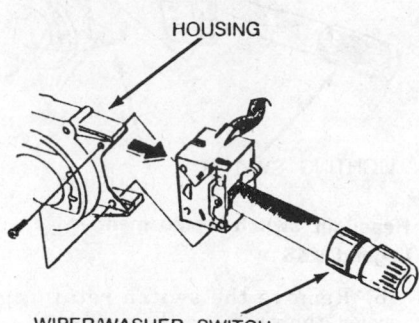

Wiper/washer switch assembly— Legend/825S

Instrument Cluster

REMOVAL & INSTALLATION

Integra

1. Remove the right and left switches from the instrument panel then disconnect the wire connecters from the switches.

2. Remove the upper instrument panel caps and the two screws, then remove the panel.

3. Remove the screws under the holes made by removing the switches.

4. Remove the rubber seal, loosen off the two screws in the column cover, then remove the instrument panel.

5. Remove the four screws retaining the gauge assembly, then lift out the gauge assembly so you can disconnect the wire connectors.

6. Disconnect the speedometer cable and remove the gauge assembly.

7. To install, reverse the removal procedure.

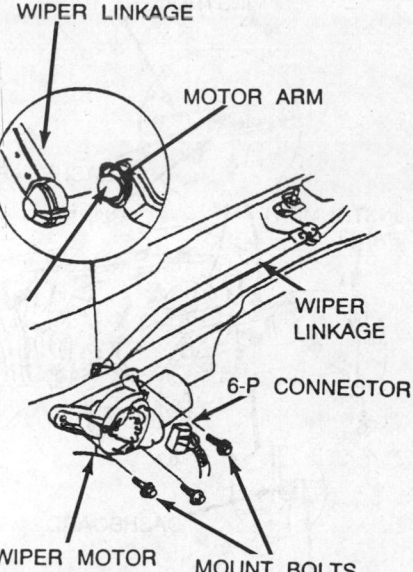

Wiper motor replacement—Integra, Legend/825S similar

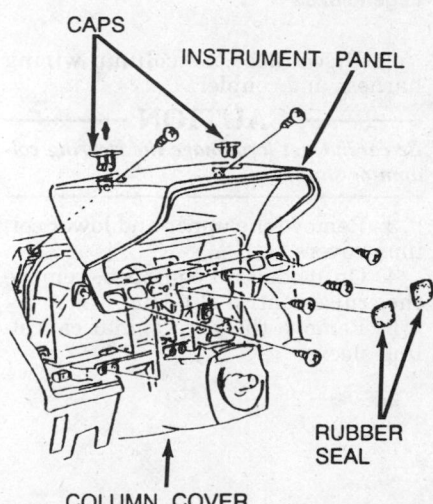

Instrument cluster replacement—Integra

Legend/825S

1. Remove the four screws, then remove the instrument panel by disconnecting the wire harness.

2. Remove the four screws retaining the gauge assembly, then lift out the gauge assembly so you can disconnect the wire connectors.

3. Disconnect the speedometer cable and remove the gauge assembly.

4. To install, reverse the removal procedure.

Headlight Switch

REMOVAL & INSTALLATION

Integra

1. Remove the steering wheel.

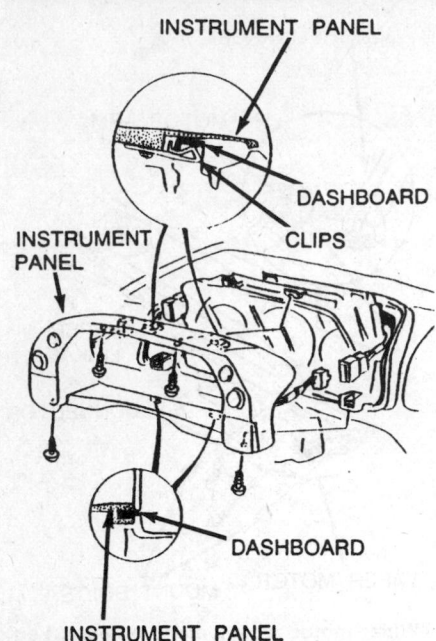

INSTRUMENT PANEL

DASHBOARD

CLIPS

INSTRUMENT PANEL

DASHBOARD

INSTRUMENT PANEL

Instrument cluster replacement— Legend/825S

2. Disconnect the column wiring harness and coupler.

— **CAUTION** —
Be careful not to damage the steering column or shaft.

3. Remove the upper and lower column covers.
4. On models so equipped, remove the cruise control slip ring.
5. Remove the turn signal cancelling sleeve.

WITHOUT CRUISE CONTROL

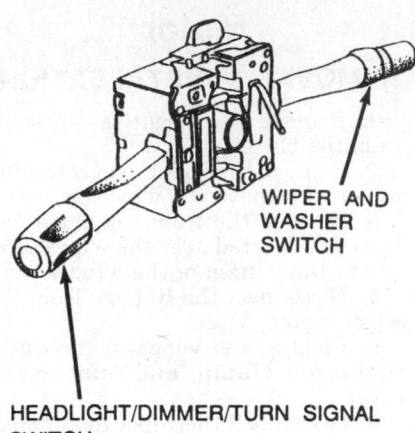

WIPER AND WASHER SWITCH

HEADLIGHT/DIMMER/TURN SIGNAL SWITCH

Headlight switch replacement—Integra

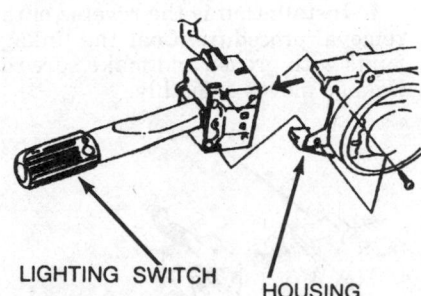

LIGHTING SWITCH

HOUSING

Headlight switch replacement— Legend/825S

6. Remove the switch retaining screws, then remove the switch.
7. To assemble and install, reverse the above procedure.

Legend/825S

1. Remove the negative (–) cable from the battery.
2. Remove the dashboard lower panel and disconnect the 14-pin connector from the lighting switch.
3. Remove the steering wheel, then remove the steering column lower cover and disconnect the 3-pin connector from the slip ring.
4. Remove the upper cover from the steering column.
5. Remove the two screws and slide the lighting switch out of the housing.
6. Installation is the reverse of removal.

Fuses and Circuit Breakers

LOCATION

Integra

The Integra fuse/relay box is located in the interior on the drivers side below the dashboard. There is also a main fuse box located in the engine compartment containing two 45 amp and one 65 amp fuse. In addition to these, there is a ten amp hazard fuse located at the positive battery terminal.

Legend/825S

The Legend/825S fuse box is located in the interior on the drivers side below the dashboard. There is also a relay box located in the left side of the engine compartment.

Audi 2

4000, 5000, Coupe, Quattro — All Models

SERIAL NUMBER LOCATION

Vehicle Identification Plate

ALL MODELS EXCEPT THE 5000 MODELS

The vehicle identification number (VIN) is located on the left (driver's side) windshield pillar and in the engine compartment on the ledge.

5000 MODELS

The vehicle identification number (VIN) is on the plate on top of the instrument panel, clearly visible through the driver's side of the windshield. It is also stamped into the upper right corner of the firewall. The vehicle identification plate is mounted on the right wheel housing.

Engine Number

ALL MODELS EXCEPT THE 5000 MODELS

The engine number is located on the left side of the cylinder block, below the cylinder head and next to the distributor.

5000 MODELS

The engine number is stamped on the left side of the engine block (clutch housing). In addition to the engine number, an engine code number is also stamped on the starter end of the cylinder block, just below the cylinder head. The number indicates the exact cylinder bore of the particular engine.

Vehicle Identification Label

The vehicle identification label is lo-

1. Production control no.
2. Vehicle identification no.
3. Type code number
4. Type designation
5. Engine and transmission code letter
6. Paint no./Interior
7. Optional equipment no.'s.

Vehicle identification label (1984 and later) showing the serial number locations

cated in the inside of the luggage compartment lid.

ENGINE IDENTIFICATION

Year	Model	Engine Displacement cu. in. (cc/liter)	Engine Series Identification	No. of Cylinders	Engine Type
1981	4000	105 (1715/1.7)	WT	4	OHC
	4000 Coupe	131 (2144/2.1)	WE	5	OHC
	5000 Turbo	131 (2144/2.1)	WK	5	OHC
	5000	131 (2144/2.1)	WD	5	OHC
	5000 Diesel	121 (1986/2.0)	CN	5	OHC

2–1

ENGINE IDENTIFICATION

Year	Model	Engine Displacement cu. in. (cc/liter)	Engine Series Identification	No. of Cylinders	Engine Type
1982	4000	105 (1715/1.7)	WT	4	OHC
	4000 Coupe	131 (2144/2.1)	WE	5	OHC
	4000 Diesel	97 (1588/1.6)	CR, CY	4	OHC
	5000 Turbo	131 (2144/2.1)	WK	5	OHC
	5000	131 (2144/2.1)	WD	5	OHC
	5000 Diesel	121 (1986/2.0)	CN	5	OHC
1983	4000	105 (1715/1.7)	WT	4	OHC
	4000 Coupe	131 (2144/2.1)	WE	5	OHC
	4000 Diesel	97 (1588/1.6)	CR, CY	4	OHC
	5000 Turbo	131 (2144/2.1)	WK	5	OHC
	5000	131 (2144/2.1)	WD	5	OHC
	5000 Diesel	121 (1986/2.0)	DE	5	OHC
	Quattro Turbo	131 (2144/2.1)	WX	5	OHC
1984	4000	109 (1780/1.8)	JN	4	OHC
	4000 Quattro	136 (2226/2.2)	KX	5	OHC
	4000 Coupe	131 (2144/2.1)	WE	5	OHC
	Coupe GT	131 (2144/2.1)	KX	5	OHC
	Quattro Coupe	131 (2144/2.1)	WU	5	OHC
	5000 Turbo	131 (2144/2.1)	KH	5	OHC
	5000	131 (2144/2.1)	WU	5	OHC
	Quattro	131 (2144/2.1)	WX	5	OHC
	Coupe	131 (2144/2.1)	KM	5	OHC
1985	4000 Coupe	136 (2226/2.2)	KX	5	OHC
	4000 S	109 (1780/1.8)	MG	4	OHC
	4000 S	136 (2226/2.2)	KX	5	OHC
	Quattro	136 (2226/2.2)	KZ	5	OHC
	Quattro Turbo	131 (2144/2.1)	WX	5	OHC
	5000 Turbo	131 (2144/2.1)	KH	5	OHC
	5000 S Wagon	136 (2226/2.2)	KX, KZ	5	OHC
	5000 S	136 (2226/2.2)	KZ	5	OHC
	5000 S Turbo	131 (2144/2.1)	MC	5	OHC
	Coupe GT	136 (2226/2.2)	KX	5	OHC
1986	4000 Coupe	136 (2226/2.2)	KX	5	OHC
	4000 S	109 (1780/1.8)	MG	4	OHC
	4000 CS Quattro	136 (2226/2.2)	JT	5	OHC
	5000 Turbo	136 (2226/2.2)	MC	5	OHC
	5000 CS Turbo	136 (2226/2.2)	MC	5	OHC
	5000 CS Quattro Turbo	136 (2226/2.2)	MC	5	OHC
	5000 CS Quattro Wagon	136 (2226/2.2)	MC	5	OHC
	5000 S	136 (2226/2.2)	MC	5	OHC
	5000 S Wagon	136 (2226/2.2)	MC	5	OHC
	Coupe GT	136 (2226/2.2)	KX	5	OHC

ENGINE IDENTIFICATION

Year	Model	Engine Displacement cu. in. (cc/liter)	Engine Series Identification	No. of Cylinders	Engine Type
1987–88	4000 Coupe	136 (2226/2.2)	KX	5	OHC
	4000 S	109 (1780/1.8)	MG	4	OHC
	4000 CS Quattro	136 (2226/2.2)	JT	5	OHC
	5000 CS Turbo	136 (2226/2.2)	MC	5	OHC
	5000 CS Quattro Turbo	136 (2226/2.2)	MC	5	OHC
	5000 CS Quattro Wagon	136 (2226/2.2)	MC	5	OHC
	5000 S	136 (2226/2.2)	MC	5	OHC
	5000 S Wagon	136 (2226/2.2)	MC	5	OHC
	Coupe GT	136 (2226/2.2)	KX	5	OHC

GENERAL ENGINE SPECIFICATIONS

Year	Model	Engine Displacement cu. in. (cc)	Fuel System Type	Net Horsepower @ rpm	Net Torque @ rpm (ft. lbs.)	Bore × Stroke (in.)	Compression Ratio	Oil Pressure @ rpm
1981	4000	105 (1715)	CIS	74 @ 5000	86.9 @ 3000	3.13 × 3.40	8.0:1	29 @ 2000
	4000 Coupe	131 (2144)	CIS	100 @ 5100	112.3 @ 3000	3.12 × 3.40	8.0:1	29 @ 2000
	5000	131 (2144)	CIS	100 @ 5100	122.3 @ 4000	3.13 × 3.40	8.0:1	29 @ 2000
	5000 Turbo	131 (2144)	CIS	130 @ 5400	142 @ 3000	3.12 × 3.40	7.0:1	29 @ 2000
	5000 Diesel	121 (1986)	DFI	67 @ 4800	86.4 @ 3000	3.09 × 3.40	23.0:1	28 @ 2000
1982	4000	105 (1715)	CIS	74 @ 5000	86.9 @ 3000	3.13 × 3.40	8.2:1	29 @ 2000
	4000 Coupe	131 (2144)	CIS	100 @ 5100	112.3 @ 3000	3.12 × 3.40	8.0:1	29 @ 2000
	4000 Diesel	97 (1588)	DFI	52 @ 4800	71.5 @ 2000	3.01 × 3.40	23.0:1	29 @ 2000
	5000	131 (2144)	CIS	100 @ 5100	122.3 @ 4000	3.13 × 3.40	8.2:1	29 @ 2000
	5000 Turbo	131 (2144)	CIS	130 @ 5400	142 @ 3000	3.12 × 3.40	7.0:1	29 @ 2000
	5000 Diesel	121 (1986)	DFI	67 @ 4800	86.4 @ 3000	3.09 × 3.40	23.0:1	28 @ 2000
1983	4000	105 (1715)	CIS	74 @ 5000	86.9 @ 3000	3.13 × 3.40	8.2:1	29 @ 2000
	4000 Coupe	131 (2144)	CIS	100 @ 5100	112.3 @ 3000	3.12 × 3.40	8.0:1	29 @ 2000
	4000 Diesel	97 (1588)	DFI	52 @ 4800	71.5 @ 2000	3.01 × 3.40	23.0:1	29 @ 2000
	5000	131 (2144)	CIS	100 @ 5100	122.3 @ 4000	3.13 × 3.40	8.2:1	29 @ 2000
	5000 Turbo	131 (2144)	CIS	130 @ 5400	142 @ 3000	3.12 × 3.40	7.0:1	29 @ 2000
	5000 Diesel	121 (1986)	DFI	67 @ 4800	86.4 @ 3000	3.09 × 3.40	23.0:1	28 @ 2000
	Quattro Turbo	131 (2144)	CIS	130 @ 5400	142 @ 3000	3.12 × 3.40	7.0:1	29 @ 2000
1984	4000	109 (1780)	CIS-E	88 @ 5500	101 @ 3000	3.19 × 3.40	8.5:1	29 @ 2000
	4000 Quattro	136 (2226)	CIS-E	115 @ 5500	126 @ 3000	3.19 × 3.40	8.5:1	29 @ 2000
	4000 Coupe	131 (2144)	CIS	100 @ 5100	112.3 @ 3000	3.12 × 3.40	8.0:1	29 @ 2000
	Coupe GT	131 (2144)	CIS-E	100 @ 5100	112.3 @ 3000	3.12 × 3.40	8.2:1	29 @ 2000
	Quattro Coupe	131 (2144)	CIS-E	160 @ 5500	170 @ 3000	3.12 × 3.40	8.2:1	29 @ 2000
	5000	131 (2144)	CIS	100 @ 5500	112 @ 3000	3.13 × 3.40	8.2:1	29 @ 2000
	5000 Turbo	131 (2144)	CIS-E	140 @ 5500	149 @ 2500	3.13 × 3.40	8.3:1	29 @ 2000
	Quattro	131 (2144)	CIS	160 @ 5500	170 @ 3000	3.12 × 3.40	7.0:1	29 @ 2000
	Coupe	131 (2144)	CIS	100 @ 5100	112.3 @ 3000	3.12 × 3.40	8.2:1	29 @ 2000

GENERAL ENGINE SPECIFICATIONS

Year	Model	Engine Displacement cu. in. (cc)	Fuel System Type	Net Horsepower @ rpm	Net Torque @ rpm (ft. lbs.)	Bore × Stroke (in.)	Compression Ratio	Oil Pressure @ rpm
1985	4000 S	109 (1780)	CIS-E	88 @ 5500	101 @ 3000	3.19 × 3.40	8.5:1	29 @ 2000
	4000 S	136 (2226)	CIS-E	110 @ 5500	122 @ 2500	3.19 × 3.40	8.5:1	29 @ 2000
	4000 Coupe	136 (2226)	CIS-E	110 @ 5500	122 @ 2500	3.19 × 3.40	8.5:1	29 @ 2000
	Quattro	136 (2226)	CIS	115 @ 5500	126 @ 3000	3.19 × 3.40	8.5:1	29 @ 2000
	Quattro Turbo	131 (2144)	CIS	160 @ 5500	170 @ 3000	3.12 × 3.40	7.0:1	29 @ 2000
	5000 S	136 (2226)	CIS-E	110 @ 5500	122 @ 2500	3.19 × 3.40	8.5:1	29 @ 2000
	5000 S Turbo	131 (2144)	CIS-E	140 @ 5500	149 @ 2500	3.19 × 3.40	8.3:1	29 @ 2000
	5000 S Wagon	136 (2226)	CIS-E	110 @ 5500	122 @ 2500	3.19 × 3.40	8.5:1	29 @ 2000
	5000 Turbo	131 (2144)	CIS-E	140 @ 5500	149 @ 2500	3.13 × 3.40	8.3:1	29 @ 2000
	Coupe GT	136 (2226)	CIS-E	110 @ 5500	110.6 @ 2500	3.19 × 3.40	8.5:1	29 @ 2000
1986	4000 S	109 (1780)	CIS-E	88 @ 5500	101 @ 3000	3.19 × 3.40	8.5:1	29 @ 2000
	4000 Coupe	136 (2226)	CIS-E	110 @ 5500	122 @ 2500	3.19 × 3.40	8.5:1	29 @ 2000
	4000 CS Quattro	136 (2226)	CIS-E	115 @ 5500	126 @ 3000	3.19 × 3.40	8.5:1	29 @ 2000
	5000 S	136 (2226)	CIS-E	110 @ 5500	122 @ 2500	3.19 × 3.40	8.5:1	29 @ 2000
	5000 S Wagon	136 (2226)	CIS-E	110 @ 5500	122 @ 2500	3.19 × 3.40	8.5:1	29 @ 2000
	5000 CS Turbo	136 (2226)	CIS-E	158 @ 5500	166 @ 3000	3.19 × 3.40	7.8:1	29 @ 2000
	5000 Turbo	136 (2226)	CIS-E	160 @ 5500	166 @ 3000	3.19 × 3.40	7.8:1	29 @ 2000
	5000 Quattro Turbo	136 (2226)	CIS-E	158 @ 5500	166 @ 3000	3.19 × 3.40	7.8:1	29 @ 2000
	5000 CS Quattro Wagon	136 (2226)	CIS-E	158 @ 5500	166 @ 3000	3.19 × 3.40	7.8:1	29 @ 2000
	Coupe GT	136 (2226)	CIS-E	110 @ 5500	122 @ 2500	3.19 × 3.40	8.5:1	29 @ 2000
1987–88	4000 S	109 (1780)	CIS-E	88 @ 5500	101 @ 3000	3.19 × 3.40	8.5:1	29 @ 2000
	4000 Coupe	136 (2226)	CIS-E	110 @ 5500	122 @ 2500	3.19 × 3.40	8.5:1	29 @ 2000
	4000 CS Quattro	136 (2226)	CIS-E	115 @ 5500	126 @ 3000	3.19 × 3.40	8.5:1	29 @ 2000
	5000 S	136 (2226)	CIS-E	110 @ 5500	122 @ 2500	3.19 × 3.40	8.5:1	29 @ 2000
	5000 S Wagon	136 (2226)	CIS-E	110 @ 5500	122 @ 2500	3.19 × 3.40	8.5:1	29 @ 2000
	5000 CS Turbo	136 (2226)	CIS-E	158 @ 5500	166 @ 3000	3.19 × 3.40	7.8:1	29 @ 2000
	5000 Turbo	136 (2226)	CIS-E	160 @ 5500	166 @ 3000	3.19 × 3.40	7.8:1	29 @ 2000
	5000 Quattro Turbo	136 (2226)	CIS-E	158 @ 5500	166 @ 3000	3.19 × 3.40	7.8:1	29 @ 2000
	5000 CS Quattro Wagon	136 (2226)	CIS-E	158 @ 5500	166 @ 3000	3.19 × 3.40	7.8:1	29 @ 2000
	Coupe GT	136 (2226)	CIS-E	110 @ 5500	122 @ 2500	3.19 × 3.40	8.5:1	29 @ 2000

GASOLINE ENGINE TUNE-UP SPECIFICATIONS

Year	Model	Engine Displacement cu. in. (cc)	Spark Plugs Type	Gap (in.)	Ignition Timing (deg.) MT	Ignition Timing (deg.) AT	Compression Pressure (psi)	Fuel Pump (psi)	Idle Speed (rpm) MT	Idle Speed (rpm) AT	Valve Clearance In.	Valve Clearance Ex.
1981	4000	105 (1715)	N8Y	.028	3A	3A	NA	64–74	850–1000	850–1000	.008–.012	.016–.020
	4000 Coupe	131 (2144)	N8Y	.028	6B	3A	NA	64–74	775–925	850–1000	.008–.012	.016–.020
	5000	131 (2144)	N8Y	.035	3A	3A	NA	64–74	850–1000	850–1000	.008–.012	.016–.020
	5000 Turbo	131 (2144)	N8Y	.028	21B	21B	NA	72–82	880–1000	880–1000	.008–.012	.016–.020

GASOLINE ENGINE TUNE-UP SPECIFICATIONS

Year	Model	Engine Displacement cu. in. (cc)	Spark Plugs Type	Spark Plugs Gap (in.)	Ignition Timing (deg.) MT	Ignition Timing (deg.) AT	Compression Pressure (psi)	Fuel Pump (psi)	Idle Speed (rpm) MT	Idle Speed (rpm) AT	Valve Clearance In.	Valve Clearance Ex.
1982	4000	105 (1715)	N8Y	.028	3A	3A	NA	64–74	850–1000	850–1000	.008–.012	.016–.020
	4000 Coupe	131 (2144)	N8Y	.028	6B	3A	NA	67–74	775–925	850–1000	.008–.012	.016–.020
	5000	131 (2144)	N8Y	.035	6B	3A	NA	64–74	850–1000	850–1000	.008–.012	.016–.020
	5000 Turbo	131 (2144)	N8Y	.028	21B	21B	NA	72–84	790–910	790–910	.008–.012	.016–.020
1983	4000	105 (1715)	N8Y	.028	3A	3A	NA	64–74	850–1000	850–1000	.008–.012	.016–.020
	4000 Coupe	131 (2144)	N8Y	.028	6B	3A	NA	64–74	725–925	850–1000	.008–.012	.016–.020
	5000	131 (2144)	N8Y	.028	6B	3A	NA	64–74	850–1000	850–1000	.008–.012	.016–.020
	5000 Turbo	131 (2144)	N8Y	.028	21B	21B	NA	72–82	790–910	790–910	.008–.012	.016–.020
	Quattro Turbo	131 (2144)	N8Y	.028	①	①	NA	68–78	790–910	790–910	.008–.012	.016–.020
1984	4000	109 (1780)	N8Y	.032	6B	6B	NA	75–85	850–1000	850–1000	Hyd.	Hyd.
	4000 Coupe	131 (2144)	N8GY	.032	8B	8B	NA	75–81	750–850	750–850	Hyd.	Hyd.
	Quattro 4000	136 (2226)	N8GY	.028	8B	8B	NA	75–81	750–850	750–850	Hyd.	Hyd.
	Coupe GT	131 (2144)	N8BY	.032	8B	8B	NA	68–78	750–850	750–850	Hyd.	Hyd.
	Quattro Coupe	131 (2144)	N8GY	.032	8B	8B	NA	75–81	750–850	750–850	Hyd.	Hyd.
	5000	131 (2144)	N8Y	.028	6B	6B	NA	68–78	730–870	730–870	Hyd.	Hyd.
	5000 Turbo	131 (2144)	N8BY	.028	6B	6B	NA	61–67	750–850	750–850	Hyd.	Hyd.
	Quattro	131 (2144)	N6GY	.028	6B	6B	NA	75–85	750–805	750–850	Hyd.	Hyd.
	Coupe	131 (2144)	N8GY	.032	6B	6B	NA	75–85	750–850	750–850	Hyd.	Hyd.
1985	4000S	109 (1780)	N8GY	.031	6B	6B	NA	75–82	800–1000	800–1000	Hyd.	Hyd.
	4000S	136 (2226)	N8GY	.032	8B	8B	NA	75–85	750–850	750–850	Hyd.	Hyd.
	4000 Coupe	136 (2226)	N8GY	.032	8B	8B	NA	75–81	750–850	750–850	Hyd.	Hyd.
	Quattro	136 (2226)	N6GY	.028	6B	6B	NA	75–85	750–850	750–850	Hyd.	Hyd.
	Quattro Turbo	131 (2144)	N8GY	.028	8B	8B	NA	75–85	750–850	750–850	Hyd.	Hyd.

GASOLINE ENGINE TUNE-UP SPECIFICATIONS

Year	Model	Engine Displacement cu. in. (cc)	Spark Plugs Type	Gap (in.)	Ignition Timing (deg.) MT	AT	Com- pression Pressure (psi)	Fuel Pump (psi)	Idle Speed (rpm) MT	AT	Valve Clearance In.	Ex.
	5000S	136 (2226)	N8GY	.028	6B	6B	NA	73–84	750–850	750–850	Hyd.	Hyd.
	5000 Turbo	131 (2144)	N8GY	.028	0	0	NA	84–91	750–850	750–850	Hyd.	Hyd.
	5000S Wagon	136 (2226)	N8GY	.028	6B	6B	NA	73–84	750–850	750–850	Hyd.	Hyd.
	5000S Turbo	131 (2226)	N8GY	.028	0	0	NA	84–91	750–850	750–850	Hyd.	Hyd.
	Coupe GT	136 (2226)	N8GY	.032	8B	8B	NA	75–81	750–850	750–850	Hyd.	Hyd.
1986	4000S	109 (1780)	N8GY	.031	6B	6B	NA	75–82	800–1000	800–1000	Hyd.	Hyd.
	4000 Coupe	136 (2226)	N8GY	.032	8B	8B	NA	75–81	750–850	750–850	Hyd.	Hyd.
	4000CS Quattro	136 (2226)	N8GY	.032	8B	8B	NA	75–81	750–850	750–850	Hyd.	Hyd.
	5000S	136 (2226)	N8GY	.028	6B	6B	NA	75–85	750–850	750–850	Hyd.	Hyd.
	5000 Wagon	136 (2226)	N8GY	.028	6B	6B	NA	75–85	750–850	750–850	Hyd.	Hyd.
	5000 S Wagon	136 (2226)	N8GY	.028	6B	6B	NA	75–85	750–850	750–850	Hyd.	Hyd.
	5000CS Turbo	136 (2226)	N8GY	.028	0	0	NA	84–91	750–850	750–850	Hyd.	Hyd.
	5000 Turbo	136 (2226)	N8GY	.028	0	0	NA	84–91	750–850	750–850	Hyd.	Hyd.
	5000 Quattro Turbo	136 (2226)	N8GY	.028	0	0	NA	84–91	750–850	750–850	Hyd.	Hyd.
	5000CS Quattro Wagon	136 (2226)	N8GY	.028	6B	6B	NA	75–85	750–850	750–850	Hyd.	Hyd.
	Coupe GT	136 (2226)	N8GY	.032	8B	8B	NA	75–85	750–850	750–850	Hyd.	Hyd.
1987	4000S	109 (1780)	N8GY	.031	6B	6B	NA	75–82	800–1000	800–1000	Hyd.	Hyd.
	4000 Coupe	136 (1780)	N8GY	.032	8B	8B	NA	75–81	750–850	750–850	Hyd.	Hyd.
	4000CS Quattro	136 (2226)	N8GY	.032	8B	8B	NA	75–81	750–850	750–850	Hyd.	Hyd.
	5000S	136 (2226)	N8GY	.028	6B	6B	NA	75–85	750–850	750–850	Hyd.	Hyd.
	5000S Wagon	136 (2226)	N8GY	.028	6B	6B	NA	75–85	750–850	750–850	Hyd.	Hyd.
	5000CS Turbo	136 (2226)	N8GY	.028	0	0	NA	84–91	750–850	750–850	Hyd.	Hyd.
	5000 Turbo	136 (2226)	N8GY	.028	0	0	NA	84–91	750–850	750–850	Hyd.	Hyd.

GASOLINE ENGINE TUNE-UP SPECIFICATIONS

Year	Model	Engine Displacement cu. in. (cc)	Spark Plugs Type	Spark Plugs Gap (in.)	Ignition Timing (deg.) MT	Ignition Timing (deg.) AT	Compression Pressure (psi)	Fuel Pump (psi)	Idle Speed (rpm) MT	Idle Speed (rpm) AT	Valve Clearance In.	Valve Clearance Ex.
1987	5000 Quattro Turbo	136 (2226)	N8GY	.028	0	0	NA	84–91	750–850	750–850	Hyd.	Hyd.
	5000CS Quattro Wagon	136 (2226)	N8GY	.028	6B	6B	NA	75–85	750–850	750–850	Hyd.	Hyd.
	Coupe GT	136 (2226)	N8GY	.032	8B	8B	NA	75–85	750–850	750–850	Hyd.	Hyd.
1988	All	SEE UNDERHOOD SPECIFICATIONS STICKER										

B Before top dead center
A After top dead center
Hyd. Hydraulic lash adjusters—no adjustment is necessary.
NA Not available
① Align the distributor housing with the timing mark.

DIESEL ENGINE TUNE-UP SPECIFICATIONS

Year	Engine Displacement cu. in. (cc)	Valve Clearance Intake (in.)	Valve Clearance Exhaust (in.)	Intake Valve Opens (deg.)	Injection Pump Setting (deg.)	Injection Nozzle Pressure (psi) New	Injection Nozzle Pressure (psi) Used	Idle Speed (rpm)	Cranking Compression Pressure (psi)
1981	121 (1986)	.008–.012	.016–.020	NA	①	1849	1706	700-800	398-483
1982	97 (1588)	.008–.012	.016–.020	NA	②	1885	1740	800-850	398-493
	121 (1986)	.008–.012	.016–.020	NA	①	1849	1706	700-800	398-483
1983	97 (1588)	.008–.012	.016–.020	NA	③	2306	2139	900-1000	493
	121 (1986)	.008–.012	.016–.020	NA	④	2306	2139	720-780	493

① The injection timing is .033 in. plunger stroke at top dead center. With the cold start knob pushed in, turn the injection pump body to adjust
② The injection timing is .034 in. plunger stroke at top dead center. With the cold start knob pushed in, turn the injection pump body to adjust
③ The injection timing is .036 in. plunger stroke at top dead center. With the cold start knob pushed in, turn the injection pump body to adjust
④ The injection timing is .037 in. plunger stroke at top dead center. With the cold start knob pushed in, turn the injection pump body to adjust

FIRING ORDER

NOTE: To avoid confusion, always replace spark plug wires one at a time.

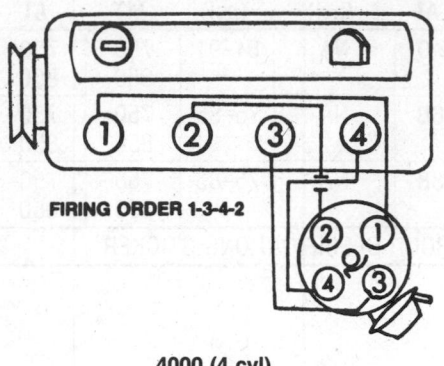

FIRING ORDER 1-3-4-2

4000 (4 cyl)

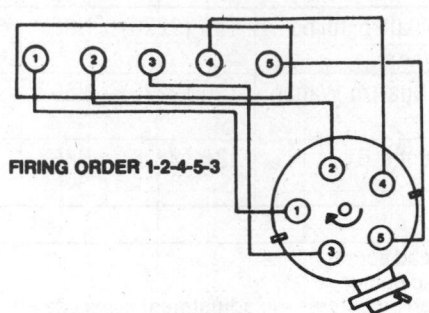

FIRING ORDER 1-2-4-5-3

Coupe (4000 5 cyl), 5000 and Quattro

CAPACITIES

Year	Model	Engine Displacement cu. in. (cc)	Engine Crankcase with Filter	Engine Crankcase without Filter	Transmission (pts) 4-Spd	Transmission (pts) 5-Spd	Transmission (pts) Auto.	Drive Axle (pts.)	Fuel Tank (gal.)	Cooling System (qts.)
1981	4000	105 (1715)	3.7	3.2	3.4	3.4	6.4	2.2	15.9	7.4
	4000 Coupe	131 (2144)	4.8	4.3	5.5	5.5	6.4	2.5	15.9	8.5
	5000	131 (2144)	4.8	4.3	3.4	5.5	6.4	2.5	19.8	8.6
	5000 Diesel	121 (1986)	4.8	4.3	—	5.5	6.4	2.5	19.8	9.9
	5000 Turbo	131 (2144)	4.8	4.3	—	—	6.4	2.5	19.8	9.9
1982	4000	105 (1715)	3.7	3.2	3.4	3.4	6.4	2.2	15.9	7.4
	4000 Diesel	97 (1588)	3.7	3.2	—	3.4	6.4	2.2	15.9	6.6
	4000 Coupe	131 (2144)	4.8	4.3	—	5.5	6.4	2.5	15.9	8.5
	5000	131 (2144)	4.8	4.3	3.4	5.5	6.4	2.5	19.8	8.6
	5000 Diesel	121 (1986)	4.8	4.3	—	5.5	6.4	2.5	19.8	9.9
	5000 Turbo	131 (2144)	4.8	4.3	—	—	6.4	2.5	19.8	9.9
1983	4000	105 (1715)	3.5	3.0	3.4	3.4	6.4	2.2	15.9	7.4
	4000 Diesel	97 (1588)	3.7	3.2	—	3.4	6.4	2.2	15.9	6.6
	4000 Coupe	131 (2144)	4.0	3.5	—	3.4	6.4	2.2	15.9	8.5
	5000	131 (2144)	4.9	4.5	3.4	5.5	6.4	2.5	19.8	8.5
	5000 Diesel	121 (1986)	4.8	4.3	—	5.5	6.4	2.5	19.8	9.9
	5000 Turbo	131 (2144)	4.5	4.5	—	—	6.4	2.5	19.8	9.9
	Quattro Turbo	131 (2144)	4.5	4.3	—	—	6.4	2.5	23.8	9.8

CAPACITIES

Year	Model	Engine Displacement cu. in. (cc)	Engine Crankcase with Filter	Engine Crankcase without Filter	Transmission (pts) 4-Spd	Transmission (pts) 5-Spd	Transmission (pts) Auto.	Drive Axle (pts.)	Fuel Tank (gal.)	Cooling System (qts.)
1984	4000	109 (1780)	4.7	4.3	3.4	3.4	6.4	2.2	15.9	9.8
	4000 Coupe	131 (2144)	4.0	3.5	—	3.4	6.4	2.2	15.9	8.5
	4000 Quattro	136 (2226)	4.0	3.5	—	5.5	—	2.5	18.5	8.5
	Quattro Coupe	131 (2144)	4.5	4.3	—	7.0	6.4	3.0	23.8	9.8
	Coupe GT	131 (2144)	5.3	5.0	—	5.0	6.4	3.0	15.8	7.4
	5000	131 (2144)	5.3	5.0	—	5.4	6.4	3.0	21.1	8.5
	5000 Turbo	131 (2144)	5.3	5.0	—	5.4	6.4	3.0	21.1	8.5
	Quattro	131 (2144)	3.7	3.5	—	7.0	6.4	2.5	18.5	8.5
	Coupe	131 (2144)	4.0	3.5	—	3.4	6.4	2.2	15.9	8.5
1985	400S	109 (1780)	3.7	3.5	—	4.2	6.4	2.2	15.8	6.9
	4000S	136 (2226)	4.0	3.7	—	7.0	6.4	2.5	18.5	8.5
	4000 Coupe	136 (2226)	4.0	3.5	—	5.5	6.4	2.2	15.9	7.4
	Quattro	136 (2226)	4.5	4.0	—	7.0	6.4	2.5	23.8	9.8
	Quattro Turbo	131 (2144)	4.5	4.0	—	7.0	6.4	2.5	23.8	9.8
	5000S	136 (2226)	5.3	5.0	—	5.4	6.4	3.0	21.0	8.5
	5000 Turbo	131 (2144)	5.0	4.5	—	5.5	6.4	3.0	21.1	8.6
	5000S Wagon	136 (2226)	5.3	5.0	—	5.4	6/4	3.0	21.0	8.5
	5000S Turbo	131 (2144)	5.3	5.0	—	5.4	6.4	3.0	21.0	8.5
	Coupe GT	136 (2226)	4.0	3.7	—	5.0	6.4	3.0	15.8	7.4
1986	4000S	109 (1780)	3.5	3.0	—	5.5	6.4	2.2	15.9	7.4
	4000 Coupe	136 (2226)	4.0	3.5	—	5.5	6.4	2.2	15.9	7.4
	4000CS Quattro	136 (2226)	4.0	3.5	—	5.5	6.4	2.2	15.9	8.6
	5000S	136 (2226)	5.3	5.0	—	5.4	6.4	3.0	21.0	8.5
	5000 Turbo	136 (2226)	5.0	4.5	—	5.5	6.4	3.0	21.0	8.6
	5000CS Turbo	136 (2226)	5.3	5.0	—	5.4	6.4	3.0	21.0	8.5
	5000S Wagon	136 (2226)	5.3	5.0	—	5.4	6.4	3.0	21.0	8.5
	5000CS Quattro Turbo	136 (2226)	5.3	5.0	—	5.4	6.4	3.0	21.0	8.5
	5000CS Quattro Wagon	136 (2226)	5.3	5.0	—	5.4	6.4	3.0	21.0	8.5
	Coupe GT	136 (2226)	4.0	3.7	—	5.0	6.4	3.0	15.8	7.4
1987-88	4000S	109 (1780)	3.5	3.0	—	5.5	6.4	2.2	15.9	7.4
	4000 Coupe	136 (2226)	4.0	3.5	—	5.5	6.4	2.2	15.9	7.4
	4000CS Quattro	136 (2226)	4.0	3.5	—	5.5	6.4	2.2	15.9	8.6
	5000S	136 (2226)	5.3	5.0	—	5.4	6.4	3.0	21.0	8.5
	5000 Turbo	136 (2226)	5.0	4.5	—	5.5	6.4	3.0	21.0	8.6
	5000CS Turbo	136 (2226)	5.3	5.0	—	5.4	6/4	3.0	21.0	8.5
	5000S Wagon	136 (2226)	5.3	5.0	—	5.4	6.4	3.0	21.0	8.5
	5000CS Quattro Turbo	136 (2226)	5.3	5.0	—	5.4	6.4	3.0	21.0	8.5
	5000CS Quattro Wagon	136 (2226)	5.3	5.0	—	5.4	6.4	3.0	21.0	8.5
	Coupe GT	136 (2226)	4.0	3.7	—	5.0	6.4	3.0	15.8	7.4

CRANKSHAFT AND CONNECTING ROD SPECIFICATIONS

All measurements are given in inches.

Year	Engine Displacement cu. in. (cc)	Crankshaft				Connecting Rod		
		Main Brg. Journal Dia.	Main Brg. Oil Clearance	Shaft End-play	Thrust on No.	Journal Diameter	Oil Clearance	Side Clearance
1981	105 (1715)	2.1247	0.0010–0.0030	0.003–0.007	3	1.8098	0.0011 0.0034	0.015
	121 (1986)	2.3187	0.0006–0.0030	0.003–0.007	4	1.9107	0.005–0.0024	0.015
	131 (2144)	2.2834	0.0006–0.0030	0.003–0.007	4	1.8110	0.0006–0.0020	0.016
1982	97 (1588)	2.1248	0.0010–0.0030	0.003–0.007	3	1.8807	0.0011–0.0034	0.014
	105 (1715)	2.1247	0.0010–0.0030	0.003–0.007	3	1.8098	0.0011–0.0034	0.015
	121 (1986)	2.3187	0.0006–0.0030	0.003–0.007	4	1.9107	0.005–0.0024	0.015
	131 (2144)	2.2822	0.0006–0.0030	0.003–0.007	4	1.8098	0.006–0.0020	0.016
1983	97 (1588)	2.1248	0.0010–0.0030	0.003–0.007	3	1.8807	0.0011–0.0034	0.014
	105 (1715)	2.1247	0.0010–0.0030	0.003–0.007	3	1.8098	0.0011–0.0034	0.015
	121 (1986)	2.3187	0.0006–0.0030	0.003–0.007	4	1.9107	0.005–0.0024	0.015
	131 (2144)	2.2822	0.0006–0.0030	0.003–0.007	4	1.8098	0.006–0.0020	0.016
1984	109 (1780)	2.1260	0.0010–0.0030	0.003–0.007	3	1.811	0.001–0.003	0.015
	131 (2144)	2.2822	0.0006–0.0030	0.003–0.007	4	1.8098	0.0006–0.0020	0.016
	136 (2226)	2.2818	0.0006–0.0030	0.003–0.007	4	1.8803	0.0006–0.0020	0.016
1985	109 (1780)	2.1260	0.0010–0.0030	0.003–0.007	3	1.811	0.001–0.003	0.015
	131 (2144)	2.2822	0.0006–0.0030	0.003–0.007	4	1.8098	0.0006–0.0020	0.016
	136 (2226)	2.2818	0.0006–0.0030	0.003–0.007	4	1.8803	0.0006–0.0020	0.016
1986	109 (1780)	2.1260	0.0010–0.0030	0.003–0.007	3	1.811	0.001–0.003	0.015
	136 (2226)	2.2818	0.0006–0.0030	0.003–0.007	4	1.8803	0.0006–0.0020	0.016
1987–88	109 (1780)	2.1260	0.0010–0.0030	0.003–0.007	3	1.811	0.001–0.003	0.015
	136 (2226)	2.2818	0.0006–0.0030	0.003–0.007	4	1.8803	0.0006–0.0020	0.016

VALVE SPECIFICATIONS

Year	Engine Displacement cu. in. (cc)	Seat Angle (deg.)	Face Angle (deg.)	Spring Test Pressure (lbs.)	Spring Installed Height (in.)	Stem-to-Guide Clearance (in.)		Stem Diameter (in.)	
						Intake	Exhaust	Intake	Exhaust
1981	105 (1715)	45	45	—	—	0.039	0.051	0.3140	0.3130
	121 (1986)	45	45	—	—	0.051	0.051	0.3140	0.3130
	131 (2144)	45	45	—	—	0.039	0.051	0.3140	0.3130
1982	97 (1588)	45	45	—	—	0.039	0.051	0.3140	0.3130
	105 (1715)	45	45	—	—	0.039	0.051	0.3140	0.3130
	121 (1986)	45	45	—	—	0.051	0.051	0.3140	0.3130
	131 (2144)	45	45	—	—	0.039	0.051	0.3140	0.3130
1983	97 (1588)	45	45	—	—	0.039	0.051	0.3140	0.3130
	121 (1986)	45	45	—	—	0.051	0.051	0.3140	0.3130
	105 (1715)	45	45	—	—	0.039	0.051	0.3140	0.3130
	131 (2144)	45	45	—	—	0.039	0.051	0.3140	0.3130
1984	109 (1780)	45	45	—	—	0.039	0.051	0.3140	0.3130
	131 (2144)	45	45	—	—	0.039	0.051	0.3140	0.3130
	136 (2226)	45	45	—	—	0.039	0.051	0.3140	0.3130
1985	109 (1780)	45	45	—	—	0.039	0.051	0.3140	0.3130
	131 (2144)	45	45	—	—	0.039	0.051	0.3140	0.3130
	136 (2226)	45	45	—	—	0.039	0.051	0.3140	0.3130
1986	109 (1780)	45	45	—	—	0.039	0.051	0.3140	0.3130
	136 (2226)	45	45	—	—	0.039	0.051	0.3140	0.3130
1987-88	109 (1780)	45	45	—	—	0.039	0.051	0.3140	0.3130
	136 (2226)	45	45	—	—	0.039	0.051	0.3140	0.3130

PISTON AND RING SPECIFICATIONS

All measurements are given in inches.

Year	Engine Displacement cu. in. (cc)	Piston Clearance	Ring Gap			Ring Side Clearance		
			Top Compression	Bottom Compression	Oil Control	Top Compression	Bottom Compression	Oil Control
1981	105 (1715)	0.0011	0.012–0.018	0.012–0.018	0.012–0.018	0.0008–0.002	0.0008–0.002	0.0008–0.002
	121 (1986)	0.0011	0.012–0.020	0.012–0.020	0.010–0.016	0.002–0.0035	0.002–0.003	0.001–0.002
	131 (2144)	0.0011	0.010–0.020	0.010–0.020	0.010–0.020	0.0008–0.003	0.0008–0.003	0.0008–0.003
1982	97 (1588)	0.0011	0.012–0.020	0.012–0.020	0.010–0.016	0.002–0.004	0.002–0.003	0.001–0.002
	105 (1715)	0.0011	0.012–0.018	0.012–0.018	0.012–0.018	0.0008–0.002	0.0008–0.002	0.0008–0.002
	121 (1986)	0.0011	0.012–0.020	0.012–0.020	0.010–0.016	0.002–0.0035	0.002–0.003	0.001–0.002
	131 (2144)	0.0011	0.010–0.020	0.010–0.020	0.010–0.020	0.0008–0.003	0.0008–0.003	0.0008–0.003

PISTON AND RING SPECIFICATIONS

All measurements are given in inches.

Year	Engine Displacement cu. in. (cc)	Piston Clearance	Ring Gap			Ring Side Clearance		
			Top Compression	Bottom Compression	Oil Control	Top Compression	Bottom Compression	Oil Control
1983	97 (1588)	0.0011	0.012–0.020	0.012–0.020	0.010–0.016	0.002–0.004	0.002–0.003	0.001–0.002
	105 (1715)	0.0011	0.012–0.018	0.012–0.018	0.012–0.018	0.0008–0.002	0.0008–0.002	0.0008–0.002
	121 (1986)	0.0011	0.012–0.020	0.012–0.020	0.010–0.016	0.002–0.0035	0.002–0.003	0.001–0.002
	131 (2144)	0.0011	0.010–0.020	0.010–0.020	0.010–0.020	0.0008–0.003	0.0008–0.003	0.0008–0.003
1984	109 (1780)	0.0011	0.012–0.018	0.012–0.018	0.012–0.018	0.0008–0.012	0.0008–0.002	0.0008–0.002
	131 (2144)	0.0011	0.010–0.020	0.010–0.020	0.010–0.020	0.0008–0.003	0.0008–0.003	0.0008–0.003
	136 (2226)	0.0011	0.010–0.020	0.010–0.020	0.010–0.020	0.0008–0.003	0.0008–0.002	0.0008–0.002
1985	109 (1780)	0.0011	0.012–0.018	0.012–0.018	0.012–0.018	0.0008–0.012	0.0008–0.002	0.0008–0.002
	131 (2144)	0.0011	0.010–0.020	0.010–0.020	0.010–0.020	0.0008–0.003	0.0008–0.003	0.0008–0.003
	136 (2226)	0.0011	0.010–0.020	0.010–0.020	0.010–0.020	0.0008–0.003	0.0008–0.002	0.0008–0.002
1986	109 (1780)	0.0011	0.012–0.018	0.012–0.018	0.012–0.018	0.0008–0.002	0.0008–0.002	0.0008–0.002
	136 (2226)	0.0011	0.010–0.020	0.010–0.020	0.010–0.020	0.0008–0.003	0.0008–0.003	0.0008–0.003
1987–88	109 (1780)	0.0011	0.012–0.018	0.012–0.018	0.012–0.018	0.0008–0.002	0.0008–0.002	0.0008–0.002
	136 (2226)	0.0011	0.010–0.020	0.010–0.020	0.010–0.020	0.0008–0.003	0.0008–0.003	0.0008–0.003

TORQUE SPECIFICATIONS

All readings in ft. lbs.

Year	Engine Displacement cu. in. (cc)	Cylinder Head Bolts	Main Bearing Bolts	Rod Bearing Bolts	Crankshaft Pulley Bolts	Flywheel Bolts	Manifold		Spark Plugs
							Intake	Exhaust	
1981	105 (1715)	①	47	33	58	54	16	16	14
	121 (1986)	②	47	33	253	54 ⑤	18	18	—
	131 (2144)	①	47	36 ③	250	54 ⑤	18	18	14
1982	97 (1588)	①	47	33	58 ④	54 ⑤	18	18	14
	105 (1715)	①	47	33	58	54	16	16	14
	121 (1986)	②	47	33	253	54 ⑤	18	18	—
	131 (2144)	①	47	36 ③	250	54 ⑤	18	18	14

TORQUE SPECIFICATIONS
All readings in ft. lbs.

Year	Engine Displacement cu. in. (cc)	Cylinder Head Bolts	Main Bearing Bolts	Rod Bearing Bolts	Crankshaft Pulley Bolts	Flywheel Bolts	Manifold Intake	Manifold Exhaust	Spark Plugs
1983	97 (1588)	①	47	33	58 ④	54 ⑤	18	18	14
	121 (1986)	②	47	33	253	54 ⑤	18	18	—
	105 (1715)	①	47	33	58	54 ⑤	16	16	14
	131 (2144)	①	47	36 ③	250	54	18	18	14
1984	109 (1780)	①	47	22 ⑥	145	54 ⑤	22	22	14
	131 (2144)	①	47	36 ③	250	54 ⑤	18	18	14
	136 (2226)	①	47	22 ⑥	253	54 ⑤	22	26	14
1985	109 (1780)	①	47	22 ⑥	145	54 ⑤	22	22	14
	131 (2144)	①	47	36 ③	250	54 ⑤	18	18	14
	136 (2226)	①	47	22 ⑥	253	54 ⑤	22	26	14
1986	109 (1780)	①	47	22 ⑥	145	54 ⑤	22	22	14
	136 (2226)	①	47	22 ⑥	253	54 ⑤	22	26	14
1987–88	109 (1780)	①	47	22 ⑥	145	54 ⑤	22	22	14
	136 (2226)	①	47	22 ⑥	253	54 ⑤	22	26	14

NOTE: Always use new rod bearing bolts.
① In sequence 29 ft. lbs., 43 ft. lbs. and then tighten it a half turn more (180°). On gasoline engines with cylinder head bolts other than M11, 54 ft. lbs. plus a 90° (a quarter turn more)
② In sequence 29 ft. lbs., 43 ft. lbs., and then tighten it a half turn more (180°) Warm the engine and tighten the head bolts an additional quarter turn more (90°)

③ Turbo and Quattro models 47 ft. lbs. Nut with notches—22 ft. lbs. plus a quarter turn.
④ Replacement bolt and washer 108 ft. lbs.
⑤ Models with a built in lug—145 ft. lbs.
⑥ Plus a quarter turn (90°)

BRAKE SPECIFICATIONS
All measurements in inches unless noted

Year	Model	Lug Nut Torque (ft. lbs.)	Master Cylinder Bore	④ Brake Disc Minimum Thickness	Maximum Runout	Standard Brake Drum Diameter	Minimum Lining Thickness Front	Rear
1981	4000	65	0.825	0.413 ①	0.002	7.910	0.078	0.098
	4000 Coupe	65	0.825	0.413 ①	0.002	7.910	0.078	0.098
	5000	80	0.875	0.807	0.004	9.094	0.078	0.098
	5000 Diesel	80	0.875	0.807	0.004	9.094	0.078	0.098
	5000 Turbo	80	0.875	0.807	0.002	9.980	0.051	0.472
1982	4000	65	0.825	0.413 ①	0.002	7.910	0.078	0.098
	4000 Coupe	65	0.825	0.413 ①	0.002	7.910	0.078	0.098
	4000 Diesel	65	0.825	0.413 ①	0.002	7.910	0.078	0.098
	5000	80	0.875	0.807	0.004	9.094	0.078	0.098
	5000 Diesel	80	0.875	0.807	0.004	9.094	0.078	0.098
	5000 Turbo	80	0.875	0.807	0.002	9.980	0.051	0.472

BRAKE SPECIFICATIONS

All measurements in inches unless noted

Year	Model	Lug Nut Torque (ft. lbs.)	Master Cylinder Bore	Brake Disc Minimum Thickness	Brake Disc Maximum Runout	Standard Brake Drum Diameter	Minimum Lining Thickness Front	Minimum Lining Thickness Rear
1983	4000	65	0.825	0.413 ①	0.002	7.910	0.078	0.098
	4000 Coupe	65	0.825	0.413 ①	0.002	7.910	0.078	0.098
	4000 Diesel	65	0.825	0.413 ①	0.002	7.910	0.078	0.098
	5000	80	0.875	0.807	0.004	9.094	0.078	0.098
	5000 Diesel	80	0.875	0.807	0.004	9.094	0.078	0.098
	5000 Turbo	80	0.875	0.807	0.002	9.980	0.051	0.472
	Quattro Turbo	80	0.875	0.807	0.002	9.980	0.051	0.472
1984	4000	65	0.825	0.413 ①	0.002	7.910	0.078	0.098
	4000 Coupe	65	0.825	0.413 ①	0.002	7.910	0.078	0.098
	4000 Quattro	80	0.810	0.472	0.002	9.981	0.276 ②	0.276 ②
	Coupe GT	80	0.810	0.472	0.002	7.894	0.078	0.098
	Quattro Coupe	80	0.875	0.807	0.002	9.980	0.051	0.472
	5000	80	0.875	0.807	0.004	9.094	0.078	0.098
	5000 Turbo	80	0.875	0.807	0.002	9.980	0.051	0.472
	Quattro	80	0.875	0.807	0.002	9.980	0.051	0.472
	Coupe	80	0.810	0.472	0.002	7.913	0.276 ②	0.098
1985	4000S	80	0.810	0.472	0.002	7.913	0.276 ②	0.098
	4000 Coupe	80	0.810	0.472	0.002	7.913	0.276 ②	0.098
	Quattro	80	0.875	0.807	0.002	9.980	0.051	0.472
	Quattro Turbo	80	0.875	0.807	0.002	9.980	0.051	0.472
	5000S	80	0.810	0.787	0.002	9.094	③	0.098
	5000S Turbo	80	0.810	0.787	0.002	9.981	③	0.281
	5000S Wagon	80	0.810	0.787	0.002	9.094	③	0.098
	5000 Turbo	80	0.875	0.807	0.002	9.980	0.051	0.472
	Coupe GT	80	0.810	0.472	0.002	7.894	0.078	0.098
1986	4000S	80	0.810	0.472	0.002	7.913	0.276 ②	0.098
	4000 Coupe	80	0.810	0.472	0.002	7.913	0.276 ②	0.098
	4000CS Quattro	80	0.810	0.728	0.003	—	③	③
	5000S	80	0.810	0.787	0.002	9.980	0.051	0.472
	5000S Wagon	80	0.810	0.787	0.002	9.980	0.051	0.472
	5000CS Turbo	80	0.810	0.807	0.002	—	③	③
	5000 Turbo	80	0.875	0.807	0.002	9.980	0.051	0.472
	5000 Quattro Turbo	80	0.810	0.807	0.002	—	③	③
	5000CS Quattro Wagon	80	0.810	0.807	0.002	—	③	③
	Coupe GT	80	0.810	0.472	0.002	7.894	0.078	0.098
1987-88	4000S	80	0.810	0.472	0.002	7.913	0.276 ②	0.098
	4000 Coupe	80	0.810	0.472	0.002	7.913	0.276 ②	0.098
	4000CS Quattro	80	0.810	0.728	0.003	—	③	③
	5000S	80	0.810	0.787	0.002	9.980	0.051	0.472
	5000S Wagon	80	0.810	0.787	0.002	9.980	0.051	0.472
	5000CS Turbo	80	0.810	0.807	0.002	—	③	③
	5000 Turbo	80	0.875	0.807	0.002	9.980	0.051	0.472

BRAKE SPECIFICATIONS
All measurements in inches unless noted

Year	Model	Lug Nut Torque (ft. lbs.)	Master Cylinder Bore	Brake Disc Minimum Thickness	Brake Disc Maximum Runout	Standard Brake Drum Diameter	Minimum Lining Thickness Front	Minimum Lining Thickness Rear
1987-88	5000 Quattro Turbo	80	0.810	0.807	0.002	—	③	③
	5000CS Quattro Wagon	80	0.810	0.807	0.002	—	③	③
	Coupe GT	80	0.810	0.472	0.002	7.894	0.078	0.098

NOTE: Minimum lining thickness is as recommended by the manufacturer. Due to variations in state inspection regulations, the minimum allowable thickness may be different than recommended by the manufacturer.

① With ventilated discs—0.768 after refinishing—0.728 discard thickness
② Included backing plate
③ Replace the pads when the indicator on the dash turns on
④ All models with rear disc brakes—
Minimum Thickness 0.335
Maximum Runout   0.002

WHEEL ALIGNMENT

Year	Model	Caster Range (deg.)	Caster Preferred Setting (deg.)	Camber Range (deg.)	Camber Preferred Setting (deg.)	Toe-in (in.)	Steering Axis Inclination (deg.)
1981	4000	0–1P	1/2P	15/32N–5/32N	21/32N	5/64	N/A
	4000 Coupe	15/16P–15/16P	17/16P	1/6N–11/6N	2/3N	1/12	N/A
	5000	1/2P–113/16P	15/32P	1N–0	1/2N	0	N/A
	5000 Diesel	1/2P–113/16P	15/32P	1N–0	1/2N	0	N/A
	5000 Turbo	1/2P–113/16P	15/32P	1N–0	1/2N	0	N/A
1982	4000	0–1P	1/2P	15/32N–5/32N	21/32N	5/64	N/A
	4000 Coupe	15/16P–15/16P	17/16P	1/6N–11/6N	2/3N	1/12	N/A
	4000 Diesel	0–1P	1/2P	15/32N–5/32N	21/32N	5/64	N/A
	5000	1/2P–113/16P	15/32P	1N–0	1/2N	0	N/A
	5000 Diesel	1/2P–113/16P	15/32P	1N–0	1/2N	0	N/A
	5000 Turbo	1/2P–113/16P	15/32P	1N–0	1/2N	0	N/A
1983	4000	0–1P	1/2P	15/32N–5/32N	21/32N	5/64	N/A
	4000 Coupe	0–1P	1/2P	15/32N–5/32N	21/32N	5/64	N/A
	4000 Diesel	0–1P	1/2P	15/32N–5/32N	21/32N	5/64	N/A
	5000	1/2P–113/16P	15/32P	1N–0	1/2N	0	N/A
	5000 Diesel	1/2P–113/16P	15/32P	1N–0	1/2N	0	N/A
	5000 Turbo	1/2P–113/16P	15/32P	1N–0	1/2N	0	N/A
	Quattro Turbo	27/32P–25/32P	11/2P	111/32N–11/32N	27/32N	0	N/A
1984	4000	0–1P	1/2P	15/32N–5/32N	21/32N	5/64	N/A
	4000 Coupe	0–1P	1/2P	15/32N–5/32N	21/32N	5/64	N/A
	4000 Quattro	15/16P–115/16P	17/16P	11/4N–1/4N	3/4N	5/64	N/A
	Coupe GT	0–1P	1/2P	15/32N–5/32N	21/32N	5/64	N/A

WHEEL ALIGNMENT

Year	Model	Caster Range (deg.)	Caster Preferred Setting (deg.)	Camber Range (deg.)	Camber Preferred Setting (deg.)	Toe-in (in.)	Steering Axis Inclination (deg.)
	Quattro Coupe	$27/32$P–$25/32$P	$1\,1/2$P	$1\,11/32$N–$11/32$N	$27/32$N	0	N/A
	5000	$1/2$P–$1\,13/16$P	$1\,5/32$P	1N–0	$1/2$N	0	N/A
	5000 Turbo	$1/2$P–$1\,13/16$P	$1\,5/32$P	1N–0	$1/2$N	0	N/A
	Quattro	$5/6$P–$2\,1/6$P	$1\,1/2$P	$1\,1/3$N–$1/3$N	$5/6$N	$1/12$	N/A
	Coupe	0–1P	$1/2$P	$1\,1/6$N–$1/6$N	$2/3$N	$1/3$	N/A
1985	4000S	$5/16$P–$1\,5/16$P	$1\,7/16$P	$1/6$N–$1\,1/6$N	$2/3$N	$1/12$	N/A
	4000 Coupe	$15/16$P–$1\,5/16$P	$1\,7/16$P	$1/6$N–$1\,1/6$N	$2/3$N	$1/12$	N/A
	Quattro	$5/6$P–$2\,1/6$P	$1\,1/2$P	$1\,1/3$N–$1/3$N	$5/6$N	$1/12$	N/A
	Quattro Turbo	$27/32$P–$2\,5/32$P	$1\,1/2$P	$1\,11/32$N–$11/32$N	$27/32$N	0	N/A
	5000S	$11/32$P–$1\,21/32$P	1P	1N–0 ①②	$1/2$N	0 ③④	N/A
	5000S Turbo	$11/32$P–$1\,21/32$P	1P	1N–0 ①②	$1/2$N	0 ③④	N/A
	5000S Wagon	$11/32$P–$1\,21/32$P	1P	1N–0 ①②	$1/2$N	0 ③④	N/A
	5000 Turbo	$11/32$P–$1\,21/32$P	1P	1N–0 ①②	$1/2$N	0 ③④	N/A
	Coupe GT	0P–1P	$1/2$P	$1\,5/32$N–$5/32$N	$21/32$N	$5/64$	N/A
1986	4000S	$15/16$P–$1\,5/16$P	$1\,7/16$P	$1/6$N–$1\,1/6$N	$2/3$N	$1/12$	N/A
	4000 Coupe	$15/16$P–$1\,5/16$P	$1\,7/16$P	$1/6$N–$1\,1/6$N	$2/3$N	$1/12$	N/A
	4000CS Quattro	$15/16$P–$1\,5/16$P	$1\,7/16$P	$1/6$N–$1\,1/6$N	$2/3$N	$1/12$	N/A
	5000S	$11/32$P–$1\,21/32$P	1P	1N–0 ①②	$1/2$N	0 ③④	N/A
	5000S Wagon	$11/32$P–$1\,21/32$P	1P	1N–0 ①②	$1/2$N	0 ③④	N/A
	5000CS Turbo	$11/32$P–$1\,21/32$P	1P	1N–0 ①②	$1/2$N	0 ③④	N/A
	5000 Turbo	$11/32$P–$1\,21/32$P	1P	1N–0 ①②	$1/2$N	0 ③④	N/A
	5000 Quattro Turbo	$11/32$P–$1\,21/32$P	1P	1N–0 ①②	$1/2$N	0 ③④	N/A
	5000CS Quattro Wagon	$11/32$P–$1\,21/32$P	1P	1N–0 ①②	$1/2$N	0 ③④	N/A
	Coupe GT	0P–1P	$1/2$P	$1\,5/32$N–$5/32$N	$21/32$N	$5/64$	N/A
1987-88	4000S	$15/16$P–$1\,5/16$P	$1\,7/16$P	$1/6$N–$1\,1/6$N	$2/3$N	$1/12$	N/A
	4000 Coupe	$15/16$P–$1\,5/16$P	$1\,7/16$P	$1/6$N–$1\,1/6$N	$2/3$N	$1/12$	N/A
	4000CS Quattro	$15/16$P–$1\,5/16$P	$1\,7/16$P	$1/6$N–$1\,1/6$N	$2/3$N	$1/12$	N/A
	5000S	$11/32$P–$1\,21/32$P	1P	1N–0 ①②	$1/2$N	0 ③④	N/A
	5000S Wagon	$11/32$P–$1\,21/32$P	1P	1N–0 ①②	$1/2$N	0 ③④	N/A
	5000CS Turbo	$11/32$P–$1\,21/32$P	1P	1N–0 ①②	$1/2$N	0 ③④	N/A
	5000 Turbo	$11/32$P–$1\,21/32$P	1P	1N–0 ①②	$1/2$N	0 ③④	N/A
	5000 Quattro Turbo	$11/32$P–$1\,21/32$P	1P	1N–0 ①②	$1/2$N	0 ③④	N/A
	5000CS Quattro Wagon	$11/32$P–$1\,21/32$P	1P	1N–0 ①②	$1/2$N	0 ③④	N/A
	Coupe GT	0P–1P	$1/2$P	$1\,5/32$N–$5/32$N	$21/32$N	$5/64$	N/A

N   Negative
P   Positive
NA   No application
① $5/6$N to $1/6$N—Rear axle
② $1/2$N—Maximum difference between left and right—Rear Axle
③ $1/30$P to $5/18$P—Up to chassis No. EN096669—Rear Axle
④ $1/30$P to $1/4$P—from chassis No. EN096670—Rear Axle

TUNE-UP PROCEDURES

All the tune-up steps should be followed, as each adjustment complements the effects of the other adjustments. If the tune-up specifications sticker in the engine compartment disagrees with the "Tune-up Specifications" chart, the sticker figures must be followed.

Ignition Timing

NOTE: Production changes are noted on the underhood specifications sticker. If the procedure differs from below, follow sticker instructions.

STATIC ADJUSTMENT

A basic timing adjustment can be made in the following manner. Turn the engine until the basic ignition timing mark is aligned with the ignition timing pointer and the distributor rotor points towards the No. 1 cylinder mark on the rim of the distributor body. Timing marks are on the flywheel on the 4000 and 5000. This will put the No. 1 cylinder at TDC (0°T). Connect a 12 volt test lamp between the ignition coil terminal, No. 1 connected to the distributor, and a ground. Rotate the distributor clockwise until the lamp goes out. Turn the distributor counterclockwise until the lamp just lights, and tighten the clamp on the distributor at that point. The ignition timing is now approximately set. As soon as possible, check the adjustment with a timing light.

DYNAMIC ADJUSTMENT

Connect a timing light to the No. 1 cylinder and connect a tachometer.

NOTE: Some tachometers, dwell-meters and oscilloscopes will not work with the capacitive discharge ignition system. Some may be damaged. Check with the manufacturer of the test equipment if there is any doubt.

Loosen the distributor clamp screw until it is just possible to turn the distributor by hand. Run the engine at idle speed and point the timing light at the timing window on the flywheel housing. Turn the distributor until the specified notch on the flywheel aligns with the pointer.

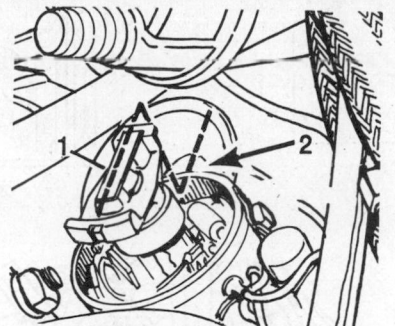

The distributor rotor (1) aligned with the No. 1 cylinder mark (2) on the rim of the distributor body. The dust cap is removed

NOTE: 5000S Turbo and Quattro models are timed by aligning the distributor housing and reference marks, 4000S and 5000S models require the vacuum hoses to be connected when checking or adjusting the timing or curb idle speed.

On most models the idle stabilizer must be bypassed. To bypass the idle stabilizer, disconnect its two electrical leads and plug them together. This must be done with the ignition turned off or it could ruin the entire system. Check the timing at 2500, 2750 or 3000 rpm, if specified. Adjust as necessary.

The idle stabilizer is located on top of the ignition control unit. The idle stabilizer controls idle speed by either advancing or retarding the distributor timing in accordance with engine load (air conditioner on, lights on, etc.) If idle speed is erratic or if the engine fails to start, try bypassing the idle stabilizer by disconnecting the two plugs at the idle stabilizer and plugging them together. If idle improves, the idle stabilizer should probably be replaced.

NOTE: Certain late models have an impedance transformer installed on top of the ignition control unit in place of an idle stabilizer. DO NOT disconnect the plugs of the transformer when setting the timing. Timing should always be checked both at idle and at 2500, 2750 or 3000 rpm if specified.

Valve Lash

ADJUSTMENT

NOTE: The 4000S (built after Jan. 1984) and 5000S series are equipped with hydraulic valve lash adjusters which eliminate

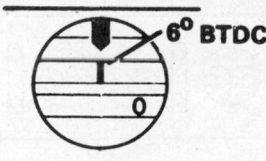

Timing mark alignment—typical of the 1.8L engine

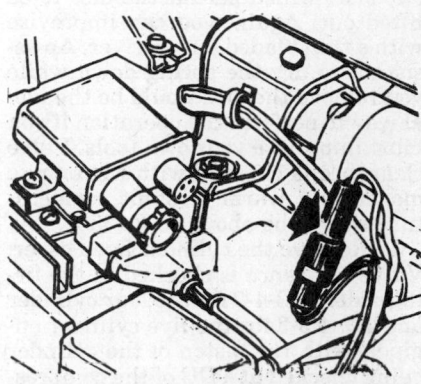

Bypass the idle stabilizer unit by connecting thye two plugs together (arrow)

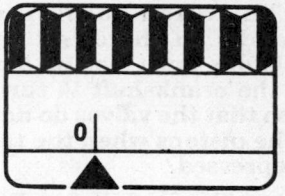

Typical timing mark alignment—4000 and 5000 series

the need for periodic valve clearance adjustment. Intermittent valve noises are normal with a cold engine. Should valve noise persist, check cam lobes and lifter for wear, replace as necessary.

Audi recommends checking the valve clearance at 1000 miles and then every 15,000 miles thereafter. The overhead cam acts directly on the valves through cam followers which fit over the springs and valves. Adjustment is made with an adjusting disc which fits into the cam follower. Different thickness discs result in changes in valve clearance.

Audi also recommends that two special tools be used to remove and install the adjustment discs. One is a pry bar (VW 546, 2078 or equivalent) to compress the valve springs and the other a pair of special pliers (US 10–208, US4476 or equivalent) to remove the disc. If the purchase of these tools is not possible, a flat metal plate can be used to compress the valve springs if you are careful not to gouge the camshaft lobes. The cam follower has

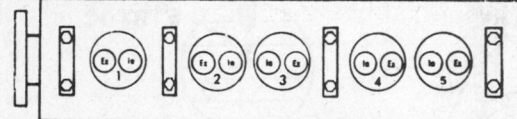

Valve location—5 cyl engine

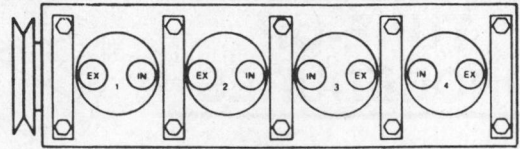

Valve location—4000, 4 cyl. engine

two slots which permit the disc to be lifted out. Again, you can improvise with a thin bladed screwdriver. An assistant to pry the spring down while you remove the disc would be the ideal way to perform the operation if you must improvise your own tools. Valve clearance is checked with the engine moderately warm (coolant temperature should be about 95°F (35°C).

1. Remove the cylinder head cover. Valve clearance is checked in the firing order (1-3-4-2 for the four cylinder and 1-2-4-5-3 for the five cylinder engines) with the piston of the cylinder being checked at TDC of the compression stroke. Both valves will be closed at this position and the cam lobes will be pointing straight up.

NOTE: When adjusting the clearances on the diesel engine, the pistons must not be at TDC. Turn the crankshaft ¼ turn past TDC so that the valves do not contact the pistons when the tappets are depressed.

2. Turn the crankshaft pulley bolt with a socket wrench to position the camshaft for checking.

CAUTION

Do not turn the camshaft by the camshaft mounting bolt, this will stretch the drive belt. When turning the crankshaft pulley bolt, turn it clockwise only.

---

3. With the No. 1 piston at TDC (¼ turn past for the diesel) of the compression stroke, determine the clearance with a feeler gauge.

4. Continue on to check the other cylinders in the firing order, turning the crankshaft to bring each piston to the top of the compression stroke (¼ turn for diesel). Record the individual clearances as you go along.

5. If measured clearance is within tolerance levels (0.002 in.), it is not necessary to replace the adjusting discs.

6. If adjustment is necessary, the discs will have to be removed and replaced with thicker or thinner ones which will yield the correct clearance. Discs are available in 0.002 in. increments from 0.12 in.– 0.17 in.

NOTE: The thickness of the adjusting discs are etched on one

Test the hydraulic lash adjuster by pushing down against the lifter with a suitable wooden dowel—if the lifter can be pushed down, replacement is indicated

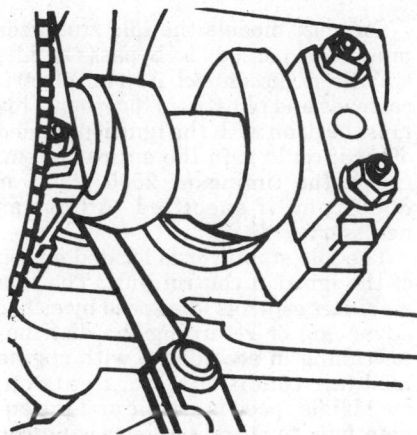

Checking valve clearance with a feeler gauge—4000, 5000 and Coupe

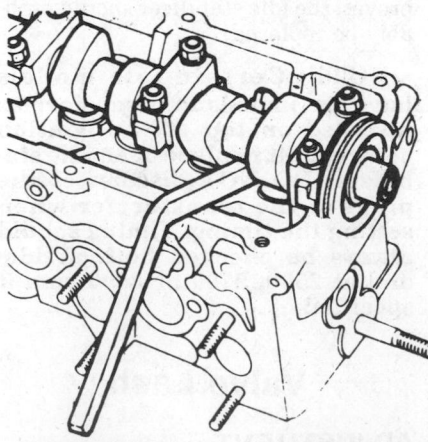

Remove the adjusting discs with a special pry bar and pliers—don't press on the disc itself, but on the lip of the disc holder. Note the position of the camshaft lobes on no. 1 cylinder. This is the correct position for measuring valve clearance

side. When installing, the marks must face the cam followers. Discs can be reused if they are not worn or damaged.

7. To remove the discs, turn the cam followers so that the grooves are accessible when the pry bar is depressed.

8. Press the cam follower down with the pry bar and remove the adjusting discs with the special pliers or the screwdriver.

9. Replace the adjustment discs as necessary to bring the clearance within the 0.002 in. tolerance level. If the measured clearance is larger than the given tolerance, remove the existing disc and insert a thicker one to bring the clearance up to specification. If it is smaller, insert a thinner one.

10. Recheck all valve clearances after adjustment.

11. Install the cylinder head cover with a new gasket.

Idle Speed and Mixture Gasoline Engines

IDLE SPEED ADJUSTMENT

NOTE: On later models, the idle speed should be adjusted in conjunction with the % CO. In these cases, it is suggested that the adjustment not be attempted unless the necessary equipment is available.

4000, Coupe Models and 5000 Except Turbo, and Calif. Models

NOTE: The timing must be set to specifications before adjusting the idle speed.

On 1984–88 4000S, 1.8L models: check idle with all vacuum hoses attached. If adjustment is necessary the oxygen sensor should be connected, the crankcase vent hose to the valve cover should be disconnected and opened to outside air. The evaporative canister cap should be removed.

On 4000S Quattro, 2.2L models: Check idle with all vacuum hoses connected. If adjustment is necessary the oxygen sensor should be connected, the crankcase vent hose to the valve cover should be disconnected and plugged and the evaporative canister cap should be removed.

On 5000S series models: Check the idle with the oxygen sensor and all vacuum hoses connected. If adjustment is necessary, disconnect the crankcase vent hoses and plug them. Remove the cap from the evaporative canister and on the 5000S (non-turbo) and 4000 Quattro, disconnect the purge line. Idle speed stabilizer is bypassed on models so equipped.

1. Connect a dwell/tachometer according to the manufacturer's instructions.

2. Run the engine until the oil temperature is above 176°F (80°C). The radiator fan must come on at least once.

3. Turn the headlights ON high beam. If equipped with A/C, DO NOT turn it ON. DO NOT connect a pressure gauge to the fuel system.

4. Disconnect the PCV valve, if equipped.

NOTE: If the fuel lines were disconnected, run the engine to 3000 rpm (several times), then idle for 2 minutes.

5. Locate the idle adjusting screw in the throttle valve housing on the back of the intake manifold and adjust the idle to specifications.

NOTE: If equipped with an idle stabilizer, disconnect both plugs and connect them together.

6. Adjust the % CO.

NOTE: The radiator fan must not run while adjusting the idle.

4000, Coupe Models, 5000 Calif. Models and All Turbocharged Models

NOTE: The timing must be set to specifications before adjusting the idle speed. Refer to above on the 4000S and 5000S models (1984-88).

1. Connect a dwell/tachometer, according to the manufacturer's instructions.

2. Turn off all electrical accessories.

3. Run the engine until the oil temperature is above 175°F (80°C). The radiator fan must come on at least once.

4. Turn the ignition off.

5. Disconnect the PCV valve.

6. Disconnect the plug for the oxygen sensor wire by the manifold.

7. Unplug both wire leads at the idle stabilizer and connect them together.

8. Start the engine.

9. Locate the idle adjusting screw

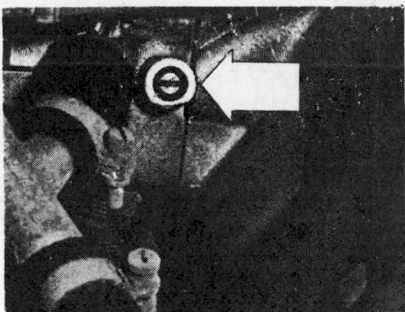
Idle speed adjustment screw—5000

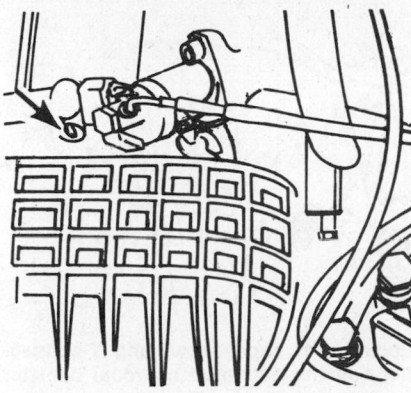
Idle speed adjustment screw—4000

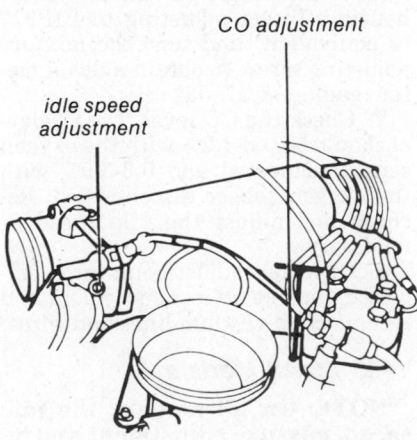
Locations of idle speed and mixture adjustment screws typical of CIS fuel injection

in the throttle valve housing on the back of the intake manifold and adjust the idle to specifications.

NOTE: The radiator fan must not run while adjusting the idle.

10. Turn off the engine and reconnect the PCV valve, the oxygen sensor wire and the idle stabilizer.

11. Recheck the idle speed. If it has changed, the idle stabilizer will probably require replacement.

12. Adjust the % CO.

CO (MIXTURE) ADJUSTMENT

NOTE: An exhaust gas analyzer or a CO meter will be required for this procedure; adjustment of the CO is impossible without one.

1981–83 Models Without Oxygen Sensor or Idle Stabilizer

1. Operate the engine at normal operating temperature.

2. Turn the high beams and A/C on. Set the ignition timing to specifications with the screw shown.

3. Adjust the idle speed to specifications with the screw shown.

4. Remove the charcoal filter hose from the air cleaner.

5. Remove the plug from the CO

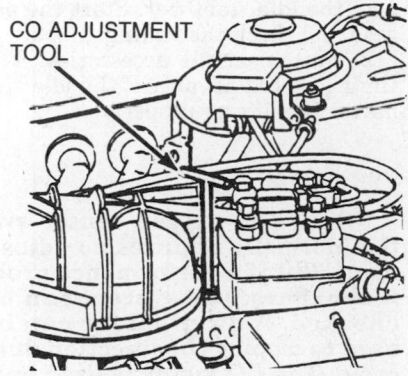
Special mixture adjustment tool installed on typical CIS air flow sensor. Do not race the engine with the tool in place

adjusting hole and insert tool VW-P377 or equivalent. Turn adjustment screw clockwise to raise the CO or counterclockwise to decrease the CO. Do not push down on the adjustment tool or accelerate the engine with the tool in place.

6. Remove the tool and accelerate the engine briefly before reading the CO.

NOTE: For 1982–88 models a CO meter is not used to adjust the idle mixture. Audi specifies using the Siemens 451 or equivalent device when making adjustments and only using the CO meter to verify the settings. The purge hose or cap on the evaporative control system must also be removed to adjust CO.

1981-83 Models With Oxygen Sensor and Idle Stabilizer

1. Connect Siemens 451 or equivalent according to manufacturers instructions.

2. Start the engine and allow it to reach operating temperature. Turn the ignition OFF.

3. Remove the multi-point connectors from the idle stabilizer and connect them together.

4. Remove and plug the crankcase breather hose.

5. Connect the hose probe to the CO test point.

6. Disconnect the oxygen sensor wire, then start the engine.

7. Insert adjusting tool P377 and adjust CO% to specifications. Check the underhood EPA sticker for the correct settings.

8. Remove the tool after each adjustments and accelerate the engine briefly before reading CO gauge.

9. Reconnect the oxygen sensor wire. Check CO.

10. Remove PCV hose and check idle speed.

11. Shut off the engine and reconnect the idle stabilizer. Start the engine and check the timing.

12. Switch on all accessories. The timing should advance if the idle stabilizer is working properly.

1984 All Models

NOTE: The oxygen sensor system normally requires no adjustment. But if a performance problem occurs, the system can be checked. A dwell meter can be used to display the injection duty cycle. The CO meter is used only to verify proper operations. The oxygen sensor should not be disconnected for this procedure.

1. Start the engine and let it run until it reaches its normal operating temperature. Disconnect and plug the crankcase ventilation hoses at the cylinder head.

2. On the 4000 (4-cyl) models, pinch the supply hose to the idle stabilizer. On the 5000S models, disconnect the canister purge hose. On the 5000S Turbo and Coupe GT, remove the cap from the "T" in the purge hose (which is usually located near the right fender well). On the Quattro, disconnect the purge hose and plug opening.

3. On the 5000S Turbo and Quattro models, disconnect the idle stabilizer signal wire from the negative side of the distributor. On all other models with idle stabilizer, connect the bypass hoses together.

4. Adjust the idle speed by adjusting the idle screw on the inside of the throttle valve housing.

5. Connect a CO meter to the test point with adapter (US-4492 or equivalent). Connect a dwell meter to the test connection. The duty cycle should fluctuate between 25–59° on the dwell meter.

6. If the idle mixture is incorrect,

Idle speed adjustment screw

Location of cap (arrow) and T-connections at the activated charcoal canister hose

remove the plug from the air sensor housing. Insert adjusting tool (P377 or equivalent) and turn the mixture adjusting screw to obtain a dwell meter reading of 37–53°.

7. Check the CO level. The CO level should be 0.3-1.2% with the oxygen sensor connected and 0.3-3.0% with the oxygen sensor disconnected. Recheck and adjust the idle speed as necessary.

8. Once the adjustments are completed, remove all test equipment and reconnect all vacuum lines and wires.

1985–88 All Models

NOTE: On all models, the idle speed, mixture adjustment and ignition timing must be checked together. Exhaust gas mixture must be checked and adjusted by measuring milliamps (mA), with a special meter and with the oxygen sensor connected. Refer to the underhood vacuum diagram for all hose locations.

4 CYLINDER MODELS

1. Start the engine and allow it to reach normal operating temperature. The radiator fan must come on at least once.

2. Switch OFF all accessories. The radiator fan and air conditioner must not be running during the test.

3. Pinch the hose to the idle speed boost valve.

4. Pull the crankcase breather hose off the valve cover and allow it to vent to the atmosphere.

5. Remove the cap from the T-piece.

6. Connect SIEMENS 451 tester (or equivalent) according to the manufacturer's instructions.

7. Remove the cap from the CO probe receptacle and insert the CO probe. The hose must fit tightly so there is no exhaust leak.

8. To measure milliamps (mA), connect a digital multimeter to the differential pressure regulator. Remove the connector from the differential pressure regulator and install adaptor VW 1515 A/1 or equivalent. Connect the multimeter to the adaptor and set the selector switch to DCA 20 mA.

NOTE: If the engine does not run after the adaptor is connected, the connections may be improper. Reverse the plug and try again.

9. Check the idle speed and adjust to specifications if necessary.

10. Check the ignition timing and adjust to specifications if necessary.

11. Read the milliamp and CO values on the testers. The multimeter should read between 4–16 mA (reading fluctuates) and the CO value should be 0.3–1.2%.

12. If the current reading is less than 4 mA or more than 16 mA, remove the CO adjustment plug as follows:

   a. Stop the engine and remove the boot on the mixture control

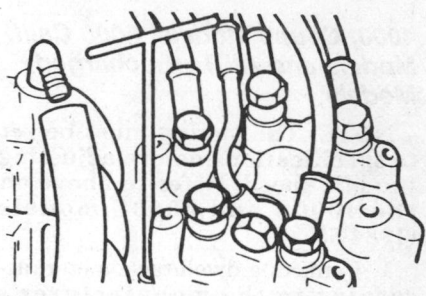

Using the special tool to adjust the mixture

unit.

   b. Centerpunch the plug in the CO adjusting hole.

   c. Drill a $\frac{3}{32}$ in. (2.5mm) hole in the center of the plug $\frac{9}{64}$–$\frac{5}{32}$ in. (3.5–4mm) deep.

   d. Carefully clean up any metal shavings and insert a $\frac{1}{8}$ in. sheet metal screw into the drilled hole, then remove the screw and plug with pliers.

13. Start the engine and allow it to idle.

14. Adjust the current reading on the multimeter by turning the CO adjusting screw with tool P377 or equivalent to obtain 8–12 mA (reading fluctuates). Turn the adjusting screw clockwise to lower the current reading (CO higher) and counterclockwise to raise the current reading (CO lower).

— **CAUTION** —

Do not push adjustment tool down when making CO adjustment and do not accelerate the engine with the tool in place. Remove the tool after each adjustment and accelerate the engine briefly before reading multimeter. Always adjust in direction from high to low.

15. After CO adjustment is complete, recheck the idle speed and adjust if necessary. Reconnect the crankcase breather hose. If, after reconnecting the breather hose, the current reading drops below specifications, an oil change may be necessary.

16. Turn the ignition OFF and drive in a new mixture plug, flush with the mixture control unit.

17. Remove all test equipment, attach CO probe cap and remove the device used to pinch the idle speed boost valve hose.

ALL 5 CYL MODELS

NOTE: Idle speed, ignition timing and oxygen sensor duty cycle (mixture) must be checked and adjusted together.

1. Check that there are no leaks in the exhaust system and connect Siemens 451 tester or equivalent according to the manufacturer's instructions. Make sure the TDC sending unit is installed snugly into the transmission housing.

2. Remove the cap from the CO probe receptacle and install CO test probe. Make sure the hose fits snugly so there is no exhaust leak.

3. Disconnect the crankcase breather hose at the cylinder head cover and plug the hose.

4. Disconnect both plugs at the idle stabilizer and plug the connectors together to bypass the unit. Make sure the connectors are tight.

5. Turn OFF all accessories. If any fuel lines were disconnected or replaced, start the engine and run it to 3000 rpm several times, then let idle for at least two minutes.

6. Start the engine and allow it to reach normal operating temperature. The radiator fan must come on at least once.

NOTE: The radiator fan must not be running during all tests and adjustments.

Plug the crankcase breather hose as shown

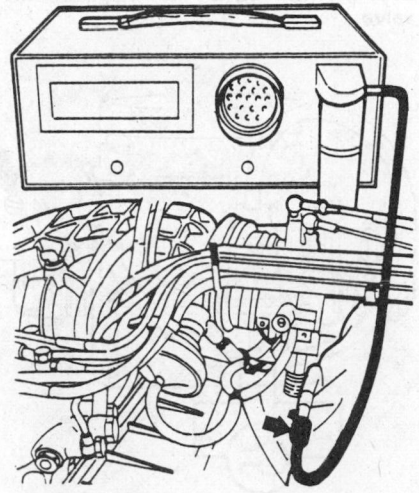

Attach the CO tester to the tap tube as shown

7. Check and adjust the idle speed if necessary.

8. Check and adjust the ignition timing if necessary. Turn ignition OFF.

9. Connect the dwell lead on the tester to the oxygen sensor blue/white test connection. Remove the cap from the charcoal canister purge line.

10. Remove the test lead from No. 1 ignition wire and TDC sending unit. Make sure the tester is on the 4 cylinder scale and press "%" button. Start the engine and check the oxygen sensor duty cycle (dwell) and CO at idle speed.

11. The OXS duty cycle should be 25–65% (reading should fluctuate) and the CO should be between 0.3–1.2%. If the CO is more than 1.2%, but the dwell range is correct, check for leaks in the intake or exhaust system, malfunctioning fuel distributor, or a faulty injector spray pattern.

12. If the OXS duty cycle is less than 25% or more than 65%, remove the tamper-proof plug as described in Step 12 of the 4 cylinder procedure, above.

13. Using adjusting tool P377 or equivalent, adjust the OXS duty cycle

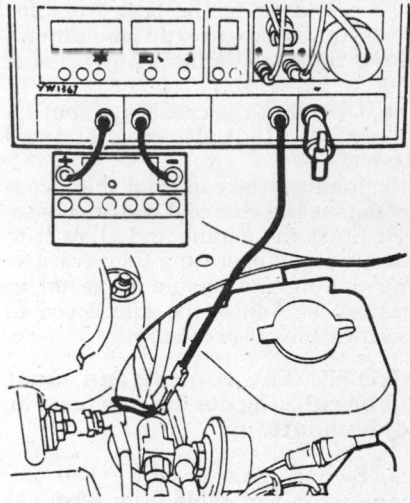

Connect a tester to the oxygen sensor to the test connector as shown

(mixture) by turning the adjusting screw clockwise to lower the meter reading, or counterclockwise to increase the reading. Adjust to 44–56% (reading should fluctuate). The radiator fan must not be running during adjustment.

— **CAUTION** —

Do not push adjustment tool down while adjusting CO level. Never accelerate the engine with the tool in place and remove the tool and accelerate the engine briefly after each adjustment.

14. Readjust the idle speed, if necessary, then turn ignition OFF and remove the test equipment. Be sure to replace the CO probe cap to prevent exhaust leaks. Reconnect the crankcase breather hose and idle stabilizer. Install the cap to the charcoal canister purge line and replace the tamper-proof adjustment plug.

TURBOCHARGED MODELS

NOTE: Idle speed, ignition timing and oxygen sensor duty cycle (mixture) must be checked and adjusted together with the engine at normal operating temperature, throttle valve in the idle position and all electrical accessories OFF. If injector lines were disconnected or replaced, start and run the engine to 3000 rpm several times, then let idle for two minutes prior to test.

1. Connect Siemens 451, VW 1367, or equivalent tester according to manufacturer's instructions. Make sure the TDC sensor is firmly seated into the transmission housing.

2. Disconnect the green wire from terminal #1 of the ignition coil.

3. Remove the cap from the CO test

tube and connect the hose from the CO tester. Make sure the hose connection is tight to eliminate any exhaust leak.

4. Disconect the crankcase ventilation hoses at the valve cover and seal the ends.

5. Remove the cap from the T-connection at the charcoal canister hose.

6. Start the engine and allow it to reach normal operating temperature. The cooling fan should come on at least once. Adjust the idle speed to specifications if necessary.

NOTE: The cooling fan must not be running during any tests or adjustments.

7. Switch ignition OFF, then disconnect the test cable from terminal #1 of the ignition coil and connect to the blue/white wire of the oxygen sensor. Disconnect the test connections from No. 1 cylinder ignition cable and TDC sensor. Push "Dwell Angle %" button on the tester.

8. Start the engine and allow it to idle. Raise the engine speed above 2000 rpm for five seconds, then check the oxygen sensor (OXS) duty cycle. Duty cycle should read 25–65% (reading should fluctuate) and the CO value should be 0.3–1.2% with the oxygen sensor connected.

9. If the CO value exceeds 1.2% with the duty cycle within 25–65%, check for a fault in the ignition system, leaks in the exhaust system or a problem with the fuel distributor. If the duty cycle is less than 25% or exceeds 65%, a CO adjustment is necessary.

10. Switch the ignition OFF and remove the CO adjustment plug as outlined in Step 12 of the 4 cylinder adjustment procedure, above.

11. Using CO adjustment tool P377 or equivalent, turn the adjustment screw clockwise to lower the OXS duty cycle, or counterclockwise to raise it to obtain a reading of 42–58% (reading should fluctuate). Do not lift or press down on the adjustment tool when making adjustments and remove the tool and briefly accelerate the engine after each adjustment. Never accelerate the engine with the tool in place.

12. Once the correct duty cycle reading is obtained, reset the idle speed if necessary.

13. Switch the ignition OFF and disconnect the CO tester. Install the cap on the CO test tube, making sure it is tight to prevent exhaust leaks. Disconnect all test equipment and restore all disconnected hoses. Install the cap on the charcoal canister T-connection and drive in a new tamper-proof mixture plug.

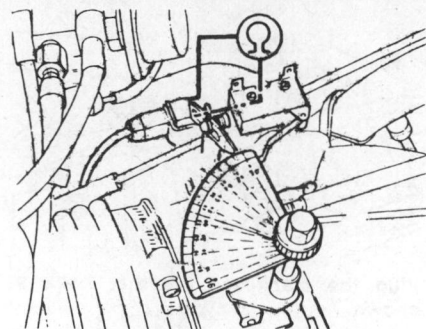
Tool mounted on the 1st stage throttle valve

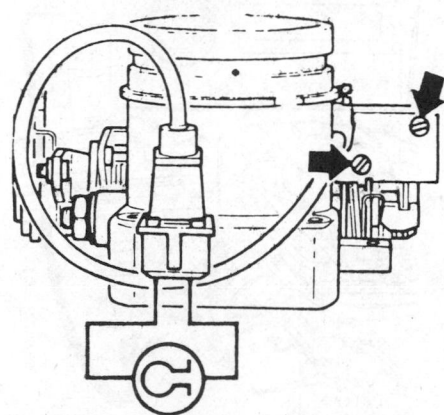
Ohmmeter connection and adjusting points for idle switch adjustment

Throttle Valve Switches

NOTE: To check and adjust the idle and full throttle switch on various 1984–88 models, Special Tool No. 3084 and an ohmmeter are necessary.

IDLE SWITCH ADJUSTMENT

1. Loosen the upper left bolt from the throttle valve housing and install the pointer for Tool 3084. Tighten bolt.

2. Attach the protractor (Tool 3084) to the first stage throttle valve shaft (remove the nut if necessary).

3. Disconnect the switch wire plug and connect the ohmmeter.

4. Adjust the protractor to "zero". Open the throttle approximately 20°, then close throttle slowly.

5. Ohmmeter should show continuity (0 ohms) when the pointer indicates the throttle position is at 1° to 2.5°. If not within specs, remove housing cover and adjust idle switch position. The ohmmeter must indicate continuity (0 ohms) before the throttle reaches the idle position.

FULL THROTTLE SWITCH ADJUSTMENT

1. Mount pointer as in Idle Switch procedure Step 1.

2. Attach the protractor (Tool

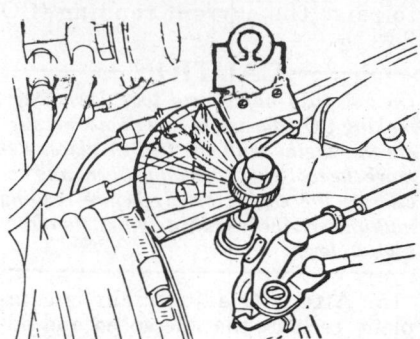
Tool 3084 mounting and ohmmeter connections for the full throttle switch adjustment

3084) to the second stage throttle valve shaft (remove the nut if necessary).

3. Remove the full throttle switch connectors and connect the ohmmeter.

4. Open the second stage throttle fully and "zero" the protractor.

5. Close the throttle to approximately 30°.

6. Open the throttle valve slowly and watch the protractor and ohmmeter. The ohmmeter should read continuity (0 ohms) when the protractor is at 12° to 8° before full throttle.

7. Adjust throttle switch position as necessary. The ohmmeter must indicate zero ohms at full throttle.

Idle Speed—Diesel Engine

ADJUSTMENTS

Diesel engines have both an idle speed and a maximum speed adjustment. The maximum engine speed adjustment prevents the engine from over-revving and self-destructing. The adjusters are located side by side on top of the injection pump. The screw closest to the engine is the idle speed adjuster, while the outer screw is the maximum speed adjuster.

The idle and maximum speed must be adjusted with the engine warm (normal operating temperature). Because the diesel engine has no conventional ignition, a special adaptor is necessary to connect the tachometer, or use the tachometer in the instrument panel, if equipped. Conventional tachometers will not work on a diesel engine. Adjust all engines to the

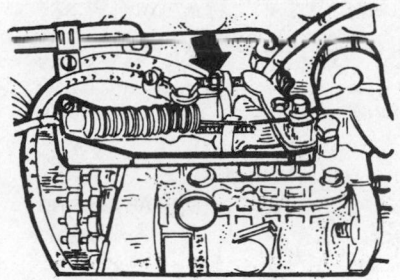

Idle speed adjustment scew—diesel

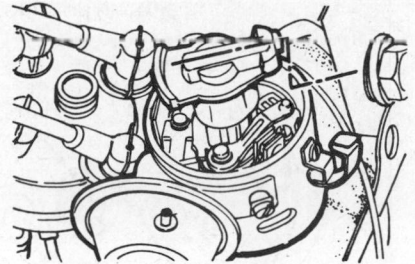

Rotor/distributor alignment for the No. 1 cylinder

specified idle speed. When adjustment is correct, lock the locknut on the screw and apply non-hardening thread sealer (Loctite® or similar) to prevent the screw from vibrating loose.

The maximum speed for all engines is between 5300–5400 rpm. If it is not in this range, loosen the screw and correct the speed (turning the screw clockwise decreases rpm). On 5000 series turn dash control knob counterclockwise until it stops prior to adjustment. Lock the nut on the adjusting screw and apply a dab of thread sealer in the same manner as you did on the idle screw.

— **CAUTION** —

Do not attempt to squeeze more power out of the engine by raising the maximum speed (rpm). Serious engine damage can occur.

ENGINE ELECTRICAL

Distributor

REMOVAL & INSTALLATION

4000, Coupe Models and 5000

1. Disconnect the wiring harness connector and any other connectors from the distributor cap.
2. Remove the static shield (if equipped).
3. Disconnect and note the position of the vacuum lines.
4. Release the two retaining spring clips and remove the distributor cap.
5. Note the position of the rotor in relation to the base. Scribe a mark on the base of the distributor and on the engine block to facilitate reinstallation. Align the marks with the direction the metal tip of the rotor is pointing. Note the approximate position of the vacuum advance unit in relation to the engine.

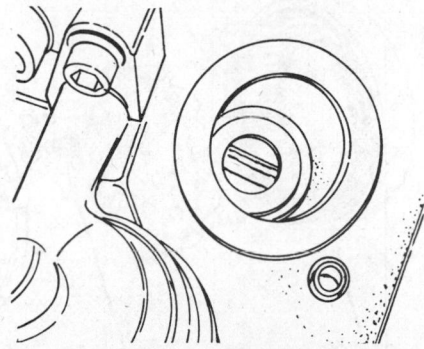

The oil pump driveshaft must be parallel to the crankshaft on the 4000

6. Remove the distributor hold-down bolt and clamp.
7. Lift the distributor assembly from the engine.
8. To install the distributor, perform one of the following procedures.

UNDISTURBED ENGINE

1. Insert the distributor shaft and assembly into the engine.
2. Line up the marks on the distributor and on the engine with the metal tip of the rotor.
3. Make sure the vacuum advance unit is pointed in the same direction as it was pointed originally. If the marks on the distributor and the engine are lined up properly, this will be done automatically.
4. Install the distributor hold-down clamp and bolt.
5. Install and secure the distributor cap.
6. Install the vacuum lines in their original places.
7. Install the static shield.
8. Install the wiring harness connector and any other connectors previously removed.
9. Start the engine. Adjust the dwell angle (breaker point ignitions) and set the ignition timing.

DISTURBED ENGINE

NOTE: If the crankshaft has been turned or the engine has been disturbed in any manner (i.e. disassembled and rebuilt)

while the distributor was removed, or if the marks were not drawn, it will be necessary to initially time the engine. Follow the procedure given below.

1. It is necessary to place the No. 1 cylinder in the firing position (TDC) to correctly install the distributor. To locate this position, the ignition timing marks on the flywheel and the clutch housing are used.
2. Remove the spark plug from the No. 1 cylinder. Turn the crankshaft until the piston in the No. 1 cylinder is moving up on the compression stroke. This can be determined by placing your thumb over the spark plug hole and feeling the air being forced out of the cylinder. Stop turning the engine when the timing mark on the flywheel is aligned with the lug on the flywheel housing.
3. Remove the upper drive belt cover.
4. Align the mark on the camshaft sprocket with the upper edge of the drive belt cover or with the upper edge of the cylinder head cover gasket.
5. Align the oil pump drive pinion lug so that it is parallel to the crankshaft (4000 only).
6. Oil the distributor housing lightly where it bears on the cylinder block.
7. Install the distributor so that the rotor, which is mounted on the shaft, points to the mark on the distributor housing for the No. 1 cylinder.
8. When the distributor shaft has reached the bottom of the hole, move the rotor back and forth slightly until the drive lug on the oil pump shaft enters the slots cut into the end of the distributor shaft, and the distributor assembly slides down into place (4000 only).
9. Clean the distributor cap and check for signs of cracking or carbon tracks. Replace the cap and continue from Step 5 of the installation procedure, undisturbed engine.

Alternator

PRECAUTIONS

All Audi models are equipped with alternators. When performing any service to the alternator or alternator system the following precautions should be observed:

• Leads or cables to any part of the charging circuit should be disconnected only after the engine has been switched Off and and has stopped running.

• When working on the electrical

system, always disconnect the lead from the negative battery terminal.

• When performing tests with the engine running, the battery must always be connected.

• Temporary connections should never be made to the alternator. Always make firm connections.

• The alternator warning light on the instrument panel should go out when the engine reaches idle speed, or shortly after.

REMOVAL & INSTALLATION

1. Disconnect the negative battery cable.

2. Disconnect all the leads to the alternator, tagging them first. Various arrangements of plug-in or bolt-on connections have been used. On some models the wiring may be unplugged from the back of the alternator.

3. Remove the belt tensioning bolt from the slotted adjusting bracket.

4. Remove the drive belt.

5. Unbolt and remove the alternator.

To install the unit:

6. Install the pivot bolts.

7. Install the drive belt and the belt tensioning bolt.

8. Adjust the belt tension.

9. Replace all the electrical connections, making sure that they are installed in their original locations.

10. Connect the battery ground strap.

BELT TENSION ADJUSTMENT

The alternator drive belt is correctly tensioned when the longest span of belt between pulleys can be depressed ⅛–½ in. by moderate thumb pressure. To adjust, loosen the slotted adjusting bracket bolt on the alternator. If the alternator hinge bolts are very tight, it may be necessary to loosen them slightly to move the alternator. Move the alternator in or out by hand to get the correct tension, then tighten the adjusting bolt.

V-belts under 39 inches in length should deflect about ⅛ in. Belts over 40 inches long should deflect about ½ in.

NOTE: Be careful not to overtighten the belt, as this may damage the alternator bearings.

Starter

REMOVAL & INSTALLATION

1. Disconnect the negative battery cable.

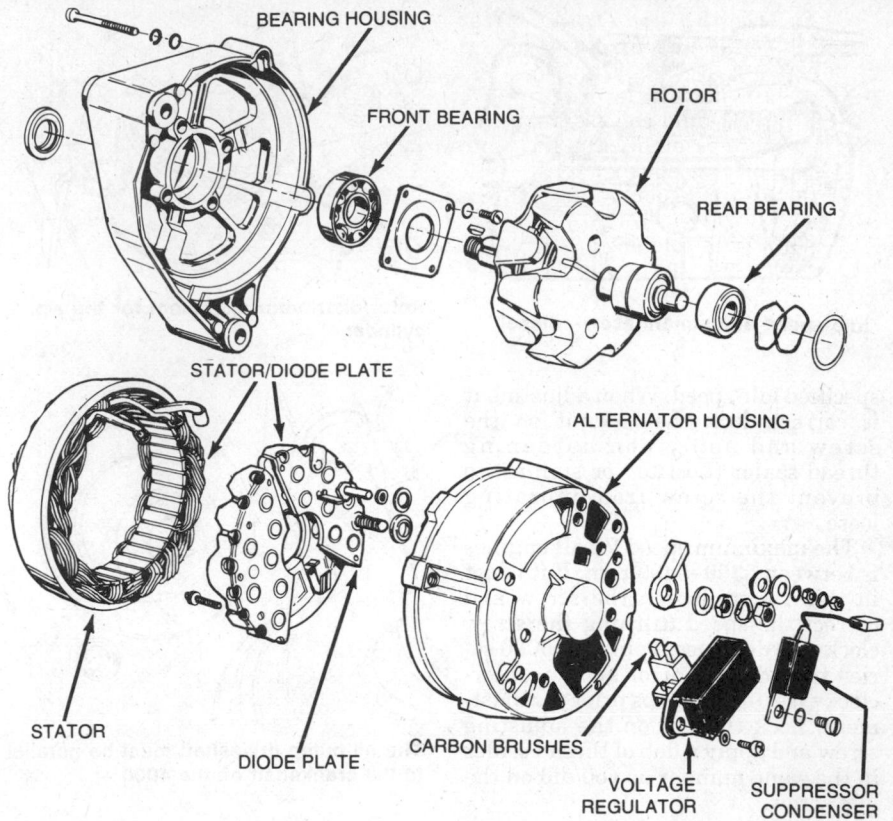

Exploded view of alternator—typical

2. Jack up the right-front of the vehicle and support it with jackstands.

3. Mark with tape and then disconnect the two small wires from the starter solenoid. One wire connects to the ignition coil and the other to the ignition switch.

4. Disconnect the large cable which comes from the battery.

5. Remove the starter support bracket bolts (4000 only). Remove the starter mounting bolts from the back of the starter (all models).

6. Remove the starter.

7. To install, reverse the removal procedures.

STARTER DRIVE REPLACEMENT

NOTE: In order to complete this procedure you will need a pair of circlip pliers and Special Tool US 1078; a gear puller.

1. Remove the starter from the vehicle.

2. Remove the solenoid.

3. Remove the two long housing screws and remove the end plate.

4. Lift the brushes to free them from the commutator and remove the brush holder.

5. Tap the field coil housing lightly

with a wooden mallet and remove it from the starter drive housing.

6. Remove the nut and bolt that serves as a pin for the shift lever. Be careful to retain all the associated washers.

7. Remove the shift lever.

8. Slide the armature/starter drive assembly out of the starter drive housing.

9. Using tool No. VW421, press the stop ring down and remove the circlip from the end of the armature shaft.

10. Remove the stop ring using the gear puller tool No. 1078.

11. Slide the starter drive off of the armature shaft.

To install the drive:

1. Lubricate the drive pinion lightly with multi-purpose grease and slide the starter drive onto the armature shaft.

2. Install the stop ring and press it over the circlip groove.

NOTE: When installing the stop ring, the groove must always be on the side closest to the front of the starter (the side nearest to the starter drive).

3. Install the circlip and, using the gear puller tool No. 1078, pull the stop ring up into place against the circlip.

4. Lightly grease the shaft.

5. Install the armature/starter drive assembly into the starter drive housing.

6. Install the shift lever.

7. Ease the field coil housing over the armature assembly and fit it into the starter drive housing.

8. Install the brush holder and the end plate.

9. Install the solenoid.

10. Install the starter.

SOLENOID REPLACEMENT

1. Remove the starter.

2. Remove the three solenoid switch retaining screws from the back of the starter drive housing.

3. Withdraw the solenoid, being careful that you unhook it from the shift lever.

4. Installation is in the reverse order of removal. In order to facilitate proper engagement of the shift lever upon installation, the drive pinion should be pulled out as far as possible.

Diesel Glow Plug

REMOVAL & INSTALLATION

1. Disconnect the electrical connector from the glow plug.

2. Using a socket wrench, remove the glow plug from the cylinder head.

3. Clean and inspect the glow plug for correct operation.

4. To install, reverse the removal procedures.

TESTING

1. Remove the electrical wire and bus-bar from the glow plugs.

2. Using a test light, connect the spring clip to the (+) positive battery terminal, then touch the probe to each glow plug.

3. If the light turns ON, the glow plug is OK; if the light does not turn ON, the glow plug is defective and must be replaced.

4. When installing the glow plug, torque the plug to 29 ft. lbs. (40 Nm).

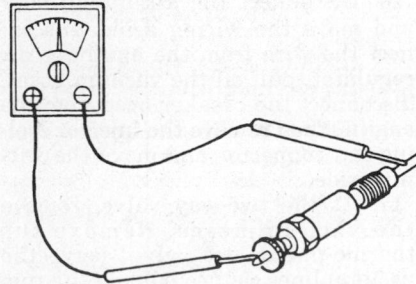

Testing glow plug continuity with an ohmmeter—typical

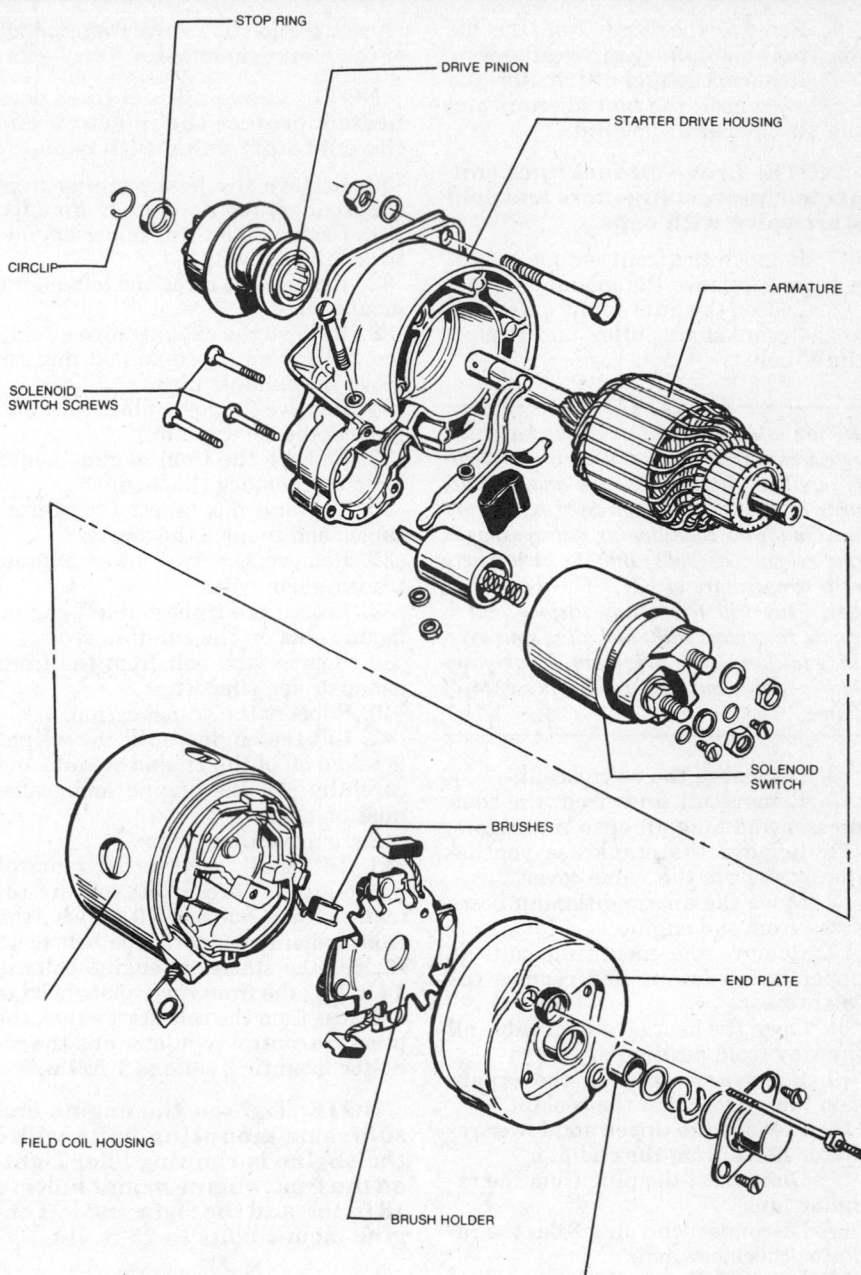

Exploded view of the starter

GASOLINE ENGINE MECHANICAL

Engine

REMOVAL & INSTALLATION
4000 (Except Coupe and Quattro)

NOTE: Though not necessary, removal of the hood will make engine removal easier. Be sure to mark the location of each hood hinge to facilitate reinstallation.

1. Disconnect the negative battery cable. Steps 2–13 refer to cars equipped with air conditioning.

2. Remove the two clips on the top of the grille. Remove the screw on the bottom and remove the grille.

3. Loosen the right and left sides of the condenser and tilt it away from the radiator.

4. Remove the air duct from the throttle valve housing.

5. Remove the hose from the air duct to the auxiliary air regulator.

6. Remove the fuel distributor, the air flow sensor, the fuel injectors and the air cleaner as one unit.

NOTE: Leave all fuel lines connected; protect injectors and cold start valve with caps.

7. Remove the front engine mount bolts and remove the mount.

8. Loosen the nuts on the outer half of the crankshaft pulley and remove the V-belt.

CAUTION

Do not attempt to charge or discharge the refrigerant system unless you are thoroughly familiar with its operation and the hazards involved. The compressed refrigerant used in the air conditioning system expands and evaporates (boils) into the atmosphere at a temperature of $-21.7°F$ ($-29.8°C$) or less. This will freeze any surface that it comes in contact with, including your eyes. In addition, the refrigerant decomposes into a poisonous gas in the presence of flame.

9. Discharge the refrigerant.

10. Remove all lines from the compressor and plug all open connectors.

11. Remove the crankcase ventilation hose from the valve cover.

12. Move the air conditioning hoses away from the engine.

13. Remove the mounting bolts (2 upper and 3 lower) and remove the compressor.

14. Open the heater control valve all the way (cold position).

15. Remove the cap on the expansion tank and drain the coolant.

16. Remove the upper and lower radiator hoses from the radiator.

17. Disconnect the plug from the radiator fan.

18. Disconnect the plug from the radiator thermoswitch.

19. Remove the radiator complete with the fan and shroud.

20. Disconnect the clutch cable.

21. Tag and disconnect all wiring from the engine.

22. Remove the control pressure regulator (above the oil filter) leaving all the fuel lines connected.

23. Remove the air hose from the back of the alternator if so equipped.

24. Unplug the blue wire from the alternator at the plug located between the battery and the rear of the engine.

25. Remove the charcoal filter hose at the intake air duct.

26. Remove the heater hoses.

27. Remove the throttle cable.

28. Tag and remove all vacuum hoses.

29. Pull out the fuel injectors and re-

move the cold start valve from the top of the intake manifold.

NOTE: Leave all fuel lines connected; protect the injectors and the cold start valve with caps.

30. Remove the hose running from the auxiliary regulator to the air duct.

31. Remove the three upper engine/transmission bolts.

32. Remove the right and left engine mount nuts.

33. Remove the exhaust pipe attaching bolts from the manifold and remove the exhaust pipe.

34. Remove the cover plate bolts and remove the cover plate.

35. Remove the front engine mount bolts and remove the mount.

36. Tag and disconnect the starter cables and remove the starter.

37. Remove the two lower engine/transmission bolts.

38. Loosen the right and left engine mount nuts on the sub-frame.

39. Remove the bolt from the front exhaust pipe support.

40. Support the transmission.

41. Lift the engine until the weight is taken off of the engine mounts and carefully pry the engine and transmission apart.

42. Remove the engine.

43. To install, reverse the removal procedures. Torque the engine-to-transmission bolts to 40 ft. lbs., the front exhaust support pipe bolt to 18 ft. lbs., the starter-to-engine bolts to 14 ft. lbs., the front cover plate bolts to 7 ft. lbs., then the cold start valve, the pressure control regulator and the radiator mounting bolts to 7 ft. lbs.

NOTE: Tighten the engine and subframe mounting bolts while the engine is running idle. Tighten the front engine mount bolts to 18 ft. lbs. and the right and left engine mount bolts to 25 ft. lbs.

4000 Quattro Turbo

1. Lift the rear seat and disconnect the negative battery terminal.

2. Open the heater control valve "Fully". Place a container under the radiator, loosen the hose clamp, pull off the radiator hose and drain the coolant into the container; save the coolant for later use.

3. Remove the blower motor (injector cooling) intake hose from the motor.

4. Remove the upper radiator cover screws and the cover. Remove the upper radiator hose from the engine.

5. Remove the electrical connector from the coolant fan. Remove the radiator-to-expansion tank hose from the tank and the bleeder hose from the auxiliary radiator.

6. Disconnect the wire from the thermostatic switch. Remove the radiator mounting bolts, the right-side radiator cover and the bottom radiator cover.

7. Remove the windshield washer reservoir.

CAUTION

Do not attempt to charge or discharge the refrigerant system unless you are thoroughly familiar with it s operation and the hazards involved. The compressed refrigerant used in the air condition system expands and evaporates (boils) into the atmosphere at a temperature of $-21.7°F$ ($-29.8°C$) or less. This will freeze any surface that it comes in contact with, including your eyes. In addition, the refrigerant decomposes into a poisonous gas in the presence of flame.

8. Discharge the A/C system and disconnect the refrigerant hoses from the A/C condenser.

9. Remove the radiator and the A/C condenser together. Remove the A/C compressor and the mounting bracket from the engine.

10. If equipped with power steering, remove the drive belt and the pump (leave the hoses attached), then move the pump aside.

11. Disconnect the coolant hose from the thermostat housing, the wires from the oil pressure switch and the temperature sender, then the wire plugs from the control pressure regulator.

12. If equipped with injector cooling, remove the air distributor, the hose and the motor. Remove the pressure control regulator (leave the fuel lines connected).

13. Remove the throttle cable circlip and the throttle cable. Remove the injector line holder, then pull out the injectors.

14. Disconnect the electrical connector from the cold start valve and remove the valve (leave the fuel line connected).

15. At the throttle body, disconnect the electrical connectors from the throttle valve switches and the intake temperature switch.

16. Disconnect the air intake hose and move the wiring aside. Disconnect the wire from the auxiliary air regulator, pull off the vacuum hoses, disconnect the breaker hose from the engine, then remove the injector cooling fan connector and move the wiring aside.

17. At the two-way valve, remove the vacuum hoses. Remove the thermo-pneumatic valve (leave the vacuum lines connected) and the rpm sensor.

18. Disconnect the speedometer cable from the transmission.

19. Remove the distributor, the No. 4 (center) ignition wire from the cap, then disconnect the Hall sender connector from the distributor.

20. Disconnect the thermo-time switch and the overheating warning lamp connectors. Disconnect the heater hoses from the engine.

21. At the engine mount, disconnect the brake booster (with the reservoir) and leave the lines connected. Disconnect the differential lock control lights connector and the backup light switch wires.

22. Disconnect the tie-rod bracket from the steering rack and the shift linkage.

23. Remove the clutch slave cylinder (leave the line attached), the bracket and pin (under the transmission bracket).

24. Disconnect the left-engine mount ground strap and the vacuum hose from the auxiliary air valve.

25. Remove the air duct from the oil cooler, then remove the intercooler.

26. Disconnect the electrical connectors from the alternator. Remove the oil cooler (leave the lines attached). Remove the starter cables.

27. Disconnect the exhaust pipe at the flange. Remove the transmission cover plates and the transmission mount (right-side). Disconnect the axle shafts (both sides) from the transmission, then the driveshaft from the rear of the transmission.

28. At the differential lock, remove the front and rear circlips, then push back the boot and disconnect the cable.

29. Remove the left-side transmission mounting bolt and the mounts from both sides.

30. At both front wheels, remove the ball joint-to-steering knuckle mounting bolts. At the subframe, remove the mounting bolts and the subframe, then press the ball joints from the strut.

31. Using the Engine Sling tool No. US 1105 and a hoist, connect the sling to the engine, then remove the left and right engine mounts. Lower the engine/transmission assembly from the vehicle.

32. Using a hoist, raise the front of the vehicle and slide the engine/transmission assembly from under the vehicle.

33. Remove the engine-to-transmission bolts and separate the engine from the transmission. Mount the engine on a work stand.

34. To install, reverse the removal procedures.

5000 (All Models) and Coupe Models

1. Disconnect the negative battery cable.

2. Open the heater control valve all the way (cold position).

3. Remove the cap on the expansion tank and drain the coolant.

4. Remove all radiator and heater hoses. Disconnect the intercooler from the turbocharger on the Quattro.

5. Remove the control pressure regulator.

— **CAUTION** —

Do not disconnect any fuel lines.

6. Remove the cold start valve.

7. Pull out the fuel injectors and lay them aside.

NOTE: Protect the fuel injectors and the cold start valve with caps.

8. Loosen the air duct and vacuum hoses from the throttle valve assembly.

9. Remove the air cleaner cover with the filter.

10. Pull the hood latch cable guide off of its bracket.

11. If equipped with A/C, proceed with the following procedures:

  a. Remove the two clips from the top of the grille and the screw from the bottom, then remove the grille.

  b. Remove the condenser-to-radiator mounting bolts.

  c. Remove the air duct-to-auxiliary air regulator hose, then the air duct from the throttle valve housing.

  d. Remove the fuel distributor, the air flow sensor, the fuel injectors and the air cleaner as a unit.

NOTE: When removing the fuel assembly, leave all of the lines connected and cover the fuel injectors/cold start valve with caps.

  e. Remove the engine stop and the stop.

  f. At the crankshaft pulley, loosen the nuts on the outer half of the pulley and remove the V-belt.

— **CAUTION** —

Do not attempt to charge or discharge the refrigerant system unless you are thoroughly familiar with its operation and the hazards involved. The compressed refrigerant used in the air conditioning system expands and evaporates (boils) into the atmosphere at a temperature of −21.7°F (−29.8°C) or less. This will freeze any surface that it comes in contact with, including your eyes. In addition, the refrigerant decomposes into a poisonous gas in the presence of flame.

  g. Discharge the refrigerant from the A/C system, then remove and plug the A/C hoses, move them away from the engine.

  h. Remove the upper/lower compressor-to-engine mounting bolts, then remove the compressor from the engine.

12. Remove the power steering pump leaving the hose connected.

13. Remove the vacuum amplifier.

14. Remove the ignition coil.

15. Remove the EGR control valve.

16. Remove the windshield washer reservoir from its holder.

17. Remove the power steering reservoir from its holder.

18. Remove the distributor cap, the rotor and the ignition wires.

NOTE: Tape the distributor dust cap on to prevent it from falling off.

19. If equipped with a manual transmission, take off the circlip and remove the throttle cable.

20. If equipped with an automatic transmission, remove the throttle pushrod.

21. Disconnect the oil pressure and the water temperature senders.

22. On air-conditioned cars, remove the compressor mounting bolts. Leaving the hoses connected, tie back the compressor with wire.

23. Remove the exhaust pipe-to-manifold bolts. On turbocharged models, remove the exhaust pipe-to-wastegate connector.

24. Remove the exhaust pipe support bracket from the transmission.

25. Remove the front engine mount bolts and remove the mount.

26. Tag and disconnect all wires from the starter and remove the starter.

27. Tag and disconnect all wires leading from the alternator and remove the alternator.

28. On cars equipped with an automatic transmission, remove the torque converter mounting bolts from the drive plate. This can be done through the starter hole.

29. Remove the lower engine/transmission bolts.

30. Support the transmission.

31. Remove the upper engine/transmission bolts.

32. Remove the left engine support bracket.

33. Loosen the right engine bracket from the right engine mount.

34. Lift the engine until the V-belt pulley is behind the grille opening.

35. Carefully detach the engine from the transmission.

36. Remove the engine completely, turning it to the right as you lift it out.

37. To install, reverse the removal procedures. Torque the engine-to-transmission bolts to 43 ft. lbs., the exhaust pipe support bracket to 22 ft. lbs., the torque converter-to-drive

plate bolts to 14 ft. lbs., the starter bolts to 14 ft. lbs., the A/C mounting bolts to 29 ft. lbs., then the power steering pump and the control pressure regulator mounting bolts to 14 ft. lbs.

NOTE: Tighten the engine and subframe mounting bolts while the engine is running at idle. Tighten all bolts to 32 ft. lbs.

Quattro, Quattro Turbo & Quattro Coupe

1. Disconnect the negative battery cable. Open the heater control valve, remove the cap from the expansion valve and drain the coolant by removing the lower radiator hose.
2. Remove the intake hose from the injector cooling blower motor. Remove the upper radiator cover screws and cover, then remove the upper radiator hose.
3. Disconnect the coolant fan electrical connector, then remove the coolant hose between the radiator and the expansion tank. Remove the bleeder hose to the auxiliary radiator, then disconnect the thermo switch electrical connector.
4. Remove the radiator mountings, then the right side and bottom radiator covers. Remove the windshield washer reservoir.
5. Disconnect the A/C lines at the condenser, then remove the radiator and the condenser as an assembly. Remove the upper compressor mounting bracket attaching bolts and the compressor to bracket attaching bolts. Remove the compressor and bracket.
6. Remove the power steering pump and its drive belt. position the pump out of the way without disconnecting the hoses. Disconnect the coolant hose at the thermostat housing.
7. Disconnect the electrical connectors at the oil pressure switch, temperature sender, and the control pressure regulator. Remove the injector cooling air distributor hose and motor.
8. Remove the control pressure regulator. leaving all the fuel lines attached. Remove the throttle cable and remove the holder foe the injector lines and pull out the injectors.
9. Disconnect the electrical connector at the cold start valve. Remove the cold start valve and leave the fuel lines connected.
10. Disconnect the electrical connectors of the two throttle valve switches and intake temperature switch, then disconnect the air intake hose and position the wiring out of the way.
11. Disconnect the electrical connector of the auxiliary air regulator, the

vacuum hoses, engine breather hose and the electrical connector of the injector cooling fan and position the wiring out of the way. Disconnect the vacuum hoses of the two way valve.
12. Remove the thermo pneumatic valve , leaving the vacuum hoses connected. Remove the rpm sensor, then disconnect the speedometer cable at the transmission.
13. Remove the distributor and the number four ignition wire from the distributor. Disconnect the electrical connector for the Hall sender at the distributor. Disconnect the connectors for the thermo time switch and the overheating warning lamp.
14. Disconnect the heater hoses from the engine. Disconnect the hydraulic brake booster with the reservoir from the motor mount, leaving the lines connected. Disconnect the electrical connector for the differential lock control lights and the back-up light switch.
15. Disconnect the tie-rod bracket on the steering rack. Disconnect the shift linkage. Remove the clutch slave cylinder, leaving the hydraulic line connected, then the bracket and pin from the transmission. Do not operate the clutch pedal after removing the slave cylinder.
16. Disconnect the ground strap from the left engine mount and the vacuum hose from the auxiliary air valve. Remove the oil cooler air duct, then the intercooler.
17. Disconnect the alternator electrical connectors. Remove the oil cooler, leaving the lines connected. Disconnect the starter electrical connectors. Disconnect the exhaust pipe at the flange.
18. Remove the transmission cover plates and the right side transmission mount. Disconnect the axle shafts at the transmission. Disconnect the differential lock cable by removing the the front and rear circlip, pushing the back the boot and disconnect the cable from the mounting.
19. Remove the transmission mounting bolts and remove the transmission mounts. Remove the attaching bolts for the ball joints. Disconnect the rear subframe mounts. Remove the subframe mounting bolts, remove the subframe and press the ball joint out of the strut.
20. Attach a suitable engine lift to the proper engine locations and slightly lift the engine. Remove the engine side mounts and lower the engine and transmission assembly.
21. Raise and support the vehicle safely. Remove the the engine and transmission assembly from underneath the vehicle. Then once the assembly is secure in a suitable engine

stand, remove the transmission from the engine.
22. The installation is the reverse order of the removal procedure.

Cylinder Head

NOTE: Before removing or installing the cylinder head, align the engine timing marks at TDC, then turn the crankshaft mark away about ¼ turn (BTDC). This will prevent the valves from hitting the piston heads. Be sure to turn the crankshaft to the proper position after cylinder head installation.

REMOVAL & INSTALLATION

All Models

NOTE: Cylinder head removal should not be attempted unless the engine is cold.

1. Disconnect the negative battery cable.
2. Drain the cooling system.
3. Disconnect the air duct from the throttle valve assembly on all models except the Turbo and Quattro. On the Turbo and Quattro, remove the hose which runs between the air duct and the turbocharger.
4. Disconnect the throttle cable from the throttle valve assembly.
5. Remove the air duct for the injector cooling fan on the Turbo and Quattro.
6. Clean and remove the fuel injectors and all other fuel lines.

NOTE: Protect the fuel injectors and the cold start valve with caps.

7. Tag and disconnect all vacuum and PCV lines.
8. Remove the hose which runs from the intake manifold to the turbocharger on the Turbo and Quattro.
9. Tag and disconnect all electrical lines leading to the cylinder head.
10. Unbolt and remove the intake manifold.
11. Disconnect all radiator and heater hoses where they are attached to the cylinder head. Position them out of the way.
12. Tag and remove all spark plug wires and then remove the spark plugs.
13. For all models but the 4000, remove the distributor. To aid in reinstallation, scribe a mark on the body of the distributor and the cylinder head.
14. Unbolt and separate the exhaust manifold from the exhaust pipe.

NOTE: Exhaust pipe detachment differs slightly on the Turbo and Quattro. First the exhaust pipe must be unbolted from the turbocharger and then it must be unbolted from the wastegate, towards the rear of the engine.

15. Disconnect the EGR valve and the oxygen sensor (if so equipped) from the exhaust manifold.

16. Remove the heat deflector shield on the 4000 models.

17. Unbolt and remove the oil lines (2) from the turbocharger.

18. Unbolt and remove the exhaust manifold.

NOTE: When removing the exhaust manifold on the Turbo and Quattro, the manifold, turbocharger and wastegate should all be removed as one unit.

19. Remove the air hose cover from the back of the alternator (if so equipped) on the 4000.

20. Tag and disconnect all wires coming from the back of the alternator and then remove the alternator and the V-belt.

21. Disconnect and plug the hoses coming from the power steering pump (if so equipped).

22. Remove the power steering pump and the V-belt (if so equipped).

23. Remove the drive belt cover and the drive belt.

24. Remove the cylinder head cover.

25. Loosen the cylinder head bolts in the reverse order of the tightening sequence.

26. Remove the bolts and lift the cylinder head straight off.

——— CAUTION ———

If the head sticks, loosen it by compression or rap it upward with a soft rubber mallet. Do not force anything between the head and the engine block to pry it upward; this may result in serious damage.

27. Clean the cylinder head and engine block mating surfaces thoroughly and then install the new gasket without any sealing compound. Make sure the words TOP or OBEN are facing up when the gasket is installed.

28. Place the cylinder head on the engine block and install bolts No. 8 and 10 first. These holes are smaller and will properly locate the gasket and the head on the engine block.

29. Install the remaining bolts. Tighten them in three stages as follows: Step 1: 29 ft. lbs.; Step 2: 43 ft. lbs.; Step 3: Tighten ½ turn more (180°).

——— CAUTION ———

Do not re-torque the cylinder head bolts at the 1000 mile maintenance nor at the 1000 mile interval following repairs.

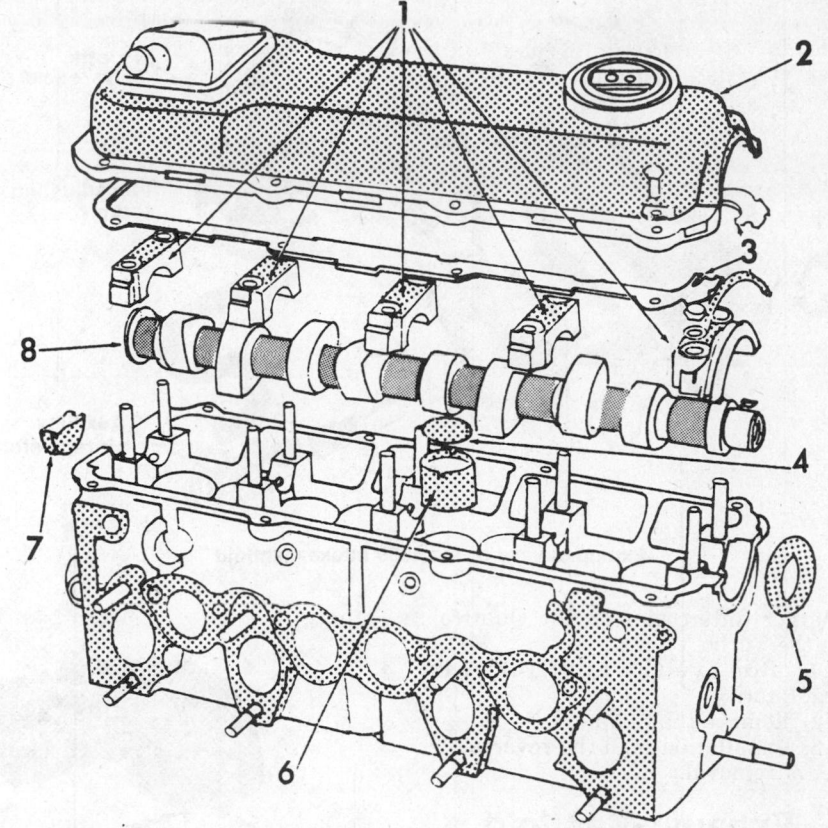

1. Camshaft bearing caps
2. Camshaft cover
3. Gasket
4. Valve adjusting disc
5. Oil seal
6. Cam follower
7. End plug
8. Camshaft

Exploded view of the 4000 cylinder head

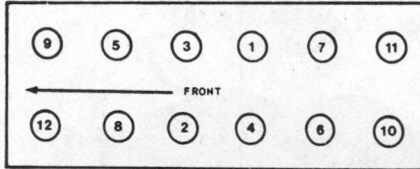

Torque sequence for all 5 cylinder engines

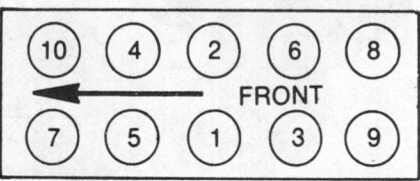

Torque sequence for all 4 cylinder engines

30. Installation of all other components is in the reverse order of removal.

OVERHAUL

For all cylinder head procedures, please refer to "Engine Rebuilding" in the Unit Repair section of this manual.

Intake Manifold

REMOVAL & INSTALLATION

All Models

1. Disconnect the negative battery cable.

2. Drain the cooling system.

3. Disconnect the air duct from the throttle valve assembly on all normally aspirated models. On turbocharged models, remove the hose which runs between the air duct and the turbocharger.

4. Disconnect the throttle cable from the throttle valve assembly.

5. Remove the air duct for the injector cooling fan on the Turbo.

6. Clean and remove the fuel injectors.

7. Disconnect the cold start valve.

NOTE: Protect the fuel injectors and the cold start valve with caps.

8. Tag and disconnect all vacuum and PCV lines.

9. Tag and disconnect all electrical lines leading to the cylinder head.

10. Remove the hose which runs from the intake manifold to the turbo-

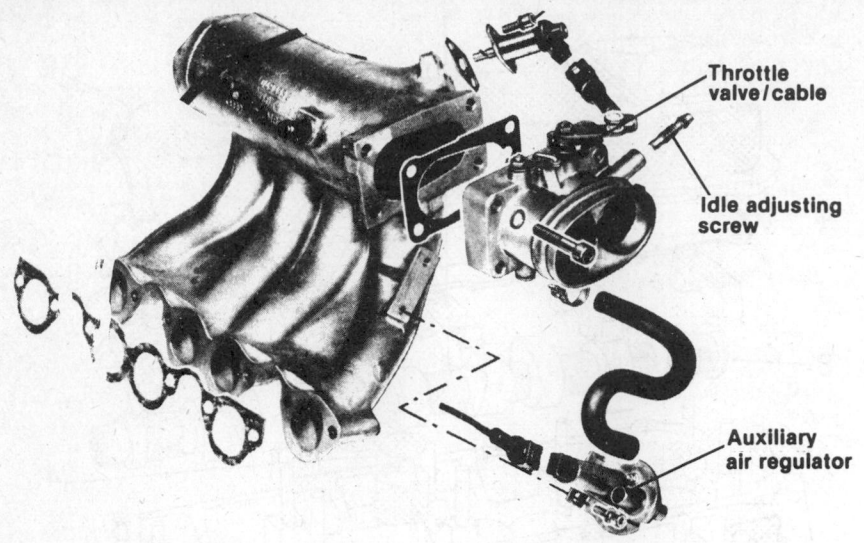

Throttle valve/cable

Idle adjusting screw

Auxiliary air regulator

Exploded view of the 4000 intake manifold

4. Unbolt the exhaust pipe from the wastegate on the rear of the manifold (gasoline engines only).

5. Disconnect the EGR valve and the oxygen sensor from the manifold on gasoline engined models.

6. Remove the oil lines (2) from the turbocharger.

7. Remove the line from the bottom of the turbocharger to the intercooler (Quattro only).

NOTE: The manifold, the turbocharger and the wastegate can all be removed as one unit.

charger (intercooler on the Quattro) on the Turbo.

11. Remove the auxiliary air regulator.

12. Remove the manifold.

13. Installation is in the reverse order of removal.

Exhaust Manifold

REMOVAL & INSTALLATION

All Except Turbocharged Models

Although it is not imperative to remove the intake manifold in order to remove the exhaust manifold, you may find that it makes everything more accessible.

1. Unbolt and separate the exhaust pipe from the exhaust manifold.

2. Disconnect the EGR valve and the oxygen sensor (if so equipped) from the manifold.

3. Remove the heat deflector shield on the 4000.

4. Disconnect the CO probe receptacle tube (if so equipped).

5. Remove the manifold.

6. Installation is in the reverse order of removal.

NOTE: Always replace old gaskets.

Turbocharged Models

1. Remove the hose which runs between the air duct and the turbocharger.

2. If the intake manifold has not been removed, disconnect the hose which runs from the intake manifold to the turbocharger or intercooler.

3. Unbolt the exhaust pipe from the turbocharger.

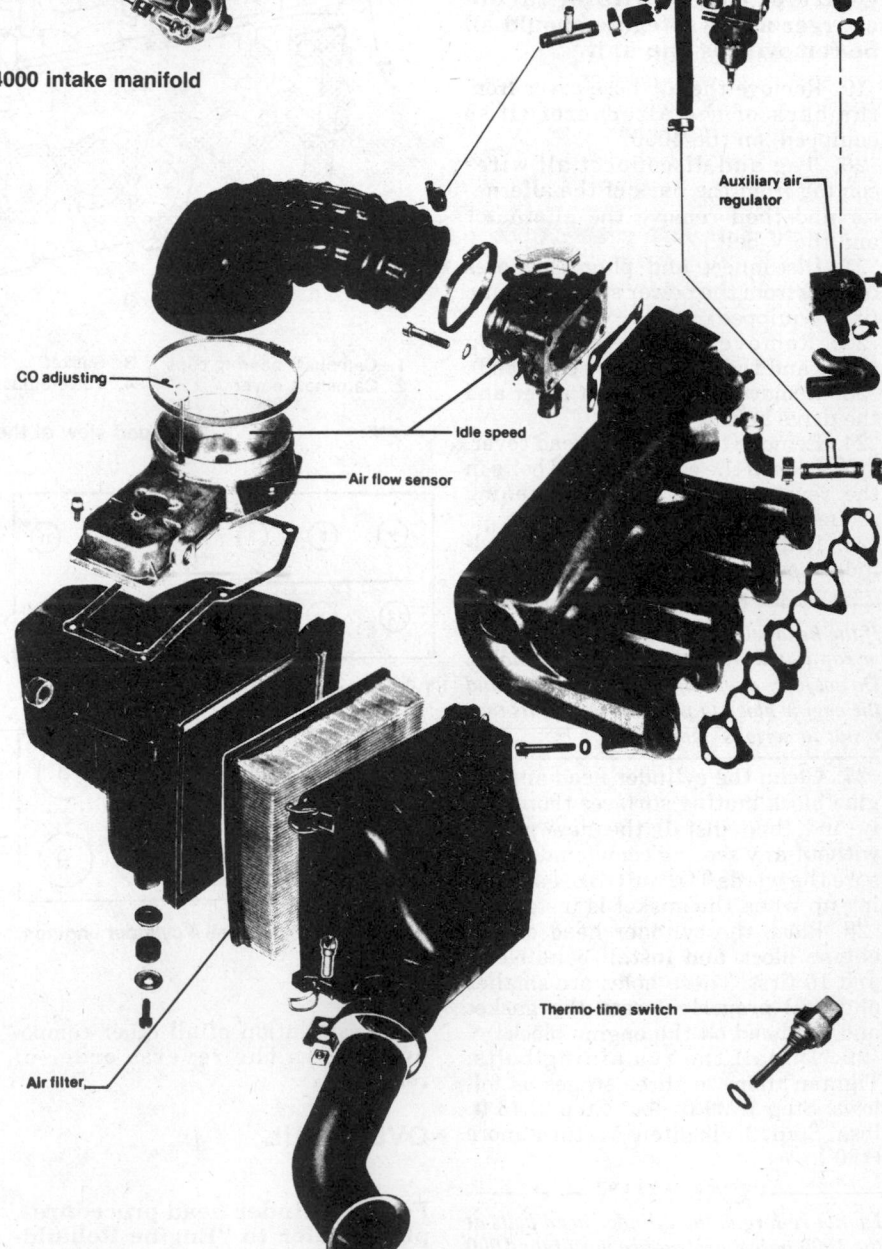

Deceleration valve (manual transm. only, not for California)

Auxiliary air regulator

CO adjusting

Idle speed

Air flow sensor

Thermo-time switch

Air filter

Exploded view of the 5000 intake manifold

8. Remove the manifold.

9. Installation is in the reverse order of removal.

Turbocharger

REMOVAL & INSTALLATION

4000 Turbo

1. Removal of the intake manifold (as detailed earlier) is not absolutely necessary but will greatly aid in the accessibility of all related nuts and bolts.

2. Loosen the hose clamps and remove the hose which leads to the intake manifold or intercooler.

3. Loosen the hose clamps and remove the hose which leads to the air cleaner.

4. Unbolt the oil supply (upper) and return (lower) lines and position them out of the way.

5. Remove the exhaust pipe mounting nuts and pull the exhaust pipe away from the turbocharger.

6. Remove the turbocharger mounting nuts and pull the turbocharger off of the exhaust manifold.

7. Installation is in the reverse order of removal. Note the following:

   a. Use new gaskets.

   b. Tighten the turbocharger-to-exhaust manifold bolts to 43 ft. lbs. (33 ft. lbs. on 4000 Turbodiesel). Coat bolt threads with high temperature grease before installation.

   c. Tighten the turbocharger-to-exhaust pipe bolts to 18–29 ft. lbs.

5000 Turbo

1. Disconnect the negative battery cable. If the battery interferes with space requirements, remove from car.

2. Spray all mounting bolts with a rust solvent.

3. Remove any components that are in the way (grille etc.).

4. Remove the vacuum tube between the intake air boot and turbocharger.

5. Remove the intake boot and crankcase ventilation hose. Remove the hose assembly between the intake manifold and throttle housing.

6. Remove the air filter housing cover.

7. Remove the engine mount heat shield.

8. Remove the oil supply pipe from the turbocharger. Remove the exhaust pipe from the corrugated pipe and loosen the exhaust pipe at the transmission mount and catalytic converter.

9. Remove the retaining clamp from the starter housing and sensor air hose.

10. Remove the exhaust pipe from the turbocharger.

11. Remove the alternator support bolt and position the alternator to the side.

12. Remove the oil return pipe from the turbocharger. Remove mounting bolts and turbocharger.

13. Install in reverse order.

NOTE: Always change the oil and oil filter after turbocharger service.

TROUBLESHOOTING

For more information on turbocharging, please refer to turbocharging in the unit repair section.

Turbocharger Wastegate

REMOVAL & INSTALLATION

1. As suggested in the turbocharger removal procedure, intake manifold removal is a prudent idea for wastegate accessibility.

2. Remove the wastegate-to-exhaust pipe connecting tube (three bolts top and three bolts bottom).

3. Remove the mounting bolt for the tube leading from the wastegate to the exhaust manifold.

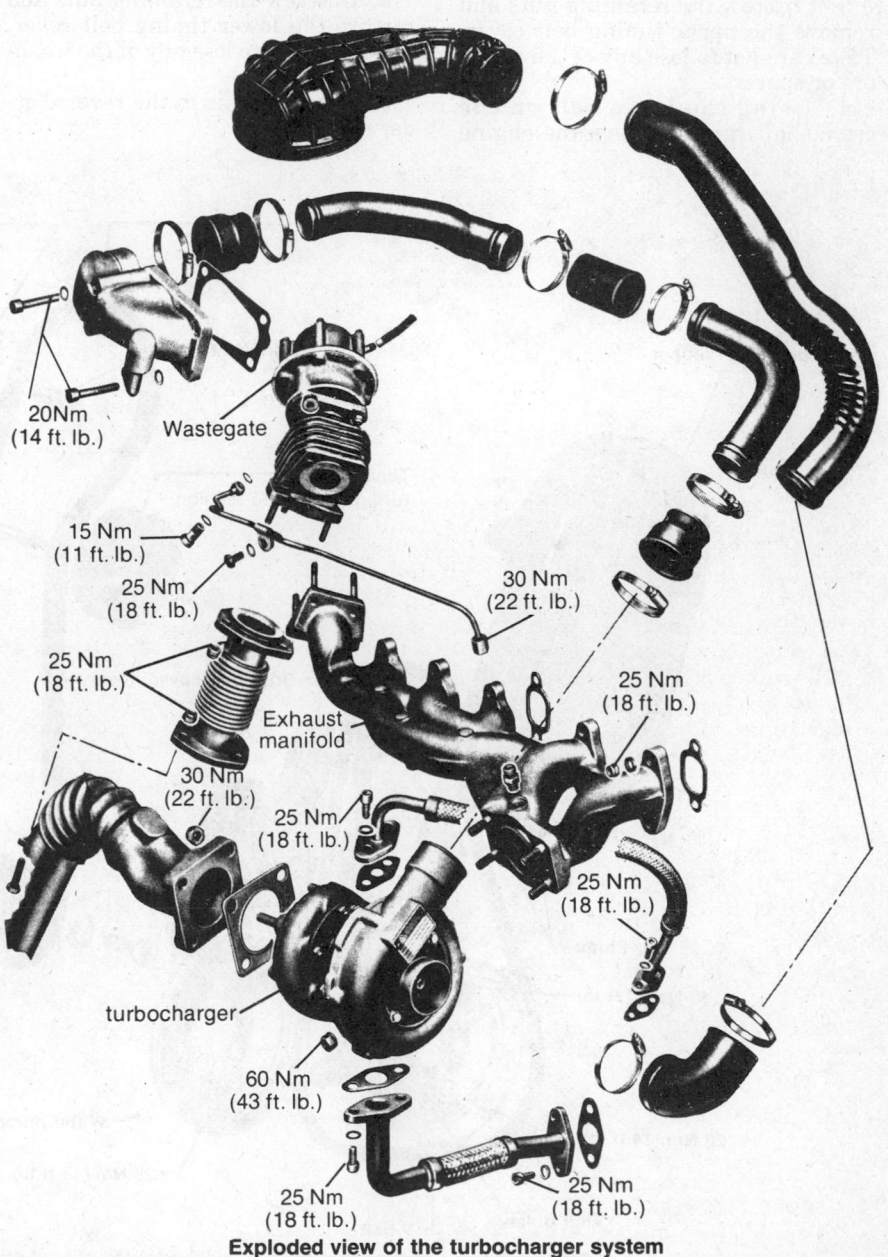

Exploded view of the turbocharger system

4. Remove the vacuum line from the end of the wastegate.

5. Remove the four mounting bolts and remove the wastegate from the exhaust manifold.

6. Installation is in the reverse order of removal.

Timing Belt Cover

REMOVAL & INSTALLATION

All 4 Cylinder Models

1. Loosen the alternator adjusting bolts. Pivot the alternator over and slip the V-belt off.

2. If equipped with air conditioning, loosen the compressor mounting bolts and slip off the V-belt.

3. Unscrew the retaining nuts and remove the upper timing belt cover. Take care not to lose any of the washers or spacers.

4. Using the large bolt on the crankshaft sprocket, turn the engine until the No. 1 cylinder is at TDC of the compression stroke. At this point, both of the valves will be closed and the "0" mark on the flywheel will be aligned with the pointer on the clutch housing.

5. Unscrew the crankshaft pulley retaining bolts (4) and then loosen the crankshaft sprocket bolt.

NOTE: To remove the crankshaft sprocket bolt, you will need an assistant, to place the car in 4th gear and apply the brake, this will enable you to loosen the bolt.

6. Remove the crankshaft pulley.

7. Unscrew the water pump pulley retaining bolts (3) and remove the pulley.

8. Unscrew the retaining nuts and remove the lower timing belt cover. Take care not to lose any of the washers or spacers.

9. Installation is in the reverse order of removal.

All 5 Cylinder Models

1. Loosen the alternator adjusting bolts and remove the V-belt.

2. Loosen the power steering pump adjusting bolts and remove the V-belt (if so equipped).

3. If equipped with air conditioning, loosen the compressor adjusting bolts and remove the V-belt.

4. Unscrew the retaining nuts and remove the timing belt cover. Take care not to lose any of the washers or spacers.

5. Installation is in the reverse order of removal.

Timing Belt

REMOVAL & INSTALLATION

All 4 Cylinder Models

1. Remove the upper and lower timing belt covers.

2. While holding the large hex nut

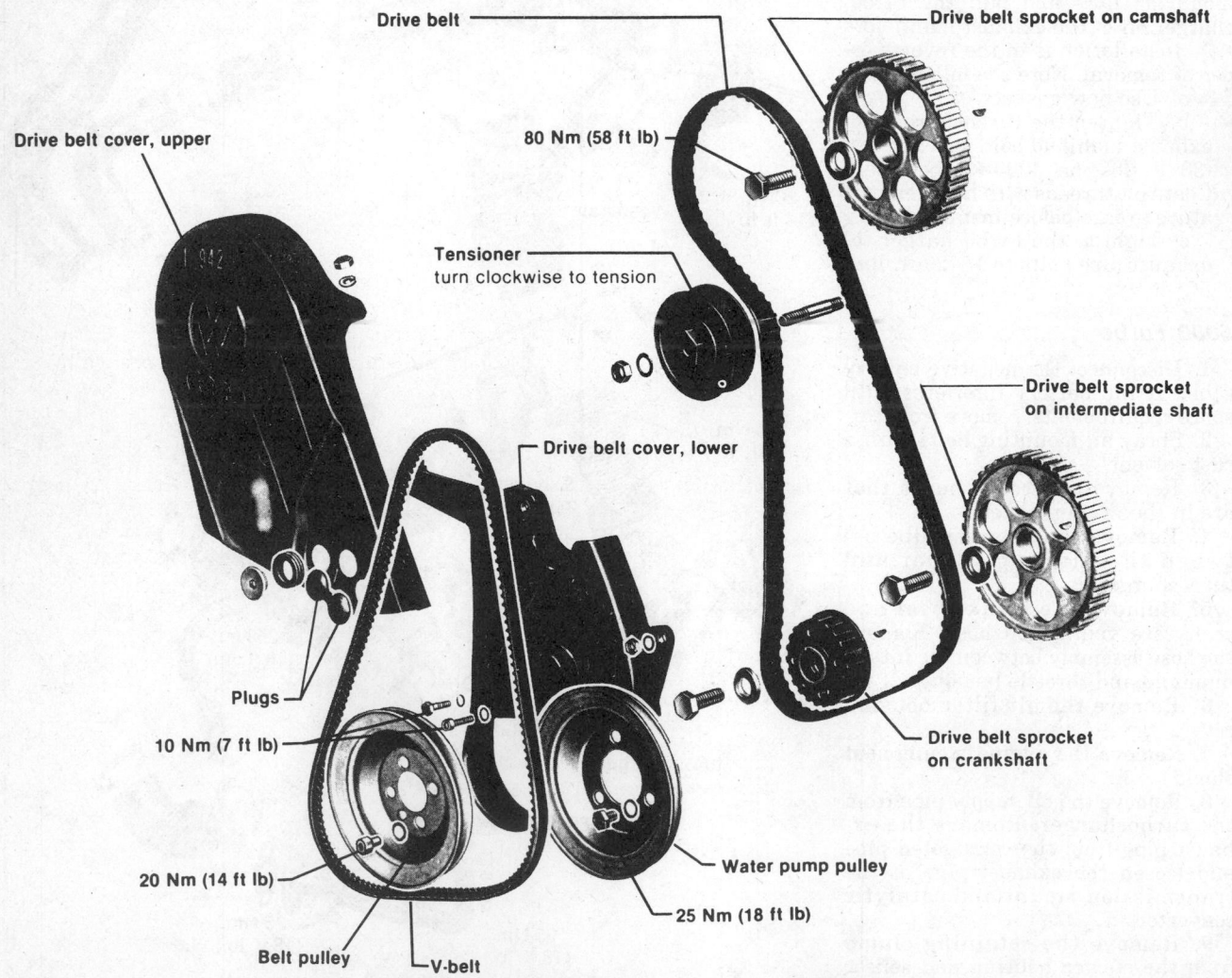

Exploded view of the front cover—4000 engine—diesel engine is similar on the tensioner pulley, loosen the smaller pulley lock nut.

3. Turn the tensioner counterclockwise to relieve the tension on the timing belt.

4. Carefully slide the timing belt off of the three sprockets and remove the belt.

5. Using the large bolt on the crankshaft sprocket, turn the engine until the No. 1 cylinder is at TDC of the compression stroke. At this point, both valves will be closed and the "0" mark on the flywheel will be aligned with the pointer on the clutch housing.

6. Check that the timing mark on the rear face of the camshaft sprocket is aligned with the upper edge of the rear timing belt cover. If it's not, turn the sprocket until they align.

7. Replace the crankshaft pulley and check that the notch on the pulley is aligned with the mark on the intermediate shaft sprocket. If not, turn them until they align.

CAUTION

If the timing marks are not correctly aligned with the No. 1 piston at TDC of the compression stroke and the belt is installed, valve timing will be incorrect. Poor performance and possible engine damage can result from the improper valve timing.

8. Remove the crankshaft pulley. Observe its location on the crankshaft sprocket so that it can be replaced in the same position. Hold the large nut on the tensioner pulley and loosen the smaller locknut. Turn the tensioner counterclockwise to loosen and remove the belt.

9. Slide the timing belt back onto the sprockets and check for the proper tension (see "Tension Adjustment").

10. Installation is in the reverse order of removal.

All 5 Cylinder Models

1. Remove the alternator and air conditioning compressor from their mounting brackets and position them out of the way.

2. Remove the front cover bolts and lift off the cover.

3. Loosen the water pump bolts and turn the pump clockwise.

4. Slide the drive off the sprockets.

5. Turn the camshaft until the notch on the back of the sprocket is in line with the left side edge of the camshaft housing flange.

6. Align the TDC "0" mark on the flywheel with the lug cast on the clutch housing.

7. Install the drive belt and turn the water pump counterclockwise to tighten the belt. Tighten the water pump bolts to 14 ft. lbs.

Crankshaft pulley and intermediate shaft sprocket alignment on the 4000

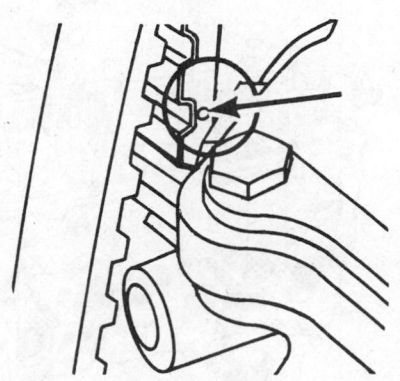

Camshaft sprocket alignment of the 4000

V-belt pulley alignment on the 5000

NOTE: The belt is correctly tensioned when it can be twisted 90° with the thumb and index finger along with the straight run between the camshaft sprocket and the water pump.

8. Install the front cover and tighten the bolts to 7 ft. lbs.

9. Install the alternator and compressor and tighten the belts. These belts are correctly tensioned when they can be depressed ⅜ in. along their longest straight run.

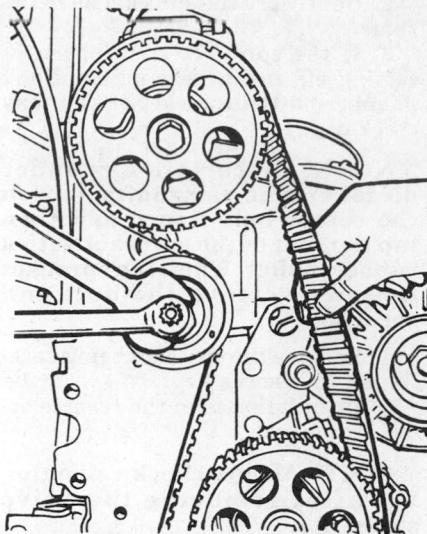

The timing belt on all models is correctly tensioned when it can be twisted 90° with the thumb and forefinger

TENSION ADJUSTMENT

All 4 Cylinder Models

1. Holding the large bolt on the tensioner pulley, loosen the small nut and turn the tensioner clockwise to tighten and counterclockwise to loosen.

2. The belt is correctly tensioned when it can be twisted 90 degrees with the thumb and forefinger, midway between the camshaft and the intermediate shaft drive sprockets.

All 5 Cylinder Engines

1. Loosen the water pump adjusting bolts (2) and turn the pump clockwise to tighten and counterclockwise to loosen.

2. The belt is correctly tensioned when it can be twisted 90 degrees with the thumb and forefinger, midway between the camshaft drive sprocket and the water pump.

Timing Sprockets

REMOVAL & INSTALLATION
All Models

All of the drive sprockets are located by keys on their respective shafts (with the exception of certain diesel engine camshaft sprockets which are a taper fit or crankshaft sprockets which have a built-in lug) and each is retained by a bolt. To remove any or all of the sprockets, first remove the timing belt covers and belts and then use the following procedure.

1. Remove the center retaining bolt for the particular drive sprocket.

2. Gently pry the sprocket off of the shaft.

3. If the sprocket is stubborn in coming off, use a gear puller. Don't hammer on the sprocket or you may crack it.

NOTE: On certain 4 cylinder diesel engine camshafts, loosen the center bolt 1 turn and then tap the rear of the sprocket with a rubber mallet. When the sprocket loosens, remove the bolt and sprocket.

4. Remove the sprocket being careful not to lose the key.

5. Installation is in the reverse order of removal.

NOTE: Always check valve timing after removing the drive sprockets.

OIL SEAL REPLACEMENT

The oil seal is a part of the oil pump, it can be removed during the "Oil Pump Removal and Installation" procedures or it can be replaced as follows:

1. Refer to the "Timing Belt Removal and Installation" procedures and remove the timing belt.

2. Using a small pry bar, pry the oil seal from the oil pump.

3. Clean out the seal seat. Using a new seal, lubricate the lip with engine oil. Using a large socket (the dia. of the seal), press the seal into the seal seat, or a depth of 0.079 in. below the outer edge of the cover.

NOTE: When installing a new seal, be careful not to damage the lip of the seal.

4. The following seal removal & installation procedure is for later Audi models with the 1700 cc engine:

   a. Insert the bolt of tool 3083 or equivalent into the crankcase to guide the seal extractor tool 2085 or equivalent and remove the old seal.

   b. Slide the sleeve of tool 3083 or equivalent onto the crankcase journal. Dip the new seal in clean engine oil and slide it over the sleeve.

   c. Slide the thrust sleeve over the guide sleeve and press in the seal with the thrust sleeve and bolt until fully seated.

5. Reinstall the timing belt. Torque the crankshaft pulley bolt to 253 ft. lbs.

Camshaft
REMOVAL & INSTALLATION

All 4 Cylinder Engines

Be sure that the camshaft end play does not exceed 0.006 in. with the cam

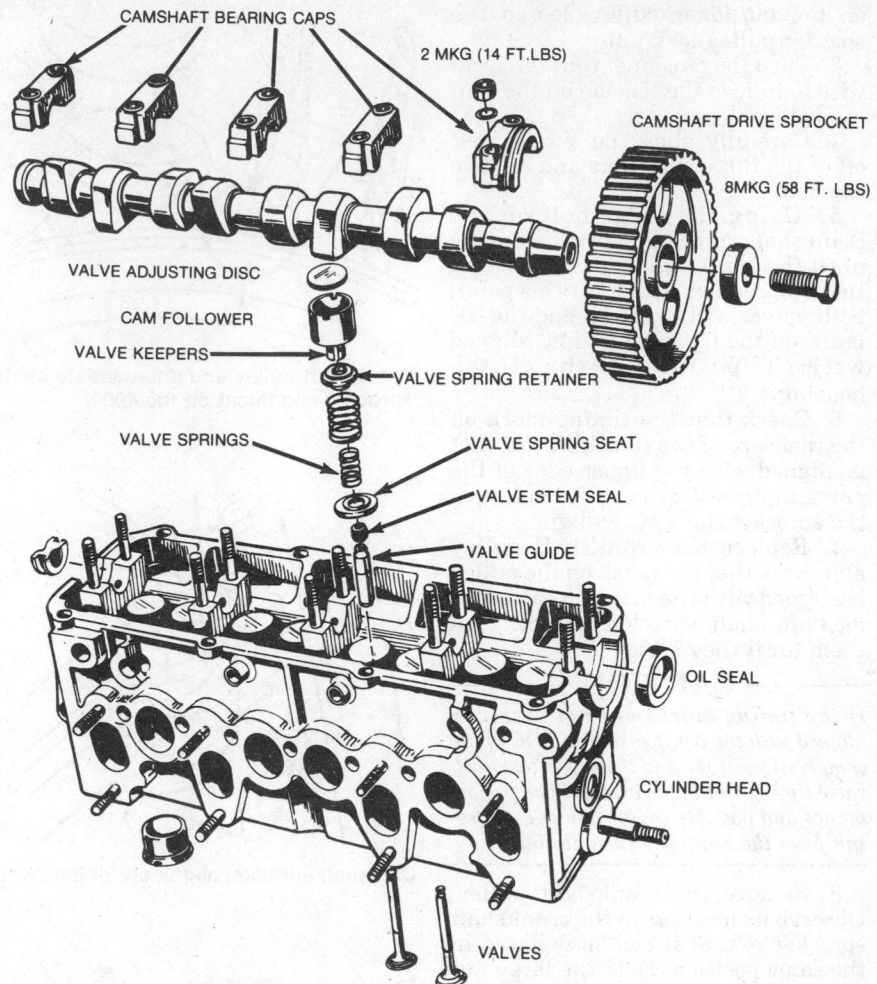

Exploded view of the 4000 4-cyl engine cylinder head

followers and hydraulic lifters removed.

1. Remove the timing belt.
2. Remove the PCV line.
3. Remove the cylinder head cover.
4. Remove the camshaft drive sprocket.
5. On the 1981-83 models, unscrew and remove the Nos. 1, 3 and 5 bearing caps (No. 1 is at the front of the engine) and then diagonally loosen bearing caps Nos. 2 and 4.
6. On the 1984–88 models, first remove bearing caps 1, 3, and 4 and then loosen bearing cap 2.
7. Remove the camshaft from the cylinder head.
8. Remove the camshaft journals, lobes, bearing shells and the contact faces of the caps with assembly lube or gear oil before reinstallation.
9. Replace the camshaft oil seal. If necessary, replace the end plug also.
10. Install the bearing caps in the proper order, observing the off center position. On the 1981-83 models, lightly tighten bearing caps 2 and 4

and diagonally, before installing bearing caps 5, 1 and 3 and torque all the cap nuts to 14 ft. lbs.

11. On the 1984–88 models, lightly tighten bearing cap number 2 before installing bearing caps 4, 1 and 3 and torque al the cap nuts to 14 ft. lbs.

NOTE: Tighten the bearing caps diagonally. Observe off center bearing position; numbers on bearing caps are not always on the same side.

12. Replace the seal in the No. 1 bearing cap.

13. Installation of the remaining components is in the reverse order of removal. When installing the crankshaft drive belt sprocket on the later Audi models equipped with the 1700 cc engine and the 1984–88 models, besure that the lug on the sprocket is properly installed into the slot on the crankshaft.

NOTE: Always recheck the valve clearance after the camshaft has been removed.

All 5 Cylinder Models

1. Remove the camshaft cover.
2. Remove the drive belt and camshaft sprocket.
3. Diagonally loosen bearing caps 2 and 4 and remove the bearing caps.
4. Diagonally loosen bearing caps 1 and 3 and remove the bearing caps.
5. Lift out the camshaft.
6. When installing, lightly oil the camshaft and bearings with clean engine oil.
7. Position the caps on the same journals from which they were removed.
8. Lightly tighten the nuts of caps 2 and 4.
9. Tighten all nuts to 14 ft. lbs.
10. Install the drive belt and sprocket and the camshaft cover. The sprocket bolt is torqued to 58 ft. lbs; the cover bolts to 7 ft. lbs.

Pistons and Connecting Rods

POSITIONING

For all piston and connecting rod overhaul procedures, please refer to "Engine Rebuilding" in the Unit Repair section.

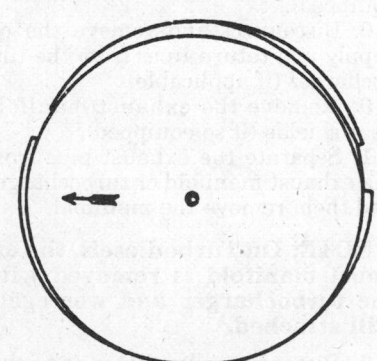

Arrow on pistons must face forward

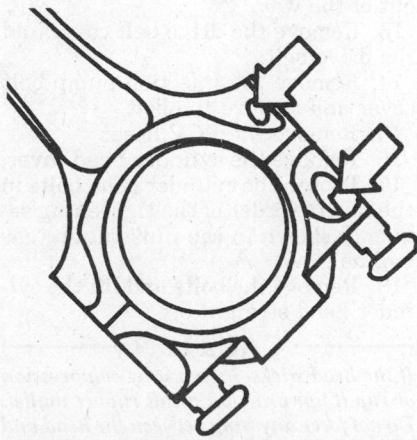

Align the forged marks when assembling the connecting rods and caps

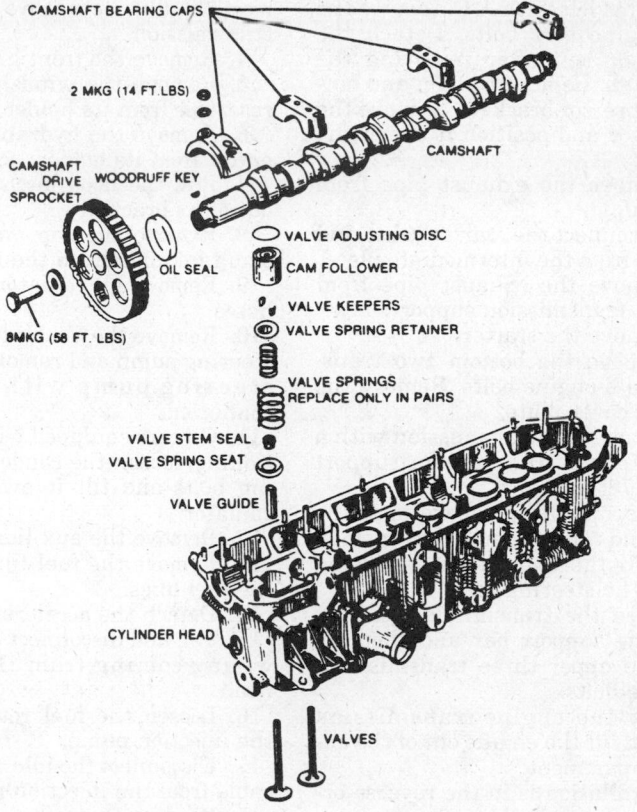

Exploded view of the 5-cyl. engine cylinder head

NOTE: Most pistons are notched or marked to indicate which way they should be installed. If your pistons are not marked, mark them before removal. Then reinstall them in the proper position.

DIESEL ENGINE MECHANICAL

Engine

REMOVAL & INSTALLATION

4000 Models

1. Disconnect the negative battery cable.
2. Remove the engine and transmission cover plates.
3. Open the heater control valve fully and then open the cap on the expansion tank.
4. Drain the coolant.
5. Detach the radiator cowl from the radiator and remove complete with both fans (A/C models only).
6. Remove the grille and then detach the condenser from the radiator (A/C models only).
7. Disconnect the plugs from the fan and the thermo-switch. Remove the radiator with the fan.
8. Disconnect and remove:
   a. Fuel supply and return lines from the injection pump.
   b. Accelerator cable from pump lever and bracket from pump body.
   c. Cold start cable at pin.
   d. Wire from fuel shut-off solenoid.
   e. Gear shift light switch complete with all wiring from the bracket.
9. Tag and disconnect the wiring from the:
   a. Oil pressure switch
   b. Coolant temperature sensors
   c. Glowplugs
   d. Thermoswitch
10. Disconnect the coolant hose.
11. Loosen the clutch cable and unhook it from the clutch lever.
12. Loosen the right and left engine mounts at top.
13. Disconnect the vacuum hose from the vacuum reservoir.
14. Disconnect and remove the alternator.
15. Remove the front engine stop bolts.

16. On models with A/C, remove the front engine stop bolts. Detach the compressor belt after removing the pulley nuts. Remove the top and bottom compressor brackets. Remove the compressor and position it out of the way.

17. Remove the exhaust pipe from the manifold.

18. Disconnect the starter cable and detach it from the intermediate plate.

19. Remove the exhaust pipe from the front transmission support.

20. Remove the starter.

21. Remove the bottom two transmissions-to-engine bolts. Remove the flywheel cover plate.

22. Support the transmission with a jack or install transmission support bar VW 785/1B.

23. Attach a lifting apparatus to the engine and raise the engine/transmission until the transmission housing touches the steering rack.

24. Raise the transmission jack or adjust the support bar and then remove the upper three transmission-to-engine bolts.

25. Pry the engine/transmission apart and lift the engine out of the engine compartment.

26. Installation is in the reverse order of removal. Please note the following:

  a. Place the intermediate plate on the dowel sleeves and stick it to engine block with grease.

  b. Place the starter on the engine carrier before installing the engine.

— CAUTION —

Do not interchange fuel supply and return pipe union screws. For identification, the fuel return pipe union screw is marked OUT on the screw head.

  c. Connect the starter cable so it cannot touch the engine.

  d. Install the engine mounts free of tension.

27. Tightening torques for installation are as follows:

  a. Cover plate-to-transmission/engine – 7 ft. lbs.

  b. Exhaust pipe-to-transmission – 18 ft. lbs.

  c. Front engine stop-to-engine block – 18 ft. lbs.

  d. Stop housing-to-front cross member – 18 ft. lbs.

  e. Engine mounts – 25 ft. lbs.

  f. Engine-to-transmission (12 M) – 40 ft. lbs.

  g. Starter bolts – 14 ft. lbs.

5000 Models

1. Disconnect the negative battery cable.

2. Remove the air cleaner.

3. Remove the cover plates underneath the engine and the transmission.

4. Remove the front grille.

5. Remove the windshield washer reservoir from its holder.

6. Remove the hydraulic fluid reservoir from its holder.

7. Pull the hood latch cable guide out of its bracket.

8. Remove the cap on the expansion tank and drain the radiator.

9. Remove all radiator and heater hoses.

10. Remove the V-belt for the power steering pump and remove the power steering pump with the hoses connected.

11. On cars equipped with air conditioning, loosen the condenser mounting bolts and tilt it away from the radiator.

12. Remove the auxiliary radiator.

13. Remove the fuel filter and plug the fuel lines.

14. Detach the accelerator cable.

15. Tag and disconnect all electrical wiring coming from the cylinder head.

16. Loosen the fuel return pipe on the injection pump.

17. Disconnect the idle speed control cable from the injection pump lever.

18. Remove the cover plate for the right engine mount.

19. Remove the front engine mount bolts and remove the mount from the crossmember.

20. Tag and disconnect all wiring from the alternator and then remove the alternator and its bracket.

21. Remove the exhaust pipes from the manifold.

22. Remove the exhaust pipe support bracket from the transmission.

23. Tag and disconnect all wiring from the starter and remove the starter.

24. On cars equipped with air conditioning, remove the compressor mounting bolts along with the mount. Leave the hoses connected and tie the compressor out of the way with wire.

25. Remove the lower engine/transmission bolts.

26. Remove the flywheel cover plate from the transmission.

27. Support the transmission.

28. Remove the left engine bracket.

29. Lift the engine/transmission up until the transmission housing touches the steering housing.

30. Remove the upper engine/transmission bolts.

31. Carefully pry the engine/transmission apart.

32. Turn the engine to the right and lift up at the same time.

33. Turn the engine 90° and lift it completely out.

34. Proceed in the reverse order for installation and note the following:

  a. Tighten the engine/transmission bolts to 43 ft. lbs.

  b. Tighten all engine mount bolts to 33 ft. lbs.

  c. Tighten the exhaust pipe-to-manifold bolts to 22 ft. lbs.

Cylinder Head

REMOVAL & INSTALLATION

NOTE: Cylinder head removal should not be attempted unless the engine is cold.

1. Disconnect the negative battery cable.

2. Drain the cooling system.

3. Remove the air cleaner.

4. Clean and disconnect the fuel (injector) lines.

5. Tag and disconnect all electrical wires and leads.

6. Disconnect and plug all lines coming from the brake booster vacuum pump and remove the pump.

7. Disconnect the air supply tubes (Turbo Diesels only) and then unbolt and remove the intake manifold.

8. Disconnect and plug all lines coming from the power steering pump and remove the pump and V-belt (if so equipped).

9. Disconnect and remove the oil supply and return lines from the turbocharger (if applicable).

10. Remove the exhaust manifold heat shields (if so equipped).

11. Separate the exhaust pipe from the exhaust manifold or turbocharger and them remove the manifold.

NOTE: On Turbodiesels, the exhaust manifold is removed with the turbocharger and wastegate still attached.

12. Disconnect all radiator and heater hoses where they are attached to the cylinder head and position them out of the way.

13. Remove the drive belt cover and the drive belt.

14. Remove the injection pump belt cover and remove the belt.

15. Remove the PCV hose.

16. Remove the cylinder head cover.

17. Loosen the cylinder head bolts in the reverse order of the tightening sequence shown in the illustration (gas engine).

18. Remove the bolts and lift the cylinder head straight off.

— CAUTION —

If the head sticks, loosen it by compression or rap it upward with a soft rubber mallet. Do not force anything between the head and the engine block to pry it upward; this may result in serious damage.

19. Clean the cylinder head and engine block mating surfaces thoroughly and then install the new gasket without any sealing compound. Make sure the words TOP or OBEN are facing up when the gasket is installed.

NOTE: Depending upon piston height above the top surface of the engine block, there are three gaskets of different thicknesses which can be used. Be sure that the new gasket has the same number of notches and the same identifying number as the one being replaced.

20. Place the cylinder head on the engine block and install bolts No. 8 and 10 first. These holes are smaller and will properly locate the gasket and the head on the engine block.

21. Install the remaining bolts. Tighten them in three stages as follows: Step 1: 29 ft. lbs.; Step 2: 43 ft. lbs.; Step 3: Tighten ½ turn more (180°).

22. Installation of all other components is in the reverse order of removal. See the appropriate section for injection timing.

23. After reassembly, start the engine and let it run until it reaches normal operating temperature (when the radiator fan switches on). Stop the engine, remove the cylinder head cover and tighten the head bolts an additional ¼ turn (90°), following the tightening sequence.

— CAUTION —

On all diesel engines using M12, 12 point cylinder head bolts, never reinstall old bolts. Always replace cylinder head bolts.

24. After about 1000 miles, remove the cylinder head cover and retighten the cylinder head bolts, turning the bolts in sequence ¼ turn (90°) WITHOUT loosening them first. This is done one bolt at a time, in the proper sequence, without interruption.

Intake Manifold

REMOVAL & INSTALLATION

1. Disconnect the negative battery cable.
2. Drain the cooling system.
3. Disconnect the hose that runs between the air duct and the turbocharger (Turbo Diesel only).
4. Remove the air cleaner.
5. Disconnect the plug all lines coming from the brake booster vacuum pump and remove the pump.
6. Disconnect the PCV line.
7. Disconnect and remove the blow-off valve and then disconnect the hose which runs from the intake manifold

to the turbocharger (Turbo Diesel only).
8. Remove the manifold.
9. Installation is in the reverse order of removal.

Exhaust Manifold

REMOVAL & INSTALLATION

All Except Turbodiesel

Although it is not imperative to remove the intake manifold in order to remove the exhaust manifold, you may find that it makes everything more accessible.

1. Unbolt and separate the exhaust pipe from the exhaust manifold.
2. Disconnect the EGR valve and the oxygen sensor (if so equipped) from the manifold.
3. Remove the heat deflector shield on the 4000.
4. Disconnect the CO probe receptacle tube (if so equipped).
5. Remove the manifold.
6. Installation is in the reverse order of removal.

Turbodiesel

1. Remove the hose which runs between the air duct and the turbocharger.
2. If the intake manifold has not been removed, disconnect the hose which runs from the intake manifold to the turbocharger or intercooler.
3. Unbolt the exhaust pipe from the turbocharger.
4. Unbolt the exhaust pipe from the wastegate on the rear of the manifold.
5. Disconnect the EGR valve.
6. Remove the old lines (2) from the turbocharger.
7. Remove the line from the bottom of the turbocharger to the intercooler.

NOTE: The manifold, the turbocharger and the wastegate can all be removed as one unit.

8. Remove the manifold.
9. Installation is in the reverse order of removal.

Turbocharger

REMOVAL & INSTALLATION

4000 Turbodiesel

1. Disconnect the neagtive battery cable. Remove the engine/transmission cover plate.
2. Removal of the intake manifold (as detailed earlier) is not absolutely necessary but will greatly aid in the accessibility of all related nuts and bolts.

3. Loosen the hose clamps and remove the hose which leads to the intake manifold or intercooler.
4. Loosen the hose clamps and remove the hose which leads to the air cleaner. Loosen the left and right stabilzer bar clamps and push the stabilizer bar down.
5. Unbolt the oil supply (upper) and return (lower) lines and position them out of the way. Remove the turbocharger heat shield.
6. Remove the exhaust pipe mounting nuts and pull the exhaust pipe away from the turbocharger.
7. Remove the turbocharger mounting nuts and pull the turbocharger off of the exhaust manifold.
8. Installation is in the reverse order of removal. Note the following:
   a. Use new gaskets.
   b. Tighten the turbocharger-to-exhaust manifold bolts to 33 ft. lbs. Coat bolt threads with high temperature grease before installation.
   c. Tighten the turbocharger-to-exhaust pipe bolts to 18–29 ft. lbs.

5000 Turbodiesel

1. Disconnect the negative battery cable. If the battery interferes with space requirements, remove from car.
2. Spray all mounting bolts with a rust solvent.
3. Remove any components that are in the way (grille etc.).
4. Remove the vacuum tube between the intake air boot and turbocharger.
5. Remove the intake boot and crank-case ventilation hose. Remove the hose assembly between the intake manifold and throttle housing.
6. Remove the air filter housing cover.
7. Remove the right side engine mount heat shield and engine cover plate.
8. Remove the oil supply pipe from the turbocharger. Remove the exhaust pipe from the corrugated pipe and loosen the exhaust pipe at the transmission mount and catalytic converter.
9. Remove the retaining clamp from the starter housing and sensor air hose.
10. Remove the exhaust pipe from the turbocharger and remove the exhaust bracket from the transmission.
11. Remove the alternator support bolt and position the alternator to the side.
12. Remove the oil return pipe from the turbocharger. Remove mounting bolts and turbocharger.
13. Install in reverse order.

NOTE: Always change the oil and oil filter after turbocharger service.

Turbocharger Wastegate

REMOVAL & INSTALLATION

The wastegate on the 4 cylinder engine is a press-fit and cannot be removed. The wastegate on the 5 cylinder engine is removed by disconnecting the air hose and then unbolting it from the turbocharger itself.

Front Cover

REMOVAL & INSTALLATION

There are two drive belts on the 5000 Diesels; one at the front on the engine and one at the rear, therefore there are two covers to remove. The front cover on all models is removed in the same manner as the gasoline engined 5000's with two exceptions, the cover has an upper and lower half. To remove the upper half, follow the procedure for the 5000 above. To remove the lower half, use the following procedure.

1. Remove the upper cover.
2. Unscrew the crankshaft pulley retaining bolts and remove the pulley.
3. Unscrew the retaining nuts and remove the lower cover.
4. Installation is in the reverse order of removal.

To remove the rear timing belt cover on 5000 Diesels, use the following procedure.

1. Remove the outside half of the vacuum pump pulley and remove the V-belt.
2. Unscrew the retaining bolts and remove the rear timing belt cover. Take care not to lose any of the washers or spacers.
3. Installation is in the reverse order of removal.

Timing Belt

REMOVAL & INSTALLATION

4000 Models

NOTE: This procedure will require a number of special tools and a certain expertise with diesel engines.

1. Remove the timing belt cover. Remove the cylinder head cover.
2. Turn the engine so that No. 1 cylinder is at TDC and fix the cam-shaft in position with tool 2065A. Align the tool as follows:

    a. Turn the camshaft until one end of the tool touches the cylinder head.

    b. Measure the gap at the other end of the tool with a feeler gauge.

    c. Take half of the measurement and insert a feeler gauge of this thickness between the tool and the cylinder head; turn the camshaft so that the tool rests on the feeler gauge.

    d. Insert a second feeler gauge of the same thickness between the other end of the tool with the cylinder head.

3. Lock the injection pump sprocket in position with pin 2064.
4. Check that the marks on the sprocket, bracket and pump body are in alignment (engine at TDC).
5. Loosen the timing belt tensioner. Remove the V-belt from the crankshaft.
6. Remove the timing belt.
7. Check that the TDC mark on the flywheel is aligned with the reference marks.
8. Loosen the camshaft sprocket bolt ½ turn and then loosen the gear from the camshaft end by tapping it with a rubber mallet.
9. Install the timing belt and remove pin 2064 from the injection pump sprocket.
10. Tension the belt by turning the tensioner to the right. Check the belt tension as detailed later in the section.
11. Tighten the camshaft sprocket bolt to 33 ft. lbs.
12. Remove the tool from the camshaft.
13. Turn the crankshaft two turns in the direction of engine rotation (clockwise) and then strike the belt once with a rubber mallet between the camshaft sprocket and the injection pump sprocket.
14. Check the belt tension again. Check the injection pump timing, as outlined under "Diesel Fuel System."

5000 Models

NOTE: This procedure will require the use of a number of special tools.

1. Remove all V-belts on the front of the engine.
2. Remove the outside half of the vacuum pump pulley and remove the V-belt.
3. Remove the front timing belt covers.
4. Remove the rear timing belt cover.
5. Remove the cylinder head cover.
6. Using the large bolt on the crank-shaft sprocket, turn the engine until the No. 1 cylinder is at TDC of the compression stroke. At this point, both of the valves will be closed and the mark on the flywheel will be aligned with the pointer on the clutch housing.
7. Align the marks on the injection pump sprocket mounting plate.
8. Using special tool 2064 (a pin), lock the injection pump sprocket in place so that it cannot move and change the valve timing.
9. Using special tool 3036, hold the remaining (inside) half of the vacuum pump pulley and the injection pump drive sprocket in place. Remove the center retaining bolt and take off the pulley half and the drive sprocket along with the timing belt.
10. Using special tool 2084 to hold the crankshaft pulley in place, attach special tool 2079 to a ratchet and loosen the crankshaft pulley center bolt.
11. Attach special tool 2065A to the rear of the camshaft so that it will not move and alter the valve timing.
12. Loosen the adjusting bolts (2) on the water pump and turn it counterclockwise to relieve the tension on the timing belt.
13. Unbolt and remove the crankshaft pulley and slide the timing belt off of the sprockets.

To install the front timing belt:

14. Check that the No. 1 cylinder is still at TDC and the mark on the flywheel is still aligned with the pointer on the clutch housing.
15. Loosen the camshaft sprocket bolt approximately 1 turn and lightly tap the gear loose from the camshaft with a rubber mallet.
16. Install the timing belt and check the tension (see "Tension Adjustment").
17. Tighten the camshaft sprocket bolt to 33 ft. lbs. and remove special tool 2065A.
18. Install the injection pump drive sprocket along with the timing belt.
19. Check that the No. 1 cylinder is still at TDC.
20. Tighten the injection pump drive sprocket retaining bolt until it is just possible to turn the sprocket by hand.
21. Check for proper tension (see "Tension Adjustment").
22. Retighten the retaining bolt to 7 ft. lbs.
23. Attach the rear timing belt cover and the outside half of the vacuum pump pulley along with the V-belt and check for proper tension.
24. Remove special tool 2064 from the injection pump.
25. Check the injection timing, and adjust if necessary.
26. Installation of the remaining components is in the reverse order of removal.

TENSION ADJUSTMENT

NOTE: Special tool VW210 will be required for this procedure.

Tension adjustment on the front timing belt is performed in the same manner as with the other four or five cylinder engines. Deflection is also checked in the same position, but with the special tool VW210 rather than your fingers. Proper tension is achieved when the scale reads 12–13.

Tension on the rear timing belt (5 cyl. engines only) is also checked with VW210, in between the two drive sprockets. The scale should read be-

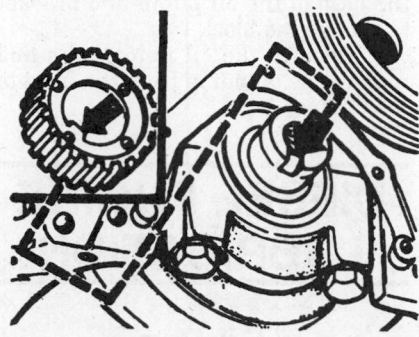

Various late models have the crankshaft pulley locating lug contained by the pulley

tween 12 and 13. To adjust the tension, loosen the injection pump mounting bracket bolts and move the pump toward the engine to loosen and away from the engine to tighten.

Timing Sprockets

REMOVAL & INSTALLATION

All of the drive sprockets are located by keys on their respective shafts (with the exception of certain diesel engine camshaft sprockets which are a taper fit or crankshaft sprockets which have a built-in lug) and each is retained by a bolt. To remove any or all of the sprockets, first remove the timing belt covers and belts and then use the following procedure.

1. Remove the center retaining bolt for the particular drive sprocket.
2. Gently pry the sprocket off of the shaft.
3. If the sprocket is stubborn in coming off, use a gear puller. Don't hammer on the sprocket as you may crack it.

NOTE: On certain 4 cylinder diesel engine camshafts, loosen the center bolt 1 turn and then tap the rear of the sprocket with a rubber mallet. When the sprocket loosens, remove the bolt and sprocket.

4. Remove the sprocket being careful not to lose the key.
5. Installation is in the reverse order of removal.

NOTE: Always check valve timing after removing the drive sprockets.

OIL SEAL REPLACEMENT

The oil seal is a part of the oil pump, it can be removed during the "Oil Pump Removal and Installation" procedures or it can be replaced as follows:

4000 Models

1. Refer to the "Timing Belt Removal and Installation" procedures and remove the timing belt.
2. Using seal extractor tool 2085 or equivalent, unscrew the inner part of the tool approximately 0.12 in. out of the outer part, then lock it in position by tightening the knurled screw.
3. Guide in the extractor by screwing the sprocket bolt in until it protrudes approximately 0.79 in.
4. Lubricate the threaded head of the oil seal extractor. place the extractor in position and screw it into the oil seal as far as possible while pushing inward.
5. Loosen the kurled screw and turn the inner part of the tool against the crankshaft until the seal is pulled out.
6. Clamp the extrtactor in a suitable vise and remove the oil seal with a suitable pair of pliers.
7. Using tool 10-203 or equivalent, press the tool in a depth of $\frac{3}{32}$ in., then install the new seal flush with the front cover.
8. The following seal removal & installation procedure is for the 4000 turbo diesel engine:
   a. Insert the bolt of tool 3083 or equivalent into the crankcase to guide the seal extractor tool 2085 or equivalent and remove the old seal.
   b. Slide the sleeve of tool 3083 or equivalent onto the crankcase journal. Dip the new seal in clean engine oil and slide it over the sleeve.
   c. Slide the thrust sleeve over the guide sleeve and press in the seal with the thrust sleeve and bolt until fully seated.

NOTE: When installing a new seal, be careful not to damage the lip of the seal.

9. Reinstall the timing belt. Torque the crankshaft pulley bolt to 253 ft. lbs.

5000 Models

1. Refer to the "Timing Belt Re-

moval and Installation" procedures and remove the timing belt.
2. Using a small pry bar, pry the oil seal from the oil pump.
3. Clean out the seal seat. Using a new seal, lubricate the lip with engine oil. Using a large socket (the dia. of the seal), drive the seal into the seal seat.

NOTE: When installing a new seal, be careful not to damage the lip of the seal.

4. Reinstall the timing belt. Torque the crankshaft pulley bolt to 253 ft. lbs.

Camshaft

REMOVAL & INSTALLATION

1. Remove the front and rear timing belts.
2. Remove the cylinder head cover.
3. Remove the camshaft drive sprocket.
4. Remove the injection pump drive sprocket.
5. Set cylinder No. 1 to TDC of the compression stroke.
6. Remove bearing cap Nos. 1 and 4.
7. Diagonally loosen bearing cap Nos. 2 and 3 and remove.
8. Remove the camshaft from the cylinder head.
9. Lubricate the camshaft journals, lobes, bearing shells and the contact faces of the caps with assembly lube or gear oil before reinstallation.
10. Replace both camshaft oil seals.

NOTE: The cam lobes for the No. 1 cylinder must face upward.

11. Install bearing caps Nos. 2 and 3 tightening alternately and diagonally.
12. Install bearing caps Nos. 1 and 4.
13. Replace the seal in the No. 1 bearing cap.
14. Installation of the remaining components is in the reverse order of removal.

NOTE: Always recheck the valve clearance after the camshaft has been removed.

Pistons and Connecting Rods

POSITIONING

NOTE: Most pistons are notched or marked to indicate which way they should be installed. If your pistons are not marked, mark them before re-

moval. Then reinstall them in the proper position.

GASOLINE ENGINE LUBRICATION

Oil Pan

REMOVAL & INSTALLATION

All Models

1. Raise and support the vehicle on jackstands.
2. Drain the oil from the crankcase. Remove the cover plate from under the engine, if so equipped.
3. Remove the four bolts from the subframe and lower the subframe. Remove the oil pan bolts while supporting the pan.
4. Lower the pan from the engine. Discard the gasket.
5. Coat both sides of a new gasket with sealer and install the gasket and oil pan.
6. Torque the bolts to 7 ft. lbs.

Rear Main Bearing Oil Seal

REPLACEMENT

NOTE: When this seal fails, the usual result is oil leakage onto the clutch. This of course, causes clutch slippage or failure to disengage.

All Models

The rear main oil seal is located at the rear of the engine block. It can be found in a housing behind the flywheel. To replace the seal it is necessary to remove the transmission.

1. Remove the transmission.
2. Unscrew the six bolts and remove the flywheel.
3. Using special tool VW2086 or a suitable tool, pry the old seal out of its housing.
4. To install, lightly oil the replacement seal then press it into place using a canister top or other circular piece of flat metal.

———— CAUTION ————
Be careful not to damage the seal or score the crankshaft.

5. Install the flywheel and the transmission.

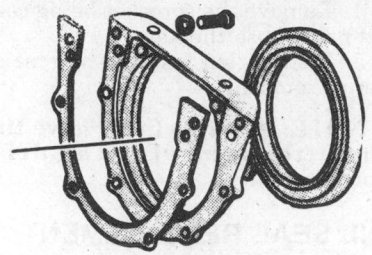

Rear main oil seal (circular)—4000 and 5000

Oil Pump

REMOVAL & INSTALLATION

4000 Models

1. Drain the oil and remove the oil pan.
2. Remove the oil pump mounting bolts and pull the pump down and out of the engine.
3. Unscrew the two bolts and separate the pump halves.
4. Clean the lower half in solvent.
5. To remove the oil strainer for cleaning, bend out the metal rim of the oil strainer cover plate and remove it.
6. Examine the gears and the driveshaft for any wear or damage. Replace them if necessary.
7. Reassemble the pump halves.

8. Prime the pump with oil and install in the reverse order of removal.

4000 (5 cyl.) and All 5 Cylinder Models

1. Loosen and remove the crankshaft pulley bolt.
2. Remove the drive belt guard.
3. Loosen the water pump bolts and turn the pump body clockwise.
4. Remove the drive belt and V-belt pulley with the drive belt sprocket.
5. Remove the dipstick and drain the engine oil.
6. Remove the front bolts on the sub frame and remove the oil pan.
7. Remove the oil suction pipe from the base of the oil pump and bracket to the engine block.
8. Remove the oil pump bolts and remove the oil pump from the front of the engine.

DIESEL ENGINE LUBRICATION

Oil Pan

REMOVAL & INSTALLATION

4 and 5 Cylinder

1. Raise and support the vehicle.

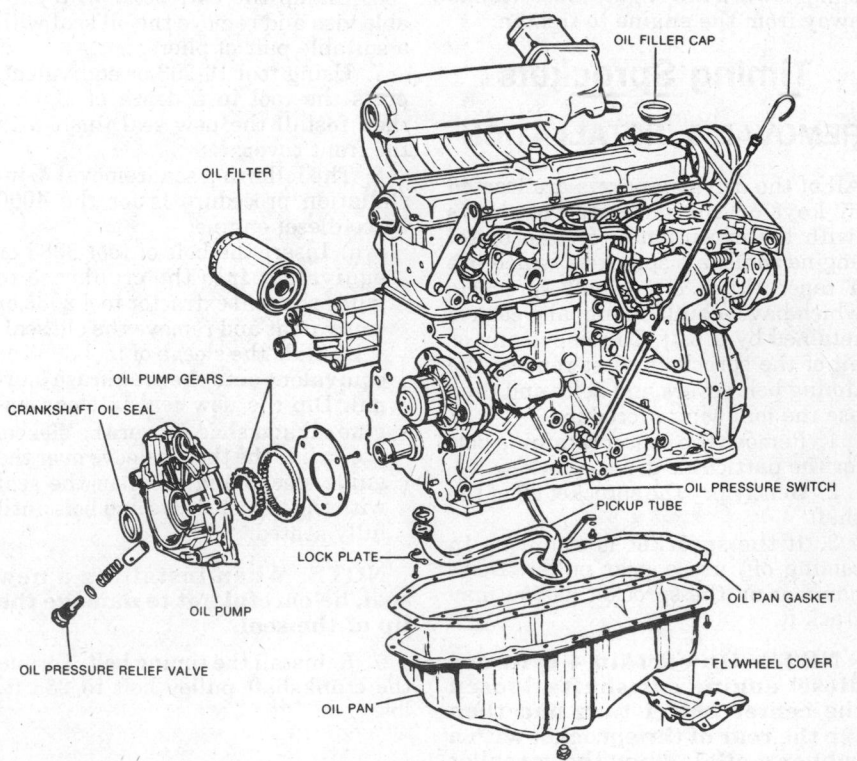

Exploded view of the 5-cyl diesel lubrication system components—gasoline engines are similar

2. Drain the oil. Remove the four bolts from the subframe and lower the subframe.

3. Remove the oil pan bolts while supporting the pan.

4. To remove the two bolts at the rear of the oil pan turn the flywheel so that the recesses are pointing down. This will afford you access to the two bolts.

5. Lower the pan from the engine. Discard the gasket.

6. Coat both sides of a new gasket with sealer and install the gasket and oil pan.

7. Torque the bolts to 14 ft. lbs. Refill the crankcase.

Rear Main Bearing Oil Seal

REPLACEMENT

NOTE: When this seal fails, the usual result is oil leakage onto the clutch. This of course, causes clutch slippage or failure to disengage.

The rear main oil seal is located at the rear of the engine block. It can be found in a housing behind the flywheel. To replace the seal it is necessary to remove the transmission.

1. Remove the transmission.

2. Unscrew the six bolts and remove the flywheel.

3. Using special tool VW 2086 or a suitable tool, pry the old seal out of its housing.

4. To install, lightly oil the replacement seal then press it into place using a canister top or other circular piece of flat metal.

— CAUTION —

Be careful not to damage the seal or score the crankshaft.

5. Install the flywheel and the transmission.

Oil Pump

REMOVAL & INSTALLATION

4 Cylinder Diesel and Turbodiesel

1. Drain the oil and remove the oil pan.

2. Remove the oil pump mounting bolts and pull the pump down and out of the engine.

3. Unscrew the two bolts and separate the pump halves.

4. Clean the lower half in solvent.

5. To remove the oil strainer for cleaning, bend out the metal rim of

the oil strainer cover plate and remove it.

6. Examine the gears and the driveshaft for any wear or damage. Replace them if necessary.

7. Reassemble the pump halves.

8. Prime the pump with oil and install in the reverse order of removal.

NOTE: Turbocharged diesel engines may use an oil cooler mounted between the oil filter and engine. Always check tightness of the cooler retaining nut when changing the oil filter. Nut should be torqued to 18 ft. lbs.

5 Cylinder Diesel and Turbodiesel

1. Loosen and remove the crankshaft bolt.

2. Remove the drive belt guard.

3. Loosen the water pump bolts and turn the pump body clockwise.

4. Remove the drive belt and V-belt pulley with the drive belt sprocket.

5. Remove the dipstick and drain the engine oil.

6. Remove the front bolts on the sub frame and remove the oil pan.

7. Remove the oil suction pipe from the base of the oil pump and bracket to the engine block.

8. Remove the oil pump bolts and remove the oil pump from the front of the engine.

GASOLINE ENGINE COOLING

NOTE: When replacing or adding coolant, use only a phosphate-free coolant/antifreeze.

Radiator

NOTE: Various late models have the radiator retained by locating tabs at the bottom and two mounting brackets at the top. Disconnect hoses, wiring connectors and top brackets. Remove the radiator and fan assembly.

REMOVAL & INSTALLATION

4000 (4 Cylinder—All Models)

1. Drain the cooling system.

2. If equipped with air conditioning, remove the grille and detach the condenser from the radiator.

3. Remove the upper and lower radiator hoses, the expansion tank sup-

ply hose and the expansion tank vent hose. Being careful not to crimp them, tie all hoses back out of the way.

NOTE: All disconnections should be done at the radiator end of the particular hose.

4. Disconnect the wiring at the temperature switch (two switches if air conditioning) and the rear of the fan motor.

5. Unscrew the fan shroud retaining bolts and remove the fan, motor and shroud as one assembly.

6. Unscrew the radiator retaining bolts and remove the radiator.

7. Installation is in the reverse order of removal.

4000 Coupe and Quattro, 5000 and All 5 Cylinder Models

1. Drain the cooling system.

2. Remove the three pieces of the radiator cowl and the fan motor assembly. Take care in removing the fan motor connectors to avoid bending them.

3. Remove the upper and lower radiator hoses and the coolant tank supply hose.

4. Disconnect the coolant temperature switch located on the lower right side of the radiator.

5. Remove the radiator mounting bolts and lift out the radiator.

6. Installation is the reverse of removal. Torque radiator mounting bolts to 14 ft. lbs. and cowl bolts to 7 ft. lbs.

Water Pump

REMOVAL & INSTALLATION

All Models

1. Drain the cooling system.

2. Remove the V-belts, timing belt covers and timing belts (5000 only) as outlined earlier in this section.

3. On the 4000, unscrew the water pump pulley retaining bolts (3) and remove the pulley. On 1.8L engine, remove the four pump retaining bolts (take note of various lengths and locations). Turn the pump slightly and lift from engine block.

4. On the 5000, unscrew the intermediate shaft drive sprocket retaining bolt and remove the sprocket.

5. Unscrew the water pump retaining bolts and remove the pump from its housing (4000) or from the engine block (5000).

6. Always replace the old gasket with a new one.

7. Installation is in the reverse order of removal.

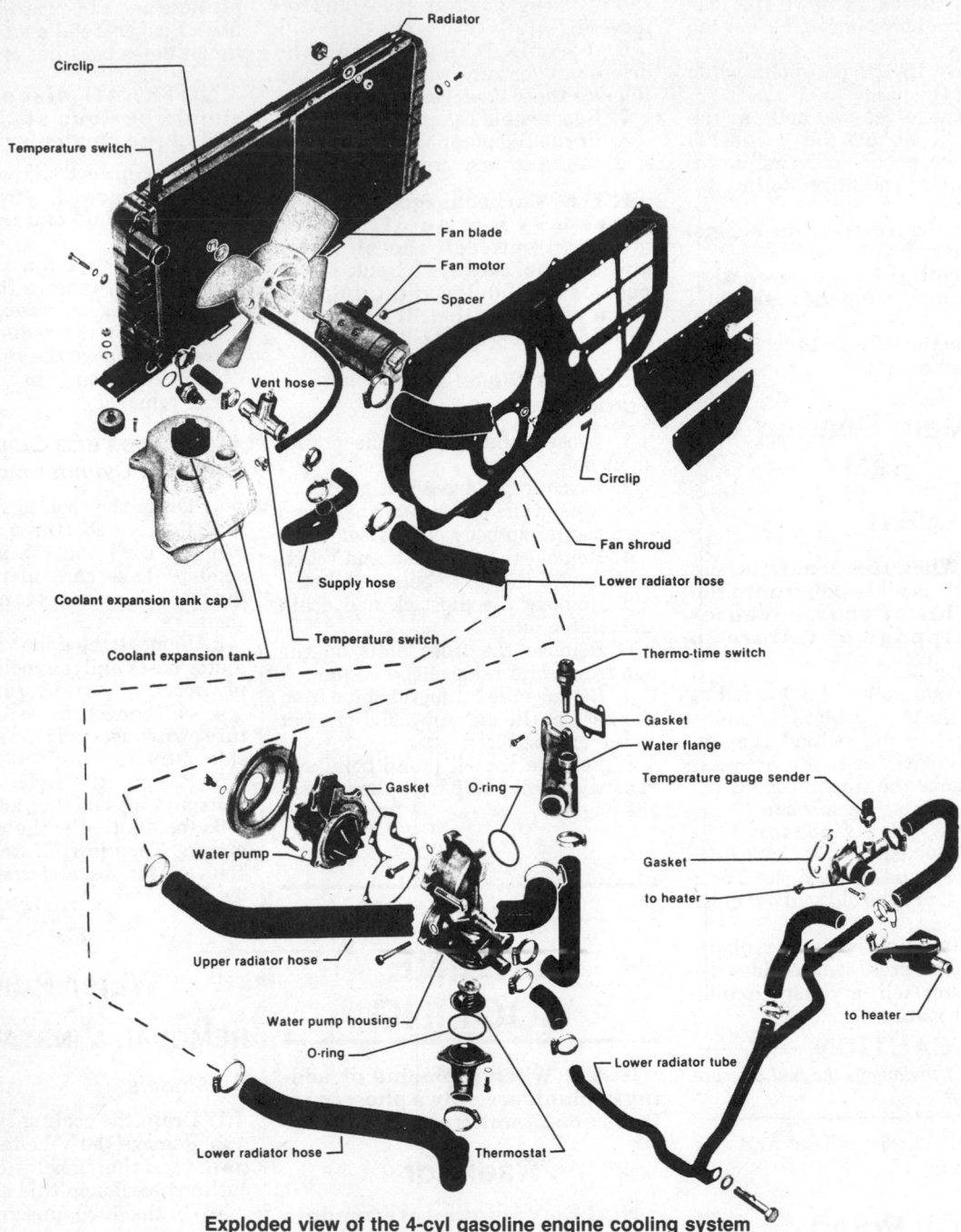

Exploded view of the 4-cyl gasoline engine cooling system

Labels in figure: Radiator, Circlip, Temperature switch, Fan blade, Fan motor, Spacer, Vent hose, Circlip, Fan shroud, Lower radiator hose, Coolant expansion tank cap, Supply hose, Temperature switch, Coolant expansion tank, Thermo-time switch, Gasket, Water flange, Temperature gauge sender, Gasket, Gasket, O-ring, Water pump, to heater, Upper radiator hose, Water pump housing, O-ring, to heater, Lower radiator tube, Lower radiator hose, Thermostat

Thermostat

REMOVAL & INSTALLATION

All 4 Cylinder Models

The thermostat is located in the lower radiator hose neck on the bottom of the water pump housing.

1. Drain the cooling system.
2. Remove the two retaining bolts from the lower water pump neck.

NOTE: **It is not necessary to disconnect the lower radiator hose.**

3. Move the neck, with the hoses attached, out of the way.
4. Carefully pry the thermostat out of the water pump housing. Install with new gasket or O-ring.

5000 and All 5 Cylinder Models

The thermostat is located in the lower radiator hose neck, on the left side of the engine block, behind the water pump housing.

Follow Steps 1–3 of the 4000 procedure.

1. Carefully pry the thermostat out of the engine block.
2. Install a new O-ring on the water pump neck.
3. Install the thermostat.

NOTE: **When installing the thermostat, the spring end should be pointing toward the engine block.**

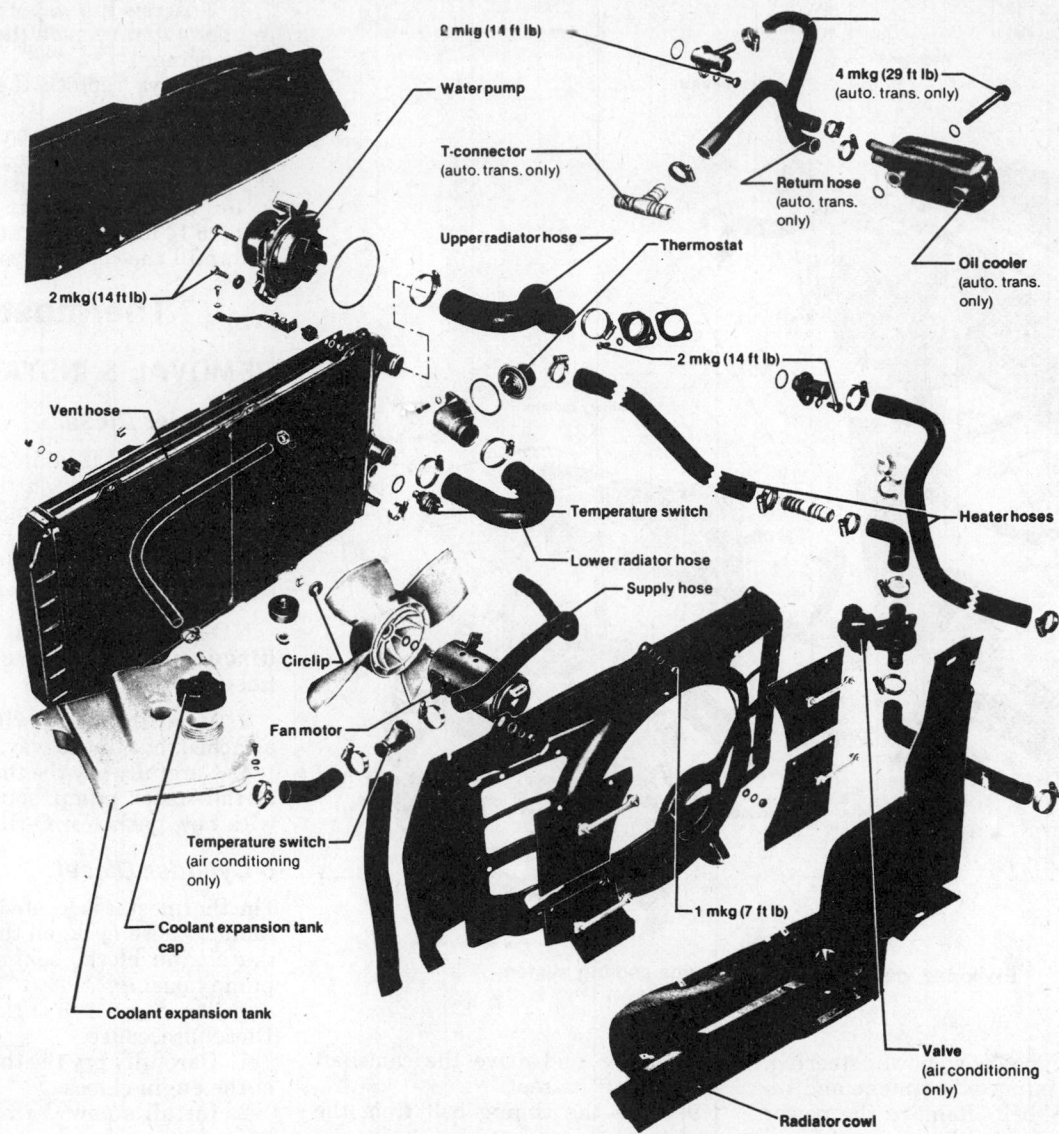

2 mkg (14 ft lb)

Water pump

T-connector
(auto. trans. only)

4 mkg (29 ft lb)
(auto. trans. only)

Return hose
(auto. trans.
only)

Upper radiator hose

Thermostat

Oil cooler
(auto. trans.
only)

2 mkg (14 ft lb)

2 mkg (14 ft lb)

Vent hose

Temperature switch

Heater hoses

Lower radiator hose

Supply hose

Circlip

Fan motor

Temperature switch
(air conditioning
only)

1 mkg (7 ft lb)

Coolant expansion tank
cap

Coolant expansion tank

Valve
(air conditioning
only)

Radiator cowl

Exploded view of the 5-cyl gasoline engine cooling system

4. Reposition the water pump neck and tighten the retaining bolts.

DIESEL ENGINE COOLING

NOTE: When replacing or adding coolant, use only a phosphate-free coolant/antifreeze.

Radiator

NOTE: The 5000 diesel and turbodiesel engine is equipped with an auxiliary radiator which is mounted at the right-front of the engine.

REMOVAL & INSTALLATION

4000 Diesel and Turbodiesel

1. Drain the cooling system.
2. Remove the three pieces of the radiator cowl and the fan motor assembly. Take care in removing the fan motor connectors to avoid bending them.
3. Remove the upper and lower radiator hoses and the coolant tank supply hose.
4. Disconnect the coolant temperature switch located on the lower right side of the radiator.
5. Remove the radiator mounting bolts and lift out the radiator.
6. Installation is the reverse of removal. Torque radiator mounting bolts to 14 ft. lbs. and cowl bolts to 7 ft. lbs.

5000 Diesel and Turbodiesel

The 5000 diesel and turbodiesel is equipped with an auxiliary radiator which must also be removed. To remove the auxiliary radiator:

1. Remove the grille and detach the condenser (air conditioning only).
2. Remove all hoses from the auxiliary radiator.
3. Remove the radiator retaining bolts and remove the radiator.
4. Installation is in the reverse order of removal.

Water Pump

REMOVAL & INSTALLATION
5000 Engine (Diesel)

1. Drain the coolant from the cooling system.

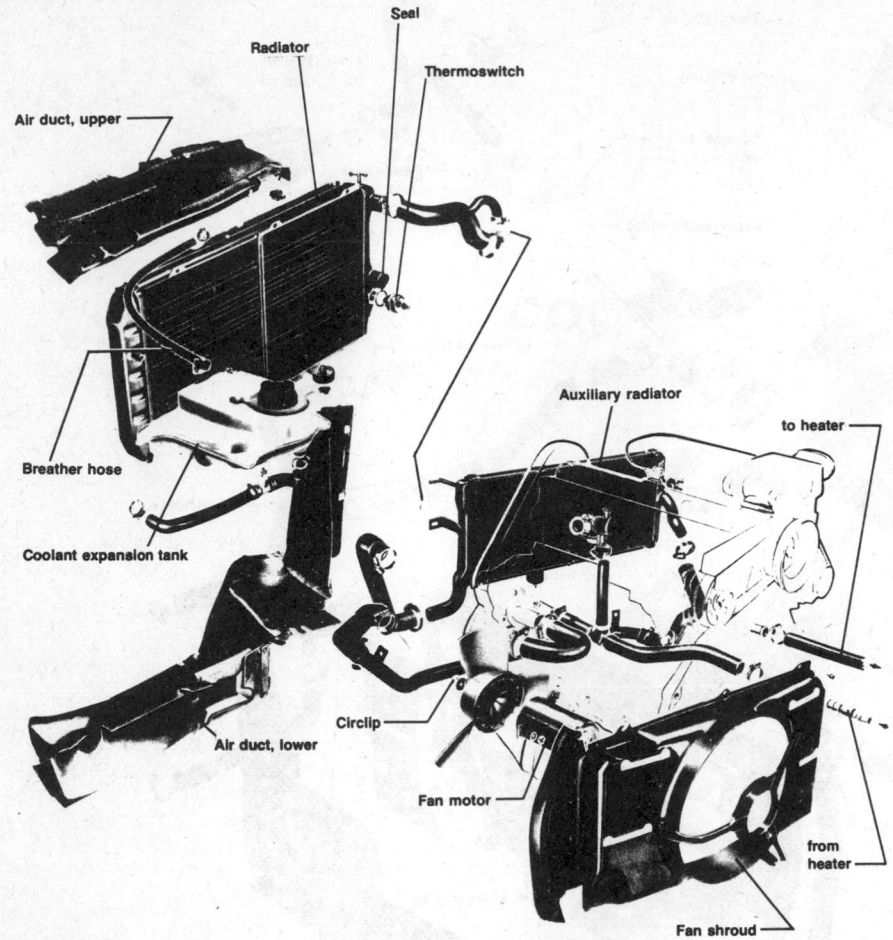

Exploded view of the diesel engine cooling system

Labels: Seal · Radiator · Thermoswitch · Air duct, upper · Breather hose · Coolant expansion tank · Air duct, lower · Circlip · Fan motor · Auxiliary radiator · to heater · from heater · Fan shroud

2. If equipped with power steering, loosen the pump adjustment and remove the V-belt. Remove the power steering pump (with the hoses) and lay it aside.

3. Remove both of the drive belt covers.

4. Turn the crankshaft, so that the No. 1 cylinder is at the TDC of the compression stroke; the mark on the flywheel aligns with the mark on the clutch housing and the mark on the injection pump aligns with the mark on the mounting plate.

5. Using tool No. 2064, secure the injection pump sprocket. Using tool No. 3036, secure the vacuum pump belt pulley and the injection pump drive sprocket.

6. Remove the injection pump drive sprocket retaining bolt, then the belt pulley, the injection pump drive sprocket and the drive belt.

7. Remove the cylinder head cover. Using tool No. 2065A, secure camshaft.

8. Loosen the camshaft sprocket retaining bolt (1 turn), then insert a drift, through the hole in the cam-shaft cover and drive the camshaft sprocket off its seat.

9. Slide the timing belt from the water pump sprocket.

NOTE: When removing the timing belt, be careful not to move the timing mark positions.

10. Remove the water pump-to-engine bolts and the pump from the engine.

11. To install, use a new gasket, sealant and reverse the removal procedures. Torque the water pump bolts to 14 ft. lbs., the camshaft sprocket bolt to 33 ft. lbs. and the injection pump drive sprocket bolt to 72 ft. lbs. Adjust the drive belts and refill the cooling system.

4000 Engine (Diesel)

1. Drain the cooling system.
2. Remove the V-belts as outlined earlier in this section.
3. Unscrew the water pump pulley retaining bolts (3) and separate the pulley. Turn the pump slightly and lift from engine block.

4. Unscrew the water pump retaining bolts and remove the pump from its housing.

5. Always replace the old gasket with a new one.

6. To install, use sealant and reverse the removal procedures. Torque the water pump-to-housing bolts to 7 ft. lbs. and the pulley-to-water pump bolts to 14 ft. lbs. Adjust the drive belt and refill the cooling system.

Thermostat

REMOVAL & INSTALLATION

4 Cylinder Diesel

The thermostat is located in the lower radiator hose neck on the bottom of the water pump housing.

1. Drain the cooling system.
2. Remove the two retaining bolts from the lower water pump neck.

NOTE: It is not necessary to disconnect the lower radiator hose.

3. Move the neck, with the hoses attached, out of the way.
4. Carefully pry the thermostat out of the water pump housing. Install with new gasket or O-ring.

5 Cylinder Diesel

The thermostat is located in the lower radiator hose neck, on the left side of the engine block, behind the water pump housing.

Follow Steps 1–3 of the 4 Cylinder Diesel procedure.

1. Carefully pry the thermostat out of the engine block.
2. Install a new O-ring on the water pump neck.
3. Install the thermostat.

NOTE: When installing the thermostat, the spring end should be pointing toward the engine block.

4. Reposition the water pump neck and tighten the retaining bolts.

EMISSION CONTROLS

Please refer to the "Emission Control" in the unit repair section for system maintenance procedures. Due to the complex nature of the modern electronic engine control systems, comprehensive diagnosis and testing procedures fall outside

the confines of this repair manual. For complete information on diagnosis, testing and repair procedures concerning all modern engine and emission control systems, please refer to the *"Chilton's Guide To Electronic Engine Controls"*.

EGR MAINTENANCE REMINDER SYSTEM

Inspect the system for leaks and deterioration every 30,000 miles. Clean the EGR valve and fittings and inspect the manifold for carbon deposits. Check the system for proper operation. The EGR maintenance reminder light will come on every 15,000 miles of operation. After the EGR system is checked and adjusted, reset the mileage counter.

If equipped with a service reminder, a dash light will illuminate at 15,000 or 30,000 mile intervals to indicate the need for EGR service. Replace the EGR valve and reset the service reminder by depressing the button marked "EGR" on the mileage counter located in the engine compartment or under the rear seat. Clean any carbon deposits from all components. If excessive carbon buildup is noted on the intake ports, the intake manifold should be removed and cleaned. Never attempt to clean the intake manifold while it is attached to the engine.

OXYGEN SENSOR MAINTENANCE REMINDER LIGHT RESET

Every 30,000 miles a maintenance reminder light in the dashboard will come on. This is an indications that the emission systems should be checked and that the oxygen sensor should be replaced.

1. To reset the 5000 non-turbo models, remove the instrument panel cluster. Remove the switch cover near

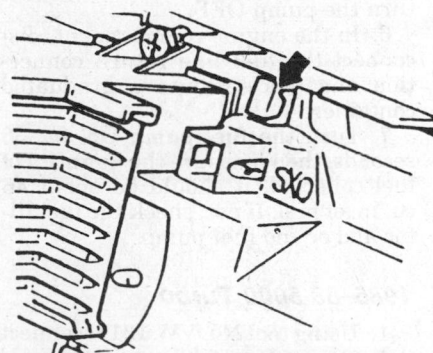

Maintenance reminder light reset button location 5000 non-turbo models

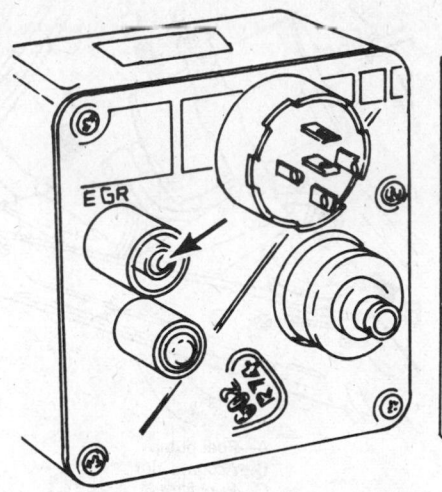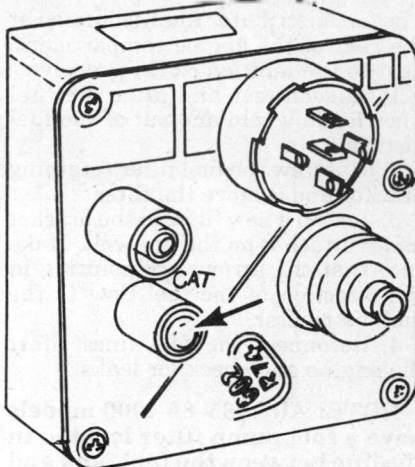

Location of reset buttons on emission system EGR/Catalyst counter assembly

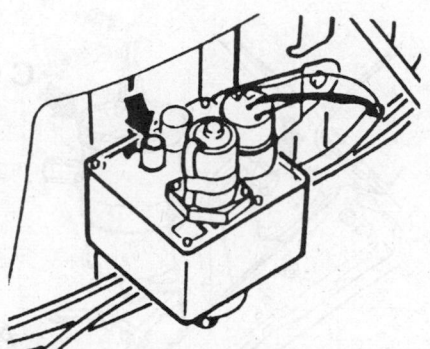

Maintenance reminder light reset button location 5000 turbo models

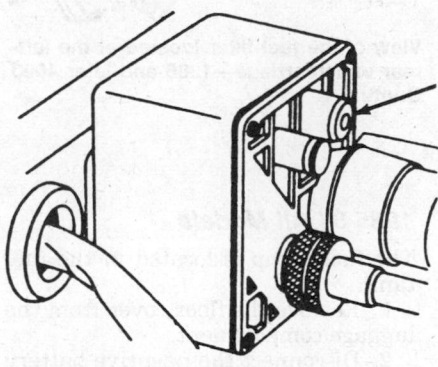

Maintenance reminder light reset button location all other models

the "OXS". Push the switch to reset the light.

2. On the 5000 turbo models, lift the rear seat and push the button marked "OXS" on the reset box.

3. On the 5000S models, depress the switch below the warning light after removing the housing cover. Place the ignition switch in the "ON" position and verify the reminder light is out.

4. On all other models, trace the speedometer cable to the mileage counter control box (usually located on the left side of the instrument panel). The control box is installed in-line with the cable, press the white button on the control box and check to see that the reminder light has gone out.

GASOLINE FUEL SYSTEM

Fuel Filter

REMOVAL & INSTALLATION

4000, 4-Cyl (1981–84) and 5-Cyl (1985–88)

NOTE: The 1981–84 4000 has two fuel filters, one for the fuel pump and one for the fuel distributor. Both should be replaced every 15,000 miles.

The fuel pump filter is underneath the car, below the fuel tank. To remove:

1. Loosen the fuel line clamps on each end of the filter and disconnect the filter from the lines.

2. Install a new filter. Make sure that the arrow points in the direction of fuel flow to the fuel pump.

3. Tighten the fuel line clamps and secure the new filter. Start the engine and check for leaks.

1981–84 ONLY

The fuel distributor filter is located at the rear of the engine compartment, next to the ignition coil. To remove.

1. Disconnect and plug the fuel lines leading into and out of the fuel distributor.

2. Unscrew the fuel filter retaining bracket and remove the filter.

3. Install a new filter in the bracket and reattach it on the fire wall. Make sure that the arrows are pointing in the direction of the fuel flow to the fuel distributor.

4. Reconnect the fuel lines, start the engine and check for leaks.

NOTE: All 1985–88 4000 models have a fuel pump filter located in the line between the fuel tank and the fuel pump. To remove: disconnect the fuel lines and remove the filter. To install, use a new filter and reverse the removal procedures.

4000 (5cyl) 1981–84 & 5000 Models

The 5 cylinder engines (gas versions only) have a fuel distributor filter which should be replaced every 15,000 miles (30,000 for the Turbo). It is located on the right wheel arch, directly behind the air cleaner housing (1981–84) or next the fuel distributor (1985–88). To remove:

1. Disconnect the fuel lines leading into and out of the fuel distributor.

2. Unscrew the filter retaining bracket and remove the filter.

3. Install a new filter in the bracket and reattach it to the wheel arch. Make sure that the arrows are pointing in the direction of the fuel flow to the distributor.

4. Reconnect the fuel lines, start the engine and check for leaks.

Electric Fuel Pump

REMOVAL & INSTALLATION

All Models Except the 1985–88 5000 Models

On all models, except the 1985–88 4000 Quattro, the fuel pump is located at the right rear of the undercarriage. On the 1985–88 4000 Quattro, the fuel pump is located at the left-rear of the undercarriage.

1. Disconnect the battery ground.

2. Clean all fuel and electrical connections.

3. Disconnect the pump wiring.

4. Disconnect the fuel lines.

5. Unbolt and dismount the pump.

6. Installation is the reverse of removal. Torque the mounting bolts to 14 ft. lbs.

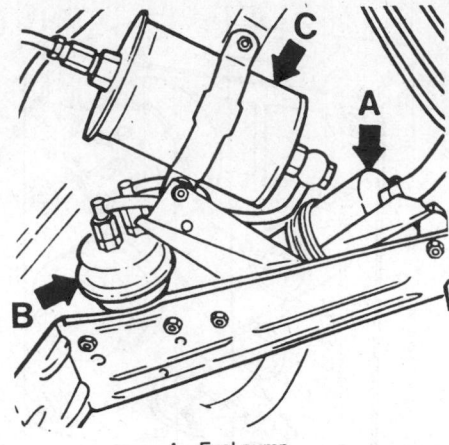

A—Fuel pump
B—Accumulator
C—Fuel filter

View of the fuel filter located at the right-rear undercarriage—1985 and later 4000S Coupe

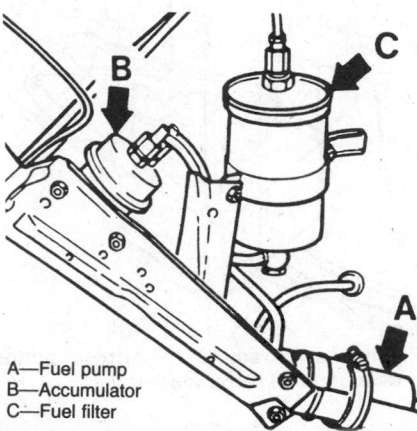

A—Fuel pump
B—Accumulator
C—Fuel filter

View of the fuel filter located at the left-rear undercarriage—1985 and later 4000 Quattro

1985-88 All Models

The fuel pump is located in the fuel tank.

1. Remove the floor cover from the luggage compartment.

2. Disconnect the negative battery cable and the electrical connector from the fuel gauge sender.

3. Mark and remove the hoses from the fuel gauge sender.

4. Using tool No. 3087, loosen the fuel gauge sender-to-fuel tank retaining ring, then pull out the fuel gauge fuel pump assembly.

5. From inside the assembly housing, pull off the fuel hoses, detach the electrical connections and remove the gravity vent valve.

6. To install, reverse the removal procedures. Start the engine and check for leaks.

TESTING THE FUEL PUMP

— CAUTION —
When performing this test, do not smoke or have any open flame around.

NOTE: Do not open the fuel tank cap until after the fuel pump delivery rate has been checked, for the tank is pressurized.

All Models Except the 1985–88 5000 Models

1. Using tool No. US 4480/3, connect it in place of the fuel pump relay with the switch OFF.

2. At the input side of the fuel filter, disconnect the fuel line and place it into a graduated flask.

3. Turn the fuel pump ON for 30 second; you should collect about 60 cubic inches of fuel.

4. If not within specifications, check the fuel pump filter. If the fuel pump filter is OK, replace the fuel pump.

5. Install the input hose onto the filter, then remove the ouput hose from the filter and place filter output into the flask.

6. Turn the fuel pump ON for 30 seconds; the amount of fuel collected should be the same, if not replace the fuel filter.

7. Replace the output line onto the fuel filter.

1985-88 5000 Non-Turbo

1. Using tool No. US 4480/3, connect it in place of the fuel pump relay with the switch OFF.

2. Remove the fuel pump cover from the floor of the trunk.

3. At the fuel pump connecting plug, pull back the rubber cover, leave the plug connected to the pump.

4. Using a voltmeter, connect the probes to terminals 1 and 2 of the fuel pump connector, then turn the fuel pump ON.

5. Check the voltage of the running pump, it should be at least 9.0 V, then turn the pump OFF.

6. In the engine compartment, disconnect the fuel line return connection and place it into a graduated container.

7. Turn the fuel pump ON for 30 seconds, then measure the quantity of fuel collected, it should be about 46 cu. in. of fuel. If not, check the fuel filter and/or the fuel pump.

1985–88 5000 Turbo

1. Using tool No. VW 1318, connect it between the fuel line at the cold start valve and the lower chamber test connection of the fuel distributor.

Position the gauge lever so that the valve is open.

2. Remove the fuel pump relay from the fuse panel and install tool No. US 4480/3 (be certain that it is turned OFF).

3. Remove the electrical connector from the differential pressure regulator.

4. Turn ON the fuel pump, the fuel pressure should be 75–82 psi.

5. If the pressure is below specifications, check the fuel pump delivery quantity.

6. If the fuel pump delivery is OK, replace the diaphragm pressure regulator.

7. If the pressure is higher than specifications, disconnect the fuel tank return line from the diaphragm pressure regulator and repeat the test.

8. If the pressure is OK, check for a plugged fuel return line.

9. If the pressure is not OK, replace the diaphragm pressure regulator.

NOTE: The system pressure is not adjustable.

Fuel Injection

Due to the complex nature of the modern electronic engine control systems, comprehensive diagnosis and testing procedures fall outside the confines of this repair manual. For complete information on diagnosis, testing and repair procedures concerning all modern engine and emission control systems, please refer to the *"Chilton's Guide To Fuel Injection And Feedback Carburetors"*.

DIESEL FUEL SYSTEM

Fuel Filter

DRAINING WATER

1. Loosen the vent screw on the fuel filter cover.

2. Open the water drain screw at the bottom of the filter and let the water drain out until only pure fuel appears.

3. Tighten the drain screw and the vent screw.

4. Start the engine and check for leaks.

REMOVAL & INSTALLATION

1. Remove and plug the fuel lines.

2. Open the vent screw on the fuel filter cover and then drain the remaining fuel from the filter using the drain screw at the bottom of the filter.

3. Remove the two filter cover mounting screws and the filter assembly.

4. Carefully clamp the filter cover in a vise and pry off the protective sleeve.

5. Loosen the filter element with a band wrench and unscrew the filter by hand.

6. Apply a thin film of diesel fuel to the gasket of the new filter element and screw it in by hand. DO NOT use the band wrench to tighten.

7. Slide the protective sleeve back on.

8. Start the engine and accelerate a few times until it is running smoothly. Check for leaks.

Diesel Injection Pump

REMOVAL & INSTALLATION

—————— CAUTION ——————
When working on diesel injection system everything must be kept extremely clean. Wipe pipe unions clean before loosening. DO NOT use cold water if degreasing a hot injection pump, the sudden contraction of the metal can cause the pump to seize.

4000 Models

1. Turn the engine until the TDC mark on the flywheel is in line with the boss on the bellhousing. Disconnect the negative battery cable.

2. Lock the camshaft with a suitable setting bar, then remove the the timing belt.

3. Lock the injection pump sprocket with pin 2064 or equivalent. Slightly loosen the injection pump sprocket retaining nut and remove the pin.

4. Attach puller 3032 or equivalent so that the jaws are at right angles to cross and point in the direction of the spindle rotation, carefully apply tension with the puller.

5. Hit the puller spindle head (with light taps) with a suitable hammer until the sprocket loosens from the injection pump shaft taper. Remove the puller and nut and the sprocket by hand.

6. Disconnect all fuel lines from the fuel pump, covering the fuel line unions with a clean shop towel. Disconnect and remove the fuel lines at the injectors.

7. Disconnect the fuel shutoff solenoid electrical connector at the injection pump, then the accelerator and the cold start cables. Remove the bolt

from the injection pump mounting plate, but do not loosen the bolts on the fuel distributor head.

8. Remove the bolts from the front injection pump mounting plate support and remove the injection pump.

9. Installation is the reverse order of the removal procedure. Be sure to note the following exceptions:

　a. During injection pump installation, align the marks on the pump and the mounting plate.

　b. Torque the pump bolts and fuel line unions to 18 ft. lbs. and the injection pump sprocket to 33 ft. lbs.

　c. Adjust the injection timing as outlined in this section. Be sure that the injection pump runout does not exceed 0.0079 in.

5000 Models

1. Remove the vacuum pump pulley and fan belt. Remove the injection pump drive belt cover.

2. Turn the engine until the TDC mark on the flywheel is in line with the boss on the clutch housing. Disconnect the negative battery cable.

3. Lock the camshaft with a suitable setting bar, then remove the the timing belt. Lock the injection pump sprocket with pin 2064 or equivalent.

4. Secure the vacuum pump belt pulley and injection pump drive sprocket with tool 3036 or equivalent.

5. Loosen and remove the drive sprocket attaching bolt and remove the drive sprocket with the timing belt.

6. Attach puller 3032 or equivalent so that the jaws are at right angles to cross and point in the direction of the spindle rotation, carefully apply tension with the puller.

7. Hit the puller spindle head (with light taps) with a suitable hammer until the sprocket loosens from the injection pump shaft taper. Remove the puller and nut and the sprocket by hand.

8. Disconnect all fuel lines from the fuel pump, covering the fuel line unions with a clean shop towel. Disconnect and remove the fuel lines at the injectors.

9. Disconnect the fuel shutoff solenoid electrical connector at the injection pump, then the accelerator and the cold start cables.

10. Remove the coolant hoses from the cold start device. Remove the four bolts from the injection pump mounting plate and one bolt from the support bracket and remove the injection pump.

NOTE: To remove the rear attaching bolt at the mounting plate, use a 6mm hex key sockey with a 8.6 inch extension.

11. Install the injection pump, aligning the marks on the pump and the mounting plate. Install the attaching bolts loosely. Align the rear support so that it contacts the cylinder block and injection pump free of tension and tighten it in this position.

12. During injection pump sprocket installation, be sure that the injection pump runout does not exceed 0.0079 in. Install the injection pump sprocket, turning it to align the marks on the gear and mounting plate.

13. Lock the pump with tool 2064 or equivalent and torque the attaching bolts to 33 ft. lbs. Install the timing belt with the injection pump drive sprocket on the camshaft.

14. Tighten the drive sprocket attaching bolt so that the drive sprocket can still be turned manually. Using tool VW210 or equivalent, check the timing belt tension.

15. If the scale of the tool does not read 12-13 adjust the drive belt tension by loosening the bolts and moving the plate pump. Be sure the TDC mark on the flywheel is aligned with the reference mark.

16. Secure the injection pump drive sprocket with the setting bar and torque the sprocket attaching bolt to 72 ft. lbs. Remove tool 2064 or equivalent.

17. Connect the coolant hoses to the cold start valve. Loosen the cold start device cable by loosening the screw on the slip collar. Do not loosen the cable clamping nut.

18. Hold the cold start lever to the left while turning the collar a ¼ turn to allow the cable clamp to slide to the left of the collar slot. Install the adapter 2066 or equivalent and a small dial indicator with a 0.0984 in. preload in place of the plug on the injection pump.

19. Remove the cover plate below the engine. Slowly turn the crankshaft counterclockwise until the dial indicator needle stops moving. Zero the dial indicator with approximately 0.03997 inch preload.

20. Turn the crankshaft clockwise until the TDC mark on the flywheel is aligned with the reference mark. The dial indictor should read, 0.0315-0.0354 in. On vehicles without a turbocharger and 0.0346-0.0386 in. on vehicles equipped with a turbocharger.

21. If it is necessary, loosen the injection pump bolts and set the lift by turning the injection pump. Set to .0327-.0343 in. On vehicles without a turbocharger and 0.0358-0.0374 in. on vehicles equipped with a turbocharger. Torque the injection pump attaching bolts to 18 ft. lbs.

22. Retention the cold start device

cable by rotating the slip collar back a ¼ turn and tightening the slip collar screw. Connect the coolant hoses to the cold start device.

23. Reconnect all fuel lines, the shutoff solenoid and all other disconnect electrical connectors. Torque the fuel injection line unions to 18 ft. lbs. Re-install the timing belt cover. Start the engine and adjust the idle speeds as necessary.

INJECTION TIMING

4 cylinder

——————— CAUTION ———————

Before checking or adjusting the injection timing, always push in the Cold Start Device completely. The knob to control the Cold Start Device is on the instrument panel.

1. Locate the plug in the center of the injection pump cover. Remove this plug. Note that the seal must always be replaced whenever the plug is removed.

2. VW has an adapter (VW tool No. 2066 or equivalent) that fits the plug opening to which a dial indicator is attached. If this tool is not available, a dial indicator that is substituted must have a range of at least (0-0.120 inch (0-3mm). Place the gauge so that the plunger will be in the hole from which the plug was removed. Preload the gauge to approximately 0.097 in. (2.5mm).

3. Turn the engine slowly counterclockwise, which is opposite the normal rotation, until the needle on the dial indicator stops moving. Zero the gauge.

——————— CAUTION ———————

DO NOT try to rotate the engine by turning the camshaft drive nut. This will only damage the drive belt.

4. With the dial indicator zeroed, turn the engine clockwise, which is the normal rotation, until the TDC mark on the flywheel is aligned with the boss on the belt housing. The gauge should read 0.032 inch on regular diesels and 0.035 inch on turbodiesels.

5. If the reading cannot be obtained, loosen the bolts on the mounting plate and injector support. Set the regular diesel lift of the pump to 0.032 inch by turning the pump; set the turbo-diesel lift to 0.035 inch by turning the pump. Tighten the mounting bolts and recheck the injection timing.

6. Replace the seal on the center plug and install the plug.

5 Cylinder

1. Set crankshaft to TDC of the

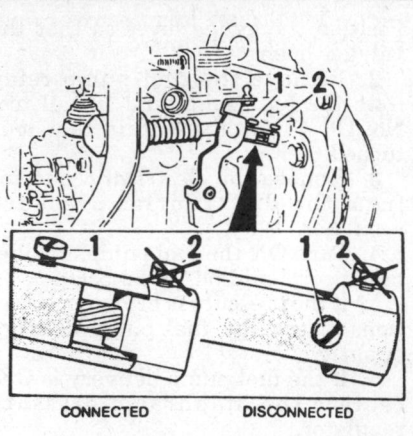

Disconnecting cold start device on diesel models—see text for details

compression stroke of the No. 1 cylinder, then align marks on the flywheel/clutch housing and injection pump sprocket mounting plate.

2. Loosen cold start device cable by loosening screw (1) on clamp and turning clamp 90°. DO NOT loosen screw (2).

3. Install adaptor and small dial indicator with 0.097 in. (2.5mm) preload in place of injection pump cover.

4. Turn the crankshaft counterclockwise slowly until the dial indicator stops moving.

5. Zero the dial indicator with about 0.04 in. (1mm) preload.

6. Turn crankshaft clockwise until TDC mark on flywheel is aligned with the reference mark. Dial indicator should read a lift of 0.031-0.035 in. (0.80-0.90mm) diesel or 0.035-0.038 in. (0.88-0.98mm) for diesel-turbo.

7. If necessary, loosen injection pump bolts and set lift to specifications by turning injection pump.

8. Turn clamp on cold start device cable back 90° to tension cable, tighten screw.

CHECKING & ADJUSTING INJECTION PUMP/VALVE TIMING

All engines

1. Remove vacuum pump pulley and V-belt.

2. Remove cylinder head cover and drive belt cover for injection pump drive sprocket.

3. Set crankshaft to TDC of the compression stroke of the No. 1 cylinder, then align marks on flywheel/clutch housing and injection pump sprocket/mounting plate.

4. Secure injection pump sprocket with Setting Pin tool No. 2064.

5. Secure injection pump drive

sprocket with bar. Remove retaining bolt, drive sprocket and drive belt.

6. Check that the TDC mark on the flywheel is still aligned with reference mark. Adjust if necessary.

7. Setting Bar tool No. 2065 A should fit in camshaft slot. If not, timing must be set as follows:

a. Turn crankshaft so that setting bar will fit.

b. Remove camshaft drive belt cover and loosen camshaft sprocket retaining bolt about one turn.

c. Loosen the camshaft sprocket by tapping with a drift inserted through hole in cover.

d. Turn crankshaft until TDC mark on flywheel and boss on clutch housing are aligned.

e. Tighten the camshaft sprocket bolt to 33 ft. lbs. and remove setting bar.

8. Install injection pump drive sprocket with drive belt. Tighten the drive sprocket retaining bolt until drive sprocket can just be turned by hand.

9. Check the drive belt tension. If necessary, adjust by loosening bolts and moving mounting plate with pump.

NOTE: The belt is correctly tensioned when it can be twisted 90° with the thumb and forefinger midway between the camshaft and intermediate shaft drive sprockets.

10. Check that the TDC mark on flywheel is aligned. Adjust if necessary.

11. Secure injection pump drive sprocket with bar and tighten retaining bolt to 72 ft. lbs.

12. Remove the Setting Pin tool No. 2064 from injection pump.

13. Check injection timing. Adjust if necessary.

14. Install belt cover and cylinder head cover.

Injection Nozzle

REMOVAL & INSTALLATION

NOTE: A loud knocking in one or more cylinders can be caused by a faulty injector. Locate by loosening pipe union on each cylinder in turn with engine at fast idle. If engine speed remains constant, that injector is faulty.

—— CAUTION ——
To avoid damage keep injector parts clean when removing, installing, disassembling and assembling.

1. Clean all injector pipe fittings.
2. Remove injector pipes.
3. Disconnect fuel return hoses.

4. Remove injectors using tool No. US 2775 or equivalent.
5. Remove heat shields from injectors and discard.
6. Install new heat shields on injectors.
7. Install injectors and tighten to 51 ft. lbs.
8. Install injector pipes and tighten to 18 ft. lbs.
9. Reconnect fuel return hoses.
10. Start engine and accelerate a few times to clear air bubbles. Check for leaks.

MANUAL TRANSAXLE

The transmission is combined with the differential in a transaxle assembly.

REMOVAL & INSTALLATION

NOTE: If the flywheel has been removed from the crankshaft for any reasons (4000 and 5000 models) torque the mounting bolts to: Bolt without shoulder — 72 ft. lbs.; bolt with shoulder — 54 ft. lbs. Coat all threads with a locking compound.

4000 Models (Except the 1984-88 Quattro)

This procedure can be performed with the engine installed.

1. Disconnect the negative battery cable.
2. Unplug the two electrical connectors for the back-up lights. They can be found between the ignition coil and the fuel distributor filter.
3. Remove the upper engine/transmission bolts.
4. Using special tool 3016 (or a pair of pliers), detach the speedometer cable from the transaxle.
5. Detach the clutch cable from the clutch lever.
6. Unbolt the exhaust pipe from the exhaust manifold.
7. Unscrew the three mounting bolts and remove the center engine mount.
8. Unbolt the front exhaust pipe from the support bracket and then unbolt it from the catalytic converter or muffler.
9. Unscrew the six screws and remove the left halfshaft from the transaxle. Wire the halfshaft up and out of the way. Repeat the procedure for the right halfshaft.

—— CAUTION ——
When wiring the halfshaft, tighten the wire only enough so as to relieve any downward pressure on them.

10. Remove the cover plate. On Quattro models, disconnect the front/rear driveshaft at the rear output shaft of the transmission and secure out of the way.
11. Tag and disconnect all wires leading to the starter and remove the starter.
12. Remove the bolt from the shift rod coupling.
13. Pry off the linkage coupling with a suitable small prybar.
14. Pull the shift rod coupling off of the shift rod. Place a transmission jack under the transmission, support it by lifting up slightly.
15. Loosen the left (chassis) bolt on the rear transmission support. Remove the two bolts (some models have one) from the right (transmission) side of the support and pivot the support out of the way.
16. Remove the rubber mounting block.
17. Unscrew three bolts and remove the front transmission support.
18. Remove the lower engine/transmission bolts.
19. Carefully pry the transmission apart from the engine and remove it.
20. Installation is in the reverse order of removal. Note the following:

a. Make sure that all engine/transmission mounts are correctly aligned and free of tension.

b. Check for proper adjustment of the gear shift lever, as detailed under "Linkage Adjustment".

c. Secure the bolt on the shift rod coupling with wire.

d. Tighten the engine/transmission bolts to 40 ft. lbs.

e. Tighten the halfshaft-to-drive flange bolts to 33 ft. lbs.

f. Tighten the subframe-to-body bolts to 51 ft. lbs.

g. Tighten the front transmission support-to-transmission bolts to 18 ft. lbs.

h. Tighten the rubber mount-to-body bolts to 29 ft. lbs. (1981–83) or 80 ft. lbs. (1984–88).

i. Tighten the rubber mount-to-transmission bolts to 40 ft. lbs.

j. Tighten the rubber mount-to-crossmember bolts to 18 ft. lbs.

4000 Quattro (1984–88)

1. Disconnect the negative battery cable.
2. Disconnect the rpm sensor.
3. Remove the upper engine-to-transmission bolts.
4. Using tool No. 3016, disconnect

the speedometer cable from the transmission.

5. Disconnect the tie rod coupling from the steering rack.

—————— CAUTION ——————
When removing the tie rod coupling, remove the self-locking nuts (first) then the mounting bolts.

6. Disconnect the transmission switch electrical connector from the transmission.

7. At the clutch slave cylinder, drive out the lock pin, remove the cylinder (leave the hydraulic line attached) and move it aside.

8. Disconnect the shift linkage from the transmission.

9. Using an Engine Support tool No 10–222, place it on the vehicle and support the engine.

10. At the right-transmission mount, remove the axle shaft deflector and the transmission mount.

11. Remove the front exhaust pipe, then disconnect the right-axle shaft from the transmission.

12. At the left-side of the transmission, remove the mount and the left-axle shaft from the transmission.

13. At the rear of the transmission, disconnect the driveshaft and the differential lock cable.

14. Remove the transmission cover plate, then turn the spindle of the engine support tool to raise the engine slightly.

15. Place a Transmission Support Lift tool No. VWAG 1383 under the transmission and secure it to the transmission.

16. Remove the lower engine-to-transmission bolts, push the transmission back and lower it from the vehicle.

—————— CAUTION ——————
When removing the transmission, make sure that the axle shafts, driveshaft, tie-rods and shift linkage do not interfere.

NOTE: If the pickup eye is still in place on the transmission housing (near the starter), remove it with a hacksaw to provide easier access to the exhaust pipe.

17. To install, reverse the removal procedures. Torque the engine-to-transmission bolts to 43 ft. lbs., the transmission mounting-to-transmission bolts to 29 ft. lbs., the transmission mount-to-frame bolts to 32 ft. lbs., the axle shafts-to-transmission bolts to 33 ft. lbs., the tie rod coupling-to-steering rack bolts to 29 ft. lbs. and the driveshaft-to-transmission bolts to 39 ft. lbs. Adjust the shift linkage.

5000 Models
The manual transaxle may be re-moved with the engine in place.

1. Disconnect the battery ground.

2. Remove the air filter (Diesel only).

3. Remove the windshield washer bottle.

4. Remove the upper engine-transmission bolts.

5. Raise and support the vehicle.

6. Disconnect the speedometer cable from the transmission.

7. Disconnect all wires and hoses connected to the transaxle.

8. Drive out the clutch slave cylinder lockpin and remove the slave cylinder. Leave the hydraulic line connected.

9. Support the engine, either from above with a hoist or from below with a jack.

10. Remove the heat shield.

11. Remove the lower engine/transmission splash shield (Diesel only).

12. Disconnect the exhaust pipe from the manifold.

13. Remove the right side guard plate.

14. Disconnect the driveshafts from the flanges and support them out of the way with wires. On the Quattro, disconnect the front/rear driveshaft at the rear output shaft on the transmission and wire it out of the way.

15. Disconnect the back-up light switch.

16. Pry off the shift and adjusting rods.

17. Remove the lower engine-transmission bolts.

18. Remove the starter.

19. Remove the sub-frame skid plate.

20. Install a jack under the transmission and lift it slightly.

21. Remove both transmission-to-sub-frame bolts.

22. Remove the right-side transmission bracket.

23. Slide the transmission back off the locating dowels and remove it from the car.

24. When installing, place the drive-shafts on top of the sub-frame; tighten the lower bolts first, then tighten the transmission bracket, sub-frame and upper bolts. Driveshaft bolts are torqued to 32 ft. lbs.; transmission bracket bolts to 29 ft. lbs.; sub-frame support bolts to 29 ft. lbs.; sub-frame to body bolts to 80 ft. lbs. and the transmission to engine bolts to 40 ft. lbs. Install all other parts in reverse order of removal.

Quattro, Quattro Turbo & Quattro Coupe

1. Disconnect the negative battery cable and disconnect the rpm sensor.

2. Remove the upper engine to transmission attaching bolts. Disconnect the speedometer.

3. Disconnect the tie-rod coupling from the steering rack, first removing the self locking nuts below the tie rod coupling, then the mounting bolts.

4. Drive out the clutch slave cylinder lock pin, then remove the clutch slave cylinder leaving the hydraulic lines attached. Disconnect the back-up light switch and shift linkage.

5. Attach tool 10-222 or equivalent and support the engine with a suitable engine hoist. Remove the deflector for the axle shaft and the right transmission mount. Remove the right transmission mount.

6. Disconnect the exhaust pipe at the flange and the right axle shaft at the transmission. Remove the left transmission mount and disconnect the left axle shaft at the transmission.

7. Disconnect the driveshaft at the transmission. Disconnect the differential lock cable and remove the transmission cover plate.

8. Raise the engine slightly and place a suitable transmission jack under the transmission. Remove the lower engine to transmission bolts.

9. Remove the transmission from underneath the vehicle. On the Quattro Turbo models, remove the transmission towards the rear of the vehicle, making sure the transmission clears the axle shafts, drive-shafts, tie rods and shift linkage.

10. Installation is the reverse order of the removal procedures. Torque the exhaust pipe flange attaching bolts to 18 ft. lbs. Torque the exhaust pipe to transmission mount attaching bolts to 22 ft. lbTorque the tie-rod couplingto the steering rack attaching bolts and thetransmission mount to transmission attaching bolts to 29 ft. lbs.

11. Torque the transmission mount to sub-frame attaching bolts and driveshaft attaching bolts to 32 ft. lbs. Torque the engine to transmission mounting bolts to 43 ft. lbs. Torque the axle shaft to the transmission mounting bolts to 58 ft. lbs.

LINKAGE ADJUSTMENTS

4000 Models (except 4000 Quattro) & All Coupe Models

4 SPEED

NOTE: This procedure will require Special Tool VW 3014.

1. Place the shift lever in the Neutral position.

2. Working under the car, loosen the clamp nut on the shift rod. Check that the shift finger slides freely on the shift rod.

3. Inside the car, remove the shift

knob and the boot. It is not necessary to remove the console.

4. Align the holes in the shifter base with the holes in the bearing plate directly below it and tighten the bolts.

5. Install the Special Tool VW 3014 with the locating pin toward the front.

6. Push the shift lever to the left side of the tool cutout and tighten the lower knurled knob to secure the tool.

7. Move the top slide of the tool to the left side stop and tighten the upper knurled knob.

8. Push the shift lever into the right cutout of the slide. Align the shift rod and the shift finger under the car and tighten the clamp nut.

9. Remove the special tool.

10. Place the shift lever in the first gear position. Press the lever to the left side against the stop. Release the lever; it should spring back ¼–½ in. If not, move the lever housing slightly sideways to correct. Check that all gears can be engaged easily.

5 SPEED

1. Place the shift lever in the Neutral position.

2. Working under the vehicle, loosen the clamp nut on the shift rod. Be certain that the shift finger slides freely on the shift rod.

3. Working inside the vehicle, remove the gearshift lever knob and the boot.

4. Loosen the shifter base plate bolts slightly, then align the holes in the plate with the holes in the bearing housing and tighten the bolts.

5. Using the Alignment tool No. 3057, slip it over the gearshift lever and make sure that the locating pin is in the front centering hole.

6. Position the shift lever to the right cut out of slide 5/R and tighten the lower knurled nut of the tool.

7. At the top of the tool, move the slide with the gearshift lever to the right stop, then tighten the upper knurled nut of the tool.

8. Position the gearshift lever into the left cut-out (¾) of the slide, then adjust the shift rod and the shift finger (with the transmission in Neutral) and tighten the clamp nut.

9. Remove the tool and check the shifting of the gears for smoothness.

5000 Models and 4000 Quattro

1. Remove the gear shift boot.

2. Position the shift lever in neutral.

3. The seam on the plastic stop bracket should line up with the center hole in the curved stop plate. If not, proceed below:

NOTE: On the 4000 Quattro, adjust the adjusting rod (center-to-center) to 5.275 in. (134mm) and install the rod.**

4. Loosen the four bolts at the base of the shifter.

5. Align the holes in the shifter base with the holes in the bearing plate directly below it.

6. Tighten the bolts.

7. Loosen the clamp between the

View of the 1985 and later shift rod coupling used on the 4000 Sedan and Coupe GT

Loosen the clamp nut on the shift rod—4000

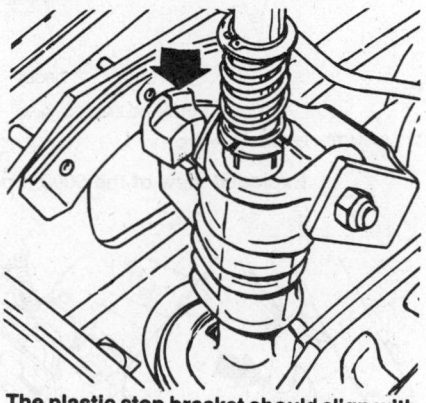

The plastic stop bracket should align with the curved stop plate—5000

front and rear shift rods; the rear shift rod must move freely.

8. Make certain that the front shift rod is in the neutral position.

9. Using the Shifter Locating tool No. 3048, place it on the stop plate with the shift lever resting in the notch, then tighten the shift rod clamp.

NOTE: On the 1984–88 models, a bearing pin is used. Adjust the projection of the bearing pin to $^{11}/_{16}$ in. The bearing pin is attached to the shift lever lower bearing and faces the rear of the vehicle.

10. Release the shifter and check its operation in all gears.

11. Install the shifter boot, making sure that the top of the boot is in contact with the shift knob.

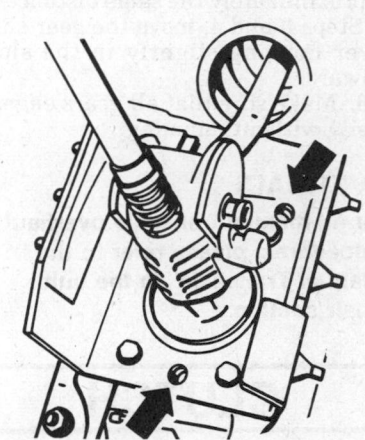

Align the centering holes of the stop lever bearing (arrows), then tighten the bolts on 5000 models

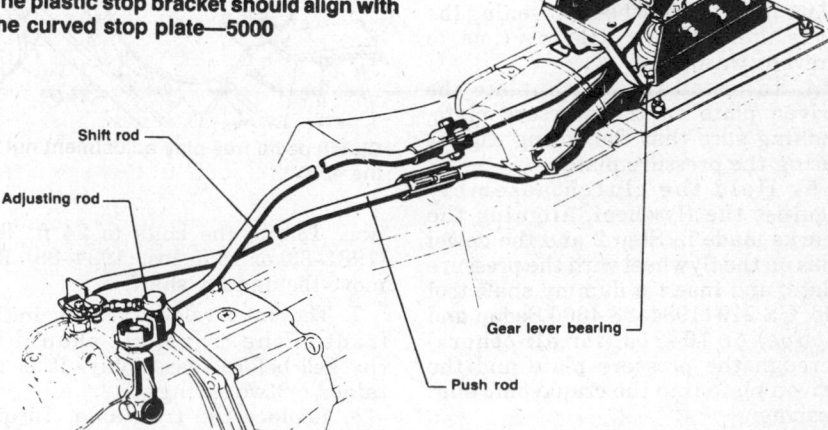

Linkage adjustment point at the transmission—5000 5-speed models

Shift rod

Adjusting rod

Gear lever bearing

Push rod

Quattro, Quattro & Quattro Coupe

1. Place the shift lever in neutral. Adjust the length of the adjusting rod so that the distance between the center point of the end holes is 5.275 in.

2. Loosen the clamp nut, making sure that the shift rod moves freely. Loosen the bolts slightly, align the centering holes of the gearshift lever housing and stop plate and tighten the bolts.

3. Intall tool 3048 or equivalent, tighten the clamp nut, and remove the tool. Engage first gear, press the shaft lever to the left, stop and release the shift lever.

4. Engage fifth gear, press the shaft lever to the right, stop and release the shift lever.

5. If the lever does not spring back approximmately the same distance as in Steps 3 and 4, move the gear shift lever housing slightly in the slots sidward.

6. Make sure that all gears engage easily without jamming.

OVERHAUL

For all manual transaxle overhaul procedures, please refer to the "Manual Transaxle" in the unit repair section.

CLUTCH

REMOVAL & INSTALLATION

1. Refer to the "Transmission, Removal and Installation" procedures in this section and remove the transmission.

2. Mark the relationship of the pressure plate to the flywheel (only if it is to be reused).

3. Using tool No. 10–201, lock the flywheel, then unbolt the pressure plate from the flywheel, loosening the bolts alternately, a little at a time, to prevent warpage.

4. To install the clutch, place the driven plate on the pressure plate, making sure that the spring cage is facing the pressure plate.

5. Hold the clutch assembly against the flywheel, aligning the marks made in Step 2 and the dowel pins on the flywheel with the pressure plate, and insert a dummy shaft tool No. US 219 (1984–88 4000 Sedan and Coupe) or 10–213 (for all others) through the pressure plate and the driven plate into the crankshaft pilot bearing.

6. Install the pressure plate bolts finger tight. Then tighten the bolts evenly, in rotation, to avoid distor-

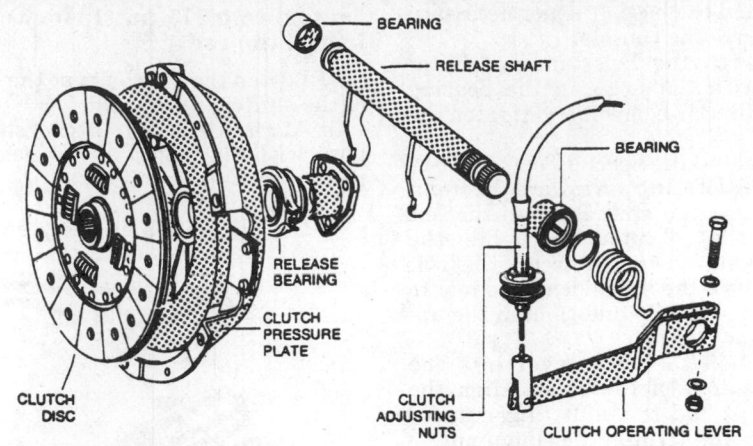

Exploded view of the 4000 models clutch, except the 4000 Quattro (1984 and later)

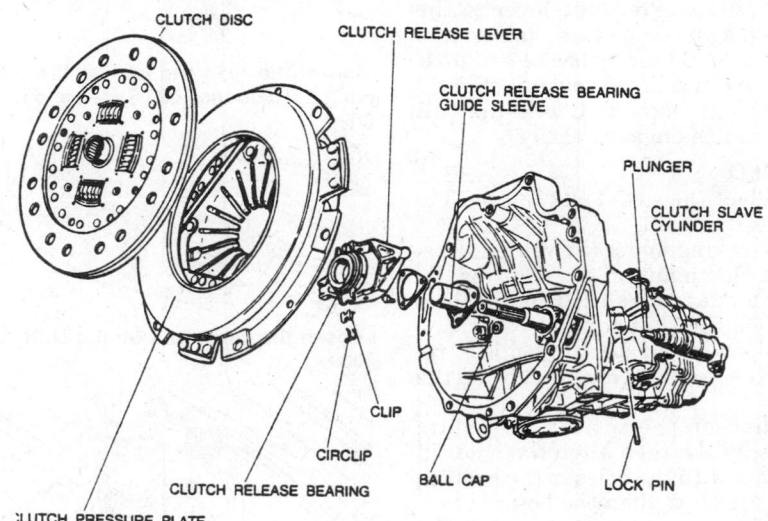

Exploded view of the 5000 models and the 4000 Quattro (1984 and later)

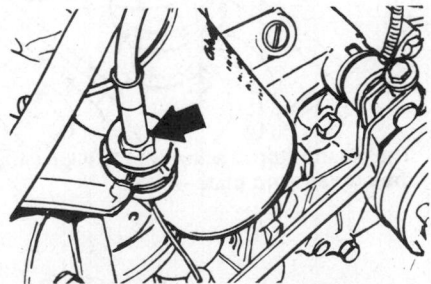

Clutch pedal free play adjustment nut on the 4000

tion. Torque the bolts to 24 ft. lbs. (1981–83) or 18 ft. lbs. (1984–88). Remove the dummy shaft.

7. The clutch release bearing in the front of the transaxle should be checked before reassembly. It is retained by two springs.

8. Replace the transaxle. Torque the engine-to-transaxle bolts to 40 ft. lbs. and the axle shaft to 28 ft. lbs. (1981–83) or 58 ft. lbs. (1984–88).

PEDAL FREE-PLAY ADJUSTMENT

4000 (1981–83 Sedan) and (1984–88, Sedan and Coupe)

Free-play is the distance that the pedal travels from the released position to the point at which clutch spring pressure can first be felt. This can be measured by placing a yardstick alongside the clutch pedal. Free-play should be ⅝ in. (1981–83 Sedan) or ⁹⁄₁₆ in. (1984–88 Sedan and Coupe), measured at the pedal.

1. Locate the clutch cable bracket by the oil filter.

2. Loosen the upper cable nut.

3. Turn both nuts clockwise to reduce pedal free-play or counterclockwise to increase it.

4. When adjustment is correct, tighten the upper nut to lock the cable in position.

PEDAL HEIGHT ADJUSTMENT

4000 (1981–83 Coupe, (1984–88 Quattro), 5000 and All Other Models

The clutch pedal should be at rest ⅜ inch above the brake pedal. To adjust the pedal height, remove the cotter pin holding the clutch master cylinder clevis to the pedal, loosen the locknut on the clevis shaft and turn the shaft to give the required pedal height. Tighten the locknut and install the clevis on the pedal.

Clutch Cable

REMOVAL & INSTALLATION

4000 (1981–83 Sedan) and (1984–88 Sedan and Coupe)

1. Loosen the adjustment.
2. Disengage the cable from the clutch arm.
3. Unhook the cable from the pedal. Remove the threaded eye from the end of the cable. Remove the adjustment nut(s).
4. Remove the C-clip which holds the outer cable at the adjustment point. Remove all the washers and bushings, first noting their locations.
5. Pull the cable out of the firewall toward the engine compartment side.
6. Install and connect the new cable. Adjust the pedal free-play.

Clutch Master Cylinder

REMOVAL & INSTALLATION

5 Cylinder Models Only

1. Locate the master cylinder under the instrument panel and behind the clutch pedal.
2. Remove and plug the line leading to the slave cylinder from the end of the master cylinder.
3. Remove the circlip and the pin which attaches the clevis to the clutch pedal.
4. Remove the two master cylinder mounting screws from the pedal mounting.
5. Remove and plug the remaining line which leads to the fluid reservoir and remove the master cylinder.
6. Installation is in the reverse order of removal. Torque the master cylinder bolts to 15 ft. lbs.
7. Bleed the system.

Clutch Slave Cylinder

REMOVAL & INSTALLATION

5 Cylinder Models Only

1. Locate the slave cylinder on top of the transaxle housing.

2. Remove the retaining yoke.
3. Drive out the slave cylinder lock pin.
4. Remove and plug the fluid line (this step is necessary only if the cylinder is to be disassembled).
5. Installation is in the reverse order of removal.
6. If the fluid line was removed, bleed the system.

BLEEDING THE SYSTEM

Audi recommends that the system be bled by means of a pressure bleeder. You may purchase one at an auto supply store. Follow the manufacturer's instructions for proper bleeding techniques with a pressure bleeder. The maximum working pressure is 36 psi.

AUTOMATIC TRANSAXLE

REMOVAL & INSTALLATION

1981–83

NOTE: If the torque converter drive plate is removed from the crankshaft for any reason, torque the mounting bolts to: Bolt without shoulder – 73 ft. lbs.; bolt with shoulder – 54 ft. lbs. Coat all threads with a locking compound.

1. Disconnect the negative battery cable.
2. Remove the windshield washer bottle.
3. Drain the cooling system.
4. Remove the hoses from the transmission cooler and cap the ends.
5. Remove the upper end of the accelerator linkage rod.
6. Disconnect the speedometer cable at the bell housing.
7. Remove the upper engine-to-transmission bolts.
8. Raise and support the car.
9. Using a chain hoist or jack, support the engine and raise it just enough to take the weight off of the mounts.
10. Remove the skid plate from the sub-frame.
11. Disconnect the exhaust pipe from the sub-frame.
12. Remove the right halfshaft guard plate.
13. Remove the right and left halfshafts.
14. Remove the starter.
15. Remove the selector lever cable and holder from the transmission.
16. Remove the lower accelerator linkage rod.
17. Remove the accelerator cable

from the transmission support.
18. Remove the right side guard plate from the sub-frame.
19. Remove both transmission mounts from the sub-frame.
20. Rotate the torque converter and remove each bolt as it appears in the starter opening.
21. Place a jack under the transmission and raise it slightly.
22. Remove the lower engine-to-transmission bolts.
23. Remove the rear sub-frame mounting bolts.
24. Swing both halfshafts rearward out of the way. Secure them with wire.
25. Separate the transmission from the engine and carefully lower the transmission on the jack.
26. Installation is basically the reverse of removal.

— CAUTION —
Be sure that the torque converter is fully seated on the one-way clutch support. When the converter is properly seated, the distance between the converter cover nose and the end of the bell housing should be 0.393 in. (10mm).

27. Install the lower engine-to-transmission bolts first, then the transmission-to-sub-frame bolts.
28. Observe the following torques: converter bolts 22 ft. lbs.; transmission-to-engine bolts 40 ft. lbs; starter bolts 40 ft. lbs.; sub-frame to body 80 ft. lbs. Proper bolt torque is important; use a suitable torque wrench to tighten all fasteners.
29. Adjust the throttle kickdown switch, as detailed below.

Model 087 (1984–88)

1. Disconnect the negative battery cable.
2. Raise and support the vehicle on jackstands.
3. At the transmission's relay lever, remove the retaining clip and disconnect the pushrod socket.
4. Using tool No. 3016, disconnect the speedometer cable from the transmission-to-engine bolts.
5. Using the Engine Support tools No. 10–222/1 and 10–222, install them to the engine and support it. Loosen the engine mounting bolts.
6. Disconnect the exhaust pipe from the exhaust manifold, the exhaust pipe from the converter, then remove the exhaust pipe from the vehicle.
7. Remove the right axle shaft guard plate and the axle shafts-to-transmission bolts; using a wire support the axle shafts.
8. Remove the starter. Through the starter hole, remove the torque converter-to-drive plate bolts.

9. Using tools No. 3094, clamp off the coolant hoses at the ATF cooler, then remove the hoses from the cooler.

10. Place an oil pan under the transmission, remove the filler tube from the oil pan and drain the fluid from the transmission.

11. At the accelerator pushrod, remove the circlip. Remove the accelerator cable support, then remove the accelerator cable from the transmission operating lever.

12. Remove the selector cable bracket, the circlip and the cable from the transmission shifting lever.

13. At the sub-frame, remove the front bolts. Using tool No. US 4470, support the transmission and raise it slightly.

14. On the 4000 models, remove the center bolt from the transmission mount; on the 5000 models, remove the mounts from both sides of the transmission, then the lower transmission-to-engine bolts.

15. Separate the transmission from the engine and lower it from the vehicle. Be sure to secure the torque converter.

NOTE: When installing the transmission, should the torque converter slip off the one-way clutch support, the oil pump shaft could be pulled from the oil pump. This may cause severe damage when bolting the transmission to the engine.

16. To install, reverse the removal procedures. Torque the engine-to-transmission bolts to 41 ft. lbs., the sub-frame bolts to 52 ft. lbs., the torque converter-to-drive plate bolts to 22 ft. lbs., the axle shaft-to-transmission bolts 33 ft. lbs. and the transmission mount center bolt to 30 ft. lbs. Refill the transmission. Adjust the accelerator linkage and align the engine-to-transmission mounts (if necessary).

Model 089 (1984–88)

1. Disconnect the negative battery cable.

2. Remove the upper engine-to-transmission bolts. Raise and support the vehicle on jackstands.

3. Using the Engine Support tool No. 10–222A, secure it to the engine and the vehicle.

4. At the front of the engine, remove both stop bolts. Remove the starter.

5. Through the starter opening, remove the torque converter-to-drive plate bolts, then remove torque converter cover plate.

6. Using tools No. 3094, clamp off the coolant hoses at the ATF cooler,

then remove the hoses from the cooler.

7. Using tool No. 3016, remove the speedometer cable from the transmission.

8. At both inner axle shaft-to-transmission bolts, then using a wire, tie up the axle shafts.

9. At the left control arm, mark the position of the ball joint, then remove the ball joint and the support.

10. Place an oil catch pan under the transmission, remove the oil filler tube from the oil pan and drain the fluid.

11. Remove the exhaust pipe-to-transmission bracket.

12. Remove the selector cable bracket from the transmission. At the transmission shift lever, remove the selector cable circlip and the cable.

13. At the transmission, remove the accelerator cable bracket and the cable from the operating lever.

14. From the transmission mount, remove the center bolt. Using the engine support tool, lift the engine slightly.

15. Remove the throttle cable bracket bolts and the bracket.

16. Using tool No. 4470, support the transmission and lift it slightly. Remove the lower transmission to engine bolts.

17. Separate the engine from the transmission and lower it from the vehicle. Be sure to secure the torque converter.

NOTE: When installing the transmission, should the torque converter slip off the one-way clutch support, the oil pump shaft could be pulled from the oil pump. This may cause severe damage when bolting the transmission to the engine.

18. To install, reverse the removal procedures. Torque the engine-to-transmission bolts to 41 ft. lbs., the sub-frame bolts to 52 ft. lbs., the torque converter-to-drive plate bolts to 22 ft. lbs., the axle shaft-to-transmission bolts to 33 ft. lbs., the ball joint-to-control arm bolts to 48 ft. lbs. and the transmission mount center bolt to 30 ft. lbs. Refill the transmission. Adjust the accelerator linkage and align the engine-to-transmission mounts (if necessary).

PAN REPLACEMENT

The automatic transmission fluid should be changed and the pan cleaned out every 20,000 miles. The interval should be shortened to 12,000 miles under severe use such as city driving or trailer towing.

1. Run the engine in Neutral for a minute or two.

2. Make sure that the vehicle is

parked on level ground. Stop the engine.

3. Place a pan of at least four quarts capacity under the transmission.

4. Remove the plug (1981–83) or the oil filler tube (1984–88) from the transmission bottom pan, after wiping the area clean.

5. Remove pan bolts and the pan, then clean out the pan.

NOTE: When removing the pan, remove the oil filter, wash it in solvent, use a new gasket and torque the assembly to 26 inch lbs.

6. Replace the pan, using a new gasket. Torque the bolts to 7 ft. lbs. (1981–83) or 15 ft. lbs. (1984–88). Wait ten minutes and retorque the bolts.

7. Clean off the plug or the filler tube, particularly the threads, and replace it.

8. Pour in fluid through the dipstick filler tube. The proper transmission fluid is Dexron® or Dexron® II.

9. Start the engine and shift through all the lever positions.

10. The level should reach the tip of the dipstick. Add fluid until the level reaches this point.

11. Take a short test drive. Fill the transmission until the level is between the marks on the dipstick. Retorque the bolts.

NOTE: If the transmission is overfilled, the excess must be drained.

KICKDOWN SWITCH ADJUSTMENT

4000 and 5000

1. Position the accelerator pedal in the fully released position.

2. Check the distance between the pedal lower edge and the pedal stop. Clearance should be 3.0 in.

3. If not, loosen the lockbolt which holds the cable at the pedal and place the pedal to give the three inch clearance. Tighten the lockbolt.

4. Press the pedal to the full throttle position but not into the kickdown detent. The kickdown take-up spring should not be compressed and the throttle valve should be wide open.

5. Press the accelerator lever to the stop (kickdown position); the operating lever must contact the stop and the pushrod's kickdown spring must be compressed to $^{13}/_{32}$ in. (4000 model 087, 1984–88), $^{5}/_{16}$ in. (4000 model 089, 1984–88) or $^{5}/_{16}$ in. (5000 model 087 and 087 E-mode, 1984–88).

6. Adjust the shift linkage, as detailed below.

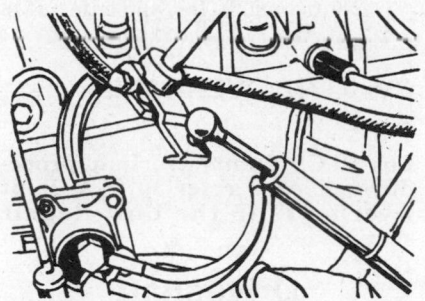

Kickdown detent linkage—4000 and 5000

NEUTRAL SAFETY SWITCH ADJUSTMENT

The neutral safety switch prevents the engine from being started with the transmission in any position other than Park or Neutral. It also activates the back-up lights. The switch is at the base of the shift lever, inside the floorshift console. To replace or adjust the switch:

1. Remove the four screws which hold the console to the floor.
2. Shift into Neutral. Remove the two screws which hold the shift position indicator plate to the console. Remove the shift knob and the console.
3. Disconnect the switch electrical leads. These are: red/black—neutral safety; black—back-up lights; blue/red—back-up lights. The back-up light wires are at the front.
4. Remove the two switch retaining screws. Remove the switch.
5. Install the new switch so that the neutral safety switch contacts are together.
6. Install the electrical connectors. Hold the footbrake while making sure that the engine will start only in Neutral and Park. Make sure that the back-up lights operate only in Reverse. If the switch does not operate properly, it may have to be moved on its slotted mounting bracket.
7. Replace the console cover when adjustment is complete.

SHIFT LINKAGE ADJUSTMENT

The function of this adjustment is to make sure that the transmission is fully engaged in each shift position. If this is not done, the transmission may be only partially engaged in a certain range position. This would result in severe damage due to slippage.

1. Remove the floor console. Place the selector lever in Park.
2. Loosen the cable clamp nut at the transmission end.
3. Press the selector lever on the transmission into the Park position to the stop.

4. Tighten the clamp nut to 6 ft. lbs. Install the console.

BAND ADJUSTMENTS

4000 and 5000

SECOND GEAR BAND

1. Loosen the locknut.
2. Tighten the adjusting screw to 7 ft. lbs.
3. Loosen the adjusting screw and retighten it to 4 ft. lbs.
4. Loosen the screw exactly 2½ turns.
5. Hold the screw and tighten the locknut.

DRIVE AXLE

Halfshaft

REMOVAL & INSTALLATION

4000 Models Except Quattro Turbo

———— CAUTION ————
Never remove or install the axle nut with the wheel off the ground. The vehicle must be resting on the ground for these operations.

1. Remove the axle nut.
2. Unbolt and remove the six halfshaft retaining bolts from the drive flange.
3. Mark the position of the ball joint on the control arm, remove the two retaining nuts and remove the ball joint.

NOTE: **On cars with manual transmissions, remove only the right side ball joint.**

4. Pull the pivot mounting outward and remove the halfshaft.
5. Installation is the reverse of removal.
6. Tighten the ball joint-to-control arm nuts to 47 ft. lbs. Torque the halfshaft-to-transmission flange bolts to 33 ft. lbs.
7. Always replace the self-locking axle nut with a new one and tighten to 167 ft. lbs.
8. Check for proper camber adjustment.

4000 Quattro Turbo (1984–88)

1. With the vehicle on the ground, loosen the axle shaft nut.
2. Raise and support the front of the vehicle on jackstands.
3. Remove the axle nut, the wheel

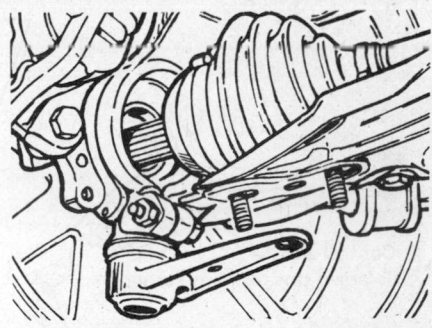

Remove the halfshafts by pivoting the control arm outward

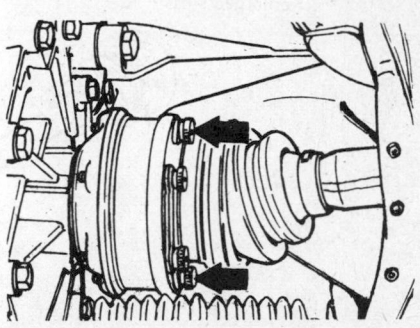

Remove the halfshaft retaining bolts at the transaxle

bolts and the wheel. Remove the right backing plate.
4. Remove the halfshaft-to-transmission bolts, then support the halfshaft on a wire.
5. Using an Axle Shaft Press, tool No. OTC 827–B attach it to the wheel hub and press the halfshaft from the hub.
6. Using the locking compound D-6, apply a ¼ in. bead around the front edge of the spline section of the halfshaft.

NOTE: **After applying the locking compound, allow it to dry for at least an hour.**

7. To install, reverse the removal procedures. Be sure to replace the inner CV gasket. Torque the halfshaft-to-transmission bolts to 58 ft. lbs., the halfshaft-to-wheel hub nut to 203 ft. lbs. and the wheel bolts to 80 ft. lbs.

5000 Models & Coupe GT

———— CAUTION ————
Never remove or install the axle shaft nut with the wheel off the ground. The vehicle must be resting on the ground for these operations. A puller is required for this job.

1. Remove the axle nut.
2. Raise and support the vehicle and remove the wheels.
3. On the right side, remove the halfshaft skid plate.
4. Disconnect the halfshaft from

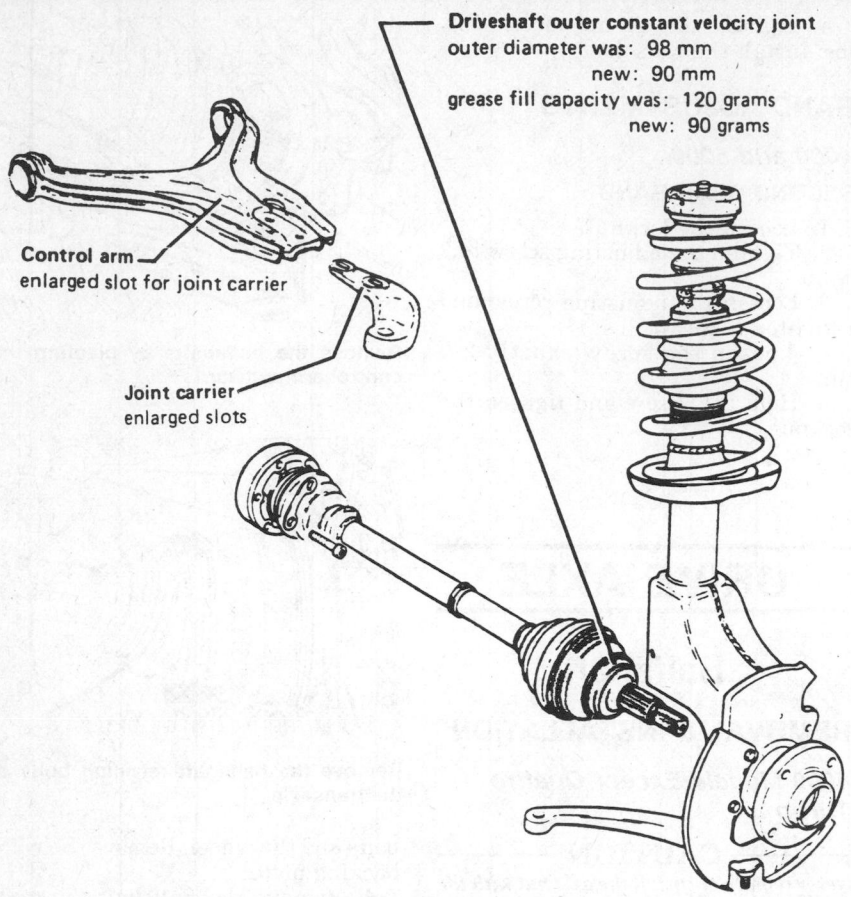

Driveshaft outer constant velocity joint
outer diameter was: 98 mm
                new: 90 mm
grease fill capacity was: 120 grams
                    new: 90 grams

Control arm
enlarged slot for joint carrier

Joint carrier
enlarged slots

View of the 1985 and later halfshaft used on the 4000 Quattro

the transmission. Using a wire, support the halfshaft.

5. Using a 4-armed puller mounted on the wheel hub, press the halfshaft out of the hub.

6. Guide the inside end of the shaft up over the transmission and out of the hub.

7. If equipped with an automatic transmission, perform the following:

   a. Remove the stabilizer bar clamps.

   b. Remove the ball joint-to-hub bolt, then remove the ball joint from the hub.

   c. Press the halfshaft from the hub.

   d. Swing the suspension strut outward and press the halfshaft from the hub.

8. When installing a shaft, make certain that the splines are clean and free of grease. Apply a ¼ inch bead of RTV silicone sealant around the leading edge of the splines, and allow it to harden at least one hour. Torque the shaft-to-transmission bolts to 32 ft. lbs. and the axle nut to 203 ft. lbs.

Quattro, Quattro Turbo & Quattro Coupe

1. Remove the wheel cover and

loosen the lug nuts. Remove the dust cover and the axle nut.

2. Raise and support the vehicle safely. remove the lug nuts and wheel assembly. Remove the right backing plate.

3. Disconnect the axle shaft at the transmission flange and position it out of the way.

4. Using a suitable puller, press out the stub axle from the hub. Use only a mechanical or hydraulic puller to remove the stub axle. Never use hot air blower or a flame to heat the stub axle.

5. Installation is the reverse order of the removal procedure, with the following exceptions:

   a. Replace the gasket on the inner CV-joint.

   b. Make sure that the splines on the stub axle and the wheel hub are free of oil, grease and old locking compound.

   c. Apply a bead of suitable locking compound approximately $^{13}/_{64}$ in. wide around the splines and install the stub axle shaft. Allow at least one hour for the locking compound to harden.

   d. Torque the axle shaft to transmission attaching bolts to 58 ft.lbs.,

lug nuts to 80 ft. lbs. and axle nut to 203 ft. lbs.

CV-JOINT OVERHAUL

For all CV-Joints overhaul procedures, please refer to "CV-Joint Overhaul" in the Unit Repair section.

Driveshaft

REMOVAL & INSTALLATION

4000 and 5000 Quattro

1. Raise and support the vehicle on jackstands.

2. Using a scribing tool, mark the position of the driveshaft to the transmission flange and the rear differential.

3. Remove the driveshaft flange mounting bolts from both ends and remove the driveshaft from the vehicle. Remove the center bearing bolts.

4. To install reverse the removal procedures. Torque the driveshaft-to-transmission/differential flange bolts to 39 ft. lbs. (4000 Quattro) or 33 ft. lbs. (5000 Quattro) and the driveshaft center bearing-to-frame bolts to 14 ft. lbs.

Rear Axle Hub and Bearings

REMOVAL & INSTALLATION

1. Depress the brake pedal approximately 1.2 in. and hold it in that position to close the master cylinder compensating bore.

2. Detach the brake lines on both sides and plug the lines.

3. Pry off the grease cap and remove the cotter pin, castellated nut and washer. Remove the wheel and brake drum.

4. Remove the bearing inner race from the brake drum.

5. Carefully (the spring can fly out) pry out the brake shoe retaining spring. Remove the brake shoes complete with pressure rod and spring, bottom bracket first. Disconnect the handbrake cable.

6. Unbolt the rear stub axle and brake backing plate.

7. Pry out the shaft seal (which must be replaced) and remove the inner race of the roller bearing.

8. Drive the roller bearing outer race from the brake drum, using a suitable mandrel or socket. Remove the snap-ring and drive the outer roller bearing race from the drum.

9. Replace the snap-ring and drive

in the outer race of the outer roller bearing.

10. Press in the outer race of the inner roller bearing. Use a brass hammer or suitable wood block to seat the race evenly.

11. Lightly coat the inner race of the inner roller bearing with wheel bearing grease and push it into the outer race.

12. Drive a new shaft seal into position (the open side of the seal should face the roller bearing). Fill the space between the two roller bearings with approximately 10 oz. of wheel bearing grease.

13. Coat the inner race of the outer roller bearing with grease and install the inner race.

14. Replace the stub axle and brake backing plate with the groove in the stub axle facing upward. Bolt torque is 14–15 ft. lbs. for 8G bolts and 22 ft. lbs. for 10 K bolts.

15. Assemble the brake shoes, connect the handbrake cable, and insert the brake shoes on the bottom bracket first, then at the wheel cylinder. Replace the retaining spring, exercising caution as before.

16. Replace the brake drum and wheel, special washer, nut, castellated nut, and a new cotter pin. Wheel bearing play should be 0.001–0.002 in. It can be measured with a dial indicator. Fill the dust cap with approximately 10 oz. of wheel bearing grease and tap lightly into place.

Rear Axle Shaft

REMOVAL & INSTALLATION

4000 Quattro – 1984–88

1. With the vehicle resting on the ground, loosen the axleshaft nut.

2. Raise and support the rear of the vehicle on jackstands.

3. Remove the axleshaft nut, the wheel bolts and the wheel.

4. Remove the ball joint nut. Using the Ball Joint Removal tool No. 1078, press the ball joint from the control arm.

5. Loosen the control arm mounting bolts at the sub-frame and swing it downwards.

6. Remove the tie rod nut. Using a tie rod puller tool, press the tie rod from the strut assembly.

7. Pull the brake hose and the parking brake cable (with the grommet) from the holding fixture.

8. Remove the axleshaft-to-differential bolts, separate the shaft from the differential and support it on a wire.

9. Using an Axle Shaft Pulling tool No. OTC 827–B, attach it to the wheel

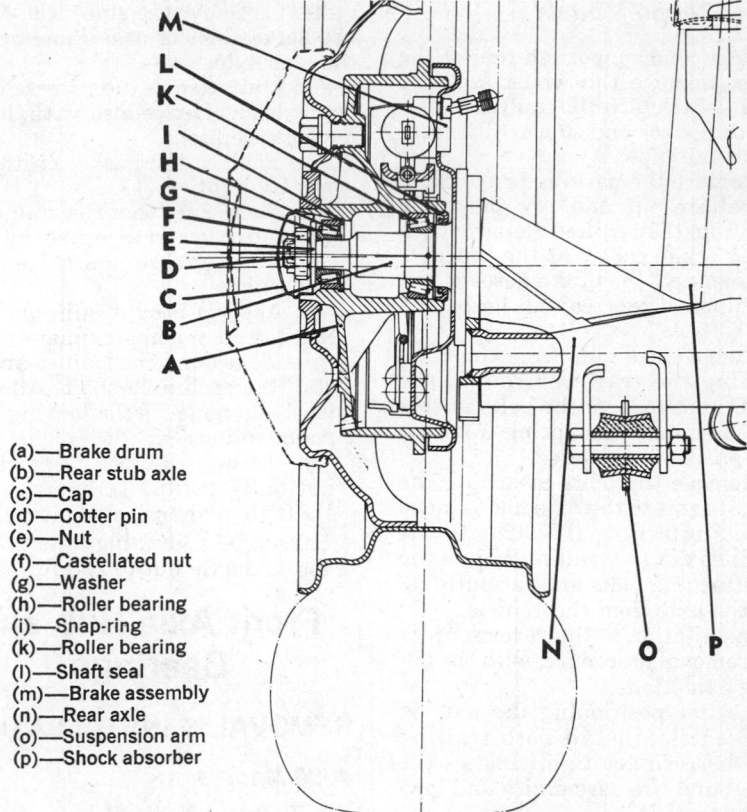

(a)—Brake drum
(b)—Rear stub axle
(c)—Cap
(d)—Cotter pin
(e)—Nut
(f)—Castellated nut
(g)—Washer
(h)—Roller bearing
(i)—Snap-ring
(k)—Roller bearing
(l)—Shaft seal
(m)—Brake assembly
(n)—Rear axle
(o)—Suspension arm
(p)—Shock absorber

Rear wheel bearing and stub axle assembly

hub and press the axleshaft from the hub.

10. Wipe the axleshaft splines free of grease and dirt. Using the locking compound D-6, apply a ¼ in. bead around the outer edge of the splines.

NOTE: Allow the locking compound to dry for an hour before installation.

11. To install, use a new CV inner gasket and reverse the removal procedures. Torque the axleshaft-to-differential bolts to 58 ft. lbs., the axleshaft-to-hub nut to 203 ft. lbs., the wheel bolts to 80 ft. lbs. and the ball joint clamp nut to 47 ft. lbs.

5000 Quattro – 1985–88

1. With the vehicle resting on the ground, loosen the axleshaft nut.

2. Raise and support the rear of the vehicle on jackstands.

3. Remove the axleshaft nut, the wheel bolts and the wheel.

4. Remove the caliper-to-strut retaining bolt and the caliper. Using a wire, support the caliper.

5. Remove the brake disc. Remove the axleshaft-to-differential bolts and support the axleshaft on a wire.

NOTE: When removing the right-side axleshaft, first, remove the fuel tank cover plate.

6. Remove the transverse link-to-wheel bearing housing nut and remove the link.

7. Remove the trapezoidal arm-to-crossmember nut/bolt, then press the arm downward.

8. Using an Axle Shaft Pulling tool No. OTC 827–B, attach it to the wheel hub and press the axleshaft from the hub.

9. Wipe the axleshaft splines free of grease and dirt. Using the locking compound D-6, apply a ¼ in. bead around the outer edge of the splines.

NOTE: Allow the locking compound to dry for an hour before installation.

10. To install, use a new CV inner gasket and reverse the removal procedures. Torque the axleshaft-to-differential bolts to 58 ft. lbs., the axleshaft-to-hub nut to 266 ft. lbs., the wheel bolts to 80 ft. lbs., the brake caliper-to-wheel bearing housing bolt to 48 ft. lbs., the trapezoidal arm-to-crossmember nut/bolt to 63 ft. lbs. and the transverse link-to-wheel bearing housing nut to 148 ft. lbs.

4000 & Coupe Models

1. Raise and support eh rear of the vehicle. Remove the wheel and tire assemblies. Detach the muffler hanger bands. Lower and support the muffler and tail pipe.

2. Remove the parking brake cable to equalizer nut and pry the cable sleeve from the bracket. Remove both parking brake cables at the brackets and disconnect the brake hoses at the brake line brakets, cap all hoses and lines.

3. Remove the nuts from the bolts attaching the trailing arms to the body. Do not remove the bolts at this time. Disconnect the spring from the brake pressure regulator.

4. Remove the bolts attaching the diagonal arms to the axle and remove the bolts attaching the strut to the axle. Slide out the trailing arm to the body attaching bolts and carefully remove the axle from the vehicle.

5. Installation is the reverse order of the removal procedure, with the following exceptions:

a. After positioning the axle in the vehicle, install both trailing arm bolts finger tight. Install the wheel and tire assemblies and lower the vehicle.

b. Torque the trailing arm attaching bolts to 72 ft. lbs. and raise the vehicle so as to install the remaining components.

c. Torque the strut attaching bolts to 43 ft. lbs. and the diagonal arm attaching bolts to 51 ft. lbs.

d. After the installation procedure has been completed, bleed the brake system and adjust the parking brake as necessary.

Quattro, Quattro Turbo & Quattro Coupe

1. Loosen the lug nuts, remove the axle nut cover and the axle nut. Raise and support the vehicle safely.

2. Remove the lug nuts and wheel assemblies. Disconnect the axle shaft from the final drive flange and position it out of the way. Using a suitable tool, press off the tie rod ends.

NOTE: The axle shafts are diagonally interchangeable. The left rear is identical with the right front and the right rear is identical to the left front.

3. Remove the ball joint clamp bolt. Disconnect the brake hose at the bracket. Pry the ball joint out of the hub and move the strut to the outside.

4. Press out the stub axle from the hub, making sure that there is sufficient clearance between the inner CV-joint and the final drive housing. Use only a mechanical or hydraulic

puller to remove the stub axle. Never use hot air blower or a flame to heat the stub axle.

5. Installation is the reverse order of the removal procedure, with the following exceptions.

a. Replace the gasket on the inner CV-joint.

b. Make sure that the splines on the stub axle and the wheel hub are free of oil, grease and old locking compound.

c. Apply a bead of suitable locking compound approximately $^{13}/_{64}$ in. wide around the splines and install the stub axle shaft. Allow at least one hour for the locking compound to harden.

d. Torque the ball joint clamp nut to 47 ft. lbs. Torque the axle shaft to transmission attaching bolts to 58 ft.lbs., lug nuts to 80 ft. lbs. and axle nut to 203 ft. lbs.

Front Axle Hub and Bearings

REMOVAL & INSTALLATION

4000 Models

1. Refer to the "Halfshafts, Removal and Installation" procedures in this section and remove the halfshafts.

2. Remove the strut housing-to-vehicle nuts and the strut/hub assembly from the vehicle.

3. Remove the disc brake caliper (suspend it on a wire), the disc and the splash shield.

4. Using an arbor press with tools No. VW 408A, VW 295A, VW 402 and Base Plate tool No. VW 401, press the wheel hub from the strut housing.

5. Using a pair of snap-ring pliers, remove the snap-rings from both sides of the wheel bearing.

6. Using an arbor press with tools No. VW 408A, VW 442, VW 401 and VW 402, press the wheel bearing from the strut housing.

7. Using the Wheel Puller tool No. VW 295A, pull the wheel bearing race from the wheel hub.

8. Place new grease inside the strut housing before installing the new bearing.

9. Using an arbor press and tools No. VW 412, VW 455 and VW 401, press the new wheel bearing and wheel hub into the strut housing. Be sure to replace the snap-rings.

10. To install the strut/wheel hub assembly, reverse the removal procedures. Torque the strut-to-vehicle nuts to 44 ft. lbs.

5000 and All Other Models

1. Refer to the "Halfshafts, Remov-

al and Installation" procedures in this section and remove the halfshafts.

2. Remove the strut-to-vehicle nut, the retainer and the strut from the vehicle.

3. Remove the disc brake caliper (suspend it on a wire), the disc and the splash shield.

4. Using an arbor press with tools No. VW 412, VW 420 and VW 295A, press the wheel hub from the strut housing.

5. Using a pair of snap-ring pliers, remove the snap-rings from both sides of the wheel bearing.

6. Using an arbor press with tool No. 40–20, press the wheel bearing from strut housing.

7. Using the tools No. VW 295A and US 1078, press the bearing race from the wheel hub.

8. Install the outer snap-ring into the strut housing. Using an arbor press with tools No. VW 411, 40–20,A and VW 402, press the new wheel bearing into the strut housing until it seats against the snap-ring, then install the inner snap-ring.

9. Using an arbor press and tool No. 40–21, press the wheel hub into the strut housing.

10. To install, reverse the removal procedures. Torque the strut-to-vehicle nut to 43 ft. lbs.

FRONT SUSPENSION

All Audi models use MacPherson struts. The strut unit, steering arm, and steering knuckle are all combined in one assembly; there is no upper control arm.

— CAUTION —

Exercise extreme caution when working with the front suspension. Coil springs and torsion bars are under great tension and can cause severe injury if released suddenly.

MacPherson Strut

REMOVAL & INSTALLATION

All Models Except the Quattro, Quattro Turbo & Quattro Coupe

1. With the car on the ground, remove the front axle nut and loosen the wheel bolts.

2. Raise and support the front of the car and remove the wheels.

3. Remove the brake caliper mounting bolts and the brake line

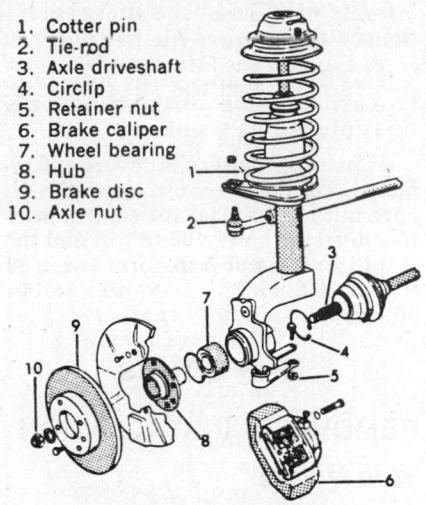

1. Cotter pin
2. Tie-rod
3. Axle driveshaft
4. Circlip
5. Retainer nut
6. Brake caliper
7. Wheel bearing
8. Hub
9. Brake disc
10. Axle nut

4000 front suspension

bracket. Remove the brake caliper with the line still attached to it and wire it out of the way.

4. Remove the wheel bearing housing-to-ball joint clamp bolt.

5. Remove the retaining nut and press off the tie rod end.

6. If equipped with a stabilizer bar, remove the retaining bolt and remove the stabilizer bar end clamps. Pivot the stabilizer bar downward (4000 only).

7. Remove the two center stabilizer bar clamps and then unbolt it from the lower control arm. Remove the stabilizer bar (5000 only).

8. Pry the lower control arm down and remove the ball joint from the wheel hub.

9. Using the removal tool No. OTC 827B, press the halfshaft from the wheel hub.

10. While holding the shock absorber piston rod with an internal socket wrench, remove the retaining bolt and then remove the strut assembly (4000 only).

11. Remove the spring strut cover (Quattro and Turbo) and remove the three strut retaining nuts, then remove the strut assembly (5000 series only).

12. Installation is in the reverse order of removal. Note the following:

   a. When installing the stabilizer bar, the position is correct if the clamps are difficult to install in the rubber bushings. Attach the clamps loosely, take a short test drive to bring the bushings into the correct position and then tighten to 18 ft. lbs.

   b. Tighten the ball joint bolt to 36 ft. lbs. (4000) or 47 ft. lbs. (5000).

   c. Tighten the axle nut to 167 ft. lbs. on the 4000, 203 ft. lbs. on the Quattro and Turbo and 207 ft. lbs. on all other 5000 models.

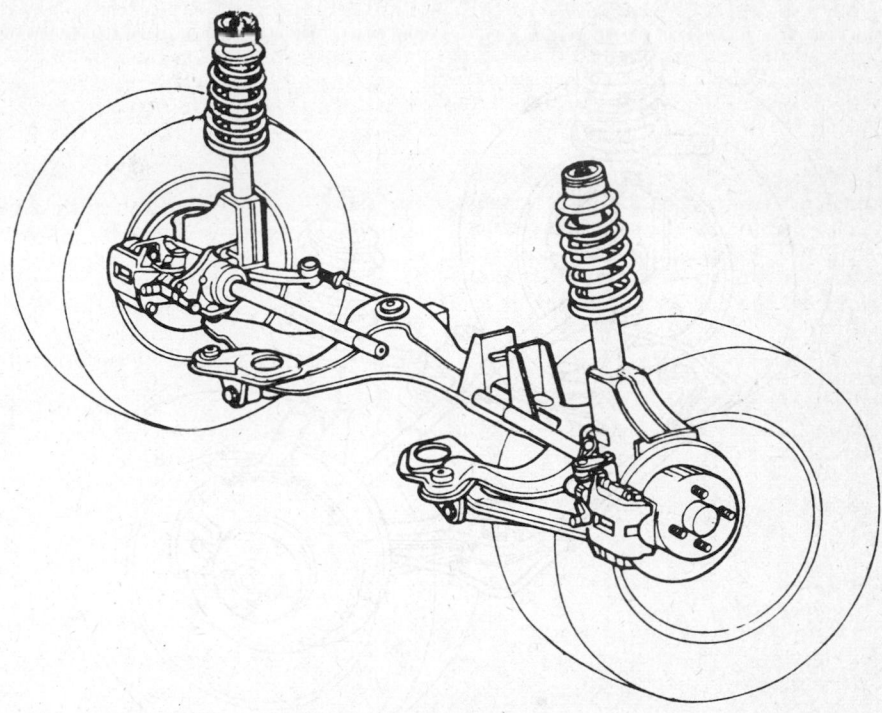

4000S Quattro front suspension

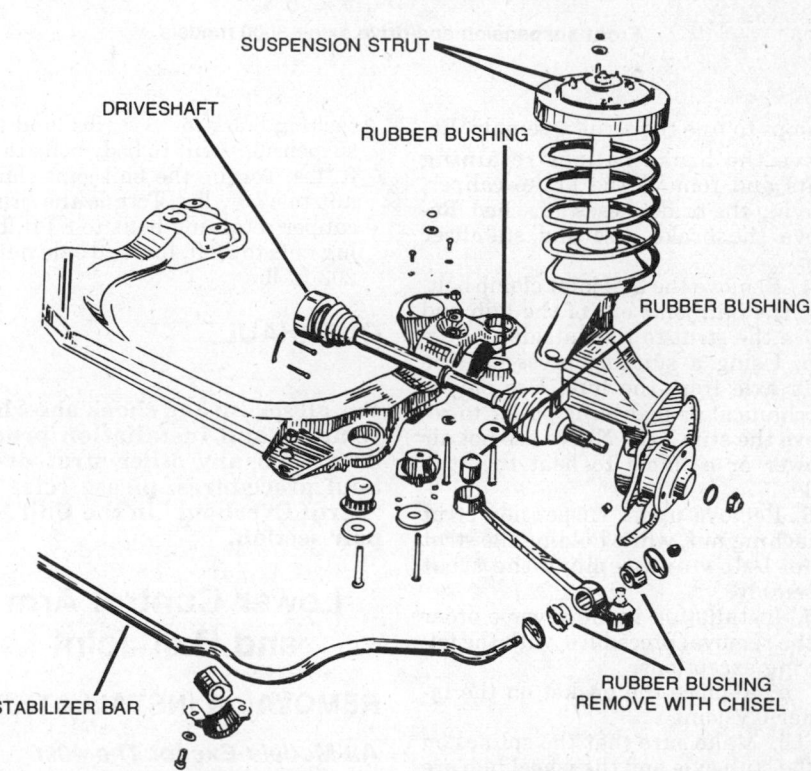

SUSPENSION STRUT

DRIVESHAFT

RUBBER BUSHING

RUBBER BUSHING

RUBBER BUSHING REMOVE WITH CHISEL

STABILIZER BAR

Front suspension and drive axle—4000 and 5000 models—5 cyl

Quattro, Quattro Turbo & Quattro Coupe

1. Loosen the lug nuts, remove the axle nut cover and the axle nut. Raise and support the vehicle safely.

2. Remove the lug nuts and wheel assemblies. Disconnect the axle shaft from the final drive flange and position it out of the way. Using a suitable tool, press off the tie rod ends.

3. Remove the necessary bolts and

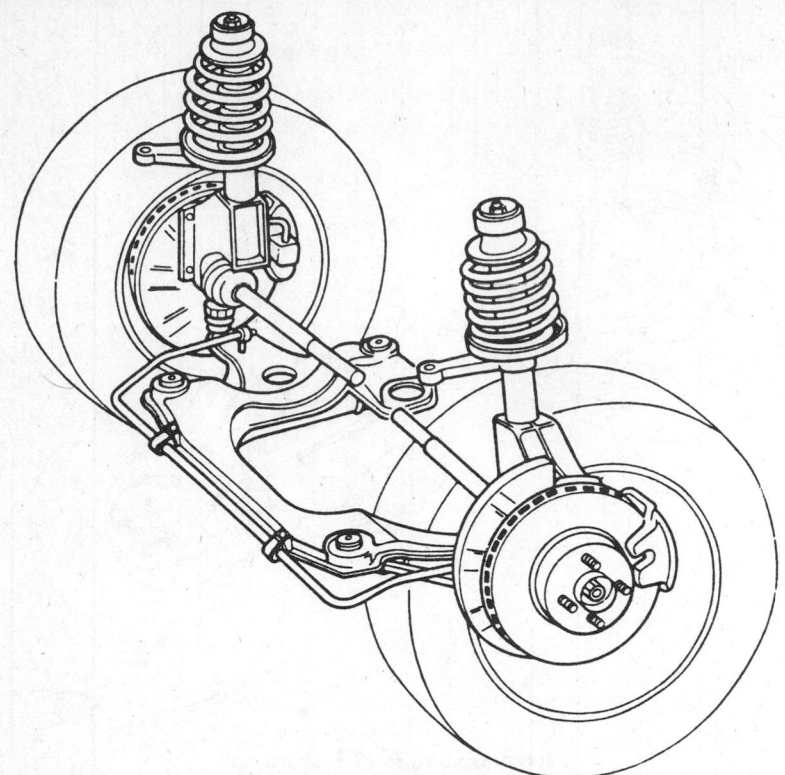

Front suspension and drive axle—5000 models

clamps to free the strut assembly. Remove the brake caliper retaining bolts and remove the brake caliper, leaving the brake hoses attached. Remove the brake disc and stabilizer bar.

4. Remove the ball joint clamp bolt. Pry the ball joint out of the hub and move the strut to the outside.

5. Using a suitable press out the stub axle from the hub. Use only a mechanical or hydraulic puller to remove the stub axle. Never use hot air blower or a flame to heat the stub axle.

6. Remove upper suspension strut attaching nut, while holding the strut from below and remove the strut assembly.

7. Installation is the reverse order of the removal procedure, with the following exceptions.

　　a. Replace the gasket on the inner CV-joint.

　　b. Make sure that the splines on the stub axle and the wheel hub are free of oil, grease and old locking compound.

　　c. Apply a bead of suitable locking compound approximately $^{13}/_{64}$ in. wide around the splines and install the stub axle shaft. Allow at least one hour for the locking compound to harden.

　　d. Torque the stabilizer bar at-

taching bolts to 18 ft. lbs. and the suspension strut to body bolts to 43 ft. lbs. Torque the ball joint clamp nut to 47 ft. lbs. Torque the brake caliper retaining bolts to 83 ft.lbs., lug nuts to 80 ft. lbs. and axle nut to 203 ft. lbs.

OVERHAUL

For all spring and shock absorber removal and installation procedures and any other strut overhaul procedures, please refer to "Strut Overhaul" in the Unit Repair section.

Lower Control Arm and Ball Joint

REMOVAL & INSTALLATION

All Models Except The 4000

1. Remove the ball joint clamp nut.
2. Pry the control arm down and out of the clamp.
3. Remove the nut on the end of the stabilizer bar.
4. Loosen the control arm-to-sub-frame mounting bolts and then pull the control arm off of the end of the stabilizer bar.

5. Remove the bolts and remove the control arm.

NOTE: The ball joint and control arm are one unit and can only be replaced as a unit.

6. Installation is the reverse of removal. Torque the control arm-to-ball joint nut to 48 ft. lbs., the control arm-to-sub-frame bolt to 63 ft. lbs. and the stabilizer bar-to-control arm nut to 81 ft. lbs. Check the toe and camber adjustments.

Ball Joints

REMOVAL & INSTALLATION

4000 Models

1. Mark the position of the ball joint flange on the lower control arm.
2. Remove the ball joint retaining clamp nut and pull the ball joint/control arm down and out of the retaining clamp.
3. Unscrew the two ball flange retaining nuts and remove the ball joint.
4. Installation is the reverse of removal. Tighten the clamp nut to 47 ft. lbs. and tighten the ball joint flange nuts to 47 ft. lbs. (Turbo) or 36 ft. lbs. (non-Turbo).

Lower Control Arm

REMOVAL & INSTALLATION

4000 Models

1. Raise the front of the vehicle and support it with jackstands.
2. Remove the ball joint as detailed earlier.
3. If equipped with a stabilizer bar, disconnect the end of the stabilizer bar and pull it down.
4. Remove the two control arm-to-sub-frame bolts and the control arm.
5. Installation is in the reverse order of removal. Check control arm bushings for cracking or undue wear. Tighten the control arm-to-subframe bolts to 43 ft. lbs. and the stabilizer bar mounting bolts to 18 ft. lbs.

Front Wheel Bearings

ADJUSTMENT

There is no front wheel bearing adjustment. The bearing is pressed into the steering knuckle. Axle nut torque is 167 ft. lbs. for the 4000, 203 ft. lbs. for the 5000 and 207 ft. lbs. for the Turbo and Quattro. The axle nut should be tightened only with the wheels resting on the ground.

REMOVAL & INSTALLATION

1. Raise the front of the car and support it with jackstands.
2. Remove the wheels.
3. Remove the caliper assembly.
4. Remove the brake disc.
5. Unscrew two retaining screws and remove the splash shield.
6. Using the removal tool No. OTC 827B, press the halfshaft from the wheel hub.
7. Press off the wheel hub.
8. Remove the inner and outer circlips and press out the wheel bearing.

NOTE: The wheel bearing will be damaged upon removal and must be replaced.

9. Installation is in the reverse order of removal.

Front Wheel Alignment

NOTE: A suitable alignment rack is necessary to check and adjust the camber and toe-in to specifications.

Before checking wheel alignment, tire pressure should be brought up to specifications and the front ride height checked. The vehicle should be bounced and settled before each alignment check or adjustment. Make camber adjustment first, then toe-in. Caster is set at the factory and is not adjustable other than the replacement of damaged suspension parts. Make all adjustments with the wheels straight ahead.

CAMBER ADJUSTMENT

1981–83 4000 & 4000 Coupe

1. Loosen both ball joint flange mounting bolts on the control arm. Using the special tool US 4490 and VW 582 or equivalents.
2. Tighten the tensioner nut to break the joint loose from the control arm. Loosen the tensioner nut until the wheel has negative camber. When the wheel nut is loosened, the weight of the vehicle on the wheels will move the wheel to the negative camber position.
3. Adjust the camber to specifications, torque the mounting bolts to 47 ft. lbs. and remove all tools.

1984-88 Models Except the 4000 Quattro and The 5000 Models

1. Loosen both ball joint flange mounting bolts on the control arm. Check so see that the ball joint breals loose from the control arm. If not, bounce the vehicle lightly and the

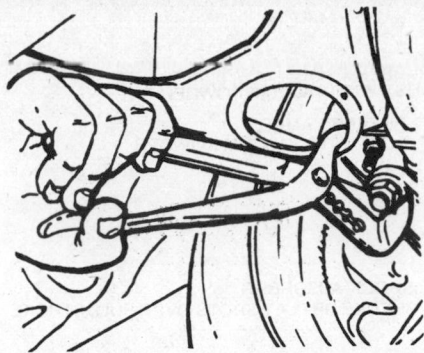

Adjusting the camber on the 4000 and Quattro without the special tool

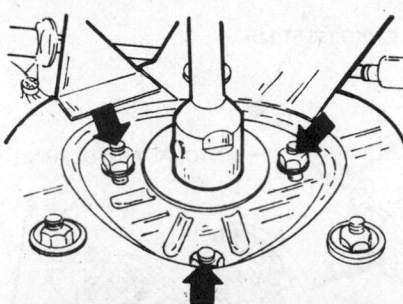

To adjust the camber on the 5000, move the strut assembly in the slots of the spring strut mounting plate

wheel should move to the negative camber position.
2. Install special tool US 4490 and VW 552 or equivalents. Tighten the tensioning nut on tool VW 552 or equivalent, to adjust the camber to specifications.
3. Torque the outboard ball joint mounting nut to 47 ft. lbs. Recheck the camber and re-adjust as necessary.
4. Torque the inboard ball joint mounting nut to 47 ft. lbs. and remove all tools.

4000 Quattro

1. Loosen both ball joint flange mounting bolts on the control arm. Using tool 3098 or equivalent, move the ball joint until the camber is within the specifications.
2. Torque the mounting nuts to 47 ft. lbs. recheck the camber and adjust if necessary.

5000 Models

Loosen the spring strut plate mounting bolts. Attach a socket wrench to the top piston rod nut and move the assembly in the slots until the camber is correct. Tighten all bolts.

TOE-IN ADJUSTMENT

Toe-in can be determined by measur-

ing and comparing the distance between the center of the tire tread, front and rear, or by measuring and comparing the distance between the inside edges of the wheel rims, front and rear. If the wheel rims are used as the basis of measurement, the car should be rolled forward slightly and a second set of measurements taken. This avoids any error induced by bent wheels. If at all possible, a toe-in gauge should be used; it will give a much more accurate measurement. Toe-in is adjusted at the steering tie-rods. Turn both rods to lengthen or shorten them an equal amount. If the tie-rods are not adjusted equally, the steering wheel will be crooked and the turning arcs of the front wheels will be changed. If the steering wheel is crooked, it must be removed and repositioned. Tighten the clamps when adjustment is complete.

REAR SUSPENSION

Shock Absorbers

REMOVAL & INSTALLATION

1981-83 5000 Models

If the vehicle is to be raised to remove the shock absorber, the spring tensioner tool 3004 or equivalent must be used to support the rear axle before removing any of the shock absorber nuts and or bolts. If the vehicle does not have to be raised, the spring tensioner tool 3004 or equivalent is not required.

1. Open the trunk and loosen the carpet trim. Remove the stem form the shock absorber upper mounting stud.
2. Remove the nut and bushing from the shock upper mounting, then remove the shock absorber lower attaching bolt and remove the shock absorber.
3. The installation is the reverse order of the removal procedure, with the following exceptions.
   a. Torque the shock absorbers upper attaching nut to 14 ft. lbs. and the lower attaching bolt to 43 ft. lbs.

MacPherson Struts

For all spring and shock absorber

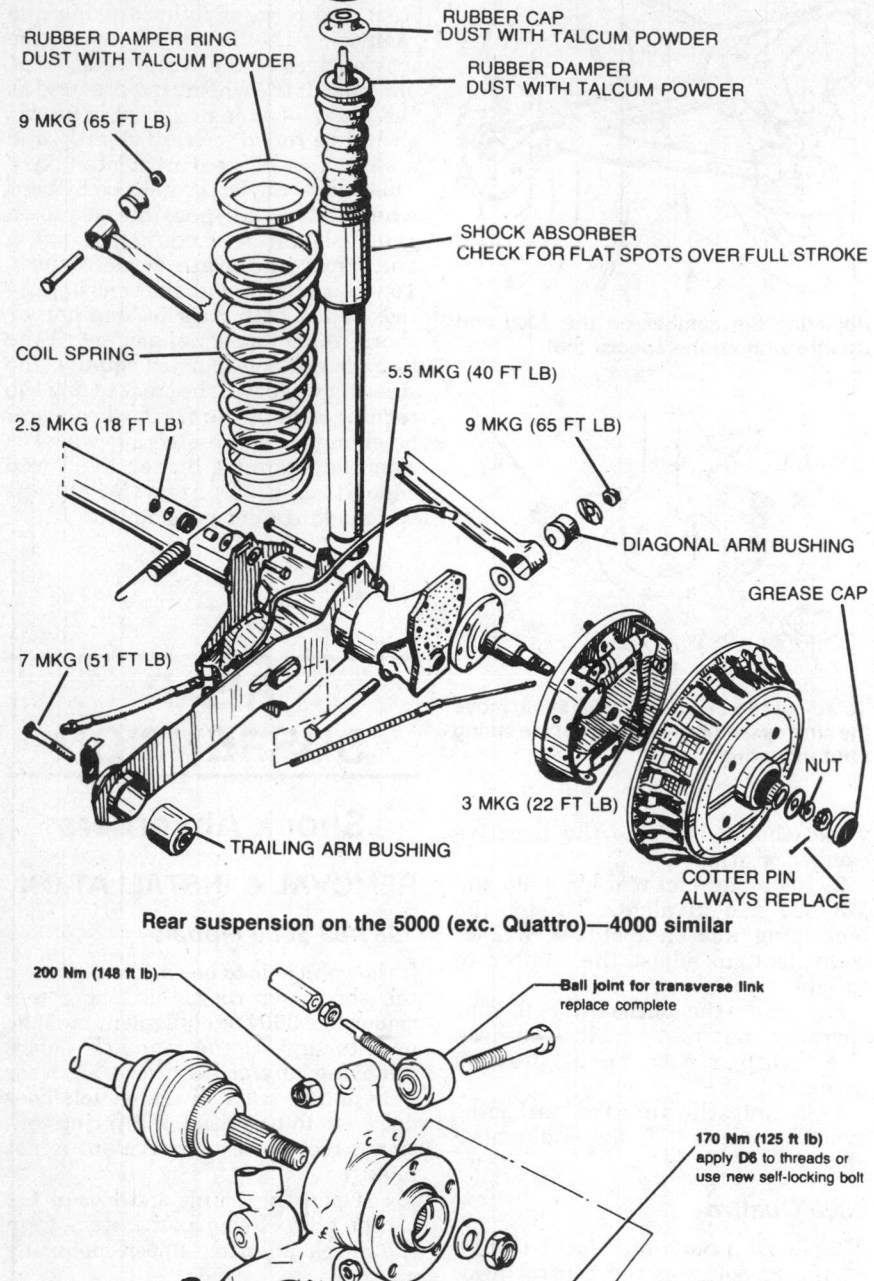

2 MKG (14 FT LB)

RUBBER CAP
DUST WITH TALCUM POWDER

RUBBER DAMPER
DUST WITH TALCUM POWDER

RUBBER DAMPER RING
DUST WITH TALCUM POWDER

9 MKG (65 FT LB)

SHOCK ABSORBER
CHECK FOR FLAT SPOTS OVER FULL STROKE

COIL SPRING

5.5 MKG (40 FT LB)

2.5 MKG (18 FT LB)

9 MKG (65 FT LB)

DIAGONAL ARM BUSHING

GREASE CAP

7 MKG (51 FT LB)

3 MKG (22 FT LB)

NUT

TRAILING ARM BUSHING

COTTER PIN
ALWAYS REPLACE

Rear suspension on the 5000 (exc. Quattro)—4000 similar

200 Nm (148 ft lb)

Ball joint for transverse link
replace complete

170 Nm (125 ft lb)
apply D6 to threads or
use new self-locking bolt

Washer
install all provided

Bonded rubber bushing
pressing out of pivot mount
pressing into pivot mount

170 Nm (125 ft lb)
apply D6 to threads or
use new self-locking bolt

Washer
install all provided

Bonded rubber bushing
pressing out of wheel bearing housing
pressing into wheel bearing housing

Exploded view of the rear suspension used on the 5000CS Turbo Quattro—1986 and later

removal and installation procedures and any other strut overhaul procedures, refer to "Strut Overhaul" in the Unit Repair section.

REMOVAL & INSTALLATION

All 4000 Models (exc. Quattro)

NOTE: Always remove and install the suspension struts one at a time. Do not allow the rear axle to hang in place as this may cause damage to the brake lines.

1. With the car at ground level, open the trunk and remove the sheel metal trim from around the shock tower.
2. Remove the rubber cap.
3. Remove the strut mounting nut.
4. Raise the rear of the car and support it with jackstands.
5. Remove the lower strut mounting bolt from the axle beam and remove the strut.
6. Installation is the reverse of removal. Torque the upper strut mounting bolt to 14 ft. lbs. and the lower strut mounting bolt to 43 ft. lbs.

5000 (exc. Quattro)

NOTE: The struts must be removed with the weight of the vehicle on the rear wheels. If not, a spring compressor must be used on the rear springs.

1. If the vehicle is not on its wheels, install the spring compressor and compress the spring. Do Not attempt to remove the shock with the rear wheels raised without a compressor.
2. Remove the upper strut mounting nut.
3. Remove the lower strut mounting nut.
4. Remove the shock absorber.
5. Installation is the reverse of removal. Torque the lower mounts to 40 ft. lbs. (1981–83) or 66 ft. lbs. (1984–86) and the upper to 14 ft. lbs.

4000 Quattro

1. Loosen the lug nuts and remove the axle nut cover.
2. Remove the axle nut and then raise and support the rear of the vehicle. Remove the wheels.
3. Using a tie-rod end puller, remove the tie-rod end.
4. Remove the brake caliper mounting bolts. Disconnect the brake line from its bracket and then position the caliper out of the way.
5. Remove the brake disc and the ball joint clamp bolt and then pry the ball joint out of the hub.
6. Using a four-armed puller tool

No. OTC 8278, press the halfshaft from the strut/wheel hub assembly.

7. Have a helper hold the strut assembly and remove the upper strut mounting nut. Remove the strut.

NOTE: The rear axle assembly must not be under tension while removing the strut.

8. Installation is in the reverse order of removal. Please note the following torque figures:

• Tie-rod nut – 29 ft. lbs. (non-Turbo) or 43 ft. lbs. (Turbo).
• Axle nut – 203 ft. lbs.
• Upper strut mounting nut – 43 ft. lbs.
• Ball joint clamp bolt – 54 ft. lbs. (non-Turbo) or 47 ft. lbs. (Turbo).

5000 Quattro

1. Raise and support the rear of the vehicle on jackstands. Remove the wheel.
2. Open the trunk and remove the shock absorber covers, the remove the shock absorber-to-body nuts/bolts.
3. Remove the shock absorber-to-rear wheel knuckle assembly. Remove the shock absorber from the vehicle.
4. To install, reverse the removal procedures. Torque the shock absorber-to-body nuts/bolts to 15 ft. lbs. and the shock absorber-to-rear wheel knuckle assembly bolt to 66 ft. lbs.

Quattro, Quattro Turbo & Quattro Coupe

1. Loosen the lug nuts, remove the axle nut cover and the axle nut. Raise and support the vehicle safely.
2. Remove the lug nuts and wheel assemblies. Using a suitable tool, press off the tie-rod ends.
3. Remove the brake caliper retaining bolts and remove the brake caliper. Disconnect the brake hose at the bracket. Remove the brake caliper and secure it out of the way.
4. Remove the brake discand the ball joint clamp bolt. Pry the ball joint out of the hub.
5. Remove the fuel tank cover. Remove the sunroof storage holder, if so equipped.
6. Remove the strut attaching nut holding the suspension strut from below to keep it from falling. Remove the suspension strut assembly.
7. Installation is the reverse order of the removal procedure, with the following exceptions:
  a. Torque the tie-rod nut and suspension strut to body attaching nuts to 43 ft. lbs. Torque the ball joint clamp nut to 47 ft. lbs. Torque the brake caliper retaining bolts to 47 ft.lbs., lug nuts to 80 ft. lbs. and axle nut to 203 ft. lbs.

OVERHAUL

For all spring and shock absorber removal and installation procedures and any other strut overhaul procedures, refer to "Strut Overhaul" in the Unit Repair section.

Rear Control Arms

REMOVAL & INSTALLATION

4000 Quattro

1. Raise and support the rear of the vehicle on jackstands, under the frame and differential.
2. Using a scribing tool, mark the position of the ball joint carrier with the control arm.
3. Remove the ball joint carrier-to-control arm nuts and the lock plate, then separate the ball joint carrier from the control arm.
4. Remove the control arm-to-sub-frame bolts and the control arm from the vehicle.
5. To install, reverse the removal procedures. Torque the control arm-to-sub-frame bolts to 43 ft. lbs. Check the rear wheel alignment.

5000 Quattro

On this vehicle, the control arm is know as the Trapezoidal Arm. It is connected to the wheel bearing housing and to two separate cross-members.

1. Raise and support the rear of the vehicle on jackstands, placed under the frame and the differential.
2. Remove the wheel. Along the trapezoidal arm, remove the speed sensor wiring bracket nuts/bolts and the guide.
3. Remove the wheel bearing housing-to-trapezoidal arm front and rear bolts.
4. Remove the trapezoidal arm-to-rear cross-member bolt.
5. At the brake pressure regulator, disconnect the spring.
6. Remove the trapezoidal arm-to-front cross-member nut and the trapezoidal arm from the vehicle.
7. To install, reverse the removal procedures. Torque the trapezoidal arm-to-front cross-member nut to 44 ft. lbs., the trapezoidal arm-to-rear cross-member bolt to 63 ft. lbs., the trapezoidal arm-to-wheel bearing housing bolts to 125 ft. lbs. and the speed sensor guide nut/bolts to 7 ft. lbs. Adjust the rear wheel alignment.

NOTE: Before installing the trapezoidal arm, be sure to coat the fasteners with locking compound D-6.

Ball Joint

REMOVAL & INSTALLTION

4000 Quattro & Quattro Turbo

1. Raise and support the vehicle safely. Remove the wheel and tire assembly.
2. Remove the ball joint attaching nut and using a suitable tool, press the ball joint out of the ball joint carrier.
3. Loosen the control arm mounting bolts at the subframe and swing the control arm downward.
4. Remove the bolts from the wheel bearing housing and insert two M8 x 40mm bolts approximately one inch into the wheel bearing housing.
5. Push the preassembled tool 40-204A or equivalent over the ball joint. Attach the ball joint mounting nut with a large washer onto the joint and tighten it as far as possible.
6. Pull out the ball joint by turning the installed bolts counterclockwise one at a time.
7. Using tool VW 415A or equivalent, drive the ball joint into the wheel bearing housing until seated. But before driving the ball joint into place, align the holes with the wheel bearing housing.
8. Torque the ball joint to 29 ft. lbs. Swivel the control arm into place and torque the ball joint nut to 54 ft. lbs. Tighten the control arm mountings with the vehicle wheels touching the ground.

Rear Wheel Bearings

ADJUSTMENT

All Models – Except Quattro

1. Raise and support the rear of the vehicle on jackstands.
2. Remove the grease cap.
3. Remove the cotter pin and the locking nut.
4. While turning the wheel (so that the wheel bearing does not jam), tighten the adjusting nut firmly.
5. Back the nut off slightly. Using a screwdriver, try to move the thrust washer with finger pressure; when the thrust washer can be moved slightly, the correct adjustment has been met.
6. To install, place new grease in the grease cap and reverse the removal procedures.

Rear Wheel Alignment

Only the 4000 and 5000 Quattro's are provided with rear wheel camber and toe adjustments.

NOTE: It is advised to take the vehicle to a qualified alignment shop to have the alignment performed correctly.

STEERING

Steering Wheel

REMOVAL & INSTALLATION

1. Center the steering wheel. Disconnect the battery ground cable.
2. Pry off the wheel pad (horn button). Mark the relationship of the steering wheel to the steering column.
3. Unbolt and remove the wheel. A steering wheel puller should not be necessary.
4. On installation, torque the bolt to 36 ft. lbs. (5000, 1981–83), 30 ft. lbs. (5000, 1984–88) and 29 ft. lbs. (4000). Do not pound on the wheel, as the collapsible column may be damaged.

Combination Switch

REMOVAL & INSTALLATION

All Models Except the 5000 Models

1. Disconnect the negative battery cable. Remove the horn cover (pry it off by hand), remove the nut and washer securing the stering wheel and remove the steering wheel, spring and horn contact.
2. Remove the screws and remove the steering column cover. Remove the screws securing the combination switch to the steering lock housing.
3. Disconnect the switch from the wiring harness and remove the combintaion switch.
4. Installation is the reverse of removal procedure.

5000 Models

1. Disconnect the negative battery cable. Remove the horn cover (pry it off by hand), remove the nut and washer securing the stering wheel and remove the steering wheel, spring and horn contact.
2. Remove the screws securing the combination switch housing through the access hole provided.
3. Pull the housing and switch assembly forward to clear the steering shaft and disconnect the wiring harness connectors. On the 5000, insert a screwdriver into the slot at the bottom right of the switch housing, loosen the

screw and pull the housing off enough to unplug the electrical connectors.
4. The switches can be removed from the housing by removing the the retaining screws.
5. Installation is the reverse of removal procedure.

Ignition Lock/Switch

REMOVAL & INSTALLATION

1981-83 5000

1. Disconnect the negative battery cable. Lower the air conditioning ducts as required and remove the combination switch assembly.
2. Disconnect the wiring harness from the switch. Support the steering column and drill out the two shear bolts using a $5/16$ in. drill bit.
3. Remove the steering lock and switch assembly from the vehicle. Remove the screw from the bottom of the lock housing and remove the ignition switch. Drill a hole in the locking housing (in the center of the locking housing), using a $1/8$ in. drill bit.
4. Insert a suitable punch into the hole to depress the spring, turn the ignition key slightly to the right and pry the locking cylinder from the housing.
5. Making sure to note the correct key position, insert a new lock cylinder into the housing until the spring snaps into position.
6. Insert the ignition switch into the housing, making sure the switch lines-up with the hole in the housing and engage the lock mechanism and secure the switch with a suitable set screw.
7. Remove the shear bolts from the upper steering column support. Install the housing on the steering column, make sure the projection on the housing engages the hole in the steering column.
8. Install the two new shear bolts and temporarily secure the housing. Check the operation of the steering lock mechanism. Tighten the shear bolts until the heads shear off.
9. Reinstall the steering column covers and air conditioner ducts as necessary.

1981-83 4000, Quattro & Coupe

1. Disconnect the negative battery cable.
2. Remove the steering wheel, the steering column covers and the steering column combination switches.
3. Pry the lock washer off the steering column and discard it.
4. Remove the spring and pull off the contact ring.

5. Unplug the electrical connector.
6. Unscrew the retaining bolt and slide the ignition switch/steering lock assembly off of the steering column tube.
7. Drill a hole in the locking housing (in the center of the locking housing), using a $1/8$ in. drill bit.
8. Insert a suitable punch into the hole to depress the spring, turn the ignition key slightly to the right and pry the locking cylinder from the housing.
9. Making sure to note the correct key position, insert a new lock cylinder into the housing until the spring snaps into position.
10. Remove the ignition switch retaining screw, and the ignition switch from the housing. Push the new steering lock and ignition assembly onto the steering column tube and install the retaining bolt.
11. Push the support ring onto the steering shaft and fit the shaft into the steering column tube. Push the contact ring onto the steering shaft and install the spring and lock washer, be sure to fully compress the spring.
12. To finish this procedure, install the rest of the components in the reverse order of the removal procedure.

1984–88 5000S Models

1. Disconnect the negative battery cable. Remove the horn pad cover and remove the steering wheel.
2. Remove the instrument cluster attaching bolts. Disconnect the speedometer cable at the transmission.
3. Pull the instrument cluster forward and detach the speedometer cable at the speedometer. Disconnect the electrical connectors at the instrument cluster and remove the instrument cluster.
4. Remove the locking compound around the ignition switch and remove the switch. To remove the ignition lock cylinder go on with this procedure.
5. Support the steering column and drill out the two shear bolts using a $1/8$ in. drill bit. Loosen the steering column bolts. Remove the left lower dash panel and the left air deflector.
6. Slide the steering column tube with the steering column downward and remove the steering lock from the steering column clamp. Drill a hole in the locking housing (in the center of the locking housing), using a $1/8$ in. drill bit.
7. Push the retaining spring in with a suitable punch and remove the lock cylinder.
8. Installation is the reverse order of the removal procedure.

1984–88 4000

1. Disconnect the negative battery cable.
2. Remove the steering wheel, the steering column covers and the steering column combination switches.
3. Pry the lock washer off the steering column and discard it.
4. Remove the spring and pull off the contact ring.
5. Unplug the electrical connector.
6. Unscrew the retaining bolt and slide the ignition switch/steering lock assembly off of the steering column tube.
7. Installation is in the reverse order of removal. Replace the old lock washer with a new one.

Manual Steering Gear

REMOVAL & INSTALLATION

4000 (1981–83)

1. Raise and support the front of the vehicle on jackstands.
2. At the steering gear, remove the tie–rods from the steering drive pawl bracket by prying them off with a small pry bar.
3. At the steering gear-to-steering column lower flange tube, push back the dust cap, then loosen the steering column-to-steering gear clamp bolt and pry the clamp back. Remove the seal ring from the steering gear.
4. Using a brass drift, drive the steering column lower flange off the steering gear.
5. Remove the steering gear-to-body bolts, turn the wheels to the right lock and remove the steering gear through the opening in the right wheel well.
6. To install, reverse the removal procedures. Torque the flange tube bolt to 18 ft. lbs., the tie-rod end ball joint nut to 22 ft. lbs. and the steering gear-to-body nuts to 25 ft. lbs.

ADJUSTMENT

The tie-rod is adjustable on the left-side ONLY for the 4 cyl. models and on both sides for the 5 cyl. models.

1. At the steering gear cover, loosen the lock nut. Tighten the adjusting screw until it touches the thrust washer. While holding the screw, tighten the lock nut.
2. If the steering rattles, is too tight or does not center, readjust the adjusting screw.

------ CAUTION ------

When turning the steering wheel with the wheels off the ground, be careful not to turn it too hard against the stops for damage may result.

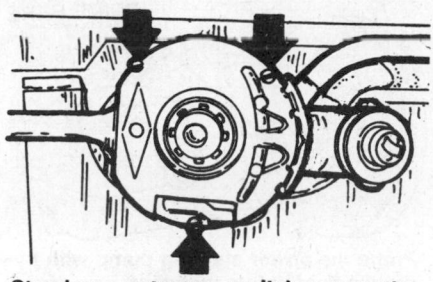

Steering column switch mounting screws—4000

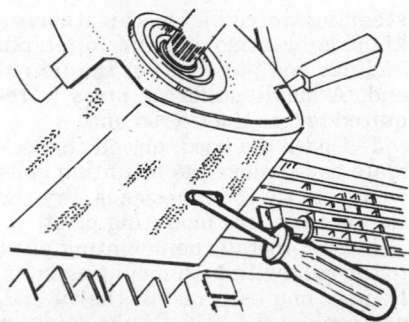

To remove the switch housing on the 5000, insert a screwdriver and loosen the screw

Power Steering Gear

REMOVAL & INSTALLATION

4000 (1981–83)

1. Raise and support the front of the vehicle on jackstands.
2. Disconnect the pressure hoses from the power steering gear and drain the fluid from the system.
3. At the power steering gear, pull the rubber cap back and disconnect the steering column clamp from the power steering gear pinion.
4. Remove the tie-rods from the steering drive pawl at the power steering gear.
5. Remove the power steering gear-to-frame bolts and the steering gear from the vehicle.
6. To install, reverse the removal procedures. Bleed the hydraulic system.

4000 (1984–87)

1. Raise and support the front of the vehicle on jackstands.
2. Remove the lower-left instrument panel cover, the steering column-to-steering gear clamp bolt and the steering column-to-dash bolts, then remove the steering column from the vehicle.
3. Using a pair of vise-grips, clamp off the fluid return line to the reservoir. Disconnect the fluid pressure line from the steering gear.

4. At the steering column boot, press in on the clips and remove the boot from the panel. From inside the vehicle, remove the fluid return line from the control valve body.
5. At the left-wheel housing, disconnect the steering gear from the frame.
6. At the steering rack, remove the tie-rod coupling lock nuts/bolts and the tie-rods from the rack. Push the rack back into the steering housing.
7. Disconnect the steering assembly from the firewall. Turn the wheels to the right, then remove the assembly between the left-wheel housing and the control arm.
8. To install, reverse the removal procedures. Bleed the hydraulic system.

All Models, Except the 4000

1. Raise and support the front of the vehicle on jackstands.
2. Pry off the lock plate and remove both tie rod mounting bolts from the steering rack, inside the engine compartment. Pry the tie rods out of the mounting pivot.
3. Remove the lower instrument panel trim.
4. Remove the pressure and return lines from the steering gear control valve body.
5. Remove the shaft clamp bolt, pry off the clip, and drive the shaft toward the inside of the car with a brass drift.
6. Remove the steering gear mounting bolts at both ends. There is a single bolt at the right end.
7. Turn the wheels all the way to the right and remove the steering gear through the opening in the right wheel housing.
8. For installation, temporarily install the tie rod mounting pivot to the rack with both mounting bolts. Remove one bolt, install the tie rod, and replace the bolt. Do the same on the other tie rod. Make sure to install the lock plate. Torque the tie rod to 39 ft. lbs., the mounting pivot bolt to 15 ft. lbs., and the steering gear-to-body mounting bolts to 15 ft. lbs. Bleed the hydraulic system.

ADJUSTMENT

All Models Equipped With Adjusting Screws

1. Position the wheels in the straight-ahead position.
2. On top of the steering gear, loosen the lock nut. Turn the adjusting nut until it bottoms against the thrust piece. While holding the adjusting screw, tighten the lock nut.
3. If the steering rattles, is too tight

or does not center, readjust the adjusting screw.

SYSTEM BLEEDING

1. Fill the reservoir to the Full mark.
2. Raise and support the front of the vehicle on jackstands.
3. Turn the steering wheel (with the engine NOT running) from lock to lock (several times) to remove the air from the system.
4. Add fluid to the reservoir until the level is maintained at 1 ³⁄₁₆ in. (30mm) below the Full mark.
5. Start the engine. As the fluid in the reservoir continues to drop, add fluid to maintain the 1 ³⁄₁₆ in. (30mm) level.

NOTE: When turning the steeing wheel, DO NOT use more force than necessary to turn it.

6. Keep bleeding the system until no more air bubbles appear in the reservoir.
7. Turn Off the engine and pump the brake pedal at least 20 times.
8. Replenish the fluid to the proper level.

Power Steering Pump

REMOVAL & INSTALLATION

All Models

1. Remove the hoses from the pump. Plug the openings.
2. Remove the belt adjusting bolt, push the pump to one side and remove the belt.
3. Support the pump, remove the mounting bolts and lift out the pump.
4. Installation is the reverse. Be sure to fill the pump suction chamber with hydraulic fluid before attaching lines or the pump may be damaged.

BELT ADJUSTMENT

1. Loosen the pump mounting bolts.
2. Turn the pump adjusting bolt until the center of the belt can be depressed ³⁄₈ in. (10mm).
3. After adjustment, tighten the mounting bolts.

Tie Rod Ends

REMOVAL & INSTALLATION

NOTE: A puller or press is required for this job.

1. Raise the car and remove the front wheels.
2. Disconnect the outer end of the

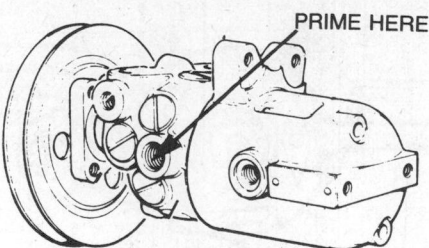

Prime the power steering pump with hydraulic fluid before installing

steering tie rod from the steering knuckle by removing the cotter pin and nut and pressing out the tie rod end. A small puller or press is required to free the tie rod end.

3. Under the hood, pry off the lock plate and remove the mounting bolts from both tie rod inner ends. Pry the tie rod out of the mounting pivot.
4. First install the mounting pivot to the rack with both mounting bolts. Remove one bolt, install the tie rod, and replace the bolt. Do the same on the other tie rod. Make sure to install the lock plate. The inner tie rod end bolts should be torqued to 40 ft. lbs. (4000, 1981–83) or 32 ft. lbs. (4000, 1984–87), 43 ft. lbs. on the 5000.
5. If you are replacing the adjustable left tie rod, adjust it to the same length as the old one. Check the toe-in when the job is done.
6. Use new cotter pins when installing the outer tie rod end. Torque the nut to 22 ft. lbs. on the 4000 and 43 ft. lbs. on the 5000.

BRAKES

Master Cylinder

REMOVAL & INSTALLATION

1. Have an assistant hold the brake pedal down about 1 ½ in. Disconnect the brake lines nearest the firewall.
2. Hold a container under the fitting disconnected in Step 1 and have the assistant release the pedal. The contents of the reservoir will drain into the container. Discard the used fluid.
3. Disconnect the other brake line.
4. Disconnect the stoplight switch from the master cylinder.
5. Unbolt and remove the master cylinder from the power brake unit. Be careful not to lose the sealing ring between the two units.
6. Installation is the reverse of removal. Master cylinder bolt torque is

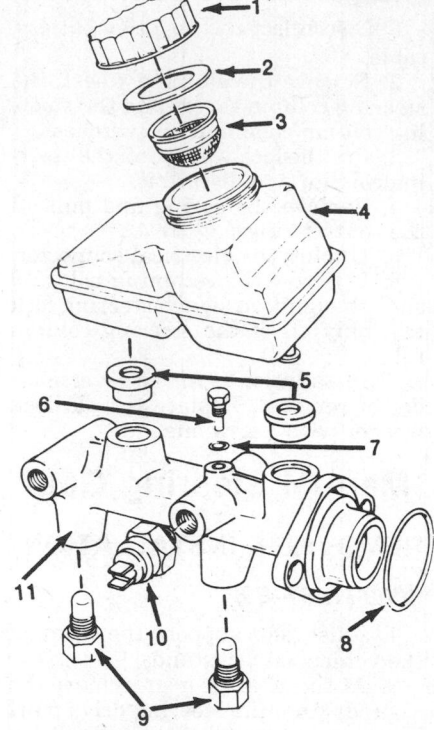

1. Reservoir cap
2. Washer
3. Filter screen
4. Reservoir
5. Master cylinder plugs
6. Stop screw
7. Stop screw seal
8. Master cylinder seal
9. Residual pressure valves
10. Warning light sender unit
11. Brake master cylinder housing

4000 master cylinder—5000 similar

17 ft. lbs. Fill and bleed the system. There should be a pedal free-play of 0.2 in. It can be adjusted on the linkage, inside the car.

Proportioning Valve

CHECKING

1981–83

1. With the wheels on the ground, depress the brake pedal firmly.
2. Release the pedal suddenly and check that the lever on the proportioning valve moves.
3. If the lever does not move, the valve will probably require replacement.

NOTE: It is normal for small quantities of brake fluid to escape through the vent hole.

REMOVAL & INSTALLATION

1981–83

1. Remove and plug the four brake lines leading from the proportioning valve.
2. Disconnect the spring which is attached to the valve and the axle beam.
3. Remove the two mounting bolts and remove the valve.

NOTE: Do not disassemble the valve.

4. Installation is in the reverse order of removal.
5. Bleed the brakes.

Brake Pressure Regulator

The brake pressure regulator is attached to the left-rear of the body and is operated by a spring attached to the rear axle (all models, except the 4000 Quattro and the 5000S Turbo). On the 4000 Quattro, it is mounted beneath the brake booster. On the 5000S Turbo, it is mounted on the left-rear of the body and is operated by a spring attached to the left-side of the rear axle arm.

BRAKE PRESSURE REGULATOR PRESSURES

Application	Front Gauge (psi)	Rear Gauge (psi)
4000 (1980–84)		
1st Reading	725	457–566
2nd Reading	1450	725–914
5000 (1980–84)		
1st Reading	725	493–566
2nd Reading	1450	827–899
4000 and 5000 (1985–87)		471–616
1st Reading	725	783–1037
2nd Reading	1450	
5000S Turbo (1985–87)		
1st Reading	725	508–653
2nd Reading	1450	827–1059

REMOVAL & INSTALLATION

All Models—Except 4000 Quattro

1. Raise and support the rear of the vehicle on jackstands.
2. Disconnect the spring from the pressure regulator.
3. Remove the brake lines from the pressure regulator.
4. Remove the bolts and the pressure regulator from the vehicle.

5000 brake proportioning valve; when checking, the lever (arrow) should move

5. To install, reverse the removal procedures. Bleed the brake system.

4000 Quattro

1. Remove the brake lines from the brake pressure regulator.
2. Remove the mounting bolts and the regulator from the vehicle.
3. To install, reverse the removal procedures. Bleed the brake system.

CHECKING AND ADJUSTING

NOTE: The brake pressure regulator on the 4000 Quattro is nonadjustable.

All Models—Except 4000 Quattro

1. Fill the fuel tank, empty out the vehicle and place a weight of 165 lbs. in the driver's seat.
2. At the rear of the vehicle, bounce it several times and allow it to come to rest.
3. Using a set of pressure gauges (1500 psi capacity), connect one (with the adapter) into the brake line at the left-front wheel brake caliper and the other into the brake line at the right-rear wheel cylinder or brake caliper. Using the bleeder screw on the gauges, bleed the brake system.
4. Depress the brake pedal firmly several times and release it quickly, the regulator should have moved.
5. Depress the brake pedal until the front gauge reads 725 psi, check the chart and compare the reading for the rear gauge.
6. If the pressures at the rear axle are HIGH, loosen the spring bolt and move it to reduce the spring pressure.
7. If the pressures at the rear axle are LOW, loosen the spring bolts and move it to increase the spring pressure.
8. Perform the checking and adjustment procedures until the readings conform with the chart.
9. If the pressures cannot be obtained or held, replace the regulator.

10. After the system has been adjusted, remove the pressure gauges. Bleed the brake system.

Power Brake Booster

REMOVAL & INSTALLATION

1. Refer to the "Master Cylinder, Removal and Installation" procedures in this section and remove the master cylinder; DO NOT remove the brake lines.
2. Disconnect the vacuum hose from the power brake booster.
3. From under the dash, disconnect the pushrod from the brake pedal, then remove the power brake booster-to-firewall nuts and the booster from the vehicle.
4. To install, reverse the removal procedures.

Wheel Cylinder

REMOVAL & INSTALLATION

1. Raise and support the rear of the vehicle on jackstands.
2. Remove the wheel, the drum and the brake shoes.
3. Depress the brake pedal about 1 ½ in. to block the master cylinder compensating port and prevent leakage. Secure the pedal in this position.
4. Disconnect the brake line and plug the opening.
5. Remove the two mounting screws from the backing plate.
6. Remove the cylinder.
7. To install, reverse the removal procedures. Bleed the brake system.

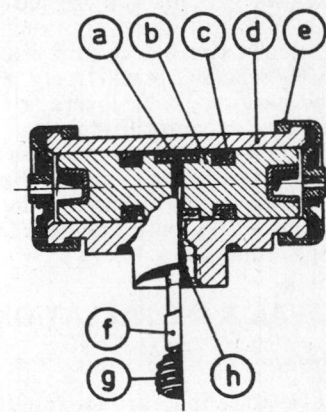

(a)—Spring
(b)—Piston
(c)—Grooved cup
(d)—Cylinder
(e)—Cap
(f)—Bleeder valve
(g)—Dust cap
(h)—Brake line

Cross-section of a rear wheel cylinder

Parking Brake Cable

ADJUSTMENT

All Models Except Turbo and Quattro

NOTE: Because of self-adjusting rear brakes, adjustment is only necessary after replacement of any of the brake components.

1. Raise the rear of the car and support it with jackstands.
2. Release the parking brake lever.
3. Depress the brake pedal once.
4. Pull the parking brake lever onto the second tooth in the 4000 and third tooth in the 5000.
5. Tighten the adjusting nut on the parking brake cable equalizer bar until the wheels can just be turned by hand.
6. Release the lever and check that both wheels rotate freely.
7. Turn the ignition switch On and check that the brake warning light comes On when the parking brake lever is pulled up to the first tooth and goes Out when it is released.

Turbo and Quattro

NOTE: Because of the self-adjusting rear brakes, adjustment is only necessary after replacement of any of the brake components.

1. Raise the rear of the car and support it with jackstands.
2. Release the parking brake lever.
3. Check that the parking brake levers at the rear calipers stay on the stop. If not, loosen the adjusting nut.
4. Depress the brake pedal approximately 40 times and pull the parking brake lever to the third tooth.
5. Tighten the adjusting nut on the parking brake equalizer bar until the rear wheels can just be turned by hand.
6. Release the brake and check that both wheels rotate freely and that the parking brake levers at the rear calipers stay on the stops.
7. Turn the ignition switch On and check that the brake warning light comes On when the parking brake is pulled to the first tooth and goes Out when it is release.

REMOVAL & INSTALLATION

All Models

1. Raise and support the rear of the car. Release the parking brake.
2. Remove the rear brake drums on all but the Turbo and Quattro.
3. Disconnect the cable from the shoe assembly by pushing the spring forward and removing the cable from the adjusting arm on all but the Turbo and Quattro.
4. Pull the parking brake cable out of its retaining clip on the caliper (Turbo and Quattro only).
5. Remove the cable compensating spring.
6. Back off the equalizer nut and guide the cable through the trailing arms and supports.
7. Installation is the reverse of removal.
8. Adjust if necessary.

NOTE: When installing the parking brake cables on the Turbo and Quattro, the long cable goes on the left side and the short one goes on the right side. The cable coupling should connect the two cables on the right side of the equalizer bar.

CHASSIS ELECTRICAL

Heater Core and Blower Motor

REMOVAL & INSTALLATION

1981-83 4000—All Models

1. Disconnect the negative battery cable.
2. Drain the engine coolant into a suitable clean container and save for re-use.
3. Trace the heater hoses coming from the firewall and disconnect them. One leads to the back of the cylinder head and the other leads to the heater valve located above and behind the oil filter.
4. Detach the cable for the heater valve.
5. Remove the center console.
6. Remove the left and right covers below the instrument panel.
7. Pull off the fresh air/heater control knobs.
8. Pull off the trim plate.
9. Remove the screws (2) for the controls.
10. Remove the center cover mounting screws (2 top and 2 bottom) and remove the cover.
11. Detach the right, left and center air ducts.
12. Remove the heater housing retaining spring.
13. Remove the cowl for the air plenum which is located under the hood and in front of the windshield.
14. Remove the heater housing mounting screws (4) and remove the heater housing. The mounting screws are under the hood where the air plenum was.
15. Remove the blower motor and the heater core from the assembly.
16. Installation is in the reverse order of removal. Be sure to replace all sealing material.

5000—All Models

NOTE: Blower or core removal requires removal and disassembly of the entire unit.

1. Disconnect the battery ground.
2. Drain the cooling system.

--- CAUTION ---

If the vehicle is equipped with air conditioning, the A/C system must be discharged. Do Not attempt to discharge the freon unless familiar with air conditioning.

---

3. Discharge the air conditioning system.
4. Disconnect the:
   a. Temperature sensor connector.
   b. Evaporator/heater connector clamp.
   c. Temperature control cable.
   d. Fresh air door vacuum hose.
5. Disconnect the main harness connector.
6. Loosen the case retaining strap.
7. Remove the coolant hoses at the heater core tubes.
8. Remove the yellow, green and red vacuum hoses from the heater case.
9. Remove the air duct hoses.
10. Remove the heater case mounting screws (two in the passenger compartment, one in the engine compartment). On A/C equipped cars, remove the four evaporator housing mounting screws in the passenger compartment.
11. Support the heater/evaporator unit and pull it away from the firewall.
12. Remove the control cable grommet to facilitate case removal.
13. The case halves may be separated by removing the clips at the top and bottom with a small pry bar.
14. Remove the blower motor and the heater core from the unit.
15. Installation is the reverse of removal. Replace all sealing material. Evacuate, charge and leak test the system.

--- CAUTION ---

Freon will freeze any surface it contacts, including skin and eyeballs. It also turns into a poisonous gas in the presence of an open flame. Wear eye protection and suitable gloves when working on or around the air conditioning system.

Heater Blower

REMOVAL & INSTALLATION

1984–88 4000 Models, Coupe & Quattro

1. Disconnect the negative battery cable.
2. Remove the air plenum from the cowl.
3. Remove the ballast resistor.
4. At the blower motor, disconnect the electrical connector.
5. Remove the blower mounting bolts and the blower from the heater assembly.
6. To install, reverse the removal procedures.

Heater Core
REMOVAL & INSTALLATION

1984–88 4000 Models, Coupe & Quattro

1. Disconnect the negative battery cable.
2. At the radiator, pull off the bottom hose and drain the coolant into a container for reuse.
3. Remove the heater hoses from the heat exchanger.
4. At the heater assembly control valve, disconnect the control wire.
5. Remove the console. Remove the left and the right heater covers from below the dashboard.
6. At the heater control unit, pull off the control knobs.
7. Remove the trim plate from the heater control unit.
8. At the heater control unit, remove the retaining screws and the center cover.
9. Remove the heater air ducts and the heater assembly retaining springs.
10. Remove the air plenum from the cowl and the heater assembly from the vehicle.
11. Separate the heater unit and remove the heater core.
12. To install, reverse the removal procedures. Refill the cooling system.

Radio

The radio is usually a dealer-installed or aftermarket unit; thus no specific removal and installation procedures can be given. The following information applies generally to all car radios.

Care should be taken during installation to avoid reversing the ground and power leads. Reversal of these leads will cause serious damage to the radio. The power lead usually has an in-line fuse.

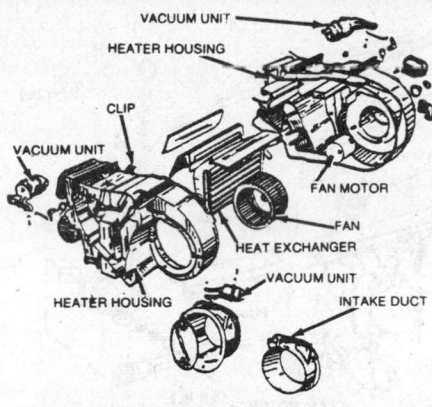

Exploded view of the 5000 heater assembly

If the speaker needs replacement, it should be replaced with one of the same impedance, measured in ohms. Mismatched impedance can cause rapid transistor failure as well as poor radio performance. This should also be taken into consideration when adding a second speaker.

The radio should never be operated without a speaker connected or with the speaker leads shorted. This will result in transistor failure.

Windshield Wiper Switch
REMOVAL & INSTALLATION

The windshield wiper switch is incorporated with the combination switch located on the steering column. On some models, if the wiper switch has to be replaced, the combination switch must be replaced.

4000S, 4000S Quattro & Coupe GT

1. Disconnect the negative battery cable. Pull off the horn pad and remove the steering wheel.

2. Remove the steering column cover. Remove the three screws on the turn signal switch.
3. Pull the turn signal switch and the wiper switch from the column.
4. Installtion is the reverse order of the removal procedure.

5000 & 5000S Turbo

1. Disconnect the negative battery cable. Pull off the horn pad and remove the steering wheel.
2. Insert a suitable (phillips head) tool into the slot at the bottom of the steering column cover and loosen the screw(s).
3. Pull the switch and the top of the cover assembly off of the steering column. Remove the two screws inside the cover to remove the wiper switch from the cover.
4. Installtion is the reverse order of the removal procedure.

Windshield Wiper Motor and Linkage

REMOVAL & INSTALLATION

All Models

1. Disconnect the negative battery cable and disconnect the wiring harness connector at the motor. Pry off the wiper arms and remove the nuts from the studs in the cowl.
2. Remove the brace-to-body screws. While holding the crank, remove the nut securing the crank to the wiper motor and remove the crank.
3. Remove the bolts securing the wiper motor to the support and remove the motor.
4. Connect the new motor to the wiring harness, run the motor two revolutions and turn the wiper switch to the off position. The wiper motor

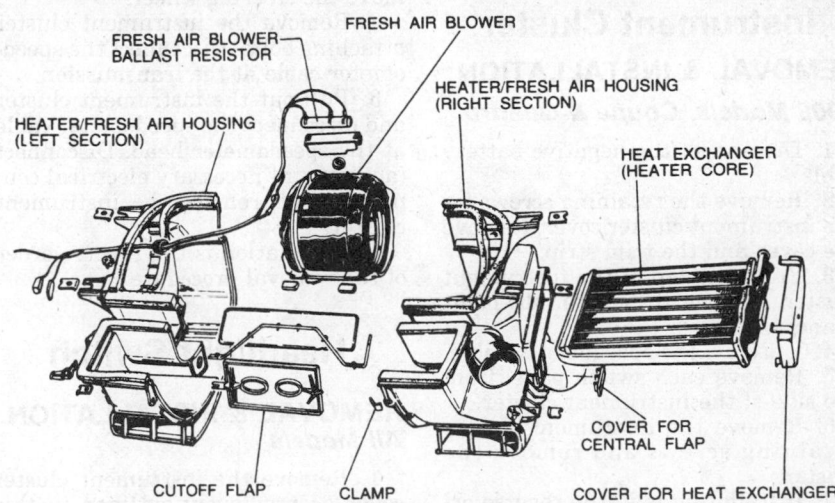

Exploded view of the 4000 heater assembly

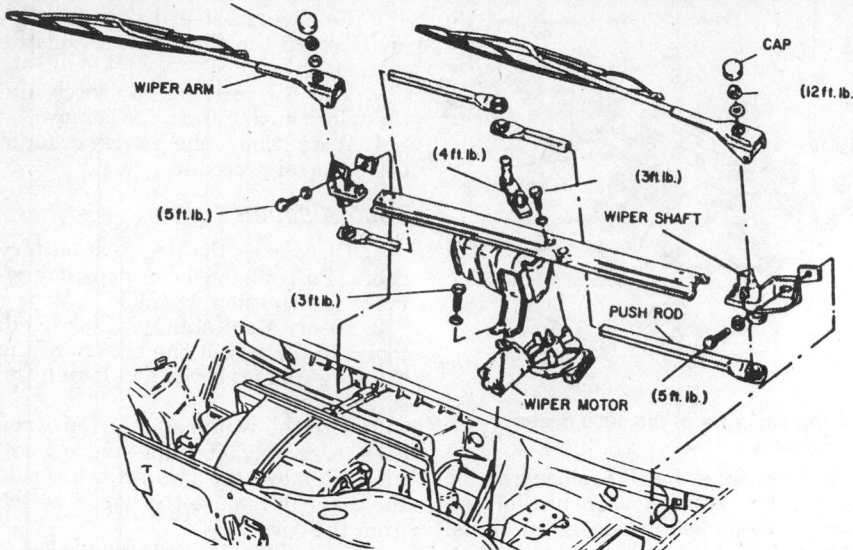

Exploded view of the windshield wiper assembly—1984 and later 5000 models

should stop in the park position. Remove the linkage followed by the motor.

6. To install, reverse the removal procedures. Make sure that the crank is installed in the proper position.

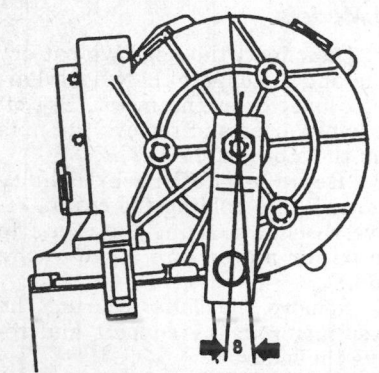

Wiper crank in the park position (at 8 degrees) for the 4000 models and the Coupe GT

Instrument Cluster

REMOVAL & INSTALLATION

4000 Models, Coupe & Quattro

1. Disconnect the negative battery cable.
2. Remove the retaining screws for the instrument cluster cover. Remove the cover and the trim strip.
3. From the top of the instrument cluster, remove the four multi-point connectors.
4. Unscrew the speedometer cable.
5. Remove each switch panel from the side of the instrument cluster.
6. Remove the instrument cluster retaining screws and remove the cluster.
7. Installation is in the reverse order of removal.

1981–83 5000 Models

1. Disconnect the negative battery cable.
2. Remove the instrument panel trim.
3. Remove the instrument cluster cover retaining screws and remove the cover.
4. Remove the upper portion of the cluster cover and then remove the lower portion.
5. Loosen the instrument cluster retaining screws and slide it forward enough to remove the multi-point connectors and the speedometer cable.
6. Remove the cluster retaining screws and remove the cluster.
7. Installation is in the reverse order of removal.

1984–88 5000 Models

1. Disconnect the negative battery cable. Pull of the the horn pad and remove the steering wheel.
2. Remove the instrument cluster attaching bolts. Disconnect the speedometer cable at the transmission.
3. Pull out the instrument cluster and disconnect the speedometer cable at the speedometer head. Disconnect (and tag) all necessary electrical connectors and remove the instrument cluster.
4. Installation is the reverse order of the removal procedure.

Headlight Switch

REMOVAL & INSTALLATION
All Models

1. Remove the instrument cluster cover as previously outlined in this section.

2. Disconnect the wiring harness connector from the headlight switch. Depress the clips on the headlight switch retainer and remove the switch from the instrument cluster.
3. Installation is the reverse order of the removal procedure.
NOTE: On some of the later models the headlight switch could be incorporated with the combination switch. If this is the case refer to the combination switch removal & installation procedure in this section.

Stoplight Switch

REMOVAL & INSTALLATION
All Models

1. Disconnect the negative battery cable.
2. Disconnect the stoplamp switch wire connector from the switch.
3. If the stoplight switch is located behind the brake pedal. Remove the hairpin retainer and outer nylon washer from the pedal pin. Slide the stoplamp switch off the brake pedal pin just far enough for the outer side plate of the switch to clear the pin. Then remove the switch.
4. If the stoplight switch is located in the master cylinder, use a suitable wrench and remove the switch from the master cylinder.
5. Installation is the reverse order of the removal procedure. If the switch was located in the master cylinder, be sure to top off the master cylinder reservoir and bleed the brake circuit.

Fuse Box

LOCATION

The fuse box for all 4000 and quattro models can be found underneath the left-side of the dashboard, behind the rear panel of the package tray. The fuse box for all 5000 models is located under the hood, at the left-rear of the engine compartment. The relays for both models are also plugged into the fuse box. In the cover of each fuse box (and in the Owner's Manual) is a chart which tells which circuit the fuse protects and its correct amperage. The chart also tells which circuit the relays are connected to. Each model also uses in-line fuses for certain circuits; fuel pump, battery, air conditioning and power door locks (if equipped), 4000; air conditioning, power windows and heated sets, 5000; glow plug, 5000 Diesel; cigar lighter, power windows and the cooling fan for the injectors, 5000 Turbo and Quattro. On the later 4000 models and the Coupe GT, the fuse/relay box is located under the hood in a protective box with a cover.

BMW 3

318, 320, 325, 524, 528, 533, 535, 633, 635, 733, 735—All Models

SERIAL NUMBER IDENTIFICATION

Vehicle Identification Plate

The manufacturer's plate is located in the engine compartment of the right side inner fender panel or support, or on the right side of the firewall.

Engine Number

The engine number is located on the left rear side of the engine, above the starter motor.

Vehicle Identification Number

The VIN is located on a plate on the upper left of the instrument panel, visible through the windshield.

Chassis Number

The chassis number can be found in the engine compartment on the right inner fender support or facing forward on the right side of the heater bulkhead. A label is also attached to the upper steering column cover inside the vehicle. On 1987 models, it appears on the left/front door jamb and on all major components.

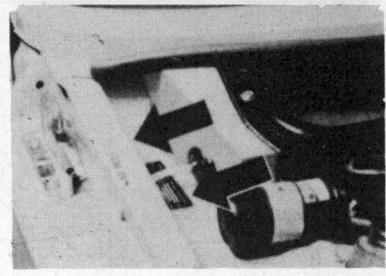

Under hood serial number location—typical

Engine serial number location

ENGINE IDENTIFICATION

Year	Model	Engine Displacement cu. in. (cc/liter)	Engine Series Identification	No. of Cylinders	Engine Type
1981	320i	108 (1766/11.8)	—	4	OHC
	528i	170 (2788/12.8)	—	6	OHC
	633CSi,733i	196 (3210/13.2)	M30B32	6	OHC
1982	320i	108 (1766/11.8)	—	4	OHC
	325e,528e	165 (2693/12.7)	M20B27	6	OHC
	533i,633CSi,733i	196 (3210/13.2)	M30B32	6	OHC

ENGINE IDENTIFICATION

Year	Model	Engine Displacement cu. in. (cc/liter)	Engine Series Identification	No. of Cylinders	Engine Type
1983	320i	108 (1766/11.8)	—	4	OHC
	325e,528e	165 (2693/12.7)	M20B27	6	OHC
	533i,633CSi,733i	196 (3210/13.2)	M30B32	6	OHC
1984	318i	108 (1766/11.8)	M10B18	4	OHC
	325e,528e	165 (2693/12.7)	M20B27	6	OHC
	533i,633CSi,733i	196 (3210/13.2)	M30B32	6	OHC
1985	318i	108 (1766/11.8)	M10B18	4	OHC
	325e,528e	165 (2693/12.7)	M20B27	6	OHC
	524td	149 (2443/12.4)	M21D24	6	OHC
	533i,633CSi,733i	196 (3210/13.2)	M30B32	6	OHC
1986	325e,528e	165 (2693/12.7)	M20B27	6	OHC
	524td	149 (2443/12.4)	M21D24	6	OHC
	535i,635CSi,735i	209 (3428/13.4)	M30B34	6	OHC
1987-88	325i,528e	165 (2693/12.7)	M20B27	6	OHC
	325i,325iS	152 (2494/12.5)	M20B25	6	OHC
	535i,635CSi,735i	209 (3428/13.4)	M30B35MZ	6	OHC
	M5,M6	210.6 (3453/13.5)	M6538Z	6	DOHC

GENERAL ENGINE SPECIFICATIONS

Year	Model	Engine Displacement cu. in. (cc)	Fuel System Type	Net Horsepower @ rpm	Net Torque @ rpm (ft. lbs.)	Bore × Stroke (in.)	Compression Ratio	Oil Pressure @ rpm
1981	320i	108 (1766)	EFI	101 @ 5800	100 @ 4500	3.504 × 2.793	8.8:1	57 @ 4000
	528i	170 (2788)	EFI	169 @ 5500	100 @ 4500	3.390 × 3.150	8.2:1	71 @ 4000
	633CSi,733i	196 (3210)	EFI	174 @ 5200	184 @ 4200	3.504 × 3.386	8.0:1	71 @ 6000
1982	320i	108 (1766)	EFI	101 @ 5800	100 @ 4500	3.504 × 2.793	8.8:1	57 @ 4000
	325e,528e	165 (2693)	EFI	121 @ 4250	170 @ 3250	3.307 × 3.189	9.0:1	71 @ 5000
	533i,633CSi,733i	196 (3210)	EFI	181 @ 6000	195 @ 4000	3.504 × 3.386	8.8:1	64 @ 4000
1983	320i	108 (1766)	EFI	101 @ 5800	100 @ 4500	3.504 × 2.793	8.8:1	57 @ 4000
	325e,528e	165 (2693)	EFI	121 @ 4250	170 @ 3250	3.307 × 3.189	9.0:1	71 @ 5000
	533i,633CSi,733i	196 (3210)	EFI	181 @ 6000	195 @ 4000	3.504 × 3.386	8.8:1	64 @ 6000
1984	318i	108 (1766)	EFI	101 @ 5800	103 @ 4500	3.504 × 2.793	9.0:1	64 @ 4000
	325e,528e	165 (2693)	EFI	121 @ 4250	170 @ 3250	3.307 × 3.189	9.0:1	71 @ 5000
	533i,633CSi,733i	196 (3210)	EFI	181 @ 6000	195 @ 4000	3.504 × 3.386	8.8:1	64 @ 6000
1985	318i	108 (1766)	EFI	101 @ 5800	103 @ 4500	3.504 × 2.793	9.0:1	64 @ 4000
	325e,528e	165 (2693)	EFI	121 @ 4250	170 @ 3250	3.307 × 3.189	9.0:1	71 @ 5000
	524td	149 (2443)	DFI	114 @ 4800	155 @ 2400	3.15 × 3.19	22:1	71 @ 6000
	533i,633CSi,733i	196 (3210)	EFI	181 @ 6000	195 @ 4000	3.504 × 3.386	8.8:1	64 @ 6000
	535i,635CSi,735i	209 (3428)	EFI	182 @ 5400	213 @ 4000	3.62 × 3.38	8.0:1	71 @ 6000
1986	325e,528e	165 (2693)	EFI	121 @ 4250	170 @ 3250	3.307 × 3.189	9.0:1	71 @ 5000
	524td	149 (2443)	DFI	114 @ 4800	155 @ 2400	3.15 × 3.19	22:1	71 @ 6000
	535i,635CSi,735i	209 (3428)	EFI	182 @ 5400	213 @ 4000	3.62 × 3.38	8.0:1	71 @ 6000

GENERAL ENGINE SPECIFICATIONS

Year	Model	Engine Displacement cu. in. (cc)	Fuel System Type	Net Horsepower @ rpm	Net Torque @ rpm (ft. lbs.)	Bore × Stroke (in.)	Compression Ratio	Oil Pressure @ rpm
1987-88	325,528e	165 (2693)	EFI	121 @ 4250	170 @ 3250	3.307 × 3.189	9.0:1	71 @ 5000
	325i,325iS	152 (2494)	EFI	167 @ 5800	164 @ 4300	3.307 × 2.953	8.8:1	71 @ 5000
	535i,635CSi,735i	209 (3428)	EFI	182 @ 5400	213 @ 4000	3.62 × 3.38	8.0:1	71 @ 6000
	M5,M6	210.6 (3453)	EFI	256 @ 6500	239 @ 4500	3.30 × 3.67	9.8:1	N/A

EFI   Electronic Fuel Injection
DFI   Diesel Fuel Injection

GASOLINE ENGINE TUNE-UP SPECIFICATIONS

Year	Model	Engine Displacement cu. in. (cc)	Spark Plugs Type	Gap (in.)	Ignition Timing (deg.) MT	AT	Compression Pressure (psi)	Fuel Pump (psi)	Idle Speed (rpm) MT	AT	Valve Clearance In.	Ex.
1981	320i	108 (1766)	WR9DS	0.024	25B @ 2200	25B @ 2200	128	64–74	850	900	0.007	0.007
	528i	170 (2788)	WR9DS	0.024	22B @ 2200	22B @ 2200	142	64–74	900	900	0.011	0.011
	633CSi,733i	196 (3210)	WR9DS	0.024	22B @ 1650	22B @ 1650	114	35	900	900	0.011	0.011
1982	320i	108 (1766)	WR9DS	0.024	25B @ 2200	25B @ 2200	128	64–74	850	900	0.007	0.007
	325e,528e	165 (2693)	WR9LS	0.024	①	①	142	33–38	①	①	0.010	0.010
	533i,633CSi,733i	196 (3210)	WR9LS	0.024	①	①	114	35	①	①	0.011	0.011
1983	320i	108 (1766)	WR9DS	0.024	25B @ 2200	25B @ 2200	128	64–74	850	900	0.007	0.007
	325e,528e	165 (2693)	WR9LS	0.024	①	①	142	33–38	①	①	0.010	0.010
	533i,633CSi,733i	196 (3210)	WR9LS	0.024	①	①	142	35	①	①	0.012	0.012
1984	318i	108 (1766)	WR9DS	0.024	①	①	142	43	①	①	0.008	0.008
	325e,528e	165 (2693)	WR9LS	0.024	①	①	142	33–38	①	①	0.010	0.010
	533i,633CSi,733i	196 (3210)	WR9LS	0.024	①	①	142	35	①	①	0.012	0.012
1985	318i	108 (1766)	WR9DS	0.033	①	①	142	43	①	①	0.008	0.008
	325e,528e	165 (2693)	WR9LS	0.029	①	①	142	33–38	①	①	0.010	0.010
	533i,633CSi,733i	196 (3210)	WR9LS	0.024	①	①	142	35	①	①	0.012	0.012
	535i,635CSi,735i	209 (3428)	WR9LS	0.029	①	①	142	43	①	①	0.012	0.012
1986	325e,528e	165 (2693)	WR9LS	0.029	①	①	142	33–38	①	①	0.010	0.010
	535i,635CSi,735i	209 (3428)	WR9LS	0.029	①	①	142	43	①	①	0.012	0.012
1987	325,528e	165 (2693)	WR9LS	0.029	①	①	142	33–38	①	①	0.010	0.010
	325i,325iS	152 (2494)	W8LCR	0.029	①	①	142	43	①	①	0.010	0.010
	535i,635CSi,735i	209 (3428)	WR9LS	0.029	①	①	142	43	①	①	0.012	0.012
	M5,M6	210.6 (3453)	X5DC	0.029	①	①	143	43	①	①	0.013	0.013
1988	All					SEE UNDERHOOD SPECIFICATIONS STICKER						

NOTE: The underhood specifications sticker often reflects tune-up specification changes made in production. Sticker figures must be used if they disagree with those in this chart.

NA   Not available
B   Before Top Dead Center
① Motronic injection system: controlled by computer, please refer to the underhood sticker for specifications.

DIESEL ENGINE TUNE-UP SPECIFICATIONS

Year	Engine Displacement cu. in. (cc)	Valve Clearance		Intake Valve Opens (deg.)	Injection Pump Setting (deg.)	Injection Nozzle Pressure (psi)		Idle Speed (rpm)	Cranking Compression Pressure (psi)
		Intake (in.)	Exhaust (in.)			New	Used		
1985	149 (2443)	0.012	0.012	NA	3.5B	2133–2247	1920	750	284
1986	149 (2443)	0.012	0.012	NA	3.5B	2133–2247	1920	750	284

B—Before Top Dead Center
NA—Not Available

FIRING ORDERS

NOTE: To avoid confusion, always replace spark plug wires one at a time.

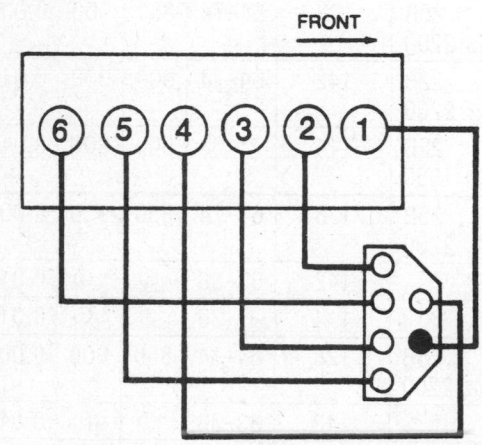

325, 325e, 325i, 528e, 533i, 535i, M5, and
1982 and later 633CSi, 635CSi, M6, and
733i, 735i
Firing order: 1–5–3–6–2–4

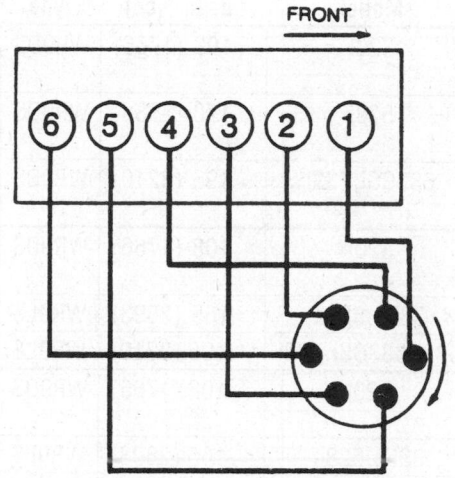

528i, 1981 633CSi and 733i
Firing order: 1–5–3–6–2–4

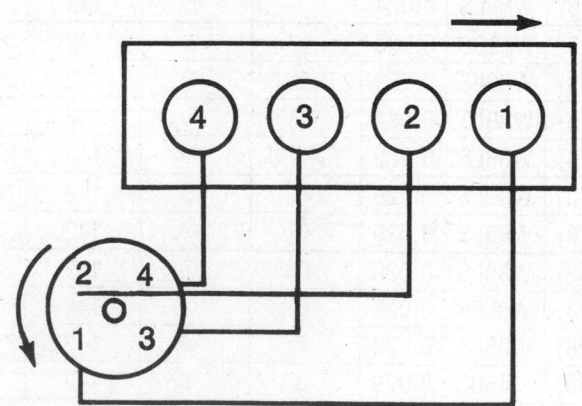

320i, 318i firing order: 1-3-4-2

CAPACITIES

Year	Model	Engine Displacement cu. in. (cc)	Engine Crankcase with Filter	Engine Crankcase without Filter	Transmission (pts) 4-Spd	Transmission (pts) 5-Spd	Transmission (pts) Auto.	Drive Axle (pts.)	Fuel Tank (gal.)	Cooling System (qts.)
1981	320i	108 (1766)	4.5 ①	4.25 ②	2.2	—	4.2	1.9	15.3	7.4
	528i	170 (2788)	6.0	5.25	2.3	—	4.2	3.4	16.4	12.7
	633CSi	196 (3210)	6.0	5.25	2.4	—	4.2	3.2	16.5	12.7
	733i	196 (3210)	6.0	5.25	2.4	—	4.0	3.8	22.5	12.7
1982	320i	108 (1766)	4.5 ①	4.25 ②	2.2	—	4.2	1.9	15.3	7.4
	528e	165 (2693)	4.5	4.2	3.4	—	4.2	3.8	16.6	12.7
	633CSi	196 (3210)	6.0	5.25	2.4	—	4.2	3.2	16.5	12.7
	733i	196 (3210)	6.0	5.25	2.4	—	4.0	3.8	22.5	12.7
1983	320i	108 (1766)	4.5 ①	4.25 ②	2.2	—	4.2	1.9	15.3	7.4
	528e	165 (2693)	4.5	4.2	—	3.4	4.2	3.8	16.6	12.7
	533i	196 (3210)	6.0	5.3	—	2.65	6.3	3.6	16.6	12.7
	633CSi	196 (3210)	6.0	5.25	2.4	—	4.2	3.2	16.5	12.7
	733i	196 (3210)	6.0	5.25	—	2.4	4.0	3.8	22.5	12.7
1984	318i	108 (1766)	4.5	4.2	—	2.4	6.3	1.9	14.5	7.4
	528e	165 (2693)	4.5	4.2	—	3.4	4.2	3.8	16.6	12.7
	533i	196 (3210)	6.0	5.3	—	2.65	6.3	3.6	16.6	12.7
	633CSi	196 (3210)	6.0	5.25	2.4	—	4.2	3.2	16.5	12.7
	733i	196 (3210)	6.0	5.25	—	2.4	4.0	3.8	22.5	12.7
1985	318i	108 (1766)	4.5	4.2	—	2.4	6.3	1.9	14.5	7.4
	325e,es	165 (2693)	4.5	4.2	—	2.4	6.3	3.4	14.5	7.4
	528e	165 (2693)	4.5	4.2	—	3.4	4.2	3.8	16.6	12.7
	524td	149 (2443)	6.1	5.3	—	3.4	6.4	4.0	16.6	12.7
	535i	209 (3428)	6.1	5.3	—	3.4	6.4	4.0	16.6	12.7
	635CSi	209 (3428)	6.1	5.3	—	3.4	6.4	4.0	16.6	12.7
	735i	209 (3428)	6.1	5.3	—	3.4	6.4	4.0	22.5	12.7
1986	325e,es	165 (2693)	4.5	4.2	—	2.4	6.3	3.4	14.5	7.4
	524td	149 (2443)	6.1	5.3	—	3.4	6.4	4.0	16.6	12.7
	528e	165 (2693)	4.5	4.2	—	3.4	4.2	3.8	16.6	12.7
	535i	209 (3428)	6.1	5.3	—	3.4	6.4	4.0	16.6	12.7
	635CSi	209 (3428)	6.1	5.3	—	3.4	6.4	4.0	16.6	12.7
	735i	209 (3428)	6.1	5.3	—	3.4	6.4	4.0	22.5	12.7
1987–88	325	165 (2693)	4.5	4.2	—	2.6	6.4	3.6	15.3	12.7
	528e	165 (2693)	4.5	4.2	—	3.4	6.4	3.8	16.6	11.6
	535i	209 (3428)	6.1	5.3	—	3.4	6.4	4.0	16.6	12.7
	635CSi	209 (3428)	6.1	5.3	—	3.4	6.4	4.0	16.6	12.7
	735i	209 (3428)	6.1	5.3	—	3.4	6.4	3.6	21.4	12.7
	M5	210.6 (3453)	6.1	5.3	—	2.6	6.4	4.0	16.6	12.7
	M6	210.6 (3453)	6.1	5.3	—	2.6	6.4	4.0	16.6	12.7

① With chrome plated guide tube for dipstick: 4.25
② With chrome plated guide tube for dipstick: 4.0

CRANKSHAFT AND CONNECTING ROD SPECIFICATIONS

All measurements are given in inches.

Year	Engine Displacement cu. in. (cc)	Crankshaft Main Brg. Journal Dia.	Main Brg. Oil Clearance	Shaft End-play	Thrust on No.	Connecting Rod Journal Diameter	Oil Clearance	Side Clearance
1981	108 (1766)	2.3622	0.0012–0.0027	0.003–0.007	3	1.8898 ②	①	0.016
	170 (2788)	2.3622	0.0012–0.0027	0.003–0.007	4	1.8898 ②	①	0.0016
	196 (3210)	2.3622	0.0012–0.0027	0.003–0.007	4	1.8898 ②	①	0.0016
1982	108 (1766)	2.3622	0.0012–0.0027	0.003–0.007	3	1.8898 ②	①	0.0016
	165 (2693)	2.3622	0.0012–0.0027	0.003–0.007	4	1.8898 ②	①	0.0016
	196 (3210)	2.3622	0.0012–0.0027	0.003–0.007	4	1.8898 ②	①	0.0016
1983	108 (1766)	2.3622	0.0012–0.0027	0.003–0.007	3	1.8898 ②	0.0012–0.0028	0.0016
	165 (2693)	2.3622	0.0012–0.0027	0.003–0.007	4	1.7717	0.0012–0.0028	0.0016
	196 (3210)	2.3622	0.0012–0.0027	0.003–0.007	4	1.8898 ②	0.0012–0.0028	0.0016
1984	108 (1766)	2.1654	0.0012–0.0027	0.003–0.007	3	1.8898 ②	0.0012–0.0028	0.0016
	165 (2693)	2.3622	0.0012–0.0027	0.003–0.007	4	1.7717	0.0012–0.0028	0.0016
	196 (3210)	2.3622	0.0012–0.0027	0.003–0.007	4	1.8898 ②	0.0012–0.0028	0.0016
1985	108 (1766)	2.1654	0.0012–0.0027	0.003–0.007	3	1.8898 ②	0.0012–0.0028	0.0016
	149 (2443)	②	0.0008–0.0018	0.0031–0.0064	4	1.7707–1.7713	0.0008–0.0022	—
	165 (2693)	2.3622	0.0012–0.0027	0.003–0.007	4	1.7717	0.0012–0.0028	0.0016
	209 (3428)	2.3622	0.0012–0.0027	0.003–0.007	4	1.8898 ②	0.0012–0.0028	0.0016
1986	149 (2443)	②	0.0008–0.0018	0.0031–0.0064	4	1.7707–1.7713	0.0008–0.0022	0.0016
	165 (2693)	2.3622	0.0012–0.0027	0.003–0.007	4	1.7717	0.0012–0.0028	0.0016
	209 (3428)	2.3622	0.0012–0.0027	0.003–0.007	4	1.8898 ②	0.0012–0.0028	0.0016
1987–88	152 (2494)	2.3622	0.0012–0.0027	0.003–0.007	4	1.8898 ②	0.0012–0.0028	0.0016
	165 (2693)	2.3622	0.0012–0.0027	0.003–0.007	4	1.7717	0.0012–0.0028	0.0016
	209 (3428)	2.3622	0.0012–0.0027	0.003–0.007	4	1.8898 ②	0.0012–0.0028	0.0016
	210.6 (3453)	2.3622	0.0012–0.0027	0.003–0.007	4	1.8898 ②	0.0012–0.0028	0.0016

① 528i, 530i, 533i, 630CSi, and 633CSi: 0.0009–0.0027; 320i, 733i: 0.0009–0.0031; 528e: 0.0013–0.0027
② Yellow: 2.3616–2.3618
   Green: 2.3613–2.3615
   White: 2.3611–2.3613

PISTON AND RING SPECIFICATIONS

All measurements are given in inches.

Year	Engine Displacement cu. in. (cc)	Piston Clearance	Ring Gap			Ring Side Clearance		
			Top Compression	Bottom Compression	Oil Control	Top Compression	Bottom Compression	Oil Control
1981	108 (1766)	0.0018	0.0120–0.0180	0.0080–0.0160	0.0100–0.0200	0.002–0.004	0.002–0.003	0.001-0.002
	170 (2788)	0.0018	0.0120–0.0180	0.0120–0.0200	0.0100–0.0200	0.0024–0.0036	0.0012–0.0024	0.0008-0.0020
	196 (3210)	0.0018	0.0120–0.0200	0.0080–0.0160	0.0024–0.0036	②	①	—
1982	108 (1766)	0.0018	0.0120–0.0180	0.0080–0.0160	0.0100–0.0200	0.002–0.004	0.002–0.003	0.001-0.002
	165 (2693)	0.0004–0.0016	0.0120–0.0200	0.0120–0.0200	0.0100–0.0200	0.0016–0.0028	0.0012–0.0024	0.0008-0.0017
	196 (3210)	0.0018	0.0120–0.0200	0.0080–0.0160	0.0024–0.0036	②	①	—
1983	108 (1766)	0.0018	0.0120–0.0180	0.0080–0.0160	0.0100–0.0200	0.002–0.004	0.002–0.003	0.001-0.002
	165 (2693)	0.0004–0.0016	0.0120–0.0200	0.0120–0.0200	0.0100–0.0200	0.0016–0.0028	0.0012–0.0024	0.0008-0.0017
	196 (3210)	0.0008–0.0020	0.0120–0.0280	0.0080–0.0160	0.0100–0.0200	0.0020–0.0032	0.0016–0.0028	0.0008-0.0028
1984	108 (1766)	0.0008–0.0020	0.0120–0.0280	0.0080–0.0160	0.0100–0.0200	0.0024–0.0035	0.0012–0.0028	0.0008-0.0024
	165 (2693)	0.0004–0.0016	0.0120–0.0200	0.0120–0.0200	0.0100–0.0200	0.0016–0.0028	0.0012–0.0024	0.0008-0.0017
	196 (3210)	0.0008–0.0020	0.0120–0.0280	0.0080–0.0160	0.0100–0.0200	0.0020–0.0032	0.0016–0.0028	0.0008-0.0028
1985	108 (1766)	0.0008–0.0020	0.0120–0.0280	0.0080–0.0160	0.0100–0.0200	0.0024–0.0035	0.0012–0.0028	0.0008-0.0024
	149 (2443)	0.0010–0.0013	0.0008–0.0016	0.0080–0.0160	0.0100–0.0200	0.0024–0.0025	0.0020–0.0031	0.0012-0.0024
	165 (2693)	0.0004–0.0016	0.0120–0.0200	0.0120–0.0200	0.0100–0.0200	0.0016–0.0028	0.0012–0.0024	0.0008-0.0017
	209 (3428)	0.0008–0.0020	0.0120–0.0020	0.0080–0.0160	0.0100–0.0200	0.020–0.032	0.0016–0.0028	0.0008-0.0020
1986	149 (2443)	0.0008–0.0020	0.0120–0.0200	0.0080–0.0160	0.0100–0.0200	0.020–0.032	0.0016–0.0028	0.0008-0.0020
	165 (2693)	0.0004–0.0016	0.0120–0.0200	0.0120–0.0200	0.0100–0.0200	0.0016–0.0028	0.0012–0.0024	0.0008-0.0017
	209 (3428)	0.0008–0.0020	0.0120–0.0200	0.0080–0.0160	0.0100–0.0200	0.020–0.032	0.0016–0.0028	0.0008-0.0020
1987-88	165 (2693)	0.0004–0.0016	0.0120–0.0200	0.0120–0.0200	0.0100–0.0200	0.0016–0.0028	0.0012–0.0024	0.0008-0.0017
	152 (2494)	0.0004–0.0016	0.0120–0.0200	0.0120–0.0200	0.0100–0.0200	0.0016–0.0028	0.0012–0.0024	0.0008-0.0017
	209 (3428)	0.0008–0.0020	0.0120–0.0200	0.0080–0.0160	0.0100–0.0200	0.020–0.032	0.0016–0.0028	0.0008-0.0020
	210.6 (3453)	0.0012–0.0024	0.0120–0.0220	0.0120–0.0220	0.0100–0.0200	0.0024–0.0035	0.0024–0.0035	0.0008-0.0020

① Mahle: 0008–.0020
 KS: .0012–.0024
② Mahle: .0020–.0032
 KS: .0016-.0028

VALVE SPECIFICATIONS

Year	Engine Displacement cu. in. (cc)	Seat Angle (deg.)	Face Angle (deg.)	Spring Test Pressure (lbs.)	Spring Installed Height (in.)	Stem-to-Guide Clearance (in.)		Stem Diameter (in.)	
						Intake	Exhaust	Intake	Exhaust
1981	108 (1766)	45	45.5	64 @ 1.48	1.71 ①	0.0010–0.0020 ②	0.0010–0.0020 ②	0.3149	0.3149
	170 (2788)	45	45.5	64 @ 1.48	1.71 ①	0.0010–0.0020 ②	0.0010–0.0020 ②	0.3149	0.3149
	196 (3210)	45	45.5	64 @ 1.48	1.71 ①	0.0010–0.0020 ②	0.0010–0.0020 ②	0.3149	0.3149
1982	108 (1766)	45	45.5	64 @ 1.48	1.71 ①	0.0010–0.0020 ②	0.0010–0.0020 ②	0.3149	0.3149
	165 (2693)	45	45	NA	NA	0.006	0.006	0.275	0.275
	196 (3210)	45	45.5	64 @ 1.48	1.71 ①	0.0010–0.0020 ②	0.0010–0.0020 ②	0.3149	0.3149
1983	108 (1766)	45	45.5	64 @ 1.48	1.71 ①	0.0010–0.0020 ②	0.0010–0.0020 ②	0.3149	0.3149
	165 (2693)	45	45	NA	NA	0.031 ③	0.031 ③	0.3149	0.3149
	196 (3210)	45	45.5	64 @ 1.48	1.71 ①	0.031 ③	0.031 ③	0.3149	0.3149
1984	108 (1766)	45	45.5	64 @ 1.48	1.71 ①	0.031 ③	0.031 ③	0.3149	0.3149
	165 (2693)	45	45	NA	NA	0.031 ③	0.031 ③	0.275	0.275
	196 (3210)	45	45.5	64 @ 1.48	1.71 ①	0.031 ③	0.031 ③	0.3149	0.3149
1985	108 (1766)	45	45.5	64 @ 1.48	1.71 ①	0.031 ③	0.031 ③	0.3149	0.3149
	149 (2443)	45	NA	NA	NA	0.031 ③	0.031 ③	0.275	0.275
	165 (2693)	45	45	NA	NA	0.031 ③	0.031 ③	0.275	0.275
	209 (3428)	45	45.5	64 @ 1.48	1.71 ①	0.031 ③	0.031 ③	0.3149	0.3149
1986	149 (2443)	45	NA	NA	NA	0.031 ③	0.031 ③	0.275	0.275
	165 (2693)	45	45	NA	NA	0.031 ③	0.031 ③	0.275	0.275
	209 (3428)	45	45.5	64 @ 1.48	1.71 ①	0.031 ③	0.031 ③	0.3149	0.3149
1987–88	152 (2494)	45	45.5	64 @ 1.48	1.71 ①	0.031 ③	0.031 ③	0.3149	0.3149
	165 (2693)	45	45	NA	NA	0.031 ③	0.031 ③	0.275	0.275
	209 (3428)	45	45.5	64 @ 1.48	1.71 ①	0.031 ③	0.031 ③	0.3149	0.3149
	210.6 (3453)	45	NA	NA	NA	0.025 ③	0.031 ③	0.276	0.276

① A dimension of 1.8110 applies to some springs, depending upon manufacturer. Figure given is free height.
② Wear limit: .006 in.
③ Tilt clearance

TORQUE SPECIFICATIONS

All readings in ft. lbs.

Year	Engine Displacement cu. in. (cc)	Cylinder Head Bolts	Main Bearing Bolts	Rod Bearing Bolts	Crankshaft Pulley Bolts	Flywheel Bolts	Manifold		Spark Plugs
							Intake	Exhaust	
1981	108 (1766)	①	42–46	38–41	101–108	72–83	15–20	22–24	18–22
	170 (2788)	①	42–46	38–41	②	72–83	—	22–24	18–22
	196 (3210)	①	42–46	38–41	②	72–83	—	22–24	18–22
1982	108 (1766)	①	42–46	38–41	101–108	72–83	15–20	22–24	18–22
	165 (2693)	③	43–48	14	282–311	71–82	—	22–24	18–22
	196 (3210)	①	42–46	38–41	②	72–83	—	22–24	18–22
1983	108 (1766)	①	42–46	38–41	101–108	72–83	15–20	22–24	15–21
	165 (2693)	⑤	42–45 ⑫	⑨	283–311	71–81	22–24	22–24	15–21
	196 (3210)	④	42–46	38–41	318–333	75–83 ⑦	16–17	22–24	15–21
1984	108 (1766)	⑩	42–46	38–41	130–145	71–81 ⑦	22–24	22–24	15–21
	165 (2693)	⑤	42–45 ⑫	⑨	283–311	71–81	22–24	22–24	15–21
	196 (3210)	④	42–46	38–41	318–333	75–83 ⑦	16–17	22–24	15–21

TORQUE SPECIFICATIONS

All readings in ft. lbs.

Year	Engine Displacement cu. in. (cc)	Cylinder Head Bolts	Main Bearing Bolts	Rod Bearing Bolts	Crankshaft Pulley Bolts	Flywheel Bolts	Manifold Intake	Manifold Exhaust	Spark Plugs
1985	108 (1766)	⑩	42–46	38–41	103–145	71–81 ⑦	22–24	22–24	15–21
	149 (2443)	⑧	44–49 ⑫	⑨	283–311	71–81	14–17	14–17	—
	165 (2693)	⑤	42–45 ⑫	⑨	283–311	71–81	22–24	22–24	15–21
	196 (3210)	④	42–46	38–41	318–333	75–83 ⑦	16–17	22–24	15–21
	209 (3428)	⑪	42–45 ⑫	38–41	311–325	71–81	22–24	22–24	15–21
1986	149 (2443)	⑧	44–49 ⑫	⑨	283–311	71–81	14–17	14–17	—
	165 (2693)	⑤	42–45 ⑫	⑨	283–311	71–81	22–24	22–24	15–21
	209 (3428)	⑪	42–45 ⑫	38–41	311–325	71–81	22–24	22–24	15–21
1987	209 (3428)	⑪	42–45 ⑫	38–41	311–325	71–81	22–24	22–24	15–21
1987–88	152 (2494)	⑪	42–45 ⑫	⑨	283–311	71–81	22–24	22–24	15–21
	165 (2693)	⑤	42–45 ⑫	⑨	283–311	71–81	22–24	22–24	15–21
	210.6 (3453)	⑬	14.5–17.5 ⑫	⑭	311–325	71–81	14–17	6.5–7	15–21

• Install with Loctite®

① 320i, 528i, 633CSi & 733i '79–'80
Step 1—25–32
2—49–52
3—56–59
4—56–59 (after warm-up)
633CSi & 733i—'81–'82
Step 1—25–32
2—49–51
3—54–59
4—20–30 degrees (after warm-up)

② Flat hex nut: 174–188
Shoulder hex nut: 318–333

③ Step 1—22–25
2—43–47

④ Step 1—25–29
2—42–45
Wait 20 minutes
3—56–59
4—20°–30°

⑤ Step 1—29–33
Wait 20 minutes
2—43–47
Warm engine fully
3—20°–30°

⑥ Then turn additional 70°

⑦ First coat w/Loctite® 270 or equivalent

⑧ Step 1—50–60
Wait 15 minutes

Step 2—70–76
Run engine hot—25 minutes
Step 3—Turn 85°–95° angle torque
Crossbolts—28–34

⑨ Torque to 14 ft. lbs.
Turn 70° angle torque

⑩ Step 1—42–44
Wait 15 minutes
Step 2—30°–36° angle torque
Run engine warm—25 minutes
Step 3—20°–30° angle torque

⑪ Step 1—42–44
Wait 15 minutes
Step 2—30–36
Run engine warm—25 minutes
Step 3—30°–40° angle torque

⑫ Step 1—Torque to figure shown
Step 2—Turn 47°–53° angle torque

⑬ Step 1—35–37
Step 2—57–59
Wait 15 minutes
Step 3—71–73

⑭ Step 1—7
Step 2—21.5
Step 3—60°–62° angle torque

BRAKE SPECIFICATIONS

All measurements in inches unless noted

Year	Model	Lug Nut Torque (ft. lbs.)	Master Cylinder Bore	Brake Disc Minimum Thickness	Brake Disc Maximum Runout	Standard Brake Drum Diameter	Minimum Lining Thickness Front	Minimum Lining Thickness Rear
1981	320i	59–65	.812	.827	0.008	10.04	—	—
	528i	59–65	.956	.840F/.340R	0.008	—	—	—
	633CSi	65–79	.936	.840F ①/.720R	0.008	—	—	—
	733i	65–79	.874	.840F ①/.360R	0.008	—	—	—
1982	320i	59–65	.812	.827	0.008	10.04	—	—
	633CSi	65–79	.936	.840F ①/.720R	0.008	—	—	—
	733i	65–79	.874	.840F ①/.360R	0.008	—	—	—

BRAKE SPECIFICATIONS
All measurements in inches unless noted

Year	Model	Lug Nut Torque (ft. lbs.)	Master Cylinder Bore	Brake Disc Minimum Thickness	Brake Disc Maximum Runout	Standard Break Drum Diameter	Minimum Lining Thickness Front	Minimum Lining Thickness Rear
1983	320i	59–65	.812	.827	0.008	10.04	—	—
	533i	65–79	—	.787	0.008	—	0.079	0.079
	633CSi	65–79	—	.906F/.315R	0.008	—	0.079	0.079
	733i	65–79	—	.906F/.315R	0.008	—	0.079	0.079
1984	318i	65–79	—	.421	0.008	9.035	0.079	0.059
	533i	65–79	—	.787	0.008	—	0.079	0.079
	633CSi	65–79	—	.906F/.315R	0.008	—	0.079	0.079
	733i	65–79	—	.906F/.315R	0.008	—	0.079	0.079
1985	318i	65–79	—	.421	0.008	9.035	0.079	0.059
	325e	65–79	—	.421	0.008	—	0.079	0.079
	528e	65–79	—	.787F/.315R	0.008	—	0.079	0.079
	524td	65–79	—	.787F/.315R	0.008	—	0.079	0.079
	535i, 635CSi	65–79	—	.906F/.315R	0.008	—	0.079	0.079
	735i	65–79	—	.906F/.315R	0.008	—	0.079	0.079
1986	325e	65–79	—	.421	0.008	—	0.079	0.079
	528e	65–79	—	.787F/.315R	0.008	—	0.079	0.079
	524td	65–79	—	.787F/.315R	0.008	—	0.079	0.079
	535i, 635CSi	65–79	—	.906F/.315R	0.008	—	0.079	0.079
	735i	65–79	—	.906F/.315R	0.008	—	0.079	0.079
1987–88	325i, is	65–79	—	.421	0.008	—	0.077	0.079
	528e	65–79	—	.787F/.315R	0.008	—	0.079	0.079
	535i, 635CSi	65–79	—	.906F/.315R	0.008	—	0.079	0.079
	735i	65–79	—	.906F/.315R	0.008	—	0.079	0.079
	M5	65–79	—	1.102F/.315R	0.008	—	0.079	0.079
	M6	65–79	—	.906F/.315R	0.008	—	0.079	0.079

F Front
R Rear
① 1984 Models—.9213F

WHEEL ALIGNMENT

Year	Model	Caster Range (deg.)	Caster Preferred Setting (deg.)	Camber Range (deg.)	Camber Preferred Setting (deg.)	Toe-in (in.)	Steering Axis Inclination (deg.)
1981	320i (F)	—	$8^5/_{16}$P	—	0	$1/_{16}$	$10^5/_{16}$P
	(R)	—	—	—	2N	$1/_{32}$P	—
	528i (F)	—	$7^{11}/_{16}$P	—	0	$1/_{16}$	$8^1/_2$P
	(R)	—	—	—	2N	$5/_{64}$P	—
	633CSi (F)	—	$7^2/_3$P	—	0	.060	8P
	(R)	—	—	—	2N	.080	—
	733i (F)	—	9P	—	0	$3/_{64}$P	$11^9/_{16}$
	(R)	—	—	—	$1^1/_2$N	$3/_{16}$P	—

WHEEL ALIGNMENT

Year	Model	Caster Range (deg.)	Caster Preferred Setting (deg.)	Camber Range (deg.)	Camber Preferred Setting (deg.)	Toe-in (in.)	Steering Axis Inclination (deg.)
1982	320i (F)	—	$8\frac{5}{16}$P	—	0	$\frac{1}{16}$	$10\frac{5}{16}$P
	(R)	—	$8\frac{5}{16}$P	—	0	$\frac{1}{16}$	$10\frac{5}{16}$P
	633CSi (F)	—	$7\frac{2}{3}$P	—	0	.060	8P
	(R)	—	—	—	2N	.080	—
	733i (F)	—	9P	—	0	$\frac{3}{64}$P	$11\frac{9}{16}$
	(R)	—	—	—	$1\frac{1}{2}$N	$\frac{3}{16}$P	—
1983	320i (F)	—	$8\frac{5}{16}$P	—	0	$\frac{1}{16}$	$10\frac{5}{16}$P
	(R)	—	—	—	2N	$\frac{1}{32}$P	—
	633CSi (F)	—	$8\frac{1}{4}$P	—	$\frac{5}{16}$N	$\frac{5}{64}$P	$12\frac{3}{16}$P
	(R)	—	—	—	$2\frac{5}{16}$N	$\frac{5}{64}$P	—
	733i (F)	—	$8\frac{1}{4}$P	—	$\frac{1}{3}$N	.078	$12\frac{2}{15}$P
	(R)	—	—	—	2N	.08	—
1984	318i (F)	$8\frac{1}{4}$P–$9\frac{1}{4}$P	$8\frac{3}{4}$P	$1\frac{1}{10}$N-$\frac{1}{10}$N	$\frac{2}{3}$N	0.079 ①	$13\frac{2}{3}$P
	(R)	—	—	—	$1\frac{13}{16}$N	0.079 ①	—
	528e, 533i (F)	$7\frac{3}{4}$P-$8\frac{3}{4}$P	$8\frac{1}{4}$P	$\frac{1}{2}$N-$\frac{1}{10}$P	$\frac{1}{3}$N	$\frac{3}{32}$P	$12\frac{3}{16}$P
	(R)	—	—	—	2N	$\frac{3}{32}$P	—
	633CSi (F)	—	$8\frac{1}{4}$P	—	$\frac{5}{16}$N	$\frac{5}{64}$P	$12\frac{3}{16}$P
	(R)	—	—	—	$2\frac{5}{16}$N	$\frac{5}{64}$P	—
	733i (F)	9P-10P	$9\frac{1}{2}$P	$\frac{1}{2}$N-$\frac{1}{12}$P	0	$\frac{1}{2}$	$11\frac{1}{3}$P
	(R)	—	—	—	2N	$\frac{3}{32}$P	—
1985	318i (F)	$8\frac{1}{4}$P-$9\frac{1}{4}$P	$8\frac{3}{4}$P	$1\frac{1}{10}$N-$\frac{1}{10}$N	$\frac{2}{3}$N	0.079 ①	$13\frac{2}{3}$P
	(R)	—	—	—	$1\frac{13}{16}$N	0.079 ①	—
	325e (F)	$8\frac{1}{4}$P-$9\frac{1}{4}$P	$8\frac{3}{4}$P	$1\frac{1}{10}$N-$\frac{1}{10}$N	$\frac{2}{3}$N	0.079 ①	$13\frac{2}{3}$P
	(R)	—	—	—	$1\frac{13}{16}$N	0.079 ①	—
	528e, 533i (F)	$7\frac{3}{4}$P-$8\frac{3}{4}$P	$8\frac{1}{4}$P	$\frac{1}{2}$N-$\frac{1}{10}$P	$\frac{1}{3}$N	$\frac{3}{32}$P	$12\frac{3}{16}$P
	(R)	—	—	—	2N	$\frac{3}{32}$P	—
	635CSi (F)	$7\frac{3}{4}$P-$8\frac{3}{4}$P	$8\frac{1}{4}$P	$\frac{1}{2}$N-$\frac{1}{10}$P	$\frac{1}{3}$N	0.079 ①	$12\frac{3}{16}$P
	(R)	—	—	—	$2\frac{1}{3}$N	0.079 ①	—
	735i (F)	9P-10P	$9\frac{1}{2}$P	$\frac{1}{2}$N-$\frac{1}{2}$P	0	0.020 ②	$11\frac{1}{3}$P
	(R)	—	—	—	$2\frac{1}{3}$N	0.079 ①	—
1986	325e (F)	$8\frac{1}{4}$P-$9\frac{1}{4}$P	$8\frac{3}{4}$P	$1\frac{1}{10}$N-$\frac{1}{10}$N	$\frac{2}{3}$N	0.079 ①	$13\frac{2}{3}$P
	(R)	—	—	—	$1\frac{13}{16}$N	0.079 ①	—
	528e, 535i (F)	$7\frac{3}{4}$P-$8\frac{3}{4}$P	$8\frac{1}{4}$P	$\frac{1}{2}$N-$\frac{1}{10}$P	$\frac{1}{3}$N	0.079 ①	$12\frac{3}{16}$P
	(R)	—	—	—	$2\frac{1}{3}$N	0.079 ①	—
	635CSi (F)	$7\frac{3}{4}$P-$8\frac{3}{4}$P	$8\frac{1}{4}$P	$\frac{1}{2}$N-$\frac{1}{10}$P	$\frac{1}{3}$N	0.079 ①	$12\frac{3}{16}$P
	(R)	—	—	—	$2\frac{1}{3}$N	0.079 ①	—
	735i (F)	9P-10P	$9\frac{1}{2}$P	$\frac{1}{2}$N-$\frac{1}{2}$P	0	0.020 ②	$11\frac{1}{3}$P
	(R)	—	—	—	$2\frac{1}{3}$N	0.079 ①	—
1987-88	325e (F)	$8\frac{1}{4}$P-$9\frac{1}{4}$P	$8\frac{3}{4}$P	$1\frac{1}{10}$N-$\frac{1}{10}$N	$\frac{2}{3}$N	0.079 ①	$13\frac{2}{3}$P
	(R)	—	—	—	$1\frac{13}{16}$N	0.079 ①	—
	528e, 535i (F)	$7\frac{3}{4}$P-$8\frac{3}{4}$P	$8\frac{1}{4}$P	$\frac{1}{2}$N-$\frac{1}{10}$P	$\frac{1}{3}$N	0.079 ①	$12\frac{3}{16}$P
	(R)	—	—	—	$2\frac{1}{3}$N	0.079 ①	—

WHEEL ALIGNMENT

Year	Model		Caster Range (deg.)	Caster Preferred Setting (deg.)	Camber Range (deg.)	Camber Preferred Setting (deg.)	Toe-in (in.)	Steering Axis Inclination (deg.)
1987-88	635CSi	(F)	$7^3/_4$P-$8^3/_4$P	$8^1/_4$P	$^1/_2$N-$^1/_{10}$P	$^1/_3$N	0.079 ①	$12^3/_{16}$P
		(R)	—	—	—	$2^1/_3$N	0.079 ①	—
	735i	(F)	9P-10P	$9^1/_2$P	$^1/_2$N-$^1/_2$P	0	0.020 ②	$11^1/_3$P
		(R)	—	—	—	$2^1/_3$N	0.079 ①	—
	M5, M6	(F)	$7^3/_4$P-$8^3/_4$P	$8^1/_4$P	$^1/_2$N-$^1/_{10}$P	$^1/_3$N	0.079 ①	$12^3/_{16}$P
		(R)	—	—	—	$1^{13}/_{16}$N	0.079 ①	—

All 300, 500 and 700 series models aligned with 150 lbs. in each front seat, 150 lbs. in rear seat and 46 lbs. in trunk.

All 600 series models aligned with 150 lbs. in each front seat and 30 lbs. in trunk on left side.
① 14P—1986 and later models
F Front
R Rear
N Negative
P Positive
① .083 with TRX Tires
② .024 with TRX Tires

TUNE-UP PROCEDURES

Electronic Ignition

AIR GAP ADJUSTMENT

Breaker points and condensers are not used with the electronic ignition. The air gap between the rotating teeth and the stator teeth can be checked with a brass or plastic feeler gauge. This is not required on 1984-88 models. No adjustment is possible. If the gap is not 0.012–0.028 in., the unit should be replaced.

--- CAUTION ---
All repair work to the electronic ignition system should be done with the engine stopped and the ignition switch Off.

For 1982-88, some models are equipped with a Motronic engine control system. This system uses various engine sensors including an oxygen sensor in the exhaust to monitor engine conditions. The monitored information is fed to a Motronic (computer) unit, which in turn controls the air/fuel mixture entering the engine.

Ignition Timing

ADJUSTMENT

The engine should be at normal operating temperature. Adjust the idle speed (except on cars with Motronic injection. See below). Remove and plug distributor vacuum lines. Connect a timing light to the No. 1 spark plug wire and start the engine. Align the marks on the flywheel with the bell housing indicator, by rotating the distributor body. Tighten the distributor body clamp.

2. Circlip   3. Expander

Measuring rotor to stator clearance (A)

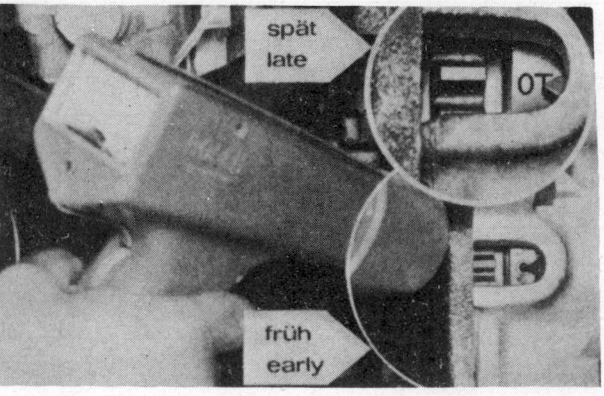

Ignition timing marks at flywheel

NOTE: The flywheel mark is either a pressed-in steel ball or a long tapered peg on the side of the starter ring gear.

On cars with the Motronic control unit, you can check the timing in a fairly straightforward manner; however, timing cannot be adjusted. The only cure for improper timing is to replace the control unit. Also, timing must be within a specified range, as the computer changes the timing slightly to allow for various changes in operating condition. In other words, the timing does not have to be right on, but anywhere within the specified range.

The engine should be at normal operating temperature and the operation should be performed at normal room temperatures. The engine rpm should be within the specified range under the control of the computer.

Look up the control unit number on the unit itself. On 3, 5, and 6 Series cars, the unit is in the glove box; on the 7 Series, it is in the right side speaker cutout. Find the control unit number on the underside of unit and then reference that number on the Computer Controlled Ignition Timing Chart.

Then connect a tachometer and a timing light to the engine (the latter to the No. 1 cylinder). Start the engine and check the rpm. If it is not correct, see the appropriate checks under Idle Speed and Mixture Adjustment below. Then, operate the timing light to see if timing is within the range specified on the chart. If it is significantly outside the range, the Motronic control unit must be replaced.

Valve Lash

ADJUSTMENT

Gasoline Engines Except M5, M6

All BMW gasoline engines except the M series, dual overhead designs are equipped with an overhead camshaft operating the intake and exhaust valves through rocker arm linkage.

NOTE: The valves must be adjusted cold.

1. Remove the rocker cover.
2. Rotate the engine until the No. 1 cylinder is at TDC on the compression stroke.

NOTE: Locate No. 1 cylinder firing position by the distributor rotor-to-cap position, or by observing the valve action in the opposite cylinder. Refer to following charts:

COMPUTER CONTROLLED IGNITION TIMING CHART

Car/Model	Unit Number	RPM	Timing BTDC
325e	0261200021	650-750	4-12
325e	0261100007	650-750	6-12
528e	0261200007	650-750	4-12
528e	0261200021	650-750	6-12
	0261200027		
533i	0261200008	650-750	6-14
535i	0261200059	750-850	10-16
M5	0261200079	800-900	–3-3 ①
633CSi	0261200008	650-750	10-16
635CSi	0261200059	750-850	10-16
M6	0261200079	800-900	–3-3 ①
733i	0261200008	600-700	6-14
735i	0261200059	700-800	10-16

① That is — 3° after top dead center to 3° before top dead center

Cylinder Firing- Piston at TDC	Exhaust Valve Closing, Intake Valve Opening On Opposite Cylinder
6 CYLINDER	
1	6
5	2
3	4
6	1
2	5
4	3
4 CYLINDER	
1	4
3	2
4	1
2	3

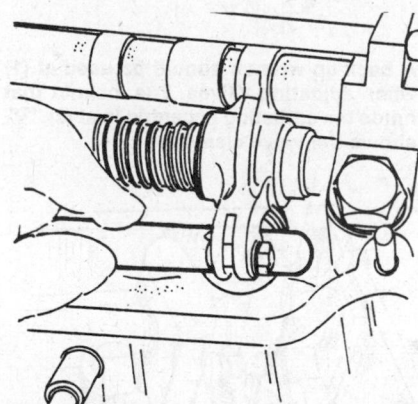

Checking valve clearance with a flat feeler gauge

3. Measure the valve clearance between the valve stem end and the rocker arm on the No. 1 cylinder (refer to the specifications for valve clearance).
4. Adjust the clearance by loosening the locknut on the rocker arm and turning the eccentric with a bent rod inserted through a hole provided on the surface of the eccentric.

5. When the proper clearance is obtained, tighten the locknut and recheck the valve clearance. Complete the adjustment on both valves.
6. Rotate the engine crankshaft to the next cylinder in the firing order, adjust the valves and repeat the procedures until all the valves are adjusted.
7. Replace the rocker cover, using a new gasket.

M5, M6

NOTE: To perform this procedure, you will need a special tool to depress the valves against spring pressure so you can gain access to the valve adjusting discs. Use BMW Tool 11 3 170 or equivalent. You will also need compressed air to lift valve adjusting discs that must be replaced out of the valve tappet, an assortment of adjusting discs of various thicknesses and a precise outside michrometer.

1. Make sure the engine is overnight cold. Remove the rocker cover.
2. Turn the engine until the No. 1 cylinder intake valve cams (The intake cam is labeled "A" on the head) are both straight up.
3. Then, slide a flat feeler gauge in between each of the cams and the adjacent valve tappet. Check to see if the clearance is within the specified range. If it is, proceed with checking the remaining clearances as described starting in Step 8. If not, switch gauges and measure the actual clearance. When you have the actual clearance, proceed with Steps 4–7.
4. Turn the tappets so the grooves machined into their edges are aligned as shown. Looking at the valves from the center of the engine, the right hand tappet's groove should be at about 5 O'Clock and the left hand tappet's groove should be at about 7 O'Clock. Use the end of the special

tool required for the camshaft involved—in this case the "A" or intake camshaft (the exhaust camshaft end is labeled "E" on the engine and tool). Slide the proper end of the tool, going from the center of the engine outward, under the cam, with the heel of the tool pivoting on the inner side of the camshaft valley. Force the handle downward until the handle rests on the protrusion on the center of the cylinder head.

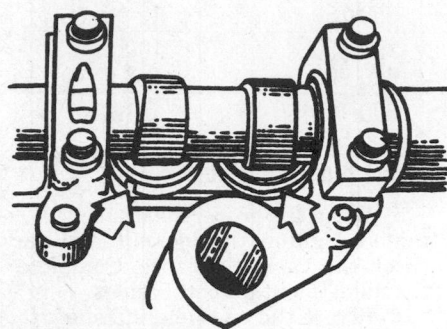

On M5 and M6 DOHC engines, rotate the valve tappets so the grooves machined in the tops are facing as shown before attempting to measure valve clearance

5. Use compressed air to pop the disc out of the tappet. Read the thickness dimension on the disc.

6. Determine the thickness required as follows:

If the valve clearance is too tight, subtract the actual, measured clearance from the minimum permissible clearance. For example, minimum clearance is 0.012 in., and let's say you measured the actual clearance as 0.010 in. If you subtract 0.010 from 0.012, the result is 0.002 in. Measure the dimension of the disc you removed with the michrometer. Since the required clearance is 0.012–0.014, you must find a disc whose thickness is 0.002–0.004 in. thinner than the disc you removed. Use michrometer measurements to find a disc of the required thickness.

If the valve clearance is too loose, subtract the maximum permissible clearance from the actual, measured clearance. For example, maximum clearance is 0.014 in., and let's say you measured the actual clearance as 0.016 in. If you subtract 0.014 from 0.016, the result is 0.002 in. Measure the dimension of the disc you removed. Since the required clearance is 0.012–0.014, you must find a disc whose thickness is 0.002–0.004 in. thicker than the disc you removed. Use michrometer measurements to find a disc of the required thickness.

7. Once you have determined the required thickness and found a disc within the specified range, slip that

disc into the tappet *with the letter facing downward*. Rock the valve spring depressing tool out and remove it. Then, recheck the clearance to make sure you calculated and measured correctly. Change the disc, if necessary.

8. Turn the engine in firing order sequence (1–5–3–6–2–4) turning the crankshaft forward ⅓ of a turn each time to get the intake cams to the upward position for each cylinder. Measure the clearance as in Step 3 and, if it is outside the specified range, follow Steps 4–7 to adjust either or both valves. Repeat this for all the intakes, and then turn the engine until No. 1 cylinder exhaust valves are upward.

9. Follow the same sequence for all the exhaust valves, going through the firing order, checking clearance as described in Step 3 and adjusting the valves as in Steps 4–7. Note that you must, however, use the opposite end of the special tool—the end marked "E" to depress the exhaust valves.

10. When all the clearances are in the specified range, replace the cam cover, start the engine, and check for leaks.

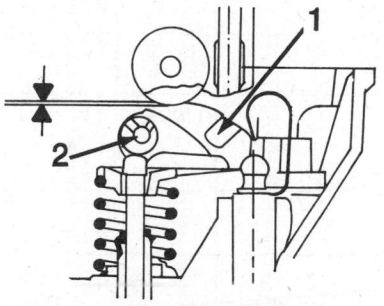

A back-up wrench should be used at (1) when adjusting valves. The locknut that holds the adjusting eccentric is at (2). "V" shows the valve clearance

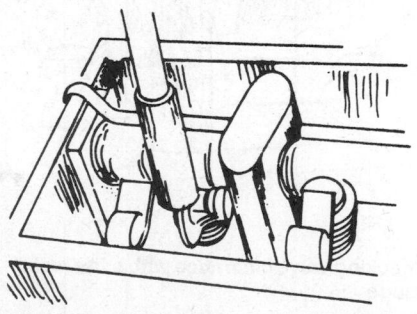

Tighten the adjusting nut with special tools 11 1 1809 and 00 2 050 or equivalent (525 td)

Diesel

1. Remove the rocker cover.
2. Rotate the engine (using a socket on the crankshaft pulley nut) until the No. 1 cylinder is at TDC on the fir-

ing stroke. Line up the timing marks and also ensure that both No. 1 cylinder valves are loose; if they are not, turn the engine 360 degrees.

3. Use the 12mm backup wrench on the nut shown in the illustration. Then, loosen the locknut. Slide a flat feeler gauge of the proper size (.012 in.) into the gap shown in the illustration. If it is necessary to change the clearance, rotate the eccentric, making sure the clearance is always taken up by turning the eccentric toward you or away from the centerline of the engine. Tighten the nut, and recheck the clearance, readjusting it if necessary. Repeat this step for the other valve on No. 1 cylinder.

4. Repeat the step above for each cylinder. Turn the engine ⅓ turn forward and adjust each cylinder in the firing order of 1–5–3–6–2–4.

5. Replace the valve rocker cover.

Idle Speed and Mixture Gasoline Engines

ADJUSTMENT

NOTE: The idle speed and mixture can be adjusted ONLY with the aid of a CO meter. If you do not have access to this tool, do not attempt any of the following procedures. The idle mixture can be adjusted ONLY with the aid of a CO meter on most models; on the 318i, it can be adjusted ONLY with a BMW digital mixture adjustment unit 12 6 400. Idle speed is not adjustable on any model with the Motronic control unit except the M5 and M6. If idle speed is incorrect, either the idle valve or the idle control unit must be replaced. See the fuel injection unit repair section.

Note that several special tools are required to drill out the anti-tamper plug for the adjustment screw and to turn the adjustment screw. You should get a new anti-tamper plug before beginning work.

318i

1. The engine must be run until is is at operating temperature. Ignition timing and valve clearances must be correct. Connect the BMW digital mixture measurement unit 12 6 400 or equivalent according to the instrument instructions. Disconnect the hose going to the active carbon filter on the throttle housing and do not plug the open connections.

2. Operate the engine at least 3000 rpm for at least 30 seconds to ensure that the oxygen sensor is at operating temperature.

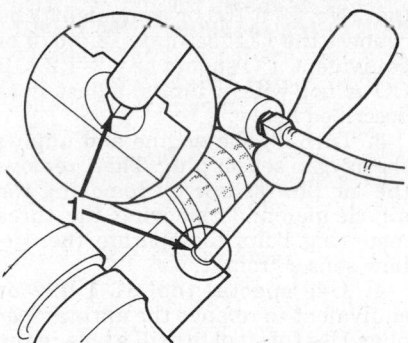

Drilling the anti-tamper plug on the 318i

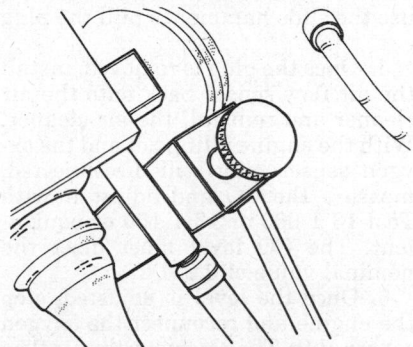

Special tool adjusting the CO on 318i

Idle speed screw location—320i

Adjusting of engine valve clearance with bent rod after loosening the locknut (1)

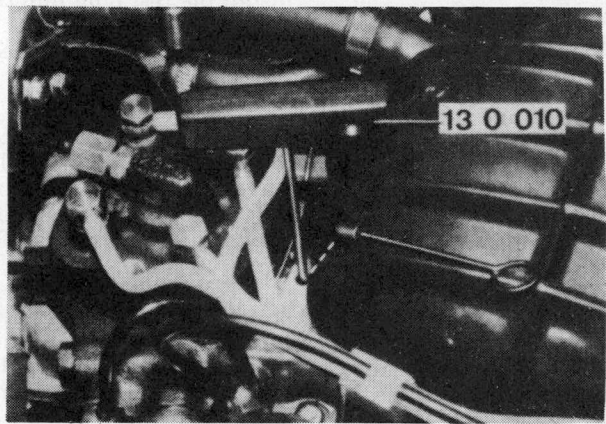

Adjusting CO level with special tool. Hole plug shown—320i

Remove plug (3) and use special tool 13-1-060 or equivalent to adjust the CO level with the screw in the bottom of the air intake sensor—530i, 528i, 528e, 630CSi, 633CSi and 733i

3. Disconnect the oxygen sensor wire, and fasten it where it cannot touch a ground. The nominal value you will be looking for will now appear in the test unit's display. Make note of it and then reconnect the oxygen sensor into the test unit. The actual value will appear in the display. If the actual value is within plug or minus 0.3 volt of the nominal value, CO is within tolerance. If not, proceed as follows.

4. Drill a hole through the tamper plug with a special tool 13 1 092 or equivalent. Then screw special tool 13 1 094 or equivalent into the plug, and use the slide hammer on the tool to draw the plug out.

5. Use a special tool 13 1 060 to turn the adjusting screw to bring the actual valve to within 0.3 volt of the nominal value plug or minus. Turn off the engine, disconnect the test unit and reconnect the oxygen sensor wire to the oxygen sensor. Replace the anti-tamper plug with a new one.

320i

1. Run the engine to normal operating temperature.

2. Adjust the engine idle speed with the screw located near the throttle-valve linkage.

3. Detach the exhaust check valve and plug the hose.

4. To adjust the CO, remove the plug from the fuel distributor and with a special wrench, adjust the CO level to a maximum of 2.0% for the 49 state vehicles or 3. 5% for California cars.

5. Reconnect the exhaust check valve hose and check the idle speed.

325, 325e, 325i and 325is

1. Disconnect the hose, leading from the throttle housing, that goes to the carbon canister. Do not plug the openings. Remove the bolts on either side of the exhaust manifold plug.

2. Remove the plug in the exhaust manifold, install the test nipple BMW part No. 13 0 100 or equivalent and connect the CO tester 13 0 070 or equivalent into the open nipple.

3. With the engine valve clearances correctly adjusted, ignition timing correct and the engine at operating temperature, measure the CO percentage at idle speed. CO nominal value is 0.2–1.2%.

4. If the CO level is within the specified range, disconnect the test unit, replace the plug in the exhaust manifold, and conclude the test. If not, adjust the CO as described below.

5. Turn off the engine and then unplug the oxygen sensor plug. Drill a hole in the anti-tamper plug in the throttle body with special tool No. 13 1 092 or equivalent. Then screw the special extractor tool 13 1 094 or equivalent into the hole drilled into the plug and draw the plug out with the impact mass. Finally, use an adjustment tool 13 1 060 or 13 1 100 or equivalent to turn the adjustment, with the engine running, until the CO meets nominal values.

6. When the adjustment is complete, install a new anti-tamer plug, and reconnect the oxygen sensor plug and the carbon canister hose. Also, remove the nipple in the exhaust manifold and replace the plug. Reinstall the exhaust manifold bolts.

528i

1. Adjust the idle speed to the proper specifications. The idle screw is on the side of the throttle body housing. Turning it clockwise will decrease the idle and counterclockwise will increase it.

2. Remove the CO test plug at the rear of the exhaust manifold and connect a CO meter. Start the engine and run it until operating temperature is

reached. Measure the CO reading. CO must be 0.2–0.8% (by volume).

3. Disconnect the connector for the oxygen sensor from the wiring harness. The connector is on the right side of the firewall in the engine compartment. The CO value should not change.

4. If CO is not to specification, adjust the mixture by turning the adjusting screw, located low on the airflow meter. Adjust for 0.5% CO.

5. Reconnect the oxygen sensor and check CO again. If CO does not meet specification, have the car checked by someone professionally trained to troubleshoot the injection system.

6. Disconnect the test probe and reinstall the test plug into the exhaust manifold.

7. Recheck the idle speed.

528e

1. Pull the canister purge hose off the solenoid shown in the illustration, leaving the connections unplugged.

2. Connect the CO meter 13 0 070 or equivalent to the manifold via the nipple 13 0 100.

3. Follow Steps 3–6 of the procedure for the 325 above. All are identical including the CO nominal value. Remember to reconnect the canister purge hose to the solenoid when you have finished.

633CSi and 733i

1981

1. Run the engine to normal operating temperature.

2. Disconnect the throttle housing-to-activated carbon filter hose. Disconnect and plug the air hose at the air pump.

3. Adjust the idle speed to specifications with the idle adjusting screw, located in the side of the throttle housing.

4. Adjust the CO to 1.5–3.0% at idle. Remove the cap from the air flow sensor and with the aid of a special tool, or short screwdriver, turn the bypass air screw located in the air flow sensor, until the CO level is as specified.

5. Reconnect the 2 hoses.

533i, 535i, 633CSi, 635CSi, 733i, 735i

1983-88

1. Make sure the idle speed is correct. The engine must be hot. Disconnect the evaporative emissions canister purge hose at the bottom of the solenoid mounted on the firewall. Leave the openings unplugged.

2. Unscrew the bolts on the exhaust manifold and install a nipple

(part No. 13 0 100 or equivalent) and connect the CO test unit 13 0 070 or equivalent. CO should be 0.2–1.2%. If CO is not within limits, adjust it as described below.

3. Turn off the engine and unplug the oxygen sensor plug. Then, remove the air flow sensor by removing the air cleaner and removing the three mounting bolts to separate the airflow sensor from it.

4. Use special tool 13 1 092 or equivalent to remove the anti-tamper plug. Use this tool to drill a hole in the plug and then use 13 1 094 or equivalent to pull it. The second tool should be screwed into the hole you drilled; use the slide hammer to pull the plug out.

5. Once the plug is removed, install the air flow sensor back onto the air cleaner and reinstall the air cleaner. With the engine idling hot and the oxygen sensor plug still disconnected, measure the CO and adjust it with Tool 13 1 060 or 13 1 100 or equivalent. The CO level must meet the nominal value of 0.2–1.2%.

6. Once the level is adjusted, stop the engine and reconnect the oxygen sensor plug. Then, remove the air flow sensor, put it on a bench, and install a new anti-tamper plug. Reinstall the airflow sensor and air cleaner. Reconnect the canister purge hose to the solenoid.

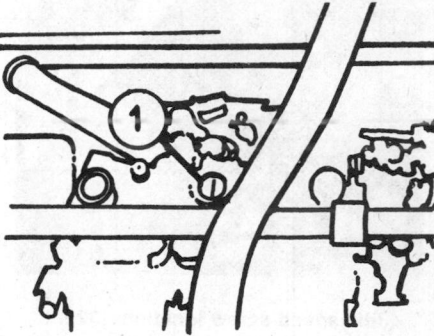

On the M5 and M6 engines, adjust idle speed by turning this screw (1)

M5 and M6

1. Make sure the engine is at operating temperature, and that the air cleaner is in reasonably clean condition. All basic engine tuning factors (spark plug condition and gap, valve adjustment, ignition timing, etc.) must be correct.

2. Adjust the idle speed by turning the screw shown in the illustration.

3. To adjust CO, first remove the cap located at the center of the top surface of the airflow sensor. Use a special tool 13 1 100 to turn the airflow control screw in the airflow sensor, accessible after the anti-tamper

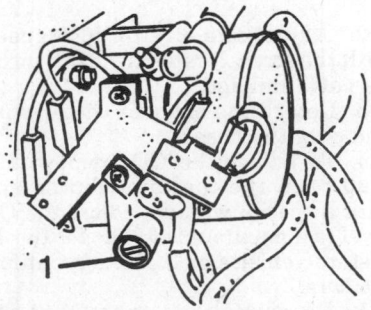

528i idle speed adjustment screw

cap is removed. CO must be 0.4–1.2%.

4. Install a new cap when CO meets specification.

Idle Speed Diesel Engines

ADJUSTMENT

1. Valve clearance must be correct. Run the engine until it reaches operating temperature. Make sure all electrical accessories are shut off. Check to make sure the throttle lever is resting on the idle adjusting screw. Shut the engine off.

2. Check the play between the throttle lever and the knurled screw. It should be 0.020–0.012 in. Hold the hexagonal nut associated with the screw with the knurled head, and then turn that screw until the play is correct.

3. Loosen the locknut (1) and turn the adjusting screw (2) to give the correct idle speed. Tighten the locknut.

4. Repeat the clearance check of Step 2. If not to specification, readjust the clearance as in Step 3. On cars with automatic transmission, check the distance from the linkage to the rear injection pump flange and adjust if necessary (see the section below covering transmission linkage adjustments).

ENGINE ELECTRICAL

Distributor

REMOVAL & INSTALLATION

4 Cylinder Engines

1. On all engines so equipped, remove the weather-proof rubber cap protecting the distributor cap and wires from moisture. Prior to removal, using paint, chalk or a sharp instrument, scribe alignment marks showing the relative position of the distributor body to its mount on the rear of the cylinder head.

2. Following the firing order illustration at the beginning of this section, mark each spark plug wire with a dab of paint or chalk noting its respective cylinder. It will be easier and faster to install the distributor and get the firing order right if you leave the plug wires in the cap.

3. Pull up and disconnect the secondary wire (high tension cable leading from the coil to the center of the distributor cap), and remove the spark plug loom retaining nut(s) from the cylinder head cover. Disconnect the vacuum line(s) from the vacuum advance unit.

4. Disconnect the primary wire (low tension wire running from one of the coil terminals to the side of the distributor) at the distributor. On electronic ignition distributors, disconnect the plug.

5. Unsnap the distributor retaining clasps and lift off the cap and wire assembly. On all engines equipped with a dust cap under the rotor, remove the rotor, remove the dust cap and reinstall the rotor.

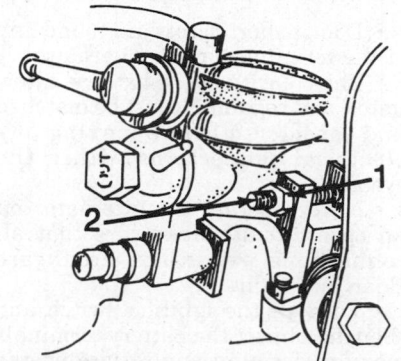

Loosen the locknut (1) and turn the adjusting screw (2) to adjust the idle on the diesel engine

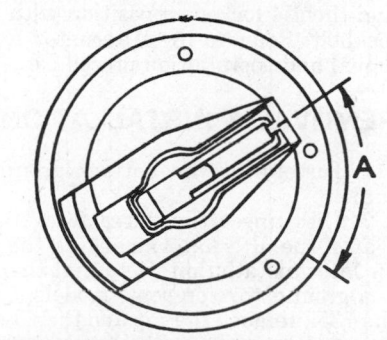

Check the play "S" between the knurled screw and the throttle lever (524 td)

Distance (A) rotor moves from the housing mark during the removal of the electronic distributor

6. Now, with the aid of a remote starter switch or a friend, "bump" the starter a few times until the No. 1 piston is at Top Dead Center (TDC) of its compression stroke. At this time, the notch scribed on the metal tip of the distributor rotor must be aligned with a corresponding notch scribed on the distributor case. Before removing the distributor, make sure that these two marks coincide as per the illustration.

7. Loosen the clamp bolt at the base of the distributor (where it slides into its mount) and lift the distributor up and out. You will notice that the rotor turns clockwise as the distributor is removed. This is because the distributor is gear driven and must be compensated for during installation.

8. Reverse the above procedure to install. Remember to rotate the rotor approximately 1.4 in. counterclockwise (see illustration) from the notch scribed in the distributor body. This will ensure that when the distributor is fully seated in its mount, the marks will coincide. Adjust the ignition timing as described earlier. Tighten the clamp bolt to 8.0 ft. lbs.

6 Cylinder Engines—1981

1. Pull the vacuum hoses for advance and retard off the distributor, as required.

2. With chalk or paint, mark the relationship between the distributor body and the cylinder head. Then, rotate the engine until the line on the tip of the rotor is directly in line with the notch in the distributor housing (this puts the engine at TDC for No. 1 cylinder). Make sure that the TDC timing marks on the flywheel or balancer pulley are in line.

3. Loosen the clamp bolt at the bottom of the distributor.

4. Unscrew the mounting bracket screw for the electrical connector on the distributor body, pulling the mounting bracket off, and unplug the connector.

5. Pull the distributor out of the cylinder head.

6. To install, first position the rotor about 1½ in. counterclockwise from the notch in the distributor housing. Then, position the distributor body so the alignment marks you made in Step 1 are aligned. Insert the distributor into the head. If necessary, shift the tip of the rotor slightly one way or the other to get the distributor and camshaft gears to mesh properly; otherwise, the distributor cannot be inserted into the head.

7. When the distributor is fully seated, reconnect the electrical connector and all vacuum lines and install the cap. Adjust the ignition timing as described earlier.

6 Cylinder Engines — 1982-88

1982-88 6 cylinder engines are equipped with the new Motronic (DME) engine control system. The distributor on these models is contained within the engine itself. Other than distributor cap and rotor removal and installation, no general service is possible.

INSTALLATION — TIMING DISTURBED

Sometimes, the engine is accidentally turned over while the distributor is removed; in this case, it will be necessary to find TDC position for No. 1 cylinder before installing the distributor. First, go to the "Valve Lash Adjustment" procedure, remove the cam cover, and set the position of the engine as described there for adjustment of the valves for No. 1 cylinder. Check the exact position of the crankshaft via the timing marks on the flywheel or front pulley, and obtain exact alignment as indicated by them. Then, proceed to install the distributor as described above.

Alternator

PRECAUTIONS

Several precautions must be observed with alternator equipped vehicles to avoid damaging the unit. They are as follows:
- If the battery is removed for any reason, make sure that it is reconnected with the correct polarity. Reversing the battery connections may result in damage to the one-way rectifiers.
- When utilizing a booster battery as a starting aid, always connect it as follows: positive to positive, and negative (booster battery) to a good ground on the engine the car being started. Note that on the 1981-82 733i, the number 5 fuse must be pulled out of the fuse panel before using a booster battery, or the onboard computer may be damaged.
- Never use a fast charger as a booster to start cars with alternating-current (AC) circuits.
- When servicing the battery with a fast charger, always disconnect the battery cables.
- Never attempt to polarize an alternator.
- Avoid long soldering times when replacing diodes or transistors. Prolonged heat is damaging to alternators.
- Do not use test lamps of more than 12 volts (V) for checking diode continuity.

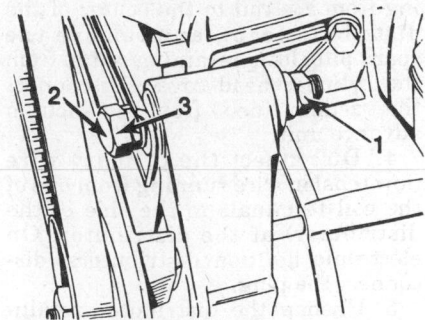

Loosen the locknut (1) at the rear of the alternator, and then turn the bolt (3) and tighten to 4.0–4.3 ft. lb. Hold the bolt in position while tightening the nut—318i

- Do not short across or ground any of the terminals on the alternator.
- The polarity of the battery, alternator, and regulator must be matched and considered before making any electrical connections within the system.
- Never operate the alternator on an open circuit. Make sure that all connections within the circuit are clean and tight.
- Turn off the ignition switch and then disconnect the battery terminals when performing any service on the electrical system or charging the battery.
- Disconnect the battery ground cable if arc welding is to be done on any part of the car.

BELT TENSION ADJUSTMENT

The fan belt tension is adjusted by moving the alternator on the slack adjuster bracket. The belt tension is adjusted to a deflection of approximately ½ in. under moderate thumb pressure in the middle of its longest span. On many late model engines, the position of the top of the alternator is adjusted via a bolt that is geared to the bracket. This bolt is turned to position the alternator and determine tension, and then is locked in position with a lockbolt. Refer to the Alternator Removal and Installation procedure.

REMOVAL & INSTALLATION

1. Disconnect the battery ground cable.
2. Disconnect the wires from the rear of the alternator, marking them for later installation. Note that there is a ground wire on some models. On the 735i, remove the cap and then disconnect the positive terminal at the junction box on the fender well. On the 633CSi, 635CSi, 733i and 735i, it

may be easier to remove the alternator mounting bolts, turn it, and then remove the wires. On the M5 and M6:
   a. Unscrew the nut and loosen the hose clamp. Pull of the plug. Then, lift out the air cleaner and airflow sensor.
   b. Make sure the engine is cool. Place a pan underneath and then disconnect the lower radiator hose. On the 528e, remove the airflow sensor.
On the 735i, make sure the engine is cool. Place a pan underneath and then disconnect the lower radiator hose.
3. Loosen the adjusting and pivot bolts, and remove the belt on those models with a standard mounting system. If the alternator has the tensioning bolt described in Step 4, remove it and then remove the belt. Remove the bolts and remove the alternator. On the 633CSi, 635CSi, 733i and 735i, it may be necessary to loosen the fan cowl to get at the mounting bolts. On the 535i, it may be necessary to disconnect a power steering line that runs near the alternator.
4. Installation is the reverse of removal. Adjust the belt tension to approximately ⅜ in., measured between the balancer and the alternator pulley. On all 1984-88 models, a unique tensioning system is used. See the illustration for the 318i — the other models are similar. You must turn the tensioning bolt on the front of the alternator so as to tension the belt, using a torque wrench, until the torque is approximately 5 ft. lbs. Then, hold the adjustment with one wrench while you tighen the locknut at the rear of the unit. Make sure that, if the unit has a ground wire on the alternator, you have reconnected it. On the M5 and M6 and 735i, make sure to reconnect the radiator hose, refill and bleed the cooling system. On the M5, M6, and 528e securely reinstall the air cleaner and airflow sensor. On the 528e, if you had to disconnect the power steering line, reconnect it securely, refill, and bleed the system.

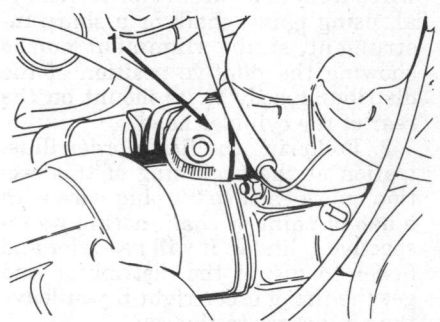

In 318i starter removal, remove the nut and detach the bracket (1)

Starter

REMOVAL & INSTALLATION

1. Disconnect the battery ground cable.

2. On fuel injection 6 cylinder models with 6 identical intake tubes, you may have to remove No. 6 intake tube for clearance. On injected 4 cylinder models, remove the intake cowl from the mixture control unit. On the 318i, remove the wire holding bracket. On the 325:

    a. Disconnect the positive terminal at the junction box on the fender well. Then, remove the air cleaner with the flow sensor.

    b. Unscrew the air collector bracket that's in the way.

    c. Unscrew the nut that fastens a wiring bracket near the starter.

    d. Make sure the engine is cool and then drain the coolant into a clean container. Disconnect the heater hose that runs near the starter. Remove the coolant pipe if doing so is necessary for clearance. On the 528e:

    a. Remove the air cleaner and airflow sensor.

    b. Disconnect the electrical leads. Remove the three bolts and remove the mounting bracket. On the 533i and 535i:

    a. Make sure the engine is cool. Drain some coolant from the cooling system and then remove the expansion tank. On the 633CSi and 635CSi:

    a. Make sure the engine is cool and drain some coolant out. Disconnect the heater hose that is near the starter.

    b. Operate the brake pedal hard 20 times. Disconnect the power steering line that would otherwise prevent access to the starter.

    c. Cut off the straps and remove the solenoid switch insulating cover, located right near the solenoid. On the M5 and M6:

    a. Remove the exhaust manifold as described later in this section.

    b. Cut off the straps and remove the solenoid switch insulating cover, located right near the solenoid.

3. Remove the starter solenoid wire leads, marking them for later installation unless they have already been removed. On 4 cylinder models, disconnect the mounting bracket at the block.

4. Unbolt and remove the starter. On the 325, the lower nut can be removed more easily from underneath. On late model 533 and 535i, 733i and 735i, M5 and M6, you may have to use a box wrench with an angled handle

to unscrew the main starter mounting bolts. On the 528e, 633CSi and 635CSi, the final mounting bolt must be removed from underneath.

NOTE: Remove the accelerator cable holder on automatic transmission equipped vehicles.

5. Installation is the reverse of removal. Make sure to reconnect all hoses and refill and bleed the cooling system or power steering system. Where the solenoid switch cover has been unstrapped, reinstall it with new straps to locate it properly for electrical safety.

STARTER DRIVE REPLACEMENT

The starter must be disassembled to replace the starter drive. A circlip retains the drive gear on the armature shaft and must be removed before the drive gear can be replaced.

1. Remove the field coil wires from the solenoid and remove the solenoid mounting bolts.

2. Disengage the solenoid plunger from the starter drive and remove the solenoid from the starter motor.

3. Remove the small dust cap from the end of the motor.

4. Remove the C-clip, shims and gasket from the end of the starter motor shaft.

5. Remove the two long pole housing screws from the housing. Lift off the pole housing cap, the brushes and the brush plate.

6. Remove the intermediate bearing screws and remove the pole housing.

7. Remove the rubber seal and washer from the engaging lever housing.

8. Remove the engaging lever screw and pull the armature out of the drive bearing.

9. Push back the thrust washer or thrust bearing race on the drive pinion end of the motor shaft in order to remove the C-clip retainer.

10. Remove the starter drive pinion and bracket.

11. Install the starter pinion and bracket. Secure them on the shaft with the thrust washer and C-clip. Lubricate the coarse threads, engaging ring and bearing with high temperature silicone grease.

12. Install the armature and shaft into the drive bearing, making sure that the tabs of the engaging lever are installed over the engaging ring. Lubricate the engaging lever with silicone grease.

13. Install the washer and rubber seal into the engaging lever housing,

making sure the tabs on the seal and washer point toward the armature.

14. Position the pole housing so that the groove faces toward the rubber pad and install the pole housing into the drive bearing. Secure the screws with Loctite® No. 270.

15. Check the commutator bearing for looseness and then guide the field coil wires into the rubber seal.

16. Install the pole housing screws through the pole housing cap and locating slots in the brush plate. Install the brushes and pole housing cap on the starter.

17. Check armature axial play to 0.004–0.006 in. (0.1–0.15mm) (0.004–0.008 in. on 1983-88 models) and correct any excessive play with additional shims.

18. Install end gasket, shims and C-clip on the end of the motor shaft. Install the dust cover on the end of the starter motor (over the shaft, end gasket and shims).

19. Install the solenoid on the starter and attach the field coil wires to the solenoid.

Measure the electrical resistance at plug (2). Plug (1) must also be unplugged before making electrical tests, however

Diesel Glow Plug

REMOVAL & INSTALLATION

Diesel

1. Unscrew the electrical connection. Unscrew the glow plug with a suitable deep well socket or BMW special socket 12 2 100.

2. Coat the threads on the replacement plug with a copper paste such as "CRC" or equivalent. Install the plug and torque it to 14–22 ft. lbs. Install leads only after the plug is fully torqued to prevent twisting the wires.

TESTING

1. Remove the cover from the heating time control unit for the flow plugs. Unplug both plugs. The engine compartment must be about 68°F.

2. Apply the test leads of an ohmmeter between the battery ground (−) and each of the lead tips G1–G6 on the No. 2 plug. Resistance must be 0.4–.6 ohms. If outside limits, replace the associated glow plug.

3. You can also test amperage draw. Connect the test leads of an ammeter between the battery (+) terminal and each of the connectors G1–G6 on plug No. 2. Connect each for 5 seconds and then read the amperage. It should be 13–15 amps.

ENGINE MECHANICAL

Engine

REMOVAL & INSTALLATION

318i

1. Remove the transmission as detailed later.

2. Scribe hood hinge locations on the hood, and then remove it.

3. Detach the two mounting bolts and remove the power steering pump with hoes attached. Suspend the pump securely so that hoses will not be damaged.

4. Looking at the top of the air conditioning compressor, loosen the two outer bolts (bolts screwing into the compressor) and remove the two bolts fastening the mounting bracket to the engine. Then, support the unit and remove the hinge nut and bolt form the bottom of the unit. Finally, support the unit to avoid putting strain on refrigerant hoses.

NOTE: Do not disconnect any air conditioning hoses!

5. Remove the radiator cap and drain coolant. Detach radiator hoses. Then, on air conditioned cars, disconnect the wires at the temperature switches. Unscrew and remove the cover located at the left side of the radiator (driver's side). Unscrew and disconnect transmission oil cooler lines at the radiator (automatic only), and plug openings. Finally, remove the mounting bolt located at the top, lift the radiator upward until it clears the rubber mounts on the bottom, and remove it.

6. Disconnect both battery leads and the battery-to-alternator wire. Disconnect the engine ground strap.

7. Open clips that hold the wiring harness running along the fender just behind the battery. Disconnect plugs

from the temperature sensor and oxygen sensor.

8. Remove the glovebox liner. Unplug plugs at the idle control and L-Jetronic units. Unplug the connector that also comes out of this harness. Then, pull the harness through into the engine compartment.

9. Disconnect all three coil wires and wire to the electronic ignition unit. Take the wires out of the clips mounted nearby.

10. At the air cleaner, disconnect the wire mounted on the side of the air cleaner housing, and disconnect

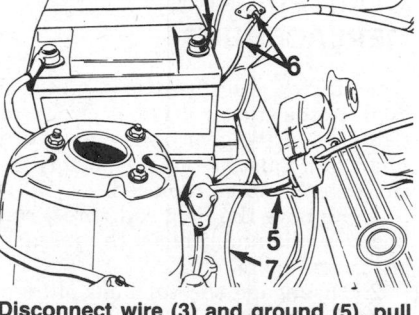

Disconnect wire (3) and ground (5), pull off plugs on temperature sensor (6), and on oxygen sensor (7)—318i

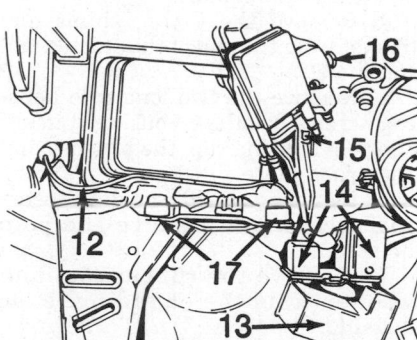

Disconnect wire (12), lift off cap (13) and remove relay (14), disconnect plug (15), open hose strap (16). Loosen nuts (17) and remove the air cleaner—318i

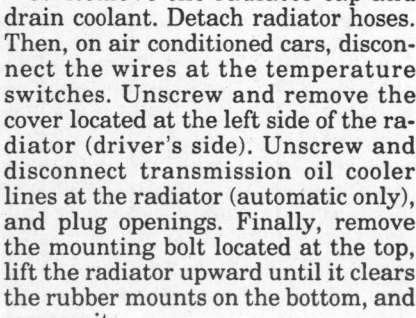

On the 318i, pull off the plug (4) and vacuum hoses (5 and 6). Detach vacuum hose (7). When installing, make sure (5) goes to the distributor, and (6) to the intake manifold.

the plug. Lift off the L-shaped cap of the plug. Lift off the L-shaped cap of the relay mounted nearby, and then remove the relay. Loosen the strap and disconnect the inlet hose. Loosen the two mounting nuts and remove the air cleaner.

11. Go to the relay box mounted in between the cowl and suspension strut on the driver's side. Remove the top of the box and lift out and disconnect the plug on the outboard side. Remove the rubber guard from the TCI control unit nearby and pull off the plug connected to that. Open both associated wire straps.

12. Going to the rear of the intake manifold, unscrew the clamp and pull off the large vacuum hose. Label and then disconnect the small vacuum hoses running to the distributor and intake manifold.

13. Disconnect the throttle cable. Remove the hose clamp and hose nearby.

14. Detach fuel hoses at the injection system, and with them the associated hose holder. Collect fuel in a metal pan.

15. Attach a suitable hoist to hooks at front and rear of the engine and support the engine securely.

16. Detach both engine mounts and the vibration damper. Lift out the engine, taking care not to permit the engine to shift and hit anything on the way out.

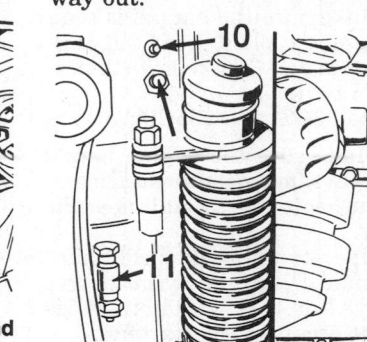

Disconnect the ground strap (9), and engine shock absorber (11) on the 318i. During installation, note that the pin (10) must fit into a bore in the axle carrier.

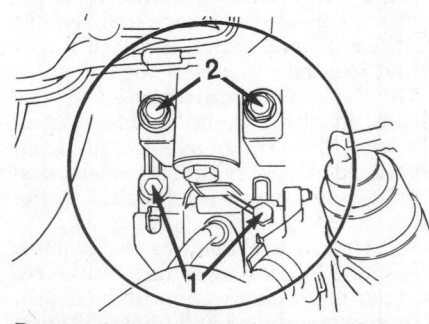

Remove bolts (1 and 2), then remove the bolt at the base of the A/C compressor—318i

17. Install the engine in reverse order, keeping these points in mind:

   a. The locating mandrel on the front of the engine must be guided into the front suspension carrier.

   b. Adjust the throttle cable for smooth operation.

   c. Adjust the fan, A/C compressor, and power steering pump drive belts.

320i

1. Remove the transmission as detailed later.

2. Scribe lines, around the hood hinges and then remove the hood.

3. Disconnect the upper and lower radiator hoses and then remove the radiator.

4. Unscrew and remove the air filter housing.

5. On models equipped with air conditioning, detach the compressor and position it out of the way with wires. Do not disconnect the refrigerant lines.

6. Disconnect the battery cables (negative cable first) and remove the battery.

7. Disconnect all fuel lines at the fuel distributor. Pull the hose off the charcoal canister. Disconnect the ground wire from the front axle carrier.

8. Unscrew the retaining nut and lift the accelerator cable from the holders toward the side. Push the nipple out toward the rear and then disconnect the calbe.

9. Tag and disconnect all remaining wires and hoses which may interfere with engine removal.

10. Lift out the relay socket and then pull out the two relays to the side of the housing. Disconnect the plug underneath and then lift out the wire harness from its holder on the wheel arch.

11. Open the glove box and disconnect the plug on the left-hand side. Pull the harness out through the hole in the firewall (into the engine compartment). Pull the harness out of its holders.

12. Attach an engine hoist or the like to the front and rear of the engine.

13. Unbolt the left engine mount and the upper engine damper.

14. Unbolt the right engine mount and lift out the engine.

15. Installation is in the reverse order of removal. When installing the accelerator cable, push the cable through the eye on the lever, attach it and then press the nipple into the eye. Attach the cable to the holder.

325, 325e, 325i and 325is

1. Disconnect the battery ground

cable. Remove the transmission as described in the appropriate section.

2. Without disconnecting hoses, loosen and remove the three power steering pump bolts and remove the pump and belts and support the pump out of the way.

3. Remove the drain plug and remove the coolant from the radiator. Then, remove the radiator (see the appropriate procedure).

4. Without disconnecting hoses, remove the three mounting bolts and remove the air conditioner compressor and drive belt and support it out of the way.

5. Disconnect and support the engine hood supports and then open the hood and support it securely.

6. Remove the trim panel inside the glovebox. Disconnect the plugs going to the engine control computer; two are located in the wiring, and one directly on the unit.

7. Unscrew the idle control unit near the main control computer and pull off its plugs. On automatic transmission-equipped cars, disconnect the plug leading to the vehicle wiring harness.

8. Lift out and disconnect the plug for the oxygen sensor and two additional wires nearby. Pull off the temperature sensor plug. Loosen the straps and pull this harness into the engine compartment.

9. Remove the coolant expansion tank. Pull off the ignition coil high tension and low tension wires. Disconnect the wiring harness.

10. Disconnect the accelerator cable and cruise control cable. Pull off the vacuum hoses going to the throttle body. Loosen the clamp and pull off the large air intake hose.

11. Disconnect the plugs near the air cleaner. Lift out the relay. Disconnect the wiring harness. Unscrew the mounting nuts and remove the air cleaner.

12. Pull off the cover and disconnect the wiring harness plug at the fusebox.

13. Unscrew the fuel lines, pull off the hose and disconnect the fuel filter.

14. Disconnect both heater hoses. Unbolt the engine mounts.

15. Lift out the engine with a suitable hoist, using hooks at front and rear.

16. To install, reverse the removal procedure, keeping these points in mind:

   a. When the engine is positioned, the guide pin must fit in the bore of the axle carrier. Torque the mounting bolts on the front axle carrier (small bolt) to 18–20 ft. lb.; the larger bolt to 31–35 ft. lb. The mount-to-bracket bolts are torqued

to 31–35 ft. lb. Engine-to-bracket mounts are torqued to (small bolt) 16–17 ft. lb., (large bolt) 31–35 ft. lb.

   b. Use new hose clamps to connect the fuel lines to the fuel lines to the fuel filter.

   c. Adjust the accelerator cable and cruise control cable.

   d. Use a new hose clamp on the coolant expansion tank.

   e. When installing hood support, make sure the plastic portion of the support connects properly to the hood.

   f. Install and adjust the V-belts on the air conditioner compressor and power steering pump.

   g. Make sure all fluid levels are correct before starting the engine. Bleed air from the cooling system.

524td

1. Remove the transmission as detailed later in this section.

2. Remove the adjusting and hinge bolts for the power steering pump support the pump out of the way securely without placing any strain on the hoses.

3. Remove the adjusting and hinge bolts for the air conditioning compressor; support the compressor out of the way without placing any strain on the hoses (do not attempt to disconnect them!)

4. Remove the drain plug from a block, and drain the coolant. Then, remove the radiator as described later in this section. Remove the circlip and disconnect the power lead, nearby.

5. Remove the ground wires from the hood. Disconnect the gas pressure hood props and then securely prop up the engine hood so it is wide open.

6. Disconnect the negative and positive battery leads.

7. Disconnect the primary electrical connection (2). Lift off the cover (3) and pull off plugs (4) and (5). Disconnect the wire (6). Remove the preheating time control (7).

8. Remove the coolant overflow tank by disconnecting wiring and the coolant hose, removing the two mounting nuts, and then pulling it off the mounting studs.

9. Remove the cover (8) and cap (9). Disconnect the plug (10). Then, pull off all three relay (11).

10. Disconnect plugs at (12) and (13). Remove the wiring harness fasteners at the body.

11. Disconnect the accelerator and cruise control cables.

12. Disconnect the fuel hoses running between the injection pump and the filter system (supply and return).

13. Disconnect the five vacuum hos-

es connecting to the rear of the engine block.

14. Disconnect the plug near the rear of the cylinder head and disconnect the ground wire nearby.

15. Disconnect the water hoses for the heater.

16. Disconnect the hoses going into the air cleaner. The large air intake hose is twisted to release it prior to removing it. Unscrew the wingnuts, release the clamps, and remove the air cleaner.

17. Place a bucket underneath the oil cooler and then disconnect both oil lines. Disconnect the manifold pressure line going to the turbo wastegate.

18. Disconnect the multi-prong plug on the control unit in the glovebox. Disconnect the engine wiring harness and pull it into the engine compartment.

19. Disconnect the wiring running near one of the engine mounts. Disconnect the engine ground strap.

20. Attach a lifting sling to the engine lifting hoods. Apply tension enough to support the engine. Pull the center-bolts out of both engine mounts and remove the engine.

21. Install in reverse order, keeping the following points in mind:

   a. The engine mounting system has a guidepin that must be fitted into a corresponding bore in the front axle to locate the engine properly for installing of the mount through-bolts.

   b. After the engine oil cooler lines are connected, refill the crankcase with the specified quantity of the proper engine oil.

   c. Make sure, when reassembling the air cleaner that the arrow faces upward.

   d. Adjust the accelerator and cruise control cables.

528i

1. Raise and support the vehicle and remove the transmission. Remove the exhaust pipe from the exhaust manifold.

2. Remove the power steering pump and place it out of the way along the inner fender panel. Leave the hoses attached.

3. Lower the vehicle, scribe the hood hinge location and remove the hood.

4. Remove the air cleaner with the duct work attached. Disconnect and remove the air volume control.

5. Disconnect and remove the battery.

6. Disconnect all electrical wires and connectors. Mark the wires and connectors for installation.

7. Disconnect all vacuum hoses, marking them for installation.

8. Drain the cooling system, disconnect the hoses and remove the radiator.

9. Disconnect the accelerator linkage.

10. Install a lifting sling on the engine.

11. Remove the left and right engine mount retaining nuts and washers.

12. Carefully lift the engine from the engine compartment.

13. Installation is the reverse of removal.

528e

1. Remove the transmission as detailed later. Disconnect the exhaust pipe from the exhaust manifold.

2. Remove the splash guard.

3. With the hoses still attached, remove the power steering pump and position it out of the way.

4. Unscrew the drain plug on the engine block, remove the upper and lower radiator hoses and drain the cooling system. After draining, remove the radiator.

5. With the refrigerant hoses still connected, remove the air conditioning compressor and position it out of the way.

6. Disconnect the gas pressure springs, scribe around the hinges and then remove the hood.

7. Disconnect the battery cables (negative first) and remove the battery.

8. Disconnect the accelerator and cruise control cables. Disconnect all hoses from the throttle housing (make sure you tag them all). Disconnect the air duct.

9. Remove the air filter housing along with the air flow sensor.

10. Tag and disconnect all remaining lines, hoses and wires which may interfere with engine removal.

11. Tag and disconnect all plugs and wires attached to the control unit in the glove box. Unscrew the straps on the firewall and pull the wire harness through to the engine compartment.

12. Disconnect the engine ground strap and then loosen both engine mounts.

13. Attach an engine lifting hoist to the front and rear of the engine, remove the engine mount bolts and then lift out the engine.

14. Installation is in the reverse order of removal.

533i, 535i, 633CSi and 635CSi

1. Disconnect both battery connections (negative first). There is a lead coming from the engine to the positive battery terminal. Disconnect it at the battery. On the 600 Series cars, disconnect the ground strap.

2. Unscrew the ground strap for the hood. Support the hood securely and then disconnect the gas props. Then, raise the hood until it is vertical and securely fasten it in place.

3. Remove the transmission as described later in this section. With the engine cool, place a clean container underneath the coolant drain plug in the side of the block. Remove the plug and drain all coolant from the block. Remove the fan and radiator.

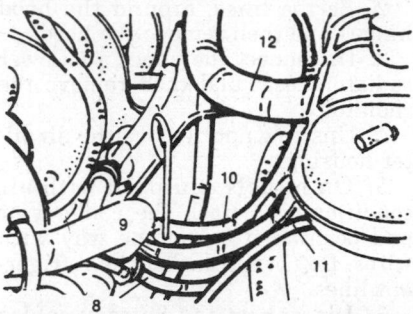

On the 630CSi and 633CSi, also disconnect the hoses shown, which are routed and coded as follows: 8—white from the booster blowoff valve to the white capped valve; 9—black from the booster blowoff valve to the blue capped valve; 10—blue from the booster blowoff valve to the blue capped valve; 11—red from the pressure converter to the EGR valve. Also detach the overflow tank hose (12)

4. Support the power steering pump. Remove the three mounting bolts and then hang the pump out of the way in a position that will not put stress on the hoses.

5. Support the air conditioning compressor. Remove the three mounting bolts and then hang the compressor out of the way in a position that will not put stress on the hoses.

6. On the 533i and 633i:

   a. Pull off the plug at the airflow sensor and remove associated wiring. Remove the hoses and pipes connected to the air cleaner and airflow sensor. If it looks like it will be confusing to reconnect all hoses to the proper connections, label them. Then, remove the nuts and remove the airflow sensor and air cleaner as an assembly.

   b. Pull off the plugs on the idle control and Digital Motor Electronics control in the glove box. Pull the wires through into the engine compartment. Disconnect the ground wire associated with the DME. Disconect the oxygen sensor. Disconnect the DME wiring harness on the firewall.

   c. Disconnect both (+) and (−) low tension and the high tension wire from the coil. Disconnect the wires from the solenoid nearby. Pull the wiring harness out of the holders. On the 633i, also disconnect the harness at the fuse box.

On the 535i and 635i:

a. Pull the wire leading to the oxygen sensor out of the clips under the floor. Disconnect the sensor at the exhaust pipe.

b. Pull off the plug at the airflow sensor and remove associated wiring. Remove the hoses and pipes connected to the air cleaner and airflow sensor. If it looks like it will be confusing to reconnect all hoses to the proper connections, label them. Then, remove the nuts and remove the airflow sensor and air cleaner as an assembly.

c. Pull the large, multiprong plug off the Digital Motor Electronics box in the glove compartment. Disconnect the smaller plug that's connected to the same harness and plugged in nearby. Then, run the entire harness back into the engine compartment.

d. Disconnect the engine ground wire located at the rear of the block. Unclip the harness for the DME from the firewall.

e. Disconnect both (+) and (−) low tension and the high tension wire from the coil. Disconnect the wires from the solenoid nearby. Pull the wiring harness out of the holders.

7. Pull off the fuse box cover and the cap nearby. Remove the three relays (they have metal covers) on one side of the fusebox. Then, disconnect the wiring harness that leads into the fusebox. On the 635i, unclamp the harness where it is clamped to the fender well and remove the diagnosis socket (located right near the fusebox).

8. Disconnect the accelerator and cruise control cables.

9. Unclamp and remove the coolant hose that leads to the expansion tank. Disconnect the fuel return line nearby, collecting any fuel in a metal container for safe disposal. Unclip the wiring harness clips on the two wires that run through this area of the engine compartment.

10. Disconnect the fuel supply line, collecting any fuel in a metal container for safe disposal. Disconnect the two heater hoses at connections nearby.

11. Pull the main vacuum supply hose off at the intake manifold.

12. Disconnect the remaining main coolant hose and plug it.

13. Install a lifting sling to the two hooks on top of the engine. Unbolt the left side engine mount. Remove the

main engine ground strap. Unbolt the right side engine mount. Carefully pull the engine out of the compartment.

14.

In installation:

a. Torque mount bolts to 31–35 ft. lbs.

b. Replenish all coolant with fresh anti-freeze/water mix appropriate for the climate. Bleed the cooling system.

M5 and M6

1. Disconnect the battery negative cable. Then, disconnect the positive cable. Scribe matchmarks and then remove the hood.

2. Remove the fan. Remove the drain plugs in the block and radiator. Disconnect the hoses and remove the radiator.

3. Support the power steering pump. Remove the three mounting bolts and then hang the pump out of the way in a position that will not put stress on the hoses.

4. Support the air conditioning compressor. Remove the three mounting bolts and then hang the compressor out of the way in a position that will not put stress on the hoses.

5. Remove the transmission as described later in this section.

6. Remove the attaching bolt and, with an appropriate puller, remove the vibration damper from the front of the engine.

7. Remove the two bolts at either end and remove the cross brace that runs under the engine. Remove the heat shield nearby.

8. Disconnect the electrical connector going to the airflow sensor. Pull the electrical leads out of the wiring holders. Loosen the hose clamp for the air intake hose. Remove the mounting nut for the air cleaner. Then, remove the air cleaner and airflow sensor as an assembly.

9. Disconnect the large vacuum hose at the bottom of the intake manifold.

10. Disconnect the PCV hoses where they connect to the top of the manifold. Disconnect the throttle cable that runs across the top of the manifold, and the hose running near the front. Remove the bolts fastening the manifold to the outer ends of the intake tubes and remove it.

11. Working inside the glove compartment, disconnect the plug that connects to the Digitial Motor Electronics control. Then, guide the leads through and into the engine compartment. Disconnect the high tension lead and the two low tension leads at the coil. Then, unfasten the wiring harness holders for the harness run-

ning to the coil where the harness runs along the fender well.

12. Disconnect the fuel hose connection at the rear of the fuel manifold on top of the engine, and collect fuel in a metal container for safe disposal. Disconnect the vacuum hose that runs along the firewall nearby.

13. Disconnect the plugs for the reference mark and speed sensors. Disconnect the hoses on the coolant expansion tank.

14. Working on the fuse box, pull off the large electrical connector. Pull off the diagnosis socket. Disconnect the remaining leads.

15. Disconnect the heater hoses near the firewall. Using a backup wrench, disconnect the two lines at the oil cooler. Disconnect the low pressure fuel line at the pressure regulator.

16. Disconnect the starter leads. Cut the straps and remove the solenoid heat shield.

17. Attach a lifting sling to the engine and support the assembly with a crane. Disconnect the ground lead. Then, disconnect the left side engine mount, removing the nut from underneath and then unscrewing the bolt out the top. Do the same for the right mount (the nut is underneath). Carefully lift the engine out of the compartment, tilting the front of the engine upward for clearance.

18. Install in reverse order, noting these points:

a. Torque the bolts and nuts for the engine mounts to 31–35 ft. lbs.

b. When reconnecting the reference mark and speed sensors, connect the gray plug to the plug with the ring underneath.

c. Check the O-rings on the intake manifold and replace any that are damaged.

d. Make sure to refill the cooling system with fresh anti-freeze/water mix and bleed the cooling system.

e. Adjust power steering and air conditioner compressor belts to the required tension.

f. Check idle speed and CO.

733i
1981-82

1. Raise and support the vehicle and remove the transmission. Remove the exhaust pipe from the exhaust manifold and reactor.

2. Remove the clutch housing from the engine.

3. Remove the power steering pump and place it out of the way. Do not disconnect the hoses.

4. If equipped with air conditioning, remove the compressor and place it out of the way. Do not disconnect the hoses.

5. Remove the damper bracket from the crankcase and lower the vehicle.

6. Scribe the hood hinge locations and remove the hood.

7. Drain the cooling system, disconnect the hoses and remove the radiator.

8. Remove the windshield washer reservoir and the air filter housing located on the inner fender panel.

9. Remove the electrical wiring from the engine components. Tag all wires.

10. Disconnect and remove the battery.

11. Remove and tag all vacuum hoses.

NOTE: Some vacuum hoses are color coded.

12. Disconnect the throttle linkage.

13. Remove the right kick panel from the passenger compartment, remove the fuel injection control unit wire connector and thread the connector and wire through the hole in the firewall.

14. Attach a lifting sling to the engine. Remove the left and right engine mount retaining nuts and washers. Lift the engine from the engine compartment.

15. Installation is the reverse of removal.

733i and 735i

1983-86 (M30 B34 Engine)

1. Scribe marks for the location of hood hinges on the hood and remove the hood.

2. Disconnect battery positive and negative cables. Unscrew the ground strap at the body. Disconnect the wire that's attached to the positive battery connector at the connector. Remove the battery.

3. Remove the transmission as described later in this section.

4. Drain the coolant, and then remove the fan and radiator (refer to the cooling system section later in this section).

5. Remove the power steering pump adjusting bolt and hinge nut and bolt. Leave the hoses connected. You'll have to suspend the pump as you remove the bolts and then wire it in a position that will keep tension off the hoses.

6. In a similar way, loosen and remove the adjusting bolt and the two hinge nuts and bolts for the air conditioning compressor. Leave the hoses connected. Suspend the compressor as you work on detaching it and then wire it in such a position that the hoses will not be stressed.

7. Disconnect the plug (2) and lift out the wiring. Pull off hoses (3 and 4). Loosen the hose clamp (5). Unscrew the air cleaner and airflow sensor.

8. Working under the dash, unscrew the right radio speaker cover. Disconnect the retaining strap for the glovebox. Then, pull off the plug for the idle control unit (located right under the glove-box), and the DME unit plug and two other plugs nearby on the right kick panel.

9. Front the front of the cowl in the engine compartment, lift out the master relay (12) and unscrew the socket (13). Take off its rubber ring (14) and lift out the oxygen sensor plug. Disconnect the wire (16). Unstrap the wiring harness. Then, disconnect the heater hose (17).

10. Remove the cover and protective cap from the fusebox. Pull off the connector and the two relays nearby. Pull off the wire and hose just below the fusebox. Then, disconnect the wiring harness. Unscrew the fuel line nearby.

11. Working near the air cleaner, remove the windshield washer fluid tank, disconnect the electrical plug at the airflow sensor, and then remove the air cleaner with the airflow sensor attached.

12. Working just in front of the right door, disconnect the additional multiprong connector for the DME control unit. Disconnect the small plug nearby.

13. Working just below the windshield on the right side of the car, lift out the master relay and unscrew the socket nearby. Disconnect the wire at the strut tower. Loosen the firewall clamps and pull the wiring harness off on this side. Disconnect the other heater hose nearby.

14. Working at the relay box near the coolant reservoir, lift off the cap and disconnect the miltiprong wiring connector. Lift the two relays from the box. Take the wiring harness out of the clamps.

15. Unscrew the fuel line at the pressure regulator. Disconnect the dipstick tube bracket. Loosen the clamp and unscrew the wiring harness for the oxygen sensor on the floor panel.

16. Disconnect the coil primary and secondary wires and the plug right nearby. Disconnect the A/C compressor wires and lift the wires out the holders.

17. Disconnect the throttle and cruise control cables. Pull off the fuel hose nearby. Disconnect the water hoses at the front of the engine.

18. Look around the engine compartment and disconnect any remaining vacuum hoses or wires.

19. Attach lifting hooks to the two lift points on the engine—you may have to disconnect a water hose to gain access to one of them. Support the engine with a crane.

20. Unscrew the attaching bolt for the left side engine mount near the steering box. Do the same for the right side mount and ground strap. Unbolt the engine vibration damper. Carefully lift the engine out of the car.

21. Install in reverse order, noting the following points:

   a. When installing the throttle and speed control cables, mount the holders carefully and adjust both.

   b. Adjust drive belt tension carefully.

   c. If you're installing a new engine, it is recommended that CO be adjusted as described above.

735i

1987-88 (M30 B35 Engine)

1. Disconnect first the negative battery cable and then the positive. Remove the transmission as described later in this section. Scribe hinge locations and remove the hood, or remove support struts and prop it securely all the way up.

2. Remove the splash guard from underneath the engine. Then, with the engine cool, remove the drain plugs in the radiator and block and drain the engine coolant.

3. Loosen the power steering pump bolts from underneath. Turn the adjusting pinion so as to loosen the belt and remove the belt. Then, remove the mounting bolts and remove the power steering pump without disconnecting the hoses. Support the pump out of the way so as to avoid stressing the hoses.

4. Do the same with the air conditioner compressor (this unit does not have the belt adjusting pinion—you merely have to loosen all the bolts and push the compressor toward the engine to remove the belt.

5. Loosen the air intake hose clamp and disconnect the hose. Remove the mounting nut and then remove the air cleaner.

6. The unit on the opposite side of the intake hose from the air cleaner contains the idle speed control valve, which must be removed next. Loosen the hose clamps and pull off the hoses. Disconnect the electrical connector. Remove the mounting nut and then pull the idle speed control out of the air intake hose.

7. Pull off the three retainers for the airflow sensor, and then pull the unit off its mountings, disconnecting the vacuum hose from the PCV system at the same time.

8. Working on the coolant expansion tank, disconnect the electrical connector. Remove the nuts on both sides. Loosen their clamps and then disconnect all three hoses and remove the tank.

9. Disconnect the heater hoses at both the control valve and at the heater core.

10. Disconnect the throttle and cruise control cables at the throttle lever. Unbolt the cable housing retainer and remove the housing and cables.

11. Pull off the four low amperage starter connectors and disconnect the high amperage connector coming from the battery.

12. Loosen its clamp and then disconnect the coolant hose the runs to the alternator.

13. Disconnect the connecting plug for the oxygen sensor, as well as the two other plugs nearby.

14. Loosen the clamps and then disconnect the fuel supply and return pipes, draining fuel into a metal container for safe disposal.

15. Disconnect the fuel pipe at the injector supply manifold. Disconnect the plug nearby. Disconnect the electrical connector at the throttle body. Lift off the protective caps and then remove the attaching nuts for the protective cover for the wiring harness for the injectors and remove it.

16. Disconnect the ground strap at the block. Remove the engine mount nut from the top on both sides.

17. Attach a lifting sling to the engine and support the assembly with a crane. Disconnect the ground lead. Carefully lift the engine out of the compartment, tilting the front of the engine upward for clearance.

18. To install, reverse the removal procedure, noting the following points:

   a. Engine mount nuts are torqued to 31–35 ft. lbs.

   b. When installing the throttle and speed control cables, mount the holders carefully and adjust both.

   b. Adjust drive belt tension carefully.

   c. Refill the cooling system with antifreeze/water mix, and bleed the cooling system.

Cylinder Head

REMOVAL & INSTALLATION

318i

NOTE: In order to perform this procedure, you must have a special tool (angle gauge) that will accurately measure the angle at which the cylinder head bolts are torqued.

Alignment of dowel pin hole and camshaft flange notch with the cast projection of the cylinder head—four cylinder engine

1. Disconnect exhaust pipes at the exhaust manifold and remove the pipe clamp on the transmission.

2. Disconnect the battery ground cable. Remove the drain plug and drain coolant.

3. Disconnect the wire and plug on the air cleaner. Loosen the clamp and disconnect the air intake hose. Then unscrew the nuts and remove the air cleaner.

4. Disconnect the throttle cable. Remove the dipstick tube locating bracket.

5. Disconnect the throttle position electronic plug. Disconnect the coolant and vacuum hoses nearby. Unscrew the support for the throttle body nearby.

6. Detach the fuel supply and return hoses and the hose mounting clamp.

7. Disconnect the intake manifold, distributor, and power brake unit vacuum hoses.

8. Disconnect the diagnosis plug, alternator wiring, and other plugs (2) nearby. Disconnect the coolant hoses at the cylinder head.

9. Disconnect any electrical plugs on the starter and injection system. This includes pulling off each injection plug and opening up the wiring straps.

10. Remove the distributor cap, disconnect distributor wiring plugs, wiring harness, and all plug wires.

11. Disconnect the coolant hoses going into the firewall.

12. Remove the cylinder head cover. Remove the bracket near the upper timing case over. Then, remove bolts and remove the upper timing case cover.

13. Rotate the engine until the TDC mark on the front pulley is aligned with the mark on the front cover and the distributor rotor is

On the final torquing step for 318i cylinder head bolts, tighten head bolts the specified angle, as shown

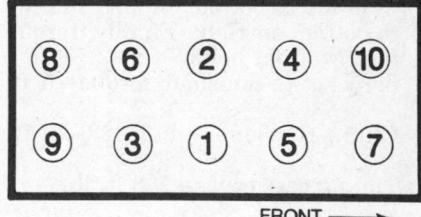

FRONT ⟶

4-cylinder head torque sequence

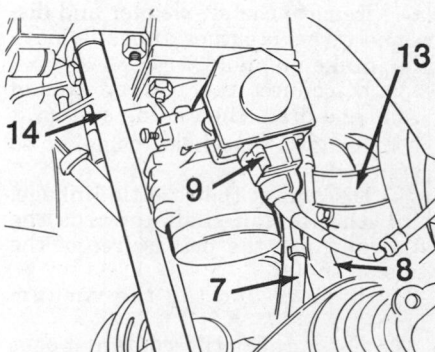

When removing the cylinder head on the 318i, disconnect the coolant hoses (7 and 8), disconnect the plug (9) and vacuum hose (13), and unscrew the support (14)

aligned with the mark on the side of the distributor (No. 1 cylinder is at TDC). Then, remove the distributor.

14. Remove the timing chain tensioner piston as described below.

15. Remove the retaining bolts and pull off the upper timing chain sprocket. *Do not rotate crankshaft while the sprocket is off!*

16. Loosen the cylinder head bolts in reverse order of the torquing sequence and remove. Lift off the cylinder head.

17. Install in reverse order, noting these points:

    a. Use a new head gasket.

    b. Lightly oil all head bolts, keeping oil out of the threaded holes in the block.

    c. Torque in the sequence shown in four stages:
- 25–29 ft. lb.
- 42–45 ft. lb.
- Wait 20 minutes — adjust the valves during this time
- 56–59 ft. lb.
- Run the engine until it is warm
- Torque bolts to 25 degrees (on the angle gauge)

    d. When installing the timing chain sprocket, fist make sure the notch in the camshaft flange is aligned with the cast tab on the cylinder head. The dowel pin will then align with the bore in the sprocket at the 6 o'clock position.

    e. When installing the upper timing cover, pack sealer into the crevices between block and the top of lower cover. Install all bolts finger tight. Tighten outer bolts first, from top to bottom on left, and top to bottom on right. Finally, torque the two front bolts.

Sprocket-to-camshaft torque — 5 ft. lb.

Chain tensioner plug — 22–29 ft. lbs.

Timing case cover — 7–8 ft. lb.

320i

1. Remove the air cleaner and disconnect the breather tube. Remove the intake manifold.

2. Disconnect the battery ground cable and drain the cooling system.

3. Remove the choke cable, if so equipped.

4. Disconnect the throttle linkage. Pull the torsion shaft towards the firewall until the ball is free of the torsion shaft.

5. Remove and tag the vacuum hoses.

6. Disconnect the coolant hoses from the cylinder head.

7. Disconnect the electrical wiring and connectors from the cylinder head and engine components.

8. Remove the cylinder head cover and the front upper timing case cover.

9. Rotate the engine until the distributor rotor points to the notch on the distributor body edge and the timing indicator points to the first notch on the belt pulley. No. 1 piston should now be at TDC on its firing stroke.

10. Remove the timing chain tensioner piston by removing the plug in the side of the block.

CAUTION
The plug is under heavy spring tension.

11. Open the lockplates, remove the retaining bolts and remove the timing chain sprocket from the camshaft.

NOTE: The dowel pin hole in the camshaft flange should be in the 6 o'clock position while the notch at the top of the cam flange should be aligned with the cast projection on the cylinder head and in the 12 o'clock position for proper installation.

12. Remove the exhaust pipe from the exhaust manifold and remove the dipstick holder.

13. Unscrew the cylinder head bolts in the reverse of the tightening sequence and remove the cylinder head.

14. Installation is the reverse of removal but note the following points:

    a. Tighten the cylinder head bolts in three stages, following the illustrated sequence. Adjust the valves, start the engine and bring to normal operating temperature. Stop the engine and allow it to cool to approximately 95°F (35°C). Retorque the cylinder head bolts to specifications and readjust the valves.

NOTE: The cylinder head bolts should be retorqued after 600 miles (1000 km) of driving.

    b. Check the projection of the cylinder head dowel sleeves in the cylinder block mating surface. Maximum height is 0.20 in.

    c. Match the cylinder head gasket to the cylinder block and head to verify coolant flow passages are correct.

    d. Adjust timing and idle speed.

Timing chain tensioner plug removal or installation—typical

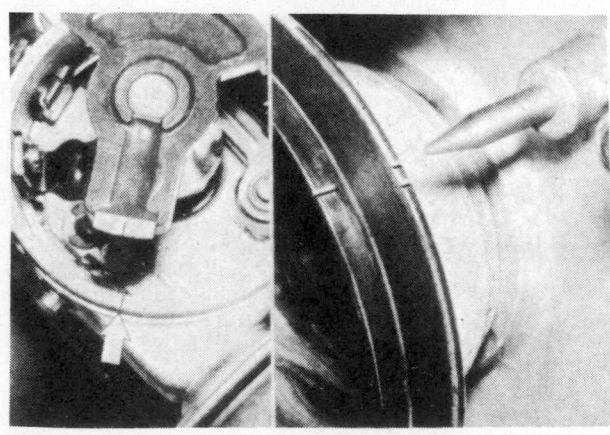

Alignment of distributor rotor and belt pulley notch—typical

e. Bleed the cooling system. Set the heater valve to the warm position and fill the cooling system. Run the engine to normal temperature and when the thermostat has opened, release the pressure cap to the first position. Squeeze the upper and lower radiator hoses in a pumping effect, to allow trapped air to escape through the radiator. Recheck the coolant level and close the pressure cap to its second catch position.

524td

NOTE: To preform this procedure, you will need a number of special tools. These include a dial indicator with a bridge that will allow the gauge to measure piston protrusion while the edges of the bridge rest on the block deck on either side of the piston; and an angle gauge for measuring turning angle of cylinder head bolts; some means of holding the camshaft in position, such as BMW tool 11 3 090.

1. Disconnect the battery ground cable. Remove the turbocharger as described later in this section.

2. Remove the fan as described under cooling system repair later in this section. Remove the drain plug from the bottom of the radiator and drain the cooling system. Then, remove the three coolant hoses connecting to the water pump.

3. Disconnect the coolant hose located at the front of the intake manifold. Disconnect the electrical plug near this hose connection. Disconnect the injector leakoff line that also connects near these connections.

4. Disconnect the heater hose nearby and under the intake manifold. Remove the bracket next to this hose connection and then disconnect the glow plug wiring.

5. Working inside the glove compartment, disconnect the multi-prong plug on the electronic control unit. Then, disconnect the engine wiring harness at the two fasteners on the firewall and pull the harness into the engine compartment.

6. Disconnect the crankcase ventilation hose at the rear of the valve cover. Then, disconnect the three electrical plugs right nearby. Disconnect the diagnostic (milti-prong) plug.

7. Disconnect the small coolant hose located to the right of the intake air box. Then, disconnect any remaining flow plug wires nearby. Disconnect the temperature sensor connectors nearby. Then, disconnect the plug at the firewall.

8. Remove the intake air box bracket located near the rear of the

intake air box. Then, disconnect the wiring harness from its retaining clips and move it downward and out of the way.

9. Disconnect the transmission dipstick tube bracket at the intake manifold. Disconnect the air hose at the manifold, nearby. Disconnect the wire at the intake pressure relief valve, nearby.

10. Remove the crankcase ventilation system oil trap from the valve cover by first disconnecting the hose and then unbolting it and removing it with its gasket.

11. Use a crowfoot wrench to unscrew and remove the injection lines at the pump and injectors. Plug all openings with clean, protective caps.

12. Remove the cam cover. Then, turn the engine until No. 1 cylinder is at Top Dead Center (No. 6 cylinder's valves overlap). Either lock the crank in position with a pin such as BMW special tool 11 2 300 or equivalent, or make sure the crankshaft is completely undisturbed until the engine is reassembled.

13. Remove the coolant hose which runs across the front of the timing belt cover and remove the timing belt cover. Then, loosen the camshaft sprocket retaining bolt. Loosen the bolt and nut which position the timing belt tensioner and then remove the timing belt.

14. Remove the cylinder head bolts in the order of 14–1, going in rotation in several stages. Lift the head off the engine.

Check the height above the block deck of each piston at the locations "A" and "B" shown

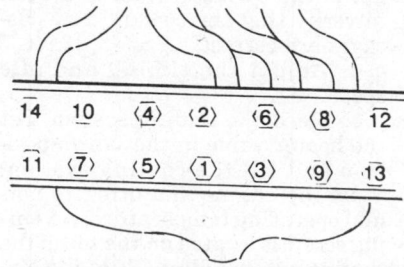

Cylinder head tightening or loosening (14–1) sequence for the 524 td

15. Clean the block deck and cylinder head lower surfaces with a solvent and wooden scraper (to avoid scoring either surface).

16. Set up and zero a dial indicator so you can measure the protrusion of the pistons above the block deck. Measure the protrusion of each piston along the center-line of the block on the flat surface at both the front and rear of the piston. Rock the engine back and forth for each cylinder until absolute maximum protrusion is obtained. Average the two readings for each piston and record the average. Return the crankshaft to No. 6 cylinder overlap position. Note the highest protrusion. Compare it to these figures and select a head gasket of the appropriate thickness from the protrusion figure:

0.025–0.030	1 hole
0.031–0.035	2 holes
0.036–0.042	3 holes

Gaskets have one, two, or three holes along one edge to indicate the thickness classification.

17. Clean all the cylinder head bolts with solvent and give them a very light coating of engine oil. Make sure the bolts are not heavily coated with oil and that the bolt holes do not contain any oil, as this will interfere with torquing and might even crack the cylinder block.

18. Turn the camshaft so that the valves on cylinder No. 6 are at the overlap position. Make sure the camshaft does not turn from this position, or the valves may be bent when the head is installed. You can use a jig such as BMW tool 11 3 090 or equivalent. Install the bolts and then torque them in the numbered order shown in the illustration (1–14) to $\frac{1}{3}$ the torque figure shown in the chart at the front of this section. Then, retorque them to $\frac{2}{3}$ that figure in the numbered order. Finally, retorque them, again in numbered order, to the full torque figure.

19. Install and adjust the timing belt as described later in this section. Adjust the valves and install the cam cover. Then, install the timing belt cover. Install the injection pump lines and torque the fittings to 14–18 ft. lbs. Bleed the fuel system as described under "Injection Pump Removal and Installation". Reconnect all electrical lines, hoses, and other fittings so the engine is ready to run. Use a new gasket on the crankcase ventilation system oil trap. Refill the cooling system.

20. Start the engine and run it at about 1,000 rpm until it is hot. Then, remove the cam cover and again in numerical order, final-torque the bolts by accurately turning them exactly another 90 degrees tighter. Use a tool designed for angle torquing

such as BMW 11 2 110. Replace the cam cover.

528i, 633CSi and 733i—1981-82

NOTE: Small variations may be encountered among models due to model changes, difference in electrical wiring, vacuum hoses and fuel line routings, but all are basically alike.

1. Disconnect the battery ground cable.

2. Disconnect the wire connectors. Loosen the clamps and remove the airflow sensor with the air filter on the fuel injected models, or remove the air cleaner from carburetor equipped models.

3. Disconnect the rocker cover vent hose, ignition line tube and electrical wiring.

4. Remove the rocker cover.

5. Drain the cooling system and remove the coolant hoses.

NOTE: Do not interchange the heater hoses.

6. Rotate the engine so that the distributor body edge and the timing indicator points to the notch on the belt pulley. This will place number one piston at TDC on its firing stroke.

7. Remove the upper timing housing cover after removing the distributor and thermostat housing.

8. Remove the timing chain tensioner piston.

--- CAUTION ---

The retaining plug is under heavy spring tension.

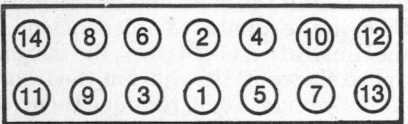

Cylinder head torque sequence for 528i and 633CSi—1981-82

Alignment of dowel pin (1) with the sprocket and upper bolt hole and cylinder head cast tab—six cylinder engines

9. Open the camshaft sprocket bolt lockplates and remove the bolts. Remove the sprocket.

NOTE: For installation purposes, the sprocket dowel pin should be located at the lower left, between 7 and 8 o'clock, while the upper bolt bore must align with the threaded bore of the camshaft and the cylinder head cast tab, visible through the two bores, when at the 12 o'clock position.

10. Remove and tag the electrical wiring and connectors.

11. Remove and tag the vacuum lines.

12. Remove the wiring harness by pulling it upward through the opening in the intake neck.

13. Disconnect the fuel lines.

14. Disconnect the exhaust line at the exhaust manifold. Remove the exhaust filter.

15. Remove the cylinder head bolts in the reverse order of the tightening sequence and install locating pins in four head bolt bores to prevent the rocker shafts from turning.

16. Remove the cylinder head.

17. Installation is the reverse or removal. Note the following points:

a. Tighten the cylinder head bolts according to the specifications chart, following the illustrated sequence. Adjust the valves before starting the engine. On those engines not using angle torque as the last torquing step, stop the engine and allow it to cool to approximately 95°F (35°C). Retorque the cylinder head bolts to specifications. Readjust the valves with the engine hot on all engines.

NOTE: The cylinder head bolts (except those on models using angle torque as the last torquing step) should be retorqued after 600 miles (1000 km) of driving.

b. Check the projection of the cylinder head dowel sleeve in the cylinder block mating surface. Maximum height is 0.20 in. (5.0mm).

c. Match the cylinder head gasket to the cylinder block and head to verify that the coolant flow passages are correct.

d. Adjust the timing and idle speed.

e. Bleed the cooling system. Set the heater valve in the Warm position and fill the cooling system. Start the engine and bring to normal operating temperature. A venting screw is located on the top of the thermostat housing. Run the engine at fast idle and open the venting screw until the coolant comes

out free of air bubbles. Close the bleeder screw and refill the reservoir with coolant.

325, 325e, 325i, 325is and 528e

1. Disconnect the battery ground cable. Make sure the engine is cool. Disconnect the exhaust pipes at the manifold and at the transmission clamp. Remove the drain plug at the bottom of the radiator and drain the coolant. Drain the engine oil.

2. Disconnect the accelerator and cruise control cables. If the car has an automatic transmission, disconect the throttle cable that goes to the transmission.

3. Working on the air cleaner/airflow sensor, disconnect the vacuum hoses, labeling them if necessary. Disconnect all electrical connectors and unclip and remove the wiring harness. Unclamp and remove the air air hose. Remove the mounting nuts and remove the assembly.

4. Working at the front of the block, disconnect the upper radiator hose, the bypass water hose, and several smaller water hoses nearby. Remove the diagnosis plug located at the front corner of the manifold. Remove the bracket located just underneath. Disconnect the fuel line and drain the contents into a metal container for safe disposal.

5. Disconnect the hoses leading to the throttle body. Remove the bracket located underneath the hoses. Disconnect the electrical connector.

6. Disconnect the heater water hoses. Press down (in the arrowed direction) on the vent tube collar shown in the illusration and install the special tool or a similar device to retain the collar in the unlocked position. Disconnect the vent tube and inspect its O-ring seal, replacing it if necessary.

7. There is a bracket with various vacuum and electrical fittings that runs from the cam cover over toward the intake manifold. Disconnect the electrical connector conntected on this bracket and the plug to its left. Remove the nuts fastening the bracket to the cam cover and the gasketed flange on the opposite end and remove the bracket. Inspect the gasket and supply a new one for use in installation, if necessary. Unplug the fuel injectors.

8. Disconnect the Digital Motor Electronics plugs nearby. Disconnect the four plugs located near the front three fuel injectors. Then, unfasten the mounting clips and pull the wiring harness out toward the left.

9. Disconnect the coil high tension wire and disconnect the high tension wires at the plugs. Then, disconnect the tube in which the wires run at the

cam cover. Disconnect the PCV hose. Then, remove the eight retaining nuts and remove the cam cover.

10. Turn the crankshaft so that the TDC line is lined up with the indicator and the valves of No. 6 clyinder are in overlapping (slightly open) position.

11. Remove the distributor cap. Then, unscrew and remove the rotor. Unscrew and remove the adapter just underneath the rotor. Remove the cover underneath the adapter. Check its O-ring and replace it if necessary.

12. Remove the distributor mounting bolts and the protective cover.

13. The 325 and 528e are equipped with a rubber drive and timing belt. Remove the belt covers as described later in this section. To loosen belt tension, loosen the tension roller bracket pivot bolt and adjusting slot bolt. Push the roller and bracket away from the belt to release the tension, hold the bracket in this position, and retighten the adjusting slot bolt to retain the bracket it this position.

14. Remove the timing belt.

NOTE: Make sure to avoid rotating both the engine and camshaft from this point onward.

15. Remove the cylinder head mounting bolts in exact reverse order of the tightening sequence shown. Then, remove the cylinder head.

16. Install the head with a new gasket. Check that all passages line up with the gasket holes. Clean the threads on the head bolts and coat with a *very light* coating of oil. Keep oil out of the bolt cavities in the head, or the head could be cracked or proper torquing affected.

17. Install the bolts and torque in three equal stages in the numbered order to the torque figure shown in specifications. Then, adjust the valves.

18. Complete the installation by reversing all removal procedures. Make sure to refill the engine oil pan and cooling system with proper fluids and to bleed the cooling system. Replace the gaskets for the exhaust system connections, if necessary. Coat the studs with CRC® copper paste or equivalent. Note that the plugs for the DME referene mark and speed signals should be connected so that the gray plug goes to the plug with a ring underneath.

NOTE: Align the timing marks when installing the timing belt. The crankshaft sprocket mark must point at the notch in the flange of the front engine cover. The camshaft sprocket arrow must point at the alignment mark

on the cylinder head. Also, the No. 1 piston must be at TDC of the compression stroke.

19. Start the engine and run it until it is hot. Stop the engine and again remove the cam cover. Using an angle gauge, tighten the head bolts 25 degrees farther in numbered order. Reinstall the cam cover.

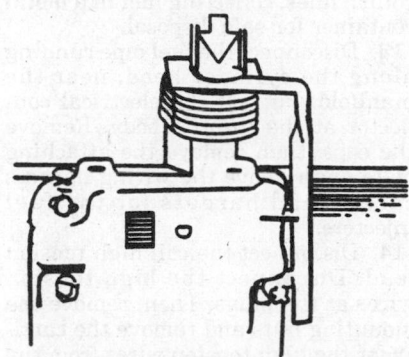

On the 325e and 528e, you'll have to press the vent tube downward (in the direction of the arrow) and then lock the collar in that position with a tool such as 11 1 290. Then, disconnect the tube.

533i, 535i, 633CSi, 635CSi, 733i and 735i—1983-86 (M30 B32 and M30 B34 engines)

1. Unbolt the exhaust pipes at the exhaust manifold. Unclamp the exhaust pipe at the transmission.

2. Disconnect the battery negative and positive cables and drain the coolant by removing the plugs from the radiator and block.

3. Disconnect the throttle, accelerator, and cruise control cables at the throttle body.

4. These engines are all virtually identical, but wiring harnesses vary from model to model. Systematically disconnect all wiring that goes to the cylinder head or would obstruct its removal. This includes: wiring to the airflow sensor; ignition wiring and, where used, the ignition wiring tube; wires to the fuel injectors; on some models you may have to disconnect the alternator wiring; on many, you'll have to disconnect the main harness to the fuse box. On 535, 635, and 735 Series cars, you'll have to disconnect the starter wiring.

5. Disconnect fuel lines, vacuum lines, and heater and coolant hoses that are in the way. Disconnect DME plugs on those models so equipped. Note that the gray plug connects to the plug with a ring underneath, for proper installation.

6. Remove the air cleaner and the windshield washer tank.

7. Remove the rocker cover. On 535, 635, and 735 Series cars, disconnect the injector electrical connections, cold start valve, and idle positioner. Disconnect the ground lead on all engines. Then, complete disconnecting the engine wiring harness by disconnecting the oil pressure sending unit and set the harness aside.

8. See the procedures below for removal of the front cover and timing chain and tensioner. Remove the upper timing case cover, tensioner piston, and then open the lockplates and remove the timing chain upper sprocket. Make sure you suspend the sprocket so the timing chain position isn't lost.

9. Loosen the cylinder head bolts following strictly the illustration in reverse order—14–1. Then, install four special pins BMW part No. 11 1 063 or equivalent. This is necessary to keep the rocker arm shafts from moving. Then, lift off the head.

10. Make checks of the lower cylinder head and block deck surface to make sure they are true. See the "Engine Rebuilding" section. Install a new head gasket, making sure that all bolt, oil, and coolant holes line up. Use a gasket marked M 30 B 34 for the larger engine used in 735i. Use a 0.3mm thicker gasket if the head has been machined.

11. Apply a very light coating of oil to the head bolts. Don't let oil get into the boltholes or apply excessive amounts of oil, or torque could be incorrect and you could crack the block. Use the newer type of bolt without a collar. Install the bolts, finger tight.

12. Torque bolts 1–6 in the order shown in the illustration to 42–44 ft. lbs. Remove the four pins holding the rocker shafts in place. Now, complete the first stage of torquing by torquing bolts 7–14 in the order shown, to the specifications shown in the Specifications chart for the first stage of torquing. Follow the remaining torquing procedures as described in the Specifications chart. Wait between steps as mentioned. Adjust the valves. Then, reassemble the engine as described below and run it until hot. Then, again remove the valve cover, and either immediately or at any time later

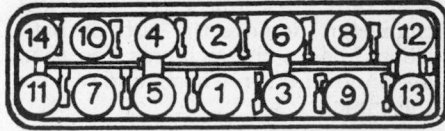

Cylinder head torque sequence for the M30B34 engine until 12/'86, and the M6 538Z engine used in the M5 and M6

(engine temperature isn't critical), turn the head bolts, in order, the number of degrees specified in the specifications chart, using special tool BMW 11 2 110 or equivalent.

13. Reinstall the timing sprocket to the camshaft. Make sure the cam is in proper time, that new lockplates are used, and that nuts are properly torqued. See the procedure for timing chain removal and installation below.

14. When reinstalling the timing cover, make sure to apply a liquid sealer to the joints between upper and lower timing covers. The remainder of installation is the reverse of removal. Note these points.

    a. Adjust throttle, speed control, and accelerator cables. Inspect and if necessary replace the exhaust manifold gasket.

    b. When reinstalling the cylinder block coolant plug, coat it with sealer. Make sure to refill the cooling system and bleed it (see the Cooling System procedure below).

535i, 635CSi and 735i—1987-88 (M30 B35 engine)

1. Unbolt the exhaust pipe connections at the manifold and at the transmission pipe clamp. Disconnect the negative battery cable.

2. Remove the splash shield from under the engine. With the engine cool, remove the drain plugs from the bottom of the radiator and block. Drain the engine oil.

3. Remove the fan. Lift out the expansion rivets on either side and remove the fan shroud.

4. Loosen the hose clamp and disconnect the air inlet hose. Remove the mounting nut and remove the air cleaner.

5. The unit on the opposite side of the intake hose from the air cleaner contains the idle speed control valve, which must be removed next. Loosen the hose clamps and pull off the hoses. Disconnect the electrical connector. Remove the mounting nut and then pull the idle speed control out of the air intake hose.

6. Pull off the three retainers for the airflow sensor, and then pull the unit off its mountings, disconnecting the vacuum hose from the PCV system at the same time.

7. Working on the coolant expansion tank, disconnect the electrical connector. Remove the nuts on both sides. Loosen their clamps and then disconnect all three hoses and remove the tank.

8. Disconnect the heater hoses at both the control valve and at the heater core.

9. Disconnect the throttle and cruise control cables at the throttle le-

ver. Unbolt the cable housing retainer and remove the housing and cables.

10. Disconnect the four plugs near the thermostat housing. Loosen the hose clamps and pull off the two coolant hoses.

11. Disconnect the plug in the line leading to the oxygen sensor. Disconnect the other two plugs nearby.

12. Disconnect the fuel supply and return lines, collecting fuel in a metal container for safe disposal.

13. Disconnect the fuel pipe running along the cylinder head, near the manifold. Pull off the electrical connector at the throttle body. Remove the caps, then remove the attaching bolts and remove the wiring harness carrier and harness for the fuel injectors.

14. Disconnect the coil high tension lead. Disconnect the high tension wires at the plugs. Then, remove the mounting nuts and remove the carrier for the high tension wires from the head.

15. Remove the attaching nuts for the cam cover and remove it.

16. Turn the engine until the timing marks are at TDC and the No. 6 valves are at overlap (both slightly open) position.

17. Remove the upper timing case cover as described below. Remove the timing chain tensioner piston as also described below.

18. Remove the four upper timing chain sprocket bolts and pull the sprocket off, *holding it upward and then supporting it securely so the relationship between the chain and sprockets top and bottom will not be lost*.

19. Disconnect the upper radiator hose at the thermostat housing. Remove the three bolts and remove the support for the intake manifold.

20. Remove the cylinder head bolts in the opposite of numbered order. Then, install four special pins BMW part No. 11 1 063 or equivalent. This is necessary to keep the rocker arm shafts from moving. Then, lift off the head.

21. Make checks of the lower cylinder head and block deck surface to

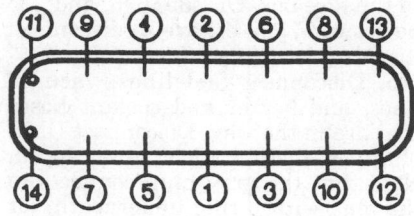

Torque head bolts in the order shown— M30 B35 engine from 12/'86 on

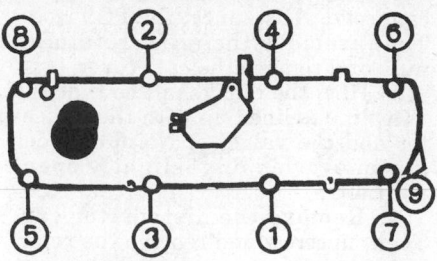

Torque the cam cover bolts on the M30 B34 and B35 engines in the order shown

make sure they are true. See the "Engine Rebuilding" section. Install a new head gasket, making sure that all bolt, oil, and coolant holes line up. Use a gasket marked M30 B35. Use a 0.3mm thicker gasket if the head has been machined.

22. Apply a very light coating of oil to the head bolts. Don't let oil get into the boltholes or apply excessive amounts of oil, or torque could be incorrect and you could crack the block. Use the newer type of bolt without a collar. Install the bolts, finger tight.

23. Torque bolts 1–6 in the order shown in the illustration to 42–44 ft. lbs. Remove the four pins holding the rocker shafts in place. Now, complete the first stage of torquing by torquing bolts 7–14 in the order shown, to the same specification. Adjust the valves after a 15 minute wait. Tighten the bolts, in the order shown, with a torque angle gauge 30–36 degrees, using special tool BMW 11 2 110 or equivalent. Then, reassemble the engine as described below and run it until hot (25 minutes). Then, again remove the valve cover, and either immediately or at any time later (engine temperature isn't critical), turn the head bolts, in order, 30–40 degrees.

24. Reinstall the timing sprocket to the camshaft. Make sure the cam is in proper time, that new lockplates are used, and that nuts are properly torqued. See the procedure for timing chain removal and installation below.

25. When reinstalling the timing cover, make sure to apply a liquid sealer to the joints between upper and lower timing covers. The remainder of installation is the reverse of removal. Note these points.

    a. Adjust throttle, speed control, and accelerator cables. Inspect and if necessary replace the exhaust manifold gasket.

    b. When reinstalling the cylinder block coolant plug, coat it with sealer. Make sure to refill the cooling system and bleed it (see the Cooling System procedure below). Make sure to refill the oil pan with the correct amount of specified oil.

c. Make sure you install the timing chain so that the down pin on the camshaft sprocket is at the lower left (8 o'Clock) when its tapped bores are at right angles to the engine. Torque the sprocket bolts to 6.5–7.5 ft. lbs.

d. Check the cam cover gasket, replacing as necessary. Retighten cam cover bolts in the order shown. Torque the bolts to 6.5–7.5 ft. lbs.

e. When reinstalling the fan shroud, make sure all guides are located properly.

f. Coat the tapered portion of the exhaust pipe connection flange with CRC® Copper Paste or equivalent. Torque the attaching nuts to 4.5 ft. lbs., and then loosen one and a half turns.

M5 and M6

NOTE: This is an extremely difficult operation involving the use of a number of special tools. You will have to remove both of the camshafts to complete it. Refer to the camshaft removal and installation procedure below for information on those special tools.

1. Disconnect the negative battery cable. Scribe matchmarks where the hood hinges attach to the hood. Then, disconnect the support struts, unbolt the hood at the hinges and remove it.

2. Disconnect the electrical connector at the airflow sensor. Loosen the hose clamp at the air intake hose going to the air cleaner, remove the air cleaner attaching nut, and remove the air cleaner and airflow senskor.

3. Disconnect the large vacuum hose that connects to the bottom of the intake manifold. Disconnect the PCV hoses where they connect to the top of the manifold. Disconnect the throttle cable that runs across the top of the manifold, and the hose running near the front. Remove the bolts fastening the manifold to the outer ends of the intake tubes and remove it.

4. With the engine cool, drain the coolant from the block. Disconnect the exhaust pipe at the manifold.

5. Working underneath, remove the heat shields. Remove the cross brace and stabilizer bar where they connect to the engine carrier. Remove the exhaust manifold as described below.

6. Disconnect the upper radiator hose. Pull the three plugs off the water manifold that connects with the upper radiator hose. Pull off the plug coming from the same harness and connecting to the top of the engine.

Then, unclip this harness and pull it out of the way.

7. Loosen the retaining straps and disconnect the electrical connector that runs directly across the front of the block. Disconnect the fuel pipe on the driver's side of the block, collecting fuel in a metal container for safe disposal.

8. Pull the electrical connector off the throttle bypass valve. Disconnect the water hose and remove the bypass valve. Disconnect the large hose just to the right of the throttle bypass valve. Remove the wiring harness clips just to the right.

9. Going to the rear of the engine, disconnect the fuel return line and collect fuel in a metal container for safe disposal. Disconnect both heater hoses. Remove the conduit for the injector wiring harness from the head. Remove the two bolts in the front of the head which run down into the timing cover.

10. See the procedures below for removal of the front timing cover and timing chain. You don't have to remove the timing chain completely, but you will have to remove the cam cover, front covers (for the camshaft drive sprockets), and the upper guide rail for the timing chain, and then turn the engine to TDC firing position for No. 1. Then, you'll be removing then timing chain tensioner. You'll be noting the relationship between the chain and both the crankshaft and camshaft sprockets, and then removing both camshaft drive sprockets. Leave the chain in a position that will not interfere with removal of the head and which will minimize disturbing its routing through the areas on the front of the block.

11. Remove the camshafts as described below.

12. You'll need a clean work area and a way to store the cam followers in order—preferably some sort of rack. Remove the cam followers one at a time, keeping them in exact order for installation in the same positions.

13. Remove the coolant pipe that runs across the front of the block. Remove the bolts (some are accessible from below) that retain the timing case to the head at the front (the timing case houses the lifters and the camshaft lower bearing saddles.) Then, go along in the area under the cam cover and remove all the remaining bolts for the timing case. Remove the timing case.

14. Loosen the head bolts in reverse of the tightening order shown. Remove the cylinder head.

15. Make checks of the lower cylinder head and block deck surface to make sure they are true. See the "En-

gine Rebuilding" section. Lubricate the head bolts with a light coating of engine oil. Make sure there is no oil or dirt in the boltholes in the block. Install a new head gasket, making sure that all bolt, oil, and coolant holes line up. Use a gasket type M6 marked 3.5M 88.3.

16. Replace the O-ring in the head at the right/rear where the coolant pipe comes up from the block. Coat the pipe with a Silastic sealer.

17. Install the head onto the block. Install the head bolts and tighten in numbered order according to Specifications.

18. When installing the timing case, replace the O-rings in the two small oil passages in the ends of the head. Inspect the six O-rings in the center of the block and replace them if necessary. Coat all sealing surfaces with Silastic sealer. Tighten the bolts evenly, torquing the smaller (M7) bolts to 10–12 ft. lbs. and the larger (M8) bolts to 14.5–15.5 ft. lbs. Install all lifters back into the same bores.

19. Install the camshafts as described below.

20. As described under the camshaft and timing chain removal and installation procedures below, reroute the timing chain as necessary and remount the drive sprockets for the camshaft. Install the tensioning rail that goes at the top of the timing chain.

21. Install the front cover according to the procedure below.

22. Continue to reverse the removal procedure. Note these points as you work:

a. When reinstalling the intake manifold, inspect the O-rings and replace as necessary.

b. Refill the cooling system with an appropriate anti-freeze/water mix for the climate and bleed the cooling system.

OVERHAUL

For all cylinder head overhaul procedures, please refer to "Engine Rebuilding" in the Unit Repair Section.

Rocker Arms/Shafts

REMOVAL & INSTALLATION

All Models Except 325, 325e, 325i, 325is, 524td, and 528e

1. Remove the cylinder head.
2. Remove the camshaft.
3. On six cylinder engines, remove the retaining bolts and remove the end cover from the rear of the cylinder

Installation of locating pins in the cylinder head bolt bores to prevent rocker shafts from turning—six cylinder engines

Removal of camshaft and rocker arm retainer plate from the cylinder head, showing the dowel pin hole on four cylinder engine

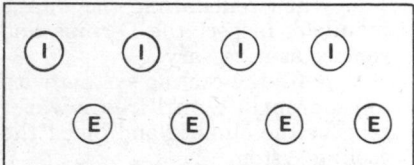

4-cylinder valve location

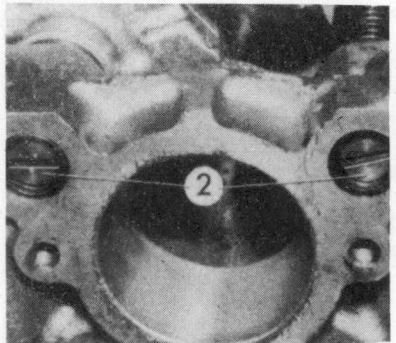

Rocker arm shaft locking bolt (2) location—six cylinder engine

Circlip location on the rocker arm shaft

Removing the rocker arm shaft with special tool—four cylinder engine

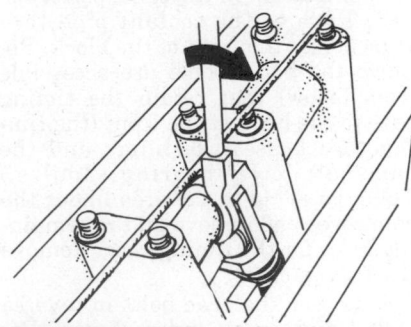

Locate the special valve spring compressing tool around the camshaft, as shown, to force the valve downward. This will give clearance to permit removal of the rocker arm

head. Slide the thrust rings and rocker arms rearward and remove the circlips from the rocker arm shafts.

4. On 4 cylinder engines:

   a. Remove the distributor flange from the rear of the cylinder head.

   b. Using a long punch, drive the rocker arm shaft from the rear to the front of the cylinder head.

NOTE: Be sure all circlips are off the shaft before attempting to drive the shaft from the cylinder head.

   c. The intake rocker shaft is not plugged at the rear, while the exhaust rocker shaft must be plugged. Renew the plug if necessary, during the installation.

5. On 6 cylinder engines:

   a. Install dowel pins BMW part No. 11 1 063 or equivalent to keep the rocker shafts from turning. Then, remove the rocker shaft retaining plugs from the front of the cylinder head. These require a hex head wrench. Then, push back the rocker arms against spring pressure and remove the circlips retaining the shafts. Remove the dowel pins. If the rocker shafts have welded plugs, the shafts will have to be pressed out of the head with a tool such as 11 3 050 or equivalent.

-------- CAUTION --------

There is considerable force on the springs positioning the rockers. They may pop out! Be cautious and wear safety glasses.

   b. Install a threaded slide hammer into the ends of the rear rocker shafts and remove.

6. The rocker arms, springs, washers, thrust rings and shafts should be examined and worn parts replaced. Special attention should be given to the rocker arm cam followers. If these are loose, replace the arm assembly. The valves can be removed, repaired or replaced, as necessary, while the shafts and rocker arms are out of the cylinder head.

7. Installation is the reverse of removal. Note the following procedures:

   a. Design changes of the rocker arms and shafts have occurred with the installation of a bushing in the rocker arm and the use of two horizontal oil flow holes drilled into the rocker shaft for improved oil supply. Do not mix the previously designed parts with the later design.

   b. When installing the rocker arms and components to the rocker shafts, install locating pins in the cylinder head bolt bores to properly align the rocker arm shafts. Note that on six cylinder engines, the longer rocker shafts go on the chain end of the engine; the openings face the bores for the cylinder head bolts; and the plug threads face outward. The order of installation is: spring, washer, rocker arm, thrust washer, circlip. Note also that newer, short springs may be used with the older design.

   c. Install sealer on the rocker arm shaft retaining plugs and rear cover.

   d. On the 4 cylinder engines, position the rocker shafts so that the camshaft retaining plate ends can be engaged in the slots of shafts during camshaft installation.

   e. Adjust the valve clearance.

524td

NOTE: To replace the rocker arms on the 524td, you will need a special tool which allows the valve involved to be opened and works against the camshaft. Use BMW Tool 11 3 120 or the equivalent. You will also need a special tool designed to remove the rocker pivots from the head. Because these are retained by an adhesive, you'll need to get an adhesive designed to retain the rocker pivots on this engine. You will also, of course, need the special tools required to adjust the valves after the rockers have been replaced.

1. Remove the cam cover. Turn the engine over with a wrench on the crankshaft pulley so the cams that drive the vacuum pump (mounted over the camshaft) are pointed downward. Then, remove the attaching nuts and remove the vacuum pump.

2. Pull off the spring clip for each rocker you are going to replace. Turn the crankshaft so the cams involved are pointing downward.

3. Locate the special valve spring compression tool around the camshaft. Make sure that if the valve will not depress easily, you turn the crankshaft. If the piston is right near top center, the valve may hit it. Also, make sure you do not depress the valve spring retainer while the valve remains stationary, which could permit the retaining collets to come loose. When there is sufficient clearance to permit the rocker to clear the ball on the top of the pivot ballstud, remove it by sliding it out from under the camshaft.

4. Remove the ballstud by clamping the special tool on it and pulling it out. Coat a new ballstud with the required adhesive and install it, pressing it in until it hits the stop. Do not replace the rocker arm without also replacing the ballstud. If re-using parts, retain ballstuds and rockers in order so the same parts will be used together.

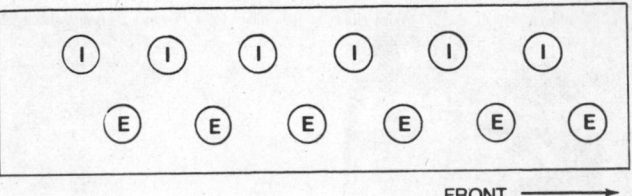

6-cylinder valve location

5. Install the rocker in reverse order. Press the spring clip into the groove in the top of the ballstud from the outboard side so the end of the clip will retain the rocker. Adjust the valves as described earlier in this section.

6. Install the vacuum pump with the cams that are under it turned downward. Make sure that the vacuum pump pipe is at the rear and that its drive cam will line up with the follower on the pump plunger. Make sure to install the seal on the pipe. Replace the cam cover in reverse or removal.

325, 325e, 325i, 325is and 528e

The cylinder head must be removed before the rocker arm shafts can be removed.

1. Remove the cylinder head.

2. Mount the head on BMW stand 11 1 060 and 00 1 490 or equivalent. Secure the head to the stand with one head bolt.

3. Remove the camshaft sprocket bolt and remove the camshaft distributor adapter and sprocket. Reinstall the adapter on the camshaft.

4. Adjust the valve play to the maximum allowable on all valves.

5. Remove the front and rear rocker shaft plugs and lift out the thrust plate.

6. Remove the spring-clips from the rocker arms by lifting them off.

7. Remove the exhaust side rocker arm shaft:

   a. Set the No. 6 cylinder rocker arms at the valve overlap position (rocker arms parallel), by rotating the engine through the firing order.

   b. Push in on the front cylinder rocker arm and turn the camshaft in the direction of the intake rocker shaft, using a ½ in. drive breaker bar and a deep well socket to fit over the camshaft adapter. Rotate the camshaft until all of the rocker arms are relaxed.

   c. Remove the rocker arm shaft.

8. Remove the intake side rocker arm shaft:

   a. Turn the camshaft in the direction of the exhaust rocker arm.

   b. Use a deep well socket and ½ in. drive breaker bar on the cam-

shaft adapter to turn the camshaft until all of the rocker arms are relaxed.

   c.. The large oil bores in the rocker shafts must be installed down to the valve guides and the small oil bores must face inward toward the center of the head.

   d. Adjust the valve clearance.

Intake Manifold

REMOVAL & INSTALLATION

318i and 320i

1. Remove the air cleaner and drain the cooling system.

2. Disconnect the accelerator cable and remove the vacuum hoses from the air collector. Tag the hoses.

3. Remove the injection line holder from No. 4 intake tube.

4. Remove the No. 3 intake tube and disconnect the vacuum and coolant lines from the throttle housing.

5. Disconnect the hoses at the EGR valve and remove the wire plugs at the temperature timing switch.

6. Remove the cold start valve from the air collector.

7. Disconnect the vacuum hose and electrical connections at the timing valve.

8. Disconnect the remaining intake tubes at the collector. Disconnect the collector brackets at the engine and remove the collector.

9. Remove the air intake tubes from the manifold and remove the injector valves.

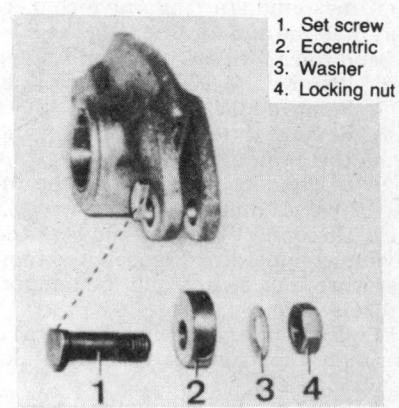

1. Set screw
2. Eccentric
3. Washer
4. Locking nut

Rocker arm valve adjusting mechanism

3. Spring   5. Rocker arm
4. Washer   6. Thrust ring

Installed position of rocker arm components

Induction system with induction tubes secured with nuts and washers

10. Remove the intake manifold.
11. Installation is the reverse of removal.

All 6 Cylinder Models Except 524td, M5 and M6

NOTE: Slight variations may exist among models due to model changes and updating but basic removal and installation remains the same.

1. Disconnect the battery ground cable and drain the cooling system.
2. Disconnect the wire harness at the air flow sensor. Remove the air cleaner and sensor as an assembly. Disconnect the air intake hose running from the air cleaner to the manifold.
3. Remove and tag the vacuum hoses and electrical plugs. Disconnect the accelerator linkage from the throttle housing.
4. Disconnect the coolant hoses from the throttle housing.
5. Working from the rear of the collector housing, disconnect the vacuum lines, and starting valve connector, fuel line and air line. Tag the hoses and lines for ease of assembly.
6. Remove the EGR valve and line.
7. Remove all intake pipes.
8. Remove the air collector housing from the engine.
9. Disconnect the plugs at the injector valves and remove the valves.
10. Disconnect the wire plugs at the coolant temperature sensor, the temperature time switch and the temperature switch.
11. Pull the wire loom upward through the opening in the intake manifold neck.
12. Remove the coolant hoses from the intake neck.

NOTE: Mark the heater hoses for proper reinstallation.

13. Remove the retaining bolts or nuts and remove either front, rear or both intake manifold necks. On later models, remove the entire assembly.
14. Installation of the manifolds in the reverse of removal. Use new gaskets on the manifolds and air intake tubes. Torque the bolts to specification (see the charts at the front of this section).

524td

1. Loosen the clamps at either end, and remove the air hose linking the turbocharger and intake air box.
2. Using a crowfoot type wrench, disconnect the injection lines at both the pump and injectors, remove the lines as an assembly, and plug all openings.
3. Remove any remaining hoses or wires interfering with manifold removal. Then, remove the retaining nuts and remove the manifold.
4. Clean both gasket surfaces, install a new gasket, and put the manifold into position. Install the retaining nuts. Torque the nuts to the figure shown in the torque chart at the beginning of this section.
5. Reinstall the injection lines, torquing the connections to 14–18 ft. lbs. Bleed the injection system as described under "Injection Pump Removal and Installation". Reconnect all hoses and wires that had to be disconnected. Reconnect the hose linking the turbocharger and manifold. Make sure connections are properly positioned and that the clamps are tight.

M5 and M6

The M5 and M6 employ a manifold chamber in combination with 6 throttle necks (one for each cylinder), each of which contains its own throttle. The throttle necks are divided into three assemblies each containing the necks for two adjacent cylinders.

1. Remove the nuts at the outer ends of the throttle necks (these attach the manifold to the outer ends of the necks). Loosen the hose clamps for the crankcase ventilation hoses and for the air intake hose. Disconnect the accelerator cable.
2. Pull the intake manifold off the throttle necks. Check O-rings and replace any that are hard or cracked.
3. Disconnect the electrical connectors to the cold start valve, throttle bypass valve, and throttle valve switch. Disconnect all the electrical connections going to the fuel injectors and remove the conduit for the injector wires from the throttle necks.
4. Disconnect the vacuum hoses for the fuel pressure regulator and the heater temperature sensor. Disconnect the fuel return pipe, and collect the fuel in a metal container for safe disposal.
5. Remove the attaching nuts and bolts, and remove the injection pipe and injectors.

NOTE: Clean the throttle shaft thoroughly and be sure not to use pliers on the shaft surface. Otherwise, needle bearings on which the shaft rides may be damaged.

6. Using a center punch, drive out the four pins locking the throttle shaft in place. Slide the shaft out of the bearings.
7. Unscrew its mounting nuts and remove the throttle bypass valve. Disconnect the air hoses from this valve.
8. Remove the nuts attaching the throttle valve necks to the head and remove them.
9. Remove the connecting pipes that run between the valve neck units. Replace O-rings if necessary. Replace all gaskets and make sure gasket surfaces on the head and inner ends of valve necks are clean.
10. Install in reverse order, providing new pins for the throttle shaft and coating its bearing surfaces with Molykote Longterm® before assem-

bly. Replace the sleeves in the intake manifold, if necessary. Replace the crankcase ventilation hose connecting the intake manifold and crankcase.

Exhaust Manifold

REMOVAL & INSTALLATION

All Except 524td, M5 and M6

The exhaust manifold are referred to as exhaust gas recirculation reactors. Refer to the "Emission Control" section for operation.

The removal and installation procedures are basically the same for all models. The four cylinder manifold (used on the 320i model), is a one piece, one outlet unit, while the six cylinder manifold assembly consists of a two piece, double outlet to the exhaust pipe. One piece can be replaced independently of the other.

1. Remove the air volume control and if necessary, air cleaner.
2. Disconnect the exhaust pipe at the reactor outlet(s).
3. Remove the guard plate from the reactor(s).
4. Disconnect the air injection pipe fitting, the EGR counterpressure line, EGR pressure line and any supports.

NOTE: An exhaust filter is used between the reactor and the EGR valve and must be disconnected. Replace the filter if found to be defective.

5. Remove the retaining bolts or nuts at the reactor and remove it from the cylinder head.
6. Installation is the reverse of removal. Use new gaskets.

524td

1. Remove the turbocharger, oil lines, and piping as described below.
2. Remove the nuts and disconnect the exhaust pipe at the manifold.
3. Remove the manifold bolts and remove the manifold. Clean both gasket surfaces.
4. Install the gasket, manifold, and attaching nuts. Torque the nuts to the figure shown in the torque chart at the beginning of this section.
5. Install the turbocharger and associated piping as described below.

M5 and M6

1. With the engine cool, remove the drain plug from the block. Remove the three electrical connectors from the front of the coolant manifold that runs along the left side of the engine. Disconnect the radiator hose from the front of this pipe. Then, remove all the

mounting bolts for this pipe and remove it. Inspect the O-rings (one for each cylinder, located in the block), and replace any that are worn or damaged.

2. Disconnect the exhaust pipe at the manifold. Remove the heat shields from underneath the engine.
3. Remove the cross brace that runs under the engine by removing the two bolts from either end and then removing it.
4. Disconnect the stabilizer bar near both ends where it is bushed to the engine carrier.
5. Attach a lifting sling to the engine. Remove the nut from the right side engine mount and lift the engine slightly for clearance.
6. Remove the mounting bolts and remove the manifold.
7. Clean all gasket material from the surfaces of the manifold and head and replace the gaskets.
8. To install, reverse the removal procedure, torquing the manifold bolts to 36–40 ft. lbs. and the coolant pipe mounting bolts to 7.5–8.5. Make sure to refill the cooling system with fresh anti-freeze/water mix and bleed it.

Turbocharger

REMOVAL & INSTALLATION

524td

1. Disconnect the connecting hoses and remove the air cleaner. Disconnect the turbo inlet and outlet air hoses.
2. Remove the EGR pipe and EGR valve.
3. Unbolt the banjo connector for the oil pressure line going to the turbocharger at the side of the block. Remove the clamps and disconnect the oil drain line from the turbo at the block. Disconnect the exhaust pipe at the turbo exhaust outlet.
4. Remove the four bolts attaching the turbocharger to the exhaust manifold, and remove it.

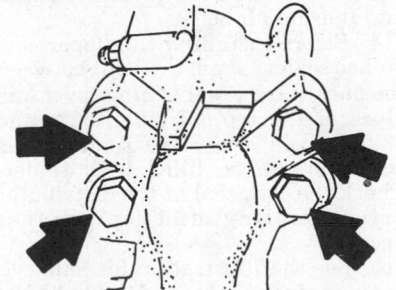

Remove the four arrowed bolts to remove the turbocharger (524 td)

5. Installation is the reverse of removal. Replace gaskets on the EGR valve and seals on the high pressure oil line. Coat EGR valve studs with a copper paste and replace the self-locking nuts.

Timing Chain (Front) Cover

REMOVAL & INSTALLATION

318i and 320i

There are two timing chain covers, one upper and one lower, which must be removed to service the timing chain and sprocket assemblies.

1. Remove the cylinder head cover. Disconnect the negative battery cable. Disconnect the air injection line at the front of the thermal reactor (if so equipped). On the 318i, disconnect the bracket located on the driver's side of the upper cover.
2. Remove 8 bolts which retain the upper timing gear cover to the cylinder head and lower timing gear cover. remove the upper cover, taking note of the placement of the alternator ground wire.
3. Drain the cooling system and remove the radiator, preheater intake air assembly (carburetor equipped cars only) and radiator hoses as outlined under "Radiator Removal and Installation".
4. Bend back the lockplates for the fan retaining bolts. Remove the bolts and lift off the fan.
5. Loosen the alternator retaining bolts. Push the alternator toward the engine and remove the fan pulley and the alternator drive (fan) belt. On the 318i, remove the alternator and tensioning bar. remove the four mounting bolts from the air pump bracket (where it attaches to the block), and remove the pump and bracket; then remove the bolt attaching the tensioning bar to the block and remove the tensioning bar.
6. Disconnect the coolant hoses from the water pump. Remove the six retaining bolts and copper sealing washers and lift off the water pump.
7. Unscrew the plug and remove the spring from the cam chain tensioner assembly, taking care to cushion the sudden release of spring tension. Remove the plunger (piston).
8. On the 320i, disconnect the multiple plug and cable lead from the alternator. Remove the alternator with its bearing block and clamping strap.
9. Remove the flywheel inspection plate and block the ring gear from turning with a small prybar.
10. Unscrew the crankshaft pulley nut and pull off the belt pulley.

11. Remove the bolts which retain the lower cover to the cylinder black and oil pan. On the 318i, remove the bolts retaining the brace plate and remove it. Also on the 318i, loosen the oil pan lower retaining bolts not directly involved with the lower cover. With a sharp knife, carefully separate the lower edge of the timing cover from the upper edge of the oil pan gasket at the front.

12. Remove the lower timing cover. At this time, it is advisable to replace the timing cover seal (sealing ring) with a new one. The sealing ring is a press fit into the cover.

13. Clean the mating surfaces of the timing covers, oil pan, cylinder head, and cylinder block. Replace all gaskets (except the oil pan gasket), and seal them at the corners with sealing compound such as Permatex® No. 2. If the oil pan gasket has been damaged, remove the oil pan and replace the gasket.

14. Reverse the above procedure to install, taking care to tighten the upper timing gear cover retaining bolts in the following sequence (as per the illustration): handtighten 1 and 2, then torque 3–8 in numerical order, and finally 1 and 2 to 6.5–7.9 ft. lbs. Note that on the 318i, the mounting web for the tensioning piston must be in the oil pocket. On the 318i, also make sure to pack the bores between the lower cover (at the top) and block with sealer.

6 Cylinder Models (Except 325, 325e, 325i, 325is, 524td, 528e, M5 andM6)

NOTE: On 533, 535, 600CS Series, and 700 Series engines, this procedure requires the use of a special gauge, to be made to a certain dimension, as in Step 16.

1. Remove the cylinder head cover. Remove the distributor as described earlier in this chapter. On all 3.3 litre models, detach the distributor guard and the air line going to the thermal reactor. On late model cars with Digital Motor Electronics, follow this procedure to remove the distributor:

   a. Remove the distributor cap, which screws onto the cover directly in front of the camshaft.

   b. Then, if the rotor is of the slide-on type, simply pull the rotor off and then remove the cover underneath it.

   c. If the rotor is of the screw-on type, unscrew it from the distributor shaft, then unscrew the adapter underneath and, finally remove the cover underneath the adapter.

2. Drain the coolant to below the level of the thermostat and remove the thermostat housing cover.

3. Remove the eight bolts and remove the upper timing case cover with the worm drive which drives the distributor (pre DME cars only).

4. Remove the piston which tensions the timing chain, working carefully because of very high spring pressure.

5. Remove the cooling fan and all drive belts. On late model 600 Series cars, the alternator must be swung aside by loosing the front bolt and removing the two side bolts. The power steering pump must be removed, leaving the pump hoses connected and supporting the pump out of the way but so that the hoses are not stressed.

6. Remove the flywheel housing cover and lock the flywheel in position with an appropriate special tool.

7. Unscrew the nut from the center of the pulley and pull the pulley/vibration damper off the crankshaft.

8. Detach the TDC position transmitter on 600CS Series, 700 Series, and certain 528i models.

9. Loosen all the oil pan bolts, and then unscrew all the bolts from the lower timing case cover. Use a knife to separate the gasket at the base of the lower timing cover. Then, remove the cover.

10. To install the lower cover, first coat the surfaces of the oil pan and block with sealer. Put it into position on the block, making sure the tensioning piston holding web (cast into the block) is in the oil pocket. Install all bolts; then tighten the lower front cover bolts evenly; finally, tighten the oil pan bolts evenly.

11. Inspect the hub of the vibration damper. If the hub is scored, install the radial seal so the sealing lip is in front of or to the rear of the scored area. Pack the seal with grease and install it with a sealer installer.

12. Install the pulley/damper and torque the bolt to specifications. When installing, make sure the key and keyway are properly aligned.

13. Remove the flywheel locking tool and reinstall the cover. Reinstall and tension all belts.

14. Before installing the upper cover, use sealer to seal the joint between the back of the lower timing cover and block at the top. On 528i, 533i and 733i models, there are sealer wells which are to be filled with sealer. Check the cork seal at the distributor drive coupling, and replace it if necessary.

15. See the illustration for four cylinder engines above, and tighten bolts 1 and 2 (the lower bolts) slightly. Then, tighten bolts 3–8. Finally, fully tighten the lower bolts.

16. Install the TDC position transmitter loosely, if so equipped. With the engine at exactly 0 degrees Top Center, as shown by the marker on the front cover, adjust the position of the transmitter with a gauge which should be made to conform to the dimensions shown in the illustration: i.e. it must fit the curve on the outside of the balancer, and incorporate a notch (for the pin on the balancer) and a ridge against which the transmitter must rest. The straight line distance between the center of the notch and bottom of the ridge must be exactly 37.5mm. Then, tighten the transmitter mounting screw.

17. If the car has the DME type distributor, inspect the sealing O-rings and replace as necessary. If it uses the DME distributor with the screw-off type rotor, make sure the bolt at the center of the rotor has its seal in place and that it is installed with a sealer designed to prevent the bolt from backing out.

18. Reverse the remaining portions of the removal procedures, making sure to bleed the cooling system.

524td

1. Disconnect the hoses and remove the air cleaner. Remove the belt driving the alternator and fan. Remove the attaching nuts and remove the fan, keeping it in the vertical position.

2. Remove the air hose running along the top edge of the cover. remove the attaching bolts and remove the cover.

3. If you are removing the cover to replace the timing belt, proceed further to remove the vibration damper:

   a. Remove the remaining accessory drive belts.

   b. Remove the belts and remove the fan drive pulley.

   c. Remove the center bolt, and pull the pulley and vibration damper off the hub.

4. Install in reverse order, torquing the center bolt for the vibration damper to the specifications shown in the torque specifications chart. Adjust belt tension.

M5 and M6

1. Disconnect the battery ground cable. Pull out the plug and remove the wiring leading to the airflow sensor. Loosen the hose clamp and disconnect the air intake hose. Remove the mounting nut and remove the air cleaner and airflow sensor as an assembly.

2. Remove the radiator and fan. See appropriate procedures below. Remove the flywheel housing cover and install a lock to lock the position of the flywheel. Remove the mounting

nut for the vibration damper with a deepwell socket. Pull the damper off with a puller.

3. Remove the pipe that runs across in front of the front cover. Remove the mounting bolts and remove the water pump pulley.

4. Loosen the top/front mounting bolt for the alternator. Remove the lower/front bolt. Loosen the two side bolts. Swing the alternator aside.

5. Remove the power steering pump mounting bolts. Make sure to retain the spacer that goes between the pump and oil pan. Swing the pump aside and support it so the hoses will not be under stress.

6. Remove the flywheel housing cover and lock the flywheel in position with an appropriate special tool.

7. Unscrew the nut from the center of the pulley and pull the pulley/vibration damper off the crankshaft.

8. Remove the bolts at the top, fastening the lower front cover to the upper front cover. Remove the bolts at the bottom, fastening the lower cover to the oil pan. Loosen the remaining oil pan mounting bolts.

9. Run a knife carefully between the upper surface of the oil pan gasket and the lower surface of the front cover to separate them without tearing the gasket.

10. Loosen and then remove the remaining front cover mounting bolts, noting the locations of the TDC sending unit on the upper/right side of the engine and the suspension position sending unit on the upper left. Also, keep track of the bolts that mount these accessories, as their lengths are slightly different. If necessary, lay the bolts out in a clean area in a pattern similar to that in which they are positioned on the engine. Remove the timing cover, pulling it off squarely.

11. Before reinstalling the cover, use a file to break or file off flashing at the top/rear of the casting on either side so the corner is smooth. Replace all gaskets, coating them with silicone sealer. Where gasket ends extend too far, trim them off. Apply sealer to the area where the oil pan gasket passes the front of the block.

12. Slide the cover straight on to avoid damaging the seal. Install all bolts in their proper positions. Tighten the bolts at the top, fastening the lower cover to the upper cover first. Then, tighten the remaining front cover bolts and, finally, the oil pan bolts. If the car has the DME type distributor, inspect the sealing O-rings and replace as necessary. If it uses the DME distributor with the screw-off type rotor, make sure the bolt at the center of the rotor has its seal in place

and that it is installed with a sealer designed to prevent the bolt from backing out.

13. Reverse the remaining portions of the removal procedures, making sure to bleed the cooling system.

Housing Cover Oil Seal

REMOVAL & INSTALLATION

All Models (Except 325, 325e, 325i, 325is, 524td and 528e)

1. Position the No. 1 piston at TDC on the beginning of its compression stroke.

2. Remove the flywheel guard and lock the flywheel with a locking tool.

3. Remove the drive belts and the fan.

4. Remove the retaining nut and remove the vibration damper from the crankshaft.

NOTE: The Woodruff key should be at the 12 o'clock position on the crankshaft.

5. Remove the seal from the timing housing cover with a small pry bar.

Position of crankshaft woodruff key (1)

6. Using a special seal installer or equivalent, lubricate and install the seal in the cover. This tool is used to press the seal into the bore with even pressure around the entire perimeter.

NOTE: If the balancer hub has serious scoring on the sealing surface, position the seal in the cover so that the sealing lip is in front of or behind the scored groove.

7. Lubricate the balancer hub and install it on the crankshaft, being careful not to damage the seal.

8. Complete the assembly, using the reverse of the removal procedure. Be sure to remove the flywheel locking tool before attempting to start the engine.

325, 325e, 325i, 325is and 528e

The 325 and 528e have two oil seals on the front engine cover. One is on the crankshaft and the other is on the intermediate shaft.

1. Remove the front engine cover (see the "Timing Belt and Front Cover" procedure).

2. Press the two radial oil seals out of the front engine cover.

3. Install the oil seals flush with the front engine cover using BMW tools 24 1 050, 33 1 180 and 005 5 500 or equivalents.

4. Install the front engine cover.

524td

NOTE: You will need a number of special tools to complete this operation. They include: A wrench designed to hold the vibration damper hub BMW 11 2 150 or equivalent; a puller for the vibration damper hub; a pin to hold the vibration damper hub 11 2 040; a puller to remove the timing belt sprocket from the crankshaft such as BMW 00 7 501 and 11 2 131; seal installer 24 1 040 and 24 1 050; and special tools designed to protect the seals when the front engine cover is installed—11 2 211 and 11 2 212. Equivalents may be available from other sources.

1. Remove the timing belt cover and vibration damper as described above.

2. Remove the radiator. Install the special wrench on the vibration damper hub. Then, unscrew the bolt at the center until it is about three turns out. Attach a puller such as 00 7 501 with bolts 11 2 132. The two outer bolts screw into holes in the outer rim of the damper hub. Then, turn the center bolt of the puller so it forces the hub off by pressing agianst the center bolt.

3. Remove the timing belt as described below. Then, use the special tool or another suitable means to hold the intermediate shaft stationary as you remove the bolt at the center. Then, remove the intermediate shaft washer and sprocket.

4. Screw the bolt into the center of the crankshaft until it is about three turns out. Screw the outer bolts for the puller into the outer edge of the crankshaft sprocket until they are secure. Then, screw in the center bolt of the puller to force the crankshaft sprocket off.

5. Remove the arrowed bolts, and oil pan bolts labeled 4, 5, and 6. Loosen the other pan bolts. Then carefully use a sharp knife to separate the oil pan gasket from the front cover. Re-

move the cover.

6. From the rear of the cover, press the oil seals outward. Then use tools such as 24 1 040 and 24 1 050 to press in new seals. Replacement seals must be pressed in until 0.039–0.079 in. indented. Apply clean engine oil to the sealing lips.

7. Install tools such as 11 2 211 (crankshaft) and 11 2 212 (intermediate shaft) to the ends of these shafts to protect the seals. Then, install the front cover.

8. Installation is the reverse of removal. Keep the following points in mind:

a. Install the crankshaft sprocket with the woodruff key in the proper position and the step forward.

b. When installing the intermediate shaft sprocket, make sure the centering pin slides into its bore.

Timing Chain and Tensioner

REMOVAL & INSTALLATION

All Models Except 325, 325e, 325i, 325is, 524td, 528e, M5 and M6

1. Rotate the crankshaft to set the No. 1 piston at TDC, at the beginning of its compression stroke.

2. Remove the distributor (6 cylinder engines only).

3. Remove the cylinder head cover, air injection pipe and guard plate.

4. Drain the cooling system and remove the thermostat housing.

5. Remove the upper timing housing cover. See the "Timing Chain Cover Removal and Installation" procedure above.

6. Remove the timing chain tensioner piston.

NOTE: The piston is under heavy spring tension.

7. Remove the drive belts and fan.

8. Remove the flywheel guard and lock the flywheel with a locking tool.

9. Remove the vibration damper assembly.

NOTE: The crankshaft woodruff key should be in the 12 o'clock position.

10. Remove upper and lower timing covers as described above.

11. Turn the crankshaft so that the No. 1 cylinder is at firing position. On the 318i, this will put the top sprocket locating pin at 6 o'clock. Open the camshaft lockplates if so equipped, remove the bolts and remove the camshaft sprocket.

Location of upper (4) and lower (3) guide rail retainers

Installation of the timing cover housing showing special sealing locations

12. On 4 cylinder engines (except 318i):

a. Remove the bottom circlip holding the chain guide rail to the block. Loosen the upper pivot pin until the guide rail rests against the forward part of the cylinder head gasket.

b. Remove the timing chain from the sprockets and remove the guide rail by pulling downward and swinging the rail to the right.

c. Remove the chain from the guide rail and remove it from the engine.

On the 318i engine:

a. Take the timing chain off top and bottom sprockets and remove carefully from the guide rail.

13. On 6 cylinder engines:

a. Remove the chain from the lower sprocket, swing the chain to the right front and out of the guide rail and remove the chain from the engine.

14. Installation is the reverse of removal, but note the following:

15. Be sure that No. 1 piston remains at the top of its firing stroke and the key on the crankshaft is in the 12 o'clock position.

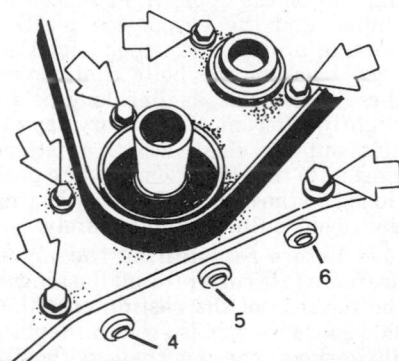

Remove the three oil pan bolts (4, 5, 6) to remove the front cover (524 td). Remove the other arrowed bolts, also

16. On 4 cylinder engines:

a. Position the camshaft flange so that the dowel pin bore is located at the 6 o'clock position and the notch in the top of the flange aligns with the cast tab on the cylinder head.

b. On all models but the 318i, position the chain in the chain guide rail and move the rail upward and to the left, engaging the lower locating pivot pin and threading the upper pivot pin into the block. Install the circlip on the lower guide pin.

On the 318i, simply locate the chain carefully in the guide rail.

c. Engage the chain on the crankshaft sprocket and fit the camshaft sprocket into the chain.

d. Align the gear dowel pin to the camshaft flange and bolt the sprocket into place. Use new lockplates (where so equipped), and secure the bolt heads.

17. On 6 cylinder engines:

a. Position the camshaft flange so that the dowel pin bore is between the 7 and 8 o'clock position and the upper flange bolt hole is aligned with the cast tab on the cylinder head.

b. Position the chain on the guide rail and swing the chain inward and to the left.

c. Engage the chain on the crankshaft gear and install the camshaft sprocket into the chain.

d. Align the gear dowel pin to the camshaft flange and bolt and sprocket into place. Torque the sprocket bolts to 5 ft. lbs. (6.5–7.5 on the M30B35 engine).

18. Install the chain tensioner piston, spring and cap plug, but do not tighten.

19. To bleed the chain tensioner, fill the oil pocket, located on the upper timing housing cover, with engine oil and move the tensioner back and forth with a screwdriver until oil is expelled at the cap plug. Tighten the cap plug securely.

20. Complete the assembly in the reverse order of removal. Check the ignition timing and the idle speed. Be sure the flywheel holder is removed before any attempt is made to start the engine.

M5 and M6

1. Remove the fan shroud and the fan. Remove the cylinder head cover. Remove the timing cover as described above.

2. Refer to the camshaft removal procedure below. Follow the procedure to the point where you unbolt the two camshaft drive sprockets and remove them.

3. Refer to the procedure below and remove the water pump.

4. Remove the two mounting bolts for the guide rail, which is located on the left (driver's) side of the engine. These are accessible from the rear. Turn the guide rail counterclockwise on its axis, looking at it from above to clear the chain and block and remove it. Be careful to retain all washers.

5. Note the relationships between timing chain and sprocket marks. Remove the timing chain.

6. Install the timing chain with the marks on all three sprockets aligned

with marked links on the chain. Make sure the chain runs on the inside of the guide sprocket on the left side of the engine and along the groove in the lower tensioning rail. Install the chain onto the camshaft drive sprockets and then install the sprockets onto the camshafts (note that the exhaust side sprocket is marked "A" and the exhaust sprocket is marked "E". Then, install the guide rail with all washers and lockwashers by rotating it into position in reverse of the removal procedure.

7. Tighten the camshaft drive sprockets, install the chain tensioner, and install the upper guide rail as described in the camshaft removal and installation procedure. Reverse the remaining removal steps to complete the procedure. Make sure to refill the cooling system with an appropriate anti-freeze/water mix and to bleed the cooling system.

Timing Belt and Front Engine Cover

REMOVAL & INSTALLATION

325, 325e, 325i, 325is and 528e

The 325 and 528e are equipped with a rubber drive and timing belt and the distributor guard plate is actually the upper timing belt cover.

1. Remove the distributor cap and rotor. Remove the inner distributor cover and seal.

2. Remove the two distributor guard plate attaching bolts and one nut. Remove the rubber guard and take out the guard plate (upper timing belt cover).

3. Rotate the crankshaft to set No. 1 piston at TDC of its compression stroke.

NOTE: At TDC of No. 1 piston compression stroke, the camshaft sprocket arrow should align directly with the mark on the cylinder head.

4. Remove the radiator.

5. Remove the lower splash guard and take off the alternator, power steering and air conditioning belts.

6. Remove the crankshaft pulley and vibration damper.

7. Hold the crankshaft hub from rotating with special BMW tool 11 2 150 or equivalent. Remove the crankshaft hub bolt.

8. Install the hub bolt into the crankshaft about three turns and use BMW tools 00 7 501 and 11 2 132 or a gear puller, to remove the crankshaft hub.

9. Remove the bolt from the engine end of the alternator bracket. Loosen the alternator adjusting bolt and swing the bracket out of the way.

10. Lift out the TDC transmitter and set it out of the way.

11. Remove the remaining bolt and lift off the lower timing belt cover.

12. Loosen the two tensioner pulley bolts and release the tension on the belt by pushing on the tensioner pulley bracket.

13. Mark the running direction of the timing belt and remove the belt.

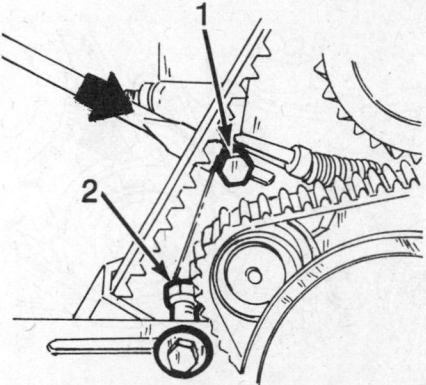

1. Tensioner adjusting slot bolt
2. Tensioner bracket pivot bolt

Releasing the tension on timing belt—528e

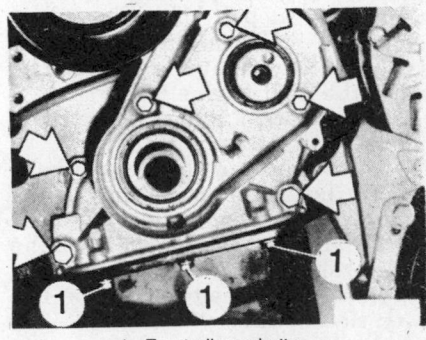

1. Front oil pan bolts

Bolt location for front engine cover—528e

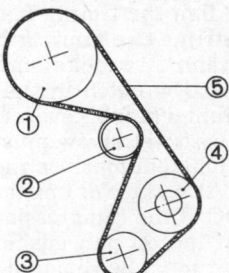

1. Camshaft sprocket
2. Tensioner roller
3. Crankshaft sprocket
4. Intermediate shaft sprocket
5. Tining drive belt

Location of timing belt sprockets and belt tensioner—528e

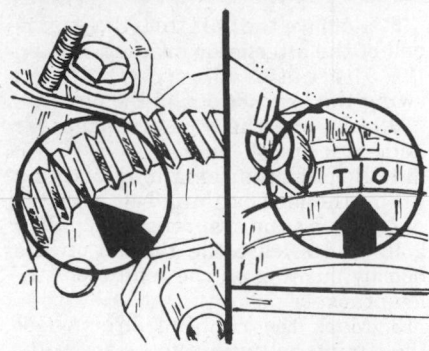

Aligning marks for timing belt installation—528e

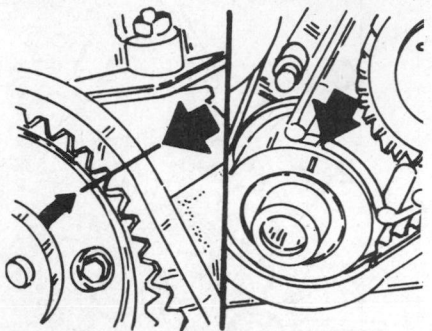

Crankshaft sprocket timing marks aligned for installation of timing belt—528e

14. Remove the three bolts across the front of the oil pan and loosen the remaining oil pan bolts. Try not to damage the oil pan gasket. Remove the six front engine cover bolts and remove the front engine cover.

15. Installation is the reverse of removal. Installation notes:

a. To tighten the timing belt, turn the engine in the direction of normal engine operation, with a ½ in. drive rachet wrench on the crankshaft bolt. When the timing belt is tight, then torque the two tensioner bolts.

b. Align the hub centering pin through the hole in the vibration damper for proper installation.

c. Align the timing marks when installing the timing belt. The crankshaft sprocket mark must point at the notch in the flange of the front engine cover. The camshaft sprocket arrow must point at the alignment mark on the cylinder head. Also, the No. 1 piston must be at TDC of the compression stroke.

d. If the oil pan gasket is damaged, it must be replaced.

e. Check and replace front cover oil seals if needed.

f. Use BMW tools 11 2 211 (crankshaft seal aligner) and 11 2 212 (intermediate shaft seal aligner) or equivalent to install the front engine cover without damaging the oil seals.

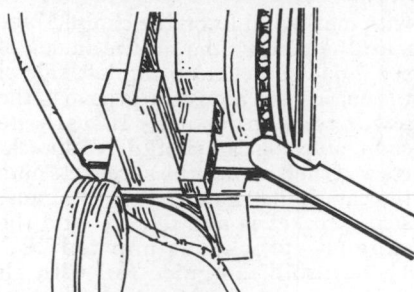

Insert a 2.5mm gauge under the exhaust side of the jig holding the camshaft for new drive belts (524 td)

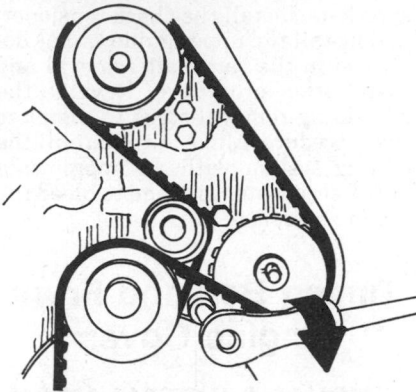

Adjusting the belt tension. Turn the torque wrench in the direction shown to apply the proper tension (see text)

g. Check the engine oil level.

h. Install engine coolant and bleed the cooling system. Bring the engine up to operating temperature and loosen the bleed screw on top of the thermostat housing. Continue to bleed until escaping coolant is free of bubbles. Add coolant to the expansion tank if needed.

524td

NOTE: To perform this procedure, you'll need a means to hold the camshaft stationary such as BMW special tool 11 3 090 and a pin to hold the injection pump gear stationary such as BMW 13 5 340. The engine must be cold.

1. Turn the engine to No. 1 cylinder at TDC, valves of No. 6 overlapping. Remove the timing belt cover and front pulley as described above. Loosen the camshaft pulley bolt, and the bolt and nut mounting the tensioner.

2. Mark the direction the belt rotates and remove it.

3. Position the camshaft at TDC No. 6 cyl. valves overlapping and lock it there. Lock the injection pump in position with the pin 13 5 340.

4. Install the new belt with the timing marks on the sprockets and belt lined up. Turn the camshaft sprocket so as to begin tensioning the belt and seat it in the grooves. When the belt is

Location of seals at hollow oil line stud

in its normal, installed position, remove the pin holding the injection pump sprocket.

5. Insert a 2.5mm thick feeler gauge under the exhaust side of the jig holding the camshaft if the belt is new or had been used less than 10,000 miles.

6. Torque the nut which rotates the tensioner (2) in the direction shown in the illustration. For belts with 10,000 miles or less on them, torque to 30.5–32.5 ft. lbs. For belts with more mileage, torque to 22–25 ft. lbs.

7. Tighten the locknut for the tensioner (3) and then tighten (1), the camshaft sprocket bolt, and (2). Remove the camshaft-holding jig.

8. Rotate the engine in the forward direction one full turn and then recheck that timing marks are all lined up.

9. Adjust the static timing of the injection pump as described below. Reinstall the timing belt cover and front pulley in the reverse of removal. Refer to the appropriate procedure above.

Camshaft

REMOVAL & INSTALLATION

All Models (Except 325, 325e, 325i, 325is, 524td, 528e, M5 and M6)

1. Remove the oil line from the top of the cylinder head.

NOTE: Observe the location of the seals when removing the hollow oil line studs. Reinstall the seals in the same position.

2. Remove the cylinder head. Support the head in such a way that the valves can be opened during camshaft removal.

3. Adjust the valve clearance to the maximum clearance on all rocker arms.

4. Remove the fuel pump and pushrod on carbureted engines.

5. On 4 cylinder engines:

a. Special tools are used to hold the rocker arms away from the camshaft lobes. On the 320i, use tool 11 1 040; on the 318i, use 11 0 040. You can use these numbers to shop for tools from independent sources also.

NOTE: The proper tool or its equivalent, must be used on fuel injection engines to avoid distorting the valve heads.

NOTE: On the 320i and 318i, the clamping bolt for the special tool is off-center. The clamp must be mounted so the shorter end faces the exhaust side of the engine, or the valve heads may contact each other. On the 318i, install two dowel pins in the head.

On 6 cylinder engines:

a. A special tool (11–2–060) except on 6 cyl. engines; on those use 11 1 060 and 00 1 490) or its equivalent, is used to hold the rocker arms away from the camshaft lobes. When installing the tool, move the intake rocker arms of No. 2 and 4 cylinders forward approximately ¼ in. and tighten the intake side nuts to avoid contact between the valve heads. On the six, turn the camshaft 15 degrees clockwise to install the tool. On these engines, to avoid contact between the valve heads, first tighten the tool mounting nuts on the exhaust side to the stop and then tighten the intake side nuts slightly. Reverse this exactly during removal.

6. Remove the camshaft.

On 4 cylinder engines:

a. Turn the camshaft until the flange is aligned with the cylinder head boss. Remove the guide plate retaining bolts and move the plate downward and out of the slots on the rocker arm shafts.

b. Carefully remove the camshaft from the cylinder head.

c. Remove the two plugs behind the guide plate (at top), coat with Loctite® No. 270 or equivalent, and replace them.

On 6 cylinder engines:

a. Rotate the camshaft so that the two cutout areas of the camshaft flange are horizontal and remove the retaining plate bolts.

b. Carefully remove the camshaft from the cylinder head.

c. The flange and guide plate can be removed from the camshaft by

removing the lockplate and nut from the camshaft end.

7. Install the camshaft and associated components in the reverse order of removal, but observe the following:

a. After installing the camshaft guide plate, the camshaft should turn easily. Measure and correct the camshaft end play.

b. The camshaft flange must be properly aligned with the cylinder head before the sprocket is installed. Refer to the disassembly procedure.

c. Install the oil tube hollow stud washer seals properly, one above and one below the oil pipe. On six cyl. engines, the arrow on the oil line must face forward.

d. Install the cylinder head. Adjust the valves.

524td

NOTE: To complete this procedure, you'll need several special tools to install a new oil seal. Use BMW tools 11 2 212, 11 3 080, and 00 5 500.

1. Remove the cam cover and vacuum pump as described below.

2. Remove the exhaust side rocker arm of cylinder No. 2 and the intake rocker arm of cylinder No. 3. See the Rocker Arm Removal & Installation procedure above. You need not disturb the rocker pedestals; keep the rockers in order of reinstallation in the same positions.

3. Turn the crankshaft until it is at TDC with No. 6 cylinder's valves in overlap position.

5. Remove the front cover as described above.

6. Remove the timing belt as described above. Make sure to loosen the camshaft sprocket bolt before releasing belt tension and removing the belt.

7. Once the belt is removed, remove the bolt and washer and remove the camshaft sprocket.

8. Disconnect the oil line that is in the way. Then, remove the camshaft bearing cap bolts and remove the caps, keeping them in order. Remove the oil seal from the front bearing cap. Remove the camshaft.

9. If you are replacing the camshaft, replace all the rocker arms as described above. Also, transfer the steels ring that drives the vacuum pump to the new camshaft.

10. Oil all bearing surfaces with clean engine oil and install the camshaft. Install the caps and bolts, and torque M6 bolts to 6–7 ft. lbs. M8 bolts should be torqued to 15–17 ft. lbs. The front bearing cap lower surface must be coated with a brush-on universal

sealing compound—Three Bond Silicone 1207 or equivalent.

11. Install a seal installer 11 2 212 or equivalent onto the end of the camshaft. Lubricate the lip of the seal with clean engine oil. Then, press the seal into the bore of the bearing, using a suitable seal installer part no. 11 3 080 and 00 5 500 or equivalent. The seal must be pressed in until it hits the stop.

12. Install the oil line. Check the end play of the camshaft with a dial indicator and compare with specifications. If end play is excessive with a new camshaft, it may be necessary to replace the cylinder head and bearing caps.

13. Install the camshaft sprocket making sure the pin in the camshaft flange fits through the bore in the sprocket and washer. Torque the bolt to 47–51 ft. lbs.

Removing camshaft thrust bearing cover—528e

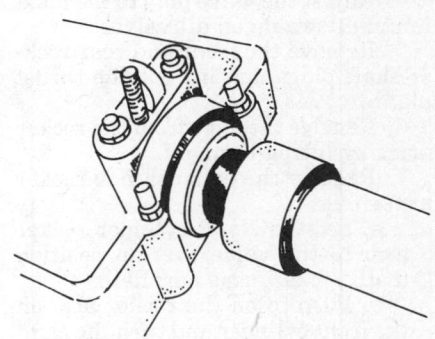
Installing the front camshaft oil seal—524 td

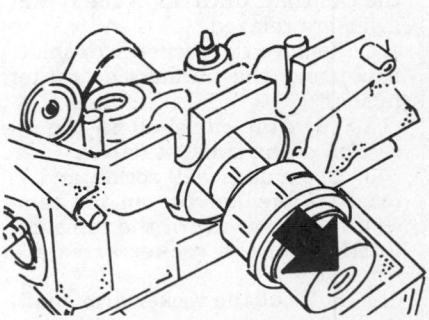
Pulling out the camshaft—528e

Location of piston in the cylinder bore with ring gaps located 180° apart

14. Install the timing belt and tension it as described above. Reverse the remaining removal procedures.

325, 325e, 325i, 325is and 528e

The cylinder head and the rocker arm shafts must be removed before the camshaft can be removed.

1. Remove the cylinder head (see "Cylinder Head Removal and Installation").

2. Mount the head on a stand. Secure the head to the stand with one head bolt.

3. Remove the camshaft sprocket bolt and remove the camshaft distributor adapter and sprocket. Reinstall the distributor adapter on the camshaft.

4. Adjust the valve play to the maximum allowable on all valves.

5. Remove the front and rear rocker shaft plugs and lift out the thrust plate.

6. Remove the clips from the rocker arms by lifting them off.

7. Remove the exhaust side rocker arm shaft:

 a. Set the No. 6 cylinder rocker arm to the valve overlap position (both rocker arms parallel).

 b. Push in on the rocker arm on the front cylinder and turn the camshaft in the direction of the intake rocker shaft, using a ½ in. breaker bar and a deep well socket to fit over the camshaft adapter. Rotate the camshaft until all of the rocker arms are relaxed.

 c. Remove the rocker arm shaft.

8. Remove the intake side rocker arm shaft:

 a. Turn the camshaft in the direction of the exhaust valves.

 b. Use a deep well socket and ½ in. drive breaker bar on the camshaft adapter to turn the camshaft until all of the rocker arms are relaxed.

 c. Pull out the rocker arm shaft.

9. Remove the camshaft thrust bearing cover. Check the radial oil seal and round cord seal, replace them if needed.

10. Pull out the camshaft.

11. Installation is the reverse of removal. Installation notes:

 a. Use BMW tool 11 2 212 or equivalent over the end of the camshaft during installation of the thrust bearing cover; this will protect the oil seals and guide the cover on.

 b. The rocker arm thrust plate must be fit into the grooves in the rocker shafts.

 c. The straight side of the springclip must be installed in the groove of the rocker arm shafts.

 d. The large oil bores in the rocker shafts must be installed down to the valve guides and the small oil bores must face inward toward the center of the head.

 e. Adjust the valve clearance.

M5 and M6

NOTE: Note that to perform this operation, you will need an expensive jig, special tool No. 11 3 010 or equivalent. This is necessary to permit you to safely remove the camshaft bearing caps and then safely release the tension the valve springs put on the camshafts. You'll also need an adapter to keep the camshaft sprockets from turning as you loosen and tighten their mounting bolts.

1. Remove the cylinder head cover. Remove the fan cowl and the fan.

2. Remove the mounting bolts and remove the distributor cap. Remove the mounting screws and remove the rotor. Unscrew the distributor adapter and the protective cover underneath. Inspect the O-ring that runs around the protective cover and replace it, if necessary.

3. Remove the two bolts and remove the protective cover from in front of the right side (intake) camshaft. Remove the bolts and remove the distributor housing from in front of the left (exhaust) side cam. Inspect the O-rings, and replace them if necessary.

4. Remove the six mounting bolts from the cover at the rear end of the cylinder head and remove it. Replace the gasket.

5. Remove the two nuts, located at the front of the head, which mount the upper timing chain guide rail. Then, remove the upper guide rail.

6. Turn the crankshaft to set the engine at No. 1 cyl. TDC (valves for No. 1 will be at overlap position – both valves just slightly open) with timing marks, of course, at TDC.

7. Remove the cap for the timing chain tensioner, located on the right side of the front timing cover. Then, slide off the damper housing. Remove the seal, discard it, and supply a new one for reassembly.

CAUTION

The next item to be removed is a plug which keeps the tensioner piston inside its hydraulic cylinder against considerable spring pressure. Use a socket wrench and keep pressure against the outer end of the plug, pushing inward, so that you can release spring pressure very gradually once the plug's threads are free of the block.

---

8. Remove the plug as described in the caution, and then release spring tension. Remove the spring and then the piston. Check the length of the spring. It must be 6.240–6.280 in. in length; otherwise, replace it to maintain stable timing chain tension.

NOTE: The timing chain should remain engaged with the crankshaft sprocket while you remove the camshafts. Otherwise, you will have to do additional work to restore proper timing. You'll need to devise a way to keep the timing chain under slight tension by supporting it at the top as you remove the camshaft sprockets in the next step.

9. Pry open the lockplates for the camshaft sprocket mounting bolts. Install an adapter to hold the sprockets still and remove the mounting bolts.

10. Using an adapter to keep the sprockets from turning and putting tension on the timing chain, loosen and remove the sprocket mounting bolts, keeping the chain supported.

11. Mount the special jig described above on the timing case (which mounts to the top of the head). Then, tighten the jig's shaft to the stop. This will hold both camshafts down against their lower bearings.

12. Remove the mounting bolts and remove the camshaft bearing caps. You can save time by keeping the

caps in order, although they are marked for installation in the same positions.

13. Once all bearing caps are removed, slowly crank backwards on the jig shaft to gradually release the tension on the camshafts. Once all tension is released, remove the camshafts.

14. Carefully remove the camshafts in such a way as to avoid nicking any bearing surfaces or cams.

15. Oil all bearing and cam surfaces with clean engine oil. Carefully install the camshafts (marked "E" for intake and "A" for exhaust) so as to avoid nicking any wear surfaces. The camshafts should be turned so that the groove between the front cam and sprocket mounting flange faces straight up. Install the special jig and tighten down on the shaft to seat the camshafts.

16. Install all bearing caps in order (or as marked). Torque the attaching bolts to 15–17 ft. lbs. Then, release the tension provided by the jig by turning the bolt and remove the jig.

17. Install the intake sprocket (marked "E"), install the lockplate, and install the mounting bolts. Use the adapter to keep the sprocket from turning, and torque the bolts to 6–7 ft. lbs. Do the same for the exhaust side sprocket. Make sure the timing chain stays in time.

18. Now, slide the timing chain tensioner piston into the opening in the cylinder in the block. Install the spring with the conically wound end facing the plug (or outward). Install the plug into the end of the sprocket and then install it over the spring and use the socket wrench to depress the spring until the plug's threads engage with those in the block. Start the threads in carefully and then torque the plug to 27–31 ft. lbs. Install a new seal, connector, damper housing, and the outside cap with a new cap seal. Torque the outside cap to 16–20 ft. lbs.

19. Crank the engine forward just one turn in normal direction of rotation. Now, one camshaft groove on each side should face toward the center of the head and one on each side should face the case boss on the front bearing cap. Lock the sprocket mounting bolts with the tabs on the lockplates.

20. Reverse the remaining removal procedures to complete the installation. Before final tightening of the mounting nuts for the guide rail for the top of the timing chain, go back and forth, measuring the clearance between the sprockets and the center of the guide rail to center it. Then, tighten the mounting nuts.

Intermediate Shaft

REMOVAL & INSTALLATION

325, 325e, 325i, 325is, 524td and 528e

1. Remove the front cover as detailed previously.

2. Remove the intermediate shaft sprocket.

3. Loosen and remove the two retaining screws and then remove the intermediate shaft guide plate.

4. Carefully slide the intermediate shaft out of the block. Turn the crankshaft if necessary to remove it. Inspect the gear on the intermediate shaft, replacing it if necessary.

5. Installation is in the reverse order of removal.

Pistons and Connecting Rods

POSITIONING

All reference numbers on the pistons and connecting rods must be located on the same side, with the arrow on the piston top facing the front of the engine. Measurement, ring fitting and installation procedures are outlined in the Engine Rebuilding section. See the section immediately below for certain specifics that apply only to BMWs.

REMOVAL & INSTALLATION

NOTE: For general piston and connecting rod overhaul procedures, please refer to "Engine Rebuilding" in the Unit Repair Section.

The pistons and connecting rods may be removed from the engine after the cylinder head, oil pan and oil pump are removed. It may be necessary to first remove a ridge worn into the cylinder above the top ring. See the engine rebuilding section. The connecting rods and caps are marked for each cylinder with No. 1 cylinder at the sprocket end of the engine. Codes pairing the connecting rods with the matching cap are located on the exhaust side of the engine. However, you should mark the exact relationship between each rod and the crankshaft to ensure replacement in the exact same position, in case the bearings can be re-used.

On the 524td engine, oil nozzles which are critically aimed must be protected from damage by studs (11 2 050) which screw into the connecting rod cap bolt holes before the rod and

piston are shoved upward and out the top of the block. Make sure each crankpin is precisely at Bottom Dead Center prior to removal.

a. To disassemble rods and pistons, remove the circlip and press out the piston pin. Note that pistons and piston pins come as a matched set. Do not mix them up.

b. A piston pin must always slide through the connecting rod under light pressure.

c. If replacing pistons, make sure all are of the same make and weight class (marked "+" or "−" on the crown).

d. Piston installed clearance must meet specifications. On the 318i, check installed clearance at a point measured up from the lower skirt edge, depending on the piston manufacturer: Mahle − 0.551 in.; KS − 1.215 in.; Alcan − 0.610 in.

On the 3.3 liter engine, measure Mahle pistons 1.024 in. up from the lower skirt edge, and KS pistons 1.340 in. up from the skirt edge. On the 3.5 liter engine, measure 0.551 in. up from the skirt edge.

On the 3.5 liter, M30 B34 engine, measure the Mahle pistons at a point 0.551 in. up from the bottom of the skirt.

On the 3.5 liter, M30 B35 engine, measure Alcan piston diameter at a point 0.531 in. from the lowest point of the skirt; measure Mahle pistons at a point 0.866 in. from the lowest point of the skirt.

On the 524td engine, the dimensions are: Alcan 0.591; KS 0.709; Mahle/Konig 0.472. Measure 0.551 in. up from the skirt edge.

On the M5, M6 engine, measure the piston at a point 0.236 in. below the deepest part of the skirt.

e. Lubricate the piston and rings with engine oil prior to installation. Offset ring gaps 120 degrees apart. The side of rings marked "TOP" must face upward 3.3 and 3.5 engines use a plain compression ring at top,

Proper piston ring installation—typical

tapered or beveled second compression ring, and an oil control ring at the bottom. The 524td uses a keystone ring at the top, a taper face lower compression ring, and a beveled oil control ring with a rubber-lined expander at the bottom.

ENGINE LUBRICATION

Oil Pan

REMOVAL & INSTALLATION

528i

1. Raise and support the vehicle. Drain the engine oil.
2. Remove the stabilizer bar.
3. Remove the alternator and remove the power steering pump, but do not disconnect the hoses.
4. Remove the lower power steering bracket bolt and remove the remaining bolts to remove the oil pan retaining bolts.
5. Loosen the engine support bracket.
6. Remove the oil pan bolts and loosen the oil pan from the engine block.
7. Rotate the crankshaft until the No. 6 crankpin is above the bottom of the engine block.
8. Lower the front of the oil pan, turn the rear of the pan towards the support bracket and remove the pan.
9. Reverse the procedure to install the oil pan, using new gaskets.

320i

1. Raise and support the vehicle. Drain the engine oil.
2. Loosen the steering gear bolts and pull the steering box off the front axle carrier.
3. Remove the oil pan bolts and separate the pan from the engine block.
4. Swing the oil pan downward while rotating the crankshaft to allow the pan to clear the crankpin and remove the pan toward the front.
5. Reverse the procedure to install the oil pan, using new gaskets.

318i

1. Remove the dipstick. Remove the lower pan by draining oil, removing pan bolts, and removing the lower pan.
2. Remove the oil pump, as described under "Oil Pump Removal and Installation", below.

3. Unscrew the ground strap, located at the right rear of the upper pan.
4. Remove the bottom three flywheel housing bolts, and two reinforcement plate bolts, and remove the reinforcement plate.
5. Remove upper pan bolts, and remove the upper pan.
6. Clean all four sealing surfaces. Replace both gaskets. Coat the mating surfaces on the timing case and end covers with sealer.
7. Install in reverse order, torquing pan bolts to 7–8 ft. lb.

524td

1. Drain the oil out of the oil pan. Disconnect the electrical connector for the wire running to the base of the oil pan.

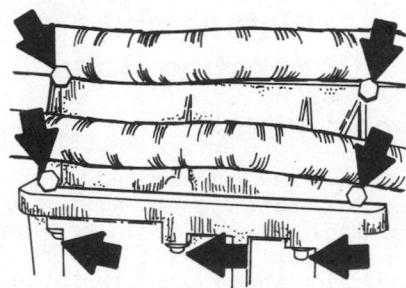
Removing the bolts (arrowed) to remove the flywheel or torque converter cover

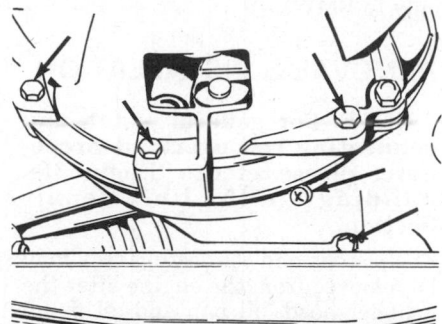
When removing the upper oil pan on the 318i, remove the arrowed bolts from the bell housing and reinforcing plate, and remove the plate

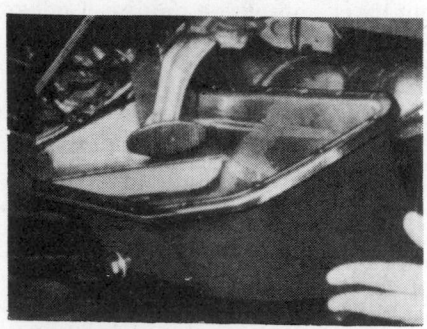
Removal of engine oil pan—typical

2. Disconnect the turbocharger drain hose running into the side of the oil pan.
3. Remove the flywheel/torque converter cover by removing the four bolts from underneath the the three from the clutch or converter housing.
4. Remove the oil pan bolts and lower it until you can access to the oil pump mounting bolts. Remove those bolts (one on one side of the crankshaft and two on the other side) then lower the pan with the pump inside it.
5. Clean all the sealing surfaces. Coat the joints between the block and timing case cover and end cover with a sealing compound. Use a new pan gasket.
6. Guide the oil pump driveshaft into the upper bearing in one side of the block. Guide the pan with the pump inside it upward until you can bolt the oil pump into position. Then, bolt the pan into position. Complete the procedure in reverse order.

533i and 633CSi — 1981-82

1. Raise and support the vehicle. Drain the engine oil.
2. Remove the front stabilizer bar.
3. Disconnect the wire terminal at the oil level switch.
4. Disconnect the power steering pump, but do not disconnect the hoses. Loosen all the power steering bracket bolts, and remove the bottom bolt.
5. Remove the engine oil pan bolts, separate the oil pan from the engine block and lower the front of the pan.
6. Rotate the crankshaft until the No. 6 crankpin is above the bottom of the engine block.
7. Lift the engine slightly at the clutch housing while removing the pan to the right side.
8. Reverse the procedure to install the oil pan, using new gaskets.

533i and 633CSi — 1983-84
535i, 635CSi, M5 and M6

1. Disconnect the engine ground lead. Disconnect the electrical connector and separate the leads from the air cleaner/air flow sensor. Loosen the hose clamp and disconnect the air intake hose. Remove the mounting nut and remove the air cleaner and the airflow sensor as a unit. Remove the fan shroud.
2. Drain the engine oil.
3. Loosen the belt tension and remove the alternator drive belt. Loosen the upper/front mounting bolt for the alternator and the two bolts on the side of the block that mount it at the rear. Remove the lower/front mounting bolt. Then, swing the alternator to the side.
4. Loosen the power steering pump mounts and remove the drive belt.

Then, remove the mounting bolts and remove the pump and pump mounting bracket. Make sure to retain spacers. If the car has air conditioning, remove the nuts and bolts that fasten the compressor to the hinge type mounting bracket. Make sure the compressor is suspended so there is no tension on the hoses. Unbolt the hinge type mounting bracket and remove it.

5. Remove the brace plate located under the oil pan. Remove those oil pan bolts that you can reach.

6. Remove the engine ground strap. Remove the engine mount through bolts. Attach a lifting sling to the hooks on top of the engine. Lift the engine slightly for clearance.

7. Shift the power steering pump out of the way and support it so no tension will be placed on the hoses.

8. Remove the remaining oil pan mounting bolts. Turn the crankshaft so the rods for cylinders 5 and 6 are as high as possible. Then, remove the pan.

9. Clean all sealing surfaces and supply a new gasket. Apply a liquid sealer to the joints between the block and the timing cover on the front and the rear main seal cover at the rear.

10. Install the oil pan in reverse order. Torque the pan bolts to 6.5–7.5 ft. lbs. Make sure to refill the pan with the required amount of the correct oil. Mount all accessories securely and adjust the drive belts.

1981–82 733i

1. Raise and support the vehicle. Drain the engine oil.

2. Remove the power steering pump, but do not disconnect the hoses.

3. Remove the lower power steering bracket bolt. Loosen the upper bracket bolts to move the bracket away from the oil pan.

4. Disconnect the oil level switch wire terminal.

5. Remove the oil pan bolts and separate the oil pan from the engine block.

6. Disconnect the left and right engine mounts.

7. Remove the engine vibration damper.

8. Lower the vehicle and remove the fan housing from the radiator.

9. Attach a lifting sling and raise the engine until the oil pan can be removed.

10. Reverse the procedure to install the oil pan, using the new gaskets.

1983–86 733i and 735i (M30 B34 engine)

1. Remove the alternator drive belt, remove the alternator mounting bolts and move it aside.

2. Loosen the adjusting and mounting bolts and remove the power steering pump belt. Remove the power steering pump hinge bolt and nut. Remove the two bolts shown, keeping any shims that may have been used in assembly together with the bolt they were on.

3. Drain coolant out of the block. Drain the oil pan. Remove the plug from the block and drain the engine of coolant.

4. Remove the two attachments fastening the stabilizer bar to the body.

5. Remove the two bolts and nuts shown and move this bracket away from the engine.

6. Remove the bolts and remove the clutch housing cover. Remove all the oil pan bolts you can reach.

7. Disconnect the oil level sending unit wire. Then, unfasten both engine mounts by removing the nuts from the ends of the bolts.

8. Disconnect the radiator hoses that's near one of the lifting hooks, and securely connect a lifting sling to the engine. Raise the engine.

9. Swing out and tie down the power steering bracket. Then, unscrew the remaining oil pan bolts.

10. Pull the oil pan down. Turn the crankshaft so the rods for cylinders 5 and 6 are in the highest position, pull the stabilizer bar away, and then remove the pan.

11. Install in reverse order, paying attention to these points:

a. Clean all gasket surfaces thoroughly. Use a new gasket and coat all mating surfaces on the timing cover and clutch housing cover with a liquid sealer.

b. Torque the stabilizer bar attachment bolts to 16 ft. lbs.

c. Make sure spacers are used on the power steering pump brace (removed in Step 2) so there will not be any torque on the bracket due to misalignment.

1987–88 735i (M30 B35 engine)

1. Loosen the hose clamp for the air intake hose. Remove the mounting nut for the air cleaner, and remove the air cleaner. Remove the fan and shroud.

2. Disconnect the electrical plug and overflow hose from the coolant expansion tank. Be careful not to kink the hose. Remove the mounting nuts and remove the tank.

3. Remove the splash guard for the power steering pump. Loosen the locknut for the pump adjustment and remove the through bolt that mounts the pump lower bracket (which contains the adjustment mechanism) to the block. Swing the bracket aside. Unscrew the bolt attaching the power steering pump lines to the block and shift them aside too.

4. Disconnect the electrical plug for the suspension leveling switch on the left side engine mounting bracket. Remove the oil pan drain plug and drain the oil.

5. Remove the bracket for the exhaust pipes located near the oil pan.

6. Disconnect the ground strap from the engine. Remove the nuts and washers attaching the engine to the mounts on both sides.

7. Attach an engine lifting sling to the hooks at either end of the cylinder head. Lift the engine as necessary for clearance.

8. Remove all oil pan mounting bolts and remove the pan. Clean both sealing surfaces and supply a new gasket. Coat the four joints (between the block and timing case cover at the front and the block and rear main seal housing cover at the rear) with a sealer such as Three Bond Silicone Sealer®. Install the oil pan bolts and torque them to 6.5–7.5 ft. lbs.

9. Reverse the remaining procedures to install the oil pan. Torque the engine mount nuts to 31–34 ft. lbs. Refill the oil pan with the required amount and type of oil.

Rear main bearing oil seal and end cover housing showing special sealing locations

325, 325e, 325i, 325is and 528e

1. Raise the vehicle and support it. Drain the engine oil.
2. Remove the front lower splash guard.
3. Disconnect the electrical terminal from the oil sending unit.
4. Remove the flywheel cover.
5. Remove the oil pan bolts and lower the oil pan. Remove the oil pump bolts and take out the oil pump and oil pan.
6. Installation is the reverse of removal. Installation notes:
   a. Clean the gasket surfaces and use a new gasket on the oil pan.
   b. Coat the joints on the ends of the front engine cover with a universal sealing compound.
   c. Install the sending unit wire and the engine oil.

Rear Main Bearing Oil Seal

REMOVAL & INSTALLATION

The rear main bearing oil seal can be replaced after the transmission, and clutch/flywheel or the converter/flywheel has been removed from the engine.

Removal and installation, after the seal is exposed, is as follows.

1. Drain the engine oil and loosen the oil pan bolts. Carefully use a knife to separate the oil pan gasket from the lower surface of the end cover housing.
2. Remove the two rear oil pan bolts.
3. Remove the end cover housing from the engine block and remove the seal from the housing.
4. Install a new seal into the end cover housing with a special seal installer BMW Tool No. 11 1 260 backed up by a mandrel, Tool No. 00 5 500 or equivalent. On 1984–86 3.3 and 3.5 liter engines, press the seal in until it is about 0.039–0.079 in. deeper than the standard seal, which was installed flush.

NOTE: Fill the cavity between the sealing lips of the seal with grease before installing. On 1984-86 engines, lubricate the seal with oil.

5. On all 1983-88 engines, coat the mating surface between the oil pan and end cover with sealer. Using a new gasket, install the end cover on the engine block and bolt it into place.
6. Reverse the removal procedure to complete the installation. If the oil pan gasket has been damaged, replace it.

Oil Pump

REMOVAL & INSTALLATION

All Models (Except 325, 325e, 325i, 325is, 524td and 528e)

1. Remove the oil pan. On the 318i, only the lower section of the pan need be removed.
2. Remove the bolts retaining the sprocket to the oil pump shaft and remove the sprocket.
3. On 4 cylinder engines:
   a. Remove the oil pump retaining bolts and lower the oil pump from the engine block.
   b. Note the location of the O-ring seal, between the housing and the pressure safety line.
   c. Be sure that the oil bore in the shim is correctly positioned during the oil pump installation.
4. On 6 cylinder engines:
   a. Remove the oil pump retaining bolts and lower the oil pump from the engine block. On 6 cyl. engines, there are three bolts at the front and two bolts attaching the rear of the oil pickup to the lower end of a support bracket. You must remove all five bolts.
   b. Do not loosen the chain adjusting shims from the two mounting locations.
5. Install the oil pump in the reverse order of removal. On 6 cylinder engines and 318i, add or subtract shims between the oil pump body and the engine block to obtain a slight movement of the chain under light thumb pressure.

─────── **CAUTION** ───────
When used, the two shim thicknesses must be the same. Tighten the pump holder at the pick-up end after shimming is completed to avoid stress on the pump.

6. On 6 cylinder engines, after the main pump mounting bolts are torqued, loosen the bolts at the bracket on the rear of the pick-up, allowing the pick-up to assume its most natural position. This will relieve tension on the bracket. Tighten the bolts.

325, 325e, 325i, 325is and 528e

1. Raise the vehicle and support it. Drain the engine oil.
2. Remove the front lower splash guard.
3. Disconnect the electrical terminal from the oil sending unit.
4. Remove the flywheel cover.
5. Remove the oil pan bolts and lower the oil pan. Remove the oil pump bolts and take out the oil pump and oil pan.

6. Installation is the reverse of removal. Installation notes:
   a. Clean the gasket surfaces and use a new gasket on the oil pan.
   b. Coat the joints on the ends of the front engine cover with a universal sealing compound.
   c. Install the sending unit wire and the engine oil.

524td

On the diesel, the pump comes down as the oil pan is removed. Refer to the Oil Pan Removal and Installation procedure which gives complete details.

ENGINE COOLING

Radiator

REMOVAL & INSTALLATION

The radiator can be removed after draining the cooling system, removal of the coolant hoses, disconnecting of the automatic transmission oil cooler lines, disconnecting of the temperature switch wire connectors and removing the shroud from the radiator core. Cover the openings of the transmission cooler and hoses. On 1983-88 3.3L and 3.5L engines, remove the plug from the bottom radiator tank. On the 318i, remove the cover from the left side of the radiator. On late model cars with the M30 B35 engine, remove the fan and shroud; then, spread the retaining clip and pull the oil cooler out to the right. Remove the radiator retaining bolts (or single bolt on some models) and lift the radiator

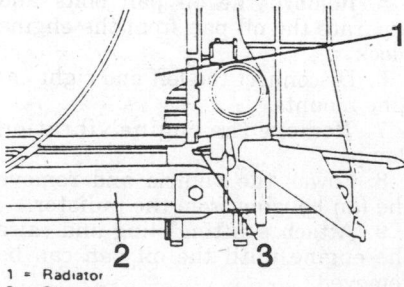

1 = Radiator
2 = Oil cooler
3 = Clip
Spread clip (3) apart and lift out the engine oil cooler to the right.
Remove radiator.

Late model 5,6,and 7 Series cars with the M30 B35 engine have an oil cooler that must be removed before removing the radiator (1). To remove the oil cooler (2), remove the clip (3) and then pull the cooler out to the right.

from the vehicle. Note that on the 1983-88 3.3L and 3.5L engines, there are two bolts at the top/rear of the radiator and two bolts at the bottom rear.

The shroud will remain in the vehicle, resting on the fan (unless already removed). The radiator is installed in the reverse order of removal. Fill and bleed the cooling system.

Water Pump

REMOVAL & INSTALLATION

All Models (Except 325, 325e, 325i, 325is, 524td and 528e)

1. Drain the cooling system and remove the radiator.
2. Remove the fan blades. Loosen the drive belts and remove as necessary. On the 318i and 1983-85 733i and 735i this requires holding the fan pulley via the locating posts, and then turning the coupling nut clockwise (left hand threads) to remove the fan and clutch. Store in a vertical position.
3. Unbolt and remove the belt pulley from the pump flange and disconnect the coolant hoses.
4. On 1983-85 3.3 and 3.5 liter engines, remove the lifting hook that's in the way before removing the two bolts. In addition, on the M5, M6 models, remove the air cleaner and airflow sensor as an assembly before removing the pump. Remove the retaining bolts and remove the water pump from the engine.
5. The installation is in the reverse of the removal procedure. Use a new gasket and bleed the cooling system.

325, 325e, 325i, 325is and 528e

1. Drain the cooling system.
2. Remove the distributor cap and rotor. Remove the inner distributor cap and rubber sealing ring.
3. Hold the fan pulley from turning with BMW tool 11 5 030 or equivalent. Remove the fan coupling nut (left hand thread—turn clockwise to remove).
4. Remove the belt and pulley.
5. Remove the rubber guard and distributor and or upper timing belt cover.
6. Compress the timing tensioner spring and clamp pin with BMW special tool 11 5 010 or equivalent.

NOTE: Observe the installed position of the tensioner spring pin on the water pump housing for reinstallation purposes.

7. Remove the water hoses, remove the three water pump bolts and remove the pump.

Measuring belt deflection

8. Clean the gasket surfaces and use a new gasket.
9. Installation is the reverse of removal.
10. Add coolant and bleed the cooling system.

524td

1. Remove the fan cowl. Hold the fan pulley with the blade of a screwdriver and remove the nut which fastens the fan in place, turning it clockwise because of the use of left hand threads. Drain the cooling system.
2. Remove the front cover as described earlier in this section. Unclamp and detach the water pump outlet hose at the pump.
3. Remove the water pump mounting bolts. Remove the pump, pushing the timing belt to one side for clearance.
4. Clean both surfaces of gasket material, and install a new gasket coated with sealer.
5. Install the water pump in reverse order. Refill the cooling system and bleed it.

Thermostat

REMOVAL & INSTALLATION

The thermostat is located near the water pump, either on the cylinder head or intake manifold on some models and is located between two coolant hose sections on other models. On the diesel, it is located right above the water pump. Remove the fan to gain access to it. See the water pump removal procedure for special procedures required to remove the fan.

The removal and installation of the thermostat is acccomplished in the conventional manner. Always drain some coolant out and save it in a clean container before removing the thermostat. On the M5, M6 engine, the

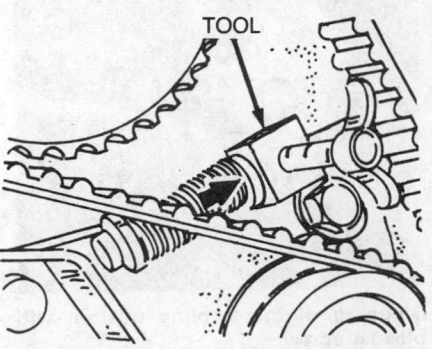
Compress tensioner spring with special tool during water pump removal—528e

1. Upper radiator hose
2. Lower radiator hose

Removing water pump retaining bolts—528e

forward (removable) portion of the housing has a hose connected to it. You need not disconnect the hose to remove the housing. Note that on the 1983-87 3.3 and 3.5 liter engines and the diesel, there is not only a thermostat housing gasket, but an inner rubber seal to keep the closed thermostat from leaking. On the engine used in the M5, M6, there is a large O-ring seal for the main portion of the housing and a small, O-ring located above it in a small passages. Replace both these seals on all models. Note that thermostats for 3.5L engines built in 1986-88 carry an "A" designation. Refill and bleed the cooling system.

Bleeding the Cooling System

WITH BLEEDER SCREW ON THERMOSTAT HOUSING

Set the heat valve in the WARM position, start the engine and bring it to normal operating temperature. Run the engine at fast idle and open the venting screw on the thermostat housing until the coolant comes out free of air bubbles. Close the bleeder screw and refill the cooling system.

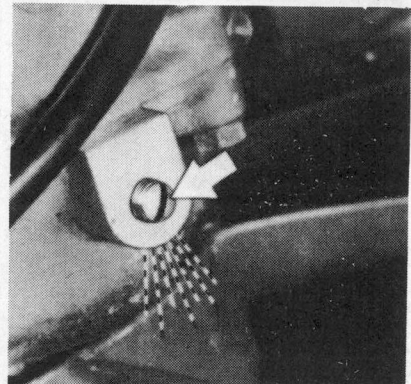

Bleeding of the cooling system with bleeder screw

WITHOUT BLEEDER SCREW

Fill the cooling system, place the heater valve in the WARM position, close the pressure cap to the second (fully closed) position. Start the engine and bring to normal operating temperature. Carefully release the pressure cap to the first position and squeeze the upper and lower radiator hoses in a pumping action to allow trapped air to escape through the radiator. Recheck the coolant level and close the pressure cap to its second position.

EMISSION CONTROLS

Please refer to "Emission Control" in the Unit Repair section for system maintenance procedures. Due to the complex nature of modern electronic engine control systems, comprehensive diagnosis and testing procedures fall outside the confines of this repair manual. For complete information on diagnosis, testing, and repair procedures concerning all modern engine and emission control systems, please refer to *"Chilton's Guide to Electronic Engine Controls"*.

EGR WARNING LIGHT

A warning light marked EGR is triggered at 25,000 miles, to alert the driver to service the exhaust gas recirculation system filter.

A triggering device, located under the dash and driven by the speedometer cable, can be reset to open the electrical contacts and extinguish the EGR warning light.

NOTE: Two different sized buttons are mounted side by side on the triggering device. The small button is for the reactor light and the large button is for the EGR light. Press the button to reset.

Triggering device with REACTOR (1) and the EGR (2) resetting buttons shown

GASOLINE ENGINE FUEL SYSTEM

Fuel Filter

REMOVAL & INSTALLATION

All Models Except 633CSi, M5 and M6

The inline fuel filters on these BMW models are easily removed. On filters that are located near the fuel tank, you must clamp the fuel lines closed before disconnecting them, or fuel will run out.

1. Disconnect the inlet and outlet hoses. Remove the hose clamps if necessary.
2. The filters will usually be attached to a frame, floor pan or wheel well by a bracket. Loosen the bracket and remove the filter.

3. Observe the instructions on the inlet and outlet during installation.

633CSi, M5 and M6

1. Disconnect the battery cables. Working under the fuel tank, pull back the protective caps and then unscrew the attaching nuts and pull off the electrical connections for the fuel pump.
2. Pinch off the inlet line to the fuel pump and the outlet from the filter. Then, loosen the clamps and disconnect these two hoses.
3. Remove the nut that clamps the fuel line near the pump. Then, remove the three bolts which mount the pump and filter to the bottom of the body and remove the assembly.
4. Remove the bolt fastening the halves of the bracket together and remove the filter from the bracket. Loosen the clamp on the inlet side of the filter and disconnect the inlet line, noting the direction of flow (arrow). Remove the rubber bushing in which the filter is mounted, and mount it on the new filter.
5. Install the filter in exact reverse order, making sure all clamps are securely tightened. Operate the engine and check for leaks.

LOCATION BY MODEL

320i, 318i, 325, 325e, 325i, 325is, 528i, 733i and 735i

The inline filter is located directly above the final drive assembly and attached to the underside of the floor pan.

528i, 533i, 535i, 633CSi, 635CSi, M5 and M6

The inline filter is located behind the passenger side wheel, near the frame, above the final driveshaft. On 1986-88 models, it is mounted on a bracket onto which the fuel pump is also mounted.

Electric Fuel Pump

PRESSURE CHECKING

318i and 320i

1. Connect a pressure gauge in the line leading from the fuel distributor on top of the injector pump to the warm-up regulator. Plug the open end of the line leading to the warm-up regulator, and make sure the gauge will read the pressure coming from the distributor.
2. Disconnect the wire plug on the mixture control unit, and turn on the ignition. The pressure should read

64–74 psi, or the fuel pump will have to be replaced.

325, 325e, 325i, 325is, 528e, 528i, 533i, 633CSi and 733i (1981-82)

1. Connect a pressure gauge in the line leading to the cold start valve from the injector feed circuit. With the engine idling, the pressure must be 33–38 psi, or the fuel pump (or filter) is defective.

533i, 535i, 633CSi, 635CSi, 733i, 735i, M5 and M6

1983-88

1. Tee a pressure gauge into the fuel feed line in front of the pressure regulator (on M5, M6, you can tee in between the cold start valve and the fuel rail). Plug the fuel return hose.

2. Pull off the pump relay. Jumper terminals 87 and 30. Measure the delivery pressure. It should be 43 psi.

REMOVAL & INSTALLATION

All Models Except 633CSi, M5 and M6

The fuel pump is an electrical unit, delivering fuel through a pressure regulator, to a fuel distributor or a ring-line for the injection valves. The fuel pump is mounted under the vehicle, near the fuel tank, or in the engine compartment.

1. Disconnect the negative battery connector. Push back any protective caps and disconnect the electrical connector(s).

2. If the fuel lines are flexible, pinch them closed with an appropriate tool. Disconnect the fuel lines and plug the ends.

3. Remove the retaining bolts and remove the pump and expansion tank as an assembly. On the 318i, the pump and mounting bracket come off together. On the 1983-88 733i and 735i, remove the clamp bolt, bend the clamp open, and remove the pump.

4. The pump can be separated from the expansion tank after removal. On the 318i, separate the pump from the mounting bracket and slide the rubber mounting ring from the pump.

5. Installation is the reverse of removal. Use similar types of hose clamps, if any need replacing. The wrong type clamp can damage the pressure lines.

633CSi, M5 and M6

1. Follow Steps 1–3 of the fuel filter removal procedure for these models, above.

Electric fuel pump assembly—typical

2. Remove the bolt fastening the halves of the bracket together and remove the filter from the bracket. Loosen the clamp on the outlet side of the fuel pump and disconnect the line. Then, slide off the rubber bushing in which the pump is mounted.

3. Check the code number on the side of the pump and make sure the replacement unit carries the same code.

4. Install the pump in exact reverse order, making sure all clamps are securely tightened. Operate the engine and check for leaks.

Fuel Pressure Regulator

REMOVAL & INSTALLATION

528i and 633CSi—1981-82 733i—1981

1. On 528i and 633CSi, remove No. 4 intake tube. Pull off the vacuum hose located on one end of the regulator. Loosen the fuel line hose clamp and pull off the fuel return line that attaches to the opposite end.

2. Using a backup wrench on the flats that are an integral part of the regulator body, loosen the coupling nut and then disconnect the fuel supply line.

3. The fitting that the fuel return line connects to is screwed into the pressure regulator and also mounts the regulator. Unscrew this fitting using an open-end wrench and remove the regulator.

4. To install the regulator, first position it so the return line connection fitting will pass through the hole in the mounting bracket, and then install that fitting. Make the other connections in reverse order. Make all connections tight and then run the engine while checking for leaks.

1982-83 733i

The regulator connections are identical with those on the unit used up to 1981. However, the mounting bracket that fits under the return line connection is bolted together. Once the lines have been disconnected, remove this bolt and remove the unit. Now, remove the return line connection and bracket parts and transfer them to the replacement unit before mounting the unit on the car. Make sure you run the engine and check for leaks.

318i, 325, 325e, 325i, 325is, 528e, 533i—1983–84 535i, 633CSi—1983–84 635CSi, 733i (1984) and 735i, M5 and M6

1. Remove the vacuum hose from the unit.

2. Loosen the clamp and pull off the fuel hose.

3. Remove the two bolts and pull the unit from the injection tube (318i, 325, all models with M30 B35 engine), or from the body (other models).

4. Inspect the seal that seals the connection with the injection tube and replace it, if necessary.

5. Install in reverse of the removal procedure.

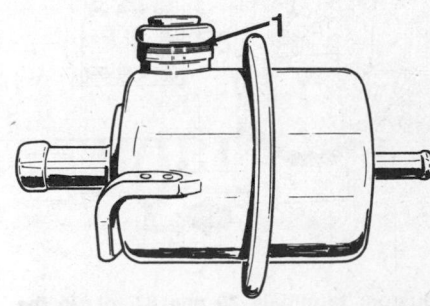

On the 318i fuel pressure regulator, check the seal (1) and replace it if necessary

Fuel Injection

Due to the complex nature of modern fuel injection systems, comprehensive diagnosis and testing procedures fall outside the confines of this repair manual. For complete information on fuel injection diagnosis, testing and repair procedures please refer to *"Chilton's Guide To Fuel Injection And Feedback Carburetors."*

DIESEL FUEL SYSTEM

Fuel Filter

REPLACEMENT

1. Loosen the bleeder screw located on top of the filter mounting fitting with a regular screwdriver. Place a container under the filter and loosen the drain cock to drain a small amount of fuel (this will keep fuel from spilling when the filter is removed).
2. Disconnect the plug on the water level sensor. Unscrew the filter with a standard oil filter strap wrench.
3. Remove the water level sensor from the old filter and move it over to the new one.
4. Thoroughly coat the seal on top of the new filter with clean fuel. Start the filter onto the threads, turn it until the gasket touches, and then turn it just one half turn more by hand.
5. Disconnect the plug for the fuel transfer pump. Open the bleeder screw. Jumper terminals 30 and 87. When fuel that is bubble-free runs out of the bleed screw, tighten it. Remove the jumper and reconnect the plug.

6. Start the engine and operate it to check for leaks. Tighten the filter just a bit further, if necessary.

DRAINING WATER FROM THE SYSTEM

Hold a half pint container under the bleeder screw and open the drain cock. See Step 5 of the procedure above for fuel filter replacement, and activate the fuel transfer pump as described there. Then, press the drain adapter in to open it. Drain until pure fuel runs out.

Diesel Injection Pump

REMOVAL & INSTALLATION

NOTE: This is a complex operation requiring several special tools. Use 13 5 020 or equivalent to remove injection lines. Use 13 5 010 and 13 5 061 or equivalent to press the injection pump off its sprocket. You'll also need two M6 x 20mm bolts and plastic caps to seal openings.

1. Remove the drain plugs from both the block and the radiator to completely drain coolant. remove the fan cowl and fan as described earlier in this section.
2. Remove the oil filler cap to watch the valves. Turn the crankshaft with a socket wrench so tha No. 1 cylinder is at TDC firing position (No. 6 valves overlapping).
3. Disconnect and remove the upper and lower radiator hoses. Remove the alternator drive belt. Remove the timing belt cover, as described earlier in this section.
4. Using a backup wrench, use the special injection line wrench to disconnect the inlet line at the injection pump. Plug the opening.
5. Disconnect the fuel return line at the connector below the pump. Remove the wiring harness clamp nearby.

6. Remove the clamp for the oil dipstick tube. Disconnect the hoses on the timing advance unit. Remove the air collector bracket near the rear of the injection pump. Remove the popoff valve air connection.
7. Disconnect the hoses for boost pressure, injection pump oil drain, vacuum, and the altitude compensator.
8. Remove the line running from the turbo to the intake manifold. Remove the oil trap from the valve cover. Then pull off the three plugs nearby.
9. Disconnect the fuel shutoff and idle switch connectors.
10. Disconnect the throttle cables at the cam and remove the cable housings from the bracket.
11. Disconnect all the coupling nuts at the injection nozzles with the special wrench, being careful not to bend the injection lines. Do the same with the lines at the injection pump end. Plug all openings and then pull the lines out of the way.
12. Remove the nut attaching the injection pump sprocket to the pump. Then, bolt the special tools for pressing the pump off the sprocket to the sprocket. Turn the crankshaft as necessary to line the boltholes up so the bolts fastening the tool to the block on either side can be installed and then install them.
13. Remove the two nuts situated directly behind the front cover. Then, remove the three bolts that fasten the pump at the rear.
14. Turn the large bolt at the center of the special tool and press the pump out of the sprocket.
15. Pull off the EGR pressure converter hoses at the converter. Remove the wiring harness for the pump out of the clips. Remove the pump. Be careful not to disturb the pump shaft. The key must remain at the top (don't lose it).
16. Install the pump so the key fits through the slot in the sprocket. Then, install and tighten the two nuts situated directly behind the front cover. Make sure the pump rests tightly

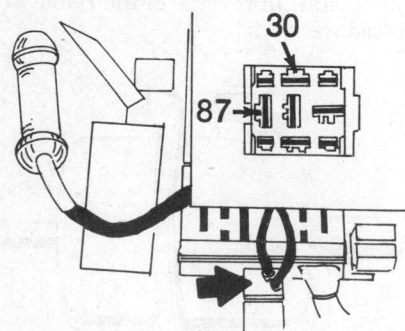

Jumper terminals 30 and 87 to run the fuel transfer pump and prime the fuel system

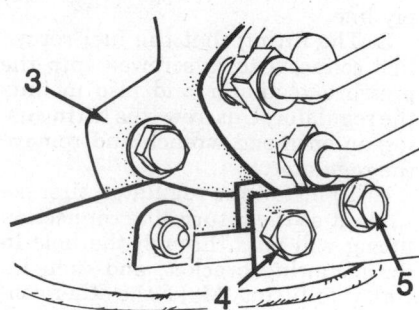

Loosen the bolts shown (3–5) before starting injection pump installation

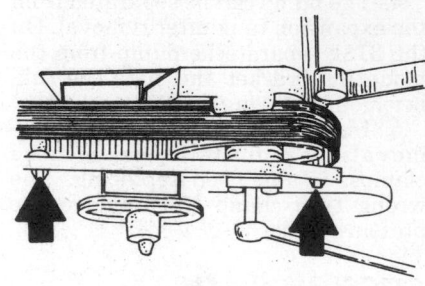

Install bolts at the arrowed point to hold the injection pump installation

against its mounting on the front cover.

17. Remove the special tool used to press the pump out of the sprocket. Then, install the sprocket bolt and torque it to 33–35 ft. lbs.

18. Adjust the static timing as described below.

19. Perform the remaining procedures in reverse order. Install the injection lines as described above under Injector Nozzle Replacement. Bleed the fuel system as described above.

INJECTION TIMING

NOTE: To perform this procedure, you will need a special dial indicator gauge and a timing pin, BMW tools 13 5 330 and 11 2 300 or equivalent.

1. Make sure the coolant temperature is above 68°F so the throttle lever will rest against the idle stop — not in the cold fast idle position.

2. Unfasten the coolant overflow tank and move it out of the way. Disconnect and plug the overflow hose.

3. Remove the plug in the injection pump head (between two of the lines going to the injectors). Install 13 5 330 or equivalent and hand tighten it. Remove the fan as described in the cooling system section. Turn the crankshaft, watching the dial gauge, in the forward direction until the gauge reaches its maximum value. Then, zero the gauge. Continue turning the engine toward TDC as you press the timing pin into the timing hole in the flywheel housing. The pin will lock into a hole in the flywheel, keeping the engine at TDC. Check that No. 6 valves are overlapping by removing the oil fill. Repeat the procedure, to set the engine at TDC firing position for No. 1, if the valves of No. 6 are not overlapping. Make sure to zero the gauge in the same way.

4. The reading should be 0.0256–.0264 in. If it is within these limits, remove the gauges and replace the plug with a new gasket, restoring other parts disturbed to their normal condition. If the reading is incorrect, follow the rest of the steps.

5. Remove the bracket for the air collector that is near the injection pump. Remove the wiring harness from its clamps.

6. Remove the bolts "3", "4" and "5" at the rear of the pump (see the illustration).

7. Loosen the hose clamp that's in the way at the front of the pump. Loosen the two nuts behind the front cover just enough to permit you to turn the pump. To increase the read-

ing or advance the timing, turn the pump toward the engine. When the figure is within tolerance, tighten the two nuts on the front cover and then tighten 3–5 in numerical order at the rear. Reverse the remaining procedures.

Injection Nozzle

REMOVAL & INSTALLATION

NOTE: To remove these injection nozzles, you'll need a special tool BMW 13 5 020 or equivalent. You should also get caps to prevent the entry of dirt.

1. Remove the oil trap located on the valve cover. Loosen the mounting clamps for the injection lines.

2. Disconnect the plugs associated with the injection system. There are a diagnostic plug and two others nearby.

3. Pull off the leakoff hoses for the injectors with a pair of pliers. Then, unscrew the coupling nuts on the injectors with the special tool 13 5 020 or equivalent.

4. Use the same tool to unscrew the coupling nuts on the injection pump. Make sure you do not hit the lines with the tool handle and bend them.

5. Unscrew the injectors using the special tool. For No. 1 injector with the wire, run the plug through the tool to protect it. Make sure it is as close as possible to the middle.

6. Install in reverse order. Coat the threads of each injector with "CRC" and torque each injector to 25–33 ft. lbs.

7. When tightening injection lines to the pump, tighten No.4 cylinder's line first. All injection line fittings (both ends) are torqued to 10–18 ft. lbs. Leave the injector ends loose for bleeding.

8. Bleed the fuel system as follows:
   a. Disconnect the electrical plug for the fuel transfer pump relay.

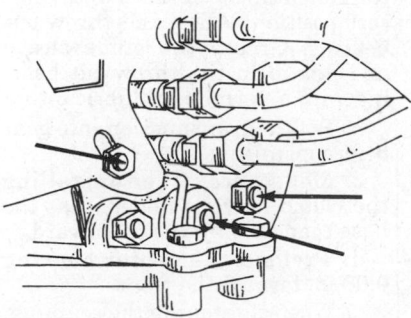

Loosen the three arrowed bolts to turn the injection pump for timing it. These are at the rear of ther pump

Jumper the terminals numbered 30 and 87 to operate the fuel transfer pump. Then, loosen the banjo fitting for the inlet fuel line on the injection pump until pure fuel runs out. Tighten the fitting. Remove the jumper wire and reconnect the plug.

   b. Loosen the bleed plug on the injection pump two turns. Then, crank the engine until air-free fuel runs out. Torque the plug to 10.5–14.5 ft. lbs.

   c. With the injection lines still loose at the nozzles, crank the engine. When fuel that is free of bubbles runs out of each line at the nozzle, stop cranking the engine. Torque the nozzles with the special tool to 10–18 ft. lbs.

MANUAL TRANSMISSION

REMOVAL & INSTALLATION

320i and 318i

1. Drain the transmission. On 320i only, unscrew all transmission mounting bolts (4) accessible from above. Swing up the bracket mounted to the top/left bolt.

2. Disconnect the exhaust system support at the rear of the transmission.

3. Detach the exhaust pipe at the manifold.

4. Detach the driveshaft at the transmission by pulling out bolts from the rear of the coupling (the coupling remains attached to the driveshaft).

5. Remove the heat shield. Remove the bolts for the center bearing bracket, and pull the bracket downward. Bend the driveshaft downward and pull it out of the bearing journal.

6. Remove the bolt and disconnect the speedometer drive cable. Disconnect the back-up light switch wire, and pull the wire out of the clips on the transmission.

7. Remove the two Allen bolts at the top and pull the console off the transmission.

8. Disconnect the gearshift selector rod by pulling off the circlip, removing the washer and pulling the rod off the pin.

9. Detach the clutch slave cylinder line bracket at the front of the transmission, remove the mounting bolts from the slave cylinder mounting, and remove the slave cylinder.

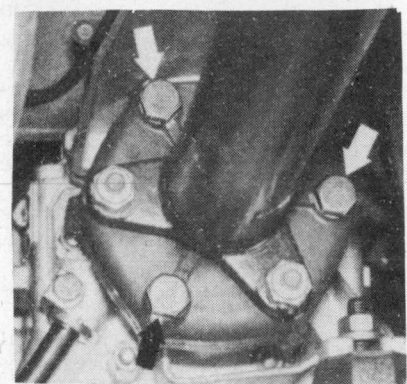

Disconnecting driveshaft at transmission

10. Remove the flywheel housing cover.

11. Support the transmission securely at the center with a floor jack and wooden block.

12. Detach the crossmember by removing the nuts attaching it to the body at either end. On 318i, remove all front mounting bolts. Remove the three remaining front mounting bolts on the 320i, and pull the transmission out toward the rear.

13. Reverse the removal procedure to install. Bear the following points in mind:

   a. Front mounting bolts are torqued to 18–19 ft. lbs. on the M8 transmissions: 34–37 on the M10 transmissions. Torque the crossmember rubber mounts to 31–35 ft. lbs.

   b. On the 318i, the console has self-locking bolts which must be replaced for reassembly.

   c. When reinstalling the clutch slave cylinder, make sure the bleeder screw faces downward.

   d. When installing the driveshaft center support bearing, preload it forward 0.078 in. on 320i, 0.079–0.157 in. on 318i.

   e. Replace the locknuts on the driveshaft coupling and tighten the nuts only – not the bolts to 31–35 ft. lbs.

   f. Inspect the gasket at the joint between the exhaust manifold and pipe and replace it if necessary.

   g. When reattaching exhaust system support at the rear, leave the attaching nut/bolt slightly loose; loosen the two nuts/bolts attaching the support via slots to the transmission; push the support toward the exhaust pipe until all tension is removed and then secure nuts and bolts.

All 6 Cylinder Models (Except Below)

1. Remove the complete exhaust system. Drain the transmission.

2. Remove the circlip and washer at the selector rod and disengage the rod at the transmission.

3. Unzip the leather boot surrounding the gearshift lever. With a pointed object such as an ice pick, release the circlip at the bottom of the gearshift lever and then pull the lever upward and out of the transmission. Lubricate the nylon bushings at the bottom of the lever mechanism with a permanent lubricant for reassembly.

4. Remove the three bolts from the coupling at the front of the driveshaft out through the rear of the coupling, leaving the nuts/bolts attaching the driveshaft to the coupling in place.

5. Remove the heat shield. Remove the mounting bolts and remove the center bearing support bracket. Bend the driveshaft downward at the front and slide the spline out of the center bearing.

6. Support the transmission securely between the front axle carrier and oil pan with a floorjack and wooden block.

7. Remove the attaching bolt and pull out the speedometer cable. Disconnect the back-up light wiring electrical connectors and pull the wire out of the clips on the transmission.

8. Loosen the connection to the rubber bushing at the transmission, remove the mounting nuts at either end, and remove the crossmember. On the 633CSi, lower the transmission to the front axle carrier.

9. On the 633CSi, disconnect the mount for the clutch hydraulic line at the front of the transmission. Then, on all models, unscrew the mounting nuts and detach the clutch slave cylinder (with the line connected).

10. Remove the mounting nuts at the clutch housing and separate the transmission and clutch housing.

11. Pull the gearbox to the rear and out of the car.

12. Install the transmission in reverse order, keeping the following points in mind:

   a. Use a slave cylinder to move the clutch throw-out arm to the correct position. Align the throw-out bearing. Grease the guide sleeve and groove in the throw-out bearing with a permanent lubricant.

   b. Put the transmission into gear before installing.

   c. Make sure, when installing the clutch slave cylinder, that the hose connection faces downward.

   d. Preload the center bearing 0.08 in. toward the front.

   e. When tightening the coupling, hold the bolt heads and torque only the nuts only to 75 ft. lbs. Use new nuts. Torque the transmission-to-engine bolts to 16–

17 ft. lbs. (M8 transmission) or 31–35 ft. lbs. (M10 transmission); torque the bolt for the rubber bushing on the crossmember to 18 ft. lbs.

325, 325e, 325i, 325is

Raise the car and support it securely.

1. Remove the exhaust system. Remove the cross brace and heat shield.

2. Hold the nuts on the front with one wrench, and remove bolts from the rear with another to disconnect the flexible coupling.

3. Loosen the threaded sleeve on the driveshaft. You'll need a special tool such as BMW 261040 to hold the splined portion of the shaft while turning the sleeve.

4. Remove its mounting bolts and remove the center mount. Support the transmission securely.

5. Remove mounting bolts and remove the crossmember holding the transmission to the body. Lower the transmission and then pull the driveshaft off the centering pin.

6. Remove the retainer and washer, and pull out the shift selector rod.

7. Lift off the gearshaft leather boot, and the insulating sheet. Pull out the cover sleeve that seals between the body and shift console. Then, lift out the circlip and remove the shift lever.

8. Remove the console supporting bolts.

9. Mark, and then unplug sensor mounting plugs (near the flywheel). Unscrew the mounting bolts for the speed sensor and reference mark sensor and remove both sensors.

10. Unscrew and remove the clutch slave cylinder and support it so the hydraulic line can remain connected.

11. Pull off wires from the reverse gear switch and pull the wiring out of the harness.

12. Using a Torx® socket, remove the Torx® bolts holding the transmission to the engine at the front. Lower the transmission.

13. Install the transmission in reverse order, keeping the following points in mind:

   a. Torque front mounting bolts to 46–58 ft. lbs.

   b. Install the clutch slave cylinder with the bleeder screw downward.

   c. Install the speed sensor with no identification ring to align with starter ring gear, while the reference mark sensor (with identification ring) aligns with the flywheel. Clean the faces of the sensors, check the O-rings and coat them with a sealer such as Molykote® Longterm 2 before installation.

   d. When installing the gearshift lever, make sure the cover sleeve is sealing all around. Coat spherical working surfaces with Molykote® Longterm.

e. When installing the driveshaft center bearing, preload it forward 0.079–0.157 in. Check the driveshaft alignment with an appropriate tool such as BMW 26 1 030. Torque the center mount bolts to 16–17 ft. lb.

f. Torque the flexible coupling bolts to 83–94 ft. lb.

g. When reinstalling the heat shield mount, install the holder on the right side.

733i – 1981-82

NOTE: This procedure requires a special tool for clamping the flexible drive coupling.

1. Remove the circlip and washer from the front end of the selector rod, and disconnect it from the lower end of the shift lever.

2. Push up the dust cover, and with needle nose pliers, remove the circlip which holds the gearshift lever in place. Lubricate the nylon bushing surrounding the socket with a permanent lubricant for reassembly.

3. Disconnect the back-up light plug near the gearshift lever. Remove the large circlip which surrounds the gearshift mount.

4. Drain the transmission. Raise the car and support it. Install the special tool (BMW 26 1 011 or equivalent) which clamps around the flexible coupling. Then, unscrew the three nuts on the forward side of the coupling, withdraw the bolts out the rear. This requires tightening the clamping tool until the bolts can be pulled out by hand.

5. Remove the web type crossmember located under the driveshaft. Then, loosen the mounting nuts for the center bearing bracket and detach it. Bend the driveshaft downward and pull it off the centering pin.

6. Support the transmission securely with a floor jack working through a wooden block. Then, remove the mounting nut from the crossmember rubber bushing, the nuts and bolts from either end of the crossmember where it bolts to the body, and remove the crossmember.

7. Detach the exhaust system bracket both at the transmission and at the exhaust pipes and remove it.

8. Detach the mounting bracket for the clutch slave cylinder hydraulic line at the transmission and then remove the two mounting bolts and remove the slave cylinder. Detach the fourth gear switch wires, if so equipped.

9. Detach the transmission at the clutch housing and remove it toward the rear.

10. Install the transmission in reverse order, keeping the following points in mind:

a. Use the clutch slave cylinder to put the release lever in position for transmission installation. Align the clutch bearing and lubricate the lubrication groove inside it with Molykote® BR2-750 or its equivalent.

b. Put the transmission into gear prior to installation.

c. Install the guide sleeve of the transmission into the bearing carefully, then turn the output flange until the driveshaft slides into the drive plate. Then, remove the slave cylinder while mounting the transmission. Torque transmission-to-clutch housing bolts to 54–59 ft. lbs.

d. When installing the clutch slave cylinder, make sure the bleeder screw faces downward.

e. When remounting the exhaust system bracket, make sure there is no torsional strain on the system.

f. Preload the center driveshaft bearing toward the front of the car 0.08 in.

g. When reassembling the flexible drive coupling, use new self-locking nuts. Leave the special tool in the compression while installing the bolts, and then install the nuts, holding the bolts in position and turning only the nuts.

h. Torque the transmission mount-to-crossmember bolt to 36–40 ft. lbs., and the crossmember-to-body nuts to 16–17 ft. lbs.

i. When install the shift lever, note that the tab on the damper plate nuts engage in the opening in the shift arm.

533i – 1983-84
535i, M5 and 633CSi – 1983-84
635CSi, M6 and 733i – 1983-84
735i

1. Raise the car and support it securely. Disconnect and lower the exhaust system to provide clearance for transmission removal. Remove the heat shield brace and transmission heat shield.

2. Support the driveshaft and then unscrew the driveshaft coupling at the rear of the transmission. Use a wrench on both the nut and the bolt.

3. Working at the front of the driveshaft center bearing, unscrew the screw-on type ring type connector which attaches the driveshaft to the center bearing. Then, unbolt the center bearing mount. Bend the drive-shaft down and pull it off the centering pin. If the car has a vibration damper, turn it and pull it back over the output flange before pulling the driveshaft off the guide pin. Suspend it from the car.

4. Pull off the wires for the backup light switch. Unscrew the passenger compartment console to disconnect it from the top of the transmission by removing the two self-locking bolts. Discard these and purchase replacements.

5. Pull out the locking clip, and disconnect the shift rod at the rear of the transmission. Take care to keep all the washers.

6. If the transmission is linked to the shift lever with an arm, use a screwdriver to lift the spring out of the holder on the bracket and then raise the arm. Pull out the shift shaft bolt.

7. If the car has a flywheel housing cover (semi-circular in shape), remove the mounting bolts and remove the cover.

8. If the car has Digital Motor Electronics, the speed sensor and reference mark sensor on the flywheel housing must be disconnected. Note their locations. The speed sensor goes in the upper bore, marked "D". The reference mark sensor, which has a ring, goes in the lower bore, marked "B". Check the O-rings for the sensors and install new ones if they are damaged.

9. Support the transmission securely. Then, unbolt and remove the rear transmission crossmember.

10. Remove the upper and lower attaching nuts and remove the clutch slave cylinder, supporting it so the hydraulic line need not be disconnected. Disconnect the reverse gear backup light switch nearby, and pull the wires out of the holders.

11. Unscrew the bolts fastening the transmission to the bell housing, using an angled box wrench. On late model cars there are some Torx® bolts; you'll have to use a special Torx® wrench for these. Pull the transmission rearward until the input shaft has disengaged from the clutch disc and then lower and remove it.

12. To install the transmission, first put it in gear. Insert the guide sleeve of the input shaft into the clutch pilot bearing carefully. Turn the output shaft to rotate the front of the input shaft until the splines line up and it engages the clutch disc.

Perform the remaining portions of the procedure in reverse of removal, observing the following points:

a. Make sure the arrows on the rear crossmember point forward.

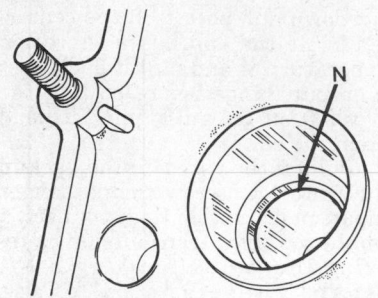

Pack the groove ("N") with Molykote® Longterm 2 or equivalent before installing the transmission used on the 733i/735i, and 633CSi/35CSi/M6

b. Preload the center bearing mount forward of its most natural position 0.079–0.157 in. On 7 Series cars with the M30 B35 engine only, and 6 Series cars with the 265/6 transmission (no integral clutch housing), preload the bearing 0.157–0.236 in.

c. In tightening the driveshaft screw on ring, use special Tool No. 26 1 040 or equivalent.

d. When reconnecting the nuts and bolt at the transmission coupling, replace the nuts with new ones and turn only the nut, holding the bolts stationary.

e. Make sure DME sensor faces are clean. Coat the sensor outside diameters with Molykote Longterm 2® or equivalent.

f. If the car has a shift arm (Step 6), lubricate the bolt with a light layer of Molykote Longterm 2® or equivalent.

g. Observe these torque figures in ft. lbs:

Transmission to bell housing—52–58 ft. lbs.

Rear/Top transmission Torx® bolts—46–58 ft. lbs.

Center mount to body—16–17 ft. lbs.

Front joint-to-transmission—83–94 ft. lbs.

OVERHAUL

For manual transmission overhaul procedures, please refer to "Manual Transmission Overhaul" in the Unit Repair section.

CLUTCH

REMOVAL & INSTALLATION

1. On cars with Digital Motor Electronics, remove the heat shield and then the two attaching bolts; disconnect the speed and reference mark sensors at the flywheel housing. Mark the plugs for reinstallation.

2. Remove the transmission and clutch housing. On late model 6 cylinder cars, you'll need a Torx® socket. If the car has a 265/6 transmission (without an integral clutch housing), remove the clutch housing.

3. Prevent the flywheel from turning, using a locking tool.

4. Loosen the mounting bolts one after another gradually (1–1½ turns at a time) to relieve tension from the clutch.

5. Remove the mounting bolts, clutch, and drive plate. Coat the spines of the transmission input shaft with Molykote® Longterm 2 or equivalent. Make sure the clutch pilot bearing, located in the center of the crankshaft, turns easily.

6. To install, reverse the removal procedure. Note that on late model six cylinder engines, the clutch pressure plate must fit over dowel pins. Torque the clutch mounting bolts to 16–17 ft. lbs. (17–19—1983-88 3.3L and 3.5L engines).

PEDAL HEIGHT AND OVER-CENTER SPRING ADJUSTMENTS

All 6 Cylinder Models (except 325, 325e, 325i, 325is)

Measure the length of the over-center spring (Dimension "A") and, if necessary, loosen the locknut and rotate the shafts as necessary to get the proper clearance. Measure the distance (Dimension "B") from the firewall to the tip of the clutch pedal and move the pedal in or out, if necessary, by loosening the locknut and rotating the shaft. Specifications for the various models are shown below:

1981–82 Models	Dimension "A" (in.)	Dimension "B" (in.)
733i	1.338	10.472–10.787
633CSi	1.138–1.358	9.644–9.960
528e, 528i	1.283–1.302	10.078–9.764

1983–88 Models	Dimension "A" (in.)	Dimension "B" (in.)
733i, 735i	1.358	10.472–10.787
633CSi, 635CSi, M6	1.358	10.669–11.102
528e, 524td, 533i, 535i, M5	1.358	9.843–10.276

All 4 Cylinder Models (and 325, 325e, 325i and 325is)

Measure the distance between the bottom edge of the clutch pedal and the firewall (A). It should be 9.920–10.197 in. except on 325. 325 – 9.961–10.394. If out of specification, loosen the locknut and rotate the piston rod (1) to correct it.

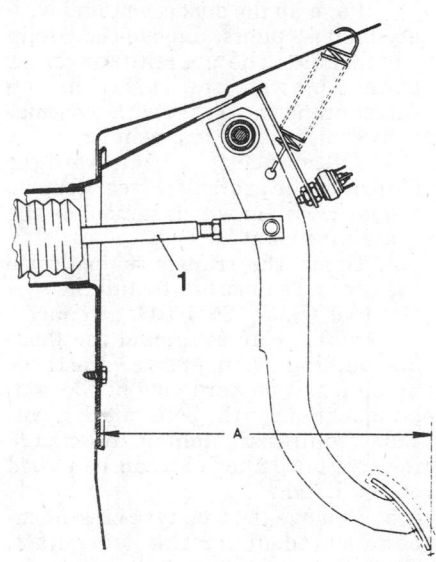

Adjusting the pedal height on the 320i

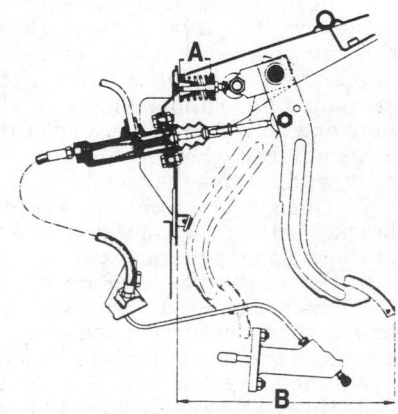

Adjusting the pedal height and over-center spring on 6 cylinder model

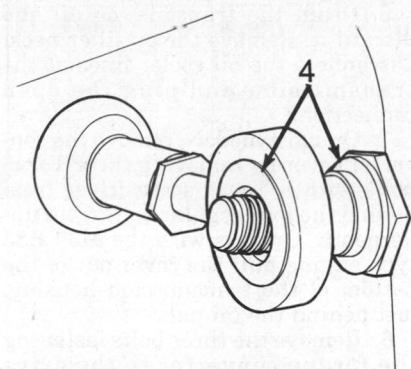

On 733i and 735i models, make sure the bushings (4) on the clutch master cylinder linkage are still in position.

Clutch Master Cylinder

REMOVAL & INSTALLATION

1. Remove the necessary trim panel or carpet.
2. On the 320i, disconnect the accelerator cable and pull it forward out of the engine firewall.
3. Disconnect the pushrod at the clutch pedal.
4. Remove the cap on the reservoir tank. On some models, there is a clutch master cylinder reservoir, while on others there is a common reservoir shared with the brake master cylinder. Remove the float container (if equipped). Remove the screen (if equipped) and remove enough brake fluid from the tank until the level drops below the refill line or the connection for the filler pipe, if there is one.
5. Disconnect the coolant expansion tank without removing the hoses on models 733i and 735i (latest models with the M30 B35 engine do not require this).
6. Disconnect the line to the slave cylinder and the fluid fill line going to the top of the master cylinder. Remove the retaining bolts and remove the master cylinder from the firewall.
7. Installation is the reverse of removal. On all 1983-88 models the piston rod bolt should be coated with Molykote® Longterm 2 or equivalent. Make sure all bushings remain in position. Bleed the system and adjust the pedal travel with the pushrod to 6 in.

Clutch Slave Cylinder

REMOVAL & INSTALLATION

1. Remove enough brake fluid from the reservoir until the level drops below the refill line connection.

2. Remove the circlip or retaining bolts depending on the model and pull the unit down.
3. Disconnect the line and remove the slave cylinder.
4. Installation is the reverse or removal. Make sure to install the cylinder with the bleed screw facing downward. When installing the front pushrod, coat it with Molykote® Longterm 2 or equivalent anti-seize compound. Bleed the system.

BLEEDING THE HYDRAULIC CLUTCH SYSTEM

1. Fill the reservoir.
2. Connect a bleeder hose from the bleeder screw to a container filled with brake fluid so that air cannot be drawn in during bleeding procedures.
3. Pump the clutch pedal about 10 times and then hold it down.
4. Open the bleeder screw and watch the stream of escaping fluid. When no more bubbles escape, close the bleeder screw and tighten it.

Remove the 4 torque convertor retaining bolts

5. Release the clutch pedal and repeat the above procedure until no more bubbles can be seen when the screw is opened.
6. If this procedure fails to produce a bubble-free stream, pull the slave cylinder off the transmission without disconnecting the fluid line.

NOTE: Do not depress the clutch pedal while the slave cylinder is dismounted.

Depress the pushrod in the cylinder until it hits the internal stop. Then, reinstall the cylinder.

AUTOMATIC TRANSMISSION

REMOVAL & INSTALLATION

3 Speed Automatic

1. Disconnect the accelerator cable.
2. On the 4 cylinder engine remove all of the transmission mounting bolts which are accessible from above.
3. Detach the oil filler neck and drain the oil.
4. On 4 cylinder engines remove the exhaust pipe support bracket and separate the pipe from the exhaust manifold. On the 318i and 325, remove the exhaust system and detach the heat shield.
5. On all 6 cylinder engines except model 733i, remove the entire exhaust system.
6. Detach the oil cooler lines from the transmission and drain fluid.
7. Disconnect the propeller shaft at the transmission, On model 733i, use special clamping tool. On the 318i and 325, disconnect the selector rod.

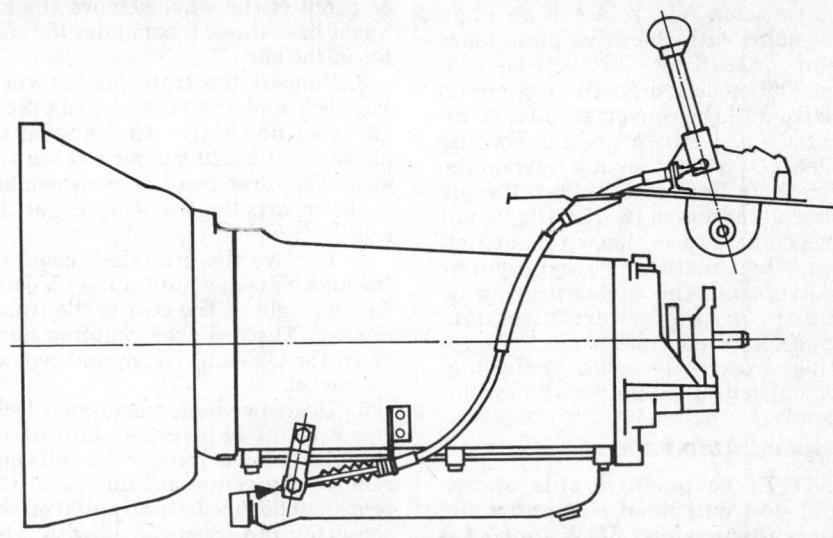

Adjusting the automatic transmission selector lever—733i and 735i

8. Disconnect the speedometer cable.

9. Remove the heat guard and center bearing and bend down and pull off the propeller shaft.

10. Remove the torque converter cover and remove the four bolts that attach the torque converter to the drive plate. Turn the engine for this procedure, using the vibration damper.

NOTE: On 1982-88 6 cyl. models, the speed transmitter and reference transmitter must be unbolted and removed from the flywheel housing. For installation, the speed transmitter faces the gear ring. The reference transmitter has a plug with a grey ring and faces the flywheel. The engine will not start if the plugs are mixed up. Coat both with anti-seize compound before installing. Make sure their tips are clean.

11. Support the transmission and disconnect the crossmember at the body.

12. Remove the remaining transmission mounting bolts.

13. Separate the transmission from the engine and take off the torque converter at the same time. On 1983-88 733i and 735i models, this is done by removing the protective grill on the side of the converter housing and gently prying it toward the transmission as the transmission is pulled rearward. On the 318i, lower the transmission onto the front axle carrier. Remove the grill from the torque converter housing and gently pry the torque converter backwards as the transmission is pulled off.

14. Installation is the reverse of removal. Push the torque converter back against the stop on the main transmission and rotate it to align bolt holes with the drive plate holes before installing. On 1983-88 733i and 735i models, drive connections on the front of the converter must be indented inside the converter housing at least 0.354 in. Use new nuts on the driveshaft flexible coupling. Torque drive plate bolts to 16–17 ft. lb. Install the exhaust suspension without twisting. When installing the propeller shaft preload the center bearing by 0.08 in. in the forward direction. Make sure the torque converter is positioned correctly before installing. Replenish drained fluid with new fluid, only.

4 Speed Automatic

NOTE: To perform this operation, you will need a support for the transmission, BMW tool 24 0 120 and 00 2 020 or equivalent and

a tool for tightening the driveshaft locking ring. BMW tool 26 1 040 or equivalent. If the car has the M30 B35 type engine, you'll need a special socket (that retains bolts) 24 1 110 or equivalent.

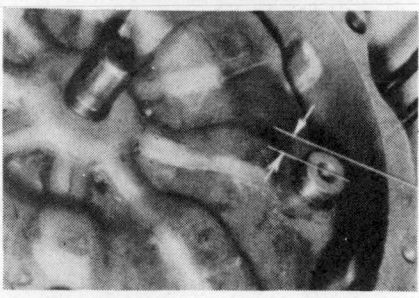

The torque converter is installed correctly if the drive shell mounting parts are located underneath the converter housing

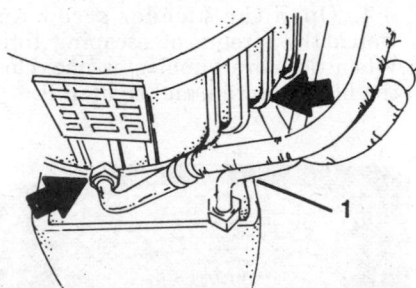

Remove the oil filler neck (1) and disconnect the arrowed hoses to drain fluid from the 4HP–22 transmission

1. On both gas and diesel engines, loosen the throttle cable adjusting nuts, release the cable tension, and disconnect the cable at the throttle lever. Then, remove (and retain) the nuts, and pull the cable housing out of the bracket.

2. Disconnect the exhaust system at the manifold and hangers, and lower it out of the way. Remove the exhaust heat shield from under the center of the car.

3. Support the transmission via a floorjack and the special tools. 24 0 120 goes under the transmission oil pan and 00 2 020 supports it via the jack. Then, remove the crossmember that supports the transmission at the rear.

4. Remove the driveshaft coupling through bolts and nuts or the CV-joint located right at the rear of the transmission. Discard used coupling nuts. Keep the CV-joint clean, and replace its gasket.

5. Unscrew the transmission locking ring at the center mount (if equipped). Then, remove the bolts and remove the center mount. Bend the propshaft downward and pull it off the centering pin. Suspend it with wire from the underside of the car.

6. Drain the transmission oil and discard it. Remove the oil filler neck. Disconnect the oil cooler lines at the transmission and plug the open connections.

7. On most models, remove the converter cover by removing three Torx® bolts with a Torx® screwdriver from behind the four regular bolts from underneath. On cars with the M30 B35 type engine pull the cover out of the bottom of the transmission housing, just behind the oil pan.

8. Remove the three bolts fastening the torque converter to the drive plate, turning the flywheel as necessary to gain access from below. Use a special socket (that retains the bolts) 24 1 110 or equivalent on cars with the M30 B35 type engine.

9. On cars so equipped, remove the guard for the speed and reference mark sensors. Remove the attaching bolt for each and remove each sensor (the diesel only has a reference mark sensor). Keep the sensors clean.

10. Disconnect the shift cable by loosening the locknut fastening it to the shift lever and disconnecting the cable at the cable housing bracket.

11. If the transmission has an electrical connection, turn the bayonet fastener to the left to release the connection, disconnect it, and pull the wire out of the ties.

12. Lower the transmission as far as possible. Then, remove all the Torx® or standard type bolts attaching the transmission to the engine.

13. Remove the small grill from the bottom of the transmission. Then, press the converter off with a large screwdriver passing through this opening as you slide the transmission out.

14. Installation is the reverse of removal. Observe the following points:

   a. Make sure the converter is fully installed onto the transmission—so the ring on the front is inside the edge of the case.

   b. When reinstalling the driveshaft, tighten the lockring with a special tool such as 26 1 040.

   c. If the driveshaft has a simple coupling (524td), rather than a CV-

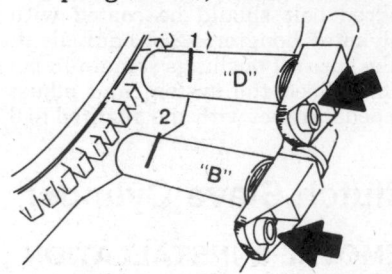

Note that the speed sensor (1) is installed into bore "D" and that the reference mark sensor (2) goes into bore "B"

joint, make sure to replace the self-locking nuts and to hold the bolts still while tightening the nuts to keep from distorting the coupling.

d. When installing the center mount, preload it forward from its most natural position 0.157–0.236 in.

e. Adjust the throttle cables.

PAN REMOVAL

1. Raise and support the car securely.

2. Remove the drain plug and drain the transmission fluid from the pan.

3. With an open-end wrench, disconnect the oil filler tube where it connects to the bottom of the pan.

4. Remove the attaching bolts and brackets and separate the pan from the transmission. Clean all gasket surfaces.

5. Note the locations of the two magnets in the sump. Clean the sump of sediment with clean rags. Replace the magnets. Position a new gasket around the outer edge of the pan.

6. Position the pan on the transmission and install the bolts and brackets. Note that the short legs of the brackets locate inward and under the pan, while the longer, outer legs rest against the transmission housing itself.

7. Tighten the bolts evenly. Torque them to 6–6.5 ft. lbs. Reconnect the filler tube and install the drain plug. Refill the pan with the amount of fluid shown in specifications.

8. Start the engine and run it with the transmission in gear (put the selector in each position for at least a few seconds) for 10 minutes or so to get the transmission fluid hot. Then,

with the engine still running, check and correct the fluid level according to the reading on the dipstick.

FILTER SERVICE

NOTE: You cannot perform this procedure without special Torx® tools BMW 00 2 100 and 00 2 050.

1. Remove the oil pan as described immediately above.

2. Remove all the Torx® head screws from both the center and the outer edges of the screen.

3. Clean the screen in a safe solvent. If the screen has a burnt residue that cannot be cleaned replace the screen.

4. Install in reverse order.

SELECTOR LEVER ADJUSTMENT

All Models Except Below

1. Detach the selector rod (1) at the selector lever lower section (2).

2. Move the selector lever (3) on the transmission to position O or N.

3. Press the selector lever (4) against the stop (5) on the shift gate.

4. Adjust the length of the selector rod (1) until the pin (6) aligns with the bore in the selector lever lower section (2). Shorten the selector rod length by: 1 turn – 320i, 1–2 turns – 318i and 325, 633CSi, 733i; 2–2½ turns – 530i, 1–2 turns – 524td and 535.

NOTE: If equipped with air conditioning on the 4 cylinder models, plates (7) must be installed between the bearing bracket and float plate and selector rod (1) must be attached in bore (K) of selector lever (3).

633CSi – 1983–84
635CSi and 733i – 1983–84
735i, M5 and M6

1. Move the selector lever (1) to "P" position. Loosen the nut (2).

2. Push the transmission lever (3) to the forward or park position. Then push the cable rod (4) in the opposite direction; tighten the nut (2) to 7.0–8.5 ft. lbs.

ACCELERATOR CABLE ADJUSTMENT

533i, 633CSi and 733i – 1981-82

1. Adjust play (S) to 0.010–0.030 in. with nuts when in Neutral.

2. Press the accelerator pedal against the stop.

3. Adjust the pressure rod (7) until the distance from the seal (3) to the end of the cable (4) is 633CSi – (1.732–2.008 in.). 733i – (1.722–2.057).

533i – 1983-84
535i and 633CSi – 1983-84
733i – 1983-84
635CSi, 735i, M5 and M6

1. On the injection system throttle body, loosen the two locknuts at the end of the throttle cable and adjust the cable until there is a play of 0.010–0.030 in.

2. Loosen the locknut and lower the kickdown stop under the accelerator pedal. Have someone depress the accelerator pedal until he can feel the transmission detent. Then, back the kickdown stop back out until it just touches the pedal.

3. Check that the distance from the seal at the throttle body end of the cable housing is at least 1.732 in. from the rear end of the threaded sleeve. If this dimension checks out, tighten all the locknuts.

524td

NOTE: For diesels, see "Idle Speed Diesel Engines" above.

320i

1. Adjust the accelerator cable at nuts (1) until the accelerator cable eye (2) has a play of 0.008–0.012 in.

2. Depress the accelerator pedal (3) to the full throttle stop screw (4).

3. There must be 0.020 in. play between the operating lever (5) and stop nut (6).

4. Adjust by the full throttle stop screw (4).

318i, 325, 325e, 325i and 325is

1. Adjust the cable for zero tension with the throttle closed and accelerator pedal released.

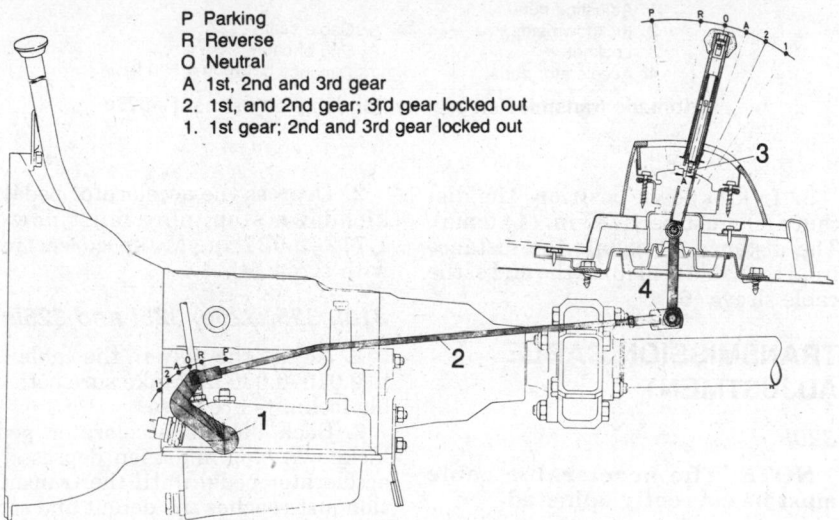

P Parking
R Reverse
O Neutral
A 1st, 2nd and 3rd gear
2. 1st, and 2nd gear; 3rd gear locked out
1. 1st gear; 2nd and 3rd gear locked out

Selector lever adjustment—typical all models

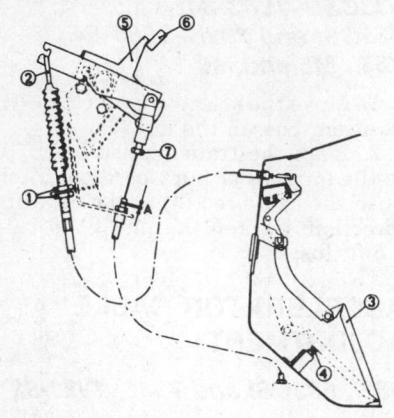

Accelerator cable and transmission cable adjustment—320i

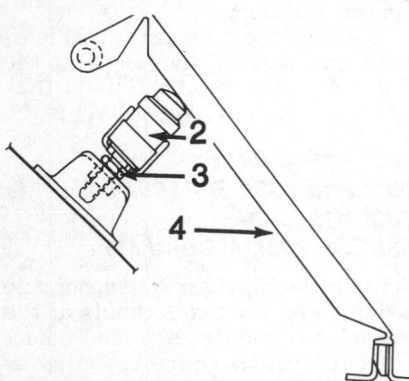

When adjusting the 318i kickdown stop, unscrew the locknut (3), screw in the stop (2) and depress the accelerator pedal (4) to kickdown—see text

2. Loosen the locknut on the throttle stop bolt. Now adjust the bolt inward just until it suspends the accelerator pedal at the point where the throttle just reaches wide open position. On automatic transmission equipped cars, make sure the throttle is in full detent position. Now, turn the stop screw 1½ turns lower to get a clearance of 0.020 in. between the accelerator pedal and stop bolt at full throttle. Tighten the locknut.

528e

1. Adjust the freeplay (s) of the cable in N position to 0.010–0.030 in. (0.25–0.75mm). Use cable adjuster nuts (1) to adjust the freeplay.

2. In the passenger compartment, loosen the kickdown switch. Screw in the kickdown stop (2) all the way in the direction of the floor pan.

3. Press down on the accelerator pedal (4) to the transmission pressure point. Unscrew the kickdown stop (2) until it contacts the accelerator pedal.

4. Press the accelerator to the kickdown (wide open throttle position.

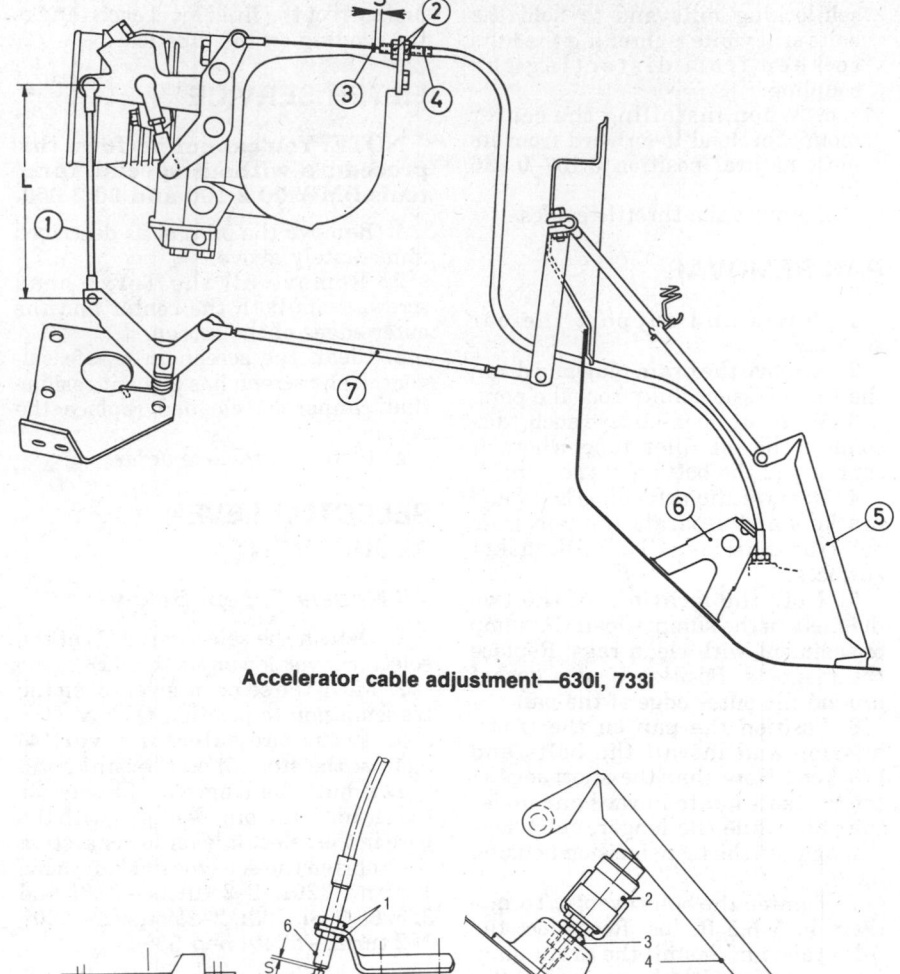

Accelerator cable adjustment—630i, 733i

1. Adjusting nuts
2. Kickdown stop
3. Locknut
4. Accelerator pedal
5. Cable seal
6. End of cable sleeve
7. Distance between 5 and 6

Automatic transmission accelerator cable adjustment—528e

5. In kickdown position, the distance (s) must be 1.732 in. (44.0mm). The distance (s) equals the distance from the cable seal (5) to the end of the cable sleeve (6).

TRANSMISSION CABLE ADJUSTMENT

320i

NOTE: The accelerator cable must be correctly adjusted.

1. With the transmission in the Neutral position, adjust play to 0.010–0.030 in. with the screw.

2. Depress the accelerator pedal to kickdown stop; play must now be 1.712–2.027 in. Make corrections with screw (4).

318i, 325, 325e, 325i and 325is

1. Adjust the play in the cable "S" to 0.010–0.030 in. Make sure both cable locknuts are loose.

2. Back off the accelerator pedal kickdown stop and then depress the accelerator pedal until the transmission just reaches the detent and some resistance is felt.

3. Run the kickdown stop out until it just touches the bottom of the pedal.

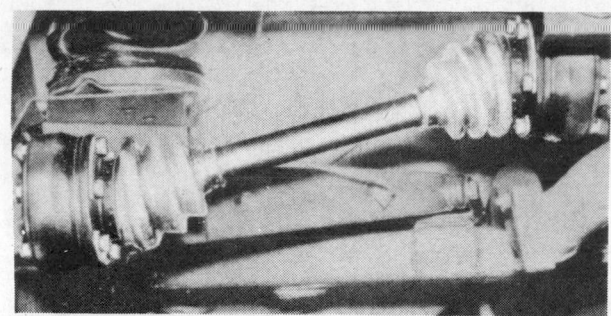

Constant velocity type output shaft

4. Depress the accelerator through the detent and hold while measuring distance "S" from the lead seal to the end of the sleeve. It must be at least 1.732 in. Adjust further, if necessary.

5. Tighten all locknuts.

524td

1. The engine must be at normal operating temperature so the operating lever on the injection pump rests on the idle stop. Adjust the play between the throttle cable stop and the end of the threads on the cable jacket to 0.010–0.030.

2. Then, loosen the nut that locks the accelerator pedal kickdown stop. Press the pedal down until it reaches the transmission detent. Screw the kickdown stop back out until it just touches the lower side of the accelerator pedal.

3. Press the accelerator pedal down until it has kicked down (extreme position). Make sure the distance measured above is at least 1.732 in. Readjust to obtain this figure, if necessary.

DRIVE AXLE

Halfshaft

REMOVAL & INSTALLATION

1. Detach the output shaft at the final drive and drive flange.

2. On the 1981-82 733i, support the control arm as the spring strut and shock absorber are detached.

3. The spring strut serves as a retaining strap and the trailing arm must be supported if the spring strut is detached.

4. Replace the bellows as follows:
   a. Take off the sealing cover.
   b. Remove the circlip.
   c. Unscrew the clamp on the dust cover. Take off the dust cover.

d. Press off the inner cover.

e. Press the output shaft out of the constant velocity joint. Make sure when you do this that the bearing inner race is supported.

f. Place the dust cover and inside cover on the output shaft.

g. Coat the splined threads with Loctite® 270 or equivalent. Keep the compound out of ball races.

h. Press the joint and cap on and install the circlip.

i. Pack the joint and bellows with CV-joint grease. Clean the sealing surfaces to remove grease. Then, coat the larger diameter end of the bellows with an adhesive and secure with new clamps. Seal the cover with Curil or equivalent and install it.

CV-JOINT OVERHAUL

NOTE: For all CV-Joint overhaul procedures, please refer to "CV-Joint Overhaul" in the unit repair section.

Driveshaft and U-Joints

REMOVAL & INSTALLATION

Except Below

1. On the 5 and 6 series cars, remove the entire exhaust system. On the 1984–86 733i and 735i remove just the muffler.

2. On the 320i, detach the outer pipe at the manifold and support it at the transmission.

3. Remove the heat shield if so equipped. On 1984-88 733i, 735i, this requires loosening the automatic transmission rear crossmember bolts slightly on the right side for clearance. On 6 and 7 Series models you must now also use BMW Special Tool 26 1 040 or equivalent to loosen the threaded sleeve attaching the rear of the driveshaft to the front of the center bearing.

4. Disconnect the propeller shaft at the transmission by removing the nuts and bolts from the flexible coupling. If the car has a vibration damper where the shaft connects to the transmission, turn the damper 60 degrees counterclockwise and remove it with the rubber coupling.

NOTE: On 1981-82 733i, install a special clamping tool (BMW-261011) or equivalent around the coupling and remove the bolts.

5. Loosen the center bearing bolts and remove them.

6. On 1981-82 733i, with manual transmission. loosen the crossmember and push the left end forward.

7. Disconnect the propeller shaft at the final drive. Bend the propeller shaft down and pull out.

8. Installation is the reverse of removal.

9. The propeller shaft is balanced in line and must only be renewed as a complete assembly.

10. Align the driveshaft with a gauge (BMW-21-1-000) (use 26 1 000 on 1984-86 733i, 735i) or equivalent by moving the center bearing sideways or by placing washers underneath the center bearing (this is not required on 6 Series cars).

11. On the 1981-83 733i, remove the special coupling tool only after the nuts have been tightened to prevent stress on the coupling.

12. Preload the center bearing by 0.078 in. in the forward direction. (.157–.236 in. on 6 Series cars).

13. Wherever self-locking nuts are used, replace them. Hold the nut or bolt in place where is runs through a U-joint, and torque at the opposite end—where the driveshaft flange is located. Check the center bearing for lubrication and if it's dry, lubricate with Molykote® Longterm 2 or equivalent.

1987-88 735i

NOTE: If the car has a front universal joint, you will need special tools 24 0 120 and 00 2 020 to support the transmission during this operation.

1. Remove the exhaust system. Remove the heat shield from the floorpan. Remove the nuts and bolts fastening the propeller shaft to the transmission at the flexible coupling. Replace the self-locking nuts.

2. If the car has a front U-joint, support the transmission from underneath with tools 24 0 120 or the equivalent. When the transmssion is securely supported, remove the six bolts and remove the rear transmission mounting crossmember.

3. Remove the self-locking nuts and then the bolts fastening the driveshaft to the final drive. Replace the self-locking nuts. Remove the propeller shaft, taking care to keep it protected from dirt.

4. Remove the bolts from the crossbrace underneath and remove the center propshaft mount. Then, bend the shaft at the middle and remove it from the car by pulling it off the centering pin on the forward end.

5. Install in reverse order, keeing the following points in mind:

   a. Repack the CV joing with approved grease and replace the gasket, if necessary.

   b. Check the center bearing for lubrication and if it's dry, lubricate with Molykote® Longterm 2 or equivalent.

   c. If the vibration damper at the forward end of the driveshaft must be replaced, turn it 60 degrees to remove it.

   d. When remounting the center mount, preload it forward from its most natural position 0.157–0.236 in.

   e. Torque U-joint bolts to 52 ft. lbs. and CV-joint bolts to 51 ft. lbs.

528e, 535i and 633CSi with CV-Joint

NOTE: To perform this procedure, you will need a set of tools designed to support the transmission via the pan BMW tools 24 0 120 and 00 2 020 or equivalent.

1. Support the transmission from underneath with the special tools and a floorjack. Remove the nuts and washers from the transmission mounts on top of the rear transmission mounting crossmember. Loosen but do not remove the nuts located underneath which fasten the crossmember to the body. Then, slide this crossmember as far to the rear as it will go.

2. Unscrew the fastening nuts on the forward end of the CV-joint and then discard them.

3. Using a prybar to keep the driveshaft from turning, remove the self locking nuts and bolts fastening the rear of the driveshaft to the final drive.

4. Remove the bolts fastening the center mount to the body. Bend the propshaft down and pull the CV-joint off the transmission flange. Cover the joint to keep it clean.

5. Replace the gasket that fits between the joint bolts. Install in reverse order, keeping these points in mind:

   a. Replace the self-locking nuts used at either end of the shaft.

   b. Preload the center mount forward by forcing the bracket 0.157–

Remove circlip (2) and dust guard (3)

Drive center bearing onto grooved ball bearing

0.197 in. forward from the neutral position on 5 Series cars and 0.157–0.236 in. forward on 6 Series cars.

318i and 325, 325e, i, is

1. Remove the mufflers. Unscrew and remove the exhaust system heat shield near the fuel tank.

2. Unbolt and remove the cross brace that runs under the driveshaft.

3. Support the transmission. The automatic transmission must be supported by the case and not the pan. BMW makes a jig and support (No. 24 0 120 and 00 2 020) for this. Loosen all transmission support bolts and remove. Remove the transmission rear support crossmember.

4. Lower the transmission and remove the driveshaft bolts from the front coupling.

5. Unscrew and remove bolts at the coupling near the final drive.

6. Loosen the threaded sleeve on the driveshaft with a tool such as BMW 26 1 040. Unbolt and remove the center mount.

7. Bend the driveshaft downward and remove it, being careful not to allow it to rest on the connecting line on the fuel tank.

8. Upon installation:

   a. Mount the holder for the oxygen sensor plug.

   b. Make sure the heat shield clears the fuel tank.

   c. Wherever self-locking nuts are used, replace them. On the transmission-end flange, tighten the nuts/bolts only on the flange side, holding the other end stationary.

   d. Preload the center mount to 0.079–0.157 in. in the forward direction before tightening the bolts. Torque the mounting bolts to 16 ft. lbs.

   e. Lubricate the center bearing with Molykote® Longterm 2 or equivalent if it is dry.

Center Bearing

REMOVAL & INSTALLATION

All 5, 6, and 7 Series Cars Except Below

1. Bend down the driveshaft and pull it out of the centering pin on the transmission (refer to "Driveshaft Removal and Installation").

2. Loosen the threaded bushing. On '83–'86 733, 735, also remove the felt ring.

3. Mark the driveshaft position on slide with a punch mark and pull the front half of the propeller shaft out of the slide.

4. Remove the circlip and dust guard.

5. Using a standard puller remove the center bearing without the dust guard.

6. Use a puller and remove the grooved ball bearing in the center bearing. On 1983-88 733i and 735i, press the grooved ball bearing into the center mount.

7. Installation is the reverse of removal. Lubricate the splines with Molykote® Longterm 2 or equivalent. Drive the center bearing onto the grooved ball bearing with tool (BMW–24–1–050) or equivalent. On 1983-88 733i and 735i, check the installed position of the dust guard—it must be flush with the center mount.

M5 and M6 — 1987-88 and 735i, 528e, 535i and 633CSi Without Splines

NOTE: This type of propshaft has the two sections bolted together just behind the center bearing. You will need a press and a puller to complete this operation.

1. Remove the propeller shaft as described above. Matchmark the relationship between the forward and rear sections of the shaft at the center bearing.
2. Remove the bolt that fastens the forward U-joint section to the center mount.
3. Using a standard puller remove the center mount and bearing without the dust guard.
4. Press the old bearing out of the mount and press a new one in. Then, use a mandrel 24 1 040 or equivalent to drive the bearing center race onto the driveshaft.
5. Assemble the driveshaft in reverse order, lining up its halves with the matchmarks. Install the bolt fastening the shaft sections together with a locking type of sealer, torquing to 72 ft. lbs.

320i

1. With the propeller shaft removed, mark the shaft's location to the coupling.
2. Remove the circlip and pull out the propeller shaft.
3. Using a standard puller remove the center bearing without its dust cover.
4. Drive the grooved ball bearing out of the center bearing.
5. Installation is the reverse of removal.

318i, 325, 325e, 325i and 325is

1. Remove the driveshaft as described above. Since the shaft is a balanced assembly, matchmark both halves so it can be reassembled in the same position.
2. Unscrew the threaded sleeve (1), and remove the front propshaft section. Remove the washer (2) and rubber ring (3). A BMW special tool is shown, but you can loosen the sleeve with an ordinary wrench, provided you carefully devise a way to hold the propshaft against the torque required to loosen the sleeve without damaging it.
3. Lift out the circlip and remove the dustguard behind it.
4. Pull out the center mount and ball bearing with a puller.
5. Lay the center mount on a flat plate and press the new ball bearing

in with even pressure all around the outer race.
6. Install the dust guard and then drive the center mount onto the splined portion of the shaft. Make sure he dust guard is installed flush with the center mount and that the center mount will operate with adequate clearance.
7. Assemble the shaft with matchmarks aligned. Push on the threaded sleeve, washer, and rubber ring (do not tighten the threaded sleeve yet).
8. Install the driveshaft as described above. Then, tighten the threaded sleeve.

Centering Ring

REMOVAL & INSTALLATION

1. Fill the center with grease and using a 14mm (0.551 in.) dia. mandrel, drive out the ring.
2. Installation is the reverse of removal.

NOTE: The shaft ring faces out.

Rear Axle Shaft, Wheel Bearings and Seals

REMOVAL & INSTALLATION

6 Cylinder Models except 325, 325e, 325i, 325is, 733i (1983-84) and 735i

1. Remove the wheel.
2. Loosen the brake caliper and leave the brake line connected.
3. Remove the brake disc.
4. Remove the driving flange as follows:
   a. Disconnect the output shaft.
   b. Remove the lockplate.
   c. Loosen the collared nut and pull off the drive flange.
5. Tighten the collared nut and drive off the rear axle shaft.
6. Drive off the wheel bearings and seals toward the outside.
7. Installation is the reverse of removal.

320i

1. Remove the wheel.
2. Remove the cotter pin from the castellated nut.
3. Apply the handbrake.
4. Loosen the castellated nut.
5. Release the handbrake.
6. Remove the brake drum.
7. Pull off the drive flange with a puller.
8. Disconnect the output shaft and tie it up.

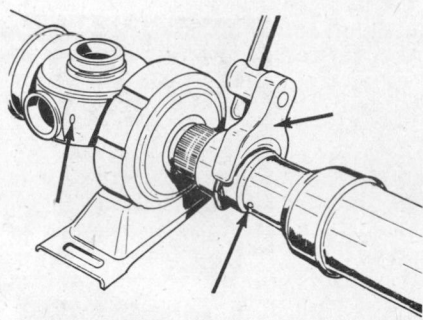

In replacing the center mount on the driveshaft on the 318i, unscrew the threaded sleeve as shown. Matchmark the assembly prior to taking it apart as shown by the arrows.

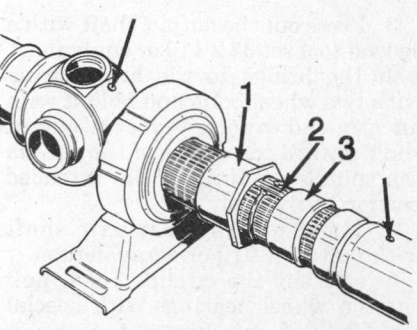

When assembling the driveshaft on the 318i, push on the threaded sleeve (1), washer (2), and rubber ring (3)

9. Drive out the halfshaft with a plastic hammer using the castellated nut to protect the end of the shaft.
10. Drive out the bearing and sealing ring.
11. Take out the spacer sleeve and shim.
12. Installation is the reverse of removal.

318i, 325, 325e, 325i and 325is

1. Lift out the lockplate and remove the retaining nut from the output flange. Remove the flange.
2. Disconnect the output shaft from the final drive and suspend it.

Wheel bearing with rear axle shaft removed—6 cylinder models

Driving out rear axle shaft—4 cylinder models

3. Press out the output shaft with a special tool set 33 2 110 or equivalent. Bolt the bridge to the brake drum with two wheel bolts and hold it with an open-end wrench. Force the output shaft toward the center of the car via the spindle by turning the threaded portion of the tool.

4. Drive out the rear axle shaft with tool 33 4 010 or equivalent.

5. Lift out the circlip. Then, pull out the wheel bearings with special tool 33 4 040 or equivalent.

6. Pull out the seal with a tool such as 33 4 045.

7. If the inner bearing shell is damaged, pull it off with a puller and thrust pad.

8. To install, pull in the wheel bearing assembly, pull in the seal, insert the circlip and then pull in the rear axle shaft, all in reverse of steps above. Install the axle shaft seal with a tool such as 33 4 045.

9. To install the output shaft, screw the threaded spindle into the shaft all the way, and then use the nut and washer against the outside of the bridge.

10. Reconnect the output shaft to the final drive.

11. Lubricate the bearing surface of the outer nut with oil. Then install and torque the nut.

12. Using installers 33 4 050 and 00 5 000 or equivalent, knock in the lockplate. Use the following torque figures:

Output shaft to drive flange — 42–46 ft. lb.

Drive flange hub to output shaft — 140–152 ft. lb.

528e, 535i, 633CSi (1981-83), M5, M6 733i (1983-84) and 735i

1. Remove the rear wheel. Disconnect the output shaft at the outer flange and suspend it with wire.

2. Unbolt the caliper and suspend it with the brake line connected. Unbolt and remove the rear disc.

Removing the output shaft on the 318i. Use two wheel bolts to fasten the bridge (33 2 112), and then press the shaft out as shown.

3. Remove the large nut and remove the lockplate. If the car has ABS, disconnect and then remove the ABS speed sensor by unscrewing it.

4. Use a special tool BMW 33 4 000 or equivalent and two M10 x 30 bolts to unscrew the collar nut. Then, pull off the drive flange with tools 00 7 501 and 00 7 502.

5. Screw on the collar nut until it is just flush with the end of the shaft and use a soft (nylon) hammer to knock out the shaft.

6. Remove the circlip. Then, use special tools 33 4 031, 33 4 032 and 33 4 038 or equivalent to pull off the wheel bearings.

7. Pull the inner bearing race off the axle shaft with special tool 00 7 500 or equivalent.

8. Pull the new bearing assembly in with special tools 33 4 036, 33 4 032, and 33 4 038 or equivalent.

9. Install special tool 33 4 037 or equivalent. Then, reinstall the circlip.

10. Pull the rear axle shaft through with special tools 23 1 300, 33 4 080 and 33 4 020 or equivalent.

11. Use special tool 33 4 000 or equivalent to tighten the collar nut.

12. Fit special tool 33 4 060 or equivalent into the lockplate and top it in

with a slide hammer 00 5 000 or equivalent.

13. Reconnect the output shaft. Remount the brake disc and caliper.

FRONT SUSPENSION

MacPherson Strut Assembly

For removal of spring from struts and all strut overhaul precedures, please refer to "Strut Overhaul" in the Unit Repair section.

——— CAUTION ———

MacPherson strut springs are under tremendous pressure and any attempt to remove them without proper tools could result in serious personal injury.

REMOVAL & INSTALLATION

318i, 325, 325e, 325i and 325is

1. Remove the front wheel. Disconnect the brake pad wear indicator plug and ground wire. Pull the wires out of the holder on the strut.

2. Unbolt the caliper and pull it away from the strut, suspending it with a piece of wore from the body. Do not disconnect the brake line.

3. Remove the attaching nut and then detach the push rod on the stabilizer bar at the strut.

4. Unscrew the attaching nut and press off the guide joint.

5. Unscrew the nut and press off the tie rod joint.

6. Press the bottom of the strut outward and push it over the guide joint pin. Support the bottom of the strut.

7. Unscrew the nuts at the top of the strut (from inside the engine compartment) and then remove the strut.

Install in reverse order, keeping the following points in mind:

a. Replace the self-locking nuts that fasten the top of the strut.

b. Tie rod and guide joints must have both pins and both bores clean for reassembly. Replace both self-locking nuts.

c. Torque the control arm to spring strut attaching nut to 43–51 ft. lb. Torque the spring strut to wheel well nuts to 16–17 ft. lb.

320i

1. Raise the vehicle and support safely. Remove the wheel.

2. Detach the bracket at the strut assembly.

3. Disconnect and suspend the bake caliper with a wire from the vehicle body. Do not disconnect the brake line.

4. Remove the cotter pin and castle nut. Press the tie rod off the steering knuckle.

5. Remove the three retaining nuts and detach the strut assembly at the wheel house.

6. Installation is the reverse of removal.

528i, 1981-82 533i and 1981-82 633CSi

1. Raise the vehicle and support safely. Remove the wheel.

2. Disconnect the bracket at the strut assembly.

3. Disconnect the brake caliper and suspend from the vehicle body with wire. Do not remove the brake hose.

4. Remove the lock wire and disconnect the tie rod arm at the strut assembly.

5. Remove the three retaining nuts and detach the strut assembly at the wheelhouse.

6. Installation is the reverse of removal.

524td, 528e, 533i (1983-84), 535i, 633CSi (1983-84), 635CSi, M5, M6 and 735i (1987-88)

1. Raise the vehicle and support it securely. Remove the front wheel.

2. Disconnect the brake caliper and suspend it with a piece of wire so there is no tension on the brake hose (do not disconnect the hose).

3. If you are removing the left side strut, lift the electrical plug out of the clip on the strut, disconnect the ground wire, and disconnect the plug.

4. On cars with ABS, disconnect the ABS pulse transmitter at the strut.

5. Disconnect the stabilizer push rod at the bracket on the side of the strut; To do this, use a wrench to hold the rod end on the flats just outside the bracket and unscrew the nut from the inside of the bracket.

6. Remove the bolts from the underside of the tie rod arm that attach the bottom of the strut to the arm. Then, move the strut outward.

7. On the 735i, remove the cap. Support the bottom of the strut and then remove the three nuts attaching the strut to the top of the fender well.

8. Installation is the reverse of removal. Use new self-locking nuts on the studs that pass through the fender well. Align the bottom of the strut with the tie rod arm so the tab on the arm fits into the notch on the bottom of the strut.

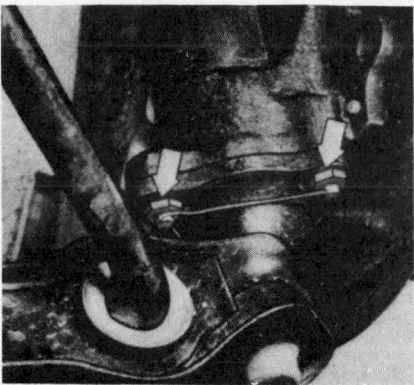

Lock wire location at strut assembly

1981-82 733i

1. Raise the vehicle and support safely. Remove the wheel.

2. Disconnect the vibration strut from the control arm.

3. Disconnect the bracket and clamps from the strut assembly.

4. Disconnect the wire connection and press out the wire from the clamp on the spring strut tube.

5. Remove the brake caliper and suspend it from the vehicle body with a wire. Do not remove the brake hose.

6. Disconnect the tie rod from the shock absorber.

7. Remove the three retaining nuts and disconnect the strut assembly from the wheelhouse.

8. Installation is the reverse of removal.

1983-84 733i and 1985-86 735i

1. Raise the vehicle and support it safely by the body. Remove the front wheel. Detach the brake line bracket and clamp from the strut.

2. Pull off the rubber cover, and then use an Allen type wrench to unbolt the antilock sensor at the rear of the caliper. Remove it.

3. Pull the antilock sensor electrical connector out of the holder and unplug it. Disconnect the ground wire.

4. Detach the caliper and suspend it from the body without disconnecting the brake line.

5. Support the strut in a secure manner at the bottom. Remove the self-locking nut and through bolt connecting the lower end of the vibration strut where it connects to the control arm.

6. Then, remove the three self-locking nuts from the top of the strut housing in the engine compartment, and remove the strut.

7. Install the strut in reverse order, noting the following points:

   a. Use new self-locking nuts on the top of the strut housing and at the connection to the control arm.

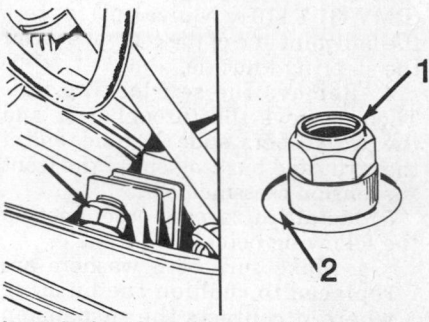

In replacing the nut located in the center of the control arm, use a replacement nut (1) and washer (2) of the type shown

   b. When reconnecting the lower strut to the track arm, clean the bolt threads and bolt holes and install the bolts with a special bolt tightener HWB No. 81 22 9 400 086 or equivalent.

OVERHAUL

NOTE: For all spring and shock absorber removal and installation procedures, and all strut overhaul procedures, please refer to "Strut Overhaul" in the unit repair section.

Control Arm

REMOVAL & INSTALLATION

528e, 528i, 533i and 633CSi 1981-82

1. Raise the vehicle and support safely. Remove the wheel.

2. Disconnect the stabilizer at the control arm.

3. Remove the tension strut nut on the control arm.

4. Disconnect the control arm at the front axle support and remove it from the tension strut.

5. Remove the lock wire, remove the bolts and take the control arm off the spring strut.

6. Remove the cotter pin and nut.

7. Using special tool BMW 00–7–500 or equivalent, pull the guide joint from the tie rod arm.

8. Installation is the reverse of removal.

524td, 533i (1982-84), 535i, 633CSi (1983-84), 635i, M5, M6 and 735i (1987-88)

1. Raise and support the vehicle securely. Remove the wheel.

2. Remove the three bolts that fasten the bottom of the strut to the steering knuckle.

3. Remove the cotter pin and castellated nut. Use a ball joint remover

(BMW 31 1 110 or equivalent) to press the ball joint end of the control arm off the steering knuckle.

4. Remove the self locking nut. Then, remove the through bolt and the two washers, slide the inner end of the strut and bushing out of the front suspension crossmember.

5. Install in reverse order, noting the following points:

   a. Make sure both washers are replaced to cushion the bushing where it contacts the suspension crossmember.

   b. Replace the bushing if it is worn or cracked.

   c. Use a new self-locking nut on the bolt fastening the inner end of the strut.

   d. Align the bottom of the strut with the steering knuckle so the tab on the arm fits into the notch on the bottom of the strut. Install the bolts with a locking type sealer.

   e. When installing the arm ball joint onto the steering knuckle, tighten the nut until a castellation lines up with the cotter pin hole and then use a new cotter pin in the nut.

   f. Final tighten the through bolt for the inner end of the arm after the car is on the ground at normal ride height.

318i, 325, 325e, 325i and 325is

1. Remove the front wheel. Disconnect the rear control arm bracket where it connects to the body by removing the two bolts.

2. Remove the nut and disconnect the thrust rod on the front stabilizer bar where it connects to the center of the control arm.

3. Unscrew the nut which attaches the front of the stabilizer bar to the crossmember and remove the nut from above the crossmember. Then, use a plastic hammer to knock this support pin out of the crossmember.

4. Unscrew the nut and press off the guide joint where the control arm attaches to the lower end of the strut.

5. Reverse the procedure to install. Keep these points in mind:

   a. Replace the self-locking nut that fastens the guide joint to the control arm.

   b. Make sure the support pin and the bore in the crossmember are clean before inserting the pin through the crossmember. Replace the original nut with a replacement nut and washer equivalent to those shown in the illustration.

   c. Torque the control arm-to-spring strut nut to 43–51 ft. lb. Torque the control arm support to crossmember nut to 29–34 ft. lb. Torque the push rod on the stabilizer bar to 29–34 ft. lb.

Vibration strut attaching bolt—733i

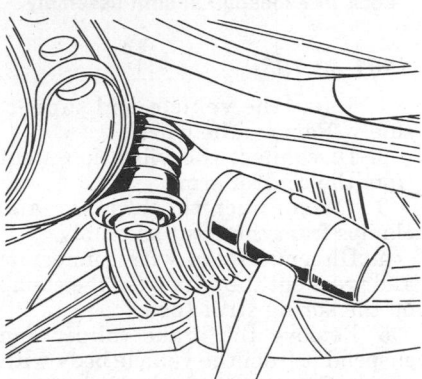

On the 318i, knock the pin loose with a soft hammer, as shown

320i

1. Disconnect the stabilizer at the control arm.

2. Disconnect the control arm at the front axle support.

3. Remove the cotter pin and castellated nut.

4. Press the control arm off the steering knuckle with special tool BMW 31–1–100 or equivalent.

5. Installation is the reverse of removal.

733i and 1985-86 735i

1. Raise the vehicle and support safely. Remove the wheel.

2. Disconnect the vibration strut from the control arm.

3. Disconnect the control arm from the axle carrier.

4. Disconnect the tie rod arm from the front strut.

5. Remove the cotter pin and castellated nut. Press off the control arm with special tool BMW 31–1–110 or equivalent.

6. Installation is the reverse of removal. Use new self-locking nuts on the connections at the vibration strut and axle carrier. On 1983-88 models, when reconnecting the arm to the tie rod arm, use a bolt tightener HBW No. 81 22 9 400 086 and make sure the threads and bolt holes are clean.

Front Wheel Bearings

ADJUSTMENT

NOTE: The wheel bearings for 318i and 325, 5 and 6 Series for 1983-88, and 7 Series for 1987-88 cannot be adjusted.

320i, 533i, 633CSi, 733i and 735i

1. Raise the vehicle, support it and remove the front wheel.

2. Remove the end cap, and then straighten the cotter pin and remove it. Loosen the castellated nut.

3. While continuously spinning the brake disc, torque the castellated nut down to 22–24 ft. lbs. Keep turning the disc thru-out this and make sure it turns at least two turns after the nut is torqued and held.

4. Loosen the nut until there is end play and the hub rotates with the nut.

5. Torque the nut to no more than 2 ft. lbs. Finally, loosen slowly just until castellations and the nearest cotter pin hole line up and insert a new cotter pin.

6. Make sure the slotted washer is free to turn without noticable resistance; otherwise, there is not end play and the bearings will wear excessively.

528i

1. Remove the wheel. Remove the locking cap from the hub by gripping it carefully on both sides with a pair of pliers.

2. Remove the cotter pin from the castellated nut, and loosen the nut.

3. Spin the disc constantly while torquing the nut to 7 ft. lbs. Continue spinning the disc a couple of turns after the nut is torqued and held.

4. Loosen the castellated nut $1/4$–$1/3$ turn-until the slotted washer can be turned readily.

5. Fasten a dial indicator to the front suspension and rest the pin against the wheel hub. Preload the meter about 0.039 in. to remove any play.

6. Adjust the position of the castellated nut while reading the play on the indicator. Make the play as small as possible while backing off the castellated nut just until a new cotter pin can be inserted. The permissible range is 0.0008–0.004 in.

7. Install the new cotter pin, locking cap, and the wheel.

REMOVAL & INSTALLATION (PACKING)

NOTE: Those vehicles listed above as not requiring adjustment have permanently sealed bearings that do not require periodic disassembly and packing.

1. Remove the wheel. Unbolt and remove the caliper. Hang it from the body. Do not disconnect or stress the hose. On models with a separate disc, remove the locking cap by gripping carefully on both sides with a pair of pliers, remove the cotter pin from the castellated nut, and remove the nut and, where equipped, the slotted washer. Then, remove the entire hub and bearing.

2. Remove the shaft sealing ring and take out the roller bearing.

3. On most models, the outer bearing race may be forced out through the recesses in the wheel hub. A BMW puller 00 8 550 or the equivalent may also be used. On the 733i, the recesses are not provided and a puller is necessary.

4. Clean all bearings and races and the interior of the hub with alcohol, and allow to air dry.

NOTE: Do not dry with compressed air as this can damage the bearings by rolling them over one another unlubricated or force one loose from the cage and injure you.

5. Replace all bearings and races if there is any sign of scoring or galling.

6. Press in the outer races with a suitable sleeve. Pack a new shaft seal with graphite grease and refill the hub with fresh grease.

7. Assemble in this order: outer race; inner race; outer race; inner race; shaft seal.

8. If necessary, adjust the wheel bearing play as described above.

318i, 325, 325e, 325i and 325is

NOTE: The bearings on the 318i and 325 are only removed if they are worn. They cannot be removed without destroying them (due to side thrust created by the bearing puller). They are not periodically disassembled, repacked and adjusted.

1. Remove the front wheel and support the car. Remove the attaching bolts and remove and suspend the brake caliper, hanging it from the body so as to avoid putting stress on the brake line.

2. Remove the setscrew with an Allen wrench. Pull off the brake disc and pry off the dust cover with a small prybar.

3. Using a chisel, knock the tab on the collar nut away from the shaft. Unscrew and discard the nut.

4. Pull off the bearing with a puller and discard.

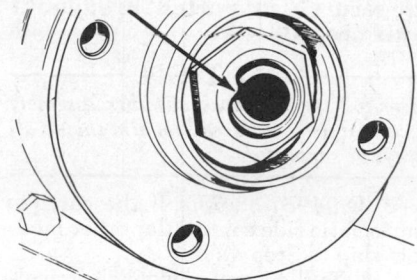

On 318i, unlock the collar nut as shown with a chisel, by applying force in the direction shown by the arrow

5. If the inside bearing inner race remains on the stub axle, unbolt and remove the dust guard. Bend back the inner dust guard and pull the inner race off with a special tool capable of getting under the race (BMW 00 7 500 and 33 1 309 or equivalent). Reinstall the dust guard.

6. Then install a special tool (BMW 31 1 120 or equivalent) over the stub axle and screw it in for the entire length of the guide sleeve's threads. Press the bearing on.

7. Reverse the remaining removal procedures to install the disc and caliper. Torque the wheel hub collar nut to 188 ft. lb. Lock the collar nut by bending over the tab.

733i and 735i — 1981-86

1. Remove the front wheel. Detach the brake line clamp and bracket on the strut. On cars with ABS, remove the rubber boot and unbolt and remove the anti-lock sensor.

2. Detach the caliper without disconnecting the brake line and suspend it.

3. Use a tool such as 21 2 000 to remove the end cap. Remove the cotter pin and unscrew the castellated nut. Then, remove the stepped washer, brake disc, and wheel hub.

4. Use an Allen type wrench to unscrew the bolt and separate the disc from the wheel hub.

5. Lift out the shaft seal. Remove the tapered roller bearings. Knock out the outer races if they show scoring with a punch by tapping all around.

6. Press in new outer races with special tools such as 31 2 061 for the inside bearings and 31 2 062 for the outside bearings. Pack the two inner races with wheel bearing grease. The order of installation is: outer race, inner race, outer race, inner race, shaft seal. To install the seal, lubricate the sealing lip of the shaft seal with grease and install the seal with a tool such as 31 2 040. Repack all bearings thoroughly with wheel bearing grease before installation.

7. Install in reverse order, adjusting the wheel bearings as described above.

524td, 528e, 535i, 1983-84 633CSi, 635CSi, M5 and M6

1. Raise the vehicle and support it securely. Unbolt and remove the caliper, suspending it so the broake line will not be stressed. Remove th Allen bolt and remove the brake disc.

2. Remove the grease cap. Use a flat punch and hammer to push the punched-in area of the retaining nut away from the groove in the axle. If necessary, chisel the nut off. Then, use a socket 31 2 080 or equivalent to unscrew the bearing retaining nut.

3. Install a puller 31 2 100 or equivalent. Screw the tool's bolt inward to pull the bearing housing out of the axle.

4. Install a new bearing assembly cover on the stub axle. Use special tool set 31 2 110 to pull the new bearing assembly into the axle.

5. Install a washer and a new retaining nut. Torque the nut to 210 ft. lbs. Use a center punch and hammer to punch the inner edge of the nut into the indentation on the axle shaft. Install a new grease cap coated with a sealer such as HWB 88 228 407 420.

1987-88 735i

1. Remove the front wheel and support the car. Remove the attaching bolts and remove and suspend the brake caliper, hanging it from the body so as to avoid putting stress on the brake line.

2. Remove the setscrew with an Allen wrench. Pull off the brake disc and pry off the dust cover with a small prybar.

3. Using a chisel, knock the tab on the collar nut away from the shaft. Unscrew and discard the nut.

4. Install a puller collar such as 31 2 105 to the bearing housing with three bolts. Install a puller such as 31 2 102 and 312 2 106 and pull off the bearing and discard it.

5. If the inside bearing inner race remains on the stub axle, unscrew and remove the dust guard. Bend back the inner dust guard and pull the inner race off with a special tool capable of getting under the race (BMW 31 2 100 and 31 2 102 or equivalent). Reinstall the dust guard and install a new dust cover.

6. Then install a special tool (BMW 31 2 110 or equivalent) over the stub axle and screw it in for the entire length of the guide sleeve's threads. Press the bearing on.

7. Reverse the remaining removal procedures to install the disc and cali-

per. Torque the wheel hub collar nut to 210 ft. lb. Lock the collar nut by bending over the tab.

8. Install a new grease cap coated with a sealer such as HWB 88 228 407 420.

Front Wheel Alignment

CASTER AND CAMBER

Caster and camber are not adjustable, except for replacement of bent or worn parts.

On the 1983-88 models, camber that is out of specification because of excessive tolerances can be corrected by installing eccentric mounts. This cannot be done to correct misalignment caused by a collision, however.

TOE-IN ADJUSTMENT

Toe-in adjusted by changing the length of the tie rod and tie rod end assembly. When adjusting the tie rod ends, adjust each by equal amount (in the opposite direction) to increase or decrease the toe-in measurement.

REAR SUSPENSION

MacPherson Strut Assembly

For all spring and shock absorber removal and installation procedures and any other strut overhaul procedures, please refer to "Strut Overhaul" in the Unit Repair section.

— CAUTION —

MacPherson strut springs are under tremendous pressure and any attempt to remove them without proper tools could result in serious personal injury.

REMOVAL & INSTALLATION

1. On model 1981-82 733i and on 1987-88 735i, remove the rear seat and back rest. On 1983-86 733i and 735i, remove the trim from over the wheel well in the trunk.
2. Jack up the car and support the control arms.

NOTE: On the 318i and 325, the spring and shock absorber are separate. The control arm must be securely supported throughout this procedures.

— CAUTION —

The coil spring, shock absorber assembly acts as a strap so the control arm should always be supported.

3. On 1987-88 735i if the car has automatic ride control (for other models skip to Step 4):
   a. Pull off and bridge (electrically) the low pressure switch electrical connection and turn on the ignition.
   b. Disconnect the control rod nut, holding the collar with an 8mm wrench against torque. Don't disconnect the rod at the ball joint.
   c. Operate the lever on the control switch in the "discharge" direction for about 20 seconds to discharge fluid from the lines.
   d. Disconnect the hydraulic line on the shock absorber.
4. Remove the lower shock retaining bolt.
5. Remove trim if necessary and disconnect the upper strut retaining nuts at the wheel arch and remove the assembly.

NOTE: On the 318i and 325, this is located behind the trim panel in the trunk. On these models only, the shock absorber, because it is separate from the spring, may now be replaced.

6. Install in reverse order, using new gaskets between the unit and the wheel arch, and new self-locking nuts on top of the strut. Torque the shock-to-body nuts to 16–17 ft. lb.; spring retainer-to-wheel house nuts (6 cyl.) to 16–17 ft. lb.; lower bolt to 52–63 ft. lb. (4 cyl.), 90–103 ft. lb. (6 cyl.). On 1983-88 733i, 735i, replace the gasket that goes between the top of the strut and the lower surface of the wheel well. Final torquing of the lower strut bolt should be done with the car in the normal riding position.

OVERHAUL

NOTE: For all spring and shock absorber removal and installation procedures, and all strut overhaul procedures, please refer to "Strut Overhaul" in the unit repair section.

Rear Spring

REMOVAL & INSTALLATION

318i, 325, 325e, 325i and 325is

1. Disconnect the rear portion of the exhaust system and hang it from the body.
2. Disconnect the final drive rubber mount, push it down, and hold it down with a wedge.
3. Remove the bolt that connects the rear stabilizer bar to the strut on the side you're working on. Be careful not to damage the brake line.

NOTE: Support the lower control arm securely with a jack or other device that will permit you to lower it gradually, while maintaining secure support.

4. Then, to prevent damage to the output shaft joints, lower the control arm only enough to slip the coil spring off the retainer.
5. Make sure, in replacing the spring, that the same part number, color code, and proper rubber ring are used. Reverse all removal procedures to install, making sure that the spring is in proper position, keeping the control arm securely supported until the shock bolt is replaced, and tightening stabilizer bar and lower shock mount bolts with the control arm in the normal ride position. Torque the stabilizer bolt to 22–24 ft. lb., and the shock bolt to 52–63 ft. lb.

Stabilizer

REMOVAL & INSTALLATION

1. Disconnect the stabilizer from the trailing arm by removing the connect bolt.
2. Disconnect the stabilizer on the crossmember.
3. Check the rubber bushings for wear and replace as necessary.

Rear Control Arm

REMOVAL & INSTALLATION

524td, 528e, 528i, 535i and M5

1. Apply the parking brake and then remove the rear wheel. Disconnect the driveshaft at the outer flange by removing the bolts.
2. Remove the parking brake lever.
3. Plug the front hose to prevent loss of brake fluid in the reservoir.
4. Support the body.
5. Disconnect the brake line at the brake hose.
6. Disconnect the stabilizer and coil spring at the control arm.
7. Disconnect the control arm at the axle carrier.
8. Installation is the reverse of removal. Bleed the system.

733i and 735i

1. Remove the rear wheel.

1. Spacer ring   2. Washer   3. Wishbone

Detaching the lower arm at front axle beam

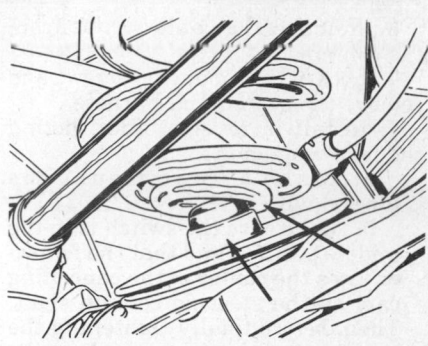

On the 318i, lower the trailing arm just enough to get the spring off the locating tang

2. Pull up the parking brake lever and disconnect the output shaft at the drive flange.

3. Remove the parking brake lever.

4. Remove the brake fluid from the reservoir.

5. Disconnect the brake line.

6. Disconnect the control arm from the rear axle carrier.

7. Disconnect the shock absorber and remove the control arm.

8. Installation is the reverse of removal. When reattaching the trailing arm, insert the bolt on the inner bracket first. Final tighten all mounting bolts with the car resting on its wheels. Bleed the brake system.

Trailing Arm

REMOVAL & INSTALLATION

528e, 533i, 633CSi through 1982

1. Raise the vehicle and remove the rear wheel. Apply the parking brake and disconnect the output shaft at the rear axle shaft. Then, disconnect the parking brake cable at the handbrake. Remove the parking brake lever.

2. Remove the rear wheel.

3. Using vise grips, clamp the front hose to prevent loss of fluid.

4. Support the body.

5. Pull the parking brake cable out of the pipe.

6. Disconnect the stabilizer and spring strut at the trailing arm.

7. Disconnect the brake line at the brake hose.

8. Disconnect the driveshaft at the outboard flange.

9. Disconnect the brake pad wear indicator wire at the right trailing arm and take the wire out of the clamps.

10. Disconnect the trailing arm at the rear axle support.

11. Installation is the reverse of removal. Bleed the system.

318i, 320i, 325, 325e, 325i and 325is

1. Raise the vehicle and remove the rear wheel. Apply the parking brake and disconnect the output shaft at the rear axle shaft. Then, on the 320i, disconnect the parking brake cable at the handbrake. On the 318i and 325, remove the parking brake lever.

2. Remove the brake fluid from the master cylinder reservoir on the 318i and 325. Disconnect the brake line connection on the rear control arm on both types of car. Plug the openings.

3. Support the control arm securely. Disconnect the shock absorber at the control arm. On 318i and 325, lower the control arm slowly and remove the spring. On the 320i, the control arm need not be lowered slowly because the spring is integral with the strut.

4. Remove the nuts and then slide the bolts out of the mounts where the control arm is mounted to the axle carrier.

5. Install in reverse order. Torque the bolts holding the trailing arm to the axle carrier to 48–54 ft. lb. On the 318i and 325, make sure the spring is positioned properly top and bottom. Torque the strut bolt to 52–63 ft. lb. Reinstall the handbrake or reconnect the cable and adjust. Then apply the brake and reconnect the output shaft. Reconnect the brake line, replenish with the proper brake fluid, and bleed the system.

Rear Wheel Bearings

ADJUSTMENT AND REMOVAL & INSTALLATION

NOTE: For these procedures, refer to "Rear Axle Shaft, Wheel Bearings, and Seals" in the Drive Axle section.

STEERING

Steering Wheel

REMOVAL & INSTALLATION

NOTE: Remove and install steering wheel in straight ahead position. Mark the relationship between the wheel and spindle.

1. Remove steering wheel pad or BMW emblem. Mark the relationship between the steering wheel and shaft for installation in the same position. On 1986-88 models, unlock the steering wheel lock with the key. Otherwise, the wheel cannot be removed.

2. Unscrew retaining nut and remove the wheel.

————— CAUTION —————

Be careful not to damage the direction signal cancelling cam, which is right under the steering wheel, in performing this operation.

3. Installation is the reverse of removal. Replace the self-locking nut on all 1983-88 models.

Turn Signal/Dimmer Switch and Wiper Switch

REMOVAL & INSTALLATION

318i, 320i, 325, 325e, 325i and 325is

1. Turn the steering wheel to the straight ahead position. Remove the steering wheel and the lower steering column cover.

2. Disconnect the (−) cable from the battery. Disconnect the direction signal switch multiple connector from under the dash by squeezing in the locks on either side and pulling it off.

3. Remove the cable straps from the column.

4. Loosen the mounting screws and remove the switch and harness.

5. Install in reverse order, noting the following points:

a. Make sure to mount the ground wire.

b. Make sure the switch is in the middle position and that the follower faces the center of the cancelling cam on the steering column shaft. Then, before finally tightening the switch mounting screws, adjust the switch on slotted mounting holes so the gap between the cam and follower is 0.118 in.

528i

1. Turn the steering wheel to the straight ahead position. Remove the steering wheel and lower column cover.

2. Disconnect the battery (–) cable. Disconnect the parking light cable connector near the column.

3. Disconnect the supply plug at the center of the connector panel on the cowl. Then, loosen the clips from the harness going from the cowl up to the switch.

4. Loosen the mounting screws and remove the switch.

5. Install in reverse order. Before final tightening of the switch mounting screws, slide the switch on its slots to adjust the gap between the cancelling cam and cam follower as follows:

a. Make sure the switch is in its middle position and that it points to the middle of the cancelling cam.

b. Adjust the gap to 0.012 in.

533i and 633CSi

1. Follow the procedure above exactly; when adjust the gap between the cancelling cam and the switch follower, use the dimension 0.118 in.

524td, 528e, 535i, 635CSi, M5 and M6

1. Disconnect the battery ground cable. Remove the steering wheel as described above.

2. Remove the instrument panel trim which is near the bottom of the steering wheel on the left side.

3. Remove the two screws from underneath and remove the steering column lower cover.

4. Disconnect the electrical connectors near the bottom of the column and at the area just under the front of the dash.

5. Unscrew the two screws fastening the switch and one ground wire to the column just to the left of the steering shaft. Pull off the plug connecting the switch to the relay on the right

side of the column. Remove the switch.

6. Installation is the reverse of removal.

1981-82 733i

1. Remove the steering wheel and disconnect the battery ground cable.

2. Remove the trim from below the steering column. Remove the mounting screws and detach the switch from the switch plate.

3. Loosen the straps holding the switch cable to the steering column. Pull the center plug out of the panel on the cowl and remove the switch.

4. Install in reverse order.

1983-85 733i and 1985-86 735i

1. Disconnect the negative battery cable. Remove the steering wheel as described above.

2. Remove the lower steering column cover.

3. Remove the two Phillips type screws located to the left of the steering shaft (the lower screw mounts a ground wire).

4. Disconnect the electrical connector for the switch and the flasher relay, located along the front of the column. Pull the flasher relay out of the holder.

Turn signal switch adjustment

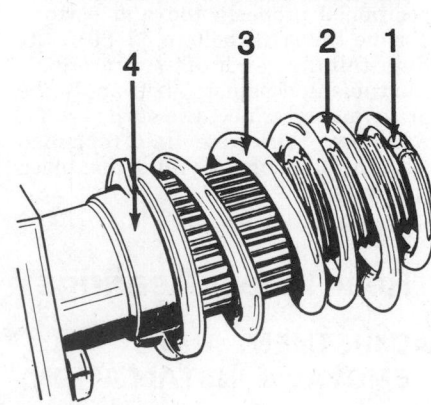

When removing the 318i steering lock, remove the snap ring (1), washer (2), spring (3), and seating ring (4)

5. Follow the wiring to the area under the dash. Open ties and unplug the electrical connector. Remove the switch.

6. Install in reverse order, making sure to retie electrical wiring going under the dash and to reconnect the ground wire to the lower switch mounting screw.

1987-88 735i

1. Disconnect the battery ground. Remove the steering wheel as described above.

2. Remove the instrument panel trim below and to the left of the steering wheel.

3. Remove the lower steering column cover.

4. Compress its retaining hook and then pull off the flasher relay socket facing downward.

5. On cars with airbags, drive out the pin and pry out the expansion rivet. Then, on all cars, remove the upper steering column cover.

6. Pull off the connector plug. This is located between the column and the dash in front of and just above where the steering wheel is normally located.

7. Compress the retaining hooks and remove the switch (located to the left of the steering shaft). Disconnect all electrical plugs and remove the switch.

8. Install in reverse order.

Ignition Switch

REMOVAL & INSTALLATION

Except Below

1. Disconnect negative battery terminal.

2. Remove lower steering column casing.

3. On 320i, 633CSi, 733i, 528i and 528e models, shear off the four tamper-proof screws with a chisel or other tool.

4. Unscrew the set screw and remove the switch.

5. Disconnect the central fuse/relay plate plug.

6. Installation is the reverse of removal.

NOTE: Turn ignition key all the way back and set the switch at the "O" position before installing. Marks on the switch must be opposite each other.

318i, 325, 325e, 325i and 325is

1. Disconnect the battery ground cable. Remove the steering wheel.

2. Remove the four screws, and re-

move the lower steering column cover.

3. Disconnect the turn signal/wiper switch by removing the four screws and disconnecting the wires.

4. Remove the collar from the steering column shaft. Then, remove the snap ring (1), washer (2), spring (3) and seating ring (4).

5. Pry off the steering spindle bearings with two screwdrivers. Pry by the inner race only.

6. Disconnect the main electrical plug at the bottom of the steering column.

7. Use a chisel to remove the tamperproof screw. Pull the lock assembly with the upper section of the casting off the outer column.

8. With a suitable tool, press downward on the lock and then slide the switch off, noting the switch position and that of the lock assembly.

9. To install, reverse the above procedure, noting these points:

   a. When installing the switch, make sure its position is the same in relationship with the lock, so the actions of the two will be synchronized.

   b. Use a Torx® screwdriver for the tamperproof screw.

   c. Drive the steering spindle bearings back on by the inner races only.

   d. When installing the seating ring that goes on the shaft, make sure the spring seat faces outward. Use a piece of pipe slightly larger than the shaft and tap it with a hammer to install the snap ring. Then, make sure the collar that goes on next locks the snap ring in place.

1985-86 524td, 528e, 535i, M5, 635i and M6

1. Disconnect the battery ground cable. Remove the steering wheel as described above.

2. Remove the instrument panel lower trim and the steering column lower cover.

3. Unplug the flasher relay and then pull the relay and holder off the front of the column. Then, remove the four Phillips screws retaining the headlight dimmer and wiper combination switch.

4. Use a hammer and chisel to shear off the five screws mounting the switch.

5. Remove the setscrew. Then, press downward on the steering column and pull the steering lock out.

6. Install in reverse order, using new shear-off type screws to mount the switch. Make sure to install the switch so it is properly positioned in relation to the steering lock. Apply

paint to the setscrew to lock it in postion after it has been installed and tightened.

1987-88 524td, 528e, 535i, M5, 635i and M6

NOTE: To perform this operation, you'll need special tools 32 3 052 and 32 3 050 or equivalent. These are a sleeve, tapered at the outer end, which permits mounting a snapring over the threaded end of the steering shaft without damaging those threads along with a pipe which fits over the sleeve and permits the snapring to be forced down the sleeve while being kept square.

1. Disconnect the battery ground cable. Remove the steering wheel as described above.

2. Remove the steering column lower cover.

3. Unplug the flasher relay and then pull the relay and holder off the front of the column. Pull the plug off the horn contact.

4. Note the location of the two ground wires. Then, remove the four Phillips screws and remove the headlight/wiper switch.

5. Pull the collar off the steering shaft. Then, remove, in order, the snap ring, washer, spring, and seating ring.

6. Press downward on the locking hook and pull the ignition switch off the column.

7. Install the switch in reverse order. Install the seating ring with the flat side outward. Use the special tools to fit the snap ring on as described in the note above. Mount the collar with the recess downward. Make sure to reconnect the ground wires to the bottom/left Phillips screw.

1983-84 733i

1. Remove the outer steering column cover.

2. Lift the flasher relay out of its holding clamp. Unscrew the attaching screw and pull out the switch.

3. Open the wire strap and pull off the plug.

4. Install in reverse order noting these points:

   a. With the ignition key in the new switch, turn the key slowly back and forth while sliding in the switch until it engages. Apply a new coating of locking sealer.

   b. Connect the black wire from the ignition switch to the black wire coming from the power saving relay. Use new straps to tie the wiring harness back in place.

1985-86 735i

1. Disconnect the battery ground cable. Remove the steering wheel as described above.

2. Remove the steering column lower cover.

3. Then, remove the four Phillips screws retaining the headlight dimmer and wiper switches.

4. Use a hammer and chisel to shear off the four screws mounting the switch to the switch plate.

5. Remove the setscrew. Then, pull the ignition switch out.

6. To synchronize the positions of the ignition lock and switch, use the key to turn the ignition lock as far back from the on position as it will go, and set the ignition switch to the "O" position. Complete the installation in reverse order, using new shear-off type screws to mount the switch. Make sure to install the switch so it is properly positioned in relation to the steering lock. Apply clear lacquer to the setscrew to lock it in postion after it has been installed and tightened.

1987-88 735i

1. Disconnect the battery ground cable. Remove the steering wheel as described above. Remove the instrument panel trim located just below the steering column.

2. Note the position of the concave collar which fits over the snapring. Then, remove the steering column cover casing by removing the two screws from underneath and the two from the front of the column.

3. Remove the bolt and nut fastening the lower end of the steering spindle (the bolt passes through a groove in the spindle). Mark alignment of the steering shaft splines with a spot of paint on each side.

4. Remove the bolts and nuts at the forked lower end of the steering column. Replace the nuts, which are self-locking.

5. Remove the two bolts fastening the upper column to the dash. Remove the column by pressing it downward.

6. Pull off the ignition switch connector. Then, compress the locking hooks and pull off the combination switch.

7. Use a screwdriver to press downward on the locking hook for the ignition switch and then pull it out of the sleeve.

8. Install in reverse order, noting the following points:

   a. Make sure to remount the spacer sleeve that goes in the column mounting bracket.

   b. After realigning the splines of the steering shaft and lower column, tighten the adjusting nut so the sliding force of the column is about 10 lbs.

c. Make sure the bolt which fastens the steering spindle in place passes through the groove in the spindle.

d. Double check to make sure you have replaced all self-locking nuts.

Manual Steering Gear

REMOVAL & INSTALLATION

320i

1. Loosen the front wheels.
2. Remove the cotter pin and castle nut.

Tie rod arm-to-shock absorber retaining bolts—733i

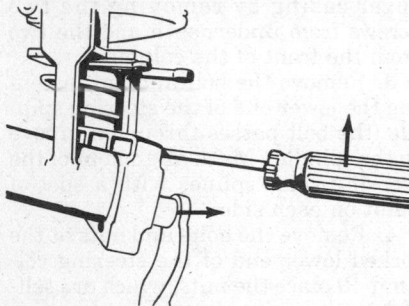

On the 318i, press down the locking hook with a screwdriver, as shown, and remove the ignition switch

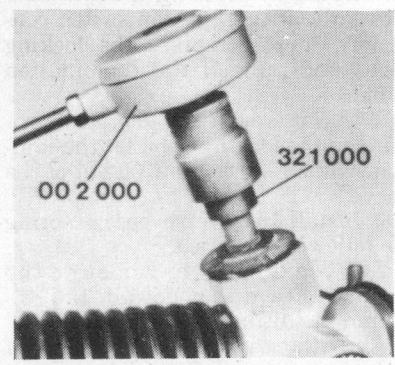

Pressure pad adjustment—320i

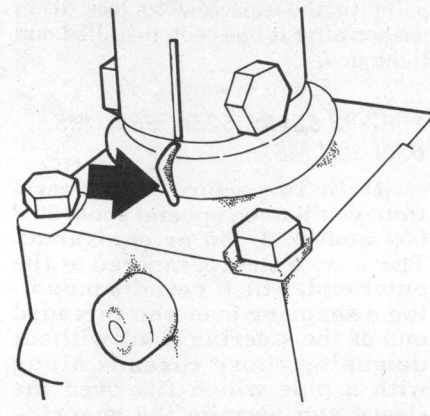

On late model 733i and 735is, line up the marks on the steering shaft and gearbox to put the steering wheel in the straight ahead position.

Steering adjustment 320i

Turning torque adjustment—320i

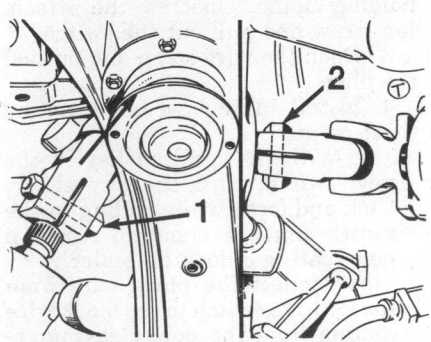

On the 318i, remove the pinch bolt (1), and through bolt (2)

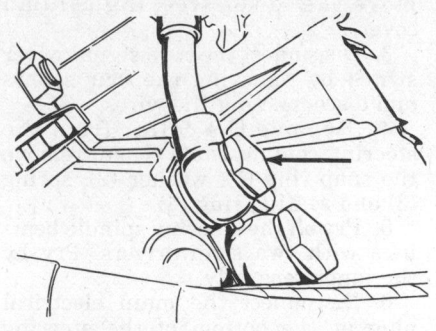

On the 318i power steering pump, disconnect the pressure line (arrowed)

3. Press the tie rods off of the steering knuckles.
4. Detach the steering at the front axle support.
5. Pull the steering gear off of the steering spindle.
6. Installation is the reverse of removal.

NOTE: Turn the steering wheel until the wheels point straight ahead. The mark on the dust seal must be between the marks on the gear box.

ADJUSTMENT

320i

1. Remove the steering gear from the car.
2. Clamp the special tool 32–1–100, or equivalent, in a vise and place the steering gear assembly into the tool.
3. Unscrew the nut on the steering damper and slide it back.
4. Remove the cap and unscrew the socket head cap about ½ in..
5. Pressure pad adjustment:

a. Remove the cotter pin. Tighten the set screw with special 32–1–100, or equivalent, and a torque wrench, to 4 ft. lbs. Loosen the set screw by one full castle slot to align the cotter pin bore.

b. Use special tools 32–1–00 and 00–2–000 or equivalent to move rack to the left and right over the entire stroke and check for sticking and hooking. If this is the case, loosen the set screw by one more castle slot and insert the cotter pin.

c. Repeat test. If there is still sticking or hooking, replace rack, drive pinion or the entire steering gear. Never loosen the screw by 2 castle slots regardless of circumstances.

6. Turning torque adjustment:

a. Move rack to the center position. Place special tools 00–2–000 and 32–1–000 or equivalent on the drive pinion, check the turning torque. If it is not between 7.8 and 11.2 ft. lbs., adjust the set screw.

b. Turn to the right to increase friction, and turn to the left to decrease friction.

c. Install cap.

Power Steering Gear

REMOVAL & INSTALLATION

All Except 318i, 325, 325e, 325i and 325is

1. Turn the steering to left lock.

2. On 1985-88 models, which share the hydraulic system with the power brakes, discharge pressure from the system by operating the brake pedal hard about 20 times. Then, drain brake fluid out of the reservoir. Remove the two mounting nuts/bolts and remove the pipe connecting the steering unit and the rest of the system.

3. On all other systems, drain the steering fluid at this point.

4. Remove the cotter pin and loosen the castellated nut. Then, press the center tie rod off the steering drop arm.

5. Remove the screw or nuts and bolts and slide the U-joint off the steering box or flange coupling the steering column and steering gear upward. Replace all self-locking nuts.

6. Disconnect the hoses at the steering gear and plug the openings.

7. Detach and remove the steering gear at the front axle carrier, working below it. Be careful to retain all washers — they are used on both side of the front axle carrier members.

8. Installation is the reverse of removal. Use new seals on the hydraulic lines. The U-joint bolts must pass through the locking grooves on the steering shaft and steering unit shaft. When reinstalling the gearbox on 1983-88 6 and 7 Series cars, line up marks on the steering shaft and gearbox so the steering wheel will be in the straight ahead position. Use a new cotter pin on the castellated nut. Replace all self-locking nuts. A new, self locking nut is available to replace the castellated nut on the steering drop arm. Use new hydraulic fluid.

NOTE: System must be bled and the front wheels must be in the straight ahead position. Marks on the housing and propeller shaft must align. Use new self locking nuts on all models.

318i, 325, 325e, 325i and 325is

1. Support the car securely and remove front wheels. Remove the pinch bolt (1) and loosen bolt (2). Press the spindle off the steering gear.

2. Loosen the clamp and pull off the hydraulic fluid return line from the power steering unit. Discard drained fluid.

3. Detach the pressure line (arrowed). Seal off openings.

4. Unscrew left and right side nuts, and press off the tie rods where they connect to the spring struts.

5. Remove the bolts attaching the steering unit to the front axle carrier and remove it.

6. Install in reverse order, keeping the following points in mind:

a. The steering unit bolts to the rear holes of the axle carrier. Use new self-locking nuts and torque them to 29–34 ft. lb.

b. When reconnecting tie rods to the spring struts, make sure tie rod pins and strut bores are clean. Replace self-locking nuts, coat threads with Loctite® 270 or equivalent, and torque to 40–48 ft. lb.

c. Replace the seals on the power steering pump connection, and torque the bolt to 29–32 ft. lb.

d. Refill the fluid reservoir with specified fluid. Idle the engine and turn the steering wheel back and forth until it has reached right and left lock two times each. Then, turn off the engine and refill the reservoir.

ADJUSTMENT

1. Remove the steering wheel center.

2. With the front wheels in the straight ahead position, remove the cotter pin and loosen the castle nut.

3. Press the center tie rod off the steering drop arm.

4. Turn the steering wheel to the left about one turn. Install a friction gauge and turn the wheel to the right, past the point of pressure and the gauge should read 0.72–0.87 ft. lbs.

5. To adjust, turn the steering wheel about one turn to the left. Loosen the counter nut and turn the adjusting screw until the specified friction is reached when passing over the point of pressure.

Power Steering Pump

REMOVAL & INSTALLATION

All Models Except 733i and 735i

NOTE: On 5, 6 and 7 Series models built in 1986-88, the power steering pump operates the power brakes. On these cars, depress the brake pedal repeatedly until all boost pressure has been discharged.

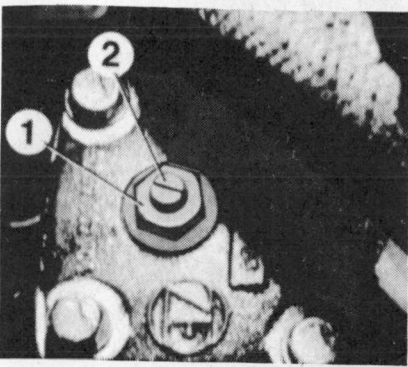

1. Locknut   2. Adjusting nut
Power steering adjustment

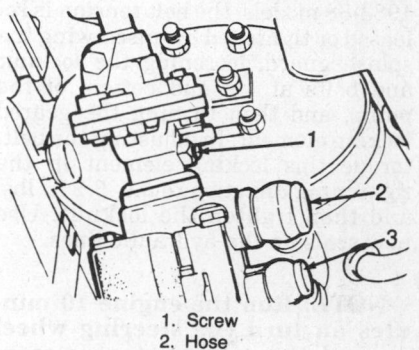

1. Screw
2. Hose
3. Hose
Coupling flange and steering box

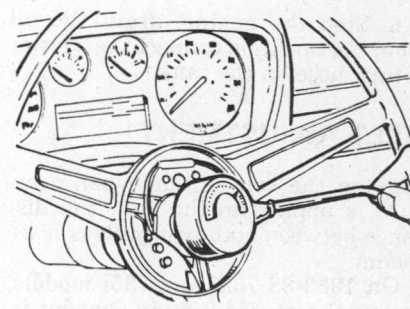

Friction gauge installation

1. Detach the steering pump hoses. Seal off all openings. Loosen the locknut and turn the adjusting bolt to release belt tension, and remove the belt.

2. On 1983-88 6 Series models, remove the splash guard. Remove bolts from the brackets holding the front and rear of the pump.

3. Installation is the reverse of removal. Torque pump mounting bolts to 16–17 ft. lbs.

NOTE: Bleed the system and torque the hose connections to 35 ft. lbs. (29–32 ft. lb – 318i and 325).

733i and 735i

NOTE: When the pump is damaged, the pressure control regulator must also be replaced.

1. Discharge the hydraulic accumulator, by depressing the brake pedal with the force required for full stop breaking (about 20 times).

2. Detach all hoses at the pump.

3. Remove bolts from the brackets holding the pump in place.

4. Remove the brake booster return hose from the accumulator tank and plug the opening.

5. Installation is the reverse of removal. Reconnect the hoses to the pump in such a way that they will not rub against body parts. Note that on 1983-88 models, the belt tension is released or tightened by unscrewing the splash guard, loosening the locknut and bolts at top and bottom of the pump, and then turning the geared locking element. In adjusting the belt, torque this locking element in the tightening direction to 5.9–6.1 ft. lbs. and then tighten the locknut. Use new seals on the hydraulic lines.

NOTE: Run the engine 10 minutes an turn the steering wheel several times from stop to stop. Operate the brake booster quickly, to obtain hard resistance, about 10 times to discard the oil leaving the return hose.

6. Stop the engine, drain the oil from the tank and connect the booster return hose on the tank.

BELT ADJUSTMENT

Tighten the belt so that when pressure is applied to the belt, the distance between both belt pulleys is 5–10mm.

On 1983-88 733i and 735i models, torque the geared locking element in the tightening direction to 5.9–6.1 ft. lbs. and then tighten the locknut.

SYSTEM BLEEDING

1. Fill the reservoir to the edge with the proper fluid.

2. Start the engine and all oil until the oil level remains constant.

3. Turn the steering wheel from lock to lock quickly until air bubbles are no longer present in the reservoir.

4. On models incorporating a combination power steering and power brake system, operate the brake pedal to discharge the hydraulic accumulator until the oil level stops rising or noticeable resistance on the brake pedal is felt.

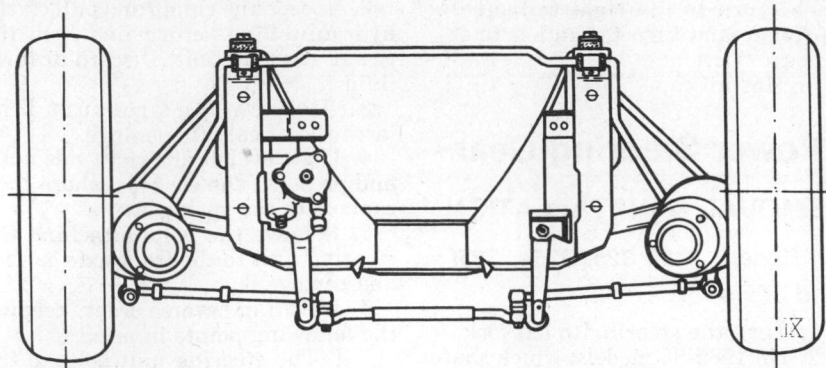

Recirculating-ball type steering linkage—all except 318i and 320i

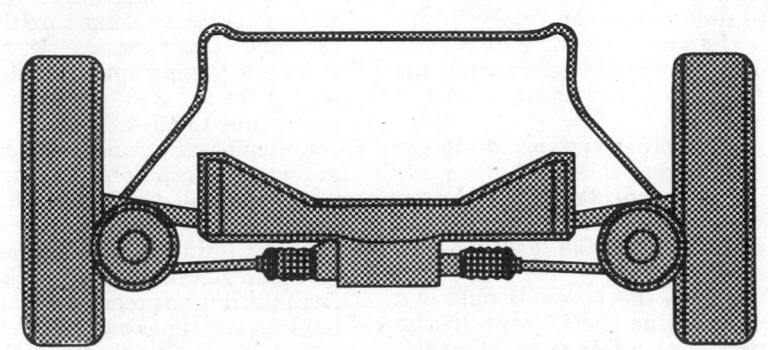

Rack and pinion steering linkage—318i and 320i

Power steering reservoir—typical

Tie Rod Ends

REMOVAL & INSTALLATION

All Models

1. Raise and support the vehicle. Loosen the clamping bolt that retains the toe-in adjustment by keeping the tie rod end from turning in relation to the tie rod.

2. Remove the cotter pin and castellated or self-locking nut from the bottom of the tie rod end. Then, press the tie rod end out of the steering knuckle with a tool such as 32 2 050. Then, unscrew the tire rod end from the tie rod and remove it, counting the number of turns required.

3. Install in reverse order, using a new cotter pin or castellated nut. Recheck the front alignment and reset the toe-in if necessary. Torque the castellated or self-locking nut to 26.5 ft. lbs. and the clamping screw to 10 ft. lbs. Final torque the clamping bolt with the car resting on its wheels.

Power steering belt adjustment

BRAKE SYSTEM

For all brake system repair and service procedures not detailed below, please refer to "Brakes" in the Unit Repair section.

Master Cylinder

REMOVAL & INSTALLATION

All Models Except Below

1. Remove the air cleaner if necessary for access.

2. Drain and disconnect the brake fluid reservoir from the master cylinder. The brake fluid reservoir will be mounted in one of two ways: (1) assembled directly on top of the master cylinder; it is removed by tilting the reservoir to one side and lifting it off of the master cylinder, or (2) the reservoir is mounted in the engine compartment where it is attached to the inner fender sheet metal by means of attaching bolts; carefully disconnect hoses leading to the master cylinder and allow the reservoir to drain.

3. Disconnect all brake lines from the master cylinder.

4. Remove the master cylinder-to-power booster attaching nuts, and remove the master cylinder.

NOTE: Observe the correct seating of the master cylinder-to-power booster seals.

To install:
1. Bench-bleed the master cylinder.

NOTE: Check for proper seating of the master cylinder-to-power booster O-ring. Check clearance between the master cylinder piston and push rod with Plastigage® or equivalent, and, if necessary, adjust to 0.002 in. by placing shims behind the head of the push rod.

2. Position the master cylinder onto the studs protruding from the power booster; install and tighten the attaching nuts.

3. Connect all brake lines.

4. Install the brake fluid reservoir and fill with brake fluid.

NOTE: An alternate method to bench bleeding the master cylinder is to bleed the master cylinder in the vehicle by opening (only slightly) the brake line fitting at the master cylinder, and allowing

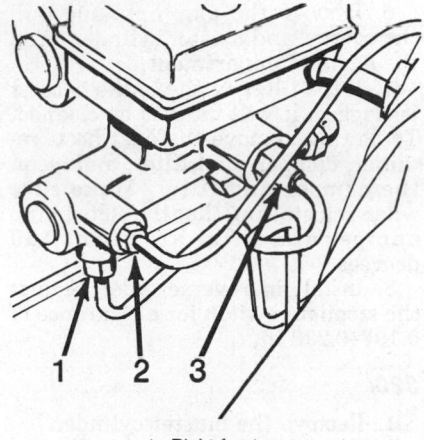

1. Right front
2. Left front
3. Rear wheels

Master cylinder—320i

the fluid to flow from the master cylinder into a container, however, this method should be considered as an ALTERNATE METHOD ONLY as it is more difficult to control the fluid leaving the master cylinder during bleeding, thereby increasing the chance of accidentally splashing brake fluid onto the painted surface of the vehicle.

5. Bleed the brake system.

318i, 320i, 325, 325e, 325i and 325is

1. Remove the fuel mixture control unit on the 320i. Disconnect the fluid level indicator plug.

2. Disconnect the hose at the clutch connection.

3. Drain and disconnect the brake fluid reservoir.

4. Disconnect the brake lines from the master cylinder.

5. On the 320i, working from the underside of the left-side inner fender panel (wheel opening area) remove the two master cylinder support bracket attaching nuts.

6. Remove the master cylinder-to-power booster attaching nuts, and remove the master cylinder.

7. Install in reverse order of removal.

NOTE: Bench bleed the master cylinder prior to installation. Refer to the aforementioned note concerning an ALTERNATE bleeding procedure.

8. Bleed the brake system.

524td, 528e, 535i, 635CSi, M5 andM6 with Vacuum Power Brakes

1. Using a syringe that is new or

has been used only for brake fluids, draw off all brake fluid from the brake fluid reservoir. Disconnect the fluid line going to the clutch master cylinder and plug it.

2. Disconnect the two brake lines connected to the side of the master cylinder.

3. Remove the two mounting bolts and remove the master cylinder from the power booster.

4. Inspect the rubber O-ring located in the groove of the rear of the master cylinder. Replace it if it is damaged.

5. Install in reverse order. Bleed the system.

524td, 528e, 535i, 635CSi, M5 andM6 with Hydraulic Power Brakes

1. Operate the brake pedal with maximum force about 20 times to remove all residual hydraulic pressure. Using a syringe that is new or has been used only for brake fluids, draw off all brake fluid from the brake fluid reservoir.

2. Disconnect the hydraulic hoses and remove the fluid storage tank from the top of the master cylinder.

3. Remove the two bolts fastening the master cylinder to the booster and remove it.

4. Install the master cylinder in reverse order. Bleed the system.

733i and 735i

1. Drain and disconnect the fluid reservoir on 733i models built through 1982 and on 1986-87 models.

2. Disconnect the two brake lines from the outboard side of the master cylinder.

3. Remove the master cylinder-to-hydraulic booster attaching bolts, and remove the master cylinder.

4. Install in the reverse order of removal.

NOTE: Bench bleed the master cylinder prior to installation. Refer to the aforementioned note concerning an ALTERNATE bleeding procedure.

Proportioning Valve

REMOVAL & INSTALLATION

318i, 325, 325e, 325i and 325is

1. Draw off hydraulic fluid from the master cylinder with a syringe or hose used only with clean brake fluid.

2. Disconnect the brake lines at the top and bottom of the proportioning valve.

3. Remove the clamp from the valve and disconnect the pressure connection at the union.

4. Check day/year codes, reduction factor, and switch over pressure to make sure the new valve is identical.

5. Install in reverse order. Bleed the system.

320i

1. Draw off brake fluid from the master cylinder with a syringe or hose used only with clean brake fluid.

2. Disconnect the four brake lines at the proportioning valve.

3. Unscrew the two mounting bolts from the inner front/left wheel well. Replace this part with one bearing the code "25" and having a piston diameter of 0.709 in.

4. Install in reverse order. Bleed the system.

Vacuum Operated Power Brake Booster

REMOVAL & INSTALLATION

318i, 325, 325e, 325i and 325is

1. Draw off brake fluid in the reservoir and discard.

2. Remove the reservoir and disconnect the clutch hydraulic hose.

3. Disconnect all brake lines from the master cylinder.

4. Remove the instrument panel trim from the bottom/left inside the passenger compartment.

5. Remove the return spring from the brake pedal. Press off the clip and remove the pin which connects the booster rod to the brake pedal.

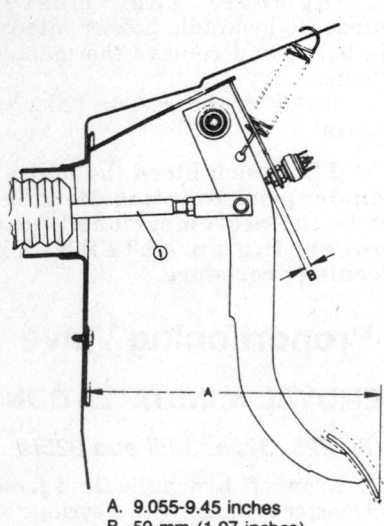

A. 9.055-9.45 inches
B. 50 mm (1.97 inches)

Brake Pedal Adjustment 528i, 528e, 630CSi, and 633CSi

6. Remove the four nuts and pull the booster and master cylinder off in the engine compartment.

7. If the filter in the brake booster is clogged, it will have to be cleaned. To do this, remove the dust boot, retainer, damper, and filter, and clean the damper and filter. Make sure when reinstalling that the slots in the damper and filter are offset 180 degrees.

8. Install in reverse order. Adjust the stoplight switch for a clearance of 0.197–0.236 in.

320i

1. Remove the master cylinder.

2. Disconnect the vacuum line at the power booster.

3. Remove the brake pedal apply-rod to power booster push rod pin.

4. Remove the power booster attaching nuts, and remove the power booster.

5. Install in the reverse order of removal.

NOTE: If the original power booster unit is to be reused, remove the dust boost and clean the silencer and filter. Position the slots in the silencer 180 degrees away from the slots in the filter.

6. Adjust the extended visible length of the brake light switch head to 0.20–0.24 in..

528e (1983-85), 528i, 533i and 633CSi

1. Remove the coolant reservoir.

2. Remove the master cylinder.

3. Disconnect the vacuum hose at the power booster.

4. Disconnect the power booster apply rod at the brake pedal.

5. Remove the power booster attaching bolts.

6. Remove the power booster.

7. Install in the reverse order of removal.

NOTE: If the original power booster unit is to be reused, remove the dust boot and clean the silencer and filter. Position the slots in the silencer 180 degrees away from the slots in the filter.

8. Adjust the brake pedal distance to 0.055–9.450 in. Adjust the stop light switch distance as described below:

   a. Disconnect the electrical connector and loosen the locknut.

   b. Measure the distance between the button on the end of the switch and the brake pedal. It must be 0.197–0.236 in. If necessary, turn

the stoplight switch to adjust the distance.

   c. Tighten the locknut and reconnect the electrical connector.

524td, 1986-88 528e, 535i, 635CSi, M5, M6

1. Remove all brake fluid from the master cylinder with a syringe or hose used only with clean brake fluid.

2. Disconnect the electrical plugs from the cap on the fluid reservoir. Disconnect the hose going to the hydraulic clutch.

3. Disconnect the two brake lines on the outboard side of the master cylinder.

4. Remove the instrument panel trim located in the bottom/left area of the panel.

5. Disconnect and remove the pedal return spring. Then, remove the retaining clip and pull out the clevis pin connecting the pedal linkage to the booster.

6. Remove the four nuts and washers from the firewall, under the brake pedal. Then, remove the booster and master cylinder from the engine compartment.

7. Remove the two mounting bolts and disconnect the master cylinder from the booster.

NOTE: If the original power booster unit is to be reused, remove the dust boot and clean the silencer and filter. Position the slots in the silencer 180 degrees away from the slots in the filter.

8. Check the O-ring located in the end of the master cylinder and replace it if it is worn or cracked.

9. Install the booster in reverse order, adjusting the stoplight switch as described in the next step and bleeding the system.

10. To adjust the stoplight switch:

   a. Disconnect the electrical connector and loosen the locknut.

   b. Measure the distance between the button on the end of the switch and the brake pedal. It must be 0.197–0.236 in. If necessary, turn the stoplight switch to adjust the distance.

   c. Tighten the locknut and reconnect the electrical connector.

Hydraulically Operated Power Brake Booster

REMOVAL & INSTALLATION

733i and 735i

1. Release the pressure in the hydraulic accumulator by operating the brake pedal (with the engine not run-

ning) with a force equivalent to that necessary to bring the vehicle to a complete stop.

2. Remove the lower left instrument panel trim.

3. Disconnect the power booster apply-rod at the brake pedal.

4. Remove the master cylinder.

5. Disconnect the fluid lines at the brake booster.

6. Remove the power booster to pedal base assembly attaching bolts, and remove the power booster.

7. Install in the reverse order of removal. On 1983-88, the hydraulic return line connection must be tightened with 34 3 153 and the pressure line with 34 3 152 or equivalent. The adjustments of Steps 8 and 9 are not required on those cars.

8. Adjust the distance between the brake pedal and the fire wall to 9.882–10.236 in.

9. Adjust the extended visible length of the brake light switch head (plunger) to 0.197–0.237 in.

Hydraulically Operated Power Brake Booster and Master Cylinder

REMOVAL & INSTALLATION

524td, 528e, 535i, 635CSi, M5 and M6

NOTE: You will need special wrenches to tighten hydraulic lines for the hydraulic booster. Use BMW tools 34 3 153 and 34 3 152 or equivalent.

1. With the engine off, discharge all pressure from the system by applying the brake pedal 20 times full force. Using a syringe or similar tool used only with brake fluids, draw excess brake fluid out of the reservoir.

2. Remove the lower/left instrument panel trim. The, lift out the spring clip and remove the clevis pin fastening the piston rod to the brake pedal.

3. Disconnect the electrical connector and then pull of the reservoir.

4. Disconnect the brake hydraulic lines at the master cylinder. Disconnect the hydraulic hoses at the brake booster.

5. Remove the bolts from the driver's side of the pedal base assembly and remove the booster and master cylinder. To separate the master cylinder and booster to replace the booster, remove the two bolts.

6. Measure the distance from the end of the threads on the piston rod to the outer end of the forked fitting for the clevis pin. Then, transfer the fit-

ting over to the new booster, screwing it on until the dimension is the same.

7. Install in reverse order, keeping the following points in mind:

a. When reattaching the hydraulic fittings to the booster, make sure everything is clean and use the special tools to tighten the fittings.

b. Check the rubber seals for the master cylinder reservoir and replace them is necessary.

c. Bleed the brakes. Test operation and boost of the system before driving the vehicle.

Rear Wheel Cylinder

REMOVAL & INSTALLATION

1. Remove the rear brake drum.

2. Loosen the wheel cylinder bleeder screw. DO NOT remove the bleeder screw.

3. Disconnect the brake line from the wheel cylinder.

4. Turn the brake shoe adjusting cams as far to the outside as possible.

5. Remove the wheel cylinder attaching bolts, and remove the wheel cylinder.

6. Install in the reverse order of removal.

Parking Brake Cable

ADJUSTMENT

Vehicles Equipped with Rear Drum Brakes

1. Support the rear of the vehicle in the raised position.

2. Fully release the handbrake.

3. On vehicles with adjustable brakes, while rotating the tire and wheel assembly, turn the left hand ec-

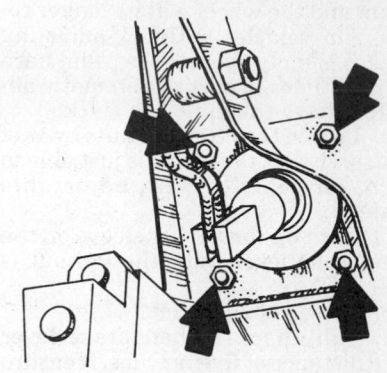

Remove the four arrowed bolts to remove the hydraulic brake booster (5–series cars

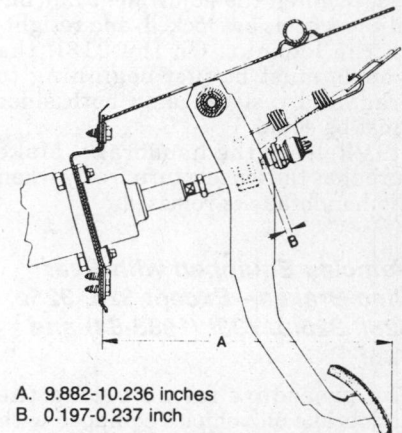

A. 9.882-10.236 inches
B. 0.197-0.237 inch

Brake pedal adjustment—733i

To disconnect the rear brake cable on the out of the housing and remove the pin at (B); pull the inner portion of the spreader 735i, pull the spreader lock assembly (A) the lower end. Disconnect the cable at lock (C) out of the housing.

centric adjustment nut counterclockwise and the right-hand eccentric adjustment nut clockwise until the brake shoes are tight against the drum and the wheel will no longer rotate. On vehicles with self-adjusting brakes, simply operate the pedal hard several times to ensure automatic adjusters have taken up the slack.

4. Loosen the eccentric nuts by ⅛ of a turn, so that the wheel is just able to turn, on vehicles with adjustable brakes.

5. Push up the rubber sleeve on the handbrake lever until the locknut is visible.

6. Loosen the locknut.

7. Pull up on the handbrake lever for a distance of five notches. Measure the distance between the middle of the handle and propeller shaft tunnel. This distance should be approximately 4.5 plus or minus 0.2 in.

8. Tighten the adjustment nut until the wheels are locked, and retighten the locknut. On the 318i, the wheels must be just beginning to drag, and resistance on both sides must be equal.

9. Release the handbrake. Make sure that the wheels turn freely when the handbrake is released.

Vehicles Equipped with Rear Disc Brakes—Except 325, 325e, 325i, 325is, 733i (1983-84) and 735i

The procedure for adjusting the handbrake on vehicles equipped with rear disc brakes is similar to the procedure for adjusting the handbrake on vehicles equipped with rear drum brakes with one exception.

The mechanism for adjusting the brake shoes is a star wheel type adjuster. Insert a screwdriver through the 0.6 in. hole, and turn the adjusting star wheel until the brake disc can no longer be moved. Proceed as though adjusting the handbrake on vehicles equipped with rear drum brakes.

325, 325e, 325i and 325is

1. Remove one bolt on each rear wheel with the vehicle securely supported. Make sure the handbrake is off and cable properly adjusted.

2. Turn the wheels until the bolt hole is about 30 degrees behind the 12 o'clock position. You can then reach the star wheel adjuster with a long screwdriver.

3. Turn the left side adjusting nut up, or the right side nut down, to tighten the adjustment until the shoes prevent the disc from being turned by hand. Now loosen the ad-

justment 3–4 threads. Make sure the disc turns easily.

733i (1983-84) and 735i

1. The parking brake should be adjusted when the lever can be pulled up more than 8 notches. First, remove the cover pate on the console (the handbrake lever protrudes through this plate). Then, loosen the locknuts and loosen the adjusting nuts (2) for the cables until they are nearly at the ends of the threads.

2. Support the car securely off the rear wheels. Remove one wheel bolt from each rear wheel. Then, rotate one wheel until the hole left by removing the bolt is about 45 degrees counterclockwise from the 6 o'clock position. This will line the hole in the wheel with the star wheel which adjusts the rear brake shoes (used for parking only). If you have trouble turning the star wheel it will help to remove the rear wheel and, if necessary, the brake disc.

3. Turn the adjusting star wheel with a screwdriver until the rear wheel or brake disc can no longer be turned. Then, back it off 4 to 6 threads.

4. In the passenger compartment, pull the handbrake up 5 notches. Then, turn the cable adjusting nuts in the tightening direction until the rear wheels can just barely be turned. Make sure the adjustment is uniform. Lock the adjusting nuts in position.

5. Release the handbrake and make sure the wheels can now be turned easily, repeating Step 4 to correct a failure to release if necessary.

REMOVAL & INSTALLATION

318i and 320i

1. Remove the brake drum as described above. Pull off the rubber boot at the handbrake lever, loosen and remove the locknuts on the appropriate side, and disconnect the cable at the handbrake lever.

2. Remove the brake shoes as described in Unit Repair.

3. Then, on 320i, pull the cable out of the holder toward the rear of the car. On 318i, disconnect the cable on the rear suspension arm, compress the locking clamp, and disconnect the cable on the backing plate and pull it out.

4. Install in reverse order, making sure the cable holders are both located properly—one in the protective tube, and the other in the backing plate. On the 318i, make sure the clamp which locates the tube is properly connected. Adjust the brakes as described at the front of this chapter.

325, 325e, 325i and 325is

1. Remove the rubber boot at the base of the handbrake by pulling up the clamp at the front and lifting it out at the rear.

2. Lift out the ashtray at the rear of the console. Remove the bolt located under the ashtray. Then, pull the console to the rear to disconnect it and remove it.

3. Unscrew and remove the parking brake cable nuts.

4. Remove the parking brake shoes. See the "Brakes" Unit Repair section. Locate the cable spread outboard of the brake disc. Pull the outer portion of the spreader to the rear and remove it. Then, press out the pin and pull the unit off.

5. Disconnect the brake cable at the trailing arm. Then, pull the cable out of the protective tube. Disconnect the cable support at the rear disc and then pull the assembly out.

6. Install in reverse order. The sliding surfaces of the cable spreader should be coated with Molykote® G paste or equivalent. Make sure the cable holder rests on the protective tube. To adjust the cable, pull the brake up just five notches, and then tighten the nuts until the right and left rear wheels just begin to drag uniformly. Release the brake and make sure the wheels turn freely.

733i (1983-84) and 735i through 1986

1. Lift out the cover plate that surrounds the handbrake lever. Remove the locknuts and adjusting nuts from the front ends of the brake cables.

2. Remove the rear brake discs. See the "Brakes" section of the Unit Repair Section.

3. Disconnect the spreader locks from the backing plates: first, rock the lower end of the spreader lock outward, and then pull out the pin. Press the cable connection out of the spreader lock. Pull the spreader lock out of the housing. Pull the cable through the backing plate.

4. Detach the parking brake cable at the trailing arm and remove it.

5. To install, reverse the removal procedures, giving the sliding surfaces and pin of the spreader lock a light coating of an lubricant such as Molykote® G paste. Adjust the handbrake as described above.

1987-88 735i

1. Remove the rear brake discs. Refer to the Brake Unit Repair Section.

2. Using brake spring pliers, disconnect the upper return spring for the parking brake shoes. Then, using a special tool 34 4 000 or the equiva-

lent, turn the retaining springs for the parking brake shoes 90 degrees to unlock them and then disconnect them.

— CAUTION —

In performing the next step, watch the pin for the expander lock and keep it if it falls out.

3. Separate the parking brake shoes at the top and then remove them from below.

4. Disconnect the spreader locks from the backing plates: first, rock the lower end of the spreader lock outward, and then pull out the pin. Press the cable connection out of the spreader lock. Pull the spreader lock out of the housing. Pull the cable through the backing plate.

5. Disconnect the parking brake cable at the trailing arm.

6. Working inside the car, remove the console cover as follows:

a. Lift out the air grille and remove the two nuts underneath.

b. Remove the cap and unscrew the mounting bolt that's located at the forward end of the console on the right side. Lift out the cover that the bolt retains.

c. Remove the bolt on the left side of the forward end of the console. If the car has power windows, disconnect the plugs. Then, lift the console and remove air ducts.

d. Turn the retainer 90 degrees and peel the rubber cover downward. Now, unscrew the adjusting nuts on the parking brake cables and pull them out.

7. Install in reverse order. Adjust the parking brake as described above.

All Others

1. Remove the parking brake shoes as described in the Unit Repair section.

2. Disconnect the negative battery cable, loosen the mounting screw and pull off the footwell nozzle.

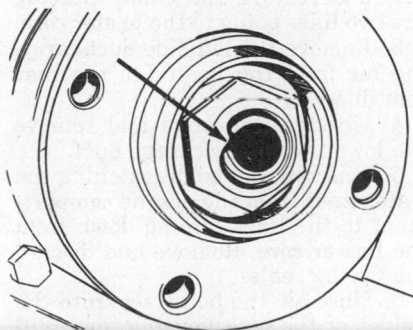

On 318i, unlock the collar nut as shown with a chisel, by applying force in the direction shown by the arrow

3. Unscrew mounting bolts, and pull the tray at the front of the footwell out far enough to disconnect the wires. Then, remove the tray.

4. Remove the rubber boot from the handbrake lever. Unscrew the locknuts and remove them and pull the cable out of the brake lever.

5. Working under the car, detach the brake cable at the suspension arm. Remove the two mounting nuts at the brake backing plate, and then pull the cable out of the protective tube.

6. Reverse the removal procedure to install.

CHASSIS ELECTRICAL

Heater Assembly, Core and Blower

REMOVAL & INSTALLATION

320i

1. Disconnect the battery ground.
2. Move the selector lever to the WARM position.
3. Drain the cooling system.
4. Loosen the hose clamp, and remove the heater core return hose.
5. Disconnect the heater hose between the hot water control valve and the engine.
6. Remove the package tray.
7. Remove outer tube casing.
8. Remove the lower center trim panel.
9. Remove the left side outer trim panel.
10. Remove the upper section of the steering tube casing.
11. Remove the heater control knobs.
12. Remove the heater control trim panel.
13. Remove the right side trim panel.
14. Disconnect the heater electrical lead.
15. Remove the heater housing retaining nuts.
16. Disconnect the left side distribution duct, and move the steering tube outer casing retaining bracket out of the way.
17. Remove the glove box lower trim panel.
18. Disconnect the left side distribution duct, and lift out the heater housing.
19. Remove the housing rivets.

20. Remove the housing clamps, and separate the housing halves.
21. Disconnect the bowden cable from the hot water control valve.
22. Remove the hot water control valve and hose from the water valve bracket on the heater housing.
23. Remove the rubber sleeves from the heater core inlet and outlet tubes.
24. Disconnect the electrical leads at the blower motor.
25. Disconnect the electrical leads at the blower resistor in the heater housing.
26. Open the blower motor support clamps, and remove the blower motor and fan as an assembly.
27. Install in the reverse order of removal.
28. Check operation of the heater controls. Adjust if necessary.

528e, 528i, 533i and 633CSi (1981-82)

1. Remove the center tray. Remove the instrument panel trim to bottom right of tray.
2. Remove the glove box and remove heater controls at water valve and at air doors. Remove center console if equipped.
3. Disconnect the battery ground.
4. Push the selector lever to the WARM position.
5. Drain the coolant and remove the air conditioning evaporator:

a. Drain the refrigerant slowly out of the low side Schraeder® valve. If you are not trained and experienced in refrigeration work, this should be left to s specialist.

b. Take off the no-drip tape type insulation and disconnect both refrigerant lines from the evaporator.

NOTE: Plug the refrigerant lines immediately to prevent moisture and contaminants from entering the system.

c. Pull the temperature sensor out of the evaporator housing.

d. Disconnect the evaporator/heater control electrical connector.

e. Remove the right and left screw from the housing (from area where the housing meets the passenger compartment carpeting).

f. Remove the floor pan to evaporator housing bracket. Lift the housing slightly and pull it from under the dash.

— CAUTION —

Do not bend the temperature sensor or it will have to be replaced.

g. Disconnect the blower wires and the blower resistor wire. Lift the evaporator slightly and pull the adapter and evaporator from under the dash.

6. Disconnect the heater hoses from the heater core, and remove the rubber seal.

7. Remove the lower instrument panel center trim.

8. Disconnect the heater controls at the instrument panel.

9. Disconnect the control shafts at the joints.

10. Disconnect the multiple electrical connector at the heater.

11. Remove the instrument panel center cover.

12. Working from inside the engine compartment, remove the upper section of the fire shield.

13. Remove the heater assembly retaining nuts, and lift out the heater.

14. Open the heater housing clips, and separate the housing halves and remove the heater core.

15. Disconnect the electrical leads at the blower motor, and remove the motor.

16. Install in the reverse order of removal.

733i and 735i — 1981-86

1. Drain the coolant from the system.

2. Discharge the refrigerant from the air conditioner or have this done by someone trained in this type of work if you are not.

3. Remove the instrument trim panel.

4. Remove the cowl fresh air grille.

5. Remove the heater assembly cover attaching screws, and remove the cover.

6. Disconnect the heater hoses at the heater core.

7. Disconnect the vacuum lines at the heater.

8. Bend open the heater duct mounting clamp.

9. Disconnect the central electrical lead.

10. Pull the duct cover downward, and remove it.

11. Remove the center strut attaching bolts (4).

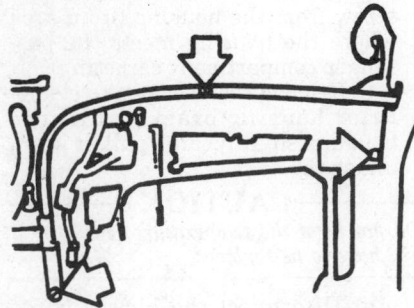

Remove the two arrowed screws to remove the heater core on 1987-88 735I

12. Remove the insulation from the refrigerant lines.

13. Disconnect the refrigerant lines from the evaporator.

14. Disconnect the evaporator drain tube.

15. Remove the heater assembly retaining bolts, remove the heater and the heater core.

16. Install in the reverse order of removal.

Heater Assembly and Core

REMOVAL & INSTALLATION

524td, 528e, 533i and 633CSi from 1983, 535i, 635CSi, M5 and M6

1. Disconnect the battery ground. Remove the instrument panel trim at bottom left. Remove the package tray.

2. If you are not trained in air conditioning work, have the air conditioning system discharged professionally. Otherwise, discharge it carefully through the Schrader® valve, and then cap the valve off.

3. Remove the two bolts and remove the trim panel underneath the evaporator unit.

4. Remove the tape type insulation. Get caps for the refrigerant lines. *Using a backup wrench*, disconnect the low and high pressure lines and cap them.

5. Disconnect the electrical connector for the evaporator. Disconnect the temperature sensor plug, accessible from the outside of the evaporator housing.

6. Remove the two bolts and then remove the bracket that braces the housing at the firewall. Remove the mounting bolt from either side of the housing.

7. Unclip both fasteners and remove the housing.

8. Now, move into the engine compartment and remove the rubber insulator from the cowl.

9. Remove the mounting bolts for the cover which is located under the windshield.

10. Remove the mounting nuts for the heater housing located on either side of the blower.

11. Drain the cooling system and disconnect the two hoses at the core.

12. Working inside the car, remove the three electrical connectors for the heater housing. Pull off the two air ducts.

13. Remove the two mounting nuts and remove the heater unit.

14. Remove the four air duct connections from the housing. Push the re-

taining bar back and then split and remove the two blower shells.

15. Remove the 13 retaining clips from the housing halves and split the housing. Then, remove the core.

16. To install, reverse the removal procedure, noting the following points:

a. Cement a new rubber seal on the core.

b. Make sure that when reassembling the halves of the housing, all the distributor door flap shafts pass through the holes in the housing.

c. Before reconnecting the refrigerant lines, coat the threads with clean refrigerant oil.

d. Refill the cooling system with clean coolant and bleed it.

e. Have the air conditioning system evacuated and recharged or do so yourself if you are qualified.

Heater Core

REMOVAL & INSTALLATION

1987-88 735i

1. Drain coolant from the cooling system (engine cooled off). Remove the center console.

2. Remove the two bolts and remove the right core mounting bracket. Lift out the front blower motor.

3. Remove the core cover screws. Loosen the wire straps and clips and remove the cover.

4. Unscrew the six mounting bolts and lift out the three heater pipes. Replace the O-rings. Then, lift out the core from the right side.

5. Install in reverse order. Refill and bleed the cooling system.

318i, 325, 325e, 325i and 325is

1. Disconnect the negative battery cable. Remove the package tray. Remove bolts and remove the left/lower dish trim panel.

2. Drain the coolant, loosen the bolt and remove the clamp bracing the two lines going to the heater core.

3. Remove the left side duct carrying air from the heater to the rear seat duct.

4. Unscrew the bolts and remove the lower heater discharge duct.

5. Unscrew the bolts fastening the water lines from the engine compartment to the lines coming down from the heater core. Remove and discard the O-ring seals.

6. Unscrew the bolts, separate the halves of the core housing, and pull the core out of the housing.

7. Installation is the reverse of removal. Replace the O-ring seals for the water lines.

Heater Blower

REMOVAL & INSTALLATION

318i, 325, 325e, 325i and 325is

1. Disconnect the negative battery cable. The blower is accessible by removing the cover at the top of the firewall in the engine compartment. To remove the cover, pull off the rubber strip, cut off the wire that runs diagonally across the cover, unscrew and remove the bolts, and pull the cover aside.
2. Open the retaining straps, swing them aside, and then remove the blower cover.
3. Pull off both connectors. Disengage the clamp that fastens the assembly in place by pulling the bottom toward you. Now, lift out the motor/fan assembly, being careful not to damage the air damper underneath.

524td, 528e, 533i and 633CSi from 1983, 535i, 635CSi, M5 and M6

1. Disconnect the battery ground cable.
2. Remove the rubber insulator from the cowl. Remove the mounting bolts for the cover which is located under the windshield.
3. Push back the three retaining tabs and remove the two shells that cover the blower wheels.
4. Disconnect the electrical connector for the motor. Unclip the retaining strap for the motor and remove the motor and blower wheels.
5. Replace the motor and blower wheels as an assembly (prebalanced). The motor will fit into the housing only one way. Reverse all procedures to install, making sure the flat surface on the inlet cowls face the body.

1987-88 735i

1. Disconnect the battery ground cable. Pull the rubber cover off the overflow tank for the cooling system. Disconnect the electrical connector and overflow hose from the overflow tank. Then, remove the mounting nuts and put the tank aside without damaging the hose leading to the radiator.
2. Cut the straps for the wiring harness running across the cowl.
3. Remove the five attaching screws and remove the blower cover from the cowl.
4. Disconnect the cable and unclip it where it is clipped to the blower cover. Then, open the plactic retainer and take off the cover.
5. Disconnect the electrical connec-

tor. Lift off the metal retainer for the blower motor and remove the blower motor.
6. Install a new, prebalanced motor and blower assembly. Install in reverse order.

Radio

REMOVAL & INSTALLATION

NOTE: The following procedure is a general one, which applies to all models.

1. Pull off the radio knobs and ornamental rings.
2. Push up on spring catches and remove them from the control shafts. Remove the radio mask.
3. Remove the bolts from supports on both sides of the radio.
4. Disconnect the automatic antenna lead, the antenna, the right and left speaker wires and the power supply.
5. Installation is the reverse of removal.

Windshield Wiper Switch

REMOVAL & INSTALLATION

All Models Except 1987-88 735i

The wiper switch is located on the steering column and in most cases the steering wheel will have to be removed, along with the lower steering column trim panels, to gain access to the switch.

After the retaining screws and electrical connectors are removed, the switch can be lifted from the plate of the steering column.

--- **CAUTION** ---

To avoid possible electrical short-circuits, the negative battery cable should be removed before the repairs are attempted.

1987-88 735i

1. Disconnect the negative battery cable. Remove the steering wheel as described earlier. Remove the lower/left instrument panel trim.
2. Remove the screws and remove the lower steering column cover.
3. Push the locking hook for the flasher back and remove the relay, socket facing downward.
4. Take off the upper steering column cover. If the car has airbags, drive out the pins and lift out the expansion rivet first.
5. Press the retaining hooks inward on both sides, pull the switch out, and then disconnect the electrical connector.

6. Installation is the reverse of removal.

Windshield Wiper Motor

The electric wiper motor assembly is located under the engine hood, at the top of the cowl panel. A few models have covers over the wiper motor assembly, while others have the motors exposed. Link rods operate the left and right wiper pivot assemblies from a drive crank bolted to the wiper motor output shaft.

REMOVAL & INSTALLATION

320i, 524td, 528e, 528i, 533i, 535i, 633CSi, 635CSi, M5 and M6

1. Remove the cowl cover to expose the wiper motor (320i and 530i and all 5 and 6 Seris cars after 1983).
2. Disconnect the wiper motor crank arm from the motor output shaft by removing the nut and pulling off the crank arm.
3. Remove the motor retaining screws and disconnect the electrical connector.
4. Remove the wiper motor from the vehicle.
5. Reverse the procedure to install the motor.

318i, 325, 325e, 325i and 325is

1. Remove the heater motor, as described above. Remove the bracket bracing the windshield wiper motor, which is now visible.
2. Disconnect the electrical connector for the motor.
3. Lift out the grill located at the top of the cowl and disconnect the linkages to both wiper arms at the left side shaft mounts.

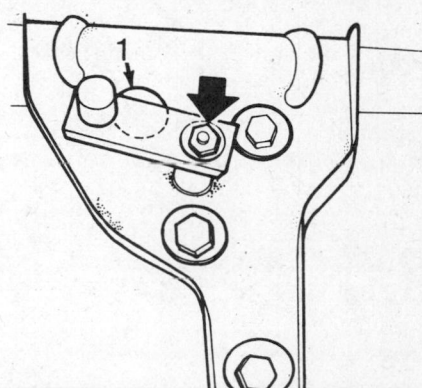

On the 735i and 733i (1983 and later), install the motor crank in the position shown, with the bolt (1) half hidden by the upper edge of the crank.

4. Disconnect both wiper arms from their shafts, by lifting the cover, unscrewing the nut, and pulling the arm off. Then, remove the cover, nut and washer surrounding the shafts and holding the console in place. Now remove the entire console and remove the motor from the console.

5. Installation is the reverse of removal.

1981-82 733i

1. Remove the cowl fresh air intake grill and tilt rearward.

2. Remove the cover from the windshield wiper motor and remove the electrical plugs.

3. Remove the left and right wiper arms. Loosen the left and right pivot bearings.

4. Turn the rubber pad at the motor, counterclockwise and disconnect the right wiper linkage.

5. Remove the motor bracket retaining screws. Separate the spacers and remove the wiper motor assembly.

NOTE: Do not lose the shims.

6. The wiper motor can be removed from the bracket after the removal.

7. Reverse the removal procedure to install.

1983-84 733i and 1985-86 735i

1. Remove the mounting screws and remove the grill from the cowl.

2. The wiper motor is located under a cover located in front of the windshield on the left side of the car. Unscrew the two mounting screws on the firewall and the two directly in front of the windshield. Pull the rubber seal out part way and move the cover slightly away from its normal position. Disconnect the hose from the cover and then tilt the cover forward.

3. Remove the wiper motor cover and unplug the electrical connector.

4. Remove both wiper arms. Unscrew the collar nuts and disconnect both wiper shaft mounts. Turn back the rubber pad and disconnect the linkage for the right wiper. Unscrew and remove the two mounting bolts and pull the spacer tube apart; remove the motor. Note the exact position of the motor crank.

5. Disconnect the linkage and pull the crank off the motor. The motor may be removed from the bracket after removing the three mounting bolts.

6. Install in reverse order, noting these points:

   a. Install the crank in the position shown to get proper parking of the wipers.

   b. When remounting the motor, make sure the bumpers that rest against the firewall are properly positioned.

   c. Situate the rubber pad so the motor has proper support.

   d. When reassembling the wiper shaft mounts, install the diaphragm spring and then the ring and torque to only 9 ft. lbs.

   e. When reinstalling the outer cover, take care not to pinch any vacuum hoses.

1987-88 735i

1. Make sure the wipers are in the parked position. Remove the heater blower as described above. Take off the cover near the blower.

2. Disconnect the heater cable and lift out the linkage. Disconnect the temperature sensor.

3. Disconnect the clips, lift the cowl cover slightly and then remove the inlet cowls on either side. Then, remove the cover.

4. Unscrew bolts and remove the mounting bracket for the wiper housing. Remove the left wiper arm by pulling up the cover, loosening the pinch bolt, and removing it. Remove the right wiper by pulling up the cover and removing the through bolt and then pulling it off.

5. Lift out the clips and remove cover for the linkage.

6. Unscrew and remove the nuts fastening the linkage to the cowl. Pull the linkage arms downward and out of the cowl.

7. Mark the relationship between the linkage lever and the motor. Remove the nut and disconnect the linkage at the motor shaft. Disconnect the electrical connector and remove the linkage.

8. Remove the three mounting bolts and remove the wiper motor. If installing a new motor, connect the motor and operate it until it reaches parked position; then install the linkage so that the shaft lever and linkage link are in a straight line.

9. Perform the remaining portions of the installation in reverse order, noting these points:

   a. Make sure the wiper arms are pressed all the way onto the linkage shafts so the contact pressure control will work.

   b. Make sure the inlet cowling is installed in proper relation to the blower housing and fresh air flap.

Chrysler Corp. **4**

Colt, Champ, Challenger, Conquest, Sapporro, Vista

SERIAL NUMBER IDENTIFICATION

Vehicle Identification Number

The vehicle identification plate is mounted on the instrument panel, adjacent to the lower corner of the windshield on the driver's side and is visible through the windshield. A standardized 17 digit Vehicle Identification Number (VIN) is used.

Vehicle Information Code

The Vehicle Information Code plate and Chassis Number plate is attached to the bulkhead (firewall) in the engine compartment.

Vehicle Safety Certification Label

A Vehicle Safety Certification Label is attached to the inside botton of the driver's door.

Engine Number

The engine number is stamped at the right front side, on the top edge of the cylinder block and contains the engine model number and engine serial number..

`J B 3 B G 3 9 D 1 H Z 0 0 0 0 0 1`

1st Digit	2nd Digit	3rd Digit	4th Digit	5th Digit	6th Digit	7th Digit	8th Digit	9th Digit	10th Digit	11th Digit	12th to 17th Digits
Country	Make	Vehicle type	Others	Line	Price class	Body	Engine	*Check digits	Model year	Plant	Serial number
J— Japan	B— Dodge P— Plymouth	3— Passenger car 4— Multi purpose vehicle	B— Manual seat belt F— 4001 lbs. or more with hydraulic brakes	G— Colt Vista H— Colt Vista 4WD	3— Medium	1— 5 door Wagon (4WD) 9— 5 door Wagon (2WD)	D— 1,997 liter (121.9 CID)	1 2 3 . . . X	H— 1987 Year	Z— Okazaki	000001 to 999999

NOTE
* "Check digit" means a single number or letter X used to verify the accuracy of transcription of vehicle identification number.

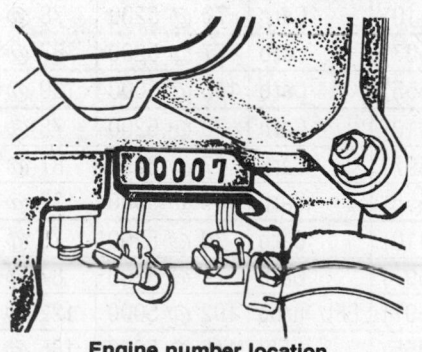

Typical Vehicle Indentification Code plate

Serial number location

Engine number location

Engine model number

4—1

ENGINE IDENTIFICATION

Year	Model	Engine Displacement cu. in. (cc/Liter)	Engine Series Identification	No. of Cylinders	Engine Type
1981	Colt, Champ	86.0 (1410/1.4)	G12B, 4G12	4	OHC
	Colt, Champ	97.5 (1597/1.6)	G32B, 4G32	4	OHC
	Challenger, Sapporo	155.9 (2555/2.6)	G54B, 4G54	4	OHC
1982	Colt, Champ	86.0 (1410/1.4)	G12B, 4G12	4	OHC
	Colt, Champ	97.5 (1597/1.6)	G32B, 4G32	4	OHC
	Challenger, Sapporo	155.9 (2555/2.6)	G54B, 4G54	4	OHC
1983	Colt, Champ	86.0 (1410/1.4)	G12B, 4G12	4	OHC
	Colt, Champ	97.5 (1597/1.6)	G32B, 4G32	4	OHC
	Challenger, Sapporo	155.9 (2555/2.6)	G54B, 4G54	4	OHC
1984	Colt	86.0 (1410/1.4)	G12B, 4G12	4	OHC
	Colt	97.5 (1597/1.6)	G32B, 4G32	4	OHC
	Colt Vista	121.9 (1997/2.0)	G63B	4	OHC
	Conquest	155.9 (2555/2.6)	G54B, 4G54	4	OHC
1985	Colt	89.6 (1468/1.5)	G15B	4	OHC
	Colt	97.5 (1597/1.6)	G32B, 4G32	4	OHC
	Colt Vista	121.9 (1997/2.0)	G63B	4	OHC
	Conquest	155.9 (2555/2.6)	G54B, 4G54	4	OHC
1986	Colt	89.6 (1468/1.5)	G15B	4	OHC
	Colt	97.5 (1597/1.6)	G32B, 4G32	4	OHC
	Colt Vista	121.9 (1997/2.0)	G63B	4	OHC
	Conquest	155.9 (2555/2.6)	G54B, 4G54	4	OHC
1987-88	Colt	89.6 (1468/1.5)	G15B	4	OHC
	Colt	97.5 (1597/1.6)	G32B, 4G32	4	OHC
	Colt Vista	121.9 (1997/2.0)	G63B	4	OHC
	Conquest	155.9 (2555/2.6)	G54B, 4G54	4	OHC

GENERAL ENGINE SPECIFICATIONS

Year	Model	Engine Displacement cu. in. (cc)	Fuel System Type	Net Horsepower @ rpm	Net Torque @ rpm (ft. lbs.)	Bore × Stroke (in.)	Compression Ratio	Oil Pressure (Psi) @ rpm
1981	Colt, Champ	86.0 (1410)	Carb	70 @ 5200	70 @ 3000	2.91 × 3.23	8.8:1	50–64
	Colt, Champ	97.5 (1597)	Carb	77 @ 5200	87 @ 3000	3.03 × 3.39	8.5:1	50–64
	Challenger, Sapporo	155.9 (2555)	Carb	105 @ 5000	139 @ 2500	3.59 × 3.86	8.2:1	50–64
1982	Colt, Champ	86.0 (1410)	Carb	70 @ 5200	78 @ 3000	2.91 × 3.23	8.8:1	50–64
	Colt, Champ	97.5 (1597)	Carb	77 @ 5200	87 @ 3000	3.03 × 3.39	8.5:1	57–71
	Challenger, Sapporo	155.9 (2555)	Carb	105 @ 5000	139 @ 2500	3.59 × 3.86	8.2:1	50–64
1983	Colt	86.0 (1410)	Carb	70 @ 5200	78 @ 3000	2.91 × 3.23	8.8:1	50–64
	Colt	97.5 (1597)	Carb	77 @ 5200	87 @ 3000	3.03 × 3.39	8.5:1	57–71
	Challenger, Sapporo	155.9 (2555)	Carb	105 @ 5000	139 @ 2500	3.59 × 3.86	8.2:1	50–64
1984	Colt	86.0 (1410)	Carb	70 @ 5200	78 @ 3000	2.91 × 3.23	8.8:1	50–64
	Colt	97.5 (1597)	Carb	77 @ 5200	87 @ 3000	3.03 × 3.39	8.5:1	57–71
	Colt Vista	97.5 (1597)	EFI/Turbo	102 @ 5000	122 @ 3000	3.03 × 3.39	7.6:1	57–71
	Conquest	155.9 (2555)	EFI	145 @ 5000	185 @ 2500	3.59 × 3.86	7.0:1	50–64

GENERAL ENGINE SPECIFICATIONS

Year	Model	Engine Displacement cu. in. (cc)	Fuel System Type	Net Horsepower @ rpm	Net Torque @ rpm (ft. lbs.)	Bore × Stroke (in.)	Compression Ratio	Oil Pressure (Psi) @ rpm
1985	Colt	89.6 (1468)	Carb	77 @ 5300	84 @ 3000	2.97 × 3.23	9.4:1	50–64
	Colt	97.5 (1597)	EFI/Turbo	102 @ 5500	122 @ 3000	3.03 × 3.39	7.6:1	57–71
	Colt Vista	121.9 (1997)	Carb	88 @ 5000	108 @ 3500	3.34 × 3.46	8.5:1	57–71
	Conquest	155.9 (2555)	EFI	145 @ 5000	185 @ 2500	3.59 × 3.86	7.0:1	50–64
1986	Colt	89.6 (1468)	Carb	68 @ 5000	84 @ 3000	2.99 × 3.23	9.4:1	50–64
	Colt	97.5 (1597)	EFI/Turbo	102 @ 5500	122 @ 3000	3.03 × 3.39	7.6:1	57–71
	Colt Vista	121.9 (1997)	Carb	88 @ 5000	108 @ 3500	3.34 × 3.46	8.5:1	57–71
	Conquest	155.9 (2555)	EFI	145 @ 5000	185 @ 2500	3.59 × 3.86	7.0:1	50–54
	Conquest	155.9 (2555)	EFI/Turbo	170 @ 5000	220 @ 2500	3.59 × 3.86	7.0:1	50–54
1987–88	Colt	89.6 (1468)	Carb	68 @ 5000	84 @ 3000	2.99 × 3.23	9.4:1	50–64
	Colt	97.5 (1597)	EFI/Turbo	102 @ 5500	122 @ 3000	3.03 × 3.39	7.6:1	57–71
	Colt Vista	121.9 (1997)	Carb	88 @ 5000	108 @ 3500	3.34 × 3.46	8.5:1	57–71
	Conquest	155.9 (2555)	EFI	145 @ 5000	185 @ 2500	3.59 × 3.86	7.0:1	50–54
	Conquest	155.9 (2555)	EFI/Turbo	170 @ 5000	220 @ 2500	3.59 × 3.86	7.0:1	50–54

TUNE-UP SPECIFICATIONS

Year	Model	Engine Displacement cu. in. (cc)	Spark Plugs Type	Gap (in.)	Ignition Timing (deg.) MT	AT	Compression Pressure (psi)	Fuel Pump (psi)	Idle Speed (rpm) MT	AT	Valve Clearance (in.) In.	Ex.
1981	Colt, Champ	86.0 (1410)	BRP6ES-11	0.039–0.043	5B	—	NA	3.7–5.1	650	—	0.006	0.010
	Colt, Champ	97.5 (1597)	BRP6ES-11	0.039–0.043	5B	5B	NA	3.7–5.1	650	700	0.006	0.010
	Challenger, Sapporo	155.9 (2555)	BPR6ES-11	0.039–0.043	5B	5B	NA	3.7–5.1	650	700	0.006	0.010
1982	Colt, Champ	86.0 (1410)	BRP6ES-11	0.039–0.043	5B	—	NA	3.7–5.1	650	—	0.006	0.010
	Colt, Champ	97.5 (1597)	BRP6ES-11	0.039–0.043	5B	5B	NA	3.7–5.1	650	700	0.006	0.010
	Challenger, Sapporo	155.9 (2555)	BPR6ES-11	0.039–0.043	7B	7B	NA	3.7–5.1	650	700	0.006	0.010
1983	Colt	86.0 (1410)	BRP6ES-11	0.039–0.043	5B	—	NA	3.7–5.1	650	—	0.006	0.010
	Colt	97.5 (1597)	BRP6ES-11	0.039–0.043	5B	5B	NA	3.7–5.1	650	700	0.006	0.010
	Challenger, Sapporo	155.9 (2555)	BPR6ES-11	0.039–0.043	7B	7B	NA	3.7–5.1	650	700	0.006	0.010
1984	Colt	86.0 (1410)	BPR6ES-11	0.039–0.043	5B	—	NA	2.7–3.7	650	650	0.006	0.010
	Colt	97.5 (1597)	BPR6ES-11	0.039–0.043	—	5B	NA	2.4–3.4	700	700	0.006	0.010
	Colt, Vista	97.5 (1597)	BPR6ES-11	0.039–0.043	8B	—	NA	35.6	650	700	0.006	0.010
	Conquest	155.9 (2555)	BPR6ES-11	0.039–0.043	10B	10B	NA	4.6–6.0	850	850	0.006	0.010

TUNE-UP SPECIFICATIONS

Year	Model	Engine Displacement cu. in. (cc)	Spark Plugs Type	Gap (in.)	Ignition Timing (deg.) MT	AT	Compression Pressure (psi)	Fuel Pump (psi)	Idle Speed (rpm) MT	AT	Valve Clearance (in.) In.	Ex.
1985	Colt	89.6 (1468)	BPR6ES-11	0.039–0.040	8B	8B	NA	NA	700	750	0.006	0.010 ①
	Colt	97.5 (1597)	BPR6ES-11	0.039–0.040	8B	8B	NA	35.6	700	700	0.006	0.010
	Colt Vista	121.9 (1997)	BPR6ES-11	0.039–0.040	5B	5B	NA	4.5–5.5	700	700	0.006	0.010
	Conquest	155.9 (2555)	BPR6ES-11	0.039–0.040	10B	10B	NA	4.6–6.0	850	850	0.006	0.010
	Conquest	155.9 (2555)	BPR6ES-11	0.039–0.043	10B	10B	NA	35.6	850	850	0.006	0.010
1986	Colt	89.6 (1468)	BPR6ES-11	0.039–0.040	5B	5B	NA	NA	700	750	0.006	0.010 ①
	Colt	97.4 (1597)	BPR6ES-11	0.039–0.040	10B	10B	NA	35.6	700	700	0.006	0.010
	Colt Vista	121.9 (1997)	BPR6ES-11	0.039–0.040	5B	5B	NA	4.5–5.5	700	700	Hyd ②	Hyd ②
	Conquest	155.9 (2555)	BPR6ES-11	0.039–0.040	10B	10B	NA	4.6–6.0	850	850	0.006	0.010
	Conquest	155.9 (2555)	BPR6ES-11	0.039–0.040	10B	10B	NA	35.6	850	850	0.006	0.010
1987	Colt	89.6 (1468)	BPR6ES-11	0.039–0.040	5B	5B	NA	NA	700	750	0.006	0.010 ①
	Colt	97.4 (1597)	BPR6ES-11	0.039–0.040	10B	10B	NA	35.6	700	700	0.006	0.010
	Colt Vista	121.9 (1997)	BPR6ES-11	0.039–0.040	5B	5B	NA	4.5–5.5	700	700	Hyd ②	Hyd ②
	Conquest	155.9 (2555)	BPR6ES-11	0.039–0.040	10B	10B	NA	4.6–6.0	850	850	0.006	0.010
	Conquest	155.9 (2555)	BPR6ES-11	0.039–0.040	10B	10B	NA	35.6	850	850	0.006	0.010
1988	All	SEE UNDERHOOD SPECIFICATIONS STICKER										

NOTE: The underhood specifications sticker often reflects tune-up specification changes in production. Sticker figures must be used if the disagree with those in this chart.
① Jet valve clearance—0.006 in.
② Jet valve clearance—0.010 in.

FIRING ORDERS

NOTE: To avoid confusion, always replace spark wires one at a time.

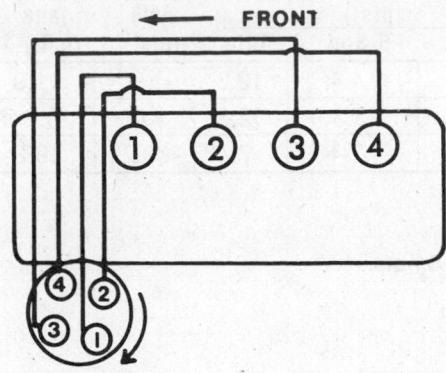

1410, 1468, 1597, 1997cc engines

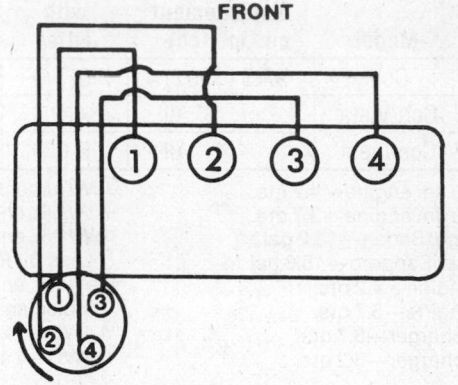

2555cc engines

CAPACITIES
U.S. Measurements.

Year	Model	Engine Displacement cu. in. (cc)	Engine Crankcase (U.S. qts.) with Filter	without Filter	Transmission (pts.) 4-Spd	5-Spd	Auto.	Drive Axle (pts.)	Fuel Tank (gal.)	Cooling System (qts.)
1981	Colt	86.0 (1410)	3.7 ①	3.2 ②	—	4.8	12	—	③	5
	Challenger	All	4.5	4.0	—	4.8	14.4	2.7	④	9.7
	Champ	86.0 (1410)	3.7 ①	3.2 ②	—	4.8	12	—	13.2	5
	Sapporo	All	4.5	4.0	—	4.8	14.4	2.7	④	9.7
1982	Colt	86.0 (1410)	3.7 ①	3.2 ②	—	4.8	12	—	③	5
	Challenger	All	4.5	4.0	—	4.8	14.4	2.7	④	9.7
	Champ	86.0 (1410)	3.7 ①	3.2 ②	—	4.8	12	—	13.2	5
	Sapporo	All	4.5	4.0	—	4.8	14.4	2.7	④	9.7
1983	Colt	86.0 (1410)	3.7 ①	3.2 ②	—	4.8	12	—	③	5
	Challenger	All	4.5	4.0	—	4.8	14.4	2.7	④	9.7
	Sapporo	All	4.5	4.0	—	4.8	14.4	2.7	④	9.7
1984	Colt	97.5 (1597)	3.7 ⑤	3.2 ⑥	—	4.8	12	—	10.6	4.1
	Colt Vista	All	4.2	3.7	—	4.9	12.3	—	13.2	7.4
	Conquest	All	4.5	4.0	—	4.8	14.8	2.7	19.8	9.7
1985	Colt	97.5 (1597)	3.2 ⑦	2.7 ⑧	—	4.4 ⑨	12.3	—	11.9	5.3
	Colt Vista	All	4.2	3.7	—	4.9	12.3	—	13.2	7.4
	Conquest	All	5.1	4.5	—	4.8	14.8	2.7	19.8	9.7
1986	Colt	97.5 (1597)	3.7 ⑩	3.2 ⑪	—	4.9 ⑨	12.3	—	11.9	5.3
	Colt Vista	All	4.2	3.7	—	4.9 ⑮	12.3	1.7	13.2 ⑭	7.4
	Conquest	All	5.1	4.5	—	4.8	14.8	2.7	19.8	9.7

CAPACITIES

U.S. Measurements.

Year	Model	Engine Displacement cu. in. (cc)	Engine Crankcase (U.S. qts.)		Transmission (pts.)			Drive Axle (pts.)	Fuel Tank (gal.)	Cooling System (qts.)
			with Filter	without Filter	4-Spd	5-Spd	Auto.			
1987-88	Colt	97.5 (1597)	3.7 ⑩	3.2 ⑪	—	4.4	12.3	—	11.9	5.3
	Colt Vista	All	4.2	3.7	—	5.3 ⑮	12.3	1.48	13.2 ⑭	7.4
	Conquest	All	5.0 ⑬	4.5	—	2.4	7.4	2.7	19.8	9.2

① W/97.5 cu. in. engine—4.2 qts.
② W/97.5 cu. in. engine—3.7 qts.
③ Colt Coupe, Sedan—13.2 gal.
④ Challenger/Sapporo—15.8 gal.
⑤ W/1.6L engine—4.2 qts.
⑥ W/1.6L engine—3.7 qts.
⑦ W/Turbocharger—3.7 qts.
⑧ W/Turbocharger—3.2 qts.

⑨ W/Turbocharger—4.9 pts.
⑩ W/1.6L engine—4.5 qts.
⑪ W/1.6L engine
   Less Oil Filter and Oil Cooler—3.7 qts.
⑫ W/1.6L engine—4.9 pts.
⑬ Including Oil Filter & Oil Cooler
⑭ 4WD—14.5 gals.
⑮ 4WD—4.4 pts.

CAMSHAFT SPECIFICATIONS

All measurements given in inches.

Year	Engine Displacement cu. in. (cc)	Journal Diameter					Lobe Life		Bearing Clearance	Camshaft End Play
		1	2	3	4	5	In.	Ex.		
1981	86.0 (1410)	1.339	1.339	1.339	1.339	1.339	1.500	1.504	.0020–.0035	.002–.008
	97.5 (1597)	1.339	1.339	1.339	1.339	1.339	1.433	1.433	.0020–.0035	.002–.008
	155.9 (2555)	1.339	1.339	1.339	1.339	1.339	1.660	1.663	.0020–.0045	.004–.008
1982	86.0 (1410)	1.339	1.339	1.339	1.339	1.339	1.500	1.504	.0020–.0035	.002–.008
	97.5 (1597)	1.339	1.339	1.339	1.339	1.339	1.433	1.433	.0020–.0035	.002–.008
	155.9 (2555)	1.339	1.339	1.339	1.339	1.339	1.660	1.663	.0020–.0045	.004–.008
1983	86.0 (1410)	1.339	1.339	1.339	1.339	1.339	1.500	1.504	.0020–.0035	.004–.008
	97.5 (1597)	1.339	1.339	1.339	1.339	1.339	1.433	1.433	.0020–.0035	.004–.008
	155.9 (2555)	1.339	1.339	1.339	1.339	1.339	1.660	1.663	.0020–.0045	.004–.008
1984	86.0 (1410)	1.339	1.339	1.339	1.339	1.339	1.500	1.504	.0020–.0035	.004–.008
	97.5 (1597)	1.339	1.339	1.339	1.339	1.339	1.433	1.433	.0020–.0035	.004–.008
	97.5 (1597) Turbo	1.339	1.339	1.339	1.339	1.339	1.660	1.663	.0020–.0045	.004–.008
1985	89.6 (1468)	1.339	1.339	1.339	1.339	1.339	1.500	1.504	.0020–.0035	.004–.008
	97.5 (1597)	1.339	1.339	1.339	1.339	1.339	1.433	1.433	.0020–.0035	.004–.008
	121.9 (1997)	1.339	1.339	1.339	1.339	1.339	1.660	1.663	.0020–.0045	.004–.008
	155.9 (2555)	1.339	1.339	1.339	1.339	1.339	1.673	1.673	.0020–.0045	.004–.008
1986	89.6 (1468)	1.339	1.339	1.339	1.339	1.339	1.500	1.504	.0020–.0035	.004–.008
	97.5 (1597)	1.339	1.339	1.339	1.339	1.339	1.433	1.433	.0020–.0035	.004–.008
	121.9 (1997)	1.339	1.339	1.339	1.339	1.339	1.660	1.663	.0020–.0045	.004–.008
	155.9 (2555)	1.339	1.339	1.339	1.339	1.339	1.673	1.673	.0020–.0045	.004–.008
1987-88	89.6 (1468)	1.339	1.339	1.339	1.339	1.339	1.500	1.504	.0020–.0035	.004–.008
	97.5 (1597)	1.339	1.339	1.339	1.339	1.339	1.433	1.433	.0020–.0035	.004–.008
	121.9 (1997)	1.339	1.339	1.339	1.339	1.339	1.660	1.663	.0020–.0045	.004–.008
	155.9 (2555)	1.339	1.339	1.339	1.339	1.339	1.673	1.673	.0020–.0045	.004–.008

CRANKSHAFT AND CONNECTING ROD SPECIFICATIONS

All measurements are given in inches.

| Year | Engine Displacement cu. in. (cc) | Crankshaft | | | | Connecting Rod | | |
		Main Brg. Journal Dia.	Main Brg. Oil Clearance	Shaft End-play	Thrust on No.	Journal Diameter	Oil Clearance	Side Clearance
1981	86.0 (1410)	1.8898	.0008–.0028	.002–.007	3	1.6535	.0004–.0024	.004–.010
	97.5 (1597)	2.2441	.0008–.0028	.002–.007	3	1.7717	.0004–.0028	.004–.010
	155.9 (2555)	2.5984	.0008–.0028	.002–.007	3	2.0866	.0008–.0028	.004–.010
1982	86.0 (1410)	1.8898	.0008–.0028	.002–.007	3	1.6535	.0004–.0024	.004–.010
	97.5 (1597)	2.2441	.0008–.0028	.002–.007	3	1.7717	.0004–.0028	.004–.010
	155.9 (2555)	2.5984	.0008–.0028	.002–.007	3	2.0866	.0008–.0028	.004–.010
1983	86.0 (1410)	1.8898	.0008–.0028	.002–.007	3	1.6535	.0004–.0024	.004–.010
	97.5 (1597)	2.2441	.0008–.0028	.002–.007	3	1.7717	.0004–.0028	.004–.010
	155.9 (2555)	2.5984	.0008–.0028	.002–.007	3	2.0866	.0008–.0028	.004–.010
1984	86.0 (1410)	1.8898	.0008–.0028	.002–.007	3	1.6535	.0004–.0024	.004–.010
	97.5 (1597)	2.2441	.0008–.0028	.002–.007	3	1.7717	.0004–.0028	.004–.010
1985	89.6 (1468)	1.8898	.0008–.0028	.002–.007	3	1.6535	.0004–.0024	.004–.010
	97.5 (1597)	2.2441	.0008–.0028	.002–.007	3	1.7717	.0004–.0028	.004–.010
	121.9 (1997)	2.2441	.0008–.0028	.002–.007	3	1.7717	.0008–.0020	.004–.010
	155.9 (2555)	2.5984	.0008–.0028	.002–.007	3	2.0866	.0008–.0028	.004–.010
1986	89.6 (1468)	1.8898	.0008–.0028	.002–.007	3	1.6535	.0004–.0024	.004–.010
	97.5 (1597)	2.2441	.0008–.0028	.002–.007	3	1.7717	.0004–.0028	.004–.010
	121.9 (1997)	2.2441	.0008–.0028	.002–.007	3	1.7717	.0008–.0020	.004–.010
	155.9 (2555)	2.5984	.0008–.0028	.002–.007	3	2.0866	.0008–.0028	.004–.010
	155.9 (2555) Turbo	2.3622	.0008–.0020	.002–.007	3	2.0866	.0008–.0024	.004–.010
1987–88	89.6 (1468)	1.8898	.0008–.0028	.002–.007	3	1.6535	.0004–.0024	.004–.010
	97.5 (1597)	2.2441	.0008–.0028	.002–.007	3	1.7717	.0004–.0028	.004–.010
	121.9 (1997)	2.2441	.0008–.0028	.002–.007	3	1.7717	.0008–.0020	.004–.010

CRANKSHAFT AND CONNECTING ROD SPECIFICATIONS

All measurements are given in inches.

Year	Engine Displacement cu. in. (cc)	Crankshaft Main Brg. Journal Dia.	Crankshaft Main Brg. Oil Clearance	Crankshaft Shaft End-play	Crankshaft Thrust on No.	Connecting Rod Journal Diameter	Connecting Rod Oil Clearance	Connecting Rod Side Clearance
1987-88	155.9 (2555)	2.5984	.0008–.0028	.002–.007	3	2.0866	.0008–.0028	.004–.010
	155.9 (2555) Turbo	2.3622	.0008–.0020	.002–.007	3	2.0866	.0008–.0024	.004–.010

VALVE SPECIFICATIONS

Year	Engine Displacement cu. in. (cc)	Seat Angle (deg.)	Face Angle (deg.)	Spring Test Pressure (lbs.)	Spring Installed Height (in.)	Stem-to-Guide Clearance (in.) Intake	Stem-to-Guide Clearance (in.) Exhaust	Stem Diameter (in.) Intake	Stem Diameter (in.) Exhaust
1981	86.0 (1410)	45	45	69 @ 1.417	1.417	.0012–.0024	.0020–.0035	.3147–.3153	.3147–.3153
	97.5 (1597)	45	45	61 @ 1.470	1.470	.0012–.0024	.0020–.0035	.3147–.3153	.3147–.3153
	155.9 (2555)	45	45	61 @ 1.590	1.590	.0012–.0024	.0020–.0035	.3147–.3153	.3147–.3153
1982	86.0 (1410)	45	45	69 @ 1.417	1.417	.0012–.0024	.0020–.0035	.3147–.3153	.3147–.3153
	97.5 (1597)	45	45	61 @ 1.470	1.470	.0012–.0024	.0020–.0035	.3147–.3153	.3147–.3153
	155.9 (2555)	45	45	61 @ 1.590	1.590	.0012–.0024	.0020–.0035	.3147–.3153	.3147–.3153
1983	86.0 (1410)	45	45	69 @ 1.417	1.417	.0012–.0024	.0020–.0035	.3147–.3153	.3147–.3153
	97.5 (1597)	45	45	61 @ 1.470	1.470	.0012–.0024	.0020–.0035	.3147–.3153	.3147–.3153
	155.9 (2555)	45	45	61 @ 1.590	1.590	.0012–.0024	.0020–.0035	.3147–.3153	.3147–.3153
1984	86.0 (1410)	45	45	69 @ 1.417	1.417	.0012–.0024	.0020–.0035	.3147–.3153	.3147–.3153
	97.5 (1597)	45	45	61 @ 1.470	1.470	.0012–.0024	.0020–.0035	.3147–.3153	.3147–.3153
	97.5 (1597) Turbo	45	45	61 @ 1.470	1.470	.0012–.0024	.0020–.0035	.3147–.3153	.3147–.3153
1985	89.6 (1468)	45	45	69 @ 1.417	1.417	.0012–.0024	.0020–.0035	.3147–.3153	.3147–.3153
	97.5 (1597)	45	45	61 @ 1.470	1.470	.0012–.0024	.0020–.0035	.3147–.3153	.3147–.3153
	121.9 (1997)	45	45	40 @ 1.591	1.591	.0012–.0024	.0020–.0035	.3147–.3153	.3147–.3153
	155.9 (2555)	45	45	61 @ 1.590	1.590	.0012–.0024	.0020–.0035	.3147–.3153	.3147–.3153
1986	89.6 (1468)	45	45	69 @ 1.417	1.417	.0012–.0024	.0020–.0035	.3147–.3153	.3147–.3153
	97.5 (1597)	45	45	61 @ 1.470	1.470	.0012–.0024	.0020–.0035	.3147–.3153	.3147–.3153
	121.9 (1997)	45	45	40 @ 1.591	1.591	.0012–.0024	.0020–.0035	.3147–.3153	.3147–.3153

VALVE SPECIFICATIONS

Year	Engine Displacement cu. in. (cc)	Seat Angle (deg.)	Face Angle (deg.)	Spring Test Pressure (lbs.)	Spring Installed Height (in.)	Stem-to-Guide Clearance (in.) Intake	Stem-to-Guide Clearance (in.) Exhaust	Stem Diameter (in.) Intake	Stem Diameter (in.) Exhaust
1986	155.9 (2555)	45	45	61 @ 1.590	1.590	.0012–.0024	.0020–.0035	.3147–.3153	.3147–.3153
1987–88	89.6 (1486)	45	45	69 @ 1.417	1.417	.0012–.0024	.0020–.0035	.3147–.3153	.3147–.3153
	97.5 (1597)	45	45	61 @ 1.470	1.470	.0012–.0024	.0020–.0035	.3147–.3153	.3147–.3153
	121.9 (1997)	45	45	40 @ 1.591	1.591	.0012–.0024	.0020–.0035	.3147–.3153	.3147–.3153
	155.9 (2555)	45	45	61 @ 1.590	1.590	.0012–.0024	.0020–.0035	.3147–.3153	.3147–.3153

PISTON AND RING SPECIFICATIONS

All measurements are given in inches.

Year	Engine Displacement cu. in. (cc)	Piston Clearance	Ring Gap Top Compression	Ring Gap Bottom Compression	Ring Gap Oil Control	Ring Side Clearance Top Compression	Ring Side Clearance Bottom Compression	Ring Side Clearance Oil Control
1981	86.0 (1410)	.0008–.0016	.0080–.0160	.0080–.0160	.0080–.0200	.0012–.0028	.0008–.0024	Snug
	97.5 (1597)	.0008–.0016	.0080–.0160	.0080–.0160	.0080–.0200	.0012–.0028	.0008–.0024	.0010–.0030
	155.9 (2555)	.0008–.0016	.0098–.0177	.0098–.0177	.0078–.0354	.0024–.0038	.0008–.0024	.0008–.0024
1982	86.0 (1410)	.0008–.0016	.0080–.0160	.0080–.0160	.0080–.0200	.0012–.0028	.0008–.0024	Snug
	97.5 (1597)	.0008–.0016	.0080–.0160	.0080–.0160	.0080–.0200	.0012–.0028	.0008–.0024	.0010–.0030
	155.9 (2555)	.0008–.0016	.0098–.0177	.0098–.0177	.0078–.0354	.0008–.0024	.0008–.0024	.0008–.0024
1983	86.0 (1410)	.0008–.0016	.0080–.0160	.0080–.0160	.0080–.0200	.0012–.0028	.0008–.0024	Snug
	97.5 (1597)	.0008–.0016	.0080–.0160	.0080–.0160	.0080–.0200	.0012–.0028	.0008–.0024	.0010–.0030
	155.9 (2555)	.0008–.0016	.0098–.0177	.0098–.0177	.0078–.0354	.0008–.0024	.0008–.0024	.0008–.0024
1984	86.0 (1410)	.0008–.0016	.0080–.0160	.0080–.0160	.0080–.0200	.0012–.0028	.0008–.0024	Snug
	97.5 (1597)	.0008–.0016	.0100–.0160	.0080–.0160	.0080–.0140	.0012–.0028	.0008–.0024	Snug
1985	89.6 (1468)	.0008–.0016	.0080–.0160	.0080–.0160	.0080–.0200	.0012–.0028	.0008–.0024	.0010–.0030
	97.5 (1597)	.0008–.0016	.0100–.0160	.0080–.0160	.0080–.0140	.0012–.0028	.0008–.0024	Snug
	121.9 (1997)	.0008–.0016	.0100–.0180	.0080–.0160	.0080–.0028	.0020–.0040	.0010–.0020	Snug
	155.9 (2555)	.0008–.0016	.0098–.0177	.0098–.0177	.0078–.0354	.0024–.0039	.0008–.0024	.0008–.0024

PISTON AND RING SPECIFICATIONS

All measurements are given in inches.

Year	Engine Displacement cu. in. (cc)	Piston Clearance	Ring Gap			Ring Side Clearance		
			Top Compression	Bottom Compression	Oil Control	Top Compression	Bottom Compression	Oil Control
1986	89.6 (1468)	.0008–.0016	.0080–.0160	.0080–.0160	.0080–.0200	.0012–.0028	.0008–.0024	.0010–.0030
	97.5 (1597)	.0008–.0016	.0100–.0160	.0080–.0140	.0080–.0280	.0012–.0028	.0008–.0024	Snug
	121.9 (1997)	.0008–.0016	.0100–.0180	.0080–.0160	.0080–.0028	.0020–.0040	.0010–.0020	Snug
	155.9 (2555)	.0008–.0016	.0098–.0177	.0098–.0177	.0078–.0354	.0024–.0039	.0008–.0024	.0008–.0024
	155.9 (2555) Turbo	.0008–.0016	.0120–.0200	.0100–.0160	.0120–.0310	.0020–.0040	.0010–.0020	Snug
1987–88	89.6 (1468)	.0008–.0016	.0080–.0160	.0080–.0160	.0080–.0200	.0012–.0028	.0008–.0024	.0010–.0030
	97.5 (1597)	.0008–.0016	.0100–.0160	.0080–.0140	.0080–.0280	.0012–.0028	.0008–.0024	Snug
	121.9 (1997)	.0008–.0016	.0100–.0180	.0080–.0160	.0080–.0028	.0020–.0040	.0010–.0020	Snug
	155.9 (2555)	.0008–.0016	.0098–.0177	.0098–.0177	.0078–.0354	.0024–.0039	.0008–.0024	.0008–.0024
	155.9 (2555) Turbo	.0008–.0016	.0120–.0200	.0100–.0160	.0120–.0310	.0020–.0040	.0010–.0020	Snug

TORQUE SPECIFICATIONS

All readings in ft. lbs.

Year	Engine Displacement cu. in. (cc)	Cylinder Head Bolts	Main Bearing Bolts	Rod Bearing Bolts	Crankshaft Pulley Bolts	Flywheel Bolts	Manifold		Spark Plugs
							Intake	Exhaust	
1981	86.0 (1410)	50–54	37–39	23–25	37–43	94–101	11–14	11–14	NA
	97.5 (1597)	50–54	36–40	23–25	44–50	94–101 ①	11–14	11–14	NA
	155.9 (2555)	65–72	55–61	33–34	80–90	94–101 ①	11–14	11–14	NA
1982	86.0 (1410)	50–54	37–39	23–25	37–43	94–101	11–14	11–14	NA
	97.5 (1597)	50–54	36–40	23–25	44–50	94–101 ①	11–14	11–14	NA
	155.9 (2555)	65–72	55–61	33–34	80–90	94–101 ①	11–14	11–14	NA
1983	86.0 (1410)	50–54	37–39	23–25	37–43	94–101	11–14	11–14	NA
	97.5 (1597)	50–54	36–40	23–25	44–50	94–101 ①	11–14	11–14	NA
	155.9 (2555)	65–72	55–61	33–34	80–90	94–101 ①	11–14	11–14	NA
1984	86.0 (1410)	50–54	37–39	23–25	37–43	94–101	11–14	11–14	NA
	97.5 (1597)	50–54	36–40	23–25	44–50	94–101 ①	11–14	11–14	NA
	97.5 (1597)	65–72	55–61	33–34	80–90	94–101 ①	11–14	11–14	NA
1985	89.6 (1468)	50–54	37–39	23–25	37–43	94–101	11–14	11–14	NA
	97.5 (1597)	50–54	36–40	23–25	44–50	94–101 ①	11–14	11–14	NA
	121.9 (1997)	65–72	37–39	33–35	80–94	94–101	11–14	11–14	NA
	155.9 (2555)	65–72	55–61	33–34	80–94	94–101	11–14	11–14	NA

TORQUE SPECIFICATIONS

All readings in ft. lbs.

Year	Engine Displacement cu. in. (cc)	Cylinder Head Bolts	Main Bearing Bolts	Rod Bearing Bolts	Crankshaft Pulley Bolts	Flywheel Bolts	Manifold		Spark Plugs
							Intake	Exhaust	
1986	89.6 (1468)	50–54	37–39	23–25	51–72	94–101	11–14	11–14	NA
	97.5 (1597)	50–54	36–40	23–25	80–93	94–101 ①	11–14	11–14	NA
	121.9 (1997)	65–72	37–39	37–38	80–94	94–101 ①	11–14	11–14	NA
	155.9 (2555)	65–72	55–61	33–34	80–94	94–101	11–14	11–14	NA
1987-88	89.6 (1468)	50–54	37–39	23–25	57–72	94–101	11–14	11–14	NA
	97.5 (1597)	50–54	36–40	23–25	80–93	94–101 ①	11–14	11–14	NA
	121.9 (1997)	65–72	37–39	37–38	80–94	94–101 ①	11–14	11–14	NA
	155.9 (2555)	65–72	55–61	33–34	80–94	94–101	11–14	11–14	NA

① W/AT—84–90 Ft. Lbs.

BRAKE SPECIFICATIONS

All measurements in inches unless noted.

Year	Model	Lug Nut Torque (ft. lbs.)	Master Cylinder Bore	Brake Disc		Standard Brake Drum Diameter	Minimum Lining Thickness	
				Minimum Thickness	Maximum Runout		Front	Rear
1981	Colt	51–58	.8125	.450	.006	7.100	.040	.040
	Challenger	51–58	.8750	.430 ②③	.006	9.000 ⑦	.040	.040
	Champ	51–58	.8125	.450	.006	7.100	.040	.040
	Sapporo	51–58	.8750	.430 ②③	.006	9.000 ⑦	.040	.040
1982	Colt	51–58	.8125	.450	.006	7.100	.040	.040
	Challenger	51–58	.8750	.430 ②③	.006	9.000 ⑦	.040	.040
	Champ	51–58	.8125	.450	.006	7.100	.040	.040
	Sapporo	51–58	.8750	.430 ②③	.006	9.000 ⑦	.040	.040
1983	Colt	51–58	.8125	.450	.006	7.100	.040	.040
	Challenger	51–58	.8750	.430 ②③	.006	9.000 ⑦	.040	.040
	Sapporo	51–58	.8750	.430 ②③	.006	9.000 ⑦	.040	.040
1984	Colt	51–58	.8125 ①	.450 ⑧	.006	7.100	.040	.040
	Colt Vista	51–58	.8750	.650 ⑥	.006	8.000 ⑤	.040	.040
	Conquest	51–58	.8750	.880 ④	.006	—	.040	.040
1985	Colt	51–58	.8125 ①	.450 ⑧	.006	7.100	.040	.040
	Colt Vista	51–58	.8750	.650 ⑥	.006	8.000 ⑤	.040	.040
	Conquest	51–58	.9400	.880 ④	.006	—	.040	.040
1986	Colt	51–58	.8125 ①	.450 ⑧	.006	7.100	.040	.040
	Colt Vista	51–58	.8750	.650 ⑥	.006	8.000 ⑤	.040	.040
	Conquest	51–58	.9400	.880 ④	.006	—	.040	.040
1987-88	Colt	51–58	.8125 ①	.450 ⑧	.006	7.100	.040	.040
	Colt Vista	51–58	.8750	.650 ⑥	.006	8.000 ⑤	.040	.040
	Conquest	51–58	.9400	.880 ④	.006	—	.040	.040

① Colt Turbo—.8750
② W/Rear disc brakes—discard at .330 in.
③ Front
④ Rear—.650 in.
⑤ 4WD—9.000 in.
⑥ 4WD—.880 in.
⑦ W/Rear drum brakes
⑧ 84–88 Turbo—.645

WHEEL ALIGNMENT

Year	Model	Caster Range (deg.)	Caster Preferred Setting (deg.)	Camber Range (deg.)	Camber Preferred Setting (deg.)	Toe-in (in.)	Steering Axis Inclination (deg.)
1981	Colt	$1/2$–$1 1/8$	$13/16$	0–1	$1/2$	$5/64$–$5/32$	$12 11/16$
	Challenger	$2 3/16$–$3 3/16$	$2 11/16$	$11/16$–$1 11/16$	$1 3/16$	0–$9/32$	$9 1/2$
	Champ	$1/2$–$1 1/8$	$13/16$	0–1	$1/2$	$5/64$–$5/32$	$12 11/16$
	Sapporo	$2 3/16$–$3 3/16$	$2 11/16$	$11/16$–$1 11/16$	$1 3/16$	0–$9/32$	$9 1/2$
1982	Colt	$1/2$–$1 1/8$	$13/16$	0–1	$1/2$	$5/64$–$5/32$	$12 11/16$
	Challenger	$2 3/16$–$3 3/16$	$2 11/16$	$11/16$–$1 11/16$	$1 3/16$	0–$9/32$	$9 1/2$
	Champ	$1/2$–$1 1/8$	$13/16$	0–1	$1/2$	$5/64$–$5/32$	$12 11/16$
	Sapporo	$2 3/16$–$3 3/16$	$2 11/16$	$11/16$–$1 11/16$	$1 3/16$	0–$9/32$	$9 1/2$
1983	Colt	$1/2$–$1 1/8$	$13/16$	0–1	$1/2$	$5/64$–$5/32$	$12 11/16$
	Challenger	$2 3/16$–$3 3/16$	$2 11/16$	$11/16$–$1 11/16$	$1 3/16$	0–$9/32$	$9 1/2$
	Sapporo	$2 3/16$–$3 3/16$	$2 11/16$	$11/16$–$1 11/16$	$1 3/16$	0–$9/32$	$9 1/2$
1984	Colt	$1/2$–$1 1/8$	$13/16$	0–1	$1/2$ ①	$5/64$–$5/32$	$12 11/16$
	Colt Vista	$5/16$–$1 5/16$	$13/16$ ⑤	$1/16$N–$15/16$P	$7/16$ ④	$1/8$	N/A
	Conquest	—	$5 5/16$	—	0	$5/64$–$13/64$	N/A
1985	Colt	$3/16$–$1 3/16$	$11/16$	$1/2$N–$1/2$P	0	0	N/A
	Colt Vista	$5/16$–$1 5/16$	$13/16$ ⑤	$1/16$N–$15/16$P	$7/16$ ④	$1/8$	N/A
	Conquest	—	$5 5/16$	—	0 ②	$5/64$–$13/64$	N/A
1986	Colt	$3/16$–$1 3/16$	$11/16$	$1/2$N–$1/2$P	0	0	N/A
	Colt Vista	$5/16$–$1 5/16$	$13/16$ ⑤	$1/16$N–$15/16$P	$7/16$ ④	$1/8$	N/A
	Conquest	—	$5 13/16$	—	$-1/2$N ③	0	N/A
1987–88	Colt	$3/16$–$1 3/16$	$11/16$	$1/2$N–$1/2$P	0	0	N/A
	Colt Vista	$5/16$–$1 5/16$	$13/16$ ⑤	$1/16$N–$15/16$P	$7/16$ ④	$1/8$	N/A
	Conquest	—	$5 13/16$	—	$-1/2$N ③	0	N/A

N—negative
P—positive
① Rear—$5/8$° camber
 0" toe-in
② Rear—$5/16$° camber
 $5/16$" toe-in
③ Rear—0° camber
 0° toe-in
④ Rear—$5/8$° camber
 0" toe-in
⑤ FWD Front—$13/16$° caster
 $13/16$° camber
 $1/8$" toe-in
⑥ FWD Rear—0° camber
 0" toe-in

TUNE–UP PROCEDURES

Ignition Timing

ADJUSTMENT

——— CAUTION ———
When performing this or any other adjustment with the engine running, be very careful of the fan belt and pulley.

1. Attach the timing light according to the manufacturer's instructions.

2. Locate the timing tab line on the front of the engine and the notch on the crankshaft pulley. Mark them so they are easily recogniziable with the timing light.
3. Start the engine and allow it to reach operating temperature.
4. Point the timing light at the crankshaft pulley marks. The marked line should align with the pulley notch.
5. If the marks do not align, loosen the distributor mounting nut and rotate the distributor slowly in either direction to align the timing marks.
6. Tighten the mounting nut when the ignition timing is correct. Stop the engine and remove the timing light.

Valve Lash

ADJUSTMENT

NOTE: The jet valve adjuster is located on the intake valve rocker arm and must be adjusted before the intake valve. The 1985–88 Vista engine has automatic lash adjusters incorporate in the rocker arms of the intake and exhaust valves. These valves are not adjustable. The Jet Valve is, however, adjustable in the same manner as other engines.

1. Start the engine and allow it to reach normal operating temperature.

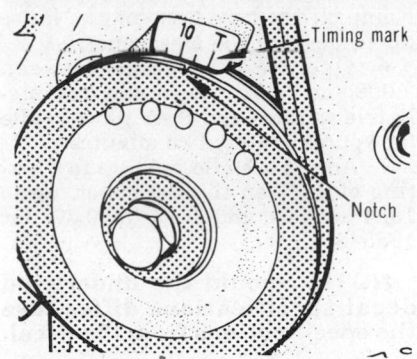

1410, 1468, 1597 and 1997cc engine timing marks

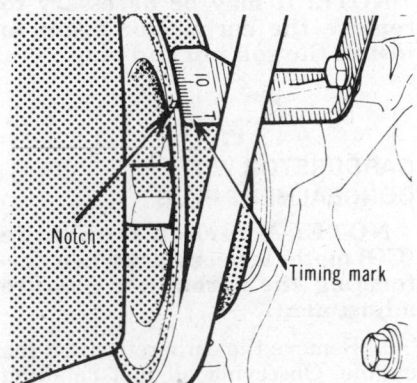

2555cc timing marks

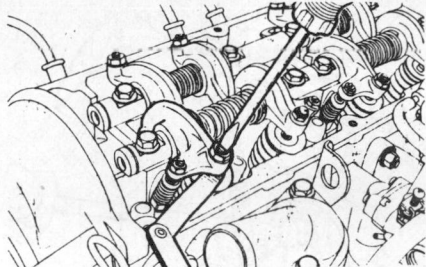

Adjusting valve clearance all engines

Exhaust Valve

Closing	Adjust
No. 1 cylinder	No. 4 cylinder valves
No. 2 cylinder	No. 3 cylinder valves
No. 3 cylinder	No. 2 cylinder valves
No. 4 cylinder	No. 1 cylinder valves

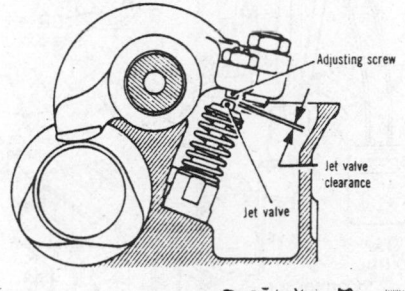

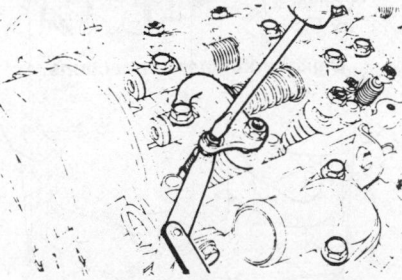

Jet valve clearance adjustment

NOTE: Do not run the engine with the rocker arm cover removed. Oil will be sprayed onto the hot exhaust manifold.

2. Shut off engine and remove the rocker arm cover.

3. Watch the valve operation on No. 1 cylinder (No. 1 cylinder on transverse mounted engines is on the driver's side) while turning the crankshaft to close the exhaust valve and have the intake valve just begin to open. This places the No. 4 cylinder on TDC of its firing stroke and permits the adjustment of the valves.

NOTE: On front wheel drive models with the "K" engine (1597cc), a crankshaft pulley access hole is located on the left side fender shield. Remove the covering plug and use a ratchet extension to turn the crankshaft when adjusting the valves.

4. Jet valves must be adjusted before the intake valve.

To adjust the jet valves:

   a. Loosen the intake valve lock nut and back off the adjustment screw two or more turns.

   b. Loosen the lock nut on the jet valve adjusting screw. Turn the jet valve adjusting screw counterclockwise and insert a 0.006 in. feeler gauge between the valve stem and the adjusting screw.

   c. Tighten the adjusting screw until it touches the feeler gauge.

NOTE: The jet valve spring is weak, be careful not to force the jet valve in.

   d. After adjustment is made, hold the adjusting screw with a screwdriver and tighten the lock nut.

5. Proceed to adjust the intake and the exhaust valves on the same cylinder as the jet valve just adjusted. Adjust by loosening the locknut and passing a feeler gauge of the correct thickness between the bottom of the rocker arm and top of the valve stem. If the clearance is too great or too small, turn the adjusting screw until the gauge will pass through with a slight drag. Tighten the locknut and proceed to the next valve. Refer to the chart for the adjusting sequence.

Idle Speed

ADJUSTMENT

Carbureted Engines

1981

1. Have the engine at normal operating temperature. Connect a tachometer.

2. Position the manual altitude compensator knob (if equipped) with the lugs and the slot in a vertical position for altitudes over 4000 ft. and the lugs and the slot in the horizontal position for less than 4000 ft.

3. Adjust the engine speed to the specifications listed on the engine compartment sticker, using the idle adjusting screw on the base of the carburetor.

1982–88

Set the idle with all accessories off and the transmission in neutral.

1. Have the engine at normal operating temperature.

2. Operate the engine at 2000–3000 rpm for over 5 seconds, then allow to idle for 2 minutes.

3. Using a tachometer, set the idle to specifications, using the idle adjusting screw on the base of the carburetor.

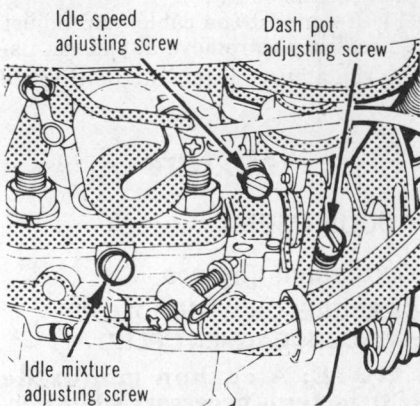

Idle speed adjusting screw

Fuel Injected Engines

NOTE: This adjustment MUST be made any time the Idle Speed Control (ISC) servo, Throttle Position Sensor (TPS), mixing body or throttle body has been removed. A digital voltmeter is essential for this operation.

1. Run the engine to normal operating temperature, then shut it off.

2. Disconnect the accelerator cable at the throttle lever on the mixing body.

3. Loosen the screws holds the TPS and turn it fully clockwise. Tighten the screws.

4. Turn the ignition switch to the ON position for at least 15 seconds, then turn if OFF. This will automatically set the ISC servo to the proper position.

5. Disconnect the ISC servo wiring connector.

6. Start the engine and check the idle speed with a tachometer. Idle speed should be 600 rpm. If not, adjust it with the adjusting screw.

7. Insert the digital voltmeter test probes in the TPS connector GW and B holes.

8. Turn the ignition switch to the ON position. DO NOT START THE ENGINE!!!

9. Read the voltage. If indicated voltage is not 0.45–0.51, loosen the PTS mounting screw and turn the sensor clockwise or counterclockwise until the indicated voltage is 0.48V. Tighten the screws and apply a thread-locking sealant.

10. Open the throttle valve fully and let it close. Recheck the indicated voltage. Adjust if necessary.

11. Remove the voltmeter and reconnect the wiring.

12. Start the engine. Recheck the idle speed. Adjust if necessary and stop the engine.

13. Turn the ignition switch to the ON position for at least 15 seconds, then turn it OFF.

14. Reconnect the cable, and adjust if necessary to remove any slack, using the adjusting nut at the throttle level.

Mixture

ADJUSTMENT

Carbureted Engines

CARBURETOR WITH ROLL PIN AND CONCEALMENT PLUG

NOTE: A carbon monoxide (CO) meter is necessary when performing the carburetor mixture adjustment.

1. Remove the carburetor from the engine. Observing all fuel handling precautions, drain the fuel from the carburetor bowl.

2. Place the carburetor upside down, in a vise and carefully tighten to hold carburetor securely.

3. With an appropriate pin punch, remove the roll pin from the carbure-

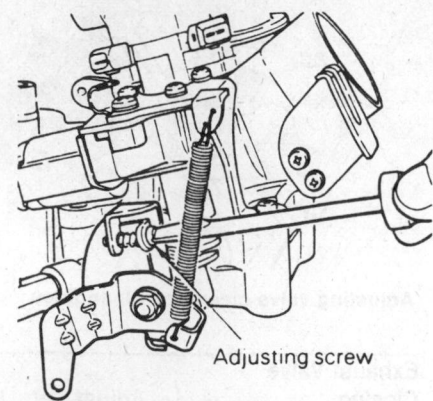
Fuel injection unit idle speed adjusting screw

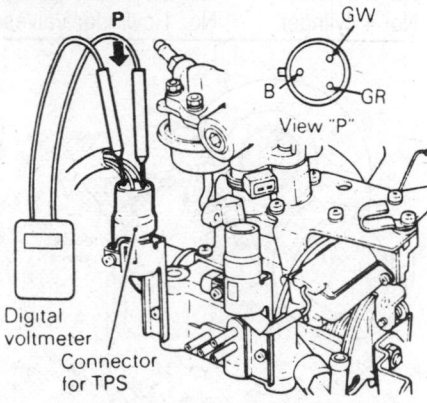
Digital voltmeter connections

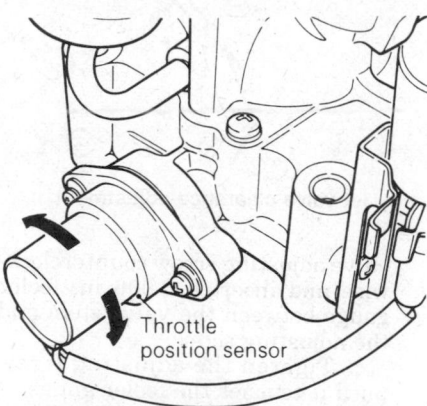
Throttle position sensor adjustment

tor base and the concealment plug from over the mixture adjustment screw.

NOTE: Some carburetors may only have a roll pin installed over the mixture adjusting screw channel to prevent tampering.

4. Reinstall the carburetor and start the engine. Bring to normal operating temperature.

5. When equipped, disconnect or

clamp off the hose between the Pulse air feeder and the air cleaner.

6. Operate the engine between 2,000 and 3,000 rpm for approximately five seconds and then allow to idle for approximately two minutes.

7. Adjust the idle mixture to a setting of 0.5% on the CO meter, up to 1984 models and 0.1% to 0.3% for 1985–88.

NOTE: Should the underhood decal specifications differ, use the specifications from the decal.

8. Replace the roll pin and if equipped, the concealment plug. Reset the engine idle speed as required.

NOTE: It may be necessary to remove the carburetor again to install the roll pin and plug.

CARBURETOR WITH CONCEALMENT PLUG

NOTE: A carbon monoxide (CO) meter is necessary when performing the carburetor mixture adjustment.

1. Remove the carburetor from the engine. Observing all fuel handling precautions, drain the fuel from the carburetor bowl.

2. Place the carburetor upside down, in a vise and carefully tighten to hold carburetor securely.

3. With a 1/64 in. pilot bit, drill a hole in the carburetor base casting to the edge of the concealment plug. Enlarge the drilled hole to 1/8 in.

4. With an appropriate pin punch, remove the concealment plug from over the mixture adjustment screw.

5. Reinstall the carburetor and start the engine. Bring to normal operating temperature.

6. When equipped, disconnect or clamp off the hose between the Pulse air feeder and the air cleaner.

7. Operate the engine between 2,000 and 3,000 rpm for approximately five seconds and then allow to idle for approximately two minutes.

8. Adjust the idle mixture to a setting of 0.5% on the CO meter, up to 1984 models and 0.1% to 0.3% for 1985–88.

NOTE: Should the underhood decal specifications differ, use the specifications from the decal.

9. Replace the concealment plug. Reset the engine idle speed as required.

NOTE: It may be necessary to remove the carburetor again to install the concealment plug.

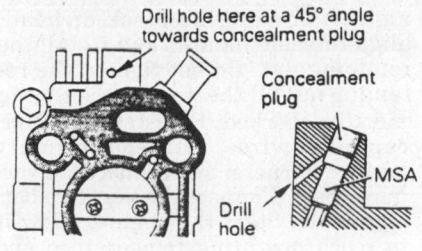

Drilling of carburetor base to remove concealment plug, exposing the mixture adjustment screw

ELECTRONIC FEEDBACK CARBURETOR

NOTE: A carbon monoxide (CO) meter is necessary when performing the carburetor mixture adjustment.

1. Remove the carburetor from the engine. Observing all fuel handling precautions, drain the fuel from the carburetor bowl.
2. Place the carburetor upside down, in a vise and carefully tighten to hold carburetor securely.
3. With a $\frac{5}{64}$ in. pilot bit, drill a hole in the carburetor base casting to the edge of the concealment plug. Enlarge the drilled hole to $\frac{1}{8}$ in.
4. With an appropriate pin punch, remove the concealment plug from over the mixture adjustment screw.
5. Reinstall the carburetor and start the engine. Bring to normal operating temperature.
6. Disconnect the oxygen sensor. 1985–88 models, disconnect the battery cable for three seconds and then reconnect.
7. Operate the engine between 2,000 and 3,000 rpm for approximately five seconds and then allow to idle for approximately two minutes.
8. Adjust the idle mixture to a setting of 0.5% on the CO meter, up to 1984 models and 0.1% to 0.3% for 1985–88.

NOTE: Should the underhood decal specifications differ, use the specifications from the decal.

9. Connect the oxygen sensor and replace the mixture adjusting screw concealment plug.

NOTE: It may be necessary to remove the carburetor again to install the concealment plug.

10. Reset the engine idle speed as required.

ELECTRONIC FEEDBACK CARBURETOR WITH IDLE SPEED CONTROL

NOTE: A carbon monoxide (CO) meter is necessary when performing the carburetor mixture adjustment.

1. Remove the carburetor from the engine. Observing all fuel handling precautions, drain the fuel from the carburetor bowl.
2. Place the carburetor upside down, in a vise and carefully tighten to hold carburetor securely.
3. With a $\frac{5}{64}$ in. pilot bit, drill a hole in the carburetor base casting to the edge of the concealment plug. Enlarge the drilled hole to $\frac{1}{8}$ in.
4. With an appropriate pin punch, remove the concealment plug from over the mixture adjustment screw.
5. Reinstall the carburetor and start the engine. Bring to normal operating temperature. Stop the engine and relax the accelerator cable.
6. Switch ON the ignition switch, wait 18 seconds and then turn the switch OFF. Disconnect the oxygen sensor and ISC actuator.
7. Start the engine and operate between 2,000 and 3,000 rpm for approximately five seconds and then allow to idle for approximately two minutes.
8. Adjust the idle mixture to a setting of 0.1% to 0.3% CO.
9. Adjust the engine rpm with the ISC adjustment screw to specifications.

NOTE: Should the underhood decal specifications differ, use the specifications from the decal.

10. Recheck the mixture and idle speed adjustments. Adjust the accelerator cable.
11. Connect the oxygen sensor, the ISC and replace the mixture adjusting screw concealment plug.

NOTE: It may be necessary to remove the carburetor again to install the concealment plug.

PROPANE IDLE ADJUSTMENT

1. Remove the carburetor from the engine and place in a vise to remove the idle mixture screw concealment plug. Observe fuel safety precautions.
2. Reinstall the carburetor on the engine.
3. Start the engine and bring to normal operating temperature.
4. Turn off the engine and disconnect the negative battery cable for five seconds, then reconnect it.
5. If equipped, disconnect the oxygen sensor connector at the main wiring harness.
6. Start the engine and operate the engine at a speed of 2,000–3,000 rpm for five seconds. Lights, cooling fan and all accessories must be off.
7. Allow the engine to operate at curb idle for two minutes.

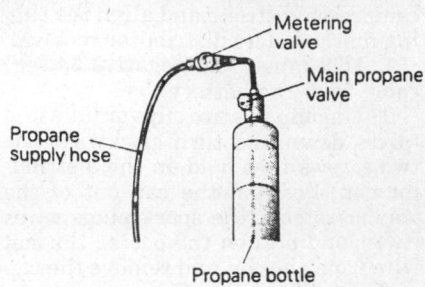

Components necessary to perform the Propane Idle Enrichment procedure

8. If necessary, adjust the ignition timing.
9. Disconnect the fresh air duct from the air cleaner and insert the propane supply hose into the air cleaner about 4–6 in.
10. Be sure both valves are closed on the propane bottle and it is in an upright and safe position.
11. Open the main propane valve and slowly open the metering valve until maximum engine speed is achieved. Excessive amounts of propane will cause engine speed to reduce. Fine tune the metering valve to obtain the highest engine rpm.
12. With the propane still flowing, adjust idle speed screw to obtain the specified enriched rpm. Fine tune the the metering valve again to obtain the highest engine rpm. If there is a change in the enriched rpm, readjust the idle speed screw to obtain the specified enriched rpm.
13. Turn off the propane main valve and allow the engine speed to stablize.
14. Slowly adjust the idle mixture screw to obtain the specified curb idle speed.
15. Recheck the maximum enriched idle speed again by using the propane metering valve. If the enriched speed varies by more than 25 rpm than the specified enriched rpm, perform the adjustment again.
16. Turn off both propane valves and remove the bottle and hose.
17. Reconnect the oxygen sensor connector to the main wiring.
18. Reinstall the idle mixture screw concealment plug and connect the fresh air duct to the air cleaner.

ENGINE ELECTRICAL

Distributor

REMOVAL & INSTALLATION

Position No. 1 cylinder at TDC on the

compression stroke and align the timing marks before distributor removal.

1. Disconnect the negative battery cable from the battery.

2. Unsnap the two clips or unfasten (press down and turn clockwise) the two screws that hold on the distributor cap. Position the cap out of the way or remove the spark plugs wires (twist and pull on the boots), the coil wire from the coil and remove the cap and wires from the car.

3. Verify the rotor points to the No. 1 cylinder position and the timing marks on the crankshaft pulley and the timing tab are aligned at TDC.

4. Mark the distributor body to the exact place the rotor points. Matchmark both the distributor mounting flange and the engine block.

5. Disconnect the distributor primary wire or wiring harness. Remove the vacuum line (lines) from the advance unit. Loosen and remove the retaining nut from the mounting stud. Lift the distributor from the engine. The rotor may turn slightly from the mark on the distributor body. Make note of how far. When the distributor is reinstalled, this is the point to position the rotor.

6. If the engine has not bee disturbed, i.e. the crankshaft was not turned, then reinstall the distributor in the reverse order or removal. Carefully align the matchmarks. Always check the ignition timing whenever the distributor has been removed.

7. If the engine has been disturbed, i.e. rotated while the distributor was out, proceed as follows:

   a. Turn the crankshaft so that the No. 1 piston is on the compression stroke and the timing marks are aligned.

8. Turn the distributor shaft so that the rotor points approximately 15 degrees before the rotor position that was marked on the distributor.

NOTE: If the distributor was not marked, line up the factory marks on the shaft and housing.

9. Insert the distributor into the engine. On block-mounted distributors, if resistance is met, slight wiggling of the rotor shaft will help seat the distributor. If unable to seat it, the oil pump gear is probably out of alignment.

NOTE: Do not force the distributor.

10. Remove the distributor, and using a long screwdriver, turn the oil pump shaft so that it is vertical to the centerline of the crankshaft on 1597 and 1997cc engines.

11. When the distributor seats

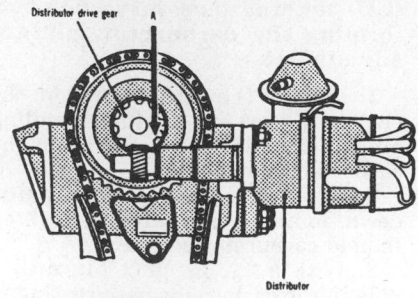

Distributor installation—cylinder head mounted distributors

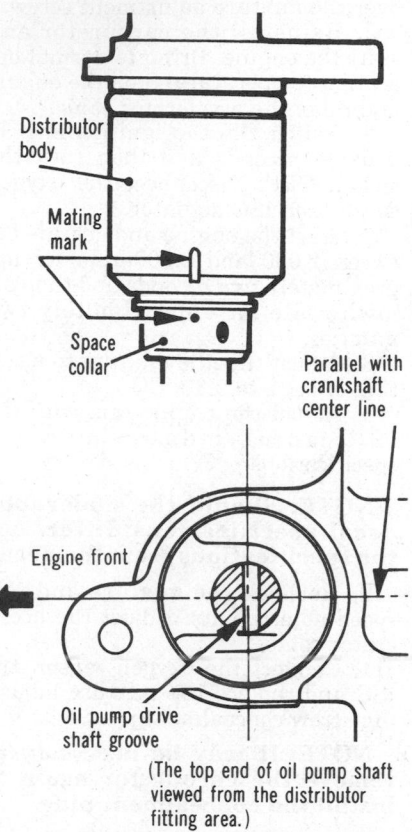

1597cc engine block-mounted distributor

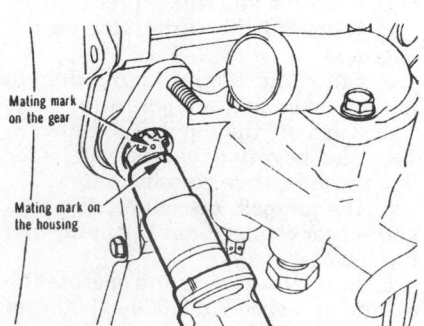

Aligning mating marks for installation of cylinder head mounted distributors

against the engine block or head, align the matchmarks and install the retaining nut. Do not tighten the retaining nut all the way, as the timing must be checked. Reinstall the rotor, cap, plug wires, coil lead, primary lead (or harness) and connect the vacuum hoses. Connect the negative battery cable. Start the engine, allow it to reach operating temperature and check the ignition timing.

Alternator

PRECAUTIONS

There are numerous precautions which must be strictly observed in order to avoid damaging the unit.

• Reversing the battery connections will result in damage to the diodes.

• Booster batteries should be connected from negative to negative and positive to positive.

• Never use a fast charger as a booster to start the car.

• When servicing the battery with a fast charger, always disconnect the car battery cables.

• Never attempt to polarize an alternator.

• Avoid long soldering times when replacing diodes or transistors. Prolonged heat is damaging to alternators.

• Do not use test lamps of more than 12 volts (V) for checking diode continuity.

• Do not short across or ground any of the terminals to the alternator.

• The polarity of the battery, alternator, and regulator must be matched and considered before making any electrical connections within the system.

• Never operate the alternator on an open circuit. Make sure that all connections within the circuit are clean and tight.

• Disconnect the battery terminals when performing any service on the electrical system. This will eliminate the possibility of accidental reversal of polarity.

• Disconnect the battery ground cable if arc welding is to be done on any part of the car.

REMOVAL & INSTALLATION

1. Disconnect the battery cables (negative first) and the alternator wires. Note or tag the wires in order to reinstall them correctly.

2. Loosen and remove the top mounting bolt.

3. Loosen the elongated lower mounting nut. Slide the alternator over in its attaching bracket and remove the fan belt.

4. Remove the lower mounting nut and bolt, being sure not to lose any mounting shims (if equipped).

5. Remove the alternator.

NOTE: Remember when installing the alternator that it is not necessary to polarize the system.

6. Trial fit the alternator on the engine. If shims are installed on the inside of both alternator mounting legs, add or subtract shims as necessary.

7. Install the lower mounting bolt and nut. Do not completely tighten it yet.

8. Fit the fan belt over the alternator and crankshaft pulleys.

9. Loosely install the top mounting bolt and pivot the alternator over until the fan belt is correctly tensioned as outlined in the next procedure.

10. Tighten the top and bottom bolts.

11. Connect the alternator wires and the battery cables.

BELT REPLACEMENT AND TENSIONING

1. Check the drive belt(s) for cracking, fraying and any other deterioration. Replace if necessary.

2. To replace the belt, loosen the mounting bolts and pivot the driven component in its bracket. Remove the old belt and slip the replacement belt over the pulleys.

3. Move the drive component over until the belt can be deflected $\frac{1}{4}$–$\frac{3}{8}$ in. at its midpoint.

4. Tighten the mounting bolts.

Regulator

REMOVAL & INSTALLATION

The voltage regulator is a solid state unit built into or mounted on the alternator. The regulator is non-adjustable and is serviced, when necessary, by replacement.

Starter

REMOVAL & INSTALLATION

1. Disconnect the battery ground cable and the starter motor wiring.

2. Loosen the two starter attaching bolts and brace (if so equipped). Remove the starter motor.

NOTE: With air conditioning or large steering gear box, disconnect the pitman arm from the starter motor attaching bolts and remove the starter from under the car.

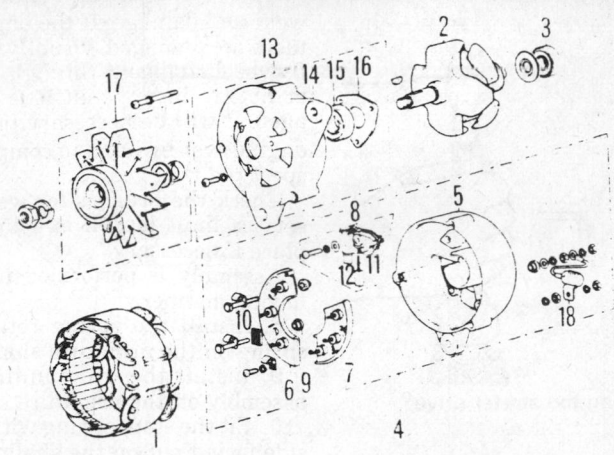

1. Stator
2. Rotor
3. Ball bearing
4. Rear bracket assembly
5. Rear bracket
6. Heat sink complete (+)
7. Heat sink complete (−)
8. Brush holder assembly
9. Insulator
10. Insulator
11. Brush spring
12. Brush
13. Front bracket assembly
14. Front bracket
15. Ball bearing
16. Bearing retainer
17. Pulley
18. Condenser

Exploded view of the typical alternator

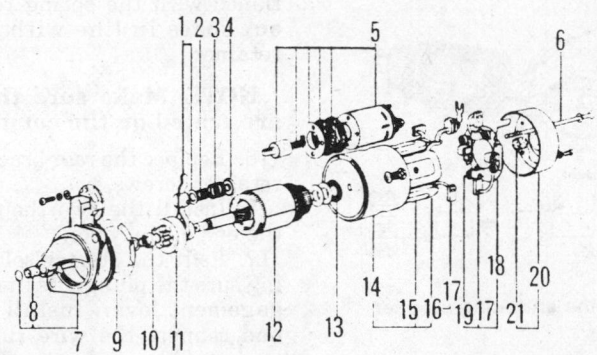

1. Lever assembly
2. Lever spring (A)
3. Lever spring (B)
4. Spring retainer
5. Electromagnetic switch
6. Through bolt
7. Front bracket
8. Front bracket bearing
9. Plate
10. Stop ring
11. Overrunning clutch
12. Armature
13. Insulating washer
14. Yoke assembly
15. Pole piece
16. Field coil
17. Brush
18. Brush holder
19. Brush spring
20. Rear bracket
21. Rear bracket bearing

Exploded view of the typical starter

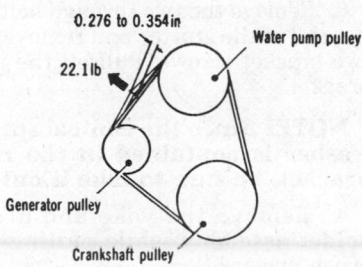

0.276 to 0.354 in

22.1 lb

Water pump pulley

Generator pulley

Crankshaft pulley

Belt tension adjustment

3. Position the starter in the housing opening.

4. Install the attaching bolts and brace (if so equipped). Tighten evenly to avoid binding.

5. Install the starter wiring and connect the battery cable.

STARTER DRIVE
Direct Drive Starter

NOTE: Starter removed from car.

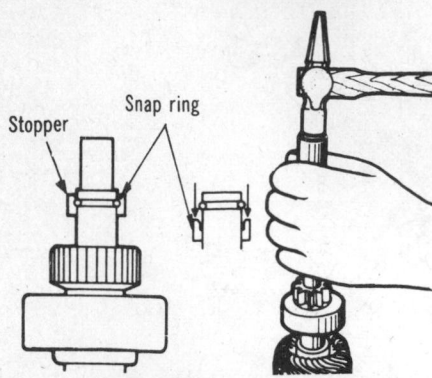

Removing the starter drive

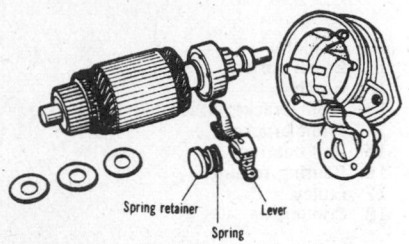

Removing the starter armature and lever

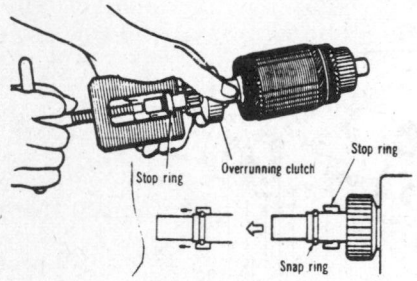

Installing the snap-ring stopper

1. Remove the wire connecting the starter solenoid to the starter.

2. Remove two screws holding the starter solenoid on the starter-drive housing and remove the solenoid.

3. Remove the two long through bolts at the rear of the starter and separate the armature yoke from the armature.

4. Carefully remove the armature and the starter drive engagement lever from the front bracket, after making a mental note of the way they are positioned along with the attendant spring and spring retainer.

5. Loosen the two screws and remove the rear bracket.

6. Tap the stopper ring at the end of the drive gear engagement shaft in towards the driver gear to expose the snap ring. Remove the snap ring.

7. Pull the stopper, drive gear and overrunning clutch from the end of the shaft.
Inspect the pinion and spline teeth for

wear and damage. If the engagement teeth are damaged, visually check the flywheel ring gear through the starter hole to insure that it is not damaged. It will be necessary to turn the engine over by hand to completely inspect the ring gear.

Check the brushes for wear. Their service limit length is 0.453 in. Replace if necessary.

Assembly is performed in the following manner.

8. Install the spring retainer and spring on the armature shaft.

9. Install the overrunning clutch assembly on the armature shaft.

10. Fit the stopper ring with its open side facing out on the shaft.

11. Install a new snap ring and , using a gear puller, pull the stopper ring into place over the snap ring.

12. Fit the small washer on the front end of the armature shaft.

13. Fit the engagement lever into the overrunning clutch and refit the armature into the front housing.

14. Fit the engagement lever spring and spring retainer into place and slide the armature yoke over the armature. Make sure the yoke is positioned with the spring retainer cutout space in line with the spring retainer.

NOTE: Make sure the brushes are seated on the commutator.

15. Replace the rear bracket and two retainer screws.

16. Install the two though bolts in the end of the yoke.

17. Refit the starter solenoid, making sure the plunger is fit over the engagement lever. Install the screws and connect the wire running from the starter yoke to the starter solenoid.

Reduction Gear Type

NOTE: Starter removed from car.

1. Remove the wire connecting the starter solenoid to the starter.

2. Remove the two screws holding the solenoid and, pulling out, unhook it from the engagement lever.

3. Remove the two through bolts in the end of the starter and remove the two bracket screws. Pull off the rear bracket.

NOTE: Since the conical spring washer is contained in the rear bracket, be sure to take it out.

4. Remove the yoke and brush holder assembly while pulling the brush upward.

5. Pull the armature assembly out of the mounting bracket.

6. On the side of the armature mounting bracket, there is a small dust shield held on by two screws, remove the shield. Remove the snap ring and washer located under the shield.

7. Remove the remaining bolts in the mounting bracket and separate the reduction case.

NOTE: Several washers will come out of the reduction case when separated. These adjust the armature end play; do not lose them.

8. Remove the reduction gear, lever and lever spring from the front bracket.

9. Use a brass drift or a deep socket to knock the stopper ring on the end of the shaft in toward the pinion. Remove the snap ring. Remove the stopper, pinion and pinion shaft assembly.

10. Remove the ball bearings at both ends of the armature.

NOTE: The ball bearings are pressed into the front bracket and are not replaceable. Replace them together with the bracket.

Inspect the pinion and spline teeth for wear or damage. If the pinion drive teeth are damaged, visually check the engine flywheel ring gear. Check the flywheel ring gear by looking through the starter motor mounting hole. It will be necessary to turn the engine over by hand to completely inspect the ring gear.

Check the starter brushes for wear. Their service limit length is 0.453 in. Replace if necessary.

Assembly is the reverse of disassembly procedure. Be sure to replace all the adjusting and thrust washers that was removed. When replacing the rear bracket, fit the conical spring pinion washer with its convex side facing out. Make sure that the brushes seat themselves on the commutator.

ENGINE MECHANICAL

Engine

REMOVAL & INSTALLATION

Rear Wheel Drive Models

The factory recommends removing the engine and transmission as a unit.

1. Drain the cooling system. Open the radiator petcock and the engine drain plug.

2. Disconnect and remove the battery.

3. Disconnect the coil, throttle positioner solenoid, fuel cut-off solenoid, alternator, starter, transmission switch, backup light switch, and temperature and oil pressure gauge sending units.

4. On cars with air conditioning, the refrigerant must be released from the system. After the system has been drained, disconnect and cap lines at the compressor and condensor.

5. Remove all air cleaners hoses. Remove the wing nut (and snap clips) and the air cleaner to cover.

6. Remove the two retaining nuts and bracket and remove the air cleaner housing.

7. Disconnect the accelerator cable.

8. Remove and plug the radiator hose.

9. Remove the exhaust manifold nuts and drop the pipe down and out of the way.

10. Disconnect and cap the fuel lines at the pump. On cars with fuel injection, see Fuel Pump Removal for the procedure necessary to bleed the pressure from the system before disconnecting the lines.

11. Disconnect the vacuum hose from the canister purge valve located on the passenger side firewall. Remove the purge hose which runs from the valve to the intake manifold.

12. Scribe a line around the hood hinges and then remove the hood. Place it away from the work area to avoid it being scratched or dented.

13. Remove the grill, radiator cross panel and the radiator. Disconnect and plug the oil cooler lines on automatic transmission equipped cars. Disconnect and plug the engine oil cooler lines (at the engine) on turbo models. Remove and secure the power steering pump (with hoses connected) out of the way.

14. Jack up the front of the car and support it on jackstands. Remove the splash shield.

15. Drain the engine oil and the transmission fluid. Remove the driveshaft.

16. Disconnect the speedometer cable and back-up switch wire. Remove the neutral switch on automatic cars.

17. Disconnect the clutch cable from the clutch lever.

18. Remove the control rod and the cross shaft that are located under the transmission.

19. Untie and open the leather shift boot. Pull the rug back. Remove the four retaining bolts and remove the shift lever.

On automatic cars:

20. Disconnect the transmission control rod from the shift linkage.

21. Attach the lifting device to the two engine brackets provided by the factory, one near the water neck at the front and the other on the passenger's side at the rear.

22. Raise the engine a slight amount and remove the retaining nuts on the side mounts and the rear crossmember mount.

23. Lift the engine out of the compartment by tilting it at approximately a 45x angle.

24. Check the condition of the engine mounts. There are three: left front, right front and rear. Replace, if required.

25. Installing the engine is basically a reverse of the removal procedure, noting the following:

a. Drape heavy rags over the rear of the cylinder head to prevent damaging the firewall when lowering the engine into place.

b. Tighten the two front mounts first and then the rear crossmember mount. All tightening torques are listed in the chart below:
• Front mount-to-crossmember: 15–17 ft. lbs.
• Front mount-to-engine bracket nut: 15–17 ft. lbs.
• Front engine block-to-bracket bolt: 29–36 ft. lbs.
• Rear mount-to-support bracket: 7–8.5 ft. lbs.
• Rear mount-to-frame bolt: 15–17 ft. lbs.
• Crossmember-to-body bolt: (Manual) 9–11 ft. lbs., (Automatic) 7–8.5 ft. lbs.

c. Refill the cooling system, engine crankcase and the transmission with the proper fluids.

d. Before stating the engine, recheck the following: fuel lines, coolant lines, electrical connections, and bolt torques. Start the engine and check for correct operation and leaks.

Front Wheel Drive Models
EXCEPT 4WD VISTA

The factory recommends that the engine and transaxle be removed as a unit.

1. Disconnect the battery cables (ground cable first) remove the battery hold down and battery. Remove the battery tray.

2. Remove the air cleaner assembly. Disconnect the purge control valve. Remove the purge control valve mounting bracket. Remove the windshield washer reservoir, radiator tank and carbon canister.

3. Drain the coolant from the radiator. Remove the radiator assembly with the electric cooling fan attached. Be sure to disconnect the fan wiring harness and the transmission cooler lines (if equipped).

4. Disconnect the following cables, hoses and wires from the engine and transaxle: Clutch, Accelerator, Speedometer, Heater Hose, Fuel lines, PCV vacuum line, High-altitude compensator vacuum hose (Calif. Models), Bowl vent valve purge hose (U.S.A. Models), Inhibitor switch (Auto Trans), Control Cable (Auto Trans), Starter, Engine Ground Cable, Alternator, Water Temperature, Ignition Coil, Water Temperature Sensor, Back-Up Light (Man. Trans.), Oil Pressure Wires, and the ISC cable on fuel injected cars.

5. Remove the ignition coil. Be sure all wires and hoses are disconnected.

6. Jack up the front of the vehicle and support safely on jackstands. Remove the splash shield (if equipped).

7. Drain the lubricant out of the transaxle.

8. Remove the right and left driveshafts from the transaxle and support them with wire. Plug the transaxle case holes so dirt cannot enter.

CAUTION

The driveshaft retainer ring should be replaced whenever the shaft is removed.

---

9. Disconnect the assist rod and the control rod from the transaxle. If the car is equipped with a range selector, disconnect the selector cable.

10. Remove the mounting bolts/bolt from the front and rear roll control rods.

11. Disconnect the exhaust pipe from the engine and secure it with wire.

12. Loosen the engine and transaxle mounting bracket nuts. On turbocharged engines, disconnect the oil cooler tube.

13. Lower the car.

14. Attach a lifting device to the engine. Apply slight lifting pressure to the engine. Remove the engine and transaxle mounting nuts and bolts.

15. Make sure the rear roll control rod is disconnected. Lift the engine and transaxle from the car.

CAUTION

Make sure the transaxle does not hit the battery bracket when the engine and transaxle are lifted.

---

16. To install, lower the engine and transaxle carefully into position and loosely install the mounting bolts. Temporarily tighten the front and rear roll control rod mounting bolts. Lower the full weight of the engine and transaxle onto the mounts and tighten the nuts and bolts. Loosen and retighten the roll control rods.

17. The rest of the engine installa-

tion is the reverse of the removal. Make sure all cables, hoses and wires are connected. Fill the radiator with coolant, the transaxle with lubricant. Adjust the clutch cable and accelerator cable. Adjust the transaxle control rod. Start the engine and check for leaks.

4WD VISTA

1. Remove the battery, battery tray and bracket.

2. Disconnect the engine oil pressure switch and power steering pump connectors.

3. Disconnect the alternator harness.

4. Remove the air cleaner.

5. Remove the high tension cable from the distributor.

6. Disconnect the engine ground wire at the firewall.

7. Remove the windshield washer bottle.

8. Disconnect the brake booster vacuum hose.

9. Disconnect and tag all other vacuum lines connected to the engine.

10. Drain the coolant.

11. Remove the coolant reservoir tank.

12. Remove the radiator.

13. Disconnect the heater hoses at the engine.

14. Disconnect the accelerator cable from the carburetor.

15. Disconnect the speed control cable at the carburetor.

16. Disconnect the speedometer cable at the transaxle.

17. If the car is equipped with air conditioning, the system must be evacuated.

18. Disconnect the hose at the air conditioning compressor and cap all openings immediately.

19. Disconnect the hoses at the power steering pump.

20. Disconnect the fuel return hose, then the fuel inlet hose, at the carburetor.

21. Disconnect the shift control cables at the transaxle.

22. Raise and support the car on jackstands.

23. Remove the lower cover and skid plate.

24. Drain the transaxle and transfer case.

25. Disconnect the exhaust pipe from the manifold.

26. See the procedures under Driveshaft, later in this section, and remove the driveshaft.

27. Remove the clutch slave cylinder as described later in this section.

28. Disconnect the halfshafts at the transaxle as described later in this section.

29. Remove the transfer case extension stopper bracket.

NOTE: The two top stopper bracket bolts are easier to get at from the engine compartment, using a T-type box wrench.

30. Lower the vehicle to the ground.

31. Remove the nuts only, from the engine mount-to-body bracket.

32. Remove the range select control valves from the transaxle insulator bracket.

33. Remove the nut only, from the transaxle mounting insulator.

34. Remove the front roll insulator nut.

35. Remove the front roll insulator nut.

36. Remove the rear insulator-to-engine nut.

37. Remove the grille and valance panel.

38. Remove the A/C condensor.

39. Take up the weight of the engine with a lifting device attached to the lifting eyes.

40. Remove all the mounting bolts.

41. Double check that all wiring, hoses and cable from the engine, transaxle and transfer case have been disconnected.. Move the assembly forward slightly to a point at which it will clear the floorpan, and lift the whole assembly clear of the car.

42. Installation is the reverse of removal. Observe the following torques:

• Transaxle stopper: 58 ft. lbs.
• Engine-to-body bracket bolts: 47 ft. lbs.
• Rear insulator: 29 ft. lbs.
• Transaxle mount nuts: 58 ft. lbs.
• Heat shield: 7 ft. lbs.
• Front roll bracket nuts: 36 ft. lbs.

Cylinder Head

The timing chain/belt and gear should be attached together in correct timing position and hung on wire except on 1410cc and 1468cc engines where only the timing belt needs to be removed. The head bolts on the 1410, 1468, 1597 and 1997cc engines require a $5/16$ in. Allen socket for removal.

--- **CAUTION** ---
Never remove the cylinder head unless the engine is absolutely cold; the cylinder head could warp.

REMOVAL & INSTALLATION

All Engines

1. Disconnect the battery ground cable, remove the air cleaner assembly and the attached hoses.

2. Drain the coolant, remove the upper radiator hose, and the heater hoses.

3. Remove the fuel line, disconnect the accelerator linkage, distributor vacuum lines, purge valve, and water temperature gauge wire.

4. Remove the spark plug wires and the fuel pump. Remove the distributor, where necessary.

5. Disconnect the exhaust pipe from the exhaust manifold flange.

6. Remove the exhaust manifold assembly.

7. Remove the intake manifold and carburetor as a unit.

8. Turn the crankshaft to No. 1 piston at TDC on the compression stroke.

NOTE: During the following procedure, do not turn the crankshaft after locating TDC.

1410 and 1468cc Engines

a. Remove the timing belt cover. Be sure that the knockout pin is at 12 o'clock and the cam sprocket mark and cylinder head pointer are aligned at 3 o'clock.

b. Loosen the timing belt tensioner mounting. Move the tensioner toward the water pump and secure it in that position.

c. Remove the rocker arm cover.

NOTE: The cam pulley need not be removed.

1597cc Engine – With or Without Silent Shaft and 1977cc Engines:

a. Align the timing mark on the upper under cover of the timing belt with that of the cam shaft sprocket.

b. Matchmark the timing belt and the timing mark on the camshaft sprocket with a felt tip pen.

c. Remove the sprocket and insert a 2 in. piece of timing belt or other material between the bottom of the camshaft sprocket and the sprocket holder on the timing belt lower front cover, to hold the sprocket and belt so that the valve timing will not be changed.

d. Remove the timing belt upper under cover and rocker arm cover.

2555cc Engine

a. Remove the rocker arm cover.

b. Position the camshaft sprocket dowel pin at the 12 o'clock position with the crankshaft pulley notch aligned with the timing mark "T" at the front of the timing chain case.

c. Match the timing chain with the timing mark on the camshaft sprocket.

d. Remove the camshaft sprocket bolt, distributor, gear and the sprocket from the camshaft.

All Engines

9. Loosen and remove the cylinder head bolts in two or three stages to avoid cylinder head warpage.

10. Remove the cylinder head from the engine block.

11. Clean the cylinder head and block mating surfaces and install a new cylinder head gasket.

12. Position the cylinder head on the engine block, engage the dowel pins front and rear and install the cylinder head bolts.

13. Tighten the head bolts in three stages and then torque to specifications.

14. Install the timing belt upper under cover on the 1597 and 1997cc engines.

15. Locate the camshaft in original position. Pull the camshaft sprocket and belt or chain upward and install on the camshaft.

NOTE: If the dowel pin and the dowel pin hole does not line up between the sprocket and the spacer or camshaft, move the camshaft by bumping either of the two projections provided at the rear of the No. 2 cylinder exhaust cam of the camshaft, with a light hammer or other tool, until the hole and pin align. Be certain the crankshaft does not turn.

16. Install the camshaft sprocket bolt and the distributor gear and tighten. (The gear is used on 2555cc engines.)

17. Install the timing belt upper front cover and spark plug cable support.

18. Apply sealant to the intake manifold gasket on both sides. Position the gasket and install the intake manifold. Tighten nuts to specifications.

——— **CAUTION** ———

Be sure that no sealant enters the jet air passages when equipped.

19. Install the exhaust manifold gaskets and the manifold assembly. Tighten the nuts to specifications.

20. Connect the exhaust pipe to the

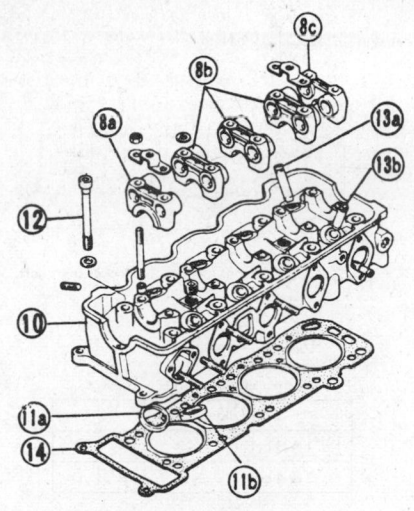

8a. Camshaft bearing cap
8b. No. 2, 3 and 4 caps
8c. Camshaft bearing cap (rear)
10. Cylinder head
11a. Intake valve seat ring
11b. Exhaust valve seat ring
12. Cylinder head bolt
13a. Exhaust valve guide
13b. Intake valve guide
14. Cylinder head gasket

Exploded view of the cylinder head

exhaust manifold and install the fuel pump. Install the purge valve.

21. Install the water temperature gauge wire, heater hoses and the upper radiator hose.

22. Connect the fuel lines, accelerator linkage, vacuum hoses and the spark plug wires.

23. Fill the cooling system and connect the battery ground cable. Install the distributor.

24. Temporarily adjust the valve clearance to the cold engine specifications.

25. Install the gasket on the rocker arm cover and temporarily install the cover on the engine.

26. Start the engine and bring it to normal operating temperature. Stop the engine and remove the rocker arm cover.

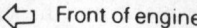
⟸ Front of engine

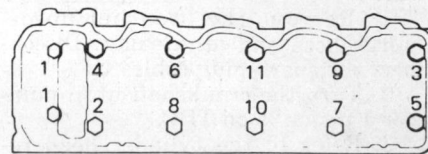

2555cc cylinder head bolt loosening sequence

Crankshaft pulley side

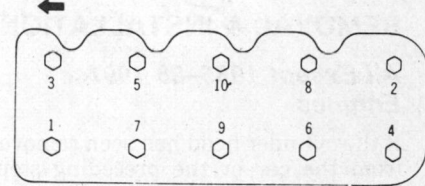

1410, 1468, 1597 and 1997cc cylinder head bolt loosening sequence

COLD ENGINE SPECIFICATIONS

	Inch	mm
Jet valve, if equipped	0.003	0.07
Intake valve	0.003	0.07
Exhaust valve	0.007	0.17

HOT ENGINE SPECIFICATIONS

	Inch	mm
Jet valve, if equipped	0.006	0.15
Intake valve	0.006	0.15
Exhaust valve	0.010	0.25

27. Adjust the valves to hot engine specifications.

28. Reinstall the rocker arm cover and tighten securely.

29. Install the air cleaner, hoses, purge valve hose and any other removed unit.

Rocker Arm/Shaft

To service the rocker arm or camshaft while the cylinder head is still mount-

← FRONT

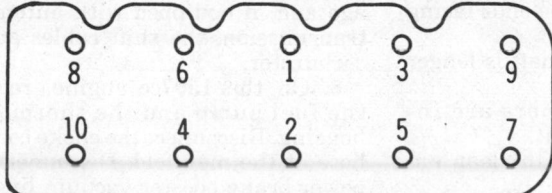

Head bolt torque sequence for the 1410, 1468, 1597 and 1997cc engines

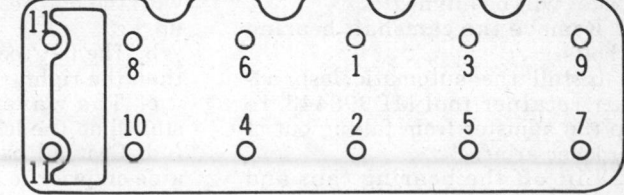

Cylinder head bolt tightening sequence— 2555cc

ed on the cylinder block and in the car:

1. Remove the breather hoses, purge hose and air cleaner. Disconnect the spark plug cables.

2. Turn the crankshaft until number 1 piston is on TDC.

3. Refer to the cylinder head removal. Remove the cam sprocket timing chain/belt and rocker arm cover.

REMOVAL & INSTALLATION

All Except 1985–88 1997cc Engines

If the cylinder head has been removed from the car or the preceding steps have been followed:

1. Matchmark the camshaft/rocker arm bearing caps to their cylinder head location. (Except 1410 and 1468cc engine).

2. Loosen the bearing cap bolts, or the rocker shaft bolts (1410 and 1468cc engine) from the cylinder head but do not remove them from the caps or shafts. Lift the rocker assembly from the cylinder head as a unit.

3. The rocker arm assembly can be disassembled by the removal of the mounting bolts (and dowel pins on some models) from the bearing caps and/or shafts.

NOTE: Keep the rocker arms and springs in the same order as disassembly. The left and right springs have different tension ratings and free length. Observe the location of the rocker arms as they are removed. Exhaust and intake, right and left, are different. Do not get them mixed up.

1985–88 1997cc Engines

NOTE: A special tool, MD998443, is required for this procedure.

1. Remove the rocker cover and gasket, and the timing belt cover.

2. Turn the crankshaft so that the #1 piston is a TDC compression. At this point, the timing mark on the camshaft sprocket and the timing mark on the head to the left of the sprocket will be aligned.

3. Remove the camshaft bearing cap bolts.

4. Install the automatic lash adjuster retainer tool MD998443, to keep the adjuster from falling out of the rocker arms.

5. Lift off the bearing caps and rocker arm assemblies.

6. The rocker arms may now be removed from the shaft.

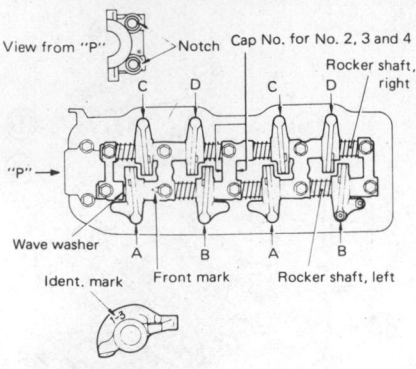

1997cc engine rocker arm shaft assembly

	Ident. mark	In.	Ex.
No. 1 & 3 cyl.	1–3	A	C
No. 2 & 4 cyl.	2–4	B	D

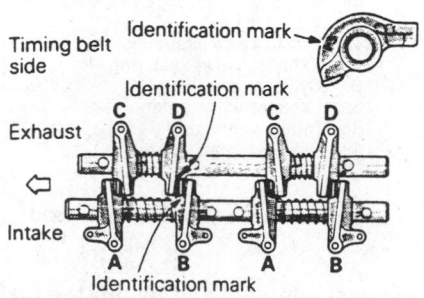

Correct assembly of rocker arm assembly, 1597cc, 1410cc and 1468cc engines

—————— CAUTION ——————
Keep all parts in the order in which they were removed. None of the parts are interchangeable.

NOTE: The lash adjusters are filled with diesel fuel, which will spill out if they are inverted. If any diesel fuel is spilled, the adjusters must be bled. The bleeding procedure can be found following this procedure.

7. Check all parts for wear or damage. Replace any damaged or excessively worn parts.

8. Assemble all parts in reverse order of removal. Note the following:

a. The rocker shafts are installed with the notches in the ends facing up.

b. The left rocker shaft is longer than the right.

c. The wave washers are installed on the left shaft.

d. Coat all parts with clean engine oil prior to assembly.

e. Insert the lash adjuster from under the rocker arm and install the special holding tool. If any of

the diesel fuel is spilled, the adjuster must be bled.

f. Tighten the bearing cap bolts, working from the center towards the ends to 15 ft. lbs.

g. Check the operation of each lash adjuster by positioning the camshaft so that the rocker arm bears on the low, or round portion of the cam (pointed part of the can faces straight down). Insert a thin steel wire, or tool MD998442, in the hole in the top of the rocker arm, over the lash adjuster and depress the check ball at the top of the adjuster. While holding the check ball depressed, move the arm up and down. Looseness should be felt. Full plunger stroke should be .0866 in. (2.2mm). If not, remove, clean and bleed the lash adjuster.

BLEEDING THE LASH ADJUSTERS

If the lash adjuster is removed and the diesel fuel contained inside is spilled, submerge the adjuster in clean diesel fuel and compress it several times to expel the air. If air is still trapped after assembly and installation and a clattering noise is heard when the engine is started, the air can be bled by increasing engine speed from idle to 3,000 rpm and back to idle over a one minute period. Do this several times, or until the clattering stops. If this does not stop the clattering, remove and submerge the lifter in clean diesel fuel, compressing it several times. If clattering continues, replace the lash adjuster.

Intake Manifold

REMOVAL & INSTALLATION

—————— CAUTION ——————
The intake manifold is case aluminum.

1. Remove the air cleaner.

2. Disconnect the fuel line and EGR lines on models so equipped.

3. Disconnect the throttle postiner solenoid and fuel cut-off solenoid wires.

4. Disconnect the accelerator linkage and, if equipped with automatic transmission, the shift cables at the carburetor.

5. On the 1597cc engine, remove the fuel pump and the thermostat housing. Disconnect the choke coolant hose at the manifold. Disconnect the power brake booster vacuum line.

6. Drain the coolant.

7. Remove the water hose from carburetor and cylinder head.

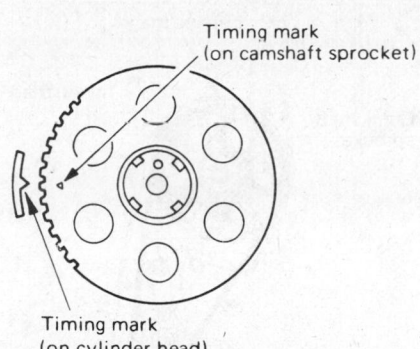

Timing mark
(on camshaft sprocket)

Timing mark
(on cylinder head)

Camshaft timing mark alignment for #1 TDC, on the 1997cc engine

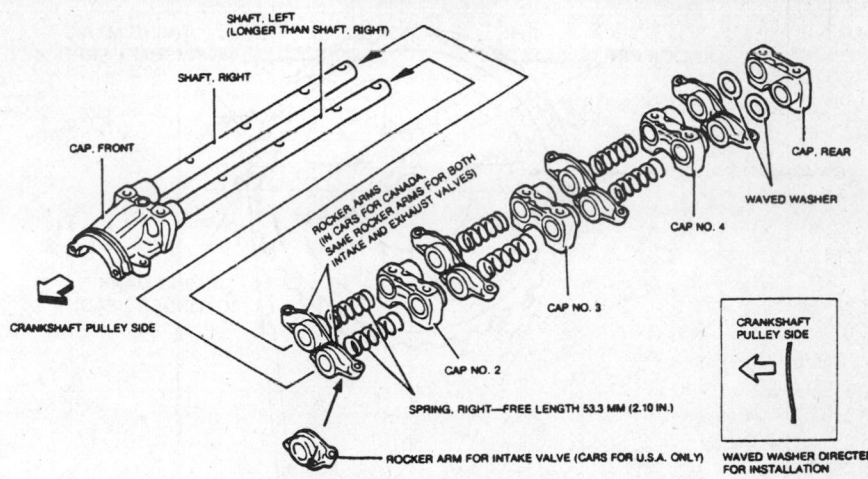

Rocker arm assembly, 1597cc engine

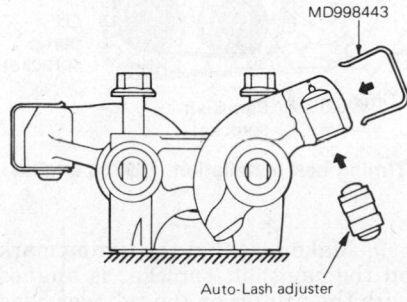

MD998443

Auto-Lash adjuster

Automatic lash adjuster installation

8. Remove the heater and water outlet hoses.

9. Disconnect the water temperature sending unit.

10. Remove the manifold and carburetor.

11. Clean all mounting surfaces. Before reinstalling the manifold, coat both side with gasket sealer.

— CAUTION —

If the engine is equipped with the jet air system, take care not to get any sealer into the jet air intake passage.

12. Installation is the reverse of removal.

Exhaust Manifold

REMOVAL & INSTALLATION

1. Remove the carburetor air cleaner assembly.

2. Remove the manifold heat stove and hose. Disconnect the EGR lines and reed valve, if equipped. On turbocharged models, remove the turborcharger as described below.

3. Disconnect the exhaust pipe bracket from the engine block.

4. Remove the exhaust pipe flange bolts (one bolt and nut may have to be removed from under the car).

5. Remove the manifold flange stud

Model	Item	Torque ft. lbs.
Colt	● Oil Pipe	11–14
	● Turbocharger-To-Manifold	38–52
	● Oil Return Pipe	6–7
	● Oil Pipe Flare Nut	21–25
	● Oxygen Sensor	30–35
	● Converter-To-Support Bracket	9–11
Conquest	● Oil Pipe Fitting	17–20
	● Turbocharger Mounting Nuts	37–50
	● Oil Return Pipe	6–7
	● Oil Pipe-To-Fitting	13–17

nuts and remove the manifold from the cylinder head.

6. Installation is the reverse of removal. Port liner gaskets may be used along with the exhaust manifold gaskets on some engine models.

Turbocharger

REMOVAL & INSTALLATION

— CAUTION —

Make sure that the engine and turbocharger are cold, preferably overnight, before removing the unit.

1. Remove the heat shield.

2. Remove the oxygen sensor from the catalytic converter.

3. Remove the converter-to-turbocharger nuts.

4. Disconnect the hose from the oil return pipe and time chain case.

5. Remove the oil pipe from the turbocharger and oil filter housing.

6. Remove the air intake pipe connecting bolt.

7. Remove the turbocharger mounting nuts and lift the unit off the engine.

8. Installation is the reverse of removal. Torque all parts to the specification. Before the oil flare nut is installed at the top of the unit, pour clean engine oil into the turbocharger. Always use new gaskets.

Timing Gear Cover, Chain/Belt, Counterbalance Shafts and Tensioner

NOTE: The timing chain case is cast aluminum, so exercise caution when handling this part.

The following outlines are the recommended removal and installation procedures for the timing chain or belt. Some modifications to the procedures may be necessary due to added accessories, sheet metal parts, or emission control units and connecting hoses.

REMOVAL & INSTALLATION

1410 and 1468cc Engine

1. Turn the engine until the No. 1 piston is on TDC with the timing marks aligned.

2. Disconnect the ground (negative) battery cable.

4–23

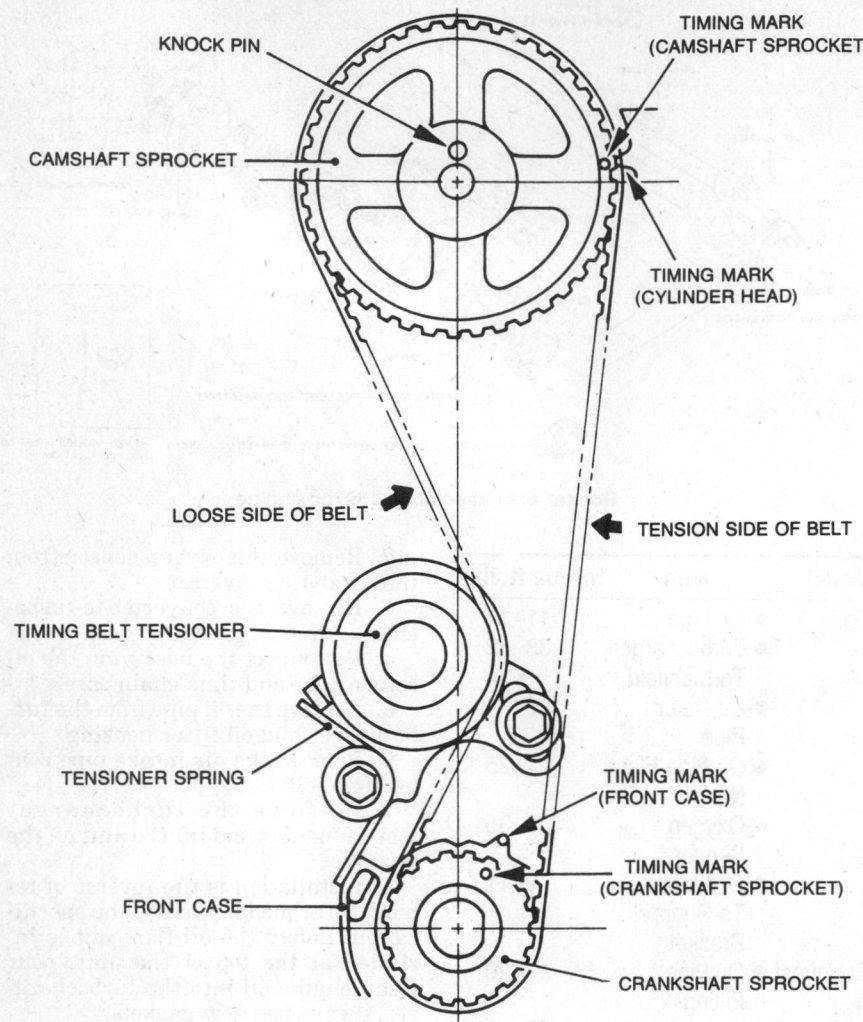

1410 and 1468cc engine timing belt installation

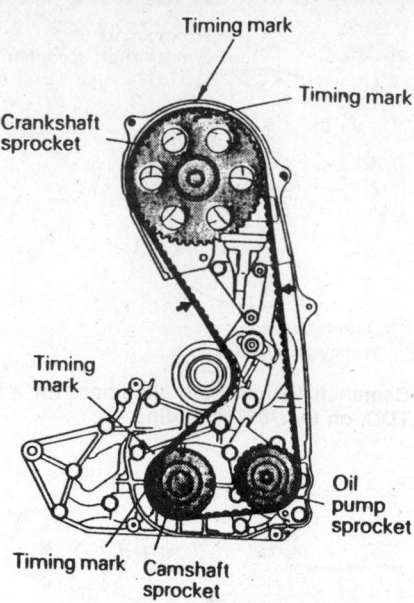

Timing belt installation, 1597cc engine

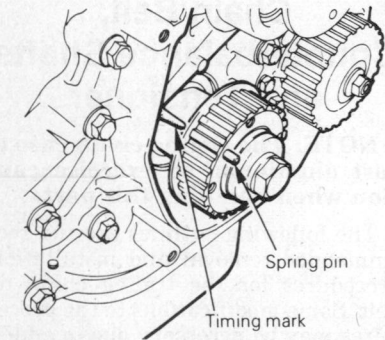

1597cc crankshaft sprocket timing mark alignment

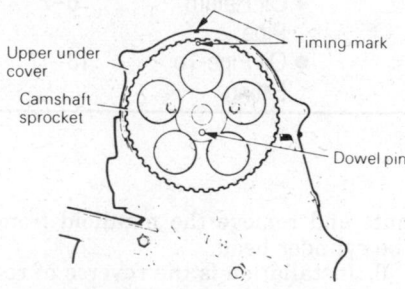

1597cc camshaft sprocket installation alignment

3. Remove the fan drive belt, the fan blades, spacer and water pump pulley.

4. Remove the timing belt cover.

5. Loosen the timing belt tensioner mounting bolt and move the tensioner toward the water pump. Temporarily secure the tensioner.

6. Remove the crankshaft pulley and slide the belt off of the camshaft and crankshaft drive sprockets.

7. Inspect the drive sprockets for abnormal wear, cracks or damage and replace if necessary. Remove and inspect the tensioner. Check for smooth pulley rotation, excessive play or noise. Replace tensioner if necessary.

8. Reinstall the tensioner, if it was removed and temporarily secure it close to the water pump.

9. Make sure that the timing mark on the camshaft sprocket is aligned with the pointer on the cylinder head and that the crankshaft sprocket mark is aligned with the mark on the engine case.

10. Install the timing belt on the crankshaft sprocket.

11. Install the belt counterclockwise over the camshaft sprocket making sure there is no play on the tension side of the belt. Adjust the belt fore and aft so that it is centered on the sprockets.

12. Loosen the tensioner from it's temporary position so that the spring pressure will allow it to contact the timing belt.

13. Rotate the crankshaft two complete turns in the normal rotation direction to remove any belt slack. Turn the crankshaft until the timing marks are lined up. If the timing has slipped, remove the belt and repeat the procedure.

14. Tighten the tensioner mounting bolts, slotted side (right) first, then the spring side.

15. Once again rotate the engine two complete revolutions until the timing marks line up. Recheck the belt tension.

NOTE: When the tension side of the timing belt and the tensioner are pushed in horizontally with a moderate force (about 11 lbs.) and the cogged side of the belt covers about a quarter of an in. of the tensioner right side mounting bolt head (across flats), the tension is correct.

16. Reinstall the timing belt cover,

the water pump pulley, spacer, fan blades and drive belt.

17. Connect the battery ground cable.

1597cc Engine – Standard
1597cc Engine – W/Silent Shaft

1. Drain the coolant and remove the radiator on rear wheel drive cars only. Disconnect the battery cable.

2. Remove the alternator and accessory belts. Remove the belt cover.

3. Rotate the crankshaft to bring No. 1 piston to TDC on the compression stroke. Align the notch on the crankshaft pulley with the "T" mark on the timing indicator scale and the timing mark on the upper under cover of the timing belt with the mark on the camshaft sprocket. Mark and remove the distributor.

4. Remove the crankshaft pulley and bolt.

5. On rear wheel drive cars, remove the fan blades.

6. Remove the timing belt covers, upper front and lower front.

7. Remove the crankshaft sprocket bolt.

8. Loosen the tensioner mounting nut and bolt. Move the tensioner away from the belt and retighten the nut to keep the tensioner in the off position. Remove the belt.

9. Remove the camshaft sprocket, crankshaft sprocket, flange and tensioner.

10. Silent shaft engines:

   a. Loosen the counterbalance shaft sprocket mounting bolt.

   b. Remove the belt tensioner and remove the timing belt.

   c. Remove the crankshaft sprocket (inner) and counterbalance shaft sprocket.

   d. Remove the upper and lower under timing belt covers.

11. The water pump or cylinder head may be removed at this point, depending upon the type of repairs needed.

12. Raise the front of the car and support it safely. Remove any interfering splash pans.

13. Drain the oil pan and remove the pan from the block.

14. Remove the oil pump sprocket and cover.

NOTE: On the silent shaft engines, remove the plug at the bottom of the left side of the cylinder block and insert a screwdriver to keep the left counterbalance shaft in position while removing the sprocket nut.

15. Remove the front cover and oil pump as a unit, with the left countershaft attached, if equipped.

16. Remove the oil pump gear and left counterbalance shaft.

NOTE: To aid in removal of the front cover, a driver groove is provided on the cover, above the oil pump housing. Avoid prying on the thinner parts of the housing flange or hammering on it to remove the case.

17. Remove the right counterbalance shaft from the engine block.

TO INSTALL – STANDARD ENGINE

1. Install a new front seal in the cover. Install a new gasket on the front of the cylinder block and using a seal protector on the front of the crankshaft, install the front cover on the engine block.

2. Tighten the front case mounting bolts to 11–13 ft. lbs.

3. Install the oil screen and using a new gasket, install the oil pan. Tighten bolts to 4.5–5.5 ft. lbs.

4. If the cylinder head and/or water pump had been removed, reinstall them, using new gaskets.

5. Install the upper and lower under covers.

6. Install the spacer, flange and crankshaft sprocket and tighten the bolt to 43.5–50 ft. lbs.

7. Align the timing mark on the crankshaft sprocket with the timing mark on the front case.

8. Align the camshaft sprocket timing mark with the upper under cover timing mark.

9. Install the tensioner spring and tensioner. Temporarily tighten the nut. Install the front end of the tensioner spring (bent at right angles) on the projection of the tensioner and the other end (straight) on the water pump body.

10. Loosen the nut and move the tensioner in the direction of the water pump. Lock it by tightening the nut.

11. Ensure that the sprocket timing marks are aligned, and install the timing belt. The belt should be installed on the crankshaft sprocket, the oil pump sprocket, and then the camshaft sprocket, in that order, while keeping the belt tight.

12. Loosen the tensioner mounting bolt and nut and allow the spring tension to move the tensioner against the belt.

NOTE: Make sure the belt comes in complete mesh with the sprocket by lightly pushing the tensioner up by hand toward the mounting nut.

13. Tighten the tensioner mounting nut and bolt.

NOTE: Be sure to tighten the

nut before tightening the bolt. Too much tension could result from tightening the bolt first.

14. Recheck all sprocket alignments.

15. Turn the crankshaft through a complete rotation in the normal direction.

— CAUTION —

Do not turn in a reverse direction or shake or push the belt.

16. Loosen the tensioner bolt and nut. Retighten the nut and then the bolt.

17. Install the lower and upper front outer covers.

18. Install the crankshaft pulley and tighten the bolts to 7.5–8.5 ft. lbs.

19. Install the alternator and belt and adjust. Install the distributor.

20. Install the radiator, fill the cooling system and inspect for leaks.

TO INSTALL – SILENT SHAFT ENGINES

1. Install a new front seal in the cover. Install the oil pump drive and driven gears in the front case, aligning the timing marks on the pump gears.

2. Install the left counterbalance shaft in the driven gear and temporarily tighten the bolt.

3. Install the right counterbalance shaft into the cylinder block.

4. Install an oil seal guide on the end of the crankshaft, and install a new gasket on the front of the engine block for the front cover.

5. Install a new front case packing, if equipped.

6. Insert the left counterbalance shaft into the engine block and at the same time, guide the front cover into place on the front of the engine block.

7. Insert a screwdriver at the bottom of the left side of the block and hold the left counterbalance shaft and tighten the bolt. Install the hole plug.

8. Install an O-ring on the oil pump cover and install it on the front cover.

9. Tighten the oil pump cover bolts and the front cover bolts to 11–13 ft. lbs.

10. Install the oil screen, and using a new gasket, install the oil pan.

11. Install the water pump and/or the cylinder head, if removed previously.

12. Install the upper and lower under covers.

13. Install the spacer on the end of the right counterbalance shaft, with the chamfered edge toward the rear of the engine.

14. Install the counterbalance shaft sprocket and temporarily tighten the bolt.

15. Install the inner crankshaft sprocket and align the timing marks on the sprockets with those on the front case.

16. Install the inner tensioner (B) with the center of the pulley on the left side of the mounting bolt and with the pulley flange toward the front of the engine.

17. Lift the tensioner by hand, clockwise, to apply tension to the belt. Tighten the bolt to secure the tensioner.

18. Check that all alignment marks are in their proper places and the belt deflection is approximately $\frac{1}{4}$–$\frac{1}{2}$ in. on the tension side.

NOTE: When the tensioner bolt is tightened, make sure the shaft of the tensioner does not turn with the bolt. If the belt is too tight there will be noise, and if the belt is too loose, the belt and sprocket may come out of mesh.

19. Tighten the counterbalance shaft sprocket bolt to 22–28.5 ft. lbs.

20. Install the flange and crankshaft sprocket. Tighten the bolt to 43.5–50.5 ft. lbs.

21. Install the camshaft spacer and sprocket. Tighten the bolt to 44–57 ft. lbs.

22. Align the camshaft sprocket timing mark with the timing mark on the upper inner cover.

23. Install the oil pump sprocket, tightening the nut to 25–28 ft. lbs. Align the timing mark on the sprocket with the mark on the case.

—————— CAUTION ——————

To be assured that the phasing of the oil pump sprocket and the left counterbalance shaft is correct, a metal rod should be inserted in the plugged hole on the left side of the cylinder block. If it can be inserted more than 2 $\frac{3}{8}$ in., the phasing is correct. If the tool can only be inserted approximately one in., turn the oil pump sprocket through one turn and realign the timing marks. Keep the metal rod inserted until the installation of the timing belt is completed. Remove the tool from the hole and install the plug, before starting the engine.

24. Refer to Step 9 of the belt installation for the standard engine.

25. If the timing belt is correctly tensioned, there should be about 0.5 in clearance between the outside of the belt and the edge of the belt cover. This is measured about halfway down the side of the belt opposite the tensioner.

26. Complete the assembly by installing the upper and lower front covers.

27. Install the crankshaft pulley, alternator, and accessory belts, and adjust to specifications.

28. Install the radiator, fill the cooling system, and start the engine.

2555cc Engines — w/Silent Shaft (Chain Equipped)

1. Drain the coolant and remove the radiator. Disconnect the battery ground cable.

2. Remove the alternator and accessory belts.

3. Rotate the crankshaft to bring No. 1 piston to TDC, on the compression stroke.

4. Mark and remove the distributor.

5. Remove the crankshaft pulley.

6. Remove the water pump assembly.

7. Remove the cylinder head, if necessary.

8. Raise the front of the car and support it safely.

9. Drain the engine oil and remove the oil pan and screen.

10. Remove the timing case cover.

11. Remove the chain guides. Side (A), Top (B), Bottom (C), from the "B" chain (outer).

12. Remove the locking bolts from the "B" chain sprockets.

13. Remove the crankshaft sprocket, counterbalance shaft sprocket and the outer chain.

14. Remove the crankshaft and camshaft sprockets and the "A" (inner) chain.

15. Remove the camshaft sprocket holder and the chain guides, both left and right. Remove the tensioner spring and sleeve from the oil pump.

16. Remove the oil pump by first removing the bolt locking the oil pump driven gear and the right counterbalance shaft, and then remove the oil pump mounting bolts. Remove the counterbalance shaft from the engine block.

NOTE: If the bolt locking the oil pump driven gear and the counterbalance shaft is hard to loosen, remove the oil pump and the shaft as a unit.

17. Remove the left counterbalance shaft thrust washer and take the shaft from the engine block.

18. Install the right counterbalance shaft into the engine block.

19. Install the oil pump assembly. Do not lose the Woodruff key from the end of the counterbalance shaft. Torque the oil pump mounting bolts to 6–7 ft. lbs.

20. Tighten the counterbalance shaft and the oil pump driven gear mounting bolt.

NOTE: The counterbalance shaft and the oil pump can be installed as a unit, if necessary.

21. Install the left counterbalance shaft into the engine block.

22. Install a new O-ring on the thrust plate and install the unit into the engine block, using a pair of bolts without heads, as alignment guides.

—————— CAUTION ——————

If the thrust plate is turned to align the bolt holes, the O-ring may be damaged.

23. Remove the guide bolts and install the regular bolts into the thrust plate and tighten securely.

24. Rotate the crankshaft to bring No. 1 piston to TDC.

25. Install the cylinder head, if removed.

26. Install the sprocket holder and the right and left chain guides.

27. Install the tensioner spring and sleeve on the oil pump body.

28. Install the camshaft and crankshaft sprockets on the timing chain, aligning the sprocket punch marks to the plated chain links.

29. While holding the sprocket and chain as a unit, install the crankshaft sprocket over the crankshaft and align it with the keyway.

30. Keeping the dowel pin hole on the camshaft in a vertical position, install the camshaft sprocket and chain on the camshaft.

NOTE: The sprocket timing mark and the plated chain link should be at the 2 to 3 o'clock position when correctly installed.

—————— CAUTION ——————

The chain must be aligned in the right and left chain guides with the tensioner pushing against the chain. The tension for the inner chain is predetermined by spring tension.

31. Install the crankshaft sprocket for the outer or "B" chain.

32. Install the two counterbalance shaft sprockets and align the punched mating marks with the plated links of the chain.

33. Holding the two shaft sprockets and chain, install the outer chain in alignment with the mark on the crankshaft sprocket. Install the shaft sprockets on the counter balance shaft and the oil pump driver gear. Install the lock bolts and recheck the alignment of the punch marks and the plated links.

34. Temporarily install the chain guides, Side (A), Top (B), and Bottom (C).

35. Tighten Side (A) chain guide securely.

36. Tighten Bottom (B) chain guide securely.

37. Adjust the position of the Top (B) chain guide, after shaking the right and left sprockets to collect any chain

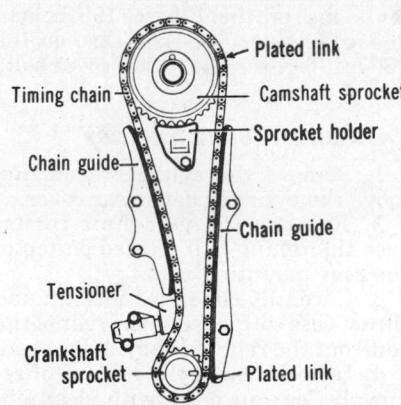

2555cc timing chain and tensioner installation

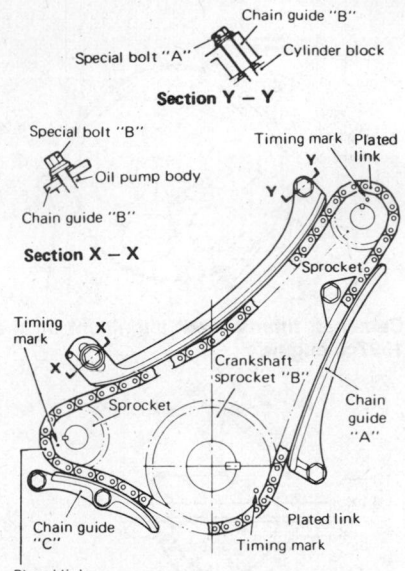

Silent shaft chain timing mark alignment, 2555cc engine

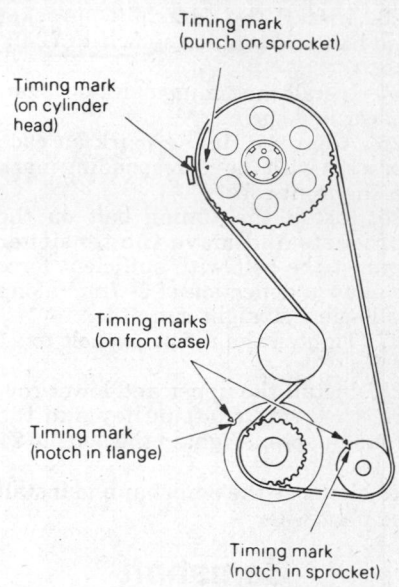

1997cc timing mark alignment

slack, so that when the chain is moved toward the center, the clearance between the chain guide and the chain links will be approximately ⁹⁄₆₄ in. Tighten the Top (B) chain guide bolts.

38. Install the timing chain cover using a new gasket, being careful not to damage the front seal.

39. Install the oil screen and the oil pan, using a new gasket. Torque the bolts to 4.5–5.5 ft. lbs.

40. Install the crankshaft pulley, alternator and accessory belts, and the distributor.

41. Install the oil pressure switch, if removed, and install the battery ground cable.

42. Install the fan blades, radiator, fill the system with coolant and start the engine.

1997cc Engine

NOTE: An 8mm diameter metal bar is needed for this procedure.

1. Remove the water pump drive belt and pulley.

2. Remove the crank adapter and crankshaft pulley.

3. Remove the upper and lower timing belt covers.

4. Move the tensioner fully in the direction of the water pump and temporarily secure it there.

5. If the timing belt is to be reused, make a paint mark on the belt to indicate the direction of rotation. Slip the belt from the sprockets.

— **CAUTION** —

Place the belt in an area where it will not be contacted by oil or other petroleum distillated.

6. Remove the camshaft sprocket bolt and pull the sprocket from the camshaft.

7. Remove the crankshaft sprocket bolt and pull the crankshaft sprocket and flange from the crankshaft.

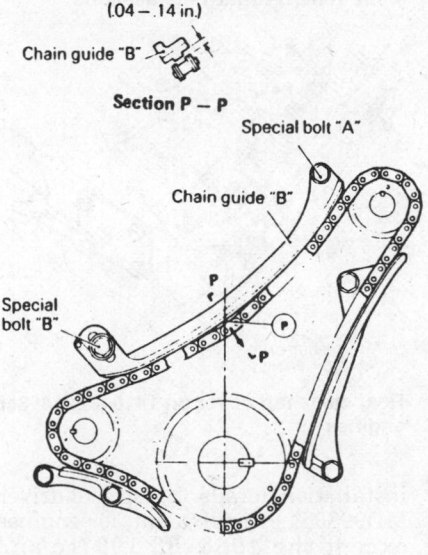

Location of special bolts for chain guide "B", 2555cc engine

8. Remove the plug on the left side of the block and insert an 8mm diameter metal bar in the opening to keep the silent shaft in position.

9. Remove the oil pump sprocket retaining nut and remove the oil pump sprocket.

10. Loosen the right silent shaft sprocket mounting bolt until it can be turned by hand.

11. Remove the belt tensioner and remove the timing belt.

NOTE: Do not attempt to turn the silent shaft sprocket or loosen its bolt while the belt is off.

12. Remove the silent shaft belt sprocket from the crankshaft.

13. Check the belt for wear, damage or glossing. Replace it if any cracks, damage, brittleness or excessive wear are found.

14. Check the tensioners for a smooth rate of movement.

15. Replace any tensioner that shows grease leakage through the seal.

16. Install the silent shaft belt sprocket on the crankshaft, with the flat face toward the engine.

17. Apply light engine oil on the outer face of the spacer and install the spacer on the right silent shaft. The side with the rounded shoulder faces the engine.

18. Install the sprocket on the right silent shaft and install the bolt fingertight.

19. Install the silent shaft belt and adjust the tension, by moving the tensioner into contact with the belt, tight enough to remove all slack. Tighten the tensioner bolt to 21 ft. lbs.

20. Tighten the silent shaft sprocket bolt to 28 ft. lbs.

21. Install the flange and crankshaft sprocket on the crankshaft. The flange conforms to the front of the silent shaft sprocket and the timing belt sprocket is installed with the flat face toward the engine.

— **CAUTION** —

The flange must be installed correctly or a broken belt will result.

22. Install the washer and bolt in the crankshaft and torque it to 94 fft. lbs.

23. Install the camshaft sprocket and bolt and torque the bolt to 72 fft. lbs.

24. Install the timing belt tensioner, spacer and spring.

25. Align the timing mark on each sprocket with the corresponding mark on the front case.

26. Install the timing belt on the sprockets and move the tensioner against the belt with sufficient force to allow a deflection of 5–7mm along its longest straight run.

27. Tighten the tensioner bolt to 21 ft. lbs.

28. Install the upper and lower covers, the crankshaft pulley and the crank adapter. Tighten the bolts to 21 ft. lbs.

29. Remove the 8mm bar and install the plug.

Camshaft

REMOVAL & INSTALLATION

All Except 1410 and 1468cc Engines

1. Match mark the rocker arm bearing caps to the cylinder head.

2. Remove the bearing cap bolts from the cylinder head, but do not remove them from the bearing caps and shafts. Lift the rocker arm assembly from the cylinder head.

3. Make sure the timing marks on the camshaft sprocket and head are properly aligned, so that No. 1 piston is at TDC of the compression stroke. If the camshaft sprocket is to be removed, do so before removing the camshaft from the head. If not, it will be difficult to remove the sprocket bolt. So, prior to removing the bearing caps or belt, remove the camshaft sprocket bolt and lift off the sprocket and belt. Discard the camshaft oil seal.

4. Remove the camshaft from the bearing saddles.

NOTE: On some engines, a distributor drive gear and spacer are used on the front of the camshaft.

5. The valves, valve springs, and valve guide seals can now be removed from the cylinder head.

NOTE: Refer to the cylinder head overhaul procedures in the "Engine Rebuilding" section. Valve guides are a shrink fit, with oversize guides available. Valve seats are replaceable, with oversize seats available.

6. Installation is the reverse of removal. Coat all parts with clean engine oil prior to installation. See Rocker Arm and Shaft procedures for

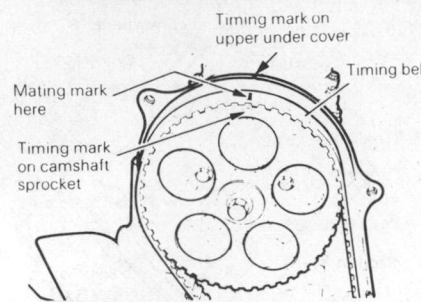

Camshaft timing mark alignment on the 1597cc engine

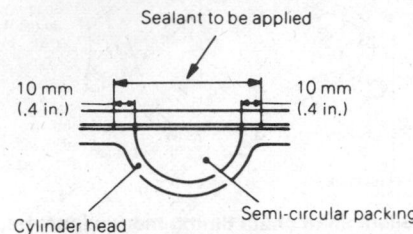

Sealant application on the rocker cover rear seal projections used for turning the shaft in hard-to-turn installations

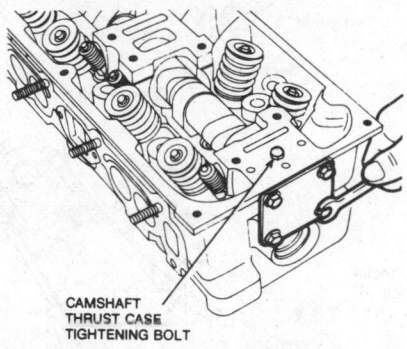

CAMSHAFT THRUST CASE TIGHTENING BOLT

Rear camshaft cover on 1410 and 1468cc engines

installation details. Using seal driver MD998364 or equivalent, for engines except the 1985–88 1997cc and MD998307 or equivalent, for 1985–88 1977cc engines, install a new oil seal after the camshaft is in place.

NOTE: If the dowel pin hole of the camshaft sprocket will not align with the dowel pin on the camshaft on the 1597cc engine, the shaft can be easily turned by striking the projections on the shaft, just behind No. 2 exhaust valve cam, with a punch. Make sure that the crankshaft does not turn. On the 1985–88 1997cc engine, turn the camshaft until the dowel pin on the shaft end is in the 12 o'clock position. This will ensure correct camshaft sprocket installation.

7. Tighten the sprocket bolt to 50–

60 ft. lbs. on the 1994cc, 1997cc and 2555cc engines; 44–55 ft. lbs. on the 1597cc. Tighten the rocker cover bolts to 5 ft. lbs.

1410 and 1468cc Engines

1. Remove the cylinder head. Remove the cylinder head rear cover.

2. Remove the camshaft thrust case tightening bolt located on top of the rear mounting boss.

3. Carefully slide the camshaft and thrust case (attached to the rear of the cam) out the rear of the cylinder head.

4. Installation is the reverse of removal. Coat all parts with clean engine oil prior to installation.

Piston and Connecting Rod

POSITIONING

NOTE: For all piston and connecting rod overhaul procedures, please refer to "Engine Rebuilding" in the Unit Repair section.

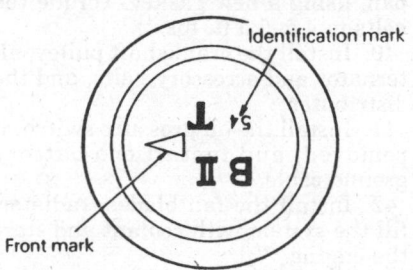

Typical piston identification and direction indicator

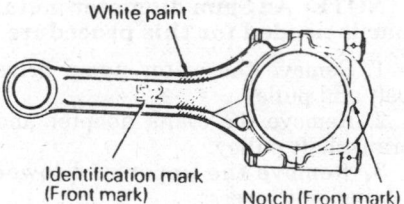

Typical connecting rod identification and front indicator

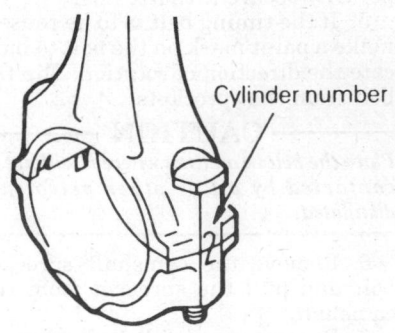

Location of cylinder number on connecting rod

ENGINE LUBRICATION

Oil Pan

REMOVAL & INSTALLATION

The engine may have be raised off its mount for the pan to clear the suspension crossmember. However, on some front wheel drive models, there is usually enough clearance without raising the engine.

1. Remove the underbody splash shield.
2. Unbolt the left and right engine mounts (except front wheel drive).
3. Jack up the engine under the the bell housing (except front wheel drive).
4. Remove the oil pan.
5. Installation is the reverse of removal.

Rear Main Bearing Oil Seal

REMOVAL & INSTALLATION

The rear main oil seal is located in a housing on the rear of the block. To replace the seal, remove the transmission and do the work from underneath the car (except front wheel drive models) or remove the end housing and do the work on the bench.

1. Remove the housing from the block.
2. Remove the separator from the housing.
3. Pry out the oil seal.
4. Lightly oil the replacement seal. The oil seal should be installed so that the seal plate fits into the inner contact surface of the seal case. Install the separator with the oil holes facing down.

Oil Pump

REMOVAL & INSTALLATION

1410 and 1468cc Engines

1. Remove the timing belt as previously described.
2. Remove the oil pan as previously described.
3. Remove the oil screen.
4. Unbolt and remove the front case assembly.
5. Remove the oil pump cover.
6. Remove the inner and outer gears from the front case.

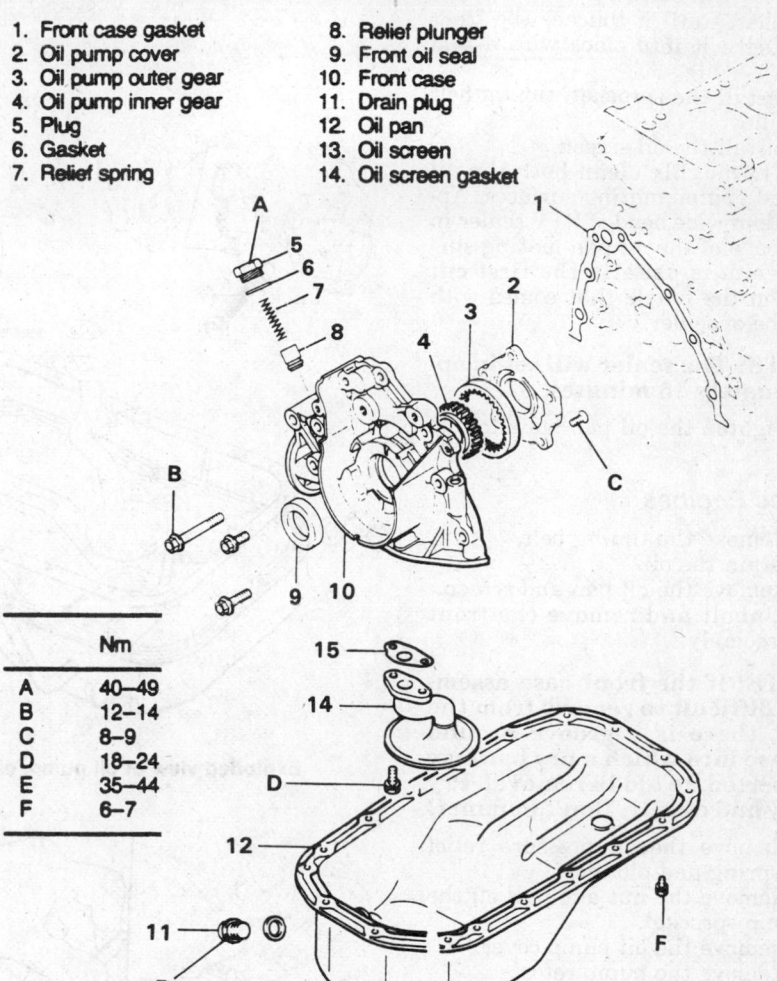

1. Front case gasket
2. Oil pump cover
3. Oil pump outer gear
4. Oil pump inner gear
5. Plug
6. Gasket
7. Relief spring
8. Relief plunger
9. Front oil seal
10. Front case
11. Drain plug
12. Oil pan
13. Oil screen
14. Oil screen gasket

	Nm
A	40—49
B	12—14
C	8—9
D	18—24
E	35—44
F	6—7

1410 and 1468cc engine oil pump, front case and oil pan

NOTE: The outer gear has no identifying marks to indicate direction of rotation. Clean the gear and mark it with an indelible marker.

7. Remove the plug, relief valve spring and relief valve from the case.
8. Check the front case for damage or cracks. Replace the front seal. Replace the oil screen O-ring. Clean all parts thoroughly with a safe solvent.
9. Check the pump gears for wear or damage. Clean the gears thoroughly and place them in position in the case to check the clearances. There is a crescent-shaped piece between the two gears. This piece is the reference point for two measurements. Use the following clearances for determining gear wear:

Outer gear face-to-case: 0.0039–0.0079 in.

Outer gear teeth-to-crescent: 0.0087–0.0134 in.

Outer gear end-play: 0.0016–0.0039 in.

Inner gear teeth-to-crescent: 0.0083–0.0126 in.

Inner gear end-play: 0.0016–0.0039 in.

10. Check that the relief valve can slide freely in the case.
11. Check the relief valve spring for damage. The relief valve free length should be 1.850 in. Load/length should be 9.5 lb. at 1.575 in.
12. Thoroughly coat both oil pump gears with clean engine oil and install them in the correct direction of rotation.
13. Install the pump cover and torque the bolts to 7 ft. lbs.
14. Coat the relief valve and spring with clean engine oil, install them and tighten the plug to 30–36 ft. lbs.
15. Position a new front case gasket, coated with sealer, on the engine and install the front case. Torque the bolts to 10 ft. lbs. Note that the bolts have different shank lengths.
16. Coat the lips of a new seal with clean engine oil and slide it along the

crankshaft until it touches the front case. Drive it into place with a seal driver.

17. Install the sprocket, timing belt and pulley.

18. Install the oil screen.

19. Thoroughly clean both the oil pan and engine mating surfaces. Apply a 4mm wide bead of RTV sealer in the groove of the oil pan mating surface. 4mm is usually the first cut mark on the nozzle that comes with the tube of sealer.

NOTE: The sealer will set in approximately 15 minutes.

20. Tighten the oil pan bolts to 5–6 ft. lbs.

1597cc Engines

1. Remove the timing belt.
2. Drain the oil.
3. Remove the oil pan and screen.
4. Unbolt and remove the front case assembly.

NOTE: If the front case assembly is difficult to remove from the block, there is a groove around the case into which a pry bar may be inserted, to aid in removal. Pry slowly and evenly. Don't hammer!

5. Remove the oil pressure relief plug, spring and plunger.
6. Remove the nut and pull off the oil pump sprocket.
7. Remove the oil pump cover.
8. Remove the pump rotor.
9. Check the case for cracks and damage.
10. Check the oil screen for damage.
11. Replace the oil screen O-ring.
12. Thoroughly clean all parts in a safe solvent.
13. Place the rotor back in the case to check clearances.
    Side clearance: 0.0024–0.0047in.
    Tip clearance: 0.0016–0.0047 in.
    Body clearance: 0.0039–0.0063 in.
    Shaft-to-cover clearance: 0.0008–0.0020 in.
14. Check that the relief valve plunger slides smoothly in its bore.
15. Check the relief valve spring. The free length should be 1.850 in.; the load/length should be 9.5 lb. @ 1.575 in.
16. Install a new oil seal, coated with clean engine oil, into the oil pump cover. Drive it into place using a hammer and flat block.
17. Install a new cover gasket in the groove in the case.
18. Coat the rotor with clean engine oil and install it in the cover.
19. Install the cover and tighten the bolts.
20. Install the sprocket and tighten the nut to 28 ft. lbs.
21. Coat the oil relief valve plunger

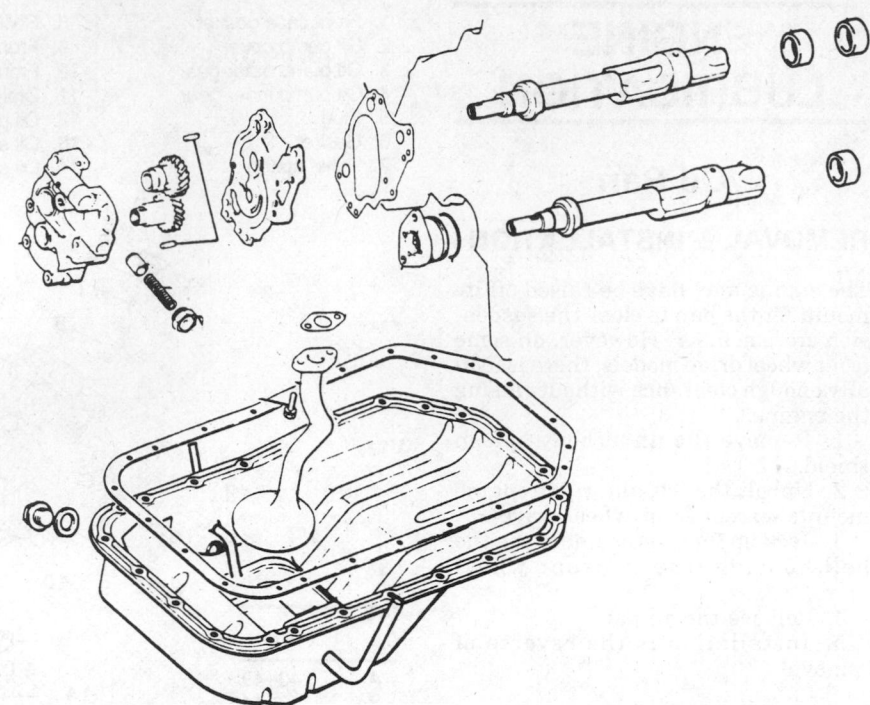

Exploded view of oil pump, oil pan and silent shafts, 2555cc engine

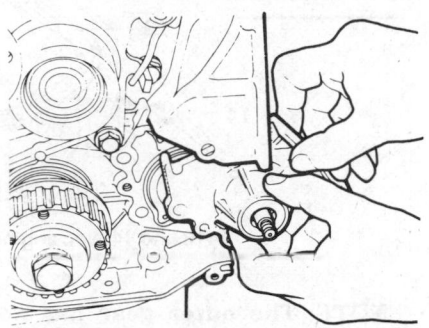

Removing the oil pump cover from 1597cc engines

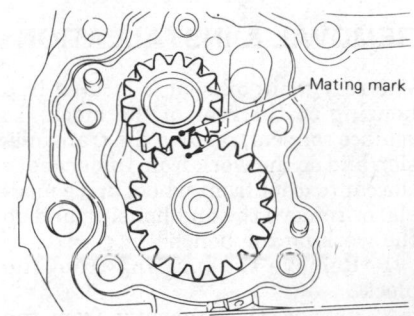

Oil pump gear mating marks on the 1997cc engine

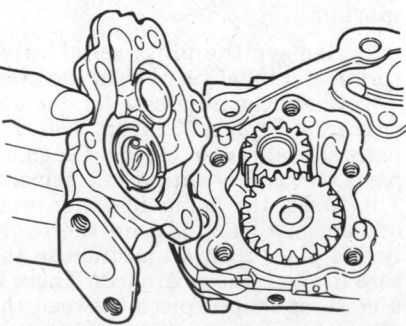

Oil pump cover removal from the 1997cc engine

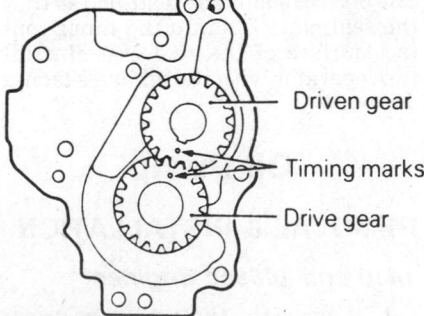

Installation of oil pump drive and driven gears and matching of timing marks, 2555cc engine

with clean engine oil and install it, along with the spring and plug.

22. Install a new case gasket, coated with sealer, on the block and install the case. Torque the case bolts to 13 fft. lbs.

NOTE: There are two different lengths of case bolts.

23. Install the screen. Tighten the bolts to 18 ft. lbs.

24. Install the oil pan as previously described.

1997 and 2555cc Engines

1. Remove the timing chain as previously described.
2. Remove the oil pump cover and gears.
3. Remove the relief valve plug, spring and plunger.
4. Thoroughly clean all parts in a safe solvent and check for wear and damage.
5. Clean all orifices and passages.
6. Place the gear back in the pump body and check clearances.
   Gear teeth-to-body: 0.0041–0.0059 in.
   Driven gear end play: 0.0024–0.0047 in.
   Drive gear-to-bearing (front end): 0.0008–0.0018 in.
   Drive gear-to-bearing (rear end): 0.0017–0.0026 in.

NOTE: If gear replacement is necesssary, the entire pump body must be replaced.

7. Check the relief valve spring for wear or damage. Free length should be 1.850 in.; load/length should be 9.5 lb @ 1.575 in.
8. Assembly is the reverse of disassembly. Make sure that the gears are installed with the mating marks aligned.

ENGINE COOLING

Radiator

REMOVAL & INSTALLATION

1. Remove the splash panel from the bottom of the car. Drain the radiator by opening the petcock. Remove the shroud on models so equipped. On the Conquest, remove the battery.
2. Disconnect the radiator hoses at the engine. On automatic transmission cars, disconnect and plug the transmission lines to the bottom of the radiator.
3. Remove the two retaining bolts from either side of the radiator. Lift out the radiator. On front wheel drive models, disconnect the electric fan wiring harness. Do not remove the fan motor, blades or bracket—remove as a unit with the radiator.
4. Install the radiator in the reverse order of removal. Tighten the retaining bolts gradually in a criss-cross pattern.

— CAUTION —

Work around the electric cooling fan when the engine is cold or disconnect the negative battery cable. On some models, the fan will run to cool the engine even when the ignition is off.

Water Pump

REMOVAL & INSTALLATION

Rear Wheel Drive

1. Drain the cooling system.
2. Remove the fan shroud and radiator if necessary for working room.
3. Remove the alternator belt and accessory belts.
4. Remove the fan blades and/or automatic hub, if equipped.
5. Remove the water pump assembly from the timing chain case or the cylinder block.
6. Installation is the reverse of removal.
7. Fill the radiator with coolant and test for leaks.

Front Wheel Drive

1. Drain the cooling system.
2. Remove the drive belt and water pump pulley.
3. Remove the timing belt covers and timing belt tensioner, as explained earlier.
4. Remove the water pump bolts and alternator bracket.
5. Remove the water pump.

NOTE: The pump is not rebuildable. If there are signs of damage, or leakage from the seals or vent hole, the unit must be replaced.

6. Discard the O-ring in the front end of the water pipe. Install a new O-ring coated with water.
7. Using a new gasket, mount the water pump and alternator bracket on the engine. Torque the bolts with a head mark "4" to 10 ft. lbs.; the bolts with a head mark "7" to 20 ft. lbs.
8. The remainder of assembly is the reverse of disassembly. Fill the system with coolant.

Thermostat

REMOVAL & INSTALLATION

Rear Wheel Drive

The thermostat is located in the intake manifold under the upper radiator hose.
1. Drain the coolant below the level of the thermostat.
2. Remove the two retaining bolts and lift the thermostat housing off the

intake manifold with the hose still attached.

NOTE: It is not necessary to remove the upper radiator hose.

3. Lift the thermostat out of the manifold.
4. Install the thermostat in the reverse order of removal. Use a new gasket and coat the mating surfaces with sealer.

Front Wheel Drive

1. Drain the cooling system to a point below the thermostat level.
2. Remove the air cleaner.
3. Disconnect the hose at the thermostat water pipe.
4. Remove the water pipe support bracket nut.

NOTE: This nut is also an intake manifold nut. It is VERY difficult to get to. A deep offset 12mm box wrench is used to remove or replace it.

5. Unbolt and remove the thermostat housing and pipe.
6. Lift out the thermostat. Discard the gasket.
7. Clean the mating surfaces of the housing and manifold thoroughly.
8. Install the thermostat with the spring facing downward and position a new gasket. The jiggle valve in the thermostat should be on the manifold side.
9. Install the housing and pipe assembly. Torque the housing bolts to 10 ft. lbs.; the intake manifold nut to 14 ft. lbs.
10. Refill the system with coolant.

EMISSION CONTROLS

NOTE: Please refer to "Emission Control" in the Unit Repair section for system maintenance procedures. Due to the complex nature of modern electronic engine control systems, comprehensive diagnosis and testing procedures fall outside the confines of this repair manual. For complete information on diagnosis, testing and repair procedures concerning all modern engine and emission control systems, please refer to 'Chilton's Guide to Electronic Engine Controls''.

MAINTENANCE REMINDER LAMP

An EGR maintenance reminder lamp

will illuminate at approximately 50,000 miles and after the EGR inspection/service has been accomplished, the lamp timer switch must be reset.

The reset button is located on the back of the instrument panel, on the left side of the speedometer cable junction or below it. It is only necessary to slide the switch from on side of the switch to the other, to reset the sensor.

FUEL SYSTEM

Fuel Filter

REPLACEMENT

The fuel filter should be replaced every 12,000 miles. The filter is usually located on the left-handed inner fender near the master cylinder. Loosen both hose clamps and remove the lines from the filter. Pull the filter from its bracket and discard it. Snap the replacement filter into the bracket. Install the lines on the filter and tighten the hose clamps. Start the engine and check for leaks.

NOTE: On models with fuel injection (Turbo), relieve fuel system pressure before removing filter. Follow Step 1 of "Fuel Pump Removal," turbocharged engines.

Fuel Pump

TESTING

Without EFI And Turbocharger

A mechanical fuel pump is used and is attached to the engine. A cartridge type fuel filter is used and is located in the engine compartment.
Disconnect the fuel line from the carburetor and attach a pressure tester to the end of the line. Crank the engine. The pressure should agree with the figure given in the "Tune-Up Specification" chart.

With EFI And Turbocharger

An electric fuel pump is used and is located either in the fuel tank or behind the left rear wheel, A high pressure fuel filter is used and is located in the engine compartment.
There is a connector for checking the fuel function in the engine compartment, under the battery. The fuel pump can be operated by connecting the terminals with jumper wires.
1. Connect jumper wires to termi-

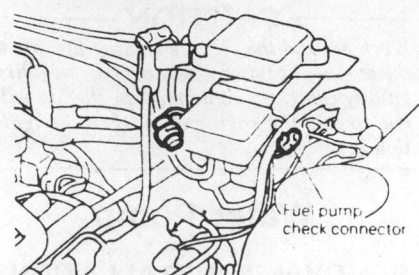

Colt Turbo fuel pump test connectors

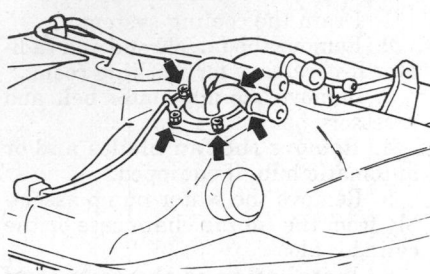

Colt Turbo electric fuel pump location. The arrows indicate the mounting bolts

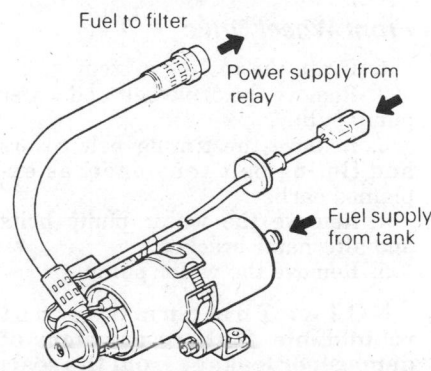

Fuel to filter
Power supply from relay
Fuel supply from tank

Conquest electric fuel pump

nals 1 and 2 of fuel pump check connector, and check to ensure that when operating, the sound of fuel pump can be heard.
2. When no operating sound can be heard, check for defective connector, wiring, etc.
3. If there is nothing wrong with connector and wiring, disconnect the fuel pump connector at the pump and energize the pump. If pump still fails to operate, replace it.

REMOVAL & INSTALLATION

Without Turbocharger

The pump is mounted on the front side of the engine and is driven by an eccentric on the camshaft.
1. Remove the fuel lines.
2. Unbolt the pump mounting bolts, remove the pump, insulator, and gasket.
3. Coat both sides of a new insula-

tor and gasket with sealer and install the pump in the reverse order of removal.

Turbocharger

COLT

─── **CAUTION** ───

Working around gasoline is extremely dangerous unless precautions are taken! NEVER smoke! Make sure the electrical system is disconnected. Avoid prolonged contact of gasoline with the skin. Wear safety glasses. Avoid prolonged breathing of gasoline vapors.

1. Reduce pressure in the fuel lines as follows:
   a. Remove the rear seat cushion and carpet. Note the fuel pump wire running along the floor. It has an in-wire connector in it.
   b. Start the engine and uncouple the connector in the wire. Let the engine stop by itself.
   c. Turn the key to OFF.
   d. Disconnect the negative battery cable.
2. Remove the fuel tank.
3. Disconnect the hoses at the pump.
4. Unbolt and remove the pump.
5. Installation is the reverse of removal. Use a new gasket. Replace any cracked or brittle fuel hoses.

CONQUEST

1. See Step 1 of the Colt procedure, above, to reduce fuel line pressure.
2. Raise and support the rear of the car on jackstands.
3. Remove the left rear wheel.
4. Loosen the fuel tank mounting strap nut and lower the tank slightly.
5. Remove the fuel pump support.
6. Disconnect the hoses from the pump and remove the pump.
7. Installation is the reverse of removal.

Carburetor

REMOVAL & INSTALLATION

1. Remove the solenoid valve wiring.
2. Disconnect the air cleaner breather hose, air duct and vacuum tube.
3. Remove the air cleaner.
4. Remove the air cleaner case.
5. Disconnect the accelerator and shift cables (automatic transmission) at the carburetor.
6. Disconnect the purge valve hose; remove the vacum compensator, and fuel lines.
7. Drain the coolant.
8. Remove the water hose between the carburetor and the cylinder head.

9. Remove the carburetor.

10. Installation is the reverse of removal.

THROTTLE LINKAGE ADJUSTMENT

Adjust the stopper bolt to a distance of 0.750–0.040 in. from inside of the bolt holding bracket, to the contact point of the pedal lever while holding the carburetor throttle plates closed. The yoke at the carburetor end of the accelerator rod is serrated to allow the yoke to be loosened and moved so that a minimal readjustment of the stopper adjusting bolt is needed to give the proper throttle release and opening.

FLOAT LEVEL ADJUSTMENT

1981–83

A sight glass is fitted at the float chamber and the fuel level can be checked without disassembling the carburetor. Normal fuel level is within the level mark on the sight glass.

The fuel level adjustment is corrected by increasing or decreasing the number of needle valve packings. The float level may be off 0.160 in., above or below the level mark and the operation of the engine would not be affected.

1984–88 (Dry Setting)

1. Invert the float chamber cover assembly without a gasket.

2. Position a universal float level gauge and measure the distance from the bottom of the float to the surface of the float chamber cover. The distance should by 0.787 in. (20mm), 0.0394 in. (1mm).

3. If the reading is not within this range, the shim under the needle seat must be changed. Shim kits are available which contain 3 shims; 0.0118 in. (0.3mm), 0.0157 in. (0.4mm) and 0.0196 in. (0.5mm).

FAST IDLE ADJUSTMENT

1. Start the engine and open the throttle valve about 45 degrees. Manually close the choke valve and slowly return the throttle valve to the stop position.

2. With a tachometer, check that the fast idle speed is 2000 rpm or lower. (Not less than 1700 rpm). Adjust the speed as necessary with the fast idle speed screw.

3. Cold start the engine and check the automatic choke and fast idle operation.

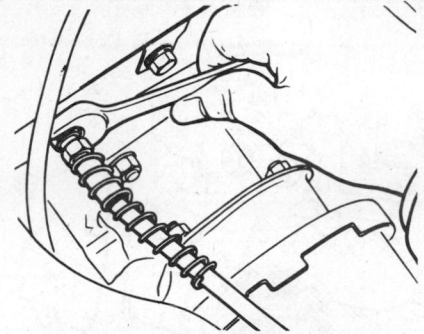

Throttle linkage adjustment (typical)

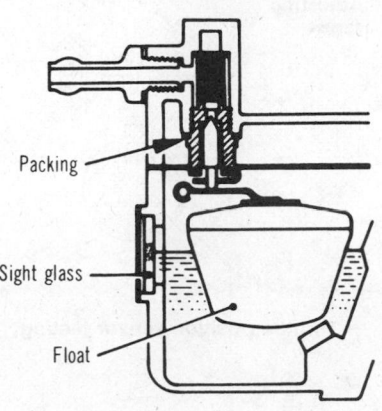

Packing

Sight glass

Float

Float level adjustment—1981–83

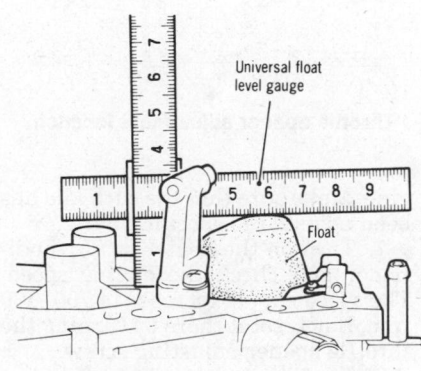

Universal float level gauge

Float

Dry float level adjustment—1984–88

AUTOMATIC CHOKE ADJUSTMENT

1981–84

The choke is adjusted by turning the screw located on the choke spring bracket. The latest model years could have a tamper resistant cover on the screw. If choke adjustment is absolutely necessary, then the cover could be removed to make the adjustment. A new cover should be installed on the screw after the adjustment is made.

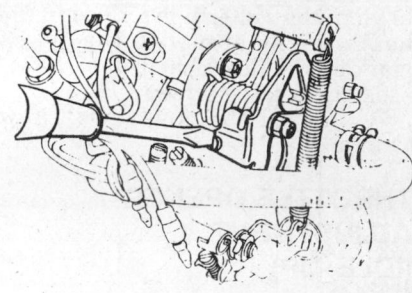

Adjustment of choke—1981–88

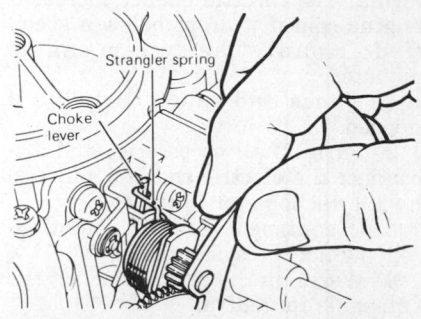

Strangler spring

Choke lever

Removing the choke bracket bridge on 1985–86 models with feedback carburetor

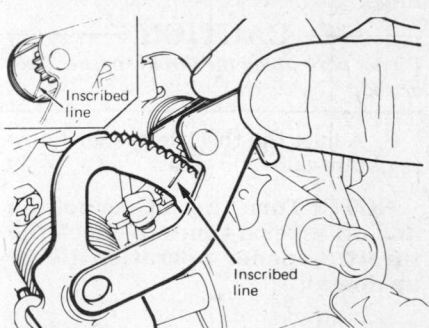

Inscribed line

Inscribed line

Aligning the choke gear and cam mating marks

1985–88

1. Remove the air cleaner and choke mechanism cover.

NOTE: Some models might have headless, tamperproof screws securing the choke mechanism cover. These have to be drilled out. In that case, it's easier to remove the carburetor.

2. Remove the bracket bridging the choke spring gear and choke actuating cam.

3. Slip the choke strangler spring from the choke lever. Align the scribed black line on the choke gear with the mark below the teeth on the actuating cam and reassemble all parts.

4. Temporarily tighten the lower bracket screw.

5. Move the arm at the upper screw

to align the center line scribed in the notch on the arm with the punch mark on the float chamber.

6. Tighten the screws.

7. Install the cover with new screws.

THROTTLE OPENER ADJUSTMENT (IDLE–UP)

1981–84

This system is not available in California. Ths throttle opener increases engine rpm if it drops below a specified amount. The system can be adjusted.

1. Check and adjust curb idle if needed.

2. Turn off all accessories and disconnect the electric radiator fan and hook a tachometer to the engine.

3. If equipped with air conditioning, switch the system on.

4. Warm up the engine and set the transaxle in neutral.

5. Remove the pressure on throttle opener by lifting on the unit with a finger.

—— CAUTION ——

Do not push up on the throttle opener lever or rod.

6. Adjust the throttle opener screw to obtain 800–900 rpm.

NOTE: Turn the A/C switch on and off several times to check the throttle opener operation (lever up/down).

1985–88

EXCEPT 4WD VISTA

1. Check the vacuum hoses and electrical connectors.

2. Disconnect the vacuum hose at the throttle opener nipple.

3. Connect a vacuum pump to the throttle opener nipple.

4. Connect a tachometer to the engine.

5. Run the engine to normal operating temperature at idle.

6. Apply 300mm Hg. (11.8 in. Hg.) vacuum with the pump. The idle speed should increase. If not, replace the throttle opener dashpot.

4WD VISTA

1. Turn all lights and accessories off.

2. Place the transaxle in neutral.

3. Disconnect the electric fan connector.

4. Apply the parking brake.

5. Make sure that the wheels are in the straight ahead position.

6. Connect a tachometer to the en-

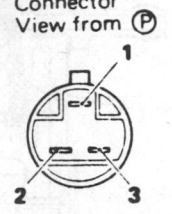

Throttle position sensor testing

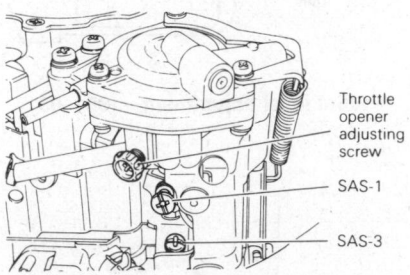

Throttle opener adjustment location

gine. Make sure that the curb idle has been adjusted to specification.

7. Turn on the heater or air conditioner and check the engine speed. The speed should increase to 700–800 rpm. If not, set it there by turning the throttle opener adjusting screw.

8. Turn the A/C or heater off and on several times to verify that the throttle opener responds.

THROTTLE POSITION SENSOR TESTING

1985–88 USA Models

1. Disconnect the TPS connector.

2. Check the resistance with an ohmmeter between terminals 2 and 3 (the bottom, adjacent terminals in the connector). With the throttle closed, resistance should be 1.2 ohms. Resistance should slowly increase to 4.9 ohms at wide open throttle.

NOTE: For all carburetor overhaul procedures, please refer to

"CARBURETOR SERVICE" in the Unit Repair section.

FUEL INJECTION

Due to the complex nature of modern fuel injection systems, comprehensive diagnosis and testing procedures fall outside the confines of this repair manual. For complete information on fuel injection diagnosis, testing and repair procedures, please refer to *"Chilton's Guide To Fuel Injection and Feedback Carburetors."*

MANUAL TRANSMISSION

REMOVAL & INSTALLATION

For all overhaul procedures, please refer to "Manual Transmission Overhaul" in the Unit Repair section.

Rear Wheel Drive—Except Conquest

NOTE: The clutch housing and transmission are removed as a unit.

1. Disconnect the battery cables, negative (ground) cable first.

2. Remove the battery cable from the starter and fasten it away from the transmission.

3. Remove the starter.

4. Remove the top two clutch housing bolts.

From inside the passenger compartment:

5. Untie the leather or rubber shift boot and pull the rug back over the shift lever. If the car is equipped with a console it is necessary to remove same for access to the shift lever retaining plate etc.

6. Place the four speed transmission in second gear and the five speed transmission in first gear. Unscrew the four retaining bolts and remove the gearshift lever from the tailshaft housing.

From underneath the car:

7. Jack up the front of the car and support it on stands.

8. Drain the transmission oil.

9. Disconnect the transmission

backup light switch and the speedometer cable.

10. Remove the driveshaft as outlined in the next chapter.

11. Disconnect the exhaust pipe at the manifold and the engine side bracket. Drop the pipe down and out of the way.

12. Disconnect the clutch cable.

13. Position a jack under the transmission cover to support it when the crossmember is removed. Use a board between the cover and the jack.

14. Remove the two attaching bolts from the transmission-to-crossmember mount.

15. Unscrew the two bolts at each side of the crossmember and remove the crossmember.

16. Remove the remaining bolts from the clutch housing.

17. Pull the transmission rearward and lower it to the floor.

--------- CAUTION ---------
When removing the transmission, pull it straight back so as not to damage the pilot bering, clutch disc, or pressure plate.

18. Installation of the transmission is basically the reverse of the removal procedure, noting the following points:

a. When installing the gearshift assembly, position the lever in First gear so that the nylon bushing is vertical. Make sure that no dirt enters the transmission housing during the installation of the shifter.

b. Refill the transmission with gear oil.

c. Adjust the clutch as described in the following "Clutch" section.

Conquest

1. Raise and support the front and rear of the car on jackstands.

2. Remove the driveshaft.

3. Drain the transmission.

4. Disconnect the speedometer cable and switch connector at the transmission.

5. Remove the clutch slave cylinder.

6. Remove the bell housing cover.

7. Remove the starter.

8. Remove the two upper transmission mounting bolts.

9. Support the transmission with a floor jack.

10. Remove the remaining transmission mounting bolts.

11. Remove the engine support bracket, insulator assembly and ground strap.

12. Place the shift lever in the NEUTRAL position. Remove the trim plate and unbolt the shifter assembly, removing it and the stopper plate underneath it.

13. Cover the rear of the cylinder head with a heavy cloth to prevent damage from contact with the firewall.

14. Slowly lower the jack, pull it rearward to disengage the transmission from the clutch.

15. Installation is the reverse of removal. Torque the transmission mounting bolts to 35 ft. lbs.; the starter bolts to 20 ft. lbs.

MANUAL TRANSAXLE

For all manual transaxle overhaul procedures, please refer to "Manual Transaxle" in the Unit Repair section.

Front Wheel Drive—Colt and Champ

1. Disconnect the battery ground (negative) cable.

2. Disconnect from the transaxle: the clutch cable, speedometer cable, back-up light harness, starter motor and the four upper bolts connecting the engine to the transaxle.

3. On cars with a turbocharger, remove the air cleaner case, the actuator mounting bolts, the pin coupling, the actuator and shaft and remove the actuator. Discard the collar used with the pin and replace it with a new collar. On cars with a 5-speed transaxle, disconnect the selector control valve.

4. Jack up the car and support on jackstands.

5. Remove the front wheels. Remove the splash shield. Drain the transaxle fluid.

6. Remove the shift rod and extension. It may be necessary to remove any heat shields that interfere.

7. On 1985–86 Colts, remove the stabilizer bar from the lower arm and disconnect the lower arm from the body side.

8. Remove the right and left driveshafts from the transaxle case. See halfshaft removal in this section.

9. Disconnect the range selector cable (if equipped). Remove the engine rear cover.

10. Support the weight of the engine from above (chain hoist). Support the transaxle and remove the remaining lower mounting bolts.

11. Remove the transaxle mount insulator bolt.

12. Remove (slide back and away from the engine) and lower the transaxle.

13. To install reverse the removal

procedure. Be sure to connect all controls and wiring. Use new retaining rings when installing the driveshafts.

2WD Vista

1. Remove the battery and tray.

2. Remove the coolant reservoir.

3. Remove the air cleaner.

4. Disconnect the clutch cable, speedometer cable, and backup light wiring from the transaxle.

5. Remove the upper 5 engine-to-transaxle bolts.

6. Disconnect the select control lever and switch harness.

7. Remove the starter.

8. Disconnect and tag all wiring from the transaxle.

9. Jack up and support the front end.

10. Remove the wheels.

11. Drain the transaxle fluid.

12. Remove the extension and shift rod from the engine compartment.

13. Remove the stabilizer and strut bar from the lower control arm.

14. Remove the left and right axle shafts.

15. Support the transaxle with a floor jack, taking care to avoid damaging the pan.

16. Remove the bell housing cover.

17. Remove the remaining transaxle-to-engine bolts.

18. Remove the transaxle mounting bolt.

19. Lower the jack and slide the transaxle from under the car.

20. Installation is the reverse of removal. Torque the mount bolt to 30 ft. lbs.; the engine-to-transaxle bolts to 45 ft. lbs.

4WD Vista

1. Disconnect the battery cables at the battery. Remove the coolant reserve tank.

2. Disconnect the speedometer cable, shift control cable and back-up light harness at the transaxle.

3. Remove the range select control valves and connectors.

4. Tag and disconnect all other wiring attached to the transaxle.

5. Remove the clutch slave cylinder.

6. Remove the vacuum reservoir tank.

7. Disconnect the starter wiring.

8. Remove the upper 5 engine-to-transaxle bolts.

9. Raise and support the car on jackstands.

10. Remove the front wheels, lower engine cover and skid plate.

11. Drain the transaxle and transfer case.

12. Remove the driveshaft.

13. Remove the transfer case extension housing.

14. Remove the left and right halfshafts.

15. Disconnect the right strut from the lower arm.

16. Remove the right fender liner.

17. Take up the weight of the transaxle with a floor jack.

NOTE: Use a wide board on the floor jack pedestal to help spread the weight over a large area of the transaxle.

18. Remove the bell housing cover bolts and remove the cover.

19. Remove the remaining engine-to-transaxle bolts.

20. Remove the transaxle mount insulator bolt.

21. Remove the transaxle mounting bracket attaching bolts.

22. Move the transaxle/transfer case assembly to the right. Tilt the right side of the transaxle down, until the transfer case is about level with the upper part of the steering rack tube, then turn it to the left and lower the assembly. Observe the following torques:

Transaxle mount insulator nut: 55–58 ft. lbs.

Transaxle mounting bracket bolts: 25–30 ft. lbs.

Engine-to-transaxle bolts: 45 ft. lbs.

CLUTCH

NOTE: All models use a cable-actuated clutch, except the Conquest and 4wd Vista, which employ hydraulically-actuated clutches.

REMOVAL & INSTALLATION

1. On the 4WD Vista, remove the slave cylinder. Remove the transmission or transaxle as outlined.

2. Insert a pilot shaft or an old input shaft into the center of the clutch disc, pressure plate, and the pilot bearing in the crankshaft.

3. With the pilot tool supporting the clutch disc, loosen the pressure plate bolts gradually and in a criss-cross pattern.

4. Remove the pressure plate and clutch disc.

5. Clean the transmission and clutch housing. Clean the flywheel surface with a non-oil based solvent.

NOTE: Before assembly, slide the clutch disc up and down on the transmission input shaft to check for any binding. Remove any rough spots with crocus cloth

and then lightly coat the shaft with Lubriplate.

To remove the throwout bearing assembly:

6. Remove the return clip and take out the throwout bearing carrier and the bearing.

7. To replace the throwout arm use a $\frac{3}{16}$ in. punch, knock out the throwout shaft spring pin and remove the shaft, springs, and the center lever.

8. Do not immerse the throwout bearing in solvent; it is permanently lubricated. Blow and wipe it clean. Check the bearing for wear, deterioration, or burning. Replace the bearing if there is any question about its condition.

9. Check the shafts, lever, and springs for wear and defects. Replace them if necessary.

10. Examine the clutch disc for the following before reusing it:
    a. Loose rivets.
    b. Burned facing.
    c. Oil or grease on the facing.
    d. Less than 0.012 in. left between the rivet head and the top of the facing.

11. Check the pressure plate and replace it if any of the following conditions exist:
    a. Scored or excessively worn.
    b. Bent or distorted diaphragm spring.
    c. Loose rivets.

12. Insert the control lever into the clutch housing. Install the two return sprins and the throwout shaft.

13. Lock the shift lever to the shaft with the spring pin.

14. Fill the shaft oil seal with multi-purpose grease.

15. Install the throwout bearing carrier and the bearing. Install the return clip.

16. Grease the carrier groove and inner surface.

17. Lightly grease the clutch disc splines.

NOTE: The clutch is installed with the larger boss facing the transmission.

18. Support the clutch disc and pressure plate with the pilot tool.

19. Turn the pressure plate so that its balance mark aligns with the notch in the flywheel.

20. Install the pressure plate-to-flywheel bolts hand-tight. Using a torque wrench and, working in a criss-cross pattern, tighten the bolts to 11–15 ft. lbs.

21. Install the transmission as outlined.

22. Adjust the clutch as described in the following section.

CLUTCH ADJUSTMENTS
Front Wheel Drive
(In.)

Model	Pedal Height
1981–84 Colt	7.10-7.30
1985–88 Colt, Vista	6.20-6.40
1985–88 4WD Vista	7.10-7.30

Model	Pedal Free-play
1981–84 Colt	0.80-1.20
1985–88 Vista	0.60-0.80
1985–88 4WD Visa	0.04-0.12

Model	Cable Free-play
1981–84 Colt	0.20-0.24
1985–88 Colt Vista	0.00-0.04

Model	Pedal-to-floorboard Clearance
1981–84 Colt	1.40-1.60
1985–88 Colt	3.10 +
1985–88 2WD, 4WD Vista	2.20 +

CLUTCH ADJUSTMENTS
Rear Wheel Drive Cars
(In.)

Model	Pedal Height
1981–83	7.1
1985–88	7.4-7.6

Model	Pedal Stroke
1981–84	6.0

Model	Pedal Free-play
1985–88	0.04-0.10

Model	Pedal Pad surface-to-floor
1985–88	1.4

ADJUSTMENTS

Pedal height Adjustment

1. Measure the distance between the floor and the top of the clutch pedal.

2. Refer to the chart above for proper distance. Loosen the clutch switch locknut and move the switch in or out as necessary.

Cable and Free–Play Adjustments

EXCEPT CONQUEST AND 4WD VISTA

1. Slightly pull the cable out from the firewall.

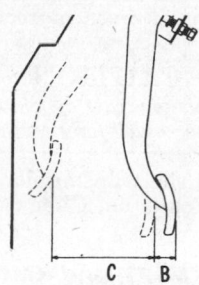

Dimension B and C

2. Turn the adjusting wheel on the cable until the play between the wheel and the cable is within the dimension listed in the accompanying chart.

3. Check the clutch free-play.

a. Jack up the front of the car and support it on stands.

b. Slide under and remove the rubber cover from the clutch housing.

c. Using a 0.030 in. feeler gauge, check the clearance between the pressure plate diaphragm spring and the throwout bearing.

4. If the free travel is not correct, make further adjustments at the cable adjusting wheel.

NOTE: Each turn of the adjusting wheel equals 0.060 in. of adjustment to the wheel and retainer clearance.

5. Lower the car and check the clutch operation.

CONQUEST AND 4WD VISTA

If free-play and pedal surface-to-floorboard adjustments are not within specification, there is air in the system. Follow the procedures listed below for bleeding the hydraulic system.

Clutch Master Cylinder

REMOVAL & INSTALLATION

1. Loosen the bleeder screw on the slave cylinder and drain the system.

2. Disconnect the pushrod from the clutch pedal.

3. Disconnect the clutch pedal from the pedal bracket.

4. Disconnect the fluid line from the master cylinder.

5. Unbolt and remove the master cylinder.

6. Installation is the reverse of removal. Bleed the system.

NOTE: On the 4WD Vista, the lower master cylnder mounting nut is accessed from inside the car.

Clutch Slave Cylinder

REMOVAL & INSTALLATION

1. Disconnect the clutch hose from the slave cylinder.

2. Unbolt and remove the cylinder from the clutch housing.

3. Installation is the reverse of removal. Bleed the system.

BLEEDING THE SYSTEM

NOTE: An assistant is needed for the bleeding operation.

1. Raise and support the car on jackstands.

2. Loosen the bleeder screw at the slave cylinder.

3. Make sure that the master cylinder is full.

4. Attach a length of rubber hose to the bleeder screw nipple and place the other end in a glass jar half full of clean brake fluid.

5. Have the assistant push the clutch pedal down slowly to the floor. If air is in the system, bubbles will appear in the jar as the pedal is being depressed.

6. When the pedal is at the floor, tighten the bleeder screw.

7. Repeat Steps 5 and 6 until no bubbles are found. Check the master cylinder level frequently to make sure of fluid level.

Clutch Cable

REMOVAL & INSTALLATION

1. Loosen the cable adjusting wheel inside the engine compartment.

2. Loosen the clutch pedal adjusting bolt locknut and loosen the adjusting bolt.

3. Remove the cable end from the clutch throwout lever.

4. Remove the cable end from the clutch pedal.

5. Installation is the reverse of removal.

NOTE: Lubricate the cable with engine oil and after installation, install pads isolating the cable from the intake manifold and from the rear side of the engine mount insulator on coupe, sedan, and hatchbacks only.

AUTOMATIC TRANSMISSION/ TRANSAXLE

REMOVAL & INSTALLATION

TorqueFlite A–904

1. The transmission and converter must be removed as an assembly; otherwise, converter drive plate, pump bushing, or the oil seal may be damaged. The drive plate will not support a load; therefore, none of the weight of the transmission should be allowed to rest on the plate during removal.

2. Disconnect negative cable from the battery for safety.

3. Remove the cooler lines at transmission.

4. Remove starter motor and cooler line bracket.

5. Loosen pan to drain transmission.

6. Rotate engine clockwise with socket wrench on crankshaft pulley bolt to position the bolts attaching torque converter to drive plate, and remove them.

7. Mark parts for reassembly then disconnect driveshaft at rear universal joint. Carefully pull shaft assembly out of the extension housing.

8. Disconnect gearshift rod and torque shaft assembly from transmission.

9. Disconnect throttle rod from lever at the left-side of trnasmission. Remove linkage bell crank from transmission if so equipped.

10. Remove the oil filter tube and speedometer cable.

11. Support the rear of the engine with jack or similar device.

12. Raise transmission slightly with service jack to relieve load on the supports.

13. Remove bolts securing transmission mount to crossmember and crossmember to frame, then remove crossmember.

14. Remove all bellhousing bolts.

15. Carefully work transmission converter assembly rearward off engine block dowels and disengage converter hub from end of crankshaft. Attach a small C-clamp to edge of bellhousing to hold coverter in place during transmission removal.

16. Lower transmission and remove assembly from under the vehicle.

17. To remove converter assembly, remove C-clamp from edge of bellhousing, then carefully slide assembly out of transmission.

18. Follow the removal procedure in

reverse order to install TorqueFlite transmission.

KM170, KM171, and KM172

NOTE: The transaxle and converter must be removed and installed as an assembly.

1. Remove the battery and tray. On cars with a turbochager, remove the air cleaner case.

2. Disconnect the throttle control cable at the carburetor and the manual control cable at te transaxle.

3. Disconnect from the transaxle: the inhibitor switch (neutral safety) connecter, fluid cooler hoses and the four upper bolts connecting the engine to the transaxle.

NOTE: Cap oil cooler hoses to prevent fluid loss.

4. Jack up the car and support on jackstands.

5. Remove the front wheels. Remove the engine splash shield.

6. Drain the transaxle fluid.

7. Disconnect the stabilizer bar at the lower arms, and disconnect the control arms from the body. Remove the right and left driveshafts from the transaxle case. See halfshaft removal in this section.

8. Disconnect the speedometer cable. Remove the starter motor.

9. Remove the lower cover from the converter housing. Remove the three bolts connecting the converter to the engine drive plate.

NOTE: Never support the full weight of the transaxle on the engine drive plate.

10. Turn and force the converter back and away from the engine drive plate.

11. Support the weight of the engine from above (chain hoist). Support the transaxle and remove the remaining mounting bolts.

12. Remove the transalxle mount insulator bolt.

13. Remove (slide away from the engine) and lower the transaxle and converter a an assembly.

14. To install reverse the removal procedure. Be sure to connect all controls, wiring and hoses. Use new retaining rings when installing the drive axles. Torque all indicated "7T" bolts to 39 ft. lbs.; all indicated "10T" bolts to 25 ft. lbs.

JM600

1. Drain the fluid.

2. Disconnect the battery ground.

3. Remove the dipstick and unbolt the filler tube.

4. Raise the front and rear of the car and support it on jackstands.

5. Remove the two topmost transmission-to-engine bolts.

6. Remove the starter.

7. Disconnect the oil cooler lines and cap them to avoid spillage.

8. Remove the bell housing cover.

9. Turn the crankshaft so that the torque converter bolts appear and remove them, turning the crankshaft for each bolt in turn.

10. Disconnect the speedometer cable at the transmission.

11. Disconnect the linkage and cross shaft.

12. Disconnect the ground strap.

13. Matchmark the flanges and remove the driveshaft.

14. Support the transmission with a transmission jack, and the engine with a floor jack.

15. Remove the rear engine support bracket.

16. Remove the remaining engine-to-transmission bolts.

17. Slowly lower the transmission while pulling it rearward to disengage it from the engine. Be careful to avoid dropping the torque converter.

18. Installation is the reverse of removal. Torque the torque converter-to-flywheel bolts to 42–46 ft. lbs.; the transmission-to-engine bolts to 32–40 ft. lbs. Adjust the linkage, fill the unit and roadtest the car.

PAN AND FILTER SERVICE

TorqueFlite A–904

1. Raise and support the vehicle.

2. Loosen the pan bolts from one end to the other allowing the fluid to drain out.

3. Unbolt the old filter from the pan.

4. Clean the pan and install a new filter. Tighten filter bolts to 35 inch lbs.

5. Install the pan and new gasket. Torque pan bolts to 6–9 ft. lbs.

6. Add four quarts of Dexron®II fluid, start the engine and move the lever through all positions, pausing momentarily in each. Add enough fluid to bring the level to the full mark on the dipstick.

JM600

1. Jack up the front of the car and support it safely on stands.

2. Slide a drain pan under the transmission. Loosen the rear oil pan bolts first, to allow most of the fluid to drain off.

3. Remove the remaining bolts and drop the pan.

4. Discard the old gasket, clean the pan, and install the pan with a new gasket.

5. Tighten the pan bolts to 4–6 ft.

lbs. in a criss-cross pattern. Lower car.

--- CAUTION ---

The transmission case is aluminum, so don't exert too much force on the bolts.

6. Refill the transmission through the dipstick tube. Check the fluid level.

KM170, KM171, and KM172

1. Jack up the front of the car and support it safely on jackstands. Remove splash shield.

2. Slide a drain pan under the differntial drain plug. Loosen and remove the plug and drain the fluid. Move the drain pan under the transaxle oil pan, remove the plug and drain the fluid. The transmission fluid cannot all be drained by just draining the oil pan.

3. Remove the pan retaining bolts and remove the pan.

4. The filter may be serviced at this time.

5. Use a new oil pan gasket and reinstall the pan in the reverse order of removal.

6. Replace both drain plugs. Lower car. Refill the transmission with 4.2 qts of Dexron®II fluid. Start the engine and allow to idle for at least two minutes. With the parking brake applied, move the selector to each position ending in neutral.

7. Add sufficient fluid to bring the level to the lower mark. Recheck the fluid level after the transmission is up to normal operating temperature.

KICKDOWN BAND ADJUSTMENT

TorqueFlite A–904

The kickdown band adjusting screw is located on the left side of the transmission case.

1. Loosen the locknut and back off approximately 5 turns. Test the adjustment screw for free turning in the transmission case.

2. Tighten the adjusting screw to 69 inch lbs. (the torque specifications shown are true torque with no adapter on the wrench).

3. Back off the adjusting screw 3½ turns.

4. Hold the adjusting screw to prevent turning and secure the locknut to 30–40 ft. lbs.

KM170

NOTE: No adjustment is possible on the KM171 and KM172.

1. Wipe all dirt and other contamination from the kickdown servo cover

and surrounding area. The cover is located to the right of the dipstick hole.

2. Remove the snap ring and then the cover.

3. Loosen the locknut.

4. Holding the kickdown servo piston from turning, tighten the adjusting screw to 7 ft. lbs. (84 inch lbs.) and then back it off. Repeat the tightening and backing off two times in order to ensure seating of the band on the drum.

5. Tighten the adjusting screw to 3.5 ft. lbs. (42 inch lbs.) and back off 3.5 times (counterclockwise).

6. Holding the adjusting screw against rotation, tighten the locknut nut to 11–15 ft. lbs.

7. Install a new seal ring (D-shaped) in the groove in the outside surface of the cover. Use care not to distort the seal ring.

8. Install the cover and then the snap ring.

KICKDOWN SWITCH ADJUSTMENT

JM600

The kickdown switch is locted on the upper post of the accelerator pedal. With the pedal fully depressed, a click should be heard just before the pedal bottoms out. If not, loosen the locknut and extend the switch until the pedal lever contacts the switch and a click is heard at the proper time.

LOW & REVERSE BAND ADJUSTMENT

TorqueFlite A–904

1. Raise and safely support the front of the car. Drain the transmission fluid and remove the oil pan.

2. The allen socket head adjusting screw is located at the servo end of the strut. Loosen and remove the locknut from the adjusting screw. Tighten the adjusting screw to 43 inch lbs. of true torque. Back off the adjusting screw 7 turns.

3. Install the locknut on the adjusting screw. Hold the adjusting screw in position and tighten the locknut to 25–35 ft. lbs.

4. Reinstall the oil pan using a new gasket. Refill the transmission with the proper amount of transmission fluid.

NEUTRAL SAFETY SWITCH ADJUSTMENT

TorqueFlite A–904

1. The inhibitor (Neutral) switch is

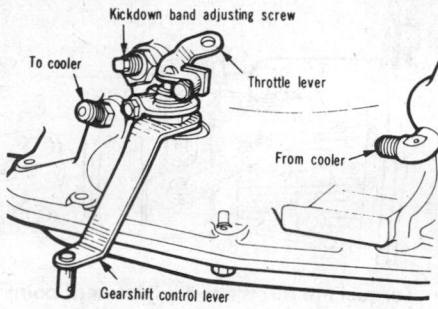

TorqueFlite kickdown band adjustment points

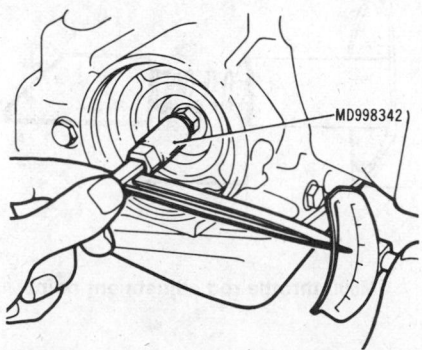

KM170 kickdown band adjustment point

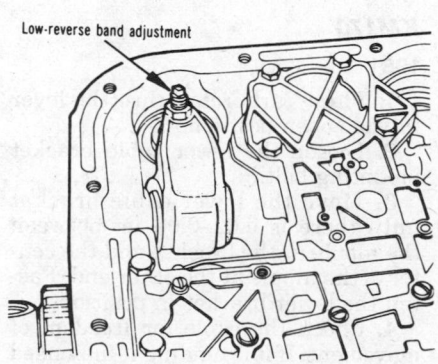

TorqueFlite low/reverse band adjustment

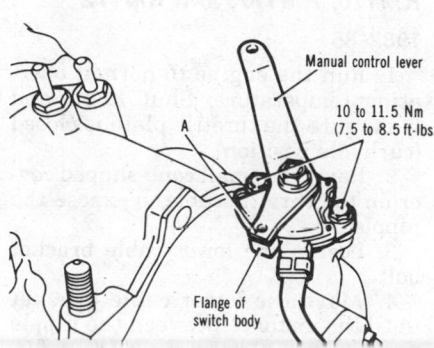

KM—170,171,172, neutral start switch adjustment

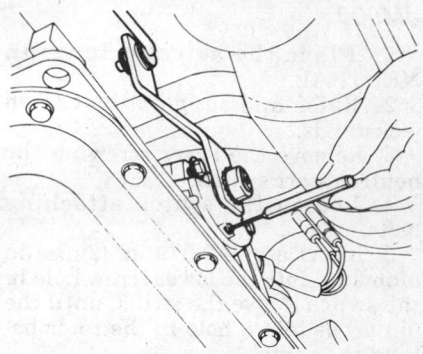

JM600 neutral start switch adjustment

located at the base of the shift control under the console cover.

2. Loosen the set screw that retains the shift lever handle to the shift lever. Remove the handle.

3. Remove the screws at the top and rear of the console, place the shift lever in "L" and remove the console. Put the lever in the "P" position.

4. Remove the top and side shift indicator panel mounting screws and pull the panel up. The inhibitor switch can now be disconnected and removed if necessary.

5. Adjust the switch by moving the selector lever to the "N" position. Loosen the mounting screws and adjust the inhibitor switch so that the pin on the forward end of the rod assembly will be in the position near the lobe of the detent plate and that this position will be at the front end of the range of the N connection of the switch. Temporarily tighten the switch mounting screws. After adjusting the selector lever clearance to 0.059 in., tighten the mounting screws.

6. To test the switch, disconnect the wiring connector and set the selector lever in each of its positions. With a continuity tester connected, current should be available in the "P," "N," and "R" positions only. Replace the switch if necessary. Install the console and shift handle.

KM170, KM171, and KM172

1. Place manual control lever in the Neutral position.

2. Loosen the two switch attaching bolts. Switch is located on side of transmission.

3. Turn the switch body until the flat end of the manual lever overlaps the square end of the switch body flange.

4. While keeping the switch body flange and manual lever aligned torque the two attaching bolts to 7.5–8.5 ft. lbs.

JM600

1. Place the selector lever in NEUTRAL.
2. Raise and support the car on jackstands.
3. Remove the lower screw on the neutral start switch.
4. Loosen the switch attaching bolts.
5. Insert a pin, 0.079 in. (2mm) in diameter, into the lower screw hole in the switch. Move the switch until the pin drops into a hole in the rotor behind the switch.
6. Hold the switch in that position and tighten the attaching bolts to 5 fft. lbs.
7. Using an ohmmeter, check the switch across the leads for continuity.

THROTTLE ROD ADJUSTMENT

TorqueFlite A-904

Warm the engine until it reaches the normal operting temperature. With the carburetor automatic choke off the fast idle cam, adjust the engine idle speed by using a tachometer. Then make the throttle rod adjustment.

1. Install each linkage. Loosen its bolts so that the rods B and C can slide properly.
2. Lightly push the rod A or the transmission throttle lever and the rod C toward the idle stopper and set the rods to idle position. In this case the carburetor automatic choke must be fully released. Tighten the bolt securely to connect the rods B and C.
3. Make sure that when the carburetor throttle valve is wide-open, the transmission throttle lever smoothly moves from idle to wide-open position (operating angle; 45-54°) and that there is some room in the lever stroke.

NOTE: Make sure that when the throttle linkage alone is returned slowly from the fully open throttle position, that the transmission throttle lever completely returns to the idle position by spring force.

JM600

1. Apply chassis lube to all sliding parts.
2. Place the selector in the NEUTRAL position.
3. Turn the adjusting cam until the distance between the adjusting cam and the selector lever end is 15–16mm.

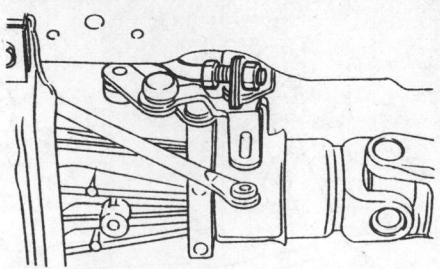

TorqueFlite throttle rod adjustment point

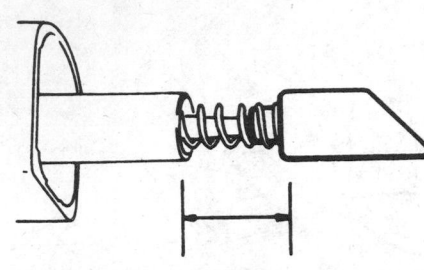

JM600 throttle rod adjustment point

THROTTLE CABLE ADJUSTMENT

KM170

1981

1. Place carburetor throttle lever in wide open position.
2. Loosen the lower cable bracket mounting bolt.
3. Move the lower cable bracket until there is 0.02–0.06 in. between the nipple at the bracket and the center of the nipple at the other end. Fasten the lower bracket in position.
4. Check the cable for freedom of movement. If it is binding it may need replacement.

KM170, KM171, and KM172

1982–88

1. Run the engine to normal operating temperature. Shut it off and make sure the throttle plate is closed (curb idle position).
2. Raise the small cone-shaped cover on the throttle cable to expose the nipple.
3. Loosen the lower cable bracket bolt.
4. Move the lower cable bracket until the distance between the nipple and the lower cover directly underneath it is 0.02–0.06 in.
5. Tighten the bracket bolt to 9–11 ft. lbs.

DOWNSHIFT SOLENOID INSPECTION

JM600

1. Raise and support the car on jackstands.
2. Uncouple the connectors on the wiring at the solenoid.

NOTE: Transmission fluid will drain from the hole after the solenoid is removed. Have a drain pan ready to catch it.

3. Remove the solenoid and O-ring.
4. Connect a 12V source across the solenoid wire to verify that the plunger is operational. If not, replace it.
5. Apply a coating of clean transmission fluid to the O-ring and install the solenoid. Refill the transmission.

TRANSFER CASE

REMOVAL & INSTALLATION

4WD Vista

1. Remove the transaxle as described above.
2. Unbolt the transfer case from the transaxle and using a small prybar, separate the two.

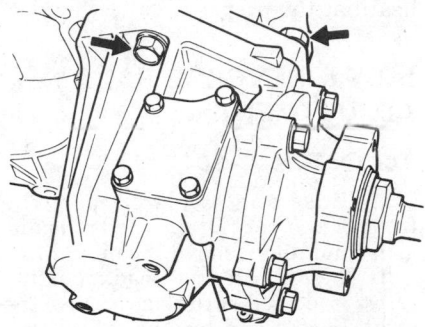

Transfer case attaching bolts

3. Installation is the reverse of removal. Torque the attaching bolts to 40–43 ft. lbs.

DRIVE AXLE

Halfshafts

REMOVAL & INSTALLATION

Except 4wd Vista

1. Remove the hub center cap and

loosen the driveshaft (axle) nut. Loosen the wheel lug nuts.

2. Lift the car and support it on jackstands. Remove the front wheels. Remove the engine splash shield.

3. Remove the lower ball joint and strut bar from the lower control arm.

4. Drain the transaxle fluid.

NOTE: On models with turbocharger, remove the snap ring which secures the center bearing.

5. Insert a pry bar between the transaxle case (on the raised rib) and the driveshaft double off-set joint case (DOJ) or tripod joint (T.J.). Do not insert the pry bar too deeply or the oil seal will be damaged. Move the bar to the right to withdraw the left driveshaft; to the left to remove the right driveshaft.

NOTE: In the case of the T.J.-R.J. driveshaft be sure to hold the T.J. case and pull out the shaft straight. Simply pulling the shaft out of position could cause damage to the T.J. boot or the spider assembly slipping from the case.

6. Plug the transaxle case with a clean rag to prevent dirt from entering the case.

7. Use a puller-driver mounted on the wheel studs to push the driveshaft from the front hub. Take care to prevent the spacer from falling out of place.

NOTE: On models with turbocharger, after forcing out the driveshaft, remove it by lightly tapping the DOJ outer race with a plastic hammer.

8. Assembly is the reverse of removal. Insert the driveshaft into the hub first, then install the transaxle end. Torque the shaft nut to 180 ft. lbs.

NOTE: Always use a new retaining ring every time the driveshaft is removed.

9. Installation of the old parts is the reverse of removal after they have been re-greased. To install the kit, use the grease supplied with the kit and apply an amount to the inner race and cage. Install the inner race and cock slightly.

10. Apply grease to the balls and install them in the cage. Place the inner race on the driveshaft and install the snap-ring. Apply grease to the outer race and install. Install the boots and bands.

11. Install the driveshaft using a new retainer ring.

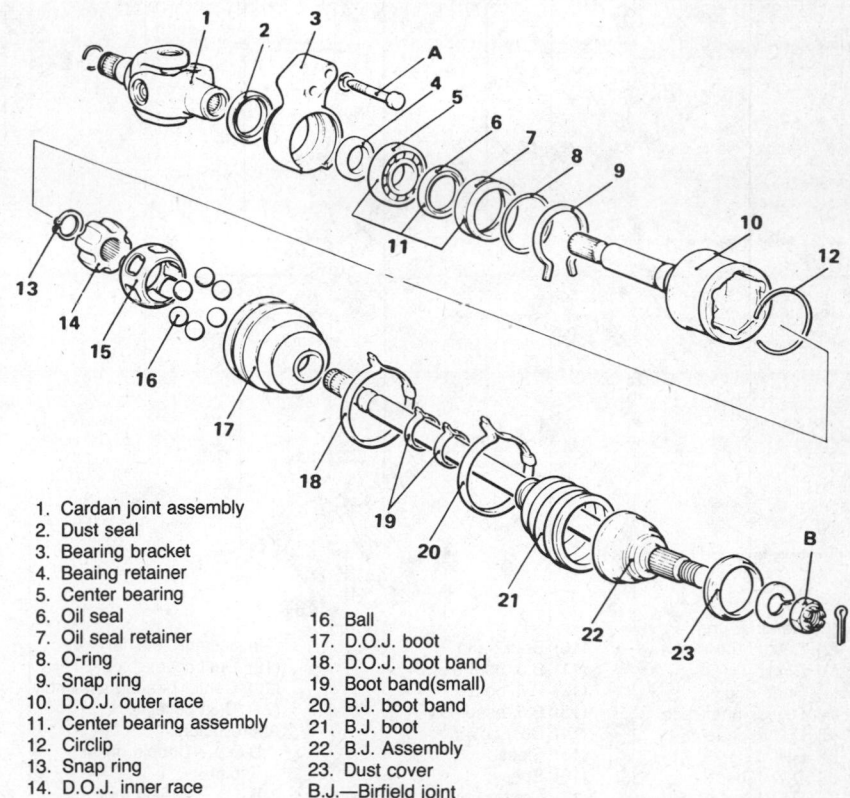

1. Cardan joint assembly
2. Dust seal
3. Bearing bracket
4. Bearing retainer
5. Center bearing
6. Oil seal
7. Oil seal retainer
8. O-ring
9. Snap ring
10. D.O.J. outer race
11. Center bearing assembly
12. Circlip
13. Snap ring
14. D.O.J. inner race
15. D.O.J. cage
16. Ball
17. D.O.J. boot
18. D.O.J. boot band
19. Boot band(small)
20. B.J. boot band
21. B.J. boot
22. B.J. Assembly
23. Dust cover
B.J.—Birfield joint
D.O.J.—Double offset joint

4-wd Vista halfshaft

4wd Vista

LEFT SIDE

1. Remove the hub cap and halfshaft nut.

2. Raise and support the car on jackstands.

3. Remove the front wheels.

4. Drain the transaxle fluid.

5. Disconnect the lower ball joint from the knuckle.

6. Remove the strut and stabilizer bar from the lower arm.

7. Remove the center bearing snapring from the bearing bracket.

8. Lightly tap the double off-set joint outer race with a wood mallet and disconnect the halfshaft from the cardan joint.

9. Disconnect the halfshaft from the bearing bracket.

10. Using a two-jawed puller secured to the hub lugs, press the halfshaft from the hub.

11. Unbolt and remove the bearing bracket.

12. Using a wood mallet, lightly tap the cardan joint yoke and remove it from the transaxle.

—— **CAUTION** ——

Never pry the cardan joint from the transaxle. Prying will damage the cardan joint dust cover.

13. Install the cardan joint.

14. Apply a coating of chassis lube on the center bearing.

15. Attach a new O-ring to the oil seal retainer.

16. Install the bearing bracket. Torque the bolts to 40 ft. lbs.

17. Insert the center bearing in the bearing bracket, making sure it is fully seated, then secure it with the snapring.

18. Coat the halfshaft splines with chassis lube and slide it into the cardan joint.

19. Slide the halfshaft into the hub and install the nut. Torque the nut to 188 ft. lbs.

RIGHT SIDE

The right side shaft is serviced in the same manner as those on other front wheel drive models. See the procedures above.

CV-JOINT OVERHAUL

For all CV-Joint removal, installation and overhaul procedures, please refer to "CV-Joint Overhaul" in the Unit Repair section.

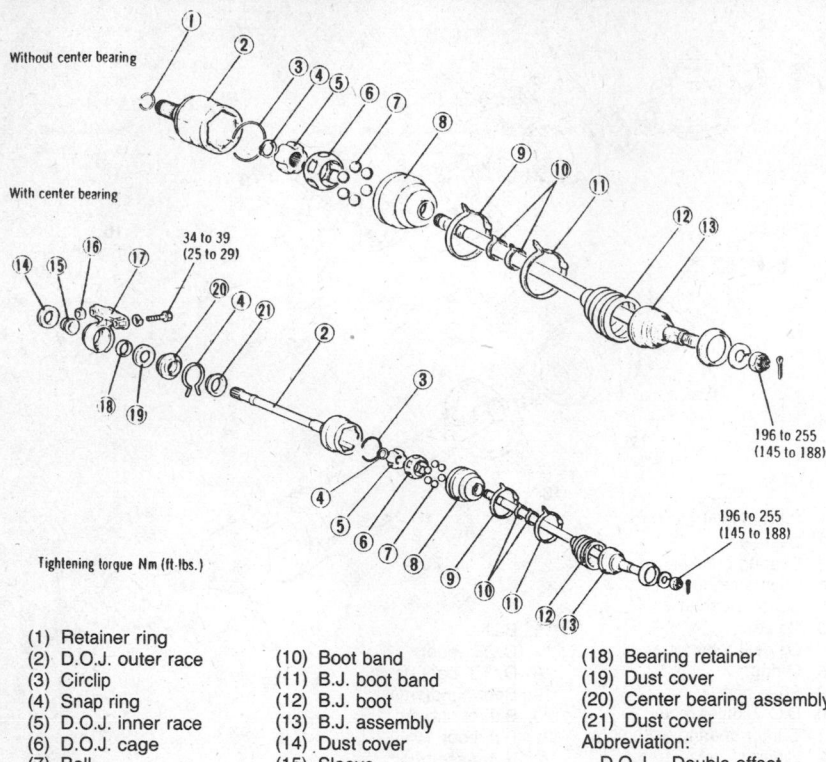

Exploded view of front drive shaft—Type D.O.J. and B.J.

(1) Retainer ring
(2) D.O.J. outer race
(3) Circlip
(4) Snap ring
(5) D.O.J. inner race
(6) D.O.J. cage
(7) Ball
(8) D.O.J. boot
(9) D.O.J. boot band
(10) Boot band
(11) B.J. boot band
(12) B.J. boot
(13) B.J. assembly
(14) Dust cover
(15) Sleeve
(16) Spacer
(17) Center bearing bracket
(18) Bearing retainer
(19) Dust cover
(20) Center bearing assembly
(21) Dust cover
Abbreviation:
D.O.J.—Double offset joint
B.J. —Birfield joint

34 to 39 (25 to 29)
Tightening torque Nm (ft.-lbs.)
196 to 255 (145 to 188)
196 to 255 (145 to 188)

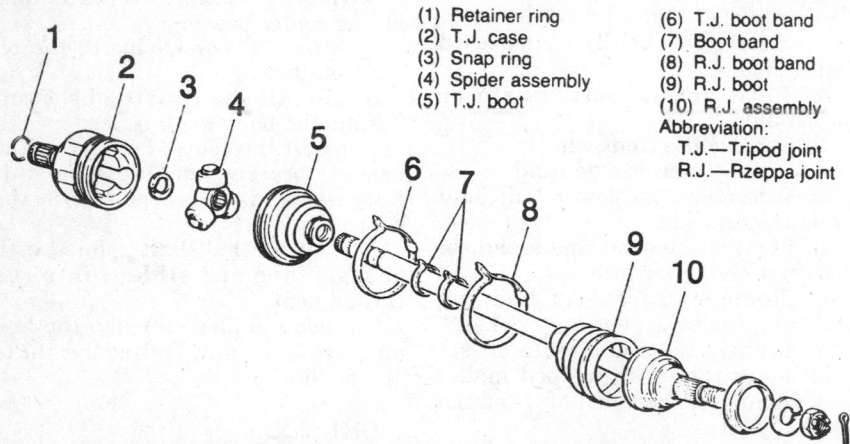

Exploded view of front drive shaft—Type T.J. and R.J.

(1) Retainer ring
(2) T.J. case
(3) Snap ring
(4) Spider assembly
(5) T.J. boot
(6) T.J. boot band
(7) Boot band
(8) R.J. boot band
(9) R.J. boot
(10) R.J. assembly
Abbreviation:
T.J.—Tripod joint
R.J.—Rzeppa joint

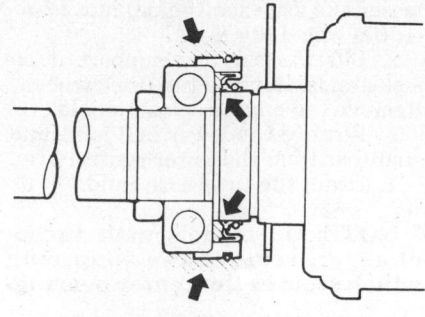

Lubricant application points

Driveshafts and U–Joints

REMOVAL & INSTALLATION

All Except 4wd Vista

1. Matchmark the rear flange yoke and the differential pinion flange.
2. On late models with a two piece driveshaft, remove the center support mounting bolts. Remove the bolts from the rear flange. Remove the driveshaft by pulling it from the rear of the transmission extension housing.

NOTE: Place a container under the transmission extension housing to collect any oil leakage when the driveshaft is removed.

3. To install the shaft, align the front sleeve yoke with the splines of the transmission output shaft and push the driveshaft into the extension housing.

NOTE: Be careful not to damage the rear transmission seal lip upon installation.

4. Align the matchmarks on the rear yokes, install the bolts, and tighten securely. Secure center support mounting bolts.
5. Inspect the oil level of the transmission.

4wd Vista

1. Raise and support the car on jackstands.
2. Drain the transfer case.
3. Matchmark the differential companion flange and the driveshaft flange yoke.
4. Unbolt the driveshaft from the differential flange.
5. Remove the two center bearing attaching nuts.

NOTE: Make sure the flat washer and the adjusting spacer are not interchanged. Keep them separate for assembly.

6. Pull the driveshaft from the transfer case. Be careful to avoid damaging the transfer case oil seal.
7. Installation is the reverse of removal. Torque the center bearing nuts to 25–30 ft. lbs.; the driveshaft-to-differential flange nuts to 20–25 ft. lbs.

Rear Axle Shaft and/or Bearing

REMOVAL & INSTALLATION

Conquest

1. Raise and support the car on jackstands.
2. Disconnect the parking brake cable from the rear calipers.
3. Remove the caliper, caliper support and rotor. Don't disconnect the

brake line from the caliper, just suspend it out of the way.

4. Remove the intermediate shaft and companion flange as described below.

5. Remove the axleshaft housing from the lower control arm.

6. Remove the strut assembly from the axleshaft housing.

7. Loosen the companion flange mounting nut and tap the axleshaft out of the housing with a plastic mallet. Be careful to avoid scratching the oil seal.

8. Remove the spacer and dust covers from inside the housing.

NOTE: Don't remove the bearings unless they are to be replaced, since they will be damaged during removal.

9. Remove the outer bearing with a puller.

10. Using a brass drift, drive the inner bearing and seal from the housing.

11. Press the new outer bearing onto the shaft with the seal side facing the flange side of the shaft.

12. Pack the housing with lithium based wheel-bearing grease.

13. Press the inner bearing onto the shaft with the seal side facing the companion flange side of the shaft.

14. Grease the seal bore in the housing and drive the new seal into position.

15. Install the dust covers.

16. Insert the axleshaft and spacer into the housing and attach the companion flange.

17. Place the housing in a vise and install and tighten the companion flange nut to 200–220 ft. lbs.

18. Install all other parts in reverse order of removal. Check axleshaft end-play with a dial indicator. End-play should be 0.031 in. If end-play exceeds the limit, either the bearing needs replacing or the shaft bearings are not assembled properly.

4wd Vista

1. Raise and support the rear of the car on jackstands placed under the frame.

2. Remove the rear wheels.

3. Remove the brake drums.

4. Remove the 3 bolts securing the axleshaft flange to the intermediate shaft flange.

5. Using special tool MB900767, remove the axleshaft flange nut.

6. Using a slidehammer connected to a two-jawed adapter secured under two lug nuts, pull the axleshaft from the housing.

7. Remove the lower arm as described later in this section.

8. Using special tool MB990560,

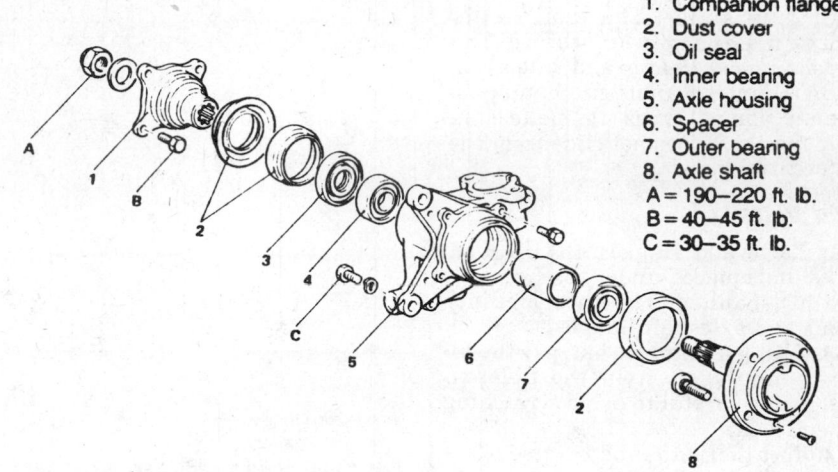

1. Companion flange
2. Dust cover
3. Oil seal
4. Inner bearing
5. Axle housing
6. Spacer
7. Outer bearing
8. Axle shaft
A = 190–220 ft. lb.
B = 40–45 ft. lb.
C = 30–35 ft. lb.

Conquest rear axle axleshaft and housing assembly

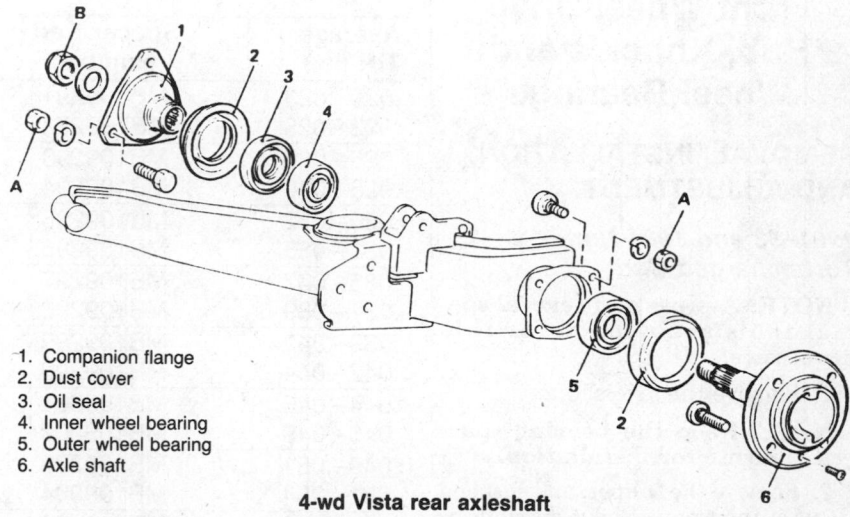

1. Companion flange
2. Dust cover
3. Oil seal
4. Inner wheel bearing
5. Outer wheel bearing
6. Axle shaft

4-wd Vista rear axleshaft

remove the dust cover and the outer wheel bearing and seal from the axleshaft at the same time. Discard the seal.

9. Using driver MB990938 and adapter MB990927, or equivalent, drive the inner bearing and seal from the housing. The new bearing should be thoroughly packed with chassis lube and driven into place with the same tools.

10. Install a new inner bearing seal with a seal driver.

11. Using a special tool MB990799, or similar driver, tape a new dust cover into place. Tap evenly around the tool to seat the cover.

12. Coat the lip of a new seal with chassis lube and pack the new outer bearing thoroughly with chassis lube.

13. Using MB990560 and a press, install the bearing and seal.

14. Mount the inner arm in a vise and, using a press, install the axleshaft.

15. Install the axleshaft and inner arm assembly.

16. Torque the axleshaft nut to 160 ft. lbs.

17. Connect the axleshaft and intermediate shaft flanges and torque the bolts to 43 ft. lbs.

Intermediate Shaft

REMOVAL & INSTALLATION

Conquest

1. Remove the 4 bolts and separate the intermediate shaft from the companion flange.

2. Using a slidehammer and adapter, remove the intermediate shaft from the differential. Be careful to avoid damaging the oil seal.

3. If the oil seal is to be replaced, pry it from the housing.

4. Installation is the reverse of removal. Coat the part of the intermedi-

ate shaft that passes through the seal, with chassis lube. The shaft can be driven into place using the slidehammer. Before and after coupling the intermediate shaft and companion flange, check to make sure that the shaft does not slide from the differential housing.

4wd Vista

1. Raise and support the rear on jackstands placed under the frame.
2. Disconnect the intermediate shaft and axleshaft flanges.
3. Using a small prybar, pry the intermediate shaft from the differential, being careful to avoid scratching the oil seal.
4. Installation is the reverse of removal. Torque the flange bolts to 43 ft. lbs.

Front Wheel Drive Hub, Knuckle and Wheel Bearings

REMOVAL, INSTALLATION AND ADJUSTMENT

1981–83 and 1984 Non-Turbocharged Cars

NOTE: A press and several special tools are needed for this procedure.

1. Remove the axle shaft.

NOTE: Keep the bearing spacers separate for installation.

2. Remove the caliper, and suspend it out of the way, without disconnecting the brake line.
3. Disconnect the tie rod end from the knuckle.
4. Disconnect the strut from the knuckle and remove the hub and knuckle assembly.
5. Pry the hub and knuckle assembly apart. If separation is difficult, mount the knuckle in a vise and drive out the hub with a plastic mallet. Drive out the oil seals, bearings and races with a brass drift.
6. Inspect all parts for wear and damage; replace any suspect parts.
7. Install the outer races of the inner and outer bearings, using a brass drift or press. If a press is used, 4,400 lb. installation pressure is necessary.
8. Apply lithium based wheel bearing grease to the inside of the knuckle, the oil seals and bearings. Thoroughly pack the bearings making sure that clean grease permeates all cavities.
9. If separated, assemble the hub and rotor. Torque the bolts to 36 ft. lbs.

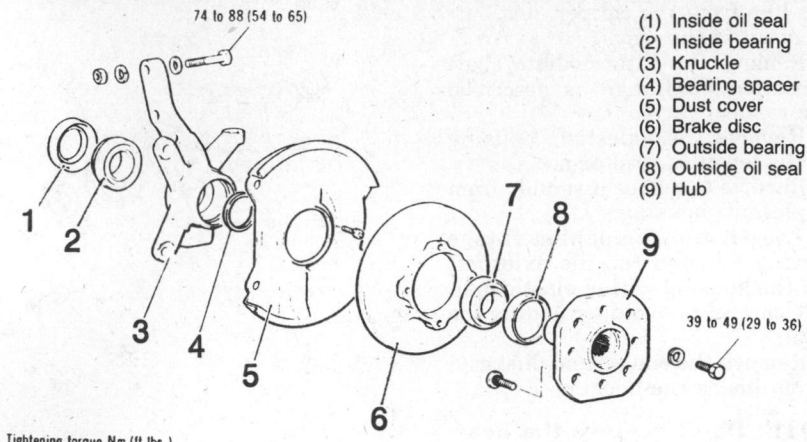

(1)	Inside oil seal
(2)	Inside bearing
(3)	Knuckle
(4)	Bearing spacer
(5)	Dust cover
(6)	Brake disc
(7)	Outside bearing
(8)	Outside oil seal
(9)	Hub

Tightening torque Nm (ft-lbs.)

Front hub and knuckle assembly, 1981–83 and non-turbocharged 1984 and later FWD vehicles

Average TIR (in.)	Spacer Part Number	Thickness (in.)	Identifying Color
.020–.023	MB109291	0.223	Pink
.023–.025	MB109292	0.226	Green
.025–.028	MB109293	0.228	Red
.028–.030	MB109294	0.230	White
.030–.032	MB109295	0.233	None
.032–.035	MB109296	0.235	Yellow
.035–.037	MB109297	0.237	Blue
.037–.039	MB109298	0.240	Orange
.039–.042	MB109299	0.242	Light Green
.042–.044	MB109300	0.244	Brown
.044–.046	MB109301	0.247	Grey
.046–.049	MB109302	0.249	Navy Blue
.049–.051	MB109303	0.252	Vermillion
.051–.054	MB109304	0.254	Purple
.137–.141	MB109126	0.139	Red
.141–.146	MB109127	0.144	White
.146–.151	MB109128	0.149	Black
.151–.156	MB109129	0.154	Yellow
.156–.160	MB109165	0.159	Blue

10. Install the inner race of the outer bearing using a brass drift. Using a driver, install the outer oil seal.
11. Using special tool MB990776–A, hold the inner race of the outer bearing, while pressing the hub into the knuckle. 1,100 lb. of press pressure is needed.
12. After installing the inner race of the inner bearing, install the inner oil seal.

NOTE: At this point, the correct spacer between the front axle and hub must be determined. The spacers are vital for establishing front wheel bearing preload.

13. Install spacer selection gauge MB990768 (1981–82) or MB9907959 (1983–84) on the hub and tighten the nut to 14–15 ft. lbs. Prevent the tool from turning while tightening the nut.
14. Rotate the hub and tool several turns to seat the bearings.
15. Install a dial indicator on the tool and load about 5mm of travel on the indicator, then zero the dial.
16. While holding the threaded stud of the tool with a wrench, back off the nut until travel no longer registers on the gauge. Note the total indicator reading.

NOTE: Be sure that the tool does not turn during this procedure. Hold it in a vise if necessary. Be sure to back off the nut SLOWLY to give an accurate indicator reading.

17. Repeat Step 16 and average the two readings. Use the averaged reading to calculate what spacers will be needed. Use the following chart as a guide:

18. Install the spacer in the hub with the chamferred side toward the knuckle.

19. Installation of the hub and knuckle is the reverse of the removal. Observe the following torques:
• Axleshaft nut: 88–130 ft. lbs.
• Knuckle-to-strut: 55–65 ft. lbs.
• Ball joint-to-arm: 70–88 ft. lbs.
• Lower arm-to-strut: 70–88 ft. lbs.
• Knuckle-to-tie rod: 11–25 ft. lbs.

1984 Turbocharged Colt, 1985–88 Colt and 2wd Vista

NOTE: The following procedure requires the use of several special tools.

1. Remove the axleshaft nut.
2. Raise and support the car with jackstands positioned so that the wheels hang freely.
3. Remove the wheels.
4. Remove the caliper and suspend it out of the way without disconnecting the brake hose.
5. Disconnect the lower ball joint from the knuckle.
6. Disconnect the tie rod end from the knuckle.
7. Using a two-jawed puller, press the axleshaft from the hub.
8. Unbolt the strut from the knuckle. Remove the hub and knuckle assembly from the car.
9. Install first the arm, then the body of special tool MB991056 (Colt) or MB991001 (Vista) on the knuckle and tighten the nut.
10. Using special tool MB990998, separate the hub from the knuckle.

NOTE: Prying or hammering will damage the bearing. Use these special tools, or their equivalent to separate the hub and knuckle.

11. Place the knuckle in a vise and separate the rotor from the hub.
12. Using special tools, C–293–PA, SP–3183 and MB990781, remove the outer bearing inner race.
13. Drive the oil seal and inner bearing inner race from the knuckle with a brass drift.
14. Drive out both outer races in a similar fashion.

NOTE: Always replace bearings

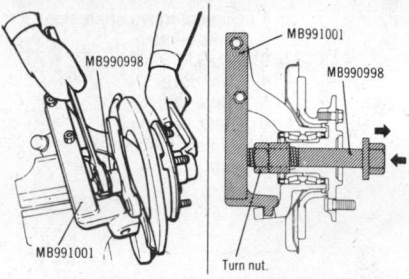

Using special tools to remove the hub from the knuckle

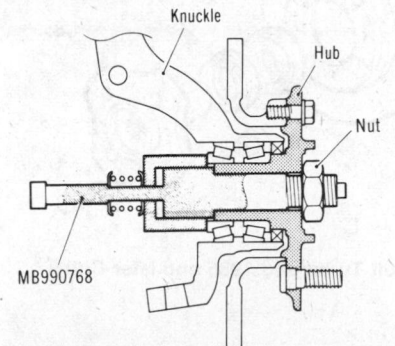

Spacer selection gauge installation on 1980–82 front wheel drive

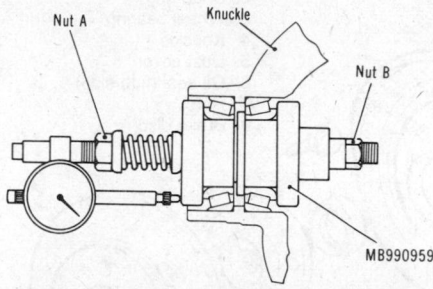

Spacer selection gauge installation on 1980—82 front wheel drive

and races as a set. Never replace just an inner or outer bearing. If either is in need of replacement, both sets must be replaced.

15. Thoroughly clean and inspect all parts. Any suspect part should be replaced.
16. Pack the wheel bearings with lithium based wheel bearing grease. Coat the inside of the knuckle with similar grease and pack the cavities in the knuckle. Apply a thin coating of grease to the outer surface of the races before installation.
17. Using special tools C–3893 and MB990776, install the outer races.
18. Install the rotor on the hub and torue the bolts to 36–43 ft. lbs.
19. Drive the outer bearing inner race into position.
20. Coat the out rim and lip of the oil seal and drive the hub side oil seal into place, using a seal driver.

21. Place the inner bearing in the knuckle.
22. Mount the knuckle in a vise. Position the hub and knuckle together. Install tool MB99098 and tighten the tool to 147–192 ft. lbs. Rotate the hub to seat the bearing.
23. With the knuckle still in the vise measure the hub starting torque with an in. lb. torque wrench and tool MB990998. Starting torque should be 11.5 inch lbs. If the starting torque is 0, measure the hub bearing axial play with a dial indicator. If axial play exceeds 0.0078 in., while the nut is tightened to 145–192 ft. lbs., the assembly has not been done correctly. Disassemble the knuckle and hub and start again.
24. Remove the special tool.
25. Place the outer bearing in the hub and drive the seal into place.
26. The remainder of installation is the reverse of removal.

4wd Vista

NOTE: The following procedure requires the use of several special tools.

1. Remove the hub cap and halfshaft nut.
2. Raise and support the car on jackstands.
3. Remove the front wheels.
4. Drain the transaxle fluid.
5. Disconnect the lower ball joint from the knuckle.
6. Remove the strut and stabilizer bar from the lower arm.
7. Remove the center bearing snapring from the bearing bracket.
8. Lightly tap the double off-set joint outer race with a wood mallet and disconnect the halfshaft from the cardan joint.
9. Disconnect the halfshaft from the bearing jacket.
10. Using a two-jawed puller secured to the hub lugs, press the halfshaft from the hub.
11. Unbolt the strut from the hub. Remove the hub and knuckle assembly from the car.
12. Install first the arm, then the body of special tool MB991001 on the knuckle and tighten the nut.
13. Using special tool MB9900998, separate the hub from the knuckle and tighten the nut.

NOTE: Prying or hammering will damage the bearing. Use these special tools, or their equivalent, to separate the hub and knuckle.

14. Matchmark the hub and rotor. The rotor should slide from the hub. If not, insert M8X 1.25 bolts in the holes between the lugs and tighten them al-

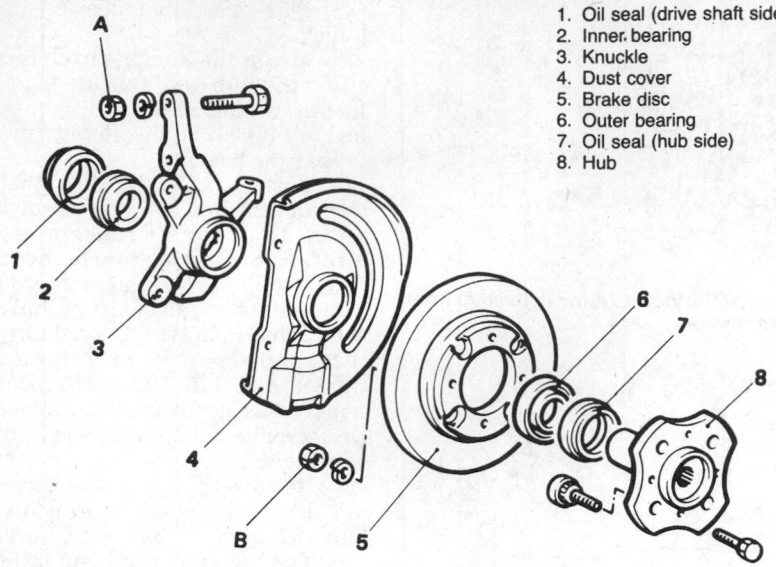

1. Oil seal (drive shaft side)
2. Inner bearing
3. Knuckle
4. Dust cover
5. Brake disc
6. Outer bearing
7. Oil seal (hub side)
8. Hub

Front hub and knuckle used on 1984 Colt Turbo and 1985 and later Colt

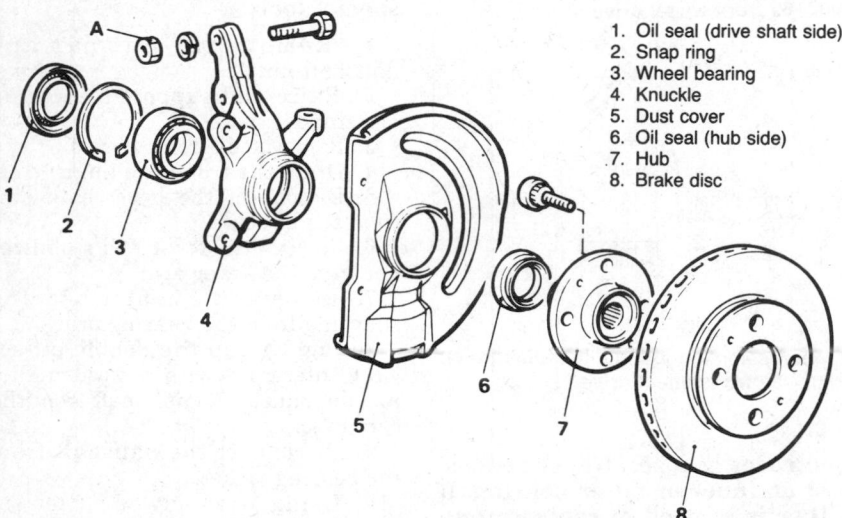

1. Oil seal (drive shaft side)
2. Snap ring
3. Wheel bearing
4. Knuckle
5. Dust cover
6. Oil seal (hub side)
7. Hub
8. Brake disc

4-wd Vista front hub, knuckle and bearing

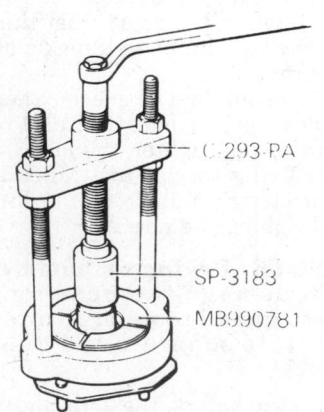

Removing the outer bearing inner race from the hub, using the special tools described

ternately to press the hub from the rotor. NEVER HAMMER THE ROTOR TO REMOVE IT!

15. Using a two-jawed puller, remove the outer bearing inner race.
16. Remove and discard the outer oil seal.
17. Remove and discard the inner oil sea.
18. Remove the bearing snapring from the knuckle.
19. Using special tools C–4628 and MB991056 or MB991001, remove the bearing from the knuckle. Using a driver, drive the bearing from the knuckle.

NOTE: Always replace bearings and races as a set. Never replace just an inner or outer bearing. If either is in need of replacement, both sets must be replaced.

20. Thoroughly clean and inspect all parts. Any suspect part should be replace.
21. Pack the wheel bearings with lithium based wheel bearing grease. Coat the inside of the knuckle with similar grease and pack the cavities in the knuckle. Apply a thin coating of grease to the outer surface of the races before installation.
22. Using special tools C–4171 and MB990985, press the bearing into place in the knuckle. Install the snapring.
23. Coat the lips of a new hub-side seal with lithium grease. Using a seal driver, install the seal. Make sure it is flush.
24. Install the rotor on the hub.
25. Using special tool MB990998, join the hub and knuckle. Torque the special tool nut to 188 ft. lbs.
26. Rotate the hub several times to seat the bearing.
27. Mount the knuckle in a vise. Using MB990998 and an inch lb. torque wrench, measure the turning torque. Turning torque should be 15.6 inch lbs. or less. Next, measure the axial play using a dial indicator. Axial play should be .008 in. If either the axial play or the turning torque are not within the specified values, the hub and knuckle have not been properly assembled. Repeat the procedure. If everything checks out okay, go on to the next step.
28. Remove all the special tools.
29. Using a seal driver, drive a new seal coated with lithium grease, into place on the halfshaft side, until it contacts the snapring.
30. The remainder of installation is the reverse of removal.

FRONT SUSPENSION

MacPherson Strut

REMOVAL & INSTALLATION

Rear Wheel Drive

ALL EXCEPT CONQUEST

1. Loosen the lug nuts, jack up the front of the car (after blocking the rear wheels) and support safely on jackstands.
2. Remove the brake caliper, hub and brake disc rotors. Disconnect the

stabilizer link from the lower arm, remove the three steering knuckle-to-strut assembly bolts. Carefully force the lower control arm down and separate the strut assembly and the steering knuckle. Unscrew the three retaining nuts at the top and remove the strut assembly.

NOTE: On some models the lower splash shield may interfere with the strut removal.

3. To install the strut, position the strut assembly in the fender. Install the upper retaining nuts hand tight.

4. Apply sealer on the mounting flange and fasten the strut assembly to the steering knuckle. Connect the brake hose if removed.

5. Tighten the upper retaining nuts to 7–11 ft. lbs. Torque the knuckle bolts to 30–36 ft. lbs.

6. Assemble the stabilizer link and fasten to the lower control arm if removed.

7. Assemble the remaining parts in the opposite order of removal. If the brake line was disconnected during the strut removal, the brake system will have to be bled.

CONQUEST

1. Raise and support the front end on jackstands. Let the wheels hang.

2. Remove the caliper and suspend it out of the way.

3. Remove the hub and rotor assembly.

4. Remove the brake dust cover.

5. Unbolt the strut from the knuckle.

6. Remove the strut-to-fender linder nuts and lift out the strut. Installation is the reverse of removal. Torque the strut-to-fender liner nuts to 18–25 ft. lbs.; the stut-to-knuckle arm bolts to 58–72 ft. lbs.

Front Wheel Drive

1981–84 COLT AND CHAMP, 1985–88 VISTA

1. Raise and support the front end.
2. Remove the front wheels.
3. Detach the brake hose from the clip on the strut.
4. Remove the three nuts securing the strut to the fender housing.
5. Unbolt the strut from the knuckle.
6. Remove the strut from the car.
7. Installation is the reverse of removal. Torque the strut-to-knuckle bolts to 55–65 ft. lbs. Torque the strut-to-fender housing nuts to 7–11 ft. lbs. on Colts and Champs; 18–25 ft. lbs. on Vistas.

1985–88 COLT

1. Raise and support the front end on jackstands.

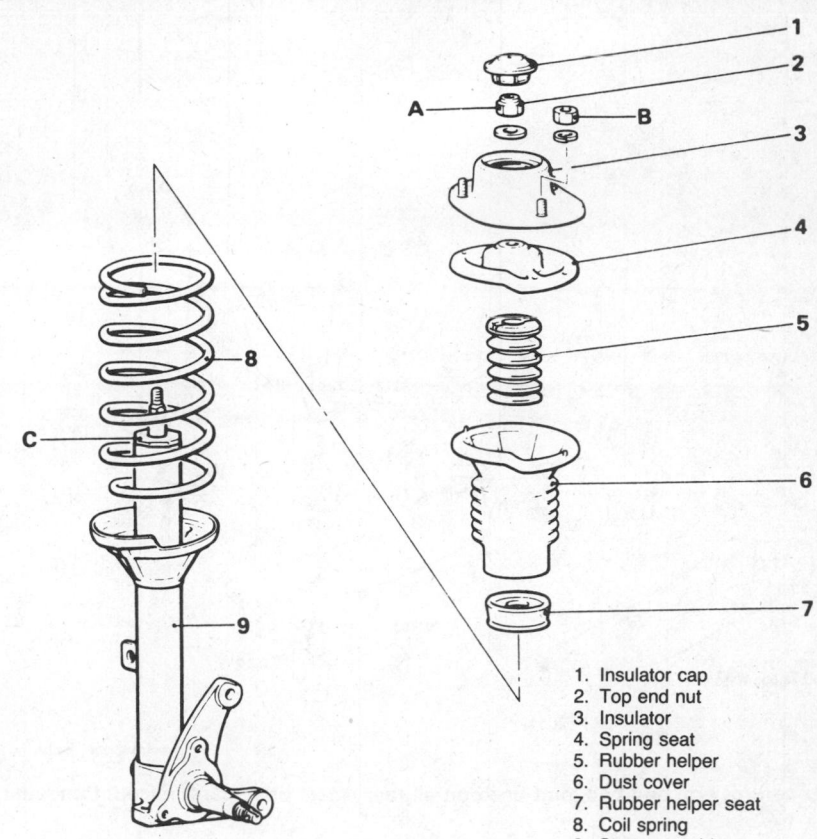

1. Insulator cap
2. Top end nut
3. Insulator
4. Spring seat
5. Rubber helper
6. Dust cover
7. Rubber helper seat
8. Coil spring
9. Strut assembly

Conquest front strut

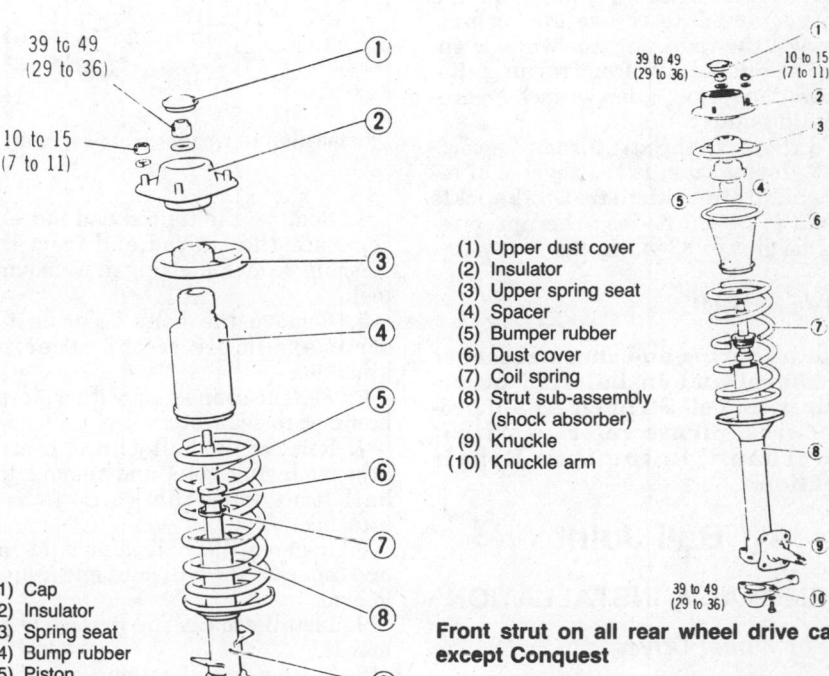

(1) Cap
(2) Insulator
(3) Spring seat
(4) Bump rubber
(5) Piston
(6) Oil seal nut
(7) Square section O-ring
(8) Spring
(9) Outer shell

Tightening torque Nm (ft-lbs.)

Colt FWD front strut–1981–84

(1) Upper dust cover
(2) Insulator
(3) Upper spring seat
(4) Spacer
(5) Bumper rubber
(6) Dust cover
(7) Coil spring
(8) Strut sub-assembly (shock absorber)
(9) Knuckle
(10) Knuckle arm

Front strut on all rear wheel drive cars except Conquest

2. Remove the front wheels.
3. Detach the brake hose from the clip on the strut.
4. Unbolt the strut from the knuckle.
5. Remove the dust cover from the upper end of the strut.

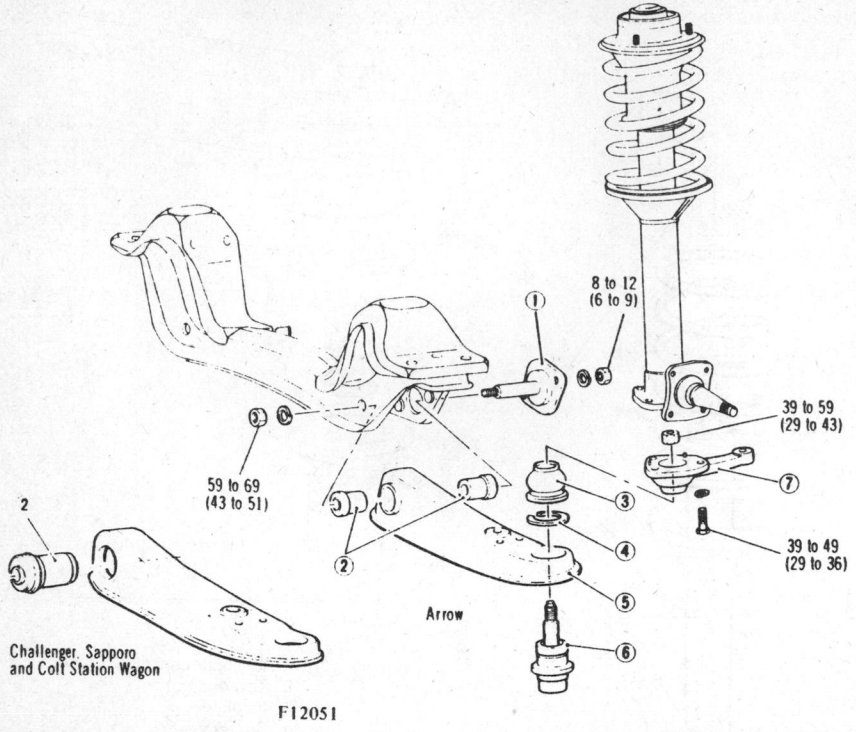

Lower control arm and ball joint used on all rear wheel drive cars, except Conquest

6. Insert a ½ in. drive socket in the top of the strut to hold the gland nut.

7. Insert an allen wrench in the socket and into the retaining nut. Loosen the retaining nut while keeping the gland nut from turning. Remove the socket, allen wrench and retaining nut.

8. Remove the strut from the car.

9. Installation is the reverse of removal. Torque the strut-to-knuckle bolts to 55–65 ft. lbs.; the upper retainer nut to 33–43 ft. lbs.

OVERHAUL

For all spring and shock absorber Removal and Installation procedures, and all Strut Overhaul procedures, please refer to "Strut Overhaul" in the Unit Repair section.

Ball Joint

REMOVAL & INSTALLATION

Rear Wheel Drive

1981–88

1. Remove the tire and wheel assembly.

2. Remove the brake caliper and support from the mounting adapter.

3. Anchor assembly out of the way with wire to the strut spring.

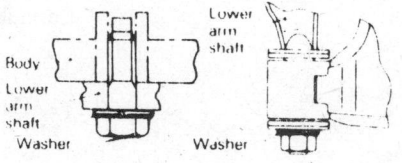

Installation of washer on lower shaft

4. Remove the tie rod end nut and separate the tie rod end from the steering knuckle using a removing tool.

5. Remove the bolts securing the strut assembly to the steering knuckle.

6. Tap the connection with a plastic hammer to separate.

7. Remove the ball joint to control arm mounting bolts and remove the ball joint with the knuckle arm attached.

8. Remove the ball joint stud nut and separate the ball joint and knuckle arm.

9. Installation is the reverse of removal.

10. Torque specifications are: Ball joint stud nut; 43–52 ft. lbs. Strut to knuckle bolts; 58–78 ft. lbs. Ball joint to control arm bolts; 43–51 ft. lbs.

--- CAUTION ---
When self-locking nuts are removed, always replace with new self-locking nuts.

Front Wheel Drive

1981–84

Unbolt the ball joint from the control arm. Use a ball joint removing tool and separate the ball joint from the steering knuckle after removing the stud retaining nut. Install in the reverse order. Torque specifications are: Ball joint to control arm; 69–87 ft. lbs. Ball joint stud nut; 40–51 ft. lbs.

1985–88 COLT

The ball joint is not replaceable. The ball joint and lower control arm must be replaced as an assembly.

1985–88 VISTA

NOTE: This procedure requires a hydraulic press.

1. See the "Lower Control Arm" procedure and disconnect the lower arm.

2. Remove the ball joint dust cover.

3. Using snapring pliers, remove the snapring from the ball joint.

4. Using an adapter plate and driver, such as tool MB990800, press the ball joint from the arm.

5. Installation is the reverse of removal, inverting the tool in the press for installation. Coat the lip and interior of the dust cover with lithium based chassis lube.

Lower Control Arm

REMOVAL & INSTALLATION

Rear Wheel Drive

EXCEPT CONQUEST

1. Loosen the lug nuts and then raise the front end of the car.

2. Remove the caliper, hub and disc.

3. Disconnect the stabilizer link and strut bar from the lower control arm. Depending on year, remove idler arm support from the chassis and move steering linkage to gain clearance.

4. Remove the three steering knuckle-to-strut assembly bolts.

5. Carefully force the lower control arm down and separate the strut assembly and the steering knuckle.

6. Unscrew the three retaining nuts at the top and withdraw the strut assembly, if necessary.

7. Using a puller, disconnect the steering knuckle arm and the tie-rod ball joint.

8. Again using a puller, disconnect the knuckle arm and the lower arm ball joint.

9. Remove the control arm-to-crossmember bolts and remove the control arm.

10. Install the lower arm on the

crossmember. Tighten the bolts to 58–69 ft. lbs. The chamfered end of the nut should be facing the round surface of the bracket.

11. Tighten the steering knuckle arm-to-control arm ball joint nut to 52–69 ft. lbs.

12. Install the strut assembly into the fender. Tighten the top mounting nuts to 18–25 ft. lbs.

13. Apply sealer to the lower end of the strut. Install and tighten the strut-to-steering knuckle arm bolts to 58–72 ft. lbs.

14. Assemble the stabilizer link and fasten it and strut bar to the lower control arm.

15. Install the backing plate, brake disc, hub, and caliper. Tighten strut bar to 18–25 ft. lbs.

16. Install the wheel and lower the car.

17. Jounce the car up and down a few times and then tighten the stabilizer bolt to 7–10 ft. lbs.

CONQUEST

NOTE: This procedure requires the use of a special tool.

1. Raise and support the front end on jackstands.

2. Remove the front wheels.

3. Remove the caliper and suspend it out of the way.

4. Remove the hub and rotor assembly.

5. Disconnect the stabilizer bar and strut bar from the lower arm.

6. Using a separator, remove the attaching nut and disconnect the tie rod from the knuckle arm.

7. Unbolt the strut from the knuckle arm.

8. Unbolt the lower control arm and knuckle arm assembly from the crossmember.

9. Using special tool MB990635, separate the knuckle arm from the lower control arm.

10. Installation is the reverse of removal. Apply sealant to the flange of the knuckle arm where it mates with the strut. Torque the lower control arm shaft bolt to 60–70 ft. lbs.; the ball joint-to-knuckle arm nut to 45–55 ft. lbs.

Front Wheel Drive Models

1981–84

1. Loosen front wheel lugs, block rear wheels, jack up the front of the car and support on jackstands.

2. Remove the front wheels. Remove the lower splash shield.

3. Disconnect the lower ball joint by unfastening the nuts and bolts mounting it to the control arm. It is not necessary to remove the ball joint from the knuckle.

4. Remove the strut bar and the control arm inner mounting nut and bolt. Remove the control arm.

5. Assembly is the reverse of removal.

Torque Specifications are:
Inner mount bolt: 69–87 ft. lbs.
Ball joint mount: 69–87 ft. lbs.
Ball joint nut: 40–51 ft. lbs.

1985–88 COLT

1. Raise and support the front end. Remove the wheels. Remove the splash shield.

2. Disconnect the stabilizer bar from the lower arm.

3. Using a ball joint separator, disconnect the ball joint from the knuckle.

4. Unbolt the lower arm from the body and remove it from the car.

NOTE: The ball joint cannot be separated from the control arm, but must be replaced as an assembly.

5. If the stabilizer bar is to be removed, disconnect the tie rod from the knuckle, and unbolt and remove the stabilizer.

6. Check all parts for wear and damage and replace any suspect part.

7. Using an inch lb. torque wrench, check the ball joint starting torque. Nominal starting effort should be 22–87 inch lbs. Replace it if otherwise.

8. Installation is the reverse of removal. Use a new dust cover, the lip and inside of which is coated with lithium based chassis lube. The dust cover should be hammered into place with a driver, such as tool MB990800. Install the stabilizer bar so that the serrations on the horizontal part protrude 6mm to the inside of the clamp and 23mm of threaded stud appear below the nut at the control arm. The washer on the lower arm shaft should be installed as shown in the accompanying illustration. The left side lower arm shaft has left-handed threads. The lower arm shaft nut must be torqued with the wheels hanging freely. Observe the following torques:
Knuckle-to-strut: 54–65 ft. lbs.
Lower arm shaft-to-body: 118–125 ft. lbs.
Stabilizer bar-to-body: 12–20 ft. lbs.
Ball joint-to-knuckle: 44–53 ft. lbs.
Lower arm-to-shaft: 70–88 ft. lbs.

1985–88 VISTA

1. Raise and support the front end.

2. Remove the wheels.

3. Disconnect the stabilizer bar and strut bar from the lower arm.

4. Remove the nut and disconnect the ball joint from the knuckle with a separator.

5. Unbolt the lower arm from the crossmember.

6. Check all parts for wear or damage and replace any suspect part.

7. Using an inch lbs. torque wrench, check the ball joint starting torque. Starting torque should be 20–86 inch lbs. If it is not within that range, replace the ball joint.

8. Installation is the reverse of removal. Tighten all fasteners with the wheels hanging freely. Observe the following torques:
Ball joint-to-knuckle: 44–53 ft. lbs.
Arm-to-crossmember: 2wd: 90–111 ft. lbs.; 4wd: 58–68 ft. lbs.
Stabilizer bar hanger brackets: 7–9 ft. lbs.

NOTE: When installing the stabilizer bar, the nut on the bar-to-crossmember bolts and the bar-to-lower arm bolts, are not torqued, but turned on until a certain length of thread is exposed above the nut:
2wd stabilizer bar-to-crossmember: 0.31–0.39 in.
2wd stabilizer bar-to-lower control arm: 0.31–0.39 in.
4wd stabilizer bar-to-crossmember: 0.31–0.39 in.
4wd stabilizer bar-to-lower arm: 0.51–0.59.

Front Wheel Bearings

NOTE: Please refer to the "Drive Axle" Section for FWD Models.

REMOVAL & INSTALLATION

Rear Wheel Drive

1. Remove the caliper (pin type) or the caliper and support (sliding type).

NOTE: On sliding type calipers, remove the caliper and support as a unit by unfastening the bolts holding it to the adapter ("backing plate"). Support the caliper with wire, do not allow the weight to be supported by the brake hose.

2. Pry off the dust cap. Tap out and discard the cotter pin. Remove the locknut.

3. Being careful not to drop the outer bearing, pull off the brake disc and wheel hub.

4. Remove the grease inside the wheel hub.

5. Using a brass drift, carefully drive the outer bearing race out of the hub.

6. Remove the inner bearing seal and bearing.

7. Check the bearings for wear or damage and replace them if necessary.

8. Coat the inner surface of the hub with grease.

9. Grease the outer surface of the bearing race and drift it into place in the hub.

10. Pack the inner and outer wheel bearings with grease. (see repacking.)

NOTE: If the brake disc has been removed and/or replaced; tighten the retaining bolts to 25–29 ft. lbs.

11. Install the inner bearing in the hub. Being careful not to distort it, install the oil seal with its lip facing the bearing. Drive the seal on until its outer edge is even with the edge of the hub.

12. Install the hub/disc assembly on the spindle, being careful not to damage the oil seal.

13. Install the outer bearing, washer, and spindle nut. Adjust the bearing as follows.

ADJUSTMENT

Rear Wheel Drive

1. Remove the wheel and dust cover. Remove the cotter pin and lock cap from the nut.

2. Torque the wheel bearing nut to 14.5 ft. lbs. (19.6 Nm) and then loosen the nut. Retorque the nut to 3.6 ft. lbs. (4.9 Nm) and install the lock cap and cotter pin.

3. Install the dust cover and the wheel.

Front Wheel Alignment

CASTER AND CAMBER

Caster is preset at the factory. It requires adjustment only if the suspension and steering linkage components are damaged, in which case, repair is accomplished by replacing the damaged part. A slight caster adjustment can be made by moving the nuts on the front anchors of the strut bars.

TOE–IN

Toe-in is the difference in the distance between the front wheels, as measured at both the front and the rear of the front tires.

Toe-in is adjusted by turning the tie rod turnbuckles as necessary. The turnbuckles should always be tightened or loosened the same amount for both tie rods; the difference in length between the two tie rods should not exceed 0.2 in. On the Challenger and Sapporo, only the left tie rod is adjustable.

REAR SUSPENSION

Leaf Springs

REMOVAL & INSTALLATION

Rear Wheel Drive Except Conquest and Station Wagons

1. Remove the hub cap or wheel cover. Loosen the lug nuts.

2. Raise the rear of the car. Install a stand at the exact point at which the two dimples locate the support point on the sill flange.

— CAUTION —
Damage to the unit body can result from installing a stand at any other location.

3. Disconnect the lower mounting nut of the shock absorber.

4. Remove the four U-bolt fastening nuts from the spring seat.

NOTE: It's not necessary to remove the shock absorber, leave the top connected.

5. Place a floor jack under the rear axle and raise it just enough to remove the load from the springs. Remove the spring pad and seat.

6. Remove the two rear shackle attaching nuts and remove the rear shackle.

7. Remove the front pin retaining nut. Remove the two pin retaining bolts and take off the pin.

NOTE: It is a good safety practice to replace used suspension fasteners with new parts.

9. Install the front spring eye bushings from both sides of the eye with the bushing flanges facing out.

10. Insert the spring pin assembly from the body side and fasten it with the bolts. Temporarily tighten the spring pin nut.

11. Install the rear eye bushings in the same manner as the front, insert the shackle pins from the outside of the car, and temporarily tighten the nut after installing the shackle plate.

12. Install the pads on both sides of the spring, aligning the pad center holes with the spring center bolt collar, and then install the spring seat with its center hole through the spring center collar.

13. Attach the assembled spring and spring seat to the axle housing with the axle housing spring center hole meeting with the spring center bolt and install the U-bolt nuts. Tighten the nuts to 33–36 ft. lbs.

14. Tighten the lower shock absorber nut to 12–15 ft. lbs. on all models.

15. Lower the car to the floor, jounce it a few times, and then tighten the spring pin and shackle pin nuts to 36–43 ft. lbs.

Coil Springs

REMOVAL & INSTALLATION

Front Wheel Drive and Station Wagons Except 4WD Vista

1. Raise and support the car safely allowing the rear axle to hang unsupported.

2. Place a jack under the rear axle, and remove the bottom bolts or nuts of the shock absorbers.

3. Lower the rear axle and remove the left and right coil springs.

4. Installation is the reverse of removal.

NOTE: When installing the spring, pay attention to the difference in shape between the upper and lower spring seats.

Torsion Bar and Control Arms

Instead of springs, the 4wd Vista uses transversely mounted torsion bars housed inside the rear crossmember, attached to which are inner and outer control arms. The conventional style shock absorbers are mounted on the inner arms.

REMOVAL & INSTALLATION

4wd Vista

1. Raise and support the car with jackstands under the frame.

2. Remove the differential as described above.

3. Remove the intermediate shafts and axleshafts.

4. Remove the rear brake assemblies.

5. Disconnect the brake lines and parking brake cables from the inner arms.

6. Remove the main muffler.

7. Raise the inner arms slightly with a floor jack and disconnect the shock absorbers.

8. Matchmark, precisely, the upper ends of the outer arms, the torsion bar ends and the top of the crossmember bracket and remove the inner and outer arm attaching bolts.

9. Remove the extension rods fixtures' attaching bolts.

10. Remove the crossmember attaching bolts and remove the rear suspension assembly from the car.

11. Unbolt and remove the damper from the crossmember.

12. Remove the front and rear insulators from both ends of the crossmember.

13. Loosen, but do not remove, the lockbolts securing the outer arm bushings at both ends of the crossmember.

14. Pull the outer arm from the crossmember. Many times, the torsion bar will slide out of the crossmember with the outer arm.

15. Remove the torsion bar from either the crossmember or outer arm.

16. Inspect all parts for wear or damage. Inspect the crossmember for bending or deformation.

17. Inner arm bushings may be replaced at this time using a press. The thicker end of the bushings goes on the inner side.

18. Prior to installation note that the torsion bars are marked with an L or R on the outer end, and are not interchangeable.

19. If the original torsion bars are being installed, align the identification marks on the torsion bar end, crossmember and outer arm, install the torsion bar and arm and tighten the lockbolts. Skip Step 20. If new torsion bars are being installed, proceed to Step 20.

20. A special alignment jib must be fabricated. See the accompanying illustration for the dimension needed to make this jig. The jig is bolted to the rear insulator hole on the crossmember bracket as shown. Insert the torsion bar into the outer arm, aligning the red identification mark on the torsion bar end with the matchmark made on the outer arm top side. Install the torsion bar and arm so that the center of the flanged bolt hole on the arm is 32mm below the lower marking line on the jig. Then, pull the outer arm off of the torsion bar, leaving the bar undisturbed in the crossmember. Reposition the arm on the torsion bar, one serration counterclockwise from its former position. This will make the previously measured dimension, 33mm above the lower line. In any event, when the outer arm and torsion bar are properly positioned, the markeing lines on the jig will run diagonally across the center of the toe-in adjustment hole as shown. When the adjustment is complete, tighten the lockbolts. The clearance between the outer arm and the crossmember bracket, at the torsion bar, should be 5.0–7.0mm.

21. The remainder of installation is the reverse of removal. Observe the following torques:
• Extension rod fixture bolts: 45–50 ft. lbs.

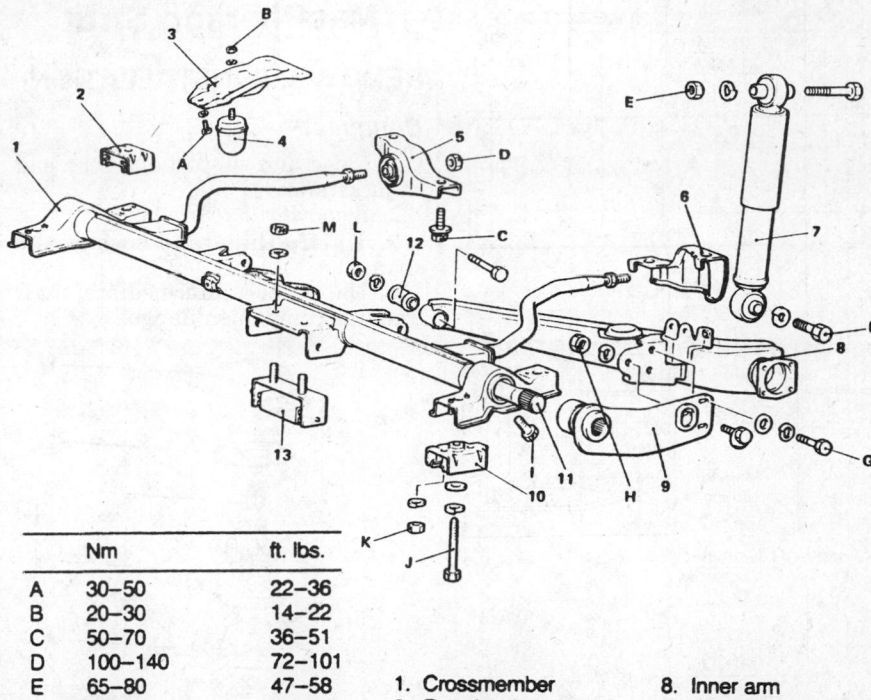

	Nm	ft. lbs.
A	30–50	22–36
B	20–30	14–22
C	50–70	36–51
D	100–140	72–101
E	65–80	47–58
F	80–110	58–79
G	80–100	58–72
H	120–140	87–101
I	22–30	16–22
J	80–120	58–87
K	10–15	7–10
L	70–90	51–65
M	19–28	14–20

1. Crossmember
2. Rear insulator
3. Stopper bracket
4. Bump stopper
5. Extension rod fixture
6. Protector
7. Shock absorber
8. Inner arm
9. Outer arm
10. Front insulator
11. Torsion bar
12. Inner arm bushing
13. Dynamic damper

4wd Vista rear suspension

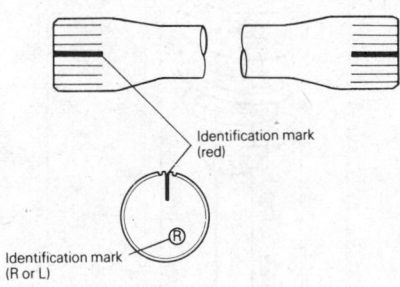

Identification mark (red)

Identification mark (R or L)

Torsion bar suspension identifying marks

• Extension rod-to-fixture nut: 95–100 ft. lbs.
• Shock absorber lower bolt: 75–80 ft. lbs.
• Outer arm attaching bolts: 65–70 ft. lbs.
• Toe-in bolt: 95–100 ft. lbs.
• Lockbolts: 20–22 ft. lbs.
• Crossmember attaching bolts: 80–85 ft. lbs.
• Front insulator nuts: 7–10 ft. lbs.
• Inner arm-to-crossmember bolts: 60–65 ft. lbs.
• Damper-to-crossmember nuts: 15–20 ft. lbs.

22. Lower the car to the ground and check the ride height. The ride height

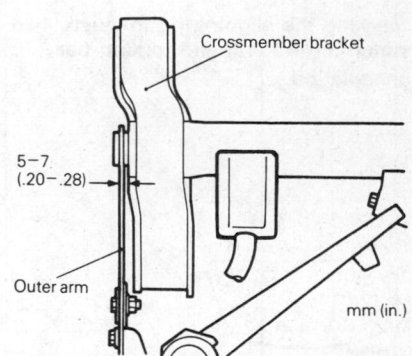

Crossmember bracket

5–7 (.20–.28)

Outer arm

mm (in.)

Outer arm-to-crossmember spacing

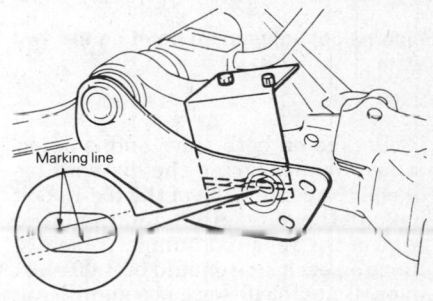

Marking line

Final alignment of the outer control arm

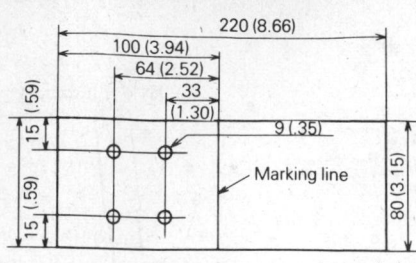

mm (in.)

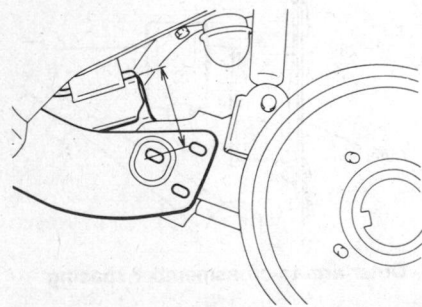

Left/right symmetrical marking

mm (in.)

Marking line

120 (4.72)

100 (3.94)

mm (in.)

Marking the aligning jig for Vista 4wd outer control arm and torsion bar installation

Ride height adjustment point on the 4wd Vista

is checked on both sides and is determined by measuring the distance between the center line of the toe-in bolt hole on the outer arm, and the lower edge of the rebound bumper. The distance on each side should be 4.00–4.11 in.es. If not, or if there is a significant difference between sides, the torsion bar(s) positioning is wrong.

MacPherson Strut

REMOVAL & INSTALLATION

Conquest

1. Raise and support the rear end on jackstands.
2. Remove the rear wheels.
3. Unclip the brake hose at the strut.
4. Unbolt the intermediate shaft from the companion flange.

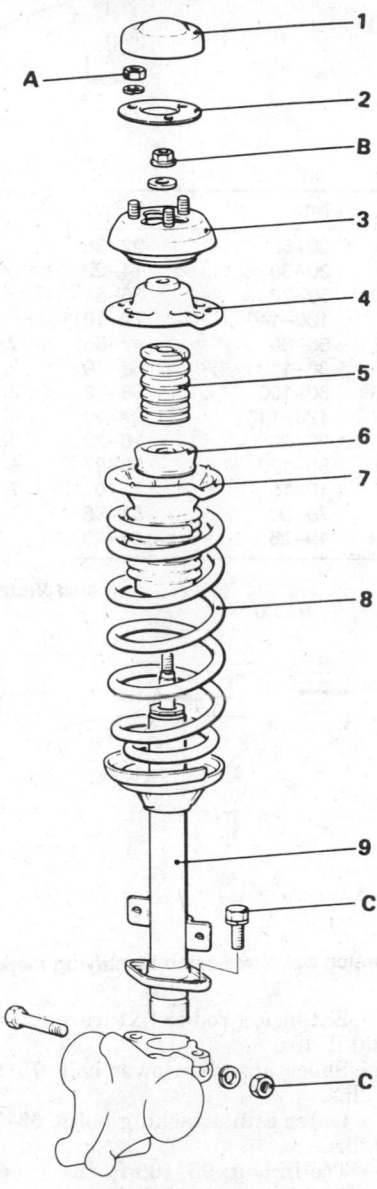

1. Strut house cap
2. Gasket
3. Strut insulator
4. Spring seat
5. Rubber helper
6. Rubber helper seat
7. Dust cover
8. Coil spring
9. Strut

Conquest rear strut

5. Unbolt the strut assembly from the axleshaft housing. Remove the housing coupling bolts. Separate the strut from the housing by pushing the housing downward while prying open the coupling on the housing.
6. Remove the strut upper end attaching nuts, found under the side trim in the cargo area.
7. Lift out the strut.
8. Installation is the reverse of removal. Torque the upper end nuts to 20–25 ft. lbs.; the strut-to-housing bolts to 50 ft. lbs.; the coupling bolt to 50 ft. lbs.

OVERHAUL

For all strut overhaul procedures, please refer to "Strut Overhaul" in the Unit Repair section.

Shock Absorbers

REMOVAL & INSTALLATION

Except 4wd Vista

1. Remove the hub cap or wheel cover. Loosen the lug nuts.
2. Raise the rear of the car. Support the car with jackstands.

NOTE: The body sill is marked with two dimples to locate the support position. Never place a stand anywhere but between these marks or the body can be damaged.

3. Remove the wheel. Remove the upper mounting bolt and nut.
4. While holding the bottom stud mount nut with one wrench, remove the locknut with another wrench.
5. Remove the shock absorber.
6. Check the shock for:
   a. Excessive oil leakage; some minor weeping is permissable.
   b. Bent center rod, damaged outer case, or other defects.
   c. Pump the shock absorber several times, if it offers even resistance on full strokes it may be considered serviceable.
7. Install the upper shock mounting nut and bolt. Hand tighten the nut.
8. Install the bottom eye of the shock over the spring stud. Tighten the lower nut to 12–15 ft. lbs. on rear wheel drive models; 47–58 ft. lbs. on front wheel drive models.
9. Finally, tighten the upper nut to 47–58 ft. lbs. on all models except station wagons, which are tightened to 12–15 ft. lbs.

4wd Vista

1. Raise and support the rear end on jackstands under the fram.

2. Remove the rear wheels.

3. Using a floor jack, raise the inner control arm slightly.

4. Unbolt the top, then the bottom of the shock absorber. Remove it from the car.

5. Installation is the reverse of removal. Torque the top nut to 55–58 ft. lbs.; the bottom bolt to 75–80 ft. lbs.

Lower Control Arm

REMOVAL & INSTALLATION

Rear Wheel Drive – Except Conquest

1. Support the vehicle body on safety stands. Use a jack under the rear axle to raise the rear axle assembly slightly.

2. Remove the wheel and the upper control arm rod.

3. Detach the parking brake rear cable from the lower arm.

4. Remove the lower arm from the rear axle housing and from the bracket attached to the body.

5. Temporarily install the lower arm (check for marking on left side arm) and torque the bolts to 94.0–108.0 ft. lbs. (127.0–147.0 Nm). Torque the assist link bushing bolt to 47.0–58.0 ft. lbs. (64.0–78.0 Nm).

6. With the special nut assembly placed securely against the rear axle housing bracket, install the upper control arm rod to the bracket. Torque the bolt to 94.0 ft. lbs. (127.0–147.0 Nm).

———— CAUTION ————

Always use new bolts.

Conquest

1. Raise and support the rear end on jackstands. Allow the wheels to hang freely.

2. Remove the rear wheels.

3. Disconnect the parking brake cable from the lower arm.

4. Disconnect the stabilizer bar.

5. Unbolt the lower control arm from the axleshaft housing.

6. Unbolt the lower control arm from the front support.

7. Unbolt the lower control arm from the crossmember and remove it.

8. Installation is the reverse of removal. Apply a thin coating of chassis lube to the cutout portion of the lower arm-to-axleshaft housing shaft. Do not allow the grease to touch the bushings. Insert the shaft with the mark on its head facing downward. When positioning the lower control arm on the crossmember, align the mark on the crossmember with the line on the plate. Torque the lower

Left side......L or white paint
Right side......R or no marking

Rear lower control arm identifying marks for all rear wheel drive cars except Conquest

control arm-to-front support bolts to 108 ft. lbs.; the arm-to-crossmember bolts to 108 ft. lb; the arm to axleshaft housing bolts to 60 ft. lbs.; the arm locking pin to 15 ft. lbs. Have the rear wheel alignment checked.

Trailing Arm

REMOVAL & INSTALLATION

Front Wheel Drive – Except 4wd Vista

1. Support the side frame on jack stands and remove the rear wheels. Remove the rear brake assembly.

2. Remove the muffler and jack the control arm just enough to raise it slightly.

3. Remove the shock absorber and lower the jack. Remove the coil spring and temporarily install the shock absorber to the control arm.

4. Disconnect the brake hoses at the rear suspension arms and remove the rear suspension from the body as an assembly.

5. Install the fixture-to-body bolts and torque to 36.0–51.0 ft. lbs. (49.0–69.0 Nm).

6. Install the coil springs and loosely install the shock absorbers. Tighten the shock absorber bolts to specification after the vehicle is lowered to the floor.

7. Install the rear brake assembly.

8. Lower the vehicle and tighten the suspension arm end nuts on all except Colt Vista: to 36.0–51.0 ft. lbs. (49.0–69.0 Nm), Colt Vista: 94–108 ft. lbs. (108–150 Nm) and the shock bolts to 47.0–58.0 ft. lbs. (64.0–78.0 Nm), for all models.

9. Install the brake drums and wheels.

10. Bleed the brake system and adjust the rear brake shoe clearance.

Rear Wheel Bearings

NOTE: For all RWD models, please refer to the "Drive Axle" section.

REMOVAL, INSPECTION AND INSTALLATION

1981–84 Colt, 1985–88

1. Loosen the lug nuts, raise the rear of the car and support it on jackstands. Remove the wheel.

2. Remove the grease cap, cotter pin, nut and washer.

3. Remove the brake drum. While pulling the drum, the outer bearing will fall out. Do not drop it.

4. Pry out the grease seal and discard it.

5. Remove the inner bearing.

6. Check the bearing races. If any scoring, heat checking or damage is noted, they should be replaced.

NOTE: When bearing or races need replacement, replace them as a set.

7. Inspect the bearings. If wear or looseness or heat checking is found replace them.

8. If the bearings and races are to be replaced, drive out the races with a brass drift.

9. Before installing new races, coat them with lithium based wheel bearing grease. The races are most easily installed using a driver made for that purpose. They can, however, be driven into place with a brass drift. Make sure that they are fully seated.

10. Thoroughly pack the bearings with lithium based wheel bearing grease. Pack the hub with grease.

11. Install the inner bering and coat the lip and rim of the grease seal with grease. Drive the seal into place with a seal driver.

12. Mount the drum onto the hub, slide the outer bearing into place, install the washer and thread the nut into place, finger-tightly.

13. Install a torque wrench on the nut. While turning the drum by hand, tighten the nut to 15 ft. lbs. Back off the nut until it is loose, then tighten it to 4 ft. lbs. If the torque wrench is not all that accurate below 10 ft. lbs., use an in. lb. torque wrench and tighten the nut to 48 inch lbs.

14. Install the lock cap and insert a new cotter pin. If the lock cap and hole don't align, and repositioning the cap can't accomplish alignment, back off the nut no more than 15°. If that won't align the holes either, try the adjustment procedure over again.

1985–88 Colt

NOTE: Special tools are needed for this procedure.

1. Loosen the lug nuts. Raise the rear of the car and support it on jackstands.

2. Remove the wheel.

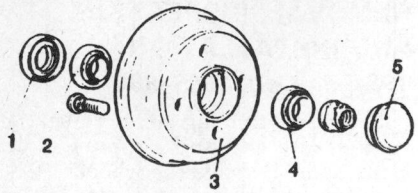

1. Oil seal
2. Inner bearing
3. Brake drum
4. Outer bearing
5. Hub cap

Rear wheel bearing assembly—1985-88 Colt

3. Remove the grease cap.
4. Remove the nut.
5. Pull the drum off. The outer bearing will fll out while the drum is coming off. Do not drop it.
6. Pry out the oil seal. Discard it.
7. Remove the inner bearing.
8. Check the bearing races. If any scoring, heat checking or damage is noted, they should be replaced.

NOTE: When bearing or races need replacement, replace them as a set.

9. Inspect the bearings. If wear or looseness or heat checking is found, replace them.
10. If the bearings and races are to be replaced, drive out the race with a brass drift.
11. Before installing new races, coat them with lithium based wheel bearing grease. The races are most easily installed using a driver made for that purpose. They can, however, be driven into place with a brass drift. Make sure that they are fully seated.
12. Thoroughly pack the bearings with lithium based wheel bearing grease. Pack the hub with grease.
13. Install the inner bearing and coat the lip and rim of the grease seal with grease. Drive the seal into place with a seal driver.
14. Mount the drum on the axleshaft. Install the outer bearing. Don't install the nut at this time.
15. Using a pull scale attached to one of the lugs, measure the starting force necessary to get the drum to turn. Starting force should be 5 lbs. If the starting torque is greater than specific, replace the bearings.
16. Install the nut on the axleshaft. Thread the nut on, by hand, to a point at which the back face of the nut is 2–3mm from the shoulder of the shaft (where the threads end).
17. Using an inch lb. torque wrench, turn the nut counterclockwise 2 to 3 turns, noting the average force needed during the turning procedure. Turning torque for the nut should be about 48 inch lb. If turning torque is not within 5 inch lb., either way, replace the nut.
18. Tighten the nut to 75–110 ft. lbs.
19. Using a stand-mounted gauge, check the axial play of the wheel bearings. Play should be less than 0.0079 in. If play cannot be brought within that figure, the unit is assembled incorrectly.
20. Pack the grease cap with wheel bearing grease and install it.

STEERING

Steering Wheel

REMOVAL & INSTALLATION

1. Pry off the steering wheel center foam pad.
2. Remove the steering wheel retaining nut.
3. Using a steering wheel puller, remove the wheel.
4. Be sure the front wheels are in a straight ahead position. Reverse the removal procedure. Tighten the nut to 30 ft. lbs.

Turn Signal Switch

REMOVAL & INSTALLATION

Rear Wheel Drive

1. Remove the steering wheel and have the tilt handle in the lowest position.
2. Remove the instrument cluster cover and column covers.
3. Remove the connectors from the column switch from the column tube.

NOTE: Early models may have the turn signal and hazard switches mounted on a base plate. Removal of the attaching screws will allow these switches to be removed without removal of the remaining switches.

4. Switch installation is the reverse of removal. Be sure that the switch is centered in the column or self-cancelling will be affected.

Front Wheel Drive

1. Remove the steering wheel.
2. Remove the lap heater duct.
3. Remove the column covers.
4. Remove the switch retaining screws, disconnect the wiring and remove the switch.
5. Installation is the reverse of removal.

Ignition Lock and Switch

REMOVAL & INSTALLATION

NOTE: When replacing the ignition switch or key reminder switch only, remove the column cover, remove the screw holding the switch, and pull out the switch.

1. Remove the turn signal switch as described above.
2. Cut a notch in the lock bracket bolt head with a hacksaw.
3. Remove the bolt and lock.
4. Remove the column cover and unbolt and remove the ignition switch.
5. Install both lock and switch in reverse of removal.

NOTE: When installing the lock, the bolt should be tightened until the head is crushed. When installing the switch, install the switch bolt loosely and insert and work the key a few times to make sure everything checks out before tightening the bolt.

Manual Steering Gear

REMOVAL & INSTALLATION

Rear Wheel Drive

1. Remove the clamp bolt connecting the steering shaft with the steering gear housing mainshaft. Check for, or make, mating marks for the assembly.
2. Using appropriate pullers, disconnect the pitman arm and the relay rod at the linkage connection.
3. Remove the gearbox from the frame by removal of the attaching bolts.
4. Remove the pitman arm from the cross shaft. Check for mating marks.
5. Installation is the reverse of removal.

Power Steering Gear

The power steering consists of a belt driven pump, a separate fluid reservoir, pressure and return lines, and a steering gear assembly with an integral control valve.

REMOVAL & INSTALLATION

Rear Wheel Drive

1. Matchmark and disconnect the steering shaft from the gearbox main shaft.

2. Disconnect the tie rod end and pitman arm from the relay rod.

3. Remove the air cleaner and disconnect the pressure and return lines from the steering gear assembly.

4. Remove any interfering splash pans from underneath the vehicle.

5. If necessary, remove the kickdown linkage splash pan shield and bolts. Move the fuel line aside to avoid damage during removal.

6. Remove the frame bolts from the gearbox and lower the unit from the vehicle.

7. Installation is the reverse of removal. Make sure that all matchmarks align. After tightening the pitman arm nut make sure that the distance between the centerline of the lowest steering gear mounting bolt and the top of the pitman arm is 19.5mm. Observe the following torques:
- Pitman arm nut: 94–109 ft. lbs.
- Steering gear mounting bolts: 40–47 ft. lbs.
- Tie rod socket and relay rod: 25–33 ft. lbs.
- High pressure hose: 22–29 ft. lbs.
- Return hose: 29–36 ft. lbs.

ADJUSTMENT

NOTE: The steering gear must be disconnected from the steering shaft.

1. Measure the mainshaft preload with an inch lbs. torque wrench. The preload should be 3.5–6.9 inch lbs., with the cross-shaft adjusting bolt backed off.

2. Adjust the valve housing top cover to obtain the proper preload. When correct, lock the top cover with the locking nut.

3. Tighten the cross-shaft adjusting bolt until zero lash is present. Check the total starting torque to rotate the main shaft. The torque should be 5.2–8.7 inch lbs.

4. Adjust the cross-shaft until the required starting torque is obtained and lock the adjusting bolt nut securely.

Rack and Pinion Steering

REMOVAL & INSTALLATION

1981–84 Colt and Champ Manual and Power Steering
1985–88 Colt Manual Steering

1. Loosen the lug nuts.
2. Raise and support the front end on jackstands under the frame.
3. Remove the wheels.

1. Steering wheel
2. Tilt bracket
3. Steering shaft
4. Gear box
5. Tie rod assembly (right)
6. Relay rod
7. Tie rod assembly (left)
8. Idler arm

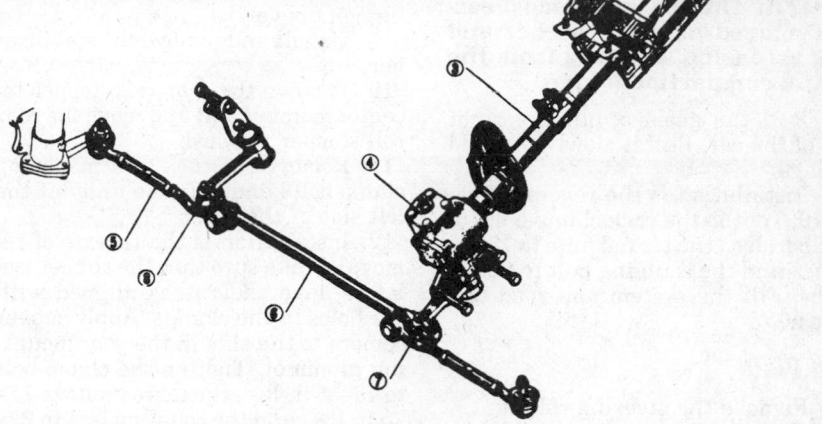

Rear wheel drive steering system

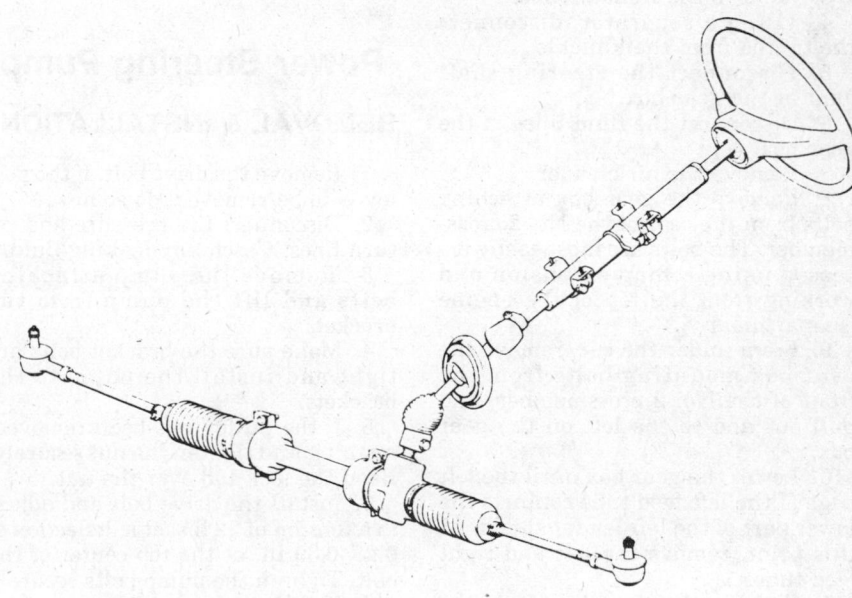

Typical rack and piston steering system

4. Remove the steering shaft-to-pinion coupling bolt.

5. Disconnect the tie rod ends with a separator. On cars with power steering, drain the fluid and disconnect the hoses at the gear unit.

6. Remove the clamps securing the rack to the crossmember and remove the unit from the car.

7. Install the rubber mount for the gear box with the slit on the downside. The remainder of installation is the reverse of removal. Torque the rack-to-crossmember bolts to 22–29 ft. lbs. on 1981–84 models, or 45–60 ft. lbs. on 1985–88 models; the cou-pling bolt to 11–14 ft. lbs. on 1981–84 models, or 22–25 ft. lbs. on 1985–88 models and the tie-rod nuts to 11–25 ft. lbs. Fill the system and road test the car.

2wd Vista

1. Loosen the lug nuts.
2. Raise and support the front end on jackstands under the frame.
3. Remove the wheels.
4. Remove the steering shaft-to-pinion coupling bolt.
5. Disconnect the tie rod ends with a separator. On cars with power steer-

ing, disconnect the hoses at the gear unit.

6. Remove the crossmember support bracket from the crossmember on the right side of the car.

7. Unbolt the gearbox from the crossmember.

NOTE: The gearbox is most easily removed using a ratchet and long extension, working from the engine compartment side.

8. Pull the gearbox out the right side of the car. Pull it slowly to avoid damage.

9. Installation is the reverse of removal. Torque the rack clamp bolts to 43–58 ft. lbs., the tie rod nuts to 17–25 ft. lbs., and the coupling bolt to 22–25 ft. lbs. Fill the system and road test the car.

4wd Vista

1. Remove the steering column.
2. Raise and suport the car on jackstands under the frame.
3. Remove the front wheels.
4. Using a separator, disconnect the tie rod from the knuckle.
5. Disconnect the steering shaft joint at the gear box.
6. Disconnect the fluid lines at the gear box.
7. Remove the air cleaner.
8. Remove the gear box attaching bolts from the rear of the No. 2 crossmember. The bolts are most easily accessed using a long extension and working from the top of the engine compartment.
9. From under the car, remove the gear box mounting bolts from the front of the No. 2 crossmember, and pull out and to the left on the gear box.
10. Lower the gear box until the left edge of the left feed tube contacts the lower part of the left fender shield. At this point, remove the left and right feed tubes.
11. Remove the gear box from the car.
12. Installation is the reverse of removal. When installing the clamps, make sure that the rubber projections are aligned with the holes in the clamps. Install the tie rods so that 191–193mm shows between the tie rod end locknut and the beginning of the boot. Torque the gear box mounting bolts to 55–60 ft. lbs.; the tie rod-to-knuckle nut to 20–25 ft. lbs.

1985–88 Colt With Power

Steering

1. Loosen the lug nuts.
2. Raise and support the front end on jackstands under the frame.
3. Remove the wheels.

4. Remove the steering shaft-to-pinion coupling bolt.
5. Disconnect the tie rod ends with a separator.
6. Drain the fluid.
7. Disconnect the hoses from the gearbox.
8. Remove the band from the steering joint cover.
9. Unbolt and remove the stabilizer bar.
10. Remove the rear roll stopper-to-center member bolt and move the rear roll stopper forward.
11. Remove the rack unit mounting clamp bolts and take the unit out the left side of the car.
12. Installation is the reverse of removal. Make sure that the rubber isolators have their nubs aligned with the holes in the clamps. Apply rubber cement to the slits in the gear mounting grommet. Tighten the clamp bolt to 43–58 ft. lbs., the tie rod nuts to 11–25 ft. lbs., and the coupling bolt to 22–25 ft. lbs.
13. Fill the system and road test the car.

Power Steering Pump

REMOVAL & INSTALLATION

1. Remove the drive belt. If the pulley is to be removed, do so now.
2. Disconnect the pressure and return lines. Catch any leaking fluid.
3. Remove the pump attaching bolts and lift the pump from the brackets.
4. Make sure the bracket bolts are tight and install the pump to the brackets.
5. If the pulley has been removed, install it and tighten the nut securely. Bend the lock tab over the nut.
6. Install the drive belt and adjust to a tension of 22 lbs. at a deflection of 0.28–0.39 in. at the top center of the belt. Tighten the pump bolts securely to hold the tension.
7. Connect the pressure and return lines and fill the reservoir with Dexron fluid.
8. Bleed the system (refer to the "Bleeding" procedure).

BLEEDING THE SYSTEM

1. The reservoir should be full of Dexron®II fluid.
2. Jack up the front wheels and support the vehicle safely.
3. Turn the steering wheel fully to the right and left until no air bubbles appear in the fluid. Maintain the reservoir level.
4. Lower the vehicle and with the engine idling, turn the wheels fully to the right and left. Stop the engine.

5. Install a tube from the bleeder screw on the steering gear box to the reservoir.
6. Start the engine, turn the steering wheel fully to the left and loosen the bleeder screw.
7. Repeat the procedure until no air bubbles pass through the tube.
8. Tighten the bleeder screw and remove the tube. Refill the reservoir as needed, and check that no further bubbles are present in the fluid.

—————— CAUTION ——————
An abrupt rise in the fluid level after stopping the engine is a sign of incomplete bleeding. This will cause noise from the pump or control valve.

Steering Linkage

NOTE: The following applies to rear wheel drive cars. For front wheel drive component service, see the Rack and Pinion procedures above.

REMOVAL & INSTALLATION

Tie Rods

1. Using a puller, disconnect the tie rod ends from the steering knuckle.
2. Loosen the jam nut and remove the tie rod ends from the tie rod. The outer end is left-hand threaded and the inner is right-hand threaded.
3. Grease the tie rod threads and install the ends. Turn each end in an equal amount.
4. Install the tie rod assembly on the steering knuckle and relay rod. Tighten the castellated nuts to 29–36 ft. lbs. Use new cotter pins.
5. Adjust the toe-in as described under "Wheel Alignment."

Relay Rod

1. Disconnect the tie rod ends from the steering knuckles with a puller.
2. Again using the puller, disconnect the relay rod from the idler arm and the pitman arm.
3. Remove the relay arm.
4. Install the rod in the reverse order of removal. Tighten the tie rod end nuts to 29–36 ft. lbs. Tighten the relay rod-to-pitman arm nut and relay rod-to-idler arm nut to 29–43 ft. lbs. Always use new cotter pins.

Idler Arm

1. Disconnect the idler arm from the relay rod using a puller.
2. Remove the retaining bolts and remove the idler arm.
3. Mount the idler arm on the frame and tighten the bolts to 25–29 ft. lbs.
4. Attach the relay rod to the idler

arm and tighten the stud nut to 29–43 ft. lbs. Use a new cotter pin.

BRAKES

For all brake system repair and service procedures not detailed below, please refer to "Brakes" in the Unit Repair section.

Master Cylinder

REMOVAL & INSTALLATION

Rear Wheel Drive Cars

——————— CAUTION ———————

Be careful not to spill brake fluid on the painted surfaces of the car. The brake fluid will cause damage to the paint.

1. Disconnect all hydraulic lines from the master cylinder. On models with remote reservoir, remove and plug the hoses from the master cylinder caps. If the master cylinder has a fluid level warning device, disconnect the wiring harness.
2. On non-power brake cars, remove the clevis pin that connects the master cylinder push rod to the brake pedal.
3. Loosen and remove the master cylinder mounting nuts, either from the firewall (manual brakes) or from the power brake booster. Remove the master cylinder.

NOTE: Before installing the master cylinder, make sure that there is less than 0.03 in. clearance between the pushrod and master cylinder piston on all but the Conquest. On Conquest, the clearance should be 0.028–0.043 in.

4. Mount the master cylinder to the firewall (manual brakes) or to the power brake booster.
5. Connect the push rod to the brake pedal (manual brakes).
6. Connect all brake lines and wiring harnesses and fill the master cylinder reservoirs with clean fluid.
7. Bleed the brake system.

Front Wheel Drive Cars

1. Disconnect the fluid level sensor.
2. Disconnect the brake tubes from the master cylinder and cap them immediately.
3. On cars with a turbocharger, remove the reservoir fromm the reservoir holder.

4. Unbolt and remove the master cylinder from the booster.
5. Installation is the reverse of removal. Measure the master cylinder pushrod clearance; it should be 0.016–0.31 in. Torque the mounting bolts to 6–9 ft. lbs. (72–108 inch lbs.).

Power Brake Booster

REMOVAL & INSTALLATION

1. Remove the master cylinder.
2. Disconnect the vacuum line from the booster.
3. Remove the pin connecting the power brake operating rod and the brake lever.
4. Unbolt and remove the booster.
5. Replace the packing on both sides of the booster-to-firewall spacer with new packing.
6. If the check valve was removed, make sure the direction of installation marking on the valve is followed.
7. Installation is the reverse of removal. Torque the booster-to-firewall nuts to 6–9 ft. lbs. (54–108 inch lbs.). Torque the master cylinder-to-booster nuts to 6–9 ft. lbs.
8. Adjust the brake pedal and master cylinder pushrod as explained earlier.

Wheel Cylinders

REMOVAL & INSTALLATION

1. Remove the brake shoes.
2. Place a container under the brake backing plate to catch the brake fluid that will run out of the wheel cylinder. Disconnect the brake line and remove the cylinder mounting bolts. Remove the cylinder from the backing plate.
3. Install new or rebuilt wheel cylinder. Install brake shoes, etc. Bleed the brake system.

Parking Brake Cable

REMOVAL & INSTALLATION

Rear Wheel Drive Models

1. Block the front wheels, jack up the rear of the car and support with jackstands.
2. Release the parking brake. Pull off the clevis pins from both sides of the rear brake. Disconnect the cable from the extension lever.
3. Remove the brake drums and disconnect the cable from the lever. Remove the retaining clip and push the cable through the hole in the backing plate. Remove the front cable after disconnecting the parking brake

lever. On rear disc brake models: Remove the clips under the floor and remove the cable.
4. Installation is the reverse of the removal. When installing, make sure that the cable clips do not interfere with a rotating part. Adjust the extension lever to stop first. Then adjust the left cable, the right on the Challenger/Sapporo and Wagons.

Front Wheel Drive Models

ALL EXCEPT VISTA

1. Block the front wheels, raise the rear of the car and support on jackstands.
2. Disconnect the brake cable at the parking brake lever (brakes released). Remove the cable clamps inside the driver's compartment (two bolts). Disconnect the clamps on the rear suspension arm.
3. Remove the rear brake drums and the brake shoe assemblies. Disconnect the parking brake cable from the lever on the trailing (rear) brake shoe. Remove the brake cables.
4. Installation is the reverse of removal.

VISTA

1. Remove the console box and parking brake cover.
2. Take out the front, second and third seats.
3. Remove the floor carpet.
4. Remove the cable adjuster, and then disconnect the front parking brake cable and parking brake lever.
5. Remove the equalizer cover, and then remove the coupling of the parking cable at the interior side.
6. Remove the parking brake cable clamp on the rear suspension arm.
7. Remove the rear brake drum.
8. Remove the snap ring of the rear side of the backing plate.
9. Disconnect the lever and cable and take out the cable.
10. Installation is the reverse of removal. The parking brake lever stroke is 5–7 clicks. The switch should be adjusted so that the light goes on when the brake lever is pulled one notch.

ADJUSTMENT

NOTE: Overtightening of the parking brake will result in dragging brakes.

Front Wheel Drive

1981–84

1. Release the parking brake.
2. Adjust the extension lever to backing plate clearance to 0.008–0.080 in., by moving the adjustment nut on the cable.

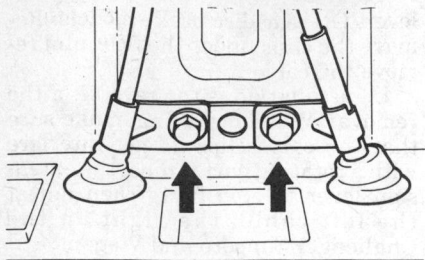

Location of cable clamp attaching bolts in passenger compartment—all except Vista

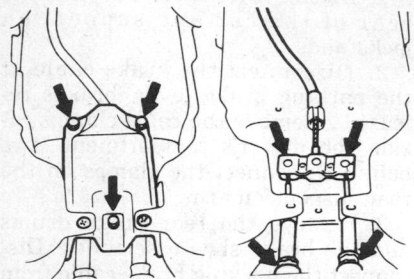

Parking brake equalizer cover bolts and cable coupler—Colt Vista

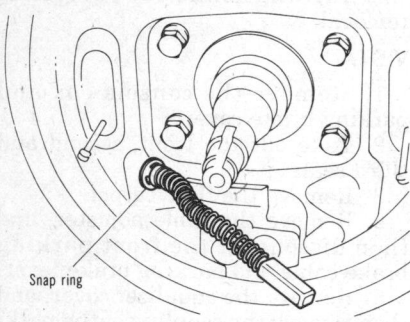

Snap ring

Cable snap ring on backing plate

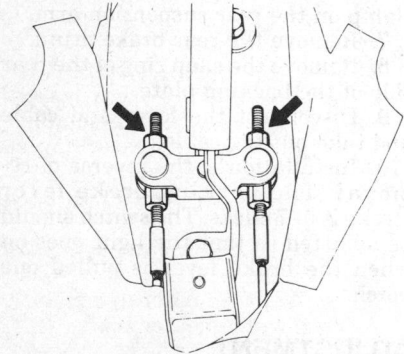

Cable adjusting nuts—front wheel drive models except Vista

3. Check the brake lever free stroke. Brake drag should occur at 6–8 notches.

1985–88

1. Pull the parking brake lever up with a force of about 45 lbs. If that value cannot be determined, just pull it

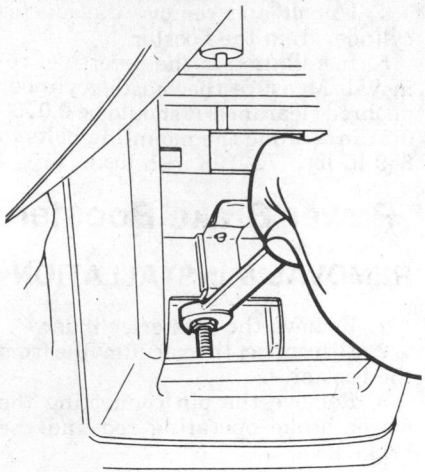

1985 and later Colt parking brake cable adjustment

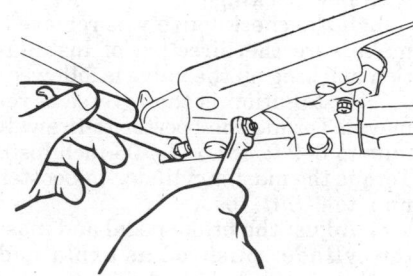

Lever adjustment—Colt Vista

up as far as possible. The total number of clicks heard should be 5–7.

2. If the number of clicks was not within that range, release the lever and back off the cable adjuster locknut at the base of the lever and tighten the adjusting nut until there is no more slack in the cable.

3. Operate the lever and brake pedal several times, until no more clicks are heard from the automatic adjuster.

4. Turn the adjusting nut to give the proper number of clicks when the lever is raised full travel.

5. Raise and support the rear of the car on jackstands.

6. Release the brake lever and make sure that the rear wheels turn freely. If not, back off on the adjusting nut until they do.

Rear Wheel Drive

EXCEPT CONQUEST

1. Release the parking brake.
2. Adjust the extension lever to stopper clearance to 0.100 in. by loosening both cable lever attaching bolts and adjusting the nut. Move the cable lever to the right. Set the left cable first and then the right.
3. Check the brake lever free

stroke. Brake drag should occur at 5–7 notches.

CONQUEST

1. Pull up on the lever, counting the number of clicks. Total travel should yield 4–5 clicks.
2. If not, remove the center console and turn the adjusting nut on the lever rod to obtain the required travel.
3. Raise and support the rear of the car on jackstands.
4. With the parking brake released, make sure that the rear wheels turn freely.

CHASSIS ELECTRICAL

Heater Blower

REMOVAL & INSTALLATION

1981–83 Colt Coupe, Sedan, and Rear Wheel Drive Hatchback

1. Remove the instrument cluster (coupe and sedan). Remove the instrument cluster and the glove box (hatchback).
2. Remove the heater control bracket assembly.
3. Remove the motor assembly and disconnect the wire connection.
4. (Coupe and sedan) Remove the motor in a horizontal position while holding the control bracket down.
5. (Hatchback) Remove the motor through the glove box opening.
6. Installation is the reverse of removal.

1981 Challenger and Sapporo

1. Remove the instrument cluster and the meter cluster.
2. Disconnect the wiring to the motor.
3. Remove the motor assembly.
4. Installation is the reverse of the removal.

1981–83 Challenger and Sapporo

1. Remove the lower instrument pad cover assembly from under the glove box.
2. Remove the passenger side console cover.
3. Remove the glove box-to-center support attaching screw.
4. Loosen the stops at either side of the glove box so that the glove box swings free.
5. Disconnect the glove box light.

6. Remove the glove compartment assembly from the instrument pad.

7. Remove the ducts, heater fan switch connector and control cables.

8. Remove three attaching bolts and lift out the blower assembly.

9. Remove the wiring bracket and the motor connector. Remove the vent tube and three motor attaching screws. Lift out the motor and remove the fan from the motor assembly.

10. Installation is the reverse of removal.

1981–84 Front Wheel Drive Models

1. Disconnect the battery ground cable. Remove the center console and parcel tray, if equipped.

2. Remove the center vent duct and defroster duct. Remove the instrument panel trim. Remove the two heater unit top bolts and loosen the bottom attaching bolt.

3. Disconnect the wiring to the motor.

4. Tilt the heater unit toward the rear of the vehicle, remove the three motor attaching bolts and remove the motor.

5. The blower fan may be removed from the shaft if necessary.

6. Installation is the reverse of the removal procedure.

1985–88 Colt

1. Remove the glove box and parcel tray.

2. Disconnect the changeover control wire and duct.

3. Remove the blower case.

4. Unbolt and remove the blower motor from the case.

5. The fan is removable from the motor shaft.

6. Installation is the reverse of removal.

Vista

1. Remove the upper and lower glove boxes.

2. Disconnect the wiring from the blower assembly.

3. Remove the blower motor mounting bolts and lift out the motor. If the entire blower case is to be removed, the instrument panel will have to be removed first.

Conquest

1. Remove the lower panel cover and the glove box.

2. Disconnect the air changeover cable from the blower.

3. Disconnect the duct from the blower.

4. Disconnect the blower wiring.

5. Unbolt and remove the blower motor.

(1) Defroster nozzle
(2) Side ventilator duct
(3) Air duct
(4) Water hose
(5) Water valve assembly
(6) Heater assembly
(7) Turbo fan
(8) Motor
(9) Heater resistor
(10) Heater core

(11) Center ventilator duct
(12) Heater control lever assembly
(13) Pad
(14) Air outlet garnish
(15) Rear ventilator duct
(16) * Rear heater duct
(17) * Rear heater cover

(18) * Rear heater nozzle
(19) ** Side defroster outlet
(20) ** Side defroster duct

NOTE: * Challenger, Sapporo and Colt Station Wagon for Canada
** Colt Station Wagon for Canada

Heater assembly used on all rear wheel drive cars except Conquest

6. Installation is the reverse of removal.

Heater Core

NOTE: The core is contained within the heater case. The core and case are removed as a unit.

REMOVAL & INSTALLATION

1981 Colt Coupe, Sedan and Rear Wheel Drive Hatchback

1. Drain the cooling system.

2. Disconnect the battery ground cable.

3. Place the water valve in the OFF position.

4. Remove the under tray, defroster nozzle and colsole box.

5. Disconnect each heater control wire and connectors at the heater assembly.

6. Disconnect the water hoses, heater duct and wiring harness.

7. Remove the heater assembly.

8. Remove the heater core.

9. Installation is the reverse of removal.

1981–83 Challenger and Sapporo, Station Wagon

1. Drain the cooling system.

2. Remove the glove box, instrument cluster and console assembly.

3. Disconnect the heater control wires at the heater box.

4. Remove the heater control assembly.

5. Disconnect all heater hoses and air ducts.

6. Remove the heater assembly.

7. Remove the heater core.

8. Installation is the reverse of removal.

NOTE: Upon removal of the heater control box, the heater core is removable. Replace all gaskets and insulation in its proper place.

1981–83 Challenger and Sapporo

1. Disconnect the negative battery terminal.

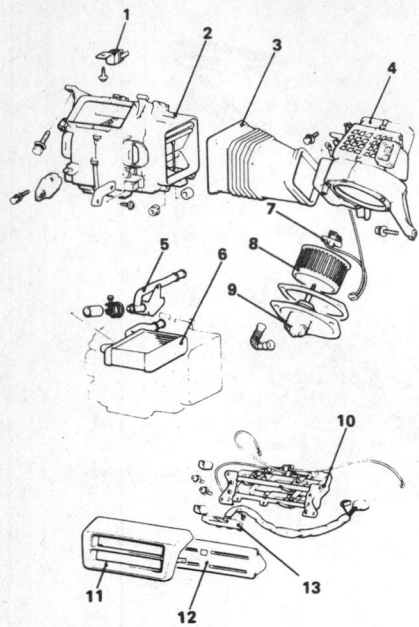

1. Heater relay
2. Heater unit
3. Duct
4. Blower case
5. Water control assembly
6. Heater core
7. Resistor
8. Fan
9. Fan motor assembly
10. Heater control assembly
11. Heater control panel
    cover
12. Heater control panel
13. Fan switch

Heating system—Colt Vista

2. Remove the steering wheel horn pad attaching screws, from the back of the steering wheel. Remove the horn pad.

3. Remove the steering wheel lock nut and remove the steering wheel using a steering wheel puller tool.

—— CAUTION ——
Do not apply impact to the column or wheel with a hammer to loosen the wheel from the column. Use the steering wheel puller tool.

4. Loosen the tilt lock lever and lower the steering column fully.

5. Remove the meter (instrument cluster) hood. Remove the meter (instrument cluster) assembly and disconnect the electrical and cable connectors.

6. Remove the inner box from the console accessory box. Press on the spring catch, to remove the remote control mirror switch from the accessory box.

7. Remove the accessory box assembly and disconnect the electrical connector.

8. Pull off the heater control knob, pull out the control panel and take out the illumination harness.

9. Pull off the radio knobs and remove the radio to panel attaching nuts. Remove the radio panel.

10. Remove the cover assembly attaching screws from below the glove box and remove the cover assembly.

11. Remove the console side covers (both sides).

12. Remove the shift knob on manual transmission vehicles and remove the center console.

13. Remove the instrument pad bolt covers at both ends of the instrument pad and remove the attaching nuts.

14. Take off the hood lock release knob and remove the release cable attaching screws. Remove the hood lock release assembly from the instrument pad.

15. Remove the defroster garnish.

16. Remove the screws attaching the glove compartment to the center dash reinforcement.

17. Remove all remaining instrument pad attaching bolts.

18. Disconnect the clock, glove box, chime and dimmer control and remove the instrument pad.

19. Disconnect the defogger switch, radio, chime driver, defogger relay connectors and the antenna feeder end.

20. Remove the center reinforcement.

21. Set the heater temperature control to "WARM" position and drain the coolant from the radiator.

22. From the engine compartment, remove the heater hoses from the heater assembly.

23. From under the dash, remove the heater ducts from the heater assembly. To remove the rear sheat heater duct, move the outlet control link to the "VENT" side, insert a finger into the outlet and remove the duct from inside heater.

24. Disconnect the power relay connector, remove three attaching bolts and remove the heater assembly. Remove the heater core.

25. The installation is the reverse of removal.

26. Connect the heater hoses in a fully seated position on the inlet and outlet fittings of the heater core assembly, so they will not leak.

27. Adjust the heater control cable by setting the control panel to "COOL" and heater unit lever on "COOL" and tighten the cable at that position.

NOTE: In order to fill the engine cooling and heating system completely it may be necssary to open the water valve fully, run the engine to circulate the cool- ant and then stop the engine and add more coolant.

1981–84 Front Wheel Drive Colt and Champ Models

1. Disconnect the battery ground cable.

2. Place the water valve lever in the HOT position. Drain the coolant.

3. Remove the center console and parcel tray, if equipped.

4. Remove the center ventilation duct and the defroster duct. Disconnect the instrument trim panel and cluster hood.

5. Disconnect all control wires at the heater unit.

6. Disconnect the heater hose from the engine. Remove the clamps from the hoses. Disconnect the heater wiring harness.

7. Remove the two top mounting bolts and the one lower nut. Remove the heater assembly.

8. Installation is the reverse of removal. Be sure the grommets through which the heater hoses pass when entering the passenger compartment are secured when reinstalling.

1985–88 Colt and Vista

1. Disconnect the battery ground cable.

2. Set the heater control lever to WARM.

3. Drain the cooling system.

4. Remove the instrument panel.

5. Remove the duct from between the heater unit and the blower case.

6. Disconnect the coolant hoses at the heater case.

7. Unbolt and remove the heater case.

8. Remove the hose and pipe clamps and remove the water valve.

9. Remove the core from the case.

10. Set the mixing damper to the closed position, and, with the damper in that position, install the rod so that the water valve is fully closed.

11. Place the damper lever in the "VENT" position, and adjust the linkage so that the "FOOT/DEF" damper opens to the "DEF" side and the "VENT" damper is level with the separator.

12. Install the hoses. They are marked for flow direction.

13. The remainder of assembly is the reverse of disassembly.

Conquest

1. Move the control lever to "WARM".

2. Drain the coolant at the radiator.

3. Disconnect the coolant hoses at the heater unit.

4. Remove the instrument panel and floor console.

5. Remove the center ventilation duct, defroster duct and lap heater duct.

6. Remove the center instrument panel brace.

7. Remove the heater control assembly.

8. Remove the three screws and lift out the heater case.

9. Check the core for leaks, clogging and bent fins. Replace or repair as necessary.

10. Installation is the reverse of removal. Replace any cracked hoses or damaged insulation. Refill the system and check for leaks.

Radio

REMOVAL & INSTALLATION

Rear Wheel Drive

1981–83

1. Remove glove box then loosen the knobs and attaching nuts on the front of the radio.

2. Remove speaker, antenna, and power wires from the back of the radio. Remove the radio attaching bracket and take out the radio.

3. Installation is the reverse of removal.

Front Wheel Drive

1981–84

1. Remove the instrument panel trim.

2. Remove the radio knobs from the radio panel.

3. Remove the nuts from behind the knobs, the screw from the bracket and remove the radio (AM radio). Remove the bolts from under the brackets and remove the radio (AM/FM radio).

NOTE: The AM radio circuit fuse block is located on the right rear side of the radio, the AM/FM circuit fuse block is installed in the line with the power cable.

1985–88 COLT

1. Remove the floor console.

2. Remove the radio and mounting bracket from the console.

NOTE: The radio fuse is on the back of the radio. The left front speaker is accessed through the corner panel. To get to the right front speaker, remove the glove box and air duct. The rear speakers are easily accessed.

VISTA

1. Remove the radio trim panel.

2. Remove the console side cover and disconnect the wiring connector and antenna cable.

3. Remove the mounting screws and slide the radio out of the panel.

4. The front speakers are accessed by removing the left or right trim panels. The rear speakers are accessed by removing the rear door trim panels.

5. Installation is the reverse of removal.

CONQUEST

1. Remove the front console box.

2. Remove the radio trim panel.

3. Remove the attaching screws and lift out the radio and mounting bracket.

4. To remove the front speaker, the instrument panel pad must first be removed.

5. The door speakers are accessed by removing the door trim panels.

6. The rear speakers are accessed by removing the rear trim panels.

7. Installation of all components is the reverse of removal.

Windshield Wiper Switch

NOTE: On all rear wheel drive cars, and Vista, the wiper switch is integral with the turn signal switch. For wiper switch service, follow the procedures listed under "Turn Signal Switch," earlier in this section.

REMOVAL & INSTALLATION

1981–82

1. Remove the instrument cluster hood screws. Leave the wiring connector as it is.

2. Remove the corner panel.

3. Disconnect the cluster hood connector and remove the hood.

4. Remove the knob from the switch and remove the switch from the hood.

5. Installation is the reverse of removal.

1983–84

1. Remove the instrument cluster.

2. Pull out on the wiper switch knob to remove it.

3. Remove the two attaching screws and pull the switch from the panel.

4. Installation is the reverse of removal.

1985–88

1. Remove the steering wheel.

2. Remove the steering column cover.

3. Pull out and remove the switch knob.

4. Remove the two mounting screws and pull the switch out.

5. Installation is the reverse of removal.

Windshield Wiper Motor

REMOVAL & INSTALLATION

All Except Vista, Conquest and 1985–88 Colt

1. Remove the motor bracket and body retaining bolts. Remove the wiper arms and unbolt and remove the cowl panel.

2. Remove the wiper arm shaft nut on the driver's side of the car and pull the motor assembly out.

3. Remove the bushing and disconnect the motor crank arm and linkage.

4. Install the motor in the reverse order of removal.

Vista and 1985–88 Colt

1. Remove the wiper arms.

2. Remove the front cowl trim plate.

3. Remove the pivot shaft mounting nuts and push the pivot shaft toward the inside.

4. Disconnect the linkage from the motor and lift out the linkage.

5. Unbolt and remove the motor.

6. Installation is the reverse of removal.

NOTE: When installing the arms, the at-rest position of the blade tips-to-windshield molding should be: Vista—passenger's side: 30mm; driver's side: 25mm. Colt—passenger's side: 20mm; driver's side: 15mm.

Conquest

1. Remove the wiper arm and pivot shaft mounting nut, remove the arms and push the pivot shaft toward the inside.

2. Remove the cover from the wiper access hole on the right side of the front deck panel.

3. Loosen the wiper motor mounting bolts, pull the motor out slightly, disconnect the motor from the linkage, then remove the motor and linkage. If the motor's crank arm is to be removed, mark its position first.

4. Installation is the reverse of removal. Install the wiper arms so that the blade tip-to-windshield molding distance, at rest, is ½ in.

Instrument Cluster

REMOVAL & INSTALLATION

Challenger/Sapporo

1. Remove the battery ground cable.
2. Remove three screws from the top and three screws from the bottom of the cluster assembly.

NOTE: Two of the bottom screws are located behind the "brake warning" and "fasten seat belt" lens and the third bottom screw is located at the ash tray opening. A thin tipped screwdriver or a wire hook is required to remove the lenses to gain access to the screws.

3. Move the instrument cluster away from the dash and disconnect the meter connections, heater fan connections, speedometer cable and any other connector or ground cables.
4. Remove the cluster assembly from the dash.
5. Installation is the reverse of removal.

1981 Station Wagon

The instrument cluster hood is removed separately to expose the instrument cluster attaching screws. Remove the screws, attaching wires and cables, and remove the cluster from the dash. Install in the reverse of the removal procedure.

1981–82 Front Wheel Drive Colt and Champ

1. Remove the 4 cluster hood mounting screws. Leave the connectors in place.
2. Remove the 5 corner panel mounting screws and remove the corner panel.
3. Pull out the hood connector, push the connector claw to disengage the connector and remove the hood.
4. Remove the 4 cluster mounting screws and lift the cluster, disconnecting the speedometer cable and wiring connectors.

5. Installation is the reverse of removal.

1983–84 Colt and Champ

1. Remove the steering wheel.
2. Remove the heater control knobs.
3. Remove the cluster panel attaching screws.
4. Remove the light switch, wiper switch, clock and indicator connectors.
5. Remove the cluster panel.
6. Remove the combination meter attaching screws.
7. Pull the combination meter out slightly and disconnect the speedometer cable and electrical connectors. Lift out the combination meter.
8. Installation is the reverse of removal.

1985–88 Colt

1. Remove the steering wheel.
2. Remove the glove box.
3. Remove the instrument panel heater duct.
4. Remove the parcel tray.
5. Remove the steering column lower cover.
6. Disconnect the light switch and wiper switch connectors.
7. Remove the steering column upper cover.
8. Remove the instrument cluster hood screws and lift off the hood.
9. Remove the cluster mounting screws and pull the cluster slightly forward. Disconnect the speedometer cable and electrical connectors and lift out the cluster.
10. Installation is the reverse of removal.

Vista

1. Remove the steering wheel.
2. Remove the ashtray.
3. Pry off (carefully) the cluster hood cover.
4. Remove the cluster hood mounting screws.
5. Pull the hood slightly toward the front and release the connectors. Lift the hood off.

6. Remove the 4 cluster mounting screws, pull the cluster slightly toward the front and disconnect the speedometer cable and electrical connectors.
7. Lift out the cluster.
8. Installation is the reverse of removal.

Conquest

──────── CAUTION ────────

The following procedure applies to both the conventional needle-type gauge cluster and to the liquid crystal display type. Because the LCD gauges are composed of very delicate components, they must not be subjected to severe shocks. Furthermore, the LCD gauges must not be disassembled.

1. Remove the cluster hood attaching screws.
2. Pull outward on both bottom side edges of the hood, and, while holding it in that position, pull it upward and off.
3. Disconnect the wiring to the hood switches.
4. Remove the cluster case attaching screws.
5. Pull both sides of the lower part of the cluster case up and toward the rear of the vehicle.
6. Disconnect the speedometer cable from the back of the case.
7. Disconnect all wiring at the back of the case and lift the case out.
8. Installation is the reverse of removal.

Fuse Box

LOCATION

Front Wheel Drive Models and Conquest

The fuse block is located up under the instrument panel on the driver's side of the steering column.

All Other Models

The fuse block is locaed on the lower part of the driver's side front pillar post.

Honda **5**

Accord, Civic, CRX, Prelude

SERIAL NUMBER IDENTIFICATION

Vehicle Identification Plate

Honda Vehicle Identification Numbers are mounted on the top edge of the instrument panel and are visible from the outside. In addition, there is a Vehicle/Engine Identification plate under the hood, on the cowl.

Engine Number

The engine number is stamped into the clutch casing. The first three dig- its indicate engine model identifica- tion. The remaining numbers refer to production sequence. This same num- ber is also stamped onto the Vehicle/Engine Identification plate mounted on the hood bracket.

Transmission Serial Number

NOTE: The transmission serial number is stamped on the top of the transmission/clutch case.

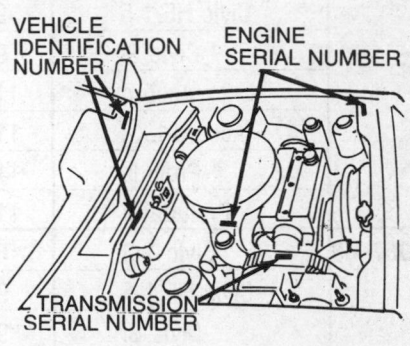

Honda identification numbers

ENGINE IDENTIFICATION

Year	Model	Engine Displacement cu. in. (cc/liter)	Engine Series Identification	No. of Cylinders	Engine Type
1981	Civic 1300	81.5 (1335/1.3)	EJ1	4	CVCC 8-valve
	Civic 1500	90.7 (1487/1.5)	EM1	4	CVCC 8-valve
	Accord	106.8 (1751/1.8)	EK1	4	CVCC 8-valve
	Prelude	106.8 (1751/1.8)	EK1	4	CVCC 8-valve
1982	Civic 1300	81.5 (1335/1.3)	EJ1	4	CVCC 8-valve
	Civic 1500	90.7 (1487/1.5)	EM1	4	CVCC 8-valve
	Accord	106.8 (1751/1.8)	EK1	4	CVCC 8-valve
	Prelude	106.8 (1751/1.8)	EK1	4	CVCC 8-valve

5 HONDA

ENGINE IDENTIFICATION

Year	Model	Engine Displacement cu. in. (cc/liter)	Engine Series Identification	No. of Cylinders	Engine Type
1983	Civic 1300	81.5 (1335/1.3)	EJ1	4	CVCC 8-valve
	Civic 1500	90.7 (1487/1.5)	EM1	4	CVCC 8-valve
	Accord	106.8 (1751/1.8)	EK1	4	CVCC 8-valve
	Prelude	111.6 (1829/1.8)	ES1	4	CVCC 12-valve
1984	Civic 1.3	81.9 (1342/1.3)	EV1	4	CVCC 8-valve
	Civic HF,1.5	90.8 (1488/1.5)	EW1	4	CVCC 12-valve
	Accord	111.6 (1829/1.8)	ES2	4	CVCC 12-valve
	Prelude	111.6 (1829/1.8)	ES1	4	CVCC 12-valve
1985	Civic 1.3	81.9 (1342/1.3)	EV1	4	CVCC 8-valve
	Civic HF,1.5	90.8 (1488/1.5)	EW1	4	CVCC 12-valve
	Civic Si	90.8 (1488/1.5)	EW3	4	Non-CVCC 12-valve
	Accord	111.6 (1829/1.8)	ES2	4	CVCC 12-valve
	Accord SE-i	111.6 (1829/1.8)	ES2	4	Non-CVCC 12-valve
	Prelude	111.6 (1829/1.8)	ET2	4	Non-CVCC 12-valve
1986	Civic 1.3	81.9 (1342/1.3)	EV1	4	CVCC 8-valve
	Civic HF,1.5	90.8 (1488/1.5)	EW1	4	CVCC 12-valve
	Civic Si	90.8 (1488/1.5)	EW4	4	Non-CVCC 12-valve
	Accord	119.3 (1955/2.0)	BS	4	Non-CVCC 12-valve
	Accord LX-i	119.3 (1955/2.0)	BT	4	Non-CVCC 12-valve
	Prelude	111.6 (1829/1.8)	ET2	4	Non-CVCC 12-valve
	Prelude Si	119.3 (1955/2.0)	BT	4	Non-CVCC 12-valve
1987–88	Civic 1.3	81.9 (1342/1.3)	EV1	4	CVCC 8-valve
	Civic HF,1.5	90.8 (1488/1.5)	EW1	4	CVCC 12-valve
	Civic Si	90.8 (1488/1.5)	EW4	4	Non-CVCC 12-valve
	Accord	119.3 (1955/2.0)	BS	4	Non-CVCC 12-valve
	Accord LX-i	119.3 (1955/2.0)	BT	4	Non-CVCC 12-valve
	Prelude	111.6 (1829/1.8)	ET2	4	Non-CVCC 12-valve
	Prelude Si	119.3 (1955/2.0)	BT	4	Non-CVCC 12-valve

GENERAL ENGINE SPECIFICATIONS

Year	Model	Engine Displacement cu. in. (cc)	Fuel System Type	Net Horsepower @ rpm	Net Torque @ rpm (ft. lbs.)	Bore × Stroke (in.)	Compression Ratio	Oil Pressure @ rpm
1981	Civic 1300	81.5 (1335)	Keihin 3 bbl	60 @ 5500	68 @ 4000	2.83 × 3.23	7.9:1	50 @ 2000
	Civic 1500	90.7 (1487)	Keihin 3 bbl	63 @ 5000	77 @ 3000	2.91 × 3.41	9.9:1	50 @ 2000
	Accord	106.8 (1751)	Keihin 3 bbl	72 @ 4500	94 @ 3000	3.03 × 3.70	8.8:1	50 @ 2000
	Prelude	106.8 (1751)	Keihin 3 bbl	72 @ 4500	94 @ 3000	3.03 × 3.70	8.8:1	50 @ 2000

GENERAL ENGINE SPECIFICATIONS

Year	Model	Engine Displacement cu. in. (cc)	Fuel System Type	Net Horsepower @ rpm	Net Torque @ rpm (ft. lbs.)	Bore × Stroke (in.)	Com-pression Ratio	Oil Pressure @ rpm
1982	Civic 1300	81.5 (1335)	Keihin 3 bbl	60 @ 5500	68 @ 4000	2.83 × 3.23	9.3:1	50 @ 2000
	Civic 1500	90.7 (1487)	Keihin 3 bbl	63 @ 5000	77 @ 3000	2.91 × 3.41	9.3:1	50 @ 2000
	Accord	106.8 (1751)	Keihin 3 bbl	72 @ 4500	94 @ 3000	3.03 × 3.70	8.8:1	50 @ 2000
	Prelude	106.8 (1751)	Keihin 3 bbl	72 @ 4500	94 @ 3000	3.03 × 3.70	8.8:1	50 @ 2000
1983	Civic 1300	81.5 (1335)	Keihin 3 bbl	60 @ 5500	68 @ 4000	2.83 × 3.23	9.3:1	50 @ 2000
	Civic 1500	90.7 (1487)	Keihin 3 bbl	63 @ 5000	77 @ 3000	2.91 × 3.41	9.3:1	50 @ 2000
	Accord	106.8 (1751)	Keihin 3 bbl	75 @ 4500	96 @ 3000	3.03 × 3.70	8.8:1	50 @ 2000
	Prelude	111.6 (1829)	Keihin Dual Sidedraft	100 @ 5000	104 @ 4000	3.15 × 3.58	9.4:1	60 @ 1500
1984	Civic 1.3 CRX 1.3	81.9 (1342)	Keihin 3 bbl	60 @ 5500	73 @ 3500	2.91 × 3.02	10.0:1	50 @ 2000
	Civic 1.5 CRX 1.5	90.8 (1488)	Keihin 3 bbl	76 @ 6000	84 @ 3500	2.91 × 3.42	9.2:1	55 @ 2000
	Accord	111.6 (1829)	Keihin 3 bbl	86 @ 5800	99 @ 3500	3.15 × 3.58	9.0:1	50 @ 2000
	Prelude	111.6 (1829)	Keihin Dual Sidedraft	100 @ 5500 ①	104 @ 4000	3.15 × 3.58	9.1:1	60 @ 1500
1985	Civic 1.3	81.9 (1342)	Keihin 3 bbl	60 @ 5500	73 @ 3500	2.91 × 3.02	10.0:1	50 @ 2000
	Civic 1.5 CRX 1.5	90.8 (1488)	Keihin 3 bbl	76 @ 6000	84 @ 3500	2.91 × 3.42	9.2:1	55 @ 2000
	Civic CRX HF	90.8 (1488)	Keihin 3 bbl	65 @ 5500	81 @ 3500	2.91 × 3.42	9.2:1	50 @ 2000
	Civic CRX Si	90.8 (1488)	Honda EFI	91 @ 5500	93 @ 4500	2.91 × 3.42	8.7:1	50 @ 2000
	Accord	111.6 (1829)	Keihin 3 bbl	86 @ 5800	99 @ 3500	3.15 × 3.58	9.0:1	50 @ 2000
	Accord SE-i	111.6 (1829)	Honda EFI	101 @ 5800	108 @ 2500	3.15 × 3.58	8.8:1	50 @ 2000
	Prelude	111.6 (1829)	Keihin Dual Sidedraft	100 @ 5500 ①	104 @ 4000	3.15 × 3.58	9.1:1	55 @ 2000

GENERAL ENGINE SPECIFICATIONS

Year	Model	Engine Displacement cu. in. (cc)	Fuel System Type	Net Horsepower @ rpm	Net Torque @ rpm (ft. lbs.)	Bore × Stroke (in.)	Compression Ratio	Oil Pressure @ rpm
1986	Civic 1.3	81.9 (1342)	Keihin 3 bbl	60 @ 5500	73 @ 3500	2.91 × 3.02	10.0:1	50 @ 2000
	Civic 1.5 CRX 1.5	90.8 (1488)	Keihin 3 bbl	70 @ 6000	84 @ 3500	2.91 × 3.41	9.2:1	50 @ 2000
	Civic CRX HF	90.8 (1488)	Keihin 3 bbl	58 @ 4500	80 @ 2500	2.91 × 3.41	8.7:1	50 @ 2000
	Civic Si CRX Si	90.8 (1488)	Honda EFI	91 @ 5500	93 @ 4500	2.91 × 3.41	8.7:1	50 @ 2000
	Accord	119.3 (1955)	Keihin 2 bbl	98 @ 5500	110 @ 3500	3.25 × 3.58	9.1:1	55 @ 2000
	Accord LX-i	119.3 (1955)	Honda EFI	110 @ 5500	114 @ 4500	3.25 × 3.58	8.8:1	55 @ 2000
	Prelude	111.6 (1829)	Keihin Dual Sidedraft	100 @ 5500	107 @ 4000	3.15 × 3.58	9.1:1	50 @ 2000
	Prelude Si	119.3 (1955)	Honda EFI	110 @ 5500	114 @ 4500	3.25 × 3.58	8.8:1	50 @ 2000
1987-88	Civic 1.3	81.9 (1392)	Keihin 3 bbl	60 @ 5500	73 @ 3500	2.91 × 3.02	10.0:1	50 @ 2000
	Civic 1.5 CRX 1.5	90.8 (1488)	Keihin 3 bbl	76 @ 6000	84 @ 3500	2.91 × 3.41	9.2:1	50 @ 2000
	Civic Si CRX Si	90.8 (1488)	Honda EFI	91 @ 5500	93 @ 4500	2.91 × 3.41	8.7:1	50 @ 2000
	Civic CRX HF	90.8 (1488)	Keihin 3 bbl	58 @ 4500	80 @ 2500	2.91 × 3.41	8.7:1	50 @ 2000
	Accord	119.3 (1955)	Keihin 2 bbl	98 @ 5500	109 @ 3500	3.25 × 3.58	9.1:1	55 @ 2000
	Accord LX-i	119.3 (1955)	Honda	110 @ 5500	114 @ 4500	3.25 × 3.58	8.8:1	55 @ 2000
	Prelude	114 (1829)	Keihin Dual Sidedraft	100 @ 5500	107 @ 4000	3.15 × 3.58	9.1:1	50 @ 2000
	Prelude Si	119.3 (1955)	Honda EFI	110 @ 5500	114 @ 4500	3.25 × 3.58	8.8:1	50 @ 2000

GASOLINE ENGINE TUNE-UP SPECIFICATIONS

Year	Model	Engine Displacement cu. in. (cc)	Spark Plugs Type	Gap (in.)	Ignition Timing (deg.) MT	AT	Com-pression Pressure (psi)	Fuel Pump (psi)	Idle Speed (rpm) MT	AT	Valve Clearance ⑬ In.	Ex.
1981	Civic 1500	90.7 (1487)	B6EB-11	0.042	10B③④	2A	180	2.5	700–800 ①	700–800 ②	0.005–0.007	0.007–0.009
	Civic 1300	81.4 (1335)	B6EB-11	0.042	2B③	—	180	2.5	700–800 ①	—	0.005–0.007	0.007–0.009
	Accord	106.8 (1751)	B6EB–L11	0.042	TDC⑧	TDC	190	2.5	750–850 ①	750–850 ②	0.005–0.007	0.010–0.012
	Prelude	106.8 (1751)	B6EB–L11	0.042	TDC⑧	TDC	190	2.5	750–850 ①	750–850 ②	0.005–0.007	0.010–0.012
1982	Civic 1500	90.7 (1487)	BR6EB–11	0.042	18B③	18B③	190	2.5	650–750 ①	650–750 ②	0.005–0.007	0.007–0.009
	Civic 1300	81.4 (1335)	BR6EB–11	0.042	20B③	—	210	2.5	650–750 ①	—	0.005–0.007	0.007–0.009
	Accord	106.8 (1751)	BR6EB–L11	0.042	16B⑤	16B	190	2.5	750–850 ①	750–850 ②	0.005–0.007	0.010–0.012
	Prelude	106.8 (1751)	BR6EB–L11	0.042	12B⑥	16B	190	2.5	700–800 ①	700–800 ②	0.005–0.007	0.010–0.012
1983	Civic 1500	90.7 (1487)	BR6EB–11	0.042	18B③	18B③	210	2.5	650–750 ①	650–750 ②	0.005–0.007	0.007–0.009
	Civic 1300	81.4 (1335)	BR6EB–11	0.042	18B ⑦③	—	210	2.5	600–750 ①	—	0.005–0.007	0.007–0.009
	Accord	106.8 (1751)	BR6EB–L11	0.042	16B⑤③	16B③	195	2.5	700–800 ①	650–750 ②	0.005–0.007	0.010–0.012
	Prelude	111.6 (1829)	BUR6EB–11	0.042	10B⑤③	12B③	215	2.5	750–850 ①	700–800 ②	0.005–0.007	0.010–0.012
1984	Civic 1.5 CRX 1.5	90.8 (1488)	BUR6EB–11	0.042	20B⑪	15B⑪	210	3.0	650–750	650–750	0.007–0.009	0.009–0.011
	Civic 1.3 CRX 1.3	81.9 (1342)	BUR6EB–11	0.042	21B⑪	—	220	3.0	650–750	—	0.007–0.009	0.009–0.011
	Accord	111.6 (1829)	BUR6EB–11	0.042	22B③	18B③	210	2.5	700–800	650–750	0.005–0.007	0.010–0.012
	Prelude	111.6 (1829)	BPR6EY–11	0.042	20B③	12B③	210	2.5	750–850	750–850	0.005–0.007	0.010–0.012

GASOLINE ENGINE TUNE-UP SPECIFICATIONS

Year	Model	Engine Displacement cu. in. (cc)	Spark Plugs Type	Gap (in.)	Ignition Timing (deg.) MT	AT	Compression Pressure (psi)	Fuel Pump (psi)	Idle Speed (rpm) MT	AT	Valve Clearance⑬ In.	Ex.
1985	Civic 1.5 CRX 1.5	90.8 (1488)	BUR5EB–11	0.042	20B⑪	15B⑩	210	3.0	650–750	650–750	0.007–0.009	0.009–0.011
	Civic CRX HF	90.8 (1488)	BUR4EB–11	0.042	21B⑥⑪	—	210	3.0	650–750	650–750	0.007–0.009	0.009–0.011
	Civic CRX Si	90.8 (1488)	BPR6EY–11	0.042	16B⑤⑪	—	190	35	550–650	—	—	0.009–0.011
	Civic 1.3	81.9 (1342)	BUR5EB–11	0.042	21B⑥⑪	—	225	3.0	650–750	—	0.007–0.009	0.009–0.011
	Accord	111.6 (1829)	BUR5EB–11	0.042	22B③⑨	18B③	190	2.5	700–800	650–750	0.005–0.007	0.010–0.012
	Accord SE-i	111.6 (1829)	BPR6EY–11	0.042	18B③	18B③	200	35	700–800	700–800	—	0.010–0.012
	Prelude	111.6 (1829)	BPR6EY–11	0.042	20B③	12B③	200	2.5	750–850	750–850	—	0.012–0.012
1986	Civic 1.3	81.9 (1342)	BUR4EB–11	0.042	21B⑥⑪	—	225	3.0	650–750	—	0.007–0.009	0.009–0.011
	Civic 1.5 CRX 1.5	90.8 (1488)	BUR4EB–11	0.042	20B⑪	15B⑩⑪	200	3.0	650–750	650–750	0.007–0.009	0.009–0.011
	Civic CRX HF	90.8 (1488)	BUR4EB–11	0.042	21B⑥⑪	—	90	3.0	650–750	650–750	0.007–0.009	0.009–0.011
	Civic Si CRX Si	90.8 (1488)	BPR6EY–11	0.042	16B⑤⑪	—	190	35	700–800	—	—	0.009–0.011
	Accord	119.3 (1955)	BPR5EY–11	0.042	24B③⑫	15B③	200	3.0	700–800	650–750	—	0.010–0.012
	Accord LX-i	119.3 (1955)	BPR5EY–11	0.042	15B③	15B③	210	35	700–800	700–800	—	0.010–0.012
	Prelude	111.6 (1829)	BPR6EY–11	0.042	20B③	12B③	200	2.5	750–850	750–850	—	0.010–0.012
	Prelude Si	119.3 (1955)	BPR5EY–11	0.042	15B③	15B③	210	35	700–800	700–800	—	0.010–0.012
1987	Civic CRX HF	90.8 (1488)	BUR4EB–11	0.042	21B⑥⑪	—	210	3.0	650–750	650–750	0.007–0.009	0.009–0.011
	Civic Si CRX Si	90.8 (1488)	BPR6EY–11	0.042	16B⑤⑪	—	200	35	700–800	—	—	0.011–0.011
	Accord	119.3 (1955)	BPR5EY–11	0.042	24B③⑫	15B③	200	3.0	700–800	650–750	—	0.010–0.012
	Accord LX-i	119.3 (1955)	BPR5EY–11	0.042	15B③	15B③	225	35	700–800	700–800	—	0.010–0.012
	Prelude	111.6 (1829)	BPR6EY–11	0.042	20B③	12B③	190	2.5	750–850	750–850	—	0.010–0.012
	Prelude Si	119.3 (1955)	BPR5EY–11	0.042	15B③	15B③	210	35	700–800	700–800	—	0.010–0.012

GASOLINE ENGINE TUNE-UP SPECIFICATIONS

Year	Model	Engine Displacement cu. in. (cc)	Spark Plugs Type	Gap (in.)	Ignition Timing (deg.) MT	AT	Compression Pressure (psi)	Fuel Pump (psi)	Idle Speed (rpm) MT	AT	Valve Clearance In.	Ex.
1988	All		SEE UNDERHOOD SPECIFICATIONS STICKER									

NOTE: The underhood specifications sticker often reflects tune-up changes made in production. Sticker figures must be used if they disagree with those in this chart.

TDC — Top Dead Center
B — Before top dead center
A — After top dead center
— Not applicable
NA — Not available

① In neutral, with headlights on
② In drive range, with headlights on
③ Aim timing light at red mark on flywheel or torque converter drive plate with the distributor vacuum hose connected at the specified idle speed.
④ Wagon/Sedan: 4B, Calif-2A
⑤ Calif: 12B
⑥ Calif: 16B
⑦ 4 speed: 20B
⑧ Aim timing light at white mark
⑨ California models: 18B
⑩ Models w/power steering: 17B
⑪ Aim timing light at red mark on crankshaft pulley
⑫ Calif:20B
⑬ All except 1342cc and 1488cc: 0.005-0.007
  1342cc and 1488cc: 0.007-0.009

FIRING ORDERS

FIRING ORDER 1-3-4-2

Front of car

Firing order—1829cc Accord

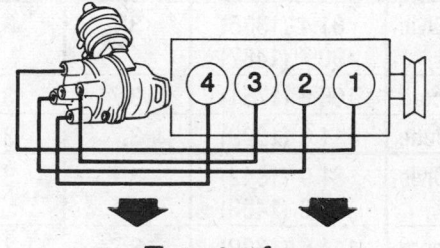

Front of car

Firing order—1342cc & 1488cc Civic

FIRING ORDERS

NOTE: To avoid confusion, always replace spark plug wires one at a time.

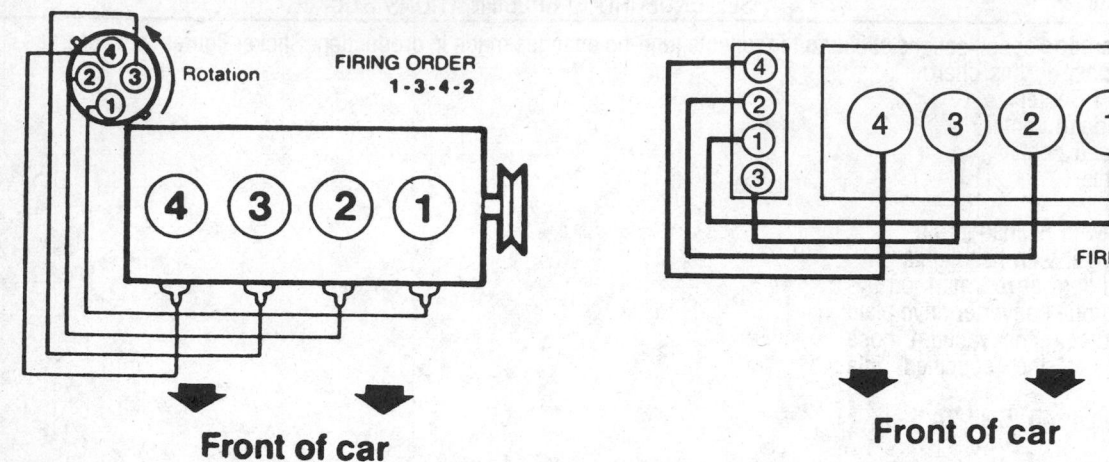

Firing order—1335cc & 1487cc Civic, 1751 cc Acord and Prelude

Firing order—1829cc Prelude, 1955cc Accord and Prelude

CAPACITIES

Year	Model	Engine Displacement cu. in. (cc)	Engine Crankcase with Filter	without Filter	Transmission (pts.) 4-Spd	5-Spd	Auto.①	Drive Axle (pts.)	Fuel Tank (gal.)	Cooling System (qts.)
1981	Civic	81.4 (1335) 90.7 (1487)	3.8	3.2	5.2	5.2	5.2	—	10.8 ②	4.8 ③
	Accord Prelude	106.8 (1751)	3.8	3.2	5.0	5.0	5.2	—	13.2	6.4
1982	Civic	81.4 (1335) 90.7 (1487)	3.7	3.2	5.2	5.2	5.2	—	10.8 ②	4.8 ③
	Accord	106.8 (1751)	3.7	3.2	5.0	5.0	5.2	—	15.8 ②	6.0
	Prelude	106.8 (1751)	3.7	3.2	5.0	5.0	5.2	—	13.2	6.0
1983	Civic	81.4 (1335) 90.7 (1487)	3.7	3.2	5.2	5.2	5.2	—	10.4 ②	4.8 ③
	Accord	106.8 (1751)	3.7	3.2	5.0	5.0	6.0	—	15.8	6.0
	Prelude	111.6 (1829)	3.7	3.2	—	5.0	5.8	—	15.9	6.3
1984	Civic	81.9 (1342) 90.8 (1488)	3.7	3.2	5.0	5.0	6.0	—	11.9 ④	4.8 ⑤
	Accord	111.6 (1829)	3.7	3.2	—	5.0	6.0	—	15.8	6.4
	Prelude	111.6 (1829)	3.7	3.2	—	5.0	5.8	—	15.9	6.3 ⑥
1985	Civic	81.9 (1342) 90.8 (1488)	3.7	3.2	5.0	5.0	6.0	—	11.9 ④	4.8 ⑤
	Accord	111.6 (1829)	3.7	3.2	—	5.0	6.0	—	15.8	6.4
	Prelude	111.6 (1829)	3.7	3.2	—	5.0	5.8	—	15.9	6.3 ⑥

CAPACITIES

Year	Model	Engine Displacement cu. in. (cc)	Engine Crankcase with Filter	Engine Crankcase without Filter	Transmission (pts.) 4-Spd	Transmission (pts.) 5-Spd	Transmission (pts.) Auto.①	Drive Axle (pts.)	Fuel Tank (gal.)	Cooling System (qts.)
1986	Civic	81.9 (1342) 90.8 (1488)	3.7	3.2	5.0	5.0	5.0 ⑦	—	11.9 ④	4.8 ⑤
	Accord	119.3 (1955)	3.7	3.2	—	5.0	5.2	—	15.9	5.2 ⑧
	Prelude	111.6 (1829) 119.3 (1955)	3.7	3.2	—	5.0	5.8	—	15.9	6.3 ⑥
1987-88	Civic	81.9 (1342) 90.8 (1488)	3.7	3.2	5.0	5.0	5.0 ⑦	—	11.9 ④	4.8 ⑤
	Accord	119.3 (1955)	3.7	3.2	—	5.0	5.2	—	15.9	5.2 ⑧
	Prelude	111.6 (1829) 119.3 (1955)	3.7	3.2	—	5.0	5.8	—	15.9	6.3 ⑥

① Does not include torque converter.
② 4-dr. sedan: 12.1
③ 1335cc: 4.0
④ 4-dr.: 12.1
   CRX: 10.8
   CRX HF: 10.0
   CRX Si: 11.9
⑤ 1342cc: 3.6
⑥ Auto.Trans.: 7.1
⑦ CRX: 6.0
⑧ Auto.Trans.: 5.8

CRANKSHAFT AND CONNECTING ROD SPECIFICATIONS
All measurements are given in inches.

Year	Engine Displacement cu. in. (cc)	Crankshaft Main Brg. Journal Dia.	Crankshaft Main Brg. Oil Clearance	Crankshaft Shaft End-play	Crankshaft Thrust on No.	Connecting Rod Journal Diameter	Connecting Rod Oil Clearance	Connecting Rod Side Clearance
1981	81.4 (1335)	1.9676– 1.9685 ②	0.0009– 0.0017	0.004– 0.014	3	1.5739– 1.5748	0.0008– 0.0015	0.006– 0.012
	90.7 (1487) 106.8 (1751)	1.9687– 1.9697 ①	0.0010– 0.0022	0.004– 0.014	3	1.6525– 1.6535	0.0008– 0.0015	0.006– 0.012
	90.7 (1487) 106.8 (1751)	1.9687– 1.9697 ①	0.0010– 0.0022	0.004– 0.014	3	1.6525– 1.6535	0.0008– 0.0015	0.006– 0.012
	81.4 (1335)	1.9676– 1.9685 ②	0.0009– 0.0017	0.004– 0.014	3	1.5739– 1.5748	0.0006– 0.0015	0.006– 0.012
1983	81.4 (1335)	1.9676– 1.9685 ②	0.0009– 0.0017	0.004– 0.014	3	1.5739– 1.5748	0.0008– 0.0015	0.006– 0.012
	111.6 (1829) 119.3 (1955)	1.9673– 1.9683 ③	0.0010– 0.0022 ②	0.004– 0.014	3	1.7707– 1.7717	0.0006– 0.0015	0.006– 0.012
	90.7 (1487) 106.8 (1751)	1.9687– 1.9697 ①	0.0010– 0.0022	0.004– 0.014	3	1.6525– 1.6535	0.0008– 0.0015	0.006– 0.012

CRANKSHAFT AND CONNECTING ROD SPECIFICATIONS
All measurements are given in inches.

| Year | Engine Displacement cu. in. (cc) | Crankshaft | | | | Connecting Rod | | |
		Main Brg. Journal Dia.	Main Brg. Oil Clearance	Shaft End-play	Thrust on No.	Journal Diameter	Oil Clearance	Side Clearance
1984	90.8 (1488)	1.9676–1.9685	0.0009–0.0017	0.004–0.014	3	1.6526–1.6535	0.0008–0.0015	0.006–0.012
	111.6 (1829) 119.3 (1955)	1.9673–1.9683 ③	0.0010–0.0022 ②	0.004–0.014	3	1.7707–1.7717	0.0006–0.0015	0.006–0.012
	81.9 (1342)	1.7707–1.7717	0.0009–0.0017	0.004–0.014	3	1.4951–1.4961	0.0008–0.0015	0.006–0.012
1985	81.9 (1342)	1.7707–1.7717	0.0009–0.0017	0.004–0.014	3	1.4951–1.4961	0.0008–0.0015	0.006–0.012
	111.6 (1829) 119.3 (1955)	1.9673–1.9683 ③	0.0010–0.0022 ②	0.004–0.014	3	1.7707–1.7717	0.0006–0.0015	0.006–0.012
	90.8 (1488)	1.9676–1.9685	0.0009–0.0017	0.004–0.014	3	1.6526–1.6535	0.0008–0.0015	0.006–0.012
1986	90.8 (1488)	1.9676–1.9685	0.0009–0.0017	0.004–0.014	3	1.6526–1.6535	0.0008–0.0015	0.006–0.012
	111.6 (1829) 119.3 (1955)	1.9673–1.9683 ③	0.0010–0.0022 ②	0.004–0.014	3	1.7707–1.7717	0.0008–0.0015	0.006–0.012
	81.9 (1342)	1.7707–1.7717	0.0009–0.0017	0.004–0.014	3	1.4951–1.4961	0.0008–0.0015	00.06–0.012
1987	81.9 (1342)	1.7707–1.7717	0.0009–0.0017	0.004–0.014	3	1.4951–1.4961	0.0008–0.0015	0.006–0.012
	111.6 (1829) 119.3 (1955)	1.9673–1.9683 ③	0.0010–0.0022 ②	0.004–0.014	3	1.7707–1.7717	0.0006–0.0015	0.006–0.012
	90.8 (1488)	1,9676–1.9685	0.0009–0.0017	0.004–0.014	3	1.6526–1.6535	0.0008–0.0015	0.006–0.012
1988	90.8 (1488)	1.9676–1.9685	0.0009–0.0017	0.004–0.014	3	1.6526–1.6535	0.0008–0.0015	0.006–0.012
	81.9 (1342)	1.7707–1.7717	0.0009–0.0017	0.004–0.014	3	1.4951–1.4961	0.0008–0.0015	0.006–0.012

① 1981 w/1487: 1.9676-1.9685
   1982-83 w/1487: 1.9687-1.9803
② 1986-88 #3: 0.0013-0.0024
③ 1983: 1.9687-1.9697

VALVE SPECIFICATIONS

Year	Engine Displacement cu. in. (cc)	Seat Angle (deg.)	Face Angle (deg.)	Spring Test Pressure (lbs.)	Spring Installed Height (in.)	Stem-to-Guide Clearance (in.)① Intake	Exhaust	Stem Diameter (in.)① Intake	Exhaust
1981	81.4 (1335) 90.7 (1487)	45	45	NA	③	0.0008–0.0020	0.0008–0.0037	0.2591–0.2594	0.2574–0.2578
	106.8 (1751)	45	45	NA	④	0.001–0.002	0.002–0.004	0.2748–0.2751	0.2732–0.2736
1982	81.4 (1335)	45	45	NA	③	0.0008–0.0020	0.0025–0.0037	0.2591–0.2594	0.2574–0.2578
	106.8 (1751)	45	45	NA	④	0.001–0.002	0.002–0.004	0.2748–0.2751	0.2732–0.2736
1983	81.4 (1335)	45	45	NA	③	0.0008–0.0020	0.0025–0.0037	0.2591–0.2594	0.2574–0.2578
	106.8 (1751)	45	45	NA	④	0.001–0.002	0.002–0.004	0.2748–0.2751	0.2732–0.2736
	111.6 (1829)	45	45	NA	⑤	0.001–0.002	0.002–0.004	0.2591–0.2594	0.2736–0.2736
1984	81.9 (1342)	45	45	NA	⑥	0.001–0.002	0.002–0.003	0.2591–0.2594	0.2579–0.2583
	111.6 (1829)	45	45	NA	⑤	0.001–0.002	0.002–0.004	0.2591–0.2594	0.2732–0.2736
1985	81.9 (1342) 90.8 (1488)	45	45	NA	⑥	0.001–0.002	0.002–0.003	0.2591–0.2594	0.2579–0.2583
	111.6 (1342) 119.3 (1955)	45	45	NA	⑤	0.001–0.002	0.002–0.004	0.2591–0.2594	0.2732–0.2736
1986	81.9 (1342) 90.8 (1488)	45	45	NA	⑥	0.001–0.002	0.002–0.003	0.2591–0.2594	0.2579–0.2583
	111.6 (1829) 119.3 (1955)	45	45	NA	⑤	0.001–0.002	0.002–0.004	0.2591–0.2594	0.2732–0.2736
1987–88	81.9 (1342) 90.8 (1488)	45	45	NA	⑥	0.001–0.002	0.002–0.003	0.2591–0.2594	0.2579–0.2583
	111.6 (1829) 119.3 (1955)	45	45	NA	⑤	0.001–0.002	0.002–0.004	0.2591–0.2594	0.2732–0.2736

NA—Not Available
① Jet Valve: 0.0009-0.0023
② Jet Valve: 0.2587-0.2593
③ 1355cc, 1487cc:
  Intake & Exhaust inner: 1.402
  Intake & Exhaust outer: 1.488
  Auxiliary: 0.906
④ 1752cc:
  Intake & Exhaust inner: 1.402
  Intake & Exhaust outer: 1.488
  Auxiliary: 0.984
⑤ 1829cc, 1955cc:
  Intake: 1.660
  Exhaust inner: 1.460
  Exhaust outer: 1.670
  Auxiliary: 0.984 (carbureted)
⑥ 1342cc, 1488cc: Intake: 1.660
  Exhaust: 1.690
  Auxiliary: 0.980 (carbureted)

PISTON AND RING SPECIFICATIONS
All measurments are given in inches.

Year	Engine Displacement cu. in. (cc)	Piston Clearance	Ring Gap			Ring Side Clearance		
			Top Compression	Bottom Compression	Oil Control	Top Compression	Bottom Compression	Oil Control
1981	81.4 (1335) 90.7 (1487)	0.0004– 0.0020	0.006– 0.014	0.006– 0.014	0.012– 0.035	0.0008– 0.0018	0.0008– 0.0018	Snug
	106.8 (1751)	0.0004– 0.0024	0.006– 0.014	0.006– 0.014	0.012– 0.035	0.0008– 0.0018	0.0008– 0.0018	Snug
1982	106.6 (1751)	0.0004– 0.0024	0.006– 0.014	0.006– 0.014	0.012– 0.035	0.0008– 0.0018	0.0008– 0.0018	Snug
	81.4 (1335) 90.7 (1487)	0.0004– 0.0020	0.006– 0.014	0.006– 0.014	0.012– 0.035	0.0012– 0.0020 ①	0.0012– 0.0020 ①	Snug
	81.4 (1335) 90.7 (1487)	0.0004– 0.0020	0.006– 0.014	0.006– 0.014	0.012– 0.035	0.0012– 0.0020 ①	0.0012– 0.0020 ①	Snug
	106.8 (1751)	0.0004– 0.0024	0.006– 0.014	0.006– 0.014	0.012– 0.035	0.0008– 0.0018	0.0008– 0.0018	Snug
	111.6 (1829)	0.0008– 0.0016	0.008– 0.014	0.008– 0.014	0.008– 0.035	0.0008– 0.0018	0.0008– 0.0018	Snug
1984	111.6 (1829)	0.0008– 0.0016	0.008– 0.014	0.008– 0.014	0.008– 0.035	0.0008– 0.0018	0.0008– 0.0018	Snug
	81.9 (1342) 90.8 (1488)	0.0004– 0.0020	0.006– 0.014	0.006– 0.014	0.006– 0.024	0.0012– 0.0024	0.0012– 0.0022	Snug
1985	81.9 (1342) 90.8 (1488)	0.0004– 0.0020	0.006– 0.014	0.006– 0.014	0.006– 0.014	0.0012– 0.024	0.0012– 0.0024	Snug
	111.6 (1829)	0.0008– 0.0016	0.008– 0.014	0.008– 0.014	0.008– 0.035	0.0008– 0.0018	0.0008– 0.0018	Snug
1986	111.6 (1829)	0.0008– 0.0016	0.008– 0.014	0.008– 0.014	0.008– 0.035	0.0008– 0.0018	0.0008– 0.0018	Snug
	119.3 (1955)	0.0008– 0.0016	0.008– 0.014	0.010– 0.015	0.008– 0.020	0.0012– 0.0022	0.0012– 0.0022	Snug
	81.9 (1342) 90.8 (1488)	0.0004– 0.0020	0.006– 0.014	0.006– 0.014	0.008– 0.024	0.0012– 0.0024	0.0012– 0.0022	Snug
1987–88	81.9 (1342) 90.8 (1488)	0.0004– 0.0020	0.006– 0.014	0.006– 0.014	0.008– 0.024	0.0012– 0.0024	0.0012– 0.0022	Snug
	111.6 (1829)	0.0008– 0.0016	0.008– 0.014	0.008– 0.014	0.008– 0.035	0.0008– 0.0018	0.0008– 0.0018	Snug
	119.3 (1955)	0.0008– 0.0016	0.008– 0.014	0.010– 0.015	0.008– 0.020	0.0012– 0.0022	0.0012– 0.0022	Snug

① 1335: 0.0012-0.0024

TORQUE SPECIFICATIONS
All readings in ft. lbs.

Year	Engine Displacement cu. in. (cc)	Cylinder Head Bolts	Main Bearing Bolts	Rod Bearing Bolts	Crankshaft Pulley Bolts	Flywheel Bolts	Manifold Intake	Manifold Exhaust	Spark Plugs
1981	81.4 (1335) 90.7 (1487)	43 ①	29-33	21	80	51	18	18	13
	106.8 (1751)	43 ①	48	23	80	51	18	18	13
1982	81.4 (1335) 90.7 (1487)	43 ①	29-33	21	80	51	18	18	13
	106.8 (1751)	43 ①	48	21	80	51	18	18	13
1983	81.4 (1335) 90.7 (1487)	43 ①	29-33	21	80	51	18	18	13
	106.8 (1751)	43 ①	48	21	80	51	18	18	13
	111.6 (1829) 119.3 (1955)	49 ①	48 ④	23	83	76 ②	16	22	13
1984	81.9 (1342) 90.8 (1488)	43 ①	33	20	83	76 ②	16	23	13
	111.6 (1829) 119.3 (1955)	49 ①	48 ④	23	83	76 ②	16	22	13
1985	81.9 (1342) 90.8 (1488)	43 ①	33	20	83	76 ②	16	23	13
	111.6 (1829) 119.3 (1955)	49 ①	48 ④	23	83	76 ②	16	22	13
1986	81.9 (1342) 90.8 (1488)	43 ①	33	20	83	76 ②	16	23	13
	111.6 (1829) 119.3 (1955)	49 ①	48 ④	23	83	76 ②	16	22	13
1987-88	81.9 (1342) 90.8 (1488)	43 ①	33	20	83	76 ②	16	23	13
	111.6 (1829)	49 ①	48 ③	23	83	76 ②	16	22	13

① 2-Step procedure; see text
② Auto Trans: 54
③ Fuel injected engine: 49

BRAKE SPECIFICATIONS

Year	Model	Lug Nut Torque (ft. lbs.)	Master Cylinder Bore	Brake Disc Minimum Thickness	Brake Disc Maximum Runout	Standard Brake Drum Diameter	Minimum Lining Thickness Front	Minimum Lining Thickness Rear
1981	Civic	51-65	NA	0.354 ①	0.006	7.066 ⑦	0.063	0.079
	Accord, Prelude	51-65 ④	NA	0.433 ③	0.006	7.066	0.039	0.079
1982	Accord, Prelude	51-65 ④	NA	0.433 ③	0.006	7.850	0.039 ②	0.079
	Civic	51-65	NA	0.354 ①	0.006	7.066 ⑦	0.063	0.079

BRAKE SPECIFICATIONS
All measurements in inches unless noted

Year	Model	Lug Nut Torque (ft. lbs.)	Master Cylinder Bore	Brake Disc Minimum Thickness	Brake Disc Maximum Runout	Standard Brake Drum Diameter	Minimum Lining Thickness Front	Minimum Lining Thickness Rear
1983	Civic	51-65	NA	0.354 ①	0.006	7.066 ⑦	0.063	0.079
	Accord	80	NA	0.60	0.006	7.850	0.063	0.079
	Prelude	80	NA	0.59	0.004	7.850	0.118	0.079
1984	Civic	80	NA	⑤	0.004	7.070 ⑦	0.120	0.080
	Accord	80	NA	0.67	0.004	7.850	0.120	0.080
	Prelude	80	NA	0.67 ⑥	0.004	7.850	0.120	0.060
1985	Prelude	80	NA	0.67 ⑥	0.004	7.850	0.120	0.060
	Civic	80	NA	⑤	0.004	7.070 ⑦	0.120	0.080
	Accord	80	NA	0.67	0.004	7.850	0.120	0.080
1986	Accord	80	NA	0.67	0.004	7.850	0.120	0.080
	Civic	80	NA	⑤	0.004	7.070 ⑦	0.120	0.080
	Prelude	80	NA	0.67 ⑥	0.004	7.750	0.120	0.060
1987–88	Prelude	80	NA	0.67 ⑥	0.004	7.850	0.120	0.060
	Civic	80	NA	⑤	0.004	7.070 ⑦	0.120	0.080
	Accord	80	NA	0.67	0.004	7.850	0.120	0.080

NA—Not available at time of publication
① '81-'83—0.394
   exc '83 1500 - 0.60
② '81-'82—0.063
③ '81-0.4134, '82-0.60
④ Prelude: 80
⑤ Civic 1300: 0.39
   Civic 1500: 0.59
   CRX: 0.67 St & Std.
   0.35 '84-'85 1300 & HF
   0.43 '86 -'88
⑥ Rear disc: 0.31
⑦ Wagon: 7.85

WHEEL ALIGNMENT

Year	Model	Caster Range (deg.)	Caster Preferred Setting (deg.)	Camber Range (deg.)	Camber Preferred Setting (deg.)	Toe-in (in.)	Steering Axis Inclination (deg.)
1981	Civic exc. SW	¾P-2¾P	1¾P	1N-1P	0	0	12⁵⁄₁₆
	Civic SW	0-2P	1P	1N-1P	0	0	12⁵⁄₁₆
	Accord	¹¹⁄₁₆P-2¹¹⁄₁₆P	1¹¹⁄₁₆	¹¹⁄₁₆N-1⁵⁄₁₆P	⁵⁄₁₆	³⁄₆₄	12½
	Prelude	½P-2½P	1½P	1N-1P	0	0	12¹³⁄₁₆
1982	Civic exc. SW	1½P-3½P	2½P	1N-1P	0	0	12¹¹⁄₃₂
	Civic SW	⁵⁄₁₆P-2⁵⁄₁₆P	1⁵⁄₁₆P	1N-1P	0	0	12¹¹⁄₃₂
	Accord	⁷⁄₁₆P-2⁷⁄₁₆P	1⁷⁄₁₆	1N-1P	0	0	12½
	Prelude	½P-2½P	1½P	1N-1P	0	0	12¹³⁄₁₆

WHEEL ALIGNMENT

Year	Model	Caster Range (deg.)	Caster Preferred Setting (deg.)	Camber Range (deg.)	Camber Preferred Setting (deg.)	Toe-in (in.)	Steering Axis Inclination (deg.)
1983	Civic exc. SW	1½P-3½P	2½P	1N-1P	0	0	$12^{11}/_{32}$
	Civic SW	$^5/_{16}$P-2$^5/_{16}$P	1$^5/_{16}$P	1N-1P	0	0	$12^{11}/_{32}$
	Accord	$^7/_{16}$P-2$^7/_{16}$P	1$^7/_{16}$	1N-1P	0	0	12½
	Prelude	1N-1P	0	1N-1P	0	0	$6^{13}/_{16}$
1984	Civic exc. SW	1$^5/_{16}$P-3$^5/_{16}$P	2$^5/_{16}$P	1N-1P	0	0	$12^{13}/_{16}$
	Civic SW	1⅛P-3⅛P	2⅛P	1N-1P	0	0	12
	Accord	$^7/_{16}$P-2$^7/_{16}$P	1$^7/_{16}$	1N-1P	0	0	12½
	Prelude	1N-1P	0	1N-1P	0	0	$6^{13}/_{16}$
1985	Civic exc. SW	1½P-3½P ①	2½P ②	1N-1P	0	0	13
	Civic SW	1P-3P	2P	1N-1P	0	0	12
	Accord	½P-2½P	1½P	1N-1P	0	0	12½
	Prelude	1N-1P	0	1N-1P	0	0	$6^{13}/_{16}$
1986	Civic exc. SW	1½P-3½P ①	2½P ②	1N-1P	0	0	13
	Civic SW	1P-3P	2P	1N-1P	0	0	12
	Accord	1N-1P	0	1N-1P	0	0	$6^{13}/_{16}$
	Prelude	1N-1P	0	1N-1P	0	0	$6^{13}/_{16}$
1987–88	Civic exc. SW	1½P-3½P ①	2½P ②	1N-1P	0	0	13
	Civic SW	1P-3P	2P	1N-1P	0	0	12
	Accord	1N-1P	0	1N-1P	0	0	$6^{13}/_{16}$
	Prelude	1N-1P	0	1N-1P	0	0	$6^{13}/_{16}$

SW Station Wagon
P Positive
N Negative
① With power steering 2P-4P
② With power steering 3P

TUNE-UP PROCEDURES

Ignition Timing

Honda recommends that the ignition timing be checked at 15,000 mile intervals. On 1342 and 1488cc engines, the timing marks are located on the crankshaft pulley, with a pointer on the timing belt cover; all visible from the driver's side of the engine compartment. On all other engines, the timing marks are located on the flywheel (manual transmission) or torque converter drive plate (automatic transmission), with a corresponding pointer on the rear of the cylinder block. All marks are visible from the front right side of the engine compartment, after removing a special rubber access plug in the timing mark window. In all cases, the timing is checked with the engine warmed to operating temperature (80°C), idling in Neutral (manual transmission.) or Drive (automatic), and with all vacuum hoses connected.

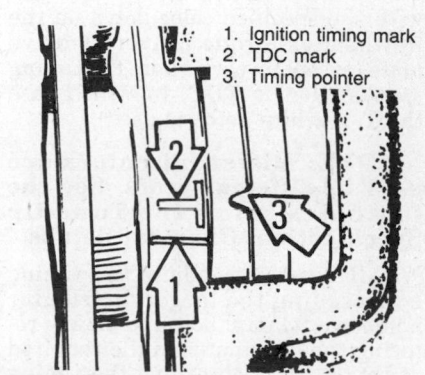

1. Ignition timing mark
2. TDC mark
3. Timing pointer

Timing marks—all except 1342 & 1488cc engines

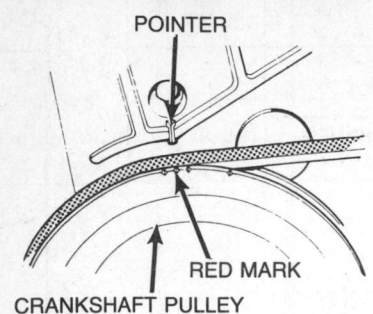

POINTER

RED MARK

CRANKSHAFT PULLEY

1342 and 1488cc timing marks

ADJUSTMENT

1. Stop the engine, and hook up a tachometer according to the manufacturer's instructions.

NOTE: On some models you will have to pull back the rubber ignition coil cover to reveal the terminals.

2. Hook up a timing light to the engine according to the manufacturer's instructions.

3. Make sure that all wires are clear of the cooling fan and hot exhaust manifolds. Start the engine. Check that the idle speed is set to specifications with the transmission in Neutral (manual transmission) or 2nd gear (Automatic). If not, adjust the idle speed as outlined later. At any engine speed other than the specified idle speed, the distributor advance or retard mechanisms will actuate, leading to an erroneous timing adjustment.

— CAUTION —

Make sure that the parking brake is firmly applied and the front wheels are blocked to prevent the car from rolling forward when the automatic transmission is engaged.

4. Point the timing light at the timing marks. On 1342cc and 1488cc engines, align the pointer with the **F** or red notch on the crankshaft pulley. On all other engines, align the pointer with the specified color notch on the flywheel or torque converter drive plate (except on cars where the timing specification is TDC, in which case the **T** or white notch is used).

NOTE: Different colors are used in different years. See the footnotes below the Tune-Up Specifications Chart for details.

5. If necessary, adjust the timing by loosening the larger distributor holddown (clamp) bolt and slowly rotating the distributor in the required direction while observing the timing marks.

— CAUTION —

Do not grasp the top of the distributor cap while the engine is running as you might get a nasty shock. Instead, grab the distributor housing to rotate it.

After making the necessary adjustment, tighten the holddown bolt, taking care not to disturb the adjustment.

NOTE: There are actually two bolts which may be loosened to adjust the ignition timing. There is a small bolt on the underside of the distributor swivel mounting plate. This smaller bolt should not be loosened unless you cannot obtain a satisfactory adjustment using the upper bolt. Its purpose is to provide an extra range of adjustment such as in cases in which the distributor was removed and then installed one tooth off.

Valve Lash

Honda recommends that the valve clearance be checked at 15,000 mile intervals.

NOTE: While all valve adjustments must be as accurate as possible, it is better to have that valve adjustment slightly loose than slightly tight, as burned valves may result from overly tight adjustments.

ADJUSTMENT

1. Make sure that the engine is cold (cylinder head temperature below 38°C).

2. Remove the valve cover.

3. Set the No. 1 cylinder (cylinder closest to the camshaft sprocket) to top dead center TDC. The word **UP**, a round mark or a cut-away in the camshaft pulley should appear at the top. You can double check this by checking the position of the distributor rotor.

4. Take some white or yellow chalk or a pencil and mark where the No. 1 spark plug wire goes into the distributor cap on the distributor body.

5. Then, remove the cap and check that the rotor points toward that mark.

6. With the No. 1 cylinder at TDC adjust the following valves:
• Intake(s) No. 1
• Auxiliary Intake (CVCC engines only) No. 1
• Exhaust No. 1
Make the valve adjustments as follows:

a. Check the valve clearance with a flat feeler gauge between the tip of the rocker arm and the top of the valve. There should be a slight drag on the feeler gauge.

b. If there is no drag or if the gauge cannot be inserted, loosen the valve adjusting screw locknut.

c. Turn the adjusting screw with a screwdriver to obtain the proper clearance.

d. Hold the adjusting screw and tighten the locknut.

e. Recheck the clearance.

7. Turn the crankshaft 180° counterclockwise (the cam pulley will turn 90°). With the No. 3 cylinder at TDC (the distributor rotor should be pointing to the No. 3 plug wire) adjust the valves on the No. 3 cylinder.

8. Turn the crankshaft 180° counterclockwise (the cam pulley will turn 90°). With the No. 4 cylinder at TDC (the distributor rotor now pointing to the No. 4 plug wire) adjust the valves on the No. 4 cylinder.

9. Turn the crankshaft 180° counterclockwise once again. The No. 2 cylinder will now be on TDC (this can be confirmed by the distributor rotor pointing to the No. 2 plug wire). The valves on the No. 2 cylinder may now be adjusted.

Idle Speed and Mixture Adjustment

CARBURETED MODELS

NOTE: All carburetor adjustments must be made with the engine fully warmed up to operating temperature (80°C).

CVCC With Keihin 3-bbl

1981-82

NOTE: This procedure requires a propane enrichment kit, and, for California cars, a special tool for fuel/air mixture adjustment.

1. Start the engine and warm it up to normal operating temperature. The cooling fan will come on.

2. Remove the vacuum tube from the intake air control diaphragm and plug the tube end.

3. Connect a tachometer.

4. Check the idle speed with the headlights, cooling fan and air conditioner OFF. Adjust the idle speed if necessary, by turning the throttle stop screw. Idle speed should be set to the specifications found in the Tune-Up Specifications Chart or on the emission control decal in the engine compartment.

INTAKE

NO.4   NO.3   NO.2   NO.1

NO.4   NO.3   NO.2   NO.1

NO.4   NO.3   NO.2   NO.1

NO.4

NO.1

AUX. INTAKE   EXHAUST

Valve locations—CVCC 12 valve engines

INTAKE

NO.4   NO.3   NO.2   NO.1

NO.4   NO.3   NO.2   NO.1

EXHAUST

Valve locations—non-CVCC 12 valve engines

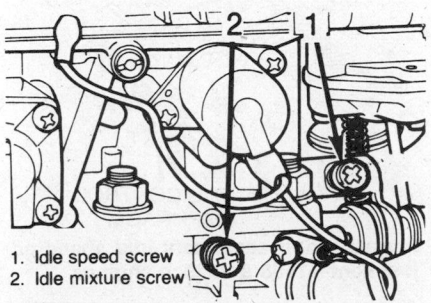

1. Idle speed screw
2. Idle mixture screw

Idle speed and mixture screws—Keihin 3 bbl carburetor

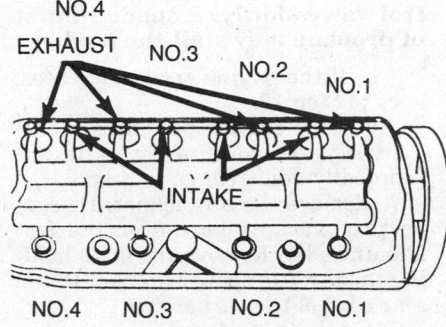

NO.4

EXHAUST   NO.3

NO.2

NO.1

INTAKE

NO.4   NO.3   NO.2   NO.1

AUX. INTAKE

Valve locations—CVCC 8 valve engines

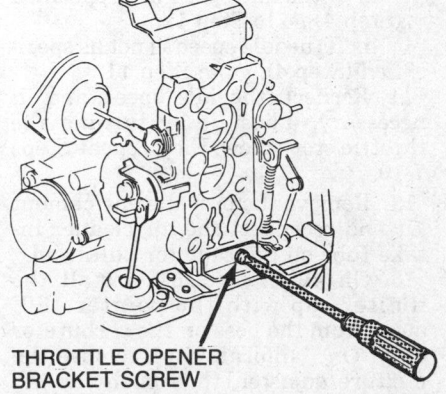

THROTTLE OPENER
BRACKET SCREW

Accord and Civic throttle opener bracket location

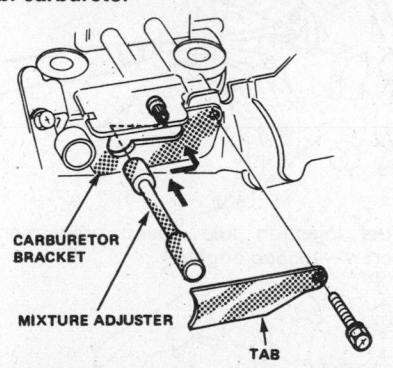

CARBURETOR
BRACKET

MIXTURE ADJUSTER

TAB

Using special tool for mixture adjustment on California models

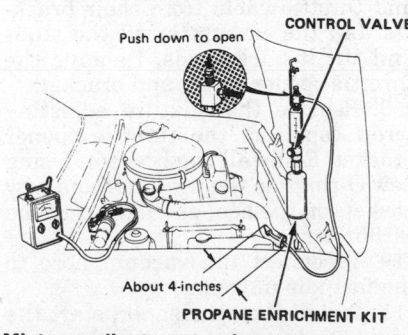
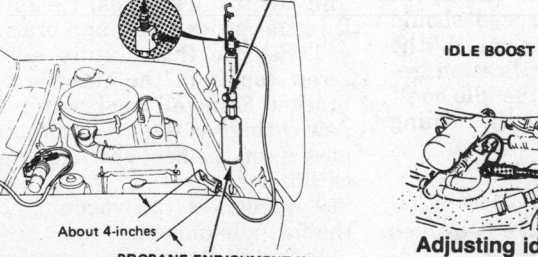

Push down to open   CONTROL VALVE

About 4-inches

PROPANE ENRICHMENT KIT

Mixture adjustment using propane enrichment method

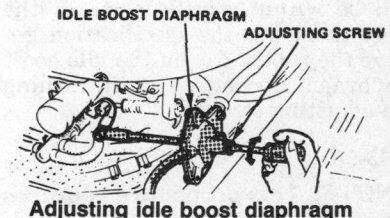

IDLE BOOST DIAPHRAGM   ADJUSTING SCREW

Adjusting idle boost diaphragm

5. Remove the air cleaner intake tube from the air duct on the radiator bulkhead.

6. Insert the tube of the propane enrichment kit into the intake tube about 4 inches.

7. With the engine idling, depress the push button on top of the propane device, then slowly open the propane control valve to obtain maximum engine speed. Engine speed should increase as the percentage of injected propane increases.

NOTE: Open the propane control valve slowly; a sudden burst of propane may stall the engine.

a. If the engine speed does not increase, the mixture screw is improperly adjusted. Go to Step 8.

b. If the engine speed increase, go to Step 9.

8. Lean out the mixture until the idle speed (with propane on) increases. On California cars remove the screws on the right side of the carburetor then swing the tab out of the way. Insert the mixture adjuster all the way to the right and slip it onto mixture the screw. Turn the mixture screw clockwise to lean out the mixture as required.

NOTE: 49 States models still have the normal mixture screw. No special tools are required for mixture adjustment.

a. If the speed increase matched the specification, go to Step 11.

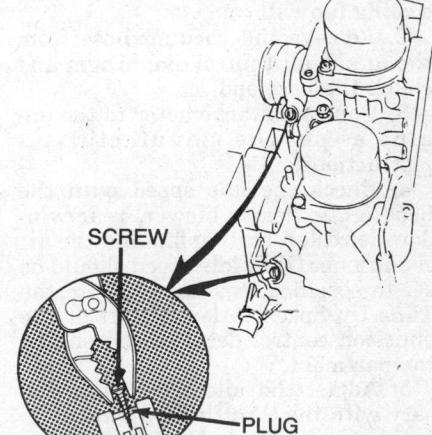

SCREW

PLUG

1983 and later Prelude mixture screw plug removal

b. If the speed increase is out of specification, go to Step 9.

9. Check the speed increase against the specifications. If adjustment is required, adjust the engine speed to the propane enriched maximum rpm by turning the mixture screw. Turn it clockwise to increase; counterclockwise to decrease. Again, adjust the propane control valve for maximum engine speed.

10. Close the propane control valve and recheck the idle speed.

NOTE: Run the engine at 2,500 rpm for 10 seconds to stabilize the condition.

    a. If the idle speed is as specified (Step 4) go to Step 12.

    b. If the idle speed is not as specified (Step 4), go to Step 11.

11. Recheck the idle speed and, if necessary, adjust it by turning the throttle stop screw, then repeat Steps 7-10.

12. Remove the propane enrichment kit and reconnect the air cleaner intake tube on the radiator bulkhead.

13. On 49 States cars, install the limiter cap with the pointer 180° away from the boss on the carburetor body. On California cars, remove the mixture adjuster, then push the tab back into place and install the screw.

14. If the car is equipped with air conditioning, recheck the idle speed with the A/C on. The speed should still be within specifications. If the speed is outside the specification, remove the rubber cap on the idle boost diaphragm and adjust it by turning the adjusting screw.

1983-88

NOTE: This procedure requires a propane enrichment kit.

1. Start the engine and warm it up to normal operating temperature. The cooling fan will come on.

2. Remove the vacuum hose from the intake air control diaphragm and clamp the hose end.

3. Connect a tachometer to the engine as per the manufacturer's instructions.

4. Check the idle speed with the headlights, heater blower, rear window defroster, cooling fan and the air conditioner OFF. Idle speed should be set to specifications according to the Tune-Up Specifications Chart or the emission control decal in the engine compartment.

5. Adjust the idle speed if necessary with the throttle stop screw.

    a. On the Prelude w/auto. trans., remove the frequency solenoid valve "A" and the control valve "A". Disconnect the vacuum tubes and connect the lower hose to the air control valve "A".

    b. On the 1986-88 Accord w/auto. trans., remove the air filter from the frequency solenoid valve "C" and plug the opening in the solenoid valve. On all models, insert the tube of the propane enrichment kit into the air intake tube about 4 inches.

6. With the engine idling, depress the push button on top of the propane device, then slowly open the propane control valve to obtain maximum engine speed. Engine speed should increase as the percentage of the propane injected goes up.

NOTE: Open the propane control valve slowly; a sudden burst of propane may stall the engine.

    a. If the engine speed increases, go to Step 13.

    b. If the engine speed does not increase, the mixture screw is improperly adjusted; go to Step 6.

7. Remove the air cleaner. Disconnect the vacuum hose from the fast idle unloader. Remove the bolts holding the throttle opener bracket to the rear edge of the carburetor.

8. On the Accord and Civic models, remove the carburetor nuts and washers. Remove the brake booster hose and throttle cable from their brackets. Lift the carburetor off the studs and tilt it backwards. Remove the throttle opener screw and bracket.

9. Remove the mixture adjusting screw cap from the throttle opener bracket. Reinstall the bracket. Using new O-rings on the insulator and new gaskets on the heat shield, install the carburetor.

10. Reconnect the vacuum hose to the fast idle unloader.

11. Install the air cleaner, start the engine and warm it to normal operating temperature. The cooling fan will come on.

12. Disconnect and plug the vacuum hose from the intake air control diaphragm.

13. On the Prelude models, label and disconnect all the lines from the carburetors. Disconnect the throttle cable and the vacuum hose from the throttle opener diaphragm. Disconnect the automatic choke lead. Drain the coolant and disconnect hoses. Remove the carburetors.

14. Place a drill stop on a 3mm drill bit, 3mm from end. Drill through the center of the mixture screw plug. Screw a 5mm sheet metal screw into the plug. Grab the screw head with a pair of pliers and remove the plug. Reinstall the carburetors in the reverse order of removal and refill the cooling system.

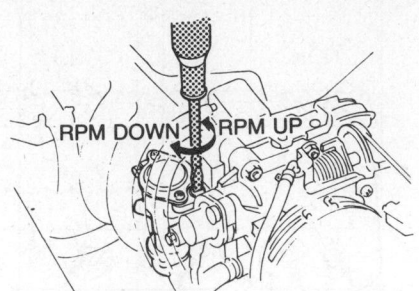

Fuel injection idle speed ajustment screw—1488 & 2829cc engines

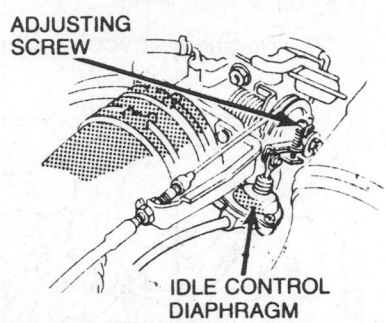

Fuel injection secondary idle speed adjustment—1488 & 1829cc engines

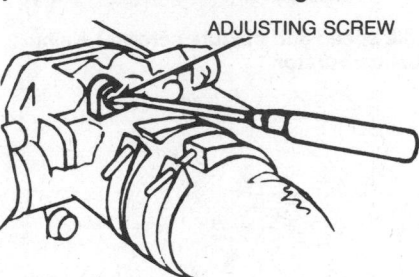

Fuel injection idle speed adjustment screw—1955cc engine

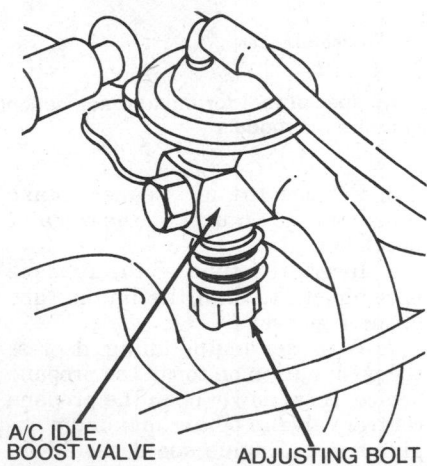

Fuel injection secondary idle speed adjustment—1955cc engine

15. On all models, install the propane enrichment kit and recheck the maximum propane enriched rpm. If the enriched rpm is too low, lean out the mixture. If it is too high, enrichen the mixture. Turn the mixture screw

clockwise to increase rpm; counter-clockwise to decrease rpm.

16. Run the engine for about 10 seconds to stabilize the mixture. Close the propane control valve and recheck the idle speed. Repeat the procedure until the idle rpm is correct. Remove the propane enrichment kit and reconnect the air cleaner intake tube.

Tailpipe Emission Inspection
CARBURETED MODELS

1. Perform Steps 1-2 of the Propane Enrichment Procedure above. If necessary adjust the idle speed. On Accord and Civic models, disconnect the air cleaner intake tube from the air duct on the radiator bulkhead.
2. Warm up and calibrate the CO meter according to the manufacturer's instructions.
3. Check the idle CO with the headlights, heater blower, rear window defroster, cooling fan and the air conditioner off. The CO reading should be 0.1% maximum. If the CO level is correct go to Step 4. If the CO level is not correct, remove the idle mixture plug as described in the Propane Enrichment Procedure and adjust the mixture screws to obtain the proper CO meter reading.
4. Recheck the idle speed and adjust it if necessary by turning the throttle stop screw. Recheck the CO level adjust if necessary. On Prelude models, check and adjust the propane enriched rpm according to Step 10 of the Propane Enrichment Procedure above.

FUEL INJECTED MODELS

NOTE: The idle mixture is electronically controlled on the fuel injected models and is not adjustable.

1. Start the engine and warm it up to normal operating temperature. The cooling fan will come on.
2. Connect a tachometer to the engine as per the manufacturer's instructions.
3. Check the idle speed with the headlights, heater blower, rear window defroster, cooling fan and the air conditioner off. Idle speed should be set to the specifications found on the "Tune-Up Specifications Chart" or the emission control decal in the engine compartment.

NOTE: To disable the idle control system, disconnect the vacuum hose from the idle control solenoid valve and plug the opening.

Adjust the idle speed, if necessary, by turning the idle adjusting screw.

4. With the air conditioning ON, check the idle control boosted speed. Adjust the idle speed, if necessary, by turning the adjusting screw.

ENGINE ELECTRICAL

Distributor

REMOVAL & INSTALLATION

1. Disconnect the high tension and primary lead wires that run from the distributor to the coil.
2. Unsnap the two distributor cap retaining clamps or remove the two holddown screws, and remove the distributor cap. Position it out of the way.
3. Using chalk or paint, carefully mark the position of the distributor rotor in relation to the distributor housing, and mark the relation of the distributor housing to the engine block. When this is done, you should have a line on the distributor housing directly in line with the tip of the rotor, and another line on the engine block directly in line with the mark on the distributor housing.

NOTE: This aligning procedure is very important because the distributor must be reinstalled in the exact location from which it was removed, if correct ignition timing is to be maintained.

4. Note the position of the vacuum line(s) on the vacuum diaphragm with masking tape and then disconnect the lines from the vacuum unit.
5. Remove the bolt which attaches the distributor to the engine block, cylinder head or distributor extension housing, and remove the distributor from the engine.

NOTE: Do not disturb the engine while the distributor is removed. If you attempt to start the engine with the distributor removed, you will have to retime the engine.

6. To install, place the rotor on the distributor shaft and align the tip of the rotor with the line that you made on the distributor housing.
7. With the rotor and housing aligned, insert the distributor into the engine while aligning the mark on the housing with the mark on the block, cylinder head or extension housing.

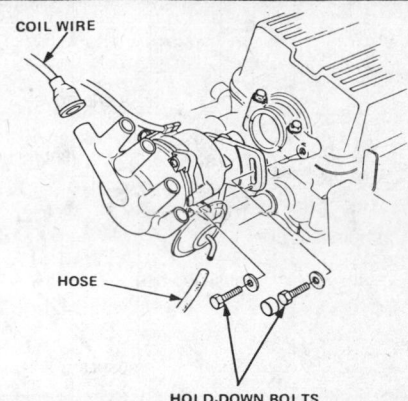
Distributor mounting—1983 and later Prelude

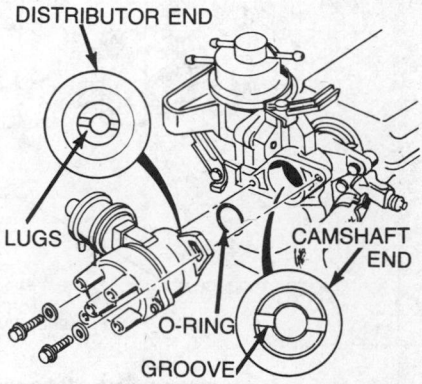
Distributor lug positioning—1342, 1488, 1829, and 1955cc engines

Since the distributor pinion gear has helical teeth on the 1335cc, 1487cc and 1751cc engines, the rotor will turn slightly as the gear on the distributor meshes with the gear on the camshaft. Allow for this when installing the distributor by aligning the mark on the distributor with the mark on the block, by positioning the tip of the rotor slightly to the side of the mark on the distributor.

On the 1342cc, 1488cc, 1829cc, and 1955cc engines, the distributors are equipped with a coupling that connect them to the camshaft. The lugs at the end of the coupling and its mating grooves in the end of the camshaft are offset to prevent installing the distributor 180° out of time.

8. When the distributor is fully seated in the engine, install and tighten the distributor retaining bolt.
9. Align and install the distributor cap and snap the retaining clamps into place or install the two holddown screws.
10. Install the high tension and primary wires onto the coil.
11. Check the ignition timing.

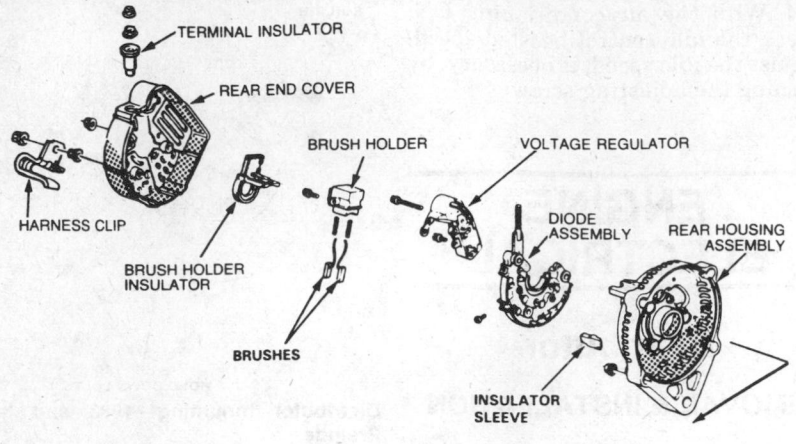

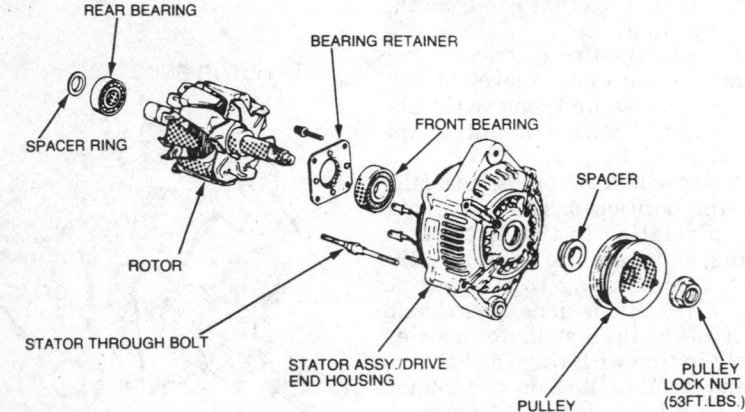

Alternator exploded view—Internal regulator type shown others similar

INSTALLATION CRANKSHAFT AND/OR CAMSHAFT ROTATED

If the engine was cranked with the distributor removed it will be necessary to retime the engine. If you have installed the distributor incorrectly and the engine will not start, remove the distributor from the engine and start from scratch.

1. Install the distributor with the No. 1 cylinder at the top dead center position on the compression stroke (the **TDC** mark on the crankshaft pulley or flywheel aligned with the index mark on the timing belt cover or crankcase and both intake and exhaust valves closed).

2. Line up the metal end of the rotor head with the protrusion on the distributor housing.

3. Carefully insert the distributor into the cylinder head opening with the attaching plate bolt slot aligned with the distributor mounting hole in the cylinder head. Then secure the plate at the center of the adjusting slot. The rotor head must face No. 1 cylinder.

4. Inspect and adjust the point gap and ignition timing.

Alternator

PRECAUTIONS

Observe the proper polarity of the battery connections by making sure that the positive (+) and negative (−) terminal connections are not reversed. Misconnection will allow current to flow in the reverse direction, resulting in damaged diodes and an overheated wiring harness.

• Never ground or short out any alternator or alternator regulator terminals.

• Never operate the alternator with any of its or the battery's leads disconnected.

• Always remove the battery or disconnect its output lead while charging it.

• Always disconnect the ground cable when replacing any electrical components.

• Never subject the alternator to excessive heat or dampness if the engine is being steam cleaned.

• Never use arc welding equipment with the alternator connected.

REMOVAL & INSTALLATION

NOTE: On the 1983-88 Prelude it is necessary to remove the air cleaner assembly.

1. Disconnect the negative (−) battery terminal.

2. Label and unplug the wires from the plugs on the rear of the alternator.

3. Loosen and remove the alternator mounting bolts and remove the V-belt and alternator assembly.

4. To install, reverse the removal procedure. Adjust the alternator belt tension according to the Belt Tension Adjustment section below.

BELT TENSION ADJUSTMENT

The initial inspection and adjustment to the alternator drive belt should be performed after the first 3,000 miles or if the alternator has been moved for any reason. Afterwards, you should inspect the belt tension every 12,000 miles. Before adjusting, inspect the belt to see that it is not cracked or worn. Be sure that its surfaces are free of grease and oil.

1. Push down on the belt halfway between pulleys with a force of about 24 lbs. The belt should deflect 10-12mm.

2. If the belt tension requires adjustment, loosen the adjusting link bolt and move the alternator with a pry bar positioned against the front of the alternator housing.

NOTE: Do not apply pressure to any other part of the alternator.

3. After obtaining the proper tension, tighten the adjusting link bolt.

NOTE: Do not overtighten the belt. Damage to the alternator bearings could result.

Voltage Regulator

REMOVAL & INSTALLATION

The regulator is inside the engine compartment, attached to the right fender liner just above the battery, except on the 1982-83 Accord, which is located just below the main fuse plate, and the 1984-88 models, which have solid state regulators mounted in the alternator.

1981-83 Except 1982-83 Accord

1. Disconnect the negative (−) terminal from the battery.

2. Remove the regulator terminal lead wires.

NOTE: You should label these wires to avoid confusion during installation.

3. Unscrew the two regulator retaining bolts and remove the regulator from the car.

4. To install, reverse the removal procedure.

1982-83 Accord

1. Disconnect the negative (–) terminal from the battery.

2. Remove the four main fuse plate retaining bolts and remove the main fuse plate to gain access to the solid state regulator.

3. Remove the regulator terminal plug from the regulator.

4. Unscrew the regulator retaining bolts and remove the regulator from the car.

5. To install, reverse the removal procedure.

Starter

REMOVAL & INSTALLATION

1. Disconnect the ground cable at the battery negative (-) terminal, and the starter motor cable at the positive terminal.

2. Disconnect the starter motor cable at the motor.

3. Remove the two attaching bolts and remove the starter.

4. Reverse the removal procedure to install the motor. Be sure to tighten the attaching bolts to 29-36 ft. lbs. and make sure that all wires are securely connected.

STARTER DRIVE REPLACEMENT

Direct Drive Type

1. Remove the solenoid by loosening and removing the attaching bolts.

2. Remove the two brush holder plate retaining screws from the rear cover. Also pry off the rear dust cover along with the clip and thrust washer(s).

3. Remove the two through bolts from the rear cover and lightly tap the rear cover with a mallet to remove it.

4. Remove the four carbon brushes from the brush holder and remove the brush holder.

5. Separate the yoke from the case. The yoke is provided with a hole for positioning, into which the gear case lock pin is inserted.

6. Pull the yoke assembly from the gear case, being sure to carefully detach the shift lever from the pinion.

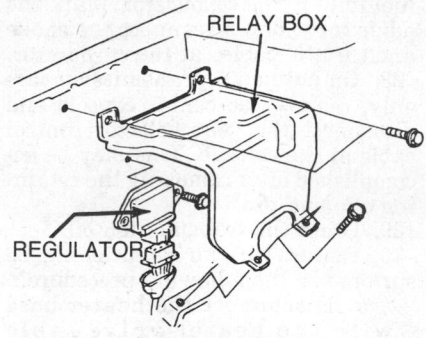

RELAY BOX

REGULATOR

1982–83 Accord voltage regulator mounting

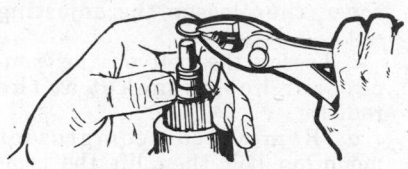

Removing pinion gear from armature

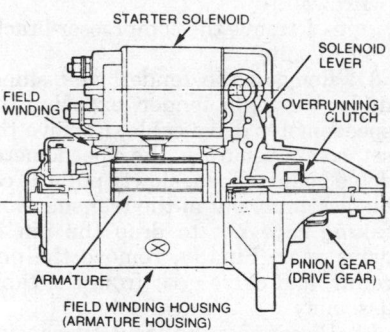

STARTER SOLENOID

SOLENOID LEVER

FIELD WINDING

OVERRUNNING CLUTCH

ARMATURE

PINION GEAR (DRIVE GEAR)

FIELD WINDING HOUSING (ARMATURE HOUSING)

Direct drive starter—typical

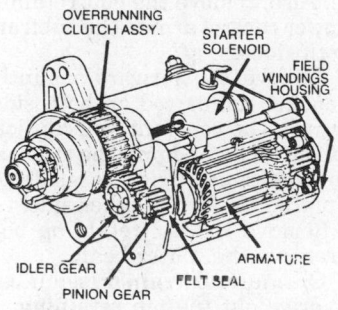

OVERRUNNING CLUTCH ASSY.

STARTER SOLENOID

FIELD WINDINGS HOUSING

IDLER GEAR

PINION GEAR

FELT SEAL

ARMATURE

Reduction gear starter—typical

7. Remove the armature unit from the yoke casing and the field coil.

8. To remove the pinion gear from the armature, first set the armature on end with the pinion end facing upward and pull the clutch stop collar downward toward the pinion. Then remove the pinion stop clip and pull the pinion stop and gears from the armature shaft as a unit.

9. To assemble and install the starter motor, reverse the disassembly and removal procedures. Be sure to install new clips, and be careful of the installation direction of the shift lever.

Reduction Gear Type

1. Remove the solenoid end cover. Pull out the solenoid. There is a spring on the shaft and a steel ball at the end of the shaft.

2. Remove the through bolts retaining the end frame to the motor and solenoid housing.

3. Remove the end frame. The overrunning clutch assembly complete with drive gear can be removed. The idler and motor pinion gears can be removed separately. The idler gear retains five steel roller bearings.

4. The clutch assembly is held together by a circlip. Push down on the gear against the spring inside the clutch assembly and remove the circlip with a circlip expander. Slide the stopper ring, gear, spring, and washer out of the clutch assembly.

5. Assembly is the reverse of disassembly. The stopper ring is installed with the smaller end lip towards the clutch. Be sure that the steel ball is in place at the end of the solenoid shaft. Grease all sliding surfaces of the solenoid before reassembly.

ENGINE MECHANICAL

Engine

REMOVAL & INSTALLATION

—————— CAUTION ——————

If any repair operation requires the removal of a component of the air conditioning system, the system should be discharged by a trained technician. The air conditioning system contains refrigerant gas under pressure. This gas can be very dangerous. Therefore, under no circumstances should an untrained person attempt to disconnect the air conditioner refrigerant lines.

1335cc and 1487cc Civic CVCC

1. Raise the front of the car and support it with jackstands.

2. Disconnect and remove the battery, holddown equipment, tray and mount.

3. Remove the headlight rim attaching screws and the rims.

4. Remove the lower grill molding and remove the six grille retaining bolts and the grille.

5. Disconnect the windshield washer hose and remove it from the underside of the hood.

6. Remove the upper torque (engine locating) arm.

7. Disconnect the vacuum hose at the power brake booster, thermosensors **A** and **B** at their wiring connectors, and the coolant temperature gauge sending unit wire.

8. Drain the radiator. After all coolant has drained, install the drain bolt finger tight.

9. Disconnect all four coolant hoses. Disconnect cooling fan motor connector and the temperature sensor. Remove the radiator hose from the overflow tank.

10. On automatic transmission cars only, remove both ATF cooler line bolts.

NOTE: Save the washers from the cooler line banjo connectors and replace them if damaged.

11. Remove the radiator.

12. Label and disconnect the starter motor wires. Remove the two starter mounting bolts (one from each end of the starter), and remove the starter.

13. Label and disconnect the spark plug wires at the plug.

14. Remove the distributor cap and scribe the position of the rotor on the side of the distributor housing.

15. Remove the top distributor swivel bolt and remove the distributor. The rotor will rotate 30° because the drive gear is beveled.

16. On manual transmission cars, remove the C-clip retaining the clutch cable at the firewall. Then, remove the end of the clutch cable from the clutch release arm and bracket. First, pull up on the cable, and then push it out to release it from the bracket. Remove the end from the release arm.

17. Disconnect the back-up light switch wires.

18. Disconnect the control valve vacuum hose, the air intake hose, and the preheat air intake hose.

19. Disconnect the air bleed valve hose from the air cleaner.

20. Label and disconnect all remaining vacuum hoses from the underside of the air cleaner. Remove the air cleaner.

21. Label and disconnect all remaining emission control vacuum hoses from the engine.

22. Disconnect the emission box wiring connector and remove the black emission box from the firewall.

23. Remove the engine mount heat shield.

24. Disconnect the engine-to-body ground strap at the valve corner.

25. Disconnect the alternator wiring connector and oil pressure sensor leads.

26. Disconnect the vacuum hose from the start control and electrical leads to both cut-off solenoid leads.

27. Disconnect the vacuum hose from the charcoal canister and both fuel lines to the carburetor. Mark the adjustment and disconnect the choke and throttle cables at the carburetor.

28. On automatic transmission cars only, remove the center console and disconnect the gear selector control cable at the console. This may be accomplished after removing the retaining clip and pin.

29. Drain the transmission oil.

30. On cars with air conditioning, be sure to use the following procedure.:

a. Disconnect the heater hose with the heater valve cable attached.

b. Remove the compressor belt cover, then loosen the adjusting nut.

c. Loosen the belt on the compressor hose bracket at the radiator.

d. Remove the compressor mounting bolt then lift the compressor out of the bracket with the hoses attached and wire it up to the firewall.

e. Remove the compressor bracket (5 bolts).

31. Remove the fender well shield under the right fender, exposing the speedometer drive cable. Remove the set screw securing the speedometer drive holder. Then, slowly pull the cable assembly out of the transmission, taking care not to drop the pin or drive gear. Finally, remove the pin, collar, and drive gear from the cable assembly.

32. Disconnect the front suspension stabilizer bar from its mounts on both sides. Also, remove the bolt retaining the lower control arm to the subframe on both sides.

33. Remove the forward mounting nut on the radius rod on both sides. Then, pry the constant velocity joint out about ½ in. and pull the stub axle out of the transmission case. Repeat this procedure for the other side.

34. Remove the six retaining bolts and remove the center beam.

35. On manual transmission cars only, drive out the pin retaining the shift linkage.

36. Disconnect the lower torque arm from the transmission.

37. On automatic transmission cars only, remove the bolt retaining the control cable stay at the transmission. Loosen the two U-bolt nuts and pull the cable out of its housing.

38. Disconnect the exhaust pipe at the manifold. Disconnect the retaining clamp also.

39. Remove the rear engine mount nut.

40. Attach a chain pulley hoist to the engine. Honda recommends using the threaded bolt holes at the extreme right and left ends of the cylinder head (with special hardened bolts) as lifting points, as opposed to wrapping a chain around the entire block and risk damaging some components.

41. Raise the engine enough to place a slight tension on the chain. Remove the nut retaining the front engine mount. Then, remove the three bolts retaining the front mount. While lifting the engine, remove the mount.

42. Remove the three retaining bolts and push the left engine support into its shock mount bracket to the limit of its travel.

43. Slowly raise the engine out of the vehicle.

44. Install the engine in the reverse order of removal, making the following checks:

a. Make sure the clip at the end of the driveshaft seats into the groove in the differential. You should hear a click as they seat themselves.

NOTE: Always use new spring clips.

b. Bleed the air from the cooling system.

c. Adjust the throttle cable tension.

d. Check the clutch for the correct free-play.

e. Make sure the transmission shifts properly.

1342cc and 1488cc Civic

1. Apply the parking brake and place blocks behind the rear wheels. Raise the front of the car and support it on jackstands.

2. Disconnect the battery cables from the battery. Remove the battery, and then remove the battery tray from the engine compartment.

3. Scribe a line where the hood brackets meet the inside of the hood. This will help realign the hood during installation.

4. Unbolt and remove the hood.

5. Remove the engine and wheelwell splash shields.

6. Drain the oil from the engine, the coolant from the radiator, and the transmission oil from the transmission.

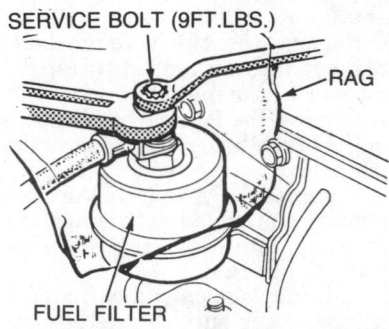

SERVICE BOLT (9FT.LBS.)

RAG

FUEL FILTER

Relieving fuel system pressure

NOTE: Removal of the filler plug or cap will speed the draining process.

7. On carbureted models:

a. Remove the air cleaner using the following procedure:

b. Disconnect and label all hoses leading to the air cleaner.

c. Remove the air cleaner cover and filter.

d. Remove the three bolts holding down the air cleaner. Lift up the air cleaner and disconnect the temperature sensor wire and the remaining two hoses. Remove the air cleaner.

8. On fuel injected models:

a. Remove the intake duct and the vacuum hose.

b. Relieve the fuel pressure by slowly loosening the service bolt on the top of the fuel filter about one turn.

—— CAUTION ——

Place a rag under the filter during this procedure to prevent fuel from spilling onto the engine.

c. Disconnect the fuel return hose from the pressure regulator. Remove the special nut and then remove the fuel hoses.

9. Disconnect the following hoses and wires:

• The engine compartment sub-harness connector.

• The engine secondary cable.

• Remove the harness cable from the fuse box.

• The brake booster vacuum hose.

• On engines with A/C, remove the idle control solenoid hoses from the valve and remove the valve.

10. Disconnect the control box connector(s). Remove the control box(es) from the bracket(s), and let it hang next to the engine.

11. Disconnect the purge control solenoid valve vacuum hose at the charcoal canister.

12. Remove the air jet controller (if so equipped).

13. Loosen the throttle cable locknut and adjusting nut, then slip the cable end out of the throttle bracket, removing the cable.

14. Disconnect the fuel line hose from the fuel pump. Remove the fuel pump cover and the pump.

15. Remove the spark plug wires and the distributor from the engine.

16. Remove the radiator and heater hoses from the engine.

NOTE: Label the heater hoses so they will be installed in their original locations.

17. On manual transmission models (except 4wd):

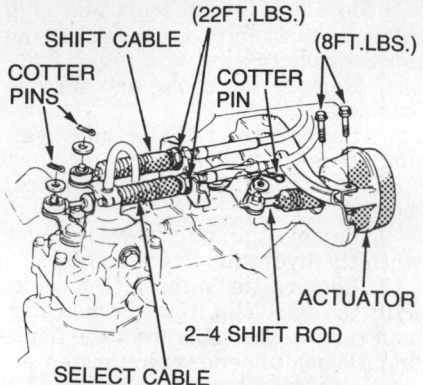

SHIFT CABLE (22FT.LBS.) (8FT.LBS.)
COTTER PINS
COTTER PIN
ACTUATOR
2–4 SHIFT ROD
SELECT CABLE

Shift and Selector control cables

a. Disconnect the transmission ground cable.

b. Loosen the clutch cable adjusting nut and remove the cable from the release arm.

c. Disconnect the shift lever torque rod from the clutch housing.

d. Slide the shift rod pin retainer out of the way, then with a pin punch, drive the pin out and remove the shift rod.

18. On 4wd models:

a. Loosen the clutch adjusting nut and disconnect the clutch cable from the release arm.

b. Disconnect the ground cable from the transmission.

c. Disconnect the shift control cables.

d. Disconnect the rear axle driveshaft at the transmission.

19. On automatic transmission cars:

a. Remove the oil cooler hoses at the transmission, let the fluid drain from the hoses then prop the hoses up out of the way near the radiator.

b. Remove the center console from the inside of the car.

c. Put the shift lever in reverse and remove the lock pin from the end of the shift cable.

d. Unbolt and remove the shift cable holder.

e. Disconnect the throttle control cable end from the throttle lever. Loosen the lower locknut on the throttle cable bracket and remove the cable from the bracket.

NOTE: Do not move the upper locknut as it will change the transmission shift points.

20. Remove the speedometer cable clip, then pull the cable out of the holder.

NOTE: Do not remove the holder from the transmission as it may cause the speedometer gear to fall into the transmission.

21. Squirt penetrating oil on the nuts holding the exhaust header pipe in place. Loosen and remove the nuts and pipe.

22. Remove the driveshaft as follows:

a. Remove the jackstands and lower the car. Loosen the 32mm spindle nuts with a socket. Raise the car and resupport it on jackstands.

b. Remove the front wheel, and the spindle nut.

c. Place a floor jack under the lower control arm, then remove the ball joint cotter pin and nut.

NOTE: Be certain the lower control arm is positioned securely on top of the floor jack so that it doesn't suddenly jump or spring off when the ball joint remover is used.

d. Using a ball joint puller, separate the ball joint from the front hub.

e. Slowly, lower the floor jack under lower the control arm. Pull the hub outward and off the driveshaft.

f. Using a small pry bar, pry out the inboard CV-joint approximately ½ in. in order to release the spring clip from the groove in the differential.

g. Pull the driveshaft out of the transmission case.

23. Attach a lifting sling to the engine block and raise the hoist to remove the slack from the chain.

24. Remove the rear transmission mount, and remove the bolts from the front transmission mount and the engine side mount.

25. On A/C equipped cars:

a. Loosen the compressor drive belt adjusting bolts and remove the belt.

b. Remove the mounting bolts from the A/C compressor, then wire it up out of the way on the front beam.

NOTE: DO NOT disconnect the A/C refrigerant lines; the compressor can be moved without discharging the system.

c. Remove the lower compressor mounting bracket.

26. Disconnect the alternator wiring harness connectors. Remove the alternator belt. Remove the alternator mounting bolts and remove the alternator.

27. Check that the engine and transaxle are free from any hoses or electrical connectors.

28. Slowly raise the engine up and out of the car.

29. To install, reverse the removal procedures. Pay special attention to the following:

a. Torque the engine mounting bolts in the proper sequence.

b. Be sure that the spring clip on the end of each driveshaft audibly clicks into the differential.

NOTE: Always use new spring clips on installation.

c. Bleed the air from the cooling system.

d. Adjust the belt(s) tension, and the throttle cable tension.

e. Check the clutch pedal free-play.

Accord/Prelude 1,751cc Engine

1. Disconnect the negative battery terminal.
2. Drain the coolant, and drain the engine oil.
3. Jack up the front of the car and remove the front wheels. Be sure to support the car with safety stands.
4. Remove the air cleaner.
5. Remove the following wires and hoses:
• The coil wire and the ignition primary wire from the distributor.
• The engine subharness and the starter wires (mark the wires before removal to ease installation).
• The vacuum tube from the brake booster.
• On Hondamatic models, remove the ATF cooler hose from the transmission.
• The engine ground cable.
• Alternator wiring harness.
• Carburetor solenoid valve connector.
• Carburetor fuel line.

• Models with California and high altitude disconnect the hoses at the air controller.
6. Remove the choke and throttle cables.
7. Remove the radiator and heating hoses.
8. Remove the emission control box.
9. Remove the clutch slave cylinder with the hydraulic line attached.
10. Remove the speedometer cable. Pull the wire clip from the housing, and remove the cable from the housing. Do not, under any circumstances, remove the housing from the transmission.
11. Attach an engine hoist to the engine block, and raise the engine just enough to remove the slack from the chain.

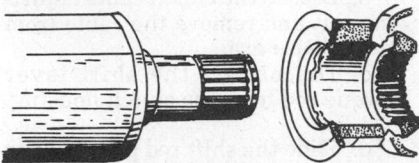

Accord driveshaft removal

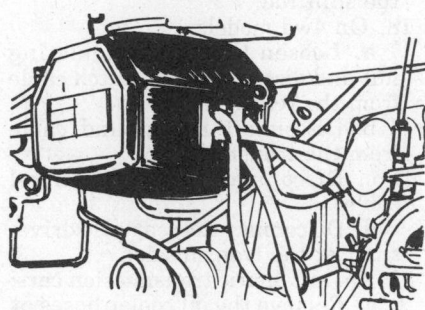

Emission control box

12. Disconnect the right and left lower ball joints, and the tie rod ends. You will need a ball joint remover tool for this operation. An alternative method is to leave the ball joints connected, and remove the lower control arm inner bolts, and the radius rods from the lower control arms.
13. Remove the driveshafts from the transmission by prying the snapring off the groove in the end of the shaft. Then, pull the shaft out by holding the knuckle.
14. Remove the center engine mount.
15. Remove the shift rod positioner from the transmission case.
16. Drive out the pin from the shift rod using a small pin driver.
17. On Hondamatics, remove the control cable.
18. Disconnect the exhaust pipe.
19. Remove the three engine support bolts and push the left engine support into the shock mount bracket.
20. Remove the front and rear engine mounts.
21. Raise the engine carefully and remove it from the car.
22. Install the engine in the reverse order of removal, making the following checks:

a. Make sure that the clip at the end of a driveshaft seats in the groove in the differential. Failure to do so may lead to the wheels falling off.

NOTE: Always use new spring clips.

b. Bleed the air from the cooling system.

c. Adjust the throttle and choke cable tension.

d. Check the clutch for the correct free-play.

e. Make sure that the transmission shifts properly.

Accord and Prelude 1829cc and 1955cc Engines

1. Apply the parking brake and place blocks behind the rear wheels. Raise the front of the car and support it on jackstands.
2. Disconnect both battery cables from the battery. Remove the battery, and then remove the battery tray from the engine compartment.
3. On the Prelude, remove the knob caps covering the headlights' manual retracting knobs, then turn the knobs to bring the headlights to the **ON** position.
4. On the Prelude, remove the five screws retaining the grille and remove the grille.
5. Remove the splash guard from under the engine. Unbolt and remove the hood.

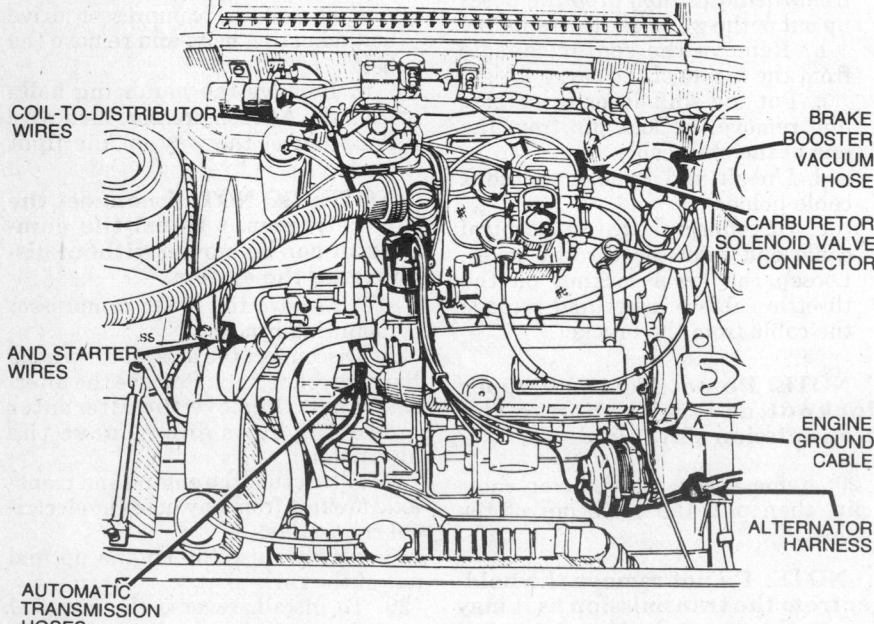

COIL-TO-DISTRIBUTOR WIRES

AND STARTER WIRES

AUTOMATIC TRANSMISSION HOSES

BRAKE BOOSTER VACUUM HOSE

CARBURETOR SOLENOID VALVE CONNECTOR

ENGINE GROUND CABLE

ALTERNATOR HARNESS

Component removal points—Accord 1751cc

6. Remove the oil filler cap and drain the engine oil.

NOTE: When replacing the drain plug be sure to use a new washer.

7. Remove the radiator cap, then open the radiator drain petcock and drain the coolant from the radiator.

8. Remove the transmission filler plug, then remove the drain plug and drain the transmission.

9. On Carbureted models:

a. Label and then remove the wires at the coil and the engine secondary ground cable located on the valve cover.

b. Remove the air cleaner cover and filter.

c. Remove the air intake ducts. Remove the two nuts and two bolts from the air cleaner, remove the air control valve, then remove the air cleaner (Accord only).

d. Loosen the locknut on the throttle cable and loosen the cable adjusting nut, then slip the cable end out of the carburetor linkage.

NOTE: Be careful not to bend or kink the throttle cable. Always replace a damaged cable.

e. Disconnect the No. 1 control box connector. Remove the control box from its bracket, and let it hang next to the engine.

f. Disconnect the fuel line at the fuel filter and remove the solenoid vacuum hose at the charcoal canister.

g. On California and high altitude models, remove the air jet controller.

10. On fuel injected models:

a. Remove the air intake duct. Disconnect the cruise control vacuum tube from the air intake duct and remove the resonator tube.

b. Remove the secondary ground cable from the top of the engine.

c. Disconnect the air box connecting tube. Unscrew the tube clamp bolt and disconnect the emission tubes.

d. Remove the air cleaner case mounting nuts and remove the air cleaner case assembly.

e. Loosen the locknut on the throttle cable and loosen the cable adjusting nut, then slip the cable end out of the bracket and linkage.

NOTE: Be careful not to bend or kink the throttle cable. Always replace a damaged cable.

f. Disconnect the following wires:
• The ground cable at the fuse box
• The engine compartment sub-harness connector and clamp

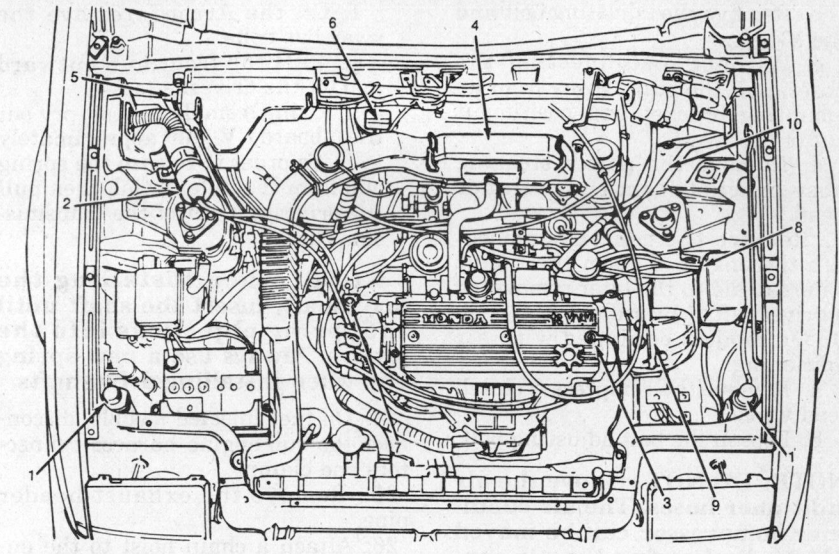

① Headlight retracting knobs
② Ignition coil wires
③ Secondary ground cable
④ Air cleaner assembly
⑤ No. 1 control box connector
⑥ Charcoal canister
⑦ Air bleed bolt for cooling system
⑧ No. 2 control box connector
⑨ Air chamber location (if so equipped)
⑩ Air jet controller location (if so equipped)

Component removal points—Prelude 1829 and 1955cc

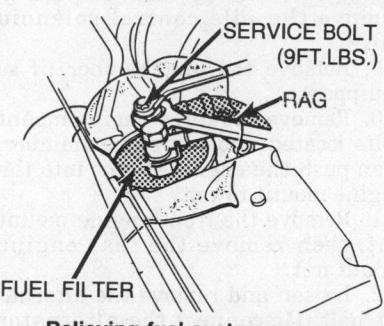

Relieving fuel system pressure

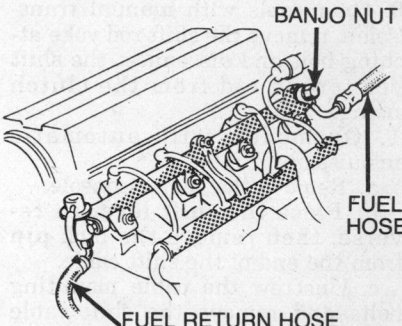

Disconnecting the fuel hoses

• The high tension wire and ignition primary leads at the coil
• The radio condenser connector at the coil.

g. Using the following procedures relieve the fuel system pressure:
•Place a shop rag over the fuel filter to absorb any gasoline which may be sprayed on the engine while relieving the pressure.
• Slowly loosen the service bolt approximately one full turn. This will relieve any pressure in the system.
• Using a new sealing washer, re-tighten the service bolt.

h. Disconnect the fuel return hose from the pressure regulator. Remove the banjo nut and then remove the fuel hose.

i. Disconnect the vacuum hose from the brake booster.

11. Disconnect the radiator and heater hoses at the engine. Label the heater hoses so they can be installed correctly.

12. On automatic transaxle models, disconnect the transmission oil cooler hoses at the transmission, let the fluid drain from the hoses, then hang the hoses up near the radiator.

13. On manual transmission models, loosen the clutch cable adjusting nut and remove the clutch cable from the release arm.

14. Disconnect the battery cable at the transmission and the starter cable at the starter motor terminal.

15. Disconnect both engine harness connectors.

16. Remove the speedometer cable clip, then pull the cable out of the holder.

NOTE: DO NOT remove the holder as the speedometer gear may drop into the transmission.

17. On models equipped with power steering:

a. Remove the speed sensor complete with hoses.

b. Remove the adjusting bolt and the V-belt.

c. Without disconnecting the hoses, pull the pump away from its mounting bracket and position it out of the way.

d. Remove the power steering hose bracket from the cylinder head.

18. Remove the center beam beneath the engine. Loosen the radius rod nuts to aid in the later removal of the driveshafts (Accord only).

19. On models equipped with air conditioning:

a. Remove the compressor clutch lead wire.

b. Loosen the belt adjusting bolt.

NOTE: DO NOT remove the air conditioner hoses. The air conditioner compressor can be moved without discharging the air conditioner system.

c. Remove the compressor mounting bolts, then lift the compressor out of the bracket with the hoses attached, and hang it on the front bulkhead with a piece of wire.

20. On models with manual transmission, remove the shift rod yoke attaching bolt and disconnect the shift lever torque rod from the clutch housing.

21. On models with automatic transmission:

a. Remove the center console.

b. Place the shift lever in reverse, then remove the lock pin from the end of the shift cable.

c. Unscrew the cable mounting bolts and remove the shift cable holder.

d. Remove the throttle cable from the throttle lever. Loosen the lower locknut, then remove the cable from the bracket.

NOTE: DO NOT loosen the upper locknut as it will change the transmission shift points.

22. Disconnect the right and left lower ball joints and the tie rod ends.

23. Remove the driveshafts as follows:

a. Remove the jackstands and lower the car. Loosen the 32mm spindle nuts with a socket. Raise the car and resupport on jackstands.

b. Remove the front wheel, and the spindle nut.

c. Remove the damper fork and the damper pinch bolts.

d. Remove the ball joint bolt and separate the ball joint from the front hub (Accord) or lower arm control (Prelude).

e. Disconnect the tie rods from the steering knuckles.

f. On the Accord, remove the sway bar bolts.

g. Pull the front hub outward and off the driveshafts.

h. Using a small pry bar, pry out the inboard CV-joint approximately ½ in. in order to release the spring clip from the differential, then pull the driveshaft out of the transmission case.

NOTE: When installing the driveshaft, insert the shaft until the spring clip clicks into the groove. Always use a new spring clip when installing driveshafts.

24. On fuel injected models, disconnect the sub-engine harness connectors and clamp.

25. Remove the exhaust header pipe.

26. Attach a chain hoist to the engine and raise it just enough to remove the slack.

27. Disconnect the No. 2 control box connector, lift the control box off its bracket, and let it hang next to the engine.

28. On models with air conditioning, remove the idle control solenoid valve.

29. Remove the air chamber (if so equipped).

30. Remove the three engine mount bolts located under the air chamber, then push the engine mount into the engine mount tower.

31. Remove the front engine mount nut, then remove the rear engine mount nut.

32. Loosen and remove the alternator belt. Disconnect the alternator wire harness and remove the alternator.

33. Remove the bolt from the rear torque rod at the engine, then loosen the bolt in the frame mount and swing the rod up and out of the way.

34. Raise the engine carefully from the car checking that all wires and hoses have been removed from the engine/transaxle. Raise the engine all the way up and remove it from the car.

35. Installation is the reverse of removal, making the following checks:

a. Torque the engine mounting bolts in the proper sequence.

b. Bleed the air from the cooling system.

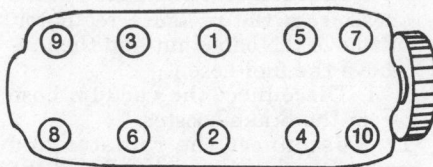

Cylinder head torque sequence—1335, 1487, and 1751cc engines

c. Adjust the clutch pedal free-play.

d. Adjust the throttle cable tension.

e. Make sure the transmission shifts properly.

Cylinder Head

REMOVAL & INSTALLATION

NOTE: You will need a 12 point socket to remove and install the head bolts on the CVCC engine.

REMOVAL PRECAUTIONS

• To prevent warping, the cylinder head should be removed when the engine is cold.

• Remove oil, scale or carbon deposits accumulated from each part. When decarbonizing take care not to score or scratch the mating surfaces.

• After washing the oil holes or orifices in each part, make sure that they are not restricted by blowing out with compressed air.

• If parts will not be reinstalled immediately after washing, spray parts with a rust preventive to protect them from corrosion.

1335cc and 1487cc Civic

NOTE: If the engine has already been removed from the car, begin with Step 12 in the following procedure.

1. Disconnect the negative battery cable.

2. Drain the radiator.

3. Disconnect the upper radiator hose at the thermostat cover.

4. Remove the distributor cap, ignition wires and primary wire. Also, loosen the alternator bracket and remove the upper mounting bolt from the cylinder head.

5. On models with A/C, remove the compressor drive belt cover, then loosen the drive belt adjusting nut. Remove the compressor mounting bolts

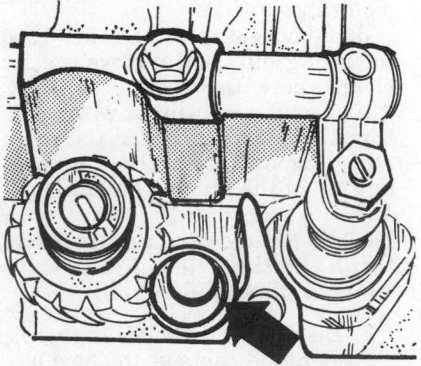

Hidden bolt next to the oil pump gear

and move the compressor to one side without discharging it. Remove the compressor bracket.

6. Remove the air cleaner case.

7. Disconnect the tube running between the canister and carburetor at the canister.

8. Disconnect the throttle and choke control cables. Label and disconnect all vacuum hoses.

9. Disconnect the heater hose at the intake manifold.

10. Disconnect the wires from both thermostats.

11. Disconnect the fuel line.

12. Disconnect the temperature gauge sending unit wire, idle cut-off solenoid valve, and primary/main cut-off solenoid valve.

13. Disconnect the engine torque rod.

14. Disconnect the exhaust pipe at the exhaust manifold.

15. Remove the valve cover bolts and the valve cover.

16. Remove the two timing belt upper cover bolts and the cover.

17. Bring No. 1 piston to TDC. Do this by aligning the notch next to the red notch you use for setting ignition timing, with the index mark on the rear of engine block.

18. Loosen, but do not remove, the timing belt adjustment bolt and pivot bolt.

NOTE: Use care when handling the timing belt. Do not use sharp instruments to remove the belt. Do not get oil or grease on the belt. Do not bend or twist the belt more than 90°.

19. Loosen and remove the cylinder head bolts in the reverse order given in the head bolt tightening sequence diagram. The number one bolt is hidden underneath the oil pump. To prevent warpage, unscrew the bolts ⅓ turn each time and repeat sequence until loose.

20. Remove the cylinder head with the carburetor and manifolds attached.

21. Remove the intake and exhaust manifolds from the cylinder heads.

NOTE: After removing the cylinder head, cover the engine with a clean cloth to prevent materials from getting into the cylinders.

22. To install, reverse the removal procedure, being sure to pay attention to the following points:

 a. Be sure that No. 1 cylinder is at top dead center before positioning the cylinder head in place.

 b. Use a new head gasket and make sure the head, engine block, and gasket are clean.

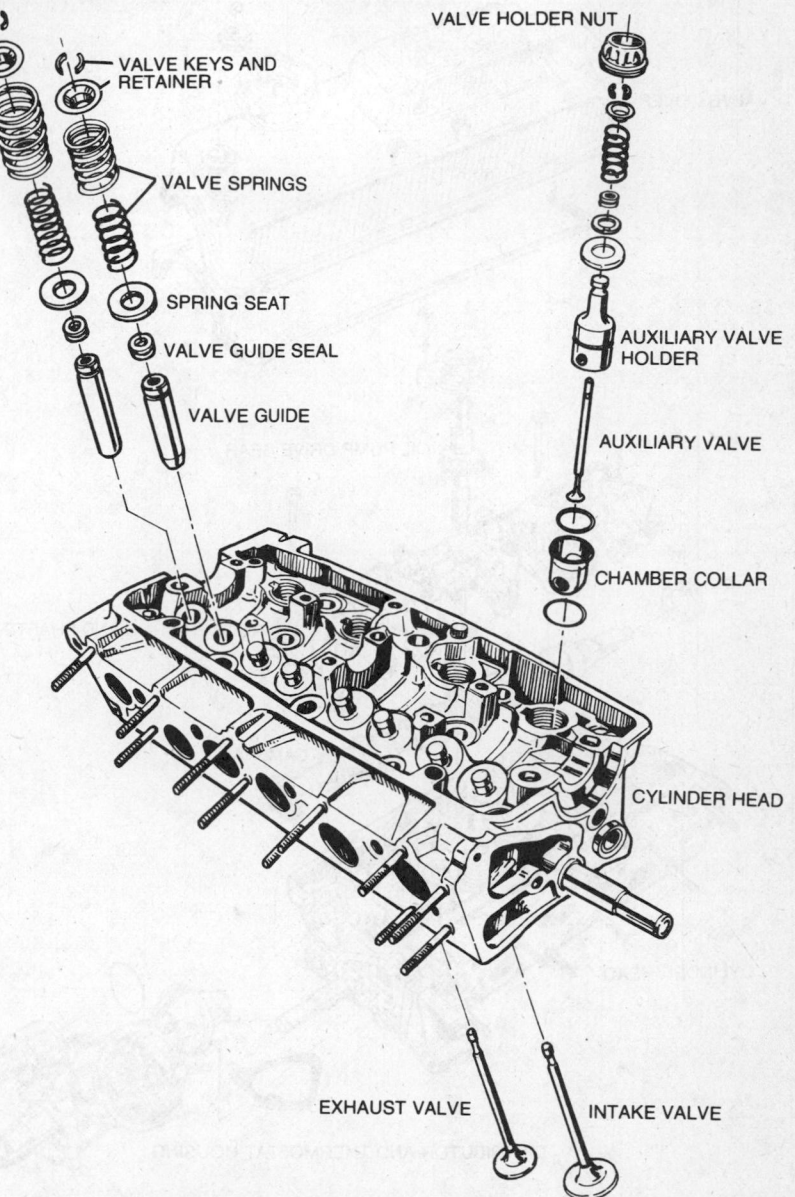

Cylinder head and valve train—8-valve engines

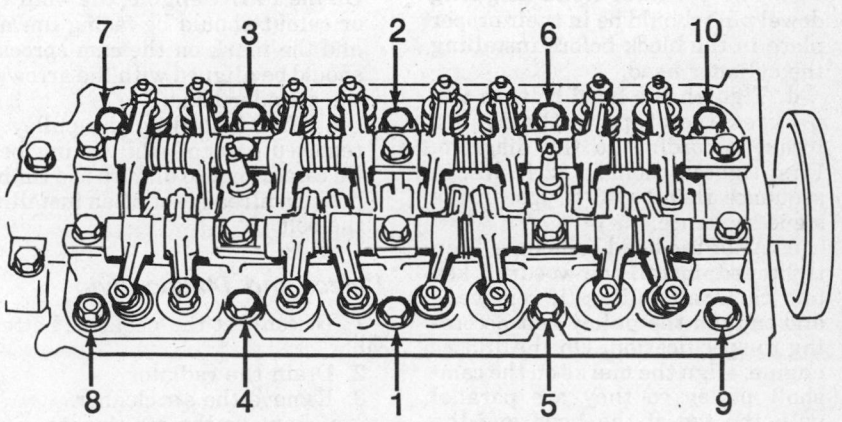

Cylinder head torque sequence—1342 and 1488cc engines

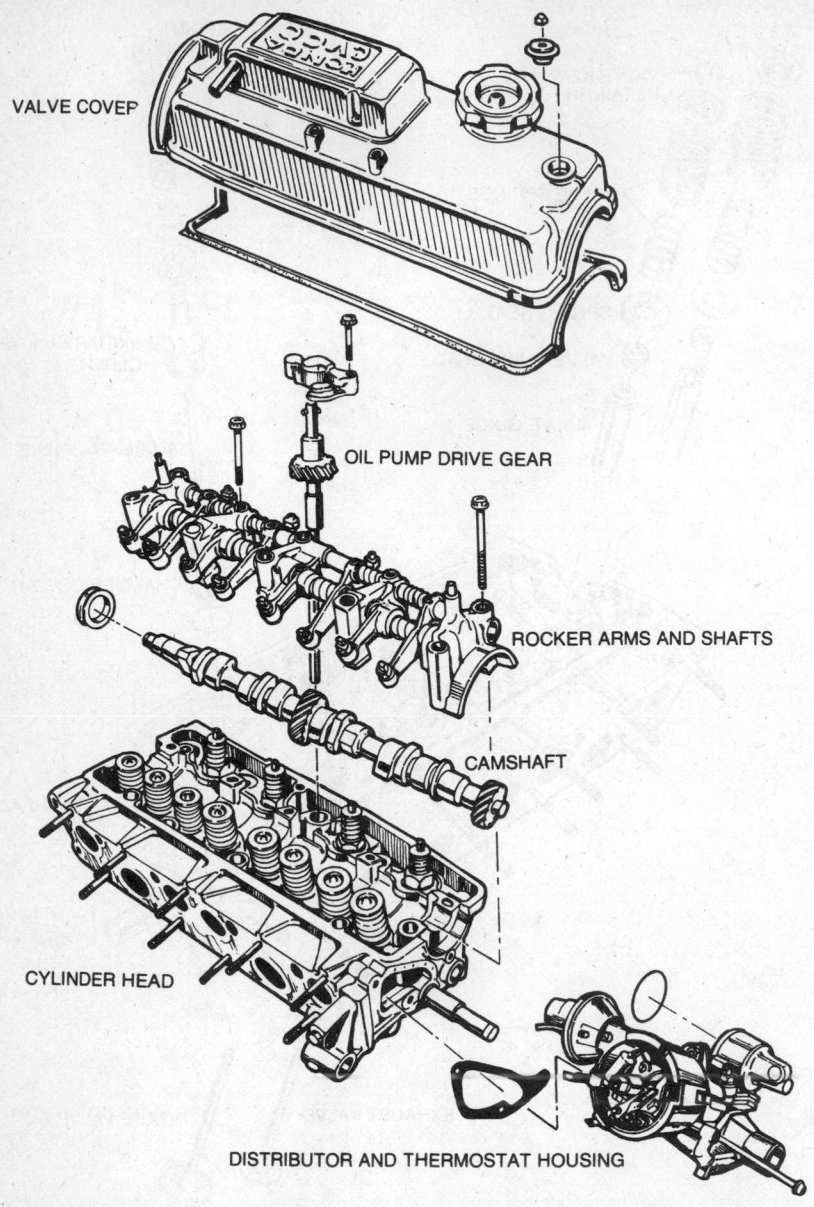

VALVE COVER

OIL PUMP DRIVE GEAR

ROCKER ARMS AND SHAFTS

CAMSHAFT

CYLINDER HEAD

DISTRIBUTOR AND THERMOSTAT HOUSING

CVCC cylinder head component

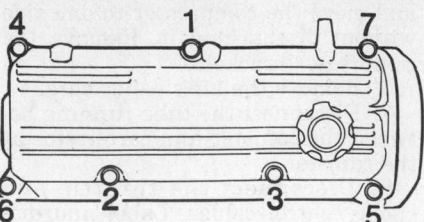

Valve cover torque sequence—1342cc engine

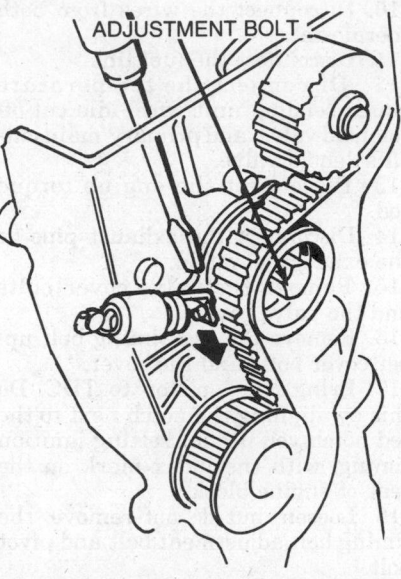

ADJUSTMENT BOLT

Timing belt tensioner adjustment bolt—1342 and 1488cc engines

c. The cylinder head aligning dowel pins should be in their proper place in the block before installing the cylinder head.

d. Tighten the head bolts in two progressive steps to the proper torque according to the diagram. First tighten them to 22 ft. lbs. in sequence then to 43 ft. lbs. in the same sequence.

e. After the head bolts have been tightened, install the woodruff key and camshaft pulley (if removed), and tighten the pulley bolt according to specification. On the 1355cc engine, align the marks on the camshaft pulley so they are parallel with the top of the head and the woodruff key or cutout is facing up.

On the 1487cc engine, the word **UP** or cutout should be facing upward and the mark on the cam sprocket should be aligned with the arrow on the cylinder head.

f. After installing the pulley (if removed), install the timing belt. Be careful not to disturb the timing position already set when installing the belt.

1342cc and 1488cc Civic

1. Disconnect the negative battery cable.

2. Drain the radiator.

3. Remove the air cleaner:

a. Remove the air cleaner cover and filter.

b. Disconnect the hot and cold air intake ducts, and remove the air chamber hose.

c. Remove the 3 bolts holding the air cleaner.

d. Lift up on the air cleaner housing, then remove the remaining hoses and the air temperature sensor wire.

e. Remove the air cleaner.

4. On fuel injected models, relieve the fuel pressure using the following procedures:

a. Slowly loosen the service bolt on the top of the fuel filter about one turn.

NOTE: Place a rag under the filter during this procedure to prevent fuel from spilling onto the engine.

b. Disconnect the fuel return hose from the pressure regulator. Remove the special nut and then remove the fuel hose.

5. Remove the brake booster vacuum tube from the intake manifold.

6. Remove the engine ground wire from the valve cover and disconnect the wires from the fuel cut-off solenoid valve, automatic choke and thermosensor.

7. Disconnect the fuel lines.

8. Disconnect the spark plug wires from the spark plugs, then remove the distributor assembly.

9. Disconnect the throttle cable from the carburetor.

10. Disconnect the hoses from the charcoal canister, and from the No. 1 control box at the tubing manifold.

11. Disconnect the air jet controller (California and high altitude only).

12. Disconnect the idle control solenoid hoses (w/air conditioning only).

13. Disconnect the upper radiator heater and bypass hoses.

14. On fuel injected models, disconnect the engine sub harness connectors and the following couplers from the head and the intake manifold.
- The four injector couplers
- The TA sensor connector
- The ground connector
- The TW sensor connector
- The throttle sensor connector
- The crankshaft angle sensor coupler

15. Remove the thermostat housing-to-intake manifold hose.

16. Disconnect the oxygen sensor coupler.

17. Remove the exhaust manifold bracket and manifold bolts, then remove the manifold.

18. Remove the bolts from the intake manifold and bracket.

19. Disconnect the breather chamber to the intake manifold hose.

20. Remove the valve and timing belt covers.

21. Loosen the timing belt tensioner adjustment bolt, then remove the belt.

22. Remove the cylinder head bolts in the reverse order given in the head bolt torque sequence.

NOTE: Unscrew the bolts ⅓ of a turn each time and repeat the sequence to prevent cylinder head warpage.

23. Carefully remove the cylinder head from the engine.

24. To install, reverse the removal procedure, being sure to pay attention to the following points:

a. Always use a new head gasket and make sure the head, engine block, and gasket are clean.

b. Be sure the No. 1 cylinder is at top dead center and the camshaft pulley **UP** mark is on the top before positioning the head in place.

c. The cylinder head dowel pins and oil control jet must be aligned.

d. Tighten the cylinder head bolts in two progressive steps as shown in the torque sequence diagram. First tighten them to 22 ft. lbs. in sequence, then to 43 ft. lbs. in the same sequence.

e. On the 1342cc engine torque

the valve cover two turns at a time in the sequence shown to 9 ft. lbs. (108 inch lbs.).

f. After installation, check to see that all hoses and wires are installed correctly.

Accord and Prelude 1751cc Engines

NOTE: Cylinder head temperature must be below 38°C.

1. Disconnect the battery ground cable.

2. Drain the cooling system.

3. Remove the air cleaner, tagging all hoses for installation.

4. Disconnect the wires from the thermosensor temperature gauge sending unit, idle cut-off solenoid valve, primary/main cut-off solenoid valve, and the automatic choke.

5. Disconnect the fuel lines and throttle cable from the carburetor.

6. Tag all emission hoses going to the carburetor then remove them and the carburetor.

7. Disconnect all wires and hoses from the distributor, tagging them for installation, and remove the distributor.

8. Remove all coolant hoses from the head.

9. Disconnect the hot air ducts and head pipe from the head. Loosen the exhaust manifold-to-engine bracket bolts to ease assembly.

10. If equipped with power steering, loosen the adjustment bolt and remove the belt. Disconnect the hoses and plug the hoses and fitting to prevent contamination. Remove the pump mounting bolt and swing the pump to the right side of the engine.

11. On cars without A/C, remove the bolt holding the alternator bracket to the head. Loosen the adjustment bolt.

12. On cars with A/C, remove the alternator and bracket from the car.

13. Disconnect the brake booster vacuum hose at the one-way valve.

14. Remove the valve cover and timing bolt upper cover.

15. Loosen the timing belt pivot and adjust bolts and slide the belt off the pulley.

16. Remove the oil pump gear cover and pull the oil pump shaft out of the head.

17. Remove the head bolts in sequence working from the ends, across the head, toward the center. This is the reverse of the tightening sequence. To prevent warpage, unscrew the bolts ⅓ turn each time and repeat the sequence until loose.

18. Carefully lift the head from the block.

19. Thoroughly clean the mating surfaces to the head and block.

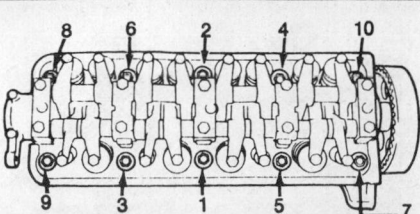

Cylinder head torque sequence—1829 & 1955cc engines

20. Always use a new gasket.

21. Install the head in reverse order of the removal procedure. Make sure the head dowel pins are aligned. Make sure that the UP mark or cutout on the timing belt pulley is at the top. Torque the cylinder head bolts in two equal steps. Tighten all bolts to 22 ft. lbs. in sequence, then to 43 ft. lbs. in the final step.

Accord and Prelude 1829cc and 1955cc Engines

NOTE: Cylinder head temperature must be below 38°C.

1. Disconnect the battery ground cable.

2. Drain the cooling system.

3. Remove the vacuum hose from the brake booster.

4. Remove the air intake ducts from the air cleaner case.

5. On fuel injected models, relieve the fuel pressure using the following procedure:

a. Slowly loosen the service bolt on the top of the fuel filter about one turn.

NOTE: Place a rag under the filter during this procedure to prevent fuel from spilling onto the engine.

b. Disconnect the fuel return hose from the pressure regulator. Remove the special nut and then remove the fuel hose.

6. Remove the secondary ground cable from the valve cover.

7. Remove the air cleaner, tagging all hoses for installation.

8. Disconnect the wires from the automatic choke and the fuel cut-off solenoid valve.

9. Disconnect the throttle cable and the fuel lines.

10. Disconnect the connector and hoses from the distributor.

11. On fuel injected models, disconnect the engine sub harness connectors and the following couplers from the head and the intake manifold.
- The four injector couplers
- The TA sensor connector
- The ground connector
- The TW sensor connector

Rocker arm assembly—8-valve engines

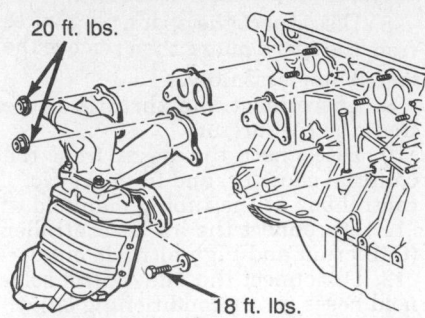

20 ft. lbs.

18 ft. lbs.

Exhaust manifold mounting—1342 and 1488cc engines

- The throttle sensor connector
- The crankshaft angle sensor coupler

12. Disconnect the No.1 control box hoses from the tubing manifold.

13. On California and high altitude models, disconnect the air jet controller hoses.

14. Disconnect the oxygen sensor coupler.

15. Disconnect the cooling system hoses at the cylinder head.

16. Remove the power steering pump (on models so equipped) but DO NOT disconnect the pump hoses. Also, remove the hose clamp bolt on the cylinder head.

17. Remove the power steering pump bracket.

18. Disconnect the No. 2 control box connector. Lift the control box from its bracket, and let it hang next to the carburetor (if so equipped).

19. Remove the air chamber, and on models with air conditioning, disconnect the idle boost solenoid hoses.

20. Remove the engine splash guard from under the car (if so equipped).

21. Remove the exhaust header pipe and pull it clear of the exhaust manifold.

22. Remove the air cleaner base mount bolts and disconnect the hose from the intake manifold to the breather chamber.

23. Remove the valve cover, upper timing belt cover and then loosen the belt tensioner to remove the belt.

24. Remove the cylinder head bolts and remove the head.

NOTE: Unscrew the cylinder head bolts ⅓ of a turn in the reverse order of the torque sequence each turn until loose to prevent warpage to the cylinder head.

25. Installation is the reverse of the removal procedure, taking note of the following items:

a. Make sure the cylinder head gasket surfaces are clean.

b. Make sure the **UP** mark on the timing belt pulley is at the top.

c. Make sure the head dowel pins are aligned.

d. Adjust the valve timing.

e. Torque the cylinder head bolts in two steps. Torque all bolts in sequence to 22 ft. lbs., then to 49 ft. lbs. in the final step.

OVERHAUL

For all cylinder head procedures, please refer to "Engine Rebuilding" in the Unit Repair section.

Camshaft and Rocker Shafts

REMOVAL & INSTALLATION

NOTE: To facilitate installation, make sure that No. 1 piston is at Top Dead Center before removal of camshaft.

1. Follow the Cylinder Head removal procedure before attempting to remove the camshaft.

2. Loosen the camshaft and rocker arm shaft holder bolts in a crisscross pattern, beginning on the outside holder.

3. Remove the rocker arms, shafts, and holders as an assembly.

4. Lift out the camshaft and right head seal (or tachometer body if equipped).

5. To install, reverse the removal procedure, being sure to install the holder bolts in the reverse order of removal.

NOTE: Back off valve adjusting screws before installing rockers. Then adjust valves as outlined earlier.

Intake Manifold

REMOVAL & INSTALLATION

1342cc, 1488cc, 1829cc and 1955cc Engines

1. Drain the coolant from the radiator.

2. Remove the air cleaner and case from the carburetor(s).

3. Remove the air valve, EGR valve, air suction valve and air chamber (if so equipped).

4. Label and remove any wires running to the intake manifold.

5. Remove the intake manifold attaching nut in a crisscross pattern, beginning from the center and moving out to both ends. Then remove the manifold.

6. Clean all the old gasket material from the manifold and the cylinder head.

7. If the intake manifold is to be replaced, transfer all the necessary components to the new manifold.

8. To install, reverse the removal procedures, being sure to observe the following points:

a. Always use a new gasket.

b. Tighten the nuts in a crisscross patter in 2-3 steps, starting with the inner nuts.

c. Be sure all hoses and wires are correctly connected.

Exhaust Manifold

REMOVAL & INSTALLATION

1342cc, 1488cc, 1829cc, and 1955cc Engines

—— **CAUTION** ——

Do not perform this operation on a warm or hot engine.

1. Remove the header pipe or catalytic converter to exhaust manifold attaching bolts.

2. Remove the oxygen sensor (if so equipped).

3. Remove the EGR and the air suction tubes (if so equipped).

4. Remove the exhaust manifold shroud.

5. Remove the exhaust manifold bracket bolts.

6. Remove the exhaust attaching nuts in a crisscross pattern starting from the center, and remove the manifold.

7. To install, reverse the removal procedure. Use new gaskets and tighten the manifold bolts in a criss-cross pattern starting from the center.

Combination Manifold

REMOVAL & INSTALLATION

1335cc, 1487cc and 1751cc Engines

1. Drain the radiator. Disconnect the manifold coolant hoses.
2. Remove the air cleaner assembly.
3. Label and disconnect all emission control vacuum hoses and electrical leads.
4. Disconnect the fuel lines, throttle, and choke linkage.
5. Remove the carburetor from the intake manifold.
6. Remove the upper heat shield. Loosen, but do not remove the four bolts retaining the intake manifold to the exhaust manifold.
7. Disconnect the exhaust pipe from the exhaust manifold.
8. Remove the nuts retaining the intake and exhaust manifolds to the cylinder head. The two manifolds are removed as a unit.
9. Reverse the above procedure to install, using new gaskets. The thick washers used beneath the cylinder head-to-manifold retaining nuts must be installed with the dished (concave), side toward the engine. Tighten in sequence shown to specifications given in the Torque Specifications chart. Adjust the choke and throttle linkage and bleed the cooling system.

Timing Belt Cover and Oil Seal

REMOVAL & INSTALLATION

1. Align the crankshaft pulley, or flywheel pointer, at Top Dead Center (TDC).
2. Remove the bolt(s) which hold the timing belt upper cover and remove the cover.
3. Loosen the alternator and air pump (if so equipped), and remove the pulley belt(s).
4. On all models except the 1984-88 and later Civic and CRX, remove the water pump pulley bolts and the water pump pulley.
5. Remove the crankshaft pulley attaching bolt. Use a two-jawed puller to remove the crankshaft pulley.

NOTE: The crankshaft bolt cannot be reused. It must be replaced whenever removed.

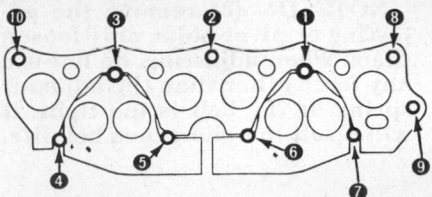

Combination manifold torque sequence—1982–83 1335 and 1487cc engines

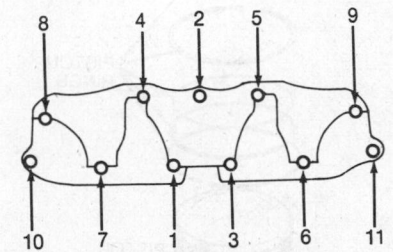

Combination manifold torque sequence—1982–83 1751cc engine

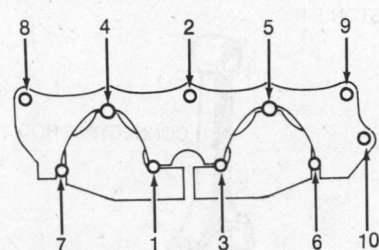

Combination manifold torque sequence—1980–81 1487cc, 1981 1335cc, 1980 1751cc (Calif.), and all 1981 1751cc engines

6. Remove the timing gear cover retaining bolts and the timing gear cover.
7. To install, reverse the removal procedure. Make sure that the timing guide plates, pulleys and the front oil seal are properly installed on the crankshaft and before replacing the cover.

Timing Belt and Tensioner

REMOVAL, INSTALLATION & ADJUSTMENT

1. Turn the crankshaft pulley until No.1 is at Top Dead Center of the compression stroke. This can be determined by observing the valves (all closed) or by feeling for pressure in the spark plug hole (with your thumb or a compression gauge) as the engine is turned.
2. Remove the pulley belt, water pump pulley (if so equipped), crankshaft pulley, and timing gear cover. Mark the direction of timing belt rotation.

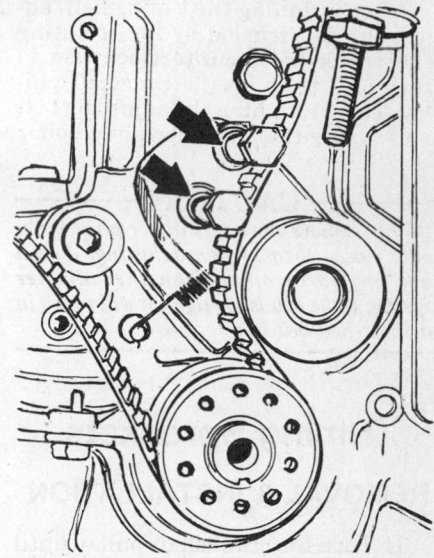

Typical timing belt tensioner adjustment

3. Loosen, but do not remove, the tensioner adjusting bolt and pivot bolt.
4. Slide the timing belt off the camshaft sprocket, crankshaft sprocket and the water pump sprocket (if so equipped), then remove it from the engine.
5. To remove the camshaft timing sprocket, first remove the center bolt and then remove the sprocket with a pulley remover or a brass hammer. This can be accomplished by simply removing the timing belt upper cover, loosening the tensioner bolts, and sliding the timing belt off to expose the sprocket for removal.

NOTE: If you remove the timing sprocket with the timing belt cover in place, be sure not to let the woodruff key fall inside the timing cover when removing the sprocket from the camshaft.

Inspect the timing belt. Replace it if it has been in service longer than 10,000 miles, if it is oil soaked (find source of oil leak also), or if it is worn on the leading edges of the belt teeth.
6. To install, reverse the removal procedure. Be sure to position the crankshaft and camshaft timing sprockets in the Top Dead Center position.

When installing the timing belt, do not allow oil to come in contact with the belt. Oil will cause the rubber to swell. Be careful not to bend or twist the belt unnecessarily, since it is made of fiberglass; nor should you use tools having sharp edges when installing or removing the belt. Be sure to install the belt with the arrow facing in the same direction it was facing during removal.

After installing the timing belt, adjust the belt tension by first rotating the crankshaft counterclockwise ¼ turn or 3 teeth on the camshaft pulley. Then, retighten the adjusting bolt and finally the tensioner pivot bolt.

—— **CAUTION** ——

Do not remove the adjusting or pivot bolts, only loosen them. When adjusting, do not use any force other than the adjuster spring. If the belt is too tight, it will result in a shortened belt life.

Timing Sprockets

REMOVAL & INSTALLATION

1. Turn the crankshaft pulley until #1 is at Top Dead Center of the compression stroke. This can be determined by observing the valves (all closed) or by feeling for pressure in the spark plug hole (with your thumb or a compression gauge) as the engine is turned.

2. Remove the pulley belt, water pump pulley (if so equipped), crankshaft pulley, and timing gear cover. Mark the direction of timing belt rotation.

3. Loosen, but do not remove, the tensioner adjusting bolt and pivot bolt.

4. Slide the timing belt off the camshaft sprocket, crankshaft sprocket and the water pump sprocket (if so equipped), then remove it from the engine.

5. To remove the either the camshaft or crankshaft timing sprocket, first remove the center bolt and then remove the sprocket with a pulley remover or a brass hammer.

6. To install, reverse the removal procedure. Be sure to position the crankshaft and camshaft timing sprockets in the Top Dead Center position. Torque the camshaft sprocket bolt to 30 ft. lbs.

When installing the timing belt, do not allow oil to come in contact with the belt. Oil will cause the rubber to swell. Be careful not to bend or twist the belt unnecessarily, since it is made of fiberglass; nor should you use tools having sharp edges when installing or removing the belt. Be sure to install the belt with the arrow facing in the same direction it was facing during removal.

After installing the timing belt, adjust the belt tension by first rotating the crankshaft counterclockwise ¼ turn or 3 teeth on the camshaft pulley. Then, retighten the adjusting bolt and finally the tensioner pivot bolt.

NOTE: Do not remove the adjusting or pivot bolts, only loosen them. When adjusting, do not use any force other than the adjuster spring. If the belt is too tight, it will result in a shortened belt life.

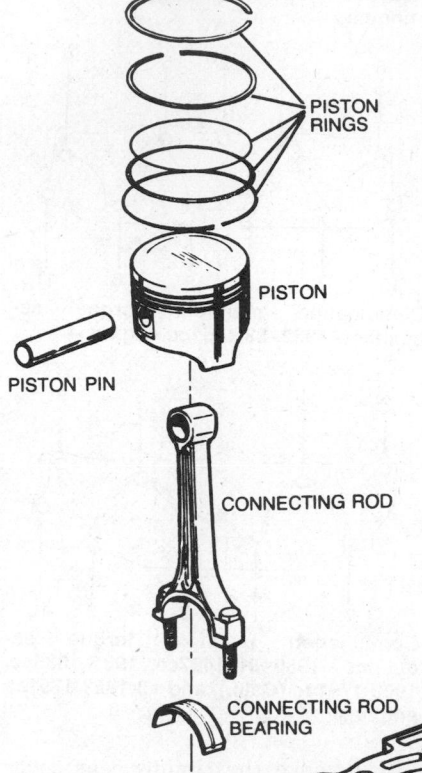
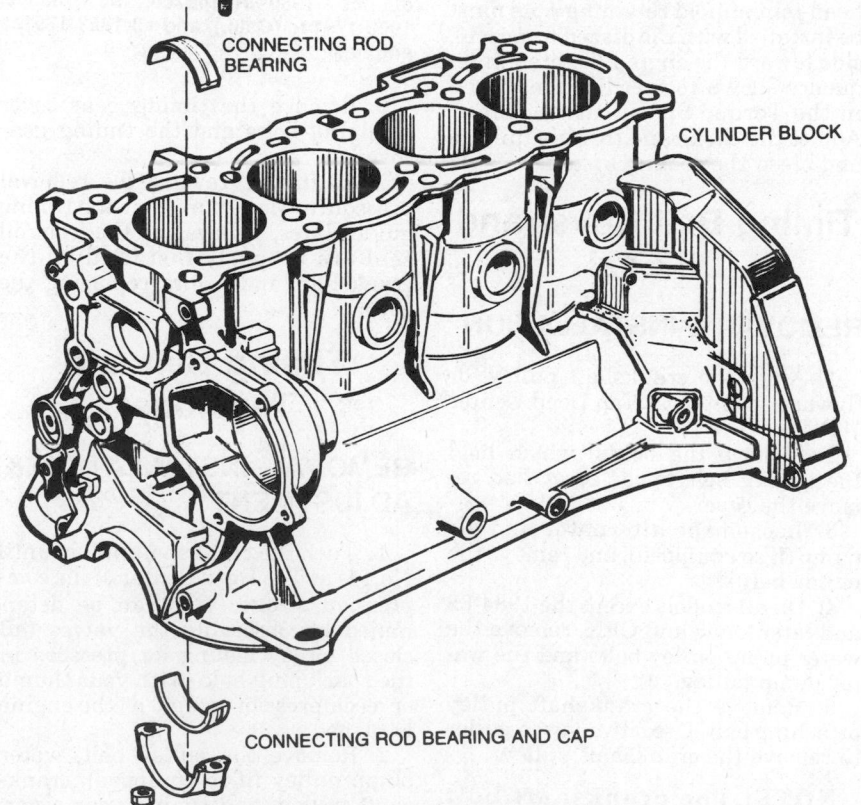

Typical CVCC engine block and piston

Pistons and Connecting Rods

POSITIONING

For all piston and connecting rod overhaul procedures, please refer to "Engine Rebuilding" in the Unit Repair section.

ENGINE LUBRICATION

Oil Pan

REMOVAL & INSTALLATION

NOTE: Removal of the oil pan on the Civic 4wd model requires transfer case removal. Please refer to Transfer Case Removal for this procedure.

1. Drain the engine oil.
2. Raise the front of the car and support it with safety stands. Remove the lower splash pan (if so equipped).

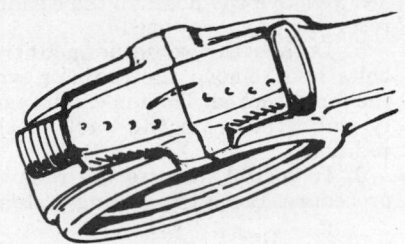

Mark the pistons and rods if they are not marked from the factory

3. Attach a chain to the bracket on the transmission case and raise just enough to take the load off the center mount.

NOTE: Do not remove the left engine mount.

4. Remove the center beam and engine lower mount.

5. Loosen the oil bolts and remove the oil pan flywheel dust shield.

NOTE: Loosen the bolts in a criss-cross pattern beginning with the outside bolt. To remove the oil pan, lightly tap the corners of the oil pan with a mallet. It is not necessary to remove the gasket unless it is damaged.

6. To install, reverse the removal procedure. Apply a coat of sealant to the entire mating surface of the cylinder block, except the crankshaft oil seal, before fitting the oil pan. Tighten the bolts in a circular sequence, beginning in the center and working out towards the ends.

Rear Main Oil Seal

REPLACEMENT

The rear oil seal is installed in the rear main bearing cap. Replacement of the seal requires the removal of the transmission, flywheel and clutch housing, as well as the oil pan. Refer to the appropriate sections for the removal and installation of the above components. Both the front and rear main seal are installed after the crankshaft bearing caps have been torqued, if the crankshaft has been removed. Special drivers must be used.

Oil Pump

REMOVAL & INSTALLATION

1335cc, 1487cc, and 1751cc Engines

To remove the oil pump, follow the procedure given for oil pan removal and installation. After the oil pan has

been dropped, simply unbolt the oil passage block and oil pump assembly from the engine. Remove the oil pump screen to find the last bolt. When installing the pump, tighten the bolts to no more than 8 ft. lbs. (96 inch lbs.).

1342cc, 1488cc, 1829cc and 1955cc Engines

To remove the oil pump, follow the procedure given to remove the timing belt cover. After removing the cover, remove the timing belt and unbolt the oil pump and remove it from the block. When installing the pump, tighten the bolts to 9 ft. lbs. (108 in.lbs.) and the nuts to 5 ft. lbs. (60 inch lbs.). To remove the oil pump pick-up screen, follow the procedure to remove the oil pan.

ENGINE COOLING

Radiator

REMOVAL & INSTALLATION

NOTE: When removing the radiator, take care not to damage the core and fins.

1. Drain the radiator.
2. Disconnect the thermo-switch wire and the fan motor wire. Remove the fan shroud (if so equipped).
3. Disconnect the upper coolant hose at the upper radiator tank and the lower hose at the water pump connecting pipe. Disconnect and plug the automatic transmission cooling lines at the bottom of the radiator (if so equipped).

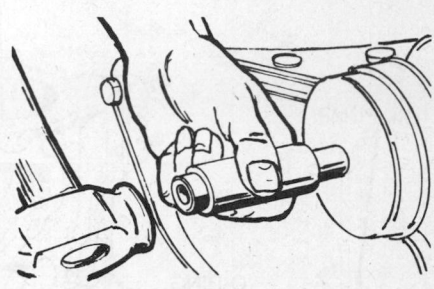

Driving in the rear main seal

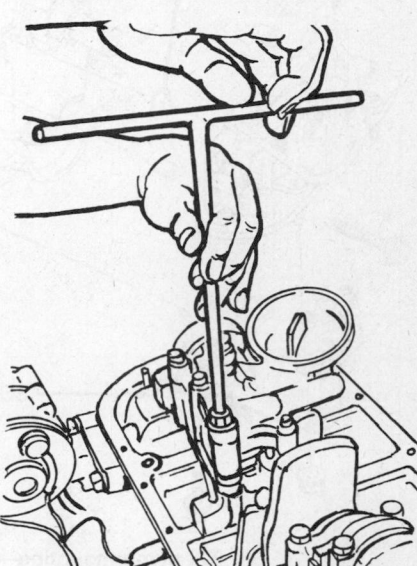

Oil pump removal—1335, 1487, and 1751cc engines

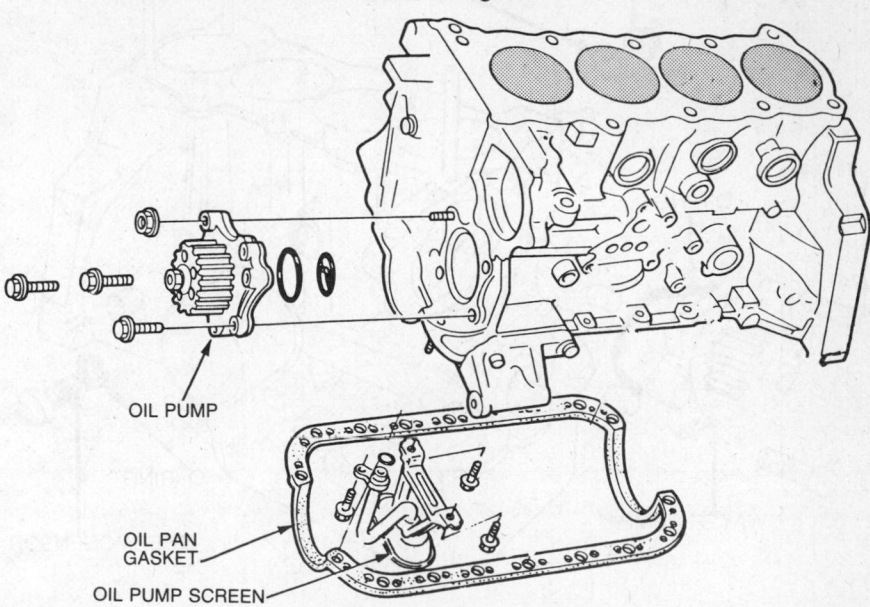

OIL PUMP

OIL PAN GASKET

OIL PUMP SCREEN

Oil pump removal—1829 and 1955cc engines

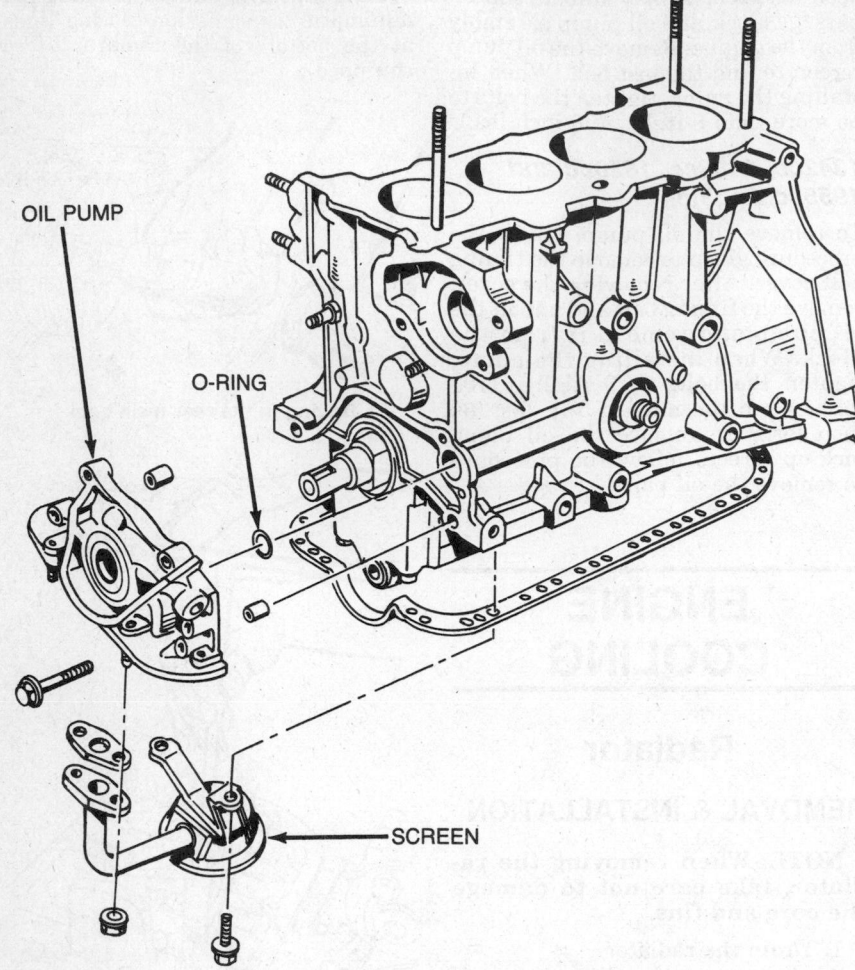

OIL PUMP

O-RING

SCREEN

Oil pump mounting—1342 and 1488cc engines

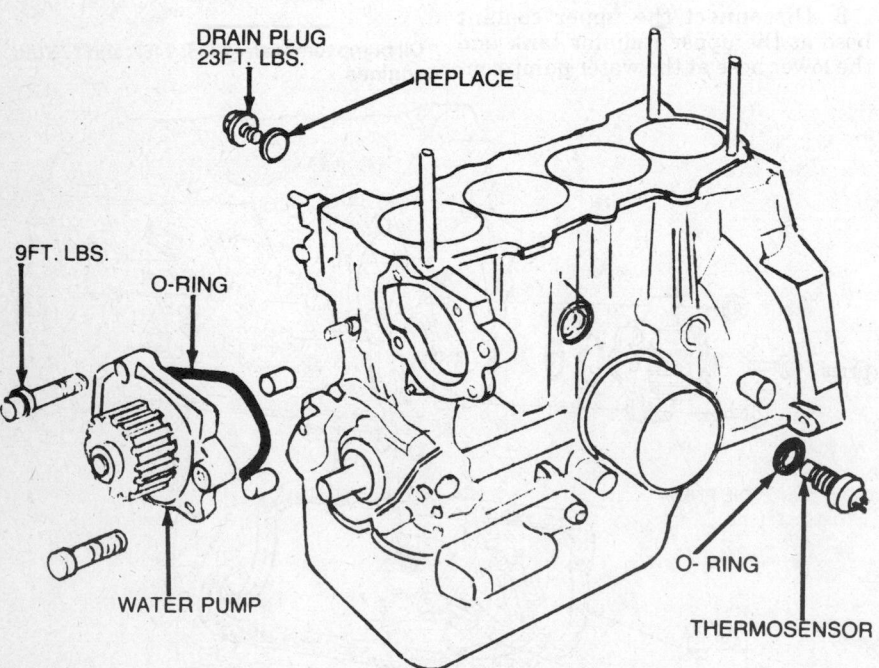

DRAIN PLUG
23FT. LBS.

REPLACE

9FT. LBS.

O-RING

WATER PUMP

O-RING

THERMOSENSOR

Water pump replacement—1342 and 1488cc engines

4. Remove the hoses to the coolant reservoir (if so equipped).

5. Detach the radiator mounting bolts and remove the radiator with the fan attached. The fan can be easily unbolted from the back of the radiator.

6. To install, reverse the removal procedure. Bleed the cooling system.

Water Pump

REMOVAL & INSTALLATION

All Except 1342cc and 1488cc Engines

1. Drain the radiator.

2. Loosen the alternator bolts. Move the alternator toward the cylinder block and remove the drive belt.

3. Loosen the pump mounting bolts and remove the pump together with the pulley and the rubber seal.

4. To install, reverse the removal procedure using a new gasket. Bleed the cooling system.

1342cc and 1488cc Engines

1. Drain the radiator.

2. Following the procedures shown under Timing Belt and Tensioner remove the timing belt from the water pump drive sprocket.

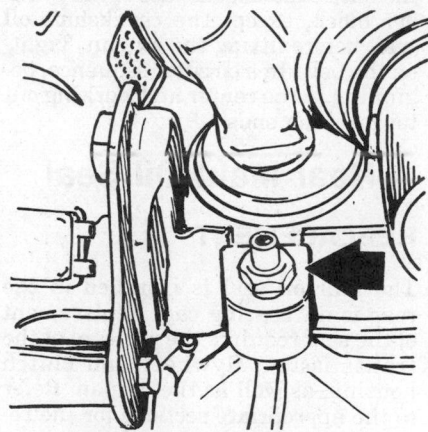

Cooling system bleed bolt

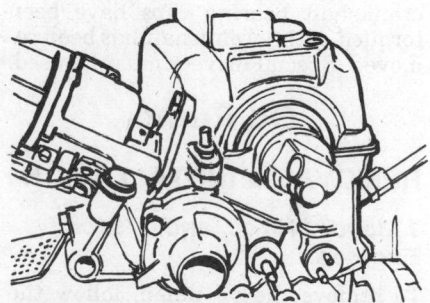

Typical thermostat housing and cooling system bleed bolt

3. Loosen the water pump mounting bolts and remove together with the drive sprocket.

4. To install, reverse the removal procedure using a new O-ring. Bleed the cooling system.

Thermostat

REMOVAL & INSTALLATION

1. The thermostat housing is located in the end of the cylinder head, with the exception of the 1342cc and 1488cc engines where it is located at the end of the water pump inlet tube.

2. Unbolt and remove the thermostat cover and pull the thermostat from the housing.

3. To install, reverse the removal procedure. Always install the spring end of the thermostat toward the engine. Tighten the two cover bolts to 7 ft. lbs. (84 inch lbs.). Always use a new gasket. Bleed the cooling system.

COOLING SYSTEM BLEEDING

1. Loosen the air bleed bolt in the water outlet, and then fill the radiator to the bottom of the filler neck with antifreeze/coolant. Tighten the bleed bolt as soon as the coolant starts to run out in a steady stream without any air bubbles in it.

2. With the radiator cap off, start the engine and allow it to warm up (the cooling fan should go on at least twice). Then if necessary add more antifreeze/coolant to bring the level back up to the bottom of the filler neck.

3. Put the radiator cap on, restart the engine and check for any leaks.

EMISSION CONTROLS

Please refer to "Emission Controls", in the Unit Repair section for system maintenance procedures. Due to the complex nature of modern electronic engine control systems, comprehensive diagnosis and testing procedures fall outside the confines of this repair manual. For complete information on diagnosis, testing and repair procedures concerning all modern engine and emission control systems, please refer to *Chilton's Guide to Electronic Engine Controls.*

FUEL SYSTEM

Fuel Filter

REPLACEMENT

Carbureted Engines

— CAUTION —
Before disconnecting any fuel lines, be sure to open the gas tank filler cap to relieve any pressure in the system. If this is not done, you may run the risk of being squirted with gasoline.

All models use a disposable type fuel filter which cannot be disassembled for cleaning. The filter is replaced after the first 15,000 miles, and every 60,000 miles thereafter.

On all 1981-83 Civic Sedan models, the rear filter is located beneath a special access cover under the rear seat on the driver's side. The rear seat can be removed after removing the bolt at the rear center of the cushion and then pivoting the seat forward from the rear. Then, remove the four screws retaining the access cover to the floor and remove the cover. The filter, together with the electric fuel pump, are located in the recess. Pinch the lines shut, loosen the hose clamps and remove the filter.

On all 1984-88 carbureted Civic Sedans, Coupes, and Wagons and the Accord and Prelude models, the rear filter is located under the car, in front of the spare tire. To replace the fuel filter, you must raise the rear of the car, support it with jackstands, and clamp off the fuel lines leading to and from the filter. Then, loosen the hose clamps and, taking note of which hose is the inlet and which is the outlet, remove the filter. Some replacement filters have an arrow embossed or printed on the filter body, in which case you want to install the new filter with the arrow pointing in the direction of the fuel flow. After installing the new filter, remember to unclamp the fuel lines. Check for leaks.

All 1982-88 carbureted models are also equipped with a front in-line disposible fuel filter, located at the carburetor. Replacement is the same as the others.

Fuel Injected Engine

The fuel filter on the fuel injected models is located on the firewall in the engine compartment. It should be replaced every 60,000 miles, or whenever the fuel pressure drops below 33-39 psi with the vacuum pressure hose disconnected, and after checking the

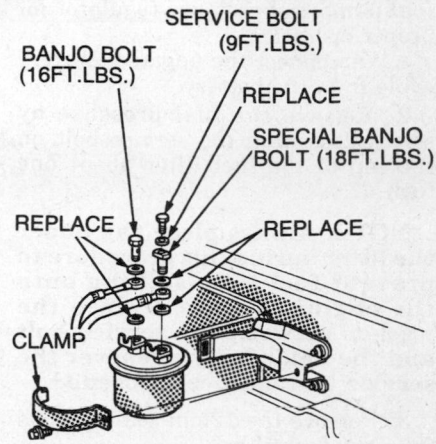
Fuel filter mounting—Accord fuel injected models

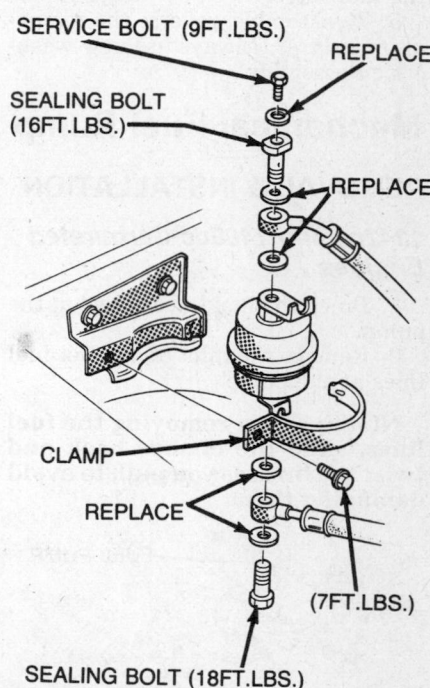
Fuel filter mounting—Civic fuel injected models

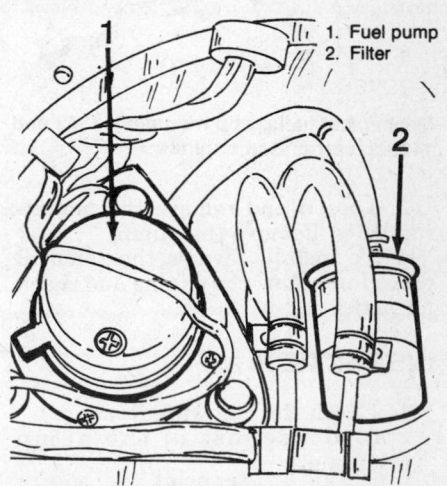
Rear fuel filter mounting—Civic sedan

fuel pump and pressure regulator for proper operation.

1. Disconnect the negative battery cable from the battery.

2. Relieve the fuel pressure by slowly loosening the service bolt on the top of the fuel filter about one turn.

NOTE: Always place rag under the filter during this procedure to prevent fuel from spilling onto the engine. Always replace the washer between the service bolt and the banjo bolt, whenever the service bolt has been loosened.

3. Remove the 12mm sealing bolts from the fuel filter.

4. Remove the fuel filter clamp and the fuel filter.

5. To assemble, reverse the removal procedures. Always use new washers on assembly.

Mechanical Fuel Pump

REMOVAL & INSTALLATION

1342cc and 1488cc Carbureted Engines

1. Pinch the fuel lines closed at the pump.

2. Remove the inlet and outlet fuel lines at the pump.

NOTE: When removing the fuel lines, slide the clamps back and twist the lines as you pull, to avoid damaging them.

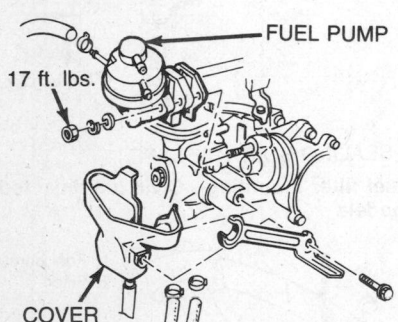

Mechanical fuel pump mounting–1342 and 1488cc carbureted engines

3. Loosen and remove the mounting bolts. Remove the pump.

4. To install, reverse the removal procedure. Start the engine and check for leaks.

INSPECTION

1. Check the following items:
   a. Looseness of the pump connector.
   b. Looseness of the upper and lower body and cover screws.
   c. Looseness of the rocker arm pin.
   d. Contamination or clogging of the air hole.
   e. Improper operation of the pump.

2. Check to see if there are signs of oil or fuel around the air hole. If so, the diaphragm is damaged and you must replace the pump.

3. To inspect the pump for operation, first disconnect the fuel line at the carburetor. Connect a fuel pressure gauge to the delivery side of the pump. Start the engine and measure the pump delivery pressure.

MECHANICAL FUEL PUMP SPECIFICATIONS

Engine rpm	Delivery Pressure (lb. in.^{2})	Vacuum (in.Hg.)	Displacement (in.^{3}/minute)
600	2.56	17.72	27
3,000	2.56	7.87–11.81	43
6,000	2.56	7.87–11.81	46

4. After measuring, stop the engine and check to see if the gauge drops suddenly. If the gauge drops suddenly and/or the delivery pressure is incorrect, check for a fuel or oil leak from the diaphragm or from the valves.

5. To test for volume, disconnect the fuel line from the carburetor and insert it into a one quart container. Crank the engine for 64 seconds at 600 rpm, or 40 seconds at 400 rpm. The bottle should be half full (1 pint).

Electrical Fuel Pump

REMOVAL & INSTALLATION

Carbureted Engines

1. Remove the gas filler cap to relieve any excess pressure in the system.

2. Obtain a pair of suitable clamps to pinch shut the fuel lines to the pump.

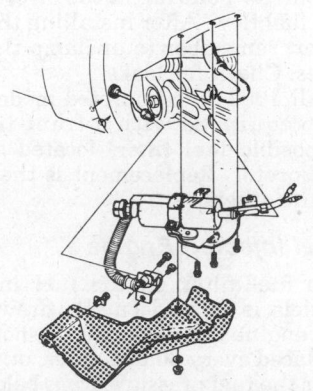

Electric fuel pump mounting–fuel injected models

3. Disconnect the negative battery cable.

4. Locate the fuel pump. On Civic sedan and hatchback models (1981-82 only) you wil first have to remove the rear seat by removing the bolt at the rear center of the bottom cushion and pivoting the seat forward from the rear. The pump and filter are located on the driver's side of the rear seat floor section beneath an access plate retained by four Phillips head screws.

On station wagon and 1983 sedan & hatchback models and the Accord and Prelude, you will probably have to raise the rear of the car to obtain access to the pump. On Accord and Prelude models, remove the left rear wheel. In all cases, make sure, if you are crawling under the car, that the car is securely supported.

5. Pinch the inlet and outlet fuel lines shut. Loosen the hose clamps. On station wagon and Accord models, remove the filter mounting clip on the left hand side of the bracket.

6. Disconnect the positive lead wire and ground wire from the pump at their quick disconnect.

7. Remove the two fuel pump retaining bolts, taking care not to lose the two spacers and bolt collars.

8. Remove the fuel lines and fuel pump.

9. Reverse the above procedure to install. The pump cannot be disassembled and must be replaced if defective. Operating fuel pump pressure is 2-3 psi.

Fuel Injected Engine

1. Disconnect the negative battery cable from the battery.

2. Relieve the fuel pressure by slowly loosening the service bolt on the top of the fuel filter about one turn.

NOTE: Place a rag under the filter during this procedure to prevent fuel from spilling onto the engine. Always replace the washer between the service bolt and the banjo bolt, whenever the service bolt has been loosened.

3. Raise the car and support on jackstands.

4. Remove the left rear wheel.

5. Remove the fuel pump cover bolts, then remove the cover.

6. Remove the mounting bolts from the fuel pump mount, then remove the fuel pump with its mount.

7. Disconnect the fuel lines and the electrical connectors.

8. Remove the clamp and remove the fuel pump from the mounting bracket.

9. Remove the fuel line and silencer from the pump.

10. To install, reverse the removal procedures. Turn on the ignition switch and check for fuel leaks.

Carburetor

REMOVAL & INSTALLATION

1. Disconnect and label the following:

   a. Hot air tube.

   b. All vacuum hoses and lines.

   c. Breather chamber (on air cleaner case) to intake manifold at the breather chamber.

   d. Hose from the air cleaner case to to the valve cover.

   e. Hose from the carbon canister to the carburetor, at the carburetor.

   f. Throttle opener hose, at the throttle opener.

   g. On the 1829cc Prelude, drain the coolant and remove the coolant hoses from the thermowax valve and the right end of the intake manifold.

2. Disconnect the fuel line at the carburetor. Plug the end of the fuel line to prevent dust entry.

3. Disconnect the choke and throttle control cables.

4. Disconnect the fuel shut-off solenoid wires.

5. Remove the carburetor retaining bolts or loosen the insulator bands and then remove the carburetor. Leave the insulator on the manifold.

NOTE: After removing the carburetor, cover the intake manifold parts to keep out foreign materials.

THROTTLE LINKAGE ADJUSTMENT

1. Remove the air cleaner assembly to provide access.

2. Check that the cable free play (deflection) is 4-10mm. This is measured right before the cable enters the throttle shaft bellcrank.

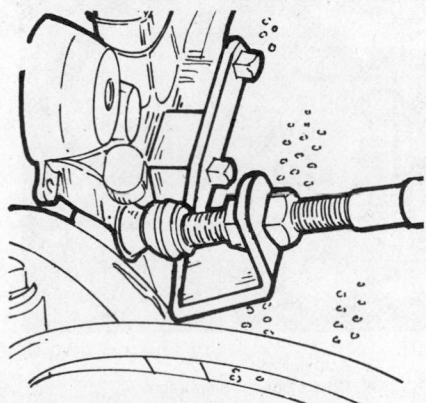

Throttle cable adjusting location

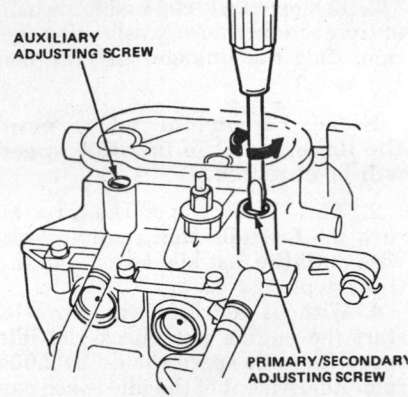

Float level adjustment—1982 and later models with the Keihn 3 bbl. carburetor

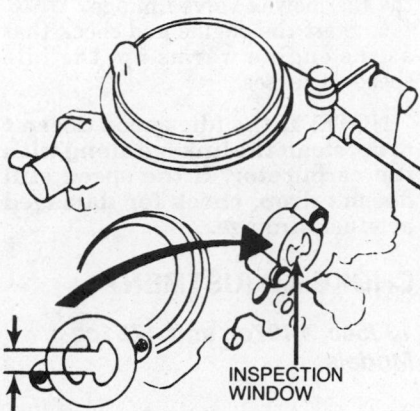

Inspection window showing the fuel level—1986 and later models with the Keihn 2 bbl. carburetor

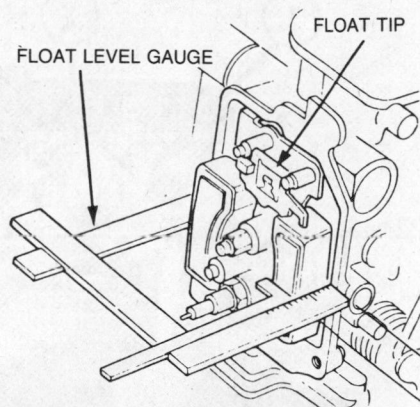

Float level measurement on the dual Keihin sidedraft carburetors—1829cc Prelude

3. If the deflection is not to specifications, rotate the cable adjusting nuts in the required direction.

4. As a final check, have an assistant press the gas pedal all the way to the floor, while you look down inside the throttle bore checking that the throttle plates reach the wide open throttle (WOT) vertical position.

5. Install the air cleaner.

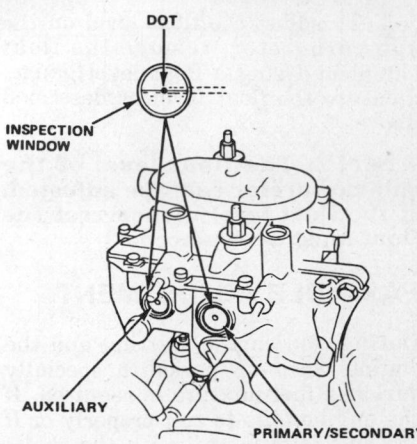

Inspection window showing the fuel level—1982 and later models with the Keihn 3 bbl. carburetor

FLOAT AND FUEL LEVEL ADJUSTMENT

1,335cc, 1342cc, 1487cc and 1751cc CVCC Models

1981

Due to the rather unconventional manner in which the Keihin 3-bbl carburetor float level is checked and adjusted, it requires the use of Honda tool No. 07501-6570000 (which is a special float level gauge/fuel catch tray/drain bottle assembly. This carburetor is adjusted while mounted on a running engine. After the auxiliary and the primary/secondary main jet covers are removed, the special float gauge apparatus is installed over the jet apertures. With the engine running, the float level is checked against a red index line on the gauge. If adjustment proves necessary, there are adjusting screws provided for both the auxiliary and the primary/secondary circuits atop the carburetor.

1982-88 Except 1829cc Prelude

With the car on level ground and at normal operating temperature, check the primary and secondary fuel level inspection windows. If the fuel level is not touching the dot, adjust it by turning the adjusting screws.

NOTE: Do not turn the adjusting screws more than ⅛ turn every 15 seconds.

1829cc Prelude

1. Remove the side draft carburetors from the engine and remove the float chambers from the carburetors.

2. Using a float level gauge, measure the float level with the float tip lightly touching the float valve and the float chamber surface tilted about 30 degrees from vertical. The float level should be 16mm.

3. To adjust the float level on the sub-carburetor, remove the float chamber. Using a float level gauge, measure the float level as described above.

NOTE: The float level of the sub-carburetor can't be adjusted. If the float level is incorrect the float must be replaced.

FAST IDLE ADJUSTMENT

During cold engine starting and the engine warm-up period, a specially enriched fuel mixture is required. If the engine fails to run properly or if the engine over-revs with the choke knob pulled out (on models so equipped) in cold weather, the fast idle system should be checked and adjusted. This is accomplished with the carburetor installed.

All except 1829cc Prelude

1. Run the engine to normal operating temperature.
2. Connect a tachometer according to the manufacturer's specifications.
3. Disconnect and plug the hose from the fast idle unloader.
4. Shut the engine off, hold the choke valve closed, and open and close the throttle to engage the fast idle cam.
5. Start the engine, run it for one minute. Fast idle speed should be 2,300-3,300 rpm for manual transmission models and 2,200-3,200 rpm for automatic transmission models.

NOTE: Underhood specifications sticker figures must be used if they differ from those above.

6. Adjust the idle by turning the fast idle screw.

1829cc Prelude

1. Start the engine and bring it to normal operating temperature. Shut off the engine.

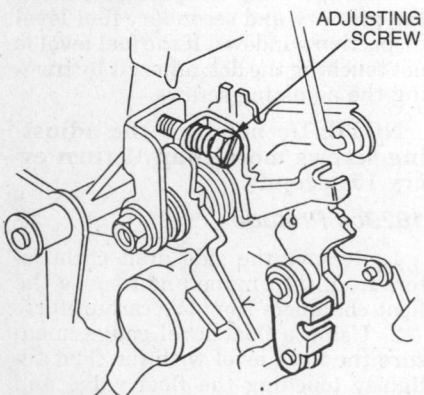

Idle speed adjustment on the dual Keihin sidedraft carburetors

2. Remove the E-clip and flat washer from the thermowax valve linkage, then slide the linkage past the fast idle cam.

NOTE: Be careful not to bend the linkage or the fast idle speed will be changed.

3. While holding open the throttle, turn the fast idle cam counterclockwise until the fast idle lever is on the third step.
4. Without touching the throttle, start the engine and check the idle speed. The idle speed should be 2,000 rpm. Adjustment of the idle speed can be made by turning the fast idle adjusting screw.
5. Stop the engine and reconnect the thermowax valve linkage.
6. Start the engine and check that as the engine warms up, the idle speed decreases.

NOTE: If the idle speed doesn't drop, clean the linkage along with the carburetor. If the speed still doesn't drop, check for damaged or stuck linkage.

CHOKE ADJUSTMENT

1335cc, 1487cc and 1751cc Models

The choke plate should close to less than 3mm clearance when the engine is cold (ignition on) on models with the automatic choke.

1. Remove the choke cover (3 screws) and check free movement of the linkage. Repair or replace as necessary.
2. Install the choke cover and adjust so that the index marks on the cover and thermostat body align. If the choke still does not close properly, replace the cover and retest.

CHOKE CABLE ADJUSTMENT

NOTE: Perform the adjustment only after the throttle plate opening has been set.

1487cc CVCC

1. Remove the air cleaner assembly.
2. Push the choke knob all the way in at the dash. Check that the choke butterfly valve (choke plate) is fully open (vertical).
3. Next, have a friend pull out the choke knob while you observe the action of the butterfly valve. When the choke knob is pulled out to the second detent position, the butterfly valve should just close. Then, when the choke knob is pulled all the way out, the butterfly valve should remain in the closed position.
4. To adjust, loosen the choke cable locknut and rotate the adjusting nut so that with the choke knob pushed flush against the dash (open position), the butterfly valve just rests against its positioning stop tab. Tighten the locknut.

1. Stop tab
2. Relief lever adjusting tang
3. Actuator rod
4. Choke opener diaphragm

CVCC choke adjustment components

5. If the choke butterfly valve is irregular in operation, or if it does not close properly, check the butterfly valve and shaft for binding. Check also the operation of the return spring.

ACCELERATOR PUMP ADJUSTMENT

1335cc, 1487cc and 1751cc Models

1. Remove the air cleaner.
2. Make sure that the pump shaft is moving freely throughout the pump stroke.
3. Check that the pump lever is in contact with the pump shaft.
4. Measure between the bottom end of the pump lever and the lever stop tang. The gap should be 11.5-12.5mm. If not, bend the tang to adjust.

OVERHAUL

For all carburetor overhaul procedures please refer to Carburetor Service in the Unit Repair section.

Fuel Injection

Due to the complex nature of modern fuel injection systems, comprehensive diagnosis and testing procedures fall outside the confines of this repair manual. For complete information on fuel injection diagnosis, testing and repair procedures, please refer to *Chilton's Guide to Fuel Injection and Feedback Carburetors.*

MANUAL TRANSAXLE

REMOVAL & INSTALLATION

Accord

1. Disconnect the battery ground cable at the battery and the transmission case. Unlock the steering column; place the transmission in neutral.
2. Drain the transmission.
3. Raise the front of the car and support it with safety stands.
4. Remove the front wheels.
5. Remove the starter motor positive battery cable and the solenoid wire. Then remove the starter.

1. Choke butterfly valve   2. Adjusting nut   3. Locknut

CVCC choke cable adjustment

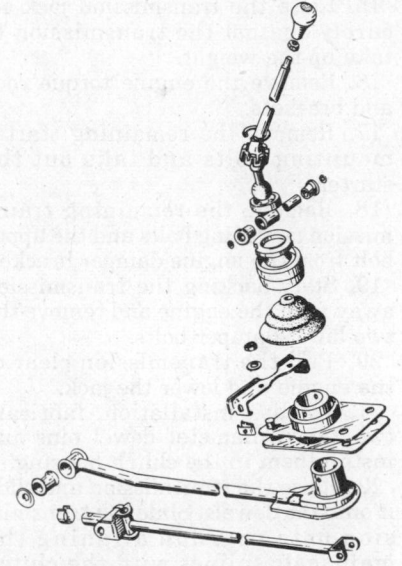

Exploded view of the gearshift mechanism

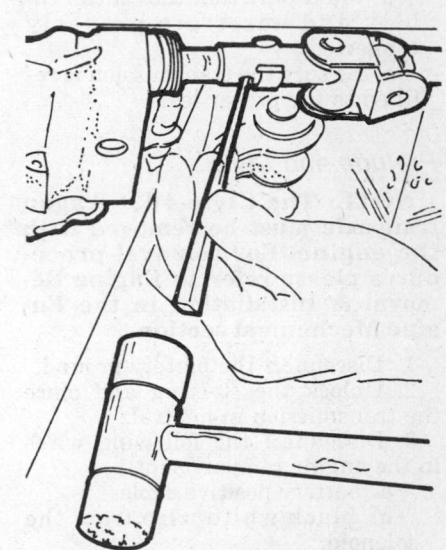

Driving out the gearshift rod pin

6. Disconnect the following cables and wires:

   a. Clutch cable at the release arm (1982-88 Accord).

   b. Back-up light switch wires.

   c. TCS (Transmission Controlled Spark) switch wires.

   d. Speedometer cable.

   e. Hydraulic hose at slave cylinder (1981 Accord).

NOTE: When removing the speedometer cable from the transmission, it is not necessary to remove the entire cable holder. Remove the end boot (gear holder seal), the cable retaining clip and then pull the cable out of the holder. In no way should you disturb the holder, unless it is absolutely necessary. For further details, see the Engine Removal section.

7. Disconnect the left and right lower ball joints at the knuckle, using a ball joint remover.

8. Pull on the brake disc and remove the left and right driveshafts from the differential case.

9. Drive out the gearshift rod pin (8mm) with a drift and disconnect the rod at the transmission case.

10. Disconnect the gearshift extension at the clutch housing.

11. Screw in the engine hanger bolts (see the Engine Removal section) to the engine torque rod bolt hole and to the hole just to the left of the distributor. Hook a chain onto the bolts and lift the engine just enough to take the load off the engine mounts.

12. After making sure that the engine is properly supported, remove the two center beam-to-lower engine mount nuts. Next, remove the center beam, followed by the lower engine mount.

13. Reinstall the center beam (without mount) and lower the engine until it rests on the beam.

14. Place a jack under the transmission and loosen the 4 attaching bolts. Using the jack to support the transmission, slide it away from the engine and lower the jack until the transmission clears the car.

15. To install, reverse the removal procedure. Be sure to pay attention to the following points:

   a. Tighten all mounting nuts and bolts.

   b. Use a new shift rod pin.

   c. After installing the driveshafts, attempt to move the inner joint housing in and out of the differential housing. If it moves easily, the driveshaft end clips should be replaced.

   d. Make sure that the control cables and wires are properly connected.

   e. Be sure the transmission is refilled to the proper level.

Prelude and Civic

NOTE: The Civic 4WD Wagon transaxle must be removed with the engine. For removal procedures please refer to Engine Removal & Installation in the Engine Mechanical section.

1. Disconnect the battery ground.

2. Unlock the steering and place the transmission in neutral.

3. Disconnect the following wires in the engine compartment:

   a. battery positive cable.

   b. black/white wire from the solenoid.

   c. temperature gauge sending unit wire.

   d. ignition timing thermo-sensor wire.

   e. back-up light switch.

   f. distributor wiring.

   g. transmission ground cable.

4. Unclip and remove the speedometer cable at the transmission. Do not disassemble the speedometer gear holder!

5. Remove the clutch save cylinder with the hydraulic line attached, or disconnect the clutch cable at the release arm.

6. Remove the side and top starter mounting bolts. Loosen the front wheel lug nuts. Remove the front wheels.

7. Raise and support the car.

8. Drain the transmission.

9. Remove the splash shields from the underside.

10. Remove the stabilizer bar.

11. Disconnect the left and right lower ball joints and tie end rods, using a ball joint remover.

CAUTION

In 1984-88 Civics use caution when removing the ball joints. Place a floor jack under the lower control arm securely at the ball joint. Otherwise, the lower control arm may jump suddenly away from the steering knuckle as the ball joint is removed!

---

12. Turn the right steering knuckle out as far as it will go. Place a prybar against the inboard CV-joint, pry the right axle out of the transmission about ½ inch. This will force the spring clip out of the groove inside the differential gear splines. Pull it out the rest of the way. Repeat this procedure on the other side.

13. Disconnect the shift lever torque rod from the clutch housing.

14. Remove the bolt from the shift rod clevis.

15. Raise the transmission jack securely against the transmission to take up the weight.

16. Remove the engine torque rods and brackets.

17. Remove the remaining starter mounting bolts and take out the starter.

18. Remove the remaining transmission mounting bolts and the upper bolt from the engine damper bracket.

19. Start backing the transmission away from the engine and remove the two lower damper bolts.

20. Pull the transmission clear of the engine and lower the jack.

21. To ease installation, fabricate two 14mm diameter dowel pins and install them in the clutch housing.

22. Raise the transmission and slide it onto the dowels. Slide the transmission onto position aligning the mainshaft splines with the clutch plate.

23. Attach the damper lower bolts when the positioning allows. Tighten both bolts until the clutch housing is seated against the block.

24. Install two lower mounting bolts and torque them to 33 ft. lbs.

25. Install the front and rear torque rod brackets. Torque the front torque rod bolts to 54 ft. lbs., the front bracket bolts to 33 ft. lbs., the rear torque rod bolts to 54 ft. lbs., and the rear bracket bolts to 47 ft. lbs.

26. Remove the transmission jack.

27. Install the starter and torque the mounting bolts to 33 ft. lbs.

28. Turn the right steering knuckle out far enough to fit the end into the transmission. Use new 26mm spring clips on both axles. Repeat procedure for the other side.

CAUTION

Make sure that the axles bottom fully so that you feel the spring clip engage the differential.

---

29. Install the lower ball joints. Torque the nuts to 32 ft. lbs.

30. Install the tie rods. Torque the nuts to 32 ft. lbs.

31. Connect the shift linkage.

32. Connect the shift lever torque rod to the clutch housing and torque the bolt to 7 ft. lbs. (84 inch lbs.).

33. Install the stabilizer bar.

34. Install the lower shields.

35. Install the front wheels and torque the lugs to specifications.

36. Install the remaining starter bolts and torque to 33 ft. lbs.

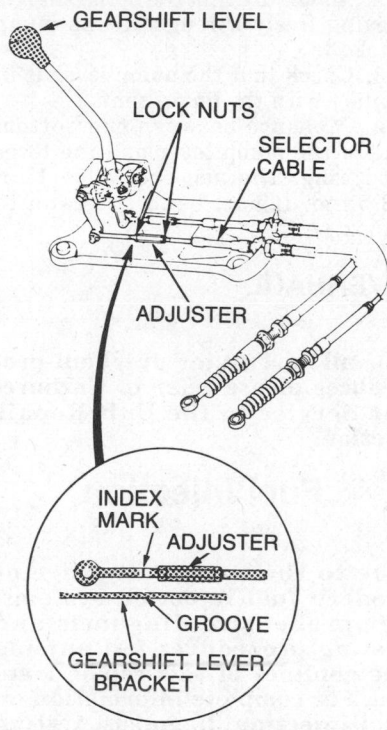

Selector cable adjustment

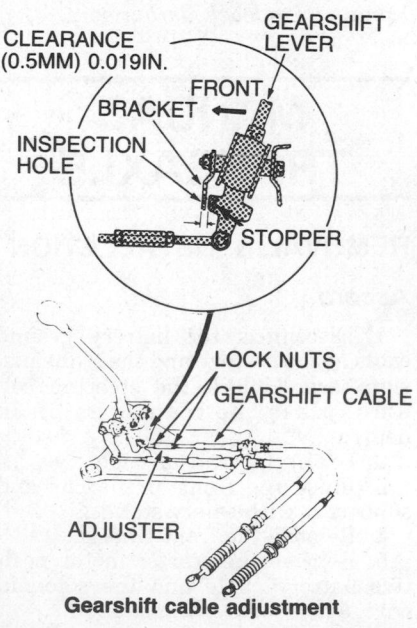

Gearshift cable adjustment

37. Install the clutch slave cylinder and or install the clutch cable at the release arm.

38. Install the speedometer cable using a new O-ring coated with clean engine oil.

39. Connect all engine compartment wiring.

40. Fill the transmission with SAE 10W-40 engine oil.

SHIFT LINKAGE ADJUSTMENT

All Except Civic 4wd Model

The Honda shift linkage on those models is non-adjustable. However, if the linkage is binding, or if there is excessive play, check the linkage bushings and pivot points. Lubricate with light oil, or replace worn bushings as necessary.

Civic 4wd Models

SELECTOR CABLE ADJUSTMENT

1. Remove the console.

2. With the transmission in neutral, check that the groove in the lever bracket is aligned with the index mark on the selector cable.

3. If the index mark is not aligned with the groove in the cable, loosen the lock nuts and turn the adjuster as necessary.

NOTE: After adjustment, check the operation of the gearshift lever. Also check that the threads of the cables do not extend out of the cable adjuster by more than 10mm.

GEARSHIFT CABLE ADJUSTMENT

1. Remove the console.

2. Place the transmission in 4th gear.

3. Measure the clearance between the gearshift lever bracket and the stopper while pushing the lever forward.

4. If the clearance is outside the specifications 4.3mm, loosen the lock nuts and turn the adjuster in or out until the correct clearance is obtained.

NOTE: After adjustment, check the operation of the gearshift lever. Also check that the threads of the cables do not extend out of the cable adjuster by more than 10mm.

OVERHAUL

For all overhaul procedures, please refer to "Manual Transaxle Overhaul" in the Unit Repair section.

CLUTCH

All models use a single dry disc with a diaphragm spring type pressure plate. The Civic, the 1982-88 Accord and the 1983-88 Prelude clutch is cable operated. However, on the 1981 Accord and 1981-82 Prelude, a hydraulic master and slave cylinder system is used.

REMOVAL & INSTALLATION

1. Follow the transaxle removal procedure, previously given. Matchmark the flywheel and clutch for easy reassembly.

2. Hold the flywheel ring gear with a tool made for the purpose, remove the retaining bolts and remove the pressure plate and clutch disc.

NOTE: Loosen the retaining bolts two turns at a time in a circular pattern. Removing one bolt while the rest are tight may warp the diaphragm spring.

3. The flywheel can now be removed, if it needs repairing or replacing. Inspect it for scoring and wear, and reface or replace as necessary. Torque to the specifications shown in the Torque Specification Chart. Tighten in a criss-cross pattern.

4. To separate the pressure plate from the diaphragm spring, remove the 4 retracting clips.

5. To remove the release, or throwout bearing, first straighten the locking tab and remove the 8mm bolt, followed by the release shaft and release arm with the bearing attached.

NOTE: It is recommended that the release bearing be removed after the release arm has been removed from the casing. Trying to remove or install the bearing with the release arm in the case will damage the retaining clip.

6. If a new release bearing is to be installed, separate the bearing from the holder, using a bearing drift.

7. To assemble and install the clutch, reverse the removal procedure. Be sure to pay attention to the following points:

a. Make sure that the flywheel and the end of the crankshaft are clean before assembling.

b. When installing the pressure plate, align the mark on the outer edge of the flywheel with the alignment mark on the pressure plate.

Failure to align these marks will result in imbalance.

c. When tightening the pressure plate bolts, use a pilot shaft to center the friction disc. The pilot shaft can be bought at any large auto supply store or fabricated from a wooden dowel. After centering the disc, tighten the bolts two turns at a time, in a criss-cross pattern to avoid warping the diaphragm springs; tighten to 7 ft. lbs. (84 inch lbs.).

d. When installing the release shaft and arm, place a lock tab washer under the retaining bolt.

e. When installing the transmission, make sure that the mainshaft is properly aligned with the disc spline and the aligning pins are in place, before tightening the case bolts to 17-22 ft. lbs.

PEDAL HEIGHT ADJUSTMENT

1981 Civic

The pedal height should be 21mm minimum from the floor.

1981 Accord and 1981-82 Prelude

1. Pedal height should be 184mm measured from the front of the pedal to the floorboard (mat removed).

2. Adjust by turning the pedal stop bolt in or out until height is correct. Tighten the locknut after adjustment.

FREE-PLAY ADJUSTMENT

Civic, Accord (1982-88) and Prelude (1983-88)

Adjust the clutch release lever so that free-play, when you move the clutch lever at the transmission with your hand, is:
Civic
- 4.4-5.4mm 1981-83
- 4.0-5.0mm 1984-88

1982-88 Accord and 1983-88 Prelude
- 5.2-6.4mm

Adjust the pedal free-play at the outer cable housing adjuster so that pedal free-play is:
Civic and 1982-83 Accord
- 10-30mm

1984-88 Accord and 1983-88 Prelude
- 23-28mm

NOTE: Less than 3mm of free-play may lead to clutch slippage, while more than 3mm clearance may cause difficult shifting. Make sure that the upper and lower adjusting nuts are tightened after adjustments.

1981 Accord and 1981-82 Prelude

1. Free-play should measure 2.0-2.6mm at the clutch release fork.
2. Adjust by loosening the locknut on the slave cylinder pushrod. Turn the pushrod in or out to adjust. Standard adjustment is made by turning the pushrod in until all play is removed, then backing out the pushrod 1¾-2 turns to achieve specified free-play. Tighten the locknut after adjustment.

Clutch Master Cylinder

REMOVAL & INSTALLATION

1981 Accord and 1981-82 Prelude

1. The clutch master cylinder is located on the firewall in the engine compartment next to the brake master cylinder. Remove the hydraulic line. Either plug the port to prevent leakage or drain the reservoir prior to removing the hydraulic line.
2. Remove the cotter pin which retains the pivot pin in the yoke of the pushrod (under the instrument panel at the clutch pedal).
3. Detach the pushrod from the clutch pedal.
4. Remove the two bolts retaining the master cylinder to the firewall. Remove the master cylinder.
5. Installation is the reverse. Bleed the system after installation.

OVERHAUL

1. Remove the snapring which retains the stopper plate. Note the installed position of the stopper plate before removal.
2. Apply compressed air to the inlet port to remove the piston assembly. Note the order of all components.
3. Check the cylinder bore for corrosion or wear. Light scores or scratches can be removed with crocus cloth or a brake cylinder hone. The cylinder should be replaced if heavily worn.

Accord slave cylinder locknut and adjusting nut

4. Replace the piston and spring with new ones. Reassemble in correct order. Coat the inside of the cylinder and the piston with clean brake fluid before installation.
5. Install the cylinder and bleed the system.

Clutch Slave Cylinder

REMOVAL & INSTALLATION

1981 Accord and 1981-82 Prelude

1. The slave cylinder is retained by two bolts. Disconnect and plug the hydraulic line at the slave cylinder and remove the two mounting bolts. Remove the return spring and remove the slave cylinder.
2. Installation is the reverse. Bleed the system after installation.

OVERHAUL

1. Apply compressed air to the inlet port to remove the piston and seal.
2. Inspect the cylinder bore for pitting, corrosion, or wear. Replace the cylinder if worn.
3. Coat the parts with clean brake fluid and reassemble.

CLUTCH HYDRAULIC SYSTEM BLEEDING

1981 Accord and 1981-82 Prelude

The hydraulic system must be bled whenever the system has been leaking or dismantled. The bleed screw is located on the slave cylinder.
1. Remove the bleed screw dust cap.
2. Attach a clear hose to the bleed screw. Immerse the other end of the hose in a clear jar half filled with brake fluid.
3. Fill the clutch master cylinder with fresh brake fluid.
4. Open the bleed screw slightly and have an assistant slowly depress the clutch pedal. Close the bleed

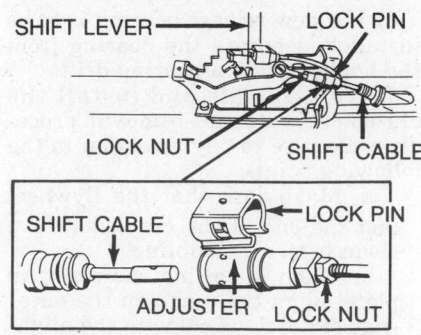

Automatic shift lever adjustment

screw when the pedal reaches the end of its travel. Allow the clutch pedal to return slowly.
5. Repeat Steps 3-4 until all air bubbles are expelled from the system.
6. Discard the brake fluid in the jar. Replace the dust cap. Refill the master cylinder.

AUTOMATIC TRANSAXLE

REMOVAL & INSTALLATION

The automatic transmission is removed in the same basic manner as the manual transmission. The following exceptions should be noted during automatic transmission removal and installation.
1. Remove the center console and control rod pin.
2. Remove the front floor center mat and control cable bracket nuts.
3. Jack and support the front of the car.
4. Remove the two selector lever bracket nuts at the front side.
5. Loosen the bolts securing the control cable holder and support beam and disconnect the control cable.
6. Disconnect the transmission cooler lines at the transmission.
7. Remove the throttle control cable, by loosening only the lower cable locknut. Otherwise the transmission shift points will be changed.

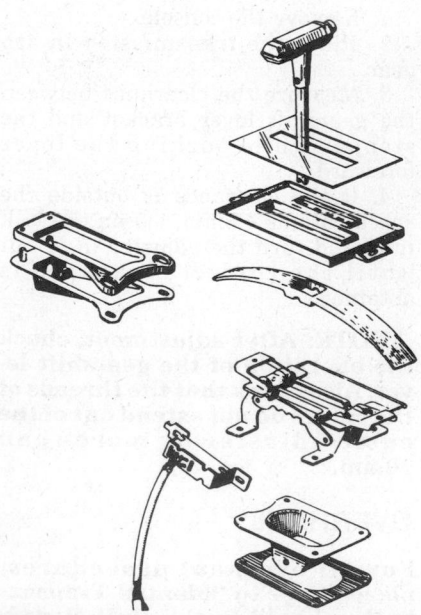

Exploded view of Hondamatic gearshift mechanism

8. Remove the engine (to transmission) mounts and torque converter case cover.

9. Remove the starter motor and separate the transmission from the engine.

10. Installation of the automatic transmission is the reverse of the removal. Close attention should be paid to the following points.

11. Be sure that the stator hub is correctly located and moves smoothly. The stator shaft can be used for this purpose.

12. Align the stator, stator shaft, main shaft and torque converter turbine serrations.

13. After installation of the engine-transmission unit in car, make all required adjustments.

Shift Lever

INSPECTION

1. Pull up fully on the parking brake lever and run the engine at idle speed, while depressing the brake pedal.

------ CAUTION ------

Be sure to check continually for car movement.

2. By moving the shift selector lever slowly forward and backward from the **N** position, make sure that the distance between the **N** and the points where the **D** clutch is engaged for the **2** and **R** positions are the same. The **D** clutch engaging point is just before the slight response is felt. The reverse gears will make a noise when the clutch engages. If the distances are not the same, then adjustment is necessary.

ADJUSTMENT

1. Remove the center console retaining screws, and pull away the console to expose the shift control cable and turnbuckle.

2. Adjust the length of the control cable by removing the lock pin, (if so equipped) loosening the lock nut and turning the turnbuckle, located at the front bottom of the shift lever assembly. After adjustment, the cable and turnbuckle should twist toward the left (driver's) side if the car when shifted toward the **R** position and toward the right side when shifted into the **2** position. The hole in the cable end should be perfectly aligned with holes in the selector lever bracket (pin removed).

TRANSFER CASE

REMOVAL & INSTALLATION

Civic Wagon 4wd

1. Raise the car and support on jackstands.

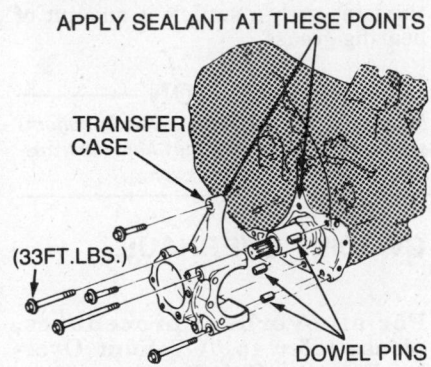

Transfer case mounting

2. Remove the splash shield from beneath the engine.

3. Drain the oil from both the engine and the transmission.

4. Remove the head pipe from the engine.

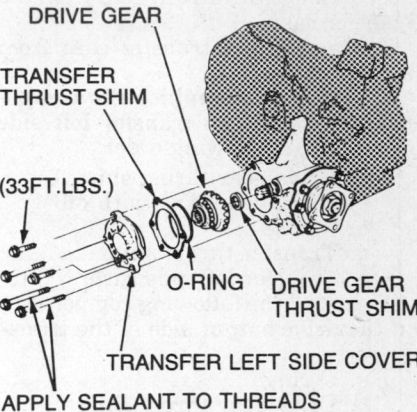

Transfer case left side assembly

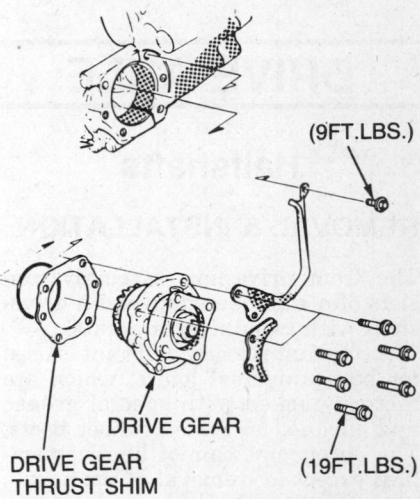

Transfer case drive gear side assembly

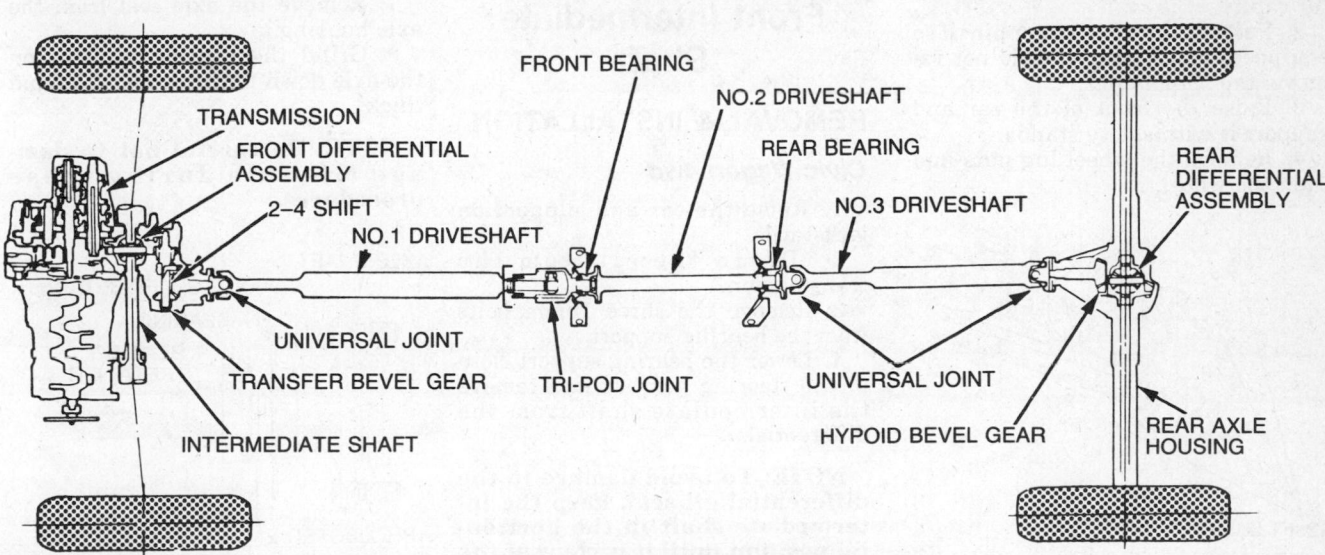

Civic 4WD Station Wagon driveline

5. Disconnect the driveshaft from the transmission.

6. Remove the splash pan from beneath the transmission.

7. Remove the left side cover from the transfer case.

8. Remove the driven gear from the transfer case.

9. Remove the transfer case from the clutch housing.

10. To install, replace the components beneath the transfer left side cover in the following order:

    a. Drive gear thrust shim

    b. Drive gear (coat with oil)

    c. O-ring

    d. Transfer thrust shim

    e. Transfer left side cover

11. Install the following components on the drive output side of the transfer case:

    a. O-ring

    b. Drive gear thrust shim

    c. Drive gear (coat with oil)

DRIVE AXLE

Halfshafts

REMOVAL & INSTALLATION

The front driveshaft assembly consists of a sub-axle shaft and a driveshaft with two universal joints.

A constant velocity ball joint is used for both universal joints, which are factory packed with special grease and enclosed in sealed rubber boots. The outer joint cannot be disassembled except for removal of the boot.

1. Remove the hubcap from the front wheel and then remove the center cap.

2. Pull out the 4mm cotter pin (if so equipped) and loosen, but do not remove, the spindle nut.

3. Raise the front of the car and support it with safety stands.

4. Remove the wheel lug nuts and then the wheel.

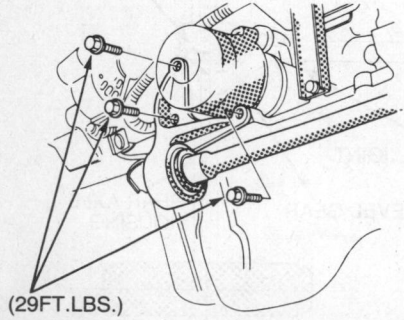

(29FT.LBS.)

Intermediate shaft bearing support

5. Remove the spindle nut.

6. Drain the transmission.

7. Remove the lower arm ball joints at the knuckle by using a ball joint remover.

— CAUTION —

On 1984-88 Civic models, make sure that a floor jack is positioned securely under the lower control arm, at the ball joint. Otherwise, the lower control arm may "jump" suddenly away from the steering knuckle as the ball joint is removed.

On 1983-88 Prelude and 1986-88 Accord models, remove the damper fork bolt and damper locking bolt. Remove the damper fork.

8. To remove the driveshaft, hold the front hub and pull it toward you. Then slide the driveshaft out of the front hub. Pry the CV-joint out about ½ in. Pull the inboard joint side of the driveshaft out of the differential case.

9. To install, reverse the removal procedure. If either the inboard or outboard joint boot bands have been removed for inspection or disassembly of the joint (only the inboard joint can be disassembled), be sure to repack the joint with a sufficient amount of bearing grease.

— CAUTION —

Make sure the CV joint sub-axle bottoms son that the spring clip may hold the transaxle securely in transmission.

CV-JOINT OVERHAUL

For all overhaul procedures, please refer to "CV-Joint Overhaul" in the Unit Repair section.

Front Intermediate Shaft

REMOVAL & INSTALLATION

Civic Wagon 4wd

1. Raise the car and support on jackstands.

2. Drain the oil from the transmission.

3. Remove the three 10mm bolts from the bearing support.

4. Lower the bearing support close to the steering gearbox and remove the intermediate shaft from the differential.

NOTE: To avoid damage to the differential oil seal, keep the intermediate shaft in the horizontal position until it is clear of the differential.

Rear Driveshafts

REMOVAL & INSTALLATION

Civic Wagon 4wd

1. Raise the car and support it on jackstands.

2. Mark the position of the driveshafts on both of the flanges for reassembly.

3. Remove the No. 1 driveshaft protector.

4. Remove the No. 3 driveshaft by disconnecting the U-joints.

5. Remove the bolts holding the rear bearing support, then remove the No. 2 driveshaft.

6. Remove the bolts holding the front bearing support, then remove the No. 1 driveshaft by disconnecting the U-joint.

7. To install, reverse the removal procedures.

Rear Axle Shafts and Bearings

REMOVAL

Civic Wagon 4wd

1. Raise the rear of the car and support it securely on jackstands.

2. Remove the rear wheel and tire assembly, then remove the brake drum.

3. Disconnect the brake line from the brake cylinder.

4. Remove the brake shoes and the parking brake cable.

5. Remove the axle shaft retainer 10mm self-locking nuts.

6. Using a slide hammer, pull the axle shaft from the axle housing.

7. Remove the axle seal from the axle housing.

8. Grind the bearing retainer on the axle down until it's about 0.5mm thick.

NOTE: Be careful not to damage the axle during these procedures.

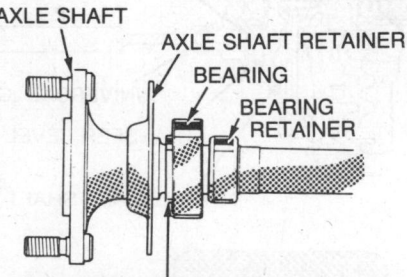

AXLE SHAFT

AXLE SHAFT RETAINER

BEARING

BEARING RETAINER

PROJECTED END OF BEARING RACE

Rear axle and bearing assembly

9. Place the axle in a vice, and split the bearing retainer using a chisel and hammer.

10. Place the axle and bearing in a hydraulic press with the appropriate adapters and press the bearing off the axle.

INSTALLATION

Civic Wagon 4wd

1. Drive a new seal into the rear axle housing.

2. Coat the sealing lip of the oil seal with grease.

3. Thoroughly clean the axle shaft; install the axle retainer, the bearing and the bearing retainer on the axle.

NOTE: DO NOT oil or grease the contact surfaces of the axle, bearing or the bearing retainer. The projected end of the bearing race must face outward.

4. Using the appropriate adapters and a hydraulic press, press the new bearing onto the axle shaft.

5. Measure the following dimensions:

    a. The width of the axle bearing outer race.

    b. The thickness of the backing plate.

    c. The depth from the edge of the axle housing to the bearing seating surface.

X	Shims required
−0.16−0.10 mm (−0.0063−0.0039 in.)	None
0.10−0.25 mm (0.0039−0.0098 in.)	Use one 0.1 mm shim
0.25−0.40 mm (0.0098−0.0157 in.)	Use one 0.25 mm shim

Part Numbers:
0.1 mm shim: 42150−SC2−000
0.25 mm shim: 42154−SC2−000

Rear axle shim chart

Using the above measurements calculate the correct shim thickness using the following formula: a - (b + c) = X.

6. Apply a thin coat of sealant to the backing plate face of the shim.

7. Apply a thin coat of sealant to the axle retainer contacting the face of the shim.

8. Push the axle into the axle housing aligning its splines with the differential side gear splines.

NOTE: Before installing the axle, coat the inner corner of the bearing housing seat with sealant.

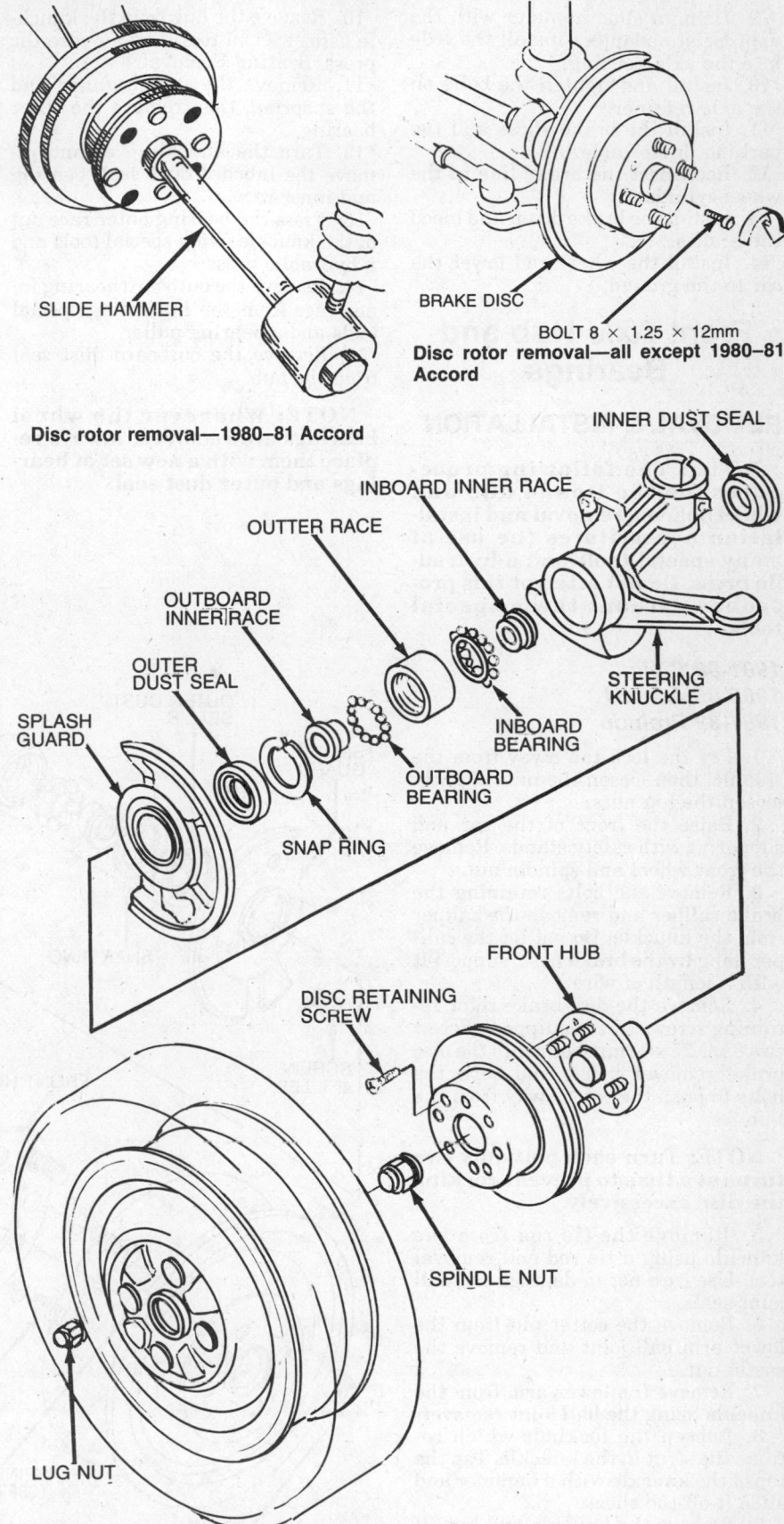

SLIDE HAMMER

Disc rotor removal—1980–81 Accord

BRAKE DISC

BOLT 8 × 1.25 × 12mm
Disc rotor removal—all except 1980–81 Accord

INNER DUST SEAL

INBOARD INNER RACE

OUTTER RACE

OUTBOARD INNER RACE

OUTER DUST SEAL

SPLASH GUARD

INBOARD BEARING

OUTBOARD BEARING

STEERING KNUCKLE

SNAP RING

FRONT HUB

DISC RETAINING SCREW

SPINDLE NUT

LUG NUT

Front steering knuckle, hub and bearing—all except 1984 and later Civic, 1980–82 Accord, 1986 and later Accord and 1983 and later Prelude

9. Using a slide hammer with the appropriate adapters install the axle into the axle housing.

10. Install and tighten the bolts on the axle retainer.

11. Install the brake shoes and the parking brake cable.

12. Reconnect the brake line to the wheel cylinder.

13. Install the brake drum and bleed the brakes.

14. Install the wheel and lower the car to the ground.

Front Axle Hub and Bearings

REMOVAL & INSTALLATION

NOTE: The following procedures for the Honda hub and wheel bearing removal and installation necessitates the use of many special tools and a hydraulic press. Do not attempt this procedure without these special tools.

1981-83 Civic
1983-85 Accord
1981-82 Prelude

1. Pry the lock tab away from the spindle, then loosen the nut. Slightly loosen the lug nuts.

2. Raise the front of the car and support it with safety stands. Remove the front wheel and spindle nut.

3. Remove the bolts retaining the brake caliper and remove the caliper from the knuckle. Do not let the caliper hang by the brake hose, support it with a length of wire.

4. Remove the disc brake rotor retaining screws (if so equipped). Screw two 8 x 1.25 x 12mm bolts into the disc brake removal holes, and turn the bolts to push the rotor away from the hub.

NOTE: Turn each bolt only two turns at a time to prevent cocking the disc excessively.

5. Remove the tie rod from the knuckle using a tie rod end removal tool. Use care not to damage the ball joint seals.

6. Remove the cotter pin from the lower arm ball joint and remove the castle nut.

7. Remove the lower arm from the knuckle using the ball joint remover.

8. Loosen the lockbolt which retains the strut in the knuckle. Tap the top of the knuckle with a hammer and slide it off the shock.

9. Remove the knuckle and hub, if still attached, by sliding the assembly off the driveshaft.

10. Remove the hub from the knuckle using special tools and a hydraulic press. Bearing Removal:

11. Remove the splash guard and the snapring, then remove the outer bearing.

12. Turn the knuckle over and remove the inboard dust seal, bearing and inner race.

13. Press the bearing outer race out of the knuckle using special tools and a hydraulic press.

14. Remove the outboard bearing inner race from the hub using special tools and a bearing puller.

15. Remove the outboard dust seal from the hub.

NOTE: Whenever the wheel bearings are removed, always replace them with a new set of bearings and outer dust seal.

16. Clean all old grease from the driveshafts and spindles on the car.

17. Remove all old grease from the hub and knuckle and thoroughly dry and wipe clean all components.

18. When fitting new bearings, you must pack them with wheel bearing grease. To do this, place a glob of grease in your left palm, then, holding one of the bearings in your right hand, drag the face of the bearing heavily through the grease. This must be done to work as much grease as possible through the ball bearings and the cage. Turn the bearing and continue to pull it through the grease, until the grease is thoroughly packed between the bearing balls and the cage, all around the bearing. Repeat this operation until all of the bearings are packed with grease.

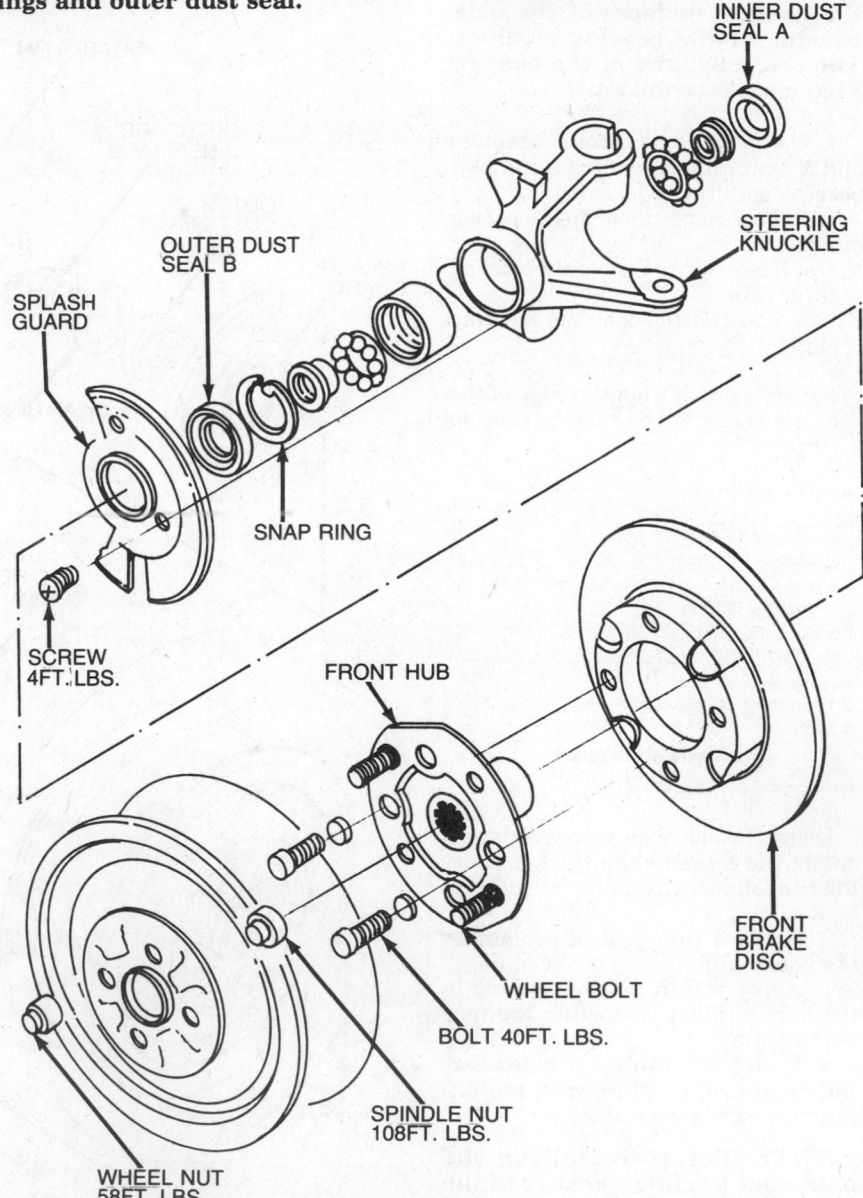

Front steering knuckle, hub and bearing—1980–81 Accord

19. Pack the inside of the rotor and knuckle hub with a moderate amount of grease. Do not overload the hub with grease.

20. Apply a small amount of grease to the spindle and to the lip of the inner seal before installing.

21. To install the bearings, press the bearing outer race into the knuckle using the special tools used as above, plus the installing base tool.

22. Install the outboard ball bearing and its inner race in the knuckle.

23. Install the snapring. Pack grease in the groove around the sealing lip of the outboard grease dust seal.

24. Drive the outboard grease seal into the knuckle, using a seal driver and hammer, until it is flush with the knuckle surface.

25. Install the splash guard, then turn the knuckle upside down and install the inboard ball bearing and its inner race.

26. Place the hub in the special tool fixture, then set the knuckle in position on the press and apply downward pressure.

27. Pack grease in the groove around the sealing lip of the inboard dust seal.

28. Drive the dust seal into the knuckle using a seal driver.

29. The remaining step are the reverse of the removal procedure. Use a new spindle nut, and stake after torquing.

1984-88 Civic

1. Pry the lock tab away from the spindle, then loosen the nut. Slightly loosen the lug nuts.

2. Raise the front of the car and support it with safety stands. Remove the front wheel and spindle nut.

3. Remove the bolts retaining the brake caliper and remove the caliper from the knuckle. Do not let the caliper hang by the brake hose, support it with a length of wire.

4. Remove the disc brake rotor retaining screws (if so equipped). Screw two 8 x 1.25 x 12mm bolts into the disc brake removal holes, and turn the bolts to push the rotor away from the hub.

NOTE: Turn each bolt only two turns at a time to prevent cocking the disc excessively.

5. Remove the tie rod from the knuckle using a tie rod end removal tool. Use care not to damage the ball joint seals.

6. Use a floor jack to support the lower control arm, then remove the cotter pin from the lower arm ball joint and remove the castle nut.

CAUTION

Be sure to place the jack securely beneath the lower control arm at the ball joint. Otherwise, the tension from the torsion bar may cause the arm to suddenly "jump" away from the steering knuckle as the ball joint is removed.

---

7. Remove the lower arm from the knuckle using the ball joint remover.

8. Loosen the pinchbolt which retains the shock in the knuckle. Tap the top of the knuckle with a hammer and slide it off the shock.

9. Remove the knuckle and hub, if still attached, by sliding the assembly off of the driveshaft.

10. Remove the hub from the knuckle using special tools and a hydraulic press. Bearing Removal:

11. Remove the splash guard and the snapring.

12. Press the bearing outer race of the knuckle using special tools and a hydraulic press.

13. Remove the outboard bearing inner race from the hub using special tools and a bearing puller.

NOTE: Whenever the wheel bearings are removed, always replace with a new set of bearings and outer dust seal.

14. Clean all old grease from the driveshafts and spindles on the car.

15. Remove the old grease from the hub and knuckle and thoroughly dry and wipe clean all components.

16. To install the bearings, press the bearing outer race into the knuckle using the special tools as used above, plus the installing base tool.

17. Install the snapring, then install the splash guard.

18. Place the hub in the special tool fixture, then set the knuckle in position on the press and apply downward pressure.

19. The remaining steps are the reverse of the removal procedure. Use a new spindle nut, and stake after torquing.

1981 Accord

1. Pry the lock tab away from the spindle, then loosen the nut. Slightly loosen the lug nuts.

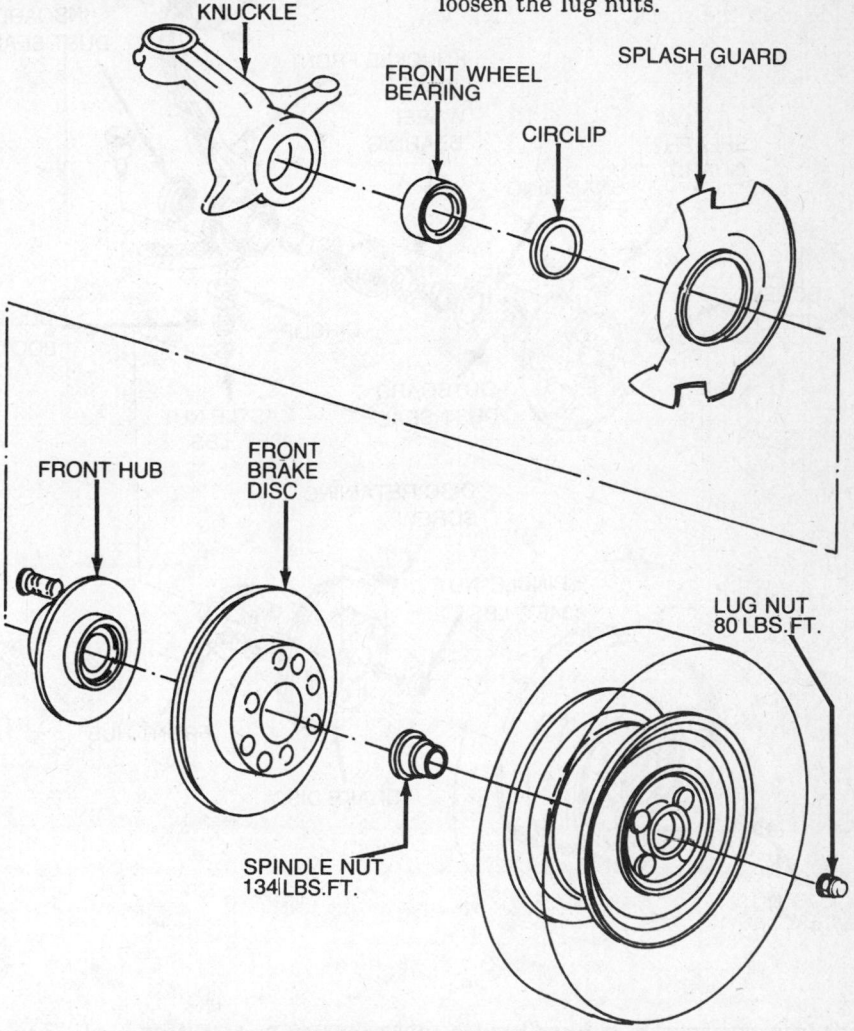

Front steering knuckle, hub and bearing—1984 and later Civic

2. Raise the front of the car and support it with safety stands. Remove the front wheel and spindle nut.

3. Remove the bolts retaining the brake caliper and remove the caliper from the knuckle. Do not let the caliper hang by the brake hose, support it with a length of wire.

4. Install a hub puller attachment against the hub and rotor with the lug nuts.

5. Attach a slide hammer in the center hole of the attachment and pull out the hub, with the disc attached, from the knuckle. Unbolt and remove the brake disc from the hub.

6. Remove the tie rod from the knuckle using a tie rod end removal tool. Use care not to damage the ball joint seals.

7. Remove the cotter pins from the lower arm ball joint and remove the castle nut.

8. Remove the lower arm from the knuckle using the ball joint remover.

9. Loosen the lockbolt which retains the strut in the knuckle. Tap the rop of the knuckle with a hammer and slide it off the shock.

10. Remove the knuckle by sliding the assembly off of the driveshaft. Bearing Removal:

11. Remove the splash guard and the snapring, then remove the outer bearing.

12. Turn the knuckle over and remove the inboard dust seal, bearing and inner race.

13. Press the bearing outer race out of the knuckle using special tools and a hydraulic press.

14. Remove the outboard bearing inner race from the hub using special tools and a bearing puller.

15. Remove the outboard dust seal from the hub.

NOTE: Whenever the wheel bearings are removed, always replace with a new set of bearings and outer dust seal.

16. Clean all old grease from the driveshafts and spindles of the car.

17. Remove all old grease from the hub and knuckle and thoroughly dry and wipe clean all components.

18. When fitting new bearings, you must pack them with wheel bearing grease. To do this, place a glob of grease in your left palm, then, holding one of the bearings in your right hand, drag the face of the bearing heavily through the grease. This must be done to work as much grease as possible through the ball bearings and the cage. Turn the bearing and continue to pull it through the grease, until the grease is thoroughly packed between the bearing balls and the cage, all around the bearing. Repeat this operation until all of the bearings are packed with grease.

19. Pack the inside of the rotor and knuckle hub with a moderate amount of grease. Do not overload the hub with grease.

20. Apply a small amount of grease to the spindle and to the lip of the inner seal before installing.

21. To install the bearings, press the bearing outer race into the knuckle using the special tools as used above, plus the installing base tool.

22. Install the outboard ball bearing and its inner race in the knuckle.

23. Install the snapring. Pack grease in the groove around the sealing lip of the outboard grease dust seal.

24. Drive the outboard grease seal into the knuckle, using a seal driver and a hammer, until its flush with the knuckle surface.

25. Install the splash guard, then turn the knuckle upside down and install the inboard ball bearing and its inner race.

26. Bolt the brake disc to the front hub and place the hub in the special tool fixture, then set the knuckle in position on the press and apply downward pressure.

27. Pack grease in the groove around the sealing lip of the inboard dust seal.

28. Drive the dust seal into the knuckle using a seal driver.

29. The remaining steps are the reverse of the removal procedure. Use a new spindle nut, and stake after torquing.

1983-88 Prelude, and 1986-88 Accord

1. Pry the lock tab away from the spindle, then loosen the nut. Slightly loosen the lug nuts.

2. Raise the front of the car and support it with safety stands. Remove the front wheel and spindle nut.

3. Remove the bolts retaining the brake caliper and remove the caliper from the knuckle. Do not let the cali-

BALL JOINT SEAL

INBOARD DUST SEAL

KNUCKLE FRONT

WHEEL BEARING

SPLASH GUARD

SNAP RING

SCREW 4FT. LBS.

CIRCLIP

DUST BOOT

OUTBOARD DUST SEAL

CASTLE NUT 40FT. LBS.

DISC RETAINING SCREW

SPINDLE NUT 134FT. LBS.

FRONT HUB

LUG NUT 79FT. LBS.

BRAKE DISC

Front steering knuckle, hub and bearing—1983 and later Prelude, 1986 and later Accord similar

per hang by the brake hose, support it with a length of wire.

4. Remove the disc brake rotor retaining screws (if so equipped). Screw two 8 x 1.25 x 12mm bolts into the disc brake removal holes, and turn the bolts to push the rotor away from the hub.

NOTE: Turn each bolt only two turns at a time to prevent cocking the disc excessively.

5. Remove the tie rod from the knuckle using a tie rod end removal tool. Use care not to damage the ball joint seals.

6. Remove the cotter pin from the lower arm ball joint and remove the castle nut.

7. Remove the lower arm from the knuckle using the ball joint remover.

8. Remove the cotter pin from the upper arm ball joint and remove the castle nut.

9. Remove the upper arm from the knuckle using the ball joint remover.

10. Remove the knuckle and hub by sliding the assembly off of the driveshaft.

11. Remove the two back splash guard screws from the knuckle.

12. Remove the hub from the knuckle using special tools and a hydraulic press. Bearing Removal:

13. Remove the splash guard, dust seal and the snapring, then remove the outer bearing race.

14. Turn the knuckle over and remove the inboard dust seal, bearing and inner race and bearing.

15. Press the bearing outer race out of the knuckle using special tools and a hydraulic press.

16. Remove the outboard bearing inner race from the hub using special tools and a bearing puller.

17. Remove the outboard dust seal from the hub.

NOTE: Whenever the wheel bearings are removed, always replace with a new set of bearings and outer dust seal.

18. Clean all old grease from the driveshafts spindles on the car.

19. Remove all old grease from the hub and knuckle and thoroughly dry and wipe clean all components.

NOTE: The bearings on 1986 and later Accord and certain replacement bearings may be sealed and cannot be packed with grease.

20. When fitting new bearings, you must pack them with wheel bearing grease. To do this, place a glob of grease in your left palm, then, holding one of the bearings in your right hand, drag the face of the bearing

heavily through the grease. This must be done to work as much grease as possible through the ball bearings and the cage. Turn the bearing and continue to pull it through the grease, until the grease is thoroughly packed between the bearing balls and the cage, all around the bearing. Repeat this operation until all of the bearings are packed with grease.

21. Pack the inside of the rotor and knuckle hub with a moderate amount of grease. Do not overload the hub with grease.

22. Apply a small amount of grease to the spindle and to the lip of the inner seal before installing.

23. To install the bearings, press the bearing outer race into the knuckle using the special tools used as above, plus the installing base tool.

24. Install the outboard ball bearing and its inner race in the knuckle.

25. Install the snapring. Pack grease in the groove around the sealing lip of the outboard grease dust seal.

26. Drive the outboard grease seal into the knuckle, using a seal driver and hammer, until it is flush with the knuckle surface.

27. Install the splash guard, then turn the knuckle upside down and install the inboard ball bearing and its inner race.

28. Place the hub in the special tool fixture, then set the knuckle in position on the press and apply downward pressure.

29. Pack grease in the groove around the sealing lip of the inboard dust seal.

30. Drive the dust seal into the knuckle using a seal driver.

31. The remaining steps are the reverse of the removal procedure. Use a new spindle nut, and stake after torquing.

FRONT SUSPENSION

Shock Absorbers

REMOVAL & INSTALLATION

1983-88 Prelude
1986-88 Accord

1. Raise the front of the car and support it on jackstands. Remove the front wheels.

2. Remove the shock absorber locking bolt.

3. Remove the shock fork bolt and remove the shock fork.

4. Remove the shock absorber assembly.

5. Installation is the reverse of the removal procedure, taking note of the following:

   a. Align the shock absorber aligning tab with the slot in the shock absorber fork.

   b. The mounting base bolt should be tightened with the weight of the car placed on the shock.

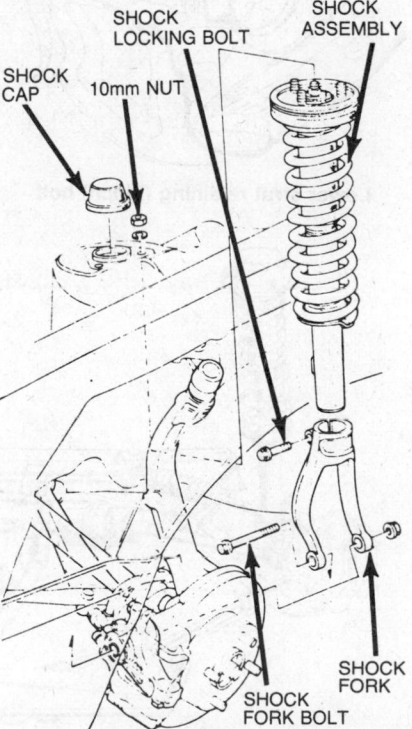

Front shock mounting—1983 and later Prelude, and 1986 and later Accord

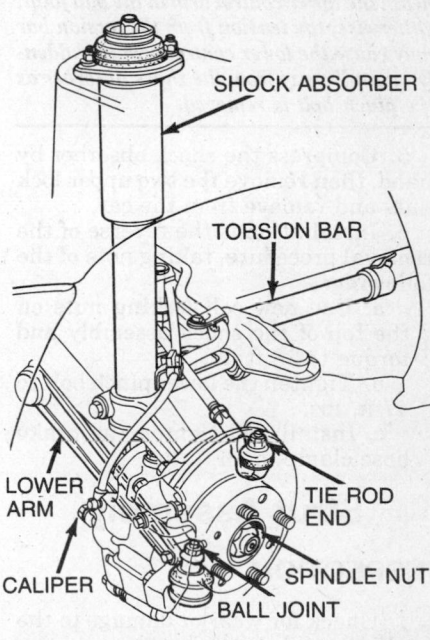

Front suspension—1984 and later Civic

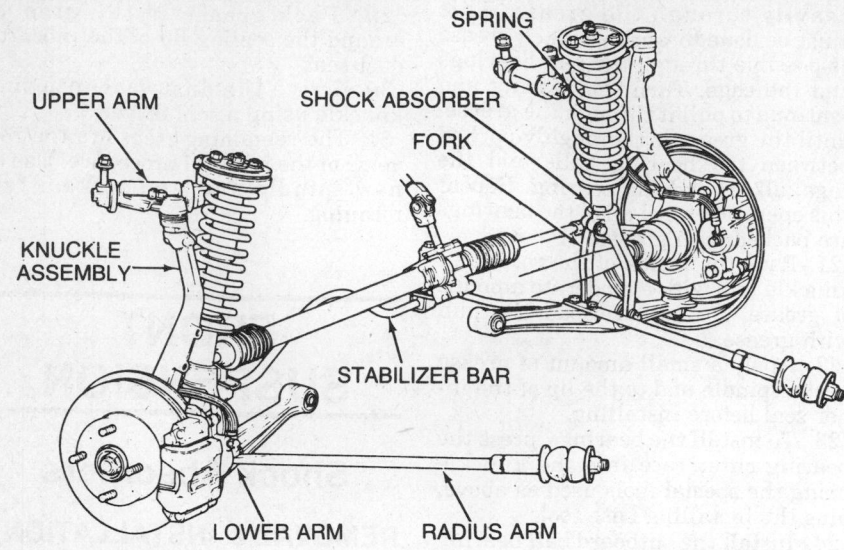

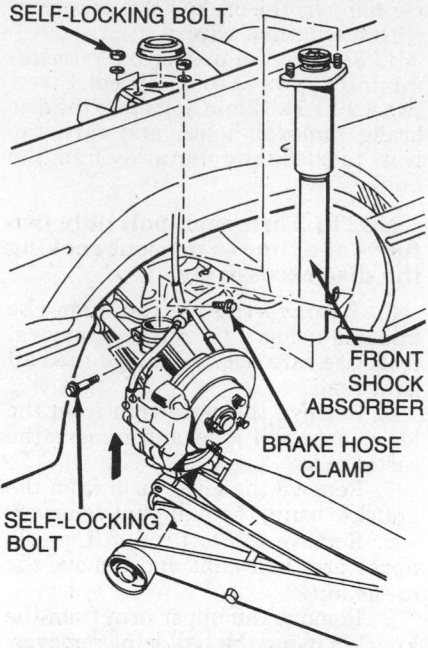

Front suspension—1983 and later Prelude, and 1986 and later Accord

c. Torque the upper mounting bolts to 29 ft. lbs., the shock locking bolt to 32 ft. lbs., and the shock fork bolt to 47 ft. lbs.

1984-88 Civic Models

1. Raise the front of the car and support it on jackstands. Remove the front wheels.
2. Remove the brake hose clamp bolt.
3. Place a floor jack beneath the lower control arm to support it.
4. Remove the lower shock retaining bolt from the steering knuckle, then slowly lower the jack.

——— **CAUTION** ———

Be sure the jack is positioned securely beneath the lower control arm at the ball joint. Otherwise, the tension from the torsion bar may cause the lower control arm to suddenly "jump" away from the shock absorber as the pinch bolt is removed.

5. Compress the shock absorber by hand, then remove the two upper lock nuts and remove from the car.
6. Installation is the reverse of the removal procedure, taking note of the following:
   a. Use new self locking nuts on the top of the shock assembly and torque to 28 ft. lbs.
   b. Tighten the lower pinch bolt to 47 ft. lbs.
   c. Install and tighten the brake hose clamp to 16 ft. lbs.

Strut Assembly

INSPECTION

1. Check for wear or damage to the bushings and needle bearings.

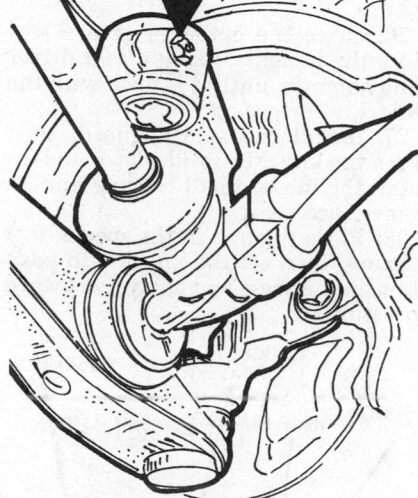

Lower strut retaining (pinch) bolt

Front shock mounting—1984 and later Civic

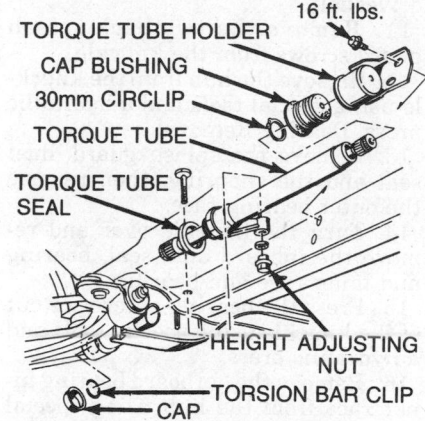

Torsion bar assembly—1984 and later Civic

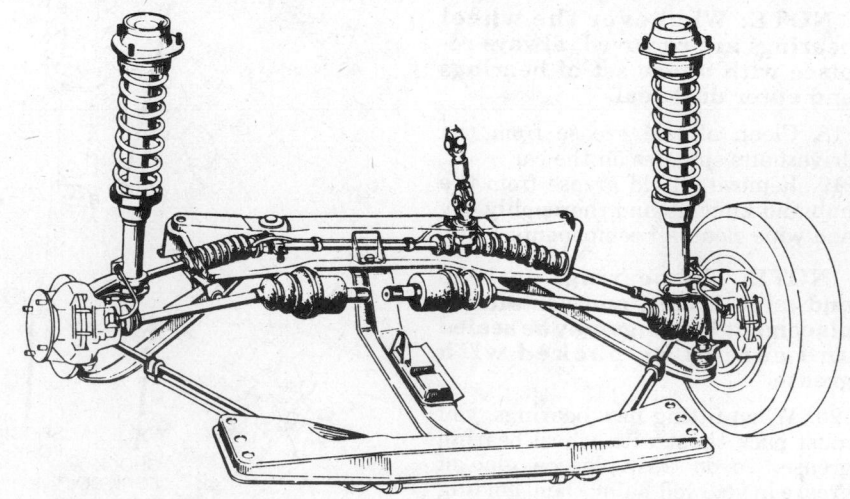

Typical front suspension and steering gear—1980–82 models

2. Check for oil leaks from the struts.

3. Check all rubber parts for wear or damage.

4. Bounce the car to check shock absorber effectiveness. The car should continue to bounce for no more than two cycles.

REMOVAL & INSTALLATION

1. Raise the front of the car and support it with safety stands. Remove the front wheels.

2. Disconnect the brake pipe at the strut and remove the brake hose retaining clip.

3. Remove the caliper and carefully hang from the undercarriage of the car with a piece of wire.

4. On 1981-85 Accord models, disconnect the stabilizer bar from the lower arm.

5. Loosen the bolt on the knuckle that retains the lower end of the shock absorber. Push down firmly while tapping it with a hammer until the knuckle is free of the strut.

6. Remove the three nuts retaining the upper end of the strut and remove the strut from the car.

7. To install, reverse the removal procedure. Be sure to properly match the matching surface of the strut and the knuckle notch. Tighten the knuckle bolt to 40 ft. lbs. (43-51 ft. lbs. on the Accord).

OVERHAUL

For all strut overhaul procedures, please refer to "Strut Overhaul" in the Unit Repair section.

Torsion Bar Assembly

REMOVAL & INSTALLATION

1984-88 Civic Models

1. Raise the front of the car and support it on jackstands.

2. Remove the height adjusting nut and the torque tube holder.

3. Remove the 33mm circlip.

4. Remove the torsion bar cap, then remove the torsion bar clip by tapping the bar out of the torque tube.

NOTE: The torsion bar will slide easier if you move the lower arm up and down.

5. Tap the torsion bar backward, out of the torque tube and remove the torque tube.

6. Install a new seal onto the torque tube. Coat the torque tube seal and torque with grease, then install them on the rear beam.

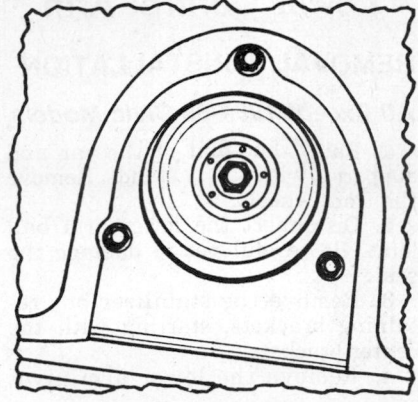

Typical strut upper mounting nuts

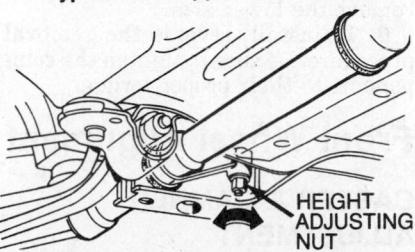

Torsion bar adjustment—1984 and later Civic

7. Grease the ends of the torsion bar and insert into the torque tube from the back.

8. Align the projection on the torque tube splines with the cutout in the torsion bar splines and insert the torsion bar approximately 10mm.

NOTE: The torsion bar will slide easier if the lower arm is moved up and down.

9. Install the torsion bar clip and cap, then install the 30mm circlip and the torque tube cap.

NOTE: Push the torsion bar to the front so there is no clearance between the torque tube and the 30mm circlip.

10. Coat the cap bushing with grease and install it on the torque tube. Install the torque tube holder.

11. Temporarily tighten the height adjusting nut.

12. Remove the jackstands and lower the car to the ground. Adjust the torsion bar spring height.

TORSION BAR ADJUSTMENT

1. Measure the torsion bar spring height between the ground and the highest point of the wheel arch:
• Coupe (CRX): 644mm ± 5mm
• Hatchback: 646mm ± 5mm
• Sedan: 651mm ± 5mm
• Wagon: 645mm ± 5mm

2. If the spring height does not meet the specifications above, make the following adjustment.

  a. Raise the front wheels off the ground.

  b. Adjust the spring height by turning the height adjusting nut. Tightening the nut raises the height, and loosening the nut lowers the height.

NOTE: The height varies 0.20 in. per turn of the adjusting nut.

  c. Lower the front wheels to the ground, then bounce the car up and down several times and recheck the spring height to see if it is within specifications.

Lower Ball Joints

INSPECTION

Check ball joint play as follows:

  a. Raise the front of the car and support it with safety stands.

  b. Clamp a dial indicator onto the lower control arm and place the indicator tip on the knuckle, near the ball joint.

  c. Place a pry bar between the lower control arm and the knuckle. Replace the lower control arm if the play exceeds 0.020 in.

REMOVAL & INSTALLATION

All Except the 1983-88 Prelude and the 1986-88 Accord

If the ball joint play exceeds 0.020 in. the ball joint and lower control arm or lower radius arm (1984-88 Civics) must be replaced as an assembly.

1983-88 Prelude 1986-88 Accord

NOTE: This procedure is performed after the removal of the steering knuckle and requires the use of the following special tools or their equivalent: Honda part no. 07965-SB00200 Ball Joint Removal Base, 07965-SB00300 Ball Joint Installation Base, and 07974-SA50700 Clip Guide Tool.

1. Pry the snapring off and remove the boot.

2. Pry the snapring out of the groove in the ball joint.

3. Install the ball joint removal tool with the large end facing out and tighten the ball joint nut.

4. Position the ball joint removal tool base on the ball joint and set the assembly in a large vise. Press the ball joint out of the steering knuckle.

5. Position the new ball joint into the hole of the steering knuckle.

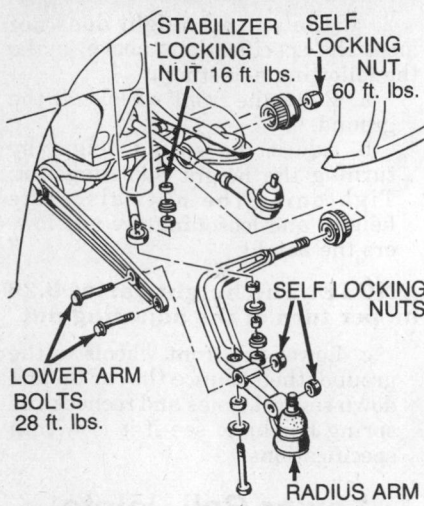

Radius arm—1984 and later Civic

6. Install the ball joint installer tool with the small end facing out.

7. Position the ball joint installation base tool on the ball joint and set the assembly in a large vise. Press the ball joint into the steering knuckle.

8. Seat the snapring in the groove of the ball joint.

9. Install the boot and snapring using the clip guide tool.

Radius Arm

REMOVAL & INSTALLATION

1984-88 Civic Models Only

1. Raise the front of the car off the ground and support it on jackstands. Remove the front wheels.

2. Place a floor jack beneath the lower control arm, then remove the ball joint cotter pin and nut.

——— **CAUTION** ———

Be sure to place the jack securely beneath the lower control arm at the ball joint. Otherwise, the tension from the torsion bar may cause the arm to suddenly "jump" away from the steering knuckle as the ball joint is removed.

3. Using a ball joint remover, remove then ball joint from the steering knuckle.

4. Remove the radius arm locking nuts and the stabilizer locking nut, then separate the radius arm from the stabilizer bar.

5. Remove the lower arm bolts and remove the radius arm by pulling it down and then forward.

6. Installation is the reverse of the removal procedure. Tighten all the rubber bushings and dampered parts only after the car is placed back on the ground.

Lower Control Arm

REMOVAL & INSTALLATION

All Except 1984-88 Civic Models

1. Raise the front of the car and support it with safety stands. Remove the front wheels.

2. Disconnect the lower arm ball joint. Be careful not to damage the seal.

3. Remove the stabilizer bar retaining brackets, starting with the center brackets.

4. Remove the lower arm pivot bolt.

5. Disconnect the radius rod and remove the lower arm.

6. To install, reverse the removal procedure. Be sure to tighten the components to their proper torque.

Front Wheel Alignment

CASTER & CAMBER ADJUSTMENT

Caster and camber cannot be adjusted on any Honda except the 1983-88 Prelude. If caster, camber or kingpin angle is incorrect or front end parts are damaged or worn, they must be replaced.

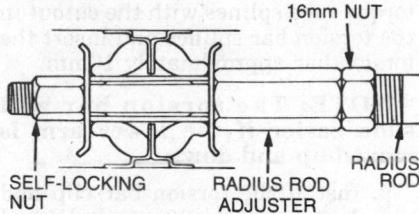

Caster adjustment—1983 and later Prelude, and 1986 and later Accord

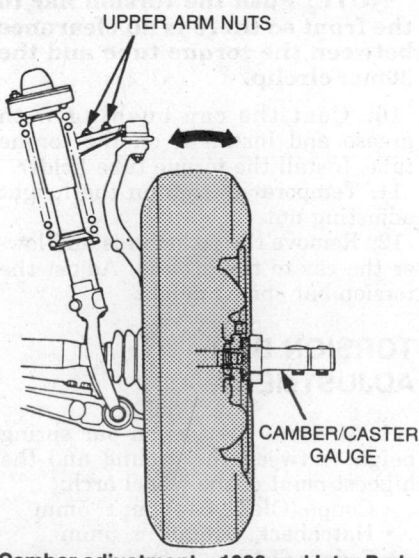

Camber adjustment—1983 and later Prelude, and 1986 and later Accord

1983-88 Prelude
1986-88 Accord

NOTE: Wheel alignment adjustments must be performed in the following order: camber, caster and then toe-in.

The camber adjustment can be made by loosening the two nuts on the upper control arm and sliding the ball joint until the camber meets specifications. The caster adjustment can be made by loosening the 16mm nuts on the front beam radius rods and then turning the locknut to make the adjustment. Turning the nut clockwise decreases the caster and turning it counterclockwise increases the caster. After adjusting to specifications, hold the nylon locknut and lightly tighten the adjuster. Tighten the 16mm nut to 58 ft. lbs., then tighten the locknut to 32 ft. lbs. while holding the 16mm nut.

TOE-OUT ADJUSTMENT

Toe is the difference of the distance between the forward extremes of the front tires and the distance between the rearward extremes of the front tires. On Hondas, the fronts of the tires are further apart than the rear to counteract the pulling together effect of front wheel drive.

Toe-out can be adjusted on all Hondas by loosening the locknuts at each end of the tie rods. To increase toe-out, turn the right tie rod in the direction of forward wheel rotation and turn the left tie rod in the opposite direction. Turn both tie rods an equal amount until toe-out meets specifications.

REAR SUSPENSION

All Civic sedan, hatchback and 1984-88 2wd station wagon models and the Accord and Prelude utilize an independent MacPherson strut arrangement for each rear wheel. Each suspension unit consists of a combined oil spring/shock absorber strut, a lower control arm, and a radius rod or arm. The Civic 4wd Station Wagon uses coil springs which are mounted directly on the axle housing independent of the rear shock absorbers. The Accord and Prelude have adjustable rear suspension.

1981-83 station wagon models use a more conventional leaf spring rear suspension with a solid rear axle. The springs are 3-leaf, semi-elliptic types located longitudinally with a pair of telescopic shock absorbers to control rebound. The solid axle and leaf springs allow for a greater load carrying capacity for the wagon.

Rear Strut Assembly

REMOVAL & INSTALLATION

1. Raise the rear of the car and support it with safety stands.
2. Remove the rear wheel.

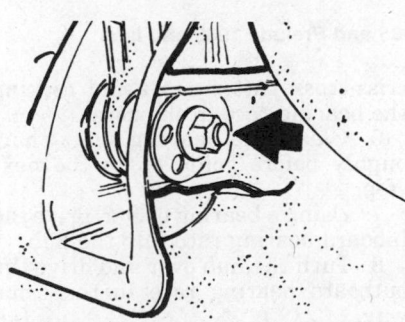

Rear toe adjustment location—Civic 1980–82

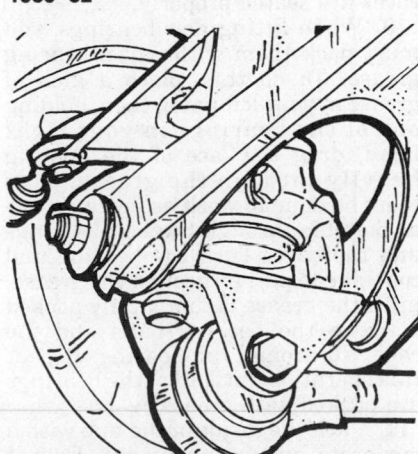

Rear toe adjustment location—Accord 1980–82

1983 Civic Sedan rear control arm

3. Disconnect the brake line at the shock absorber (if so equipped). Remove the retaining clip and separate the brake hose from the shock absorber.
4. Disconnect the parking brake cable at the backing plate lever.
5. Remove the lower strut retaining bolt or pinch bolt and hub carrier pivot bolt. To remove the pivot bolt, you first have to remove the castle nut and its cotter pin.
6. Remove the upper strut retaining nuts and remove the strut from the car.

7. To install, reverse the removal procedure. Be sure to install the top of the strut in the body first. After installation, bleed the brake lines.

OVERHAUL

For all strut overhaul procedures, please refer to "Strut Overhaul" in the Unit Repair section.

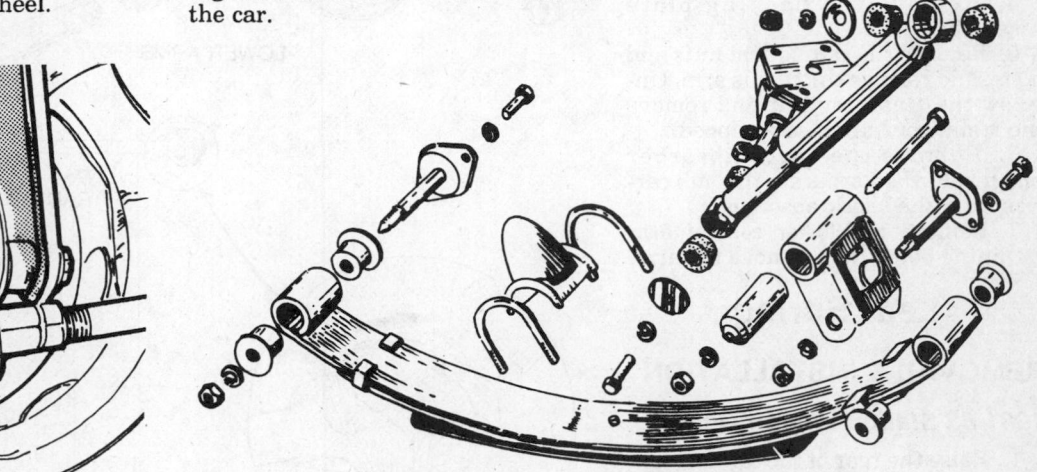

Rear suspension—Civic station Wagon 1980–83

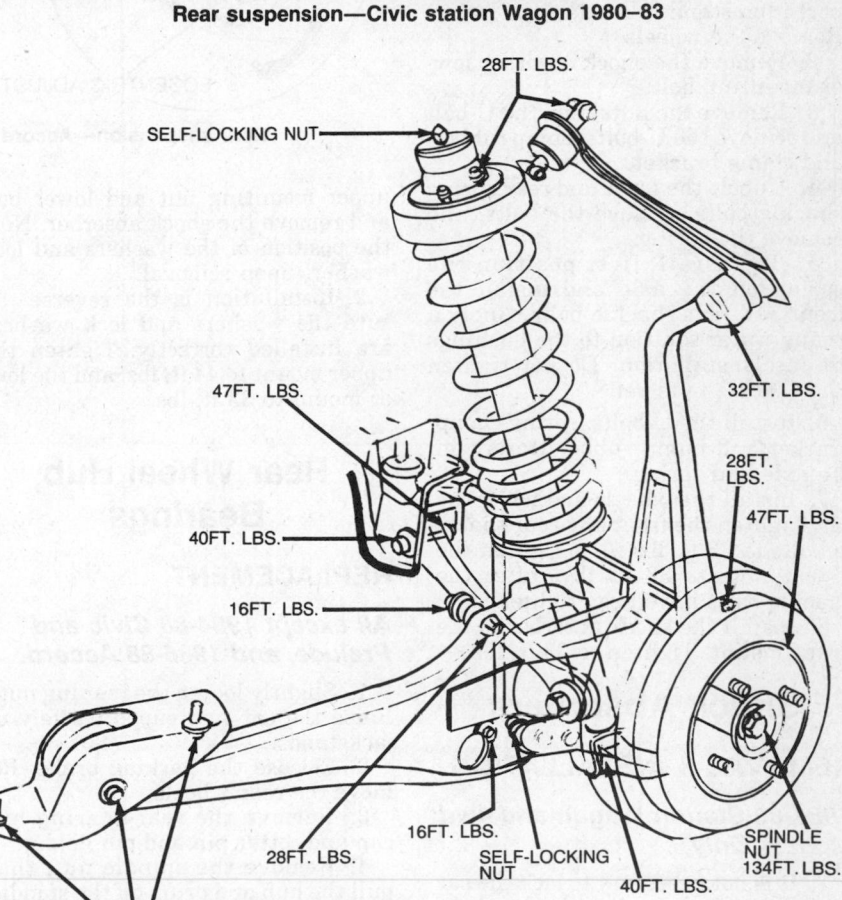

Rear suspension—Accord 1986 and later

Lower Control Arm and Radius Arm

REMOVAL & INSTALLATION

Except 1981-83 Station Wagon

1. Raise the rear of the car and support it with safety stands.
2. Remove the rear wheels and brake drums.
3. Disconnect the hydraulic brake line and parking brake cable.
4. Remove the backing plate assembly.
5. Remove the radius arm nuts and bolts, and remove the radius arm. Unscrew the stabilizer bolt and remove the stabilizer bar (if so equipped).
6. Remove the shock absorber pinch bolt, then separate the hub carrier from the shock absorber.
7. Remove the lower control arm retaining bolts, then remove the arm.

Leaf Spring

REMOVAL & INSTALLATION

1981-83 Station Wagon Only

1. Raise the rear of the car and support it on stands placed on the frame. Remove the wheels.
2. Remove the shock absorber lower mounting bolt.
3. Remove the nuts from the U-bolt and remove the U-bolts, bump rubber, and clamp bracket.
4. Unbolt the front and rear spring shackle bolts, remove the bolts, and remove the spring.
5. To install, first position the spring on the axle and install the front and rear shackle bolts. Apply a soapy water solution to the bushings to ease installation. Do not tighten the shackle nuts yet.
6. Install the U-bolts, spring clamp bracket and bump rubber loosely on the axle and spring.
7. Install the wheels and lower the car. Tighten the front and rear shackle bolts to 33 ft. lbs. Also tighten the U-bolt nuts to 33 ft. lbs., after the shackle bolts have been tightened.
8. Install the shock absorber to the lower mount. Tighten to 33 ft. lbs.

Shock Absorbers

REMOVAL & INSTALLATION

1981-83 Station Wagon and 4wd Models Only

1. It is not necessary to jack the car or remove the wheels unless you require working clearance. Unbolt the

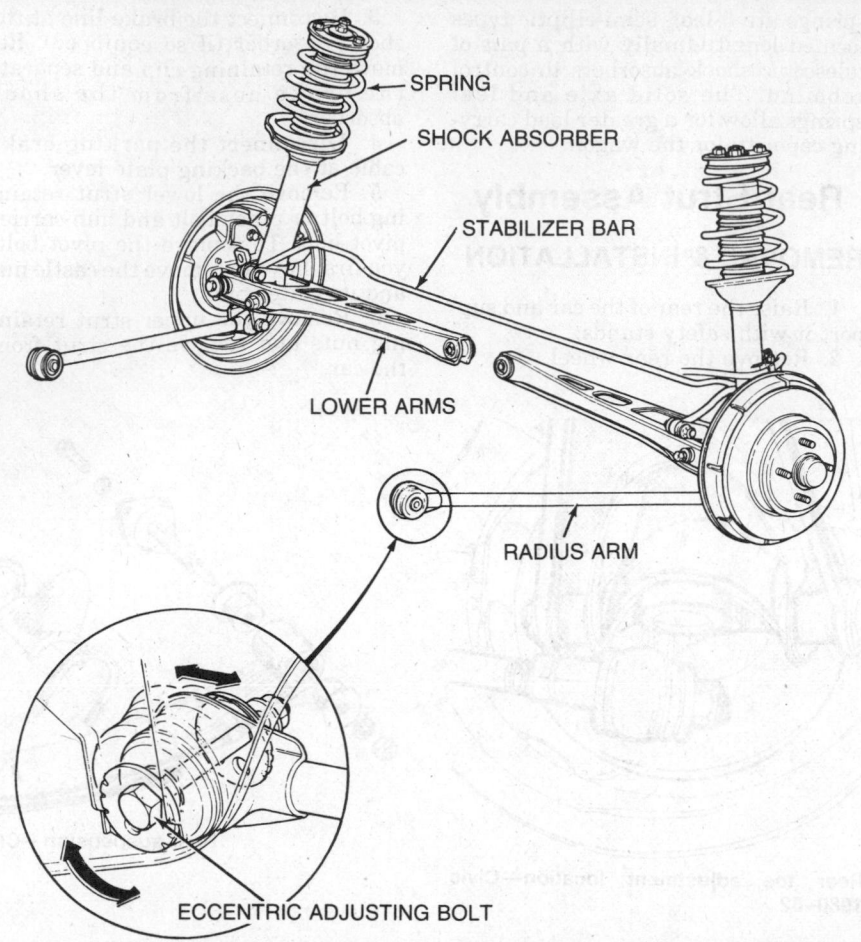

Rear suspension—Accord 1980–85 and Prelude 1983 and later

upper mounting nut and lower bolt and remove the shock absorber. Note the position of the washers and lock washers upon removal.
2. Installation is the reverse. Be sure the washers and lock washers are installed correctly. Tighten the upper mount to 44 ft. lbs. and the lower mount to 33 ft. lbs.

Rear Wheel Hub Bearings

REPLACEMENT

All except 1984-88 Civic and Prelude, and 1986-88 Accord.

1. Slightly loosen the rear lug nuts. Raise the car and support safely on jackstands.
2. Release the parking brake. Remove the rear wheels.
3. Remove the rear bearing hub cap and cotter pin and pin holder.
4. Remove the spindle nut, then pull the hub and drum off the spindle.
5. Drive the outboard inboard bearing races out of the hub. Punch in a

criss-cross pattern to avoid cocking the bearing race in the bore.
6. Clean the bearing seats thoroughly before going on to the next step.
7. Using a bearing driver, drive the inboard bearing race into the hub.
8. Turn the hub over and drive the outboard bearing race in the same way.
9. Check to see that the bearing races are seated properly.
10. When fitting new bearings, you must pack them with wheel bearing grease. To do this, place a glob of grease in your left palm, then, holding one of the bearings in your right hand, drag the face of the bearing heavily through the grease. This must be done to work as much grease as possible through the ball bearings and the cage. Turn the bearing and continue to pull it through the grease, until the grease is thoroughly packed between the bearing balls and the cage, all around the bearing. Repeat this operation until all of the bearings are packed with grease.
11. Pack the inside of the hub with a moderate amount of grease. Do not overload the hub with grease.

12. Apply a small amount of grease to the spindle and to the lip of the inner seal before installing.

13. Place the inboard bearings into the hub.

14. Apply grease to the hub seal, and carefully tap into place. Tap in a crisscross pattern to avoid cocking the seal in the bore.

15. Slip the hub and drum over the spindle, then insert the outboard bearing, hub, washer, and spindle nut.

16. Follow the procedures below under, "Adjustment".

1984-88 Prelude

1. Slightly loosen the rear lug nuts. Raise the car and support safely on jackstands.

2. Release the parking brake. Remove the rear wheels.

3. Remove the bolts retaining the brake caliper and remove the caliper from the knuckle. Do not let the caliper hang by the brake hose, support it with a length of wire.

4. Remove the rear bearing hub cap and cotter pin and pin holder. Remove the spindle nut, then pull the hub and disc off of the spindle.

5. Drive the outboard and inboard bearing races out of the disc. Punch in a criss-cross pattern to avoid cocking the bearing race in the bore.

6. Clean the bearing seats thoroughly before going on to the next step.

7. Using a bearing driver, drive the inboard bearing race into the disc.

8. Turn the disc over and drive the outboard bearing race in the same way.

9. Check to see that the bearing races are seated properly.

10. When fitting new bearings, you must pack them with wheel bearing grease. To do this, place a glob of grease in your left palm, then, holding one of the bearings in your right hand, drag the face of the bearing heavily through the grease. This must be done to work as much grease as possible through the ball bearings and the cage. Turn the bearing and continue to pull it through the grease, until the grease is thoroughly packed between the bearing balls and the cage, all around the bearing. Repeat this operation until all of the bearings are packed with grease.

11. Pack the inside of the hub with a moderate amount of grease. Do not overload the hub with grease.

12. Apply a small amount of grease to the spindle and to the lip of the inner seal before installing.

13. Place the inboard bearing into the hub.

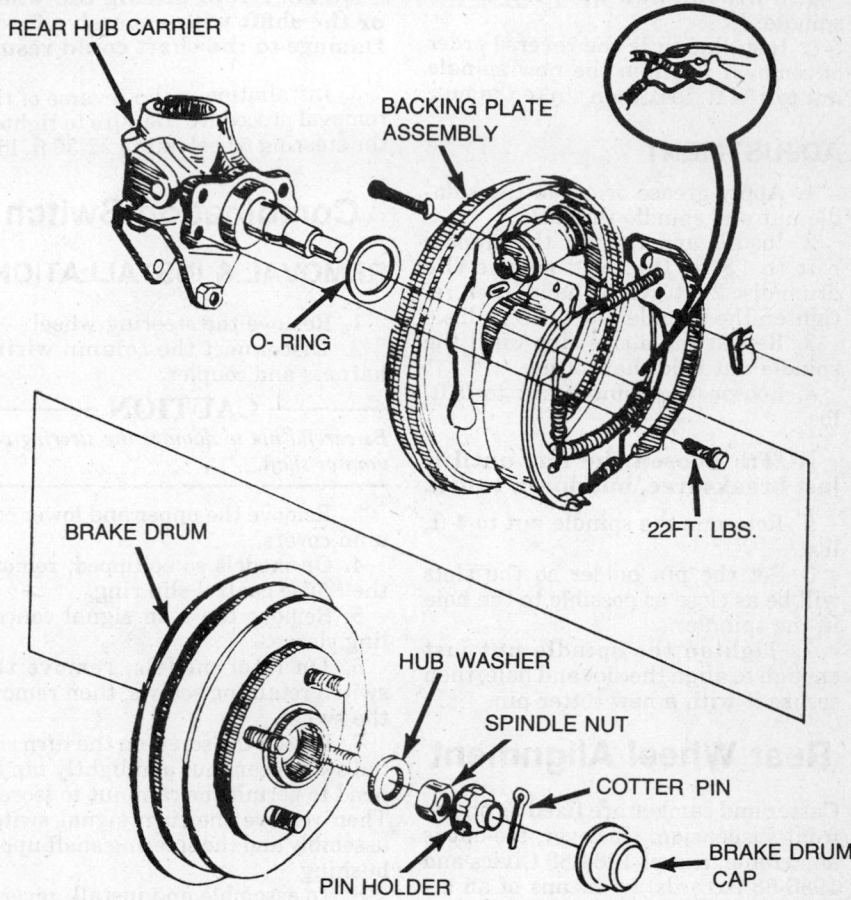

Rear hub and bearing—all except 1984 and later Civic and Prelude, and 1986 and later Accord

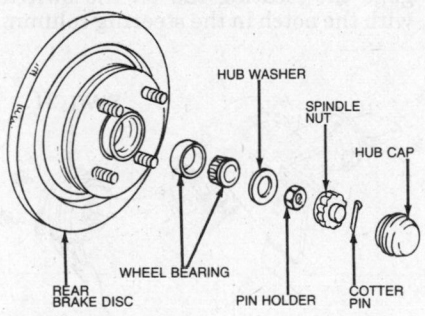

Rear hub and bearing–Prelude 1984 and later

14. Apply grease to the hub seal, and carefully tap into place. Tap in a crisscross pattern to avoid cocking the seal in the bore.

15. Slip the hub and disc over the spindle, then insert the outboard bearing, hub washer, and spindle nut.

16. Follow the procedures below for adjustment.

1984-88 Civic
1986-88 Accord

1. Slightly loosen the rear lug nuts. Raise the car and support safely on jackstands.

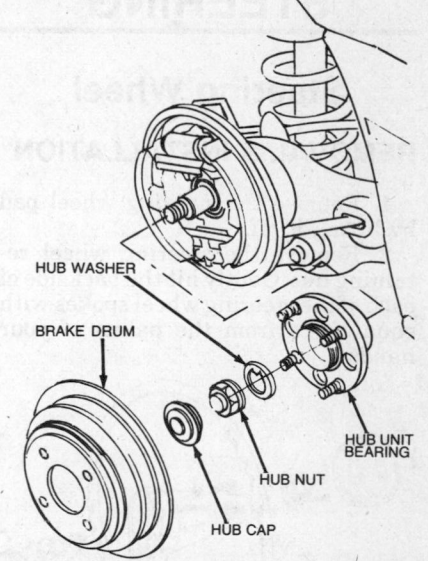

Rear hub and bearing—Civic 1984 and later, and Accord 1986 and later

2. Release the parking brake. Remove the rear wheel and the brake drum.

3. Remove the rear bearing hub cap and nut.

4. Pull the hub unit off of the spindle.

5. Installation is the reverse order of removal. Tighten the new spindle nut to 134 ft. lbs., then stake the nut.

ADJUSTMENT

1. Apply grease or oil on the spindle nut and spindle threads.

2. Install and tighten the spindle nut to 18 ft. lbs. and rotate the drum/disc 2-3 turns by hand, then retighten the spindle nut to 18 ft. lbs.

3. Repeat the above step until the spindle nut hold that torque.

4. Loosen the spindle nut to 0 ft. lbs.

NOTE: Loosen the nut until it just breaks free, but doesn't turn.

5. Retorque the spindle nut to 4 ft. lbs.

6. Set the pin holder so the slots will be as close as possible to the hole in the spindle.

7. Tighten the spindle nut just enough to align the slot and hole, then secure it with a new cotter pin.

Rear Wheel Alignment

Caster and camber are fixed as on the front suspension. However, toe-out is adjustable (except 1984-88 Civics and 1986-88 Accords) by means of an eccentric adjusting bolt at the forward anchor of the radius rod.

STEERING

Steering Wheel

REMOVAL & INSTALLATION

1. Remove the steering wheel pad by lifting it off.

2. Remove the steering wheel retaining nut. Gently hit the backside of each of the steering wheel spokes with equal force from the palms of your hands.

NOTE: Avoid hitting the wheel or the shaft with excessive force. Damage to the shaft could result.

3. Installation is the reverse of the removal procedure. Be sure to tighten the steering wheel nut to 22-36 ft. lbs.

Combination Switch

REMOVAL & INSTALLATION

1. Remove the steering wheel.
2. Disconnect the column wiring harness and coupler.

——————— CAUTION ———————

Be careful not to damage the steering column or shaft.

3. Remove the upper and lower column covers.

4. On models so equipped, remove the cruise control slip ring.

5. Remove the turn signal cancelling sleeve.

6. On later models, remove the switch retaining screws, then remove the switch.

7. Loosen the screw on the turn signal switch cam nut and lightly tap its head to permit the cam nut to loosen. Then remove the turn signal switch assembly and the steering shaft upper bushing.

8. To assemble and install, reverse the above procedure. When installing the turn signal switch assembly, engage the locating tab on the switch with the notch in the steering column.

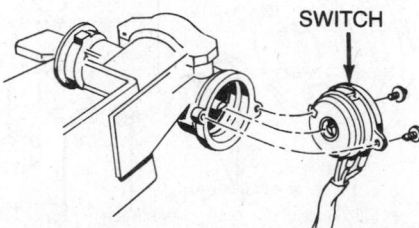

Ignition switch removal—1982 and later Accord, 1984 and later Civic and 1983 and later Prelude.

The steering shaft upper bushing should be installed with the flat side facing the upper side of the column. The alignment notch for the turn signal switch will be centered on the flat side of the bushing.

NOTE: On earlier models, if the cam nut has been removed, be sure to install it with the small end up.

Ignition Switch

REMOVAL & INSTALLATION

1. Remove the steering column housing lower cover.

2. Disconnect the ignition switch wiring at the couplers.

3. The ignition switch assembly is held onto the column by two shear bolts. Remove these bolts, using a drill, to separate and remove the ignition switch.

4. To install, reverse the removal procedure. You will have to replace the shear bolts with new ones.

On 1982-88 Accords, 1983-88 Preludes, and 1984-88 Civics, the mechanical part of the switch does not have to be removed to replace the electrical part. To remove the electrical part or base of the switch proceed as follows:

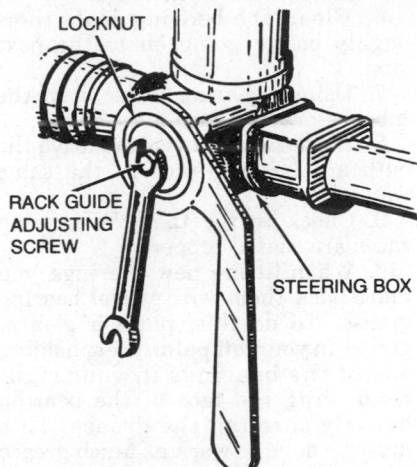

Steering box adjustment

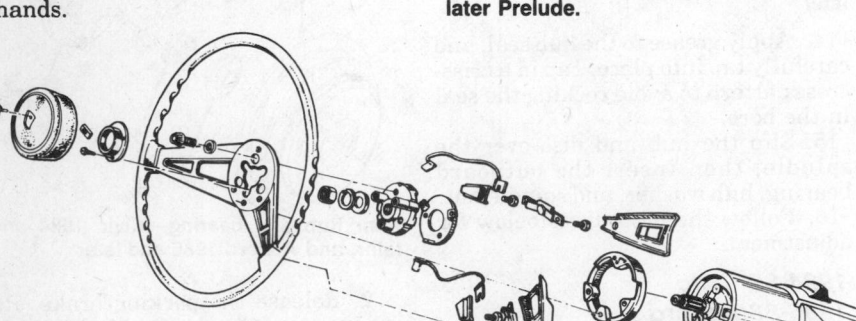

Typical exploded view of steering wheel and related parts

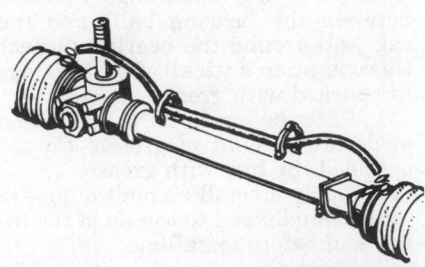

Separate the air tube from the dust boot

1. Remove the steering column lower cover.

2. Disconnect the electrical connector at the switch.

3. Insert the key and turn it to lock position.

4. Remove the two switch retaining screws, then remove the switch (base) from the rest of the switch.

Manual Steering Gear

TESTING

1. Remove the dust seal bellows retaining bands and slide the dust seals off the left and right side of the gearbox housing.

2. Turn the front wheels full left and using your hand, attempt to move the steering rack in an up-down direction.

3. Repeat with the wheel turned full right.

4. If any movement is felt, the steering gearbox must be adjusted.

ADJUSTMENT

Civic

1. Make sure that the rack is well lubricated.

2. Loosen the rack guide adjusting locknut.

3. Tighten the adjusting screw just to less than 36 inch lbs. (less than 48 inch lbs. on variable ration steering).

4. Back off the adjusting screw 25° ± 5° (15° –3° on variable ratio steering) and hold it in that position while adjusting the locknut to 18 ft. lbs. (60 ft. lbs. on variable ratio steering).

5. Recheck the play, and then move the wheels lock-to-lock, to make sure that the rack moves freely.

6. Check the steering force by first raising the front wheels and then placing them in a straight ahead position. Turn the steering wheel with a spring scale to check the steering force. Steering force should be no more than 3.3 lbs.

CRX

1. Make sure that the rack is well lubricated.

2. Loosen the rack guide adjusting locknut.

3. Tighten the adjusting screw just to 36 inch lbs.

4. Back off the adjusting screw 1/10 of a turn and hold it in that position while adjusting the locknut to 18 ft. lbs.

5. Recheck the play, and then move the wheels lock-to-lock, to make sure that the rack moves freely.

6. Check the steering force by first raising the front wheels and then placing them in a straight ahead position. Turn the steering wheel with a spring scale to check the steering force. Steering force should be no more than 3.3 lbs.

REMOVAL & INSTALLATION

Civic and CRX

1. Raise and support the front end on jackstands.

2. Unbolt and separate the steering shaft at the coupling.

3. Remove the front wheels.

4. Using a ball joint tool disconnect the tie rod ends.

5. On cars with manual transmissions:

• Disconnect the shift lever torque rod from the clutch housing.

• Slide the pin retainer out of the way, drive out the spring pin and disconnect the shift rod.

6. On cars with automatic transmissions, remove the shift cable guide from the floor and pull the shift cable down by hand.

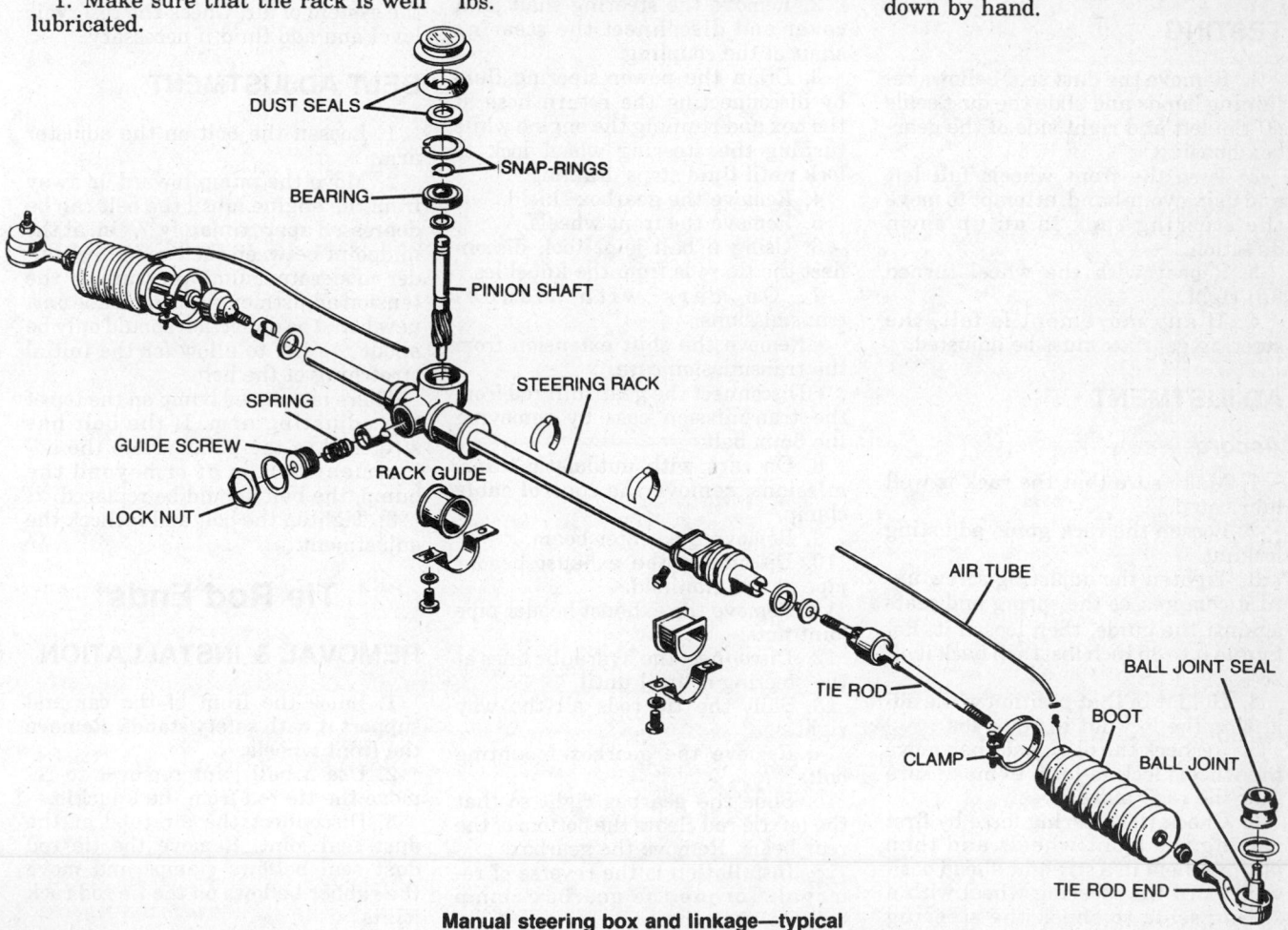

Manual steering box and linkage—typical

Tie rod lockwasher removal

7. Remove the two nut connecting the exhaust header pipe to the exhaust pipe and move the exhaust pipe out of the way.

8. Push the rack all the way to the right and remove the gearbox brackets.

9. Drop the gearbox far enough to permit the end of the pinion shaft to come out of the hole in the frame channel, then rotate it forward until the shaft is pointing rearward.

10. Slide the gearbox to the right until the left tie rod clears the exhaust pipe, then drop it down and out of the car to the left.

11. Installation is the reverse of removal. Torque the mounting bracket bolts to 29 ft. lbs.

Power Steering Gear

TESTING

1. Remove the dust seal bellows retaining bands and slide the dust seals off the left and right side of the gearbox housing.

2. Turn the front wheels full left and using your hand, attempt to move the steering rack in an up-down direction.

3. Repeat with the wheel turned full right.

4. If any movement is felt, the steering gearbox must be adjusted.

ADJUSTMENT

Accord

1. Make sure that the rack is well lubricated.

2. Loosen the rack guide adjusting locknut.

3. Tighten the adjusting screw until it compresses the spring and seats against the guide, then loosen it. Retorque it to 35 inch lbs. then back it off 25°.

4. Hold it in that position while adjusting the locknut to 18 ft. lbs.

5. Recheck the play, and then move the wheels lock-to-lock, to make sure that the rack moves freely.

6. Check the steering force by first raising the front wheels and then placing them in a straight ahead position. Turn the steering wheel with a spring scale to check the steering force. Steering force should be no more than 4 lbs.

Prelude

1. Make sure that the rack is well lubricated.

2. Loosen the rack guide adjusting locknut.

3. Tighten the adjusting screw until it compresses the spring and seats against the guide, then loosen it. Retorque it to 24 inch lbs. then back it off 25°.

4. Hold it in that position while adjusting the locknut to 18 ft. lbs.

5. Recheck the play, and then move the wheels lock-to-lock, to make sure that the rack moves freely.

6. Check the steering force by first raising the front wheels and then placing them in a straight ahead position. Turn the steering wheel with a spring scale to check the steering force. Steering force should be no more than 4 lbs.

REMOVAL & INSTALLATION

Accord and Prelude

1. Raise and support the front end on jackstands.

2. Remove the steering shaft joint cover and disconnect the steering shaft at the coupling.

3. Drain the power steering fluid by disconnecting the return hose at the box and running the engine while turning the steering wheel lock to lock until fluid stops draining.

4. Remove the gearbox shield.

5. Remove the front wheels.

6. Using a ball joint tool, disconnect the tie rods from the knuckles.

7. On cars with manual transmissions:
• Remove the shift extension from the transmission case.
• Disconnect the gear shift rod from the transmission case by removing the 8mm bolt.

8. On cars with automatic transmissions, remove the control cable clamp.

9. Remove the center beam.

10. Disconnect the exhaust header pipe at the manifold.

11. Remove the exhaust header pipe joint nuts.

12. Disconnect the hydraulic lines at the steering control until.

13. Shift the tie rods all the way right.

14. Remove the gearbox mounting bolts.

15. Slide the gearbox right so that the left tie rod clears the bottom of the rear beam. Remove the gearbox.

16. Installation is the reverse of removal. Torque the gearbox clamp bolts to 16 ft. lbs.

Power Steering Pump

REMOVAL & INSTALLATION

1. Drain the fluid from the system: Disconnect the cooler return hose from the reservoir and place the end in a large container. Start the engine and allow it to run at fast idle. Turn the steering wheel from lock to lock several times, until fluid stops running from the hose. Shut off the engine and discard the fluid. Reattach the hose.

2. Disconnect the inlet and outlet hoses at the pump.

3. Remove the drive belt.

4. Remove the bolts and remove the pump.

5. To install, install the pump on its mounts, install the belt, adjust belt tension, and install the fluid hoses.

6. Fill the reservoir with fresh fluid, to the full mark. Use only genuine Honda power steering fluid; ATF or other brands of fluid will damage the system.

7. Start the engine and allow to fast idle. Turn the steering wheel from side to side several times, lightly contacting the stops. This will bleed the system of air. Check the reservoir level and add fluid if necessary.

BELT ADJUSTMENT

1. Loosen the bolt on the adjuster arm.

2. Move the pump toward or away from the engine, until the belt can be depressed approximately $9/16$ in. at the midpoint between the two pulleys under moderate thumb pressure. If the tension adjustment is being made on a new belt, the deflection should only be about $7/16$ in., to allow for the initial stretching of the belt.

There is a raised bump on the top of the adjusting arm. If the belt has stretched to the point where the adjustment bolt is at or beyond the bump, the belt should be replaced.

3. Tighten the bolt and recheck the adjustment.

Tie Rod Ends

REMOVAL & INSTALLATION

1. Raise the front of the car and support it with safety stands. Remove the front wheels.

2. Use a ball joint remover to remove the tie rod from the knuckle.

3. Disconnect the air tube at the dust seal joint. Remove the tie rod dust seal bellows clamps and move the rubber bellows on the tie rod rack joints.

4. Straighten the tie rod lockwasher tabs at the tie rod-to-rack joint and remove the tie rod by turning it with a wrench.

5. To install, reverse the removal procedure. Always use a new tie rod lockwasher during reassembly. Fit the locating lugs into the slots on the rack and bend the outer edge of the washer over the flat part of the rod, after the tie rod nut has been properly tightened.

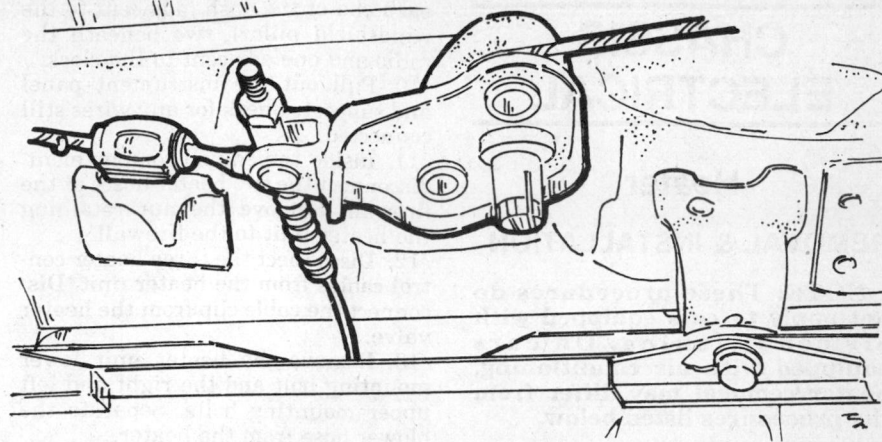

Parking brake equalizer assembly

BRAKE SYSTEM

For all brake system repair and service procedures not detailed below, please refer to "Brakes" in the Unit Repair section.

Master Cylinder

REMOVAL & INSTALLATION

———— CAUTION ————
Before removing the master cylinder, cover the body surfaces with fender covers and rags to prevent damage to painted surfaces by brake fluid.

1. Disconnect and plug the brake lines at the master cylinder.
2. Remove the master cylinder-to-vacuum booster attaching bolts and remove the master cylinder from the car.
3. To install, reverse the removal procedure. Before operating the car, you must bleed the brake system.

Power Brake Booster

INSPECTION

A preliminary check of the vacuum booster can be made as follows:
a. Depress the brake pedal several times using normal pressure. Make sure that the pedal height does not vary.
b. Hold the pedal in the depressed position and start the engine. The pedal should drop slightly.
c. Hold the pedal in the above position and stop the engine. The pedal should stay in the depressed position for approximately 30 seconds.
d. If the pedal does not drop when the engine is started or rises after the engine is stopped, the booster is not functioning properly.

REMOVAL & INSTALLATION

1. Disconnect the vacuum hose at the booster.
2. Disconnect and plug the brake lines at the master cylinder.
3. Remove the brake pedal-to-booster link pin and the four nuts retaining the booster. The pushrod and nuts are located inside the car under the instrument panel.
4. Remove the booster with the master cylinder attached.
5. To install, reverse the removal procedure. Check the vacuum booster pushrod-to-master cylinder piston clearance as outlined in the master cylinder removal procedure. Don't forget to bleed the brake system before operating the car.

Wheel Cylinder

REMOVAL & INSTALLATION

1. Remove the brake drum and shoes.
2. Disconnect the parking brake cable and brake lines at the backing plate. Be sure to have a drip pan to catch the brake fluid.
3. Remove the two wheel cylinders retaining nuts on the inboard side of the backing plate and remove the wheel cylinder.
4. To install, reverse the removal procedure. When assembling, apply a thin coat of grease to the grooves of the wheel cylinder piston and the sliding surfaces of the backing plate. Bleed the brakes.

Parking Brake Cable

REMOVAL & INSTALLATION

1. Remove the adjusting nut from the equalizer mounted on the rear axle, or in the console on (1982-88 Accords, 1983-88 Preludes, and 1984-88 Civics) and separate the cable from the equalizer.
2. Set the parking brake lever to a fully released position and remove the cotter pin from the side of the brake lever.
3. After removing the cotter pin, pull out the pin which connects the cable and the lever.
4. Detach the cable from the guides at the front and right side of the fuel tank and remove the cable.
5. To install, reverse the removal procedure, making sure that grease is applied to the cable and the guides.

ADJUSTMENT

Inspect the following items:
a. Check the ratchet for wear.
b. Check the cables for wear or damage and the cable guide and equalizer for looseness.
c. Check the equalizer cable where it contracts the equalizer and apply grease if necessary.
d. Check the rear brake adjustment.
1. Block the front wheels and jack up the rear of the car. Support the car on jackstands.
2. Loosen the adjusting nut, located in the console on (1982-88 Accords, 1983-88 Preludes, and 1984-88 Civics) and at the equalizer, between the lower control arms on the other models.
3. Pull the parking brake lever up one notch.
4. Tighten the adjusting nut until the rear brakes drag slightly.
5. Release the brake lever and check that the rear brakes do not drag.
6. The rear brakes should be locked when the handbrake lever is pulled 4-8 notches on the Civic, CRX and Prelude; 7-11 notches on the Accord.

CHASSIS ELECTRICAL

Heater

REMOVAL & INSTALLATION

NOTE: These procedures do not apply to cars equipped with air conditioning. On cars equipped with air conditioning, heater removal may differ from the procedures listed below.

Civic

1. Drain the radiator.
2. Remove the dashboard.
3. Disconnect both heater hoses at the firewall and drain the coolant into a container.
4. Remove the heater lower mounting nut on the firewall.
5. Remove the two heater duct retaining clips or bolts.
6. Disconnect the control cables from the heater.
7. Remove the heater valve cable cover and remove the heater assembly.
8. Installation is the reverse of removal. Bleed cooling system and make sure cables are properly adjusted.

Accord

1981-85

NOTE: To remove the heater core, it is necessary to first remove the entire instrument panel and heater assemblies.

1. Drain the cooling system.
2. Remove the steering column lower trim cover.
3. Remove the two nuts and two bolts retaining the column to the firewall support.
4. Remove the instrument wire harnesses from cabin wire harness couples.
5. Reach behind the instrument cluster and disconnect the speedometer cable and four wiring harness connectors at rear of cluster. Pry out the lock tabs to disconnect.
6. Disconnect radio lead and antenna wire.
7. Remove the heater fan switch knob, heater lever knobs and heater control bezel. Remove heater control center panel. Disconnect cigarette lighter and blower motor leads.
8. Disconnect clock leads.
9. Remove the seven sheet metal screws retaining the instrument panel to the firewall. There are two at

each end of the dash (adjacent to the windshield pillar), two beneath the radio and one adjacent to the clock.
10. Pull out the instrument panel and support. Check for any wires still connected.
11. Inside the engine compartment, disconnect the two heater hoses at the firewall. Remove the nut retaining the heater unit to the firewall.
12. Disconnect the three heater control cables from the heater unit. Disconnect the cable clip from the heater valve.
13. Remove the heater unit lower mounting bolt and the right and left upper mounting bolts. Separate the blower hose from the heater.
14. Lay some towels underneath to catch residual coolant leakage. Remove the heater unit.
15. To service the heater core, separate the heater housing halves.
16. Reverse the above to install. Bleed the cooling system using the bleed bolt located near the ignition distributor.

1986-88

1. Drain coolant from the bottom of the radiator and collect it for re-use. Put a drain pan underneath the hose connections at the firewall, carefully note hose locations, and then disconnect those two connections.
2. Disconnect the heater valve cable from the heater valve. Remove the two lower heater mounting nuts.
3. On pushbutton type heaters, disconnect the cool vent cable at the heater. On lever type heaters, disconnect the function cable and the air mix cable at the heater.
4. Remove the dashboard.
5. Remove the heater duct (lever type) or ducts (pushbutton type).
6. On pushbutton type heaters, disconnect the air mix cable at the heater and the wiring harness at the connector.
7. Remove the four heater mounting bolts and pull the heater away from its mounts.
8. Install in reverse order, noting these points:

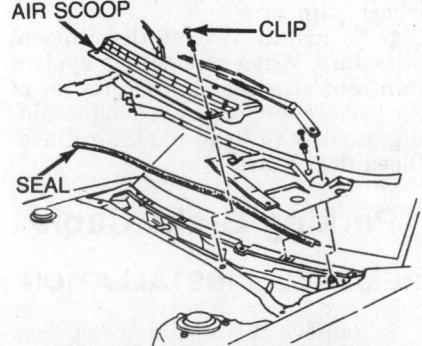

Front air scoop removal—typical

a. Apply sealant to all grommets.
b. Check routing of inlet and outlet hoses to the heater core to make sure they are not reversed. Install clamps in proper positions and make sure they are securely tightened.
c. Refill and then bleed the cooling system with the bleed bolt.
d. Make sure all door operating cables are securely connected and adjusted for proper door operation.

Prelude

1981-82

1. Remove the blower by removing the instrument panel slide cover.
2. Remove the glove box and the three blower mounting bolts.
3. Remove the blower from the heater case.
4. Drain the coolant.
5. Remove the lower dash panel.
6. Place a drain pan under the case and disconnect both heater hoses at the core tubes.
7. Remove the heater lower mount nut on the firewall.
8. Disconnect the cable at the water valve.
9. Remove the control cables from the heater case.
10. Remove the upper mount bolts and remove the heater.

Heater Core

REMOVAL & INSTALLATION

NOTE: Only the 1983-88 Prelude models may have the heater core replaced without removing the heater assembly.

1983-88 Prelude

1. Drain the cooling system. Remove the heater pipe cover and heater pipe clamps.
2. Remove the heater core retaining plate.
3. Pull the cotter pin out of the hose clamp joint and separate the heater pipes.

NOTE: Engine coolant will drain from the heater pipes when they are disconnected. Place a drip pan under the pipes to catch the coolant.

4. When all the coolant has drained from the heater core, remove it from the heater housing.
5. Installation is the reverse of the removal procedure, please note the following:
a. Replace the hose clamps with new ones.

b. Turn the cotter pin in the hose clamps tightly to prevent leaking coolant.

c. Fill the cooling system with coolant and open the bleed bolt until coolant begins to flow from it. Tighten the bolt when all the air has escaped from the system.

Blower Motor

REMOVAL & INSTALLATION

1983-88 Prelude
1986-88 Accord

1. Remove the three lower retaining screws for the glovebox. Then, push down and remove the glovebox. Remove the three screws for the glovebox ceiling, and remove the ceiling.

2. Disconnect the fresh air control cable from the blower housing. Disconnect the blower leads.

3. Remove the three bolts retaining the blower housing to the firewall. Separate the heater duct hose from the blower housing, and remove the blower housing.

4. To service the blower motor, separate the blower housing halves.

5. Reverse the above procedures to install.

Radio

REMOVAL & INSTALLATION

NOTE: Never operate the radio without a speaker; severe damage to the output transistors will result. If the speaker must be replaced, use a speaker of the correct impedance (ohms) or else the output transistors will be damaged and require replacement.

Civic

1. Remove the screw which holds the rear radio bracket to the back tray underneath the instrument panel. Then remove the wing nut which holds the radio to the bracket and remove the bracket.

2. Remove the control knobs, hex nuts, and trim plate from the radio control shafts.

3. Disconnect the antenna and speaker leads, the bullet type radio fuse, and the white lead connected directly over the radio opening.

4. Drop the radio out, bottom first, through the package tray.

5. To install, reverse the removal procedure. When inserting the radio

through the package tray, be sure the bottom side is up and the control shafts are facing toward the engine. Otherwise, you will not be able to position the radio properly through its opening.

Accord and Prelude

1. Remove the center lower trim panel beneath the radio. Then remove the three radio lower bracket retaining screws.

2. Pull off the radio knobs and remove the radio shaft nuts.

3. Remove the heater fan switch knob, the heater lever knobs, the heater control bezel, and the heater control center trim panel. Disconnect the cigarette lighter leads.

4. Pull out the radio from the front, and disconnect the power, speaker, and antenna leads.

5. Reverse the above to install.

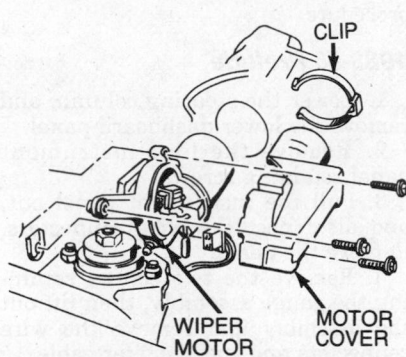

Windshield wiper motor installation

Windshield Wiper Motor

REMOVAL & INSTALLATION

1. Remove the negative (–) cable from the battery.

2. Remove the wiper arm retaining nuts and remove the wiper arms.

3. Remove the front air scoop (if so equipped) and hood seal located over the wiper linkage at the bottom of the windshield.

4. Disconnect the linkage from the wiper motor.

5. Remove the wiper motor water seal cover clamp, and remove the cover (if so equipped).

6. Disconnect the wiper motor electrical connector, remove the motor mounting bolts and remove the motor.

7. Installation is the reverse of the removal procedure. Coat the linkage joints with grease and make sure the linkage moves smoothly.

Windshield Wiper Switch

REMOVAL & INSTALLATION

The windshield wiper switch is a function of the Combination Switch, details for which are included above.

Instrument Cluster

REMOVAL & INSTALLATION

All except Civics, 1982-88
Accord and 1983-88 Prelude

METER CASE ASSEMBLY

1. Remove the three meter case mounting wing nuts from the rear of the instrument panel.

2. Disconnect the speedometer and tachometer drive cables at the engine.

3. Pull the meter case away from the panel. Disconnect the meter wires at the connectors.

NOTE: Be sure to label the wires to avoid confusion during reassembly.

4. Disconnect the speedometer and tachometer cables at the meter case and remove the case from the car.

5. To install, reverse the removal procedure.

SWITCH PANEL

1. Loosen the four steering wheel column cover screws and remove the upper and lower covers.

2. Remove the four steering column bolts (remove the upper two bolts first) and rest the steering assembly on the floor.

3. Remove the four switch panel screws from the rear of the instrument panel.

4. To release the switch panel, remove the switches in the following manner:

a. Remove the light switch by prying the cover off the front of the knob. Pinch the retaining tabs together and pull off the knob.

b. Remove the wiper switch by pushing the knob in and turning counterclockwise. Then remove the retaining nut.

c. Remove the choke knob by loosening the set screw. Then remove the retaining nut.

5. To install, reverse the removal procedure.

Civic 1981-83

1. On 1981 models remove the steering column.

2. On 1982-83 models lower the steering column.

3. On 1981 models remove the bulb access panel and remove the two upper mounting screws through the access panel; then the lower mounting bolt and screws.

4. On 1982-83 models, remove the four screws and trim cover.

5. Disconnect the speedometer cable and tachometer cable if so equipped.

6. Disconnect any remaining mount screws and wire connectors and remove the instrument panel.

7. Installation is the reverse of removal.

1984-88 Civic Coupe (CRX)

1. Remove the screws and clips that retain the lower dash panel and remove the panel.

2. Remove the heater lower control knob and the lower panel.

3. Remove the heater control mount screws and the upper screws in the instrument panel.

4. Pull the panel out and disconnect the wire connectors. Remove the instrument panel.

5. Remove the 4 screws, then lift out the gauge assembly so that you can disconnect the wire connectors.

6. Disconnect the speedometer cable, then remove the gauge assembly.

7. To install, reverse the removal procedure.

1984-88 Civic Hatchback and Sedan
1986-88 Accord

1. Remove the upper instrument panel caps and the 4 screws, then remove the panel.

2. Remove the 4 screws retaining the gauge assembly, then lift out the gauge assembly so you can disconnect the wire connectors.

3. Disconnect the speedometer cable and remove the gauge assembly.

4. To install, reverse the removal procedure.

1984-88 Civic Wagon

1. Remove the screws and the dashboard lower panel, this allows access to the four instrument panel retaining bolts.

2. Remove the four instrument panel retaining bolts, raise the panel

and disconnect the wire connectors and the speedometer cable. Remove the instrument panel with the gauge assembly.

3. The gauge assembly may be separated from the instrument panel by removing the four screws.

4. To install, reverse the removal procedure.

1982-85 Accord

1. Lower the steering column.

2. Remove the three screws at the top of the instrument panel.

3. Pull the instrument panel out, then disconnect the wire connectors and remove the panel.

4. Remove the four screws that hold the gauge assembly in place, then lift up on the panel so you can reach the wire connectors.

5. Disconnect the wire connectors and the speedometer cable, then remove the gauge assembly.

6. To install, reverse the removal procedure.

1983-88 Prelude

1. Lower the steering column, and remove the lower dashboard panel.

2. Remove the four instrument panel retaining screws.

3. Pull the instrument panel out, and disconnect the wire connectors. Remove the panel.

4. Remove the two screws retaining the gauge assembly, then lift out the assembly and remove the wire connectors and speedometer cable.

5. Installation is the reverse of the removal procedure.

Headlight Switch

REMOVAL & INSTALLATION

The headlight switch is a function of the Combination Switch, details for which are included above.

Stoplight Switch

REMOVAL & INSTALLATION

The brake light switch is mounted on a bracket at the top of the brake pedal. Switch action is controlled by pedal movement. To remove the switch,

simply disconnect the wires, loosen the locknut and unscrew the switch.

However, the position of the switch control the brake pedal height. If the switch is removed, pedal height must be adjusted when the switch is installed. Adjust the pedal height as follows:

1. Position the switch in the bracket, with the locknut loose and the plunger not touching the pedal arm.

2. Turn the plunger with pliers until the height of the pedal pad above the nearest point of the floor is:
• Civic hatchback and sedan: 174mm
• Civic wagon: 168mm
• CRX: 174mm
• Accord: 205mm
• Prelude: 176mm

Fuses and Fusible Links

LOCATION

All models are equipped with a fusible link connected between the starter relay and the main wiring harness of the car, located next to the battery.

The 1981-83 Civic fuse box is located below the glove compartment, on the right bulkhead. The 1984 and later Civic fuse box is located under a flip down door, under the dashboard on the left side of the instrument panel. The rating and function of each fuse is posted inside the fuse box cap for quick reference.

The 1981-82 Accord and Prelude fuse box is a flip down door, located under the left side of the instrument panel. The 1983-88 Accord and Prelude fuse box is located behind a flip down door, under the dashboard on the left side of the instrument panel.

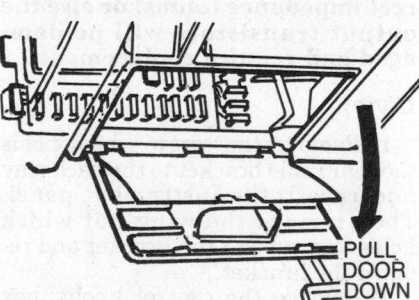

Fuse box location—1982 and later Accord, 1984 and later Civic

Hyundai
Excel

6

SERIAL NUMBER IDENTIFICATION

Vehicle Identification Plate

The vehicle identification number (VIN) is located on a plate attached to the left front of the dash panel so it can be seen through the windshield when you stand beside the car, in front of the driver's door.

The letters and numbers in the VIN digits can be interpreted according to their positions in the sequence as follows:
1. Manufacturing country
2. Make
3. Vehicle type
4. Type of seat belt system
5. Vehicle line
6. Trim Code/Price Class
7. Body type
8. Engine displacement

9. Check digit—a special letter or number code used to verify the serial number. This contains no useful information for the car owner.
10. Model year
11. Plant where the car was built
12. Transmission code

Engine number location

Engine Identification

The engine model and serial numbers in all cases are stamped on the top edge of the block near the front of the engine. In most cases, they are located on the right side of the engine.

Vehicle Identification Label

The Vehicle Identification Lable is located on the top center of the firewall in the engine compartment.

Transmission Number

On all models, the basic transmission model number is stamped on the Vehicle Information Code Plate, located on the engine compartment side of the firewall.

The manual transaxle serial number is stamped on the clutch of the transaxle case.

On automatic transaxle models, the number is on a plate attached to the side of the transmission, or stamped on the boss of the oil pan flange.

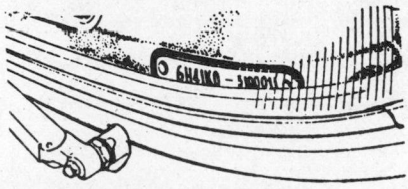

Serial number location

Engine model number

ENGINE IDENTIFICATION

Year	Model	Engine Displacement cu. in. (cc/liter)	Engine Series Identification	No. of Cylinders	Engine Type
1986	Excel	89.6 (1468/1.5)	—	4	OHC
1987-88	Excel	89.6 (1468/1.5)	—	4	OHC

GENERAL ENGINE SPECIFICATIONS

Year	Model	Engine Displacement cu. in. (cc)	Fuel System Type	Net Horsepower @ rpm	Net Torque @ rpm (ft. lbs.)	Bore × Stroke (in.)	Compression Ratio	Oil Pressure @ rpm
1986	Excel	89.6 (1468)	2 bbl	77 @ 5300	84 @ 3000	2.97 × 3.38	9.4:1	45@2000
1987-88	Excel	89.6 (1468)	2 bbl	77 @ 5300	84 @ 3000	2.97 × 3.38	9.4:1	45@2000

TUNE-UP SPECIFICATIONS

Year	Model	Engine Displacement cu. in. (cc)	Spark Plugs Type	Gap (in.)	Ignition Timing (deg.) MT	Ignition Timing (deg.) AT	Compression Pressure (psi)	Fuel Pump (psi)	Idle Speed (rpm) MT	Idle Speed (rpm) AT	Valve Clearance In.	Valve Clearance Ex.
1986	Excel	89.6 (1468)	RN9YC4	①	②	②	NA	2.5-3.5	③	③	0.059	0.098
1987	Excel	89.6 (1468)	RN9YC4	①	②	②	NA	2.5-3.5	③	③	0.059	0.098
1988	SEE UNDERHOOD SPECIFICATIONS STICKER											

NOTE: Valve clearance is set with the engine at normal operating temperature. On the USA Excel, the jet valve must be set before the intake valve. Jet valve clearance is 0.098 in.
① USA: 0.39-0.43; Canada: 0.27-0.31
② 49 states: 5B; California: 3B; Canada: 4B
③ USA MT: 700; AT: 750; Canada: 850

FIRING ORDERS

NOTE: To avoid confusion, always replace spark wires one at a time.

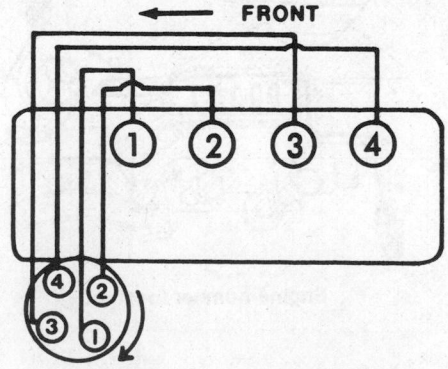

Firing order for the 1468cc engine

CAPACITIES

Year	Model	Engine Displacement cu. in. (cc)	Engine Crankcase with Filter	Engine Crankcase without Filter	Transmission (pts.) 4-Spd	Transmission (pts.) 5-Spd	Transmission (pts.) Auto.	Drive Axle (pts.)	Fuel Tank (gal.)	Cooling System (qts.)
1986	Excel	89.6 (1468)	4.0	—	3.5	3.5	4.0	—	10.4	4.1
1987-88	Excel	89.6 (1468)	3.5	—	3.5	3.5	4.0	—	10.4	4.1

CAMSHAFT SPECIFICATIONS
All measurements given in inches.

Year	Engine Displacement cu. in. (cc)	Journal Diameter 1	Journal Diameter 2	Journal Diameter 3	Journal Diameter 4	Journal Diameter 5	Lobe Lift In.	Lobe Lift Ex.	Bearing Clearance	Camshaft End Play
1986	89.6 (1468)	1.338	1.338	1.338	1.338	1.338	1.500	1.503	0.0019–0.0035	0.0019–0.0078
1987-88	89.6 (1468)	1.338	1.338	1.338	1.338	1.338	1.500	1.503	0.0019–0.0035	0.0019–0.0078

CRANKSHAFT AND CONNECTING ROD SPECIFICATIONS
All measurements are given in inches.

Year	Engine Displacement cu. in. (cc)	Crankshaft Main Brg. Journal Dia.	Crankshaft Main Brg. Oil Clearance	Crankshaft Shaft End-play	Crankshaft Thrust on No.	Connecting Rod Journal Diameter	Connecting Rod Oil Clearance	Connecting Rod Side Clearance
1986	89.6 (1468)	1.8897	0.00078–0.00279	0.0019–0.0070	3	1.6535	0.00039–0.00236	0.00393–0.00984
1987-88	89.6 (1468)	1.8897	0.00078–0.00279	0.0019–0.0070	3	1.6535	0.00039–0.00236	0.00393–0.00984

VALVE SPECIFICATIONS

Year	Engine Displacement cu. in. (cc)	Seat Angle (deg.)	Face Angle (deg.)	Spring Test Pressure (lbs. @ in.)	Spring Installed Height (in.)	Stem-to-Guide Clearance (in.) Intake	Stem-to-Guide Clearance (in.) Exhaust	Stem Diameter (in.) Intake	Stem Diameter (in.) Exhaust
1986	89.6 (1468)	45	45	53 @ 1.07	1.41	.00118–.00236	.00196–.00354	.2598	.2598
1987-88	89.6 (1468)	45	45	53 @ 1.07	1.41	.00118–.00236	.00196–.00354	.2598	.2598

PISTON AND RING SPECIFICATIONS
All measurments are given in inches.

Year	Engine Displacement cu. in. (cc)	Piston Clearance	Ring Gap Top Compression	Ring Gap Bottom Compression	Ring Gap Oil Control	Ring Side Clearance Top Compression	Ring Side Clearance Bottom Compression	Ring Side Clearance Oil Control
1986	89.6 (1468)	.00078–.00157	.0078–.0137	.0078–.0137	.0078–.0275	.00118–.0275	.00078–.00236	Snug
1987-88	89.6 (1468)	.00078–.00157	.0078–.0137	.0078–.0137	.0078–.0275	.00118–.0275	.00078–.00236	Snug

TORQUE SPECIFICATIONS
All readings in ft. lbs.

Year	Engine Displacement cu. in. (cc)	Cylinder Head Bolts	Main Bearing Bolts	Rod Bearing Bolts	Crankshaft Pulley Bolts	Flywheel Bolts	Manifold Intake	Manifold Exhaust	Spark Plugs
1986	89.6 (1468)	①	38	24	40	101	13	13	18
1987-88	89.6 (1468)	①	38	24	40	101	13	13	18

① Cold: 52 ft. lbs; warm: 60 ft. lbs.

BRAKE SPECIFICATIONS
All measurements in inches unless noted

Year	Model	Lug Nut Torque (ft. lbs.)	Master Cylinder Bore	Brake Disc Minimum Thickness	Brake Disc Maximum Runout	Standard Brake Drum Diameter	Minimum Lining Thickness Front	Minimum Lining Thickness Rear
1986	Excel	50-58 ②	.8125	.4488	.0059	7.086	.45	.04
1987-88	Excel	50-58 ②	.8125	.4488	.0059	7.1700	.45	.04

① Aluminum wheels: 67
② Aluminum wheels: 58-72

WHEEL ALIGNMENT

Year	Model	Caster Range (deg.)	Caster Preferred Setting (deg.)	Camber Range (deg.)	Camber Preferred Setting (deg.)	Toe-in (in.)	Steering Axis Inclination (deg.)
1986	Excel	½-1⅛	13/16	0-1P	½P	1/16-5/32	①
1987-88	Excel	½-1⅛	13/16	0-1P	½P	1/16-5/32	①

① Inside wheel: 35⅝; outside wheel: 29¼

TUNE-UP PROCEDURES

Electronic Ignition

RELUCTOR GAP ADJUSTMENT

The reluctor gap is adjustable on the Hitachi Electric distributor used in these engines. While service is not required as a part of normal maintenance, if you have worked on the distributor or if you suspect the reluctor gap might be incorrect because of ignition problems, you can check and adjust it.

1. Get a feeler gauge of non-magnetic material (brass, plastic or wood) of 0.031 in. thickness. Remove the distributor cap and rotor.

2. Rotate the engine (you can use a large socket wrench on the bolt that attaches the front pulley) until one of the prongs of the rotor is directly across from the igniter pickup.

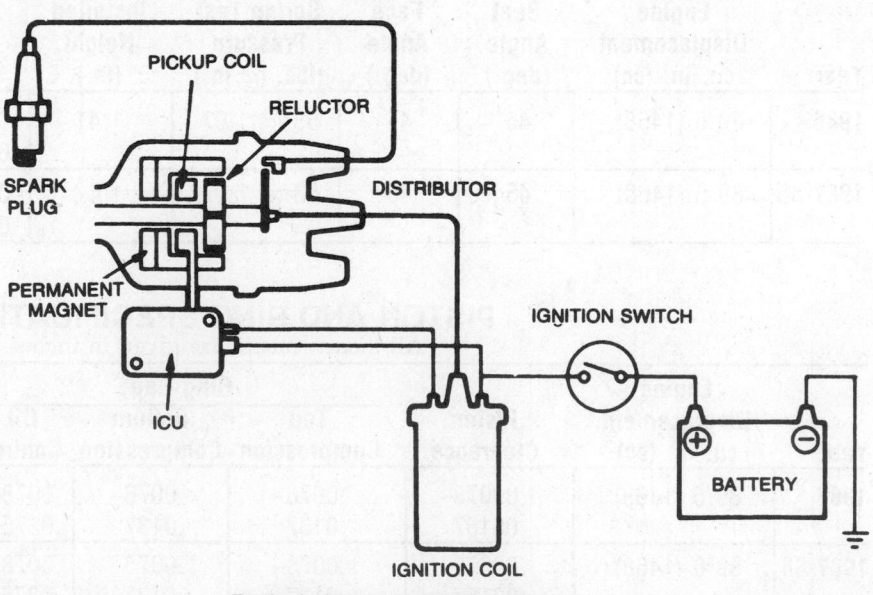

Typical electronic ignition circuit

3. Insert or attempt to insert the feeler gauge between the prong and pickup. If the gap is correct, there will be a very slight drag. If the gauge fits loosely or cannot be inserted, loosen both mounting screws and then (if necessary widen the gap) and insert the gauge. Slowly close the gap by pivoting the igniter assembly on the left screw and rotating it at the right side, where it's slotted. When the gauge is just touching, tighten first the right side screw and then the screw on the left. Recheck the gap and readjust (if necessary). Reinstall the cap and rotor.

Ignition Timing

ADJUSTMENT

1. Drive the car until the engine is hot; the temperature gauge indicates normal operating temperature. This is necessary as parts dimensions, and therefore timing may change slightly with temperature.

2. Leave the engine idling, apply the handbrake and put the transmission in neutral (manual) or Park (automatic). Turn off all accessories.

3. Install a tachometer, connecting the red lead to the (–) terminal of the coil and the black lead to a clean ground (the battery minus terminal works well). Verify that the engine idle speed is correct. If not adjust it, because incorrect idle speed will change the timing.

4. Stop the engine, and connect the timing light high voltage pickup into the No. 1 spark plug circuit (unless you have an inductive type of timing light, see the instructions that came with it). To do this, carefully pull the front spark plug wire off by the rubber boot at the spark plug end. Then, connect the timing light pickup to the end of the plug and install the other end of the pickup into the plug wire. On inductive timing lights, you'll have a device that looks like a clothespin which must simply be clamped around the wire. You won't have to disconnect the wire at all on these lights.

5. On all powered timing lights, connect the red lead to the battery (+) terminal and the black lead to the (–) terminal.

6. If the front pulley and timing mark are dirty, wipe them clean with a rag. If they are hard to see, you might want to put a small drop of white paint on both the timing scale and groove in the pulley. You may have to turn the engine over using a wrench on the bolt in the front of the crankshaft to do this. Check the timing setting in degrees Before Top

Dead Center and verify that this is the correct setting by checking on the engine compartment sticker. Make sure you know where the correct setting is on the front cover. Then, make sure all wires are clear of any rotating parts and the light is in a secure place. Make sure you haven't left any rags or tools near the engine.

7. Start the engine and allow it to idle. Point the timing light at the mark on the front cover and read the timing by noting the position of the groove in the front pulley in relation to the timing mark or scale on the front cover. If the timing is incorrect, loosen the distributor mounting bolt. Turn the distributor slightly clockwise to retard the timing or counterclockwise to advance it (advance means turning to a setting representing more degrees Before Top Dead Center). Read the timing light as you turn the distributor. When the reading is correct, tighten the distributor mounting bolt back up and then verify that the setting has not changed. If necessary readjust the position of the distributor until the setting is correct after the bolt is tight.

8. Turn the engine off, disconnect the timing light and tachometer and, if necessary, reconnect the ignition wire.

Valve Lash

ADJUSTMENT

Models with a Jet Valve

1. Start the engine and allow it to reach normal operating temperature.

2. Remove the wing nut and remove the air cleaner. Disconnect the large crankcase ventilation hose from the front of the air cleaner. Disconnect the two smaller hoses from the rear of the rocker arm cover and the intake manifold.

3. Loosen and remove the nuts and bracket which secure the air cleaner to the rocker arm cover.

4. Lift the bottom housing of the air cleaner off of the carburetor, with the hose from the exhaust manifold heat stove attached.

5. Unsnap the spark plug wires from their clips on the rocker arm cover.

6. Remove the two rocker arm cover bolts.

7. Carefully lift the rocker arm cover off the cylinder head. Using an $5/16$ in.(8mm) allen socket and a torque wrench, torque the cylinder head bolts. Observe the sequence in the appropriate illustration. Turn each bolt in the sequence back just until it breaks loose, and then torque it to 58–

61 ft. lbs. After the first bolt in the sequence has been torqued, move on to the second one, repeating the procedure. Continue, in order, until all the bolts have been torqued. Make sure that the cylinder head bolts are all tightened, in sequence, to specification.

8. Remove the spark plugs.

9. Remove the distributor cap.

NOTE: On front wheel drive models, a crankshaft pulley access hole is located on the left side finder shield. Remove the covering plug and use a ratchet extension to turn the crankshaft when adjusting the valves.

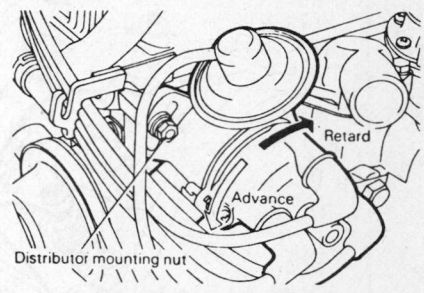

Adjusting ignition timing

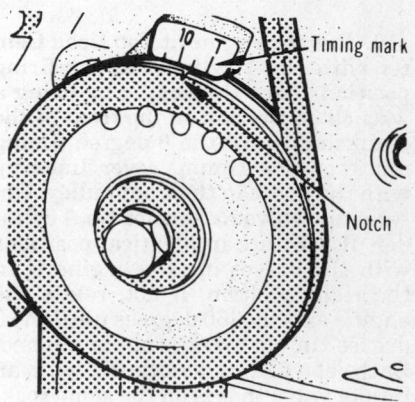

Timing marks

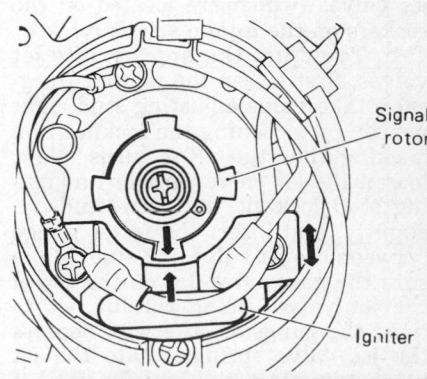

Reluctor gap adjustment

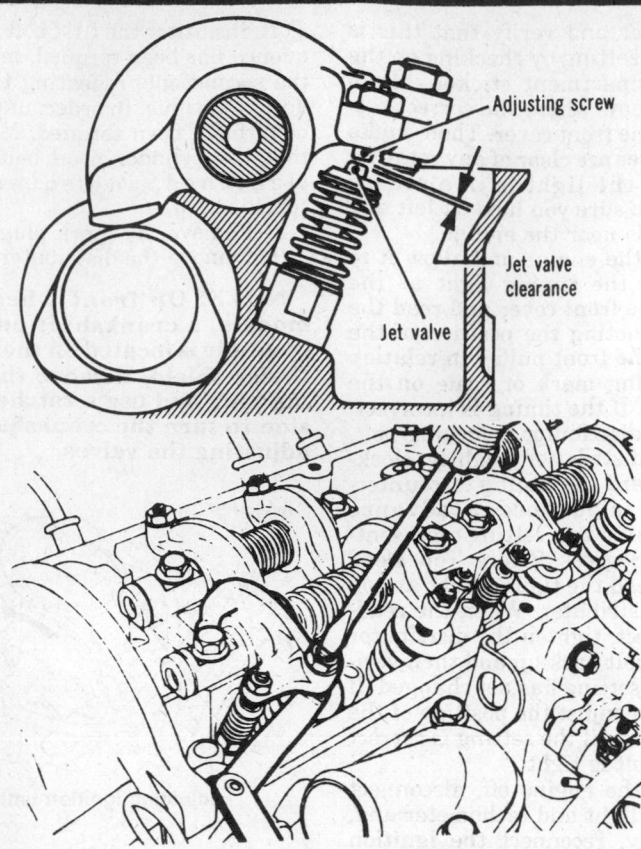

Jet valve clearance adjustment

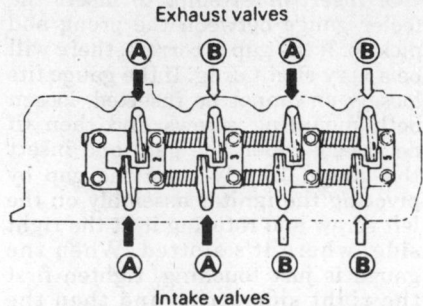

"A" and "B" valve adjusting positions

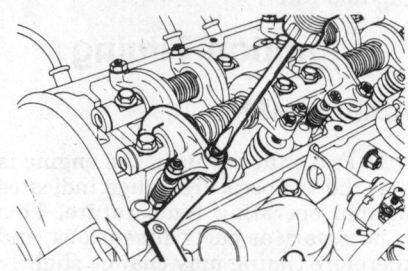

Adjusting the valves

10. Put the engine at Top Dead Center with No. 1 cylinder at the firing position. Turn the engine by using a wrench on the bolt in the front of the crankshaft until the 0 degree timing mark on the timing cover lines up with the notch in the front pulley. Observe the valve rockers for No. 1 cylinder. If both are in identical positions with the valves up, the engine is in the right position. If not, rotate the engine exactly 360 degrees until the 0 degree timing mark is again aligned. Each jet valve is associated with an intake valve that is on the same rocker lever. In this position you'll be able to adjust all the valves marked "A" in the illustration, including associated jet valves (which are located on the rockers on the intake side only).

11. To adjust the appropriate jet valves, first loosen the regular (larger) intake valve adjusting stud right nearby by loosening the locknut and backing the stud off 2 turns. Now, loosen the jet valve (smaller) adjusting stud locknut, back the stud out slightly, and insert the feeler gauge between the jet valve and stud. Make sure the gauge lies flat on the top of the jet valve. Being careful not to twist the gauge or otherwise depress the jet valve spring, rotate the jet valve adjusting stud back in until it just touches the gauge. Now, tighten

the locknut. Make sure the gauge still slides very easily between the stud and jet valve and that they both are still just touching the gauge. Readjust if necessary. Note that, especially with the jet valve, the clearance MUST NOT be too tight. Just make sure you are not clamping the gauge in between the stud and valve, but that the parts JUST TOUCH. Repeat entire the procedure for the other jet valves associated with rockers labeled "A". Then, repeat the procedure for the intake valves labeled "A".

12. Change the thickness of the feeler gauge (if necessary), and repeat the basic adjustment procedure for exhaust valves labeled "A".

13. Turn the engine exactly 360 degrees, until the timing marks are again aligned at 0 degrees BTDC. First, perform Step 4 for all the jet valves on rockers labeled "B" (intake side only). Complete Step 4 for the regular intake valves labeled "B". Finally, repeat Step 5 for exhaust valves labeled "B".

14. Apply non-hardening sealer to the rocker arm cover gasket. Always use a new gasket.

15. Install the cover, hoses, spark plug wires and the air cleaner in the reverse order of removal. Tighten the rocker arm cover bolts to 4–5 ft. lbs.

16. Start the engine and check for leaks. It's best to install new gaskets and seals wherever they are used, and to observe torque specifications for the cam cover bolts.

Models Without A Jet Valve

Valve clearance is adjusted with the engine OFF.

1. Run the engine until it reaches normal operating temperature and then turn it off.

2. Remove the air cleaner. Pull the large crankcase ventilation hose off the front of the air cleaner. Disconnect the two smaller hoses, one goes to the rear of the rocker arm cover and the other to the intake manifold.

3. Loosen and remove the nuts and bracket which attach the air cleaner to the rocker arm cover.

4. Lift the bottom housing of the air cleaner off of the carburetor and the hose coming up from the exhaust manifold heat stove.

5. Remove the spark plug wires from their clips on the rocker arm cover.

6. Using a deep socket or box wrench, remove the two rocker arm cover bolts.

7. Carefully lift the rocker arm cover off the cylinder head. Using an $\frac{5}{16}$ in. (8mm) allen socket and a torque wrench, make sure that the cylinder head bolts are all tightened to specification.

8. Hot valve clearance is 0.006 in. (0.15mm) for the intake valves and 0.010 in. (0.25mm) for the exhaust.

9. Turn the crankshaft pulley to bring the piston to top dead center (TDC) of the compression stroke on the cylinder being adjusted.

10. Loosen the two rocker arm adjusting screw lock nuts.

11. Using the correct thickness feeler gauge, turn the adjusting screw until the gauge just snaps through the valve stem and the rocker arm.

12. Repeat the procedure to adjust the valves of each cylinder.

---- **CAUTION** ----

Loose valve clearances will result in excessive wear and valve train chatter. Tight valve clearance will result in burnt valve seats. Make sure to set the valve clearence to the exact specifications.

---

13. Apply non-hardening sealer to the rocker arm cover gasket. Always use a new gasket.

14. Install the cover, hoses, spark plug wires and the air cleaner in the reverse order of removal. Tighten the rocker arm cover bolts to 4-5 ft. lbs.

15. Start the engine and check for leaks.

Idle Speed and Mixture

ADJUSTMENT

Idle speed is adjusted periodically to compensate for engine wear. Idle mixture adjustments are not required as a matter of routine, but only when major carburetor work is required. The emission control system compensates as required to ensure a stable idle mixture. If you suspect trouble because of a rough idle, check the idle mixture with a CO meter.

Also, Hyundais have an idleup solenoid that operates to prevent stalling under certain conditions. This does not require adjustment as a matter of routine either, but may be adjusted if you suspect the system is not functioning properly.

NOTE: The idle mixture adjustment is preset at the factory. The mixture adjusting screw is inaccessible without removing and modifying the carburetor. Since this adjustment is preset, it should not be changed unless major unscheduled maintenance has been performed on the carburetor. This adjustment can only be made with a CO meter.

The idle adjustment is made with all electrical accessories Off, the electric cooling fan Off, the transmission in neutral and parking brake applied.

1. Start and run the engine at idle until normal operating temperature is reached.

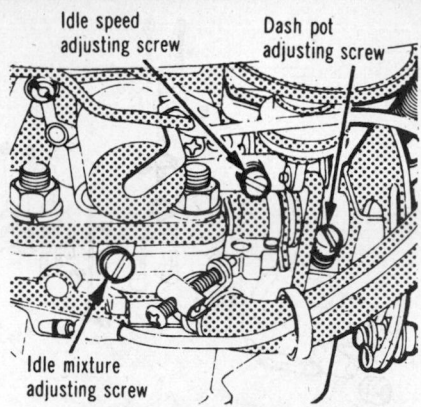

Idle speed adjusting screw

2. Check the underhood decal or the tune-up specification charts for the correct curb idle speed.

3. Connect a tachometer and adjust the idle speed screw until the correct rpm is reached.

4. Run the engine for at least 5 seconds at 2,000-3,000 rpm. Then reduce the speed to idle rpm for at least 2 minutes. If the idle speed is not at the specified rpm, turn the idle speed adjusting screw until the proper rpm is reached. Check either your underhood specifications sticker or the tune-up specifications charts for the correct idle speed rpm.

MIXTURE ADJUSTMENT (USA)

1. Remove the carburetor. The idle mixture screw is located in the base of the carburetor, just to the left of the PCV hose. Mount the carburetor, carefully, in a softjawed vise, protecting the gasket surface, and with the mixture adjusting screw facing upward.

2. Drill a $\frac{5}{64}$ in. hole through the casting from the underside of the carburetor. Make sure that this hole intersects the passage leading to the mixture adjustment screw just behind the plug. Now, widen that hole with a $\frac{1}{8}$ in. drill bit.

3. Insert a blunt punch into the hole and tap out the plug. Install the carburetor on the engine and connect all hoses, lines, etc.

4. Start the engine and run it at fast idle until it reaches normal operating temperature. Make sure that all accessories are OFF and the transaxle is in neutral. Turn the ignition switch OFF and disconnect the battery ground cable for about 3 seconds, then, reconnect it. Disconnect the oxygen sensor.

5. Start the engine and run it for at least 5 seconds at 2,000–3,000 rpm. Then, allow the engine to idle for about 2 minutes.

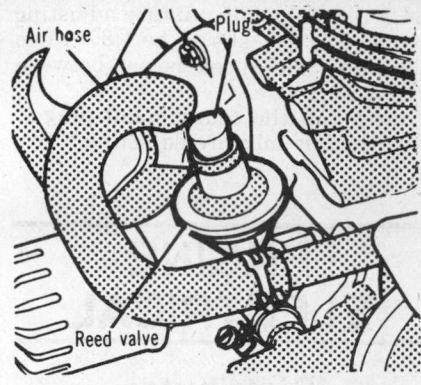

Air hose removal (typical)

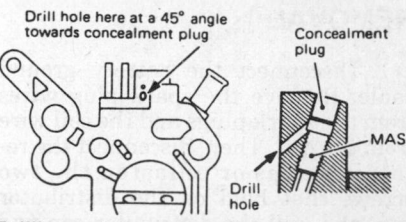

Drilling out the concealment plug to adjust CO

6. Connect a tachometer and allow the engine to operate at the specified curb idle speed. Adjust it, if necessary, to obtain this speed. Connect a CO meter to the exhaust pipe. A reading of 0.1–0.3% is necessary. Adjust the mixture screw to obtain the reading. If, during this adjustment, the idle speed is varied more than 100 rpm in either direction, reset the idle speed and readjust the CO until both specifications are met simultaneously. Shut off the engine, reconnect the oxygen sensor and install a new concealment plug.

MIXTURE ADJUSTMENT (CANADA)

1. Turn off all of the electrical accessories and place the transmission in the neutral position. Then remove the carburetor from the engine.

2. Position the carburetor in a vice with idle mixture adjusting screw facing up. Make sure that the gasket surface does not become damaged when the carburetor is placed in the the vise.

3. Drill a $\frac{5}{64}$ in. (2mm) pilot hole in the casting surrounding the idle mixture adjusting screw, then redrill the hole to $\frac{1}{8}$ in. (3mm). Insert a blunt punch into the hole and drive out the plug.

4. Reinstall the carburetor. Run the engine until it reaches normal operating temperature.

5. Run the engine for 5 seconds or more at 2000–3000 rpm. Allow the engine to idle for 2 minutes.

7. Set the idle CO and the engine speed to specifications, by adjusting the idle speed adjusting screw No. 1

SAS-1 and the idle mixture adjusting screw. Idle CO. should be 1.8% when the curb idle speed is set between 850–900 rpm.

8. Install the concealment plug to seal the idle mixture adjusting screw

ENGINE ELECTRICAL

Distributor

REMOVAL

1. Disconnect the battery ground cable. Remove the spark plug wires from the spark plugs and the coil wire from the coil. Then, disconnect the retaining clips or unfasten the two screws that hold on the distributor cap, and pull the distributor cap and seal off the distributor. Locate the cap and wires away from the distributor. Disconnect the vacuum advance line. Disconnect the distributor wiring connector.

2. Turn the engine until the rotor points to number one cylinder position and the timing marks on the crankshaft pulley and the timing tab are aligned at TDC.

3. Mark the distributor body to the exact place the rotor points. Matchmark both the distributor mounting flange and the cylinder head.

4. Now, carefully pull the distributor out of the engine, noting the direction and degree to which the rotor turns as you pull it out. Mark the location of the rotor after it has turned, too.

5. If the engine has been rotated while the distributor is out, proceed to the next step. To install the distributor, position it so the distributor and matchmarks are lined up. Now, position the rotor so it is lined up with the matchmark on the distributor body after the distributor was pulled part way out. Insert the distributor into the engine until the gears at the bottom engage and then begin turning the rotor. If there is resistance, turn the rotor back and forth slightly so the gears mesh. Once the gears engage and inserting the distributor causes the rotor to turn, push the distributor in until it seats and the rotor is lined up with the first mark made on the body.

6. If the engine has been rotated while the distributor was out, you'll have to first put the No. 1 cylinder at Top Dead Center firing position. You

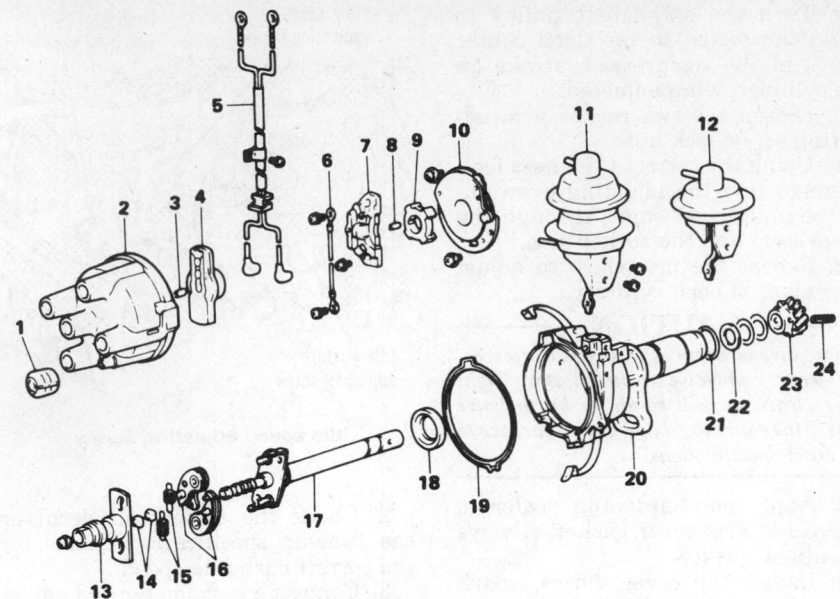

1. Breather
2. Cap
3. Contact carbon
4. Rotor
5. Lead wire
6. Earth wire
7. Igniter
8. Pin
9. Rotor
10. Breaker base
11. Vacuum controller for dual diaphragm
12. Vacuum controller for single diaphragm
13. Rotor shaft
14. Spring retainer (2)
15. Governor spring (2)
16. Governor weight (2)
17. Distributor shaft
18. Oil seal
19. Packing
20. Distributor housing
21. O-ring
22. Washer
23. Gear
24. Pin

Exploded view of the distributor

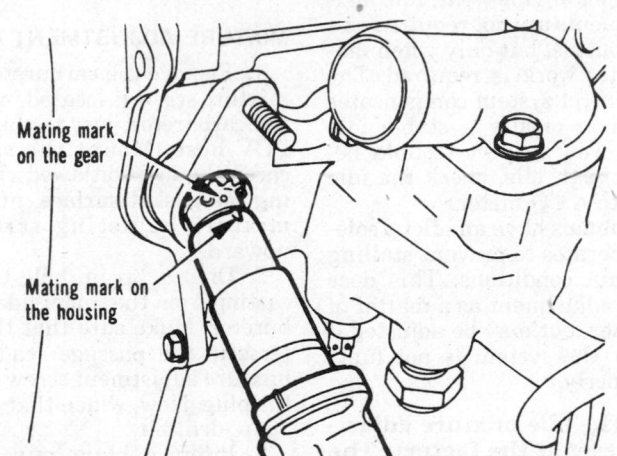

Mating mark on the gear

Mating mark on the housing

Aligning mating marks for installation of cylinder head mounted distributors

can either remove the valve cover or No. 1 spark plug to determine engine position. Rotate the engine with a socket wrench on the nut at the center of the front pulley in the normal direction of rotation. Either feel for air being expelled forcefully through the spark plug hole or watch for the engine to rotate up to the Top Center mark without the valves moving (both valves will be closed or all the way up). If the valves are moving as

you approach TDC or there is no air being expelled through the plug hole, turn the engine another full turn until you get the appropriate indication as the engine approaches TDC position.

7. Start the distributor into the engine with the matchmarks lined up. Turn the rotor slightly until the matchmarks on the bottom of the distributor body and the bottom of the distributor shaft near the gear are

aligned. Then, insert the distributor all the way into the head. If you have trouble getting the distributor and camshaft gears to mesh, turn the rotor back and forth very slightly until the distributor can be inserted easily. If the rotor is not now lined up with the position of No. 1 plug terminal, you'll have to pull the distributor back out slightly, shift the position of the rotor appropriately, and then reinstall it.

8. Align the matchmarks between the distributor and. Install the distributor mounting bolt and tighten it finger tight. Reconnect the vacuum advance line and distributor wiring connector, and reinstall the gasket and cap. Reconnect the negative battery cable. Adjust the ignition timing. Then, tighten the distributor mounting bolt securely.

Alternator

PRECAUTIONS

To prevent damage to the alternator and regulator, the following precautions should be taken when working with the electrical system.

• Never reverse the battery connections.

• Booster batteries for starting must be connected properly: positive-to-positive and negative-to-negative.

• Disconnect the battery cables before using a fast charger; the charger has a tendency to force current through the diodes in the opposite direction for which they were designed. This burns out the diodes.

• Never use a fast charger as a booster for starting the vehicle.

• Never disconnect the voltage regulator while the engine is running.

• Avoid long soldering times when replacing diodes or transistors. Prolonged heat is damaging to AC generators.

• Do not use test lamps of more than 12 volts (V) for checking diode continuity.

• Do not short across or ground any of the terminals on the AC generator.

• The polarity of the battery, generator, and regulator must be matched and considered before making any electrical connections within the system.

• Never operate the alternator on an open circuit. Make sure that all connections within the circuit are clean and tight.

• Disconnect the battery terminals when performing any service on the electrical system. This will eliminate the possibility of accidental reversal of polarity.

• Disconnect the battery ground cable if arc welding is to be done on any part of the car.

REMOVAL & INSTALLATION

1. Turn off the ignition switch and disconnect both battery cables.

2. Loosen the support bolt and adjusting bolt, and then shift the alternator toward the engine so belt tension is lost. Remove the belt.

3. Note the locations of all connectors. Make a drawing, if necessary. Unplug the plug type connectors and unscrew the fastening nuts for terminal type connectors. Clean any dirty connections.

4. Remove the adjusting bolt. Remove the nut from the rear of the mounting bolt.

5. To install the alternator, first position it so the mounting bolt can be inserted. Install the mounting bolt loosely.

6. Install the adjusting bolt loosely. Install the belt and turn the alternator to put tension on the belt. Tighten the adjusting bolt 10 ft. lbs. and the mounting bolt and nut to 15–18 ft. lbs.

Voltage Regulator

The voltage regulator is built into the alternator, if the regulator is found to be defective, the alternator and regulator must be replaced as a unit.

Starter

REMOVAL & INSTALLATION

1. Disconnect the negative battery cable. Then, mark and disconnect all wiring connectors at the starter.

NOTE: It my be helpful to remove the battery and battery tray, as well as the engine underside shield.

2. Raise and support the front end of the vehicle safely. Then remove the two starter mounting bolts and remove the starter.

3. Clean the surfaces of the starter motor flange and the flywheel housing where the starter attaches. Then, install the starter motor in reverse order. Torque the bolts to 16–23 ft. lbs.

STARTER DRIVE REPLACEMENT

1. Remove the starter from the car as described above. Remove the solenoid.

2. Remove the two through bolts and two Phillips screws from the rear

starter bracket. Remove the rear bracket.

3. Pry the retaining springs back and slide the two brushes out of the brush holder. Then, pull the brush holder off the rear of the starter. Remove the field coil assembly from the front frame. Remove the armature.

4. Remove the pinion shaft end cover from the center frame. Measure the clearance between the spacer and center cover and record it. If the pinion shaft is replaced, you'll have to insert or subtract spacer washers until the clearance is the same as that recorded. Use a screwdriver to remove the retaining clip and then remove the washers. Remove the retaining bolt and then separate the center frame from the front frame.

5. Remove the spring retainer and spring for the yoke from the front frame. Then, remove the washer, reduction gear, shift yoke lever, and two lever supports.

6. Turn the front frame so the pinion gear is at the top and support it securely. Then, use a socket that fits tight over the pinion shaft to force the snapring collar downward. Tap the socket lightly at the top or use a press to do this. Then, use a screwdriver to work the snapring out of its groove and remove it from the shaft. Remove the collar. Remove the pinion and the spring behind it from the shaft.

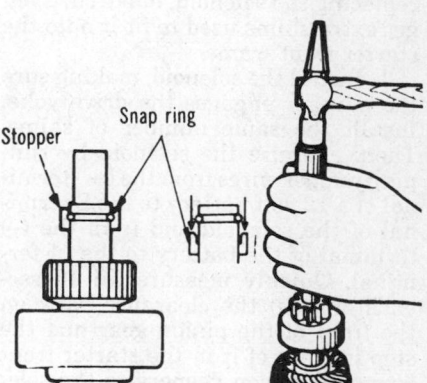

Removing the starter drive

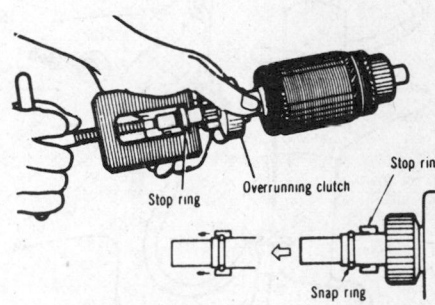

Installing the snap-ring stopper

7. Now, pull the overrunning clutch and pinion shaft assembly out of the rear of the front frame. Replace the pinion if its teeth are damaged (check the flywheel ring gear as well).

Replace the overrunning clutch if the pinion gear is damaged or if the oneway action of the clutch is not precise.

8. To install, first coat the splines of the pinion shaft with a light coating of a high temperature grease designed for this purpose. Then, reverse all the removal procedures to install. When reassembling the washer and clip at the rear of the pinion shaft, note that the clearance must be corrected by changing the thickness or number of washers if the overrunning clutch and pinion shaft assembly have been replaced.

STARTER SOLENOID REPLACEMENT

1. Remove the starter from the car as described above. Then, disconnect the starter motor wire at the M terminal of the solenoid.

2. Remove the Phillips screws from the front end of the solenoid. Disengage the solenoid plunger from the yoke inside the front of the starter and then remove the solenoid and the shims located between the solenoid and the starter front frame. If you're replacing the solenoid, make sure you get extra shims used to fit it onto the starter front frame.

3. Install the solenoid, making sure the plunger engages the drive yoke. Install the same number of shims. Then, energize the solenoid by running jumper wires from the (+) terminal of a 12 volt battery to the S terminal of the solenoid and from the (−) terminal of the battery to the M terminal. Quickly measure (in 10 seconds or less) the clearance between the front of the pinion gear and the stop in front of it in the starter front frame, and then deenergize the sole-

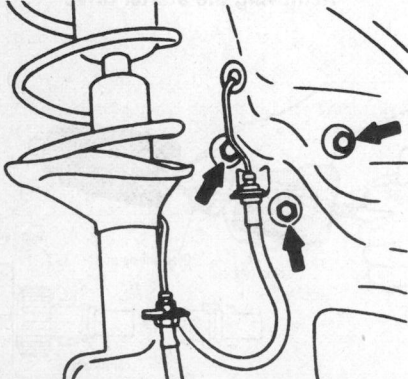

Removing the transaxle mounting bolts

noid before it overheats. The pinion gear should be pushed back against the drive mechanism when you do this. Perform the remaining steps in reverse of the removal procedure. Make sure all connections are clean and tight.

ENGINE MECHANICAL

Engine

REMOVAL & INSTALLATION

1. Remove the air cleaner assembly. Disconnect the purge control vacuum hose from the purge valve. Remove the purge control valve mounting bracket. Remove the windshield washer reservoir, radiator tank and carbon canister.

2. Drain the coolant from the radiator. Remove the radiator assembly with the electric cooling fan attached. Be sure to disconnect the fan wiring harness.

3. Disconnect the electrical connectors for the backup lights and engine harness, located near the battery tray. If the car has a 5-speed, disconnect the select control valve connector. Disconnect the two alternator harness connectors and the oil pressure sending unit.

4. First label and then disconnect the automatic transmission oil cooler hoses. Avoid spilling oil and cap the openings.

Remove the front roll stop nut and the bolt; or, you may remove the attaching bolts from the engine damper

5. Label and then disconnect all low tension wires and the one high tension wire going to the coil from the distributor. Disconnect the engine ground.

6. Disconnect the brake booster vacuum hose at the intake manifold.

7. Disconnect the fuel supply, return, and vapor hoses at the side of the engine. Avoid spilling fuel.

8. Disconnect the heater hoses from the side of the engine.

9. Remove the clutch control cable (manual transmission) or transmission shifter control cable (automatic transmissions) from the transaxle.

10. Unscrew and disconnect the speedometer cable at the transaxle.

11. Raise and securely support the vehicle. Remove the splash shield. Remove the drain plug and drain the transmission fluid. Disconnect the exhaust pipe at the manifold. Then, suspend the pipe securely with wire.

12. If the car has manual transmission, remove the shift control rod and extension rod.

13. Disconnect the stabilizer bar at both lower control arms. Remove the bolts that attach the lower control arms to the body on either side. Support the arms from the body.

14. Disconnect the driveshafts at the transmission on both sides. Then, seal off the openings in the transaxle. Make sure you replace the circlips holding the driveshafts in the transaxle. Support the driveshafts from the body.

15. Attach a crane type lift, via chains or cables, to both the engine lifting hooks. Put just a little tension on the cables. Then, remove the nut and bolt from the front roll stopper; unbolt the brace from the top of the engine damper.

16. Separate the rear roll stopper from the crossmember. Remove the attaching nut from the left mount insulator bolt, but do not remove the bolt.

17. Raise the engine just enough that the crane is supporting its weight. Check that everything is disconnected from the engine.

18. Remove the blind cover from the inside of the right fender inner shield. Remove the transaxle mounting bracket bolts.

19. Remove the left mount insulator bolt. Then, press downward on the transaxle while lifting the engine-transaxle assembly to guide it up and out of the car.

--- **CAUTION** ---
Make sure the transaxle does not hit the battery bracket during engine and transaxle removal.

20. Lower the engine and transaxle

carefully into position and loosely install the mounting bolts. Temporarily tighten the front and rear roll control rods mounting bolts. Lower the full weight of the engine and transaxle onto the mounts and tighten the nuts and bolts. Loosen and retighten the roll control rods.

21. The rest of installation is generally performed in reverse of the removal procedure. During installation, first install all nuts and bolts with the weight of the engine carried by the crane. Tighten just slightly. Then, allow the weight of the engine to sit on the mounts, and torque parts as follows:

- Left mount large insulator nut: 65–80 ft. lbs.
- Left mount small insulator nut: 22–29 ft. lbs.
- Left mount bracket-to-engine nuts/bolts: 36–47 ft. lbs.
- Transaxle mount insulator nut: 65–80 ft. lbs.
- Transaxle insulator bracket-to-side frame bolts: 22–29 ft. lbs.
- Transaxle bracket assembly-to-automatic transaxle nuts: 65–80 ft. lbs.
- Transaxle mount bracket to manual transaxle bolts: 40–43 ft. lbs.
- Rear roll insulator nut: 33–43 ft. lbs.
- Rear roll stopper bracket-to-crossmember assembly bolts: 22–29 ft. lbs.
- Front roll insulator nut: 33–43 ft. lbs.
- Front roll stopper bracket-to-crossmember assembly bolts: 33–40 ft. lbs.
- Lower roll insulator-to-roll damper bracket bolt: 22–29 ft. lbs.
- Center crossmember to body: 43–58 ft. lbs.

22. Finally, replenish all fluids. Adjust the transmission and accelerator linkages. Start the engine and check for leaks as well as proper gauge operation. Replace the hood and have the air conditioner recharged.

Cylinder Head

——— CAUTION ———

Never remove the cylinder head unless the engine is COLD, or the cylinder head will warp.

REMOVAL & INSTALLATION

1. Drain the cooling system and then disconnect the upper radiator hose. Remove the PCV hose that runs between the air cleaner and the rocker cover.

2. Remove the air cleaner. Disconnect the fuel lines. Label and disconnect any vacuum lines running to the cylinder head, manifold, or carburetor from other parts of the engine compartment. Disconnect the heater hoses going to the head.

3. Label and disconnect the spark plug wires. Remove the rocker cover. Turn the crankshaft over until the Top Dead Center timing marks line up and both No. 1 cylinder valves are closed (both rockers are off the cams). Then, remove the distributor.

4. Remove the carburetor. Remove the intake manifold. Remove the exhaust manifold.

5. Remove the timing belt cover. Note the location of the camshaft sprocket timing mark. Loosen both timing belt tensioner mounting bolts and then lever it over toward the water pump as far as it will go. Retighten the adjusting bolt to hold the tensioner in this position. Pull the timing belt off the camshaft sprocket but leave it engaged with the other sprockets.

6. Using a hex type wrench, loosen the head bolts in the sequence shown. When all have been loosened, remove them. Then, pull the head off the engine block, rocking it slightly top break it loose.

7. Inspect the head with a straightedge and a flat feeler gauge of 0.002 in. (0.05mm) thickness. The tolerance for warping of a used head is 0.002 in. (0.05mm). The block deck must be flat within the same tolerance. The height of the head should be 3.5 in. (88.5mm) with a maximum machining limit of 0.012 in. (0.3mm).

8. Clean the combustion chambers of carbon with a scraper that is not excessively sharp, being carefully not to damage the aluminum surface. Sharp edges in the combustion chambers can cause detonation.

9. The oil and water passages should be cleaned thoroughly, if necessary by taking the head to a machine shop that can clean it in some sort of solvent or hot tank that is compatible with aluminum. You should also blow compressed air through all the small oil passages to ensure that they are clear. Check that the EGR and air pump passages are also clear. Both gasket surfaces must be completely free of dirt.

10. Install a new head gasket (without any sealer) and then position the head on the block deck. Install all the bolts finger tight. Then, torque them, in the illustrated sequence, first to 25 ft. lbs. Then, torque again, in the same sequence, to 58–61 ft. lbs.

11. Install the timing belt on the camshaft tensioner and rotate the camshaft sprocket backward so the belt is tight on what is normally the tension side. Makes sure all the timing marks are now lined up. That is, timing marks on the crankshaft sprocket and front case must line up; and the marks on the camshaft sprocket and the tab on the cylinder head must be simultaneously lined up with the side of the belt away from the tensioner under tension. Now, loosen the timing belt tensioner adjusting bolt and allow spring tension to tension the belt. Make sure all timing marks are still lined up. If not, the belt is out of time and must be shifted

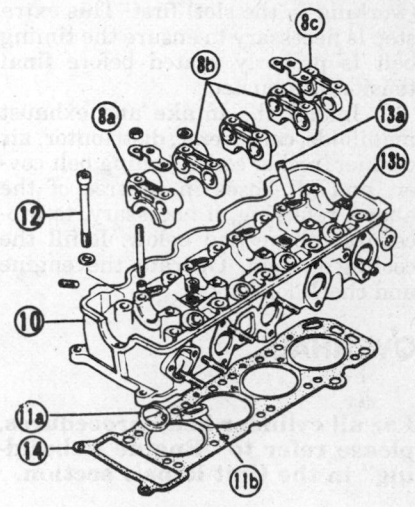

8a. Camshaft bearing cap
8b. No. 2, 3 and 4 caps
8c. Camshaft bearing cap (rear)
10. Cylinder head
11a. Intake valve seat ring
11b. Exhaust valve seat ring
12. Cylinder head bolt
13a. Exhaust valve guide
13b. Intake valve guide
14. Cylinder head gasket

Exploded view of the cylinder head

Crankshaft pulley side

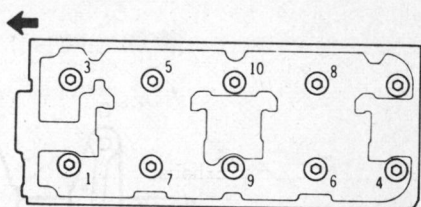

Cylinder head removal sequence for the 1468cc engine

Crankshaft pulley side

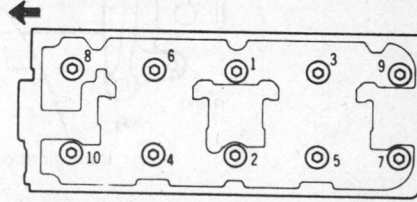

Cylinder head torque sequence for the 1468cc engine

with the tensioner shifted back toward the water pump and locked there. Now, torque the adjusting bolt (on the right side and working through a slot) to 15–18 ft. lbs. Now, after the tensioner adjusting bolt is torqued, torque the hinged mounting bolt located on the opposite side. Don't torque the mounting bolt first, or the tension on the belt will be too great!

Turn the crankshaft one full turn in the normal direction of rotation. Loosen first the tensioner pivot bolt and then the adjusting bolt. Now torque them exactly as before, adjusting bolt (working in the slot) first! This extra step is necessary to ensure the timing belt is properly seated before final tension is adjusted.

12. Install the intake and exhaust manifolds, carburetor, distributor, air cleaner, rocker cover, timing belt cover, and all hoses in reverse of the above, referring, if necessary, to procedures above and below. Refill the cooling system. Operate the engine and check for leaks.

OVERHAUL

For all cylinder head procedures, please refer to "Engine Rebuilding" in the Unit Repair section.

Rocker Arms/Shafts

REMOVAL & INSTALLATION

1. Remove the PCV hose running from the rocker cover and the air cleaner. Remove the air cleaner.
2. Remove the upper timing belt cover. Remove the rocker cover.
3. Loosen the bearing cap bolts, or the rockershaft mounting bolts, but do not remove them and remove each rocker shaft, rocker arms and springs as an assembly. Disassemble the whole assembly by progressively removing each bolt, and then the associated springs and rockers, keeping all parts in the exact order of disassembly. The left and right springs have different tension ratings and free length. Observe the location of the rocker arm as they are removed. Exhaust and intake, right and left are different. Do not mix them up.
4. Check the rocker arm face contacting the cam lobe and the adjusting screw that contacts the valve stem for excess wear. Inspect the fit of the rockers on the shaft. Replace adjusting screws, rockers, and/or shafts that show excessive wear. Pay special attention to the contact pad ends of the rocker arms and the ball surface of the adjustings studs. Check the diam-

eter of the shaft at the rocker mounting points and subtract that number from the measured inside diameter of the corresponding rocker arm. Clearance should be 0.0005–0.0017 in. (0.012-0.043mm). The service limit is 0.004 in. (0.1mm). Check the rocker shaft bend. Total rocker shaft bend should be 0.002 in. (0.05mm). Check the spring free length. Maximum free length should be 2.1 in. (53.3mm) for the exhaust side springs; 2.6 in. (65.3mm) for intake side springs.

5. Assemble all the parts, noting the differences between intake and exhaust parts. The intake rocker shaft is much longer; the intake rocker shaft springs are over three in. long, while those for the exhaust side are less than two in. long; intake rockers have the extra adjusting screw for the jet valve; rockers are labeled "1–3" and "2–4" for the cylinder with which they are associated. See the illustration. Torque the rocker shaft mounting bolts to 15–19 ft. lbs.

6. Adjust the valve clearances. This step may be omitted only if all parts are being reused. Install the rocker cover with a new gasket, torquing the bolts to 1–1.5 ft. lbs. Install the air cleaner and PCV valve. Remember that there is no timing belt cover in place, and keep your fingers clear. Run the engine at idle speed until it is hot. Then (unless valves did not require adjustment), remove the valve cover again and adjust the valve clearances with the engine hot. Finally, replace the rocker cover and timing belt cover, air cleaner, and PCV valve.

Intake Manifold

REMOVAL & INSTALLATION

——— CAUTION ———

The intake manifold is made from cast aluminum and should not be removed until the engine is cold.

1. Remove the air cleaner assembly.
2. Disconnect the fuel line and the EGR lines (models equipped with EGR) and tag and disconnect all vacuum hoses.
3. Disconnect the throttle positioner and fuel cut-off solenoid wires.
4. Disconnect the throttle linkage. On automatic transmission equipped cars, disconnect the shift cable linkage.
5. Disconnect the carburetor choke water hose at the manifold.
6. Disconnect the power brake booster vacuum line.
7. Drain the engine coolant.

Identification mark	Installation position
1-3	No. 1 and 3 cylinders (positions A and C in illustration shown below)
2-4	No. 2 and 4 cylinders (positions B and D in illustration shown below)

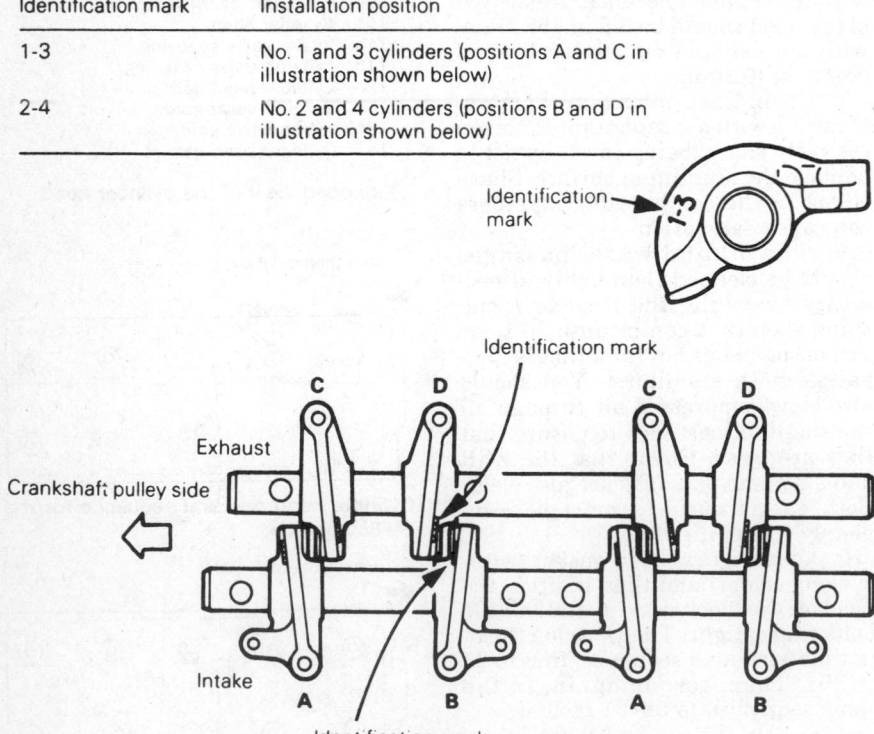

Rocker arm installation and identification

8. Remove the water hose from the carburetor.

9. Remove the heater and water outlet hoses, disconnect the water temperature sending unit.

10. Remove the mounting nuts that hold the manifold to the cylinder head. Remove the intake manifold and carburetor as a unit.

11. Clean all mounting surfaces. Before installing the manifold, coat both sides of a new gasket with a gasket sealer.

─────── **CAUTION** ───────
If the engine is equipped with jet air system, take care not to get any sealer into the jet air intake passage.
─────────────────────────

12. The rest of the installation is the reverse of removal.

Exhaust Manifold

REMOVAL & INSTALLATION

1. Remove the air cleaner. Remove the heat stove and/or heat shield on the exhaust manifold, if so equipped. With the manifold cool, soak all manifold nuts and studs with a liquid penetrant.

2. Disconnect the exhaust pipe at the exhaust manifold. Disconnect and remove the oxygen sensor. If there is a secondary air line connected to the exhaust manifold, disconnect that. First remove the exhaust pipe, then the secondary air supply pipe.

3. Now, support the manifold and re move all attaching nuts and washers. Slide the manifold from the cylinder head so you have enough room to remove the converter mounting bolts. When the converter is disconnected, remove the exhaust manifold, if necessary rock it to break it loose.

4. Thoroughly clean the sealing surfaces on the cylinder head and manifold. Replace any nuts, washers, or studs that are excessively rusted or may have been damaged during removal. Studs may sometimes be removed by installing two nuts and twisting them in opposite directions to lock them, and then using your wrench on the inner nut. Use a straightedge to check the manifold and cylinder head sealing surfaces for flatness. Correct problems by replacing the manifold or machining the cylinder head surface.

5. Install new gaskets in such a way that all bolt holes and ports are lined up. Make sure all the nuts turn freely, oiling them lightly if necessary. Also, make sure all the studs are screwed all the way into the block. Now, put the manifold in position and support it while you install all the

washers and nuts hand tight. Refer to the "Torque Specifications Chart", and torque all the nuts to specification, alternately and in several stages. Install piping, heat stoves, and shields. Connect the exhaust pipe or primary catalytic converter.

6. Operate the engine and check for leaks.

Timing Belt Cover and Timing Belt

REMOVAL & INSTALLATION

1. Remove the timing belt cover.

2. Turn the crankshaft until the timing marks on the camshaft sprocket and cylinder head are aligned. Loosen the tensioning bolt (it runs in the slotted portion of the tensioner) and the pivot bolt on the timing belt tensioner and lever the tensioner as far as it will go toward the water pump. Tighten the adjusting bolt. Mark the timing belt with an arrow showing direction of rotation if you may be reusing it.

3. Pull the timing belt off the camshaft sprocket. Remove the camshaft sprocket.

4. Remove the crankshaft pulley. Then, remove the timing belt.

5. Remove the crankshaft sprocket bolts and remove the crankshaft sprocket and flange, noting the direction of installation for each. Remove the timing belt tensioner.

6. Inspect the belt thoroughly. The back surface must be pliable and rough. If it is hard and glossy, the belt should be replaced. Any cracks in the belt backing or teeth or missing teeth mean the belt must be replaced. The canvas cover should be intact on all the teeth. If rubber is exposed anywhere, the belt should be replaced.

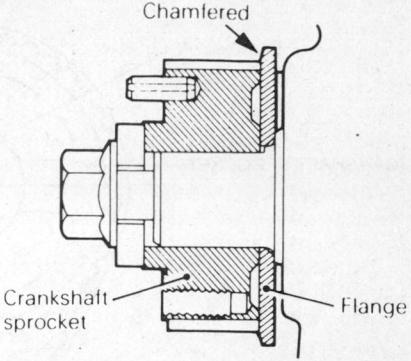

Installing the crankshaft sprocket

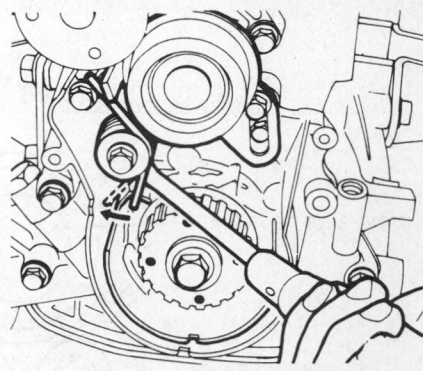

Installing the belt tensioner spring

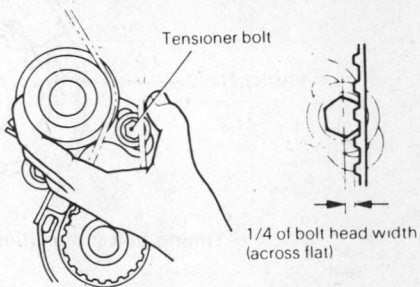

Checking the belt tension

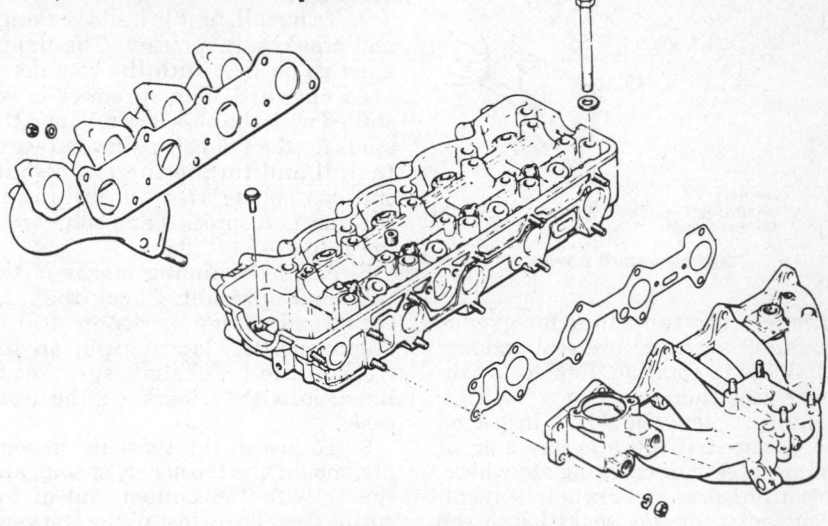

Intake and exhaust manifolds

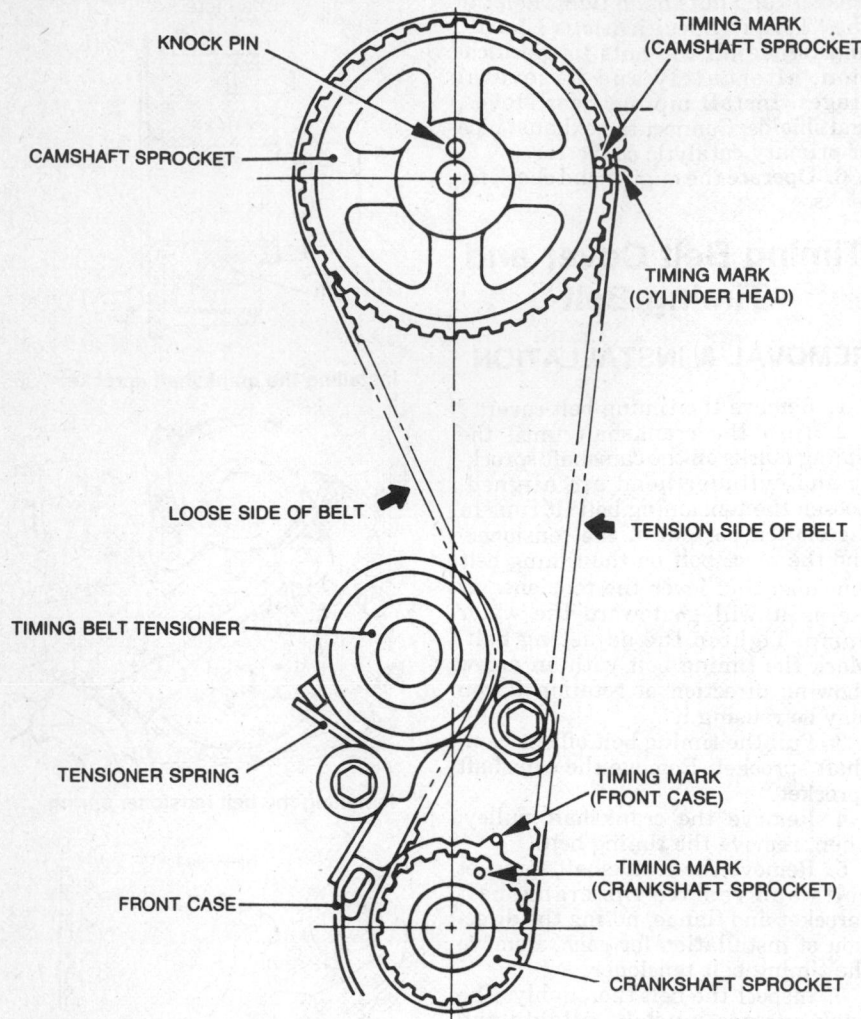

KNOCK PIN

TIMING MARK (CAMSHAFT SPROCKET)

CAMSHAFT SPROCKET

TIMING MARK (CYLINDER HEAD)

LOOSE SIDE OF BELT

TENSION SIDE OF BELT

TIMING BELT TENSIONER

TENSIONER SPRING

TIMING MARK (FRONT CASE)

TIMING MARK (CRANKSHAFT SPROCKET)

FRONT CASE

CRANKSHAFT SPROCKET

Timing belt installation and timing mark alignment

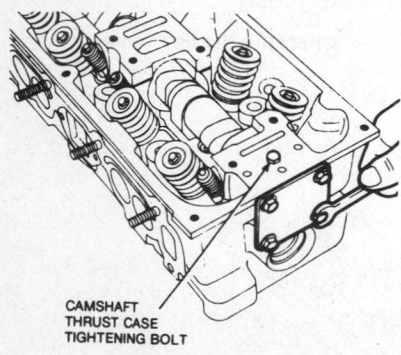

CAMSHAFT THRUST CASE TIGHTENING BOLT

Rear camshaft cover

Inspect the tensioner for grease leaking from the grease seal and any roughness in rotation. Replace a tensioner for either defect.

The sprockets should be inspected and replaced if there is any sign of damaged teeth or cracking anywhere. Do not immerse sprockets in solvent, as solvent that has soaked into the metal may cause deterioration of the

timing belt later. Do not clean the tensioner in solvent either, as this may wash the grease out of the bearing.

7. To install, first install the flange and crankshaft sprocket. The flange must go on first with the chamfered area outward. The sprocket is installed with the boss forward, and the studs for the fan belt pulley outward. Install and torque the crankshaft sprocket bolt to 37–43 ft. lbs. Install the camshaft sprocket and bolt, torquing it to 47–54 ft. lbs.

8. Align the timing marks of the camshaft sprocket. Check that the crankshaft timing marks are still in alignment (the locating pin on the front of the crankshaft sprocket is lined up with a mark on the front case).

9. To install the tensioner assembly, mount the tensioner, spring, and spacer with the bottom end of the spring free. Then, install the bolts and tighten the adjusting bolt slightly

with the tensioner moved as far as possible away from the water pump. Install the free end of the spring into the locating tang on the front case. Position the belt over the crankshaft sprocket and then over the camshaft sprocket. Make sure the belt is straight on the right side (where there's no tensioner as you do this. Slip the back of the belt over the tensioner wheel. Turn the camshaft sprocket in the opposite of its normal direction of rotation until the straight side of the belt is tight, and make sure the timing marks line up. If not, shift the belt one tooth at a time in the appropriate direction until this occurs.

10. Loosen the tensioner mounting bolts so the tensioner works, without the interference of any friction, under spring pressure. Make sure the belt follows the curve of the camshaft pulley so that the teeth are engaged all the way around.

Correct the path of the belt if necessary. Torque the tensioner adjusting bolt to 15–18 ft. lbs. Then, torque the tensioner pivot bolt to the same figure. Bolts must be torqued in that order, or tension won't be correct.

11. Turn the crankshaft one turn clockwise until timing marks again line up to seat the belt. Then loosen both tensioner attaching bolts and let the tensioner position itself under spring tension as before. Finally, torque the bolts in the proper order exactly as before. Check belt tension by putting your fingers on the water pump side of the tensioner wheel and pull the belt toward it with your thumb. The belt should move toward the pump until the teeth are about ¼ of the way across the head of the tensioner adjusting bolt. Retension the belt if necessary.

12. Install the timing belt covers.

13. Install the crankshaft pulley, making sure the pin on the crankshaft sprocket fits through the hole in the rear surface of the pulley. Install the bolts and torque to 7.5–8.5 ft. lbs.

Camshaft

REMOVAL & INSTALLATION

1468cc

1. Remove the rocker cover. Remove the timing belt cover. Remove the distributor.

2. Loosen the two bolts and move the timing belt tensioner toward the water pump as far as it will go, then retighten the timing belt tensioner adjusting bolt. Disengage the timing belt from the camshaft sprocket and unbolt and remove the sprocket. The timing belt may be left engaged with

the crankshaft sprocket, and tensioner.

3. Remove the rocker shaft assembly as described earlier. Remove the small, square cover that sits directly behind the camshaft on the transaxle side of the head. Remove the camshaft thrust case tightening bolt that sits on the top of the head right near that cover.

4. Carefully slide the camshaft out of the head through the hole in the camshaft side of the head, being carefull that the cam lobes do not strike the bearing bores in the head.

5. Lubricate all journal and thrust surfaces with clean engine oil.

6. Carefully insert the camshaft into the engine. Make sure the camshaft goes in with the threaded hole in the top of the thrust case straight upward.

7. Align the bolt hole in the trust case and the cylinder head surface.

8. Install the thrust case bolt and tighten firmly.

9. Install the rear cover with a new gasket and install and tighten the four bolts.

10. Coat the external surface of the front oil seal with engine oil.

11. With special installer Part No. MD 998306-01 or equivalent, drive the a new front camshaft oil seal into the clearance between the cam and head at the forward end, making sure the seal seats fully.

12. Install the camshaft sprocket and torque the bolt to 47–54 ft. lbs.

13. Reconnect the timing belt, check the timing and adjust the belt tension.

14. Reinstall the rocker shaft assembly. Adjust the valves and install the rocker and timing belt covers.

Pistons and Connecting Rods

POSITIONING

For all piston and connecting rod overhaul procedures, please refer to "Engine Rebuilding" in the Unit Repair section.

Rods and caps should be installed in numbered order. If the pistons and rods were assembled properly in the piston pin installation procedure the arrows on the piston tops will face the crankshaft pulley as will the markings on the sides of the rods. Numbers stamped on the sides of rods and caps should be on the same side; if necessary, proper positioning of the cap on the rod can be checked during assembly by making sure the two bearing notches (one on rod and one on cap) are on the same side.

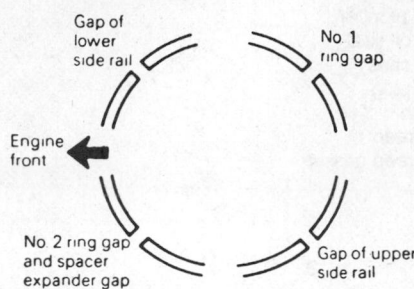

Piston ring positioning

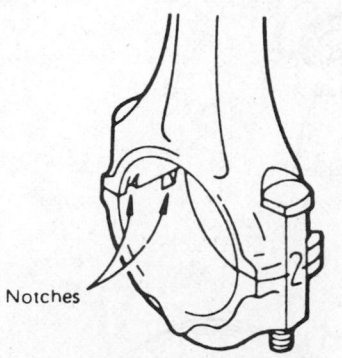

Connecting rod cap installation

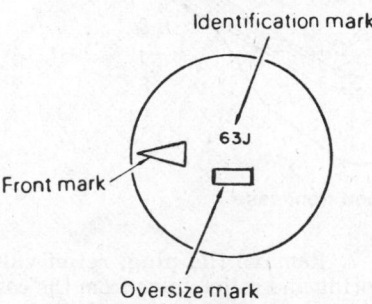

Piston installation

Engine Lubrication

Oil Pan

REMOVAL & INSTALLATION

The engine must be raised off its mounts to provide for the pan to clear the suspension crossmember. However, most of the front wheel drive models have enough clearance to provide for pan removal without raising the engine.

1. Jack up the front of the car and support it on stands.

2. Drain the oil.

3. Remove the underbody splash shield.

4. Remove the oil pan bolts, drop the pan, and slide it out from under the car.

5. Clean the mating surfaces of the oil pan and the engine block.

6. Apply a 0.15 in. (4mm) bead of RTV sealer along the groove in the oil pan.

7. Using non-hardening sealer, glue a new gasket to the oil pan.

8. Install the oil pan. Hand tighten the retaining bolts.

9. Starting at one end of the pan, gradually tighten the retaining bolts to 4–6 ft. lbs. in a criss-cross pattern.

10. Lower the engine and tighten the mount retaining nuts.

11. Install the oil pan drain plug.

12. Install the splash shield and lower the car.

13. Refill the crankcase with oil. Start the engine and check for leaks.

Rear Main Bearing Oil Seal

REMOVAL & INSTALLATION

The rear main seal is located in a housing on the rear of the block. To replace the seal, it is necessary to remove the transmission and perform the work from underneath the car or remove the engine and perform the work on an engine stand.

NOTE: The engine must be removed from the car.

1. Unscrew the retaining bolts and remove the housing from the block.

2. Remove the separator from the housing.

3. Using a small pry bar, pry out the old seal.

4. Clean the housing and the separator.

5. Lightly oil the replacement seal.

Tap the seal into the housing using a canister top or other circular piece of metal. The oil seal should be installed so that the seal plate fits into the inner contact surface of the seal case.

6. Install the separator into the housing so that the oil hole faces down.

7. Oil the lips of the seal and install the housing on the rear of the engine block.

Oil Pump

REMOVAL & INSTALLATION

1. Remove the timing belt as previously described.

6 HYUNDAI

1. Front case gasket
2. Oil pump cover
3. Oil pump outer gear
4. Oil pump inner gear
5. Plug
6. Gasket
7. Relief spring
8. Relief plunger
9. Front oil seal
10. Front case
11. Drain plug
12. Oil pan
13. Oil screen
14. Oil screen gasket

	Nm
A	40–49
B	12–14
C	8–9
D	18–24
E	35–44
F	6–7

Oil pan, pump and front case

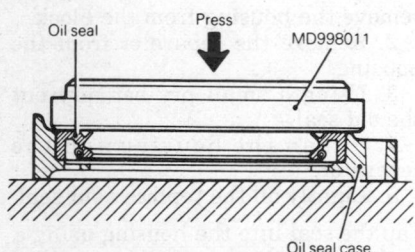

Oil seal — Press — MD998011

Oil seal case

Pressing a new rear main seal into place

2. Remove the oil pan as previously described.
3. Remove the oil screen.
4. Unbolt and remove the front case assembly.
5. Remove the oil pump cover.
6. Remove the inner and outer gears from the front case.

NOTE: The outer gear has no identifying marks to indicate direction of rotation. Clean the gear and mark it with an indelible marker.

7. Remove the plug, relief valve spring and relief valve from the case.
8. Check the front case for damage or cracks. Replace the front seal. Replace the oil screen O-ring. Clean all parts thoroughly with a safe solvent.
9. Check the pump gears for wear or damage. Clean the gears thoroughly and place them in position in the case to check the clearances. There is a crescent-shaped piece between the two gears. This piece is the reference point for two measurements. Use the following clearances for determining gear wear.
• Outer gear outer face-to-case: 0.003–0.007 in. (0.10–0.20mm)
• Outer gear teeth-to-crescent: 0.008–0.013 in. (0.22–0.34mm)
• Outer gear end-play: 0.001–0.003 in. (0.04–0.10mm)
• Inner gear teeth-to-crescent: 0.008–0.012 in. (0.21–0.32mm)
• Inner gear end-play: 0.001–0.004 in. (0.04–0.10mm)
10. Check that the relief valve can slide freely in the case.

11. Check the relief valve spring for damage. The relief valve free length should be 1.8 in. (47mm). Load length should be 10 ft. lbs. at 1.6 in.es (4.3 kg at 40mm).
12. Throughly coat both oil pump gears with clean engine oil and install them in the correct direction of rotation.
13. Install the pump cover and torque the bolts. to 7 ft. lbs.
14. Coat the relief valve and spring with clean engine oil, install them and tighten the plug to 30–36 ft. lbs.
15. Position a new front case gasket, coated with sealer, on the engine and install the front case. Torque the bolts to 10 ft. lbs. Note that the bolts have different shank lengths. Use the following guide and the accompanying illustration to determine which bolts go where.
   Bolts marked A: 0.8 in. (20mm) B: 1.2 in. (30mm) C: 2.4 in. (60mm)
16. Coat the lips of a new seal with clean engine oil and slide it along the crankshaft until it touches the front case. Drive it into place with a seal driver.
17. Install the sprocket, timing belt and pulley.
18. Install the oil screen.
19. Thoroughly clean both the oil pan and engine mating surfaces. Apply a 0.15 in. (4mm) wide bead of RTV sealer in the groove of the oil pan mating surface. 0.15 (4mm) is usually the first cut mark on the nozzle that comes with the tube of sealer.

NOTE: You have only 15 minutes before the sealer sets.

20. Tighten the oil pan bolts to 5–6 lbs.

ENGINE COOLING

Radiator

REMOVAL & INSTALLATION

1. Remove the splash shield from under the car.
2. Drain the radiator.
3. Remove the fan shroud and disconnect the fan motor wiring harness.
4. Disconnect the radiator hoses and, if equipped, the automatic transmission cooler hoses.
5. Disconnect the expansion tank hose.
6. Remove the radiator mounting bolts and lift out the radiator and fan assembly. The fan and motor may be left attached to the radiator and removed with the radiator as one unit.

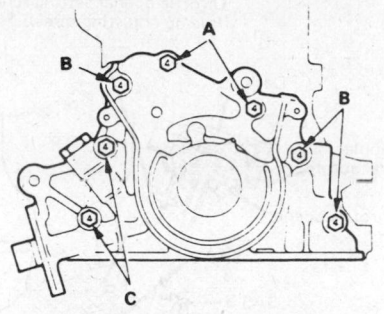

Installing the bolts for the 1468cc engine's oil pump. Bolts of .79 in. length are at location A; of 1.18 in. length are at location B; and those of 2.36 in. length are at C.

7. Installation is the reverse of removal. Tighten the retaining bolts gradually in a criss-cross pattern.

Water Pump

REMOVAL & INSTALLATION

1. Loosen the four bolts attaching the water pump pulley to the pulley flange. Loosen the alternator mounting bolts, slide the alternator toward the engine and remove the belt. Remove the radiator cap, open the drain cock at the bottom of the radiator, and drain the coolant from the radiator into a clean container.
2. Remove the timing belt covers, timing belt and tensioner.
3. Remove the water pump mounting bolts, noting the three different lengths and locations. Remove the pump and gasket, disconnecting the outlet at the water pipe (don't lose the O-ring).
4. Clean gasket surfaces and coat a new gasket with sealer. Then, position the gasket on the front of the block with all bolt holes lined up. Replace the O-ring for the outlet water pipe.
5. Install the pump connecting the outlet water pipe. Install the bolts with the shortest at the bottom; two just slightly longer at the one and four o'clock positions on the right side of the pump; next-to-longest bolt at the eight o'clock position just under the outlet; and the longest bolt at the eleven o'clock position and also attaching the alternator brace. Torque the bolts with a head mark, 4, to 10 ft. lbs.; those with a head mark 7, to 20 ft. lbs.
6. Install the remaining parts in reverse order. Final tightening of the water pump pulley bolts is done most easily after the V-belt has been installed and tensioned somewhat. Recheck tension after the pulley bolts

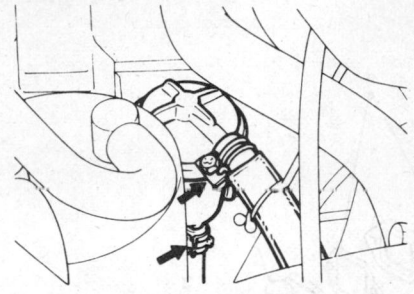

Fuel filter

are tightened. Close the radiator drain and refill the system. Run the engine until the thermostat opens and then add coolant until the level stabilizes before replacing the radiator cap. Check for leaks.

Thermostat

REMOVAL & INSTALLATION

1. To replace the unit, remove the air cleaner and then drain the cooling system down well below the level of the tubes in the top tank of the radiator.
2. Disconnect the hose at the thermostat housing.
3. Unbolt and remove the thermostat housing.
4. Lift out the thermostat and discard the gasket.
5. Clean both mating surfaces thoroughly.
6. Install the thermostat. The jiggle valve MUST be on the intake manifold side.
7. Install the housing. Torque the housing bolts to 10 ft. lbs.
8. Refill the system.

EMISSION CONTROLS

Please refer to "Emission Control" in the Unit Repair section for system maintenance procedures. Due to the complex nature of the modern electronic engine control systems, comprehensive diagnosis and testing procedures fall outside the confines of this repair manual. For complete information on diagnosis, testing and repair procedures concerning all modern engine and emission control systems, please refer to "Chilton's Guide to Electronic Engine Controls".

FUEL SYSTEM

Fuel Filter

REPLACEMENT

The fuel filter is of the in-line type. The filter is located at low center of the firewall.
1. Turn off the engine and allow it to cool. Using a pair of pliers, force open the clamps on the fuel lines and back them well away from the connections.
2. Work the fuel lines back and off the filter connections. If they are difficult to remove, it may help to pull them off with a twisting motion. Remove the filter from its mounting clip.
3. Inspect the fuel lines for cracks or breaks and replace them if necessary.
4. Install the new filter in the same position the old one was in in the clamp. Connect the inlet fuel line to the inlet fitting on the bottom of the filter. Connect the outlet to the outlet fitting on top. Make sure the hoses are fully installed over the bulged-out portions of the fittings. Then, with pliers, move the clamps over the filter fittings so they are beyond the bulged-out sections of the fittings but a small distance away from the ends of the hoses.

Fuel Pump

REMOVAL & INSTALLATION

The mechanical fuel pump operates directly off of a camshaft eccentric. A fuel return valve is located in the upper body of the pump. If the fuel temperature rises above 50°C, the valve opens and routes fuel back to the tank, preventing percolation.
1. Remove the two screws and remove the plastic heat shield.
2. Disconnect the three fuel pump lines.
3. Unscrew the two retaining nuts and remove the fuel pump.
4. Remove the gasket, insulator, and gasket.
5. Clean the fuel pump.
6. Apply non-hardening sealer to both sides of the gaskets. Position a gasket, the insulator and the other gasket on the head studs.
7. Install the pump and torque the nuts to 25 ft.lb.

TESTING

1. Disconnect the inlet line (coming from the filter) at the pump.

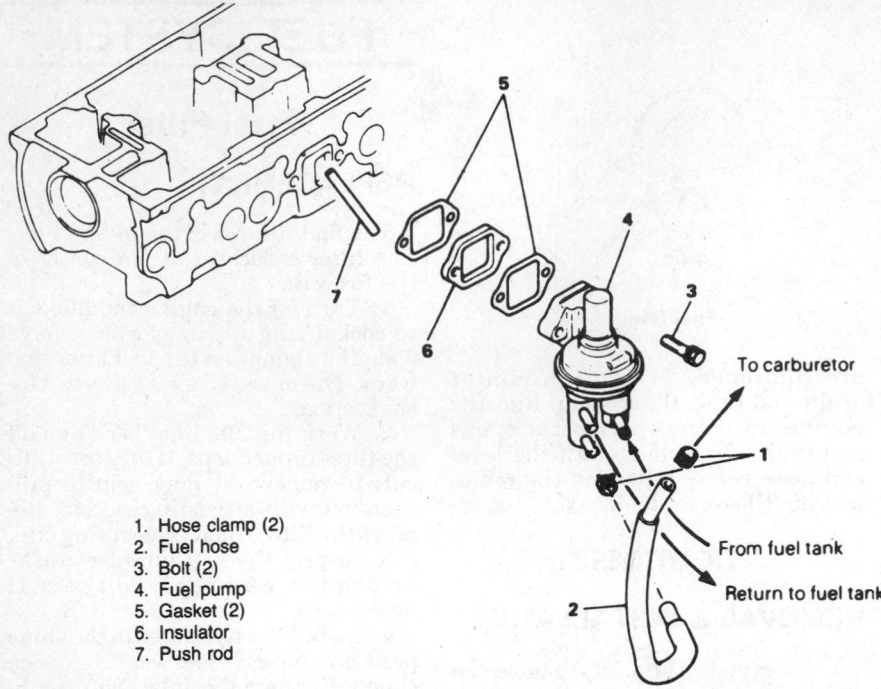

1. Hose clamp (2)
2. Fuel hose
3. Bolt (2)
4. Fuel pump
5. Gasket (2)
6. Insulator
7. Push rod

Fuel pump

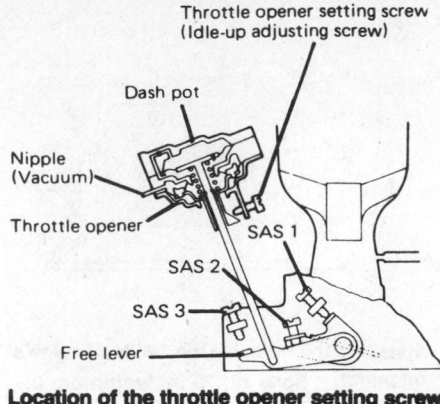

Location of the throttle opener setting screw

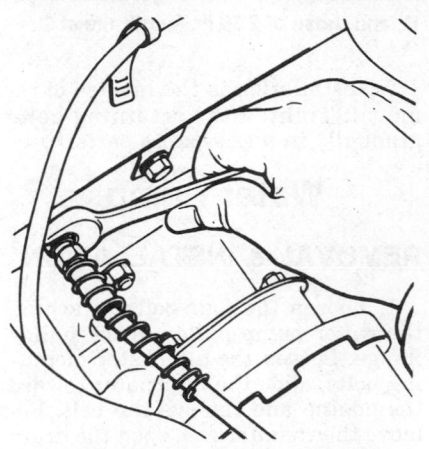

Accelerator cable adjustment

2. Connect a vacuum gauge to the pump nipple.

3. Remove the high tension cable at the coil. Then, have someone crank the engine as you watch the gauge.

4. A vacuum of 2.7-3.7 psi should be produced. If there is blowback of pressure, the inlet valve on the pump is leaking and the unit must be replaced.

Carburetor

REMOVAL & INSTALLATION

USA

1. Disconnect the negative battery connector. Drain the coolant down to below the level of the intake manifold.

2. Remove the air cleaner. Disconnect the throttle cable at the carburetor.

3. Make a drawing to show vacuum hose locations or label each vacuum hose, and then disconnect them all.

4. Disconnect the connectors for the solenoid valves and the Throttle Position Sensor.

5. Place a pan of some sort under the fuel connections and then disconnect them. Remove the container, avoiding the spilling of fuel.

6. Remove the mounting bolts. Three of the four bolts are VERY hard to get at. An offset, open-ended wrench is a great help. Lift the carburetor off the engine and remove it to a workbench, keeping it level to avoid the spilling of fuel from the float bowl.

7. To install, first inspect the mating surfaces of the carburetor and manifold. They should be clean and free of nicks or burrs. Clean and, if necessary, remove any slight imperfections with crocus cloth. Put a new carburetor gasket on the surface of the manifold.

8. Position the carburetor on top of the gasket with all holes lined up. Install the carburetor bolts and tighten them alternately and evenly.

9. Connect the throttle linkage. Have someone depress the accelerator pedal and make sure the throttle blade opens all the way. Adjust, as described below, if necessary.

10. Connect the vacuum hoses according to your drawing or labeling. Make sure all are soft and free of cracks to make a good seal. Replace hoses that are hard and cracked. Reconnect the fuel hoses.

11. Install the remaining parts in reverse order. To start the engine, merely set the choke in the usual way and operate the starter. Don't attempt to prime the engine by pouring gas into the carburetor inlet. Check for leaks with the engine running.

Canada

1. Disconnect the battery ground cable.

2. Drain the coolant to a level just below the intake manifold.

3. Remove the air cleaner.

4. Disconnect the wiring from the fuel cutoff solenoid.

5. Disconnect the accelerator rod and, on cars equipped with automatic transmissions, the shift rod.

6. Tag and disconnect the vacuum hoses from the carburetor.

7. Place suitable rags or a container under the fuel inlet and return hoses to catch a fuel, and disconnect the hoses.

8. Disconnect the water hose which runs between the carburetor and the cylinder head.

9. Unscrew the four retaining nuts and remove the carburetor. Hold the carburetor level to avoid an unwanted fuel spill.

10. Installation is the reverse of removal.

THROTTLE LINKAGE ADJUSTMENT

1. Run the engine to operating temperature and allow it to idle at curb idle speed.

2. There should be no slack in the exposed part of the throttle cable near the carburetor.

3. Make sure that there are no sharp bends in the cable.

4. Loosen the cable adjusting nut lock nut and turn the adjusting nut until the throttle just starts to open.

5. Back off the adjusting nut one full turn and lock it with the locknut.

ACCELERATOR CABLE ADJUSTMENT

1. The engine must be hot so the fast idle cam will not interfere with throttle position; warm it if necessary.

2. Inspect the inner cable to see if there is slack. If there is no slack, the adjustment is ok. If there is slack, loosen the adjusting nuts until the throttle is free to assume idle position with no effect by the accelerator cable.

3. Make sure there are no sharp bends in the cable. Then, turn the adjusting nut that's farther away from the carburetor until you can see the throttle start to move; now, back the nut off one turn. Secure the locknut.

FLOAT LEVEL ADJUSTMENT

A sight glass is fitted in the float chamber and the fuel level can be checked without disassembling the carburetor. Normal fuel level is within the level mark on the sight glass.

1. Invert the float chamber cover and remove the gasket. Use a float level gauge or depth gauge to measure the distance between what is normally the bottom of the float (the top surface in this position) and what is normally the lower surface of the float chamber cover. This dimension must be 0.79–0.82 in. (20–21mm).

2. If the dimension is not to specification, the shim under the needle seat must be changed. Use a thicker seat to raise the dimension (lower the float level). You can use a Hyundai shim kit or equivalent. The kit contains shims of 0.012 in. (0.3mm), 0.4mm, and 0.5mm. The change in float level will be three times the change in shim thickness. You can use multiple shims if that is what is necessary to get the right dimension.

3. To change the shim, first pull out the float hinge pin. Then, remove the float and the needle. Finally, use a pair of pliers to unscrew the needle seat by the widest dimensioned area of the seat. Slip the shim(s) over the narrow portion of the seat and then reinstall it, tightening it gently by the same portion of the assembly. Reassemble the needle, float, and hinge pin and retest the dimension. Reshim if necessary.

FUEL LEVEL ADJUSTMENT

The fuel level adjustment is corrected by increasing or decreasing the number of needle valve packings between the valve and top cover.

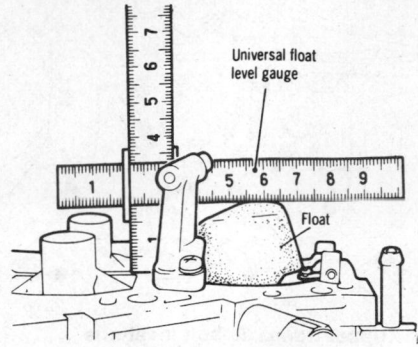

Dry float level adjustment

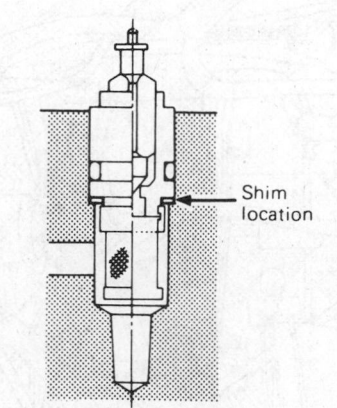

Float needle seat shim location

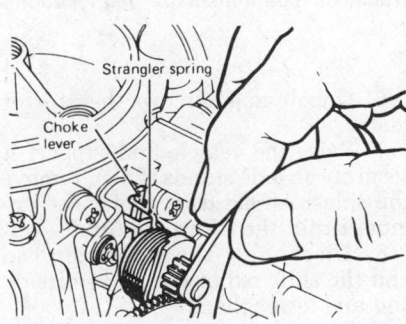

Removing the choke bracket bridge

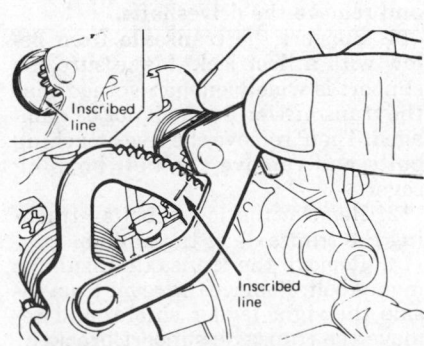

Aligning the choke gear and cam mating marks

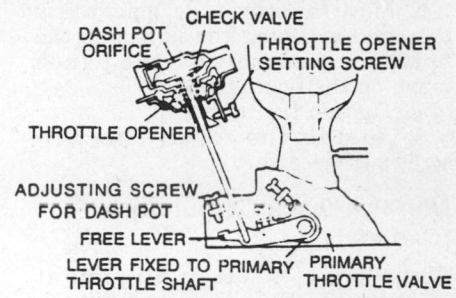

Fast idle adjustment

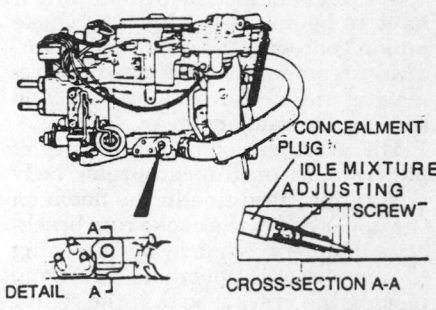

Idle mixture adjustment screw

FAST IDLE ADJUSTMENT

1. Start the engine and open the throttle valve about 45 degrees. Manually close the choke valve and slowly return the throttle valve to the stop position.

2. With a tachometer connected, check that the fast idle speed at 2,000 rpm maximum but not less than 1,700 rpm). Adjust the speed, using the fast idle speed screw.

3. Cold start the engine and check the automatic choke and fast idle operation.

AUTOMATIC CHOKE ADJUSTMENT

Feedback Carburetors (USA)

1. Remove the air cleaner.
2. Remove the choke cover.

NOTE: Some cars might have headless screws securing the cover. These screws will have to be drilled out. To do this, you should remove the carburetor.

3. Remove the bracket bridging the choke spring gear and the choke actuating cam.

4. Remove the choke strangler spring from the choke lever. Align the scribed mark on the choke gear with the mark below the teeth on the actuating cam, and reassemble the parts.

5. Temporarily tighten the lower bracket screw.

6. Move the arm at the upper screw to align the center line scribed in the notch on the arm with the punch mark on the float chamber.

7. Tighten the screws.

8. Install the cover with new screws (if necessary).

Non-Feedback Carburetors (Canada)

There are two sets of alignment marks on the Canadian non-feedback carburetors.

One set has inscribed lines which have to be mated to align the choke pinion gear with the choke cam lever. This alignment is performed by removing the choke cam bracket and moving the cam and gear.

The other set of marks consist of punch mark on the carburetor body and an inscribed line in the notch on the upper end of the choke cam bracket. Alignment is made by loosening the cam bracket upper end screw and moving the bracket so that the center inscribed line aligns with the punch mark.

OVERHAUL

For all carburetor overhaul procedures, please refer to "Carburetor Service" in the Unit Repair section.

MANUAL TRANSAXLE

LINKAGE ADJUSTMENT

Hyundai manual transaxle linkages are not adjustable. If the shifter does not work properly, transmission mounting, lubrication, or parts wear problems are indicated.

Transaxle

REMOVAL & INSTALLATION

1. Remove the battery and battery tray.

2. On five speed transaxles, disconnect the electrical connector for the selector control valve.

3. Disconnect and remove the speedometer and clutch cables.

4. Disconnect the backup lamp electrical connector. Remove the starter motor electrical harness.

5. Remove the six transaxle mounting bolts accessible from the top side of the transaxle.

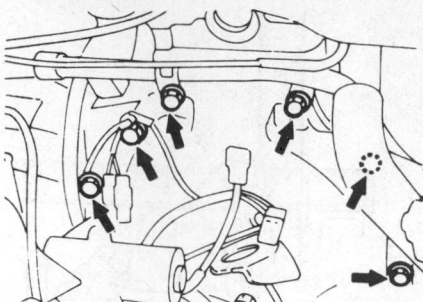

Upper transaxle bolt locations

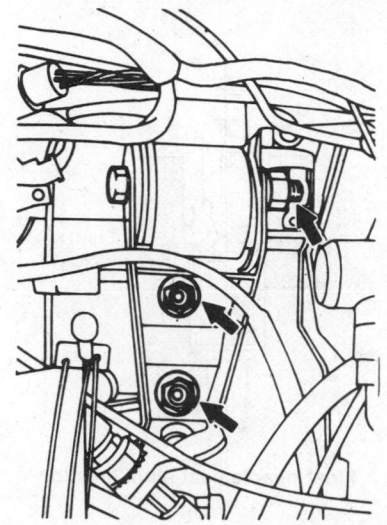

Transaxle mount insulator bolt locations

6. Unbolt and remove the starter motor.

7. Raise the vehicle and support it securely on axle stands. Then, remove the splash shield from under the engine. Drain the transaxle fluid.

8. Disconnect the extension rod and the shift rod at the transmission end and lower them.

9. Disconnect the stabilizer bar at the lower control arm.

10. Refer to the procedure on "Halfshaft Removal & Installation" and remove the driveshafts.

11. Support the transaxle from below with a floor jack. Make sure the support is widely enough spread that the transmission pan will not be damaged. Then, remove the five attaching bolts and remove the bell housing cover.

12. Remove the lower bolts attaching the transaxle to the engine.

13. Remove the transaxle insulator mount bolt. Remove the cover from inside the right fender shield, and remove the transaxle support bracket.

14. Remove the transaxle mount bracket.

15. Pull the assembly away from the engine and then lower it from the vehicle.

16. Installation is the reverse of removal. Torque the M10–7T engine-to-transaxle bolts to 35 ft. lbs.; the M8–10T engine-to-transaxle bolts to 25 ft. lbs. Torque the 8 x 20 bell housing cover bolts to 15 ft. lbs.; the 8 x 14 bell housing cover bolts to 9 ft. lbs. Torque the transaxle mounting bracket bolt to 40 ft. lbs. Refill the transmission pan with the specified fluid to the level of the filler plug. Adjust the clutch cable, as described below. Make sure the gearshift lever works correctly.

OVERHAUL

For all manual transaxle overhaul procedures, please refer to "Manual Transaxle" in the unit repair section.

CLUTCH

REMOVAL & INSTALLATION

1. Remove the transaxle as described above. Insert the forward end of an old transaxle input shaft or a clutch disc guide tool into the splined center of the clutch disc, pressure plate, and the pilot bearing in the crankshaft. This will keep the disc from dropping when the pressure plate is removed from the flywheel.

2. Loosen the clutch mounting bolts alternately and diagonally in very small increments (no more than two turns at a time) so as to avoid warping the cover flange. When all bolts are free, remove the pressure plate and disc.

3. Remove the snapring. Remove the clevis pin.

4. Remove the return clip and then remove the release bearing.

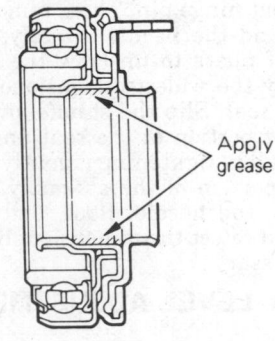

Apply grease

Grease the groove in the throwout bearing as shown

5. Use a center punch and hammer to remove the spring pins from the clutch release fork and shaft. Discard the spring pins.

6. Remove the release shaft. Remove the release fork, seals, and return spring.

7. To install, first grease the bearing areas for the release shaft. Then, install the release shaft, seals, return spring, and the release fork. Apply grease to the throwout bearing contacting surfaces of the release fork.

8. Align the lock pin holes of the release fork and shaft and drive in two new spring pins, using a tool such as MD998245-01. You may be able to simply fashion an appropriate tool, a device similar to a center punch with a tip the same diameter as the lock pins but flat on its front surface. Make sure the spring pin slot is a right angles to the centerline of the control shaft.

9. Apply grease into the groove in the release bearing and install it into the front bearing retainer in the transaxle. Install the return clip to the release bearing and fork.

10. Make sure the surfaces of the pressure plate and flywheel are wiped clean of grease and lightly sand them with crocus cloth. Lightly grease the clutch disc and transmission input shaft splines.

11. Locate the clutch disc on the flywheel with the stamped mark facing outward. Use a clutch disc guide or old input shaft to center the disc on the flywheel, and then install the pressure plate over it. Install the bolts and tighten them evenly. Tighten them in increments of two turns or less to avoid warping the pressure plate. Torque to 11–15 ft. lbs.

12. Remove the clutch disc centering tool. Install the transaxle. Adjust the clutch free play.

PEDAL HEIGHT ADJUSTMENT

Measure the pedal height from the top of the pedal pad to the closest point on the floor. The distance should be 7.3 in. (185mm). Loosen the clutch switch locknut and move the pedal stop bolt. Then, tighten the locknut.

PEDAL PLAY ADJUSTMENT

Slightly pull the cable away from the firewall. Turn the adjusting wheel on the cable until the play between the wheel and the cable retainer is 2–2.3 in. (5–6mm). Release the cable and make sure that the end of the tension spring engages the adjusting wheel, so that the wheel won't turn.

Check the clutch pedal free-play. Free-play should be 7.8–1.2 in. (20–30mm). If it is outside specification, adjust it by means of the adjusting wheel on the cable.

Clutch Cable

REMOVAL & INSTALLATION

1. Completely back-off the cable adjusting wheel in the engine compartment.

2. Raise and support the front end on jackstands.

3. Pull out the split pin from the end of the clutch control lever and disconnect the cable from the lever.

4. Disconnect the cable at the clutch pedal.

5. Installation is the reverse of removal. Make sure that the cable doesn't touch any hot or moving parts. Lubricate the cable with clean engine oil. Adjust the clutch.

AUTOMATIC TRANSAXLE

Transaxle

REMOVAL & INSTALLATION

NOTE: The transaxle and converter must be removed and installed as an assembly.

1. Remove the battery and battery tray. Remove the air cleaner and housing.

2. Disconnect the throttle control cable at the carburetor and the manual control cable at the transaxle. To do this, loosen the locknut which uses a star washer and locates the cable housing on the bracket. Also, remove the locknut at the very end of the cable, where it connects with the neutral start switch.

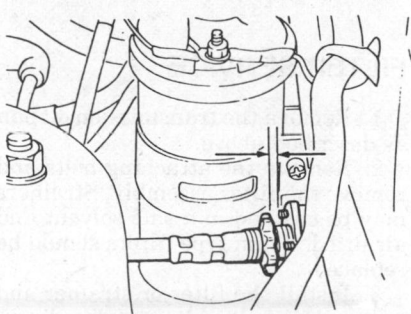

Clutch cable adjustment

3. Disconnect the inhibitor switch connector, pulse generator connector, oil cooler hoses, solenoid valve connector, and speedometer cable from the transaxle. Immediately install clean caps in the open ends of the hoses. Keep the hoses pointed up so fluid will not escape until the caps are installed.

4. Remove the five bolts attaching the converter housing to the engine that are accessible from above.

5. Jack up the car and support on jackstands. Label and then disconnect the starter motor wiring. Then, remove the mounting bolts, and the starter.

6. Remove the front wheels. Remove the engine splash shield.

7. Drain the transmission fluid by removing the drain plug. Remove the transmission pan bolts and remove the pan and drain it as described earlier in this section.

9. Remove the under cover. Disconnect the strut bars and stabilizer bar from the lower control arm. Disconnect the lower arm at the crossmember.

10. Disconnect both driveshafts from the transmission. Then, suspend them in a secure manner.

11. Remove the bell housing cover. Turn the engine for access and remove the three bolts connecting the drive plate to the front of the torque converter. Make sure to push the converter as far as it will go toward the transaxle after the bolts have been removed.

12. Support the weight of the engine from above, using a chain hoist. Support the transmission from underneath with a floor jack in such a way that the support will be spread out and will not dent the transmission pan. Remove the remaining bolts connecting the transmission to the engine.

NOTE: Never support the full weight of the transaxle on the engine drive plate.

13. Remove the transaxle mount insulator bolts. Remove the transaxle insulator mount bracket from the transaxle.

14. Slide the transaxle and converter away from the engine, to the right and then lower and remove it as an assembly.

15. Installation is the reverse of removal. Torque the torque converter-to-driveplate mounting bolts to 30 ft. lbs. The transaxle assembly mounting bolts are torqued to 35 ft. lbs. Torque the 7T engine-to-transaxle bolts to 35 ft. lbs.; the 10T engine-to-transaxle bolts to 25 ft. lbs. Adjust the throttle control cable and neutral

safety switch according to the procedures above. Test the neutral safety switch. Refill the transmission to the proper level and refill it hot according to the procedure for fluid change above. Make sure the neutral safety switch wiring does not rub against the insulator mount bracket.

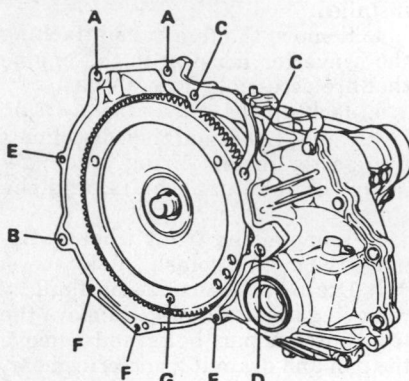

Bolt torques in ft. lbs. for the automatic transaxle: A—31-40; B—31-40; C—16-2?; D—22-25; E—7-9; F—11-16; G—25-3C

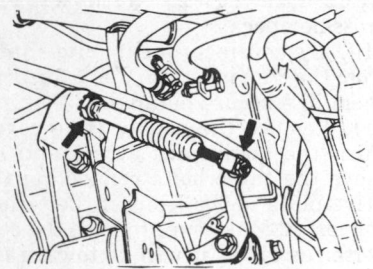

Disconnecting the throttle control cable at the trans axle

PAN REMOVAL

1. Remove the transmission pan and differential drain plugs to drain the fluid.

2. Remove the splash shield. Unbolt and remove the pan. It may be necessary to tap the pan lightly, with a soft mallet, to break the seal. Discard the gasket.

3. Clean all the gasket surfaces thoroughly. Then, put the pan and gasket in position with bolt holes lined up. Replace the bolts, tightening them with your fingers.

4. Then, tighten them diagonally in several stages to 7.5–8.5 ft. lbs. Torque the drain plug to 22–25 ft. lbs. Pour 4.2 qts. of fluid into the transmission. Start the engine, put the gear selector in each of the positions for several seconds, and then go back to Park. Check the fluid level again and make sure it's above the lower mark. Drive the vehicle until the transmission is hot and add fluid to the full mark.

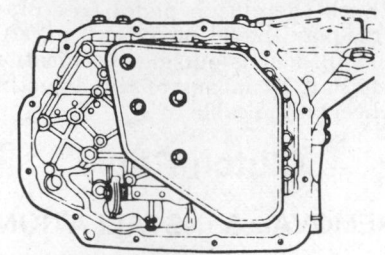

The automatic transaxle filter

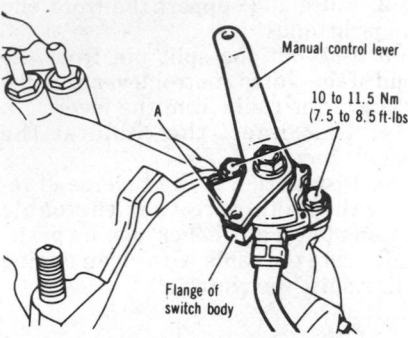

Neutral start switch adjustment

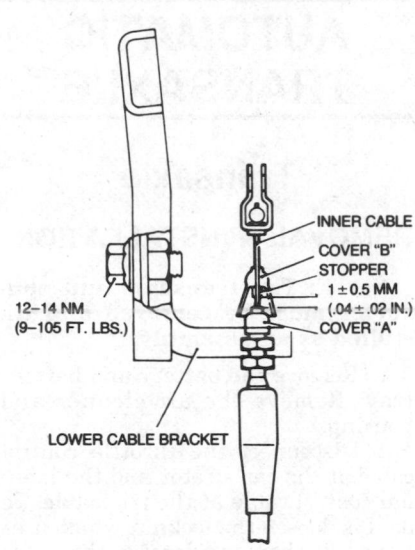

Throttle cable adjustment

FILTER SERVICE

1. Remove the transmission oil pan as described above.

2. Remove the attaching bolts and remove the filter assembly. Strainers may be cleaned in a safe solvent and air dried. Foam type filters should be replaced.

3. Install the filter or strainer and torque the bolts alternately (diagonally) is several stages to 4–5 ft. lbs.

NEUTRAL SAFETY SWITCH ADJUSTMENT

1. Apply the parking brake. Place the gearshift lever in NEUTRAL position.

2. Loosen the two mounting screws of the neutral switch so that it can be rotated. Now, rotate it so that the end of the operating lever is directly over the flange on the switch body and the holes in that flange and the outer end of the lever are lined up.

3. Hold the switch securely in place while torquing the mounting screws to 7.5–8.5 ft. lbs.

4. Recheck the function of the switch by attempting to start the engine in all selector positions. It should start only in Park and Neutral.

THROTTLE CONTROL CABLE ADJUSTMENT

1. Make sure the engine is warm with the throttle in normal idling position.

2. Loosen the lower cable bracket mounting bolt. Pull the small rubber cover located near the transmission back toward the housing to expose the nipple. Now, move the cable bracket until the distance between the nipple and the outer end of the cover next to the bracket is 0.02–0.05 in. (0.5–1.5mm). Then, torque the bracket mounting bolt to 9–10.5 ft. lbs.

3. With the engine off, have someone open the throttle all the way and hold it there. Then, pull the cable further upward to make sure it still has freedom of movement; that it has not bottomed out. If necessary, repeat the adjustment.

DRIVE AXLE

Halfshafts

REMOVAL & INSTALLATION

1. Remove the hub center cap, remove the cotter pin, and loosen the halfshaft nut. Loosen the wheel lug nuts. Then, raise the car and support it on jackstands under the crossmember.

2. Drain the transaxle fluid (you need not drain the pan on auto transaxles, just remove the drain plug from the housing).

3. Disconnect the steering knuckle from the lower control arm by removing the ballstud from the knuckle.

4. Disconnect the tie rod end from the knuckle.

5. If the halfshaft has a center bearing, remove the circlip from the center bearing. Then, gently tap on the outer part of the constant velocity joint with a plastic hammer on this type halfshaft so as to pull the halfshaft out of the transaxle. Where the halfshaft runs directly into the transaxle, insert a prybar in such a way as to avoid damaging the seal

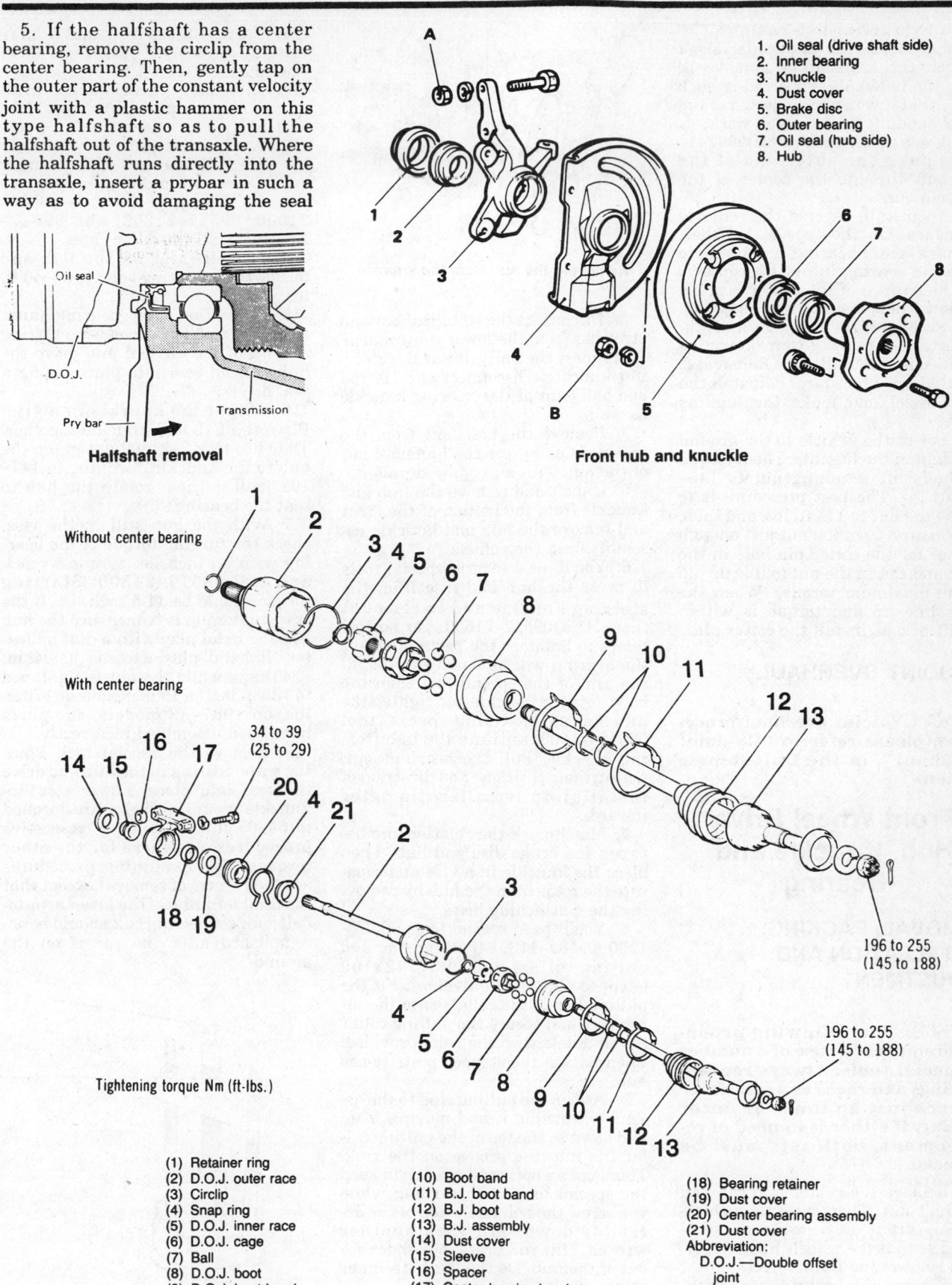

Oil seal

D.O.J.

Pry bar

Transmission

Halfshaft removal

1. Oil seal (drive shaft side)
2. Inner bearing
3. Knuckle
4. Dust cover
5. Brake disc
6. Outer bearing
7. Oil seal (hub side)
8. Hub

A B

Front hub and knuckle

Without center bearing

With center bearing

34 to 39
(25 to 29)

196 to 255
(145 to 188)

196 to 255
(145 to 188)

Tightening torque Nm (ft-lbs.)

(1) Retainer ring
(2) D.O.J. outer race
(3) Circlip
(4) Snap ring
(5) D.O.J. inner race
(6) D.O.J. cage
(7) Ball
(8) D.O.J. boot
(9) D.O.J. boot band

(10) Boot band
(11) B.J. boot band
(12) B.J. boot
(13) B.J. assembly
(14) Dust cover
(15) Sleeve
(16) Spacer
(17) Center bearing bracket

(18) Bearing retainer
(19) Dust cover
(20) Center bearing assembly
(21) Dust cover
Abbreviation:
  D.O.J.—Double offset
    joint
  B.J. —Birfield joint

Exploded view of front drive shaft—Type D.O.J. and B.J.

and pry outward to remove the halfshaft from the transaxle. Don't pull on the halfshaft to remove it! Keep the halfshaft supported in such a way that it won't be subjected to unusual bending stress as you work.

6. Use a puller such as MB990241–01 to push the outer end of the halfshaft through the center of the hub and out.

7. To install, reverse the removal procedure. On the type of halfshaft having a center bearing, make sure to press the bearing in until it contacts the the surface of the center bearing bracket. Then, install a new snapring.

8. Reconnect the ball joint and other parts to the lower control arm as specified in the "Ball Joint Removal & Installation" procedure. Reinstall the front wheel and make the lugnuts snug.

9. Lower the vehicle to the ground and tighten the lugnuts. Then, torque the halfshaft retaining nut to 145–188 ft. lbs. The best procedure is to torque the nut to 145 ft. lbs. and then, if necessary, turn the nut just enough further for the cotter pin hole in the shaft and slot in the nut to line up (up to the maximum torque). When the holes line up and torque is within specifications, install the cotter pin.

CV-JOINT OVERHAUL

For all CV-Joint overhaul procedures, please refer to "CV-Joint Overhaul", in the Unit Repair section.

Front Wheel Drive Hub, Knuckle and Bearing

REMOVAL, PACKING, INSTALLATION AND ADJUSTMENT

NOTE: The following procedure requires the use of a number of special tools. Always replace bearings and races as a set. Never replace just an inner or outer bearing. If either is in need of replacement, both sets must be replaced.

1. Remove the center hub cap and halfshaft nut. Then raise the vehicle and support it on floor stands, positioned so that the wheels hang freely. Then remove the front wheel.

2. Remove the brake caliper without disconnecting the hydraulic line (see the procedure above) and suspend it out of the way with a piece of wire.

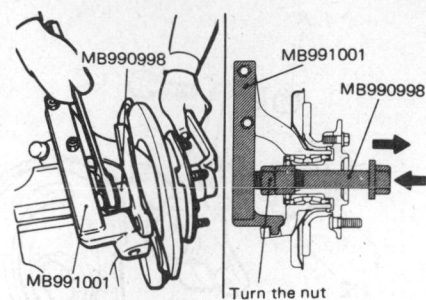

Removing the hub from the knuckle

3. Disconnect the stabilizer bar and strut bar from the lower control arm. Disconnect the ball joint at the steering knuckle. Disconnect the tie rod end ball joint at the steering knuckle as well.

4. Remove the halfshaft from the transaxle and press the halfshaft out of the hub with a two jawed puller.

5. Unbolt and remove the hub and knuckle from the bottom of the strut and remove the hub and knuckle assembly from the vehicle.

6. You'll need several special tools to press the hub and disc from the steering knuckle and to remount them. Use 09517–21600. Do not attempt to hammer the parts apart, or the bearing will be damaged! Install the arm of the special tool then the body onto the knuckle and tighten the nut manually. Using special tool 09517–21500, separate the hub from the knuckle. Pull the bearings out, noting their positions and direction of installation (smaller diameter inward).

7. Matchmark the relationship between the brake disc and hub. Then place the knuckle in a vise and separate the rotor from the hub by removing the 4 attaching bolts.

8. You'll need special tools 09532–1100, 09532–11301 (pulling ring and pulling collar) and 09517–21100 (stepped plate) or equivalent. Fit the pulling lips of the collets onto the inner race and secure the pulling collar to the collets with the bolts provided. Then, attach the stepped plate to the hub.

9. Attach the pulling ring to the assembly, turning it and moving it up and down so the top of the pulling collar fits into the groove on the ring. Then, use an open-end wrench to keep the special tools from turning while you screw the bolt at the top of the assembly downward with another wrench. This will press the inner race out of the hub. Do this for both inner races.

10. Drive the oil seal and inner bearing inner race from the knuckle with a brass drift.

11. Using a brass drift and a hammer, tap the bearing outer races out of the knuckle.

12. Thoroughly clean and inspect all parts. Any suspect part should be replaced.

13. Apply multipurpose grease to the OUTSIDE surfaces of the bearing outer races to make them easy to press in. Using special tools 09500–21000, 09517–21300, and 09517–21200, install the outer races.

14. Install rotor on the hub and torque the mounting bolts to 36–43 ft. lbs.

15. Drive the outer bearing inner race into position. Coat the out ring and lip of the oil seal and drive the hub side oil seal into place, using a seal driver.

16. Mount the knuckle in a vise. Place the hub and knuckle together. Then use 09517–21500 to tighten the hub to the knuckle, torquing to 147–192 ft. lbs. Then, rotate the hub to seat the bearing.

17. With the hub still in the vise, check the turning torque of the bearing with an inch lbs. torque wrench and tool 09517–21500. Starting torque should be 11.5 inch lbs. If the starting torque is 0, measure the hub bearing axial play with a dial indicator. If axial play exceeds 0.004 in. (0.11mm), while the nut is tightened to 188 ft. lbs. on 1986 models or 170 ft. lbs. on 1987–88 models, the parts have been assembled incorrectly.

18. Remove the special tool. Place the outer bearing in the hub and drive the seal into place. Lower strut-to-knuckle mounting bolts are torqued to 54–65 ft. lbs. Refer to respective procedures elsewhere for the other torques. The remaining procedures are the reverse of removal except that the final torquing of the lower arm-to-ball joint connecting bolt should be accomplished after the car is on the ground.

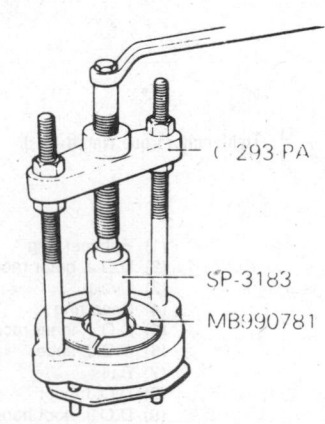

Removing the outer bearing inner race from the hub

FRONT SUSPENSION

MacPherson Strut

REMOVAL & INSTALLATION

1. Raise the vehicle and support it by the body or crossmembers. Remove the front wheels. Detach the brake hose bracket at the strut.
2. Remove the four nuts securing the strut to the fender well.
3. Unbolt the strut lower end from the knuckle.
4. Remove the strut from the car.
5. Installation is the reverse of removal. Torque the strut-to-knuckle bolts to 55–65 ft. lbs.; the strut-to-fender well nuts to 7–11 ft. lbs.

OVERHAUL

For all spring and shock absorber removal and installation procedures, and all strut overhaul procedures, please refer to "Strut Overhaul" in the Unit Repair section.

Stabilizer Bar

REMOVAL & INSTALLATION

1. Raise and support the front end on jackstands.
2. Unbolt the stabilizer clamps from the crossmember.
3. Unbolt the stabilizer bar from the strut bar.
4. Examine the bushings for cracks and wear, if one is worn or cracked all the bushings must be replaced.
5. Installation is the reverse of removal. Torque the chassis clamp bolts to 29 ft. lbs.; the strut bar clamps to 50 inch lbs.

Ball Joints

INSPECTION

Support the vehicle on axle stands. Disconnect the ball joint at the lower end of the strut as described below; you need not remove the lower control arm entirely. Install the nut back onto the ballstud. Then, with an inch lbs. torque wrench, measure the torque required to start the ball joint rotating. The figures are 26–86 inch lbs. If the figures are within specification, the ball joint is satisfactory. If the figure is too high, the joint should be replaced. If the figure is too low, you can still reuse the joint, provided its rotation is smooth and even. If there is roughness, or play, it must be replaced.

REMOVAL & INSTALLATION

1. Raise and support the front end on jackstands placed under the frame.
2. Unbolt the ball joint from the control arm.
3. Remove the stud retaining nut.
4. Use a ball joint removing tool and separate the ball joint from the steering knuckle.
5. Install is the reverse of removal. Torque the ball joint to control arm to 69–87 ft. lbs. Torque the ball joint stud nut 43–52 ft. lbs.

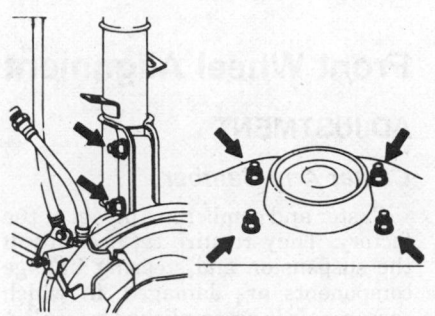

Strut attaching points

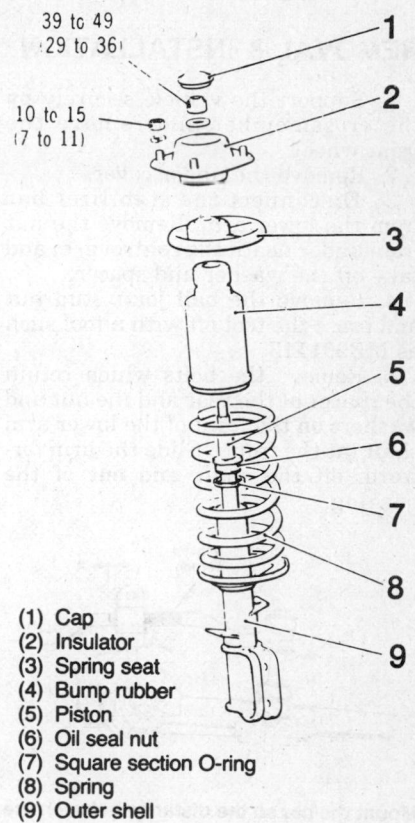

(1) Cap
(2) Insulator
(3) Spring seat
(4) Bump rubber
(5) Piston
(6) Oil seal nut
(7) Square section O-ring
(8) Spring
(9) Outer shell

Front strut assembly

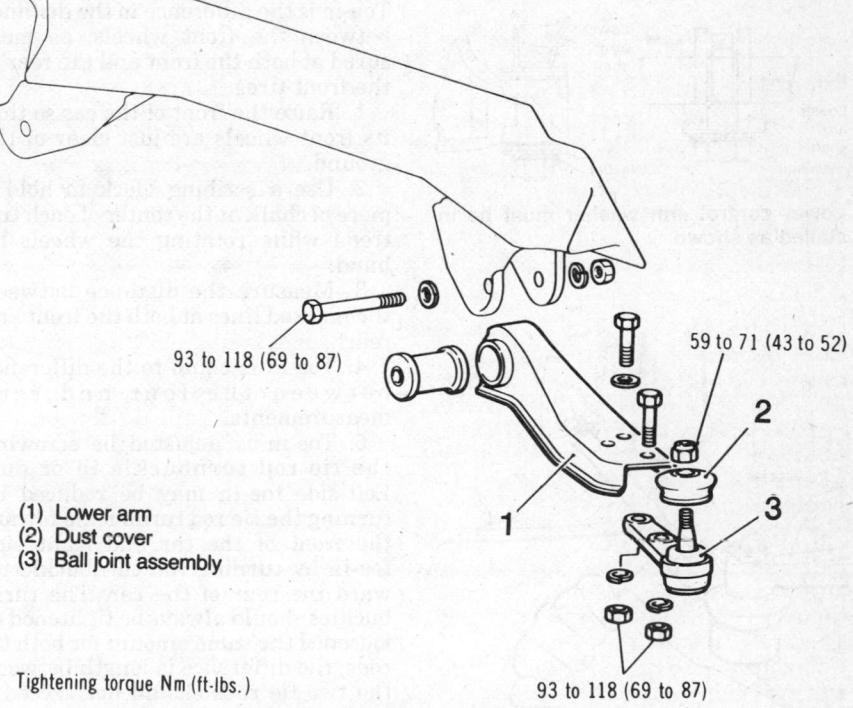

(1) Lower arm
(2) Dust cover
(3) Ball joint assembly

Tightening torque Nm (ft-lbs.)

93 to 118 (69 to 87)
59 to 71 (43 to 52)
93 to 118 (69 to 87)

Lower control arm and ball joint

Control Arm

REMOVAL & INSTALLATION

1. Support the vehicle securely by the crossmember and remove the front wheel.

2. Remove the under cover.

3. Disconnect the stabilizer bar from the lower arm. Remove the nut from under neath the control arm and take off the washer and spacer.

4. Remove the ball joint stud nut and press the tool off with a tool such as MB991113.

5. Remove the bolts which retain the spacer at the rear and the nut and washers on the front of the lower arm shaft (at the front). Slide the arm forward, off the shaft and out of the bushing.

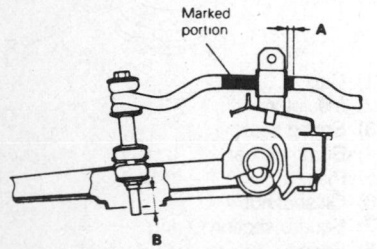

Mount the bar so the distance between the inner end of the retaining bracket and the inner edge of the marked portion is .16–.24 in. Torque the link at either amount of threads exposed is .83–.91 in.

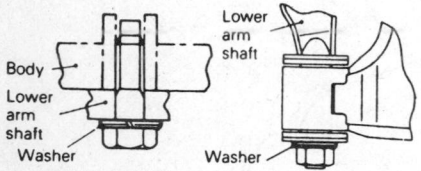

Lower control arm washer must be installed as shown

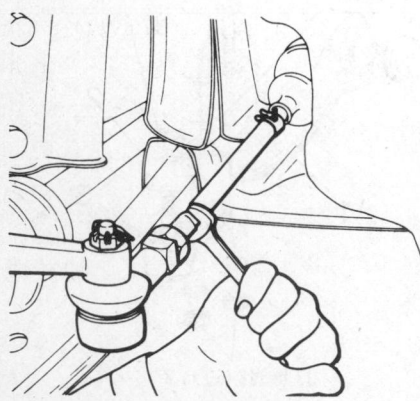

Adjusting the toe-in

6. Replace the dust cover on the ball joint. The new cover must be greased on the lip and inside with #2 EP Multipurpose grease and pressed on with a tool such as MB990800 and a hammer until it is fully seated.

7. Installation is the reverse of removal. The nut on the stabilizer bar bolt must be torqued until the link shows 0.8–0.9 in. (21–23mm) of threads below the bottom of the nut. Also, the washer for the lower arm must be installed as shown. The left side arm shaft has a left hand thread. Finally, tighten the arm shaft to the lower arm with the weight of the car with no passengers or luggage on the front suspension. Torque the nut for the lower arm shaft to 69–87 ft. lbs.; the bolts for the spacer at the rear to 43–58 ft. lbs.; the ball stud nut to 43–52 ft. lbs.

Front Wheel Alignment

ADJUSTMENT

Caster And Camber

Caster and camber are preset at the factory. They require service only if the suspension and steering linkage components are damaged, in which case, repair is accomplished by replacing the damaged part. Caster, however, can be adjusted slightly by moving the strut bar nut.

Toe

Toe-in is the difference in the distance between the front wheels, as measured at both the front and the rear of the front tires.

1. Raise the front of the car so that its front wheels are just clear of the ground.

2. Use a scribing block to hold a piece of chalk at the center of each tire tread while rotating the wheels by hand.

3. Measure the distance between the marked lines at both the front and rear.

4. Toe-in is equal to the difference between the font and rear measurements.

5. Toe-in is adjusted be screwing the tie rod turnbuckle in or out. Left-side toe-in may be reduced by turning the tie rod turnbuckle toward the front of the car and right side toe-in by turning the turnbuckle toward the rear of the car. The turnbuckles should always be tightened or loosened the same amount for both tie rods; the difference is length between the two tie rods should not exceed 2 in.(5mm). Tighten the locknuts to 36–40 ft. lbs.

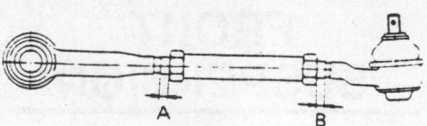

Toe-in adjustment points

REAR SUSPENSION

Shock Absorbers

REMOVAL & INSTALLATION

1. Remove the wheel cover. Loosen the lug nuts.

2. Raise the rear of the car. Support the car with jackstands. Remove the wheel.

3. Remove the upper mounting bolt/nut or nut.

4. While holding the bottom stud mount nut with one wrench, remove the locknut with another wrench, or on some models remove the nut and bolt from the mounting bracket.

5. Remove the shock absorber.

6. Check the shock for:

   a. Excessive oil leakage, some minor weeping is permissible;

   b. Bent center rod, damaged outer case, or other defects;

   c. Pump the shock absorber several times, if it offers even resistance on full strokes it may be considered serviceable.

7. Install the upper shock mounting nut and bolt. Hand-tighten the nut.

8. Install the bottom eye of the shock over the spring stud or into the mounting bracket and insert the bolt and nut. Tighten the nut to 52 ft. lbs. on the 1986 Excel and 58 ft. lbs. on the 1987–88 Excel.

9. Tighten the upper fasteners to 52 ft. lbs. on the 1986 Excel and 58 ft. lbs. on the 1987–88 Excel.

Coil Spring

REMOVAL & INSTALLATION

1. Support the car securely at the rear of the body at approved points and remove the rear wheels.

2. Support the rear suspension arm with a floorjack. Then, remove the lower shock absorber attaching bolt, nut, and lockwasher.

3. Slowly lower the jack just to the point where the spring can be removed and remove the spring. If the spring is being replaced, transfer the spring seat to the new spring.

4. Install the spring in reverse order of the removal procedure, making sure the smaller diameter is upward. Make sure the spring identification and load markings match up.

5. Torque the lower shock mounting nut/bolt to 65–80 ft. lbs.

Rear Suspension Alignment

All Hyundai models have independent rear suspension systems on which unusual wear can cause alignment problems. Alignment cannot be adjusted, but camber can be checked in case handling or tire wear problems should occur. Alignment problems can be corrected only by replacement of major suspension components that have become severely worn or bent through abuse. In all cases, camber must be corrected through parts replacement.

Rear Wheel Bearings

REMOVAL, INSPECTION, PACKING, INSTALLATION & ADJUSTMENT

1. Loosen the lug nuts and raise and support the rear of the car.

2. Remove the grease cap, cotter pin serrated nut cap, axle shaft nut and washer.

3. Pull outward on the brake drum, positioning your hand to catch the outer bearing when it fall out.

4. Pry the inner grease seal from the hub and discard it.

5. Remove the inner bearing. If the bearings are being replaced, drive the bearing races from the hub.

6. Clean all old grease from the hub and bearings. If the old bearing are beings reused, clean them in a safe solvent and inspect them thoroughly.

7. If the bearings are being replaced, coat the new races with EP lithium wheel bearing grease and drive them into the hub, making sure they are fully and squarely seated.

8. Pack the hub cavity with new EP lithium wheel bearing grease, until the cavity is full.

9. Pack the bearings completely.

10. Install the inner bearing and drive a new grease seal into place.

11. Install the drum on the spindle and install the outer bearing, washer and shaft nut. Tighten the nut to 15 ft. lbs. while turning the drum, to seat

the bearings. Back off on the nut until it is loose, then torque it to 48 inch lbs. (4 ft. lbs.).

12. Install the serrated nut cap and a new cotter pin. If the cotter pin holes have to be aligned, back off on the nut no more than 15 degrees. If that won't align the holes, repeat the adjustment procedure.

STEERING

Steering Wheel

REMOVAL & INSTALLATION

1. Pull off the horn cover at the center of the wheel by grasping the upper edge with your fingers to release it.

Then, disconnect the horn wire connector.

2. Remove the steering wheel retaining nut. Matchmark the relationship between the wheel and shaft.

3. Screw the two bolts of a steering wheel puller into the wheel. Then, turn the bolt at the center of the puller to force the wheel off the steering shaft. Do not pound on the wheel to

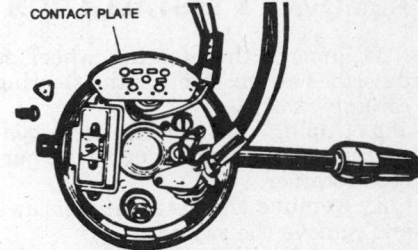

Turn signal switch removal

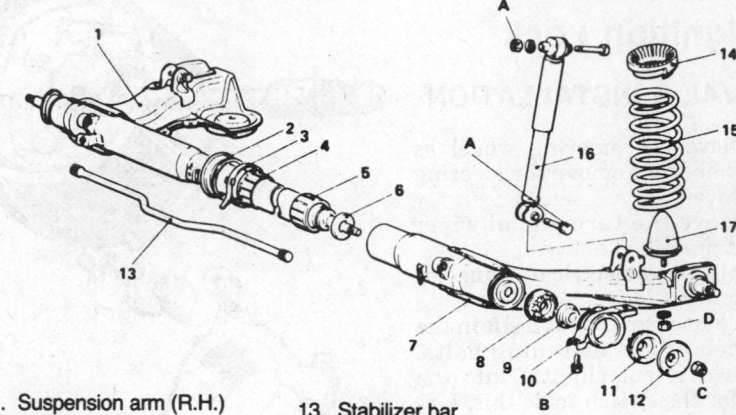

1. Suspension arm (R.H.)
2. Dust cover
3. Clamp
4. Bushing A
5. Bushing B
6. Rubber stopper
7. Suspension arm (L.H.)
8. rubber bushing (inner)
9. Rubber stopper
10. Fixture
11. Rubber bushing (outer)
12. Washer
13. Stabilizer bar
14. Spring seat
15. Coil spring
16. Shock absorber
17. Bump stopper

	Nm	ft. lbs.
A	65–80	46–56
B	50–70	36–51
C	80–100	56–70
D	18–25	13–18

Rear suspension

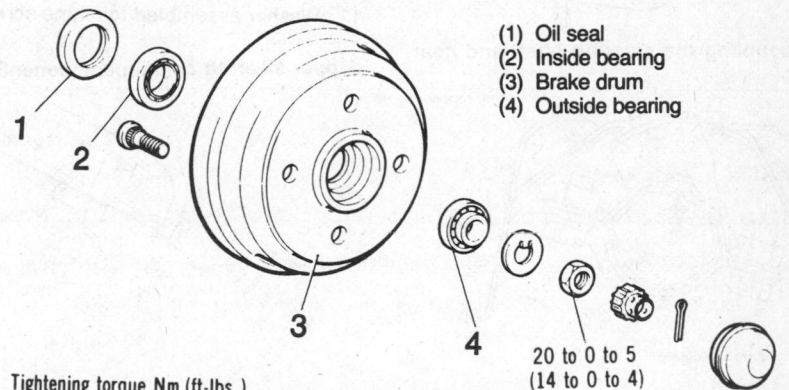

(1) Oil seal
(2) Inside bearing
(3) Brake drum
(4) Outside bearing

20 to 0 to 5
(14 to 0 to 4)

Tightening torque Nm (ft-lbs.)

Rear wheel bearings and hub

remove it, or the collapsible steering shaft may be damaged.

4. Install the wheel in reverse order (it can be pushed onto the shaft splines by hand far enough to start the retaining nut). Install the retaining nut and torque it to 26–32 ft. lbs.

Combination Switch

REMOVAL & INSTALLATION

1. Remove the steering wheel as described above. Remove the steering column cover.

2. Unplug the two electrical connectors. If necessary, remove the harness retainer.

3. Remove the retaining screws and remove the switch.

4. Installation is the reverse of the removal procedure.

Ignition Lock

REMOVAL & INSTALLATION

1. Remove the steering wheel as described above. Remove the steering column cover.

2. Remove the turn signal/wiper switch as described above.

3. Unplug the electrical connector for the ignition lock.

4. Use a hacksaw to cut a slit in the top of each of the fastening bolts. You'll have to cut slightly into the housing for the switch to do this. Unscrew the bolts and remove the switch.

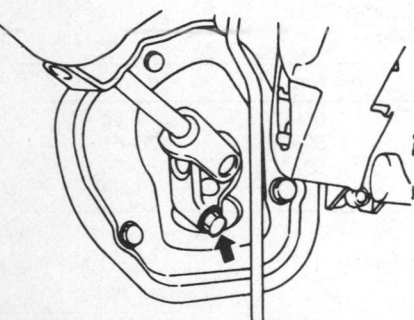

Uncoupling the steering shaft and gearbox

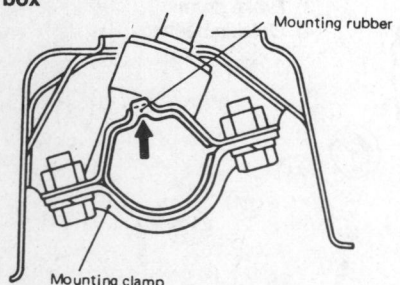

Locate the steering box rubber mount in the indentation in the crossmember as shown

5. Install the new switch in reverse order. Align the halves of the assembly around the steering column, align the assembly with the column boss, and then install the special new installation bolts just loosely. Verify that the ignition switch works and then tighten the bolts until their heads break off to prevent removal.

Manual Steering Gear

REMOVAL & INSTALLATION

1. Loosen the lug nuts.

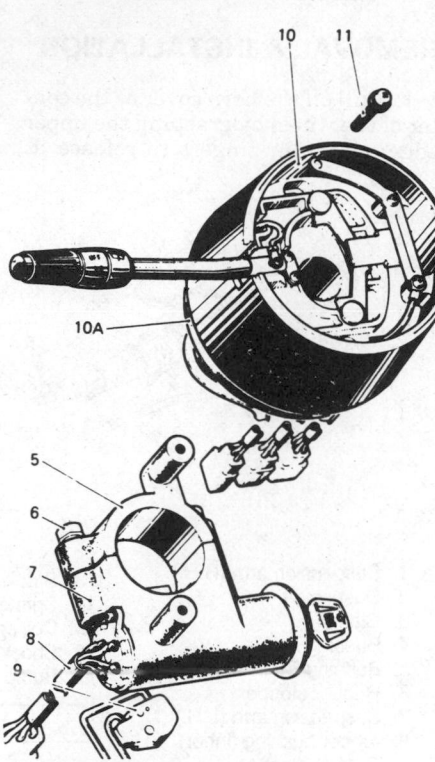

5. Bracket
6. Bolt
7. Body and cylinder
8. Ignition and starter switch
9. Door warning switch
10. Column switch
10A. Column switch rubber ring
11. Washer assembled machine screw

Upper steering column components

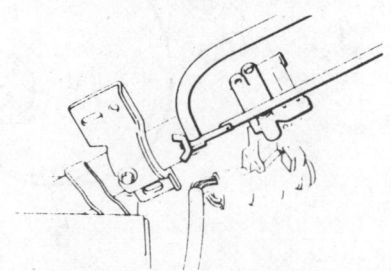

Using a hacksaw to cut screwdriver grooves into the ignition lock fastening

2. Raise and support the front end on jackstands under the frame.

3. Remove the wheels.

4. Remove the steering shaft-to-pinion coupling bolt.

5. Disconnect the tierod ends with a separator.

6. Removing the clamps securing the rack to the crossmember and remove the unit from the car. The tie rod ends can now be removed. Prior to removal, count the exact number of exposed threads on the tie rod ends, then loosen the locknut and unscrew the tie rod end. When installing new tie rod ends, oil the threads and screw them into place so that the previously noted number of threads is visible with the locknut tight. As a further reference, the distance between the end of the tie rod boot and the centerline of the tie rod ball stud should be 9.6 in. (243.5mm). Torque the locknut to 38 ft. lbs.

7. Install the rubber mount for the gear box with the slit on the downside. The remainder of installation is the reverse of removal. Torque the rack-to-crossmember bolts to 22–29 ft. lbs.; the coupling bolt to 11–14 ft. lbs. and the tierod nuts to 11–25 ft. lbs.

ADJUSTMENT

1. Mount the rack and pinion assembly in a soft jawed vise, clamping on the rack mounting area, only.

2. Using a spline adapter on an in.-pound torque wrench, turn the pinion shaft at the rate of one full turn every 4–6 seconds, turning the steering from lock-to-lock. Measure the total preload lock-to-lock. Preload should be 3.6–9.6 inch lbs.

3. Place a pull scale on each tie rod end, in turn, and pull straight away. The rack starting force should be 11–66 lbs.

4. If the specifications in either Steps 2 or 3 or not met, the rubber cushion and yoke spring behind the pinion shaft nut will have to be replaced.

ADJUSTMENT

1. Mount the steering rack in a soft-jawed vise with the steering coupling (pinion) shaft horizontal and the rack preload plate on the upside.

2. Remove the preload plate, shim pack and gasket.

3. Remove the spring and slipper bearing.

4. Remove the pinion shaft cover plate and gasket.

5. Position a dial gauge on a mounting block and zero the gauge by placing the block on a flat surface.

Zero the gauge with the stylus just touching the glass.

6. Place the block on the rack slipper opening gasket surface and position the stylus on the pinion housing body.

7. Using the pinion shaft, turn the rack from lock-to-lock and measure the deflection.

8. Using a micrometer, measure the thickness of the shim pack, including gasket. Assemble the shim pack, so that its thickness, including gasket, is 0.0019–0.0049 in. (0.050–0.125mm) greater than the recorded deflection.

9. Place this shim pack and gasket on the rack slipper opening and install the preload cover plate. Coat the bolt threads with sealer and torque them to 54–80 inch lbs.

10. Place a spline adapter on an in.-pound torque wrench, position it on the pinion shaft and measure the turning torque lock-to-lock. Turning torque should be 5–18 inch lbs. An incorrect torque reading indicates that either the shim pack thickness is off, or there is damage or lack of lubricant within the rack.

Power Steering Gear

REMOVAL & INSTALLATION

1. Loosen the lug nuts.
2. Raise and support the front end on jackstands under the frame.
3. Remove the wheels.
4. Remove the steering shaft-to-pinion coupling bolt.
5. Disconnect the tie rod ends with a separator.
6. Drain the fluid.
7. Disconnect the hoses from the gear box.
8. Remove the band from the steering joint cover.
9. Unbolt and remove the stabilizer bar.
10. Remove the rear roll stopper-to-center member bolt and move the rear roll stopper forward.
11. Remove the rack unit mounting clamp bolts and take the unit out the left side of the car. The tie rod ends can now be removed. Prior to removal, count the exact number of exposed threads on the tie rod ends, then loosen the locknut and unscrew the tie rod end. When installing new tie rod ends, oil the threads and screw them into place so that the previously noted number of threads is visible with the locknut tight. As a further reference, the distance between the end of the tie rod boot and the point at which the locknut touches the tie rod ball socket body should be 6.1–6.2 in. (155.5–157.5mm). Torque the locknut to 38 ft. lbs.

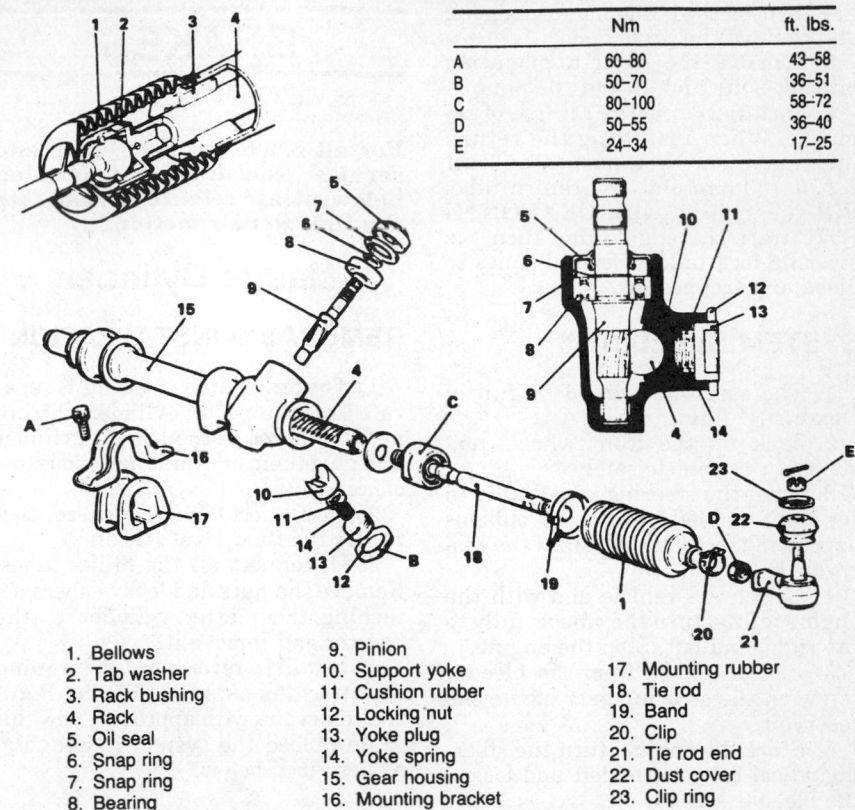

	Nm	ft. lbs.
A	60–80	43–58
B	50–70	36–51
C	80–100	58–72
D	50–55	36–40
E	24–34	17–25

1. Bellows
2. Tab washer
3. Rack bushing
4. Rack
5. Oil seal
6. Snap ring
7. Snap ring
8. Bearing
9. Pinion
10. Support yoke
11. Cushion rubber
12. Locking nut
13. Yoke plug
14. Yoke spring
15. Gear housing
16. Mounting bracket
17. Mounting rubber
18. Tie rod
19. Band
20. Clip
21. Tie rod end
22. Dust cover
23. Clip ring

Manual rack and pinion steering assembly

12. Installation is the reverse of removal. Make sure that the rubber isolators have their nubs aligned with the holes in the clamps. Apply rubber cement to the slits in the gear mounting grommet. Tighten the clamp bolt to 43–58 ft. lbs., the tie rod nuts to 11–25 ft. lbs., and the coupling bolt to 22–25 ft. lbs.

13. Fill the system with DEXRON®II ATF.

ADJUSTMENTS

Total Pinion Preload

1. Mount the rack in a soft jawed vise, clamping the vise on the rack mounting areas, only.
2. Using a spline adapter on an in.-pound torque wrench, rotate the pinion shaft several times, lock-to-lock, and note the total pinion preload. Preload should be 5–11 inch lbs.
3. If the preload is note within specifications, adjust the position of the rack support cover and recheck the preload. If that doesn't work, the rack support cover components are defective.

Tie Rod Swing Resistance

1. With the rack assembly mounted in a soft jawed vise, clamped on the rack mounting areas, only, give 10 hard swings on the tie rod.

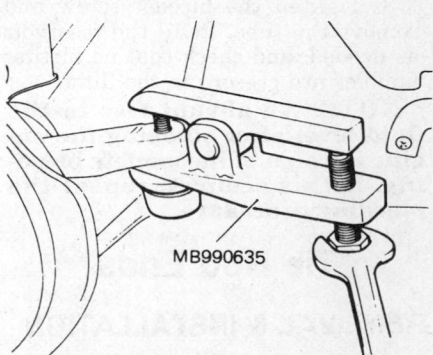

MB990635

Freeing the tie rod end ball stud

2. Attach a pull scale to the tie rod end and check the swing resistance. Resistance should be 2–4½ lbs. If resistance is excessive, replace the tie rod. If resistance is below 2 lbs. the tie rod may be used if resistance is smooth and even.

Power Steering Pump

REMOVAL & INSTALLATION

1. Place a drain pan under the pump.
2. Disconnect the pressure hose from the pump.
3. Disconnect the return hose from the pump.

4. Loosen the pump mounting bolts and remove the drive belt.

5. Remove the pump-to-mounting bracket bolts and lift out the pump.

6. Installation is the reverse of removal. When installing the return line, make sure you push it at least 1.2 in. (30mm) onto the return tube. Fill the system with DEXRON®II ATF, start the engine and turn the steering lock-to-lock several times to bleed any trapped air.

SYSTEM BLEEDING

1. The reservoir should be full of Dexron® II fluid.

2. Jack up the front wheels and support the vehicle safely.

3. Turn the steering wheel fully to the right and left until no air bubbles appear in the fluid. Maintain the reservoir level.

4. Lower the vehicle and with the engine idling, turn the wheels fully to the right and left. Stop the engine.

5. Install a tube from the bleeder screw on the steering gear box to the reservoir.

6. Start the engine, turn the steering wheel fully to the left and loosen the bleeder screw.

7. Repeat the procedure until no air bubbles pass through the tube.

8. Tighten the bleeder screw and remove the tube. Refill the reservoir as needed. and check that no further bubbles are present in the fluid.

NOTE: An abrupt rise in the fluid level after stopping the engine is a sign of incomplete bleeding. If this occures, repeat the bleeding procedure.

Tie Rod Ends

REMOVAL & INSTALLATION

1. Raise the car and support it securely at the front via axle stands. Remove the front wheels.

2. Remove the cotter pin and then remove the ball stud retaining nut. Use a vice-like tool (MB991113 or equivalent) to press the ballstud down and out of the steering knuckle.

3. Using a backup wrench on the flats at the inner end of the tie rod end, loosen the nut that retains the end to the tie rod coming out of the steering box. Now, unscrew the tie rod end, counting the turns required to remove it.

4. Install the new tie rod end in reverse order. Torque the castellated nut retaining the ballstud to 17 ft. lbs. Then, turn it just far enough to line up the castellations with the hole in the stud, and install a new cotter pin. Torque the inner nut to 36–40 ft. lbs.

BRAKES

For all brake system repair and service procedures not detailed below, please refer to "Brakes" in the Unit Repair section.

Master Cylinder

REMOVAL & INSTALLATION

1. The brake fluid reservoir is separate from the master cylinder. Disconnect the hoses at the master cylinder and plug them or drain the fluid into a clean container.

2. Disconnect the electrical connector for the fluid level sensor.

3. Disconnect all the brake tubes. Remove the nuts and lockwashers attaching the master cylinder to the booster and remove it.

4. Install in reverse order, torquing the attaching nuts to 6–9 ft. lbs. Refill the reservoirs with approved, new fluid and bleed the system thoroughly, as described below.

Proportioning Valve

The proportioning valve is located under the master cylinder and supported by the brake lines to which it is connected and a throughbolt. It does not require routine check or adjustment; however, if the car exhibits slightly unstable braking in a hard stop due to rear wheel lockup, it is best to have it tested with special high pressure gauges by a reputable mechanic.

REMOVAL & INSTALLATION

1. Disconnect the brake lines at the valve.

NOTE: Use a flare nut wrench to avoid damage to the lines and fittings.

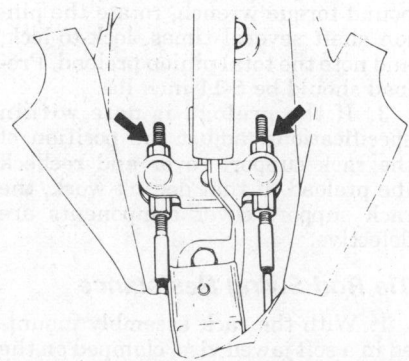

Parking brake cable adjusting nuts

2. Remove the mounting bolts and remove the valve.

NOTE: If the proportioning valve is found to be defective, it must be replaced.

3. Installation is the reverse of removal. Torque the mounting bolts to 15 ft. lbs.

4. Refill the system with fluid and bleed the brakes.

Power Brake Booster

REMOVAL & INSTALLATION

1. Slide back the clip and disconnect the vacuum supply line at the brake booster. Pull gently in order to avoid damaging the check valve.

2. Remove the master cylinder as described above.

3. Disconnect the pushrod at the brake pedal. This requires pulling the lockpin out of the pedal clevis pin and then pulling the latter out of the pedal lever and clevis rod.

4. Remove the mounting bolts and nuts from the firewall and remove the booster.

5. Install in reverse order, torquing the mounting nuts to 6–9 ft. lbs. Bleed the system.

Wheel Cylinders

REMOVAL & INSTALLATION

1. Remove the brake drums and shoes as described above. Disconnect the brake line where it connects to the wheel cylinder behind the backing plate, and plug the open end of the brake line.

2. Remove the two bolts that fasten the wheel cylinder to the backing plate from behind it, and remove the wheel cylinder.

3. Installation is the reverse of the removal procedure. Torque the mounting bolts for the wheel cylinder to 6–9 ft. lbs. Bleed the system as described above. Make sure the self-adjusters have taken up play so the brakes actuate normally before operating the vehicle.

Parking Brake Cable

ADJUSTMENT

1. Apply the brake with about 45 lbs. tension and count the number of clicks required. 5–7 clicks should be required. If the number of clicks is incorrect, proceed with the remaining steps.

2. Remove the rear console box. Remove the parking brake cover and the

ashtray. Then, remove the console mounting screws and remove the console.

3. Release the brake and then adjust the cable adjusting nuts until all cable slack is just removed. Then, apply the footbrake (the engine should be idling) and release it, apply the handbrake and release it, apply the footbrake and release it, etc. in a continuous cycle until the automatic adjusters stop clicking.

4. Recheck the number of clicks required to apply the brake, adjust the cable adjuster, and repeat the check until the number of clicks required is correct.

5. Reinstall the console in reverse of the removal procedure.

6. Raise the rear of the car and support it safely. Release the handbrake and rotate each rear wheel to make sure the brakes are not dragging.

REMOVAL & INSTALLATION

1. Block the front wheels, loosen the rear lugnuts, raise the car and support it on jackstands, and remove the rear wheels and brake drums.

2. Remove the console box and rear seat (see the adjustment procedure above).

3. Release the handbrake and then disconnect the cable connectors at the equalizer. It may be necessary to loosen the cable adjusting nuts to do this.

4. Disconnect all cable clamps from the body. Remove the mounting bolts for the large mounting clamp located just forward of where the cables pass through the body grommets.

5. Pull the cables and grommets out of the body.

6. Disconnect the cables at the rear brakes.

7. Install in reverse order. Make sure the grommets are installed in the body completely and that the concave side faces to the rear. Adjust the handbrake mechanism as described above. Adjust the switch for the indicator light so the light comes on when the lever is pulled one notch.

CHASSIS ELECTRICAL

Heater Blower

REMOVAL & INSTALLATION

NOTE: To remove either the blower or core, the heater case must be removed.

1. Disconnect the battery ground.
2. Place the control in the HOT position.
3. Drain the cooling system.
4. Remove the heater hoses from the core tubes.
5. Remove the lower instrument panel section.
6. Remove the center console and on-board computer.
7. Loosen the heater duct mounting screw. Then, pushing downward and pulling, remove the heater ducts.
8. Disconnect the heater control cable.
9. Disconnect the wiring at the motor.
10. Remove the five heater case mounting bolts and remove the heater case from under the dash.
11. Separate the case halves and remove the blower.
12. Installation is the reverse of removal. Adjust the control cable and refill the cooling system.

Heater Core

REMOVAL & INSTALLATION

1. Disconnect the battery ground cable.
2. Set the heater control to HOT and drain the cooling system.
3. Disconnect the coolant hoses at the heater core tubes, in the engine compartment.
4. Remove the lower instrument panel section.
5. Remove the center console and on-board computer.
6. Loosen the heater duct mounting screw.

7. Pushing downward and pull, remove the heater ducts.
8. Disconnect the heater control cable.
9. Disconnect the wiring at the motor.
10. Remove the five heater case mounting bolts and remove the heater case from under the dash.
11. Separate the case halves and remove the blower.
12. Installation is the reverse of removal. Refill the cooling system.

Radio

REMOVAL & INSTALLATION

1. Remove the panel that surrounds the parking brake. Remove the ashtray.

2. Remove the two console mounting screws from each side, two near the handbrake, and one at the rear of the ashtray. Then, remove the console.

3. Remove the four mounting screws from the radio bracket, and remove the radio and bracket as an assembly. Now, separate the radio and bracket. Note that the radio fuses are located behind the radio and are now accessible.

4. Installation is the reverse of removal.

Windshield Wiper Switch

REMOVAL & INSTALLATION

Front Wiper Switch

NOTE: The windshield wiper switch is part of a combination (multi-function) switch.

1. Heater unit
2. Blower unit
3. Duct
4. Cover
5. Cover

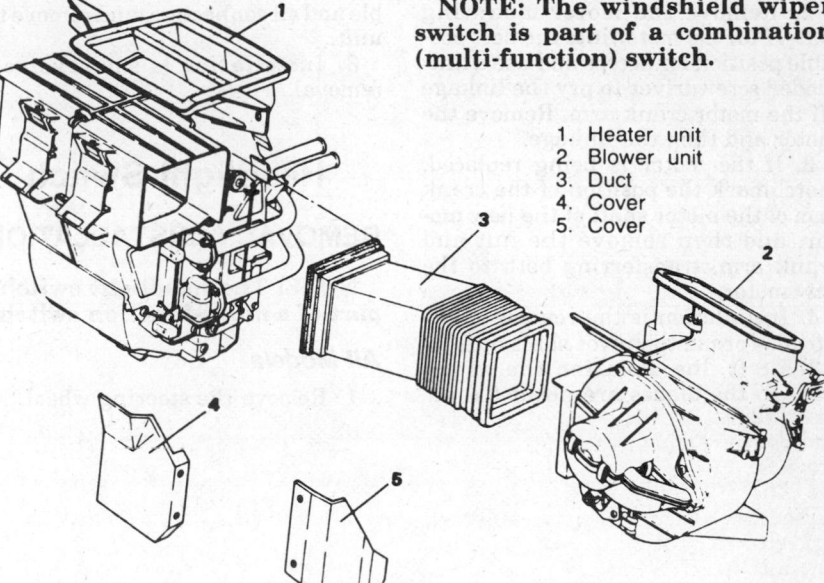

Heater and blower assembly

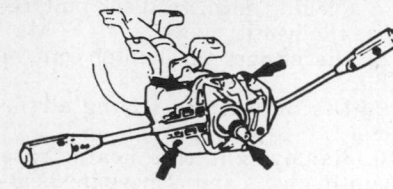

Windshield wiper switch mounting

All Models

1. Remove the steering wheel.
2. Remove the steering column cover.
3. Remove the two mounting screws and pull the switch out.
4. Installation is the reverse of removal.

Rear Wiper Switch

1. Pry the switch bezel from the panel.
2. Reach behind the panel and disconnect the wiring from the switch.
3. Depress the two retainers and pull the switch from the panel.
4. Installation is the reverse of removal.

Windshield Wiper Motor

REMOVAL & INSTALLATION

Front Wiper Motor

1. Remove the air inlet and cowl front center trim panels. Remove the three pivot shaft mounting nuts and push the pivot shafts into the area under the cowl.
2. Remove the motor mounting bolts. Pull the motor into the best possible position for access and use a flat-bladed screwdriver to pry the linkage off the motor crank arm. Remove the motor and then the linkage.
3. If the motor is being replaced, matchmark the position of the crank arm of the motor shaft of the new motor, and then remove the nut and crank arm, transferring both to the new motor.
4. Installation is the reverse of removal. Torque the pivot shaft nuts to 4.3–5.8 ft. lbs. Position the wiper arms so the blades are about 0.6 in.

(15mm) above the lower windshield molding on the driver's side and 0.7 in. (20mm) above it on the passenger's side. Torque the wiper arm mounting nuts to 7.2–12 ft. lbs. Make sure the wiper motor is securely grounded.

Rear Wiper Motor

1. Remove the wiper blade and arm by lifting the wiper blade lock nut cover and removing the locknut. Then, pull the arm from the shaft.
2. Remove the lift gate trim panel and disconnect the wiring harness connector.
3. Match mark the relationship of the crank arm to the motor and remove the crank arm.
4. Remove the inside and outside motor mounting nuts and remove the motor.
5. Installation is the reverse of the removal procedure.

NOTE: When installing the wiper arm, the distance between the tip of the blade and the lower window molding should be 1.6 in. (40mm).

Instrument Cluster

REMOVAL & INSTALLATION

1. Remove the two meter hood attaching screws, located at the bottom, and tilt the lower meter hood outward. Pull the hood downward to release the locking tangs at the top and remove it.
2. Remove the four meter assembly mounting screw (two at top and two at the bottom) and pull the unit outward. Disconnect the speedometer cable and all connectors, and remove the unit.
3. Installation is the reverse of removal.

Headlight Switch

REMOVAL & INSTALLATION

NOTE: The headlight switch is part of a multi-function switch.

All Models

1. Remove the steering wheel.

2. Remove the steering column cover.
3. Remove the two mounting screws and pull the switch out.
4. Installation is the reverse of removal.

Stoplight Switch

REMOVAL & INSTALLATION

All Models

The switch is located on a bracket above the brake pedal arm. To replace the switch, loosen the locknut, unplug the wiring connector and unscrew the switch.

ADJUSTMENT

Loosen the locknut and adjust the switch so that the distance between the switch outer case and the pedal arm is 0.02–0.04 in. (0.5–1.0mm).

Fuses
LOCATION

The fuse box is located behind a snap-off cover in front of the driver's left knee. The sunroof fuse is located in the electrical harness for the roof circuit—at the extreme right side of the dashboard, directly behind the right windshield pillar. The radio fuse is located behind the radio and is accessible after the radio is removed.

The hazard and turn signal flashers are located in the relay box on the left fender in the engine compartment, and are replaced by simply unplugging the burnt out flasher and plugging a new one in with all the prongs properly lined up.

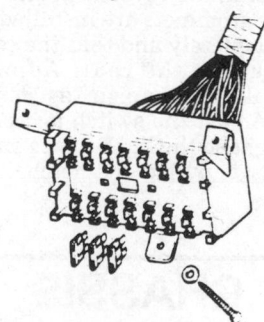

Fuse box assembly

Isuzu

I-Mark, Impulse

SERIAL NUMBER IDENTIFICATION

Vehicle Identification Plate

The vehicle identification number is embossed on a plate, that is attached to the top left corner of the instrument panel. The number is visible through the windshield from the outside of the vehicle. The eighth digit of the number, indicates the engine model and the tenth digit represents the model year (example is G for 1986).

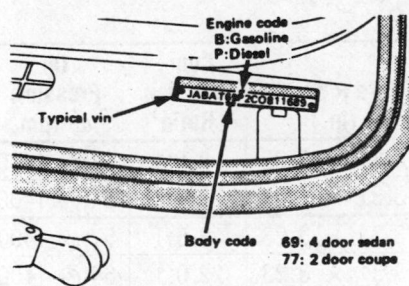

Vehicle identification plate location

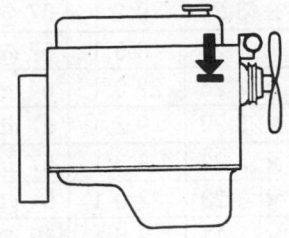

G200Z engine serial number location

Engine Number

The Impulse equipped with the G200Z engine, has the engine serial number stamped on the top right corner of the engine block.

4ZC1-T engine serial number location

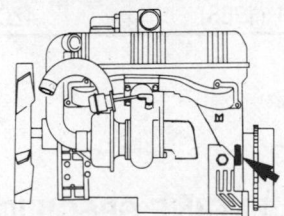

G180Z engine serial number location

The Impulse equipped with the 4ZC1-T engine, has the number stamped on the left rear corner of the engine block, near the engine to transaxle mounting. On the I-Mark equipped with the G180Z engine, the number is stamped on the top right corner of the engine block. The I-Mark equipped with the 4FB1 diesel

Engine serial number location—diesel

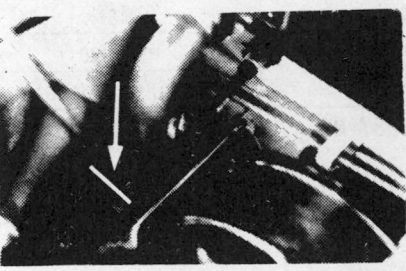

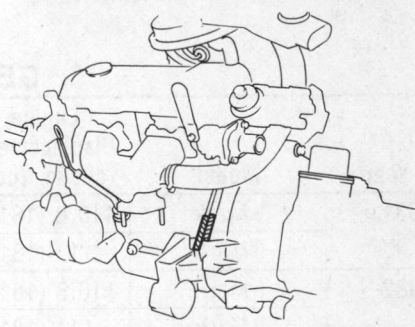

4XC1-U engine serial number location

engine, has the number stamped on the left rear corner of the engine block. The I-Mark (FWD) equipped with the 4XC1-U engine, has the number stamped on the flange near the transaxle mounting, toward the front of the vehicle.

Transmission

Both manual transmissions have their serial numbers on the side of the main case. The automatic location is similar.

ENGINE IDENTIFICATION

Year	Model	Engine Displacement cu. in. (cc)	Engine Series Identification	No. of Cylinders	Engine Type
1981	I-Mark	110.8 (1816)	G1080Z	4	OHC
	I-Mark	111 (1815)	4FBI-Diesel	4	OHC
1982	I-Mark	110.8 (1816)	G1080Z	4	OHC
	I-Mark	111 (1815)	4FBI-Diesel	4	OHC
1983	I-Mark	110.8 (1816)	G1080Z	4	OHC
	I-Mark	111 (1815)	4FBI-Diesel	4	OHC
	Impulse	118.9 (1949)	G200Z	4	SOHC
1984	I-Mark	110.8 (1816)	G1080Z	4	OHC
	I-Mark	111 (1815)	4FBI-Diesel	4	OHC
	Impulse	118.9 (1949)	G200Z	4	SOHC
1985	I-Mark (RWD)	110.8 (1816)	G1080Z	4	OHC
	I-Mark (RWD)	111 (1815)	4FBI-Diesel	4	OHC
	I-Mark (FWD)	90 (1471)	4XCI-U	4	OHC
	Impulse	118.9 (1949)	G200Z	4	SOHC
	Impulse (Turbo)	121 (1983)	4ZCI-T	4	Turbo SOHC
1986	I-Mark	90 (1471)	4XCI-U	4	OHC
	Impulse	118.9 (1949)	G200Z	4	SOHC
	Impulse (Turbo)	121 (1983)	4ZCI-T	4	Turbo SOHC
1987–88	I-Mark	90 (1471)	4XCI-U	4	OHC
	Impulse	118.9 (1949)	G200Z	4	SOHC
	Impulse (Turbo)	121 (1983)	4ZCI-T	4	Turbo OHC

GENERAL ENGINE SPECIFICATIONS

Year	Model	Engine Displacement cu. in. (cc)	Fuel System Type	Net Horsepower @ rpm	Net Torque @ rpm (ft. lbs.)	Bore × Stroke (in.)	Compression Ratio	Oil Pressure @ rpm
1981	I-Mark	110.8 (1816)	2 bbl	80 @ 4800	95 @ 3000	3.31 × 3.23	8.5:1	57 @ 1400
	I-Mark	111 (1815)	Diesel	51 @ 5000	72 @ 3000	3.31 × 3.23	22.0:1	64 @ 1400
1982	I-Mark	110.8 (1816)	2 bbl	80 @ 4800	95 @ 3000	3.31 × 3.23	8.5:1	57 @ 1400
	I-Mark	111 (1815)	Diesel	51 @ 5000	72 @ 3000	3.31 × 3.23	22.0:1	64 @ 1400
1983	I-Mark	110.8 (1816)	2 bbl	80 @ 4800	95 @ 3000	3.31 × 3.23	8.5:1	57 @ 1400
	I-Mark	111 (1815)	Diesel	51 @ 5000	72 @ 3000	3.31 × 3.23	22.0:1	64 @ 1400
	Impulse	118.9 (1949)	EFI	90 @ 5000	108 @ 3000	3.43 × 3.29	9.2:1	57 @ 1400
1984	I-Mark	110.8 (1816)	2 bbl	80 @ 4800	95 @ 3000	3.31 × 3.23	8.5:1	57 @ 1400
	I-Mark	111 (1815)	Diesel	51 @ 5000	72 @ 3000	3.31 × 3.23	22.0:1	64 @ 1400
	Impulse	118.9 (1949)	EFI	90 @ 5000	146 @ 3000	3.43 × 3.29	9.2:1	57 @ 1400
1985	I-Mark (RWD)	110.8 (1816)	2 bbl	80 @ 4800	95 @ 3000	3.31 × 3.23	8.5:1	57 @ 1400
	I-Mark (RWD)	111 (1815)	Diesel	51 @ 5000	72 @ 3000	3.31 × 3.23	22.0:1	64 @ 1400
	I-Mark (FWD)	90 (1471)	2 bbl	70 @ 5400	87 @ 3400	3.03 × 3.11	9.6:1	49 @ 5200
	Impulse	118.9 (1949)	EFI	90 @ 5000	146 @ 3000	3.43 × 3.29	9.2:1	57 @ 1400
	Impulse (Turbo)	121 (1983)	EFI	140 @ 5400	166 @ 3000	3.47 × 3.29	7.9:1	60 @ 1400

GENERAL ENGINE SPECIFICATIONS

Year	Model	Engine Displacement cu. in. (cc)	Fuel System Type	Net Horsepower @ rpm	Net Torque @ rpm (ft. lbs.)	Bore × Stroke (in.)	Compression Ratio	Oil Pressure @ rpm
1986	I-Mark	90 (1471)	2 bbl	70 @ 5400	87 @ 3400	3.03 × 3.11	9.6:1	49 @ 5200
	Impulse	118.9 (1949)	EFI	90 @ 5000	146 @ 3000	3.43 × 3.29	9.2:1	57 @ 1400
	Impulse (Turbo)	121 (1983)	EFI	140 @ 5400	166 @ 3000	3.47 × 3.29	7.9:1	60 @ 1400
1987–88	I-Mark (S)	90 (1471)	2 bbl	70 @ 5400	87 @ 3400	3.03 × 3.11	9.6:1	49 @ 5200
	I-Mark (RS)	90 (1471)	EFI	110 @ 5400	120 @ 3500	3.03 × 3.11	8.0:1	49 @ 5200
	Impulse	118.9 (1949)	EFI	90 @ 5000	146 @ 3000	3.43 × 3.29	9.2:1	57 @ 1400
	Impulse (Turbo)	121 (1994)	EFI	140 @ 5400	166 @ 3000	3.47 × 3.29	7.9:1	60 @ 1400

GASOLINE ENGINE TUNE-UP SPECIFICATIONS

Year	Model	Engine Displacement cu. in. (cc)	Spark Plugs Type	Spark Plugs Gap (in.)	Ignition Timing (deg.) MT	Ignition Timing (deg.) AT	Compression Pressure (psi)	Fuel Pump (psi)	Idle Speed (rpm) MT	Idle Speed (rpm) AT	Valve Clearance In.	Valve Clearance Ex.
1981	I-Mark	110.8 (1816)	BPR6ES11	.040	6B	6B	170.6	3.6	900	900	.006	.010
1982	I-Mark	110.8 (1816)	BPR6ES11	.040	6B	6B	170.6	3.6	900	900	.006	.010
1983	I-Mark	110.8 (1816)	BPR6ES11	.040	6B	6B	170.6	3.6	900	900	.006	.010
	Impulse	118.9 (1949)	BPR6ES11	.040	12B	12B	178.0	3.6	900	900	.006	.010
1984	I-Mark	110.8 (1816)	BPR6ES11	.040	6B	6B	170.6	3.6	900	900	.006	.010
	Impulse	118.9 (1949)	BPR6ES11	.040	12B	12B	178.0	3.6	900	900	.006	.010
1985	I-Mark (RWD)	110.8 (1816)	BPR6ES11	.040	6B	6B	170.6	3.6	900	900	.006	.010
	I-Mark (FWD)	90 (1475)	BPR6ES11	.040	3B	3B	177.8	3.6	750	1000	.006	.010
	Impulse	118.9 (1949)	BPR6ES11	.040	12B	12B	178.0	3.6	900	900	.006	.010
	Impulse	121 (1983)	BPR6ES11	.040	12B	12B	178.0	3.6	900	900	.006	.010

FIRING ORDERS

NOTE: To avoid confusion, always replace spark wires one at a time.

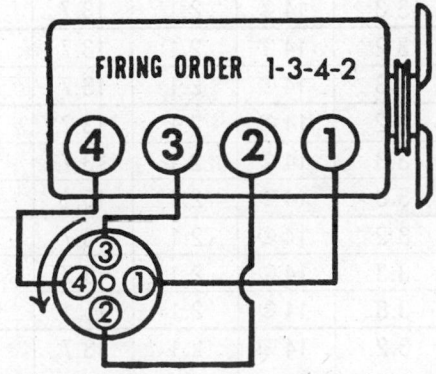

FIRING ORDER 1-3-4-2

Firing order—gasoline engine

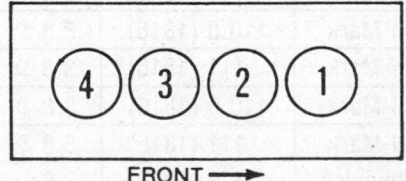

FRONT →

Firing order—diesel engine, 1-3-4-2

GASOLINE ENGINE TUNE-UP SPECIFICATIONS

Year	Model	Engine Displacement cu. in. (cc)	Spark Plugs Type	Gap (in.)	Ignition Timing (deg.) MT	AT	Compression Pressure (psi)	Fuel Pump (psi)	Idle Speed (rpm) MT	AT	Valve Clearance In.	Ex.
1986	I-Mark	90 (1475)	BPR6ES11	.040	3B	3B	177.8	3.6	750	1000	.006	.010
	Impulse	118.9 (1949)	BPR6ES11	.040	12B	12B	178.0	3.6	900	900	.006	.010
	Impulse	121 (1983)	BPR6ES11	.040	12B	12B	178.0	3.6	900	900	.006	.010
1987	I-Mark	90 (1475)	BPR6ES11	.040	3B	3B	177.8	3.6	750	100	.006	.010
	Impulse	118.9 (1949)	BPR6ES11	.040	12B	12B	178.0	3.6	900	900	.006	.010
	Impulse	121 (1983)	BPR6ES11	.040	12B	12B	178.0	3.6	900	900	.006	.010
1988	All	SEE UNDERHOOD SPECIFICATIONS STICKER										

DIESEL ENGINE TUNE-UP SPECIFICATIONS

Year	Engine Displacement cu. in. (cc)	Valve Clearance Intake (in.)	Exhaust (in.)	Intake Valve Opens (deg.)	Injection Pump Setting (deg.)	Injection Nozzle (psi)	Idle Speed (rpm)	Cranking Compression Pressure (psi)
1981	111 (1815)	0.010	0.014	32B	18B	1706-1848	625 ①	441
1982	111 (1815)	0.010	0.014	32B	18B	1706-1848	625 ①	441
1983	111 (1815)	0.010	0.014	32B	18B	1706-1848	625 ①	441
1984	111 (1815)	0.010	0.014	32B	12B	1706-1848	②	441
1985	111 (1815)	0.010	0.014	32B	12B	1706-1848	②	441

B—Before Top Dead Center
① Auto. Trans.: 725 rpm
② Man. Trans.: 575–675 rpm
   Auto. Trans.: 675–775 rpm

CAPACITIES

Year	Model	Engine Displacement cu. in. (cc)	Engine Crankcase with Filter	without Filter	Transmission (pts) 4-Spd	5-Spd	Auto.	Drive Axle (pts.)	Fuel Tank (gal.)	Cooling System (qts.)
1981	I-Mark	110.8 (1816)	3.8 ①	3.4	2.8	3.2	14 ②	2.1	13.7	6.8
	I-Mark	111 (1815)	3.8 ①	3.4	2.8	3.3	14 ②	2.1	13.7	7.4
1982	I-Mark	110.8 (1816)	3.8 ①	3.4	2.8	3.2	14 ②	2.1	13.7	6.8
	I-Mark	111 (1815)	3.8 ①	3.4	2.8	3.3	14 ②	2.1	13.7	7.4
1983	I-Mark	110.8 (1816)	3.8 ①	3.4	2.8	3.2	14 ②	2.1	13.7	6.8
	I-Mark	111 (1815)	3.8 ①	3.4	2.8	3.3	14 ②	2.1	13.7	7.4
	Impulse	118.9 (1949)	3.8 ①	3.4	—	3.8	14 ②	2.1	15.1	8.0
1984	I-Mark	110.8 (1816)	3.8 ①	3.4	2.8	3.2	14 ②	2.1	13.7	6.8
	I-Mark	111 (1815)	3.8 ①	3.4	2.8	3.3	14 ②	2.1	13.7	7.4
	Impulse	118.9 (1949)	3.8 ①	3.4	—	3.8	14 ②	2.1	15.1	8.0
1985	I-Mark (RWD)	110.8 (1816)	3.8 ①	3.4	2.8	3.2	14 ②	2.1	13.7	6.8
	I-Mark	111 (1815)	3.8 ①	3.4	2.8	3.3	14 ②	2.1	13.7	7.4

CAPACITIES

Year	Model	Engine Displacement cu. in. (cc)	Engine Crankcase with Filter	Engine Crankcase without Filter	Transmission (pts) 4-Spd	Transmission (pts) 5-Spd	Transmission (pts) Auto.	Drive Axle (pts.)	Fuel Tank (gal.)	Cooling System (qts.)
1985	I-Mark (FWD)	90 (1471)	3.2	2.8	—	2.8	14 ②	2.1	11.1	6.8
	Impulse	118.9 (1949)	3.8 ①	3.4	—	3.8	14 ②	2.1	15.1	8.0
	Impulse (Turbo)	121 (1983)	3.8 ①	3.4	—	3.3	14 ②	3.1	15.1	9.5
1986	I-Mark	90 (1471)	3.8	2.8	—	2.8	14 ②	2.1	11.1	6.8
	Impulse	118.9 (1949)	3.8 ①	3.4	—	3.8	14 ②	2.1	15.1	9.3
	Impulse (Turbo)	121 (1983)	3.8 ①	3.4	—	3.3	14 ②	3.1	15.1	9.5
1987–88	I-Mark	90 (1471)	3.2	2.8	—	2.8	14 ②	2.1	11.1	6.4
	Impulse	118.9 (1949)	3.8 ①	3.4	—	3.8	14 ②	2.1	15.1	9.3
	Impulse (Turbo)	121 (1983)	3.8 ①	3.4	—	3.3	14 ②	3.1	15.1	9.5

① The original fill is 5.0 qts., except for the diesel which is 5.5 qts.
② 26.8 pts. with torque converter

CAMSHAFT SPECIFICATIONS

All measurements given in inches.

Year	Engine Displacement cu. in. (cc)	Journal Diameter 1	Journal Diameter 2	Journal Diameter 3	Journal Diameter 4	Journal Diameter 5	Lobe Lift In.	Lobe Lift Ex.	Bearing Clearance	Camshaft End Play
1981	110.8 (1816)	1.3362-1.3368	1.3362-1.3368	1.3362-1.3368	1.3362-1.3368	1.3362-1.3368	1.451	1.451	0.0400-0.0900	0.0020-0.0059
	111 (1815)	1.1004-1.1010	1.1004-1.1010	1.1004-1.1010	1.1004-1.1010	1.1004-1.1010	1.451	1.451	0.0008-0.0035	—
1982	110.8 (1816)	1.3362-1.3368	1.3362-1.3368	1.3362-1.3368	1.3362-1.3368	1.3362-1.3368	1.451	1.451	0.0400-0.0900	0.0020-0.0059
	111 (1815)	1.1004-1.1010	1.1004-1.1010	1.1004-1.1010	1.1004-1.1010	1.1004-1.1010	1.451	1.451	0.0008-0.0035	—
1983	110.8 (1816)	1.3362-1.3368	1.3362-1.3368	1.3362-1.3368	1.3362-1.3368	1.3362-1.3368	1.451	1.451	0.0400-0.0900	0.0020-0.0059
	111 (1815)	1.1004-1.1010	1.1004-1.1010	1.1004-1.1010	1.1004-1.1010	1.1004-1.1010	1.451	1.451	0.0008-0.0035	—
	118.9 (1949)	1.3390	1.3390	1.3390	1.3390	1.3390	1.451	1.451	0.0030-0.0043	0.0020-0.0060
1984	110.8 (1816)	1.3362-1.3368	1.3362-1.3368	1.3362-1.3368	1.3362-1.3368	1.3362-1.3368	1.451	1.451	0.0400-0.0900	0.0020-0.0059
	111 (1815)	1.1004-1.1010	1.1004-1.1010	1.1004-1.1010	1.1004-1.1010	1.1004-1.1010	1.451	1.451	0.0008-0.0035	—
	118.9 (1949)	1.3390	1.3390	1.3390	1.3390	1.3390	1.451	1.451	0.0030-0.0043	0.0020-0.0060
1985	110.8 (1816)	1.3362-1.3368	1.3362-1.3368	1.3362-1.3368	1.3362-1.3368	1.3362-1.3368	1.451	1.451	0.0400-0.0900	0.0020-0.0059
	111 (1815)	1.1004-1.1010	1.1004-1.1010	1.1004-1.1010	1.1004-1.1010	1.1004-1.1010	1.451	1.451	0.0008-0.0035	—

CAMSHAFT SPECIFICATIONS

All measurements given in inches.

Year	Engine Displacement cu. in. (cc)	Journal Diameter 1	2	3	4	5	Lobe Lift In.	Ex.	Bearing Clearance	Camshaft End Play
1985	118.9 (1949)	1.3390	1.3390	1.3390	1.3390	1.3390	1.451	1.451	0.0030-0.0043	0.0020-0.0060
	121 (1983)	1.3390	1.3390	1.3390	1.3390	1.3390	1.451	1.451	0.0026-0.0043	0.0002-0.0059
	90 (1471)	1.0210-1.0220	1.0210-1.0220	1.0210-1.0220	1.0210-1.0220	1.0210-1.0220	1.426	1.426	0.0024-0.0044	0.0039-0.0071
1986	118.9 (1949)	1.3390	1.3390	1.3390	1.3390	1.3390	1.451	1.451	0.0030-0.0043	0.0020-0.0060
	121 (1983)	1.3390	1.3390	1.3390	1.3390	1.3390	1.451	1.451	0.0026-0.0043	0.0002-0.0059
	90 (1471)	1.0210-1.0220	1.0210-1.0220	1.0210-1.0220	1.0210-1.0220	1.0210-1.0220	1.426	1.426	0.0024-0.0044	0.0039-0.0071
1987-88	118.9 (1949)	1.3390	1.3390	1.3390	1.3390	1.3390	1.451	1.451	0.0030-0.0043	0.0020-0.0060
	121 (1983)	1.3390	1.3390	1.3390	1.3390	1.3390	1.451	1.451	0.0026-0.0043	0.0002-0.0069
	90 (1471)	1.0210-1.0220	1.0210-1.0220	1.0210-1.0220	1.0210-1.0220	1.0210-1.0220	1.426	1.426	0.0024-0.0044	0.0039-0.0071

CRANKSHAFT AND CONNECTING ROD SPECIFICATIONS

All measurements are given in inches.

Year	Engine Displacement cu. in. (cc)	Crankshaft Main Brg. Journal Dia.	Main Brg. Oil Clearance	Shaft End-play	Thrust on No.	Connecting Rod Journal Diameter	Oil Clearance	Side Clearance
1981	110.8 (1816)	2.2016-2.2022	0.0008-0.0025	0.012	3	1.929	0.0007-0.0030	0.0137
	111 (1815)	2.2016-2.2022	0.0012-0.0027	0.012	3	1.925	0.0016-0.0027	0.0137
1982	110.8 (1816)	2.2016-2.2022	0.0008-0.0025	0.012	3	1.929	0.0007-0.0030	0.0137
	111 (1815)	2.2016-2.2022	0.0012-0.0027	0.012	3	1.925	0.0016-0.0027	0.0137
1983	110.8 (1816)	2.2016-2.2022	0.0008-0.0025	0.012	3	1.929	0.0007-0.0030	0.0137
	111 (1815)	2.2016-2.2022	0.0012-0.0027	0.012	3	1.925	0.0016-0.0027	0.0137
	118.9 (1949)	2.2016-2.2022	0.0008-0.0025	0.012	3	1.929	0.0007-0.0029	0.0137
1984	110.8 (1816)	2.2016-2.2022	0.0008-0.0025	0.012	3	1.929	0.0007-0.0030	0.0137
	111 (1815)	2.2016-2.2022	0.0012-0.0027	0.012	3	1.925	0.0016-0.0027	0.0137
	118.9 (1949)	2.2016-2.2022	0.0008-0.0025	0.012	3	1.929	0.0007-0.0029	0.0137

CRANKSHAFT AND CONNECTING ROD SPECIFICATIONS
All measurements are given in inches.

Year	Engine Displacement cu. in. (cc)	Crankshaft				Connecting Rod		
		Main Brg. Journal Dia.	Main Brg. Oil Clearance	Shaft End-play	Thrust on No.	Journal Diameter	Oil Clearance	Side Clearance
1985	110.8 (1816)	2.2016-2.2022	0.0008-0.0025	0.012	3	1.929	0.0007-0.0030	0.0137
	111 (1815)	2.2016-2.2022	0.0012-0.0027	0.012	3	1.925	0.0016-0.0027	0.0137
	118.9 (1949)	2.2016-2.2022	0.0008-0.0025	0.012	3	1.929	0.0007-0.0029	0.0137
	121 (1983)	2.2032-2.2038	0.0008-0.0025	0.012	3	1.929	0.0007-0.0029	0.0078-0.0130
	90 (1471)	1.8865-1.8873	0.0008-0.0020	0.012	3	1.5720-1.5726	0.0010-0.0029	0.0790-0.0138
1986	118.9 (1949)	2.2016-2.2022	0.0008-0.0025	0.012	3	1.929	0.0007-0.0029	0.0137
	121 (1983)	2.2032-2.2038	0.0008-0.0025	0.012	3	1.929	0.0007-0.0029	0.0078-0.0130
	90 (1471)	1.8865-1.8873	0.0008-0.0020	0.012	3	1.5720-1.5726	0.0010-0.0029	0.0790-0.0138
1987-88	118.9 (1949)	2.2016-2.2022	0.0008-0.0025	0.012	3	1.929	0.0007-0.0029	0.0137
	121 (1983)	2.2032-2.2038	0.0008-0.0025	0.012	3	1.929	0.0007-0.0029	0.0078-0.0130
	90 (1471)	1.8865-1.8873	0.0008-0.0020	0.012	3	1.5720-1.5726	0.0010-0.0029	0.0790-0.0138

VALVE SPECIFICATIONS

Year	Engine Displacement cu. in. (cc)	Seat Angle (deg.)	Face Angle (deg.)	Spring Test Pressure (lbs.)	Spring Installed Height (in.)	Stem-to-Guide Clearance (in.)		Stem Diameter (in.)	
						Intake	Exhaust	Intake	Exhaust
1981	110.8 (1816)	45 ①	45	②	③	0.0009-0.0022	0.0015-0.0031	0.315	0.315
	111 (1815)	45 ①	45	②	④	0.0015-0.0027	0.0020-0.0030	0.313	0.313
1982	110.8 (1816)	45 ①	45	②	③	0.0009-0.0022	0.0015-0.0031	0.315	0.315
	111 (1815)	45 ①	45	②	④	0.0015-0.0027	0.0020-0.0030	0.313	0.313
1983	110.8 (1816)	45 ①	45	②	③	0.0009-0.0022	0.0015-0.0031	0.315	0.315
	111 (1815)	45 ①	45	②	④	0.0015-0.0027	0.0020-0.0030	0.313	0.313
	118.9 (1949)	45	45	55 @ 1.60	1.60	0.0009-0.0022	0.0015-0.0031	0.315	0.315

VALVE SPECIFICATIONS

Year	Engine Displacement cu. in. (cc)	Seat Angle (deg.)	Face Angle (deg.)	Spring Test Pressure (lbs.)	Spring Installed Height (in.)	Stem-to-Guide Clearance (in.)		Stem Diameter (in.)	
						Intake	Exhaust	Intake	Exhaust
1984	110.8 (1816)	45 ①	45	②	③	0.0009-0.0022	0.0015-0.0031	0.315	0.315
	111 (1815)	45 ①	45	②	④	0.0015-0.0027	0.0020-0.0030	0.313	0.313
	118.9 (1949)	45	45	55 @ 1.60	1.60	0.0009-0.0022	0.0015-0.0031	0.315	0.315
1985	110.8 (1816)	45 ①	45	②	③	0.0009-0.0022	0.0015-0.0031	0.315	0.315
	111 (1815)	45 ①	45	②	④	0.0015-0.0027	0.0020-0.0030	0.313	0.313
	118.9 (1949)	45	45	55 @ 1.60	1.60	0.0009-0.0022	0.0015-0.0031	0.315	0.315
	121 (1983)	45	45	55 @ 1.60	1.60	0.0009-0.0022	0.0015-0.0031	0.315	0.315
	90 (1471)	45	45	49 @ 1.57	1.57	0.0009-0.0022	0.0012-0.0025	0.272	0.272
1986	118.9 (1949)	45	45	55 @ 1.60	1.60	0.0009-0.0022	0.0015-0.0031	0.315	0.315
	121 (1983)	45	45	55 @ 1.60	1.60	0.0009-0.0022	0.0015-0.0031	0.315	0.315
	90 (1471)	45	45	49 @ 1.57	1.57	0.0009-0.0022	0.0012-0.0025	0.272	0.272
1987-88	118.9 (1949)	45	45	55 @ 1.60	1.60	0.0009-0.0022	0.0015-0.0031	0.315	0.315
	121 (1983)	45	45	55 @ 1.60	1.60	0.0009-0.0022	0.0015-0.0031	0.315	0.315
	90 (1471)	45	45	49 @ 1.57	1.57	0.0009-0.0022	0.0012-0.0025	0.272	0.272

① Because of the aluminum head and valve seat inserts, cut the valve seat with 15, 45 or 75 degree cutters. Use the minimum necessary to remove dents or damage, leaving the contact width inside the 0.0472-0.063 range
② Outer: 34.5 @ 1.614
Inner: 20 @ 1.516
③ Outer: 1.61
Inner: 1.51
④ Outer: 1.85
Inner: 1.51

PISTON AND RING SPECIFICATIONS

All measurements are given in inches.

Year	Engine Displacement cu. in. (cc)	Piston Clearance	Ring Gap			Connecting Rod		
			Top Compression	Bottom Compression	Oil Control	Top Compression	Bottom Compression	Oil Control
1981	110.8 (1816)	0.0018-0.0026	0.0120-0.0180	0.0080-0.0350	0.0080-0.0350	0.0059	0.0059	0.0059
	111 (1815)	0.0002-0.0017	0.0078-0.0157	0.0078-0.0157	0.0078-0.0157	0.0059	0.0059	0.0059

PISTON AND RING SPECIFICATIONS

All measurements are given in inches.

Year	Engine Displacement cu. in. (cc)	Piston Clearance	Ring Gap			Connecting Rod		
			Top Compression	Bottom Compression	Oil Control	Top Compression	Bottom Compression	Oil Control
1982	110.8 (1816)	0.0018–0.0026	0.0120–0.0180	0.0080–0.0350	0.0080–0.0350	0.0059	0.0059	0.0059
	111 (1815)	0.0002–0.0017	0.0078–0.0157	0.0078–0.0157	0.0078–0.0157	0.0059	0.0059	0.0059
1983	110.8 (1816)	0.0018–0.0026	0.0120–0.0180	0.0080–0.0350	0.0080–0.0350	0.0059	0.0059	0.0059
	111 (1815)	0.0002–0.0017	0.0078–0.0157	0.0078–0.0157	0.0078–0.0157	0.0059	0.0059	0.0059
	118.9 (1949)	0.0018–0.0026	0.0140–0.0190	0.0140–0.0190	0.0080–0.0350	0.0010–0.0024	0.0010–0.0024	0.0008
1984	110.8 (1816)	0.0018–0.0026	0.0120–0.0180	0.0080–0.0350	0.0080–0.0350	0.0059	0.0059	0.0059
	111 (1815)	0.0002–0.0017	0.0078–0.0157	0.0078–0.0157	0.0078–0.0157	0.0059	0.0059	0.0059
	118.9 (1949)	0.0018–0.0026	0.0140–0.0190	0.0140–0.0190	0.0080–0.0350	0.0010–0.0024	0.0010–0.0024	0.0008
1985	110.8 (1816)	0.0018–0.0026	0.0120–0.0180	0.0080–0.0350	0.0080–0.0350	0.0059	0.0059	0.0059
	111 (1815)	0.0002–0.0017	0.0078–0.0157	0.0078–0.0157	0.0078–0.0157	0.0059	0.0059	0.0059
	118.9 (1949)	0.0018–0.0026	0.0140–0.0190	0.0140–0.0190	0.0080–0.0350	0.0010–0.0024	0.0010–0.0024	0.0008
	121 (1983)	0.0018–0.0026	0.0120–0.0180	0.0100–0.0160	0.0080–0.0280	0.0059	0.0059	0.0059
	90 (1471)	0.0110–0.0190	0.0098–0.0138	0.0098–0.0138	0.0039–0.0236	0.0059	0.0059	0.0059
1986	118.9 (1949)	0.0018–0.0026	0.0140–0.0190	0.0140–0.0190	0.0080–0.0350	0.0010–0.0024	0.0010–0.0024	0.0008
	121 (1983)	0.0018–0.0026	0.0120–0.0180	0.0100–0.0160	0.0080–0.0280	0.0059	0.0059	0.0059
	90 (1471)	0.0110–0.0190	0.0098–0.0138	0.0098–0.0138	0.0039–0.0236	0.0059	0.0059	0.0059
1987–88	118.9 (1949)	0.0018–0.0026	0.0120–0.0180	0.0100–0.0160	0.0080–0.0280	0.0059	0.0059	0.0059
	121 (1983)	0.0018–0.0026	0.0120–0.0180	0.0100–0.0160	0.0080–0.0280	0.0059	0.0059	0.0059
	90 (1471)	0.0110–0.0190	0.0098–0.0138	0.0098–0.0138	0.0039–0.0236	0.0059	0.0059	0.0059

TORQUE SPECIFICATIONS

All readings in ft. lbs.

Year	Engine Displacement cu. in. (cc)	Cylinder Head Bolts	Main Bearing Bolts	Rod Bearing Bolts	Crankshaft Pulley Bolts	Flywheel Bolts	Manifold Intake	Manifold Exhaust	Spark Plugs
1981	110.8 (1816)	①	72	43	87	69	13	15	11–14
	111 (1815)	②	65–72	54–61	108	36–43	25–32	11–18	11–14
1982	110.8 (1816)	①	72	43	87	69	13	15	11–14
	111 (1815)	②	65–72	54–61	108	36–43	25–32	11–18	11–14
1983	110.8 (1816)	①	72	43	87	69	13	15	11–14
	111 (1815)	②	65–72	54–61	108	36–43	25–32	11–18	11–14
	118.9 (1949)	①	65–79	42–45	87	72–79	13–18	13–18	11–14
1984	110.8 (1816)	①	72	43	87	76	13	15	11–14
	111 (1815)	②	65–72	54–61	108	36–43	25–32	11–18	11–14
	118.9 (1949)	①	65–79	42–45	87	72–79	13–18	13–18	11–14
1985	110.8 (1816)	①	72	43	87	76	13	15	11–14
	111 (1815)	②	65–72	54–61	108	36–43	25–32	11–18	11–14
	118.9 (1949)	①	65–79	42–45	87	72–79	13–18	13–18	11–14
	121 (1983)	①	72	43	87	43	13–18	16	11–14
	90 (1471)	③	68	25	108	22 ④	17	17	11–14
1986	118.9 (1949)	①	65–79	42–45	87	72–79	13–18	16	11–14
	121 (1983)	①	72	43	87	43	13–18	16	11–14
	90 (1471)	③	68	25	108	22 ④	17	17	11–14
1987–88	118.9 (1949)	①	65–79	42–45	87	72–79	13–18	16	11–14
	121 (1983)	①	72	43	87	43	13–18	16	11–14
	90 (1471)	③	68	25	108	22 ④	17	17	11–14

① 1st step: 62 ft. lbs.
　2nd step: 72 ft. lbs.
② Tighten in sequence: New bolts–90 ft. lbs., Used bolts–97 ft. lbs.
③ 1st step: 29 ft. lbs.
　2nd step: 58 ft. lbs.
④ Turn the bolt an additional 45 degrees

BRAKE SPECIFICATIONS

All measurements in inches unless noted.

Year	Model	Lug Nut Torque (ft. lbs.)	Master Cylinder Bore	Brake Disc		Standard Brake Drum Diameter	Minimum Lining Thickness	
				Minimum Thickness	Maximum Runout		Front	Rear
1981	I-Mark	50 ①	0.875	0.338	0.0060	9.00	0.067	0.039
1982	I-Mark	50 ①	0.875	0.338	0.0060	9.00	0.067	0.039
1983	I-Mark	50 ①	0.875	0.338	0.0060	9.00	0.067	0.039
	Impulse	80–94	0.874	0.654	0.0051	—	0.120	0.120
1984	I-Mark	50 ①	0.875	0.338	0.0060	9.00	0.067	0.039
	Impulse	80–94	0.874	0.654	0.0051	—	0.120	0.120
1985	I-Mark (RWD)	50 ①	0.875	0.338	0.0060	9.00	0.067	0.039
	I-Mark (FWD)	87	0.810	0.378	0.0059	7.09	0.039	0.039
	Impulse	80–94	0.874	0.654	0.0051	—	0.120	0.120
1986	I-Mark	87	0.810	0.378	0.0059	7.09	0.039	0.039
	Impulse	80–94	0.874	0.654	0.0051	—	0.120	0.120
1987–88	I-Mark	65 ①	0.810	0.378	0.0059	7.09	0.039	0.039
	Impulse	80–94	0.874	0.654	0.0051	—	0.120	0.120

① Aluminum wheels: 86 ft. lbs.

WHEEL ALIGNMENT

Year	Model	Caster		Camber		Toe-in (in.)	Steering Axis Inclination (deg.)
		Range (deg.)	Preferred Setting (deg.)	Range (deg.)	Preferred Setting (deg.)		
1981	I-Mark	3¹¹/₁₆P–6³/₁₆P	5³/₁₆P	⁷/₈N–⁵/₈P	¹/₈P	¹/₈P	7⁷/₈
1982	I-Mark	3¹¹/₁₆P–6³/₁₆P	5³/₁₆P	⁷/₈N–⁵/₈P	¹/₈P	¹/₈P	7⁷/₈
1983	I-Mark	3¹¹/₁₆P–6³/₁₆P	5³/₁₆P	⁷/₈N–⁵/₈P	¹/₈P	¹/₈P	7⁷/₈
	Impulse	3¹/₂P–6P	4³/₄P	1N–¹/₂P	0	¹/₁₆P	8
1984	I-Mark	3¹¹/₁₆P–6³/₁₆P	5³/₁₆P	⁷/₈N–⁵/₈P	¹/₈P	¹/₈P	7⁷/₈
	Impulse	3¹/₂P–6P	4³/₄P	1N–¹/₂P	0	¹/₁₆P	8
1985	I-Mark (RWD)	3¹¹/₁₆P–6³/₁₆P	5³/₁₆P	⁷/₈N–⁵/₈P	¹/₈P	¹/₈P	7⁷/₈
	I-Mark (FWD)	1³/₄P–2³/₄P	2¹/₄P	¹¹/₁₆N–1⁵/₁₆P	⁵/₁₆P	0	NA
	Impulse	3¹/₂P–6P	4³/₄P	1N–¹/₂P	0	¹/₁₆	8
1986	I-Mark	1³/₄P–2³/₄P	2¹/₄P	¹¹/₁₆N–1⁵/₁₆P	⁵/₁₆P	0	NA
	Impulse	3¹/₂P–6P	4³/₄P	1N–¹/₂P	0	¹/₁₆	8
1987–88	I-Mark	1³/₄P–2³/₄P	2¹/₄P	¹¹/₁₆N–1⁵/₁₆P	⁵/₁₆P	0	NA
	Impulse	3¹/₂P–6P	4³/₄P	1N–¹/₂P	0	¹/₁₆	8

N—Negative
P—Positive
Note: Caster angle is pre-set and cannot be serviced
NA—Not available

TUNE-UP PROCEDURES

All Isuzu models come equipped with a tune-up label in the engine compartment. This label has information developed during production. Should the preceding information in any way disagree with the specifications label, follow the label information for proper settings.

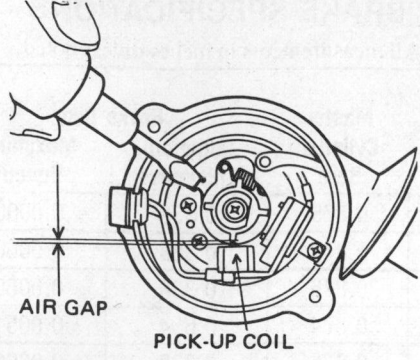

AIR GAP

PICK-UP COIL

Distributor air gap adjustment

Timing Mark

Timing mark location for the 4XC1-U engine

Electronic Ignition

AIR GAP ADJUSTMENT

All models of gasoline engines have electronic ignition. The only adjustment possible on this ignition system is the setting of the air gap inside the distributor.

1. Remove the distributor cap and O-ring.
2. Remove the rotor.
3. Use a feeler gauge (brass) to measure the air gap at the pick up coil projection. The gap should be 0.008–0.016 in. Adjust if necessary.
4. Loosen the screws and move the signal generator until the gap is correct. Tighten the screws and recheck the gap.

NOTE: The electrical parts in this system are not repairable. If found to be defective they must be replaced.

The signal generator can be checked for proper operation by using an ohmmeter to determine its resistance. It should be 140–180 ohms. If the resistance is not correct, replace the signal generator.

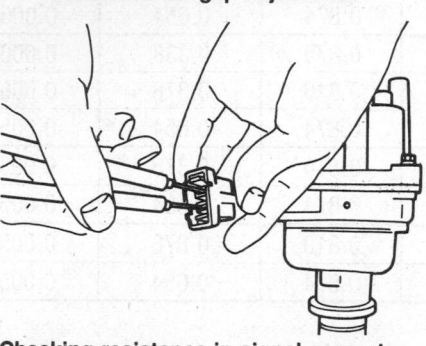

Checking resistance in signal generator with ohmmeter

Ignition Timing

ADJUSTMENT

All Models Except I-Mark (FWD) with 4XC1-U Engine

NOTE: The timing marks are located at the front of the crankshaft pulley and consist of a graduated scale attached to the engine block and a notch in the crankshaft pulley. Check and adjust the timing every 30,000 miles.

1. Locate and clean off the timing marks. Highlight the marks with paint or chalk.
2. Connect a timing light according to the manufacturer's instructions. The spark plug connection may be made at either No. 1 or No. 4 cylinder.
3. Start the engine and allow it to

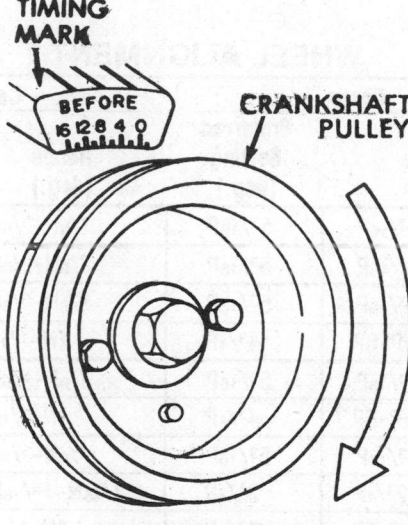

TIMING MARK

BEFORE
16 12 8 4 0

CRANKSHAFT PULLEY

Ignition timing marks

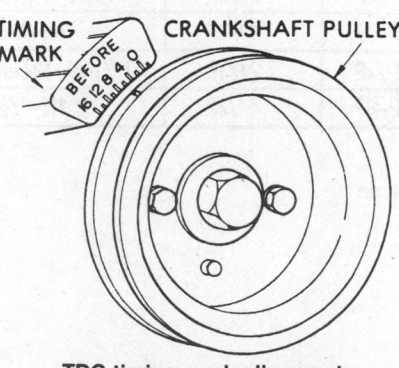

TIMING MARK

BEFORE
16 12 8 4 0

CRANKSHAFT PULLEY

TDC timing mark alignment

reach operating temperature. Make sure the engine is idling smoothly.

4. Aim the timing light at the marks and check the position of the crankshaft pulley notch on the timing scale. If necessary, adjust the timing by loosening the distributor clamping bolt and turning the distributor to the specification in the Tune-Up chart.

5. After timing is set to specifications, tighten the distributor clamping bolt and remove the timing light connections.

I-Mark (FWD) 4XC1-U Engine

1. Set the parking brake and block the drive wheels. Disconnect and plug the distributor vacuum line from the intake manifold.
2. Connect the timing light lead to the number one spark plug wire. Loosen the distributor hold down bolt (slightly).
3. Start the engine and let it run until it reaches normal operating temperature. Check the idle speed and make any adjustments if necessary. Align the notched line on the crankshaft pulley with the mark on the timing cover using the timing light.
4. While aligning the notched line on the crankshaft pulley, advance or retard the timing as necessary by turning the distributor clockwise or counterclockwise.
5. After the timing has been set to specifications, tighten the distributor hold down bolt and re-check the timing.

NOTE: Be sure the distributor body does not move together with the hold down bolt.

6. Reconnect the distributor vacuum line and remove all test equipment, except for the tachometer.
7. Re-check the idle speed and adjust as necessary.

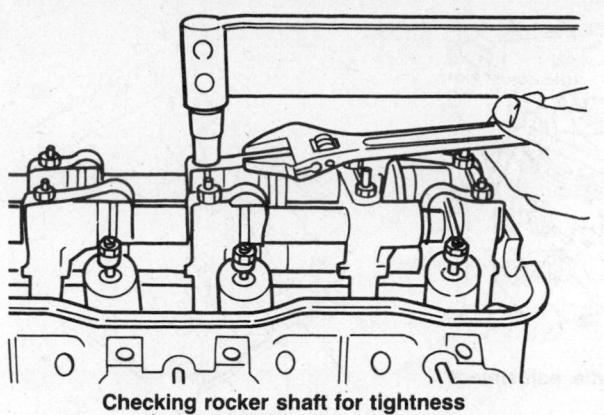

Checking rocker shaft for tightness

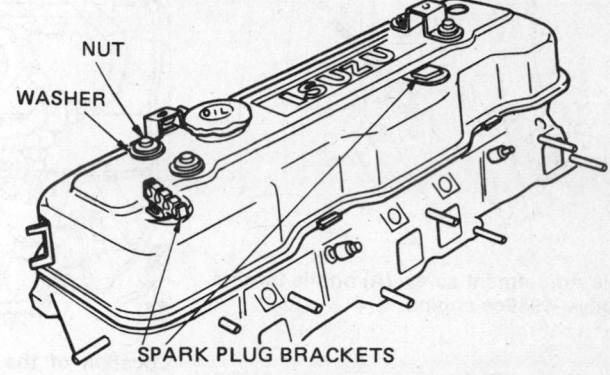

NUT

WASHER

SPARK PLUG BRACKETS

Rocker arm cover showing attaching bolts

Valve Lash

ADJUSTMENT

1. Remove the air cleaner and rocker shaft cover.

NOTE: Engine should be cold for adjustment. Adjust the valves every 15,000 miles.

2. Check the rocker arm shaft bracket nuts for tightness before adjusting the valves. Torque the bracket nuts to 16 ft. lbs.

	Diesel	Gasoline
Intake	0.25mm (0.010 in)	0.15mm (0.006 in)
Exhaust	0.35mm (0.014 in)	0.25mm (0.010 in)

3. Bring either NO. 1 or No. 4 piston up to top dead center on the compression stroke. Align the timing mark with the pointer on the crankshaft pulley by turning the crankshaft.

4. Once the engine is set up at TDC, adjust the valves for the cylinder at TDC, the move down in order after turning the crankshaft one revolution for each cylinder.

5. Measurements should be taken at the clearance between the rocker arm and valve stem. Standard valve clearances at low temperatures are:

6. To adjust the clearance, loosen the locknut and use a screwdriver to turn the adjusting stud until a slight drag is felt on the feeler gauge.

NOTE: While all valve adjustments must be made accurately, it's better to have the valve adjustment slightly loose than slightly tight. A burned valve or warped valve stem can result from overly tight adjustments.

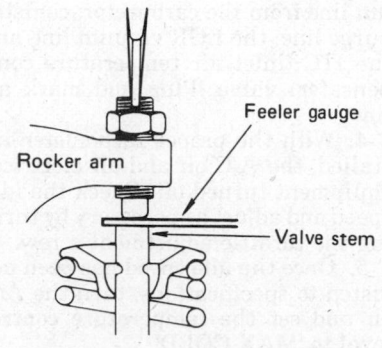

Feeler gauge

Rocker arm

Valve stem

Adjusting the valve clearance

Valve \ Cylinder	1	2	3	4
Intake	○	○	●	●
Exhaust	○	●	○	●

Note:

○ When piston in No. 1 cylinder is at TDC on compression stroke.

● When piston in No. 4 cylinder is at TDC on compression stroke.

Valve adjustment sequence (gas engine)

7. Tighten the locknut and recheck the adjustment.

8. When all valves are correctly adjusted, replace the rocker arm cover using a new gasket. Check for oil leaks.

NOTE: On the diesel engine, adjust the clearances of the valves marked with '0' when the piston in the number one cylinder is at top dead center on its compression stroke. Turn the crankshaft one full turn to bring the piston in the number four cylinder to top dead center on its compression

CYLINDER NO.	1		2		3		4	
VALVES	I	E	I	E	I	E	I	E
STEP. 1	○	○	○			○		
STEP. 2				○	○		○	○

I : INTAKE VALVE

E : EXHAUST VALVE

Valve adjustment sequence (diesel engine)

stroke and adjust the clearances of the valves marked with the '0' as shown in the illustration.

Idle Speed

ADJUSTMENT

Gasoline Engine (G180Z)

NOTE: Idle speed should be adjusted every 30,000 miles.

1. Set the parking brake and block the drive wheels.

2. Place the transmission in Neutral, start the engine and allow it to reach normal operating temperature.

NOTE: If the engine is idling for more than five minutes, precede all adjustments with a clear-out blip of the throttle for a few seconds.

3. The adjustments should be made with the choke open, air conditioner off, air cleaner installed, and distributor vacuum line, canister purge line and EGR vacuum line disconnected and plugged, and the idle compensator vacuum line closed by bending the rubber hose.

4. Turn the throttle adjusting screw to adjust the engine to 900 ± 50 rpm if the car is an automatic, and 800 ± 50 rpm the car has a manual transmission.

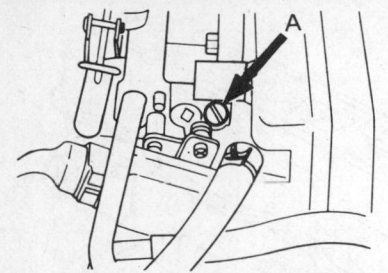

Idle Adjustment screw (A) on the throttle body—1949cc engine

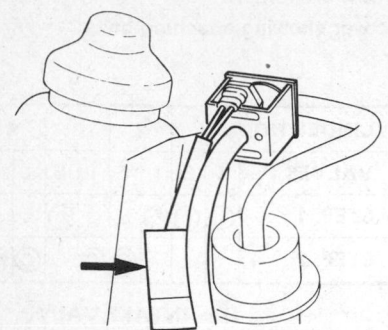

VSV wire connection—1949cc engine

5. If the car has an air conditioner, turn the A/C on Max Cold and High blower. Open the throttle to approximately 1/3 and allow the throttle to close. (This allows the speed-up solenoid to reach full travel.) Adjust the speed-up solenoid adjusting screw to set the idle at 900 ± 50 rpm.

Gasoline Engine (G200Z & 4ZC1-T)

1. Run the engine to the normal operating temperature.
2. Set the parking brake and block the drive wheels.
3. Place the transmission in neutral or park.
4. With the air conditioner turned off and the harness of the pressure regulator V.S.V. disconnected, adjust the idle adjustment screw to specifications.

NOTE: It is important to check and clean the idle port as necessary, as restrictions in the port can cause fluctuations in idle speed.

Gasoline Engine 4XC1-U

1. Set the parking brake and block the drive wheels.
2. Place the transmission in neutral or park and start the engine.
3. Let the engine run until it reaches normal operating temperature. Leave the air cleaner installed and disconnect the distributor vacu-

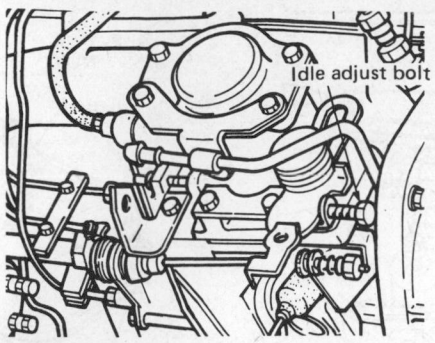

Location of the diesel idle adjustment screw

um line from the carburetor, canister purge line, the EGR vacuum line and the ITC (inlet air temperature compensator) valve. Plug and mark all lines.

4. With the proper tachometer installed, the A/C off and all electrical equipment turned off. Check the idle speed and adjust as necessary by turning the throttle adjustment screw.
5. Once the idle speed has been adjusted to specifications, turn the A/C on and set the temperature control level to 'MAX COLD'.
6. Set the blower to its highest position. Using the fast idle adjusting screw, located at the tip of the carburetor lever set the fast idle speed to the correct specifications.

Diesel Engines

NOTE: Idle speed should be adjusted every 30,000 miles.

1. Set the parking brake and block the drive wheels.
2. Place the transmission in neutral.
3. Start the engine and allow it to warm up to operating temperature.
4. Connect a tachometer according to the manufacturer's instructions.
5. If the idle speed deviates from the specified range, loosen the idle adjusting screw lock nut and turn the screw in or out until the idle speed is correct.

Idle Mixture

ADJUSTMENT

Carburetted Engines Only

1. Set the parking brake and block the drive wheels.
2. Place the transmission in neutral or park and remove the carburetor assembly.
3. On all engines except the 4XC1-U engine, remove the plug for the idle mixture screw by inserting a suitable

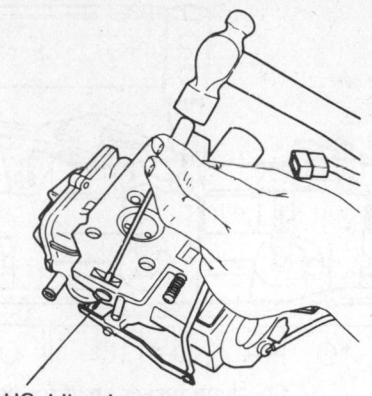

PLUG; Idle mixture screw

Removing mixture plug

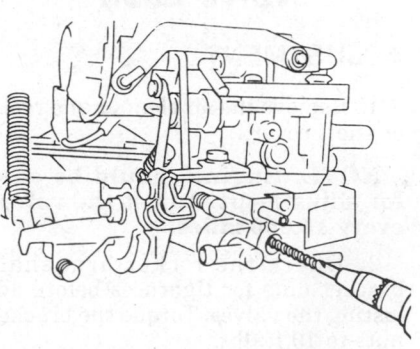

Idle mixture screw concealment plug removal (4XC1-U engine)

tool into the slit of the lower carburetor.

4. On the 4XC1-U engine, remove the idle mixture screw plug by drilling a small hole in the plug and remove the plug by inserting a suitable tool into the drilled hole and pry the mixture screw plug out.
5. Re-install the carburetor assembly and on the 4XC1-U engine re-install the air cleaner assembly and related rubber hoses.
6. Make the idle speed adjustment by following the procedures previously outlined.
7. On all the engines, turn the idle mixture screw all the way in and back it out one turn on all the California models (1981). On the 1982 models, back the idle mixture screw out 1½ turns.
8. On all 1983-88 engines, use the idle mixture screw to set the dwell angle to 36° on the 4 cyl. scale of the tachometer (24° on the 6 cyl. scale.).
9. Apply a suitable adhesive to the new mixture screw concealment plug and install the plug.
10. Adjust the fast idle using the procedures previously outlined and re-check all adjustment. Remove all test equipment.

Fuel Injected Engines

Idle mixture is controlled electronically by the I-TEC Fuel Injection System. No adjustments are necessary.

Fast Idle Speed

ADJUSTMENT

Diesel Only

1. Start and warm up the engine.
2. Connect a tachometer according to the manufacturer's instructions.
3. Disconnect the hoses from the vacuum switch valve, then connect a pipe (4mm diameter) in position between the hoses.
4. Loosen the adjusting nut and adjust the idle speed. Fast idle should be around 900–950 rpm.
5. Tighten the adjusting nut and remove the tachometer.

ENGINE ELECTRICAL

Distributor

REMOVAL & INSTALLATION

NOTE: Every 30,000 miles, the distributor should be checked for proper operation. Check the cap and wires, rotor, air gap, vacuum advance mechanism and lubricate all working parts lightly.

1. Disconnect the battery cable.
2. Tag the wires and remove the distributor cap with the ignition wires attached.
3. Disconnect the coil and vacuum lines.
4. Remove the distributor clamp bolt and bracket and lift out the distributor.

——— CAUTION ———
Never hammer on the distributor housing to tap it loose.

5. Installation is the reverse of removal. Check the timing and adjust if necessary.

Alternator

REMOVAL & INSTALLATION

Removing the alternator is simply a matter of loosening the mounting and adjustment bolts, removing the belt and lifting out the assembly. Diesel

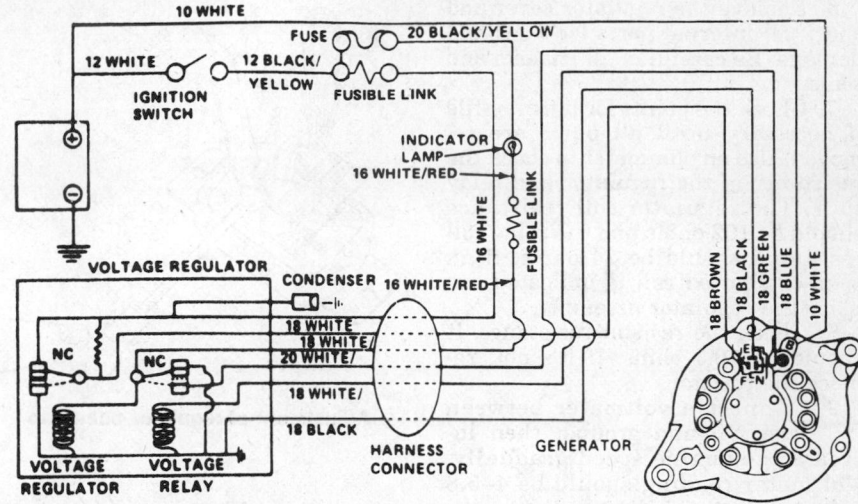

Alternator and regulator wiring schematic

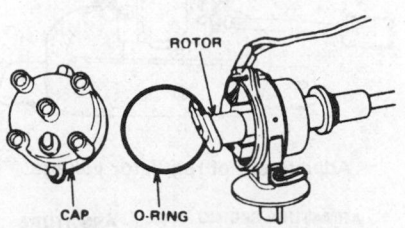

Distributor cap, O-ring and rotor

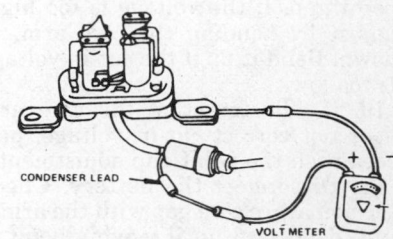

Regulator test connections

models have a vacuum pump mounted on the front of the alternator assembly. It must be removed along with the alternator for service.

1. Disconnect the battery.
2. Loosen all the mounting and adjusting bolts and remove the drive belt.
3. Remove mounting bolts and lift out the alternator.

NOTE: Tag all wires before removing them from the alternator.

4. Installation is the reverse of removal. Proper belt deflection is 0.4 in. (10mm).

Voltage Regulator

TESTING AND ADJUSTING

Externally Mounted Regulator

1. Perform this test with the regulator on the car and the engine running.
2. Connect a voltmeter between the condenser lead and ground with all electrical loads disconnected, including the blower relay connector.
3. The voltage regulator is working properly when the lower side points are closed while the engine is turned off, and when the upper points are closed when the engine is running at

Voltage regulator adjustments

idle. If the points are not working normally, chances are that the regulator is out of adjustment, or the voltage coil is open.

4. Check the coil resistance and replace the regulator assembly if found to be malfunctioning. If the coil resistance is normal, adjust the regulator.
5. Start the engine and increase the engine speed gradually. Voltage should increase with engine rpm up to 1400–1850 rpm. A normal condition is indicated when the voltage is within the range of 13.8–14.8 volts. Reconnect the blower relay connector.

6. Remove the regulator cover and check all internal parts for wear and damage. Be careful of all gaskets and seals.

7. Check the points for burning-file if necessary until all burrs are removed. Use an ohmmeter to check the resistance of the regulator and relay coils. The regulator coil resistance should be 102 ohms and the relay coil resistance should be 24 ohms. If an open or shorted coil is indicated, replace the regulator assembly.

8. Check the resistor resistance. It should be 10.5 ohms. If it's not, replace the resistor.

9. Connect a voltmeter between "N" terminal and ground, then increase the engine speed gradually. Voltmeter reading should be 4–5.8 volts when the indicator light goes out. Adjust the cut-in voltage by adjusting the armature core gap and point gap. If the voltage is too high, adjust by bending the core arm 'A' down. Bend it up if the cut-in voltage is too low.

10. If adjustment of the core arm does not correct cut-in voltage, proceed with the point gap adjustment.

11. Disconnect the battery. Check the armature core gap with the armature depressed until moving point is in contact with the "B" side point. Armature core gap should be 0.012 in. (0.0mm) or more. Adjust by bending the point arm "B".

12. Release the armature and adjust the gap between the "B" side point and the moving point by bending the point arm "C". Point gap should be 0.016–0.04 in. (0.4–1.2mm).

13. After the point gap adjustment, recheck the cut-in voltage. If not within 4–5.8 volts, repeat the cut-in voltage adjustment.

14. If the no load regulated voltage is not within the 13.8–14.8 range, adjust the voltage regulator setting. If the voltage is low, bend it up.

15. If the core arm adjustment does not correct the voltage problem, adjust the regulator point gap. Make sure the battery ground cable is disconnected.

16. Depress the armature until the moving point contacts the "E" side point. Bend the point arm "E" to obtain an armature gap of 0.012 in. (0.3mm).

17. Release the armature and adjust the gap between the "E" side point and the moving point by bending the point arm "F". The gap should be 0.012–0.016 in. (0.3–0.46mm).

18. After the gap adjustment is made, recheck the no load regulated voltage and repeat the core arm adjustment if necessary.

19. Adjust the point gap by loosen-

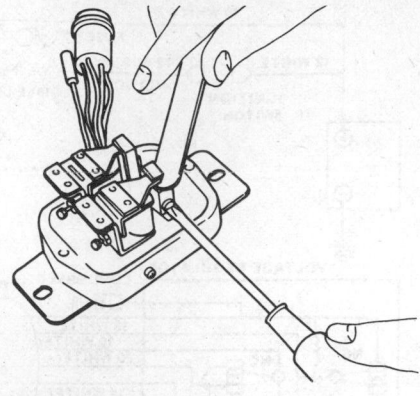

Adjustment of regulator point gap

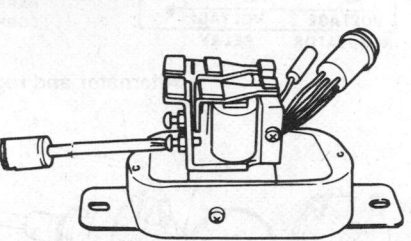

Adjustment of regulator voltage

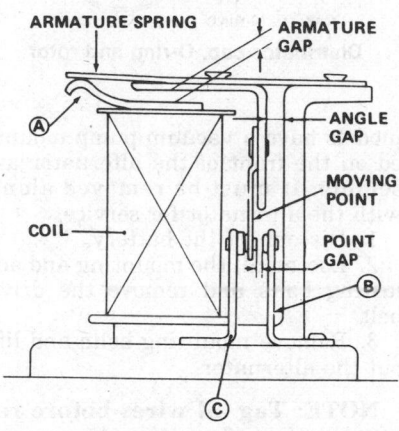

Voltage relay adjustment

ing the 3mm screw attaching the upper contact. Move the contact up and down as desired.

20. Adjust the regulated voltage with the adjusting screw. Turn clockwise to decrease it. Be sure to tighten the lock nut when adjustments are complete.

IC Regulator

NOTE: In order to test the IC regulator, a 12 volt test light, a DC (20V) voltmeter and a variable (10–20V) DC power source will be needed.

1. Take voltage readings at the following points with the instruments connected as shown in the illustration provided.

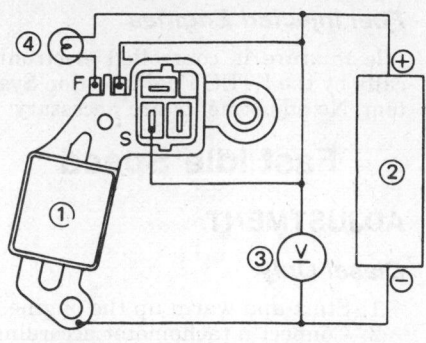

Installation of the IC regulator test equipment

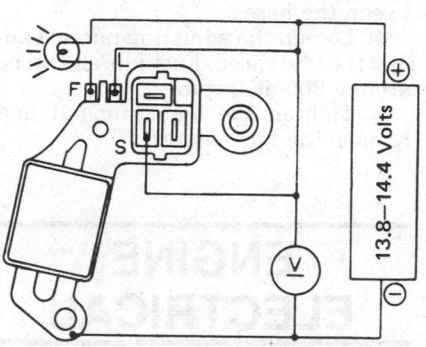

Appling the voltage to the IC regulator

2. Connect the circuit to the power source in the final step. Do not connect the "L" terminal to the power source with the 'S' terminal disconnect. This will cause damage to the IC regulator.

3. While increasing the voltage from 10 volts, check to see if the test light turns off at the specified voltage of 13.8–14.4 volts.

4. If the test light does not turn off at the specified voltage, replace the IC regulator.

Starter

REMOVAL & INSTALLATION

Gasoline Engines

1. Disconnect the battery cables at the battery posts.

2. Disconnect the EGR pipe from the EGR valve and exhaust manifold, then remove the EGR pipe.

3. Disconnect the wiring from the starter magnetic switch.

NOTE: Tag all wires before disconnecting.

4. Remove the bolts and nuts attaching the starter to the motor.

5. Remove the starter assembly

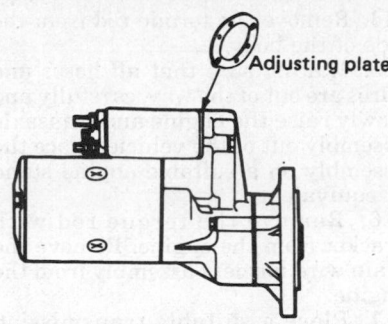

Typical diesel engine starter assembly showing adjustment shims

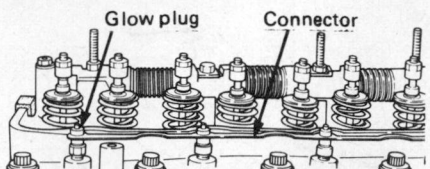

Glow plugs and connector locations

through the clearance under the intake manifold.

6. Installation is the reverse of removal.

Diesel Engines

1. Open the hood and disconnect the battery cables at the posts.

2. Disconnect the magnetic switch wiring at the connector.

NOTE: Label all wires before disconnecting.

3. Remove the starter motor attaching nut and bolt and remove the starter motor.

4. Installation is the reverse of removal.

Diesel Glow Plugs

REMOVAL & INSTALLATION

The glow plugs are designed to preheat the combustion chambers so that the diesel engine will have sufficient temperature to fire the fuel on initial starting. They resemble spark plugs and are removed much the same way. Disconnect the wire leads and use a deep socket to remove the glow plug from the cylinder head. Care must be taken not to damage the glow plug in any way or to strip the threads in the cylinder head. If a tight glow plug is encountered, coat the threads with some light weight oil and allow it to soak for a while. Be sure to use the correct glow plug for the engine. They are not interchangeable.

TESTING

NOTE: If the glow plugs should fail to work, check the fusible link before removing the glow plugs. The fusible link wire can be found near the battery, at the left side of the engine compartment.

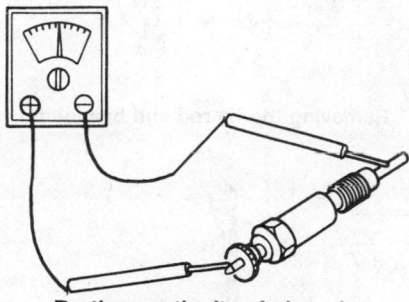

Testing continuity of glow plug

1. Remove the glow plug.

2. Using a circuit tester, check for continuity across the plug terminals and the body. If no continuity exists, the glow plug should be replaced.

GASOLINE ENGINE MECHANICAL

Engine

REMOVAL & INSTALLATION

I-MARK (RWD)

1. Remove the battery cables.

2. Scribe the position of the hood hinges on the underside of the hood. Remove the four attaching bolts and lift off the hood.

3. Remove the bottom shrouds and drain the crankcase and cooling system.

4. Disconnect the PCV hose from the air cleaner body. Disconnect the air hose from the air pump and remove the air duct from the air cleaner.

5. Remove the bolts attaching the air cleaner and loosen the clamp bolt.

6. Disconnect the thermostatic air cleaner (TAC) hot air hose and remove the manifold cover.

7. Tag and disconnect the generator valves at the connector.

8. Remove the two nuts connecting the exhaust pipe to the exhaust manifold and disconnect the exhaust pipe.

9. Take the tension off the clutch control cable by loosening the adjusting nut.

10. Disconnect the heater hose from the engine to the heater control valve at the engine side.

11. Disconnect the heater hose from the heater unit and joint.

12. Disconnect the control cable from the heater temperature valve and remove the control valve together with the hose.

13. Remove the engine mounting nut.

14. Support the engine with special tool J–26555 or equivalent. Attach the engine hanger using the exhaust manifold stud bolts.

15. Disconnect the cable grounding the cylinder block to the frame.

16. Disconnect the fuel lines and vapor lines from the carburetor and charcoal canister.

17. Remove the high tension cable from the coil. Disconnect the vacuum hose from the rear of the intake manifold at the connector.

18. Disconnect the accelerator control cable from the carburetor.

19. Disconnect the starter motor wiring.

NOTE: Tag all wires before disconnecting.

20. Disconnect the thermo-unit, oil pressure switch and distributor wiring at the connectors.

21. Disconnect the carburetor solenoid valve and the automatic choke wiring at the connectors.

22. Disconnect the back-up light switch and transmission switch wiring at the connector on the rear part of the engine.

23. Disconnect the emission control hose from the oil pan.

24. Remove the engine mounting nut.

— **CAUTION** —
Make sure the engine is well-supported from above.

25. Remove the stopper plate.

26. Connect the engine hoist. Raise the engine slightly and disconnect the left side engine mounting stopper plate.

27. Disconnect the air conditioner hoses.

— **CAUTION** —
Discharge the A/C system before attempting to disconnect any hoses.

28. Disconnect the radiator upper and lower hoses. Remove the bolts attaching the fan shroud and remove the shroud.

29. Remove the radiator attaching

bolts and remove the radiator by lifting straight upward.

30. Remove the fan blades from the pulley.

31. Remove the gearshift lever assembly.

32. Disconnect the parking brake return spring and disconnect the cable.

33. Disconnect the propeller shaft from the transmission. Remove the clutch return spring.

34. Disconnect the clutch control cable from the clutch withdraw lever and remove it from the engine stiffener.

35. Remove the front side exhaust pipe bracket from the transmission.

36. Disconnect the front and rear side exhaust pipes at the joint, then remove the front side exhaust pipe.

37. Disconnect the speedometer cable.

38. Remove the rear engine mounting bolts.

NOTE: Check that the engine is slightly lifted before removing the rear mounting bolts.

39. Check to make certain all the parts have been removed or disconnected from the engine and that the parts are tied safely out of the way so as not to snag when the engine is being lifted clear.

40. Lift the engine and slide it toward the front of the car. Remove the transmission from the engine and set it on the floor.

41. Slowly lift the engine clear.

42. Installation is the reverse of removal. Fill the crankcase and cooling system. Check and adjust the clutch pedal free play and check the carburetor and clutch linkage for smooth operation. Start the engine and check for leaks.

I-Mark (FWD)

1. Disconnect the battery cables and remove engine hood.

2. Drain the oil from the transaxle case and engine oil pan into a suitable drain pan.

3. Drain the cooling system and if the vehicle is equipped with air conditioning, discharge the refrigerant from the A/C system.

4. Remove the air cleaner assembly and the throttle cable at the carburetor.

5. Remove, plug and tag the fuel pump inlet and return hoses.

6. Remove the power steering hoses, A/C hose assembly, radiator and heater hoses and automatic transmission cooler hoses (if so equipped).

7. Remove the brake booster hose, clutch cable and select/shift cables (if so equipped), speedometer cable and high tension cable.

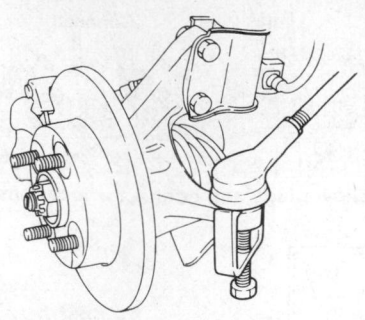
Removing the tie rod end ball joints

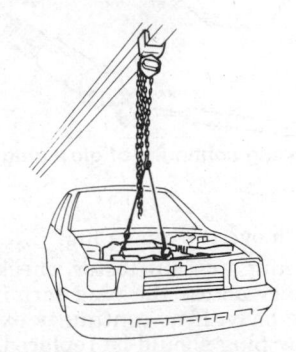
Removing the engine with transaxle as an assembly

8. Remove and tag all necessary electrical wires and remove the distributor from the engine.

9. Remove the battery and battery tray. Remove all the necessary wiring connectors from their respective sensor. Be sure to tag all connectors.

10. Remove and tag all necessary vacuum lines and remove the engine control cable.

11. Remove the drive shafts as follows:

    a. Raise and support safely the front of the vehicle. Remove the front wheels.

    b. Disconnect the tie rod end ball joints from the steering knuckles using special remover tool No. J–21687–02 or equivalent.

    c. Disconnect the lower arm end ball joints from the lower arm. Loosen but do not remove the nuts attaching the strut to the body.

    d. Using a suitable tool, pull out the driveshafts and be careful not to damage the transaxle oil seals when removing the driveshafts.

12. Remove the front exhaust pipe. Attach a suitable engine chain hoist to the engine hanger located on the top of the engine.

13. Raise the engine just enough to remove the weight from the engine mounts, while putting a slight tension on the rubber in the engine mounts.

14. Remove the torque rod from the side of the body.

15. Making sure that all hoses and wires are out of the way, carefully and slowly raise the engine and transaxle assembly out of the vehicle. Place the assembly on a suitable engine stand or equivalent.

16. Remove the torque rod with bracket from the engine. Remove the main wire harness assembly from the engine.

17. Place a suitable transmission jack or equivalent under the transaxle and separate the transaxle assembly from the engine.

18. Installation is the reverse order of the removal procedure. Make all necessary adjustments and refill the engine, transaxle, cooling system, power steering reservoir and recharge the A/C system with the proper lubricants and to the specified amount.

19. When installing the engine pay close attention to the following torque specifications.

    a. Transaxle to engine mounting bolts 56 ft. lbs.

    b. Torque rod bracket to frame bolt 40 ft. lbs.

    c. Torque rod to bracket bolt 56 ft. lbs.

    d. Engine mount bracket to block 28 ft. lbs.

    e. Front and rear engine mounting through bolts and nuts 60 ft. lbs. (always use new bolts and nuts).

    f. Right hand mounting rubber — body side 30 ft. lbs. engine side 45 ft. lbs.

    g. Torque rod to body frame 42 ft. lbs.

    h. Nuts attaching the strut to body 40 ft. lbs.

    i. Tie rod end ball joints to steering knuckle 42 ft. lbs.

    j. Front wheel lug nuts 65 ft. lbs.

20. After the installation is complete, connect the battery cables and start the engine. Check for leakage of any kind, perform all engine adjustments, road test the vehicle and then re-check the fluid levels, add as necessary.

Impulse

NOTE: The engine removal and installation for the 4ZC1-T engine are the same as the procedure used for the G200Z engine. The main difference is the electrical wiring and vacuum hose routing.

1. Remove the battery cables.

2. Disconnect the headlight cover motor harness, remove the strut-to-hood bolt and the engine hood side bolt and remove the hood.

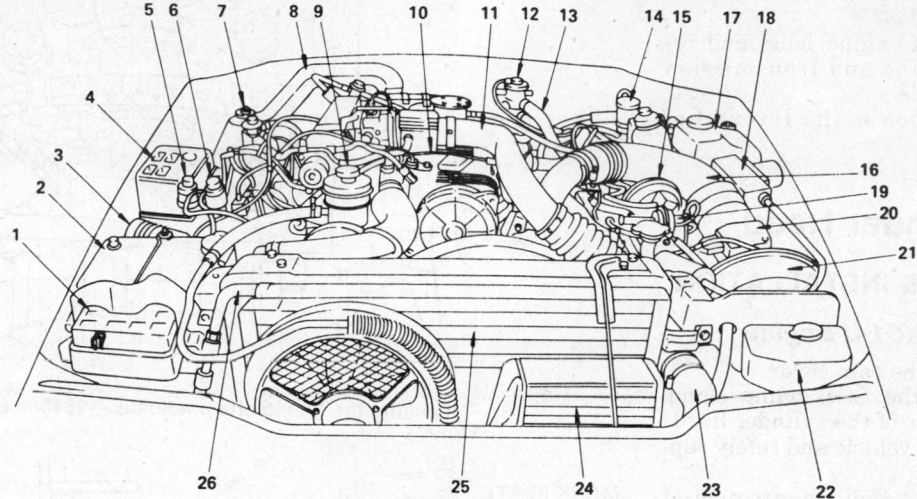

Main engine parts removal and installation position diagram

1. Relay box
2. Battery
3. Ignition coil
4. Relay box
5. Fast idel solenoid (only for models with digital meter)
6. Booster sensor (only for models with digital meter)
7. Pressure regulator
8. Blower duct
9. Power steering fluid reservoir tank
10. Accelerator cable
11. Air duct (intercoller to common chamber)
12. Air switching valve
13. Air hose-air switching valve to air manifold
14. Brake fluid reservoir tank
15. Cruise control actuator
16. Air duct (air cleaner to turbocharger)
17. Windshield washer surge tank
18. Stepping motor
19. Water valve
20. Air flow sensor
21. Air cleaner
22. Radiator reservoir
23. Air duct (to engine intercooler)
24. Intercooler
25. Radiator
26. A/C pipe

3. Drain the crankshaft and cooling systems.

4. Disconnect the upper radiator hose.

5. Disconnect the oil cooler line for the automatic transmission (if so equipped).

6. On models with air conditioning, remove the compressor mounting bracket from the engine and position the compressor out of the way without disconnecting the refrigerant lines.

NOTE: If the compressor lines do not have enough slack to move the compressor out of the way without disconnecting the refrigerant lines, the air conditioning system must be evacuated, using the required tools, before the refrigerant lines can be disconnected.

——— CAUTION ———

Do not disconnect any refrigerant lines unless you have experience with air conditioning systems. Escaping refrigerant will freeze any surface it contacts, including your skin and eyes.

7. Remove the rubber air duct hose to the cylinder head cover.

8. Disconnect the accelerator cable.

9. Disconnect and tag the rubber hoses at the following connections:

   a. Between the injection pipe and the pressure regulator.

   b. Fuel pipe to injection pipe.

   c. Canister (purge) to common chamber.

   d. Canister (VC) to 3-way.

   e. VSV to common chamber.

   f. VSV to 3-way.

   g. Solenoid fast idle to common chamber.

   h. Solenoid fast idle to thermal valve.

10. Disconnect the cable harness between the fender skirt and the cylinder head.

11. Disconnect and tag the connectors at the following locations.

   a. Oil pressure switch.

   b. Water temperature sensor.

   c. Knock sensor.

   d. I-TEC harness.

   e. Crank angle distributor sensor.

   f. Starter terminal.

   g. Cable harness, engine rear to cross-member front.

   h. Automatic transmission control.

   i. O_2 Sensor.

12. Remove the R.H. engine mounting nut.

13. Remove the air intake nut.

14. Disconnect the following rubber hoses.

   a. Radiator reservoir.

   b. Auto cruise to common chamber.

   c. Master vac to intake manifold.

   d. Heater hoses.

   e. Radiator hoses.

   f. Power steering hoses.

15. Remove the L.H. mounting bolt and heat shield.

16. Remove the cover from under the engine.

17. Disconnect the propeller shaft and install a plug in the transmission rear cover to prevent the oil from draining.

18. On models with automatic transmission remove the pin from the transmission select lever.

19. Disconnect the speedometer cable.

20. On models equipped with manual transmissions remove the clutch slave cylinder.

21. Remove the converter mounting bracket.

22. Remove the exhaust pipe nut to manifold.

23. Disconnect the rear engine mounting bracket.

24. Install an engine hoist and remove the engine and transmission from the vehicle.

25. Installation is the reversal of removal.

Cylinder Head

REMOVAL & INSTALLATION

All Except 4XC1-U Engine

1. Remove the cam cover.

2. Remove the EGR pump clamp bolt at the rear of the cylinder head.

3. Raise the vehicle and safely support it.

4. Disconnect the exhaust pipe at the exhaust manifold.

5. Drain the cooling system.

6. Lower the car.

7. Disconnect the heater hoses at the intake manifold and at the rear of the cylinder head.

8. Disconnect the accelerator linkage, all necessary electrical connections, spark plug wires and necessary vacuum lines.

NOTE: Tag all wires and hoses before disconnecting them from the engine.

9. Raise the camshaft until No.4 cylinder is in firing position. Remove the distributor cap and mark the rotor-to-housing relationship. This simple act will save untold grief when trying to get the distributor back in correctly.

10. Lock the timing chain adjuster by depressing and turning the automatic chain adjuster slide pin 90° clockwise.

11. Remove the timing sprocket-to-camshaft bolt and remove the sprocket from the camshaft. Keep the sprocket on the chain damper and tensioner. Do not remove the sprocket from the chain.

12. Disconnect the air pump hose and check valve at the exhaust manifold.

13. Remove the cylinder head-to-timing cover bolts.

14. Remove the cylinder head bolts using an extension bar with socket. Remove bolts in progressive sequence, beginnning with the outer bolts.

NOTE: Use light oil to free frozen bolts.

15. With the aid of an assistant, remove the cylinder head, intake and exhaust manifolds as an assembly.

16. Clean all gasket material from the cylinder head and block surfaces.

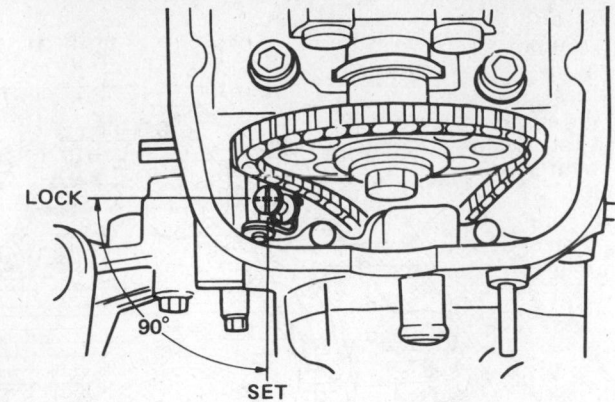

Locking the timing chain adjuster—1816cc engine

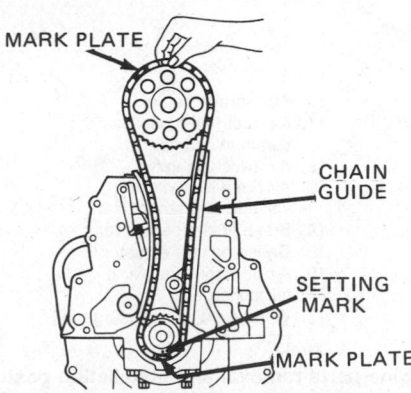

Keep the timing sprocket attached to the chain while aligning or removing

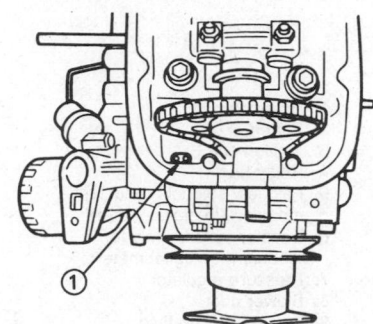

Timing chain automatic adjuster lock level—(1) 1949cc gasoline engine

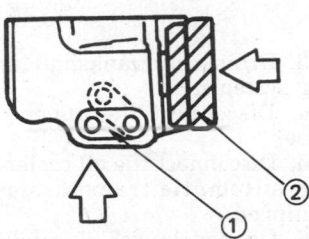

Push in on the automatic adjuster shoe (1) and lock it in the retracted position by releasing lever (2)—118.9 cu. in. gasoline engine

Check for nicks or heavy scratches on the mating surfaces.

17. Installation is the reverse of removal. Cylinder bolt threads in the block and threads on the bolts must be cleaned. Dirt will affect head torque.

18. Torque all head bolts to specifications according to the sequence in the illustration. Torque bolts to half normal value in sequence, then to specifications on the second pass.

CYLINDER HEAD BOLT TORQUE

First Pass	61 ft. lbs.
Second Pass	72 ft. lbs.

4XC1-U Engine

1. Disconnect the negative battery cable and drain the cooling system into a suitable drain pan.

2. Remove the air cleaner assembly and disconnect the flex hose along with the oxygen sensor at the exhaust manifold.

3. Disconnect the exhaust pipe bracket at the block and the exhaust pipe at the manifold.

4. Disconnect the spark plug wires and remove the thermostat housing.

5. Scribe some marks on the distributor housing and cylinder head. Rotate the engine until the engine is at TDC on the compression stroke of the No. 1 cylinder. Remove the distributor hold down bolt and remove the distributor.

6. Remove the vacuum advance hoses and the ground cable at the cylinder head.

7. Disconnect the fuel lines at the fuel pump and at the carburetor remove the secondary hoses and throttle cable.

8. Disconnect the vacuum switching valve electrical connector and the heater hoses.

9. Remove the alternator, power

steering pump and A/C adjusting bolts, brackets and drive belts. Remove and tag all necessary electrical and vacuum lines.

10. Support the engine using a suitable vertical hoist. Remove the right hand motor mount and the bracket at the front cover.

11. Rotate the engine to align the timing marks. Remove the crankshaft bolt and remove the boss and the crank pulley.

12. Remove the timing cover and be sure the mark on the cam pulley is aligned with the upper surface of the cylinder head. Also the dowel pin on the camshaft should be positioned at the top.

13. Disconnect the PCV hoses and remove the valve cover. If the cover sticks to the head, carefully strike the valve cover with a soft mallet.

14. Insert a hex wrench into the tension pulley hexagonical hole. Loosen the timing belt tension by rotating the tension pulley clockwise and remove the timing belt.

15. Remove the fuel pump and disconnect the intake manifold coolant hoses.

16. Remove the cylinder head bolts, remove the bolts from both ends at the same time, working toward the middle and remove the cylinder head.

17. To install, use new seals and gaskets, apply oil to the head bolt threads and torque the head bolts.

NOTE: When torquing the cylinder head bolts, work from the middle toward both ends at the same time.

CYLINDER HEAD BOLT TORQUE

| First Pass | 29 ft. lbs. |
| Second Pass | 58 ft. lbs. |

18. After torquing the head bolts, adjust the valve clearance and complete the installation procedure, by reversing the removal procedure.

OVERHAUL

NOTE: For all cylinder head overhaul procedures, please refer to "Engine Rebuilding" in the Unit Repair Section.

Rocker Arms/Shaft

REMOVAL & INSTALLATION

All Engines

1. Remove the cam cover.
2. On the 118.9 cu. in. engine re-

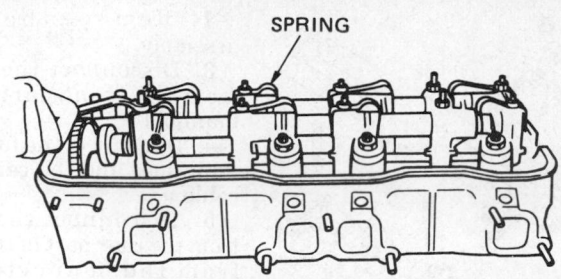
Rocker arm assembly—gasoline engine

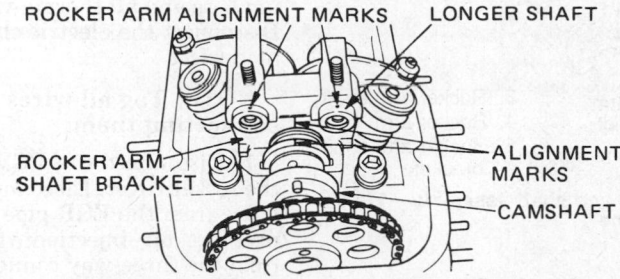
Rocker arm shaft installation—gasoline engine

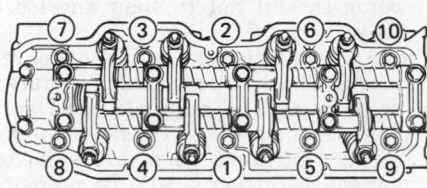
Cylinder head bolt torque sequence for the 4XC1-U engine

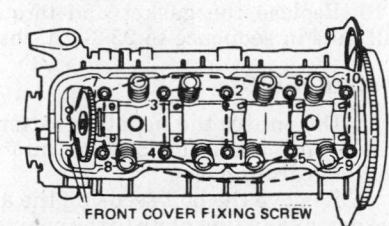
Cylinder head bolt torque sequence—gasoline engine

lease the tension on the automatic adjuster prior to the removal of the rocker shaft assembly as follows:

    a. With a suitable tool depress the lock lever on the automatic adjuster rearward.

    b. Push on the automatic adjuster shoe and lock it in the retracted position by releasing the lever.

3. Loosen the rocker arm shaft bracket nuts a little at a time, in sequence, commencing with the outer brackets.

4. Remove the nuts from the rocker arm shaft brackets.

5. Disassemble the rocker arm shaft assembly by removing the spring from the rocker arm shaft and then removing the rocker arm brackets and arms.

6. Inspect the rocker arm shaft for runout. Support the shaft on V-blocks at each end and check runout by slowly turning it with the probe of a dial indicator. Replace the shaft with a new one if the runout exceeds 0.0156 in. (0.4mm). Runout should not exceed 0.0079 in. (0.2mm).

7. Inspect the rocker arm shaft for wear, replace the shaft if obvious signs of wear are encountered.

8. Installation is the reverse of removal. Use a liberal amount of clean engine oil to coat the shaft, rocker arms and valve stems. Install the longer shaft on the exhaust valve side, shorter shaft on the intake side, so that the aligning marks on the shafts are turned to the front of the engine.

9. Torque the rocker arm shaft bracket and stud nuts to 16–22 ft. lbs. (1816cc gas engine), 15–17 ft. lbs. (Impulse engines) and 16 ft. lbs. (1475cc gas engine). Hold the rocker arm springs with an adjustable wrench while torquing the nuts to prevent damage to the springs. Torque the nuts a little at a time in sequence, beginning with the center bracket and working outward.

NOTE: On the 4XC1-U engine in the (FWD) I-Mark, the rocker arm shafts are different from each other, make sure they are installed in the same position that they were removed. Install the rocker arms with the identification marks toward the front of the engine. Apply a sealant to the bracket and cylinder head mating surfaces of the front and rear rocker brackets.

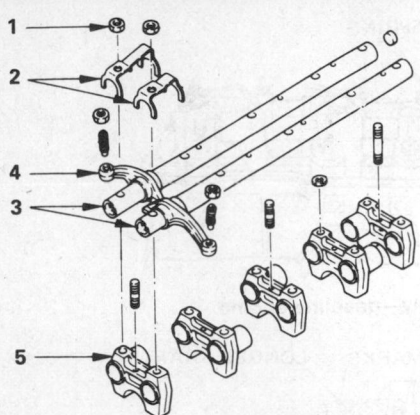

1. Rocker arm bracket nut
2. Rocker arm spring
3. Rocker arm shaft
4. Rocker arm
5. Rocker arm shaft bracket

Rocker arm and shaft assembly—118.9 cu. in. engine

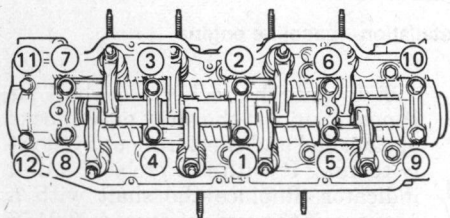

Rocker arm bolt torque sequence for the 4XC1-U engine

Rocker arm and shaft assembly—1949cc engine

10. Adjust valve clearances, reinstall the cam cover and check for leaks.

Intake Manifold

REMOVAL & INSTALLATION

I-Mark(RWD)

1. Drain the cooling system.

NOTE: Before removing the intake manifold, check to make certain the engine coolant is completely drained. If any water remains in the block it will flow into the cylinders when the intake manifold is removed.

2. Remove the air cleaner assembly.
3. Disconnect the radiator hose from the front part of the intake manifold.
4. Disconnect the fuel lines, all vacuum lines and the carburetor control cable.
5. Disconnect the heater hoses from the rear part of the manifold and from the connector under the dashboard.
6. Disconnect the distributor vacuum hose and all thermo-valve wiring. Disconnect the electric choke or solenoid wires.

NOTE: Tag all wires before disconnecting them.

7. Disconnect the PCV hose from the rocker cover. Disconnect the EGR valve from the EGR pipe and disconnect the air injection vacuum hose from the three-way connector.
8. Remove the eight nuts attaching the intake manifold and lift it clear, being careful not to snag any loose lines.
9. Installation is the reverse of removal. Check the manifold for cracks or damage. The manifold head surfaces can be checked for distortion by using a straight edge and a feeler gauge. Distortion should be no more than 0.0157 in. (0.4mm), if it is beyond the limit, the distortion has to be corrected with a surface grinder.
10. Replace the gasket and torque all nuts in sequence to 25–32 ft. lbs.

I-Mark (FWD)

1. Disconnect the negative battery cable and drain the coolant into a suitable drain pan.
2. Remove the bolt securing the alternator adjusting plate to the engine.
3. Disconnect and tag all hoses attached to the air cleaner assembly and remove the air cleaner.
4. Disconnect the air inlet temperature switch wiring connector. Disconnect and tag all the hoses, electrical connectors and control cable attached to the carburetor.
5. If equipped with A/C disconnect the fast idle control vacuum hose, the pressure tank control valve hose, the distributor/3-way connector hose and the vacuum switching valve wiring connector.
6. Remove the carburetor attaching bolts, which are located underneath the intake manifold. Remove the carburetor and the EFE heater.
7. At the intake manifold, remove the PCV hose, the water bypass hose, the two heater hoses, the EGR valve canister hose, the distributor vacuum advance hose and the ground wires.
8. Disconnect the thermometer

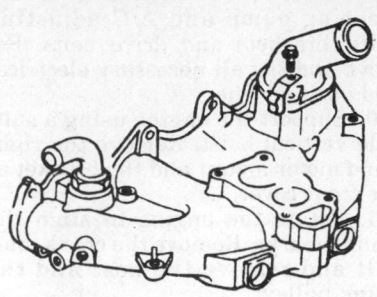

Intake manifold—1816cc gasoline engine

unit switch wiring connector (if so equipped).
9. Remove the intake manifold attaching nuts and bolts and remove the intake manifold.
10. Clean the sealing surfaces of the intake manifold and the cylinder head.
11. Use a straight-edge and a feeler gauge to check the surfaces containing the cylinder head for excessive warpage. The inlet manifold must be replaced if the warpage is in excess of 0.0157 in. (0.4mm).
12. To install, use new gaskets and reverse the removal procedure. Torque the intake manifold to 17 ft. lbs; then adjust the engine control cable and the alternator belt tension. Refill the engine with coolant, run the engine and check for leaks. Make all necessary adjustments and road test the vehicle, be sure to check for and vacuum leaks around the intake manifold sealing surfaces.

Impulse

1. Drain the cooling system.
2. Remove the air cleaners.
3. Disconnect the linkage to the throttle valve.
4. Tag and disconnect all wires and hoses.
5. Remove the eight manifold attaching bolts and remove the manifold and common chamber as an assembly.
6. Installation is the reverse of removal.

Exhaust Manifold

REMOVAL & INSTALLATION

All Except 4XC1-U Engine

1. Remove the bolts attaching the air cleaner and loosen the clamp bolt.
2. Lift the air cleaner slightly and remove the air hose.
3. Remove the bolts attaching the manifold cover and remove the manifold cover.
4. Remove the EGR pipe clip from

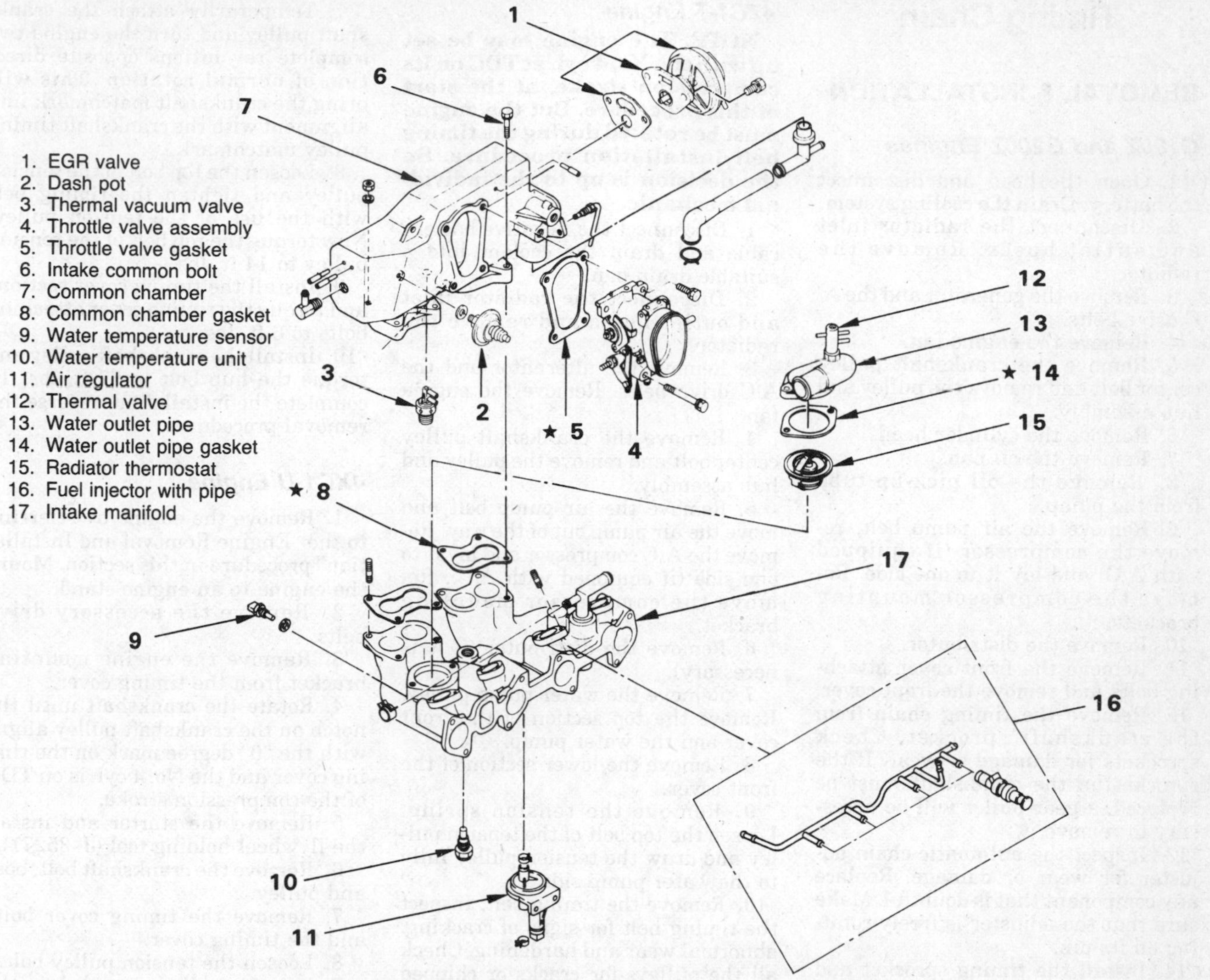

1. EGR valve
2. Dash pot
3. Thermal vacuum valve
4. Throttle valve assembly
5. Throttle valve gasket
6. Intake common bolt
7. Common chamber
8. Common chamber gasket
9. Water temperature sensor
10. Water temperature unit
11. Air regulator
12. Thermal valve
13. Water outlet pipe
14. Water outlet pipe gasket
15. Radiator thermostat
16. Fuel injector with pipe
17. Intake manifold

Intake manifold and common chamber—1949cc engine

the upper portion of the transmission and disconnect the EGR pipe from the exhaust manifold. On the 4ZC1-T engine, disconnect and tag all necessary wires, coolant hoses and pipes from the turbocharger. Also disconnect the oxygen sensor wiring connector.

5. Remove the two nuts connecting the exhaust pipe with the exhaust manifold and disconnect the exhaust pipe from the manifold.

6. Remove the seven nuts mounting the exhaust manifold and remove the manifold.

7. Installation is the reverse of removal. Use a straightedge to check for distortion as described in the intake section. Use new gaskets and torque to specifications.

4XC1-U Engine

1. Disconnect the negative battery

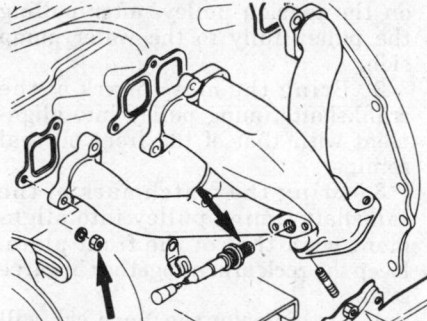

Exhaust manifold showing oxygen sensor mounting—1949cc engine

cable and the oxygen sensor wiring connector.

2. Disconnect and tag all of the hoses attached to the air cleaner assembly and remove the air cleaner.

3. Remove the manifold hot air cov-

er. Raise the vehicle and support safely.

4. Disconnect the exhaust pipe from the exhaust manifold and lower the vehicle.

5. Remove the nuts and bolts securing the exhaust manifold to the cylinder head. Clean the gasket mounting surfaces.

6. Check the exhaust manifold for cracks or other damage. Use a straight-edge and a feeler gauge to check the surfaces contacting the cylinder head for excessive warpage. The exhaust manifold must be replaced if the measured warpage exceeds 0.0157 in. (0.4mm).

7. To install, use a new gasket and reverse the removal procedure. Torque the exhaust manifold to 17 ft. lbs. and the exhaust pipe to 42 ft. lbs. then start

the engine and check for any exhaust leaks.

Timing Chain

REMOVAL & INSTALLATION

G180Z and G200Z Engines

1. Open the hood and disconnect the battery. Drain the cooling system.
2. Disconnect the radiator inlet and outlet hoses. Remove the radiator.
3. Remove the generator and the A/C drive belts.
4. Remove the engine fan.
5. Remove the crankshaft pulley center bolt and remove the pulley and hub assembly.
6. Remove the cylinder head.
7. Remove the oil pan.
8. Remove the oil pick-up tube from the pump.
9. Remove the air pump belt, remove the compressor (if equipped with A/C) and lay it to one side. Remove the compressor mounting brackets.
10. Remove the distributor.
11. Remove the front cover attaching bolts and remove the front cover.
12. Remove the timing chain from the crankshaft sprocket. Check sprockets for damage or wear. If the sprocket on the crankshaft must be replaced, a gear puller will be necessary to remove it.
13. Inspect the automatic chain adjuster for wear or damage. Replace any component that is doubtful. Make sure that the adjuster is freely rotating on its pin.
14. Install the timing sprocket and pinion gear (groove side toward front cover). Align the key grooves with the key on the crankshaft and then drive it into position with special tool J–26587 or equivalent.
15. Turn the crankshaft so that the key is turned toward the cylinder head side (No. 1 and No. 4 pistons at TDC).
16. Install the timing chain by aligning the mark plate on the chain with the mark on the crankshaft timing sprocket. The side of the chain with the mark plate is on the front side.
   The side of the chain with the most links between mark plates is on the chain guide side.
17. Keep the timing chain engaged with the camshaft timing sprocket until the sprocket is installed on the camshaft. Install the sprocket so that the marked side faces forward and so that the triangular mark aligns with the chain mark plate.
18. Install the front cover and reverse the removal instructions from Steps 1–10.

4ZC1-T Engine

NOTE: **The engine may be set up with the No. 4 cyl. at TDC on its compression stroke, at the start of this procedure. But the engine must be rotated during the timing belt installation procedure. So the decision is up to the individual mechanic.**

1. Disconnect the negative battery cable and drain the coolant into a suitable drain pan.
2. Disconnect the radiator inlet and outlet hoses and remove the radiator.
3. Remove the alternator and the A/C drive belts. Remove the engine fan.
4. Remove the crankshaft pulley center bolt and remove the pulley and hub assembly.
5. Remove the air pump belt and move the air pump out of the way. Remove the A/C compressor and lay it to one side (if equipped with A/C). Remove the compressor mounting bracket.
6. Remove the distributor (if it is necessary).
7. Remove the water pump pulley. Remove the top section of the front cover and the water pump.
8. Remove the lower section of the front cover.
9. Remove the tension spring. Loosen the top bolt of the tension pulley and draw the tension pulley fully to the water pump side.
10. Remove the timing belt. Inspect the timing belt for signs of cracking, abnormal wear and hardening. Check all the pulleys for cracks or chipped teeth.

To install:
1. Set the tension spring in its plate and temporarily tighten the top bolt on the tension pulley, after pulling the pulley fully to the water pump side.
2. Bring the matchmark of the crankshaft timing pulley into alignment with that of the front oil seal retainer.
3. Bring the matchmark of the camshaft timing pulley into alignment with that of the front plate. Keep the rock arm altogether in a free state.
4. At this point the No. 4 cyl. will come to its compression stroke at top dead center.
5. Lay the timing belt over the crankshaft pulley, oil pump pulley, cam pulley and tension pulley (in that order) while avoiding loosening between them.
6. Loosen the top bolt of the tension pulley to allow the tension spring to tighten the belt and to temporarily tighten the bolt.

7. Temporarily attach the crankshaft pulley and turn the engine two complete revolutions opposite direction of normal rotation. This will bring the crankshaft matchmark into alignment with the crankshaft timing pulley matchmark.
8. Loosen the top bolt of the tension pulley and tighten the timing belt with the use of the tension pulley. Now torque the top bolt of the tension pulley to 14 ft. lbs.
9. Install the timing cover sections and torque the timing cover attaching bolts to 6 ft. lbs.
10. Install the crankshaft pulley and torque the hub bolt to 87 ft. lbs. To complete the installation, reverse the removal procedures.

4XC1-U Engine

1. Remove the engine by referring to the "Engine Removal and Installation" procedure in this section. Mount the engine to an engine stand.
2. Remove the accessory drive belts.
3. Remove the engine mounting bracket from the timing cover.
4. Rotate the crankshaft until the notch on the crankshaft pulley aligns with the "0" degree mark on the timing cover and the No. 4 cyl. is on TDC of the compression stroke.
5. Remove the starter and install the flywheel holding tool (J–35271).
6. Remove the crankshaft bolt, boss and pulley.
7. Remove the timing cover bolts and the timing cover.
8. Loosen the tension pulley bolt.
9. Insert an allen wrench into the tension pulley hexagonical hole and loosen the timing belt by turning the tension pulley clockwise.
10. Remove the timing belt.

NOTE: **Inspect the timing belt for signs of cracking, abnormal wear and hardening. Never expose the belt to oil, sunlight or heat. Avoid excessive bending, twisting or stretching.**

To install:
1. Position the woodruff key on the crankshaft followed by the crankshaft timing gear. Align the groove on the timing gear with the mark on the oil pump.
2. Align the timing gear mark with the upper surface of the cylinder head and the dowel pin in its uppermost position.
3. Place the timing belt arrow in the direction of the engine rotation and install the timing belt. Tighten the tension pulley bolt.
4. Insert a hex wrench into the tension pulley hexagonal hole and hold

the pulley stationary while tightening the bolt temporarily.

5. Turn the crankshaft two complete reverse revolutions and align the crankshaft timing pulley groove with the mark on the oil pump. Loosen the tension pulley bolt and apply tension to the timing belt.

6. Insert a hex wrench into the tension pulley hexagonal hole and hold the pulley stationary while torquing the bolt to 37 ft. lbs.

7. Move the crankshaft back to about 50° before TDC and re-adjust the timing belt. Use a drive belt tension gauge to check the timing belt tension. The tension should be 38 (±4) ft. lbs.; if the belt is not at the proper tension it must be re-adjusted.

8. Adjust the valve clearance and to complete the installation, reverse the removal procedures.

Timing Cover Seal

REPLACEMENT

1. Once the timing cover is exposed, the seal can be pried out with a suitable tool.
2. Replace the seal using tool J-26587 or equivalent.

Camshaft

REMOVAL & INSTALLATION

G180Z and G200Z Engines

1. Remove the cam cover.
2. Rotate the camshaft until No. 4 cyl. is in firing position. Remove the distributor cap and mark the rotor-to-housing position.
3. On the G180Z engine, lock the timing chain adjuster by depressing and turning the automatic adjuster slide pin 90° in a clockwise direction. After locking the chain adjuster, check that the chain is loose.
4. On the G200Z engine, release the tension on the automatic adjuster as follows.
    a. With a suitable tool depress the lock lever on the automatic adjuster rearward.
    b. Push in the automatic adjuster shoe and lock in the retracted position by releasing the lever.
5. Remove the timing sprocket-to-camshaft bolt and remove the sprocket on the chain damper and tensioner without removing the chain from the sprocket.
6. Remove the rocker arm, shaft and the bracket assembly.
7. Remove the camshaft.
8. Installation is the reverse of removal. Use a liberal amount of clean

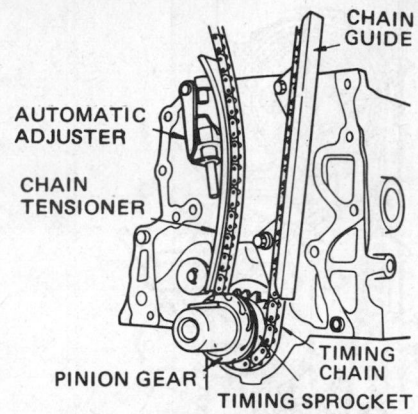

Removing the timing chain

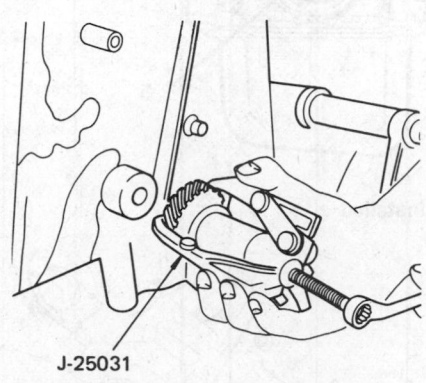

J-25031

Using a puller to remove crankshaft sprocket

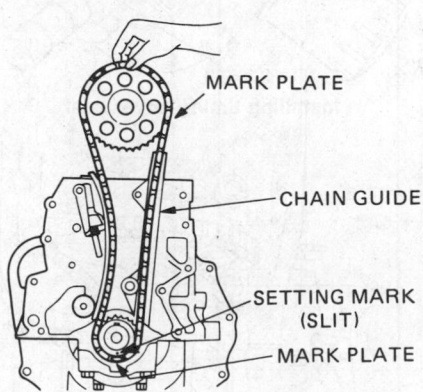

Timing chain alignment—gasoline engines

oil to coat the camshaft before installing. Check that the mark on the No. 1 rocker arms shaft bracket is in alignment with the mark on the camshaft and that the crankshaft pulley groove is aligned with the TDC mark("0" mark) on the front cover.

9. Assemble the timing sprocket to the camshaft by aligning it with the pin on the camshaft. Use care not to remove the chain from the sprocket.

10. Install the sprocket retaining bolt. Remove the half-moon seal in the front end of the head, insert a torque wrench and torque the bolt to

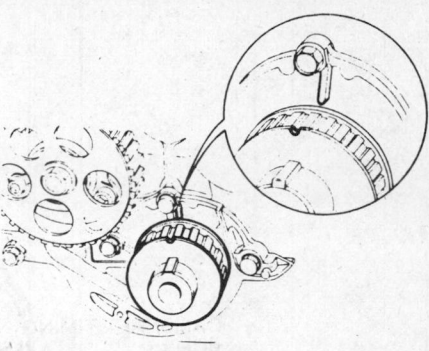

Aligning the crankshaft timing pulley— timing marks

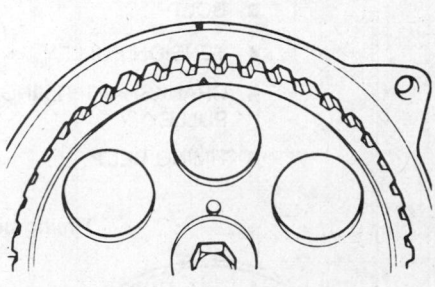

Aligning the camshaft timing pulley—timing marks

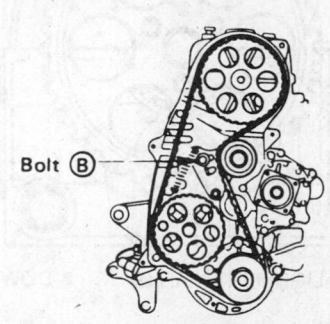

Installation of the timing belt and location of the top tension pulley bolt

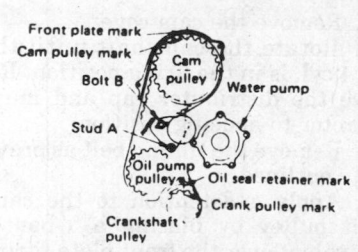

The finished timing belt installation

58 ft. lbs. Apply sealant and replace the half-moon seal in the head.

11. Set the automatic adjuster by turning the adjuster slide pin 90° counterclockwise with a screwdriver.

12. Check the valve timing and the rotor mark alignment on the distributor. Reinstall the distributor cap.

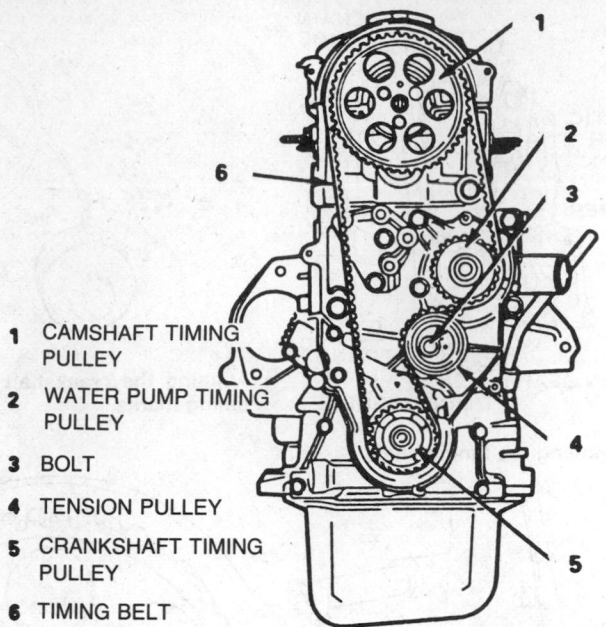

1 CAMSHAFT TIMING PULLEY
2 WATER PUMP TIMING PULLEY
3 BOLT
4 TENSION PULLEY
5 CRANKSHAFT TIMING PULLEY
6 TIMING BELT

Timing belt installed

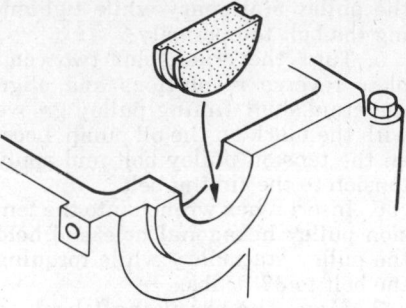

Half-moon seal

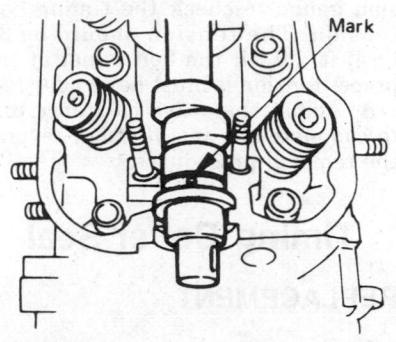

Camshaft alignment mark for the 4ZC1-T engine

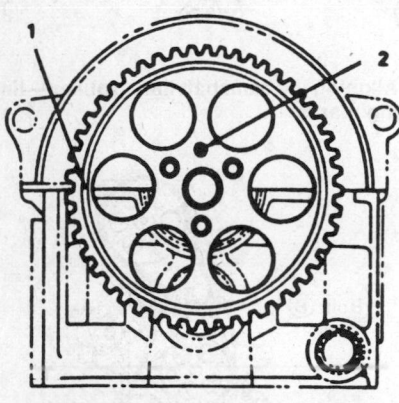

1 ALIGNMENT MARKS   2 DOWEL

Alignment of the camshaft pulley

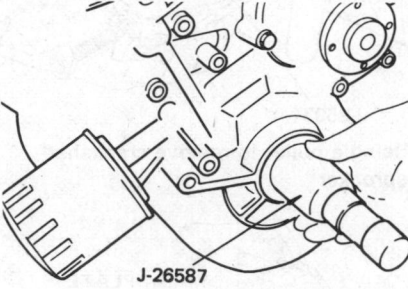

Installing timing cover seal

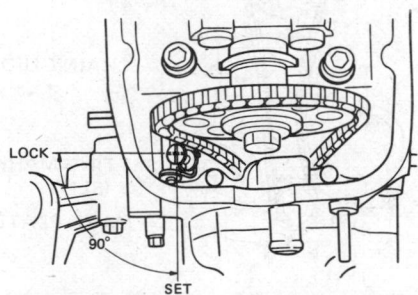

Locking the timing chain adjuster—1816cc gasoline engine

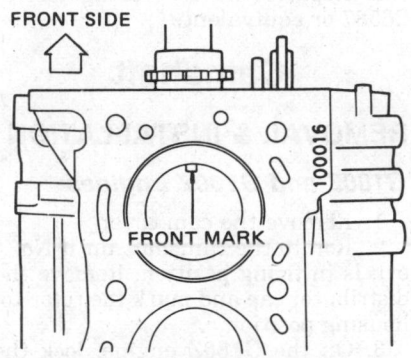

Piston correctly installed

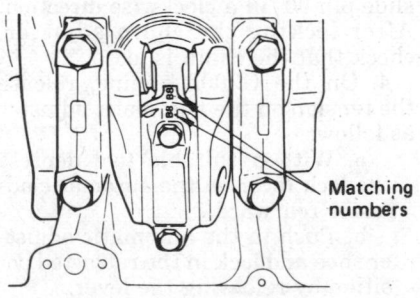

Cylinder identification on connecting rod and bearing cap

4ZC1-T Engine

1. Remove the cam cover.
2. Rotate the camshaft until the No. 4 cyl. is in the firing position. Remove the distributor cap and mark the rotor-to-housing position.
3. Remove the timing belt as previously outlined.
4. Apply a detention to the camshaft pulley by placing a T-bar or equivalent over the front plate fitting bolt and loosen the pulley fitting bolt. Remove the camshaft pulley, do not lose the camshaft boss or key.
5. Sequentially loosen and remove the outermost one and remove the rocker arm shaft with the bracket as an assembly.
6. Remove the camshaft.
7. Installation is the reverse of the removal procedure. Use a liberal

amount of oil to coat the camshaft before installing it. Be sure that the mark on the camshaft is facing upward when it is being installed.
8. Use the timing belt removal and installation procedure previously outlined in this section to finish the installation.

4XC1-U Engine

1. Disconnect the negative battery cable.

2. Align the crankshaft pulley notch with the "0" degree mark on the timing cover.
3. Remove the cylinder head cover.
4. Remove the timing cover.

5. Loosen the camshaft timing gear bolts (DO NOT rotate the engine).

6. Loosen the timing belt tensioner and remove the timing belt from the camshaft timing gear.

7. Remove the rocker arm shaft/rocker arm assembly.

8. Remove the distributor bolt and the distributor.

9. Remove the camshaft and the camshaft seal.

10. To install, drive a new camshaft seal onto the camshaft using seal installation tool No. J–35268 or equivalent. Place the camshaft in the cylinder head with the dowel pin in the camshaft facing forward. Reverse the removal procedure to finish this installation. Re-adjust the valves and the timing belt.

Piston and Connecting Rod

All Engines

It is not advisable to remove the piston from the connecting rod unless part replacement is necessary. Whenever a piston is removed, the piston pin should be replaced. When examining a piston, look for scuffs, cracking or wear. The rings should be removed with a ring expander and should be kept separately to avoid interchanging parts. All clearances should be checked with a micrometer or comparable precision gauge. Assemble the piston rings to the piston so that the NPR or TOP marks are turned up. Every piston has a mark to designate proper installation, this "Front Mark" is located on the top edge, in line with the piston pin bore. In addition, the cylinder number that the piston came from is stamped on the connecting rod and the bearing cap.

OVERHAUL

NOTE: For all piston and connecting rod overhaul procedures, please refer to "Engine Rebuilding" in the Unit Repair Section.

DIESEL ENGINE MECHANICAL

Engine

REMOVAL & INSTALLATION
I-Mark (RWD)

1. Open the hood and remove the battery cables at the posts. Remove the battery.

2. Scribe the position of the hinges on the underside of the hood and remove the hood.

3. Remove the bottom shrouds.

4. Drain the radiator and crankcase.

5. Remove the fan shroud attaching screws and remove the shroud. Remove the radiator attaching bolts and remove the radiator after disconnecting the upper and lower hoses.

6. Remove the air connecting hose.

7. Disconnect the heater hoses at the thermostat housing pipe and water inlet pipe.

8. Disconnect the quick start and silent idle (Q.S.S.I.) thermo switch, fast idle thermo switch, thermo unit wiring at the connector on the thermostat housing.

9. Tag and disconnect the generator wiring at the connector.

10. Disconnect the vacuum hose from the connector at the rear of the vacuum pump.

11. Disconnect the vacuum hose from the actuator of fast idle.

12. Remove the two nuts connecting the exhaust pipe to the exhaust manifold and separate the pipe from the manifold, then remove the two nuts connecting the exhaust front pipe to the exhaust mounting bracket and separate the front pipe from the bracket and remove the front pipe.

13. Disconnect the accelerator cable from the injection pump lever.

14. Disconnect the fuel cut solenoid valve switch wiring at the connector. Disconnect the tachometer pickup sensor wiring at the connector (if equipped).

15. Tag and disconnect the starter motor wiring at the connector. Disconnect the oil pressure switch, oil pressure unit wiring at the connector.

16. Disconnect the fuel hoses at the injection pump.

17. Disconnect the sensing resistor wiring at the connector.

18. Disconnect the back-up lamp switch and the top/third switch wiring at the connector on the rear of the engine.

19. Remove the return spring and disconnect the clutch control cable from the hook on the withdraw lever.

20. Disconnect the speedometer cable at the transmission side.

21. Remove the four bolts connecting the propeller shaft with the extension shaft and disconnect the propeller shaft flange yoke from the extension shaft, then pull the propeller shaft rearward. When the propeller shaft has been removed, wrap a small plastic bag around the rear transmission housing to prevent any leakage of fluid.

22. Untie the strings on the console boot and remove the screws on each side of the console box. Remove the grommets between the floor carpet and floor panel.

23. Pry off the edge of the gearshift lever dust boot and remove the gearshift lever assembly upward.

NOTE: Plug the gearshift lever fitting hole to prevent entry of dust or foreign material.

24. Remove the bolts and nuts attaching the rear mounting bracket, then remove the bolts attaching the exhaust mounting bracket.

25. Using a chain, engine lifting fixtures or other suitable means, lift the engine slightly.

26. Remove the engine mount nuts and disconnect the engine damper from the frame.

27. Check to make certain all parts have been removed or disconnected and tied out of the way so as not to snag on the motor when it is lifted clear.

28. Attach the engine hoist and remove the engine assembly with the transmission attached. Slowly lift the engine clear of the chassis.

29. Installation is the reverse of removal. Fill the crankcase, cooling system and check all cable adjustments.

30. Bleed the fuel system by filling the filter with diesel fuel and operating the primer pump handle several times. The force needed to operate the priming pump becomes greater as the filter fills up.

31. Start the engine and check for leaks.

Cylinder Head

REMOVAL & INSTALLATION

1. Drain the cooling system by opening the drain plug on the cylinder block.

2. Remove the camshaft.

3. Remove the sensing resistor assembly.

4. Remove the six screws attaching the injection pipe clip and remove the injection pipe clip.

5. Remove the eight sleeve nuts attaching the injection pipes and separate the infection pipes.

6. Remove the clip attaching the fuel leak off hose and separate the hose from the return pipe.

7. Remove the two nuts connecting the exhaust manifold to the exhaust pipe and separate the pipe from the manifold.

8. Disconnect the joint bolt attaching the oil feed line to the head side.

9. Disconnect the heater hose at the thermostat housing pipe.

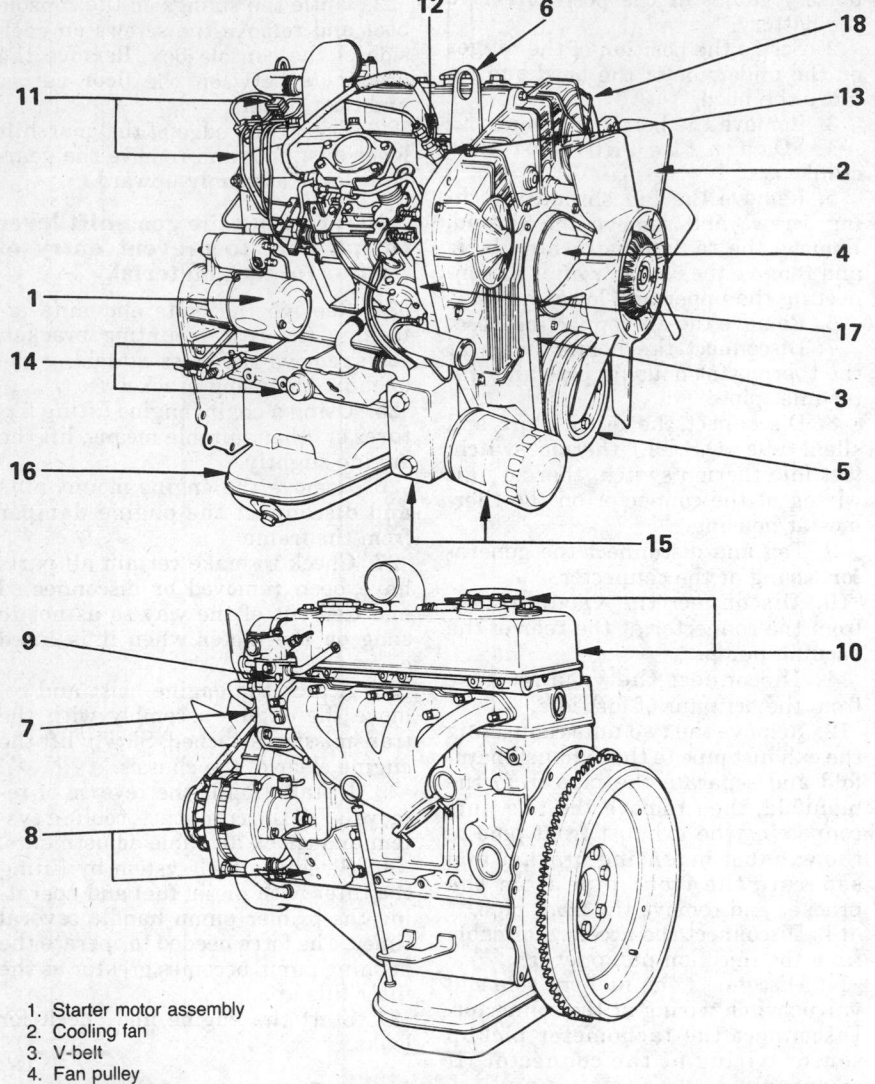

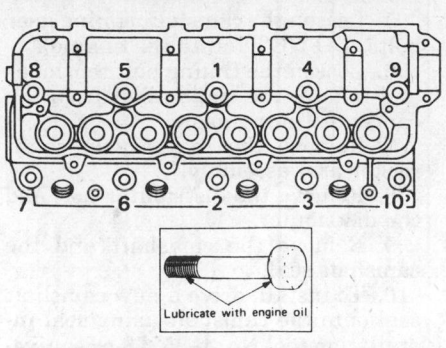

Cylinder head bolt torque sequence—diesel engine

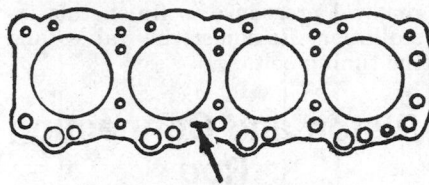

Location of TOP mark

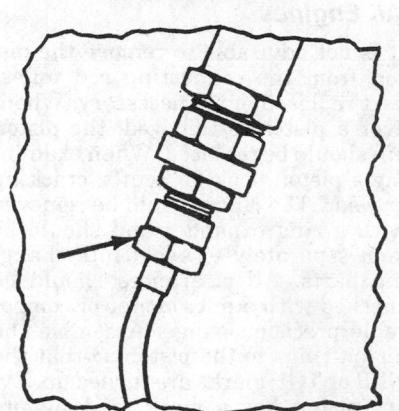

Diesel fuel injector showing injection pipe union

1. Starter motor assembly
2. Cooling fan
3. V-belt
4. Fan pulley
5. Damper pulley
6. Engine hanger
7. Water by-pass hose
8. Generator assembly and engine foot
9. Thermostat housing
10. Cam cover with positive crankcase ventilation valve
11. Injection pipe and clip
12. Nozzle holder assembly
13. Glow plug and connector
14. Oil pressure switch, unit and oil pipe
15. Oil cooler and oil filter
16. Oil pan
17. Tension spring
18. Dust cover

Diesel engine major components

10. Remove the cylinder head bolts by loosening them in sequence, then remove the cylinder head and gasket.

NOTE: Use light oil to free stubborn bolts.

11. Clean the head and block of all gasket material before reassembly.

12. Installation is the reverse of removal. Refill the cooling system. Torque all bolts in the sequence given at the front of this section. Apply oil to the bolt threads and clean them thoroughly before reinstalling them in the head.

NOTE: Make sure that the cylinder head gasket is properly placed before lowering the head. Look for the "TOP" mark to assure proper placement.

CYLINDER HEAD BOLT TORQUE

First Pass	21–36 ft. lbs.
Second Pass	83–98 ft. lbs.
Reused Bolt	90–105 ft. lbs.

13. Reinstall the camshaft and rocker arm assembly. Reinstall the timing belt and adjust the valve clearance.

14. Start the engine and check for leaks.

OVERHAUL

NOTE: For all cylinder head overhaul procedures, please refer to "Engine Rebuilding" in the Unit Repair Section.

Rocker Arms/Shaft

REMOVAL & INSTALLATION

1. Remove the cam cover.
2. Loosen the rocker arm shaft bracket nuts a little at a time, in sequence, commencing with the outer brackets.
3. Remove the nuts from the rocker arm shaft brackets.
4. Disassemble the rocker arm shaft assembly by removing the spring from the rocker arm shaft and then removing the rocker arm brackets and arms.
5. Inspect the rocker arm shaft for runout. Support the shaft on V-blocks at each end and check runout by slowly turning it with the probe of a dial indicator. Replace the shaft with a new one if the runout exceeds 0.0156 in. (0.4mm). Runout should not exceed 0.0079 in. (0.2mm).

6. Inspect the rocker arm shaft for wear, replace the shaft if obvious signs of wear are encountered.

7. Installation is the reverse of removal. Use a liberal amount of clean engine oil to coat the shaft, rocker arms and valve stems. Install the longer shaft on the exhaust valve side, shorter shaft on the intake side, so that the aligning marks on the shafts are turned to the front of the engine.

8. Torque the rocker arm shaft bracket and stud nuts to 15–22 ft. lbs. Hold the rocker arm springs with an adjustable wrench while torquing the nuts to prevent damage to the springs. Torque the nuts a little at a time in sequence, beginning with the center bracket and working outward.

9. Adjust valve clearances, reinstall the cam cover and check for leaks.

Intake Manifold

REMOVAL & INSTALLATION

1. Open the hood and disconnect the battery. Remove the air cleaner assembly.

2. Remove the connecting hose and PCV hose.

3. Remove the sensing resistor assembly.

4. Remove the six screws attaching the injection pipe clips and remove the injection pipe.

5. Remove the ten bolts attaching the upper dust cover and remove the upper dust cover.

6. Remove the two bolts attaching the engine hanger and remove the engine hanger.

7. Remove the two bolts attaching the stay and remove the stay. Remove the three bolts and two nuts attaching the intake manifold and lift off the manifold.

8. Installation is the reverse of removal. Use a new manifold gasket. Torque to 25–32 ft. lbs.

Exhaust Manifold

REMOVAL & INSTALLATION

1. Disconnect the negative battery cable and remove the connecting hose plus the PCV hose from the intake manifold.

2. Remove the sensing resistor assembly.

3. Remove the six screws holding the injection pipe clips and remove the injection pipe clips.

4. Remove the eight sleeve nuts holding the injection pipe and remove the injection pipe.

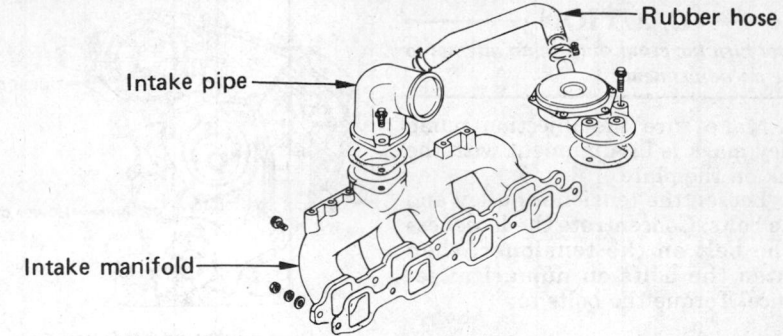

Intake manifold—diesel engine

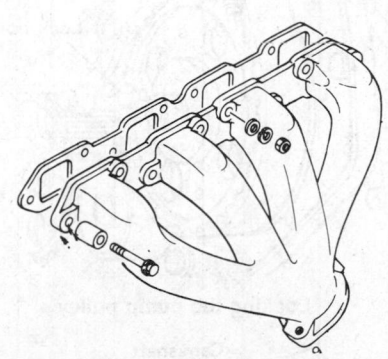

Exhaust manifold—diesel engine

5. Remove the ten bolts attaching the upper dust cover and remove the upper dust cover.

6. Remove the two bolts attaching the engine hanger and remove the engine hanger.

7. Remove the two bolts attaching the stay and remove the stay.

8. Remove the three bolts and two nuts holding the intake manifold to the block and remove the manifold.

9. Check the intake manifold for any cracks, warpage or any other kind of damage.

10. Place a new gasket over the manifold studs and the manifold installation is the reverse order of the removal procedure. Torque the intake manifold bolts and nuts to 25–32 ft. lbs.

Timing Cover Seal

REPLACEMENT

1. Once the timing cover is exposed, the seal can be pried out with a suitable tool.

2. Replace the seal using tool J-26587 or equivalent.

Timing Belt

REMOVAL & INSTALLATION

1. Open the hood and disconnect

the battery. Drain the radiator system.

2. Remove the lower engine shrouds.

3. Remove the fan shroud, V-belt, cooling fan and pulley.

4. Remove the ten retaining bolts on the upper dust cover and remove the cover.

5. Remove the bypass hose.

6. With the piston in the No. 1 cylinder at TDC, make sure the setting mark on the pump pulley is in alignment with the front plate, then lock the pulley with an 8mm 1.25 pitch bolt.

7. Remove the cam cover. Loosen the adjusting screws so that the rocker arms are held in a free state. Lock the camshaft by fitting a plate to the slit in the rear end of the camshaft.

8. Remove the damper pulley after making sure the piston in No. 1 is at TDC.

9. Remove the lower dust cover, then remove the timing belt holder.

10. Remove the tension spring. Loosen the tension pulley and plate bolts and remove the timing belt.

11. Remove the bolt locking the camshaft pulley and remove the pulley from the camshaft. Put the pulley back on the shaft, but only tighten the bolts enough to allow the pulley to be turned by hand.

12. Install the new timing belt, making sure the cogs on the pulley and the belt are engaged properly. The crankshaft should not be turned.

13. Concentrate belt looseness on the tension pulley, then depress the tension pulley with your fingers and install the tension spring. Semi-tighten the bolts in numerical sequence to prevent movement of the tension pulley.

14. Tighten the camshaft pulley bolts.

15. Remove the injection pump pulley lock bolt.

16. Remove the locking plate on the end of the camshaft.

17. Install the damper pulley on the hub and make sure the No. 1 piston is still at TDC.

18. Make sure the injection pump pulley mark is in alignment with the mark on the plate.

19. Loosen the tensioner pulley and plate bolts. Concentrate the looseness of the belt on the tensioner, then tighten the bolts on numerical sequence. Torque the bolts to:

Bolt No.	Torque
1	11–18 ft. lbs.
2	11–18 ft. lbs.
3	47–61 ft. lbs.

20. Check valve adjustment and install the cam cover.

21. Remove the damper pulley and install the belt holder in position away from the timing belt.

22. Install the bypass hose and dust covers.

23. Install the damper pulley and reverse removal Steps 1–5.

24. Refill the cooling system.

Camshaft

REMOVAL & INSTALLATION

1. Remove the cam cover.

2. Remove the timing belt.

3. Remove the rear plug and hold the shaft by attaching the fixing plate (J–29761 or equivalent) into the slit at the rear of the camshaft.

4. Remove the camshaft pulley bolt, then remove the pulley with a gear puller.

5. Remove the rocker arm and shaft.

6. Remove the bolts attaching the front head plate and remove the plate.

7. Remove the bolts attaching the camshaft bearing caps. Remove the caps and bearings.

8. Remove the camshaft oil seal, then remove the camshaft.

9. Installation is the reverse of removal. Use a liberal amount of clean oil to coat the camshaft and journals during assembly.

10. Install a new oil seal and apply Permatex® or equivalent gasket compound to the cylinder head fitting face of the No. 1 camshaft bearing cap.

11. Torque the rocker arm shafts and camshaft bearing caps to specifications.

Piston and Connecting Rod

All Engines

It is not advisable to remove the pis-

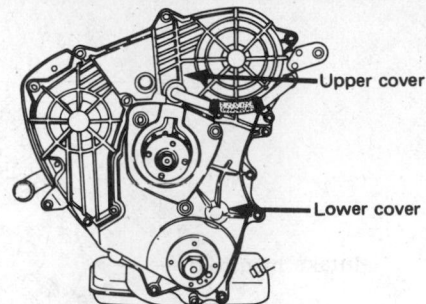

Dust covers on diesel engine

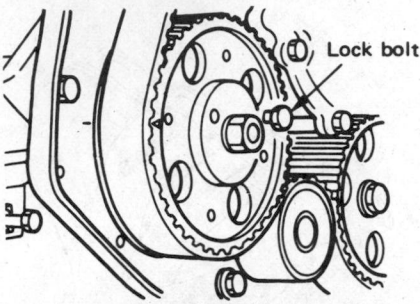

Locking the pump pulley

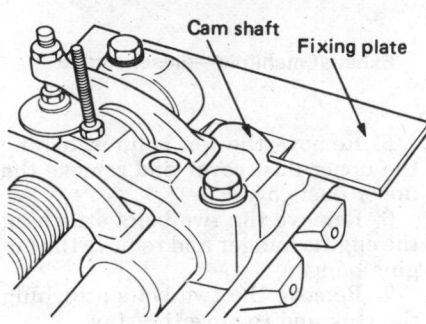

Locking the camshaft with fixing plate

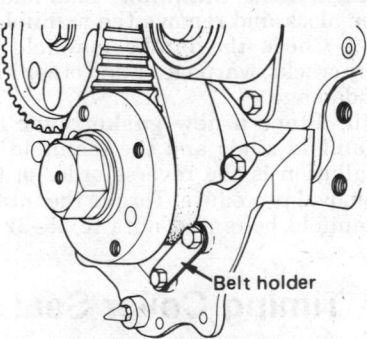

Location of timing belt holder

Install timing belt in numerical sequence

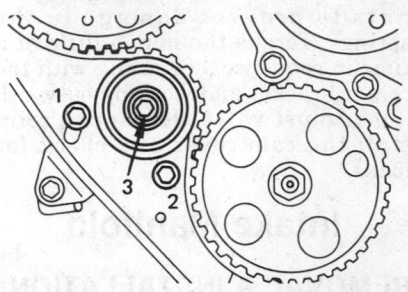

Tensioner pulley bolt tightening sequence

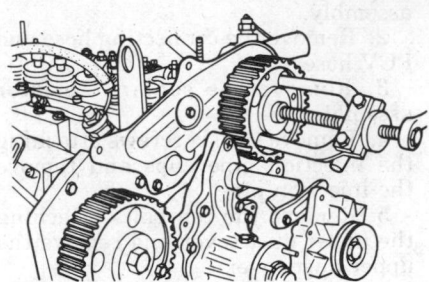

Removing camshaft pulley with gear puller

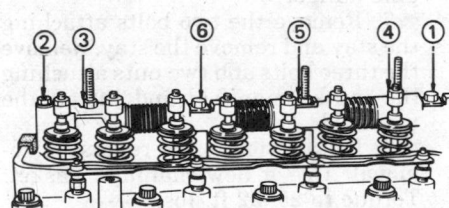

Bolt loosening sequence for removing rocker arm assembly

ton from the connecting rod unless part replacement is necessary. Whenever a piston is removed, the piston pin should be replaced. When examining a piston, look for scuffs, cracking or wear. The rings should be removed with a ring expander and should be kept separately to avoid interchanging parts. All clearances should be checked with a micrometer or comparable precision gauge. Assemble the piston rings to the piston so that the NPR or TOP marks are turned up. Every piston has a mark to designate proper installation, this "Front Mark" is located on the top edge, in line with the piston pin bore. In addition, the cylinder number that the piston came from is stamped on the connecting rod and the bearing cap.

NOTE: For all piston and connecting rod overhaul procedures, please refer to "Engine Rebuilding" in the Unit Repair Section.

ENGINE LUBRICATION

Oil Pan

REMOVAL & INSTALLATION

All Engines

NOTE: Isuzu recommends removing the engine (or at least raising it up) to service the oil pan. There isn't sufficient clearance to remove the pan with the engine bolted down.

1. Remove or raise the engine to allow sufficient room to clear the oil pan.

NOTE: On the diesel engine it may be necessary to remove the engine in order to remove the oil pan because of lack of clearance. Also on the 4XC1-U engine, disconnect the exhaust pipe bracket and the exhaust pipe at the manifold. Disconnect the right hand tension rod located under the front bumper to gain access to the oil pan.

2. Remove the bolts and nuts attaching the oil pan to the engine block. Remove the oil pan and gasket.
3. Clean the oil pan and engine block gasket surface carefully to remove all traces of the old gasket.
4. Install in reverse order of removal, using a thin coat of Permatex® No. 2 or equivalent to hold the gasket in place while installing the bolts and to prevent any oil leaks.
5. Torque the oil pan bolts evenly to 4 ft. lbs. Check the edges of the gasket to ensure that it is sealed properly. If the gasket projects unevenly around the oil pan flange, remove the gasket and reinstall carefully.

NOTE: Do not overtighten the oil pan bolts. Bolts that are too tight cause as many leaks as bolts that are too loose.

6. Start the engine and check for leaks.

Rear Main Bearing Oil Seal

REMOVAL & INSTALLATION

1. Remove the transmission and oil pan.
2. On manual transmission models, remove the clutch cover and pressure plate assembly.

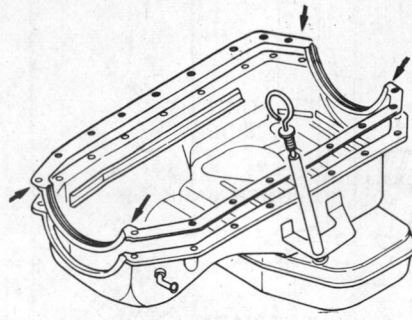

Oil pan and gasket—diesel engine

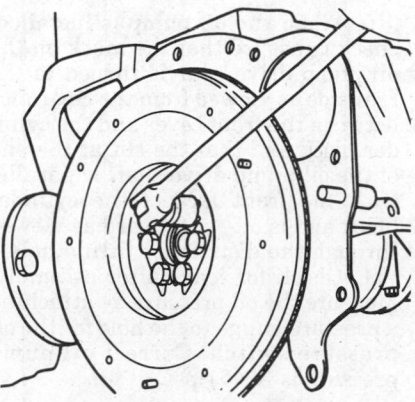

Removing flywheel assembly

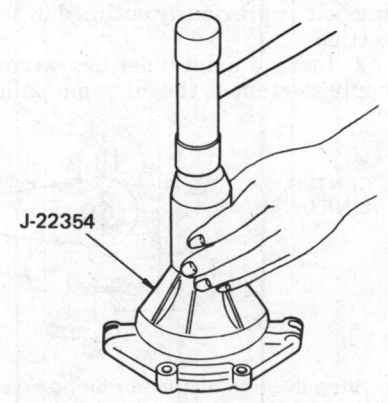

J-22354

Installing crankshaft rear seal with special tool

3. Remove the starter and lay to one side or wire to the frame.

NOTE: Disconnect the battery before removing starter.

4. Remove the six flywheel bolts and the flywheel assembly.
5. Remove the four rear crankshaft seal retainer bolts and remove the retainer seal assembly.
6. Pry the old seal out of the retainer and discard.
7. Place a new seal in position in the retainer. Fill the clearance between the lips of the seal with grease and lubricate the seal lip with engine oil.
8. Place the retainer on a flat surface and drive the seal into place using installer tool No. J-22354 or equivalent.
9. Installation is the reverse of removal steps 1–6. When installing the flywheel, install washer and bolts and torque to 69 ft. lbs.
10. Start the engine and check for leaks.

NOTE: Diesel engines use a different number seal installing tool (J-29818), and the seal is installed on the No. 5 crankshaft bearing cap. Other than that, the removal and replacement procedures are identical for all engines.

Oil Pump

REMOVAL & INSTALLATION

G180Z and G200Z Engines

NOTE: The oil pump can be serviced with the engine in or out of the vehicle. The procedure below is for the engine in the car.

1. Remove the cam cover.
2. Remove the distributor assembly.
3. Remove the engine oil pan.
4. Remove the bolt attaching the

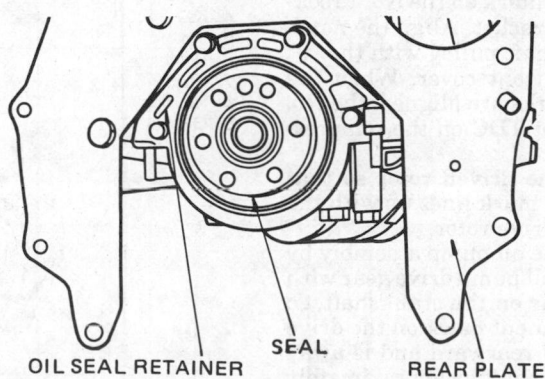

OIL SEAL RETAINER   SEAL   REAR PLATE

Rear main oil seal assembly

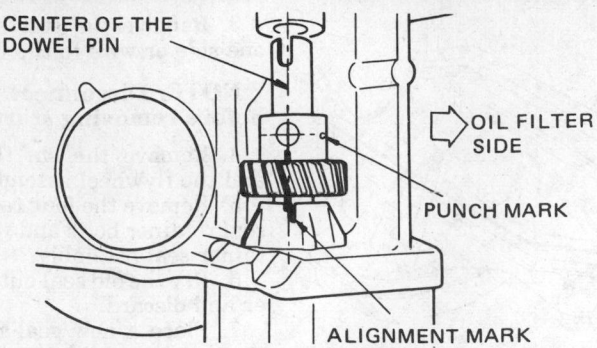

Oil pump alignment

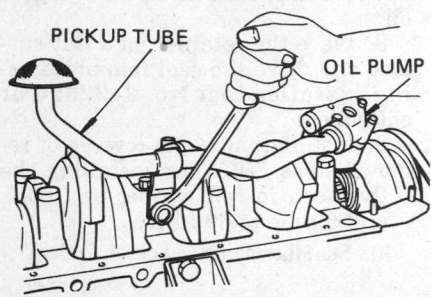

Oil pump assembly (engine upside down)

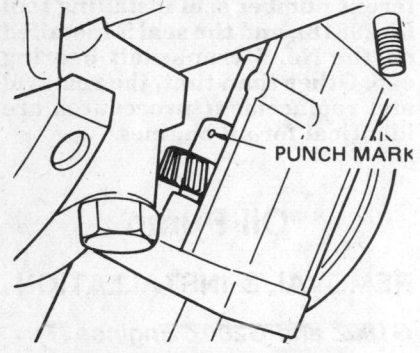

Checking oil pump alignment

oil pick-up tube to the block and remove the tube from the oil pump.

5. Remove the oil pump mounting bolts and remove the pump assembly.

6. Remove the rubber hose and relief valve from the oil pump.

7. Installation is in reverse order of removal. Align the mark on the camshaft with the mark on the No. 1 rocker arm shaft bracket. Align the notch on the crankshaft pulley with the "0" mark on the front cover. When the two sets of marks are aligned, the No. 4 cylinder is at TDC on the compression stroke.

8. Install the driven rotor so that the alignment mark lines up with the mark on the drive rotor.

9. Install the oil pump assembly by engaging the oil pump drive gear with the pinion gear on the crankshaft, so that the alignment mark on the drive gear is turned rearward and is away from the crankshaft by approximately 20° in a clockwise direction.

10. When the oil pump is installed, check to assure that the mark on the oil pump drive gear is turned to the rear side as viewed from the clearance between the front cover and the cylinder block and that the slit at the end of the oil pump drive shaft is parallel with the front face of the cylinder block and is off-set forward as viewed through the distributor fitting hole.

11. Check for leaks after assembly. Measure the oil pressure by attaching a pressure gauge to the hole for the oil pressure switch. Correct oil pump pressure is 56–71 psi.

4ZC1-T Engine

1. Remove the front cover and timing belt as previously outlined in this section.

2. Using a 6mm inner hex wrench apply a detent to the oil pump pulley

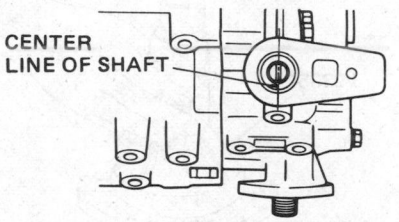

View through distributor fitting hole

1. Nut
2. Oil pump pulley
3. Vane
4. Key
5. Pin
6. Rotor
7. Shaft
8. Housing
9. Oil seal

and loosen the oil pump pulley bolt, remove the oil pump pulley.

3. Using the same hex head wrench, remove the allen bolts attaching the oil pump to the engine and remove the pump.

4. Installation is the reverse order of the removal procedure. Apply a liberal amount of oil to all components before installation. Install the rotor with the chamfered side turned towards the cylinder body.

5. Apply a light coat of oil to the O-ring and insert the O-ring into the groove of the oil pump housing. Install the oil pump onto the engine and torque the Allen bolts to 14 ft. lbs.

6. Check and make sure that the oil pump turns smoothly, if it does not, replace the cartridge assembly.

7. Install the oil pump pulley and torque the pulley bolt to 58 ft. lbs. Follow the timing belt procedure previously outlined to finish the installation.

4XC1-U Engine

1. Refer to the "Engine Removal &

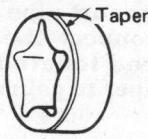

Install vane with taper side toward the cylinder body

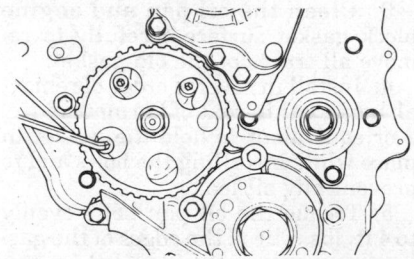

Using special tool to remove Allen bolts on oil pump

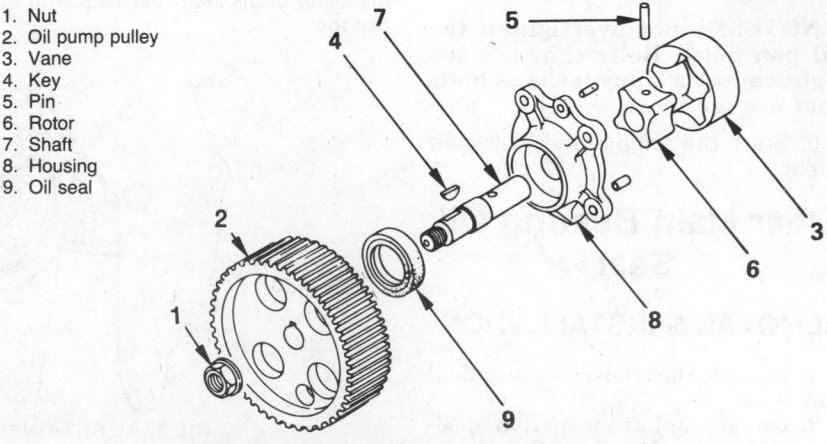

Exploded view of diesel oil pump and pulley assembly

Installation" procedure in this section and remove the engine.

2. Drain the crankcase.

3. Remove the alternator belt and the starter.

4. Install the flywheel holding tool (J–35271) to secure the flywheel.

5. Remove the crankshaft pulley and boss.

6. Remove the timing cover bolts and the timing cover.

7. Loosen the tension pulley and remove the timing belt.

8. Remove the crankshaft timing gear and the tension pulley.

9. Remove the oil pan bolts, oil pan, oil strainer fixing bolt and the oil strainer assembly.

10. Remove the oil pump bolts and the oil pump assembly.

11. Remove the sealing material from the oil pump and engine block sealing surfaces.

12. To install, use seal installer J–35269 or equivalent and install a new oil seal in the oil pump housing, lubricate the oil pump, use new gaskets, apply sealant to the sealing surfaces and reverse the removal procedure. The final torque for the oil pump attaching bolts is 7 ft. lbs.

Diesel Engine

1. Remove the timing belt.

2. Remove the Allen bolts attaching the oil pump and remove the pump together with the pulley.

NOTE: The special tool for the Allen bolts is J–29767

3. Disassemble the oil pump on the workbench. A gear puller may be necessary to remove the pulley.

4. Installation is the reverse of removal. Apply generous amounts of clean engine oil to all components before installation. Install the vane with the taper side toward the cylinder body.

5. Install a new O-ring into the groove in the housing. Lubricate with oil. Install the rotor and then the pump body together with the pulley. Torque the Allen bolts to 11–18 ft. lbs.

ENGINE COOLING

Radiator

REMOVAL & INSTALLATION

All Models

1. Open the hood and disconnect the battery.

2. Remove the radiator cap and drain the cooling system.

— **CAUTION** —
The engine should be cold for removal procedures.

3. Loosen the top and bottom hose clamps and remove the radiator hoses.

4. Remove the fan shroud.

5. Remove the bolts and nuts attaching the radiator and remove the radiator assembly.

6. Installation is the reverse of removal. Fill the cooling system with

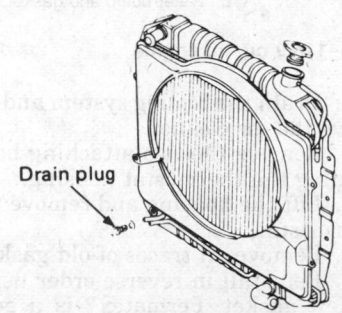

Radiator with shroud attached

water and the proper proportion of antifreeze solution. Start the engine and check for leaks.

Water Pump

REMOVAL & INSTALLATION

Gasoline Engines

I-MARK (RWD)

1. Open the hood and disconnect the battery. Remove the lower engine cover.

2. Drain the cooling system.

3. On cars without A/C, remove the fan.

4. On cars with A/C, remove the air pump and generator mounting bolts, then remove the fan and air pump drive belt (pivot the generator and air pump in toward the engine). Remove the fan and pulley with set plate. Remove the hoses to the pump.

5. Remove the six bolts attaching the water pump and remove the water pump assembly. Clean all gasket surfaces carefully.

6. Installation is the reverse of removal. Fill the cooling system with the correct anti-freeze and water solution and adjust all drive belts. Use a new gasket.

7. Start the engine and check for leaks.

I-MARK (FWD)

1. Disconnect the negative battery

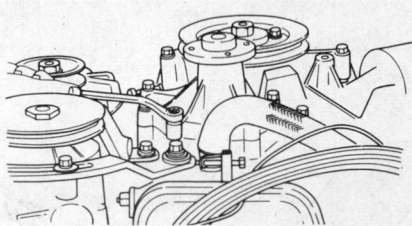

Water pump on gasoline engines

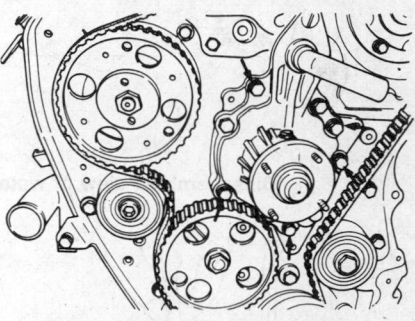

Water pump attaching bolts

cable and drain the coolant into a suitable drain pan.

2. Loosen the power steering pump adjustment bolts and remove the belt. (Remove all necessary drive belts).

3. Remove the timing belt as previously outlined in this section.

4. Remove the tension pulley and spring. Remove the water pump pulley.

5. Remove the water pump mounting bolts, water pump and gasket from the engine. Clean the mounting surfaces of all gasket material.

6. To install, reverse the removal procedures. Apply a suitable sealant to the mounting surfaces of the pump and torque the pump to 17 ft. lbs.

IMPULSE

1. Disconnect the battery and drain the radiator.

2. Remove the fan belt, plate, spacer, and pulley.

3. Remove the water pump and gasket.

4. Before installation, clean the gasket surfaces carefully and torque the water pump retaining bolts to 18 ft. lbs.

Diesel Engines

1. Open the hood and disconnect the battery. Remove the radiator cap.

2. Drain the cooling system and remove the hoses from the pump.

3. Remove the fan and pulley.

4. Remove the four attaching bolts holding the damper pulley. Remove the damper pulley.

5. Remove the engine dust covers.

6. Remove the bypass hose.

7. Remove the five bolts attaching

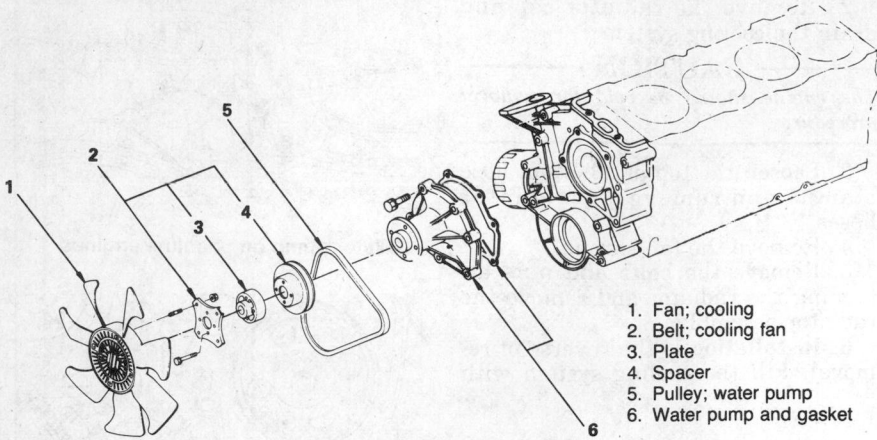

1. Fan; cooling
2. Belt; cooling fan
3. Plate
4. Spacer
5. Pulley; water pump
6. Water pump and gasket

Disassembled view of water pump—118.9 cu. in. engine

Due to the complex nature of modern electronic engine control systems, comprehensive diagnosis and testing procedures fall outside the confines of this repair manual. For complete information on diagnosis, testing and repair procedures concerning all modern engine and emission control systems, please refer to *"Chilton's Guide to Electronic Engine Controls"*.

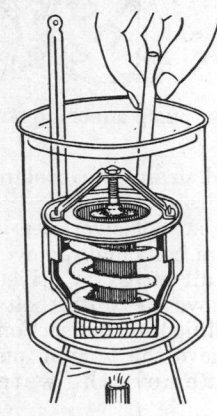

Testing thermostat operation in hot water

1. Drain the cooling system and remove the air cleaner.
2. Remove the two attaching bolts holding the thermostat housing.
3. Lift the housing and remove the thermostat.
4. Remove all traces of old gasket.
5. Reinstall in reverse order using a new gasket. Permatex® is a good idea to avoid leaks. Make sure the thermostat is installed properly (it doesn't work upside-down).

GASOLINE FUEL SYSTEM

Fuel Filter

REPLACEMENT

I-Mark (RWD) & Impulse

The fuel system has a cartridge type, inline filter installed on the left side panel in the luggage compartment on all models except the Impulse. On the Impulse it is located in the engine compartment.

1. Remove the bolts attaching the cover on the side of the fuel tank in the luggage compartment, then remove the cover.
2. Disconnect the hoses from the filter.
3. Remove the fuel filter from the clip.
4. Installation is the reverse of removal.

I-Mark (FWD)

The fuel filter is located under the

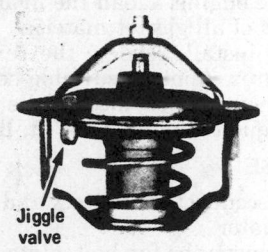

Jiggle valve

Thermostat—typical for all models

EMISSION CONTROLS

NOTE: Please refer to the "Emission Control" in the Unit Repair section for system maintenance procedures.

the water pump and remove the pump and gasket.
8. Clean all gasket surfaces carefully and inspect for nicks, cracks or deep scratches.
9. Installation is the reverse of removal. Use a new gasket. Torque all water pump mounting bolts to 11–18 ft. lbs.

Thermostat

REMOVAL & INSTALLATION

All Models

NOTE: Engine should be cold for this procedure.

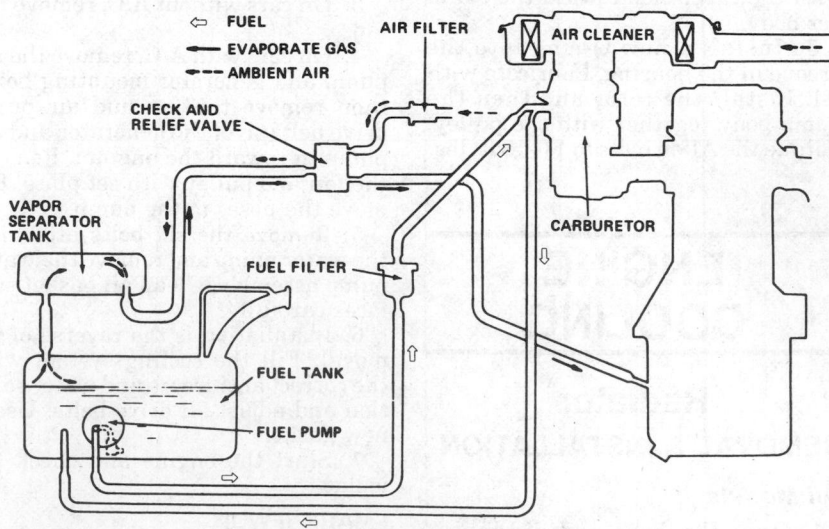

⇦ FUEL
← EVAPORATE GAS
⇠ AMBIENT AIR

AIR FILTER
AIR CLEANER
CHECK AND RELIEF VALVE
VAPOR SEPARATOR TANK
FUEL FILTER
CARBURETOR
FUEL TANK
FUEL PUMP

Fuel system schematic

Vacuum Booster of the Power Brake System and should be replaced every 15,000 miles.

1. Remove the fuel tank cap.

2. Disconnect and plug the fuel hoses from the fuel filter.

3. Remove the fuel filter and reinstall the fuel tank cap.

4. Installation is the reverse of the removal procedure. Be sure to securely attach the fuel filter clips and start the engine to check for any leaks.

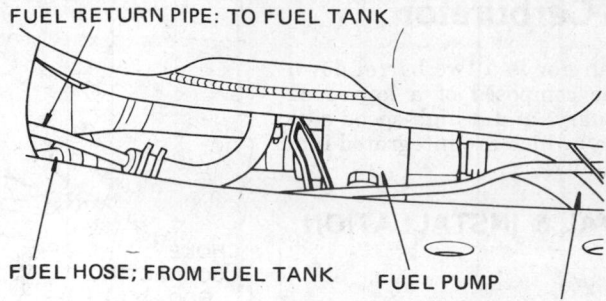

Fuel pump location—1949cc gasoline engine

Fuel Pump

OPERATION

I-Mark (RWD)

The fuel pump is a lightweight, motor-driven centrifugal typemounted near the bottom of the fuel tank. The pump will shut off immediately if the generator belt breaks, if there is a loss of voltage signal from the generator, or if the fusible link is open. At idle, the shut down is immediate; at fast idle or if the accelerator is partially depressed, the shut down is delayed 30–45 seconds to use up the fuel in the carburetor float bowl.

Impulse

The Impulse engines use an electrical fuel pump, which is located near the fuel tank and can be reached by removing the rear seat. There is also an optional sub-fuel pump available in this model and it is installed in line with the main fuel pump.

I-Mark (FWD)

The mechanical fuel pump is located at the left rear side of the cylinder head intake manifold. It is a diaphragm-type pump which is operated by an eccentric on the camshaft. No adjustment or repairs are possible, it is serviced by replacement only.

TESTING DELIVERY PRESSURE

I-Mark (RWD)

1. Disconnect the main fuel hose at the carburetor side and connect a fuel pump pressure gauge using a T-fitting.

2. Start the engine and note the pressure reading on the gauge.

3. Delivery pressure at 900–4800 rpm is 2.40–3.3 psi.

4. If the measured value is different from specifications, replace the fuel pump.

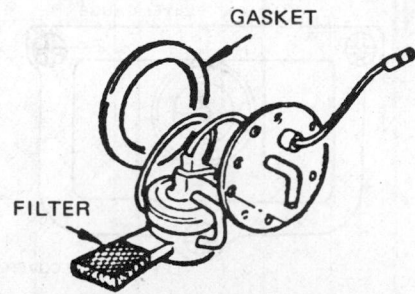

Fuel pump—1816cc gasoline engine

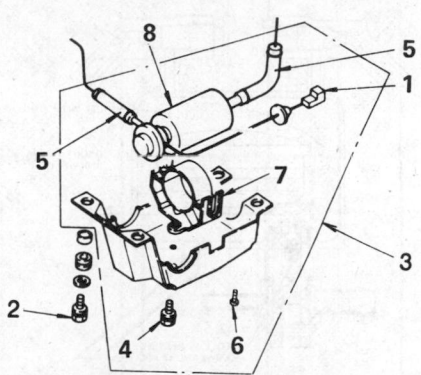

1 Connector; fuel pump harness
2. Bolt; guard to body
3. Bracket; fuel pump, guard and fuel pump assembly.
4. Bolt; guard to fuel pump bracket
5. Hose; rubber
6. Screw; fuel pump bracket
7. Bracket; fuel pump
8. Pump assembly; fuel

Exploded view of fuel pump and attaching parts—118.9 cu. in. engine

───── **CAUTION** ─────

Do not operate the fuel pump under no-load conditions and perform all tests with the filter installed.

REMOVAL & INSTALLATION

I-Mark (RWD)

1. Disconnect the fuel return hose from the pipe and drain the fuel.

───── **CAUTION** ─────

Fire hazard. Take precautions to avoid igniting any spilled fuel. Be particularly careful when using a work light around the fuel system.

2. Remove the fuel tank cover.

3. Remove the two screws holding the fuel pipe cover and remove the cover.

4. Disconnect the fuel hose from the fuel pump.

5. Disconnect the fuel pump wiring.

6. Remove the nine screws attaching the fuel pump and remove the fuel pump assembly from the fuel tank.

7. Installation is the reverse of removal. Check for leaks and cracked hoses.

Impulse

1. Raise the rear seat by hand and disconnect the electrical harness connector under the right side of the seat.

2. Remove the bolts connecting the fuel pump guard to the body.

3. Disconnect and cap the rubber hose at the fuel pump.

4. Remove the fuel pump bracket and fuel pump.

NOTE: The fuel pump cannot be disassembled and must be replaced if found to be defective.

5. Installation is the reverse of removal.

I-Mark (FWD)

1. Disconnect the fuel and air hoses from the fuel pump.

2. Remove the bolts, fuel pump and heat insulator assembly.

3. After removing the fuel pump, cover the mounting surface of the cylinder head to prevent oil discharge.

4. To install, reverse the removal procedure and replace the heat insulator assembly. Start the engine and check for fuel leaks.

Carburetor

The carburetor is a two barrel down draft type composed of a low-speed side (primary) and a high-speed side (secondary) which are integrated into a single unit.

REMOVAL & INSTALLATION

I-Mark

1. Disconnect the PCV hose from the cylinder head cover.
2. Disconnect the ECS hose from the air cleaner body.
3. Disconnect the AIR hose from the air pump.
4. Remove the bolts attaching the air cleaner and loosen the clamp bolts.
5. Lift the air cleaner slightly and disconnect the TCA vacuum hose and air duct, then remove the air cleaner.
6. Disconnect the vacuum signal hose from the EGR valve.
7. Disconnect the electrical leads connector.
8. Disconnect the accelerator cable.
9. Disconnect the fuel line at the carburetor.

--- CAUTION ---

Fire hazard. Use rags to catch any fuel and be careful with work lights. A broken light bulb landing on raw fuel can be quite spectacular.

10. Disconnect the ECS hose from the carburetor.
11. Remove the four nuts and lockwashers securing the carburetor to the intake manifold and remove the carburetor.
12. Installation is the reverse of removal. Clean all gasket surfaces before installation and always use a new gasket.
13. Start the engine and adjust the carburetor. Any time the carburetor is removed for inspection or overhaul, the emissions levels must be reset using an exhaust gas analyzer.

I-Mark

1. Disconnect the negative battery cable and drain the engine coolant into a suitable drain pan.
2. Remove the air cleaner assembly.
3. Disconnect the harness connector, vacuum lines and fuel lines from the carburetor.
4. Remove the accelerator cable from the carburetor.
5. Remove the bolts securing the carburetor to the intake manifold.
6. Remove the carburetor and place a cover over the intake manifold.
7. Installation is the reverse order of the removal procedure.

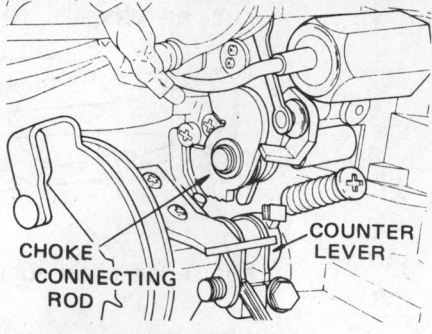

Choke components

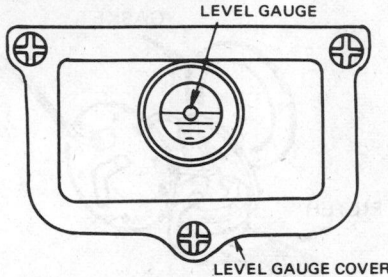

Checking float level

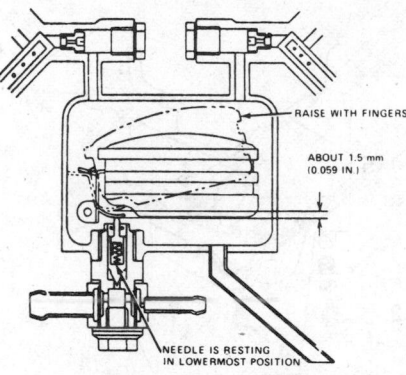

Adjusting float level

LINKAGE ADJUSTMENTS

When the primary throttle valve is opened to an angle of 57° (about half way) the adjust plate, which is interlocked with the primary throttle valve, is brought into contact with the kick lever. When the primary throttle valve is opened further, the return plate is pulled apart from the stopper, allowing the secondary throttle valve to open. To measure just when the secondary is opening:

1. Measure the clearance between the primary throttle valve and the wall of the throttle chamber at the center of the throttle valve when the adjust plate is brought into contact with the kick lever.
2. Standard clearance is 0.20–0.30 in. (6.1–7.6mm) and 0.23 in. on the I-

Mark (FWD). If necessary, make adjustments by bending the kick lever.

PRIMARY THROTTLE VALVE OPENING ADJUSTMENT

Check and make necessary adjustment so that the primary throttle valve is opened, by means of the fast idle adjusting screw, to an angle of 16° MT or 17° AT (1982 and later) when the choke valve is completely closed. On the I-Mark (FWD) it is 20° AT and 18°. To check the opening angle of the primary throttle valve:

1. Close the choke valve completely and measure the clearance between the throttle valve and the wall of the throttle valve chamber at the center part of the valve.
2. Standard clearance is 0.050–0.059 in. (1.28–1.51mm) for manual and 0.055–0.064 in. (1981) or 0.059–0.069 in. (1982 and later) for automatic transmissions. The Standard Clearance on the I-Mark (FWD) is 0.0323 in. AT and 0.0256 in. MT. If necessary, adjust by bending the kick lever.

FLOAT LEVEL ADJUSTMENT

The fuel level is normal if it is within the marks on the window glass of the float chamber when the engine is off. If the fuel level is outside of the lines, make adjustment by bending the float seat. The needle valve should have an effective stroke of about 0.59 in. (1.5mm).

The needle valve is adjusted by bending the float stopper, but accomplishing that simple task requires the removal and disassembly of the carburetor. See the Unit Repair Section.

AUTOMATIC CHOKE ADJUSTMENT (FAST IDLE)

--- CAUTION ---

The automatic choke fast idle is adjusted by opening the angle of the throttle valve on the carburetor, NOT by engine speed.

The adjusted throttle valve opening at the first step of the fast idle cam is 16° ± 1°(AT). The engine fast idle speed becomes approximately 3200 rpm after the engine is warmed up, or if the vacuum line to the distributor, idle compensator and EGR valve is plugged.

OVERHAUL

For all carburetor overhaul procedures, please refer to "Carburetor Service" in the Unit Repair

Fuel Injection

Due to the complex nature of modern fuel injection systems, comprehensive diagnosis and testing procedures fall outside the confines of this repair manual. For complete information on fuel injection diagnosis, testing and repair procedures please refer to *"Chilton's Guide To Fuel Injection And Feedback Carburetors"*.

DIESEL ENGINE FUEL SYSTEM

Fuel Filter

REPLACEMENT

1. Disconnect the water separator sensor wiring at the connector and the water drain hose.
2. Using special filter wrench J–22700 or equivalent, remove the fuel filter. Be careful when removing the filter cartridge so as not to spill fuel within the cartridge.
3. Drain the cartridge into a suitable drain pan and remove the sensor from the filter cartridge.
4. Install the sensor on the new filter and apply some clean diesel fuel to the O-ring before installation.
5. Apply clean diesel fuel to the filter O-ring and turn in the filter until the sealing surface is brought in contact with the O-ring. Then tighten the filter ⅔ of a turn.
6. Connect the sensor connector and install the water drain hose.
7. Fill the filter cartridge with fuel by using the priming pump handle 30–40 times. The force needed to operate the priming pump increases when the filter is full.
8. Start the engine and check for any fuel leaks.

DRAINING THE WATER

1. Place a suitable container at the end of the vinyl hose under the drain plug of the water separator.
2. Loosen the drain plug approximately four turns.
3. Pump the priming pump ten times by hand. Tighten the drain plug and continue to pump the priming pump another ten times.
4. Start the engine and check for fuel leaks. Also check to see that the "FILTER" indicator light has turned off.

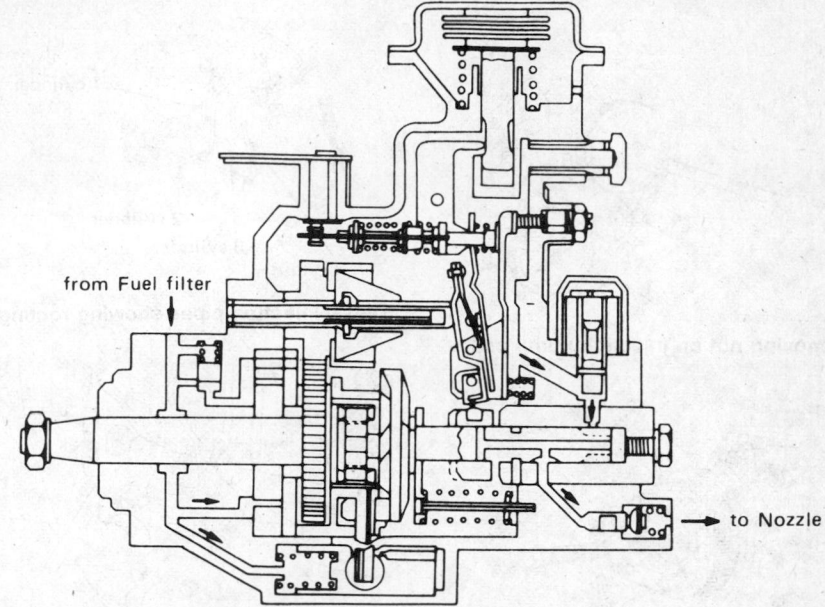

Cross section of diesel injection pump

Removing the water separator sensor

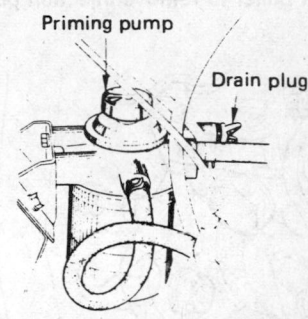

Priming pump and drain plug location

Injection Nozzle

REMOVAL & INSTALLATION

1. Loosen the screws attaching the injection pipe clips.
2. Remove the sleeve nut attaching injection pipe and separate the injection pipe.
3. Remove the injection nozzle assembly, corrugated washer and nozzle gasket.
4. Installation is the reverse order of the removal procedure. Do not reuse the old corrugated washer. The new corrugated washer should be installed with the blue collar painted side turned toward the nozzle. Torque the nozzle assembly to 47–61 ft. lbs.

NOTE: The diesel injection pump is an extremely complicated device, built to tolerances of millionths of an inch. Servicing should be left to a qualified diesel specialist. Never use cold water to clean a hot engine or the diesel injection pump may seize.

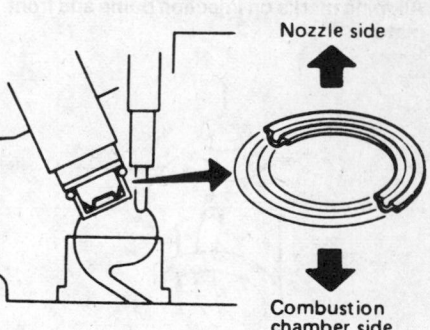

Installation of the injection nozzle

Injection Pump

REMOVAL & INSTALLATION

1. Remove the timing belt as previously described.
2. Remove the nut attaching the injection pump pulley.
3. Remove the pulley using a suitable puller and remove the lock bolt.

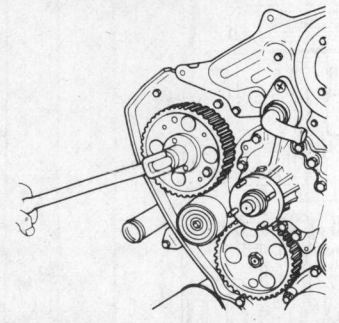

Removing nut on injection pump pulley

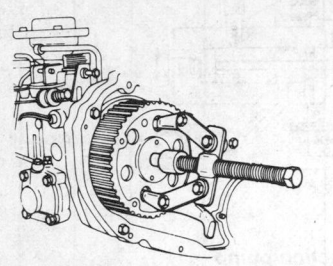

Using a puller to remove injection pump pulley

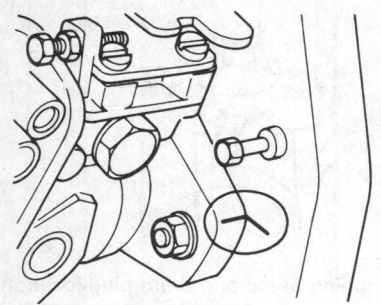

Aligning marks on injection pump and front plate

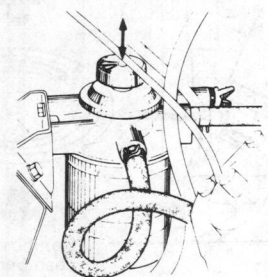

Diesel fuel filter with priming pump (arrows)

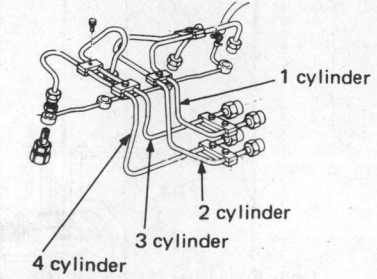

Diesel injection pipes showing routing

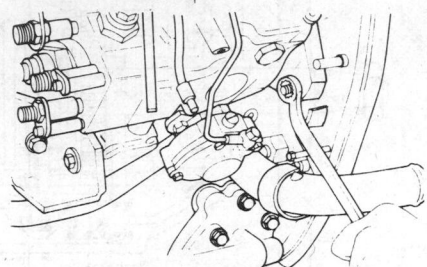

Removing pump flange nuts

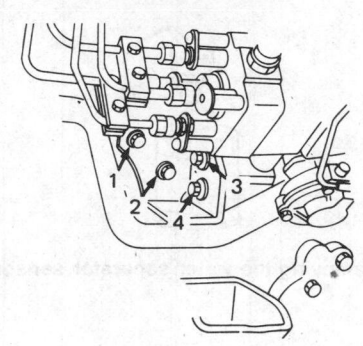

Bolt tightening sequence for injection pump mount

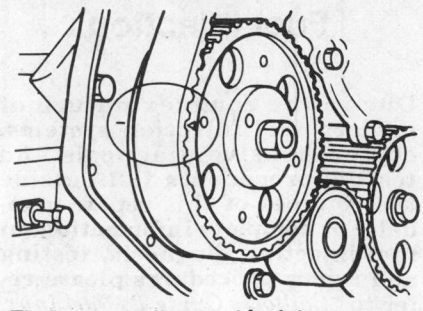

Timing mark alignment for injection pump pulley

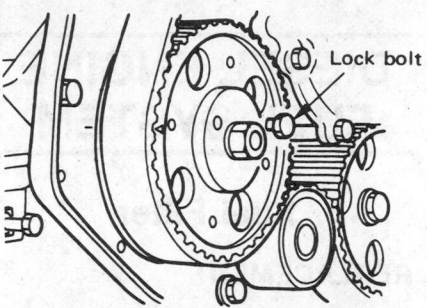

Securing injection pump pulley

4. Disconnect the fuel cut-off solenoid valve switch wiring and tachometer sensor wiring, if equipped.

5. Disconnect the accelerator cable from the pump lever. (A/T models only).

6. Disconnect the vacuum hose from the actuator of the fast idle device.

7. Disconnect the fuel hoses at the injection pump.

8. Remove the six screws attaching the injection pipe clips and remove the clips.

9. Remove the eight sleeve nuts attaching the injection pipes and remove the pipes.

10. Remove the four bolts attaching the pump rear bracket and remove the rear bracket. Disconnect the spring of the control lever.

11. Remove the two nuts attaching the injection pipe flange and remove the injection pump together with the fast idle device.

12. Install the injection pump together with the fast idle device by aligning the notched line on the flange with the line on the front plate.

13. Tighten the bolts in sequence. No clearance should be between the rear bracket and injection pump bracket.

14. Install the injection pump pulley by aligning it with the key groove. Align the mark on the pulley with the mark on the front plate, the tighten the nut using the lock bolt to prevent the pulley from turning.

15. Reinstall the timing belt as previously described and set the injection timing.

16. Install the injection pipes, clips and the vacuum hose for the actuator. Connect all control cables and wiring.

17. Fill the filter with fuel by operating the priming handle several times. Adjust the idle speed.

Diesel Injection Timing

ADJUSTMENT

1. Check that the notched line on the injection pump flange is in alignment with the notched line on the injection pump front bracket.

2. Bring the piston in No. 1 cylinder to TDC on the compression stroke by turning the crankshaft as necessary.

3. With the timing pulley housing cover removed, check that the timing belt is properly tensioned and that the timing marks are aligned (see timing belt adjustment).

4. Disconnect the injection pipe from the injection pump and remove the distributor head screw, then install a static timing gauge (special tool J-29763).

5. Use a wrench to hold the delivery holder when loosening the sleeve nuts on the injection pump side.

6. Bring the piston in No. 1 cylin-

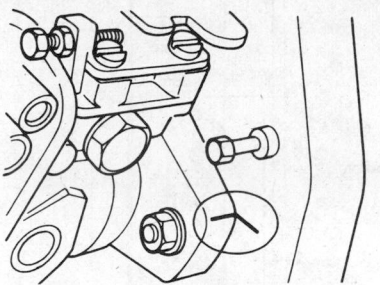

Correct injection pump alignment

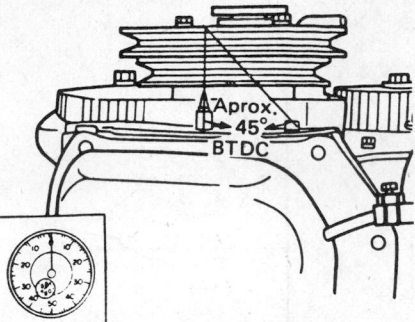

Calibrating the dial indicator

Static timing gauge J-29763

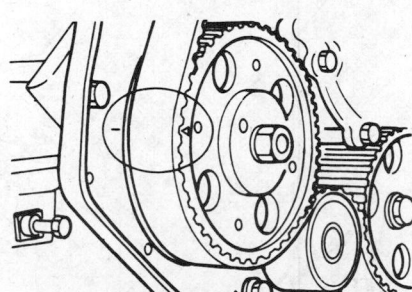

Correct alignment of timing marks

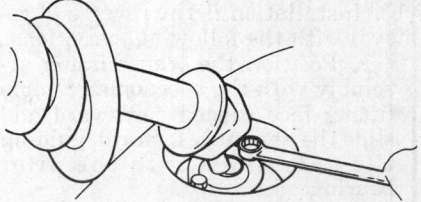

Typical removal of manual shifter assembly—except Impulse

Installing the static gauge

der to a point 45–60° BTDC by turning the crankshaft, then calibrate the dual indicator to zero.

7. Turn the crankshaft pulley slightly in both directions and check that gauge indication is stable.

8. Turn the crankshaft in the normal direction of rotation (clockwise) and take the reading on the dial indicator when the timing mark on the crankshaft pulley is in alignment with the pointer.

9. If the reading on the dial indicator deviates from the specified range, hold the crankshaft in position 12° BTDC (18°–1981) and loosen the two nuts on the injection pump flange.

10. Move the injection pump to a point where the dial indicator gives a reading of 0.5mm (0.020 in.) then tighten the pump flange nuts to 42–52 ft. lbs.

MANUAL TRANSMISSION

REMOVAL & INSTALLATION

I-Mark (RWD)

1. Disconnect the battery ground cable.

2. Remove the shift lever assembly from inside the car.

3. Loosen the clutch cable adjusting nuts at the left side of the engine compartment.

4. Remove the upper starter mounting nut and disconnect the starter wiring.

5. Raise the car and safely support it.

6. Remove the driveshaft.

7. Disconnect the speedometer cable.

8. Remove the clutch cable.

9. Remove the starter lower bolt and remove the starter.

10. Disconnect the exhaust pipe from the manifold.

11. Remove the exhaust pipe from the manifold.

12. Remove the flywheel inspection cover.

13. Remove the rear transmission support mounting bolt.

14. Support the transmission under the case and remove the rear transmission support from the frame.

15. Lower the transmission approxi-

mately four inches. Disconnect the back-up light and coasting fuel cut-off switch (gasoline models only) wires.

16. Remove the transmission housing-to-engine block bolts.

— **CAUTION** —

Make sure transmission is supported by a suitable jack.

17. Move the transmission slowly back and lower it clear of the car.

18. Installation is the reverse of removal. Lubricate the drive gear shaft spline with a light coat of grease before installing.

19. Adjust the clutch as described in the clutch section. Fill the transmission with SAE 30 engine oil until it begins to run out the filler hole.

Impulse

1. Disconnect the negative battery cable.

2. Drain the transmission oil.

3. Remove the gearshift control lever knob, cover assembly and console.

4. Disconnect the front exhaust pipe.

5. Disconnect the propeller shaft.

6. Disconnect the speedometer cable assembly.

7. Disconnect the clutch slave cylinder.

8. Remove the cover under the transmission case.

9. Position a jack under the transmission case, remove the engine rear mounting nuts, lower the transmission case slightly, then remove the bolts attaching the quadrant box cover to the transmission case.

10. Disconnect all electrical harness connectors.

11. Remove the control box assembly.

12. Remove the transmission to engine retaining bolts.

NOTE: The starter assembly is mounted in position with the bolts that are used for installing the transmission assembly to the engine. It may be necessary to move the starter assembly forward to prevent it from falling out when the bolts are removed.

13. Installation is the reverse of removal with the following exceptions:

a. Position the transmission assembly with the speedometer cable fitting face turned downward and slide the assembly forward, guiding the gear shaft into the pilot bearing.

b. Install and tighten the quadrant box cover to the transmission case bolts with a gasket fitted in position between the quadrant box cover and the transmission case, then install the engine rear mounting.

c. When reconnecting the propeller shaft, install the bolts from the extension shaft side and the nuts and washers on the propeller shaft side and torque to 20 ft. lbs.

d. After tightening the rear engine mounting nuts to 20 ft. lbs., raise the tab of the washers to prevent the nuts from loosening.

LINKAGE ADJUSTMENT

The shift lever is mounted on top of the transmission extension housing and requires no adjustment. For further details, see the Unit Repair Section.

OVERHAUL

For all overhaul and disassembly procedures, please refer to "Manual Transmission Overhaul" in the Unit Repair section.

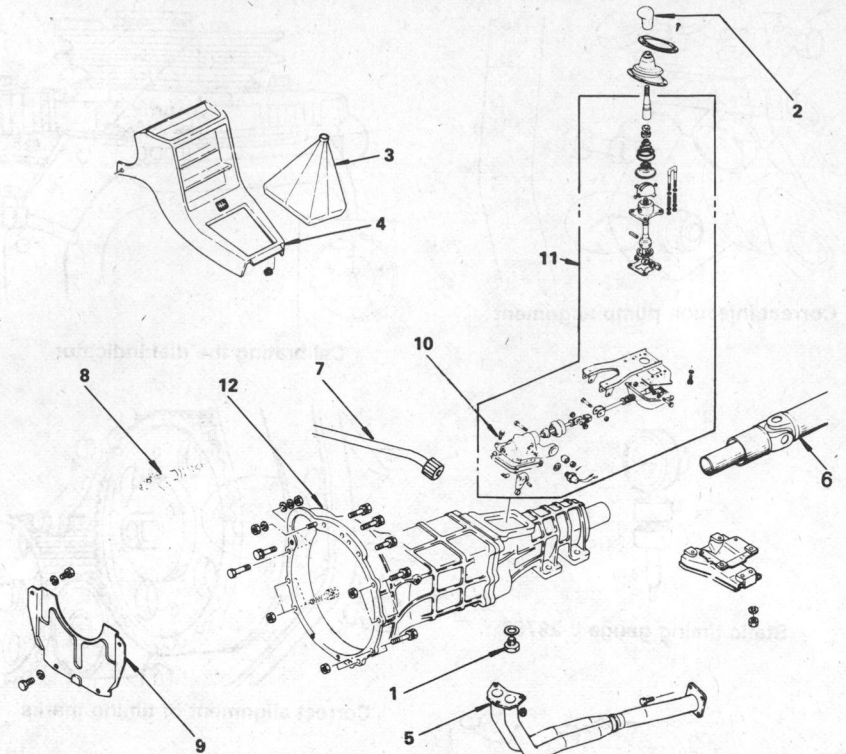

1. Plug; magnet, oil drain
2. Knob; gear shift control lever
3. Cover assembly; shift lever
4. Console assembly
5. Pipe assembly; exhaust front
6. Shaft assembly; propeller
7. Cable assembly; speedometer
8. Cylinder assembly; slave
9. Cover; under, transmission case
10. Bolts; quadrant cover to case
11. Box assembly; control
12. Transmission assembly

Transmission removal and installation—Impulse

MANUAL TRANSAXLE

REMOVAL & INSTALLATION

I-Mark (FWD)

1. Disconnect the negative battery cable.

2. Drain the transaxle oil. Remove the shift lever assembly from inside the vehicle. Remove the upper transaxle to engine retaining bolts.

3. Remove the engine hood and the negative cable from the transaxle unit.

4. Remove the air duct assembly. Disconnect and tag the wiring connectors from the transaxle.

5. Disconnect the speedometer cable from the transaxle and disconnect the clutch cable from the transaxle.

6. Disconnect the shift cables from the transaxle.

7. Raise the front of the vehicle and support it safely with suitable jack stands. Remove the front wheel assemblies.

8. Disconnect the right control arm end at the knuckle. Remove the left tension rod with bracket. Disconnect both tie rod ends at the knuckle using tool J–21687–02 or equivalent.

9. Use a suitable tool and pull out the drive shafts. Be careful with the transaxle oil seals when pulling out the drive shafts. Remove the motor mount bolts.

10. Using a suitable engine lift, raise the engine. Remove the bolts of the center beam and then lower the engine and slant the engine from the engine support fixture.

11. Remove the mounting bolts of the clutch housing to engine. Remove the transaxle assembly from underneath the vehicle.

12. Installation is the reverse order of the removal procedure. Use these following torque specifications during installation:

a. Clutch housing to engine bolts 56 ft. lbs.

b. Center beam bolts 51 ft. lbs.

c. Driveshaft/tie rod to knuckle 42 ft. lbs.

d. Tension rod bracket bolts 48 ft. lbs.

e. Right control arm end bolts 80 ft. lbs.

f. Front wheel lugs aluminum 87 ft. lbs. and steel are 65 ft. lbs.

LINKAGE ADJUSTMENT

I-Mark (FWD)

Shift and Select Cable Linkage Adjustment

1. Place the transaxle in neutral. Turn the adjusting nuts on the left side of the shift housing, until the shift changer lever is at the right angle to the pivot case, as viewed from the side of the gear control.

2. After the adjustment tighten those two adjusting nuts securely.

3. Turn the adjusting nuts on the right side of the shift housing, until the shift change lever is at right angle to the pivot case as viewed from the front or rear gear control. After the adjustment tighten those two adjusting nuts securely.

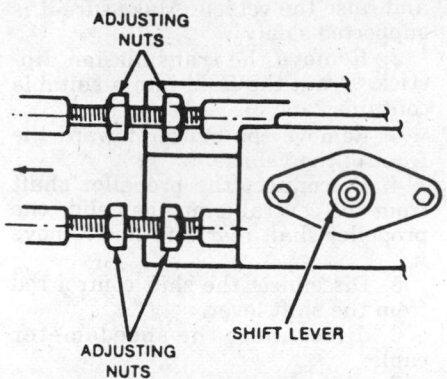

Making the shift linkage adjustment

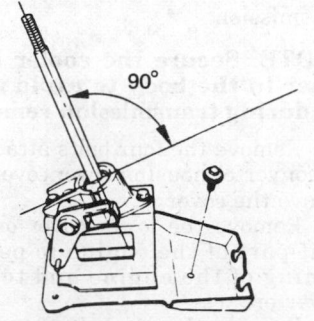

Adjusting the shift changer lever to the right angle

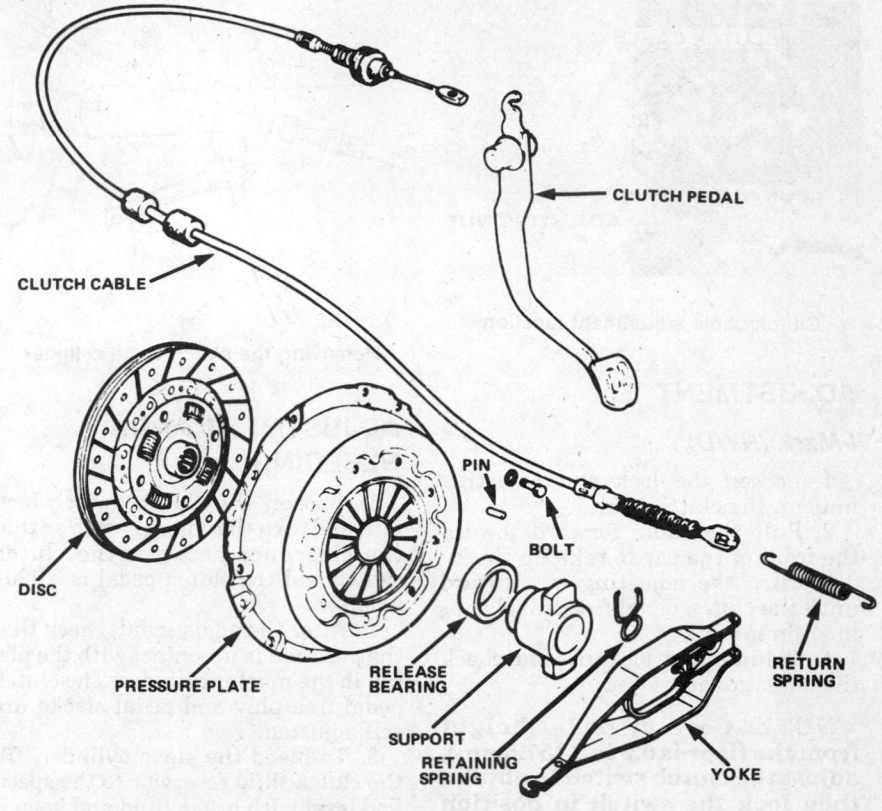

Exploded view of clutch components—all except Impulse

OVERHAUL

For all manual transaxle overhaul procedures, please refer to "Manual Transaxle Overhaul" in the unit repair section.

CLUTCH

REMOVAL & INSTALLATION

1. Remove the transmission as previously described.
2. Mark the clutch assembly position on the flywheel with paint or a scribe.
3. Install clutch aligning tool J–24547 or equivalent and remove the six retaining bolts. Remove the clutch assembly.
4. Remove the release bearing-to-yoke retaining springs, and then remove the release bearing with its support.
5. Remove the release yoke from the transmission ball stud.
6. Wash all metal parts of the clutch assembly, except the release

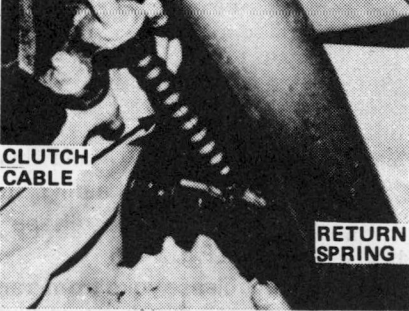

Location of clutch cable under car —typical

bearing and friction plate in suitable cleaning solution.

—— CAUTION ——
Soaking the release bearing in cleaning solution will ruin the bearing, soaking the clutch plate in cleaning solution will damage the facings.

7. Inspect all parts for wear or deep scoring. Replace any parts that show excessive wear.
8. Installation is the reverse of removal. Lubricate the ball stud when installing the release yoke. Align the clutch with scribe marks and use an aligning tool to assure proper positioning of the clutch.

Clutch Cable

REMOVAL & INSTALLATION

I-Mark (RWD)

1. Loosen the clutch lock and adjusting nuts.
2. Raise the car and support it safely with jackstands.
3. From under the car, remove the clutch cable from the release yoke and slide it forward through the retaining bracket.
4. Disconnect the cable from the pedal and remove.
5. Installation is the reverse of removal.

I-Mark (FWD)

1. Disconnect the negative battery cable.
2. Raise and support safely the front of the vehicle.
3. Disconnect the clutch cable from the clutch housing and transaxle. Remove all necessary snap rings and lock nuts to free the clutch cable.
4. Remove the clutch cable from the clutch pedal and pull the cable out from the engine compartment.
5. Installation is the reverse of the removal procedure.

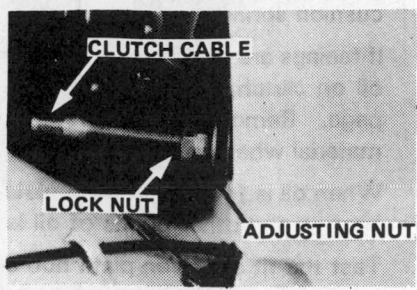

Clutch cable adjustment location

ADJUSTMENT

I-Mark (RWD)

1. Loosen the lock and adjusting nuts on the clutch cable.
2. Pull the cable forward toward the front of the car to take up slack.
3. Turn the adjusting nut inward until the clutch pedal free travel is $\frac{5}{8}$ in. (16mm).
4. Tighten the locknut and check the adjustment.

NOTE: Correct pedal height from the floor is 6.2 in. (157.5mm), adjust the clutch switch to obtain, then lock the switch in position with the lock nut.

I-Mark (FWD)

1. Loosen the clutch cable adjusting nut and pull the cable to the rear of the vehicle until the adjustment nut turns freely.
2. Turn the adjusting nut either clockwise or counterclockwise to adjust the cable length.
3. When the clutch pedal free play travel reaches 0.59 ± 0.20 in. release the cable.
4. Check the adjustment and then tighten the lock nut.

Clutch Slave Cylinder

REMOVAL & INSTALLATION

Impulse

1. Disconnect the negative battery cable.
2. Raise and support the front of the vehicle safely.
3. Remove and cap the hydraulic lines from the slave cylinder.
4. Remove the slave cylinder push rod from the clutch release bearing fork.
5. Remove the slave cylinder retaining bolts and remove the slave cylinder.
6. Installation is the reverse order of the removal procedure.

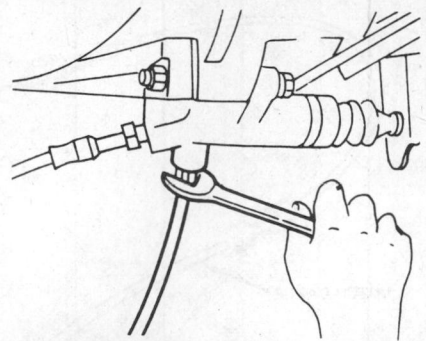

Removing the clutch slave cylinder

ADJUSTMENT AND BLEEDING

1. Loosen the clutch switch lock nut, and turn the clutch switch so that the clearance between the clutch switch and the clutch pedal is 0.020–0.059 in.
2. After the adjustment, check that the push rod is in contact with the piston in the master cylinder. The clutch pedal free play and pedal stroke are self-adjusted.
3. To bleed the slave cylinder, fill the clutch fluid reservoir to the specified level with brake fluid and keep it filled during the bleeding procedure.
4. Remove the bleeder rubber cap and connect a vinyl pipe to the bleeder and hold the free end of the pipe in a transparent container.
5. Pump the clutch pedal several times and hold the pedal in the depressed stage. With the pedal depressed, loosen the bleeder on the slave cylinder a ½ of turn and then tighten it immediately.
6. Repeat the above step until the air bubbles are no longer a part of the brake fluid being bled.
7. After completion of the bleeding operation, check for pedal free play and clutch disengagement, then check the brake fluid in the clutch reservoir.

NOTE: Removing the clutch master cylinder is only a simple matter of disconnecting the hydraulic lines and removing the retaining bolts.

AUTOMATIC TRANSMISSION

REMOVAL & INSTALLATION

All Models Except I-Mark (FWD)

1. Disconnect the battery cables and raise the vehicle. Make sure it is supported safely.
2. Remove the transmission dipstick. Drain the fluid into a suitable container and discard.
3. Remove the starter toward the front of the vehicle.
4. Disconnect the propeller shaft from the central joint, then slide the propeller shaft rearward and remove it.
5. Disconnect the shift control rod from the shift lever.
6. Disconnect the speedometer cable.
7. Remove the exhaust pipe bracket.
8. Disconnect the oil cooler lines by loosening the joint nuts at the transmission.

NOTE: Secure the cooler lines closer to the body to avoid damage during transmission removal.

9. Remove the four bolts attaching the converter housing lower cover and remove the cover.
10. Remove the lower cover on the front part of the engine to permit turning of the engine and torque converter.
11. Remove the six bolts fastening the torque converter and drive plate by turning the crankshaft pulley.
12. Remove the bolt on the center part of the rear mounting from bracket.
13. Raise the engine and transmission using a suitable jack and support the rear end of the engine to hold it in position when the transmission is removed.
14. Remove the four bolts or nuts securing the rear mounting frame bracket, then remove the bracket.
15. Lower the transmission slightly then remove the bolts and nuts fixing the converter housing, then remove the transmission toward the rear.

——— **CAUTION** ———
When removing the transmission, exercise care so as not to let the torque converter slide out.

16. Installation is the reverse of removal. Refill the transmission with fluid according to the capacities chart. Adjust the throttle valve control cable.

THROTTLE CABLE ADJUSTMENT

I-Mark (RWD) and Impulse

1. Check that the throttle valve is held closed completely.
2. Adjust the setting of the adjustment nut as necessary so that the

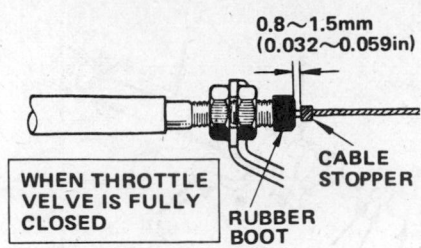

Throttle valve cable adjustment—
gasoline engine

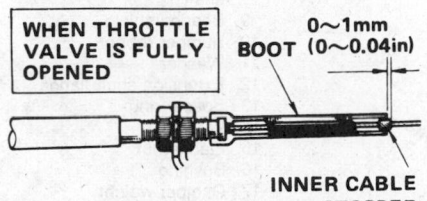

Throttle valve cable adjustment—
diesel engine

clearance between the inner cable stopper and the end of the rubber boot on the outer cable is adjusted to 0.0315–0.0591 in. (0.8–1.5mm).

3. Open the throttle valve fully and check that the inner cable stroke is within the range of 1.30–1.34 in. (33–34mm).

AUTOMATIC TRANSAXLE

REMOVAL & INSTALLATION

I-Mark (FWD)

1. Disconnect the negative battery cable.
2. Remove the air duct tube from the air cleaner.
3. At the transaxle, disconnect the shift cable, speedometer cable, vacuum diaphragm hose, engine wiring harness clamp and the ground cable.
4. At the left fender, disconnect the inhibitor switch and the kickdown solenoid wiring connectors.
5. Disconnect the oil cooler lines from the transaxle.
6. Remove the 3 upper transaxle-to-engine mounting bolts and raise the vehicle.
7. Remove both front wheels and the left front fender splash shield.
8. Disconnect both tie rod ends at the steering knuckles.
9. Remove both front tension rod brackets and disconnect the rods from the control arms.
10. Disengage the axle shafts from the transaxle.

11. Remove the flywheel dust cover and the converter-to-flywheel attaching bolts.
12. Remove the transaxle rear mount through bolt.
13. Disconnect the starter wiring and the starter. Support the transaxle.
14. Remove the lower transaxle-to-engine mounting bolts and remove the transaxle.
15. To install, reverse the removal procedure, torque the converter-to-flywheel at 30 ft. lbs., transaxle-to-engine at 56 ft. lbs., adjust the shift linkage and fill the transaxle with automatic transmission fluid.

KICKDOWN SWITCH ADJUSTMENT

I-Mark (FWD)

1. Connect a multi-purpose tester to the kickdown switch solenoid terminals.
2. Make sure there is continuity when depressing the throttle pedal fully.
3. If continuity does not exist, adjust the kickdown switch. To adjust the switch, turn the switch so that continuity exists when depressing the throttle pedal more than ⅛ of its stroke.

DRIVE AXLE

Halfshafts

REMOVAL & INSTALLATION

I-Mark (FWD)

1. Refer to the "Front Hub Removal and Installation" procedure in this section and remove the front hub. Support the axle shaft on a wire.

2. Remove the drain plug and drain the oil from the transaxle.
3. Place a large pry bar between the differential case and the inboard constant velocity joint. Pry the axle shaft from the differential case.
4. Remove the front axle assembly.
5. To install, reverse the removal procedure. When installing the axle shaft, press it into the differential case until it locks with snap ring.

CV-JOINT OVERHAUL

For all CV-joint overhaul procedures, please refer to "CV-Joint Overhaul" in the Unit Repair section.

Driveshaft and U-Joint

REMOVAL & INSTALLATION

I-Mark (RWD) and Impulse

1. Raise the rear of the car and support it safely on jack stands at the rear jack brackets.
2. Disconnect the parking brake return spring from the rod.
3. Mark the mating parts of the U-joint and the drive pinion extension shaft flange.
4. Remove the bolts and nuts connecting the U-joint and the extension shaft flange.
5. Work the propeller shaft slightly forward, lower the rear end of the shaft and slide the assembly rearward. Remove the thrust spring from the front of the shaft.
6. Install a plug (or wrap a small plastic bag) on the transmission ex-

REAR U-JOINT

FRONT U-JOINT

COIL SPRING

Driveshaft assembly

tension housing to prevent the loss of oil.

CAUTION

When replacing any fasteners or attaching bolts, be sure to use the proper grade bolt. Substitution of lesser quality hardware could cause failure and serious damage.

7. Installation is the reverse of removal. Make sure that the transmission rear seal is not damaged. Align all marks and torque the bolts to 18 ft. lbs.

8. Connect the parking brake return spring.

Central Joint

REMOVAL & INSTALLATION

I-Mark (RWD) and Impulse

1. Raise and support the rear of the car safely under the axle tubes.
2. Disconnect the parking brake return spring from the brake rod.
3. Unhook the exhaust system bracket from the central joint support bracket.
4. Mark the universal joint and flange, then disconnect the propeller shaft from the flange and support it out of the way.
5. Support the torque tube with a floor jack using minimum pressure.
6. Remove the central joint support bracket to underbody attaching bolts.
7. Allow the floor jack to lower the torque tube.
8. Disconnect the torque tube from the differential carrier by removing the attaching bolts.
9. Installation is the reverse of removal. Align all marks, torque all bolts to specifications.

Rear Axle Shaft

REMOVAL & INSTALLATION

I-Mark (RWD) and Impulse

1. Raise the car and support it safely with jackstands at the jack brackets.
2. Remove the wheel and brake drum assembly.
3. Working through the access holes in the axle shaft flange, remove the four nuts and washers that retain the axle shaft and bearing retainer.
4. Install an axle shaft puller (slaphammer) and remove the axle shaft.
5. To replace the bearing parts, first remove the retaining ring by cutting it off with a chisel. The bearing must be pressed off with a suitable bench press.
6. Installation is the reverse of removal. Press the new bearing on to

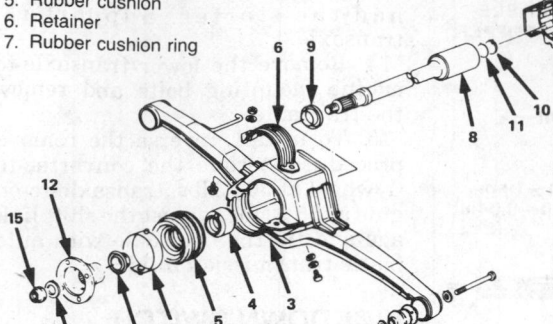

1. Torque tube
2. Rubber support cushion
3. Support bracket
4. Bearing Assembly
5. Rubber cushion
6. Retainer
7. Rubber cushion ring
8. Drive pinion extension shaft
9. Bearing shield
10. Bumper rubber
11. Washer
12. Extension shaft flange
13. Spacer ring
14. Washer
15. Flange nut
16. Bushing
17. Damper weight

Exploded view of central joint

BOLT TORQUE SPECIFICATIONS

Location	Torque (ft. lbs.)
Extension shaft flange nut	87
Extension shaft flange-to-universal joint	18
Central joint support bracket-to-under body	30
Torque tube-to-carrier	20
Central joint support bracket-to-support cushion	15
Rubber cushion retainer-to-central joint support	10

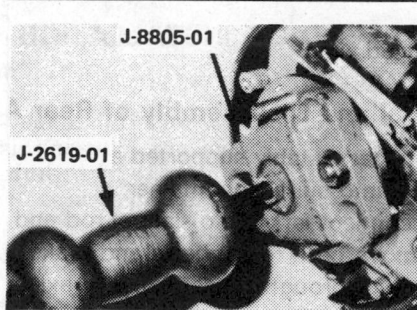

J-8805-01
J-2619-01

Removing axle shaft with slide hammer and adaptor

the axle shaft with a suitable press.

7. Check the axle shaft end play by using a depth gauge to measure the depth of the rear axle bearing seat in the axle housing with the backing plate in place.

8. Measure the width of the bearing outer race. The difference between the two measurements indicates the required thickness of the shims. If necessary to increase endplay, add shims. To decrease endplay, remove shims. Standard end play is 0–0.008 in. (0.2mm) thickness. Shims are only available in 0.006 in. (0.15mm) thickness.

9. Coat all rear axle components with gear oil before installation. Torque the lock washers and nuts to 28 ft. lbs.

Front Axle Hub and Bearings

REMOVAL & INSTALLATION

I-Mark (FWD)

DO NOT remove the hub from the steering knuckle unless it is absolutely necessary.

1. Loosen the wheel nuts. Remove the grease cap, cotter pin, hub nut and thrust washer.
2. Remove the caliper and support it on a wire.
3. Remove the rotor.
4. Remove the tie rod nut. Using a ball joint removal tool, separate the tie rod from the steering knuckle.
5. Remove the two ball joint-to-control arm/tension rod retaining nuts and bolts.
6. Remove the two strut-to-steering knuckle retaining nuts/bolts.
7. Remove the steering knuckle. When removing the axle shaft from the steering knuckle, be careful not to drop it and support it with a wire.
8. To install, reverse the removal procedure and bleed the brake system.

Steering Knuckle, Hub and Bearing

DISASSEMBLY & REASSEMBLY

I-Mark (FWD)

1. Remove the inner seal and snap ring.

2. Using an arbor press, press the hub from the steering knuckle. If necessary, press the spacer from the hub.

3. Remove the outer seal and snap ring.

4. Using an arbor press, press the bearing from the steering knuckle. Clean and inspect all parts.

5. To assemble, reverse the disassembly procedure.

NOTE: Replace the seals and bearings. Lubricate all parts.

FRONT SUSPENSION

Front Wheel Bearings

REPLACEMENT, REPACKING & ADJUSTMENT

I-Mark (RWD) and Impulse

1. Raise the car and safely support it with jackstands. Remove the front wheel.

2. Remove the grease cap. Remove and discard the cotter pin, then remove the spindle nut and washer.

3. Wiggle the hub and the wheel bearing will pop out enough to grab it. Wipe any dirt or old grease off of the spindle.

NOTE: If the rear wheel bearing is to be inspected, the hub will have to be removed. Remove and tie up the brake caliper as outlined in the brake section and the hub will be free to be removed.

4. Inspect the wheel bearing for signs of wear, nicks or obvious damage. Clean the bearings in solvent and blow dry with compressed air.

--- CAUTION ---
Do not give in to the impulse of spinning the clean bearing with the air nozzle. Running a dry bearing at high rpm while holding it in your hand can damage the bearing.

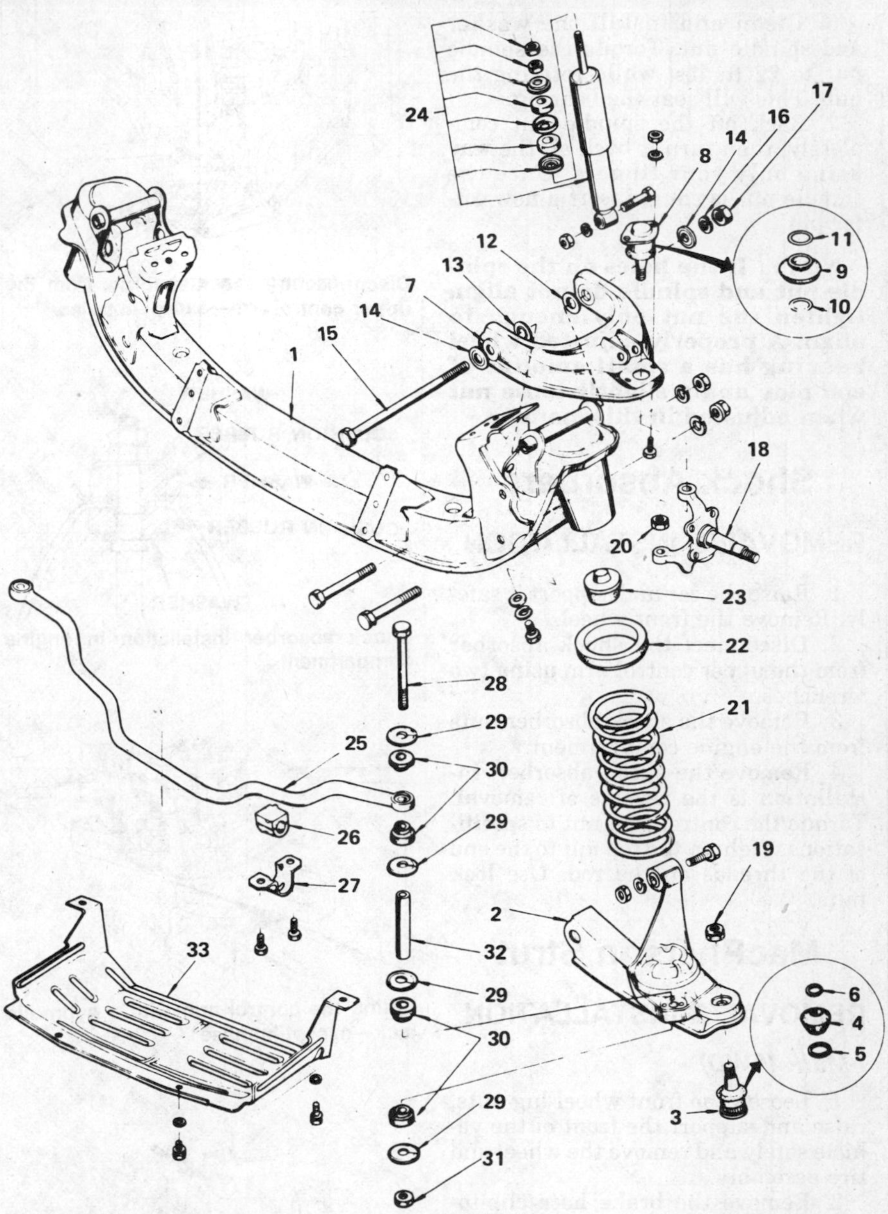

1. Cross member assembly	12. Washer	23. Bumper rubber
2. Lower control arm assembly	13. Washer	24. Shock absorber
3. Lower ball joint assembly	14. Washer	25. Stabilizer bar
4. Boot	15. Through-bolt	26. Rubber bushing
5. Clamp ring	16. Spring washer	27. Clamp
6. Clamp ring	17. Nut	28. Bolt
7. Upper control arm assembly	18. Steering knuckle	29. Retainer
8. Upper ball joint	19. Nut	30. Grommet
9. Boot	20. Nut	31. Nut
10. Clamp ring	21. Front coil spring	32. Distance tube
11. Clamp ring	22. Damper rubber	33. Under cover

Exploded view of front suspension system—all except Impulse

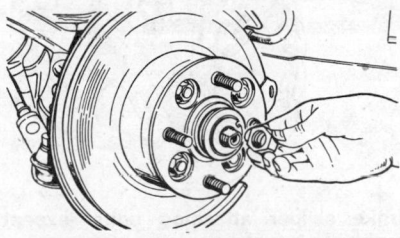

Removing spindle nut on front hub

5. Carefully repack the front wheel bearings with new high temperature wheel bearing grease. Put a glob of grease in your palm and force it into the bearing with a scraping motion until the grease comes out the top. Coat the packed bearing with a covering of grease and install it with the taper side in.

6. Clean and install the washer and spindle nut. Torque the spindle nut to 22 ft. lbs. while rotating the hub. This will seat the bearing.

7. Back off the spindle nut completely, then turn it back all the way using only your fingers. Once the spindle nut is snug, insert a new cotter pin.

NOTE: If the holes on the spindle nut and spindle do not align, tighten the nut only enough to align. A properly adjusted wheel bearing has a small amount of end-play and a slightly loose nut when adjusted in this manner.

Shock Absorbers

REMOVAL & INSTALLATION

1. Raise the car and support it safely. Remove the front wheel.
2. Disconnect the shock absorber from the upper control arm using two wrenches.
3. Remove the shock absorber nuts from the engine compartment.
4. Remove the shock absorber. Installation is the reverse of removal. Torque the control arm nut to specifications. Tighten the top nut to the end of the threads on the rod. Use lock nuts.

MacPherson Strut

REMOVAL & INSTALLATION

I-Mark (FWD)

1. Loosen the front wheel lug nuts, raise and support the front of the vehicle safely and remove the wheel and tire assembly.
2. Remove the brake hose clip-to-strut bolt (if so equipped). Install a drive axle cover, to protect the axle boot.
3. Remove the bolts attaching the strut to the steering knuckle.
4. Remove the two strut tower nuts and remove the strut assembly from the vehicle.
5. Installation is the reverse order of the removal procedure. The two strut tower nuts must be tightened before the lower strut bolts. The strut tower nuts should be torqued to 40 ft. lbs. and the lower strut bolts should be torqued to 80 ft. lbs.

OVERHAUL

For all spring and shock absorber removal and installation procedures, and all strut overhaul procedures, please refer to "Strut Overhaul" in the Unit Repair section.

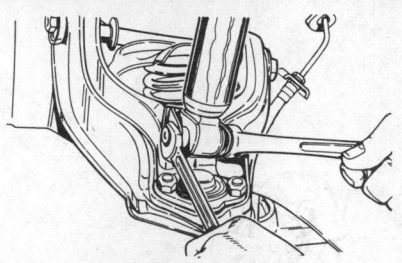
Disconnecting shock absorber from the upper control arm—except Impulse

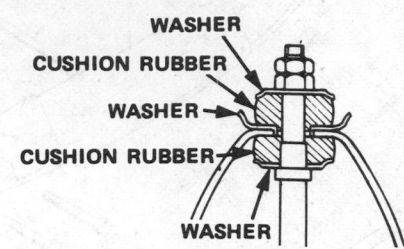
Shock absorber installation in engine compartment

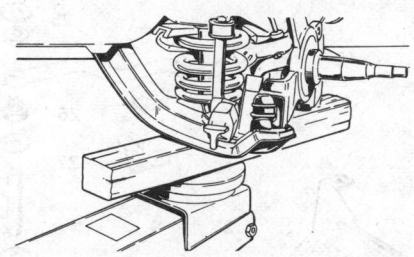
Lifting the control arm with a hydraulic jack—except Impulse

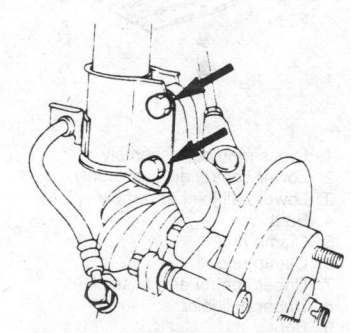
Removing the lower strut bolts

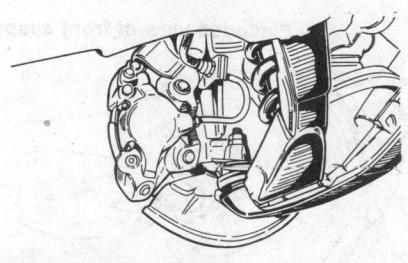
Brake caliper attaching bolts—except Impulse

Coil Springs

REMOVAL & INSTALLATION

All Models Except Impulse and I-Mark (FWD)

1. Raise the car and safely support it with jackstands. Remove the wheel.
2. Remove the tie rod end cotter pin and castle nut. Discard the cotter pin.
3. Use a suspension fork to separate the tie rod end from the steering knuckle.
4. Remove the lower shock absorber bolt and push the shock up as far as possible.
5. Remove the stabilizer bar bolt and grommet assembly from the lower control arm.
6. Remove the upper brake caliper bolt and slide the hose retaining clip back about ½ in.
7. Place the lifting pad of a hydraulic floor jack under the outer extreme of the control arm and raise the lower control arm until it is level.

——————— CAUTION ———————
Secure a safety chain through one coil near the top of the spring and attach it to the upper control arm to prevent the spring from coming out unexpectedly. The coil spring will come out with a lethal force, so don't take any chances.

8. Loosen the lower ball joint lock nut until the top of the nut is flush with the top of the ball joint. Using tool J–26407 or equivalent, disconnect the lower ball joint from the steering knuckle.
9. Remove the hub assembly and steering knuckle from the lower ball joint and support with a wire or rope out of the way.
10. Pry the lower control arm down, using extreme caution so as not to injure yourself. Remove the spring.
11. Installation is the reverse of removal. Properly seat the spring and use the safety chain. Use the hydraulic jack to compress the new spring until the control arm is stable.
12. Torque the ball joint lock nut to 58 ft. lbs. Torque the lower shock absorber mounting nuts and all other attaching hardware according to the specifications chart at the end of the section.

Front Stabilizer Bar

REMOVAL & INSTALLATION

I-Mark (RWD)

1. Raise and support safely the front of the vehicle.

2. Remove the engine dust cover from underneath the engine.

3. Remove the stabilizer bar bolt and grommet assemblies from the lower control arms.

4. Remove the clamps securing the stabilizer bar.

5. Installation is the reverse order of the removal procedure.

I-Mark (FWD)

1. Raise and support the front of the vehicle safely.

2. Remove the nuts, bolts and insulators retaining the stabilizer bar to the tension rod.

3. Remove the stabilizer bar.

4. To install, reverse the removal procedure. Align the front side of the insulator edge with the paint mark on the upper rear edge of the tension bar.

Tension Bar

REMOVAL & INSTALLATION

I-Mark (FWD)

1. Raise and support the vehicle on jackstands.

2. If equipped with a stabilizer bar, remove the nuts, bolts and insulators retaining it to the tension rod.

3. Remove the nut and washer retaining the tension rod to the body.

4. Remove the nuts and bolts retaining the tension rod to the control rod.

5. Remove the tension rod.

6. To install, reverse the removal procedure.

Ball Joints

INSPECTION

The maximum permissible axial play in the ball joint is 0.008 in. (0.2mm). Replace any joint that exceeds this value.

NOTE: The lower ball joint is splined to the lower control arm. The upper ball joints are offset to allow for camber setting.

REMOVAL & INSTALLATION

NOTE: For Impulse models please refer to "Control Arms, Knuckles And Coil Springs."

I-Mark (RWD)

UPPER BALL JOINT

1. Raise the car and support it safely. Remove the wheel.

2. Remove the upper brake caliper bolt and slide the hose retaining clip back about ½ in.

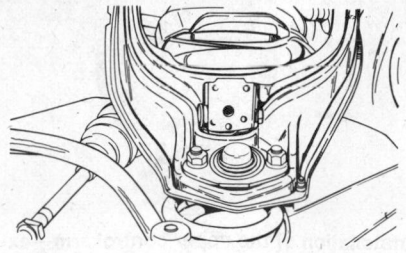

Installing the upper ball joint in the control arm—except Impulse

3. Remove the lower shock absorber nut and bolt and push the shock absorber up.

4. Place a hydraulic jack under the outer extreme of the lower control arm and raise until level.

5. Loosen the upper ball joint nut until the top of the nut is flush with the top of the ball joint.

6. Using special tool J-26407 or equivalent, disconnect the upper ball joint from the steering knuckle.

7. Remove the two bolts connecting the upper ball joint to the upper control arm. Remove the ball joint.

8. Installation is the reverse of removal. Install the new ball joint in the control arm so that the cut-off portion is facing outward. Torque all attaching nuts and bolts. For specifications, see the torque chart at the end of the section.

NOTE: The car should be aligned whenever any suspension components are replaced.

LOWER BALL JOINT

1. Raise the car and support it safely. Remove the front wheel.

2. Remove the tie rod end cotter pin and castle nut. Discard the pin and separate the tie rod end with a suspension fork. Remove the tie rod from the steering knuckle.

3. Remove the stabilizer bar bolt and grommet assembly from the lower control arm.

4. Remove the upper brake caliper bolt and slide the brake hose retaining clip back about ½ in.

5. Remove the shock absorber lower bolt and push the shock up.

───── **CAUTION** ─────

Secure a safety chain through the upper and lower control arms to prevent the possibility of the spring coming out and causing serious damage or injury. Allow enough room to get the ball joint out.

6. Place a hydraulic jack under the outer extremity of the lower control arm and raise it until level.

7. Loosen the ball joint lock nut until the top of the nut is flush with the top of the ball joint.

8. Using special tool J-26407 or equivalent, disconnect the lower ball joint from the steering knuckle.

9. Remove the hub assembly and steering knuckle from the lower ball joint and support with a wire or rope.

10. Remove the lower ball joint from the control arm using tool J-9519-03 or equivalent.

11. Installation is the reverse of removal. Do not strike the ball joint bottom. Torque the ball joint nut to 50 ft. lbs.

12. Torque all bolts to specifications as listed in the chart at the end of the section.

REMOVAL & INSTALLATION

I-Mark (FWD)

1. Loosen the wheel nuts.

2. Raise the vehicle and support it on jackstands.

3. Remove the wheel and tire assembly.

4. Remove the two nuts retaining the ball joint to the tension rod and control arm assembly.

5. Remove the pinch bolt retaining the ball joint to the steering knuckle.

6. Remove the ball joint.

7. To install, reverse the removal procedure.

Control Arms
REMOVAL & INSTALLATION

I-Mark (RWD)

UPPER

1. Raise the car and support it safely. Remove the front wheel.

2. Remove the upper brake caliper bolt and slide the brake hose retainer clip back about ½ in.

3. Remove the lower shock bolt and push the shock absorber up.

4. Place a hydraulic jack under the control arm on the outer extreme and raise the control arm until it is level.

5. Loosen the upper ball joint lock nut until the top of the nut is flush with the top of the ball joint. Disconnect the upper ball joint from the steering knuckle using tool J-26407 or equivalent.

6. Disconnect and remove the through bolt connecting the upper control arm to the crossmember. Remove the upper control arm.

7. Installation is the reverse of removal. On installation, make sure the smaller washer is on the inner face of the front arm and larger washer is on the inner face of the rear arm.

8. Torque all attaching hardware to the specifications in the chart at the end of the section. Align the front end.

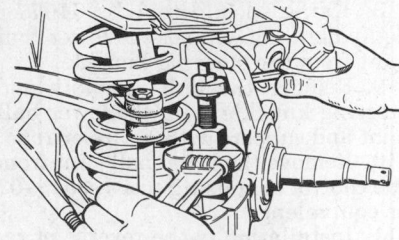

Disconnecting the lower ball joint with the special tool—except Impulse

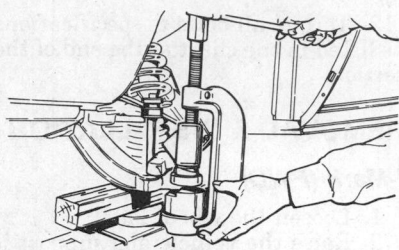

Removing the lower ball joint from the control arm—except Impulse

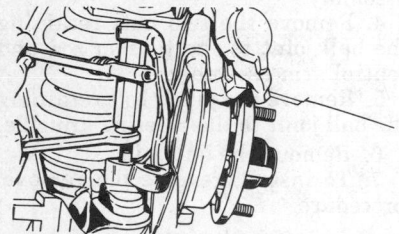

Removing the lower ball joint from the steering knuckle—except Impulse

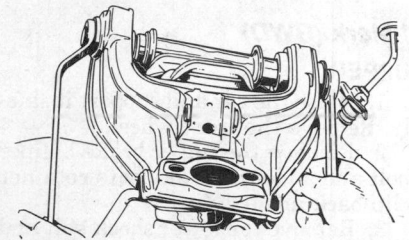

Removing the upper control arm from the crossmember—except Impulse

NOTE: Always check the camber when working around the upper control arm area.

LOWER

1. Follow Steps 1–10 for removal of coil springs.
2. Remove the bolts connecting the lower control arm to the crossmember and the body.
3. Installation is the reverse of removal. Torque all bolts and nuts to specifications.

NOTE: When reinstalling front end components, it's best to snug all the bolts and nuts first, then lower the car so that there is weight on the suspension when final torque adjustments are made.

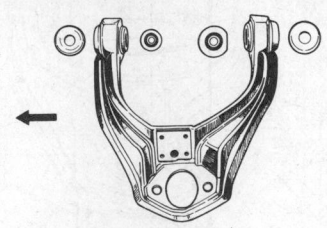

Installation of the upper control arm—except Impulse

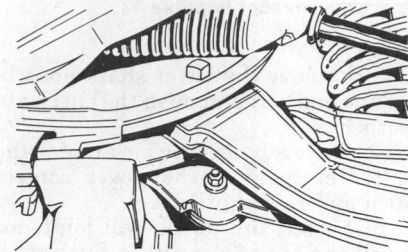

Removing the lower control arm—except Impulse

I-Mark(FWD)

1. Raise and support the front of the vehicle.
2. Remove the control arm to tension arm retaining nuts and bolts.
3. Remove the nut/bolt securing the control arm to the body.
4. Remove the control arm and check for cracking or distortion.
5. To install, reverse the removal procedure.

NOTE: Raise the control arm to a distance of 15.18 in. from the top of the wheel well to the center of the hub. Use 41 ft. lbs. of torque to fasten the control arm to the body and 80 ft. lbs. to secure the control arm to the tension rod. This procedure aligns the bushing arm to the body.

Control Arms, Knuckles and Coil Springs

REMOVAL & INSTALLATION

Impulse

1. Raise the car and support it safely. Remove the front wheel.
2. Remove the tie rod end cotter pin and castle nut and remove the tie rod end using tool J–21687–02.
3. Using coil spring compressor J–33992, compress the coil spring.

— CAUTION —
Secure a safety chain through one coil near the top of the spring and attach it to the upper control arm to prevent the spring from coming out.

4. Compress the coil spring until its top end releases from the cushion rubber at the center of the upper link, then remove the coil spring.
5. Remove the lower link bolt, then remove the coil spring together with the lower link.
6. Remove the lower ball joint assembly.
7. Press out the lower link bushing.
8. Remove the upper ball joint assembly.
9. Press out the upper link bushings.
10. Installation is the reverse of removal with the following precautions:
   a. When installing the upper control arm washers install the small washer on the inboard side of the rear end.
   b. Leave the upper and lower control arm link bolts semi-tight as they are to be torqued to specifications after completion of installation with the wheels lowered to the floor. Upper—47 ft. lbs., lower—61 ft. lbs.
   c. When installing the upper ball joint to the control arm the cutaway portion of the ball joint should be turned outward.

Front Wheel Alignment

NOTE: Steering problems are not always the result of improper alignment. Before aligning the car, check the tire pressure and check all suspension components for damage or excessive wear.

CAMBER ADJUSTMENT

On all models except the Impulse, camber angle can be increased approximately 1° by removing the upper ball joint, rotating it ½ turn and reinstalling it with the cut-off portion of the upper flange on the inboard side of the control arm. On the Impulse, camber is not adjustable. Replace parts as necessary to correct alignment.

CASTER ADJUSTMENT

The caster angle is pre-set at the factory and cannot be adjusted.

TOE-IN ANGLE ADJUSTMENT

Toe-in is controlled by adjusting the tie rod. To adjust the toe-in setting loosen the nuts at the steering knuckle end of the tie rod. Rotate the rod as required to adjust the toe-in. Retighten the cover and locknuts, check that the rubber bellows is not twisted. For all specifications, see the Alignment Specs in the front of the section.

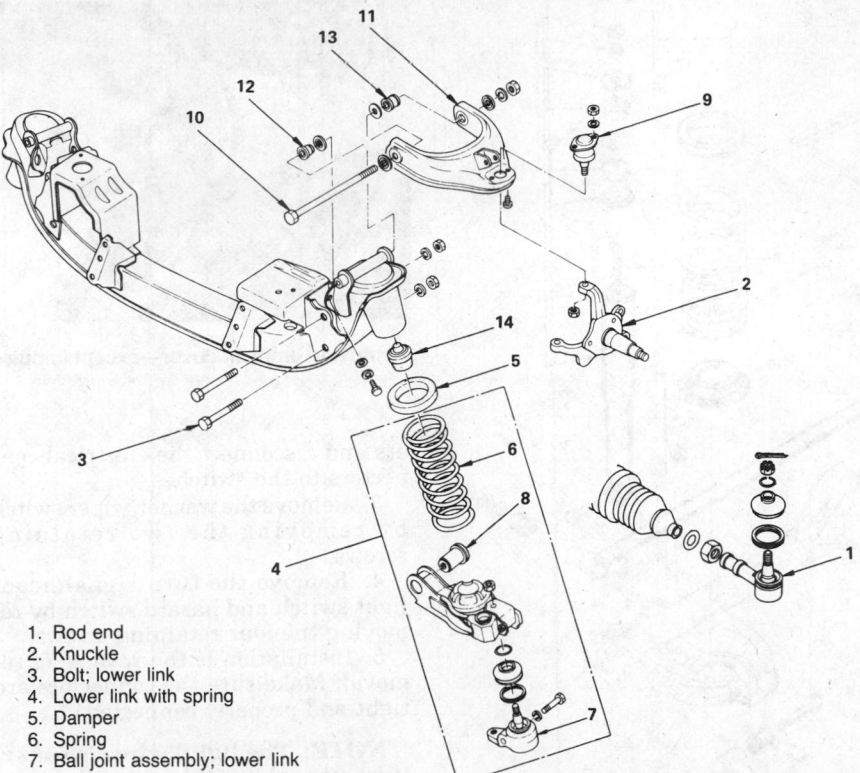

1. Rod end
2. Knuckle
3. Bolt; lower link
4. Lower link with spring
5. Damper
6. Spring
7. Ball joint assembly; lower link

Exploded view of front suspension—Impulse

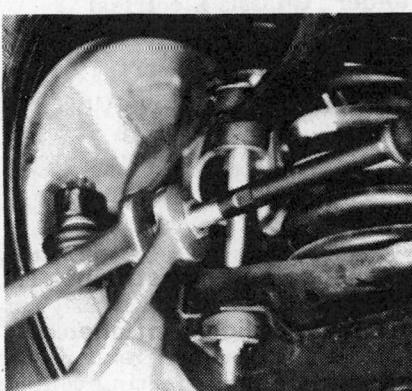

Toe-in adjustment

REAR SUSPENSION

Shock Absorbers

REMOVAL & INSTALLATION

1. Raise the car and support it safely under the axle housing.
2. Disconnect the lower end of the shock absorber from the axle.
3. Remove the fuel tank cover from inside the trunk on all models except the Impulse and disconnect the upper end of the shock absorber.
4. Working from under the car, remove the shock absorber.
5. Installation is the reverse of removal. Use lock nuts at each end. Torque all shock absorber nuts to specifications.

Coil Springs

REMOVAL & INSTALLATION

1. Raise the rear of the car on the axle housing and support it at the jack side brackets with jackstands.
2. Position a hydraulic jack under the differential housing, but use a light contact pressure.
3. Disconnect the shock absorber lower mounting bolts.
4. Slowly lower or separate the axle assembly from the car body to the point where the spring becomes loose enough to allow removal.

--- CAUTION ---
Do not stress the brake hoses when lowering the axle.

5. Installation is the reverse of removal. Position the spring correctly. Make sure that the insulator is in position on top of the spring.

---

6. Torque the shock absorber lower bolts to 29 ft. lbs.

Rear Control Arm

REMOVAL & INSTALLATION

1. Raise the car and support it safely.
2. Remove the bolt connecting the control arm to the axle case.
3. Remove the bolt connecting the control arm to the body.
4. Remove the control arm assembly.
5. Installation is the reverse of removal. Torque the bolts to specifications.

NOTE: When reinstalling the control arm assembly, leave the bolts semi-tight. Lower the car before torquing any nuts. The vehicle weight should be on all suspension components when torquing the nuts.

Rear axle side
Body side

Installing rear control arm—all except Impulse

Rear Axle Hub

REMOVAL & INSTALLATION

I-Mark (FWD)

1. Raise the rear end of the vehicle and support it on jackstands. Remove the rear wheels.
2. Remove the hub cap, cotter pin, hub nut, washer and outer bearing.
3. Remove the hub.
4. To install, reverse the removal procedure.

NOTE: If the cotter pin holes are out of alignment upon reassembly, use a wrench to tighten the nut until the hole in the shaft and a slot of the nut align.

Rear Wheel Bearings

REMOVAL & INSTALLATION

I-Mark (FWD)

1. Refer to the "Rear Axle Hub Removal and Installation" procedure in this section, then remove the hub.
2. Using a slide hammer puller and attachment, pull the oil seal from the hub. Remove the inner bearing.
3. Using a brass drift and a ham-

1. Control arm
2. Bushing
3. Bushing
4. Lateral rod
5. Bushing
6. Bushing
7. Sleeve
8. Spring
9. Insulator
10. Insulator
11. Shock Absorber assembly
12. Rear stabilizer bar
13. Bushing
14. Clamp
15. Bracket
16. Bushing
17. Sleeve

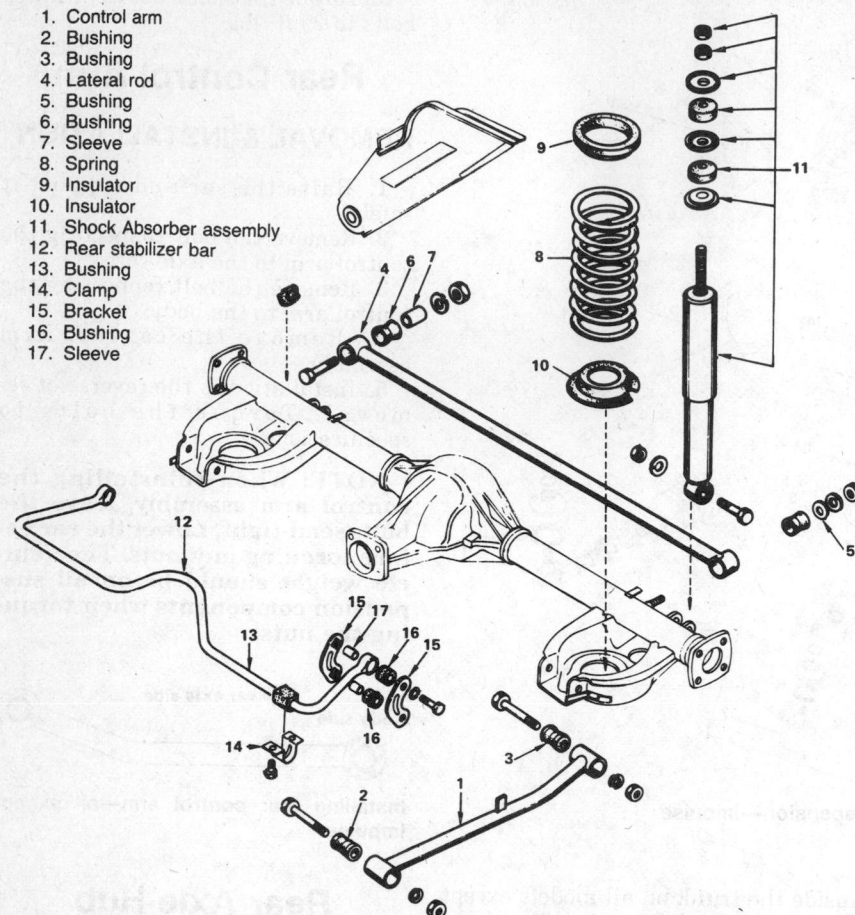

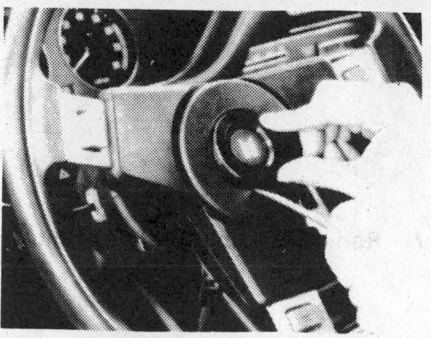

Removing emblem cover—except Impulse

Exploded view of rear suspension system—all except Impulse

mer, drive both bearing races from the hub.

4. Clean, inspect and/or replace all parts.

5. To install, pack the bearings with grease, coat the oil seal lips with grease and reverse the removal procedure.

ADJUSTMENT

I-Mark (FWD)

1. Torque the rear hub nut to 22 ft. lbs.

2. Rotate the hub two or three times, then untighten the nut completely.

3. Tighten the nut fully by hand and insert the cotter pin.

4. If the cotter pin holes are not aligned, tighten the nut just enough to align the holes.

STEERING

Steering Wheel

REMOVAL & INSTALLATION

1. Raise the hood and disconnect the battery ground cable.

2. On models with the 2-spoke wheel, remove the two screws retaining the horn shroud and disconnect the horn contact.

3. On models with the 3-spoke wheel, remove the medallion cover from the center of the wheel by prying lightly around the edge with a small screwdriver.

4. Remove the steering wheel nut and washer. Mark the steering wheel and shaft to assure proper positioning later.

5. Using a steering wheel puller, remove the steering wheel. Installation is the reverse of removal. Align the marks you made earlier.

6. Torque the steering wheel nut to specifications.

Combination Switch

REMOVAL & INSTALLATION

All Except Impulse

1. Remove the steering wheel as previously described.

2. Remove the steering column cov-

ers and disconnect the electrical connectors to the switches.

3. Remove the washer/wiper switch by removing the two retaining screws.

4. Remove the turn signal/headlight switch and hazard switch by removing the four retaining screws.

5. Installation is the reverse of removal. Make sure the connectors are tight and properly connected.

NOTE: The light, wiper/washer, turn signal switches etc. on the Impulse, are contained in a control panel which is removed as an assembly. Refer to the procedure under "Chassis Electrical"

Ignition Lock Switch

REMOVAL & INSTALLATION

All Models

1. Disconnect the negative battery cable. Using the steering wheel removal procedure, (as previously outlined), remove the steering wheel.

2. Remove the screws retaining the upper and lower steering column covers.

3. Disconnect all the electrical connectors.

4. On the I-Mark models, remove the combination windshield wiper and washer switch by removing the two retaining screws. Then remove the combination turn signal, headlight dimmer and hazard warning switch by removing the two retaining screws.

5. Remove the ignition lock cylinder housing by removing the snap ring and washer, along with the lock cylinder housing retaining bolts on the column flange.

6. Remove the lock cylinder housing from the steering column shaft.

7. Installation is the reverse order of the removal procedure.

Manual Steering Gear

REMOVAL & INSTALLATION

I-Mark (RWD)

1. Raise the car and safely support it with jackstands. Remove the lower engine shrouds.

2. Remove the steering shaft coupling bolt.

3. Remove both tie rod ends cotter pin and castle nut. Discard the pins and use tool J–21687–02 or equivalent to disconnect the tie rod ends from the steering knuckles.

4. Disconnect the rack retaining bolts from the crossmember. Expand the steering shaft coupling and remove the assembly.

5. Installation is the reverse of removal. Before installing the rack assembly, set the steering gear to the high point by positioning the front wheels straight ahead with the steering wheel centered.

6. Torque the crossmember retaining bolts to 14 ft. lbs. Torque the steering shaft coupling bolt to 19 ft. lbs.

I-Mark (FWD)

1. Disconnect the negative battery cable and remove the engine hood.

2. Loosen the front wheel lugs and raise and support the front of the vehicle safely. Remove both front tires.

3. Remove the tie rod ends from the steering knuckles.

4. Using a suitable engine hoist, slightly raise the engine. Support the lower part of the engine with a suitable engine jack or jack stand.

5. Remove the engine mounting bolts.

6. Remove the front exhaust pipe hange mounting rubber nut. Detach the mounting rubber from the beam. Remove the intermediate shaft mounting bolt (steering shaft side bolt).

7. Remove the bracket nut(s) holding the manual steering unit.

8. Remove the steering unit and when removing the right and left steering unit boots through the body be careful not to damage the boots.

9. Installation is the reverse order of the removal procedure. Be sure to use the following torque specifications when installing the steering unit.

    a. Steering unit bracket nut – 30 ft. lbs.

    b. Steering shaft side bolt – 19 ft. lbs.

    c. Support beam bolts – 51 ft. lbs.

    d. Engine mounting bolts – 61 ft. lbs.

    e. Tie rod end nut – 29 ft. lbs.

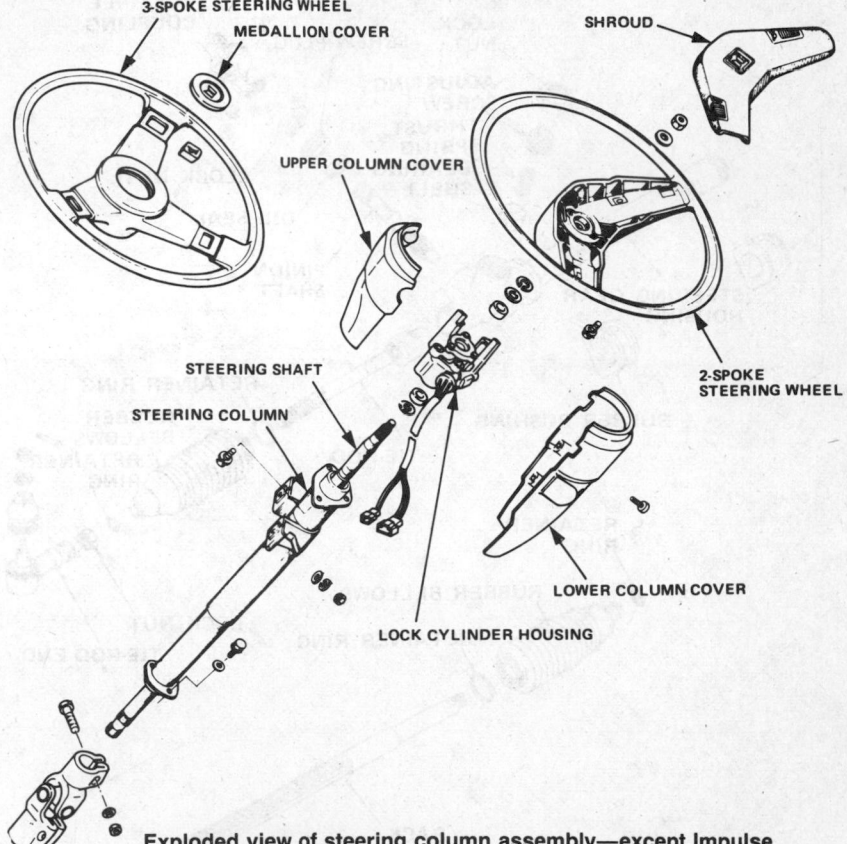

Exploded view of steering column assembly—except Impulse

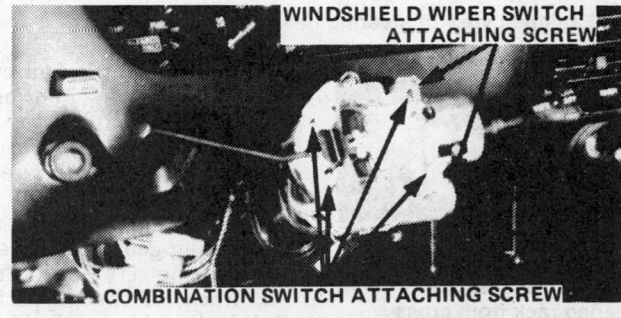

Removing combination switches

Power Steering Gear

1. Disconnect the negative battery cable and remove the engine hood.

2. Loosen the front wheel lugs and raise and support the front of the vehicle safely. Remove both front tires.

3. Remove the tie rod ends from the steering knuckles.

4. Using a suitable engine hoist, slightly raise the engine. Support the lower part of the engine with a suitable engine jack or jack stand.

5. Remove the engine mounting bolts.

6. Remove the exhaust pipe hanger rubber mounting and separate the mounting rubber and the beam.

7. Remove the intermediate shaft

Removing tie rod end from knuckle

mounting bolt and remove the intermediate shaft.

8. Remove the power steering unit oil line and place the lines in a suit-

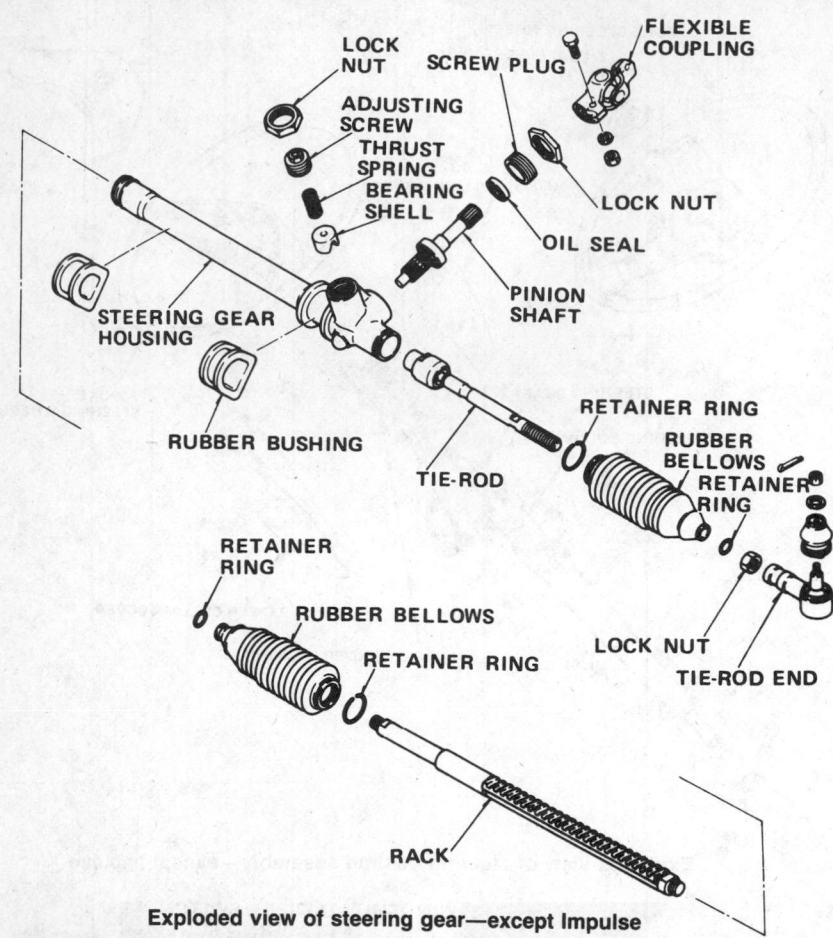

LOCK NUT
SCREW PLUG
FLEXIBLE COUPLING
ADJUSTING SCREW
THRUST SPRING
BEARING SHELL
LOCK NUT
OIL SEAL
PINION SHAFT
STEERING GEAR HOUSING
RETAINER RING
RUBBER BELLOWS
RETAINER RING
RUBBER BUSHING
TIE-ROD
RETAINER RING
RUBBER BELLOWS
RETAINER RING
LOCK NUT
TIE-ROD END
RACK

Exploded view of steering gear—except Impulse

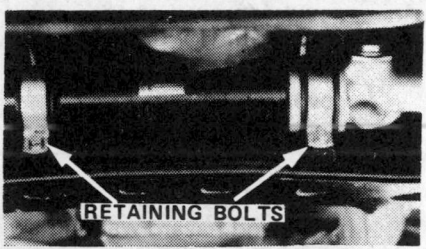

RETAINING BOLTS

Removing steering rack from cross member

able container. Turn the steering wheel fully to the left and right to force the oil out of the cylinder.

9. Remove the bracket nut(s) holding the power steering unit in the vehicle. Remove the unit from the vehicle and be careful not to damage the boots.

10. Installation is the reverse order of the removal procedure. Use the same torque specifications as the manual steering unit. The feed oil line is torqued to 25 ft. lbs. and the return line is torqued to 33 ft. lbs.

11. After installation is completed, realign the front end.

ADJUSTMENTS

Adjustment of the steering gear as-sembly is accomplished by turning the adjusting screw in or out.

1. Set the steering to the high point by positioning the front wheels straight ahead with the steering wheel centered.

2. Thread the adjusting screw into the steering gear housing and torque the adjusting screw to 11 ft. lbs.

3. Back off the adjusting screw slightly, then torque the locknut to 58 ft. lbs.

Power Steering Unit

REMOVAL & INSTALLATION

Impulse

1. Remove the front disc brake hub and rotor.

2. Remove the outer tie rod end with tool J–21687–02.

3. Disconnect and plug the return and feed pipes.

4. Unbolt the brackets at the cross-member and remove the power steering unit.

5. Installation is the reverse of removal.

Power Steering Pump

REMOVAL & INSTALLATION

All Models

1. Disconnect the negative battery cable. Remove all necessary drive belts.

2. Disconnect the high pressure lines from the power steering pump and let them and the pump drain out into a suitable drain pan. On the Impulse G200Z engine it is necessary to remove the under the engine dust cover in order to reach the high pressure lines and to remove the drive belt.

4. In the I-Mark models, remove the power steering pump adjusting plate, brackets and retaining bolts. Then remove the power steering pump from the vehicle.

5. On the G200Z Impulse, remove the power steering pump pulley, brackets and retaining bolts and remove the pump from the vehicle.

6. On the 4ZCI-T Impulse, remove the V-belt, pump pulley, idler pulley, brackets and retaining bolts. Then remove the pump from the vehicle.

7. Installation is the reverse order of the removal procedure. Tighten the drive belts to specifications, refill the power steering reservoir, bleed the system and start the car and check for leaks.

BLEEDING

1. Turn the wheels to the extreme left.

2. With the engine stopped, add power steering fluid to the "MIN" mark on the fluid indicator.

3. Start the engine and run it for 15 seconds at fast idle.

4. Stop the engine, recheck the fluid level and refill to the "MIN" mark.

5. Start the engine and turn the wheels from side to side (3 times).

6. Stop the engine check the fluid level.

NOTE: If air bubbles are still present in the fluid, the procedure must be repeated.

Tie Rod Ends

REMOVAL & INSTALLATION

All Models

1. Raise the vehicle and remove the front wheel.

2. Remove the castle nut from the ball joint. Using a ball joint removal tool, separate the tie rod from the steering knuckle.

3. Disconnect the retaining wire

1. Disc brake; front
2. Hub and rotor; front brake
3. Rod end assembly; outer
4. Shaft; steering, 2nd
5. Pipe assembly; return
6. Pipe assembly; feed
7. Bolt; bracket to crossmember
8. Washer; spring, bracket to crossmember
9. Bracket; steering unit to crossmember

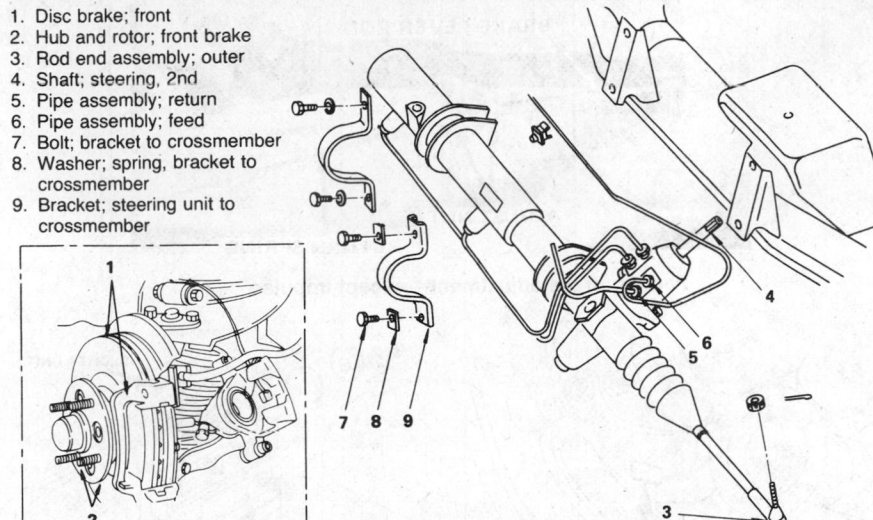

Power steering unit removal and installation—Impulse

1. Tandem master cylinder assembly
2. Cylinder body
3. Primary piston assembly
4. Secondary piston assembly
5. Primary piston spring
6. Secondary piston spring
7. Check valve
8. Connector
9. Check valve spring
10. Washer
11. Gasket
12. Stop—bolt
13. Gasket
14. Snap-ring
15. Connector
16. Clip
17. Gasket
18. Bracket
19. Bolt
20. Washer
21. Fluid reservoir assembly
22. Body
23. Filter
24. Cover
25. Bracket
26. Screw
27. Washer
28. Bolt
29. Washer
30. Front rubber hose
31. Rear rubber hose
32. Clip
33. Nut
34. Washer

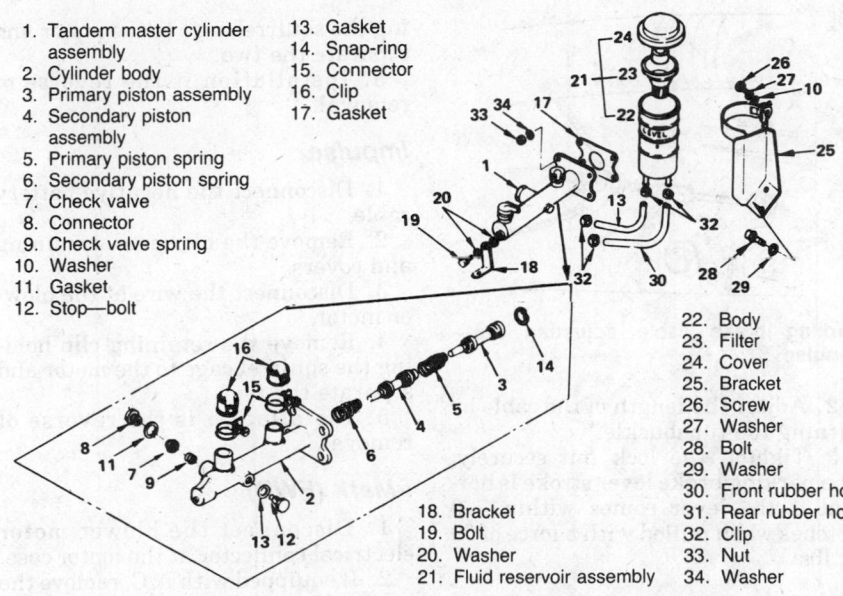

Exploded view of master cylinder—except Impulse

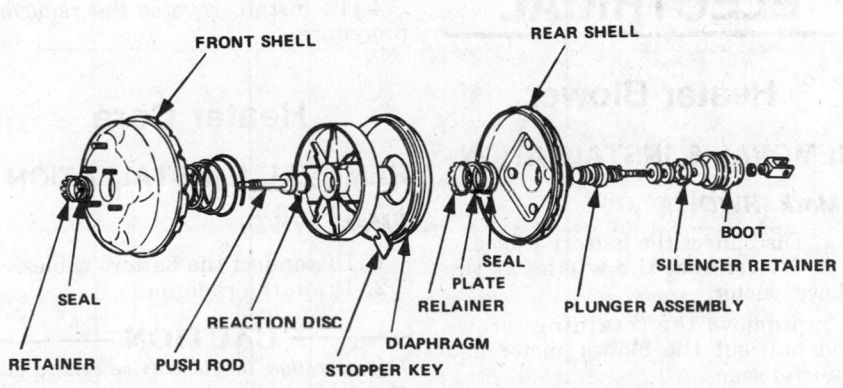

Exploded view of power brake unit—typical

FRONT SHELL
REAR SHELL
BOOT
SILENCER RETAINER
SEAL
PLATE
RETAINER
SEAL
RETAINER
REACTION DISC
PLUNGER ASSEMBLY
DIAPHRAGM
STOPPER KEY
PUSH ROD

---

from the inner boot and pull back the boot.

4. Using a chisel, straighten the staked part of the locking washer between the tie rod and the rack.

5. Remove the tie rod from the rack.

6. To install, reverse the removal procedure.

BRAKES

For all brake system repair and service not detailed below, please refer to "Brakes" in the Unit Repair section.

Master Cylinder

REMOVAL & INSTALLATION

1. Set the parking brake and chock the wheels to prevent the car from rolling.

2. Open the hood and disconnect the front and rear brake lines from the master cylinder.

3. Remove the nuts securing the master cylinder to the power brake unit and the support bracket.

4. Remove the nuts securing the fluid reservoir bracket and remove the master cylinder and fluid reservoir as an assembly. (remove the fluid hoses, too)

NOTE: Be careful not to spill brake fluid on any painted surface. Brake fluid acts exactly like paint remover.

5. Installation is the reverse of removal.

For information on bleeding the master cylinder and brake system, see "Brakes" in the Unit Repair section.

Power Brake Booster

REMOVAL & INSTALLATION

1. Wipe the master cylinder, power unit and lines clean with a clean rag. Use rags to catch any leaking fluid.

2. Disconnect the hydraulic lines at the master cylinder, and cover the lines with a clean, lint-free material to prevent dirt from contaminating the system.

3. Remove the master cylinder bracket bolts to the cylinder and fender skirt and remove the bracket.

4. Remove the bolts securing the fluid reservoir bracket.

5. Remove the vacuum hose clip and the hose from the check valve.

6. Remove the clevis pin from the brake pedal and separate the clevis and pedal.

7. Remove the power unit retaining nuts holding it to the dash panel and lift out the power unit and master cylinder/reservoir as an assembly.

8. Installation is the reverse of removal. Bleed the brake system and top up the fluid level.

Wheel Cylinder

REMOVAL & INSTALLATION

1. Remove the brake shoes.

2. Disconnect the hydraulic brake line at the wheel cylinder.

3. Remove the wheel cylinder attaching bolts from the backing plate.

4. Cap or tape the openings of the brake line and wheel cylinders.

5. Installation is the reverse of removal. Bleed the brake system.

Parking Brake Cable

ADJUSTMENT

All Models Except Impulse and I-Mark (FWD)

NOTE: Adjustment of the parking brake is necessary every time the rear brake cables are disconnected for any reason.

1. Fully release the parking brake lever and check the cable for free movement.

2. Remove the cable play by turning the brake lever rod adjusting nut.

3. When adjustment is complete, check that the travel of the parking brake lever is within 8–10 notches from full off to full on. If the travel is incorrect, readjust to specifications.

Impulse

1. The parking brake shoes can be adjusted by turning the adjuster until contact can be felt when turning the wheel manually, then backing off six notches.

2. The parking brake cable can be adjusted by pulling the parking brake lever from full off to full on. The lever travel should be within 11–12 notches. If the travel is incorrect adjust by turning the rod adjusting nut. Make sure the brakes do not drag after adjustment.

I-Mark (FWD)

1. Release the parking brake lever.

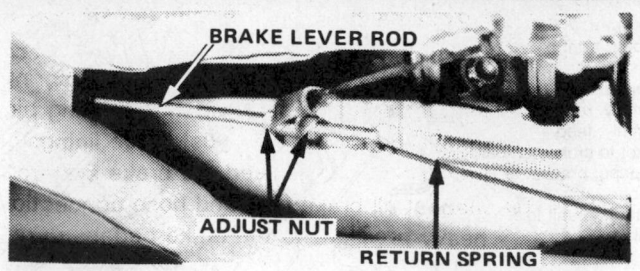
Parking brake adjustment—except Impulse

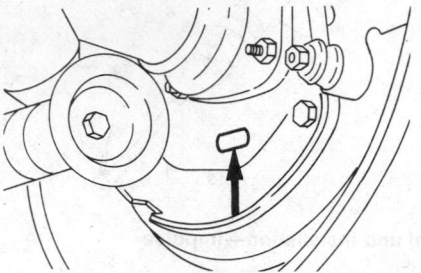
Parking brake shoe adjuster hole—Impulse

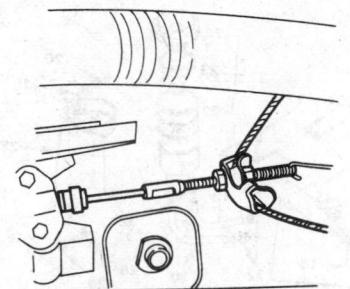
Parking brake cable adjusting nut—Impulse

2. Adjust the length of the cable by turning the turnbuckle.

3. Tighten the lock nut securely. The parking brake lever stroke is normal if the lever comes within 7–9 notches when pulled with a force of 60 ft. lbs.

CHASSIS ELECTRICAL

Heater Blower

REMOVAL & INSTALLATION

I-Mark (RWD)

1. Disconnect the battery cables.

2. Disconnect the wiring at the blower motor.

3. Remove the retaining screws and pull out the blower motor and squirrel cage.

4. Remove the retaining clip hold-

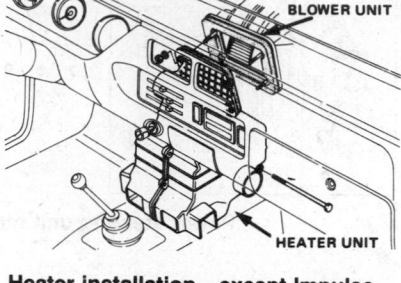
Heater installation—except Impulse

ing the squirrel cage to the motor and separate the two.

5. Installation is the reverse of removal.

Impulse

1. Disconnect the negative battery cable.

2. Remove the blower motor lining and covers.

3. Disconnect the wire at the blower motor.

4. Remove the retaining clip holding the squirrel cage to the motor and separate the two.

5. Installation is the reverse of removal.

I-Mark (FWD)

1. Disconnect the blower motor electrical connector at the motor case.

2. If equipped with A/C, remove the rubber hose from the blower case.

3. Rotate the blower motor case counterclockwise and remove the blower motor assembly.

4. To install, reverse the removal procedure.

Heater Core

REMOVAL & INSTALLATION

I-Mark (RWD)

1. Disconnect the battery cables.

2. Drain the radiator.

— CAUTION —
This operation should only be carried out on a cold engine.

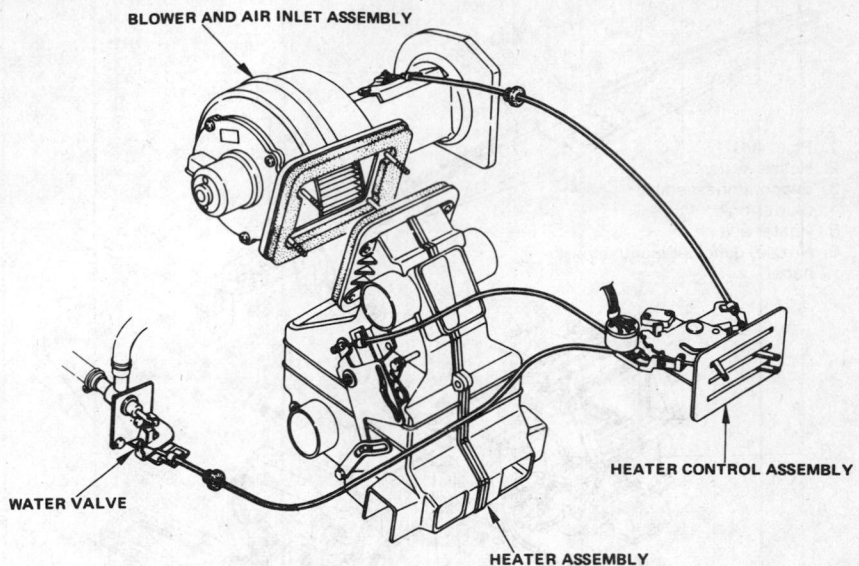

Heater system components—except Impulse

3. Disconnect the heater hoses at the core connections and plug the core tubes to prevent the spillage of coolant when removing the core inside the car.

4. Remove the outer blower unit case cover and disconnect the fresh air door control cable.

5. Disconnect the temperature cable at the water valve.

6. Remove the steering wheel as previously described.

7. Remove the instrument cluster as described.

8. Disconnect the wiring for the console gauges, remove the console retaining screws, untie the shift lever leather boot and remove the console.

9. Remove the heater control and radio face plate.

10. Remove the glovebox.

11. Remove the radio as described.

12. Disconnect the selector mode cable from the driver's side of the heater assembly.

13. Carefully pull the temperature and fresh air door cables through the cowl and remove the control panel through the cluster opening.

14. Remove the instrument panel assembly as described.

15. Remove the heater unit assembly through-bolt located at the rear and bottom of the heater.

16. Remove the four attaching nuts holding the heater unit and blower unit together and remove the heater unit assembly.

17. Remove the bolts holding the heater unit case halves together and remove the heater core.

18. Installation is the reverse of removal. Refill and bleed the cooling system.

I-Mark (FWD)

1. Disconnect the heater hoses in the engine compartment.

2. At the lower part of the heater unit case, remove the six retaining clips.

3. Using a small pry bar, pry open the lower part of the case and remove it.

4. Remove the core assembly insulator and the core assembly.

5. To install, reverse the removal procedure.

Heater And Evaporator Assembly

REMOVAL & INSTALLATION

Impulse

1. Remove the instrument panel and compartment box.

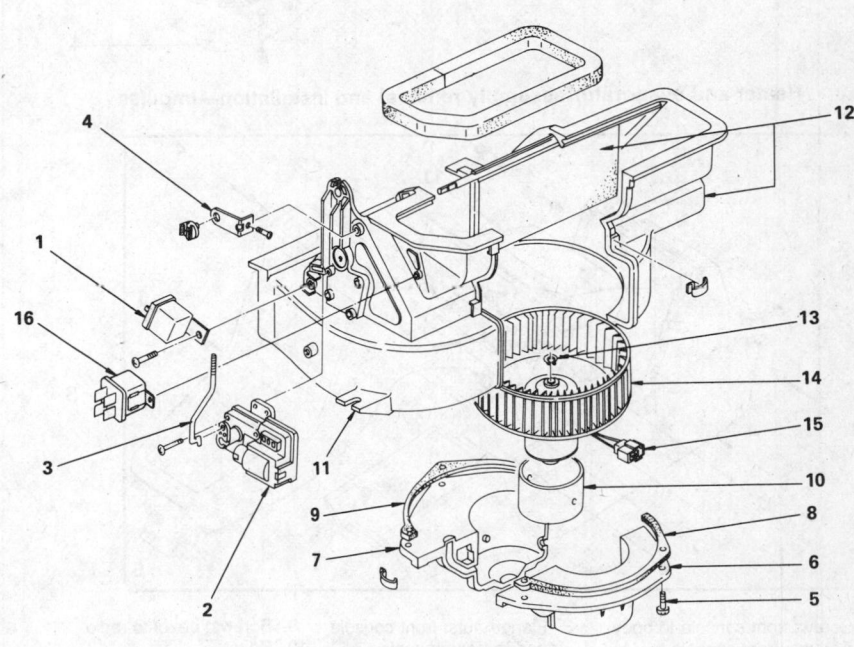

1. Relay; fresh-circulation
2. Actuator; blower unit
3. Rod; actuator
4. Lever; shutter
5. Screw; cover to case
6. Cover; blower unit
7. Cover; blower unit
8. Lining; blower unit
9. Lining; blower unit
10. Isolator; blower unit
11. Case; blower unit rear
12. Case; blower unit front
13. Ring; snap
14. Impeller; motor
15. Motor assembly; fan
16. Relay; blower unit

Blower motor removal—Impulse

2. Disconnect the A/C lines at the evaporator.

NOTE: The air conditioning system must be discharged and evacuated, using the required tools, before the refrigerant lines can be disconnected.

─────── CAUTION ───────
Do not disconnect any refrigerant lines unless you have experience with air conditioning systems. Escaping refrigerant will freeze any surface it contacts, including your skin and eyes.

3. Disconnect and plug the heater

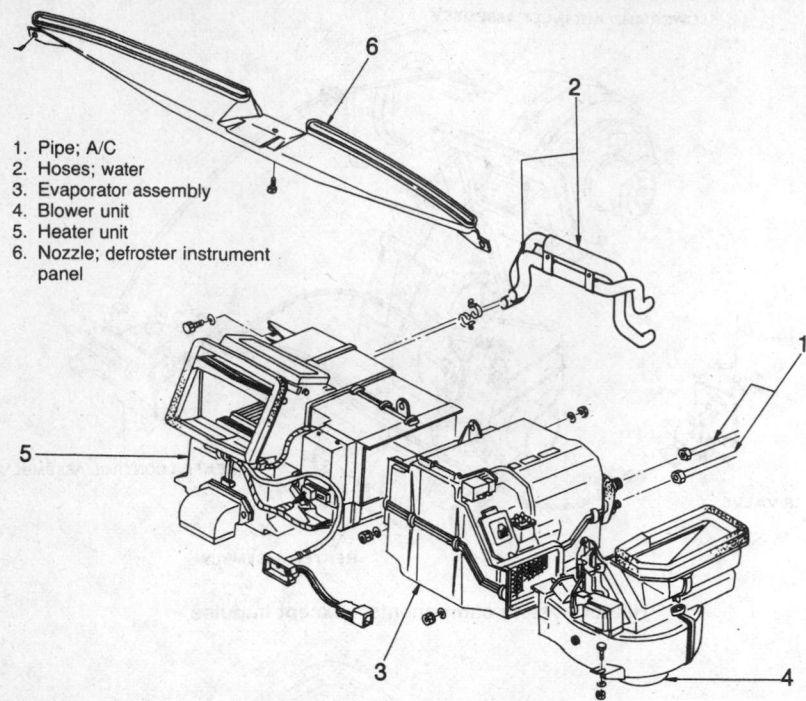

1. Pipe; A/C
2. Hoses; water
3. Evaporator assembly
4. Blower unit
5. Heater unit
6. Nozzle; defroster instrument panel

Heater and evaporator assembly removal and installation—Impulse

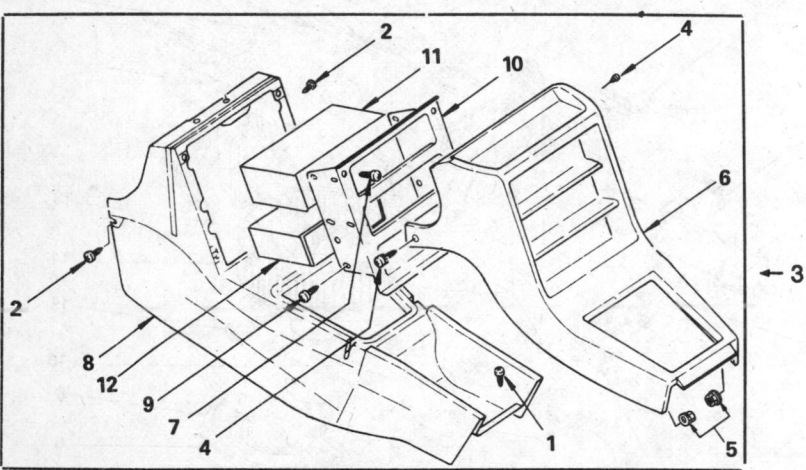

1. Screw; front console to body	5. Flange nuts; front console pad to front console
2. Screws; front console to bracket	6. Front console pad
3. Console assembly	7. Screws; bezel to front console
4. Screws; front console pad to front console	8. Front console
9. Screws; bezel to radio	
10. Bezel	
11. Cassette deck with FM/AM radio or FM/AM radio	
12. Graphic equalizer or cassette deck	

Radio and front console removal and installation—Impulse

hoses, then remove the blower motor and heater assemblies.

4. The heater core may now be removed by removing the retaining screws.

5. Installation is the reverse of removal.

Radio

REMOVAL & INSTALLATION

I-Mark (RWD)

1981

1. Remove the battery cables.

2. Remove the ash tray and ash tray support.

3. Remove the radio knobs and heater control knobs by pulling them straight back.

4. Remove the radio shaft nuts and trim panel.

5. Remove the radio retainer screws from under the dash board.

6. Disconnect the electrical and speaker connections and antenna cable.

7. Remove the radio down through the back of the dash.

8. Installation is the reverse of removal.

1982-88

1. Disconnect the battery cables.

2. Pull off the radio knobs.

3. Remove the radio shaft nuts and trim panel.

4. Remove the ash tray.

5. Pull off the A/C control knobs, if so equipped.

6. Remove the four screws, then remove the control panel.

7. Remove the two panel lights.

8. Remove the two radio retaining screws.

9. Disconnect the electrical connectors and lead-in cable.

10. Installation is the reverse of removal.

I-Mark (FWD)

1. Remove the screws retaining the radio cover and remove the cover.

2. Remove the radio and bracket.

3. Disconnect the electrical connector, speaker connectors and the antenna cable.

4. To install, reverse the removal procedure.

Impulse

1. Remove the front console retaining screws and disconnect the wiring harnesses at the front console and also at the radio main feed connection. Disconnect the antenna cable and the bolt retaining the ground cable.

2. Remove the flange nuts retaining the front console pad to the front console.

3. Remove the screws retaining the bezel to the radio.

4. Disconnect any remaining harnesses and remove the radio assembly.

5. Installation is the reverse of removal. Be sure to properly connect all harnesses and cables before installing the console assembly.

Windshield Wiper Switch

REMOVAL & INSTALLATION

All Models

On the I-Mark (RWD), remove the switch by following the ignition switch removal procedure previously outlined in this section. On the I-Mark (FWD) and the Impulse, follow the "Instrument Cluster" removal procedure as outlined in this section and remove the switch from the instrument cluster.

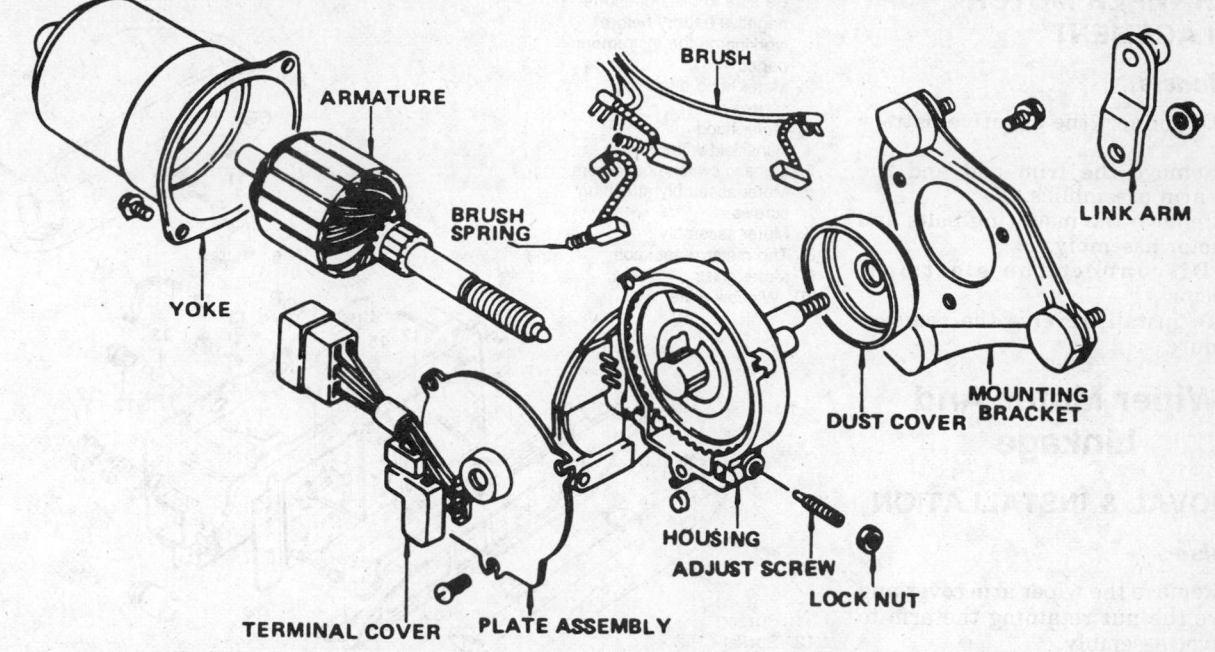

Exploded view of wiper components—except Impulse

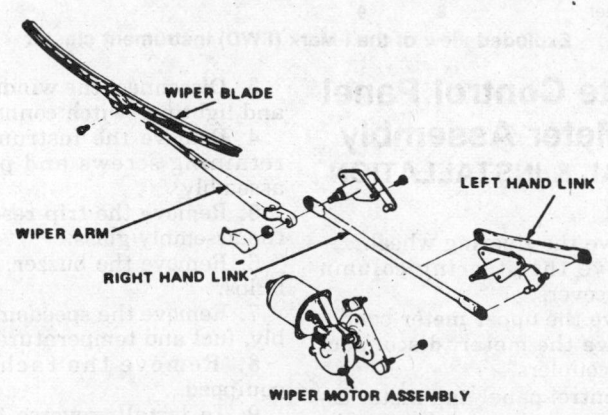

Wiper system components—except Impulse

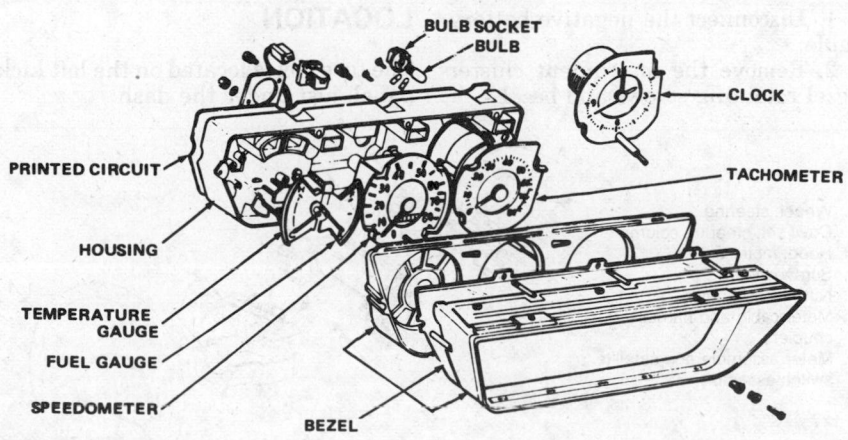

Exploded view of instrument cluster—1981 except Impulse

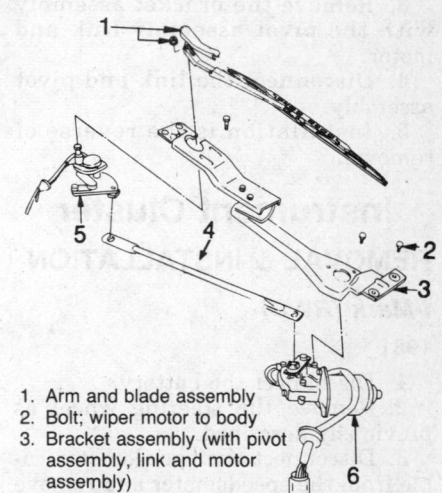

1. Arm and blade assembly
2. Bolt; wiper motor to body
3. Bracket assembly (with pivot assembly, link and motor assembly)
4. Link; wiper
5. Pivot assembly; wiper link
6. Motor assembly; wiper

Front wiper motor and linkage—Impulse

Wiper Motor

REMOVAL & INSTALLATION

All Except Impulse

1. Disconnect the battery cables.
2. Working under the instrument panel, remove the nut and crank-arm from motor.
3. Disconnect the wiring connector.
4. Remove the three nuts securing the wiper motor and remove the motor.
5. Installation is the reverse of removal.

REAR WIPER MOTOR REPLACEMENT

All Models

1. Disconnect the negative battery cable.

2. Remove the trim pad and the wiper arm assemblies.

3. Remove the mounting bolts and the motor assembly.

4. Disconnect the electrical connector.

5. To install, reverse the removal procedure.

Wiper Motor And Linkage

REMOVAL & INSTALLATION

Impulse

1. Remove the wiper arm cover and remove the nut retaining the arm to the pivot assembly.

2. Remove the two bolts retaining the wiper motor to the body.

3. Remove the bracket assembly with the pivot assembly link and motor.

4. Disconnect the link and pivot assembly.

5. Installation is the reverse of removal.

Instrument Cluster

REMOVAL & INSTALLATION

I-Mark (RWD)

1981

1. Disconnect the battery.

2. Remove the steering wheel as previously described.

3. Disconnect the speedometer cable from the speedometer and remove wing nut.

4. Remove the instrument cluster attaching screws and remove the cluster assembly outward.

5. Disconnect the connectors and clock harness (if equipped). Disconnect the harness connecting to the speedometer reed switch on diesel models.

6. Installation is the reverse of removal.

1982-88

1. Disconnect the battery.

2. Remove the cluster panel.

3. Remove the instrument cluster attaching screws.

4. Rotate the cluster outwards and disconnect the electrical connectors and the speedometer cable.

5. Installation is the reverse of removal.

1. Be sure to disconnect the negative battery before working on the instrument panel.
2. Meter hood attaching screws
3. Meter hood
4. Winshield wiper switch
5. Lighting switch connectors
6. Meter assembly attaching screws
7. Meter assembly
8. Trip meter reset knob
9. Meter glass
10. Window plate

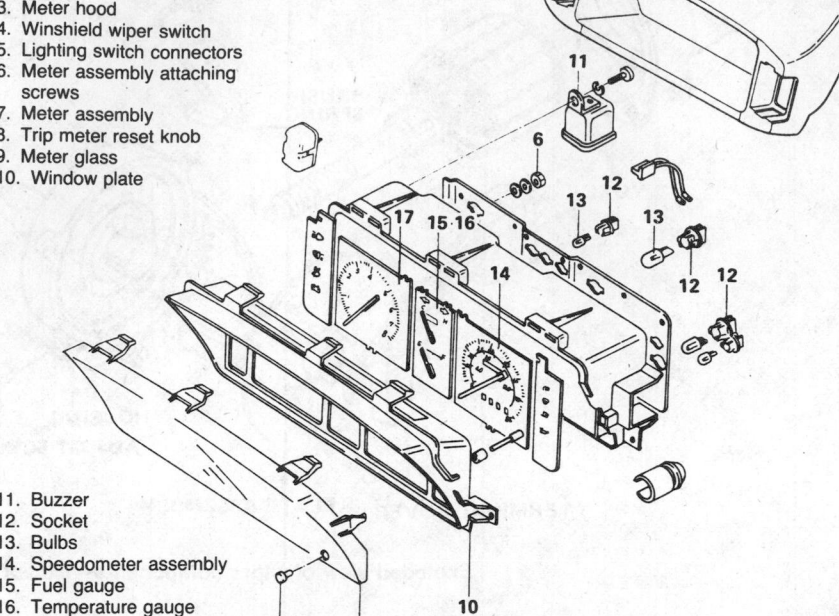

11. Buzzer
12. Socket
13. Bulbs
14. Speedometer assembly
15. Fuel gauge
16. Temperature gauge
17. Tachometer

Exploded view of the I-Mark (FWD) instrument cluster

Satellite Control Panel and Meter Assembly

REMOVAL & INSTALLATION

Impulse

1. Remove the steering wheel.

2. Remove the steering column cowl set or covers.

3. Remove the upper meter bond.

4. Remove the meter, disconnect the wiring couplers.

5. The control panel and meter assembly can now be removed as a unit.

6. Installation is the reverse of removal.

I-Mark (FWD)

1. Disconnect the negative battery cable.

2. Remove the instrument cluster bezel retaining screws and bezel.

3. Disconnect the windshield wiper and lighting switch connectors.

4. Remove the instrument cluster retaining screws and pull out the assembly.

5. Remove the trip reset knob and the assembly glass.

6. Remove the buzzer, sockets and bulbs.

7. Remove the speedometer assembly, fuel and temperature gauge.

8. Remove the tachometer, if equipped.

9. To install, reverse the removal procedure.

Fuse Box

LOCATION

The fuse box is located on the left kick panel, just under the dash.

1. Wheel; steering
2. Cowl set; steering column
3. Hood; meter upper
4. Screw; meter
5. Nut; flange, meter
6. Meter cable and harness couplers
7. Meter assemble and satellite switch assembly

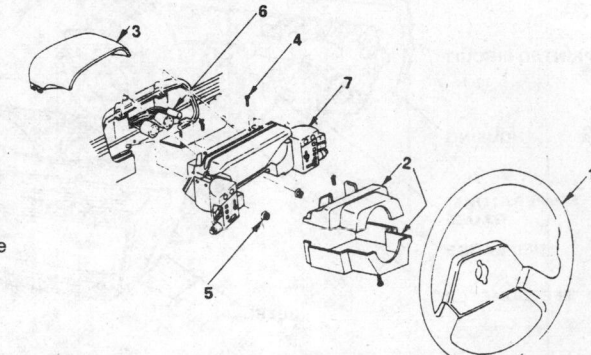

Satellite control panel and meter assembly removal and installation—Impulse

Mazda **8**
323, 626, GLC, RX–7

SERIAL NUMBER IDENTIFICATION

Vehicle Identification Plate

The serial number is on a plate located on the driver's side windshield pillar and is visible through the glass.

A vehicle identification number (VIN) plate, bearing the serial number and other data, is attached to the cowl.

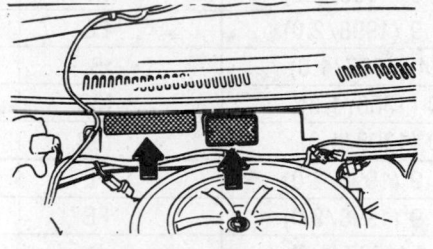

Chassis number (left) and model plate (right) location

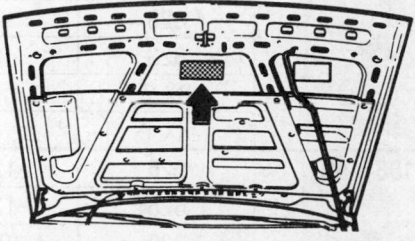

Emission control information label location

Engine Number

The engine number is located on a plate which is attached to the engine

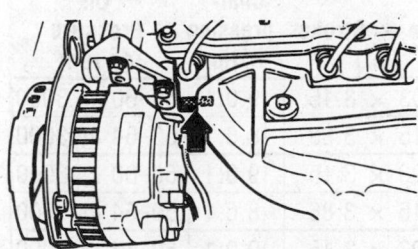

Engine number location

housing, just behind the distributor or on a machined pad at the right front side of the engine block.

The engine number consists of an identification number followed by a 6-digit production number.

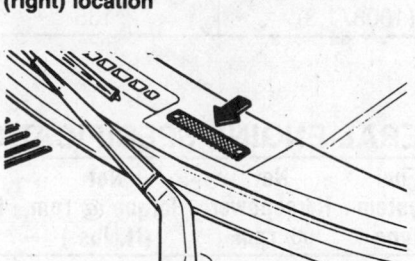

Vehicle identification plate location

The Mazda 626 and RX-7 engine serial number is located on the rear of the alternator bracket, stamped on the engine block. The 626 diesel engine serial number is located between the first and second fuel injectors, stamped on the engine block. The GLC and 323 engine serial number is stamped on the left hand side of the engine block, just below the cylinder head.

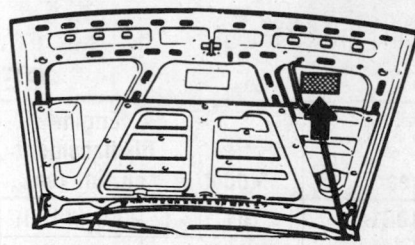

Vacuum hose routing label location

Vehicle Identification Labels

In addition to the serial numbers, other important vehicle information and specifications can be found on the underhood emission sticker, vacuum hose routing diagram, tire pressure label and motor vehicle safety certification label.

ENGINE IDENTIFICATION

Year	Model	Engine (1490/1.5) Displacement cu. in. (cc/liter)	Engine Series Identification	No. of Cylinders	Engine Type Type
1981	GLC	90.9 (1490/1.5)	E5	4	SOHC
	626	120.2 (1970/2.0)	MA	4	SOHC
	RX7	70 (1146/1.1)	12A	2	Rotary
1982	GLC	90.9 (1490/1.5)	E5	4	SOHC
	626	120.2 (1970/2.0)	MA	4	SOHC
	RX7	70 (1146/1.1)	12A	2	Rotary
1983	GLC	90.9 (1490/1.5)	E5	4	SOHC
	626	121.9 (1998/2.0)	FE	4	SOHC
	RX7	70 (1946/1.1)	12A	2	Rotary
1984	GLC	90.9 (1490/1.5)	E5	4	SOHC
	662	121.9 (1998/2.0)	FE	4	SOHC
	RX7	70 (1146/1.1)	12A	2	Rotary
1985	GLC	90.9 (1490/1.5)	E5	4	SOHC
	626	121.9 (1998/2.0)	FE	4	SOHC
	626	121.9 (1998/2.0)	RF	4	Diesel
	RX7	70 (1146/1.1)	12A	2	Rotary
	RX7	80 (1308/1.3)	13B	2	Rotary
1986	626	121.9 (1998/2.0)	FE	4	SOHC
	626	121.9 (1998/2.0)	FE	4	SOHC-Turbo
	323	97.4 (1597/1.6)	B	4	SOHC
	RX-7	80 (1308/1.3)	13B	2	Rotary
	RX-7	80 (1308/1.3)	13B	2	Rotary-Turbo
1987-88	626	121.9 (1998/2.0)	FE	4	SOHC
	626	121.9 (1998/2.0)	FE	4	SOHC-Turbo
	323	97.4 (1597/1.6)	B	4	SOHC
	RX-7	80 (1308/1.3)	13B	2	Rotary
	RX-7	80 (1308/1.3)	13B	2	Rotary-Turbo

GENERAL ENGINE SPECIFICATIONS

Year	Model	Engine Displacement cu. in. (cc)	Fuel System Type	Net Horsepower @ rpm	Net Torque @ rpm (ft. lbs.)	Bore × Stroke (in.)	Com-pression Ratio	Oil Pressure @ rpm
1981	GLC	90.9 (1490)	2 bbl	68 @ 5000	82 @ 3000	3.03 × 3.15	9.0:1	50–60 @ 3000
	626	120.2 (1970)	2 bbl	75 @ 4500	105 @ 2500	3.15 × 3.86	8.6:1	50–64 @ 3000
1982	GLC	90.9 (1490)	2 bbl	68 @ 5000	82 @ 3000	3.03 × 3.15	9.0:1	50–60 @ 3000
	626	120.2 (1970)	2 bbl	75 @ 4500	105 @ 2500	3.15 × 3.86	8.6:1	50–64 @ 3000
1983	GLC	90.9 (1490)	2 bbl	68 @ 5000	82 @ 3000	3.03 × 3.15	9.0:1	50–64 @ 3000
	626	121.9 (1998)	2 bbl	83 @ 4800	110 @ 2500	3.39 × 3.39	8.6:1	43–57 @ 3000
1984	GLC	90.9 (1490)	2 bbl	68 @ 5000	82 @ 3000	3.03 × 3.15	9.0:1	50–60 @ 3000
	626	121.9 (1998)	2 bbl	83 @ 4800	110 @ 2500	3.39 × 3.39	8.6:1	43–51 @ 3000
1985	GLC	90.9 (1490)	2 bbl	68 @ 5000	82 @ 3000	3.03 × 3.15	9.0:1	50–60 @ 3000
	626	121.9 (1998)	2 bbl	83 @ 4800	110 @ 2500	3.39 × 3.39	8.6:1	43–57 @ 3000
	626 Diesel	121.9 (1998)	DFI	NA	NA	3.39 × 3.39	22.7:1	58–10 @ 3000

GENERAL ENGINE SPECIFICATIONS

Year	Model	Engine Displacement cu. in. (cc)	Fuel System Type	Net Horsepower @ rpm	Net Torque @ rpm (ft. lbs.)	Bore × Stroke (in.)	Compression Ratio	Oil Pressure @ rpm
1986	323	97.4 (1597)	EFI ①	82 @ 5000	92 @ 2500	3.07 × 3.29	9.3:1	43–57 @ 3000
	626	121.9 (1998)	EFI	93 @ 5000	115 @ 2500	3.39 × 3.39	8.6:1	43–57 @ 3000
	626 Turbo	121.9 (1998)	EFI	120 @ 5000	150 @ 3000	3.39 × 3.39	7.8:1	43–57 @ 3000
1987–88	323	97.4 (1597)	EFI ①	82 @ 5000	92 @ 2500	3.07 × 3.39	9.3:1	43–57 @ 3000
	626	121.9 (1998)	EFI	93 @ 5000	115 @ 2500	3.39 × 3.39	8.6:1	43–57 @ 3000
	626 Turbo	121.9 (1998)	EFI	120 @ 5000	150 @ 3000	3.39 × 3.39	7.8:1	43–57 @ 3000

NA—Information not available
DFI—Diesel Fuel Injection
EFI—Electronic Fuel Injection
① Canadian models use 2 bbl carburetor

GENERAL ENGINE SPECIFICATIONS—ROTARY ENGINE

Year	Model	Engine Displacement cu. in. (cc)	Carburetor Type	Net Horsepower @ rpm	Net Torque @ rpm	Rotor Displacement (cu. in.)	Compression Ratio	Oil Pressure @ rpm (psi)
1981–83	RX-7	70 (1146)	4-bbl	101 @ 6000	105 @ 4000	35	9.4:1	64–78 @ 3000
1984–85	RX-7	80 (1308)	EFI	135 @ 6000	133 @ 2750	40	9.4:1	64–78 @ 3000
	RX-7	70 (1146)	3-bbl	101 @ 6000	105 @ 4000	35	9.4:1	64–78 @ 3000
1986–87	RX-7	80 (1308)	EFI	146 @ 6500	138 @ 3500	40	9.4:1	64–78 @ 3000
	Turbo	80 (1308)	EFI	182 @ 6500	183 @ 3500	40	8.5:1	64–78 @ 3000

EFI Electronic Fuel Injection

GASOLINE ENGINE TUNE-UP SPECIFICATIONS

Year	Model	Engine Displacement cu. in. (cc)	Spark Plugs Type	Gap (in.)	Ignition Timing (deg.) MT	AT	Compression Pressure (psi)	Fuel Pump (psi)	Idle Speed (rpm) MT	AT	Valve Clearance In.	Ex.
1981	GLC	90.9 (1490)	BPR-5ES	0.031	8B	8B	NA	2.8–3.8	850	750	0.010	0.012
	626	120.2 (1970)	BRP-5ES	0.031	5B	5B	NA	2.8–3.8	750	650	0.012	0.012
1982	GLC	90.9 (1490)	BPR-5ES	0.031	8B	8B	NA	2.8–3.8	850	750	0.010	0.012
	626	120.2 (1970)	BRP-5ES	0.031	5B	5B	NA	2.8–3.8	750	650	0.012	0.012
1983	GLC	90.9 (1490)	BPR-5ES	0.031	8B	8B	NA	2.8–3.8	850	750	④	⑤
	626	121.9 (1998)	BRP-5ES	0.031	6B	6B	NA	2.8–3.5	750	700	0.012	0.012
1984	GLC	90.9 (1490)	BPR-5ES	0.031	6B	6B	NA	4.2–6.0	850	750	④	⑤
	626	121.9 (1998)	BPR-5ES	0.031	6B	6B	NA	2.8–4.3	750	700	0.012	0.012
1985	GLC	90.9 (1490)	BPR-5ES	0.031	6B	6B	NA	4.2–6.0	850	750	④	⑤
	626	121.9 (1998)	BPR-5ES	0.031	6B	6B	NA	2.8–4.3	750	700	0.012	0.012
1986	323	97.4 (1597)	BPR-5ES-11	0.040	2B ①	2B	NA	②	800–900	900–1050	③	③
	626	121.9 (1998)	BPR-5ES	0.031	6B	6B	NA	64–85	750	900	③	③
	626 Turbo	121.9 (1998)	BRP-6ES	0.031	6B	6B	NA	64–85	750	900	③	③

GASOLINE ENGINE TUNE-UP SPECIFICATIONS

Year	Model	Engine Displacement cu. in. (cc)	Spark Plugs Type	Gap (in.)	Ignition Timing (deg.) MT	AT	Compression Pressure (psi)	Fuel Pump (psi)	Idle Speed (rpm) MT	AT	Valve Clearance In.	Ex.
1987	323	97.4 (1597)	BPR-5ES-11	0.040	2B ①	2B	NA	②	800–900	900–1050	③	③
	626	121.9 (1998)	BPR-5ES	0.031	6B	6B	NA	64–85	750	900	③	③
	626 Turbo	121.9 (1998)	BRP-6ES	0.031	6B	6B	NA	64–85	750	900	③	③
1988			SEE UNDERHOOD SPECIFICATION STICKER									

NA—Not Available
B—Before top dead center
① 7B with the vacuum hose connected on EFI models
② Carburetor—4.0–5.0 psi
  EFI—64–85 psi

③ Valve side—0.012 in.
  Cam side—0.008 in.
④ Intake Valve Side—0.010 in.
  Intake Cam Side—0.007 in.
⑤ Exhaust Valve Side—0.012 in.
  Exhaust Cam Side—0.009 in.

TUNE-UP SPECIFICATIONS—ROTARY ENGINE

When analyzing compression test results, look for uniformity among cylinders, rather than specific pressures.

Year	Engine Displacement (cc)	Spark Plugs Type	Gap (in.)	Distributor	Ignition Timing (deg) Leading	Trailing	Idle Speed (rpm) MT	AT ①
1981–83	70 (1146)	②	0.039–0.043	Electronic	0	20A	725–775	725–775
1984–85	70 (1146)	③	0.053–0.057	Electronic	0	20A	750	750
1985	80 (1308)	③	.055	Electronic	5A	20A	800	800
1986–87	80 (1308)	S-29A, S-31A	.080	Electronic	5A	20A	750	750
1988	All		SEE UNDERHOOD SPECIFICATIONS STICKER					

NOTE: The underhood specifications sticker often reflects tune-up specification changes made in production. Sticker figures must be used if they disagree with those in this chart.
TDC—Top dead center
A—After top dead center
B—Before top dead center
MT—Manual transmission
AT—Automatic transmission
deg—degrees
① Transmission in Drive
② BR7ET, BR8ET, BR9ET
③ BR7EQ14, BR8EQ14, BR9EQ 14

DIESEL ENGINE TUNE-UP SPECIFICATIONS

Year	Engine Displacement cu. in. (cc)	Valve Clearance Intake (in.)	Exhaust (in.)	Intake Valve Opens (deg.)	Injection Pump Setting (deg.)	Injection Nozzle Pressure (psi) New	Used	Idle Speed (rpm)	Cranking Compression Pressure (psi)
1985	121.9 (1998)	0.008–0.012	0.012–0.016	13B	0 ①	1920	NA	800–850	426 @ 200 rpm

B—Before top dead center
① @ 0.039 in. lift of cam.

FIRING ORDERS

NOTE: To avoid confusion, always replace spark plug wires one at a time.

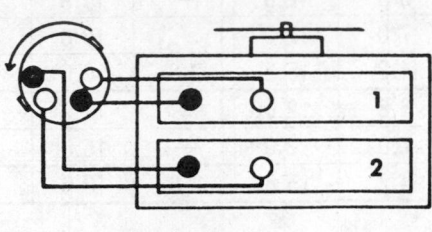

Rotary engine

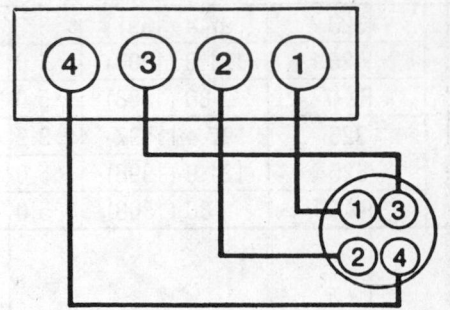

1415 cc engine—GLC 1979–80 and 1970 cc engine—626 1979–82

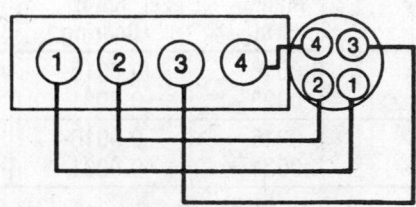

1490cc engine—1981–85 GLC 1597cc engine—323 1998cc engine—1983 and later 626

CAPACITIES

Year	Model	Engine Displacement cu. in. (cc)	Engine Crankcase with Filter	Engine Crankcase without Filter	Transmission (pts.) 4-Spd	Transmission (pts.) 5-Spd	Transmission (pts.) Auto.	Drive Axle (pts.)	Fuel Tank (gal.)	Cooling System (qts.)
1981	GLC	90.9 (1490)	4.0	3.5	2.8	6.8	12.0	—	11.1	5.8
	626	120.2 (1970)	4.1	3.8	3.0	3.6	13.2	2.6	14.5	7.9
	RX-7	70 (1146)	5.0	4.5	—	4.2	13.2	2.6	16.4	10.0
1982	GLC	90.9 (1490)	4.0	3.5	2.8	6.8	12.0	—	11.1	5.8
	626	120.2 (1970)	4.1	3.8	3.0	3.6	13.2	2.6	14.5	7.9
	RX-7	70 (1146)	5.0	4.5	—	4.2	13.2	2.6	16.4	10.0
1983	GLC	90.9 (1490)	4.0	3.5	2.8	6.8	12.0	—	11.1	5.8
	626	121.9 (1998)	5.0	4.5	—	7.0	12.0	—	15.6	7.4
	RX-7	70 (1146)	5.0	4.5	—	4.2	13.2	2.6	16.4	10.0
1984	GLC	90.9 (1490)	4.0	3.5	2.8	6.8	12.0	—	11.1	5.8
	626	121.9 (1998)	5.0	4.5	—	7.0	12.0	—	15.6	7.4
	RX-7	70 (1146)	5.0	4.5	—	4.2	15.8	2.6	16.4	10.0
1985	GLC	90.9 (1490)	4.0	3.5	2.8	6.8	12.0	—	11.1	5.8
	626	121.9 (1998)	5.0	4.5	—	7.0	12.0	—	15.6	7.4
	626 Diesel	121.9 (1998)	6.8	6.3	—	7.0	12.0	—	15.8	9.5
	RX-7	70 (1146)	5.0	4.5	—	4.2	15.8	2.6	16.4	10.0
	RX-7	80 (1308)	5.0	4.5	—	4.2	15.8	2.8	16.6	9.2

CAPACITIES

Year	Model	Engine Displacement cu. In. (cc)	Engine Crankcase with Filter	Engine Crankcase without Filter	Transmission (pts.) 4-Spd	Transmission (pts.) 5-Spd	Transmission (pts.) Auto.	Drive Axle (pts.)	Fuel Tank (gal.)	Cooling System (qts.)
1986	323	97.4 (1597)	3.2	2.9	6.8	6.8	12.0	—	11.9	6.3
	626	121.9 (1998)	5.0	4.5	—	7.0	12.0	—	15.6	7.4
	RX-7	80 (1308)	5.0	4.5	—	4.2	15.8	2.8	16.6	9.2
1987-88	323	97.4 (1597)	3.2	2.9	6.8	6.8	12.0	—	11.9	6.3
	626	121.9 (1998)	5.0	4.5	—	7.0	12.0	—	15.6	7.4
	RX-7	80 (1308)	5.0	4.5	—	4.2	15.8	2.8	16.6	9.2

ECCENTRIC SHAFT SPECIFICATIONS—ROTARY ENGINE

All measurements are given in inches.

Engine Type	Journal Diameter Main Bearing	Journal Diameter Rotor Bearing	Oil Clearance Main Bearing	Oil Clearance Rotor Bearing	Eccentric Shaft End-Play Normal	Eccentric Shaft End-Play Limit	Min. Shaft Run-Out
12A	1.6929	2.9134	0.0016-0.0028	0.0016-0.0031	0.0016-0.0028	0.0035	0.0024
13B	1.6918-1.6923	2.9122-2.9128	0.0016-0.0031	0.0016-0.0031	0.0016-0.0028	0.0035	0.0047

CAMSHAFT SPECIFICATIONS

All measurements given in inches.

Year	Engine Displacement cu. in. (cc)	Journal Diameter 1	Journal Diameter 2	Journal Diameter 3	Journal Diameter 4	Journal Diameter 5	Lobe Lift In.	Lobe Lift Ex.	Bearing Clearance	Camshaft End Play
1981	90.9 (1490) ④	1.6536	1.6536	1.6536	1.6536	1.6536	1.7367	1.7367	0.0014-② 0.0030	0.001-① 0.007
	120.2 (1970)	1.7117	1.7117	1.7117	1.7117	1.7117	1.7731	1.7718	0.0007-③ 0.0027	0.001-① 0.007
1982	90.9 (1490)	1.6515-1.6522	1.6504-1.6510	1.6504-1.6510	1.6504-1.6510	1.6515-1.6522	1.7368	1.7368	0.0014-② 0.0030	0.001-① 0.007
	120.2 (1970)	1.7717	1.7717	1.7717	1.7717	1.7717	1.7731	1.7718	0.0007-③ 0.0027	0.001-① 0.007
1983	90.9 (1490)	1.6515-1.6522	1.6504-1.6510	1.6504-1.6510	1.6504-1.6510	1.6515-1.6522	1.7368	1.7368	0.0014-② 0.0030	0.001-① 0.007
	121.9 (1998)	1.257-1.258	1.256-1.257	1.256-1.257	1.256-1.257	1.257-1.258	1.5023	1.5024	0.0014-② 0.0033	0.003-① 0.007
1984	90.9 (1490)	1.6515-1.6522	1.6504-1.6510	1.6504-1.6510	1.6504-1.6510	1.6515-1.6522	1.7368	1.7368	0.0014-② 0.0030	0.001-① 0.001
	121.9 (1998)	1.257-1.258	1.256-1.257	1.256-1.257	1.256-1.257	1.257-1.258	1.5023	1.5024	0.0014-③ 0.0030	0.003-① 0.007
1985	90.9 (1490)	1.6515-1.6522	1.6504-1.6510	1.6504-1.6510	1.6504-1.6510	1.6515-1.6522	1.7368	1.7368	0.0014-② 0.0030	0.001-① 0.007
	121.9 (1998)	1.257-1.258	1.256-1.257	1.256-1.257	1.256-1.257	1.257-1.258	1.5023	1.5024	0.0014-② 0.0030	0.003-① 0.007
	Diesel 121.9 (1998)	1.258-1.259	1.258-1.259	1.258-1.259	1.258-1.259	1.258-1.259	1.744	1.783	0.00098-0.00260	0.006-0.008

CAMSHAFT SPECIFICATIONS

All measurements given in inches.

| Year | Engine Displacement cu. in. (cc) | Journal Diameter | | | | | Lobe Lift | | Bearing Clearance | Camshaft End Play |
		1	2	3	4	5	In.	Ex.		
1986	97.4 (159)	1.710–1.711	1.709–1.710	1.709–1.710	1.709–1.710	1.710–1.711	1.439–1.443	1.439–1.443	0.001– ③ 0.003	0.0020–0.0071
	121.9 (1998)	1.257–1.258	1.256–1.257	1.256–1.257	1.256–1.257	1.257–1.258	1.5023	1.5024	0.0014– ② 0.0033	0.003– ① 0.006
1987–88	97.4 (1597)	1.710–1.711	1.709–1.710	1.709–1.710	1.709–1.710	1.710–1.711	1.439–1.443	1.439–1.443	0.001– ⑤ 0.003	0.0020–0.0071
	121.9 (1998)	1.257–1.258	1.256–1.257	1.256–1.257	1.256–1.257	1.257–1.258	1.5023	1.5024	0.0014– ② 0.0033	0.003– ① 0.006

ROTOR AND HOUSING SPECIFICATIONS—ROTARY ENGINE

All measurements are given in inches.

| Engine Type | Rotor | | Housings | | | | | |
| | Side Clearance | Width | Front and Rear | | Rotor | | Intermediate | |
			Distortion Limit	Wear Limit	Width	Distortion Limit	Distortion Limit	Wear Limit
12A	0.0047–0.0075	2.7481	0.0016	0.0039	2.7559	0.0024	0.0016	0.0039
13B	0.0047–0.0083	3.142–3.144	0.0016	0.0039	3.1485–3.1500	0.0024	0.0016	0.0039

SEAL CLEARANCES—ROTARY ENGINE

All measurements are given in inches.

| Engine Type | Apex Seals | | | | Side Seal | | | |
| | To Side Housing | | To Rotor Groove | | To Rotor Groove | | To Corner Seal | |
	Normal	Limit	Normal	Limit	Normal	Limit	Normal	Limit
12A	0.0051–0.0075	—	0.0020–0.0035	0.0059	0.0012–0.0031	0.0039	0.0020–0.0059	0.0157
13B	0.0051–0.0075	—	0.0024–0.0040	0.0059	0.0011–0.0031	0.0039	0.0020–0.0059	0.016

SEAL SPECIFICATIONS—ROTARY ENGINE

All measurements are given in inches.

| Engine Type | Apex Seal | | Corner Seal Width (OD) | Side Seal | | Oil Seal Contact Width of Lip |
	Normal Height	Height Limit		Thickness	Height	
12A	0.33470	0.27560	0.4331	0.0394	0.1378	0.0197
13B	0.31500	0.25600	0.4327–0.4336	0.0260–0.0270	0.1122–0.1240	0.020

OD Outside diameter

CRANKSHAFT AND CONNECTING ROD SPECIFICATIONS
All measurements are given in inches.

Year	Engine Displacement cu. in. (cc)	Crankshaft Main Brg. Journal Dia.	Crankshaft Main Brg. Oil Clearance	Crankshaft Shaft End-play	Thrust on No.	Connecting Rod Journal Diameter	Connecting Rod Oil Clearance	Connecting Rod Side Clearance
1981	90.9 (1490)	1.9661–1.9668	0.0009–0.0017	0.004–0.006	5	1.5724–1.5734	0.0009–0.0019	0.004–0.010
	120.2 (1970)	2.4804	0.0012–0.0020	0.003–0.009	5	2.0866	0.001–0.003	0.004–0.008
1982	90.9 (1490)	1.9661–1.9668	0.0009–0.0017	0.004–0.006	5	1.5724–1.5734	0.0009–0.0019	0.004–0.010
	120.2 (1970)	2.4804	0.0012–0.0020	0.003–0.009	5	2.0866	0.001–0.003	0.004–0.008
1983	90.9 (1490)	1.9661–1.9668	0.0009–0.0017	0.004–0.006	5	1.5724–1.5734	0.0009–0.0019	0.004–0.010
	121.9 (1998)	2.359–2.360	0.0012–0.0019	0.0031–0.0071	3	2.005–2.006	0.0010–0.0026	0.004–0.010
1984	90.9 (1490)	1.9661–1.9668	0.0009–0.0017	0.004–0.006	5	1.5724–1.5734	0.0009–0.0019	0.004–0.010
	121.9 (1998)	2.359–2.360	0.0012–0.0019	0.0031–0.0071	3	2.005–2.006	0.0010–0.0026	0.004–0.010
1985	90.9 (1490)	1.9661–1.9668	0.0009–0.0017	0.004–0.006	5	1.5724–1.5734	0.0009–0.0019	0.004–0.010
	121.9 (1998)	2.359–2.360	0.0012–0.0019	0.0031–0.0071	3	2.005–2.006	0.0010–0.0026	0.004–0.010
	121.9 (1998) Diesel	2.360–2.361	0.0012–0.0019	0.0016–0.0110	3	2.0055–2.0063	0.0012–0.0024	0.0043–0.0102
1986	97.4 (1597)	1.9662–1.9668	0.0011–0.0027	0.0031–0.0071	4	1.7693–1.7699	0.0011–0.0027	0.0043–0.0103
	121.9 (1998)	2.359–2.360	0.0012–0.0019	0.0031–0.0071	3	2.005–2.006	0.0010–0.0026	0.004–0.010
1987–88	97.4 (1597)	1.9662–1.9668	0.0011–0.0027	0.0031–0.0071	4	1.7693–1.7699	0.0011–0.0027	0.0043–0.0103
	121.9 (1998)	2.359–2.360	0.0012–0.0019	0.0031–0.0071	3	2.005–2.006	0.0010–0.0026	0.004–0.010

VALVE SPECIFICATIONS—PISTON ENGINE
(All measurements in inches unless noted.)

Year	Engine Displacement cu. in. (cc)	Seat Angle (deg.)	Face Angle (deg.)	Spring Square-ness Limit	Spring Free Length Outer	Spring Free Length Inner	Stem-to-Guide Clearance Intake	Stem-to-Guide Clearance Exhaust	Stem Diameter Intake	Stem Diameter Exhaust
1981	90.9 (1490)	45	45	0.059	1.705	1.705	0.0007–0.0021	0.0007–0.0021	0.3164	0.3163
	120.2 (1970)	45	45	①	②	②	0.0007–0.0021	0.0007–0.0021	0.3150	0.3150
1982	90.9 (1490)	45	45	0.059	1.705	1.705	0.0007–0.0021	0.0007–0.0021	0.3164	0.3163
	120.2 (1970)	45	45	①	②	②	0.0007–0.0021	0.0007–0.0021	0.3150	0.3150

VALVE SPECIFICATIONS—PISTON ENGINE
(All measurements in inches unless noted.)

Year	Engine Displacement cu. in. (cc)	Seat Angle (deg.)	Spring Face Angle (deg.)	Spring Squareness Limit	Free Length Outer	Free Length Inner	Stem-to-Guide Clearance Intake	Stem-to-Guide Clearance Exhaust	Stem Diameter Intake	Stem Diameter Exhaust
1983	90.9 (1490)	45	45	0.059	1.705	1.705	0.0007–0.0021	0.0007–0.0021	0.3164	0.3163
	121.9 (1998)	45	45	0.071	2.047	1.732	0.0010–0.0024	0.0010–0.0024	0.3177–0.3185	0.3159–0.3165
1984	90.9 (1490)	45	45	0.059	1.705	1.705	0.0007–0.0021	0.0007–0.0021	0.3164	0.3163
	121.9 (1998)	45	45	0.071	2.047	1.732	0.0010–0.0024	0.0010–0.0024	0.3177–0.3185	0.3159–0.3165
1985	90.9 (1490)	45	45	0.059	1.705	1.705	0.0007–0.0021	0.0007–0.0021	0.3164	0.3163
	121.9 (1998)	45	45	0.071	2.047	1.732	0.0010–0.0024	0.0010–0.0024	0.3177–0.3185	0.3159–0.3165
	121.9 (1998) Diesel	45	45	0.071	2.047	1.732	0.0016–0.0031	0.0020–0.0031	0.3138–0.3144	0.3136–0.3142
1986	97.4 (1597)	45	45	0.059	1.717	1.717	0.0018–0.0051	0.0019–0.0053	0.274–0.275	0.274–0.275
	121.9 (1998)	45	45	0.071	2.047	1.732	0.0010–0.0024	0.0010–0.0024	0.3177–0.3185	0.3159–0.3165
1987–88	97.4 (1597)	45	45	0.059	1.717	1.717	0.0018–0.0051	0.0019–0.0053	0.274–0.275	0.274–0.275
	121.9 (1998)	45	45	0.071	2.047	1.732	0.0010–0.0024	0.0010–0.0024	0.3177–0.3185	0.3159–0.3165

Test Pressure (lbs. @ in.)
Outer: 31.4 @ 1.339
Inner: 17.9 @ 1.260
Installed Height (in.)
Outer: 1.339
Inner: 1.260

PISTON AND RING SPECIFICATIONS
All measurements are given in inches.

Year	Engine Displacement cu. in. (cc)	Piston Clearance	Ring Gap Top Compression	Ring Gap Bottom Compression	Ring Gap Oil Control	Ring Side Clearance Top Compression	Ring Side Clearance Bottom Compression	Ring Side Clearance Oil Control
1981	90.9 (1490)	0.0010–0.0026	0.0012–0.0028	0.0012–0.0028	—	0.008–0.016	0.008–0.016	0.012–0.035
	120.2 (1970)	0.0014–0.0030	0.0012–0.0028	0.0012–0.0028	—	0.008–0.016	0.008–0.016	0.012–0.035
1982	90.9 (1490)	0.0010–0.0026	0.0012–0.0028	0.0012–0.0028	—	0.008–0.016	0.008–0.016	0.012–0.035
	120.2 (1970)	0.0019–0.0025	0.0012–0.0028	0.0012–0.0028	—	0.008–0.016	0.008–0.016	0.012–0.035
1983	90.9 (1990)	0.0010–0.0026	0.0012–0.0028	0.0012–0.0028	—	0.008–0.016	0.008–0.016	0.012–0.035
	121.9 (1998)	0.0014–0.0030	0.0012–0.0028	0.0012–0.0028	—	0.008–0.014	0.006–0.012	0.012–0.035

PISTON AND RING SPECIFICATIONS

All measurements are given in inches.

| Year | Engine Displacement cu. in. (cc) | Piston Clearance | Ring Gap | | | Ring Side Clearance | | |
			Top Compression	Bottom Compression	Oil Control	Top Compression	Bottom Compression	Oil Control
1984	90.9 (1490)	0.0010–0.0026	0.0012–0.0028	0.0012–0.0028	—	0.008–0.016	0.008–0.016	0.012–0.035
	121.9 (1998)	0.0014–0.0030	0.0012–0.0028	0.0012–0.0028	—	0.008–0.014	0.006–0.012	0.012–0.035
1985	90.9 (1490)	0.0010–0.0026	0.0012–0.0028	0.0012–0.0028	—	0.008–0.016	0.008–0.016	0.012–0.035
	121.9 (1998)	0.0014–0.0030	0.0012–0.0028	0.0012–0.0028	—	0.008–0.014	0.006–0.012	0.012–0.035
	121.9 (1998) Diesel	0.0012–0.0020	0.0020–0.0035	0.0016–0.0031	—	0.0079–0.0157	0.0079–0.0157	0.0079–0.0157
1986	97.4 (1597)	0.0015–0.0020	0.0010–0.0030	0.0010–0.0030	—	0.0080–0.0160	0.0060–0.0120	0.0120–0.0350
	121.9 (1998)	0.0014–0.0030	0.0012–0.0028	0.0012–0.0028	—	0.008–0.014	0.006–0.012	0.012–0.035
1987–88	97.4 (1597)	0.0015–0.0020	0.0010–0.0030	0.0010–0.0030	—	0.0080–0.0160	0.0060–0.0120	0.0120–0.0350
	121.9 (1998)	0.0014–0.0030	0.0012–0.0028	0.0012–0.0028	—	0.008–0.014	0.006–0.012	0.012–0.035

TORQUE SPECIFICATIONS—ROTARY ENGINE

All figures in ft. lbs.

| Engine Displacement cu. in. (cc) | Front Cover | Bearing Housing | Rear Stationary Gear | Eccentric Shaft Pulley Bolt | Flywheel-to-Eccentric Shaft Nut | Manifolds | | Oil Pan | Tension Bolts |
						Intake	Exhaust		
70 (1146)	15	15	15	72–87	289–362	14–19	23–34	6–8	23–27
80 (1308)	12–17	12–17	12–17	80–98	290–360	14–19	23–34	6–8	23–29

TORQUE SPECIFICATIONS

All readings in ft. lbs.

| Year | Engine Displacement cu. in. (cc) | Cylinder Head Bolts | Main Bearing Bolts | Rod Bearing Bolts | Crankshaft Pulley Bolts | Flywheel Bolts | Manifold | | Spark Plugs |
							Intake	Exhaust	
1981	90.9 (1490)	56–59	48–51	22–26	80–87	65–69	14–19	14–19	11–17
	120.2 (1970)	59–64	61–65	29–33	101–108	112–118	14–19	16–21	11–17
1982	90.9 (1490)	56–59	48–51	22–26	80–87	65–69 ①	14–19	14–19	11–17
	120.2 (1970)	65–69	61–65	29–33	101–108	112–118	14–19	16–21	11–17
1983	90.9 (1490)	56–59	48–51	22–26	80–87	65–69 ①	14–19	14–19	11–17
	121.9 (1998)	59–64 ②	61–65	37–41	80–87	71–76	14–19	16–20	11–17
1984	90.9 (1490)	56–59	48–51	22–26	80–87	65–69 ①	14–19	14–19	11–17
	121.9 (1998)	59–64 ②	61–65	37–41	80–87	71–76	14–19	16–20	11–17
1985	90.9 (1490)	56–59	48–51	22–26	80–87	65–69 ①	14–19	14–19	11–17
	121.9 (1998)	59–64 ②	61–65	37–41	108–112	71–76	14–19	16–20	11–17
	121.9 (1998) Diesel	③	61–65	51–54	116–123	130–137	14–19	16–20	N/A

TORQUE SPECIFICATIONS
All readings in ft. lbs.

Year	Engine Displacement cu. in. (cc)	Cylinder Head Bolts	Main Bearing Bolts	Rod Bearing Bolts	Crankshaft Pulley Bolts	Flywheel Bolts	Manifold Intake	Manifold Exhaust	Spark Plugs
1986	121.9 (1998)	59–64 ②	61–65	37–41	108–112	71–76	14–19	16–20	11–17
	97.4 (1597)	56–60	40–43	37–41	36–45	71–76	14–19	12–17	11–17
1987-88	121.9 (1998)	59–64 ②	61–65	37–41	108–112	71–76	14–19	16–20	11–17
	97.4 (1597)	56–60	40–43	37–41	36–45	71–76	14–19	12–17	11–17

① Auto Trans: 51–61
② Warm: 69–80
③ Torque to 22 ft. lbs. Then turn 90° + 90° more.

BRAKE SPECIFICATIONS
All measurements in inches unless noted.

Year	Model	Lug Nut Torque (ft. lbs.)	Master Cylinder Bore	Brake Disc Minimum Thickness	Brake Disc Maximum Runout	Standard Brake Drum Diameter	Minimum Lining Thickness Front	Minimum Lining Thickness Rear
1981	GLC	65–80	¹³⁄₁₆	0.390	0.0040	7.090	0.040	0.040
	626	65–80	⁷⁄₈	0.4724	0.0040	9.0001	0.040	0.039
	RX7	65–87	0.8125	0.6693	0.0039	7.8741	0.039	0.039
1982	GLC	65–80	¹³⁄₁₆	0.390	0.0040	7.090	0.040	0.040
	626	65–80	⁷⁄₈	0.4724	0.0040	9.0001	0.040	0.039
	RX7	65–87	0.8125	0.6693	0.0039	7.8741	0.039	0.039
1983	GLC	65–80	¹³⁄₁₆	0.390	0.0040	7.090	0.118	0.040
	626	65–80	⁷⁄₈	0.550	0.0040	7.8741	0.040	0.040
	RX7	65–87	0.8130	0.6693 ①	0.0039	7.8741	0.039	0.039
1984	GLC	65–80	¹³⁄₁₆	0.390	0.0040	7.090	0.118	0.040
	626	65–80	⁷⁄₈	0.550	0.0040	7.8741	0.040	0.040
	RX7	65–80	0.8130	0.6693 ①	0.0039	7.8741	0.039	0.039
1985	GLC	65–80	¹³⁄₁₆	0.390	0.0040	7.090	0.118	0.040
	626	65–80	⁷⁄₈	0.550	0.0040	7.8741	0.040	0.040
	626 Diesel	65–80	⁷⁄₈	0.710	0.0040	7.8741	0.040	0.040
	RX7	65–87	0.8130	0.6693 ①	0.0039	7.8741	0.039	0.039
1986	323	65–87	0.8750	0.630 ②	0.0030	7.870	0.120	0.040
	626	65–87	⁷⁄₈	0.710 ②	0.0040	7.870	0.118	0.040
	RX7	65–87	0.8750	0.790 ③	0.0040	—	0.120	0.040
1987-88	323	65–87	0.8750	0.630 ②	0.0030	7.870	0.120	0.040
	626	65–87	⁷⁄₈	0.710 ②	0.0040	7.870	0.118	0.040
	RX7	65–87	0.8750	0.790 ③	0.0040	—	0.120	0.040

NOTE: Minimum lining thickness is as recommended by the manufacturer. Due to variations in state inspection regulations, the minimum allowable thickness may be different than specified.

① Rear rotor:
 Solid—0.3543
 Ventilated—0.7870
② Rear disc: 0.350
③ Rear disc:
 14 in. wheels—0.310
 15 in. wheels—0.710

WHEEL ALIGNMENT

Year	Model	Caster Range (deg.)	Caster Preferred Setting (deg.)	Camber Range (deg.)	Camber Preferred Setting (deg.)	Toe-in (in.)	Steering Axis Inclination (deg.)
1981	GLC Wagon	3/4P–1 3/4P	1 1/4P	3/4P–2 1/4P	1 1/2P	0–1/4	8 1/4
	GLC	7/16P–1 7/16P	15/16P	1 3/16P–2 11/16P	1 15/16P	1/8–1/8	12 3/16
	626	3/4P–1 3/4P	1 1/4P	2 15/16P–3 15/16P	3 7/16P	0–1/4	10 9/16
	RX-7	1/2P–1 1/2P	1P	①	②	0–1/4	10 3/4
1982	GLC Wagon	3/4P–1 3/4P	1 1/4P	3/4P–2 1/4P	1 1/2P	0–1/4	8 1/4
	GLC	7/16P–1 7/16P	15/16P	1 3/16P–2 11/16P	1 15/16P	1/8–1/8	12 3/16
	626	3/4P–1 3/4P	1 1/4P	2 15/16P–3 15/16P	3 7/16P	0–1/4	10 9/16
	RX-7	1/2P–1 1/2P	1P	①	②	0–1/4	10 3/4
1983	GLC Wagon	1/4P–1 1/4P	3/4P	13/16P–2 5/16P	1 9/16P	0–1/4	8 1/4
	GLC	7/16P–1 7/16P	15/16P	1 3/16P–2 11/16P	1 15/16P	1/8–1/8	12 3/16
	626	3/16N–13/16P	5/16P	15/16P–2 7/16P	1 11/16P	0–1/4 ⑤	12 15/16
	RX-7	1/2P–1 1/2P	1P	①	②	0–1/4	10 3/4
1984	GLC	7/16P–1 7/16P	15/16P	1 3/16P–2 11/16P	1 15/16P	1/8–1/8	12 3/16
	626	3/16N–13/16P	5/16P	15/16P–2 7/16P	1 11/16P	0–1/4 ⑤	12 15/16
	RX-7 ③	1/2P–1 1/2P	1P	①	②	0–1/4	10 3/4
	RX-7 ④	1/16P–1 1/16P	9/16P	①	②	0–1/4	11 5/16
1985	GLC	7/16P–1 7/16P	15/16P	1 3/16P–2 11/16P	1 15/16P	1/8–1/8	12 3/16
	626	3/16N–1 11/16P	5/16P	15/16P–2 7/16P	1 11/16P	0–1/4 ⑤	12 15/16
	RX-7 ③	1/2P–1 1/2P	1P	①	②	0–1/4	10 3/4
	RX-7 ④	1/16P–1 1/16P	9/16P	①	②	0–1/4	11 5/16
1986	626	3/16N–1 11/16P	5/16P	15/16P–2 7/16P	1 11/16P	0–1/4 ⑤	12 15/16
	323	1/16P–1 9/16P	13/16P	13/16P–2 5/16P	1 9/16P	3/64–13/16	12 3/8
	RX-7	⑦	5/16P	4 5/8	—	0–1/4 ⑧	13 3/4
1987–88	626	3/16N–1 11/16P	5/16P	15/16P–2 7/16P	1 11/16P	0–1/4 ⑤	12 15/16
	323	1/16P–1 9/16P	13/16P	13/16P–2 5/16P	1 9/16P	3/64–13/16	12 3/8
	323 Wagon	3/4N–3/4P	0P	—	—	3/64–13/64	12 3/8
	RX-7	⑦	5/16P	4 5/8	—	0–1/4 ⑧	13 3/4

① Right side wheel 3 11/16P–4 11/16P
   Left side wheel 3 3/16P–4 3/16P
② Right side wheel 4 13/16P
   Left side wheel 3 11/16P
③ 13 inch tires
④ 14 inch tires
⑤ 1/8 in. rear
⑥ Rear: 7/16N–9/16P
⑦ Rear: 1 1/4N–1/4N–3/4 preferred
⑧ Rear: 0 in.

TUNE-UP PROCEDURES

Ignition Timing

ROTARY ENGINE

1. Warm the engine up until it reaches operating temperature. Connect a tachometer as per the manufacturer's instructions. On automatic transmission cars, securely apply the handbrake, block the wheels, and put the car in "Drive". Reading the tach as for a conventional four cylinder engine, verify that the engine is running at its normal idle speed. If not, adjust idle speed to specification.

2. Stop the engine and connect a timing light to the leading (lower) spark plug on the front rotor. Then, restart the engine. Aim the timing light at the pin on the front housing cover and observe the timing. If the timing pointer does not line up with the first (yellow) notch on the pulley, loosen the locknut and rotate the distributor or crank angle sensor either way until the timing is correct. Tighten the locknut and check that the timing is still correct.

3. Stop the engine and connect the timing light to the trailing (upper) spark plug on the front rotor. Start the engine (putting automatic transmission cars in Drive), and check the trailing timing. The timing pointer should line up with the second (red) notch in the pulley.

4. If the trailing timing is not correct, loosen the vacuum unit attaching screws (manual transmission) or the adjusting lever attaching screws (automatic transmission) and move

Timing marks—1146cc rotary engine

Timing marks—1308cc rotary engine

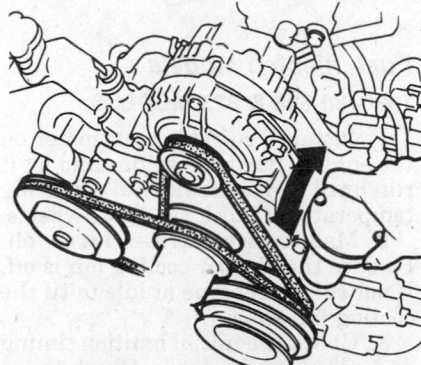

Turn the crank angle sensor to adjust the ignition timing on 1986 and later RX-7

the vacuum unit (manual transmission) or adjusting lever (automatic transmission) in or out until the timing pointer lines up with the second mark on the pulley, then tighten the screws and recheck the timing.

PISTON ENGINE

NOTE: Most models require the ignition timing adjusted with the vacuum line connected to the distributor. Refer to the emission sticker (under the hood) to determine if the vacuum line is to be connected or disconnected and plugged.

1. If required, disconnect and plug the distributor vacuum line.
2. Set the parking brake and block the front wheels. Start and run the engine until it reaches the normal operating temperature. Shut off the engine and connect a tachometer. Restart and check engine idle speed. Adjust if necessary. Shut OFF the engine. On 323 models and fuel injected models, disconnect the black connector at the distributor.

NOTE: Prior to starting the engine, clean off any grease or oil that will prevent seeing the timing marks on the crankshaft pulley. Mark the pulley notches with chalk or paint.

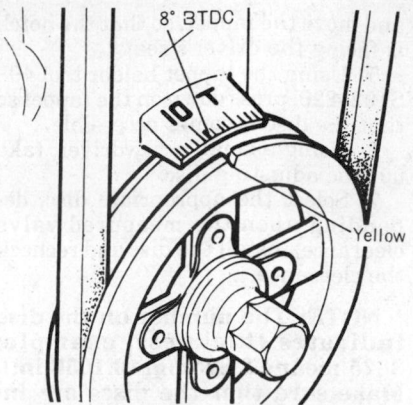

Timing marks—1981 and later GLC

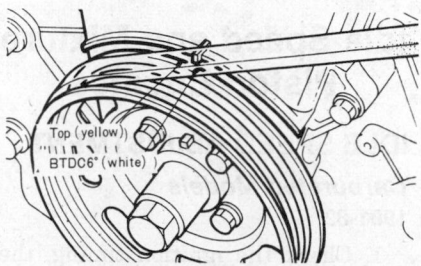

Timing marks—1983–85 626

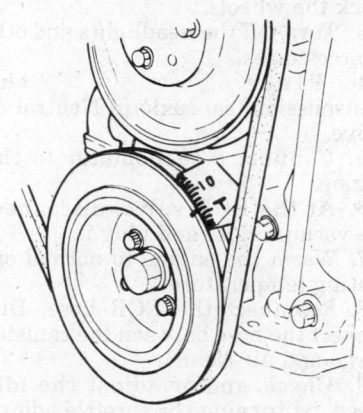

Timing marks—1986 and later 323

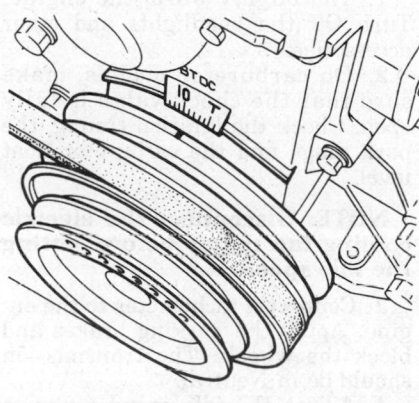

Timing marks—1986 and later 626

3. Connect a timing light to the engine following the manufacturer's instructions. Start the engine and observe the timing by pointing the light at the timing marks on the crankshaft pulley.

NOTE: If the car is equipped with an automatic transmission put the lever in Drive; check emission sticker or tune-up "specs" for requirement.

4. If the timing is not correct, loosen the distributor mounting bolt and rotate the distributor as necessary to produce the correct timing mark alignment. Recheck and/or readjust the timing after tightening the lock bolt, if necessary. Check the idle speed.
5. Reconnect the vacuum line, accelerator switch or bullet connectors, if disconnected. Recheck the idle speed and readjust, if necessary.

Valve Lash

ADJUSTMENT

Gasoline Piston Engines

1. Warm-up the engine and tighten the cylinder head bolts in the proper sequence.
2. Rotate the engine until the No. 1 piston is at top dead center.
   a. Adjust No. 1 and No. 2 cylinder intake valve clearance.
   b. Adjust No. 1 and No. 3 cylinder exhaust valve clearance.
3. Rotate the engine one turn, so that the No. 4 piston is at top dead center.
   a. Adjust the No. 3 and No. 4 cylinder intake valve clearance.
   b. Adjust the No. 2 and No. 4 cylinder exhaust valve clearance.
4. On the 1987–88 626 models, rotate the engine until the No. 1 piston is at top dead center and adjust the valves as follows.
   a. Adjust No. 3 and No. 4 cylinder intake valve clearance.
   b. Adjust No. 2 and No. 4 cylinder exhaust valve clearance.
5. Rotate the engine one turn, so that the No. 4 piston is at top dead center.
   a. Adjust the No. 1 and No. 2 cylinder intake valve clearance.
   b. Adjust the No. 1 and No. 3 cylinder exhaust valve clearance.

Diesel Engines

The camshaft lobes are in direct contact with the valves. The adjustment of the valves is performed by removing the tappet discs and replace the discs with ones of the appropriate thickness.

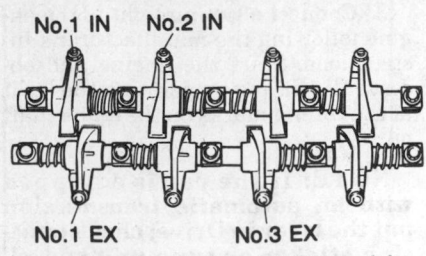

Valve location on 626 and 323 models

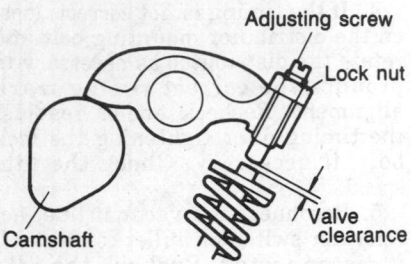

Adjusting valve clearance—typical

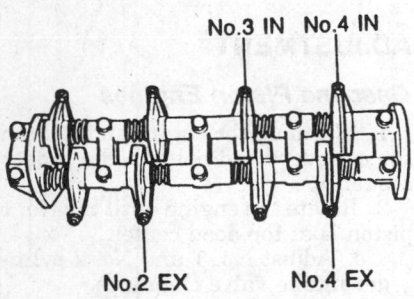

Valve location for the 1987-88 626 models

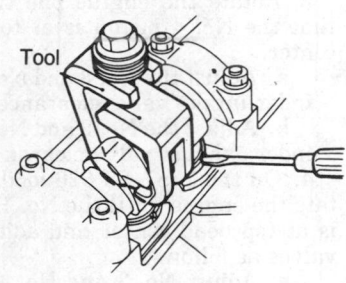

Compressing the valve tappets—626 diesel

1. Remove the cylinder head cover.
2. Turn the crankshaft so that the cylinder being worked on, is positioned with the piston at TDC of the compression stroke (the intake and exhaust cam lobes must be standing up).
3. Using a feeler gauge, check the clearance between the cam lob and tappet disc.

NOTE: On a COLD engine the intake clearance is 0.008–0.012 in. and exhaust is 0.012–0.016.

4. Face the cam intake lobe upward

and move the tappet, so that the notch is facing the driver's seat.
5. Using the tappet holder tool 49–S102–220, press down on the tappet so that the disc becomes accessible.
6. Using a small screwdriver, take out the adjusting disc.
7. Select the appropriate disc, depending upon the measured valve clearance, install the disc and recheck the clearance.

NOTE: The number on the disc indicates thickness, example: 3825 means 3.825mm (0.1056 in.). Make sure that the discs are installed with the numbered side facing down.

Idle Speed and Mixture Piston Engines

IDLE SPEED ADJUSTMENT

Carbureted Models

1981-82

1. Check the ignition timing, the spark plugs and the carburetor float level.
2. Apply the parking brakes and block the wheels.
3. Turn Off the headlights and other accessories.
4. Place the transmission/transaxle in Neutral or Drive.
5. Connect a tachometer to the engine.
6. At the EGR valve, disconnect the vacuum hose and plug it.
7. Warm the engine to normal operating temperature.
8. Reconnect the EGR hose. Disconnect the hose between the canister purge and air cleaner.
9. Check and/or adjust the idle speed, by turning the throttle adjusting screw.

1983-88

1. Thoroughly warm the engine. Turn Off the headlights and other accessories.
2. On carburetor models, make sure that the check valve is fully open. Check the ignition timing, the park plugs and the carburetor float level.

NOTE: Disconnect the electric cooling fan motor before setting the idle speed.

3. Connect a tachometer to the engine. Apply the parking brakes and block the wheels. The transmission should be in Neutral.
4. Adjust the idle speed screw to specifications.
5. Disconnect the tachometer.

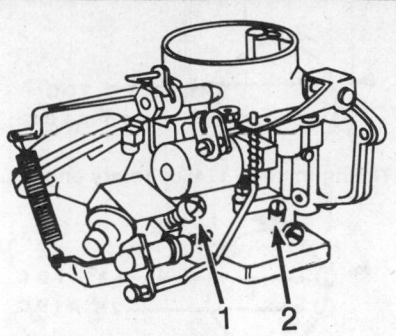

Idle speed (1) and mixture (2) screws—1980–82 piston engine

Fuel Injected Models

1986–88 626 & 323 MODELS

1. Install a suitable tachometer on the engine. Start the engine and let it run until it reaches normal operating temperature. Block the drive wheels.
2. Make sure all accessories are off. Be sure the electric cooling fan is off, if not run the engine at idle until the cooling fan stops.
3. Check the initial ignition timing and adjust as necessary. Check to see if the idle speed is within specifications.

NOTE: Disconnect the air by-pass solenoid connector when checking and adjusting the idle speed at sea level (lower than 3,280 ft.)

4. If the idle speed is not within specifications, adjust it by turning the air adjusting screw.

MIXTURE ADJUSTMENT

Carbureted Models

1981-82

NOTE: Adjustment of the idle mixture requires the use of an exhaust gas analyzer.

1. Adjust the throttle angle opening to specifications. Make the adjustment from the fully closed position.
2. Adjust the idle speed.
3. Using the gas analyzer, check the CO (carbon monoxide) readings. If the CO is between 0.1–2.0%, no further adjustment is needed.
4. Disconnect the air hose between the air silencer and the reed valve, plug the reed valve port.
5. If the CO is not within specification, adjust the CO reading to as close to 0.1% as possible. Use the mixture adjust screw to make this adjustment.
6. Reconnect the air hose and the canister purge hose.
7. Recheck the idle speed, if it shifts from specifications, repeat the above procedures.

1983-85 626 MODELS

NOTE: The following procedures apply to carburetors only. On fuel injected models, mixture is computer-controlled and not adjustable.

NOTE: Before adjusting the idle mixture, check the the idle mixture with a tachometer as described below.

1. Start the engine and let it run until it reaches normal operating temperature.

2. Connect a dwell meter (90 degrees, 4 cylinder) to the BrY wire in the check connector.

3. Check the idle mixture. With the idle speed set at specifications, the idle mixture should be 20–70 degrees on the dwell meter. If the idle mixture is not within specifications, adjust the idle mixture as follows.

4. Remove the carburetor from the vehicle and remove the spring pin from the base of the carburetor.

5. Install the carburetor on the vehicle and start the engine, letting it run until it reaches normal operating temperature.

6. Be sure that the air cleaner is installed and the idle compensator is closed. Connect a tachometer to the engine.

7. Connect a dwell meter (90 degrees, 4 cylinder) to the BrY wire in the check connector of the A/F solenoid valve and read the meter.

8. The reading should be 32–40 degrees at idle. If the reading is not within specification, adjust the idle mixture by turning the idle mixture adjustment screw.

NOTE: If the adjustment cannot be made, it is possible the oxygen sensor is not operating properly or either a broken wire or short in the the wiring between the oxygen sensor and the control unit.

9. Drive the spring pin back into to position in the carburetor.

1983–88 GLC AND 323 (CARBURETED) MODELS

NOTE: The following procedures apply to carburetors only. On fuel injected models, mixture is computer-controlled and not adjustable.

NOTE: Do not fix the spring pin to lock the mixture adjust screw until the adjustment is performed.

1. Start the engine, letting it run until it reaches normal operating temperature. Connect a tachometer to the engine. On the 323 models,

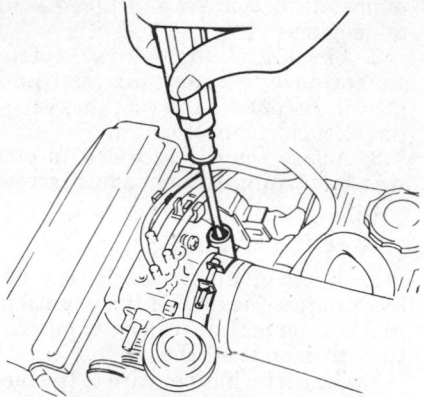

Idle speed adjustment screw on fuel injected engines

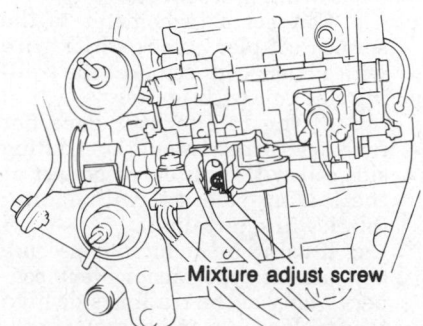

Mixture adjust screw

Mixture adjusting screw location - 1983-88 models

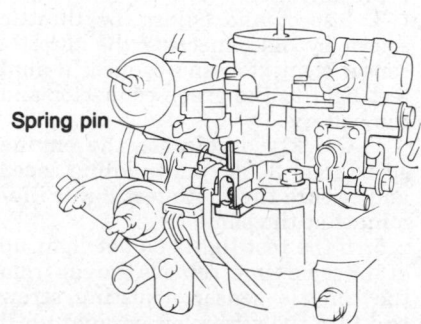

Spring pin

Location of spring pin on carburetor

siconnect and plug the secondary hoses from the reed valves.

2. Connect a dwell meter (90 degrees, 4 cylinder) to the Y wire in the check connector of the A/F solenoid valve and read the meter.

3. The reading should be 32–40 degrees at idle. If the reading is not within specification, adjust the idle mixture by turning the idle mixture adjustment screw.

NOTE: If the adjustment cannot be made, it is probably because of a faulty O_2 sensor, or either a broken wire or a short in the wiring between the O_2 sensor and the control unit.

4. On the 323 models, insert an ex-

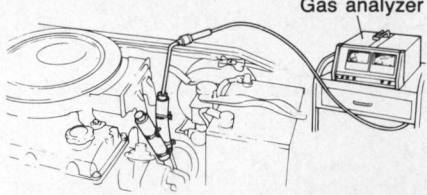

Gas analyzer

Adjusting idle mixture on 323 models. Insert the probe into the secondary air hose as shown

haust gas analyzer probe into the secondary air hose and plug the opening to prevent leakage. Adjust the CO to 1.5–2.5% by turning the idle mixture screw.

5. Be sure that the idle speed is set at specification. If not, adjust as necessary by using the throttle adjust screw. Fix the spring pin to lock the mixture adjustment screw.

Fuel Injected Models

Because a automatic compensation function of the air fuel mixture has been built into the the Electronic Gasoline Injection (EGI) control unit, it is not necessary to check and adjust the idle mixture.

Idle Speed and Mixture Rotary Engine

Idle speed changes with air temperature. It is suggested by Mazda that the idle adjustment be made indoors with a floor fan blowing through the radiator to assist in cooling. Whenever operating an engine indoors, make certain that provision is made for removal of exhaust gases. Idle speed should be adjusted with the engine at normal operating temperature, all accessories off and fuel tank cap removed. If equipped with an automatic transmission, place it in Drive, with the parking brake set firmly.

IDLE SPEED ADJUSTMENT

Carbureted Models

1981-85 12A ENGINE

1. Start the engine and let it run until it reaches normal operating temperature.

2. Connect a tachometer to the engine and adjust the idle speed as necessary, by turning the throttle adjusting screw.

3. Inspect and adjust the throttle sensor by disconnecting the brown connector and connect a dual test light to the green connector and the battery.

4. Quickly decelerate the engine speed from 3000 rpm to idling speed

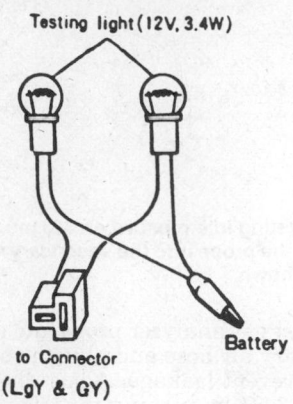

Testing light (12V, 3.4W)

to Connector
(LgY & GY)

Battery

Connecting the test lights to the green connector

Idle speed adjustment screw location on the 13B engine

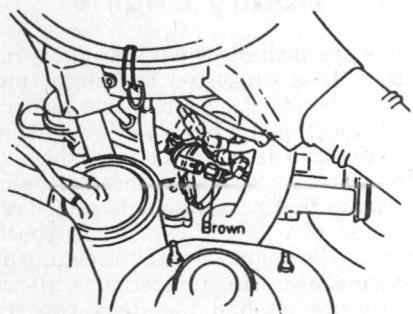

Brown

Disconnecting the brown connector

and be sure that both test lights illuminate at the same time.

5. If the test lights do not light up at the same time, remove the cap from the throttle sensor adjusting screw and turn the screw left or right until both test light illuminate at the same time.

6. Disconnect the test light and reconnect the brown connector.

7. If the idle speed is not within specifications, adjust the idle speed by turning the throttle adjusting screw until the idle speed is within specifications.

Fuel Injected Models

1985 13B ENGINE

1. Start the engine and let it run until it reaches normal operating

temperature, connect a tachometer to the engine.

2. Check and adjust the throttle sensor as necessary (as outlined above), disconnect the vent and vacuum solenoid connector.

3. Adjust the idling speed to 800 rpm by turning the air adjust screw (AAS).

1986-88 13B ENGINE

1. Switch off all accessories engine. Start the engine and let it run until it reaches normal operating temperature, then shut off the engine.

2. Connect a jumper wire to the terminals of the initial set coupler. Before adjusting the idle speed complete the foloowing procedures:

   a. Connect a tachometer to the service coupler (black/white wire with a black connector) at the trailing side coil with igniter.

   b. If the tachometer does not function correctly on the trailing side coil with igniter, reconnect at the leading side coil with igniter (black/white terminal).

   c. If using an inductive (secondary pick-up type tachometer), connect it only at the trailing side high tension leads (spark wires). If connected on the leading side coil with igniter, it will not function properly.

3. Inspect and adjust the throttle sensor by disconnecting the throttle sensor connector and connect a dual test light to the green connector and the battery.

4. Quickly decelerate the engine speed from 3000 rpm to idling speed and be sure that both test lights illuminate at the same time.

5. If the test lights do not light up at the same time, remove the cap from the throttle sensor adjusting screw and turn the screw left or right until both test light illuminate at the same time.

6. Disconnect the test light and reconnect the throttle sensor connector.

7. Remove the blind cap and adjust the idle speed by turning the air adjust screw.

8. Install the blind cap and disconnect the jumper wire from the initial coupler. Be sure to remove the jumper wire, otherwise the engine performance will be reduced.

IDLE MIXTURE ADJUSTMENT

Carbureted Models

1981-83 12A ENGINE

1. Disconnect the vacuum line at the idle compensator in the air cleaner and plug the line.

2. Check the dash pot rod and the A/C throttle opener. Make certain these devices are not stopping the throttle linkage from returning to a fully seated idle stop position.

3. Connect a tachometer to the negative terminal of the leading coil and a good ground. The leading coil is the rear coil on the driver's side fender well. Disconnect the richer solenoid connector, if equipped.

4. Bring the engine up to operating temperature.

5. Set vehicles equipped with automatic transmissions in the Drive position. Adjust the idle stop screw to obtain 750 rpm in drive. Adjust manual transmission equipped vehicles to 750 rpm in Neutral.

6. Remove the throttle body. Using a hacksaw, cut the idle limiter cap from the idle mixture screw. Remove and install a new idle mixture screw.

7. Adjust the idle mixture to obtain the highest rpm before it starts to drop. Reset the idle speed to specification. Repeat these procedures until both the highest rpm and the idle speed are correct. Install a replacement limiter cap on the idle mixture screw.

NOTE: After adjusting the speed, adjust the throttle sensor on the carburetor.

1983-85 12A ENGINE

1. Remove the carburetor from the vehicle. Separated the the main body from the throttle body.

2. Use a hack saw and cut through the limiter cap and mixture screw about 0.4 in. (10mm) from the end of the cap.

3. Remove the mixture screw. Install a new mixture screw and tighten it until it is fully seated. Back the screw out three turns.

4. Install the carburetor back on the vehicle and start the engine, letting it run until normal operating temperature has been reached. Check the idle speed and adjust as necessary by turning the throttle adjust screw.

5. Set the idle speed at the highest rpm by backing out the mixture adjusting screw.

6. Reset the idle speed by turning the throttle adjust screw, 770 rpm in neutral for manual transmission 870 rpm in neutral for automatic transmission.

7. Screw in the idle mixture screw and adjust the idle speed to 750 rpm for manual transmission and 840 rpm for automatic transmission.

8. On vehicles equipped with automatic transmission, shift the selector to the drive position and adjust the idle speed to 750 rpm by turning the throttle adjust screw.

Throttle adjusting screw—RX-7 models

Mixture adjusting screw—RX-7 models

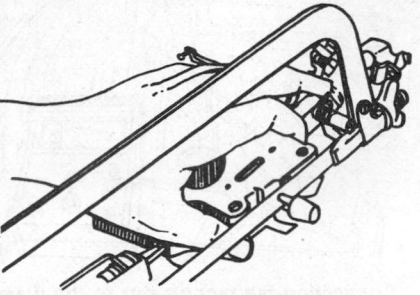

Cutting through the mixture limiter cap

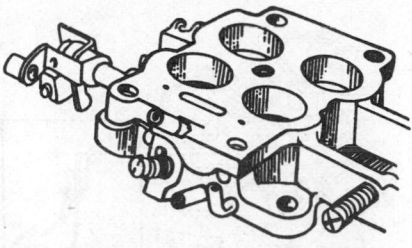

New mixture screw installation

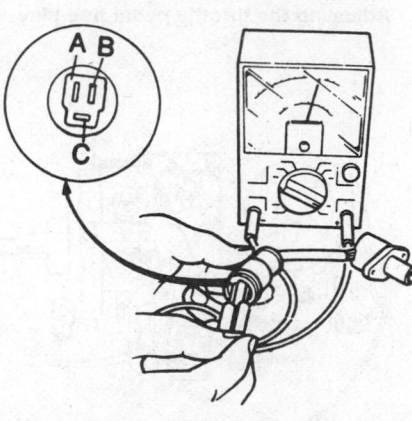

Connecting the ohmmeter to the variable resistor

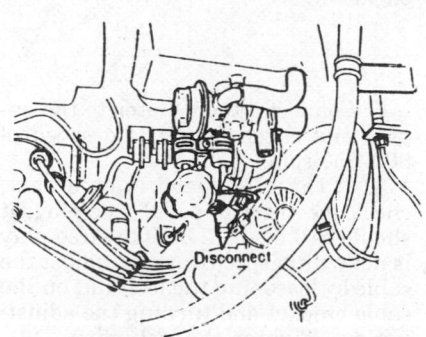

Disconnecting the vent/vacuum solenoid valve connector

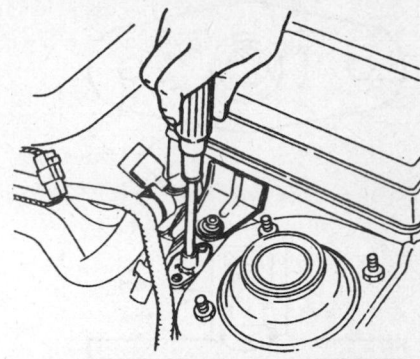

Adjusting the variable resistor

Connecting the jumper wire to the initial coupling

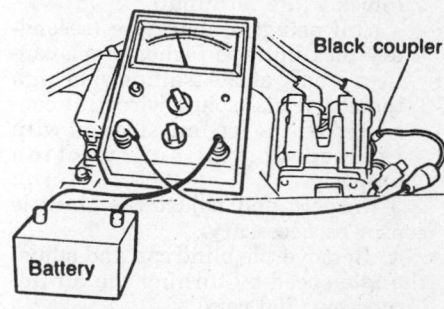

Connecting the tachometer to the black connector

9. After the idle mixture adjustment is completed, fit an idle limiter cap onto the mixture adjust screw securely.

10. After adjusting the idle speed, the throttle sensor on the carburetor should be adjusted as previously outlined in this section.

Fuel Injected Models

NOTE: The idle mixture adjustment usually is not necessary. The idle mixture adjustment should be adjusted when the variable resistor is replaced. Disconnect the variable resistor connector and connect an ohmmeter to the variable resistor. If the continuity (resistance) does not exist, replace the variable resistor and adjust the idle mixture. Resistance from terminal A to C should be 0.5–4.5 ohms and from terminal B to C, 0.5–4.5 ohms.

1981–85 13B ENGINE

1. Start the engine and let it run until it reaches normal operating temperature, connect a tachometer to the engine.

2. Check and adjust the throttle sensor as necessary. Disconnect the vent and vacuum solenoid connector.

3. Adjust the idling speed to 800 rpm by turning the air adjust screw (AAS).

4. Set the idle speed at the highest by turning the variable resistor and then readjust the idle speed to 800 rpm by turning the air adjust screw (AAS).

5. Turn the variable resistor counter-clockwise until the engine speed reaches 780 rpm then turn it clockwise until the engine speed reaches 800 rpm.

6. Connect the vent and vacuum solenoid connector, fill up the head of the adjust screw with the adhesive agent part # N304–23–795 or equivalent.

1986–88 13B ENGINE

1. Switch off all accessories engine. Start the engine and let it run until it reaches normal operating temperature, then shut off the engine.

2. Connect a jumper wire to the terminals of the initial set coupler. Be-

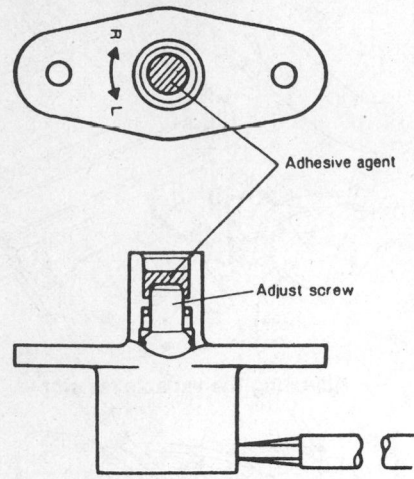

Sealing the mixture adjustment screw

fore adjusting the idle speed complete the folowing procedures:

   a. Connect a tachometer to the service coupler (black/white wire with a black connector) at the trailing side coil with igniter.

   b. If the tachometer does not function correctly on the trailing side coil with igniter, reconnect at the leading side coil with igniter (black/white terminal).

   c. If using an inductive (secondary pick-up type tachometer), connect it only at the trailing side high tension leads (spark wires). If connected on the leading side coil with igniter, it will not function properly.

3. Inspect and adjust the throttle sensor as necessary.

4. Remove the blind cap and adjust the idle speed by turning the air adjust screw (750 rpm).

5. Set the variable speed to its highest rpm by turning the varibale resistor. Reset the idle speed to 750 rpm.

6. Turn the variable resistor counter-clockwise until the engine speed reaches 730 rpm then turn it clockwise until the engine speed reaches 750 rpm.

7. Install the blind cap and disconnect the jumper wire from the initial coupler. Be sure to remove the jumper wire, otherwise the engine performance will be reduced.

8. Plug up the head of the adjust screw with the adhesive agent part # N304-23-795 or equivalent.

Idle Speed Diesel Engine

ADJUSTMENT

1. Warm the engine to normal operating temperatures.

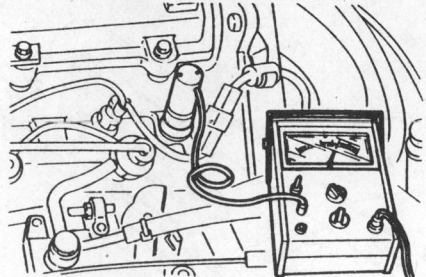

Connecting the tachometer to the diesel engine

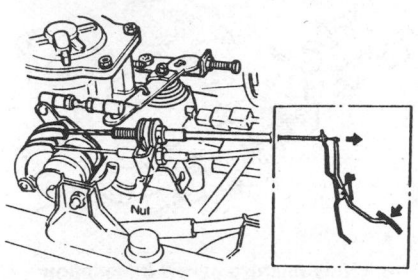

Adjusting the throttle pedal free-play

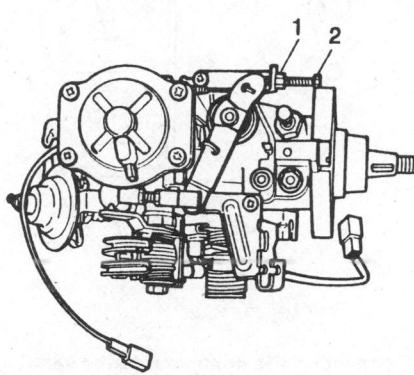

Adjusting the idle speed on the 626 diesel engine

2. Connect a tachometer to the engine and check for an idle speed of 800–850 rpm.

3. If the idle speed is incorrect, check the throttle pedal free-play, it should be 0.04–0.12 in. If the free-play is not within specifications, adjust the cable by loosening the lock-nut on the cable bracket and turning the adjusting nut. Tighten the lock-nut.

4. Check the idle speed. Adjust the idle speed to 800–850 rpm, by loosening the lock-nut on the idle adjusting bolt. Turn the bolt clockwise to increase the idle speed and counterclockwise to decrease the idle speed. Tighten the lock-nut.

5. Remove the tachometer.

ENGINE ELECTRICAL

Distributor

REMOVAL & INSTALLATION

Rotary Engines

NOTE: 1986-88 13B engines use a crank angle sensor in place of the electronic distributor. Removal procedures are similar.

1. Rotate the engine in the normal direction of rotation until the first ("TDC" or "Leading") timing mark aligns with the pin on the front cover. Matchmark the body of the distributor (or crank angle sensor) and the engine rotor housing.

2. The easiest way to clear the high tension wires out of the way is to simply remove the cap and set it aside with the wires still attached. However, if you wish to keep the cap with the distributor, tag the wires and then pull the wires out of the cap, observing markings.

3. Disconnect the vacuum advance and, if equipped, retard hoses. Disconnect the primary electrical connector.

4. Remove the distributor adjusting bolt. Pull the distributor vertically out of the engine.

5. To install the distributor, first make sure the engine has not been disturbed. If it has been moved, turn the crankshaft until the first timing mark (yellow) aligns with the pin on the front cover. Then align the dimple in the distributor gear with the notch or line cast into the body of the distributor.

6. Insert the distributor carefully and slowly into the engine with the distributor body and rotor housing matchmarks aligned. Avoid allowing the shaft to turn and be careful not to damage the housing when inserting the hear into it.

7. Install the adjusting bolt, but do not tighten. Turn the distributor until the protrusion of the signal rotor aligns with the core of the pick-up coil, and then tighten the locking bolt.

8. Install vacuum hoses, electrical connectors and high tension wires in reverse of the removal procedure.

9. Set the ignition timing.

Piston Engines

1. Unfasten the clips which hold the distributor cap to the top of the distributor, and remove the cap. Note the location of the wire going to the No. 1 (the front) cylinder where it enters the cap.

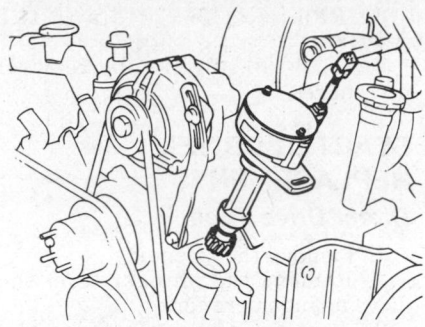

1986-88 13B engine crank angle sensor

2. Rotate the engine with the starter or by using a socket wrench on the bolt which retains the front pulley until the timing mark on the pulley is aligned with the pin on the front cover. Check to see if the contact on the rotor is pointing toward the No. 1 spark plug wire. If the rotor is half a turn away from the No. 1 plug wire, turn the crankshaft ahead 1 full turn until the timing mark is again aligned with the pin. Match mark the distributor body with the cylinder head.

3. Disconnect the vacuum advance line at the advance unit and disconnect the primary wire at the connector near the distributor.

4. Remove the adjusting bolt and pull the distributor out of the engine.

5. To install the distributor, first align the dimple on the distributor drive gear with the mark cast into the base of the distributor body by rotating the shaft. Then, being careful not to rotate the shaft, insert the distributor back into the cylinder head with the distributor body and cylinder head match marks aligned and seat it. On the 1597cc engine, align the distributor blade with the oil hole. Lubricate the O-ring with engine oil.

6. Install the mounting bolt, but do not tighten it.

7. Install the distributor cap, reconnect the vacuum advance line and the primary connector.

8. Set the timing.

NOTE: If the engine has been rotated while the distributor was removed, it will be necessary to turn the crankshaft until the point where the No. 1 cylinder is just about to fire. To do this, remove the No. 1 spark plug and rotate the engine until you can feel compression pressure building (with your finger over the spark plug hole) as the engine is turned forward. Then, turn the engine until the timing mark on the front pulley is aligned with the pin on the front cover and proceed with Step 5.

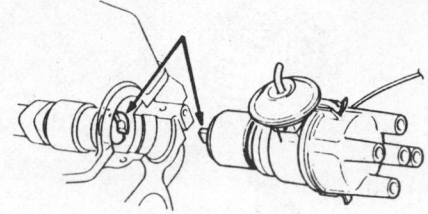

When installing the distributor on the 1490 cc engine front wheel drive, make sure the distributor shaft fits into the groove in the camshaft

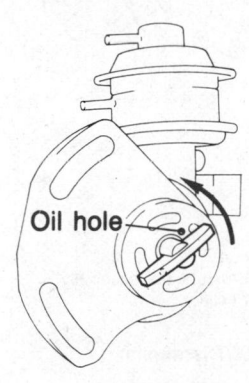

Oil hole

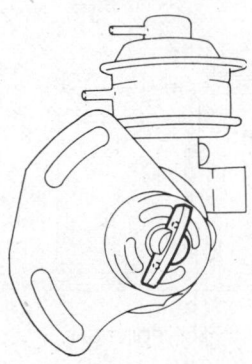

Align the blade with the oil hole when installing distributor on 323 models

Alternator

PRECAUTIONS

There are several precautions which must be strictly observed in order to avoid damaging the unit. They are:

• Reversing the battery connections will result in damage to the diodes.

• Booster batteries should be connected from negative to negative, and positive to positive.

• Never use a fast charger as a booster to start the car.

• When servicing the battery with a fast charger, always disconnect the car battery cables.

• Never attempt to polarize an alternator.

• Avoid long soldering times when replacing diodes or transistors. Prolonged heat is damaging to alternators.

• Do not use test lamps of more than 12 volts (V) for checking diode continuity.

• Do not short across or ground any of the terminals on the alternator.

• The polarity of the battery, alternator, and regulator must be matched and considered before making any electrical connections within the system.

• Never operate the alternator on an open circuit. Make sure that all connections within the circuit are clean and tight.

• Disconnect the battery terminals when performing any service on the electrical system. This will eliminate the possibility of accidental reversal of polarity.

• Disconnect the battery ground cable if arc welding is to be done on any part of the car.

REMOVAL & INSTALLATION

1. Disconnect the negative battery cable and all electrical leads from the alternator.

2. Remove the alternator adjusting link bolt. Do not remove the adjusting link.

3. On the diesel engine, remove the drive belts, the vacuum hoses and the oil tubes.

4. Remove the drivebelt and the alternator.

5. To install, reverse the removal procedures. Adjust the drive belt.

NOTE: The alternator is removed from under the vehicle on 1981-87 GLC models. If necessary to raise the vehicle, make sure it is safely supported with jack stands.

BELT TENSION ADJUSTMENT

Check tension by applying thumb pressure to the belt, midway between the eccentric shaft and alternator pulleys. The belt should deflect about ½ in.

1. To adjust the alternator drive belt use the following procedure:

  a. Loosen the alternator mounting bolt and adjusting bar bolt.

  b. Move the alternator to obtain the correct belt tension and tighten the bolts. Recheck the belt tension.

2. To adjust the power steering oil pump drive belt use the following procedure:

  a. Loosen the mounting bolt and

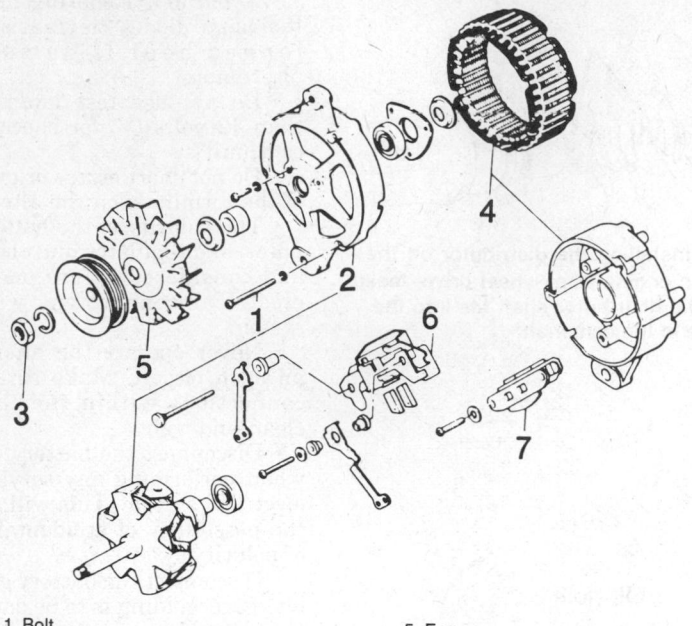

1 Bolt
2 Front bracket and rotor
3 Lock nut
4 Rear bracket and stator

5 Fan
6 Brush-holder assembly
7 Rectifier

Exploded view of the alternator—RX-7 is similar

lock nut. Turn the adjusting bolt (if so equipped) or manuaaly move the pump until the correct belt tension is obtained.

b. Tighten the lock nut and re-check the belt tension.

3. To adjust the A/C drive belt use the following procedure:

a. Loosen the lock nut on the idler pulley (if so equipped) and turn the adjusting bolt until the correct belt tension is obtained.

b. Tighten the lock nut and re-check the belt tension.

Voltage Regulator

REMOVAL & INSTALLATION

Externally Mounted

Disconnect the wiring and remove the regulator mounting screws. Remove the regulator. To install, reverse the removal procedures.

VOLTAGE ADJUSTMENT

1. Remove the cover. Check the air gap, the point gap and the back gap with a feeler gauge.
2. Adjust the gaps by bending the stationary contact support.
3. Conduct the Constant Voltage Relay Test in this section.
4. Bend the upper plate down to decrease the voltage setting or up to increase the setting, as required.
5. If the regulator cannot be

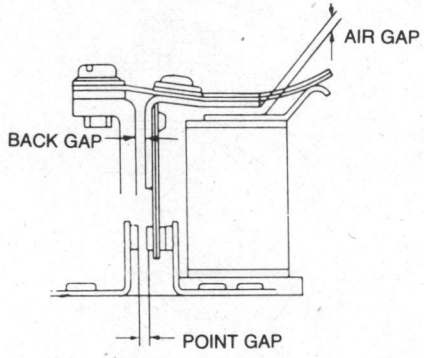

Regulator mechanical adjustments

brought within specifications, replace it.

Internally Mounted

Most of the later Mazda models, are equipped with a IC voltage regulator. This regulator is incorporated with the alternator and therefore the alternator must be removed and disassembled in order to gain access to the IC voltage regultor. No adjustments can be made to this regulator assembly.

Starter

REMOVAL & INSTALLATION

1. Disconnect the negative battery cable.
2. Disconnect the wiring from the starter.

3. Remove the bolts and the starter.
4. To install, reverse the removal procedures.

STARTER DRIVE REPLACEMENT

Direct Drive Type

1. Remove the solenoid.
2. Remove the plunger from the drive engagement fork.
3. Remove the nuts from the thru-bolts.
4. Remove the drive housing.
5. Remove the engagement fork, spring and spring seat.
6. Place a deep socket over the drive end of the armature shaft and drive the over-running clutch stopper toward the clutch.
7. Remove the spring retainer from the armature.
8. Withdraw the over-running clutch from the armature shaft.
9. To assemble, reverse the disassembly procedures. Check the clearance between the pinion and the stop collar with the solenoid closed. It should be 0.020–0.079 in.

NOTE: If the pinion gap is not to specifications, adjust the gap by altering the number of washers between the solenoid and the front bracket.

Reduction Type

1. Remove the solenoid and the plunger from the drive engagement fork.
2. Remove the thru-housing bolts and separate the front housing from the armature housing.
3. At the rear of the center bracket, remove the 2 cover screws, the cover, the C-washer and the adjustment washer.
4. Remove the center bracket bolts and separate the center bracket from the front housing. Remove the reduction gear and washer.
5. Remove the packing, the spring, and the lever.
6. At the front housing, tap the stop ring to reveal the retaining ring. Remove the retaining ring from the drive shaft.
7. Remove the gear assembly from the drive shaft and remove the drive assembly from the front housing.
8. To install, reverse the removal procedures. Adjust the pinion shaft thrust gap to 0.020 in. max., by adjust the washer numbers at the center bracket housing.

STARTER INTERLOCK SWITCH

On models equipped with a starter

lock swithc the following is a switch inspection procedure.

1. Disconnect the electrical connector at the starter interlock switch (located on the clutch pedal bracket).

2. Using a suitable ohmmeter, check the continuity between the terminals by pushing the rod.

3. The switch should show continuity when the rod is pushed into the switch and should show no continuity when the rod is released from the switch.

Diesel Glow Plugs

REMOVAL & INSTALLATION

626 Diesel Engine

1. Remove the glow plug connector nut and remove the glow plug connector.

2. Using a suitable tool, remove the glow plug from the engine.

3. Installation is the reverse order of the removal procedure.

Glow Plug Inspection

1. Disconnect the wiring from the glow plug.

2. Using an ohmmeter, check the continuity between each terminal of the glow plug and the cylinder head.

3. If continuity does not exist, remove and replace the glow plug.

Glow Plug Relay Inspection

1. Disconnect the glow plug relay connector. Using a suitable jumper wire, connect the wire to the battery and the relay connector. Also connect a suitable ohmmeter to the relay connector.

2. If the ohmmeter shows continuity when the battery is connected. The relay is good.

3. If the ohmmeter shows no continuity when the battery is connected then the relay is not good and should be replaced.

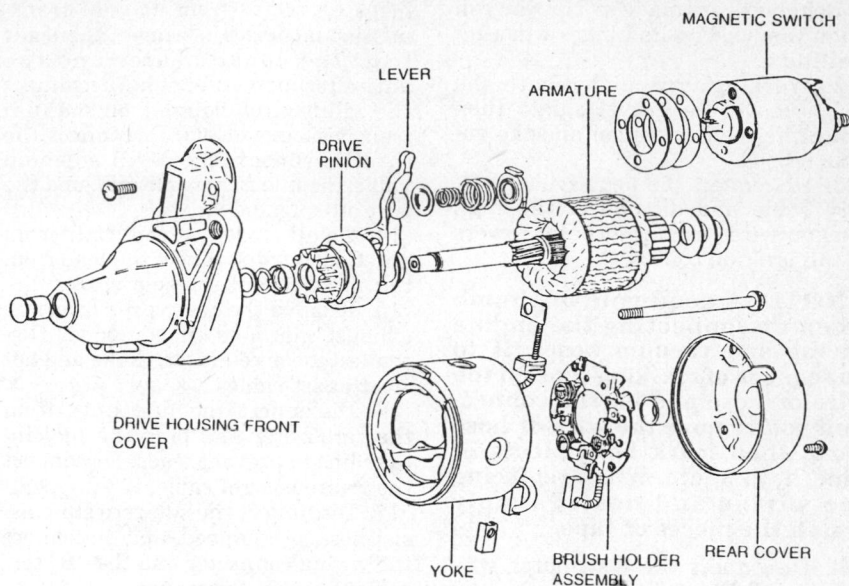

Exploded view of a conventional type of starter

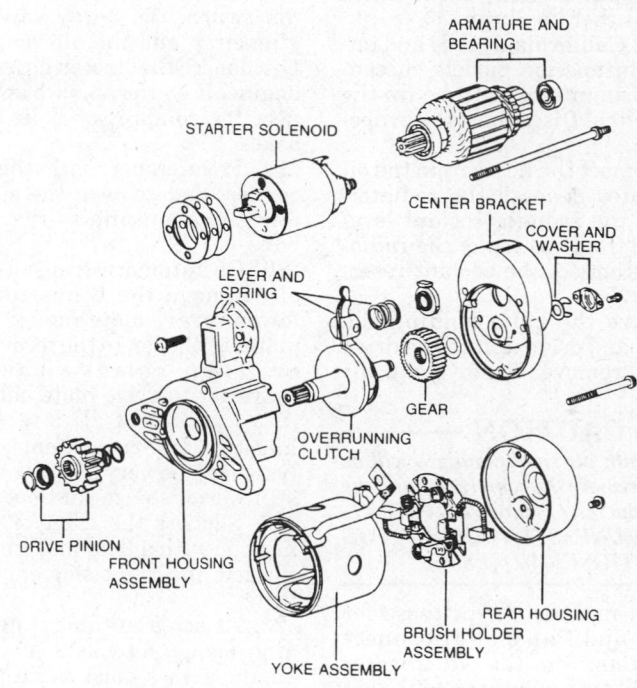

Exploded view of a reduction type of starter

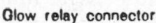

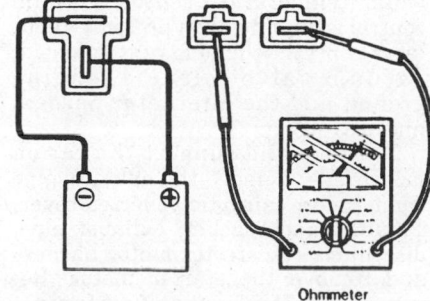

Making the glow plug relay inspection

ENGINE MECHANICAL— ROTARY

NOTE: Because of the unique design of the Mazda rotary engine, some procedures require the use of special factory tools. The text notes where these tools are necessary.

Engine

REMOVAL & INSTALLATION

RX-7

12A ENGINE

——— **CAUTION** ———
Be sure that the engine has completely cooled before attempting to remove it.

1. Scribe matchmarks on the hood and hinges and remove the hood. The

matchmarks are made so that you can align the hood on its hinges when installing it.

2. Working from underneath the car, remove the gravel shield then drain the cooling system and the engine oil.

3. Disconnect the negative (−) battery cable and disconnect the high tension wires from the center towers of the ignition coils.

NOTE: A good rule of thumb when disconnecting the engine wiring and vacuum hoses, it to put a piece of masking tape on the wire or hose and on the connection you remove the wire or hose from, then mark both pieces of tape, 1, 2, 3, etc. When replacing the wiring and hoses, simply match the pieces of tape.

4. Disconnect the distributor wiring, the oil level sensor lead, the water temperature lead and, on all except California models, the coupler from the oil thermosensor.

5. On all California models and automatic transmission models, disconnect the vacuum sensing tube fro the vacuum switch. Disconnect the evaporative hose.

6. Disconnect the hoses from the oil cooler, located beneath the radiator. Disconnect the radiator coolant level sensor lead from the top of the radiator and disconnect the coolant reservoir hose.

7. Remove the bolts holding the coolant fan and drive unit to the drive pulley and remove. Remove the air cleaner.

─────── CAUTION ───────

On models with air conditioning it will be necessary to remove the compressor and the condensor from their mounts. DO NOT ATTEMPT TO UNFASTEN ANY OF THE AIR CONDITIONER HOSES.

8. On all models, except those for California and Canada, disconnect the connectors from the No. 2 water temperature sensor, located on the radiator next to the radiator cap.

9. Remove the lower and upper radiator hoses. Disconnect the transmission fluid pipes from the radiator (automatic transmission only).

10. Remove the cooling fan, the drive assembly, the radiator and shroud assembly.

11. Remove the vacuum hose for the brake booster. Disconnect the heat exchanger pipe from the rear of the intake manifold.

12. Disconnect the coupler from the power valve solenoid on all models, except Canadian manual transmission.

13. Disconnect the coasting enrich-

ment connector from manual transmission models. Disconnect the leads from the choke heater and the anti-afterburn solenoid. Disconnect the idle switch coupler on manual transmission models. Disconnect the throttle sensor, the MAB solenoid valve, the idle richer solenoid, and the port air solenoid valve.

14. On all models, except California and Canada, disconnect the lead from the choke return solenoid valve.

15. Remove the rear cover from the exhaust manifold, if equipped. Disconnect the accelerator, choke and hot start assist cables.

16. Disconnect the fuel lines from the carburetor and plug the fuel intake line to prevent leads. Disconnect the cruise control cable, if equipped.

17. Disconnect the sub-zero start assist hose, if equipped, and disconnect the wiring connector and the "B" terminal from the alternator.

18. Disconnect the wiring from the No. 1 water temperature switch vacuum switch, the 3-way valve, the engine strap and the air vent solenoid. Disconnect the heater hoses from the engine. If equipped with A/C, disconnect the compressor bolts and move aside.

19. From underneath the car, disconnect and remove the starter. Remove the engine-to-transmission bolts.

20. On automatic transmission models, remove the converter housing lower cover, matchmark the drive plate in relation to the torque converter, then remove the torque converter-to-drive plate bolts.

21. Disconnect all interfering exhaust system components. The catalysts may be very hot if the engine is still warm, so use caution.

22. Support the front of the transmission with a floor jack, then remove the left and right side engine mount bolts.

23. Attach a suitable sling to the engine hanger brackets and raise the engine with a hoist slightly.

24. Pull the engine forward until it clears the clutch shaft or torque converter, then lift it out of the car.

25. Mount the engine on a stand. Remove the valve and piping assemblies from the engine.

NOTE: A special hanger and work stand are available from Mazda (engine stand tool number 49 0107 680A, hanger tool number 49 1114 005).

26. To install, reverse the removal procedures. Be sure to refill the engine with all fluids and check the engine timing.

13B NON TURBO ENGINE

NOTE: Do not disconnect any air conditioner lines unless the system has been properly discharged.

1. Scribe mark the hinge locations and remove the hood. Drain the coolant and engine oil.

2. Disconnect the negative battery cable.

3. From the left side of the engine compartment, remove the spark plug wires, distributor cap and the rotor. Disconnect the oil pressure gauge and oil temperature gauge wire harnesses. Disconnect the accelerator cable, fuel lines and evaporator lines. Plug the lines.

4. Disconnect the air conditioner compressor drive belt and remove the compressor. Remove the power steering pump and mounting brackets. Remove the rear oil hose and drain the engine oil into a container. Remove the starter wire harness bracket. Disconnect the heater hoses and temperature gauge unit wiring.

5. From the right side of the engine remove or disconnect the following: Remove the air pump hose, the air funnel, air flow meter connector and the air cleaner assembly. Remove the radiator hoses and heater hoses.

6. Disconnect the fan harness. Remove the fan and cover. Disconnect the coolant level sensor. Remove the radiator. Disconnect the oil cooler hoses. Disconnect the cruise control cable and the oil pump metering rod connector. Remove water hoses, brake booster hose and air pump hoses. On turbocharged engines, remove the intercooler assembly.

7. From the top of the engine, remove or disconnect the eight vacuum sensor tubes from the chamber to sensing pipes. Disconnect the intake air sensor connector, the air supply valve connector and the throttle sensor. Remove the mounting nut and disconnect the terminal cover wire. Remove the dynamic chamber from the engine.

8. Disconnect the following wiring connectors: Oxygen sensor, injectors, water temperature sensor, vacuum control solenoid valve, pressure regulator control solenoid, vent solenoid, vacuum valve solenoid, engine ground and the alternator harness and wires.

9. Raise and support the car on jackstands. Remove the exhaust pipe front cover, catalytic coverter cover, exhaust pipe bracket, exhaust pipe, disconnect the starter motor harness and remove the starter motor. Remove the turbocharger, if equipped.

10. Remove the converter cover and remove the converter to flywheel

mounting bolts. Remove the transmission to engine mounting bolts and engine mount nuts.

11. Lower the vehicle, attach a suitable lifting sling to a hoist and carefully remove the engine after pulling it forward slightly to disengage the transmission.

12. To install, reverse the removal procedures. Replace the coolant and lubricant. Check the ignition timing.

13B TURBO ENGINE

1. Disconnect the negative battery cable. Drain the engine oil and coolant into suitable containers.

2. Starting from the front and right side of the engine, remove the following components:

  a. Air intake pipe and air cleaner assembly.

  b. Battery and battery box.

  c. Cooling fan and upper and lower radiator hoses.

  d. Heater return hose. Coolant level sensor connector and radiator switch connector.

  e. Radiator, cowling and intercooler.

  f. Accelerator cable and cruise control cable. Brake vacuum hose, pressure sensor vacuum hose, relief silencerhose and spilt air pipe.

  g. Oxygen sensor connector. Insulator covers, front converter upper nut and engine harness connector.

3. Working from the left side of the engine, remove the following components:

  a. Power steering pump and drive belt. Leave the hoses connected to the power steering pump and secure it out of the way.

  b. A/C compressor and drive belt. Leave the hoses connected to the A/C compressor and secure it out of the way.

  c. Remove the spark plug wires, crank angle sensor connector and alternator connector.

  d. Remove the canister hose. Remove and plug the fuel hose.

  e. Remove the oil pressure connector, heater hose, clutch release cylinder, engine ground and oil cooler pipe and bracket.

4. Raise and support the vehicle and working from underneath the vehicle, remove the following components:

  a. Remove the under cover, catalytic converter insulator, split air pipe, exhaust pipe bracket and catalytic converter.

  b. Remove the exhaust pipe and front converter, starter, transmission attaching bolts and engine mounting nuts.

5. Lower the vehicle, attach a suitable lifting sling to a hoist and carefully remove the engine after pulling it forward slightly to disengage the transmission.

6. To install, reverse the removal procedures. Replace the coolant and lubricant. Check the ignition timing.

DISASSEMBLY

NOTE: Because of the design of the rotary engine, it is not practical to attempt component removal and installation. It is best to disassemble and assemble the entire engine, or go as far as necessary with the disassembly procedure. Refer to the specification charts for measurements of the components.

12A Engine

1. Mount the engine on a stand.

2. Remove the oil hose support bracket from the front housing.

3. Disconnect the vacuum hoses, air hoses and remove the decel valve.

4. Remove the air pump and drive belt. Remove the air pump adjusting bar.

5. Remove the alternator and drive belt.

6. Disconnect the metering oil pump connecting rod, oil tubes and vacuum sensing tube from the carburetor.

7. Remove the exhaust manifold cover, if equipped. Remove the carburetor and intake manifold as an assembly.

8. Remove the gasket and two rubber rings.

9. Remove the thermal reactor and gaskets, if equipped. Remove the exhaust manifold and engine mount.

10. Remove the distributor.

11. Remove the water pump.

12. Proceed to "ALL ENGINES" procedures in this section.

13B Non Turbo Engine

1. Mount the engine on a stand.

2. Remove components in the following order:

3. Remove the A/C compressor and the power steering pump bracket.

4. Remove the left engine mount, spark plugs, oil level gauge, oil filler pipe, oil filter and filter body.

5. Remove the oil pressure gauge, crank angle sensor, air pump and drive belt, air pump bracket, alternator and drive belt, clutch cover and clutch disc.

6. Remove the metering oil connectiong rod, second vacuum piping, throttle and dynamic chamber.

7. Primary fuel injector and distribution pipe. Air contro valve, switching actuator, water pipe and air hose.

8. Housing oil nozzle and manifold oil nozzle. intake manifold, exhaust manifold and insultor.

9. Metering oil pump, eccentric shaft pulley, water pump, dynamic chamber bracket, engine harness and vaccum piping and the oil inlet pipe.

10. Proceed to "ALL ENGINES" procedures in this section.

13B Turbo Engine

1. Mount the engine on a stand.

2. Remove components in the following order:

3. Remove the A/C compressor and the power steering pump bracket.

4. Remove the left engine mount, spark plugs, oil level gauge, oil filler pipe, oil filter and filter body.

5. Remove the oil pressure gauge, crank angle sensor, air pump and drive belt, air pump bracket, alternator and drive belt, clutch cover and clutch disc.

6. Remove the metering oil connectiong rod, second vacuum piping, throttle and dynamic chamber.

7. Primary fuel injector and distribution pipe. Air contro valve, switching actuator, water pipe, turbocharger and insulator and air hose.

8. Housing oil nozzle and manifold oil nozzle. intake manifold, exhaust manifold and insultor.

9. Metering oil pump, eccentric shaft pulley, water pump, dynamic chamber bracket, engine harness and vaccum piping and the oil inlet pipe.

10. Proceed to "ALL ENGINES" procedures in this section.

ALL ENGINES

1. Invert the engine.

2. Remove the oil pan.

3. Remove the oil strainer and gasket.

4. Identify the front and rear rotor housing with a felt tip pen. These are common parts and must be identified to be reassembled in their respective locations.

5. Turn the engine on the stand so that the top of the engine is up.

6. Remove the engine mounting bracket from the front cover.

7. Remove the eccentric shaft pulley. Remove the eccentric shaft bypass valve and spring.

8. Turn the engine on a stand so that the front end of the engine is up.

9. Remove the front cover.

10. Remove the O-ring from the oil passage on the front housing.

11. Remove the oil slinger and distributor drive gear from the shaft.

12. Unbolt and remove the chain adjuster.

13. Remove the locknut and washer from the oil pump driven sprocket.

14. Slide the oil pump drive sprocket

and driven sprocket, together with the drive chain off the eccentric shaft and oil pump, simultaneously.

15. Remove the keys from the eccentric and oil pump shaft. Remove the oil pump.

16. Slide the balance weight, thrust washer and needle bearing from the shaft.

17. Unbolt the bearing housing and slide the bearing housing, needle bearing, spacer and thrust plate off the shaft.

18. Turn the engine on the stand so that the top of the engine is up.

19. If equipped with a manual transmission, remove the clutch pressure plate and clutch disc. Remove the flywheel with a puller. Remove the key from the shaft.

20. If equipped with an automatic transmission, remove the drive plate. Remove the counterweight. Block the weight and remove the mounting nut. Remove the counterweight with a suitable puller.

21. Working at the rear of the engine, loosen the tension bolts.

NOTE: Do not loosen the tension bolts one at a time. Loosen the bolts evenly in small stages to prevent distortion. Mark tension bolts to replace in original holes during reassembly.

22. Lift the rear housing off the shaft.

23. Remove any seals that are stuck to the rotor sliding surface of the rear housing and reinstall them in their original locations.

24. Remove all the corner seals, corner seal spring, side seal and side seal springs from the rear side of the rotor. Mazda has a special tray which holds all the seals and keeps them segregated to prevent mistakes during reassembly. Each seal groove is marked to prevent confusion.

25. Remove the two rubber seals and two O-rings from the rear rotor housing.

26. Remove the dowels from the rear rotor housing.

27. Lift the rear rotor housing away from the rear rotor, being very careful not to drop the apex seals on the rear rotor.

28. Remove each apex seal, side piece and spring from the rear rotor and segregate them.

29. Remove the rear rotor from the eccentric shaft and place it upside down on a clean rag.

— **CAUTION** —
Do not place the rotor on a hard surface.

30. Remove each seal and spring from the other side of the rotor and segregate these.

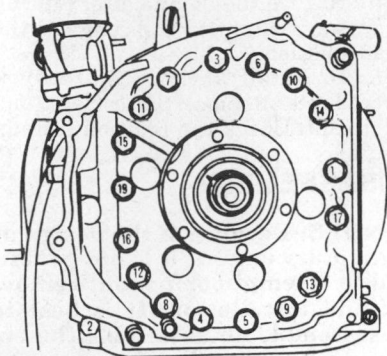

12A engine tension bolt loosening sequence

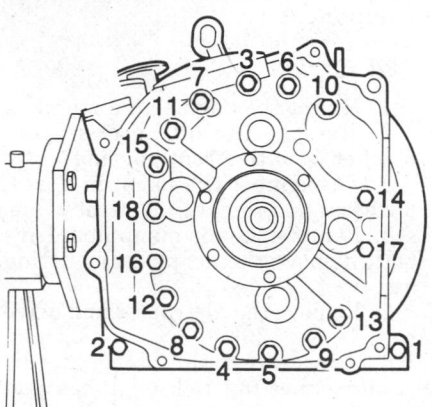

13B engine tension bolt loosenting sequence

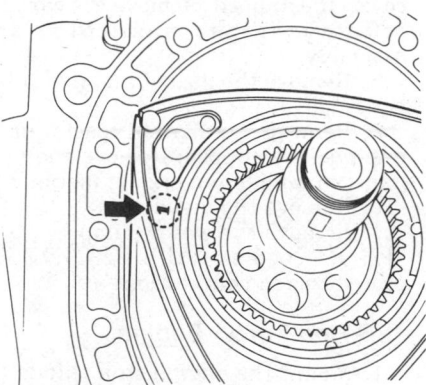

Seal groove number mark—typical

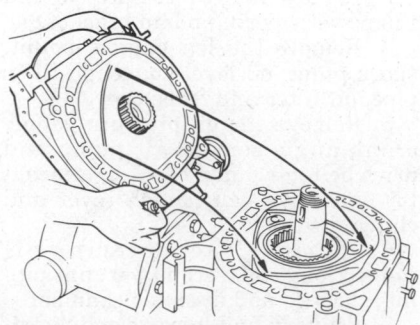

Remove any side seals adhering to the surface

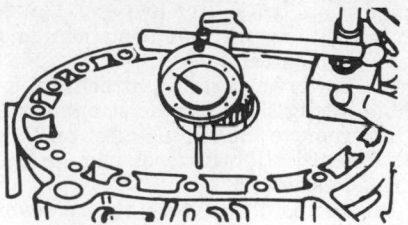

Measuring housing wear with a dial indicator

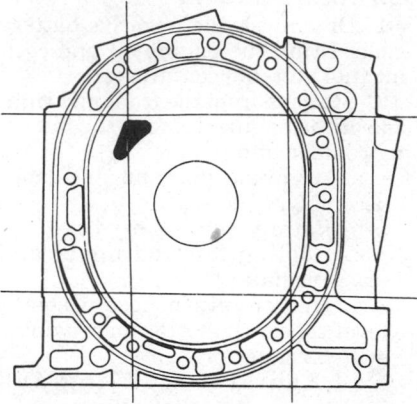

Measure housing distortion along the lines

31. If some of the seals fall off the rotor, be careful not to change the original position of each seal.

32. Identify the bottom of each apex seal with a felt tip pen.

33. Remove the oil seals and the spring. Do not exert heavy pressure at only one place on the seal, since it could be deformed. Replace the O-rings in the oil seal when the engine is overhauled.

34. Hold the intermediate housing down and remove the dowels from it.

35. Lift off the intermediate housing being careful not to damage the eccentric shaft. It should be removed by sliding it beyond the rear rotor journal on the eccentric shaft while holding the intermediate housing up and, at the same time, pushing the eccentric shaft up.

36. Lift out the eccentric shaft.

37. Repeat the above procedures to remove the front rotor housing and front rotor.

INSPECTION AND REPLACEMENT

Front, Intermediate and Rear Housings

1. Check the housing for signs of gas or water leakage.

2. Remove the carbon deposits from the front housing with extra fine emery cloth.

3. Remove any of the old sealer which is adhering to the housing, us-

ing a brush or a cloth soaked in Ketone.

4. Check for distortion by placing a straightedge on the surface of the housing. Measure the clearance between the straightedge and the housing with a feeler gauge. If the clearance is greater than 0.0016 in. at any point, replace the housing.

5. Use a dial indicator to check for wear on the rotor contact surfaces of the housing. If the wear is greater than 0.004 in., replace the housing.

NOTE: The wear at either end of the minor axis is greater than at any other point on the housing. However, this is normal and should be not cause for concern.

Front Stationary Gear and Main Bearing

1. Examine the teeth of the stationary gear for wear or damage.
2. Be sure that the main bearing shows no signs of excessive wear, scoring, or flaking.
3. Check the main bearing-to-eccentric journal clearance by measuring the journal with a vernier caliper and the bearing with a pair of inside calipers.

Main Bearing Replacement

1. Unfasten the securing bolts, if used. Remove stationary gear and main bearing assembly, out of the housing, using a suitable puller/installer tool, such as Mazda tool 49-0813-235.
2. Press the main bearing out of the stationary gear.
3. Press a new main bearing into the stationary gear so that it is in the same position that the old bearing was.
4. Align the slot in the stationary gear flange with the dowel pin in the housing and press the gear into place. Install the securing bolts, if required.

NOTE: To aid in stationary gear and main bearing removal and installation, Mazda manufactures a special tool, part No. 49-0813-235.

Rear Stationary Gear and Main Bearing

Inspect the rear stationary gear and main bearing in a similar manner to the front. In addition, examine the O-ring, which is located in the stationary gear, for signs of wear or damage. Replace the O-ring, if necessary.

To replace the stationary gear, use the following procedure.

1. Remove the rear stationary gear securing bolts.

2. Drive the stationary gear out of the rear housing with a brass drift.
3. Apply a light coating of grease to a new O-ring and fit it into the groove on the stationary gear.
4. Apply sealer to the flange of the stationary gear.
5. Install the stationary gear on the housing so that the slot on its flange aligns with the pin on the rear housing.

------- CAUTION -------

Use care not to damage the O-ring during installation.

6. Tighten the stationary gear bolts evenly, in several stages, to 15 ft. lbs.

Rotor Housings

1. Examine the inner margin of both housings for signs of gas or water leakage.
2. Wipe the inner surface of each housing with a clean cloth to remove the carbon deposits.

NOTE: If the carbon deposits are stubborn, soak the cloth in a solution of Ketone. Do not scrape or sand the chrome plated surfaces of the rotor chamber.

3. Clean all of the rust deposits out of the cooling passages of each rotor housing.
4. Remove the old sealer with a cloth soaked in Ketone.
5. Examine the chromium plated inner surfaces for scoring, flaking, or other signs of damage. If any are present, the housing must be replaced.
6. Check the rotor housings for distortion by placing a straightedge on the axes.
7. If distortion exceeds 0.002 in., replace the rotor housing.
8. Check the widths of both rotor housings, at a minimum of eight points near the trochoid surfaces of each housing, using a vernier caliper.

If the difference between the maximum and minimum values obtained is greater than 0.0024 in., replace the housing. A housing in this condition will be prone to gas and coolant leakage.

Rotors

1. Check the rotor for signs of blow-by around the side and corner seal areas.
2. The color of the carbon deposits on the rotor should be brown, just as in a piston engine.

NOTE: Usually the carbon deposits on the leading side of the rotor are brown, while those on

the trailing side tend toward black, as viewed from the direction of rotation.

3. Remove the carbon on the rotor with a scraper or extra fine emery paper. Use the scraper carefully when doing the seal grooves so that no damage is done to them.
4. Wash the rotor in solvent and blow it dry with compressed air.
5. Examine the internal gear for cracks or damaged teeth.

NOTE: If the internal gear is damaged, the rotor and gear must be replaced as a single assembly.

6. With the oil seal removed, check the land protrusions by placing a straightedge over the lands. Measure the gap between the rotor surface and the straightedge with a feeler gauge.
7. Check the gaps between the housings and the rotor on both of its sides.

   a. Measure the rotor width with a vernier caliper.

   b. Compare the rotor width against the width of the rotor housing which was measured above.

   c. Replace the rotor, if the difference between the two measurements is not within 0.0047–0.0074 in. (12A engines); 0.0047–0.0083 in. (13B engine).

8. Check the rotor bearing for flaking, wearing, or scoring and proceed as indicated in the next section, if any of these are present.

Rotor Bearing Replacement

------- CAUTION -------

The use of the special service tools, as indicted in the text, is mandatory, if damage to the rotor is to be avoided.

Check the clearance between the rotor bearing and the rotor journal on the eccentric shaft. Measure the inner diameter of the rotor bearing and the outer diameter of the journal. The wear limit is 0.0039 in.; replace the bearing if it exceeds this.

1. Place the rotor on the support so that the internal gear is facing downward. Using the puller/installer tool 49-0813-240 without adaptor ring, press the bearing out of the rotor. Being careful not to damage the internal gear.
2. Place the rotor on the support with internal gear faced upward.
3. Place the new rotor bearing on the rotor so that the bearing lug is in line with the slot of the rotor bore.
4. Remove the screws attaching the adaptor ring to the puller/installer. Using the puller/installer and adaptor ring, press fit the new bearing until the bearing is flush with the rotor boss.

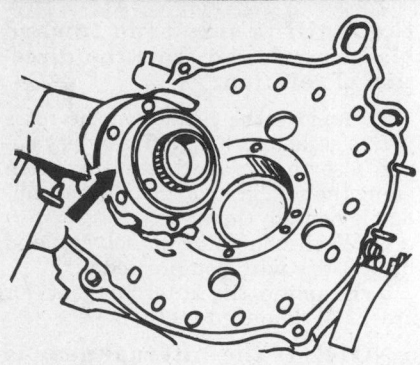

Position the O-ring in the groove on the stationary gear (arrow)

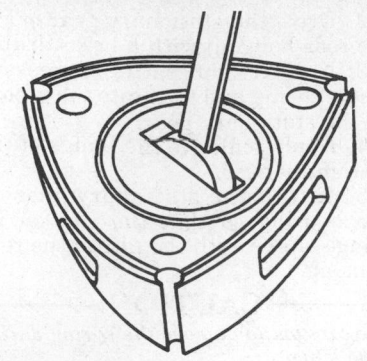

Insert the special bearing expander into the rotor

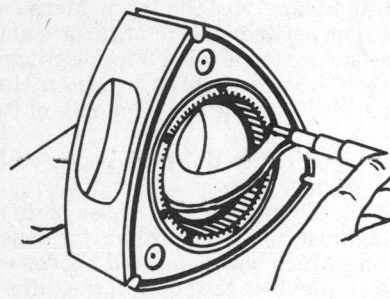

Measure the rotor width at the point indicated

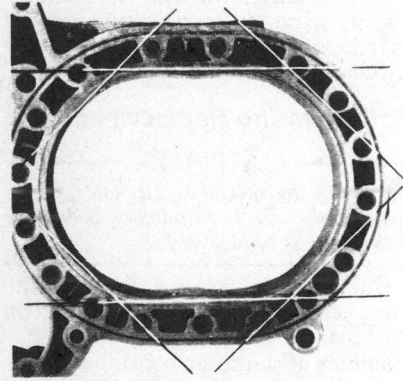

Measure the rotor housing distortion along the axes indicated

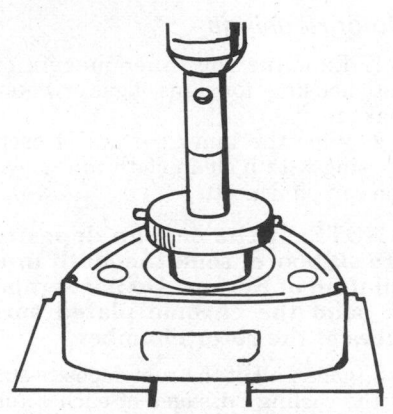

Installing a new rotor bearing

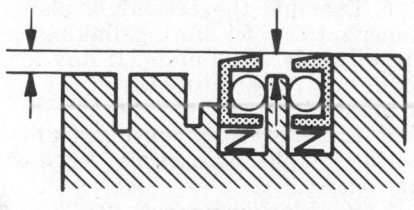

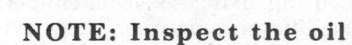

Measuring oil seal protrusion

Oil Seal Inspection

NOTE: Inspect the oil seal while it is mounted in the rotor.

1. Examine the oil seal.
2. If the width of the oil seal lip is greater than 0.020 in., replace the oil seal.
3. If the protrusion of the oil seal is greater then 0.020 in., replace the seal.

Oil Seal Replacement

NOTE: Replace the rubber O-ring in the oil seal as a normal part of the engine overhaul.

1. Pry the seal out by inserting a small prybar into the slots on the rotor.

CAUTION

Be careful not to deform the lip of the oil seal if it is to be reinstalled.

2. Fit both the oil seal springs into their respective grooves, so that their ends are facing upward and their gaps are opposite each other on the rotor.
3. Insert a new O-ring into each of the oil seals.

NOTE: before installing the O-rings into the oil seals, fit each of the seals into its proper groove on the rotor. Check to see that all of the seals move smoothly and freely.

4. Coat the oil seal groove and the oil seal with engine oil.
5. Gently press the oil seal into the groove with your fingers. Be careful not to distort the seal.

NOTE: Be sure that the white mark is on the bottom side of each seal when it is installed.

6. Repeat the installation procedure for the oil seals on both sides of each rotor.

Apex Seals

CAUTION

Although the apex seals are extremely durable when in service, they are easily broken when they are being handled. Be careful never to drop them.

1. Remove the carbon deposits from the apex seals and their springs. Do not use emery cloth on the seals as it will damage their finish.
2. Wash the seals and the springs in cleaning solution.
3. Check the apex seals for cracks.
4. Test the seal springs for weakness.
5. Use a micrometer to check the seal height. Refer to the specifications chart.
6. With a feeler gauge, check the side clearance between the apex seal and the groove in the rotor. Insert the gauge until its tip contacts the bottom of the groove. If the gap is greater than 0.0035 in. (12A engines), or .0059 in. (13B engines), replace the seal.
7. Check the gap between the apex seals and the side housing in the following manner:
   a. Use a vernier caliper to measure the length of each apex seal.
   b. Compare this measurement to the minimum figure obtined when the rotor housing width was being measured.
   c. If the seal is too long, sand the ends of the seal with emery cloth until the proper length is reached.

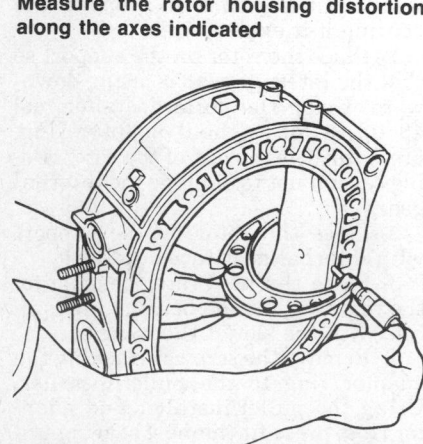

Checking rotor housing width

CAUTION

Do not use the emery cloth on the faces of the seal.

Side Seals

1. Remove the carbon deposits from the side seals and their springs.
2. Check the side seals for cracks.
3. Check the clearance between the side seals and their grooves with a feeler gauge.
4. Check the clearance between the side seals and the corner seals with both installed in the rotor.

   a. Insert a feeler gauge between the end of the side seal and the corner seal.

   NOTE: Insert the gauge against the direction of the rotor's rotation.

   b. Replace the side seal if the clearance is greater than 0.016 in.
5. If the side seal is replaced, adjust the clearance between it and the corner seal as follows:

   a. File the side seal on its reverse side, in the same rotational direction of the rotor, along the outline made by the corner seal.

   b. The clearance obtained should be 0.002–0.006 in. If it exceeds this, the performance of the seals will deteriorate.

CAUTION

There are four different types of side seals, depending upon location. Do not mix the seals up and be sure to use the proper type of seal for replacement.

Corner Seals

1. Clean the carbon deposits.
2. Examine each of the seals.
3. Measure the clearance between the corner seal and its groove. The clearance should be 0.008–0.0019 in. The wear limit of the gap is 0.031 in.
4. If the wear between the corner seal and the groove is uneven, check the clearance with the special "bar limit gauge" tool 49–0839–165. The gauge has to "go" end and a "no go" end.

   a. If neither end of the gauge goes into the groove, the clearance is within specifications.

   b. If the "go" end of the gauge fits into the groove, but the "no go" end does not, replace the corner seal with one that is 0.0012 in. oversize.

   c. If both ends of the gauge fit into the groove, then the groove must be reamed out. Replace the corner seal with one which is 0.0072 in. oversize, after reaming.

   NOTE: Take the measurement of the groove in the direction of maximum wear, i.e., that of rotation.

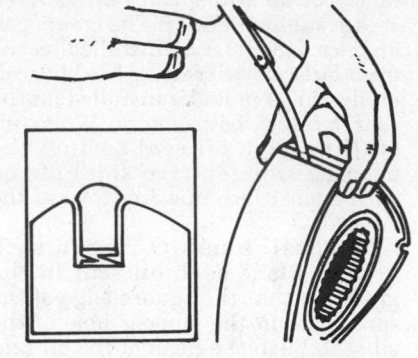

Check the gap between the apex seal and groove with a feeler gauge

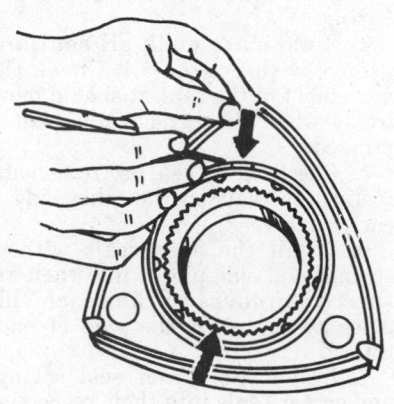

Position the oil seal spring gaps at arrows

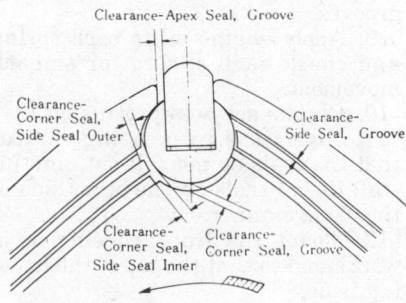
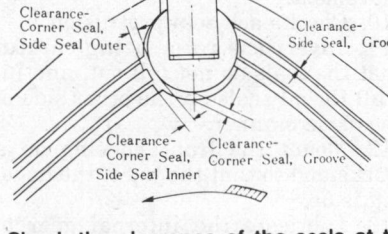

Check the clearance of the seals at the points indicated

Seal Springs

Check the seal springs for damage or weakness. Be exceptionally careful when checking the spring areas which contact either the rotor or the seal.

Eccentric Shaft

1. Wash the eccentric shaft in solvent and blow the oil passages dry with compressed air.
2. Check the shaft for wear, cracks, or other signs of damage. Make sure that none of the oil passages are clogged.

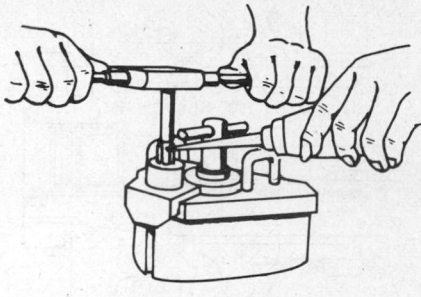

Reaming the corner seal groove

Corner seal installation

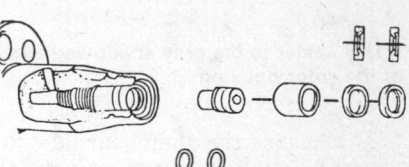

Needle bearing components

Position the dial indicator as shown to measure shaft run-out

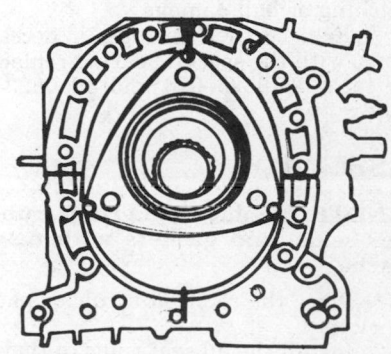

The rear rotor must be positioned as shown during engine assembly

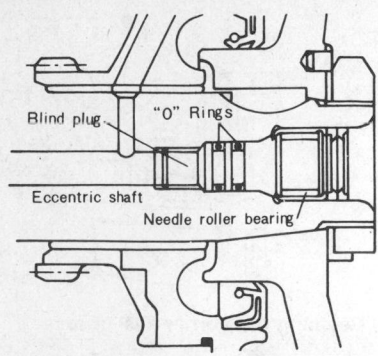

Eccentric shaft blind plug assembly

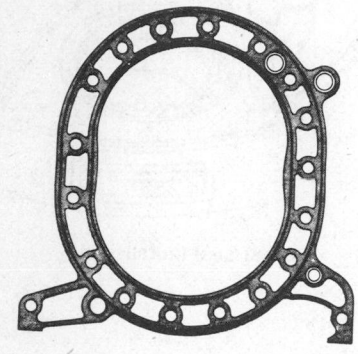

Apply sealer to the grey shadowed areas of the rotor housing

3. Measure the shaft journals. Replace the shaft if any of its journals shows excessive wear.

4. Check eccentric shaft run-out. Rotate the shaft slowly and note the dial indicator reading. If run-out is more than specifications, replace the eccentric shaft.

5. Check the blind plug at the end of the shaft. If it is loose or leaking, remove it with an Allen wrench and replace the O-ring.

6. Check the operation of the needle roller bearing for smoothness by inserting a mainshaft into the bearing and rotating it. Examine the bearing for signs of wear or damage. Check the oil jet for spring weakness, sticking or ball damage.

7. Replace the bearings, if necessary, with the special bearing replacer tools 49–0823–073 and 49–0823–072.

ASSEMBLY

NOTE: Replace all O-rings, rubber seals, and gaskets with new parts.

1. Place the rotor on a rubber pad or cloth.

2. Install the oil seal rings in their respective grooves in the rotors with the edge of the spring in the stopper hole. The oil seal springs are painted cream or blue in color. The cream colored springs must be installed on the front faces of both rotors. The blue colored springs must be installed on the rear faces of both rotors. When installing each oil seal spring, the painted side (square side) of the spring must face upward (toward the oil seal).

3. Install a new O-ring in each groove. Place each oil seal in the groove so that the square edge of the spring fits in the stopper hole of the oil seal. Push the head of the oil seal slowly with the fingers, being careful that the seal is not deformed. Be sure that the oil seal moves smoothly in the groove before installing the O-ring.

4. Lubricate each oil seal and groove with engine oil. Check the movement of the seal. It should move freely when the head of the seal is pressed.

5. Check the oil seal protrusion and install the seals on the other side of each rotor.

6. Install the apex seals without springs and side pieces into their respective grooves so that each side piece positions on the side of each rotor.

7. Install the corner seal springs and corner seals into their respective grooves.

8. Install the side seal springs and side seals into their respective grooves.

9. Apply engine oil to each spring and check each spring for smooth movement.

10. Check each seal protrusion.

11. Invert the rotor being careful that the seals do not fall out, and install the oil seals on the other side of the same manner.

12. Mount the front housing on a workstand so that the top of the housing is up.

13. Lubricate the internal gear of the rotor with engine oil.

14. Hold the apex seals with used O-ring to keep the apex seals installed and place the rotor on the front housing. Be careful not to drop the seals. Turn the front housing so that the sliding surface faces upward.

15. Mesh the internal and stationary gears so that one of the rotor apexes is at any one of the four places shown and remove the old O-ring which is holding the apex seals in position.

16. Lubricate the front rotor journal of the eccentric shaft with engine oil and lubricate the eccentric shaft main journal.

17. Insert the eccentric shaft. Be careful that you do not damage the rotor bearing and main bearing.

18. Apply sealing agent to the front side of the front rotor housing.

19. Apply a light coat of petroleum jelly onto new O-rings and rubber seals (to prevent them from coming off) and install the O-rings and rubber seals on the front side of the rotor housing.

NOTE: The inner rubber seal is of the square type. The wider white line of the rubber seal should face the combustion chamber and the seam of the rubber seal should be positioned as shown. Do not stretch the rubber seal.

20. If the engine is being overhauled, install the seal protector to only the inner rubber seal to improve durability.

21. Invert the front rotor housing, being careful not to let the rubber seals and O-rings fall from their grooves, and mount it on the front housing.

22. Lubricate the dowels with the engine oil and insert them through the front rotor housing holes and into the front housing.

23. Apply sealer to the front side of the rotor housing.

24. Install new O-rings and rubber seals on the front rotor housing in the same manner as for the other side.

25. Insert each apex spring seal, making sure that the seal is installed in the proper direction.

26. Install each side piece in its original position and be sure that the springs seat on the side piece.

27. Lubricate the side pieces with engine oil. Make sure that the front rotor housing is free of foreign matter and lubricate the sliding surface of the front housing with engine oil.

28. Turn the front housing assembly with the rotor, so that the top of the housing is up. Pull the eccentric shaft about 1 in.

29. Position the eccentric portion of the eccentric shaft diagonally, to the upper right.

30. Install the intermediate housing over the eccentric shaft onto the front rotor housing. Turn the engine so that the rear of the engine is up.

31. Install the rear rotor and rear rotor housing following the same steps as for the front rotor and the front housing.

32. Turn the engine so that the rear of the engine is up.

33. Lubricate the stationary gear and main bearing.

34. Install the rear housing onto the rear rotor housing. If necessary, turn the rear rotor slightly to mesh the rear housing stationary gear with the rear rotor internal gear.

35. Install a new washer on each tension bolt, and lubricate each bolt with engine oil.

36. Install the tension bolts and tighten them evenly, in several stages following the sequence shown. The specified torque is 23–27 ft. lbs. (23–29 ft. lbs. on the 13B engine).

NOTE: Be sure bolts are installed in their original positions. Longer bolts are used in later engines and are not interchangeable.

37. After tightening the bolts, turn the eccentric shaft to be sure that the shaft and rotors turn smoothly and easily.

38. Lubricate the oil seal in the rear housing.

39. On vehicles with manual transmission, install the flywheel on the rear of the eccentric shaft so that the keyway of the flywheel fits the key on the shaft.

40. Apply sealer to both sides of the flywheel lockwasher and install the lockwasher.

41. Install the flywheel locknut. Hold the flywheel SECURELY and tighten the nut to THREE HUNDRED AND FIFTY FT. LBS. (350 ft. lbs.) of torque.

NOTE: 350 ft. lbs. is a great deal of torque. In actual practice, it is practically impossible to accurately measure that much torque on the nut. At least a 3 ft. bar will be required to generate sufficient torque. Tighten it as tight as possible, with no longer than 3 ft. of leverage. Be sure the engine is held SECURELY.

42. On vehicles with automatic transmission, install the key, counterweight, lockwasher and nut. Tighten the nut to 350 ft. lbs. SEE STEP 41 AND THE NOTE FOLLOWING STEP 41. Install the drive plate on the counterweight and tighten the attaching nuts.

43. Turn the engine so that the front faces up.

44. Install the thrust plate with the tapered face down, and install the needle bearing on the eccentric shaft. Lubricate with engine oil.

45. Install the bearing housing on the front housing. Tighten the bolts and bend up the lockwasher tabs. The spacer should be installed so that the center of the needle bearing comes to the center of the eccentric shaft and the spacer should be seated on the thrust plate.

46. Install the needle bearing on the shaft and lubricate it with engine oil.

47. Install the balancer and thrust washer on the eccentric shaft.

48. Install the oil pump drive chain over both of the sprockets. Install the sprocket and chain assembly over the eccentric shaft and oil pump shaft simultaneously. Install the key on the eccentric shaft.

NOTE: Be sure that both of the sprockets are engaged with the chain before install them over the shafts.

49. Install the distributor drive gear onto the eccentric shaft with the "F" mark on the gear facing the front of the engine. Slide the spacer and oil slinger onto the eccentric shaft.

50. Align the keyway and install the eccentric shaft pulley. Tighten the pulley bolt to 72–87 ft. lbs.

51. Turn the engine until the top of the engine faces up.

52. Check the eccentric shaft end-play in the following manner:

    a. Attach a dial indicator to the flywheel. Move the flywheel forward and backward.

    b. Note the reading on the dial indicator: it should be 0.0016–0.0028 in.

    c. If the end-play is not within specifications, adjust it by replacing the front spacer. Spacers come in four sizes, ranging from 0.3150–0.3181 in. If necessary, a spacer can be ground on a surface plate with emery paper.

    d. Check the end-play again and, if it is now within specifications, proceed with the next Step.

53. Remove the pulley from the front of the eccentric shaft. Tighten the oil pump drive sprocket nut and bend the locktabs on the lockwasher.

54. Fit a new O-ring over the front cover oil passage.

55. Install the chain tensioner, if equipped, and tighten its securing bolts.

56. Position the front cover gasket and the front cover on the front housing, then secure the front cover with its attachment bolts.

57. Install the eccentric shaft pulley again. Tighten its bolt to required torque.

58. Turn the engine so that the bottom faces up.

59. Cut off the excess gasket on the front cover along the mounting surface of the oil pan.

60. Install the oil strainer gasket and strainer on the front housing and tighten the attaching bolts.

61. Apply sealer to the joint surfaces of each housing.

62. Install the oil pan.

63. Turn the engine so that the top if up.

NOTE: On 13B engines, go to Step 74.

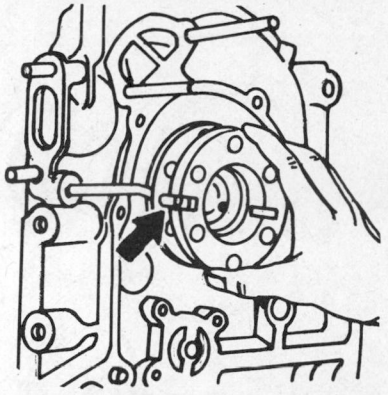

Align the slot in the stationary gear flange with the pin in the housing (arrow)

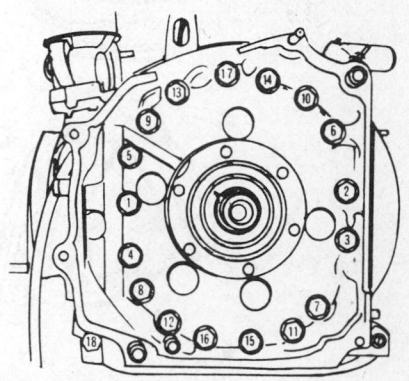

12A engine tension bolt tightening sequence

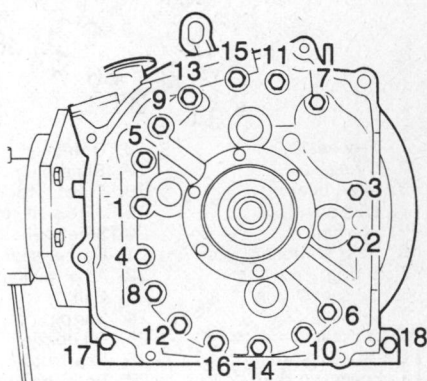

13B engine tension bolt tightening sequence

64. Install the water pump.

65. Rotate the eccentric shaft until the yellow mark (leading side mark) aligns with the pointer on the front cover.

66. Align the marks on the distributor gear and housing and install the distributor so that the lockbolt is in the center of the slot.

67. Rotate the distributor until the leading points start to separate and tighten the distributor locknut.

68. Install the gaskets and thermal reactor.

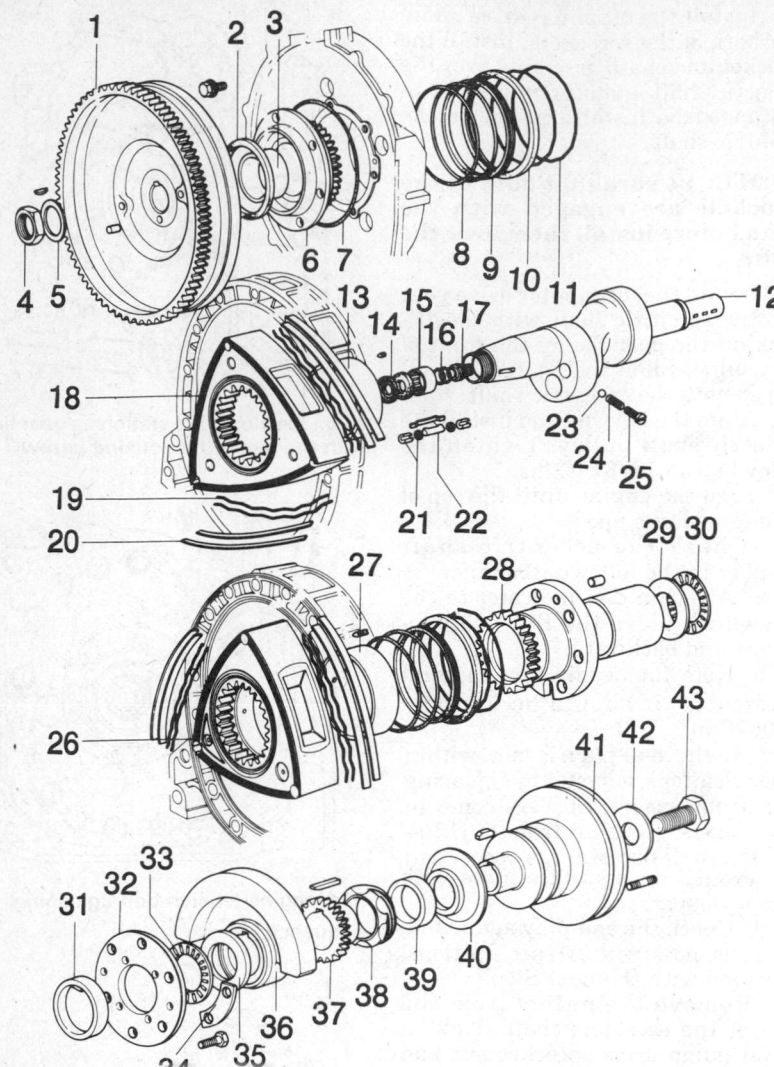

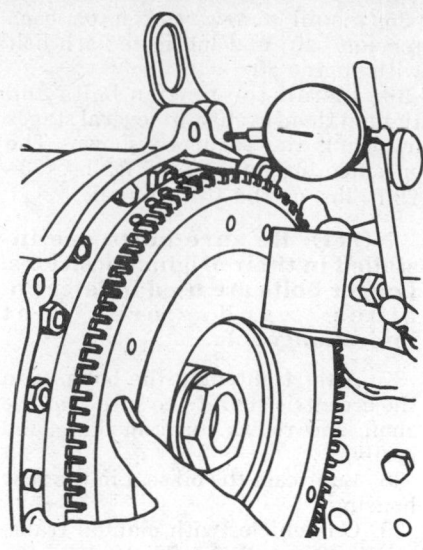

Use a dial indicator attached to the flywheel to measure eccentric shaft end-play

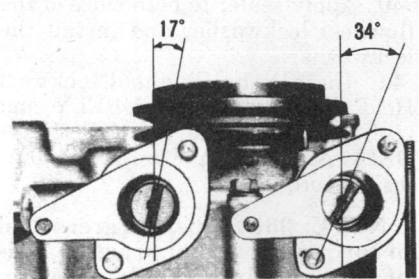

Position the slots in the distributor drive as shown

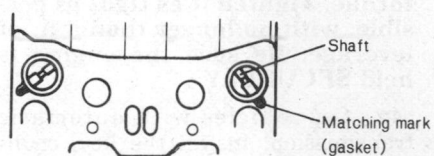

Shaft

Matching mark (gasket)

Auxiliary port valve and mounting gasket marks must match

1. Flywheel	16. O-ring	31. Spacer
2. Oil seal	17. Blind plug	32. Bearing housing
3. Main bearing	18. Front rotor	33. Needle bearing
4. Locknut	19. Side seal spring	34. Washer
5. Washer	20. Side seal	35. Thrust plate
6. Rear stationary gear	21. Corner seal and spring	36. Balance weight
7. O-ring	22. Apex seal and spring	37. Oil pump drive sprocket
8. Oil seal O-ring	23. Ball	38. Distributor drive gear
9. Oil seal	24. Spring	39. Spacer
10. Oil seal	25. Oil nozzle	40. Oil slinger
11. Oil seal spring	26. Rear rotor	41. Eccentric shaft pulley
12. Eccentric shaft	27. Rotor bearing	42. Washer
13. Rotor bearing	28. Front stationary gear	43. Pulley bolt
14. Grease seal	29. Thrust washer	
15. Needle bearing	30. Thrust bearing	

Typical rotor and eccentric shaft components—12A engine shown

---
CAUTION

Do not forget to use shims on the side housing contact surfaces. If shims are not used, coolant will leak.

75. Attach two O-rings to the oil filter body. Install the oil filter body.

76. Align the leading timing mark (yellow painted) on the eccentric shaft pulley with the indicator pin on the front cover.

77. Align the tally marks on the distributor housing and driven gear. Install the distributor and lock nut. Turn the distributor housing until the projection of the signal rotor aligns with core of the leading side pick-up coil. Tighten the lock nut. Install the distributor rotor and cap.

78. Place the exhaust manifold gas-

69. Install the hot air duct.

70. Install the carburetor and intake manifold assembly.

71. Connect the oil tubes, vacuum tube and metering oil pump connecting rod to the carburetor.

72. Install the decel valve and connect the vacuum lines, air hoses and wires.

73. Install the alternator bracket, alternator and bolt and check the clearance. If the clearance is more than 0.006 in., adjust the clearance using a shim. Shims are available in 3 sizes: 0.0059 in., 0.0118 in., and 0.0197 in.

74. On 13B Engines: Install the water pump and tighten the nuts in a crisscross sequence. Tighten to 13–20 ft. lbs.

ket in position and install the exhaust manifold. Tighten to 23–34 ft. lbs.

79. Install the hot air duct and absorber plate.

80. Install the intake manifold auxiliary ports.

NOTE: Installation should be made so that the bigger sides of the auxiliary port valve shaft align the matching mark on the gasket as shown in the figure.

81. Install the O-rings. Install the intake manifold and gasket.

82. Connect the metering oil pump pipes. Tighten to 14–19 ft. lbs.

83. Install the fuel injection nozzles.

84. Refer to the illustration and install the delivery pipe assembly, the chamber, and the emission device assembly as one piece. Tighten delivery pipe body to 14–19 ft. lbs.; emission device assembly to 14–19 ft. lbs.

85. Refer to the illustration and check to be sure that the vacuum sensing tube is not installed incorrectly.

86. On all engines, install the alternator drive belt.

87. Install the air pump.

88. Install the engine hanger bracket.

89. Remove the engine from the stand.

90. Install the engine in the vehicle.

Intake Manifold

REMOVAL & INSTALLATION

12A Engine

To remove the intake manifold and carburetor assembly with the engine remaining in the automobile, proceed in the following manner:

1. Perform Steps 2–7 "Engine Removal and Installation." Do not remove the engine. Do not drain the engine oil; merely remove the metering oil pump hose from the carburetor.

2. Perform Steps 1–4 of "Engine Disassembly."

3. Install the intake manifold and carburetor assembly in the reverse order of removal.

Intake Manifold and Auxiliary Port Valve

REMOVAL & INSTALLATION

13B Engine

1. Remove the dynamic chamber by removing or disconnecting the following parts:

a. Negative battery cable; Air funnel; accelerator cable and throttle sensor connector.

1. Dynamic chamber
2. Fuel hose
3. Vacuum sensing tube
4. Injector connector
5. Delivery pipe
6. Injector

Dynamic chamber, removal and installation

b. Metering oil pump connecting rod and water hoses.

c. Terminal cover; vacuum sensing tubes (label for correct reinstallation).

d. Air supply connector; intake air temperature sensor connector.

e. Retaining bolts and nuts and the dynamic chamber.

2. Cover the intake manifold port opening with a clean cloth to prevent dust or dirt from entering.

3. remove the incline check valve assemblies and vacuum lines.

4. Remove the air hoses from the manifold mounted solenoids.

5. Remove the actuator from the intake manifold.

6. Remove the nuts and bolts that mount the intake manifold to the engine, remove the manifold. Clean all gaskets mounting surfaces.

7. Remove the auxiliary port valve. Check the valve for cracks and breakage.

8. Install the auxiliary valve. Make sure that the bigger side of the valve shafts align with the matching mark on the mounting gasket.

9. Install the remaining parts in the reverse order of removal.

Thermal Reactor

REMOVAL & INSTALLATION

1981-87

On 1981-87 models, the thermal reactor/heat exchanger system is replace by two catalytic converters and a special reactive exhaust manifold. See "Emission Control" section for explanation.

ENGINE LUBRICATION— ROTARY

A conventional oil pump, which is chain driven, circulates oil through the rotary engine. A full-flow filter is mounted on the top of the rear housing and an oil cooler is used to reduce the temperature of the engine oil.

An unusual feature of the rotary engine lubrication system is a metering oil pump which injects oil into the float chamber of the carburetor on 12A engines, or directly into the cylinder on 13B engines. Once there, it is mixed with the fuel which is to be burned, thus providing extra lubrication for the seals. The metering oil pump is designed to work only when the engine is working under a load.

Oil Pan

REMOVAL & INSTALLATION

NOTE: The only component(s) that can be serviced by removing the oil pan are the oil strainer and the oil pressure control valve.

1. Drain the engine oil.

2. Disconnect the oil level sensor and oil thermo unit, if so equipped. On 13B engines, raise and support the vehicle safely and remove the engine under cover. Support the engine from above, remove the engine mount nuts and lift the engine slightly to gain working clearance.

3. Remove the pan bolts and lower the pan.

4. To install, clean all of the old gasket material off the pan and engine mating surfaces, then apply a continuous bead sealer (part no. 8527 77 739) to the pan surface. The bead should be from 0.16–0.24 in. (4–6mm)

wide and should overlap at the end.

5. Fit the gasket on the pan, then apply an identical bead of sealer on top of the gasket.

6. Fit the gasket and torque the bolts to 6–8 ft. lbs. (0.6–0.9 Nm).

7. Fill the crankcase with oil.

Oil Pump

REMOVAL & INSTALLATION

Oil pump removal and installation is contained in the engine overhaul section above. Perform only those steps needed to remove the oil pump.

Metering Oil Pump

OPERATION

A metering oil pump, mounted on the top of the engine, is used to provide additional lubrication to the engine when it is operating under a load. The metering pump is a plunger type and is controlled by throttle opening. A cam arrangement, connected to the throttle lever, operates a plunger. The plunger, in turn, acts as a differential plunger, the stroke of which determines the amount of oil flow.

When the throttle opening is small, the amount of the plunger stroke is small; as the throttle opening increases, so does the amount of the plunger stroke.

TESTING

12A Engines

1. At the carburetor, disconnect the oil lines which run from the metering oil pump to the carburetor.

2. Use a container which has a scale calibrated in cubic centimeters (cc) on its side to catch the pump discharge from the oil lines.

3. Run the engine at 2000 rpm for six minutes.

4. At the end of this time, 2.4–2.9cc should be collected in the container. If not, adjust the pump.

13B Engine

1. Start the engine and allow it to reach normal operating temperature. Shut off the engine.

2. Connect a tachometer to the engine according to the manufacturer's instructions.

3. Disconnect the two housing oil hoses from the metering oil pump.

------- CAUTION -------
Only disconnect two hoses at one time.

4. Connect suitable hoses to the metering oil pump for measurement.

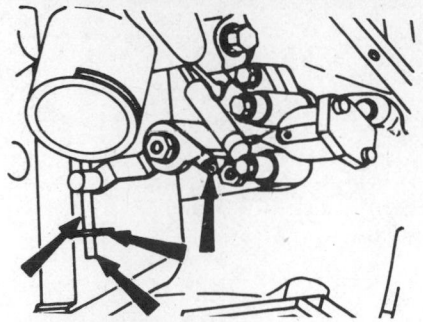

Arrow (right) indicates the metering oil pump adjusting screw. The 3 arrows (left) indicate the connecting rod adjusting holes

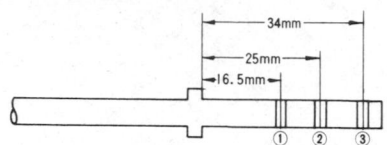

① : 248cc / 6,000rpm / Hr
② : 174cc / 6,000rpm / Hr
③ : 104cc / 6,000rpm / Hr

Connecting rod adjusting holes

5. Pull the metering pump rod up to its maximum stop. Make sure to lift the rod fully while the engine is running.

6. Start and run the engine at 2000 rpm for five minutes and measure the oil discharge; it should be 4.5–5.5cc.

7. Install the housing hoses and measure the manifold metering oil discharge in the same manner.

ADJUSTMENTS

Rotate the adjusting screw on the metering oil pump to obtain the proper oil flow. Clockwise rotation of the screw increases the flow; counterclockwise rotation decreases the oil flow.

If necessary, the oil discharge rate may be further adjusted by changing the position of the cam in the pump connecting rod. The shorter the rod throw, the more oil will be pumped. Adjust the throw by means of the three holes provided.

Oil Cooler

REMOVAL & INSTALLATION

The oil cooler is easily removed after removing the gravel shield and disconnecting the lines. Unbolt the cooler from the radiator.

Installation is the reverse of removal.

ENGINE COOLING – ROTARY

Radiator

REMOVAL & INSTALLATION

1. Disconnect the negative battery cable. Drain the coolant from the radiator drain plug into a suitable container.

2. Remove the cooling fan, air intake pipe, battery and bracket.

3. Remove the lower radiator hose, heater hoses and upper radiator hose.

4. Disconnect the coolant level sensor connector, radiator switch connector and the automatic transmission lines from the radiator.

5. Remove the radiator attaching bolts and remove the radiator along with the radiator cowling.

6. Installation is the reverse order of the removal procedure.

Water Pump

REMOVAL & INSTALLATION

1. Remove the air cleaner and disconnect the water temperature switch wiring from the radiator. Disconnect the negative battery cable.

2. Remove the air conditioner, air pump, power steering, and alternator drive belts.

3. Remove the cooling fan and drive assembly. On 13B engines, turn the eccentric shaft so that the top mark of the pulley is aligned with the indicator pin.

4. Remove the drive pulley for the air conditioner compressor from in front of the alternator/air pump drive pulleys (the pulley on the eccentric shaft, not the one on the front of the compressor).

5. Place a pan under the lower radiator hose then disconnect the hose (or remove the drain plug) and allow the coolant to drain out of the system.

6. Remove the upper radiator hose, coolant reservoir hose and coolant bypass hose. Disconnect the water thermo sensor connector and the water thermo switch connector (on the A/T models only).

7. Remove the attaching bolts and remove the water pump along witht eh cooling fan pulley.

8. When installing, clean the old gasket from the mating surfaces, and install a new gasket with sealer. Torque the attaching bolts evenly and in the order shown to 13–20 ft. lbs. Remaining installation is the reverse of removal.

Thermostat

REMOVAL & INSTALLATION

——— CAUTION ———

The thermostat is equipped with a plunger which covers and uncovers a by-pass hole at its bottom. Because of this unusual construction, only the specified Mazda thermostat should be used for replacement. A standard thermostat will cause the engine to overheat.

1. Drain the engine coolant. Remove the upper hose from thermostat housing.
2. Disconnect the water thermo switch connector. Remove the thermostat housing and the thermostat.
3. Installation is the reverse or removal procedure, always install a new mounting gasket.

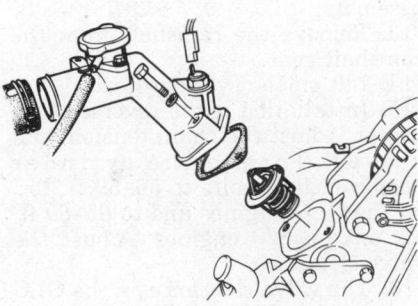

13B engine thermostat mounting

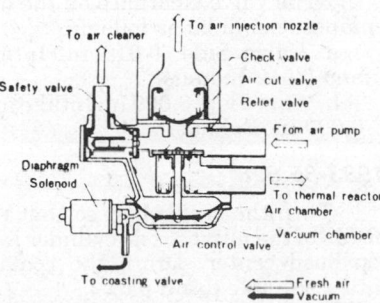

Thermostat installation and by-pass circuit

ENGINE MECHANICAL— GASOLINE PISTON ENGINE

Engine

REMOVAL & INSTALLATION

Rear Wheel Drive GLC and 626

The engine is removed separately, leaving the transmission in place.
1. Remove the hood.
2. Remove the engine splash shield.
3. Drain the coolant.
4. Drain the engine oil.
5. Disconnect all electrical wires and leads. Remove the battery.
6. Disconnect all fluid lines and hoses.
7. Remove the air cleaner.
8. Unbolt and remove the radiator and cowling.
9. Disconnect the throttle cable from the carburetor and remove the throttle linkage from the rocker cover.
10. Disconnect the choke cable.
11. remove the starter.
12. Disconnect the exhaust pipe.
13. remove the clutch cover plate. Support the transmission.
14. Unbolt the right and left engine mounts.
15. Attach a lifting sling to the engine and pull the engine forward until it clears the clutch shaft.
16. Lift the engine from the vehicle.
17. Installation is the reverse of removal.

GLC—Front Wheel Drive

NOTE: The factory recommends that the engine and transaxle be removed from the car as a unit.

1. Mark the outline of the hood hinges for reinstallation alignment. Remove the hood.
2. Disconnect the negative battery cable and remove the battery, if necessary.
3. Loosen the front wheel lugs. Jack up the vehicle and safely support it one jackstands.
4. Remove the two front wheels. Remove the bottom and side splash shields. Drain the coolant, engine oil and transaxle fluid.
5. Remove the air cleaner assembly. remove the radiator hoses and the

radiator shroud and electric fan assembly.
6. Connect an engine lifting sling to the engine. Connect a chain hoist or portable engine crane to the lifting sling and apply slight upward pressure to the engine and transaxle assembly.
7. Remove the mounting bolts from the engine crossmember. Remove the crossmember.
8. Disconnect the lower ball joints. Dismount the steering knuckles and drive axles.
9. Vehicles equipped with manual transaxles: disconnect the shifting rod and extension bar. Vehicles equipped with an automatic transaxle: disconnect the selector rod and counter rod.
10. Remove the front and rear transaxle mounting bushings. Disconnect the exhaust pipe from the catalytic converter. Remove the transaxle crossmember.
11. Disconnect all wires and hoses from under the engine and transaxle. Label them for identification.
12. Disconnect all wires, heater hoses and vacuum hoses from the upper side of the engine and transaxle. Label them for correct installation.
13. Disconnect the accelerator cable, speedometer cable, clutch cable, power brake booster line and fuel lines.
14. Check to be sure all remaining hoses and wiring are disconnected. remove the evaporative canister. Remove the right side upper engine mount through bolt.
15. Lift the engine and transaxle assembly from the vehicle. Take care not to allow the assembly to swing forward into the radiator.
16. If the vehicle must be moved from underneath the engine; remount the steering knuckles, secure the drive axles so that they can still turn, mount the front wheels and lower the vehicle from the jackstand.
17. Installation is in the reverse order of removal.

626—Front Wheel Drive

NOTE: The factory recommends that the engine and transaxle be removed from the car as a unit.

1. Mark the outline of the hood hinges for reinstallation alignment. Remove the hood.
2. Disconnect the negative battery cable. Remove the battery, if necessary.
3. Loosen the front wheel lugs. Jack up the vehicle and safely support it on jackstands.
4. Drain the coolant, engine oil and transaxle fluid.

5. Remove the air cleaner assembly. Remove the radiator hoses and the radiator shroud and electric fan assembly.

6. Remove the fuel hose, fuel return hose, accelerator cable and speedometer cable.

7. On vehicles with a manual transaxle, remove the clutch cable along with the clutch slave cylinder, and on those with an automatic transaxle, remove the control cable.

8. Remove the engine ground wire, engine harness, power brake vacuum hose and three-way valve vacuum switch with bracket.

9. Remove the heater hoses, duty solenoid valve and the vacuum sensor.

10. Remove any additional engine or transaxle wiring.

11. Remove the air vent hose and vacuum canister hose.

12. Remove the electric cooling fan and radiator.

13. Remove the washer tank and the radiator overflow tank.

14. On air conditioned models, remove the alternator and the A/C compressor.

NOTE: Do not disconnect the high and low pressure hoses from the compressor. Secure the compressor in the fender well area with a piece of wire or rope.

15. Remove the front wheels and the splash shields.

16. Remove the power steering pump.

NOTE: Do not remove the pressure and return hoses from the pump. Raise the pump and allow it to rest on the crossmember.

17. Remove the drive axles and change rod.

18. Disconnect the shift control rod on manual transaxle models. Remove the shift control extension bar. Install a suitable engine hoist to the engine and lift the engine slightly.

19. Remove the transmission and engine mounting bolts and nuts. Disconnect the exhaust pipe and turbo charger, if equipped.

20. Remove the torque stopper mount from the right wheel house area and inside the engine compartment.

21. Carefully remove the engine and transaxle from the vehicle.

22. Installation is the reverse of removal. Refill the engine coolant, engine oil and transaxle fluid.

323—Front Wheel Drive

1. Disconnect the negative battery cable. Drain the engine oil, transaxle

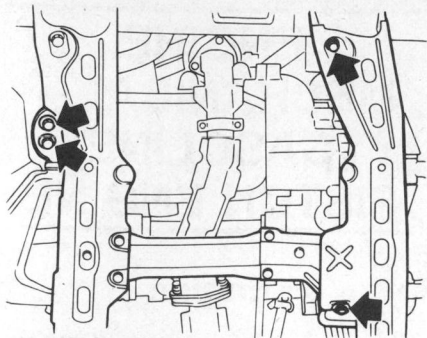

1983-88 626 engine mounting bolt locations

oil and coolant into suitable drain pans.

2. Remove the battery and battery box. Remove the air cleaner assembly, oil level gauge and cooling fan with the radiator assembly (on the A/T models, just remove the radiator shroud, do not remove the radiator).

3. Remove the accelerator cable and cruise control cable (if so equipped). Remove the speedometer cable and fuel hoses. On A/T models, remove the upper and lower radiator hoses.

4. Remove the heater hose, brake vacuum hose, 3-way solenoid vacuum hoses, canister hose and the engine harness connectors along with the engine ground.

5. Remove the upper and lower radiator hoses. Remove the exhaust pipe (on A/T models, remove the secondary air pipe).

6. Rempove the A/C compressor anf power steering pump (if so equipped).

NOTE: Do not disconnect the high and low pressure hoses from the compressor. Secure the compressor in the fender well area with a piece of wire or rope. Do not remove the pressure and return hoses from the pump. Raise the pump and store it out of the way.

7. Remove the driveshafts, clutch control cable, shift control rod, engine under cover and side cover.

8. Install a suitable engine hoist to the engine and lift the engine slightly. Remove the engine mounts.

9. Carefully remove the engine and transaxle from the vehicle.

10. Installation is the reverse of removal. Refill the engine coolant, engine oil and transaxle fluid.

Cylinder Head

NOTE: On all models, refer to the "Front Cover, Timing Belt, Tensioner and Timing Pulleys,

Removal and Installation" procedures in this section for the correct camshaft pulley removal and timing belt installation procedure

REMOVAL & INSTALLATION

GLC and 1981-82 626

Be sure that the cylinder head is cold before removal. This will prevent warpage. Do not remove the cam gear from the timing chain.

1. Drain the cooling system.
2. Remove the air cleaner.
3. Disconnect all applicable electrical wires and leads.
4. Rotate the crankshaft to put the No. 1 cylinder at TDC on the compression stroke.
5. Remove the distributor.
6. Remove the rocker arm cover.
7. Raise and support the vehicle. Disconnect the exhaust pipe from the manifold.
8. Remove the accelerator linkage.
9. Remove the nut, washer and the distributor gear from the camshaft.
10. Remove the nut, washer and camshaft gear. On front-wheel drive 1490cc models, remove the tensioner from the timing case cover. Fasten the gear and chain together.
11. Remove the cylinder head bolts and cylinder head-to-front cover bolt. Loosen the head bolts in reverse of the torque sequence.
12. Remove the rocker arm assembly.
13. Remove the camshaft from the camshaft gear.
14. Lift off the cylinder head.
15. Installation is the reverse of removal. Adjust the chain tension, and valves. Torque the cylinder head/camshaft bolts to 56–59 ft. lbs. on the GLC engines and to 65–69 ft. lbs on the 626 engines. Adjust the valve clearance.
16. The valve clearance on the GLC engines shoud be as follows:
  a. Valve Side: 0.010 in. Intake and 0.012 Exhaust.
  b. Cam Side: 0.007 in. Intake and 0.009 in. Exhaust.
17. The valve clearance on the 626 engines should be as follows:
  a. Valve Side: 0.012 in. Intake and 0.012 Exhaust.
  b. Cam Side: 0.009 in. Intake and 0.009 in. Exhaust.

1983-85 626

1. Turn the crankshaft so that the piston of the number one cylinder is at top dead center. Drain the coolant into a suitable drain pan.
2. Remove the air cleaner, distributor, thermostat, fuel pump and accelerator cable.

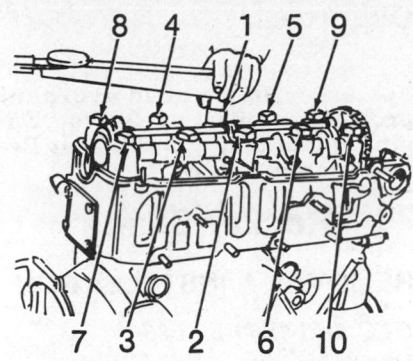

Piston engine cylinder head torque sequence—GLC and 1980–82 626

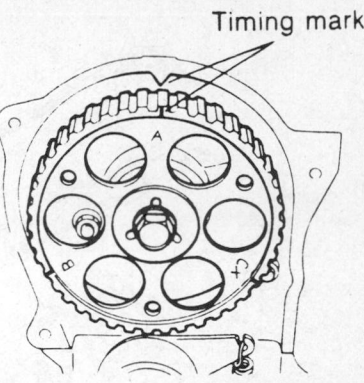

Timing mark

Camshaft pulley timing marks—626 engine

3. Remove the intake manifold and carburetor. Remove the alternator and alternator strap. Remove the A/C compressor and alternator bracket installation bolts.

NOTE: Do not disconnect the high and low pressure hoses from the compressor. Secure the compressor in the fender well area with a piece of wire or rope.

4. Remove the engine ground wire. Remove the upper timing belt cover and timing belt.

NOTE: Before removing the timing belt, turn the crankshaft to align the timing mark (A) of the camshaft pulley with the front timing mark. Be sure to mark the direction of rotation on the timing belt. The reason to mark the belt is so that the belt can be reinstalled in the same direction. If the camshaft pulley has to be removed, use a suitable tool to lock the pulley in place so as to keep it from turning and remove the pulley retaining nut or bolt.

5. Remove the secondary pipes and disconnect the oxygen sensor connector.

6. Remove the insulator assembly along with the nuts and gaskets. Remove the exhaust pipe from the exhaust manifold.

7. Remove the rear housing and gaskets. Remove the cylinder head cover and gaskets.

8. Remove the cylinder head bolts. Loosen the head bolts in reverse of the torque sequence.

9. Remove the cylinder head and exhaust manifold as an assembly. Remove the cylinder head gasket.

10. Clean and inspect the gasket mating surfaces. Check for wear and/or damage, replace the parts, if necessary.

11. To install, use new gaskets and reverse the removal procedures.

Torque the cylinder head bolts to 59–65 ft. lbs.(and do not forget to insert the plain washer) and the rocker arm assembly to 13–19 ft. lbs. Adjust the valve clearances and check the timing. Refill the cooling system.

12. The valve clearance on the 626 engines should be as follows:

a. Valve Side: 0.012 in. Intake and 0.012 Exhaust.

b. Cam Side: 0.009 in. Intake and 0.009 in. Exhaust.

1986–88 626

1. Turn the crankshaft so that the piston of the number one cylinder is at top dead center. Drain the coolant into a suitable drain pan.

2. Remove the accelerator cable, secondary air pipe, distributor and rear housing.

3. Remove the air hose, secondary air pipe, oil pipe and insulator number one, two and three.

4. Remove the turbo bracket and the front catalytic converter.

5. Remove the oil return hose, water inlet hose, water outlet hose and the EGR pipe.

6. Remove the exhaust manifold and turbocharger assembly with gasket.

7. Remove the intake manifold assembly and gasket.

8. Remove the timing belt cover and timing belt.

NOTE: Before removing the timing belt, turn the crankshaft to align the timing mark (A) of the camshaft pulley with the front timing mark. Be sure to mark the direction of rotation on the timing belt. The reason to mark the belt is so that the belt can be reinstalled in the same direction. If the camshaft pulley has to be removed, use a suitable tool to lock the pulley in place so as to keep it from turning and remove the pulley retaining nut or bolt.

9. Remove the cylinder head cover and gaskets. Remove the cylinder head bolts. Loosen the head bolts in reverse of the torque sequence.

10. Remove the cylinder head and cylinder head gasket.

11. Clean and inspect the gasket mating surfaces. Check for wear and/or damage, replace the parts, if necessary.

12. To install, use new gaskets and reverse the removal procedures. Torque the cylinder head bolts to 59–65 ft. lbs.(and do not forget to insert the plain washer) and the rocker arm assembly to 13–19 ft. lbs. Adjust the valve clearances and check the timing. Refill the cooling system.

13. The valve clearance on the 626 engines should be as follows:

a. Intake: 0.012 in.

b. Exhaust: 0.012 in.

1986–88 323

1. Turn the crankshaft so that the piston of the number one cylinder is at top dead center. Drain the coolant into a suitable drain pan.

2. Remove the air cleaner assembly, and remove the following components:

a. Remove the oil level gauge, accelerator cable and cruise control cable (if so equipped).

b. Remove the fuel hoses, fuel pump (carbureted models only), heater hoses, brake vacuum hose and canister hose.

c. Remove the engine harness connectors, spark plug wires, distributor, spark plugs and secondary air pipe assembly (for carbureted models only).

d. Remove the front hanger and engine ground wire. Remove the upper radiator hose, water bypass hose and bracket.

e. Remove the intake manifold assembly. Remove the exhaust manifold insulator and the exhaust manifold.

f. Remove the engine side cover. Remove the upper and lower timing belt cover. Remove the timing belt tensioner with spring and remove the timing belt.

NOTE: Before removing the timing belt, turn the crankshaft to align the timing matching mark on the camshaft pulley with the matching mark on the cylinder head cover. Be sure to mark the direction of rotation on the timing belt. The reason to mark the belt is so that the belt can be reinstalled in the same direction.

g. To remove the camshaft pulley, use a suitable tool to lock the

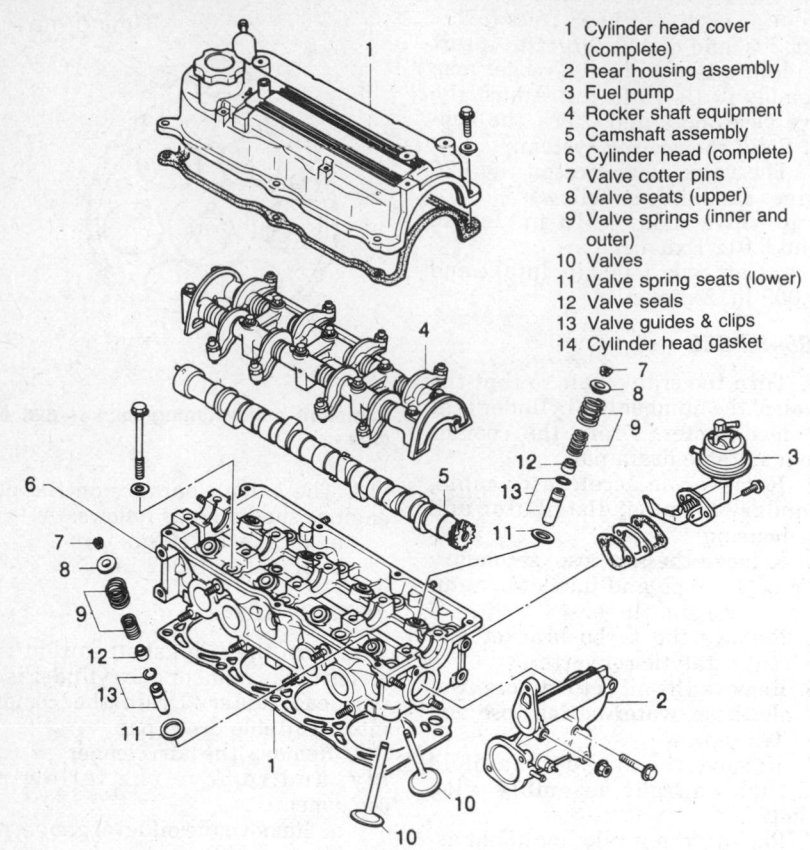

1 Cylinder head cover
(complete)
2 Rear housing assembly
3 Fuel pump
4 Rocker shaft equipment
5 Camshaft assembly
6 Cylinder head (complete)
7 Valve cotter pins
8 Valve seats (upper)
9 Valve springs (inner and
outer)
10 Valves
11 Valve spring seats (lower)
12 Valve seals
13 Valve guides & clips
14 Cylinder head gasket

Exploded view of 1983 and later 626 cylinder head—323 similar

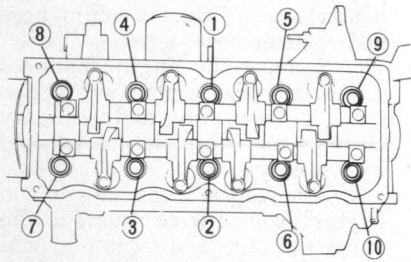

Head bolt torque sequence—323 and 626
models

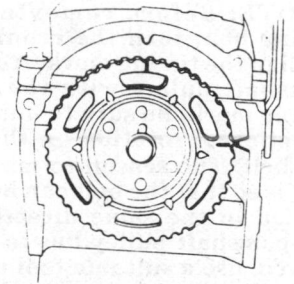

Camshaft pulley timing marks—323 engine

OVERHAUL

For all cylinder head overhaul procedures, please refer to "Engine Rebuilding" in the Unit Repair section.

Rocker Shafts

REMOVAL & INSTALLATION

GLC and 1981-82 626

This operation should only be performed on a cold engine; the bolts which hold the rocker shafts in place also hold the cylinder head to the block.

1. Disconnect the choke cable.
2. If equipped, disconnect the air bypass valve cable.
3. Remove the rocker cover.
4. Remove the rocker arm shaft attaching bolts and the rocker arm assemblies.
5. Installation is the reverse of removal. Install the rocker arm assemblies on the cylinder head. Temporarily tighten the cylinder head bolts to specifications and offset each rocker arm support 0.04 in.(0.039 in on the 1984–85 GLC) from the valve stem center. Torque the cylinder head/camshaft bolts to 56–59 ft. lbs. on the GLC engine and 65–69 ft. lbs. on the 626 engine. Adjust the valve clearance.

1983-88 626

1. Refer to the "Front Cover, Timing Belt, Tensioner and Timing Pulleys, Removal and Installation" procedures in this section and remove the camshaft pulley.
2. Remove the front housing assembly from the cylinder head.
3. Remove the distributor hold down bolt and the distributor from the cylinder head.
4. Remove the rear housing assembly from the rear of the cylinder head.
5. Remove the cylinder head cover and gasket.
6. Loosen the rocker arm assembly bolts, a little at a time, in the reverse order of installation (from the outer ends, toward the center).

NOTE: DO NOT remove the bolts, remove them with the rocker arm assembly. When disassembling the rocker arm assembly, keep the part in order.

7. Inspect the parts for wear and/or damage, replace as necessary.
8. Clean and inspect the gasket mounting surfaces.
9. To install, use new gaskets/sealant and reverse the re-

pulley in place so as to keep it from turning and remove the pulley retaining nut or bolt.
h. Remove the rear engine hanger and cylinder head cover and gaskets.
i. Remove the cylinder head bolts. Loosen the head bolts in reverse of the torque sequence.
j. Remove the cylinder head and cylinder head gasket.
3. Clean and inspect the gasket mating surfaces. Check for wear and/or damage, replace the parts, if necessary.
4. To install, use new gaskets and reverse the removal procedures.

Torque the cylinder head bolts to 50–60 ft. lbs. (and do not forget to insert the plain washer) and the rocker arm assembly to 16–21 ft. lbs. Adjust the valve clearances and check the timing. Refill the cooling system.
5. The valve clearance on the 323 engines should be as follows:
a. Intake: 0.012 in.
b. Exhaust: 0.012 in.
6. Be sure to install the camshaft pulley onto the dowel pin and keyway with the matching mark straight up, so that the timing marks on the camshaft pulley and cylinder head align. Tighten the camshaft pulley to 36–45 ft. lbs.

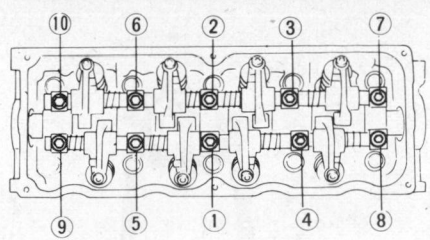

Rocker shaft torque sequence—323 and 626 models

moval procedures. Torque the rocker arm assembly bolts to 13–19 ft. lbs. Adjust the valve clearances and check the timing.

1986–88 323

1. Disconnect the negative battery cable. Drain the coolant into a suitable drain pan.
2. Remove the air cleaner assembly, and remove the following components:

   a. Remove the oil level gauge, accelerator cable and cruise control cable (if so equipped).

   b. Remove the fuel hoses, fuel pump (carbureted models only), heater hoses, brake vacuum hose and canister hose.

   c. Remove the engine harness connectors, spark plug wires, distributor, spark plugs and secondary air pipe assembly (for carbureted models only).

   d. Remove the front hanger and engine ground wire. Remove the upper radiator hose, water bypass hose and bracket.

   e. Remove the intake manifold assembly. Remove the exhaust manifold insulator and the exhaust manifold.

   f. Remove the engine side cover. Remove the upper timing belt cover.
3. Remove the cylinder head cover and gaskets.
4. Remove the rocker arm and rocker shaft assembly by gradually loosening the bolts evenly, until they are all free (do not remove the bolt from the rocker arm assembly).
5. Plug the oil drain hole with a shop rag to prevent the possibility of the spring retainers falling into the oil pan.
6. Install the rocker arm and rocker shaft assembly on the cylinder head and tighten it gradually to a torque of 16–21 ft. lbs. Adjust the valves and install the cylinder head cover and gasket (be sure to use a suitable sealant on the cylinder head cover).
7. The rest of the installation is the reverse order of the removal procedure.

Intake Manifold

REMOVAL & INSTALLATION

Due to the lack of information available on the intake manifold removal and installation at the time of this publication, a general intake manifold removal and installation procedure is outlined below. The removal steps can be altered as required by the technician.

1. Drain the cooling system.
2. Remove the air cleaner, air intake, or turbo ducts.
3. Remove the accelerator linkage.
4. Disconnect the choke cable and fuel line on carbureted models. On engines with fuel injection, disconnect the fuel line, vacuum hoses and electrical connectors.
5. Disconnect the PCV valve hose.
6. Disconnect the heater return hose and by-pass hose.
7. Remove the intake manifold-to-cylinder head attaching nuts.
8. Remove the manifold and carburetor or throttle body and injectors as an assembly.
9. To install, use a new gasket and reverse the removal procedures. Torque the intake manifold to specifications.

Exhaust Manifold

REMOVAL & INSTALLATION

Due to the lack of information available on the exhaust manifold removal and installation at the time of this publication, a general exhaust manifold removal and installation procedure is outlined below. The removal steps can be altered as required by the technician.

1. Remove the heat shield cover (if equipped). Remove the tow attaching nuts from the exhaust pipe at the manifold. On turbo models, remove the air duct and turbocharger-to-manifold mounting bolts.
2. Remove all necessary exhaust brackets and hangers. Remove the retaining nuts and remove the manifold.
3. To install, use a new gasket and reverse the removal procedures. Torque the exhaust manifold to specifications.

Turbocharger

REMOVAL & INSTALLATION

NOTE: This procedure should only be attempted on a cold engine.

1. Drain the cooling system.
2. Align the No. 1 cylinder at TDC/compression, then remove the distributor and spark plug wires.
3. Remove the turbo air duct and secondary air pipe from the exhaust manifold.
4. Remove the lower insulator cover. Remove the secondary air pipe and nipple.
5. Disconnect the oil feed pipe from the turbocharger.
6. Remove the upper insulator cover.
7. Disconnect the exhaust pipe from the front catalytic converter.
8. Disconnect the EGR pipe and water hoses.
9. Remove the oxygen sensor from the exhaust manifold. Remove the front pipe from the catalytic converter.
10. Remove the turbocharger-to-bracket mounting bolts.
11. Remove the exhaust manifold mounting bolts and lift off the manifold turbocharger and front catalytic converter as an assembly. Continue disassembly on a workbench.
12. Installation is the reverse or removal. Add 25cc of oil to the turbocharger oil passage before installing and replace all gaskets or sealant. Disconnect the coil and crank the engine for 20 seconds to insure that oil reaches the center bearings. Reconnect the coil and start the engine, letting it idle for 30 seconds to endure the proper operation of the turbocharger.

TROUBLESHOOTING

For more information on turbocharging, please refer to "Turbocharging" in the Unit Repair Section.

Front Cover, Timing Chain/Belt and Tensioner

REMOVAL & INSTALLATION

GLC and 1981-82 626

NOTE: On front wheel drive GLC models, the engine must be removed from the car. Start procedure at Step 5.

1. Bring the No. 1 piston to TDC (timing marks aligned). Drain the cooling system. Remove the radiator

hoses, thermostat housing, thermostat, fan, water pump and radiator.

2. Remove all lower and side splash or skid shields. Remove the crankshaft pulley and any driven units (alternator, air pump, etc.) that will interfere with front cover removal.

3. Remove the blind cover (small plate retained by two or three bolts that covers the chain adjuster). Install the special clamping tool or make a simple device to prevent the slipper head of the chain adjuster from popping out.

4. Remove the cylinder head, oil pan and timing chain front cover.

5. On GLC front wheel drive models: Remove the chain tensioner (located on the left upper corner of the timing cover) before removing the cylinder head. Remove the crankshaft pulley and proceed as follows.

6. If equipped, remove the oil slinger from the crankshaft. Depending on the engine, remove the oil pump pulley and chain or the timing chain with sprockets first, the remaining sprockets and chain second. Loosen the timing chain guide strip and remove the chain tensioner, if necessary.

7. Installation is in the reverse order of removal.

8. When installing the oil pump sprocket and chain, check for excessive slack. Replace the chain if necessary. On the 626 models slack should be 0.015 in. Adjusting shims (between the oil pump and mounting) are available in thicknesses of 0.006 in.

9. Inspect the slipper head of the chain adjuster, the chain guide strip and the vibration damper for wear or damage. Check the adjuster spring for loss of tension. Replace parts as necessary.

10. Place the camshaft sprocket into the timing chain as shown on appropriate illustration. Wire the sprocket and chain in position.

11. Install the timing chain onto the crankshaft sprocket as illustrated. Tighten the chain guide. Install the timing chain tensioner (except GLC front wheel drive). Make sure the snubber spring is fully compressed. Install clamping tool.

12. Install a new timing cover oil seal. Install the timing chain front cover, oil pan and cylinder head. When installing the front cover, be sure tension is applied to the timing chain to prevent it from coming off of the crankshaft sprocket. If the chain comes off of the sprocket, incorrect timing and engine damage will occur.

13. Install the sprocket and timing chain on the camshaft. Refer to the illustrations. Adjust the timing chain tension.

14. To complete the installation, reverse the removal procedures.

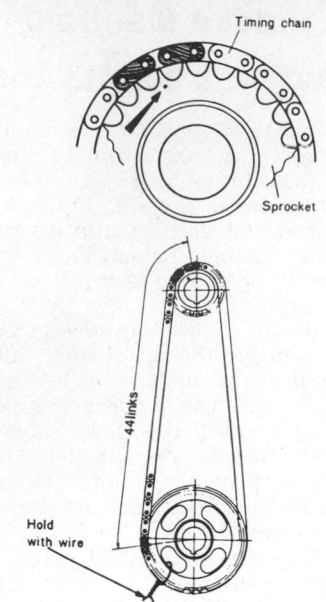

Timing chain installation 1970cc engine 1981-82 626

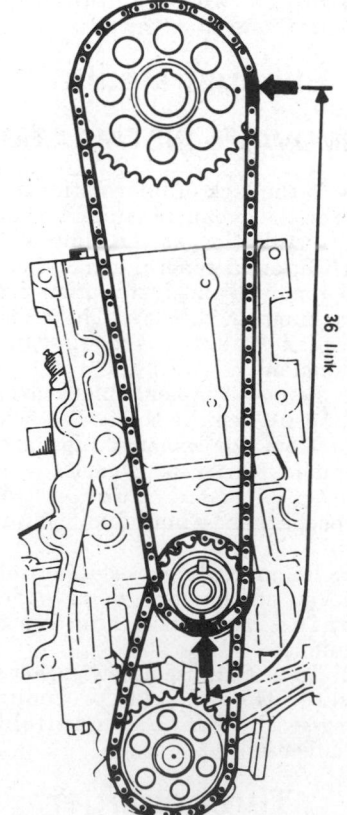

Timing chain installation 1981-85 GLC (FWD). Match the ring plate mark (shiny white) of the timing chain with the timing mark on the crankcase sprocket

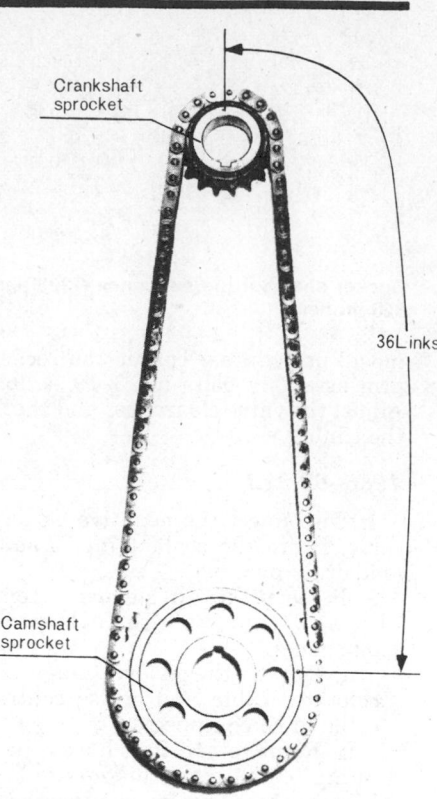

Alignment of the timing chain and timing gear marks 1981–83 GLC wagon

1983-88 626

1. Remove the alternator belt and the power steering pump belt.

2. Remove the upper and the lower timing belt cover.

3. Turn the crankshaft to position the "A" mark on the camshaft pulley with the mark on the housing.

4. Remove the crankshaft pulley mounting bolts and the pulley.

5. Remove the tensioner pulley lock bolt, the pulley and the spring.

6. Remove the timing belt and mark an arrow in the direction of rotation on the timing belt.

7. To remove the camshaft pulley, insert a T-wrench through the camshaft pulley onto a housing bolt, place another wrench on the pulley center bolt, hold the T-wrench securely and remove the pulley center bolt.

8. Pull the camshaft pulley from the camshaft.

9. To remove the crankshaft pulley, remove the center bolt and the pulley.

10. To install, Reinstall the camshaft and crankshaft pulleys if they where removed. Install the timing belt as follows, be sure the timing mark on the timing belt pulley is aligned with the matching mark. Make sure that the mark (A) of the

camshaft pulley is aligned with the timing mark. If it is not, turn the camshaft to align it.

11. Install the timing belt tensioner and spring. Temporarily secure it as the spring is fully extended.

12. Install the timing belt, if using the old timing belt, be sure it is reinstalled in the same direction of previous rotation. Also make sure there is no oil, grease or dirt on the timing belt.

13. Loosen the tensioner lock bolt. Turn the crankshaft twice in the diretion of rotation. Align the timing marks.

14. Make sure the timing marks are correctly aligned, if they are not aligned, remove the timing belt tensioner and timing belt and repeat Steps 10–14.

15. Tighten the timing belt tensioner lock bolt to 28–38 ft. lbs. Check the timing belt tension. The timing belt deflection should be 0.43–0.51 in. at 22 lbs.

16. Complete the installation by reversing the removal procedure.

1986–88 323

1. Remove the engine side cover. Remove the A/C belt and the power steering pump belt.

2. Remove the alternator drive belt and alternator. Remove the water pump pulley. Remove the upper and the lower timing belt cover.

3. Turn the crankshaft to position the matching mark of the camshaft pulley is aligned with the cylinder head and the cylinder head cover timing mark.

4. Remove the crankshaft pulley mounting bolts and the pulley along with the baffle plate.

5. Remove the tensioner pulley lock bolt, the pulley and the spring.

6. Remove the timing belt and mark an arrow in the direction of rotation on the timing belt.

7. To remove the camshaft pulley, use a suitable tool to lock the pulley in place so as to keep it from turning and remove the pulley retaining nut or bolt. To remove the crankshaft pulley, remove the center bolt and the pulley.

8. To install, Reinstall the camshaft and crankshaft pulleys if they where removed. Install the timing belt as follows, be sure the timing mark on the timing belt pulley is aligned with the matching mark. Make sure that the matching mark of the camshaft pulley is aligned with the cylinder head and the cylinder head cover timing mark. If it is not, turn the camshaft to align it.

9. Install the timing belt tensioner and spring. Temporarily secure it as the spring is fully extended.

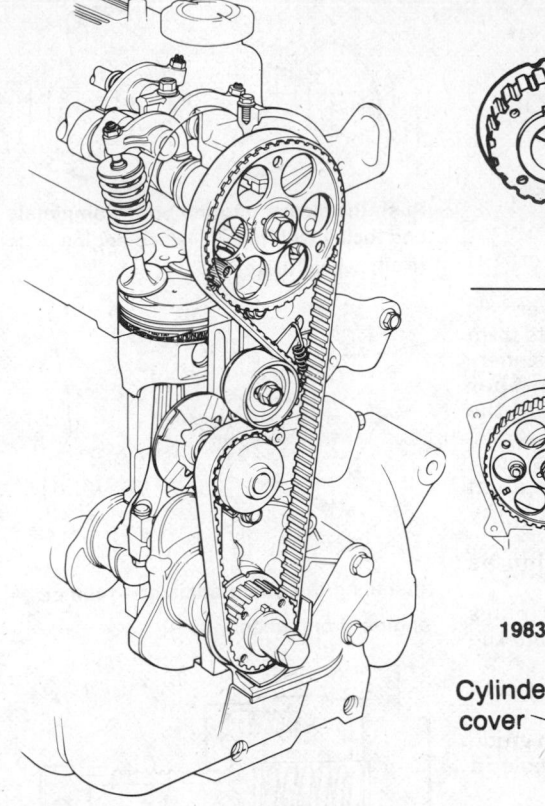

Cutaway view of the 1983-88 626 timing belt

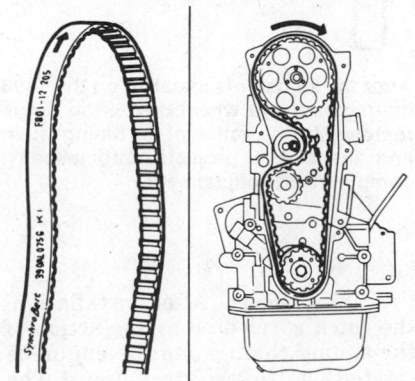

Cutaway view of the 1983-88 626 timing belt

10. Install the timing belt, if using the old timing belt, be sure it is reinstalled in the same direction of previous rotation. Also make sure there is no oil, grease or dirt on the timing belt.

11. Loosen the tensioner lock bolt. Turn the crankshaft twice in the diretion of rotation. Align the timing marks.

12. Make sure the timing marks are correctly aligned, if they are not aligned, remove the timing belt tensioner and timing belt and repeat Steps 8 to 12.

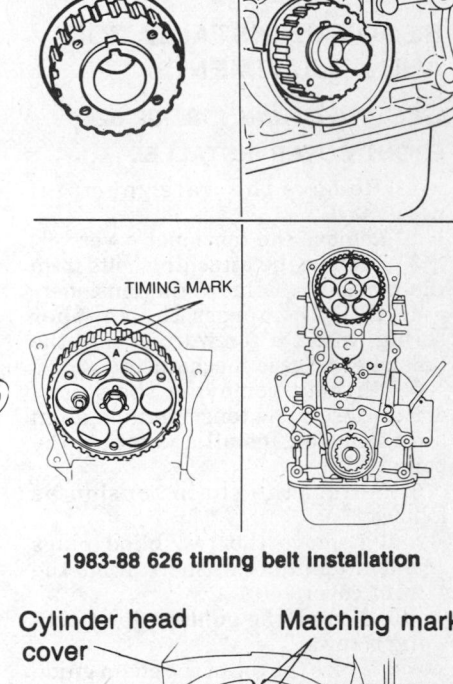

1983-88 626 timing belt Installation

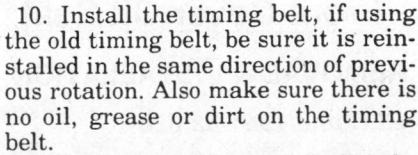

Timing mark alignment on 323 models

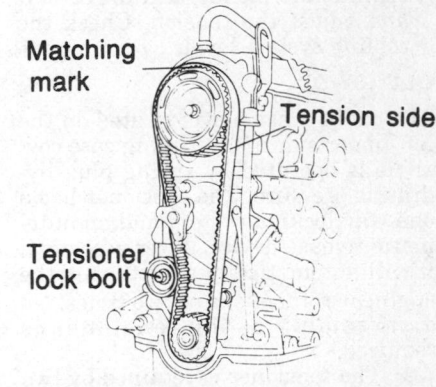

Timing belt and tensioner on 323 models

13. Tighten the timing belt tensioner lock bolt to 14–19 ft. lbs. Check the timing belt tension. The timing belt deflection should be 0.35–0.51 in. at 22 lbs.

14. Complete the installation by reversing the removal procedure.

Timing Chain Tensioner

REMOVAL, INSTALLATION AND ADJUSTMENT

GLC (RWD) and 1981-82 626
FRONT COVER INSTALLED

1. Remove the water pump, if necessary.
2. Remove the tensioner cover.
3. Remove the attaching bolts from the tensioner. Remove the tensioner.
4. Fully compress the snubber spring. Insert a screwdriver into the tensioner release mechanism.
5. Without removing the screwdriver, insert the tensioner and align the bolt holes. Install and torque the bolts.
6. Adjust the chain tension as follows:
   a. Remove the two blind plugs and aluminum washers from the front cover.
   b. Loosen the guide strip attaching screws.
   c. Press the top of the chain guide strip through the adjusting hole in the cylinder head.
   d. Tighten the guide strip attaching screws.
   e. Remove the screwdriver from the tensioner and let the snubber take up the slack in the chain.
   f. Install the blind plugs and aluminum washers.
   g. Install the tensioner cover and gasket.
   h. Install a new gasket and water pump, if removed. Install the crankshaft pulley and drive belt and adjust the tension. Check the cooling system level.

GLC (FWD)

The chain tensioner is located on the left upper side of the timing case cover. It is operated by spring plug hydraulic pressure. The tensioner has a one-way locking system and an automatic release device. After assembly, it will automatically adjust when the engine is rotated one or two times. No disassembly of the tensioner is required.

1. The tensioner is retained by two bolts. Remove the bolts and the tensioner.
2. Check the number of teeth showing on the sleeve of the tensioner. If thirteen or more notches are showing the timing chain is stretched and must be replaced.
3. To install the tensioner, push the sleeve back into the body and lock it with the swivel catch on the tensioner body. Install the tensioner into

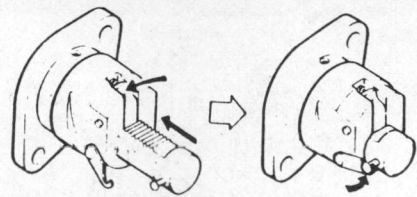

Push the sleeve into the body completely and lock it with pin— 1490 cc engine (front wheel drive)

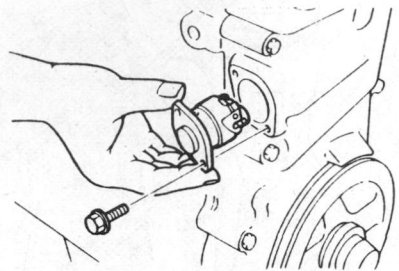

Installing the chain adjuster—1490 cc engine (front wheel drive)

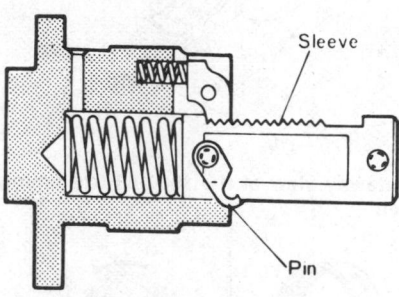

After the adjuster is installed on the 1490 cc engine (front wheel drive), the pin is removed by the action of the timing chain and the sleeve projects automatically, completing the adjustment

the timing cover. After installation, the catch is released by the action of the timing chain when the engine is rotated one to two revolutions. The sleeve projects automatically providing the proper chain adjustment.

Front Cover Oil Seal

REMOVAL & INSTALLATION

GLC and 1981-82 626

The front cover oil seal can be replaced, in most cases, without removing the front cover.
1. Drain the cooling system (except GLC front wheel drive).
2. Remove the radiator (except GLC front wheel drive).
3. Remove the drive belts and crankshaft pulley.

4. Pry the front oil seal carefully from the timing case cover.
5. Install the new oil seal. The rest of the installation is in the reverse order of removal.

1983-88 626 and 323

The oil seal is part of the oil pump assembly, it can be removed ONLY after the oil pump has been removed from the engine.

NOTE: Refer to the "Oil Pump, Removal & Installation" procedures in this section and remove the oil seal from the oil pump.

Camshaft

REMOVAL & INSTALLATION

GLC and 1981-82 626

Perform this operation on a cold engine only. Do not remove the camshaft gear from the timing chain. Be sure that the gear teeth and chain relationship is not disturbed. Wire the chain and cam gear to a place so that they will not fall into the front cover.

1. Remove the water pump, if necessary.
2. Rotate the crankshaft to place the No. 1 cylinder on TDC of the compression stroke.
3. Remove the distributor.
4. Remove the valve cover.
5. Release the tension on the timing chain.
6. Remove the cylinder head bolts.
7. Remove the rocker arm assembly.
8. Remove the nut, washer and distributor gear from the camshaft.
9. Remove the nut and washer holding the camshaft gear.
10. Remove the camshaft.
11. Installation is the reverse of removal. The camshaft end-play (The clearance between the sprocket and the thrust plate) should be 0.001–0.008 in. Check the timing and adjust the valve clearances.

1983-88 626 and 323

1. Refer to the "Front Cover, Timing Belt, Tensioner & Timing Pulleys, Removal and Installation" procedures in this section and remove the timing belt.
2. Drain the coolant.
3. Remove the air cleaner. Remove the thermostat housing and distributor.
4. Remove the cylinder head cover

and gasket. On the 626 models, remove the rear housing, on the 1983-85 626 engine, remove the fuel pump.

5. Remove the rocker shaft/arm assembly. Remove the rocker arm shaft a little at a time, in the reverse order of installation. Remove the trust plate, if so equipped.

6. Remove the camshaft and the cylinder head bolts (if necessary).

— CAUTION —

Do not remove the head bolts when the engine is hot.

7. Installation is the reverse of removal. Install a new seal in the front cover housing and new gaskets as necessary. Torque the front cover and the rear housing bolts to 14–19 ft. lbs. and the rocker arm assembly to 13–19 ft. lbs. on the 626 models and 16–21 ft. lbs on the 323 models.

Piston and Connecting Rod

POSITIONING

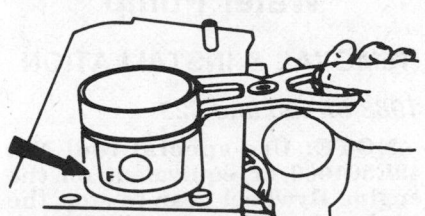

The "F" marks (arrow) face the front of the engine

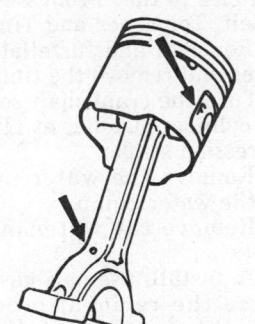

Piston and connecting rod positioning

When assembling the piston and connecting rod, the big end of the rod and the "F" mark on the piston must face in the same direction. The pistons should be installed in the block with the "F" facing the front of the engine. The oil hole of the connecting rod must face the intake manifold.

ENGINE LUBRICATION — GASOLINE PISTON ENGINE

Oil Pan

REMOVAL & INSTALLATION

1983-88 626

1. Jack up the vehicle and use safety stands to support it.
2. Drain the engine oil and remove the torque stopper.
3. Remove the right wheel and splash shield.
4. Remove the front exhaust pipe and raise the passenger side of the engine slightly.

NOTE: A chain, block and tackle may be used to raise the engine.

5. Remove engine mount No. 3.
6. Remove the front engine lower cover and the oil pan.

NOTE: Remove the oil pan by turning the front end to the left.

7. To install, use a new

gasket/sealant and reverse the removal procedures. Torque the oil pan bolts to 6 ft. lbs. Refill the crankcase.

GLC and 1981-82 626

1. Jack up the front of the vehicle and safely support on jackstands. Disconnect negative battery cable. Remove the engine splash shield or skid plate.
2. Remove the engine rear brace attaching bolts and loosen the bolts on the left side, if equipped.
3. Loosen the front motor mounts, raise the front of the engine and block up to gain clearance, if necessary (except GLC front wheel drive).
4. Remove the oil pan and allow it to rest on the crossmember. Remove

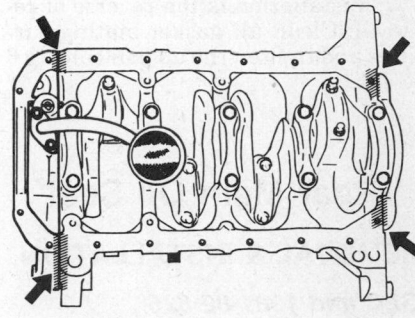

Use sealer at these locations when installing the oil pan

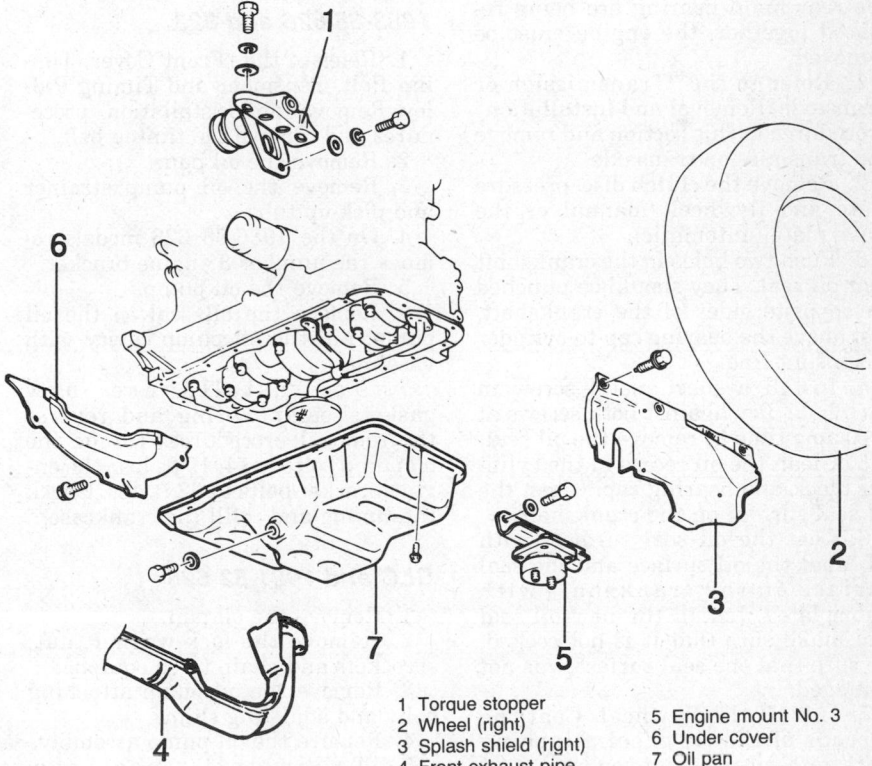

1 Torque stopper
2 Wheel (right)
3 Splash shield (right)
4 Front exhaust pipe
5 Engine mount No. 3
6 Under cover
7 Oil pan

1983-88 626 oil pan removal and installation

the oil pump pickup tube, if necessary, to remove the oil pan.

5. To install, use a new gasket/sealant and reverse the removal procedures. Torque the oil pan bolts to 6 ft. lbs. Refill the crankcase.

323 Models

1. Disconnect the negative battery cable.

2. Raise the car and support it safely.

3. Drain the engine oil into a suitable container.

4. Remove the engine splash shields.

5. Disconnect and lower the exhaust pipe. Remove the stiffener.

6. Remove the oil pan mounting bolts and lower the oil pan.

7. Installation is the reverse of removal. Clean all gasket mating surfaces and tighten the oil pan bolts to 6 ft. lbs.

Rear Main Oil Seal

REMOVAL & INSTALLATION

GLC and 1981-82 626

If the rear main oil seal is being replaced independently of any other parts, it can be done with the engine in place. If the rear main oil seal and the rear main bearing are being replaced together, the engine must be removed.

1. Refer to the "Transmission or Transaxle, Removal and Installation" procedures in this section and remove the transmission/transaxle.

2. Remove the clutch disc, pressure plate and flywheel (manual or the drive plate (automatic).

3. Push two holes in the crankshaft rear oil seal. They should be punched on opposite sides of the crankshaft, just above the bearing cap-to-cylinder block split line.

4. Install a sheet metal screw in each hole. Pry against both screws at the same time to remove the oil seal.

5. Clean the oil recess in the cylinder block and bearing cap. Clean the oil seal surface on the crankshaft.

6. Coat the oil seal surfaces with oil. Coat the oil surface and the seal surface on the crankshaft with Lubriplate®. Install the new oil seal and make sure that it is not cocked. Be sure that the seal surface was not damaged.

7. Install the flywheel. Coat the threads of the flywheel attaching bolts with oil-resistant sealer.

8. To complete the installation, reverse the removal procedures.

1983-88 626 and 323

1. Refer to the "Transaxle, Removal and Installation" procedures in this section and remove the transaxle.

2. If equipped with a manual transaxle, remove the pressure plate, the clutch disc and the flywheel. If equipped with an automatic transaxle, remove the drive plate from the crankshaft.

3. Remove the rear oil pan-to-seal housing bolts.

4. Remove the rear main seal housing bolts and the housing from the engine.

5. Remove the oil seal from the rear main housing.

6. Clean the gasket mounting surfaces.

7. To install, use a new seal, coat the seal and the housing with oil. Press the seal into the housing, using an arbor press.

8. To complete the installation, use new gaskets, apply sealant to the oil pan mounting surface and reverse the removal procedures. Torque the rear seal housing to 8 ft. lbs.

Oil Pump

REMOVAL & INSTALLATION

1983-88 626 and 323

1. Refer to the "Front Cover, Timing Belt, Tensioner and Timing Pulley, Removal and Installation" procedures and remove the timing belt.

2. Remove the oil pan.

3. Remove the oil pump strainer and pick-up tube.

4. On the 1986-88 626 models remove the number 3 engine bracket.

5. Remove the oil pump.

6. Replace the oil seal in the oil pump. Fill the oil pump cavity with vasoline.

7. To install, use new gaskets/sealant/O-ring and reverse the removal procedures. Torque the oil pump bolts to 14–19 ft. lbs., the engine bracket bolts to 32 ft. lbs. Check the timing and refill the crankcase.

GLC and 1981-82 626

1. Remove the oil pan.

2. Remove the lock washer, nut, sprockets and chain (if so equipped).

3. Remove the oil pump attaching bolts and adjusting shims.

4. Remove the oil pump assembly.

5. To install, use new gaskets/sealant/O-ring and reverse the removal procedure.

ENGINE COOLING—GASOLINE PISTON ENGINE

Radiator

REMOVAL & INSTALLATION

1. Drain the coolant from the radiator.

2. Remove the fan blades and shroud or disconnect the electrical harness from the electric fan motor and remove the fan and cowling mount.

3. Remove the upper/lower hoses and coolant reservoir tank hose. Disconnect the transmission cooler lines, (if equipped).

4. Remove the radiator mounting bolts and remove the radiator.

5. Install the radiator by reversing the removal procedure. Refill the cooling system.

Water Pump

REMOVAL & INSTALLATION

1983-87 626 and 323

NOTE: Use special tool No. 49E301060 or equivalent on the engine flywheel gear to stop the engine from rotating during removal and installation of the crankshaft pulley.

1. Refer to the "Front Cover, Timing Belt, Tensioner and Timing Pulleys, Removal and Installation" procedures and remove the timing belt.

2. Turn the crankshaft so that the No. 1 cylinder piston is at TDC on the compression stroke.

3. Remove the water inlet pipe from the water pump.

4. Remove the water pump and gasket.

5. To install, use new gaskets and reverse the removal procedures. Torque the water pump bolts to 13.7–18.8 ft. lbs. on 626 models, and 14–29 ft. lbs. on 323 models; torque the water inlet tube to 18 ft. lbs. Refill the cooling system and check the timing.

GLC and 1981-82 626

1. Drain the coolant from the radiator.

2. On GLC front wheel drive models, jack up the front of the car and safely support it on jackstands. Re-

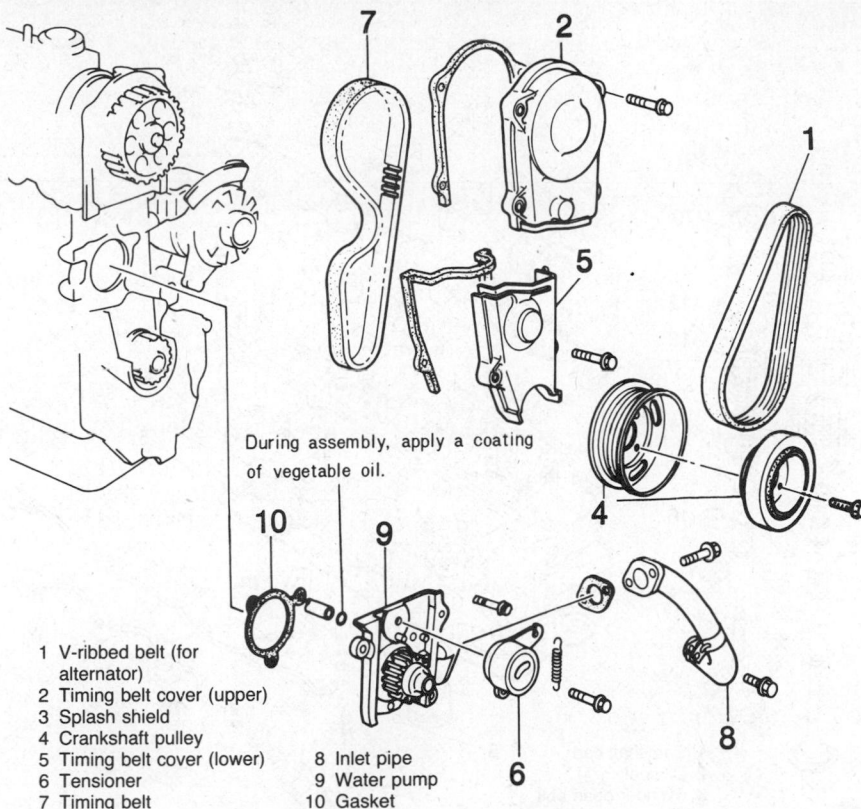

During assembly, apply a coating of vegetable oil.

1 V-ribbed belt (for alternator)
2 Timing belt cover (upper)
3 Splash shield
4 Crankshaft pulley
5 Timing belt cover (lower)
6 Tensioner
7 Timing belt
8 Inlet pipe
9 Water pump
10 Gasket

Water pump removal 1983-88 626

move the splash shield. Remove the drive belt, lower hose and by-pass pipe with O-ring. Remove the water pump.

3. On other models, remove all drive belts. Remove the cooling fan and fan drive assembly. Remove the radiator cowling. Remove the air pump, if necessary. Remove the radiator lower hose, heater hose (if so equipped) and by-pass hose.

4. Loosen and remove the water pump mounting bolts, remove the water pump.

5. Clean all gasket surfaces. Mount the new water pump and gasket. Tighten the mounting bolts evenly in several stages. The rest of the installation is in the reverse order of removal.

Thermostat

REMOVAL & INSTALLATION

1. Drain several quarts of coolant from the radiator so that the coolant level is below the thermostat.
2. On the 1981–82 626 models remove the air pump assembly. Disconnect the radiator hose from the thermostat housing.
3. Remove the thermostat housing mounting bolts, housing, gasket and thermostat.

4. Clean all gasket surfaces. Install the new thermostat with the temperature sensing pellet downwards or toward the engine block. Use a new mounting gasket and install the housing.

5. To complete the installation, reverse the removal procedures. When installing the thermostat into the housing, be sure the jiggle pin is positioned upward. Fill the cooling system.

ENGINE MECHANICAL – DIESEL

Engine

REMOVAL & INSTALLATION

1. Disconnect the negative battery cable.
2. Drain the engine oil, the transaxle oil and the engine coolant. Remove the hood.
3. Raise and support the front of the vehicle. Remove both front wheels.

4. Disconnect the wires from the starter, the alternator, the cooling fan and the backup light switch connector at the transaxle.
5. Remove the oil pressure switch connector, the OSS and the after flow relays from the air cleaner bracket.
6. Disconnect the water level sensor and the temperature switch wiring connectors.
7. Disconnect the glow plug, the revolution sensor, the fuel cut relay and the water temperature sensor (at the thermostat body) wiring connectors.
8. Remove the air cleaner assembly and the air cleaner bracket.
9. Remove the radiator hoses, the heater hoses, the radiator coolant tank hose, the radiator and the mounts.
10. Remove the two fuel hoses from the fuel injection pump.
11. Remove the vacuum hose from the brake vacuum pipe, the two heater and the two oil bypass hoses from the oil cooler.
12. Remove the accelerator cable and the CSD wire from the fuel injection pump.
13. Remove the clutch release cylinder, the ground cable and speedometer cable from the transaxle.
14. Remove the exhaust pipe rubber supports, the brackets and the exhaust pipe from the exhaust manifold.
15. Separate the shift rod(s) and the extension bars from the transaxle.
16. Remove the lower ball joint clamp bolts and separate the control arms from the steering knuckles.
17. Remove the tie rod ends from the steering knuckles.
18. Separate the axleshafts from the front wheels.
19. Place a pry bar between the right axleshaft to disconnect it from the joint shaft, pull out the axleshaft.
20. Remove the mounting nuts from the engine/transaxle mounts. Lower the vehicle.
21. Place a pry bar between the left axleshaft and the transaxle. Pry on the axleshaft to disconnect it from the transaxle.

NOTE: DO NOT damage the oil seal of the axleshaft.

22. Connect a differential side gear holder tool 49–G030–455 to the transaxle case.

23. Connect a engine lift to the engine.

24. Remove the torque stopper from the front of the engine, the engine mounting bolts and the engine/transaxle assembly from the vehicle.

25. Installation is the reverse of removal procedures.

Cylinder Head

REMOVAL & INSTALLATION

1. Disconnect the negative battery cable.

2. Remove the air cleaner tube. Drain the engine coolant and the engine oil.

3. Disconnect the heater outlet hose from the oil cooler and the upper radiator hose.

4. Remove the fuel inlet and return hoses from the fuel injection pump.

5. Disconnect the water temperature gauge wire, the flow plug connector and the ground strap from the engine.

6. Remove the fuel injection pipes.

7. Disconnect the exhaust pipe from the exhaust manifold.

8. Remove the right splash shield and the drive belts.

9. Remove the cylinder head cover with the gasket.

10. Remove the rear timing belt cover, the timing belt and the rear camshaft pulley bolt. Using the puller tool 49–S120–215A, pull the rear pulley from the camshaft.

11. Install two bolts (M8 x 1.25 x 45mm) through the injection pump pulley-to-bracket, to lack the pulley. Remove the injection pump pulley bolt, the two holding bolts and the pulley (using tool 49–S120–215A).

12. Remove the tensioner, the spring, the lock bolt and the rear seal plate.

13. Remove the right timing belt cover and the top bolt of the left timing belt cover.

14. Align the camshaft pulley's mark with the mark on the front seal plate and turn the crankshaft 45 degrees in the direction of rotation.

15. Loosen the tensioner pulley lock bolt, push on the timing belt (between the camshaft and the water pump pulley), then straighten.

16. Rotate the camshaft pulley slightly and remove the timing belt from the pulley.

17. Using an adjustable wrench to hold the camshaft, remove the camshaft pulley bolt.

18. Using the puller tool 49–S120–215A, pull the camshaft pulley from the camshaft.

19. Remove the front seal plate lock bolts.

20. Loosen the camshaft bearing cap bolts, a little at a time, working from the outer caps, towards the center caps.

21. Remove the camshaft bolts, the camshaft bearing caps, the oil seals and the camshaft.

22. Loosen the cylinder head bolts, a little at a time, working from the out-

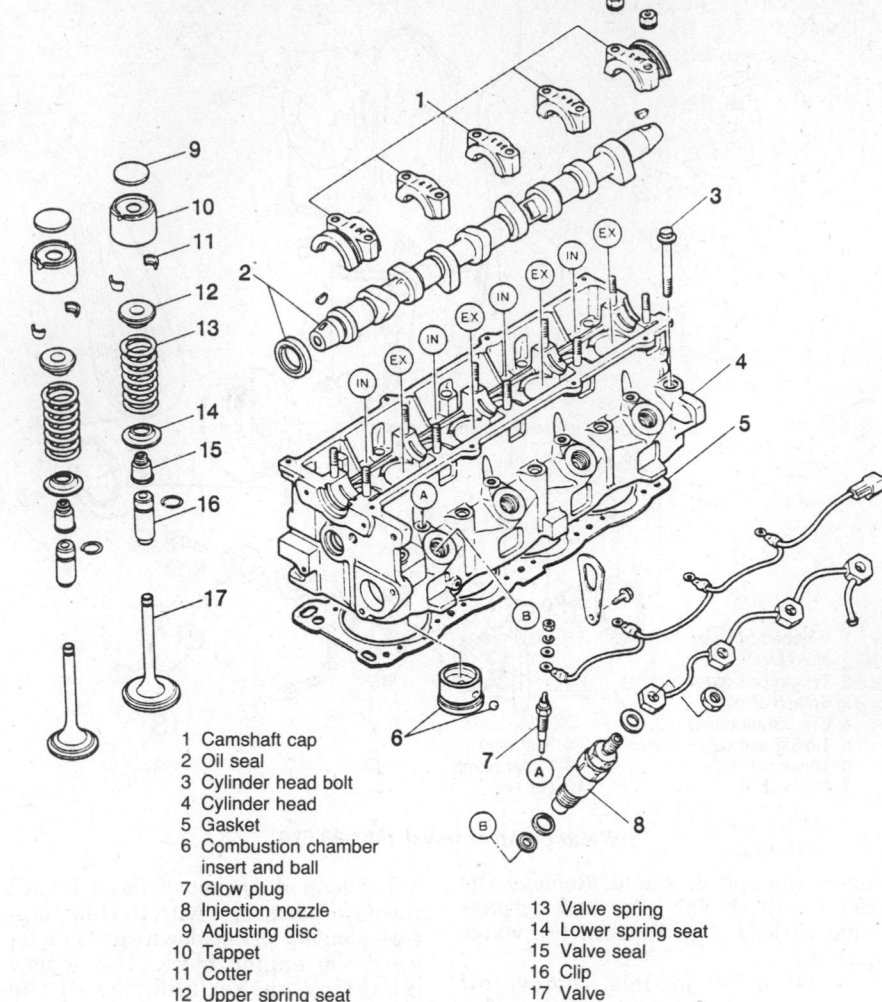

1 Camshaft cap
2 Oil seal
3 Cylinder head bolt
4 Cylinder head
5 Gasket
6 Combustion chamber insert and ball
7 Glow plug
8 Injection nozzle
9 Adjusting disc
10 Tappet
11 Cotter
12 Upper spring seat
13 Valve spring
14 Lower spring seat
15 Valve seal
16 Clip
17 Valve

Exploded view of the cylinder head—626 diesel

er bolts, towards the center bolts.

23. Remove the cylinder head from the engine. Remove the intake and the exhaust manifolds, if necessary. Clean the gasket mating surfaces.

24. To install, use a new head gasket, measure the cylinder head bolt lengths (4.4371–4.4607 in.) and make sure that the crankshaft is turned 45 degrees past the TDC of the No. 1 cylinder firing position.

25. Apply engine oil to the cylinder head bolt threads and torque them in sequence to 22 ft. lbs. Apply a paint or punch mark to the bolt heads. Retorque the bolts by turning 90 degrees and after the sequence, add another 90 degree turn.

26. Lubricate the camshaft and the bearing caps. Install the camshaft, the bearing caps and new oil seals. Torque the camshaft bearing caps bolts to 15–20 ft. lbs., starting at the center, tighten towards both ends.

27. Install the front seal plate, the front camshaft key and the pulley.

Torque the pulley lock bolt to 41–48 ft. lbs.

28. Align the camshaft pulley mark with the alignment mark of the front seal plate.

29. Remove the inspection hole cover on the clutch housing. Position the timing indicator to the 45 degree mark on the flywheel.

30. Position the tensioner pulley near the water pump pulley and tighten the lock bolt.

31. Install the timing belt. Release the tensioner lock bolt.

32. Turn the crankshaft clockwise, twice and torque the tensioner lock bolt to 28 ft. lbs. Recheck the timing marks on the camshaft pulley and the flywheel.

33. Check the timing belt deflection, by pressing between the water pump pulley and the camshaft pulley, it should be 0.4434 in.

34. Install the rear camshaft and the fuel injection pump pulleys and torque the pulleys to 45 ft. lbs.

35. Install the rear tensioner pulley assembly, align the timing marks on the rear camshaft and the fuel injection pulleys, and install the rear timing blet. Adjust the rear timing belt deflection to ⅜ in., between the longest span between the two pulleys.

36. Install the rear timing cover and adjust the valve clearances.

37. To complete the installation, apply sealant to the cylinder head gasket and reverse the removal procedures.

OVERHAUL

For all cylinder head overhaul procedures, please refer to "Engine Rebuilding" in the Unit Repair Section.

Intake Manifold

REMOVAL & INSTALLATION

NOTE: Drain some of the engine coolant.

1. Remove the air cleaner assembly tube, the top radiator hose and the oil cooler hose, from the intake manifold.

2. Remove the exhaust manifold insulator from the exhaust manifold.

3. Disconnect the cylinder head cover-to-intake manifold PCV hose.

4. Remove the intake manifold mounting bolts/nuts, the manifold, the gasket and the engine hanger.

5. Clean the gasket mounting surfaces.

6. To install, use a new gasket and reverse the removal procedures. Torque the manifold nuts/bolts to 15 ft. lbs. and the engine hanger to 20 ft. lbs.

Exhaust Manifold

REMOVAL & INSTALLATION

1. Remove the exhaust manifold insulator from the exhaust manifold.

2. Disconnect the exhaust pipe from the exhaust manifold.

3. Remove the exhaust manifold bolts and the manifold.

4. Clean the gasket mounting surfaces.

5. To install, use a new gasket and reverse the removal procedures. Torque the manifold to 18 ft. lbs.

Front Timing Covers, Belt, Tensioner and Pulleys

REMOVAL & INSTALLATION

1. Disconnect the negative battery cable.

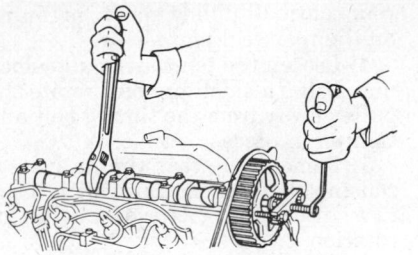

Removing the rear camshaft pulley—626 diesel

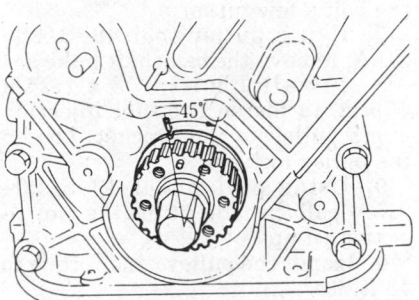

Turning the crankshaft 45 degrees—626 diesel

Removing the front camshaft pulley—626 diesel

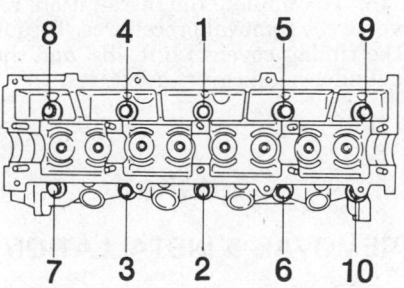

Cylinder head torquing sequence—626 diesel

2. Loosen the alternator and remove the drive belts.

3. Remove the right-side splash shield, the cylinder head cover/gasket and the crankshaft pulley.

4. Remove the right and left timing belt covers/gaskets.

--- **CAUTION** ---

Before loosening the tensioner pulley, turn the crankshaft to align the camshaft pulley with the seal plate timing mark.

5. Loosen the tensioner, push it back and tighten place.

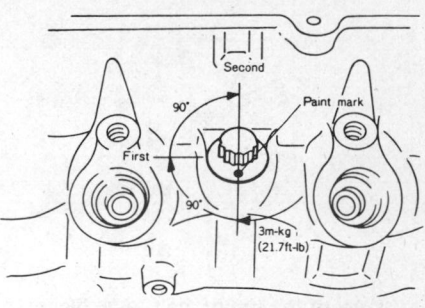

Cylinder bolt torquing procedure—626 diesel

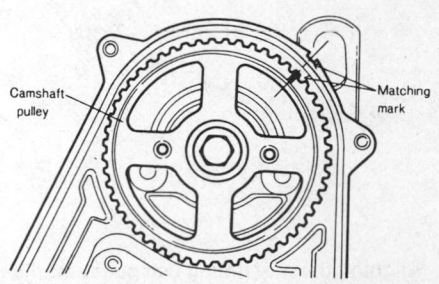

Timing the front camshaft pulley—626 diesel

6. Remove the torque stopper and the timing belt.

NOTE: If reusing the timing belt, mark the direction of rotation on the belt.

7. Turn the crankshaft 45 degrees in the direction of rotation, from the timing mark of the oil pump (this prevents damage to the pistons and valves).

8. Place an adjustable wrench on a camshaft lobe, hold the camshaft and loosen the camshaft pulley lock bolt (back out of the bolt a few turns).

9. Using the puller tool 49–S120–215, pull the camshaft pulley from the camshaft.

10. Remove the crankshaft timing belt pulley, by holding the flywheel ring gear and removing the pulley bolt, washer and the pulley.

11. To install, torque the camshaft pulley bolt to 45 ft. lbs. and the crankshaft pulley bolt to 120 ft. lbs.

12. Align the camshaft pulley mark with the seal plate mark and the crankshaft pulley mark with the mark on the oil pump housing.

13. Install the tensioner pulley in the retracted position.

14. Install the timing belt with the directional arrow aligned with the rotation of the engine.

15. Release the tensioner pulley to put spring pressure on the timing belt.

16. Turn the crankshaft, twice in the direction of rotation to equalize the belt. DO NOT turn in reverse.

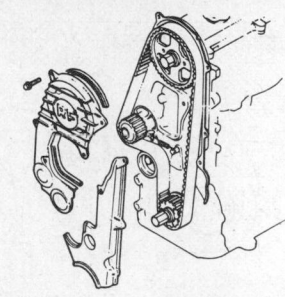

View of the timing belt—626 diesel

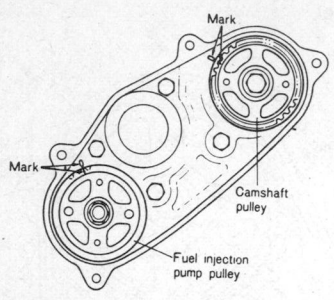

Aligning the rear timing belt pulley marks-626 diesel

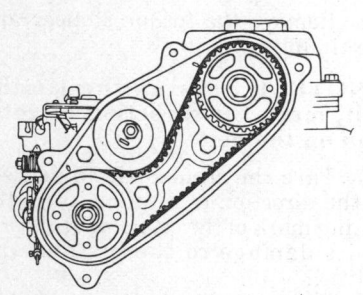

Installing the timing belt—626 diesel

17. Torque the tensioner pulley bolt to 28 ft. lbs. Check the belt deflection between the camshaft pulley and the water pump pulley, it should be $7/16$ in.

18. To complete the installation and reverse the removal procedures. Torque the timing cover bolts to 6 ft. lbs.

Rear Timing Cover, Belt, Tensioner & Pulleys

REMOVAL & INSTALLATION

1. Disconnect the negative battery cable.

2. Remove the rear timing belt cover, the cylinder head cover and gasket.

3. Turn the crankshaft to align the rear camshaft pulley mark the timing on the rear seal plate.

4. Loosen the tensioner pulley lock nut. Using a small pry bar, rotate the pulley away from the timing belt and tighten in place.

5. Remove the rear timing belt. If reusing the belt, mark it with a arrow, indicating the direction of rotation.

6. Using an adjustable wrench, hold the camshaft lobe and loosen the rear camshaft pulley bolt (back out the bolt a few turns).

7. Using puller tool 49–S120–215A, remove the camshaft pulley.

8. Install 2 bolts (M8 x 1.25 x 45mm) to fasten the fuel injection pump pulley to the bracket. Loosen the pulley lock bolt.

9. Using puller tool 49–S120–215A, pull the pulley from the fuel injection pump.

10. Install the pulleys and torque to 45 ft. lbs.

11. Align the pulley marks with the timing marks on the rear seal plate.

12. Install the timing belt on the fuel injection pump (first) and on the camshaft pulley. Remove the 2 bolts holding the lower pulley.

13. Loosen the tensioner pulley and allow it to put pressure on the timing belt.

14. Turn the crankshaft, twice in the direction of rotation to equalize the belt.

15. Torque the tensioner lock nut to 18 ft. lbs. and check the belt deflection, it should be $3/8$ in. between the longest span of the 2 pulleys.

16. To complete the installation, reverse the removal procedures. Torque the timing cover to 6 ft. lbs. and the cylinder head cover to 6 ft. lbs.

Camshaft

REMOVAL & INSTALLATION

1. Refer to the "Front/Rear Timing Cover, Belt, Tensioner & Pulley Removal & Installation" procedures in this section. Remove the front and rear camshaft pulleys.

2. Loosen each camshaft cap bolt, a little at a time, working from both ends, towards the center.

3. Remove the bearing caps, the oil seals and the camshaft.

4. Check for wear and/or distortion, replace the parts, if necessary.

5. To install, lubricate the parts, use new gaskets/seals and reverse the removal procedures. Torque the camshaft bearings, starting at the center, working toward both ends, to 18 ft. lbs.

Piston & Connecting Rods

POSITIONING

For all piston and connecting rod service procedures, please refer to "Engine Rebuilding" in the Unit Repair section.

ENGINE LUBRICATION – DIESEL

The diesel engine uses a crescent type oil pump that is directly driven by the front of the crankshaft. An oil bypass filter is provided to eliminate carbon/sludge in the engine oil and to improve efficiency. A water-cooled oil cooler, attached to the right-side of the engine, and oil jets, built into the engine crankcase, enable the pistons to run cooler.

Oil Pan

REMOVAL & INSTALLATION

1. Disconnect the negative battery cable.

2. Drain the engine oil and the coolant.

3. Raise and support the front of the vehicle.

4. Remove the No. 3 engine mount nuts.

5. Remove the engine hanger at the front of the engine and attach it to the right-front top corner. Using engine support 49–G030–025 or a vertical lift, take the weight off of the engine.

6. Remove the right-front wheel and the splash shield.

7. Remove the five crossmember nuts/bolts, the crossmember, the No. 3 engine mount and bracket.

8. Remove the under cover, the water return pipe and the oil pan.

9. Clean the gasket mating surfaces.

10. To install, use a new gasket/sealer and reverse the removal procedures. Torque the oil pan bolts to 6 ft. lbs. Fill the engine with oil and coolant; check for leaks. Lower the vehicle.

Rear Main Oil Seal

REMOVAL & INSTALLATION

1. Refer to the "Transaxle Removal & Installation" procedures in this section and remove the transaxle.

2. Attach the clutch disc center tool 49–SE01–310 to the clutch assembly and the flywheel ring gear brake tool 49–V101–060 to the flywheel.

3. Remove the mounting bolts, the clutch cover assembly and the clutch disc.

4. Remove the flywheel mounting bolts and the flywheel.

5. Using a screwdriver, place a rag to protect the end of the flywheel, pry the oil seal from the oil seal housing.

6. To install, use a new seal, lubricate the seal with engine oil, place the new seal over the end of the crankshaft, place a piece of pipe (the same diameter as the seal) against the seal and drive it into the oil seal housing. To complete the installation, reverse the removal procedures.

Camshaft Oil Seals

REMOVAL & INSTALLATION

The camshaft has an oil seal located at each end of the shaft; the seals are of two sizes and are not interchangeable.

1. Refer to the "Camshaft Removal & Installation" procedures in this section, remove the necessary camshaft pulley and the oil seal.

NOTE: It may be necessary to remove the end camshaft bearing cap, to remove the oil seal.

2. To install the new seal, lubricate the seal and press onto the end of the camshaft. Replace the bearing cap, if it was removed.

3. To complete the installation, reverse the removal procedures.

Front Main Bearing Oil Seal

REMOVAL & INSTALLATION

1. Please refer to the "Timing Cover, Belt, Tensioner & Pulley Removal & Installation" procedures in this section, to remove the timing belt.

2. Remove the crankshaft pulley bolt and the crankshaft pulley.

3. Using a suitable tool, pry the oil seal from the front of the oil pump.

4. To install, lubricate the new seal, place it on the crankshaft, use a piece of pipe of the same diameter to drive the seal into the oil pump housing and reverse the removal procedures.

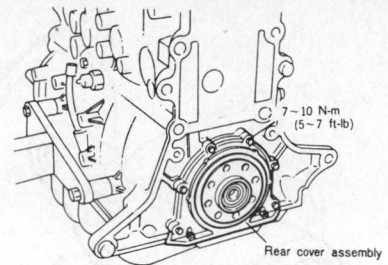

7~10 N·m
(5~7 ft-lb)

Rear cover assembly

View of the rear main oil seal—626 diesel

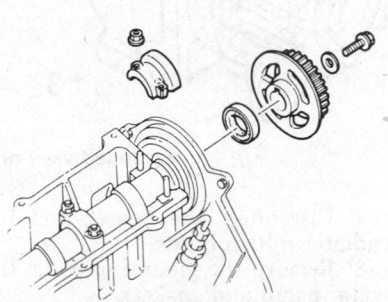

View of the rear oil seal—626 diesel

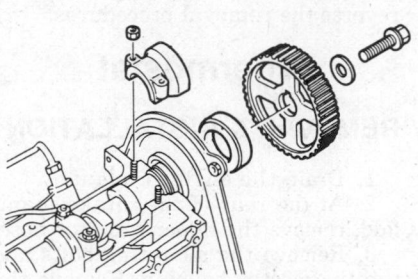

View of the front oil seal—626 diesel

Oil Jet

REMOVAL & INSTALLATION

1. Refer to "Oil Pan Removal & Installation" procedures in this section and remove the oil pan.

2. At the base of each cylinder bore, an oil jet is located. Remove the mounting bolt and the oil jet.

3. Make sure that the oil passage is not clogged.

4. To install, use new mounting washers and reverse the removal procedures.

Oil Pump

REMOVAL & INSTALLATION

1. Refer to the "Timing Cover, Belt, Tensioner & Pulley Removal & Installation" procedures and remove the timing belt.

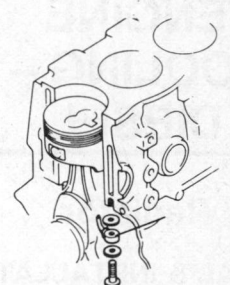

Oil jet assembly—626 diesel

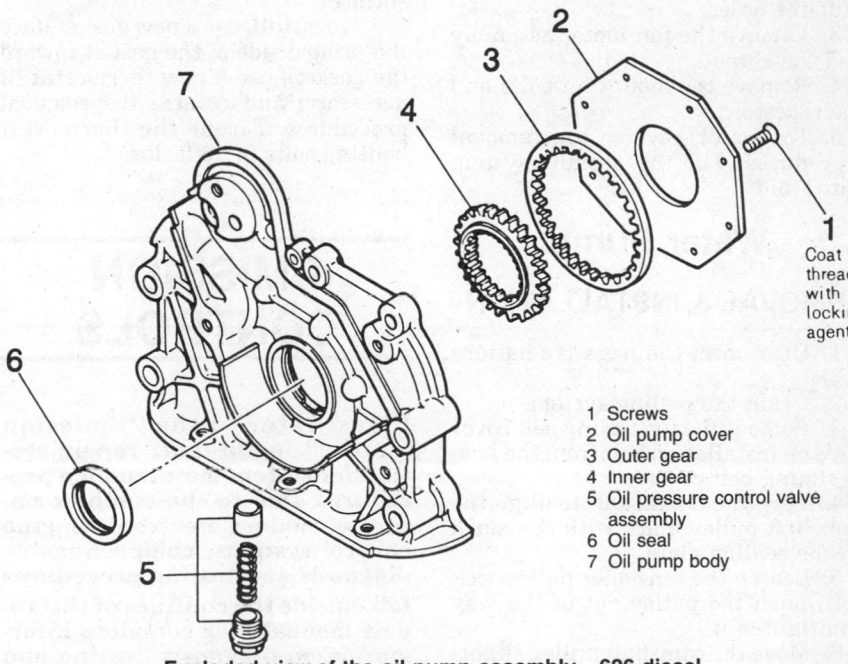

Coat thread with locking agent

1 Screws
2 Oil pump cover
3 Outer gear
4 Inner gear
5 Oil pressure control valve assembly
6 Oil seal
7 Oil pump body

Exploded view of the oil pump assembly—626 diesel

2. Remove the oil pan and the oil pick up tube from the oil pump.

3. Remove the crankshaft pulley center bolt, the washer and the pulley.

4. Remove the oil pump mounting bolt and the oil pump.

5. If necessary, remove the oil pump cover plate, using a impact driver to loosen the screws. Remove the cover plate, the inner ring and the outer ring.

6. Check for wear and replace the parts as necessary.

7. To assembly, pack the oil pump cavity with vasoline and install the outer gear ring with the punch marks facing forward.

8. When installing the cover plate, coat the locking screws with a locking agent.

9. To install the oil pump, use new gaskets/O-ring and reverse the removal procedures. Fill the engine with oil and coolant.

ENGINE COOLING – DIESEL

Radiator

REMOVAL & INSTALLATION

1. Drain the engine coolant.
2. Remove the upper and the lower radiator hoses.
3. Remove the fan motor assembly and the shroud.
4. Remove the mounting bolts and the radiator.
5. To install, reverse the removal procedures. Fill the coolant system with fluid.

Water Pump

REMOVAL & INSTALLATION

1. Disconnect the negative battery cable.
2. Drain the cooling system.
3. Remove the top timing belt cover and the installation bolt from the lower timing belt cover.
4. Turn the crankshaft to align the camshaft pulley mark with the mark on the sealing plate.
5. Loosen the tensioner pulley lock bolt, push the pulley out of the way and tighten it.
6. Move the camshaft pulley slightly to remove the timing belt.

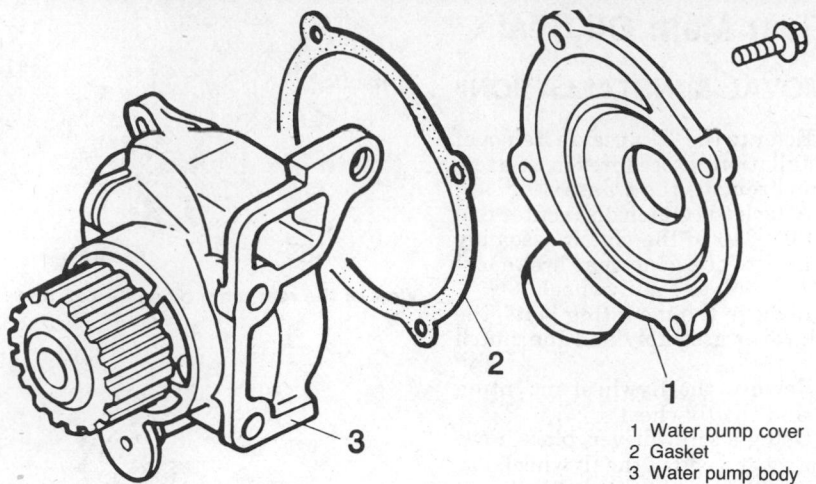

1 Water pump cover
2 Gasket
3 Water pump body

Exploded view of the water pump—626 diesel

7. Disconnect the heater and the radiator return hoses.
8. Remove the mounting bolts, the water pump and gaskets.
9. Clean the gasket mounting surfaces.
10. To install, use new gaskets and reverse the removal procedures.

Thermostat

REMOVAL & INSTALLATION

1. Drain the engine coolant.
2. At the rear of the intake manifold, remove the upper radiator hose.
3. Remove the mounting bolts and the thermostat housing. Remove the thermostat.
4. Clean the gasket mounting surfaces.
5. To install, use a new gasket (face the printed side of the gasket toward the gasket), use a new thermostat (if necessary) and reverse the removal procedures. Torque the thermostat housing bolts to 18 ft. lbs.

EMISSION CONTROLS

Please refer to the "Emission Control" in the unti repair section for system maintenance procedures. Due to the complex nature of modern electronic engine control systems, comprehensive diagnosis and testing procedures fall outside the confines of this repair manual. For complete information on diagnosis, testing and repair procedures concerning all modern engine and emissions control systems, please refer to *"Chilton's Guide to Electronic Engine Controls.*

EGR WARNING SYSTEM

Some Mazda models are equipped with a EGR warning system. This system is used to alert the operater to either perform or have performed, the EGR maintenance service on the system. A warning lamp on the dashboard will illuminate every 12,500 miles of operation.

To reset the EGR maintenance interval detector, located under the left side of the dash panel, simply reverse the connector to the detector terminals.

GASOLINE ENGINE FUEL SYSTEM

Fuel Filter

REMOVAL & INSTALLATION

GLC (RWD)

1. The fuel filter is an in-line type, located under the hood in the engine compartment.
2. Detach both hoses from the filter.
3. Unfasten the filter from its mounting bracket.
4. To install, reverse the removal procedures. Start the engine and check for leaks.

RX-7 and 1981-82 626

The fuel filter is located under the rear of the vehicle just in front of the fuel tank.

NOTE: On fuel injected models relieve the fuel pressure in the fuel system by starting the engine and disconnecting the fuel pump connector with the engine running. After stalling the engine, turn the ignition switch to the off position.

1. Raise the rear of the vehicle and support it on jackstands. Locate the filter by following ther fuel lines out of the fuel tank.
2. Loosen the clips at both ends of the filter and place a collection pan beneath it to catch any of the fuel that is in the lines.
3. Disconnect the fuel filter lines and remove the filter from its retainer.
4. Install the new filter, paying close attention to the direction of the filter in relation to the direction of the fuel flow. See the illustration for correct positioning.
5. Turn the starter to ON to activate the fuel pump and check the fuel filter connections for leaks.

NOTE: If the filter is held by spring tension clamps, it would be wise to replace them with new clamps when the filter is changed.

GLC (FWD) and 1983-88 626 and 323

The fuel filter is located in the engine compartment, next to the driver's side shock tower.

NOTE:On fuel injected models relieve the fuel pressure in the fuel system by starting the engine and disconnecting the fuel pump connector with the engine running. After stalling the engine, turn the ignition switch to the off position.

1. Remove the screw and wire retainer bracket.
2. Remove the inlet and outlet fuel lines.
3. Remove the fuel filter. On some models it may be necessary to remove the bracket with the fuel filter.

NOTE: Install the filter in the proper direction.

4. To install, reverse the removal procedures. Start the engine and check for leaks.

Mechanical Fuel Pump

The GLC (RWD) fuel pump is mount-

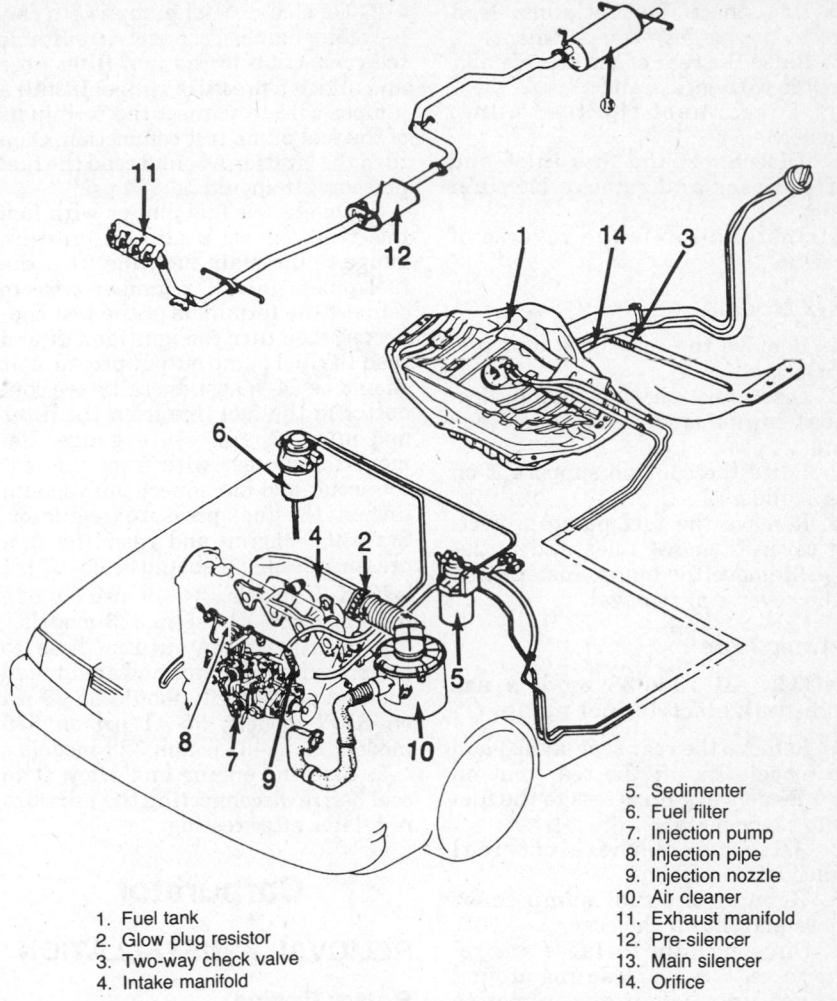

1. Fuel tank
2. Glow plug resistor
3. Two-way check valve
4. Intake manifold
5. Sedimenter
6. Fuel filter
7. Injection pump
8. Injection pipe
9. Injection nozzle
10. Air cleaner
11. Exhaust manifold
12. Pre-silencer
13. Main silencer
14. Orifice

View of the fuel system—626 diesel

ed on the right front-side of the engine block.

NOTE: The 1981-85 GLC (FWD) and the 1983-85 626 fuel pump is mounted on the right rear of the cylinder head.

REMOVAL & INSTALLATION

GLC

1. Slide the two fuel line clips from the pump inlet and outlet hoses. Remove the hoses.
2. Remove the fuel pump mounting bolts and remove the pump, gasket and spacer.
3. The installation is the reverse of the removal procedure.

1983-85 626 and 323 Carbureted Engine

1. Remove the fuel inlet and return hoses from the pump.
2. Remove the fuel outlet hose and two fuel pump-to-engine attaching bolts.

3. Remove the fuel pump, two gaskets and a spacer.
4. Installation is the reverse of removal. Start the engine and check for leaks.

Electric Fuel Pump

REMOVAL & INSTALLATION

NOTE: On fuel injected models relieve the fuel pressure in the fuel system by starting the engine and disconnecting the fuel pump connector with the engine running. After stalling the engine, turn the ignition switch to the off position.

Chassis-Mounted Type

NOTE: The fuel pump is located under the left rear of the vehicle, in front of the fuel tank.

1. Disconnect the negative battery cable at the battery.

2. Disconnect the fuel pump lead wire in the luggage compartment.

3. Raise the rear of the vehicle and support with jack stands.

4. Disconnect the fuel pump bracket.

5. Disconnect the fuel inlet and outlet hoses and remove the fuel pump.

6. Installation is the reverse of removal.

RX-7 Models

1. Remove the rear floor mat and floor plate.

2. Disconnect the fuel pump electrical connection under the floor plate.

3. Raise the car and support it on jack stands.

4. Remove the fuel pump protecting cover. Remove inlet and outlet lines. Remove the pump. Installation is the reverse of removal.

In-Tank Type

NOTE: All 1986-88 models use an in-tank electric fuel pump.

1. Remove the rear seat on 323 and 626 models, or lift the rear mat on RX-7 models to gain access to the fuel pump cover plate.

2. Disconnect the electrical connector.

3. Remove the fuel pump cover screws and lift off the cover.

4. Disconnect the fuel feed and return hoses. Wrap a clean rag around the fuel lines when disconnect to catch any fuel spray, then plug the lines to prevent leakage.

—————— CAUTION ——————

Take precautions to avoid the risk of fire while working on the fuel system.

5. Remove the mounting screws and lift the fuel pump and gauge assembly from the fuel tank. Continue disassembly on a clean workbench.

6. Installation is the reverse of the removal procedures. Be careful not to allow any dirt or other foreign material to contaminate the fuel tank while the gauge unit is removed.

FUEL PRESSURE TESTING

NOTE: Allow the engine to cool before disconnecting any fuel lines. Wrap a clean rag around the fuel fitting to catch any fuel spray and take precautions to avoid the risk of fire.

1. On mechanical fuel pumps, connect a suitable fuel pressure gauge to the main fuel feed from the fuel pump, then crank the engine and read the fuel pressure. It should be 4–6 psi.

2. On electric fuel pumps with carburetor engines, connect a suitable tee connection to the fuel filter hose and attach a pressure gauge. Install a jumper wire to connect the terminals of the fuel pump test connection, then turn the ignition ON and read the fuel pressure. It should be 3–4 psi.

3. On electric fuel pumps with fuel injection, connect a suitable pressure gauge to the main fuel line from the fuel pump. Install a jumper wire to connect the terminals of the test connector, then turn the ignition ON and read the fuel pump output pressure. It should be 64–85 psi. Install a tee connector in the fuel line from the filter and attach the pressure gauge. Remove the jumper wire from the test connector and disconnect the vacuum line at the fuel pressure regulator. Start the engine and read the fuel pressure at idle. It should be 35–37 psi on RX-7 models, 44–49 psi on 626 models, or 36–41 psi on 323 models.

4. Reconnect the vacuum hose to the pressure regulator and again read the fuel pressure. It should be 28 psi on RX-7 models, 35–41 psi on 626 models, or 28–31 psi on 323 models.

5. Stop the engine and allow it to cool before disconnecting the pressure regulator after testing.

Carburetor

REMOVAL & INSTALLATION

Rotary Engine

1. Remove the air cleaner.

2. Detach the choke and accelerator cables.

3. Label and disconnect the fuel and vacuum lines and plug the main fuel line to prevent leakage.

4. Remove the oil line.

5. Remove all electrical wiring from carburetor.

6. Remove the carburetor.

7. To install, reverse the removal procedures.

Piston Engine

GLC (FWD), 1983-85 626 and 1986-88 323

1. Remove the negative battery cable.

2. Remove the air cleaner and the accelerator cable.

3. Remove the cruise control cable (if equipped).

4. Remove the vacuum hoses and disconnect the fuel line.

5. Disconnect the air/fuel solenoid harness at the wiring connector and the bullet connector. Remove the connector for the bi-metal heater).

6. Remove the carburetor, gasket and PTC heater. Cover the carburetor inlet with a clean cloth to prevent dust or dirt from entering the engine.

7. Installation is the reverse of removal. Inspect the base gasket and use a new one if needed.

GLC (RWD) and 1981-82 626

1. Remove the air cleaner and duct.

2. Disconnect the accelerator shaft. Disconnect the cruise control cable if necessary. Remove all necessary wiring and vacuum lines.

3. Disconnect the fuel supply and fuel return lines.

4. Disconnect the leads from the throttle solenoid and deceleration valve at the quick-disconnects.

5. Disconnect the throttle return spring.

6. Disconnect the choke cable.

7. Remove the carburetor. Cover the carburetor inlet with a clean cloth to prevent dust or dirt from entering the engine.

8. To install, reverse the removal procedures.

ACCELERATOR LINKAGE ADJUSTMENT

All Models

1. Check the pedal position. The accelerator pedal should be lower than the brake pedal.

2. If necessary, adjust the nut on the linkage above the pedal to obtain the proper height.

3. Check the free-play of the cable at the carburetor. It should be 0.04–0.12 in. If not, adjust by turning the clevis nut.

4. The accelerator pedal distance below the brake pedal (in.) should be as follows:

   a. 1981–84 GLC – 2.0 ± 0.2 in.
   b. 1981–85 RX-7 – 1.7 ± 0.2 in.
   c. 1981–82 626 – 1.7 ± 0.2 in.
   d. All other models, depress the accelerator pedal to the floor and confirm that the throttle valve is fully open. Adjust as necessary, by using the adjusting boltor nut on the linkage above the accelerator pedal.

FLOAT AND FUEL LEVEL ADJUSTMENTS

GLC and 626

1. Remove the carburetor air horn assembly.

2. Invert the air horn and allow the float to hang so that the needle valve contacts the seat.

3. Measure the clearance between the float and the air horn without the air horn gasket in place.

4. The clearance should be 0.453 in. for 626 (1981–82); 0.394 in. 626 (1983);).530 in. 626 (1984-87); 0.476 in. GLC (1984), 0.390 in. GLC (1985-87) or 0.433 in. All others.

5. Adjust by bending the float seat lip.

6. Reassemble and recheck idle.

RX-7

1. Remove the carburetor air horn assembly.

2. Invert the air horn to a position with the float facing upward. The air horn gasket surface must be level. Place the air horn on a carburetor work stand, if available, in order to insure a level position.

3. The distance between the float and the air horn gasket should be 0.63 plus/minus 0.02 in., measured at the top of the float.

4. Install the air horn assembly.

323

1. Remove the carburetor air horn assembly.

2. Invert the air horn and allow the float to hang so that the needle valve contacts the seat.

3. Measure the clearance between the float and the air horn without the air horn gasket in place.

4. The clearance should be 1.811–1.890 in.

5. Turn the air horn upside down on a stand and allow the float to lower by its own weight. measure the clearance between the float and the air horn, the clearnace shouls be 0.236–0.276 in.

6. If the clearance is not correct, bend the arm until the proper clearnace is obtained.

FLOAT DROP ADJUSTMENTS

Piston Engines

1. Remove the carburetor air horn and hold it in its normal position.

2. Measure the distance between the air horn (without gasket) and the bottom of the float.

3. The distance should be 1.811 in. 626 (1981-82); 1.929 in. 626 (1983-87); 1.77 in. GLC (1983-87) FWD.

4. If the distance is not correct, bend the float stopper until the distance is correct.

5. To install, use new gaskets and remove the removal procedures.

RX-7

1. Remove the carburetor air horn assembly.

2. Position the air horn in the nor-

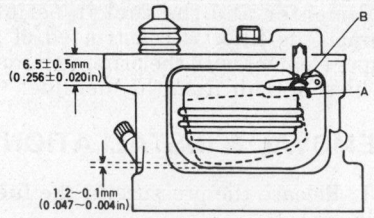

Piston engine float adjustment: bend tab "A" to adjust float drop and bend tab "B" to adjust float level

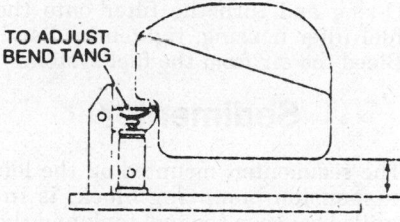

Float level adjustment, float bowl inverted and gasket installed

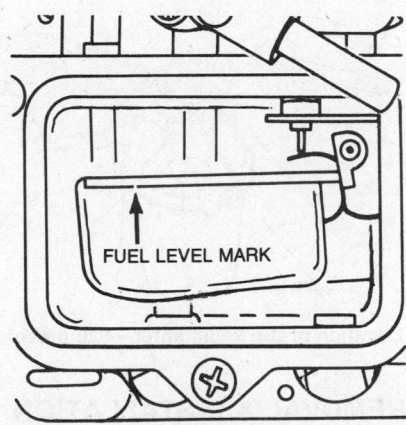

Fuel level mark on sight glass: piston engine

mal installed position. The air horn gasket surface should be level.

3. The float should be in a fully dropped position. Measure the distance between the lowest part of the float and the air horn gasket.

4. The measured distance should be 2.0 ± 0.02 in. If the distance is not correct, bend the tab on the float to obtain the correct distance.

5. Install the air horn.

FAST IDLE CAM ADJUSTMENT

RX-7 Engines

1. Remove the carburetor from the engine.

2. With the choke valve fully closed, adjust the clearance between the primary throttle valve and the wall of the throttle bore by bending the connecting rod between the choke

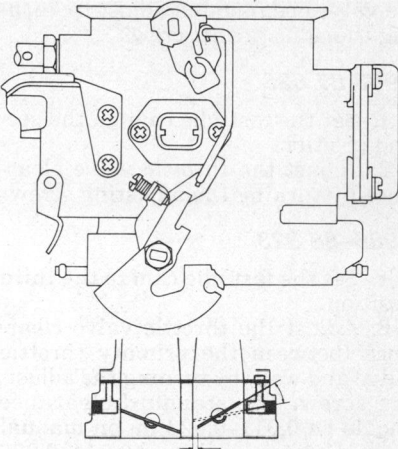

Fast idle adjustments: measure the angle "A" and clearance "B"—rotary engines

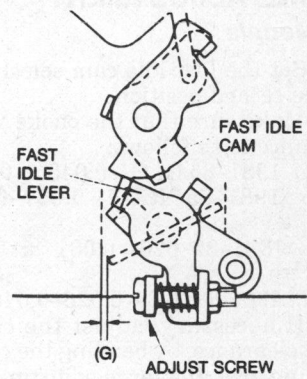

Fast idle cam adjustment—1970 cc engine

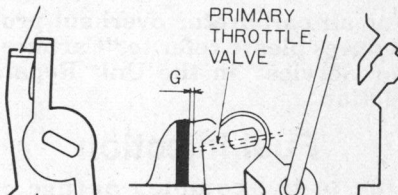

Fast idle cam adjustment showing cam lever in the first position (see text)—1415, and 1490 cc engine

valve and the throttle valve to the following specifications:

GLC and 1981-82 626

1. On the 1415cc engine, remove the bi-metal cover.

2. Using your fingers, close the choke valve fully.

3. Make sure the fast idle cam is on the first position. (Third position—GLC with 1490cc engine).

4. Check the clearance at the throt-

tle valve opening and adjust by turning the adjustment screw.

1983-87 626

1. Set the fast idle cam on the second position.
2. Adjust the throttle valve clearance by turning the adjusting screw.

1986–88 323

1. Set the fast idle cam to the third position.
2. Adjust the throttle valve clearance (between the primary throttle valve and wall) by turning the adjusting screw. The standard clearance shoule be 0.011–0.023 in. on manual transmission models and 0.014–0.026 in. on automatic transmission models.

CHOKE ADJUSTMENT
All Models

1. Set the fast idle cam select arm on the second position.
2. Make sure that the choke valve clearance is as follows:
    a. 1981–85 GLC – 0.043 ± 0.008.
    b. 1981–85 RX-7 – 0.057–0.070 in.
    c. 1981–82 626 – 0.031 ± 0.008 in.
    d. 1986–88 323 – 0.026–0.046 in.
3. If necessary, adjust the choke valve clearance, by bending the choke Starting arm. If a large adjustment is required, the choke rod should be bent.

OVERHAUL

For all carburetor overhaul procedures please refer to "Carburetor Service" in the Unit Repair section.

Fuel Injection

Due to the complex nature of modern fuel injection systems, comprehensive diagnosis and testing procedures fall outside the confines of this repair manual. For complete information on fuel injection diagnosis, testing and repair procedures please refer to *"Chilton's Guide To Fuel Injection and Feedback Carburetors".*

DIESEL FUEL SYSTEM

Fuel Filter

The fuel filter installed between the

sedimenter and the fuel injection pump. The filter is constructed of a paper element with the priming pump to bleed the air from the fuel line.

REMOVAL & INSTALLATION

1. Release the pressure in the fuel line.
2. Using a fuel filter wrench, remove the filter from the fuel filter housing.
3. To install, apply fuel to the O-ring and turn the filter onto the fuel filter housing, tighten by hand. Bleed the air from the fuel system.

Sedimenter

The sedimenter, mounted on the left suspension mounting block, is installed between the fuel tank and the fuel filter, it is used to separate the water from the fuel.

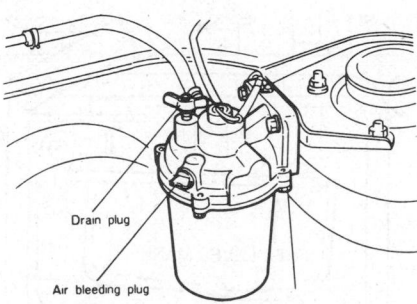

Drain plug

Air bleeding plug

Location of the sedimenter—626 diesel

REMOVAL & INSTALLATION

1. Release the pressure in the fuel system.
2. Remove the fuel lines and the electrical connectors from the sedimenter.
3. Remove the mounting bolts and sedimenter.
4. To install, reverse the removal procedures. Bleed the fuel system.

DRAINING WATER

The water drain light will turn ON, when the sedimenter is full of water, every 3,750 miles or every 3¾ months.
1. Loosen the drain plug.
2. Loosen the air bleed screw, if it is hard to drain the water.
3. After the water is drained, tighten the drain plug.
4. If the air bleed screw has been opened, bleed the air from the fuel line.
5. Make sure the plugs of the sedimenter are closed and the fuel hoses are connected.

6. Loosen the fuel filter air vent plug. Pump the fuel filter head in and UP and DOWN motion, until solid fuel flows from the air vent plug hole.
7. Depress the fuel filter pump head and close the air vent plug.

Injection Pump

The injection pump is a distributor (VE) type, located at the left-rear of the engine and driven by the rear camshaft timing belt; it is manufactured by Nippondenso.

REMOVAL & INSTALLATION

1. Disconnect the negative battery cable.
2. Disconnect the accelerator control, the cold start device control and the cruise control (if equipped) cables.
3. Disconnect the fuel out valve and the pickup coil couplers.
4. Remove the fuel injection tubes, the fuel and vacuum hoses from the pump.
5. Remove the rear timing belt cover, the tensioner and the timing belt.
6. Remove the fuel injection pulley from the fuel injection pump. Use puller tool 49–S120–215, to remove the pulley (DO NOT hit the pulley).

NOTE: Be careful not to drop the semi-circular (woodruff) key.

7. If the matching marks are not present on the pump flange and the rear seal plate, use a cold chisel to mark them.
8. Remove the mounting nuts/bolts and the fuel injection pump from the rear seal plate.
9. To install, align the matching marks of the pump flange and the rear seal plate. Install the pump's mounting nuts/bolts and the pulley.
10. To complete the installation, reverse the removal procedures. Time the rear timing belt. Torque the pump's mounting nuts to 16 ft. lbs. and the bolt to 28 ft. lbs. Torque the fuel pump pulley to 46 ft. lbs. Bleed the air from the fuel injection pump and system.

BLEEDING THE FUEL INJECTION PUMP

1. At the fuel filter, open the air vent plug.
2. Use a pumping motion on top of the fuel filter to bleed air from the fuel line, until a steady stream of fluid flows.
3. Close the air bleed valve and continue to pump (about 15 times), until the pump works hard.

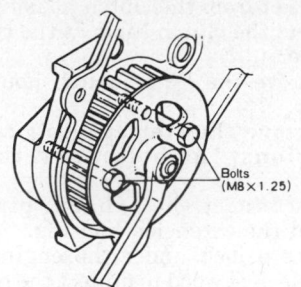

Removing the fuel injection pump pulley—626 diesel

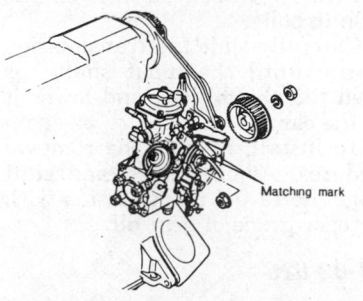

Removing the fuel injection pump—626 diesel

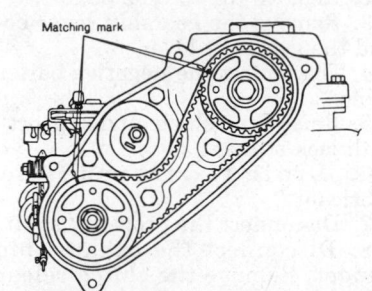

Aligning the timing marks—626 diesel

INJECTION TIMING

1. Remove the fuel injection pipes and remove the service hole cover on the clutch housing.

2. Align the timing mark (TDC) on the flywheel with the indicator pin by turning the crankshaft.

3. Remove the hydraulic head plug on the injection pump, mount the measuring device # 49-9140-074 (dial indicator) or equivalent into the plug hole on the hydraulic head, so the tip of the dial gauge touches the plunger end of the pump and the dial gauge indicates approximately 0.008 in. (2.0mm).

NOTE: The delivery valve should be removed as an assembly shown in order to mount the measuring device. When installing the delivery valve, the gasket should be replaced and the valve should be torqued 3-4 ft. lbs.

4. Turn the flywheel slowly counterclockwise (in the reverse direction of the engine rotation), until the timing mark on the crankshaft pulley moves from the original position (TDC) to the counterclockwise side by 30–50 degrees and make sure the dial indicator pointer stops.

5. Set the dial indicator to zero. When setting the dial indicator to zero, confirm that the pointer does not deviate from the scale mark of zero, by slightly turning the crankshaft to the right and left.

6. Turn the flywheel clockwise (in direction of the engine rotation), to align the timing mark (TDC) on the flywheel with the indicator pin.

7. If the dial indicator pointer indicates 0.004 ± 0.0008 in. (1.0 ± 0.02mm) when the timing mark (TDC) is aligned with the indicator pin, the injection timing is correctly adjusted. If it does not, adjust the pump timing as outlined in Steps 8 and 9.

8. Start the engine and run it until it reaches normal operating temperature.

9. Stop the engine and loosen the injection pump attaching nuts and bolts. Adjust the injection timing by moving the pump until the cam lift becomes 0.004 ± 0.0008 in. (1.0 ± 0.02mm) on the dial indicator.

10. Tighten the injection pump nuts and bolts, recheck the cam lift and remove all test equipment.

Cold Start Device

When pulling the cold start device knob, the injection timing is advanced and the idle speed is increased.

ADJUSTMENT

1. Check the CSD cable deflection of 0.04–0.12 in.

NOTE: If the deflection is not correct, turn the cable adjusting nuts of the CSD.

2. Warm the engine to the normal operating temperatures.

3. Connect a tachometer to the engine.

4. Pull the CSD knob fully OUT.

5. The engine speed should be 1350–1650 rpm.

6. If the engine speed is not correct, turn the connecting lever on the fuel injection pump, to adjust.

7. Remove the tachometer and push the CSD knob IN.

Fast Idle Control Device (A/C Only)

When the A/C and the blower motor

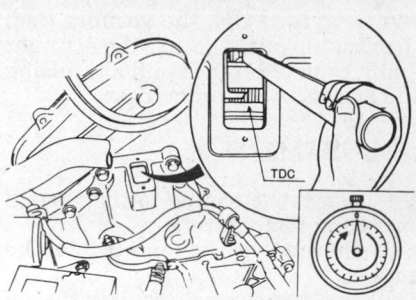

Timing the engine—626 diesel

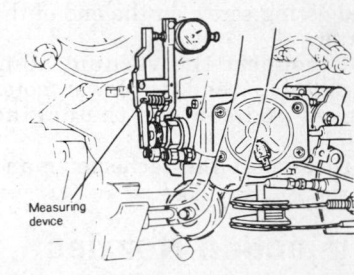

Measuring the fuel injector plunger—626 diesel

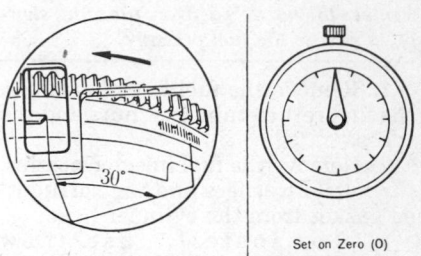

Adjusting the timing—626 diesel

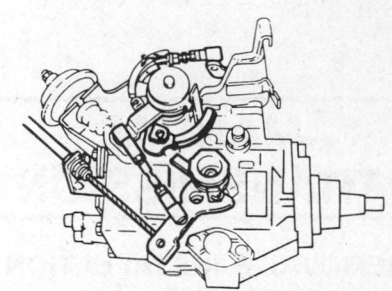

Adjusting the cold start device 626 diesel

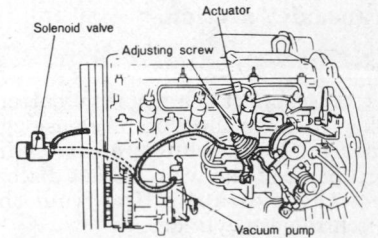

Adjusting the fast idle control device (for A/C)—626 diesel

8-53

switches, turn ON, the vacuum from the vacuum pump goes to the actuator and a control lever is pulled, causing the engine speed to increase.

ADJUSTMENT

1. Warm the engine to the normal operating temperature.
2. Connect a tachometer to the engine.
3. Apply vacuum directly to the actuator and check the engine speed, it should be 900–950 rpm.
4. If the speed is not correct, turn the adjusting screw on the end of the actuator.
5. Reconnect the vacuum hose, turn on the A/C and the blower motor switches and confirm the engine speed.
6. Disconnect the tachometer and turn the A/C switches.

Injection Nozzles

REMOVAL & INSTALLATION

——— CAUTION ———
Remove the nozzle's delivery tube nut, slowly, to release the fuel pressure.

1. Remove the fuel injection tubes, the fuel return tube lock nuts and the tubes.
2. Remove the fuel injector nozzles, the nozzle washers and the corrugated gasket from the cylinder head.
3. To install, use new copper/corrugated washers (face the red side of the corrugated washer toward the nozzle) and reverse the removal procedures. Torque the nozzles to 48 ft. lbs.

MANUAL TRANSMISSION

REMOVAL & INSTALLATION

NOTE: The GLC (front wheel drive) and the 1983-87 626 and 323 are detailed in the "Manual Transaxle" section.

RX-7

1. Disconnect the negative battery cable. Remove the clutch release cylinder and tie the clutch release cylinder up out of the way. Do not disconnect the hydraulic line from the clutch release cylinder.
2. Remove the air cleaner assembly, on the 12A engine only.

3. Remove the bolts attaching the transmission to the rear end of the engine. Unscrew and remove the gear shift lever knob. Remove the console box, if so equipped.
4. Remove the gear shift lever boot and boot plate. Remove the gear shift lever and retainer assembly.
5. Raise the vehicle and support it safely. Remove the front engine under cover and rear engine under cover. Remove the converter under cover and disconnect the air pipe.
6. Remove the converter brackets. Remove the rear exhaust pipe and converter assembly. Remove the front exhaust pipe and monolith converter assembly.
7. Remove the floor under covers. Drain the transmission oil into a suitable drain pan. Remove the drive shaft.
8. Disconnect the wiring and remove the starter motor. Remove the bolts attaching the transmission to the rear end of the engine. Disconnect the couplers from the back-up lamp switch.
9. Place a suitable transmission jack under the transmission. Disconnect the speedometer. Remove the nuts attaching the transmission support to the vehicle. On the 1986–88 RX-7 models, remove the transmission crossmember. On the 1981-85 RX-7 models, place a suitable piece of wood approximately 1 in. in height between the oil pan and the center link. This will prevent the engine from interfering with the dash panel.
10. Slide the transmission rearward until the main shaft clears the clutch disc and carefully remove the transmission from under the vehicle.
11. Installation is the reverse order of the removal procedure. Adjust the clutch and shift linkage as detailed elsewhere. Refill the transmission and road test the vehicle.

GLC (RWD)

1. Disconnect the negative (–) battery cable.
2. Put the transmission in neutral and remove the shift lever.
3. Remove the two upper bolts from the clutch housing.
4. Raise the vehicle and support it securely on axle stands or a lift.
5. Drain the transmission oil and replace the plug.
6. Remove the driveshaft, and plug or cover the hole in the extension housing.
7. Disconnect the speedometer cable and back-up light switch wires.
8. Disconnect the exhaust pipe hanger from the bracket on the clutch housing.
9. Remove the exhaust pipe sup-

port bracket from the clutch housing. Disconnect the clutch cable at the release lever.
10. Remove the lower clutch housing cover.
11. Remove the starter electrical connections, the bolts, and the starter.
12. Disconnect the exhaust pipe hanger at the extension housing.
13. Place a jack under the engine, using a block of wood to protect the oil pan. Make sure the jack can securely support the weight of the engine.
14. Disconnect the transmission support member at the transmission.
15. Remove transmission-to-engine attaching bolts.
16. Carefully slide the transmission rearward until the input shaft has cleared the clutch disc, and lower it from the car.
17. To install, reverse the removal procedures. Adjust clutch and shift linkage. Refill the transmission with the proper grade of gear oil.

1981-82 626

1. Remove the gearshift lever knob.
2. Remove the console box.
3. Remove the gearshift lever boot and the gearshift lever.
4. Disconnect the negative battery cable.
5. Raise the vehicle and support it with jack stands.
6. Drain the transmission lubricant.
7. Disconnect the propeller shaft.
8. Disconnect the exhaust pipe hanger. Remove the clutch release cylinder and tie the clutch release cylinder up out of the way. Do not disconnect the hydraulic line from the clutch release cylinder.
9. Remove the starter motor.
10. Disconnect the back-up switch wire.
11. Disconnect the speedometer cable.
12. Place a jack under the engine, protecting the oil pan with a block of wood.
13. Remove the transmission attaching bolts and remove the transmission.
14. To install, reverse the removal procedures. Add lubricant until the level reaches the bottom of the filler plug hole.

SHIFT LEVER ADJUSTMENT

The shift lever may be adjusted during transmission installation by means of the adjusting shims on the three bolts between the cover plate and the packing. The force required to move the shift knob should be 4.4–8.8 lbs.

OVERHAUL

For all transmission overhaul procedures, please refer to "Manual Transmission Overhaul" in the Unit Repair section.

MANUAL TRANSAXLE

REMOVAL & INSTALLATION

GLC (FWD)

1. Raise the vehicle and support it safely. Disconnect the negative battery cable. Disconnect the speedometer cable.
2. Disconnect all electrical wiring and connections, control linkages from the transaxle. Mark these units to aid in reassembling.
3. Remove the water pipe bracket and the harness clips. Raise the vehicle and support it safely. Remove the front wheels. Remove the under cover and side cover. Disconnect the lower ball joints from the steering knuckles. Pull the axle shafts from the differential gears as follows:

   a. The drive shaft can be removed by puling the caliper toward the operator, appling impact to the shaft.

   b. Never give a sharp impact, just gradually increase the force. Pull the shaft straight out of the axle, be careful not to damage the oil seal.

   c. Be sure the driveshaft's ball joint is bent to its maximum extent.

NOTE: Do not allow the axle shafts to drop. Damage may occur to the ball and socket joints and to the rubber boots. Wire the shafts to the vehicle body when released from the differential.

4. Support the engine with the support tool 49–E301–025.
5. At the transaxle, separate the shift control rod from the shift rod.
6. Remove the extension bar from the transaxle. Remove the crossmember.
7. Remove the transaxle rubber mounts.
8. Remove the starter.
9. Support the transaxle on a jack.
10. Remove the mounting bolts and the transaxle.
11. Installation is the reverse of removal.

12. To properly install the axle shafts in the differential side gears, position the axle shaft in a horizontal position, push the axle shaft into the side gear. To be sure the axle shaft engages the groove, a sound may be head or attempt to pull the driveshaft from the differential. Reconnect the ball joints at the lower arms.

1983-88 626

1. Disconnect the negative battery cable and remove the speedometer cable from the transaxle.
2. Remove the clutch cable bracket mounting bolts and disconnect the clutch cable from the release lever.
3. Remove the ground wire and wiring harness clip. Remove any pipe brackets attached to the case.
4. Remove the starter.
5. Install the engine support 49–G030–025 (626), or 49–E301–025A (323), or equivalent and support the weight of the engine on the hook.
6. Remove the transaxle-to-engine mounting bolts.
7. Jack up the vehicle and support it with jackstands. Drain the transaxle oil.
8. Remove the front wheels and the splash shields.
9. Remove the stabilizer bar control link. Remove the under cover (if so equipped).
10. Remove the lower arm ball joint and the knuckle coupling bolt, pull the arm downward and separate the lower arm from the knuckle.
11. Remove the left-side axle shaft from the transaxle. Insert a lever between the axle shaft and the transaxle case. Tap the end of the lever to uncouple the axle shaft from the differential side gear. Pull the front hub forward and separate the axle shaft from the transaxle.

12. Remove the right-side axle shaft and joint shaft. Insert a lever between the driveshaft and the joint shaft. Pry the lever to uncouple the shafts.
13. Pull the front hub forward and then separate the axle shaft from the joint shaft.
14. Remove the joint shaft bracket mounting bolts. Remove the joint

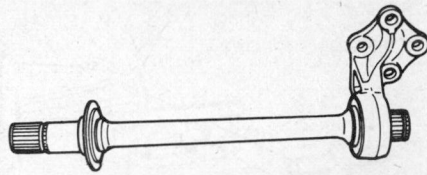

Joint shaft—1983 and later 626

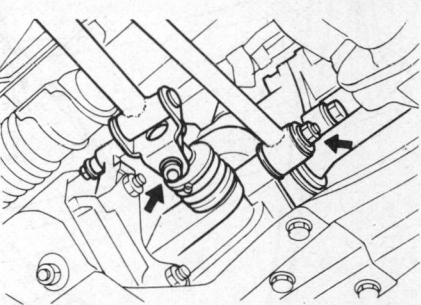

Shift change control rod and extension bar on 1983 and later 626 with manual transaxle—323 similar

shaft and bracket from the transaxle as an assembly.
15. Remove the transaxle mounting bracket nuts at the crossmember.
16. Remove the crossmember and the left lower arm as an assembly.
17. Separate the shift change control rod from the shift change rod.
18. Remove the shift control extension bar from the transaxle. Remove the transaxle undercover.
19. Attach a rope to the transaxle mount bracket at two places and to the engine support.
20. Place a board on a garage floor jack and use this to support the transaxle.

21. Remove the two remaining transaxle-to-engine bolts and separate the transaxle from the engine.

NOTE: To prevent the transaxle from falling off the jack, loosen the rope while removing the transaxle.

22. Remove the transaxle mounting brackets from the transaxle.
23. To install, reverse the removal procedures.

1986-88 323

1. Disconnect the negative battery cable. Remove the air cleaner and loosen the front whell lug nuts.
2. Disconnect the speedometer from the transaxle. Disconnect the clutch cable from the release lever and remove the clutch cable braket mounting bolts.
3. Remove the ground wire instal-

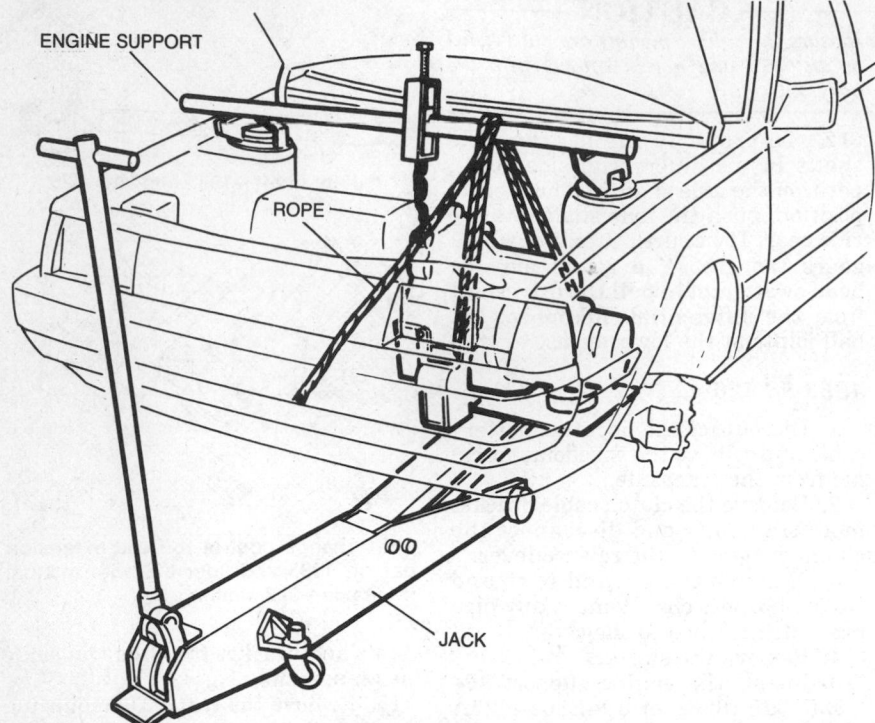

Lowering the transaxle from the car with a rope and floor jack arrangement 1983-88 626 and 323 models

lation boot. Remove the water pipe bracket. Remove the secondary air pipe and the EGR pipe bracket.

4. Remove the wire harness clip. Disconnect the coupler for the neutral switch and back-up lamp switch. Disconnect the body ground connector.

5. Remove the two upper transaxle mounting bolts. Mount the engine support (49-ER301-025A) or equivalent to the engine hanger.

6. Raise and support the vehicle safely. Drain the transaxle oil into a suitable container and remove the front wheels.

7. Remove the engine under cover and side covers. Remove the front stabilizer.

8. Remove the lower arm ball joints and the knuckle clinch bolts, pull the lower arm downward and separate the lower arms from the knuckles.

9. Separate the driveshaft by pulling the front hub outward. Make sure not to use too much force at once, increase the force gradually. Be sure the driveshaft's ball joint is bent to its maximum extent. Do not allow the axle shafts to drop. Damage may occur to the ball and socket joints and to the rubber boots. Wire the shafts to the vehicle body when released from the differential.

10. Remove the transaxle crossmember. Separate the change control rod from the transaxle. Remove the extension bar from the transaxle. Re-

move the wiring and the starter motor.

11. Remove the end plates. Lean the engine toward the transaxle side to lower the transaxle by loosening the engine support hook bolt. Support the transaxle with a suitbale transaxle jack.

12. Remove the necessary engine brackets. Remove the remaining transaxle mounting bolt. Lower the jack and slide the transaxle out from under the vehicle.

13. To install, reverse the removal procedures. Adjust clutch and shift linkage. Refill the transaxle with the proper grade of gear oil.

OVERHAUL

For all manual transaxle overhaul procedures, please refer to "Manual Transaxle Overhaul" in the Unit Repair section.

CLUTCH AND FLYWHEEL

REMOVAL & INSTALLATION

The flywheel nut on rotary engine

models is tighten to 289–362 ft. lbs. with no more than a 3 foot extension on the wrench.

1. Remove the transmission or transaxle.

2. To remove the pressure plate and clutch disc, use ring gear brake tool 49-E301-060 on all models (49-V101-060 for 626 Diesel) excpet the RX-7, use tool 49-F011-101 or equivalent on ther RX-7. Remove the clutch cover, using the clutch centering tool 49-E310-310 (for GLC) or 49-SE01-310 (for 626, 323 and RX-7).

3. Remove the clutch disc.

NOTE: Remove the flywheel only if the flywheel surface is damaged or there is trouble in removing the pilot bearing. On the RX-7, use the flywheel box wrench tool 49-0820-035, to remove the flywheel nut and the flywheel. On all others, remove the bolts and the flywheel.

4. From the Clutch Housing, unhook the return spring from the throw-out bearing and remove the bearing.

5. Remove the bolt holding the release fork and release lever together. Pull the release lever and remove the key and the release fork. until the retaining spring frees itself from the ball stud.

6. Installation is the reverse of removal. If removed, install the flywheel fasteners and tighten it to specifcations. Torque the pressure plate to 13–20 ft. lbs.

PEDAL HEIGHT ADJUSTMENT

RX-7, GLC and 1981-82 626

Loosen the locknut on the adjusting bolt. Turn the adjusting bolt until the clearance between the pedal pad and the floormat is as specified below:

1. 1981–83 GLC – 7.48 ± 0.2 in.
2. 1984–85 GLC – 9.05–9.25 in.
3. 1981–85 RX-7 – 7.5–7.7 in.
4. 1986–88 RX-7 – 8.66 ± 0.20 in.
5. 1981–88 626 – 8.44–8.64 in.
6. 1986–88 323 – 8.44–8.64 in.
7. After the adjustment has been made, tighten the locknut.

PEDAL FREE-PLAY ADJUSTMENT

Cable Clutch

Loosen the locknut and pull the outer cable away from the engine side of the firewall. Turn the adjusting nut on the cable to obtain a 0.06–0.010 in. clearance between the adjusting nut and the firewall. Tighten the locknut.

Adjust the free-play to the following specifications:

   1. 1981–85 GLC – 0.43–0.67 in.

   3. 1981–88 626 – 0.43–0.67 in. non-turbo models.

   4. 1986–88 626 – 0.20–0.51 in. turbo models.

   5. 1981–88 RX-7 – 0.02–0.12 in. at the pedal.

   6. 1986–88 323 – 0.35–0.59 in.

Hydraulic Clutch

Loosen the locknut on the clutch master cylinder pushrod. Turn the push-rod to obtain 0.02–0.12 in. free play between the pedal and the pushrod. Tighten the locknut on the pushrod. 1983-87 626 free play is 0.08–0.12 in. The 626 turbo and diesel free play is 0.20–0.51 in. 1981-85 GLC free play is 0.08–0.12 in. The RX-7 free play is 0.02–0.12 in.

Clutch Master Cylinder

REMOVAL & INSTALLATION

   1. Disconnect the hydraulic line at the master cylinder.

   2. Remove the blower duct.

   3. Remove the two mounting nuts and the master cylinder.

   4. To install, reverse the removal procedures. Bleed the hydraulic system.

Clutch Slave Cylinder

REMOVAL & INSTALLATION

   1. Remove the air cleaner. Unscrew the hydraulic line at the body mounting bracket.

   2. Unhook the release fork return spring from the cylinder.

   3. Remove the clutch cylinder mounting bolts and the cylinder.

   4. Installation is the reverse of removal. Bleed the hydraulic system. Adjust the release fork free-play.

BLEEDING THE CLUTCH HYDRAULIC SYSTEM

   1. Remove the rubber cap from the bleeder screw on the release cylinder.

   2. Place a bleeder tube over the end of the bleeder screw.

   3. Submerge the other end of the tube in a jar half-filled with hydraulic (brake) fluid.

   4. Slowly pump the clutch pedal fully and allow it to return slowly, several times.

   5. While pressing the clutch pedal to the fllor, loosen the bleeder screw until the fluid starts to run out. Then close the bleeder screw. Keep repeat-

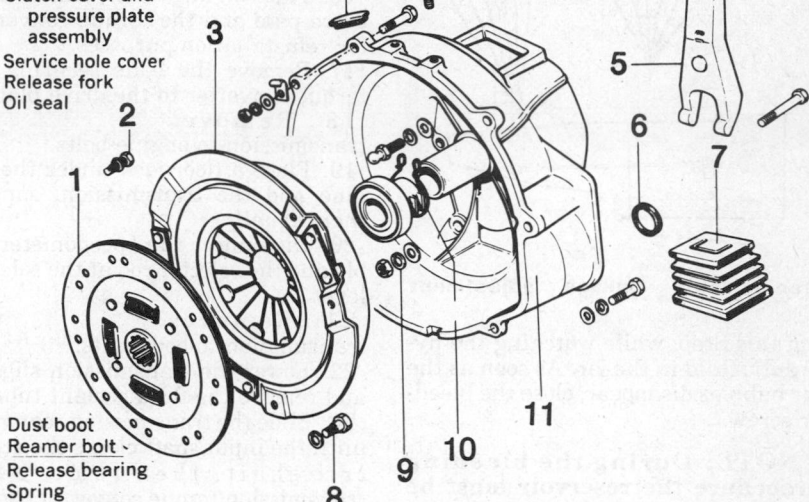

1. Clutch disc
2. Bolt
3. Clutch cover and pressure plate assembly
4. Service hole cover
5. Release fork
6. Oil seal
7. Dust boot
8. Reamer bolt
9. Release bearing
10. Spring
11. Clutch housing

Clutch components

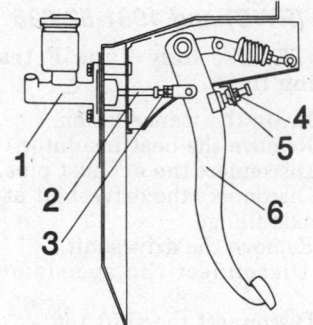

1. Master cylinder
2. Rod
3. Locknut
4. Adjusting bolt
5. Locknut
6. Clutch pedal

Clutch pedal height adjustment

1.5~2.25mm (0.06~0.09in)

GLC clutch cable adjustment

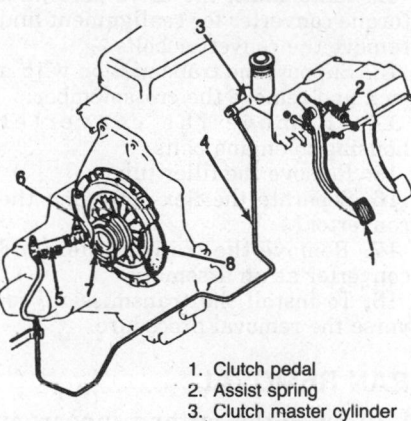

1. Clutch pedal
2. Assist spring
3. Clutch master cylinder
4. Clutch pipe
5. Clutch release cylinder
6. Release lever
7. Clutch fork
8. Clutch disc

Hydraulic clutch system—626 and RX-7 models

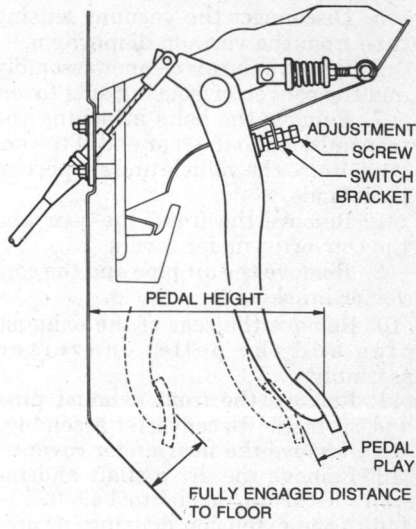

ADJUSTMENT SCREW
SWITCH BRACKET
PEDAL HEIGHT
PEDAL PLAY
FULLY ENGAGED DISTANCE TO FLOOR

1983 and later 626 clutch pedal arrangement—pedal height and pedal free play shown

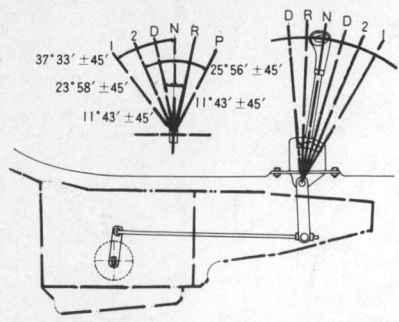

Transmission linkage adjustment

ing this Step, while watching the hydraulic fluid in the jar. As soon as the air bubbles disappear, close the bleeder screw.

NOTE: During the bleeding procedure the reservoir must be kept at least ¾ full.

AUTOMATIC TRANSMISSION

REMOVAL & INSTALLATION

RX-7

NOTE: The transmission is filled with Type F fluid.

1. Disconnect the negative battery cable.
2. Disconnect the inhibitor switch connector.
3. Apply the parking brake and block the wheels.
4. Remove the converter housing upper cover.
5. Disconnect the vacuum sensing tube from the vacuum diaphragm.
6. Remove the air cleaner assembly and the converter housing side cover.
7. Remove the bolts attaching the transmission to the rear end of the engine. Raise the vehicle and support on jackstands.
8. Remove the front, the rear and the converter under covers.
9. Remove the air pipe and the converter brackets.
10. Remove the rear of the exhaust pipe and the pellet converter assembly.
11. Remove the front exhaust pipe and the monolith converter assembly.
12. Remove the floor under covers.
13. Remove the drive shaft and install the turning holder tool 49–0259–440 to the extension housing, to prevent the fluid from leaking from the housing.
14. Disconnect the starter wiring connectors.

15. Remove the starter and the lower converter housing cover.
16. Place an alignment mark on the drive pate and the torque converter, for reinstallation purposes.
17. Remove the bolts securing the torque converter to the drive plate.
18. Remove the transmission-to-engine bolts.
19. Place a floor jack under the engine and the transmission, support them equally.
20. Disconnect the speedometer cable and the selector rod at the selector lever.
21. Remove the transmission-to-body nuts.
22. Lower the transmission slightly and remove the fluid coolant tubes.
23. Slide the transmission rearward, until the input shaft clears the eccentric shaft, then remove the transmission/torque converter assembly from under the vehicle.
24. To install, reverse the removal procedures.

GLC (RWD) and 1981-82 626

NOTE: Use only Type F transmission fluid.

1. Drain the transmission.
2. Remove the heat insulator.
3. Disconnect the exhaust pipe.
4. Disconnect the driveshaft at the rear axle flange.
5. Remove the driveshaft.
6. Disconnect the speedometer cable.
7. Disconnect the shift rod.
8. Disconnect all vacuum hoses.
9. Disconnect all wiring.
10. Disconnect the oil cooler lines.
11. Remove the access cover from the lower end of the converter housing.
12. Matchmark the drive plate and torque converter for realignment and remove the converter bolts.
13. Support the transmission with a jack and remove the crossmember.
14. Remove the converter housing-to-engine bolts.
15. Remove the filler tube.
16. Separate the flex-plate and the converter.
17. Remove the transmission and converter as an assembly.
18. To install the transmission, reverse the removal procedure.

PAN REMOVAL

1. Raise the car and support it safely.
2. Place a suitable container to catch the transmission fluid when the pan is loosened.
3. Slowly loosen the oil pan mounting bolts and allow the pan to tip downward.

4. Support the oil pan and slowly remove the mounting bolts as the fluid drains from the edge of the pan.
5. Remove the oil pan and clean all gasket mating surfaces. Wipe the inside of the oil pan with a clean rag. Remove any deposits with solvent and dry the inside of the pan.
6. Installation is the reverse of removal. Use a new gasket and torque the oil pan mounting bolts to 5 ft. lbs.

SHIFT LINKAGE ADJUSTMENT

GLC (RWD) and 1981-82 626

1. Place the transmission selector lever in Neutral.
2. Disconnect the clevis from the lower end of the selector arm.
3. Move the manual lever to the Neutral position.

NOTE: The Neutral position is the third detent from the back.

4. Loosen the two clevis retaining nuts and adjust the clevis so that it freely enters the lever hole.
5. Tighten the retaining nuts.
6. Connect the clevis to the lever and secure with the spring washer, flat washer and retaining clip.

1981-85 RX-7

Before adjusting the linkage, be sure that the idle speed is adjusted properly.

1. Remove the boot plate.
2. Place the shifting lever in the Park position.
3. Loosen the selector lever plate setting bolt.
4. Raise and support the vehicle on jackstands.
5. Place the selector rod at the Park position, the 1st detent position from the rear of the transmission.
6. Torque the selector lever plate setting bolt to 30 ft. lbs. Check the operation after adjustment.

1986-87 RX-7

1. Remove the shifter cover.
2. Turn locknuts A and B to the position shown in the illustration.
3. Move the shifter level to the park position.
4. Shift the transmission. Make sure the car is supported safely when working underneath.
5. Turn locknut A by hand until it just touches the shifter lever, then back it off one full turn.
6. Torque locknut B to 8 ft. lbs.
7. Move the shifter and make sure there is a click at each gear when shifting from Park through First. The positions of the selector lever and the

indicator should be exact. The release button should return smoothly when used to shift the selector.

NEUTRAL SAFETY SWITCH ADJUSTMENT

RX-7

1. Check the shift linkage.
2. Remove the nut from the gear selector lever and the neutral safety switch attaching bolts.
3. Unfasten the screw underneath the switch body.
4. Place the selector shaft in Neutral by using the gear selector lever.

NOTE: If the linkage is adjusted properly, the slot in the selector shaft should be vertical.

5. Move the switch body so that the screw hole in the case aligns with the hole in the internal rotor.
6. Check the alignment by inserting an 0.08 in. diameter pin through the holes.
7. Once the proper alignment is obtained, tighten the switch mounting bolts.
8. If it still is not operating properly, i.e., the car starts in position other than Park or Neutral or the back-up lights come on in gears other than Reverse, replace the switch.

GLC (RWD)

1. Place the manual lever in Neutral. Neutral is the third detent from the back.
2. Remove the manual lever.
3. Loosen the neutral switch attaching bolts and remove the screws from the alignment hole at the bottom of the switch.
4. Rotate the switch so that the hole in the switch aligns with the hole in the internal rotor. The 0.078 in. diameter pin should be inserted while tightening switch.
5. Install the alignment hole screw and manual lever.

1981-82 626

1. Place the transmission selector lever in the neutral position.
2. Loosen the neutral switch attaching screws.
3. Position the manual shift lever shaft in the neutral position by adjusting the range select lever. The proper neutral position is where the slot of the manual shaft is positioned vertically and the detent positions in the shaft correctly with a click sound.
4. Move the neutral switch so that the identification marks on the switch body and the sliding plate are aligned.

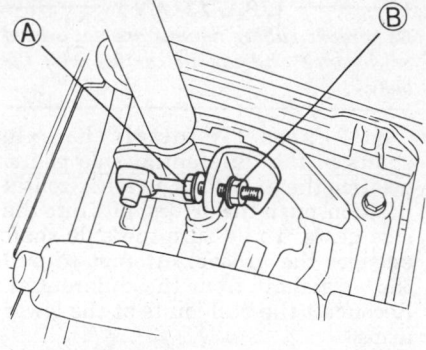

Shifter adjustment on 1986 and later RX–7 models

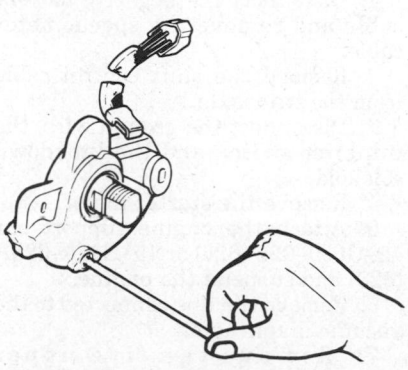

Align the neutral safety switch by inserting a drill through the holes on it.

5. Tighten the neutral switch adjusting screws.
6. Check the adjustment by trying to start the engine in all gears. It should only start in Park and Neutral.

KICKDOWN SWITCH AND DOWNSHIFT SOLENOID ADJUSTMENT

GLC (RWD)

1. Check the accelerator linkage for smooth operation.
2. Turn the ignition on but do not start the engine.
3. Depress the accelerator pedal fully to the floor. As the pedal nears the end of its travel, a light "click" should be heard from the downshift solenoid.
4. If the kickdown switch operates too soon, loosen the locknut on the switch shaft. Adjust the shaft so that the accelerator linkage make contact with it when the pedal is depressed $7/8$–$15/16$ of the way to the floor. Tighten the locknut.
5. If no noise comes from the solenoid at all, then check the wiring for the solenoid and the switch.
6. If the wiring is in good condition, remove the wire from the solenoid and connect it to a 12V power source. If

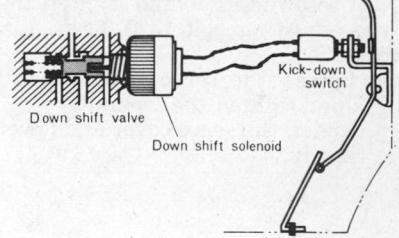

Kickdown switch the downshift solenoid circuit

the solenoid does not click when connected, it is defective and should be replaced.

NOTE: When the solenoid is removed, about two pints of transmission fluid will leak out.

1981-82 626 and RX-7

1. Disconnect the wiring connectors from the kickdown switch.
2. Screw out the kick-down switch at few turns.
3. Fully depress the accelerator pedal.
4. Gradually screw in the kick-down switch until you hear a clicking sound then screw it in ½ turn more.

NOTE: On the 1984-88 RX-7 screw the switch stopper just to where it makes contact with the accelerator pedal.

5. Tighten the locknut and connect the wiring connectors.

BAND ADJUSTMENT

JATCO Models 3N71B and l4N71B

1. Raise the vehicle and support safely.
2. Drain the transmission fluid and remove the transmission pan.
3. Loosen the locknut and torque the servo adjusting bolt to 9–11 ft. lbs.
4. Back off the servo bolt 2(3N71B) or 3(L4N71B) full turns and tighten the locknut.

NOTE: On the L4N71B, an overdirve brake band is used. Loosen the locknut and torque the stem to 5–7 ft. lbs., then back off the stem two full turns.

5. Install the pan assembly and fill with fluid.

JATCO Models R3A

1. Raise the vehicle and support safely.
2. Locate the servo cover and remove from the right side of the transmission case.

3. Loosen locknut and tighten the servo adjusting bolt to 9–11 ft. lbs. torque.

4. Loosen the servo bolt two full turns and tighten the locknut.

5. Install the servo cover and lower the vehicle.

AUTOMATIC TRANSAXLE

REMOVAL & INSTALLATION

GLC (FWD)

1. Raise the vehicle on a hoist and support it safely. Disconnect the negative battery cable.

NOTE: When removing or installing the transaxle assembly the rear end of the power plant (engine) must be lifted and secured with the aid of a chain, or special engine support.

2. Disconnect all electrical wiring and connections, control linkages from the transaxle. Mark these units to aid in reassembling.

3. Remove the front wheels. Disconnect the lower ball joints from the steering knuckles. Pull the driveshafts from the differential gears.

— CAUTION —

Separate the driveshaft by pulling the front hub outward. Make sure not to use too much force at once, increase the force gradually. Be sure the driveshaft's ball joint is bent to its maximum extent. Do not allow the axle shafts to drop. Damage may occur to the ball and socket joints and to the rubber boots. Wire the shafts to the vehicle body when released from the differential.

4. Remove the undercover. Hook the engine support hoist 49–E301-025 or equivalent on the engine hanger and hoist the engine up slightly. Disconnect the control cable. Remove the crossmember and disconnect the cooler lines.

5. Disconnect the oil hose from the oil pipe, plug both the pipe and the hose to prevent fluid lose. Remove the starter motor. Remove the end covers and remove the bolts holding the torgue converter to the drive plate.

6. Support the transaxle with a jack. Remove the transaxle-to-engine mounting bolts. Remove the unit from the vehicle.

7. Installation is the reverse of removal.

— CAUTION —

Be sure the rubber mounts are not twisted or distorted and not in contact with the body.

8. To properly install the axle shafts in the differential side gears, position the axle shaft in a horizontal position, push the driveshafts into the side gears. To be sure the axle shaft engages the groove, attempt to pull the axle shaft from the differential. Reconnect the ball joints at the lower arms.

1983-85 626

1. Disconnect the negative battery cable and remove the speedometer cable.

2. Remove the shift control cable from the transaxle.

3. Disconnect the ground wire, the inhibitor switch and the kickdown solenoid.

4. Remove the starter motor.

5. Attach the engine support bar 49–G030–025 (626) or 49–E310–025A (323) and suspend the engine.

6. Remove the line connected to the vacuum diaphragm.

7. Remove the five upper transaxle-to-engine attaching bolts.

8. Remove the transmission cooler lines from the transaxle.

9. Jack up the vehicle and support it with safety stands.

10. Remove the front wheels and the left and right splash shields.

11. Remove the stabilizer bar control link. Remove the undercover.

12. Remove the pinch bolt and separate the ball joint from the steering knuckle.

13. Pull the left axle shaft from the transaxle:

   a. Insert a chisel between the driveshaft and the bearing housing. Tap the end of the chisel lightly in order to uncouple the axle shaft and differential side gear.

— CAUTION —

Do not insert the chisel too far between the shaft and the housing, doing so might damage the lip of the oil seal or the dust cover.

   b. Pull the front hub outward and remove the axle shaft from the transaxle.

NOTE: Support the axle shaft during and after removal to avoid damaging the CV-joints and boots.

14. Pull the right axle shaft from transaxle:

   a. Insert a prybar between the axle shaft and the joint shaft and force the axle shaft coupling open.

   b. Pull the front hub out and re-move the axle shaft from the joint shaft.

NOTE: Support the axle shaft during and after removal to avoid damaging the CV-joints and boots.

   c. Remove the joint shaft assembly from the transaxle.

15. Remove the transaxle undercover and torque converter-to-drive plate bolts.

16. Remove the crossmember and the left-side lower arm together as an assembly.

17. Attach a rope to the transaxle mounting brackets in two places and secure the rope over the engine support bar.

18. Place a board on a floor jack and use it to support the transaxle.

19. Remove the lower two transaxle-to-engine bolts.

20. Lower the transaxle with the floor jack while guiding it with a rope.

NOTE: Do not separate the torque converter from the transaxle during removal.

21. Installation is the reverse of removal. Torque the transaxle-to-engine bolts to specifications.

1986-88 626 & 323

1. Disconnect the negative battery cable. Remove the air cleaner and loosen the front whell lug nuts. On the 626 models, remove the cruise control actuator and the battery.

2. Disconnect the speedometer and throttle cable from the transaxle. Disconnect the change control cable from the transaxle.

3. Remove the ground wire installation boot. Remove the water pipe bracket. Remove the secondary air pipe and the EGR pipe bracket.

4. Remove the wire harness clip. Disconnect the coupler for the inhibitor switch, the kick-down solenoid and any other necessary solenoids or switches. Disconnect the body ground connector and selector cable.

5. Remove the two or four upper transaxle mounting bolts. Disconnect the neutral switch connector and ther vacuum line from the vacuum diaphragm. Disconnect the transaxle oil cooler lines. Mount the engine support (49-ER301-025A) or equivalent to the engine hanger.

6. Raise and support the vehicle safely. Drain the transaxle oil into a suitable container and remove the front wheels.

7. Remove the engine under cover and side covers. Remove the front stabilizer.

8. Remove the lower arm ball joints and the knuckle clinch bolts, pull the lower arm downward and separate the lower arms from the knuckles.

9. Separate the driveshaft from the transaxle by prying with a suitable pry bar inserted between the shaft and the case. Be sure not to damage the oil seals.

10. Remove the transaxle cross-member. Remove the wiring and the starter motor.

11. Remove the end plates. Lean the engine toward the transaxle side to lower the transaxle by loosening the engine support hook bolt. Support the transaxle with a suitbale transaxle jack.

12. Remove the necessary engine brackets. Remove the remaining transaxle mounting bolt. Lower the jack and slide the transaxle out from under the vehicle.

13. To install, reverse the removal procedures. Adjust the shift linkage. Refill the transaxle with the proper grade of gear oil.

PAN REMOVAL

1. Raise the car and support it safely.

2. Place a suitable container to catch the transmission fluid when the pan is loosened.

3. Slowly loosen the oil pan mounting bolts and allow the pan to tip downward.

4. Support the oil pan and slowly remove the mounting bolts as the fluid drains from the edge of the pan.

5. Remove the oil pan and clean all gasket mating surfaces. Wipe the inside of the oil pan with a clean rag. Remove any deposits with solvent and dry the inside of the pan.

6. Installation is the reverse of removal. Use a new gasket and torque the oil pan mounting bolts to specifications.

SHIFT LEVER ADJUSTMENT

1. Set the parking brake.
2. Loosen locknuts A and B.
3. Move the gearshaft to the Park position.
4. Shift the selector lever on the transaxle to the Neutral position. This is the third detent from the rear of the transaxle.
5. Turn locknut A by hand until it lightly contacts the T-joint.
6. Tighten locknut B to 8 ft. lbs.
7. Move the selector lever through all gear positions and make sure it operates smoothly.

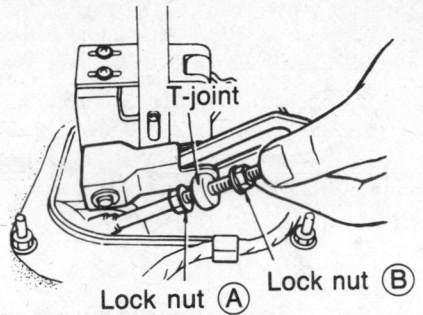

Shifter adjustment on 323 and 626 models

KICK-DOWN SWITCH ADJUSTMENT

1. Connect an ohmmeter between the terminals of the kick-down switch.

2. Depress the accelerator to the floor and check for continuity.

3. To adjust, loosen the locknut and turn the switch to make contact with the depressed accelerator ($\frac{7}{8}$ or more of the full stroke).

4. With the adjustment completed, torque the locknut.

DOWNSHIFT SOLENOID

When the accelerator pedal is fully depressed, the kickdown switch becomes active and the downshift solenoid gets power. The downshift valve in the control valve is pushed up to kickdown position 3-to-2 and position 2-to-1 at an given speed.

NEUTRAL SAFETY/REVERSE LAMP SWITCH

The switch contacts should operate when the switch plunger is moved into its respective operating positions. The switch operates from closed (starter solenoid on) to the neutral (or Off) position and then to the reverse light ("On" position). The switch plunger must operate smoothly otherwise the gear selector will be affected.

DRIVE AXLE

Halfshafts

REMOVAL & INSTALLATION

1981-85 GLC

1. Raise and support the front of the vehicle. Remove both front wheels

and splash shields. Drain the transaxle fluid.

2. Loosen the driveaxle locknut at the center of the disc brake hub after raising the lock tab. Apply brake pressure while loosening.

3. Remove the lower ball joint from the steering knuckle.

4. Remove the axle shaft from the transaxle case by pulling the brake caliper outward with increasing force. While applying outward force, hit the driveaxle shaft with a brass hammer, if necessary, to help in removal.

5. Remove the locknut and pull the axle shaft from the steering knuckle. Remove the axle shaft and plug the transaxle case with a clean rag to prevent dirt from entering.

6. Installation is in the reverse order of removal. Before installing the axle shaft into the transaxle case, check the oil seals for cuts or damage. Replace the oil seals if necessary. Insert the axle into the transaxle case by pushing on the wheel hub assembly.

1983-88 626 and 323

1. Raise and support the front of the vehicle. Drain the transaxle fluid and remove the splash shield.

2. Operate the brakes to secure the wheel hub and then loosen the axle shaft lock nut. Remove the front wheels.

NOTE: Raise the tabs before loosening the locknut.

3. Remove the stabilizer bar control link from the lower arm.

4. Remove the pinch bolt and remove the ball joint from the steering knuckle.

5. Remove the left-side axle shaft:

a. On manual transaxles, insert a prybar between the axle shaft and the transaxle case. Remove the axle shaft from the side gear by lightly tapping the end of the prybar.

--- CAUTION ---

Do not insert the prybar too far, doing so, could damage the lip of the oil seal or the dust cover.

b. For automatic transaxle, insert a prybar between the axle shaft and the bearing housing. Tap the end of the prybar in order to uncouple the axle shaft and differential side gear.

c. After removing the axle shaft lock nut, pull the front hub outward and toward the rear. Disconnect the axle shaft from the wheel and the transaxle.

6. Remove the right-side axle shaft and joint shaft:

a. Insert a prybar between the

axleshaft and the joint shaft and separate them.

b. Remove the axle shaft lock nut and pull the front hub outward and to the rear, disconnecting the axle shaft from the front hub. Remove the axle shaft from the joint shaft.

NOTE: If the driveshaft is stuck to the front hub and can not be removed, install bearing puller tool 49-0839-425C or equivalent, to push the shaft out. After removing the driveshaft, install differential side gear holder 49G-030-455 into the transaxle, thus preventing dirt from getting into the transaxle.

7. Installation is the reverse of removal.

CV-JOINT OVERHAUL

On GLC, the joint on the wheel side of the axle shaft is non-rebuildable. If worn, the joint and axle must be replaced. The boot may be changed if necessary. Do not interfere with the balancer found on the right axle unless necessary for wheel/joint boot replacement. If balancer is removed it must be reinstalled in the same position 14.45 in. from the front of the wheel joint.

For all CV-joint overhual procedures, please refer to "CV-Joint Overhaul" in the Unit Repair Section.

Driveshaft and U-Joints

REMOVAL & INSTALLATION

GLC (RWD) and RX-7

Do not remove the oil seals from models with a center bearing unless they are defective.

1. Raise and support the vehicle safely. Matchmark the flanges on the driveshaft and pinion so that they may be installed in their original position.
2. Remove all necessary exhaust pipes and remove the nuts that attach the drive shaft to the companion flange of the rear axle. Lower the back end of the driveshaft and slide the front end out of the transmission.
3. Plug up the hole in the transmission with the main shaft turning holder 49-0259-440, to prevent it from leaking.
4. Driveshaft installation is the reverse of removal.

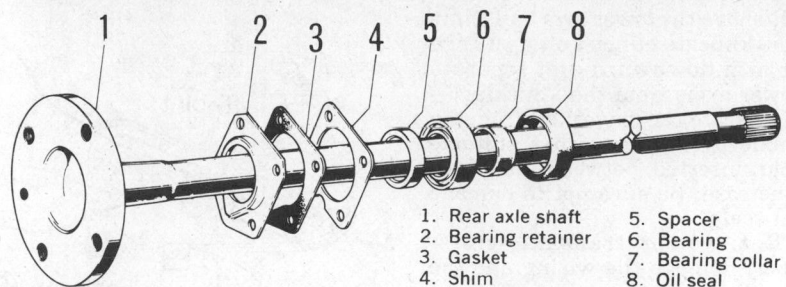

1. Rear axle shaft
2. Bearing retainer
3. Gasket
4. Shim
5. Spacer
6. Bearing
7. Bearing collar
8. Oil seal

Components of the rear wheel drive axle shaft assembly

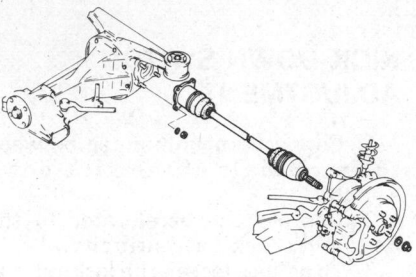

1986-88 RX-7 rear axle shaft

1981-82 626

Perform this operation only when the exhaust system is cold.

1. Raise and support the vehicle safely. Remove the front heat insulator.
2. Remove the nuts which secure the downpipe to the thermal reactor flange.
3. Remove the downpipe from the main muffler flange.
4. Matchmark the pinion and driveshaft flange bolts.
5. Unfasten the center bearing.
6. Remove the driveshaft.
7. Driveshaft installation is the reverse of removal. Tighten the yoke-to-front driveshaft locknut to 116–130 ft. lbs.

Rear Axle Shafts

REMOVAL & INSTALLATION

All 1981-85 Rear Drive Models

1. Raise and support the rear of the vehicle on jackstands.
2. Remove the rear wheel assembly.
3. If equipped with brake drums, remove the brake drum, the return spring, the brake shoe assembly, the parking brake cable, the brake tube and the backing plate nuts.
4. If equipped with disc brakes, remove the brake caliper, the disc rotor and the dust cover retaining nuts.
5. Connect the axle shaft puller 49-0223-630B and the attachment 49-8501-631 to the axle shaft, then

pull the axle/backing plate assembly from the housing.
6. To install, reverse the removal procedures.

1986-87 RX-7

1. Raise the rear of the car and support it safely on jackstands.
2. Remove the rear tire. Using a blunt drift, uncrimp the lock nut on the axle shaft. Depress the brake pedal to hold the hub secure and then remove the axle nut.
3. Remove the caliper assembly and tie it back with a piece of rope. Remove the setting screws and the disc plate.
4. Remove the knuckle assembly.
5. Remove the nuts attaching the drive shaft to the companion flange ot the transaxle and remove the drive shaft.
6. When installing, insert the wheel side of the driveshaft to the axle flange and then install the differential side of the driveshaft. Tighten the drive shaft attaching nuts to 40–47 ft. lbs.
7. The rest of the installation procedure is the reverse order of the removal procedure. Torque the lock nut to 174–231 ft. lbs. Be sure to measure the play of the wheel bearing. If the play exceeds the 0.004 in. or less, replace the wheel bearing. Crimp the driveshaft lock nut to the drive shaft groove.

Axle Bearing & Oil Seal

REMOVAL & INSTALLATION

All 1981-85 Rear Drive Models

1. Refer to the "Axle Shafts, Removal & Installation" procedures in this section and remove the axle shaft.
2. Using a grinder, grind a portion of the bearing collar down to 0.020 in., then using a chisel, cut through the collar.

3. Remove the bearing and the backing plate from the axle shaft.

4. Using a screwdriver, remove the oil seal from the axle housing.

5. Using the installer tool 49-0180-321A, oil the axle housing and drive a new seal into the housing.

6. Assemble the backing plate, bearing and the bearing collar onto the axle shaft, press the assembly together with an arbor press and the installation tool 49-1011-748.

7. Align and slide the axle assembly into the axle housing. Be careful not to damage the oil seal.

8. To complete the installation, reverse the removal procedures.

Output Shaft Oil Seal

REMOVAL & INSTALLATION

1986-87 RX-7

1. Remove the axle shaft as described above.

2. Insert two prybars between the differential case and the output shaft, then remove the output shaft by applying pressure to both bars evenly. Exercise caution as the shaft may suddenly pop out.

3. Pry out the old seal using a suitable tool.

4. Coat the lip of the new seal with a thin coat of grease and install using installer tool 49-F027-004, or equivalent.

5. Install the output shaft and axle shaft.

Front Axle Hub and Bearing

REMOVAL & INSTALLATION

Front Wheel Drive

1. Loosen the lug nuts, raise the front of the car and safely support it on jackstands. Remove the tire and wheel.

2. Raise the staked tab from the hub center nut, remove the nut from the axle. Apply the brake to help hold the rotor while loosening the nut.

3. Using a ball joint puller (49-0118-850C), remove the tie rod end from the steering knuckle. Disconnect the horseshoe clip that retains the brake line to the strut.

NOTE: On the 626 model, remove the stabilizer bar control link from the control arm.

4. Remove the mounting bolts that hold the caliper assembly to the knuckle. Wire the caliper out of the way, do not allow the caliper to be supported by the brake hose.

5. Remove the thru-bolt and nut that retains the lower ball joint to the steering knuckle and disconnect the ball joint.

6. Remove the 2 bolts and nuts retaining the strut to the steering knuckle. Separate the steering knuckle and hub from the strut and axle shaft.

7. The hub is pressed through the wheel bearings into the knuckle. Replacement of the hub removal requires a wheel hub puller 49-B001-726 (GLC) or 49-G030-725/49-G030-727 (626 and 323), to remove the hub from the steering knuckle.

8. Remove the inner oil seal and bearing. Remove the outer bearing using a press and Mazda tools 49-F401-368/49-F401-365 (GLC) or 49-G030-725/49-G030-728 (626 and 323), to remove the bearing from the steering knuckle. Drive the outer and inner race from the knuckle with a brass drift and hammer.

9. Install new inner and outer races. Pack the inner and outer bearing and install in knuckle. Use Mazda tool 49-B001-727 (GLC) or 49-G030-728 (626 and 323), press the hub into the steering knuckle. Measure the preload with a scale connected to the caliper mounting hole on the knuckle. Various spacers are available to increase or decrease the preload. Preload should be 1.7-6.9 ft. lbs.

10. Install the inner and outer grease seals. Press fit the hub through the bearings into the knuckle.

11. Installation of the knuckle and hub is in the reverse order of removal. Always use a new axle locknut. On the GLC and 323, torque axle shaft locknut to 116-174 ft. lbs. or 626 to 116-124 ft. lbs. Stake the locknut after tightening. Torque the knuckle-to-strut 58-86 ft. lbs. (GLC) or 69-86 ft. lbs. (626 and 323), the knuckle-to-ball joint to 33-40 ft. lbs. and the knuckle-to-tie rod end to 22-33 ft. lbs.

FRONT SUSPENSION

MacPherson Struts

REMOVAL & INSTALLATION

1. Remove the wheel cover and loosen the lug nuts.

2. Raise the front of the vehicle and support it with jackstands. Do not jack it or support it by any of the front suspension members. Remove the wheel.

—— CAUTION ——
Be sure the car is securely supported. Remember, you will be working underneath it.

3. Remove the brake caliper and disc on all models except the GLC and 626 with front wheel drive.

4. Unfasten the nuts which secure the upper shock mount to the top of the wheel arch.

5. Unfasten the two bolts that secure the lower end of the shock to the steering knuckle arm.

6. Remove the shock and coil spring as a complete assembly.

7. To remove the shock absorber or strut cartridge, compress the coil spring with coil spring holder 49-0223-640B and 49-0370-641 or equivalent. Remove the strut lock nut and washer, mounting block, spring upper seat, spring seat, coil spring, bound stopper, spring lower seat and shock absorber or strut cartridge.

—— CAUTION ——
The coil springs are retained under considerable pressure. They can exert enough force to cause serious injury. Exercise extreme caution when servicing.

8. Installation is in the reverse order. Be sure to keep the coil spring compressed until the strut assembly is completely assembled.

OVERHAUL

For all spring removal and installation procedures and any other strut overhaul procedures, please refer to "Strut Overhaul" in the Unit Repair section.

Front Control Arm

REMOVAL & INSTALLATION

1981-85 Rear Wheel Drive

Remove the control arm and steering knuckle as an assembly.

1. Remove the wheel.

2. Remove the cotter pin and nut, which secure the tie-rod end, from the knuckle arm; then use a puller to separate them.

3. Unbolt the lower end of the shock absorber.

4. Remove the nut, then withdraw the rubber busing and washer which secure the stabilizer bar to the control arm.

5. Unfasten the nut and bolt which secure the control arm to the frame member.

6. Push outward on the strut assembly while removing the end of the control arm from the frame member.

1. Front side bushing
2. Spindle
3. Lower arm
4. Ball joint
5. Mounting block
6. Spring upper seat
7. Rubber seat
8. Dust cover
9. Coil spring
10. Shock absorber
11. Knuckle

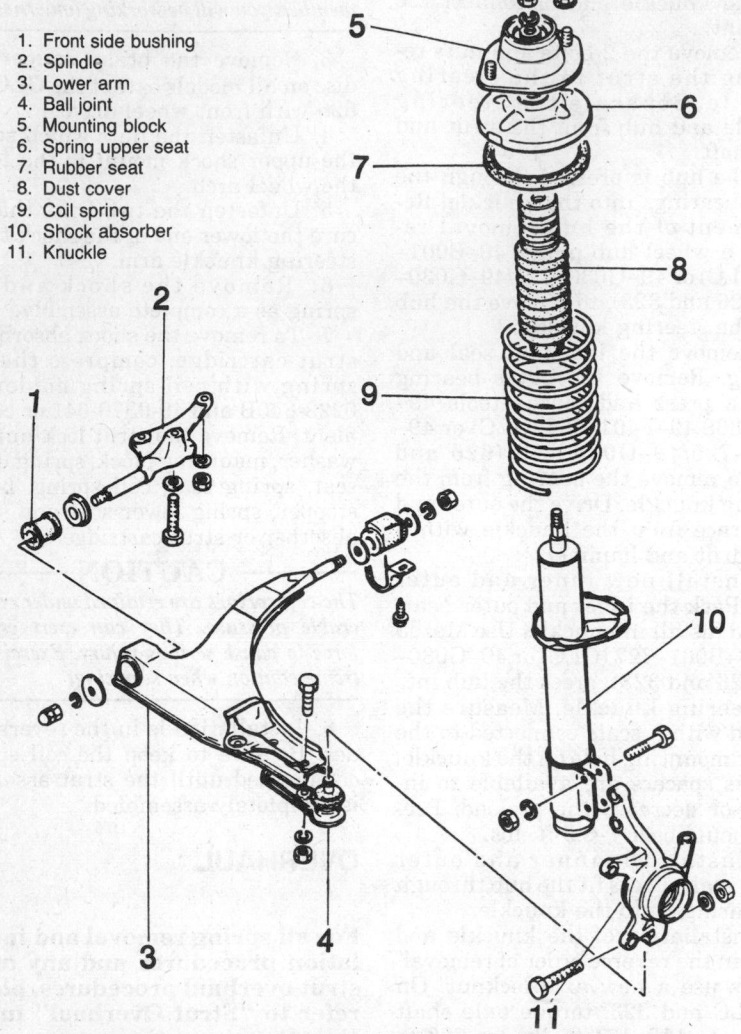

Typical front suspension assembly—front wheel drive models

7. Remove the control arm and steering knuckle arm as an assembly.

8. Separate the knuckle arm from the control arm with a puller.

9. Installation of the control arm is the reverse of removal.

1986-88 RX-7

1. Raise the front of the car and support it safely with jackstands.
2. Remove the lower splash shield.
3. Disconnect the front stabilizer link from the control arm.
4. Remove the pinch bolt, then separate the lower ball joint from the steering knuckle.
5. Remove the front control arm mounting bolt.
6. Remove the control arm bushing bracket bolts and lower the control arm from the car.
7. Installation is the reverse of removal. Check the front end alignment.

Front Wheel Drive

GLC

1. Loosen the wheel lugs, raise the car and safely support it on jackstands. Remove the front wheel.
2. Remove the thru-bolt connecting the lower arm to the steering knuckle.
3. Remove the bolts and nuts mounting control arm to the body (two inner and three outer).
4. Remove the lower control arm. The ball joint can be serviced at this time if necessary.
5. Installation is in the reverse order or removal.
Mounting Torque:
Ball Joint-to-Steering Knuckle: 32–40 ft. lbs.
Outer Bolts: 43–54 ft. lbs.
Inner Bolts: 69–86 ft. lbs.

1983-88 626 AND 323

1. Raise the front end and support it with safety stands.

2. Remove the wheel and splash shield.

3. Remove the stabilizer link from the control arm.

4. Remove the lower control arm-to-frame attaching bolts.

5. Remove the pinch bolt and separate the ball joint from the steering knuckle.

6. Remove the lower control arm.

7. Installation is the reverse of removal. Torque the lower arm mounting bolts to 69–86 ft. lbs.

Ball Joints

INSPECTION

All Except GLC

1. Perform Steps 1–5 of the "Control Arm Removal" procedure.

2. Check the ball joint dust boot.

3. Check the amount of pressure required to turn the ball stud, by hooking a pull scale into the tie rod hole in the knuckle arm. Pull the spring scale until the arm just begins to turn; this should require 4.4–7.7 lbs. on 626 models; 1–2.2 lbs. on 323 models.

If the reading is lower than 14 oz. on the 1981-85 RX-7, replace the ball joint and the suspension arm as a unit.

GLC

1. Check the dust boot for wear.

2. Raise the wheels off the ground and grip the tire at the top and bottom and alternately push and pull to check ball joint end-play. Wear limit is 0.04 in. If necessary, replace the ball joint and control arm assembly.

REMOVAL & INSTALLATION

1981-85 RX-7 and 1981-82 626

1. Remove the control arm.

2. Remove the set-ring and the dust boot.

3. Press the ball joint out of the control arm.

4. Clean the ball joint mounting bore and coat it with kerosene.

5. Press the ball joint into the control arm.

NOTE: If the pressure required to press the new ball joint into place is less than 3,300 lbs., the bore is worn and the control arm must be replaced.

GLC

The ball joint may be removed during lower control arm removal. See "Control Arm Removal and Installation." Torque the ball joint nut, check the revolving torque of the ball joint on 1981-85 models (63–109 ft. lbs.)

1983-88 626

The ball joint and control arm assembly is replaced as a unit.

1986-88 323 and RX-7

The ball joint can be unbolted from the control arm after separation from the steering knuckle.

Wheel Bearings—Front Discs

REMOVAL & INSTALLATION

All 1981-85 Rear Drive Models

1. Remove the brake disc/hub.
2. Drive the seal out and remove the inner bearing.
3. Drive the outer bearing races out.
4. Installation is the reverse of removal. Repack the bearings and the hub cavity with lithium grease. Adjust the bearing.

ADJUSTMENT

NOTE: This operation is performed with the wheel, grease cap, nut lock, and cotter pin removed.

1. To seat the bearings, back off on the adjusting nut three turns and then rotate the hub/dics assembly while tightening the adjusting nut.
2. Back off on the adjusting nut about ⅙ of a turn.
3. Hook a spring scale in one of the bolt holes on the hub.
4. Pull the spring scale squarely, until the hub just begins to rotate. The scale reading should be 0.9–2.2 lbs.-all passenger cars exc. GLC, 626 and RX-7. GLC: 0.33–1.32 lbs.; 626: 0.77–1.92 lbs.; RX-7: 0.99–1.43 lbs. Tighten the adjusting nut until the proper spring scale reading is obtained.
5. Place the castellated nut lock over the adjusting nut. Align one of the slots on the nut-lock with the hole in the spindle and fit the cotter pin into place.

Front Wheel Alignment

CASTER AND CAMBER

Caster and camber are preset by the manufacturer. They require adjustment only if the suspension and steering linkage components are damaged. In this case, adjustment is accomplished by replacing the damaged

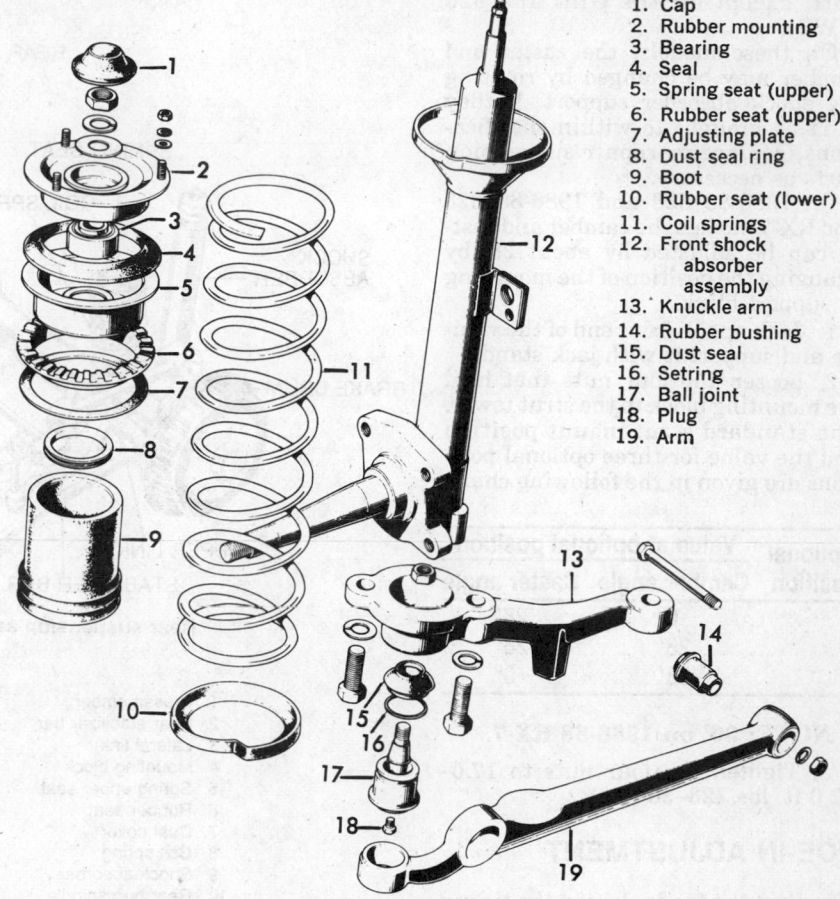

1. Cap
2. Rubber mounting
3. Bearing
4. Seal
5. Spring seat (upper)
6. Rubber seat (upper)
7. Adjusting plate
8. Dust seal ring
9. Boot
10. Rubber seat (lower)
11. Coil springs
12. Front shock absorber assembly
13. Knuckle arm
14. Rubber bushing
15. Dust seal
16. Setring
17. Ball joint
18. Plug
19. Arm

Typical front suspension assembly—rear wheel drive models

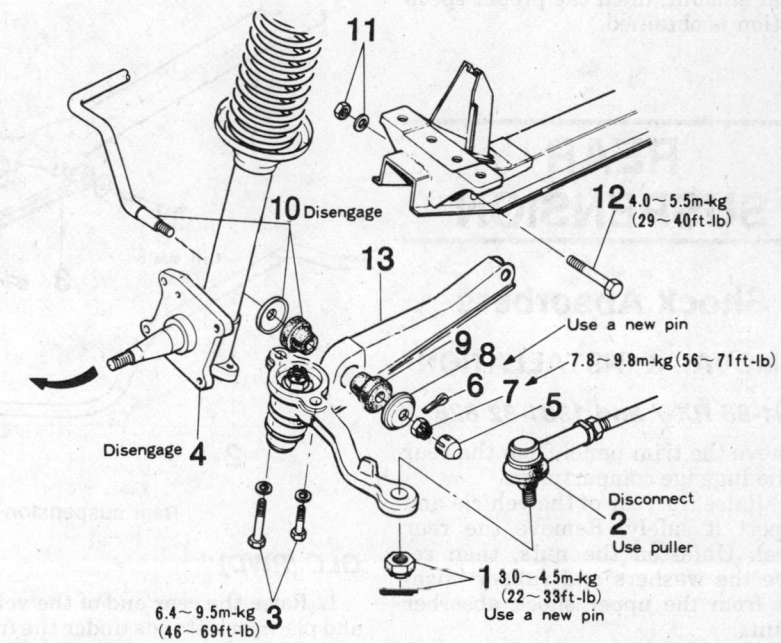

1. Castle nut and cotter pin
2. Tie-rod end
3. Strut to lower arm bolts
4. Strut and wheel spindle
5. Cap nut
6. Cotter pin
7. Castle nut
8. Washer
9. Bushing
10. Anti-roll bar and bushing
11. Nut and washer
12. Suspension arm bolt
13. Suspension arm

GLC rear wheel drive—strut and lower control arm

part, except for the GLC and 626 (FWD).

On these models, the caster and camber may be changed by rotating the shock absorber support. If they can't be brought to within specifications, replace or repair suspension parts as necessary.

On 1983-88 626 and 1986-88 323 and RX-7 models the camber and caster can be adjusted by about 28' by changing the position of the mounting or support block.

1. Jack up the front end of the vehicle and support it with jack stands.

2. Loosen the four nuts that hold the mounting block to the strut tower. The standard strut mount position and the value for three optional positions are given in the following chart:

| Optional position | Value at optional position | |
	Camber angle	Caster angle
A	0°	28'
B	28'	28'
C	28'	0°

NOTE: 30' on 1986-88 RX-7.

3. Tighten the four nuts to 17.0–22.0 ft. lbs. (23–30 Nm).

TOE-IN ADJUSTMENT

To adjust the toe-in, loosen the tie rod locknuts and turn both tie rods an equal amount, until the proper specification is obtained.

REAR SUSPENSION

Shock Absorbers

REMOVAL & INSTALLATION

1981-85 RX-7 and 1981-82 626

Remove the trim panel from the rear of the luggage compartment.

1. Raise the rear of the vehicle and support it safely. Remove the rear wheel. Unfasten the nuts, then remove the washers and rubber bushings from the upper shock absorber mounts.

2. Unfasten the nut and bolt which secure the end of the rear shock to the axle housing.

3. Remove the shock.

4. Installation is the reverse of removal. Torque the shock absorber bolts to 54 ft. lbs.

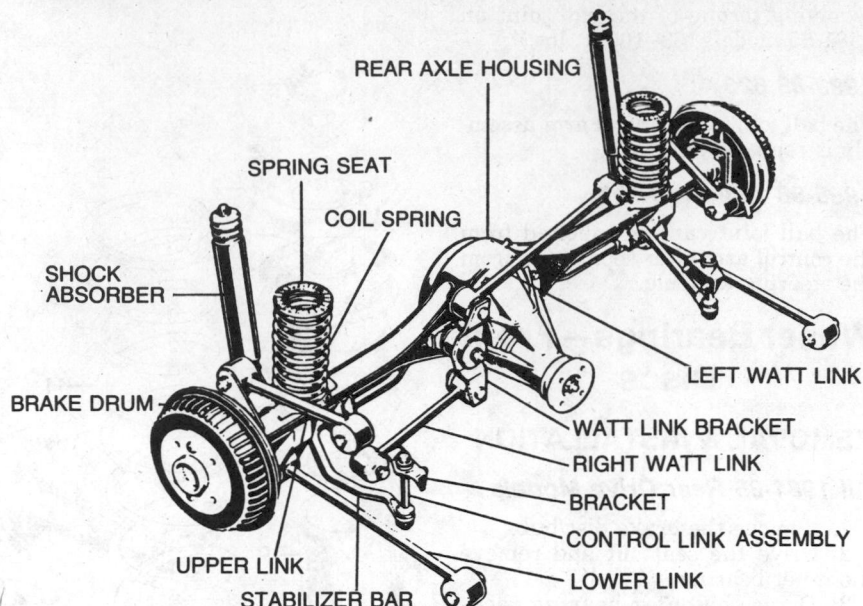

Rear suspension assembly—1980–85 RX–7

1. Crossmember
2. Rear stabilizer bar
3. Lateral link
4. Mounting block
5. Spring upper seat
6. Rubber seat
7. Dust cover
8. Coil spring
9. Shock absorber
10. Rear hub spindle
11. Trailing link

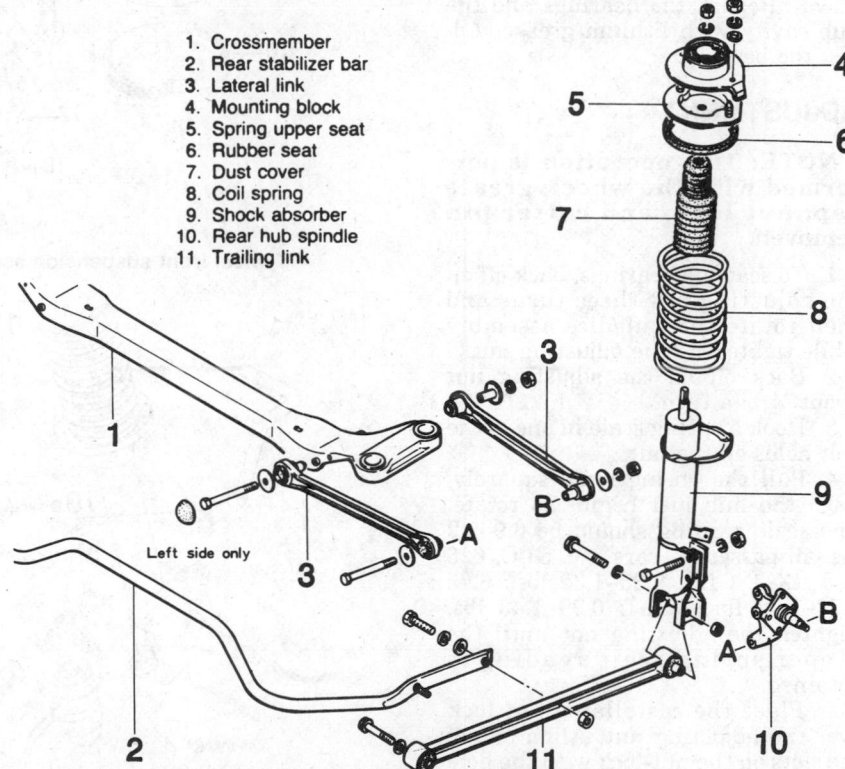

Rear suspension assembly—GLC front wheel drive

GLC (RWD)

1. Raise the rear end of the vehicle and place jack stands under the frame side rails.

2. Remove the rear wheel.

3. Remove the upper and lower shock absorber bolts and nuts and remove the shock absorber.

4. Install the shock absorber in the reverse order of removal.

MacPherson Strut

REMOVAL & INSTALLATION

1981-85 GLC and 1983-88 626 and 323

1. Remove the side trim panels from inside the "trunk," or the rear seat and trim. Loosen and remove the

top mounting nuts from the strut mounting block assembly.

2. Loosen the rear wheel lugs, raise the car and safely support it on jackstands.

3. Remove the rear wheels. Disconnect the flexible brake hose from the strut.

4. Disconnect the trailing arm from the lower side of the strut: Separate the lateral link and strut by removing the bolt assembly.

5. Remove the strut from the lower unit by removing the two through nuts and bolts.

6. Remove the strut and brake assembly.

7. To remove the shock absorber or strut cartridge, compress the coil spring with coil spring holder 49-0223-640B and 49-0370-641 or equivalent. Remove the strut lock nut and washer, mounting block, spring upper seat, spring seat, coil spring, bound stopper, spring lower seat and shock absorber or strut cartridge.

————— CAUTION —————

The coil springs are retained under considerable pressure. They can exert enough force to cause serious injury. Exercise extreme caution when servicing.

8. Installation is in the reverse order. Be sure to keep the coil spring compressed until the strut assembly is completely assembled.

1986-88 RX-7

1. Raise the rear of the car and support it safely with jackstands.

2. Remove the two top shock flange mounting bolts, actuator, nut and actuator bracket.

3. Remove the bottom shock absorber mounting bolt and remove the shock and spring assembly from the car.

4. To remove the shock absorber or strut cartridge, compress the coil spring with coil spring holder 49-0223-640B and 49-0370-641 or equivalent. Remove the strut lock nut and washer, stopper, mounting block, rubber bushing, spring seat, rubber bushing, set plate, spacer, coil spring, bound stopper and shock absorber or strut cartridge.

————— CAUTION —————

The coil springs are retained under considerable pressure. They can exert enough force to cause serious injury. Exercise extreme caution when servicing.

5. Installation is in the reverse order. Be sure to keep the coil spring

compressed until the strut assembly is completely assembled.

NOTE: If equipped with adjustable shock absorbers, disconnect the electrical connector from the top shock absorber tower before removal.

OVERHAUL

For all strut overhaul procedures, please refer to "Strut Overhaul" in the Unit Repair section.

Springs

REMOVAL & INSTALLATION

GLC (RWD)

1. Raise the rear end of the vehicle and place jackstands under the frame side rails.

2. Remove the rear wheel.

3. Remove the upper and lower shock absorber bolts and nuts and remove the shock absorber.

4. Place a jack under the lower arm to support it.

5. Remove the pivot bolt and nut that secures the rear end of the lower arm to the axle housing.

6. Slowly lower the jack to relieve the spring pressure on the lower arm, then remove the spring.

7. Install the spring in the reverse order of removal.

1981-85 RX-7 and 1981-82 626

1. Raise the rear of the vehicle and support it safely.

2. Remove the rear wheel.

3. Position any hydraulic floor jack under the rear axle housing.

4. Disconnect the shock absorber lower end of the lower link bolt (just to the front of the lower shock bolt). Remove the rear bolt from the upper link.

NOTE: These trailing control arm links run parallel from the front to rear on the vehicle, with the smaller watt links running side to side on the vehicle.

5. Disconnect the front ends of the stabilizer bar (if equipped).

6. Remove the right and left watt links at the rear axle housing.

7. Carefully lower the rear axle housing and remove the coil spring and the rubber seat.

8. The installation is the reverse of the removal.

Trailing Arm

REMOVAL & INSTALLATION

1986-88 RX-7

1. Raise the rear of the car and support it safely.

2. Remove the axle shaft locknut.

3. Remove the brake caliper and wire it out of the way. Do not let the caliper hang by its brake hose.

4. Remove the brake caliper mounting bracket and the brake rotor.

5. Remove the shock absorber.

6. Disconnect the rear stabilizer bar from the trailing arm.

7. Remove the drive axle shaft and rear hub assembly.

8. Disconnect the lateral link. Remove the inner trailing arm mounting bolt.

9. Remove the outer trailing arm bolt and remove the trailing arm from the car.

10. Installation is the reverse of removal.

Rear Wheel Bearings

REPLACEMENT

All front wheel drive models use a conventional roller bearing with the race pressed into the rotor or brake drum. To replace the bearing, remove the rear brake drum or rotor and lift out the bearing cage assembly. Use a blunt drift to knock the bearing race out, then press in a new race using a bench press and suitable mandrel. When the drum or rotor is installed, torque the center nut to 18–22 ft. lbs. (25–29 Nm) to preload the bearing, then crimp the nut collar using a suitable drift to lock the nut in place.

STEERING

Steering Wheel

REMOVAL & INSTALLATION

1. Remove the crash pad/horn button assembly. On four-spoke steering wheels, pull the center cap toward the wheel top.

2. Punch matchmarks on the steering wheel and steering shaft.

————— CAUTION —————

Never strike the steering shaft on collapsible steering columns. Always use a suitable puller to remove the steering wheel.

3. Remove the wheel using a suitable puller.

4. Installation is the reverse of removal.

Combination Switch

REPLACEMEMT

1981-85 RX-7

1. Remove the steering wheel.
2. Remove the steering column shroud.
3. Remove the retaining ring from the combination (turn signal) switch, or remove the mounting screws.
4. Carefully draw the switch over the steering column.
5. Installation is the reverse of removal.

1981-82 626

1. Remove the steering wheel.
2. Loosen the nut which secures the vent knob (left side) and allow the knob assembly to drop away from its mounting bracket.
3. Remove choke knob. Remove the choke retaining nut and separate the choke from the panel.
4. Remove the upper column cover.
5. Disconnect the panel light dimmer switch wiring.
6. Disconnect the exhaust temperature warning light wiring.
7. Loosen, but don't remove the screws at either end of the lower panel cover.

NOTE: The left-hand screw is located in the hole which was covered by the upper column cover and the right-hand screw is above the ashtray opening (ashtray removed).

8. Pull the upper column cover away from the instrument panel.
9. Disconnect the combination switch connector.
10. Remove the retaining ring from the steering column.
11. Unfasten the combination switch retaining screw and remove the switch.
12. Installation is the reverse of removal.

GLC and 1983-88 626 and 323

1. Disconnect the negative battery cable.
2. Remove the horn cap and steering wheel.
3. Remove the steering column covers.
4. Disconnect the wire connectors.
5. Remove the stop ring from the shaft.
6. Remove the attaching screw and remove the combination switch.

7. To install reverse the removal procedure.

Ignition Lock/Switch

REMOVAL & INSTALLATION

RX-7

1. Disconnect the negative battery cable.
2. Remove the horn cover and the steering wheel, using a steering wheel puller.

NOTE: Mark the steering wheel and steering shaft before removing the steering wheel.

3. Remove the steering wheel covers.
4. Remove the air duct and disconnect the couplers of the combination switch.
5. Remove the combination switch assembly.
6. Place a protector under the steering lock assembly to protect the steering shaft from the shock of the hammer blows.
7. Using a chisel, loosen the steering lock body to the column jacket.
8. To install, tighten the switch's retaining bolts, until their heads break off.
9. To complete the installation, reverse the removal procedures.

GLC, 323 and 626

1. Follow steps under "Combination Switch Replacement".
2. Remove the instrument frame brace.
3. Disconnect the switch wires.
4. Use a chisel to make slots in the lockscrews. Remove the screws with a screwdriver. Install the new screws until the head twists off.
5. Installation is the reverse of removal.

Steering Linkage

REMOVAL & INSTALLATION

1981-85 Rear Wheel Drive Models

The front wheels should point straight ahead. Align the marks on the pitman arm and the sector shaft to ensure proper steering linkage alignment.

1. Remove the cotter pins and the castellated nuts which secure the ends of the tie rods to the center link and the steering knuckle.
2. Remove the tie rods.
3. Remove the idler arm.
4. Remove the pitman arm. Remove the center link.

5. Unfasten the nut which secures the pitman arm to the sector shaft and use a puller to separate them.
6. Installation is the reverse of removal.

Tie Rod

REMOVAL & INSTALLATION

All 1981-85 Rear Wheel Drive Models

1. Disconnect the tie rod from the center link and knuckle arm. A puller will be necessary.
2. Install the tie rod to the center link and knuckle arm. Tighten the nuts to 22–32 ft. lbs. and install new cotter pins.

Steering Gear

REMOVAL & INSTALLATION

1981–85 RX-7

1. Remove the steering wheel.
2. Remove the column covers.
3. Remove the combination switch assembly.
4. Remove the steering lock and ignition switch assembly.
5. Remove the steering column support bracket.
6. Raise and support the front end.
7. Remove the front wheel.
8. Remove the cotter pin and nut and disconnect the center link from the pitman arm using a ball joint puller.
9. Unbolt the steering gear from the frame, taking note of the presence of any shim for realigning the gear with the shaft.
10. Remove the steering column dust cover and remove the gear housing, column jacket and aligning shim.
11. Reverse the removal for installation. Place the shim in its original position for realignment. Gear housing-to-frame bolt torque is 32–40 ft. lbs.

1981-82 626

1. Remove the front wheel.
2. Remove the nut and cotter pin and disconnect the center link from the pitman arm with a ball joint puller.
3. Unbolt the flexible coupling from the worm shaft.
4. Unclip the speedometer cable from the gear housing and the power brake unit.
5. Unbolt and remove the gear housing.
6. Install in reverse of the above.

ADJUSTMENT

Worm Bearing Preload

1. Check the torque of the worm shaft by rotating it with a torque wrench, or the RX-7 it should be 4.3–7.7 inch lbs., 5–10 inch lbs. on GLC and 1.74–2.60 inch lbs. on 626.
2. If the torque is not correct, loosen the locknut and adjust the rear cover nut.
3. Torque the locknut.

Backlash

1. Loosen the locknut.
2. Torque the adjustment cover to 7.2 ft. lbs., loosen it again.
3. Torque it to 2.60 inch lbs. and loosen 0–15 degrees from that position.
4. Torque the locknut to 29–43 ft. lbs.

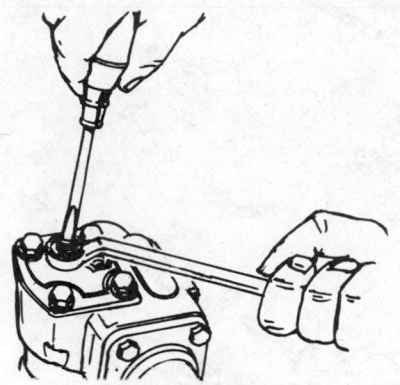

Adjusting backlash

Steering Gear and Linkage

REMOVAL & INSTALLATION

GLC (FWD)

1. Raise the front of the vehicle and support it with safety stands.
2. Remove the wheels.
3. Disconnect the tie rod ends from the knuckles.

NOTE: **On models with power steering, place a pan underneath to catch fluid and disconnect the return and pressure lines.**

4. Remove the boot band and attaching bolts and remove the gear and linkage from the engine compartment through the tie rod hole.
5. Installation is the reverse of removal. Make sure the steering wheel is straight forward and tighten the following torques: Mounting bracket bolts: 23–34 ft. lbs.; tie rod end and knuckle bolts: 21–35 ft. lbs.; Intermediate shaft and pinion connecting bolt: 13–19.5 ft. lbs.

1986-88 RX-7

1. Raise the front of the car and support it with jackstands.
2. Disconnect the battery cables and remove the battery. Drain the coling system into a suitable drain pan.
3. Remove the radiator cooling fan, shroud and radiator.
4. Disconnect the front stabilizer bar from the steering rack assembly.
5. Remove the cotter pin and tie rod end castle nut. Separate the tie rod from the steering knuckle.
6. Remove the pinch bolt at the steering column U-joint.
7. Remove the steering rack mounting bolts and power steering lines, if equipped with power steering.
8. Remove the rack and separate the steering column U-joint.
9. Installation is the reverse of removal. If equipped with power steering, see the procedures under power steering system bleeding. Check the front end alignment.

1983-88 626 & 323

1. Raise the front of the vehicle and support it with safety stands.
2. Remove the wheels.
3. Remove the steering gear to steering column coupler pinch bolt na d separate the coupler from the steering gear. Disconnect the tie rod end nuts and cotter pin. Remove the knuckle arm/tie rod connections.
4. On power steering models remove and plug the pressure hose going tp the power steering pump.

NOTE: **On models with power steering, place a pan underneath to catch fluid and disconnect the return and pressure lines.**

5. Remove the boot band and all attaching and retaining bolts from the steering gear. Remove the gear and linkage from the engine compartment through the tie rod hole.
6. Installation is the reverse of removal. Be sure to bleed the air out of the system if equipped with a power steering pump.

Power Steering Pump

REMOVAL & INSTALLATION

1. Disconnect and plug the fluid hoses from the pump.
2. Remove all necessary drive belts in order to get to the power steering belt. Remove the alternator and or the A/C compressor if necessary.
3. Loosen the pump belt adjusting bolt, slide the pump to one side and remove the belt.
4. Support the pump, remove the mounting bolts and lift out the pump.
5. Installation is the reverse of removal. Adjust belt to give a ½ in. deflection at the mid-point of its longest stretch. Fill the reservoir and bleed the system.

SYSTEM BLEEDING

1. Check the fluid level.
2. Start the engine.
3. Turn the steering wheel completely to the left and the right, several times until the air bubbles leave the oil.
4. Top off the fluid reservoir.

BRAKE SYSTEM

For all brake system repair and service procedures not detailed below, please refer to "Brakes" in the Unit Repair section.

Master Cylinder

REMOVAL & INSTALLATION

NOTE: **On models which have a fluid reservoir located separately from the master cylinder, remove the lines which run between the two and plug the lines to prevent leakage.**

1. Disconnect the oil level sensor if so equipped.
2. Using a suitable line wrench, disconnect and plug the brake fluid lines from the master cylinder.
3. Remove the proportioning bypass valve attaching bolts and valve, if so equipped.
4, Remove the bolts attaching the master cylinder to the power brake unit. Remove the master cylinder from the vehicle.
5. Installation is the reverse of removal. Bleed the brake system.

Power Brake Booster

REMOVAL & INSTALLATION

1. Remove the blower air duct, if so equipped. Disconnect the vacuum hose from the power booster assembly.
2. Disconnect and plug the brake lines from the master cylinder.
3. Remove the master cylinder from the brake booster.
4. Remove the cotter pin and disconnect the clevis pin from the booster yoke at the brake pedal.

5. Remove the booster mounting nuts and remove the booster from the car.

6. Installation is the reverse of removal. Bleed the brake system and grease the pedal clevis pin before installing.

Wheel Cylinder

REMOVAL & INSTALLATION

1. Remove the wheel.
2. Remove the brake drum and brake shoes.
3. Disconnect and plug the brake lines.
4. Remove the stud nuts and bolt attaching the wheel cylinder to the backing plate and remove the wheel cylinder.
5. Installation is the reverse of removal. Be sure to bleed the system after installation.

Parking Brake Cable

ADJUSTMENT

1. Adjust the rear brake shoes.
2. Adjust the front cable with the nut located at the rear of the parking brake handle. The handle should require 6–8 notches for 1981-85 RX-7; 5–7 for the 1981-82 626 and 5–9 for the GLC (1981-85) to apply the parking brake. Adjust the 1983-88 626 to 7–9 notches, the 1986-88 323 is 7–11 notches for drum brakes and 9–15 notches for disc brakes and 1986-87 RX-7 to 4–5 notches.
3. Operate the parking brake several times; check to see that the rear wheels do not drag when it is fully released.

CHASSIS ELECTRICAL

Heater Blower Motor

REMOVAL & INSTALLATION

All Models

1. Disconnect the negative battery cable.
2. Remove the dash undercover located in the passenger side, if equipped. Remove the glove box. Disconnect the multi-connector to the blower motor.
3. Remove the stay of the steel plate provided in the upper part of the glove box. Remove the right side de-

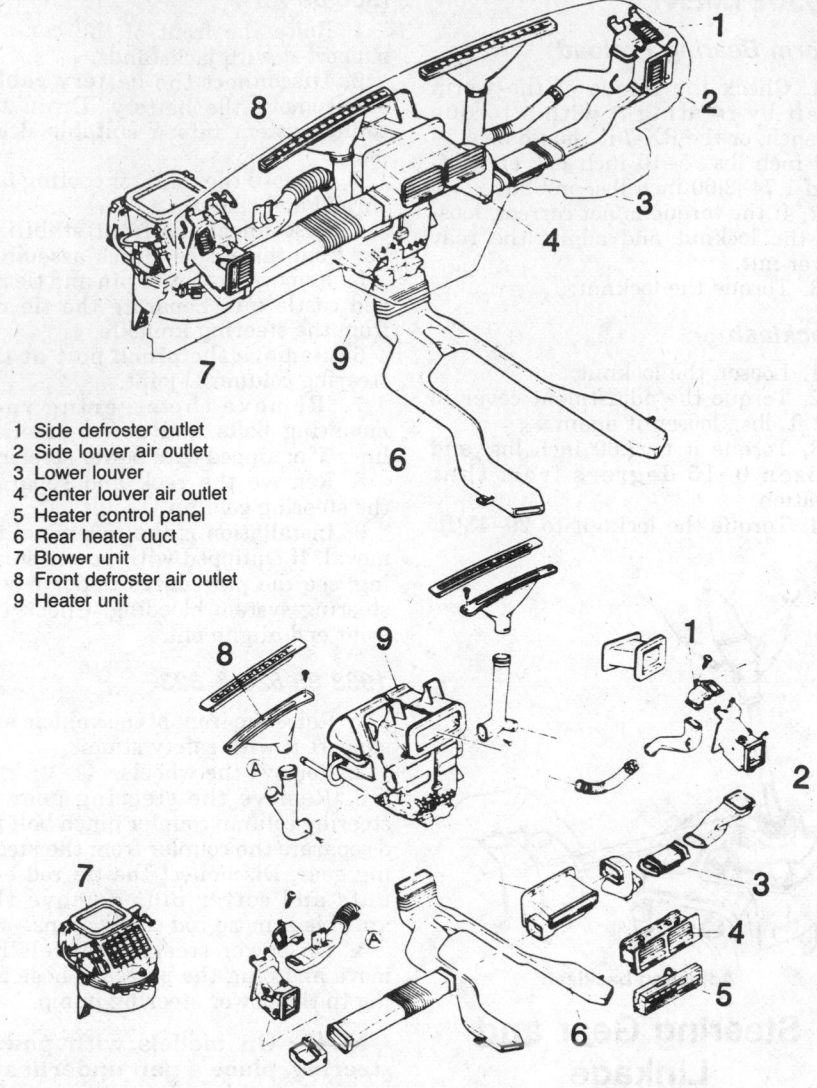

1 Side defroster outlet
2 Side louver air outlet
3 Lower louver
4 Center louver air outlet
5 Heater control panel
6 Rear heater duct
7 Blower unit
8 Front defroster air outlet
9 Heater unit

323 Heater assembly

froster hose for clearance if necessary.

4. Remove the air duct in between the blower unit and the heater unit. If equipped with sliding heater controls, move the control to the HOT position and disconnect the control wire if in the way.
5. Remove the mounting screws and remove the Fresh-Rec air selector wire harness connector. Remove the blower motor.
6. Installation is the reverse of removal.

Heater Core

REMOVAL & INSTALLATION

All Models

NOTE: On models equipped with air conditioning access to the heater core will be more difficult.

— CAUTION —

Do not attempt to discharge the air conditioning system unless you are thoroughly familiar with the system. Escaping refrigerant will freeze any surface it contacts. If you do not have the proper training, have the system discharged and recharged by a professional.

1. Disconnect the negative battery cable. Drain the coolant from the radiator.
2. Disconnect the heater hoses at the engine firewall.
3. Disconnect the duct which runs between the heater box and the blower motor or, depending on the model, remove the crash pad and instrument panel pad from the dash.
4. Disconnect the defroster hose(s) if necessary, set the control to the DEF and HOT position and disconnect the control wires if they are in the way.

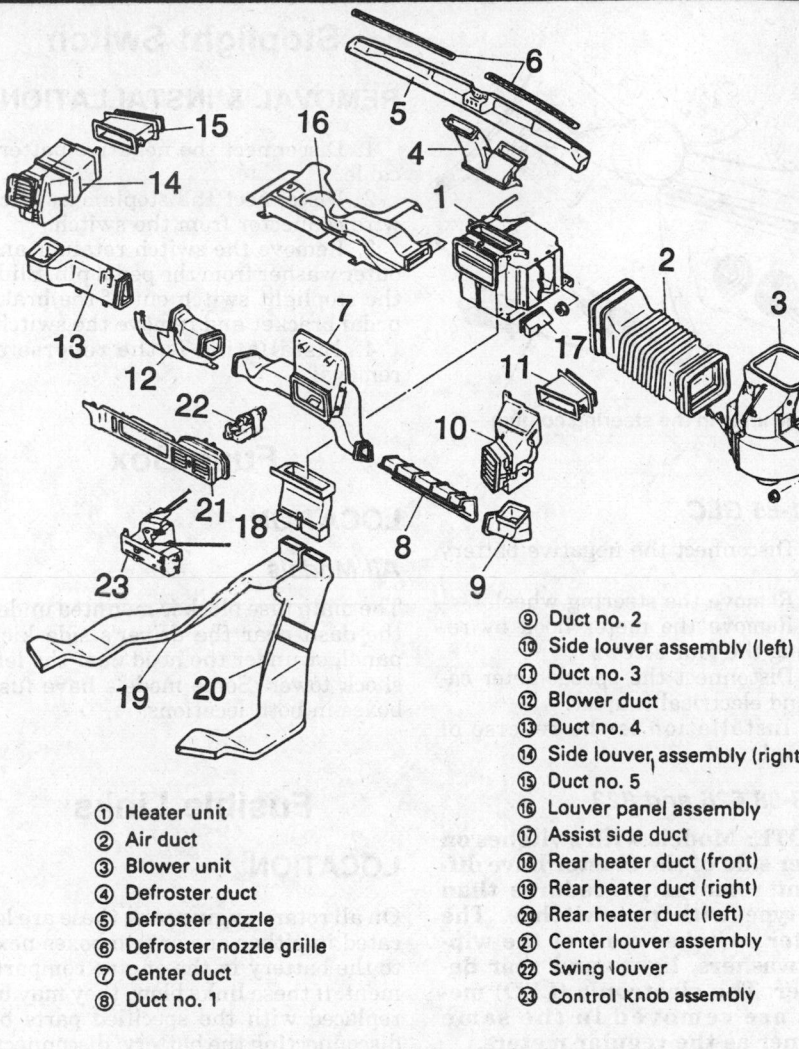

① Heater unit
② Air duct
③ Blower unit
④ Defroster duct
⑤ Defroster nozzle
⑥ Defroster nozzle grille
⑦ Center duct
⑧ Duct no. 1

⑨ Duct no. 2
⑩ Side louver assembly (left)
⑪ Duct no. 3
⑫ Blower duct
⑬ Duct no. 4
⑭ Side louver assembly (right)
⑮ Duct no. 5
⑯ Louver panel assembly
⑰ Assist side duct
⑱ Rear heater duct (front)
⑲ Rear heater duct (right)
⑳ Rear heater duct (left)
㉑ Center louver assembly
㉒ Swing louver
㉓ Control knob assembly

Heater assembly 626

5. Unfasten the retaining screws that secure the halves of the heater box together or remove the heater unit and separate the heater box for access to the heater core.

6. Detach the hoses if not already disconnected. Remove the mounting clips and the heater core. Reverse the removal procedure for installation.

Radio

REMOVAL & INSTALLATION

1. Disconnect the negative battery cable. Remove the ashtray.

2. Remove the center console trim plate.

3. Remove the radio securing bracket bolts. Disconnect the antenna and remove the radio.

4. Installation is the reverse order of the removal procedure.

Windshield Wiper Switch

REMOVAL & INSTALLATION

The windshield wiper switch is incorporated in the multi-function combination switch. To remove the switch the combination switch must also be removed. Refer to the combination switch removal and installation procedure in this section.

Front Windshield Wiper Motor

REMOVAL & INSTALLATION

1. Disconnect the neagtive battery cable. Remove the wiper arms.

2. Remove the cowl plate screws,

move the cowl plate up at the front and disconnect the washer hose. Remove the cowl plate.

3. Disconnect the wires from the wiper motor.

4. Unbolt and remove the motor.

5. Installation is the reverse of removal.

Rear Windshield Wiper Motor

REMOVAL & INSTALLATION

1. Disconnect the neagtive battery cable. Remove the wiper arms.

2. Remove the trunk room light. Remove the service hole cover on the back door.

3. Disconnect the coupler from the wiper motor and remove the wiper motor retaining bolts. Remove the wiper assembly.

4. Installation is the reverse of removal.

Instrument Cluster

REMOVAL & INSTALLATION

1981-85 RX-7

1. Pull the knob off of the steering column-mounted headlight switch. Remove the halves of the steering column shroud.

2. open the left-hand (driver's side) door, to gain access to the screw located on the side of the instrument cluster.

3. Remove the three retaining screws which are located underneath the instrument cluster.

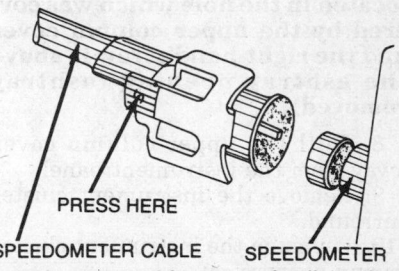

PRESS HERE

SPEEDOMETER CABLE   SPEEDOMETER

Speedometer cable removal, all models

4. Tip the top of the cluster toward the steering wheel.

5. Disconnect the wiring and the speedometer cable from the back of the instrument cluster.

6. Remove the cluster.

7. Installation is the reverse of removal.

1986-88 RX-7

The instrument cluster front bezel contains the switches for headlamps and lighting, cruise control, turn signals and high beams, windshield wiper controls and dimmer knobs. The bezel and switch assembly is removed by unscrewing the seven attaching screws, then pulling the cluster gently and disconnecting the instrument cluster wiring harness from the switch assemblies. Once the bezel is removed, the switch assemblies can be removed from the rear on a workbench. The gauges can be removed once the bezel is clear by simply unscrewing the mounting screws and disconnecting the speedometer cable and wiring connectors.

NOTE: The turn signal cancelling sensor is mounted behind the steering wheel. It is similar to the combination switch mounting and may be removed by following the procedure under "Combination Switch Removal & Installation."

1981-82 626

1. Remove the steering wheel.
2. Loosen the nut which secures the vent knob (left side) and allow the knob assembly to drop away from its mounting bracket.
3. Remove choke knob. Remove the choke retaining nut and separate the choke from the panel.
4. Remove the upper column cover.
5. Disconnect the panel light dimmer switch wiring.
6. Disconnect the exhaust temperature warning light wiring.
7. Loosen, but don't remove the screws at either end of the lower panel cover.

NOTE: The left-hand screw is located in the hole which was covered by the upper column cover and the right-hand screw is above the ashtray opening (ashtray removed).

8. Pull the upper column cover away from the instrument panel.
9. Remove the instrument cluster surround.
10. Unfasten the instrument cluster wiring harness(es).
11. Disconnect the speedometer cable.
12. Tilt the top of the cluster forward, and lift the cluster out.
13. Installation is the reverse of removal.

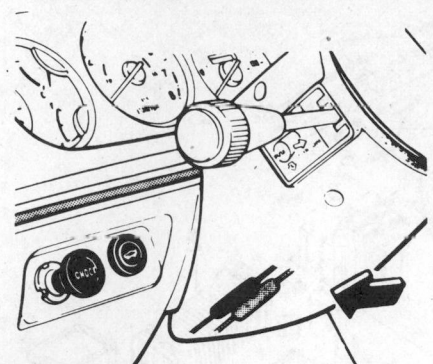

Fusible links in the steering column—RX–7

1981-85 GLC

1. Disconnect the negative battery cable.
2. Remove the steering wheel.
3. Remove the meter hood by removing the four screws.
4. Disconnect the speedometer cable and electrical coupler.
5. Installation is the reverse of removal.

1983-88 626 and 323

NOTE: Models with switches on either side of the cluster have different removal procedures than the type with no switches. The cluster switches control the wipers, washers, lights and rear defogger. The electronic (LED) meters are removed in the same manner as the regular meters.

WITH CLUSTER SWITCHES

1. Disconnect the negative battery cable and remove the upper meter cover.
2. Remove the meter hood, take out the meter light and wires and cables.
3. Remove the meter cluster screws and lift out the meter cluster.
4. Installation is the reverse of removal.

WITHOUT CLUSTER SWITCHES

1. Remove the light and meter cover.
2. Remove the wire connectors and meter cables.
3. Remove the meter screws and lift out the meter cluster.
4. Installation is the reverse of removal.

Stoplight Switch

REMOVAL & INSTALLATION

1. Disconnect the negative battery cable.
2. Disconnect the stoplamp switch wire connector from the switch.
3. Remove the switch retainer and outer washer from the pedal pin. Slide the stoplight switch out of the brake pedal bracket and remove the switch.
4. Installation is the reverse of removal.

Fuse Box

LOCATION

All Models

The main fuse block is mounted under the dash near the driver's side kick panel, or under the hood near the left shock tower. Some models have fuse boxes in both locations.

Fusible Links

LOCATION

On all rotary engine cars, these are located in either one or two boxes next to the battery in the engine compartment. If these links blow, they may be replaced with the specified parts by disconnecting the battery, disconnecting wiring to each link requiring replacement, removing the attaching screws and the link, and install the new link or link in the reverse of the removal procedures.

On the GLC, there is a connector block located in the radiator panel on the right side of the radiator inside the engine compartment. Two links connected there are color coded red and green and may simply be unplugged to remove the, and replace by plugging in replacement parts. Make sure to disconnect the battery before replacing them.

NOTE: Late models use circuit breakers to protect computer-controlled systems and accessories. Circuit breakers are located in the fuse box.

Mercedes-Benz 9

190, 240, 260, 300, 380, 420, 500, 560 — All Models

SERIAL NUMBER IDENTIFICATION

Vehicle Identification Plate

The Vehicle Identification Plate is located in the left window post and consists of a 17 digit number.

Engine Number

The Engine Number is located in rear of the engine block and consists of a 10 digit number.

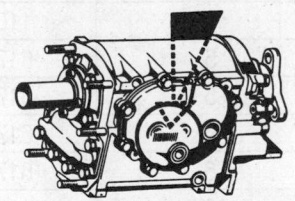

Transmission identification number

Transmission Identification

Mercedes-Benz cars for the U.S. market have been equipped with either a 4 or 5 speed manual transmission or with a fully automatic 3 or 4 speed unit. The automatic transmissions are equipped with a torque converter.

Example: 560 SL = WDB B A 48 D X G A 123456

VIN code group	1	2	3	4	5	6	7	8	9
	WDB	B	A	48	D	X	G	A	123456

Manufacturer

Model
B = 107, C = 126, D = 201, E = 124

Engine type
A = Gasoline, B = Diesel

Model designation
107.048

Restraint system
D = Seat belts + Supplemental Restraint System

Check digit

Model year
G = 1986, H = 1987

Manufacturing plant
A–E = Sindelfingen, F–H = Bremen

Chassis end number

The key to engine identification is a 10 digit number

Serial numbers on the manual transmission are located on a pad on the side cover of the transmission (left side).

Automatic transmission serial numbers are located on a metal plate which is attached to the driver's side of the transmission.

Example: 560 SL = WDB B A 48 D X G A 123456

VIN code group	1	2	3	4	5	6	7	8	9
	WDB	B	A	48	D	X	G	A	123456

Manufacturer

Model
B = 107, C = 126, D = 201, E = 124

Engine type
A = Gasoline, B = Diesel

Model designation
107.048

Restraint system
D = Seat belts + Supplemental Restraint System

Check digit

Model year
G = 1986, H = 1987

Manufacturing plant
A–E = Sindelfingen, F–H = Bremen

Chassis end number

The key to vehicle identification is a 17 digit number

ENGINE IDENTIFICATION

Year	Model	Engine Displacement cu. in. (cc/liter)	Engine Series Identification	No. of Cylinders	Engine Type
1981	240D	146 (2399/2.4)	OM616	4	616.912
	280E	168 (2746/2.8)	M110	6	110.984
	280CE	168 (2746/2.8)	M110	6	110.984
	300D	183 (2996/3.0)	OM617	5	617.912
	300CD	183 (2996/3.0)	OM617	5	617.912
	300SD	183 (2996/3.0)	OM617	5	617.951
	300TD	183 (2996/3.0)	OM617	5	617.952
	380SEL	234 (3839/3.8)	M116	8	116.961
	380SL	234 (3839/3.8)	M116	8	116.962
	380SLC	234 (3839/3.8)	M116	8	116.960
1982	240D	146 (2399/2.4)	OM616	4	616.912
	300D	183 (2996/3.0)	OM617	5	617.912
	300CD	183 (2996/3.0)	OM617	5	617.912
	300SD	183 (2996/3.0)	OM617	5	617.951
	300TD	183 (2996/3.0)	OM617	5	617.952
	380SEC	234 (3839/3.8)	M116	8	116.963
	380SEL	234 (3839/3.8)	M116	8	116.961
	380SL	234 (3839/3.8)	M116	8	116.962
	380SLC	234 (3839/3.8)	M116	8	116.960

ENGINE IDENTIFICATION

Year	Model	Engine Displacement cu. in. (cc/liter)	Engine Series Identification	No. of Cylinders	Engine Type
1983	240D	146 (2399/2.4)	OM616	4	616.912
	300D	183 (2996/3.0)	OM617	5	617.912
	300CD	183 (2996/3.0)	OM617	5	617.912
	300SD	183 (2996/3.0)	OM617	5	617.951
	300TD	183 (2996/3.0)	OM617	5	617.952
	380SEC	234 (3839/3.8)	M116	8	116.963
	380SEL	234 (3839/3.8)	M116	8	116.961
	380SL	234 (3839/3.8)	M116	8	116.962
1984	190D	134 (2197/2.2)	OM601	4	601.921
	190E	140 (2299/2.3)	M102	4	102.961
	300D	183 (2996/3.0)	OM617	5	617.912
	300CD	183 (2996/3.0)	OM617	5	617.912
	300SD	183 (2996/3.0)	OM617	5	617.951
	300TD	183 (2996/3.0)	OM617	5	617.952
	380SE	234 (3839/3.8)	M116	8	116.963
	380SL	234 (3839/3.8)	M116	8	116.962
	500SEC	303 (4973/5.0)	M117	8	117.963
	500SEL	303 (4973/5.0)	M117	8	117.963
1985	190D	134 (2197/2.2)	OM601	4	601.921
	190E	140 (2299/2.3)	M102	4	102.961
	300D	183 (2996/3.0)	OM617	5	617.912
	300CD	183 (2996/3.0)	OM617	5	617.912
	300SD	183 (2996/3.0)	OM617	5	617.951
	300TD	183 (2996/3.0)	OM617	5	617.952
	380SE	234 (3839/3.8)	M116	8	116.963
	380SL	234 (3839/3.8)	M116	8	116.962
	500SEC	303 (4973/5.0)	M117	8	117.963
	500SEL	303 (4973/5.0)	M117	8	117.963
1986	190D	152 (2497/2.5)	OM602	5	602.911
	190E	140 (2299/2.3)	M102	4	102.961
	190E-16	140 (2299/2.3)	M102	4	102.983
	300E	181 (2962/3.0)	M103	6	103.983
	300SDL	183 (2996/3.0)	OM603	6	603.961
	420SEL	256 (4196/4.2)	M116	8	116.965
	560SL	338 (5547/5.6)	M117	8	117.967
	560SEC	338 (5547/5.6)	M117	8	117.968
	560SEL	338 (5547/5.6)	M117	8	117.968
1987-88	190D	152 (2497/2.5)	OM602	5	602.911
	190D	152 (2497/2.5)	OM602	5	602.961
	190E	140 (2299/2.3)	M102	4	102.985
	190E	159 (2599/2.6)	M103	6	103.940
	190E-16	140 (2299/2.3)	M102	4	102.983
	260E	159 (2599/2.6)	M103	6	103.942
	300D	183 (2996/3.0)	M603	6	603.962

ENGINE IDENTIFICATION

Year	Model	Engine Displacement cu. in. (cc/liter)	Engine Series Identification	No. of Cylinders	Engine Type
1987-88	300SDL	183 (2996/3.0)	M603	6	603.961
	300TD	183 (2996/3.0)	M603	6	603.962
	300E	181 (2962/3.0)	M103	6	103.983
	420SEL	256 (4196/4.2)	M116	8	116.965
	560SL	338 (5547/5.6)	M117	8	117.967
	560SEC	338 (5547/5.6)	M117	8	117.968
	560SEL	338 (5547/5.6)	M117	8	117.968

GENERAL ENGINE SPECIFICATIONS

Year	Model	Engine Displacement cu. in. (cc)	Fuel System Type	Net Horsepower @ rpm	Net Torque @ rpm (ft. lbs.)	Bore × Stroke (in.)	Compression Ratio	Oil Pressure @ rpm
1981	240D	147 (2399)	DFI	64 @ 4000	97 @ 2400	3.58 × 3.64	21:1	55 @ 2000
	280E	168 (2746)	CIS	142 @ 5750	149 @ 4600	3.39 × 3.10	8.0:1	55 @ 2000
	280CE	168 (2746)	CIS	142 @ 5750	149 @ 4600	3.39 × 3.10	8.0:1	55 @ 2000
	300D	183 (2996)	DFI	80 @ 4000	120 @ 2400	3.58 × 3.64	21:1	55 @ 2000
	300CD	183 (2996)	DFI	80 @ 4000	120 @ 2400	3.58 × 3.64	21:1	55 @ 2000
	300SD	183 (2996)	Turbo	115 @ 4200	169 @ 2400	3.58 × 3.64	21:1	55 @ 2000
	300TD	183 (2996)	Turbo	120 @ 4350	170 @ 2400	3.58 × 3.64	21:1	55 @ 2000
	380SEL	234 (3839)	CIS	155 @ 4750	196 @ 2750	3.46 × 3.11	8.3:1	55 @ 2000
	380SL	234 (3839)	CIS	155 @ 4750	196 @ 2750	3.46 × 3.11	8.3:1	55 @ 2000
	380SLC	234 (3839)	CIS	155 @ 4750	196 @ 2750	3.46 × 3.11	8.3:1	55 @ 2000
1982	240D	147 (2399)	DFI	64 @ 4000	97 @ 2400	3.58 × 3.64	21:1	55 @ 2000
	300D	183 (2996)	Turbo	120 @ 4350	170 @ 2400	3.58 × 3.64	21:1	55 @ 2000
	300SD	183 (2996)	Turbo	115 @ 4200	169 @ 2400	3.58 × 3.64	21:1	55 @ 2000
	300CD	183 (2996)	Turbo	120 @ 4350	170 @ 2400	3.58 × 3.64	21:1	55 @ 2000
	300TD	183 (2996)	Turbo	120 @ 4350	170 @ 2400	3.58 × 3.64	21:1	55 @ 2000
	380SEC	234 (3839)	CIS	155 @ 4750	196 @ 2750	3.46 × 3.11	8.3:1	55 @ 2000
	380SEL	234 (3839)	CIS	155 @ 4750	196 @ 2750	3.46 × 3.11	8.3:1	55 @ 2000
	380SL	234 (3839)	CIS	155 @ 4750	196 @ 2750	3.46 × 3.11	8.3:1	55 @ 2000
	380SLC	234 (3839)	CIS	155 @ 4750	196 @ 2750	3.46 × 3.11	8.3:1	55 @ 2000
1983	240D	147 (2399)	DFI	64 @ 4000	97 @ 2400	3.58 × 3.64	21:1	55 @ 2000
	300D	183 (2996)	Turbo	120 @ 4350	170 @ 2400	3.58 × 3.64	21:1	55 @ 2000
	300SD	183 (2996)	Turbo	115 @ 4200	169 @ 2400	3.58 × 3.64	21:1	55 @ 2000
	300CD	183 (2996)	Turbo	120 @ 4350	170 @ 2400	3.58 × 3.64	21:1	55 @ 2000
	300TD	183 (2996)	Turbo	120 @ 4350	170 @ 2400	3.58 × 3.64	21:1	55 @ 2000
	380SEC	234 (3839)	CIS	155 @ 4750	196 @ 2750	3.46 × 3.11	8.3:1	55 @ 2000
	380SEL	234 (3839)	CIS	155 @ 4750	196 @ 2750	3.46 × 3.11	8.3:1	55 @ 2000
	380SL	234 (3839)	CIS	155 @ 4750	196 @ 2750	3.46 × 3.11	8.3:1	55 @ 2000
1984	190D	134 (2197)	DFI	72 @ 4200	96 @ 2800	3.43 × 3.64	22:1	55 @ 2000
	190E	140 (2299)	CIS	113 @ 5000	133 @ 3500	3.76 × 3.16	8.0:1	55 @ 2000
	300D	183 (2996)	Turbo	120 @ 4350	170 @ 2400	3.58 × 3.64	21:1	55 @ 2000

GENERAL ENGINE SPECIFICATIONS

Year	Model	Engine Displacement cu. in. (cc)	Fuel System Type	Net Horsepower @ rpm	Net Torque @ rpm (ft. lbs.)	Bore × Stroke (in.)	Compression Ratio	Oil Pressure @ rpm
1984	300SD	183 (2996)	Turbo	115 @ 4200	169 @ 2400	3.58 × 3.64	21:1	55 @ 2000
	300CD	183 (2996)	Turbo	120 @ 4350	170 @ 2400	3.58 × 3.64	21:1	55 @ 2000
	300TD	183 (2996)	Turbo	120 @ 4350	170 @ 2400	3.58 × 3.64	21:1	55 @ 2000
	380SE	234 (3839)	CIS	155 @ 4750	196 @ 2750	3.46 × 3.11	8.3:1	55 @ 2000
	380SL	234 (3839)	CIS	155 @ 4750	196 @ 2750	3.46 × 3.11	8.3:1	55 @ 2000
	500SEC	303 (4973)	CIS	184 @ 4500	247 @ 2000	3.80 × 3.35	8.0:1	55 @ 2000
	500SEL	303 (4973)	CIS	184 @ 4500	247 @ 2000	3.80 × 3.35	8.0:1	55 @ 2000
1985	190D	134 (2197)	DFI	72 @ 4200	96 @ 2800	3.43 × 3.64	22:1	55 @ 2000
	190E	140 (2299)	CIS	113 @ 5000	133 @ 3500	3.76 × 3.16	8.0:1	55 @ 2000
	300D	183 (2996)	Turbo	120 @ 4350	170 @ 2400	3.58 × 3.64	21:1	55 @ 2000
	300SD	183 (2996)	Turbo	115 @ 4200	169 @ 2400	3.58 × 3.64	21:1	55 @ 2000
	300CD	183 (2996)	Turbo	120 @ 4350	170 @ 2400	3.58 × 3.64	21:1	55 @ 2000
	300TD	183 (2996)	Turbo	120 @ 4350	170 @ 2400	3.58 × 3.64	21:1	55 @ 2000
	380SE	234 (3839)	CIS	155 @ 4750	196 @ 2750	3.46 × 3.11	8.3:1	55 @ 2000
	380SL	234 (3839)	CIS	155 @ 4750	196 @ 2750	3.46 × 3.11	8.3:1	55 @ 2000
	500SEC	303 (4973)	CIS	184 @ 4500	247 @ 2000	3.80 × 3.35	8.0:1	55 @ 2000
	500SEL	303 (4973)	CIS	184 @ 4500	247 @ 2000	3.80 × 3.35	8.0:1	55 @ 2000
1986	190D	152 (2497)	DFI	93 @ 4600	122 @ 2400	3.43 × 3.31	22:1	55 @ 2000
	190E	140 (2299)	CIS	113 @ 5000	133 @ 3500	3.76 × 3.16	8.0:1	55 @ 2000
	190E-16	140 (2299)	CIS	167 @ 5800	162 @ 4750	3.76 × 3.16	9.7:1	55 @ 2000
	300D	183 (2996)	Turbo	148 @ 4600	201 @ 2400	3.43 × 3.31	22:1	55 @ 2000
	300SDL	183 (2996)	Turbo	148 @ 4600	201 @ 2400	3.43 × 3.31	22:1	55 @ 2000
	300TD	183 (2996)	Turbo	148 @ 4600	201 @ 2400	3.43 × 3.31	22:1	55 @ 2000
	420SEL	256 (4196)	CIS	201 @ 5200	228 @ 3600	3.62 × 3.11	9.0:1	55 @ 2000
	560SL	338 (5547)	CIS	227 @ 4750	279 @ 3250	3.80 × 3.73	9.0:1	55 @ 2000
	560SEC	338 (5547)	CIS	238 @ 4800	287 @ 3500	3.80 × 3.73	9.0:1	55 @ 2000
	560SEL	338 (5547)	CIS	238 @ 4800	287 @ 3500	3.80 × 3.73	9.0:1	55 @ 2000
1987–88	190D	152 (2497)	DFI	93 @ 4600	122 @ 2400	3.43 × 3.31	22:1	55 @ 2000
	190D	152 (2497)	Turbo	123 @ 4600	168 @ 2400	3.43 × 3.31	22:1	55 @ 2000
	190E	140 (2299)	CIS	130 @ 5100	146 @ 3500	3.76 × 3.16	9.0:1	55 @ 2000
	190E	159 (2599)	CIS	158 @ 5800	162 @ 4600	3.26 × 3.16	9.2:1	55 @ 2000
	190E-16	140 (2299)	CIS	167 @ 5800	162 @ 4750	3.76 × 3.16	9.7:1	55 @ 2000
	260E	159 (2599)	CIS	158 @ 5800	162 @ 4600	3.26 × 3.16	9.2:1	55 @ 2000
	300D	183 (2996)	Turbo	148 @ 4600	201 @ 2400	3.43 × 3.31	22:1	55 @ 2000
	300E	181 (2962)	Turbo	177 @ 5700	188 @ 4400	3.16 × 3.48	9.2:1	55 @ 2000
	300SDL	183 (2996)	Turbo	148 @ 4600	201 @ 2400	3.43 × 3.31	22:1	55 @ 2000
	300TD	183 (2996)	Turbo	148 @ 4600	201 @ 2400	3.43 × 3.31	22:1	55 @ 2000
	420SEL	256 (4196)	CIS	201 @ 5200	228 @ 3600	3.62 × 3.11	9.0:1	55 @ 2000
	560SL	338 (5547)	CIS	227 @ 4750	279 @ 3250	3.80 × 3.73	9.0:1	55 @ 2000
	560SEC	338 (5547)	CIS	238 @ 4800	287 @ 3500	3.80 × 3.73	9.0:1	55 @ 2000
	560SEL	338 (5547)	CIS	238 @ 4800	287 @ 3500	3.80 × 3.73	9.0:1	55 @ 2000

CIS Continuous Injection System
DFI Diesel Fuel Injection
Turbo Turbocharged

GASOLINE ENGINE TUNE-UP SPECIFICATIONS

Year	Model	Engine Displacement cu. in. (cc)	Spark Plugs Type	Gap (in.)	Ignition Timing (deg.) MT	AT	Compression Pressure (psi)	Fuel Pump (psi)	Idle Speed (rpm) MT	AT	Valve Clearance In.	Ex.
1981	280D	168 (2746)	N10Y	.032	—	10B	125	8	750	750	.004	.010
	280CE	168 (2746)	N10Y	.032	—	10B	125	8	750	750	.004	.010
	380SEL	234 (3839)	N10Y	.032	—	5B	125	8	500	500	Hyd.	Hyd.
	380SL	234 (3839)	N10Y	.032	—	5B	125	8	500	500	Hyd.	Hyd.
	380SLC	234 (3839)	N10Y	.032	—	5B	125	8	500	500	Hyd.	Hyd.
1982	380SEL	234 (3839)	N10Y	.032	—	5B	125	8	550	550	Hyd.	Hyd.
	380SL	234 (3839)	N10Y	.032	—	5B	125	8	550	550	Hyd.	Hyd.
	380SLC	234 (3839)	N10Y	.032	—	5B	125	8	550	550	Hyd.	Hyd.
1983	380SEL	234 (3839)	N10Y	.032	—	TDC	125	8	550	550	Hyd.	Hyd.
	380SL	234 (3839)	N10Y	.032	—	TDC	125	8	550	550	Hyd.	Hyd.
	380SLC	234 (3839)	N10Y	.032	—	TDC	125	8	550	550	Hyd.	Hyd.
1984	190E	140 (2299)	S12YC	.032	5B	5B	125	8	650	650	Hyd.	Hyd.
	380SEL	234 (3839)	N10Y	.032	—	TDC	125	8	550	550	Hyd.	Hyd.
	380SL	234 (3839)	N10Y	.032	—	TDC	125	8	550	550	Hyd.	Hyd.
	380SLC	234 (3839)	N10Y	.032	—	TDC	125	8	550	550	Hyd.	Hyd.
	500SEC	303 (4973)	N10Y	.032	—	TDC	125	8	650	650	Hyd.	Hyd.
	500SEL	303 (4973)	N10Y	.032	—	TDC	125	8	650	650	Hyd.	Hyd.
1985	190E	140 (2299)	S12YC	.032	5B	5B	125	8	650	650	Hyd.	Hyd.
	380SEL	234 (3839)	N10Y	.032	—	TDC	125	8	550	550	Hyd.	Hyd.
	380SL	234 (3839)	N10Y	.032	—	TDC	125	8	550	550	Hyd.	Hyd.
	380SLC	234 (3839)	N10Y	.032	—	TDC	125	8	550	550	Hyd.	Hyd.
	500SEC	303 (4973)	N10Y	.032	—	TDC	125	8	650	650	Hyd.	Hyd.
	500SEL	303 (4973)	N10Y	.032	—	TDC	125	8	650	650	Hyd.	Hyd.
1986	190E	140 (2299)	S12YC	.032	5B	5B	125	8	650	650	Hyd.	Hyd.
	190E16	140 (2299)	S7YC	.032	TDC	TDC	125	8	890	890	.006	.012
	300E	181 (2962)	S9YC	.032	TDC	TDC	125	8	650	650	Hyd.	Hyd.
	420SEL	256 (4196)	N9YC	.032	—	5B	125	8	650	650	Hyd.	Hyd.
	560SL	338 (5547)	N9YC	.032	—	5B	125	8	650	650	Hyd.	Hyd.
	560SEC	338 (5547)	N9YC	.032	—	5B	125	8	650	650	Hyd.	Hyd.
	560SEL	338 (5547)	N9YC	.032	—	5B	125	8	650	650	Hyd.	Hyd.
1987–88	190E	140 (2299)	S9YC	.032	10B	10B	125	8	750	750	Hyd.	Hyd.
	190E	159 (2599)	S12YC	.032	9B	9B	125	8	700	700	Hyd.	Hyd.
	190E16	140 (2299)	S7YC	.032	TDC	TDC	125	8	890	890	.006	.012
	260E	159 (2599)	S12YC	.032	9B	9B	125	8	700	700	Hyd.	Hyd.
	300E	181 (2962)	S9YC	.032	TDC	TDC	125	8	650	650	Hyd.	Hyd.
	420SEL	256 (4196)	N9YC	.032	—	5B	125	8	650	650	Hyd.	Hyd.
	560SL	338 (5547)	N9YC	.032	—	5B	125	8	650	650	Hyd.	Hyd.
	560SEC	338 (5547)	N9YC	.032	—	5B	125	8	650	650	Hyd.	Hyd.
	560SEL	338 (5547)	N9YC	.032	—	5B	125	8	650	650	Hyd.	Hyd.

Hyd. Hydraulic lifters
TDC Top Dead Center

DIESEL ENGINE TUNE-UP SPECIFICATIONS

Year	Engine Displacement cu. in. (cc)	Valve Clearance Intake (in.)	Valve Clearance Exhaust (in.)	Intake Valve Opens (deg.)	Injection Pump Setting (deg.)	Injection Nozzle Pressure (psi) New	Injection Nozzle Pressure (psi) Used	Idle Speed (rpm)	Cranking Compression Pressure (psi)
1981	147 (2399) D	.004	.016	13.5B	24B	1564–1706	1422–1706	750–800	284–327
	183 (2996) D	.004	.012	13.5B	24B	1635–1706	1422	700–800	284–327
	183 (2996) CD	.004	.012	13.5B	24B	1635–1706	1422	700–800	284–327
	183 (2996) SD	.004	.014	13.5B	24B	1958–2074	1740	650–850	284–327
	183 (2996) TD	.004	.012	13.5B	24B	1958–2074	1740	650–850	284–327
1982	147 (2399) D	.004	.016	13.5B	24B	1564–1706	1422–1706	750–800	284–327
	183 (2996) D	.004	.014	13.5B	24B	1958–2074	1740	650–850	284–327
	183 (2996) CD	.004	.014	13.5B	24B	1958–2074	1740	650–850	284–327
	183 (2996) SD	.004	.014	13.5B	24B	1958–2074	1740	650–850	284–327
	183 (2996) TD	.004	.014	13.5B	24B	1958–2074	1740	650–850	284–327
1983	147 (2399) D	.004	.016	13.5B	24B	1564–1706	1422–1706	750–800	284–327
	183 (2996) D	.004	.014	13.5B	24B	1958–2074	1740	650–850	284–327
	183 (2996) CD	.004	.014	13.5B	24B	1958–2074	1740	650–850	284–327
	183 (2996) SD	.004	.014	13.5B	24B	1958–2074	1740	650–850	284–327
	183 (2996) TD	.004	.014	13.5B	24B	1958–2074	1740	650–850	284–327
1984	134 (2197) D	Hyd.	Hyd.	12A	15A	1564–1706	1422–1706	700–800	284–327
	183 (2996) D	.004	.014	13.5B	24B	1958–2074	1740	650–850	284–327
	183 (2996) CD	.004	.014	13.5B	24B	1958–2074	1740	650–850	284–327
	183 (2996) SD	.004	.014	13.5B	24B	1958–2074	1740	650–850	284–327
	183 (2996) TD	.004	.014	13.5B	24B	1958–2074	1740	650–850	284–327
1985	134 (2197) D	Hyd.	Hyd.	12A	15A	1564–1706	1422–1706	700–800	284–327
	183 (2996) D	.004	.014	13.5B	24B	1958–2074	1740	650–850	284–327
	183 (2996) CD	.004	.014	13.5B	24B	1958–2074	1740	650–850	284–327

DIESEL ENGINE TUNE-UP SPECIFICATIONS

Year	Engine Displacement cu. in. (cc)	Valve Clearance Intake (in.)	Exhaust (in.)	Intake Valve Opens (deg.)	Injection Pump Setting (deg.)	Injection Nozzle Pressure (psi) New	Used	Idle Speed (rpm)	Cranking Compression Pressure (psi)
1985	183 (2996) SD	.004	.014	13.5B	24B	1958–2074	1740	650–850	284–327
	183 (2996) TD	.004	.014	13.5B	24B	1958–2074	1740	650–850	284–327
1986	152 (2497) D	Hyd.	Hyd.	12A	15A	1564–2103	1740	660–700	284–327
	183 (2996) SDL	Hyd.	Hyd.	12A	15A	1958–2103	1740	610–650	284–327
1987-88	152 (2497) D	Hyd.	Hyd.	12A	15A	1564–2103	1740	660–700	284–327
	152 (2497) D	Hyd.	Hyd.	12A	15A	1564–2103	1740	660–700	284–327
	183 (2996) D	Hyd.	Hyd.	12A	15A	1958–2103	1740	610–650	284–327
	183 (2996) TD	Hyd.	Hyd.	12A	15A	1958–2103	1740	610–650	284–327
	183 (2996) SDL	Hyd.	Hyd.	12A	15A	1958–2103	1740	610–650	248–327

Hyd. Hydraulic lifters

FIRING ORDERS

NOTE: To avoid confusion, always replace spark wires one at a time.

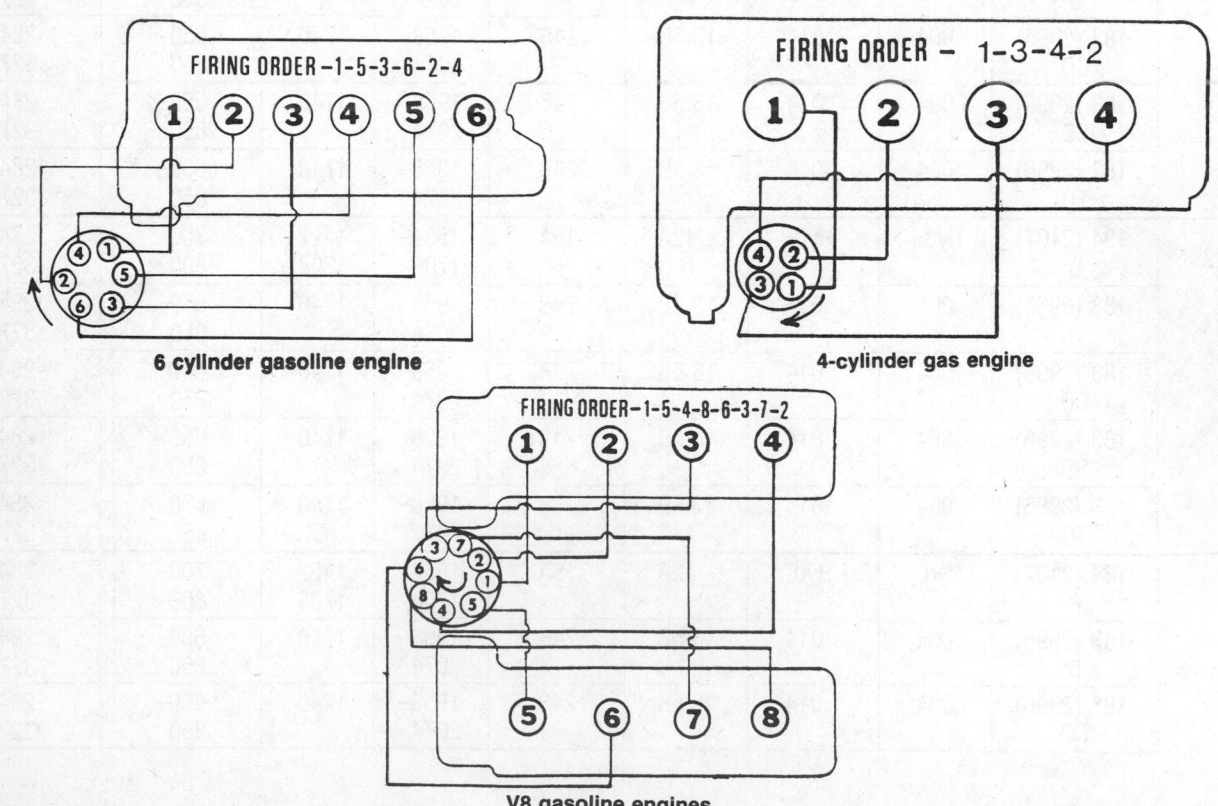

FIRING ORDER – 1-5-3-6-2-4

6 cylinder gasoline engine

FIRING ORDER – 1-3-4-2

4-cylinder gas engine

FIRING ORDER – 1-5-4-8-6-3-7-2

V8 gasoline engines

CAPACITIES

Year	Model	Engine Displacement cu. in. (cc)	Engine Crankcase with Filter	Engine Crankcase without Filter	Transmission (pts.) 4-Spd	Transmission (pts.) 5-Spd	Auto.	Drive Axle (pts.)	Fuel Tank (gal.)	Cooling System (qts.)
1981	240D	147 (2399)	6.3	5.3	3.4	—	11.5	2.1	18.5	10.5
	280E	168 (2746)	6.3	5.3	—	—	12.3	2.1	18.5	11.5
	280CE	168 (2746)	6.3	5.3	—	—	12.3	2.1	18.5	11.5
	300D	183 (2996)	6.8	5.3	—	—	11.5	2.1	18.5	11.7
	300CD	183 (2996)	6.8	5.3	—	—	11.5	2.1	18.5	11.7
	300SD	183 (2996)	8.5	8.0	—	—	13.2	2.2	20.3	13.2
	300TD	183 (2996)	8.5	8.0	—	—	13.2	2.2	18.5	13.2
	380SL	234 (3839)	8.5	8.0	—	—	13.0	2.7	22.4	13.7
	380SEL	234 (3839)	8.5	8.0	—	—	13.0	2.7	23.8	13.7
	380SLC	234 (3839)	8.5	8.0	—	—	13.0	2.7	22.4	13.7
1982	240D	147 (2399)	6.3	5.3	3.4	—	11.5	2.1	18.5	10.5
	300D	183 (2996)	6.8	5.3	—	—	13.2	2.2	18.5	13.2
	300CD	183 (2996)	6.8	5.3	—	—	13.2	2.2	18.5	13.2
	300SD	183 (2996)	8.5	8.0	—	—	13.2	2.2	20.3	13.2
	300TD	183 (2996)	8.5	8.0	—	—	13.2	2.2	18.5	13.2
	380SL	234 (3839)	8.5	8.0	—	—	16.2	2.8	22.4	13.2
	380SEC	234 (3839)	8.5	8.0	—	—	13.0	2.7	23.8	13.2
	380SEL	234 (3839)	8.5	8.0	—	—	13.0	2.7	23.8	13.2
	380SLC	234 (3839)	8.5	8.0	—	—	13.0	2.7	22.4	13.7
1983	240D	147 (2399)	6.3	5.3	—	—	11.5	2.1	18.5	10.5
	300D	183 (2996)	6.8	5.3	—	—	13.2	2.2	18.5	13.2
	300CD	183 (2996)	6.8	5.3	—	—	13.2	2.2	18.5	13.2
	300SD	183 (2996)	8.5	8.0	—	—	13.2	2.2	20.3	13.2
	300TD	183 (2996)	8.5	8.0	—	—	13.2	2.2	18.5	13.2
	380SL	234 (3839)	8.5	8.0	—	—	16.2	2.7	22.4	13.2
	380SEL	234 (3839)	8.5	8.0	—	—	13.0	2.7	23.8	13.2
	380SEC	234 (3839)	8.5	8.0	—	—	13.0	2.7	23.8	13.2
1984	190D	134 (2197)	6.9	6.4	—	3.2	12.5	1.5	14.5	9.0
	190E	140 (2299)	4.8	4.3	—	3.2	11.6	1.5	14.5	9.0
	300D	183 (2996)	6.8	5.3	—	—	13.2	2.2	18.5	13.2
	300CD	183 (2996)	6.8	5.3	—	—	13.2	2.2	18.5	13.2
	300SD	183 (2996)	8.5	8.0	—	—	13.2	2.2	20.3	13.2
	300TD	183 (2996)	8.5	8.0	—	—	13.2	2.2	18.5	13.2
	380SL	234 (3839)	8.5	8.0	—	—	16.2	2.7	22.5	13.2
	380SE	234 (3839)	8.5	8.0	—	—	16.2	2.7	23.8	13.2
	500SEC	303 (4973)	8.5	8.0	—	—	16.2	2.8	23.8	13.7
	500SEL	303 (4973)	8.5	8.0	—	—	16.2	2.8	23.8	13.7
1985	190D	134 (2197)	6.9	6.4	—	3.2	11.6	1.4	14.5	9.0
	190E	140 (2299)	5.3	4.8	—	3.2	11.6	1.4	14.5	9.0
	300D	183 (2996)	6.8	5.3	—	—	13.2	2.2	18.5	13.2
	300CD	183 (2996)	6.8	5.3	—	—	13.2	2.2	18.5	13.2
	300SD	183 (2996)	8.5	8.0	—	—	13.2	2.2	20.3	13.2
	300TD	183 (2996)	8.5	8.0	—	—	13.2	2.2	18.5	13.2

CAPACITIES

Year	Model	Engine Displacement cu. in. (cc)	Engine Crankcase with Filter	Engine Crankcase without Filter	Transmission (pts.) 4-Spd	Transmission (pts.) 5-Spd	Transmission (pts.) Auto.	Drive Axle (pts.)	Fuel Tank (gal.)	Cooling System (qts.)
1985	380SL	234 (3839)	8.5	8.0	—	—	16.2	2.7	22.4	13.2
	380SE	234 (3839)	8.5	8.0	—	—	16.2	2.7	23.8	13.2
	500SEC	303 (4973)	8.5	8.0	—	—	16.2	2.8	23.8	13.7
	500SEL	303 (4973)	8.5	8.0	—	—	16.2	2.8	23.8	13.7
1986	190D	152 (2497)	7.5	7.0	—	3.2	11.6	1.5	14.5	8.5
	190E	140 (2299)	5.3	4.8	—	3.2	11.6	1.4	14.5	9.0
	190E-16	140 (2299)	5.3	4.8	—	3.4	12.6	2.3	18.5	8.5
	300E	181 (2962)	6.4	5.9	—	3.2	13.1	2.3	18.5	8.5
	300SDL	183 (2996)	8.5	8.0	—	3.2	13.1	2.3	23.8	13.3
	420SEL	256 (4196)	8.5	8.0	—	—	16.2	2.7	18.5	13.8
	560SL	338 (5547)	8.5	8.0	—	—	16.2	2.7	22.4	13.8
	560SEL	338 (5547)	8.5	8.0	—	—	16.2	2.7	23.8	13.8
	560SEC	338 (5547)	8.5	8.0	—	—	16.2	2.7	23.8	13.8
1987-88	190D	152 (2497)	8.0	7.5	—	3.2	11.6	1.5	14.5	8.5
	190D	152 (2497)	8.0	7.5	—	3.2	11.6	1.5	14.5	8.5
	190E	140 (2299)	4.8	4.3	—	3.2	12.7	2.3	14.5	9.0
	190E	159 (2599)	6.4	5.9	—	3.2	12.7	2.3	14.5	9.5
	190E16	140 (2299)	5.3	4.8	—	3.4	12.6	2.3	18.5	8.5
	260E	159 (2599)	6.4	5.9	—	3.2	13.1	2.3	18.5	9.5
	300E	181 (2962)	6.4	5.9	—	3.2	13.1	2.3	18.5	8.5
	300D	183 (2996)	8.5	8.0	—	—	13.1	2.3	18.5	10.6
	300TD	183 (2996)	8.5	8.0	—	—	13.1	2.3	19.0	10.6
	300SDL	183 (2996)	8.5	8.0	—	3.2	13.1	2.3	23.8	13.3
	420SEL	256 (4196)	8.5	8.0	—	—	16.2	2.7	18.5	13.8
	560SL	338 (5547)	8.5	8.0	—	—	16.2	2.7	22.4	13.8
	560SEL	338 (5547)	8.5	8.0	—	—	16.2	2.7	23.8	13.8
	560SEC	338 (5547)	8.5	8.0	—	—	16.2	2.7	23.8	13.8

CAMSHAFT SPECIFICATIONS

All measurements given in inches.

Year	Engine Displacement cu. in. (cc)	Journal Diameter 1	2	3	4	5	Lobe Lift In.	Lobe Lift Ex.	Bearing Clearance	Camshaft End Play
1981	147 (2399)	1.378	1.831	1.831	1.831	1.831	.394	.413	.002	.004
	168 (2746) R	0.944	1.966	2.025	2.084	2.123	NA	NA	.003	.007
	L	0.944	1.966	2.025	2.084	2.084				
	168 (2746) R	0.944	1.966	2.025	2.084	2.123	NA	NA	.003	.007
	L	0.944	1.966	2.025	2.084	2.084				
	183 (2996)	1.378	1.831	1.831	1.831	1.831	.394	.413	.002	.004
	183 (2996)	1.378	1.831	1.831	1.831	1.831	.394	.413	.002	.004
	183 (2996)	1.378	1.831	1.831	1.831	1.831	.394	.413	.002	.004
	183 (2996)	1.378	1.831	1.831	1.831	1.831	.394	.413	.002	.004
	234 (3839)	1.377	1.936	1.936	1.944	1.944	NA	NA	.0016	.004

CAMSHAFT SPECIFICATIONS

All measurements given in inches.

Year	Engine Displacement cu. in. (cc)	Journal Diameter					Lobe Lift		Bearing Clearance	Camshaft End Play
		1	2	3	4	5	In.	Ex.		
1981	234 (3839)	1.377	1.936	1.936	1.944	1.944	NA	NA	.0016	.004
	234 (3839)	1.377	1.936	1.936	1.944	1.944	NA	NA	.0016	.004
1982	147 (2399)	1.378	1.831	1.831	1.831	1.831	.394	.413	.002	.004
	183 (2996)	1.378	1.831	1.831	1.831	1.831	.394	.413	.002	.004
	183 (2996)	1.378	1.831	1.831	1.831	1.831	.394	.413	.002	.004
	183 (2996)	1.378	1.831	1.831	1.831	1.831	.394	.413	.002	.004
	183 (2996)	1.378	1.831	1.831	1.831	1.831	.394	.413	.002	.004
	234 (3839)	1.377	1.936	1.936	1.944	1.944	NA	NA	.0016	.004
	234 (3839)	1.377	1.936	1.936	1.944	1.944	NA	NA	.0016	.004
	234 (3839)	1.377	1.936	1.936	1.944	1.944	NA	NA	.0016	.004
1983	147 (2399)	1.378	1.831	1.831	1.831	1.831	.394	.413	.002	.004
	183 (2996)	1.378	1.831	1.831	1.831	1.831	.394	.413	.002	.004
	183 (2996)	1.378	1.831	1.831	1.831	1.831	.394	.413	.002	.004
	183 (2996)	1.378	1.831	1.831	1.831	1.831	.394	.413	.002	.004
	183 (2996)	1.378	1.831	1.831	1.831	1.831	.394	.413	.002	.004
	234 (3839)	1.377	1.936	1.936	1.944	1.944	NA	NA	.0016	.004
	234 (3839)	1.377	1.936	1.936	1.944	1.944	NA	NA	.0016	.004
	234 (3839)	1.377	1.936	1.936	1.944	1.944	NA	NA	.0016	.004
1984	134 (2197)	1.218	1.218	1.218	1.218	1.218	NA	NA	NA	NA
	140 (2299)	1.260	1.260	1.260	1.260	1.260	NA	NA	NA	NA
	183 (2996)	1.378	1.831	1.831	1.831	1.831	.394	.413	.002	.004
	183 (2996)	1.378	1.831	1.831	1.831	1.831	.394	.413	.002	.004
	183 (2996)	1.378	1.831	1.831	1.831	1.831	.394	.413	.002	.004
	183 (2996)	1.378	1.831	1.831	1.831	1.831	.394	.413	.002	.004
	234 (3839)	1.377	1.936	1.936	1.944	1.944	NA	NA	.0016	.004
	234 (3839)	1.377	1.936	1.936	1.944	1.944	NA	NA	.0016	.004
	303 (4973)	1.377	1.936	1.936	1.944	1.944	NA	NA	.0016	.004
	303 (4973)	1.377	1.936	1.936	1.944	1.944	NA	NA	.0016	.004
1985	134 (2197)	1.218	1.218	1.218	1.218	1.218	NA	NA	NA	NA
	140 (2299)	1.260	1.260	1.260	1.260	1.260	NA	NA	NA	NA
	183 (2996)	1.378	1.831	1.831	1.831	1.831	.394	.413	.002	.004
	183 (2996)	1.378	1.831	1.831	1.831	1.831	.394	.413	.002	.004
	183 (2996)	1.378	1.831	1.831	1.831	1.831	.394	.413	.002	.004
	183 (2996)	1.378	1.831	1.831	1.831	1.831	.394	.413	.002	.004
	234 (3839)	1.377	1.936	1.936	1.944	1.944	NA	NA	.0016	.004
	234 (3839)	1.377	1.936	1.936	1.944	1.944	NA	NA	.0016	.004
	303 (4973)	1.377	1.936	1.936	1.944	1.944	NA	NA	.0016	.004
	303 (4973)	1.377	1.936	1.936	1.944	1.944	NA	NA	.0016	.004
1986	140 (2299)	1.260	1.260	1.260	1.260	1.260	NA	NA	NA	NA
	140 (2299)	1.102	1.102	1.102	1.102	1.102	NA	NA	NA	NA
	152 (2497)	1.260	1.260	1.260	1.260	1.260	NA	NA	NA	NA
	181 (2962)	1.378	1.831	1.831	1.831	1.831	.394	.413	.002	.004
	183 (2996)	1.378	1.831	1.831	1.831	1.831	.394	.413	.002	.004

CAMSHAFT SPECIFICATIONS
All measurements given in inches.

Year	VIN	No. Cylinder Displacement cu. in. (liter)	Journal Diameter 1	2	3	4	5	Lobe Lift In.	Ex.	Bearing Clearance	Camshaft End Play
1986	256 (4196)	1.377	1.936	1.936	1.944	1.944	NA	NA	.0016	.004
	338 (5547)	1.377	1.936	1.936	1.944	1.944	NA	NA	.0016	.004
	338 (5547)	1.377	1.936	1.936	1.944	1.944	NA	NA	.0016	.004
	338 (5547)	1.377	1.936	1.936	1.944	1.944	NA	NA	.0016	.004
1987–88	140 (2299)	1.260	1.260	1.260	1.260	1.260	NA	NA	NA	NA
	140 (2299)	1.102	1.102	1.102	1.102	1.102	NA	NA	NA	NA
	159 (2599)	1.378	1.831	1.831	1.831	1.831	.394	.413	.002	.004
	152 (2497)	1.260	1.260	1.260	1.260	1.260	NA	NA	NA	NA
	152 (2497)	1.260	1.260	1.260	1.260	1.260	NA	NA	NA	NA
	159 (2599)	1.378	1.831	1.831	1.831	1.831	.394	.413	.002	.004
	181 (2962)	1.378	1.831	1.831	1.831	1.831	.394	.413	.002	.004
	183 (2996)	1.378	1.831	1.831	1.831	1.831	.394	.413	.002	.004
	183 (2996)	1.378	1.831	1.831	1.831	1.831	.394	.413	.002	.004
	183 (2996)	1.378	1.831	1.831	1.831	1.831	.394	.413	.002	.004
	256 (4196)	1.377	1.936	1.936	1.944	1.944	NA	NA	.0016	.004
	338 (5547)	1.377	1.936	1.936	1.944	1.944	NA	NA	.0016	.004
	338 (5547)	1.377	1.936	1.936	1.944	1.944	NA	NA	.0016	.004
	338 (5547)	1.377	1.936	1.936	1.944	1.944	NA	NA	.0016	.004

NA Not Available at time of publication

CRANKSHAFT AND CONNECTING ROD SPECIFICATIONS

All measurements are given in inches.

Year	Engine Displacement cu. in. (cc)	Crankshaft Main Brg. Journal Dia.	Main Brg. Oil Clearance	Shaft End-play	Thrust on No.	Connecting Rod Journal Diameter	Oil Clearance	Side Clearance
1981	147 (2399)	2.754–2.755	0.002–0.003	0.004–0.009	①	2.045–2.046	0.001–0.002	0.004–0.010
	168 (2746)	2.360–2.361	0.001–0.003	0.004–0.009	①	1.887–1.888	0.006–0.020	0.004–0.009
	168 (2746)	2.360–2.361	0.001–0.003	0.004–0.009	①	1.887–1.888	0.006–0.020	0.004–0.009
	183 (2996)	2.754–2.755	0.002–0.003	0.004–0.009	①	2.045–2.046	0.001–0.002	0.004–0.010
	183 (2996)	2.754–2.755	0.002–0.003	0.004–0.009	①	2.045–2.046	0.001–0.002	0.004–0.010
	183 (2996)	2.754–2.755	0.002–0.003	0.004–0.009	①	2.045–2.046	0.001–0.002	0.004–0.010
	183 (2996)	2.754–2.755	0.002–0.003	0.004–0.009	①	2.045–2.046	0.001–0.002	0.004–0.010
	234 (3839)	2.517–2.518	0.002–0.003	0.004–0.009	①	1.887–1.888	0.004–0.009	0.009–0.014
	234 (3839)	2.517–2.518	0.002–0.003	0.004–0.009	①	1.887–1.888	0.004–0.009	0.009–0.014
	234 (3839)	2.517–2.518	0.002–0.003	0.004–0.009	①	1.887–1.888	0.004–0.009	0.009–0.014

CRANKSHAFT AND CONNECTING ROD SPECIFICATIONS

All measurements are given in inches.

Year	Engine Displacement cu. in. (cc)	Crankshaft Main Brg. Journal Dia.	Main Brg. Oil Clearance	Shaft End-play	Thrust on No.	Connecting Rod Journal Diameter	Oil Clearance	Side Clearance
1982	147 (2399)	2.754–2.755	0.002–0.003	0.004–0.009	①	2.045–2.046	0.001–0.002	0.004–0.010
	183 (2996)	2.754–2.755	0.002–0.003	0.004–0.009	①	2.045–2.046	0.001–0.002	0.004–0.010
	183 (2996)	2.754–2.755	0.002–0.003	0.004–0.009	①	2.045–2.046	0.001–0.002	0.004–0.010
	183 (2996)	2.754–2.755	0.002–0.003	0.004–0.009	①	2.045–2.046	0.001–0.002	0.004–0.010
	183 (2996)	2.754–2.755	0.002–0.003	0.004–0.009	①	2.045–2.046	0.001–0.002	0.004–0.010
	234 (3839)	2.517–2.518	0.002–0.003	0.004–0.009	①	1.887–1.888	0.004–0.009	0.009–0.014
	234 (3839)	2.517–2.518	0.002–0.003	0.004–0.009	①	1.887–1.888	0.004–0.009	0.009–0.014
	234 (3839)	2.517–2.518	0.002–0.003	0.004–0.009	①	1.887–1.888	0.004–0.009	0.009–0.014
1983	147 (2399)	2.754–2.755	0.002–0.003	0.004–0.009	①	2.045–2.046	0.001–0.002	0.004–0.010
	183 (2996)	2.754–2.755	0.002–0.003	0.004–0.009	①	2.045–2.046	0.001–0.002	0.004–0.010
	183 (2996)	2.754–2.755	0.002–0.003	0.004–0.009	①	2.045–2.046	0.001–0.002	0.004–0.010
	183 (2996)	2.754–2.755	0.002–0.003	0.004–0.009	①	2.045–2.046	0.001–0.002	0.004–0.010
	183 (2996)	2.754–2.755	0.002–0.003	0.004–0.009	①	2.045–2.046	0.001–0.002	0.004–0.010
	234 (3839)	2.517–2.518	0.002–0.003	0.004–0.009	①	1.887–1.888	0.004–0.009	0.009–0.014
	234 (3839)	2.517–2.518	0.002–0.003	0.004–0.009	①	1.887–1.888	0.004–0.009	0.009–0.014
	234 (3839)	2.517–2.518	0.002–0.003	0.004–0.009	①	1.887–1.888	0.004–0.009	0.009–0.014
1984	134 (2197)	2.281–2.282	0.001–0.003	0.004–0.010	①	1.887–1.888	0.001–0.003	0.003 0.012
	140 (2299)	2.281–2.282	0.001–0.003	0.004–0.010	①	1.887–1.888	0.001–0.003	NA
	183 (2996)	2.754–2.755	0.002–0.003	0.004–0.009	①	2.045–2.046	0.001–0.002	0.004–0.010
	183 (2996)	2.754–2.755	0.002–0.003	0.004–0.009	①	2.045–2.046	0.001–0.002	0.004–0.010
	183 (2996)	2.754–2.755	0.002–0.003	0.004–0.009	①	2.045–2.046	0.001–0.002	0.004–0.010
	183 (2996)	2.754–2.755	0.002–0.003	0.004–0.009	①	2.045–2.046	0.001–0.002	0.004–0.010
	234 (3839)	2.517–2.518	0.002–0.003	0.004–0.009	①	1.887–1.888	0.004–0.009	0.009–0.014
	234 (3839)	2.517–2.518	0.002–0.003	0.004–0.009	①	1.887–1.888	0.004–0.009	0.009–0.014

CRANKSHAFT AND CONNECTING ROD SPECIFICATIONS

All measurements are given in inches.

Year	Engine Displacement cu. in. (cc)	Crankshaft				Connecting Rod		
		Main Brg. Journal Dia.	Main Brg. Oil Clearance	Shaft End-play	Thrust on No.	Journal Diameter	Oil Clearance	Side Clearance
1984	303 (4973)	2.517–2.518	0.002–0.003	0.004–0.009	①	1.887–1.888	0.004–0.009	0.009–0.014
	303 (4973)	2.517–2.518	0.002–0.003	0.004–0.009	①	1.887–1.888	0.004–0.009	0.009–0.014
1985	134 (2197)	2.281–2.282	0.001–0.003	0.004–0.010	①	1.887–1.888	0.001–0.003	0.003 0.012
	140 (2299)	2.281–2.282	0.001–0.003	0.004–0.010	①	1.887–1.888	0.001–0.003	NA
	183 (2996)	2.754–2.755	0.002–0.003	0.004–0.009	①	2.045–2.046	0.001–0.002	0.004–0.010
	183 (2996)	2.754–2.755	0.002–0.003	0.004–0.009	①	2.045–2.046	0.001–0.002	0.004–0.010
	183 (2996)	2.754–2.755	0.002–0.003	0.004–0.009	①	2.045–2.046	0.001–0.002	0.004–0.010
	183 (2996)	2.754–2.755	0.002–0.003	0.004–0.009	①	2.045–2.046	0.001–0.002	0.004–0.010
	234 (3839)	2.517–2.518	0.002–0.003	0.004–0.009	①	1.887–1.888	0.004–0.009	0.009–0.014
	234 (3839)	2.517–2.518	0.002–0.003	0.004–0.009	①	1.887–1.888	0.004–0.009	0.009–0.014
	303 (4973)	2.517–2.518	0.002–0.003	0.004–0.009	①	1.887–1.888	0.004–0.009	0.009–0.014
	303 (4973)	2.517–2.518	0.002–0.003	0.004–0.009	①	1.887–1.888	0.004–0.009	0.009–0.014
1986	140 (2299)	2.281–2.282	0.001–0.003	0.004–0.010	①	1.887–1.888	0.001–0.003	NA
	140 (2299)	2.281–2.282	0.001–0.003	0.004–0.010	①	1.887–1.888	0.001–0.003	NA
	152 (2497)	2.281–2.282	0.001–0.003	0.004–0.010	①	1.887–1.888	0.001–0.003	NA
	183 (2996)	2.754–2.755	0.002–0.003	0.004–0.009	①	2.045–2.046	0.001–0.002	0.004–0.010
	256 (4196)	2.517–2.518	0.002–0.003	0.004–0.009	①	1.887–1.888	0.004–0.009	0.009–0.014
	338 (5547)	2.517–2.518	0.002–0.003	0.004–0.009	①	1.887–1.888	0.004–0.009	0.009–0.014
	338 (5547)	2.517–2.518	0.002–0.003	0.004–0.009	①	1.887–1.888	0.004–0.009	0.009–0.014
	338 (5547)	2.517–2.518	0.002–0.003	0.004–0.009	①	1.887–1.888	0.004–0.009	0.009–0.014
1987–88	140 (2299)	2.281–2.282	0.001–0.003	0.004–0.010	①	1.887–1.888	0.001–0.003	NA
	140 (2299)	2.281–2.282	0.001–0.003	0.004–0.010	①	1.887–1.888	0.001–0.003	NA
	159 (2599)	2.360–2.361	NA	NA	①	2.031–2.032	0.001–0.002	NA
	152 (2497)	2.281–2.282	0.001–0.003	0.004–0.010	①	1.887–1.888	0.001–0.003	NA

CRANKSHAFT AND CONNECTING ROD SPECIFICATIONS

All measurements are given in inches.

| Year | Engine Displacement cu. in. (cc) | Crankshaft | | | | Connecting Rod | | |
		Main Brg. Journal Dia.	Main Brg. Oil Clearance	Shaft End-play	Thrust on No.	Journal Diameter	Oil Clearance	Side Clearance
1987–88	152 (2497)	2.281– 2.282	0.001– 0.003	0.004– 0.010	①	1.887– 1.888	0.001– 0.003	NA
	159 (2599)	2.360– 2.361	NA	NA	①	2.031– 2.032	0.001– 0.002	NA
	181 (2962)	2.360– 2.361	NA	NA	①	2.031– 2.032	0.001– 0.002	NA
	183 (2996)	2.754– 2.755	0.002– 0.003	0.004– 0.009	①	2.045– 2.046	0.001– 0.002	0.004– 0.010
	183 (2996)	2.754– 2.755	0.002– 0.003	0.004– 0.009	①	2.045– 2.046	0.001– 0.002	0.004– 0.010
	183 (2996)	2.754– 2.755	0.002– 0.003	0.004– 0.009	①	2.045– 2.046	0.001– 0.002	0.004– 0.010
	256 (4196)	2.517– 2.518	0.002– 0.003	0.004– 0.009	①	1.887– 1.888	0.004– 0.009	0.009– 0.014
	338 (5547)	2.517– 2.518	0.002– 0.003	0.004– 0.009	①	1.887– 1.888	0.004– 0.009	0.009– 0.014
	338 (5547)	2.517– 2.518	0.002– 0.003	0.004– 0.009	①	1.887– 1.888	0.004– 0.009	0.009– 0.014
	338 (5547)	2.517– 2.518	0.002– 0.003	0.004– 0.009	①	1.887– 1.888	0.004– 0.009	0.009– 0.014

NA Not Available at the time of publication
① Center main on 5 main bearing engines; rear main on 7 main bearing engines; 3rd from front on 300D (5-cylinder)

VALVE SPECIFICATIONS

| Year | Engine Displacement cu. in. (cc) | Seat Angle (deg.) | Face Angle (deg.) | Spring Test Pressure (lbs.) | Spring Installed Height (in.) | Stem-to-Guide Clearance (in.) | | Stem Diameter (in.) | |
						Intake	Exhaust	Intake	Exhaust
1981	147 (2399)	30 ①	30 ①	12.90	1.178	0.004	0.004	0.391	0.391
	168 (2746)	45 ①	45 ①	194	1.200	0.004	0.004	0.353	0.352
	168 (2746)	45 ①	45 ①	194	1.200	0.004	0.004	0.353	0.352
	183 (2996)	30 ①	30 ①	119	2.008	0.004	0.004	0.391	0.391
	183 (2996)	30 ①	30 ①	119	2.008	0.004	0.004	0.391	0.391
	183 (2996)	30 ①	30 ①	119	2.008	0.004	0.004	0.391	0.391
	183 (2996)	30 ①	30 ①	119	2.008	0.004	0.004	0.391	0.391
	234 (3839)	45	45	194	1.200	0.004	0.004	0.353	0.352
	234 (3839)	45	45	194	1.200	0.004	0.004	0.353	0.352
	234 (3839)	45	45	194	1.200	0.004	0.004	0.353	0.352
1982	147 (2399)	30 ①	30 ①	12.90	1.178	0.004	0.004	0.390	0.391
	183 (2996)	30 ①	30 ①	119	2.008	0.004	0.004	0.391	0.391
	183 (2996)	30 ①	30 ①	119	2.008	0.004	0.004	0.391	0.391
	183 (2996)	30 ①	30 ①	119	2.008	0.004	0.004	0.391	0.391
	183 (2996)	30 ①	30 ①	119	2.008	0.004	0.004	0.391	0.391
	234 (3839)	45	45	194	1.200	0.004	0.004	0.353	0.352
	234 (3839)	45	45	194	1.200	0.004	0.004	0.353	0.352
	234 (3839)	45	45	194	1.200	0.004	0.004	0.353	0.352
	234 (3839)	45	45	194	1.200	0.004	0.004	0.353	0.352

VALVE SPECIFICATIONS

Year	Engine Displacement cu. In. (cc)	Seat Angle (deg.)	Face Angle (deg.)	Spring Test Pressure (lbs.)	Spring Installed Height (in.)	Stem-to-Guide Clearance (in.)		Stem Diameter (in.)	
						Intake	Exhaust	Intake	Exhaust
1983	147 (2399)	30 ①	30 ①	12.90	1.178	0.004	0.004	0.390	0.391
	183 (2996)	30 ①	30 ①	119	2.008	0.004	0.004	0.391	0.391
	183 (2996)	30 ①	30 ①	119	2.008	0.004	0.004	0.391	0.391
	183 (2996)	30 ①	30 ①	119	2.008	0.004	0.004	0.391	0.391
	183 (2996)	30 ①	30 ①	119	2.008	0.004	0.004	0.391	0.391
	234 (3839)	45	45	194	1.200	0.004	0.004	0.353	0.352
	234 (3839)	45	45	194	1.200	0.004	0.004	0.353	0.352
	234 (3839)	45	45	194	1.200	0.004	0.004	0.353	0.352
1984	134 (2197)	45 ①	45 ①	169	2.000	0.004	0.004	0.314	0.353
	140 (2299)	45 ①	45 ①	191	1.929	0.004	0.004	0.314	0.353
	183 (2996)	30 ①	30 ①	119	2.008	0.004	0.004	0.391	0.391
	183 (2996)	30 ①	30 ①	119	2.008	0.004	0.004	0.391	0.391
	183 (2996)	30 ①	30 ①	119	2.008	0.004	0.004	0.391	0.391
	183 (2996)	30 ①	30 ①	119	2.008	0.004	0.004	0.391	0.391
	234 (3839)	45	45	194	1.200	0.004	0.004	0.353	0.352
	234 (3839)	45	45	194	1.200	0.004	0.004	0.353	0.352
	303 (4973)	45	45	194	1.200	0.004	0.004	0.353	0.352
	303 (4973)	45	45	194	1.200	0.004	0.004	0.353	0.352
1985	134 (2197)	45 ①	45 ①	169	2.000	0.004	0.004	0.314	0.353
	140 (2299)	45 ①	45 ①	191	1.929	0.004	0.004	0.314	0.353
	183 (2996)	30 ①	30 ①	119	2.008	0.004	0.004	0.391	0.391
	183 (2996)	30 ①	30 ①	119	2.008	0.004	0.004	0.391	0.391
	183 (2996)	30 ①	30 ①	119	2.008	0.004	0.004	0.391	0.391
	183 (2996)	30 ①	30 ①	119	2.008	0.004	0.004	0.391	0.391
	234 (3839)	45	45	194	1.200	0.004	0.004	0.353	0.352
	234 (3839)	45	45	194	1.200	0.004	0.004	0.353	0.352
	303 (4973)	45	45	194	1.200	0.004	0.004	0.353	0.352
	303 (4973)	45	45	194	1.200	0.004	0.004	0.353	0.352
1986	140 (2299)	45 ①	45 ①	191	1.929	0.004	0.004	0.314	0.353
	140 (2299)	45	45	191	1.929	0.004	0.004	0.274	0.313
	152 (2497)	45 ①	45 ①	169	2.000	0.004	0.004	0.314	0.353
	183 (2996)	45	45	191	1.929	0.004	0.004	0.314	0.353
	183 (2996)	45	45	NA	NA	0.004	0.004	0.314	0.352
	256 (4196)	45	45	194	1.200	0.004	0.004	0.353	0.352
	338 (5547)	45	45	194	1.200	0.004	0.004	0.353	0.352
	338 (5547)	45	45	194	1.200	0.004	0.004	0.353	0.352
	338 (5547)	45	45	194	1.200	0.004	0.004	0.353	0.352
1987–88	140 (2299)	45 ①	45 ①	191	1.929	0.004	0.004	0.314	0.353
	140 (2299)	45	45	191	1.929	0.004	0.004	0.274	0.313
	152 (2497)	45 ①	45 ①	169	2.000	0.004	0.004	0.314	0.353
	152 (2497)	45 ①	45 ①	169	2.000	0.004	0.004	0.314	0.353
	159 (2599)	45	45	NA	NA	0.004	0.004	0.314	0.353
	159 (2599)	45	45	NA	NA	0.004	0.004	0.314	0.353

VALVE SPECIFICATIONS

Year	Engine Displacement cu. in. (cc)	Seat Angle (deg.)	Face Angle (deg.)	Spring Test Pressure (lbs.)	Spring Installed Height (in.)	Stem-to-Guide Clearance (in.)		Stem Diameter (in.)	
						Intake	Exhaust	Intake	Exhaust
1987–88	183 (2996)	45	45	191	1.929	0.004	0.004	0.314	0.353
	183 (2996)	45	45	NA	NA	0.004	0.004	0.314	0.352
	256 (4196)	45	45	194	1.200	0.004	0.004	0.353	0.352
	338 (5547)	45	45	194	1.200	0.004	0.004	0.353	0.352
	338 (5547)	45	45	194	1.200	0.004	0.004	0.353	0.352
	338 (5547)	45	45	194	1.200	0.004	0.004	0.353	0.352

NA Not Available at the time of publication
① Plus 15′

PISTON AND RING SPECIFICATIONS

All measurements are given in inches.

Year	Engine Displacement cu. in. (cc)	Piston Clearance	Ring Gap			Ring Side Clearance		
			Top Compression	Bottom Compression	Oil Control	Top Compression	Bottom Compression	Oil Control
1981	147 (2399)	0.001–0.002	0.008–0.016	0.008–0.016	0.010–0.016	0.004–0.005	0.003–0.004	0.001–0.002
	168 (2746)	0.001–0.002	0.012–0.018	0.012–0.018	0.010–0.016	0.002–0.003	0.001–0.002	0.001–0.002
	168 (2746)	0.001–0.002	0.012–0.018	0.012–0.018	0.010–0.016	0.002–0.003	0.001–0.002	0.001–0.002
	183 (2996)	0.001–0.002	0.008–0.016	0.008–0.016	0.010–0.016	0.004–0.005	0.003–0.004	0.001–0.002
	183 (2996)	0.001–0.002	0.008–0.016	0.008–0.016	0.010–0.016	0.004–0.005	0.003–0.004	0.001–0.002
	183 (2996)	0.001–0.002	0.008–0.016	0.008–0.016	0.010–0.016	0.004–0.005	0.003–0.004	0.001–0.002
	183 (2996)	0.001–0.002	0.008–0.016	0.008–0.016	0.010–0.016	0.004–0.005	0.003–0.004	0.001–0.002
	234 (3839)	0.001	0.010–0.017	0.010–0.017	0.010–0.016	0.004–0.005	0.001–0.002	0.001–0.002
	234 (3839)	0.001	0.010–0.017	0.010–0.017	0.010–0.016	0.004–0.005	0.001–0.002	0.001–0.002
	234 (3839)	0.001	0.010–0.017	0.010–0.017	0.010–0.016	0.004–0.005	0.001–0.002	0.001–0.002
1982	147 (2399)	0.001–0.002	0.008–0.016	0.008–0.016	0.010–0.016	0.004–0.005	0.003–0.004	0.001–0.002
	183 (2996)	0.001–0.002	0.008–0.016	0.008–0.016	0.010–0.016	0.004–0.005	0.003–0.004	0.001–0.002
	183 (2996)	0.001–0.002	0.008–0.016	0.008–0.016	0.010–0.016	0.004–0.005	0.003–0.004	0.001–0.002
	183 (2996)	0.001–0.002	0.008–0.016	0.008–0.016	0.010–0.016	0.004–0.005	0.003–0.004	0.001–0.002
	183 (2996)	0.001–0.002	0.008–0.016	0.008–0.016	0.010–0.016	0.004–0.005	0.003–0.004	0.001–0.002
	234 (3839)	0.001	0.010–0.017	0.010–0.017	0.010–0.016	0.004–0.005	0.001–0.002	0.001–0.002
	234 (3839)	0.001	0.010–0.017	0.010–0.017	0.010–0.016	0.004–0.005	0.001–0.002	0.001–0.002

PISTON AND RING SPECIFICATIONS

All measurements are given in inches.

Year	Engine Displacement cu. in. (cc)	Piston Clearance	Ring Gap			Ring Side Clearance		
			Top Compression	Bottom Compression	Oil Control	Top Compression	Bottom Compression	Oil Control
1982	234 (3839)	0.001	0.010–0.017	0.010–0.017	0.010–0.016	0.004–0.005	0.001–0.002	0.001–0.002
1983	147 (2399)	0.001–0.002	0.008–0.016	0.008–0.016	0.010–0.016	0.004–0.005	0.003–0.004	0.001–0.002
	183 (2996)	0.001–0.002	0.008–0.016	0.008–0.016	0.010–0.016	0.004–0.005	0.003–0.004	0.001–0.002
	183 (2996)	0.001–0.002	0.008–0.016	0.008–0.016	0.010–0.016	0.004–0.005	0.003–0.004	0.001–0.002
	183 (2996)	0.001–0.002	0.008–0.016	0.008–0.016	0.010–0.016	0.004–0.005	0.003–0.004	0.001–0.002
	183 (2996)	0.001–0.002	0.008–0.016	0.008–0.016	0.010–0.016	0.004–0.005	0.003–0.004	0.001–0.002
	234 (3839)	0.001	0.010–0.017	0.010–0.017	0.010–0.016	0.004–0.005	0.001–0.002	0.001–0.002
	234 (3839)	0.001	0.010–0.017	0.010–0.017	0.010–0.016	0.004–0.005	0.001–0.002	0.001–0.002
	234 (3839)	0.001	0.010–0.017	0.010–0.017	0.010–0.016	0.004–0.005	0.001–0.002	0.001–0.002
1984	134 (2197)	0.001–0.002	0.008–0.016	0.008–0.016	0.008–0.016	0.004–0.005	0.002–0.003	0.001–0.003
	140 (2299)	0.001–0.002	0.008–0.016	0.008–0.016	0.008–0.016	0.004–0.005	0.002–0.003	0.001–0.002
	183 (2996)	0.001–0.002	0.008–0.016	0.008–0.016	0.010–0.016	0.004–0.005	0.003–0.004	0.001–0.002
	183 (2996)	0.001–0.002	0.008–0.016	0.008–0.016	0.010–0.016	0.004–0.005	0.003–0.004	0.001–0.002
	183 (2996)	0.001–0.002	0.008–0.016	0.008–0.016	0.010–0.016	0.004–0.005	0.003–0.004	0.001–0.002
	183 (2996)	0.001–0.002	0.008–0.016	0.008–0.016	0.010–0.016	0.004–0.005	0.003–0.004	0.001–0.002
	234 (3839)	0.001	0.010–0.017	0.010–0.017	0.010–0.016	0.004–0.005	0.001–0.002	0.001–0.002
	234 (3839)	0.001	0.010–0.017	0.010–0.017	0.010–0.016	0.004–0.005	0.001–0.002	0.001–0.002
	303 (4973)	0.001	0.010–0.017	0.010–0.017	0.010–0.016	0.004–0.005	0.001–0.002	0.001–0.002
	303 (4973)	0.001	0.010–0.017	0.010–0.017	0.010–0.016	0.004–0.005	0.001–0.002	0.001–0.002
1985	134 (2197)	0.001–0.002	0.008–0.016	0.008–0.016	0.008–0.016	0.004–0.005	0.002–0.003	0.001–0.003
	140 (2299)	0.001–0.002	0.008–0.016	0.008–0.016	0.008–0.016	0.004–0.005	0.002–0.003	0.001–0.002
	183 (2996)	0.001–0.002	0.008–0.016	0.008–0.016	0.010–0.016	0.004–0.005	0.003–0.004	0.001–0.002
	183 (2996)	0.001–0.002	0.008–0.016	0.008–0.016	0.010–0.016	0.004–0.005	0.003–0.004	0.001–0.002
	183 (2996)	0.001–0.002	0.008–0.016	0.008–0.016	0.010–0.016	0.004–0.005	0.003–0.004	0.001–0.002

PISTON AND RING SPECIFICATIONS

All measurements are given in inches.

Year	Engine Displacement cu. in. (cc)	Piston Clearance	Ring Gap			Ring Side Clearance		
			Top Compression	Bottom Compression	Oil Control	Top Compression	Bottom Compression	Oil Control
1985	183 (2996)	0.001–0.002	0.008–0.016	0.008–0.016	0.010–0.016	0.004–0.005	0.003–0.004	0.001–0.002
	234 (3839)	0.001	0.010–0.017	0.010–0.017	0.010–0.016	0.004–0.005	0.001–0.002	0.001–0.002
	234 (3839)	0.001	0.010–0.017	0.010–0.017	0.010–0.016	0.004–0.005	0.001–0.002	0.001–0.002
	303 (4973)	0.001	0.010–0.017	0.010–0.017	0.010–0.016	0.004–0.005	0.001–0.002	0.001–0.002
	303 (4973)	0.001	0.010–0.017	0.010–0.017	0.010–0.016	0.004–0.005	0.001–0.002	0.001–0.002
1986	140 (2299)	0.001–0.002	0.008–0.016	0.008–0.016	0.008–0.016	0.004–0.005	0.002–0.003	0.001–0.003
	140 (2299)	0.001–0.002	0.008–0.016	0.008–0.016	0.008–0.016	0.004–0.005	0.002–0.003	0.001–0.002
	152 (2497)	0.001–0.002	0.008–0.016	0.008–0.016	0.010–0.016	0.004–0.005	0.003–0.004	0.001–0.002
	181 (2962)	0.001–0.002	0.008–0.016	0.008–0.016	0.010–0.016	0.004–0.005	0.003–0.004	0.001–0.002
	183 (2996)	0.001–0.002	0.008–0.016	0.008–0.016	0.010–0.016	0.004–0.005	0.003–0.004	0.001–0.002
	183 (2996)	0.001–0.002	0.008–0.016	0.008–0.016	0.010–0.016	0.004–0.005	0.003–0.004	0.001–0.002
	256 (4196)	0.001	0.008–0.016	0.008–0.016	0.010–0.016	0.004–0.005	0.003–0.004	0.001–0.002
	338 (5547)	0.001	0.010–0.017	0.010–0.017	0.010–0.016	0.004–0.005	0.001–0.002	0.001–0.002
	338 (5547)	0.001	0.010–0.017	0.010–0.017	0.010–0.016	0.004–0.005	0.001–0.002	0.001–0.002
	338 (5547)	0.001	0.010–0.017	0.010–0.017	0.010–0.016	0.004–0.005	0.001–0.002	0.001–0.002
1987–88	140 (2299)	0.001–0.002	0.008–0.016	0.008–0.016	0.008–0.016	0.004–0.005	0.002–0.003	0.001–0.003
	140 (2299)	0.001–0.002	0.008–0.016	0.008–0.016	0.008–0.016	0.004–0.005	0.002–0.003	0.001–0.002
	152 (2497)	0.001–0.002	0.008–0.016	0.008–0.016	0.010–0.016	0.004–0.005	0.003–0.004	0.001–0.002
	152 (2497)	0.001–0.002	0.008–0.016	0.008–0.016	0.010–0.016	0.004–0.005	0.003–0.004	0.001–0.002
	159 (2599)	0.001–0.002	0.008–0.016	0.008–0.016	0.010–0.016	0.004–0.005	0.003–0.004	0.001–0.002
	159 (2599)	0.001–0.002	0.008–0.016	0.008–0.016	0.010–0.016	0.004–0.005	0.003–0.004	0.001–0.002
	181 (2962)	0.001–0.002	0.008–0.016	0.008–0.016	0.010–0.016	0.004–0.005	0.003–0.004	0.001–0.002
	183 (2996)	0.001–0.002	0.008–0.016	0.008–0.016	0.010–0.016	0.004–0.005	0.003–0.004	0.001–0.002
	183 (2996)	0.001–0.002	0.008–0.016	0.008–0.016	0.010–0.016	0.004–0.005	0.003–0.004	0.001–0.002

PISTON AND RING SPECIFICATIONS

All measurements are given in inches.

Year	Engine Displacement cu. in. (cc)	Piston Clearance	Ring Gap			Ring Side Clearance		
			Top Compression	Bottom Compression	Oil Control	Top Compression	Bottom Compression	Oil Control
1987–88	183 (2996)	0.001–0.002	0.008–0.016	0.008–0.016	0.010–0.016	0.004–0.005	0.003–0.004	0.001–0.002
	256 (4196)	0.001	0.008–0.016	0.008–0.016	0.010–0.016	0.004–0.005	0.003–0.004	0.001–0.002
	338 (5547)	0.001	0.010–0.017	0.010–0.017	0.010–0.016	0.004–0.005	0.001–0.002	0.001–0.002
	338 (5547)	0.001	0.010–0.017	0.010–0.017	0.010–0.016	0.004–0.005	0.001–0.002	0.001–0.002
	338 (5547)	0.001	0.010–0.017	0.010–0.017	0.010–0.016	0.004–0.005	0.001–0.002	0.001–0.002

TORQUE SPECIFICATIONS

All readings in ft. lbs.

Year	Engine Displacement cu. in. (cc)	Cylinder Head Bolts	Main Bearing Bolts	Rod Bearing Bolts	Crankshaft Pulley Bolts	Flywheel Bolts	Manifold		Spark Plugs
							Intake	Exhaust	
1981	147 (2399)	④ ①	65	33	155	⑥	NA	20	—
	168 (2746)	58	58	33	216	⑥	NA	NA	15
	168 (2746)	58	58	33	216	⑥	NA	NA	15
	183 (2996)	65 ⑨	65	33	218	⑥	NA	18	—
	183 (2996)	65 ⑨	65	33	218	⑥	NA	18	—
	183 (2996)	65 ⑨	65	33	218	⑥	NA	18	—
	183 (2996)	65 ⑨	65	33	218	⑥	NA	18	—
	234 (3839)	44 ⑧	③	33	289	⑥	NA	NA	15
	234 (3839)	44 ⑧	③	33	289	⑥	NA	NA	15
	234 (3839)	44 ⑧	③	33	289	⑥	NA	NA	15
1982	147 (2399)	④ ①	65	33	155	⑥	NA	20	—
	183 (2996)	65 ⑨	65	33	218	⑥	NA	18	—
	183 (2996)	65 ⑨	65	33	218	⑥	NA	18	—
	183 (2996)	65 ⑨	65	33	218	⑥	NA	18	—
	183 (2996)	65 ⑨	65	33	218	⑥	NA	18	—
	234 (3839)	44 ⑧	③	33	289	⑥	NA	NA	15
	234 (3839)	44 ⑧	③	33	289	⑥	NA	NA	15
	234 (3839)	44 ⑧	③	33	289	⑥	NA	NA	15
	234 (3839)	44 ⑧	③	33	289	⑥	NA	NA	15
1983	147 (2399)	④ ①	65	33	155	⑥	NA	20	—
	183 (2996)	65 ⑨	65	33	218	⑥	NA	18	—
	183 (2996)	65 ⑨	65	33	218	⑥	NA	18	—
	183 (2996)	65 ⑨	65	33	218	⑥	NA	18	—
	183 (2996)	65 ⑨	65	33	218	⑥	NA	18	—
	234 (3839)	44 ⑧	③	33	289	⑥	NA	NA	15
	234 (3839)	44 ⑧	③	33	289	⑥	NA	NA	15
	234 (3839)	44 ⑧	③	33	289	⑥	NA	NA	15
	234 (3839)	44 ⑧	③	33	289	⑥	NA	NA	15

TORQUE SPECIFICATIONS
All readings in ft. lbs.

Year	Engine Displacement cu. in. (cc)	Cylinder Head Bolts	Main Bearing Bolts	Rod Bearing Bolts	Crankshaft Pulley Bolts	Flywheel Bolts	Manifold Intake	Manifold Exhaust	Spark Plugs
1984	134 (2197)	④ ①	65	⑤	218	25	18	NA	—
	140 (2299)	51 ⑦	65	⑥	218	25	NA	NA	15
	183 (2996)	65 ⑨	65	33	218	⑥	18	18	—
	183 (2996)	65 ⑨	65	33	218	⑥	18	18	—
	183 (2996)	65 ⑨	65	33	218	⑥	NA	18	—
	183 (2996)	65 ⑨	65	33	218	⑥	NA	18	—
	234 (3839)	44 ⑧	③	33	289	⑥	NA	NA	15
	234 (3839)	44 ⑧	③	33	289	⑥	NA	NA	15
	303 (4973)	44 ⑧	②	33	187	⑥	NA	20	15
	303 (4973)	44 ⑧	②	33	187	⑥	NA	20	15
1985	134 (2197)	④ ①	40	⑤	218	25	18	NA	—
	140 (2299)	51 ⑦	65	⑥	145	25	NA	NA	15
	183 (2996)	65 ⑨	65	33	218	⑥	18	18	—
	183 (2996)	65 ⑨	65	33	218	⑥	18	18	—
	183 (2996)	65 ⑨	65	33	218	⑥	NA	18	—
	183 (2996)	65 ⑨	65	33	218	⑥	NA	18	—
	234 (3839)	44 ⑧	③	33	289	⑥	NA	NA	15
	234 (3839)	44 ⑧	③	33	289	⑥	NA	NA	15
	303 (4973)	44 ⑧	②	33	187	⑥	NA	20	15
	303 (4973)	44 ⑧	②	33	187	⑥	NA	20	15
1986	140 (2299)	51 ⑦	65	⑥	145	25	NA	NA	15
	140 (2299)	51 ⑦	65	⑥	145	25	NA	NA	15
	152 (2497)	④ ①	40	⑤	218	25	18	NA	—
	181 (2962)	65 ⑨	65	33	218	⑥	18	18	15
	183 (2996)	65 ⑨	65	33	218	⑥	18	18	—
	183 (2996)	65 ⑨	65	33	218	⑥	NA	18	—
	256 (4196)	44 ⑧	③	33	289	⑥	NA	NA	15
	338 (5547)	44 ⑧	②	33	187	⑥	NA	20	15
	338 (5547)	44 ⑧	②	33	187	⑥	NA	20	15
	338 (5547)	44 ⑧	②	33	187	⑥	NA	20	15
1987–88	140 (2299)	51 ⑦	65	⑥	145	25	NA	NA	15
	140 (2299)	51 ⑦	65	⑥	145	25	NA	NA	15
	152 (2497)	④ ①	40	⑤	218	25	18	NA	—
	152 (2497)	④ ①	40	⑤	218	25	18	NA	—
	159 (2599)	70 ⑩	65	22	217	22	NA	NA	15
	159 (2599)	70 ⑩	65	22	217	22	NA	NA	15
	181 (2962)	65 ⑨	65	33	218	⑥	NA	18	15
	183 (2996)	65 ⑨	65	33	218	⑥	18	18	—
	183 (2996)	65 ⑨	65	33	218	⑥	18	18	—
	183 (2996)	65 ⑨	65	33	218	⑥	NA	18	—
	256 (4196)	44 ⑧	③	33	289	⑥	NA	NA	15
	338 (5547)	44 ⑧	②	33	187	⑥	NA	20	15
	338 (5547)	44 ⑧	②	33	187	⑥	NA	20	15

TORQUE SPECIFICATIONS

All readings in ft. lbs.

Year	Engine Displacement cu. in. (cc)	Cylinder Head Bolts	Main Bearing Bolts	Rod Bearing Bolts	Crankshaft Pulley Bolts	Flywheel Bolts	Manifold		Spark Plugs
							Intake	Exhaust	
1987-88	338 (5547)	44 ⑧	②	33	187	⑥	NA	20	15

NA Not Available at the time of publication

① See text

② M 10 bolts—37 ft. lbs.
M 12 bolts—72 ft. lbs.

③ M 10 bolts—43 ft. lbs.
M 12 bolts—58 ft. lbs.

④ M 10 bolts—1st step—18 ft. lbs., 2nd step—29 ft. lbs., setting time 10 min., 3rd step—90 degrees torquing angle, 4th step—29 degrees torquing angle
M 8 bolts—18 ft. lbs.

⑤ 1st step—22-25 ft. lbs., 2nd step—90 degrees-100 degrees torquing angle

⑥ 1st step—22-25 ft. lbs., 2nd step—90 degrees-100 degrees torquing angle

⑦ M 12 bolts—29 ft. lbs., 2nd step—51 ft. lbs., setting time 10 min., 3rd step—90 degrees torquing angle, 4th step—90 degrees toruqing angle
M 8 bolts—18 ft. lbs.

⑧ 1st step—22 ft. lbs., 2nd step—44 ft. lbs., setting time 10 min., 3rd step—loosen bolts and retighten to 44 ft. lbs.

⑨ 1st step—29 ft. lbs., 2nd step—51 ft. lbs., setting time 10 min., 3rd step—90 degrees torquing angle, 4th step—90 degrees torquing angle

⑩ 1st step—70 ft. lbs., 2nd step—90 degrees torquing angle, 3rd step—90 degrees torquing angle

BRAKE SPECIFICATIONS

All measurements in inches unless noted.

Year	Model	Lug Nut Torque (ft. lbs.)	Master Cylinder Bore	Brake Disc		Maximum Brake Drum Diameter	Minimum Lining Thickness	
				Minimum Thickness	Maximum Runout		Front	Rear
1981	240D	75	②	① ⑤	0.005 ⑦	—	0.08	0.08
	280E	75	②	① ⑤	0.005 ⑦	—	0.08	0.08
	280CE	75	②	① ⑤	0.005 ⑦	—	0.08	0.08
	300D	75	②	① ⑤	0.005 ⑦	—	0.08	0.08
	300CD	75	②	① ⑤	0.005 ⑦	—	0.08	0.08
	300SD	75	②	③ ⑤	0.005	—	0.08	0.08
	300TD	75	②	① ⑤	0.005 ⑦	—	0.08	0.08
	380SEL	75	②	③ ⑤	0.005	—	0.08	0.08
	380SL	75	②	③ ⑤	0.005	—	0.08	0.08
	380SLC	75	②	③ ⑤	0.005	—	0.08	0.08
1982	240D	75	②	① ⑤	0.005 ⑦	—	0.08	0.08
	300D	75	②	① ⑤	0.005 ⑦	—	0.08	0.08
	300CD	75	②	① ⑤	0.005 ⑦	—	0.08	0.08
	300SD	75	②	③ ⑤	0.005	—	0.08	0.08
	300TD	75	②	① ⑤	0.005 ⑦	—	0.08	0.08
	380SL	75	②	③ ⑤	0.005	—	0.08	0.08
	380SEC	75	②	③ ⑤	0.005	—	0.08	0.08
	380SEL	75	②	③ ⑤	0.005	—	0.08	0.08
	380SLC	75	②	③ ⑤	0.005	—	0.08	0.08
1983	240D	75	②	① ⑤	0.005 ⑦	—	0.08	0.08
	300D	75	②	① ⑤	0.005 ⑦	—	0.08	0.08
	300CD	75	②	① ⑤	0.005 ⑦	—	0.08	0.08
	300SD	75	②	③ ⑤	0.005	—	0.08	0.08
	300TD	75	②	① ⑤	0.005 ⑦	—	0.08	0.08
	380SL	75	②	③ ⑤	0.005	—	0.08	0.08

BRAKE SPECIFICATIONS

All measurements in inches unless noted.

Year	Model	Lug Nut Torque (ft. lbs.)	Master Cylinder Bore	Brake Disc Minimum Thickness	Brake Disc Maximum Runout	Maximum Brake Drum Diameter	Minimum Lining Thickness Front	Minimum Lining Thickness Rear
1983	380SEC	75	②	③ ⑤	0.005	—	0.08	0.08
	380SEL	75	②	③ ⑤	0.005	—	0.08	0.08
1984	190D	75	④	0.35 ⑥	0.005 ⑦	—	0.08	0.08
	190E	75	④	0.35 ⑥	0.005 ⑦	—	0.08	0.08
	300D	75	②	① ⑤	0.005 ⑦	—	0.08	0.08
	300CD	75	②	① ⑤	0.005 ⑦	—	0.08	0.08
	300SD	75	②	③ ⑤	0.005	—	0.08	0.08
	300TD	75	②	① ⑤	0.005 ⑦	—	0.08	0.08
	380SE	75	②	③ ⑤	0.005	—	0.08	0.08
	380SL	75	②	③ ⑤	0.005	—	0.08	0.08
	500SEC	75	②	③ ⑤	0.005	—	0.08	0.08
	500SEL	75	②	③ ⑤	0.005	—	0.08	0.08
1985	190D	75	④	0.35 ⑥	0.005 ⑦	—	0.08	0.08
	190E	75	④	0.35 ⑥	0.005 ⑦	—	0.08	0.08
	300D	75	②	① ⑤	0.005 ⑦	—	0.08	0.08
	300CD	75	②	① ⑤	0.005 ⑦	—	0.08	0.08
	300SD	75	②	③ ⑤	0.005	—	0.08	0.08
	300TD	75	②	① ⑤	0.005 ⑦	—	0.08	0.08
	380SE	75	②	③ ⑤	0.005	—	0.08	0.08
	380SL	75	②	③ ⑤	0.005	—	0.08	0.08
	500SEC	75	②	③ ⑤	0.005	—	0.08	0.08
	500SEL	75	②	③ ⑤	0.005	—	0.08	0.08
1986	190D	75	④	0.35 ⑥	0.005 ⑦	—	0.08	0.08
	190E	75	④	0.35 ⑥	0.005 ⑦	—	0.08	0.08
	190E-16	75	④	0.35 ⑥	0.005 ⑦	—	0.08	0.08
	300D	75	②	① ⑤	0.005 ⑦	—	0.08	0.08
	300TD	75	②	① ⑤	0.005 ⑦	—	0.08	0.08
	300SDL	75	②	③ ⑤	0.005	—	0.08	0.08
	420SEL	75	②	③ ⑤	0.005	—	0.08	0.08
	560SL	75	②	③ ⑤	0.005	—	0.08	0.08
	560SEC	75	②	③ ⑤	0.005	—	0.08	0.08
	560SEL	75	②	③ ⑤	0.005	—	0.08	0.08
1987-88	190D	75	④	0.35 ⑥	0.005 ⑦	—	0.08	0.08
	190D	75	④	0.35 ⑥	0.005 ⑦	—	0.08	0.08
	190E	75	④	0.35 ⑥	0.005 ⑦	—	0.08	0.08
	190E	75	④	0.35 ⑥	0.005 ⑦	—	0.08	0.08
	190E-16	75	④	0.35 ⑥	0.005 ⑦	—	0.08	0.08
	260E	75	②	① ⑤	0.005 ⑦	—	0.08	0.08
	300D	75	②	① ⑤	0.005 ⑦	—	0.08	0.08
	300E	75	②	① ⑤	0.005 ⑦	—	0.08	0.08
	300TD	75	②	① ⑤	0.005 ⑦	—	0.08	0.08

BRAKE SPECIFICATIONS

All measurements in inches unless noted.

Year	Model	Lug Nut Torque (ft. lbs.)	Master Cylinder Bore	Brake Disc Minimum Thickness	Brake Disc Maximum Runout	Maximum Brake Drum Diameter	Minimum Lining Thickness Front	Minimum Lining Thickness Rear
	300SDL	75	②	③ ⑤	0.005	—	0.08	0.08
	420SEL	75	②	③ ⑤	0.005	—	0.08	0.08
	560SL	75	②	③ ⑤	0.005	—	0.08	0.08
	560SEC	75	②	③ ⑤	0.005	—	0.08	0.08
	560SEL	75	②	③ ⑤	0.005	—	0.08	0.08

① Caliper w/57 mm piston diameter: 0.44 in.
　Caliper w/60 mm piston diameter: 0.42 in.
② Pushrod circuit: 15/16 in.
　Floating circuit: 3/4 in.
③ Caliper w/57 mm piston diameter: 0.81 in.
　Caliper w/60 mm piston diameter: 0.79 in.

④ Pushrod circuit: 7/8 in.
　Floating circuit: 11/16 in.
⑤ Rear disc: 0.33 in.
⑥ Rear disc: 0.30 in.
⑦ Rear disc: 0.006 in.

WHEEL ALIGNMENT

Year	Model	Caster Range (deg.)	Caster Preferred Setting (deg.)	Camber Range (deg.)	Camber Preferred Setting (deg.)	Toe-in (in.)	Steering Axis Inclination (deg.)
1981	240D	8 1/4–9 1/4	8 3/4	5/16N–3/16P	0	1/8	NA
	280E	8 1/4–9 1/4	8 3/4	5/16N–3/16P	0	1/8	NA
	280CE	8 1/4–9 1/4	8 3/4	5/16N–3/16P	0	1/8	NA
	300D	8 1/4–9 1/4	8 3/4	5/16N–3/16P	0	1/8	NA
	300CD	8 1/4–9 1/4	8 3/4	5/16N–3/16P	0	1/8	NA
	300SD	10 3/4–9 3/4	10 1/4	5/16N–3/16P	0	1/8	NA
	300TD	8 1/4–9 1/4	8 3/4	5/16N–3/16P	0	1/8	NA
	380SL	4–3 3/8	3 11/16	5/16N–3/16P	0	1/16	NA
	380SEL	10 3/4–9 3/4	10 1/4	5/16N–3/16P	0	1/8	NA
	380SLC	4–3 3/8	3 11/16	5/16N–3/16P	0	1/16	NA
1982	240D	8 1/4–9 1/4	8 3/4	5/16N–3/16P	0	1/8	NA
	300D	8 1/4–9 1/4	8 3/4	5/16N–3/16P	0	1/8	NA
	300CD	8 1/4–9 1/4	8 3/4	5/16N–3/16P	0	1/8	NA
	300SD	10 3/4–9 3/4	10 1/4	5/16N–3/16P	0	1/8	NA
	300TD	8 1/4–9 1/4	8 3/4	5/16N–3/16P	0	1/8	NA
	380SL	4–3 3/8	3 11/16	5/16N–3/16P	0	1/16	NA
	380SEC	10 3/4–9 3/4	10 1/4	5/16N–3/16P	0	1/8	NA
	380SEL	10 3/4–9 3/4	10 1/4	5/16N–3/16P	0	1/8	NA
	380SLC	4–3 3/8	3 11/16	5/16N–3/16P	0	1/16	NA
1983	240D	8 1/4–9 1/4	8 3/4	5/16N–3/16P	0	1/8	NA
	300D	8 1/4–9 1/4	8 3/4	5/16N–3/16P	0	1/8	NA
	300CD	8 1/4–9 1/4	8 3/4	5/16N–3/16P	0	1/8	NA
	300SD	10 3/4–9 3/4	10 1/4	5/16N–3/16P	0	1/8	NA
	300TD	8 1/4–9 1/4	8 3/4	5/16N–3/16P	0	1/8	NA
	380SL	4–3 3/8	3 11/16	5/16N–3/16P	0	1/16	NA
	380SEC	10 3/4–9 3/4	10 1/4	5/16N–3/16P	0	1/8	NA
	380SEL	10 3/4–9 3/4	10 1/4	5/16N–3/16P	0	1/8	NA

WHEEL ALIGNMENT

Year	Model	Caster Range (deg.)	Caster Preferred Setting (deg.)	Camber Range (deg.)	Camber Preferred Setting (deg.)	Toe-in (in.)	Steering Axis Inclination (deg.)
1984	190D	$9^{11}/_{16}$–$10^{11}/_{16}$	$10^3/_{16}$	0–$^1/_2$P	$^5/_{16}$	$^3/_{16}$	NA
	190E	$9^{11}/_{16}$–$10^{11}/_{16}$	$10^3/_{16}$	0–$^1/_2$P	$^5/_{16}$	$^3/_{16}$	NA
	300D	$8^1/_4$–$9^1/_4$	$8^3/_4$	$^5/_{16}$N–$^3/_{16}$P	0	$^1/_8$	NA
	300CD	$8^1/_4$–$9^1/_4$	$8^3/_4$	$^5/_{16}$N–$^3/_{16}$P	0	$^1/_8$	NA
	300SD	$10^3/_4$–$9^3/_4$	$10^1/_4$	$^5/_{16}$N–$^3/_{16}$P	0	$^1/_8$	NA
	300TD	$8^1/_4$–$9^1/_4$	$8^3/_4$	$^5/_{16}$N–$^3/_{16}$P	0	$^1/_8$	NA
	380SL	4–$3^3/_8$	$3^{11}/_{16}$	$^5/_{16}$N–$^3/_{16}$P	0	$^1/_{16}$	NA
	380SE	$10^3/_4$–$9^3/_4$	$10^1/_4$	$^5/_{16}$N–$^3/_{16}$P	0	$^1/_8$	NA
	500SEC	$10^3/_4$–$9^3/_4$	$10^1/_4$	$^5/_{16}$N–$^3/_{16}$P	0	$^1/_8$	NA
	500SEL	$10^3/_4$–$9^3/_4$	$10^1/_4$	$^5/_{16}$N–$^3/_{16}$P	0	$^1/_8$	NA
1985	190D	$9^{11}/_{16}$–$10^{11}/_{16}$	$10^3/_{16}$	$^1/_{16}$N–$^9/_{16}$P	$^5/_{16}$	$^3/_{32}$	NA
	190E	$9^{11}/_{16}$–$10^{11}/_{16}$	$10^3/_{16}$	$^1/_{16}$N–$^9/_{16}$P	$^5/_{16}$	$^3/_{32}$	NA
	300D	$8^1/_4$–$9^1/_4$	$8^3/_4$	$^5/_{16}$N–$^3/_{16}$P	0	$^1/_8$	NA
	300CD	$8^1/_4$–$9^1/_4$	$8^3/_4$	$^5/_{16}$N–$^3/_{16}$P	0	$^1/_8$	NA
	300SD	$10^3/_4$–$9^3/_4$	$10^1/_4$	$^5/_{16}$N–$^3/_{16}$P	0	$^1/_8$	NA
	300TD	$8^1/_4$–$9^1/_4$	$8^3/_4$	$^5/_{16}$N–$^3/_{16}$P	0	$^1/_8$	NA
	380SL	4–$3^3/_8$	$3^{11}/_{16}$	$^5/_{16}$N–$^3/_{16}$P	0	$^1/_{16}$	NA
	380SE	$10^3/_4$–$9^3/_4$	$10^1/_4$	$^5/_{16}$N–$^3/_{16}$P	0	$^1/_8$	NA
	500SEC	$10^3/_4$–$9^3/_4$	$10^1/_4$	$^5/_{16}$N–$^3/_{16}$P	0	$^1/_8$	NA
	500SEL	$10^3/_4$–$9^3/_4$	$10^1/_4$	$^5/_{16}$N–$^3/_{16}$P	0	$^1/_8$	NA
1986	190D	10–11	$10^1/_2$	$^1/_2$N–0	$^3/_{16}$N	$^3/_{32}$	NA
	190E	10–11	$10^1/_2$	$^1/_2$N–0	$^3/_{16}$N	$^3/_{32}$	NA
	190E-16	10–11	$10^1/_2$	$^{11}/_{16}$N–$^3/_{16}$N	$^5/_{16}$N	$^3/_{32}$	NA
	300D	$9^{11}/_{16}$–$10^{11}/_{16}$	$10^3/_{16}$	$^5/_{16}$N–$^3/_{16}$P	0	$^3/_{16}$	NA
	300E	$9^{11}/_{16}$–$10^{11}/_{16}$	$10^3/_{16}$	$^5/_{16}$N–$^3/_{16}$P	0	$^3/_{16}$	NA
	300SDL	10–11	$10^1/_2$	$^1/_2$N–0	$^3/_{16}$N	$^3/_{32}$	NA
	420SEL	10–11	$10^1/_2$	$^1/_2$N–0	$^3/_{16}$N	$^3/_{32}$	NA
	560SL	10–11	$10^1/_2$	$^1/_2$N–0	$^3/_{16}$N	$^3/_{32}$	NA
	560SEC	10–11	$10^1/_2$	$^1/_2$N–0	$^3/_{16}$N	$^3/_{32}$	NA
	560SEL	10–11	$10^1/_2$	$^1/_2$N–0	$^3/_{16}$N	$^3/_{32}$	NA
1987-88	190D	10–11	$10^1/_2$	$^1/_2$N–0	$^3/_{16}$N	$^3/_{32}$	NA
	190E	10–11	$10^1/_2$	$^1/_2$N–0	$^3/_{16}$N	$^3/_{32}$	NA
	190E-16	10–11	$10^1/_2$	$^{11}/_{16}$N–$^5/_{16}$N	$^5/_{16}$N	$^3/_{32}$	NA
	300D	$9^{11}/_{16}$–$10^{11}/_{16}$	$10^3/_{16}$	$^5/_{16}$N–$^3/_{16}$P	0	$^3/_{16}$	NA
	300E	$9^{11}/_{16}$–$10^{11}/_{16}$	$10^3/_{16}$	$^5/_{16}$N–$^3/_{16}$P	0	$^3/_{16}$	NA
	300SDL	10–11	$10^1/_2$	$^1/_2$N–0	$^3/_{16}$N	$^3/_{32}$	NA
	300TD	10–11	$10^1/_2$	$^1/_2$N–0	$^3/_{16}$N	$^3/_{32}$	NA
	420SEL	10–11	$10^1/_2$	$^1/_2$N–0	$^3/_{16}$N	$^3/_{32}$	NA
	560SL	10–11	$10^1/_2$	$^1/_2$N–0	$^3/_{16}$N	$^3/_{32}$	NA
	560SEC	10–11	$10^1/_2$	$^1/_2$N–0	$^3/_{16}$N	$^3/_{32}$	NA
	560SEL	10–11	$10^1/_2$	$^1/_2$N–0	$^3/_{16}$N	$^3/_{32}$	NA

NA Not Available at time of publication
N   Negative
P   Positive

TUNE-UP PROCEDURES

Ignition Timing

ADJUSTMENT

Before attempting to set the timing, read the "Ignition Timing Specifications" chart carefully and determine at what speed the timing should be set and whether the vacuum should be connected or disconnected.

NOTE: It is a good idea to paint the appropriate timing mark with dayglow or white paint to make it quickly and easily visible.

On engines with transistorized coil ignition, the timing light may or may not work depending on the construction of the light.

All Gas Engines

NOTE: All gasoline engines as of 1986–88 utilize the new EZL electronic ignition system. Although service checking of ignition timing is possible, no adjustment is either possible or necessary.

1. Raise the hood and connect a tachometer.
2. Connect a timing light.
3. Run the engine at the specified speed and read the firing point on the balancing plate or vibration damper while shining the light on it.

The typical vibration damper is marked like this (note the pin)

NOTE: The balancer on some engines has 2 timing scales. If in doubt as to which scale to use, rotate the crankshaft (in the direction of rotation only) until the distributor rotor is aligned with the notch on the distributor housing (No. 1 cylinder). In this position, the timing pointer should be at TDC on the proper timing scale.

4. Adjust the ignition timing by loosening the distributor clamp bolt and rotating the distributor. To advance the timing, rotate the distributor in the opposite direction of normal

rotation. To retard the timing, rotate the distributor in the direction of normal rotation.

5. Once the timing has been adjusted, recheck the timing once more to be sure that it has not been disturbed.

6. Remove the timing light and tachometer and connect any wires that were removed.

Diesel Engines

The diesel uses no distributor, so requires no ignition timing adjustment.

Valve Lash

ADJUSTMENT

4 Cylinder Gasoline Engines

190 SERIES

The 190E (SOHC) utilizes hydraulic valve clearance compensation. No adjustment is either possible or necessary. The 190E–16 (DOHC) uses mechanical lash adjusters, adjustable by means of tappets and thrust washers.

Valve clearance on the 190E–16 is measured between the cam base circle and the cup-type valve tappet (see illustration).

1. Tag and disconnect the spark plug wires and position them out of the way.
2. Remove the spark plugs and then remove the cylinder head cover.
3. Note the position of the intake and exhaust valves. Viewed from the front of the vehicle, the exhaust valves are on the left and the intake valves are on the right.
4. Using a wrench on the crankshaft pulley bolt, rotate the crankshaft until the heel of the camshaft lobe is in the position shown in the illustration.

NOTE: Do not rotate the engine using the camshaft sprocket bolt. The strain will distort the timing chain tensioner rail. Always rotate the engine in the direction of normal rotation only.

5. To measure the valve clearance, insert a feeler gauge of the specified thickness between the heel of the camshaft lobe and the top of the valve tappet. Clearance is correct if the blade can be inserted and withdrawn with a very slight drag.

6. If all measured clearances are within specifications, install the cylinder head cover, spark plugs and their wires; you're done!
If any clearances are not within specifications, continue checking until you find what the actual clearance is. Write it down, you'll need it later.

7. Remove the camshafts as detailed later in this section.

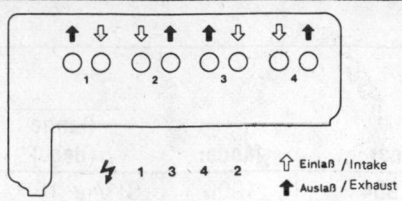

Valve location—SOHC 4 cylinder engines

8. Lift out the valve tappet. Directly under the tappet is a thrust plate. The thrust plate is held in place by means of the valve keepers; it is also your means of changing the tappet height and thus the valve clearance.

9. Pry the thrust plate from the valve keepers and check to see what thickness it is; it should be stamped on the surface.

10. Check what the clearance was from Step 6 for the valve that is being worked on. The difference between the measured clearance and the specified clearance is amount by which the existing thrust plate thickness must be increased to obtain the proper valve clearance. New thrust plates are available in increments of 0.05mm.

11. When the proper thickness of the new thrust plate has been determined, press it into the valve keepers and drop the tappet into position over the valve stem/spring.

12. Install the camshafts and then recheck the valve clearance.

13. Installation of the remaining components is as detailed in Step 6.

6 Cylinder Gasoline Engines

NOTE: The 190E with 2.6L engine, 260E and 300E utilizes hydraulic valve clearance compensation. No adjustment is either possible or necessary.

1. Threaded bushing
2. Adjusting screw
3. Pressure piece

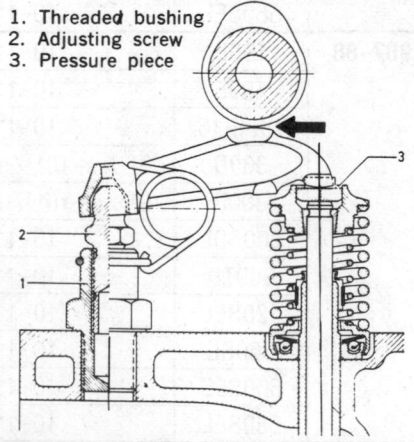

Measure the valve clearance between the sliding surface of the rocker arm and the heel of the camshaft lobe on 4 cylinder engines (except 190)

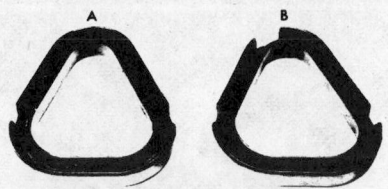

(a)—Spark plug holes 1, 3 and 5
(b)—Spark plug holes 2 and 4
Two versions of rubber gaskets

The valve clearance is measured between the sliding surface of the rocker arm and the heel of the camshaft lobe. The highest point of the camshaft lobe should be at a 90 degree angle to the sliding surface of the rocker arm.

NOTE: Prior to rotating 6 cylinder engine manually, disconnect the transmitter-ignition distributor plug (green cable) from the switching unit.

1. Remove the air vent hose and air cleaner from the valve cover. Remove the spark plugs.
2. Remove the valve cover and gasket.
3. Note the position of the intake and exhaust valves.
4. Rotate the crankshaft, using a socket wrench on the crankshaft pulley bolt, until the heel of the camshaft lobe is perpendicular to the sliding surface of the rocker arm.

NOTE: Do not rotate the engine using the camshaft sprocket bolt. The strain will distort the timing chain tensioner rail. Always rotate the engine in the direction of normal rotation only.

5. Some models have holes in the vibration damper plate to assist in crankshaft rotation. In this case, a large drift can be used to carefully rotate the crankshaft.
6. To measure the valve clearance, insert a feeler blade of the specified thickness between the heel of the camshaft lobe and the sliding surface of the rocker arm. The clearance is correct if the blade can be inserted and withdrawn with a very slight drag.
7. If adjustment is necessary, it can be done by turning the ball pin head at the hex collar. If the clearance is too small, increase it by turning the ball pin head in. If the clearance is too large, decrease it by turning the ball pin head out. if the adjuster turns too easily or the proper clearance can't be obtained, check the torque of the adjuster.

NOTE: This adjustment is ideally made with a special adapter and a torque wrench. By using it,

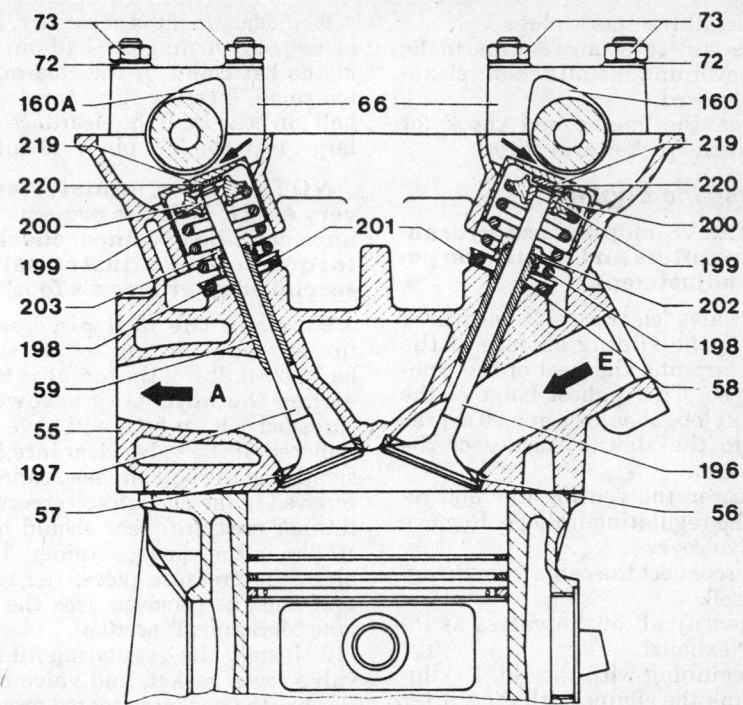

55	Cylinder head	196	Intake valve	203	Valve stem seal, exhaust
56	Valve seat ring, intake	197	Exhaust valve		valve
57	Valve seat ring, exhaust	198	Valve spring	219	Valve tappet
58	Valve guide, intake	199	Valve keeper	220	Thrust plate
59	Valve guide, exhaust	200	Valve spring retainer	E	Intake
160E	Camshaft, intake	201	Thrust ring	A	Exhaust
160A	Camshaft, exhaust	202	Valve stem seal, intake valve		

On the 190E-16 (DOHC), measure valve clearance between the valve tappet and the heal of the camshaft lobe (small arrow)

the torque wrench can be directly aligned with the ball pin head.

8. When the ball pin head is turned, the adjusting torque should be 14–25 ft. lbs. If the torque is less than 14 ft. lbs., the ball pin head will vibrate and the clearance will not remain as set. If the valve clearance is too small, and the ball pin head cannot be screwed in far enough to correct it, a thinner pressure piece should be installed in the spring retainer. To replace the pressure piece, the rocker arm must be removed.
9. After all the valves have been checked and adjusted in the manner described above, install the valve cover. Be sure that the gasket is seated properly. It is best to use a new gasket whenever the valve cover is removed.

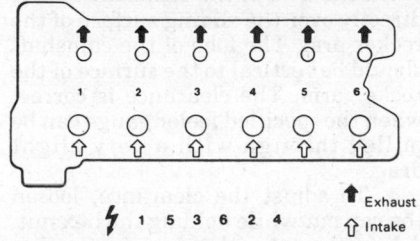

Valve location—DOHC 6-cylinder engine

⚡ 1 5 3 6 2 4

↑ Exhaust
⇧ Intake

NOTE: Two types of triangular rubber gaskets are used on 6 cylinder engines, buy only the later type with 3 notches are supplied for service.

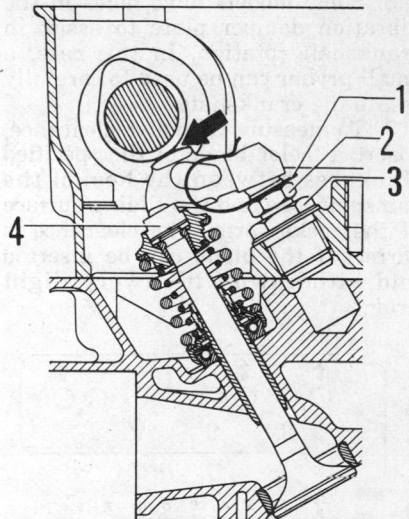

1. Tension spring   3. Threaded bushing
2. Adjusting screw   4. Pressure piece

Check the valve clearance between the sliding surface of the rocker arm and the heel of the camshaft lobe on DOHC—6-cylinder engines

10. Install the spark plugs.

11. Reconnect the air vent line to the valve cover and install the air cleaner, if removed.

12. Run the engine and check for leaks at the rocker arm cover.

V8 Gasoline Engines

NOTE: V8 engines use hydraulic valve lifters and require no periodic adjustment.

The valve clearance is measured between the sliding surface of the rocker arm and the heel of the camshaft lobe. The highest point of the camshaft lobe should be at a 90 degree angle to the sliding surface of the rocker arm.

1. Loosen the venting line and remove the regulating linkage. Remove the valve cover.

2. Disconnect the cable from the ignition coil.

3. Identify all of the valves as intake or exhaust.

4. Beginning with the No. 1 cylinder, crank the engine with the starter to position the heel of the camshaft approximately over the sliding surface of the rocker arm.

5. Rotate the crankshaft by means of a socket wrench on the crankshaft pulley bolt until the heel of the camshaft lobe is perpendicular to the sliding surface of the rocker arm.

NOTE: Do not rotate the engine using the camshaft sprocket bolt. The strain will distort the timing chain tensioner rail. Always rotate the engine in the direction of normal rotation only.

6. Some models have holes in the vibration damper plate to assist in crankshaft rotation. In this case, a small prybar can be used to carefully rotate the crankshaft.

7. To measure the valve clearance, insert a feeler blade of the specified thickness between the heel of the camshaft lobe and the sliding surface of the rocker arm. The clearance is correct if the blade can be inserted and withdrawn with a very slight drag.

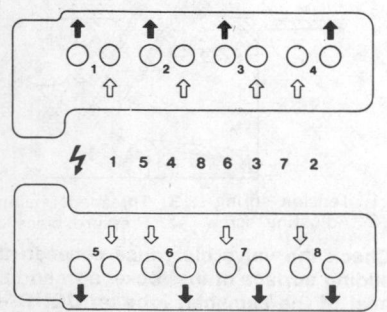

Valve location—V8 engines

8. If adjustment is necessary, it can be done by turning the ball pin head at the hex collar. If the clearance is too small, increase it by turning the ball pin head in. If the clearance is too large, turn the ball pin head out.

NOTE: If the adjuster turns very easily, or it the proper clearance can't be obtained, check the torque on the adjuster using a special adapter (crow's foot").

9. When the ball pin head is turned, the adjusting torque should be 14–29 ft. lbs. If the torque is lower, either the adjusting screw, the threaded bolt, or both will have to be replaced. If the valve clearance is too small, and the ball pin head cannot be screwed in far enough to correct it, a thinner pressure piece should be installed in the spring retainer. To replace the pressure piece, the rocker arm must be removed. (see the "Engine Mechanical" section).

10. Install the regulating linkage valve cover gasket, and valve cover. Be sure the gasket is seated properly.

11. Connect the cable to the coil and the venting line. Run the engine and check for leaks at the valve cover.

All Diesel Engines

NOTE: The 190D and the 1986–88 300D, 300TD and 300SDL utilize hydraulic valve clearance compensators. No adjustment is either necessary or possible.

1. Remove the valve cover and note the position of the intake and exhaust valves.

2. Turn the engine with a socket and breaker bar on the crankshaft pulley or by using a remote starter, hooked to the battery (+) terminal and the large, uppermost starter solenoid terminal. Due to the extremely high compression pressures in the diesel engine, it will be considerably easier to use a remote starter. If a remote starter is not available, the engine can be bumped into position with the normal starter.

NOTE: Do not turn the engine backwards or use the camshaft sprocket bolt to rotate the engine.

3. Measure the valve clearance when the heel of the camshaft lobe is directly over the sliding surface of the rocker arm. The lobe of the camshaft should be vertical to the surface of the rocker arm. The clearance is correct when the specified feeler gauge can be pulled through with a very slight drag.

4. To adjust the clearance, loosen the cap nut while holding the hex nut. Adjust the valve clearance by turning the hex nut.

A valve adjusting wrench (crow's foot) is required to accurately measure torque on all models

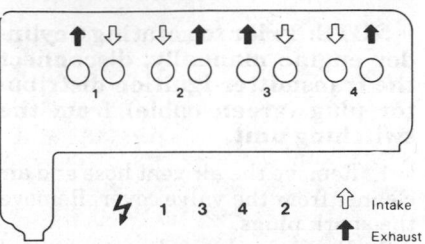

Valve arrangement—4-cylinder diesels

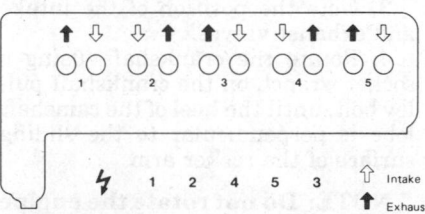

Valve arrangement—5-cylinder diesels

7. Capnut		14. Holding wrench
8. Locknut		16. Adjusting wrench

Adjusting valve clearance on diesel engine

5. After adjustment, hold the cap nut and lock it in place with the hex nut. Recheck the clearance.

6. Check the gasket and install the rocker arm cover.

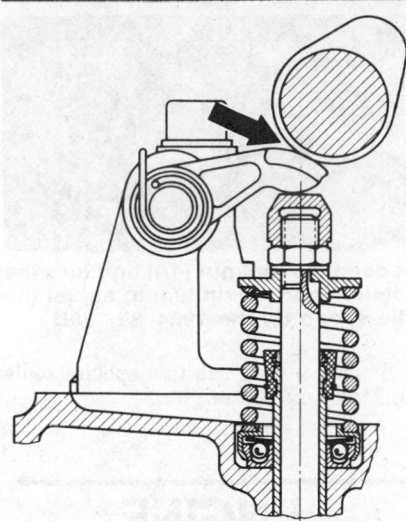

Measure valve clearance on diesel engines at arrow

Idle Speed and Mixture Gasoline Engines

ADJUSTMENT

Fuel Injection Models
280E AND 280CE MODELS

1. Run the engine to normal operating temperature (167°–185°F oil temperature) and connect the tachometer.
2. The automatic transmission should be in Park and A/C off.
3. Be sure the throttle valve lever rests against the idle speed stop.
4. Be sure the cruise control actuating rod rest against the idle speed stop. Disconnect the connecting rod and push the lever of the actuating lever clockwise to the idle speed position.
5. Reconnect the connecting rod; make sure that the actuating element is approximately 0.04 in. from the idle speed stop. Adjust this clearance with the pull rod.
6. Check and adjust the idle speed. Idle speed is adjusted at the idle speed air screw.

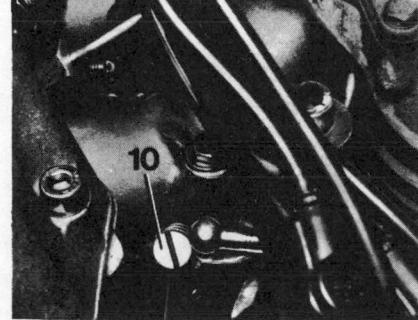

Idle speed adjusting screw — DOHC 6 cylinder engines

ALL OTHER MODELS
These engines have electronically controlled idle speed, using a solenoid connected to terminals 1 and 5 of the control unit. Idle speed an mixture adjustments are not recommended.

Idle Speed Diesel Engine

ADJUSTMENT
ALL 1981–85 DIESELS EXCEPT 1982–83 240D, 1984–85 190D AND ALL 1986–88 DIESELS

1. Run the engine to normal operating temperature.
2. On normally aspirated engines (non-turbocharged), turn the idle speed adjuster on the dash completely to the right.
3. Disconnect the pushrod at the angle lever.
4. Check the idle speed. Adjust by loosening the locknut and adjusting the idle speed screw. Tighten the locknut.
5. On all except turbodiesels, adjust the pushrod so that a clearance of approximately 0.2 in. exists between the cam on the lever and the actuator on the switchover valve. The lever on the fuel injection pump must rest against the idle stop.
6. On all models except the 1981 turbodiesel, depress the stop lever as far as possible. The cruise control Bowden cable should be free of tension against the angel lever. Use the adjusting screw to alter the tension. Let go of the stop lever. The Bowden cable should have a slight amount of play.
7. On turbodiesels, adjust the pushrod so that the roller in the guide lever rests free of tension against the stop.
8. Put the automatic transmission in Drive and turn the steering wheel to full lock. The engine should run smoothly. If not, adjust the idle speed. Disconnect the cruise control connecting rod, and push the lever clockwise to the idle stop. Attach the connecting rod, making sure the lever is about 0.04 in. from the idle speed stop.

─── **CAUTION** ───
If the engine speed is adjusted higher, it will be above the controlled idle speed range of the governor and the engine can increase in speed to maximum rpm.
───────────────

1982–83 240D
1. Run the engine to normal operating temperature.
2. Turn the idle speed adjuster knob on the dashboard completely to the right.

Idle speed adjusting screw — V8 engine

The switching unit (2), cable connector (1) and diagnostic socket (3) distinguish the 190E electronic ignition from that of the 1981 6 cylinder

Adjusting nut for dashboard idle speed knob

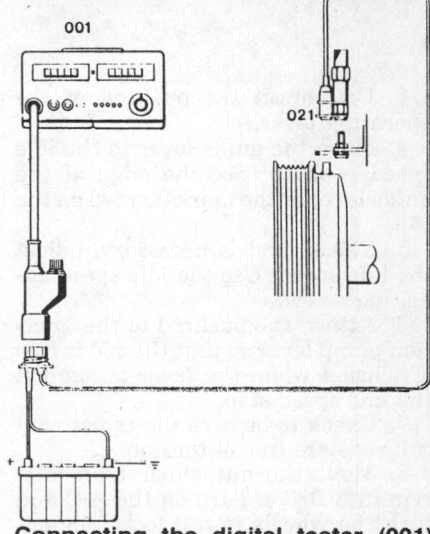

Connecting the digital tester (001) and the TDC impulse transmitter (021) on the 1984–85 190D

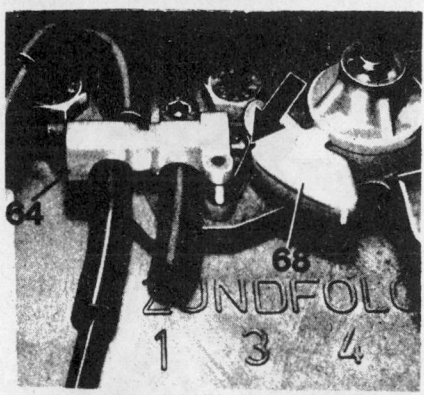

Clearance between cam and actuator on switch-over valve—all except turbodiesel

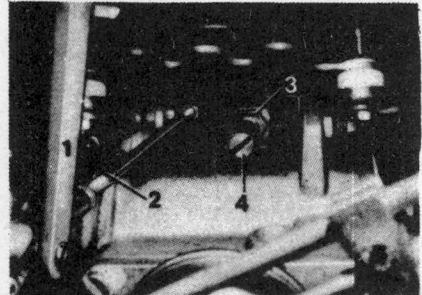

Idle speed adjustment—1981–85 5 cylinder engines

Idle speed adjustment—240D

3. Disconnect the pushrod at the operating lever.

4. Move the guide lever to the idle speed position. Set the edge of the guide lever at the mark (arrow) on the cap.

5. Check, and is necessary, adjust the idle speed. Use the idle speed adjusting screw.

6. Attach the pushrod to the injection pump lever so that the rod is free of tension when the lever is against the idle speed stop.

7. Check to be sure the cruise control rods are free of tension.

8. Move the automatic transmission into Drive. Turn on the A/C and turn the wheels to full lock. The engine should run smoothly. Adjust the idle speed if necessary.

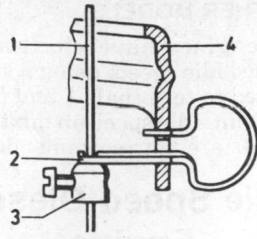

1. Cable
2. Spring
3. Adjusting barrel
4. Lever

Be sure the specially shaped spring is installed as shown

1984–85 190D

NOTE: Testing the idle speed on the 190D will require two special tools. A digital tester (SUN-1019, 2110 or All-Test 3610–MB) and a TDC impulse transmitter; not commonly available tools. Without these special tools, idle speed adjustment is impossible and should not be attempted.

1. Run the engine until it reaches normal operating temperature.

2. Connect the digital tester and the TDC impulse transmitter as indicated in the illustration.

3. Check all linkages for ease of operation.

4. Disconnect the pushrod from the adjusting lever.

5. Start the engine and check the idle speed. If required, adjust by loosening the locknut on the vacuum control unit and turning the unit itself in or out.

Adjusting the idle—1985 190D

NOTE: 1985 models with electronic idle speed control have no vacuum control unit. To adjust idle speed, loosen the locknut and turn the shaft until the idle speed is 670 rpm.

6. After the idle speed is correct, tighten the vacuum control unit locknut and reconnect the pushrod so that it is tension-free when the lever is against the idle speed stop.

7. Switch on all auxiliary power accessories and check that the engine continues to run smoothly. Readjust the idle speed if necessary.

Loosen the locknut (4A) and turn the vacuum control unit (4) to adjust the idle speed on the 1984–85 190D

8. Disconnect the two special tools and turn off the engine.

ENGINE ELECTRICAL

Distributor

REMOVAL & INSTALLATION

NOTE: The distributor on the 190E with 2.6L engine, 260E and 300E is part of the cylinder head. With the exception of the cap and rotor, it is not readily removable.

The removal and installation proce-

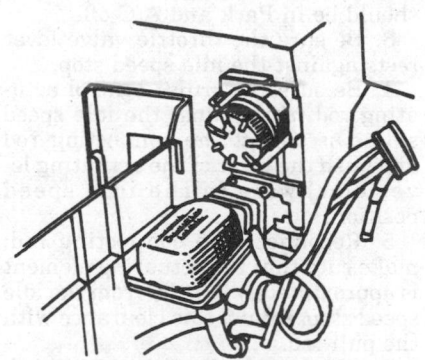

Idle speed trimming plug—190D (2.5L) shown, other similar

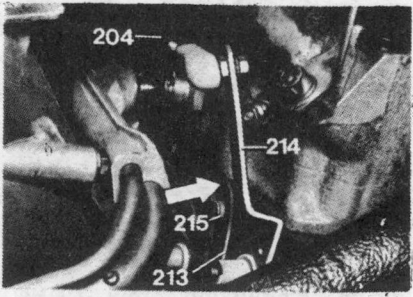

Throttle linkage on the 1984–85 190D

dures for all distributors on Mercedes-Benz vehicles are basically similar. Certain minor differences may exist from model to model.

1. The distributor is usually located on the front side or front of the engine.

2. Remove the dust, cover, distributor cap, cable plug connections, and vacuum line.

3. Rotating the engine in the normal direction, crank it around until the distributor rotor points to the mark on the rim of the distributor housing. This indicates the No. 1 cylinder.

4. The engine can be cranked with a socket wrench on the balancer bolt or with a pry bar inserted in the balancer.

5. Matchmark the distributor body and the engine so that the distributor can be returned to its original position.

6. Remove the distributor hold-down bolt and withdraw the distributor from the engine.

NOTE: Do not crank the engine while the distributor is removed.

7. Installation is the reverse of removal. Insert the distributor so that the matchmarks on the distributor and engine are aligned.

8. Tighten the clamp bolt and check the dwell angle and ignition timing.

Alternator

All Mercedes-Benz cars covered in this book use 12 volt electrical systems with alternators, in conjunction with the transistor or electronic ignition system.

PRECAUTIONS

Some precautions that should be taken into consideration when working on this, or any other, AC charging system are as follows:

1. Never switch battery polarity.
2. When install a battery, always connect the grounded terminal first.
3. Never disconnect the battery while the engine is running.
4. If the molded connector is disconnected from the alternator, do not ground the hot wire.
5. Never run the alternator with the main output cable disconnected.
6. Never electric weld around the car without disconnecting the alternator.
7. Never apply any voltage in excess of battery voltage during testing.
8. Never "jump" a battery for starting purposes with more than 12 volts.

REMOVAL & INSTALLATION

Viewing the engine from the front, the alternator is located on either side, usually down low. Because of the location, it is sometimes easier to remove the alternator from below the vehicle. The following is a general procedure for all models.

1. Locate the alternator and disconnect and identify all wires.

2. Loosen the adjusting (pivot) bolt or the adjusting mechanism and swing the alternator in toward the engine.

3. Remove the drive belt from the alternator pulley.

4. The alternator can now be removed from its mounting bracket or the bracket and alternator can be removed from the engine.

5. Installation is the reverse of removal.

6. Tighten all of the drive belts that were loosened.

BELT TENSION ADJUSTMENT

All alternator dive belts should be tensioned to approximately ½ in. deflection under thumb pressure at the middle of the longest span.

NOTE: The 190D, 1985–88 190E and all 1986–88 models utilize a single V-belt with automatic tensioning. No adjustment is necessary.

Starter

All Mercedes-Benz passenger cars are equipped with 12 volt Bosch electric starters of various rated outputs. The starter is actuated and the pinion engaged by an electric solenoid mounted on top of the starter motor.

When removing the starter, note the exact position of all wires and washers since they should be installed in their original locations. On some models it may be necessary to position the front wheels to the left or right to provide working clearance.

REMOVAL & INSTALLATION

1. Remove all wires from the starter and tag them for location.

2. Disconnect the battery cable.

3. Unbolt the starter from the bellhousing and remove the ground cable.

4. Remove the starter from underneath the car.

5. Installation is the reverse of removal. Be sure to replace all wires and washers in their original location.

ENGINE MECHANICAL

NOTE: Care should be taken when working on Mercedes-Benz engines, since there are many aluminum parts which can be damaged if carelessly handled.

Engine
REMOVAL & INSTALLATION

NOTE: In all cases, Mercedes-Benz engines and transmissions are removed as a unit.

— CAUTION —

Air conditioner lines should not be indiscriminately disconnected without taking proper precautions. It is best to swing the compressor out of the way while still connected to its hoses. Never do any welding around the compressor-heat may cause an explosion. Also, the refrigerant, while inert at normal room temperature, breaks down under high temperature into hydrogen fluoride and phosgene (among other products), which are highly poisonous.

All 4, 5 and 6 Cylinder Engines (Except 280E and 280CE Models)

1. First, remove the hood, then drain the cooling system and disconnect the battery. While not strictly necessary, it is better to remove the battery completely to prevent breakage by the engine as it is lifted out.

2. Remove the fan shroud, radiator, and disconnect all heater hoses and oil cooler lines. Plug all openings to keep out dirt.

3. Remove the air cleaner and all fuel, vacuum and oil hoses (e.g., power steering and power brakes). Plug all openings to keep out dirt.

4. Remove the viscous coupling and fan.

5. On diesel engines, disconnect the idle control starting cables. On the 300SD, loosen the oil filter cover slightly; siphon off the power steering fluid and disconnect the hoses.

6. On all engines, disconnect the accelerator linkage.

7. Disconnect all ground straps and electrical connections. It is a good idle to tag each wire for easy reassembly.

8. Detach the gearshift linkage and the exhaust pipes from the manifolds.

9. Loosen the steering relay arm and pull it down out of the way, along with the center steering rod and hydraulic steering damper.

10. The hydraulic engine shock absorber should be removed.

1 U-joint flange
2 U-joint plate
3 Wooden block

Supporting a V8 engine

11. Remove the hydraulic line from the clutch housing and the oil line connectors from the automatic transmission.

12. Unbolt the clutch slave cylinder from the bellhousing after removing the return spring.

13. Remove the exhaust pipe bracket attached to the transmission and place a woodpadded jack under the bellhousing, or place a cable sling under the oil pan, to support the engine. On turbocharged models, disconnect the exhaust pipes at the turbocharger.

14. Mark the position of the rear engine support and unbolt the two outer bolts, then remove the top bolt at the transmission and pull the support out.

15. Disconnect the speedometer cable and the front driveshaft U-joint. Push the driveshaft back and wire it out of the way.

16. Unbolt the engine mounts on both sides and, on four-cylinder engines, the front limit stop.

17. Unbolt the power steering fluid reservoir and swing it out of the way; then, using a chain hoist and cable, lift the engine and transmission upward and outward. An angle of about 45 degrees will allow the car to be pushed backward while the engine is coming up.

18. Reverse the procedure to install, making sure to bleed the hydraulic clutch, power steering, power brakes and fuel system.

280E and 280CE

1. Scribe alignment marks on the hood hinges and remove the hood. Drain the coolant from the radiator and block.

2. Remove the radiator.

3. Disconnect the lines from the vacuum pump.

4. On vehicles with air conditioning, remove the compressor and place it aside.

─────── CAUTION ───────

Do not remove the refrigerant lines from the compressor. Physical harm could result.

5. Disconnect and tag all electrical connections from the engine.

6. Disconnect all coolant and vacuum lines from the engine.

7. Disconnect and plug the oil pressure lines from the power steering pump after draining the pump reservoir.

8. Remove the accelerator linkage control rod by pulling off the lockring and pushing the shaft in the direction of the firewall.

9. Loosen and remove the exhaust pipes from the manifold and transmission support.

10. Disconnect the transmission linkage and all other connections.

11. Loosen the front right (driving direction) shock absorber from the front axle carrier.

12. Remove the left hand engine shock absorber from the engine mount.

13. Attach a lifting device to the engine and tension the cables.

14. Unbolt the engine and transmission mounts and remove the engine at a 45 degree angle.

15. Installation is the reverse of removal. Be sure to check all fluids and fill as necessary. Check all adjustments on the engine.

V8 Engines

NOTE: Removal of a V8 engine equipped with air conditioning, may require discharging the air conditioning system. Use caution; Freon is lethal.

1. Remove the hood. On the 380SEC, the hood can be tilted back 90 degrees and does not have to be removed.

2. Drain the cooling system.

3. Remove the radiator and fan shroud.

4. Remove the cable plug from the temperature switch.

5. Remove the battery, battery frame and air filter.

6. Drain the power steering reservoir and windshield washer reservoir.

7. Disconnect and plug the high pressure and return lines on the power steering pump.

8. Detach the fuel lines from the fuel filter, pressure regulator, and pressure sensor.

9. If equipped, loosen the line to the supply and anti-freeze tanks. On models so equipped, disconnect the lines to the hydro-pneumatic suspension.

10. Disconnect the cables from the ignition coil and transistor ignition switchbox.

11. Disconnect the brake vacuum lines.

12. Detach the cable connections for the following:
   a. venturi control unit
   b. temperature sensor
   c. distributor
   d. temperature switch
   e. cold starting valve
   f. speedometer inductance transmitter (3.8l only)

13. Remove the regulating shaft by pushing it in the direction of the firewall.

14. Disconnect the thrust and pullrods.

15. Disconnect the heater lines.

16. Detach the lines to the oil pressure and temperature gauges.

17. Remove the ground strap from the vehicle.

18. Detach the cables from the alternator, terminal bridge, and battery. Remove the battery.

19. Position a lifting sling on the engine and take up the slack in the chain.

20. Remove the left-hand engine mount and loosen the hex nut on the right-hand mount.

21. Remove the exhaust system. Remove the connecting rod chain on the rear level control valve and loosen the torsion bar slightly. Raise the vehicle slightly at the rear and remove the exhaust system in the rearward direction.

22. Disconnect the handbrake cable.

23. Remove the shield plate from the transmission tunnel.

24. Place a block of wood between the transmission and cross-yoke so the engine will not sag when the rear mount is removed.

25. Loosen the driveshaft intermediate bearing and the driveshaft slide.

26. Support the transmission with a jack.

27. Mark the installation of the crossmember and remove the crossmember. Remove the rear engine carrier with the engine mount.

28. Unbolt the front U-joint flange on the transmission and push it back. Do not loosen the clamp nut on the intermediate bearing. Support the driveshaft.

29. Disconnect the speedometer shaft, shift rod, control pressure rod, regulating linkage (on automatic transmissions), kickdown switch cable, starter lockout switch cable, and the cable for the back-up light switch.

30. Remove the front engine mounting bolt and remove the engine at approximately a 45 degree angle.

31. Installation is the reverse of re-

moval. Lower the engine until it is behind the front axle carrier. Place a jack under the transmission and lower the engine into its compartment. While lowering the engine, install the right-hand shock mount.

32. Fill the engine with all required fluids and start the engine. Check for leaks.

Cylinder Head

REMOVAL & INSTALLATION

4 and 5 Cylinder Engines

EXCEPT 190E-16 (DOHC)

This is fairly straightforward but some caution must be observed to ensure that the valve timing is not disturbed.

1. Drain the radiator and remove all hoses and wires. Tag all wires to ensure easy reassembly.

2. Remove the camshaft cover and associated throttle linkage, then press out the spring clamp from the notch in the rocker arm (all except 190).

NOTE: The cylinder head cover on the 190E is removed with the spark plug cables and distributor cap still attached to it.

3. Push the clamp outward over the ball cap of the rocker, then depress the valve with a large prying tool and lift the rocker arm out of the ball pin head (all except 190).

4. Remove the rocker arm supports (all except 190) and the camshaft sprocket nut.

5. On all 5 cylinder engines and the 190E, the rockers and their supports must be removed together.

6. Using a suitable puller, remove the camshaft sprocket, after having first marked the chain, sprocket and cam for ease of assembly.

7. Remove the sprocket and chain and wire it out of the way.

------ **CAUTION** ------

Make sure the chain is securely wired so that it will not slide down into the engine.

8. Unbolt the manifolds and exhaust header pipe and push them out of the way.

9. Loosen the cylinder head holddown bolts in the reverse order of that shown in torque diagrams for each model. It is good practice to loosen each bolt a little at a time, working around the head, until all are free. This prevents unequal stresses in the metal.

10. Reach into the engine compartment and gradually work the head loose from each end by rocking it.

Never, under any circumstances, use a screwdriver between the head and block to pry, as the head will be scarred badly and may be ruined.

11. Installation is the reverse of removal.

------ **CAUTION** ------

The dowel pin used for cylinder head alignment has been moved in 1985–88 190D models. Due to this change, the cylinder head and/or the gasket are NOT interchangeable with the 1984 190D.

NOTE: All diesel engines utilize cylinder head stretch-bolts. These bolts undergo a permanent stretch each time they are tightened. When a maximum length is reached, they must be discarded and replace with new bolts. When tightening the head bolts on these engines, it is imperative that the steps listed under "Torque Specifications" are followed exactly. Maximum stretch lengths for the different models are as follows:

Model	Length when new (mm)	Maximum (mm)
190E	119	122
190D	80	83.6
	102	105.6
	115	118.6
240D, 300D,	104	105.6
300CD, 300SD,	119	120.5
300TD (1980-85)	144	145.6

Under no circumstances may the older type cylinder head bolts be exchanged with the newer "stretch" bolts.

190E-16 (DOHC)

1. Drain the engine coolant and disconnect the radiator and heater hoses at the cylinder head.

2. Tag and disconnect the intake air temperature sensor lead and the crankcase ventilation hose where they connect to the air cleaner.

3. Remove the two air cleaner mounting nuts. Lift the housing at the rear until it releases from its holding studs, slide it backwards slightly and then remove it from the air flow sensor.

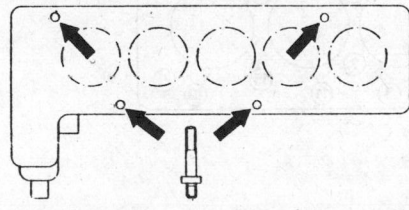

Studs (arrows) on the 1981–85 5 cylinder engine are for attaching the rocker cover

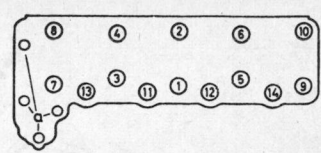

Cylinder head torque sequence—4 cylinder gasoline engines (except 190E)

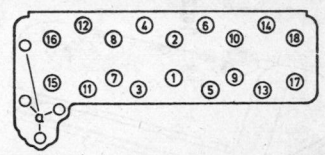

Cylinder head torque sequence—4 cylinder diesel engines (except 190D)

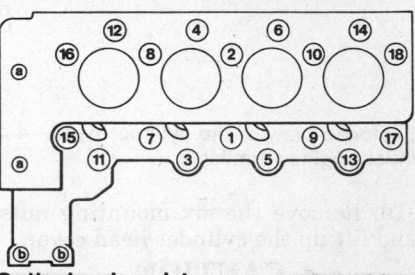

Cylinder head torque sequence—190E SOHC (bolts "A" are tightened to 25 Nm)

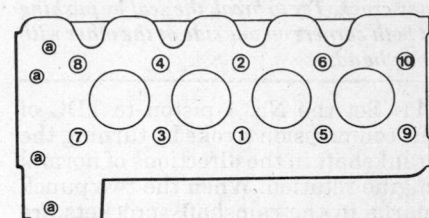

Cylinder head torque sequence—1984–85 190D (bolts "A" and "B" are tightened to 25 Nm)

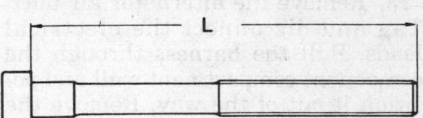

Cylinder head bolt stretch is measured at "L"

4. Loosen the oil dipstick mounting bracket screw and pull the dipstick out of the crankcase.

5. Loosen the screw in the center of the serpentine belt tensioner ¼–½ turn, loosen the tensioning nut by turning it counterclockwise and then remove the belt.

6. Remove the exhaust manifold.

7. Remove the four screws holding the ignition cable cover to the cylinder head cover. Remove the cover, tag and disconnect the cables and position them out of the way.

8. Loosen the clamp on the rear heater hose and pull it off the water outlet.

9. Disconnect the breather line at the cylinder head cover.

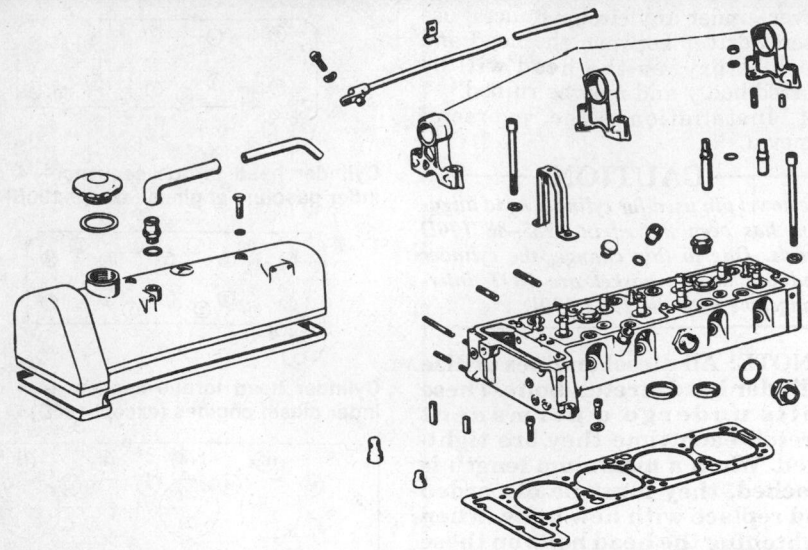

Exploded view of the cylinder head—4 cylinder diesel engines (except 190D); 5 cylinder engines similar

10. Remove the six mounting nuts and lift up the cylinder head cover.

CAUTION

If the cylinder head cover sticks to the head, DO NOT use a hammer to loosen it as it may crack. Try to break the seal by pushing at both corners on one side or the other with your hands.

---

11. Set the No. 1 piston to TDC of the compression stroke by turning the crankshaft in the directions of normal engine rotation. When the two punch marks in the camshaft sprockets are aligned, the engine will be at TDC.

12. Place matchmarks on the camshaft sprocket and the timing chain.

13. Remove the alternator air duct. Tag and disconnect the electrical leads. Pull the harness through the component compartment wall and position it out of the way. Remove the alternator.

14. Using a 32mm wrench, unscrew the chain tensioner.

15. Tag and disconnect the tow pump lines and then remove the pump from the exhaust-side camshaft. Remove the three screws and pull the pump flange from the end of the camshaft.

16. Remove the two mounting nuts and lift the chain slide from the front of the engine.

NOTE: If so equipped, remove the sheet metal bracket that is attached to the two front cylinder head bolts and the two eyes at the timing chain housing cover.

17. Remove the four mounting screws from each camshaft sprocket. Knock the camshaft back slightly with a rubber mallet. Be careful! Remove the front bearing caps and pull off the two sprockets.

CAUTION

Secure the timing chain in such a way that it will not slip down into the crankcase.

---

18. Loosen the water by-pass hose clamp. Remove the mounting screws and pull out the water inlet/thermostat housing.

19. Use a Allen wrench to remove the two return pipe mounting screws and then pull it out of the cylinder head. If the pipe sticks, rotate it clockwise slightly and force it out with a suitable prybar.

20. Unbolt the intake manifold and push it out of the way.

21. Loosen the cylinder head bolts in the reverse order of the tightening sequence. Loosen each bolt a little at a time, working around the head until all are free; this will prevent unequal stress on the aluminum head.

22. Reach into the engine compartment and gradually work the head loose from the cylinder block. NEVER, under any circumstances us a screwdriver or the like to pry the head free.

23. Installation is in the reverse order of removal. Please note the following:

a. Measure the cylinder head bolts prior to installation. A new bolt is 110mm long from the bottom of bolt head to the end of the bolt. If it has stretched to more than 113mm, replace it.

b. Tighten the cylinder head bolts a little at a time, in the order shown in the illustration.

c. Use new O-rings and a new flange gasket when installing the return pipe.

d. Install the intake camshaft sprocket first (right side when facing the vehicle). Be certain that the matchmarks made earlier are aligned.

e. Make sure that the two punch marks in the sprockets are in alignment.

Return pipe—190E-16 (DOHC)

V8 Engines

NOTE: Before removing the cylinder head from a V8, be sure you have the 4 special tools necessary to torque the head bolts; without them it will be impossible. Do not confuse the left and right-hand head gaskets—the left side has 2 attaching holes in the timing chain cover, the right side has only 1 hole. Cylinder heads on 3.8 and 5.0 liter V8's are not interchangeable.

NOTE: Cylinder heads can only be removed with the engine cold.

Cylinder head torque sequence—1981–85 5 cylinder engines (bolts marked "A" are tightened with a Hex bit)

When the two punch marks are in alignment on the 190E-16 camshaft sprockets, the engine is at TDC

1. Drain the cooling system.
2. Remove the battery.
3. Remove the air cleaner. Remove the fan and fan shroud.
4. Pull the cable plug from the temperature sensor.
5. Detach the vacuum hose from the venturi control unit.
6. Remove the following electrical connections:
    a. injection valves.
    b. distributor
    c. venturi control unit
    d. temperature sensor and temperature switch
    e. starting valve
    f. temperature switch for the auxiliary fan.
7. Loosen the ring line on the fuel distributor.
8. Loosen the screws on the injection valves and pressure regulator or mixture regulator. Remove the ring line with the injection valves and pressure regulator.
9. Plug the holes for the injection valves in the cylinder head.
10. Remove the regulating shaft by disconnecting the pull rod and the thrust rod.
11. Remove the ignition cable plug.
12. Loosen the vacuum connection on the intake manifold.
13. Loosen the vacuum connection for the central lock at the transmission.
14. Remove the oil filler tube from the right hand cylinder head and remove the temperature connector.
15. Remove the oil pressure gauge line from the left hand cylinder head.
16. Loosen the coolant connection on the intake manifold.
17. Remove the intake manifold. This is not necessary on 3.8, 4.2, 5.0 and 5.6 liter V8's although the intake manifold bolts must be removed.
18. Loosen the alternator belt and remove the alternator and mounting bracket.

19. Remove the electrical connections from the distributor and electronic ignition switch-gear.
20. Drain some fluid from the power steering reservoir and disconnect and plug the return hose and high pressure supply line.
21. Disconnect the exhaust system. On 3.8, 4.2, 5.0 and 5.6 liter V8's, remove the exhaust manifolds.
22. Loosen the right hand holder for the engine damper.
23. Remove the right hand chain tensioner.
24. Matchmark the camshaft, camshaft sprocket, and chain. Remove the camshaft sprocket and chain after removing the cylinder head cover. Be sure to hang the chain and sprocket to prevent it from falling into the timing chain case.
25. Remove the upper slide rail. On 3.8, 4.2, 5.0 and 5.6 liter V8's, remove the distributor and remove the inner slide rail on the left cylinder head. Remove the rail after the camshaft sprocket.
26. Unscrew the cylinder head bolts. This should be done with a cold engine. Unscrew the bolts in the reverse order of the torque sequences. Unscrew all the bolts a little at a time and proceed in this manner until all the bolts have been removed.

NOTE: Cylinder head bolts on the 3.8 and 5.0 liter V8's are nickel plated and 10mm longer than those for previous engines.

27. Remove the cylinder head. Do not pry on the cylinder head.
28. Remove the cylinder head gasket.
29. Clean the cylinder head and cylinder block joint faces.
30. To install, position the cylinder head gasket.

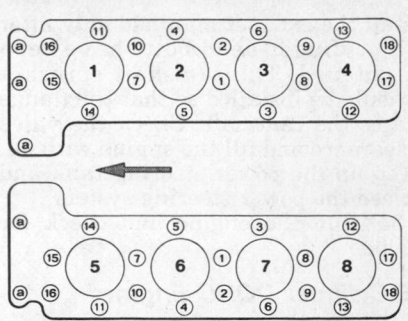

Cylinder head torque sequence—V8 engines

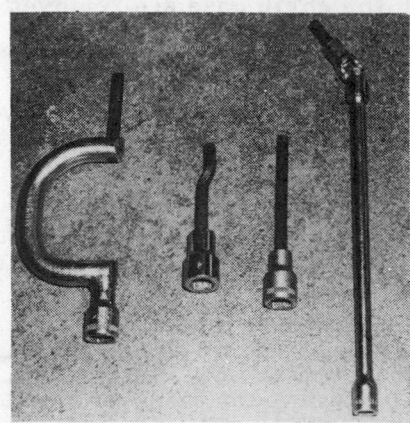

You need these tools to remove or install the V8 cylinder head. Without them it is practically impossible.

31. Do not confuse the cylinder head gaskets. The left hand head has two attaching holes in the timing chain cover while the right hand has three.
32. Install the cylinder head and torque the bolts according to the illustrated torque sequence.
33. Further installation is the reverse of removal. On 3.8, 4.2, 5.0 and 5.6 liter V8's, insert the rear cam bearing cylinder head bolt before positioning the cylinder head. Also, in-

Be careful removing the cylinder head bolts on a V8. The inner row of cam bolts are the only bolts NOT holding the head on. Note the angle of the bolts.

stall the exhaust manifold only after the cylinder head bolts have been tightened. The camshaft sprocket should be installed so that the flange faces the camshaft. Check the valve clearance and fill the engine with oil. Top up the power steering tank and bleed the power steering system.

34. Run the engine and check for leaks.

6 Cylinder DOHC Engine

NOTE: The head must be removed STRAIGHT up. The 2 bolts in the chain case are removed with magnet.
Two people are best for this job.

To install use 2 pieces of wood ½ in. x 1½ x 9 in. to support the head while aligning the bolt holes. The exhaust camshaft gear bolt is 0.2 in. shorter.

1. Completely drain the cooling system.
2. Remove the air filter.
3. Remove the radiator.
4. Remove the rocker arm cover.
5. Remove the battery. Remove the idler pulley and the holding bracket for the compressor.
6. Remove the compressor and bracket and lay it aside without disconnecting any of the lines.

----- **CAUTION** -----
Disconnecting any of the refrigerant lines could result in physical harm.

7. Unbolt the cover from the camshaft housing.
8. Disconnect the heating water line from the carburetor, the vacuum line on the starter housing, and the distributor vacuum line.
9. Disconnect all electrical connections, water lines, fuel lines, and vacuum lines which are connected to the cylinder head. Tag these for reassembly.

10. Remove the regulating linkage shaft.
11. Remove the EGR line between the exhaust return valve and the exhaust pipe.
12. Disconnect and plug the oil return line at the cylinder head.
13. At the thermostat housing, loosen the hose which passes between the thermostat housing and the water pump. Unscrew the bypass line on the water pump.
14. Loosen the oil dipstick tube from the clamp and bend it slightly sidewards.
15. Unbolt the exhaust pipes from the exhaust manifolds and bracket on the transmission.
16. Force the tension springs out of the rocker arm with a small pry bar.
17. Remove all of the rocker arms.
18. Crank the engine to TDC. This can be done with a socket wrench on the crankshaft pulley bolt. The marks on the camshaft sprockets and bearing housings must be aligned.
19. Hold the camshafts and remove the bolt which holds each camshaft gear to the camshaft.
20. Remove the upper slide rail. Knock out the bearing bolts with a puller.
21. Remove the chain tensioner.
22. Push both camshafts toward the rear and remove the camshaft sprockets.
23. Remove the spacer sleeves on both camshaft. The sleeves are located in front of the camshaft bearings.
24. Remove the guide wheel by unscrewing the plug and removing the bearing bolt.
25. Lift off the timing chain and suspend the chain from the hood with a piece of wire. Pull out the guide gear.

While the head is removed from a 6 cylinder DOHC engine, always replace this rubber hose, whether it needs it or not; it is impossible to replace with the cylinder head in position

26. Remove the slide rail in the cylinder head by removing the bearing pin with a puller.
27. Loosen the cylinder head bolts in small increments, using the reverse order of the tightening sequence. This should be done on a cold engine to prevent the possibility of head warpage.
28. Pull out the two bolts in the chain case with a magnet. Be careful not to drop the washers.
29. Pull up on the timing chain and force the tensioning rail toward the center of the engine.
30. Lift the cylinder head up in a vertical direction.

NOTE: Mercedes-Benz recommends two people for this job.

31. Remove the cylinder head gasket and clean the joint faces of the block and head.
32. To install, cut two pieces of wood ½ in. x 1½ in. x 9½ in. Lay one piece upright between cylinders 1 and 2; lay the other flat between cylinders 5 and 6.
33. Install the cylinder head in an inclined position so that the timing chain and tensioning rail can be inserted.
34. Lift the cylinder head at the front and remove the front piece of wood toward the exhaust side. Carefully lower the cylinder head until the bolt holes align.
35. Lift the head at the rear so that the board can be removed toward the exhaust side. Carefully lower the cylinder head until all the bolt holes align.
36. Tighten the cylinder head bolts in gradual steps until they are fully tightened. Follow the torque sequence.
37. Check to be sure that both camshafts rotate freely after the bolts are tight.
38. The remainder of installation is the reverse of removal. Be sure that

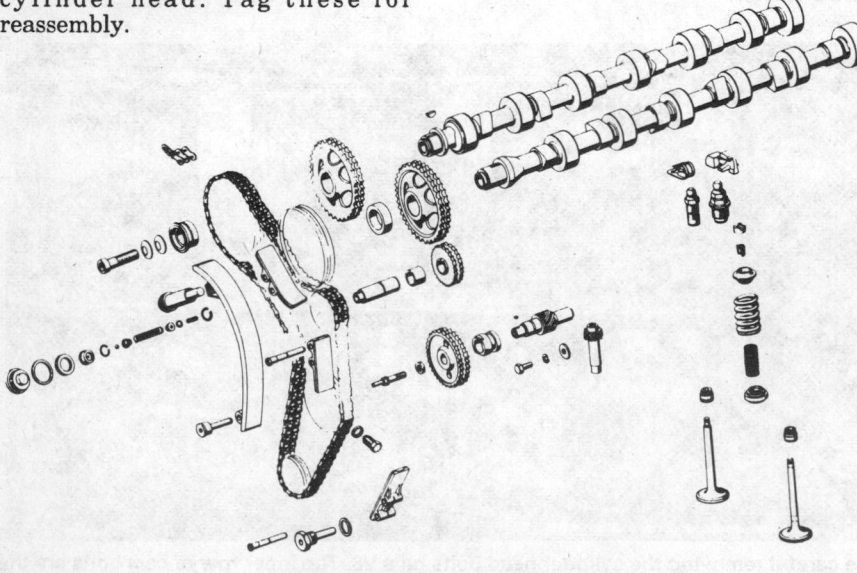

DOHC camshafts and related parts

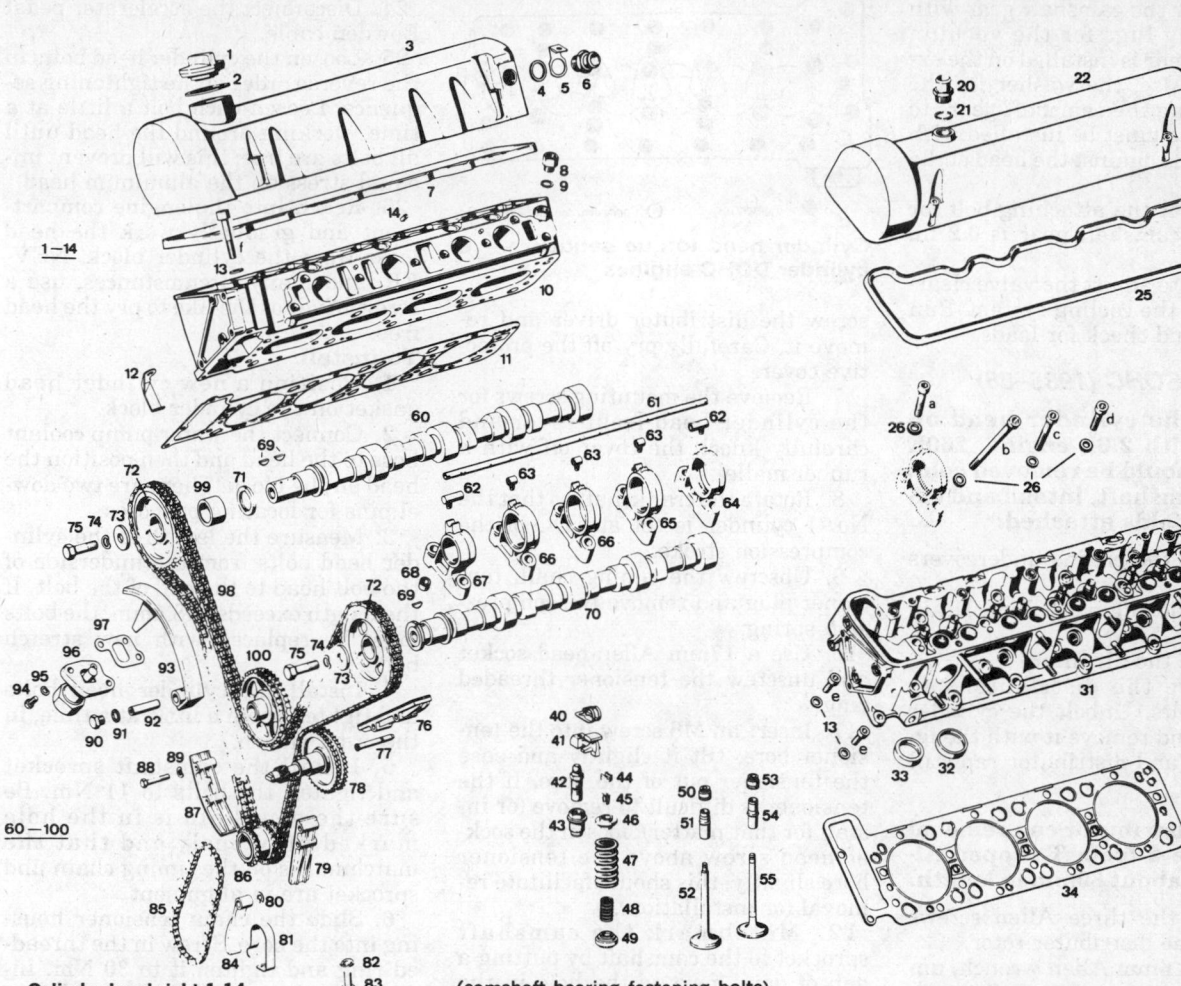

Cylinder head right 1-14

1. Filler plug
2. Sealing ring
3. Cylinder head cover
4. Sealing ring
5. Holder for cable to injection valves
6. Connection
7. Valve cover gasket
8. Connection to temperature sensor
9. Sealing ring
10. Cylinder head
11. Cylinder head gasket
12. Cable holder
13. 5 Washers
14. Hollow dowel pins

Cylinder head left 20-34

20. Connection
21. Sealing ring
22. Cylinder head cover
23. 8 Screws
24. 8 Sealing rings
25. Cylinder head cover gasket
26. 36 Washers
27. Sealing ring
28. Screw connection oil pressure gauge
29. 3 Studs
30. 13 Studs
31. Cylinder head
32. Valve seat ring—intake
33. Valve seat ring—exhaust
34. Cylinder head gasket

Cylinder head bolts

(a)—10 M 10 x 50chrauben)

(camshaft bearing fastening bolts)
(b)—10 M 10 x 155
(c)—18 M 10 x 80
(d)—8 M 10 x 55
(e)—4 M 8 x 30
(f)—1 M 8 x 70

Valve arrangement 40-55

40. Tensioning spring
41. Rocker arm
42. Adjusting screw
43. Threaded bushing
44. Thrust piece
45. Valve cone piece
46. Valve spring retainer
47. Outer valve spring
48. Inner valve spring
49. Rotator
50. Intake valve seal
51. Exhaust valve guide
52. Intake valve
53. Exhaust valve seal
54. Exhaust valve guide
55. Exhaust valve

Engine timing 60-100

60. Camshaft-right
61. Oil pipe (external lubrication)   Oil pipe to
62. Connecting piece   camshaft
63. Connecting piece   bearing
64. Camshaft bearing-flywheel end
65. Camshaft bearing 4

Exploded view of the V8 cylinder head

66. Camshaft bearing 2 and 3
67. Camshaft bearing-cranking end
68. 5 Hollow dowel pins
69. Spring washer
70. Camshaft-left
71. Compensating washer
72. Camshaft gear
73. Washer-camshaft gear
74. Spring washer
75. Bolt
76. 3 Slide rails
77. 6 Bearing bolts
78. Drive gear ignition distributor
79. Guide rail
80. Lockwasher
81. Spring—chain tensioner, oil pump
82. Washer
83. Screw
84. Clamp
85. Single roller chain (oil pump drive)
86. Crankshaft gear
87. Slide rail
88. 4 Screws
89. 4 Spring washers
90. Plug
91. Sealing ring
92. Bearing bolt
93. Tensioning lever
94. 2 Bolts
95. 2 Spring washers
96. Chain tensioner
97. Gasket
98. Double roller chain
99. Spacer ring
100. Idler gear

the spacer for the camshaft gear with the engaging lugs for the vacuum pump drive gear is installed on the exhaust side. Also, the washer for the bolts attaching the camshaft gears to the camshafts must be installed with the domed side against the head of the bolt.

39. Note that the attaching bolt for the exhaust camshaft gear is 0.2 in. shorter.

40. Be sure to adjust the valve clearance and fill the cooling system. Run the engine and check for leads.

6 Cylinder SOHC (1986–88)

NOTE: The cylinder head on the 190E with 2.6L engine, 260E and 300E should be removed cold, with the camshaft, intake and exhaust manifolds attached.

1. Remove the engine undercovers from below.

2. Drain the engine coolant. Drain the engine oil.

3. Remove the air filter.

4. Remove the distributor cap mounting bolts. Unbolt the cylinder head cover and remove it with the ignition wires and distributor cap still attached.

NOTE: Distributor cap removal will require a 5mm T-shaped Allen wrench about 80mm in length.

5. Loosen the three Allen screws and lift off the distributor rotor.

6. Using a 6mm Allen wrench, un-

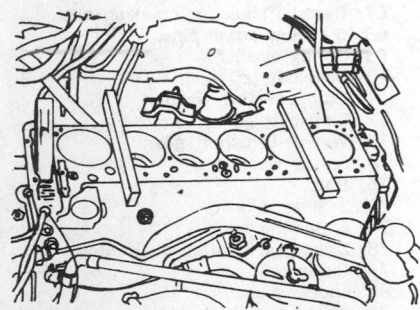

Fabricated tools for installing the cylinder head on DOHC 6-cylinder engines

The marks on the camshaft and bearing housing must align on DOHC 6-cylinder engines when the engine is at TDC

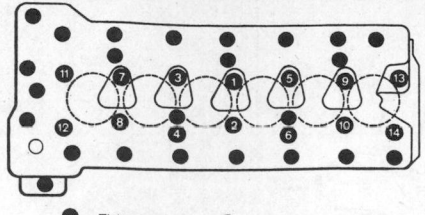

- ● Tighten   ○ Concealed, cannot be tightened

Cylinder head torque sequence— 6 cylinder DOHC engines

screw the distributor driver and remove it. Carefully pry off the protective cover.

7. Remove the mounting screws for the cylinder head front cover and carefully knock the cover off with a rubber mallet.

8. Rotate the crankshaft so that the No. 1 cylinder is set at TDC of the compression stroke.

9. Unscrew the timing chain tensioner plug and remove the compression spring.

10. Use a 17mm Allen-head socket and unscrew the tensioner threaded ring.

11. Insert an M8 screw into the tensioner bore, tilt it slightly and ease the tensioner out of the bore. If the tensioner is difficult to remove (or install for that matter), loosen the socket head screw above the tensioner bore slightly; this should facilitate removal (or installation).

12. Matchmark the camshaft sprocket to the camshaft by putting a dab of paint next to the hole in the sprocket with the dowel pin.

13. Matchmark the camshaft sprocket to the timing chain.

14. Remove the mounting screws and pull off the camshaft sprocket. Secure the timing chain in such a way that it will not slip down into the crankcase.

15. Remove the slide rail bolt with an impact puller.

16. Unscrew the oil dipstick guide tube bracket and then pull out the dipstick and tube.

17. Unscrew the upper intake manifold mounting bolt. Loosen the lower bolt.

18. Loosen the hose clamp and remove the coolant hose at the water pump.

19. ... 20. Unscrew the exhaust pipe at both flanges.

21. Disconnect the automatic transmission dipstick tube at the cylinder head and position it out of the way.

22. Tag and disconnect all wiring, electrical leads and vacuum hoses connected to, or in the way of the cylinder head.

23. Disconnect the fuel feed and return lines, plug them and position them out of the way.

24. Disconnect the accelerator pedal Bowden cable.

25. Loosen the cylinder head bolts in the reverse order of the tightening sequence. Loosen each bolt a little at a time, working around the head until all bolts are free; this will prevent unequal stress on the aluminum head.

26. Reach into the engine compartment and gradually work the head loose from the cylinder block. NEVER, under any circumstances, use a screwdriver or the like to pry the head free.

To install:

1. Position a new cylinder head gasket on the cylinder block.

2. Connect the water pump coolant hose to the head and then position the head on the block. There are two dowel pins for locating purposes.

3. Measure the length of the cylinder head bolts from the underside of the bolt head to the end of the bolt. If the length exceeds 108.4mm, the bolts must be replaced with new stretch bolts.

4. Install the cylinder head bolts and tighten them a little at a time, in the order shown.

5. Install the camshaft sprocket and tighten the bolts to 11 Nm. Be sure the dowel pin is in the hole marked previously and that the matchmarks on the timing chain and sprocket are in alignment.

6. Slide the chain tensioner housing into the bore. Screw in the threaded ring and tighten it to 30 Nm. Install the thrust bolt with the detent spring. Position the compression spring and a new seal. Tighten the plug to 50 Nm.

7. Check the alignment of the timing marks on the camshaft bearing cap and the camshaft. When they are aligned, the engine should be at TDC of the compression stroke.

8. Install a new elastic gasket into the groove of the timing chain housing cover and then mount the front cover. Tighten the two lower screws first. Torque all screws to 21 Nm.

9. Install the protective cover with a new seal. Install the distributor driver so that the groove engages the pin on the camshaft. Tighten the screw to 21 Nm.

10. Installation of the remaining components is in the reverse order of removal.

NOTE: When refilling the coolant system on the 300E, always remove the hexhead plug on the left side of the cylinder head and fill the hole with coolant until it overflows. Install the plug and then fill the coolant system. When filling the coolant system on the 190E with 2.6 liter engine and

260E, open the vent screw approximately two turns, start the engine and run at idle.

OVERHAUL

For all cylinder head procedures, please refer to "Engine Rebuilding" in the Unit Repair Section.

Rocker Arms

REMOVAL & INSTALLATION

Diesel Engines

NOTE: The 190D does not use rocker arms. The camshaft acts directly on the hydraulic valve tappet.

Rocker arms on diesel engines can only be removed as a unit with the respective rocker arm blocks.

1. Detach the connecting rod for the venturi control unit from the bearing bracket lever and remove the bearing bracket from the rocker arm cover.

The timing marks on the camshaft bearing cap (1) and the camshaft (2) should be in alignment when the No. 1 cylinder is at TDC

The groove (arrow) on the driver (5) must engage the pin in the camshaft—260E and 300E

2. Remove the air vent line from the rocker arm cover and remove the rocker arm cover.

3. Remove the stretch-bolts from the rocker arm blocks and remove the blocks with the rocker arms. Turn the crankshaft in each case so that the camshaft does not put any load on the rocker arms.

NOTE: Turn the crankshaft with a socket wrench on the crankshaft pulley bolt. Do not rotate the engine by turning the camshaft sprocket.

4. Before installing the rocker arms, check the sliding surfaces of the ball cup and rocker arms. Replace any defective parts.

5. To install, assembly the rocker arm blocks and insert new stretch-bolts.

6. Tighten the stretch-bolts. In each case, position the camshaft so that there is no load on the rocker arms. See the previous NOTE.

7. Check to be sure that the tension clamps have engaged with the notches of the rocker arm blocks.

8. Adjust the valve clearance.

9. Reinstall the rocker arm cover, air vent line, and bearing bracket for the reverse lever. Attach the connecting rod for the venturi control unit to the reversing lever.

10. Make sure that during acceleration, the control cable can move freely without binding.

11. Start the engine and check the rocker arm cover for leaks.

Gasoline Engines—All Except 190E, 260E and 300E

NOTE: All V8's use hydraulic valve lifters.

Before removing the rocker arm(s), be sure that they are identified as to their position relative to the camshaft lobe. They should be installed in the same place as they were before disassembly.

Be very careful removing the thrust pieces. They can easily fall into the engine.

1. Remove the rocker arm cover or covers.

2. Force the clamping spring out of the notch in the top of the rocker arm. Slide it in an outward direction across the ball socket or the rocker arm.

Removing the chain tensioner on the 260E and 300E

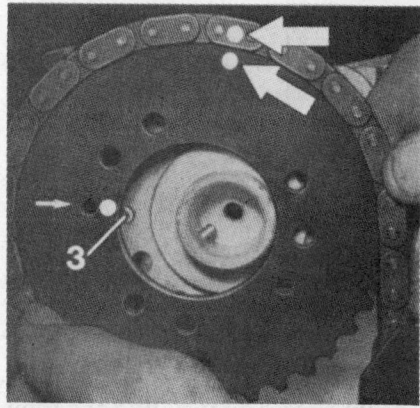

Matchmark the camshaft sprocket on the 260E and 300E before removal (note the dowel pin, 3)

NOTE: Turn the engine over each time to relieve any load from the rocker arm.

3. On V8 models, the clamping spring must be forced from the adjusting screw with a small prybar.

4. Force the valve down to remove load from the rocker arm.

NOTE: Don't depress the spring too far. When the piston is up as it should be, the valve will hit the piston. As the spring goes down, the thrust piece will fall off into the engine.

5. Lift the rocker arm from the ball pin and remove the rocker arm.

6. To install the rocker arm(s), force the rocker arm down until the rocker arm and its ball socket can be installed in the top of the pin.

7. Install the rocker arms.

8. Slide the clamping spring across

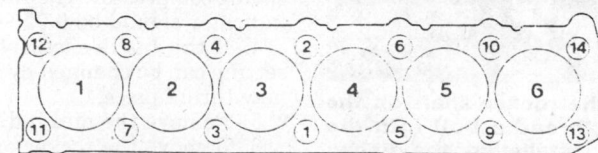

Cylinder head tightening sequence on the 260E and 300E

the ball socket of the rocker arm until it rests in the notch of the rocker arm.

9. On V8 models, engage the clamping spring into the recess of the adjusting screw.

10. Check and, if necessary, adjust the valve clearance.

11. After completion of the adjustment, check to be sure that the clamping springs are correctly seated.

12. Install the rocker arm cover and connect any hoses or lines that were disconnected.

13. Run the engine and check for leaks at the rocker arm cover.

190E, 260E and 300E

NOTE: The 190E-16 utilizes double overhead camshafts acting directly on valve tappets. There are no rocker arms on this engine.

Rocker arms on this engine are individually mounted on rocker arm shafts that fit into either side of the camshaft bearing brackets.

1. Remove the cylinder head cover. The cover is removed with the spark plug wires and distributor cap still connected.

2. Tag each rocker arm and shaft so that they are identified as to their position relative to the camshaft. They should always be install in the same place as they were before disassembly.

3. The rocker arm shaft is held axially and rotationally by a bearing bracket fastening bolt. Remove the bolt on the side of the bearing bracket that allows access to the exposed end of the rocker shaft.

4. Thread a bolt (M8) into the end of the rocker arm shaft and slowly ease the shaft out of the bearing bracket.

CAUTION
Support the rocker arm/lifter assembly while removing the shaft so it will not drop onto the cylinder head.

To remove the rocker shaft on the 190E SOHC, thread a bolt into the hole (D). On installation, the dished groove (arrow) must always line up with the mounting bolt shank

NOTE: Carefully forcing the valve down with a small prybar will remove the load on the hydraulic valve tappet and ease the removal of the shaft. Don't depress the spring too far. When the piston is up as it should be, the valve will hit the piston. As the spring goes down the thrust piece will fall off into the engine.

5. Replace the bearing bracket bolt and tighten it to 11 ft. lbs. (15 Nm) until ready to replace the rocker shaft.

6. To install, position the rocker arm between the two bearing brackets and slide the shaft into place.

NOTE: The circular groove on the end of the rocker shaft must line up with the mounting bolt shank to ensure proper positioning.

7. Replace the bearing bracket mounting bolt.

8. Repeat Steps 3–7 for all remaining rocker arm/shaft assemblies. Turn the engine over each time to relieve any load from the rocker arm.

9. Replace the cylinder head cover.

Hydraulic Valve Lifters

V8 ENGINES
Hydraulic valve lifters are used with overhead cams. The rocker arm is always in contact with the cam, reducing noise and eliminating operating clearance.

Checking Base Setting

The base setting is the clearance between the upper edge of the cylindrical part of the plunger and the lower edge of the retaining cap (dimension A) when the cam lobe is vertical.

NOTE: A dial indicator with an extension and a measuring thrust piece (MBNA *100 589 16 63 00), 0.187 in. thick are necessary to perform this adjustment.

1. Turn the cam lobe to a vertical position, relative to the rocker arm.

2. Attach a dial indicator and tip extension and insert the extension through the bore in the rocker arm onto the head plunger. Preload the dial indicator by 0.08 in. and zero the instrument.

3. Depress the valve with a valve spring compressor. The lift on the dial indicator should be 0.028–0.075 in.

4. If the lift is excessive, the base setting can be changed by installing a new thrust piece.

5. Remove the dial indicator.

6. Remove the rocker arm.

7. Remove the thrust piece and insert the measuring disc.

8. Install the rocker arm and repeat Steps 1–3.

9. Select a thrust piece according to the table. If the measured valve was 0–0.002 in. and the 0.2146 in. thrust piece will not give the proper base setting, use the 0.2283 in. thrust piece.

10. Remove the dial indicator and the rocker arm. Install the selected thrust piece.

11. Reinstall the rocker arm and dial indicator and repeat Steps 1–3.

Removal & Installation
Temporarily removed valve lifters must be reinstalled in their original locations. When replacing worn rocker arms, the camshaft must also be replace. If the rocker arm, or hydraulic lifter is replaced, check the base setting.

Remove the rocker arm and unscrew the valve lifter with a 24mm socket.

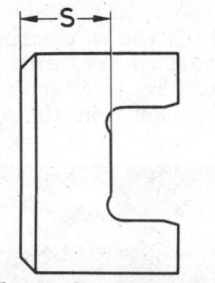

Thrust piece thickness

SELECTIVE THRUST PIECES

Measured Value (in.)	Thrust Piece Thickness(s) (in.)
0–0.002	0.2146/0.2283
0.002–0.034	0.2008
0.035–0.066	0.1870
0.067–0.099	0.1732
0.099–0.131	0.1594
above 0.131	0.1457

Intake Manifold

REMOVAL & INSTALLATION

V8 Engine

1. Partially drain the coolant.

2. Remove the air cleaner.

3. Disconnect the regulating linkage and remove the longitudinal regulating shaft.

4. Pull off all cable plug connections.

5. Disconnect and plug the fuel lines on the pressure regulator and starting valve.

6. Unscrew the nuts on the injec-

tion valves and set the injection valves aside.

7. Remove the 16 attaching bolts from the intake manifold.

8. Loosen the hose clip on the thermostat housing hose and disconnect the hose.

9. Remove the intake manifold. If a portion of the manifold must be replaced, disassembly the intake manifold. Replace the rubber connections during reassembly.

10. Intake manifold installation is the reverse of removal. Replace all seals and gaskets. Adjust the linkage and idle speed.

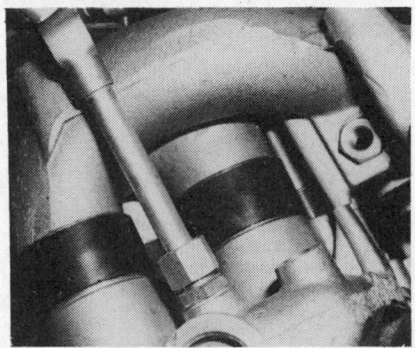

Replace the rubber connecting pieces on the intake manifold, anytime the manifold is removed.

Exhaust Manifold

REMOVAL & INSTALLATION

V8 Engine

1. Unbolt the exhaust pipes from the manifolds.

2. Disconnect the rubber mounting ring from the exhaust system.

3. Loosen the shield plate on the exhaust manifold.

4. When removing the lift hand exhaust manifold, remove the shield plate for the engine mount together with the engine damper.

5. Unbolt the manifold from the engine.

6. Pull the manifold off of the mounting.

7. Installation is the reverse of removal.

Turbocharger

REMOVAL & INSTALLATION

1. Remove the air filter.

2. Disconnect the electrical cable from the temperature switch.

3. Loosen the lower hose clamp on the air duct that connects the air filter with the compressor housing.

4. Remove the vacuum line and crankcase breather pipe.

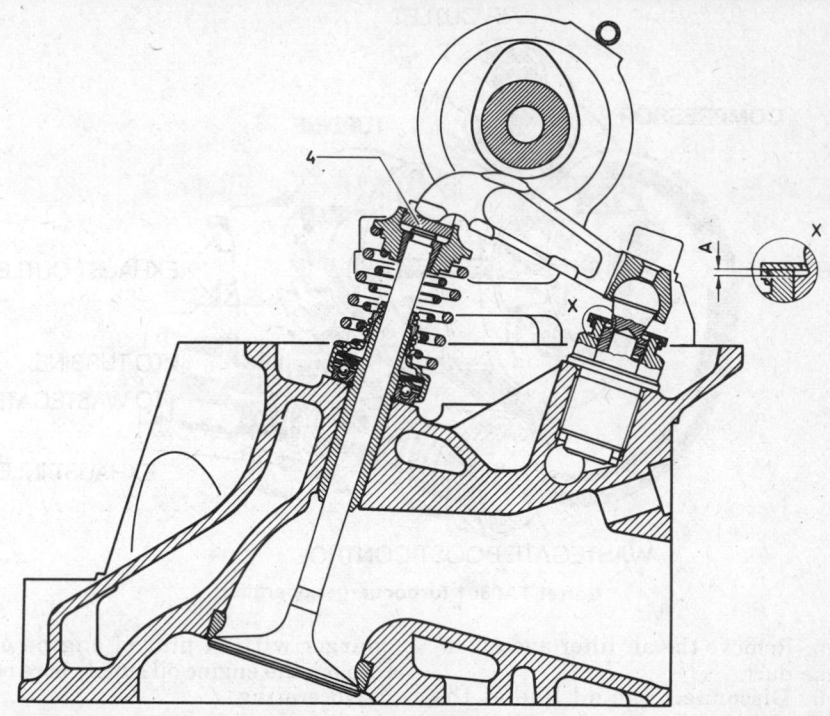

Cutaway of valve train showing hydraulic valve lifter. Dimension "A" is base setting clearance.

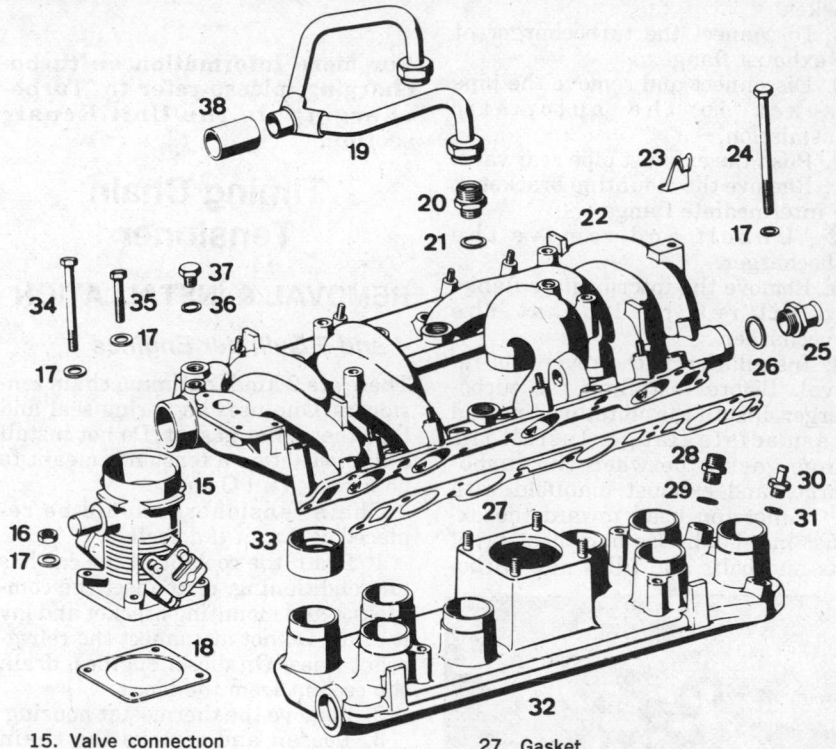

15. Valve connection
16. Nut
17. Washer
18. Gasket
19. Idle speed air line
20. Screw connection
21. Sealing ring
22. Upper Intake manifold
23. Holder
24. Hex bolt
25. Connection
26. Sealing ring
27. Gasket
28. Screw connection
29. Sealing ring
30. Screw connection
31. Sealing ring
32. Bottom intake manifold
33. Rubber connecting piece
35. Hex bolt
34. Hex bolt
36. Sealing ring
37. Plug
38. Hose

V8 intake manifold

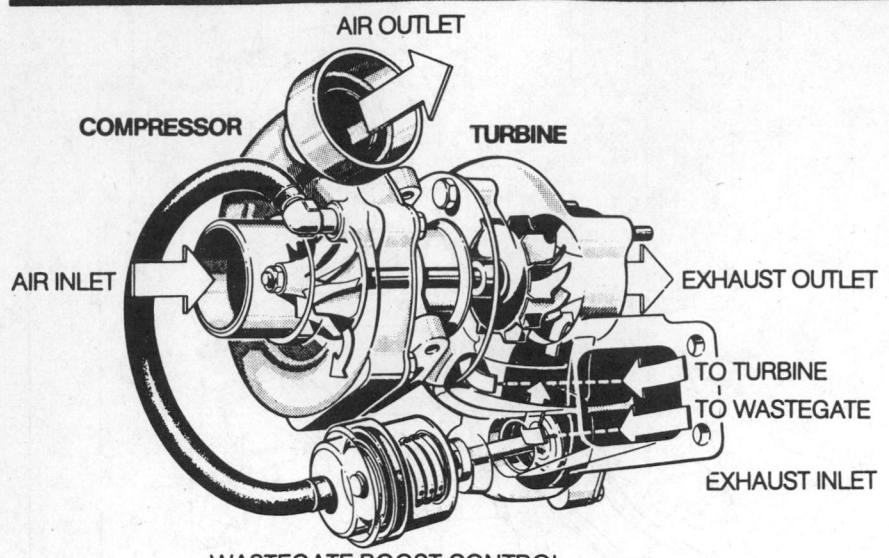

AIR OUTLET

COMPRESSOR   TURBINE

AIR INLET

EXHAUST OUTLET

TO TURBINE

TO WASTEGATE

EXHAUST INLET

WASTEGATE BOOST CONTROL

Garret TA0301 turbocharger operation

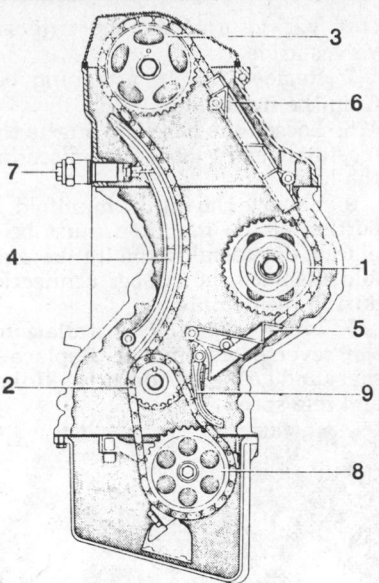

1. Injection timing advance mechanism
2. Crankshaft sprocket
3. Camshaft sprocket
4. Tensioning rail
5. Slide rail
6. Slide rail
7. Chain tensioner
8. Oil pump drive gear
9. Tensioning lever, chain, oil pump drive

Timing chain assembly—1984–85 190D

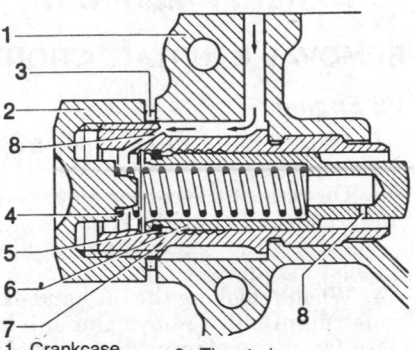

1. Crankcase
2. Cap nut
3. Seal ring
4. Compression
5. Detent spring
6. Thrust pin
7. Chain tensioner housing
8. Supply hole 1.1 mm dia.
9. Orifice 1.2 mm dia.

Cross section of the timing chain tensioner—190E (190D similar)

5. Remove the air filter and air intake duct.

6. Disconnect the oil line at the turbocharger.

7. Remove the air filter mounting bracket.

8. Disconnect the turbocharger at the exhaust flange.

9. Disconnect and remove the pipe bracket on the automatic transmission.

10. Push the exhaust pipe rearward.

11. Remove the mounting bracket at the intermediate flange.

12. Unbolt and remove the turbocharger.

13. Remove the intermediate flange and oil return line at the turbocharger.

14. Installation is the reverse of removal. Before installing the turbocharger, install the oil return line and intermediate flange. Install the flange gasket between the turbocharger and exhaust manifold with the reinforcing bead toward the exhaust manifold. Use only heat proof nuts and bolts and fill a new turbo-

1. Mounting bracket
2. Intermediate flange
3. Turbocharger

Remove the mounting nuts (arrow) to remove the turbocharger

charger with ¼ pint of engine oil through the engine oil supply bore before operating.

TROUBLESHOOTING

For more information on turbocharging, please refer to "Turbocharging" in the Unit Repair section.

Timing Chain Tensioner

REMOVAL & INSTALLATION

4 and 5 Cylinder Engines

There are 2 kinds of timing chain tensioners. One uses an O-ring seal and the other a flat gasket. Do not install a flat gasket on a tensioner meant to be use with an O-ring.

Chain tensioners should be replaced as a unit if defective.

1. Drain the coolant. If the car has air conditioning, disconnect the compressor and mounting bracket and lay it aside. Do not disconnect the refrigerant lines. On diesel engines, drain the coolant from the block.

2. Remove the thermostat housing.

3. Loosen and remove the chain tensioner. Be careful of loose O-rings. On the 190, you must first remove the tensioner capnut and the tension spring. The tensioner body can then be unscrewed with an Allen wrench.

4. Check the O-rings or gasket and replace if necessary.

5. To fill the chain tensioner, place the tensioner (pressure bolt down) in a container of SAE 10 engine oil, at least up to the flat flange. Using a

drill press, depress the pressure bolt slowly, about 7–10 times. Be sure this is done slowly and uniformly.

6. Install the chain tensioner. Tighten the bolts evenly. Tighten the capnut on the 190 to 51 ft. lbs. (70 Nm).

V8 Engines

The chain tensioner is connected to the engine oil circuit. Bleeding occurs once oil pressure has been established and the tensioner is filling with oil.

A venting hole has been installed in the tensioner to prevent oil foaming.

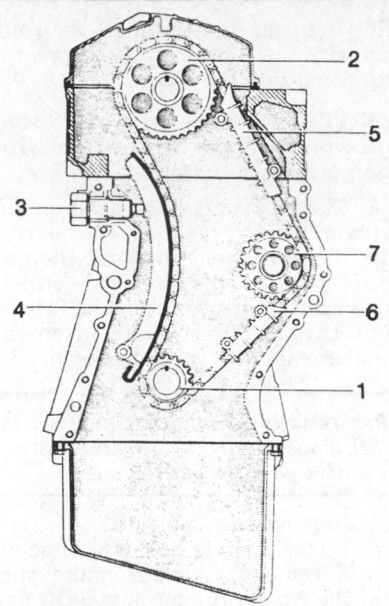

1. Crankshaft sprocket
2. Camshaft sprocket
3. Chain tensioner
4. Tensioning rail
5. Slide rail
6. Slide rail
7. Idler gear

Timing chain assembly — 190E SOHC

If there is a lot of timing chain noise, use this type of tensioner, which is identified by a white paint dot on the cap.

Service procedures for tensioners and rails on the different V8's are similar. Arrangement and shape and size of parts however, is slightly different.

1. On California models, disconnect the line from the tensioner.
2. Remove the attaching bolts and remove the tensioner. The inside bolts will probably require a long, straight 6mm Allen key to bypass the exhaust manifold. It is a tight fit.
3. Place the tensioner vertically in a container of engine oil. Operate the pressure bolt to fill the tensioner. After filling, it should permit compression very slowly under considerable force. If not, replace the tensioner with a new unit.
4. Install the tensioner and tighten the bolts evenly.

6 Cylinder Engines (DOHC)

1. On A/C vehicles, remove the battery. Unbolt the refrigerant compressor and lay it aside. Do not disconnect the refrigerant lines.
2. Remove the plug with a 17mm Allen key.
3. Tighten the threaded ring and loosen the ball seat ring.
4. Remove the threaded ring.
5. Remove the chain tensioner with a 10mm Allen key.
6. Be sure the tight side of the chain is tight.

7. Compress the tensioner and install the chain tensioner with a 10mm Allen key. Do not bump the Allen key or the tensioner will release.
8. Screw in the threaded ring and tighten it to 44 ft. lbs.
9. Tighen the ball seat ring to 18 ft. lbs. The pressure bolt should jump forward with an audible click. If it does not, the assembly must be removed and the installation repeated until it does click.
10. Install the plug.
11. Reinstall the A/C compressor, battery and air cleaner.

Timing Chain

REPLACEMENT

All Models

An endless timing chain is used on production engines, buy a split chain with a connecting link is used for service. The endless chain can be separated with a "chain breaker." Only one master link (connecting link) should be used on a chain.

1. Remove the spark plugs.
2. Remove the valve cover(s).
3. Clamp the chain to the camshaft gear and cover the opening of the timing chain case with rags. On 6 cylinder and V8 engines, remove the rocker arms from the right hand camshaft.
4. Separate the chain with a chain breaker.
5. Attach a new timing chain to the old chain with a master link.
6. Using a socket wrench on the crankshaft. slowly rotate the engine in the direction of normal rotation. Simultaneously, pull the old chain through until the master link is uppermost on the camshaft sprocket. Be

The inside bolt (arrow) on the V8 chain tensioner can only be reached by inserting a long, straight allen key underneath the exhaust manifold.

sure to keep tension on the chain throughout this procedure.

7. Disconnect the old timing chain and connect the ends of the new chain with the master link. Insert the new connecting link from the rear so that the lockwashers can be seen from the front.

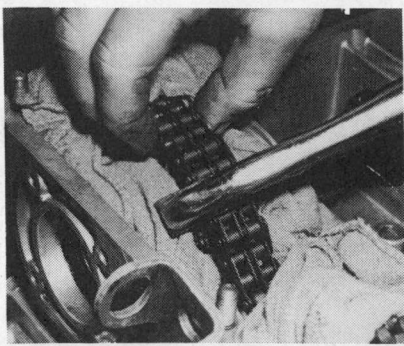

Clamp the chain to the gear and cover the opening with rags

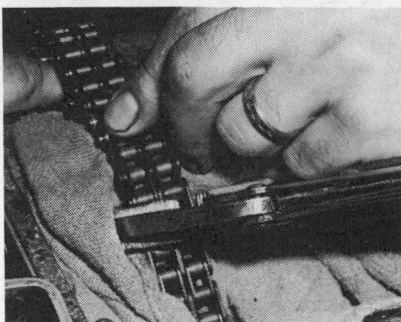

Clamp the chain again, cover the opening and remove the old chain from the master link. Connect both ends of the new chain.

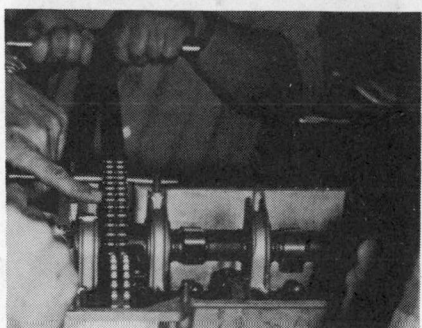

Crank the engine by hand until the new chain has come all the way through the engine. Be sure to keep tension on chain.

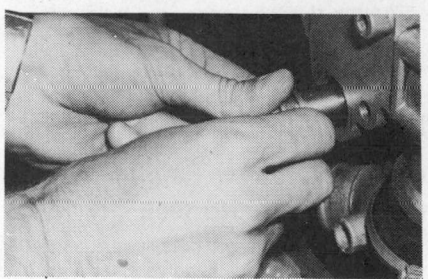

Install the chain tensioner

8. Rotate the engine until the timing marks align. Check the valve timing. Once the new chain is assembled, rotate the engine (by hand) through a least one complete revolution to be sure everything is OK. See valve timing for illustrations.

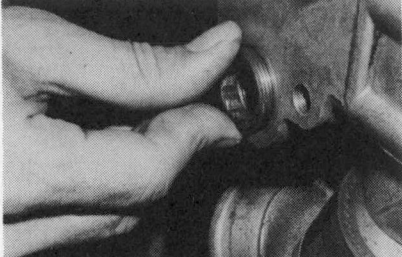

Remove the threaded plug.

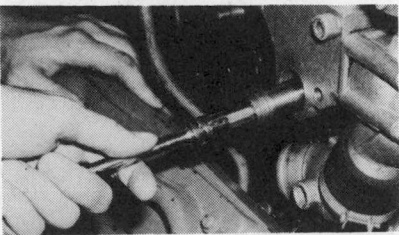

Remove the chain tensioner with a 10 mm allen key

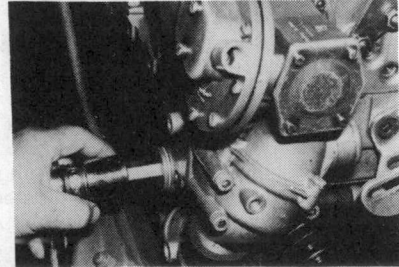

Remove the plug with a 17 mm allen key

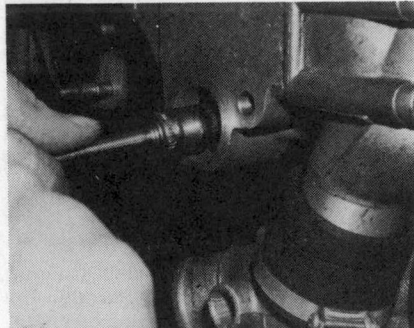

Tighten the tensioner until it "clicks"

Camshaft

REMOVAL & INSTALLATION

4 and 5 Cylinder Engines

EXCEPT 190D AND 190E

When the camshaft is replaced, be sure the rocker arms are also replaced.

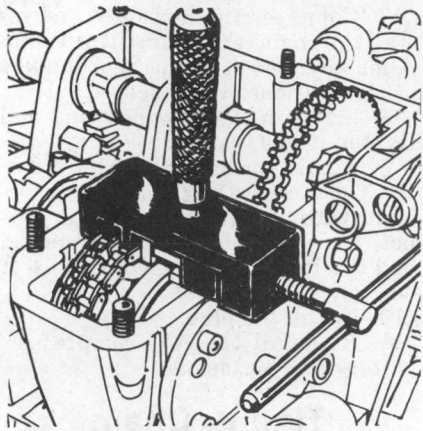

Remove the link with a chain breaker

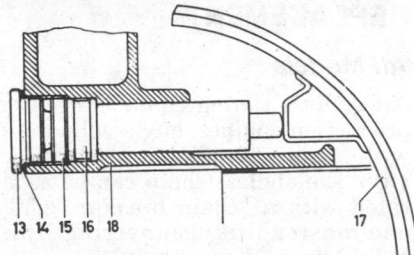

13. Closing plug
14. Sealing ring
15. Threaded ring
16. Chain tensioner
17. Tension rail
18. Cylinder head

Timing chain tensioner—6 cylinder DOHC engine

1. Remove the valve cover.
2. Remove the chain tensioner.
3. Remove the rocker arms.
4. Set the crankshaft at TDC for the No. 1 cylinder and be sure that the camshaft timing marks are aligned.
5. Hold the camshaft and loosen the cam gear bolt. Remove the cam gear and wire it securely so that the chain does not lose tension nor slip down into the chain case.
6. Remove the camshaft.
7. Installation is the reverse of removal. Be sure to check that the valve timing marks align when the No. 1 cylinder is at TDC. Check the valve clearance.

190D AND 190E

NOTE: On the 190E it is always a good idea to replace the rocker arms and shafts whenever the camshaft is replaced.

1. Remove the valve cover.
2. Remove the chain tensioner.
3. On the 190E, remove the rocker arms and shafts.
4. Set the crankshaft at TDC for the No. 1 piston and make sure that the timing marks on the camshaft are in alignment.
5. Using a 24mm open-end wrench, hold the rear of the camshaft (flats are provided) and then loosen and remove the camshaft retaining bolt. Carefully

slide the gear and chain off the shaft and wire them securely so they won't slip down into the case.

NOTE: Be careful not to lose the woodruff key while removing the gear on the 190E.

6. The camshaft is secured on the cylinder head by means of the bearing caps. Remove them and keep them in their proper order. Each cap is marked by a number punched into its side; this number must match the number cast into the cylinder head.

CAUTION

When removing the bearing caps on the 190D, always loosen the center two first and then move on to the outer ones.

---

7. Remove the camshaft.
8. Installation is in the reverse order of removal. Always make sure that the No. 1 cylinder is at TDC and all timing marks are aligned. Tighten the bearing caps to 15 ft. lbs. (21 Nm) on the 190E and 18 ft. lbs. (25 Nm) on the 190D. The camshaft gear retaining bolt should be tightened to 58 ft. lbs. (80 Nm) on the 190E and 33 ft. lbs. (45 Nm) on the 190D.

NOTE: Be certain not to forget the woodruff key on the 190E.

NOTE: The camshaft on the 1985–88 190D utilizes a new lobe design, allowing the valves to close softer. The code number is "06" and it can be retrofitted to 1984 engines. The timing has not changed.

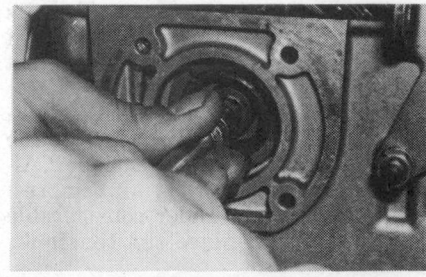

Loosen the camshaft bolts.

On the 190E SOHC, the mark (arrow) on the camshaft collar (B) must always be aligned

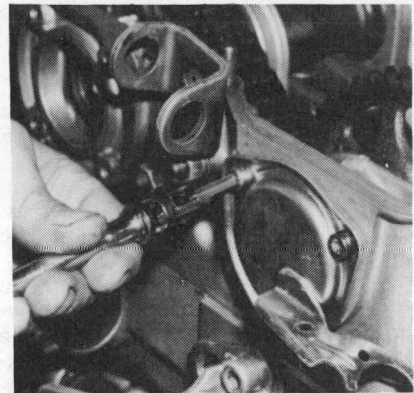

Remove the vacuum pump and camshaft cover.

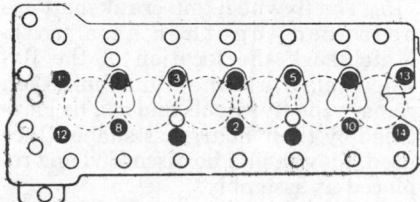

○ Unscrew M 8 bolts

① Unscrew cylinder head bolts in reverse order

● Do not loosen bolts

Bolts to be removed during the camshaft housing removal

6 CYLINDER ENGINES (DOHC)

With the engine installed in the car, the camshafts can only be removed together with the camshaft housing. If a new camshaft is installed, be sure to use new rocker arms.

1. Remove the refrigerant compressor but do not disconnect the refrigerant lines.

2. Remove the battery.

3. Remove the vacuum pump from the right-hand cylinder head.

4. Drain the coolant and remove the water hoses.

5. Remove the rocker arm cover.

6. Remove the cover from the front of the camshaft housing.

7. Remove the rocker arm springs.

8. Remove the rocker arms.

9. Crank the engine around in the normal direction of rotation (using the crankshaft bolt) until the No. 1 piston is at TDC, the pointer aligns with the TDC mark on the crankshaft pulley and the camshaft timing marks are aligned.

10. Hold the camshaft(s) and loosen the camshaft bolts.

NOTE: Wire the camshaft gears up so that tension is applied to the chain. The chain must not be allowed to slip off the camshaft or crankshaft gears.

Using a puller, remove the pins from the slide rails and remove the slide rails.

11. Remove the chain tensioner.

12. Remove the slide rail from the camshaft housing. A small puller is needed for this.

13. Loosen the cover at the right hand rear side of the camshaft housing and push the right hand camshaft toward the rear. Remove the camshaft gear.

14. Loosen the camshaft housing retaining bolts. Do not loosen the 5 lower cylinder head bolts or the 2 M8 bolts.

15. Remove the camshaft housing with the camshafts.

16. Remove the rear covers from the camshaft housing.

17. Hold the left hand camshaft and loosen the attaching bolt.

18. Push the camshaft rearward and remove the camshaft gear. Remove the spacer from the intake camshaft.

19. Remove both camshafts from the housing.

20. Oil the bearings and install the intake camshaft (left hand) with cam gear and spacer. Use a retaining bolt and washer (not springs).

21. Install the exhaust (right hand) camshaft. Do not install the gear until the housing is installed.

22. Install the rear camshaft covers. Do not tighten the one on the right hand side.

23. Install the camshaft housing.

24. Lubricate the bolts and tighten them in 3 stages:
• Starting with bolt No. 2, tighten to 30 ft. lbs.
• Starting with bolt No. 2, tighten to 44 ft. lbs.
• Starting with bolt No. 1, tighten to 67 ft. lbs. First, slightly loosen the 5 lower cylinder head bolts.

25. After torquing the camshaft housing bolts, torque the cylinder head bolts. When all bolts have finally been tightened, the camshafts should rotate easily and freely.

26. Install the righthand camshaft gear. Be sure the cam timing is accurate and the engine is set at TDC on the No. 1 cylinder.

---CAUTION---

Some engines have a scale for BDC as well as one for TDC. The TDC marks is next to the pin in the balancer.

Remove the rocker arm springs, rocker arms and thrust pieces.

27. Install the timing chain rail.
28. Install the rockers and tension springs. Adjust the valve.
29. Crank the engine by hand and check the valve timing.
30. Tighten the camshaft gear bolts to 59 ft. lbs.
31. Install the chain tensioner.
32. Install the camshaft rear housing covers (if not already done) and the vacuum pump.
33. Install the rocker covers.

V8 ENGINES

Experience shows that the right hand camshaft is always the first one to require replacement. When the V8 camshaft is removed, keep the pedestals with the camshaft. In particular, make sure that the 2 left hand rear cam pedestals are not swapped. The result will be no oil pressure. Always replace the oil gallery pipe with the camshaft.

NOTE: Arrangement of parts on the 3.8 and 5.0 liter V8 is slightly different compared to other V8 engines. Service procedures are the same.

1. Remove the valve cover.
2. Remove the tensioning springs and rocker arms.
3. Using a wrench on the crankshaft pulley, crank the engine around until the No. 1 piston is at TDC on the compression stroke. Using some stiff wire, hang the camshaft gear so that the chain will not slip off the gears.
4. Remove the camshaft gear.
5. Unbolt the camshaft, camshaft bearing pedestals and the oil pipe. Note the angle of the bolts that do not hold the head to the block.
6. Install the bearing pedestals and camshaft. On the left hand camshaft, the outer bolt on the rear bearing must be inserted prior to installing the bearings or it will not clear the

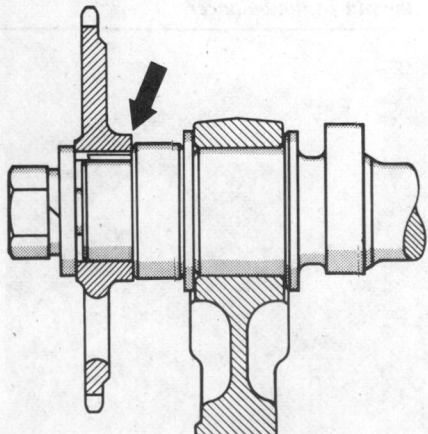

The camshaft flange (arrow) on 3.8 liter V-8's faces rearward

power brake until. Tighten the bolts from the inside out. When finished tightening, the camshaft should rotate freely.
7. Check the oil pipes for obstructions and replace if necessary.
8. When install the oil pipes, also check the 3 inner connecting pipes.
9. Install the compensating washer so that the keyway below the notch slides over the Woodruff key of the camshaft.
10. Install the rocker arms and tensioning springs.
11. Adjust the valve clearance and check the valve timing.

Engine Overhaul
DISSASSEMBLY

NOTE: This procedure is general and intended to apply to all Mercedes-Benz engines. It is suggested, however, that you be entirely familiar with Mercedes-Benz engines and be equipped with the numerous special tools before attempting an engine rebuild.

1. Remove the engine and support it on an engine stand or other suitable support.
2. Set the engine at TDC and matchmark the timing chain and timing gear(s). Remove the cylinder head(s) and gasket(s).
3. Remove the oil pan bolts and the pan and, on most models, the lower crankcase section.
4. Remove the oil pump.
5. Matchmark the connecting rod bearing caps to identify the proper cylinder for reassembly. Matchmark the sides of the connecting rod and side of the bearing cap for proper alignment. Pistons should bear an arrow indicating the front. If not, mark the front of the piston with an arrow using a magic marker. Also identify pistons as to cylinder so they may be replaced in their original location.
6. Remove the connecting rod nuts, bearing caps and lower bearing shells.
7. Place small pieces of plastic tubing on the rod bolts to prevent crankshaft damage.
8. Inspect the crankshaft journals for nicks and roughness and measure diameters.
9. Turn the engine and ream the ridge from the top of the cylinders to remove all carbon deposits.
10. Using a hammer handle or other piece of hardwood, gently tap the pistons and connecting rods out from the bottom.
11. The cylinder bores can be inspected at this time for taper and general wear.

12. Check the pistons for proper size and inspect the ring grooves. If any rings are cracked, it is almost certain that the grooves are no longer true, because broken rings work up and down. It is best to replace any such worn pistons.
13. The pistons, pins and connecting rods are marked with a color dot assembly code. Only parts having the same color may be used together.
14. If the cylinders are bored, make sure the machinist has the pistons before hand, cylinder bore sizes are nominal, and the pistons must be individually fitted to the block. Maximum piston weight deviation in any one engine is 4 grams.
15. The flywheel and crankshaft are balanced together as a unit. Matchmark the location of the flywheel relative to the crankshaft, then remove the flywheels and can be identified by their hourglass shape. Once used, they should be discarded and replaced at assembly.
16. Remove the water pump, alternator, and fuel pump, if not done previously.
17. Unbolt and remove the vibration damper and crankshaft pulley. On certain models, it is necessary to clamp the vibration damper with C-clamps before removing the bolts. Otherwise, the vibration damper will come apart.
18. Remove the timing chain tensioner and chain cover.
19. Matchmark the position of the timing chain on the timing gear of the crankshaft.
20. Matchmark the main bearing caps for number and position in the block. It is important that they are installed in their original positions. Most bearing caps are numbered for position. Remove the bearing caps.
21. Lift the crankshaft out of the block in a forward direction.
22. With the block completely disassembled, inspect the water passages and bearing webs for cracks. If the water passages are plugged with rust, they can be cleaned out be boiling the block at a radiator shop.

CAUTION
Aluminum parts must not be boiled out. They will be eroded by chemicals.

23. Measure piston ring end gap by sliding a new ring into the bore and measuring. Measure the gap at the top, bottom, and midpoint of piston travel and correct by filling or grinding the ring ends.
24. To check bearing clearances, use Plastigage® inserted between the bearing and the crankshaft journal. Blow out all crankshaft oil passages before measuring; torque the bolts to

specification. Plastigage® is a thin plastic strip that is crushed by the bearing end cap and spreads out an amount in proportion to clearance. After torqueing the bearing cap, remove the cap and compare the width of the Plastigage® with the scale.

NOTE: Do not rotate the crankshaft. Bearing shells of various thicknesses are available and should be used to correct clearance; it may be necessary to machine the crankshaft journals undersize to obtain the proper oil clearance.

— CAUTION —

Use a shim stock between bearings and caps to decrease clearance is not a good practice.

25. Check crankshaft end-play using a feeler gauge.

26. When installing new piston rings, ring grooves must be cleaned out, preferably using a special groove cleaner, although a broken ring will work as well. After installing the ring, check ring side clearance.

ASSEMBLY

1. Assemble the engine using all new gaskets and seals and make sure all parts are properly lubricated. Bearing shells and cylinder walls must be lubricated with engine oil before assembly. Make sure no metal clips remain in the cylinder bores or crankcase.

2. To install pistons and rods, turn the engine right side up and insert the rods into the cylinders. Clamp the rings to the piston, with their gaps equally spaced around the circumference, using a piston ring compressor. Gently tap the piston into the bore, using a hammer handle or similar hard wood, making sure the rings clear the edge.

NOTE: Pistons on the 3.8 and 5.0 liter V8 are installed with the arrow facing in the driving direction.

3. Torque the connecting rod bearing and main bearing caps to specification and try to turn the crankshaft by hand. It should turn with moderate resistance, not spin freely or be locked up. Main bearing caps use standard bolts (exc. 1985–88 190D; see NOTE below); stretch-bolts are used for the connecting rods (see this step for torquing procedure). These bolts are tightened by angle of rotation rather than by use of a torque wrench.

NOTE: Bearing cap bolts on 1985–88 190D's undergo a permanent stretch and must be replaced

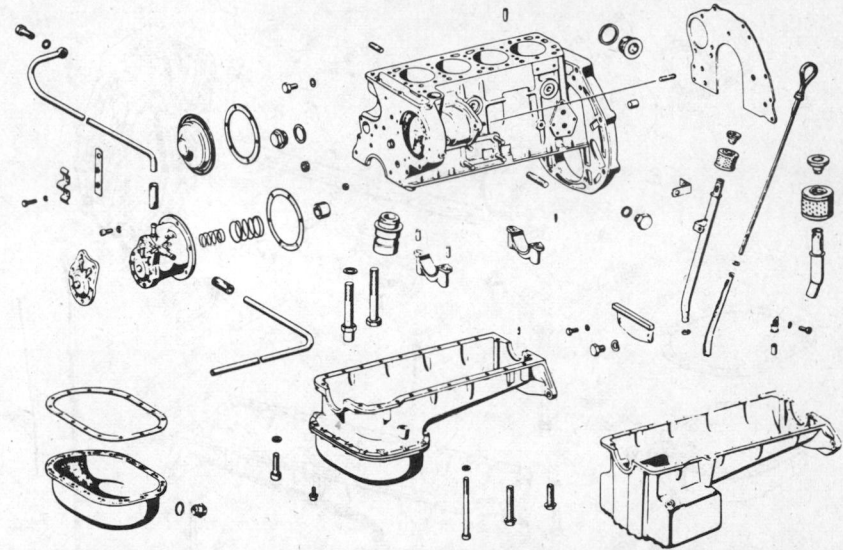

4-cylinder diesel engine cylinder block components (5-cylinder 300D is similar)

if the length (L) exceeds 2.5 in. (63.8mm)

Make sure the stretch section diameter is greater than 0.35 in. (0.003 in.). Remove the bolt from the rod and measure the diameter at the point normally covered by the rod; it should be at least 0.31 in. For reasons of standardization, the angle of rotation for all the screw connections tightened according to angle of rotation has been set to 90 degrees + 10 degrees. Initially the bolts should be torqued to 22–35 ft. lbs., then an additional 90 degrees.

NOTE: The bearing shells on the 3rd main bearing of the 190 series engines are fitted with thrust washers. The thrust washers in the bearing cap have two locating tabs to keep them from rotating. During assembly the

Before removing the flywheel, mark its position. It should be returned to its original position

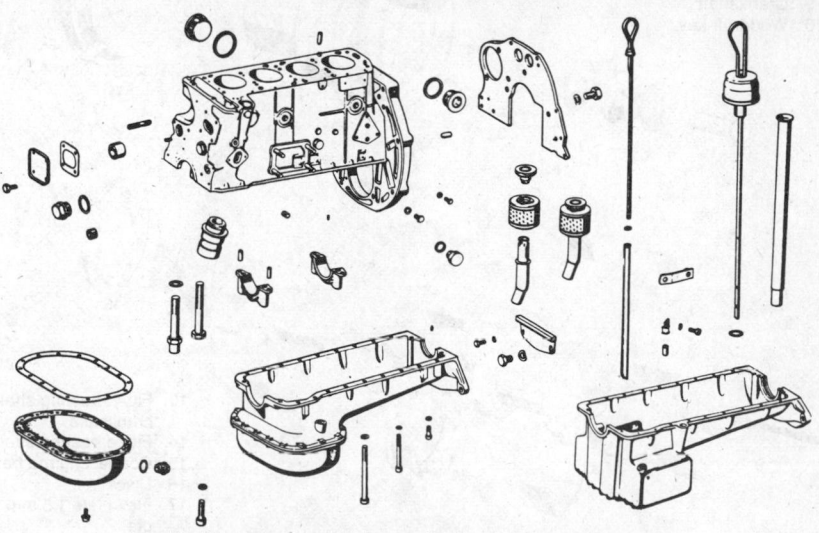

4-cylinder gasoline engine cylinder block components

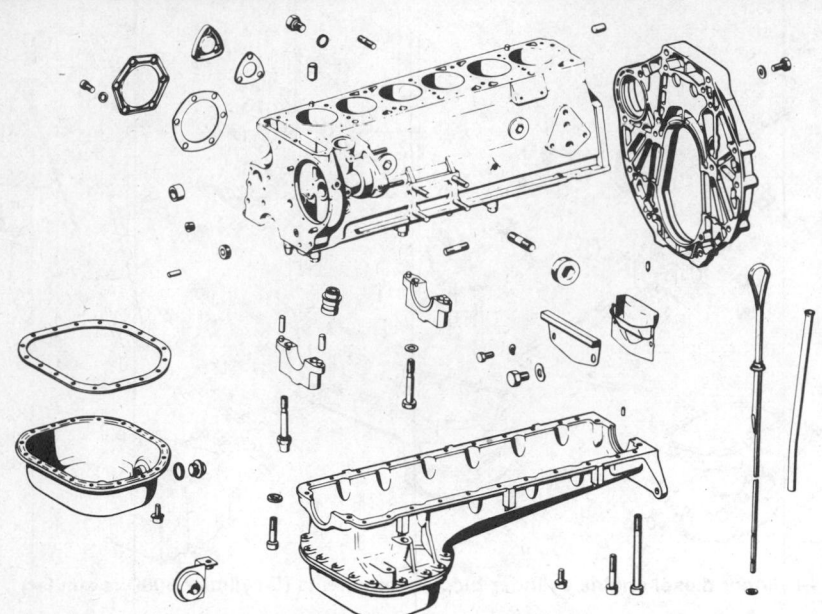

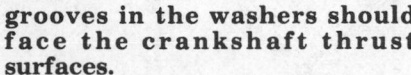

6-cylinder engine block components

Check the oil pipes (arrow) on a V8 engine.

grooves in the washers should face the crankshaft thrust surfaces.

4. Disassembly the oil pump and check the gear backlash. Place a straightedge on the cover and check for warpage. Deep scoring on the cover usually indicates that metal or dirt particles have been circulating through the oil system. Covers can be machined, but it is best to replace them is damaged.

5. Install the oil pump.

6. Install the oil pan and lower crankcase and tighten the bolts even-ly all around, then turn the engine right side up and install the cylinder head gasket and head. Make sure the gasket surfaces are clean before installation; a small dirt particle could cause gasket failure. Tighten the cylinder head bolt in sequence, in stages, to insure against distortion. Don't forget the small bolts at the front of the head.

7. Install the engine into the vehicle.

NOTE: It is a good practice to use a good break-in oil after an engine overhaul. Be sure that all fluids have been replaced and perform a general tune-up. Check the valve timing.

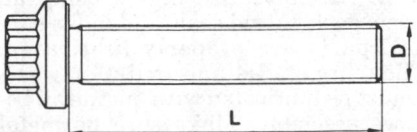

Measure the distance (L) to determine the main bearing cap bolt "stretch" on the 1985–88 190D

1. Screw
2. Cup washers
3. Screw
4. Pulley
5. Vibration damper
6. Hub
7. Crankshaft sprocket
8. Crankshaft
9. Woodruff key
10. Crankshaft bearing shell in cylinder crankcase
11. Crankshaft bearing shell in cylinder crankcase
12. Crankshaft bearing shell in bearing cap

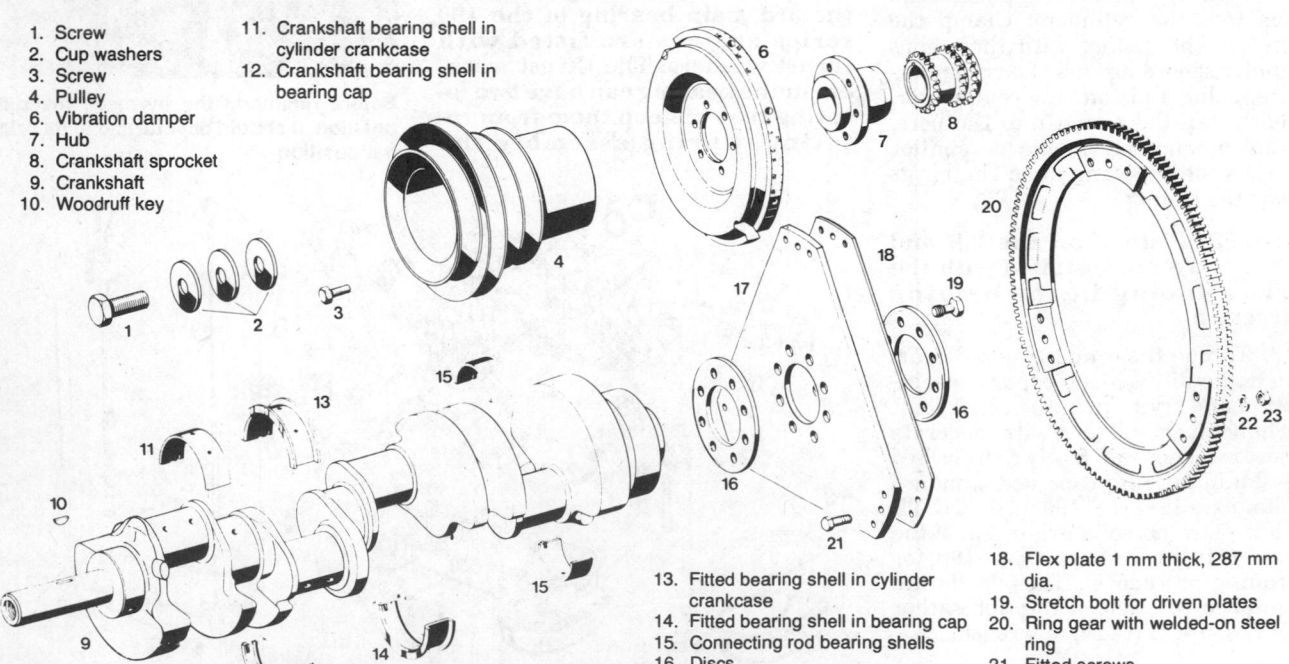

13. Fitted bearing shell in cylinder crankcase
14. Fitted bearing shell in bearing cap
15. Connecting rod bearing shells
16. Discs
17. Flex plate 1.5 mm thick, 296 mm dia.
18. Flex plate 1 mm thick, 287 mm dia.
19. Stretch bolt for driven plates
20. Ring gear with welded-on steel ring
21. Fitted screws
22. Spring washer
23. Nut

Exploded view of the V8 crankshaft assembly

On V8 models, dress the inside of the vibration damper hub before reinstalling. This will allow you to "feel" the key when installing. On early models, the key extends only 1/3 of the length of the keyway; on later models, ½ the length of the keyway.

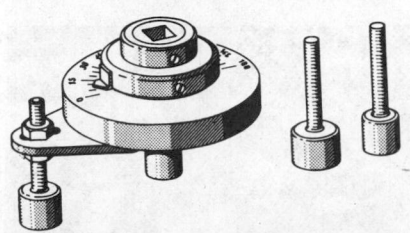

Preferred tools for torquing by angle rotation. A torque wrench is also needed.

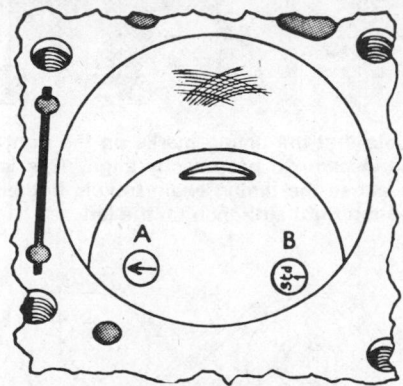

Pistons normally are marked with an arrow (a) indicating front and a weight or size marking (b).

Valve Timing

Ideally, this operation should be performed by a dealer who is equipped with the necessary tools and knowledge to do the job properly.

Checking valve timing is too inaccurate at the standard tappet clearance; therefore timing values are given for an assumed tappet clearance of 0.4mm. The engines are not measured at 0.4mm but rather at 2mm.

1. To check the timing, remove the rocker arm cover and spark plugs. Remove the tensioning springs. On the 6 cylinder engine install the testing thrust pieces. Eliminate all valve clearance.

2. Install a degree wheel.

Check the connecting rod bolts

NOTE: If the degree wheel is attached to the camshaft as shown, values read from it must be doubled.

3. A pointer must be made out of a bent section of $3/16$ in. brazing rod or coathanger wire, and attached to the engine.

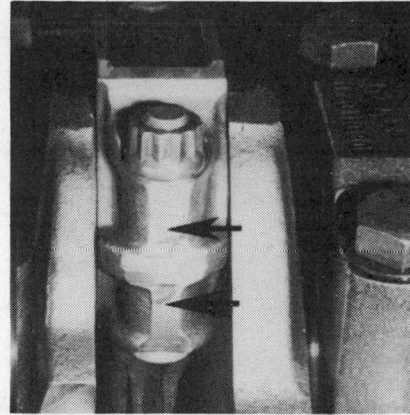

Match mark the connecting rod bearing caps.

4. With a 22mm wrench on the crankshaft pulley, turn the engine in the direction of rotation until the TDC mark on the vibration damper registers with the pointer and the distributor rotor points to the No. 1 cylinder mark on the housing. The camshaft timing marks should align at this point.

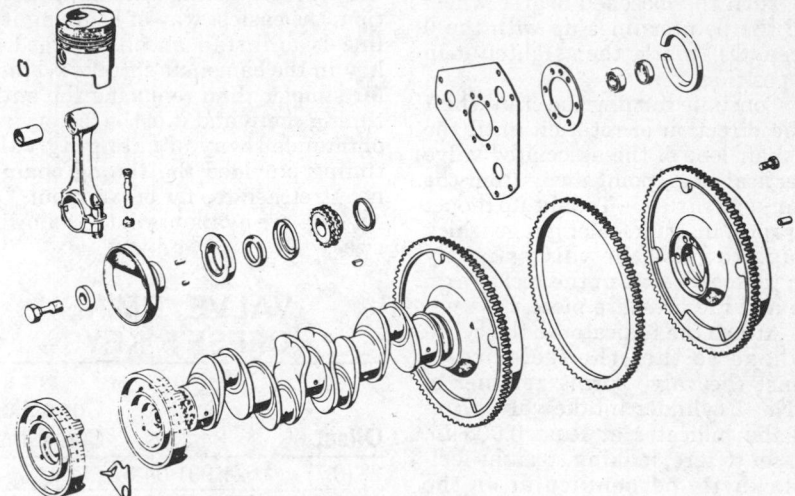

4-cylinder diesel engine components (5-cylinder is similar).

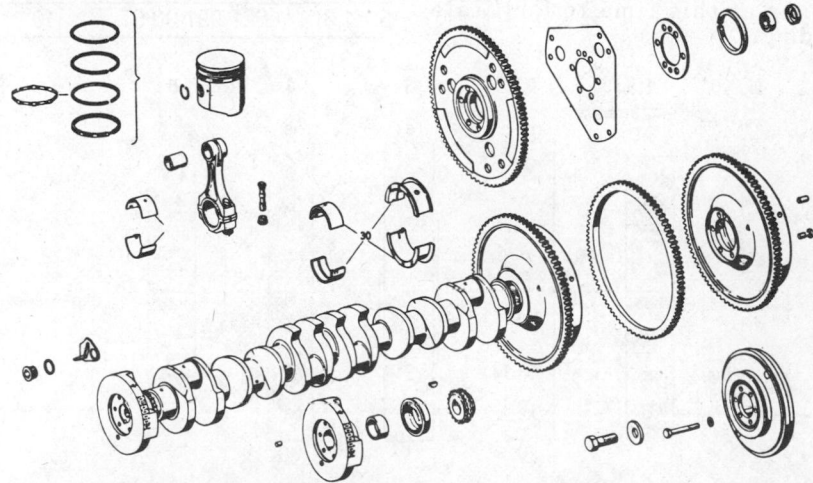

6 cylinder DOHC crankshaft and components (other engine similar)

Piston marking on 3.8 V8

NOTE: Due to the design of the chain tensioner on V8 engines, the right side of the chain travels slightly farther than the left side. This means the right-side cam will be almost 7 degrees retarded compared to the left side, and both marks will not simultaneously align.

5. Turn the loosened degree wheel until the pointer lines up with the 0 degree (OT) mark, then tighten it in this position.

6. Continue turning the crankshaft in the direction of rotation until the camshaft lobe of the associated valve is vertical (e.g., point away from the rocker arm surface). To take up tappet clearance, insert a feeler gauge (thick enough to raise the valve slightly from its seat) between the rocker arm cone and the pressure piece.

7. Attach the indicator to the cylinder head so that the feeler rests against the valve spring retainer of the No. 1 cylinder intake valve. Preload the indicator at least 0.008 in. then set to zero, making sure the feeler is exactly perpendicular on the valve spring retainer. It may be necessary to bleed down the chain tensioner at this time to facilitate readings.

8. Turn the crankshaft in the normal direction of rotation, again using a wrench on the crankshaft pulley, until the indicator reads 0.016 in. less than zero reading.

9. Note the reading of the degree wheel at this time, remembering to double the reading if the wheel is mounted to the camshaft sprocket.

10. Again turn the crankshaft until the valve is closing and the indicator again reads 0.016 in. less than zero reading. Make sure, at this time, that preload has remained constant, then note the reading of the degree wheel. The difference between the two degree wheel reading is the timing angle (number of degrees the valve is open) for that valve.

11. The other valves may be checked in the same manner, comparing them against each other and the opening values given in "Tune-Up Specifications." It must be remembered that turning the crankshaft contrary to the normal direction of rotation results in inaccurate readings and damage to the engine.

12. If valve timing is not to specification, the easiest way of bringing it in line is to install an offset Woodruff key in the camshaft sprocket. This is far simpler than replacing the entire timing chain and it is the factory-recommended way of changing valve timing provided the timing chain is not stretched too far or worn out. Offset keys are available in the following sizes:

VALVE TIMING OFFSET KEYS

Offset	Part No.	For a Correction at Crankshaft of
2° (0.7)	621 991 04 67	4°
3°20⁺ (0.9)	621 991 02 67	6½°
4° (1.1)	621 991 01 67	8°
5° (1.3)	621 991 00 67	10°

The V8 timing marks on the left-hand cam

Note that the timing marks on the right-hand cam do not exactly align. This is because the timing chain travels farther on the right side than on the left.

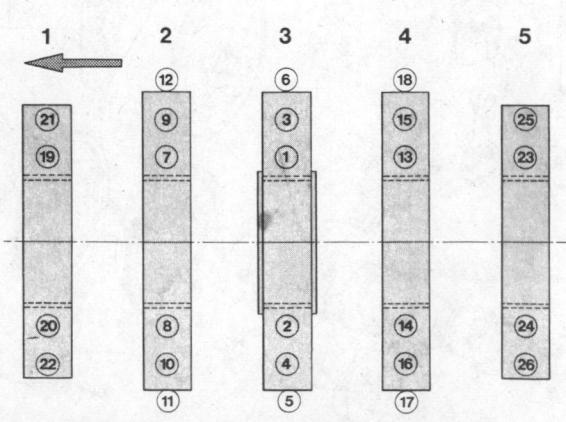

Main bearing cap torque sequence—3.8 liter V-8's

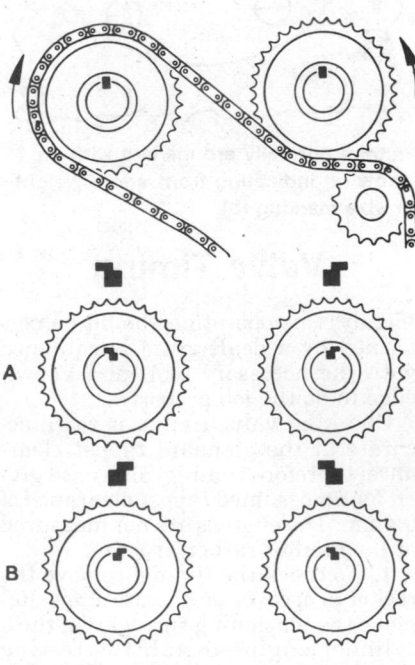

Offset woodruff keys for 6 cylinder DOHC engines

13. The Woodruff key must be installed with the offset toward the right, in the normal direction of rotation, to effect advanced valve opening; toward the left to retard.

14. Advancing the intake valve opening too much can result in piston and/or valve damage (the valve will hit the piston). To check the clearance between the valve head and the piston, the crankshaft must be positioned at 5 degrees ATDC (on intake stroke). The procedure is essentially the same as for measuring valve timing.

15. As before, the dial indicator is set to zero after being preloaded, then the valve is depressed until it touches the top of the piston. As the normal valve head-to-piston clearance is approximately 0.035 in., you can see that the dial indicator must be preloaded at least 0.042 in. so there will be enough movement for the feeler.

If the clearance is much less than 0.035 in., the cylinder head must be removed and checked for carbon deposits. If none exist, the valve seat must be cut deeper into the head. Always set the ignition timing after installing an offset key.

On 6 cylinder DOHC engines, always replace the thrust piece (arrow) if the front seal is replaced. If you don't it will almost always leak. If a new thrust piece is not available, at least remove it and turn it around. This provides a new surface for the seal because the seal does not ride on the centerline of the thrust piece

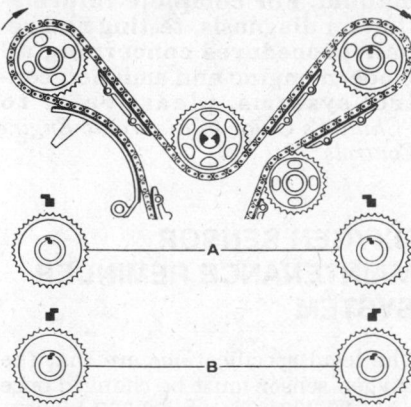

With installation position "A" opening begins earlier
With installation position "B" opening begins later

Offset woodruff keys for V8 engine

ENGINE COOLING

Radiator
REMOVAL & INSTALLATION

1. Remove the radiator cap.
2. Unscrew the radiator drain plug and drain the coolant from the radiator. If all of the coolant in the system is to be drained, move the heater controls to WARM and open the drain cocks on the engine block.

3. If the car is equipped with an oil cooler, drain the oil from the cooler.
4. If equipped, loosen the radiator shell.
5. Loosen the hose clips on the top and bottom radiator hoses and remove the hoses from the connections on the radiator.
6. Unscrew and plug the bottom line on the oil cooler.
7. If the car is equipped with an automatic transmission, unscrew and plug the lines on the transmission cooler.
8. Disconnect the right hand and left hand rubber loops and pull the radiator up and out of the body.
9. Inspect and replace any hoses which have become hardened or spongy.
10. Install the radiator shell and radiator (if the shell was removed) from the top and connect the top and bottom hoes to the radiator.
11. Bolt the shell to the radiator.
12. Attach the rubber loops or position the retaining spring, as applicable.

13. Position the hose clips on the top and bottom hoses.
14. Attach the lines to the oil cooler.
15. On cars with automatic transmissions, connect the lines to the transmission cooler.
16. Move the heater levers to the WARM position and slowly add coolant, allowing air to escape.
17. Check the oil level and fill if necessary. Run the engine for about one minute at idle with the filler neck open.
18. Add coolant to the specified level. Install the radiator cap and turn it until it seats in the second notch. Run the engine and check for leaks.

Water Pump
REMOVAL & INSTALLATION

All Except V8

1. Drain the water from the radiator.
2. Loosen the radiator shell and remove the radiator.

The valve timing marks must align (6 cylinder DOHC shown)

3. Remove the fan with the coupling and set it aside in an upright position.

4. Loosen the belt around the water pump pulley and remove the belt.

5. Remove the bolts from the harmonic balancer and remove the balancer and pulley.

6. Unbolt and remove the water pump.

7. Installation is the reverse of removal. Tighten the belt and fill the cooling system.

NOTE: The coolant feed connection on the 190E–16 is different from that on the other 190E's. The water pump is not interchangeable.

V8 Models

1. Drain the water from the radiator and block.

2. Remove the air cleaner.

3. Loosen and remove the drive belt.

4. Disconnect the upper water hose from the radiator and thermostat housing.

5. Remove the fan and coupling.

6. Remove the hose from the intake (top) connection of the water pump.

7. Set the engine at TDC. Matchmark the distributor and engine and remove the distributor. Crank the engine with a socket wrench on the crankshaft pulley bolt or with a small prybar inserted in the balancer. Crank in the normal direction of rotation only.

8. Turn the balancer so that the recesses provide access to the mounting bolts. Remove the mounting bolts. Rotate the engine in the normal direction of rotation only.

9. Remove the water pump.

10. Clean the mounting surfaces of the water pump and block.

11. Installation is the reverse of removal. Always use a new gasket. Set the engine at TDC and install the distributor rotor points to the notch on the distributor housing. Fill the cooling system and check and adjust the ignition timing.

Thermostat
REMOVAL & INSTALLATION

4 and 5 Cylinder Engines and 6 Cylinder (SOHC) Engines

The thermostat housing is a light metal casting attached directly to the cylinder head, except on the 190D where it is attached to the side of the water pump housing; and the 190E with the 2.6 liter engine, 260E and 300E where it is under a plastic cover atop the water pump.

1. Open the radiator cap and depressurize the system.

2. Open the radiator drain cock and partially drain the coolant. Drain enough coolant to bring the coolant level below the level of the thermostat housing.

3. Remove the four bolts on the thermostat housing cover and remove the cover.

4. Note the installation position of the thermostat and remove it.

5. Installation is the reverse of removal. Be sure that the thermostat is positioned with the ball valve at the highest point and that the 4 bolts are tightened evenly against the seal. On the 190D, the recess in the thermostat casing should be located above the lug in the thermostat housing. On the 190E with 2.6 liter engine, 260E and 300E, the ball valve must be at its highest point in the housing to allow complete venting of gas bubbles.

6. Refill the cooling system and check for leaks.

NOTE: When refilling the coolant system on the 300E, always remove the hex-head plug on the left side of the cylinder head and fill the hole with coolant until it overflows. Install the plug and then fill the coolant system. When filling the coolant system on the 190E with 2.6L and the 260E, open the vent screw on top of the thermostat housing approximately two turns, start the engine run the engine at idle.

6 Cylinder Engines (DOHC)

1. Drain the coolant from the radiator.

2. Remove the vacuum pump and put the pump aside.

3. Remove the three bolts on the thermostat housing.

4. Remove the cover and the thermostat.

5. Installation is the reverse of removal. Install the thermostat so that the ball valve is at the highest point. Refill the cooling system.

V8 Engines

1. Drain the coolant from the radiator and block.

2. Remove the air cleaner.

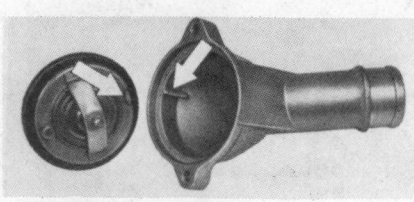

Aligning the thermostat on the 190D

3. Disconnect the battery and remove the alternator.

4. Unscrew the housing cover on the side of the water pump and remove the thermostat.

5. If a new thermostat is to be installed, always install a new sealing ring.

6. Installation is the reverse of removal. Be sure to tighten the screws on the housing cover evenly to prevent leaks. Refill the cooling system and check of leaks.

EMISSION CONTROLS

Please refer to "Emission Control" in the Unit Repair section for system maintenance procedures. Due to the complex nature of modern electronic engine control systems, comprehensive diagnosis and testing procedures fall outside the confines of this repair manual. For complete information on diagnosis, testing and repair procedures concerning all modern engine and emission control systems, please refer to *"Chilton's Guide to Electronic Engine Controls".*

OXYGEN SENSOR MAINTENANCE REMINDER SYSTEM

The legal specifications are that the oxygen sensor must be changed once after 30,000 miles or 50,000 kilometers for Canada vehicles. An "OX-SENSOR" light has been provided to indicate the required change. Once the sensor has been changed, the reminder system is deactivated.

280E and 280CE Models

After replacing the oxygen sensor, locate the in-line mileage counter, under the instrument panel. Disconnect the wiring plug from the counter and leave it disconnected. There is no reset switch provided.

All Other Models

After replacing the oxygen sensor, partially remove the instrument cluster and make the O_2 warning system inoperative by removing the bulb.

GASOLINE FUEL SYSTEM

Fuel Filter

REMOVAL & INSTALLATION

Two types of filters are used, depending on the car model. Both are located between the rear axle and the fuel tank.

1. Unscrew the cover box.
2. Remove the pressure hoses.
3. Loosen the attaching screws and remove the filter. Remove the connecting plug from the old filter and install it on a new filter using a new gasket.
4. Install a new filter in the direction of flow.
5. Replace the attaching screws.
6. Install the pressure hoses.
7. Install the fuel filter in the holder by positioning it in the center of the transparent holder. Be sure the plastic sleeve between the fuel filter and fuel pump is installed. Galvanic corrosion may occur in cases of direct contact between these components.
8. Replace the cover box and check for proper sealing.

TESTING DELIVERY

1. Remove the wire from the coil to prevent starting.
2. Connect a pressure gauge into the output line of the fuel pump.
3. Crank the engine and read the delivery pressure on the pressure gauge. The pressure should be a constant 1.5–2.5 psi.
4. If the pressure is not within specifications or is erratic, remove the pump for service or for replacement with a new or rebuilt unit. No adjustment is provided.

Electric Fuel Pump

NOTE: Do not confuse the electric fuel pump with the injection pump.

All Mercedes-Benz fuel injected engines are equipped with electric fuel pumps. The electric fuel pump is located underneath the rear floor panel. The fuel return line was also eliminated and a check ball installed in its place. The fuel pump uses a replaceable check valve on the outside of the pump which can be replaced separately.

Two types of fuel pumps have been used. One, the large pump, has been replaced with a new small design

which has a bypass system to prevent vapor lock.

REMOVAL & INSTALLATION

1. Jack the left rear of the car and support it on jack stands. This will provide sufficient working clearance.
2. Remove and plug the intake, outlet and bypass lines from the pump.
3. Disconnect the electrical leads.
4. Unbolt and remove the fuel pump and vibration pads.

NOTE: 1986–88 V8s utilize two fuel pumps connected in series.

5. Install the fuel pump in the reverse order of removal. Be sure that the electrical leads are connected to the proper terminals. The negative wire (brown) is connected to the negative terminal (brown plastic plate) and the positive wire (black/red) is connect to the positive terminal (red plastic plate). If the terminals are reversed, the pump will operate in the reverse direction of normal rotation and will deliver no fuel.

TESTING FUEL PUMP DELIVERY PRESSURE

Remove the fuel return hose from the fuel distributor. Connect a fuel line

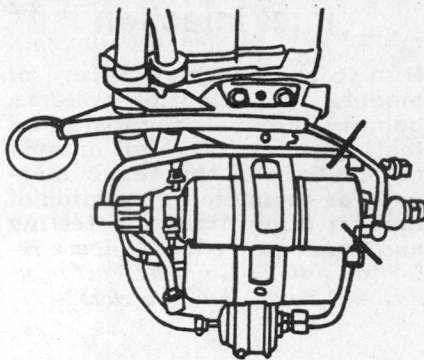

Fuel pump/filter assembly—190E-16 shown, others similar

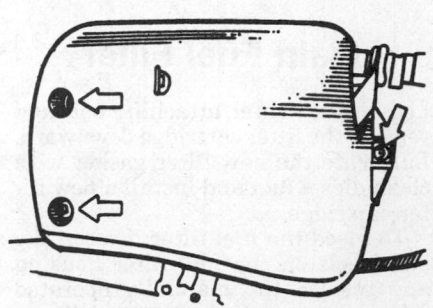

Fuel pump package cover—190 series, 260E and 300E

Some diesel injection pumps have a manually operated delivery pump (1)

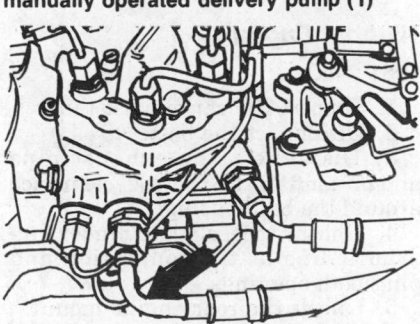

Testing fuel pump pressure

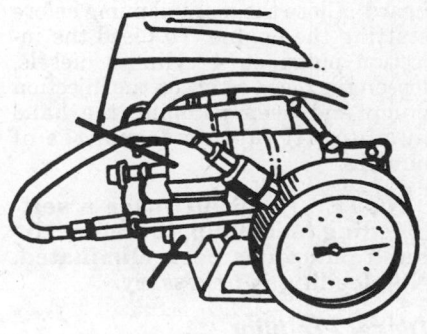

Fuel pump pressure test

and hold the end in the measuring cup. Disconnect the plug from the safety switch on the mixture regulator and turn on the ignition for 30 seconds. If the delivery rate is less than 1 liter in 30 seconds, check the voltage at the fuel pump (11.5v) and the fuel lines for kinks. Disconnect the leak off line between the fuel accumulator and the suction damper. Check the delivery rate again. If it is low, replace the accumulator.

Replace the fuel filter and test again. If still low, replace the fuel pump.

Fuel Injection

Due to the complex nature of modern fuel injection systems, comprehensive diagnosis and testing procedures fall outside the confines of this repair manual. For complete information of fuel injection diagnosis, testing and repair procedures, please refer to *Chilton's Guide To Fuel Injection And Feedback Carburetors.*

DIESEL FUEL SYSTEM

Main Fuel Filter

Loosen the center attaching bolt and remove the filter cartridge downward. Lubricate the new filter gasket with clean diesel fuel and install a new filter cartridge.

To bleed the fuel filter: Loosen the bleed bolt on the fuel filter housing and release the manually operated delivery pump. Operate the delivery pump until the fuel emerges free of bubbles at the bleed screw. Close the bleed bolt and operate the pump until the overflow valve on the injection pump opens (a buzzing noise will be heard). Close the manual pump before starting the engine. To bleed the injection pump on 4 cylinder diesels, loosen the bleed screw on the injection pump and keep pumping the hand pump until fuel emerges free of bubbles.

NOTE: The 190D uses a self-bleeding fuel pump, therefore the hand pump has been eliminated. No bleeding is necessary.

Diesel Pre-filter

Diesel engines use a pre-filter in addition to the main fuel filter, since even

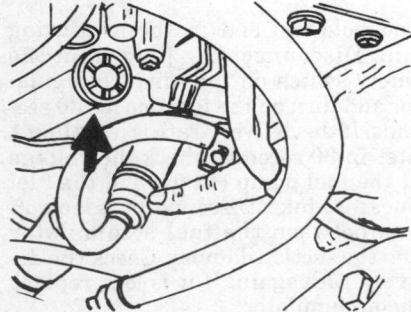

Diesel engines use a pre-filter in addition to the main fuel filter. The arrow indicates the hard operated delivery pump

the most minute particle of dirt will clog the injection system. The pre-filter is located in the line just before it enters the injection pump.

To replace it, simply unscrew the clamps on each end and remove the old filter. Install a new filter and bleed the system (see Main Fuel Filter).

MANUAL TRANSMISSION

REMOVAL & INSTALLATION

With Engine

ALL MODELS

The transmission should only be removed with the engine as a unit, since the transmission-to-clutch housing bolts can only be reached from the inside. Once the engine/transmission unit has been removed from the vehicle, the transmission and bellhousing must be separated from the engine, as follows:

See the "Engine" section to remove the engine/transmission.

1. After removing the engine/transmission unit, unbolt the bellhousing from the engine. The bolts which hold the transmission to the bellhousing cannot be reached except from inside the bellhousing.

2. Remove the starter from its mounting position and pull the transmission and bellhousing from the engine.

3. The bolts which secure the bellhousing to the transmission are now visible and can be removed to separate the bellhousing and transmission.

4. To install, connect the engine, bellhousing, and transmission, after coating the splines of the mainshaft with grease.

5. Install the starter.

6. Further installation is the reverse of removal.

Without Engine

1981 240D

1. Support the car on jackstands.
2. Disconnect the battery.
3. Disconnect the exhaust pipe and/or muffler to provide clearance around the bellhousing.
4. Unhook the slave cylinder hydraulic line at the connection and plug both openings.
5. Unbolt the rear engine mount.
6. Slightly raise the transmission with a jack and remove the lower

plate covering the transmission panel.

7. Disconnect the speedometer cable from the rear of the transmission.

8. Disconnect the shift rods from the transmission shift leavers.

9. Loosen, but do not remove, the intermediate bearing bolts.

10. Matchmark the U-joint and driveshaft coupling and loosen the U-joint.

11. Matchmark the driveshaft flange and adaptor. Loosen the 3 driveshaft bolts. Remove 2 of the bolts and pivot the driveshaft around enough to reinstall the 2 bolts. Remove the third bolt and position the driveshaft rearward as far as the center bearing permits. Use a piece of wood to block the driveshaft up in the driveshaft tunnel. Reinstall the third bolt. The adaptor plate should remain on the 3-legged transmission flange.

12. Remove the starter.

13. Remove all bolts attaching the transmission to the intermediate flange, but remove the upper 2 bolts last.

NOTE: The clutch housing is heavily ribbed. Because of this, most of the bolts can only be reached with a 17 or 19mm insert and extension.

14. Turn the transmission 45 degrees to the left so that the starter domes on both sides of the clutch housing do not scrape the transmission tunnel.

15. Keep the transmission level and slide it out.

16. The clutch housing bolts can only be reached from inside. Unbolt the housing and remove it.

17. Installation is the reverse of removal.

1982–83 240D

1. Disconnect the battery.
2. Disconnect the regulating shaft in the engine compartment.
3. Support the transmission with a floor jack.
4. Unbolt the rear engine mount.
5. Unbolt each side of the engine carrier on the floor frame.
6. Unscrew the exhaust mounting bracket on the transmission. Note the number and positioning of all washers.
7. Unbolt the retaining strap and remove the exhaust pipe bracket.
8. Loosen the clamp nut on the driveshaft.
9. Loosen, but do not remove, the intermediate bearing bolts.
10. Unbolt the driveshaft on the transmission so that the companion plate remains with the driveshaft.
11. Carefully push the driveshaft as far to the rear as permitted.

12. Loosen and remove the tachometer drive shaft on the rear transmission case cover. Unclip the clip for the tachometer drive shaft from its holder.

13. Unscrew the holder for the line to the clutch housing. Unscrew the clutch slave cylinder and move it toward the rear until the pushrod is clear of the housing.

14. Push off the clip locks and then remove the shift rods from the intermediate levers on the shift bracket. Note the position of the disc springs.

> ── **CAUTION** ──
> *When the shift rods are disconnected, do not move the shift lever into reverse or you risk damaging the back-up light switch.*

15. Unbolt the starter and remove it.

16. Remove all transmission-to-intermediate flange screw. Remove the upper two last.

17. Carefully pull the transmission toward the rear of the vehicle and then remove it downward.

> ── **CAUTION** ──
> *Make sure that the input shaft has cleared the clutch plate before tilting the transmission.*

To install:

1. Lightly grease the centering lug and splines on the transmission input shaft.

NOTE: Position the clutch slave cylinder and line above the transmission before beginning installation.

2. Move the transmission into the clutch so that one gear step engages. Rotate the mainshaft back and forth until the splines on the input shaft and clutch plate are aligned.

3. Move the transmission all the way in and then tighten the transmission-to-intermediate flange screws.

4. Install the starter.

5. Install the clutch slave cylinder with the proper plastic shims.

6. Installation of the remaining components is in the reverse order of removal. Please note the following:

   a. After installing the driveshaft, roll the car back and forth and then tighten the intermediate bearing free of tension.

   b. Tighten the driveshaft clamp nut to 22–29 ft. lbs. (30–40 Nm).

   c. Make sure of the proper positioning of all washers, spacers and shims.

190D, 190E, 260E AND 300E

1. Disconnect the battery.

2. Cover the insulation mat in the engine compartment to prevent damage.

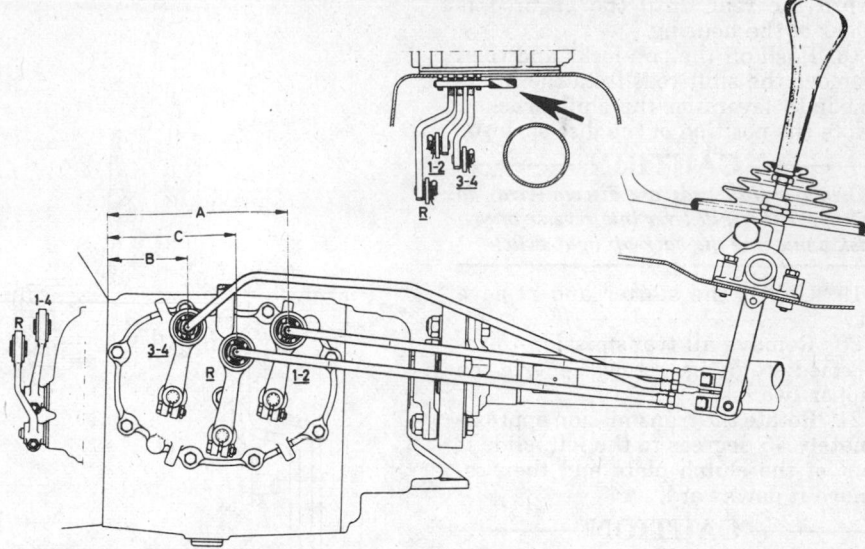

Transmission linkage — 1981 240D. Arrow at top shows locking pin installed prior to adjustment

3. On vehicles equipped with a auxiliary heater, be sure that the water hose is out of the way.

4. Support the transmission with a floor jack.

5. Unbolt the engine mounts at the rear transmission cover.

6. Unbolt the engine carrier on the floor frame.

7. Unscrew the exhaust holder at the transmission. Note the number and positioning of all washers.

8. Unscrew the clamping strap and remove the exhaust pipe holder.

9. Remove the intermediate bearing shield plate.

10. Loosen the clamp nut on the driveshaft.

11. Loosen, but do not remove, the intermediate bearing bolts.

12. Unbolt the driveshaft on the transmission so that the companion plate remains with the driveshaft.

13. Carefully push the driveshaft as far to the rear as permitted.

NOTE: On the 190E, the fitted sleeves on the universal flange must be loosened before separating the flange from the companion plate. This will require a cylindrical mandrel.

14. Disconnect the exhaust system at the rear suspension and suspend it with wire.

15. Loosen and remove the input shaft for the tachometer.

16. Loosen and remove the tachometer drive shaft on the rear transmission case cover. Unclip the clip for the tachometer drive shaft from its holder.

17. Unscrew the holder for the line to the clutch housing. Unscrew the clutch slave cylinder and move it to-

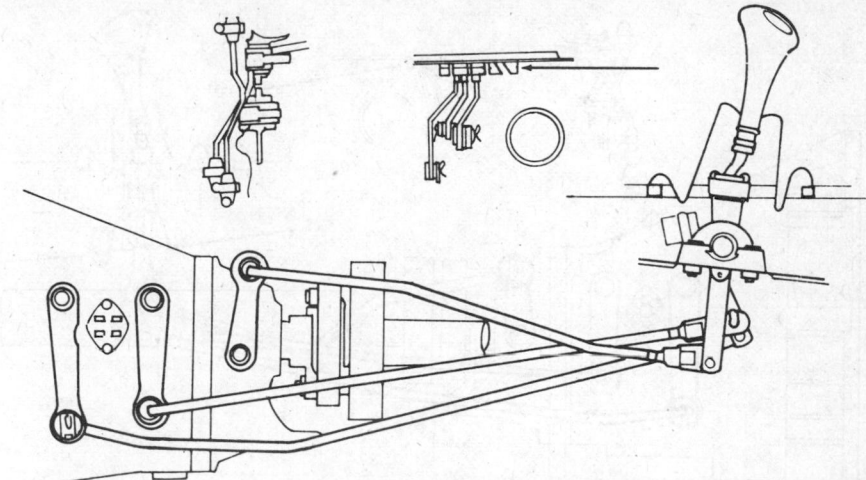

Transmission linkage—1982–83 240D. Arrow at top shows locking rod installed prior to adjustment

ward the rear until the pushrod is clear of the housing.

18. Push off the clip locks and then remove the shift rods from the intermediate levers on the shift bracket. Note the position of the disc springs.

—— CAUTION ——

When the shift rods are disconnected, do not move the shift lever into reverse or you risk damaging the back-up light switch.

19. Unbolt the starter and remove it.

20. Remove all transmission-to-intermediate flange screw. Remove the upper two last.

21. Rotate the transmission approximately 45 degrees to the left, slide it out of the clutch plate and then remove it downward.

—— CAUTION ——

Make sure that the input shaft has cleared the clutch plate before tilting the transmission.

To install:

1. Lightly grease the centering lug and splines on the transmission input shaft.

NOTE: Position the clutch slave cylinder and line above the transmission before beginning installation.

2. Move the transmission into the clutch so that one gear step engages.

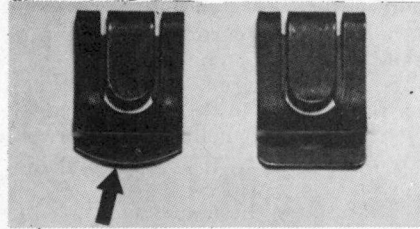

Always use clip locks with curved edges when installing the shift rods on the 190

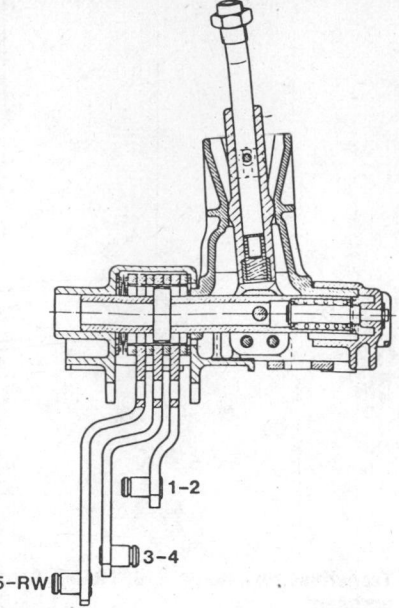

Intermediate lever positioning on the 5 speed 190

Rotate the mainshaft back and forth until the splines on the input shaft and clutch plate are aligned.

3. Move the transmission all the way in and then tighten the transmission-to-intermediate flange screws.

4. Install the starter.

5. Install the clutch slave cylinder with the proper plastic shims.

6. Installation of the remaining components is in the reverse order of removal. Please note the following:

   a. After installing the driveshaft, roll the car back and forth and then tighten the intermediate bearing free of tension.

   b. Tighten the driveshaft clamp nut to 22–29 ft. lbs. (30–40 Nm).

   c. Make sure of the proper positioning of all washers, spacers and shims.

LINKAGE ADJUSTMENT

The only type of shifter used is a floor mounted type.

—— CAUTION ——

On all types of transmissions, never hammer or force a new shift knob on with the shifter installed, as the plastic bushing connected to the lever will be damaged and caused hard shifting.

Proper adjustment of the shift linkage is dependent on both the position of the shift levers at the transmission and the length of the shift rods. The shift levers, rods and bearing block are all located underneath the floor tunnel; the driveshaft shield may have to be removed to gain access to them.

1. With the transmission in neutral and the driveshaft shield removed (if so equipped), remove the clip locks and disconnect the shift rods from the intermediate shift levers under the floor shift bearing bracket.

2. With the shifter still in the neutral position, lock the three intermediate shift levers by inserting a 0.2156 in. rod (a No. 3 drill bit will do, or any other tool of approximately the same diameter) through the levers and the holes in the bearing bracket.

3. Check the position of the shift levers at the transmission (see illustrations). Adjust by loosening the clamp bolts and moving the levers.

4. With the intermediate levers locked and the shift levers adjusted properly, try hooking the shift rods back onto their respective intermediate levers. The shift rods may be adjusted by loosening the locknut and turning the ball socket on the end until they are the proper length.

NOTE: When hooking up the shift rods to the intermediate levers, be very careful not to move the transmission shift levers out of their adjusted position.

When reattaching the shift rods on 190 models, use only clip locks which have a radius edge. If the old style clip locks with a square edge are used, there is a possibility that the locks will pop out and the shift rods will drop down.

5. Remove the locking rod from the bearing bracket, start the engine and then shift through the gears a few times. Occasionally slight binding may call for VERY slight further adjustments.

OVERHAUL

For all manual transmission overhaul procedures, please refer to the "Manual Transmission" in the Unit Repair section.

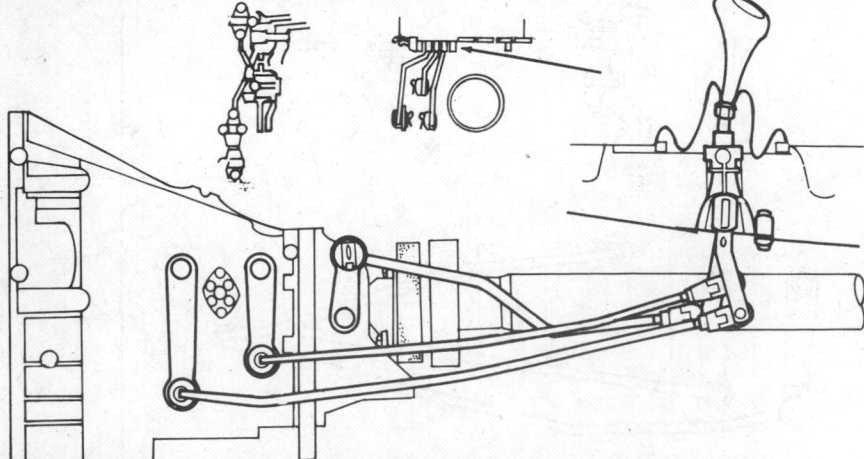

Transmission linkage—190 (4 speed shown, 5 speed similar). Arrow at top shows locking rod installed prior to adjustment

CLUTCH

REMOVAL & INSTALLATION

1. To remove the clutch, first remove the transmission and bell housing.

2. Loosen the clutch pressure plate holddown bolts evenly, 1–1½ turns at a time, until tension is relieved. Never remove one bolt at a time, as damage to the pressure plate is possible.

3. Examine the flywheel surface for blue heat marks, scoring, or cracks. If the flywheel is to be machined, always machine both sides.

4. To reinstall, coat the splines with high temperature grease and place the clutch disc against the flywheel, centering it with a clutch pilot shaft. A wooden shaft, available at automotive jobbers, is satisfactory, but an old transmission mainshaft works best.

5. Tighten the pressure plate holddown bolts evenly, 1–1½ turns at a time, until tight, then remove the pilot shaft.

——————— CAUTION ———————

Most clutch plates have the flywheel side marked as such (Kupplungsseite). Do not assume that the pressure springs always face the transmission.

Clutch Master Cylinder

REMOVAL & INSTALLATION

1. Remove cover under instrument panel at left.
2. Remove floor mat at left.
3. To prevent contamination inside vehicle, draw fluid from respective chamber of combination clutch and expansion tank.
4. Unscrew line on master cylinder.
5. Pull off connecting hose on combination brake and clutch expansion tank.
6. Loosen piston rod for brake unit (brake booster) on brake pedal.
7. Pull cable plug from stop light switch.
8. Unscrew nuts for attaching pedal carrier to fire wall.
9. Move pedal assembly to the rear until screw plate of pedal carrier is free from threaded bolt of brake unit (brake booster) and holder at top on water tank.
10. Remove pedal assembly in downward direction, while paying attention to connecting hose for master cylinder and remove master cylinder.
11. To install, return any fallen rubber mounts, reverse removal procedure and bleed clutch actuation.

Clutch Slave Cylinder

REMOVAL & INSTALLATION

1. Detach and plug the pressure line from the slave cylinder.
2. Remove the attaching screws from the slave cylinder.
3. Remove the slave cylinder, pushrod, and spacer.
4. To install, place the grooved side of the spacer in contact with the housing and hold it in position.
5. Install the slave cylinder and pushrod into the housing. Be sure that the dust cap is properly seated.
6. Install the attaching screws.
7. Connect the pressure line to the slave cylinder.
8. Bleed the slave cylinder.

BLEEDING THE SLAVE CYLINDER

The same principle is used as in bleeding the brakes.

1. Check the brake fluid level in the compensating tank and fill to maximum level.
2. Put a hose on the bleeder screw of the right front caliper and open the bleeder screw.
3. Have a helper depress the brake pedal until the hose is full and there are no air bubbles. Be sure that the bleeder screw is closed each time the pedal is released.
4. Put the free end of the hose on the bleeder screw of the slave cylinder and open the bleeder screw.
5. Keep stepping on the brake pedal. Close the bleeder screw on the caliper and release the brake pedal. Open the bleeder screw and repeat the process until no air bubbles show up at the mouth of the inlet line of the compensating tank. Between operations, check and, if necessary, refill the compensating tank.
6. Close the bleeder screws on the caliper and slave cylinder and remove the hose.
7. Check the clutch operation and the fluid level.

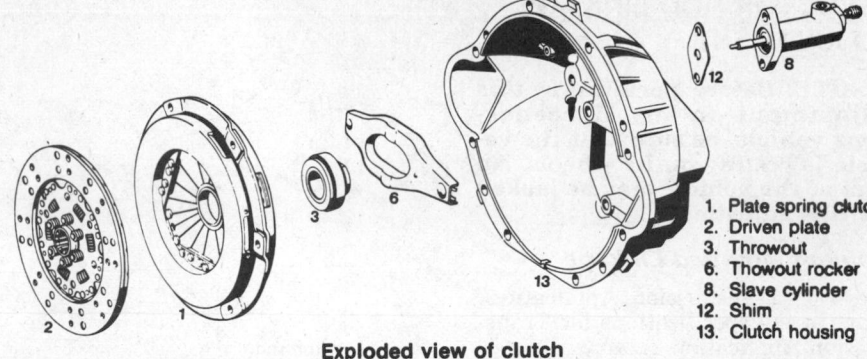

Exploded view of clutch

1. Plate spring clutch
2. Driven plate
3. Throwout
6. Thowout rocker
8. Slave cylinder
12. Shim
13. Clutch housing

AUTOMATIC TRANSMISSION

REMOVAL & INSTALLATION

Mercedes-Benz automatic transmissions are removed as a unit with the engine. Consult the "Engine Mechanical" section for removal and installation procedures concerning a given engine.

PAN AND FILTER REPLACEMENT

1. Drain the transmission of all fluid by loosening the dipstick tube.
2. Remove the transmission pan.
3. Remove the bolt or bolts which retain the filter to the transmission.
4. Remove the filter and replace it with a new one.
5. Install the transmission pan, using a new gasket.
6. Refill the transmission to the proper level with the specified brand of fluid.

Bottom view of automatic transmission showing dipstick tube (1), converter drain plug (2) and pan (3)

SELECTOR ROD LINKAGE ADJUSTMENT

NOTE: Before performing this adjustment on any Mercedes-Benz vehicle, be sure that the vehicle is resting on its wheels. No part of the vehicle may be jacked for this adjustment.

Column Mounted Linkage

See the "Transmission Application" chart in the specifications for Transmission Application.

W3A 040 (380SEL ONLY) AND W4A 040

1. Loosen the counternut on the rear selector rod while holding both recesses of the front selector rod with an open end wrench.
2. Disconnect the selector rod from the selector lever.
3. Set the selector lever on the transmission and on the column to Neutral.
4. Adjust the selector rod until the bearing pin is aligned with the bearing bushing in the selector lever.
5. Connect the rear selector lever to the selector rod and secure it with the lock. Be sure that the clearance of the selector lever in D and S is equal.
6. Tighten the locknut on the rear selector rod while holding the front selector rod as in Step 1.

Floor Mounted Linkage

NOTE: The vehicle must be standing with the weight normally distributed on all four wheels. No jacks may be used.

1. Disconnect the selector rod from the selector lever.

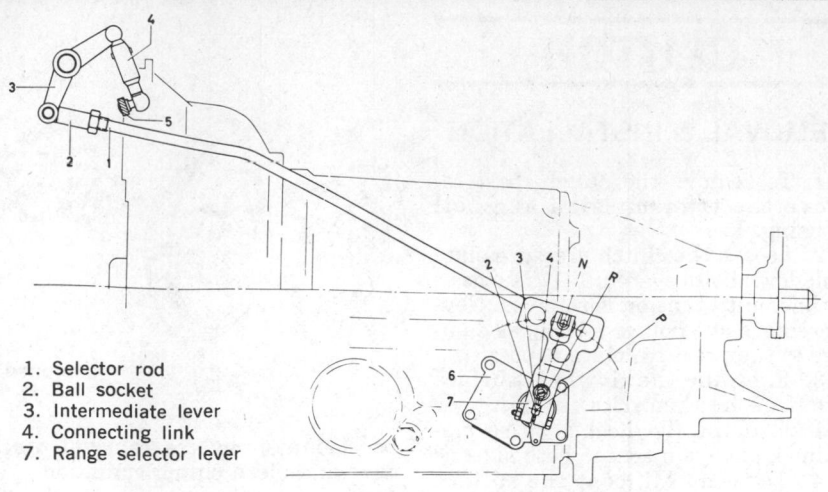

1. Selector rod
2. Ball socket
3. Intermediate lever
4. Connecting link
7. Range selector lever

Column mounted selector rod linkage—W3A 040

2. Set the selector lever in Neutral and make sure that there is approximately 1mm clearance between the selector lever and the N stop of the selector gate.
3. Adjust the length of the selector rod so that it can be attached free of tension.
4. Retighten the counternut.

STARTER LOCKOUT AND BACK-UP LIGHT SWITCH ADJUSTMENT

1. Disconnect the selector rod and move the selector lever on the transmission to position Neutral.
2. Tighten the clamping screw prior to making adjustments.
3. Loosen the adjusting screw and insert the locating pin through the driver into the locating hole in the shift housing.

4. Tighten the adjusting screw and remove the locating pin.
5. Move the selector lever to position N and connect the selector rod so that there is no tension.
6. Check to be sure that the engine cannot be started in Neutral or Park.

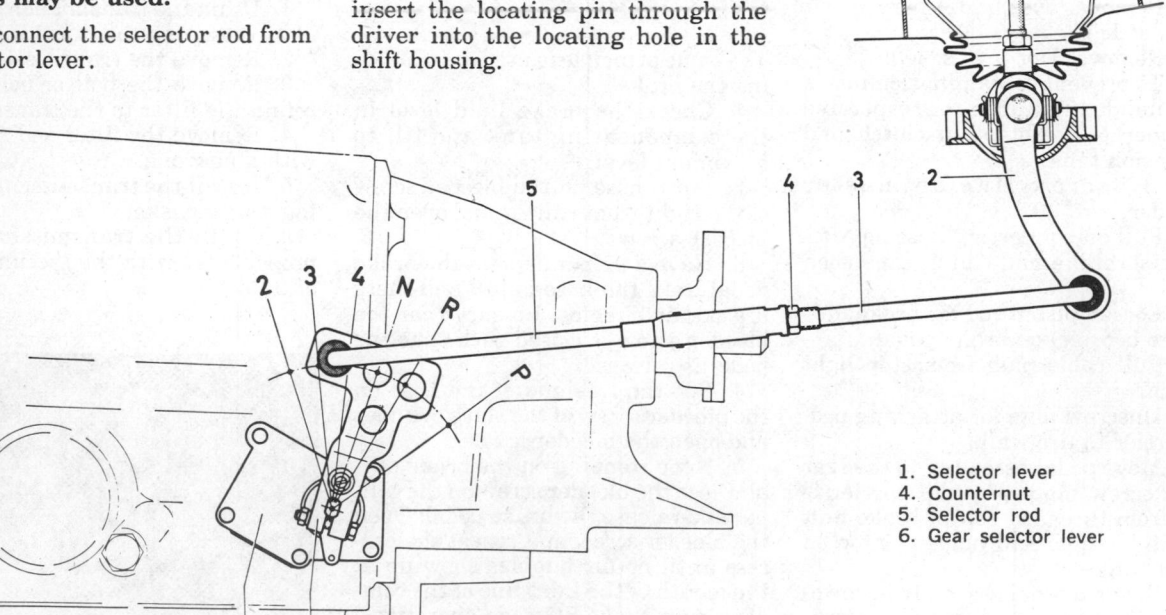

1. Selector lever
4. Counternut
5. Selector rod
6. Gear selector lever

Floor mounted selector rod linkage

KICKDOWN SWITCH

1. The kickdown position of the solenoid valve is controlled by the accelerator pedal.

2. Push the accelerator pedal against the kickdown limit stop. In this position the throttle lever should rest against the full load stop of the venturi control unit.

3. Adjustments are made by loosening the clamping screw on the return lever on the accelerator pedal shaft and turning the shaft. Tighten the clamping screw again.

CONTROL PRESSURE ROD

280E and 280CE

1. Disconnect the control pressure rod.

9. Accelerator pedal
10. Kickdown switch
11. Return lever

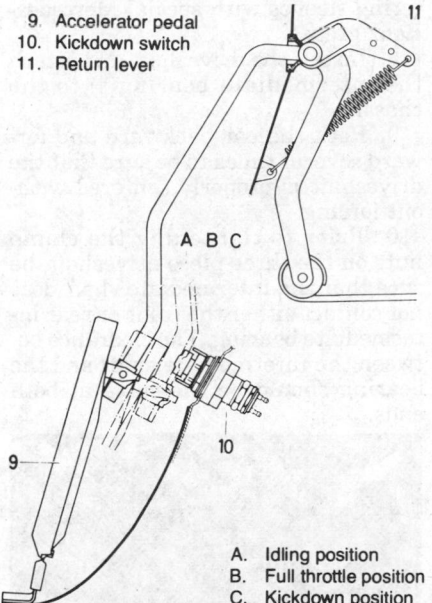

A. Idling position
B. Full throttle position
C. Kickdown position

Kickdown switch adjustment

57. Control pressure rod
58. Ball socket
59. Counternut
120. Angle lever
144. Connecting rod

Control pressure rod adjustment — 6 cylinder DOHC engines

5. Bearing bracket
6. Starter and backup light switch
7. Selector lever
8. Rear selector rod

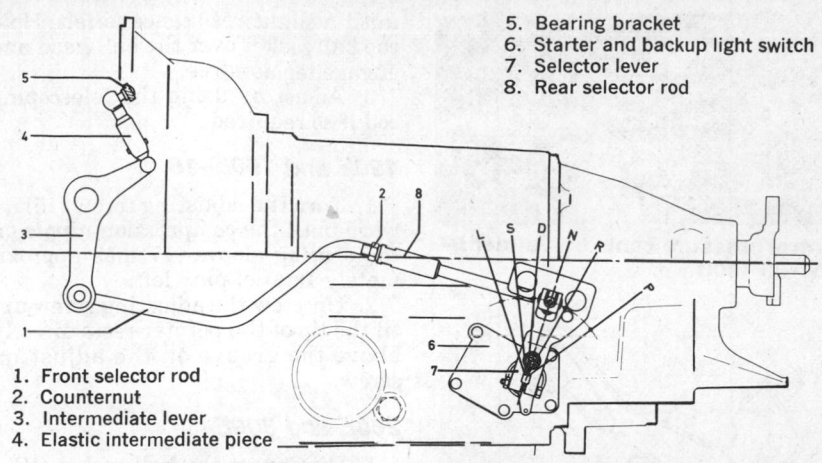

1. Front selector rod
2. Counternut
3. Intermediate lever
4. Elastic intermediate piece

Selector rod linkage on the W4A 040 and W4B 025

2. Push the angle lever in the direction of the arrow.

3. Push the control pressure rod rearward against the stop and adjust its length so there is no binding.

4. Tighten the counternut after adjustment.

CONTROL PRESSURE CABLE

380SE, 380SEC, 380SEL, 380SL, 380SLC, 420SEL, 500SEC, 500SEL, 560SEC, 560SEL and 560SL

1. Remove the air cleaner.
2. Loosen the clamping screw.
3. Push the ball socket back, then carefully forward until a slight resistance is felt. At this point, tighten the clamp screw.
4. Install the air cleaner.

Turbodiesels

1. Pry off the ball socket.
2. Push the ball socket back, then pull carefully forward until a slight resistance is felt.
3. Hold the ball socket above the ball head. The drag lever should rest against the stop.

1. Selector range lever
2. Washer
3. Adjusting screw
4. Shaft
5. Locating pin
6. Clamping screw

(a)—Column shift for left-hand and right-hand drive vehicles 220/8, 220 D/8, 230/8, 280 S/8, 280 SE/8 and 300 SEL/8.

(b)—Steering wheel shift for left-hand drive vehicles (220/8, 220 D/8, 230/8, 250/8)

(c)—Steering wheel shift for right-hand drive vehicles (220/8, 220 D/8, 230/8, 250/8)

(d)—Steering wheel shift for left-hand drive vehicles (280S/8, 280 SE/8, 300 SEL/8, 280 SE/3.5 and 300 SEL/3.5)

7. Roller
11. Connecting rod
12. Bearing bracket
13. Control pressure rod
17. Regulating lever
18. Stop pin
19. Gate lever
20. Angle lever
31. Connecting rod

Control pressure rod adjustment — V8 engines

4. Adjust the cable at the adjusting screw so that the ball socket can be attached with no strain.

190D

1. Remove the ball socket (19) and extend the telescoping rod (8) to its full length.

2. Pull the control cable forward

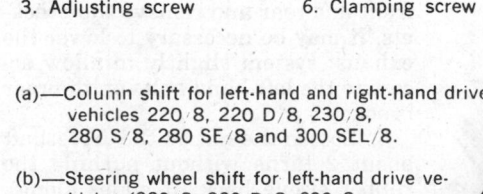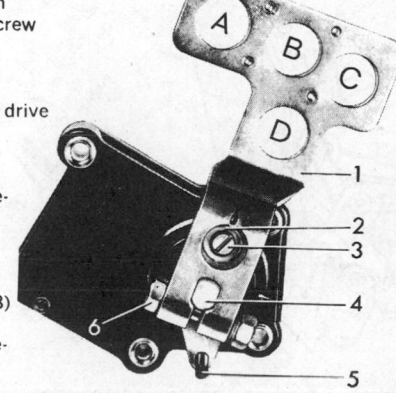

Starter lockout and backup light switch adjustment

Control pressure cable adjustment—1984–85 190D

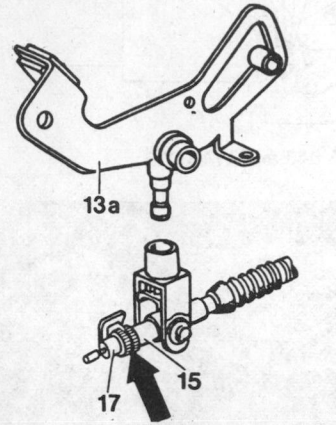

Control pressure cable adjustment—190E SOHC

Control pressure cable adjustment on the 260E and 300E

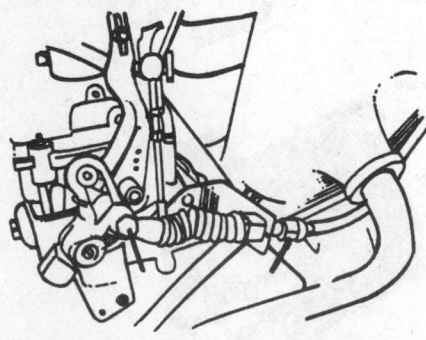

Control pressure cable adjustment—1986–88 300 series turbodiesel

until a slight resistance is felt. Hold the ball socket over the ball head and engage tension free.

3. Adjust by using the telescoping rod if so required.

190E and 190E–16

1. Turn the adjusting screw (15) inward until the compression nipple on the spacing sleeve (17) has approximately 1mm of play left.

2. Unscrew the adjusting screw until the tip of the pointer rests directly above the groove on the adjusting screw.

260E and 300E

1. Disconnect the ball socket (19).

2. Pull the control pressure cable forward until a slight resistance is felt. In this position, hold the ball socket above the ball and engage the two, free of tension.

3. Adjust by turning the screw (15) if required.

DRIVE AXLE

Mercedes-Benz automobiles use either two or three piece driveshaft to connect the transmission to a hypoid independent rear axle. All models covered in this book use independent rear suspension with open or enclosed driveshaft to the rear wheels.

Driveshaft and U-Joints

REMOVAL & INSTALLATION

1981–85 240D, 300D, 300CD, 300TD, 280E and 280CE

Matchmark all dirveshaft connections prior to removal.

1. Remove the equalizer and disconnect the parking brake cables.

2. Remove the bolts which secure the two brackets to the chassis at the front and rear and remove the brackets. It may be necessary to lower the exhaust system slightly to allow access to the left hand bolts on the rear bracket.

3. Loosen the nut on the driveshaft about 2 turns without pushing the rubber sleeve back (it slides along). On a two-piece shaft, only loosen the front clamp nut.

4. Remove the nuts which secure the attaching plate to the transmission flange and rear axle.

NOTE: A new coupling flange is used on 1981 280E and 280CE models. The new coupling flanges uses a thinner washer in place of the previous self-locking hex nut and thicker washers. Do not mix the two types.

5. Remove the bolts which secure the intermediate bearing (s) to the chassis. Push the driveshaft together and slightly down, and remove the driveshaft from the vehicle.

NOTE: If possible, do not separate the parts of the driveshaft since each driveshaft is balanced at the factory. If separation is necessary, all parts must be marked and reassembled in the same relative positions to assure that the driveshafts will remain reasonably well balanced.

6. Installation is the reverse of removal.

7. Pack the cavities of the two centering sleeves with special Mercedes-Benz grease.

8. Install the driveshaft and attach the intermediate bearing(s) to the chassis.

9. Rock the car backward and forward several times to be sure that the driveshaft is properly centered without forcing.

10. Prior to tightening the clamp nuts on the three piece driveshaft, be sure that the intermediate shaft does not contact either the front or rear intermediate bearing. The clearance between the intermediate shaft and the bearing should be the same at both ends.

1981 driveshafts use a new design coupling flange with thinner washers

All Other Models

NOTE: Steps 1–3 apply to 4 cylinder and V8 models. Matchmark all driveshaft connections prior to removal.

1. Fold the torsion bar down after disconnecting the level control linkage (if equipped).

2. Remove the exhaust system.

3. Remove the heat shield from the frame.

4. Support the transmission with a jack and completely remove the rear engine mount crossmember.

5. Without sliding the rubber

sleeve back, loosen the clamp nut approximately two turns (the rubber sleeve will slide along).

NOTE: On 3 piece driveshafts, only the front clamp nut need be loosened.

6. Unscrew the U-joint mounting flange from the U-joint plate.

NOTE: The 1981–83 380SEL and 380SEC uses a new design coupling flange with thinner washers under a new hex nut. The previous design used thicker washers. Do not mix the two types.

7. Bend back the locktabs and remove the bolts that attach the driveshaft to the rear axle pinion yoke.

8. Remove the bolts which attach the intermediate bearing(s) to the frame. Push the driveshaft together slightly and remove it from the vehicle.

9. Try not to separate the driveshafts. If it is absolutely necessary, matchmark all components so that they can be reassembled in the same order.

10. Installation is the reverse of removal. Always use new self-locking nuts. After the driveshaft is installed, rock the car back and forth several times to settle the driveshaft. Make sure that neither intermediate shaft is binding against either intermediate bearing, and that the clearance between the intermediate bearing and the driveshaft is the same at both ends.

Rear Axle Shafts

NOTE: The rubber covered joints are filled with special oil. If they are disassembled for any reason, they must be refilled with special oil.

REMOVAL & INSTALLATION

All Except 190D, 190E, 260E, 300E, 300SDL, 420SEL, 380SEC, 500SEC, 560SEC, 560SEL, 1987–88 300D and 300TD

MODELS WITHOUT TORQUE COMPENSATOR (TORSION BAR)

NOTE: On the 280E only, axle shafts identified with a yellow paint dot or part No. 107 350 07 10 (left) or Part No. 107 350 0810 (right) can be installed.

Most models do not use a torque compensator (torsion bar) which is actually a steel bar used to locate the rear axle under acceleration. In general, only the large sedans use a torque compensator, but it is wise to check for one prior to servicing the axle shaft. The illustrations apply to either type.

1. Jack up the rear of the car and remove the wheel and center axle hold-down bolt (in hub).
2. Remove the brake caliper and suspend it from a hook.
3. Drain the differential oil and place a jack under the differential housing.
4. Unbolt the rubber mount from the chassis and the differential housing, then remove the differential housing cover to expose the ring and pinion gears.
5. Press the shaft from the axle flange. If necessary, loosen the shock absorber.
6. Using a pry bar, remove the axle lock ring inside the differential case.
7. Pull the axle from the housing by pulling the splined end from the side gears, with the spacer.

NOTE: Axle shafts are stamped R and L for right and left units. Always use new lockrings.

8. Installation is the reverse of removal. Fill the rear axle. New radial seal rings are used on all models. Lubricate the outside diameter of rubber covered radial sealing rings with hypoid gear lubricant prior to installation.

———— **CAUTION** ————

Check end-play of the lockring in the groove. If necessary, install a thicker lockring or spacer to eliminate all end-play, while still allowing the lockring to rotate. Do not allow the joints in the axle shaft to hang free or the joint bearing may be damaged and leak.

MODELS WITH TORQUE COMPENSATOR (TORSION BAR)

1. Drain the oil from the rear axle.
2. Disconnect and plug the brake lines.
3. Loosen the connecting rod and unscrew the torsion bar bearing bracket. Lower the exhaust system slightly and remove the torsion bar.
4. Loosen the shock absorber.
5. Remove the bolt which attaches the rear axle shaft to the rear axle shaft flange.
6. Disconnect the brake cable control. Remove the bracket from the wheel carrier, remove the rubber sleeve, and push back the cover.
7. Force the rear axle shaft out of the flange with a suitable tool.
8. Support the rear axle with a jack.
9. Remove the rubber mount.
10. Clean the axle housing and remove the cover fan from the housing.

NOTE: The axle shafts are the floating type and can be compressed in the constant velocity joints.

11. Remove the locking ring from the end of the axle shafts which engage the side gears in the differential.
12. Disengage the axle shaft from the side gear and remove the axle shaft together with the spacer.

———— **CAUTION** ————

Do not hang the outer constant velocity joint in a free position (without any support) as the shaft may be damaged and the constant velocity joint housing may leak.

13. Installation is the reverse of removal.
14. If either axle shaft is replace, be sure that the proper replacement shaft is installed. Axle shafts are marked L and R for left and right.
15. Check the end-play between the lock-ring on the axle shaft and the side gear. There should be no noticeable end-play, but the lock-ring should be able to turn in the groove.
16. Be sure to bleed the brakes and fill the rear axle with the proper quantity and type of lubricant. New radial seal rings are used on all models. Lubricate the outside diameter of rubber covered radial seal rings with hypoid gear lubricant prior to installation.

Removing the lock-ring (26) from the axle shaft with pliers (1) or a screwdriver

Lock the collar nut on the 190 at the crush flange (arrow)

190D, 190E, 260E, 300E, 300SDL, 380SEC, 420SEL, 500SEC, 560SEC, 560SEL, 1987–88 300D and 300TD

1. Loosen, but do not remove, the axle shaft collar nut.
2. Raise the rear of the vehicle and support it on jackstands.
3. Disconnect the axle shaft from the hub assembly. On the 190, make sure that while loosening the locking screws, the bit is seated properly in the multi-tooth profile of the screws.
4. Remove the self-locking screws that attach the inner CV-joint to the connecting flange on the differential. Always loosen the screws in a crosswise manner.

NOTE: Make sure that the end cover on the inner CV-joint is not damaged when separated from the connecting flange.

5. While supporting the axle shaft, use a slide hammer or the like and press the axle shaft out of the hub assembly.
6. Tilt the axle shaft down and remove it.

— **CAUTION** —
Make sure that the CV-joint boots are not damaged during the removal process.

7. Installation is in the reverse order of removal. Please note the following:
   a. Always clean the connecting flanges before installation.
   b. Always use new self-locking screws. On the 190, 260E and 300E, lubricate the screw threads and contact faces with oil before installing. Tighten the screws to 51 ft. lbs. (70 Nm) on the 190, 260E and 300E; 51 ft. lbs. (70 Nm)—M10 bolts, 135 Nm (M12 x 1.5 bolts) on the 300D, 300TD, 300SDL, 420SEL, 560SEC and 560SEL and 90–105 ft. lbs. (125–145 Nm) on the others. Always tighten the screws in a crosswise pattern.

Axle shaft markings (r)

c. Tighten the axle shaft collar nut to 203–230 ft. lbs. (280–320 Nm) on the 190 and 22 ft. lbs. (30 Nm) on the others. On the 190, lock the collar nut at the crush flange.

CV-JOINT OVERHAUL
For all CV-joint overhaul procedures, please refer to "CV-Joint Overhaul" in the Unit Repair section.

FRONT SUSPENSION

Shock Absorbers

REMOVAL & INSTALLATION

380SL, 380SLC and 560SL

1. Jack up the front of the car until the weight is off of the wheels and support the car securely on jack stands.
2. When removing the shock absorbers, it is also wise to draw a simple diagram of the location of parts such as lockrings, rubber stops, locknuts and steel plates, since many shock absorbers require their own peculiar installation of these parts.
3. Raise the hood and locate the upper shock absorber mount.
4. Support the lower control arm with a jack.
5. Unbolt the mount for the shock absorber at the top. Remove the coolant expansion tank to allow access to the right front shock absorber.
6. Remove the nuts which secure the shock absorber to the lower control arm.
7. Push the shock absorber piston rod in, install the stirrup, and remove the shock absorber.
8. Remove the stirrup, since this must be install on replacement shock absorber.
9. Installation is the reverse of removal. Always use new bushing when installing replacement shock absorber.

All Other Models (Except 190D, 190E, 260E and 300E)

1. Jack and support the car. Support the lower control arm.
2. Loosen the nuts on the upper shock absorber mount. Remove the plate and ring.
3. Place the shock absorber vertical to the lower control arm and remove the lower mounting bolts.

4. Remove the shock absorber. Be sure to disconnect and plug the pressure line on models with level control.
5. Installation is the reverse or removal. On Bilstein shocks, do not confuse the upper and lower plates.

NOTE: The 1981–83 380SEL shock absorber uses a protective plastic sleeve that must be installed between the lower retainer and lower rubber ring. Also, a slot is provided for holding the piston rod, in place of the 2 flats used previously.

NOTE: 380SEC shock absorbers have the same part number regardless of manufacturer. However, the shock absorbers of these cars have a larger diameter and narrower lower mounting eye than other models.

Damper Strut

REMOVAL & INSTALLATION

190D, 190E, 260E and 300E

1. Raise the front of the vehicle and support it with jackstands. Remove the wheel.
2. Using a spring compressor, compress the spring until any load is removed from the lower control arm.

NOTE: When using a spring compressor, be sure that a least 7½ coils are engaged before applying tension.

3. Support the lower control arm with a floor jack. Loosen the retaining bolt for the upper end of the damper strut by holding the inner piston rod with an Allen wrench and then unscrewing the nut. NEVER use an impact wrench on the retaining nut.

— **CAUTION** —
Never unscrew the nut with the axle half at full rebound — the spring may fly out with considerable force. causing personal injury.

4. Unbolt the two screws and one nut and then disconnect the lower damper strut from the steering knuckle.
5. Remove the strut down and forward. Be sure to disconnect and plug the pressure line on models with level control. Secure the steering knuckle in position so that it won't tilt.
6. Installation is in the reverse order of removal. Please note the following:
   a. When attaching the lower end of the damper strut to the steering knuckle, first position all three screws; next tighten the two lower screws to 72 ft. lbs. (100 Nm); finally, tighten the nut on the upper

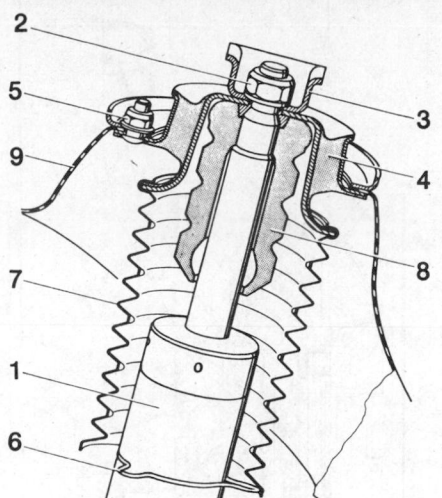

1. Damper strut
2. Hex. nut
3. Rebound stop
4. Rubber mount
5. Hex. nuts
6. Stop ring
7. Sleeve
8. Additional PU spring
9. Front end

Upper damper strut mounting — 190D, 190E, 260E and 300E

clamping connection screw to 54 ft. lbs. (75 Nm).

b. Tighten the retaining nut on the upper end of the damper strut to 44 ft. lbs. (60 Nm).

Springs

REMOVAL & INSTALLATION

190D, 190E, 260E and 300E

1. Raise the front of the vehicle and support it jackstands. Remove the wheel.

2. Remove the engine compartment lining underneath the vehicle (if so equipped).

3. Install a spring compressor so that at least 7½ coils are engaged.

4. Support the lower control arm with a floor jack and then loosen the retaining nut at the upper end of the damper strut.

—— CAUTION ——

NEVER loosen the damper strut retaining nut unless the wheels are on the ground, the control arm is supported or the springs have been removed.

5. Lower the jack under the control arm slightly and then remove the spring toward the front.

6. On installation, position the spring between the control arm and the upper mount so that when the control arm is raised, the end of the lower coil will be seated in the impression in the control arm.

7. Use the jack and raise the control arm until the spring is held securely.

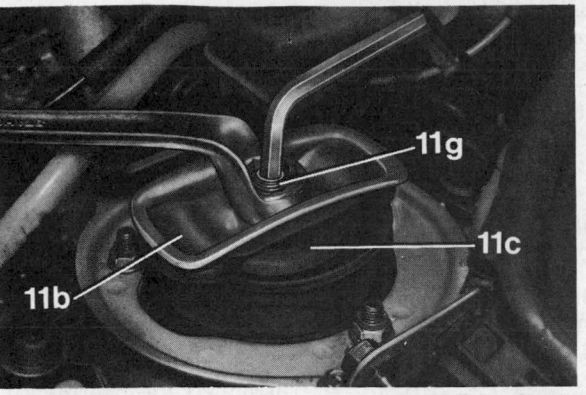

11b Rebound limiter
11c Rubber mount
11g Piston rod

Remove the upper damper strut retaining nut by locking the piston rod with an Allen wrench — 190D, 190E, 260E and 300E

8. Using a new nut, tighten the upper end of the damper strut to 44 ft. lbs. (60 Nm).

9. Slowly ease the tension on the spring compressor until the spring is seated properly and then remove the compressor.

10. Installation of the remaining components is in the reverse order of removal.

380SL, 380SLC and 560SL

NOTE: Be extremely careful when attempting to remove the front springs as they are compressed and under considerable load.

1. Raise the front of the vehicle and support it with jackstands. Remove the wheels.

2. Remove the front shock absorber and disconnect the sway bar.

3. First punchmark the position of the eccentric adjusters, then loosen the hex bolts.

4. Support the lower control arm with a jack.

5. Knock out the eccentric pins and gradually lower the arm until spring tension is relieved.

6. The spring can now be removed.

NOTE: Check caster and camber after installing a new spring.

7. Installation is the reverse of removal.

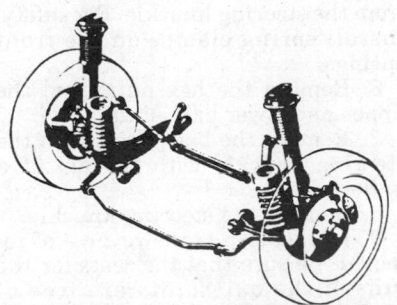

Front suspension — 190D, 190E, 260E and 300E

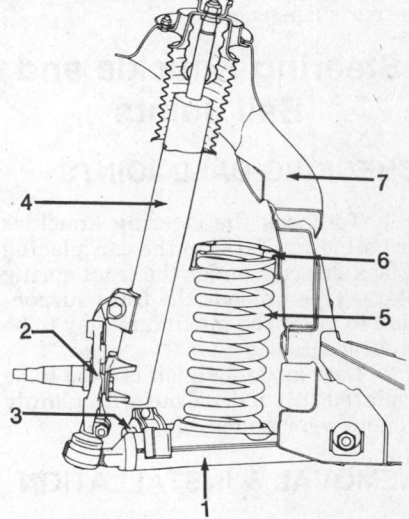

1. Wishbone
2. Steering knuckle
3. Torsion bar
4. Damper strut
5. Front spring
6. Spring-rubber mount
7. Front end

Front spring — 190D, 190E, 260E and 300E

1. Front axle carrier
3. Lower control arm
4. Upper control arm
10. Front spring
11. Front shock absorber
12. Torsion bar
29. Rubber mounting
31. Rubber mounting for front spring

Front spring removal — 380SL, 380SLC and 560SL

8. For ease of installation, tape the rubber mounts to the springs.

9. If the eccentric adjusters were not matchmarked, install the eccentric bolts as illustrated under "Front End Alignment".

All Other Models

1. Raise and support the front of the car and support the lower control arm.

2. Remove the wheel. Unbolt the upper shock absorber mount.

3. Install a spring compressor and compress the spring.

4. Remove the front spring with the lower mount.

5. Installation is the reverse of removal. Tighten the upper shock absorber suspension.

Steering Knuckle and Ball Joints

CHECKING BALL JOINTS

1. To check the steering knuckles or ball joints, jack up the car, placing a jack directly under the front spring plate. This unloads the front suspension to allow the maximum play to be observed.

2. Late model ball joints need to be replaced only if dried out with plainly visible wear and/or play.

REMOVAL & INSTALLATION

190D, 190E, 260E and 300E

1. Raise the front of the vehicle and support it with jackstands. Remove the wheel.

2. Install a spring compressor on the spring.

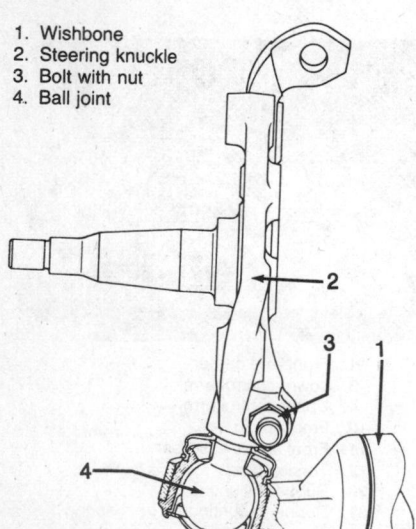

1. Wishbone
2. Steering knuckle
3. Bolt with nut
4. Ball joint

Steering knuckle/ball joint—190D, 190E, 260E and 300E

3. Remove the brake caliper and then wire it out of the way. Be careful not to damage the brake line.

4. Remove the brake disc and wheel hub.

NOTE: On vehicles equipped with ABS, remove the speed sensor.

5. Unscrew the three socket-head bolts and then remove the brake backing plate from the steering knuckle.

6. Tighten the spring compressor until all tension and/or lead has been removed from the lower control arm.

7. Disconnect the steering knuckle arm from the steering knuckle (this is the arm attached to the tie rod).

— **CAUTION** —

There must be no tension on the lower control arm.

8. Unscrew the three bolts and disconnect the lower end of the damper strut from the steering knuckle.

9. Remove the hex-head clamp nut at the supporting joint (lower ball joint).

10. Remove the steering knuckle.

11. Installation is in the reverse order of removal. Please note the following:

a. Tighten the supporting joint clamp nut to 70 ft. lbs. (125 Nm).

b. Refer to the "Damper Strut Removal and Installation" procedure when connecting the lower end of the damper strut to the steering knuckle.

380SL, 380SLC and 560SL

1. This should only be done with the front shock absorber installed. If, however, the front shock absorber has been removed, the lower control arm should be supported with a jack and the spring should be clamped with a spring tensioner. In this case, the hex nut on the guide joint should not be loosened without the spring tensioner installed.

2. Jack up the front of the car and support it on jack stands.

3. Remove the wheel.

4. Remove the brake caliper.

5. Unbolt the steering relay lever from the steering knuckle. For safety, install spring clamps on the front springs.

6. Remove the hex nuts from the upper and lower ball joints.

7. Remove the ball joints from the steering knuckle with the aid of a puller.

8. Remove the steering knuckle.

9. Installation is the reverse of removal. Be sure that the seats for the pins of the ball joints are free of grease.

10. Bleed the brakes.

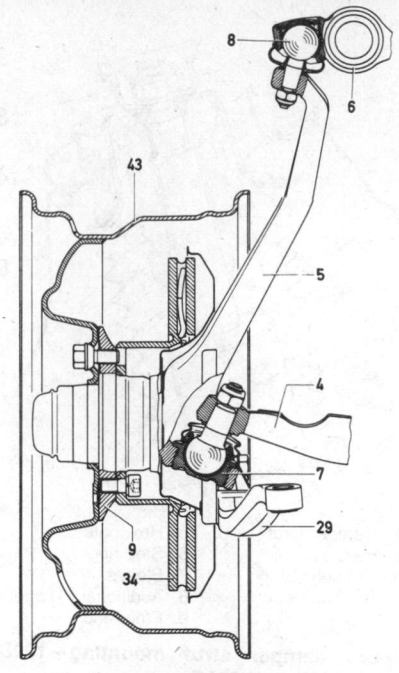

4. Lower control arm
5. Steering knuckle
6. Upper control arm
7. Support joint
8. Guide joint
9. Front wheel hub
29. Steering knuckle arm
34. Brake disc
43. Wheel

Steering knuckle/ball joint—all except 190 series, 260E, 300 series (1986–88), 380SL, 380SLC and 560SL

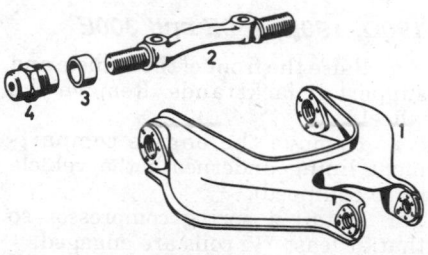

1. Upper control arm
2. Pivot pin
3. Rubber sealing ring
4. Threaded bushing

Upper control arm and pivot shaft

All Other Models

1. Raise and support the car. For safety, it's a good idea to install some type of clamp on the front spring. Position jack stands at the outside front against the lower control arms.

2. Remove the wheel.

3. Remove the steering knuckle arm from the steering knuckle.

4. Remove and suspend the brake caliper.

5. Remove the front wheel hub.

NOTE: On vehicles equipped with ABS, disconnect the speed sensor.

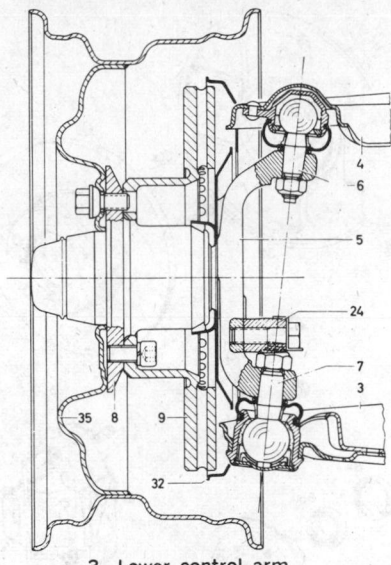

3. Lower control arm
4. Upper control arm
5. Steering knuckle
6. Guide joint
7. Supporting joint
8. Front wheel hub
9. Brake disc
24. Steering knuckle arm
32. Cover plate
35. Wheel

Steering knuckle/ball joint—380SL, 380SLC and 560SL

6. Loosen the brake hose holder on the cover plate.
7. Loosen the nut on the guide joint and remove the joint from the steering knuckle.
8. Loosen the nut on the support joint.
9. Swivel the steering knuckle outward and force the ball joint from the lower control arm.
10. Remove the steering knuckle.
11. If necessary, remove the cover plate from the steering knuckle.
12. Installation is the reverse of removal. Use self-locking nuts and adjust the wheel bearings.

Upper Control Arm

NOTE: The 190D, 190E, 260E and 300E models have no upper control arm.

REMOVAL & INSTALLATION

All Models Except 380SL, 380SLC and 560SL

1. Raise and support the car. Position jack stands at the outside front against the lower control arms.
2. Remove the wheel.
3. Loosen the nut on the guide joint.
4. Remove the guide joint from the steering knuckle.
5. Secure the steering knuckle

with a hook on the upper control arm stop to prevent it from tilting.
6. Loosen the clamp screw and separate the upper control arm from the torsion bar.
7. Loosen the upper control arm bearing at the front and remove the upper control arm.
8. Installation is the reverse of removal. Use new self-locking nuts and check the front wheel alignment.

380SL, 380SLC and 560SL

1. The front shock absorbers should remain installed. Never loosen the hex nuts of the ball joints with the shock absorber removed, unless a spring clamp is installed.
2. Jack the front of the car and remove the wheel.
3. Support the front end on jack stands.
4. Remove the steering arm from the steering knuckle.
5. Separate the brake line and brake hose from each other and plug the openings.
6. Support the lower control arm and unscrew the nuts from the ball joints.
7. Remove the ball joints from the steering knuckle.
8. Loosen the bolts on the upper control arm and remove the upper control arm.
9. Installation is the reverse of removal.

--- CAUTION ---
Mount the front hex bolt from the rear in a forward direction, and the rear hex bolt from the front in a rearward direction.

---

10. Bleed the brakes.

Lower Control Arm
REMOVAL & INSTALLATION

All Models Except 190D, 190E, 260E , 300E, 380SL, 380SLC and 560SL

The lower control arm is the same as the front axle half. For safety install a spring compressor on the coil spring.
1. Raise and support the front of the car and remove the wheels.
2. Remove the front shock absorber. Loosen the top mount first.
3. Remove the front springs.
4. Separate and plug the brake lines.
5. Remove the track rod from the steering knuckle arm.
6. Matchmark the position of the eccentric bolts on the bearing of the lower control arm in relation to the crossmember.
7. Remove the shield from the cross yoke.

8. Support the front axle half.
9. Loosen the eccentric bolt on the front and rear bearing of the lower control arm and knock them out.
10. Remove the bolt from the cross yoke bearing.
11. Loosen the screw at the opposite end of the cross yoke bearing.
12. Pull the cross yoke bearing down slightly.
13. Loosen the support of the upper control arm on the torsion bar. Remove the clamp screw from the clamp.
14. Remove the upper control arm bearing on the front end.
15. Remove the front axle half.
16. Installation is the reverse of removal. Tighten the eccentric bolts on the lower control arm bearing with the car resting on the wheels. Bleed the brakes and check the front end alignment.

190D, 190E, 260E and 300E

1. Remove the engine compartment lining at the bottom of the vehicle (if so equipped).
2. Raise the front of the vehicle and support it with jackstands. Remove the wheel.
3. Support the lower control arm

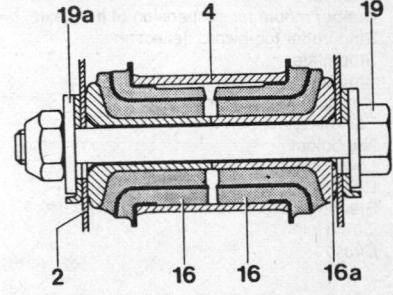

1. Frame cross member
2. Wishbone
3. Torsion rubber bushing
4. Clamping sleeve
5. Eccentric bolt (camber adjustment)
6. Eccentric washer

Cross section of the front lower control arm bushing on 190 models, 260E, and 300E

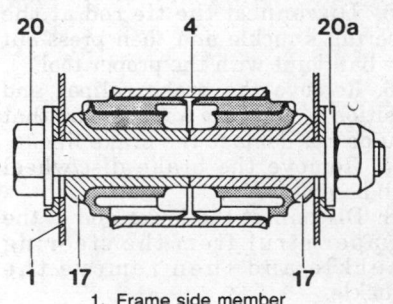

1. Frame side member
2. Wishbone
3. Torsion rubber bushing
4. Eccentric bolt (caster adjustment)
5. Eccentric washer

Cross section of the rear lower control arm bushing on 190 models, 260E and 300E

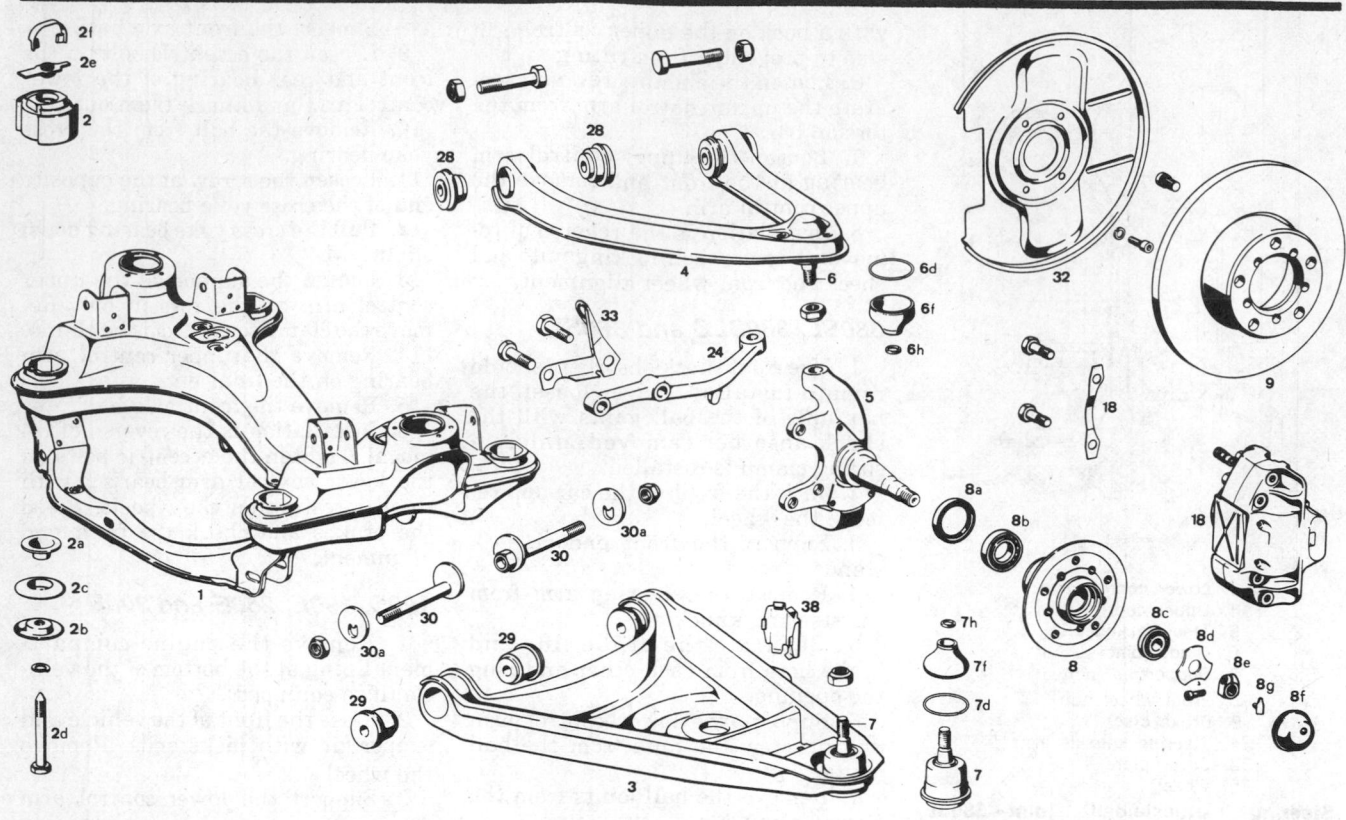

1. Front axle carrier
2. Rubber mount for suspension of front axle
2a. Stop buffer for inward deflection
2b. Stop plate
2c. Stop buffer for outward deflections
2d. Hex. bolt with snap-ring
2e. Fastening nut
2f. Nut holder
3. Lower control arm
4. Upper control arm
5. Steering knuckle
6. Guide joint
6d. Circlip

6f. Sleeve
6h. Clamping ring
7. Supporting joint
7d. Circlip
7f. Sleeve
7h. Clamping ring
8. Front wheel hub
8a. Radial sealing ring
8b. Inside tapered roller bearing
8c. Outside tapered roller bearing
8d. Washer
8e. Clamp nut
8f. Wheel cap

8g. Contact spring
9. Brake disc
18. Brake caliper
18a. Lockwasher
24. Steering knuckle arm
28. Rubber slide bearing
29. Rubber bearing (torsion bearing)
30. Cam bolt
30a. Cam washer
32. Cover plate
33. Holder for brake hose
38. Protective cap for steering lock

Lower control arm and pivot shaft

with jackstands and then disconnect the torsion bar bearing at the control arm.

4. Remove the spring as detailed earlier in this chapter.

5. Disconnect the tie rod at the steering knuckle and then press out the ball joint with the proper tool.

6. Remove the brake caliper and position it out of the way. Be sure that you do not damage the brake line.

7. Remove the brake disc/wheel hub assembly.

8. Disconnect the lower end of the damper strut from the steering knuckle and then remove the knuckle.

9. Mark the position of the inner eccentric pins, relative to the frame, on the bearing of the control arm.

10. Unscrew and remove the pins.

11. Remove the jackstands and remove the lower control arm.

12. Installation is in the reverse order of removal. Please note the following:

a. Tighten the eccentric bolts on the inner arm to 130 ft. lbs. (180 Nm).

b. To facilitate torsion bar installation, raise the opposite side of the lower control arm with a jack.

c. Tighten the clamp nut on the tie rod ball joint to 25 ft. lbs. (35 Nm).

d. When installing the rear torsion bar bushing, on the 300E, the flats on the cone must be vertical.

380SL, 380SLC and 560SL

1. Since the front shock absorber acts as a deflection stop for the front wheels, the lower shock absorber attaching point should not be loosened unless the vehicle is resting on the wheels or unless the lower control arm is supported.

2. Jack up the front of the vehicle and support it on jack stands.

3. Support the lower control arm.

4. Loosen the lower shock absorber attachment.

5. Unscrew the steering arm from the steering knuckle.

6. Separate the brake line and brake hose and plug the openings.

7. Remove the front spring.

8. Unscrew the hex nuts on the ball joints.

9. Remove the lower ball joint and remove the lower control arm.

10. Installation is the reverse of removal. Bleed the brakes and check the front end alignment.

Front Wheel Bearings

REMOVAL & INSTALLATION

If the wheel bearing play is being checked for correct setting only, it is not necessary to remove the caliper. It is only necessary to remove the brake pads.

1. Remove the brake caliper.
2. Pull the cap from the hub with a pair of channel-lock pliers. Remove the radio suppression spring, if equipped.
3. Loosen the socket screw of the clamp nut on the wheel spindle. Remove the clamp nuts and washer.
4. Remove the front wheel hub and brake disc.
5. Remove the inner race with the roller cage of the outer bearing.
6. Using a brass or aluminum drift, carefully tap the outer race of the inner bearing until it can be removed with the inner race, bearing cage, and seal.
7. In the same manner, tap the outer race of the bearing out of the hub.
8. Separate the front hub from the brake disc.
9. To assemble, press the outer races into the front wheel hub.
10. Pack the bearing cage with bearing grease and insert the inner race with the bearing into the wheel hub.
11. Coat the sealing ring with sealant and press it into the hub.
12. Pack the front wheel hub with 45–55 grams of wheel bearing grease. The races of the tapered bearing should be well packed and also apply grease to the front faces of the rollers. Pack the front bearings with the specified amount of grease. Too much grease will cause overheating of the lubricant and it may lose its lubricity. Too little grease will not lubricate properly.
13. Coat the contact surface of the sealing ring on the wheel spindle with Molykote paste.
14. Press the wheel hub onto the wheel spindle.
15. Install the inner race and cage of the outer bearing.
16. Install the steel washer and the clamp nut.

ADJUSTMENT

1. Tighten the clamp nut until the hub can just be turned.
2. Slacken the clamp nut and seat the bearings on the spindle by rapping the spindle sharply with a hammer.
3. Attach a dial indicator, with the pointer indexed, onto the wheel hub.
4. Check the end-play of the hub by pushing and pulling on the flange. The end-play should be approximately 0.0004–0.0008 in.
5. Make an additional check by rotating the washer between the inner race of the outer bearing and the clamp nut. It should be able to be turned by hand.

Dial indicator set-up for checking wheel bearing play

6. Check the position of the suppressor pin in the wheel spindle and the contact spring in the dust cap.
7. Pack the dust cap with 20–25 grams of wheel bearing grease and install the cap.
8. Install the brake caliper and bleed the brakes.

Front Wheel Alignment

Caster and camber are critical to proper handling and tire wear. Neither adjustment should be attempted without the specialized equipment to accurately measure the geometry of the front end.

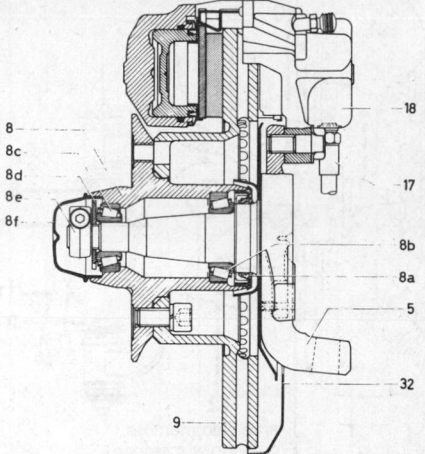

5. Steering knuckle
8. Wheel hub
8a. Radial sealing ring
8b. Tapered roller bearing, outside
8c. Tapered roller bearing, inside
8d. Washer
8e. Clamping nut
8f. Wheel cap
9. Brake disc
17. Brake hose
18. Brake caliper
32. Cover plate

Wheel bearing cutaway – 380SL, 380SLC and 560SL

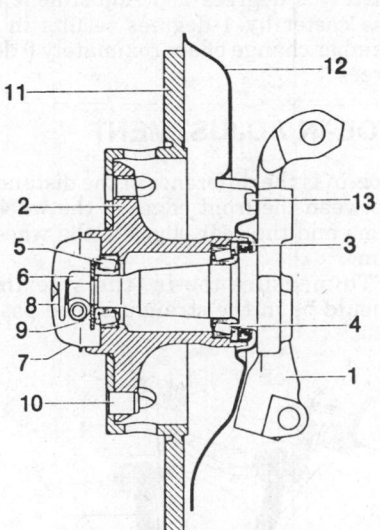

1. Steering knuckle
2. Front wheel hub
3. Radial seal ring
4. Tapered roller bearing, inner
5. Tapered roller bearing, outer
6. Clamping nut
7. Grease cap
8. Contact spring
9. Washer
10. Clamping sleeve
11. Brake disk
12. Brake backing plate
13. Allen screws

Wheel bearing cutaway – 190 series, 260E and 300E

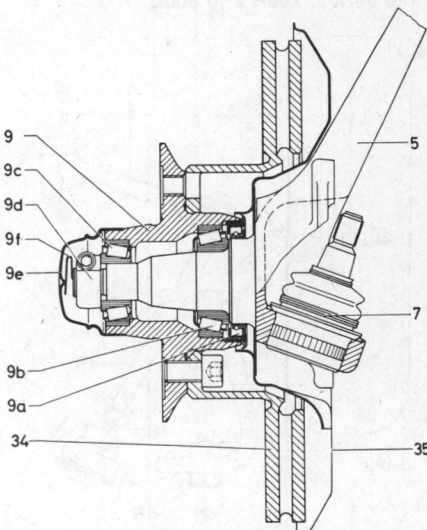

5. Steering knuckle
7. Supporting joint
9. Front wheel hub
9a. Radial sealing ring
9b. Tapered roller bearing, inside
9c. Tapered roller bearing, outside
9d. Clamping nut
9e. Wheel cap
9f. Contact spring
34. Brake disc
35. Cover plate

Wheel bearing cutaway – all except 190 series, 260E, 300E, 380SL, 380SLC and 560SL

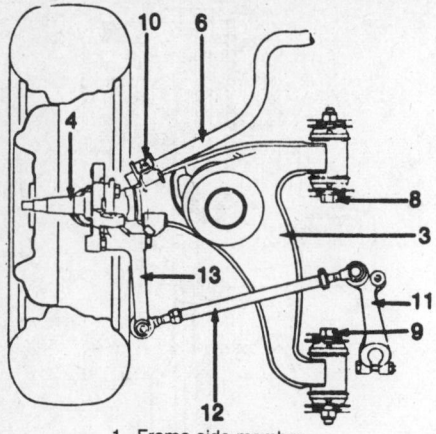

1. Frame side member
2. Frame cross member
3. Wishbone
4. Steering knuckle
5. Supporting ball joint
6. Torsion bar
7. Damper strut
8. Eccentric bolt of front bushing (camber adjusment)
9. Eccentric bolt of rear bushing (caster adjustment)
10. Torsion bar bushing on wishbone
11. Pitman arm
12. Tie rod
13. Steering knuckle arm

Caster and camber adjustment points—190 series, 260E and 300E

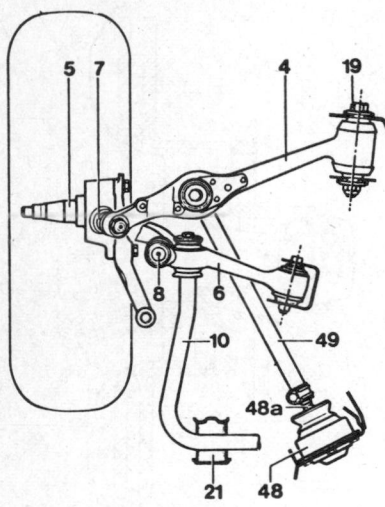

1. Frame side member
2. Frame cross member for front axle
4. Lower control arm
5. Steering knuckle
6. Upper control arm
7. Supporting joint
8. Guide joint
10. Torsion bar
19. Eccentric bolt (camber adjustment)
21. Torsion bar mounting on front end
48. Supporting joint
48a. Ball pin (caster adjustment)
49. Supporting tube

Caster and camber adjustment points on all other models

CASTER/CAMBER ADJUSTMENT

All Models Except 380SL, 380SLC and 560SL

The front axle provides for caster and camber adjustment, but both wheel adjustments can only be made together. Adjustment are made with cam bolts on the lower control arm bearings.

The front bearing cam bolt is used to set caster, while the rear bearing cam bolt is used for camber.

380SL, 380SLC and 560SL

Caster and camber are dependent upon each other and cannot be adjusted independently. They can only be adjusted simultaneously.

Caster is adjusted by turning the lower control arm around the front mounting, using the eccentric bolt.

Camber is adjusted by turning the lower control arm about the rear mounting, using the eccentric bolt. Bear in mind that caster will be changed accordingly.

When the camber is adjusted in a positive direction, caster is changed in a negative camber by 0 degrees 15' results in a caster change of approximately 0 degrees 20'. Adjustment of the caster by 1 degrees results in a camber change of approximately 0 degrees 7'.

TOE-IN ADJUSTMENT

Toe-in is the difference of the distance between the front edges of the wheel rims and the rear edges of the wheel rims.

To measure toe-in, the steering should be in the straight ahead posi-

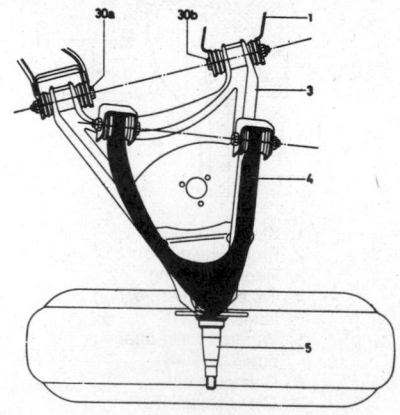

1. Front axle carrier
3. Lower control arm
4. Upper control arm
5. Steering knuckle
30a. Cam bolt front (caster)
30b. Cam bolt rear (camber)

Caster and camber adjustment points—380SL, 380SLC and 560SL

tion and the marks on the pitman arm and pitman shaft should be aligned.

Toe-in is adjusted by changing the length of the two tie rods or track rods with the wheels in the straight ahead position. Some older models have a hex nut locking arrangement rather than the newer clamp, but adjustment is the same.

NOTE: Install new tie rods so that the left-handed thread points toward the left-hand side of the car.

REAR SUSPENSION

Shock Absorber

REMOVAL & INSTALLATION

190D, 190E, 260E, 300E, 380SL, 380SLC and 560SL

1. Jack up the rear of the car and support the control arm.
2. From inside the trunk (sedans), remove the rubber cap, locknut, and hex nut from the upper mount of the shock absorber. On 380SL, the upper mount of the rear shock absorber is accessible after removing the top, top flap, rear seat, backrest and lining. On the 380SLC, remove the rear seat, backrest and cover plate.
3. Unbolt the mounting for the rear shock absorber at the bottom and remove the shock absorber. Be sure to disconnect and plug the pressure line on the 190E-16.
4. Installation is the reverse of removal.

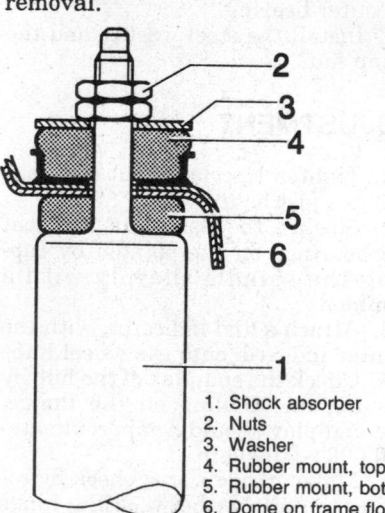

1. Shock absorber
2. Nuts
3. Washer
4. Rubber mount, top
5. Rubber mount, bottom
6. Dome on frame floor

Rear shock absorber upper mount—190D, 190E, 260E and 300E

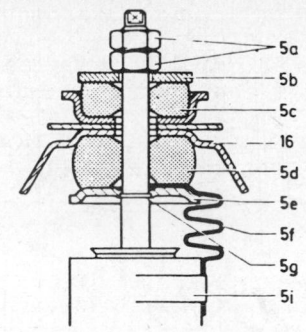

5a. Nut
5b. Washer
5c. Upper rubber ring
5d. Lower rubber ring
5e. Plate
5f. Dust protection
5g. Lockring
5i. Clamping strap
16. Dome on frame floor

Rear shock absorber lower mount—300SDL, all 380 models, 420SEL, all 500 models and 560 models

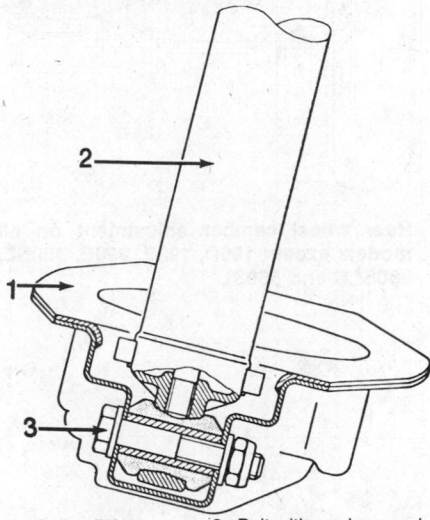

1. Spring link
2. Shock absorber
3. Bolt with washers and self-locking nut

Rear shock absorber lower mount—190D and 190E

All Other Models

1. Remove the rear seat and backrest.
2. Remove the cover from the rear wall.
3. Raise and support the car and the trailing arm.
4. Loosen the nuts on the upper mount. Remove the washer and rubber ring.
5. Loosen the lower mount and remove the shock absorber downward.
6. Installation is the reverse of removal. Tighten the upper mounting nut to the end of the threads.

Springs

REMOVAL & INSTALLATION

190D, 190E, 260E and 300E

1. Raise the rear of the vehicle and support it with jackstands. Remove the wheel.

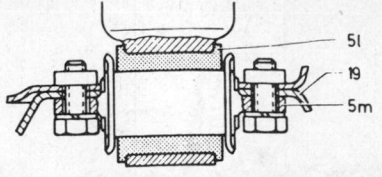

5l. Rubber mounting
5m. Fastening clip
19. Semi-trailing arm

Rear shock absorber upper mount—1981–85 300SD, 300SDL, 380SE, 380SEC, 380SEL, 380SL, 380SLC, 420SEL, 500SEC, 500SEL, 560SEC, 560SEL and 560SL

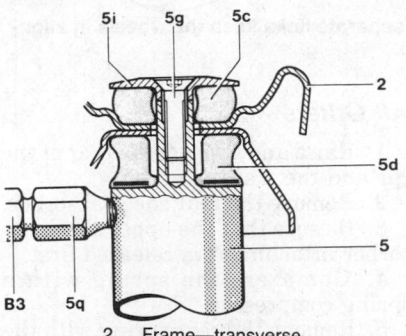

2. Frame—transverse member
5. Suspension strut
5c. Upper rubber mount
5d. Lower rubber mount
5g. Special screw
5i. Plate
5q. Stud
B3. Pressure line (pressure hose), pressure reservoir—suspension strut

Rear shock absorber upper mount—1983–85 300TD. Retrofitting is not possible

2. Disconnect the holding clamps for the spring link cover and then remove the cover.
3. Install a spring compressor and compress the spring until the spring link is free of all load.
4. Disconnect the lower end of the shock absorber.
5. Increase the tension on the spring compressor and remove the spring.
6. Installation is in the reverse order of removal. Please note the following:
   a. Position the spring so that the end of the lower coil is seated in the

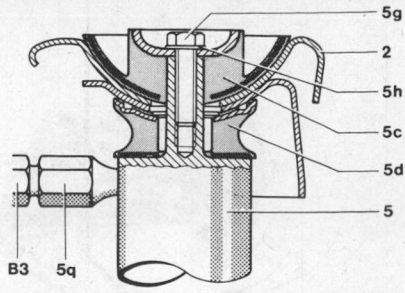

Rear shock absorber upper mount—1981–82 300TD

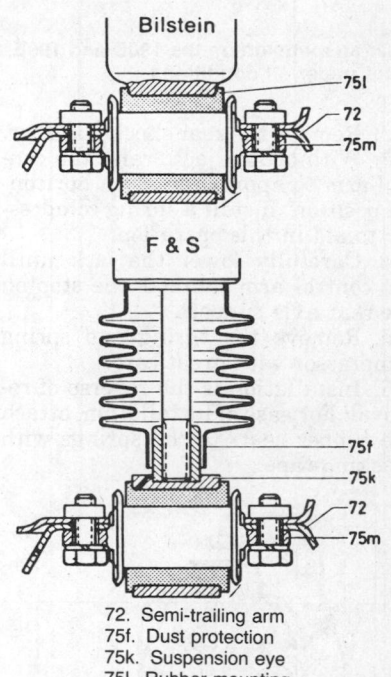

72. Semi-trailing arm
75f. Dust protection
75k. Suspension eye
75l. Rubber mounting
75m. Fastening stirrup

Rear shock absorber lower mount—240D, 280E and 280CE

impression of the spring seat and the upper coil seats properly in the rubber mount in the frame floor.
   b. Do not release tension on the spring compressor until the lower end of the shock absorber is connected and tightened to 47 ft. lbs. (65 Nm).

380SL, 380SLC and 560SL

1. Jack up the rear of the car.

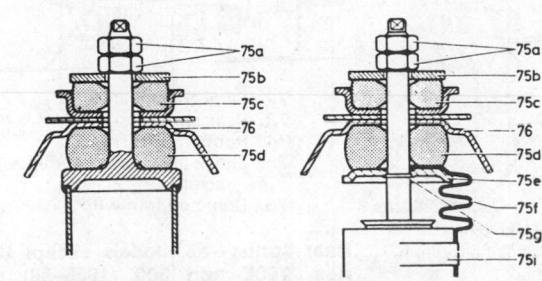

75a. Nuts
75b. Washer
75c. Upper rubber ring
75d. Lower rubber ring
75e. Plate
75f. Dust protection
75g. Locking ring
75i. Clamping strap
76. Dome on frame floor

Rear shock absorber upper mount—240D, 280E and 280CE (75f not used in U.S.)

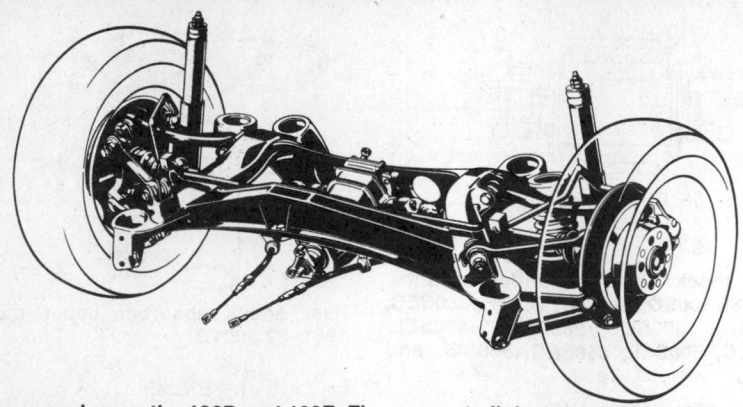

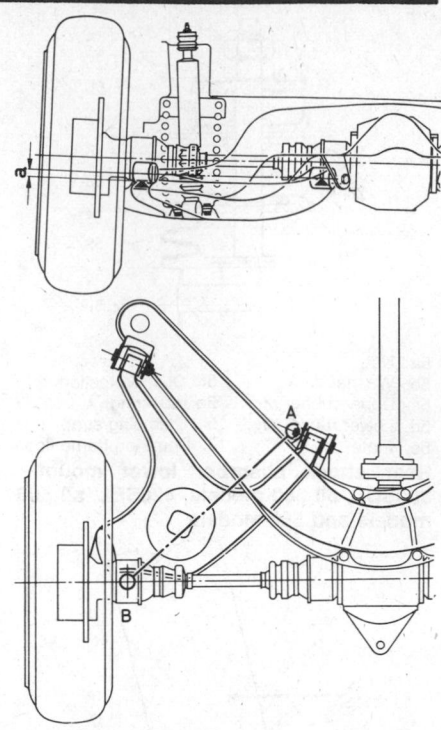

Rear suspension on the 190D and 190E. Five separate links keep the wheels in alignment under all conditions.

2. Remove the rear shock absorber.

3. With a floor jack, raise the control arm to approximately a horizontal position. Install a spring compressor to aid in this operation.

4. Carefully lower the jack until the control arm contacts the stop on the rear axle support.

5. Remove the spring and spring compressor with great care.

6. Installation is the reverse of removal. For ease of installation, attach the rubber seats to the springs with masking tape.

All Others

1. Raise and support the rear of the car and the trailing arm.

2. Remove the rear shock absorber.

3. Be sure that the upper shock absorber attachment is released first.

4. Compress the spring with a spring compressor.

5. Remove the rear spring with the rubber mount.

6. Installation is the reverse or removal. When installing the shock absorber, tighten the lower mount first.

Rear wheel camber adjustment on all models except 190D, 190E, 260E, 380SL, 380SLC and 560SL

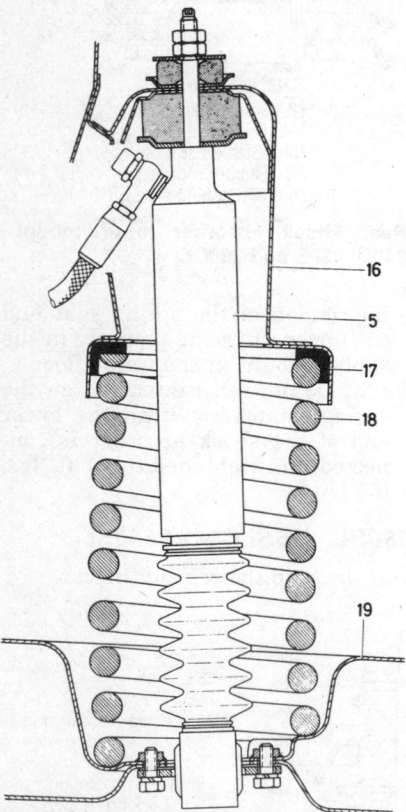

5. Spring strut
16. Dome on frame floor
17. Rubber mount
18. Rear spring
19. Semi-trailing arm

Rear spring—380SL and 380SLC

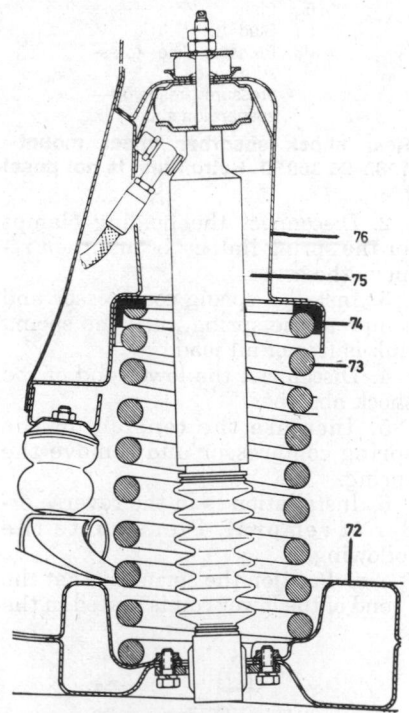

72. Semi-trailing arm
73. Rear spring
74. Rubber mounting
75. Shock absorber or spring strut
76. Dome on frame floor

Rear spring—all models except 190 series, 260E and 300 (1986–88) series, 380SL, 380SLC and 560SL

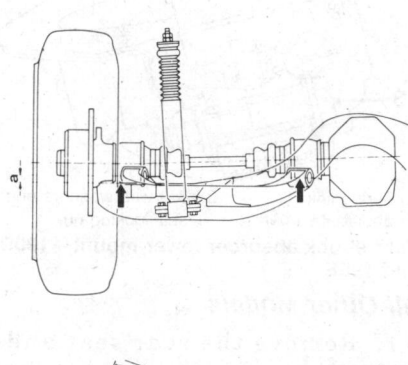

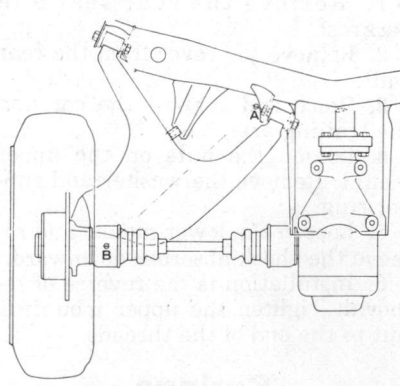

Rear wheel camber measurement on the 380SL, 380SLC and 560SL. The control arm position (difference in height between the axis of the rear control arm mount (A) and the lower edge of the cup on the outer edge of the CV-joint

Independent Rear Suspension Adjustments

Suspension adjustments should only be checked when the vehicle is resting on a level surface and is carrying the required fluids (full tank of gas, engine oil, etc.).

CAMBER

All Models

Rear wheel camber is determined by the position of the control arm. The difference in height between the axis of the control arm mounting point on the rear axle subframe and lower edge of the cup on the constant velocity joint is directly translated in degrees of camber.

TOE-IN

Toe-in, on the rear wheels, is dependent on the camber of the rear wheels.

STEERING

Steering Wheel

REMOVAL & INSTALLATION

Models Without Airbag

NOTE: 380SEC uses a bolt and spring that pushes the power piston into the teeth of the Pitman shaft when the steering is in the center position. Any backlash (play at the steering wheel) is taken up.

1. On 380SL, 380SLC and 560SL, pry the three-pointed star trademark from the center padding. On all other models, remove the padded plate. Pull at one corner near the wheel spokes.
2. Unscrew the hex nut from the steering shaft and remove the spring washer and the steering wheel.

NOTE: All models use an Allen screw in place of the hex nut. The Allen screw must be replaced if removed.

3. Installation is the reverse of removal. Be sure that the alignment mark on the steering shaft is pointing upward and be sure that the slightly curved spoke of the steering wheel is down.

Models Equipped With Airbag

──────── CAUTION ────────
The airbag passive restraint system is charged with a gas generator (explosive capsule) and should be handled with extreme care. Mishandling of the airbag unit could result in serious injury.

1. Disconnect the ground cable of the battery, cover pole and turn ignition key into 0 position.
2. Remove floor mat in righthand legroom of driver.
3. Disconnect foot support on front wall and pull out plug connection of release unit on foot support.
4. Remove both oval head screws with Intorx out of generator carrier by means of a screwdriver socket to release generator carrier from contact bridges.
5. Remove complete airbag unit from steering wheel.
6. Pull plug connection out of gas generator.

NOTE: Pulling off of the plug connection will make a short circuit bridge in the gas generator automatically effective.

7. Remove the airbag from the steering wheel.

──────── CAUTION ────────
After airbag removal, always position the airbag unit in such a manner that the padded side is facing upward and must be stored under lock and key and personal supervision. Do not expose the airbag unit to temperatures above 212°F (100°C), not even temporarily. Never apply grease, cleaning compound or like products to the airbag unit. If the unit is dropped on a hard base from a height of 18 in. or more, do not reinstall the unit but return it to a Mercedes-Benz representative. Before installing the airbag unit, check that the grounding cable is disconnected from battery, that the pole is covered and that the ignition key is in 0 position.

8. Installation is the reverse of removal.

Power Steering Gear
REMOVAL & INSTALLATION

1. Suck the oil from the power steering reservoir using a syringe.
2. Detach the high-pressure hose and oil return hose from the steering assembly.
3. Cap both lines to prevent entry of dirt, then remove the clamp screw from the lower part of the coupling flange.
4. Remove the rubber plug from the cover plate and remove the U-joint socket screw. On LS90 power steering units, remove the steering spindle. Pull the steering spindle up only until the coupling is no longer engaged with the worn gear.
5. The tailpipe and left side exhaust pipe may have to be removed for access.
6. Detach the tie rod and center tie rod (or drag link and track rod). from the pitman arm, using pullers or a tie rod splitter.
7. Remove the hex-head bolts that hold the gearbox to the frame, then press the worm shaft stub from the steering coupling and remove the gearbox from underneath the car.
8. To install, first install the pitman arm (if it has been removed) aligning the matchmarks. Tighten the pitman arm nut to 110 ft. lbs. and install the cotter pin. Use new self-locking nuts to attach the gear to the frame.
9. Remove the screw plug from the steering box. Turn the wormshaft until the center of the power piston is directly below the bore in the housing. Check dimension (a) which can be altered by changing the position of the pitman arm on its shaft.
10. Center the steering wheel.
11. Press the worm shaft stub into the steering shaft coupling, making sure not to damage the serrations.

NOTE: Install assembly pin as for manual steering.

12. Install and tighten the hex-head screws that hold the gearbox to the chassis, then install and tighten the coupling clamp screw.
13. Install the plug in the gearbox, using a new gasket; attach the tie rods to the pitman arm and make sure that the steering knuckle arms rest against their stops at full left and right lock.
14. Check toe-in and correct if necessary. Remove the dust covers from the fluid lines, then reconnect the high and low pressure lines.
15. Fill the reservoir and connect a hose between the bleed screw on the steering and the reservoir.
16. Open the bleed screw and, with engine running, bleed the system and top up.

Power Steering Pump
REMOVAL & INSTALLATION

All Models

1. Remove the nut from the supply tank.
2. Remove the spring and damping plate.
3. Drain the oil from the tank with a syringe.
4. Loosen and remove the expand-

ing and return hoses from the pump. Plug all connections and pump openings.

5. If necessary for clearance, loosen the radiator shell. Loosen the mounting bolts, and move the pump toward the engine by using the toothed wheel. Remove the belt. Remove the pulley, and then remove the pump.

6. Loosen the nut on the attaching plate and the bolt on the support.

7. Push the pump toward the engine and remove the belts from the pulley.

8. Unscrew the mounting bolts and remove the pump and carrier.

9. Installation is the reverse of removal.

Steering Linkage

REMOVAL & INSTALLATION

All Models
TRACK ROD

1. Remove the cotter pins and castellated nuts from the track rod joints. The 190D, 190E, 260E and 300E use only a self-locking nut.

2. Remove the track rod from the steering arms with a puller.

3. Check the track rod ends. The rods use 22mm ball joints and should be replaced if either ball joint is defective.

4. Check the rubber sleeves. The ball joint should be replaced if the sleeve is defective.

5. Installation is the reverse of removal. Install the track rods so that the end with the left hand threads is on the left side. Use new locknuts on the 190D, 190E, 260E and 300E.

DRAG LINK

1. Remove the castle nuts from the drag link joints.

2. Unbolt the steering damper and force it from the bracket.

3. Remove the drag link with a puller.

4. Installation is the reverse of removal.

5. Check the front wheel alignment.

Reset pin (arrow) on master cylinder with pressure warning differential

BRAKES

For all brake system service and repair procedures not detailed below, please refer to "Brakes" in the Unit Repair section.

Master Cylinder

REMOVAL & INSTALLATION

1. To remove the master cylinder, first open a bleed screw at one front, and one rear, wheel.

2. Pump the pedal to empty the reservoir completely. Make sure both reservoirs are completely drained.

3. Disconnect the switch connectors using a small screwdriver. Disconnect the brake lines at the master cylinder. Plug the ends with bleed screw caps or the equivalent.

4. Unbolt the master cylinder from the power brake unit and remove. Be careful you do not lose the O-ring in the flange groove of the master cylinder.

5. Installation is the reverse of removal. Be sure to replace the O-ring between the master cylinder and the power brake unit, since this must be absolutely tight. Torque the nuts to 12–15 ft. lbs. Be sure that both chambers are completely filled with brake fluid and bleed the brakes.

Parking Brake Cable

FRONT CABLE

Removal & Installation
190D, 190E, 260E AND 300E

1. Disconnect the return spring at the cable control compensator.

2. Unbolt the brake cable from the intermediate lever and pull the cable away.

3. Remove the parking brake lever.

4. Loosen the brake cable at the lever and then pull it out toward the rear, through the floor.

5. Installation is in the reverse order of removal.

240D, 280CE, 300D, 300CD AND 300TD

1. Remove the spring from the equalizer.

2. Back off the adjusting screw completely.

3. Detach the relay lever from the bracket on the frame and from the adjusting shackle.

4. Detach the cable from the relay lever by pulling the cotter pin out of the bolt.

5. Remove the clip from the cable guide. Remove the clips from the chassis.

6. Detach the brake cable from the parking brake link. Remove the clip from the cable guide and detach the brake cable from the parking brake.

7. Pull the cable downward from the chassis.

8. Installation is in the reverse of removal.

380SL, 380SLC AND 560SL

1. Remove the exhaust system.

2. Disconnect the return spring.

3. Remove the bolts which attach the guide to the intermediate lever.

4. Remove the adjusting screw from the adjusting bracket.

5. Loosen the brake control cables on the intermediate lever and pull the cotter pin from the flange bolt. Remove the flange bolt.

6. Remove the spring clamp from the cable guide and remove the cable control from the bracket.

7. Remove the tunnel cover.

8. Disconnect the brake control from the parking brake and remove the spring clamp from the cable guide. Remove the cable control from the parking brake.

9. Remove the brake control cable out of the frame toward the rear.

10. Installation is the reverse of removal.

ALL OTHER MODELS

1. Remove the floor mat.

2. Remove the legroom cover (upper and lower).

3. Remove the air duct.

4. Disconnect the 4 rubber rings and lower and support the exhaust system.

5. Remove the shield above the exhaust pipes.

6. Disconnect and return spring from the bracket.

7. Back off the adjusting screw on the bracket.

8. Disconnect the intermediate lever from the adjusting bracket.

9. Loosen the brake cable controls on the intermediate lever while pulling the cotter pin from the flange bolt. Remove the flange bolt.

10. Remove the spring clip from the cable guide on the floor pan.

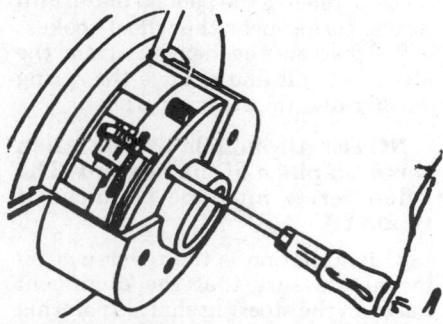

Cut-away view of rear brake shoe adjustment

11. Disconnect the brake cable control from the parking brake bracket.

12. Remove the spring clip from the cable and remove the cable control from the parking brake.

13. Pull the cable away upward.

14. Installation is the reverse of removal. Adjust the parking brake.

REAR BRAKE CABLE

Removal & Installation

240D, 280CE, 280E, 300D, 300CD AND 300TD

1. Remove the parking brake shoes after removing the wheel.

2. Remove the screws from the wheel support and detach the brake cable.

3. Back off the adjusting screw from the adjusting shackle.

4. Remove the spring clips, detach the cable, and remove the equalizer.

5. Installation is the reverse of removal.

ALL OTHER MODELS

1. Remove the parking brake shoes.

2. Remove the bolt from the wheel carrier and remove the cable.

3. Remove the exhaust system. On some models the exhaust system can be lowered and supported after removing the rubber rings. If equipped, remove the heat shield from above the exhaust pipes.

4. Disconnect the draw spring from the holder.

5. Detach the guide from the intermediate lever.

6. Remove the adjusting screw from the bracket.

7. Disconnect the intermediate lever on the bearing and remove it from the adjusting bracket.

8. Remove the holder, compensating lever, cable control plates and intermediate lever from the tunnel.

9. Remove the spring clamps and disconnect the cable from the plate.

10. Installation is the reverse of removal.

Adjustment

260E AND 300E

1. Loosen the parking brake cable slack adjusting screw. The expanders in the rear wheel should not be preloaded via the cable.

2. Raise the rear of the vehicle and support it with jackstands.

3. Remove one of the wheel bolts and then rotate the wheel until you have access to the star wheel adjuster through the hole. Positioning of the hole should be around 2 o'clock.

4. Use a screwdriver to run the star wheel adjuster until wheel locks.

Turn the adjuster back about 4 or 5 teeth until the wheel turns freely.

NOTE: To tighten the star wheel adjuster on the left wheel, move the screwdriver upwards; on the right wheel, move it downwards.

5. Turn the parking brake cable slack adjuster screw into the bracket until the cables have no slack.

6. Depress the parking brake hand (400 N), several times.

7. Turn the adjusting screw until the brake pedal can be depressed by one tooth at a force of approximately 170–200 N.

ALL OTHER MODELS

1. If the floor pedal can be depressed more than two notches before actuating the brakes, adjust by jacking up the rear of the car, then removing one lug bolt and adjusting the star wheel with a screwdriver.

2. Move the screwdriver upward on the left (driver's) side, downward on the right (passenger's) side to tighten the shoes.

3. When the wheel is locked, back off about 2–4 clicks.

4. With this type system, the adjusting bolt on the cable relay lever only serves to equalize cable length; therefore, do not attempt to adjust the brakes by turning this bolt.

CHASSIS ELECTRICAL

Heater Blower
REMOVAL & INSTALLATION

240D, 260E, 280E, 280CE, 300D, 300E, 300CD and 300TD

1. Remove the cover from under the right side of the instrument panel.

2. Disconnect the plug from the blower motor.

3. Unscrew the contact plate screw, lift the contact plate and disconnect both wires to the series resistor.

4. Loosen the blower motor flange screws and lift out the blower motor.

5. Installation is in the reverse order or removal.

380SL, 380SLC and 560SL

1. Working in the engine compartment, unscrew the eight (8) mounting screws and remove the panel which covers the blower motor.

2. Disconnect the plug from the series resistor at the firewall.

3. Remove the mounting bolts and then remove the series resistor.

4. Unscrew the four (4) blower motor retaining nuts and lift out the motor.

5. Installation is in the reverse order of removal. Be sure that the rubber sealing strip is not damaged.

300SD, 380SE, 380SEL, 380SEC, 420SEL, 500SEL, 500SEC, 560SEC and 560SEL

1. Remove the cover from under the right side of the instrument panel.

2. Remove the cover for the blower motor and disconnect the two-prong plug.

3. Remove the retaining bolts on the blower motor flange and then remove the blower motor.

4. Installation is in the reverse order of removal.

190D and 190E

1. Open the hood to a 90 degree position and then remove the wiper arms.

2. Disconnect the retaining clips for the air intake cover at the firewall.

3. Remove the rubber sealing strip from the cover and then remove the retaining screw. Slide the cover out of the lower windshield trim strip and remove it.

4. Disconnect the vacuum line from the heater valve.

5. Remove the heater cover retaining screws.

6. Pull up the rubber sealing strip from the engine side of the defroster plenum (firewall), unscrew the retaining screws and pull up and out on the blower motor cover.

7. Loosen the cable straps on the connecting cable and then disconnect the plug.

8. Unscrew the mounting bolts and then remove the blower motor.

9. Installation is in the reverse order of removal.

Instrument Cluster

REMOVAL & INSTALLATION

380SL and 380SLC

1. Remove the steering wheel.

NOTE: The instrument cluster is held in the instrument panel by means of a molded rubber strip. When pulling out the cluster, the panel can be slightly raised above the cluster. NEVER force the cluster with a screwdriver or the like.

2. Pull the instrument cluster out as much as possible and loosen or remove the tachometer shaft, all electri-

cal connections and the oil pressure line.

3. Remove the instrument cluster to the left.

---— **CAUTION** ---—

Do not bend the oil pressure line.

4. Installation is in the reverse order of removal. Make sure that the speedometer cable is not bent excessively or it will vibrate when running.

190D, 190E, 420SEL, 560SEC, 560SEL and 560SL

1. Remove the cover under the left side of the instrument panel.
2. Disconnect the defroster ducting which runs behind the instrument cluster.
3. Unscrew the speedometer cable from below and then push the cluster out far enough to disconnect all connections on the back of the instrument cluster.
4. Remove the five clips which secure the instrument cluster and then remove it.
5. Installation is in the reverse order of removal.

260E and 300E

1. Remove the instrument panel undercover.
2. Remove the speedometer cable from the slips on the panel under the instrument cluster. This will allow the cable come out when the cluster is removed.
3. Fabricate a removal tool (hook) and insert it between the padding and the cluster at the top of the left side of the cluster. Rotate the tool and then pull out until it rests against the detent.
4. Pull the instrument cluster out evenly on both sides. Be sure the speedometer cable slides into the recess on the brake pedal cover.
5. Reach behind the cluster, unscrew the speedometer cable and disconnect all electrical leads (don't forget to tag them).
6. Remove the instrument cluster.
7. When installing, position the cluster and reconnect the speedometer cable and all electrical leads.
8. Push the cluster backwards into its recess.

NOTE: Be certain that the speedometer cable slides back into the footwell area without buckling behind the cluster.

240D, 280E, 280CE, 300D, 300CD, 300SD (1981–85), 300TD, 380SE, 380SEC, 380SEL, 500SEC and 500SEL

1. Remove the steering wheel

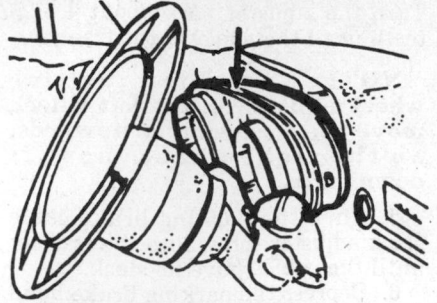

Instrument panel removal showing rubber retaining strip

(300SD, 380SE, 380SEC, 380SEL, 500SEC and 500SEL only).

2. Remove the instrument cluster slightly by hand. Don't pull on the edge of the glass.
3. A removal hook can be fabricated and inserted between the instrument cluster and the dashboard.
4. Guide the removal hook up to the right to the recess (arrow) and pull the instrument cluster out.

NOTE: The 1981–85 300SD, 380SE, 380SEC, 380SEl, 500SEC and 500SEL models use 5 clips to hold the instrument cluster in place.

5. Pull it out as far as possible and disconnect the speedometer cable, electrical connections and oil pressure line.
6. To install, reconnect the electrical connections, oil pressure line and speedometer cable. To avoid speedometer cable noise, guide it into the largest radius possible.
7. Push the instrument cluster firmly into the dashboard.

Combination Switch

REMOVAL & INSTALLATION

190D, 190E, 240D, 260E, 280E, 280CE, 300D, 300E, 300CD, 300TD, 380SL, 380SLC and 560SL

1. Remove the rubber sleeve on the switch and then unscrew the retaining screws.

Recess slot in the instrument cluster

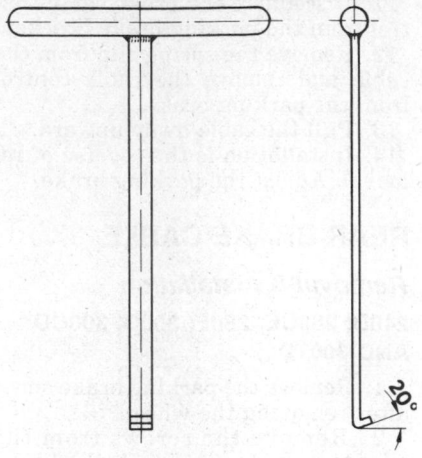

Fabricated tool for removing the instrument cluster

2. Pull the switch out slightly, loosen the screws for the cable connection of the twin carbon contacts and pull out the cable.
3. Remove the cover underneath the left side of the instrument panel.
4. Disconnect the plug and then remove the switch.
5. Installation is in the reverse order of removal.

300SD (1981–85), 380SE, 380SEC, 380SEL, 420SEL, 500SEC, 500SEL, 560SEC and 560SEL

1. Remove the steering wheel.
2. Remove the cover underneath the left side of the instrument panel.
3. Unscrew the switch retaining screws.
4. Disconnect the 14-prong plug underneath the instrument panel.
5. Remove the switch.
6. Installation is in the reverse order of removal.

Ignition Switch

REMOVAL & INSTALLATION
All Models With Ignition Switch In Dashboard (Except 190D, 190E, 260E and 300E)

1. Remove the instrument cluster.
2. Remove the right-hand cover plate under the dashboard.
3. Remove the plug connection from the ignition switch.
4. Remove the screws which hold the ignition switch to the rear of the lock cylinder and remove the ignition switch.
5. To install the ignition switch, attach the plug connection, after fastening the switch to the steering lock.
6. Install the instrument cluster.
7. Check the switch for proper function and install the lower cover.

190D, 190E, 260E and 300E

1. Remove the cover plate under the left side of the instrument panel.
2. Remove the steering wheel. Remove the instrument cluster.
3. Pry the cylinder rosette (trim ring) upwards and then remove it.
4. Insert the ignition key and turn it to position 1.
5. Disconnect the plug at the rear of the ignition switch.

NOTE: The plug can only be disconnected when the key is in position 1.

6. Loosen the screws and then remove the steering column jacket (upper and lower halves).
7. Release the clamp on the jacket tube. Press in the lock-pin in position 1 and then pull the steering lock out slightly from the jacket tube holder.
8. Pull off the ignition key at the right bottom section, slightly to the rear. Swivel the steering lock so that the lock cylinder clears its hole in the instrument panel.
9. Unscrew the retaining screws and remove the ignition switch from the back of the steering lock.
10. Installation is in the reverse order of removal. Remember to reconnect the switch to the steering lock.

Lock Cylinder (Key can be removed in position 1)

REMOVAL & INSTALLATION

1. Turn the key to position 1 and remove the key.
2. Pry the cover sleeve from the lock cylinder with a small screwdriver.
3. Using a bent paper clip, hook onto the cover sleeve and remove the

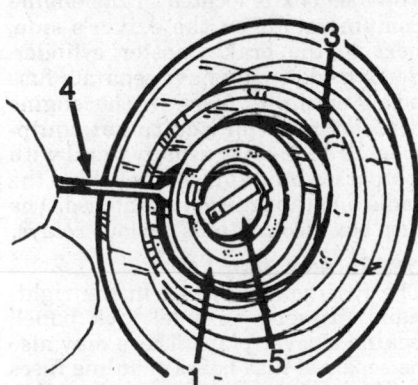

1. Steering lock   4. Steel wire (paper clip)
3. Rosette   5. Locking cylinder

Ignition lock cylinder removal from the instrument panel (both types)

sleeve. Be sure that you do not remove the rosette in the dashboard also.
4. Insert the paper clip between the rosette and the steering lock and push in the lock pin. Remove the lock cylinder slightly with the key.
5. Insert the paper clip into the locking hole and pull the lock cylinder completely out.
6. Installation is the reverse or removal. Turn the lock cylinder to position 1 and insert it into the steering lock, making sure that the lock pin engages. Push the cover sleeve into position 1.
7. Make sure that the cylinder operates properly.

Lock Cylinder (Key cannot be removed in position 1)

REMOVAL & INSTALLATION

All Models Except 190D, 190E, 260E and 300E

Because of legal requirements, the lock was changed from the previous version, so that the key can only be removed in position 0.

1. Turn the key to position 1.
2. Lift the cover sleeve to the edge of the key and turn the key to position 0.
3. Remove the key and cover sleeve.
4. Insert the key into the lock cylinder and turn to position 1 (90 degrees to the right), push in the lock pin and remove the lock cylinder.
5. To install the lock cylinder, turn the lock cylinder to position 1 and insert the lock cylinder, making sure that the locking pin engages.
6. Turn the key to position 0 and remove the key.
7. Place the cover sleeve on the steering lock, insert and turn the key, and push in the cover sleeve in position 1.
8. Check the locking cylinder for proper function.

190D, 190E, 260E and 300E

1. Pry the cylinder rosette (trim ring) upwards and then remove it.
2. Insert the ignition key and turn it to position 1.
3. Using a bent paper clip, insert each end into the holes on either side of the lock cylinder. Press the clip ends inward; the pressure will unlock the cylinder from the steering lock.
4. Grasp the key and with pressure still on the paper clip, pull the ignition key/lock cylinder assembly out of the steering lock.

5. Remove the paper clip, turn the key to position 0 and remove it. Slide the lock cylinder out of the cover.
To install:
6. Insert the lock cylinder just enough so that the ridge on the cylinder body engages the groove in the steering lock.
7. Slide the cover onto the lock cylinder so that the detent is on the left side.
8. Insert the ignition key, turn it to position 1 and then push the lock cylinder and its cover into the steering lock.

NOTE: When the ignition key is in position 1 and is aligned with the mark on the cover, the detent on the cover is also aligned with the ridge on the steering lock. This is the only manner in which the lock cylinder/cover can be installed in the steering lock.

9. Check that the lock cylinder functions properly, if so, install the rosette.

Steering Lock

REMOVAL & INSTALLATION

All Models Except 190D, 190E, 260E and 300E

1. Disconnect the ground cable from the battery.
2. Remove the instrument cluster.
3. Remove the plug connection from the ignition switch behind the dashboard.
4. Pull the ignition key to position 1.
5. Loosen the attaching screw for the steering lock.
6. Remove the cover sleeve from the steering lock.
7. On vehicles with the latest version of the steering lock, pull the connection for the warning buzzer.
8. Push in the lock pin with a small punch.
9. Turn the steering lock and remove it from the holder in the column jacket. Be sure that the rosette is not damaged.

—— **CAUTION** ——
The lock pin can only be pushed in when the cylinder is in position 1.

10. To install the steering lock, connect the warning buzzer if so equipped.
11. Place the steering lock in position 1 and insert the lock into the steering column while pushing the lock pin in. Be sure that the lock pin engages.
12. Tighten the attaching clamp screw.

13. Attach the plug connection to the ignition switch.

14. Push the cover sleeve onto the lock in position 1.

15. Install the instrument cluster.

16. Check to be sure that the steering lock works properly.

190D, 190E, 260E and 300E

1. Follow Steps 1–8 of "Ignition Switch Removal and Installation."

2. Unplug the switch and remove the steering lock.

3. Installation is in the reverse order of removal.

Wiper Motor and Linkage
REMOVAL & INSTALLATION
240D, 280E, 280CE, 300D, 300CD and 300TD

1. Remove the wiper arms.

2. Remove the air intake grille on the right side.

3. Remove the covering cap and nut on the left and right side bearing shafts.

4. Remove the four expanding rivets and then remove the left side air intake grille.

5. Remove the center air plenum cover (four expanding rivets and a Phillips screw).

6. Carefully pull the left and right side connecting rods off of the wiper motor crank.

7. Remove the water drain tube from the right side bearing shaft.

8. Disconnect the coupler plug in the engine compartment. Unclip the plug from the firewall and pull it all the way through.

9. Unbolt the wiper motor and remove it toward the right side.

10. Installation is in the reverse order of removal.

300SD (1981–85), 300SE, 380SEC, 380SEL, 420SEL, 500SEC, 500SEL, 560SEC and 560SEL

1. Remove the wiper arms.

2. Remove the air intake cover. Unscrew the fastening screws and then disconnect the front plug connector.

3. Compress the mounting flange on the rear plug connector. Push the plug out of the firewall toward the front of the car, twist it and then insert it toward the rear of the car.

4. Remove the wiper motor and linkage.

5. Unscrew the nut on the wiper motor shaft.

6. Swivel the wiper linkage and then unscrew the bolts for the wiper motor underneath.

7. Remove the wiper motor.

To install:

8. Mount the wiper motor in the base plate.

9. Push the crank arm on the wiper motor shaft and position the nut. Make sure that the lever on the right hand wiper shaft is pointing down.

10. Align the crank arm so that the upper edge is parallel with the wiper motor shaft.

11. Tighten the nut on the wiper motor shaft.

12. Attach the wiper motor and linkage assembly to the vehicle.

13. Installation of the remaining components is in the reverse order of removal.

260E and 300E

1. Open the hood.

2. Remove the air inlet cover.

3. Pry open the cover plate on the lower end of the wiper arm and remove the Allen screw.

4. Pull the wiper arm off the shaft.

5. Remove the motor assembly mounting nuts and clamp.

6. Disconnect the electrical lead and then remove the wiper assembly.

7. Unscrew the nut on the motor shaft and pry off the driver lever.

8. Unbolt the wiper motor and remove it.

9. Tighten the wiper motor-to-mount bracket nuts to 5 Nm. The motor must be in the park position; if unsure, connect the electrical lead temporarily and operate the switch to the park position. Disconnect the lead.

10. Position the drive arm onto the motor shaft and tighten the nut to 19 Nm.

11. Installation of the remaining components is the reverse order of removal.

190D and 190E

1. Open the hood all the way and disconnect the battery.

2. Remove the wiper arm.

3. Remove the round cover from the wiper shaft.

4. Remove the two clips, the rubber seal and the two screws and then remove the air intake cover.

5. Pull the three-piece air intake pan from the windshield and remove it.

6. Unscrew the wiper motor/linkage assembly.

7. Remove the cover and unscrew the four mounting bolts for the fuse box. Pull the fuse box slightly forward and up and then unplug the wiper motor connection.

8. Remove the wiper motor/linkage assembly.

9. Remove the nut on the wiper motor shaft and then pull off the crank arm and linkage.

10. Unscrew and remove the wiper motor.

To install:

11. Attach the wiper motor to the base plate.

12. Press the crank arm onto the wiper motor shaft. Make sure that the crank arm and the pushrod are parallel.

13. Attach the crank arm to the wiper motor and install the wiper motor/linkage assembly.

14. Installation of the remaining components is in the reverse order of removal.

Fuses

A listing of the protected equipment and the amperage of the fuse is printed in the lid of the fuse box. Spare fuses and a tool for removing and installing fuses are contained in the vehicle tool kit.

Fuses cannot be repaired; they must be replaced. Always determine the cause of the blown fuse before replacing it with a new one.

FUSE BOX LOCATION
240D, 300D, 300TD, 280E, 280CE and 300CD

On early models, the fuse box may be found in the kick panel on the driver's side. On later models the fuse box is located in the engine compartment on the driver's side, next the the brake master cylinder. Some models have separate fuse boxes or inline fuses for additional equipment. The radio is usually fused with a separate inline glass fuse behind the radio and the ignition is unfused.

190D, 190E, 260E, 300E, 300SD, 380SE, 380SEC, 380SEL, 420SEL, 500SEC, 500SEL, 560SEC, 560SEL, and 560SEC

The fuse box is located in the engine compartment, on the driver's side, next to the brake master cylinder. Some models may have separate fuse boxes or inline fuses in the engine compartment for additional equipment. The radio is usually fused with a separate inline glass fuse behind the radio and the ignition is unfused. The fuse box also contains various relays.

380SL and 380SLC

The fuse box is located in the right-hand (passenger's side) kick panel, behind a cover plate. There may also be separate fuse boxes or inline fuses in the engine compartment for additional equipment. The radio is usually fused with a separate inline glass fuse behind the radio and the ignition is unfused. The kick panel area also contains various relays and switches.

Merkur

XR4Ti, Scorpio

SERIAL NUMBER IDENTIFICATION

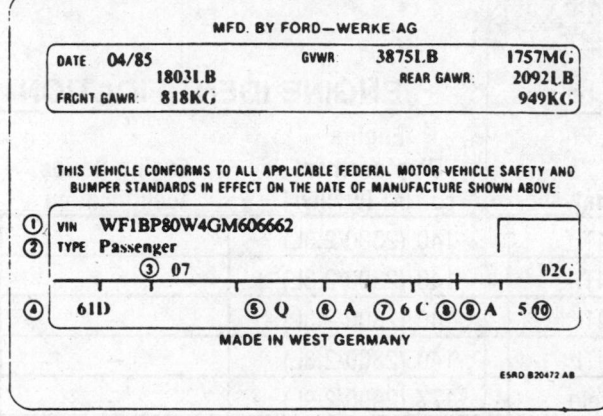

MFD. BY FORD—WERKE AG

DATE	04/85		GVWR	3875LB	1757MG
		1803LB	REAR GAWR:		2092LB
FRONT GAWR:	818KG				949KG

THIS VEHICLE CONFORMS TO ALL APPLICABLE FEDERAL MOTOR VEHICLE SAFETY AND BUMPER STANDARDS IN EFFECT ON THE DATE OF MANUFACTURE SHOWN ABOVE

① VIN WF1BP80W4GM606662
② TYPE Passenger
　　　　③ 07　　　　　　　　　02G
④ 61D　　　　⑤ Q　⑥ A ⑦ 6 C ⑧ A　5 ⑩

MADE IN WEST GERMANY

ESRD B20472 AB

Typical Vehicle Identification Label

1. Vehicle identification number
2. Vehicle type
3. Paint
4. Body type code
5. Interior trim
6. Air conditioning
7. Radio
8. Sunroof
9. Axle ratio
10. Transmission

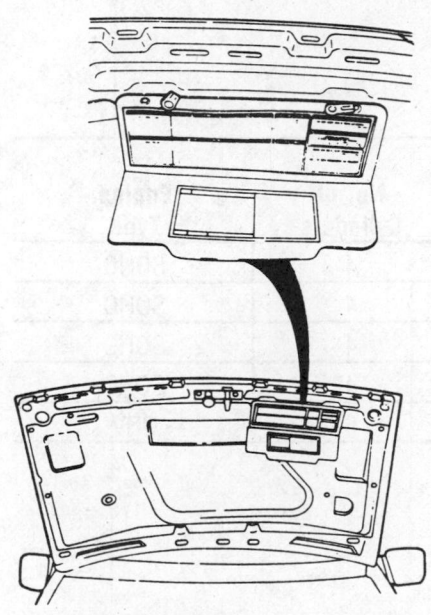

Location of emission control information folder under the hood

Vehicle Identification Plate

The official Vehicle Identification Number (VIN) for title and registration purposes is stamped on a metal tab that is fastened to the instrument panel close to the windshield on the driver's side of the vehicle.

Engine Number

Refer to Vehicle Certification Label for engine identification and consecu-

tive unit numbers. The engine calibration number is located on a sticker affixed to the front of the engine. Engine code information is also contained on this sticker.

Vehicle Identification Label

The vehicle identification/ certification label is attached to the left front door lock panel. The upper half of the label contains the name of the manufacturer, Gross Vehicle Weight (GVWR) and Gross Axle Weight (GAWR) ratings, and the certification statement. A seventeen character VIN number is also shown. The number indicates; manufacturer, type of restraint system, line, series, body type, engine, model year and consecu-

tive unit number. The last six digits of the VIN label indicate the consecutive unit number of each vehicle built at each assembly plant. Also shown on the label are the color code, body type and interior trim codes. The remaining numbers are special equipment, axle and transmission codes.

Emission Control Information Label

Every vehicle is equipped with a decal containing emission control information that applies specifically to that vehicle and engine. The specifications provided on the decal are important to servicing emission systems. In addition to the tune-up specifications and procedures, the emission decal shows

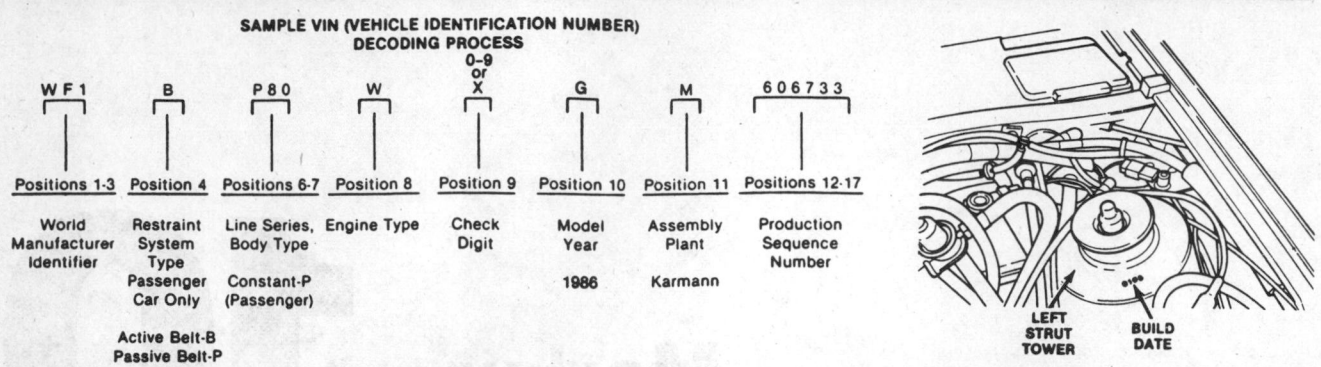

SAMPLE VIN (VEHICLE IDENTIFICATION NUMBER)
DECODING PROCESS

W F 1	B	P 80	W	0-9 or X	G	M	606733
Positions 1-3	Position 4	Positions 6-7	Position 8	Position 9	Position 10	Position 11	Positions 12-17
World Manufacturer Identifier	Restraint System Type Passenger Car Only	Line Series, Body Type Constant-P (Passenger)	Engine Type	Check Digit	Model Year 1986	Assembly Plant Karmann	Production Sequence Number
	Active Belt-B Passive Belt-P						

VIN number interpretation

The build date is stamped in ink on the left strut tower

a color coded schematic of the engine vacuum system. The color coding on the schematic represents the actual color coding of the vacuum hoses, however, there will be instances where the individual hose color will not agree. The emission information label is located under the hood in the service information folder.

ENGINE IDENTIFICATION

Year	Model	Engine Displacement cu. in. (cc/liter)	Engine Series Identification	No. of Cylinders	Engine Type
1985	XR4Ti	140 (2300/2.3L)	—	4	SOHC
1986	XR4Ti	140 (2300/2.3L)	—	4	SOHC
1987	XR4Ti	140 (2300/2.3L)	—	4	SOHC
1988	XR4Ti	140 (2300/2.3L)	—	4	SOHC
	Scorpio	177 (2900/2.9L)	—	6	OHV

SOHC Single Overhead Camshaft
OHV Overhead Valves

GENERAL ENGINE SPECIFICATIONS

Year	Model	Engine Displacement cu. in. (cc)	Fuel System Type	Net Horsepower @ rpm	Net Torque @ rpm (ft. lbs.)	Bore × Stroke (in.)	Com-pression Ratio	Oil Pressure @ rpm
1985	XR4Ti	140 (2300)	EFI	175 @ 5000 ①	200 @ 3000 ②	3.78 x 3.12	8.0:1	50 @ 2000
1986	XR4Ti	140 (2300)	EFI	175 @ 5000 ①	200 @ 3000 ②	3.78 x 3.12	8.0:1	50 @ 2000
1987	XR4Ti	140 (2300)	EFI	175 @ 5000 ①	200 @ 3000 ②	3.78 x 3.12	8.0:1	50 @ 2000
1988	XR4Ti	140 (2300)	EFI	175 @ 5000 ①	200 @ 3000 ②	3.78 x 3.12	8.0:1	50 @ 2000
	Scorpio	177 (2900)	EFI	144 @ 5500	162 @ 3000	3.66 x 2.83	9.0:1	35 @ 2000

EFI Electronic Fuel Injection
① 145 @ 4400 w/AT
② 180 @ 3000 w/AT

GASOLINE ENGINE TUNE-UP SPECIFICATIONS

Year	Model	Engine Displacement cu. in. (cc)	Spark Plugs Type	Spark Plugs Gap (in.)	Ignition Timing (deg.) MT	Ignition Timing (deg.) AT	Compression Pressure (psi)	Fuel Pump (psi)	Idle Speed (rpm) MT	Idle Speed (rpm) AT	Valve Clearance In.	Valve Clearance Ex.
1985	XR4Ti	140 (2300)	AWSF-32C	.034	13B ①	10B ①	NA	39 ②	900 ①	900 ①	Hyd.	Hyd.
1986	XR4Ti	140 (2300)	BSFC-32	.034	13B ①	10B ①	NA	39 ②	900 ①	900 ①	Hyd.	Hyd.
1987	XR4Ti	140 (2300)	BSFC-32	.034	13B ①	10B ①	NA	39 ②	900 ①	900 ①	Hyd.	Hyd.
1988			SEE UNDERHOOD SPECIFICATIONS STICKER									

NOTE: The Underhood Specifications sticker often reflects tune-up specification changes made in production. Sticker figures must be used if they disagree with those in this chart.

MT—Manual transmission
AT—Automatic transmission
NA— Not available at time of publication
A—After Top Dead Center
B—Before Top Dead Center
Hyd.—Hydraulic valve lash adjusters

① Ignition timing and idle speed are computer-controlled by the EEC-IV engine control system. See text for details
② Specification is fuel system pressure. Two fuel pumps are used. See text for details

FIRING ORDERS

NOTE: To avoid confusion, always replace spark wires one at a time.

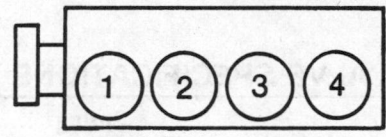

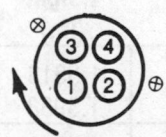

FORD MOTOR CO. 2300 cc 4-cyl.
Engine firing order: 1-3-4-2
Distributor rotation: clockwise

CAPACITIES

Year	Model	Engine Displacement cu. in. (cc)	Engine Crankcase with Filter	Engine Crankcase without Filter	Transmission (pts.) 4-Spd	Transmission (pts.) 5-Spd	Transmission (pts.) Auto.	Drive Axle (pts.)	Fuel Tank (gal.)	Cooling System (qts.)
1985	XR4Ti	140 (2300)	5.0	4.5	—	2.6	16①	1.9	15	10.5
1986	XR4Ti	140 (2300)	5.0	4.5	—	2.6	16①	1.9	15	10.5
1987	XR4Ti	140 (2300)	5.0	4.5	—	2.6	16①	1.9	15	10.5
1988	XR4Ti	140 (2300)	5.0	4.5	—	2.6	16①	1.9	15	10.5
	Scorpio	177 (2900)	4.5	4.0	—	2.6	18.5①	2.8	17	9.0

① Specification is for total refill. Check fluid level with dipstick

CAMSHAFT SPECIFICATIONS
All measurements given in inches.

Year	Engine Displacement cu. in. (cc)	Journal Diameter					Lobe Lift		Bearing Clearance	Camshaft End Play
		1	2	3	4	5	In.	Ex.		
1985	140 (2300)	1.7713–1.7720	1.7713–1.7720	1.7713–1.7720	1.7713–1.7720	1.7713–1.7720	0.400	0.400	0.001–0.003	0.001–0.007
1986	140 (2300)	1.7713–1.7720	1.7713–1.7720	1.7713–1.7720	1.7713–1.7720	1.7713–1.7720	0.400	0.400	0.001–0.003	0.001–0.007
1987-88	140 (2300)	1.7713–1.7720	1.7713–1.7720	1.7713–1.7720	1.7713–1.7720	1.7713–1.7720	0.400	0.400	0.001–0.003	0.001–0.007

CRANKSHAFT AND CONNECTING ROD SPECIFICATIONS
All measurements are given in inches.

Year	Engine Displacement cu. in. (cc)	Crankshaft				Connecting Rod		
		Main Brg. Journal Dia.	Main Brg. Oil Clearance	Shaft End-play	Thrust on No.	Journal Diameter	Oil Clearance	Side Clearance
1985	140 (2300)	2.3990–2.3982	0.0008–0.0015	0.004–0.008	3	2.0465–2.0472	0.0008–0.0015	0.0035–0.0105
1986	140 (2300)	2.3990–2.3982	0.0008–0.0015	0.004–0.008	3	2.0465–2.0472	0.0008–0.0015	0.0035–0.0105
1987-88	140 (2300)	2.3990–2.3982	0.0008–0.0015	0.004–0.008	3	2.0465–2.0472	0.0008–0.0015	0.0035–0.0105

VALVE SPECIFICATIONS

Year	Engine Displacement cu. in. (cc)	Seat Angle (deg.)	Face Angle (deg.)	Spring Test Pressure (lbs.)	Spring Installed Height (in.)	Stem-to-Guide Clearance (in.)		Stem Diameter (in.)	
						Intake	Exhaust	Intake	Exhaust
1985	140 (2300)	45	44	71–79 ①	1.5313–1.5938	0.0010–0.0027	0.0015–0.0032	0.3416–0.3423	0.3411–0.3418
1986	140 (2300)	45	44	71–79 ①	1.5313–1.5938	0.0010–0.0027	0.0015–0.0032	0.3416–0.3423	0.3411–0.3418
1987–88	140 (2300)	45	44	71–79 ①	1.5313–1.5938	0.0010–0.0027	0.0015–0.0032	0.3416–0.3423	0.3411–0.3418

① @ 1.52 inches

PISTON AND RING SPECIFICATIONS
All measurments are given in inches.

Year	Engine Displacement cu. in. (cc)	Piston Clearance	Ring Gap			Ring Side Clearance		
			Top Compression	Bottom Compression	Oil Control	Top Compression	Bottom Compression	Oil Control
1985	140 (2300)	0.0030–0.0038	0.010–0.020	0.010–0.020	0.015–0.055	0.002–0.004	0.002–0.004	Snug
1986	140 (2300)	0.0030–0.0038	0.010–0.020	0.010–0.020	0.015–0.055	0.002–0.004	0.002–0.004	Snug
1987-88	140 (2300)	0.0030–0.0038	0.010–0.020	0.010–0.020	0.015–0.055	0.002–0.004	0.002–0.004	Snug

TORQUE SPECIFICATIONS
All readings in ft. lbs.

Year	Engine Displacement cu. in. (cc)	Cylinder Head Bolts	Main Bearing Bolts	Rod Bearing Bolts	Crankshaft Pulley Bolts	Flywheel Bolts	Manifold		Spark Plugs
							Intake	Exhaust	
1985	140 (2300)	80–90 ①	80–90 ①	30–36 ②	100–120	50–04	14–21	③	10–15
1986	140 (2300)	80–90 ①	80–90 ①	30–36 ②	100–120	56–64	14–21	③	10–15
1987-88	140 (2300)	80–90 ①	80–90 ①	30–36 ②	100–120	56–64	14–21	③	10–15

① Torque in two steps: 1st to 50–60 and 2nd to 80–90
② Torque in two steps: 1st to 25–30 and 2nd to 30–36
③ Torque in two steps: 1st to 5–7 and 2nd to 16–23

BRAKE SPECIFICATIONS
All measurements in inches unless noted

Year	Model	Lug Nut Torque (ft. lbs.)	Master Cylinder Bore	Brake Disc		Standard Brake Drum Diameter	Minimum Lining Thickness	
				Minimum Thickness	Maximum Runout		Front	Rear
1985	XR4Ti	75–101	0.940	0.950	0.003	10.0	①	①
1986	XR4Ti	75–101	0.940	0.950	0.003	10.0	①	①
1987-88	XR4Ti	75–101	1.000	0.950	0.003	10.0	①	①

① $\frac{1}{8}$ in. above metal shoe
$\frac{1}{16}$ in. above rivets

WHEEL ALIGNMENT

Year	Model	Caster		Camber		Toe-in (in.)	Steering Axis Inclination (deg.)
		Range (deg.)	Preferred Setting (deg.)	Range (deg.)	Preferred Setting (deg.)		
1985	XR4Ti	$\frac{15}{16}$P–$2\frac{15}{16}$P	$1\frac{15}{16}$P	$1\frac{1}{2}$N–$\frac{1}{2}$P	$\frac{1}{2}$N ①	②	$13\frac{11}{16}$
1986	XR4Ti	$\frac{15}{16}$P–$2\frac{15}{16}$P	$1\frac{15}{16}$P	$1\frac{1}{2}$N–$\frac{1}{2}$P	$\frac{1}{2}$N ①	②	$13\frac{11}{16}$
1987	XR4Ti	$\frac{15}{16}$P–$2\frac{15}{16}$P	$1\frac{15}{16}$P	$1\frac{1}{2}$N–$\frac{1}{2}$P	$\frac{1}{2}$N ①	②	$13\frac{11}{16}$
1988	XR4Ti	$\frac{15}{16}$P–$2\frac{15}{16}$P	$1\frac{15}{16}$P	$1\frac{1}{2}$N–$\frac{1}{2}$P	$\frac{1}{2}$N ①	②	$13\frac{11}{16}$
	Scorpio	$\frac{7}{7}$P–$2\frac{7}{8}$P	$1\frac{7}{8}$P	$1\frac{3}{8}$N–$\frac{3}{8}$P	$\frac{3}{8}$N ③	④	$13\frac{11}{16}$

① Rear: $2\frac{3}{4}$N–$2\frac{3}{16}$P; dependent upon ride height
② Front: $\frac{1}{16}$N–$\frac{3}{4}$P; dependent upon ride height
  Rear: $\frac{1}{32}$N–$\frac{5}{16}$P; dependent upon ride height
③ Rear: $4\frac{5}{16}$N–$1\frac{1}{8}$P; dependent upon ride height
④ Rear: $\frac{1}{2}$N–$\frac{5}{8}$P; combined wheel-to-wheel

Tune-Up Procedures

Ignition Timing

BASE TIMING ADJUSTMENT

NOTE: Make all adjustments with the engine at normal operating temperature, transmission in neutral (manual) or park (automatic), parking brake applied, wheels blocked and all accessories turned off.

1. With engine off, clean and highlight the timing marks on the crankshaft pulley and belt cover. Connect a timing light and tachometer to the engine. The ignition coil connector allows a tachometer connection using an alligator clip without removing the coil connector.

2. Disconnect the single wire spark output (SPOUT) connector near (within six inches of the TFI module) the distributor. Restart the previously warmed up engine.

3. Check the idle rpm. The engine is equipped with an electronic idle speed control and the idle should be between 825–975 rpm for manual transmission. 925–1075 rpm for automatic transmissions. If idle adjustment is necessary, shut off the engine and disconnect the electrical connector at the idle bypass valve. Restart the engine and run at approximately 2000 rpm, briefly. Allow the engine to return to idle and adjust the idle speed to 725–775 rpm by turning the throttle plate stop screw. Shut off the engine and reconnect the electrical connector to the bypass valve. Restart engine and proceed with ignition timing check.

NOTE: If the underhood calibration/emissions sticker specifications differ from this procedure, follow the specs and directions on the sticker as they will reflect product changes. If the cooling fan comes on during idle speed adjustment, wait until it shuts off or disconnect it temporarily before making adjustment.

4. Point the timing light at the marks. Timing should be 13 degrees BTDC (before top dead center) for manual transmission models, or 10 degrees BTDC for automatic transmission models. Loosen the distributor holddown bolt and adjust the timing as required by twisting the distributor assembly clockwise or

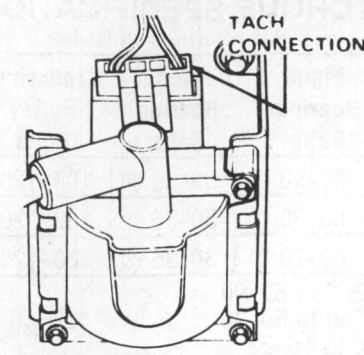

Tachometer connection

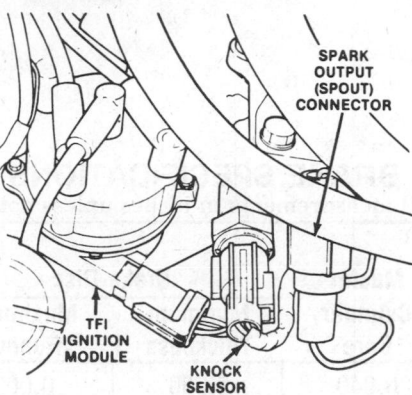

The SPOUT connector must be disconnected to set base timing

counterclockwise. Tighten the holddown bolt and recheck timing.

NOTE: Some distributor holddown bolts made have a special Torx® head which requires a special wrench.

5. After base timing has been set, shut off the engine and remove all test equipment. Reconnect the single SPOUT wire harness at the distributor.

INITIAL TIMING CHECK

An initial timing check should be performed if there is reason to believe the distributor is no longer timed to the engine. This condition can result from incorrect installation of the distributor or a timing belt that has jumped timing.

1. Remove the No. 1 spark plug from the engine.

2. Install a compression gauge in the No. 1 spark plug hole.

3. Connect a remote starter switch between the battery positive terminal and the starter relay S terminal.

4. Using the starter switch, bump the engine around until the compression gauge indicates the No. 1 piston is on its compression stroke.

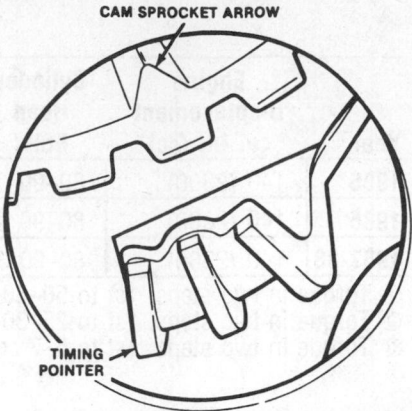

Correct timing mark alignment as viewed through the access plug on the timing belt outer cover

5. Continue bumping the engine with the starter switch until the timing mark on the crankshaft (pulley notch) is aligned with the Top Dead Center (TDC) mark on the timing scale.

6. Remove the distributor cap and check that the rotor tip is pointing to the No. 1 spark plug wire terminal in the distributor cap. If the rotor and cap are correctly aligned, initial timing is OK, proceed to the next step. If the rotor and distributor cap do not align, remove the distributor and reinstall it so the rotor is pointing to No. 1 plug tower.

7. Remove the access plug from the timing belt outer cover and check that the timing mark on the cam sprocket is aligned with the timing pointer. If the cam sprocket timing mark is aligned with the pointer, the engine is properly timed. If the cam sprocket timing mark does not align with the pointer, the timing belt has jumped time and must be replaced. Refer to the procedures under "Timing Belt" for removal and installation.

8. Check and adjust the base ignition timing as previously described.

Valve Lash

Hydraulic valve lash adjusters are used in the valve train. The last adjusters are placed at the fulcrum point of the rocker arms and operation is similar to the hydraulic lifters used in pushrod equipped engines. Oil is provided to the lash adjusters under pressure via passages drilled in the cylinder head. The lash adjusters require no periodic manual adjustment.

ADJUSTMENT

4 Cylinder

If a lash adjuster becomes noisy or valve service has been performed on

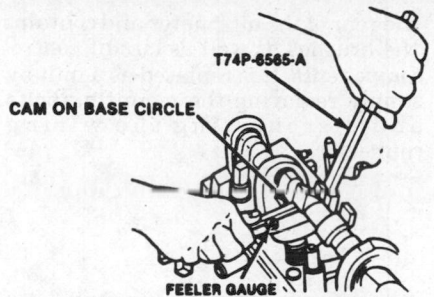

CAM ON BASE CIRCLE

T74P-6565-A

FEELER GAUGE

Measuring clearance between the base circle of the camshaft and the follower with a feeler gauge and spring compressor tool

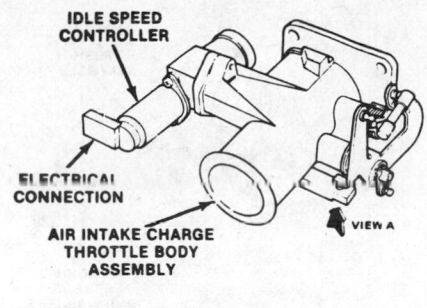

IDLE SPEED CONTROLLER

ELECTRICAL CONNECTION

AIR INTAKE CHARGE THROTTLE BODY ASSEMBLY

VIEW A

THROTTLE PLATE STOP SCREW — VIEW A

Adjust the idle speed by turning the throttle plate stop screw after unplugging the idle speed controller connector. Disconnect or reconnect all electrical connections with the ignition switch off.

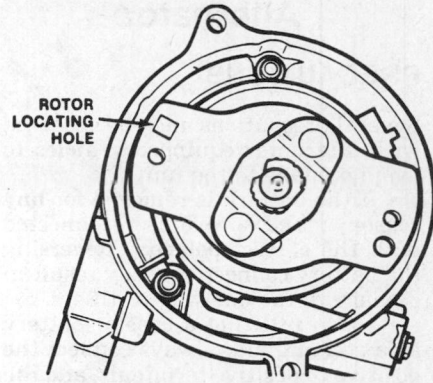

ROTOR LOCATING HOLE

Note the position of the shaft plate, armature and rotor locating holes when removing the distributor.

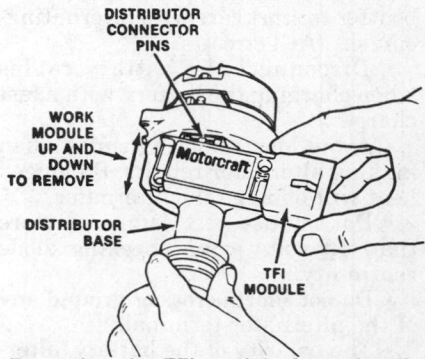

DISTRIBUTOR CONNECTOR PINS

WORK MODULE UP AND DOWN TO REMOVE

DISTRIBUTOR BASE

TFI MODULE

Removing the TFI module from the distributor. If attempting this with the distributor installed, be careful not to bend any connector pins

the cylinder head, valve train clearance should be checked as follows:

1. Remove the valve cover as described under "Cam Follower Removal & Installation". Turn the engine in the normal direction of rotation until the base circle (round part) of camshaft lobe is against the rocker arm of the valve being checked. Do not attempt to rotate the engine backwards; if you miss the base circle alignment, rotate the engine around and try again.

2. Use a valve spring compressor tool (T74P-6565-A or equivalent) to slowly apply pressure to the cam follower, until the lash adjuster is completely collapsed. Hold the rocker arm in this position and check the clearance between the base circle of the cam lobe and the rocker arm with a feeler gauge. Allowable clearance is 0.035–0.055 in. (0.89–1.4mm). Desired clearance is 0.040–0.050 in. (1.0–1.27mm).

3. If the clearance is excessive, remove the cam follower and inspect for wear. If the follower is not worn, measure the assembled height of the valve spring. If the assembled height of the spring is correct, check for camshaft wear. If the camshaft is not worn, the lash adjuster should be removed and checked.

4. Replace worn parts as required and recheck clearance.

Idle Speed and Mixture

ADJUSTMENT

Refer to the ignition timing procedure for checking and adjusting the idle speed. Mixture is controlled by the EEC IV(electronic engine control) system and is not adjustable. EEC IV system testing is required if an ignition or air/fuel mixture problem is suggested.

NOTE: If the engine speed is excessive while driving the vehicle with the throttle at the idle position, turn the ignition switch off until the engine has stopped, then restart the engine. If the engine speed is still excessive, do not drive the vehicle until the condition is repaired.

ENGINE ELECTRICAL

Distributor

REMOVAL & INSTALLATION

1. Disconnect the negative battery cable.

2. Disconnect the wiring harness to the TFI module on the side of the distributor. Disconnect the coil wire.

3. Loosen the attaching screws, then remove the distributor cap and position it to the side with the spark plug wires attached.

4. Remove the screws that retain the rotor and remove the rotor.

5. Note the position of the shaft plate, armature and rotor aligning holes. Mark reference lines on the distributor body and engine block for installation alignment.

6. Remove the distributor holddown bolt and clamp, located under the distributor bowl between the distributor base and cylinder block. If the holddown bolt has a Torx® head, a special wrench will be required.

7. Remove the distributor from the engine by grasping the base and pulling straight out. Check that the base O-ring is in position and not damaged or cut. Once the distributor is removed, the TFI module can be replaced by simply removing the two mounting bolts and working the module back and forth until the pin connectors are free. Make sure there are no bent pin connectors when installing the TFI module.

NOTE: When installing a new TFI module, coat the metal base plate uniformly with a 1/32 in. thick cover of silicone dielectric compound. Failure to do so will result in premature module failure due to excessive heat buildup.

8. Install the distributor in the reverse order of removal. Lubricate the base O-ring lightly with engine oil. Make sure the reference marks previously scribed are aligned and the TFI module is in the same position to the engine as it was when the distributor was removed.

9. Install the holddown clamp and bolt. Tighten the bolt until the distributor can barely be rotated.

10. Install the rotor and distributor cap. Reconnect the coil wire and TFI harness connector, then reconnect the negative battery cable.

11. Check and adjust the ignition timing as required. Once the ignition timing is set, tighten the holddown bolt to 6–8 ft. lbs. (8–11 Nm).

Alternator

PRECAUTIONS

Several precautions must be observed with alternator equipped vehicles to avoid damage to the unit.

• If the battery is removed for any reason, make sure it is reconnected with the correct polarity. Reversing the battery connections may result in damage to the one-way rectifiers.

• When utilizing a booster battery as a starting aid, always connect the positive to positive terminals, and the negative terminal from the booster battery to a good engine ground on the car being started.

• Never use a fast charger as a booster to start cars with alternating-current (AC) circuits.

• Disconnect the battery cables when charging the battery with a fast charger.

• Avoid long soldering times when making alternator repairs. Prolonged heat will damage the alternator.

• Do not use test lamps of more than 12 volts when checking diode continuity.

• Do not short across or ground any of the alternator terminals.

• The polarity of the battery, alternator and regulator must be matched and considered before making any electrical connections within the system.

• Never separate the alternator on an open circuit. Make sure all connections within the circuit are clean and tight.

• Disconnect the battery ground terminal when performing any service on electrical components.

• Disconnect the battery if arc welding is to be done on the vehicle.

REMOVAL & INSTALLATION

1. Disconnect the negative battery cable.
2. Loosen the alternator pivot bolt and remove the adjustment arm-to-alternator bolt. Pivot the alternator to release belt tension.
3. Remove the drive belts.
4. Tag and disconnect the wiring terminals from the alternator.
5. Remove the alternator pivot bolt and the alternator.
6. Install the alternator in the reverse order of removal. Adjust the drive belt tension so that there is approximately ¼–½ in. of deflection on the longest span of belt between pulleys. Apply pressure to the square rib on the alternator housing using the proper size open end wrench to maintain pressure when adjusting belt ten-

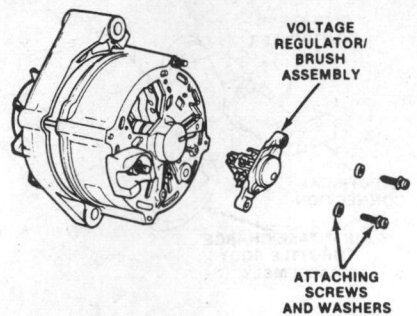

Voltage regulator mounting at rear of alternator housing

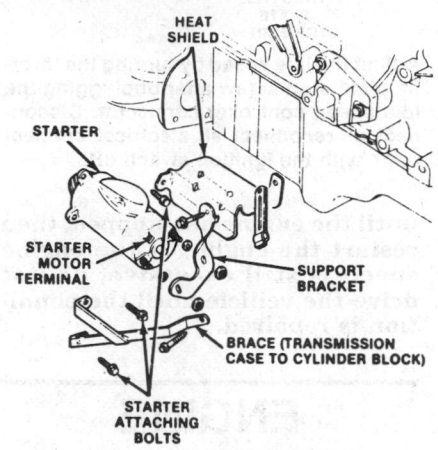

Typical starter motor mounting

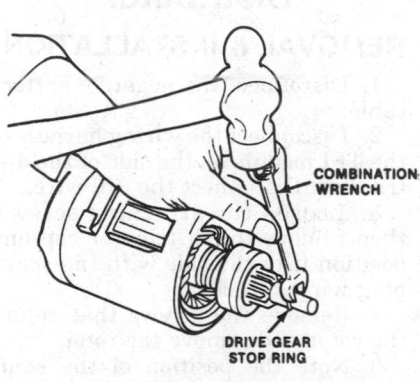

Removing the starter drive gear stop ring. Tap lightly and discard the ring.

sion. Tighten the adjuster pivot bolt to 44–60 ft. lbs. (60–81 Nm); the adjuster nut to 30–46 ft. lbs. (40–62 Nm); and the pulley attaching nut to 25–35 ft. lbs. (34–45 Nm).

Voltage Regulator

REMOVAL & INSTALLATION

The voltage regulator is mounted to the rear of the alternator and contains the brushes as well as circuit control components. It is replaced as a unit by simply removing the mounting bolts and disconecting the wiring connector.

Starter

REMOVAL & INSTALLATION

4 Cylinder

1. Disconnect the negative battery cable.
2. Raise the vehicle and support it safely with jackstands.
3. Disconnect the starter cable from the starter.
4. Remove the bolt attaching the heat shield to the cylinder block.
5. Remove the starter mounting bolts, the heat shield rear support bracket, transmission-to-block brace and the starter motor.
6. Manipulate the starter so that it can be lowered and removed from below the vehicle.
7. The installation of the starter assembly is the reverse of the removal procedure. Tighten the mounting bolts to 15–20 ft. lbs. (20–27 Nm).

STARTER DRIVE REPLACEMENT

1. Remove the top (drive yoke) cover from the starter motor.
2. Remove the through bolts, taking care to hold the brush end plate and armature in position.
3. Remove the pivot pin that retains the drive yoke, using a 0.218 in. (5.5mm) pin punch or small drift.
4. Remove the drive end housing, yoke return spring and drive yoke from the starter.
5. Remove the thrust washer and stop ring retainer from the armature shaft.
6. Remove the drive gear stop ring using a combination wrench and hammer. Discard the stop ring, then slide the starter drive gear off the armature shaft.
7. Apply Lubriplate® on the armature splines and install the starter drive in the reverse order or removal. Install a new stop ring by holding it with needle nosed pliers and tapping it onto the armature shaft with a hammer. Install the starter to the engine as previously described.

ENGINE MECHANICAL

Engine

REMOVAL & INSTALLATION

4 Cylinder

NOTE: Depressurize the fuel system, then disconnect the negative battery cable before beginning any work. Always label all disconnected hoses, vacuum lines and wires, to prevent incorrect reassembly. Do not disconnect any air conditioning lines unless you are throughly familiar with A/C systems and the hazards involved; escaping refrigerant (freon) will freeze any surface it contacts including skin and eyes.

1. Mark the hood hinge positions on the hood. Make sure the ground strap near the right hinge is disconnected, then remove the hood.

2. Disconnect the battery and remove it from the vehicle. Drain the cooling system.

3. Remove the air cleaner and duct assembly from the turbocharger.

4. Remove the upper and lower radiator hoses. If the vehicle is equipped with an automatic transmission, disconnect and plug the transmission fluid cooler lines from the radiator. If equipped with a manual transmission, disconnect the radiator air vent hose at the radiator.

5. Disconnect the electric cooling fan wire harness and remove the fan and shroud as an assembly. Remove the radiator.

6. Disconnect the heater hoses from the engine. Separate the oil level sensor wiring connector and remove the engine oil level dipstick.

7. Disconnect the wiring form the alternator and starter motor. Disconnect the air bypass valve connector and throttle position sensor connector from the throttle body. Disconnect the vacuum hose at the EGR valve, then separate the fuel injection wiring harness connector located between the upper intake manifold and the engine oil dipstick.

8. Disconnect the throttle cable and transmission kickdown cable (if equipped) at the pivot ball connections on the bracket. Remove the accelerator cable bracket attaching screws and the bracket from the upper intake manifold, then place the bracket and the accelerator and kickdown cables aside.

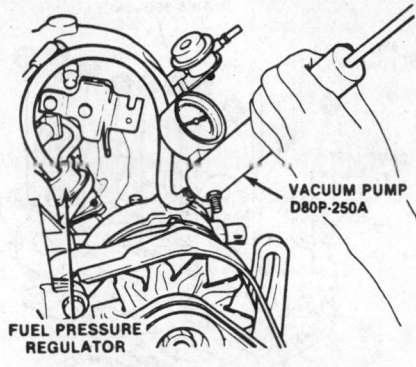

Depressurize the fuel system by applying vacuum to the fuel pressure regulator

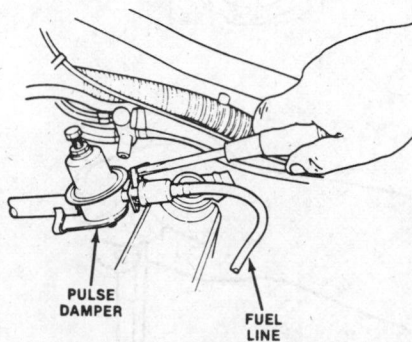

Disconnect the fuel line at the pulse damper

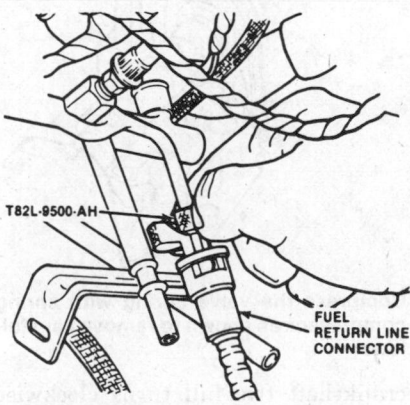

Disconnecting the quick-connect fuel line with removal tool

9. Depressurize the fuel system, if not already done, and disconnect the fuel line at the pulse damper. Disconnect the fuel return line using quick-connector removal tool T82L-9500-A or equivalent. Plug the fuel line and rail immediately to prevent contamination of the fuel system by dirt or grease during service.

10. Disconnect the wiring to the ignition coil, TFI module, oil pressure switch, temperature sending unit and all other sensors. Tag all connectors for installation. Tag and disconnect the supply hose at the vacuum tree mounted on the dash panel.

11. Remove the turbocharger air inlet tube, then disconnect the orange ground wire and vacuum hose at the turbocharger air inlet elbow.

12. Raise and safely support the front of the vehicle. Remove the air conditioner compressor from the mounting brackets with lines attached and wire it to the fender apron to position it out of the way.

13. Drain the engine oil. Remove the starter motor. Remove the flywheel or converter housing upper mounting bolts and the side braces.

14. Disconnect the muffler inlet pipe from the turbocharger. Disconnect any exhaust system mounting brackets from the engine. Remove the right and left side engine mount-to-crossmember studs and nuts.

15. Remove the flywheel or converter housing lower plate cover.

16. On models equipped with a manual transmission, remove the lower flywheel housing mounting bolts. On models with an automatic transmission, disconnect the converter from the driveplate (turn the engine in normal direction of rotation to gain access to the mountings). Remove the converter housing lower mounting bolts.

17. Lower the vehicle. Support the tranmission with a jack.

18. Attach an engine lifting sling to the existing engine lifting brackets. Slowly raise the engine and separate it from the transmission. Be sure the converter (auto trans) remains on the transmission shaft.

19. Slowly raise the engine from the vehicle, being careful not to snag any hoses, lines or wire harness connectors on the way out. Watch for any engine sensor connectors that may not have been disconnected.

20. Install the engine in the reverse order of removal. On models with an automatic transmission, be sure the converter mountings are aligned with the driveplate and the converter hub fits flush into the crank pilot. On models with a manual transmission be sure that the transmission main shaft is aligned with the clutch disc. If necessary turn the engine with the transmission in gear until the shaft splines engage the disc.

NOTE: Whenever self-locking motor mount bolts are nuts are removed, they must be replaced with new self-locking nuts or bolts. Clean old locking adhesive from the bolt or hole threads prior to installation.

Cylinder Head

REMOVAL & INSTALLATION

4 Cylinder

NOTE: The engine should be "overnight" cold before removing the cylinder head to prevent warpage or distortion. Depressurize the fuel system and always label all disconnected hoses and wires to assure proper assembly. Set the engine with No. 1 cylinder at TDC (top dead center) on the compression stroke with the timing marks aligned prior to cylinder head removal. This will make installation much easier.

1. Disconnect the negative battery cable. Drain the cooling system.
2. Disconnect the air intake cast tube from the turbocharger to the throttle body. Remove the valve rocker cover.
3. Remove the upper radiator hose and disconnect the heater hose if it interferes with cylinder head removal. Remove the alternator drive belts and the alternator and mounting brackets.
4. Depressurize the fuel system. Remove the intake and exhaust manifolds from the cylinder head.
5. Remove the camshaft drive belt cover.
6. Loosen the drive belt tensioner and remove the drive belt.
7. Remove the water outlet from the cylinder head.
8. Remove the cylinder head bolts evenly, and remove the cylinder head.
9. Position new cylinder head gasket on the block. Rotate the camshaft so that the drive sprocket locating pin is at the five o'clock position, to avoid valve or piston damage when reinstalling the cylinder head on the engine.
10. Position the cylinder head and camshaft assembly on the block. Install the bolts finger tight, then torque to specifications in two stages. The first to 50–60 ft. lbs. (68–81 Nm), the second step to 80–90 ft. lbs. (108–122 Nm).

NOTE: If difficulty in positioning the head on the block is encountered, guide pins may be fabricated by cutting the heads off two extra cylinder head bolts.

11. Set the crankshaft at TDC (if rotated) and be sure that the camshaft drive gear is positioned correctly as explained under "Timing Belt Replacement".
12. Install the camshaft drive belt and release the tensioner. Rotate the

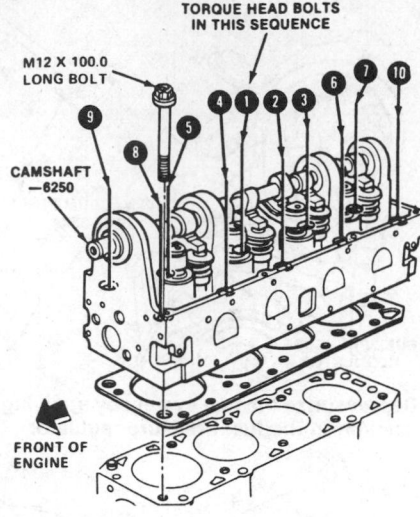

TORQUE HEAD BOLTS IN THIS SEQUENCE

M12 X 100.0 LONG BOLT

CAMSHAFT —6250

FRONT OF ENGINE

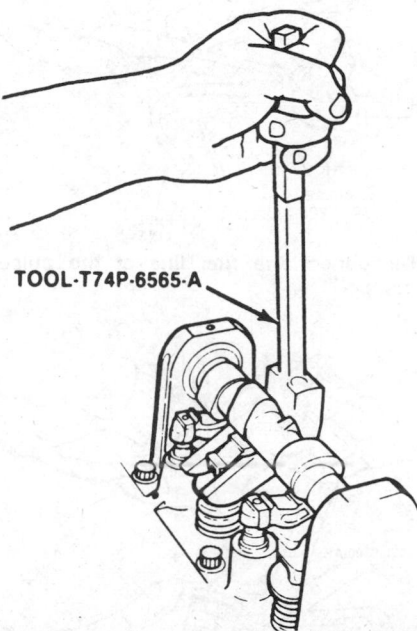

TOOL-T74P-6565-A

Compress the valve spring with spring compressor as shown to remove cam follower

crankshaft two full turns clockwise (facing the engine) to remove all slack from the belt. The timing marks should again be aligned. Tighten the tensioner lockbolt and pivot bolts.

13. Install the camshaft drive belt cover.
14. Apply sealer to the water outlet and new gasket, and install.
15. Install the intake and exhaust manifolds and torque the mounting nuts and bolts to specifications.
16. Install a new valve cover gasket and install the valve cover.
17. Install all removed components, hoses and wiring.
18. Complete the rest of the cylinder head installation in the reverse order of removal.

OVERHAUL

For all cylinder head overhaul procedures, please refer to "Engine Rebuilding" in the Unit Repair Section.

Cam Follower

REMOVAL & INSTALLATION

4 Cylinder

1. Loosen the clamp on the PCV hose at the oil separator on the rocker arm cover and disconnect the hose. Do not attempt to remove the oil separator from the valve cover; it is pressed into the cover and sealed with Locktite®.
2. Disconnect the coolant hose that passes over the rear of the rocker arm cover. Remove the coolant pipe retaining clip screw from the right front side of the valve cover.
3. Remove the throttle body from the upper intake manifold. Tag all connectors, hoses and linkage for installation in their original locations.
4. Disconnect the spark plug wires at the spark plugs and at the valve cover studs, then lay the wires out of the way.
5. Remove the remaining valve cover bolts, then lift the valve cover and gasket off the cylinder head. Tap the valve cover with a rubber mallet to break it loose, if necessary.
6. Rotate the camshaft so that the base circle of the cam is against the cam follower you intend to remove.
7. Using a valve spring compressor tool (T74P-6565-A or equivalent), depress the valve spring and slide the cam follower over the lash adjuster and out from under the camshaft.
8. Once the cam follower is removed, the hydraulic lash adjuster can be lifted out, if necessary. Make sure the lash adjuster bore is clean before installing the adjuster into the cylinder head.
9. Install the cam follower in the reverse order of removal. Make sure that the lash adjuster is collapsed and released before rotating the camshaft.

Upper Intake Manifold

REMOVAL & INSTALLATION
4 Cylinder

1. Disconnect the negative battery cable. Tag and disconnect the electronic connectors at the air bypass valve, the throttle position sensor, injector wiring harness, knock sensor, fan temperature sensor and coolant temperature sensor.

2. Tag and disconnect the upper intake manifold vacuum fitting connections at the manifold fitting, the rear vacuum line at the dash panel tree, the vacuum line to the EGR valve, and the vacuum line to the fuel pressure regulator. Disconnect the PCV hose at the intake manifold fitting.

3. Disconnect the accelerator cable and kickdown cable (automatic only) from the throttle linkage at the pivot ball connection. Unbolt the accelerator cable bracket from the upper intake manifold, then lay the bracket and cables aside.

4. Loosen the hose clamps and remove the turbocharger outlet hose flexible connection to the throttle body.

5. Remove the EGR flange attaching bolts, then remove the flange and EGR valve as an assembly. Remove the flange gasket and discard.

6. Remove the nut attaching the pulse damper to its bracket, then disconnect the low oil level sensor and remove the engine oil level dipstick.

7. Remove the engine oil dipstick bracket mounting bolt. If necessary, cut the fuel injection wiring harness routing strap at the pulse damper bracket.

8. Remove the two pulse damper bracket attaching nuts and remove the bracket.

9. The throttle body can either be removed at this point by removing the mounting bolts, or left attached and removed with the upper intake manifold as an assembly.

10. Loosen and remove the upper intake manifold mounting bolts. Lift the upper intake manifold upward and off the lower intake manifold. Remove the gasket.

11. Make sure both gasket surfaces on the upper and lower intake manifolds are clean and free from all old gasket material. Clean the EGR flange gasket surfaces and the throttle body mounting surface, if removed.

12. Installation is the reverse of removal. Tighten the upper intake manifold mounting nuts and bolts in the sequence shown to 15–22 ft. lbs. (18–26 Nm). Tighten the EGR flange mounting bolts to 13–19 ft. lbs. (18–26 Nm). If the throttle body was removed, tighten the mounting bolts to 12–15 ft. lbs. (16–20 Nm). Install the remaining components in reverse order of removal.

Lower Intake Manifold

REMOVAL & INSTALLATION
4 Cylinder

1. Drain the cooling system and

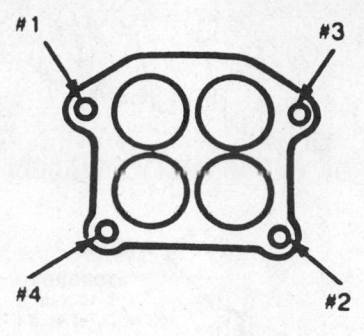

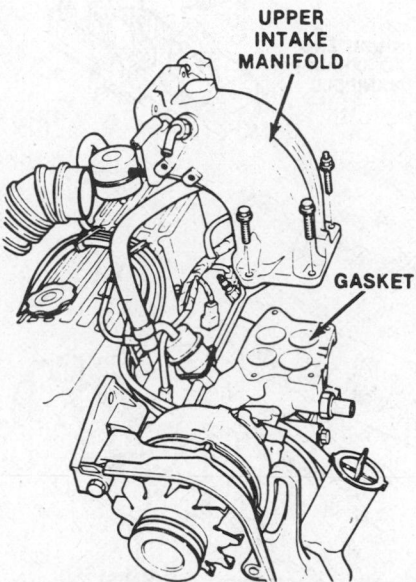

Upper intake manifold removal

disconnect the negative battery cable.

2. Tag and disconnect the wire harness connectors at the knock sensor, fan temperature sensor, fuel injection wiring harness and coolant temperature sender. The sender is located on the left side at the rear of the cylinder block below the oil pressure sender/turbocharger oil feed fitting.

3. Disconnect the coolant bypass line from the lower intake manifold.

4. Depressurize the fuel system by connecting a hand vacuum pump to the fuel pressure regulator and applying 25 in. Hg of vacuum. Disconnect the fuel supply line from the fuel supply manifold, then disconnect the push-connect fuel return line (See "Push-Connect Fittings" in the Fuel Section).

5. Remove the nut attaching the pulse damper to its bracket and place the pulse damper and fuel supply line aside.

6. Remove the upper intake manifold as previously described.

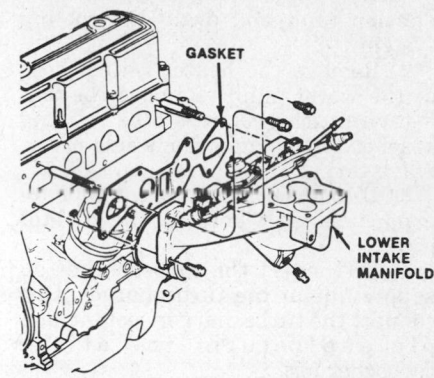

Lower intake manifold mounting

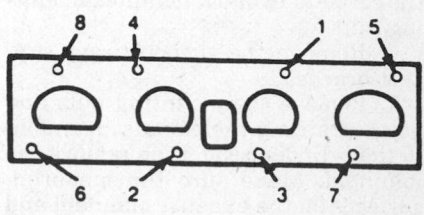

7. Disconnect the coolant temperature sensor, then remove the upper and lower mounting bolts from the lower intake manifold and lift the manifold off the engine with the fuel injectors and fuel supply manifold installed.

8. Remove the fuel supply manifold retaining bolts and remove the manifold carefully. Injectors can be removed at this time by exerting a slight twisting/pulling motion.

9. Clean and inspect all mounting surfaces of the upper and lower manifolds and cylinder head. All surfaces must be clean and flat.

10. Clean and oil all stud threads. Install a new mounting gasket over the studs.

11. Install the lower manifold to the cylinder head with lift bracket in position. Install the four upper manifold nuts finger-tight. Install the four remaining nuts, then tighten all nuts in sequence to 12–15 ft. lbs. (16–20 Nm).

12. Install the remaining components in the reverse order of removal. Refer to the "Upper Intake Manifold" procedures for installation and torque specifications. Make sure all wiring harness connectors are securely fastened and locked.

Exhaust Manifold

REMOVAL & INSTALLATION
4 Cylinder

1. Loosen the cap on the coolant ex-

pansion tank and drain the cooling system.

2. Remove the heater return hose at the water pump. Remove the bolt attaching the coolant pipe routing bracket to the right front side of the valve cover.

3. Disconnect the coolant pipe-to-expansion tank hose at the coolant pipe.

4. Disconnect the turbocharger oil supply line at the turbocharger. Disconnect the turbocharger coolant supply and return line at the turbocharger.

5. Disconnect the PCV tube at the turbo air inlet adapter, then remove the turbo-to-exhaust manifold mounting nuts.

6. Remove the turbocharger support bracket.

7. Remove the mounting nuts and bolts retaining the exhaust manifold to the cylinder head, then remove the manifold. Make sure the mounting surfaces on the exhaust manifold and cylinder head are clean.

8. Install the attaching nuts and tighten them in sequence, in two steps; first to 14–17 ft. lbs. (20–23 Nm), then to 20–30 ft. lbs. (27–41 Nm). Be sure to follow the torque sequence on each pass.

9. Complete the installation of the exhaust manifold in the reverse order of removal. Refer to the Turbocharger procedures for torque specifications. Refill the cooling system and crank the engine a few times without starting to build oil pressure back up in the turbocharger.

Turbocharger

REMOVAL & INSTALLATION

1. Turbocharger servicing is by replacement only. Prior to starting the removal procedure, clean the turbocharger and area around the turbo with a noncaustic solution. Maintain clean as possible working conditions while removing and installing the turbocharger. When disconnecting lines and feed pipes always cover or plug openings to prevent contamination by dirt or grease.

2. Disconnect the negative battery cable. Drain the cooling system.

3. Disconnect the oxygen sensor wiring connector from the harness.

4. Remove the bolts retaining the cast air tube to the turbocharger. Loosen the clamp on the intake hose at the throttle body, then disconnect the flexible hose.

5. Label for identification and disconnect all vacuum hoses and tubes that will interfere with turbocharger removal. Disconnect the boost control

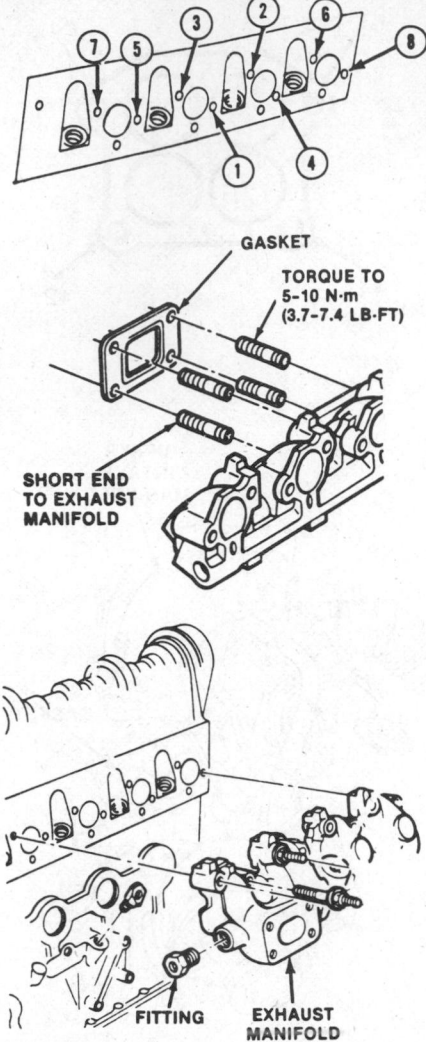

GASKET

TORQUE TO 5–10 N·m (3.7–7.4 LB·FT)

SHORT END TO EXHAUST MANIFOLD

FITTING   EXHAUST MANIFOLD

Exhaust manifold assembly showing torque sequence

solenoid hose at the turbocharger outlet fitting.

6. Disconnect the PCV tube from the turbocharger air inlet elbow. Disconnect the boost control solenoid hose from the turbocharger inlet fitting.

7. Remove the cast air tube and hose assembly from between the turbo and throttle body assembly.

8. Disconnect the electrical ground wire from the turbocharger outlet fitting.

9. Disconnect the oil supply line routing bracket, then disconnect the oil supply line from the turbocharger fitting. Disconnect the coolant outlet line from the turbocharger housing. Loosen the hose clamp and disconnect the coolant inlet line from the turbocharger fitting.

10. Loosen the nut attaching the heat shield to the top of the right engine mount.

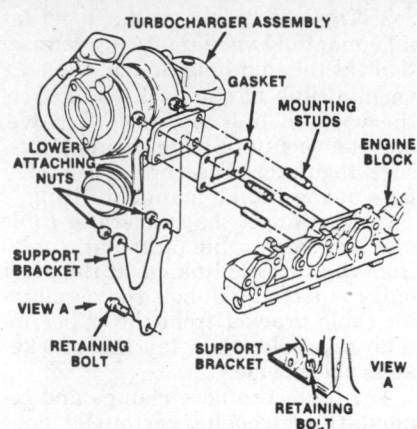

Turbocharger mounting on the 4 cylinder engine

11. Raise and support the front of the vehicle with jackstands. Remove the transmission mount center plate.

12. Disconnect the exhaust pipe from the turbocharger. Disconnect the oil return line from the bottom of the turbocharger. Be careful when handling the oil line, do not kink or damage it. Remove and discard the gasket.

13. Remove the lower turbocharger mounting nuts and bolts. Remove the turbocharger support bracket bottom attaching bolt and remove the bracket.

14. Lower the vehicle. If equipped with an automatic transmission, remove the attaching nut and disconnect the dipstick tube support bracket from the cast tube flange.

15. Remove the upper turbocharger mounting nuts.

16. Loosen the other turbocharger mounting nuts a little at a time and slide the turbo on the mounting studs until the nuts can be removed. Remove the turbocharger, gasket, outlet tube and hose as an assembly. Continue disassembly on a clean workbench to transfer components to the new turbocharger.

17. Clean all gasket mounting surfaces. Install the turbocharger in the reverse order of removal. Use new mounting gasket on the turbo and oil return line. Use new mounting nuts when installing the turbocharger. Torque is as follows: Lower bracket bolt: 28–40 ft. lbs. (38–54 Nm). Oil return line: 14–21 ft. lbs. (19–28 Nm). Exhaust pipe: 25–35 ft. lbs. (34–47 Nm). Turbo mounting nuts: 28–40 ft. lbs. (38–54 Nm). Cast air pipe to turbo: 15–22 ft. lbs. (20–30 Nm).

TROUBLESHOOTING

For further information on turbochargers, please refer to "Turbocharging" in the Unit Repair Section.

Timing Belt/Cover

REMOVAL & INSTALLATION

4 Cylinder

Should the camshaft drive belt jump timing by a tooth or two, the engine could still run; but very poorly. To visually check for correct timing of the crankshaft, auxiliary shaft and the camshaft, follow this procedure.

An access plug is provided in the cam drive belt cover so that the camshaft timing can be checked without removing the drive belt cover. Remove the access plug, turn the crankshaft until the timing mark on the crankshaft damper indicates TDC, and observe that the timing mark on the camshaft drive sprocket is aligned with the pointer on the inner belt cover. Also, the rotor of the distributor must align with No. 1 cylinder firing position.

—————— CAUTION ——————

Never turn the crankshaft of any of the overhead cam engines in the opposite direction of normal rotation. Backward rotation of the crankshaft may cause the timing belt to slip and alter the timing.

1. Set the engine at TDC as described above for checking valve timing. The crankshaft and camshaft timing marks should align with their respective pointers and the distributor rotor should point to the No. 1 plug tower.

2. Loosen the adjustment bolts on the alternator and accessories and remove the drive belts. To provide clearance for removing the camshaft belt, remove the fan and shroud assembly.

3. Remove the water pump pulley attaching bolts and remove the pulley from the water pump shaft. Remove the four bolts holding the cover, then remove the timing belt outer cover.

4. Remove the crankshaft damper and pulley center bolt. Using a crankshaft damper puller tool (T74P-6312-A or equivalent), remove the crankshaft damper from the crankshaft.

5. Loosen the belt tensioner adjustment and pivot bolts. Using tensioner tool T74P-6254-A, or equivalent, lever the tensioner away from the belt and retighten the adjustment bolt to hold it away.

6. Remove the camshaft drive belt.

7. Install the new belt over the crankshaft pulley first, then counterclockwise over the auxiliary shaft sprocket and the camshaft sprocket. Adjust the belt before and after so that it is centered on the sprockets.

8. Loosen the tensioner adjustment bolt, allowing it to spring back against the belt.

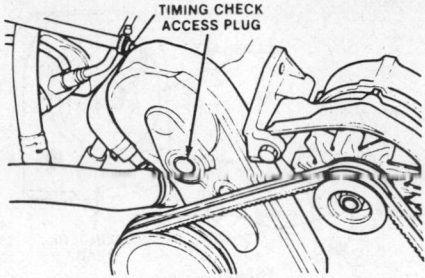

Location of access plug for checking valve timing visually

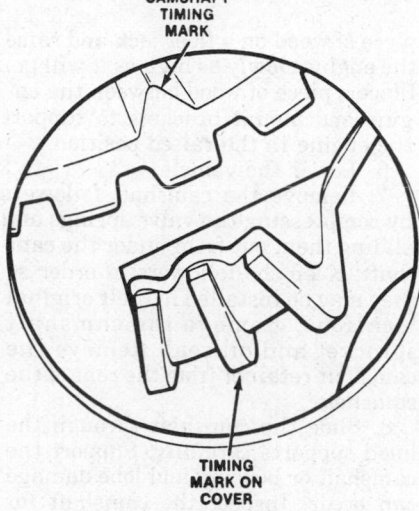

Correct timing mark alignment as viewed through the access hole

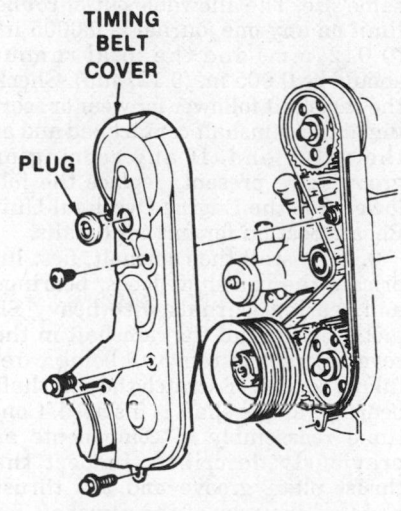

Timing belt cover assembly

9. Rotate the crankshaft two complete turns in the normal rotation direction to remove any belt slack. Turn the crankshaft until the timing check marks are lined up. If the timing has

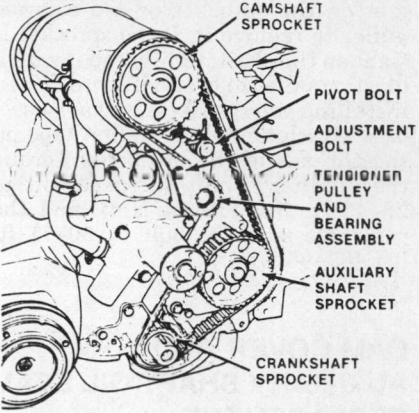

Location of timing belt tensioner, adjustment and pivot bolts

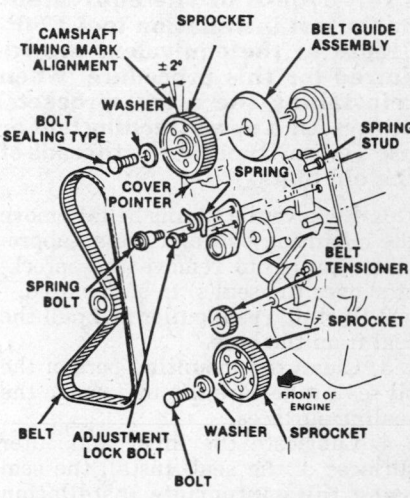

Exploded view of timing belt and sprocket assemblies

slipped, remove the belt and repeat the procedure.

10. Tighten the tensioner adjustment bolt to 14–21 ft. lbs. (19–28 Nm), and the pivot bolt to 28–40 ft. lbs. (38–54 Nm).

11. Replace the belt guide and crankshaft pulley, belt outer cover, fan and pulley, drive belts and accessories. Adjust the accessory drive belt tension. Start the engine and check the ignition timing.

Timing Belt Sprockets

REMOVAL & INSTALLATION

4 Cylinder

The camshaft and crankshaft timing belt sprockets can be removed once the timing belt is removed. A sprocket holding/removal tool such as T74P-6256-B is necessary to hold the sprockets during the center bolt removal and installation. Do not hammer on the sprocket or use a jawed puller to remove it. If the sprocket is tight on the shaft, lightly tap it with a plastic mallet to break it loose. When installing the sprockets, always use a new attaching bolt or Teflon tape on the threads of the old bolts. Torque the auxiliary shaft sprocket bolt to 28–40 ft. lbs. (38–54 Nm), and the camshaft sprocket bolt to 50–71 ft. lbs. (68–96 Nm).

CAM COVER AND AUXILIARY SHAFT OIL SEAL REPLACEMENT

NOTE: A seal puller tool such as T74P-6700-B or the equivalent and a seal installation tool T74P-6150-A or the equivalent are required for this procedure. When reinstalling the drive sprockets, always use a new attaching bolt or use Teflon® tape on the threads of the old bolts.

1. Remove the timing belt. Remove the mounting bolt and use an appropriate puller to remove the sprocket(s) over the seal(s) to be replaced.
2. Install a seal puller and pull the seal from the bore.
3. Clean the mounting bore of the oil seal, take care not to damage the sealing surfaces.
4. Lubricate the inner and outer surfaces of the seal. Install the seal using the appropriate installation tool.
5. Reinstall the drive sprocket(s) and timing belt as previously described.

Camshaft

REMOVAL & INSTALLATION

4 Cylinder

1. Disconnect the negative battery cable. Drain the cooling system.
2. Remove the camshaft drive belt, and the rocker arm (valve) cover (see various procedure sections).
3. Remove the fan and shroud assembly (if not previously removed). Remove the upper and lower radiator hoses. Disconnect and plug the transmission fluid cooler lines (if automatic transmission).
4. Raise and support the front of the vehicle.
5. If clearance is a problem when removing the camshaft from the cylinder head, remove the front motor mount upper center nut. Position a

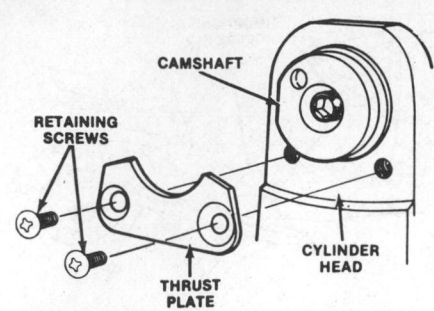

Camshaft retainer at rear of cylinder head

piece of wood on a floor jack and raise the engine slowly as high as it will go. Place a piece of wood between the engine and mount brackets to support the engine in the raised position.

6. Lower the vehicle.
7. Remove the camshaft followers by compressing the valve springs and sliding them out from under the camshaft. Keep the followers in order so they may be installed in their original locations. Remove the camshaft sprocket and oil seal. Remove the camshaft retainer from the rear of the camshaft.
8. Slide the camshaft through the head supports carefully. Support the camshaft or bearing and lobe damage can occur. Inspect the camshaft for wear or damage and check the lobes and journals with a micrometer. All of the camshaft bearing journals are the same size. The allowable out-of-round limit on any one journal is 0.0005 in. (0.0127mm) and the total runout should be 0.005 in. (0.127mm). Check the camshaft follower for wear or scoring at the camshaft contact pad and at the valve end. If any scoring or grooves are present, replace the follower. See the Engine Overhaul Unit Repair Section for further details.
9. To install the camshaft, first lubricate the camshaft lobes, bearings and bearing journals with heavy SF motor oil. Install the camshaft in the reverse order of removal, being careful not to nick or scratch the camshaft bearings as the shaft is inserted. Continue reassembly of components as previously described. Inspect the thrust plate groove and the thrust plate on the rear of the camshaft for scoring or wear. Camshaft endplay has a maximum service limit of 0.009 in. (0.2286mm).

CAUTION

After any procedure requiring removal of the rocker arms, each lash adjuster must be fully collapsed after assembly, then released. This must be done before the camshaft is turned.

Auxiliary Shaft

REMOVAL & INSTALLATION

4 Cylinder

1. Remove the camshaft drive belt cover as previously described.
2. Remove the drive belt, then remove the auxiliary shaft sprocket. A puller/holding tool may be necessary to remove the sprocket.
3. Remove the auxiliary shaft seal using a front cover seal remover tool T74P-6700-B or equivalent.
4. Remove the auxiliary shaft cover and thrust plate.
5. Withdraw the auxiliary shaft from the block, being careful not to damage the bearing surfaces or shaft journals during removal.

NOTE: The distributor drive gear and the fuel pump eccentric on the auxiliary shaft must not be allowed to touch the auxiliary shaft bearings during removal and installation. Completely coat the shaft with heavy SF engine oil before sliding it into place.

6. Slide the auxiliary shaft into the housing and insert the thrust plate to hold the shaft.
7. Install a new gasket and auxiliary shaft cover. Torque the cover bolts to 6–9 ft. lbs. (8–12 Nm)

NOTE: Install the auxiliary shaft cover without the oil seal. Once the cover is in place, install a new oil seal using installer tool T74P-6150-A. Lubricate the seal and cover seat with engine oil and make sure the seal bottoms in its bore.

8. Install the auxiliary shaft sprocket and remaining components in reverse order of removal.
9. Align the timing marks and install the drive belt.
10. Install the drive belt cover.
11. Check the ignition timing.

Pistons and Connecting Rods

For all piston and connecting rod overhaul procedures, please refer to "Engine Rebuilding" in the Unit Repair section.

IDENTIFICATION AND POSITIONING

The connecting rods should be factory marked with cylinder location numbers on the rod and bearing cap edges. If factory marks are not present,

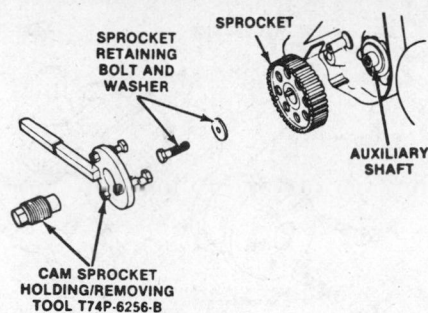

Auxiliary shaft sprocket removal showing puller/holder tool

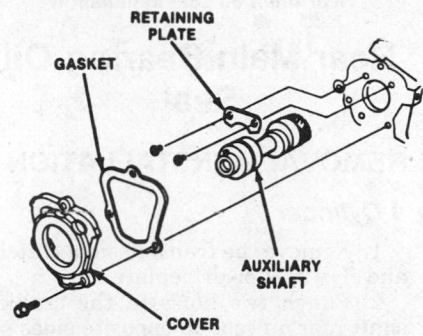

Auxiliary shaft and cover assembly

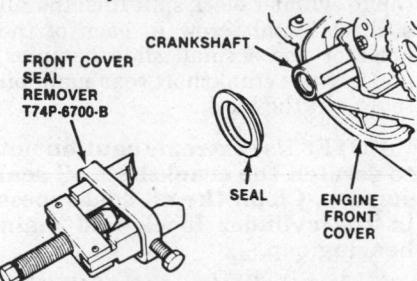

Front crankshaft oil seal showing remover tool

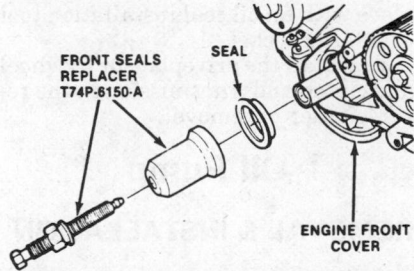

Install front cover oil seal using tool as shown

match mark both the rod and cap numerically and in sequence from the front to the back of the engine. The numbers not only tell from which cylinder the piston and rod came from but also insures that the rod caps are installed in correct matching position with the connecting rod. The piston is marked with a notch indicating front position for installation. Ring gaps should be spaced with the compression rings approximately 2 in. (50mm) apart on opposite sides of the oil ring gaps.

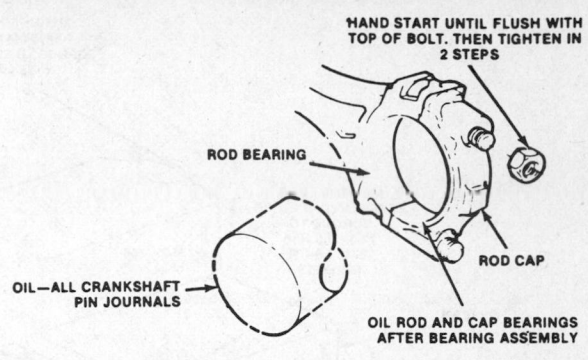

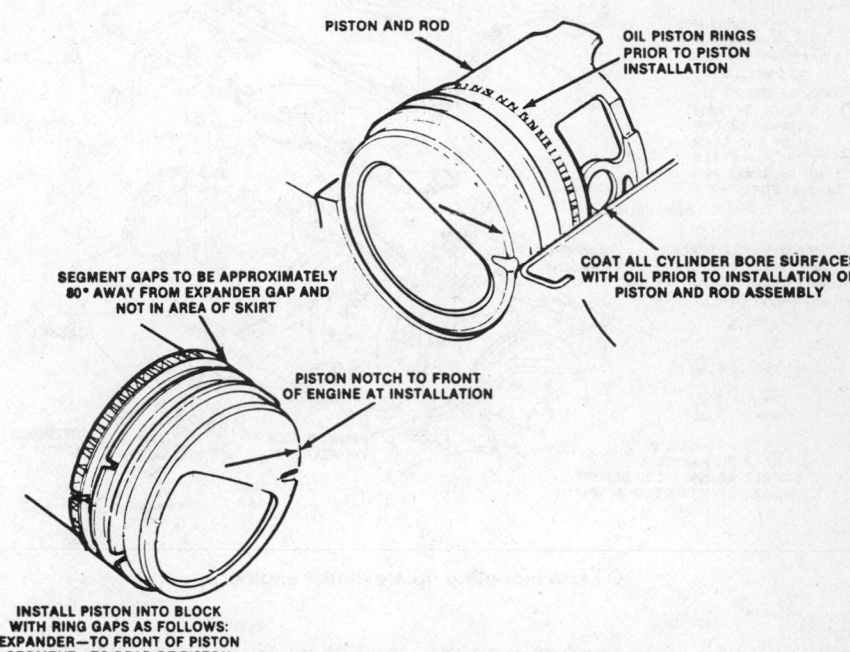

Correct piston and connecting rod installation

ENGINE LUBRICATION

Oil Pan

REMOVAL & INSTALLATION

4 Cylinder

1. Disconnect the negative battery cable.

2. Separate the oil level sensor wiring connector and remove the engine oil level dipstick.

3. Drain the crankcase into a suitable container and dispose of waste oil properly. Install a suitable engine support fixture to take the weight off of the motor mounts.

4. Remove the right and left engine mount through bolts and/or nuts.

5. Remove the starter, then remove the pinch bolt at the steering column-to-steering gear coupling.

6. Raise the engine as high as it will go with the support fixture. Be careful if using a shop crane not to raise the engine too high.

7. Remove the steering gear-to-crossmember attaching bolts.

8. Disengage the steering gear from the steering column and pull forward, away from the crossmember. Exercise caution to prevent stretching or bending the power steering gear hoses and lines.

9. Position a transmission jack under the crossmember, then remove the crossmember-to-side rail attaching bolts.

10. Carefully lower the transmission jack and crossmember.

11. Remove the oil pan retaining bolts and lower the pan. Remove the pan, turn the engine in normal direc-

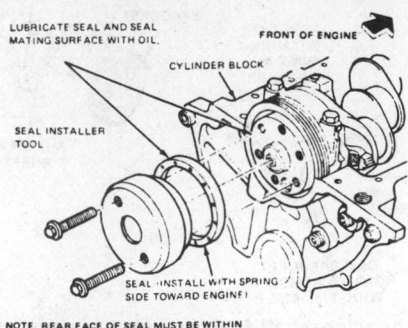

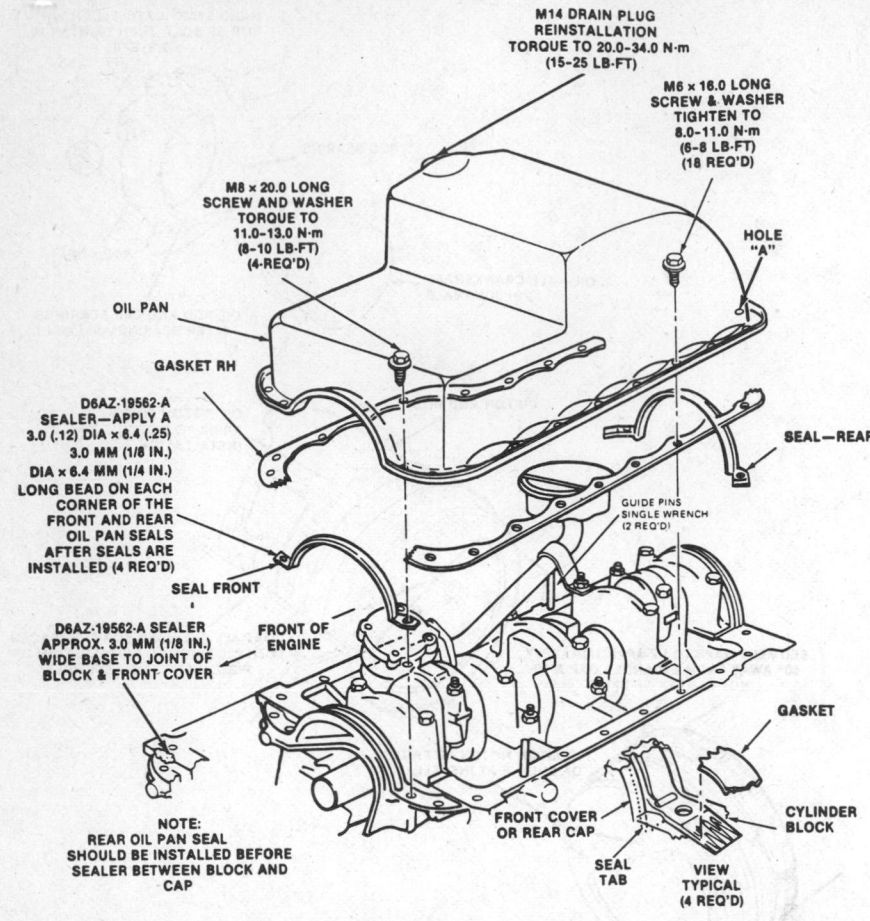

Oil pan mounting on 4 cylinder engine

Rear main oil seal installation

Rear Main Bearing Oil Seal

REMOVAL & INSTALLATION

4 Cylinder

1. Remove the transmission, clutch and flywheel or driveplate.
2. Punch two holes in the crankshaft rear oil seal on opposite sides of the crankshaft just above the bearing cap to cylinder block split line. Install a sheet metal screw in each of the holes or use a small slide hammer, and pry the crankshaft rear main oil seal from the block.

NOTE: Use extreme caution not to scratch the crankshaft oil seal surface. Clean the oil seal recess in the cylinder block and main bearing cap.

3. Coat the seal and all of the seal mounting surfaces with oil and install the seal in the recess, driving it in place with an oil seal installation tool or a large socket.
4. Install the driveplate or flywheel and clutch and transmission in the reverse order of removal.

Oil Pump

REMOVAL & INSTALLATION

4 Cylinder

1. Remove the oil pan as previously described.
2. Remove the oil pump inlet tube and screen support bracket nut from the No. 4 main bearing cap.
3. Remove the oil pump attaching bolts and remove oil pump gasket and intermediate shaft.
4. Prime oil pump by filling inlet and outlet port with engine oil and rotating shaft of pump to distribute it.
5. Position intermediate driveshaft and retaining clip into the cylinder block guide hole or into the oil pump.
6. Position new gasket on pump

---

tion of rotation if the pan hangs up on the crankshaft throws. Clean the pan with solvent and carefully remove all traces of old gasket material or sealer from all gasket mating surfaces. Inspect the pan for cracks and damage.

12. Install new oil pan gasket and end seals, using adhesive sealer to hold the gaskets in place. Apply a ¼ in. bead of sealer along the seam between the cylinder block and the front cover. Apply another ¼ in. bead of sealer along the seam between the cylinder block and the rear main bearing cap.

13. Position the oil pan to the cylinder block and install the retaining bolts. Torque the four pan-to-front cover bolts to 8–10 ft. lbs. (11–13 Nm), and the remaining oil pan bolts to 6–8 ft. lbs. (8–11 Nm). The oil pan plug torque is 15–25 ft. lbs. (20–34 Nm).

14. Raise the crossmember back into position and install the crossmember-to-side member mounting bolts. Tighten the attaching bolts to 38–47 ft. lbs. (56–64 Nm). Reposition the steering gear and install bolts and nuts. Tighten the steering gear attaching bolts to 10 ft. lbs. (15 Nm),

and then an additional 90 degrees. Tighten the steering column pinch bolt to 12–15 ft. lbs. (16–20 Nm).

15. Install the starter.

16. Slowly lower the engine and line up the engine mount studs with the holes in the crossmember and install the mounting bolts. Tighten the motor mount nuts to 50–70 ft. lbs. (68–95 Nm).

17. Fill the crankcase with oil. Reconnect the oil level sensor wiring connector and replace the dipstick. Check the engine oil level and crank the engine over a few times before starting to allow oil pressure to build up in the turbocharger.

18. Connect the battery cable, start the engine and check for leaks.

Oil Cooler

An oil coller is installed, on four cylinder models, between the engine block and oil filter to reduce oil temperature to improve high-speed durability. The cooler is of the water cooled design. The cooler is retained on the engine by the oil filter adapter stud.

body and insert intermediate drive-shaft into pump body.

7. Install pump and intermediate shaft as an assembly.

NOTE: Do not force pump if it does not seat readily. The drive-shaft may be misaligned with the distributor shaft. To align, rotate intermediate driveshaft into a new position.

8. Install and torque oil pump attaching bolts to 14–21 ft. lbs. (19–28 Nm). Tighten the strap nut to 28–40 ft. lbs. (38–54 Nm).

9. Install the oil pan as previously described.

ENGINE COOLING

Radiator

REMOVAL & INSTALLATION

1. Drain the cooling system.
2. Disconnect the upper, lower and overflow hoses at the radiator and overflow reservoir.
3. If equipped with an automatic transmission, disconnect and plug the fluid cooler lines at the radiator.
4. Remove the fan and shroud assembly. If the air conditioner condenser is attached to the radiator, remove the retaining bolts and position the condenser out of the way. DO NOT disconnect the refrigerant lines.
5. Remove the radiator attaching bolts or top brackets and lift out the radiator.
6. If a new radiator is to be installed, transfer the petcock from the old radiator to the new one. On cars equipped with automatic transmissions, transfer the fluid cooler line fittings from the old radiator.
7. Position the radiator and install, but do not tighten, the radiator support bolts. On models equipped with an automatic transmission, connect the fluid cooler lines. Then tighten the radiator support bolts and install the fan and shroud assembly.
8. Connect the radiator hoses. Close the radiator petcock. Fill and bleed the cooling system.
9. Start the engine and bring to operating temperature. Check for leaks.
10. On cars equipped with automatic transmission, check the cooler lines for leaks and interference. Check transmission fluid level.

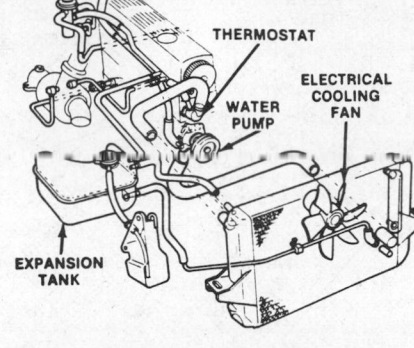

Engine and turbocharger cooling system components

Water Pump

REMOVAL & INSTALLATION

4 Cylinder

1. Drain the cooling system.
2. Disconnect the negative battery cable.
3. Remove all drive belts. Remove the outer timing belt cover.
4. Disconnect the lower radiator hose and heater hose from the water pump.
5. Remove the electric fan and shroud assembly if necessary for clearance.
6. Remove the water pump retaining bolts and the water pump. Clean all gasket mounting surfaces.
7. Coat both sides of the new gasket with a water-resistant sealer, then install the pump by reversing the removal procedures. Torque the water pump mounting bolts to 14–21 ft. lbs. (19–29 Nm).

Thermostat

REMOVAL & INSTALLATION

1. Open the drain cock and drain the radiator so the coolant level is below the coolant outlet elbow which houses the thermostat.
2. Remove the outlet elbow retaining bolts and position the elbow sufficient clear of the intake manifold or cylinder head to provide access to the thermostat.
3. Remove the thermostat and the gasket.
4. Clean the mating surfaces of the outlet elbow and the engine to remove all old gasket material and sealer. Coat the new gasket with water resistant sealer. Position the gasket on the engine, and install the thermostat in the coolant elbow. Be sure the full width of the heater outlet tube is visible within the thermostat port.

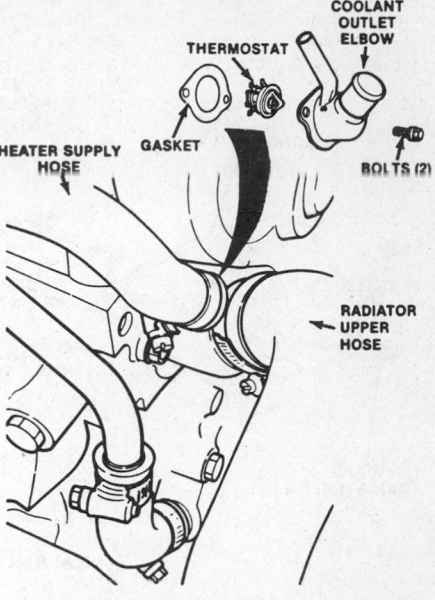

Thermostat and housing assembly

5. Install the outlet elbow and retaining bolts on the engine. Torque the bolts to 14–21 ft. lbs. (19–28 Nm).
6. Refill the radiator. Run the engine at operating temperature and check for leaks. Recheck the coolant level.

EMISSION CONTROLS

Due to the complex nature of modern electronic engine control systems, comprehensive diagnosis and testing procedures fall outside the confines of this repair manual. For complete information on diagnosis, testing and repair procedures concerning all modern engine and emission control systems, please refer to *Chilton's Guide To Electronic Engine Controls.*

FUEL SYSTEM

Quick Connect Fittings

"Quick Connect" (push) type fuel fittings are used on all models equipped with a pressurized fuel system. The fittings must be disconnected using proper procedures or the fitting may be damaged. Two types of retainers

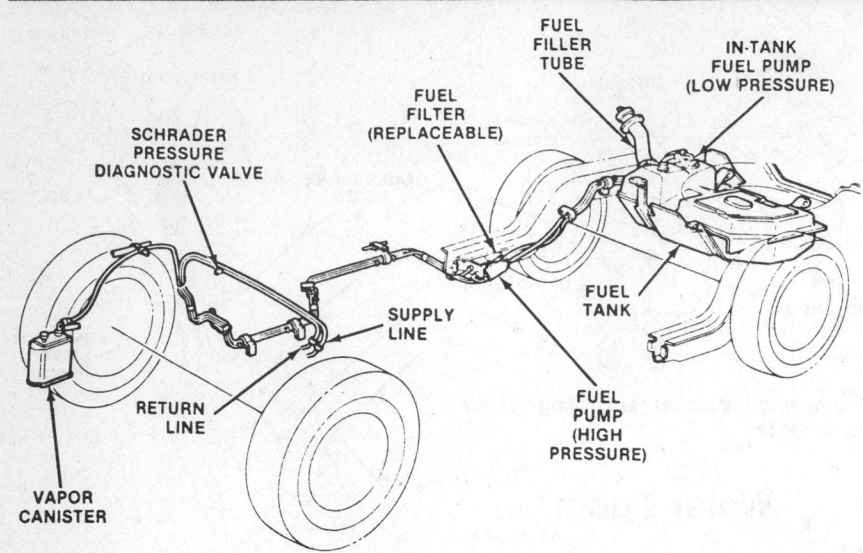

Typical fuel supply system

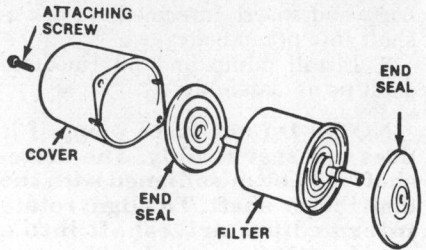

Exploded view of fuel filter showing location on fuel pump bracket

are used on the push-connect fittings. Line sizes of $\frac{3}{8}$ in. and $\frac{5}{16}$ in. use a "hairpin" clip retainer. $\frac{1}{4}$ in. line connectors use a "duck bill" clip retainer. In either case, a special connector tool must be used to separate the quick connect fittings or they may be damaged.

REMOVAL & INSTALLATION

—————— CAUTION ——————
Depressurize the fuel system before disconnecting any fuel system lines or components or attempting any service procedures. Connect a hand vacuum pump to the fuel pressure regulator vacuum connection and apply 25 in. Hg of vacuum for at least three minutes to allow the fuel system to depressurize. Never replace high pressure fuel line with ordinary fuel hose and replace all clamps.

Hairpin Clip

1. Clean all dirt and/or grease from the fitting. Spread the two clip legs about an $\frac{1}{8}$ inch each to disengage from the fitting and pull the clip outward from the fitting. Use finger pressure only, do not use any tools.
2. Grease the fitting and hose assembly and pull away from the steel line. Twist the fitting and hose assembly slightly while pulling, if necessary, when a sticking condition exists.
3. Inspect the hairpin clip for damage, replace the clip if necessary. Reinstall the clip in position on the fitting.
4. Inspect the fitting and inside of the connector to insure freedom of dirt or obstruction. Install fitting in to the connector and push together. A click

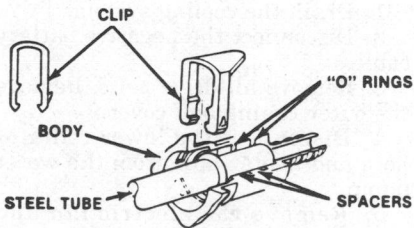

Hairpin clip fitting used on quick connect fuel lines

will be heard when the hairpin snaps into proper connection. Pull on the line to insure full engagement.

Duck Bill Clip

1. A special tool is available for removing the retaining clips (Ford Tool No. T82L-9500-AH). If the tool is not on hand see Step 2. Align the slot on the push connector disconnect tool with either tab on the retaining clip. Pull the line from the connector.
2. If the special clip tool is not available, use a pair of narrow 6 in. channel lock pliers with a jaw width of 0.2 in. or less. Align the jaws of the pliers with the openings of the fitting case and compress the part of the retaining clip that engages the case. Compressing the retaining clip will release the fitting which may be pulled form the connector. Both sides of the clip must be compressed at the same time to disengage.
3. Inspect the retaining clip, fitting end and connector. Replace clip if any damage is apparent.
4. Push the line into the steel connector until a click is heard, indicating clip is in place. Pull on line to check engagement.

Fuel Filter

REMOVAL & INSTALLATION

—————— CAUTION ——————
Depressurize the fuel system before disconnecting any fuel system lines or components or attempting any service procedures. Connect a hand vacuum pump to the fuel pressure regulator vacuum connection and apply 25 in. Hg of vacuum for at least three minutes to allow the fuel system to depressurize. Never replace high pressure fuel line with ordinary fuel hose and replace all clamps.

Models equipped with EFI actually have four fuel filters; a nylon mesh "sock" at the fuel pump inlet in the fuel tank; a large paper element filter mounted in the fuel line under the car; a small canister filter mounted in the engine compartment; and individual mesh filters at each injector fuel inlet. Of these, only the undercar paper element filter is scheduled for regular replacement. Filter replacement requires discharging of the fuel injection system pressure prior to filter change. Discharge pressure, disconnect the fuel lines and remove the fuel filter retainer from its mounting bracket beneath the fuel pump. Note the direction of the fuel flow arrow on filter. Install new filter in reverse order, making sure the arrow points in the direction of fuel flow (toward the engine).

Fuel Pump

REMOVAL & INSTALLATION

—————— CAUTION ——————
Depressurize the fuel system before disconnecting any fuel system lines or components or attempting any service procedures. Connect a hand vacuum pump to the fuel pressure regulator vacuum connection and apply 25 in. Hg of vacuum for at least three minutes to allow the fuel system to depressurize. Never replace high pressure fuel line with ordinary fuel hose and replace all clamps.

Low Pressure Tank Pump

1. Run the car until the fuel tank is about ¼ full. Disconnect the negative battery cable.

2. Depressurize the fuel system and drain as much gas from the tank by pumping it out through the filler neck into an approved safety container, then seal the can(s) tightly for temporary storage during service procedures. Place the gasoline away from the work area and take precautions to avoid the risk of fire.

3. Chock the front wheels, then raise the rear of the car and support it safely on jackstands. Rock the vehicle a bit to make sure the car is firmly supported before working underneath it.

4. Working under the vehicle at the rear frame rails near the fuel tank, disconnect the fuel supply, return and vent lines at the right and left side of the frame.

5. Disconnect the wiring to the fuel pump.

6. Support the fuel tank, loosen and remove the mounting straps, then lower the tank carefully.

7. Disconnect the fuel and vapor lines and wire harness connectors at the pump flange.

8. Clean the outside of the mounting flange and retaining ring. Turn the fuel pump lock ring counterclockwise and remove it from the top of the tank.

9. Remove the seal ring, fuel pump and fuel sending unit as an assembly from the fuel tank. Once removed, the fuel pump can be separated from the sending unit assembly on a clean workbench. Cut the hose clamps securing the pump and discard the clamps and hoses.

10. Clean the mounting surfaces. Put a light coat of grease on the mounting surfaces and on the new sealing ring. Install the new fuel pump to the sending unit assembly.

NOTE: If the low pressure fuel pump is removed from the sending unit assembly for any reason, the rubber hoses and clamps must be replaced along with any gaskets.

11. Installation is in the reverse order of removal. Coat the seal ring with heavy duty grease before installing the pump and sending unit and make sure the lock ring lugs are engaged properly. After the tank is secured and all connections are complete, fill the tank with at least 10 gals. of fuel. Turn the ignition key ON for three seconds. Repeat 6 or 7 times until the fuel system is pressurized. Check for any fitting leaks. Start the engine and check for leaks.

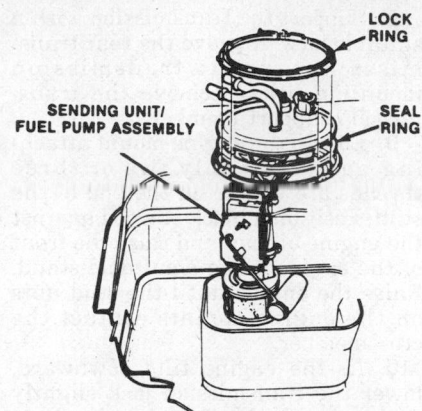

Low pressure fuel pump assembly located in the fuel tank

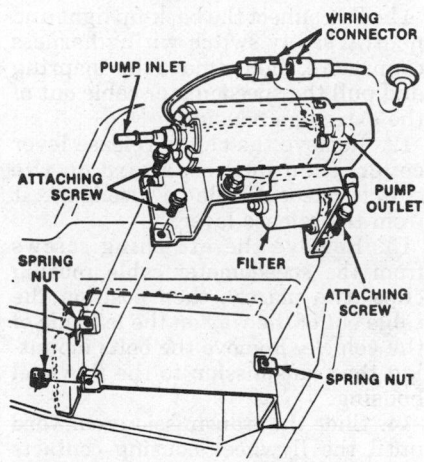

High pressure fuel pump assembly located on a mounting bracket attached to the frame near the fuel tank

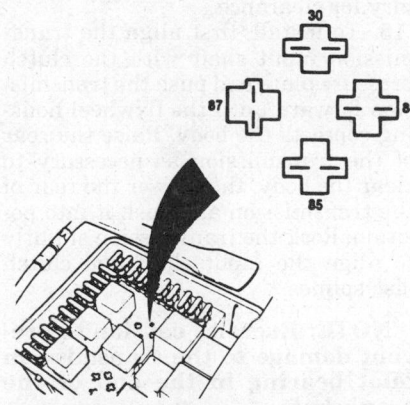

Location of fuel pump relay and terminal identification for testing

High Pressure Chassis Pump

1. Disconnect the negative battery cable.

2. Depressurize the fuel system by attaching a hand vacuum pump to the fuel pressure regulator and applying 25 in. Hg of vacuum for three minutes.

3. Chock the front wheels, then raise the rear of the car and support it safely on jackstands. Rock the vehicle a bit to make sure the car is firmly supported before working underneath it.

4. Working under the vehicle at the rear frame rail just ahead of the fuel tank, locate the external fuel pump and filter bracket and disconnect the inlet and outlet fuel lines. Separate the fuel pump electrical connector.

5. Remove the fuel pump bracket attaching screws and lower the fuel pump and bracket as an assembly. Working on a clean workbench, remove the pump and foam insulator from the mounting bracket. Disconnect the wiring harness from the pump.

6. Install in reverse order, making sure the pump is indexed correctly in the mounting bracket insulator. Position the insulator ends in the opening at the base of the mounting bracket. Route the wire harness between the insulator ends, then position the pump on the body mounting bracket and install the attaching bolts. Reconnect all fuel lines and harness connectors. Fill the tank with at least 10 gals. of fuel. Turn the ignition key ON for three seconds. Repeat 6 or 7 times until the fuel system is pressurized. Check for any fitting leaks. Start the engine and check for leaks.

FUEL SYSTEM PRESSURE/VOLUME TEST

1. Connect a compatible fuel pressure gauge to the Schrader® valve on the fuel supply manifold. An adapter may be required to tap into the valve.

2. Start the engine. If the engine will not start, remove the fuel pump relay from the circuit protection panel, then connect a jumper wire from relay terminal 87 in the panel to the alternator output terminal.

3. With the pump running, check the pressure reading on the gauge. Normal fuel pressure is 35–45 psi at idle.

4. Insert the test volume hose in a graduated container and open the flow control valve for 10 seconds. If the pump delivers 7.5 ounces in 10 seconds, the fuel volume is correct.

5. Disconnect the jumper wire to stop the pumps and observe the pressure gauge. If the pressure holds at a minimum of 30 psi, the system is holding pressure. Install the fuel pump relay and disconnect the pressure gauge.

FUEL INJECTION

Due to the complex nature of modern fuel injection systems, comprehensive diagnoses and testing procedures fall outside the confines of this repair manual. For complete information on fuel injection diagnoses, testing and repair procedures please refer to *Chilton's Guide to Fuel Injection and Feedback Carburetors.*

MANUAL TRANSMISSION

REMOVAL & INSTALLATION

1. Wedge a block of wood approximately 7 in. long under the clutch pedal. Holding the pedal above its normal position will disengage the clutch cable self-adjuster. Disconnect the negative battery cable, then raise and support the vehicle safely with jackstands. Allow enough working clearance to remove the transmission from below the vehicle.

2. Drain the transmission fluid. Matchmark the driveshaft and rear companion flange so that the driveshaft may be installed in the same position for proper balance.

3. Disconnect and remove the driveshaft. Install a suitable plug in the extension housing seal to prevent fluid leakage during service.

4. Remove the nuts attaching the catalytic converter inlet pipe to the turbocharger. Remove the attaching nuts at the catalytic converter outlet-to-muffler inlet flange and the catalytic converter support bracket. Remove the catalytic converter and inlet pipe as an assembly.

——— CAUTION ———

If the engine is started for any reason just prior to transmission removal, allow sufficient time for the catalytic converter to cool before attempting removal procedures. The normal converter operating temperature can cause severe burns.

5. Remove the starter.

6. Remove the front stabilizer bar to body U-brackets and the body stiffener rod.

7. Remove the transmission air baffle, if equipped, then position a block of wood between the stabilizer bar and the body side rail.

8. Support the transmission with a suitable jack. Remove the rear transmission mount to transmission mounting bolts. Remove the transmission support member.

9. Loosen the engine mount attaching nuts until only two or three threads are visible on the end of the stud. Position a block of wood against the engine oil pan and raise the front of the engine using a suitable stand. Raise the engine until the stud nuts on the engine mounts contact the crossmember.

10. As the engine tilts downward, lower the transmission jack slightly and remove the Torx® bolts that mount the shift lever. Remove the shift lever from the extension housing.

11. Disconnect the back-up light and neutral safety switch wiring harness connectors, then remove the snapring and pull the speedometer cable out of the extension housing.

12. Remove the clutch release lever cover, then pull rearward on the clutch release cable to disengage it from the release lever.

13. Remove the attaching screws from the speedometer cable routing clips (two places), then position the cable out of the way on the left side of the vehicle. Remove the bolts mounting the transmission to the flywheel housing.

14. Slide the transmission rearward until the flywheel housing contacts the body. Raise the rear of the transmission and pull it rearward to clear the body, then back and away from the engine and lower to the ground. Lower the engine slightly, if necessary for clearance.

15. To install, first align the transmission input shaft with the clutch pressure plate and push the transmission forward until the flywheel housing contacts the body. Raise the rear of the transmission as necessary to clear the body, then lower the rear of the transmission and push it into position. Rock the transmission slightly to align the input shaft and clutch disc splines.

NOTE: Exercise caution to prevent damage to the transmission pilot bearing in the end of the crankshaft.

16. Install the shifter into the extension housing and tighten the mounting bolts to 16–19 ft. lbs. (21–26 Nm).

17. Continue installation in the reverse order of removal. Make sure the mounting surface of the transmission and flywheel housing are free of dirt and burrs. Install two guide pins in the lower flywheel housing bolt holes (bolts with the heads cut off). Raise the transmission and move it forward on the guide pins until the input shaft splines enter the clutch hub splines and the case is against the flywheel housing. Tighten the flywheel housing and engine rear cover attaching bolts to 28–38 ft. lbs. (38–51 Nm); engine mount stud nuts to 50–70 ft. lbs. (68–95 Nm); and the rear transmission mount to 25–35 ft. lbs. (34–48 Nm). See the Suspension section for front stabilizer bar torque specifications.

OVERHAUL

For all manual transmission overhaul procedures, please refer to "Manual Transmission" in the Unit Repair Section.

CLUTCH

ADJUSTMENTS

The clutch free play is self-adjusting during normal operation. The self-adjusting feature should be checked every 5000 miles. This is accomplished by insuring that the clutch pedal travels to the top of its upward position. Grasp the clutch pedal with your hand or put your foot under the pedal, then pull up on the pedal until it stops. Very little effort is required (about 10 lbs.) During the application of upward pressure, a click may be heard which means an adjustment was necessary and has been accomplished.

REMOVAL & INSTALLATION

1. Lift the clutch pedal to its uppermost position to disengage the pawl and quadrant. Push the quadrant forward, unhook the clutch cable and allow the quadrant to slowly swing rearward.

2. Disconnect the negative battery cable. Raise and support the vehicle safely.

3. Disconnect the cable from the clutch release lever.

4. Remove the clutch cable form the flywheel housing.

5. Disconnect the starter motor cable and remove the starter motor. Remove the lower shield from the flywheel housing.

6. Remove the transmission as previously described.

7. Remove the flywheel housing. If the pressure plate is being reused, paint or scribe alignment marks on the pressure plate and flywheel so they may be assembled in their original positions.

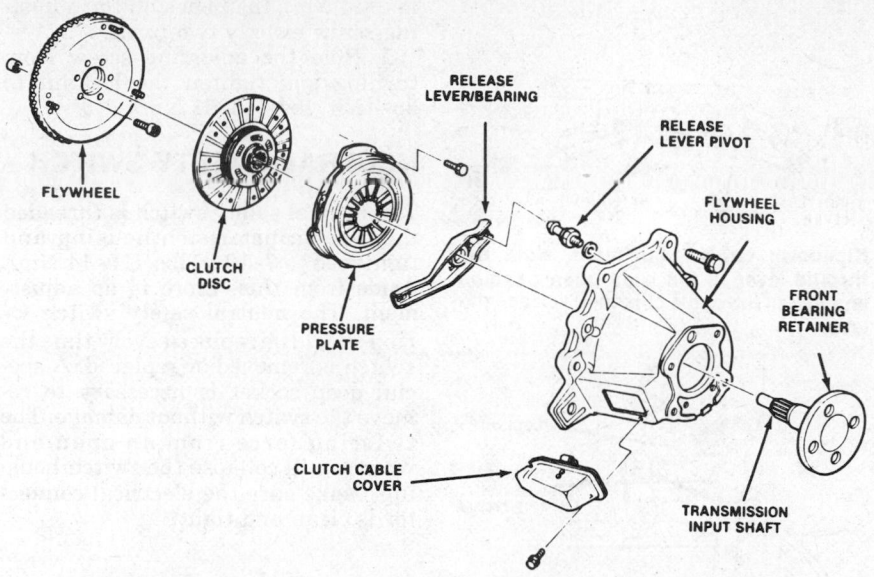

RELEASE LEVER/BEARING

RELEASE LEVER PIVOT

FLYWHEEL

CLUTCH DISC

PRESSURE PLATE

FLYWHEEL HOUSING

FRONT BEARING RETAINER

CLUTCH CABLE COVER

TRANSMISSION INPUT SHAFT

Exploded view of the clutch assembly used on 4 cylinder engines

8. Loosen the six pressure plate cover mounting bolts evenly in rotation to release the spring pressure gradually. Remove the pressure plate and clutch disc.

9. Remove the clutch release bearing from the release lever. Inspect the lever and bearing for wear and replace as necessary.

NOTE: The clutch release bearing is lubricated and permanantly sealed during manufacture. Never wash or soak the bearing in cleaning solvent or it will ruin the bearing.

10. Install the clutch disc and pressure plate in the reverse order of removal. Make sure the clutch disc is installed with the correct side facing the flywheel. A new disc will be stamped "flywheel" to indicate the correct installation, but the disc is installed properly if the damper springs face away from the flywheel. The three dowel pins on the flywheel must be properly aligned with the pressure plate. Avoid touching the disc surface and start the pressure plate mounting bolts slowly and evenly to avoid distortion. Align the clutch disc using the proper aligning tool, then tighten the pressure plate bolts evenly in sequence. Tighten the bolts to 15–19 ft. lbs. (20–25 Nm), then remove the clutch disc alignment tool and continue installation procedures.

Clutch Cable

REMOVAL & INSTALLATION

Holding the clutch pedal above its normal position will disengage the clutch cable self-adjuster. Raise the vehicle, then remove the clutch release lever cover. Pull rearward on the cable to disengage it from the release lever. The sound panels under the left side of the dashboard must be removed to gain access to the clutch cable routing through the body. Install the replacement cable using the same routing as the old cable, unless the reason for cable replacement was binding or wear due to sharp turns in the cable.

AUTOMATIC TRANSMISSION

REMOVAL & INSTALLATION

1. Disconnect the negative battery cable and remove the transmission dipstick. Raise and support the vehicle safely.

2. Place a drain pan under the transmission fluid pan. Starting at the rear of the pan and working toward the front, loosen the attaching bolts and allow the fluid to drain. Then remove all of the pan attaching bolts except two at the front, to allow the fluid to further drain. After all the fluid has drained, install two bolts on the rear side of the pan to temporarily hold it in place.

3. Remove the starter motor and the nuts attaching the catalytic converter inlet pipe to the turbocharger.

Remove the support bracket attaching bolt and then the catalytic converter and inlet pipe as an assembly.

4. Remove the stabilizer bar U-brackets and the body stiffener rod, then position a block of wood between the stabilizer bar and the body side rail.

5. Remove the torque converter drain plug access cover and adapter plate bolts from the lower end of the converter housing.

6. Remove the torque converter-to-drive plate attaching nuts through the starter opening. Remove the converter drain plug and drain the converter. Reinstall the plug. Turn the engine in normal direction of rotation to gain access to the converter mounting nuts and drain plug, using a wrench on the crankshaft pulley attaching bolt.

CAUTION

Do not turn the engine counterclockwise. Backward engine rotation may cause the valve timing belt to jump time.

7. Remove the driveshaft and plug the extension housing to prevent dirt entry and fluid loss during service.

8. Support the transmission with a suitable jack and secure it with a safety chain. Remove the bolts attaching the rear mount to the transmission support bracket. Remove the nuts attaching the rear mount to the body and remove the mount.

9. Disconnect the shift rod at the transmission lever, then disconnect the downshift rod at the transmission downshift lever.

10. Disconnect the neutral start switch wires from the switch. Disconnect the speedometer cable from the transmission.

11. Remove the vacuum line from the transmission vacuum modulator. Remove the transmission filler tube.

12. Disconnect the transmission cooler lines using quick connect removal tool T82L-9500-AH or equivalent.

13. Remove the converter housing attaching bolts located at the top of the housing.

14. Remove the crossmember-to-frame side support attaching bolts and remove the crossmember.

15. Lower the transmission slightly. Place a piece of wood on a floorjack and support the engine.

16. Pull the transmission back and away from the engine slowly. Make sure the converter is mounted fully on the transmission and not stuck on the driveplate.

17. Lower the transmission and converter and remove it from beneath the vehicle.

18. Install the transmission in the reverse order of removal. Make sure the torque converter hub is fully engaged in the pump gear. Converter housing to engine mounting bolt torque is 28–38 ft. lbs. (38–51 Nm). Tighten the torque converter-to-flywheel nuts to 12–16 ft. lbs. (27–46 Nm). If the transmission was completely drained, add two quarts of fluid before starting the engine and five more immediately after engine start-up. Check the fluid level with the dipstick and top off as necessary.

PAN AND FILTER REMOVAL

1. Raise the vehicle and support it safely.

2. Place a drain pan under the oil pan, then start at the rear of the pan and work forward loosening the pan attaching bolts until the fluid starts to drain. Slowly remove the pan bolts, leaving two on one side for last, until the pan tilts down and the remaining fluid drains.

3. Remove the remaining bolts and lower the oil pan.

4. Remove the transmission filter attaching screws and lower the filter from the valve body.

5. Clean all gasket mating surfaces on the transmission case and pan. Install the oil filter gasket and the new oil filter, then tighten the attaching bolts to 6–8 ft. lbs. (8–11 Nm).

6. Install the oil pan and gasket, then tighten the attaching bolts to 12–17 ft. lbs. (16–23 Nm).

LINKAGE ADJUSTMENTS

1. Raise the vehicle and support it safely.

2. Remove the retaining clip and disengage the shift rod from the selector lever.

3. Rotate the transmission shift lever as far as possible toward the front of the engine. This is the Drive 1 or manual Low position.

4. Rotate the transmission shift lever two detent positions toward the rear of the vehicle. This is the Drive position.

5. Move the gearshift lever to the Drive position as indicated by the shifter. Without moving the transmission or gearshift levers, attempt to slide the shift rod clevis over the selector lever pin. If the clevis slides on the pin, the linkage is properly adjusted.

6. If the clevis does not slide onto the pin, loosen the locknut and thread the clevis in or out to obtain the proper fit. After making the adjustment, tighten the clevis locknut.

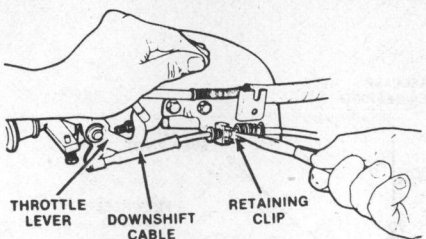

Kickdown cable adjustment. Hold the throttle lever in the wide open position and install the cable clip, then release the lever

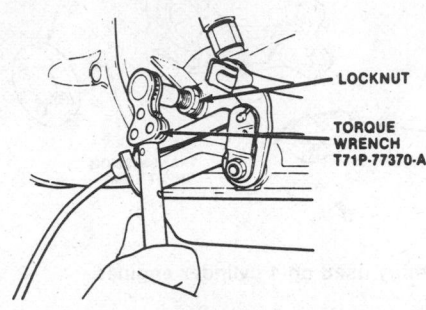

Front band adjustment

7. Install the selector rod retaining clip and lower the vehicle.

8. Check transmission in each selector position.

—————— CAUTION ——————

Make sure the linkage adjustment has not affected the operation of the neutral safety switch. With the parking brake set and service brakes applied firmly, try to start the engine in each gearshift position. The engine should crank over only in the Neutral and Park positions. If the engine cranks in any other shifter position, check the linkage adjustment and neutral safety switch.

KICKDOWN ADJUSTMENT

Using a pair of pliers, remove the kickdown cable retaining clip located near the throttle body routing bracket. Rotate the throttle body lever to the wide open position and hold it there. While holding the throttle open, install the cable retaining clip, then release the throttle lever.

FRONT BAND ADJUSTMENT

1. Raise and support the vehicle safely.

2. Clean all of the dirt and grease from around the band adjusting screw area.

3. Remove and discard the band adjusting screw locknut. Install a new locknut on the screw, but do not tighten it.

4. Use an accurate torque wrench to tighten the adjusting screw to 10 ft

lbs. (14 Nm), then back off the adjusting screw exactly two turns.

5. Hold the adjusting screw from turning and tighten the locknut to 35–45 ft. lbs. (48–61 Nm).

NEUTRAL SAFETY SWITCH

The neutral safety switch is threaded into the transmission housing and tightened to 7–10 ft. lbs. (10–14 Nm). Aside from this, there is no adjustment. The neutral safety switch O-ring should be replaced every time the switch is removed or replaced. A special deep socket is necessary to remove the switch without damage. The twisting force from an open end wrench will collapse the switch housing. Make sure the electrical connector is clean and tight.

DRIVE AXLE

Halfshafts

Power is transferred to the rear wheels by independent axle halfshafts. Each shaft is equipped with both an inner and an outer constant velocity joint. CV-joints require care during servicing to avoid causing damage to machined surfaces and splines. Never allow a CV-joint to hang by its own weight; wire the shaft to the underbody to support it during service procedures.

REMOVAL & INSTALLATION

1. Raise the vehicle and support it safely with the rear wheels hanging freely. Make sure the transmission is in Neutral and the parking brake is fully released.

2. Remove the flange bolts on the outside joint at the wheel stub shaft. Rotate the halfshaft to bring the flange bolts around.

3. Remove the flange bolts at the differential stub shaft only after securing the outer end of the halfshaft with wire or rope to the vehicle underbody.

4. Use a wide, flat-bladed prybar to separate the flanges, if necessary, but be careful not to damage any mating surfaces.

5. Carefully lower the axle driveshaft down and out. Handle the CV-joints with care; they can be damaged if dropped.

NOTE: The halfshafts are different lengths, and so must be in-

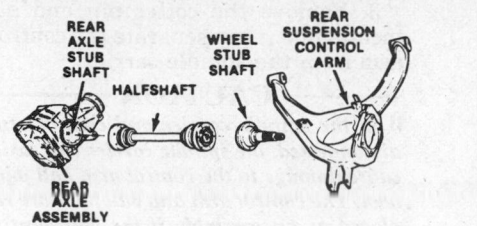
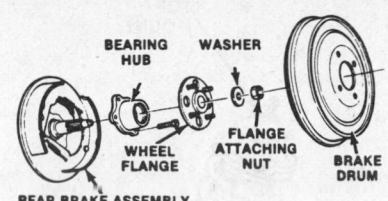

Exploded view of the rear axle, halfshaft and hub assembly.

stalled on the correct side of the vehicle. Be careful not to confuse the two; the longer shaft is installed on the right side of the vehicle.

6. Pack the constant velocity joints with grease before installation.

7. Installation is the reverse of removal. Tighten the halfshaft flange bolts to 28–31 ft. lbs. (38–43 Nm).

CV-JOINT OVERHAUL

For all CV-Joint overhaul procedures, please refer to "CV-Joint Overhaul" in the Unit Repair section.

Driveshaft and U-Joints

REMOVAL & INSTALLATION

1. Raise the vehicle and support it safely.

2. Scribe alignment marks on the driveshaft and pinion flanges before removal. If the driveshaft is not indexed properly when installed, it could ruin driveline balance and cause vibrations.

3. Place the transmission gear selector in Neutral to allow rotation of the driveshaft.

4. Detach any exhaust system components interfering with driveshaft removal.

5. Remove the pinion flange-to-driveshaft mounting bolts.

6. Remove the bolts mounting the center bearing support to the floorpan. Be careful not to lose the spacers that are installed between the support bearing bracket and the floor pan. Note the position and number of the spacers so they may be installed in their original location. Failure to do so could result in driveline vibration.

7. Remove the bolts that retain the driveshaft to the transmission flange.

8. Install the driveshaft in the reverse order of removal. Tighten the flange bolts to 42–49 ft. lbs. (57–67

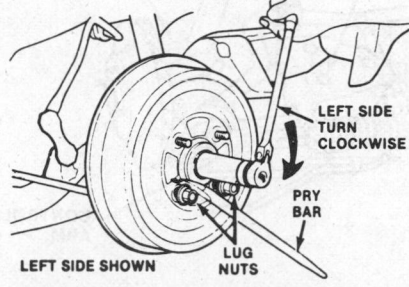

Use a prybar as shown when removing or installing the rear axle flange locknut.

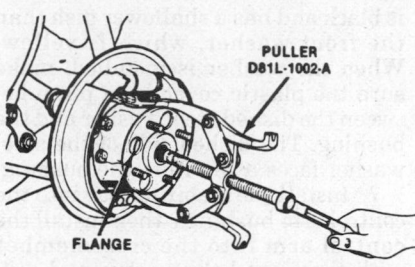

Remove the rear axle drive flange with a puller

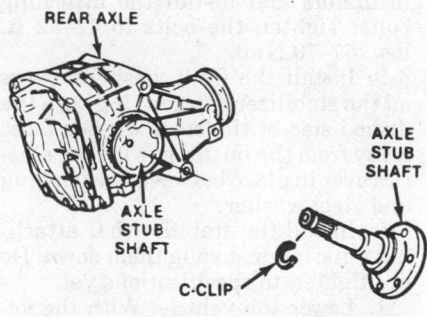

The axle shafts are held in position by C-clips installed on the end of the shaft

Nm), and the center bearing support mounting bolts to 13–17 ft. lbs. (18–23 Nm).

Rear Axle Bearing

REMOVAL & INSTALLATION

NOTE: The rear axle flange locknuts are not interchangeable; they have different threads. The

right side has right-handed threads, and the left side has left-handed threads. Be sure to turn the nuts in the proper direction when removing or installing.

1. Prior to raising the rear of the vehicle, loosen the rear axle locknut and wheel lugs. Raise and support the rear of the vehicle.

2. Remove the rear wheel and the brake drum. There is a drum retaining clip which must be removed. The self-adjusters may have to be backed off in order to allow drum removal. See the Brake Section for details.

3. Remove the axle locknut. Use a suitable three-jawed puller and slide hammer to remove the rear axle flange from the axleshaft.

4. Remove the bearing hub attaching bolts and remove the bearing hub.

5. The hub contains a set of inner and outer bearings and races similar to conventional front wheel bearings. The cups are replaceable and the inner and outer bearings should be packed with grease in the normal manner. A grease seal is installed on either side of the hub.

6. Service the bearings as required and install the hub in the reverse order of removal. Tighten the hub mounting bolts to 45–48 ft. lbs. (52–64 Nm). Install the axle flange and brake drum.

7. Install a new locknut on the axle, being careful not to mix sides. Tighten the locknuts to 185–214 ft. lbs. (250–290 Nm).

FRONT SUSPENSION

MacPherson Strut

REMOVAL & INSTALLATION

1. Raise and support the front of the vehicle safely, after loosening the front wheel lug nuts.

2. Remove the tire assembly. Position a floor jack under the lower control arm, then raise the jack until it is slightly lower than the control arm.

3. Remove the pinch bolt that secures the strut to the lower control arm. Use a small pry bar to spread the mounting flange ears and push down on the lower control arm to separate the arm and strut. Lower the jack if necessary, but do not allow the brake hose to stretch. When separated, rest the control arm on the jack.

4. Hold the top of the strut by in-

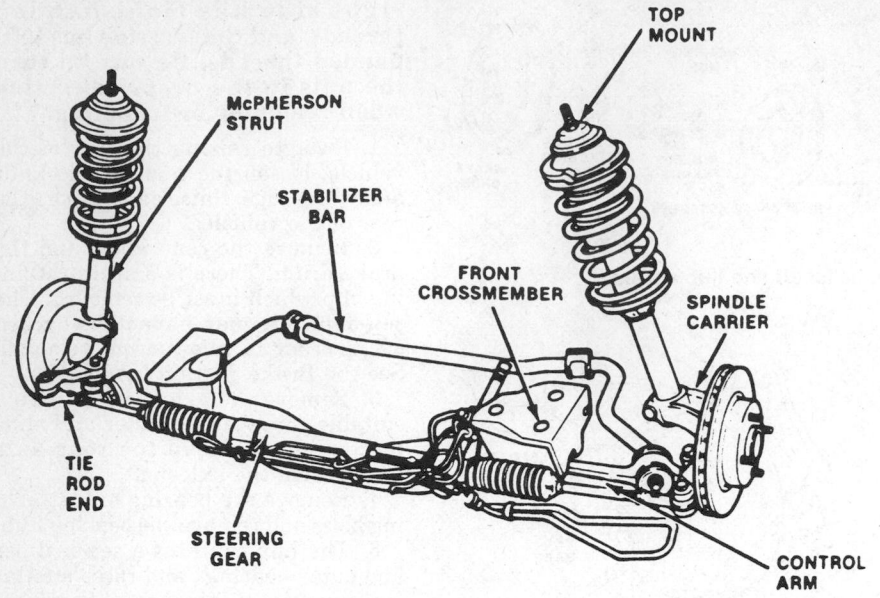

XR4Ti front suspension assembly

serting a 6mm hex wrench in the slot provided and remove the locknut.

5. Remove the strut assembly from the vehicle.

6. Install the replacement strut assembly in the reverse order of removal.

OVERHAUL

For all strut overhaul procedures, please refer to "Strut Overhaul" in the Unit Repair section.

Stabilizer Bar

REMOVAL & INSTALLATION

1. Remove the attaching nuts and front washers/covers from the ends of the stabilizer bar.

2. Remove the four bolts securing the two U-brackets and torque brace to the body.

3. Detach one control arm pivot bolt and pull the control arm out of the crossmember.

4. Pull the stabilizer out of the lower control arms and remove it from the vehicle. Remove the rear washers/covers from the stabilizer bar, along with the insulators.

5. To install: coat the inside of the stabilizer bar bushings and the bushing surfaces on the stabilizer bar with rubber lube. Do not use engine oil. Install the insulators on the stabilizer bar.

6. Install the rear washers/covers on the stabilizer bar. The rear washer is black and has a shallower dish than the front washer, which is yellow. When the washer is installed, make sure the plastic cover is in place between the dished steel washer and the bushing. The dished side of the steel washer faces away from the bushing.

7. Install the stabilizer bar into the control arm bushings, then install the control arm into the crossmember with the pivot bolt, washer and nut. Snug the attaching nut, but do not tighten.

8. Install the U-bolts on the insulators and install the attaching bolts. Tighten the bolts to 42–52 ft. lbs. (57–70 Nm).

9. Install the front washers/covers on the stabilizer bar, making sure the dished side of the steel washer faces away from the bushing, with the plastic cover in place between the bushing and steel washer.

10. Install the stabilizer bar attaching nuts, but just snug them down. Do not tighten to specifications yet.

11. Lower the vehicle. With the vehicle weight on the tires, tighten the stabilizer bar attaching nut to 52–81 ft. lbs. (70–110 Nm). Tighten the control arm pivot bolt and nut to 11 ft. lbs. (15 Nm), and then turn an additional 90 degrees.

Lower Control Arm

REMOVAL & INSTALLATION

1. Raise the front of the vehicle and support it safely.

2. Remove the front tire.

3. Remove the cotter pin and attaching nut, then separate the control arm from the spindle carrier.

─────── **CAUTION** ───────
With the spindle carrier and control arm disconnected, the spindle carrier can easily cause damage to the control arm ball joint boot. The control arm and ball joint are replaced as an assembly if the ball joint is worn or damaged.
──────────────────────────

4. Remove the pivot bolt attaching the control arm to the crossmember.

5. Remove the nut attaching the stabilizer bar to the control arm.

6. Remove the front washer/cover from the end of the stabilizer bar.

7. Remove the control arm and bushing as an assembly. Remove the rear washer/cover from the end of the stabilizer bar. Remove the bushings if replacement is necessary; the bushings are pressed into the control arm.

8. Installation is the reverse of removal. The stabilizer bar bushings are designed to allow the control arm to move forward and rearward somewhat; this movement should not be interpreted as a suspension problem. Tighten the control arm ball joint stud nut to 48–63 ft. lbs. (65–85 Nm) and install a new cotter pin. The castle nut may be tightened slightly to align the cotter pin hole with the castellations, but do not loosen the nut for alignment. Tighten the control arm pivot bolt to 11 ft. lbs. (15 Nm), then tighten an additional 90 degrees.

Front Wheel Bearing and Spindle

REMOVAL & INSTALLATION

1. Raise and safely support the vehicle. Remove the front wheels and brake calipers. Suspend the calipers on wire to prevent brake hose damage.

2. Matchmark the rotor and wheel stud. The unit is balanced by the factory and must be installed in the same position to maintain balance.

3. Remove the cotter pin and the tie rod end attaching nut. Remove the tie rod from the spindle.

4. Remove the cotter pin and control arm attaching nut and remove the control arm from the knuckle.

5. Remove the strut mounting to knuckle pinch bolt. Spread the ears and remove the knuckle from the strut assembly.

6. Place the spindle and hub in a vise, wheel studs pointing downward and clamped between two pieces of wood and the vise jaws.

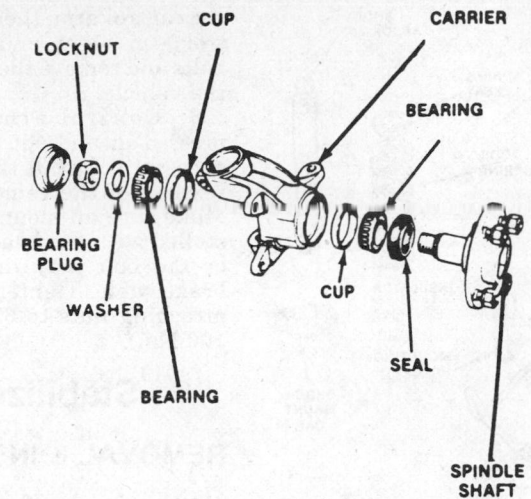

LOCKNUT CUP CARRIER

BEARING

BEARING
PLUG

WASHER

CUP

BEARING

SEAL

SPINDLE
SHAFT

Exploded view of the front hub and bearing assembly

7. Remove the bearing plug from the rear of the knuckle using a flat drift.

8. Use a 27mm socket and remove the spindle bearing locknut.

NOTE: Spindles form the right side of the vehicle are equipped with left handed threads and are loosened by turning clockwise. Spindles from the left side of the vehicle are equipped with right handed threads which are loosened by turning counterclockwise. The spindles are marked with an R or L on the large hexagonal recess.

9. Lift the spindle carrier and inner bearing off the (hub) spindle shaft. Remove the inner bearing and splined washer. If the bearing is to be reused, tag for location identification.

10. Clamp the spindle carrier (knuckle) in a vise and remove the grease seal using a flat prybar. Remove the outer bearing and tag for location identification.

11. Remove bearing cups from the spindle, if necessary, using a bearing puller jaws on a slide hammer.

12. Clean and inspect all parts. Press new bearing cups into the spindle. Pack the wheel bearing with high temperature grease.

13. Install the outer bearing and grease seal in the spindle (knuckle). Install the spindle shaft (hub).

14. Install the inner bearing and splined washer. Install the spindle bearing locknut and tighten to 202–232 ft. lbs. (274–315 Nm). Install the bearing cover plug.

NOTE: Be sure the spindle is mounted secure in the vise but do not damage the studs. The amount of torque required for the locknut is extremely important. If a higher or lower torque is applied bearing failure is likely to occur.

15. Install the spindle (knuckle) in the reverse order of removal. Torque the attaching parts as follows:
• Strut to Spindle Pinch Bolt: 59–66 ft. lbs. (80–90 Nm)
• Lower Control Arm Nut: 48–63 ft. lbs. (65–85 Nm)
• Tie Rod End Nut: 15–23 ft. lbs. (20–32 Nm)

Front Wheel Alignment

CASTER & CAMBER

Caster and Camber are not adjustable. If out of specifications, the vehicle body should be checked for distortion at suspension mounting points. The tires should be properly inflated and any abnormal loads removed from the vehicle when checking or adjusting alignment.

TOE

Toe-in should be adjusted to $\frac{1}{64}$ in. (0.5mm), out to $\frac{3}{16}$ in. (4.5mm), with a preferred setting of $\frac{5}{64}$ in. (2mm). To adjust the toe, loosen the jam nuts at the tie rod ends and release the clips at the small ends of the steering gear boots. Make sure the boots are free on the tie rods so they won't be twisted when the tie rods are turned.

Turn the tie rods in or out an equal amount on each side. Turning the tie rods in (shortening) will increase the toe, while moving the tie rods out (lengthening) decreases toe. When the toe setting is correct, tighten the jam nuts to 42–50 ft. lbs. (57–68 Nm). Make sure the steering gear boot ends are positioned correctly and install the boot clips.

REAR SUSPENSION

NOTE: The entire rear axle and suspension can be removed as an assembly by supporting the body and disconnecting the brake lines and the crossmember, rear axle mount, stabilizer bar and upper shock absorber mounting bolts.

Shock Absorber

REMOVAL & INSTALLATION

1. Remove the rear parcel shelf or luggage compartment cover, then remove the upper shock mount trim cover.

2. Raise and support the rear of the vehicle safely.

3. Position a floor jack under the lower control arm of the side requiring shock replacement. Raise the jack until it contacts the control arm.

4. Remove the upper shock mount through bolt and nut.

5. Remove the cap from the lower shock mount, then loosen and remove the through bolt and nut. Remove the shock absorber.

6. Install the replacement shock in reverse order. Install the lower through bolt with the head facing inboard, then tighten the lower mounting bolt head to 33–40 ft. lbs. (45–55 Nm), or the nut to 30–37 ft. lbs. (40–50 Nm). Install the upper mounting bolt and tighten the attaching nut to 30–37 ft. lbs. (40–50 Nm).

Coil Spring

REMOVAL & INSTALLATION

1. Loosen the rear wheel lug nuts. Raise and support the rear of the vehicle safely, with the rear suspension hanging freely. Remove the rear tire and the brake drum.

NOTE: The rear brake self-adjusters may have to be backed off in order to remove the brake drum.

2. Position a floor jack under the rear control arm and take a slight amount of weight off of the spring.

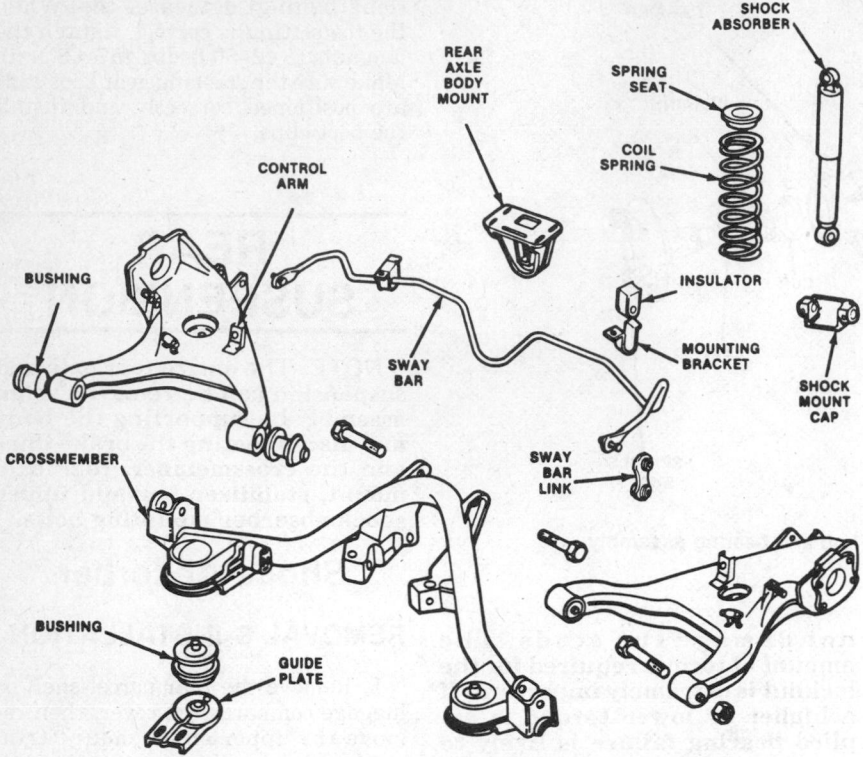

Exploded view of the rear suspension components

(Labels on diagram: REAR AXLE BODY MOUNT, CONTROL ARM, BUSHING, CROSSMEMBER, BUSHING, GUIDE PLATE, SWAY BAR, SWAY BAR LINK, SHOCK ABSORBER, SPRING SEAT, COIL SPRING, INSULATOR, MOUNTING BRACKET, SHOCK MOUNT CAP)

3. Disconnect the rear brake hose at the body bracket (rubber line from steel line).

4. Remove the bolts that attach the rear axle flange and brake backing plate to the control arm.

5. Remove the axle halfshaft from the vehicle, as described under "Halfshaft Removal & Installation". Secure the backing plate in its installed position with two bolts to prevent damage to the steel brake line.

6. Remove the lower shock mounting cap and the bolt that secures the lower mounting eye of the shock absorber to the control arm.

—————— CAUTION ——————

Make sure that the lower arm and spring tension is securely supported by a floor jack before removing the lower shock absorber mounting bolt. Exercise caution, as the energy stored in a compressed coil spring is dangerous if suddenly released.

7. Remove the bolts attaching the rear axle mount to the body and disconnect the axle vent tube.

8. Carefully lower the suspension arm on the jack and remove the coil spring and rubber spring seat. Do not remove the support from the rear axle; lower the assembly just enough to allow removal of the coil spring.

9. Install the rear spring upper seat onto the spring end with the color code and plastic sleeve. Make sure the

end of the coil seats against the step in the spring seat and that the seat tabs are positioned between the first and second coil.

NOTE: The coil spring and seat must be installed dry. Do not lubricate with spray silicone or any other type of lubricant.

10. Raise the jack slowly and make sure the spring and seat are correctly located. Raise the rear axle into position and install the body mount attaching bolts. Clean the body mount bolts and apply Locktite®, then tighten to 14–18 ft. lbs. (20–25 Nm). Install the remaining components in reverse order of removal.

Lower Control Arm

REMOVAL & INSTALLATION

1. Remove the coil spring as previously described.

2. Use a screwdriver to open the routing clamp and disengage the parking brake cable from the control arm.

3. Disconnect the sway stabilizer link from the control arm.

4. Remove the rear bearing hub and suspend the brake backing plate on a length of wire.

5. Pull the wheel stub shaft out of

the control arm, then remove the control arm inner and outer attaching bolts and remove the control arm from the vehicle.

6. Control arm bushings are pressed in and out if replacement is necessary. Install the control arm in reverse of the removal procedures. Make sure all mounting bolts are installed with the heads facing inboard or the bolt may interfere with the brake cable. Tighten the control arm attaching nuts to 63–74 ft. lbs. (85–100 Nm).

Stabilizer Bar

REMOVAL & INSTALLATION

1. Loosen the wheel lug nuts on one side of the vehicle.

2. Raise and support the rear of the vehicle.

3. Remove one wheel and tire assembly.

4. Use a small pry bar and unclip the connector from the end of the bar to lower control arm. Repeat on the other side of the vehicle.

5. Remove the bushing bracket retaining bolts from the floor pan and remove the stabilizer bar assembly. Place a piece of tape on the stabilizer bar next to the U-bracket and insulator for alignment reference during assembly.

6. Install in the reverse order or removal. Tighten the U-bracket mounting bolts to 15–18 ft. lbs. (20–25 Nm).

STEERING

Steering Wheel

REMOVAL & INSTALLATION

1. Disconnect the negative battery cable.

2. Turn the ignition switch to the RUN position and center the steering wheel with the front tires in a straight-ahead position. Remove the steering wheel hub cover assembly by carefully prying it up with a small screwdriver.

3. Loosen the center hub nut a few turns, then pull the steering wheel straight up to release it from the tapered steering shaft. Remove the wheel hub nut and lift off the steering wheel.

4. Make sure the turn signal cam is aligned with the turn signal switch cancelling lever.

5. To install, position the steering

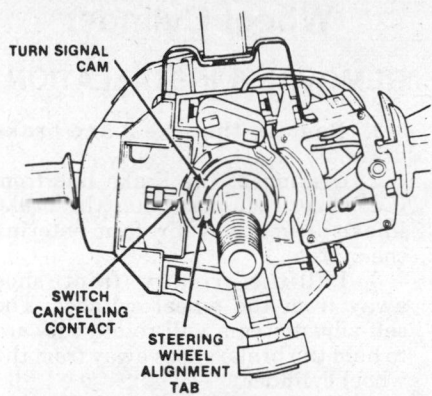

Make sure the turn signal cam is aligned with the cancelling lever before installing the steering wheel

wheel over the column shaft and align the slot on the underside of the steering wheel hub with the tab on the turn signal switch. Install the center hub nut on the shaft and tighten it to 33–40 ft. lbs. (45–55 Nm).

6. Turn the ignition key to LOCK and remove it, then check that the steering wheel locks properly. Install the hub trim pad and connect the negative battery cable, then verify horn function.

Turn Signal and Combination Switch

The combination switch contains the controls for windshield wiper/washer and headlamp high beam operation. Although mounted next to one another in the steering column, the turn signal and combination switches are replaced separately.

REMOVAL & INSTALLATION

1. Disconnect the negative battery cable.

2. Remove the steering wheel, then remove the upper and lower steering column shrouds. There is one screw near the hazard flasher switch and two underneath the column, on either side of the hood release lever.

3. Remove the sound panels from the underside of the dash. Be careful to disconnect courtesy lights and radio speaker connectors before removing the column completely.

4. Remove the screws mounting the switch to the column. Disengage the switch from the column, disconnect the wire connectors and remove the switch from the steering column.

5. To install, align the switch mounting holes with the corresponding holes in the housing and continue in the reverse order of removal.

Ignition Lock/Switch

REMOVAL & INSTALLATION

1. Disconnect the negative battery cable.

2. Remove the steering wheel, sound panels and column shrouds.

3. Turn the ignition key switch to the "I" position. Use a suitable tool and depress the lock spring (hole provided), then remove the lock cylinder from the ignition switch.

4. Remove the ignition switch mounting screws and disengage the switch from the steering column.

5. Installation is the reverse of removal.

Power Steering Gear

REMOVAL & INSTALLATION

1. Disconnect the negative battery cable, then turn the ignition switch to the ON position. Center the steering wheel with the front tires in the straight-ahead position.

2. Raise and support the front of the vehicle safely.

3. Remove the lower pinch bolt that secures the flexible coupler to the steering gear input shaft.

4. Remove the front wheels.

5. Remove the cotter pin and castle nut from the tie rod ends. Disconnect the tie rod ends from the steering knuckles using a suitable puller.

6. Position a drain pan, then disconnect the power steering pressure and return lines from the steering gear assembly by removing the routing clamp and the washer-head screw securing the pump line plate assembly to the gear housing. Plug the lines and connections at the steering gear to prevent the entry of dirt or contaminants during service.

7. Remove the mounting bolts attaching the steering gear to the crossmember and remove the gear.

8. Install the steering gear in the reverse order of removal. Replace the mounting bolts and tighten them to 11 ft. lbs. (15 Nm), then tighten an additional 90 degrees. Tighten the steering shaft pinch bolt to 18–22 ft. lbs. (25–30 Nm).

NOTE: Tie rod ends may be replaced by separating them from the steering knuckle after releasing the boot, loosening the locknut and unscrewing the tie rods from the gear assembly. Always count the number of turns for reinstallation reference.

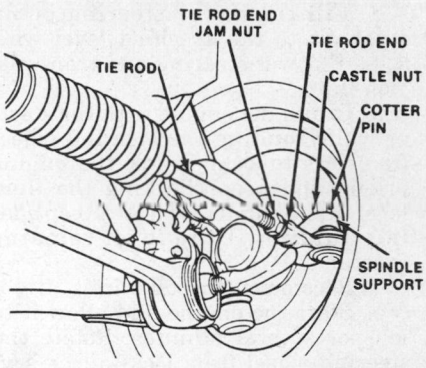

Tie rod end and steering knuckle assembly

Power Steering Pump

REMOVAL & INSTALLATION

NOTE: Special power steering pump pulley removal and installer tools are required for this procedure. The pulley remover is tool T69L-10300-B and the installer is tool T65P-3A733-E.

1. Disconnect the power steering fluid return line from the pump fitting and drain the fluid into a suitable container.

2. Remove the pressure line from the pump.

3. Remove the drive belts from the pump.

4. Remove the pump drive pulley using a suitable puller. Unbolt the pump from the mounting bracket and lift it clear.

5. Install the power steering pump in the reverse order or removal. A pulley installer tool will be necessary to attach the pump pulley. Tighten the pump mounting bolts to 30–45 ft. lbs. (41–61 Nm). Tighten the pressure and return hose fittings to 10–25 ft. lbs. (14–34 Nm). Hose swivel and/or end play in the fitting is normal and does not indicate a loose fitting. Overtightening the tube nut can result in a leak and require replacement of the hose assembly.

BLEEDING POWER STEERING SYSTEM

After any service procedure that requires draining the power steering pump, perform the following procedure to remove any trapped air in the system. Failure to bleed the power steering pump can cause excessively noisy operation.

1. Disconnect the ignition coil wire, then raise and safely support the front of the vehicle with the front wheels off the ground.

2. Fill the power steering pump reservoir to the specified level with Type F power steering and transmission fluid.

3. Crank the engine with the starter while rotating the steering wheel from lock-to-lock. Crank the engine briefly and keep checking the fluid level in the pump reservoir. Keep adding fluid until the level remains constant.

4. Reconnect the coil wire.

5. Start the engine and allow it to idle for several minutes. Rotate the steering wheel from lock-to-lock several times, then turn off the engine and recheck the fluid level. Add fluid as necessary.

BRAKES

For all brake system repair and service procedures not detailed below, please refer to "Brakes" in the Unit Repair Section.

Master Cylinder

REMOVAL & INSTALLATION

1. Disconnect the low fluid indicator connector from the filler cap.

2. Disconnect the brake lines from the master cylinder.

3. Remove the two nuts and lockwashers and attach the master cylinder to the brake booster.

4. Remove the master cylinder from the booster.

5. Reverse the procedure to install. Tighten the master cylinder mounting nuts to 16–20 ft. lbs. (21–27 Nm).

6. Fill the master cylinder reservoir with brake fluid and bleed the entire brake system.

Proportioning Valve

REMOVAL & INSTALLATION

1. Raise the vehicle and support it safely.

2. Disconnect the brake lines from the proportioning valve, located just under the master cylinder/booster assembly.

3. Remove the attaching bolt and remove the proportioning valve from the vehicle.

4. Installation is the reverse of removal. Bleed the brake system.

Power Brake Booster

The 1985–86 models are equipped with a single-diaphragm brake booster, while 1987–88 models use a dual-diaphragm booster. Although different in appearance, the two boosters function the same way and service procedures are similar.

REMOVAL & INSTALLATION

1. Depress the brake pedal several times to deplete the vacuum reserve in the brake booster. Depressurize the fuel system by connecting a hand vacuum pump to the fuel pressure regulator and applying 25 in. Hg of vacuum for about three minutes.

2. Disconnect the fuel line at the pulse damper. Disconnect the fuel return line using a quick-disconnect tool.

3. Disconnect the low oil level sensor connector and remove the engine oil level dipstick. The dipstick connector is only used on 1985–86 models.

4. Remove the screw attaching the engine oil dipstick tube to the pulse damper bracket. Remove the stud nuts attaching the pulse damper bracket to the intake manifold. Disconnect the pulse damper from the fuel manifold and remove the damper/bracket assembly.

5. Tag and disconnect the vacuum lines at the vacuum tree. Disconnect the low fluid warning light connector from the master cylinder cap and pull the vacuum check valve from the booster body.

6. Working inside the car below the instrument panel, disconnect booster valve operating rod from the brake pedal assembly. To do this, disconnect the stop light switch wires at the connector. Remove the hairpin retainer and nylon washer from the pedal pin. Slide the switch off just enough for the outer arm to clear the pin. Remove the switch. Slide the booster push rod, bushing and inner nylon washer off the pedal pin.

7. Disconnect the brake lines at the master cylinder outlet fittings.

8. On cars equipped with speed control, remove the left cowl screen in the engine compartment. Remove three nuts retaining the the speed control servo to the firewall and move the servo out of the way.

9. Remove the four bracket-to-firewall attaching bolts.

10. Remove the booster and bracket assembly from the firewall, sliding the valve operating rod out from the engine side.

11. Installation is the reverse of removal. Bleed the brakes after installation is complete.

Wheel Cylinder

REMOVAL & INSTALLATION

1. Remove the wheel and brake drum.

2. Disconnect the brake line from the wheel cylinder. Plug the brake line to prevent any dirt from entering the system.

3. Pull the primary (front) shoe away from the wheel cylinder. The self-adjuster cam will rotate outward to hold the brake shoes away from the wheel cylinder.

4. Remove the wheel cylinder mounting bolts, O-ring and the wheel cylinder from the brake backing plate.

5. To install, mount the O-ring on the wheel cylinder, then position the wheel cylinder on the brake backing plate and install the mounting bolts. Tighten the bolts to 5–7 ft. lbs. (7–10 Nm). Connect the brake line.

6. Use a suitable tool and push the adjuster cam to the release position.

7. Install the brake drum. Bleed the rear brakes and install the wheel.

NOTE: If a pressure bleeder is used, push the brake pedal hard twice to set the self-adjuster cam position. The cam will make a ratcheting sound as it resets.

Parking Brake Cable

ADJUSTMENT

NOTE: Parking brake stop plungers are installed in both rear backing plates. These plungers are used to determine correct parking brake cable adjustments.

1. Fully release the parking brake. Pump the brake pedal to make sure the brake lining self-adjuster is properly set.

2. Place the transmission in Neutral and raise the rear axle until the rear wheels clear the floor.

3. Loosen the adjuster locknut, located on the cable at the routing bracket under the vehicle, and rotate the adjuster sleeve along the cable casing until in and out movement can be felt at both parking brake stop plungers.

─────── **CAUTION** ───────

Both the adjuster and locknut are threaded onto the cable casing. Any attempt to pry them apart will result in damage to the sleeve and/or locknut. To loosen the locknut, hold the adjuster with pliers and turn the locknut counterclockwise with another set of pliers.

4. Tighten the adjuster against the retaining bracket until a slight movement is felt at each stop plunger. When added together, the total movement of the plungers should not exceed 0.16 in. (4mm).

5. Tighten the locknut by hand against the sleeve as much as possible, then tighten the locknut an additional two "clicks" using suitable pliers. Turn the rear wheels by hand to make sure the brake linings are not dragging against the drum.

6. Lower the rear of the vehicle and check the operation of the parking brake.

REMOVAL & INSTALLATION

1. Release the parking brake, raise the vehicle and support it safely.

2. Loosen the brake cable adjuster locknut as described above.

3. Remove the rear wheels and brake drums. Remove the brake shoes on both sides of the vehicle.

4. Using a screwdriver, spread the retaining clip and pull the cable out of the backing plate.

5. Remove the clip and clevis pin attaching the cable equalizer to the parking brake lever in the passenger compartment.

6. Using a screwdriver, open the routing clamps and disengage the cable from both control arms, then thread the cable through the body brackets and remove it from the vehicle.

7. Installation is the reverse of removal. Make sure the cable adjuster is on the left (driver's) side of the vehicle. Adjust the parking brake cable.

CHASSIS ELECTRICAL

Heater Blower

REMOVAL & INSTALLATION

NOTE: Evaporator case removal is required for blower motor replacement.

1. Remove the evaporator case from the vehicle.

2. Remove the three access cover retaining screws and remove the cover.

3. Remove the screws retaining the scrolls to the lower case assembly. Remove the screws retaining the thermostat.

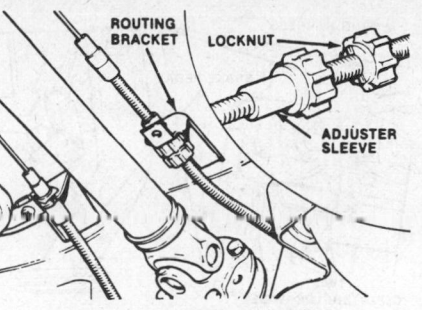

Parking brake adjustment

4. Separate the evaporator case halves after removing the retaining clips.

5. Remove the blower motor mounting screw and the blower motor.

6. Install the blower motor in the reverse order of removal. Be sure to correctly align the thermostat sensor during installation.

Heater Core

REMOVAL & INSTALLATION

1. Disconnect the negative battery cable.

2. Drain the cooling system. Remove the heater hoses from the heater core tubes at the firewall. Plug the core tubes.

3. Remove the screws retaining the tube cover and remove the cover and plate from the firewall.

4. From inside the vehicle; remove the center console and move it toward the rear of the vehicle. Remove the right side footwell trim panel.

5. Disconnect the heater control lever. Disconnect the electrical leads from the glove compartment lamp, A/C blower switch and cigarette lighter.

6. Remove the right hand dash panel.

7. Remove all duct hoses from the heater housing.

8. Detach the control cables from the heater housing.

9. Remove the screws that mount the heater housing to the firewall. Pull the heater into the vehicle until the core tubes are clear of the firewall and then pull the housing toward the right side of the vehicle for removal.

10. Remove the heater core from the housing. Install the heater core and housing in the reverse order of removal.

Radio

REMOVAL & INSTALLATION

1. Disconnect the negative battery cable.

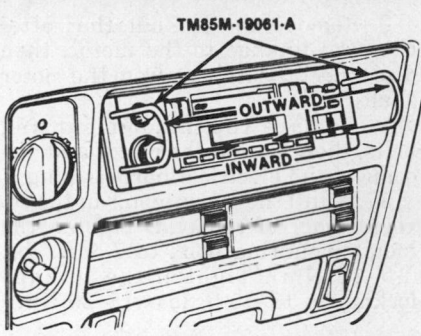

Removing the radio with special tools

2. Insert two radio removal tools T85M-19061-A, one on each side, into the access holes on the front of the radio until a click is heard.

3. Apply an outward side pressure to release the locking tangs, then slide the radio forward from the dash.

4. Disconnect the antenna, speaker, ground and power leads from the radio.

5. Disengage the special removal tools by depressing the locking tangs on the side of the radio while applying a slight inward pressure on the tool, then pull the tool from the access holes.

6. Installation is the reverse of removal. Remove the plastic support bracket from the rear of the radio and install it on the replacement unit.

Windshield Wiper Switch

REMOVAL & INSTALLATION

Follow the procedures under "Combination Switch Removal" in the Steering Section for wiper/washer switch removal procedures.

Windshield Wiper Motor

REMOVAL & INSTALLATION

Front Motor

The internal magnets used in the wiper motor are a ceramic material. Exercise care when handling the motor to avoid damaging the magnets by dropping or striking with metal tools. The ceramic magnets cannot tolerate sharp impacts.

1. Operate the wiper motor and shut off key when the linkage mounting nut is exposed, then remove the arm and blade assembly.

2. Disconnect the negative battery cable.

3. Remove the locknut that attaches the linkage to the motor, then disconnect the linkage from the motor shaft.

4. Remove the motor mounting bolts, then remove the motor and disconnect the electrical harness plug.

5. Install the wiper motor in the reverse order of removal. Tighten the motor mounting bolts to 7–9 ft. lbs. (10–12 Nm). Tighten the linkage locknut to 13–15 ft. lbs. (18–20 Nm).

Rear Motor

1. Lift the plastic cover at the base of the wiper arm to expose the mounting nut. Remove the nut, then lift the wiper arm and blade assembly from the pivot shaft.

2. Open the hatch and remove the trim panel by carefully prying out the panel clips from their locations.

3. Remove the bolts that attach the wiper motor bracket to the liftgate. Remove the screw attaching the ground lead, then disconnect the wire harness plug and remove the motor and bracket as an assembly. Disconnect the rear washer supply hose from the wiper.

4. Install the motor in the reverse order of removal. Tighten the wiper motor bracket bolts to 4–5 ft. lbs. (6–7 Nm), and the wiper arm attaching nut to 7–9 ft. lbs. (10–12 Nm).

Instrument Cluster

REMOVAL & INSTALLATION

1. Disconnect the negative battery cable.

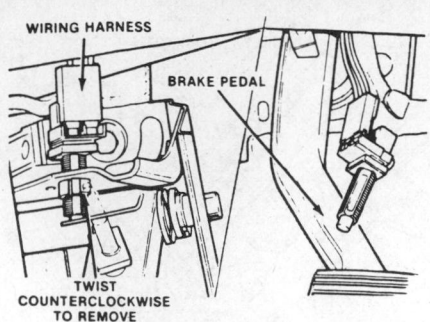

Stoplight switch mounting

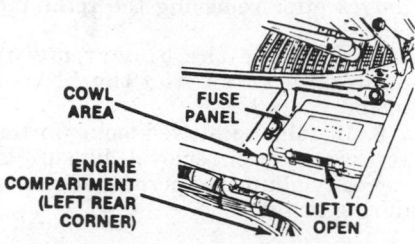

Location of fuse panel and relay block

2. Remove the screws from the upper steering column shroud and remove the shroud.

3. Remove the rheostat and intermittent wiper control from the instrument panel, if equipped.

4. Remove the four bezel mounting screws, then remove the bezel.

5. Remove the screws that attach the cluster panel to the dash.

6. Pull the cluster forward and disconnect the speedometer cable and wiring harness connectors from the instrument cluster, then remove the cluster.

7. Install the cluster in the reverse order of removal.

Headlight Switch

REMOVAL & INSTALLATION

Follow the procedures under "Combination Switch Removal" in the Steering Section for headlamp/dimmer switch removal procedures.

Stoplight Switch

REMOVAL & INSTALLATION

The stoplight switch is mounted on the brake pedal assembly. To replace the switch, first remove the left lower instrument panel. Disconnect the wiring harness connector at the switch, then twist the switch counterclockwise to remove it from its mounting bracket. Installation is the reverse of removal.

Fuses & Circuit Breakers

LOCATION

The fuse box is located in the engine compartment on the driver's side cowl. Open the fuse box by pressing the retaining handle inward and removing the cover. Replace any blown fuse or relay with the same approved amp rating for that particular circuit. Replacing a blown fuse with one of a higher rating can lead to serious wiring damage and a possible fire.

Mitsubishi

Cordia, Galant, Mirage, Precis,
Starion, Tredia, Wagon

SERIAL NUMBER IDENTIFICATION

Vehicle Identification Plate

The vehicle identification number (VIN) is mounted on the instrument panel, adjacent to the lower corner of the windshield on the driver's side and is visible through the windshield.

A standard 17 digit VIN code is used, the tenth digit identifies model year D represents 1983, E represents 1984, F represents 1985, G represents 1986, H represents 1987, I represents 1988. The eighth digit identifies the installed engine.

A vehicle information code plate is riveted onto the front of the right side wheelhouse or onto the firewall (depending on model). The plate shows model code, engine model, transaxle model and body color code.

A chassis number plate is located on the top center of the firewall in the engine compartment.

Engine Number

The engine model and serial numbers in all cases are stamped on the block near the front of the engine. In most cases, they are located on the right side.

Engine number location

Model codes for all years are as follows. G45B for the 2555cc (155.9 CID) engine, G62B for the 1795cc (109.5 CID) engine, G63B for the 1997cc (121.9 CID) engine, G15B for the 1468cc (89.6 CID) engine, G32B for the 1597ccL (97.4 CID) engine and G64B for the 2350cc (143.4 CID) engine.

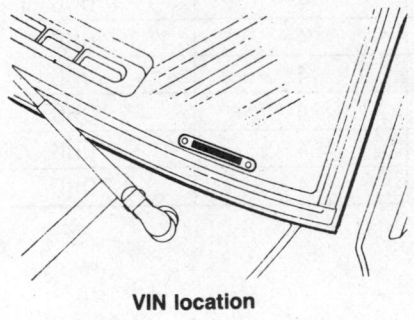

VIN location

ENGINE IDENTIFICATION

Year	Model	Engine Displacement cu. in. (cc/liter)	Engine Series Identification	No. of Cylinders	Engine Type
1983	Cordia	109.5 (1795/1.8)	G62B	4	OHC
	Tredia	109.5 (1795/1.8)	G62B	4	OHC
	Starion	155.9 (2555/2.5)	G54B	4	OHC
1984	Cordia	109.5 (1795/1.8)	G62B	4	OHC
	Cordia	121.9 (199/2.0)	G63B	4	OHC

ENGINE IDENTIFICATION

Year	Model	Engine Displacement cu. in. (cc/liter)	Engine Series Identification	No. of Cylinders	Engine Type
1984	Tredia	109.5 (1795/1.8)	G62B	4	OHC
	Tredia	121.9 (1997/2.0)	G63B	4	OHC
	Starion	155.9 (2555/2.5)	G54B	4	OHC
1985	Cordia	109.5 (1795/1.8)	G62B	4	OHC
	Cordia	121.9 (1997/2.0)	G63B	4	OHC
	Tredia	109.5 (1795/1.8)	G62B	4	OHC
	Tredia	121.9 (1997/2.0)	G63B	4	OHC
	Starion	155.9 (2555/2.5)	G54B	4	OHC
	Mirage	89.6 (1468/1.5)	G15B	4	OHC
	Mirage	97.4 (1597/1.6)	G32B	4	OHC
	Galant	143.4 (2350/2.3)	G64B	4	OHC
1986	Cordia	109.5 (1795/1.8)	G62B	4	OHC
	Cordia	121.9 (1997/2.0)	G63B	4	OHC
	Tredia	109.5 (1795/1.8)	G62B	4	OHC
	Tredia	121.9 (1997/2.0)	G63B	4	OHC
	Starion	155.9 (2555/2.5)	G54B	4	OHC
	Mirage	89.6 (1468/1.5)	G15B	4	OHC
	Mirage	97.4 (1597/1.6)	G32B	4	OHC
	Galant	143.4 (2350/2.3)	G64B	4	OHC
1987-88	Cordia	109.5 (1795/1.8)	G62B	4	OHC
	Cordia	121.9 (1997/2.0)	G63B	4	OHC
	Tredia	109.5 (1795/1.8)	G62B	4	OHC
	Tredia	121.9 (1997/2.0)	G63B	4	OHC
	Starion	155.9 (2555/2.5)	G54B	4	OHC
	Mirage	89.6 (1468/1.5)	G15B	4	OHC
	Mirage	97.4 (1597/1.6)	G32B	4	OHC
	Galant	143.4 (2350/2.3)	G64B	4	OHC
	Precis	89.6 (1468/1.5)	G15B	4	OHC
	Wagon	143.4 (2350/2.3)	G64B	4	OHC

GENERAL ENGINE SPECIFICATIONS

Year	Model	Engine Displacement cu. in. (cc)	Fuel System Type	Net Horsepower @ rpm	Net Torque @ rpm (ft. lbs.)	Bore × Stroke (in.)	Compression Ratio	Oil Pressure @ rpm
1983	Cordia	109.5 (1795)	Carb	82 @ 5000	93 @ 3000	3.17 × 3.46	7.5:1	63 ①
	Tredia	109.5 (1795)	Carb	82 @ 5000	93 @ 3000	3.17 × 3.46	7.5:1	63 ①
	Starion	155.9 (2555)	ECI ②	145 @ 5000	185 @ 2500	3.59 × 3.86	7.0:1	63 ①
1984	Cordia	109.5 (1795)	ECI ②	120 @ 5500	110 @ 2600	3.17 × 3.46	7.5.1	63 ①
	Cordia	121.9 (1997)	Carb	110 @ 5000	117 @ 3000	3.35 × 3.46	8.5:1	63 ①
	Tredia	109.5 (1795)	ECI ②	120 @ 5500	110 @ 2600	3.17 × 3.46	7.5:1	63 ①
	Tredia	121.9 (1997)	Carb	110 @ 5000	117 @ 3000	3.35 × 3.46	8.5:1	63 ①
	Starion	155.9 (2555)	ECI ②	145 @ 5000	185 @ 2500	3.59 × 3.86	7.0:1	63 ①

GENERAL ENGINE SPECIFICATIONS

Year	Model	Engine Displacement cu. in. (cc)	Fuel System Type	Net Horsepower @ rpm	Net Torque @ rpm (ft. lbs.)	Bore × Stroke (in.)	Compression Ratio	Oil Pressure @ rpm
1985	Cordia	109.5 (1795)	ECI ②	116 @ 5500	129 @ 3000	3.17 × 3.46	7.5:1	63 ①
	Cordia	121.9 (1997)	Carb	88 @ 5000	108 @ 3500	3.35 × 3.46	8.5:1	63 ①
	Tredia	109.5 (1795)	ECI ②	116 @ 5500	129 @ 3000	3.17 × 3.46	7.5:1	63 ①
	Tredia	121.9 (1997)	Carb	88 @ 5000	108 @ 3500	3.35 × 3.46	8.5:1	63 ①
	Starion	155.9 (2555)	ECI ②	145 @ 5000	185 @ 2500	3.59 × 3.86	7.0:1	63 ①
	Mirage	89.6 (1468)	Carb	68 @ 5500	82 @ 3500	2.97 × 3.23	9.4:1	63 ①
	Mirage	97.4 (1597)	ECI ②	102 @ 5500	122 @ 3000	3.03 × 3.39	7.6:1	63 ①
	Galant	143.4 (2350)	ECI ②	101 @ 5000	131 @ 2500	3.41 × 3.94	8.5:1	63 ①
1986	Cordia	109.5 (1795)	ECI ②	116 @ 5500	129 @ 3000	3.17 × 3.46	7.5:1	63 ①
	Cordia	121.9 (1997)	Carb	88 @ 5000	108 @ 3500	3.35 × 3.46	8.5:1	63 ①
	Tredia	109.5 (1795)	ECI ②	116 @ 5500	129 @ 3000	3.17 × 3.46	7.5:1	63 ①
	Tredia	121.9 (1997)	Carb	88 @ 5000	108 @ 3500	3.35 × 3.46	8.5:1	63 ①
	Starion	155.9 (2555)	ECI ②	145 @ 5000	185 @ 2500	3.59 × 3.86	7.0:1	63 ①
	Mirage	89.6 (1468)	Carb	68 @ 5000	82 @ 3500	2.97 × 3.23	9.4:1	63 ①
	Mirage	97.4 (1597)	ECI ②	102 @ 5500	122 @ 3000	3.03 × 3.39	7.6:1	63 ①
	Galant	143.4 (2350)	MPI ③	110 @ 4500	138 @ 3500	3.41 × 3.94	8.5:1	63 ①
1987-88	Cordia	109.5 (1795)	ECI ②	116 @ 5500	129 @ 3000	3.17 × 3.46	7.5:1	63 ①
	Cordia	121.9 (1997)	Carb	88 @ 5000	108 @ 3500	3.35 × 3.46	8.5:1	63 ①
	Tredia	109.5 (1795)	ECI ②	116 @ 5500	129 @ 3000	3.17 × 3.46	7.5:1	63 ①
	Tredia	121.9 (1997)	Carb	88 @ 5000	108 @ 3500	3.35 × 3.46	8.5:1	63 ①
	Starion	155.9 (2555)	ECI ②	145 @ 5000	185 @ 2500	3.59 × 3.86	7.0:1	63 ①
	Mirage	89.6 (1468)	Carb	68 @ 5000	82 @ 3500	2.97 × 3.23	9.4:1	63 ①
	Mirage	97.4 (1597)	ECI ②	102 @ 5500	122 @ 3000	3.03 × 3.39	7.6:1	63 ①
	Galant	143.4 (2350)	MPI ③	110 @ 4500	138 @ 3500	3.41 × 3.94	8.5:1	63 ①
	Precis	89.6 (1468)	Carb	68 @ 5000	82 @ 3500	2.97 × 3.23	9.4:1	63 ①
	Wagon	143.4 (2350)	MPI ③	107 @ 5000	132 @ 3500	3.41 × 3.94	8.5:1	63 ①

① Relief Valve Opening Pressure
② Electronic Controlled Injection
③ Multi-Point Injection

TUNE-UP SPECIFICATIONS

Year	Model	Engine Displacement cu. in. (cc)	Spark Plugs Type	Spark Plugs Gap (in.)	Ignition Timing (deg.) MT	Ignition Timing (deg.) AT	Compression Pressure (psi)	Fuel Pump (psi)	Idle Speed (rpm) MT	Idle Speed (rpm) AT	Valve Clearance ① In.	Valve Clearance ① Ex.
1983	Cordia	109.5 (1795)	BUR6EA-11	.039–.043	5B	5B	170 ③	2.4–3.4	650	750	.006	.010
	Tredia	109.5 (1795)	BUR6EA-11	.039–.043	5B	5B	170 ③	2.4–3.4	650	750	.006	.010
	Starion	155.9 (2555)	BUR6EA-11	.039–.043	10B	—	170 ③	35–47	850	—	.006	.010
1984	Cordia	109.5 (1795)	BPR7ES-11	.039–.043	5B	5B	170 ③	35–47	750	—	.006	.010
	Cordia	121.9 (1997)	BPR6ES-11	.039–.043	5B	5B	170 ③	2.4–3.4	700 ②	750 ②	.006	.010
	Tredia	109.5 (1795)	BPR7ES-11	.039–.043	5B	5B	170 ③	35–47	750	—	.006	.010
	Tredia	121.9 (1997)	BPR6ES-11	.039–.043	5B	5B	170 ③	2.4–3.4	700 ②	750 ②	.006	.010
	Starion	155.9 (2555)	BUR6EA-11	.039–.043	10B	10B	170 ③	35–47	750	850	.006	.010

TUNE-UP SPECIFICATIONS

Year	Model	Engine Displacement cu. in. (cc)	Spark Plugs Type	Gap (in.)	Ignition Timing (deg.) MT	AT	Compression Pressure (psi)	Fuel Pump (psi)	Idle Speed (rpm) MT	AT	Valve Clearance ① In.	Ex.
1985	Cordia	109.5 (1795)	BPR7ES-11	.039–.043	5B	5B	170 ③	35–47	750	750	.006	.010
	Cordia	121.9 (1997)	BPR6ES-11	.039–.043	5B	5B	170 ③	2.4–3.4	700 ②	750 ②	Hyd.	Hyd.
	Tredia	109.5 (1795)	BPR7ES-11	.039–.043	5B	5B	170 ③	35–47	750	750	.006	.010
	Tredia	121.9 (1997)	BPR6ES-11	.039–.043	5B	5B	170 ③	2.4–3.4	700 ②	750 ②	Hyd.	Hyd.
	Starion	155.9 (2555)	BUR6EZ-11	.039–.043	10B	10B	170 ③	35–47	750	850	.006	.010
	Mirage	89.6 (1468)	W20EP-U10	.039–.043	3B	3B	170 ③	—	700	750	.006	.010
	Mirage	97.4 (1597)	BUR7EA-11	.039–.043	8B	8B	170 ③	36	700	—	.006	.010
	Galant	143.4 (2350)	BPR6ES-11	.039–.043	—	5B	170 ③	36	—	750	Hyd.	Hyd.
1986	Cordia	109.5 (1795)	BUR7EZ-11	.035–.039	5B	5B	170 ③	35–47	750	750	.006	.010
	Cordia	121.9 (1997)	BPR6ES-11	.035–.039	5B	5B	170 ③	2.4–3.4	700 ②	750 ②	Hyd.	Hyd.
	Tredia	109.5 (1795)	BUR7EZ-11	.035–.039	5B	5B	170 ③	35–47	750	750	.006	.010
	Tredia	121.9 (1997)	BPR6ES-11	.035–.039	5B	5B	170 ③	2.4–3.4	700 ②	750 ②	Hyd.	Hyd.
	Starion	155.9 (2555)	BP6ES-11	.039–.043	10B	10B	170 ③	35–47	750	850	.006	.010
	Mirage	89.6 (1468)	W20EP-U10	.039–.043	3B	3B	170 ③	—	700	750	.006	.010
	Mirage	97.4 (1597)	BUR7EZ-11	.035–.039	8B	8B	170 ③	36	700	—	.006	.010
	Galant	143.4 (2350)	BPR6ES-11	.039–.043	—	5B	170 ③	36	—	750	Hyd.	Hyd.
1987	Cordia	109.5 (1795)	BUR7EZ-11	.035–.039	5B	5B	170 ③	35–47	750	750	.006	.010
	Cordia	121.9 (1997)	BPR6ES-11	.035–.039	5B	5B	170 ③	2.4–3.4	700 ②	750 ②	Hyd.	Hyd.
	Tredia	109.5 (1795)	BUR7EZ-11	.035–.039	5B	5B	170 ③	35–47	750	750	.006	.010
	Tredia	121.9 (1997)	BPR6ES-11	.035–.039	5B	5B	170 ③	2.4–3.4	700 ②	750 ②	Hyd.	Hyd.
	Starion	155.9 (2555)	BP6ES-11	.039–.043	10B	10B	170 ③	35–47	750	850	.006	.010
	Mirage	89.6 (1468)	W20EP-10	.039–.043	3B	3B	170 ③	—	700	750	.006	.010
	Mirage	97.4 (1597)	BUR7EZ-11	.035–.039	8B	8B	170 ③	36	700	—	.006	.010
	Galant	143.4 (2350)	BPR6ES-11	.039–.043	—	5B	170 ③	36	—	750	Hyd.	Hyd.
	Precis	89.6 (1468)	W20EP-10	.039–.043	3B	3B	170 ③	—	700	750	.006	.010
	Wagon	143.4 (2350)	BPR6ES-11	.039–.043	—	5B	170 ③	36	—	750	Hyd.	Hyd.
1988	ALL	SEE UNDERHOOD STICKER										

① Jet Valve .010   ② With a/c : 750 M/T   ③ Standard Valve; 136 Limit
850 A/T

FIRING ORDERS

NOTE: To avoid confusion, always replace spark wires one at a time.

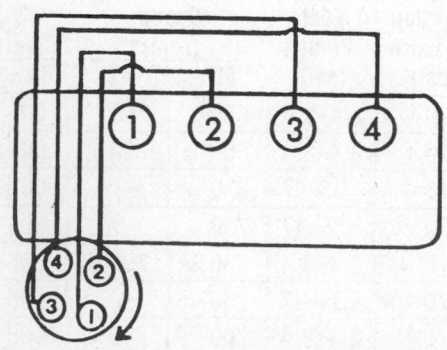

1468, 1597, 1795, 1997 and 2350cc engines

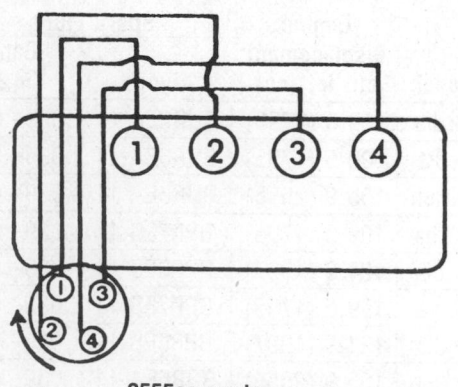

2555cc engine

CAPACITIES

Year	Model	Engine Displacement cu. in. (cc)	Engine Crankcase with Filter	Engine Crankcase without Filter	Transmission (pts) 4-Spd	Transmission (pts) 5-Spd	Transmission (pts) Auto.	Drive Axle (pts.)	Fuel Tank (gal.)	Cooling System (qts.)
1983	Cordia	109.5 (1795)	4.5	4.0	4.4	4.4	12.2	NA	13.2	7.4
	Iredia	109.5 (1795)	4.5	4.0	4.4	4.4	12.2	NA	13.2	7.4
	Starion	155.9 (2555)	5.0	4.5	4.8	—	14.8	2.7	19.8	9.7
1984	Cordia	109.5 (1795)	4.5	4.0	4.4	4.4	12.2	NA	13.2	7.4
	Cordia	121.9 (1997)	4.5	4.0	4.4	4.4	12.2	NA	13.2	7.4
	Tredia	109.5 (1795)	4.5	4.0	4.4	4.4	12.2	NA	13.2	7.4
	Tredia	121.9 (1997)	4.5	4.0	4.4	4.4	12.2	NA	13.2	7.4
	Starion	155.9 (2555)	5.0	4.5	4.8	—	14.8	2.7	19.8	9.7
1985	Cordia	109.5 (1795)	4.5	4.0	4.4	4.4	12.2	NA	13.2	7.4
	Cordia	121.9 (1997)	4.5	4.0	4.4	4.4	12.2	NA	13.2	7.4
	Tredia	109.5 (1795)	4.5	4.0	4.4	4.4	12.2	NA	13.2	7.4
	Tredia	121.9 (1997)	4.5	4.0	4.4	4.4	12.2	NA	13.2	7.4
	Starion	155.9 (2555)	5.5	5.0	4.8	—	14.8	2.7	19.8	9.7
	Mirage	89.6 (1468)	3.7	3.2	—	4.4	12.4	NA	11.9	5.3
	Mirage	97.4 (1597)	4.5	4.0	—	4.8	12.4	NA	11.9	5.3
	Galant	143.4 (2350)	4.5	4.0	—	—	12.4	NA	15.9	7.4
1986	Cordia	109.5 (1795)	4.5	4.0	4.4	4.4	12.2	NA	13.2	7.4
	Cordia	121.9 (1997)	4.5	4.0	4.4	4.4	12.2	NA	13.2	7.4
	Tredia	109.5 (1795)	4.5	4.0	4.4	4.4	12.2	NA	13.2	7.4
	Tredia	121.9 (1997)	4.5	4.0	4.4	4.4	12.2	NA	13.2	7.4
	Starion	155.9 (2555)	5.0	4.5	4.8	—	14.8	2.7	19.8	9.7
	Mirage	89.6 (1468)	3.7	3.2	—	4.4	12.4	NA	11.9	5.3
	Mirage	97.4 (1597)	4.5	4.0	—	4.8	12.4	NA	11.9	5.3
	Galant	143.4 (2350)	4.5	4.0	—	—	12.4	NA	15.9	7.4
1987-88	Cordia	109.5 (1795)	4.5	4.0	4.4	4.4	12.2	NA	13.2	7.4
	Cordia	121.9 (1997)	4.5	4.0	4.4	4.4	12.2	NA	13.2	7.4
	Tredia	109.5 (1795)	4.5	4.0	4.4	4.4	12.2	NA	13.2	7.4
	Tredia	121.9 (1997)	4.5	4.0	4.4	4.4	12.2	NA	13.2	7.4
	Starion	155.9 (2555)	5.0	4.5	4.8	—	14.8	2.7	19.8	9.7
	Mirage	89.6 (1468)	3.7	3.2	—	4.4	12.4	NA	11.9	5.3
	Mirage	97.4 (1597)	4.5	4.0	—	4.8	12.4	NA	11.9	5.3
	Galant	143.4 (2350)	4.5	4.0	—	—	12.4	NA	15.9	7.4
	Precis	89.6 (1468)	3.7	3.2	—	4.4	—	NA	11.9	5.3
	Wagon	143.4 (2350)	4.5	4.0	—	—	14.0	2.7	14.3	8.5

CRANKSHAFT AND CONNECTING ROD SPECIFICATIONS

All measurements are given in inches.

Year	Engine Displacement cu. in. (cc)	Crankshaft Main Brg. Journal Dia.	Crankshaft Main Brg. Oil Clearance	Crankshaft Shaft End-play	Crankshaft Thrust on No.	Connecting Rod Journal Diameter	Connecting Rod Oil Clearance	Connecting Rod Side Clearance
1983	109.5 (1795)	2.244	0.0008-0.0020	0.0020-0.0071	3	1.772	0.0008-0.0020	0.004-0.010
	155.9 (2555)	2.362	0.0008-0.0020	0.0020-0.0071	3	2.087	0.0008-0.0024	0.004-0.010

CRANKSHAFT AND CONNECTING ROD SPECIFICATIONS

All measurements are given in inches.

Year	Engine Displacement cu. in. (cc)	Crankshaft Main Brg. Journal Dia.	Crankshaft Main Brg. Oil Clearance	Crankshaft Shaft End-play	Thrust on No.	Connecting Rod Journal Diameter	Connecting Rod Oil Clearance	Connecting Rod Side Clearance
1984	109.5 (1795)	2.244	0.0008–0.0020	0.0020–0.0071	3	1.772	0.0008–0.0020	0.004–0.010
	121.9 (1997)	2.244	0.0008–0.0020	0.0020–0.0071	3	1.772	0.0008–0.0020	0.004–0.010
	155.9 (2555)	2.362	0.0008–0.0020	0.0020–0.0071	3	2.087	0.0008–0.0024	0.004–0.010
1985	109.5 (1795)	2.244	0.0008–0.0020	0.0020–0.0071	3	1.772	0.0008–0.0020	0.004–0.010
	121.9 (1997)	2.244	0.0008–0.0020	0.0020–0.0071	3	1.772	0.0008–0.0020	0.004–0.010
	155.9 (2555)	2.362	0.0008–0.0020	0.0020–0.0071	3	2.087	0.0008–0.0024	0.004–0.010
	89.6 (1468)	1.889	0.0008–0.0020	0.0020–0.0071	3	1.653	0.0004–0.0024	0.004–0.010
	97.4 (1597)	2.244	0.0008–0.0020	0.0020–0.0071	3	1.772	0.0004–0.0024	0.004–0.010
	•143.4 (2350)	2.244	0.0008–0.0020	0.0020–0.0071	3	2.087	0.0008–0.0024	0.004–0.010
1986	109.5 (1795)	2.244	0.0008–0.0020	0.0020–0.0071	3	1.772	0.0008–0.0020	0.004–0.010
	121.9 (1997)	2.244	0.0008–0.0020	0.0020–0.0071	3	1.772	0.0008–0.0020	0.004–0.010
	155.9 (2555)	2.362	0.0008–0.0020	0.0020–0.0071	3	2.087	0.0008–0.0024	0.004–0.010
	89.6 (1468)	1.889	0.0008–0.0020	0.0020–0.0071	3	1.653	0.0004–0.0024	0.004–0.010
	97.4 (1597)	2.244	0.0008–0.0020	0.0020–0.0071	3	1.772	0.0004–0.0024	0.004–0.010
	143.4 (2350)	2.244	0.0008–0.0020	0.0020–0.0071	3	2.087	0.0008–0.0024	0.004–0.010
1987–88	109.5 (1795)	2.244	0.0008–0.0020	0.0020–0.0071	3	1.772	0.0008–0.0020	0.004–0.010
	121.9 (1997)	2.244	0.0008–0.0020	0.0020–0.0071	3	1.772	0.0008–0.0020	0.004–0.010
	155.9 (2555)	2.362	0.0008–0.0020	0.0020–0.0071	3	2.087	0.0008–0.0024	0.004–0.010
	89.6 (1468)	1.889	0.0008–0.0020	0.0020–0.0071	3	1.653	0.0004–0.0024	0.004–0.010
	97.4 (1597)	2.244	0.0008–0.0020	0.0020–0.0071	3	1.772	0.0004–0.0024	0.004–0.010
	143.4 (2350)	2.244	0.0008–0.0020	0.0020–0.0071	3	2.087	0.0008–0.0024	0.004–0.010

VALVE SPECIFICATIONS

Year	Engine Displacement cu. in. (cc)	Seat Angle (deg.)	Face Angle (deg.)	Spring Test Pressure (lbs. @ in.)	Spring Installed Height (in.)	Stem-to-Guide Clearance (in.)		Stem Diameter (in.)	
						Intake	Exhaust	Intake	Exhaust
1983	109.5 (1795)	45	45	62 @ 1.591	1.591	0.0010–0.0022	0.0020–0.0035	0.315	0.315
	155.9 (2555)	45	45	62 @ 1.591	1.591	0.0012–0.0024	0.0020–0.0035	0.315	0.315
1984	109.5 (1795)	45	45	62 @ 1.591	1.591	0.0010–0.0022	0.0020–0.0035	0.315	0.315
	121.9 (1997)	45	45	62 @ 1.591	1.591	0.0010–0.0022	0.0020–0.0035	0.315	0.315
	155.9 (2555)	45	45	62 @ 1.591	1.591	0.0012–0.0024	0.0020–0.0035	0.315	0.315
1985	109.5 (1795)	45	45	62 @ 1.591	1.591	0.0010–0.0022	0.0020–0.0035	0.315	0.315
	121.9 (1997)	45	45	62 @ 1.591	1.591	0.0010–0.0022	0.0020–0.0035	0.315	0.315
	155.9 (2555)	45	45	62 @ 1.591	1.591	0.0012–0.0024	0.0020–0.0035	0.315	0.315
	89.6 (1468)	45	45	53 @ 1.469	1.417	0.0012–0.0024	0.0020–0.0035	0.315	0.315
	97.4 (1597)	45	45	62 @ 1.469	1.469	0.0012–0.0024	0.0020–0.0035	0.315	0.315
	143.4 (2350)	45	45	72 @ 1.591	1.591	0.0012–0.0024	0.0024–0.0035	0.322	0.315
1986	109.5 (1795)	45	45	62 @ 1.591	1.591	0.0010–0.0022	0.0020–0.0035	0.315	0.315
	121.9 (1997)	45	45	72 @ 1.591	1.591	0.0010–0.0022	0.0020–0.0035	0.315	0.315
	155.9 (2555)	45	45	72 @ 1.591	1.591	0.0012–0.0024	0.0020–0.0035	0.315	0.315
	89.6 (1468)	45	45	53 @ 1.469	1.417	0.0008–0.0020	0.0020–0.0035	0.315	0.315
	97.4 (1597)	45	45	62 @ 1.469	1.469	0.0012–0.0024	0.0020–0.0035	0.315	0.315
	143.4 (2350)	45	45	72 @ 1.591	1.591	0.0012–0.0024	0.0020–0.0035	0.322	0.315
1987–88	109.5 (1795)	45	45	62 @ 1.591	1.591	0.0010–0.0022	0.0020–0.0035	0.315	0.315
	121.9 (1997)	45	45	72 @ 1.591	1.591	0.0010–0.0022	0.0020–0.0035	0.315	0.315
	155.9 (2555)	45	45	72 @ 1.591	1.591	0.0012–0.0024	0.0020–0.0035	0.315	0.315
	89.6 (1468)	45	45	53 @ 1.469	1.417	0.0008–0.0020	0.0020–0.0035	0.315	0.315
	97.4 (1597)	45	45	62 @ 1.469	1.469	0.0012–0.0024	0.0020–0.0035	0.315	0.315
	143.4 (2350)	45	45	72 @ 1.591	1.591	0.0012–0.0024	0.0020–0.0035	0.322	0.315

PISTON AND RING SPECIFICATIONS
All measurements are given in inches.

| Year | Engine Displacement cu. in. (cc) | Piston Clearance | Ring Gap | | | Ring Side Clearance | | |
			Top Compression	Bottom Compression	Oil Control	Top Compression	Bottom Compression	Oil Control
1983	109.5 (1795)	0.0008–0.0016	0.0100–0.0180	0.0080–0.0160	0.0080–0.0200	0.002–0.004	0.001–0.002	—
	155.9 (2555)	0.0008–0.0016	0.0120–0.0200	0.0100–0.0160	0.0120–0.0310	0.002–0.004	0.001–0.002	—
1984	109.5 (1795)	0.0008–0.0016	0.0100–0.0180	0.0080–0.0160	0.0080–0.0200	0.002–0.004	0.001–0.002	—
	121.9 (1997)	0.0008–0.0016	0.0100–0.0180	0.0080–0.0160	0.0080–0.0200	0.002–0.004	0.001–0.002	—
	155.9 (2555)	0.0008–0.0016	0.0120–0.0200	0.0100–0.0160	0.0120–0.0310	0.002–0.004	0.001–0.002	—
1985	109.5 (1795)	0.0008–0.0016	0.0100–0.0180	0.0080–0.0160	0.0080–0.0200	0.002–0.004	0.001–0.002	—
	121.9 (1997)	0.0008–0.0016	0.0100–0.0180	0.0080–0.0160	0.0080–0.0200	0.002–0.004	0.001–0.002	—
	155.9 (2555)	0.0008–0.0016	0.0120–0.0200	0.0100–0.0160	0.0120–0.0310	0.002–0.004	0.001–0.002	—
	89.6 (1468)	0.0008–0.0016	0.0080–0.0160	0.0080–0.0160	0.0080–0.0280	0.0012–0.0028	0.0008–0.0024	—
	97.4 (1597)	0.0008–0.0016	0.0080–0.0160	0.0080–0.0160	0.0080–0.0280	0.0012–0.0028	0.0008–0.0024	—
	143.4 (2350)	0.0008–0.0016	0.0100–0.0180	0.0080–0.0160	0.0080–0.0280	0.002–0.004	0.001–0.002	—
1986	109.5 (1795)	0.0008–0.0016	0.0100–0.0180	0.0080–0.0160	0.0080–0.0200	0.002–0.004	0.001–0.002	—
	121.9 (1997)	0.0008–0.0016	0.0100–0.0180	0.0080–0.0160	0.0080–0.0200	0.002–0.004	0.001–0.002	—
	155.9 (2555)	0.0008–0.0016	0.0120–0.0200	0.0100–0.0160	0.0120–0.0310	0.002–0.004	0.001–0.002	—
	89.6 (1468)	0.0008–0.0016	0.0080–0.0160	0.0080–0.0160	0.0080–0.0280	0.0012–0.0028	0.0008–0.0024	—
	97.4 (1597)	0.0008–0.0016	0.0080–0.0160	0.0080–0.0160	0.0080–0.0280	0.0012–0.0028	0.0008–0.0024	—
	143.4 (2350)	0.0008–0.0016	0.0100–0.0180	0.0080–0.0160	0.0080–0.0280	0.002–0.004	0.001–0.002	—
1987–88	109.5 (1795)	0.0008–0.0016	0.0100–0.0180	0.0080–0.0160	0.0080–0.0200	0.002–0.004	0.001–0.002	—
	121.9 (1997)	0.0008–0.0016	0.0100–0.0180	0.0080–0.0160	0.0080–0.0200	0.002–0.004	0.001–0.002	—
	155.9 (2555)	0.0008–0.0016	0.0120–0.0200	0.0100–0.0160	0.0120–0.0310	0.002–0.004	0.001–0.002	—
	89.6 (1468)	0.0008–0.0016	0.0080–0.0160	0.0080–0.0160	0.0080–0.0280	0.0012–0.0028	0.0008–0.0024	—
	97.4 (1597)	0.0008–0.0016	0.0080–0.0160	0.0080–0.0160	0.0080–0.0280	0.0012–0.0028	0.0008–0.0024	—
	143.4 (2350)	0.0008–0.0016	0.0100–0.0180	0.0080–0.0160	0.0080–0.0280	0.0012–0.0028	0.0008–0.0024	

TORQUE SPECIFICATIONS
All readings in ft. lbs.

Year	Engine Displacement cu. in. (cc)	Cylinder Head Bolts ①	Main Bearing Bolts	Rod Bearing Bolts	Crankshaft Pulley Bolts	Flywheel Bolts	Manifold Intake	Manifold Exhaust	Spark Plugs
1983	109.5 (1795)	73–79	38	37	80–94	94–101	11–14	11–14	NA
	155.9 (2555)	73–79 ②	55–61	33	80–94	94–101	11–14	11–14	NA
1984	109.5 (1795)	73–79	38	37	80–94	94–101	11–14	11–14	NA
	121.9 (1992)	73–79	38	37	80–94	94–101	11–14	11–14	NA
	155.9 (2555)	73–79 ②	55–61	33	80–94	94–101	11–14	11–14	NA
1985	109.5 (1795)	73–79	38	37	80–94	94–101	11–14	11–14	NA
	121.9 (1997)	73–79	38	37	80–94	94–101	11–14	11–14	NA
	155.9 (2555)	73–79 ②	55–61	33	80–94	94–101	11–14	11–14	NA
	89.6 (1468)	58–61	38	24	51–72	94–101	11–14	11–14	NA
	97.4 (1597)	58–61	38	24	80–93	94–101	11–14	11–14	NA
	143.4 (2350)	73–79	38	33	80–94	94–101	11–14	11–14	NA
1986	109.5 (1795)	73–79	38	37	80–94	94–101	11–14	11–14	NA
	121.9 (1997)	73–79	38	37	80–94	94–101	11–14	11–14	NA
	155.9 (2555)	73–79 ②	55–61	33	80–94	94–101	11–14	11–14	NA
	89.6 (1468)	58–61	38	24	51–72	94–101	11–14	11–14	NA
	97.4 (1597)	58–61	38	24	80–93	94–101	11–14	11–14	NA
	143.4 (2350)	73–79	38	33	80–94	94–101	11–14	11–14	NA
1987–88	109.5 (1795)	73–79	38	37	80–94	94–101	11–14	11–14	NA
	121.9 (1997)	73–79	38	37	80–94	94–101	11–14	11–14	NA
	155.9 (2555)	73–79 ②	55–61	33	80–94	94–101	11–14	11–14	NA
	89.6 (1468)	58–61	38	24	51–72	94–101	11–14	11–14	NA
	97.4 (1597)	58–61	38	24	80–93	94–101	11–14	11–14	NA
	143.4 (2350)	73–79	38	33	80–94	94–101	11–14	11–14	NA

① All figures are hot torques. For cold engine figures see text.
② No. 11 in text diagram 11–15.

BRAKE SPECIFICATIONS
All measurements in inches unless noted.

Year	Model	Lug Nut Torque (ft. lbs.)	Master Cylinder Bore	Brake Disc Minimum Thickness	Brake Disc Maximum Runout	Maximum Brake Drum Diameter	Minimum Lining Thickness Front	Minimum Lining Thickness Rear
1983	Cordia	50–57 ①	.87	—	.450	8.000	.040	.040
	Tredia	50–57 ①	.87	—	.450	8.000	.040	.040
	Starion	50–57 ①	.94	—	.880	—	.040	—
1984	Cordia	50–57 ②	.87	—	.650	8.000	.040	.040
	Tredia	50–57 ②	.87	—	.650	8.000	.040	.040
	Starion	50–57 ②		—	.880		.040	—
1985	Cordia	50–57 ②	.87	—	.650	8.000	.040	.040
	Tredia	50–57 ②	.87	—	.650	8.000	.040	.040
	Starion	50–57 ②	.94	—	.880	—	.040	—
	Mirage	50–57 ②	.81 ④	—	.450 ③	7.100	.040	.040
	Galant	50–57 ②	.94	—	.650	8.000	.040	.040

BRAKE SPECIFICATIONS
All measurements in inches unless noted.

Year	Model	Lug Nut Torque (ft. lbs.)	Master Cylinder Bore	Brake Disc Minimum Thickness	Brake Disc Maximum Runout	Maximum Brake Drum Diameter	Minimum Lining Thickness Front	Minimum Lining Thickness Rear
1986	Cordia	50–57 ②	.87	—	.650	8.000	.040	.040
	Tredia	50–57 ②	.87	—	.650	8.000	.040	.040
	Starion	50–57 ②	.94	—	.880	—	.040	—
	Mirage	50–57 ②	.81 ④	—	.450 ③	7.100	.040	.040
	Galant	50–57 ②	.94	—	.650	8.000	.040	.040
1987–88	Cordia	50–57 ②	.87	—	.650	8.000	.040	.040
	Tredia	50–57 ②	.87	—	.650	8.000	.040	.040
	Starion	50–57 ②	.94	—	.880	—	.040	—
	Mirage	50–57 ②	.81 ④	—	.450 ③	7.100	.040	.040
	Galant	50–57 ②	.94	—	.650	8.000	.040	.040
	Precis	—	.81	—	.450	7.100	.040	.040
	Wagon	N/A	—	—	.803	—	.040	.040

① With aluminum wheels 57–72
② With aluminum wheels 66–81
③ Turbo .650
④ Turbo .87

WHEEL ALIGNMENT

Year	Model	Caster Range (deg.)	Caster Preferred Setting (deg.)	Camber Range (deg.)	Camber Preferred Setting (deg.)	Toe-in (in.)	Steering Axis Inclination (deg.)
1983	Cordia	$5/16$–$1^5/16$	$13/16$	$1/16$N–$15/16$P	$7/16$	$1/8$N–$1/8$P	$7^1/16$
	Tredia	$5/16$–$1^5/16$	$13/16$	$1/16$N–$15/16$P	$7/16$	$1/8$N–$1/8$P	$7^1/16$
	Starion	—	$5^1/3$	—	0	$5/64$N–$13/64$P	—
1984	Cordia	$5/16$–$1^5/16$	$13/16$	$1/16$N–$15/16$P	$7/16$	$1/8$N–$1/8$P	$7^1/16$
	Tredia	$5/16$–$1^5/16$	$13/16$	$1/16$N–$15/16$P	$7/16$	$1/8$N–$1/8$P	$7^1/16$
	Starion	—	$5^1/3$	—	0	$5/64$N–$13/64$P	—
1985	Cordia	$5/16$–$1^5/16$	$13/16$	$1/16$N–$15/16$P	$7/16$	$1/8$N–$1/8$P	$7^1/16$
	Tredia	$5/16$–$1^5/16$	$13/16$	$1/16$N–$15/16$P	$7/16$	$1/8$N–$1/8$P	$7^1/16$
	Starion	—	$5^1/3$	—	0	$5/64$N–$13/64$P	—
	Mirage	$7/32$–$1^7/32$	$23/32$	$1/2$N–$1/2$P	0	$1/8$N–$1/8$P	$5^3/4$
	Galant	$5/32$–$1^5/32$	$21/32$	0–1P	$1/2$	$1/8$N–$1/8$P	$6^5/8$
1986	Cordia	$5/16$–$1^5/16$	$13/16$	$1/16$N–$15/16$P	$7/16$	$1/8$N–$1/8$P	$7^1/16$
	Tredia	$5/16$–$1^5/16$	$13/16$	$1/16$N–$15/16$P	$7/16$	$1/8$N–$1/8$P	$7^1/16$
	Starion	—	$5^1/3$	—	0	$5/64$N–$13/64$P	—
	Mirage	$7/32$–$1^7/32$	$23/32$	$1/2$N–$1/2$P	0	$1/8$N–$1/8$P	$5^3/4$
	Galant	$5/32$–$1^5/32$	$21/32$	0–1P	$1/2$	$1/8$N–$1/8$P	$6^5/8$
1987–88	Cordia	$5/16$–$1^5/16$	$13/16$	$1/16$N–$5/16$P	$7/16$	$1/8$N–$1/8$P	$7^1/16$
	Tredia	$5/16$–$1^5/16$	$13/16$	$1/16$N–$15/16$P	$7/16$	$1/8$N–$1/8$P	$7^1/16$
	Starion	—	$5^1/3$	—	0	$5/64$N–$13/64$P	—
	Mirage	$7/32$–$1^7/32$	$23/32$	$1/2$N–$11/12$P	0	$1/8$N–$1/8$P	$5^3/4$

WHEEL ALIGNMENT

Year	Model	Caster Range (deg.)	Caster Preferred Setting (deg.)	Camber Range (deg.)	Camber Preferred Setting (deg.)	Toe-in (in.)	Steering Axis Inclination (deg.)
1987-88	Galant	$^5/_{32}$–$1^5/_{32}$	$^{21}/_{32}$	0–1P	$^1/_2$	$^1/_8$N–$^1/_8$P	$6^5/_8$
	Precis	—	$^5/_6$	$^1/_2$	0	—	—
	Wagon	N/A	N/A	N/A	N/A	N/A	N/A

N—Negative
P—Positive

TUNE-UP PROCEDURES

Ignition Timing

ADJUSTMENT

1. Run the engine until operating temperature is reached.
2. Leave the engine idling, apply the handbrake and put the transmission in Neutral (manual) or Park (automatic). Turn off all accessories.
3. Install a tachometer, connecting the red lead to the (−) terminal of the coil and the black lead to a clean ground. Verify that the engine idle speed is correct. If not adjust it.
4. Stop the engine and connect the timing light according to manufacturers instructions. Disconnect and plug the vacuum advance hose, as required.
5. Start the engine and allow it to idle. Point the timing light at the mark on the front cover and read the timing by noting the position of the groove in the front pulley in relation to the timing mark or scale on the front cover. If the timing is incorrect, loosen the distributor mounting bolt. Turn the distributor slightly clockwise to retard the timing or counterclockwise to advance it.
6. When the reading is correct, tighten the distributor mounting bolt back up and then verify that the setting has not changed.
7. Turn the engine off, disconnect the timing light and tachometer and, if necessary, reconnect the vacuum advance hose.

Valve Lash

ADJUSTMENT

Valve lash must be adjusted on all en-

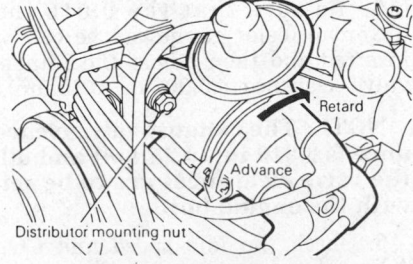

Adjusting ignition timing

Adjusting valve clearance

gines not equipped with hydraulic lash adjusters. All the engines except 1985–88 1997cc and 2350cc engines have solid valve train systems requiring valve adjustments.

Every engine covered by this section has an unusual third valve of very small size called a Jet Valve. The Jet Valve must be adjusted on all engines, whether the engine uses hydraulic lash adjusters for the normal intake and exhaust valves or not. Thus, on most engines, there are three valves per cylinder that must be adjusted. On the two engines equipped with hydraulic lash adjusters, only one valve must be adjusted per cylinder.

1. Run the engine until operating temperature is reached. Turn off the engine and block the wheels. Remove the cam cover.
2. Torque the cylinder head bolts in the proper sequence to specification. Turn each bolt in the sequence back

just until it breaks loose and then torque it to specification.

3. Now, put the engine at TDC with No. 1 cylinder at the firing position. Turn the engine by using a wrench on the bolt in the front of the crankshaft until the 0 degree timing mark on the timing cover lines up with the notch in the front pulley. Observe the valve rockers for No. 1 cylinder. If both are in identical positions with the valves up, the engine is in the right position. If not, rotate the engine exactly 360° until the 0° timing mark is again aligned. Each jet valve is associated with an intake valve that is on the same rocker lever. In this position you'll be able to adjust all the valves marked "A" in the illustration, including associated jet valves (which are located on the rockets on the intake side only).

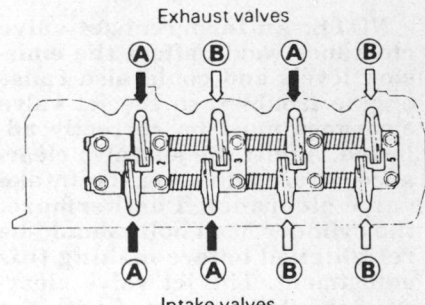

"A" and "B" valve adjusting positions

4. To adjust the appropriate jet valves, first loosen the regular (larger) intake valve adjusting stud right nearby by loosening the locknut and backing the stud off two turns. Note that this particular step is not required on the two engines that have hydraulic lash adjusters. Now, loosen the jet valve (smaller) adjusting stud locknut, back the stud out slightly and insert the feeler gauge between the jet valve and stud. Make sure the gauge lies flat on the top of the jet valve. Be careful not to twist the

gauge or otherwise depress the jet valve spring, rotate the jet valve adjusting stud back in until it just touches the gauge. Now, tighten the locknut. Make sure the gauge still slides very easily between the stud and jet valve and that they both are still just touching the gauge. Readjust if necessary. Note that, especially with the jet valve, the clearance must not be too tight.

5. Repeat the entire procedure for the other jet valves associated with rockets labeled "A".

6. Then, on engines not equipped with hydraulic lash adjusters repeat the procedure for the intake valves labeled "A".

7. Repeat the basic adjustment procedure for exhaust valves labeled "A" on engines without hydraulic lash adjusters.

8. Turn the engine exactly 360°, until the timing marks are again aligned at 0° BTDC. First, perform Step 4 for all the jet valves on rockets labeled "B" (intake side only). On engines equipped with hydraulic lash adjusters, once jet valves on rockers on the intake side and labeled "B" are adjusted, the valve adjustment procedure is completed and you can proceed to the last step. On other engines, complete Step 4 for the regular intake valves labeled "B". Finally, repeat Step 7 for exhaust valves labeled "B".

9. Reinstall the cam cover. Run the engine to check for oil leaks.

JET VALVE ADJUSTMENT

NOTE: An incorrect jet valve clearance would affect the emission levels and could also cause engine troubles, so the jet valve clearance must be correctly adjusted. Adjust the jet valve clearance before adjusting the intake valve clearance. Furthermore, the cylinder head bolts should be retightened before making this adjustment. The jet valve clearance should be adjusted with the adjusting screw on the intake valve side fully loosened.

1. Start the engine and let it run at idle until it reaches normal operating temperature.

2. With the piston in the cylinder positioned at top dead center on the compression stroke, loosen the adjusting screw for the intake valve two or more turns.

3. Loosen the locknut on the adjusting screw for the jet valve. Turn the adjusting screw counterclockwise and insert a 0.010 in. (0.25mm) feeler gauge between the jet valve stem and the adjusting screw.

4. Tighten the adjusting screw un-

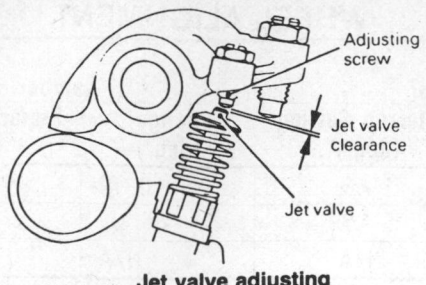

Jet valve adjusting

til it touches the feeler gauge. Turn the locknut to secure it, while holding the rocker arm adjusting screw with a suitable tool to keep it from turning.

5. Be sure that the 0.010 in. (0.25mm) feeler gauge can be easily inserted and then adjust the intake valve clearance to 0.006 in. (0.15mm).

NOTE: The exhaust valve clearance is 0.010 in. (0.25mm) and all the valve clearances are to be set with the engine hot.

6. Check the idle speed and CO. Adjust if necessary.

Idle Speed and Mixture

IDLE SPEED ADJUSTMENT

Carbureted Engines

1983–84

1. Run the engine at fast idle until normal operating temperature is reached. Turn off all lights and accessories. The electric cooling fan must not be operating. Set the parking brake, block the wheels and place the transmission in neutral.

2. Run the engine between 2000 and 3000 rpm for about five seconds, then allow it to idle for two minutes.

3. Check the idle speed adjustment screw on the carburetor linkage arm.

1985–88

NOTE: The improper setting (throttle valve opening) will increase the exhaust gas temperature and deceleration, which in turn will reduce the life of the catalyst greatly and deteriorate the exhaust gas cleaning performance. It will also effect the fuel consumption and the engine braking.

1. With the vehicle in park, the drive wheels blocked and all the accessories off. Run the engine until it reaches normal operating temperature.

2. Bring the engine rpm up to 2000–3000 rpm for about ten seconds, then let the engine idle for at least two minutes.

3. Connect a tachometer to the en-

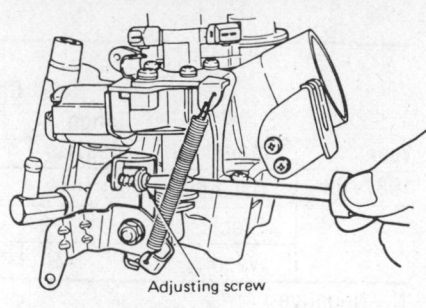

Idle Speed adjusting screw for '84 Cordia/Tredia

gine and check the idling speed. If it does not meet specifications, readjust the idle speed to the nominal specification, using the idle speed adjusting screw, which is located closest to the primary throttle valve shaft.

Fuel Injected Engines

1. Run the engine until normal operating temperature is reached. Make sure all lights and accessories are turned off.

2. Apply the parking brake and block the wheels. Place the transmission in neutral and stop the engine.

3. Attach a tachometer and timing light. Start the engine and increase the engine speed to 2000–3000 rpm several times, return to idle and check the ignition timing, adjust if necessary.

4. Remove the rubber cap covering the idle speed adjuster switch, leaving the cable connector connected. The idle adjuster switch is located on the throttle linkage. Adjust the idle speed.

5. If the idle adjustment screw must be turned more than 1 turn during adjustment, disconnect the connector from the speed adjust switch and plug it into the dummy terminal on the injector base. Adjust to correct idle speed and reconnect to the idle switch. Remove the tachometer and timing light.

IDLE SPEED CONTROL ADJUSTMENT

1984 Cordia and Tredia

1. Run the engine at fast idle until it reaches normal operating temperature. Turn the engine Off at that point.

2. Turn the ignition switch On for at least 15 seconds, then turn it Off. Disconnect the ISC servo harness connector.

3. Start the engine. Connect a tachometer and check the idle speed. Adjust it to 600 rpm, using the adjust-

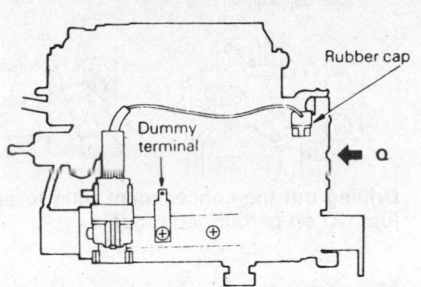

Idle speed adjustment for fuel injection

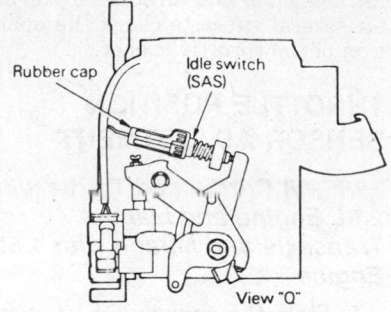

View "Q"

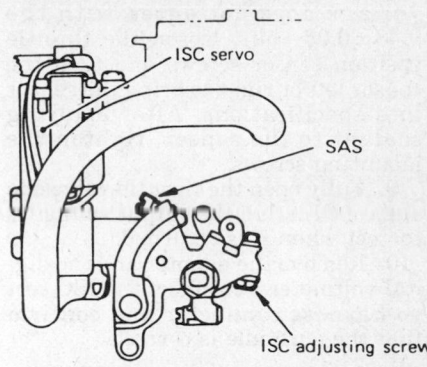

Adjusting the Idle Speed Control and CO on the 2.0L automatic. Adjust the ISC adjusting screw and then the SAS (Speed Adjusting Screw)

ing screw on the ISC servo. Reconnect the servo.

1985–88 Cordia and Tredia

NOTE: When replacing the ISC servo, the engine speed should be adjusted.

1. With the vehicle in park, the drive wheels blocked and all the accessories off. Run the engine until it reaches normal operating temperature.

2. Remove the carburetor from the engine. Remove the concealment plug from the carburetor.

3. Reinstall the carburetor onto the engine and relax the tension on the accelerator cable.

4. Place the ignition switch to the one position and wait for at least 18 seconds. Turn the ignition switch off and disconnect the ISC actuator connector and the oxygen sensor connector.

5. Start the engine check the ignition timing and adjust if necessary. Increase the engine speed between 2000–3000 rpm, two or three times and then let the engine idle for 30 seconds.

6. Adjust the mixture adjusting screw (MAS) for a CO concentration of 0.1–0.3%. Adjust the engine rpm to the specified speed by using the ISC adjustment screw.

7. Turn the idle mixture screw (secondary air supply screw) until the engine reaches its highest rpm. Turn the screw 2/3 of turn in the reverse direction from that point.

8. Race the engine two or three times. Check to be sure that the CO and engine rpm are still adjusted to specifications. If they are not, readjust as necessary.

9. Adjust the tension of the accelerator cable. The cable should have enough play so as not to interfere with idle switch.

10. Reconnect the ISC actuator connector and the oxygen sensor connector.

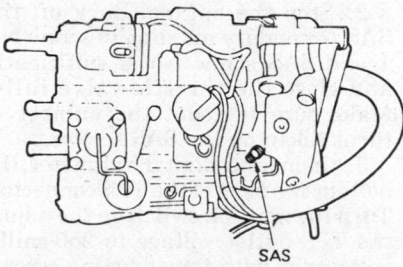

Idle speed adjusting screw (SAS)

Precis

1. Make sure the transmission is in Neutral or Park. Run the engine at fast idle until the cooling system reaches 185°F or more (not to exceed 205°F). Then, race the engine at 2000–3000 rpm for more than five seconds. Release the throttle. All accessories including the electric cooling fan must be off.

2. Idle the engine for a full two minutes. Connect a tachometer between the (−) terminal of the coil and a good ground while the engine is idling. If the idle speed is not to the specification, adjust the idle speed screw.

IDLE SPEED CONTROL (ISC) SERVO AND THROTTLE POSITION SENSOR ADJUSTMENT

1985–88 with Turbocharged Engine

NOTE: This adjustment is very important, since the vehicle driveability depends upon it. If the ISC servo, throttle position sensor, mixing body, or throttled body has been replaced or removed for any reason, use the following procedure to make the adjustments.

1. With the vehicle in park, the drive wheels blocked and all the accessories off, run the engine until it

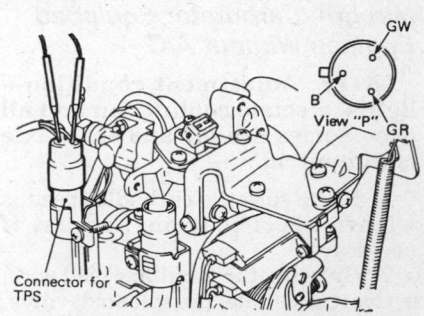

Connect the digital voltmeter to the "GW" and "B" pins of the Throttle Position sensor connector—1985 and later turbocharged vehicles

reaches normal operating temperature.

2. Stop the engine and disconnect the accelerator cable from the throttle lever of the injection mixer. Loosen the two throttle position sensor mounting screws, turn the throttle position sensor clockwise as far as it will go and then temporarily tighten the screws.

3. Turn the ignition switch to the ON position for 15 seconds and then turn it off. This will set the ISC servo to the specified position.

4. Disconnect the ISC servo harness connector. Start the engine, check the engine speed and adjust to specifications.

5. Stop the engine and disconnect the throttle position sensor harness connector.

6. Connect an adapter and a digital voltmeter between the throttle position sensor connector. Insert the probes of the digital voltmeter into the GW lead (TPS outlet) and the B lead (ground) of the body side harness. Place the ignition switch to the ON position, but do not start the engine.

7. Read the throttle position sensor output voltage.

8. If the measurement of the output

voltage does not agree with the 0.48 ± 0.03 volts, loosen the throttle position sensor screws and turn the sensor left or right to bring the sensor into specifications. After applying sealant to the sensor, tighten the mounting screws.

9. Fully open the throttle valve one and confirm that the output voltage is correct when it is returned.

10. Remove the adapter and the digital voltmeter, reconnect the ISC servo harness connector and confirm that the curb idle is correct.

IDLE SPEED-UP ADJUSTMENT

1985–88 Cordia, Tredia and Mirage – Carburetor Equipped Engines Without A/C

NOTE: Adjustment condition – lights, electric cooling fan and all accessories are off and transaxle is in neutral.

1. Make sure the curb idle speed is within specifications, adjust if necessary.

2. By using the auxiliary lead wire, activate the idle up solenoid valve. Apply the intake manifold vacuum to the throttle opener and activate the throttle opener.

3. Open the throttle slightly (to engine speed of about 2000 rpm) and then slowly close it.

4. Adjust the engine speed to the specifications with the idle-up adjusting screw.

5. After repeating Step 3, check the engine speed.

6. Remove the auxiliary lead wire used in Step 2 and reconnect the idle-up solenoid valve wiring.

1985–88 Cordia, Tredia and Mirage – Carburetor Equipped Engines

1. With the vehicle in park, the drive wheels blocked and all the accessories off. Run the engine until it reaches normal operating temperature.

2. Disconnect the electric cooling fan connector. On vehicles equipped with power steering, set the tires in the straight ahead position to prevent the pump from being loaded. Set the steering wheel in the stationary position.

3. Be sure that the curb idle speed is within the specifications, adjust if necessary.

4. With the air conditioner on, adjust the engine speed to the specified speed with the throttle opener setting screw (idle-up adjusting screw).

5. Reconnect the electric cooling fan connector and turn the A/C on and off several times to check the operation of the throttle opener.

THROTTLE POSITION SENSOR ADJUSTMENT

1985–88 Cordia and Tredia with 2.0L Engine and Manual Transaxle and Mirage with 1.5L Engine

1. Start the engine and let it run until the engine reaches normal operating temperature. Be sure that the fast idle cam is released.

2. Stop the engine. Back off the SAS (secondary air supply) screw No. 1 and SAS screw No. 2 sufficiently and close the throttle valve fully. Make sure to count the number of turns taken on the SAS screws.

3. Connect a digital voltmeter the bottom two slots of the TPS connector. Turn the ignition switch on the adjust the TPS outlet voltage to 250 millivolts (mV) with the adjusting screw.

4. Tighten the SAS screws by giving the same number of turns to the screws as recorded in Step 2.

NOTE: The Cordia and Tredia 2.0L engine with automatic transaxle TPS adjustment is the same, except for the following:
a. Make the idle speed control adjustment first.
b. The TPS outlet voltage should be 445 millivolts (mV).

IDLE MIXTURE ADJUSTMENT

All Carbureted Engines except 1985–88 Cordia, Tredia and Mirage w/Automatic Transmission and 1987–88 Precis

1. Remove the carburetor from the engine. The idle mixture screw is located in the base of the carburetor, just to the left of the PCV hose. Mount the carburetor, carefully, in a softjawed vise, protecting the gasket surface and with the mixture adjusting screw facing upward.

2. Drill a $\frac{5}{64}$ inch hole through the casting from the underside of the carburetor. Make sure that this hole intersects the passage leading to the mixture adjustment screw just behind the plug. Now, widen that hole with a $\frac{1}{8}$ inch drill bit.

3. Insert a blunt punch into the hole and tap out the plug. Install the carburetor on the engine and connect all hoses, lines, etc.

4. Start the engine and run it at fast idle until it reaches normal oper-

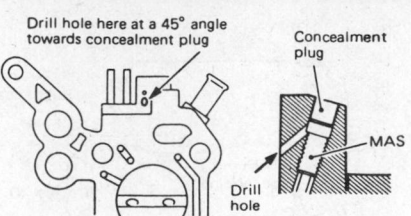

Drilling out the concealment plug to adjust CO on carbureted models

ating temperature. Make sure that all accessories are Off and the transaxle is in Neutral. Turn the ignition switch off and disconnect the battery ground cable for about 3 seconds, then, reconnect it. Disconnect the oxygen sensor.

5. Start the engine and run it for at least 5 seconds at 2000–3000 rpm. Then, allow the engine to idle for about 2 minutes.

6. Connect a tachometer and allow the engine to operate at the specified curb idle speed. Adjust it if necessary, to obtain this speed. Connect a CO meter to the exhaust pipe. A reading of 0.1–0.3% is necessary. Adjust the mixture screw to obtain the reading. If, during this adjustment, the idle speed is varied more than 100 rpm in either direction, reset the idle speed and readjust the CO until both specifications are met simultaneously. Shut off the engine, reconnect the oxygen sensor and install a new concealment plug.

1985–88 Cordia, Tredia and Mirage with Automatic Transaxle

1. Remove the carburetor from the engine and place the carburetor in a suitable fixture in order to remove the concealment plug.

2. Drill a $\frac{5}{64}$ in. (2mm) pilot hole in the casting surrounding the idle mixture adjusting screw. Then redrill the hole to $\frac{1}{8}$ in. (3mm) and insert a punch into the hole to drive out the concealment plug.

3. Reinstall the carburetor on the engine without the concealment plug.

4. With the vehicle in park, the drive wheels blocked and all the accessories off, run the engine until it reaches normal operating temperature.

5. Turn off the engine and disconnect the negative battery cable for about three seconds and reconnect the cable.

6. Disconnect the connector of the exhaust oxygen sensor. Run the vehicle for five minutes at a speed of 30 rpm or run the engine for more than five minutes at the engine speed of 2000–3000 rpm.

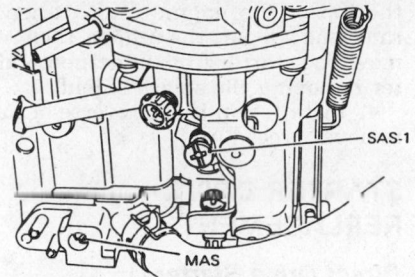

The location of the MAS (Mixture Adjusting Screw

7. Run the engine at idle for two minutes and set the idle CO and the engine speed to specification (the idle CO: 0.1–0.3% at nominal curb idle speed).

8. Reconnect the oxygen sensor connector. Readjust the engine speed, if necessary and install the concealment plug into the hole to seal the idle mixture adjusting screw.

1987–88 Precis

1. Remove the carburetor. The idle mixture screw is located in the base of the carburetor, just to the left of the PCV hose. Mount the carburetor, carefully, in a softjawed vise, protecting the gasket surface, and with the mixture adjusting screw facing upward.

2. Drill a $\frac{5}{16}$ in. hole through the casting from the underside of the carburetor. Make sure that this hole intersects the passage leading to the mixture adjustment screw just behind the plug. Now, widen that hole with a $\frac{1}{8}$ in. drill bit.

3. Insert a blunt punch into the hole and tap out the plug. Install the carburetor on the engine and connect all hoses, lines, etc.

4. Start the engine and run it at fast idle until it reaches normal operating temperature. Make sure that all accessories are off and the transaxle is in neutral. Turn the ignition switch off and disconnect the battery ground cable for about 3 seconds, then, reconnect it. Disconnect the oxygen sensor.

5. Start the engine and run it for at least 5 seconds at 2000–3000 rpm. Then, allow the engine to idle for about 2 minutes.

6. Connect a tachometer and allow the engine to operate at the specified curb idle speed. Adjust it, if necessary, to obtain this speed. Connect a CO meter to the exhaust pipe. A reading of 0.1–0.3% is necessary. Adjust the mixture screw to obtain the reading. If, during this adjustment, the idle speed is varied more than 100 rpm in either direction, reset the idle speed and readjust the CO until both specifications are met simultaneously. Shut

off the engine, reconnect the oxygen sensor and install a new concealment plug.

ENGINE ELECTRICAL

Distributor

REMOVAL & INSTALLATION

1. Rotate the engine until the No. 1 piston is at TDC of the compression stroke. Disconnect the negative battery cable. Remove all necessary components in order to gain access to the distributor assembly.

NOTE: On the Wagon it will be necessary to remove the drivers seat and the seat underframe as follows. Remove the drivers seat. Remove the parking brake lever and fuel tank filler door release lever. Remove the battery cover. Remove the bolts retaining the seat underframe in place. Remove the seat underframe.

2. Remove the distributor cap with the spark plug wires attached and position it out of the way. Disconnect the distributor wiring connector and vacuum hoses.

3. Remove the distributor base retaining nut. Remove the distributor.

4. Before installation check that the No. 1 piston is at TDC of the compression stroke, then align the marks on the bottom of the distributor housing (just above the drive gear) with the punch mark on the distributor drive gear.

5. Install the distributor to the cylinder head while aligning the mark on the base attaching flange with center of the holddown stud. Install the retaining nut, distributor cap and vacuum hoses. Start the engine and adjust the ignition timing.

Alternator

PRECAUTIONS

In order to prevent damage to the alternator observe the following precautions:

• Reversing the battery connections will result in damage to the diodes.

• Booster cables should be connected from positive to positive and the negative cable from the booster battery connected to a good ground on the

engine of the vehicle with the dead battery.

• Never use a fast charger as a booster to start the vehicle.

• When servicing the battery with a fast charger always disconnect the battery cables.

• Never attempt to polarize an alternator.

• Avoid long soldering times when replacing diodes or transistors. Prolonged heat is damaging to alternators.

• Do not use test lamps of more than 12V (volts) for checking diode continuity.

• Do not short across or ground any of the alternator terminals.

• The polarity of the battery, alternator and regulator must be matched and considered before making any electrical connections within the system.

• Never operate the alternator on an open circuit. Make sure all connections within a circuit are clean and tight.

• Disconnect the negative (or both) battery terminals when performing any service on the electrical system.

• Disconnect the negative battery cable if arc welding is to be done on any part of the vehicle.

BELT TENSION ADJUSTMENT

1. Check the drive belt(s) for cracking, fraying or any other deterioration. Replace the drive belt if suspect.

2. To replace the drive belt, loosen the fixed point mounting nut and bolt. Loosen the slotted bracket mounting nut and bolt and pivot the driven component to loosen and/or tighten the belt. When adjusting the belt, loosen the mounting bolts (see above) and pull on the driven component to increase tension. When proper tension is present, tighten the slotted bracket nut and bolt and then the fixed point nut and bolt.

3. Belt tension is proper when the belt can be deflected at midpoint $\frac{9}{32}$–$\frac{11}{32}$ in.

REMOVAL & INSTALLATION

1. Disconnect the negative battery cable. Remove all necessary components in order to gain access to the alternator assembly.

2. Disconnect the alternator electrical. Note or tag the wires so that you can reinstall them correctly.

3. Remove the top mounting bolt. Loosen the lower mounting nut. Slide the alternator over in its attaching bracket and remove the fan belt.

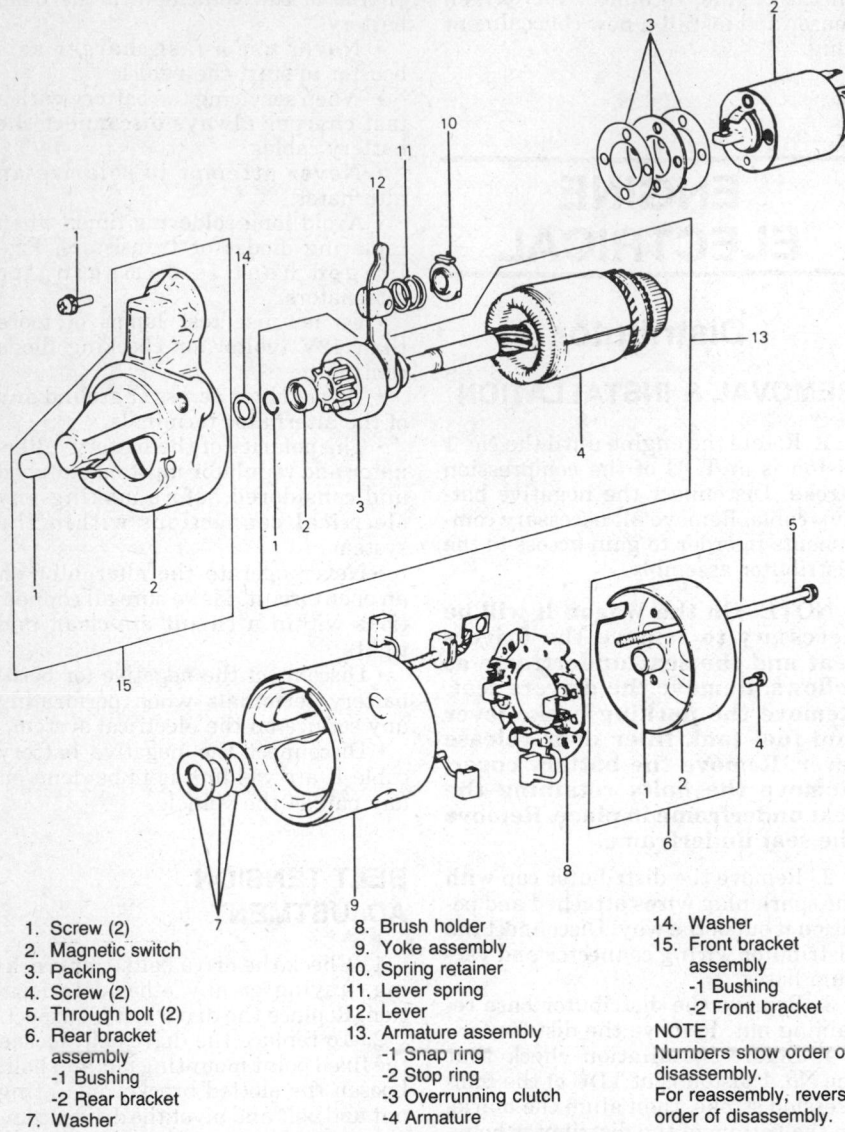

1. Screw (2)
2. Magnetic switch
3. Packing
4. Screw (2)
5. Through bolt (2)
6. Rear bracket assembly
   -1 Bushing
   -2 Rear bracket
7. Washer
8. Brush holder
9. Yoke assembly
10. Spring retainer
11. Lever spring
12. Lever
13. Armature assembly
    -1 Snap ring
    -2 Stop ring
    -3 Overrunning clutch
    -4 Armature
14. Washer
15. Front bracket assembly
    -1 Bushing
    -2 Front bracket

NOTE
Numbers show order of disassembly.
For reassembly, reverse order of disassembly.

Typical starter motor components

Voltage Regulator

The voltage regulator is of solid state design and built into the alternator. No normal maintenance is necessary.

Starter

REMOVAL & INSTALLATION

1. Disconnect the negative battery cable. Remove the necessary components in order to gain access to the starter assembly. Disconnect the electrical connections from the starter motor.
2. Remove the starter motor to engine mounting bolts. Remove the starter motor from the vehicle.
3. If various components make starter motor removal difficult from

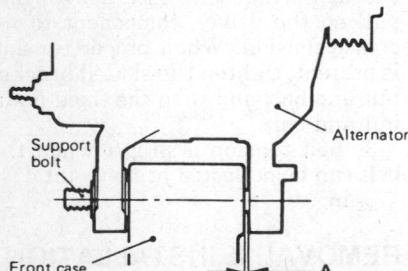

Gap "A" shows where you should measure the clearance for installation of alternator mounting shims

4. Remove the lower mounting nut and bolt. Remove the alternator from the vehicle.
5. Installation is the reverse of the removal procedure. Replace shims as required in their respective places. Adjust the drive belt as required.

the top of the engine compartment, raise and support the vehicle, then remove the starter from underneath after removing the splash shield.
4. Installation is the reverse of the removal procedure.

STARTER DRIVE REPLACEMENT

Direct Drive Starter

1. Remove the starter. Remove the solenoid.
2. Remove the through bolts and screws from the rear bracket. Remove the rear bracket.
3. Pry back the retaining rings and slide the brushes out of the brush holder. Remove the brush holder and the yoke assembly.
4. Remove the washer from the rear of the armature. Remove the field coil assembly from the front frame. Remove the spring retainer, spring and spring seat from the starter front frame. Separate the armature from the front bracket by first pulling the armature back out of the front bearing and then shifting the armature so the starter drive is pulled out of the yoke. Make sure you don't lose the washer located in the front frame.
5. Invert the armature so the starter drive is on top and rest the rear of the armature on a solid surface. Use a deep well socket wrench that is just slightly larger than the diameter of the armature shaft to press the snapring collar back. Install the socket over the top of the shaft and then press it downward or tap it very lightly to force the ring downward. Once the snapring is exposed, use snapring pliers to open it until it will slide upward, out of the groove and off the shaft. Now, pull the starter drive and snapring collar upward and off the armature shaft.
6. To install, first coat the front of the armature shaft with a very light coating of a high temperature grease approved for this purpose. Then, install the starter drive, snapring collar, and snapring. Make sure the snapring seats in its groove. Then, use a puller to pull the snapring collar up and over the snapring until the bottom of the collar touches the snapring. The rest of installation is the reverse of removal.

Reduction Gear Starter

1. Remove the starter. Remove the solenoid.
2. Remove the through bolts and screws from the rear starter bracket. Remove the rear bracket.
3. Pry the retaining springs back and slide the two brushes out of the

brush holder. Then, pull the bush holder off the rear of the starter. Remove the field coil assembly from the front frame. Remove the armature.

4. Remove the pinion shaft end cover from the center frame. Measure the clearance between the spacer and center cover and record it. If the pinion shaft is replaced, you'll have to insert or subtract spacer washers until the clearance is the same as that recorded. Use a suitable tool to remove the retaining clip and then remove the washers. Remove the retaining bolt and then separate the center frame from the front frame.

5. Remove the spring retainer and spring for the yoke from the front frame. Then, remove the washer, reduction gear, shift yoke lever and two lever supports.

6. Turn the front frame so the pinion gear is at the top and support it securely. Then, use a socket that fits tight over the pinion shaft to force the snapring collar downward. Tap the socket lightly at the top or use a press to do this. Then, use a suitable tool to work the snapring out of its groove and remove it from the shaft. Remove the collar. Remove the pinion and the spring behind it from the shaft.

7. Now, pull the overrunning clutch and pinion shaft assembly out of the rear of the front frame. Replace the pinion of its teeth are damaged (check the flywheel ring gear as well). Replace the overrunning clutch if the pinion gear is damaged or if the one way action of the clutch is not precise.

8. To install, first coat the splines of the pinion shaft with a light coating of a high temperature grease designed for this purpose. Then, reverse all the removal procedures to install. When reassembling the washer and clip at the rear of the pinion shaft, note that the clearance must be corrected by changing the thickness or number of washers if the overrunning clutch and pinion shaft assembly have been replaced.

ENGINE MECHANICAL

Engine

REMOVAL & INSTALLATION

NOTE: All engine and transaxle assemblies are removed as a unit, using a crane type lift.

Cordia and Tredia

NOTE: Use care when disconnecting the refrigerant lines. Escaping refrigerant will freeze any surface it contacts, including your skin and eyes.

1. Matchmark and then unbolt and remove the hood. Disconnect both battery connectors and remove the battery.
2. Drain the engine coolant and transaxle fluid. Disconnect the heater hoses from the engine, as required.
3. Disconnect the power steering fluid return hose at the reservoir and drain the fluid into a clean container.
4. Drain and remove the radiator overflow and windshield washer tanks.
5. Disconnect the upper and lower radiator hoses at both ends and remove them. If the vehicle has air conditioning, disconnect the hoses as close as possible to the condenser unit in front of the radiator and cap the openings securely. Then, remove the radiator or radiator and condenser assemble.
6. Remove the battery tray. Disconnect both heater hoses from the side of the engine.
7. Remove the air cleaner. On turbocharged vehicles, disconnect the turbocharger intake hose.
8. Disconnect the brake booster vacuum hose. On turbocharged vehicles only, disconnect the oil cooler hoses at the engine. On vehicles with an automatic transmission, disconnect the transmission cooler lines.
9. On vehicles with a manual transmission, disconnect the clutch cable on the side of the transaxle, on vehicles with an automatic, disconnect the shift control cable on the side of the unit. On all vehicles, disconnect the speedometer cable from the transaxle.
10. Disconnect the accelerator cable at the side of the engine. Disconnect the engine ground strap at the right front fender. On vehicles with an air conditioner, disconnect the hoses at the compressor and cap all openings securely.
11. Disconnect the power steering hoses at the side of the pump. Cap all openings. Disconnect the coil low and high tension wires. Label the low tension wires for reassembly to the proper terminals. Disconnect the battery negative cable from the engine.
12. Label and disconnect the alternator connectors. Disconnect the oil pressure sending unit wire.
13. Remove the mounting screws for the vacuum unit and solenoid valve and disconnect the electrical connector. Move the unit aside.

14. Disconnect the two smaller vacuum hoses from the purge control valve, remove the mounting screw and move the unit aside.
15. Loosen the clamps and disconnect the vacuum hoses going to the evaporative emissions canister.
16. Disconnect the fuel return hose from the carburetor or injection mixer. Disconnect the fuel supply hose at the fuel filter.
17. Raise the vehicle and support it safely. Then, disconnect the exhaust pipe at the manifold. Fasten the exhaust pipe with wire to keep it from falling.
18. On manual transmission vehicles, disconnect the shift control rod and extension and remove them.
19. Disconnect the left and right side strut bars and stabilizer bars where they connect to the lower control arms. Then, remove the bolts fastening the control arms on both sides to the rearward crossmember.
20. Disconnect the lower arm ball joint at the steering knuckle on both sides. Then, disconnect the strut bar and stabilizer bar at the lower control arm. Now, using a prybar inserted between the transaxle case and driveshaft, carefully pry the driveshaft out of the transaxle on each side. Plug the openings in the transaxle to prevent dirt from getting in.
21. Carefully lower all parts to the crossmember. Discard the retaining clips for the driveshafts. They must be replaced.
22. Attach a cable securely supported by a lift and pulley arrangement to each engine lifting point. Put tension on all the cables to support the engine securely.
23. Remove the nut from the left side engine mount insulator. Remove the four front roll bracket mounting bolts located on the side of the front crossmember.
24. Remove the mounting bolt from the rear roll insulator. Remove the nuts attaching the left engine mount insulator to the fender.
25. From inside the right fender shield, detach the protective cap and then remove the transaxle insulator bracket mounting bolts. Remove the bolts connecting the transaxle mount insulator.
26. Remove the bolts to the shift control selector. Remove the wiring connector going to the transaxle. Disconnect vacuum hoses.
27. Remove the transaxle insulator bracket. Now, increase the tension on the lifting cables so the engine weight is supported entirely by the cables and none of the weight is on the mounts. Remove the bolts passing through the insulators of the rear roll

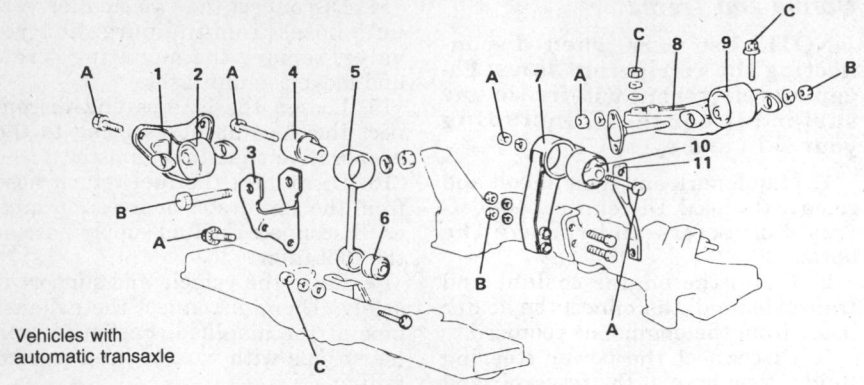

Vehicles with automatic transaxle

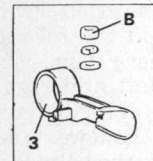

1. Transaxle insulator bracket
2. Transaxle mount insulator
3. Transaxle mount bracket
4. Upper roll insulator
5. Front roll rod
6. Lower roll insulator
7. Rear roll stopper bracket
8. Left mount bracket
9. Left mount insulator
10. Rear roll insulator
11. Rear roll stopper stay

	Nm	ft.lbs.
A	30–40	22–29
B	60–80	43–58
C	50–65	36–47

Cordia, Tredia engine/transaxle mounting

stop and left mounting bracket.

28. Check to make sure that all items are disconnected from the engine/transaxle assembly. Press downward on the transaxle to guide the assembly and lift it carefully out of the vehicle.

29. Installation is the exact reverse of removal. When installing the engine, be careful to ensure that engine compartment wiring and hoses do not catch on engine wiring and hoses do not catch on engine parts. Torque mounting bolts as follows:

Left engine mount insulator nut (large): 43–58 ft. lbs.

Left engine mount insulator nuts (small): 22–29 ft. lbs.

Left engine mount bracket to engine bolts/nuts: 36–47 ft. lbs.

Transaxle mount insulator nut: 43–58 ft. lbs.

Transaxle insulator bracket to fender shield bolts: manual 40–43 ft. lbs.

Transaxle insulator bracket to fender shield bolts: automatic 22–29 ft. lbs.

Transaxle mounting bracket to automatic transaxle nuts: 43–58 ft. lbs.

Transaxle mounting bracket bolts: 22–29 ft. lbs.

Rear roll stop insulator nut: 22–29 ft. lbs.

Rear roll stop to rear crossmember nuts: 43–58 ft. lbs.

Rear roll stop bracket to rear roll stop stay bolt: 22–29 ft. lbs.

Front roll stop insulator nut: 36–47 ft. lbs.

Front roll bracket to front crossmember nuts: 29–36 ft. lbs.

After the engine is securely mount-ed, replenish all fluids. Operate the engine checking carefully for leaks. Check all gauges for proper readings. Adjust clutch and shift linkage. Adjust the accelerator cable. Have the air conditioner recharged.

Starion

NOTE: Use care when disconnecting the refrigerant lines. Escaping refrigerant will freeze any surface it contacts, including your skin and eyes.

1. Matchmark and then unbolt and remove the hood. Drain the cooling system. Disconnect the accelerator cable at the injection mixer. Disconnect both battery cables.

2. Disconnect the two heater hoses at the block and the brake booster vacuum hose at the intake manifold.

3. Disconnect the fuel hoses at the injection system.

4. Disconnect the high tension wire at the center of the distributor. Disconnect the temperature sensor wire. Disconnect the intake manifold ground cable connector. First label the wires for reassembly and then disconnect the starter motor wiring harness.

5. Disconnect the power steering pump hoses. Remove the power steering pump.

6. Unbolt and disconnect the two engine oil cooler hoses at the oil filter adapter. Plug all openings to prevent the entry of dirt and leakage of oil.

7. Label and then disconnect the alternator wiring. Disconnect the engine ground cable. Disconnect the two plugs for the electronic injection wiring harness.

8. Disconnect the vacuum hose from the boost sensor, located on the firewall.

9. Remove the rear catalytic converter.

10. Unscrew and disconnect the speedometer cable at the transmission. Disconnect the wiring for the oil pressure gauge sending unit on the block.

11. On automatic transmission equipped vehicles, disconnect both oil cooler hoses and plug all openings. On all vehicles, disconnect the backup light switch harness at the plug located under the transmission.

12. Remove the propeller shaft.

13. Remove the clutch slave cylinder.

14. Put the gearshift in neutral. Unbolt the gearshift lever assembly.

15. Securely support the engine using a suitable engine crane. Support the transmission with a jack. Then, remove the front and rear engine mounting nuts and bolts, and the rear crossmember. Raise the assembly slightly and remove all the front support brackets and insulators. Then, gradually lower the transmission jack and pull the engine and transmission assembly out by raising the front of the engine so the transmission will clear the firewall.

16. Install in exact reverse order. When reassembling mounts, make sure all holes are properly aligned and that mounts are not distorted. On both front insulators, make sure the locating boss and hole in the insulator are in alignment. Torques are as follows.

Mounts	ft. lbs.
Crossmember mounting belts	7.2

Mounts	ft. lbs.
Bolts assm. front mounting brackets to front crossmember	22–29
Nuts assm. front mounts and bolt attaching rear mounts to rear crossmember	9.4–14
Nuts atop rear mount, attaching it to transmission	14–17

17. On the rear crossmember insulators, after bolts are torqued, turn them until a flat will line up with lockwasher tabs and then bend the tabs up against the flats to keep the bolts from unscrewing. Refill all fluids and adjust all linkages.

Mirage

NOTE: Use care when disconnecting the refrigerant lines. Escaping refrigerant will freeze any surface it contacts, including your skin and eyes.

1. Remove the hood. Remove the air cleaner assembly. Disconnect both battery cables and then remove the batter. Unbolt and remove the battery tray.

2. Disconnect the electrical connectors for the backup lights and engine harness, located near the battery tray. If the vehicle has a five speed, disconnect the select control valve connector. Disconnect the two alternator harness connectors and the oil pressure sending unit.

3. First label and then disconnect the automatic transmission oil cooler hoses. Avoid spilling oil and cap the openings.

4. Drain the cooling system. Then disconnect and remove the upper and lower hoses and remove them. Remove the radiator.

5. Label and then disconnect all low tension wires and the one high tension wire going to the coil from the distributor. Disconnect the engine ground.

6. Disconnect the brake booster vacuum hose at the intake manifold. Disconnect the cap power steering lines, as required. Remove pump as needed.

7. Disconnect the fuel supply, return and vapor hoses at the side of the engine.

8. If the vehicle has a turbocharger, you'll have to disconnect three electrical connectors — one for the idle speed control system and two for the injection system. All are located on the injection mixer.

9. Disconnect the heater hoses from the side of the engine. Disconnect the accelerator cable at the side of the injection mixer and the block.

10. Remove the clutch control cable (manual transmission) or transmission shifter control cable (automatic transmissions) from the transaxle.

11. Unscrew and disconnect the speedometer cable at the transaxle.

12. Raise and securely support the vehicle. Remove the drain plug and drain the transmission fluid. Disconnect the exhaust pipe at the manifold. Then, suspend the pipe securely with wire.

13. If the vehicle has manual transmission, remove the shift control rod and extension rod.

14. Disconnect the stabilizer bar at both lower control arms. Remove the bolts that attach the lower control arms to the body on either side. Support the arms from the body.

15. If the vehicle is turbocharged, disconnect and remove the oil cooler tube from the side of the engine.

16. Disconnect the driveshaft at the transmission on both sides. Then, seal off the openings in the transaxle. Make sure you replace the circlips holding the driveshafts in the transaxle. Support the driveshafts from the body.

17. Attach a crane type lift, via chains or cables, to both the engine lifting hooks. Put just a little tension on the cables. Then, remove the nut and bolt from the front roll stopper; unbolt the brace from the top of the engine damper.

18. Separate the rear roll stopper from the crossmember. Remove the attaching nut from the left mount insulator bolt, but do not remove the bolt.

19. Raise the engine just enough that the crane is supporting its weight. Check that everything is disconnected from the engine.

20. Remove the blind cover from the inside of the right fender inner shield. Then, remove the blind cover from the inside of the right front fender inner shied. Remove the transaxle mounting bracket bolts.

21. Remove the left mount insulator bolt. Then, press downward on the transaxle while lifting the engine/transaxle assembly to guide it up and out of the vehicle.

22. Installation is generally performed in reverse of the removal procedure. During installation, first install all nuts and bolts with the weight of the engine carried by the crane. Tighten just slightly. Then, allow the weight of the engine to sit on the mounts and torque parts as follows.

Mounts	ft. lbs.
Left mount large insulator nut	65–80
Left mount small insulator nut	22–29
Left mount bracket-to-engine nuts/bolts	36–47
Transaxle mount insulator nut	65–80
Transaxle insulator bracket-to-side frame bolts	22–29
Transaxle bracket assem.-to-auto. transaxle nuts	65–80
Transaxle mount bracket to manual transaxle bolts	40–43
Rear roll insulator nut	33–43
Rear roll stopper bracket-to-crossmember assem. bolts	22–29

Mounts	ft. lbs.
Front roll insulator nut	33–43
Front roll stopper bracket-to-crossmember assem. bolts	33–40
Lower roll insulator-to-roll damper bracket bolt	22–29
Center crossmember to body	43–58

23. Finally, replenish all fluids. Adjust the transmission and accelerator linkages. Start the engine and check for leaks as well as proper gauge operation. Replace the hood and recharge the air conditioner if necessary.

Galant

NOTE: Use care when disconnecting the refrigerant lines. Escaping refrigerant will freeze any surface it contacts, including your skin and eyes.

1. Matchmark the position of the hood hinges on the hood and remove it. Drain the engine coolant. Remove the drain plug and drain the transaxle fluid.

2. Remove the air cleaner. Disconnect the battery cables, remove the battery and then unbolt and remove the battery tray.

3. Carefully label and then disconnect each of three connectors of the engine wiring harness.

4. Disconnect the ground wire at the right side wheelhouse. Drain the power steering fluid by disconnecting a hose at the low point of the system. Plug all openings.

5. On vehicles with the electronically controlled suspension, remove the compressor and reserve tank.

6. Disconnect the transaxle control cable by moving the adjusting nut on the transaxle end of the cable and pulling the cable out of the fitting on the transaxle. Keep the rearward nut from moving to preserve the adjustment.

7. Disconnect the alternator connectors and the oil pressure sending unit. Disconnect the high tension cable at the coil.

8. Disconnect the engine ground cable at the firewall. Disconnect the brake booster vacuum hose.

9. Label and then disconnect the eight connectors for the sensors of the electronic fuel injection at the injection mixing body. Disconnect the accelerator and speed control cables nearby.

10. Disconnect the fuel supply and return hoses at the electronic injection mixing body.

11. Mark and then disconnect the transmission oil cooler hoses. Cap the openings to keep oil in and dirt out.

Disconnect both radiator hoses and both heater hoses at the engine.

12. Unscrew and then disconnect the speedometer cable at the transaxle. Disconnect the power steering hoses at the pump and cap all openings.

13. Raise and securely support the vehicle. Disconnect the exhaust pipe at the exhaust manifold. Then, hang the pipe to the body with wire.

14. Disconnect the steering knuckles from the lower arm ball joints. Disconnect the tie rods from the steering knuckle. Remove the driveshafts from the transaxle. Make sure to cap all openings to keep fluid in and dirt out. Discard the retaining clips that hold the shafts in the transmission and replace them.

15. Attach your lifting crane to both engine lifting hooks and put very slight tension on the chains or cables. Then remove the nut, but not the bolt, coupling the engine mount bracket to the body. Remove the upper installation nuts of the front and rear roll stopper brackets.

16. Detach the protective cap from inside the right fender shield and then remove the transaxle mounting bracket bolts. Then, remove the bolts connecting the transaxle mount insulator to the bracket and remove the bracket.

17. Now, increase the tension on the engine lifting mechanism until the weight of the engine is borne by the lift instead of its mounts. Now, remove the bolts of the rear roll stopper bracket, the engine mount bracket and the front roll stopper bracket. Confirm that all cable, wires and linkages are disconnected.

18. Tilting the transaxle side downward, carefully life the engine/transaxle assemble out of the vehicle.

19. Install in exact reverse order. Make sure that nothing gets pinched or bent as you're putting the engine back in position. When installing rubber insulators, make sure they are not twisted. Observe the following torques.

Mounts	ft. lbs.
Transaxle mount bracket bolts and front roll stopper mounting bracket bolts	29–36
Transaxle mount bracket through bolts and nuts	43–58
Front roll stopper bracket through bolts and nuts, and engine mount bracket attaching nuts and bolts	36–47
Rear roll stopper bracket through bolt, and engine mount bracket through bolt flange attaching nut	22–29

20. Check the operation of all linkages, adjusting if necessary, Replenish all fluids and then operate the engine, checking for leaks.

Precis

NOTE: Use care when disconnecting the refrigerant lines. Escaping refrigerant will freeze any surface it contacts, including your skin and eyes.

1. Remove the air cleaner assembly by disconnecting all hoses, unbolting it and removing it. Disconnect both battery cables and then remove the battery. Unbolt and remove the battery tray.

2. Disconnect the electrical connectors for the backup lights and engine harness, located near the battery tray. If the vehicle has a 5–speed, disconnect the select control valve connector. Disconnect the two alternator harness connectors and the oil pressure sending unit.

3. First label and then disconnect the automatic transmission oil cooler hoses. Avoid spilling oil and cap the openings.

4. Drain the cooling system through the cock on the bottom of the radiator and the plug in the block. Then disconnect and remove the upper and lower hoses and remove them. Remove the radiator.

5. Label and then disconnect all low tension wires and the one high tension wire going to the coil from the distributor. Disconnect the engine ground.

6. Disconnect the brake booster vacuum hose at the intake manifold.

7. Disconnect the fuel supply, return, and vapor hoses at the side of the engine. Avoid spilling fuel.

8. Disconnect the heater hoses from the side of the engine.

9. Remove the clutch control cable (manual transmission) or transmission shifter control cable (automatic transmissions) from the transaxle.

10. Unscrew and disconnect the speedometer cable at the transaxle.

11. Raise and securely support the vehicle. Remove the drain plug and drain the transmission fluid. Disconnect the exhaust pipe at the manifold. Then, suspend the pipe securely with wire.

12. If the vehicle has manual transmission, remove the shift control rod and extension rod.

13. Disconnect the stabilizer bar at both lower control arms. Remove the bolts that attach the lower control arms to the body on either side. Support the arms from the body.

14. Disconnect the driveshafts at the transmission on both sides. Then, seal off the openings in the transaxle. Make sure you replace the circlips holding the driveshafts in the transaxle. Support the driveshafts from the body.

15. Attach a crane type lift, via chains or cables, to both the engine lifting hooks. Put just a little tension on the cables. Then, remove the nut and bolt from the front roll stopper; unbolt the brace from the top of the engine damper.

16. Separate the rear roll stopper from the crossmember. Remove the attaching nut from the left mount insulator bolt, but do not remove the bolt.

17. Raise the engine just enough that the crane is supporting its weight. Check that everything is disconnected from the engine.

18. Remove the blind cover from the inside of the right fender inner shield. Remove the transaxle mounting bracket bolts.

19. Remove the left mount insulator bolt. Then, press downward on the transaxle while lifting the engine/transaxle assembly to guide it up and out of the vehicle.

20. Installation is generally performed in reverse of the removal procedure. During installation, first install all nuts and bolts with the weight of the engine carried by the crane. Tighten just slightly. Then, allow the weight of the engine to sit on the mounts, and torque parts as follows:

• Left mount large insulator nut: 65–80 ft. lbs.
• Left mount small insulator nut: 22–29 ft. lbs.
• Left mount bracket to engine nuts/bolts: 36–47 ft. lbs.
• Transaxle mount insulator nut: 65–80 ft. lbs.
• Transaxle insulator bracket to side frame bolts: 22–29 ft. lbs.
• Transaxle bracket assembly to automatic transaxle nuts: 65–80 ft. lbs.
• Transaxle mount bracket to manual transaxle bolts: 40–43 ft. lbs.
• Rear roll insulator nut: 33–43 ft. lbs.
• Rear roll stopper bracket to crossmember assembly bolts: 22–29 ft. lbs.
• Front roll insulator nut: 33–43 ft. lbs.
• Front roll stopper bracket to crossmember assembly bolts: 33–40 ft. lbs.
• Lower roll insulator to roll damper bracket bolt: 22–29 ft. lbs.
• Center crossmember to body: 43–58 ft. lbs.

21. Finally, replenish all fluids. Adjust the transmission and accelerator linkages. Start the engine and check for leaks as well as proper gauge operation. Replace the hood and have the air conditioner recharged.

Wagon

NOTE: Use care when disconnecting the refrigerant lines. Escaping refrigerant will freeze any surface it contacts, including your skin and eyes.

1. Disconnect the negative battery cable. Drain the engine oil. Drain the coolant.

NOTE: In order to remove the engine the seat underframe must be removed from the vehicle. Remove the drivers seat. Remove the parking brake lever and fuel tank filler door release lever. Remove the battery cover. Remove the bolts retaining the seat underframe in place. Remove the seat underframe.

2. As required, remove the radiator. Remove the radiator fan shroud. Remove the fan assembly. Remove the power steering pump assembly.
3. Remove the upper and lower radiator hoses. Disconnect all electrical connections from the engine. Disconnect the oxygen sensor harness connector connections.
4. Disconnect the accelerator cable connection. Disconnect the kickdown cable connection, if equipped.
5. Disconnect all vacuum hoses. Disconnect the power brake vacuum hose line. Remove the air condition compressor.
6. Raise and support the vehicle safely. Remove the strut bars. Remove the starter asembly.
7. Disconnect the speedometer cable at the transmission assembly. Disconnect the exhaust pipe at the exhaust manifold.
8. Disconnect the alternator and oil pressure switch electrical connectors. Disconnect and plug the automatic transmission lines, if equipped.
9. Disconnect the fuel line hose. Disconnect the heater hoses. Disconnect the transmission control cable.
10. Remove the driveshaft. Remove the engine mount bolts. Remove the transmission crossmember bolt.
11. Lower the vehicle. Using the proper lifting equipment remove the assembly from the vehicle.
12. Installation is the reverse of the removal procedure.

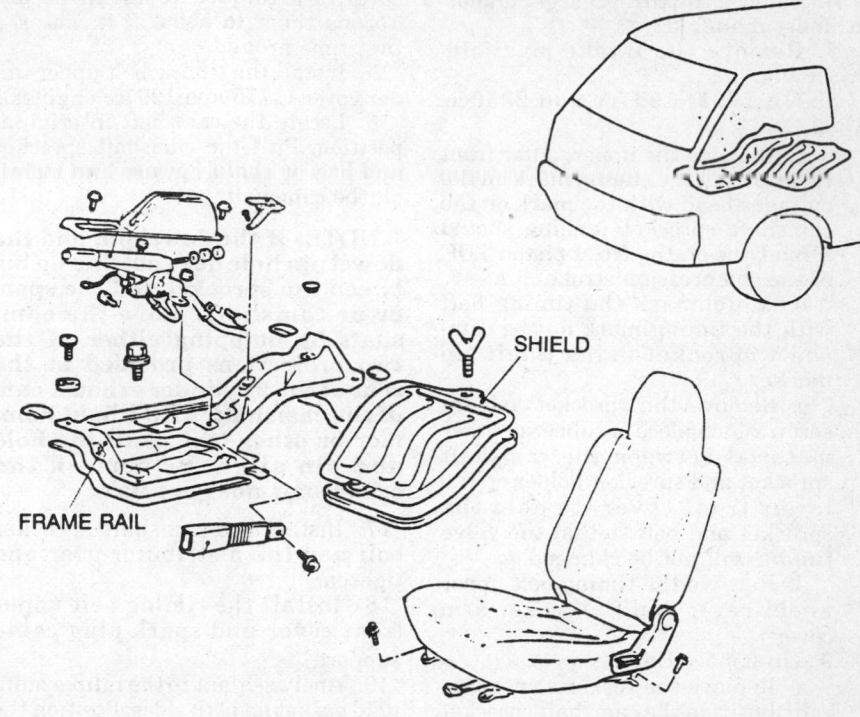

Wagon underseat frame and related components

Cylinder Head

REMOVAL & INSTALLATION

Cordia, Tredia, Starion, Galant and Wagon

NOTE: On the Wagon it will be necessary to remove the drivers seat and the seat underframe as follows. Remove the drivers seat. Remove the parking brake lever and fuel tank filler door release lever. Remove the battery cover. Remove the bolts retaining the seat underframe in place. Remove the seat underframe.

1. Turn the engine until the No. 1 piston is at TDC on the compression stroke. Disconnect the negative battery cable. Remove the air cleaner assembly.
2. Drain the engine coolant. Remove the upper radiator hose and disconnect the heater hoses.
3. Disconnect the fuel lines, wiring harnesses, distributor vacuum lines, spark plug wires (from plugs), purge valves, accelerator linkage and water temperature unit wire.
4. Remove the distributor and (if necessary) the fuel pump from the cylinder head.
5. Remove the nuts connecting the exhaust pipe to the manifold or turbocharger. Lower the exhaust pipe.

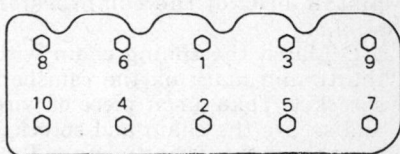

Engine head bolt torque sequence for 1795, 1997 and 2350cc engines

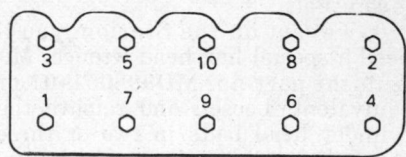

Engine head bolt removal sequence for 1795, 1997 and 2350cc engines

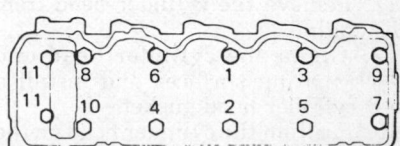

Engine head bolt torque sequence for the 2555cc engine

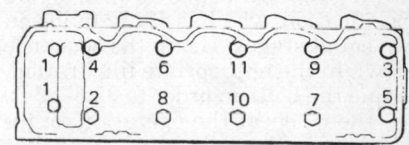

Engine head bolt removal sequence for the 2555cc engine

6. Remove the turbocharger and/or exhaust manifold.

7. Remove the intake manifold assembly.

8. On 1795, 1997cc and 2350cc Engines:

a. Remove the upper, outer front cover. Align the timing mark on the cylinder head with the mark on the camshaft sprocket (engine should already be on the No. 1 piston TDC of the compression stroke).

b. Matchmark the timing belt with the timing mark on the camshaft sprocket using a felt tip marker.

c. Remove the sprocket and insert a 2 inch piece of rubber or other material between the camshaft sprocket and sprocket holder on the lower front cover, to hold the sprocket and belt so that the valve timing will not be changed.

d. Remove the timing belt upper under cover and the rocker arm cover.

9. On 2555cc Engines:

a. Remove the rocker arm cover.

b. Position the camshaft sprocket dowel pin at the 12 o'clock position with the timing mark TDC at the front of the timing case cover (engine should already be on the No. 1 piston TDC of the compression stroke).

c. Match the timing chain with the timing mark on the camshaft sprocket. Take a soft piece of wire and secure the chain and sprocket together at the timing mark and opposite side.

d. Remove the camshaft sprocket bolt, gear and sprocket from the camshaft.

10. Except on the Starion, you'll need a special hex head wrench. Mitsubishi part no. MD998051-01 or equivalent. Loosen and remove the cylinder head bolts in two or three stages to avoid cylinder head warpage. Follow the sequence shown in the appropriate illustration.

11. Remove the cylinder head from the engine.

12. Clean the cylinder head and block mating surfaces and install a new cylinder head gasket.

13. Position the cylinder head on the engine block, engage the dowel pins front and rear and install the cylinder head bolts.

14. The bolts must be torqued to cold specification, which is 65–72 ft. lbs. in two equal stages. Using the sequence shown in the appropriate illustration, torque the bolts in order to 32.5–36 ft. lbs. then, repeat the operation torquing them to the full torque. Note that on the Starion, the front head bolts, attaching the head only to the timing cover, are torqued to 11–15 ft. lbs. Torque them to about 7 ft. lbs. the first time around.

15. Install the timing belt upper under cover (1775 and 1997cc engines).

16. Locate the camshaft in original position. Pull the camshaft sprocket and belt or chain upward and install on the camshaft.

NOTE: If the dowel pin and the dowel pin hole does not line up between the sprocket and the spacer or camshaft, move the camshaft by bumping either of the two projections provided at the rear of No. 2 cylinder exhaust cam of the camshaft, with a light hammer or other tool, until the hole and pin align. Be certain the crankshaft does not turn.

17. Install the camshaft sprocket bolt and the distributor gear and tighten.

18. Install the timing belt upper front cover and spark plug cable support.

19. Apply sealant to the intake manifold gasket on both sides. Position the gasket and install the intake manifold. Tighten the nuts to specifications. Be sure that no sealant enters the jet air passages, when equipped

20. Install the exhaust manifold gaskets and the manifold assembly. Tighten the nuts to specifications.

21. Connect the exhaust pipe to the exhaust manifold and install the fuel pump. Install the purge valve.

22. Install the water temperature gauge wire, heater hoses and the upper radiator hose.

23. Connect the fuel lines, accelerator linkage, vacuum hoses and the spark plug wires.

24. Fill the cooling system and connect the batter ground cable. Install the distributor.

25. Temporarily adjust the valve clearance to the cold engine specifications.

26. Install the gasket on the rocker arm cover and temporarily install the cover on the engine.

27. Start the engine and bring it to normal operating temperature. Stop the engine and remove the rocker arm cover.

28. Adjust the valves to hot engine specifications.

29. Reinstall the rocker arm cover and tighten securely.

30. Install the air cleaner, hoses, purge valve hose, and any other removed unit.

Mirage and Precis

1468cc ENGINE

1. Disconnect the negative battery cable. Drain the cooling system and then disconnect the upper radiator hose. Remove the PCV hose that runs between the air cleaner and the rocker cover.

2. Remove the air cleaner. Disconnect the fuel lines. Label and disconnect any vacuum lines running to the cylinder head, manifold, or carburetor from other parts of the engine compartment. Disconnect the heater hoses going to the head.

3. Label and disconnect the spark plug wires. Remove the rocker cover. Turn the crankshaft over until the TDC timing marks line up and both No. 1 cylinder valves are closed (both rockers are off the cams). Then, remove the distributor.

4. Remove the carburetor, intake manifold and the exhaust manifold.

5. Remove the timing belt cover. Note the location of the camshaft sprocket timing mark. Loosen both timing belt tensioner mounting bolts and then lever it over toward the water pump as far as it will go. Retighten the adjusting bolt to hold the tensioner in this position. Pull the timing belt off the camshaft sprocket but leave it engaged with the other sprockets.

6. Using a hex type wrench, part No. MD998360 loosen the head bolts in the sequence shown. When all have been loosened, remove them. Then, pull the head off the engine block, rocking it slightly to break it loose, if necessary.

7. Remove the gasket. If pieces of the gasket adhere to the head or block deck, scrape them off carefully, using a scraper that will not scratch the surfaces. Make sure none of the pieces gets into the engine.

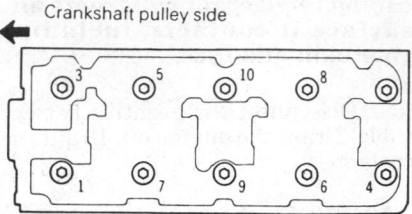

Crankshaft pulley side

Engine head bolt torque sequence for 1468 and 1597cc engines

Crankshaft pulley side

Engine head bolt removal sequence for 1468 and 1597cc engines

8. Install a new head gasket (without any sealer) and then position the head on the block deck. Install all the bolts finger tight. Then, torque them, in the illustrated sequence, first to 25 ft. lbs. Then, torque again, in the same sequence, to 58–61 ft. lbs.

9. Install the timing belt on the camshaft tensioner and rotate the camshaft sprocket backward so the belt is tight on what is normally the tension side. Make sure all the timing marks are now lined up.

10. Now, loosen the timing belt tensioner adjusting bolt and allow spring tension to tension the belt. Make sure all timing marks are still lined up. If not, the belt is out of time and must be shifted with the tensioner shifted back toward the water pump and locked there. Now, torque the adjusting bolt (on the right side and working through a slot) to 15–18 ft. lbs. Now, after the tensioner adjusting bolt is torqued, torque the hinged mounting bolt located on the opposite side. Don't torque the mounting bolt first, or the tension on the belt will be too great!

11. Now, turn the crankshaft one full turn in the normal direction of rotation. Now, loosen first the tensioner pivot bolt and then the adjusting bolt. Now torque them exactly as before — adjusting bolt (working in the slot) first! This extra step is necessary to ensure the timing belt is properly seated before final tension is adjusted.

12. Install the intake and exhaust manifolds, carburetor, distributor, air cleaner, rocker cover, timing belt cover, and all hoses in reverse of the above procedures. Refill the cooling system. Operate the engine and check for leaks.

Mirage

1597cc ENGINE

1. Disconnect the negative battery cable. Drain engine coolant and then disconnect the upper radiator hose at the thermostat. Remove PCV and canister purge hoses.

2. Remove the air cleaner. Disconnect the fuel line. Disconnect vacuum hoses at the distributor and canister purge control valve.

3. Label and then disconnect the spark plug wires. Remove the rocker cover. Turn the crankshaft over until the TDC timing marks line up and both No. 1 cylinder valves are closed (both rockers are off the cams). Then, remove the distributor.

4. Disconnect the heater hose at the intake manifold. Disconnect the water hose leading from the cylinder head and carburetor water jacket.

5. Disconnect the temperature gauge sending unit wire at the head. Remove the fuel pump.

6. Remove the exhaust manifold. Turn the crankshaft until No. 1 piston is at TDC of its compression stroke. Align the timing mark on the upper cover at the rear of the timing belt with the mark on the camshaft sprocket to do this. Use some sort of marker to mark the relationship between the timing belt and the mark on the cam sprocket.

7. Loosen and remove the bolt fastening the sprocket to the camshaft, holding the sprocket in position as you work to keep the belt from slipping off. Then, rest the sprocket on the sprocket holder provided on the lower front cover. If necessary, slip a short piece of used timing belt or other thin, flexible object between the holder and the sprocket to keep tension and avoid losing belt timing. Be sure not to turn the crankshaft throughout this work.

8. Remove the bolts from the timing belt rear cover and remove the cover.

9. Remove the cylinder head bolts. Loosen in three stages, going from bolt to bolt in the sequence shown. This requires a special hex wrench, Part No. MD998360 or equivalent.

10. Once the bolts are removed, the head may be rocked to break it loose. Do not slide it as there are dowel pins on the block deck.

11. Install a new head gasket without sealant, and install the head over the dowel pins. Install the cylinder head bolts. Then, in the sequence shown, torque the bolts first to 25 ft. lbs. Then, repeat the sequence, torquing to 51–54 ft. lbs.

12. Install the intake manifold, exhaust manifold and carburetor. Install the fuel pump and reconnect all fuel lines.

13. Install the distributor. Reconnect the plug wires in the proper firing order. Reconnect the temperature gauge wire and all water hoses. Reconnect the distributor, PCV and evaporative emissions system vacuum hoses.

14. Reconnect the top radiator hose and refill the cooling system. Operate the engine and check for leaks.

OVERHAUL

For all cylinder head procedures, please refer to "Engine Rebuilding" in the Unit Repair section.

Rocker Arms/Shafts

REMOVAL & INSTALLATION

Cordia, Tredia, Starion, Galant and Wagon

NOTE: On 1985–88 models which have hydraulic lash adjusters, you'll need eight special holders, Mitsubishi special tool NO. MD998443 to retain the hydraulic lash adjusters when you disassemble the valve train.

On the Wagon it will be necessary to remove the drivers seat and the seat underframe as follows. Remove the drivers seat. Remove the parking brake lever and fuel tank filler door release lever. Remove the battery cover. Remove the bolts retaining the seat underframe in place. Remove the seat underframe.

1. Disconnect the negative battery cable. Remove the rocker cover and, on the Cordia, Tredia, Galant and Wagon the upper timing belt cover. Loosen the camshaft sprocket bolt until you can turn it with your fingers. Turn the engine over until the camshaft sprocket timing mark lines up with the timing mark on the cylinder head on the Cordia, Tredia, Galant and Wagon. On the Starion, the timing mark on the sprocket ends up on the extreme right of the sprocket bolt as viewed from the front. In both cases the TDC mark on the front crankshaft pulley must line up with the timing scale on the front cover.

2. Remove the camshaft sprocket bolt and without allowing tension on the timing chain or belt to be lost, place the sprocket in the sprocket holder of the front cover or lower timing belt cover. Make sure you don't lose tension on the belt/chain as this will require a lot of additional labor! Make sure, also, that you do not turn the crankshaft throughout the work. On the 1985–88 Cordia/Tredia, Galant and Wagon with hydraulic lash adjusters, put the special clips on the eight hydraulic adjusters at the outer ends of all eight rocker arms. Note that these clips go over the lash adjusters that actuate the large intake valves, not on the small adjusting screw for the smaller jet valves.

3. Loosen but do not remove the camshaft bearing cap bolts. After all bolts have been loosened, remove them and then, holding the ends so the assembly stays together, remove the rocker shaft assembly from the cylinder head. Note that the rearmost cam bearing cap is not associated with the rocker shafts on the Starion and need not be removed.

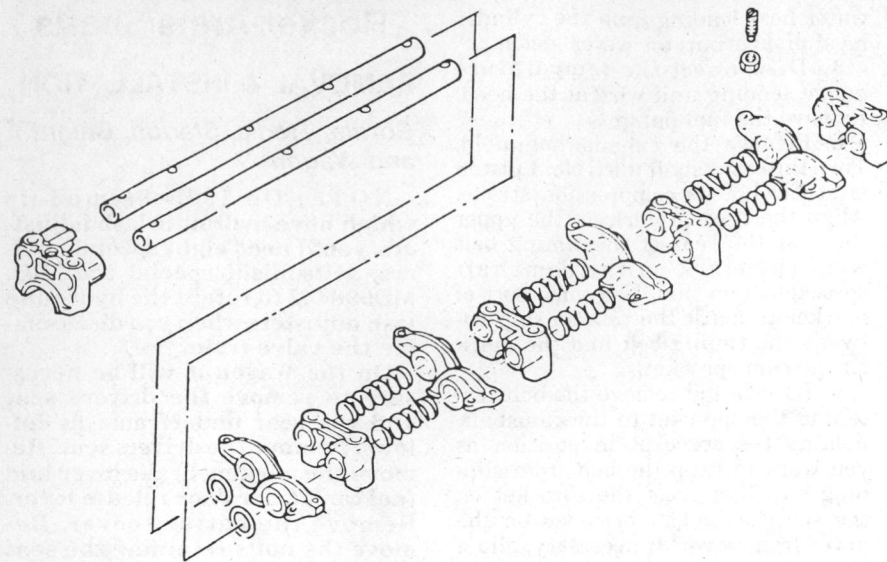

Typical rocker arm and shaft assembly

4. Keep all parts in original order. Assemble the parts of the rocker assembly as follows:

Cordia, Tredia, Galant and Wagon—Install left and right side rocker shafts into the front bearing cap. Notches in the ends of the shaft must be upward. Install the bolts for the front cap to retain the shafts in place. Note that the left rocker shaft is longer than the right rocker shaft. Install the wave washer onto the left rocker shaft with the bulge forward. Then, coat the inner surfaces of the rockers and the upper bearing surfaces of the bearing caps with clean engine oil and assemble rockers, springs and the remaining bearing caps in the order in which removed. Note that the intake rockers are the only ones with the jet valve actuators. Note also that the rockers are labeled for cylinders 1–3 and 2–4 because the direction the jet valve actuator faces changes. Use mounting bolts to hold the caps in place after each is assembled. When the assembly is complete, install it onto the head and start all mounting bolts into the head and tighten finger tight.

5. On the Starion—Install the right and left rocker shafts into the front bearing cap. Note that shafts can be identified by the fact that the rear end of the left side shaft has a notch. Align the mating marks of the front of the rocker shaft with that on the front bearing cap. Insert the front bolts. Install the waved washers on both sides with the bulge in the washers facing forward. Then, install the rockers, shafts, caps and bolts in their original positions, using the bolts to hold each cap in place after it is in-

stalled. Oil the inner surfaces of the rockers and the upper bearing surfaces of the caps with clean engine oil prior to assembly. Note that the valve actuating ends of the rockers must face outward and that only the intake side rockers have the jet valve actuator. When the assembly is complete, install it onto the head and start all the bolts into the threads, tightening them finger tight.

6. Now torque the attaching bolts for the rocker assembly 14–15 ft. lbs. going from the center outward.

7. Without removing tension from the timing chain or belt, lift the sprocket out of the holder and position it against the front of the cam. Make sure the locating tang on the sprocket goes into the hole in the front of the cam. Install the bolt. Torque it to 37–43 ft. lbs. on the Starion and 59–72 on the Cordia, Tredia, Galant and Wagon.

8. Adjust the valves.

9. Apply sealant to the top surface of the semicircular seals in the head and then install the valve cover. Install the upper timing belt cover on the Cordia, Tredia, Galant and Wagon.

Mirage and Precis

1468cc ENGINE

1. Disconnect the negative battery cable. Remove the PCV hose running from the rocker cover and the air cleaner. Remove the air cleaner.

2. Remove the upper timing belt cover. Remove the rocker cover.

3. Loosen the rocker shaft mounting bolts, but do not remove them. After all bolts are loosened remove the

rocker shaft, rocker arms and springs as an assembly.

4. Be sure to keep all parts in original order, for reinstallation.

5. Assemble all the parts, noting the differences between intake and exhaust parts. The intake rocker shaft is much longer; the intake rocker shaft springs are over three inches long, while those for the exhaust side are less than two inches long; intake rockers have the extra adjusting screw for the jet valve; rockers are labeled "1–3" and "2–4" for the cylinder with which they are associated. Torque the rocker shaft mounting bolts to 15–19 ft. lbs.

6. Adjust the valve clearances. This step may be omitted only if all parts are being reused. Install the rocker cover with a new gasket, torquing the bolts to 1–1.5 ft. lbs. Install the air cleaner and PCV valve. Remember that there is no timing belt cover in place and keep your fingers clear. Run the engine at idle speed until it is hot. Then remove the valve cover again and adjust the valve clearances with the engine hot. Finally, replace the rocker cover and timing belt cover, air cleaner and PCV valve.

Mirage

1597cc ENGINE

1. Disconnect the negative battery cable. Remove the air cleaner assembly. Label and then disconnect the spark plug high tension wires. Remove the upper front timing belt cover.

2. Turn the crankshaft until No. 1 piston is at TDC of its compression stroke. Align the timing mark on the upper cover at the rear of the timing belt with the mark on the camshaft sprocket to do this. Use some sort of marker to mark the relationship between the timing belt and the mark on the cam sprocket.

3. Loosen and remove the bolt fastening the sprocket to the camshaft, holding the sprocket in position as you work to keep the belt from slipping off. Then, rest the sprocket on the sprocket holder provided on the lower front cover. If necessary, slip a short piece of used timing belt or other thin, flexible object between the holder and the sprocket to keep tension and avoid losing belt timing. Be sure not to turn the crankshaft throughout this work.

4. Remove the upper cover located behind the timing belt. Remove the rocker cover. Loosen the camshaft bearing cap bolts without pulling them out of the caps and remove the caps, rockers and shafts as an assembly.

5. Be sure to keep all parts in original order, for reinstallation.

6. To reassemble, first lubricate all wear surfaces with clean engine oil and then insert the two rocker shafts into the front bearing cap with the cuts at the top/front of the caps at the tops. Note that the longer shaft goes on the left side (facing the crankshaft pulley). Note that the intake rockers only have the jet valve actuators and that the waved washers are installed behind the last set of rockers with the bulge at the center of the washer facing the crankshaft pulley. After each cap goes on and the holes are lined up, install the bolts to keep it in place. Note that if the camshaft front oil seal has been damaged it must be replaced.

7. Lubricate the wear surfaces of the cam bearing caps and then install them. Torque the bolts to 14–15 ft. lbs.

8. Install the timing belt rear cover. Pull the camshaft sprocket upward and install it to the camshaft. Turn the camshaft slightly if necessary to make the dowel pin fit into the hole in the sprocket. Make sure that the mating mark made when these parts were disassembled are still aligned so the camshaft will be in time. Make corrections as necessary. Install the sprocket attaching bolt, torquing it to 44–57 ft. lbs.

9. Install the timing belt upper cover and spark plug high tension wire supports. Adjust the valve clearances. Apply sealant to the top of the front bearing cap and rear of the head where the rocker cover seals and then install the rocker cover. Install new gaskets and install the rocker cover, torquing the bolts to 4–5 ft. lbs. Reconnect the spark plug wires and install the air cleaner and PCV and evaporative emissions hoses. Run the engine at idle speed until it is hot. Then, remove the rocker cover and again set the valves with the engine hot.

Intake Manifold

REMOVAL & INSTALLATION

NOTE: On the Wagon it will be necessary to remove the drivers seat and the seat underframe as follows. Remove the drivers seat. Remove the parking brake lever and fuel tank filler door release lever. Remove the battery cover. Remove the bolts retaining the seat underframe in place. Remove the seat underframe.

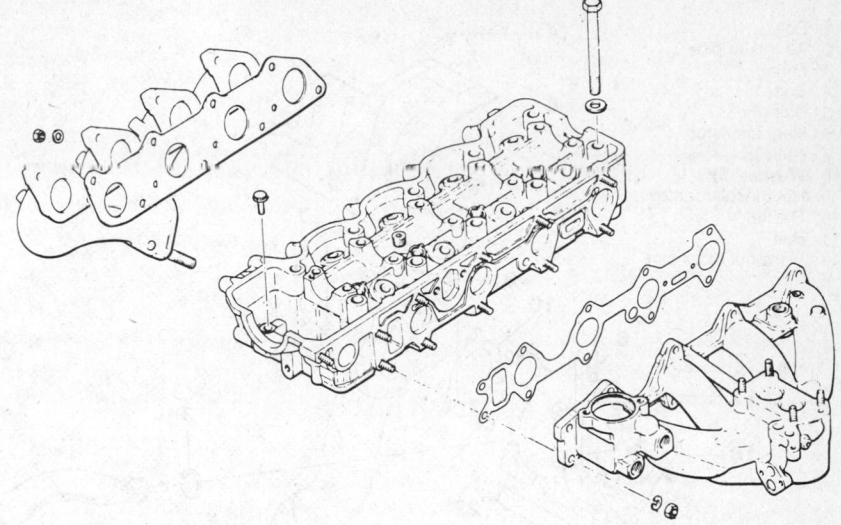

Typical intake and exhaust manifold installation

1. Disconnect the negative battery cable. Remove the air cleaner and duct hose assembly.

2. Disconnect the fuel line(s), EGR lines and other vacuum hoses and wire harness connectors.

3. Disconnect the throttle positioner solenoid and fuel cutoff solenoid wires.

4. Disconnect the accelerator linkage and, if equipped with automatic transmission, the shift cables at the carburetor/injector.

5. Drain the coolant.

6. Remove the water hose from carburetor and cylinder head.

7. Remove the heater and water outlet hoses.

8. Disconnect the water temperature sending unit.

9. Remove the manifold and carburetor/injector assembly. Remove mounting nuts/bolts from the ends toward the middle.

10. Clean all mounting surfaces. Before reinstalling the manifold, coat both sides with gasket sealer. Install mounting nuts/bolts starting from the center toward the ends.

Exhaust Manifold

REMOVAL & INSTALLATION

1. Disconnect the negative battery cable. Remove the air cleaner and duct hose assembly.

2. Remove the manifold heat stove and hose. Disconnect the EGR lines and reed valve, if equipped.

3. Disconnect the exhaust pipe bracket from the engine block.

4. Remove the exhaust pipe flange bolts from the manifold or turbocharger. (One bolt and nut may have to be removed from under the vehicle.)

5. Remove the manifold flange stud nuts starting from the ends toward the middle and remove the manifold from the cylinder head.

6. Installation is the reverse of removal. Install mounting nuts starting from the middle toward the ends.

Turbocharger

REMOVAL & INSTALLATION

1. Disconnect the negative battery cable. Remove the air cleaner and turbocharger inlet ducting. Unbolt the turbocharger discharge hose going to the injection mixer.

2. Disconnect the oxygen sensor at the catalytic converter to protect it.

3. Unbolt and remove the large heat shield that covers the top of the turbocharger.

4. Remove the three nuts fastening the turbo to the catalytic converter. On the Cordia, Tredia and Mirage, disconnect the oil return pipe at the oil pan. On the Starion, disconnect the oil return hose at the oil return pipe and the timing chain cover.

5. Disconnect the oil supply line at the turbo and at the oil filter bracket.

6. Disconnect the turbocharger from the exhaust manifold and remove the unit from the vehicle.

7. Installation is the reverse of the removal procedure. Replace all gaskets as required. Pour clean engine oil into the oil supply fitting before connecting the oil supply pipe.

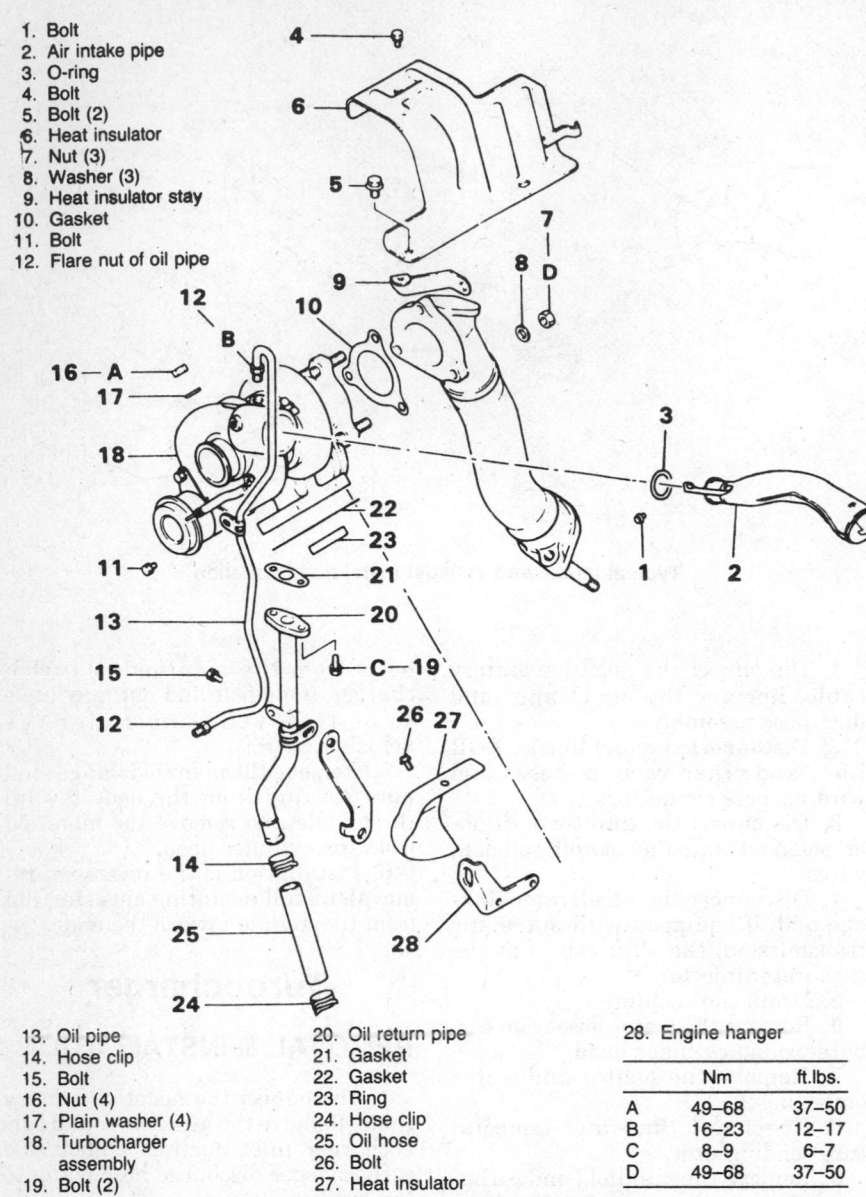

1. Bolt
2. Air intake pipe
3. O-ring
4. Bolt
5. Bolt (2)
6. Heat insulator
7. Nut (3)
8. Washer (3)
9. Heat insulator stay
10. Gasket
11. Bolt
12. Flare nut of oil pipe

13. Oil pipe
14. Hose clip
15. Bolt
16. Nut (4)
17. Plain washer (4)
18. Turbocharger assembly
19. Bolt (2)
20. Oil return pipe
21. Gasket
22. Gasket
23. Ring
24. Hose clip
25. Oil hose
26. Bolt
27. Heat insulator
28. Engine hanger

	Nm	ft.lbs.
A	49–68	37–50
B	16–23	12–17
C	8–9	6–7
D	49–68	37–50

Turbocharger mounting components

	ft. lbs.
Cordia, Tredia and Mirage	
Oil supply pipe banjo fitting at the block	10–13
Turbo-to-converter bolts	36–50
Turbo-to-exhaust manifold nuts	36–50
Oil return pipe connection bolts	6–7
Oil supply pipe banjo fitting at the turbo	21–24
Starion	
Oil supply pipe to turbo fitting	13–17
Oil supply pipe fitting to turbo	16.5–19.5
Turbo-to-exhaust manifold	37–50
Turbo-to-catalytic converter	37–50
Oil drain pipe to turbo	6–7

TROUBLESHOOTING

For more information on turbocharging, please refer to "Turbocharging" in the Unit Repair section.

Front Cover

REMOVAL & INSTALLATION

Except Starion

1. Disconnect the negative battery cable. Remove the alternator drive belt.

2. Unbolt and remove the water pump drive pulley. Remove the bolt from the crankshaft pulley. Then, with a puller, remove the crankshaft pulley.

3. Remove the bolts from the cover (1468cc—Mirage and Precis) or upper and lower covers and remove them. If the engine has two covers, the upper cover comes off first.

4. Install in reverse order, using new gaskets under the cover(s).

Starion

1. Disconnect the negative battery cable. Unbolt the clutch fan. Unbolt the fan shroud and then remove the shroud and clutch fan together. Remove the pulley and belt.

2. Remove the crankshaft bolt. With a puller, remove the crankshaft pulley.

3. Remove the rocker cover. Then, remove the two front bolts from the cylinder head; these screw into and seal the top of the timing cover.

4. Remove the oil pan bolts (front and side) that screw into the timing cover.

5. Drain the cooling system and remove the coolant hose leading to the water pump. Remove the alternator or other accessories that are in the way of the timing cover.

6. Unbolt and remove the timing cover.

7. Clean all the gasket surfaces. If the oil pan gasket was damaged in removing the front cover, carefully cut the oil pan gasket off flush with the front of the block on both sides and remove the cutoff piece of gasket.

8. Carefully pry the old oil seal out of the cover without scratching the bore into which the seal fits. Then, install a new seal with an installer such as Part Nos. MD998376-01 and MB990938-01.

9. Install new gaskets to the cylinder block. Cut an exact replacement for the section of oil pan gasket you removed from a new pan gasket, if necessary. Insert this piece of gasket onto the front of the pan in the exact position of the old piece and then use liquid sealer on the joint between the two sections of gasket on both sides. Install the chain cover. Install the cover bolts and torque them to 9–10.5 ft. lbs. Lightly coat the outside diameter of the crankshaft pulley boss with clean engine oil. Then install the pulley onto the crankshaft, install the bolt and turn it to force the pulley all the way on. Torque it to 80–94 ft. lbs.

10. Install the front head bolts (2) and torque to 11–15 ft. lbs. Install the oil pan bolts and torque them to 4.5–5.5 ft. lbs.

11. Install all hoses and accessories and refill the cooling system.

Timing Chain and Sprockets

REMOVAL & INSTALLATION

Starion

1. Disconnect the negative battery cable. Remove the rocker cover. Put the engine on TDC No. 1 cylinder firing position by turning the crankshaft until the TDC timing marks line up and both front valves are fully closed (rockers off the cams). Remove the timing cover.

2. Unbolt and remove the three silent shaft chain guides. Then, unscrew and remove the oil pump drive sprocket bolt and the left silent shaft sprocket bolt. When the bolts are removed, pull these two sprockets off and then disengage the chain from the crankshaft sprocket. Make sure you don't lose the keys. Note that the two sprockets are identical, but that the oil pump drive sprocket is installed with the concave side toward the engine while the left silent shaft sprocket has the concave side out. Remove the sprockets and the chain. Remove the crankshaft sprocket for the silent shaft chain.

3. The timing chain tensioner maintains constant spring pressure on the chain, so you must fasten the follower plunger so it will not be forced out of the body of the oil pump. Securely run wire around the follower and the left side of the oil pump.

4. Now, remove the camshaft sprocket bolt and pull the sprocket off the camshaft. You can now separate the chain from the sprockets and remove it. Finally, pull the sprocket for the camshaft timing chain that is on the crankshaft off, keeping it and the silent shaft drive sprockets in order for correct installation.

5. Inspect the tensioner follower and replace it if the follower shows a deep grooving where the chain was ridden against it. To replace it, remove the wire holding it in place and allow the spring to gradually push it out of the oil pump body. Replace the rubber seal that goes in the oil pump body and the spring behind it when you replace the tensioner follower. Make sure the thinner part of the follower faces downward. Wire the new follower in place just as the old one was. If the timing chain right and left

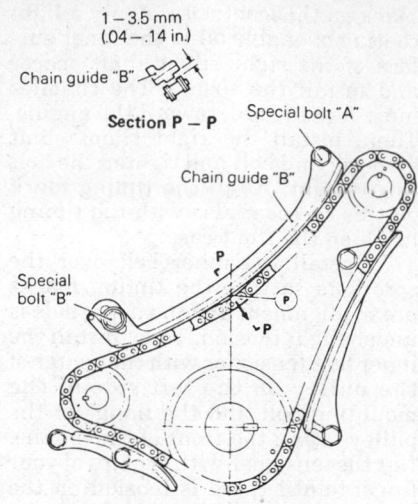

2555cc silent shaft timing mark alignment

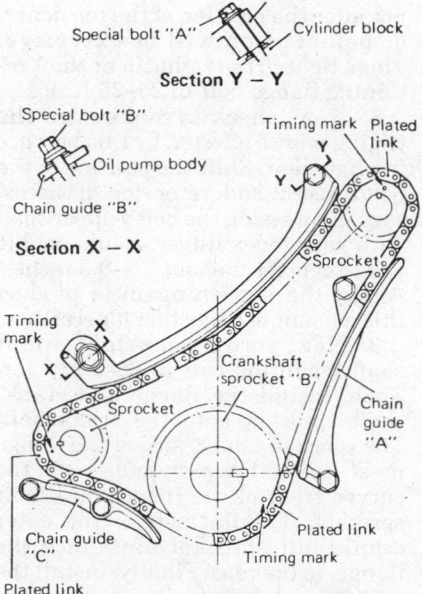

2555cc silent shaft chain timing marks

guides show heavy grooving, they should be replaced by unbolting them. Sprockets should be replaced if the teeth are deformed from wear or there are any obvious cracks.

6. To install first install the crankshaft sprocket for the camshaft timing chain onto the crankshaft. Install the sprocket so that the teeth are on the crankshaft or inner end of the sprocket. Then, engage the camshaft timing chain with the camshaft sprocket so the chrome plated link straddles the timing mark on the front of the sprocket. Wrap the lower end of the chain around the crankshaft sprocket so the chrome link straddles the timing mark there and make sure the chain rides inside the chain guides on both sides. Rest the

camshaft sprocket on the sprocket holder and get the camshaft bolt. Engage the cam shaft sprocket with the front of the camshaft so the prong on the camshaft flange fits into the hole in the sprocket, install the bolt and torque to 37–43 ft. lbs. Remove the wire holding the tensioner follower.

7. Now, install the crankshaft silent shaft chain sprocket, facing so that the teeth are on the outer end of the sprocket. Assemble the oil pump drive gear and left silent shaft sprockets to the left silent shaft chain with the chrome plated links straddling the timing marks on each. Make sure the concave side of the oil pump sprocket is toward the oil pump, but that the concave side of the left silent shaft sprocket faces outward. Carry the chain and sprockets over to the engine and engage the chain with the crankshaft sprocket so the chrome plated link straddles the timing mark on the front of the sprocket. Then, install each sprocket on its shaft. Install and tighten the bolts finger tight.

8. Install the three chain guides, turning bolts finger tight. Then torque the sprocket bolts. Then, tighten the right side and bottom chain guide bolts fully. Now, rotate the silent shaft sprockets slightly, the oil pump sprocket clockwise and the left silent shaft sprocket counter clockwise so the slack in the chain all goes to the span between the oil pump and left silent shaft sprockets, near the adjustable guide that is still loose. Adjust the position of the Chain guide "B", the adjustable guide, by positioning it and then tightening the bolts until the play in the center of the chain near the adjustable guide is 0.04–1.4 in. Pull the chain away from the guide at the center of the guide at the center of the guide and measure the distance between the outer edge of the guide and edge of the chain to do this. When the play is correct, torque, first, the guide adjusting bolt (the one that runs in the slot) to 11–15 ft. lbs. Then, torque the upper guide bolt to 6–7 ft. lbs.

9. Now, reinstall the timing chain cover and front pulley.

10. Continue the installation in the reverse order of the removal.

Timing Belt and Sprockets

REMOVAL & INSTALLATION

Cordia, Tredia, Galant and Wagon

NOTE: Timing belt and sprocket removal procedures are combined because the procedures are interrelated. **Belts are kept in place to permit sprocket bolts to be loosened. If you intention is to replace only the belt(s) simply skip the steps related to removing or replacing the sprockets, unless it is noted that a sprocket must be removed to gain access to a belt related part.**

1. Disconnect the negative battery cable. Remove the timing belt cover. Rotate the engine until the timing marks on the camshaft sprocket and cylinder head or rear belt cover and the crankshaft sprocket and front cover are perfectly aligned.

2. Loosen the timing belt tensioner adjusting bolt and the mounting bolt, shift the tensioner as far as it will go toward the left or water pump side (so belt tension is lost) and then retighten the adjusting bolt. If the belt is to be reused, draw an arrow on it in the direction of rotation. Now, remove the belt. Then, hold the tensioner in position as you remove the tensioner adjusting bolt. Slowly release tension, remove the mounting bolt, and then remove the tension, spring and spacer.

3. Remove the bolt and remove the camshaft sprocket.

4. If you need to replace the inner timing belt which drives the oil pump and right silent shaft or need to remove the sprockets, proceed as follows; otherwise, proceed with Step 5:

a. Remove the crankshaft front sprocket bolt and remove the front crankshaft sprocket and flange. Remove the plug from the left side of the block. Insert a suitable tool about .3 inch in diameter and about 2.5 inches long or longer into the hole to keep the left silent shaft in position.

b. Remove the oil pump sprocket retaining nut and remove the nut and the sprocket. Loosen the right silent shaft sprocket bolt until you can turn it with your fingers.

c. Then, remove the inner tensioner bolts and remove the tensioner. Remove the inner timing belt. Then, remove the large crankshaft sprocket from the crankshaft and the right silent shaft bolt, sprocket and spacer.

5. Inspect all components as required. Replace defective parts as needed.

6. Install the larger crankshaft sprocket onto the crankshaft with the flatter or flanged side forward and the boss which is there to extend the sprocket forward from the front of the crankshaft at the rear. Align the timing mark on the sprocket with the

mark on the front case. Apply a light coating of engine oil to the inner surface of the right silent shaft spacer and install the spacer. The chamfer must face inward, toward the engine. Then, install the right silent shaft sprocket and bolt and tighten the bolt finger tight. Align the timing mark on this sprocket also with the timing mark on the front case.

7. Install the inner belt over the sprockets so that the timing marks are in alignment and the upper side is under slight tension. Then, install the inner belt tensioner with the center of the pulley on the left side of the mounting bolt and the flange of the pulley facing the front of the engine. Lift the tensioner with the tips of your fingers until there is tension on the inner belt's upper length. Hold the tensioner in exactly this position and tighten the tensioner mounting bolt. Make sure the turning of the bolt does not alter the position of the tensioner, or belt tension will be excessive. Then, tighten the right silent shaft retaining flange bolt to 25–28 ft. lbs.

8. Now, check to make sure the timing marks effected by this belt are in alignment. Shift the position of the belt's teeth and retension if necessary. Depressing the belt's upper span with your index finger should enable you to depress it about 0.2–0.3 inches. Adjust the tension again to product this amount of deflection if necessary.

9. Now, torque the right silent shaft mounting bolt to 25–28 ft. lbs. Then, install the flange and crankshaft sprocket onto the crankshaft. The concave (inner) side of the flange must face to the rear so as to fit the curved front of the inner crankshaft sprocket. The flat side of the outer crankshaft sprocket must face the flange, to the rear. Finally, install the washer and bolt to the front of the crankshaft and torque it to 80–94 ft. lbs.

10. Install the camshaft sprocket to the camshaft and torque the bolt to 58–72 ft. lbs.

11. Install the spacer and main timing belt tensioner, installing the bolts finger tight. Now, install the spring between the locking tang on the right side of the tensioner and the tang on the right side of the water pump, just above the tensioner. This will force the tensioner to turn counterclockwise on the pivot bolt. Push the tensioner all the way toward the water pump and lock it by tightening the adjusting bolt.

12. Check alignment of all timing marks: the mark on the camshaft sprocket must align with the mark on the head; the mark on the crankshaft sprocket must align with that on the front case; and the mark on the oil

pump sprocket must align with that on the front case.

13. Install the timing belt. The belt should be fitted over the sprockets in order: first the crankshaft, then the oil pump and then the camshaft sprocket. The (right) side of the belt which is normally straight must be straight during installation so the timing marks will remain lined up when the belt is actually tensioned. Remove the suitable tool installed to keep the silent shaft in position and replace the plug. Making sure there is no tension on the pivot bolt, loosen the tensioner adjusting bolt so the spring applies tension to the belt. Make sure the belt remains completely engaged with the teeth on the camshaft sprocket and that all timing marks remain aligned. Correct if necessary. Then, tighten the adjusting bolt. Finally, tighten the pivot bolt. Make sure to tighten the bolts in that order, or tension will not be correct. Recheck alignment of the timing marks.

14. Now, turn the engine one full turn clockwise only. Loosen the tensioner pivot bolt and then the adjusting bolt. Allow the tensioner spring to again position the tensioner without interference from bolt friction. Then, tighten the adjusting bolt. Tighten the pivot bolt. Try to pry the belt outward by placing your thumb under the belt and your fingers on the seal line at the right side of the timing belt rear cover. The distance between the back of the belt and seal line will be about .55 in. if the tension is correct.

15. Continue the installation in the reverse order of the removal procedure.

Mirage and Precis

1468cc ENGINE

1. Disconnect the negative battery cable. Remove the cooling fan, spacer, water pump pulley and belt. Remove the timing belt cover.

2. Turn the crankshaft until the timing marks on the camshaft sprocket and cylinder head are aligned. Loosen the tensioning bolt (it runs in the slotted portion of the tensioner) and the pivot bolt on the timing belt tensioner and lever the tensioner as far as it will go toward the water pump. Tighten the adjusting bolt. Mark the timing belt with an arrow showing direction of rotation if you may be reusing it.

3. Pull the timing belt off the camshaft sprocket. Remove the camshaft sprocket.

4. Remove the crankshaft pulley. Then, remove the timing belt.

5. Remove the crankshaft sprocket bolts and remove the crankshaft

sprocket and flange, noting the direction of installation for each. Remove the timing belt tensioner.

6. Inspect all components, as required. Replace defective parts as needed.

7. To install, first reinstall the flange and crankshaft sprocket. The flange must go on first with the chamfered area outward. The sprocket is installed with the boss forward and the studs for the fan belt pulley outward. Install and torque the crankshaft sprocket bolt to 51–72 ft. lbs. Install the camshaft sprocket and bolt, torquing it to 47–54 ft. lbs.

8. Align the timing marks of the camshaft sprocket. Check that the crankshaft timing marks are still in alignment (the locating pin on the front of the crankshaft sprocket is lined up with a mark on the front case).

9. To install the tensioner assembly, mount the tensioner, spring and spacer with the bottom end of the spring free. Then, install the bolts and tighten the adjusting bolt slightly with the tensioner moved as far as possible away from the water pump. Install the free end of the spring into the locating tang on the front case. Position the belt over the crankshaft sprocket and then over the camshaft sprocket. Make sure the belt is straight on the right side (where there's no tensioner as you do this. Slip the back of the belt over the tensioner wheel. Turn the camshaft sprocket in the opposite of its normal direction of rotation until the straight side of the belt is tight and make sure the timing marks line up. If not, shift the belt one tooth at a time in the appropriate direction until this occurs.

10. Install the crankshaft pulley, making sure the pin on the crankshaft sprocket fits through the hole in the rear surface of the pulley. Install the bolts and torque to specification.

11. Loosen the tensioner mounting bolts so the tensioner works, without the interference of any friction, under spring pressure. Make sure the belt follows the curve of the camshaft pulley so that the teeth are engaged all the way around. Correct the path of the belt if necessary. Torque the tensioner adjusting bolt to 15–18 ft. lbs. Then, torque the tensioner pivot bolt to the same figure. Bolts must be torqued in that order, or tension won't be correct.

12. Turn the crankshaft one turn clockwise until timing marks again line up to seat the belt. Then loosen both tensioner attaching bolts and let the tensioner position itself under spring tension as before. Finally, torque the bolts in the proper order

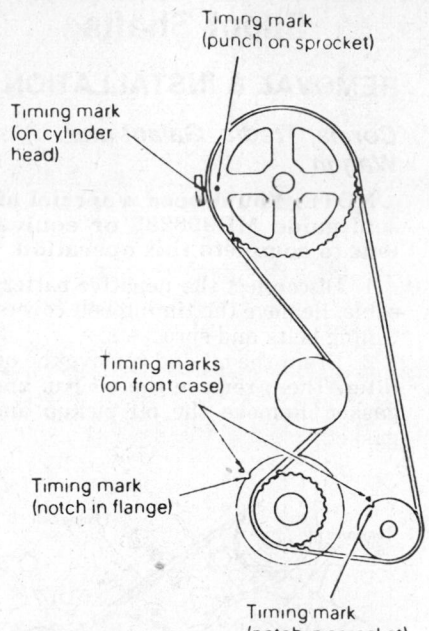

1795 and 1997cc camshaft drive belt timing marks

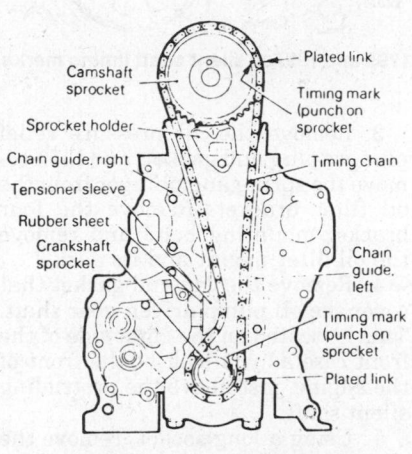

2555cc cam drive timing marks

exactly as before. Check belt tension by putting your fingers on the water pump side of the tensioner wheel and pull the belt toward it with your thumb. The belt should move toward the pump until the teeth are about ¼ of the way across the head of the tensioner adjusting bolt. Retension the belt if necessary.

13. Install the timing belt covers and remaining cooling system parts in the reverse of the removal procedure.

Mirage

1597cc ENGINE

1. Disconnect the negative battery cable. Remove the crankshaft pulley. Remove the upper and lower timing belt covers. Rotate the crankshaft un-

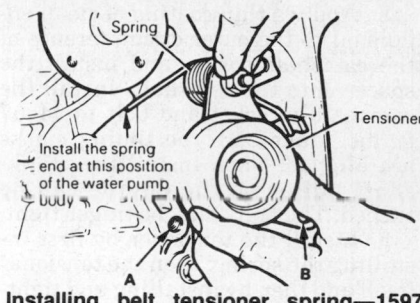

Installing belt tensioner spring—1597 engine

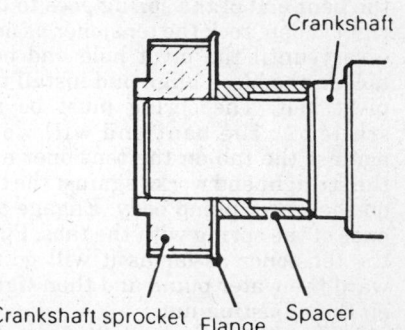

Installation of the crankshaft sprocket—1597 engine

til all timing marks are lined up. There is a pin on the crankshaft sprocket which serves as the timing mark. It lines up with a pin protruding from the block behind the sprocket.

2. Remove the crankshaft sprocket bolt and loosen the other sprocket bolts.

3. Loosen the tensioner mounting and adjusting bolts, shift the tensioner all the way to the left and retighten the adjusting bolt. Mark the timing belt with an arrow in the direction of rotation if it may be reused. Remove the timing belt.

4. Remove the camshaft sprocket, crankshaft sprocket and flange. If necessary, the crankshaft sprocket may be pulled off with a puller such as Mitsubishi part No. MD998311.

5. Remove the tensioner.

6. Inspect all components, as required. Replace defective parts as required.

7. Install the spacer, flange and crankshaft sprocket. The spacer is installed with the larger opening to the rear, so it fits tightly over the crankshaft at the front. Then install the flange with the slightly concave side backward. Finally, install the sprocket with the flat side rearward and boss forward. Install the sprocket bolt and torque to 80–93 ft. lbs. Make sure the sprocket and block timing marks are still lined up. Also check the timing marks for the oil pump drive sprocket and make sure they are lined. up.

8. Apply a thin coating of clean engine oil to the outer circumference of the camshaft spacer and install the spacer onto the camshaft. Install the camshaft sprocket and bolt to 44–57 ft. lbs. Make sure the timing marks are aligned. Then install the crankshaft pulley so the engine can be turned. The bolts may be finger tight.

9. Install the tensioner by first installing the spring, then the tensioner itself and then by installing and tightening the nut (finger tight) used for adjusting the tensioner. Make sure the bent end of the spring goes to the right. Then, rock the tensioner as necessary until the pivot hole and bolt hole in the block align and install the pivot bolt. The spring must be installed so the bent end will work against the tab on the tensioner and the straight end works against the tab on the water pump body. Engage the ends of the spring with the tabs. Push the tensioner as far as it will go toward the water pump and then tighten the adjusting nut.

10. Install the timing belt, first over the crankshaft sprocket and then onto the oil pump sprocket. With the right side straight, engage the belt with the camshaft sprocket. Then, loosen the tensioner adjusting nut so the tensioner will tension the belt.

11. Push the tensioner slightly toward the adjusting nut so that the belt teeth will be forced to mesh with the sprocket teeth. Check to make sure that all teeth have meshed. Finally, with the tensioner under spring tension only, tighten the adjusting nut and then the pivot bolt. Check to make sure all timing marks are in alignment and make corrections if necessary.

12. Turn the crankshaft one full turn in the normal direction of rotation, until all timing marks again align. Turn the engine smoothly and do not allow it to turn backwards. Don't grab the belt to test tension during this procedure. Again loosen the tensioner adjusting nut and mounting bolt, again allowing it to adjust under spring pressure along. Then, torque the tensioner adjusting nut to 16–21 ft. lbs. Finally, tighten the mounting bolt.

13. Test the tension on the belt by grasping the right edge of the rear timing belt cover and using your thumb to pull the center of the belt span toward it. With reasonable pressure, the belt should move to within just under half an inch (0.47 in.) from the seal line. Repeat Steps 11 and 12 if the tension isn't correct.

14. Remove the crankshaft pulley. Install the timing belt lower front cover. Then install the upper cover.

Silent Shafts

REMOVAL & INSTALLATION

Cordia, Tredia, Galant and Wagon

NOTE: You'll need a special oil seal guide MD998285 or equivalent to complete this operation.

1. Disconnect the negative battery cable. Remove the timing belt covers, timing belts and sprockets.

2. Drain the oil and remove the oil filter. Then, remove the oil pan and gasket. Remove the oil pickup and gasket.

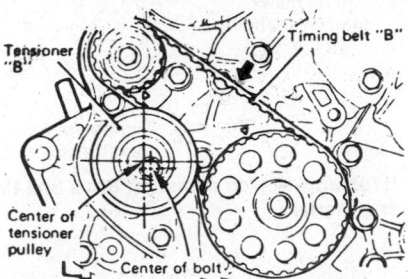

1795 and 1997cc silent shaft timing marks

3. Remove the oil pressure relief plunger plug and gasket, and then remove the spring and plunger from the oil filter bracket. Remove the four bracket mounting bolts and remove the oil filter mount and its gasket.

4. Remove the cap and gasket that cover the oil pump driven gear shaft. This is located on the right side of the front case as you look at the front of the engine, just above the protruding silent shaft.

5. Using a long socket, remove the retaining bolt from the oil pump driven gear (behind the plug removed earlier).

6. Remove the mounting bolts for the front case and remove it from the block. Remove the front case gasket. Then, slide the silent shafts from the block, noting their installation angles.

7. Inspect the silent shaft bearing journals for signs of excessive wear of seizure. If there are signs of critical wear problems, the bushings should also be inspected. The bushings may be replaced by pulling them out and pressing new ones in, using special tools. This is done with the crankshaft removed, since it normally is required only at time of major engine overhaul.

8. Lubricate the silent shaft bearing journals with clean engine oil and install the shafts into the block. Insert the shafts so they are positioned as they were when you removed them (a

suitable tool in the left side of the block will ensure that the left side shaft will be in position).

9. Install a special seal guide to the crankshaft (MD998285–01 or equivalent) so the smaller diameter faces outward. Coat the outer diameter of the seal with clean engine oil. Install a new front case gasket. Then, install the front case by carefully positioning its crankshaft seal over the seal guide and lining up all bolt holes; then, install all eight mounting bolts. Tighten the bolts just finger tight.

10. Install the oil filter mounting bracket gasket and then the mounting bracket and four bolts; torque the front case bolts to 15–19 ft. lbs. and the oil filter mounting bracket bolts to 11–15 ft. lbs.

11. Install the remaining parts in reverse of the removal procedure.

Starion

NOTE: You'll need two long, 8mm bolts to pull out the silent shaft thrust plates and two guides, made by cutting the heads off 6mm bolts about 2 in. long.

1. Disconnect the negative battery cable. Remove the timing cover, chains and sprockets. Before removing the two sprocket bolts, put a wrench on the flange bolt which attaches the upper oil pump gear to the center of the right side silent shaft and turn it just enough to break it loose.

2. Screw 8mm bolts into the bolt holes in the thrust plate and turn them evenly to pull the thrust plate out of the block. Then, remove the left silent shaft.

3. Remove the oil pump mounting bolts. Then, pull the oil pump and gasket straight off the front of the block. The right side silent shaft will come out with the pump. Be careful to support the pump and shaft in such a way that the rear shaft bearing will not be damaged. Remove the bolt from the center of the oil pump driven (upper) gear. Now, separate the silent shaft and key from the oil pump driven gear by sliding it out. Remove the oil pump gasket.

4. Inspect the silent shaft bearing journals for signs of excessive wear or seizure. If there are signs of critical wear problems, the bushings should also be inspected. The busings may be replaced by pulling them out and pressing new ones in , using special tools. This is done with the crankshaft removed, since it normally is required only at time of major engine overhaul.

5. Lubricate the left silent shaft bearing journals with clean engine oil and install the shaft into the block. Insert the shaft so it is positioned as it

was when you removed it (a suitable tool in the left side of the block will ensure that the shaft will be in position).

6. Screw the two guides (made from 6mm headless bolts) into the holes in the block above and below the left side silent shaft. Install a new O-ring with engine oil. Then, install the thrust plate over the guides and into the block. Finally, remove the guides and install the thrust plate mounting bolts, torquing to 7.5–8.5 ft. lbs.

7. Pull the cover off the oil pump housing and verify that the oil pump gears still positioned so the timing marks are aligned. Install the cover over the guide pins and pour about 0.6 cu. in. of clean engine oil into the oil pump outlet (which is at top right as you look at the pump cover). Install the oil pump gasket to the rear of the pump (you may want to use grease to hold it in position). Then, position the pump in its installed direction and engage the key of the right silent shaft to the slot in the oil pump driven gear. Slide the shaft all the way into the pump driven gear and then install the bolt and torque to 44–50 ft. lbs. Lubricate the right side silent shaft bearing journals with clean engine oil and then insert the shaft into the block and install the oil pump. Install the oil pump mounting bolts and torque to 7.5–8.5 ft. lbs.

8. Install the sprockets, timing chains, tensioners and front cover.

Camshaft

REMOVAL & INSTALLATION

Cordia, Tredia, Galant and Wagon

NOTE: On the Wagon it will be necessary to remove the drivers seat and the seat underframe as follows. Remove the drivers seat. Remove the parking brake lever and fuel tank filler door release lever. Remove the battery cover. Remove the bolts retaining the seat underframe in place. Remove the seat underframe.

1. Disconnect the negative battery cable. Remove the distributor. Remove the rocker cover, disconnect the camshaft sprocket and remove the rocker arm shaft and cam bearing assembly. The camshaft may then be lifted off the top of the cylinder head.

2. Check and replace defective components as required.

3. Thoroughly lubricate the camshaft bearing journals, the bear saddles in the cylinder head and the inner surfaces of the caps with clean en-

gine oil. Then continue the installation in the reverse order of the removal procedure.

Starion

1. Disconnect the negative battery cable. Remove the distributor. Remove the rocker cover and rocker shaft assembly. Remove also the rear bearing cap bolts and the cap.

2. Remove the camshaft from the head.

3. Check and replace defective components as required.

4. Thoroughly lubricate the camshaft bearing journals, the bearing saddles in the cylinder head and the inner surfaces of the caps with clean engine oil. Then, install the camshaft onto the cylinder head, being careful not to damage any of the camshaft journals. Apply a sealer to the outside diameter of the circular seal for the rear bearing and install it in the head with one side directly in contact with the rear of the camshaft. The packing will end up under the rearmost portion of the rear bearing cap. Then, install and torque the rocker shaft/bearing cap assembly. Include the rear bearing cap, using the same torque. Refit the cam sprocket and chain to the camshaft.

5. Also inspect the semicircular seal that goes in the front of the timing chain cover and seal the top with an adhesive such as 3M Super Weatherstrip Adhesive 801® or equivalent.

6. Adjust the valve clearances. Install the rocker cover and all other parts removed earlier. Start the engine and idle it until after the temperature gauge indicates normal operating temperature. Then, remove the rocker cover again and adjust the valves with the engine hot.

Mirage and Precis

1468cc ENGINE

1. Disconnect the negative battery cable. Remove the rocker cover, timing belt cover and the distributor.

2. Loosen the two bolts, move the timing belt tensioner toward the water pump as far as it will go and then retighten the timing belt tensioner adjusting bolt. Disengage the timing belt from the camshaft sprocket and then unbolt and remove the sprocket. The timing belt may be left engaged with the crankshaft sprocket and tensioner.

3. Remove the rocker shaft assembly. Remove the small, square cover that sits directly behind the camshaft on the transaxle side of the head. Remove the camshaft thrust case tightening bolt that sits on the top of the head right near that cover.

4. Now, very carefully slide the entire camshaft out of the head through the hold in the camshaft side of the head, being sure the cam lobes do not strike the bearing bores in the head.

5. Check and replace defective components as required.

6. Lubricate all journal and thrust surfaces with clean engine oil and then insert the camshaft into the engine, again keeping the cam lobes from touching the bearing bores. Make sure the camshaft goes in with the threaded hole in the top of the thrust case straight upward and align the bolt hole in the thrust case and the cylinder head surface once the camshaft is all the way inside the head. Install the thrust case bolt and tighten firmly. Finally, install the rear cover with a new gasket and install and tighten the four bolts.

7. Coat the external surface of the front oil seal with engine oil. With a special installer part No. MD998306–01 or equivalent, drive the reusable or new front camshaft oil seal into the clearance between the cam and head at the forward end. Make sure the seal seats fully.

8. Install the camshaft sprocket and torque the bolt to 47–54 ft. lbs. Reconnect the timing belt, check timing and adjust the belt tension. Reinstall the rocker shaft assembly. Adjust the valves. Install the rocker and timing belt covers.

Mirage

1597cc ENGINE

1. Disconnect the negative battery cable. Remove the distributor and remove the rocker cover. Remove the upper timing cover. Turn the engine over until the timing mark on the rear timing belt cover aligns with the mark on the camshaft sprocket. It's a good idea to mark the timing belt itself to align with the marks on the sprocket and rear timing belt cover to make precise reassembly easier. Now, remove the camshaft sprocket from the camshaft and remove the rocker arms and shafts assembly.

2. Pull the camshaft front oil seal off the front of the camshaft. Remove the camshaft.

3. Check and replace defective components as required.

4. Thoroughly lubricate the camshaft bearing journals, the bearing saddles in the cylinder head and the inner surfaces of the caps with clean engine oil.

5. Then, install the camshaft onto the cylinder head, being careful not to damage any of the camshaft journals. Install the rocker arm and shaft as-

sembly to the head, torquing the bolts to 14–15 ft. lbs.

6. Coat the outside diameter of the front end of the camshaft with clean engine oil. Then, with a special tool such as MD998354–01 or equivalent, tap a new front seal in, using a hammer. Install the rear timing belt cover.

7. Turn the camshaft so the dowel pin on the front lines up with the hole in the sprocket. If you need to turn the cam, you can do so by exerting force on either of the two projections behind the No. 2 cylinder exhaust valve cam. Reconnect the camshaft drive sprocket by lifting it off the rest and installing it to the camshaft with the dowel pin going through the hole in the sprocket. Torque the sprocket bolt to 44–57 ft. lbs.

8. Install the remaining parts and adjust the valves.

Piston and Connecting Rod

For all piston and connecting rod overhaul procedures, please refer to "Engine Rebuilding" in the Unit Repair section.

POSITIONING

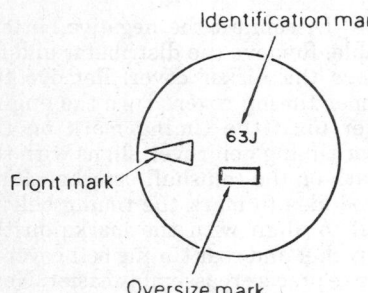

Piston installation

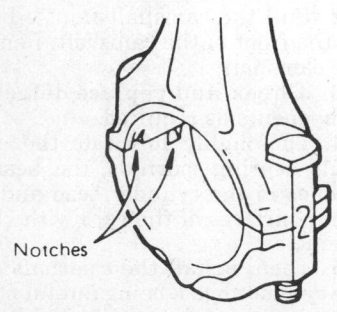

Connecting rod cap installation

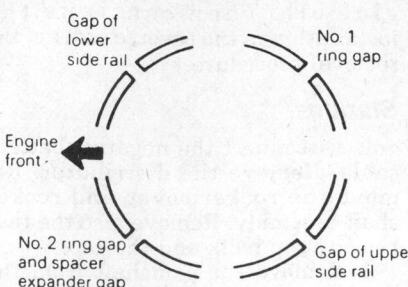

Piston ring positioning

ENGINE LUBRICATION

Oil Pan

REMOVAL & INSTALLATION

1. The oil pan must be pulled downward as much as six inches to clear the oil pickup. In nearly all applications, this requires that the engine mounts be disconnected and the engine raised to clear a crossmember underneath the shallower section of the pan. First, survey the area under the engine to determine whether or not there is clearance, in case, in your particular model the engine can be left in place.

2. Disconnect the negative battery cable. Disconnect all those hoses and wires that would prevent the engine from being lifted the requisite distance for removal of the pan.

3. Support the vehicle in a secure manner far enough above ground for you to get underneath and remove the oil pan bolts. Hook a lift to the hooks on the cylinder head and support the engine. Drain the oil pan.

4. Remove the attaching through bolts from the engine mounts. Raise the engine far enough to gain clearance, as necessary. Remove the oil pan from the vehicle.

5. Installation is the reverse of the removal procedure.

6. On the Mirage 1597cc engine, coat the four seams on the gasket surface for the block with a liquid sealer. These are the joints between the front cover and block on the front and the rear oil seal case and the block at the rear.

7. On the vehicles using gasketless pans, you'll need a tube of liquid sealer part No. MD997110 or equivalent. Cut the end of the tube off at the smallest diameter and run a bead of

sealer around the entire groove in the oil pan. It should be about .16 inch thick. Run the head in back of the bolt holes. The pan should be installed within 15 minutes of the time you apply the sealer. Position the pan, install the bolts and tighten finger tight.

8. Torque the bolts alternately and in several stages.

Rear Main Bearing Oil Seal

REMOVAL & INSTALLATION
Cordia, Tredia, Galant, Wagon and Starion

1. Remove the transaxle or transmission and clutch from the vehicle. Remove the flywheel or driveplate and adapter plate.

2. Unbolt and remove the lower bell housing cover from the rear of the engine. Remove the rear plate from the upper portion of the rear of the block.

3. The lower surface of the oil seal case seals against the oil pan gasket or sealer at the rear. On engines with a gasket, carefully separate the gasket from the bottom of the seal case with a moderately sharp instrument. You may want to loosen the oil pan bolts slightly at the rear to make it easier to separate the two surfaces. If the gasket is damaged, the oil pan will have to be removed and the gasket replaced. On vehicles employing sealer, you'll have to unbolt and lower the oil pan now, and then clean both surfaces, apply new sealer and reinstall the oil pan after Step 7 is completed.

4. Remove the oil seal case bolts and pull it straight off the rear of the crankshaft. Remove the case gasket.

5. Remove the seal retainer or oil separator from the case, and then pry out the seal. Inspect the sealing surface at the rear of the crankshaft. If a deep groove is worn into the surface, the crankshaft will have to be replaced. Lubricate the sealing surface with clean engine oil.

6. Using a seal installer such as MD998376–01 and MD990938–01, install the new seal into the bore of rear oil seal case in such a way that the flat side of the seal will face outward when the case is installed on the engine. The inside of the seal must be flush with the inside surface of the seal case.

7. Install the retainer or oil separator directly over the seal with the small hole located directly at the bottom. Then, install a new gasket onto the block surface and install the seal case to the rear of the block. Retorque

pan bolts, as necessary. Refill the oil pan if necessary.

8. Install the rear plate and bell housing cover. Install the flywheel or drive plate and the transaxle in reverse of the removal procedure.

Mirage and Precis

1. Remove the transaxle or manual transaxle and clutch from the vehicle. Remove the flywheel or driveplate and adapter plate.

2. Unbolt and remove the rear plate from the rear of the block. On the Mirage with the 1597cc engine, use a moderately sharp instrument and separate the rear portion of the oil pan gasket from the lower surface of the rear main seal case on the back of the block. You may want to loosen the oil pan bolts slightly at the rear to make it easier to separate the two surfaces. If the gasket is damaged, drain the oil pan and remove it. On the 1468cc engine, drain the oil pan and remove it, as the sealing surfaces must be cleaned and new sealer applied all around.

3. Unbolt the oil seal case and then pull it straight back and off the crankshaft. Remove the case gasket. Pry the old seal out of the case.

4. Inspect the sealing surface at the rear of the crankshaft. If a deep groove is worn into the surface, the crankshaft will have to be replaced. Press a new seal into the case with a special seal installing tool such as MD998011. The seal must be pressed in square until it bottoms in the case.

5. Oil the crankshaft sealing surfaces and the lips of the new seal. On the Mirage with the 1597cc engine spread a liquid sealer thoroughly around those areas which butt up against the block and oil pan gasket at the bottom surface and on the front at both sides. Then, install the seal, gasket and seal case straight over the crankshaft sealing surface. Install and tighten the five case bolts.

6. On the 1468cc engine, install sealer and reinstall the oil pan. On the Mirage with the 1597cc engine reinstall the pan with a new gasket, if necessary, or retorque pan bolts, as necessary.

7. Reinstall the transaxle. Make sure the engine oil pan is refilled with clean engine oil, if necessary.

Oil Pump

REMOVAL & INSTALLATION

Cordia, Tredia, Galant and Wagon

1. Disconnect the negative battery cable. Remove the timing belt cover, timing belts and sprockets. Drain the oil pan.

2. The front oil pan bolts screw into the front case, onto which the oil pump is mounted. On 1983–84 models, you may be able to loosen the oil pan bolts, use a sharp instrument to separate the gasket and front cover and remove the cover without replacing the gasket. This avoids lifting the engine. On 1985–88 models using sealer, you'll have to remove the oil pan.

3. Remove the oil filter. Remove the oil screen and gasket. Remove the oil relief plunger plug and gasket. Then, remove the relief spring and plunger from the oil filter bracket.

4. Remove the four oil filter bracket mounting bolts and remove the bracket.

5. Remove the cap from the oil pump area of the front case. This is slightly to the right and above the silent shaft on the driver's side of the vehicle. Remove the plug from the left side of the block (near the front case) and insert a suitable tool at least 2.4 in. long to retain the position of the silent shaft.

6. Remove the retaining bolt for the left silent shaft retaining bolts. Use a deep well socket. Now, remove the mounting bolts and remove the front case from the front of the block.

7. Remove the oil pump cover mounting bolts from the rear of the front case and remove the oil pump cover. Remove the gears from the front case.

8. Install the oil pump cover to the front case and torque the five bolts to 11–13 ft. lbs.

9. Install a special oil seal guide, Part No. MD998285–01 to the front of the crankshaft, with the smaller diameter facing outward. Install a new front case gasket to the block. Install the front case and install and tighten the eight mounting bolts just slightly. Remove the seal guide.

10. Install the oil pump gear and left silent shaft retaining bolt and torque to 25–28 ft. lbs.

11. Install the oil filter bracket and gasket. Tighten all the front case mounting bolts to 15–19 ft. lbs. and those going through the oil filter bracket to 11–15 ft. lbs. Install the cap that covers the oil pump shaft.

12. Coat the oil pressure relief plunger with clean engine oil and insert it into the bore, followed by the spring. Install the plug and gasket and torque the plug to 29–36 ft. lbs.

13. Install the oil screen and gasket.

14. Install the oil pan in reverse of removal. Install the sprockets, tensioners and timing belts and tension

them to specification. Install the timing covers and engine accessories. Make sure to refill the oil pan with the full capacity of clean engine oil. Idle the engine and make sure oil pressure builds up within a reasonable length of time.

Starion

1. Disconnect the negative battery cable. Remove the front cover. Follow the procedure above for removal of timing chains and sprockets up to Step 3, but make sure you unscrew and remove the bolt for the right side silent shaft (just above the oil pump drive sprocket) before you remove the chain. In other words, you'll be removing the timing chain for the silent shafts and securing the plunger for the camshaft timing chain tensioner, but you won't be disturbing the camshaft timing chain. You may also leave the crankshaft sprocket that drives the silent shaft chain in place.

2. Remove the oil pump relief valve plug, spring and plunger. Then, remove the oil pump mounting bolts and remove the pump assembly and gasket. Remove the cover from the rear of the oil pump.

3. Oil the oil pump gears and the inner walls of the pump housing thoroughly with engine oil. Install the gears into the oil pump housing with the two timing marks directly across from one another. If the timing marks aren't lined up, the silent shaft will be out of phase and the engine will vibrate severly!

4. Install the pump cover over the two pins on the rear of the pump. Pour about 0.6 cu. in. of oil into the pump outlet (at top right, looking at the rear cover). Place the gasket over the two locator pins.

5. Install the pump onto the front of the block, engaging the keyway slot in the upper oil pump gear with the key on the right silent shaft and fitting the locating pins into the holes in the front of the block. Install the oil pump mounting bolts and torque in several stages and alternately to 7.5–8.5 ft. lbs. Install the bolt that attaches the right silent shaft to the upper oil pump gear.

6. Remove the securing wire from the timing chain tensioner. Reinstall the oil pump relief valve spring, plunger and cap and torque the cap to 22–32 ft. lbs.

7. Install the timing chains and sprockets. When the timing chain for the silent shafts is installed, torque the bolt that attaches the right silent shaft gear to 44–50 ft. lbs.

8. Install the front cover. Make sure the engine oil pan is full to the correct level. Start the engine, idling

it and making sure oil pressure is built up within a reasonable length of time. Check for leaks and repair as necessary.

Mirage and Precis

NOTE: On the 1468cc engine, the front case must be removed to gain access to the oil pump. On the Mirage with the 1597cc engine, the oil pump is bolted to the front of the front case. You may wish to leave the front case in place and simply remove the timing belt covers and belts to gain access to the pump. If you are doing a complete overhaul, you may want to follow the procedure as written in order to replace the oil pan gasket and other parts.

1. Disconnect the negative battery cable. Remove the timing belt cover and timing belt.

2. Drain the oil and then remove the oil pan. Unbolt the oil pickup and screen from the front case and remove it.

3. Remove the front cover with the oil pump assembled to it. On the 1468cc engine, pull the cover straight off to avoid damaging the crankshaft seal.

4. Put the cover on a clean bench. Remove the oil pump relief valve plug and gasket, spring and plunger.

5. Remove the attaching nut and then remove the oil pump sprocket on the Mirage with the 1597cc engine. On the 1468cc engine, turn the cover over. Then, remove the bolts and remove the oil pump cover from the case.

6. Installation is the reverse of the removal procedure. Repair or replace defective components as required.

ENGINE COOLING

Radiator

REMOVAL & INSTALLATION

Cordia, Tredia, Mirage and Galant

1. Disconnect the negative battery cable. Disconnect the electrical connector for the fan motor. Drain the coolant into a clean container.

2. Disconnect the upper and lower radiator hoses and the overflow tank at the radiator. If the vehicle has an automatic transaxle, disconnect the

two hoses for the transmission cooler at the lower tank and plug all openings. Then, remove the two mounting bolts from the rear of the radiator, lift the unit out of the bushings at the front crossmember and remove it. On Galant note that the radiator is held at the top by two brackets which must be unbolted from the top of the panel in front of the radiator.

3. Remove the fan and electric motor from the radiator, transferring it to a new unit, if necessary.

4. Install the unit in reverse order, making sure the prongs on the lower tank fit securely into the bushings on the crossmember. Refill the radiator with clean coolant and run the engine until the thermostat opens. Refill the radiator with coolant as necessary, install the cap and then fill the overflow tank. If the vehicle has an automatic transmission, check the fluid level and if necessary refill the transmission.

Starion

1. Disconnect and remove the battery. Drain the coolant into a clean container.

2. Remove the two bolts on either side of the radiator and remove the upper and lower fan shrouds. Disconnect the upper and lower hoses at the radiator. Disconnect the overflow tank hose at the filler cap opening.

3. Then, remove the four radiator mounting bolts, two on either side and remove the radiator.

4. Install the unit in reverse order. Refill the radiator with clean coolant and run the engine until the thermostat opens. Refill the radiator with coolant as necessary, install the cap and then fill the overflow tank.

Precis

1. Disconnect the negative battery cable. Remove the splash shield from under the vehicle.

2. Drain the radiator.

3. Remove the fan shroud and disconnect the fan motor wiring harness.

4. Disconnect the radiator hoses and, if equipped, the automatic transmission cooler hoses.

5. Disconnect the expansion tank hose.

6. Remove the radiator mounting bolts and lift out the radiator and fan assembly.

7. Installation is the reverse of removal.

Wagon

NOTE: It will be necessary to remove the drivers seat and the seat underframe as follows. Remove the drivers seat. Remove

the parking brake lever and fuel tank filler door release lever. Remove the battery cover. Remove the bolts retaining the seat underframe in place. Remove the seat underframe.

1. Disconnect the negative battery cable. Drain the cooling system.

2. Remove the radiator shroud. Disconnect and plug the transmissions lines if equipped with automatic transmission.

3. Disconnect the upper and lower radiator hoses. Remove the overflow tank.

4. Remove the radiator retaining bolts. Remove the radiator from the vehicle.

5. Installation is the reverse of the removal procedure.

Water Pump

REMOVAL & INSTALLATION

Cordia, Tredia, Galant, Mirage and Precis

1. Disconnect the negative battery cable. Loosen the four bolts attaching the water pump pulley to the pulley flange. Loosen the alternator mounting bolts, slide the alternator toward the engine and remove the belt. Drain the radiator.

2. Remove the four bolts attaching the water pump pulley to the pump flange and remove the pulley. Remove the timing belt covers and timing belt tensioner.

3. Remove the five water pump mounting bolts. Remove the pump and gasket, disconnecting the outlet at the water pipe (don't lose the O-ring).

4. Clean gasket surfaces and coat a new gasket with sealer. Then, position the gasket on the front of the block with all bolt holes lined up. Replace the O-ring for the outlet water pipe.

5. Install the pump over a new gasket, connecting the outlet water pipe.

6. Install the remaining parts in reverse order. Final tigtening of the water pump pulley bolts is done most easily after the V-belt has been installed and tensioned somewhat. Recheck tension after the pulley bolts are tightened. Close the radiator drain and refill the system. Run the engine until the thermostat opens and then add coolant until the level stabilizes before replacing the radiator cap. Check for leaks.

Starion

1. Disconnect the negative battery cable. Drain the radiator.

2. Loosen the four nuts attaching the clutch fan to the water pump studs; then, loosen the adjusting and mounting bolts for the alternator, rock it toward the engine and remove the belt. Remove the four bolts for the fan shrouds from the rear of the radiator and romovo tho upper and lower shrouds. Now, loosen the nuts and remove them together with the lockwashers. Then, remove the fan clutch unit, storing the fan clutch in its normal altitude to keep the fluid from migrating to the wrong portions of the unit. Remove the pulley from the studs.

3. Disconnect the lower radiator hose at the pump by loosening the clamp and pulling the hose off. Then, remove the mounting bolts from the pump and then remove the pump and gasket from the front of the block.

4. Clean both gasket surfaces thoroughly and coat both sides of a new gasket and both gasket surfaces with sealer.

5. Install the gasket onto the block and then position the water pump over the gasket. Install the bolts in the proper positions.

6. Install the remaining parts in reverse order.

7. Refill the radiator with clean antifreeze and water mixed 50/50. Run the engine until the thermostat opens, refill the radiator as necessary, install the cap and check for leaks.

Wagon

NOTE: It will be necessary to remove the drivers seat and the seat underframe as follows. Remove the drivers seat. Remove the parking brake lever and fuel tank filler door release lever. Remove the battery cover. Remove the bolts retaining the seat underframe in place. Remove the seat underframe.

1. Disconnect the negative battery cable. Drain the cooling system.

2. Remove the radiator shroud. Remove the drive belts. Remove the cooling fan.

3. Remove the water pump pulley. Remove the tension pulley bracket if the vehicle is equipped with air condition. Disconnect the lower radiator hose.

4. Remove the crankshaft pulley. Remove the upper and lower timing belt covers. Remove the timing belts.

5. Remove the water pipe connection. Remove the water pump retaining bolts. Remove the water pump from the engine.

6. Installation is the reverse of the removal procedure.

Thermostat

REMOVAL & INSTALLATION

NOTE: On the Wagon it will be necessary to remove the drivers seat and the seat underframe as follows. Remove the drivers seat. Remove the parking brake lever and fuel tank filler door release lever. Remove the battery cover. Remove the bolts retaining the seat underframe in place. Remove the seat underframe.

1. Disconnect the negative battery cable. Drain the coolant below the level of the thermostat.

2. Remove the two retaining bolts and lift the thermostat housing off the intake manifold with the hose still attached. If you are careful, it is not necessary to remove the upper radiator hose.

3. Lift the thermostat out of the manifold.

4. Installation is the reverse of the removal procedure.

EMISSION CONTROLS

Please refer to "Emission Control" in the unit repair section for system maintenance procedures. Due to the complex nature of modern electronic engine control systems, comprehensive diagnosis and testing procedures fall outside the confines of this repair manual. For complete information on diagnosis, testing and repair procedures concerning all modern engine and emission control systems, please refer to "Chilton's Guide to Electronic Engine Controls".

FUEL SYSTEM

Fuel Filter

REMOVAL & INSTALLATION

1. On carbureted models, remove the inlet and outlet fuel lines from the filter connections after loosening the fuel line clamps. Remove the old filter. Install the new filter in the reverse order.

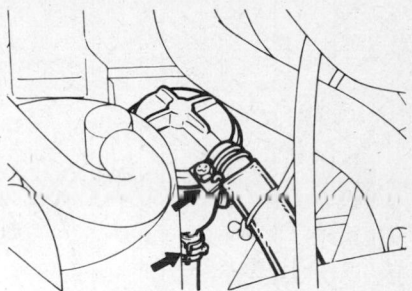
Fuel filter with carbureted engines

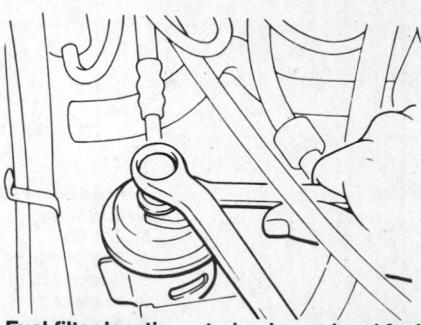
Fuel filter location—turbocharged and fuel injected engines

2. On fuel injected and turbocharged models, the underhood filter is replaced after first reducing fuel line pressure. Hold the side filter nut securely and remove the mounts. Disconnect the lines and remove the filter. Install the new filter in reverse order.

Mechanical Fuel pump

PRESSURE TESTING

1. Disconnect the fuel line from the carburetor. Attach a pressure tester to the end of the line.

2. Crank the engine. If fuel pump pressure is not within specification replace the fuel pump.

REMOVAL & INSTALLATION

1. Disconnect the negative battery cable. Remove the distributor cap to check the direction of the rotor, and then turn the engine over until the pointer near the front pulley is at Top Dead Center and the rotor points to the ignition wire for No. 1 cylinder, indicating that No. 1 is at firing position. Disconnect the negative battery cable.

2. Disconnect the fuel lines by using a pair of pliers to shift clamps away from the nipples on the pump and then pulling the lines off with a twisting motion. Note the locations at which lines connect.

3. Remove the two mounting bolts

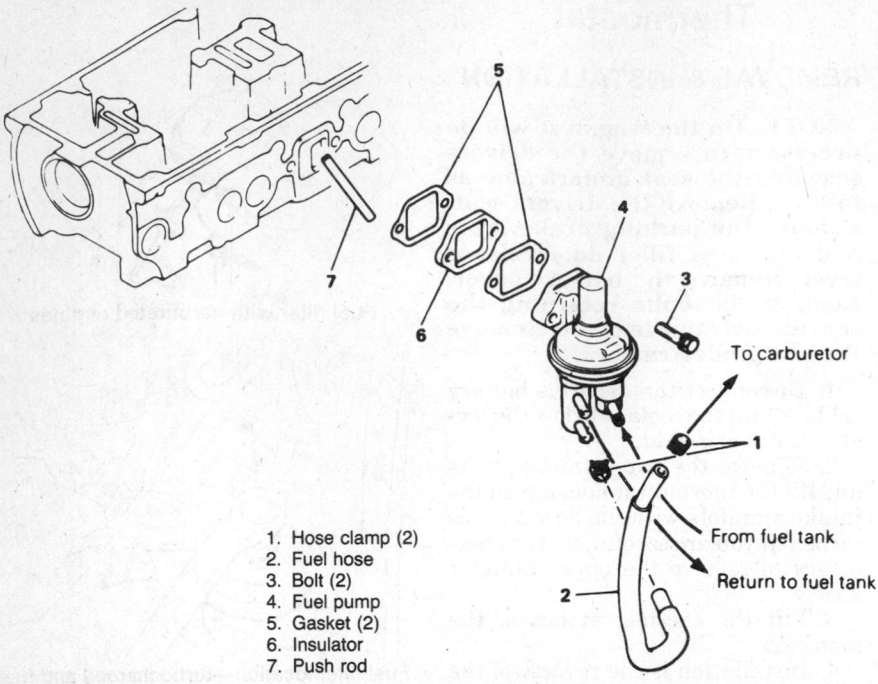

1. Hose clamp (2)
2. Fuel hose
3. Bolt (2)
4. Fuel pump
5. Gasket (2)
6. Insulator
7. Push rod

Mechanical fuel pump

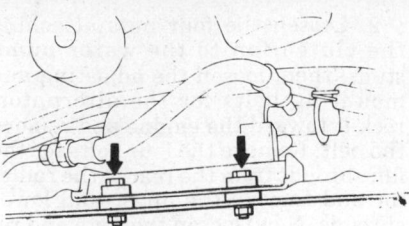

Externally mounted electric fuel pump mounting bolts

from the head, and then remove the pump, spacer, and gasket(s) from the head. As you pull the pump off the head, catch the pushrod which is located just behind the pump.

4. Inspect the pump as follows: There is a small breather hole in the area of the pump above the diaphragm which vents the pump's upper chamber. Leakage of fuel or oil here indicates that the pump's diaphragm or oil seal is leaking and that the unit should be replaced. Also, inspect the end of the pushrod and the wear surface where the pushrod engages with the pump operating lever. Replace the pushrod or pump if there is obvious wear. If the camshaft end of the pushrod is badly worn you should remove the cam cover and inspect the camshaft eccentric which operates the fuel pump for excessive wear.

5. Clean the gasket surfaces of the insulator, pump and cylinder head. Insert the two bolts through the pump's mounting base. Slide a new gasket, the insulator, and a second new gasket into position over the two bolts. Turn the pump so its mounting surface faces the cylinder head.

6. Locate the pump pushrod against the cupped surface of the operating lever and angle it upward in the position it was in during removal. Hold the pushrod at that angle as you insert it into the bore in the head. Once the pushrod is in the bore in the cylinder head, you can release it with your fingers and move the pump toward the head following the installa-

tion angle of the pushrod. Start the two bolts into the bores in the head and tighten them finger tight.

7. Tighten the mounting bolts alternately and evenly. Inspect the hoses for cracks (even hairline cracks can leak) and replace if necessary. Then, reconnect the fuel hoses. Make sure the hoses are installed all the way onto the nipples and then work the clamps into position. Make sure the clamps are located well past the bulged portion of the nipples but do not sit at the extreme inner ends of the hoses. Replace the distributor cap. Start the engine and check for leaks.

Electric Fuel Pump

REMOVAL & INSTALLATION

1. Start the engine and allow it to idle. Disconnect the electric fuel pump connector (accessible by removing a panel in the floor of the trunk). Allow the engine to continue running until it stalls to relieve the pressure in the fuel lines.

2. If the vehicle is equipped with a drain plug remove it and drain the fuel into a suitable container. Support the vehicle safely. Remove the left rear wheel.

3. Support the fuel tank with a floor jack. Loosen the fuel tank band mounting nuts and lower the tank for access to the pump support. Then, remove the nut and bolt attaching the pump clamp to the support.

4. Disconnect the fuel lines, noting their locations and remove the pump. If the pump is being replaced, switch the mounting clamp to the new pump and install it at the same angle. Installation is the reverse of the removal procedure. Make sure fuel line connections are tight and secure. Operate the pump and check for leaks.

Carburetor

REMOVAL & INSTALLATION

1. Disconnect the negative battery cable. Remove the solenoid valve wiring.

2. Disconnect the air cleaner breather hose, air duct and vacuum tube.

3. Remove the air cleaner.

4. Remove the air cleaner case.

5. Disconnect the accelerator and shift cables (automatic transmission) at the carburetor.

6. Disconnect the purge valve hose; remove the vacuum compensator and fuel lines.

7. Drain the coolant.

8. Remove the water hose between the carburetor and the cylinder head.

9. Remove the carburetor.

10. Installation is the reverse of removal.

ACCELERATOR CABLE ADJUSTMENT

1983 Cordia and Tredia, 1983-88 Starion

1. Run the engine until it is hot so the fast idle cam will not effect the throttle setting.

2. Check the action of the accelerator pedal. There should be minimal play between the normal, resting position of the pedal and the point where play in the cable is taken up and the throttle starts to move 0–0.08 in. (0–0.04 in. for Starion).

3. If there is excessive play, loosen the cable adjusting nuts located on the cable mount on the carburetor and shift their position on the outer cable as necessary to remove the play.

Then, tighten them together in opposite directions on the cable mount.

1984–88 Cordia and Tredia, 1985–88 Mirage and 1987–88 Precis

1. The engine must be hot so the fast idle cam will not interfere with throttle position; warm it if necessary.

2. Inspect the inner cable to see if there is slack. If there is no slack, the adjustment is okay. If there is slack, loosen the adjusting nuts until the throttle is free to assume idle position with no effect by the accelerator cable.

3. Make sure there are no sharp bends in the cable. Then, turn the adjusting nut that's farther away from the carburetor until you can see the throttle start to move; now, back the nut off ½ turn on the Cordia and Tredia and one turn on the Mirage. Secure the locknut.

FLOAT/FUEL LEVEL ADJUSTMENT

1983 Cordia and Tredia

Checking and adjusting the float level on this carburetor requires that you use a special tool that resembles an eyedropper. You can use Mitsubishi special tool MD998161 or equivalent.

1. Float level is checked with the carburetor mounted in the normal position on the vehicle. Start and run the engine at idle speed for a short time before checking the level. Fuel may evaporate out of the carburetor, lowering the level, especially when the engine is very hot or the vehicle sits for a long time.

2. Remove the air cleaner and then, remove the plug that gives access to the float bowl. The plug is located just to one side of the fuel inlet fitting.

3. Hold the top of the special tool and turn the lower portion, the guide collar. The top of the threads inside the guide collar must be four lines (0.16 in.) below the bold line on the upper portion of the tool.

4. Now, insert the gauge into the level checking hole until the bottom end of the guide collar touches the plug seat. Make sure it goes in straight. Push the top of the rubber squirt head down a little to verify that fuel is being drawn up. If there is no gasoline in the gauge, remove it and turn the collar half a turn upward and reinsert the tool into the carburetor. When gas comes up into the tool, remove it, turn the collar half a turn downward to permit you to read the fuel level and read it. It should be be-

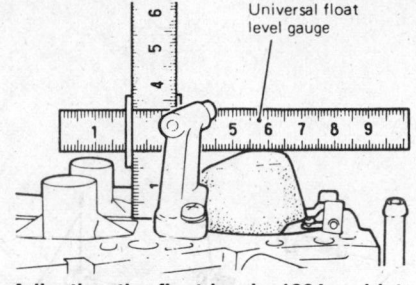

Adjusting the float level—1984 and later models

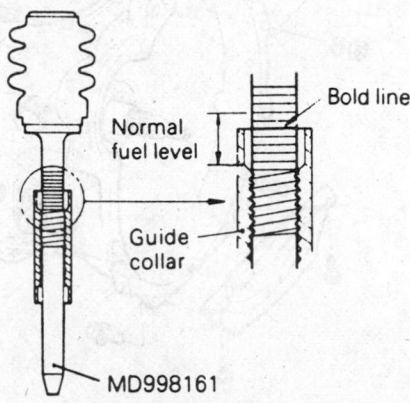

Adjusting the special took for checking float level on '83 carburetors

tween 0.08 in. below the bold line and 0.04 in. above it. If the fuel level is correct, replace the plug. Otherwise, proceed with the steps that follow.

5. Remove the screws and remove the float chamber cover. Invert it, pull out the float lever pin and remove it and the float. Remove the needle valve.

6. Remove the float seat retainer and then gently pull out the seat with a pair of pliers (squeezing the seat too hard could distort it). You'll need a shim set, Mitsubishi part MD606952. To raise the float level, use a thinner shim; to lower it, increase the thickness of the shim. Shims in the kit are 0.008, 0.012 and 0.02 in. in thickness.

7. Install the parts in reverse order, including the cover plug and air cleaner. Start the engine and allow it to idle briefly. Recheck the float level with the special tool and make further adjustments as necessary.

1984–88 Cordia and Tredia, 1985–88 Mirage and 1987–88 Precis

1. Invert the float chamber cover and remove the gasket. Use a float level gauge or depth gauge to measure the distance between that is normally the bottom of the float (the top surface in this position) and what is

normally the lower surface of the float chamber cover. This dimension must be 0.7476–0.8204 in.

2. If the dimension is not to specification, the shim under the needle seat must be changed. Use a thicker seat to raise the dimension (lower the float level). You can use a Mitsubishi shim kit MD606952 or equivalent. The kit contains shims of 0.0118, 0.0157 and 0.0196 in. The change in float level will be three times the change in shim thickness. You can use multiple shims if that is what is necessary to get the right dimension.

3. To change the shim, first pull out the float hinge pin. Then, remove the float and the needle. Finally, use a pair of pliers to unscrew the needle seat by the widest dimensioned area of the seat. Slip the shim(s) over the narrow portion of the seat and then reinstall it, tightening it gently by the same portion of the assembly. Reassemble the needle, float and hinge pin and retest the dimension. Reshim if necessary.

THROTTLE OPENER ADJUSTMENT

1984–88 Cordia and Tredia (1997cc Engine with Manual Transmission), 1985–88 Mirage and 1987–88 Precis (1468cc Engine)

1. Check and if necessary adjust the normal idle speed.

2. Locate the throttle opener on the top of the carburetor. The throttle return spring is attached to a bracket right on top of the throttle opener. Follow the vacuum line leading out of the throttle opener to the throttle opener to the throttle opener solenoid. The engine should be idling at normal operating temperature with the transmission in neutral. Connect a tachometer.

3. Connect a jumper wire to the positive battery terminal. Then, disconnect the electrical lead at the throttle opener solenoid and connect the other end of the jumper wire to the solenoid connector. Open the throttle until the engine reaches about 200 rpm and then slowly release the throttle.

4. Check the engine speed. It should be 750 rpm on 1985–88 Cordia and Tredia and 850 rpm on the Mirage and Precis; 1984 Cordia and Tredia figures are 700 with Tredia and 850 rpm on the Mirage; 1984 Cordia and Tredia figures are 700 with manual transaxle and 750 automatic. Adjust the throttle opener adjusting screw to achieve the correct rpm. This

screw has finger grips on it and is located on the lower portion of the throttle opener. Check that the rpm remains at the correct level. Readjust it, as necessary, until it remains at the correct level.

5. Disconnect the jumper wire and reconnect the throttle opener solenoid wire.

IDLE-UP ADJUSTMENT

1984 Cordia and Tredia (1997cc Engine with Air Conditioning)

1. The engine must be at normal operating temperature. Wheels must be in straight ahead position so there is no load on the power steering pump. Disconnect the electric fan motor connector. Apply the parking brake and make sure the transmission is in neutral. Turn the air conditioner on.

2. Connect a tachometer. Using the throttle opener adjust screw located near the throttle return spring mount on top of the carburetor, adjust the rpm to 850. Make sure the rpm stays steady at this level, readjusting it if necessary. Reconnect the cooling fan electrical connector.

AUTOMATIC CHOKE ADJUSTMENT

All carburetors have a tamper proof choke assembly which is factory adjusted. Choke adjustment is not required during service, except when major carburetor overhaul or choke calibration is required.

OVERHAUL

For all carburetor overhaul procedures, please refer to "Carburetor Service" in the Unit Repair section.

Fuel Injection

Due to the complex nature of modern fuel injection systems, comprehensive diagnosis and testing procedures fall outside the confines of this repair manual. For complete information on fuel injection diagnosis, testing and repair procedures please refer to *"Chilton's Guide to Fuel Injection and Feedback Carburetors"*.

MANUAL TRANSMISSION

REMOVAL & INSTALLATION

1. Disconnect the negative battery

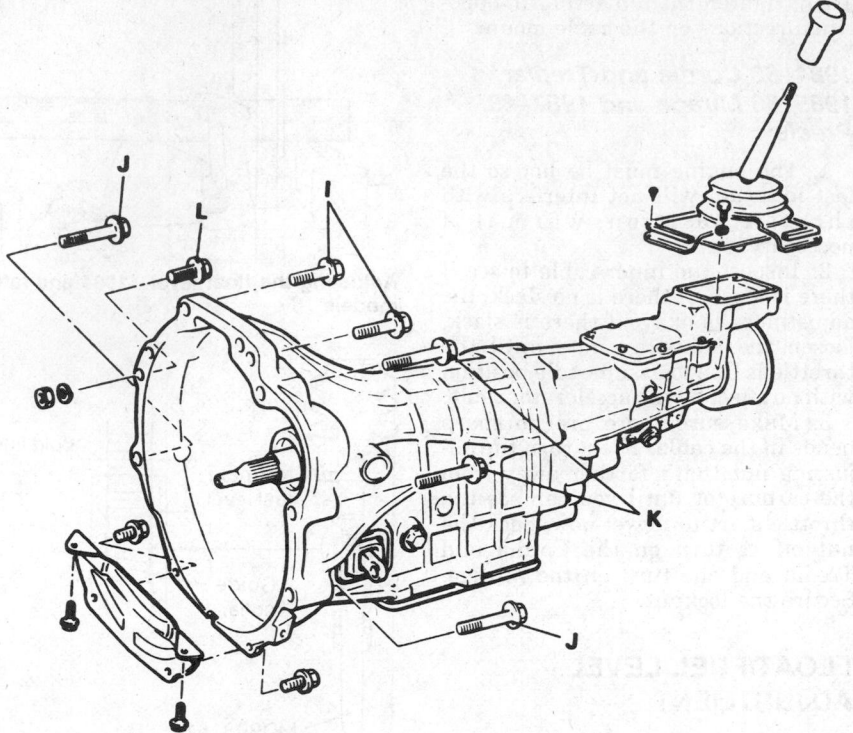

Torque labeled bolts as follows on the Starion transmission: I and J—31-40 ft. lbs; K—16-23 ft. lbs.; L—14-20 ft. lbs.

cable. Remove the air cleaner. Remove the starter.

2. Remove the top transmission mounting bolts from the bell housing.

3. From inside the vehicle, raise the console assembly and remove the dust cover retaining plate at the shift lever.

4. Place the transmission in the neutral position. Remove the control lever assembly.

5. Raise the vehicle and support it safely. Drain the transmission. Disconnect the speedometer and the backup light switch.

6. Remove the driveshaft. Disconnect the exhaust pipe. Remove the clutch cable or slave cylinder and linkage.

7. Support the engine and transmission and remove the engine rear support bracket. Drain the transmission, as required.

8. Remove the bell housing cover and bolts, move the transmission rearward and lower it carefully to the floor. Remove the transmission from under the vehicle.

9. To install the transmission, reverse the removal procedure. Torque the transmission to engine bolts to the figures shown in the illustration. Make sure the transmission is in the proper gear before installing the gear shift lever.

OVERHAUL

For all manual transmission overhaul procedures, please refer to "Manual Transmission" in the unit repair section.

MANUAL TRANSAXLE

REMOVAL & INSTALLATION

Cordia, Tredia and Galant

1. Disconnect the negative battery cable. Remove the battery and battery tray. Remove the coolant and windshield reservoir tanks. Remove the air cleaner and housing.

2. Disconnect from the transaxle; the clutch cable or slave cylinder, speedometer cable, backup light harness, starter motor and the upper bolts connecting the engine to the transaxle.

3. Raise and support the vehicle safely.

4. Remove the front wheels, Remove the engine splash shield.

5. Remove the shift rod and extension. It may be necessary to remove any heat shields that interfere with your progress.

6. Drain the transaxle fluid.

7. Remove the right and left driveshafts from the transaxle case.

8. Disconnect the range selector cable (if equipped). Remove the engine rear cover.

9. Support the weight of the engine from above. Remove the bell housing cover. Support the transaxle and remove the remaining lower mounting bolts.

10. Remove the transaxle mount insulator bolt and the cover from inside the front fender shield. Remove the insulator bracket mounting bolts and remove the bracket. Remove the transaxle mount bracket.

11. Remove (slide away from the engine) and lower the transaxle.

12. Reverse the removal procedure in install. Torque the mounting bolts to specification. Use new driveshaft retaining rings. Adjust the gearshift lever and range selector lever.

Mirage and Precis

1. Remove the battery and battery tray. On turbocharged vehicles, remove the air cleaner housing assembly.

2. On five speed transaxles, disconnect the electrical connector for the selector control valve. On turbocharged vehicles, remove the actuator mounting bolts, remove the actuator to shaft pin and then remove the actuator. Replace the collar with a new part.

3. Disconnect and remove the speedometer and clutch cables.

4. Disconnect the backup lamp electrical connector. Remove the starter motor electrical harness.

5. Remove the six transaxle mounting bolts accessible from the top side of the transaxle.

6. Unbolt and remove the starter motor.

7. Raise the vehicle and support it safely. Then, remove the splash shield from under the engine. Drain the transaxle fluid.

8. Disconnect the extension rod and the shift rod at the transaxle end and lower them.

9. Disconnect the stabilizer bar at the lower control arm.

10. Remove the driveshafts.

11. Support the transaxle from below with a floorjack or similar device. Make sure the support is widely enough spread that the transmission pan will not be damaged. Then, remove the five attaching bolts and remove the bell housing cover.

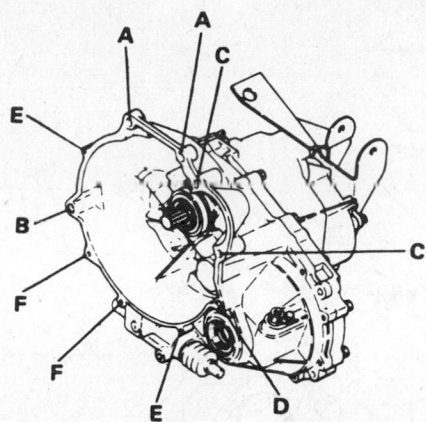

Torque Cordia/ Tredia and Mirage transaxle bolts as follows (all figs. in ft. lbs.): A—31-40; B—31-40; C—16-23; D—22-25; E—7-9; F—11-16.

12. Remove the lower bolts attaching the transaxle to the engine.

13. Remove the transaxle insulator mount bolt. Remove the cover from inside the right fender shield and remove the transaxle support bracket.

14. Remove the transaxle mount bracket.

15. Pull the assembly away from the engine and then lower it from the vehicle.

16. Installation is the reverse of removal. Refill the transmission with the specified fluid to the level of the filler plug. Adjust the clutch cable. Make sure the gearshift lever works correctly.

OVERHAUL

For all manual transmission or transaxle overhaul procedures, please refer to "Manual Transaxle" in the Unit Repair section.

CLUTCH

REMOVAL & INSTALLATION

1. Disconnect the negative battery cable. Remove the transmission. It is recommended that a clutch aligning tool be inserted in the clutch disc during disassembly.

2. Diagonally remove pressure plate bolts a little at a time each. Then remove the pressure plate and driven disc.

3. From inside the transmission bell housing, remove the return spring clip and remove the release

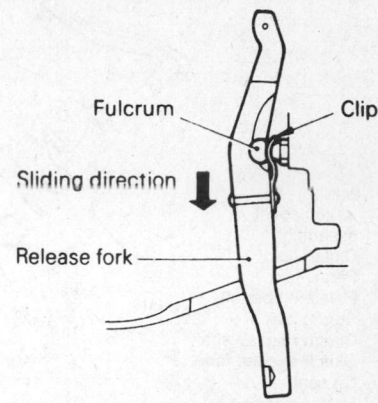

Release fork removal—Starion

bearing assembly. On the Starion, remove the release fork by sliding it in the direction of the arrow to disengage the fulcrum from the clip. Attempting to remove it any other way will damage the clip.

4. If necessary, remove the release control lever and spring pin with a 3/16 inch punch. Always replace spring pins, as they should not be reused. Remove the control lever shaft assembly and clutch shift arm, two felt packings and two return springs.

5. Installation is the reverse of removal. Torque the pressure plate bolts, diagonally, to 11–15 ft. lbs.

FREEPLAY ADJUSTMENT

Cable Type

1. Depress the clutch pedal by hand, freeplay (until tension is felt) should be 0.8–1.2 in. on 1983 models and 0.6–0.8 in. on 1984–88 models.

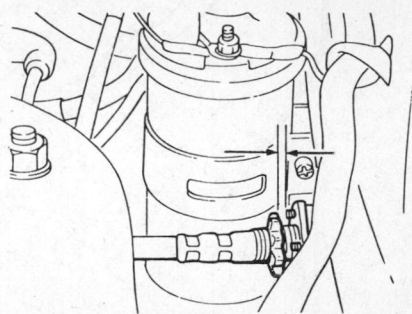

Clutch cable adjustment—front wheel drive

2. If the freeplay is too great or too little, turn the outer cable adjusting nut for adjustment.

3. After adjustment is made, depress the clutch pedal several times and recheck.

Hydraulic Type

1. Measure the clutch pedal clevis pin play at the pedal pad, it should be

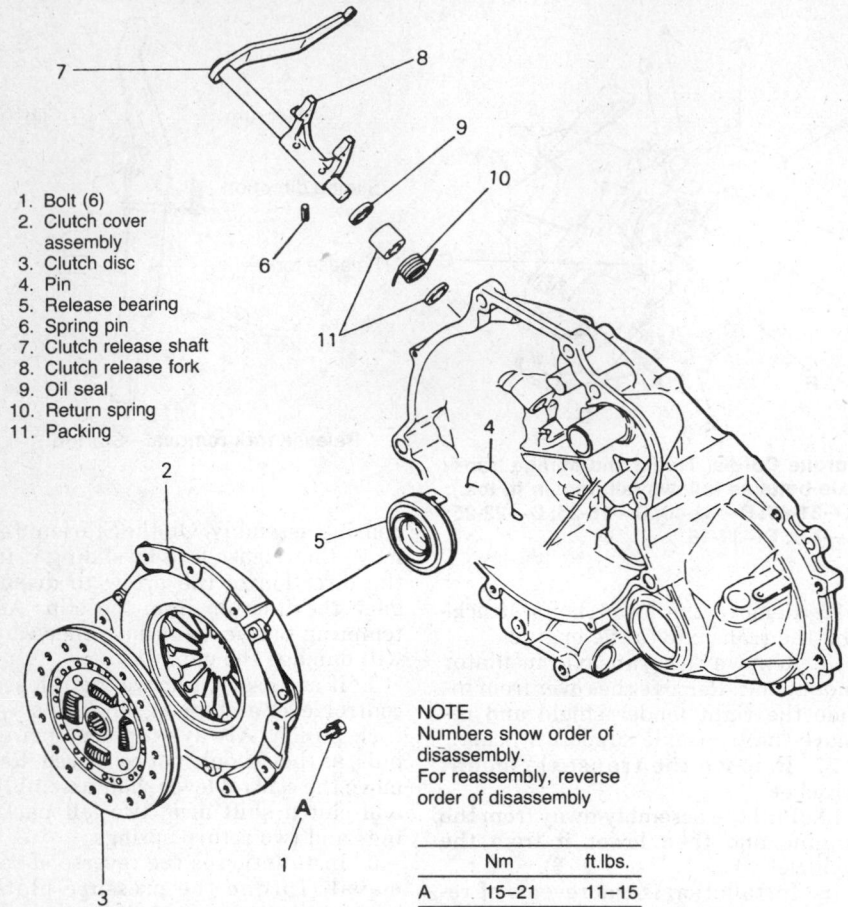

1. Bolt (6)
2. Clutch cover assembly
3. Clutch disc
4. Pin
5. Release bearing
6. Spring pin
7. Clutch release shaft
8. Clutch release fork
9. Oil seal
10. Return spring
11. Packing

NOTE
Numbers show order of disassembly.
For reassembly, reverse order of disassembly

	Nm	ft.lbs.
A	15–21	11–15

Clutch assembly—front wheel drive

Clutch pedal height

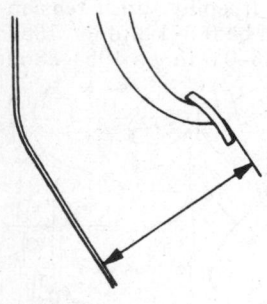

Clutch pedal clevis pin play

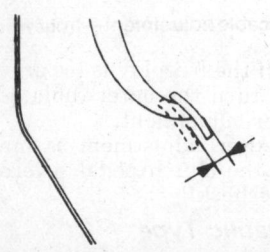

Adjustment measurments—hydraulic type clutch

6.9–7.1 in. for Cordia and Tredia (7.4–7.6 in. for Starion).

2. Measure the clutch pedal height from the surface of the pad to the floor, it should be 0.04–0.12 inch.

3. If adjustment is required, turn the clutch switch to adjust the pedal height then tighten the locknut.

4. To adjust the clevis pin play turn the pushrod and then tighten the locknut.

5. If adjustment can not be made there is probably either air in the system or the clutch cylinder or clutch disc is defective.

6. Bleed the air from the system as follows.

7. Loosen the bleeder screw at the clutch slave cylinder.

8. Push the clutch pedal down slowly while the bleeder screw is opened.

9. Hold the pedal down and tighten the bleeder screw.

10. Check the clutch master cylinder and refill with fluid if necessary. Repeat the bleeding procedure several times until all air is dispelled from the system.

Clutch Master Cylinder

REMOVAL & INSTALLATION

1. Disconnect the negative battery cable. Loosen the bleeder screw and drain the clutch fluid. Disconnect the pushrod at the clutch pedal by removing the cotter pin.

2. Disconnect the hydraulic tube at the master cylinder. Remove the clutch master cylinder.

3. Installation is the reverse of removal. Use a new cotter pin. Bleed the system. Torque the mounting bolts or nuts to 7–11 ft. lbs. Torque the clutch tube connection at the master cylinder to 9.4–12.3 ft. lbs.

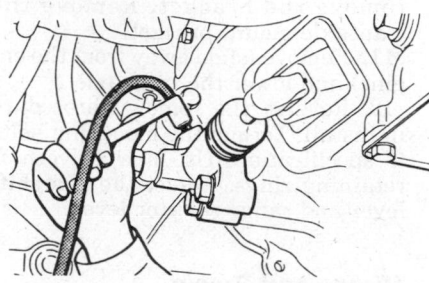

Clutch slave cylinder location; cylinder is being bled

Clutch Slave Cylinder

REMOVAL & INSTALLATION

1. Disconnect the negative battery cable. Loosen the bleeder screw and drain the fluid.

2. Disconnect the clutch tube or hose from the slave cylinder.

3. Unbolt and remove the slave cylinder.

4. Installation is the reverse of removal. Torque the clutch tube eye bolt to 14–18 ft. lbs.

BLEEDING THE HYDRAULIC CLUTCH SYSTEM

Make sure the clutch master cylinder is filled with the correct fluid. Then, loosen the bleeder screw at the slave cylinder. Now, push the clutch pedal down slowly until all air is expelled and do not release, but hold it depressed. Retighten the bleeder screw. Release the clutch pedal. Refill the master cylinder to the correct level.

AUTOMATIC TRANSMISSION

REMOVAL & INSTALLATION

1. Loosen the oil pan mounting

screws, tap the oil pan at one corner to break it loose and then allow the fluid to drain out one side. Remove the pan and remove the remaining fluid.

2. Disconnect the battery negative cable. Remove its attaching bolt and then remove the transmission pan filler tube by pulling it upward and out of the transmission case.

3. Raise and support the vehicle safely. Remove the two top transmission attaching bolts from the converter housing.

4. Disconnect the starter wiring and remove the starter.

5. Disconnect the oil cooler hoses at the metal tubes near the engine block. Then, unbolt and remove the tubes and their mountings from the block.

6. Remove the four bolts and remove the converter housing cover. Remove the torque converter bolts.

7. Disconnect the speedometer cable. Disconnect the transmission control rod and the connection lever at the cross shaft assembly.

8. Disconnect the transmission ground cable. Remove the driveshaft.

9. Support the rear of the transmission with a floor jack. Unbolt the transmission rear support bracket by removing two bolts on either side. Then, unbolt the bracket from the transmission.

10. Remove the remaining mounting bolts from the area of the converter housing. Separate the transmission from the engine and remove it.

11. Installation is the reverse of the removal procedure. Before beginning, check the distance between the front of the bell housing and the torque converter driveplate bolts with a straightedge and ruler. The distance must be at least 1.38 in. After installation, refill the transmission with the approved fluid. Check that the transmission will start only in N and P positions and that the backup light lights in R position. Torque the driveplate to crankshaft bolts to 94–100 ft. lbs. Torque the converter housing to engine bolts to 31–39 ft. lbs.

PAN AND FILTER REPLACEMENT

1. Raise and support the vehicle safely..

2. Loosen and remove the transmission pan drain plug. As required, remove the splash shield.

3. Remove the pan mounting bolts and pan. Remove the filter.

4. Install a new filter, as required. Reinstall the oil pan using a new gasket. Add the proper amount of transmission fluid after. Start the engine and move the selector lever through

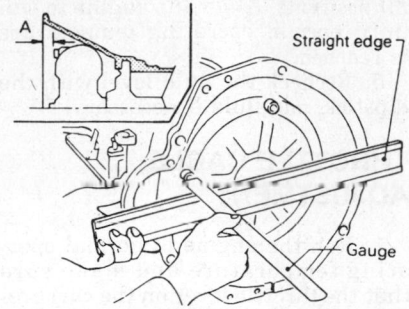

Measuring the distance between the front surface of the Starion automatic and the converter drive plate

all positions. Allow the engine to run until normal operating temperature is reached.

5. Recheck the fluid level with the dipstick, add fluid if necessary.

LINKAGE ADJUSTMENT

Wagon

1. Disconnect the negative battery cable.

2. Remove the floor console assembly.

3. Shift the selector lever into the neutral position. Unfasten the adjusting bolt.

4. Shift the transmission side lever to the neutral position. Tighten the adjusting bolt.

KICKDOWN BAND ADJUSTMENT

1. Remove the transmission oil pan.

2. Loosen the band adjusting stem locknut and turn the stem outward. Then, turn the stem inward with a torque wrench until the required torque reaches 5–7 ft. lbs. Then, back the stem off exactly two turns.

3. Hold the adjustment and torque the locknut to 11–29 ft. lbs.

NEUTRAL SAFETY SWITCH ADJUSTMENT

1. Place the control lever in the Neutral position.

2. Make sure the short end of the manual control lever covers the switch body flange. Loosen the switch mounting bolts and adjust switch as necessary. Tighten the bolts.

3. Check the switch operation by attempting to start engine in gears other than the Park and Neutral positions.

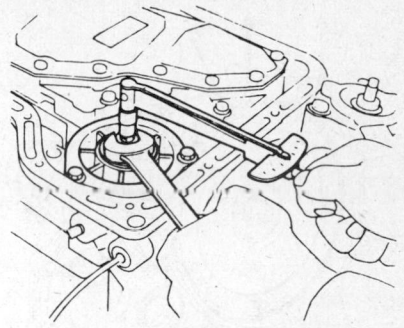

Adjusting the Starion automatic transmission band

AUTOMATIC TRANSAXLE

REMOVAL & INSTALLATION

NOTE: The transaxle and converter must be removed and installed as an assembly.

1. Disconnect the negative battery cable. Remove the battery tray. Remove the coolant reservoir and windshield washer tank. Remove the air cleaner and housing. Where so equipped, disconnect also the pulse generator connector and solenoid valve connector.

2. Disconnect the throttle control cable at the carburetor and the manual control cable at the transaxle.

3. Disconnect from the transaxle; the neutral safety switch connector, fluid cooler hose and the four upper bolts connecting the engine to the transaxle.

4. Raise and support the vehicle safely.

5. Remove the front wheels. Remove the engine splash shield.

6. Drain the transaxle fluid.

7. Remove the right and left driveshafts from the transaxle case. Remove the strut bars and the stabilizer bar from the lower arms.

8. Disconnect the speedometer cable. Disconnect and plug the oil cooler hoses. Remove the starter motor.

9. Remove the lower cover from the converter housing. Remove the three bolts that connect the converter to the engine drive plate.

NOTE: Never support the full weight of the transaxle on the engine drive plate.

10. Turn and force the converter back and away from the engine drive plate.

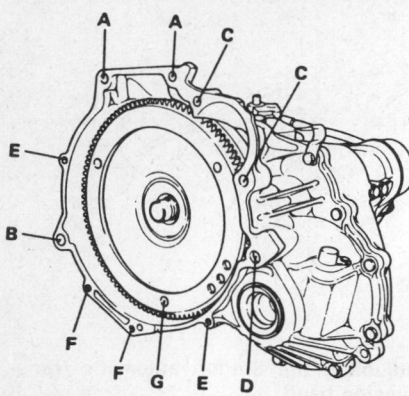

Bolt torques in ft. lbs. for the automatic transaxle: A—31-40; B—31-40; C—16-23; D—22-25; E—7-9; F—11-16; G—25-30

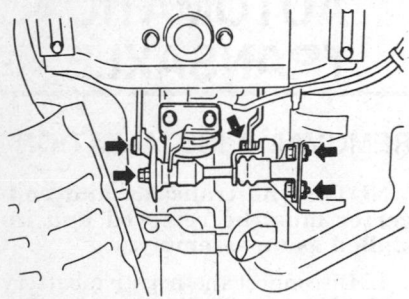

Disconnecting the control rod and connection lever from the crosshaft—Starion

11. Support the weight of the engine from above. Support the transaxle and remove the remaining mounting bolts.

12. Remove the transaxle mount insulator bolt.

13. Remove and lower the transaxle and converter as an assembly.

14. To install reverse the removal procedure. Torque the converter housing bolts according to the illustration. Torque the drive plate bolts to 25–30 ft. lbs. Be sure to connect all controls, wiring and hoses. Use new retaining rings when installing the drive axles. Refill the transmission to the proper level with the recommended fluid.

PAN AND FILTER REPLACEMENT

1. Raise and support the vehicle safely.

2. Loosen and remove the transmission pan drain plug. As required, remove the splash shield.

3. Remove the pan mounting bolts and pan. Remove the filter.

4. Install a new filter, as required. Reinstall the oil pan using a new gasket. Add the proper amount of transmission fluid after. Start the engine and move the selector lever through

all positions. Allow the engine to run until normal operating temperature is reached.

5. Recheck the fluid level with the dipstick, add fluid if necessary.

THROTTLE CABLE ADJUSTMENT

1. Run the engine to normal operating temperature and make sure that the throttle lever on the carburetor is in the curb idle position.

2. Raise the cover on the throttle cable to expose the nipple.

3. Loosen the lower cable mounting bolt.

4. Move the lower cable bracket until the distance between the nipple and the top of the cable end is 0.5mm.

5. Tighten the lower cable bracket mounting bolt and check the adjustment by pulling the cable upward with the throttle plate in the wide open position. The cable should move freely.

KICKDOWN BAND ADJUSTMENT

1. Wipe all dirt and other contamination from the kickdown servo cover and surrounding area.

2. Remove the snapring and then the cover.

3. Loosen the locknut.

4. Holding the kickdown servo piston from turning tighten the adjusting screw to 7 ft. lbs. and then back it off. Repeat the tightening and backing off two times in order to ensure seating of the band on the drum.

5. Tighten the adjusting screw to 3.5 ft. lbs. and back it off 3.5 turns (counterclockwise).

6. Holding the adjusting screw against rotation, tighten the locknut to 11–15 ft. lbs.

7. Install a new seal ring (D shaped) in the groove in the outside surface of the cover. Use care not to distort the seal ring.

8. Install the cover and then install the snapring.

NEUTRAL SAFETY SWITCH ADJUSTMENT

1. Place the control lever in the Neutral position.

2. Make sure the short end of the manual control lever covers the switch body flange. Loosen the switch mounting bolts (2) and adjust switch as necessary. Tighten the bolts.

3. Check the switch operation by attempting to start engine in gears other than the Park and Neutral positions.

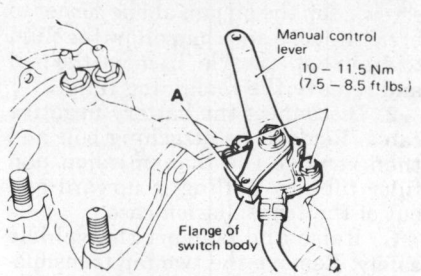

Neutral start switch adjustment. "A" denotes the small end of the lever

DRIVE AXLE

Halfshaft

REMOVAL & INSTALLATION

Except Center Bearing

1. Remove the hub center cap and loosen the driveshaft (axle) nut. Loosen the wheel lug nuts.

2. Lift the vehicle and support it on jack stands. Remove the front wheels. Remove the engine splash shield.

3. Remove the lower ball joint and strut bar from the lower control arm.

4. Drain the transaxle fluid.

5. Insert a pry bar between the transaxle case (on the raised rib) and the driveshaft double offset joint case (DOJ). Do not insert the pry bar too deeply or you will damage the oil seal. Move the bar to the right to withdraw the left driveshaft; to the left to remove the right driveshaft.

6. Plug the transaxle case with a clean rag to prevent dirt from entering the case.

7. Use a puller driver mounted on the wheel studs to push the driveshaft from the front hub. Take care to prevent the spacer from falling out of place.

8. Assembly is the reverse of removal. Insert the driveshaft into the hub first, then install the transaxle end.

NOTE: Always use a new DOJ retaining ring every time you remove the driveshaft.

Center Bearing

1. Remove the hub center cap and loosen the driveshaft (axle) nut. Loosen the wheel lug nuts.

2. Lift the vehicle and support it on jack stands. Remove the front wheels. Remove the engine splash shield.

3. Remove the lower ball joint and strut bar from the lower control arm.

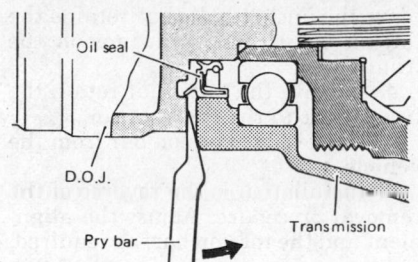

Half shaft removal—except Mirage with center bearing

3. To install the shaft, align the front sleeve yoke with the splines of the transmission output shaft and push the driveshaft into the extension housing.

NOTE: Be careful not to damage the rear transmission seal lip upon installation

4. Align the matchmarks on the rear yokes, install the bolts, and Torque to 36–43 ft. lbs.

5. Inspect the oil level of the transmission.

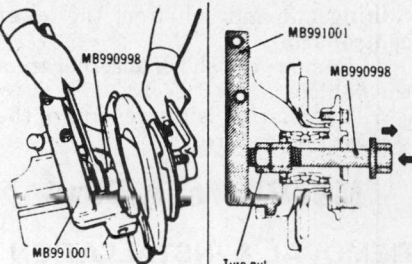

Using special tools to remove the hub from the knuckle

4. Drain the transaxle fluid.

5. Before removing the driveshaft remove the center bearing snapring.

6. Remove the driveshaft from the transaxle by lightly tapping the outer race with a plastic hammer.

7. Do not insert a pry bar between the transaxle case and the driveshaft, as damage to the dust cover of the shaft will occur.

8. If the driveshaft is pulled out from the birthfield joint side there is danger of causing damage to the joint.

9. Drive the shaft out of the hub by lightly tapping the driveshaft end with a plastic hammer.

10. Plug the transaxle case with a clean rag to prevent dirt from entering the case.

11. Use a puller driver mounted on the wheel studs to push the driveshaft from the front hub. Take care to prevent the spacer from falling out of place.

12. Assembly is reverse of removal. Insert the driveshaft into the hub first, then install the transaxle end. Always use a new DOJ retaining ring every time you remove the driveshaft.

CV JOINT OVERHAUL

For all CV-joint overhaul procedures, please refer to "CV-Joint Overhaul" in the Unit Repair section.

Driveshaft and/U-Joints

REMOVAL & INSTALLATION

1. Raise and support the vehicle safely. Matchmark the rear flange yoke and the differential pinion flange.

2. Remove the bolts from the rear flange. Remove the driveshaft by pulling it from the rear of the transmission extension housing. Place a container under the transmission extension housing to collect any oil leakage when the driveshaft is removed.

Rear Axle/Axle Shafts

REMOVAL & INSTALLATION

1. Raise and support the vehicle safely. Remove the tire and wheel.

2. Remove the brake drum and brake shoes. Remove the four wheel side flange mounting nuts and bolts.

3. Connect a flanged slide hammer to the axle flange and "pull" the axle from the differential. Take care not to damage the side differential seals.

4. Repair or replace defective components, as required. Install a new circlip on the differential side and install the axle shaft in the reverse order of removal. Tighten the mounting nuts and bolts to 36–43 ft. lbs.

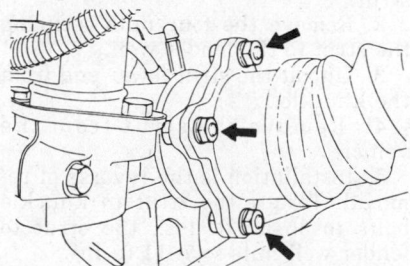

Rear drive axle flange mounting

Rear axle removal with slide hammer

Front Wheel Drive Hub Knuckle and Bearings

REMOVAL & INSTALLATION

1. Raise and support the vehicle safely. Remove the tire and wheel. Re-

move the grease cap and drive shaft nut.

2. Remove the brake caliper and suspend it from the body without disconnecting the hydraulic line.

3. Disconnect the stabilizer bar and strut bar from the lower arm.

4. Loosen but do not remove the ball joint stud nut and press the ball joint stud out of the knuckle; then remove the nut.

5. Press the driveshaft out of the hub.

6. Disconnect the tie rod end ball joint from the knuckly in the same way as the lower ball joint was disconnected.

7. Remove the nuts and bolts connecting the knuckle to the strut and remove the hub and knuckle.

8. The hub must now be pressed out of the knuckle using a special tool set such as MB990998–01 and MB991001.

9. Assembly is the reverse of removal.

10. Front wheel drive models require no bearing adjustment. The axle washer must be installed, "taper side" facing out. Tighten the axle nut to 144–148 ft. lbs. Align the nearest cotter pin hole and install cotter pin.

FRONT SUSPENSION

Shock Absorbers

REMOVAL & INSTALLATION

1. Disconnect the negative battery cable. Remove the shock absorber retaining nut from the upper control arm.

2. Raise and support the vehicle safely. Remove the front under cover spoiler.

3. Remove the shock absorber re-

taining nut and bolt from the lower control arm.

4. Remove the shock absorber from the vehicle.

5. Installation is the reverse of the removal procedure.

MacPherson Strut

REMOVAL & INSTALLATION

Cordia and Tredia

1. Raise and support the vehicle safely.

2. Remove the front wheel. Remove the brake line from the strut.

3. Disconnect the strut assembly from the steering knuckle by removing the two bolts/nuts. Support the strut and remove the two nuts and washers fastening it to the wheel well. Remove the strut.

4. Installation is the reverse of the removal procedure. When installing the strut, apply a non hardening sealer to the mating surfaces of the strut and knuckle arm.

Starion

1. Raise and support the vehicle safely. Remove the tire and wheel. Remove the caliper. Remove the front hub with disc and dust cover.

2. Disconnect the stabilizer linkage and the lower. Remove the strut assembly, knuckle arm and strut insulator retaining bolts and remove the strut assembly from the wheelhouse.

3. Installation is the reverse of the removal procedure. When installing the strut, apply a non hardening sealer to the mating surfaces of the strut and knuckle arm.

Mirage and Galant

1. Raise and support the vehicle safely. Remove the front wheels. On the Mirage, detach the brake hose bracket at the strut.

2. Remove the two nuts, bolts and lockwashers attaching the lower end of the strut to the steering knuckle.

3. Remove the dust cover from the top of the strut on the wheel well. Support the strut from underneath. Install the socket wrench on the nut at the top of the strut and a box or open end wrench on the socket. Then, install the Allen wrench through the center of the socket, long part downward. Hold the Allen wrench in place, if necessary by using a small diameter pipe as a cheater. Turn the socket to loosen the nut. Remove the nut and the lower and remove the strut.

4. To install, reverse the removal procedure. Torque the bolts attaching the bottom of the strut to the knuckle to 53–63 ft. lbs. on the Mirage and 65–

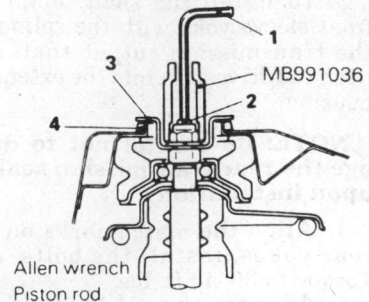

1 Allen wrench
2 Piston rod
3 Stopper
4 Stopper rubber

Removing the upper strut attaching nut with a socket wrench and Allen wrench on the Galant and Mirage

76 ft. lbs. on the Galant. The nut at the top of the strut must be torqued with the shaft of the shock held from turning with the Allen wrench, as during the loosening process. Since it is not usually possible to use a torque wrench on the flats of a socket, you'll have to estimate the torque you're applying. It should be 36–43 ft. lbs.

Precis

1. Raise and support the vehicle safely. Remove the front wheels. Detach the brake hose bracket at the strut.

2. Remove the four nuts securing the strut to the fender well.

3. Unbolt the strut lower end from the knuckle.

4. Remove the strut from the vehicle.

5. Installation is the reverse of removal. Torque the strut to knuckle bolts to 55–65 ft. lbs.; the strut to fender well nuts to 7–11 ft. lbs.

OVERHAUL

For all spring and shock absorber removal and installation procedures and all strut overhaul procedures, please refer to "Strut Overhaul" in the Unit Repair section.

Torsion Bars

REMOVAL & INSTALLATION

1. Raise and support the vehicle safely.

2. Remove the torsion bar locknut. Remove the torsion bar adjusting nut. Remove the seat holding nut.

3. Before removing the anchor bolt measure the protrusion through the assembly, this will aid in reinstallation of the assembly. Re-

move the anchor bolt that retains the torsion bar to its mounting on the frame.

4. Remove the nuts that retain the torsion bar to the control arm.

5. Remove the torsion bar from the vehicle.

6. Installation is the reverse of the removal procedure. Adjust the alignment and the torsion bar, as required.

Ball Joint

REMOVAL & INSTALLATION

Front Wheel Drive

1. Raise and support the vehicle safely. Remove the tire and wheel.

2. Disconnect the stabilizer bar and strut from the lower arm.

3. Remove the ball joint mounting nut and separate the ball joint from the front knuckle. The ball joint stud must be pressed off. You can use special tool MB991113 or equivalent.

4. Remove the lower control arm by removing the bolt(s)/nut(s) attaching it to the crossmember.

5. Remove the dust cover from the ball joint. Remove the mounting snapring.

6. Press the ball joint out of the lower control arm.

7. Press the new ball joint into place. Install a new snapring with snapring pliers.

8. Apply multipurpose grease to the lip and to the inside of the dust cover. Use a special tool (and hammer) such as MB990800-3-01 to drive a new dust cover. It must go in and make contact with the snapring.

9. Install the lower control arm to the corssmember, making sure there is not torque on it. Install and tighten the bolt and nut.

Rear Wheel Drive

1. Raise and support the vehicle safely. Remove the tire and wheel.

2. Remove the strut end from the steering knuckle.

3. Remove the ball joint to knuckle arm mounting nut. You'll need a tool which can be bolted to the holes in the knuckle arm and which will then press downward on the center of the Ball Stud—MB990241-01 or equivalent.

4. Remove the ball joint to control arm nuts and bolts and remove the ball joint.

5. Install in reverse order. Torques in ft. lbs.: Ball joint mounting bolts—43–51; strut to knuckle arm bolts—58–72; ballstud nut—43–52.

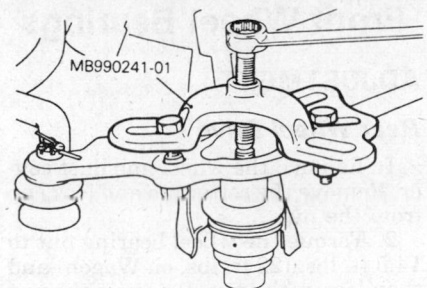

Pressing the ball joint off—Starion

Upper Control Arm

REMOVAL & INSTALLATION

1. Disconnect the negative battery cable. Remove the shock absorber retaining bolt from the upper control arm. Remove the rubber dust shield.

2. Raise and support the vehicle safely.

3. Remove the nuts that retains the torsion bar to the control arm. Remove the cotter pin and nut from the ball joint.

4. Remove the upper control arm retaining bolts. Use the proper tool to separate the ball joint from the spindle. Remove the upper control arm from the vehicle.

5. Installation is the reverse of the removal procedure.

Lower Control Arm

REMOVAL & INSTALLATION

Cordia and Tredia

1. Raise and support the vehicle. Remove the tire and wheel.

2. Disconnect the stabilizer bar and strut bar from the lower control arm by removing the one attaching bolt for the stabilizer bar and the two bolts for the strut bar.

3. Remove the ballstud nut and then press the ball joint stud out of the knuckle with a tool such as MB991113.

4. Remove the nut and bolt attaching the inner end of the stabilizer bar to the crossmember and pull the stabilizer bar and bushing out of the crossmember.

5. Installation is the reverse of removal. Install all parts and tighten nuts and bolts just snug. Then, complete tightening, torquing the lower arm to crossmember attaching nut/bolt to 87–108 ft. lbs. and the ball joint stud nut to 43–52 ft. lbs. Torque the strut rod to stabilizer bar bolt/nut to 43–50 ft. lbs.

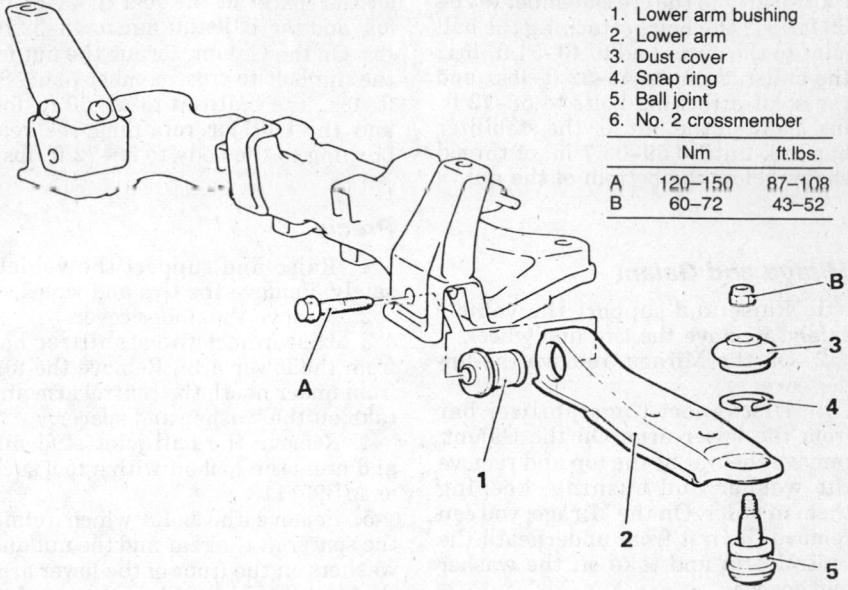

1. Lower arm bushing
2. Lower arm
3. Dust cover
4. Snap ring
5. Ball joint
6. No. 2 crossmember

	Nm	ft.lbs.
A	120–150	87–108
B	60–72	43–52

Cordia, Tredia lower front control arm and ball joint

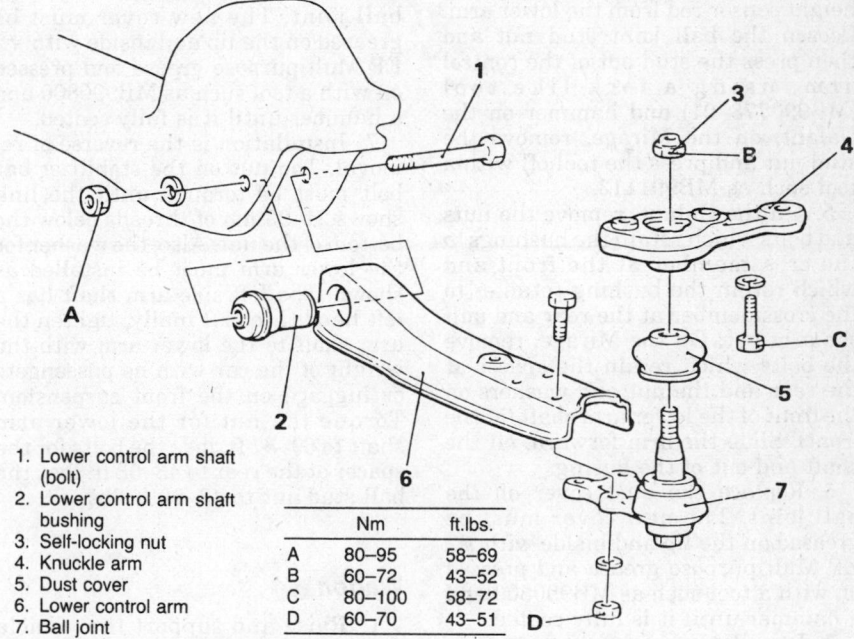

1. Lower control arm shaft (bolt)
2. Lower control arm shaft bushing
3. Self-locking nut
4. Knuckle arm
5. Dust cover
6. Lower control arm
7. Ball joint

	Nm	ft.lbs.
A	80–95	58–69
B	60–72	43–52
C	80–100	58–72
D	60–70	43–51

Starion lower front control arm and ball joint

Starion

1. Raise and support the vehicle safely. Remove the tire and wheel.

2. Disconnect the stabilizer bar where the link bolts to the control arm by removing the nut underneath the arm. Remove the nut and bolt attaching the strut bar to the control arm.

3. Disconnect the tie rod at the knuckly arm. Use a fork like tool such as MB990778–01, a standard type tool for pulling ball joint studs. First, loosen the stud nut until it is near the top of the threads and then hammer the tool between the ball joint of the tie rod end and the knuckle arm. When the ballstud comes loose, remove the nut and disconnect the stud.

4. Unbolt the MacPherson strut from the knuckle arm.

5. Unbolt the inner end of the ball joint assembly to disconnect it from the outer end of the control arm.

6. Remove the nut, bolt and lockwasher and pull the inner end of the control arm out of the crossmember.

7. Installation is the reverse of removal. Torque the bolt fastening the

control arm to the crossmember to 58–69 ft. lbs.; the bolts attaching the ball joint to the outer end to 43–51 ft. lbs.; the ballstud nut to 43–52 ft. lbs.; and the strut attaching bolts to 58–72 ft. lbs. Tighten the nut for the stabilizer bar link until 0.59–0.67 in. of thread shows below the bottom of the nut.

Mirage and Galant

1. Raise and support the vehicle safely. Remove the tire and wheel.
2. On the Mirage, remove the under cover.
3. Disconnect the stabilizer bar from the lower arm. On the Galant, remove the nut at the top and remove the washer and bushing, keeping them in order. On the Mirage, you can remove the nut from underneath the control arm and take off the washer and spacer.
4. On the Galant with electronically controlled suspension, if you're removing the right arm, disconnect the height sensor rod from the lower arm. Loosen the ball joint stud nut and then press the stud out of the control arm, using a fork like tool (MB990778–01) and hammer on the Galant; on the Mirage, remove the stud nut and press the tool off with a tool such as MB991113.
5. On the Galant, remove the nuts and bolts which retain the bushings to the crossmember at the front and which retain the bushing retainer to the crossmember at the rear and pull the arm out. On the Mirage, remove the bolts which retain the spacer at the rear and the nut and washers on the front of the lower arm shaft (at the front). Slide the arm forward, off the shaft and out of the busing.
6. Replace the dust cover on the ball joint. The new cover must be greased on the lip and inside with #2 EP Multipurpose grease and pressed on with a tool such as MB990800 and a hammer until it is fully seated.
7. Installation is the reverse of removal. On the Galant, make sure the nut on the stabilizer bar bolt is torqued to give 0.63–0.7 in. of thread exposed between the top of the nut and the end of the link. On the Mirage, the nut must be torqued until the link shows 0.83–0.91 in. of threads below the bottom of the nut. Also on the Mirage, the washer for the lower arm must be installed as shown. The left side arm shaft has a left hand thread. Finally tighten the arm shaft to the lower arm with the weight of the vehicle with no passengers or luggage on the front suspension. On the Mirage, torque the nut for the lower arm shaft to 69–87 ft. lbs.; the bolts

for the spacer at the rear to 43–58 ft. lbs. and the ballstud nut to 43–52 ft. lbs. On the Galant, torque the nut for the nut/bolt to crossmember to 69–87 ft. lbs., the ballstud to 42–50 ft. lbs. and the bolt for retaining the rear bushing to the body to 58–72 ft. lbs.

Precis

1. Raise and support the vehicle safely. Remove the tire and wheel.
2. Remove the under cover.
3. Disconnect the stabilizer bar from the lower arm. Remove the nut from under neath the control arm and take off the washer and spacer.
4. Remove the ball joint stud nut and press the tool off with a tool such as MB991113.
5. Remove the bolts which retain the spacer at the rear and the nut and washers on the front of the lower arm shaft (at the front). Slide the arm forward, off the shaft and out of the bushing.
6. Replace the dust cover on the ball joint. The new cover must be greased on the lip and inside with #2 EP Multipurpose grease and pressed on with a tool such as MB990800 and a hammer until it is fully seated.
7. Installation is the reverse of removal. The nut on the stabilizer bar bolt must be torqued until the link shows 21–23mm of threads below the bottom of the nut. Also, the washer for the lower arm must be installed as shown. The left side arm shaft has a left hand thread. Finally, tighten the arm shaft to the lower arm with the weight of the car with no passengers or luggage on the front suspension. Torque the nut for the lower arm shaft to 69–87 ft. lbs.; the bolts for the spacer at the rear to 43–58 ft. lbs.; the ball stud nut to 43–52 ft. lbs.

Wagon

1. Raise and support the vehicle safely. Remove the tire and wheel.
2. Remove the shock absorber bolt that retains the shock to the lower control arm. Remove the strut bar retaining nut. Remove the stabilizer bar nut and bolt.
3. Remove the cotter pin and nut that secures the lower ball joint to the lower control arm.
4. As required properly support the lower control arm. Use the proper tool and separate the lower ball joint from the lower control arm.
5. Remove the lower control arm retaining bolts. Remove the lower control arm from the vehicle.
6. Installation is the reverse of the removal procedure.

Front Wheel Bearings

ADJUSTMENT

Rear Wheel Drive

1. Remove the wheel and dust cover. Remove the cotter pin and lock cap from the nut.
2. Torque the wheel bearing nut to 14.5 ft. lbs. (22 ft. lbs. on Wagon) and then loosen the nut. Retorque the nut to 3.6 ft. lbs (6.0 ft. lbs. on Wagon) and install the lock cap and cotter pin.
3. Install the dust cover and the wheel.

REMOVAL & INSTALLATION

1. Raise and support the vehicle safely. Remove the tire and wheel. Remove the caliper.
2. Pry off the dust cap. Tap out and discard the cotter pin. Remove the locknut.
3. Being careful not to drop the outer bearing, pull off the brake disc and wheel hub.
4. Remove the grease inside the wheel hub.
5. Using a brass drift, carefully drive the outer bearing race out of the hub.
6. Remove the inner bearing seal and bearing.
7. Check the bearings for wear or damage and replace them if necessary.
8. Coat the inner surface of the hub with grease.
9. Grease the outer surface of the bearing race and drift it into place in the hub.
10. Pack the inner and outer wheel bearings with grease. If the brake disc has been removed and/or replaced, tighten the retaining bolts to specification.
11. Install the inner bearing in the hub. Being careful not to distort it, install the oil seal with its lip facing the bearing. Drive the seal on until its outer edge is even with the edge of the hub.
12. Install the hub/disc assembly on the spindle, being careful not to damage the oil seal.
13. Install the outer bearing, washer and spindle nut. Adjust the bearing.

Front Wheel Alignment

ADJUSTMENT

Except Wagon

Camber is preset at the factory and cannot be adjusted. Caster should not require adjustment, although adjustment (to a certain extent) is possible by adjusting the length of the strut bar. Loosen both nuts and turn in or out as required. Toe adjustment is possible by adjusting both tie rod end turnbuckles (the same amount) on the Cordia and Tredia, or the left tierod end turnbuckle on the Starion.

Before turning the turnbuckles on the Cordia and Tredia, unfasten the clips for the rubber boots on the inner ends of the turnbuckles. Using a wrench from below on the flats in the middle of the turnbuckle, the toe will move out as the left side turnbuckle is turned toward the front of the vehicle and the right toward the rear.

On the Mirage, Galant and Precis, toe in is adjusted as for the Cordia and Tredia, neither caster nor camber can be adjusted.

On the Starion, toe in can usually be adjusted by turning the one turnbuckle. You should, however, check to make sure that the difference between the length of right and left tie rods is not greater than 0.2 in. If it is, you should remove the tight tie rod at the knuckle and bring the length within specifications; and then toe-in is brought to correct values also.

Wagon

Measure the wheel alignment with the vehicle parked on level ground and with the front wheels placed in the straight ahead position. Front suspension, steering system, wheels and tires should be serviced to normal operating condition before attempting to measure wheel alignment.

Measure the toe in, it should be 0.024 inch if not within specification adjust it by turning the turnbuckels of the right and left tie rods the same amount in opposite directions. Turn the left turnbuckle in the forward direction of the vehicle and the right one in the reverse direction in order to reduce toe in. Toe in can be adjusted about 0.12 inch by turning both turnbuckles half a turn each.

Adjust camber and caster after first checking that the vehicle tire pressure is within specification. Position the front wheel on the turning radius gauge and level the vehicle. Remove the hubcap and cotter pin. Measure the camber and caster with the camber/caster/kingpin attached. The proper specification for camber is 0°31'±30' (difference in camber between right hand and left hand wheels is within 30'). The proper specification for caster is 0°08±30' (difference in caster between right hand and left hand wheels is within 30').

If the camber is not within specification adjust it by rotating the lower arm's shaft assembly. One marking

	Nm	ft.lbs.
A	65–80	47–58
B	70–90	51–65
C	80–100	58–72
D	18–25	13–18

1. Suspension arm (R.H.)
2. Dust cover
3. Clamp
4. Bushing A
5. Bushing B
6. Rubber stopper
7. Suspension arm (L.H.)
8. Fixture
9. Rubber bushing
10. Washer
11. Spring upper seat
12. Coil spring
13. Spring lower seat
14. Shock absorber
15. Bump stopper

Rear suspension—front wheel drive models

on the control is a change of 2°18' of the camber. Turn the control away from the lower control arm.

REAR SUSPENSION

Shock Absorbers

REMOVAL & INSTALLATION

1. Raise and support the vehicle safely. Remove the tire and wheel.
3. Position a floor jack under the lower control arm (rear axle assembly on Wagon). Remove the upper shock mounting bolt and nut.
4. Compress the shock slightly and remove the lower mounting bolt.
5. Remove the shock absorber.
6. Installation is the reverse of the removal procedure.

MacPherson Strut

REMOVAL & INSTALLATION

Starion

1. Support the rear of vehicle on jackstands at the frame rails. Position a floor jack under the lower control arm and raise it slightly.
2. Disconnect the rear brake hose from the strut assembly.
3. Disconnect the axle shaft from the wheel side flange.
4. Remove the strut assembly to axle housing mounting bolts. Sepa-

rate the strut assembly from the axle housing. Lower the floor jack and push down on the housing while opening the coupling with a small pry bar.
5. Remove the upper strut mounting nuts from under the side trim in rear hatch.
6. Remove the strut assembly.
7. Install in reverse order. Tighten the top mounting nuts to 18–25 ft. lbs. and the lower mounting to 36–51 ft. lbs.

Galant

1. Support the vehicle on jackstands. Remove the rear wheels.
2. Place a floor jack under the axle/arm assembly and raise it slightly. Then, remove the forward trim from the trunk and remove the cap and strut mounting nuts and washers.
3. Remove the nut, pull the throughbolt out where the strut connects with the axle/arm assembly and remove the strut assembly.
4. Installation is the reverse of removal. Torque the upper strut mounting nuts to 33–40 ft. lbs. and the lower throughbolt to 72–87 ft. lbs.

OVERHAUL

For all spring and shock absorber removal and installation procedures and all strut overhaul procedures, please refer to the "Strut Overhaul" in the Unit Repair section.

Coil Spring

REMOVAL & INSTALLATION

1. Raise and support the vehicle

safely allowing the rear axle to hang unsupported.

2. Place a jack under the work side control arm and remove the bottom bolts of the shock absorbers.

3. Lower the arm and remove the coil spring.

4. Installation is the reverse of removal.

Leaf Spring

REMOVAL & INSTALLATION

1. Raise and support the vehicle safely. Remove the tire and wheel.

2. Properly support the rear axle assembly.

3. Carefully remove the leaf spring front and rear retaining bolts.

4. Disconnect the shock absorber from its mounting on the rear axle. Remove the U-bolts and clamps retaining the assembly to the rear axle.

5. Disconnect the parking brake cable connection from the leaf spring.

6. Remove the leaf spring from the vehicle.

7. Installation is the reverse of the removal procedure.

Rear Control Arm

REMOVAL & INSTALLATION

Cordia, Tredia and Mirage and Precis

1. Raise and support the vehicle. Remove the rear wheels. Remove the rear brake assemblies. As required, remove the muffler.

2. Disconnect the parking brake cable from the suspension arm on both sides.

3. Jack up the suspension arm on both sides just slightly. Then remove both lower shock absorber attaching bolts. Then, lower the jack carefully and, when it can be disengaged, remove the spring. Keep the spring in the position it was in when installed so it can be installed in the same direction.

4. Disconnect the brake hoses at the suspension arms. Then, support the rear suspension assembly while you remove the two mounting bolts on either side and remove the assembly.

5. Installation is the reverse of removal. Lower shock mounting bolts are torqued to 47–58 ft. lbs. Suspension assembly to body mounting bolts are torqued to 51–65 ft. lbs. on the Cordia and Tredia and to 36–51 ft. lbs. on the Mirage.

Starion

1. Raise and support the vehicle safely.

2. Disconnect the parking brake from the control arm brackets. Disconnect the stabilizer bar.

3. Remove the nut and bolt connecting the lower control arm to the front support.

4. Matchmark the relationship between the crossmember and the eccentric bushing so alignment can be restored at assembly. Remove the nut and bolt connecting the lower control arm to the crossmember.

5. Remove the lower control arm from the vehicle.

6. Install in reverse order.

Rear Wheel Bearings

REMOVAL & INSTALLATION

1. Raise and support the vehicle safely. Loosen the lug nuts.

2. Remove the tire and wheel. Remove the grease cap. Remove the nut.

3. Pull the drum off. The outer bearing will fall out while the drum is coming off, so position your hand to catch it.

4. Pry out the oil seal. Discard it. Remove the inner bearing.

5. Check the bearing races and bearings. If any scoring, heat checking or damage is noted, they should be replaced. When bearings or races need replacement, replace them as a set.

6. If the bearings and races are to be replaced, drive out the race with a brass drift.

7. Before installing new races, coat them with lithium based wheel bearing grease. The races are most easily installed using a driver made for that purpose. They can, however, be driven into place with a brass drift. Make sure that they are fully seated.

8. Thoroughly pack the bearings with lithium based wheel bear grease. Pack the hub with grease.

9. Install the inner bearing and coat the lip and rim of the grease seal with grease. Drive the seal into place with a seal driver.

10. Mount the drum on the axleshaft. Install the outer bearing. Don't install the nut at this point.

11. Using a pull scale attached to one of the lugs, measure the starting force necessary to get the drum to turn. Starting force should be 5 lbs. If the starting torque is greater than specified, replace the bearings.

12. Install the nut on the axleshaft. Thread the nut on, by hand, to a point at which the back face of the nut is 2–3mm from the shoulder of the shaft (where the threads end).

13. Using an inch lb. torque wrench, turn the nut counterclockwise 2 to 3 turns, noting the average force needed during the turning procedure. Turning torque for the nut should be about 48 inch lbs. If turning torque is not within 5 inch lbs., wither way, replace the nut.

14. Tighten the nut to 75–110 ft. lbs. Using a stand mounted gauge, check the axial play of the wheel bearings. Play should be less than 0.0079 in. If play cannot be brought within that figure, you probably have assembled the unit incorrectly. Pack the grease cap with wheel bearing grease and install it.

STEERING

Steering Wheel

REMOVAL & INSTALLATION

1. Disconnect the negative battery cable. Pry off the steering wheel center foam pad or remove the mounting screws from the back (depending on model). Disconnect the electrical connector for the horn.

2. Remove the steering wheel retaining nut after marking the wheel and shaft position.

3. Using a steering wheel puller, remove the steering wheel.

4. Installation is the reverse of the removal procedure. Be sure the front wheels are in a straight ahead position.

Combination Switch

REMOVAL & INSTALLATION

1. Disconnect the negative battery cable. Remove the steering wheel and have the tilt handle in the lowest position.

2. Remove the combination meter and column cover.

3. Remove the connectors from the column switch and the column switch from the column tube.

NOTE: Some models may have the turn signal and hazard switches mounted on a base plate. Removal of the attaching screws will allow these switches to be removed without removal of the remaining switches.

4. Switch installation is the reverse of removal. Be sure that the switch is centered in the column or self cancelling will be affected.

Ignition Switch

REMOVAL & INSTALLATION

1. Disconnect the negative battery cable. Cut a notch in the lock bracket bolt head with a hacksaw.

2. Remove the bolt and lock.

3. Remove the column cover and unbolt and remove the ignition switch.

4. Install both lock and switch in reverse of removal.

NOTE: When installing lock, the bolt should be tightened until the head is crushed. When installing switch, install the switch bolt loosely and insert and work the key a few times to make sure everything checks out before tightening the bolt.

Manual Steering Gear

REMOVAL & INSTALLATION

Cordia and Tredia

1. Raise and support the vehicle safely. Remove the front wheels.

2. Remove the bolt connecting the steering shaft universal joint with the steering gear. Before removing the bolt, mark its location and be sure the wheels are pointed straight.

3. Remove the tie rod ends from the hub knuckles. Disconnect mounting bolts located near the inner tie rods on the crossmember. Remove right side submember from the No. 2 crossmember. Remove the gearbox from the No. 2 crossmember. Pull the gear box out from the right side of the vehicle.

4. Installation is the reverse of removal. Observe the following torques:
Gear box to No. 2 crossmember: 43–58 ft. lbs.
Tie rod to rack: 58–72 ft. lbs.
Tie rod end locknut: 36–40 ft. lbs.
Tie rod to knuckle: 17–25 ft. lbs.

Mirage

1. Support the vehicle. Remove front wheels.

2. Uncouple the shaft assembly from the gearbox from inside the passenger compartment.

3. Press the tie rod ends off the steering knuckles.

4. Cut the retaining band off the rubber boot that covers the joint connecting the box with the steering shaft.

5. Remove the four attaching bolts for the two main steering box clamps. Pull the gearbox out toward the left side of the vehicle.

6. Install in reverse order, making sure that the projections on the rub-

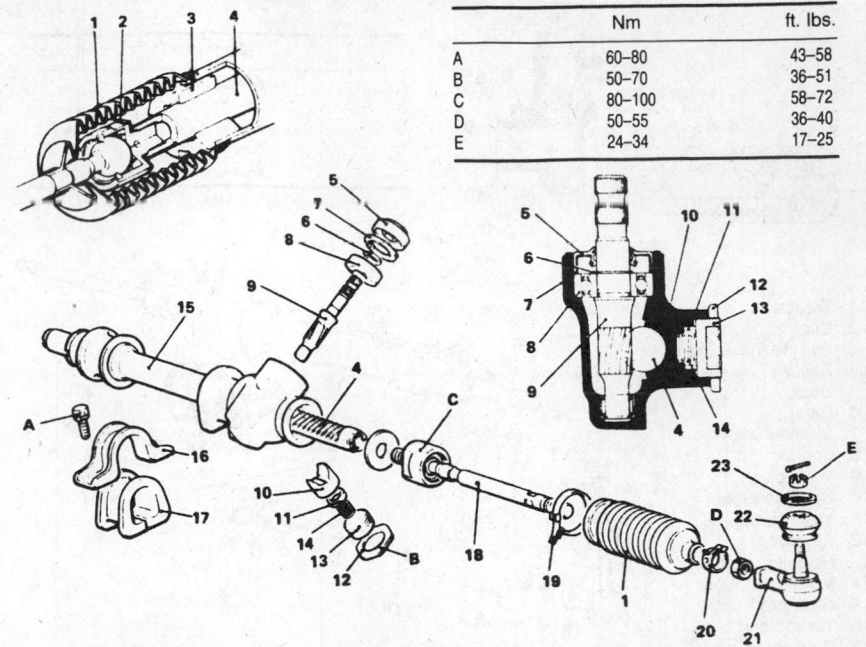

	Nm	ft. lbs.
A	60–80	43–58
B	50–70	36–51
C	80–100	58–72
D	50–55	36–40
E	24–34	17–25

1. Bellows
2. Tab washer
3. Rack bushing
4. Rack
5. Oil seal
6. Snap ring
7. Snap ring
8. Bearing
9. Pinion
10. Support yoke
11. Cushion rubber
12. Locking nut
13. Yoke plug
14. Yoke spring
15. Gear housing
16. Mounting bracket
17. Mounting rubber
18. Tie rod
19. Band
20. Clip
21. Tie rod end
22. Dust cover
23. Clip ring

Manual steering gear assembly

ber mounting fit into the holes in the housing bracket and clamps.

7. Replace the band attaching the steering joint rubber boot. Make sure the steering wheel rotates smoothly throughout its travel. Adjust toe-in. Torque the steering box mounting bolts to 43–58 ft. lbs. and the tie rod end attaching nuts to 11–25 ft. lbs.

Precis

1. Raise and support the vehicle safely. Remove the bolt which secures the universal joint in the steering shaft to the gearbox. It's just inside the car where the steering linkage passes through the toeboard.

2. Remove the cotter pin from the tie rod end ballstud and loosen the nut. Press the ballstud out of the steering knuckle with a vice like tool such as MB991113 or equivalent; then remove the nut. Do the same on the other side.

3. Cut the band off the steering joint rubber boot.

4. Remove the two attaching bolts from the gearbox housing clamp on either side and pull the gearbox out the left side of the vehicle. Work slowly to keep the unit from being damaged.

5. Install the unit in reverse order. There are rubber tabs on the inside

and outside of the sleeve. The larger tab must go on the inside. Use a new band for the steering joint rubber boot. Adjust toe-in. Use the following torques: mounting bracket attaching bolts, 43–58 ft. lbs.; ball stud nut, 17 ft. lbs. (then turn farther to align castellations with the cotter pin hole and install a new cotter pin). Turn the steering wheel back and forth to test steering operation.

Wagon

1. Raise and support the vehicle safely.

2. Remove the splash guard plate. Disconnect the right and left tie rod connection using the proper tools.

3. Remove the steering gear housing retaining clamps.

4. Separate the steering gear from the steering shaft.

5. Remove the steering gear from the vehicle.

6. Installation is the reverse of the removal procedure.

Power Steering Gear

REMOVAL & INSTALLATION

Cordia and Tredia

1. Raise and support the vehicle

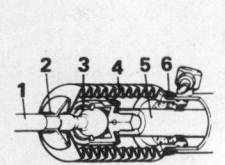

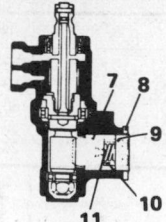

	Nm	ft. lbs.
A	60–80	43–58
B	50–70	36–51
C	80–100	58–72
D	50–55	36–39
E	24–34	17–25

1. Tie rod
2. Clip
3. Tab washer
4. Bellows
5. Rack
6. Band
7. Support yoke
8. Locking nut
9. Yoke plug
10. Cushion rubber
11. Yoke spring
12. Air tube
13. Mounting bracket
14. Mounting rubber
15. Gear box
16. Tie rod end
17. Dust cover

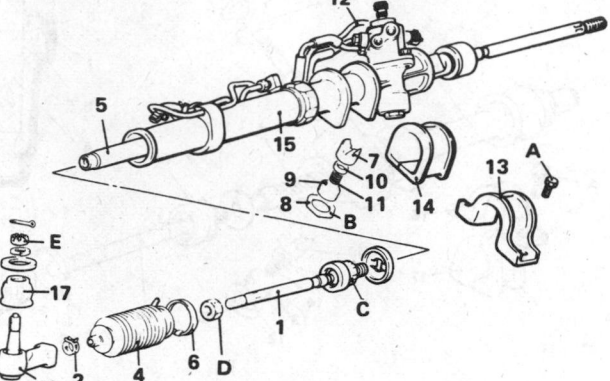

Power steering gear assembly

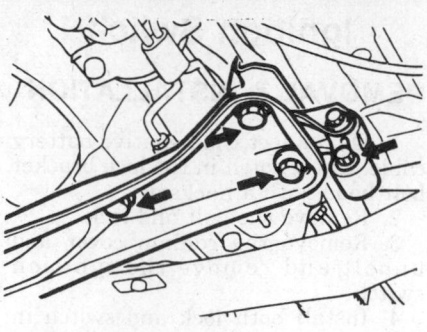

Removing the center memberfront mounting bolts to remove the steering box—Galant

safely. Remove the bolt attaching the steering shaft universal joint to the gearbox.

2. Remove the cotter pin from the tie rod end ballstud and then loosen the nut. Press the ballstud out of the steering knuckle with a vice like tool such as MB991113 or equivalent. Remove the nut and pull the stud out of the knuckle.

3. Place a drain pan under the gearbox and then disconnect the pressure and return hose connectors with a flare nut wrench and allow the fluid to drain.

4. Disconnect the hose from the bottom of the fuel filter and plug it.

5. Remove the fuel line clips to permit the fuel line to move.

6. Remove the brace from the rear engine roll stop.

7. Remove the crossmember support bracket from the No. 2 crossmember, located on the right side of the vehicle.

8. Unbolt and remove the two bolts in each gearbox mounting clamp, working from the engine compartment side.

9. Pull the gearbox out the right side of the vehicle, working carefully to keep the unit from being damaged.

10. Installation is the reverse of the removal procedure.

Starion

1. Raise and support the vehicle safely. Remove the clamp bolt which connects the steering box input shaft to the steering shaft.

2. Place a drain pan underneath and then disconnect the pressure and return hoses at the gearbox.

3. Press the pitman arm off the gearbox with the special tool.

4. Remove the four attaching nuts and remove the steering box.

5. Install in reverse order, torquing the steering box mounting nuts/bolts to 40–47 ft. lbs. and the pitman arm shaft retaining nut to 94–108 ft. lbs. Fill the power steering pump with fluid, as required.

Mirage

1. Raise and support the vehicle safely. Remove the bolt which secures the universal joint in the steering shaft to the gearbox. It's just inside the vehicle where the steering linkage passes through the toeboard.

2. Remove the cotter pin from the tie rod end ballstud and loosen the nut. Press the ballstud out of the steering knuckle with a vice like tool such as MB991113 or equivalent; then remove the nut. Do the same on the other side.

3. Cut the bad off the steering joint rubber boot. Place a drain pan under the steering box. Then, disconnect the pressure and return hoses at the gearbox.

4. Remove the stabilizer bar.

5. Remove the rear roll stopper to center member bolt and then move the rear roll stopper forward.

6. Remove the two mounting bolts in the clip on either side of the gearbox and remove the unit carefully out

the left of the vehicle. Avoid damaging the rubber boots.

7. Installation is the reverse of the removal procedure.

Galant

1. Raise and support the vehicle safely. If the vehicle has electronically controlled suspension, remove the stabilizer bar.

2. Remove the cotter pin from the tie rod and ballstud and loosen the nut. Press the ballstud out of the steering knuckle with a vice like tool such as MB991113 or equivalent; then remove the nut. Do the same on the other side.

3. Drain the fluid from the system. Then, disconnect the pressure and return hoses at the gearbox.

4. Remove the bolt attaching the steering shaft universal joint to the gearbox. Disconnect the connector for the solenoid valve.

5. Remove the front mounting bolt from the center crossmember. Remove the exhaust pipe hanger from the crossmember. Then, remove the front roll stopper bolt.

6. Disconnect the exhaust pipe at the front and lower it out of the way. Press the rear of the center crossmember downward.

7. Move the rack all the way to the right. Then, remove the mounting bolts from the brackets. Tilt the gearbox downward and remove it toward the left. Avoid damaging the rubber boots.

8. Installation is the reverse of the removal procedure.

Wagon

1. Raise and support the vehicle safely.

2. Remove the splash guard plate. Remove the power steering tube protector. Disconnect the right and left tie rod connection using the proper tools.

3. Disconnect and cap the power

steering lines. Remove the steering gear housing retaining clamps.

4. Separate the steering gear from the steering shaft.

5. Remove the steering gear from the vehicle.

6. Installation is the reverse of removal procedure.

Power Steering Pump

REMOVAL & INSTALLATION

1. Disconnect the negative battery cable. Remove the reservoir cap and disconnect the return hose at the reservoir. Drain the fluid into a clean container.

2. As required, raise and support the vehicle safely. Loosen the pulley nut if the pulley is to be removed. Loosen the mounting bolts and remove the belt. Turn the pump over to pump remaining fluid into the container. Now disconnect the pressure hose at the top of the pump. Disconnect the suction hose at the side of the pump and drain the fluid.

3. Remove the pump attaching bolts and lift the pump from the brackets.

4. Make sure the bracket bolts are tight and install the pump to the brackets.

5. If pulley had been removed, install it and tighten the nut securely. Bend the lock tab over the nut.

6. Install the drive belt and adjust to a tension of 22 lbs. at a deflection of 0.28–0.39 inches at the top center of the belt. Tighten the pump bolts securely to hold the tension.

7. Connect the pressure and return lines and fill the reservoir with approved fluid.

SYSTEM BLEEDING

1. The reservoir should be full with the proper grade and type power steering fluid.

2. Jack up the front wheels and support the vehicle safely.

3. Turn the steering wheel fully to the right and left until no air bubbles appear in the fluid. Maintain the reservoir level.

4. Lower the vehicle and with the engine idling, turn the wheels fully to the right and left. Stop the engine.

5. If equipped, install a tube from the bleeder screw on the steering gear box to the reservoir.

6. Start the engine, turn the steering wheel fully to the left and loosen the bleeder screw.

7. Repeat the procedure until no air bubbles pass through the tube.

8. Tighten the bleeder screw and

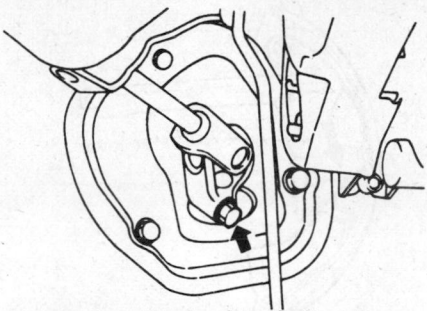

Uncoupling the steering shaft and gearbox on the Mirage

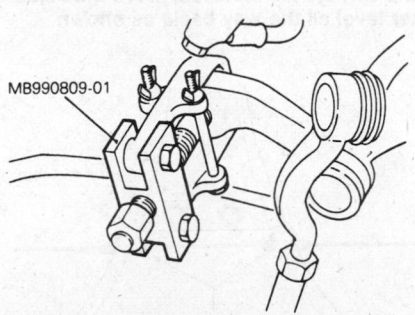

Pressing the pitman arm off to remove the Starion steering box

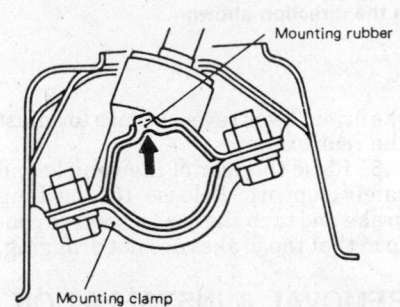

Locate the steering box rubber mount in the indentation in the crossmember as shown—Mirage

remove the tube. Refill the reservoir as needed and check that no further bubbles are present in the fluid. An abrupt rise in the fluid level after stopping the engine is a sign of incomplete bleeding. This will cause noise from the pump or control valve.

Tie Rod Ends

REMOVAL & INSTALLATION

Starion

1. Raise and support the vehcile safely.

2. Remove the cotter pin and locknut from the tie rod end.

3. Using the proper tools separate the tie rod end from its mounting.

4. Unscrew the tie rod end from the relay rod.

5. .Installation is the reverse of the removal procedure. Adjust the toe in as required.

BRAKES

For all brake system repair and service procedures not detailed below, please refer to "Brakes" in the Unit Repair section.

Master Cylinder

REMOVAL & INSTALLATION

Except Wagon

1. Disconnect the negative battery cable. On the Starion, Mirage with turbocharger and Precis, the brake fluid reservoir is separate from the master cylinder. Disconnect the hoses at the master cylinder and plug them or drain the fluid into a container.

2. Disconnect the electrical connector for the fluid level sensor.

3. Disconnect all the brake tubes. Remove the nuts and lockwashers attaching the master cylinder to the booster. Remove the master cylinder from the vehicle.

4. Install the reverse order, torquing the attaching nuts to 6–9 ft. lbs. Refill the reservoirs with approved, new fluid and bleed the system thoroughly.

Wagon

1. Disconnect the negative battery cable. Remove the instrument cluster assembly.

2. The brake fluid reservoir is separate from the master cylinder. Disconnect the hoses at the master cylinder and plug them or drain the fluid into a container.

3. Disconnect all the brake tubes. Remove the nuts and lockwashers attaching the master cylinder to the booster. Remove the master cylinder from the vehicle.

4. Install the reverse order, torquing the attaching nuts to 6–9 ft. lbs. Refill the reservoirs with approved, new fluid and bleed the system thoroughly.

Power Brake Booster

REMOVAL & INSTALLATION

Except Wagon

1. Disconnect the negative battery

cable. Disconnect the vacuum supply line from the brake booster.

2. Remove the master cylinder. It may be possible to position the master cylinder out of the way rather then disconnect the fluid lines.

3. Disconnect the pushrod from the brake pedal.

4. Remove the mounting bolts from the firewall. Remove the power brake booster.

5. Installation is the reverse of the removal procedure. Bleed the brake system.

Wagon

1. Disconnect the negative battery cable. Remove the lap heater duct. Remove the steering column cover.

2. Remove the steering column switch connector. Remove the steering column assembly.

3. Remove the master cylinder from the vehicle.

4. Remove the stop lamp switch connector. Remove the brake tube, vacuum hose and pipe.

5. Remove the pedal assembly retaining bolts. Remove the power brake booster along with the pedal assembly.

6. Installation is the reverse of the removal procedure.

Wheel Cylinder

REMOVAL & INSTALLATION

1. Raise and support the rear of the vehicle. Remove the wheel and brake drum. Remove the brake shoes.

2. Place a container under the brake backing plate to catch the brake fluid that will run out of the wheel cylinder.

3. Disconnect the brake line and remove the cylinder mounting bolts. Remove the cylinder from the backing plate.

4. Installation is the reverse of the removal procedure. Bleed the brake system.

Parking Brake Cable

ADJUSTMENT

1. Remove the center console, rear seat and rear console box if necessary.

2. Apply the parking brake and count the number of clicks (notches) until fully applied.

3. Proper adjustment is 5–7 notches for front wheel drive and 4–5 for rear drive models.

4. Adjust the parking lever stroke by turning the cable adjusting nut after attempting to tighten by applying

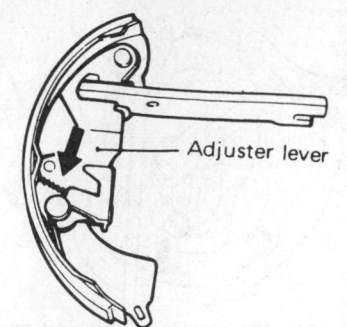

When installing new rear brake shoes, after the springs are installed, move the adjuster level all the way back, as shown

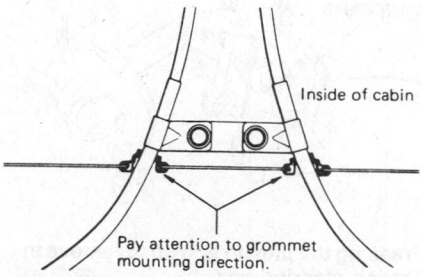

Install the grommets through which the parking brake cable passes into the car in the direction shown

the brake lever several times to adjust the rear brakes.

5. Raise the rear of the vehicle and safely support. Release the parking brake and turn the rear wheels to confirm that the brakes are not dragging.

REMOVAL & INSTALLATION

Front Wheel Drive

1. Raise rear of vehicle and support it safely.

2. Remove the console and rear seat. Disconnect the brake cable at the parking brake lever (brakes released). Remove the cable clamps inside the driver's compartment (two bolts). Disconnect the clamps on the rear suspension arm.

3. Remove the rear brake drums and the brake shoe assemblies. Disconnect the parking brake cable from the lever on the trailing (rear) brake shoe by removing the snapring. Remove the brake cables.

4. Installation is the reverse of removal. Make sure the grommets through which the cables pass into the passenger compartment are installed with the concave side outward. Adjust the parking brake. Adjust the switch so the indicator light comes on when the parking brake lever is pulled one notch.

Rear Wheel Drive

EXCEPT WAGON

1. As required, remove the console and rear seat.

2. Raise and support the rear of the vehicle.

3. Disconnect all clevis pin connecting and the cable ends.

4. Pull the cable through the floor.

5. Install in reverse order.

6. Adjust the cable. Apply sealer to the edge of the grommet at the floor opening. Check the parking brake indicator, the light should come on when the brake is applied one notch.

WAGON

1. Disconnect the enagtive battery cable.

2. Remove the parking brake lever cover. Disconnect the parking brake cable from the parking brake lever. Remove the electrical switch connector. Remove the parking brake lever.

3. Remove the front cable retaining bolts from under the vehicle. Remove the front cable after removing the heat protector.

4. Remove the fuel tank.

5. Remove the left and right parking brake cables. Remove the lever assembly.

6. Installation is the reverse of the removal procedure.

CHASSIS ELECTRICAL

Heater Blower

REMOVAL & INSTALLATION

Cordia and Tredia

1. Disconnect the negative battery cable. Unscrew the one attaching bolt and remove the lower cover from under the right side of the instrument panel. Remove the mounting screws at the front and remove the glovebox. Remove the cowl side trim.

2. Disconnect the air selector control wire. Disconnect the discharge duct at the blower.

3. Disconnect the electrical connector. Remove the four mounting bolts and remove the blower assembly.

4. Installation is the reverse of the removal procedure.

Starion

1. Disconnect the negative battery cable. Remove the under cover from

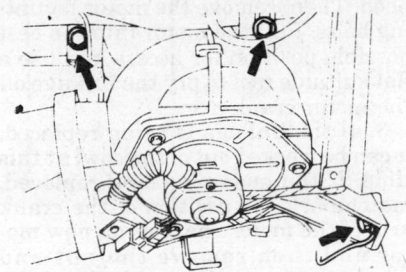

Remove the arrowed bolts and remove the blower motor (Cordia and Tredia)

the bottom of the dash panel, under the glovebox. Then, open the glovebox door and pull the glovebox forward while pressing inward on both sides of the glovebox. This will allow the door to drop downward.

2. Remove the screws attaching the glovebox door hinge to the bottom of the dashboard and then remove the assembly.

3. Disconnect the fresh air/recirculated air changeover cable from the blower housing. Disconnect the blower electrical connector.

4. Remove the three mounting bolts and remove the blower assembly. The blower motor and fan may now be removed from the case.

5. Installation is the reverse of removal.

Mirage

1. Disconnect the negative battery cable. Open the glovebox door, release the hinges and remove the glovebox.

2. Remove the four Phillips screws and remove the parcel tray.

3. Disconnect the recirculation/fresh air changeover control wire. Disconnect the electrical connector. Disconnect the duct leading out of the blower assembly.

4. Remove the three mounting bolts and remove the blower assembly. You can now remove the blower motor mounting screws and remove the motor from the blower assembly.

5. Installation is the reverse of the removal procedure.

Galant

1. Disconnect the negative battery cable. Remove the screw covers and then remove the two screws from the under cover (located at the bottom of the instrument panel on the right side). Remove the under cover.

2. Remove the installation screws and remove the instrument under cover (located under the steering column). Then, remove the underframe installation screws located under that

cover and remove the passenger side underframe.

3. Remove the two stops from the bottom of the glovebox at the front. Then, remove the glovebox installation screws and remove the glovebox. Remove the duct leading into the blower unit, which is accessible through the glovebox door.

4. Remove the four mounting bolts and remove the blower assembly. Disconnect the electrical connector and the inside/outside air changeover control vacuum hose before pulling the unit all the way out.

5. Installation is the reverse of removal.

Precis

NOTE: To remove either the blower or core, the heater case must be removed.

1. Disconnect the battery ground.

2. Place the control in the HOT position.

3. Drain the cooling system.

4. Remove the heater hoses from the core tubes.

5. Remove the lower instrument panel section.

6. Remove the center console.

7. Disconnect the ducts at the heater case.

8. Disconnect the heater control cable at the case.

9. If equipped with air conditioning, discharge the system and remove the evaporator.

10. Unbolt and remove the heater case.

11. Installation is the reverse of removal. Adjust the control cable. If, necessary, charge the refrigerant system.

Heater Core

REMOVAL & INSTALLATION

Cordia, Tredia, Mirage and Galant

1. Disconnect the battery ground cable.

2. Set the heater control lever to WARM.

3. Drain the cooling system.

4. Remove the instrument panel.

5. Remove the duct from between the heater unit and the blower case.

6. Disconnect the coolant hoses at the heater case.

7. Unbolt and remove the heater case.

8. Remove the hose and pipe clamps and remove the water valve, if equipped.

9. Remove the core from the case.

10. Set the mixing damper to the closed position and, with the damper in that position, install the rod so that the water valve is fully closed.

11. Place the damper lever in the VENT position and adjust the linkage so that the FOOT/DEF damper opens to the DEF side and the VENT damper is level with the separator.

12. Install the hoses. They are marked for flow direction.

13. The remainder of assembly is the reverse of disassembly.

Starion

1. Drain the cooling system and disconnect the negative battery cable.

2. Place the heater control in the "warm" position.

3. Disconnect the heater hose at the engine firewall.

4. Remove the instrument panel and the center console.

5. Remove the center ventilator duct, defroster duct and lap duct.

6. Remove the center reinforcement and heater control assembly.

7. Remove the heater assembly mounting bolts and the heater assembly.

8. Remove the heater core.

9. Install in reverse order.

Radio

REMOVAL & INSTALLATION

Cordia and Tredia

1. Disconnect the negative battery cable. Pry the radio cover panel out with a thin object. Pry from the right on Cordia and the left on Tredia.

2. Remove the mounting screws, disconnect the antenna and electrical connector and remove the radio.

3. Installation is the reverse of removal.

Starion

1. Disconnect the negative battery cable. Insert a flat tool between the tray in the rear console and its cover and twist it to release the tray. Then, remove it. Now, remove the side console cover screws. Push the cover downward and slightly forward to release it and then remove it.

2. Remove the radio mounting screws from the center reinforcement. Put the shift lever into fourth gear and then unscrew and remove the gearshift knob.

3. Pull the front console box slightly to the rear. Then, disconnect the electrical connector and antenna at the radio. Now, pull the front console box out toward the passenger seat.

4. Now, remove the four Phillips

screws and then remove the radio panel. Remove the radio and bracket as a assembly. Remove the bracket from the radio.

5. Installation is the reverse of removal.

Mirage

1. Disconnect negative battery cable. Remove the panel that surrounds the parking brake. Remove the ashtray.

2. Remove the two console mounting screws from each side, two near the handbrake and one at the rear of the ashtray. Then, remove the console.

3. Remove the four mounting screws from the radio bracket, and remove the radio and bracket as an assembly. Now, separate the radio and bracket. Note that the radio fuses are located behind the radio and are now accessible.

4. Installation is the reverse of removal.

Galant

1. Disconnect the negative battery cable. Use a suitable tool to pry on the lower part of the radio panel and remove it. Then, remove the four Phillips screws from the sides of the radio (and tape player) mounting bracket and pull the units out. Disconnect the electrical connectors and the antenna and then remove the unit.

2. Installation is the reverse of the removal procedure.

Precis

1. Disconnect the negative battery cable.

2. Remove the trim cover retaining screws. Remove the trim cover.

3. Remove the radio retaining screws. Remove the radio support brace, if equipped.

4. Pull the radio forward and disconnect the electrical connectors and the antenna wire. Remove the radio from the vehicle.

5. Installation is the reverse of the removal procedure.

Wagon

1. Disconnect the negative battery cable.

2. Remove the trim cover retaining screws. Remove the trim cover.

3. Remove the radio retaining screws. Remove the radio support brace, if equipped.

4. Pull the radio forward and disconnect the electrical connectors and the antenna wire. Remove the radio from the vehicle.

5. Installation is the reverse of the removal procedure.

Windshield Wiper Switch

REMOVAL & INSTALLATION

Except Galant and Mirage

1. Disconnect the negative battery cable.

2. Remove the steering column lower trim panel.

3. Remove the steering wheel. Remove the steering column cable band.

4. Disconnect the electrical connections from the switch assembly.

5. Remove the switch retaining screws. Remove the switch assembly from the vehicle.

6. Installation is the reverse of the removal procedure.

Galant and Mirage

1. Disconnect the negative battery cable.

2. If equipped with tilt wheel lower the steering wheel to its lowest position.

3. Remove the steering wheel. Remove the steering column lower trim panel. Remove the steering column upper trim panel. Remove the steering column cable band.

4. Disconnect the electrical connections from the switch assembly.

5. Remove the switch retaining screws. Remove the switch assembly from the vehicle.

6. Installation is the reverse of the removal procedure.

Windshield Wiper Motor

REMOVAL & INSTALLATION

Cordia and Tredia

1. Remove the wiper blade and arm assembly.

2. Remove the cover from the access hole or the deck panel, guide panel and garnish depending on mode.

3. Remove the wiper drive mounting bolts at the arm pivots. On the Tredia, remove the washer nozzle.

4. Loosen the wiper motor mounting bolts. Disconnect the wiper motor and linkage and remove. Install in reverse order.

Starion

1. Remove the wiper arms. Remove the pivot shaft mounting nuts and washers and push the pivot shafts into the area behind the cowl.

2. Remove the cover from the access hole for the wiper motor on the right side of the cowl, underneath the hood. Then, remove the motor mounting bolts. Pull the motor into the best possible position for access and use a flat suitable tool to pry the linkage off the motor crank arm.

3. If the linkage is being replaced, it can be worked out of the cowl at this time. If the motor is being replaced, matchmark the position of the crank arm of the motor shaft of the new motor and then remove the nut and crank arm, transferring both to the new motor.

4. Installation is the reverse of removal. Make sure the wiper blades stop about 0.5 in. from the lower windshield molding. Torque the wiper arm attaching nuts to 7–12 ft. lbs.

Mirage and Precis

1. Remove the wiper arms. Remove the air inlet and cowl front center trim panels. Remove the three pivot shaft mounting nuts and push the pivot shafts into the area under the cowl.

2. Remove the motor mounting bolts. Pull the motor into the best possible position for access and use a flat suitable tool to pry the linkage off the motor crank arm. Remove the motor and then the linkage.

3. If the motor is being replaced, matchmark the position of the crank arm of the motor shaft of the new motor and then remove the nut and crank arm, transferring both to the new motor.

4. Installation is the reverse of removal. Torque the pivot shaft nuts to 4.3–5.8 ft. lbs. Position the wiper arms so the blades are about .6 in. above the lower windshield molding on the driver's side and .8 in. above it on the passenger's side. Torque the wiper arm mounting nuts to 7.2–12 ft. lbs. Make sure the wiper motor is securely grounded.

Galant

1. Remove the wiper arms. Remove the front deck and inlet trim.

2. Then, remove the three mounting bolts for each pivot shaft and push the shafts into the area behind the panel. Disconnect the electrical connector. Loosen and remove the three motor mounting bolts and then remove the motor and linkage as an assembly.

3. If the motor is being replaced, matchmark the relationship between linkage and motor, as it is critical. If the linkage only is being replaced, pry the connection off the end of the motor crank arm with a flat suitable tool.

4. Install in reverse order. Make sure the wiper arms sit in their original positions when in parked position. Make sure the wiper motor is securely grounded.

HEATER COMPONENTS

CORDIA

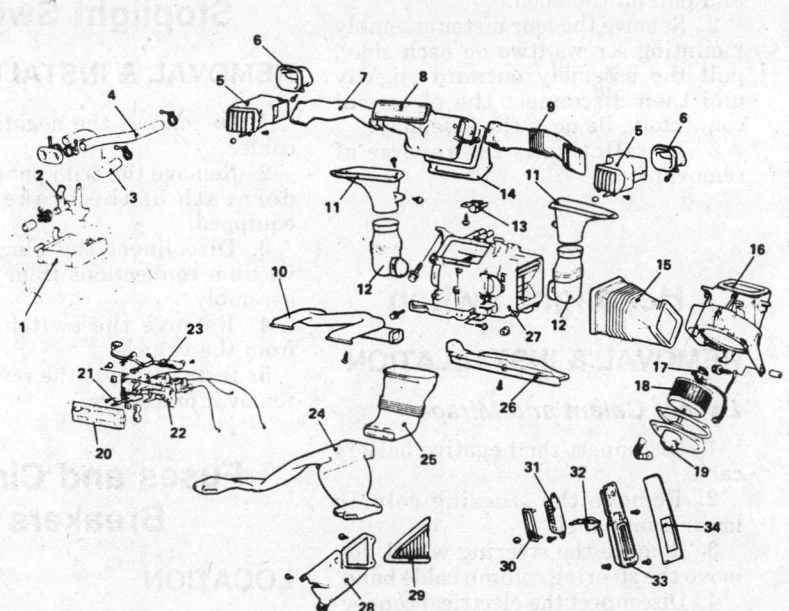

1. Heater core
2. Water valve assembly
3. Heater hose (B)
4. Heater hose (A)
5. Side duct
6. Side ventilator duct
7. Air duct (A)
8. Distribution duct
9. Air duct (B)
10. Lap heater duct
11. Defroster duct (B)
12. Defroster duct (A)
13. Heater relay
14. Center ventilator duct
15. Duct
16. Blower case
17. Resistor
18. Fan
19. Blower motor assembly
20. Heater control panel
21. Blower switch
22. Heater control assembly
23. Slide switch
24. Rear heater duct (B)
25. Rear heater duct (A)
26. Instrument under cover
27. Heater unit
28. Rear ventilator duct
29. Air outlet garnish
30. Center pillar outlet cover
31. Center pillar outlet assembly
32. Lever assembly
33. Center pillar ventilator duct
34. Center pillar garnish

1. Water valve assembly
2. Heater core
3. Heater hose (B)
4. Heater hose (A)
5. Side duct
6. Side ventilator duct
7. Air duct (A)
8. Distribution duct
9. Air duct (B)
10. Side defroster hose
11. Defroster duct (B)
12. Heater relay
13. Center ventilator duct
14. Heater unit
15. Side defroster duct
16. Defroster duct (A)
17. Duct
18. Fan
19. Resistor
20. Blower case
21. Blower motor assembly
22. Blower switch
23. Slide switch
24. Heater control panel
25. Heater control assembly
26. Instrument lower cover
27. Lap heater duct
28. Rear heater duct (B)
29. Rear heater duct (A)
30. Instrument under cover
31. Rear ventilator duct
32. Air outlet garnish

TREDIA

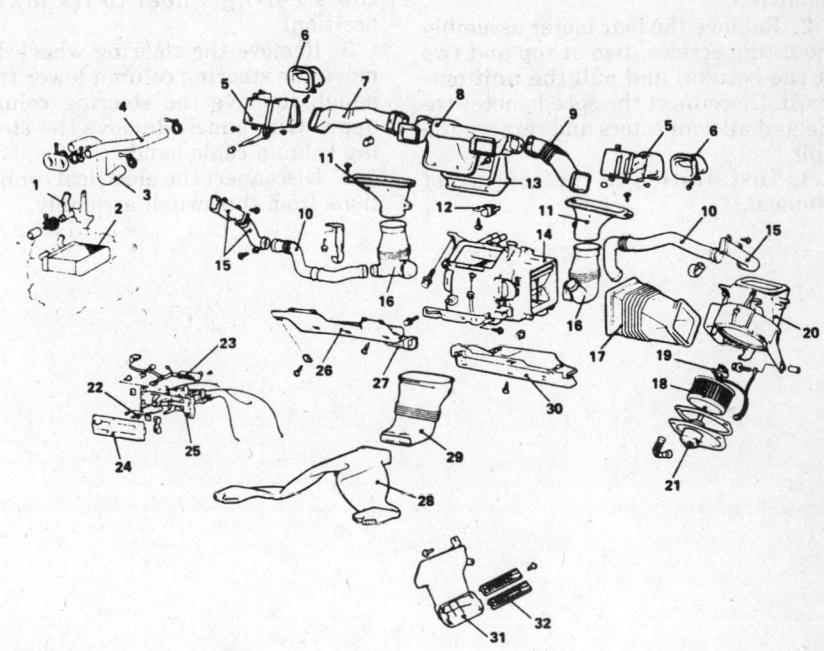

Instrument Cluster

REMOVAL & INSTALLATION

Cordia and Tredia

1. Disconnect the negative battery cable.

2. Remove the screws at the top of the instrument cluster trim panel. Remove the trim panel.

3. Disconnect the speedometer cable from the back of the speedometer.

4. Remove the cluster mounting screws and pull the cluster forward.

5. Disconnect the electrical connectors and remove the cluster. Install in reverse order.

Starion

1. Disconnect the negative battery cable.

2. Remove the meter trim hood mounting screws. Pull out and down on the side of the hood.

3. Disconnect the plug connectors on both sides of the cluster.

4. Remove the cluster mounting screws and nuts. Pull the lower sides of the cluster up and disconnect the speedometer cable.

5. Disconnect the plug connectors at the rear of the cluster and remove the cluster. Install in reverse order.

Mirage

1. Disconnect the negative battery cable. Remove the two meter hood attaching screws, located at the bottom and tile the lower meter hood outward. Pull the hood downward to release the locking tangs at the top and remove it.

2. Remove the four meter assembly mounting screws (two at top and two at the bottom) and pull the unit outward. Disconnect the speedometer cable and all connectors and remove the unit.

3. Installation is the reverse of removal.

Galant

1. Disconnect the negative battery cable. Remove the two meter hood mounting screw covers located along the bottom of the hood using a suitable tool. Then, remove the screws and pull off the hood.

2. Remove the four meter assembly mounting screws (two on each side), pull the assembly outward slightly and then disconnect the electrical connectors. Remove the assembly.

3. Installation is the reverse of removal.

Headlight Switch

REMOVAL & INSTALLATION

Except Galant and Mirage

1. Disconnect the negative battery cable.

2. Remove the steering column lower trim panel.

3. Remove the steering wheel. Remove the steering column cable band.

4. Disconnect the electrical connections from the switch assembly.

5. Remove the switch retaining screws. Remove the switch assembly from the vehicle.

6. Installation is the reverse of the removal procedure.

Galant and Mirage

1. Disconnect the negative battery cable.

2. If equipped with tilt wheel lower the steering wheel to its lowest position.

3. Remove the steering wheel. Remove the steering column lower trim panel. Remove the steering column upper trim panel. Remove the steering column cable band.

4. Disconnect the electrical connections from the switch assembly.

5. Remove the switch retaining screws. Remove the switch assembly from the vehicle.

6. Installation is the reverse of the removal procedure.

Stoplight Switch

REMOVAL & INSTALLATION

1. Disconnect the negative battery cable.

2. Remove the trim panel from underneath of the brake pedal, if equipped.

3. Disconnect the electrical and vacuum connections from the switch assembly.

4. Remove the switch assembly from the vehicle.

5. Installation is the reverse of the removal procedure.

Fuses and Circuit Breakers

LOCATION

The fuse box on every is located under the instrument panel on the left (driver's side) above the cowl side trim. On the Galant, there are also secondary fuses in the relay box in the engine compartment. The sunroof fuse is located in the electrical harness for the roof circuit—at the extreme right side of the dashboard, directly behind the right windshield pillar. The radio fuse is located behind the radio and is accessible after the radio is removed.

There is a checker knob in the fuse box that make it easy to find a blown fuse. Slide the check knob until it is lined up with the fuse you want to check. Turn on the ignition switch and lighting switch and the light will cone on, indicating the fuse is functioning.

Nissan/Datsun

200SX, 210, 280ZX, 300ZX, 310, 510, 810, Maxima, Pulsar, Sentra, Stanza, Van

12

SERIAL NUMBER IDENTIFICATION

Vehicle Identification Plate

The vehicle identification plate is attached to the hood ledge or the firewall. This plate is mounted on the front of the left strut housing on the 300ZX and on the right side of the firewall, behind the battery, on the 280ZX. On the Van, this plate is attached to the floor under the right front seat. The identification plate gives the vehicle model, engine displacement in cc., SAE horsepower rating, wheelbase, engine number and chassis number.

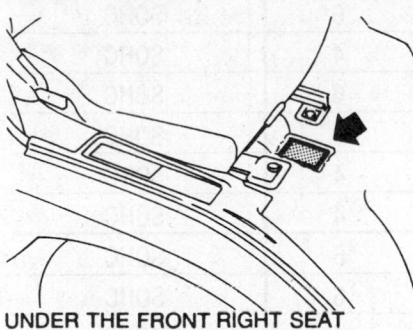

UNDER THE FRONT RIGHT SEAT

Vehicle identification plate—Van

Engine Number

The engine number is stamped on the right side top edge of the cylinder block, except on the 1984-88 200SX, Van, 300ZX and 1985-88 Maxima (VG30E, VG30ET V6). On the 300ZX, the number is stamped on the right

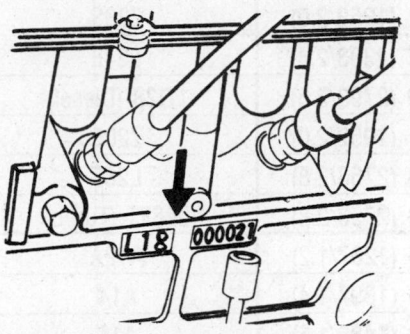

Engine serial and code number, all except V6, CD17 and CA20/CA18ET

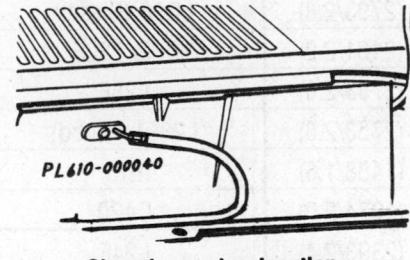

PL610-000040

Chassis number location

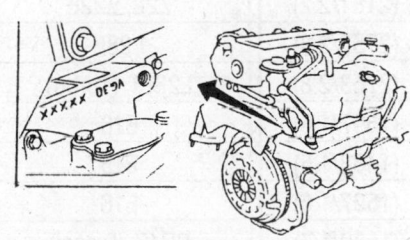

Engine identification number location— VG30E and VG30ET

VIN location

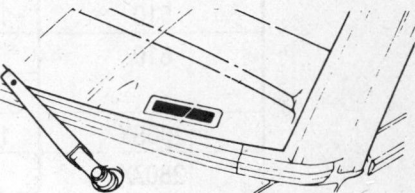

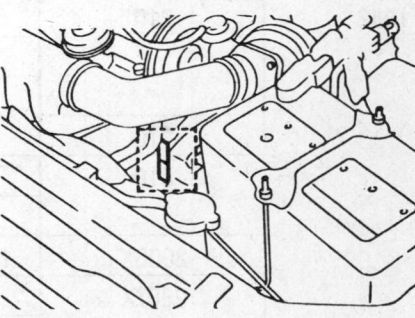

CD17 1.7L diesel engine serial number location

rear edge of the right cylinder bank, facing up. On the Maxima, the number can be found on the driver's side edge of the front cylinder bank, facing up. On the 1984-88 200SX (CA20E and CA18ET engines), the number is stamped on the left rear edge of the block, next to the bell housing. On the Van, the number can be located on the lower left edge of the cylinder head. The engine serial number is preceded by the engine model code.

Chassis Number

The chassis number is on the firewall

12–1

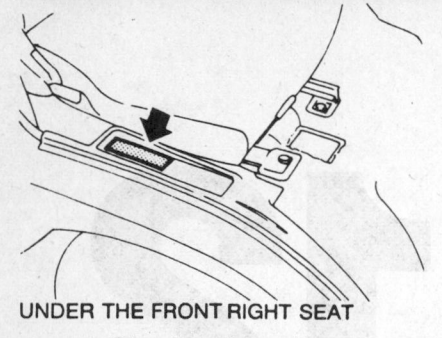

UNDER THE FRONT RIGHT SEAT

Chassis number—Van

DATSUN	TYPE	HLS30
ENGINE CAPACITY		2,393 cc
MAX. HP at RPM		151 HP at 5,600 rpm
WHEEL BASE		2,305 mm
ENGINE NO.	L24-	☐☐☐☐☐☐
CAR NO.	HLS30-	☐☐☐☐☐

NISSAN MOTOR CO., LTD.
YOKOHAMA JAPAN

Vehicle identification plate

under the hood on all models except the Van where it is stamped into the floor by the inside edge of the front passenger seat. All vehicles also have the chassis number (also known as the vehicle identification number) on a plate attached to the top of the instrument panel on the driver's side, visible through the windshield. The chassis serial number is preceded by the model designation. All models have an Emission Control information label on the firewall or on the underside of the hood.

ENGINE IDENTIFICATION

Year	Model	Engine Displacement cu. in. (cc/liter)	Engine Series Identification	No. of Cylinders	Engine Type
1981	210	75.5 (1237/1.2)	A12A	4	OHV
		85.3 (1397/1.4)	A14	4	OHV
		90.8 (1488/1.5)	A15	4	OHV
	310	90.8 (1488/1.5)	A15	4	OHV
	510	119.1 (1952/2.0)	Z20S	4	SOHC
	810	146 (2393/2.4)	L24E	6	SOHC
		170 (2793/2.8)	LD28 (Diesel)	6	SOHC
	200SX	119.1 (1952/2.0)	Z20E	4	SOHC
	280ZX	168 (2753/2.8)	L28E	6	SOHC
		168 (2753/2.8)	L28ET (Turbo)	6	SOHC
1982	210	75.5 (1237/1.2)	A12A	4	OHV
		85.3 (1397/1.4)	A14	4	OHV
		90.8 (1488/1.5)	A15	4	OHV
	310	90.8 (1488/1.5)	E15	4	SOHC
	810	146 (2393/2.4)	L24E	6	SOHC
		170 (2793/2.8)	LD28 (Diesel)	6	SOHC
	200SX	133.4 (2181/2.2)	Z22, Z22E	4	SOHC
	280ZX	168 (2753/2.8)	L28E	6	SOHC
		168 (2753/2.8)	L28ET (Turbo)	6	SOHC
	Sentra	90.8 (1488/1.5)	E15	4	SOHC
	Stanza	120.4 (1974/2.0)	CA20	4	SOHC
1983	810	146 (2393/2.4)	L24E	6	SOHC
		170 (2793/2.8)	LD28 (Diesel)	6	SOHC
	200SX	133.4 (2181/2.2)	Z22, Z22E	4	SOHC
	280ZX	168 (2753/2.8)	L28E	6	SOHC
		168 (2753/2.8)	L28ET (Turbo)	6	SOHC
	Pulsar	97.6 (1597/1.6)	E16	4	SOHC
	Sentra	90.8 (1488/1.5)	E15	4	SOHC
		97.6 (1597/1.6)	E16	4	SOHC
		103.7 (1680/1.7)	CD17 (Diesel)	4	SOHC
	Stanza	120.4 (1974/2.0)	CA20	4	SOHC

ENGINE IDENTIFICATION

Year	Model	Engine Displacement cu. in. (cc/liter)	Engine Series Identification	No. of Cylinders	Engine Type
1984	200SX	120.4 (1974/2.0)	CA20E	4	SOHC
		110.3 (1809/1.8)	CA18ET (Turbo)	4	SOHC
	300ZX	180.6 (2960/3.0)	VG30E	V6	SOHC
		180.6 (2960/3.0)	VG30ET (Turbo)	V6	SOHC
	Maxima	146 (2393/2.4)	L24E	6	SOHC
		170 (2793/2.8)	LD28 (Diesel)	6	SOHC
	Pulsar	97.6 (1597/1.6)	E16S	4	SOHC
		90.8 (1488/1.5)	E15ET (Turbo)	4	SOHC
	Sentra	97.6 (1597/1.6)	E16, E16S	4	SOHC
		103.7 (1680/1.7)	CD17 (Diesel)	4	SOHC
	Stanza	120.4 (1974/2.0)	CA20S, CA20E	4	SOHC
1985	200SX	120.4 (1974/2.0)	CA20E	4	SOHC
		110.3 (1809/1.8)	CA18ET (Turbo)	4	SOHC
	300ZX	180.6 (2960/3.0)	VG30E	V6	SOHC
		180.6 (2960/3.0)	VG30ET (Turbo)	V6	SOHC
	Maxima	180.6 (2960/3.0)	VG30E	V6	SOHC
	Pulsar	97.6 (1597/1.6)	E16S	4	SOHC
		90.8 (1488/1.5)	E15ET (Turbo)	4	SOHC
	Sentra	97.6 (1597/1.6)	E16, E16S	4	SOHC
		103.7 (1680/1.7)	CD17 (Diesel)	4	SOHC
	Stanza	120.4 (1974/2.0)	CA20S, CA20E	4	SOHC
1986	200SX	120.4 (1974/2.0)	CA20E	4	SOHC
		110.3 (1809/1.8)	CA18ET (Turbo)	4	SOHC
	300ZX	180.6 (2960/3.0)	VG30E	V6	SOHC
		180.6 (2960/3.0)	VG30ET (Turbo)	V6	SOHC
	Maxima	180.6 (2960/3.0)	VG30E	V6	SOHC
	Pulsar	97.6 (1597/1.6)	E16S	4	SOHC
	Sentra	97.6 (1597/1.6)	E16, E16S	4	SOHC
		103.7 (1680/1.7)	CD17 (Diesel)	4	SOHC
	Stanza	120.4 (1974/2.0)	CA20E	4	SOHC
1987-88	200SX	120.4 (1974/2.0)	CA20E	4	SOHC
		110.3 (1809/1.8)	CA18ET (Turbo)	4	SOHC
		180.6 (2960/3.0)	VG30E	V6	SOHC
	300ZX	180.6 (2960/3.0)	VG30E	V6	SOHC
		180.6 (2960/3.0)	VG30ET (Turbo)	V6	SOHC
	Maxima	180.6 (2960/3.0)	VG30E	V6	SOHC
	Pulsar	97.6 (1597/1.6)	E16i	4	SOHC
		97.7 (1598/1.6)	CA16DE	4	DOHC
	Sentra	97.6 (1597/1.6)	E16S, E16i	4	SOHC
		103.7 (1680/1.7)	CD17 (Diesel)	4	SOHC

ENGINE IDENTIFICATION

Year	Model	Engine Displacement cu. in. (cc/liter)	Engine Series Identification	No. of Cylinders	Engine Type
1987–88	Stanza	120.4 (1974/2.0)	CA20E	4	SOHC
	Van	146 (2389/2.4)	Z24i	4	SOHC

OHV—Pushrod-activated overhead valves
SOHC—Single overhead camshaft
DOHC—Double overhead camshaft

GENERAL ENGINE SPECIFICATIONS

Year	Model	Engine Displacement cu. in. (cc)	Fuel System Type	Net Horsepower @ rpm	Net Torque @ rpm (ft. lbs.)	Bore × Stroke (in.)	Compression Ratio	Oil Pressure @ rpm
1981	210	75.5 (1237)	2 bbl	58 @ 5600	67 @ 3600	2.95 × 2.75	8.5:1	64 @ 3000
		85.3 (1397)	2 bbl	65 @ 5600	75 @ 3600	2.99 × 3.03	8.9:1	64 @ 3000
		90.8 (1488)	2 bbl	67 @ 5200	82 @ 3200	2.99 × 3.23	8.9:1	64 @ 3000
	310	90.8 (1488)	2 bbl	67 @ 5200	82 @ 3200	2.99 × 3.23	8.9:1	64 @ 3000
	510	119.1 (1952)	2 bbl	92 @ 5200	112 @ 2800	3.35 × 3.39	8.5:1	—
	810	146 (2393)	EFI	120 @ 5200	134 @ 2800	3.27 × 2.90	8.9:1	43 @ 2000
		170 (2793)	DFI	80 @ 4600	120 @ 2400	3.33 × 3.27	22.7:1	—
	200SX	119.1 (1952)	EFI	100 @ 5200	112 @ 3200	3.35 × 3.39	8.5:1	—
	280ZX	168 (2753)	EFI	145 @ 5200	156 @ 4000	3.39 × 3.11	8.8:1	43 @ 2000
		168 (2753)	EFI①	180 @ 5600	202 @ 2800	3.39 × 3.11	7.4:1	43 @ 2000
1982	210	75.5 (1237)	2 bbl	58 @ 5600	67 @ 3600	2.95 × 2.75	8.5:1	64 @ 3000
		85.3 (1397)	2 bbl	65 @ 5600	75 @ 3600	2.99 × 3.03	8.9:1	64 @ 3000
		90.8 (1488)	2 bbl	67 @ 5200	82 @ 3200	2.99 × 3.23	8.9:1	64 @ 3000
	310	90.8 (1488)	2 bbl	67 @ 5200	85 @ 3200	2.92 × 3.23	9.0:1	43 @ 1700
	810	146 (2393)	EFI	120 @ 5200	134 @ 2800	3.27 × 2.90	8.9:1	43 @ 2000
		170 (2793)	DFI	80 @ 4600	120 @ 2400	3.33 × 3.27	22.7:1	—
	200SX	133.4 (2181)	EFI	102 @ 5200	129 @ 2800	3.43 × 3.62	8.5:1	—
	280ZX	168 (2753)	EFI	145 @ 5200	156 @ 4000	3.39 × 3.11	8.8:1	43 @ 2000
		168 (2753)	EFI①	180 @ 5600	202 @ 2800	3.39 × 3.11	7.4:1	43 @ 2000
	Sentra	90.8 (1488)	2 bbl	67 @ 5200	85 @ 3200	2.92 × 3.23	9.0:1	43 @ 1700
	Stanza	120.4 (1974)	2 bbl	88 @ 5200	112 @ 2800	3.33 × 3.46	8.5:1	43 @ 2000
1983	810	146 (2393)	EFI	120 @ 5200	134 @ 2800	3.27 × 2.90	8.9:1	43 @ 2000
		170 (2793)	DFI	80 @ 4600	120 @ 2400	3.33 × 3.27	22.7:1	—
	200SX	133.4 (2181)	EFI	102 @ 5200	129 @ 2800	3.43 × 3.62	8.5:1	—
	280ZX	168 (2753)	EFI	145 @ 5200	156 @ 4000	3.39 × 3.11	8.8:1	43 @ 2000
		168 (2753)	EFI①	180 @ 5600	202 @ 2800	3.39 × 3.11	7.4:1	43 @ 2000
	Pulsar	97.6 (1597)	2 bbl	69 @ 5200	93 @ 3200	2.99 × 3.46	9.4:1	43 @ 1700
	Sentra	90.8 (1488)	2 bbl	67 @ 5200	85 @ 3200	2.92 × 3.23	9.0:1	43 @ 1700
		97.7 (1597)	2 bbl	69 @ 5200	93 @ 3200	2.99 × 3.46	9.4:1	43 @ 1700
		103.7 (1680)	DFI	55 @ 4800	104 @ 2800	3.15 × 3.31	22.2:1	—
	Stanza	120.4 (1974)	2 bbl	88 @ 5200	112 @ 2800	3.33 × 3.46	8.5:1	43 @ 2000

GENERAL ENGINE SPECIFICATIONS

Year	Model	Engine Displacement cu. in. (cc)	Fuel System Type	Net Horsepower @ rpm	Net Torque @ rpm (ft. lbs.)	Bore × Stroke (in.)	Compression Ratio	Oil Pressure @ rpm
1984	200SX	120.4 (1974)	EFI	102 @ 5200	116 @ 3200	3.33 × 3.46	8.5:1	43 @ 2000
		110.3 (1809)	EFI①	120 @ 5200	134 @ 3200	3.27 × 3.29	8.0:1	43 @ 2000
	300ZX	180.6 (2960)	EFI	160 @ 5200	174 @ 4000	3.43 × 3.27	9.0:1	43 @ 2000
		180.6 (2960)	EFI①	200 @ 5200	227 @ 3600	3.43 × 3.27	7.8:1	43 @ 2000
	Maxima	146 (2393)	EFI	120 @ 5200	134 @ 2800	3.27 × 2.90	8.9:1	43 @ 2000
		170 (2793)	DFI	80 @ 4600	120 @ 2400	3.33 × 3.27	22.7:1	—
	Pulsar	97.6 (1597)	2 bbl	69 @ 5200	93 @ 3200	2.99 × 3.46	9.4:1	43 @ 1700
		90.8 (1488)	EFI①	100 @ 5200	152 @ 3200	2.92 × 3.23	7.8:1	43 @ 1700
	Sentra	97.6 (1597)	2 bbl	69 @ 5200	93 @ 3200	2.99 × 3.46	9.4:1	43 @ 1700
		103.7 (1680)	DFI	55 @ 4800	104 @ 2800	3.15 × 3.31	22.2:1	
	Stanza	120.4 (1974)	2 bbl	88 @ 5200	112 @ 2800	3.33 × 3.46	8.5:1	43 @ 2000
		120.4 (1974)	EFI	97 @ 5200	114 @ 3200	3.33 × 3.46	8.5:1	43 @ 2000
1985	200SX	120.4 (1974)	EFI	102 @ 5200	116 @ 3200	3.33 × 3.46	8.5:1	43 @ 2000
		110.3 (1809)	EFI①	120 @ 5200	134 @ 3200	3.27 × 3.29	8.0:1	43 @ 2000
	300ZX	180.6 (2960)	EFI	160 @ 5200	174 @ 4000	3.43 × 3.27	9.0:1	43 @ 2000
		180.6 (2960)	EFI①	200 @ 5200	227 @ 3600	3.43 × 3.27	7.8:1	43 @ 2000
	Maxima	180.6 (2960)	EFI	152 @ 5200	167 @ 3600	3.43 × 3.27	9.0:1	43 @ 2000
	Pulsar	97.6 (1597)	2 bbl	69 @ 5200	93 @ 3200	2.99 × 3.46	9.4:1	43 @ 1700
		90.8 (1488)	EFI①	100 @ 5200	152 @ 3200	2.92 × 3.23	7.8:1	43 @ 1700
	Sentra	97.6 (1597)	2 bbl	69 @ 5200	93 @ 3200	2.99 × 3.46	9.4:1	43 @ 1700
		103.7 (1680)	DFI	55 @ 4800	104 @ 2800	3.15 × 3.31	22.2:1	—
	Stanza	120.4 (1974)	2 bbl	88 @ 5200	112 @ 2800	3.33 × 3.46	8.5:1	43 @ 2000
		120.4 (1974)	EFI	97 @ 5200	114 @ 3200	3.33 × 3.46	8.5:1	43 @ 2000
1986	200SX	120.4 (1974)	EFI	102 @ 5200	116 @ 3200	3.33 × 3.46	8.5:1	43 @ 2000
		110.3 (1809)	EFI①	120 @ 5200	134 @ 3200	3.27 × 3.29	8.0:1	43 @ 2000
	300ZX	180.6 (2960)	EFI	160 @ 5200	174 @ 4000	3.43 × 3.27	9.0:1	43 @ 2000
		180.6 (2960)	EFI①	200 @ 5200	227 @ 3600	3.43 × 3.27	7.8:1	43 @ 2000
	Maxima	180.6 (2960)	EFI	152 @ 5200	167 @ 3600	3.43 × 3.27	9.0:1	43 @ 2000
	Pulsar	97.6 (1597)	2 bbl	69 @ 5200	93 @ 3200	2.99 × 3.46	9.4:1	43 @ 1700
	Sentra	97.6 (1597)	2 bbl	69 @ 5200	93 @ 3200	2.99 × 3.46	9.4:1	43 @ 1700
		103.7 (1680)	DFI	55 @ 4800	104 @ 2800	3.15 × 3.31	22.2:1	—
	Stanza	120.4 (1974)	2 bbl	88 @ 5200	112 @ 2800	3.33 × 3.46	8.5:1	43 @ 2000
		120.4 (1974)	EFI	97 @ 5200	114 @ 3200	3.33 × 3.46	8.5:1	43 @ 2000
1987-88	200SX	120.4 (1974)	EFI	102 @ 5200	116 @ 3200	3.33 × 3.46	8.5:1	43 @ 2000
		110.3 (1809)	EFI①	120 @ 5200	134 @ 3200	3.27 × 3.29	8.0:1	43 @ 2000
		180.6 (2960)	EFI	160 @ 5200	174 @ 4000	3.43 × 3.27	9.0:1	43 @ 2000
	300ZX	180.6 (2960)	EFI	160 @ 5200	174 @ 4000	3.43 × 3.27	9.0:1	43 @ 2000
		180.6 (2960)	EFI①	200 @ 5200	227 @ 3600	3.43 × 3.27	7.8:1	43 @ 2000
	Maxima	180.6 (2960)	EFI	160 @ 5200	174 @ 4000	3.43 × 3.27	9.0:1	43 @ 2000
	Pulsar	97.6 (1597)	EFI	70 @ 5000	94 @ 2800	2.99 × 3.46	9.4:1	43 @ 1700
		97.7 (1598)	EFI	113 @ 6400	99 @ 4800	3.07 × 3.29	10.0:1	67 @ 2000

GENERAL ENGINE SPECIFICATIONS

Year	Model	Engine Displacement cu. in. (cc)	Fuel System Type	Net Horsepower @ rpm	Net Torque @ rpm (ft. lbs.)	Bore × Stroke (in.)	Compression Ratio	Oil Pressure @ rpm
1987–88	Sentra	97.6 (1597)	2 bbl	70 @ 5000	92 @ 2800	2.99 × 3.46	9.4:1	43 @ 1700
		103.7 (1680)	DFI	55 @ 4800	104 @ 2800	3.15 × 3.31	22.2:1	50 @ 2000
	Stanza	120.4 (1974)	EFI	97 @ 5200	114 @ 3200	3.33 × 3.46	8.5:1	43 @ 2000
	Van	146 (2389)	EFI	106 @ 4800	NA	3.50 × 3.78	9.0:1	43 @ 2000

NA Not available at time of publication
① Turbocharged

GASOLINE ENGINE TUNE-UP SPECIFICATIONS

Year	Model	Engine Displacement cu. in. (cc)	Spark Plugs Type	Gap (in.)	Ignition Timing (deg.) MT	AT	Compression Pressure (psi)	Fuel Pump (psi)	Idle Speed (rpm) MT	AT	Valve Clearance In.	Ex.
1981	210,310	75.5 (1237)	BP5ES-11	0.041	10B	5B	192	3.8	700	650	0.014	0.014
		85.3 (1397)	BP5ES-11	0.041	5B ①	5B	192	3.8	700	650	0.014	0.014
		90.8 (1488)	BP5ES-11	0.041	5B ①	5B	192	3.8	700	650	0.014	0.014
	510	119.1 (1952)	BP6ES ②	0.033	6B	6B	171	3.8	600	600	0.012	0.012
	810	146 (2393)	BP6ES	0.041	10B	10B	171	36	700	650	0.010	0.012
	200SX	119.1 (1952)	BP6ES ②	0.033	6B	6B	171	37	750	700	0.012	0.012
	280ZX	168 (2753)	BPR6ES-11	0.041	8B	8B	171	36	700	700	0.010	0.012
		168 (2753) ⑥	BPR6ES-11	0.041	20B	20B	171	36	650	650	0.010	0.012
1982	210	75.5 (1237)	BP5ES-11	0.041	10B	5B	192	3.8	700	650	0.014	0.014
		85.3 (1397)	BP5ES-11	0.041	5B ①	5B	192	3.8	700	650	0.014	0.014
		90.8 (1488)	BP5ES-11	0.041	5B ①	5B	192	3.8	700	650	0.014	0.014
	310	90.8 (1488)	BPR5ES-11	0.041	2A ③	2A ③	181	3.8	750	750	0.011	0.011
	810	146 (2393)	BP6ES	0.041	8B	8B	171	36	700	650	0.010	0.012
	200SX	133.4 (2181)	BPR6ES ⑤	0.033	8B	8B	171	37	750	700	0.012	0.012
	280ZX	168 (2753)	BPR6ES-11	0.041	8B	8B	171	36	700	700	0.010	0.012
		168 (2753) ⑥	BPR6ES-11	0.041	20B	20B	171	36	650	650	0.010	0.012
	Sentra	90.8 (1488)	BPR5ES-11	0.041	2A ③	2A ③	181	3.8	750	750 ④	0.011	0.011
	Stanza	120.4 (1974)	BPR6ES-11 ⑦	0.041	0	0	171	3.8	750	700	0.012	0.012

GASOLINE ENGINE TUNE-UP SPECIFICATIONS

Year	Model	Engine Displacement cu. in. (cc)	Spark Plugs Type	Gap (in.)	Ignition Timing (deg.) MT	AT	Compression Pressure (psi)	Fuel Pump (psi)	Idle Speed (rpm) MT	AT	Valve Clearance In.	Ex.
1983	810	146 (2393)	BP6ES	0.041	8B	8B	171	36	700	650	0.010	0.012
	200SX	133.4 (2181)	BPR6ES [5]	0.033	8B	8B	171	37	750	700	0.012	0.012
	280ZX	168 (2753)	BPR6ES-11	0.041	8B	8B	171	36	700	700	0.010	0.012
		168 (2753) [6]	BPR6ES-11	0.041	24B	24B	171	36	650	650	0.010	0.012
	Pulsar	97.6 (1597)	BPR5ES-11 [8]	0.041	[9]	[9]	181	3.8	750	650	0.011	0.011
	Sentra	90.8 (1488)	BPR5ES-11	0.041	2A	2A	181	3.8	750	750	0.011	0.011
		97.6 (1597)	BPR5ES-11 [8]	0.041	[9]	[9]	181	3.8	750	650	0.011	0.011
	Stanza	120.4 (1974)	BPR6ES-11 [7]	0.041	0	0	171	3.8	750	700	0.012	0.012
1984	200SX	120.4 (1974)	BCPR6ES-11 [10]	0.041	0 [20]	0	171	37 [11]	750	700 [12]	0.012	0.012
		110.3 (1809) [6]	BCPR6ES-11 [10]	0.041	15B	15B	171	37	750	700 [12]	0.012	0.012
	300ZX	180.6 (2960)	BCPR6ES-11	0.041	20B	20B	173	37	700	650	Hyd.	Hyd.
		180.6 (2960) [6]	BCPR6E-11	0.041	20B	20B	165	37	700	650	Hyd.	Hyd.
	Maxima	146 (2393)	BPR6ES-11	0.041	8B	8B	171	36	700	650	0.010	0.012
	Pulsar	97.6 (1597)	BPR5ES-11 [8]	0.041	[9]	[9]	181	3.8	750	650	0.011	0.011
		90.8 (1488) [6]	BPR6ES-11	0.041	15B	15B	181	37	750	650	0.011	0.011
	Sentra	97.6 (1597)	BPR5ES-11 [8]	0.041	[9]	[9]	181	3.8	750	650	0.011	0.011
	Stanza	120.4 (1974)	BPR6ES-11 [7]	0.041	0	0	171	3.8	750	700	0.012	0.012
		120.4 (1974) (14)	BCPR6ES-11 [10]	0.041	0	0	171	37	750 [11]	700 [12]	0.012	0.012
1985	200SX	120.4 (1974)	BCPR6ES-11 [10]	0.041	4B	0	171	37	750	700	0.012	0.012
		110.3 (1809)	BCPR6ES-11 [10]	0.041	15B	15B	171	37	750	750 [12]	0.012	0.012
	300ZX	180.6 (2960)	BCPR6ES-11	0.041	20B	20B	173	37	700 [12]	700 [12]	Hyd.	Hyd.
		180.6 (2960) [6]	BCPR6E-11	0.041	20B	20B	165	37	700	650	Hyd.	Hyd.
	Maxima	180.6 (2960)	BCPR6ES-11	0.041	20B	20B	173	37	700 [12]	700 [12]	Hyd.	Hyd.
	Pulsar	97.6 (1597)	BPR5ES-11 [8]	0.041	[9]	[9]	181	3.8	750	650	0.011	0.011

GASOLINE ENGINE TUNE-UP SPECIFICATIONS

Year	Model	Engine Displacement cu. in. (cc)	Spark Plugs Type	Gap (in.)	Ignition Timing (deg.) MT	AT	Compression Pressure (psi)	Fuel Pump (psi)	Idle Speed (rpm) MT	AT	Valve Clearance In.	Ex.
1985		90.8 (1488) ⑥	BPR6ES-11	0.041	15B	15B	181	37	750	650	0.011	0.011
	Sentra	97.6 (1597)	BPR5ES-11 ⑧	0.041	⑨	⑨	181	3.8	750	650	0.011	0.011
	Stanza	120.4 (1974) ⑬	BPR6ES-11 ⑦	0.041	0	0	171	3.8	650	650	0.012	0.012
		120.4 (1974) ⑭	BCPR6ES-11 ⑩	0.041	4B	0	171	37	750	700	0.012	0.012
1986	200SX	120.4 (1974) ⑩	BCPR6ES-11	0.041	4B ⑯	0 ⑯	171	37	750	700	0.012 ⑰	0.012 ⑰
		110.3 (1809) ⑥	BCPR6ES-11	0.041	15B	15B	171	37	750 ⑫	750 ⑫	0.012	0.012
	300ZX	180.6 (2960)	BCPR6ES-11	0.041	20B	20B	173	37	700 ⑫	700 ⑫	Hyd.	Hyd.
		180.6 (2960) ⑥	BCPR6E-11	0.041	20B	20B	165	37	700	650	Hyd.	Hyd.
	Maxima	180.6 (2960)	BCPR6ES-11	0.041	20B	20B	173	37	700 ⑫	700 ⑫	Hyd.	Hyd.
	Pulsar	97.6 (1597)	BPR5ES-11 ⑧	0.041	⑮	⑮	181	3.8	800	650	0.011	0.011
	Sentra	97.6 (1597)	BPR5ES-11 ⑧	0.041	⑯	⑯	181	3.8	800	650	0.011	0.011
	Stanza	120.4 (1974)	BCPR6ES-11 ⑩	0.041	4B	0	171	37	750	700	0.012	0.012
1987	200SX	120.4 (1974)	BCPR6ES-11 ⑩	0.041	15B	15B	171	37	750	700	Hyd.	Hyd.
		110.3 (1809) ⑥	BCPR5ES-11	0.041	15B	15B	171	37	750	—	0.012	0.012
		180.6 (2960)	BCPR6ES-11 ⑩	0.041	20B	20B	173	37	700	700	Hyd.	Hyd.
	300ZX	180.6 (2960)	BCPR6ES-11	0.041	20B	20B	173	37	700	650	Hyd.	Hyd.
		180.6 (2960) ⑥	BCPR6E-11	0.041	15B	15B	165	37	700	650	Hyd.	Hyd.
	Maxima	180.6 (2960)	BCPR6ES-11	0.041	20B	20B	173	37	750	700	Hyd.	Hyd.
	Pulsar	97.6 (1597)	BPR5ES-11	0.041	7B	7B	181	14	800	700	0.011	0.011
		97.8 (1598)	PFR6A-11	NA	15B	—	199	28	800	—	Hyd.	Hyd.
	Sentra	97.6 (1597)	BPR5ES-11	0.041	7B	7B	181	14 ⑱	800	700	0.011	0.011
	Stanza	120.4 (1974)	BCPR6ES-11 ⑩	0.041	15B	15B	171	37	750	700	Hyd. ⑲	Hyd. ⑲
	Van	146 (2389)	BPR5ES	0.041	10B	10B	173	36	800	700	0.012	0.012

GASOLINE ENGINE TUNE-UP SPECIFICATIONS

Year	Model	Engine Displacement cu. in. (cc)	Spark Plugs Type	Gap (in.)	Ignition Timing (deg.) MT	AT	Compression Pressure (psi)	Fuel Pump (psi)	Idle Speed (rpm) MT	AT	Valve Clearance In.	Ex.
1988					SEE UNDERHOOD SPECIFICATIONS STICKER							

NOTE: The Underhood Specifications sticker often reflects tune-up specification changes made in production. Sticker figures must be used if they disagree with those in this chart.

MT Manual transmission
AT Automatic transmission
NA Not adjustable
A After Top Dead Center
B Before Top Dead Center
Hyd. Hydraulic valve lash adjusters
① Canada—6B
② Canada—BPR6ES-11
③ Canada—4A
④ Canada—650 rpm
⑤ Intake side; Exhaust side—BPR5ES
⑥ Turbocharged model

⑦ Intake side; Exhaust side—BPR5ES-11
⑧ Canada—BPR5ES; Gap—0.033
⑨ 5A @ 750 rpm MT; Calif. & Can.
 5A @ 650 rpm AT; Calif. & Can.
 15B @ 800 rpm MT; 49 States
 8B @ 650 rpm AT; 49 States
⑩ Intake side; Exhaust side—BCPR5ES-11
⑪ 49 States Stanza—800 rpm
⑫ High Altitude Models—680 rpm
⑬ CA20S

⑭ CA20E
⑮ 5A @ 800 rpm MT; Calif. & Can.
 5A @ 650 rpm AT; Calif. & Can.
 10B @ 800 rpm MT; 49 States
 10B @ 650 rpm AT; 49 States
⑯ Mid-year models—15B
⑰ Mid-year models—Hyd.
⑱ E16S—3.8
⑲ Station wagon—0.012
⑳ Models built after 6/1/84: 4B

DIESEL ENGINE TUNE-UP SPECIFICATIONS

Year	Engine Displacement cu. in. (cc)	Valve Clearance Intake (in.)	Exhaust (in.)	Intake Valve Opens (deg.)	Injection Pump Setting (deg.)	Injection Nozzle Pressure (psi) New	Used	Idle Speed (rpm)	Cranking Compression Pressure (psi)
1981	170 (2793)	0.010	0.012	—	align marks	1,920–2,033	1,178–1,920	650	455
1982	170 (2793)	0.010	0.012	—	align marks	1,920–2,033	1,178–1,920	650	455
1983	170 (2793)	0.010	0.012	—	align marks	1,920–2,033	1,178–1,920	650	455
	103.7 (1680)	0.012	0.020	—	see text	1,920–2,033	1,178–1,920	750	455
1984	170 (2793)	0.010	0.012	—	align marks	1,920–2,033	1,178–1,920	650	455
	103.7 (1680)	0.008–0.012	0.016–0.020	—	see text	1,920–2,033	1,178–1,920	750	455
1985	103.7 (1680)	0.008–0.012	0.016–0.020	—	see text	1,920–2,033	1,178–1,920	750	455
1986	103.7 (1680)	0.008–0.012	0.016–0.020	—	see text	1,920–2,033	1,178–1,920	750	455
1987-88	103.7 (1680)	0.008–0.012	0.016–0.020	—	see text	1,920–2,033	1,178–1,920	700	455

NOTE: The Underhood Specifications sticker often reflects tune-up specification changes made in production. Sticker figures must be used if they disagree with those in this chart.

FIRING ORDERS

NOTE: To avoid confusion when replacing spark plug wires, always remove them one at a time.

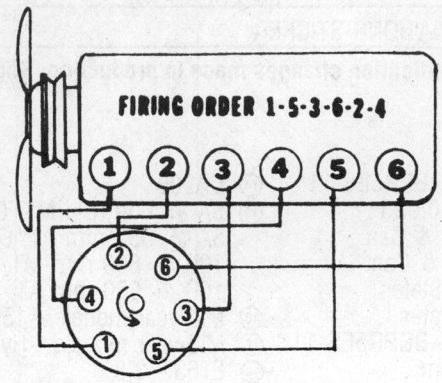

L24, L28 engines

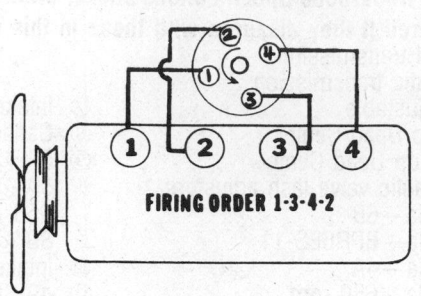

A-series engines

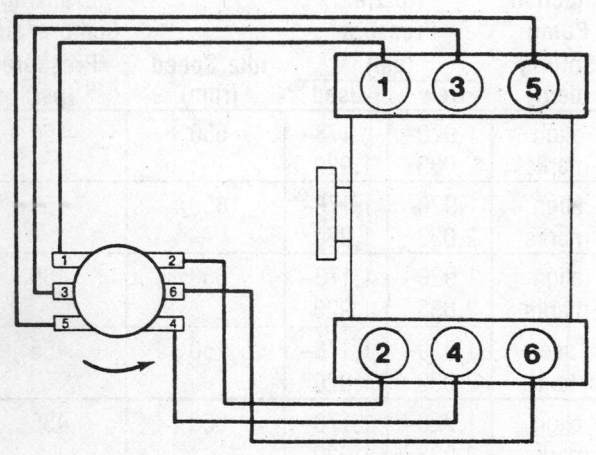

V6 engine firing order: 1–2–3–4–5–6

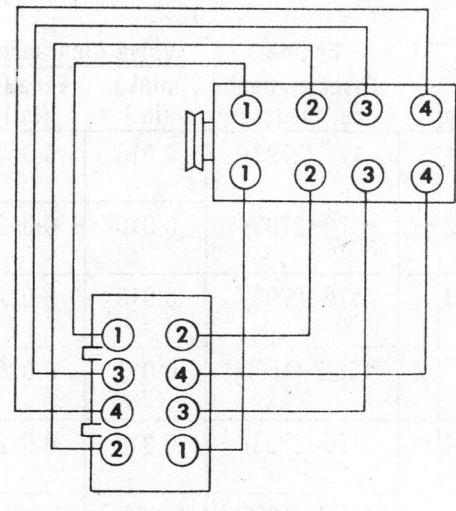

C-Series engines

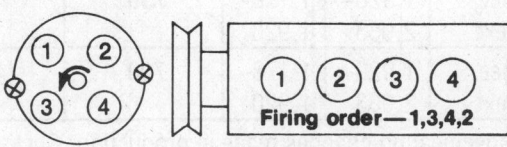

E-Series engines

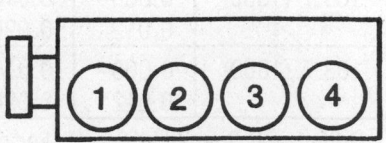

Firing order 1-3-4-2—CD 17

FIRING ORDERS

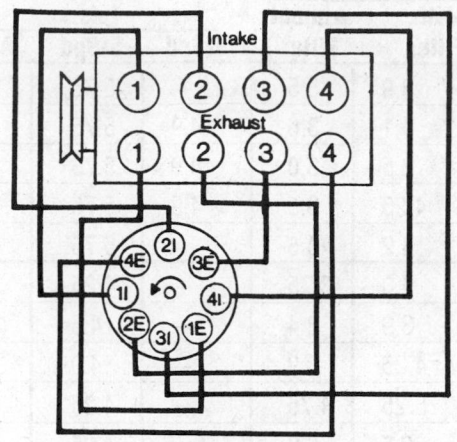

Z-Series engines

CAPACITIES

Year	Model	Engine Displacement cu. in. (cc)	Engine Crankcase with Filter	Engine Crankcase without Filter	Transmission (pts.) 4-Spd	Transmission (pts.) 5-Spd	Transmission (pts.) Auto.■	Drive Axle (pts.)	Fuel Tank (gal.)	Cooling System (qts.)
1981	210	75.5 (1237)	3.4	2.8	2.5	—	11.8	1.8	13.25	6.25①
		85.3 (1397)	3.4	2.8	2.5	—	11.8	1.8	13.25	6.25①
		90.8 (1488)	3.25	2.5	—	2.5	11.8	1.8	13.25	6.25①
	310	90.8 (1488)	3.4	2.8	4.9	4.9	—	—	13.25	6.25
	510	119.1 (1952)	4.65	4.0	3.15	3.6	11.8	2.4	13.25	9.25
	810	146 (2393)	5.25	4.75	—	4.25	11.8	2.1	16.4②	11.6
		170 (2793)	6.5	6.0	—	4.25	11.8	2.1	16.4②	11.0
	200SX	119.1 (1952)	4.4	4.1	—	4.25	11.8	2.4	14②	10.0
	280ZX	168 (2753)	4.75	4.25	—	4.25	11.8	2.75	21.12	11.12
1982	210	75.5 (1237)	3.4	2.8	2.5	—	11.8	1.8	13.25	6.25①
		85.3 (1397)	3.4	2.8	2.5	—	11.8	1.8	13.25	6.25①
		90.8 (1488)	3.25	2.5	—	2.5	11.8	1.8	13.25	6.25①
	310	90.8 (1488)	4.12	3.16	4.9	5.7	12.8	—	13.25	6.50
	810	146 (2393)	5.25	4.75	—	4.25	11.8	2.1	16.4②	11.0
		170 (2793)	6.5	6.0	—	4.25	11.8	2.1	16.4②	10.0
	200SX	119.1 (1952)	4.4	4.1	—	4.25	11.8	2.4	14②	10.0
	280ZX	168 (2753)	4.75	4.25	—	4.25	11.8	2.75	21.12	11.12
	Sentra	90.8 (1488)	4.1	3.6	4.9	5.75	13.0	—	13.25	5.5
	Stanza	120.4 (1974)	4.2	3.75	—	5.75	13.0	—	14.25③	7.2
1983	810	146 (2393)	5.25	4.75	—	4.25	11.8	2.1	16.4②	11.0
		170 (2793)	6.5	6.0	—	4.25	11.8	2.1	16.4②	10.0
	200SX	133.4 (2181)	4.4	4.1	—	4.25	11.8	2.4	14②	10.0
	280ZX	168 (2753)	4.75	4.25	—	4.25	11.8	2.75	21.12	11.12

CAPACITIES

Year	Model	Engine Displacement cu. in. (cc)	Engine Crankcase with Filter	without Filter	Transmission (pts.) 4-Spd	5-Spd	Auto.	Drive Axle (pts.)	Fuel Tank (gal.)	Cooling System (qts.)
1983	Pulsar	97.6 (1597)	3.9	3.5	—	5.75	13.0	—	13.25	5.5
	Sentra	90.8 (1488)	4.1	3.6	4.9	5.75	13.0	—	13.25	5.5
		97.6 (1597)	3.5	3.0	4.9	5.75	13.0	—	13.25	5.5
		103.7 (1680)	4.25	3.5	4.9	5.75	13.0	—	13.25	7.5
	Stanza	120.4 (1974)	4.2	3.5	—	5.75	13.0	—	14.25③	7.2
1984	200SX	120.4 (1974)	4.0	3.75	—	4.25	14.5	④	14	9.1
		110.3 (1809)	3.9	3.4	—	4.5	14.6	④	14	9.1
	300ZX	180.6 (2960)	4.25	3.9	—	4.0	14.5	2.75	19	11.1⑤
	Maxima	146 (2393)	5.25	4.75	—	4.25	11.8	2.1	16.4②	11.0
		170 (2793)	6.5	6.0	—	4.25	11.8	2.1	16.4②	10.0
	Pulsar	97.6 (1597)	3.9	3.5	—	5.75	13.0	—	13.25	5.5
		90.8 (1488)	4.75	4.25	—	5.75	13.0	—	13.25	5.5
	Sentra	97.6 (1597)	3.5	3.0	4.9	5.75	13.0	—	13.25	5.5
		103.7 (1680)	4.25	3.5	4.9	5.75	13.0	—	10.75	7.5
	Stanza	120.4 (1974)	4.2	3.75	—	5.75	13.0	—	14.25③	7.2
1985	200SX	120.4 (1974)	3.9	3.4	—	4.5	14.6	④	14	9.1
		110.3 (1809)	3.9	3.4	—	4.5	14.6	④	14	9.1
	300ZX	180.6 (2960)	4.25	3.9	—	4.0	14.5	2.75	19	11.1⑤
	Maxima	180.6 (2960)	4.5	4.1	—	10.0	14.5	—	15.9	9.75
	Pulsar	97.6 (1597)	3.5	3.1	—	5.75	13.0	—	13.25	5.5
		90.8 (1488)	4.25	3.85	—	5.75	13.0	—	13.25	5.5
	Sentra	97.6 (1597)	3.5	3.0	4.9	5.75	13.0	—	13.25	5.5
		103.7 (1680)	4.25	3.5	4.9	5.75	13.0	—	10.75	7.5
	Stanza	120.4 (1974)	3.75	3.25	—	5.75	13.0	—	14.25③	7.2
1986	200SX	120.4 (1974)	3.9	3.4	—	4.5	14.6	④	14	9.1
		110.3 (1809)	3.9	3.4	—	4.5	14.6	④	14	9.1
	300ZX	180.6 (2960)	4.25	3.9	—	4.0	14.5	2.75	19	11.1⑤
	Maxima	180.6 (2960)	4.5	4.1	—	10.0	14.5	—	15.9	9.75
	Pulsar	97.6 (1597)	3.5	3.1	—	5.75	13.0	—	13.25	5.5
	Sentra	97.6 (1597)	3.5	3.0	4.9	5.75	13.0	—	13.25	5.5
		103.7 (1680)	4.25	3.5	4.9	5.75	13.0	—	10.75	7.5
	Stanza	120.4 (1974)	3.75	3.25	—	5.75	13.0	—	14.25③	7.2
1987-88	200SX	120.4 (1974)	3.9	3.4	—	4.25	14.6	④	14	9.1
		110.3 (1809)	3.9	3.4	—	4.25	14.6	④	14	9.1
		180.6 (2960)	4.5	4.0	—	4.25	14.6	2.75	14	9.6
	300ZX	180.6 (2960)	4.25	3.9	—	4.25	14.5	2.75	19	11.1⑤
	Maxima	180.6 (2960)	4.5	4.1	—	10.0	14.5	—	15.9	9.75
	Pulsar	97.6 (1597)	3.4	2.9	—	5.75	13.0	—	13.25	⑥
		97.8 (1598)	3.75	3.25	—	5.75	—	—	13.25	5.9

CAPACITIES

Year	Model	Engine Displacement cu. in. (cc)	Engine Crankcase with Filter	Engine Crankcase without Filter	Transmission (pts.) 4-Spd	Transmission (pts.) 5-Spd	Transmission (pts.) Auto.	Drive Axle (pts.)	Fuel Tank (gal.)	Cooling System (qts.)
1987-88	Sentra	97.6 (1597)	3.5	3.0	—	5.75	13.0	—	13.75⑦	⑥
		103.7 (1680)	4.25	3.5	—	5.75	13.0	—	13.75	6.9
	Stanza	120.4 (1974)	3.75	3.25	—	10	14.5	—	15.9⑧	7.75
	Van	146 (2389)	4.5	3.9	—	4.25	14.6	—	17.2	7.5⑨

■ Figure is for drain and refill
— Not applicable
① AT—6 qts.
② Hatchback or station wagon—15.9
③ Station wagon—15.9
④ Solid rear axle—2.1
   IRS—2.75
⑤ Turbo—11.5
⑥ MT—4.9; AT—5.5
⑦ 4wd—12.4
⑧ 4wd—13.25
⑨ With rear heater—9.7

CAMSHAFT SPECIFICATIONS
All measurements given in inches.

Year	Engine Displacement cu. in. (cc)	Journal Diameter 1	Journal Diameter 2	Journal Diameter 3	Journal Diameter 4	Journal Diameter 5	Lobe Lift In.	Lobe Lift Ex.	Bearing Clearance	Camshaft End Play
1981	A-Series 75.5 (1237) 85.3 (1397) 90.8 (1488)	1.7237–1.7242	1.7041–1.7046	1.6844–1.6849	1.6647–1.6652	1.6224–1.6229	NA	NA	①	0.0004–0.0020
	L-Series 146 (2393) 168 (2753) 170 (2793)	1.8878–1.8883	1.8878–1.8883	1.8878–1.8883	1.8878–1.8883	1.8878–1.8883	0.262	0.262	0.0015–0.0026	0.0031–0.0150
	Z20S 119.1 (1952)	1.2967–1.2974	1.2967–1.2974	1.2967–1.2974	1.2967–1.2974	—	NA	NA	0.0018–0.0035	0.0080
1982	A-Series 75.5 (1237) 85.3 (1397) 90.8 (1488)	1.7237–1.7242	1.7041–1.7046	1.6844–1.6849	1.6647–1.6652	1.6224–1.6229	NA	NA	①	0.0004–0.0020
	CA20 120.4 (1974)	1.8085–1.8092	1.8085–1.8092	1.8085–1.8092	1.8085–1.8092	1.8077–1.8085	0.354	0.354	0.0040 ②	0.0028–0.0055
	E15 90.8 (1488)	1.6515–1.6522	1.6498–1.6505	1.6515–1.6522	1.6498–1.6505	1.6515–1.6522	NA	NA	0.0014–0.0030 ③	0.0160
	L-Series 146 (2393) 168 (2753) 170 (2793)	1.8878–1.8883	1.8878–1.8883	1.8878–1.8883	1.8878–1.8883	1.8878–1.8883	0.262	0.262	0.0015–0.0026	0.0031–0.0150
	Z-Series 119.1 (1952)	1.2967–1.2974	1.2967–1.2974	1.2967–1.2974	1.2967–1.2974	—	NA	NA	0.0018–0.0035	0.0080

CAMSHAFT SPECIFICATIONS
All measurements given in inches.

Year	Engine Displacement cu. in. (cc)	Journal Diameter 1	2	3	4	5	Lobe Lift In.	Ex.	Bearing Clearance	Camshaft End Play
1983	CA20 120.4 (1974)	1.8085–1.8092	1.8085–1.8092	1.8085–1.8092	1.8085–1.8092	1.8077–1.8085	0.354	0.354	0.0040 ②	0.0028–0.0055
	CD17 103.7 (1680)	1.1795–1.1803	1.1795–1.1803	1.1795–1.1803	1.1795–1.1803	1.1795–1.1803	NA	NA	0.0008–0.0024	0.0024–0.0067
	E15 90.8 (1488)	1.6515–1.6522	1.6498–1.6505	1.6515–1.6522	1.6498–1.6505	1.6515–1.6522	NA	NA	0.0014–0.0030 ③	0.0160
	E16 90.8 (1488)	1.6515–1.6522	1.6498–1.6505	1.6515–1.6522	1.6498–1.6505	1.6515–1.6522	NA	NA	0.0014–0.0030 ③	0.0059–0.0114
	L-Series 146 (2393) 168 (2753) 170 (2793)	1.8878–1.8883	1.8878–1.8883	1.8878–1.8883	1.8878–1.8883	1.8878–1.8883	0.262	0.262	0.0015–0.0026	0.0031–0.0150
	Z-Series 119.1 (1952)	1.2967–1.2974	1.2967–1.2974	1.2967–1.2974	1.2967–1.2974	–	NA	NA	0.0018–0.0035	0.0080
1984	C-Series 110.3 (1809) 120.4 (1974)	1.8085–1.8092	1.8085–1.8092	1.8085–1.8092	1.8085–1.8092	1.8077–1.8085	0.354	0.354	0.0040 ②	0.0028–0.0055
	CD17 103.7 (1680)	1.1795–1.1803	1.1795–1.1803	1.1795–1.1803	1.1795–1.1803	1.1795–1.1803	NA	NA	0.0008–0.0024	0.0024–0.0067
	E15ET 90.8 (1488)	1.6515–1.6522	1.6498–1.6505	1.6515–1.6522	1.6498–1.6505	1.6515–1.6522	NA	NA	0.0014–0.0030 ③	0.0160
	E16, E16S 90.8 (1488)	1.6515–1.6522	1.6498–1.6505	1.6515–1.6522	1.6498–1.6505	1.6515–1.6522	NA	NA	0.0014–0.0030 ③	0.0059–0.0114
	L-Series 146 (2393) 170 (2793)	1.8878–1.8883	1.8878–1.8883	1.8878–1.8883	1.8878–1.8883	1.8878–1.8883	0.262	0.262	0.0015–0.0026	0.0031–0.0150
	V-Series 180.6 (2960)	1.8472–1.8480	1.8472–1.8480	1.8472–1.8480	1.8472–1.8480	1.8472–1.8480	NA	NA	0.0024–0.0041	0.0012–0.0024
1985	C-Series 110.3 (1809) 120.4 (1974)	1.8085–1.8092	1.8085–1.8092	1.8085–1.8092	1.8085–1.8092	1.8077–1.8085	0.354	0.354	0.0040 ②	0.0028–0.0055
	CD17 103.7 (1680)	1.1795–1.1803	1.1795–1.1803	1.1795–1.1803	1.1795–1.1803	1.1795–1.1803	NA	NA	0.0008–0.0024	0.0024–0.0067
	E15ET 90.8 (1488)	1.6515–1.6522	1.6498–1.6505	1.6515–1.6522	1.6498–1.6505	1.6515–1.6522	NA	NA	0.0014–0.0030 ③	0.0160
	E16, E16S 90.8 (1488)	1.6515–1.6522	1.6498–1.6505	1.6515–1.6522	1.6498–1.6505	1.6515–1.6522	NA	NA	0.0014–0.0030 ③	0.0059–0.0114
	V-Series 180.6 (2960)	1.8472–1.8480	1.8472–1.8480	1.8472–1.8480	1.8472–1.8480	1.8472–1.8480	NA	NA	0.0024–0.0041	0.0012–0.0024

CAMSHAFT SPECIFICATIONS
All measurements given in inches.

Year	Engine Displacement cu. in. (cc)	Journal Diameter					Lobe Lift		Bearing Clearance	Camshaft End Play
		1	2	3	4	5	In.	Ex.		
1986	C-Series 110.3 (1809) 120.4 (1974)	1.8085–1.8092	1.8085–1.8092	1.8085–1.8092	1.8085–1.8092	1.8077–1.8085	0.354	0.354	0.0040 ②	0.0028–0.0055
	CD17 103.7 (1680)	1.1795–1.1803	1.1795–1.1803	1.1795–1.1803	1.1795–1.1803	1.1795–1.1803	NA	NA	0.0008–0.0024	0.0024–0.0067
	E16, E16S 90.8 (1488)	1.6515–1.6522	1.6498–1.6505	1.6515–1.6522	1.6498–1.6505	1.6515–1.6522	NA	NA	0.0014–0.0030 ③	0.0059–0.0114
	V-Series 180.6 (2960)	1.8472–1.8480	1.8472–1.8480	1.8472–1.8480	1.8472 1.8480	1.8472–1.8480	NA	NA	0.0024–0.0041	0.0012–0.0024
1987-88	CA16DE 97.7 (1598)	1.0998–1.1006	1.0998–1.1006	1.0998–1.1006	1.0998–1.1006	1.0998–1.1006	0.335	0.335	0.0018–0.0035	0.0028–0.0059
	C-Series 110.3 (1809) 120.4 (1974)	1.8085–1.8092	1.8085–1.8092	1.8085–1.8092	1.8085–1.8092	1.8077–1.8085	0.354	0.354	0.0040 ②	0.0028–0.0055
	CD17 103.7 (1680)	1.1795–1.1803	1.1795–1.1803	1.1795–1.1803	1.1795–1.1803	1.1795–1.1803	NA	NA	0.0008–0.0024	0.0024–0.0067
	E-Series 90.8 (1488)	1.6515–1.6522	1.6498–1.6505	1.6515–1.6522	1.6498–1.6505	1.6515–1.6522	NA	NA	0.0014–0.0030 ③	0.0059–0.0114
	V-Series 180.6 (2960)	1.8472–1.8480	1.8472–1.8480	1.8472–1.8480	1.8472 1.8480	1.8472–1.8480	NA	NA	0.0024–0.0041	0.0012–0.0024
	Z24i 146 (2389)	1.2961–1.2968	1.2961–1.2968	1.2961–1.2968	1.2961–1.2968	1.2961–1.2968	NA	NA	0.0024–0.0041	0.0080

NA Not available   ① No. 1 & 5: 0.0015–0.0024   ② Clearance limit
       No. 2 & 4: 0.0011–0.0020   ③ Journals No. 1, 3 & 5.
       No. 3: 0.0016–0.0025   No. 2 & 4: 0.0031–0.0047

CRANKSHAFT AND CONNECTING ROD SPECIFICATIONS
All measurements are given in inches.

Year	Engine Displacement cu. in. (cc)	Crankshaft				Connecting Rod		
		Main Brg. Journal Dia.	Main Brg. Oil Clearance	Shaft End-play	Thrust on No.	Journal Diameter	Oil Clearance	Side Clearance
1981	A-Series 75.7 (1237) 85.3 (1397) 90.8 (1488)	1.9666–1.9671	0.0010–0.0035	0.0020–0.0059	3	1.7701–1.7706	0.0012–0.0031	0.0080–0.0120
	L24E 146 (2393)	2.1631–2.1636	0.0010–0.0030	0.0020–0.0070	Center	1.9670–1.9675 ①	0.0010–0.0030	0.0080–0.0120
	L28E, L28ET 168 (2753)	2.1631–2.1636	0.0008–0.0026	0.0020–0.0070	Center	1.9670–1.9675	0.0009–0.0026	0.0079–0.0118
	LD28 170 (2793)	2.1631–2.1636	0.0008–0.0024	0.0020–0.0071	Center	1.9670–1.9675	0.0008–0.0024	0.0080–0.0120
	Z20 119.1 (1952)	2.1631–2.1636	0.0008–0.0024	0.0020–0.0071	3	1.9670–1.9675	0.0010–0.0022	0.0080–0.0120

CRANKSHAFT AND CONNECTING ROD SPECIFICATIONS
All measurements are given in inches.

Year	Engine Displacement cu. in. (cc)	Crankshaft				Connecting Rod		
		Main Brg. Journal Dia.	Main Brg. Oil Clearance	Shaft End-play	Thrust on No.	Journal Diameter	Oil Clearance	Side Clearance
1982	A-Series 75.7 (1237) 85.3 (1397) 90.8 (1488)	1.9666– 1.9671	0.0010– 0.0035	0.0020– 0.0059	3	1.7701– 1.7706	0.0012– 0.0031	0.0080– 0.0120
	CA20 120.4 (1974)	2.0847– 2.0852	0.0016– 0.0024	0.0120	3	1.7701– 1.7706	0.0008– 0.0024	0.0080– 0.0120
	E15 90.8 (1488)	1.9663– 1.9671	②	0.0020– 0.0070	3	1.5730– 1.5738	0.0012– 0.0024	0.0040– 0.0146
	L24E 146 (2393)	2.1631– 2.1636	0.0010– 0.0030	0.0020– 0.0070	Center	1.9670– 1.9675 ①	0.0010– 0.0030	0.0080– 0.0120
	L28E,L28ET 168 (2753)	2.1631– 2.1636	0.0008– 0.0026	0.0020– 0.0070	Center	1.9670– 1.9675	0.0009– 0.0026	0.0079– 0.0118
	LD28 170 (2793)	2.1631– 2.1636	0.0008– 0.0024	0.0020– 0.0071	Center	1.9670– 1.9675	0.0008– 0.0024	0.0080– 0.0120
	Z-Series 119.1 (1952)	2.1631– 2.1636	0.0008– 0.0024	0.0020– 0.0071	3	1.9670– 1.9675	0.0010– 0.0022	0.0080– 0.0120
1983	CA20 120.4 (1974)	2.0847– 2.0852	0.0016– 0.0024	0.0120	3	1.7701– 1.7706	0.0008– 0.0024	0.0080– 0.0120
	CD17 103.7 (1680)	2.0847– 2.0852	0.0015– 0.0026	0.0020– 0.0071	Center	1.7701– 1.7706	0.0009– 0.0026	0.0080– 0.0120
	E-Series 90.8 (1488)	1.9663– 1.9671	②	0.0020– 0.0070	3	1.5730– 1.5738	0.0012– 0.0024	0.0040– 0.0146
	L24E 146 (2393)	2.1631– 2.1636	0.0010– 0.0030	0.0020– 0.0070	Center	1.9670– 1.9675 ①	0.0010– 0.0030	0.0080– 0.0120
	L28E,L28ET 168 (2753)	2.1631– 2.1636	0.0008– 0.0026	0.0020– 0.0070	Center	1.9670– 1.9675	0.0009– 0.0026	0.0079– 0.0118
	LD28 170 (2793)	2.1631– 2.1636	0.0008– 0.0024	0.0020– 0.0071	Center	1.9670– 1.9675	0.0008– 0.0024	0.0080– 0.0120
	Z-Series 119.1 (1952)	2.1631– 2.1636	0.0008– 0.0024	0.0020– 0.0071	3	1.9670– 1.9675	0.0010– 0.0022	0.0080– 0.0120
1984	C-Series 120.4 (1974)	2.0847– 2.0852	0.0016– 0.0024	0.0120 ③	3	1.7701– 1.7706	0.0008– 0.0024	0.0080– 0.0120
	CD17 103.7 (1680)	2.0847– 2.0852	0.0015– 0.0026	0.0020– 0.0071	Center	1.7701– 1.7706	0.0009– 0.0026	0.0080– 0.0120
	E-Series 90.8 (1488)	1.9663– 1.9671	②	0.0020– 0.0070	3	1.5730– 1.5738	0.0012– 0.0024	0.0040– 0.0146
	L24E 146 (2393)	2.1631– 2.1636	0.0010– 0.0030	0.0020– 0.0070	Center	1.9670– 1.9675 ①	0.0010– 0.0030	0.0080– 0.0120
	LD28 170 (2793)	2.1631– 2.1636	0.0008– 0.0024	0.0020– 0.0071	Center	1.9670– 1.9675	0.0008– 0.0024	0.0080– 0.0120

CRANKSHAFT AND CONNECTING ROD SPECIFICATIONS
All measurements are given in inches.

Year	Engine Displacement cu. in. (cc)	Crankshaft				Connecting Rod		
		Main Brg. Journal Dia.	Main Brg. Oil Clearance	Shaft End-play	Thrust on No.	Journal Diameter	Oil Clearance	Side Clearance
1984	V-Series 180.6 (2960)	2.4790– 2.4793	0.0011– 0.0022	0.0020– 0.0067	4	1.9670– 1.9675	0.0004– 0.0020	0.0079– 0.0138
1985	C-Series 120.4 (1974)	2.0847– 2.0852	0.0016– 0.0024	0.0120 ③	3	1.7701– 1.7706	0.0008– 0.0024	0.0080– 0.0120
	CD17 103.7 (1680)	2.0847– 2.0852	0.0015– 0.0026	0.0020– 0.0071	Center	1.7701– 1.7706	0.0009– 0.0026	0.0080– 0.0120
	E-Series 90.8 (1488)	1.9663– 1.9671	②	0.0020– 0.0070	3	1.5730– 1.5738	0.0012– 0.0024	0.0040– 0.0146
	V-Series 180.6 (2960)	2.4790– 2.4793	0.0011– 0.0022	0.0020– 0.0067	4	1.9670– 1.9675	0.0004– 0.0020	0.0079– 0.0138
1986	C-Series 120.4 (1974)	2.0847– 2.0852	0.0016– 0.0024	0.0120 ③	3	1.7701– 1.7706	0.0008– 0.0024	0.0080– 0.0120
	CD17 103.7 (1680)	2.0847– 2.0852	0.0015– 0.0026	0.0020– 0.0071	Center	1.7701– 1.7706	0.0009– 0.0026	0.0080– 0.0120
	E-Series 90.8 (1488)	1.9663– 1.9671	②	0.0020– 0.0070	3	1.5730– 1.5738	0.0004– 0.0017	0.0040– 0.0146
	V-Series 180.6 (2960)	2.4790– 2.4793	0.0011– 0.0022	0.0020– 0.0067	4	1.9670– 1.9675	0.0004– 0.0020	0.0079– 0.0138
1987-88	CA16DE 97.7 (1598)	2.0847– 2.0856	0.0008– 0.0019	0.0120	3	1.7698– 1.7706	0.0007– 0.0018	0.0007– 0.0018
	C-Series 120.4 (1974)	2.0847– 2.0852	0.0016– 0.0024	0.0120 ③	3	1.7701– 1.7706	0.0008– 0.0024	0.0080– 0.0120
	CD17 103.7 (1680)	2.0847– 2.0852	0.0015– 0.0026	0.0020– 0.0071	Center	1.7701– 1.7706	0.0009– 0.0026	0.0080– 0.0120
	E-Series 90.8 (1488)	1.9661– 1.9671	②	0.0020– 0.0071	3	1.5730– 1.5738	0.0004– 0.0017	0.0040– 0.0146
	V-Series 180.6 (2960)	2.4790– 2.4793	0.0011– 0.0022	0.0020– 0.0067	4	1.9670– 1.9675	0.0004– 0.0020	0.0079– 0.0138
	Z24i 146 (2389)	2.3599– 2.3604	④	0.0020– 0.0071	3	1.9670– 1.9675	0.0005– 0.0021	0.0080– 0.0012

① L24E: 1.7701–1.7706
② No. 1 & 5:0.0012–0.0022
   No. 2, 3 & 4:0.0012–0.0036
③ CA18ET: 0.0020–0.0071
④ No. 1 & 5:0.0008–0.0024
   No. 2, 3 & 4:0.0008–0.0030

VALVE SPECIFICATIONS

Year	Engine Displacement cu. in. (cc)	Seat Angle (deg.)	Face Angle (deg.)	Spring Test Pressure (lbs.)	Spring Installed Height (in.)	Stem-to-Guide Clearance (in.)		Stem Diameter (in.)	
						Intake	Exhaust	Intake	Exhaust
1981	A-Series 75.5 (1237) 85.3 (1397) 90.8 (1488)	44°30'	45°30'	52.7 @ 1.19	1.83	0.0006–0.0018	0.0016–0.0028	0.3138–0.3144	0.3128–0.3134
	L24E 146 (2393)	44°30'	45°30'	①	1.575 ②	0.0010–0.0020	0.0020–0.0030	0.3136–0.3142	0.3128–0.3134
	L28E,L28ET 168 (2753)	45	45	108 @ 1.16 ③	1.575 ②	0.0008–0.0021	0.0016–0.0029	0.3136–0.3142	0.3128–0.3134
	LD28 170 (2793)	45	45	115.3 @ 1.18	1.575	0.0008–0.0021	0.0016–0.0029	0.3136–0.3142	0.3128–0.3134
	Z-Series 119.1 (1952)	45	45	115.3 @ 1.16 ④	1.575 ②	0.0008–0.0021	0.0016–0.0029	0.3136–0.3142	0.3128–0.3134
1982	A-Series 75.5 (1237) 85.3 (1397) 90.8 (1488)	44°30'	45°30'	52.7 @ 1.19	1.83	0.0006–0.0018	0.0016–0.0028	0.3138–0.3144	0.3128–0.3134
	CA20 120.4 (1974)	44°30'	45°30'	108 @ 1.16 ④	1.575 ②	0.0008–0.0021	0.0016–0.0029	0.2742–0.2748	0.2734–0.2740
	E15 90.8 (1488)	44°30'	45°30'	—	1.543	0.0008–0.0020	0.0018–0.0030	0.2744–0.2750	0.2734–0.2740
	L24E 146 (2393)	44°30'	45°30'	①	1.575 ②	0.0010–0.0020	0.0020–0.0030	0.3136–0.3142	0.3128–0.3134
	L28E,L28ET 168 (2753)	45	45	108 @ 1.16 ③	1.575 ②	0.0008–0.0021	0.0016–0.0029	0.3136–0.3142	0.3128–0.3134
	LD28 170 (2793)	45	45	115.3 @ 1.18	1.575	0.0008–0.0021	0.0016–0.0029	0.3136–0.3142	0.3128–0.3134
	Z-Series 119.1 (1952)	45	45	115.3 @ 1.16 ④	1.575 ②	0.0008–0.0021	0.0016–0.0029	0.3136–0.3142	0.3128–0.3134
1983	CA20 120.4 (1974)	44°30'	45°30'	108 @ 1.16 ④	1.575 ②	0.0008–0.0021	0.0016–0.0029	0.2742–0.2748	0.2734–0.2740
	CD17 103.7 (1680)	44°30'	45°30'	—	1.555 ⑤	0.0008–0.0021	0.0016–0.0029	0.2742–0.2748	0.2734–0.2740
	E-Series 90.8 (1488) 97.6 (1597)	44°30'	45°30'	—	1.543	0.0008–0.0020	0.0018–0.0030	0.2744–0.2750	0.2734–0.2740
	L24E 146 (2393)	44°30'	45°30'	①	1.575 ②	0.0010–0.0020	0.0020–0.0030	0.3136–0.3142	0.3128–0.3134
	L28E,L28ET 168 (2753)	45	45	108 @ 1.16 ③	1.575 ②	0.0008–0.0021	0.0016–0.0029	0.3136–0.3142	0.3128–0.3134
	LD28 170 (2793)	45	45	115.3 @ 1.18	1.575	0.0008–0.0021	0.0016–0.0029	0.3136–0.3142	0.3128–0.3134
	Z-Series 119.1 (1952)	45	45	115.3 @ 1.16 ④	1.575 ②	0.0008–0.0021	0.0016–0.0029	0.3136–0.3142	0.3128–0.3134

VALVE SPECIFICATIONS

Year	Engine Displacement cu. in. (cc)	Seat Angle (deg.)	Face Angle (deg.)	Spring Test Pressure (lbs.)	Spring Installed Height (in.)	Stem-to-Guide Clearance (in.)		Stem Diameter (in.)	
						Intake	Exhaust	Intake	Exhaust
1984	C-Series 110.3 (1809) 120.4 (1974)	44°30'	45°30'	108 @ 1.16 ④	1.575 ②	0.0008–0.0021	0.0016–0.0029	0.2742–0.2748	0.2734–0.2740
	CD17 103.7 (1680)	44°30'	45°30'	—	1.555 ⑤	0.0008–0.0021	0.0016–0.0029	0.2742–0.2748	0.2734–0.2740
	E-Series 90.8 (1488) 97.6 (1597)	44°30'	45°30'	—	1.543	0.0008–0.0020	0.0018–0.0030	0.2744–0.2750	0.2734–0.2740
	L24E 146 (2393)	44°30'	45°30'	①	1.575 ②	0.0010–0.0020	0.0020–0.0030	0.3136–0.3142	0.3128–0.3134
	LD28 170 (2793)	45	45	115.3 @ 1.18	1.575	0.0008–0.0021	0.0016–0.0029	0.3136–0.3142	0.3128–0.3134
	V-Series 180.6 (2960)	44°30'	45°30'	118 @ 1.18 ④	1.575 ②	0.0008–0.0021	0.0016–0.0029	0.2742–0.2748	0.3128–0.3134
1985	C-Series 110.3 (1809) 120.4 (1974)	44°30'	45°30'	108 @ 1.16 ④	1.575 ②	0.0008–0.0021	0.0016–0.0029	0.2742–0.2748	0.2734–0.2740
	CD17 103.7 (1680)	44°30'	45°30'	—	1.555 ⑤	0.0008–0.0021	0.0016–0.0029	0.2742–0.2748	0.2734–0.2740
	E-Series 90.8 (1488) 97.6 (1597)	44°30'	45°30'	—	1.543	0.0008–0.0020	0.0018–0.0030	0.2744–0.2750	0.2734–0.2740
	V-Series 180.6 (2960)	44°30'	45°30'	118 @ 1.18 ④	1.575 ②	0.0008–0.0021	0.0016–0.0029	0.2742–0.2748	0.3128–0.3134
1986	C-Series 110.3 (1809) 120.4 (1974)	44°30'	45°30'	108 @ 1.16 ④	1.575 ②	0.0008–0.0021	0.0016–0.0029	0.2742–0.2748	0.2734–0.2740
	CD17 103.7 (1680)	44°30'	45°30'	—	1.555 ⑤	0.0008–0.0021	0.0016–0.0029	0.2742–0.2748	0.2734–0.2740
	E-Series 97.6 (1597)	44°30'	45°30'	—	1.543	0.0008–0.0020	0.0018–0.0030	0.2744–0.2750	0.2734–0.2740
	V-Series 180.6 (2960)	44°30'	45°30'	118 @ 1.18 ④	1.575 ②	0.0008–0.0021	0.0016–0.0029	0.2742–0.2748	0.3128–0.3134
1987-88	CA16DE 97.7 (1598)	44°30'	45°30'	—	—	0.0008–0.0021	0.0016–0.0021	0.2348–0.2354	0.2341–0.2346
	C-Series 110.3 (1809) 120.4 (1974)	44°30'	45°30'	108 @ 1.16 ④	1.575 ②	0.0008–0.0021	0.0016–0.0029	0.2742–0.2748	0.2734–0.2740
	CD17 103.7 (1680)	44°30'	45°30'	—	1.555 ⑤	0.0008–0.0021	0.0016–0.0029	0.2742–0.2748	0.2734–0.2740
	E-Series 97.6 (1597)	44°30'	45°30'	—	1.543	0.0008–0.0020	0.0018–0.0030	0.2744–0.2750	0.2734–0.2740
	V-Series 180.6 (2960)	44°30'	45°30'	118 @ 1.18 ④	1.575 ②	0.0008–0.0021	0.0016–0.0029	0.2742–0.2748	0.3128–0.3134

VALVE SPECIFICATIONS

Year	Engine Displacement cu. in. (cc)	Seat Angle (deg.)	Face Angle (deg.)	Spring Test Pressure (lbs.)	Spring Installed Height (in.)	Stem-to-Guide Clearance (in.) Intake	Stem-to-Guide Clearance (in.) Exhaust	Stem Diameter (in.) Intake	Stem Diameter (in.) Exhaust
1987-88	Z24i 146 (2389)	45	45	—	1.575 ②	0.0008–0.0021	0.0016–0.0029	0.3136–0.3142	0.3128–0.3134

① Exhaust:
   Outer—108 @ 1.16
   Inner—56 @ 0.965
Intake:
   Outer—105.2 @ 1.18
   Inner—54.9 @ 0.984

② Outer; Inner:1,378
③ Outer; Inner:56 @ 0.965
④ Outer; Inner:57 @ 0.98
⑤ Outer; Inner:1.417

PISTON AND RING SPECIFICATIONS
All measurments are given in inches.

Year	Engine Displacement cu. in. (cc)	Piston Clearance	Ring Gap Top Compression	Ring Gap Bottom Compression	Ring Gap Oil Control	Ring Side Clearance Top Compression	Ring Side Clearance Bottom Compression	Ring Side Clearance Oil Control
1981	A-Series 75.5 (1237) 85.3 (1397) 90.8 (1488)	0.0010–0.0020	0.0080–0.0140	0.0060–0.0120	0.0120–0.0350	0.0020–0.0030	0.0010–0.0020	Combined ring
	L24E 146 (2393)	0.0010–0.0020	0.0090–0.0150	0.0060–0.0120	0.0120–0.0350	0.0020–0.0030	0.0010–0.0030	0.0010–0.0030
	L28E 168 (2753)	0.0010–0.0018	0.0098–0.0157	0.0050–0.0118	0.0120–0.0350	0.0016–0.0029	0.0012–0.0025	—
	L28ET 168 (2753)	0.0010–0.0018	0.0075–0.0130	0.0050–0.0118	0.0120–0.0350	0.0016–0.0029	0.0012–0.0025	0.0009–0.0028
	LD28 170 (2793)	0.0020–0.0028	①	0.0079–0.0138	0.0118–0.0177	0.0024–0.0039	0.0016–0.0031	0.0012–0.0028
	Z-Series 119.1 (1952)	0.0010–0.0020	0.0098–0.0160	0.0060–0.0120	0.0120–0.0350	0.0020–0.0030	0.0010–0.0025	0
1982	A-Series 75.5 (1237) 85.3 (1397) 90.8 (1488)	0.0010–0.0020	0.0080–0.0140	0.0060–0.0120	0.0120–0.0350	0.0020–0.0030	0.0010–0.0020	Combined ring
	CA20 120.4 (1974)	0.0009–0.0017	0.0079–0.0138	0.0059–0.0118	0.0118–0.0354	0.0016–0.0029	0.0012–0.0025	0.0020–0.0057
	E15 90.8 (1488)	0.0009–0.0017	0.0079–0.0138	0.0059–0.0118	0.0118–0.0354	0.0016–0.0029	0.0012–0.0025	0.0020–0.0057
	L24E 146 (2393)	0.0010–0.0020	0.0090–0.0150	0.0060–0.0120	0.0120–0.0350	0.0020–0.0030	0.0010–0.0030	0.0010–0.0030
	L28E 168 (2753)	0.0010–0.0018	0.0098–0.0157	0.0050–0.0118	0.0120–0.0350	0.0016–0.0029	0.0012–0.0025	—
	L28ET 168 (2753)	0.0010–0.0018	0.0075–0.0130	0.0050–0.0118	0.0120–0.0350	0.0016–0.0029	0.0012–0.0025	0.0009–0.0028
	LD28 170 (2793)	0.0020–0.0028	①	0.0079–0.0138	0.0118–0.0177	0.0024–0.0039	0.0016–0.0031	0.0012–0.0028
	Z-Series 119.1 (1952)	0.0010–0.0020	0.0098–0.0160	0.0060–0.0120	0.0120–0.0350	0.0020–0.0030	0.0010–0.0025	0

PISTON AND RING SPECIFICATIONS
All measurments are given in inches.

Year	Engine Displacement cu. in. (cc)	Piston Clearance	Ring Gap			Ring Side Clearance		
			Top Compression	Bottom Compression	Oil Control	Top Compression	Bottom Compression	Oil Control
1983	CA20 120.4 (1974)	0.0009–0.0017	0.0079–0.0138	0.0059–0.0118	0.0118–0.0354	0.0016–0.0029	0.0012–0.0025	0.0020–0.0057
	CD17 103.7 (1680)	0.0020–0.0028	0.0079–0.0138	0.0079–0.0138	0.0118–0.0177	0.0024–0.0039	0.0016–0.0031	0.0012–0.0028
	E-Series 90.8 (1488) 97.6 (1597)	0.0009–0.0017	0.0079–0.0138	0.0059–0.0118	0.0118–0.0354	0.0016–0.0029	0.0012–0.0025	0.0020–0.0057
	L24E 146 (2393)	0.0010–0.0020	0.0090–0.0150	0.0060–0.0120	0.0120–0.0350	0.0020–0.0030	0.0010–0.0030	0.0010–0.0030
	L28E 168 (2753)	0.0010–0.0018	0.0098–0.0157	0.0050–0.0118	0.0120–0.0350	0.0016–0.0029	0.0012–0.0025	–
	L28ET 168 (2753)	0.0010–0.0018	0.0075–0.0130	0.0050–0.0118	0.0120–0.0350	0.0016–0.0029	0.0012–0.0025	0.0009–0.0028
	LD28 170 (2793)	0.0020–0.0028	①	0.0079–0.0138	0.0118–0.0177	0.0024–0.0039	0.0016–0.0031	0.0012–0.0028
	Z-Series 119.1 (1952)	0.0010–0.0020	0.0098–0.0160	0.0060–0.0120	0.0120–0.0350	0.0020–0.0030	0.0010–0.0025	0
1984	CA18ET 110.3 (1809)	0.0010–0.0018	②	0.0059–0.0098	0.0079–0.0236	0.0016–0.0029	0.0012–0.0025	–
	CA20S, CA20E 120.4 (1974)	0.0010–0.0018	0.0098–0.0138	0.0059–0.0098	0.0079–0.0236	0.0016–0.0029	0.0012–0.0025	–
	CD17 103.7 (1680)	0.0020–0.0028	0.0079–0.0138	0.0079–0.0138	0.0118–0.0177	0.0024–0.0039	0.0016–0.0031	0.0012–0.0028
	E15ET 90.8 (1488)	0.0016–0.0024	③	0.0059–0.0098	0.0079–0.0236	0.0016–0.0029	0.0012–0.0025	0.0020–0.0049
	E16, E16S 97.6 (1597)	0.0009–0.0017	0.0079–0.0138	0.0059–0.0118	0.0118–0.0354	0.0016–0.0029	0.0012–0.0025	0.0020–0.0057
	L24E 146 (2393)	0.0010–0.0020	0.0090–0.0150	0.0060–0.0120	0.0120–0.0350	0.0020–0.0030	0.0010–0.0030	0.0010–0.0030
	LD28 170 (2793)	0.0020–0.0028	①	0.0079–0.0138	0.0118–0.0177	0.0024–0.0039	0.0016–0.0031	0.0012–0.0028
	V-Series 180.6 (2960)	0.0010–0.0018	0.0083–0.0173	0.0071–0.0173	0.0079–0.0299	0.0016–0.0029	0.0012–0.0025	0.0006–0.0075
1985	CA18ET 110.3 (1809)	0.0010–0.0018	②	0.0059–0.0122	0.0079–0.0299	0.0016–0.0029	0.0012–0.0025	–
	CA20S, CA20E 120.4 (1974)	0.0010–0.0018	0.0098–0.0201	0.0059–0.0122	0.0079–0.0299	0.0016–0.0029	0.0012–0.0025	–
	CD17 103.7 (1680)	0.0020–0.0028	0.0079–0.0138	0.0079–0.0138	0.0118–0.0177	0.0008–0.0024	0.0016–0.0031	0.0012–0.0028
	E15ET 90.8 (1488)	0.0016–0.0024	③	0.0059–0.0098	0.0079–0.0236	0.0016–0.0029	0.0012–0.0025	0.0020–0.0049
	E16, E16S 97.6 (1597)	0.0009–0.0017	0.0079–0.0138	0.0059–0.0118	0.0118–0.0354	0.0016–0.0029	0.0012–0.0025	0.0020–0.0057
	V-Series 180.6 (2960)	0.0010–0.0018	0.0083–0.0173	0.0071–0.0173	0.0079–0.0299	0.0016–0.0029	0.0012–0.0025	0.0006–0.0075

PISTON AND RING SPECIFICATIONS
All measurments are given in inches.

Year	Engine Displacement cu. in. (cc)	Piston Clearance	Ring Gap			Ring Side Clearance		
			Top Compression	Bottom Compression	Oil Control	Top Compression	Bottom Compression	Oil Control
1986	CA18ET 110.3 (1809)	0.0010–0.0018	②	0.0059–0.0122	0.0079–0.0299	0.0016–0.0029	0.0012–0.0025	—
	CA20E 120.4 (1974)	0.0010–0.0018	0.0098–0.0201	0.0059–0.0122	0.0079–0.0299	0.0016–0.0029	0.0012–0.0025	—
	CD17 103.7 (1680)	0.0020–0.0028	0.0079–0.0138	0.0079–0.0138	0.0118–0.0177	0.0008–0.0024	0.0016–0.0031	0.0012–0.0028
	E16,E16S 97.6 (1597)	0.0009–0.0017	0.0079–0.0138	0.0059–0.0118	0.0118–0.0354	0.0016–0.0029	0.0012–0.0025	0.0020–0.0057
	V-Series 180.6 (2960)	0.0010–0.0018	0.0083–0.0173	0.0071–0.0173	0.0079–0.0299	0.0016–0.0029	0.0012–0.0025	0.0006–0.0075
1987-88	CA16DE 97.7 (1598)	0.0006–0.0014	0.0087–0.0154	0.0075–0.0177	0.0079–0.0299	0.0016–0.0029	0.0012–0.0025	0.0010–0.0033
	CA18ET 110.3 (1809)	0.0010–0.0018	②	0.0059–0.0122	0.0079–0.0299	0.0016–0.0029	0.0012–0.0025	—
	CA20E 120.4 (1974)	0.0010–0.0018	0.0098–0.0201	0.0059–0.0122	0.0079–0.0299	0.0016–0.0029	0.0012–0.0025	—
	CD17 103.7 (1680)	0.0010–0.0018	④	④	⑤	0.0008–0.0024	0.0016–0.0031	0.0012–0.0028
	E16i 97.6 (1597)	0.0009–0.0017	⑥	⑦	0.0079–0.0236	0.0016–0.0029	0.0012–0.0025	⑧
	E16S 97.6 (1597)	0.0009–0.0017	0.0079–0.0138	0.0059–0.0118	0.0118–0.0354	0.0016–0.0029	0.0012–0.0025	0.0020–0.0057
	V-Series 180.6 (2960)	0.0010–0.0018	0.0083–0.0173	0.0071–0.0173	0.0079–0.0299	0.0016–0.0029	0.0012–0.0025	0.0006–0.0075
	Z24i 146 (2389)	0.0010–0.0018	0.0110–0.0150	0.0098–0.0138	0.0079–0.0236	0.0016–0.0029	0.0012–0.0025	—

① Without mark — 0.0079–0.0114
With mark — 0.0055–0.0087
② Piston grades No.1 & No. 2: 1984 — 0.0098–0.0126; 1985-88 — 0.0098–0.0150
Piston grades No.3, 4, & 5: 1984 — 0.0075–0.0102; 1985-88 — 0.0110–0.0165
③ Piston grades No.1 & No. 2: 0.0079–0.0102 (yellow)
Piston grades No.3, 4, & 5: 0.0055–0.0079
④ Grade 1: 0.0079–0.0091
Grade 2: 0.0091–0.0106
Grade 3: 0.0106–0.0118
Grade 4: 0.0118–0.0130
Grade 5: 0.0130–0.0146
⑤ Grade 1: 0.0118–0.0130
Grade 2: 0.0130–0.0142
Grade 3: 0.0142–0.0154
Grade 4: 0.0154–0.0165
Grade 5: 0.0165–0.0181
⑥ Type 1: 0.0055–0.0102
Type 2: 0.0079–0.0118
⑦ Type 1: 0.0110–0.0146
Type 2: 0.0059–0.0098
⑧ Type 1: 0.0026–0.0055
Type 2: 0.0002–0.0069

TORQUE SPECIFICATIONS
All readings in ft. lbs.

Year	Engine Displacement cu. in. (cc)	Cylinder Head Bolts	Main Bearing Bolts	Rod Bearing Bolts	Crankshaft Pulley Bolts	Flywheel Bolts	Manifold Intake	Manifold Exhaust	Spark Plugs
1981	A-Series 75.5 (1237) 85.3 (1397) 90.8 (1488)	51–54 ①	36–43	23–27	108–145	58–65	11–14	11–14	11–14
	L24E 146 (2393)	51–61	33–40	33–40	101–116	94–108	②	②	11–14
	L28E, L28ET 168 (2753)	54–61 ③	33–40	33–40	101–116	94–108	④	④	11–14
	LD28 170 (2793)	87–94	51–61	33–40	101–116	101–116	⑤	⑤	—
	Z-Series 119.1 (1952)	51–58	33–40	33–40	87–116	101–116	12–15	12–15	11–14
1982	A-Series 75.5 (1237) 85.3 (1397) 90.8 (1488)	51–54 ①	36–43	23–27	108–145	58–65	11–14	11–14	11–14
	CA20 120.4 (1974)	51–61 ⑥	33–40	22–27	90–98	72–80	13–16	13–17	11–14
	E15 90.8 (1488)	51–54 ①	36–43	23–27	83–108	58–65	11–14	11–14	11–14
	L24E 146 (2393)	51–61	33–40	33–40	101–116	94–108	②	②	11–14
	L28E, L28ET 168 (2753)	54–61 ③	33–40	33–40	101–116	94–108	④	④	11–14
	LD28 170 (2793)	87–94	51–61	33–40	101–116	101–116	⑤	⑤	—
	Z-Series 119.1 (1952)	51–58	33–40	33–40	87–116	101–116	12–15	12–15	11–14
1983	CA20 120.4 (1974)	51–61 ⑥	33–40	22–27	90–98	72–80	13–16	13–17	11–14
	CD17 103.7 (1680)	72–80	33–40	23–27	90–98	72–80	13–16	13–16	—
	E15, E16 90.8 (1488) 97.6 (1597)	51–54 ①	36–43	23–27	83–108	58–65	11–14	11–14	11–14
	L24E 146 (2393)	51–61	33–40	33–40	101–116	94–108	②	②	11–14
	L28E, L28ET 168 (2753)	54–61 ③	33–40	33–40	101–116	94–108	④	④	11–14
	LD28 170 (2793)	87–94	51–61	33–40	101–116	101–116	⑤	⑤	—
	Z-Series 119.1 (1952)	51–58	33–40	33–40	87–116	101–116	12–15	12–15	11–14

TORQUE SPECIFICATIONS
All readings in ft. lbs.

Year	Engine Displacement cu. in. (cc)	Cylinder Head Bolts	Main Bearing Bolts	Rod Bearing Bolts	Crankshaft Pulley Bolts	Flywheel Bolts	Manifold Intake	Manifold Exhaust	Spark Plugs
1984	CA18ET,CA20E 110.3 (1809)	⑥	33–40	24–27	90–98	72–80	14–19	14–22	14–22
	CA20S 120.4 (1974)	51–61 ⑥	33–40	22–27	90–98	72–80	13–16	13–17	14–22
	CD17 103.7 (1680)	72–80	33–40	23–27	90–98	72–80	13–16	13–16	—
	E-Series 90.8 (1488) 97.6 (1597)	51–54 ①	36–43	23–27	83–108	58–65	12–15	12–15	14–22
	L24E 146 (2393)	51–61	33–40	33–40	101–116	94–108	②	②	11–14
	LD28 170 (2793)	87–94	51–61	33–40	101–116	101–116	⑤	⑤	—
	V-Series 180.6 (2960)	40–47 ⑦	67–74	33–40	90–98	72–80	⑧	13–16	14–22
1985	CA18ET,CA20E 110.3 (1809)	⑥	33–40	24–27	90–98	72–80	14–19	14–22	14–22
	CA20S 120.4 (1974)	51–61 ⑥	33–40	22–27	90–98	72–80	13–16	13–17	14–22
	CD17 103.7 (1680)	72–80	33–40	23–27	90–98	72–80	13–16	13–16	—
	E-Series 90.8 (1488) 97.6 (1597)	51–54 ①	36–43	23–27	83–108	58–65	12–15	12–15	14–22
	V-Series 180.6 (2960)	40–47 ⑦	67–74	33–40	90–98	72–80	⑧	13–16	14–22
1986	C-Series 110.3 (1809)	⑥	33–40	24–27	90–98	72–80	14–19	14–22	14–22
	CD17 103.7 (1680)	72–80	33–40	23–27	90–98	72–80	13–16	13–16	—
	E-Series 97.6 (1597)	51–54 ①	36–43	23–27	80–94	58–65	12–15	12–15	14–22
	V-Series 180.6 (2960)	40–47 ⑦	67–74	33–40	90–98	72–80	⑧	13–16	14–22
1987-88	CA16DE 97.7 (1598)	76 ⑦	33–40	30–33	105–112	61–69	14–19	27–35	14–22
	CA18ET,CA20E 110.3 (1809)	⑥	33–40	24–27	90–98	72–80	14–19	14–22	14–22
	CD17 103.7 (1680)	72–80	33–40	23–27	90–98	72–80	13–16	13–16	—
	E-Series 97.6 (1597)	51–54 ①	36–43	23–27	80–94	58–65	12–15	12–15	14–22
	V-Series 180.6 (2960)	40–47 ⑦	67–74	33–40	90–98	72–80	⑧	13–16	14–22

TORQUE SPECIFICATIONS
All readings in ft. lbs.

Year	Engine Displacement cu. in. (cc)	Cylinder Head Bolts	Main Bearing Bolts	Rod Bearing Bolts	Crankshaft Pulley Bolts	Flywheel Bolts	Manifold Intake	Manifold Exhaust	Spark Plugs
1987-88	Z24i 146 (2389)	54–61 ⑦	33–40	33–40	105–112	101–116	12–15	12–15	14–22

① Tighten in two steps:
    1st – 33 ft. lbs.
    2nd – 51–54 ft. lbs.
② 8mm bolts: 11–18 ft. lbs.
    8mm nut: 9–12 ft. lbs.
    10mm bolts: 25–33 ft. lbs.
③ Tighten in three steps:
    1st – 30 ft. lbs.
    2nd – 44 ft. lbs.
    3rd – 54–61 ft. lbs.
④ 8mm bolts: 10–13; 10mm bolts: 25–36 ft. lbs.
⑤ Upper bolt (M10): 24–27 ft. lbs.
    Lower nut & bolt (M8): 12–18 ft. lbs.
⑥ Tighten in two steps: 1st – 22 ft. lbs.; 2nd – 58 ft. lbs. Then loosen all bolts completely. Final torque is in two steps: 1st – 22 ft. lbs.; 2nd – 54–61 ft. lbs. If angle torquing, turn all bolts 90–95 degrees clockwise
⑦ See text
⑧ Intake bolt: 12–14 ft. lbs.; intake nut: 17–20 ft. lbs.

BRAKE SPECIFICATIONS
All measurements in inches unless noted

Year	Model	Lug Nut Torque (ft. lbs.)	Master Cylinder Bore	Brake Disc Minimum Thickness	Brake Disc Maximum Runout	Standard Brake Drum Diameter	Minimum Lining Thickness Front	Minimum Lining Thickness Rear
1981	210	58–65	0.8125	0.331	0.0047	8.000	0.063	0.059
	310	58–72	0.8125	0.339	0.0047	8.000	0.079	0.059
	510	58–72	0.8125	0.331	0.0047	9.000	0.080	0.059
	810	58–72	0.8125	0.630 ①	0.0059 ②	9.000	0.079	0.059
	200SX	58–72	0.8750	0.413 ③	0.0047 ④	—	0.079	0.079
	280ZX	58–72	0.9375	0.709 ①	0.0039 ②	—	0.080	0.080
1982	210	58–65	0.8125	0.331	0.0047	8.000	0.063	0.059
	310	58–72	0.8125	0.339	0.0047	8.000	0.079	0.059
	810	58–72	0.8125	0.630 ①	0.0059 ②	9.000	0.079	0.059
	200SX	58–72	0.8750	0.413 ③	0.0047 ④	—	0.079	0.079
	280ZX	58–72	0.9375	0.709 ①	0.0039 ②	—	0.080	0.080
	Sentra	58–72	0.7500	0.433	0.0047	7.09	0.079	0.059
	Stanza	58–72	0.8125	0.633	0.0028	8.000	0.080	0.059

BRAKE SPECIFICATIONS
All measurements in inches unless noted

Year	Model	Lug Nut Torque (ft. lbs.)	Master Cylinder Bore	Brake Disc		Standard Brake Drum Diameter	Minimum Lining Thickness	
				Minimum Thickness	Maximum Runout		Front	Rear
1983	810	58–72	0.8125	0.630 ①	0.0059 ②	9.000	0.079	0.059
	200SX	58–72	0.8750	0.413 ③	0.0047 ④	—	0.079	0.079
	280ZX	58–72	0.9375	0.709 ①	0.0039 ②	—	0.080	0.080
	Pulsar	58–72	0.7500	0.394	0.0028	7.09	0.079	0.059
	Sentra	58–72	0.7500	0.394	0.0028	7.09	0.079	0.059
	Stanza	58–72	0.8125	0.633	0.0028	8.000	0.080	0.059
1984	200SX	58–72	0.9380	0.630 ⑤	0.0028 ⑥	9.000	0.079	0.059 ⑦
	300ZX	58–72	0.9380	0.787 ⑤	0.0028 ⑥	—	0.080	0.080
	Maxima	58–72	0.8125	0.630 ①	0.0059 ②	9.000	0.079	0.059
	Pulsar	58–72	0.7500	0.394	0.0028	8.000	0.079	0.059
	Sentra	58–72	0.7500	0.394	0.0028	8.000	0.079	0.059
	Stanza	58–72	0.8125	0.633	0.0028	8.000	0.080	0.059
1985	200SX	58–72	0.9380	0.630 ⑤	0.0028 ⑥	—	0.080	0.080
	300ZX	58–72	0.9380	0.787 ⑤	0.0028 ⑥	—	0.080	0.080
	Maxima	58–72	0.9380	0.787 ⑤	0.0028 ⑥	—	0.079	0.079
	Pulsar	58–72	0.7500	0.394	0.0028	8.000	0.079	0.059
	Sentra	58–72	0.7500	0.394	0.0028	8.000	0.079	0.059
	Stanza	58–72	0.8125	0.633	0.0028	8.000	0.080	0.059
1986	200SX	58–72	0.9380	0.630 ⑤	0.0028 ⑥	—	0.080	0.080
	300ZX	58–72	0.9380	0.787 ⑤	0.0028 ⑥	—	0.080	0.080
	Maxima	58–72	0.9380	0.787 ⑤	0.0028 ⑥	—	0.079	0.079
	Pulsar	58–72	0.7500	0.433	0.0028	8.000	0.079	0.059
	Sentra	58–72	0.7500	0.394	0.0028	8.000	0.079	0.059
	Stanza	58–72	0.8125 ⑪	0.630 ⑫	0.0028	8.000 ⑬	0.079	0.059
1987-88	200SX	87–108	0.9380	0.630 ⑤	0.0028 ⑥	—	0.080	0.080
	300ZX	72–87	0.9380	0.787 ⑧	0.0028 ⑥	—	0.079	0.079

BRAKE SPECIFICATIONS
All measurements in inches unless noted

Year	Model	Lug Nut Torque (ft. lbs.)	Master Cylinder Bore	Brake Disc Minimum Thickness	Brake Disc Maximum Runout	Standard Brake Drum Diameter	Minimum Lining Thickness Front	Minimum Lining Thickness Rear
1987-88	Maxima	72–87	1.0000	0.787 ⑤	0.0028 ⑥	—	0.079	0.079
	Pulsar	72–87	⑨	⑩	0.0028	8.000	0.079	0.059
	Sentra	72–87	⑨	⑩	0.0028	8.000 ⑭	0.079	0.059
	Stanza	72–87	⑨	0.787	0.0028	10.24 ⑮	0.079	0.059
	Van	72–87	1.0000	0.945	0.0028	10.24	0.079	0.059

NOTE: Minimum lining thickness is as recommended by the manufacturer. Due to variation in state inspection regulations, the minimum allowable thickness may be different than recommended.

— Not applicable
① Rear disc: 0.339
② Rear disc: 0.0059
③ Rear disc: 0.339
④ Rear disc: 0.0059
⑤ Front disc on V6 models: 0.787; rear disc on all models: 0.354
⑥ Rear disc: 0.0028
⑦ Rear disc: 0.0079
⑧ Front disc on Turbo: 0.945; rear disc on all models: 0.709

⑨ Pulsar
   W/CA16DE: 1.0000
   W/E16i: 0.9380
Stanza
   All exc. 2wd wagon: 1.0000
   2wd wagon: 0.9380
⑩ Pulsar
   W/CA16DE: 0.630
   W/E16i: 0.394
Sentra
   Gas engine exc. wagon: 0.394
   Gas engine wagon & all diesel models: 0.630

Sentra
   W/diesel engine: 1.0000
   W/gasoline engine: 0.9380

⑪ 2wd wagon: 0.9380
   4wd wagon: 1.0000
⑫ Wagon: 0.787
⑬ 2wd wagon: 9.000
   4wd wagon: 10.24
⑭ 4wd: 9.000
⑮ Wagon: 9.000

WHEEL ALIGNMENT

Year	Model	Caster Range (deg.)	Caster Preferred Setting (deg.)	Camber Range (deg.)	Camber Preferred Setting (deg.)	Toe-in (in.)	Steering Axis Inclination (deg.)
1981	210 Exc. Wagon, Canada	$1\frac{11}{16}$P–$3\frac{7}{16}$P	$2\frac{9}{16}$P	0–$1\frac{1}{2}$P	$\frac{3}{4}$P	$\frac{3}{64}$–$\frac{1}{8}$	$8\frac{19}{32}$
	Wagon	$1\frac{15}{16}$P–$3\frac{7}{16}$P	$2\frac{11}{16}$P	0–$1\frac{1}{2}$P	$\frac{3}{4}$P	$\frac{3}{64}$–$\frac{1}{8}$	$8\frac{19}{32}$
	Canada	$1\frac{11}{16}$–$3\frac{3}{16}$P	$2\frac{7}{16}$P	$\frac{1}{4}$N–$1\frac{3}{32}$P	$1\frac{27}{64}$P	0–$\frac{3}{32}$	$8\frac{13}{32}$
	310 (Front)	$\frac{7}{16}$P–$1\frac{15}{16}$P	$1\frac{1}{4}$P	$\frac{1}{4}$P–$1\frac{3}{4}$P	$\frac{1}{2}$P	$\frac{1}{16}$	$8\frac{27}{32}$
	(Rear)	—	—	$\frac{1}{4}$N–$1\frac{3}{4}$P	$\frac{1}{4}$P	0	—
	510 Exc. Wagon	$1\frac{1}{16}$P–$2\frac{9}{16}$P	$1\frac{13}{16}$P	$\frac{1}{4}$N–$1\frac{1}{4}$P	$\frac{1}{2}$P	$\frac{1}{16}$	$8\frac{27}{32}$
	Wagon	$\frac{15}{16}$P–$2\frac{7}{16}$P	$1\frac{9}{16}$P	$\frac{1}{16}$P–$1\frac{9}{16}$P	$\frac{3}{4}$P	$\frac{1}{16}$	$8\frac{5}{32}$
	810 (Front)	$2\frac{15}{16}$P–$4\frac{7}{16}$P	$3\frac{11}{16}$P	$\frac{5}{16}$N–$1\frac{3}{16}$P	$\frac{7}{16}$P	$\frac{1}{32}$	$12\frac{1}{8}$
	(Rear)	—	—	$\frac{15}{16}$P–$2\frac{7}{16}$P	$1\frac{11}{16}$P	$\frac{7}{32}$	—
	200SX	$1\frac{3}{4}$P–$3\frac{1}{4}$P	$2\frac{1}{2}$P	$\frac{11}{16}$N–$1\frac{13}{16}$P	$\frac{1}{16}$P	$\frac{3}{64}$	$8\frac{5}{32}$
	280ZX (Front)	$4\frac{3}{16}$P–$5\frac{11}{16}$P	$4\frac{15}{16}$P	$\frac{9}{16}$N–$\frac{15}{16}$P	$\frac{3}{16}$P	$\frac{3}{64}$–$\frac{1}{8}$	$9\frac{11}{32}$
	(Rear)	—	—	$\frac{1}{16}$N–$1\frac{7}{16}$P	$\frac{3}{4}$P	$\frac{5}{64}$–$\frac{5}{32}$	—

WHEEL ALIGNMENT

Year	Model	Caster Range (deg.)	Caster Preferred Setting (deg.)	Camber Range (deg.)	Camber Preferred Setting (deg.)	Toe-in (in.)	Steering Axis Inclination (deg.)
1982	210 Exc. Wagon, Canada	$1\frac{11}{16}$P–$3\frac{7}{16}$P	$2\frac{9}{16}$P	0–$1\frac{1}{2}$P	$\frac{3}{4}$P	$\frac{3}{64}$–$\frac{1}{8}$	$8\frac{19}{32}$
	Wagon	$1\frac{15}{16}$P–$3\frac{7}{16}$P	$2\frac{11}{16}$P	0–$1\frac{1}{2}$P	$\frac{3}{4}$P	$\frac{3}{64}$–$\frac{1}{8}$	$8\frac{19}{32}$
	Canada	$1\frac{11}{16}$–$3\frac{3}{16}$P	$2\frac{7}{16}$P	$\frac{1}{4}$N–$1\frac{3}{32}$P	$1\frac{27}{64}$P	0–$\frac{3}{32}$	$8\frac{13}{32}$
	310 (Front)	$\frac{7}{16}$P–$1\frac{15}{16}$P	$1\frac{1}{4}$P	$\frac{1}{4}$P–$1\frac{3}{4}$P	$\frac{1}{2}$P	$\frac{1}{16}$	$8\frac{27}{32}$
	(Rear)	—	—	$\frac{1}{4}$N–$1\frac{3}{4}$P	$\frac{1}{4}$P	0	—
	810 (Front)	$2\frac{15}{16}$P–$4\frac{7}{16}$P	$3\frac{11}{16}$P	$\frac{5}{16}$N–$1\frac{3}{16}$P	$\frac{7}{16}$P	$\frac{1}{32}$	$12\frac{1}{8}$
	(Rear)	—	—	$\frac{15}{16}$P–$2\frac{7}{16}$P	$1\frac{11}{16}$P	$\frac{7}{32}$	—
	200SX	$1\frac{3}{4}$P–$3\frac{1}{4}$P	$2\frac{1}{2}$P	$\frac{11}{16}$N–$\frac{13}{16}$P	$\frac{1}{16}$P	$\frac{3}{64}$	$8\frac{5}{32}$
	280ZX (Front)	$4\frac{3}{16}$P–$5\frac{11}{16}$P	$4\frac{15}{16}$P	$\frac{9}{16}$N–$\frac{15}{16}$P	$\frac{3}{16}$P	$\frac{3}{64}$–$\frac{1}{8}$	$9\frac{11}{32}$
	(Rear)	—	—	$\frac{1}{16}$N–$1\frac{7}{16}$P	$\frac{3}{4}$P	$\frac{5}{64}$–$\frac{5}{32}$	—
	Sentra	$\frac{3}{4}$P–$2\frac{1}{4}$P	$1\frac{1}{2}$P	$\frac{9}{16}$N–$1\frac{1}{16}$P	$\frac{1}{4}$P	$\frac{1}{8}$–$\frac{3}{16}$	$12\frac{15}{16}$
	Stanza (Front)	$\frac{11}{16}$P–$2\frac{3}{16}$P	$1\frac{3}{8}$P	$\frac{3}{4}$N–$\frac{3}{4}$P	0	0–$\frac{5}{64}$	$14\frac{13}{32}$
	(Rear)	—	—	0–$1\frac{1}{2}$P	$\frac{3}{4}$P	0–$\frac{5}{64}$	—
1983	810 (Front)	$2\frac{15}{16}$P–$4\frac{7}{16}$P	$3\frac{11}{16}$P	$\frac{5}{16}$N–$1\frac{3}{16}$P	$\frac{7}{16}$P	$\frac{1}{32}$	$12\frac{1}{8}$
	(Rear)	—	—	$\frac{15}{16}$P–$2\frac{7}{16}$P	$1\frac{11}{16}$P	$\frac{7}{32}$	—
	200SX	$1\frac{3}{4}$P–$3\frac{1}{4}$P	$2\frac{1}{2}$P	$\frac{11}{16}$N–$\frac{13}{16}$P	$\frac{1}{16}$P	$\frac{3}{64}$	$8\frac{5}{32}$
	280ZX (Front)	$4\frac{3}{16}$P–$5\frac{11}{16}$P	$4\frac{15}{16}$P	$\frac{9}{16}$N–$\frac{15}{16}$P	$\frac{3}{16}$P	$\frac{3}{64}$–$\frac{1}{8}$	$9\frac{11}{32}$
	(Rear)	—	—	$\frac{1}{16}$N–$1\frac{7}{16}$P	$\frac{3}{4}$P	$\frac{5}{64}$–$\frac{5}{32}$	—
	Pulsar	$\frac{3}{4}$P–$2\frac{1}{4}$P	$1\frac{1}{2}$P	$\frac{9}{16}$N–$1\frac{1}{16}$P	$\frac{1}{4}$P	0–$\frac{5}{64}$	$12\frac{3}{4}$
	Sentra	$\frac{3}{4}$P–$2\frac{1}{4}$P	$1\frac{1}{2}$P	$\frac{9}{16}$N–$1\frac{1}{16}$P	$\frac{1}{4}$P	$\frac{1}{8}$–$\frac{3}{16}$	$12\frac{15}{16}$
	Stanza (Front)	$\frac{11}{16}$P–$2\frac{3}{16}$P	$1\frac{3}{8}$P	$\frac{3}{4}$N–$\frac{3}{4}$P	0	0–$\frac{5}{64}$	$14\frac{13}{32}$
	(Rear)	—	—	0–$1\frac{1}{2}$P	$\frac{3}{4}$P	0–$\frac{5}{64}$	—
1984	200SX (Front)	$2\frac{3}{4}$P–$4\frac{1}{4}$P	$3\frac{1}{2}$P	$\frac{7}{16}$N–$1\frac{1}{16}$P	$\frac{1}{4}$P	$\frac{1}{32}$N–$\frac{1}{32}$P	$11\frac{11}{16}$
	(Rear)	—	—	$1\frac{1}{4}$N–$\frac{1}{4}$P	$\frac{1}{2}$N	$\frac{1}{16}$N–0	—
	300ZX (Front)	$5\frac{13}{16}$P–$7\frac{5}{16}$P	$6\frac{9}{16}$P	$\frac{9}{16}$N–$\frac{15}{16}$P	$\frac{3}{16}$P	$\frac{1}{32}$–$\frac{1}{8}$	13
	(Rear)	—	—	$1\frac{15}{16}$N–$\frac{7}{16}$N	$1\frac{3}{16}$N	$\frac{1}{16}$–$\frac{1}{16}$	—

WHEEL ALIGNMENT

Year	Model	Caster Range (deg.)	Caster Preferred Setting (deg.)	Camber Range (deg.)	Camber Preferred Setting (deg.)	Toe-in (in.)	Steering Axis Inclination (deg.)
1984	Maxima (Front)	$2^{15}/_{16}$P–$4^7/_{16}$P	$3^{11}/_{16}$P	$^5/_{16}$N–$1^3/_{16}$P	$^7/_{16}$P	$^1/_{32}$	$12^1/_8$
	(Rear)	–	–	$1^1/_4$P–$2^3/_4$P	2P	$^5/_{32}$	–
	Pulsar	$^3/_4$P–$2^1/_4$P	$1^1/_2$P	$^9/_{16}$N–$1^1/_{16}$P	$^1/_4$P	0–$^5/_{64}$	$12^3/_4$
	Sentra (Front)	$^3/_4$P–$2^1/_4$P	$1^1/_2$P	$^7/_{16}$N–$1^1/_{16}$P	$^1/_4$P	$^1/_{16}$–$^3/_{32}$	$12^3/_{16}$
	(Rear)	–	–	$1^3/_4$N–$^1/_4$N	1N	$^1/_8$N–$^1/_8$P	–
	Stanza (Front)	$^{11}/_{16}$P–$2^3/_{16}$P	$1^3/_8$P	$^3/_4$N–$^3/_4$P	0	0–$^5/_{64}$	$14^{13}/_{32}$
	(Rear)	–	–	0–$1^1/_2$P	$^3/_4$P	0–$^5/_{64}$	–
1985	200SX (Front)	$2^3/_4$P–$4^1/_4$P	$3^1/_2$P	$^7/_{16}$N–$1^1/_{16}$P	$^1/_4$P	$^1/_{32}$N–$^1/_{32}$P	$11^{11}/_{16}$
	(Rear)	–	–	$1^1/_4$N–$^1/_4$P	$^1/_2$N	$^1/_{16}$N–0	–
	300ZX (Front)	$5^{13}/_{16}$P–$7^5/_{16}$P	$6^9/_{16}$P	$^9/_{16}$N–$^{15}/_{16}$P	$^3/_{16}$P	$^1/_{32}$–$^1/_8$	13
	(Rear)	–	–	$1^{15}/_{16}$N–$^7/_{16}$N	$1^3/_{16}$N	$^1/_{16}$–$^1/_{16}$	–
	Maxima (Front)	$1^1/_4$P–$2^3/_4$P	2P	$^7/_{16}$N–$1^1/_{16}$P	$^5/_{16}$P	$^1/_{32}$–$^1/_8$	$13^3/_4$
	(Rear — Sedan)	–	–	$^1/_2$N–1P	$^1/_4$P	$^{15}/_{64}$–$^5/_{64}$	–
	(Rear — Wagon)	–	–	$^{23}/_{64}$N–$1^5/_{32}$P	–	$^9/_{32}$–$^1/_8$	–
	Pulsar (Front)	$^3/_4$P–$2^1/_4$P	$1^1/_2$P	$^7/_{16}$N–$1^1/_{16}$P	$^1/_4$P	$^1/_{16}$–$^3/_{32}$	$12^3/_{16}$
	(Rear)	–	–	$1^3/_4$N–$^1/_4$N	1N	$^1/_8$N–$^1/_8$P	–
	Sentra (Front)	$^3/_4$P–$2^1/_4$P	$1^1/_2$P	$^7/_{16}$N–$1^1/_{16}$P	$^1/_4$P	$^1/_{16}$–$^3/_{32}$	$12^3/_{16}$
	(Rear)	–	–	$1^3/_4$N–$^1/_4$N	1N	$^1/_8$N–$^1/_8$P	–
	Stanza (Front)	$^{11}/_{16}$P–$2^3/_{16}$P	$1^3/_8$P	$^7/_{16}$N–$1^1/_{16}$P	$^1/_4$P	0–$^5/_{64}$	$14^{13}/_{32}$
	(Rear)	–	–	0–$1^1/_2$P	$^3/_4$P	0–$^5/_{64}$	–
1986	200SX (Front)	$2^3/_4$P–$4^1/_4$P	$3^1/_2$P	$^7/_{16}$N–$1^1/_{16}$P	$^1/_4$P	$^1/_{32}$N–$^1/_{32}$P	$11^{11}/_{16}$
	(Rear)	–	–	$1^1/_4$N–$^1/_4$P	$^1/_2$N	$^1/_{16}$N–0	–
	300ZX (Front)	$5^{13}/_{16}$P–$7^5/_{16}$P	$6^9/_{16}$P	$^9/_{16}$N–$^{15}/_{16}$P	$^3/_{16}$P	$^1/_{32}$–$^1/_8$	13
	(Rear)	–	–	$1^{15}/_{16}$N–$^7/_{16}$N	$1^3/_{16}$N	$^1/_{16}$N–$^3/_{32}$P	–
	Maxima (Front)	$1^1/_4$P–$2^3/_4$P	2P	$^7/_{16}$N–$1^1/_{16}$P	$^5/_{16}$P	$^1/_{32}$–$^1/_8$	$13^3/_4$
	(Rear, Sdn)	–	–	$^1/_2$N–1P	$^1/_4$P	$^{15}/_{64}$–$^5/_{64}$	–
	(Rear — Wgn)	–	–	$^{23}/_{64}$N–$1^5/_{32}$P	–	$^9/_{32}$–$^1/_8$	–
	Pulsar (Front)	$^3/_4$P–$2^1/_4$P	$1^1/_2$P	$^7/_{16}$N–$1^1/_{16}$P	$^1/_4$P	$^1/_{16}$–$^3/_{32}$	$12^3/_{16}$
	(Rear)	–	–	$1^3/_4$N–$^1/_4$N	1N	$^1/_8$N–$^1/_8$P	–

WHEEL ALIGNMENT

Year	Model	Caster Range (deg.)	Caster Preferred Setting (deg.)	Camber Range (deg.)	Camber Preferred Setting (deg.)	Toe-in (in.)	Steering Axis Inclination (deg.)
1986	Sentra (Front)	$3/4$P–$2\,1/4$P	$1\,1/2$P	$7/16$N–$1\,1/16$P	$1/4$P	$1/16$–$3/32$	$12\,3/16$
	(Rear)	—	—	$1\,3/4$N–$1/4$N	1N	$1/8$N–$1/8$P	—
	Stanza (Front)	$11/16$P–$2\,3/16$P	$1\,3/8$P	$7/16$N–$1\,1/16$P	$1/4$P	0–$5/64$	$14\,13/32$
	(Rear)	—	—	0–$1\,1/2$P	$3/4$P	$9/32$N–$1/4$P	—
	Stanza Wagon (Front-2wd)	$3/4$P–$2\,1/4$P	$1\,1/2$P	$1/4$N–$1\,1/4$P	$1/2$P	$1/16$–$1/8$	12
	(Front-4wd)	$9/16$P–$2\,1/16$P	$1\,5/16$P	$9/16$N–$1\,1/16$P	$5/16$P	$1/32$N–$1/16$P	$11\,3/4$
	(Rear-2wd)	—	—	1N–1P	0	$5/64$–$5/16$	—
	(Rear-4wd)	—	—	0–$1\,1/2$P	$3/4$P	$5/32$N–0	—
1987-88	200SX (Front)	$2\,3/4$P–$4\,1/4$P	$3\,1/2$P	$7/16$N–$1\,1/16$P	$1/4$P	$1/32$N–$1/32$P	$11\,11/16$
	(Rear)	—	—	$1\,1/4$N–$1/4$P	$1/2$N	$5/64$N–0	—
	300ZX (Front)	$5\,13/16$P–$7\,5/16$P	$6\,9/16$P	$9/16$N–$15/16$P	$3/16$P	$1/32$–$1/8$	13
	(Rear)	—	—	$1\,15/16$N–$7/16$N	$1\,3/16$N	$1/16$N–$3/32$P	—
	Maxima (Front)	$1\,1/4$P–$2\,3/4$P	2P	$7/16$N–$1\,1/16$P	$5/16$P	$1/32$–$1/8$	$13\,3/4$
	(Rear)	—	—	$1\,3/16$N–$5/16$P	$7/16$N	$5/64$–$15/64$	—
	Pulsar (Front)	$1\,3/16$P–$2\,11/16$P	$1\,15/16$P	$1\,1/4$N–$1/4$P	$1/2$N	$1/32$N–$1/32$P	$14\,7/16$
	(Rear)	—	—	2N–$1/2$N	$1\,1/4$N	$1/16$N–$3/32$P	—
	Sentra—2wd (Front exc Cpe)	$1\,1/16$P–$2\,9/16$P	$1\,13/16$P	$15/16$N–$9/16$P	$3/16$N	$1/32$N–$1/32$P	14
	(Front—Cpe)	$1\,1/4$P–$2\,3/4$P	2P	$1\,1/16$N–$1/4$P	$7/16$N	$1/32$N–$1/32$P	$14\,1/4$
	(Rear exc Cpe)	—	—	$1\,3/4$N–$1/4$N	1N	$1/32$–$3/16$	—
	(Rear Cpe)	—	—	$1\,15/16$N–$7/16$N	$1\,3/16$N	$1/32$–$3/16$	—
	Sentra—4wd (Front)	$3/16$P–$1\,11/16$	$15/16$P	$13/16$N–$11/16$P	$1/16$N	$1/32$N–$1/16$P	$13\,9/16$
	(Rear)	—	—	$15/16$N–$9/16$P	$3/16$N	0–$5/32$	—
	Stanza (Front)	$1\,1/4$P–$2\,3/4$P	2P	$1/4$N–$1\,1/2$P	$5/8$P	$1/32$–$1/8$	$14\,9/16$
	(Rear)	—	—	$1\,3/16$N–$5/16$P	$7/16$N	$5/64$–$16/64$	—
	Stanza Wagon (Front-2wd)	$3/4$P–$2\,1/4$P	$1\,1/2$P	$1/4$N–$1\,1/4$P	$1/2$P	$1/16$–$1/8$	12
	(Front-4wd)	$9/16$P–$2\,1/16$P	$1\,5/16$P	$7/16$N–$1\,1/16$P	$3/16$P	$1/32$N–$1/16$P	$11\,3/4$
	(Rear-2wd)	—	—	1N–1P	0	$5/64$–$5/16$	—
	(Rear-4wd)	—	—	0–$1\,1/2$P	$3/4$P	$5/32$N–0	—
	Van	1P–2P	$1\,1/2$P	$1/4$N–$3/4$P	$1/4$P	$1/32$N–$1/32$P	$9\,1/2$

N — Negative
P — Positive

TUNE-UP PROCEDURES

Electronic Ignition

AIR GAP ADJUSTMENT

WITH RING-TYPE PICK-UP

All models, with the exception of those listed under "With Stator", use the ring-type of electronic ignition system.

Adjustment of these models is made by simply loosening the pick-up coil (toothed stator ring) retaining screws and centering the ring around the reluctor until the proper gap is achieved.

WITH STATOR

NOTE: On the Van, 300ZX, 1985-88 Maxima, 200SX Turbo, 1987-88 200SX (CA20E and VG30E), 1987-88 Stanza, 1985-86 49 States versions of the Pulsar/Sentra and all 1987-88 Pulsar/Sentra models, no air gap adjustment is either necessary or possible.

Models using this type of electronic ignition system include: 510 and 200SX (W/Z-Series engines), 1984-86 200SX (CA20E engine only) 1982 210 (USA models only), 1982-84 310, Pulsar, Sentra and 1982-86 Stanza. Adjustment of these models is made by simply loosening the stator mounting screws and moving the stator until the proper gap is achieved.

Ignition Timing

Timing settings for each model are given in the "Tune-Up Specifications" chart.

NOTE: The Van, 200SX, 200SX Turbo and Stanza models use a dual electronic ignition. The firing order is 1–3–4–2 and the rotor is designed with a 135 degree offset to fire both spark plugs at the same time.

NOTE: Datsun/Nissan does not give ignition timing adjustments for any models (U.S.), except those specified below as the timing is continually adjusted by the engine control system. These models (exc. below) are not covered in this section. If the ignition timing requires adjustment, please refer to the underhood specifications sticker for applicable procedures.

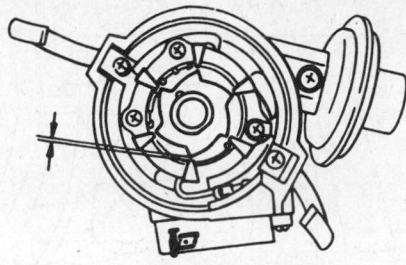

Checking the air gap—ring-type pick-up

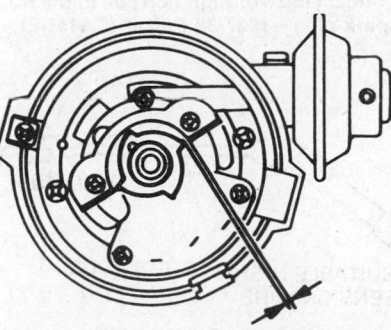

Checking the air gap—stator type

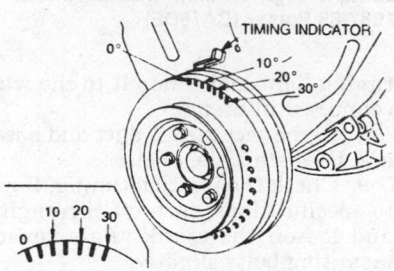

300ZX V6 timing marks

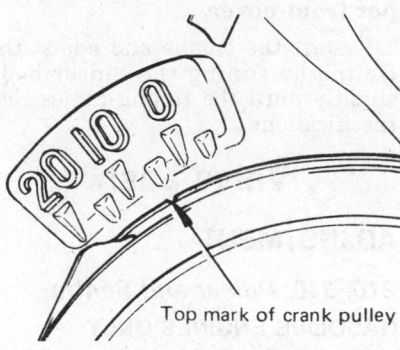

Top mark of crank pulley

Typical timing marks

ADJUSTMENT

All Except 1983-86 200SX and 1987-88 Pulsar (CA16DE)

1. Locate the timing marks on the crankshaft pulley and the front of the engine.
2. Clean off the timing marks so that you can see them.
3. Use chalk or white paint to color the mark on the crankshaft pulley

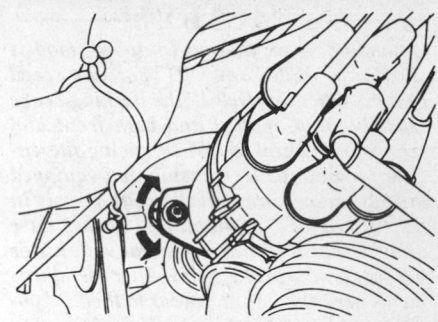

Loosen the distributor lockbolt and turn the distributor slightly to advance (upper arrow) or retard (lower arrow) the timing

and the mark on the scale which will indicate the correct timing when aligned with the notch on the crankshaft pulley.

4. Attach a tachometer to the engine.
5. Attach a timing light to the engine, according to the manufacturer's instructions.
6. Leave the vacuum line connected to the distributor vacuum diaphragm on all models except the A series engines; disconnect and plug the hose on those models.
7. Check to make sure that all of the wires clear the fan and then start the engine. Allow the engine to reach normal operating temperature.
8. Check that the idle speed is set to specifications.
9. Aim the timing light at the timing marks. If the marks that you put on the pulley and the engine are aligned when the light flashes, the timing is correct. Turn off the engine and remove the tachometer and the timing light. If the marks are not in alignment, proceed with the following steps.
10. Turn off the engine.
11. Loosen the distributor lockbolt(s) just enough so that the distributor can be turned with a little effort.
12. Start the engine. Keep the wires of the timing light clear of the fan.
13. With the timing light aimed at pulley and the marks on the engine, turn the distributor in the direction of rotor rotation to retard the spark, and in the opposite direction of rotor rotation to advance the spark. Align the marks on the pulley and the engine with the flashes of the timing light. Tighten the hold-down bolt.

1983-86 200SX

NOTE: When checking ignition timing on air conditioner-equipped cars, make sure that the air conditioner is "off" when proceding with the check.

CAUTION

Automatic transmission-equipped models should be shifted into "D" for idle speed checks. When in 'Drive" the parking brake must be fully applied and both front and rear wheels checked. When racing the engine on automatic transmission-equipped models, make sure that the shift lever is in the "N" or "P" position, and always have an assistant in the driver's seat with his or her foot on the brake pedal. After all adjustments are made, shift the car to the "P" position and remove the wheel chocks.

1. Run the engine until it reaches normal operating temperature.

2. Open the hood, and run the engine up to 2,000 rpm for about 2 minutes under no-load (all accessories "off").

3. Run the engine at idle speed. Disconnect the hose from the air induction pipe, and cap the pipe.

4. Race the engine two or three times under no-load, then run the engine for one minute at idle.

5. Check idle speed. Manual transmission cars should be idling at 750 rpm (plus 50 rpm, or minus 150). Automatic transmission cars should be idling in the "D" position at 750 rpm (plus 50 rpm, or minus 150 rpm). Adjust the idle speed by turning the idle speed adjusting screw.

6. Connect the timing light according to the light's manufacturer's instructions. Ignition timing should be 8° plus or minus 2° BTDC. Adjust the timing by loosening the distributor hold-down bolts and turning the distributor clockwise to advance and counter-clockwise to retard.

7. Reconnect the air induction pipe hose.

1987-88 Pulsar (CA16DE)

NOTE: The CA16DE does not utilize a conventional distributor and high tension wires. Instead it uses 4 small ignition coils fitted directly to each spark plug. The ECU controls the coils by means of a crankangle sensor.

1. Run the engine until it reaches normal operating temperature.

2. Check that the idle speed is at specifications.

3. Disconnect the air duct and both air hoses at the throttle chamber.

4. Remove the ornament cover between the camshaft covers. It has 8 screws and says "Twin Cam".

5. Remove the ignition coil at the No. 1 cylinder.

6. Connect the No. 1 ignition coil to the No. 1 spark plug with a suitable high tension wire.

7. Use an inductive pick-up type

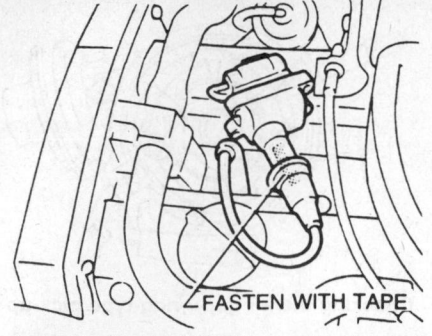

Connect the No. 1 ignition coil to the No. 1 spark plug—1987-88 Pulsar (CA16DE)

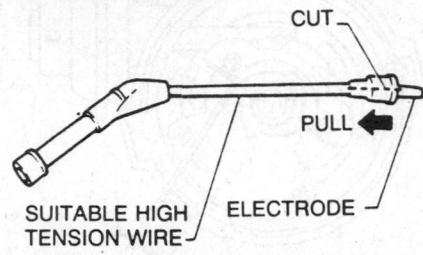

For ignition timing adjustment, prepare a suitable high tension wire as shown—1987-88 Pulsar (CA16DE)

timing light and clamp it to the wire connected in Step 6.

8. Reconnect the air duct and hoses and then start the engine.

9. Check the ignition timing. If not to specifications, turn off the engine and loosen the crank angle sensor mounting bolts slightly.

NOTE: The crank angle sensor can be found attached to the upper front cover.

Restart the engine and adjust the timing by tuning the sensor body slightly until the timing comes into specifications.

Valve Lash

ADJUSTMENT

210, 310, Pulsar and Sentra
GASOLINE ENGINES ONLY

NOTE: The CA16DE engine utilizes hydraulic lash adjusters. No adjustment is either necessary or possible.

1. Run the engine until it reaches normal operating temperature. Oil temperature, not water temperature, is critical to valve adjustment. With this in mind, make sure the engine is fully warmed up since this is the only way to make sure the parts have reached their full expansion. Generally speaking, this takes around fifteen minutes. After the engine has

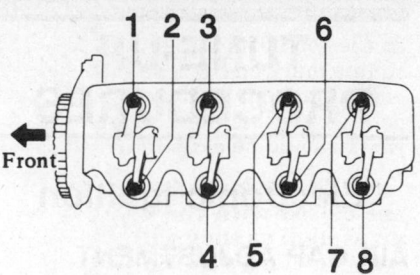

Valve adjustment sequence—E-Series engines

Valve adjustment sequence—A-Series engines

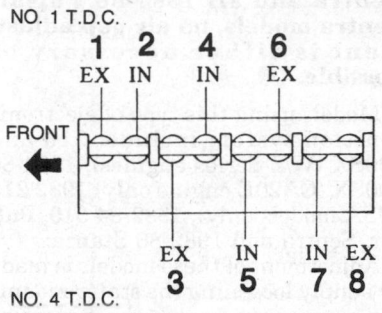

Valve adjustment sequence—CD17 diesel engines

reached normal operating temperature, shut if off.

2. Purchase a new valve cover gasket before removing the valve cover. The new silicone gasket sealers are just as good or better if you can't find a gasket.

3. Note the location of any hoses or wires which may interfere with valve cover removal, tag and disconnect them and move them aside. Then, remove the bolts which hold the valve cover in place.

4. After the valve cover has been removed, the next step is to get the No. 1 piston at TDC on the compression stroke. There are at least two ways to do it; you can bump the engine over with the starter or turn it over by using a wrench on the front pulley attaching bolt. The easiest way to find TDC is to turn the engine over slowly with a wrench (after first removing No. 1 plug) until the piston is

at the top of its stroke and the TDC timing mark on the crankshaft pulley is in alignment with the timing mark pointer. At this point, the valves for No. 1 should be closed.

NOTE: Make sure both valves are closed with the valve springs up as high as they will go. An easy way to find the compression stroke is to remove the distributor cap and see toward which spark plug lead the rotor is pointing. If the rotor points to the No. 1 spark plug lead, the No. 1 cylinder is on its compression stroke. When the rotor points to the No. 2 spark plug lead, the No. 2 cylinder is on its compression stroke etc.

5. With No. 1 piston at TDC of the compression stroke, check the clearance on valves No. 1, 2, 3 and 5 (counting from the front to the rear). Adjust valves No. 1, 2, 3 and 6 on 1982-88 310, Pulsar and Sentra.

6. To adjust the clearance, loosen the locknut and turn the adjuster with a screwdriver while holding the locknut. The correct size feeler gauge should pass with a slight drag between the rocker arm and the valve stem.

7. Turn the crankshaft one full revolution to position the No. 4 piston at TDC of the compression stroke. Adjust valves No. 4, 6, 7 and 8 in the same manner as the first four. Adjust valves No. 4, 5, 7 and 8 on 1982-88 310, Pulsar and Sentra.

8. Replace the valve cover.

CD17 DIESEL ENGINES

NOTE: The CD17 diesel valve train differs from the other Datsun/Nissan engines in that the valves are operated directly off of the camshaft via bucket-type cam followers; valve adjustment is performed by compressing the follower removing the adjust shim and replacing it with either a thicker shim (when clearance is too large) or a thinner shim (when clearance is small). The shim is located on top of the bucket directly underneath each cam lobe. A valve spring compressor, Kent-Moore part no. KV 101092S0, is necessary for this job. A magnet is also very useful for removing the shims.

1. Warm the engine up to operating temperature.

2. Set the No. 1 piston at TDC following the procedure under "210, etc." valve adjustment.

3. Remove the camshaft (valve) cover.

4. Measure the clearance between the cam follower (actually the top of

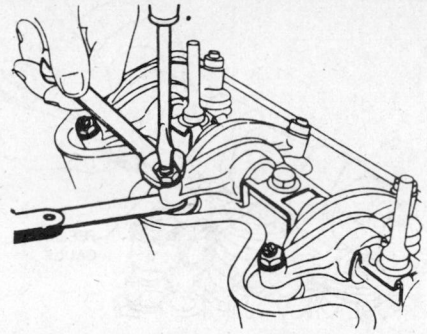

Adjusting the valves on the E-series engine

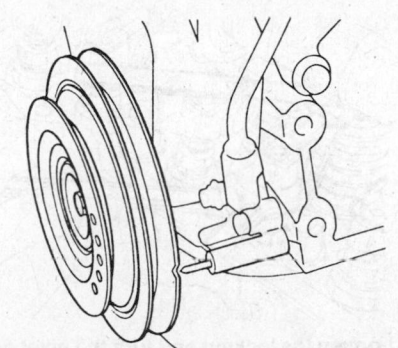

Timing marks and pointer at TDC—CD17 diesel

the shim) and the cam lobe using a feeler gauge. If clearance is beyond specification (see the "Tune-Up Specifications" chart), install a new adjustment shim according to the amount of clearance needed or in excess. Shims are available in varying thicknesses from Datsun/Nissan dealers. Mike up the old shims and mark down the measurement of each, or keep the shims in order and take them to the dealer for miking so you'll know the proper sizes to buy.

NOTE: Please refer to the following chart when computing replacement shim sizes.

5. After replacing the adjustment shims, recheck valve clearances.

NOTE: The adjustment shims that have been removed may be reused if not excessively worn or

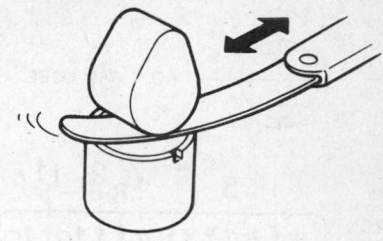

Insert the feeler gauge between the cam lobe and the top of the cam follower on the CD17

damaged. Mark the sizes on each for later reference.

280ZX and 1981-84 810/Maxima

1981-84 810/Maxima engines and all 280ZX engines are adjusted hot.

NOTE: The procedures given below are applicable to the LD28 Diesel engine also.

1. Note the locations of all hoses or wires that would interfere with valve cover removal disconnect them and move them aside. Then, remove the six bolts which hold the valve cover in place.

2. Bump one end of the cover sharply to loosen the gasket and then pull the valve cover off the engine vertically.

3. Place a wrench on the crankshaft pulley bolt and turn the engine over until the first cam lobe is pointing straight up. The timing marks on the crankshaft pulley should be lined up approximately where they would be when the No. 1 spark plug fires.

NOTE: If you decide to turn the engine by "bumping" it with the starter, be sure to disconnect the high tension wire from the coil to prevent the engine from accidentally starting and spewing oil all over the engine compartment

—— CAUTION ——

Never attempt to turn the engine by using a wrench on the camshaft sprocket bolt; this would put a tremendous strain on the timing chain.

	Intake	Exhaust
Specified clearance	0.20–0.30mm (0.008–0.012 in)	0.40–0.50mm (0.016–0.020 in)
Measured clearance	0.32mm (0.013 in)	0.36mm (0.014 in)
Clearance	0.02–0.12mm (0.001–0.005 in) large	0.04–0.14mm (0.002–0.006 in) small
Thickness of shim that was used	3.60mm (0.142 in)	3.55mm (0.140 in)
Thickness of shim to be used	3.65 or 3.70mm (0.144 or 0.146 in)	3.45 or 3.50mm (0.136 or 0.138 in)

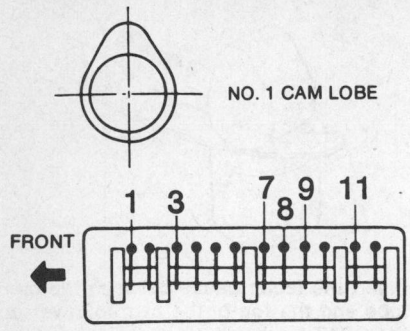

Primary valve adjustment, No. 1 cam lobe pointing up—1981-82 810/Maxima and 280ZX

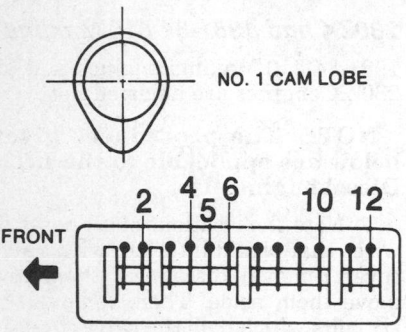

Secondary valve adjustment, No. 1 cam lobe pointing down—1981-82 810/Maxima and 280ZX

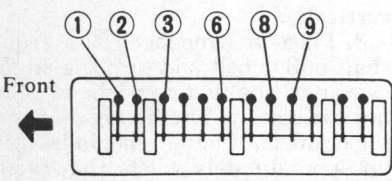

Primary valve adjustment—1983–84 810/Maxima and 1983 280ZX

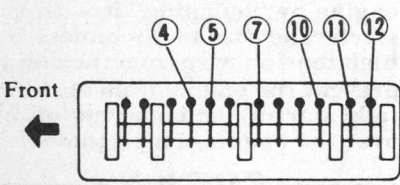

Secondary valve adjustment—1983–84 810/Maxima and 1983 280ZX

4. See the illustration for primary adjustment and check the clearance for valves (1), (3), (7), (8), (9) and (11) using a flat-bladed feeler gauge, on 1981-82 models. On the 1983 280ZX and 1983-84 810/Maxima, adjust valves (1), (2), (3), (6), (8) and (9). The feeler gauge should pass between the cam and the cam follower with a very slight drag. Insert the feeler gauge straight, not at an angle.

5. If the clearance is not within the specified limits, loosen the pivot locking nut and then insert the feeler

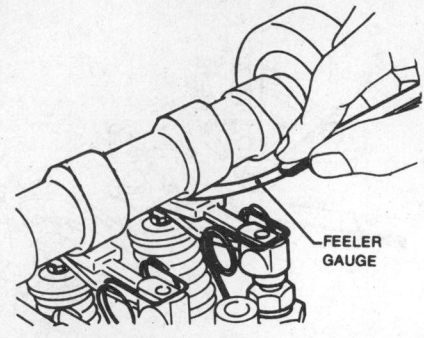

Checking the valve lash with a flat feeler gauge—L-series engines

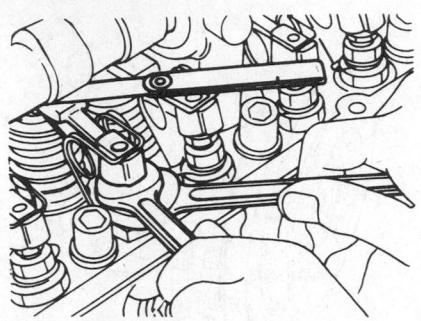

Loosen the locknut and turn the pivot adjuster to change the clearance

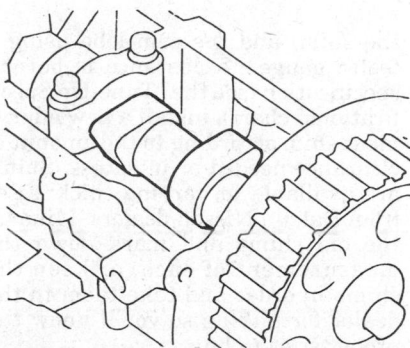

Position of No. 1 cylinder camshaft lobes at TDC

gauge between the cam and the cam follower. Adjust the pivot screw until there is a very slight drag on the gauge, tighten the locking nut, recheck the adjustment and correct as necessary.

6. Turn the engine over so that the first cam lobe is pointing straight down. See the illustration for secondary adjustment and then check the clearance on valves (2), (4), (5), (6), (10) and (12), on 1981-82 models. On the 1983 280ZX and the 1983-84 810/Maxima, adjust valves (4), (5), (7), (10), (11) and (12). If clearance is not within specifications, adjust as detailed in Step 5.

1981-83 510/200SX (W/Z-Series engines) and 1982-83 Stanza

1. The valves must be adjusted

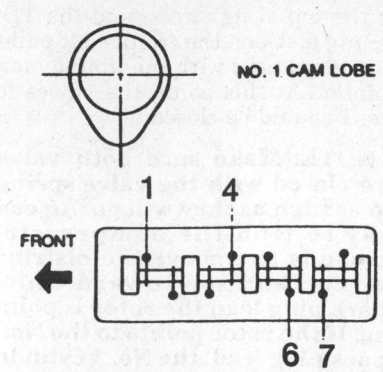

Primary valve adjustment, No. 1 cam lobe pointing down—1981-83 Z-Series and 1982-83 CA20 engines

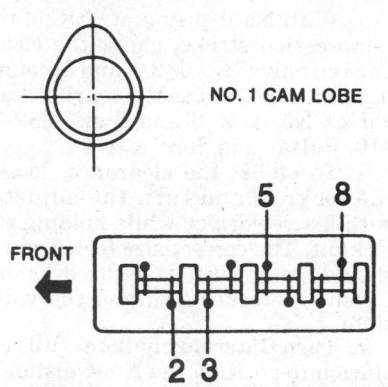

Secondary valve adjustment, No. 1 cam lobe pointing up—1981-83 Z-Series and 1982-83 CA20 engines

with the engine warm, so start the car and run the engine until the needle on the temperature gauge reaches the middle of the gauge. After the engine is warm, shut it off.

2. Purchase either a new gasket or some silicone gasket sealer before removing the camshaft cover. Counting on the old gasket to be in good shape is a losing proposition; always use new gaskets. Note the location of any wires and hoses which may interfere with cam cover removal, tag and disconnect them and move them to one side. Remove the bolts holding the cover in place and remove the cover. Remember, the engine will be hot, so be careful.

3. Place a wrench on the crankshaft pulley bolt and turn the engine over until the first cam lobe behind the camshaft timing chain sprocket is pointing straight down.

NOTE: If you decide to turn the engine by "bumping" it with the starter, be sure to disconnect the high tension wire from the coil(s) to prevent the engine from accidentally starting and spewing oil all over the engine compartment.

CAUTION

Never attempt to turn the engine by using a wrench on the camshaft sprocket bolt; there is a one-to-two turning ratio between the camshaft and the crankshaft which will put a tremendous strain on the timing chain.

4. See the illustration for primary adjustment and adjust valves (1), (4), (6) and (7) using a flat-bladed feeler gauge. The feeler gauge should pass between the valve stem end and the rocker arm screw with a very slight drag. Insert the feeler gauge straight, not an angle.

5. If the clearance is not within specified value, loosen the rocker arm lock nut and turn the rocker arm screw to obtain the proper clearance. After correct clearance is obtained, tighten the lock nut.

6. Turn the engine over so that the first cam lobe behind the camshaft timing chain sprocket is pointing straight up and adjust valves marked (2), (3), (5) and (8) in the secondary adjustment illustration. They, too, should be adjusted to specification as in Step 5.

7. Install the cam cover gasket, the cam cover and any wires and hoses which were removed.

1984-86½ 200SX, 1987-88 200SX (CA18ET), 1984-86 Stanza, 1986-88 Stanza Wagon and Van

Follow the procedure above for 1981-83 models, with the following exceptions: on Step 4, check and adjust the clearance on valves 1, 2, 4 and 6 as shown in the accompanying illustration. This is with No. 1 cylinder at TDC on compression. On Step 6, check and adjust the clearance on valves 3, 5, 7 and 8 with the No. 4 cylinder at TDC on compression.

1986½-88 200SX (Exc. W/ CA18ET), 1987-88 Stanza (Exc. Wagon), 300ZX and 1985-88 Maxima

The VG30E and VG30ET V6 engines and the 1986½-88 CA20E engines in these models are equipped with hydraulic lash adjusters, which continually take up excess clearance in the valve train. No routine adjustment is necessary or possible.

Idle Speed & Mixture Gasoline Engines

ADJUSTMENT

1981-82

1. Start the engine and allow it to

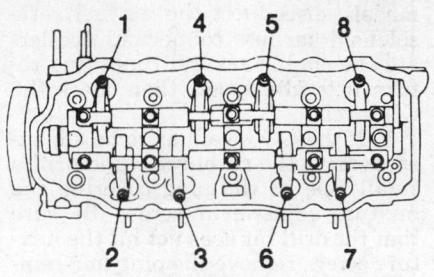

Valve adjustment sequence – 1984-86½ 200SX, 1987-88 200SX (CA18ET), 1984-86 Stanza, 1986-88 Stanza wagon and Van

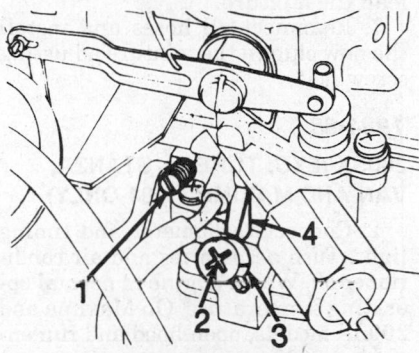

1 Throttle adjusting screw
2 Idle adjusting screw
3 Idle limiter cap
4 Stopper

Adjustment screws on a typical down draft carburetor

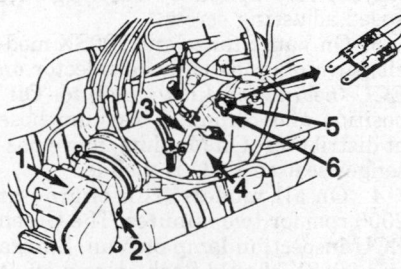

1. Air flow meter
2. Air by-pass screw
3. Throttle chamber
4. Throttle valve switch
5. Connector of throttle valve switch harness
6. Leading wire

Installing a jumper wire for a CO adjustment

run until it reaches normal operating temperature.

2. With the engine idle stabilized, check the ignition timing and adjust if necessary.

3. Shut off the engine and connect a tachometer, disconnect and plug the air hose between the three way connector and the check valve, if so equipped.

4. Disconnect the air induction hose and plug the pipe.

5. Adjust the idle speed screw to obtain the idle speed given in the Tune-Up Specifications.

6. Turn the mixture screw inward until the idle speed starts to drop and the engine just about stalls due to an overly lean mixture.

7. Slowly back off the mixture screw (½ turn at a time) until the fastest smooth idle is obtained.

8. Open the throttle suddenly, the engine should accelerate immediately, without hesitation. If the engine stumbles or stalls, richen the mixture slightly.

9. Reinstall all vacuum lines and hoses and recheck the idle speed adjustment.

NOTE: On models equipped with limiter caps on the mixture screw, remove the limiter cap and reinstall it after adjustments have been made. Also, on some of the later models, the idle speed and idle mixture is controlled by an electronic control unit, which is programmed at the factory and should not be tampered with.

IDLE ADJUSTMENT WITH CO METER

1981-82

1. Have engine warmed to normal operating temperature and the CO meter properly calibrated. The probe should be inserted into the tail pipe at least 16 inches.

2. Remove the air hose between the 3 or 4-way connector and the air check valve. Plug the disconnected hose at the air check valve side.

3. Increase the engine speed between 1,500 and 2,000 rpm at least three times and allow the engine to idle for approximately one minute under no load.

4. Adjust the engine idle speed and ignition timing to specifications.

5. Allow the engine to operate for approximately ten minutes from the Step 3 procedure. Adjust the idle adjusting screw so that the CO percentage is at the specified level.

6. Repeat Steps 3 and 5 so that the CO percentage is maintained.

7. Remove the plug from the air hose and connect the air hose to the three or four way connector.

8. If the engine speed increases, adjust the engine speed to specifications as necessary.

NOTE: Mixture adjustments are not a part of a normal tune-up procedure. Adjustments should not be attempted, unless the mixture control unit is replaced, the carburetor overhauled or the vehicle does not pass the emission test.

1983

810/MAXIMA, 200SX, 280ZX AND 280ZX TURBO

1. Connect a tachometer to engine. Start engine and run at 2000 rpm for two minutes to stabilize operating condition.

2. Accelerate engine 2–3 times and return to idle. Turn idle speed adjusting screw to obtain specified idle rpm.

3. Turn ignition switch off. Disconnect throttle valve switch harness connector. Disconnect and plug distributor vacuum hose.

4. Disconnect air injection hose and canister purge hose at intake manifold. Plug air induction pipe and purge hose fitting on intake manifold.

5. Start engine, accelerate 2–3 times and allow to idle for one minute. Check and, if necessary, adjust ignition timing.

6. Connect a jumper wire between throttle valve switch harness connector terminals #24 and #30. Install CO meter probe into tailpipe at least 16 inches.

7. With engine idling, check CO level. If necessary to adjust CO, remove air flow meter and drill a small hole in plug covering air by-pass screw. Do not allow drill to contact screw.

8. Clean up metal shavings. Install self tapping screw into hole and remove plug from bore. Install air flow meter. Adjust CO level by turning air bypass screw clockwise to enrich mixture and counterclockwise to lean mixture.

9. Remove air flow meter. Tap new seal plug, with convex side up, into air by-pass screw bore. Install air flow meter.

10. Stop engine. Remove jumper wire from throttle valve switch harness connector. Reconnect harness and all hoses. Reset idle speed to specified rpm.

PULSAR, SENTRA AND STANZA

1. Connect a tachometer to the engine and run the engine at idle speed or at 2000 rpm for the Stanza for at least two minutes.

2. Install the CO meter probe 16 inches or more into the tailpipe and disconnect and plug the distributor vacuum and air induction hoses. Accelerate the engine to 2000–3000 rpm several times under a no load condition.

3. Let the engine return to and run at idle speed for at least a minute. Check the ignition timing and adjust if necessary, reconnect the distributor vacuum hoses.

4. Check the idle speed and adjust if necessary and on the Sentra MPG

models, disconnect the air/fuel ratio solenoid harness connector. Accelerate the engine several times and return it to idle speed, then check the CO level.

5. If the CO level has to be adjusted, remove the carburetor and drill a small hole in the plug covering the mixture adjustment screw. Be sure that the drill bit does not hit the mixture screw, remove the plug and reinstall the carburetor.

6. Adjust the CO level by turning the mixture adjustment screw inward to enrich the mixture and outward to lean the mixture.

7. Reconnect all hoses and install the new plug in the mixture adjusting screw hole.

1984-88

200SX (EXC. TURBO), STANZA, VAN AND MAXIMA (1984 ONLY)

1. Connect tachometer and timing light. Turn accessories and air conditioner off. Warm engine to normal operating temperature. On Maxima and 200SX models, open hood and run engine at 2000 rpm for ten minutes.

2. Stop engine, disconnect and plug vacuum hose at distributor. On Maxima models, disconnect Gray harness connector at distributor. Accelerate engine 2–3 times and return to idle. Adjust idle speed by turning idle speed adjusting screw.

3. On Van, Stanza and 200SX models, turn diagnostic mode selector on ECU (behind left kick panel) to "Off" position and reconnect vacuum hose at distributor. On Maxima, move passenger seat so ECU is visible.

4. On all models, run engine at 2000 rpm for two minutes. The Green ECU inspection lamp on Van, Stanza and 200SX should flash on and off at least nine times in ten seconds at 2000 rpm. The lamp on Maxima should flash at least five times in ten seconds. If lamp flashed, go to next step.

5. On Maxima models, turn ignition off and reconnect Gray connector and vacuum hose at distributor. Start and race engine 2–3 times and return to idle. Recheck idle speed and remove test equipment.

6. On Van, Stanza and 200SX models, accelerate engine 2–3 times and return to idle. If Red and Green ECU inspection lamps flash together, mixture is okay and adjustment is complete. Recheck idle speed and remove test equipment

200SX TURBO, MAXIMA (1985-88), 300ZX AND 300ZX TURBO

1. Connect the tachometer (coil adapter must be used on most models)

and timing light. Turn accessories and air conditioner off. Start and warm engine to operating temperature.

2. On 300ZX and Maxima models, disconnect harness connect at idle-up solenoid valve. Accelerate engine 2–3 times and return to idle. Check and adjust idle speed and ignition timing. To adjust idle speed on all models except 300ZX Turbo, turn idle speed adjusting screw. Reconnect idle-up solenoid on 300ZX and Maxima models.

3. To adjust idle speed on 300ZX Turbo models, stop engine and disconnect harness connect at auxiliary air control valve. Start engine and adjust idle speed to specifications. Stop engine and reconnect control valve. Start engine and ensure idle speed is correct.

4. Locate ECU behind left kick panel on 200SX Turbo, and right kick panel on other models. Turn diagnostic mode selector screw on ECU fully counterclockwise. Start and run engine at 2000 rpm for two minutes. Green ECU inspection lamp should flash on and off at least nine times in ten seconds at 2000 rpm and 200SX Turbo and at least 5 times in other models. If lamp flashes, go to next step.

5. On Maxima, 300ZX and 300ZX Turbo models, disconnect harness connector at throttle valve switch. On all models, accelerate engine 2–3 times and return to idle. If Red and Green ECU inspection lamps flash together, mixture adjustment is okay. Recheck idle speed and remove test equipment.

SENTRA AND PULSAR

1. Connect a tachometer to the engine and run the engine at idle speed for at least two minutes.

2. Install the CO meter probe 16 inches or more into the tailpipe and disconnect and plug the distributor vacuum and air induction hoses. Accelerate the engine to 2000–3000 rpm several times under a no load condition.

3. Let the engine return to and run at idle speed for at least a minute. Check the ignition timing and adjust if necessary, reconnect the distributor vacuum hoses.

4. Check the idle speed and adjust if necessary and disconnect the air/fuel ratio solenoid harness connector. Accelerate the engine several times and return it to idle speed, check the CO level.

5. If the CO level has to be adjusted, remove the carburetor and drill a small hole in the plug covering the mixture adjustment screw. Be sure that the drill bit does not hit the mix-

ture screw, remove the plug and reinstall the carburetor.

6. Adjust the CO level by turning the mixture adjustment screw inward to enrich the mixture and outward to lean the mixture.

7. Reconnect all hoses and install the new plug in the mixture adjusting screw hole.

Idle Speed — Diesel Engines

NOTE: A special tachometer compatible with diesel engines will be required for this procedure. A normal tachometer will not work.

ADJUSTMENT

For further information on diesel engines, please refer to "Diesel Service" in the Unit Repair section.

1. Turn off lights, heater fan and all electrical accessories.

2. On automatic transmission equipped models, checks should be carried out while shaft lever is in "D" position.

3. Start engine and warm it up until water temperature indicator points to the idle of gauge.

4. Attach a diesel tachometer tester's pick-up to the No. 1 injection tube.

NOTE: In order to obtain a more accurate reading of engine speed, remove clamps on No. 1 injection tube.

5. Run engine at about 2000 rpm for two minutes under no load. Race engine two or three times. Make sure that it returns to idle speed. If not, check acceleration linkage for binding.

6. Run engine for one minute at idle speed.

7. Check idle speed.

NOTE: The idle speed on the CD17 engine should be 750 rpm ±.

8. Stop the engine.

9. Disconnect accelerator wire from injection pump control lever.

10. Move control lever to full acceleration side, and loosen idle screw lock nut while holding control lever (LD28 only).

11. Turn idle adjusting screw to obtain the specified value.

12. Stop the engine.

13. Tighten idle adjusting screw

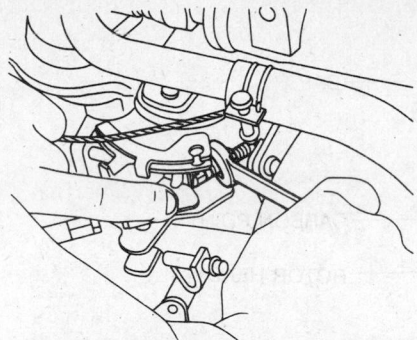

Loosen the idle screw locknut while holding the control lever—diesel engine

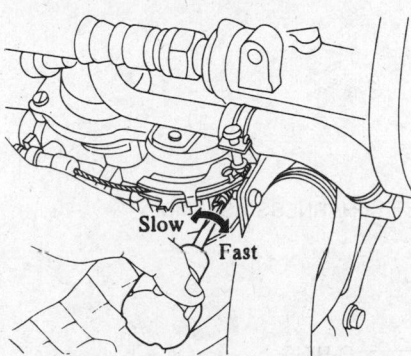

Idle speed adjusting screw—LD28

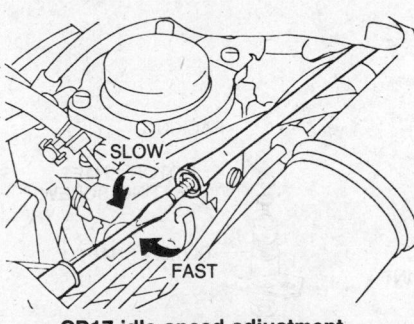

CD17 idle speed adjustment

lock nut while holding control lever at full acceleration side.

14. Connect accelerator wire.

ENGINE ELECTRICAL

Distributor

NOTE: The CA16DE (used in the 1987-88 Pulsar) does not utilize a conventional distributor and high tension wires. Instead it uses 4 small ignition coils fitted directly to each spark plug. The ECU controls the coils by means of a crankangle sensor.

REMOVAL

1. Unfasten the retaining clips and lift the distributor cap straight up. 'It will be easier to install the distributor if the wiring is not disconnected form the cap.' If the wires must be removed from the cap, mark their positions to aid in installation.

2. Disconnect the distributor wiring harness.

3. Disconnect the vacuum lines.

4. Note the position of the rotor in relation to the base. Scribe a mark on the base of the distributor and on the engine block to facilitate reinstallation. Align the marks with the direction the metal tip of the rotor is pointing.

5. Remove the bolt(s) which hold the distributor to the engine.

6. Lift the distributor assembly from the engine.

INSTALLATION

1. Insert the distributor shaft and assembly into the engine. Line up the mark on the distributor and the one on the engine with the metal tip of the rotor. Make sure that the vacuum advance diaphragm is pointed in the

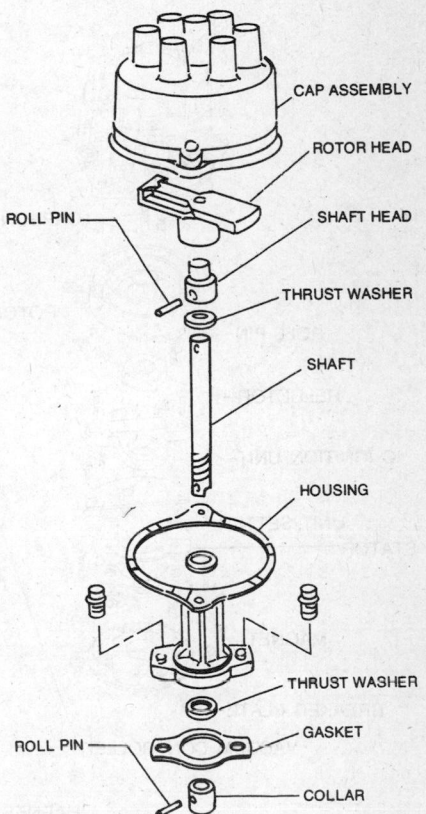

Exploded view of the electronic distributor—280ZX Turbo

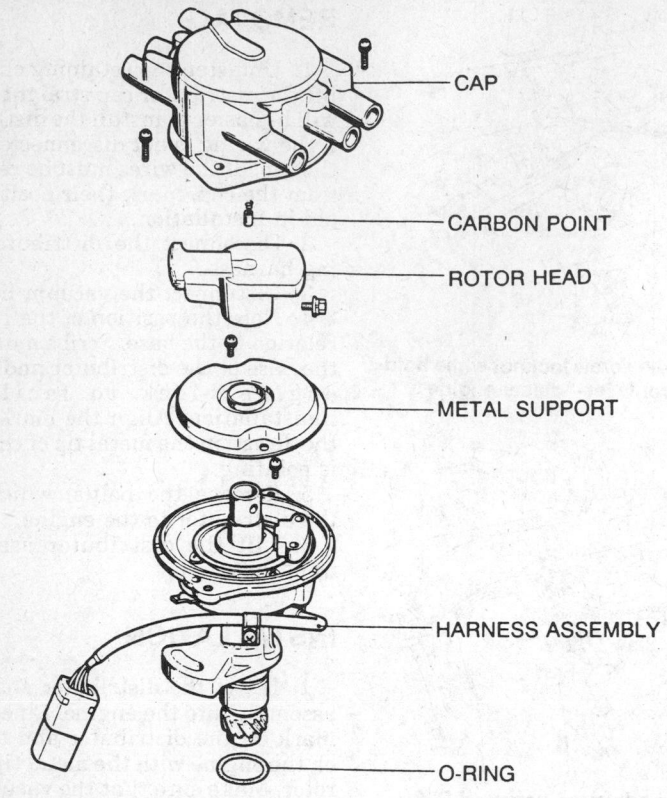

CAP

CARBON POINT

ROTOR HEAD

METAL SUPPORT

HARNESS ASSEMBLY

O-RING

Exploded view of a typical distributor – V6 shown (most late models similar)

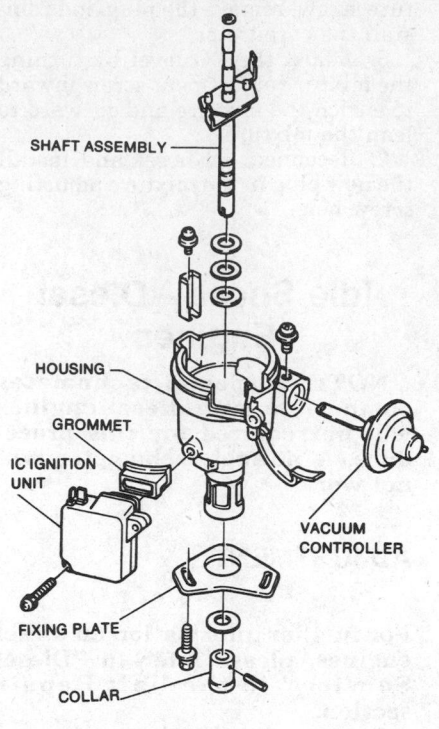

SHAFT ASSEMBLY

HOUSING

GROMMET

IC IGNITION UNIT

VACUUM CONTROLLER

FIXING PLATE

COLLAR

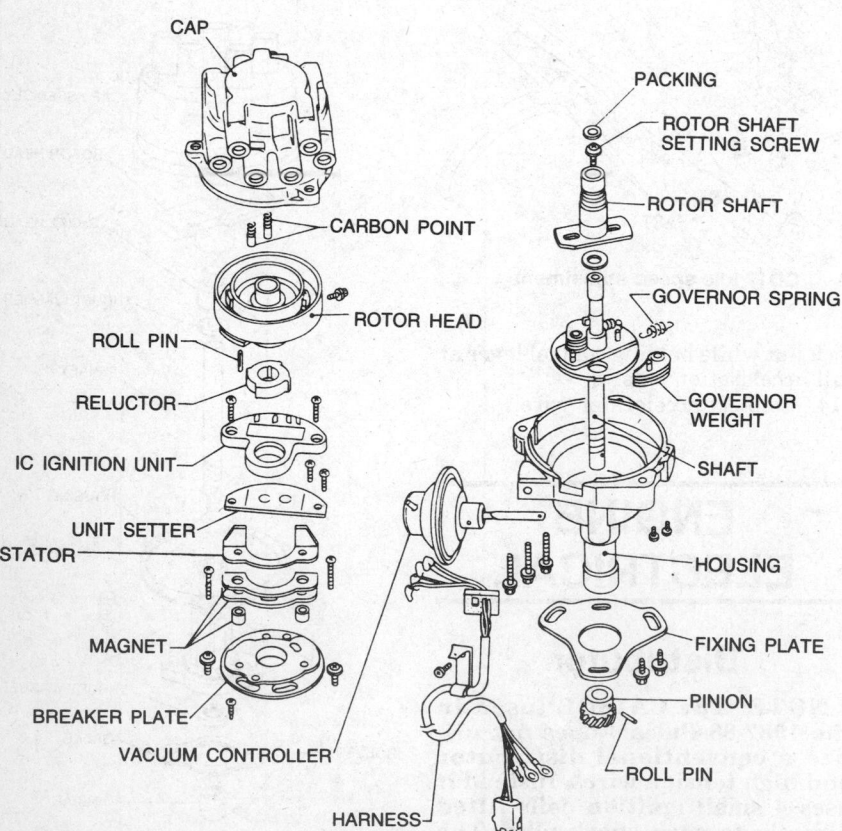

CAP

CARBON POINT

ROTOR HEAD

ROLL PIN

RELUCTOR

IC IGNITION UNIT

UNIT SETTER

STATOR

MAGNET

BREAKER PLATE

VACUUM CONTROLLER

HARNESS

PACKING

ROTOR SHAFT SETTING SCREW

ROTOR SHAFT

GOVERNOR SPRING

GOVERNOR WEIGHT

SHAFT

HOUSING

FIXING PLATE

PINION

ROLL PIN

Exploded view of a typical distributor – 1984-86 4 cyl. engines (1987-88 similar)

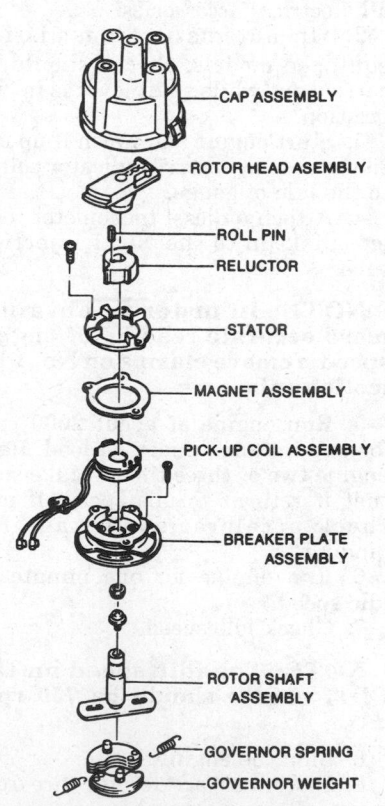

CAP ASSEMBLY

ROTOR HEAD ASEMBLY

ROLL PIN

RELUCTOR

STATOR

MAGNET ASSEMBLY

PICK-UP COIL ASSEMBLY

BREAKER PLATE ASSEMBLY

ROTOR SHAFT ASSEMBLY

GOVERNOR SPRING

GOVERNOR WEIGHT

Exploded view of the electronic distributor—with ring-type pick-up

coil. Install the distributor cap on the distributor housing. Secure the distributor cap with the spring clips.

4. Install the spark plug wires if removed. Make sure that the wires are pressed all the way into the top of the distributor cap and firmly onto the spark plug.

5. Adjust the point dwell and set the ignition timing.

NOTE: If the crankshaft has been turned or the engine disturbed in any manner (i.e., disassembled and rebuilt) while the distributor was removed, or if the marks were not drawn, it will be necessary to initially time the engine. Follow the procedure given below.

INSTALLATION—ENGINE DISTURBED

1. It is necessary to place the No. 1 cylinder in the firing position to correctly install the distributor. To locate this position, the ignition timing marks on the crankshaft front pulley are used.

2. Remove the No. 1 cylinder spark plug. Turn the crankshaft until the piston in the No. 1 cylinder is moving up on the compression stroke. This can be determined by placing your thumb over the spark plug hole and feeling the air being forced out of the cylinder. Stop turning the crankshaft when the timing marks that are used to time the engine are aligned.

3. Oil the distributor housing lightly where the distributor housing lightly where the distributor bears on the cylinder block.

4. Install the distributor so that the rotor, which is mounted on the shaft, points toward the No. 1 spark plug terminal tower position when the cap is installed. Of course, you won't be able to see the direction in which the rotor is pointing if the cap is on the distributor. Lay the cap on the top of the distributor and make a mark on the side of the distributor housing just below the No. 1 spark plug terminal. Make sure that the rotor points toward that mark when you install the distributor.

5. When the distributor shaft has reached the bottom of the hole, move the rotor back and forth slightly until the driving lug on the end of the shaft enters the slots cut in the end of the oil pump shaft and the distributor assembly slides down into place.

6. When the distributor is correctly installed, the reluctor teeth should be aligned with the pick-up coil. This can be accomplished by rotating the distributor body after it has been in-

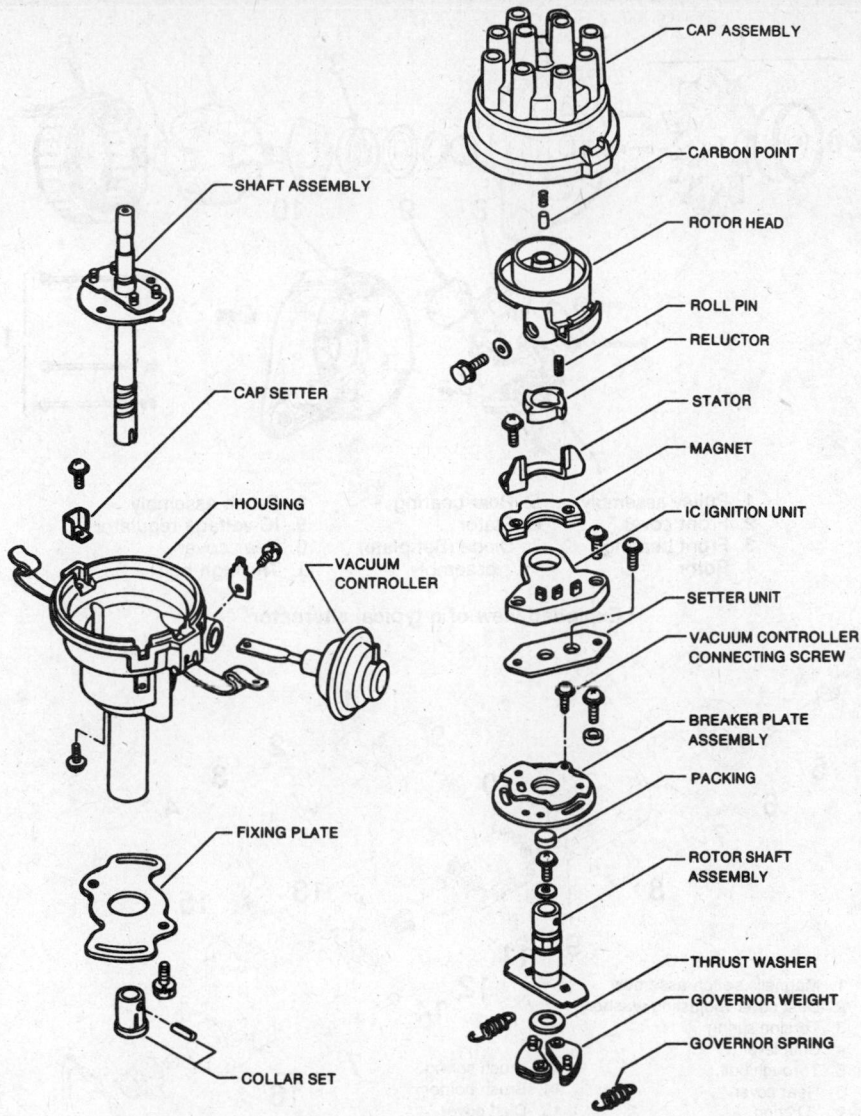

Exploded view of the electronic distributor—with stator

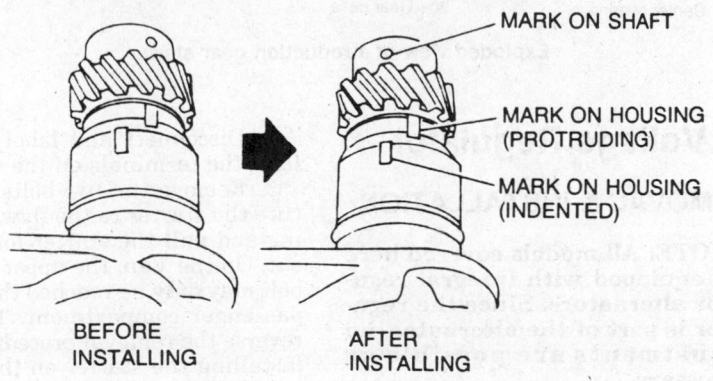

SHAFT ASSEMBLY

CAP SETTER

HOUSING

VACUUM CONTROLLER

FIXING PLATE

COLLAR SET

CAP ASSEMBLY

CARBON POINT

ROTOR HEAD

ROLL PIN

RELUCTOR

STATOR

MAGNET

IC IGNITION UNIT

SETTER UNIT

VACUUM CONTROLLER CONNECTING SCREW

BREAKER PLATE ASSEMBLY

PACKING

ROTOR SHAFT ASSEMBLY

THRUST WASHER

GOVERNOR WEIGHT

GOVERNOR SPRING

MARK ON SHAFT

MARK ON HOUSING (PROTRUDING)

MARK ON HOUSING (INDENTED)

BEFORE INSTALLING

AFTER INSTALLING

Distributor gear position on the VG30E and VG30ET

same direction as it was pointed originally. This will be done automatically if the marks on the engine and the distributor are lined up with the rotor.

2. Install the distributor hold-down bolt and clamp. Leave the screw loose enough so that you can move the distributor with heavy hand pressure.

3. Connect the primary wire to the

stalled in the engine. Once again, line up the marks that you made before the distributor was removed.

7. Install the distributor hold-down bolt.

8. Install the spark plug into the No. 1 spark plug hole and continue from Step 3 of the preceding distributor installation procedure.

Alternator

PRECAUTIONS

An alternator is used on all models. The following precautions must be observed to prevent alternator and regulator damage:

• Be absolutely sure of correct polarity when installing a new battery, or connecting a battery charger.

• Do not short across or ground any alternator or regulator terminals.

• Disconnect the battery ground cable before replacing any electrical unit.

• Never operate the alternator with any of the leads disconnected.

• When steam cleaning the engine, be careful not to subject the alternator to excessive heat or moisture.

• When charging the battery, remove it from the car or disconnect the alternator output terminal.

BELT TENSION ADJUSTMENT

The correct belt tension for all alternators give about ½ in. play on the longest span of the belt.

1. Loosen the alternator pivot and mounting bolts.

2. Pry the alternator toward or away from the engine until the tension is correct. Use a hammer handle or wooden prybar.

3. When the tension is correct, tighten the bolts and check the adjustment. Be careful not to over-tighten the belt, which will lead to bearing failure.

REMOVAL & INSTALLATION

1. Disconnect the negative battery terminal.

2. Disconnect the two lead wires and connector from the alternator.

3. Loosen the drive belt adjusting bolt and remove the belt.

4. Unscrew the alternator attaching bolts and remove the alternator from the vehicle. On the 300ZX, first remove the front stabilizer bar bolts and pull the stabilizer bar down.

5. Installation is in the reverse order of removal.

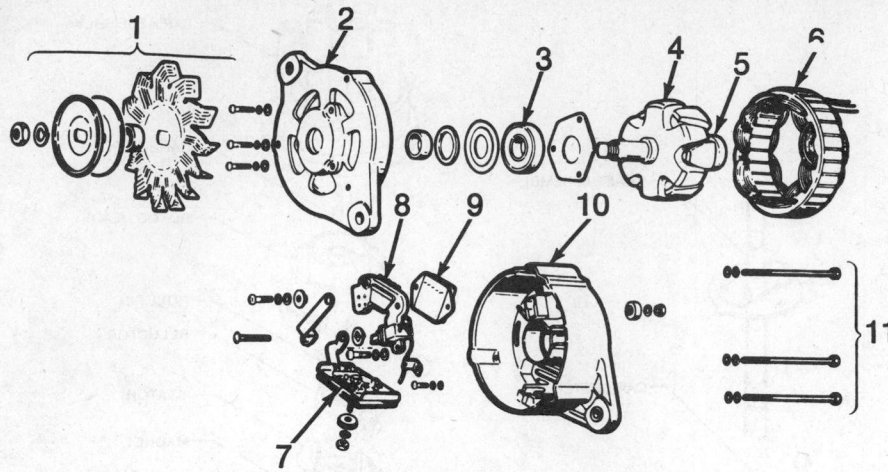

1. Pulley assembly
2. Front cover
3. Front bearing
4. Rotor
5. Rear bearing
6. Stator
7. Diode (Set plate) assembly
8. Brush assembly
9. IC voltage regulator
10. Rear cover
11. Through bolt

Exploded view of a typical alternator

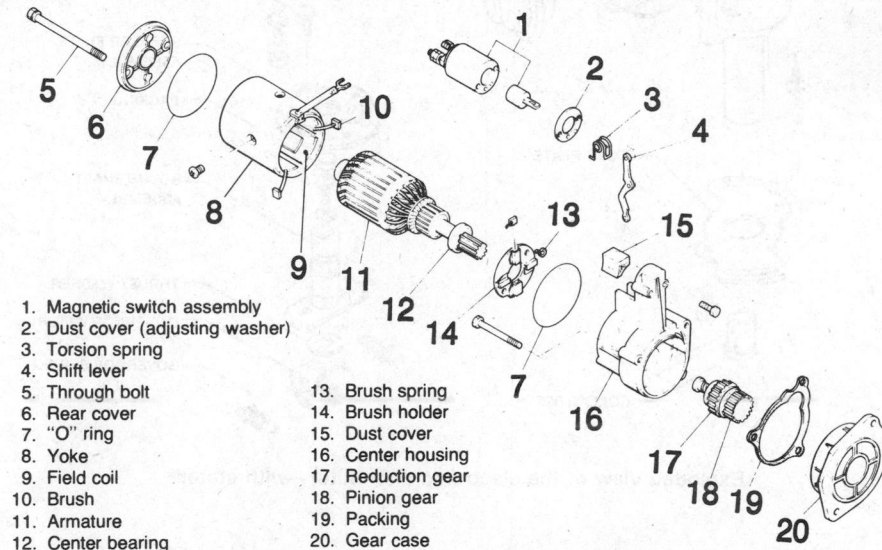

1. Magnetic switch assembly
2. Dust cover (adjusting washer)
3. Torsion spring
4. Shift lever
5. Through bolt
6. Rear cover
7. "O" ring
8. Yoke
9. Field coil
10. Brush
11. Armature
12. Center bearing
13. Brush spring
14. Brush holder
15. Dust cover
16. Center housing
17. Reduction gear
18. Pinion gear
19. Packing
20. Gear case

Exploded view of a reduction gear starter

Voltage Regulator

REMOVAL & INSTALLATION

NOTE: All models covered here are equipped with integral regulator alternators. Since the regulator is part of the alternator, no adjustments are possible or necessary.

Starter

REMOVAL & INSTALLATION

1. Disconnect the negative battery cable.

2. Disconnect and label the wires from the terminals on the solenoid.

3. Remove the two bolts which secure the starter to the flywheel housing and pull the starter forward and out. On the Van, the upper mounting bolt may only be reached through the passenger compartment. To install, reverse the removal procedure. When installing the starter on the Van, be certain to set the rubber cap onto the stater motor body.

DRIVE REPLACEMENT

Non-Reduction Gear Type

1. Loosen the locknut and remove

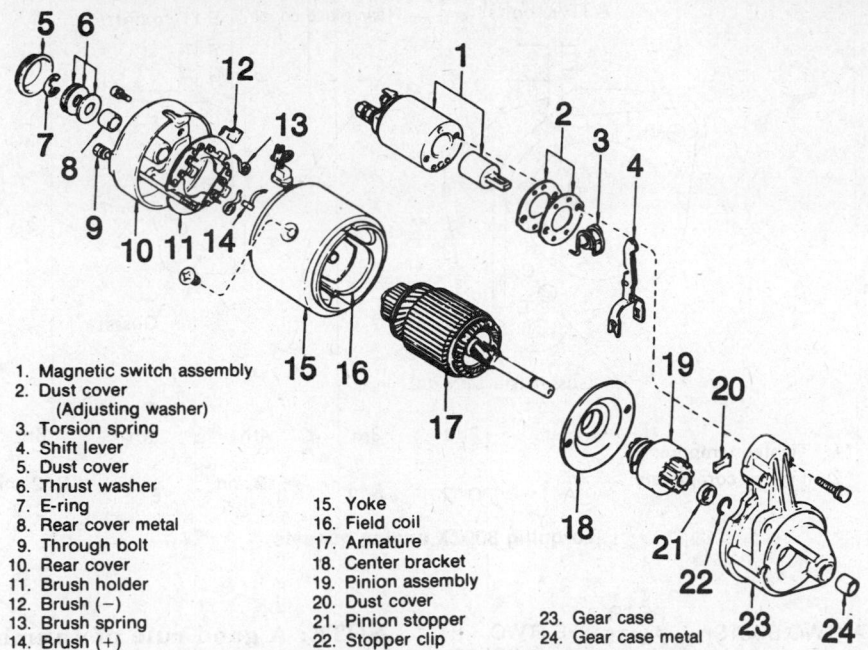

1. Magnetic switch assembly
2. Dust cover
   (Adjusting washer)
3. Torsion spring
4. Shift lever
5. Dust cover
6. Thrust washer
7. E-ring
8. Rear cover metal
9. Through bolt
10. Rear cover
11. Brush holder
12. Brush (−)
13. Brush spring
14. Brush (+)
15. Yoke
16. Field coil
17. Armature
18. Center bracket
19. Pinion assembly
20. Dust cover
21. Pinion stopper
22. Stopper clip
23. Gear case
24. Gear case metal

Exploded view of a non-reduction gear starter

ing the engine. This heat, combined with the first "squirt" of fuel from the injectors and the extremely high cylinder pressures, fires the engine during cold starts. After normal operating temperature is reached, the water temperature sensor wired in the glow plug system changes the system's electrical resistance and cancels glow plug operation during hot starting.

Glow Plug

REMOVAL

LD28 and CD17 Engines

1. Disconnect the glow plug electrical leads. Remove the glow plug connecting plate.
2. Remove the glow plugs by unscrewing them from the cylinder head.
3. Inspect the tips of the plugs for any evidence of melting. If even one glow plug tip looks bad, all the glow plugs must be replaced. This is a general rule-of-thumb which applies to all diesel engines.

TESTING

Glow plugs are tested by checking their resistance with an ohmmeter. The plugs can be tested either while removed from the cylinder head or while still in position. To test them while removed, connect the ground side of the ohmmeter to the threaded section of the plug, and the other side to the plug's tip. If a minimum of continuity is shown on the meter, the plug is OK. If no continuity whatsoever is shown, the plug must be replaced. To check the glow plugs without removing them from the cylinder head, connect the ground side of the ohmmeter to the engine block (or any other convenient ground) and the other end to the glow plug tip. Likewise, a minimum of continuity shown signifies that the plug is OK; a lack of continuity and the plug must be replaced.

INSTALLATION

To install the glow plugs, reverse the removal procedure. Torque the glow plugs to 14–18 ft. lbs. and the glow plug connecting plate bolts to 1 ft. lb.

CHECKING GLOW PLUG CONNECTIONS

A diesel engine's reluctance to start can often be traced to the glow plug busbar (the wire connections to the plugs). Because diesel engines have a certain degree of vibration when run-

---

the connection going to the "M" terminal of the solenoid. Remove the securing screws and remove the solenoid.

2. Remove the dust cover, E-ring, thrust washers, and the two screws retaining the brush holder assembly. Remove the brush cover thru-bolts and remove the cover assembly (all models).

3. Lift the brushes to free them from the commutator and remove the brush holder.

4. Tap the yoke assembly lightly with a wooden hammer and remove it from the field and case.

5. Remove the nut and bolt which serve as a pin for the shift lever, carefully retaining the associated washers.

6. Remove the armature assembly and shift lever.

7. Push the stop ring (located at the end of the armature shaft) toward the clutch and remove the snap ring. Remove the stop ring.

8. Remove the clutch assembly from the armature shaft.

To install the drive:

1. Install the clutch assembly onto the armature shaft.

2. Put the stop ring on and hold it toward the clutch while installing the snap ring.

3. Install the armature assembly and shift lever into the yoke.

4. Install the washers, nut and bolt which serve as a shift lever pivot pin.

5. Install the field back onto the yoke assembly.

6. Life the brushes and install the

brush holder. Install the brush cover and thru-bolts.

7. Replace the brush holder set screws, the thrust washers, E-ring, and the dust cover.

8. Install the solenoid. Reconnect the wire to the "M" terminal of the solenoid.

Reduction Gear Type

1. Remove the starter.
2. Remove the solenoid and the shift lever.
3. Remove the bolts securing the center housing to the front cover and separate the parts.
4. Remove the gears and the starter drive.
5. Installation is the reverse.

SOLENOID REPLACEMENT

All Models

1. Loosen the locknut and remove the connection going to the "M" terminal of the solenoid.

2. Remove the three securing screws and remove the solenoid.

3. To install, reverse the removal procedures.

Auto-Glow System Diesel Engines

The glow plug circuit is used on diesel engines to initially start the engine from cold. The glow plugs heat up the combustion chambers prior to crank-

ning, they tend to loosen the glow plug busbars. This causes hard starting, as the plugs are not receiving their full current. Periodically tighten the wire connection to all glow plugs.

CAUTION

The Datsun/Nissan glow plug system is a 12 volt system equipped with a dropping resistor and fast glow control unit. The resistor reduces the amount of current flowing through the plugs during the after-glow period, and the glow plug control unit stops the after-glow when more than 7 volts is detected flowing through the glow plugs.

ENGINE MECHANICAL

Engine

REMOVAL & INSTALLATION

All Datsun/Nissan engines, except the V6 (VG30E and VG30ET) in the 1987-88 200SX, 300ZX and the 1985-88 Maxima are inline, with either four or six cylinders. Some have overhead valves with rocker arm valve gear and others have a single overhead camshaft. The CA16DE has a double overhead camshaft. The engine in the 1987-88 200SX, 300ZX and 1985-88 Maxima is a single overhead cam V6, with rocker arm-type valve gear. Refer to the "Engine Identification" chart for identification of engines by model, number of cylinders, displacement, and camshaft location. Engines are referred to by model designation codes throughout this section.

Rear Wheel Drive

It is best to remove the engine and transmission as a unit, except on 300ZX; the engine and transmission are separated before engine removal.

1. Mark the location of the hinges on the hood. Unbolt and remove.
2. Disconnect the battery cable. Remove the battery on California models with the Z20E and Z22E engine with air conditioning.
3. Drain the coolant and automatic transmission fluid, if so equipped.
4. Remove the grille on 510 models. Remove the radiator after disconnecting the automatic transmission coolant tubes.
5. Remove the air cleaner.
6. Remove the fan and pulley.

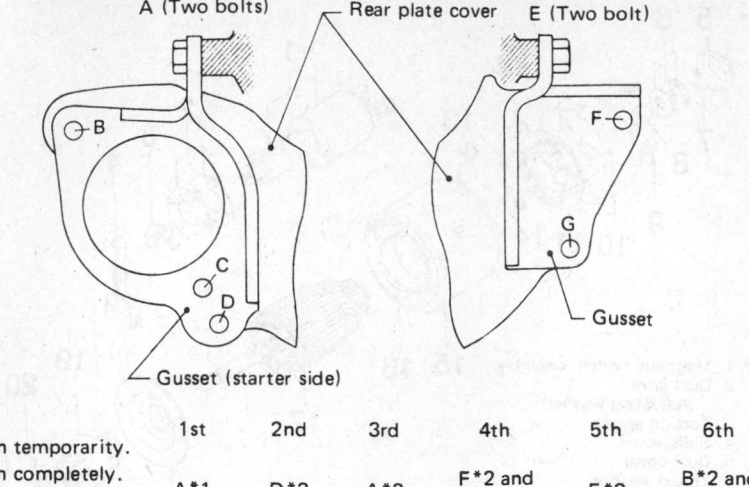

*1: Tighten temporarity.
*2: Tighten completely.

	1st	2nd	3rd	4th	5th	6th
	A*1	D*2	A*2	F*2 and G*2	E*2	B*2 and C*2

Torquing 300ZX engine gussets

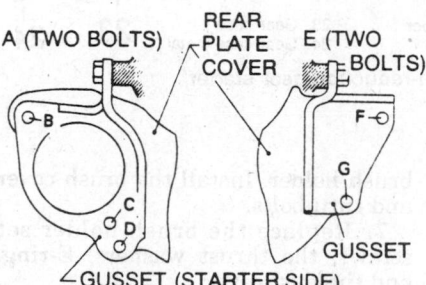

Torquing the 200SX (V6) engine gussets

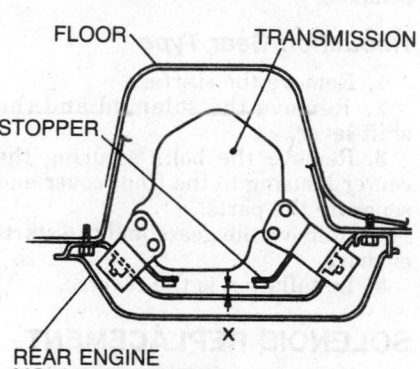

Adjust the rear mount stopper clearance (X) to 13 ± 1.5mm — 200SX (4 cyl.) with AT

7. Disconnect:
   a. water temperature gauge wire
   b. oil pressure sending unit wire
   c. ignition distributor primary wire
   d. starter motor connections
   e. fuel hose
   f. alternator leads
   g. heater hoses
   h. throttle and choke connections
   i. engine ground cable.

NOTE: A good rule of thumb when disconnecting the rather complex engine wiring of today's cars is to put a piece of masking tape on the wire and on the connection you removed the wire from, then mark both pieces of tape 1, 2, 3, etc. When replacing wiring, simply match the pieces of tape.

CAUTION

On models with air conditioning, it is necessary to remove the compressor and the condenser from their mounts. DO NOT ATTEMPT TO UNFASTEN ANY OF THE AIR CONDITIONER HOSES.

8. Disconnect the power brake booster hose from the engine.
9. Remove the clutch operating cylinder and return spring.
10. Disconnect the speedometer cable from the transmission. Disconnect the back up light switch and any other wiring or attachments to the transmission.
11. Disconnect the column shift linkage. Remove the floorshift lever. On the Z20, Z20E and Z22E models, remove the boot, withdraw the lock pin, and remove the lever from inside the car.
12. Detach the exhaust pipe from the exhaust manifold. Remove the front section of the exhaust system.
13. Mark the relationship of the driveshaft flanges and remove the driveshaft.
14. Place a jack under the transmission. Remove the rear crossmember.
15. Attach a hoist to the lifting hooks on the engine (at either end of the cylinder head). Support the engine.

16. Unbolt the front engine mounts. Tilt the engine by lowering the jack under the transmission and raising the hoist.

17. Reverse the procedure to install the engine.

On the 200SX (V6) and 300ZX, torque the engine gusset bolts in six stages, as shown in the accompanying illustration. When installing the engine on A/T equipped 200SXs (4 cyl.), adjust the rear mounting insulator to 0.51 ± 0.059 in. (13 ± 1.5mm) ("x" in the illustration).

——— CAUTION ———

Never loosen the front engine mount insulator cover nuts on a 200SX (4 cyl.); if removed, the insulator will malfunction due to oil loss.

Front Wheel Drive

It is recommended that the engine and transmission be removed as a unit. If need be, the units may be separated after removal.

1. Mark the location of the hinges on the hood. Remove the hood by holding at both sides and unscrewing bolts. This requires two people.

2. Remove the battery and drain radiator coolant.

3. Remove the air cleaner and disconnect the accelerator wire from the carburetor.

4. Disconnect the following wires and hoses:

    a. Ignition wire from the coil to the distributor.

    b. Ignition coil ground wire and the engine ground cable.

    c. Disconnect the block connector from the distributor.

    d. Remove fusible links.

    e. Unplug all engine harness connectors.

    f. Remove the fuel and fuel return hoses.

    g. Disconnect the upper and lower radiator hoses.

    h. Detach the heater inlet and outlet.

    i. Remove the Master-Vac vacuum hose.

    j. Disconnect the carbon canister hoses and the air pump air cleaner hose.

5. Remove the air pump air cleaner.

6. Remove the carbon canister.

7. Remove the auxiliary fan and the washer tank.

8. Remove the grille and radiator with the fan assembly.

9. Remove the clutch cylinder from the clutch housing.

10. Remove both buffer rods (do not alter the length of the rods) and disconnect the speedometer cable.

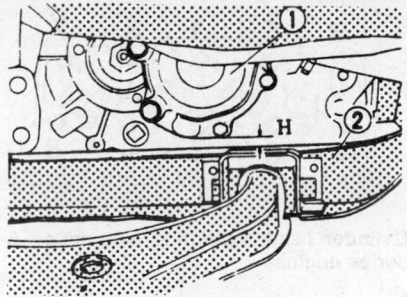

1. Clutch housing
2. Sub-frame

Clearance between the frame and clutch housing—310

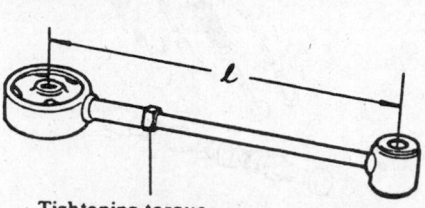

Tightening torque
0.8 to 1.2 kg-m (5.8 to 8.7 ft-lb)

Adjusting the buffer rod length—310

11. Remove the spring pins from the transmission gear selection rods.

12. Attach suitable engine slingers to the block and attach chain or cable. Keep the lifting source slack at this point.

13. Disconnect the exhaust pipe at both the manifold connection and the clamp holding the pipe to the engine.

14. On the Sentra, Stanza and Pulsar, remove the lower ball joint.

15. Drain the gear oil.

16. Disconnect the right and left side drive shafts from their side flanges and remove the bolt holding the radius link support.

NOTE: When drawing out the halfshafts on the Sentra, Stanza and Pulsar, it is necessary to loosen the strut head bolts.

17. Lower the shifter and selector rods and remove the securing bolts from the motor mounts.

    a. Remove the nuts holding the front and rear motor mounts to the frame.

    b. On the Sentra, Stanza and Pulsar, disconnect the clutch and accelerator wires and remove the speedometer cable with its pinion from the transaxle.

18. Lift the engine up and away from the car.

Installation is the reverse of removal with the following cautions and observations.

1. When lowering the engine into the car and onto the frame, make sure to keep it as level as possible.

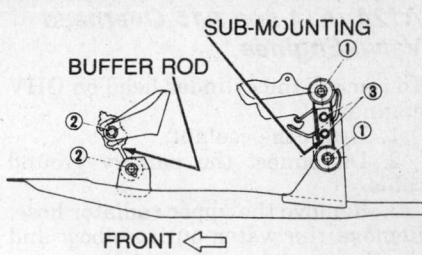

On the 1986 Stanza wagon (2wd) and all 1987-88 models, tighten the buffer rod and the sub-mounting bolts in the order shown

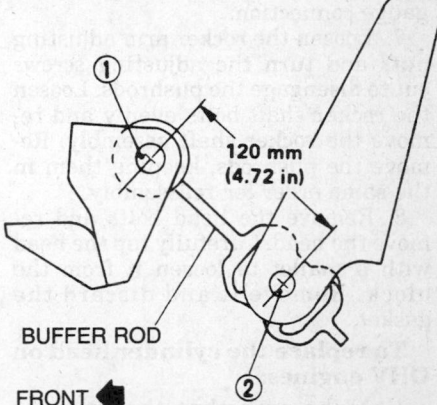

On the 1986 Stanza wagon (4wd), tighten the buffer rod and the sub-mounting bolts in the order shown

2. Check the clearance between the frame and clutch housing and make sure that the engine mount bolts are seated in the groove of the mounting bracket.

    a. Distance "H" should be 0.394–0.472 in. (310).

3. After installing the motor mounts, adjust and install the buffer rods. The right side should be 8.23–8.31 in. and the left 5.39–5.47 in. (310); on the 1987-88 Pulsar: front should be 3.50–3.58 in., and the rear, 3.90–3.98 in.

4. On the 1986 Stanza Wagon and all 1987-88 Stanzas, tighten the engine mount bolts first, then apply a load to the mounting insulators before tightening the buffer rod and sub-mounting bolts. See illustrations for tightening order.

Cylinder Head

REMOVAL & INSTALLATION

NOTE: To prevent distortion or warping of the cylinder head, allow the engine to cool completely before removing the head bolts.

A12A, A14 and A15 Overhead Valve Engines

To remove the cylinder head on OHV engines:

1. Drain the coolant.
2. Disconnect the battery ground cable.
3. Remove the upper radiator hose. Remove the water outlet elbow and the thermostat.
4. Remove the air cleaner, carburetor, rocker arm cover, and both manifolds.
5. Remove the spark plugs.
6. Disconnect the temperature gauge connection.
7. Loosen the rocker arm adjusting nuts and turn the adjusting screws out to disengage the pushrods. Loosen the rocker shaft bolts evenly and remove the rocker shaft assembly. Remove the pushrods, keeping them in the same order for reassembly.
8. Remove the head bolts and remove the head. Carefully tap the head with a mallet to loosen it from the block. Remove it and discard the gasket.

To replace the cylinder head on OHV engines:

1. Make sure that the cylinder head and block mating surfaces are clean. Check the cylinder head surface with a straightedge and a feeler gauge for flatness. If the head is warped more than 0.003 in., it must be trued. If this is not done, there will probably be a leak. The block surface should also be checked in the same way. If the block is warped more than 0.003 in., it must be trued (machined flat).
2. Install a new head gasket. Most gaskets have a TOP marking. Make sure that the proper head gasket is used so that no water passages are blocked off.
3. Install the cylinder head. Install the pushrods in their original locations. Install the rocker arm assembly. Loosen the rocker arm adjusting screws to prevent bending the pushrods when tightening the head bolts. Tighten the head bolts finger tight. The single bolt marked T must go in the No. 1 position on the center right side of the engine.
4. Refer to the "Torque Specifications" chart for the correct head bolt torque. Tighten the bolts to one third of the specified torque in the order shown in the head bolt tightening sequence illustration. Torque the rocker arm mounting bolts to 15–18 ft. lbs.
5. Tighten the bolts to two thirds of the specified torque in sequence.
6. Tighten the bolts to the full specified torque in sequence.
7. Adjust the valves. If no cold set-

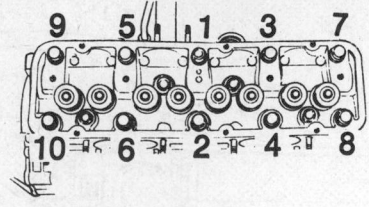

Cylinder head tightening sequence—A-series engines

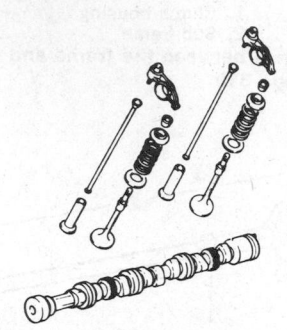

Pushrod, cam and valve assemblies—A series engines

ting is given, adjust the valves to the normal hot setting.

8. Reassemble the engine. Intake and exhaust manifold bolt torque is 11–14 ft. lbs. Fill the cooling system. Start the engine and run it until normal temperature is reached. Remove the rocker arm cover. Torque the bolts in sequence once more. Check the valve clearances.
9. Retorque the head bolts after 600 miles of driving. Check the valve clearances after torquing, as this may disturb the settings.

E15, E15ET, E16, E16S and E16i Single Overhead Camshaft

1. Crank the engine until the No. 1 piston is at Top Dead Center on its compression stroke and disconnect the negative battery cable. Drain the cooling system and remove the air cleaner assembly.
2. Remove the alternator.
3. Number all spark plug wires as to their respective cylinders and remove the distributor, with all wires attached.
4. Remove the EAI pipes bracket and EGR tube at the right (EGR valve) side. Disconnect the same pipes on the front (exhaust manifold) side from the manifold.
5. Remove the exhaust manifold cover and the exhaust manifold, taking note that the center manifold nut has a different diameter than the other nuts.
6. Remove the A/C compressor

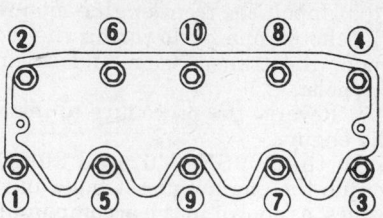

Loosen the cylinder head bolts, in stages, in the order shown—E-series engines

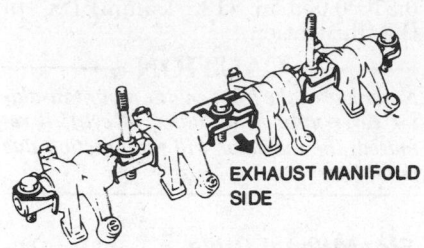

Make sure the cutout on the E-series engine rocker shaft faces the exhaust manifold

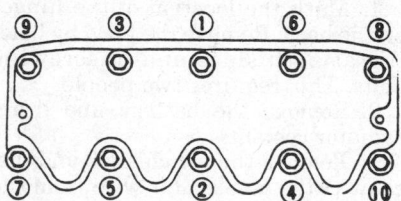

TIGHTEN IN NUMERICAL ORDER

Cylinder head torque sequence—E-Series engines

bracket and the power steering pump bracket (if equipped).

7. Label and disconnect the carburetor throttle linkage, fuel line, and all vacuum and electrical connections.
8. Remove the intake manifold with carburetor or throttle body.
9. Remove water pump drive belt and pulley. Remove crankshaft pulley.
10. Remove the rocker (valve) cover.
11. Remove upper and lower dust cover on the camshaft timing belt shroud.
12. With the shroud removed, the cam sprocket, crankshaft sprocket, jackshaft sprocket, tensioner pulley, and toothed rubber timing belt are exposed.
13. Mark the relationship of the camshaft sprocket to the timing belt and the crankshaft sprocket to the timing belt with paint or a grease pencil. This will make setting everything up during reassembly much easier if the engine is disturbed during disassembly.

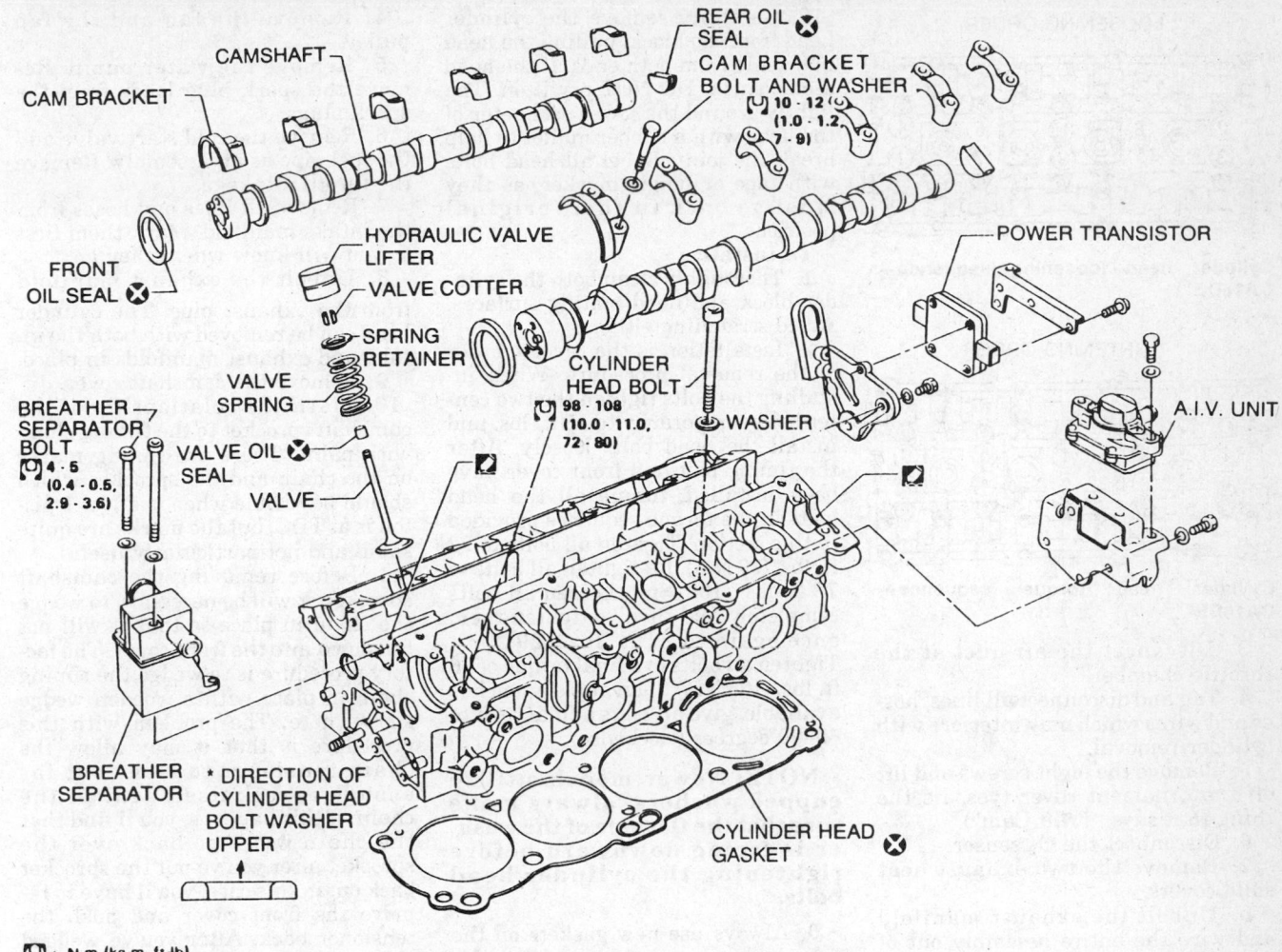

CAM BRACKET — CAMSHAFT — REAR OIL SEAL — CAM BRACKET BOLT AND WASHER [U] 10 - 12 (1.0 - 1.2, 7 - 9)

FRONT OIL SEAL ⊗

HYDRAULIC VALVE LIFTER

VALVE COTTER

SPRING RETAINER

VALVE SPRING

BREATHER SEPARATOR BOLT [U] 4 - 5 (0.4 - 0.5, 2.9 - 3.6)

VALVE OIL SEAL ⊗

VALVE

CYLINDER HEAD BOLT [U] 98 - 108 (10.0 - 11.0, 72 - 80)

WASHER

POWER TRANSISTOR

A.I.V. UNIT

BREATHER SEPARATOR

* DIRECTION OF CYLINDER HEAD BOLT WASHER UPPER

CYLINDER HEAD GASKET ⊗

[U] : N·m (kg-m, ft-lb)

Exploded view of the cylinder head—CA16DE

14. Remove the belt tensioner pulley.

15. Mark an arrow on the timing belt showing direction of engine rotation, because the belt wears a certain way and should be replaced the way it was removed. Slide the belt off the sprockets.

16. Carefully remove the cylinder head from the block, pulling the head up evenly from both ends. If the head seems stuck, DO NOT pry it off. Tap lightly around the lower perimeter of the head with a rubber mallet to help break the joint. Label all head bolts with tape or magic marker, as they must go back in their original positions.

To install:

1. Thoroughly clean both the cylinder block and head mating surfaces. Avoid scratching either.

2. Turn the crankshaft and set the No. 1 cylinder at TDC on its compression stroke. This causes the crankshaft timing sprocket mark to be aligned with the cylinder block cover mark.

3. Align the camshaft sprocket mark with the cylinder head cover mark. This causes the valves for No. 1 cylinder to position at TDC on the compression stroke.

4. Place a new gasket on the cylinder block.

5. E15 engines: Install the cylinder head on the block and tighten the bolts in two stages: first 29–33 ft. lbs. on all bolts, then go around again and torque them all up to 51–54 ft. lbs. After the engine has been warmed up, check all bolts and re-torque if necessary.

E16 engines:

Install the cylinder head on the block and tighten the bolts in two stages: first tighten all bolts to 22 ft. lbs. (29 Nm), then retighten them all to 51 ft. lbs. (69 Nm). Next, loosen all bolts completely, and then retighten them again to 22 ft. lbs. (29 Nm). Tighten all bolts to a final torque of 51–54 ft. lbs. (69–74 Nm); or if an angle wrench is available, turn each bolt until they have achieved the specified number of degrees—bolts 1, 3, 6, 8 & 9: 45–50°; bolt 7: 55–60° and bolts 2, 4, 5 & 10: 40–45°.

NOTE: Be sure to use washers when installing the cylinder head bolts on the E16 engines.

6. Reassemble in the reverse order of disassembly, making sure all timing marks are in proper alignment.

CA16DE Double Overhead Camshaft Engines

1. Crank the engine until the No. 1 piston is at Top Dead Center on its compression stroke and disconnect the negative battery cable. Drain the cooling system and remove the air cleaner assembly.

2. Loosen the alternator and remove all drive belts. Remove the alternator.

LOOSENING ORDER

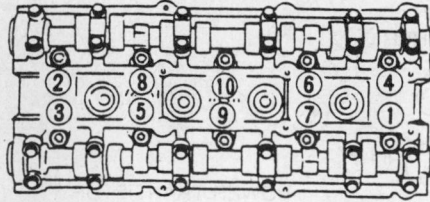

Cylinder head loosening sequence—CA16DE

TIGHTENING ORDER

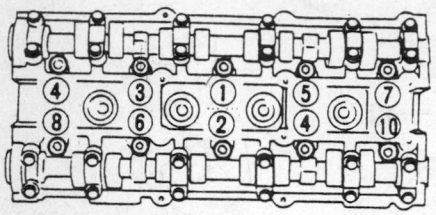

Cylinder head torque sequence—CA16DE

3. Disconect the air duct at the throttle chamber.

4. Tag and disconnect all lines, hoses and wires which may interfere with cylinder removal.

5. Remove the eight screws and lift off the ornament cover (yes, its the thing that says "Twin Cam").

6. Disconnect the O_2 sensor.

7. Remove the two exhaust heat shild covers.

8. Unbolt the exhaust manifold and wire the entire assembly out of the way.

9. Disconnect the EGR tube at the passage cover and then remove the passage cover and its gasket.

10. Disconnect and remove the crank angle sensor from the upper front cover.

11. Remove the support stay from under the intake manifold assembly.

12. Unbolt the intake manifold and remove it along with the collector and throttle chamber.

13. Disconnect and remove the fuel injectors as an assembly.

14. Remove the upper and lower front covers.

15. Remove the timing belt and camshaft sprockets as detailed later in this section.

NOTE: When the timing belt has been removed, NEVER rotate the crankshaft and camshaft separately because the valves will hit the pistons!

16. Remove the camshaft cover.

17. Remove the breather separator.

18. Gradually loosen the cylinder head bolts in several stages, in the sequence illustrated.

19. Carefully remove the cylinder head from the block, pulling the head up evenly from both ends. If the head seems stuck, DO NOT pry it off. Tap lightly around the lower perimeter of the head with a rubber mallet to help break the joint. Label all head bolts with tape or magic marker, as they must go back in their original positions.

To install:

1. Thoroughly clean both the cylinder block and head mating surfaces. Avoid scratching either.

2. Installation is the reverse order of the removal procedure. When installing the bolts tighten the two center bolts temporarily to 15 ft. lbs. and install the head bolts loosely. After the timing belt and front cover have been installed, torque all the head bolts in the torque sequence provided in this section. Tighten all bolts to 22 ft. lbs. (29 Nm). Re-tighten all bolts to 76 ft. lbs. (103 Nm). Loosen all bolts completely and then re-tighten them once again to 22 ft. lbs. (29 Nm). Tighten all bolts to a final torque of 76 ft. lbs. (103 Nm). If an angle wrench is available, give all bolts a final turn to 85–90 degrees (clockwise).

NOTE: Newer models utilize cupped washers, always make sure that the flat side of the washer is facing downward before tightening the cylinder head bolts.

3. Always use new gaskets on the cylinder head, manifolds and cylinder head cover (camshaft cover).

L24E, L28E, L28ET and LD28 Single Overhead Camshaft Engines

1. Crank the engine until the No. 1 piston is at TDC of the compression stroke, disconnect the battery, and drain the cooling system.

NOTE: To set the No. 1 piston at TDC of the compression stroke on the LD28 engine, remove the blind plug from the rear plate. Rotate the crankshaft until the marks on the flywheel and rear plate are in alignment. The No. 1 piston should now be at TDC.

2. Remove the radiator hoses and the heater hoses. Unbolt the alternator mounting bracket and move the alternator to one side.

3. If the car is equipped with air conditioning or power steering, unbolt the compressor or pump and position it out of the way. *Do not disconnect the compressor lines. Severe injury could result.*

4. Remove the fan and the fan pulley.

5. Remove the water pump. Remove the spark plug leads from the spark plugs.

6. Remove the cold start valve and the fuel pipe as an assembly. Remove the throttle linkage.

7. Remove all lines and hoses from the intake manifold. Mark them first so you will know where they go.

8. Unbolt the exhaust manifold from the exhaust pipe. The cylinder head can be removed with both the intake and exhaust manifolds in place.

9. Remove the camshaft cover.

10. Mark the relationship of the camshaft sprocket to the timing chain with paint. There are timing marks on the chain and the sprocket which should be visible when the No. 1 piston is at TDC, but the marks are quite small and not particularly useful.

11. Before removing the camshaft sprocket, it will be necessary to wedge the chain in place so that it will not fall down into the front cover. The factory procedure is to wedge the timing chain in place with a wooden wedge shown here. The problem with this procedure is that it may allow the chain tensioner to move out far enough to cock itself against the chain. If this happens, you'll find that the chain won't go back over the sprocket after you've put the sprocket back on. In this case, you'll have to remove the front cover and push the tensioner back. After you've wedged the chain, unbolt the camshaft sprocket and remove it.

12. Remove the cylinder head bolts; they require an Allen wrench type socket adapter. Keep the bolts in order as two different sizes are used.

13. Lift off the cylinder head. You may have to tap it lightly with a ruber mallet.

14. Clean the block and head mating surfaces thoroughly and check for warpage according to the procedure described in the A-series engine section. Install a new head gasket on the block and lower the head into position.

15. Install a new head gasket and place the head in position on the block.

16. Install the head bolts in their original locations.

17. Torque the head bolts in three stages: first to 29 ft. lbs., then to 43 ft. lbs., then to 62 ft. lbs.

18. Reinstall the camshaft sprocket in its original location. The chain is installed at the same time as the sprocket. Make sure the marks made earlier line up. If the chain has slipped, or the engine has been disturbed, correct the timing as de-

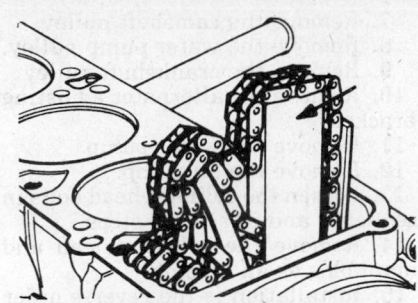

On overhead cam engines, the wedge shown by the arrow can be used to prevent the timing chain from slipping off the crankshaft sprocket.

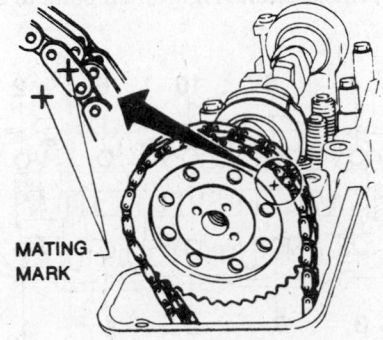

Matchmark the timing chain to the camshaft sprocket

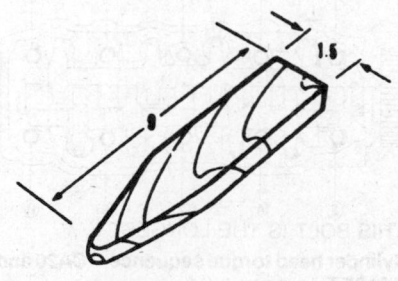

Dimensions of wooden wedge used to hold chain in place

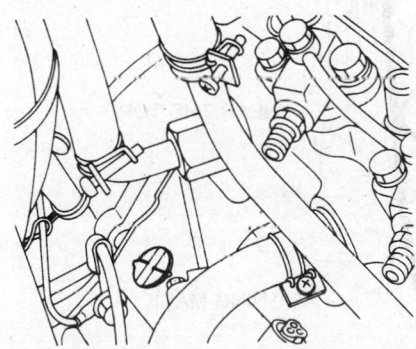

Remove the plug in the rear plate to set the No. 1 piston at TDC—diesel engines

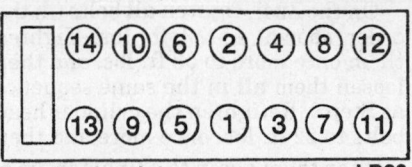

Cylinder head torque sequence—LD28 engines

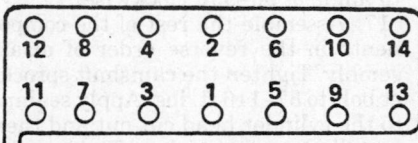

Cylinder head torque sequence—L24 and L28 engines

scribed under "Timing Chain Removal and Installation".

19. Reinstall all remaining parts, coolant, etc.

20. Adjust the valves.

21. After 600 miles of driving, retorque the head bolts and readjust the valves.

Z20E, Z20S, Z22, Z22E and Z24 Single Overhead Camshaft

Engines

1. Complete Steps 1–5 under "L24 Overhead Camshaft Engine." Observe the following note for Step 5.

NOTE: The spark plug leads should already be marked. However, it would be wise to mark them yourself, especially the dual spark plug models.

2. Disconnect the throttle linkage, the air cleaner or its intake hose assembly (fuel injection). Disconnect the fuel line, the return fuel line and any other vacuum lines or electrical leads. On the Z20S, remove the carburetor to avoid damaging it while removing the head.

NOTE: A good rule of thumb when disconnecting the rather complex engine wiring of today's automobiles is to put a piece of masking tape on the wire or hose and on the connection from which you removed the wire or hose, then mark both pieces of tape 1, 2, 3, etc. When replacing wiring, simply match the pieces of tape.

3. Remove the EGR tube from around the rear of the engine.

4. Remove the exhaust air induction tubes from around the front of the engine on Z20S engines and from the exhaust manifold on Z20E engines.

5. Unbolt the exhaust manifold

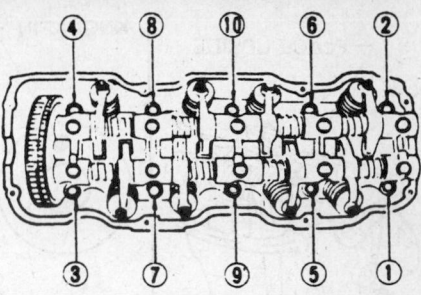

Cylinder head loosening sequence—Z-Series engines

from the exhaust pipe. On the Z20S, remove the fuel pump.

6. On the Z20E, remove the intake manifold supports from under the manifold. Remove the PCV valve from around the rear of the engine if necessary.

7. Remove the spark plugs to protect them from damage. Remove the cylinder head (rocker) cover.

8. Mark the relationship of the camshaft sprocket to the timing chain with paint or chalk. If this is done, it will not be necessary to locate the factory timing marks. Before removing the camshaft sprocket, it will be necessary to wedge the chain in place so that it will not fall down into the front cover. The factory procedure is to wedge the timing chain in place with the wooden wedge shown here. The problem with this procedure is that it may allow the chain tensioner to move out far enough to cock itself against the chain. If this happens, you'll find that the chain won't go back over the sprocket after you've put the sprocket back on. In this case, you'll have to remove the front cover and push the tensioner back. After you've wedged the chain, unbolt the camshaft sprocket and remove it.

9. Working from both ends in, loosen the cylinder head bolts and remove them. Remove the bolts securing the cylinder head to the front cover assembly.

10. Lift the cylinder head off the engine block. It may be necessary to tap the head lightly with a rubber mallet to loosen it.

To install the cylinder head:

11. Thoroughly clean the cylinder block and head surfaces and check both for warpage. See "A12, etc. Overhead Valve Engines" cylinder head removal section for procedure (Step 1 of assembly process).

12. Fit the new head gasket. Don't use sealant. Make sure that no open valves are in the way of raised pistons, and do not rotate the crankshaft or camshaft separately because of possible damage which might occur to the valves.

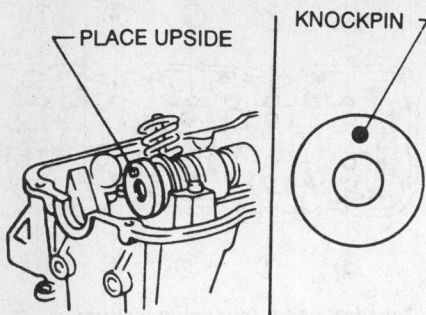

The camshaft knockpin on the Z24i must be facing up

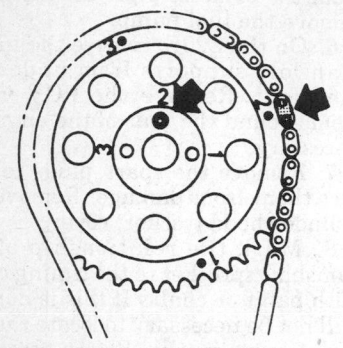

Camshaft sprocket installation on the Z24i

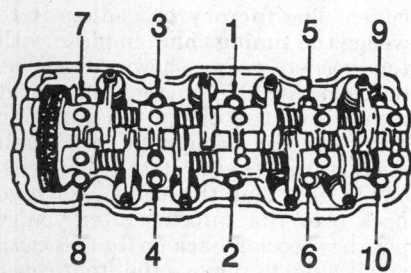

Cylinder head torque sequence—Z-Series engines

13. Temporarily tighten the two center right and left cylinder head bolts to 14 ft. lbs.

14. On the Z24i, make sure that the camshaft knockpin is pointing upward.

15. Install the camshaft sprocket together with the timing chain to the camshaft. Make sure the marks you made earlier line up with each other. When fitting the sprocket on the Z24i engine, camshaft knockpin should fit into the sprocket's No. 1 hole; the No. 2 timing mark must also be used. If you get into trouble, see "Timing Chain Removal and Installation" for timing procedures.

16. Install the cylinder head bolts and torque them to 20 ft. lbs., then 40 ft. lbs., then 58 ft. lbs. in the order shown in the illustration.

On the Z24i, tighten all bolts (in the order shown) to 22 ft. lbs. Tighten them once more to 58 ft. lbs. and then loosen them all in the same sequence as Step 9. Retighten the cylinder head bolts to 22 ft. lbs. once more and then tighten them again to a final torque of 74–80 ft. lbs. If an angle wrench is available, turn all bolts on final time to angle of 90–95°, clockwise.

17. Assemble the rest of the components in the reverse order of disassembly. Tighten the camshaft sprocket bolt to 87–116 ft. lbs. Apply sealant to the cylinder head cut-out and then install the rubber plug. Tighten the cylinder head-to-upper front cover bolts to 2.9–7.2 ft. lbs. Adjust the valves.

NOTE: It is always wise to drain the crankcase oil after the cylinder head has been installed to avoid coolant contamination.

CA18ET, CA20, CA20E and CA20S Single Overhead Camshaft Engines

1. On the CA18ET and CA20E models, remove the air intake pipe.
2. Remove the cooling fan and radiator shroud (all models).
3. Remove the alternator drive belt, power steering pump drive belt and the A/C compressor drive belt if so equipped.
4. Position the No. 1 cylinder at TDC of the compression stroke and remove the upper and lower timing belt covers.
5. Loosen the timing belt tensioner and return spring, then remove the timing belt.

NOTE: When the timing belt has been removed, do not rotate the crankshaft and the camshaft separately, because the valves will hit the piston heads.

6. Remove the exhaust manifold.

7. Remove the camshaft pulley.
8. Remove the water pump pulley.
9. Remove the crankshaft pulley.
10. Remove the alternator adjusting bracket.
11. Remove the water pump.
12. Remove the oil pump.
13. Loosen the cylinder head bolts in sequence and in several steps.
14. Remove the cylinder head and manifolds as an assembly.
15. Installation is the reverse order of the removal procedure. When installing the bolts tighten the two center bolts temporarily to 15 ft. lbs. and install the head bolts loosely. After the timing belt and front cover have been installed, torque all the head bolts in the torque sequence provided in this section. Tighten all bolts to 22

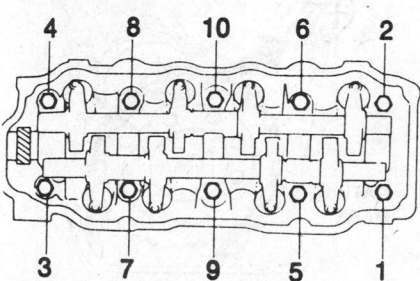

Cylinder head bolt loosening sequence—CA20 and CA 18ET engines

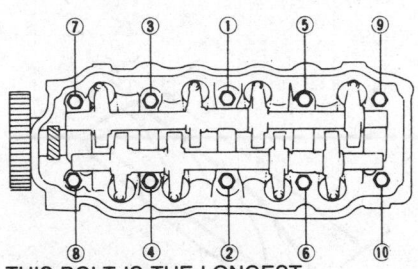

THIS BOLT IS THE LONGEST

Cylinder head torque sequence—CA20 and CA18ET engines

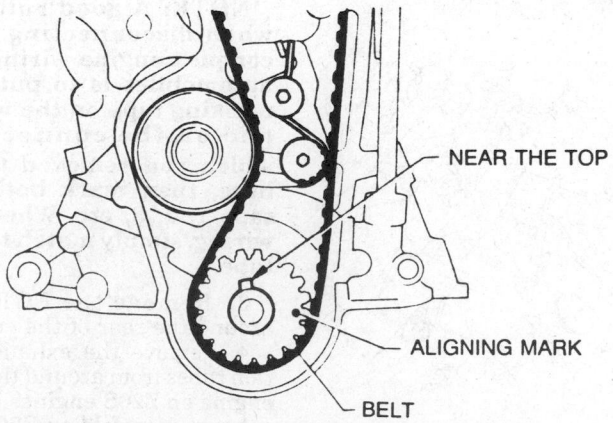

Make sure the crankshaft pulley key is near the top—C-Series engines

ft. lbs. (29 Nm). Re-tighten all bolts to 58 ft. lbs. (78 Nm). Loosen all bolts completely and then re-tighten them once again to 22 ft. lbs. (29 Nm). Tighten all bolts to a final torque of 54–61 ft. lbs. (74–83 Nm). If an angle wrench is available, give all bolts a final turn to 90–95 degrees (clockwise). On 1986-88 models; 75–80° except bolt #8 which is 83–88°.

NOTE: Newer models utilize cupped washers, always make sure that the flat side of the washer is facing downward before tightening the cylinder head bolts.

————— CAUTION —————
Before installing the timing belt, be certain that the crankshaft pulley key is near the top and that the camshaft knock pin or sprocket aligning mark is at the top.

VG30E and VG30ET V6 Engines
REMOVAL

NOTE: Includes camshaft, intake manifold, exhaust manifold, rocker shaft removal procedures.

1. Remove the engine assembly.
2. Remove the timing belt.

NOTE: NEVER rotate the crankshaft and camshaft separately after the timing belt has been removed or the valves will hit the pistons!

3. Set the No. 1 cylinder at TDC on its compression stroke.
4. Drain the coolant from the cylinder block.
5. Remove the collector cover and collector. On the 200SX, remove the collector together with the throttle chamber, EGR valve and I.A.A. unit.
6. Remove the intake manifold with fuel tube assembly.
7. Remove the power steering pump bracket.
8. Remove the exhaust manifold covers.
9. Disconnect the exhaust manifold connecting tube.
10. Remove the bolts securing the camshaft pulleys and rear timing cover.
11. Remove the compressor and rocker covers.
12. Remove the cylinder head with exhaust manifold.
13. Remove the right and left exhaust manifolds. Loosen the bolts in numerical order as illustrated.
14. Loosen the bolts in two or three stages and remove the rocker shafts with the rocker arms.
15. Remove the hydraulic valve lifters and lifter guide.

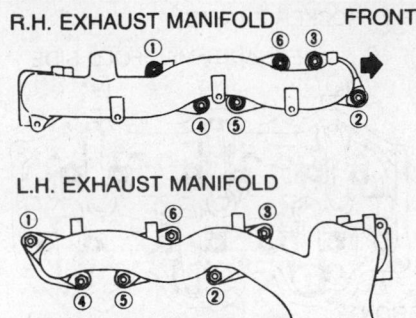

Exhaust manifold loosening sequence—VG30E (Maxima and 200SX)

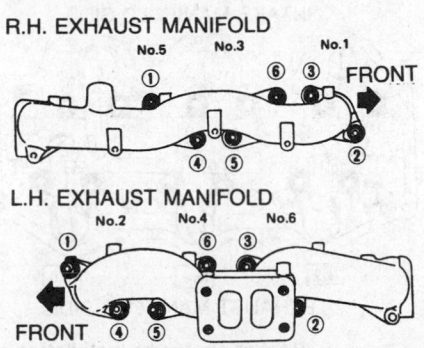

Exhaust manifold loosening sequence—VG30E and VG30ET (300ZX)

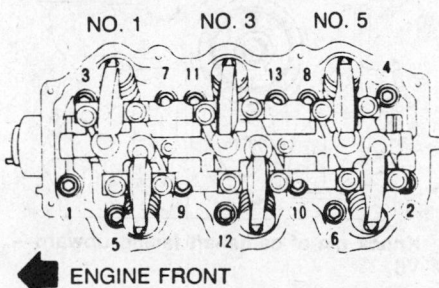

LOOSEN IN NUMERICAL ORDER
Cylinder head loosening sequence—VG30E (200SX)

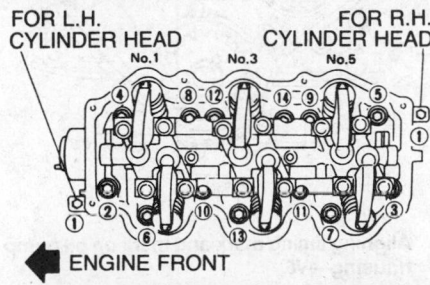

Cylinder head loosening sequence—VG30E and VG30ET (Maxima and 300ZX)

NOTE: Hold the valve lifters with wire so that they will not drop from the lifter guide. Put an identification mark on the lifters to avoid mixing them up.

16. Remove the camshaft from the front side of the engine.

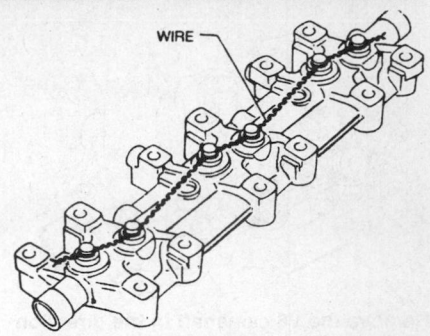

Holding the V6 valve lifters with a wire

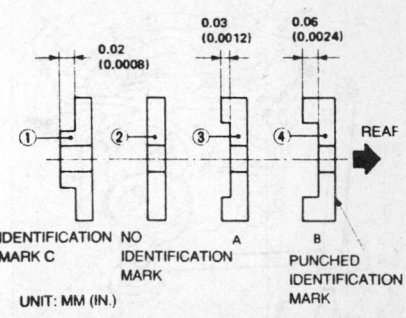

Select shim thickness so that camshaft end play is withing specs—V6

INSPECTION

Camshaft End Play

Using a dial gauge measure the camshaft end play. If the camshaft end play exceeds the limit (0.0012–0.0024 in.), select the thickness of a cam locate plate so that the end play is within specification.

Example:
If camshaft end play measures 0.08mm (0.0031 in.) with shim 2 used, then change shim 2 to shim 3 so that the camshaft end play is 0.05mm (0.0020 in.).

Camshaft Journal Clearance

Measure the inside diameter of the camshaft journals in the head and the outside diameter of the camshaft.

Standard Inside Diameter:
• 47.00–47.025mm (1.8504–1.8514 in.) Standard Outside Diameter:
• 46.94–46.96mm (1.8480–1.8488 in.)
• Wear Limit: 0.15mm (0.0059 in.)
• Valve Dimensions

Check the valve dimensions in each valve. When the valve head has been worn down to .05mm (0.020 in.) in margin thickness, replace the valve.

Grinding allowance for the valve stem tip is 0.2mm (0.008 in.) or less.

ASSEMBLY

1. Install the valve component parts.

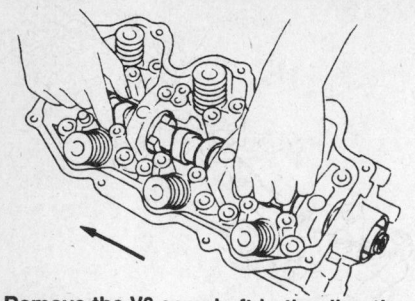

Remove the V6 camshaft in the direction of the arrow

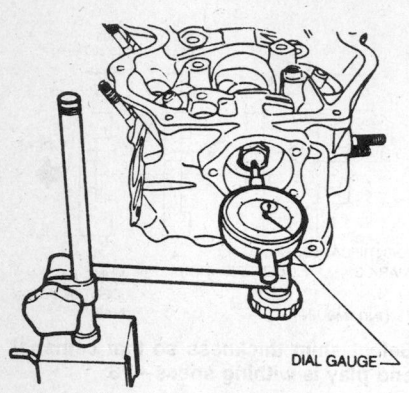

DIAL GAUGE

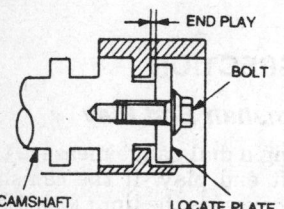

END PLAY

BOLT

CAMSHAFT   LOCATE PLATE

Using a dial indicator to measure camshaft end play—V6

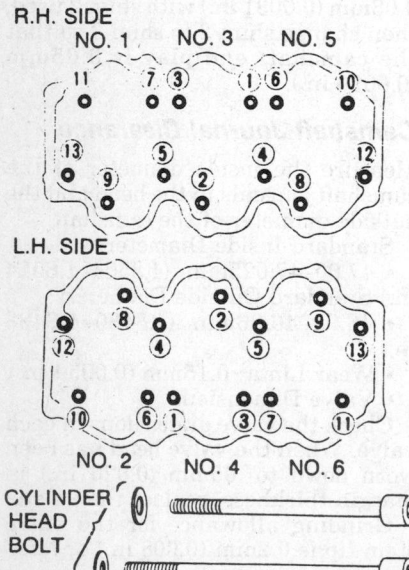

R.H. SIDE

NO. 1   NO. 3   NO. 5

L.H. SIDE

NO. 2   NO. 4   NO. 6

CYLINDER HEAD BOLT

Cylinder head torque sequence—VG30E (200SX)

R.H. ROCKER SHAFTS

EXHAUST MANIFOLD SIDE

No 1   No 3   No 5

FRONT   INTAKE MANIFOLD SIDE

L.H. ROCKER SHAFTS

INTAKE MANIFOLD SIDE

No.2   No.4   No.6

EXHAUST MANIFOLD SIDE

ROCKER SHAFT DIRECTION

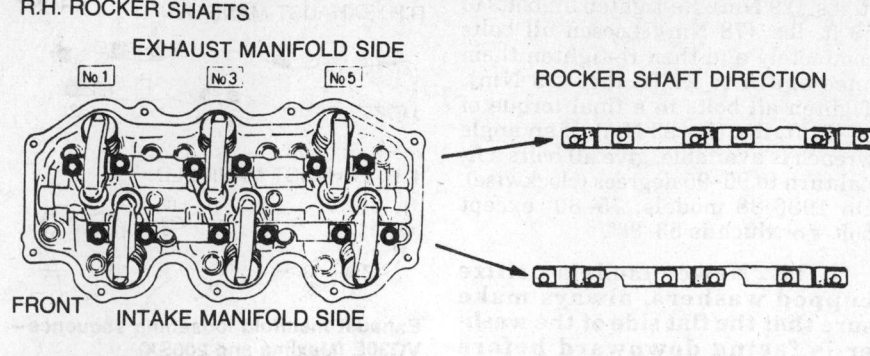

Rocker shaft/arm installation procedure—VG30E and VG30ET

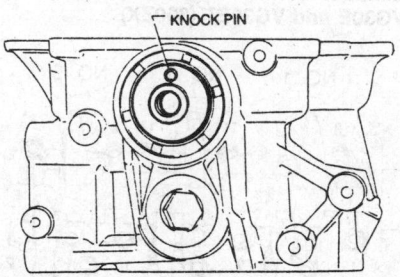

KNOCK PIN

Knock pin of camshaft facing upward—V6

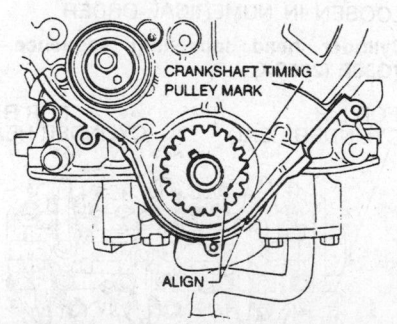

CRANKSHAFT TIMING PULLEY MARK

ALIGN

Aligning timing mark and mark on oil pump housing—V6

NOTE: Install the outer valve spring (uneven pitch type) with its narrow pitch side toward the cylinder head side.

2. Install the camshaft.
3. Apply engine oil to the camshaft oil seal and install it in place.

4. Adjust the camshaft end play with the locate plate installed.

INSTALLATION

1. On the 200SX, install the exhaust manifold to the cylinder head.
2. Make sure the No. 1 cylinder is set at TDC on its compression stroke as follows:

   a. Align the crankshaft timing mark with the mark on the oil pump housing.

   b. The knock pin in the front end of the camshaft should be facing upward.

NOTE: Do not rotate crankshaft and camshaft separately because valves will hit piston head.

3. Position the cylinder head on the block and tighten the cylinder head bolts in five steps in the numerical sequence illustrated.

   1st Tighten all bolts to 29 Nm (3.0 kg-m, 22 ft. lb.)
   2nd Tighten all bolts to 59 Nm (6.0 kg-m, 43 ft. lb.)
   3rd Loosen all bolts completely.
   4th Tighten all bolts to 29 Nm (3.0 kg-m, 22 ft. lb.)
   5th Tighten all bolts to 54–64 Nm (5.5–6.5 kg-m, 40–47 ft. lbs.)
or if you have an angle wrench, turn all bolts 60–65 degrees clockwise.

4. Tighten the rear timing belt cover.
5. Install the camshaft pulley and tighten to 58–65 ft lbs.

NOTE: The R.H. and L.H. camshaft pulleys are different parts. Install them in the correct positions. The R.H. pulley has an R3 identification mark and the L.H. has an L3.

6. Install the timing belt and adjust the tension.

7. Install the front upper and lower belt covers.

8. Install the valve lifters and lifter guide. Hold all valve lifters with a wire as was done during disassembly and install to their original position.

9. Install the rocker shafts with the rocker arms and tighten the rocker shaft bolts to 13–16 ft. lbs. in two or three stages.

10. Install the rocker cover.

11. Install the intake manifold and fuel tube and tighten in two or three stages.

Nut

　1st 3–5 Nm

　　(0.3–0.5 kg-m, 2.2–3.6 ft lbs.)

　2nd 24–27 Nm

　　(2.4–2.8 kg-m, 17–20 ft lbs.)

Bolt

　1st 3–5 Nm

　　(0.3–0.5 kg-m, 2.2–3.6 ft. lbs.)

　2nd 24–27 Nm

　　(2.4–2.8 kg-m, 17–20 ft. lbs.)

12. On the 300ZX and Maxima, install the exhaust manifolds and connecting tube and torque in sequence to 13–16 ft. lbs. Tighten the connecting tube to 16–20 ft. lbs.

13. The remainder of the installation is the reverse of removal. When installing the collector cover, always use a new gasket. On the 200SX, tighten the throttle chamber-to-collector bolts in two stages; 6.5–8 ft. lbs. (9–11 Nm) and then to 13–16 ft. lbs. (18–22 Nm).

CD17 Single Overhead Camshaft Diesel Engines

1. Drain the coolant and disconnect the battery.

2. Disconnect the exhaust pipe.

3. Set the No. 1 cylinder at TDC on the compression stroke. Tag and disconnect all hoses and electrical connections.

4. Remove the valve timing belt on the camshaft pulley side of the engine.

5. Remove the injection pump timing belt.

6. Loosen the injection pump pulley and remove it with a suitable puller.

7. Remove the rear engine cover.

8. Tag and remove all fuel injection lines from the injectors.

9. Remove the camshaft (valve) cover and loosen the cylinder head bolts in the reverse of the torque se-

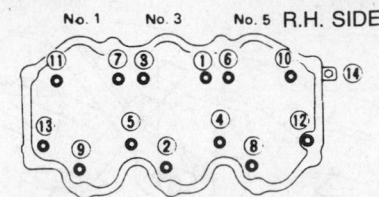

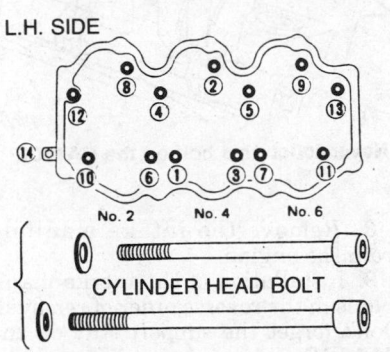

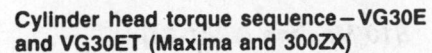

Cylinder head torque sequence—VG30E and VG30ET (Maxima and 300ZX)

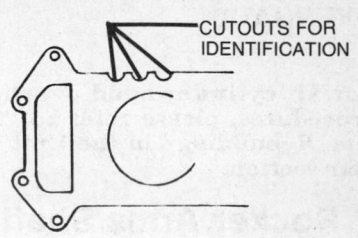

Cylinder head gasket identification—280ZX

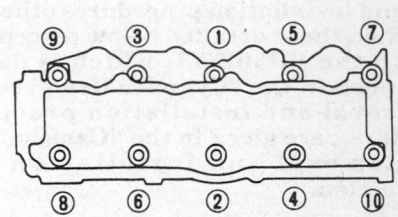

Cylinder head torque sequence—CD17 diesel engines; reverse for loosening

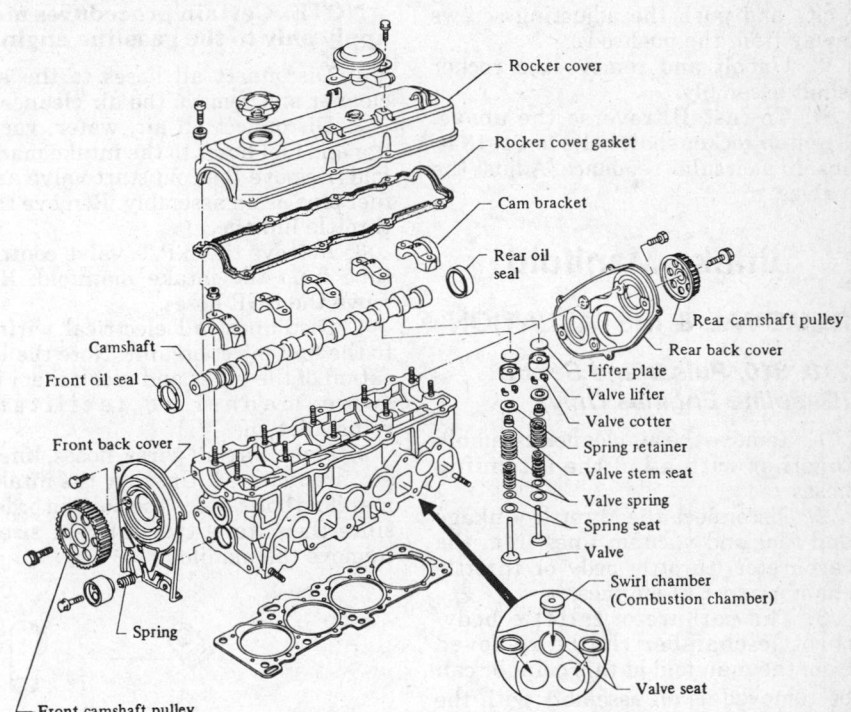

Exploded view of CD17 cylinder head assembly

quence given in this section.

10. Remove the cylinder head, with the manifolds still attached. If the head will not budge, tap around the head-to-block mating surface with a rubber mallet. The manifolds can be removed on a bench.

11. Installation is in the reverse order of removal. Head gaskets are selected by measuring the piston projection. See "Piston and Connecting Rod" for an application chart. Torque the head bolts to 29 ft. lbs. (39 Nm) in

sequence. Tighten them once more to 72–80 ft. lbs. (98–108 Nm) and then loosen all bolts completely. Tighten them once again as already detailed or if an angle wrench is available, turn all bolts to a final torque of 82–87°. Tighten the injection pump pulley nut to 43–51 ft. lbs. (59–69 Nm). Install the valve and injection timing belts and check that timing is correct as detailed later in this section. Adjust the valve clearance and check the plunger lift.

OVERHAUL

For all cylinder head overhaul procedures, please refer to "Engine Rebuilding" in the Unit Repair section.

Rocker Arms/Shaft

REMOVAL & INSTALLATION

NOTE: All rocker shaft removal and installation procedures other than those detailed below (except on the VG30E/ET, which is detailed in the "Cylinder Head" removal and installation procedure), are given in the "Camshaft Removal and Installation" section.

A12A, A14 and A15 Engines

1. Remove the rocker cover.
2. Loosen the rocker adjusting bolts and push the adjusting screws away from the pushrods.
3. Unbolt and remove the rocker shaft assembly.
4. To install, reverse the above. Tighten rocker shaft bolts to 14–18 ft. lbs. in a circular sequence. Adjust the valves.

Intake Manifold

REMOVAL & INSTALLATION

210, 310, Pulsar and Sentra (Gasoline Engines Only)

1. Remove the air cleaner assembly together with all of the attending hoses.
2. Disconnect the throttle linkage and fuel and vacuum lines from the carburetor (throttle body or throttle chamber on EFI engines).
3. The carburetor/throttle body/throttle chamber can be removed from the manifold at this point or can be removed as an assembly with the intake manifold.
4. On A-Series engines, disconnect the intake and exhaust manifold unless both are being removed.
5. Remove the manifold support stay on the CA16DE.
6. Remove the EGR valve assembly, air regulator and F.I.C.D valve from the manifold on the CA16DE.
7. Loosen the intake manifold attaching nuts, working from the two ends toward the center, and then remove them.

NOTE: NEVER tighten or loosen the power valve adjusting screw on the CA16DE.

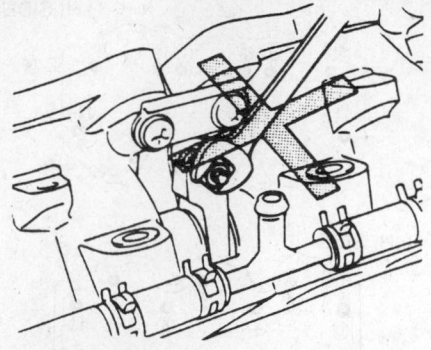

Never touch this bolt on the CA16DE

8. Remove the intake manifold from the engine.
9. Installation of the intake manifold is in the reverse order of removal. Don't forget the support stay on the CA16DE.

810/Maxima (1981-84)

NOTE: Certain procedures may apply only to the gasoline engine.

1. Disconnect all hoses to the air cleaner and remove the air cleaner.
2. Disconnect all air, water, vacuum and fuel hoses to the intake manifold. Remove the cold start valve and fuel pipe as an assembly. Remove the throttle linkage.
3. Remove the B.P.T. valve control tube from the intake manifold. Remove the EGR hoses.
4. Disconnect all electrical wiring to the fuel injection unit. Note the location of the wires and mark them in some manner to facilitate reinstallation.
5. Make sure all wires, hoses, lines, etc. are removed. Unscrew the intake manifold bolts. Keep the bolts in order since they are of two different sizes. Remove the manifold.

6. Installation is the reverse of removal. Use a new gasket, clean both sealing surfaces, and torque the bolts in several stages, working from the center outward.

510/200SX, Sentra (Diesel Engines Only) and Stanza

1. Drain the coolant.
2. On the fuel injected engine, remove the air cleaner hoses. On the carbureted engine, remove the air cleaner.
3. Remove the radiator hoses from the manifold.
4. For the carbureted engine, remove the fuel, air and vacuum hoses from the carburetor. Remove the throttle linkage and remove the carburetor.

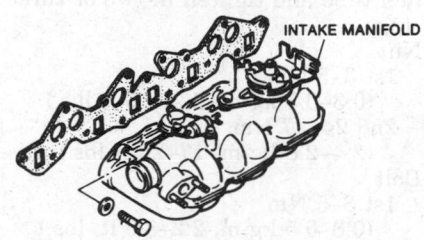

LD28 diesel intake manifold—810 and Maxima

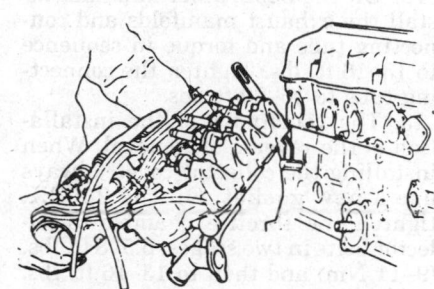

Removing the manifold with injectors, etc., still attached—Z20E, Z22E

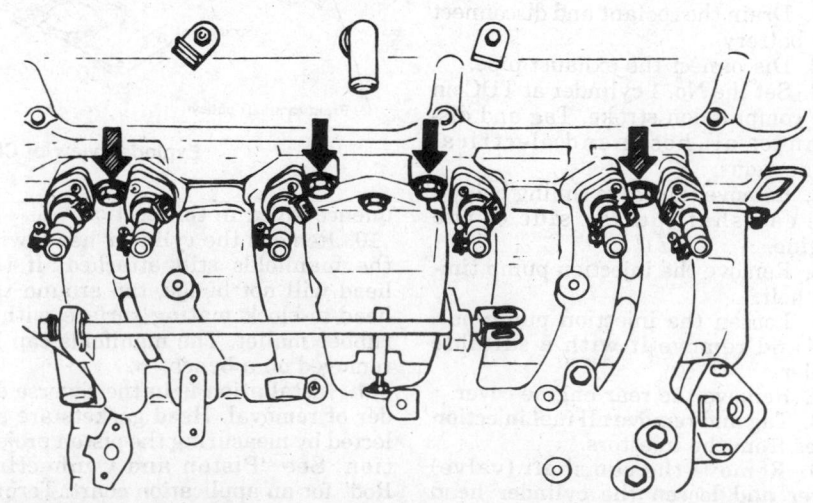

810/Maxima (1981-84) intake manifold mounting bolt locations—gasoline engines

5. Remove the throttle cable and disconnect the fuel pipe and the fuel return line on fuel injected engines. Plug the fuel pipe to prevent spilling fuel.

NOTE: When unplugging wires and hoses, mark each hose and its connection with a piece of masking tape, then match code the two pieces of tape with the numbers 1, 2, 3, etc. When assembling, simply match up the pieces of tape.

6. Remove all remaining wires, tubes, the air cleaner bracket (carbureted engines) and the EGR and PCV tubes from the rear of the intake manifold. On carbureted engines, remove the air induction pipe. On fuel injected engines, remove the manifold supports.

7. Unbolt and remove the intake manifold. On fuel injected engines, remove the manifold with the fuel injectors/injection body, EGR valve, fuel pipes, etc. still attached.

8. Installation is in the reverse order of removal. Always use a new gasket. Tighten the mounting bolts from the outside, in; in two or three stages.

200SX (V6), 300ZX and Maxima (1985-88)

1. Disconnect the negative battery cable and drain the cooling system.

2. Disconnect the valve cover-to-throttle chamber hose at the valve cover.

3. Disconnect the heater housing to water inlet tube at the water inlet.

4. Remove the bolt holding the water and fuel tubes to the head.

5. Relieve the fuel pressure from the fuel system, and remove the heater housing to thermostat housing tube.

6. Remove the intake collector cover and then remove the collector itself.

7. Disconnect the fuel line and remove the intake manifold mount bolts. Remove the intake manifold assembly (with the fuel tube, assembly still attached) from the vehicle.

8. Installation is the reverse order of the removal procedure. Also be sure to use new gaskets when re-installing the manifold and torque the manifold bolts to 11–18 ft. lbs. in two stages, in the sequence shown.

Exhaust Manifold

REMOVAL & INSTALLATION

NOTE: You may find that removing the intake manifold first on many models will provide bet-

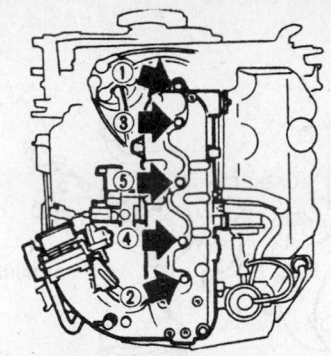

Intake manifold collector cover bolt removal sequence—V6

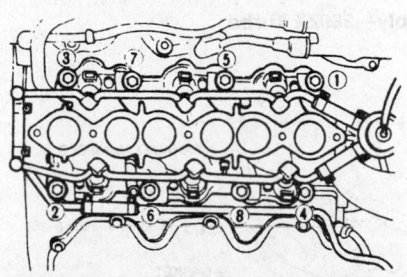

Intake manifold bolt removal sequence—V6

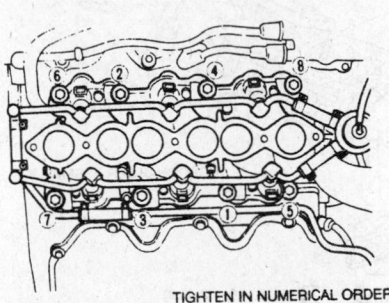

TIGHTEN IN NUMERICAL ORDER.

Intake manifold torque sequence—V6

ter access to the exhaust manifold.

1. Remove the air cleaner assembly, if necessary for access. Remove the heat shield, if present.

2. Disconnect the exhaust pipe from the exhaust manifold. Disconnect the intake manifold from the exhaust manifold (A-series engines only) unless removing both.

3. Remove all temperature sensors, air induction pipes and other attachments from the manifold. Disconnect the EAI and EGR tubes from their fittings on the E-series manifold.

4. Loosen and remove the exhaust manifold attaching nuts and remove the manifold from the engine.

5. Installation of the exhaust manifold is in the reverse order of removal. Tighten all bolts from the center outward.

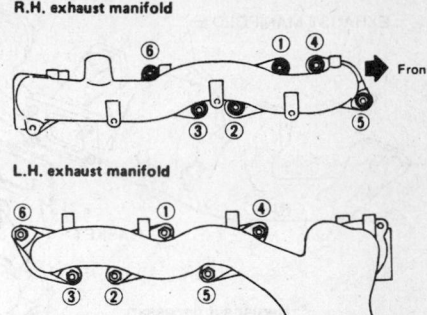

Exhaust manifold torque sequence—VG30E (Maxima and 200SX)

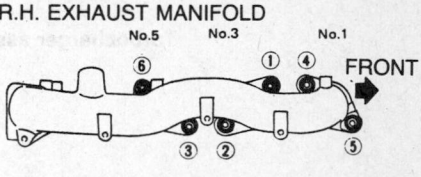

Exhaust manifold torque sequence—VG30E and VG30ET (300ZX)

Combination Manifold

REMOVAL & INSTALLATION

280ZX

NOTE: It is important to replace the gasket whenever either manifold is removed. Because the manifolds share a common gasket, it is necessary to remove both manifolds for access to the gasket. Be sure to get the correct replacement gasket for the car.

1. Disconnect the air and vacuum hoses from the air cleaner.

2. Remove the air cleaner.

3. On fuel injected models: relieve fuel line pressure as outlined in the fuel filter replacement procedure. Disconnect the fuel injection wiring harness. Disconnect the hose from the rocker cover to the throttle chamber at the rocker cover. Drain the coolant into a clean container. Disconnect the coolant hose which runs from the heater to the coolant inlet at the inlet. Remove the bolt securing the coolant pipe/fuel pipe to the cylinder head. Remove the tube connecting the heater to the thermostat housing. Disconnect the fuel lines.

4. Disconnect the vacuum hose to

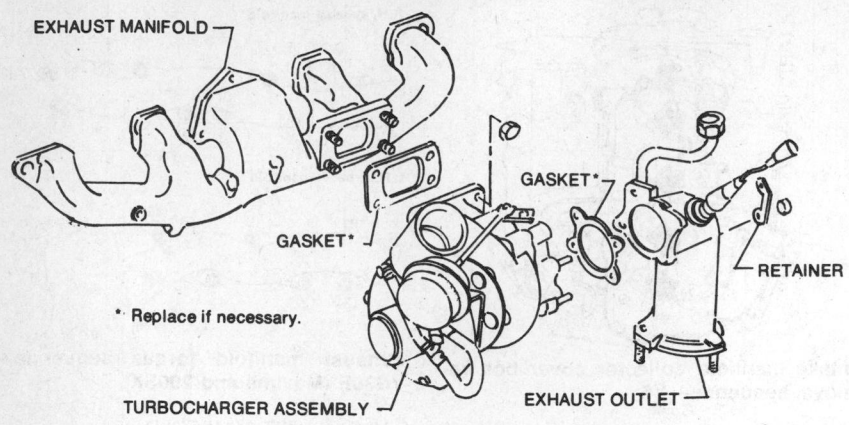

EXHAUST MANIFOLD

GASKET*

GASKET*

RETAINER

* Replace if necessary.

TURBOCHARGER ASSEMBLY

EXHAUST OUTLET

Turbocharger assembly—280ZX Turbo

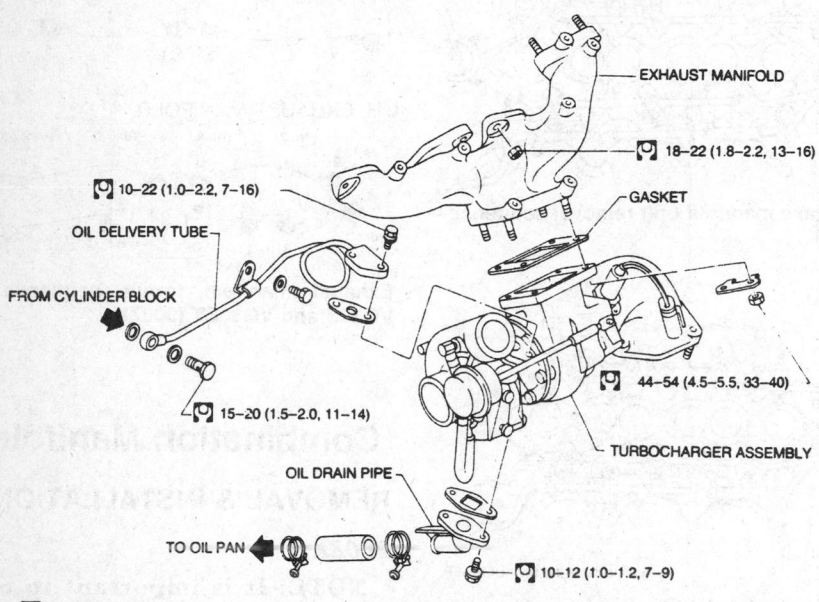

EXHAUST MANIFOLD

18—22 (1.8—2.2, 13—16)

10—22 (1.0—2.2, 7—16)

GASKET

OIL DELIVERY TUBE

FROM CYLINDER BLOCK

44—54 (4.5—5.5, 33—40)

15—20 (1.5—2.0, 11—14)

TURBOCHARGER ASSEMBLY

OIL DRAIN PIPE

TO OIL PAN

10—12 (1.0—1.2, 7—9)

: N·M (KG-M, FT. LB.)

V6 turbocharger assembly

the EGR valve, and the EGR tube from the exhaust manifold.

5. On models with an air pump, disconnect the air injection hose from the air injection gallery on the exhaust manifold at the check valve.

6. Disconnect the exhaust pipe from the exhaust manifold or from the exhaust outlet of the turbocharger if so equipped. Remove the exhaust manifold heat shield.

7. Remove the intake and exhaust manifold.

8. Install the manifolds in the reverse order of removal. *Always use a new gasket*: air leaks will cause burnt valves and misfiring. Tighten the manifold bolts from the center outwards, in two progressive steps, to the proper torque.

Turbocharger

The turbocharger is installed on the exhaust manifold. This system utilizes exhaust gas energy to rotate the turbine wheel which drives the compressor turbine installed on the other end of the turbine wheel shaft. The compressor supplies compressed air to the engine to increase the charging efficiency so improving engine output and torque.

REMOVAL & INSTALLATION

Pulsar NX Turbo

1. Remove the heat insulator, inlet tube, air duct hose, suction air pipe

and turbocharger temperature sensor.

2. Disconnect the exhaust gas sensor harness connector, from tube, oil delivery tube, and oil drain pipe.

3. Remove the catalyzer supporting bracket and disconnect the front exhaust tube.

4. Remove the exhaust outlet and catalyzer as an assembly.

5. Remove the turbocharger and exhaust manifold as an assembly and then remove the turbocharger from the exhaust manifold.

6. Installation is the reverse order of the removal procedure.

200SX Turbo

1. Drain the engine coolant.

2. Remove the air duct and hoses, and the air intake pipe.

3. Disconnect the front exhaust pipe at the exhaust manifold (exhaust outlet in the illustration).

4. Remove the heat shield plates.

5. Tag and disconnect the oil delivery tube and return hose.

6. Disconnect the water inlet tube.

7. Unbolt and remove the turbocharger from the exhaust manifold.

NOTE: The turbocharger unit should only be serviced internally by an engine specialist trained in turbocharger repair.

8. Reverse the above procedure to install. Torque the turbocharger outlet-to-housing bolts to 16–22 ft. lbs.

280ZX Turbo

1. Remove the heat insulator, inlet tube, air duct hose and suction air pipe.

2. Disconnect the exhaust gas sensor harness connector, front tube, oil delivery tube and oil drain pipe.

3. Loosen the nuts which attach the turbocharger unit to the exhaust manifold, then remove the turbocharger.

NOTE: The turbocharger should not be disassembled. The turbocharger is replaced as a unit if found to be defective.

300ZX Turbo

1. Remove the following:
   a. Compressor and compressor bracket.
   b. Exhaust front tube.
   c. Center cable.
   d. Heat insulator for the brake master cylinder.
   e. Air duct and hoses.
   f. Exhaust manifold connecting tube and heat shield plate.
   g. Oil delivery tube and return hose.

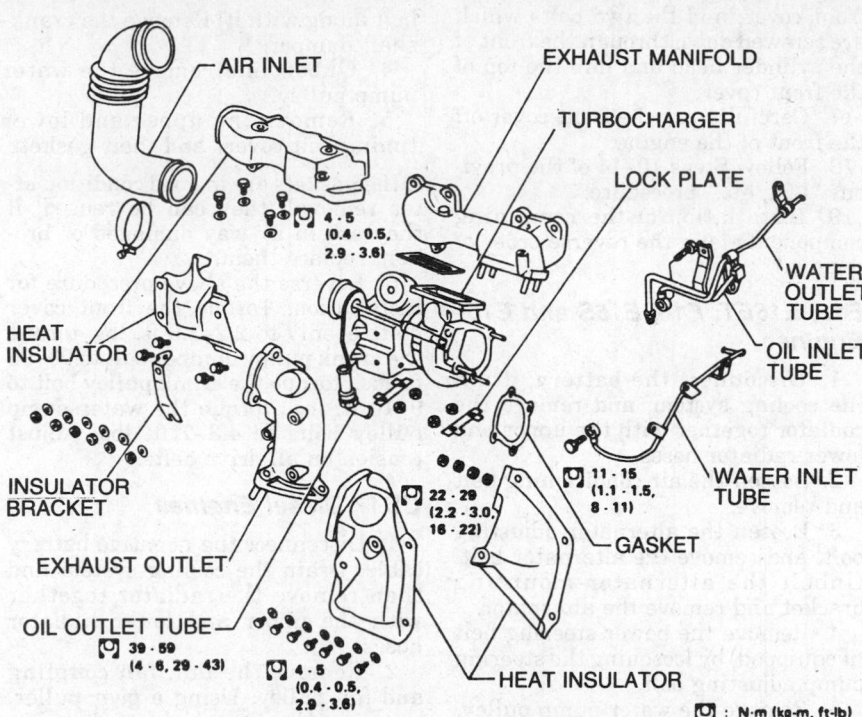

Turbocharger assembly—200SX

AIR INLET

EXHAUST MANIFOLD

TURBOCHARGER

LOCK PLATE

WATER OUTLET TUBE

OIL INLET TUBE

WATER INLET TUBE

GASKET

HEAT INSULATOR

HEAT INSULATOR

INSULATOR BRACKET

EXHAUST OUTLET

OIL OUTLET TUBE

4 - 5 (0.4 - 0.5, 2.9 - 3.6)

11 - 15 (1.1 - 1.5, 8 - 11)

22 - 29 (2.2 - 3.0, 16 - 22)

39 - 59 (4 - 6, 29 - 43)

4 - 5 (0.4 - 0.5, 2.9 - 3.6)

[ ] : N·m (kg-m, ft-lb)

2. Remove the exhaust manifold and the turbocharger as an assembly.

NOTE: The turbocharger unit should not be disassembled.

3. Installation is the reverse of removal.

TROUBLESHOOTING

For more information on turbochargers, please refer to "Turbocharging" in the Unit Repair section.

Front Cover

REMOVAL, INSTALLATION & OIL SEAL REPLACEMENT

A12A, A14 and A15 Engines

1. Remove the radiator, Loosen the alternator and remove the belt. Loosen the air pump and remove the belt on engines with the air pump system.

2. Remove the fan. Unbolt and remove water pump.

3. Bend back the lock tab from the crankshaft pulley nut. Remove the nut with a heavy wrench. If the nut will not come loose without turning the pulley with it, you may have to fabricate a wooden wedge to place between the pulley and cover in order to hold the pulley. The nut must be un-

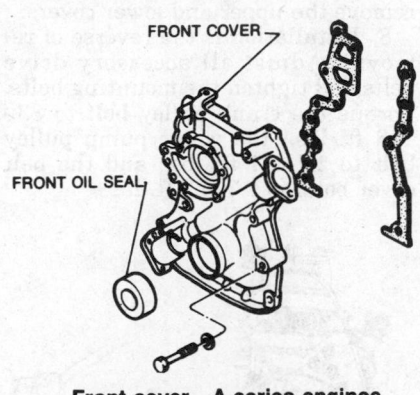

FRONT COVER

FRONT OIL SEAL

Front cover—A-series engines

screwed opposite normal engine rotation. Pull off the pulley.

4. It is recommended that the oil pan be removed or loosened before the front cover is removed.

5. Unbolt and remove the timing chain cover.

6. Replace the crankshaft oil seal in the cover. Most models use a felt seal.

7. Reverse the procedure to install, using new gaskets. Apply sealant to both sides of the timing cover gasket. Front cover bolt torque is 4 ft. lbs., water pump bolt torque is 7–10 ft. lbs., and oil pan bolt torque is 4 ft. lbs.

L24E, L28E, L28ET, Z20S, Z20E, Z22, Z22E and Z24i Engines

NOTE: It may be necessary to remove the cylinder head to per-

form this operation if you cannot cut the front of the head gasket cleanly as described in Step 10. If so, you will need a new head gasket.

1. Disconnect the negative battery cable from the battery, drain the cooling system, and remove the radiator together with the upper and lower radiator hoses.

2. Loosen the alternator drive belt adjusting screw and remove the drive belt. Remove the bolts which attach the alternator bracket to the engine and set the alternator aside out of the way.

3. Remove the distributor.

4. Remove the oil pump attaching screws, and take out the pump and its drive spindle.

5. Remove the cooling fan and the fan pulley together with the drive belt.

6. Remove the water pump.

7. Remove the crankshaft pulley bolt and remove the crankshaft pulley.

8. Remove the bolts holding the front cover to the front of the cylinder block, the four bolts which retain the front of the oil pan to the bottom of the front cover, and the two bolts which are screwed down through the front of the cylinder head and into the top of the front cover.

NOTE: The oil pan must be removed on the Van.

9. Carefully pry the front cover off the engine.

10. Cut the exposed front section of the oil pan gasket away from the oil pan. Do the same to the gasket at the top of the front cover. Remove the two side gaskets and clean all of the mating surfaces.

11. Cut the portions needed from a new oil pan gasket and top front cover gasket.

12. Apply sealer to all of the gaskets and position them on the engine in their proper places.

13. Apply a light coating of grease to the crankshaft oil seal and carefully mount the front cover to the front of the engine and install all of the mounting bolts. Tighten the 8mm bolts to 7–12 ft. lbs. and the 6mm bolts to 3–6 ft. lbs. Tighten the oil pan attaching bolts to 4–7 ft. lbs.

14. Before installing the oil pump, place the gasket over the shaft and make sure that the mark on the drive spindle faces (is aligned with) the oil pump hole. Install the oil pump so that the projection on the top of the shaft is located in the exact position as when it was removed or in the 11:25 o'clock position with the piston

in the No. 1 cylinder placed at TDC on the compression stroke, if the engine was disturbed since disassembly. Tighten the oil pump attaching screws to 8–10 ft. lbs. See "Oil Pump Removal and Installation".

LD28 Diesel Engine

NOTE: It may be necessary to remove the cylinder head to perform this procedure if you cannot cut the front of the head gasket cleanly as described in Step 16. If so, you will need a new head gasket.

— CAUTION —

This procedure requires the removal and subsequent installation of the diesel injection pump. It is a good idea to read through the "Diesel Fuel Injection" section before you continue with this procedure.

1. Disconnect the negative battery cable. Drain the cooling system and then remove the radiator together with the upper and lower radiator hoses.
2. Remove the fan, fan coupling and fan pulley.
3. Unscrew the retaining bolts on the crankshaft damper pulley. Use a plastic mallet and lightly tap around the outer edges of the pulley, this should loosen it enough so that you can pull it off. If not, use a two-armed gear puller.
4. Remove the power steering pump, bracket and idler pulley (if so equipped).
5. Unscrew the five mounting bolts and remove the front dust cover.
6. Remove the thermostat housing and the bottom bypass inlet with the hose.
7. Remove the engine slinger.
8. Tag and disconnect all hoses and lines running from the injection pump. Make sure to plug any hoses or lines to prevent dust or dirt from entering.
9. Drain the engine oil.
10. Remove the oil cooler and coolant hose together with the oil filter.
11. Remove the water inlet, the oil dipstick and the right side engine mounting bracket.
12. Remove the oil pump.
13. Remove the injection pump (refer to "Diesel Fuel Injection", found later in this section).
14. Remove the water pump.
15. Loosen the mounting bolt and remove the injection pump drive crank pulley. You will need a two armed gear puller.
16. Remove the bolts holding the front cover to the front of the cylinder block, the four bolts which retain the front of the oil pan to the bottom of the

front cover, and the two bolts which are screwed down through the front of the cylinder head and into the top of the front cover.
17. Carefully pry the front cover off the front of the engine.
18. Follow Steps 10–14 of the previous "L24, etc." procedure.
19. Installation of the remaining components is in the reverse order of removal.

E15, E15ET, E16, E16S and E16i Engines

1. Disconnect the battery, drain the cooling system, and remove the radiator together with the upper and lower radiator hoses.
2. Loosen the air conditioning belt and remove.
3. Loosen the alternator adjusting bolt, and remove the alternator belt. Unbolt the alternator mounting bracket and remove the alternator.
4. Remove the power steering belt (if equipped) by loosening the steering pump adjusting bolt.
5. Remove the water pump pulley.
6. Remove crankshaft pulley.
7. Loosen and remove the eight bolts securing the timing covers and remove the upper and lower covers.
8. Installation is the reverse of removal. Adjust all accessory drive belts and tighten the mounting bolts. Torque the crank pulley bolt to 83–108 ft. lbs.; the water pump pulley bolt to 2.7–3.7 ft. lbs.; and the belt cover bolts to 2.7–3.7 ft. lbs.

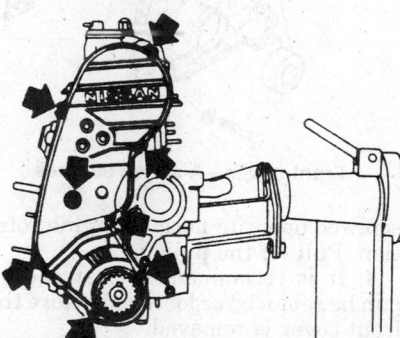

Front cover removal—E-series engines

CA18ET, CA20, CA20E and CA20S Engines

1. Losen the upper and lower alternator securing bolts until the alternator can be moved enough to remove the drive belt from the pulley.
2. Loosen the idler pulley locknut and turn the adjusting bolt until the air conditioner compressor belt can be removed.
3. Unbolt and remove the crankshaft pulley, removing the alternator

belt along with it. Remove the crankshaft damper.
4. Unbolt and remove the water pump pulley.
5. Remove the upper and lower timing belt covers and their gaskets.

If the gaskets are in good condition after removal, they can be reused; if they are in ay way damaged or broken, replace them.

6. Reverse the above procedure for installation. Torque the front cover bolts evenly to 2.2–3.6 ft. lbs; torque the crank pulley damper bolt to 90–98 ft. lbs.; torque the crank pulley bolt to 9–10 ft. lbs.; torque the water pump pulley bolts to 4.3–7 ft. lbs. Adjust tension on all drive belts.

CD17 Diesel Engines

1. Disconnect the negative battery cable. Drain the cooling system and then remove the radiator together with the upper and lower radiator hoses.
2. Remove the fan, fan coupling and fan pulley. Using a gear puller, remove the crankshaft damper pulley.
3. Remove the power steering pump, bracket and idler pulley.
4. Remove the front belt cover. Remove the valve timing belt (see "Timing Belt and Camshaft" removal in this section).
5. Remove the front oil seal by tapping the end of a thin prybar and *care-*

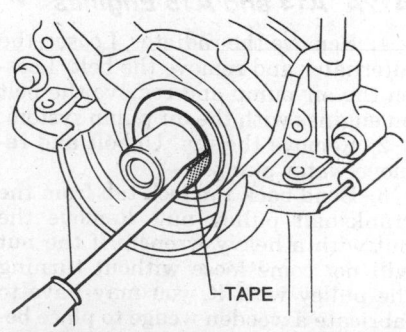

Correct installation of the crankshaft pulley plate—CD17 diesel engines

Carefully pry out the front oil seal—CD17 diesel engines

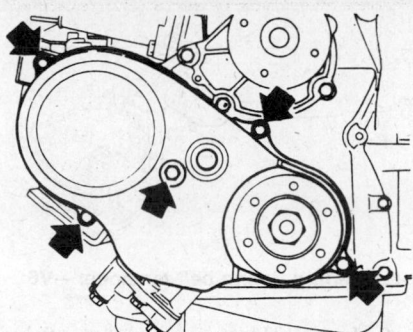

Remove the dust cover on the diesel

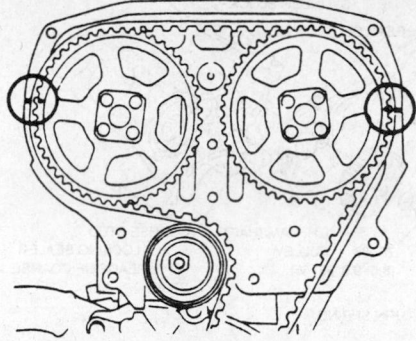

Align the camshaft pulley timing marks—CA16DE

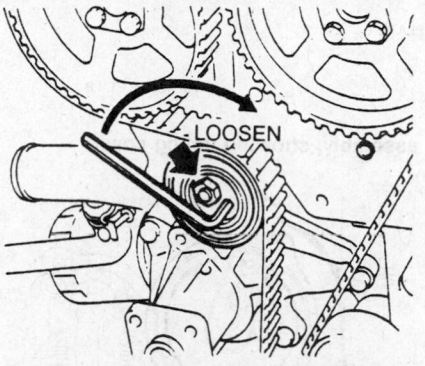

Loosen the tensioner pulley nut before removing the timing belt—CA16DE

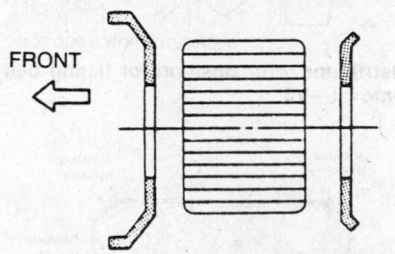

Crankshaft sprocket plate installation—CA16DE

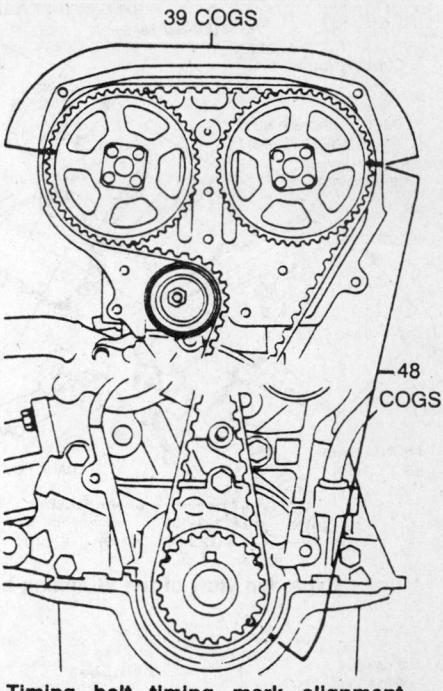

Timing belt timing mark alignment—CA16DE

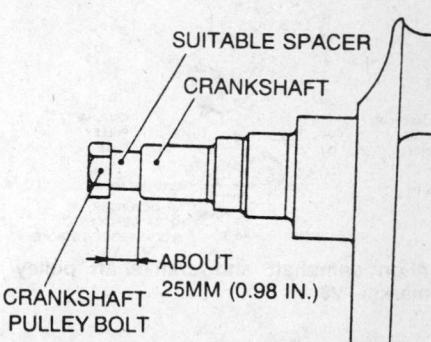

A spacer must be installed between the crankshaft and crankshaft pulley bolt head before rotating the engine—CA16DE

fully prying the old seal out from around the end of the crankshaft. Do not scratch the shaft with the prybar.

6. Coat a new seal with clean engine oil. Slide it onto the crankshaft end and back into place in the front of the block. Use a small drift to evenly drive the seal back until it seats in position.

7. Installation is the reverse of removal. Follow the "Timing Belt and Camshaft" removal and installation procedure when installing the timing belt.

Front Cover/Timing Belt

REMOVAL & INSTALLATION

CA16DE Engines

1. Disconnect the negative battery cable. Drain the cooling system.
2. Disconnect the upper radiator hose at the elbow and then position it out of the way.
3. Remove the right side engine undercover.
4. Loosen the power steering pump and the A/C compressor and then remove the drive belts.
5. Remove the water pump pulley.
6. Matchmark the crank angle sensor to the upper front cover and the remove it. Carefully position it out of the way.
7. Position a floor jack under the engine and raise it just enough to support the engine.
8. Remove the upper engine mount bracket at the right side of the upper front cover.
9. Remove the upper front cover.
10. Align the timing marks on the camshaft pulley sprockets and then remove the crankshaft pulley.

NOTE: The crankshaft pulley may be reached by removing the side cover from inside the righthand wheel opening.

11. Remove the lower front cover.

12. Loosen the tensioner pulley nut to slacken the timing belt and then slide off the belt.

To install:

— CAUTION —

Do not bend or twist the timing belt. NEVER rotate the crankshaft and camshaft separately with the timing belt removed.

Be sure the timing belt is free of any oil, water or debris.

1. Install the crankshaft sprocket with the sprocket plates.
2. Before installing the timing belt, ensure that the No. 1 piston is at TDC of the compression stroke (all sprock-

et timing marks will be in alignment with the marks on the case).

When the timing belt is on and in position, there should be 39 cogs between the timing mark on each of the camshaft sprocket and 48 cogs between the mark on the right camshaft sprocket and the mark on the crankshaft sprocket.

3. Loosen the timing belt tensioner pulley nut.
4. Temporarily install the crankshaft pulley bolt and then rotate the engine two complete revolutions.

— CAUTION —

Fabricate and install a suitable 25mm (0.98 in.) thick spacer between the end of the crankshaft and the head of the crankshaft pulley bolt to prevent bolt damage.

5. Tighten the tensioner pulley bolt to 16–22 ft. lbs. (22–29 Nm).

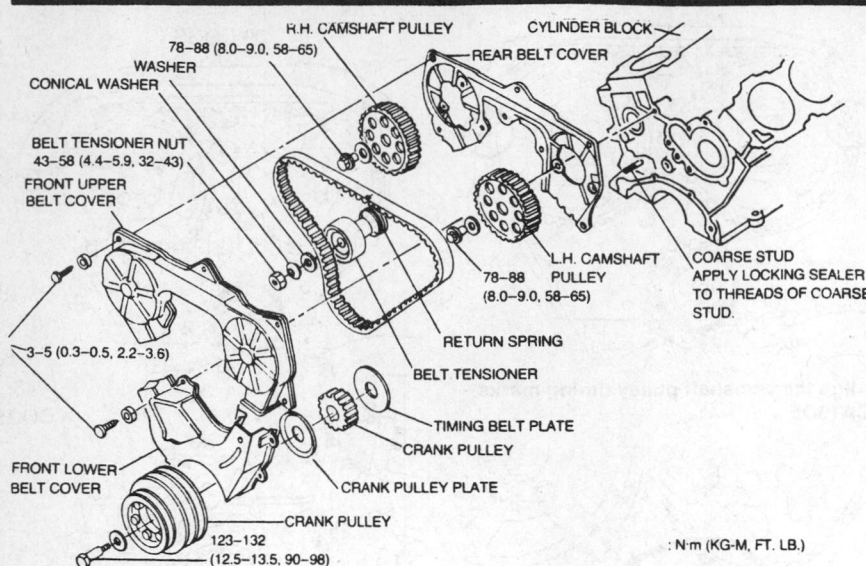

Exploded view of the V6 timing belt assembly, showing timing cover

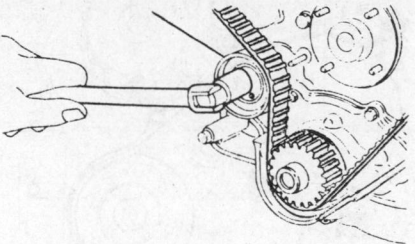

Loosening timing belt tensioner—V6

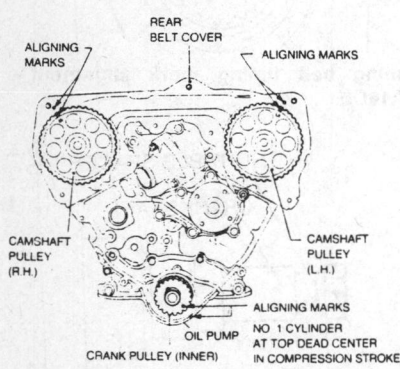

Align camshaft and crankshaft pulley marks—V6

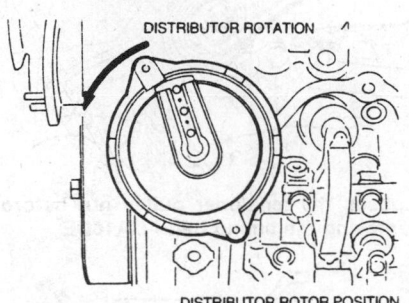

Distributor rotor position for timing belt removal—V6

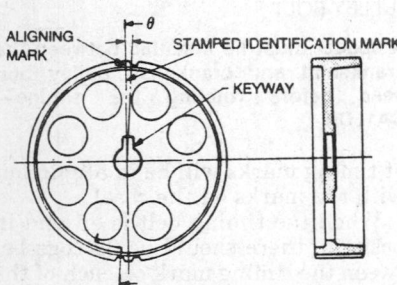

Camshaft pulley alignment marks—V6

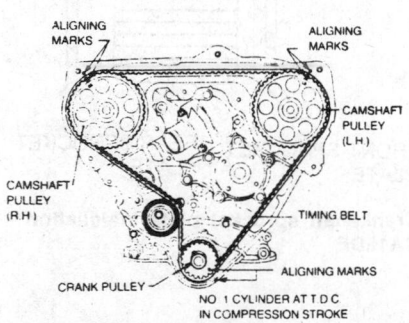

Aligning timing belt white lines with marks on camshaft and crankshaft pulleys—V6

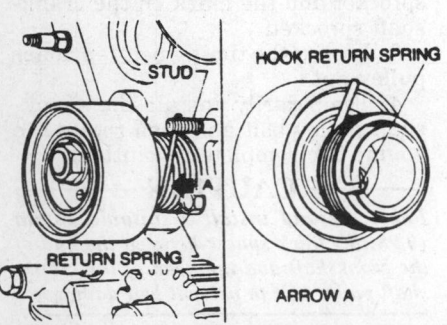

Installation of the tensioner and return spring—VG30E and VG30ET

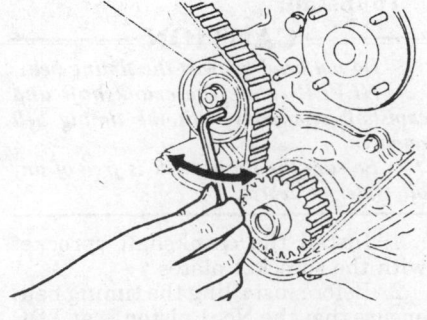

Tightening tensioner locknut—V6

6. Install the upper and lower front covers.

7. Install the crankshaft pulley with its washer and tighten it to 105–112 ft. lbs. (145–152 Nm).

8. Install the engine mount bracket.

9. Install the water pump pulley. Install the crank angle sensor so that the matchmarks made previously line up and tighten the bolts to 5.1–5.8 ft. lbs. (7–8 Nm).

10. Installation of the remaining components is in the reverse order of removal. Check the tension on all drive belts and fill the engine with coolant.

VG30E and VG30ET Engines

1. Remove the radiator shroud, fan and pulleys.

2. Drain the coolant from the radiator and remove the water pump hose.

3. Remove the power steering, compressor and alternator drive belts.

4. Set the No. 1 cylinder at TDC on its compression stroke.

5. Remove the idler bracket of the compressor drive belt and crankshaft pulley.

6. Remove the front upper and lower belt covers.

7. Using chalk or paint, mark the relationship of the timing belt to the camshaft and the camshaft sprockets; also mark the timing belt's direction of rotation.

8. Loosen the timing belt tensioner and return spring then remove the timing belt.

NOTE: After Step 7, the camshaft oil seal can be replaced by removing the camshaft sprockets and lifting the oil seal off the shaft. Apply clean engine oil to the new oil seal and install it on the camshaft along with the camshaft sprockets.

9. Before installing the timing belt confirm that the No. 1 cylinder is set at TDC on its compression stroke.

10. Remove both rocker covers and loosen all rocker shaft retaining bolts.

NOTE: The rocker arm shaft bolts MUST be loosened so that

the correct belt tension can be obtained.

11. Install tensioner and return spring. Using an Allen wrench, turn the tensioner clockwise and temporarily tighten the locknut.

12. Make sure that the timing belt is clean and free from oil or water.

13. When installing the timing belt align the white lines on the belt with the punch mark on the camshaft pulleys and crankshaft pulley. Have the arrow on the timing belt pointing toward the front belt covers.

14. Using a hexagon wrench, loosen the tensioner lock bolt, then slowly turn the tensioner clockwise and counterclockwise 2–3 times.

NOTE: If the coarse tensioner stud has been removed, be sure to apply locking sealer to the threads before installing it.

15. Torque the tensioner lock nut to 32–43 ft. lbs., the rocker arm shaft retaining bolts (in 2–3 stages) to 13–16 ft. lbs.

NOTE: Before tightening, be sure to set the camshaft lobe at the position where the lobe is not lifted.

16. Install the lower and upper belt covers.

17. The remainder of the installation is the reverse of removal.

Timing Chain and Camshaft

REMOVAL & INSTALLATION

A12A, A14 and A15 Engines

This operation can only be performed with the engine out of the car.

1. Remove the engine.
2. Remove the rocker cover and rocker shaft assembly.
3. Remove the pushrods.
4. Invert the engine.
5. Remove the timing chain cover.
6. Remove the chain tensioner.
7. Remove the camshaft sprocket retaining bolt.
8. Remove the camshaft sprocket, crankshaft sprocket, and timing chain as an assembly. Be careful not to lose the shims (if present) and oil slinger from behind the crankshaft sprocket.
9. Remove the distributor, and distributor drive spindle. Remove the oil pump and pump driveshaft.
10. Unbolt and remove the camshaft locating plate. Remove the camshaft carefully. The engine must be inverted to prevent the lifters from falling

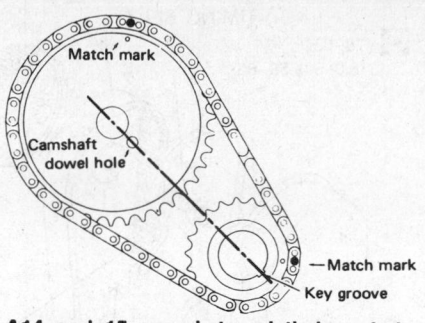

A14 and 15 sprocket and timing chain assembly

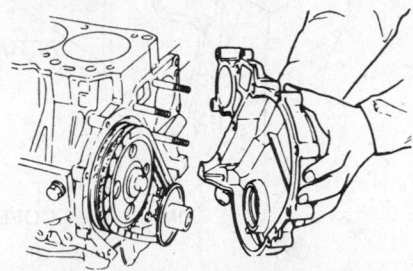

Installing the A-series timing chain cover. Note slinger on end of crankshaft

down into the engine. If the lifters must be removed, remove the oil pan and remove them after withdrawing the camshaft. Keep the lifters in order and return them to their original positions.

11. The camshaft bearings can be pressed out and replaced. They are available in undersizes, should it be necessary to regrind the camshaft journals. The bearings must be line-bored after installation.

12. Coat the bearings and camshaft with engine oil. Reinstall the camshaft. If the locating plate has an oil hole, it should be to the right of the engine. The locating plate is marked with the word LOWER and an arrow. The engine locating plate bolt torque is 3–4 ft. lbs. Be careful to engage the drive pin in the rear end of the camshaft with the slot in the oil pump driveshaft.

13. Camshaft end-play can be measured after temporarily replacing the camshaft sprocket and securing bolt. If end-play is excessive, replace the locating plate. They are available in several sizes.

14. If the crankshaft or camshaft has been replaced, install the sprockets temporarily and make sure that they are parallel. Adjust by shimming under the crankshaft sprocket.

15. Assemble the sprockets and chain, aligning them.

16. Turn the crankshaft until the keyway and No. 1 piston are at top dead center. Install the sprockets and chain. The oil slinger behind the crankshaft sprocket must be replaced

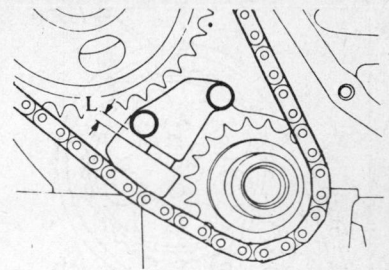

Checking projection of tensioner spindle—A-series engines

with the concave surface to the front. If the chain and sprocket installation is correct, the sprocket marks must be aligned between the shaft centers when the No. 1 piston is at TDC. Check the projection ("L") of the timing chain tensioner spindle. If the projection exceeds 0.59 in., replace the timing chain. Engine camshaft sprocket retaining bolt torque is 33–36 ft. lbs.

17. The rest of the reassembly procedure is the reverse of disassembly. Engine chain tensioner bolt torque is 4–6 ft. lbs.

Timing Belt

REMOVAL & INSTALLATION

E15, E15ET, E16, E16i and E16S

1. Removal of the cylinder head from the engine is necessary. Crank the engine until the No. 1 piston is at TDC on its compression stroke.

2. Follow the "Front Cover" removal procedure and remove the cover. Mark the relationship of the camshaft sprocket to the timing belt and the crankshaft sprocket to the timing belt with paint or a grease pencil. This will make setting everything up during reassembly much easier if the engine is disturbed during disassembly.

3. Remove the distributor.
4. Remove the thermostat housing.
5. Remove the water pump and crankshaft pulleys.
6. Position a floor jack under the engine and raise it just enough to support the engine. Remove the right side engine mounting bracket.
7. Remove the upper and lower front covers.
8. Loosen the timing belt tensioner locknut and rotate the tensioner clockwise. Retighten the locknut.
9. Mark a rotational, direction arrow on the timing belt and then remove the belt.

——— **CAUTION** ———
After removing the timing belt, NEVER rotate the crankshaft or camshaft separately or the valves will hit the pistons.

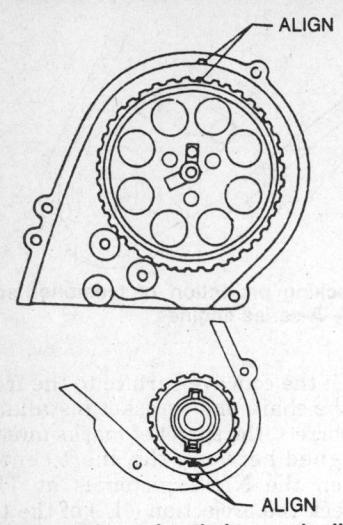

E-series engine valve timing mark alignment

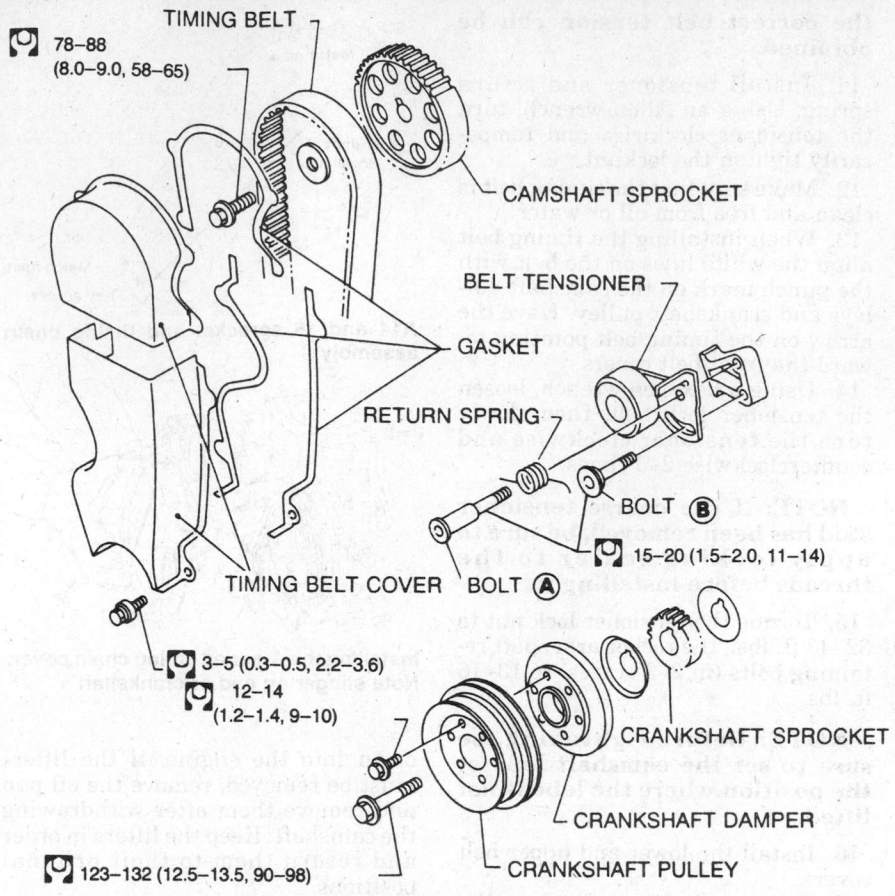

78–88
(8.0–9.0, 58–65)

TIMING BELT

CAMSHAFT SPROCKET

BELT TENSIONER

GASKET

RETURN SPRING

BOLT **B**

15–20 (1.5–2.0, 11–14)

TIMING BELT COVER   BOLT **A**

3–5 (0.3–0.5, 2.2–3.6)

12–14
(1.2–1.4, 9–10)

CRANKSHAFT SPROCKET

CRANKSHAFT DAMPER

123–132 (12.5–13.5, 90–98)

CRANKSHAFT PULLEY

Timing belt assembly—C-Series engines

10. Remove the belt tensioner and its return spring.

To install:

1. Check that the timing marks on the camshaft sprocket and upper front cover and on the crankshaft sprocket and lower front cover are in alignment. This will ensure that the No.1 piston is at TDC of its compression stroke.

2. Install the timing belt tensioner and return spring temporarily.

3. Rotate the tensioner about 70–80° clockwise and then tighten the locknut.

4. Install the timing belt.

5. Loosen the tensioner locknut so that the tensioner pushes on the timing belt and then turn the camshaft sprocket about 20° clockwise (2 cogs).

—————— CAUTION ——————

All spark plugs MUST be removed before turning the camshaft sprocket.

6. Prevent the tensioner from spinning and tighten the locknut to 12–15 ft. lbs. (16–21 Nm).

7. Installation of the remaining components is in the reverse order of removal. Adjust all drive belts and fill the engine with coolant.

CA18ET, CA20, CA20E and CA20S Engines

1. Disconnect the negative battery cable. Drain the coolant from the engine.

2. Remove the air intake ducts on the CA20E.

3. Remove the cooling fan.

4. Remove the power steering, alternator and A/C drive belts.

5. Set the No. 1 piston at TDC of the compression stroke. The timing marks will all be aligned.

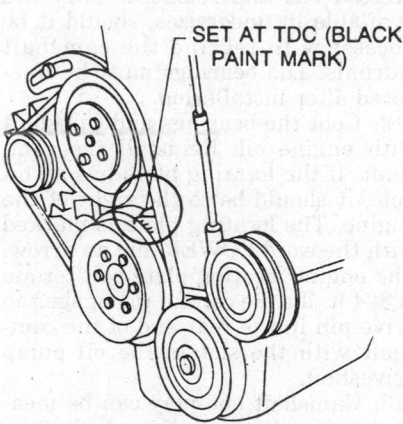

SET AT TDC (BLACK PAINT MARK)

Timing marks for finding TDC—C-Series engines

6. Remove the upper and lower front covers.

7. Loosen the timing belt tensioner and return spring. Remove the timing belt.

8. Carefully inspect the condition of the timing belt. There should be no breaks or cracks anywhere on the belt. Be particularly careful when checking around the bottom of the cog teeth, where they the main belt; cracks often show up here first. Evi-

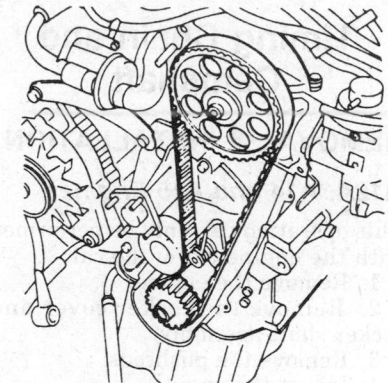

Timing belt with covers removed—C-Series engines

dence of any wear or damage on the belt call for replacement.

To install:

1. Check to make certain that the No. 1 piston is still at TDC on the compression stroke.

2. Install the timing belt tensioner and return spring.

NOTE: If the coarse stud has been removed, apply Loctite® or another locking thread sealer to the stud threads prior to installation.

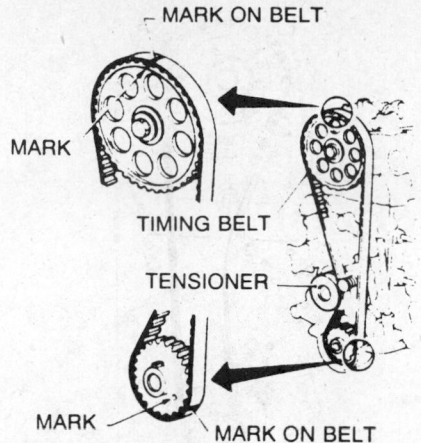

Timing belt installation—C-Series engines

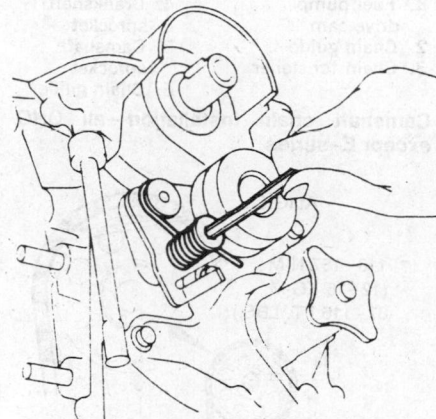

Installing the belt tensioner and return spring—C-Series engines

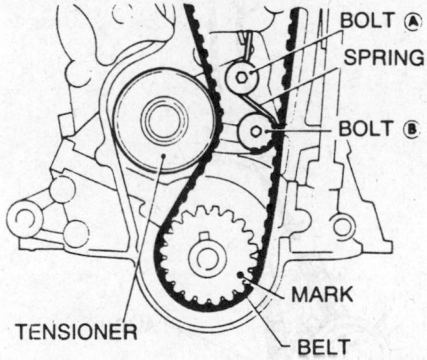

Setting the tensioner spring—C-Series engines

3. Make sure the tensioner mounting bolts are not securely tightened before installing the timing belt. The tensioner pulley should rotate smoothly.

4. Place the timing belt into position, aligning the lines on the belt with the punchmarks on the camshaft and crankshaft pulleys. The arrow on

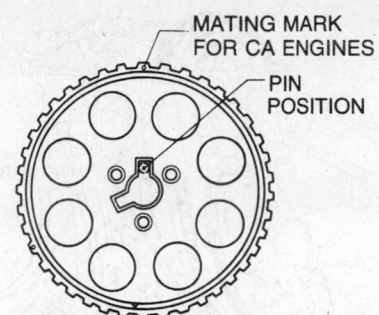

Camshaft sprocket installation—CA20

the belt should be pointing toward the front belt covers.

5. Tighten the belt tensioner and assemble the spring. Hook one end of the spring around bolt B and then hook the othe end over the tensioner bracket pawl. Rotate the crankshaft two complete revolutions clockwise, tighten bolt B and then bolt A.

6. Installation of the remaining components is in the reverse order of removal. Adjust the tension an all drive belts and fill the engine with coolant.

Timing Belt And Camshaft

REMOVAL & INSTALLATION

CD17 Diesel Engines

NOTE: The camshaft is removed with the cylinder head removed from the engine. Follow the procedure below for timing belt removal, then follow the "Cylinder Head Removal" procedure earlier in this section; the camshaft removal procedure follows timing belt removal. The injection pump has its own belt drive and is covered later in this section.

1. Support the engine with a jack and remove the right side engine mount, then jack the engine up to allow working clearance.

2. Set the No. 1 cylinder at TDC on its compression stroke.

3. Remove the alternator and A/C compressor (if equipped) drive belts.

4. Using a puller, remove the crankshaft damper pulley.

5. Loosen the tensioner pulley and set it to the "free" position. Remove the idler pulley.

6. Remove the crankshaft pulley with the timing belt.

7. Check the belt for damage, missing teeth, wear or saturation with oil or grease. If damage is evident or if you are in doubt as to the belt's condition, replace the belt.

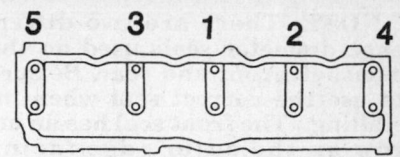

CD17 camshaft bearing cap torque sequence

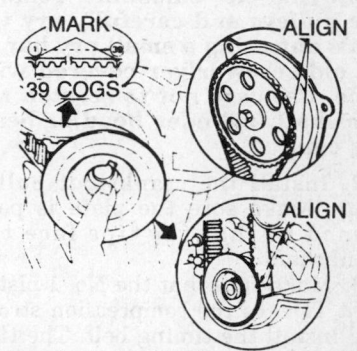

Timing belt installation—CD17 diesel engines

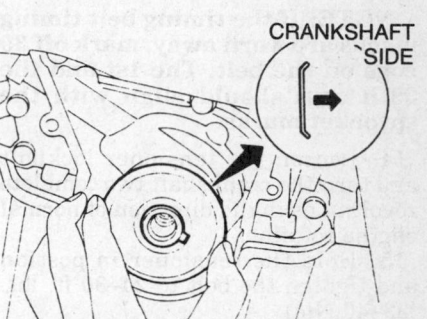

Crankshaft pulley plate installation—CD17 diesel engines

NOTE: Do not bend, twist or turn the timing belt inside out. Do not allow the belt to come into contact with any grease, oil or solvents.

8. Remove the cylinder head and manifolds.

9. Remove the camshaft bearing caps and check the clearance with Plastigage®. Do not turn the camshaft. If the bearing clearance exceed 0.1mm (0.004 in.) replace the bearing caps, camshaft or cylinder head.

10. After checking clearances, remove the bearing caps and remove the camshaft with both oil seals. Have the camshaft run-out and lobe height checked; if worn beyond specification, replace the camshaft.

11. To install the camshaft, assemble in the reverse order of removal. Before installing the oil seals, lubricate with clean engine oil. Reinstall the cylinder head and check valve clearances; adjust if necessary.

NOTE: There are two difference diameter seals used on the camshaft front and rear. Be sure to use the correct seal when installing. (The front seal has an arrow on the outer edge facing clockwise; the rear seal arrow points counterclockwise). If you are replacing the oil seals without removing the camshaft, remove the pulleys and carefully pry the seals out using a small pry bar or an old screwdriver covered with tape. Use care not to scratch the camshaft, cylinder head or bearing cap.

12. Install the crankshaft pulley plate. Make sure the plate is positioned so that the lips face the crankshaft.

13. Make sure that the No. 1 piston is at TDC os the compression stroke and install the timing belt. The timing marks on the belt should be in alignment with those on the camshaft and crankshaft sprockets.

NOTE: If the timing belt timing marks are worn away, mark off 39 cogs on the belt. The 1st and the 39th cogs should align with the sprocket marks.

14. Loosen the tensioner lockbolt and turn the crankshaft two complete revolutions in the direction of normal engine rotation.

15. Hold the tensioner in postion and tighten the bolt to 24–30 ft. lbs. (32–40 Nm).

16. Install the front cover.

17. Install the crankshaft damper pulley and tighten it to 90–98 ft. lbs. (123–132 Nm).

Timing Chain and Tensioner

REMOVAL & INSTALLATION

L24E, L28E, L28ET, Z20E, Z20S, Z22, Z22E and Z24i Engines

1. Before beginning any disassembly procedures, position the No. 1 piston at TDC on the compression stroke.

2. Remove the front cover as previously outlined. Remove the camshaft cover and remove the fuel pump if it runs off a cam lobe in front of the camshaft sprocket.

3. With the No. 1 piston at TDC, the timing marks on the camshaft sprocket and the timing chain should be visible. Mark both of them with paint. Also mark the relationship of the camshaft sprocket to the camshaft. There are three sets of timing marks and locating holes in the sprocket for making adjustments to

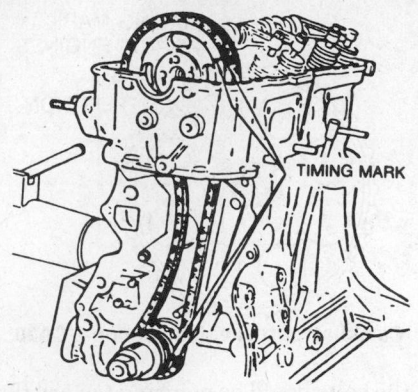

Timing chain and sprocket alignments—Z20 engines

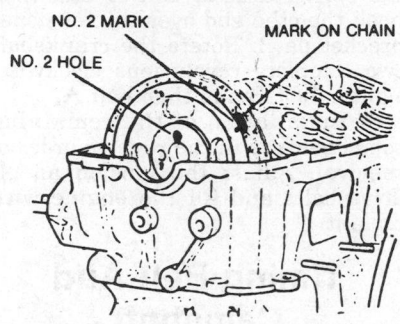

Use the No. 2 mark and hole to align the camshaft—Z20, Z22 series engines

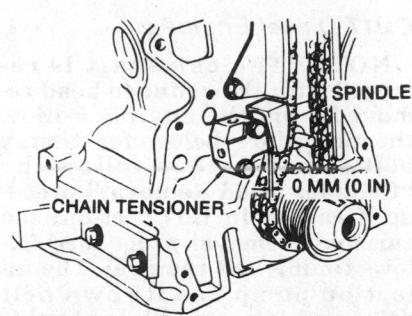

Chain tensioner mounting—Z-Series and L28 engines

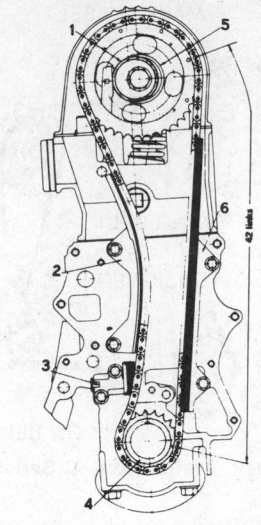

1. Fuel pump drive cam
2. Chain guide
3. Chain tensioner
4. Crankshaft sprocket
5. Camshaft sprocket
6. Chain guide

Camshaft chain installation—all OHC except E–series

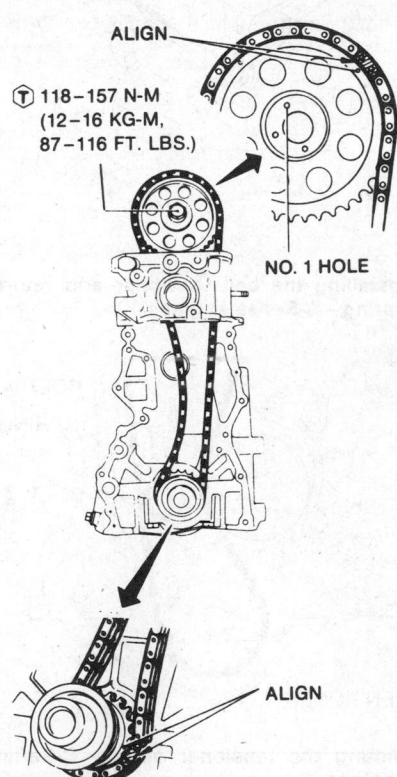

ⓣ 118–157 N-M (12–16 KG-M, 87–116 FT. LBS.)

Timing chain and sprocket alignment—L28 engines

compensate for timing chain stretch. See the following "Timing Chain Adjustment" for more details.

4. With the timing marks on the cam sprocket clearly marked, locate and mark the timing marks on the crankshaft sprocket. Also mark the chain timing mark. Of course, if the chain is not to be re-used, marking it is useless.

5. Unbolt the camshaft sprocket and remove the sprocket along with the chain. As the chain is removed, hold it where the chain tensioner contacts it. When the chain is removed, the tensioner will come apart; *hold on to it and you won't lose any of the parts.* There is no need to remove the

chain guide unless it is being replaced.

6. Using a two-armed gear puller, remove the crankshaft sprocket.

7. Install the timing chain and the camshaft sprocket together after first positioning the chain over the crank-

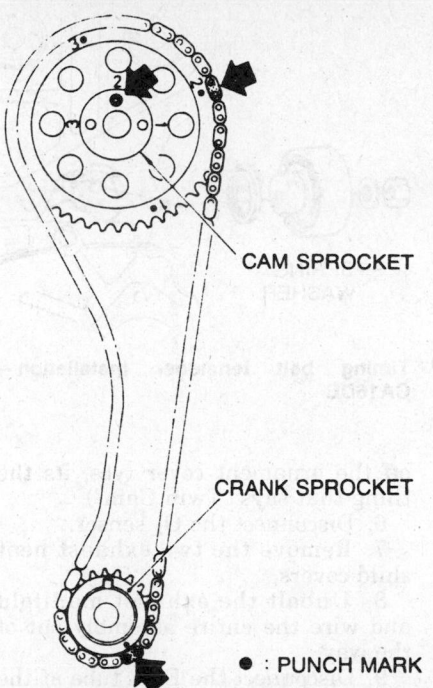

CAM SPROCKET

CRANK SPROCKET

● : PUNCH MARK

Alignment marks on the Z-Series engines

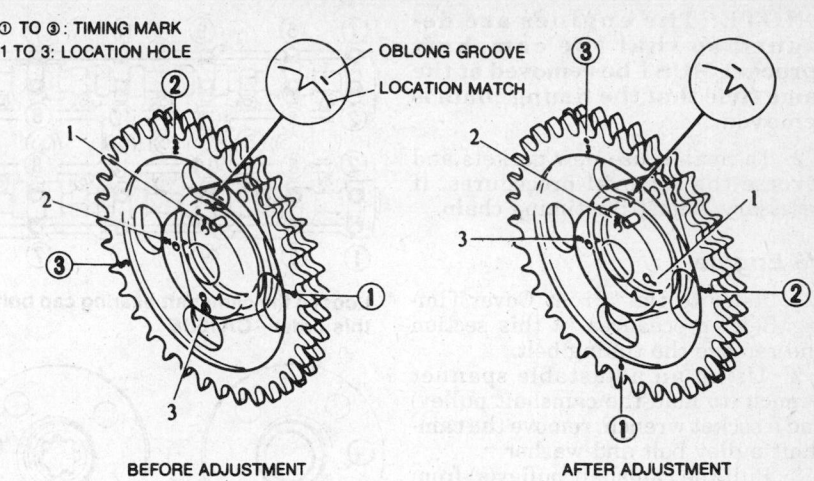

① TO ③ : TIMING MARK
1 TO 3: LOCATION HOLE

OBLONG GROOVE

LOCATION MATCH

BEFORE ADJUSTMENT

AFTER ADJUSTMENT

Timing chain adjustment

shaft sprocket. Position the sprocket so that the marks made earlier line up. This is assuming that the engine has not been disturbed. The camshaft and crankshaft keys should both be pointed upward. If a new chain and/or gear is being installed, position the sprocket so that the timing marks on the chain align with the marks on the crankshaft sprocket and the camshaft sprocket (with both keys pointing up). The marks are on the right-hand side of the sprockets as you face the engine. The L24, L28, Z20, Z22 and Z24i engines do not use the pin counting method for finding correct valve timing. Instead, position the key in the crankshaft sprocket so that is pointing upward and install the camshaft sprocket on the camshaft with its dowel pin at the top using the No. 2 (No. 1—L24 and L28) mounting hole and timing mark. The painted links of the chain should be on the right hand side of the sprockets as you face the engine. See the illustration.

NOTE: On Z-series engines, make sure that the crankshaft mating marks face forward.

8. Install the chain tensioner. Adjust the protrusion of the tensioner spindle to zero clearance. Install the remaining components in the reverse order of disassembly. Tighten the camshaft sprocket bolt to 87–116 ft. lbs. (118–157 Nm). Tighten the chain guide and tensioner bolts to 4.3–7.2 ft. lbs. (6–10 Nm).

LD28 Diesel Engines

1. Follow Steps 1–6 of the preceding "L24E, etc." procedure. You need not remove the fuel pump as detailed in Step 2.

2. Install the crankshaft sprocket. Make sure that the mating marks on the sprocket face the front of the car.

3. Install the timing chain and the camshaft sprocket together after first positioning the chain over the crankshaft sprocket. Position the cam sprocket so that the marks made earlier line up. This is assuming that the engine has not been disturbed. The camshaft and crankshaft keys should be pointing upward. If a new chain and/or gear is being installed, position the sprocket so that the timing marks on the chain align with the marks on the crankshaft and camshaft sprockets (with both keys pointing up). The marks are on the right-hand side of the sprockets as you face the engine. Insert the camshaft dowel pin into the No. 1 hole in the camshaft sprocket. Install and tighten the camshaft sprocket bolt.

4. Install the chain guide (if removed) and the chain tensioner. Tighten the slack side (left side when facing the engine) chain guide mounting bolt so that the protrusion of the chain tensioner spindle is 0 in.

5. Installation of the remaining components is in the reverse order of removal.

TIMING CHAIN ADJUSTMENT

When the timing chain stretches excessively, the valve timing will be adversely affected. There are three sets of holes and timing marks on the camshaft sprocket.

If the stretch of the chain roller links is excessive, adjust the camshaft

sprocket location by transferring the set position of the camshaft sprocket from the factory position of No. 1 or No. 2 to one of the other positions as follows:

1. Turn the crankshaft until the No. 1 piston is at TDC on the compression stroke. Examine whether the camshaft sprocket location notch is to the left of the oblong groove on the camshaft retaining plate. If the notch in the sprocket is to the left of the groove in the retaining plate, then the chain is stretched and needs adjusting.

2. Remove the camshaft sprocket together with the chain and reinstall the sprocket and chain with the locating dowel on the camshaft inserted into either the No. 2 or 3 hole of the sprocket. The timing mark on the timing chain must be aligned with the mark on the sprocket. The amount of modification is 4 degrees of crankshaft rotation for each mark.

3. Recheck the valve timing as outlined in Step 1. The notch in the sprocket should be to the right of the groove in the camshaft retaining plate.

4. If and when the notch cannot be brought to the right of the groove, the timing chain is worn beyond repair and must be replaced.

Camshaft Sprocket/ Pulleys

REMOVAL & INSTALLATION

All Engines—Except V6

1. Refer to the "Timing Belt/Chain and Tensioner, Removal and Installation" procedures, in this section and remove the timing chain/belt with the camshaft sprocket.

NOTE: The engines are designed so that the camshaft sprocket MUST be removed at the same time that the timing chain is removed.

2. To install, use new gaskets and reverse the removal procedures. If necessary, adjust the timing chain.

V6 Engine

1. Refer to the "Front Cover/Timing Belt" procedures in this section and remove the timing belt.

2. Using an adjustable spanner wrench (to hold the camshaft pulley) and a socket wrench, remove the camshaft pulley bolt and washer.

3. Pull the camshaft pulley(s) from the camshaft(s). Be careful not to loose the woodruff key.

NOTE: The R.H. and L.H. camshaft pulleys are different parts. Install them in their correct positions. The R.H. pulley has an R3 identification mark and the L.F. has an L3.

4. To install the camshaft pulleys, perform the following:
   a. Remove the rocker arm covers.
   b. Loosen the rocker arm shaft assembly bolts.
   c. Remove the spark plugs.
   d. Install the camshaft pulleys by reversing the removal procedures.

5. Install and adjust the timing belt.

6. To complete the installation, reverse the removal procedures.

Camshaft

REMOVAL & INSTALLATION

NOTE: For camshaft removal and installation procedures on the V6 engine (VG30E, VG30ET), please refer to "Cylinder Head Removal & Installation".

CA16DE Engines

1. Crank the engine until the No. 1 piston is at Top Dead Center on its compression stroke and disconnect the negative battery cable. Drain the cooling system and remove the air cleaner assembly.

2. Loosen the alternator and remove all drive belts. Remove the alternator.

3. Disconect the air duct at the throttle chamber.

4. Tag and disconnect all lines, hoses and wires which may interfere with cylinder removal.

5. Remove the eight screws and lift

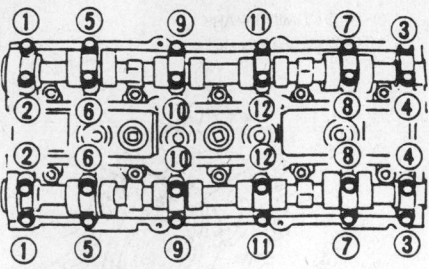

Loosen the camshaft bearing cap bolts in this order—CA16DE

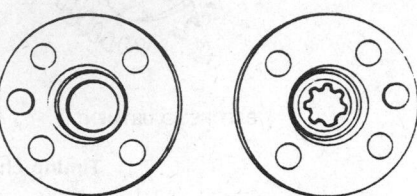

INTAKE SIDE   EXHAUST SIDE

The exhaust side camshaft is splined—CA16DE

INSTALL CAMSHAFT AS SHOWN

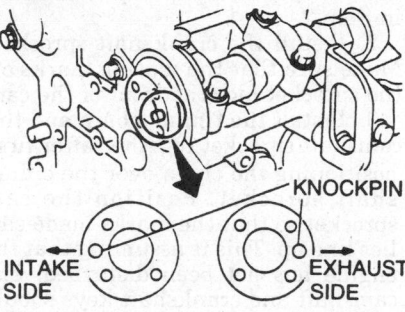

KNOCKPIN

INTAKE SIDE   EXHAUST SIDE

Install the camshafts as shown—CA16DE

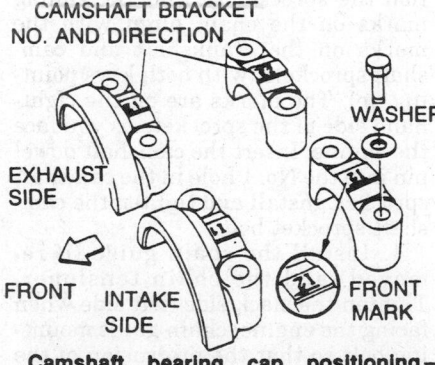

CAMSHAFT BRACKET NO. AND DIRECTION

WASHER

EXHAUST SIDE

FRONT   INTAKE SIDE   FRONT MARK

Camshaft bearing cap positioning—CA16DE

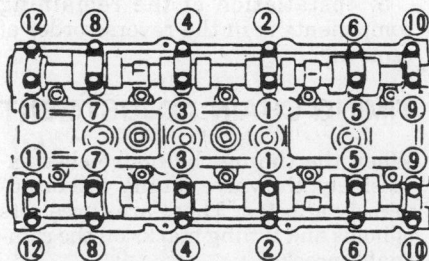

Tighten the camshaft bearing caps in this order—CA16DE

SPRING WASHER

Timing belt tensioner installation—CA16DE

off the ornament cover (yes, its the thing that says "Twin Cam").

6. Disconnect the O_2 sensor.

7. Remove the two exhaust heat shild covers.

8. Unbolt the exhaust manifold and wire the entire assembly out of the way.

9. Disconnect the EGR tube at the passage cover and then remove the passage cover and its gasket.

10. Disconnect and remove the crank angle sensor from the upper front cover.

11. Remove the support stay from under the intake manifold assembly.

12. Unbolt the intake manifold and remove it along with the collector and throttle chamber.

13. Disconnect and remove the fuel injectors as an assembly.

14. Remove the timing belt.

15. Remove the camshaft cover.

16. Remove the breather separater.

17. While holding the camshaft sprockets, remove the four mounting bolts and then remove the sprockets themselves.

18. Remove the timing belt tensioner pulley. Remove the rear timing belt cover.

19. Loosen the camshaft bearing caps in several stages, in the order shown. Remove the bearing caps, but be sure to keep them in order.

20. Remove the front oil seals and then lift out the camshafts.

21. Check the camshaft runout, endplay, wear and journal clearance.

To install:

1. Position the camshafts in the cylinder head so the knockpin on each is on the outboard side.

NOTE: The exhaust side camshaft has splines to accept the crank angle sensor.

2. Position the camshaft bearing caps and finger-tighten them. Each cap has an ID mark and a directional arrow stamped into its top surface.

3. Coat a NEW oil seal with engine

oil (on the lip) and install it on each camshaft end.

4. Tighten the camshaft bearing cap bolts to 7–9 ft. lbs. (9–12 Nm) in the order shown.

5. Install the rear timing cover and tighten the four bolts to 5–6 ft. lbs. (7–8 Nm).

6. Install the timing belt tensioner and tighten it to 16–22 ft. lbs. (22–29 Nm).

7. Install the camshaft sprockets and tighten the bolts to 10–14 ft. lbs. (14–19 Nm) while holding the camshaft in place.

8. Installation of the remaining components is in the reverse order of removal as detailed in the "Cylinder Head" and "Timing Belt" procedures.

CA18ET, CA20, CA20E and CA20S Engines

1. Set the No. 1 piston to TDC of the compression stroke and then remove the timing belt.

2. Remove the valve rocker cover.

3. Fully loosen all rocker arm adjusting screws (the valve adjusting screws). Loosen the rocker shaft mounting bolts in two or three stages and then remove the rocker shafts as an assembly. Keep all components in the correct order for reassembly.

4. Hold the camshaft pulley and remove the pulley mounting bolt. Remove the pulley.

5. Carefully pry the camshaft oil seal out of the front of the cylinder head.

6. Slide the camshaft out the front of the cylinder head, taking extreme care not to score any of the journals.

To install:

1. Coat the camshaft with clean engine oil.

2. Carefully slide the camshaft into the cylinder head, coat the end with oil and install a NEW oil seal.

3. Lubricate the rocker shafts lightly and install them, with the rocker arms, into the head. Both shafts have punchmarks on their leading edges, while the intake shaft is also marked with two slits on its leading edge.

NOTE: To prevent the rocker shaft springs from slipping out of the shaft, insert the bracket bolts into the shaft prior to installation.

4. Tighten the rocker shaft bolts gradually, in two or three stages.

5. Install the camshaft pulley and then install the timing belt.

6. Adjust the valves and install the cylinder head cover.

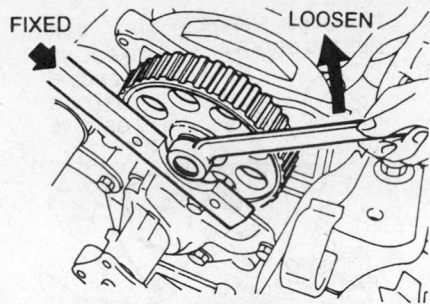

Loosening the camshaft sprocket—C-Series engines

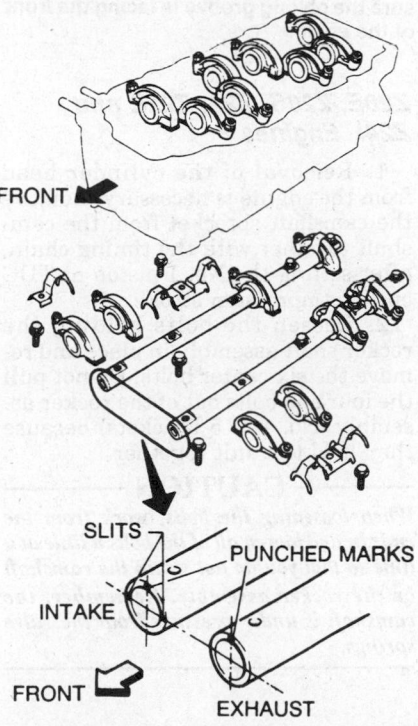

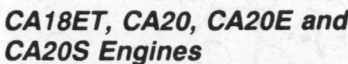

Rocker shaft assembly—C-Series engines

E15, E15ET, E16, E16S and E16i Engines

1. Follow Steps 1–15 of the "Cylinder Head Removal & Installation" procedure.

2. Remove the rocker shaft along with the rocker arms. Loosen the bolts gradually, in two or three stages.

3. Carefully slide the camshaft out the front of the cylinder head.

4. Check the camshaft runout, endplay, wear and journal clearance.

To install:

1. Slide the camshaft into the cylinder head carefully and then install a NEW oil seal.

2. Install the rear timing belt cover.

3. Set the camshaft so that the knockpin faces upward and then install the camshaft sprocket so its tim-

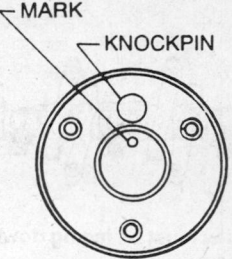

Camshaft positioning—E-Series engines

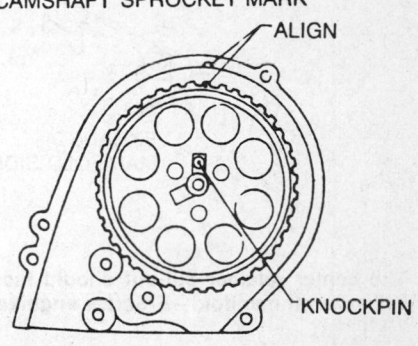

Camshaft sprocket alignment—E-Series engines

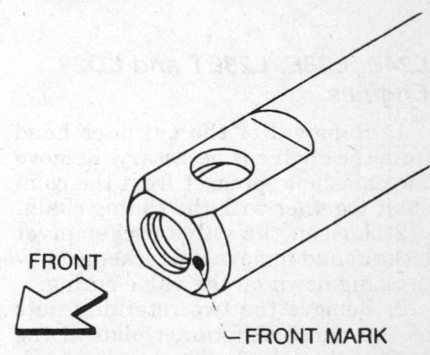

The punch mark on the rocker shaft should face forward—E-Series engines

ing mark aligns with the one on the rear timing cover.

4. Install the timing belt. Refer to "Timing Belt Removal & Installation".

5. Coat the rocker shaft and the interior of the rocker arm with engine oil. Install them so the punchmark on the shaft faces forward and the oil holes in the shaft face down. The cutout in the center retainer on the shaft should face the exhaust manifold side of the engine.

6. Make sure tha valve adjusting screws are loosened and then tighten the shaft bolts to 13–15 ft. lbs. (18–21 Nm) in several stages, from the center out. The first and last mounting bolts should have a new bolt stopper installed.

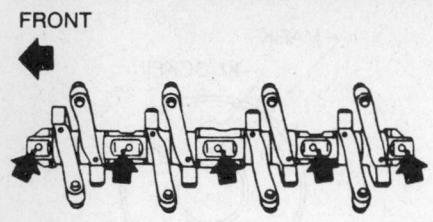

The oil holes must be facing down—E-Series engines

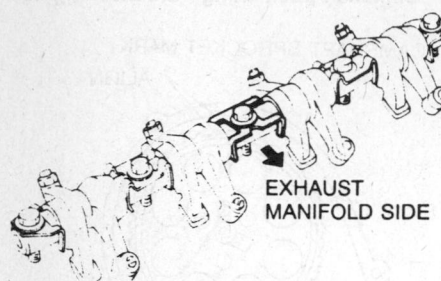

The center retainer cut-out should face the exhaust manifold—E-Series engines

EXHAUST MANIFOLD SIDE

7. Adjust the valves and then complete the installation procedure as detailed in the "Cylinder Head" section.

L24E, L28E, L28ET and LD28 Engines

1. Removal of the cylinder head from the engine is necessary. Remove the camshaft sprocket from the camshaft together with the timing chain.

2. Loosen the valve rocker pivot locknut and remove the rocker arm by pressing down on the valve spring.

3. Remove the two retaining nuts on the camshaft retainer plate at the front of the cylinder head and carefully slide the camshaft out of the camshaft carrier.

4. Lightly coat the camshaft bearings with clean motor oil and carefully slide the camshaft into place in the camshaft carrier.

5. Install the camshaft retainer plate with the oblong groove in the face of the plate facing toward the front of the engine.

6. Check the valve timing as outlined under "Timing Chain Removal and Installation" and install the timing sprocket on the camshaft, tightening the bolt together with the fuel pump cam to 86–116 ft. lbs.

7. Install the rocker arms by pressing down the valve springs with a screwdriver and install the valve rocker springs.

8. Install the cylinder head, if it was removed, and assemble the rest of the engine in the reverse order of removal.

When installing the retaining plate, make sure the oblong groove is facing the front of the engine

FOR DIESEL ENGINE OBLONG GROOVE

FOR GASOLINE ENGINE OBLONG GROOVE

Z20E, Z20S, Z22, Z22E and Z24i Engines

1. Removal of the cylinder head from the engine is necessary. Remove the camshaft sprocket from the camshaft together with the timing chain, after setting the No. 1 piston at TDC on its compression stroke.

2. Loosen the bolts holding the rocker shaft assembly in place and remove the six center bolts. Do not pull the four end bolts out of the rocker assembly (No. 1 & 5 brackets) because they hold the unit together.

CAUTION

When loosening the bolts, work from the ends in and loosen all of the bolts a little at a time so that you do not strain the camshaft or the rocker assembly. Remember, the camshaft is under pressure from the valve springs.

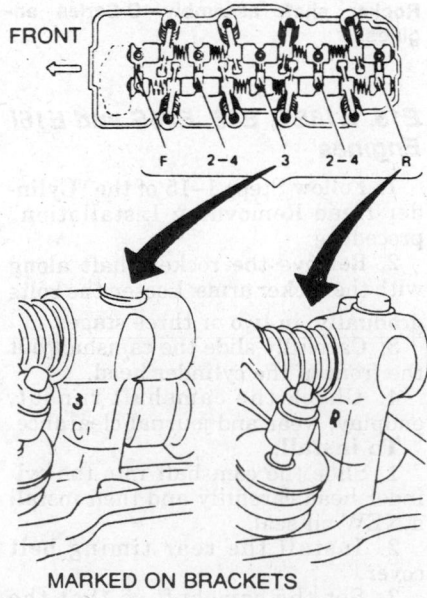

FRONT

F 2–4 3 2–4 R

MARKED ON BRACKETS

Rocker shaft installation—Z24i

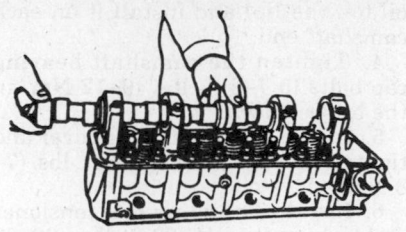

Carefully slide the camshaft out of the carrier

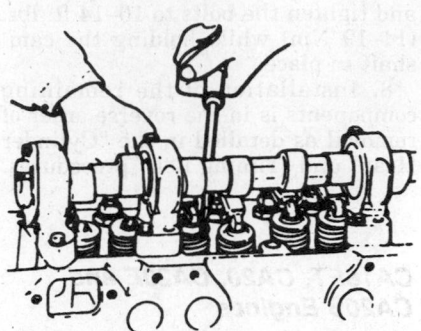

Remove the rocker arm by pressing down on the valve spring

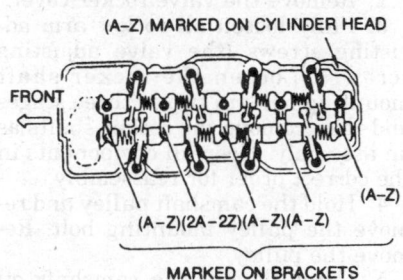

(A–Z) MARKED ON CYLINDER HEAD

FRONT

(A–Z)

(A–Z)(2A–2Z)(A–Z)(A–Z)

MARKED ON BRACKETS

Rocker shaft mounting brackets are assembled in this order—Z20, Z22 series engines

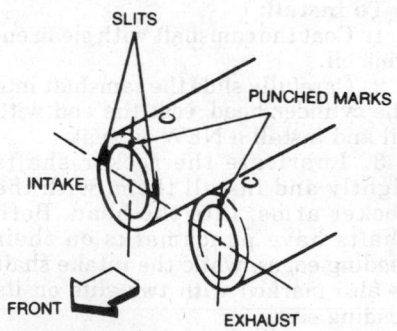

SLITS

PUNCHED MARKS

INTAKE

FRONT

EXHAUST

Note the difference in rocker shafts—Z-Series engines

3. After removing the rocker assembly, remove the camshaft.

NOTE: Keep the disassembled parts in order.

If you need to disassemble the rocker unit, assemble as follows:

4. Install the mounting brackets,

valve rockers and springs observing the following considerations.

The two rocker shafts are different. Both have punch marks in the ends that face the front of the engine. The rocker shaft that goes on the side of the intake manifold has two slits in its end just below the punch mark. The exhaust side rocker shaft does not have slits.

The rocker arm for the intake and exhaust valves are interchangeable between cylinders one and three and are identified by the mark "1". Similarly, the rockers for cylinders two and four are interchangeable and are identified by the mark "2".

The rocker shaft mounting brackets are also coded for correct placement with either an "A" or an "Z" plus a number code.

To install the camshaft and rocker assembly:

5. Place the camshaft on the head with its dowel pin pointing up.

6. Fit the rocker assembly on the head, making sure you mount it on its knock pin.

7. Torque the bolts to 11–18 ft. lbs., in several stages working from the middle bolts and moving outwards on both sides.

NOTE: Make sure the engine is on TDC of the compression stroke for the No. 1 piston or you may damage some valves.

See the section on timing chain installation. Adjust the valves.

Pistons and Connecting Rods

REMOVAL & INSTALLATION

For all piston and connecting rod overhaul procedures, please refer tp "Engine Rebuilding" in the Unit Repair section

All Engines

1. Remove the cylinder head.
2. Remove the oil pan.
3. Remove any carbon buildup from the cylinder wall at the top of the piston travel with a ridge reamer tool.
4. Position the piston to be removed at the bottom of its stroke so that the connecting rod bearing cap can be reached easily from under the engine.
5. Unscrew the connecting rod bearing cap nuts and remove the cap and lower half of the bearing. Attach a length of rubber hose to each of the connecting rod bolts. These will pro-

LD28

Piston projection mm (in)	Cylinder head gasket thickness mm (in)	No. of cutouts in cylinder head gasket
Below 0.487 (0.0192)	1.12 (0.0441)	1
0.487–0.573 (0.0192–0.0226)	1.2 (0.047)	2
Above 0.573 (0.0226)	1.28 (0.0504)	3

CD17

Piston projection mm (in)	Cylinder head gasket thickness mm (in)	No. of cutouts in cylinder head gasket
Below 0.52 (0.0205)	1.15 (0.0453)	1
0.52–0.57 (0.0205–0.0224)	1.20 (0.0472)	2
Above 0.57 (0.0224)	1.25 (0.0492)	3

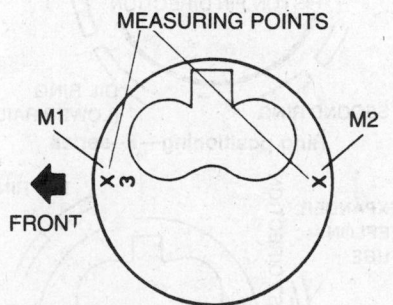

Piston projection measuring points—CD17 diesel engines

tect the cylinder bore from being scratch by the rod bolts.

6. Push the piston and connecting rod up and out of the cylinder block with a length of wood. Use care not to scratch the cylinder wall with the connecting rod or the wooden tool.

7. Keep all of the components from each cylinder together and install them in the cylinder from which they were removed.

8. Coat the bearing face of the connecting rod and the outer face of the pistons with engine oil. Attach a length of rubber hose to each of the connecting rod bolts. These will pro-

tect the cylinder bore from being scratched by the rod bolts.

9. See the illustrations for the correct placement of the piston rings.

10. Turn the crankshaft until the rod journal of the particular cylinder you are working on is brought to the TDC position.

NOTE: On diesel engines, the amount of projection of each piston crown above the deck of the block must be measured.

11. On diesel engines, clean the deck of the cylinder block completely. Set a dial gauge on the cylinder block surface to zero. For every cylinder, measure the piston projection and record the length. Be sure to measure the length of piston projection at least three points for every cylinder. Determine the maximum length of piston projection and select the suitable head gasket according to the chart below. The head gaskets have cut-outs in them for identification purposes. When the gasket is replaced, always install a gasket of the same thickness.

12. With the piston and rings clamped in a ring compressor, the notched mark on the head of the piston toward the front of the engine, and the oil hole side of the connecting rod toward the fuel pump side of the engine, push the piston and connecting rod assembly into the cylinder bore until the big bearing end of the connecting rod contacts and is seated on the rod journal of the crankshaft. Use the lengths of rubber hose as guides in seating the connecting rod onto the crankpin. Use care not to scratch the cylinder wall with the connecting rod.

13. Push down farther on the piston and turn the crankshaft while the connecting rod rides around on the crankshaft rod journal. Turn the crankshaft until the crankshaft rod journal is at BDC (bottom dead center).

14. Align the mark on the connecting rod bearing cap with that on the connecting rod and tighten the bearing cap bolts to the specified torque.

15. Install all of the piston/connecting rod assemblies in the manner outlined above and assemble the oil pan and cylinder head to the engine in the reverse order of removal.

IDENTIFICATION & POSITIONING

The pistons are marked with a notch (or F) in the piston head. When installed, the notch (or F) markings are to be facing toward the front of the engine.

The connecting rods are installed

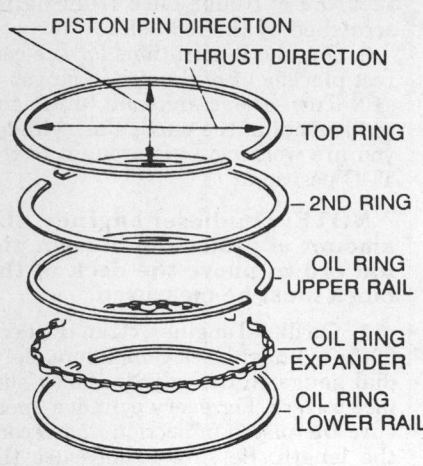

MARK SHOULD BE FACING UPWARD

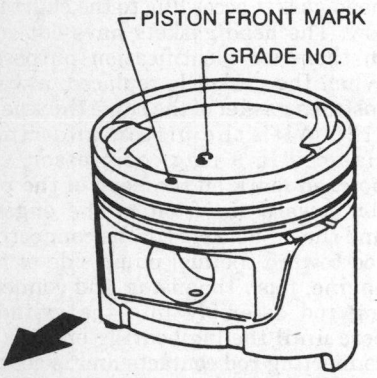

INSTALL TOWARDS ENGINE FRONT

Piston and ring identification and positioning—VG30E and VG30ET

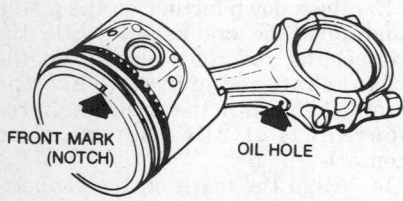

Piston and rod positioning

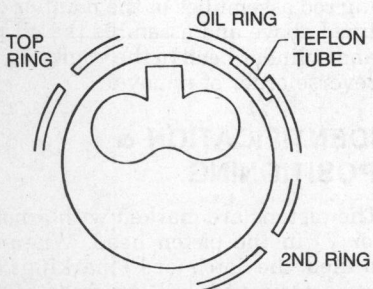

Space CD17 ring gaps 120° apart when installing piston

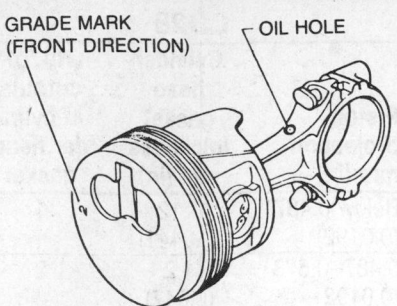

CD17 piston identification marks

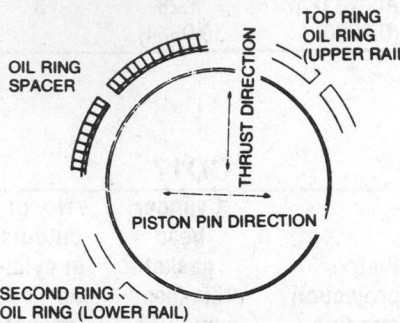

Piston ring placement—A–series engines; L28, 1981 and later L24E similar

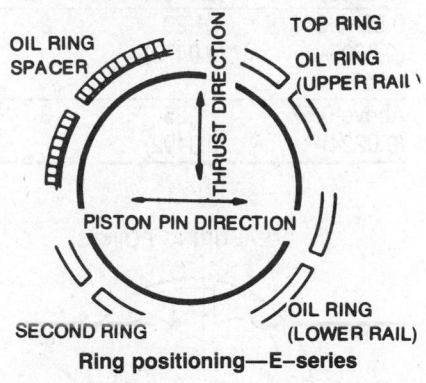

Ring positioning—E–series

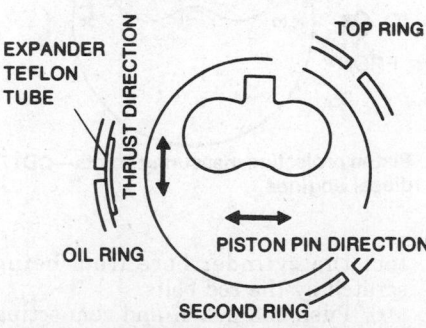

Piston ring placement—LD28 diesel; note Teflon expander tube

with the oil hole facing toward the right side of the engine.

NOTE: It is advisable to number the pistons, connecting rods, and bearing caps in some manner so that they can be reinstalled in the same cylinder, facing the same direction, from which they are removed.

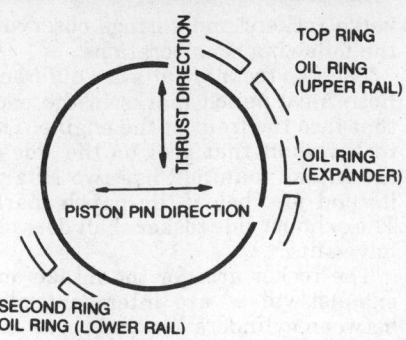

Piston ring placement—L24E, C-Series and Z-Series engines

ENGINE LUBRICATION

Oil Pan

REMOVAL & INSTALLATION

All Models Except 1987-88 Pulsar/Sentra (Gasoline Engines), Van, 1985-88 Maxima and 300ZX

1. If the engine is in the vehicle, attach a lift, support the engine, and remove the engine mounting bolts as described in "Engine Removal and Installation".
2. Raise the engine slightly, watching to make sure that no hoses or wires are damaged.
3. Drain the engine oil.
4. Remove the oil pan bolts and slide the pan out to the rear.

To install the pan:

1. Use a new gasket, coated on both sides with sealer.
2. Apply a thin bead of silicone seal to the engine block at the junction of the block and front cover, and the junction of the block and rear main bearing cap. Then apply a thin coat of silicone seal to the new oil pan gasket, install the gasket to the block and install the pan.
3. Tighten the pan bolts in a circular pattern from the center to the ends, to 4–7 ft. lbs. Overtightening will distort the pan lip, causing leakage.
4. Reinstall the engine mounting bolts as described under "Engine Removal and Installation", using the specified torque and maintaining support until all mounts are secure.
5. Refill the oil pan to the specified level.

1987-88 Pulsar/Sentra (Gasoline Engines) and Van

1. Drain the engine oil.
2. Raise the vehicle and support it with safety stands.
3. Remove the right side splash cover. Remove the right side under cover.
4. Remove the center member.
5. Remove the forward section of the exhaust pipe.
6. Remove the front buffer rod and its bracket.
7. Remove the engine gussets.
8. Insert a seal cutter (SST KV10111100) between the oil pan and the cylinder block.

NOTE: DO NOT use a screwdriver!

9. Tapping the cutter with a hammer, slide it around the oil pan.
10. Remove the oil pan.
11. Remove all old liquid gasket from the pan and block mating surfaces.
12. Apply a continuous bead (3.5–4.5mm) of liquid gasket around the oil pan. Apply the sealer to the *inner* surface around the bolt holes where there is no groove.
13. Wait five minutes and then install the pan.

1985-88 Maxima

1. Drain the engine oil.
2. Raise the vehicle and support it safely with jack stands.
3. Scribe around the hood support brackets and then remove the hood.
4. Position a block of wood between a floor jack and the engine and then raise the engine slightly in its mounts.
5. Remove the lower engine splash pans.
6. Remove the insulator bolt and nuts from the engine mounts.
7. Remove the center crossmember assembly.
8. Unbolt the front exhaust pipe and wire it out of the way.
9. Remove the oil pan.
10. To install, carefully scrape the old gasket material away from the pan and cylinder block mounting surfaces and then apply gasket sealer to the four corners of the cylinder block mounting surface. Do the same to the oil pan gasket; both upper and lower surfaces.
11. Install the oil pan and tighten the mounting bolts from the inside, out, to 3.6–5.1 ft. lbs. (5–7 Nm)

300ZX

1. Drain the engine oil.
2. Raise the vehicle and support it safely with jack stands.

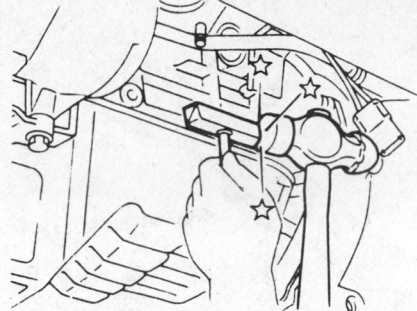

Using a seal cutter on the oil pan

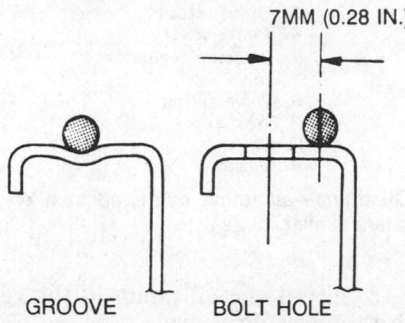

Apply sealer on the inside of the bolt holes

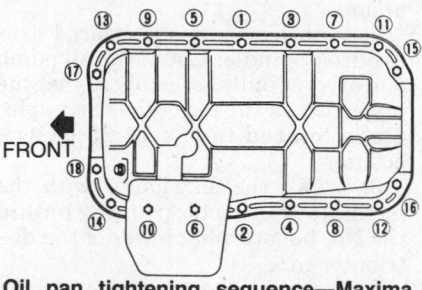

Oil pan tightening sequence—Maxima (1985 and later)

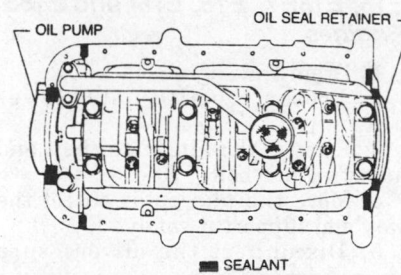

Apply sealant to these areas before installing the oil pan gasket—V6

3. Remove the front stabilizer bar retaining bolts and nuts from the suspension crossmember.
4. Remove the steering column shaft from the gear housing.
5. Remove the tension rod retaining nuts from the transverse link.
6. Lift and support the engine.
7. Remove the rear plate cover from the transmission case.

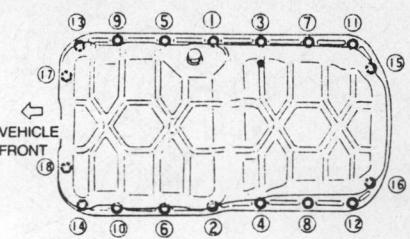

Oil pan tightening sequence—V6

8. Remove the oil pan retaining bolts.
9. Remove the suspension crossmember retaining bolts.
10. Remove the strut mounting insulator retaining nuts.
11. Remove the screws retaining the refrigerant lines and power steering tubes to the suspension crossmember.
12. Lower the suspension crossmember.
13. Remove the oil pan from the rear side.
14. Installation is the reverse of removal. Apply sealant to the surface points indicated in the illustration and torque the pan retaining bolts in numerical sequence to 3.5–5.1 ft. lbs.

Rear Main Oil Seal

REPLACEMENT

All Engines Except CA16DE, CA18ET, CA20, CA20E and CA20S

In order to replace the rear main oil seal, the rear main bearing cap must be removed. Removal of the rear main bearing cap requires the use of a special rear main bearing cap puller. Also, the oil seal is installed with a special crankshaft rear oil seal drift.

1. Remove the engine and transmission assembly from the vehicle.
2. Remove the transmission from the engine. Remove the oil pan.
3. Remove the clutch from the flywheel.
4. Remove the flywheel from the crankshaft.
5. Remove the rear main bearing cap together with the bearing cap side seals (except on CD17).
6. Remove the rear main oil seal from around the crankshaft.
7. Apply lithium grease around the sealing lip of the oil seal and install the seal around the crankshaft using a suitable tool.
8. Apply sealer to the rear main bearing cap, install the rear main bearing cap, and tighten the cap bolts to the proper specification.

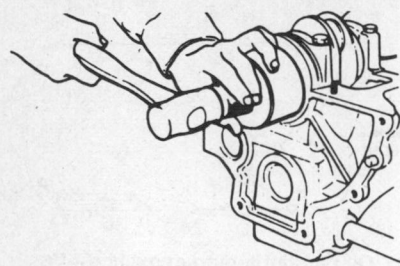

Rear oil seal installation—A-Series engines (L-Series and Z-Series engines similar)

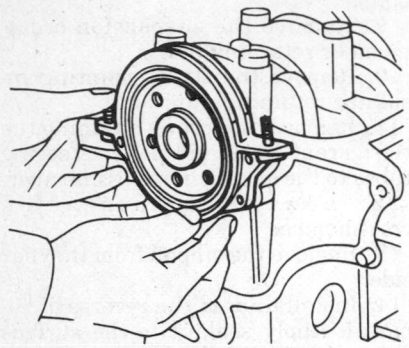

Installing the E—series rear oil seal retainer

9. Apply sealant to the rear main bearing cap side seals and install by driving the seals into place with a suitable drift.

10. Assemble the engine and install it in the vehicle in the reverse order of removal.

CA16DE, CA18ET, CA20, CA20E and CA20S Engines

1. Remove the transmission.
2. Remove the flywheel.
3. Remove the rear oil seal retainer.
4. Using a pair of pliers, remove the oil seal from the retainer.
5. Liberally apply clean engine oil to the new oil seal and carefully install it into the retainer.
6. Install the rear oil seal retainer into the engine, along with a new gasket. Torque the bolts to 2.9–4.3 ft. lbs. Install the flywheel and transmission in the reverse order of removal.

Oil Pump

REMOVAL & INSTALLATION

A12A, A14 and A15 Engines

1. Drain the engine oil.
2. Remove the front stabilizer bar if it is in the way of removing the oil pump.
3. Remove the splash shield.
4. Remove the oil pump body with the drive spindle assembly.

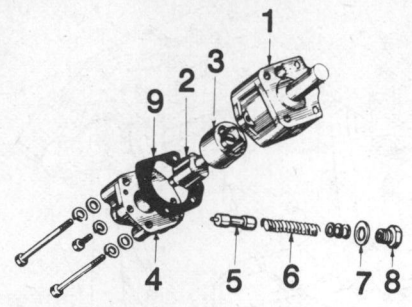

1. Pump body
2. Inner rotor and shaft
3. Outer rotor
4. Pump cover
5. Pressure regulator valve
6. Valve spring
7. Washer
8. Cap
9. Gasket

Oil pump—all inline overhead cam engines similar

5. Install the oil pump in the reverse order of removal.
6. Fill the pump housing with engine oil, then align the punch mark on the spindle with the hole in the oil pump.
7. With a new gasket placed over the drive spindle, install the oil pump and drive spindle assembly so that the projection on the top of the drive spindle is located in the 11:25 o'clock position.
8. Install the distributor with the metal tip of the rotor pointing toward the No. 1 spark plug tower of the distributor cap.
9. Assemble the remaining components in the reverse order of removal.

E15, E15ET, E16, E16i and E16S Engines

1. Drain the engine oil.
2. Loosen the alternator lower bolts.
3. Remove the alternator belt and adjusting bar bolt.
4. Move the alternator out of the way and support it safely.
5. Disconnect the oil pressure gauge harness.
6. Remove the oil filter.
7. Remove the pump assembly.
8. For installation, fill the pump with clean engine oil and rotate it several times.
9. Install the pump on the engine using a new gasket. Torque the pump mounting bolts to 7–9 ft. lbs.

CA16DE, CA18ET, CA20, CA20E and CA20S Engines

1. Remove all accessory drive belts and the alternator.

2. Remove the timing (cam) belt covers and remove the timing belt.
3. On 1984-88 200SX and the Stanza wagon, unbolt the engine from its mounts and lift or jack the engine up from the unibody. On the Stanza (exc. wagon) and Pulsar, remove the center member from the body.
4. Remove the oil pan.
5. Remove the oil pump assembly along with the oil strainer.
6. If installing a new or rebuilt oil pump, first pack the pump full of petroleum jelly to prevent the pump from cavitating when the engine is started. Apply RTV sealer to the front oil seal end of the pan prior to installation. Install the pump in the reverse order of removal, torquiing the mounting bolts to 9–12 ft. lbs.

CD17 Diesel Engines

1. Remove the valve timing belt.
2. Drain the engine oil and remove the oil pan.
3. The oil pump is bolted to the front of the engine block, at the front of the crankshaft. Loosen the mounting bolts and remove the oil pump assembly.

— CAUTION —

Remove the crankshaft key in order to avoid damage to the oil seal on the pump.

4. Remove the oil pump rear cover and check the gear clearance using a feeler gauge.
5. Installation is in the reverse order of removal. Apply sealer to the four corners of the oil pan and use a new oil pump gasket. Tighten the pump mounting bolts to 9–12 ft/ lbs.

L24E, L28E, L28ET, LD28, Z20E, Z20S, Z22, Z22E and Z24i Engines

1. Drain the crankcase.
2. Turn the crankshaft so that the No. 1 piston is at TDC on its compression stroke.
3. Remove the distributor cap and mark the position of the distributor base with a piece of chalk.
4. Remove the front stabilizer bar (if so equipped).
5. Remove the splash shield.
6. Remove the oil pump body with the drive spindle assembly.
7. When installing the pump on the Van, align the punch mark on the drive spindle with the oil hole on the pump.
Tighten the long mounting bolts to 8–11 ft. lbs. (11–15 Nm). Tighten the short mounting bolts to 4.3–7.2 ft. lbs. (6–10 Nm).

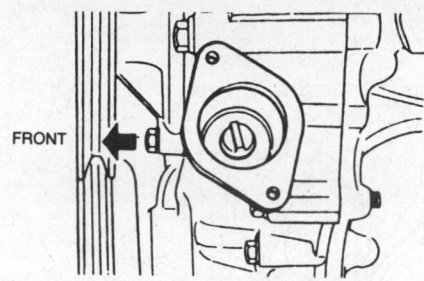

Position of the distributor drive spindle—L-series gas engines

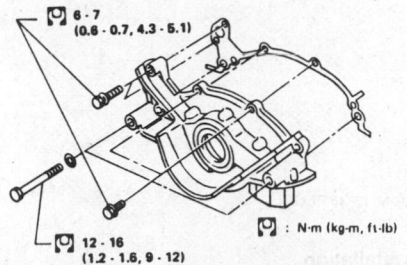

Oil pump installation—V6

VG30E and VG30ET Engines

1. Remove the oil pan and timing belt as detailed previously in this section.
2. Remove the crankshaft timing sprocket (you may need a puller!).
3. Remove the timing belt plate.
4. Remove the oil pump strainer and pick-up tube from the oil pump.
5. Remove the mounting bolts and remove the oil pump.
6. To install, use new gaskets (silicone sealant), a new oil seal and reverse the removal procedures. Refill the engine with oil.

NOTE: Before installing the oil pump, be sure to pack the pump's cavity with petroleum jelly, then make sure the O-ring is fitted properly.

ENGINE COOLING

Radiator

REMOVAL & INSTALLATION

1. Disconnect the negative battery cable.
2. Remove the front bumper on the 1985-88 Maxima and 300ZX.
3. Disconnect the transmission cooling lines from the bottom of the radiator, if so equipped.

4. Remove the retaining bolts at each of the four corners of the fan shroud and position the shroud over the fan and clear of the radiator.
5. Disconnect the upper and lower hoses from the radiator.
6. Remove the radiator retaining bolts or the upper supports and lift the radiator out of the vehicle.
7. Install the radiator in the reverse order of the removal, fill the cooling system and check for leaks.

Water Pump

REMOVAL & INSTALLATION

All Engines Except CD17, E15, E15ET, E16, E16i, E16S, VG30E and VG30ET

1. Drain the engine coolant.

NOTE: Be sure to drain the cylinder block also. Most models have a drain plug on the left side of the block.

2. Loosen the bolts retaining the fan shroud to the radiator and remove the shroud.
3. Loosen the belt, then remove the fan and pulley from the water pump hub.
4. Remove the bolts retaining the pump and remove the pump together with the gasket from the front cover.
5. Remove all traces of gasket material and install the pump in the reverse order. Use a new gasket and sealer. Tighten the bolts uniformly.

CD17 Diesel Engines

1. Disconnect the negative battery cable. Drain the cooling system.
2. Remove the alternator and A/C compressor drive belts, if equipped.
3. Remove the front crankshaft

pulley after first setting the No. 1 cylinder at TDC on the compression stroke.
4. Remove the front engine covers.
5. Remove the timing belt.
6. Loosen the mounting bolts and remove the water pump.
7. Installation is the reverse of removal. Clean all gasket surfaces before reassembly.

NOTE: The water pump cannot be disassembled and must be replaced as a unit. Inspect the timing belt for wear or damage and replace if necessary.

E15, E15ET, E16, E16i and E16S Engines

1. With the engine cold, raise the hood and open the drain cock on the radiator and drain the coolant into a suitable drain pan. Remove the radiator cap to relieve the pressure in the system.
2. Remove the power steering belt and power steering pump, do not let the power steering fluid drain out.
3. Remove the water pump drive belts, loosen the alternator mounting bolts and slide the alternator toward the engine.
4. Remove the water pump pulley and the water pump securing bolts.
5. Remove the water pump with the gasket.
6. Installation is the reverse order of the removal procedure. Be sure to check for coolant leaks after the installation is completed and the engine is funning.

NOTE: Check water pump for excessive end play and rough operation. The pump cannot be disassembled and must be replaced as a unit.

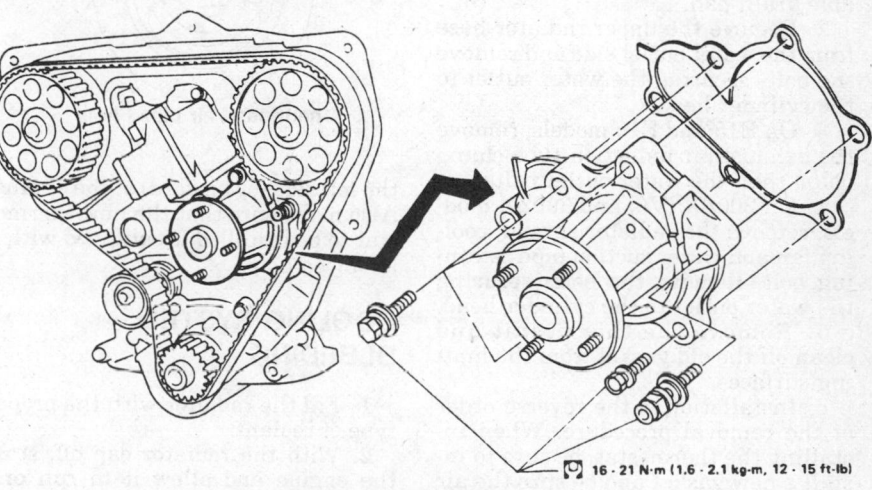

16 - 21 N·m (1.6 - 2.1 kg-m, 12 - 15 ft-lb)

Water pump installation—V6

VG30E and VG30ET Engines

1. Drain the coolant from the left side drain cocks on the cylinder block and radiator.

2. Remove the radiator shroud fan and pulleys.

3. Remove the power steering, compressor and alternator drive belts.

4. Disconnect the water pump hose.

5. Remove the upper and lower timing covers.

6. On the Maxima, if the vehicle is equipped with cruise control, remove the unit from the fender well to improve access.

7. Remove the thermostat housing and gasket.

NOTE: Be careful not to get coolant on the timing belt and to avoid deforming the timing cover, make sure there is enough clearance between the timing cover and the hose clamp.

8. Remove the water pump retaining bolts (note different lengths) and remove the pump.

9. Installation is the reverse of removal. Scrape the gasket surfaces, install a new gasket and reinstall the pump. Torque the retaining bolts to 12–15 ft. lbs.

NOTE: Check water pump for excessive end play and rough operation. The pump cannot be disassembled and must be replaced as a unit.

Thermostat

REMOVAL & INSTALLATION

NOTE: The engine thermostat is housed in the water outlet casting on the cylinder head.

1. Open the drain cock on the radiator and drain the coolant into a suitable drain pan.

2. Remove the upper radiator hose from the water outlet side and remove the bolts securing the water outlet to the cylinder head.

3. On E15 and E16 models, remove the exhaust air induction tube clamp bolts, then the water outlet bolts.

4. On 200SX (V6) and 300ZX models, remove the radiator shroud, cooling fan and water suction pipe retaining bolt. Remove the bolts securing the water outlet to the cylinder head.

5. Remove the thermostat and clean off the old gasket from the mating surfaces.

6. Installation is the reverse order of the removal procedure. When installing the thermostat, be sure to install a new gasket and be sure the air bleed hole in the thermostat is facing

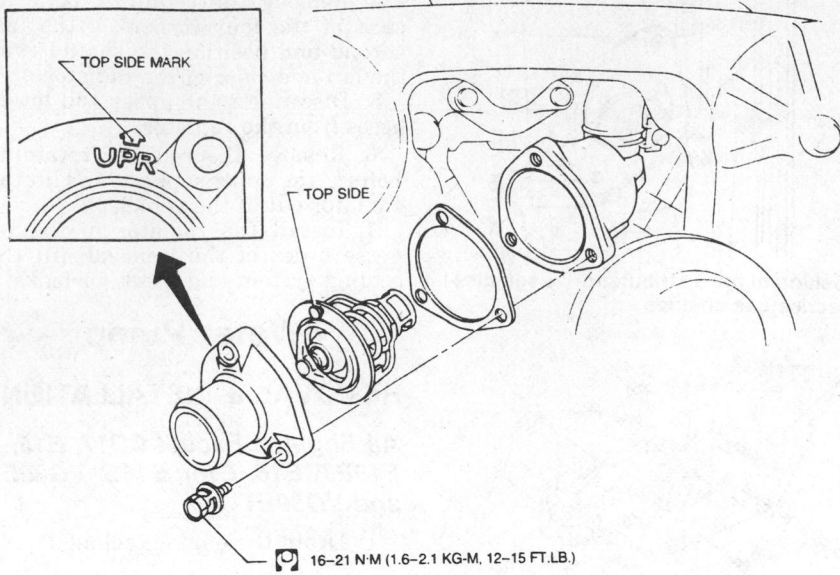

V6 thermostat installation

16–21 N·M (1.6–2.1 KG-M, 12–15 FT.LB.)

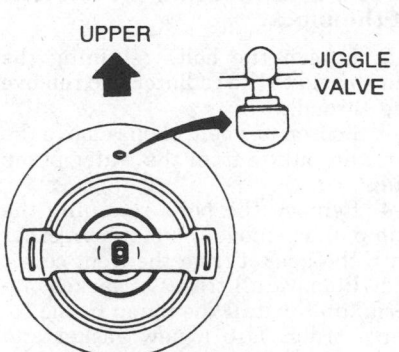

Always be sure the jiggle valve is facing upward when installing the thermostat

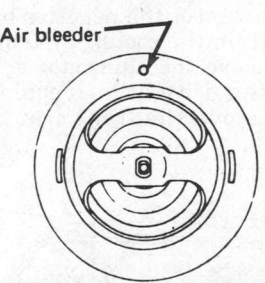

Thermostat air bleed hole

the left side (or upward) of the engine. Also make sure that the new thermostat to be installed is equipped with a air bleed hole.

COOLING SYSTEM BLEEDING

1. Fill the radiator with the proper type of coolant.

2. With the radiator cap off, start the engine and allow it to run and reach normal operating temperature.

3. Run the heater at full force and with the temperature lever in the hot position. Be sure that the heater control valve is functioning.

4. Shut the engine off and recheck the coolant level, refill as necessary.

EMISSION CONTROLS

Please refer to "Emission Control" in the Unit Repair section for system maintenance procedures. Due to the complex nature of modern electronic engine control systems, comprehensive diagnosis and testing procedures fall outside the confines of this repair manual. For complete information on diagnosis, testing and repair procedures concerning all modern engine and emission control systems, please refer to *"Chilton's Guide to Electronic Engine Controls".*

RESETTING MAINTENANCE REMINDER LIGHTS

1981-84

NOTE: The later model Datsuns use an oxygen sensor and after 30,000 miles of operation, the warning light on the dash panel for the oxygen sensor will come on. When this light comes on and remains on, it is indicating that the oxygen sensor should be

inspected and replaced if it is not operating properly.

1. Disconnect the negative battery cable and remove the oxygen sensor, which is located on the exhaust manifold.

2. Coat the thread of the new sensor with a suitable anti-seize compound and reinstall it into the exhaust manifold.

3. After the new sensor has been installed or the old sensor passes inspection and has been re-installed into the exhaust manifold. The sensor light can be turned off by disconnecting the wiring harness connecter for the sensor.

4. On the 200SX and 280ZX models, the wiring harness is located under the right side of the instrument panel.

5. On all other models, the wiring harness is located in the area under the left side of the dash next to the hood release handle.

6. On all models, the harness is a single wire which will be green and white on the 200SX, green and yellow on the 280ZX and blue and yellow on all others. Trace the wire to the connector and unplug the connector. The mileage counter can not be reset.

1985-88

NOTE: There is no warning light on the Van, therefore it cannot be reset! O₂ sensor replacement at 60,000 miles is the only regular service.

Procedures for 1985-88 models are basically similar to those already given for 1981-84 models in so far as the testing and replacement of the sensor is concerned. The difference arises in the resetting procedures.

U.S. models should be reset after the warning light comes on at 30,000 miles (43,000 km) and then again at 60,000 miles (96,000 km). When the warning light comes on a third time, at 90,000 miles (144,000 km), it should then be disconnected.

On Canadian models, when the warning light comes on at 30,000 miles (43,000 km), it should be disconnected. There is no provision for resetting the warning light on models sold in Canada.

For resetting and disconnection procedures, please see the following:

NOTE: Refer to illustrations for exact location of reset boxes and wiring harness disconnect points.

1. On the Maxima, reset the warning light by pressing the reset button on the small box found under the left side of the instrument panel. To dis-

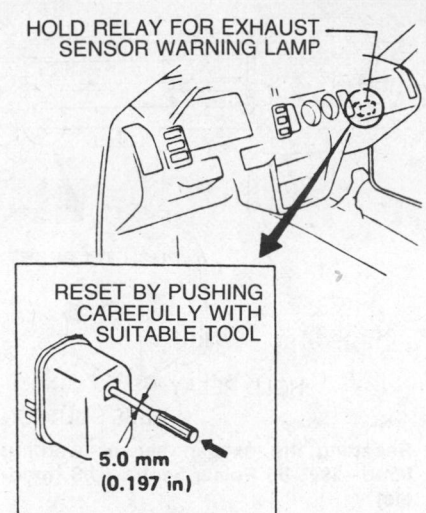

Resetting the oxygen sensor warning lamp—1985-86 300ZX (U.S. models)

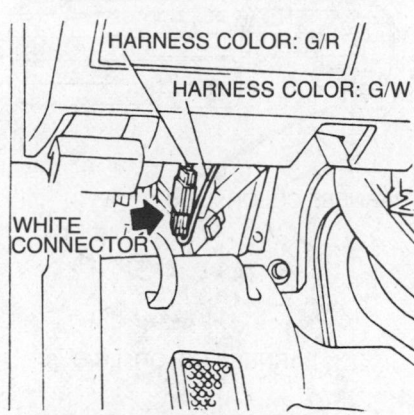

Disconnecting the oxygen sensor warning lamp—1985-88 Maxima

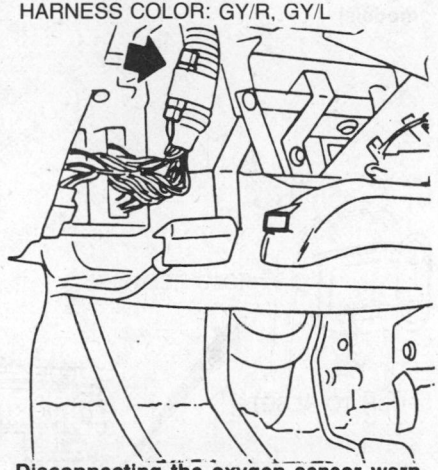

Disconnecting the oxygen sensor warning lamp—1985-88 300ZX

connect the warning, unplug the white connector behind and above the reset box. On the 1985 Maxima, unplug the connector only.

2. On the 300ZX, locate the reset box underneath and behind the glove

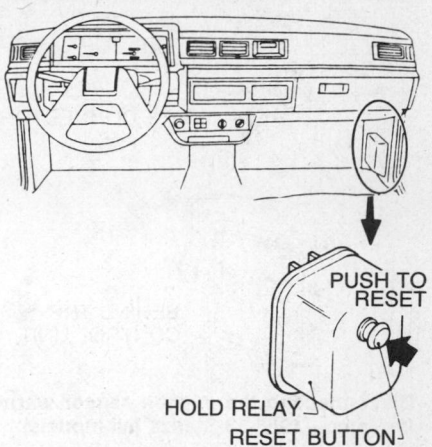

Resetting the oxygen sensor warning lamp—1985-88 Stanza sedan (U.S. models)

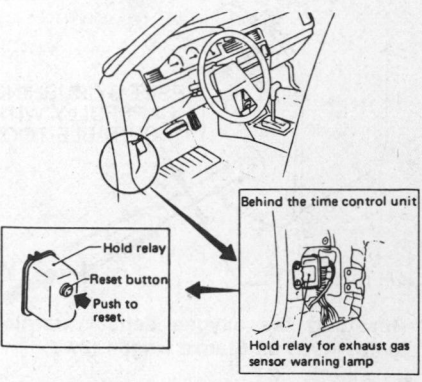

Resetting the oxygen sensor warning lamp—1986-88 Maxima (U.S. models)

compartment, insert a suitable 5mm (0.197 in.) diameter tool and push lightly one time. On 1987-88 models with an analog meter, switch off the lamp after every inspection by disconnecting one of the three connectors found behind the glove box. Disconnect the warning light by unplugging the white connector found under the left side of the instrument panel.

3. On the Stanza sedan, locate the reset box behind the right side kick panel and push the button one time.

On the 1986 Stanza wagon (2wd), the box is under the passenger seat and is reset in the same manner as the 1985-86 300ZX.

On the 1986 Stanza wagon (4wd) and all 1987-88 Stanza wagons, the reset box is also under the passenger seat, but is reset with a push button, similar to the sedan.

On all models, the warning light is disconnected by unplugging the white connector found behind the Electronic Control Unit, underneath the left side of the instrument panel.

4. On the 200SX, the reset box may be found behind the right side of the center console. It uses a push button

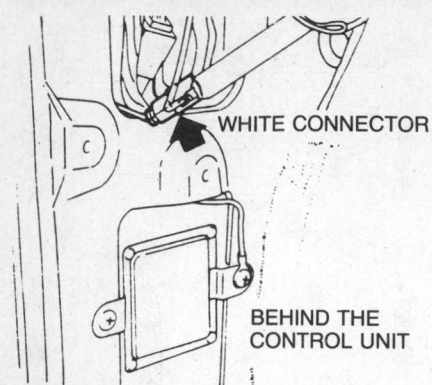

WHITE CONNECTOR

BEHIND THE
CONTROL UNIT

Disconnecting the oxygen sensor warning lamp—1985-88 Stanza (all models)

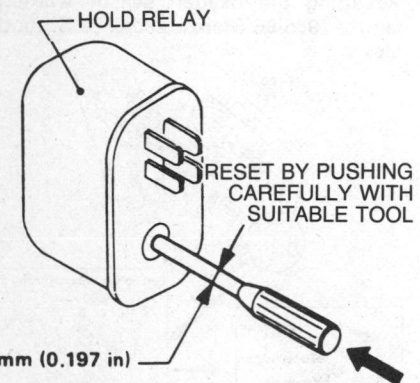

HOLD RELAY

RESET BY PUSHING CAREFULLY WITH SUITABLE TOOL

mm (0.197 in)

Resetting the oxygen sensor warning lamp—1985-86 Stanza wagon (2wd)

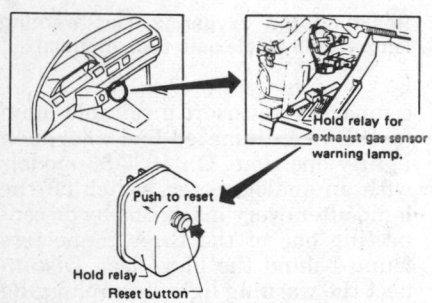

Hold relay for exhaust gas sensor warning lamp.

Push to reset

Hold relay

Reset button

Resetting the oxygen sensor warning lamp—1985-88 200SX (U.S. models)

BEHIND FUSE BOX

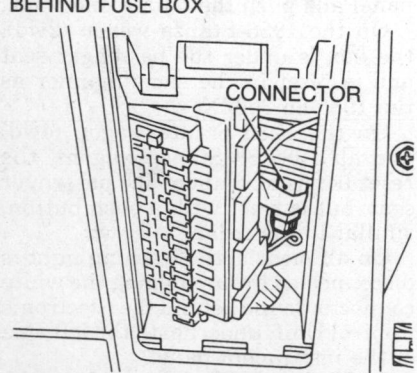

CONNECTOR

Disconnecting the oxygen sensor warning lamp—1985-88 200SX (all models)

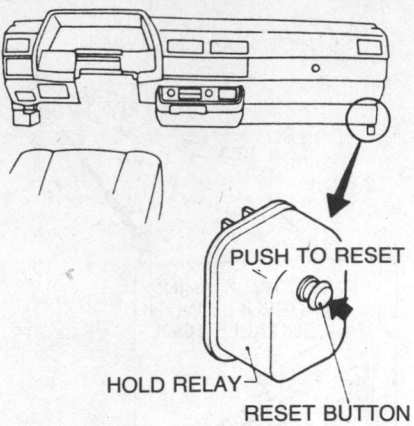

PUSH TO RESET

HOLD RELAY

RESET BUTTON

Resetting the oxygen sensor warning lamp—1985-86 Pulsar/Sentra (U.S. models)

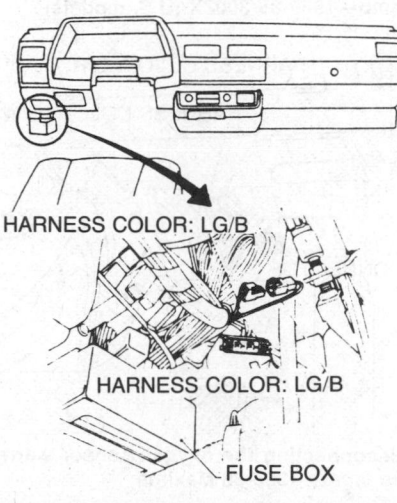

HARNESS COLOR: LG/B

HARNESS COLOR: LG/B

FUSE BOX

Disconnecting the oxygen sensor warning lamp—1985-86 Pulsar/Sentra (all models)

HOLD RELAY

PUSH TO RESET

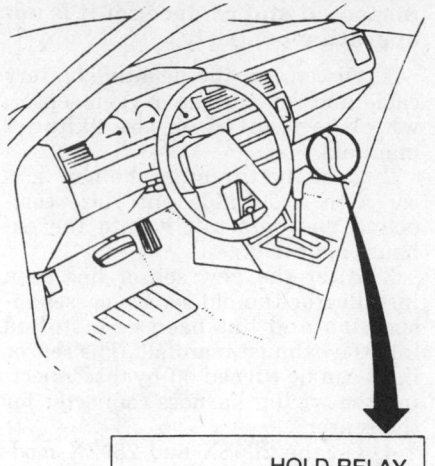

HOLD RELAY

RESET BUTTON

PUSH TO RESET

Resetting the oxygen sensor warning lamp—1985-88 Maxima

HOLD RELAY FOR EXHAUST GAS SENSOR WARNING LAMP

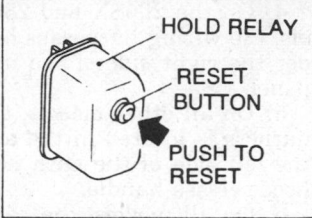

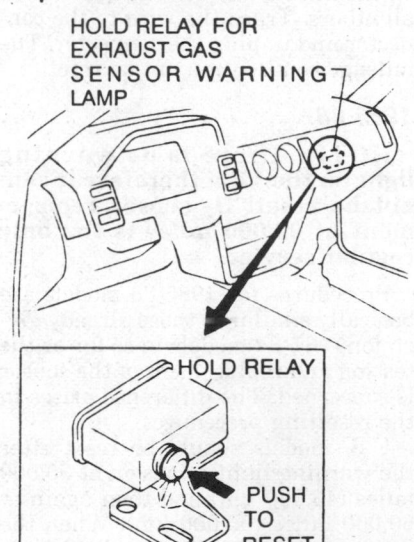

HOLD RELAY

PUSH TO RESET

Resetting the oxygen sensor warning lamp—1987-88 300ZX (U.S. models)

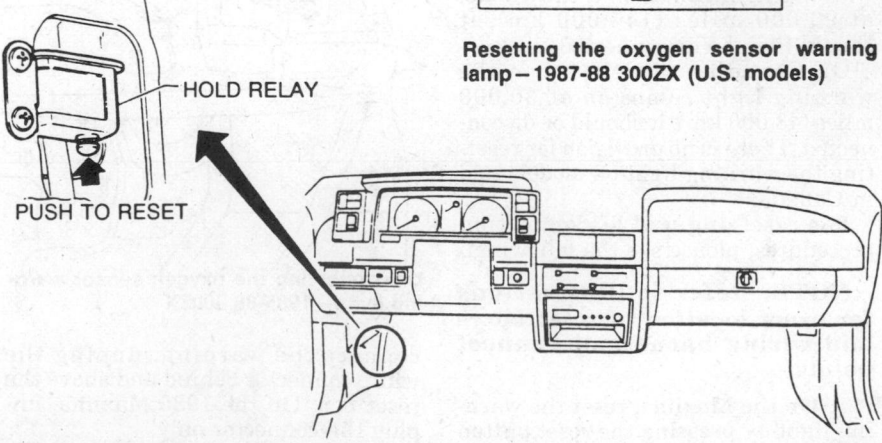

Disconnecting the oxygen sensor warning lamp—1987-88 Pulsar/Sentra (all models)

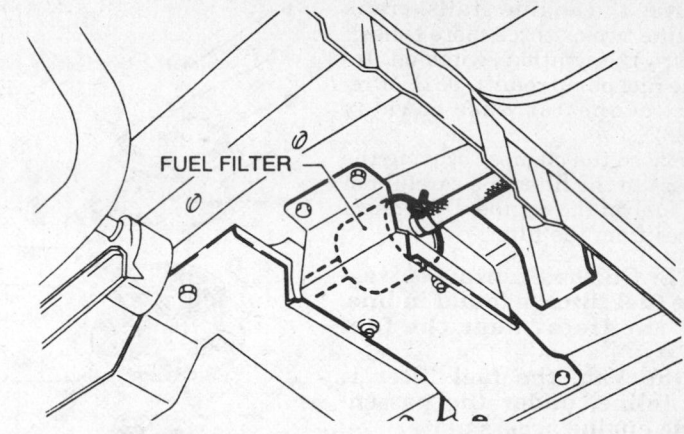

HARNESS COLOR:
● W [30,000 miles (48,000 km)]
● W/L [60,000 miles (96,000 km)]
● W/R [90,000 miles (144,000 km)]

RIGHT DOOR

Switch off the warning lamp after each inspection — 1987-88 300ZX w/analog meter

The fuel filter is found under the floor on Stanza wagons (4wd)

for resetting. To disconnect the warning light, unplug the white connector behind the main fuse box.

5. On the Pulsar and Sentra, the reset box is located behind the right side kick panel; 1987-88 Pulsar—left side kick panel. It is actuated by means of a push button. Warning light disconnection may be accomplished by unplugging the white connector behind the slightly above the main fuse box.

GASOLINE ENGINE FUEL SYSTEM

Fuel Filter

REMOVAL & INSTALLATION

All Carburetor Models

1. Locate fuel filter on right-side of the engine compartment.
2. Disconnect the inlet and outlet hoses from the fuel filter. Make certain that the inlet hose (bottom) doesn't fall below the fuel tank level or the gasoline will drain out.
3. Pry the fuel filter from its clip and replace the assembly.
4. Replace the inlet and outlet lines; secure the hose clamps to prevent leaks.
5. Start the engine and check for leaks.

Fuel Injected Models

The fuel filter is of the same type as that used on the other fuel injected models, but the method for discharging the fuel injection system is different.

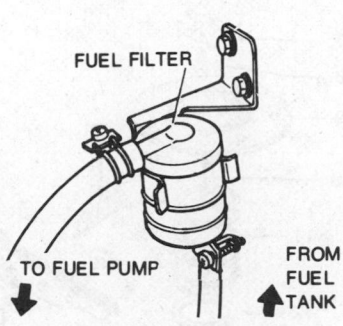

FUEL FILTER

TO FUEL PUMP   FROM FUEL TANK

Typical fuel filters - all models

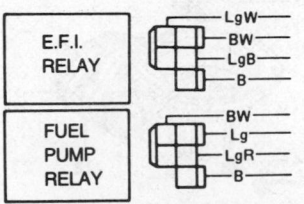

E.F.I. RELAY — LgW, BW, LgB, B
FUEL PUMP RELAY — BW, Lg, LgR, B

Both of the above relays are green, but can be distinguished by the color of harness.

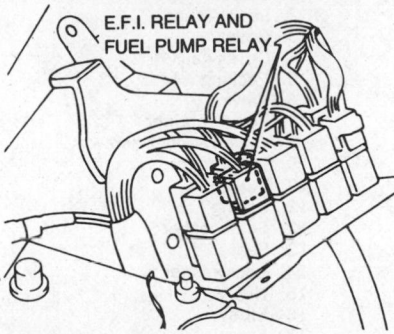

E.F.I. RELAY AND FUEL PUMP RELAY

810/Maxima (1981-84) fuel pump relay is located in the engine compartment near the battery

1. Start the engine.
2. On 1981 models remove the fuel pump relay (#2 in the diagram) from the relay connector while the engine is running. The relay is located on the right front fender in the engine com-

The fuel pump harness connector is in the tool box on the rear right side — 1984-86 200SX

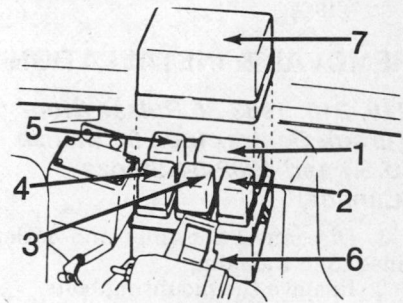

1. Fuel pump relay #2
2. Lighting relay
3. Bulb check relay
4. Air conditioning relay
5. Inhibitor relay
6. Relay box
7. Relay cover

Location of fuel pump relay #2 — 1981

partment, just aft of the windshield washer reservoir. On 1982-88 models except those noted below, disconnect the fuel pump electrical connector while the engine is running. This is usually found in-line, near the pump.

On the 1987-88 Pulsar/Sentra, 1987-88 Stanza sedans, 1986½-88 200SX, 1986-88 Maxima, Van and 300ZX, remove the fuel pump fuse. On the 1986-88 Stanza wagons, pull out the fuel pump relay (first one on left, above fuse box).

3. After the engine stalls, crank the engine two or three more times.

4. Turn the ignition switch off. Install the fuel pump relay (1981), or reconnect connector, fuse or relay (1982-88).

5. Release the clamps securing the fuel hoses to the filter. Be careful not to spill fuel on the engine. Disconnect the hoses from the filter.

NOTE: On the Stanza 4x4 wagon, the fuel filter is found in-line, under the floor, near the fuel pump.
On the Van, the fuel filter is found inline, under the passenger-side engine access plate.

6. Remove the bolt securing the filter to the bracket; remove the filter.

7. Install the new filter. Connect the fuel hoses and secure them with new clamps.

8. Start the engine and check for leaks.

Mechanical Fuel Pump

The mechanical fuel pump is driven from the camshaft on all engines. It is mounted on the side of the engine on OHV engines and on the side of the cylinder head or block on OHC engines. The pump is on the right side of all engines.

REMOVAL & INSTALLATION

210, 310, 1983-86 Pulsar (Non-Turbo), Sentra, 1982-83 Stanza (U.S.) and 1982-84 Stanza (Canada)

1. Disconnect the inlet and outlet lines from the pump.

2. Remove the mounting bolts.

3. Remove the pump and discard the gasket.

4. Lubricate the pump rocker arm, rocker arm pin, and lever pin before reinstallation.

5. Bolt the pump into position, using a new gasket.

6. Connect the fuel lines.

FUEL PUMP TESTS

Static Pressure Test

1. Disconnect the fuel line at the carburetor.

2. Attach an adapter and tee to the fuel line and connect a pressure gauge.

3. Run the engine at varying speeds. Pressure should remain constant, 3–4 psi. (2.8–3.8 psi on Pulsar/Sentra).

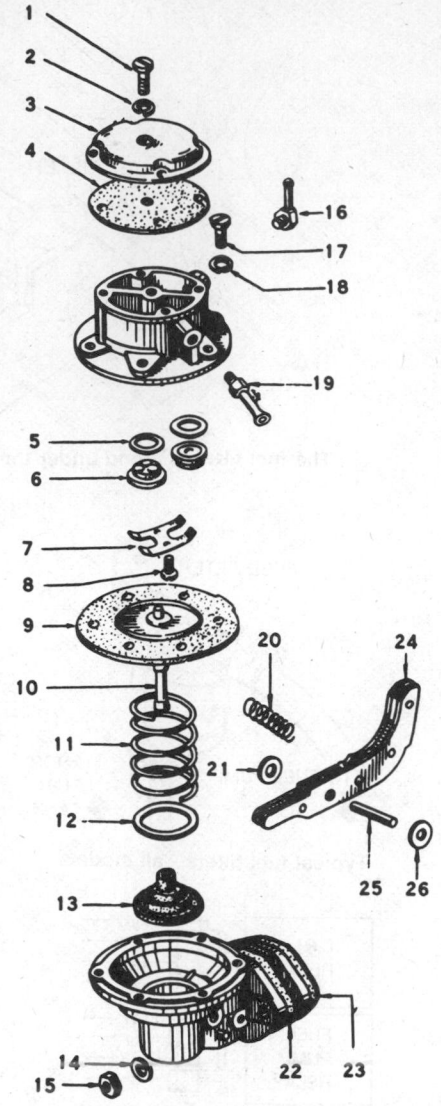

1. Screw
2. Lockwasher
3. Cover
4. Cover gasket
5. Packing
6. Valve
7. Valve retainer
8. Valve retainer screw
9. Diaphragm
10. Pull rod
11. Spring
12. Seal washer
13. Seal
14. Lockwasher
15. Nut
16. Elbow
17. Screw
18. Lockwasher
19. Connector
20. Spring
21. Rocker arm slide spacer
22. Spacer
23. Gasket
24. Rocker arm
25. Pin
26. Rocker arm slide spacer

Typical mechanical fuel pump

Electric Fuel Pump

DESCRIPTION AND LOCATION

280ZX

All 280ZX models are equipped with one electric fuel pump mounted near the fuel tank and the right rear wheel.

1981-84 810/Maxima, 200SX, 1984-85 Pulsar Turbo, 1987-88 Pulsar/Sentra, 1984-88 Stanza and Van

These models use an electric fuel pump of wet type construction. A vane pump and roller are directly coupled to a motor filled with fuel. A relief valve in the pump is designed to open when the pressure in the fuel lines rises over 64 psi. The pump is automatically activated when the ignition switch is turned on to the start position. If the engine stalls for some reason, the fuel pump is cut off even though the ignition switch remains in the on position. The fuel pump on the 810/Maxima is located near the fuel tank; the 1980-83 200SX is located near the center of the vehicle; the 1984-88 200SX is located in the fuel tank; and all others can be found in or near the fuel tank.

300ZX and 1985-88 Maxima

The electric fuel pump on the 300ZX is mounted on the fuel tank on the top left side. On the Maxima it can be found under the rear seat.

PRESSURE TEST

280ZX, 300ZX and 1985-88 Maxima

1. Reduce the fuel pressure to zero. For 1981-88 models, follow Step 1 of the 1981 fuel pump replacement procedure.

2. Connect a fuel pressure gauge into the fuel line in the engine compartments between the fuel pipe and the fuel filter outlet hose.

3. Start the engine and read the fuel pressure. It should be approximately 30 psi ($2.1 kg/cm_2$) at idle, and approximately 37 psi ($2.6 kg/cm_2$) at any speed above idle.

4. If the pressure is incorrect, replace the pressure regulator, following the replacement procedure given later in this chapter. After replacement of the regulator, repeat the pressure test. If still incorrect, check the fuel lines for kinks or blockage, and replace the pump as necessary.

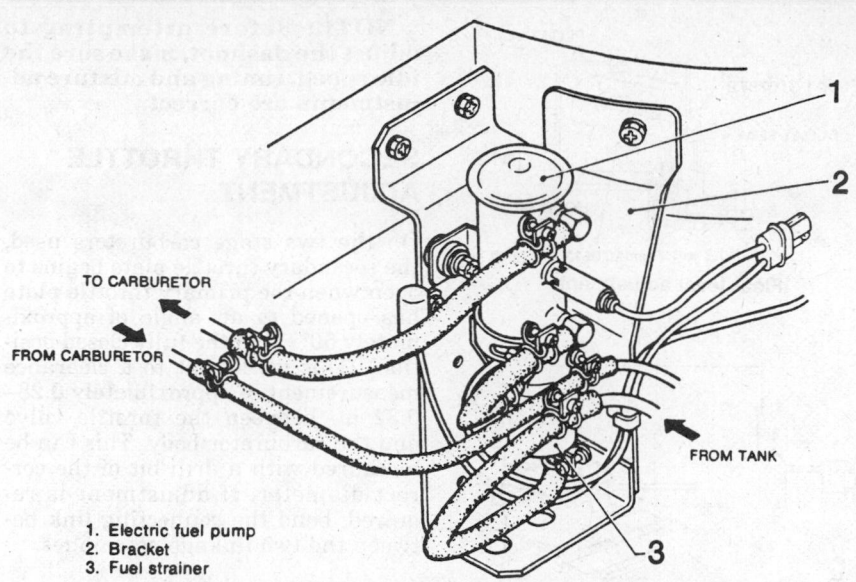

1. Electric fuel pump
2. Bracket
3. Fuel strainer

280Z electric fuel pump and strainer—typical through 1983

1981-84 810/Maxima, Pulsar/Sentra, Stanza, 200SX and Van

1. Fuel pressure must be reduced to zero.

2. Connect a fuel pressure gauge between the fuel feed pipe and the fuel filter outlet.

3. Start the engine and read the pressure. It should be 30 psi at idle, and 37 psi at the moment the accelerator pedal is fully depressed.

4. If pressure is not as specified, replace the pressure regulator and repeat the test. If the pressure is still incorrect, check for clogged or deformed fuel lines, then replace the fuel pump.

FUNCTIONAL TEST

280ZX

1. Disconnect either the wire to the alternator "L" terminal, or the oil pressure switch connector.

2. Turn the ignition key to Start. You should be able to hear the fuel pump running. If not, check the wiring circuits and fuses; if they are in order replace the fuel pump.

1981-84 810/Maxima, Pulsar/Sentra, Stanza, 200SX and Van

Fuel pressure must be reduced to zero before tests are made.

Start the engine, disconnect the harness connector of fuel pump relay-2 while the engine is running. On 1984-88 200SXs, the fuel pump connector is inside the tool box on the rear right-hand side of the car. After the engine stalls, crank it over two or three times to make sure all of the fuel pressure is released.

NOTE: If the engine will not start remove the fuel pump relay-2 harness connector and crank the engine for about 5 seconds.

REMOVAL & INSTALLATION

280ZX

1. Reduce the fuel line pressure to zero: start the engine and remove the fuel pump relay No. 2 while the engine is running. After the engine stalls, crank the engine with the starter two or tree times. Turn the ignition off.

2. Disconnect the negative battery cable.

3. Remove the luggage compartment mat. Disconnect the fuel pump harness airing at the connector at the rear of the compartment. Push the wires and the grommet through the floor.

4. Raise and support the rear of the car.

5. Clamp the hose between the fuel tank and the pump.

6. Loosen the fuel line clamps and disconnect the hoses from the pump. Have a metal container ready to catch the fuel which will spill from the lines.

7. Remove the bolts which secure the pump bracket to the body and remove the pump.

8. Installation is the reverse.

300ZX and 1985-88 Maxima

NOTE: Before disconnecting the fuel line, the fuel pressure must be released from the fuel line. Start the engine and then refer to the fuel filter removal procedure.

1. Remove the fuel tank as described later in this section.

2. Remove the retaining bolt and remove the fuel pump.

3. Installation is the reverse of removal. Run the engine and check for leaks.

1981-84 810/Maxima, 200SX, Pulsar, Stanza and Van

1. Relieve the pressure from the fuel system (refer to "Fuel Filter") and disconnect the electrical harness connector at the pump.

2. On the 1984-88 200SX, open the trunk, remove the mat and flip up the fuel pump access plate in the trunk floor.

On the Van, lift up the carpet under the rear-most seat and unscrew the fuel pump inspection cover.

3. On models not located in the fuel

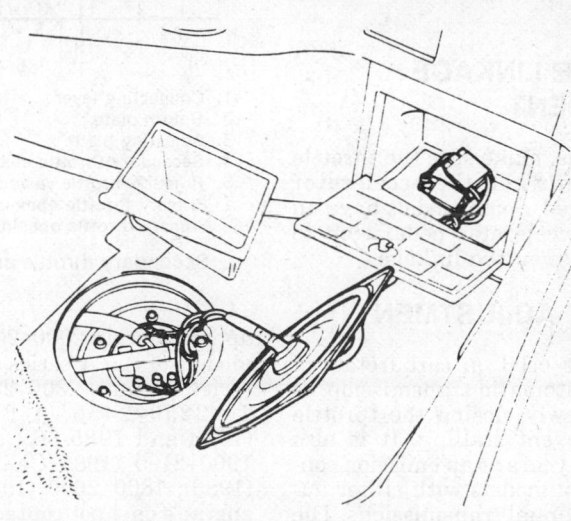

Fuel pump access plate—1987 200SX shown

tank, clamp the hose between the fuel tank and the fuel pump to prevent gas from spilling out of the tank.

4. Remove the inlet and outlet tubes at the fuel pump. Unclamp the inlet hose and allow the fuel lines to drain into a suitable container.

5. Unbolt and remove the pump and on models equipped with fuel dampers, remove the dampers at the same time as the pump.'

6. Installation is the reverse order of removal procedure. Be sure to use new clamps and that all hoses are properly seated on the fuel pump body.

Carburetor

REMOVAL & INSTALLATION

1. Remove the air cleaner.
2. Disconnect the fuel and vacuum lines from the carburetor.
3. Remove the throttle lever.
4. Remove the four nuts and washers retaining the carburetor to the manifold.
5. Lift the carburetor from the manifold.
6. Remove and discard the gasket used between the carburetor and the manifold.
7. Install the carburetor in the reverse order of removal, using a new carburetor base gasket.

FUEL LEVEL ADJUSTMENT

All Nihonkikaki (Nikki) and Hitachi carburetors have a glass float chamber side cover marked with a fuel level line (some have a small window in the side of the float chamber). Fuel level is adjusted by bending the float seat tab with the float cover removed and inverted, and the float fully raised.

THROTTLE LINKAGE ADJUSTMENT

On all models, make sure the throttle is wide open when the accelerator pedal is floored. Some models have an adjustable accelerator pedal stop to prevent strain on the linkage.

DASHPOT ADJUSTMENT

A dashpot is used on carburetors of cars with automatic transmission as means of slowly closing the throttle valve to prevent stalling. It is also used in later years as an emission control device on models with either automatic or manual transmissions. The dashpot should be adjusted to contact the throttle lever on deceleration at

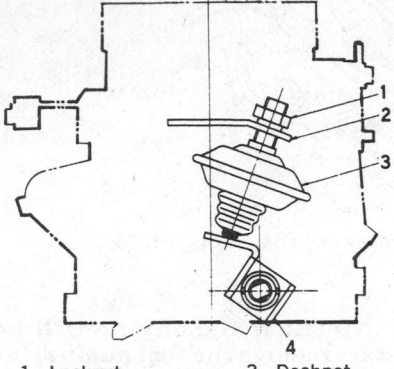

1.3 to 1.7 mm (0.0512 to 0.0669 in)

Float level adjustment

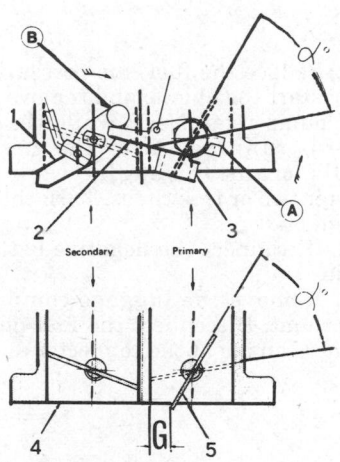

1. Locknut	3. Dashpot
2. Mounting arm	4. Throttle lever

Typical dashpot

1. Connecting lever
2. Return plate
3. Adjusting plate
4. Secondary throttle chamber
5. Primary throttle valve
a. Primary throttle opening in degrees
G. Primary throttle opening in inches

Secondary throttle adjustment

approximately 2000–2300 rpm for all models of the A series engine. For E-series engines: 2300–2500 (1983); M/T – 2250–2450, A/T – 1900–2100 (1984 and 1985-86 Canada); A/T – 1900–2100 (1985 Calif.); 1600–2400 (1986); 1800–2600 (1987). The Z20S engine's dashpot contact point should be between 1400–1600 rpm for automatic transmissions.

NOTE: Before attempting to adjust the dashpot, make sure the idle speed, timing and mixture adjustments are correct.

SECONDARY THROTTLE ADJUSTMENT

On the two stage carburetors used, the secondary throttle plate begins to open when the primary throttle plate has opened to an angle of approximately 50° (from the fully closed position). This works out to a clearance measurement of approximately 0.28-0.32 in. between the throttle valve and the carburetor body. This can be measured with a drill bit of the correct diameter. If adjustment is required, bend the connecting link between the two linkage assemblies.

AUTOMATIC CHOKE ADJUSTMENT

1. With the engine cold, make sure the choke is fully closed (press the gas pedal all the way to the floor and release).

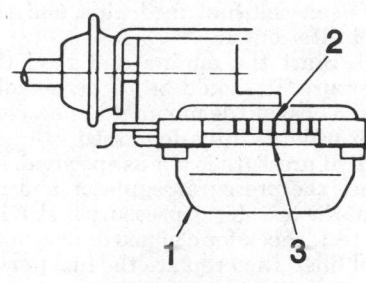

1. Thermostat cover
2. Thermostat housing
3. Groove

Choke index setting

2. Check the choke linkage for binding. The choke plate should be easily opened and closed with your finger. If the choke sticks or binds, it can usually be freed with a liberal application of a carburetor cleaner made for the purpose. A couple of quick squirts of the right stuff normally does the trick.

If not, the carburetor will have to be disassembled for repairs.

3. The choke is correctly adjusted when the index mark on the choke housing (notch) aligns with the center mark on the carburetor body. If the setting is incorrect, loosen the three screws clamping the choke body in place and rotate the choke cover left or right until the marks align. Tighten the screws carefully to avoid cracking the housing.

CHOKE UNLOADER ADJUSTMENT

1. Close the choke valve completely.

2. Hold the choke valve by stretching a rubber band between the choke shaft lever and the carburetor.

3. Pull the throttle lever until it completely opens.

4. Adjust the gap between the choke plate and the carburetor body to:

A-Series engines:
1980: 0.0929 in. except:
Non-Cal. 5 speed hatchback 210, and Canada manual trans. A12A: 0.0854 in.

E-series engines:
1982-84: 0.0929 in. (E15)
1983-85: 0.1165 in. (E16)

CA-series engines:
1982-85: 0.0965 in.

FAST IDLE ADJUSTMENT

1. With the carburetor removed from the vehicle, place the upper side of the fast idle screw on the second step (first step for 1981 Z-Series engines) of the fast idle cam and measure the clearance between the throttle valve and the wall of the throttle valve chamber at the center of the throttle valve. Check it against the following specifications:

1981-82 210, A12A engine:
0.0248–0.0315 in. M/T
A14 engine:
0.0283–0.0350 in. M/T
A15 engine:
0.0386–0.0461 in. A/T
1981 510:
0.0299–0.0354 in. M/T
0.0378–0.0433 in. M/T
1981 310:
0.0287–0.0343 in.
1982 310:
0.0287–0.0343 in. M/T
0.0393–0.0449 in. A/T
1982 Stanza:
0.0260–0.0315 in.
1983-85 Stanza:
0.0260–0.0315 M/T
0.0319–0.0374 A/T
1982-83 Sentra (E15):
0.0315–0.0343 in. M/T
0.0421–0.0449 in. A/T
1983-84 Sentra, Pulsar (E16):
USA:
0.0311–0.0367 in. M/T
0.0425–0.0481 in. A/T
Canada:
0.0255–0.0311 in. M/T
0.0366–0.0422 in. A/T
1984-85 Sentra, Pulsar (E16):
USA:
0.0339–0.0378 in. M/T
0.0453–0.0492 in. A/T

Canada:
0.0283–0.0433 in. A/T
0.0394–0.0433 in. A/T
1986-87 Pulsar/Sentra:
Calif.:
0.0268–0.0039 in. M/T
0.0378–0.0039 in. A/T
Canada:
0.0268–0.0039 in. M/T
0.0378–0.0039 in. A/T
"M/T" means manual transmission.
"A/T" means automatic transmission.

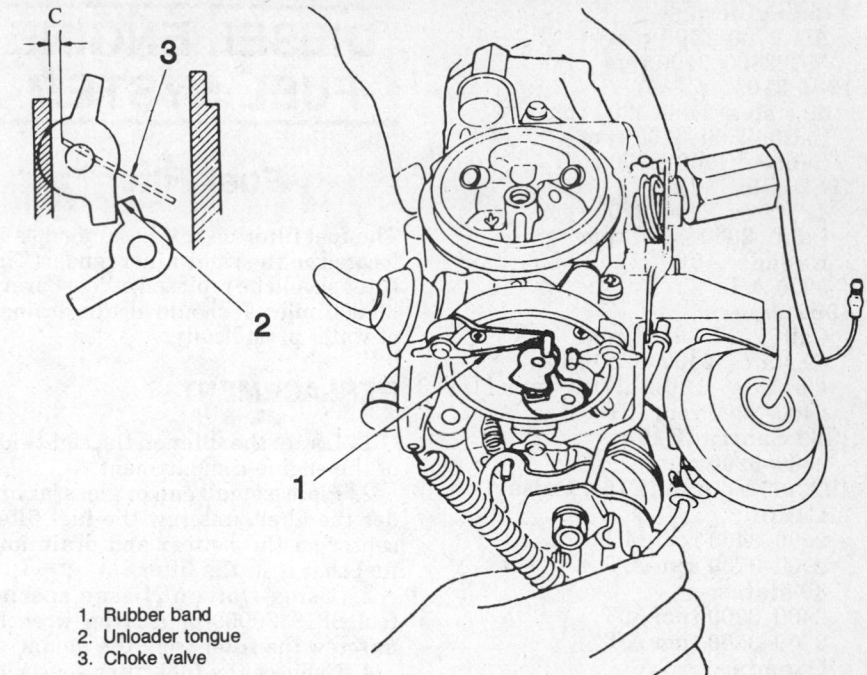

1. Rubber band
2. Unloader tongue
3. Choke valve

Typical choke unloader adjustment

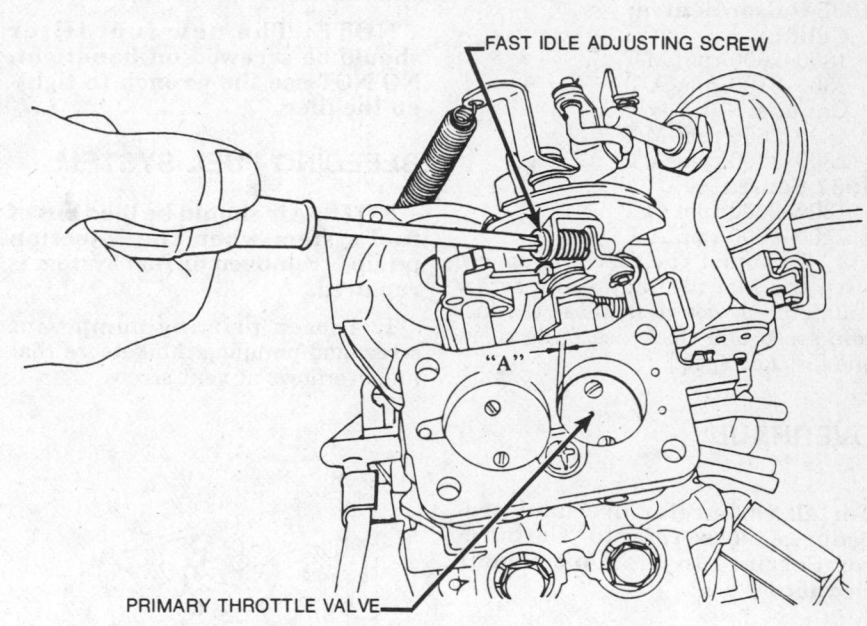

FAST IDLE ADJUSTING SCREW

"A"

PRIMARY THROTTLE VALVE

Fast idle adjustment—E-series engines

NOTE: The first step of the fast idle adjustment procedure is not absolutely necessary.

2. Install the carburetor on the engine.

3. Start the engine and measure the fast idle rpm with the engine at operating temperature. The cam should be at the 2nd step.

210, A12A, A14 engines:
49 states: M/T 2400 and 3200 rpm
California: M/T 2300–3100 rpm

A15 engines:
  A/T 2700–3500 rpm
  M/T 2300–3100 rpm
1981 310:
  49 states: 2400–3200 rpm
  Calif.: 2300–3100 rpm
  Canada: 1900–2700 rpm
1982 310:
  49 states: 2400–3200 rpm
  Calif.: 2300–3100 rpm
  Canada: 1900–2700 M/T; 2400–3200 A/T
1982 Sentra:
  Calif.: 2300–3100 rpm
  49 states: 2400–3200 rpm
  Canada: 1900–2700 rpm M/T; 2400–3200 rpm A/T
1983 Sentra (E15):
  2400–3200 rpm
1983-85 Sentra (E16), Pulsar:
  Calif.:
  2600–3400 rpm M/T
  2900–3700 rpm A/T
  49 states:
  2400–3200 rpm M/T
  2700–3500 rpm A/T
  Canada:
  1900–2700 rpm M/T
  2400–3200 rpm A/T
1986 Pulsar/Sentra:
  Calif.:
  1800–2600 rpm M/T
  2300–3100 rpm A/T
  Canada:
  1800–2600 rpm M/T
  2300–3100 rpm A/T
1987 Sentra
  1800–2600 rpm M/T
  2100–2900 rpm A/T
4. To adjust the fast idle speed, turn the fast idle adjusting screw counterclockwise to increase the fast idle speed and clockwise to decrease the fast idle speed.

OVERHAUL

For all carburetor overhaul procedures, please refer to "Carburetor Service" in the Unit Repair Section.

Fuel Injection

Due to the complex nature of modern fuel injection systems, comprehensive diagnosis and testing procedures fall outside the confines of this repair manual. For complete information on fuel injection diagnosis, testing and repair procedures (other than found below) please refer to *Chilton's Guide to Fuel Injection And Feedback Carburetors.*

DIESEL ENGINE FUEL SYSTEM

Fuel Filter

The fuel filter on all diesel models is located on the right inner fender. The filter should be replaced at least every 30,000 miles. It should also be drained of water periodically.

REPLACEMENT

1. Locate the filter on the right side of the engine compartment.
2. Place a small pan or glass jar under the filter, unscrew the fuel filter sensor on the bottom and drain any fuel that is in the filter.
3. Using Datsun/Nissan special tool SP19320000 or a strap wrench, unscrew the filter from the mount.
4. Connect the fuel filter sensor to the new filter and then install the new filter.

NOTE: The new fuel filter should be screwed on handtight. NO NOT use the wrench to tighten the filer.

BLEEDING FUEL SYSTEM

NOTE: Air should be bled out of fuel system when the injection pump is removed or fuel system is repaired.

1. Loosen priming pump vent screw and pumping. Make sure that fuel overflows at vent screw.

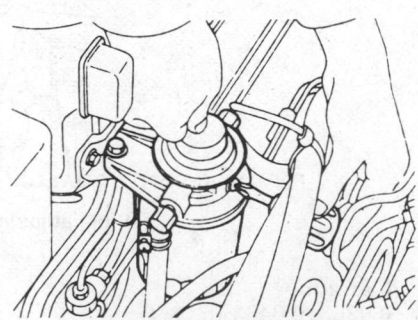

Bleeding the fuel system

2. Tighten vent screw.
3. Disconnect fuel return hose and install suitable hose at overflow connector. Place a container beneath hose end.
4. Prime priming pump to make sure that fuel overflows at hose end.
5. Remove suitable hose and install fuel return hose.

DRAINING WATER FROM FUEL SYSTEM

1. Set a container or rag under fuel filter.
2. Remove fuel filter sensor and drain water.

NOTE: Pumping priming pump will quicken water draining.

3. When fuel overflows, install fuel filter sensor.
4. Bleed fuel system

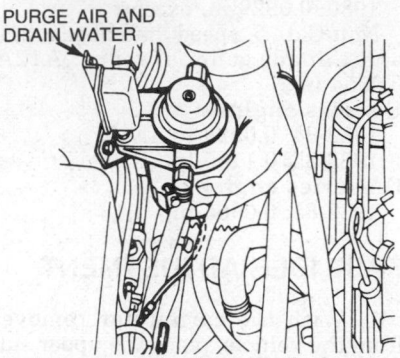

Draining the water from the fuel system

Diesel Injection Pump

For further information on diesel injection systems, please refer to "Diesel Service" in the Unit Repair Section.

NOTE: The diesel injection pump is located at the right front side of the engine. In case of pump failure or damage, the pump must be replaced as an assembly, except for certain simple parts on the outside of the pump.

REMOVAL & INSTALLATION

LD28 Six Cylinder

1. Disconnect the negative battery cable.
2. Remove the air cleaner duct. Remove the engine under cover.
3. Drain the engine coolant and then remove the radiator and its shroud.
4. Loosen the fan pulley nuts and then remove the drive belts (air conditioning, alternator and power steering pump).
5. Disconnect the power steering oil pump and position it out of the way.
6. Tag and disconnect the accelerator wire, the overflow hose (on the spill tube side), the fuel cut solenoid connector and the fuel return hose.
7. Tag and disconnect the potenti-

ometer, the injection timing control solenoid valve wire, the cold start device water hoses (at the 4-way connector side) and the vacuum modulator (A/T models only).

8. Remove the crank damper pulley. Use a plastic mallet and tap lightly around the sides, if this does not loosen the pulley you will need a two-armed gear puller.

9. Remove the pulley bracket and the idler pulley (if so equipped) and then remove the front dust cover.

10. Loosen the spring set pin, set the tensioner pulley to the "free tension" position and then tighten them.

11. Slide the injection pump drive belt off its pulleys.

12. Loosen the retaining nut and remove the injection pump drive gear. You may need a two-armed gear puller.

13. Disconnect the injection tubes at the injection nozzle side.

14. Unscrew the injection pump fixing nuts and the bracket bolt.

15. Remove the injection pump assembly with the injection tubes attached.

NOTE: If you plan to measure plunger lift, remove the injection tubes before removing the pump.

Installation is in the reverse order of removal. Observe the following:

1. Set the No. 1 cylinder at TDC of the compression stroke. Make sure that the grooves in the rear plate and the flywheel align and that the No. 1 cam lobe on the camshaft is in the position shown.

2. Install the injection pump and temporarily tighten the mounting bolts.

3. Use the alignment marks as shown in the illustration and install the injection pump drive gear. Tighten the nut to 43–51 ft. lbs. (59–69 Nm).

NOTE: The injection pump drive shaft is tapered. If the drive gear is difficult to install, use a plastic mallet and drive it into place.

4. Make sure that the tensioner pulley is still in the free position and slide the injection pump drive belt over the pulley.

5. The drive belt should have two timing marks on it. Align one with the mark on the crank pulley and the other with the mark on the drive gear. If the timing marks on the drive belt are not clear enough to read, set the marks on the drive gear and the crank pulley so that there are 20 cogs of the drive belt between them when it is installed.

6. Loosen the spring set pin and the

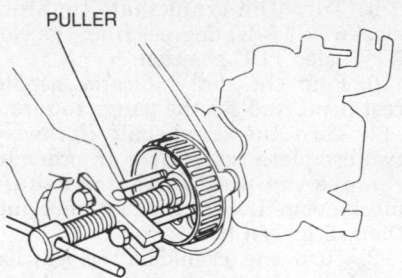

Removing injection pump pulley using puller

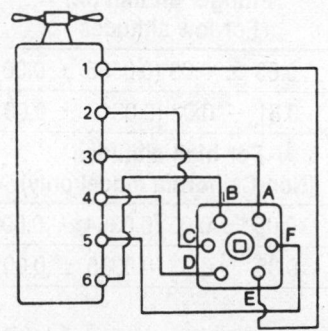

Injection tube routing—LD28 engines

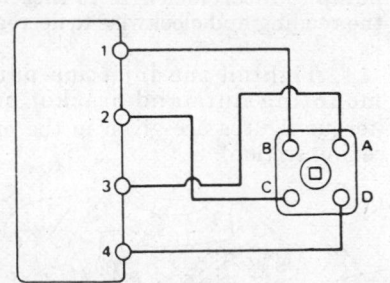

Injection tube routing—CD17 diesel engines

tensioner so that the belt is automatically set to the "tension" position.

7. Adjust the injection timing as detailed later in this section.

8. Tighten the injection pump nuts to 12–15 ft. lbs. (16–21 Nm) and the bracket bolt to 22–26 ft. lbs. (30–35 Nm).

9. Reconnect the injection tubes. Connect them to the cylinders in this order: 4, 2, 6, 1, 5, 3.

10. Bleed the air from the fuel system as detailed later in this section.

CD17 Four Cylinder

1. Disconnect the negative battery cable.

2. Drain the radiator coolant. Remove the air cleaner assembly.

3. Tag and disconnect all wires and hoses attached to the injection pump.

4. Remove the injection timing belt by first setting the No. 1 cylinder at TDC on its compression stroke.

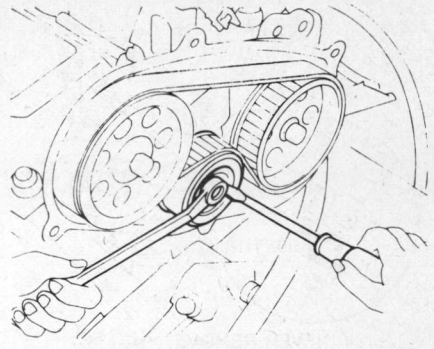

Move the belt tensioner to the free position—CD17 diesel engines

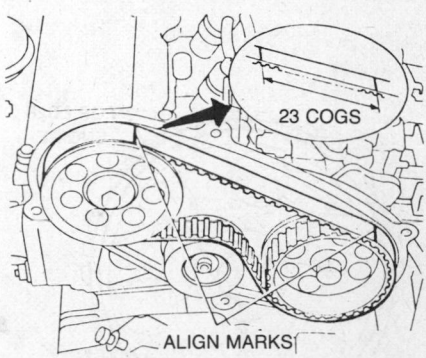

Mark the timing belt before removal—CD17 diesel engines

Matchmark the timing belt to both pulleys using paint or a crayon for later installation. Set the belt tensioner to the "free" position and remove the timing belt.

5. Loosen the nut and remove the injection pump pulley. Remove all injection tubes. Remove the injection pump fixing nuts and bracket bolt, and remove the injection pump.

6. To install the pump, reverse the removal procedure. Make sure the No. 1 cylinder is at TDC on its compression stroke. Install the pump and temporarily tighten the bolts. Torque the pump pulley nut to 43–51 ft. lbs. Install the belt by aligning the match marks on the belt and pulleys. Loosen the tensioner and turn the crankshaft two times in its normal direction of rotation. Tighten the tensioner while holding it.

7. Set the injection timing, and tighten the pump securely. Connect the injection tubes in the order shown. Bleed the injection pump as explained below.

INJECTION PUMP TIMING

LD28 Six Cylinder

1. Remove the under cover and drain the coolant.

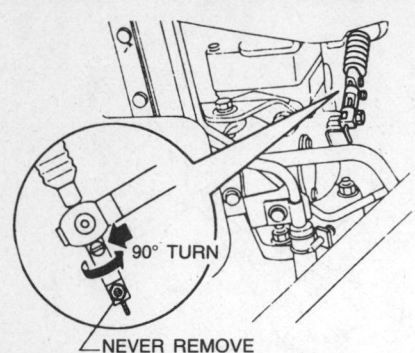

Setting the fork screw on the cold start device—LD28 diesel engines

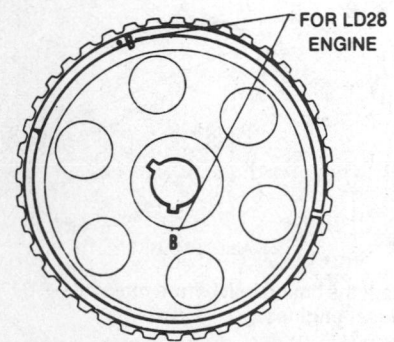

Injection pump drive gear alignment marks—LD28 diesel engines

2. Remove the coolant hoses that are connected to the coldstart device.

3. Remove the power steering pump.

4. Set the No. 1 cylinder at TDC of its compression stroke. Make sure that the grooves in the rear plate and the drive plate are aligned with each other. Make sure that the No. 1 camshaft lobe is in the position shown in the illustration.

5. Using two wrenches, remove the fuel injection tubes.

6. Loosen the fork retaining screw on the cold start device. Turn the fork 90° and then set the cold start device in the free position.

— CAUTION —

Never remove the screw on the cold start device wire. If it should be removed accidentally, the pump assembly should be readjusted at a service shop specified by the manufacturer.

7. Remove the plug bolt from the rear side of the injection pump and, in its place, attach a dial indicator.

8. Loosen the injection pump mounting nuts and bracket bolt.

9. Turn the crankshaft counterclockwise 15–20 degrees from the No. 1 cylinder TDC position.

10. Find the dial indicator needle rest point and set the gauge to zero.

11. Turn the crankshaft clockwise two complete revolutions in order to remove the play in the camshaft mechanism. Loosen the tensioner and then retighten it.

12. Turn the crankshaft clockwise until the No. 1 cylinder is again at TDC and then read the dial indicator.

Plunger lift mm (in) For low altitudes	
M/T	0.85 ± 0.03 (0.0335 ± 0.0012)
A/T	0.81 − 0.03 (0.0319 ± 0.0012)
For high altitudes (Non-California model only)	
M/T	0.09 ± 0.03 (0.0354 ± 0.0012)
A/T	0.85 ± 0.03 (0.0335 ± 0.0012)

13. If the dial indicator is not within the above range, turn the injection pump counterclockwise to increase the reading and clockwise to decrease it.

14. Tighten the injection pump mounting nuts and bracket bolt (torque figures are given in the preceding section).

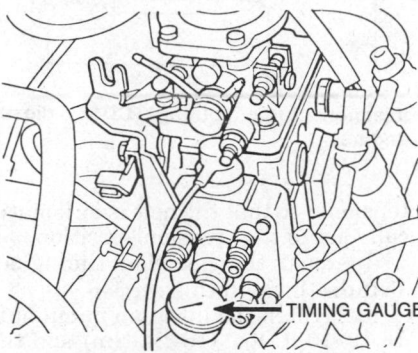

Timing gauge installed in injection pump

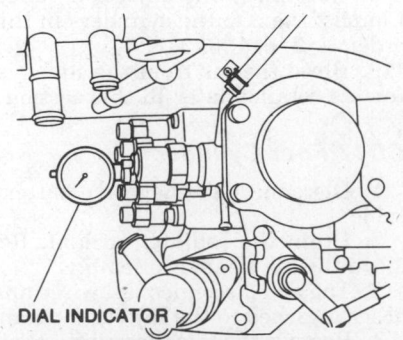

Remove the plug bolt and attach a dial indicator—diesel engines

Position a block between the cold start device and the linkage—CD17 diesel engines

15. Remove the dial indicator and reinstall the plug bolt with a new washer. Tighten the plug bolt to 10–14 ft. lbs. (14–20 Nm).

16. Set the fork at the cold start device in its original position by pulling on the cold start device wire and then tighten the fork screw.

17. Connect the injection tubes as detailed in the preceding section.

18. Install the power steering pump, connect the cold start device water hoses, refill the pump with coolant and replace the under cover.

CD17 Four Cylinder

1. Set the No. 1 cylinder to TDC on its compression stroke. Make sure the timing indicator and crank damper pulley marks are aligned with each other.

2. Tag and remove the fuel injection lines.

3. Turn the cold start device linkage clockwise and set a 0.59 in. block between the cold start device and the linkage.

4. Remove the plug bolt from the fuel injection pump and insert a dial gauge.

5. Turn the crankshaft clockwise 15–20 degrees from TDC. Find the dial gauge needle rest point, then zero the dial gauge.

6. Turn the crankshaft clockwise until the No. 1 cylinder is again at TDC and read the gauge measurement.

Plunger lift for low altitudes	
M/T	0.94 ± 0.03 mm (0.0370 ± 0.0012 in.)
A/T	0.88 ± 0.03 mm (0.0346 ± 0.0012 in.)
Plunger lift for high altitudes	
M/T	1.00 ± 0.03 mm (0.0394 ± 0.0012 in.)
A/T	0.94 ± 0.03 mm (0.0370 ± 0.0012 in.)

7. If the dial gauge does not read within the proper range, turn the injection pump body until it is within specifications.

8. Install the plug bolt and tighten it to 10–14 ft. lbs. (14–20 Nm). Tight-

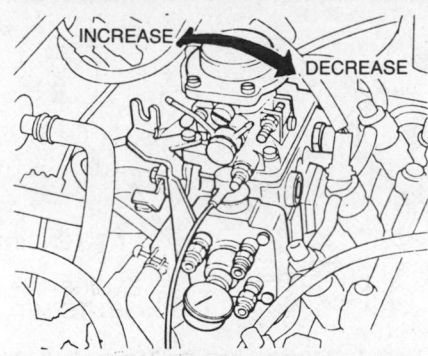

Move the injection pump to adjust the plunger lift—CD17 diesel engines

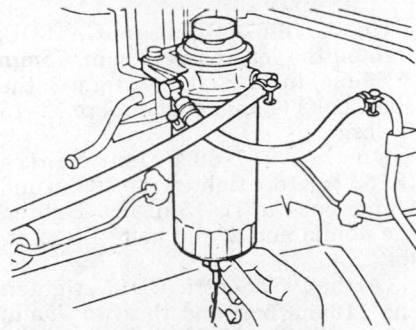

Drain the fuel filter here

en the injection pump nut to 9–13 ft. lbs. (13–18 Nm) and the pump-to-bracket bolt to 36–43 ft. lbs. (49–59 Nm).

9. Connect the injection tubes and tighten the flare nuts to 16–18 ft. lbs. (22–25 Nm).

10. Bleed the system.

BLEED THE FUEL SYSTEM

NOTE: Air should be bled from the fuel system whenever the injection pump is removed or the fuel system is repaired.

1. Loosen the priming pump vent screw and pump a few times. Make sure that the fuel overflows at the vent screw.

2. Tighten the vent screw.

3. Disconnect the fuel return hose and install a suitable hose over the overflow connector. Place a small pan under the over flow hose.

4. Prime the priming pump to make sure that the fuel overflows at the open end of the hose.

5. Remove the pan and the overflow hose and then install the return hose.

Injector/Injection Nozzle

REMOVAL & INSTALLATION

1. Remove the injection tubes at

the injector and then remove the spill tube assembly.

CAUTION

To prevent the spill tube from breaking, remove it by grabbing the nozzle holder,

2. Unscrew the two mounting bolts and pull out the injectors and their washers.

3. Installation is in the reverse order of removal. Tighten the injector mounting nuts to 12–15 ft. lbs. (16–21 Nm). Tighten the injection tube-to-injector nut to 16–18 ft. lbs. (22–25 Nm). Always use a new injector small washer.

MANUAL TRANSMISSION/ TRANSAXLE

REMOVAL & INSTALLATION

The transmission may be removed separately from under the vehicle. Transmission removal and replacement procedure for most models is generally similar.

Rear Wheel Drive

1. Raise and support the vehicle. Disconnect the battery. Disconnect the back-up light switch on all models and neutral switch, if equipped.

2. On the Z and ZX, remove the exhaust system. On models with the A14, Z20, Z22 and Z24i engine, disconnect the exhaust pipe from the manifold. On the 280ZX, 810/Maxima and the 200SX, disconnect the accelerator linkage. Remove the heat shield plate on the 280ZX.

3. Unbolt the driveshaft at the rear and remove. If there is a center bearing, unbolt it from the crossmember. Seal the end of the transmission extension housing to prevent leakage.

4. Disconnect the speedometer drive cable from the transmission.

5. Remove the shift lever.

NOTE: On the 300ZX, the shifter boot must not be removed from the shift lever.

6. Remove the clutch operating cylinder from the clutch housing.

7. Support the engine with a large wood block and a jack under the oil pan.

8. Unbolt the transmission from the crossmember. Support the transmission with a jack and remove the crossmember.

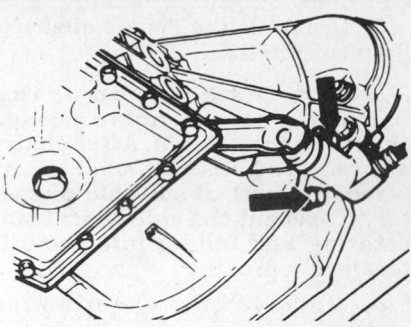

Removing the clutch slave cylinder

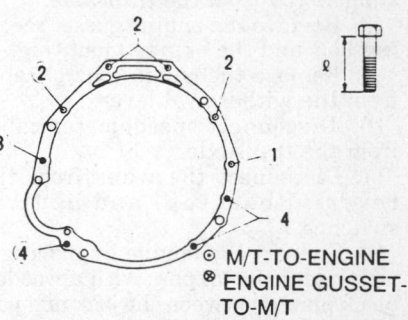

On the 300ZX and 200SX (V6), bolts 1 & 2 are long; bolts 3 & 4 are short

9. Lower the rear of the engine to allow clearance.

10. Remove the starter.

11. Unbolt the transmission. Lower and remove it to the rear.

NOTE: Tagging the transmission-to-engine bolts upon removal will facilitate proper tightening during installation.

12. Reverse the procedure for reintallation. Check the clutch linkage adjustment. On the 200SX (V6), Van and 300ZX, tighten the long mounting bolts (65mm & 60mm) to 29–36 ft. lbs. (39–49 Nm). Tighten the short bolts (55mm & 25mm; 40mm on Van) to 22–29 ft. lbs. (29–39 Nm).

On the 1984-88 200SX (4 cyl.), tighten the 4 longer bolts to 29–36 ft. lbs. and the 4 shorter bolts to 22–29 ft. lbs.

Front Wheel Drive

NOTE: You must remove the engine/transmission as a unit.

1. Remove the battery and battery holding plate.

2. Jack up the front of the car and safely support with jack stands.

3. Remove the radiator reservoir tank.

4. Drain the transmission gear oil.

NOTE: Remove the transfer case on the Stanza wagon (4wd) and Sentra (4wd).

5. Draw out the drive halfshafts from the transaxle.

NOTE: When removing halfshafts, use care not to damage the lip of the oil seal. After shafts are removed, insert a steel bar or wooden dowel of suitable diameter to prevent the side gears from rotating and falling into the differential case.

6. Remove the wheel house protector.

7. Separate the control rod and support rod from the transaxle.

8. Remove the engine gusset securing bolt and the engine mounting.

9. Remove the clutch control cable from the withdrawal lever.

10. Disconnect speedometer cable from the transaxle.

11. Disconnect the wires from the reverse (back-up) and neutral switches.

12. Support the engine by placing a jack under the oil pan, with a wooden block placed between the jack and pan for protection.

13. Support the transaxle with a hydraulic floor jack.

14. Remove the engine mounting securing bolts.

15. Remove the bolts attaching the transaxle to the engine.

16. Using the hydraulic floor jack as a carrier, carefully lower the transaxle down and away from the car.

— CAUTION —

Be careful not to strike any adjacent parts or input shaft (the shaft protruding from the transaxle which fits into the clutch assembly) when removing the transaxle from the car.

Installation of the transaxle is in the reverse order of removal, but pay attention to the following points:

1. Before installing, clean the mating surfaces on the engine rear plate and clutch housing.

2. Apply a light coat of a lithium-based grease (which includes molybdenum-disulfide) to the spline parts of the clutch disc and the transaxle input shaft.

3. Remove the filler plug and fill the transaxle with 4⅞ U.S. pints (four speed) and 5¾ U.S. pints (five speed) of a quality API GL–4 rating. Fill to the level of the plug hole (refer to "Capacities" chart at the beginning of this section).

4. Apply a thread sealant to the threads of the filler plug and install the plug in the transaxle case. Tighten the bolts securing the transaxle to the engine to 12–15 ft. lbs.

On the 1987-88 Stanza sedan, tighten the long bolts (120mm, 70mm &

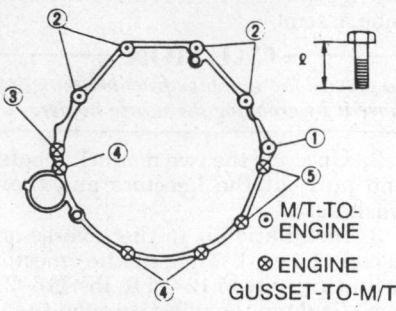

On the Maxima, bolts 1–3 are long; bolts 4 & 5 are short

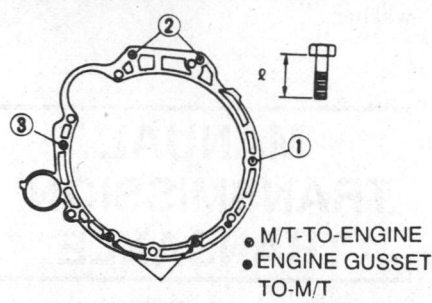

On the 1987-88 Stanza sedan, bolts 1–3 are long (#1 has a nut); bolts 4 are short

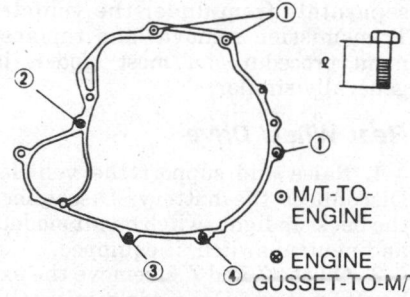

Bolt 1: 70mm, bolt 2: 40mm, bolt 3: 25mm, bolt 4: 20mm – 1987-88 Pulsar/ Sentra (E-Series engines)

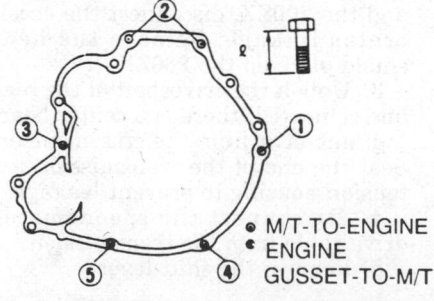

Bolts 1–3 are long, bolts 4 & 5 are short – 1987-88 Pulsar (CA16DE)

65mm) to 32–43 ft. lbs. Tighten the short bolts (25mm) to 22–30 ft. lbs.

On the Maxima, tighten the long bolts (65mm, 60mm &55mm) to 32–43 ft. lbs. Tighten the short bolts (25mm) to 22–30 ft. lbs. (#4 in the illustration) or 12–15 ft. lbs. (#5 in the illustration).

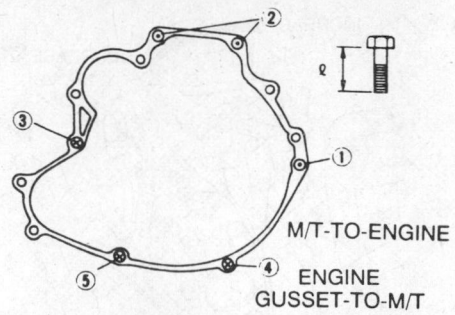

On the Maxima, bolts 1–3 are long; bolts 4 & 5 are short

Bolt 1: 110mm, bolt 2: 75mm, bolt 3: 75mm, bolt 4: 40mm, bolt 5: 25mm –1987-88 Sentra (CD17)

On the 1987-88 Pulsar (CA16DE, tighten the long bolts (90mm, 75mm & 55mm) to 22–30 ft. lbs.; tighten the short bolts (40mm & 25mm) to 12–15 ft. lbs.

On the 1987-88 Pulsar/Sentra (E16S & E16i), tighten the 70mm and 25mm bolts to 12–15 ft. lbs. Tighten the 40mm and 20mm bolts 14–22 ft. lbs.

On the 1987 Sentra (CD17), tighten the 110mm bolt and the two 75mm bolts on top to 22–30 ft. lbs.; tighten the 75mm bolt on the side to 33–40 ft. lbs. and tighten the short bolts (40mm & 25mm) to 12–16 ft. lbs.

— CAUTION —

If the clutch has been removed, it will have to be re-aligned Then connecting drive-shafts, insert O-rings between the differential side flanges and driveshafts.

Shift Linkage Adjustment

FRONT WHEEL DRIVE MODELS

310 4 and 5 Speed (1981)

Adjustment can be made by adjusting the select lever.

1. Loosen the adjusting nuts at each end of the control rod lever near the bottom of the linkage.

2. Set the shift control lever in the Neutral position.

3. Fully push the shift lever (transmission side) in the direction P1, as shown in the illustration. On the four speed transmission, pull the lever back about 8mm (0.31 in.). On the five speed, pull the shift lever back 11.5mm (0.453 in.) With the select lever held in the above position, move the shift lever in direction P2, which engages third gear on four speed transmissions and second gear on five speed transmissions.

4. Push the control rod select lever as far as it will go in direction P3,

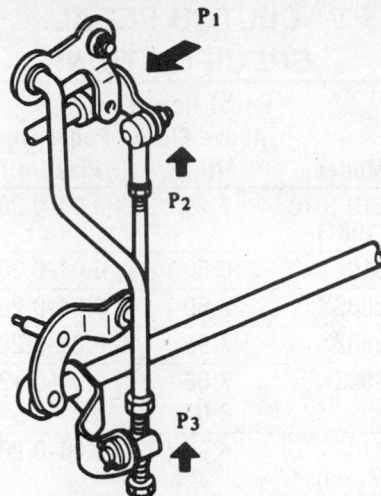

310 4 speed linkage—1981

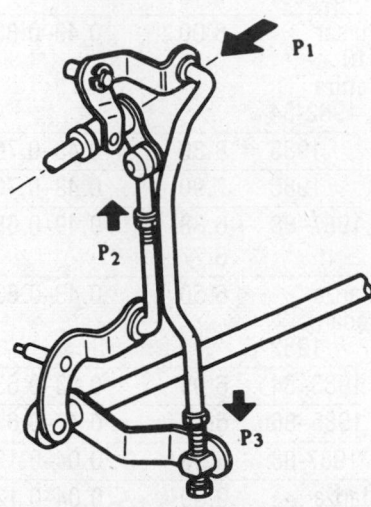

310 5 speed linkage—1981

then turn the upper adjusting nut until it touches the trunnion. Turn the nut a quarter turn more, and lock the select lever with the other adjusting nut.

5. Operate the shift control lever in the car to see if it shifts smoothly through the gears.

Sentra, Pulsar, Stanza, 310 (1982-84) and Maxima (1985-88)

No linkage adjustment is either possible or necessary.

REAR WHEEL DRIVE MODELS

Van

1. Loosen the adjuster locknut on the select cable.
2. Set the cross shaft (shift change lever) on the transmission to the third or fourth gear position.

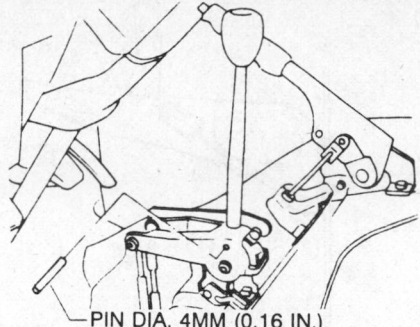

—PIN DIA. 4MM (0.16 IN.)

Shift cable adjustment on the Van

3. Adjust the length of the select cable by turning the adjuster.
4. Tighten the locknut.
5. Loosen the trunnion locknut at the end of the shift cable.
6. Disconnect the shidt cable trunnion from the cross shaft.
7. Set the cross shaft so that the transmission is in NEUTRAL.
8. Insert a 4mm (0.16 in.) pin into each adjustment hole, through the control lever and roller bearing.
9. Adjust the position of the trunnion and reinstall it on the cross shaft.
10. Tighten the trunnion locknut.

OVERHAUL

For all manual transmission/ transaxle overhaul procedures, please refer to "Manual Transmission/Transaxle Overhaul" in the Unit Repair section.

CLUTCH

All models in all years use diaphragm spring pressure plates.

Rear Wheel Drive

REMOVAL & INSTALLATION

1. Remove the transmission from the engine.
2. Insert a clutch aligning bar or similar tool all the way into the clutch disc hub. This must be done so as to support the weight of the clutch disc during removal. Mark the clutch assembly-to-flywheel relationship with paint or a center punch so that the clutch assembly can be assembled in the same position from which it is removed.
3. Loosen the bolts in sequence, a turn at a time. Remove the bolts.
4. Remove the pressure plate and clutch disc.
5. Remove the release mechanism. Apply multi-purpose grease to the bearing sleeve inside groove, the contact point of the withdrawal lever and bearing sleeve, the contact surface of the lever ball pin and lever. Replace the release mechanism.
6. Inspect the pressure plate for wear, scoring, etc., and reface or replace as necessary. Inspect the release bearing and replace as necessary. Ap-

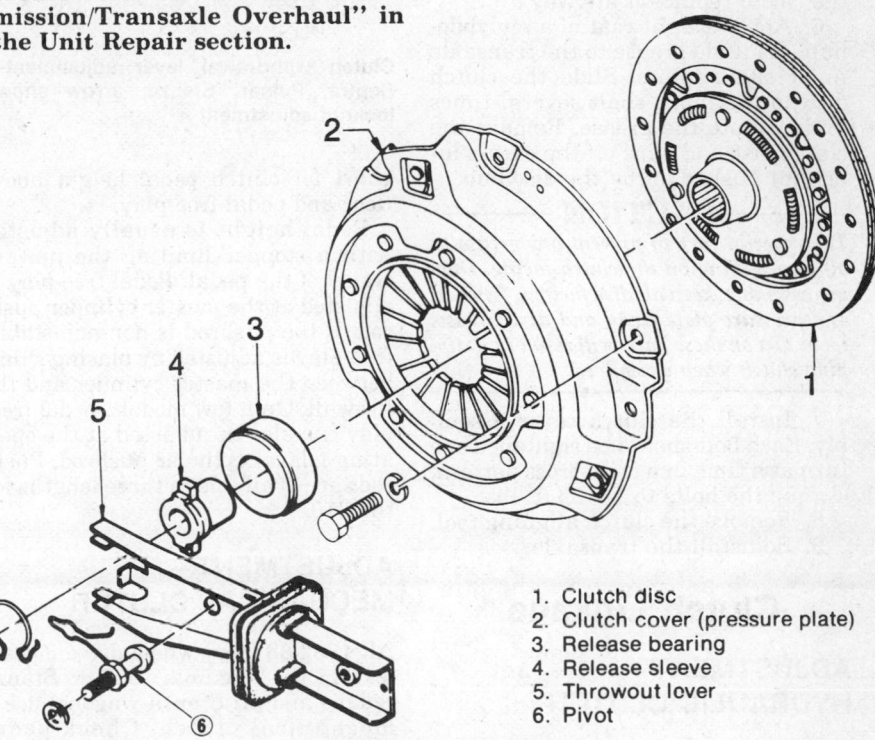

1. Clutch disc
2. Clutch cover (pressure plate)
3. Release bearing
4. Release sleeve
5. Throwout lever
6. Pivot

Typical clutch assembly

ply a small amount of grease to the transmission splines. Install the disc on the splines and slide it back and forth a few times. Remove the disc and remove any excess grease on the hub. Be sure no grease contacts the disc or pressure plate.

7. Install the disc, aligning it with a splined dummy shaft.
8. Install the pressure plate and torque the bolts to 16–22 ft. lbs.
9. Remove the dummy shaft.
10. Replace the transmission.

Front Wheel Drive

REMOVAL & INSTALLATION

1. Remove transaxle from engine.
2. Insert Nissan clutch aligning tool or a similar splined clutch tool into the clutch disc hub.
3. Loosen the bolts attaching the clutch cover to the flywheel, one turn each at a time, until the spring pressure is released.

NOTE: Be sure to turn them out in a crisscross pattern.

4. Remove the clutch disc and cover assembly.
5. Inspect the pressure plate or scoring for roughness, and reface or replace as necessary (slight roughness can be smoothed with a fine emery cloth). Inspect the clutch disc for worn or oily facings, loose rivets and broken or loose springs, and replace. (You probably have the clutch out of the car to replace it anyway).
6. Apply a light coat of a molybdenum-disulfide grease to the transaxle input shaft spline. Slide the clutch disc on the input shaft several times to distribute the grease. Remove the clutch disc and wipe off the excess lubricant pushed off by the disc hub.

—————— **CAUTION** ——————
Take special care to prevent any grease or oil from getting on the clutch facing. During assembly, keep all disc facings, flywheel and pressure plate clean and dry. Grease, oil or dirt on these parts will result in a slipping clutch when assembled.
————————————————

7. Install the clutch cover assembly. Each bolt should be tightened one turn at a time in a criss-cross pattern. Torque the bolts to 16–22 ft. lbs.
8. Remove the clutch aligning tool.
9. Reinstall the transaxle.

Clutch Linkage

ADJUSTMENT— HYDRAULIC CLUTCH

Refer to the "Clutch Specifications"

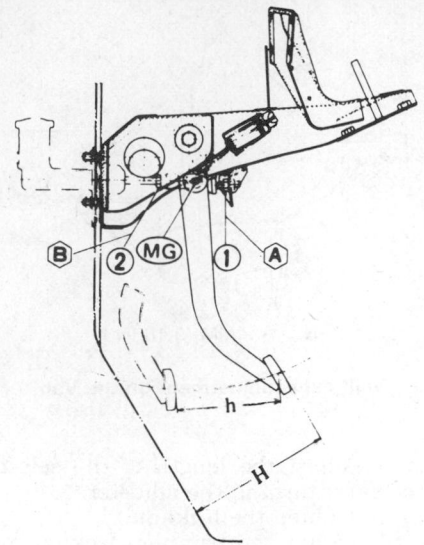

1. Adjust pedal height here
2. Adjust pedal free-play here
MG. Lubricate with multipurpose grease here
H. is pedal height
h. is free play

Clutch adjusting points

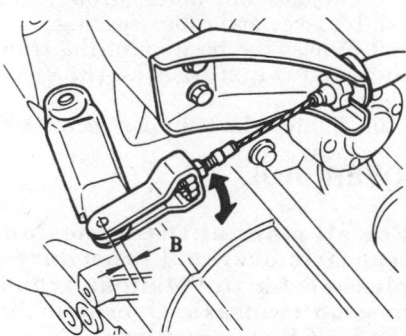

Clutch withdrawal lever adjustment— Sentra, Pulsar, Stanza; arrow shows locknut adjustment

chart for clutch pedal height above floor and pedal free-play.

Pedal height is usually adjusted with a stopper limiting the upward travel of the pedal. Pedal free-play is adjusted at the master cylinder pushrod. If the pushrod is non-adjustable, free-play is adjusted by placing shims between the master cylinder and the firewall. On a few models, pedal free-play can also be adjusted at the operating (slave) cylinder pushrod. Pushrods are available in three lengths for the 310.

ADJUSTMENT— MECHANICAL CLUTCH

All 1982-88 front wheel drive models (except the Maxima, 1987-88 Stanza sedans and all Stanza wagons) use a mechanical clutch. Check pedal height and free travel, adjust if neces-

CLUTCH PEDAL SPECIFICATIONS

Model	Pedal Height Above Floor (in.)	Pedal Free Play (in.)
210, 310 (1981)	7.29	0.04–0.20
510	6.50	0.04–0.20
200SX	7.60	0.04–0.20
280ZX	7.99	0.04–0.20
300ZX	7.68–8.07	0.04–0.12
810/ Maxima (1981–84)	6.90	0.04–0.20
Maxima (1985–88)	6.73–7.13	0.04–0.12
Pulsar 310 Sentra 1982-84	8.00	0.43–0.83
1985	8.30	0.43–0.70
1986	7.90	0.43–0.70
1987–88	6.38–6.77	0.49–0.68
Stanza Sedan 1982	6.50	0.43–0.63
1983–84	6.05	0.43–0.63
1985–86	6.22	0.47–0.67
1987-88	6.93	0.04–0.12
Stanza Wagon	9.50	0.04–0.12
Van	6.47–7.25	0.04–0.12

sary. Refer to the "Clutch Specifications" chart for proper adjustment specifications.

1. Loosen the locknut and adjust the pedal height by means of the pedal stopper. Tighten the locknut.
2. Adjust withdrawal lever play at the lever tip end with the locknuts.
3. Depress and release the clutch pedal several times and then recheck the withdrawal lever play again. Readjust if necessary.
4. Measure the pedal free travel at the center of the pedal pad.

Clutch Master Cylinder

REMOVAL & INSTALLATION

1. Disconnect the clutch pedal arm from the pushrod.

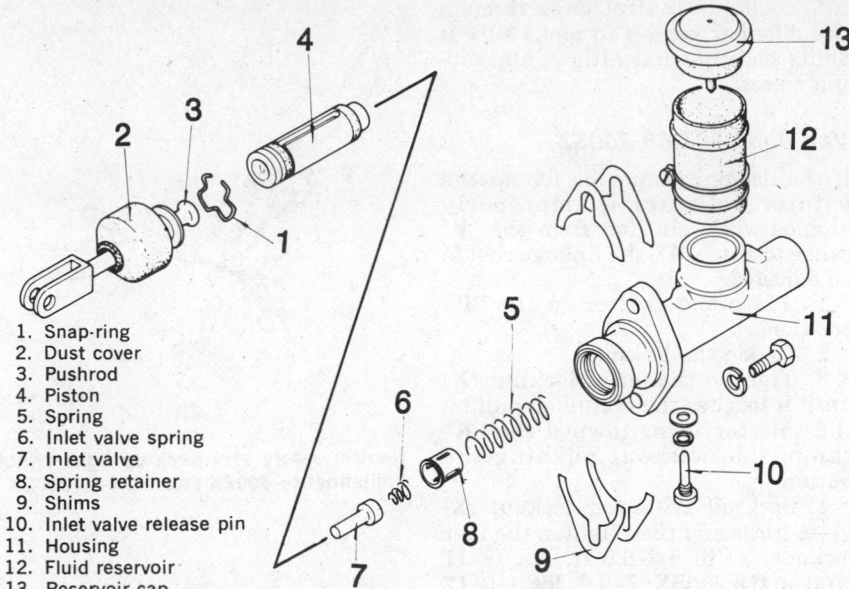

1. Snap-ring
2. Dust cover
3. Pushrod
4. Piston
5. Spring
6. Inlet valve spring
7. Inlet valve
8. Spring retainer
9. Shims
10. Inlet valve release pin
11. Housing
12. Fluid reservoir
13. Reservoir cap

Clutch master cylinder—210 shown; others similar

2. Disconnect the clutch hydraulic line from the master cylinder.

NOTE: Take precautions to keep brake fluid from coming in contact with any painted surfaces.

3. Remove the nuts attaching the master cylinder and remove the master cylinder and pushrod toward the engine compartment side.

NOTE: The master cylinder on the Van is located inside the passenger compartment, under the dashboard. Remove toward the front seat.

4. Install the master cylinder in the reverse order of removal and bleed the clutch hydraulic system.

Clutch Slave Cylinder

REMOVAL & INSTALLATION

1. Remove the slave cylinder attaching bolts and the pushrod from the shift fork.
2. Disconnect the flexible fluid hose from the slave cylinder and remove the unit form the vehicle.
3. Install the slave cylinder in the reverse order of removal and bleed the clutch hydraulic system.

HYDRAULIC SYSTEM BLEEDING

Bleeding is required to remove air trapped in the hydraulic system. This operation is necessary whenever the

system has been leaking or dismantled. The bleed screw is usually located on the clutch operating (slave) cylinder.

1. Remove the bleed screw dust cap.
2. Attach a tube to the bleed screw, immersing the free end in a clean container of brake fluid.
3. Fill the master cylinder with fluid.
4. Open the bleed screw about ¾ turn.
5. Depress the clutch pedal quickly. Hold it down. Have an assistant tighten the bleed screw. Allow the pedal to return slowly. Bleeder screw torque is 5–6 ft. lbs.
6. Repeat Steps 2 and 5 until no more air bubbles are seen in the fluid container.
7. Remove the bleed tube. Replace the dust cap. Refill the master cylinder.

AUTOMATIC TRANSMISSION

Only external transmission adjustments and repairs, and transmission removal and replacement, are covered in this section.

All models use a JATCO automatic transmission, either model 3N71B, L4N71B (four speed overdrive) or E4N71B. This transmission uses Dexron® fluid.

REMOVAL & INSTALLATION

1. Disconnect the battery cable.
2. Remove the accelerator linkage.
3. Detach the shift linkage.
4. Disconnect the neutral safety switch and downshift solenoid wiring.
5. Remove the drain plug and drain the torque converter. If there is no converter drain plug, drain the transmission. If there is no transmission drain plug, remove the pan to drain. Replace the pan to keep out dirt.
6. Remove the front exhaust pipe.
7. Remove the vacuum tube and speedometer cable.
8. Disconnect the fluid cooler tubes.
9. Remove the drive shaft and starter.
10. Support the transmission with a jack under the oil pan. Support the engine also.
11. Remove the rear crossmember.
12. Mark the relationship between the torque converter and the drive plate. Remove the four bolts holding the converter to the drive plate through the hole at the front, under the engine. Unbolt the transmission from the engine.
13. Reverse the procedure for installation. If warped, make sure the drive plate has no more than 0.020 in. run-out. Torque the drive plate-to-torque converter and converter housing-to-engine bolts to 29–35 ft. lbs. Drive plate-to-crankshaft bolt torque is 101–116 ft. lbs.
14. Refill the transmission and check the fluid level.

SHIFT LINKAGE ADJUSTMENT

All Models Except 300ZX, Van and 1984-88 200SX

Adjustment is made at the locknuts at the base of the shifter, which control the length of the shift control rod.

1. Place the shift lever in "D".
2. Loosen the locknuts and move the shift lever until it is firmly in the "D" range, the pointer is aligned, and the transmission is in "D" range.
3. Tighten the locknuts.
4. Check the adjustment. Start the car and apply the parking brake. Shift through all the ranges, starting in "P". As the lever is moved from "P" to "I", you should be able to feel the detents in each range. If proper adjustment is not possible, the grommets are probably worn and should be replaced.

300ZX and 1984-86 200SX

If the detents cannot be felt or the pointer indicator is improperly

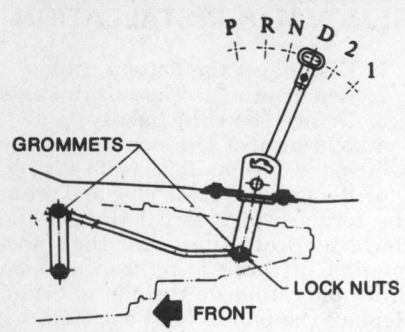

Automatic transmission linkage adjustment

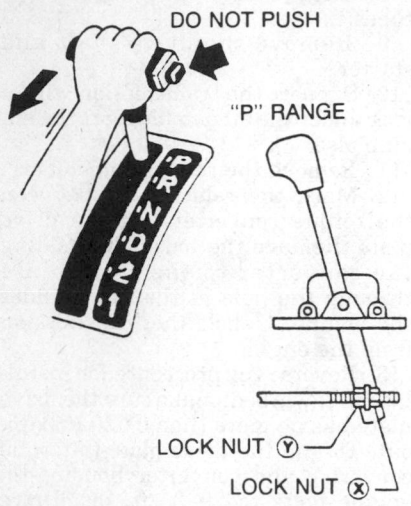

Linkage adjustment — 1987-88 300ZX and 200SX

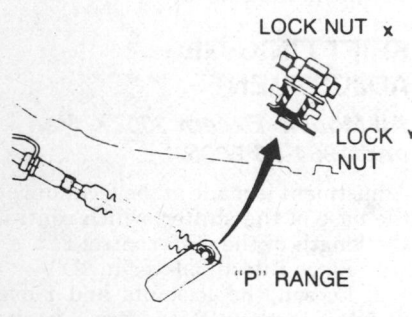

Linkage adjustment — Van

aligned while shifting from the "P" range to range "1", the linkage should be adjusted.

1. Place the shifter in the "N" position.
2. Loosen the locknuts.
3. Move the range selector lever at the transmission to the "N" range.
4. Tighten the locknuts when the floor control lever is in the "N" range and pushed against the "P" range side.

5. Shift the control lever through the different ranges to make sure it shifts smoothly and without any sliding noises.

Van and 1987-88 200SX

If the detents cannot be felt or the pointer indicator is improperly aligned while shifting from the "P" range to range "1", the linkage should be adjusted.

1. Place the shifter in the "P" position.
2. Loosen the locknuts.
3. Tighten the outer locknut (X) until it touches the trunnion, pulling the selector lever toward the "R" range side without pushing the button.
4. Back off the outer locknut (X) ¼–½ turns and then tighten the iner locknut (Y) to 5.8–8.0 ft. lbs. (8–11 Nm) on the 200SX; 7–9 ft. lbs. (10–12 Nm) on the Van.
5. Move the selector lever from "P" to "1". Make sure it moves smoothly.

DOWNSHIFT SOLENOID CHECK

The solenoid is controlled by a downshift switch on the accelerator linkage inside the car. To test the switch and solenoid operation:

1. Turn the ignition on.
2. Push the accelerator all the way down to actuate the switch.
3. The solenoid should click when actuated. The solenoid is screwed into the outside of the case. If there is no click, check the switch, wiring, and solenoid.
4. To remove the solenoid, first drain 2–3 pints of fluid, then unscrew the unit

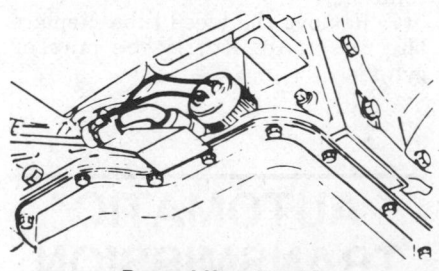

Downshift solenoid

NEUTRAL SAFETY AND BACK-UP LIGHT SWITCH ADJUSTMENT

The switch unit is bolted to the left side of the transmission shift lever. The switch prevents the engine from being started in any transmission po-

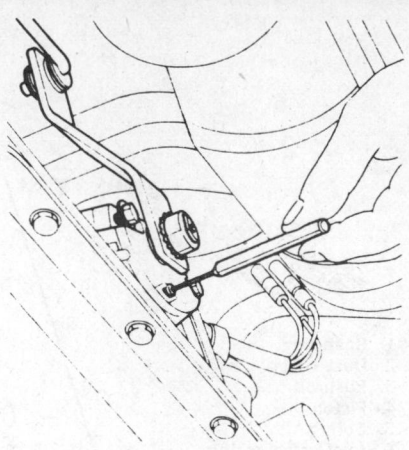

Neutral safety and back-up light switch adjustment — 300ZX and 1984-88 200SX

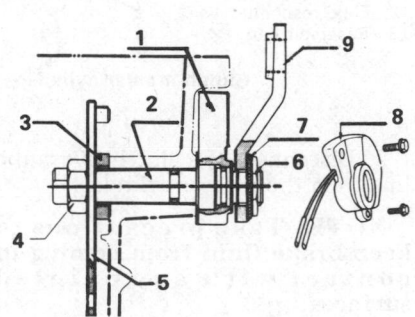

1. Neutral safety switch
2. Manual shaft
3. Washer
4. Nut
5. Manual plate
6. Nut
7. Washer
8. Neutral safety switch
9. Transmission shift lever

Neutral safety and back-up light switch —JATCO transmission

sition except Park or Neutral. It also controls the back-up lights.

1. Remove the transmission shift lever retaining nut and the lever.
2. Remove the switch.
3. Remove the machine screw in the case under the switch.
4. Align the switch to the case by inserting a 0.059 in. (0.079 in. on Van, 300ZX and 1984-88 200SX) diameter pin through the hole in the switch into the screw hole. Mark the switch location.
5. Remove the pin, replace the machine screw, install the switch as marked, and replace the transmission shift lever and retaining nut.
6. Make sure while holding the brakes on, that the engine will start only in Park or Neutral. Check that the back-up lights go on only in reverse.

AUTOMATIC TRANSAXLE

REMOVAL & INSTALLATION

Pulsar, Sentra and Stanza

1. Disconnect the negative battery cable. Raise and support the vehicle safely.

2. Remove the left front tire and drain the transmission fluid into a suitable container.

3. Remove the left side fender protector and disconnect the halfshafts.

NOTE: Be careful not to damage the oil seals when removing the driveshafts. After removing the halfshafts, install a suitable bar so that the side gears will not rotate and fall into the differential case.

4. On Stanza wagon, disconnect and remove the forward exhaust pipe.

5. Disconnect the speedometer cable. Disconnect the throttle wire from the carburetor throttle lever on carbureted models.

6. Remove the control cable rear end from the unit and remove the oil level gauge tube.

7. Place a suitable transmission jack under the transaxle and engine (do not place the jack under the oil pan drain plug).

8. Disconnect the oil cooler tubes and remove the engine motor mount securing bolts.

9. Remove the starter motor and the bolts holding the transaxle to the engine.

10. Slide the rear plate to remove the bolts holding the torque converter, then install 2 or 3 bolts to secure the transaxle to the engine for safety purposes.

11. Remove the bolts securing the torque converter to the drive plate.

12. Before removing the torque converter, place chalk marks on two parts for alignment purposes during installation.

13. Move the jack gradually until the transaxle can be lowered and removed from the vehicle through the left side wheel house.

14. Installation is the reverse order of the removal procedure.

15. After installation be sure to add the proper amount of transmission fluid to the transaxle and road test the vehicle to make sure the job was done properly.

1985-88 Maxima

NOTE: The engine/transaxle unit must be removed and installed as a unit. After removal, the transaxle may be separated from the engine.

1. Remove the transaxle/engine as an assembly.

2. Remove the transaxle-to-engine mounting bolts and then carefully draw out the rear plate.

3. Remove the bolts securing the torque converter to the drive plate.

4. Before removing the torque converter, use chalk or paint to matchmark at least two parts so that they may be replaced in their original positions during installation. Remove the torque converter.

5. Installation is in the reverse order of removal. Take note of the following:

6. When installing the torque converter to the drive plate, be certain that the matchmarks made during removal are in alignment. Apply Loctite® or a similar sealing compound to the converter-to-drive plate bolts before installation.

7. After the torque converter has been reinstalled, rotate the crankshaft a few times to ensure that the transaxle rotates freely, with no binding.

8. Adjust the control cable and check the inhibitor switch as detailed later in this section.

9. After installation of the engine/transaxle assembly into the vehicle, fill the transaxle (and engine!) with the proper amounts of vital fluids and then road test the vehicle.

THROTTLE WIRE ADJUSTMENT

The throttle wire is adjusted by means of double nuts on the carburetor or throttle side.

1. Loosen the adjusting nuts.

2. With the throttle fully opened (P_1), turn the threaded shaft (Q) inward as far as it will go (T) and then tighten the first nut (B) against the bracket (S).

3. Back off the first nut (B) 1–1½ turns on the 1982–86 Stanza; ¾–1¼ turns on the Maxima; and 2¾–3¼ turns on the 1987–88 Stanza (inc. 1986 wagon) and then tighten the second nut (A) against the bracket.

4. Tighten both double nuts to 5.8–7.2 ft. lbs. (8–10 Nm). The throttle drum should be held securely in the full open position.

5. On pre-1985 models, check that the throttle wire stroke between the threaded shaft and the throttle drum is 1.079–1.236 in.

On 1987–88 Stanza and Maxima models, check that the throttle wire

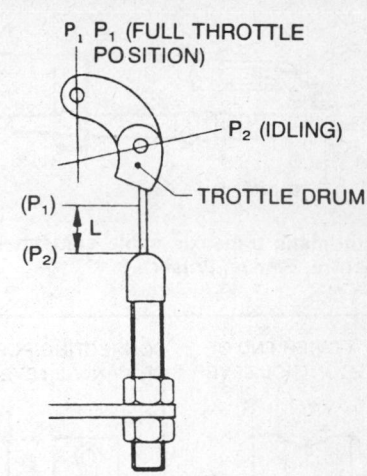

Throttle wire stroke—1987–88 Maxima, Pulsar, Sentra and Stanza

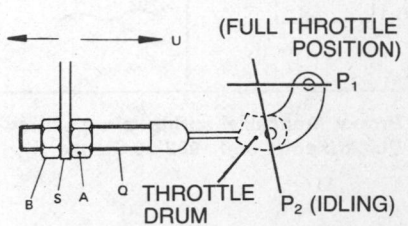

Throttle wire adjustment—typical

stroke (L) between full throttle and idling is 1.54–1.69 in. (39–43mm).

On the 1987–88 Pulsar/Sentra it should be 1.079–1.236 in. (27.4–31.4mm).

CONTROL CABLE ADJUSTMENT

Pulsar, Sentra, Stanza and 1987-88 Maxima

1. Position the control lever (gear selector) in Park.

2. Connect the control cable end to the lever in the transaxle unit and tighten the cable securing bolt.

3. Move the control lever to the "1" position. Be certain that the lever works smoothly and quietly.

4. Position the lever in Park once again.

5. Make sure that the lever locks into the Park position. Remove the outer cable adjustment nut and loosen the inner nut. Connect the control cable to the trunnion and reinstall the outer nut.

6. Pull on the cable a couple of times, then tighten the outer nut until it just contacts the bracket. Tighten the inner nut securely.

7. Move the control lever through all of its detents again and check for smooth and quiet operation.

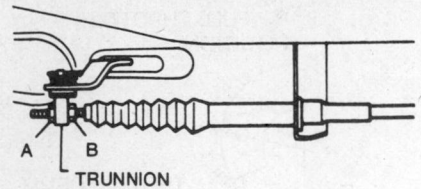

Automatic transaxle cable adjustment—
Sentra, Stanza, Pulsar

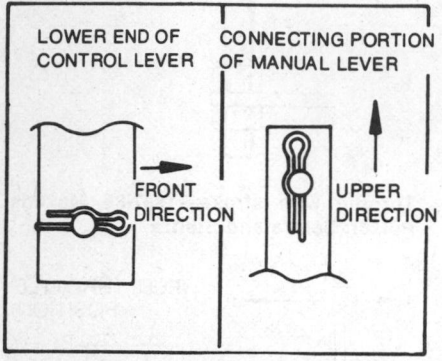

Proper transaxle spring pin position—
Pulsar/Sentra and 1982-86 Stanza

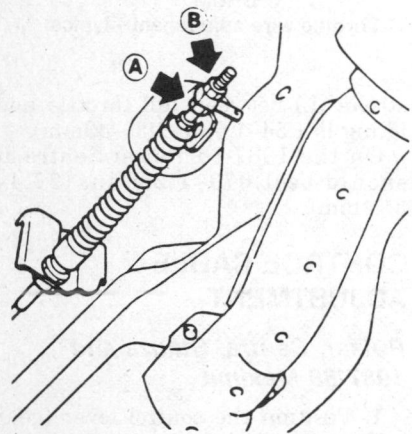

Control cable adjustment—1985-86 Maxima

8. Grease the spring washer at the end of the cable.

9. Check the spring pin to make sure it is assembled as illustrated.

1985-86 Maxima

1. Release the parking brake.

2. Disconnect the control cable from the gear selector lever and then pull it forward so as to place the manual lever on the transaxle in the "P" position.

3. Make certain that the halfshafts will not rotate. To do this, attempt to rotate both shafts in the same direction at the same time.

4. Loosen the two trunnion nuts at the forward edge of the cable.

5. Check that the selector lever moves smoothly and quietly through its range of detents, place it in the "P" position and then reconnect the control cable to the lever.

6. Tighten the two trunnion nuts. Be careful not to move the cable or selector lever from their previous position.

BRAKE BAND ADJUSTMENT

NOTE: The 1985-88 Maxima and the 1987-88 Stanza (inc. 1986 wagon) have no provision for brake band adjustment.

1. Raise and support the vehicle safely and disconnect the negative battery cable.

2. Drain the oil from the transmission or transaxle and remove the oil pan with the gasket.

3. Loosen the brake band adjustment locknut.

4. Torque the end pin locknut to 4.3 ft. lbs.

5. Back off the anchor end pin locknut two and a half complete turns.

6. While holding the anchor end pin locknut in place, torque the brake band locknut to 12–16 ft. lbs.

7. Reinstall the oil pan with a new gasket and torque the oil pan nuts to 4–6 ft. lbs. (do not forget the drain plug for the oil pan).

8. Refill the transmission or transaxle with the specified amount of transmission fluid and road test the vehicle.

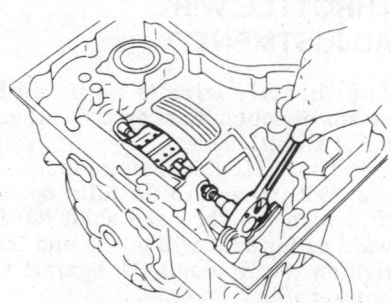

Brake band adjustment

KICKDOWN SWITCH ADJUSTMENT

1. Depress the accelerator pedal, a click should be heard just before the pedal bottoms out.

2. If the click is not heard, loosen the kickdown switch locknut and extend the switch until it makes contact with the accelerator pedal and the switch clicks on and off with the travel of the pedal.

NEUTRAL SAFETY SWITCH ADJUSTMENT

1. Locate the neutral safety switch on the side of the transaxle and loosen (but don't remove) the mounting screws.

2. Set the manual selector shaft (NOT the gear selector lever) on the transaxle to the "N" position.

3. Insert a small pin (0.16 in Maxima and 1987-88 Stanza (inc. 1986 wagon); 0.098 in.—all others) through the adjustment holes of both the switch and the switch lever so that it is perpendicular to them.

4. Tighten the switch mounting screws.

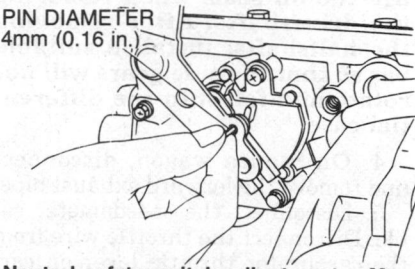

Neutral safety switch adjustment— Maxima shown; others typical

TRANSFER CASE

REMOVAL & INSTALLATION

Sentra (4wd) and Stanza Wagon (4wd) Only

1. Drain the gear oil from the transaxle and the transfer case.

2. Disconnect and remove the forward exhaust pipe.

3. Using chalk or paint, matchmark the flanges on the driveshaft and then unbolt and remove the driveshaft from the transfer case as detailed later in this section.

4. Unbolt and remove the transaxle support rod from the transfer case on the Sentra.

5. Unbolt and remove the transfer control actuator from the side of the transfer case.

6. Disconnect and remove the right side halfshaft.

7. Unscrew and withdraw the speedometer pinion gear from the transfer case. Position it out of the way and secure it with wire.

8. Unbolt and remove the front, rear and side transfer case gussets (support members).

9. Use an hydraulic floor jack and a

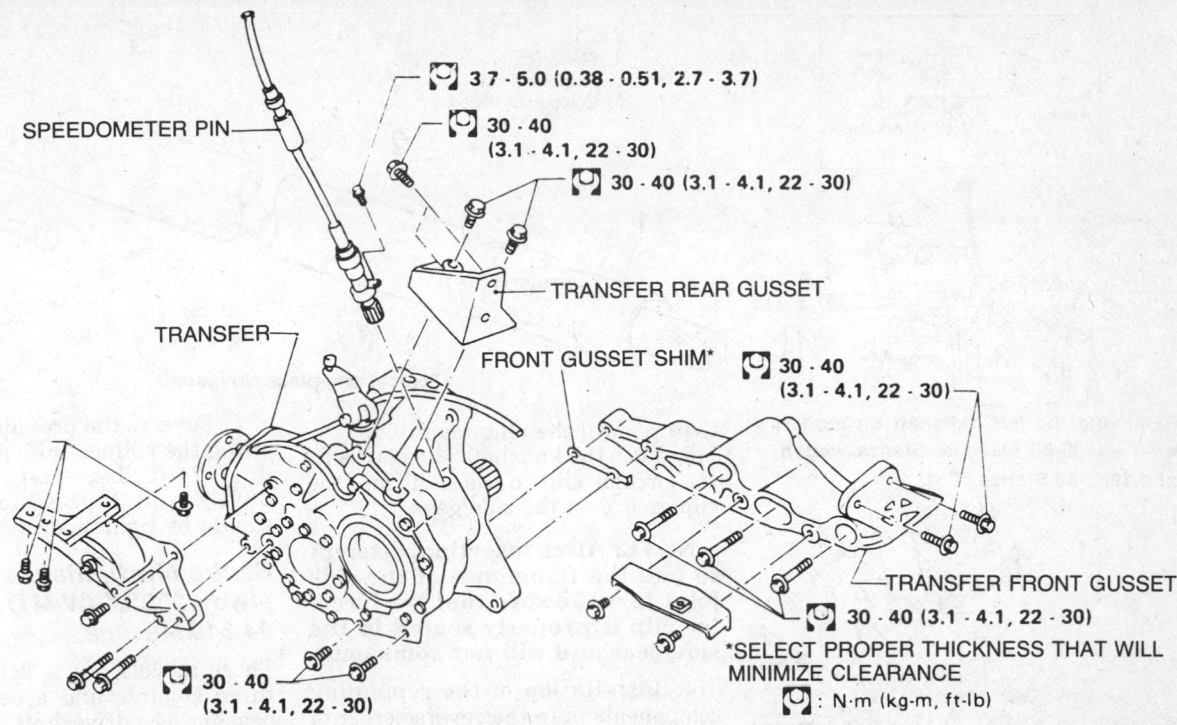

- 3 7 - 5.0 (0.38 - 0.51, 2.7 - 3.7)

SPEEDOMETER PIN

- 30 - 40 (3.1 - 4.1, 22 - 30)

- 30 - 40 (3.1 - 4.1, 22 - 30)

TRANSFER REAR GUSSET

TRANSFER

FRONT GUSSET SHIM*

- 30 - 40 (3.1 - 4.1, 22 - 30)

TRANSFER FRONT GUSSET

30 - 40 (3.1 - 4.1, 22 - 30)

*SELECT PROPER THICKNESS THAT WILL MINIMIZE CLEARANCE

30 - 40 (3.1 - 4.1, 22 - 30)

: N·m (kg-m, ft-lb)

Transfer case removal—Stanza wagon 4wd (Sentra 4wd similar)

block of wood to support the transfer case, remove the transfer case-to-transaxle mounting bolts and then remove the case itself. Be careful when moving it while supported on the jack.

10. Installation is in the reverse order of removal. Tighten the transfer case-to-transaxle mounting bolts and the transfer case gusset mounting bolts to 22–30 ft. lbs. (30–40 Nm).

Be sure to use a multi-purpose grease to lubricate all oil seal surfaces prior to reinstallation, and don't forget that the transfer case and the transaxle use different types and weights of lubricant.

DRIVE AXLE

Halfshafts

REMOVAL & INSTALLATION

Front Wheel Drive Only

ALL EXCEPT 1987-88 PULSAR/ SENTRA, STANZA WAGON, 1987-88 STANZA AND 1985-88 MAXIMA

1. Jack up the car and support it with jack stands.
2. Remove the wheel and tire assembly.
3. Remove the brake caliper assembly.

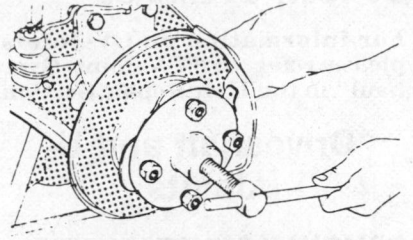

Removing halfshaft

4. Pry off the cotter pin from the castellated nut on the wheel hub.
5. Loosen, but do not remove, the wheel hub nut from the halfshaft while holding the wheel hub with a suitable tool.
6. Remove the tie rod ball joint. Remove the lower ball joint. 'Do not reuse the nut once it has been removed;' install a new nut during assembly.
7. Drain the gear oil from the transaxle.
8. Remove the bolts holding the halfshaft flange to the transaxle. Remove the halfshaft, along with the wheel hub and knuckle.
9. Insert a suitable bar, wooden dowel or similar tool into the transaxle to prevent the side gear from dropping inside.

CAUTION

When removing the transaxle, be very careful not to damage the grease seal on the transaxle side.

10. Installation is the reverse of re-

moval. Coat the transaxle-end halfshaft spline with a molybdenum-disulfide grease before insertion. Make sure the rubber gaiters on both ends of the halfshaft are in good shape; it not, replace them (use new metal bands to retain the gaiters).

1987-88 PULSAR/SENTRA, STANZA WAGON, 1987-88 STANZA AND 1985-88 MAXIMA

NOTE: Installation of the halfshafts will require a special tool for the spline alignment of the halfshaft end and the transaxle case. Do not perform this procedure without access to this tool.

1. Raise the front of the vehicle and support it with jack stands.
2. Remove the wheel and tire assembly.
3. Pull out the cotter pin from the castellated nut on the wheel hub and then remove the wheel bearing lock nut.
4. Separate the halfshaft from the steering knuckle by tapping it with a block of wood and a mallet.
5. Remove the tie rod ball joint. Remove the three mounting nuts for the lower ball joint and then pull it down.

NOTE: Always use a new nut when replacing the tie rod ball joint.

6. Using a suitable tool, reach through the engine crossmember and

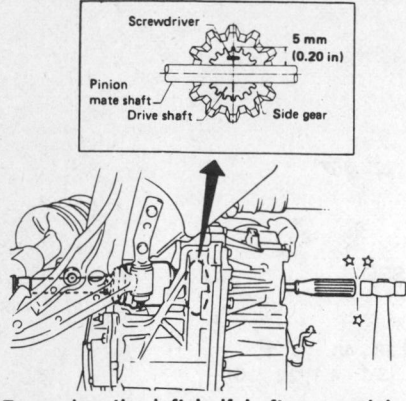

Removing the left halfshaft on models w/AT—1985-88 Maxima, Stanza wagon and 1987-88 Stanza

Separating the halfshaft from the steering knuckle

carefully tap the right side inner CV-joint out of the transaxle case.

7. Using a block of wood on an hydraulic floor jack, support the engine under the oil pan.

8. Remove the support bearing bracket from the engine and then withdraw the right halfshaft (exc. Pulsar w/E16i and Sentra).

9. On models with manual transmissions, carefully insert a small prybar between the left CV-joint inner flange and the transaxle case mounting surface and pry the half shaft out of the case. Withdraw the shaft from the steering knuckle and remove it.

10. On models with automatic transmissions, insert a dowel through the right side halfshaft hole and use a small mallet to tap the left halfshaft out of the transaxle case. Withdraw the shaft from the steering knuckle and remove it.

— CAUTION —

Be careful not to damage the pinion mating shaft and the side gear while tapping the left halfshaft out of the transaxle case.

11. When installing the shafts into the transaxle, use a new oil seal and then install an alignment tool along the inner circumference of the oil seal.

12. Insert the halfshaft into the transaxle, align the serrations and

then remove the alignment tool.

13. Push the halfshaft, then press-fit the circular clip on the shaft into the clip groove on the side gear.

NOTE: After insertion, attempt to pull the flange out of the side joint to make sure that the circular clip is properly seated in the side gear and will not come out.

14. Installation of the remaining components is in the reverse order of removal.

CV-JOINT OVERHAUL

For information on CV-Joints, please refer to "CV-Joint Overhaul" in the Unit Repair Section.

Driveshaft and U-Joints

REMOVAL & INSTALLATION

510, 200SX (W/AT), Van, 280ZX and 300ZX

These driveshafts are the one piece type with a U-joint and flange at the rear, and a U-joint and a splined sleeve yoke which fits into the rear of the transmission, at the front. The U-joints must be disassembled for lubrication at 24,000 mile intervals if no grease fittings are present. The splines are lubricated by transmission oil.

1. Release the handbrake.

2. The front pipe and the heat shield plate must come off on 280ZX models sold in California, and all 300ZXs.

3. Matchmark the flanges on the driveshaft and differential so that the driveshaft can be reinstalled in its original orientation; this will help maintain driveline balance.

4. Unbolt the rear flange.

5. Pull the driveshaft down and back.

6. Plug the transmission extension housing.

1. Sleeve yoke
2. Propeller shaft
3. Companion flange

Typical one-piece driveshaft

7. Reverse the procedure to install, oiling the splines. Flange bolt torque is 17–24 ft. lbs., except for the Van, 280ZX and 300ZX models, which should be tightened to 25–33 ft. lbs.

Sentra (4wd), Stanza Wagon (4wd), 200SX (W/MT) and 1981-84 810/Maxima

These models use a driveshaft with three U-joints and a center support bearing. The driveshaft is balanced as an assembly. It is not recommended that it be disassembled.

1. Mark the relationship of the driveshaft flange to the differential flange.

2. Unbolt the center bearing bracket.

3. Unbolt the driveshaft flange from the differential flange.

4. Pull the driveshaft back under the rear axle. Plug the rear of the transmission to prevent oil or fluid loss.

5. On installation, align the marks made in Step 1. Torque the flange bolts to 17–24 ft. lbs. Center bearing bracket both torque is 26–35 ft. lbs.

CENTER BEARING REPLACEMENT

The center bearing is a sealed unit which must be replaced as an assembly if defective.

1. Remove the driveshaft.

2. Paint a matchmark across where the flanges behind the center yoke are joined. This is for assembly purposes. If you don't paint or somehow mark the relationship between the two shafts, they may be out of balance when you put them back together.

3. Remove the bolts and separate the shafts. Make a matchmark on the front driveshaft half which lines up with the mark on the flange half.

4. Devise a way to hold the driveshaft while unbolting the companion flange from the front driveshaft. Do not place the front driveshaft tube in a vise. The best way is to grip the

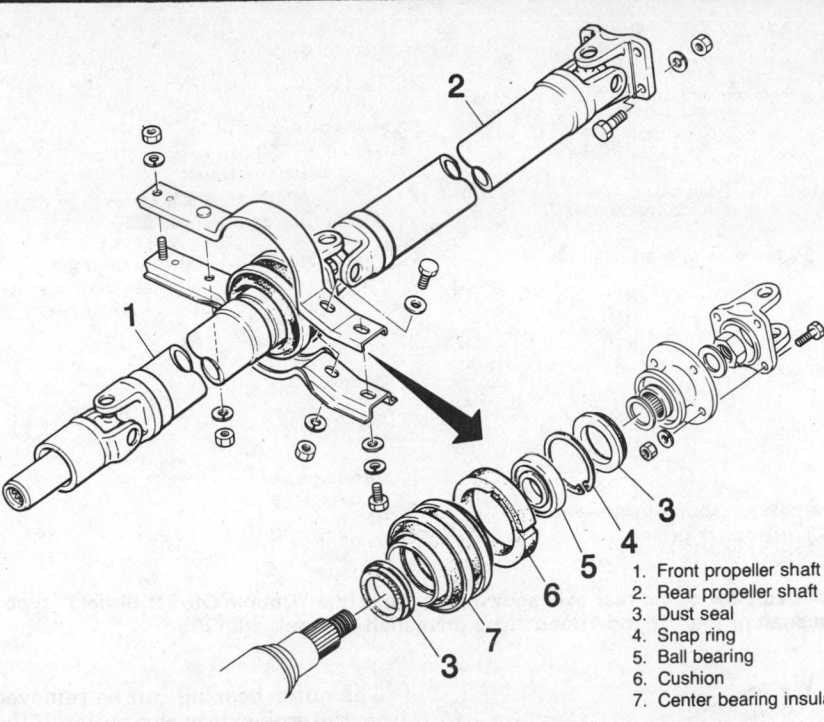

1. Front propeller shaft
2. Rear propeller shaft
3. Dust seal
4. Snap ring
5. Ball bearing
6. Cushion
7. Center bearing insulator

Two piece driveshaft with center bearing and three U–joints

flange while loosening the nut. It is going to require some strength to remove.

5. Press the companion flange off the front driveshaft and press the center bearing from its mount.

6. The new bearing is already lubricated. Install it into the mount, making sure that the seals and so on are facing the same way as when removed.

7. Slide the companion flange onto the front driveshaft, aligning the marks made during removal. Install the washer and locknut. If the washer and locknut are separate pieces, tighten them to 145–175 ft. lbs. If they are a unit, tighten it to 180–217 ft. lbs. Check that the bearing rotates freely around the driveshaft. Stake the nut.

8. Connect the companion flange to the other half of the driveshaft, aligning the marks made during removal. Tighten the bolts securely.

9. Install the driveshaft.

Final Drive Unit— Independent Rear Suspension

REMOVAL & INSTALLATION

280ZX and 1981-84 810/Maxima Sedan

1. Jack up the rear of the car and drain the oil from the differential.

2. Disconnect the driveshaft.
3. Disconnect the halfshafts.
4. Remove the side flange fixing bolts, and disconnect the flange yokes together with the halfshafts. Support the case with a jack.
5. Remove the four bolts retaining the case to the suspension carrier.
6. Pull the case backwards on the jack until clear of the car.
7. After the case is removed, support the suspension on a stand to prevent damage.
8. Installation is the reverse. Tighten the rear cover-to-insulator nuts to 65–87 ft. lbs., the case-to-suspension bolts to 43–58 ft. lbs., and the side flange and driveshaft bolts to 36–43 ft. lbs.

Sentra (4wd), Stanza Wagon (4wd) and 300ZX

1. Jack up the rear of the car and drain the oil·from the differential. Support with jack stands. Position the floor jack underneath the differential unit.
2. Disconnect the brake hydraulic lines and the parking brake cable.
3. Disconnect the sway bar from the control arms on either sides.
4. Remove the rear exhaust tube.
5. Disconnect the driveshaft and the rear axle shafts.
6. Remove the rear shock absorbers from the control arms.
7. Unbolt the differential unit from the chassis, at the differential mounting insulator.

8. Lower the rear assembly out of the car using the floor jack. It is best to have at least one other person helping to balance the assembly.

9. Reverse the procedure to install. Torque the rear cover-to-insulator nuts to 72–87 ft. lbs.; the mounting insulator-to-chassis bolts to 22–29 ft. lbs.; the non-turbo driveshaft-to-flange bolts to 43–51 ft. lbs. Torque the strut nuts to 51–65 ft. lbs.; and the sway bar-to-control arm nuts to 12–15 ft. lbs.

Rear Wheel Drive Axle Shaft/Wheel Bearing

REMOVAL & INSTALLATION

Solid Rear Axle

210, 510, 810 WAGON, VAN AND 1981-84 200SX

NOTE: Bearings must be pressed on and off the shaft with an arbor press. Unless you have access to one, it is inadvisable to attempt any repair work on the axle shaft and bearing assemblies.

1. Remove the hubcap or wheel cover. Loosen the lug nuts.
2. Raise the rear of the car and support it safely on stands.
3. Remove the rear wheel. Remove the four brake backing plate retaining nuts. Detach the parking brake linkage from the brake backing plate.
4. Attach a slide hammer to the axle shaft and remove it. Use the slide hammer and a two-pronged puller to remove the oil seal from the housing.

NOTE: If a slide hammer is not available, the axle can sometimes be pried out using pry bars on opposing sides of the hub.

If end-play is found to be excessive, the bearing should be replaced. Shimming the bearing is not recommended as this ignores end-play of the bearing itself and could result in improper seating of the bearing.

5. Using a chisel, carefully nick the bearing retainer in three or four places. The retainer does not have to be cut, only collapsed enough to allow the bearing retainer to be slid off the shaft.
6. Pull or press the old bearing off and install the new one by pressing it into position.
7. Install the outer bearing retainer with its raised surface facing the wheel hub, and then install the bearing an the inner bearing retainer in that order on the axle shaft.
8. With the smaller chamfered side

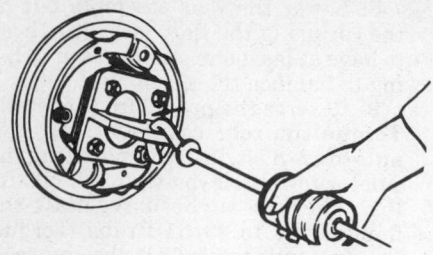

Use a slide hammer to remove the axle shaft—solid rear axle models

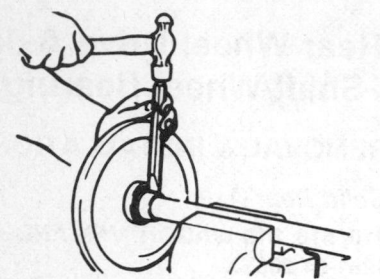

Use a chisel to collapse the bearing retainer

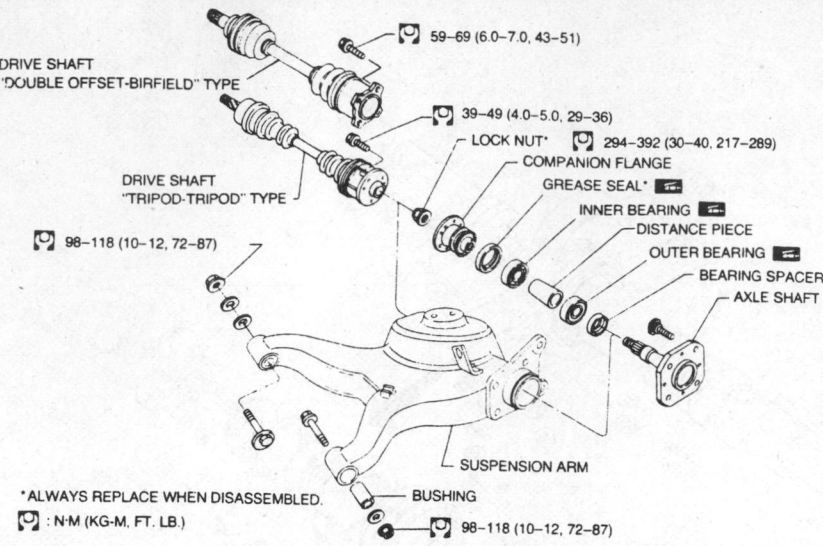

DRIVE SHAFT "DOUBLE OFFSET-BIRFIELD" TYPE

DRIVE SHAFT "TRIPOD-TRIPOD" TYPE

59–69 (6.0–7.0, 43–51)

39–49 (4.0–5.0, 29–36)
LOCK NUT* 294–392 (30–40, 217–289)
COMPANION FLANGE
GREASE SEAL*
INNER BEARING
DISTANCE PIECE
OUTER BEARING
BEARING SPACER
AXLE SHAFT

98–118 (10–12, 72–87)

SUSPENSION ARM

*ALWAYS REPLACE WHEN DISASSEMBLED.
BUSHING
: N·M (KG-M, FT. LB.)
98–118 (10–12, 72–87)

Exploded view of the rear axle shown with either the "Double Off-Set Birfield" type driveshaft or the "Tripod-Tripod" type driveshaft—models with IRS

of the inner bearing retainer facing the bearing, press on the retainer. The edge of the retainer should fully touch the bearing.

9. Clean the oil seal seat in the rear axle housing. Apply a thin coat of chassis grease.

10. Using a seal installation tool, drive the oil seal into the rear axle housing. Wipe a thin coat of bearing grease on the lips of the seal.

11. Determine the number of retainer gaskets which will give the correct bearing-to-outer retainer clearance of 0.01 in.

12. Insert the axle shaft assembly into the axle housing, being careful not to damage the seal. Ensure that the shaft splines engage those of the differential pinion. Align the vent holes of the gasket and the outer bearing retainer. Install the retaining bolts.

13. Install the nuts on the bolts and tighten them evenly, and in a crisscross pattern, to 20 ft. lbs. (33–40 ft. lbs. on the Van).

Independent Rear Suspension

1984-88 200SX, 1981-84 810/ MAXIMA, 280ZX and 300ZX

1. Block the front wheels. Loosen the wheel nuts, raise and support the car, and remove the wheel.

2. Apply the parking brake firmly. This will help hold the stub axle while you remove the axle nut. You will probably also have to hold the stub axle at the outside while removing the nut from the axle shaft side. The

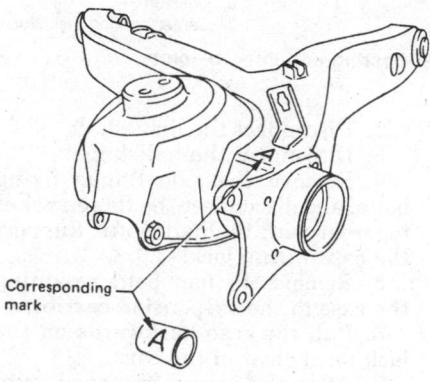

Corresponding mark

A

Match the bearing housing to the spacer with the proper letter

nut will require a good deal of force to remove, so be sure to hold the stub axle firmly.

3. On cars with rear disc brakes, unbolt the caliper and move it aside. Do not disconnect the hose from the caliper. Do not allow the caliper to hang by the hose; support the caliper with a length of wire or rest it on a suspension member.

4. Remove the brake disc on models with rear disc brakes. Remove the brake drum on cars with drum brakes.

5. Remove the stub axle with a slide hammer and an adapter. The outer wheel bearing will come off with the stub axle.

6. Remove the companion flange from the lower arm.

7. Remove and discard the grease seal and inner bearing from the lower arm using a drift made for the purpose or a length of pipe of the proper diameter.

The outer bearing can be removed from the stub axle with a puller. If the grease seal or the bearings are removed, new parts must be used on assembly.

8. Clean all the parts to be reused in solvent.

9. Sealed-type bearings are used. When the new bearings are installed, the sealed side must face out. Install the sealed side of the outer bearing facing the wheel, and the sealed side of the inner bearing facing the differential.

10. Press the outer bearing onto the stub axle.

11. The bearing housing is stamped with an "N", "M", or "P". Select a spacer on the stub axle.

12. Install the stub axle into the lower arm.

13. Install the new inner bearing into the lower arm with the stub axle in place. Install a new grease seal.

14. Install the companion flange onto the stub axle.

15. Install the stub axle nut. Tighten to 181–239 ft. lbs. (217–289 ft. lbs. on 300 ZX).

16. Install the brake disc or drum, and the caliper if removed. Install the wheel and lower the car.

Rear Wheel Drive Halfshaft

REMOVAL & INSTALLATION

Independent Rear Suspension

1981 810 and 1981-83 280ZX

1. Raise and support the car.
2. Remove the U-joint yoke flange

bolts at the outside. Remove the U-joint center bolt at the differential.

3. Remove the axle shaft.

4. Installation is the reverse. Torque the outside flange bolts to 36–43 ft. lbs. (5.0–6.0 kg-m). Tighten the four differential side flange bolts to 36–43 ft. lbs. (5.0–6.0 kg-m). On axle shafts retained to the differential with a single center bolt, tighten the bolt to 23–31 ft. lbs.

1984-88 200SX, 1982-84 810/MAXIMA, 1982-83 280ZX and 300ZX

1. Raise and support the rear of the car.

2. Remove the spring seat stay on 1984-88 200SX and 300ZX.

3. Disconnect the halfshaft on the wheel side by removing the four flange bolts.

4. Grasp the halfshaft at the center and extract if from the differential carrier by prying it with a suitable pry bar.

5. Installation is in the reverse order of removal. Install the differential end first and then the wheel end. Tighten the four flange bolts to 20–27 ft. lbs. (2.3–3.8 kg).

— CAUTION —

Take care not to damage the oil seal or either end of the halfshaft during installation.

Four Wheel Drive Rear Halfshafts

REMOVAL & INSTALLATION

Sentra (4wd) and Stanza Wagon (4wd) Only

1. Raise the rear of the vehicle and support it with jack stands.

2. Remove the wheel and tire assembly.

3. Pull out the wheel bearing cotter pin and then remove the adjusting cap and insulator.

4. Set the parking brake and then remove the wheel bearing lock nut.

5. Disconnect and plug the hydraulic brake lines. Disconnect the parking brake cable.

6. Using a block of wood and a small mallet, carefully tap the halfshaft out of the knuckle/backing plate assembly.

7. Unbolt the radius rod and the transverse link at the wheel end.

— CAUTION —

Before removing the transverse link mounting bolt, matchmark the toe-in adjusting plate to the link.

8. Using a suitable pry bar, care-

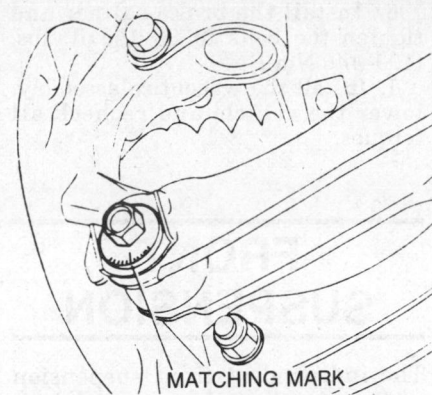

MATCHING MARK

Matchmark the toe adjustment bolt to the transverse link on the Stanza wagon (4 × 4)

fully remove the halfshaft from the final drive.

9. On installation , position the halfshaft into the knuckle and then insert it into the final drive; makeing sure the serrations are properly aligned.

10. Push the shaft into the final drive and then press-fit the circlip on the halfshaft into the groove on the side gear.

11. After insertion, pull the halfshaft by hand to be certain that it is properly seated in the side gear and will not come out.

12. Installation of the remaining components is in the reverse order of removal.

Front Axle Hub & Steering Knuckle

REMOVAL & INSTALLATION

1981 310

1. Raise and support the front of the vehicle safely and remove the wheels.

2. Disconnect and plug the brake line at the caliper, and remove the caliper assembly.

3. Remove the cotter pin and hub nut from the driveshaft while holding the hub from turning.

4. Remove the wheel hub with special tool #ST35100000, or equivalent, and remove the splash shield or baffle plate.

5. Remove the driveshaft and separate the ball joints from the steering knuckle, using a ball joint fork or equivalent.

6. Remove the steering knuckle-to-strut attaching bolts and remove the steering knuckle from the vehicle.

7. Installation is the reverse order of the removal procedure.

1982 310

1. Raise and support the front of the vehicle safely and remove the wheels.

2. While holding the hub from turning, remove the cotter pin and hub nut.

3. Remove the lower ball joint from the transverse link and drain the transaxle fluid.

4. Disconnect the side rod ball stud and disconnect the driveshaft from the transaxle.

5. Insert a suitable rod into the transaxle to prevent the side gear from falling off.

6. Disconnect the brake line, then remove the steering knuckle-to-strut attaching bolts.

7. Remove the driveshaft, wheel hub, steering knuckle and caliper as an assembly.

8. Remove the hub nut first, then the driveshaft using special tool #ST35100000 or equivalent.

9. Remove the snap ring, then the caliper assembly and wheel hub.

10. Installation is the reverse order of the removal procedure.

200SX, 1981-84 810/Maxima, 280ZX and 300ZX

1. Raise and support the front of the vehicle safely and remove the wheels.

2. Remove the brake hose and plug the hose (if necessary).

3. Remove the caliper retaining bolts and remove the caliper from the axle.

4. Remove the bolts holding the strut to the knuckle arm.

5. Remove the knuckle arm away from the strut arm and remove the stabilizer, tension rod, and transverse link.

6. Remove the ball joint from the knuckle arm by pressing it out of the knuckle arm.

7. Installation is the reverse order of the removal procedure.

Pulsar, Sentra, Stanza and 1985-88 Maxima

1. Raise and support the front of the vehicle safely and remove the wheels.

2. Disconnect the plug the brake line at the caliper and then remove the caliper and axle nut.

3. Disconnect the side rod ball stud and remove the lower ball joint from the transverse link.

4. Drain the transaxle and disconnect the driveshaft from the transaxle.

5. Insert a suitable rod into the transaxle to prevent the side gear from falling off.

NOTE: On 1983-88 models, remove the transaxle oil seal.

6. Remove the wheel hub, steering knuckle and driveshaft as an assembly.

7. Remove the hub nut and separate the driveshaft and wheel hub.

8. Using a suitable puller, remove the ball joint from the steering knuckle.

9. Using a ball joint fork or equivalent, separate the wheel hub and steering knuckle.

10. Installation is the reverse order of the removal procedure.

Van

1. Raise the front of the vehicle and support it on safety stands. Remove the wheel/tire assembly.

2. Remove the wheel bearing locknut.

3. Unbolt the brake caliper without disconnecting the brake line and suspend it out of the way.

4. Using a four armed puller if necesary, slide the wheel hub/brake disc assembly off the knuckle spindle.

5. Separate the tie rod from the knuckle spindle with a removal tool. Temporarily reinstall the stud nut upside down on the tie rod stud to prevent damage to the stud.

6. Loosen, but do not remove, the upper and lower ball joint securing nuts.

7. Using a ball joint removal tool, separate the knuckle spindle from the upper ball joint stud and then remove the upper ball joint securing nut.

8. Position the ball joint removal tool on the lower ball joint and then reinstall the knuckle spindle to the upper ball joint stud. Finger-tighten the nut only.

9. Separate the knuckle spindle from the lower ball joint stud and then remove both the upper and lower ball joint nuts.

10. Remove the knuckle spindle from the upper and lower links.

To install:
1. Position a floor jack under the lower link.

2. Insert the knuckle spindle and then raise the floor jack enough to support the spindle in position.

3. Tighten the upper ball joint stud nut to 40–72 ft. lbs. (54–98 Nm). Tighten the lower ball joint stud nut to 124–141 ft. lbs. (169–191 Nm). Always use new cotter pins.

4. Tighten the tie rod-to-knuckle arm nut to 40–72 ft. lbs. (54–98 Nm).

5. Install the wheel hub/brake disc assembly on the knuckle assembly and tighten the hub nut to 195–260 ft. lbs. (265–363 Nm). Always use a new cotter pin.

6. Install the brake caliper and tighten the bolts to 80–108 ft. lbs. (109–146 Nm).

7. Install the wheel/tire assembly, lower the vehicle and recheck all torques.

FRONT SUSPENSION

The independent front suspension system on all models covered here (with the exception of the Van) uses MacPherson struts. Each strut combines the function of coil spring and shock absorber. The spindle is mounted to the lower part of the strut which has a single ball joint. No upper suspension arm is required in this design. The spindle and lower suspension transverse link (control arm) are located fore and aft by the tension rods to the front part of the chassis on most models. A cross-chassis sway bar is used on all models.

The Van utilizes an unique leaf spring system with an upper and lower link (control arm) connected to the knuckle spindle by means of ball joints and the suspension crossmember or body by means of bushings. Single shock absorbers are situated aft of the crossmember while the leaf spring is sandwiched between the under side of the suspension crossmember and the top of the lower links.

Shock Absorber

REMOVAL & INSTALLATION

Van Only

1. Raise the front of the vehicle and support it with safety stands. Remove the wheel/tire assembly.

2. Position a floor jack under the lower link and then remove the upper shock mounting bolt.

3. Remove the lower shock-to-link nut and remove the shock absorber.

4. Position the shock absorber on the mounting stud and install the lower mounting nut. Tighten to 22–30 ft. lbs. (30–40 Nm).

5. Install the upper mounting bolt and tighten the nut to 43–58 ft. lbs. (59–78 Nm).

Leaf Spring And Spring Support Rubber

REMOVAL & INSTALLATION

Van Only

1. Remove the one of the lower links as detailed in this section.

2. Unbolt the support rubber-to-lower link nuts on the side opposite that to which you have removed the lower link.

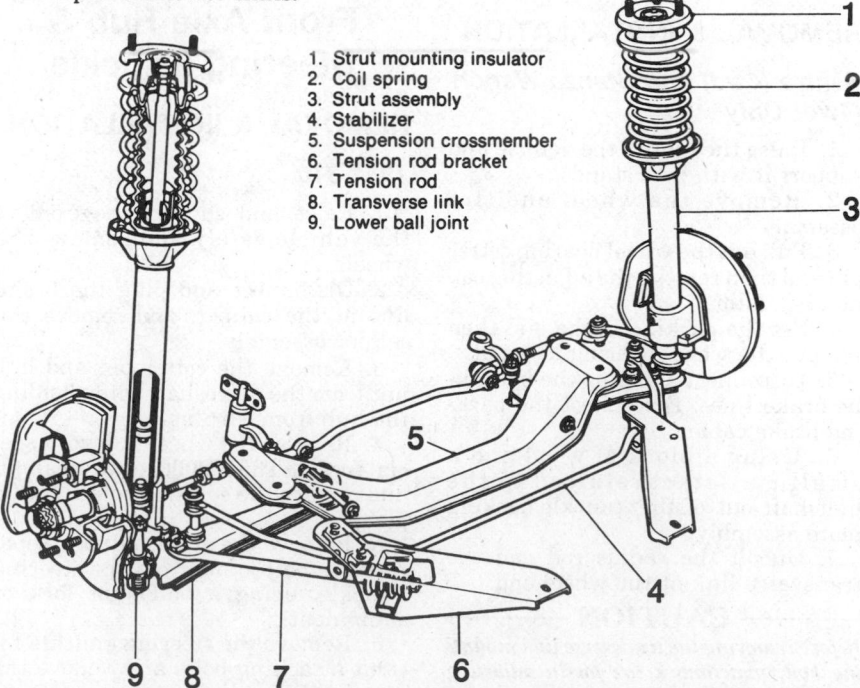

1. Strut mounting insulator
2. Coil spring
3. Strut assembly
4. Stabilizer
5. Suspension crossmember
6. Tension rod bracket
7. Tension rod
8. Transverse link
9. Lower ball joint

Typical MacPherson strut-type front suspension—front wheel drive models

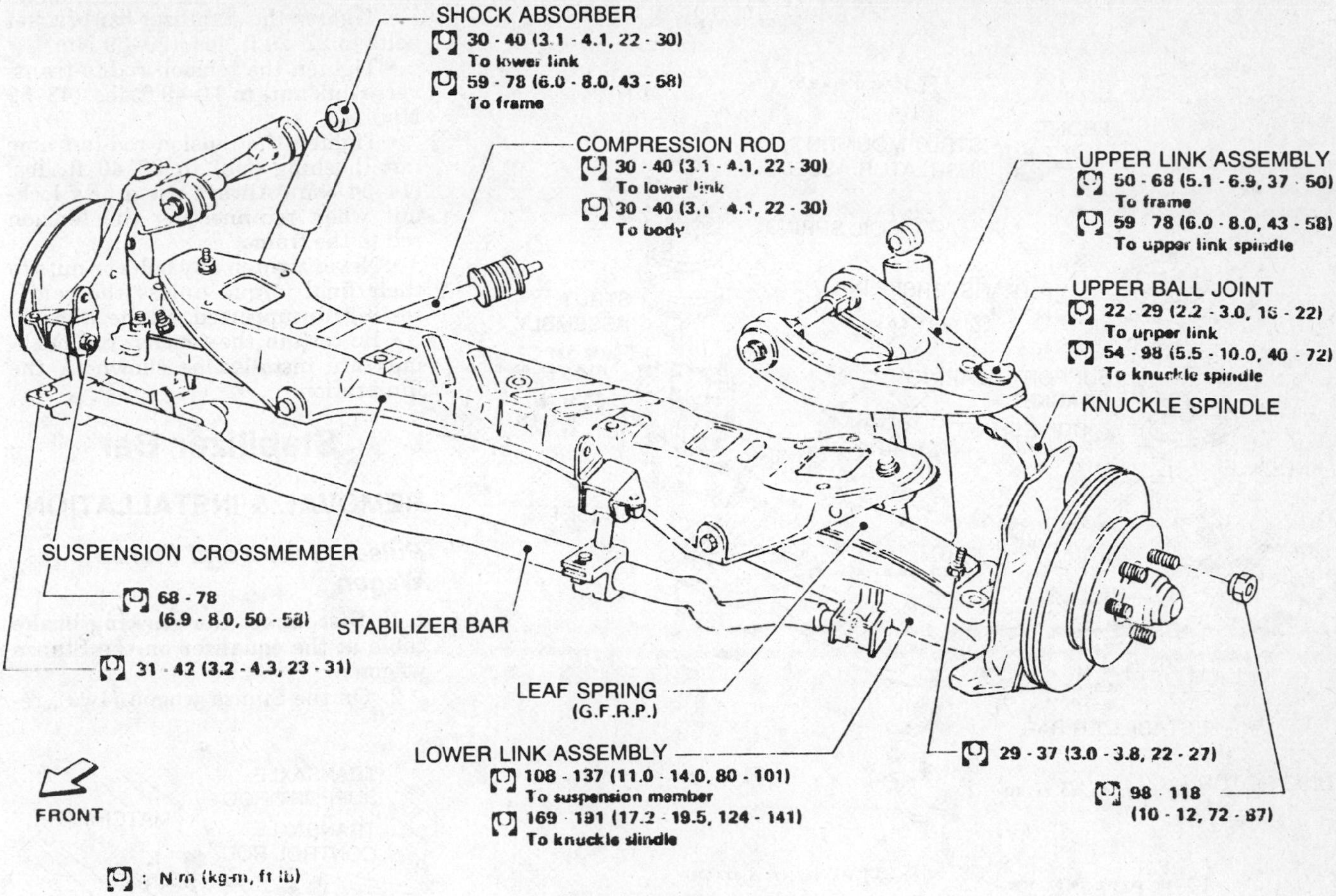

SHOCK ABSORBER
- 🔧 30 - 40 (3.1 - 4.1, 22 - 30)
  To lower link
- 🔧 59 - 78 (6.0 - 8.0, 43 - 58)
  To frame

COMPRESSION ROD
- 🔧 30 - 40 (3.1 - 4.1, 22 - 30)
  To lower link
- 🔧 30 - 40 (3.1 - 4.1, 22 - 30)
  To body

UPPER LINK ASSEMBLY
- 🔧 50 - 68 (5.1 - 6.9, 37 - 50)
  To frame
- 🔧 59 - 78 (6.0 - 8.0, 43 - 58)
  To upper link spindle

UPPER BALL JOINT
- 🔧 22 - 29 (2.2 - 3.0, 16 - 22)
  To upper link
- 🔧 54 - 98 (5.5 - 10.0, 40 - 72)
  To knuckle spindle

KNUCKLE SPINDLE

SUSPENSION CROSSMEMBER
- 🔧 68 - 78
  (6.9 - 8.0, 50 - 58)

STABILIZER BAR
- 🔧 31 - 42 (3.2 - 4.3, 23 - 31)

LEAF SPRING
(G.F.R.P.)

LOWER LINK ASSEMBLY
- 🔧 108 - 137 (11.0 - 14.0, 80 - 101)
  To suspension member
- 🔧 169 - 191 (17.2 - 19.5, 124 - 141)
  To knuckle slindle

- 🔧 29 - 37 (3.0 - 3.8, 22 - 27)
- 🔧 98 - 118
  (10 - 12, 72 - 87)

FRONT

🔧 : N·m (kg-m, ft lb)

Front suspension—Van

3. Slide out the leaf spring toward the side where the lower link has been removed.

4. Unbolt the support rubber from each end of the leaf spring. Don't lose the shim!

5. On installation, slide the leaf spring back through the suspension crossmember and install the lower link. Make sure that the spring pivot seats fit into the recesses in the crossmember. When installing more than one support rubber shim, make sure that their locking tongues are positioned left and right alternately. The standard number of shims is one; never use more than three as each shim changes the ride height by about 4mm (0.16 in.). Tighten the support rubber-to-link nuts to 22–30 ft. lbs. (30–40 Nm). Tighten the support rubber-to-leaf spring nut to 22–27 ft. lbs. (29–37 Nm). Check wheel alignment and ride height.

MacPherson Strut

REMOVAL & INSTALLATION

All Models Except Van

1. Jack up the car and support it safely. Remove the wheel.

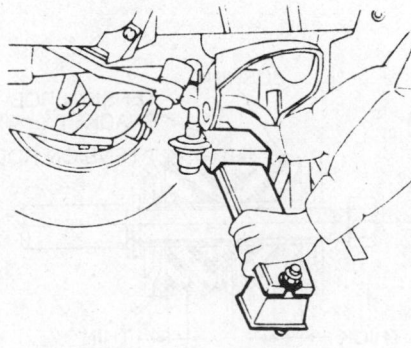

Sliding the leaf spring out through the suspension crossmember—Van

2. Disconnect and plug the brake line.

3. Disconnect the tension rod (compression rod on the "Z" series) and stabilizer bar from the transverse link.

4. Unbolt the steering arm from the lower end of the strut..

5. Place a jack under the bottom of the strut.

6. Open the hood and remove the nuts holding the top of the strut. If your 300ZX or 1985-88 Maxima is equipped with adjustable shocks, disconnect the electrical lead.

7. Lower the jack slowly and cautiously until the strut assembly can be removed.

8. Reverse the procedure to install. The self locking nuts holding the top of the strut must be replaced.

OVERHAUL

For all spring and shock absorber removal and installation procedures and any other strut overhaul procedures, please refer to "Strut Overhaul" in the Unit Repair Section.

Compression Rod

REMOVAL & INSTALLATION

Van Only

1. Raise the front of the vehicle and support it with safety stands. Remove the wheel and tire assembly.

2. Position a floor jack under the lower link and raise it just enough to support the link.

3. Remove the two lower link-to-compression rod nuts.

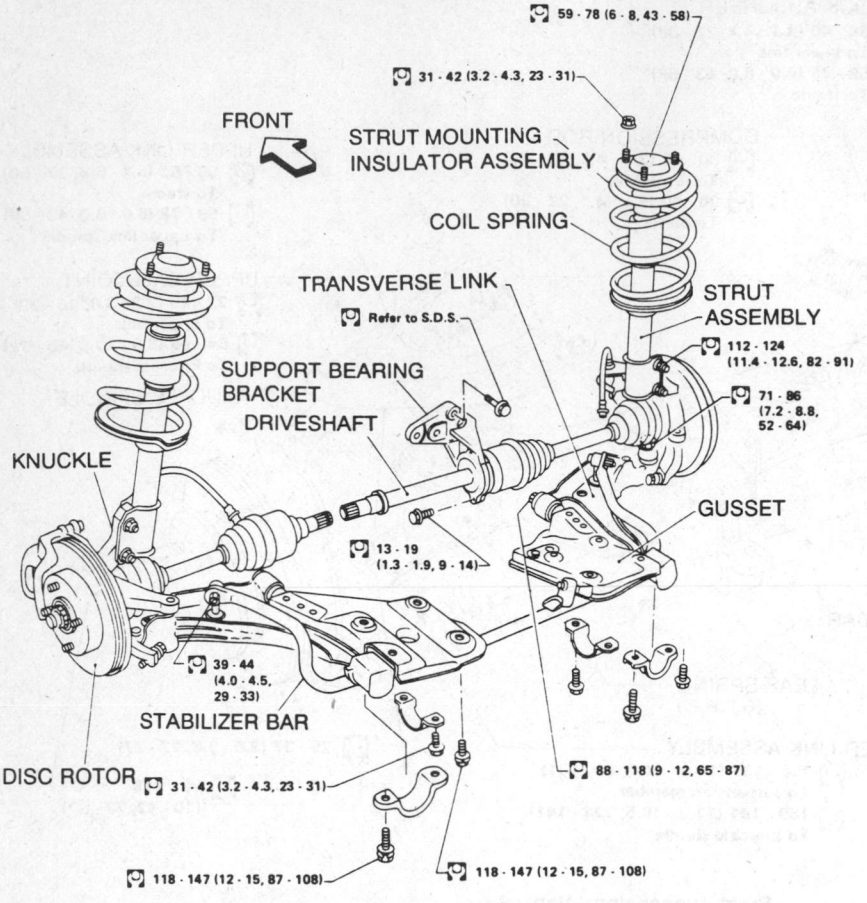

Strut-type front suspension — front wheel drive models

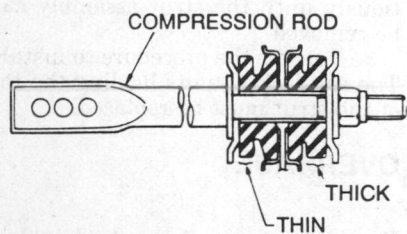

Correct compression rod bushing positioning — Van

4. Remove the rod-to-frame nut and remove the rod.

5. Installation is in the reverse order of removal. Make sure that the link-to-frame bushings are installed correctly. Tighten the two rod-to-link nuts and the rod-to-frame nut to 22–30 ft. lbs. (30–40 Nm).

Tension Rod And Stabilizer Bar

REMOVAL & INSTALLATION

Rear Wheel Drive Models Only

1. Support and set the load of the vehicle.

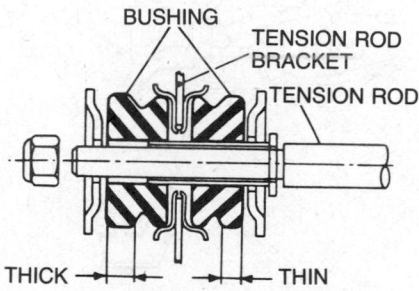

Tension rod bushing positioning — rear wheel drive models

2. Remove the tension rod-to-frame lock nuts. Remove the two mounting bolts at the transverse link (lower control arm) and then slide out the tension rod.

3. Unbolt the stabilizer bar at each transverse link.

4. Remove the four stabilizer bar bracket bolts, and remove the stabilizer bar.

5. Installation is in the reverse order of removal.

• Tighten the stabilizer bar-to-transverse link bolts to 12–16 ft. lbs. (16–22 Nm)

• Tighten the stabilizer bar bracket bolts to 22–29 ft. lbs. (29–39 Nm)

• Tighten the tension rod-to-transverse link nuts to 31–43 ft. lbs. (42–59 Nm)

• Tighten the tension rod-to-frame nut (bushing end) to 33–40 ft. lbs. (44–54 Nm). Always use a new lock-nut when reconnecting the tension rod to the frame

• Never tighten any bolts or nuts to their final torque unless the car is resting, unsupported, on the wheels

• Be certain the tension rod bushings are installed as shown in the illustration.

Stabilizer Bar

REMOVAL & INSTALLATION

Pulsar, Sentra and Stanza Wagon

1. Disconnect the parking brake cable at the equalizer on the Stanza wagon.

2. On the Stanza wagon (4wd), re-

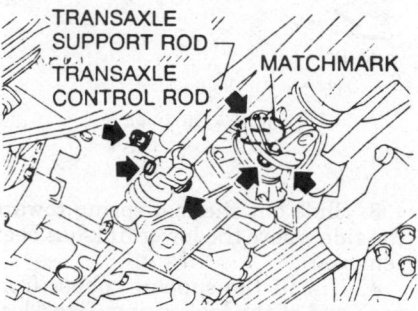

Removing the stabilizer bar on the Stanza wagon (4wd)

VIEW FROM B

O.K.

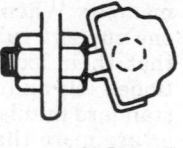

N.G.

Ball joint socket positioning — 1987-88 Pulsar/Sentra

move the mounting nuts for the transaxle support rod and the transaxle control rod.

3. Disconnect the front exhaust pipe at the manifold and position it out of the way.

4. On the Stanza wagon (4wd), matchmark the flanges and then separate the driveshaft from the transfer case.

5. Remove the stabilizer bar-to-transverse link (lower, control arm) mounting bolts.

6. Remove the four stabilizer bar bracket mounting bolts and then pull the bar out, around the link and exhaust pipe.

7. Installation is in the reverse order of removal. Never tighten the mounting bolts unless the car is resting on the ground with normal weight upon the wheels. On the 1987-88 Pulsar/Sentra, be sure the stabilzer bar ball joint socket is properly positioned.

Ball Joint

INSPECTION

The upper and lower ball joint should be replaced when play becomes excessive. Datsun does not publish specifications for this, giving instead a rotational torque figure for the ball joint. However, this requires removal for measurement. An effective way to determine play is to jack up the car until the wheel is clear of the ground. Do not place the jack under the ball joint; it must be unloaded. Place a long bar under the tire and move the wheel up and down. Keep one hand on top of the tire while doing this. If 1/4 in. or more of play exists at the top of the tire, the ball joint should be replaced. Be sure the wheel bearings are properly adjusted before making this measurement. A double check can be made; while the tire is being moved up and down, observe the ball joint. If play is seen, replace the ball joint.

REMOVAL & INSTALLATION

Lower Ball Joint

REAR WHEEL DRIVE MODELS

NOTE: On most late-model vehicles, the transverse link (lower control arm) must be removed and then the ball joint must be pressed out.

On the Van, the lower ball joint cannot be pressed out, it must be replaced as an assembly with the lower link

The ball joint should be greased every 30,000 miles. There is a plugged hole in the bottom of the joint for installation of a grease fitting.

1. Raise and support the car so the wheels hang free. Remove the wheel.

2. Unbolt the tension rod (compression rod on "Z" series) and stabilizer bar from transverse link.

3. Unbolt the strut from the steering arm.

4. Remove the cotter pin and ball joint stud nut. Separate the ball joint and steering arm.

5. Unbolt the ball joint from the transverse link.

6. Reverse the procedure to install a new ball joint. Grease the joint after installation.

FRONT WHEEL DRIVE MODELS

1. Jack up the car and support it on stands.

2. Remove the wheel.

3. Remove the halfshaft.

4. Separate the ball joint from the steering knuckle with a ball joint remover, being careful not to damage the ball joint dust cover if the ball joint is to be used again.

5. Remove the other ball joint from the transverse link and remove the ball joint.

Installation is the reverse of removal. Tighten the ball stud attaching nut (from ball joint-to-steering knuckle) to 22–29 ft. lbs., and the ball joint-to-transverse link bolts to 40–47 ft. lbs. (56–80 ft. lbs.—1987-88 Stanza).

Upper Ball Joint

VAN ONLY

1. Raise the front of the vehicle and support it on safety stands. Remove the wheel/tire assembly.

2. Remove the wheel bearing locknut.

3. Unbolt the brake caliper without disconnecting the brake line and suspend it out of the way.

4. Using a four armed puller if necesary, slide the wheel hub/brake disc assembly off the knuckle spindle.

5. Separate the tie rod from the knuckle spindle with a removal tool. Temporarily reinstall the stud nut upside down on the tie rod stud to prevent damage to the stud.

6. Loosen the upper joint securing nut. Separate the knuckle spindle from the upper ball joint stud and then remove the upper ball joint securing nut.

7. Remove the two upper link-to-ball joint bolts and the nut and then lift out the upper ball joint.

To install:

1. Install the upper ball joint into position and tighten the two bolts and the nut to 16–22 ft. lbs. (22–29 Nm).

2. Position a floor jack under the lower link.

3. Insert the knuckle spindle over the ball joint stud and then raise the floor jack enough to support the spindle in position.

4. Tighten the upper ball joint stud nut to 40–72 ft. lbs. (54–98 Nm). Always use new cotter pins.

5. Tighten the tie rod-to-knuckle arm nut to 40–72 ft. lbs. (54–98 Nm).

6. Install the wheel hub/brake disc assembly on the knuckle assembly and tighten the hub nut to 195–260 ft. lbs. (265–363 Nm). Always use a new cotter pin.

7. Install the brake caliper and tighten the bolts to 80–108 ft. lbs. (109–146 Nm).

8. Install the wheel/tire assembly, lower the vehicle and recheck all torques.

Lower Control Arm (Transverse Link)

REMOVAL & INSTALLATION

1985-88 Maxima

1. Raise the vehicle and support it securely on jackstands. Remove the nut fastening the link between the stabilizer bar and the control arm to the control arm.

2. Remove the three nuts fastening the ball joint to the lower control arm.

3. Remove the two bolts attaching the front and rear hinge joints of the control arm to the body.

4. Remove the control arm.

5. Installation is in the reverse order of removal. Tighten all bolts and nuts until they are snug enough to support the weight of the vehicle, but not quite fully tightened.

6. Lower the vehicle so it rests on the ground.

7. Tighten the forward bolts attaching the hinge joint to the body to 65–87 ft. lbs. Tighten the rear hinge joint bolts to 87–108 ft. lbs. and the ball joint mounting nuts to 56–80 ft. lbs.

1982-86 Pulsar/Sentra and Stanza

CAUTION
Always use new nuts when installing the ball joint to the control arm.

1. Raise and support the vehicle on safety stands.

2. Remove the wheel/tire assembly.

3. Remove the lower ball joint bolts from the control arm.

NOTE: If equipped with a stabilizer bar, disconnect it at the control arm.

4. Remove the control arm-to-body bolts.

5. Remove the gusset.

6. Remove the control arm from the vehicle.

7. Installation is in the reverse order of removal. Tighten the gusset-to-body bolts to 65–87 ft. lbs. (1982-86 Stanza), 87–108 ft. lbs. (1987-88 Stanza) or 65–80 ft. lbs. (Pulsar/Sentra);

the control arm securing nut to 65–80 ft. lbs. (1982-86 Stanza), 87–108 ft. lbs. (1987-88 Stanza) or 72–87 ft. lbs. (Pulsar/Sentra); the lower ball joint-to-control arm nuts to 40–51 ft. lbs. (1982-86 Stanza), 56–80 ft. lbs. (1987-88 Stanza) or 40–47 ft. lbs. (Pulsar/Sentra) and the stabilizer bar-to-control arm to 6.7–8.7 ft. lbs. (2wd Stanza and Pulsar/Sentra) or 12–16 ft. lbs. (4wd Stanza).

NOTE: When installing the link, tighten the nut securing the link spindle to the gusset. Final tightening should be made with the weight of the vehicle on the wheels.

Lower Control Arm (Transverse Link) and Ball Joint

REMOVAL & INSTALLATION

Rear Wheel Drive Models

You'll need a ball joint remover for this operation.

1. Jack up the vehicle and support it with jack stands; remove the wheel.
2. Remove the splash board, if so equipped.
3. Remove the cotter pin and castle nut from the side rod (steering arm) ball joint and separate the ball joint from the side rod. You'll need either a fork type or puller type ball joint remover.
4. Separate the steering knuckle arm from the MacPherson strut.
5. Remove the tension rod and stabilizer bar from the lower arm. Front wheel drive models do not have tension rods.
6. Remove the nuts or bolts connecting the lower control arm (transverse link) to the suspension crossmember on all models.
7. On the 810 and Maxima, to remove the transverse link (control arm) on the steering gear side, separate the gear arm from the sector shaft and lower steering linkage; to remove the transverse link on the idler arm side, detach the idler arm assembly from the body frame and lower steering linkage.
8. Remove the lower control arm (transverse link) with the suspension ball joint and knuckle arm still attached. Installation is the reverse of removal with the following notes:
9. When installing the control arm, temporarily tighten the nuts and/or bolts securing the control arm to the suspension crossmember. Tighten

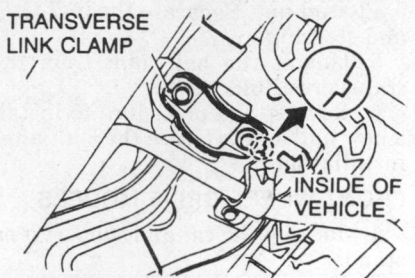

Transverse link clamp positioning – 1987-88 Pulsar/Sentra

them fully only after the car is sitting on its wheels.

10. Lubricate the ball joints after assembly.

1987-88 Pulsar/Sentra

A ball joint removal tool will be required for this operation.

1. Raise the vehicle and support it with safety stands. Remove the wheel.
2. Remove the wheel bearing locknut.
3. Remove the tie rod ball joint with a puller.
4. Remove the lower strut-to-knuckle mounting bolts and separate the strut from the knuckle.
5. Separate the outer end of the halfshaft from the steering knuckle by carefully tapping it with a rubber mallet.

— **CAUTION** —
Be sure to cover the CV-joints with a shop rag.

6. Using a ball joint removal tool, separate the lower ball joint stud from the steering knuckle.
7. Unbolt and remove the transverse link and ball joint as an assembly.
8. Installation is in the reverse order of removal. Make sure the tab on the transverse link clamp is pointing in the proper direction. Final tightening of all bolts should take place with the weight of the vehicle on the wheels. Check wheel alignment.

Lower Control Arm (Lower Link) And Ball Joint

REMOVAL & INSTALLATION

Van

You'll need a ball joint remover for this operation.

1. Jack up the vehicle and support it with jack stands; remove the wheel.
2. Loosen (not remove) the lower ball joint stud nut.

3. Remove the two bolts and nut attaching the upper ball joint to the upper link.
4. Position an ball joint separater over the lower ball joint and then reinstall the upper joint mounting bolts again; finger-tighten them only.
5. Separate the knuckle spindle from the lower ball joint stud.
6. Remove the stabilizer bar brackets from the lower links and then swing the bar down and away from the links.
7. Support the lower link with a floor jack and remove the shock absorber and compression rod.
8. Remove the nut that attaches the spring support rubber to the leaf spring.
9. Slowly lower the floor jack until the leaf spring is completely tension free. Pivot the lower link downward and then position the jack under the leaf spring and raise it.
10. Remove the nut securing the lower link pin to the suspension crossmember and then lift out the link/ball joint assembly itself.
11. Installation is in the reverse order of removal. Tighten the lower link pin nut to 80–101 ft. lbs. (108–137 Nm). Tighten the support rubber-to-spring bolt to 22–27 ft. lbs. (29–37 Nm) and make sure that the washer does not protrude past the edge of the leaf spring. Tighten the stabilizer bar bracket bolt to 23–31 ft. lbs. (31–42 Nm); make sure that the thick portion of the bushing is facing forward. Tighten the upper ball joint-to-upper link bolts and nut to 16–22 ft. lbs. (22–29 Nm). Tighten the upper ball joint stud nut to 40–72 ft. lbs. (54–98 Nm) and the lower ball joint stud nut to 124–141 ft. lbs. (169–191 Nm); always use new cotter pins.
12. Lower the vehicle and recheck all torque figures with the wheels on the ground and the car unladen.

Upper Control Arm (Upper Link)

REMOVAL & INSTALLATION

Van Only

1. Raise the front of the vehicle and support it with safety stands. Remove the wheel.
2. Position a floor jack under the lower link and raise it just enough to support the link.
3. Remove the bolts and nut connecting the upper ball joint to the upper link.
4. Remove the bolts connecting the upper link spindle to the frame and lift out the upper link.

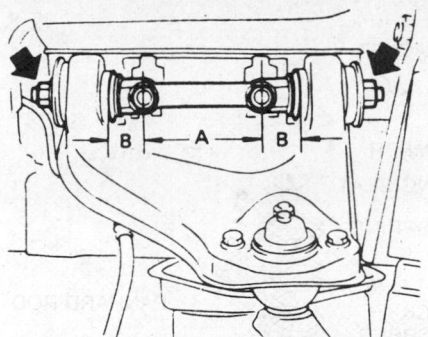

Upper link spindle installation – Van

5. To install, position the upper link at the frame with the camber adjusting shims installed and tighten the link spindle mounting bolts to 37–50 ft. lbs. (50–68 Nm).

6. Reconnect the upper link to the ball joint and tighten the bolts and nut to 16–22 ft. lbs. (22–29 Nm).

7. Check dimensions A and B (as shown) on the upper link spindle. A: 90mm (3.54 in.); B: 27.5mm (1.083 in.).

8. Lower the car and recheck all torque figures. Check the front end alignment.

Front Wheel Bearing

ADJUSTMENT

NOTE: For wheel bearing adjustment on front wheel drive models, please refer to "Drive Axles".

Rear Wheel Drive Only

1. Raise and support the vehicle safely, remove the front wheels and the brake shoes.

2. While rotating the brake disc, torque wheel bearing lock nut to 18–22 ft. lbs. on all models.

3. Loosen lock nut approximately 60 degrees on all models. Install adjusting cap and align groove of nut with hole in spindle. If alignment cannot be obtained, change position of adjusting cap. Also, if alignment cannot be obtained, loosen lock nut slightly but not more than 15 degrees.

4. Install brake shoes.

Front Wheel Alignment

CASTER AND CAMBER

Caster is the forward or rearward tilt of the upper end of the kingpin, or the upper ball joint, which results in a slight tilt of the steering axis forward or backward. Rearward tilt is referred

to as a positive caster, while forward tilt is referred to as a negative caster.

Camber is the inward or outward tilt from the vertical, measured in degrees, of the front wheels at the top. An outward tilt gives the wheel positive camber. Proper camber is critical to assure even tire wear.

Since caster and camber are adjusted traditionally by adding or subtracting shims behind the upper control arms, and the models covered in this guide have replaced the upper control arm with the MacPherson strut, the only way to adjust caster and camber is to replace bent or worn parts of the front suspension.

NOTE: Camber is adjustable on the 1987-88 Pulsar/Sentra, while both camber and caster are adjustable on the Van.

Adjustment

1987-88 PULSAR/SENTRA ONLY

1. Camber is adjusted by means of a pin on the top-most lower strut mounting bolts.

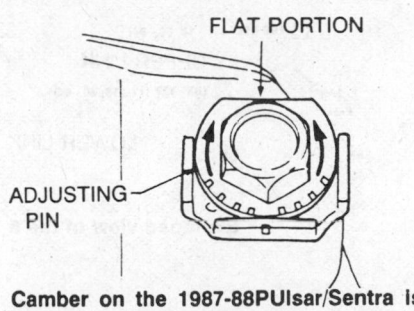

Camber on the 1987-88 Pulsar/Sentra is set by means of an adjusting pin on the lower end of the strut

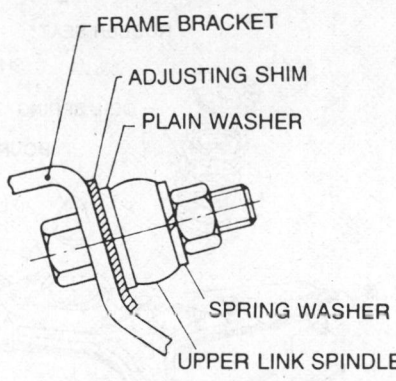

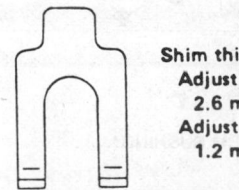

Shim thickness
Adjusting shim A:
2.6 mm (0.102 in)
Adjusting shim B:
1.2 mm (0.047 in)

Camber and caster on the Van are adjusted by means of shims

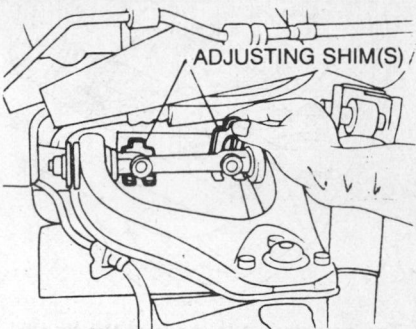

Camber and caster adjustment – Van

2. The pin is installed with the flat side facing downward at the factory. Remove the pin and then reinstall it with the flat side facing up.

3. Turn the pin to adjust camber. Camber changes about 15' with each gradation of the adjusting pin.

4. Tighten the pin to 72–87 ft. lbs. (98–118 Nm).

VAN

1. Camber and caster are both adjusted by means of shims positioned between the upper link spindle and the frame.

2. The standard number for the adjusting shims is Shim A: 1 piece; Shim B: nothing. Refer to "Upper Link" for shim identification.

3. The number of shims inserted in the same position should not be more than two pieces; meaning shim A would be two pieces maximum and shim B would be one piece maximum.

4. When installing shims, always make sure the pawl faces the spindle and that they are inserted from the bracket side.

TOE

Toe is the amount, measured in a fraction of an inch, that the wheels are closer together at one end than the other. Toe-in means that the front wheels are closer together at the front than the rear, toe-out means the rears are closer than the front. Most models are adjusted to have slight amount of toe-in. Toe-in is adjusted by turning the tie rod, which has a right-hand thread on one and a left-hand thread on the other.

You can check your vehicle's toe-in yourself without special equipment if you make careful measurements. The wheels must be straight ahead.

1. Toe-in can be determined by measuring the distance between the center of the tire treads, at the front of the tire and at the rear. If the tread pattern of your car's tires make this impossible, you can measure between

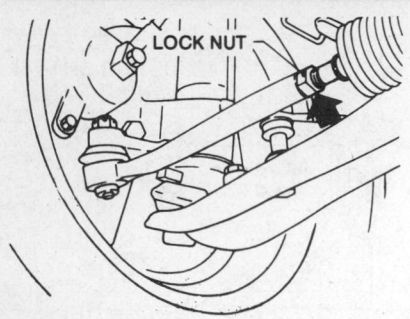

Toe adjustment is made at the tie rod

the edges of the wheel rims, but make sure to move the car forward and measure in a couple of places to avoid errors caused by bent rims or wheel runout.

2. If the measurement is not within specifications, loosen the lock nuts at both ends of the tie rod (the driver's side lock nut is left-hand threaded).

3. Turn the top of the tie rod toward the front of the car to reduce toe-in, or toward the rear to increase it. When the correct dimension is reached, tighten the lock nuts and check the adjustment.

NOTE: The length of the tie rods must always be equal to each other.

STEERING ANGLE ADJUSTMENT

The maximum steering angle is adjusted by stopper bolts on the steering arms. Loosen the lock nut on the stopper bold, turn the stopped bold in or out as required to obtain the proper maximum steering angle and retighten the lock nut.

REAR SUSPENSION

Shock Absorber

REMOVAL & INSTALLATION

210, 510 Sedan, 200SX and 1986-88 Stanza Wagon (2WD)

1. Open the trunk and remove the cover panel (if necessary) to expose the shock mounts. Pry off the mount covers, if so equipped. On leaf spring models, jack up the rear of the vehicle and support the rear axle on stands.

2. Remove the two nuts holding the

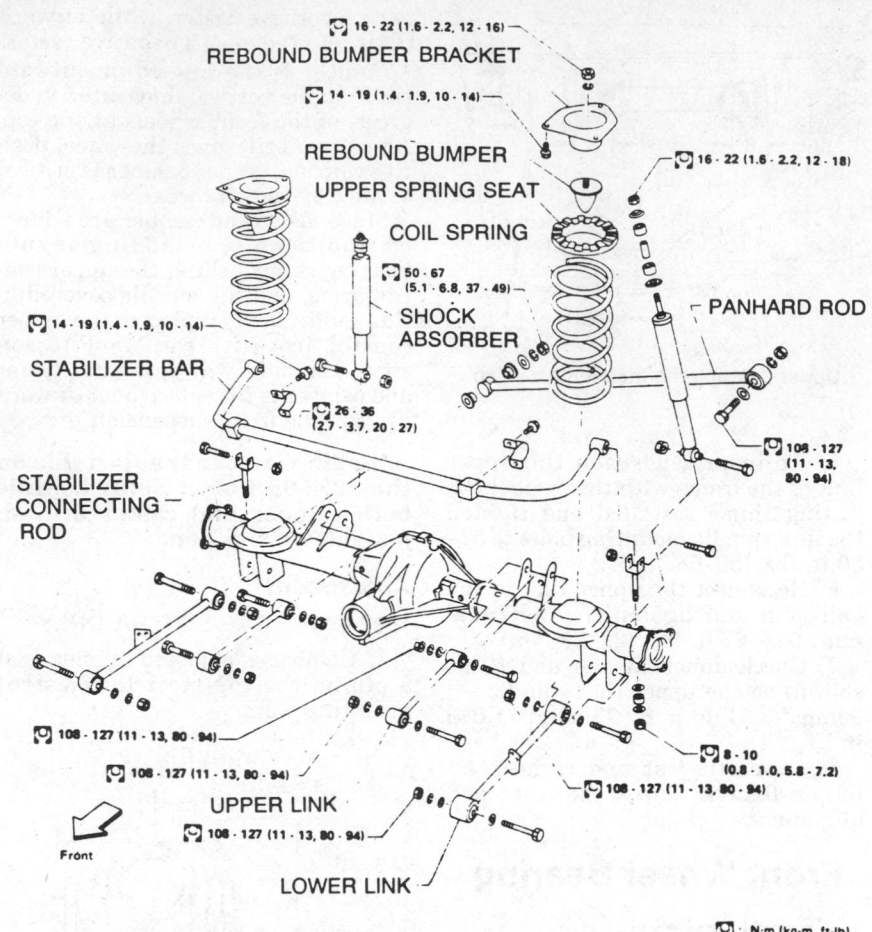

Exploded view of the 5 link rear suspension — Van

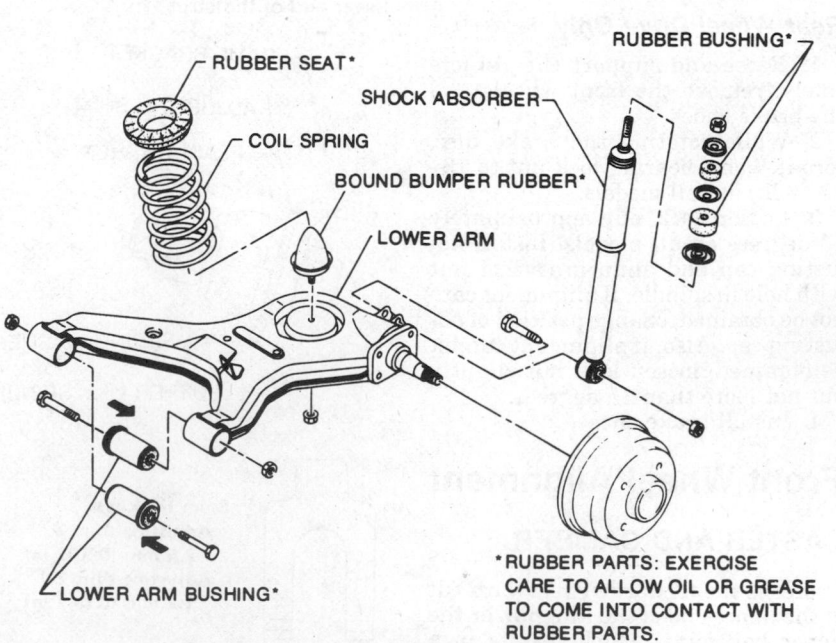

One side of a typical trailing arm rear suspension

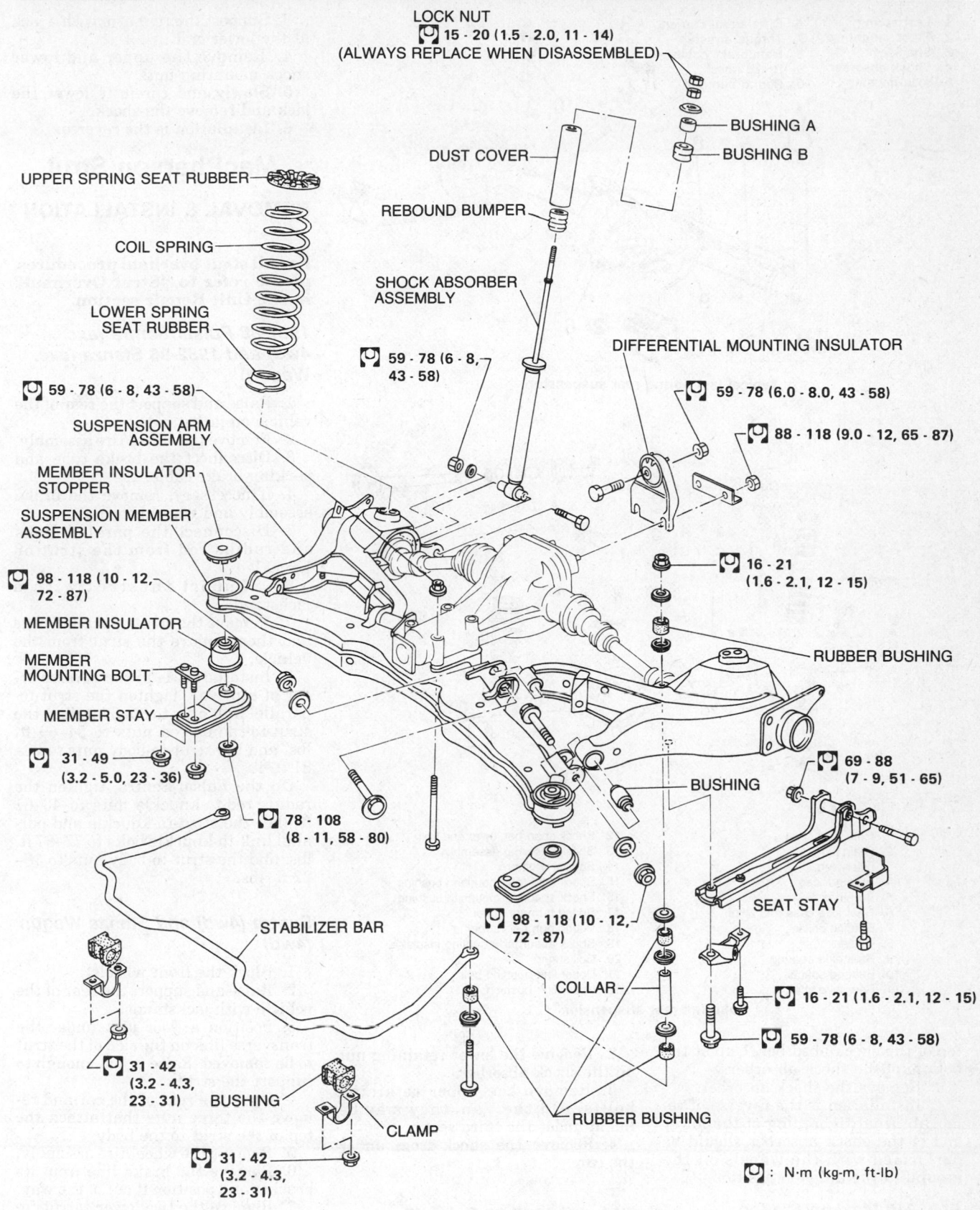

LOCK NUT
🔧 15 - 20 (1.5 - 2.0, 11 - 14)
(ALWAYS REPLACE WHEN DISASSEMBLED)

BUSHING A

BUSHING B

DUST COVER

UPPER SPRING SEAT RUBBER

REBOUND BUMPER

COIL SPRING

SHOCK ABSORBER
ASSEMBLY

LOWER SPRING
SEAT RUBBER

DIFFERENTIAL MOUNTING INSULATOR

🔧 59 - 78 (6 - 8,
43 - 58)

🔧 59 - 78 (6.0 - 8.0, 43 - 58)

🔧 59 - 78 (6 - 8, 43 - 58)

🔧 88 - 118 (9.0 - 12, 65 - 87)

SUSPENSION ARM
ASSEMBLY

MEMBER INSULATOR
STOPPER

SUSPENSION MEMBER
ASSEMBLY

🔧 16 - 21
(1.6 - 2.1, 12 - 15)

🔧 98 - 118 (10 - 12,
72 - 87)

MEMBER INSULATOR

RUBBER BUSHING

MEMBER
MOUNTING BOLT

MEMBER STAY

🔧 31 - 49
(3.2 - 5.0, 23 - 36)

🔧 69 - 88
(7 - 9, 51 - 65)

BUSHING

🔧 78 - 108
(8 - 11, 58 - 80)

SEAT STAY

STABILIZER BAR

🔧 98 - 118 (10 - 12,
72 - 87)

COLLAR

🔧 16 - 21 (1.6 - 2.1, 12 - 15)

🔧 59 - 78 (6 - 8, 43 - 58)

🔧 31 - 42
(3.2 - 4.3,
23 - 31)

BUSHING

CLAMP

RUBBER BUSHING

🔧 : N·m (kg-m, ft-lb)

🔧 31 - 42
(3.2 - 4.3,
23 - 31)

IRS coil spring rear suspension—200SX shown; others similar

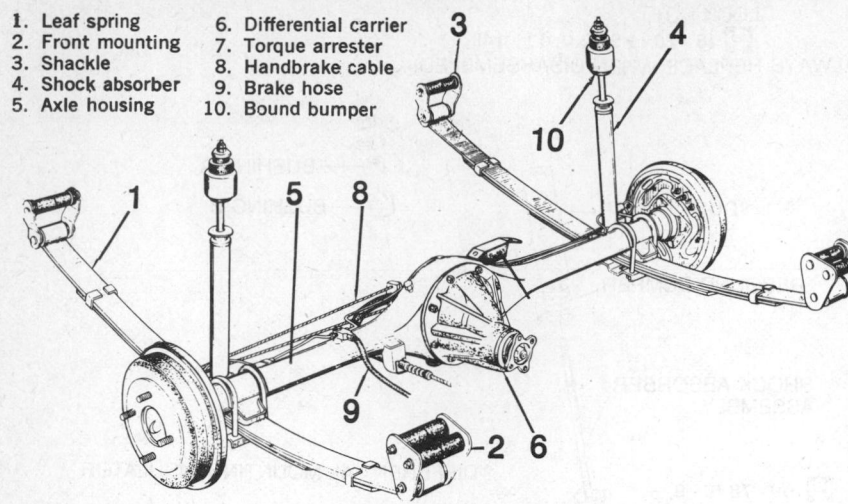

1. Leaf spring
2. Front mounting
3. Shackle
4. Shock absorber
5. Axle housing
6. Differential carrier
7. Torque arrester
8. Handbrake cable
9. Brake hose
10. Bound bumper

Typical leaf spring rear suspension

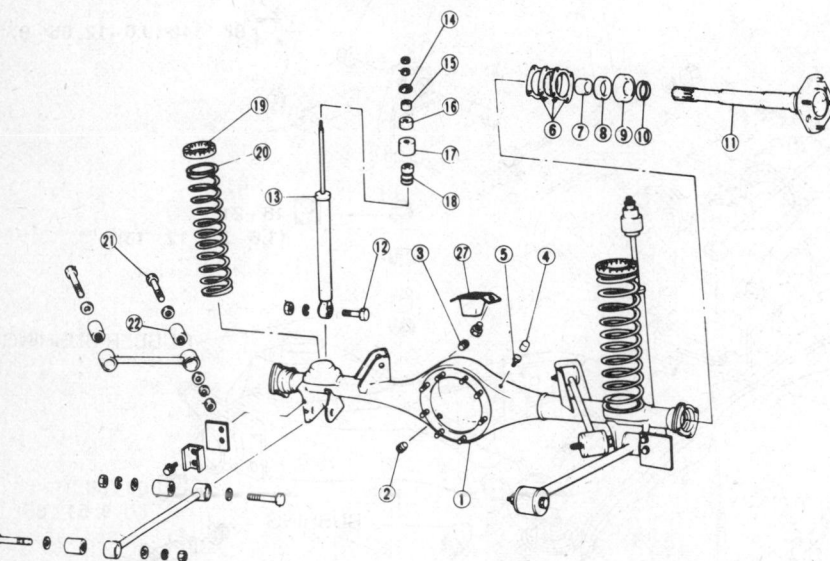

1. Rear axle case
2. Drain plug
3. Filler plug
4. Breather cap
5. Breather
6. Rear axle case end shim
7. Bearing collar
8. Oil seal
9. Rear axle bearing
10. Bearing spacer
11. Rear axle shaft
12. Shock absorber lower end bolt
13. Shock absorber assembly
14. Special washer
15. Shock absorber mounting bushing
16. Shock absorber mounting bushing
17. Bound bumper cover
18. Bound bumper rubber
19. Shock absorber mounting insulator
20. Coil spring
21. Upper link bushing bolt
22. Upper link bushing

Four link rear suspension

top of the shock absorber. Unbolt the bottom of the shock absorber.

3. Remove the shock absorber.

4. Installation is the reverse of removal. Final tightening of the lower end of the shock absorber should be performed with the wheels on the ground in the unladen position.

510, 810/Maxima Station Wagons and Van

1. Raise the rear of the car and support the axle on jack stands.

2. Remove the lower retaining nut on the shock absorber.

3. Remove the upper retaining bolt(s). On the Van, they may be found under the third seat.

4. Remove the shock from under the car.

310 and 1987-88 Pulsar/Sentra

1. Raise and support the rear of the car.

2. Remove the wheels.

3. Support the rear arm with a jack at the lower end.

4. Remove the upper and lower shock mounting nuts.

5. Slowly and carefully lower the jack and remove the shock.

6. Installation is the reverse.

MacPherson Strut

REMOVAL & INSTALLATION

For all strut overhaul procedures, please refer to "Strut Overhaul" in the Unit Repair section.

1987-88 Pulsar/Sentra (exc. 4wd) and 1982-86 Stanza (exc. Wagon)

1. Raise and support the rear of the vehicle on jackstands.

2. Remove the wheel/tire assembly.

3. Disconnect the brake tube and parking brake cable.

4. If necessary, remove the brake assembly and wheel bearing.

5. Disconnect the parallel links and radius rod from the strut or knuckle.

6. Support the strut with a jachstand.

7. Remove the strut upper end nuts and then remove the strut from the vehicle.

8. Installation is in the reverse order of removal. Tighten the strut-to-parallel link nuts to 65–87 ft. lbs., the strut-to-radius rod nuts to 54–69 ft. lbs. and the strut-to-body nuts to 23–31 ft. lbs.

On the Pulsar/Sentra, tighten the radius rod-to-knuckle nuts to 43–61 ft. lbs., the strut-to-knuckle and parallel link-to-knuckle bolts to 72–87 ft. lbs. and the strut-to-body nuts to 18–22 ft. lbs.

Sentra (4wd) and Stanza Wagon (4wd)

1. Block the front wheels.

2. Raise and support the rear of the vehicle with jackstands.

3. Position a floor jack under the transverse link on the side of the strut to be removed. Raise it just enough to support the strut.

4. Open the rear of the car and remove the three nuts that attach the top of the strut to the body.

5. Remove the wheel/tire assembly.

6. Remove the brake line from its bracket and position it out of the way.

7. Remove the two lower satrut-to-knuckle mounting bolts.

8. Carefully lower the floor jack and remove the strut.

9. Installation is the reverse order

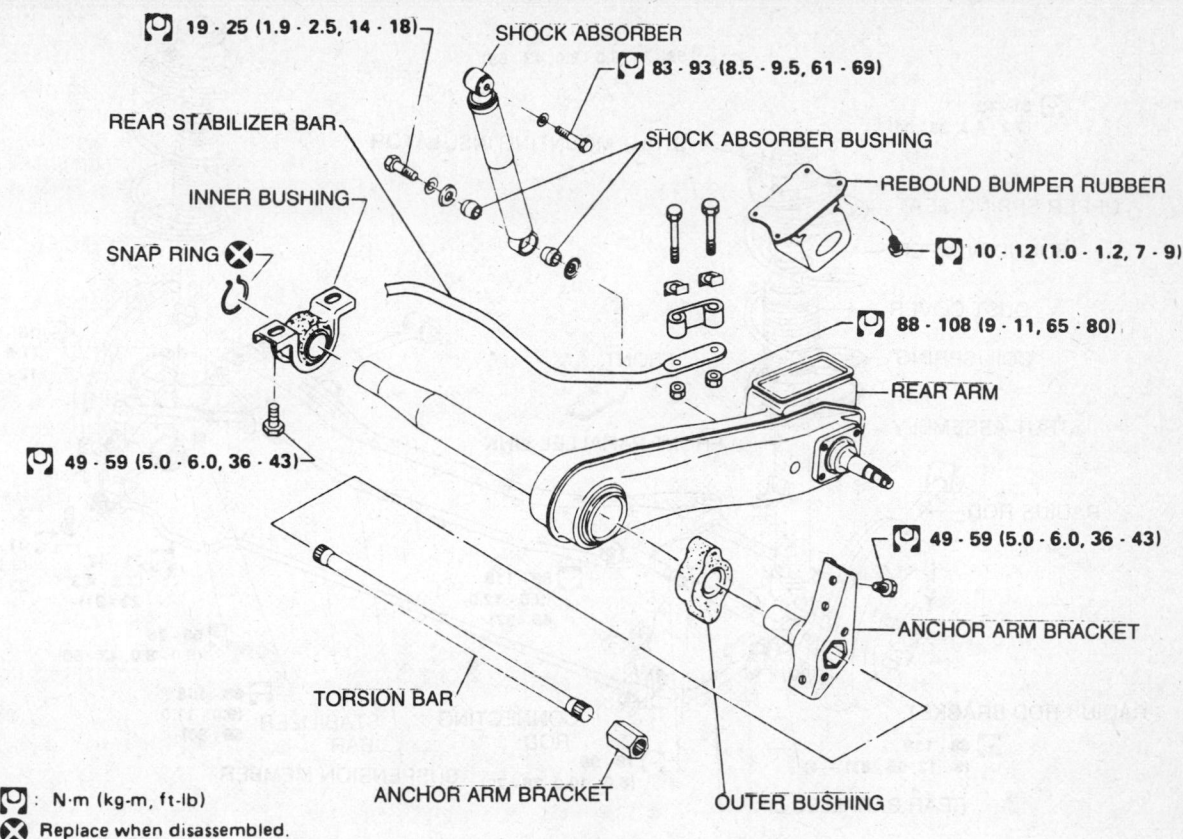

19 · 25 (1.9 · 2.5, 14 · 18)

SHOCK ABSORBER

83 · 93 (8.5 · 9.5, 61 · 69)

REAR STABILIZER BAR

SHOCK ABSORBER BUSHING

INNER BUSHING

REBOUND BUMPER RUBBER

SNAP RING

10 · 12 (1.0 · 1.2, 7 · 9)

88 · 108 (9 · 11, 65 · 80)

REAR ARM

49 · 59 (5.0 · 6.0, 36 · 43)

49 · 59 (5.0 · 6.0, 36 · 43)

ANCHOR ARM BRACKET

TORSION BAR

ANCHOR ARM BRACKET

OUTER BUSHING

: N·m (kg-m, ft-lb)

Replace when disassembled.

Typical torsion bar rear suspension—Stanza wagon (2wd)

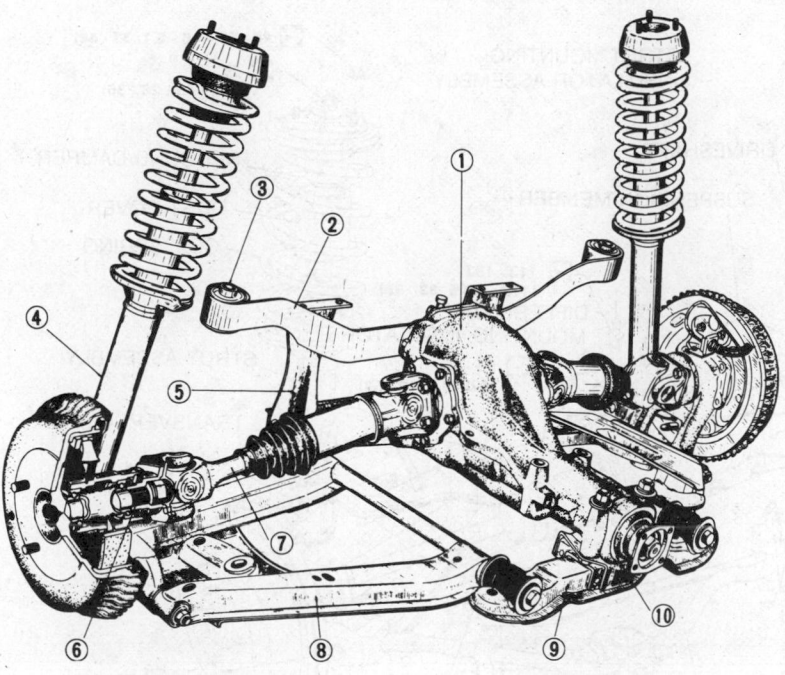

1. Differential carrier
2. Differential case mount rear member
3. Differential case mount rear insulator
4. Strut assembly
5. Link mount brace
6. Rear axle shaft
7. Drive shaft
8. Transverse link
9. Differential case mount front member
10. Differential case mount front insulator

Typical MacPherson strut-type rear suspension—rear wheel drive models

of removal. Final tightening of the strut mounting bolts should take place with the wheels on the ground and the vehicle unladen. Tighten the upper strut-to-body nuts to 33–40 ft. lbs. (45–60 Nm). Tighten the lower strut-to-knuckle bolts to 111–120 ft. lbs. (151–163 Nm).

1981-84 810/Maxima

1. Raise the car and safely support the rear with jackstands and a floor jack.
2. Open the trank and remove the three nuts which secure the top of the dtrut to the body.
3. Disconnect the strut at the bottom by removing the bolt at the suspension arm.
4. Installation is in the reverse order of removal. Install the strut so that the larger hole on the lower end faces outward.

1987-88 Stanza (exc. Wagon) and 1985-88 Maxima

1. Unclip the rear brake line at the strut. Unbolt and remove the brake assembly, wheel bearings and backing plate. Position the brake caliper out of the way and suspend it so as not to stress the brake line.

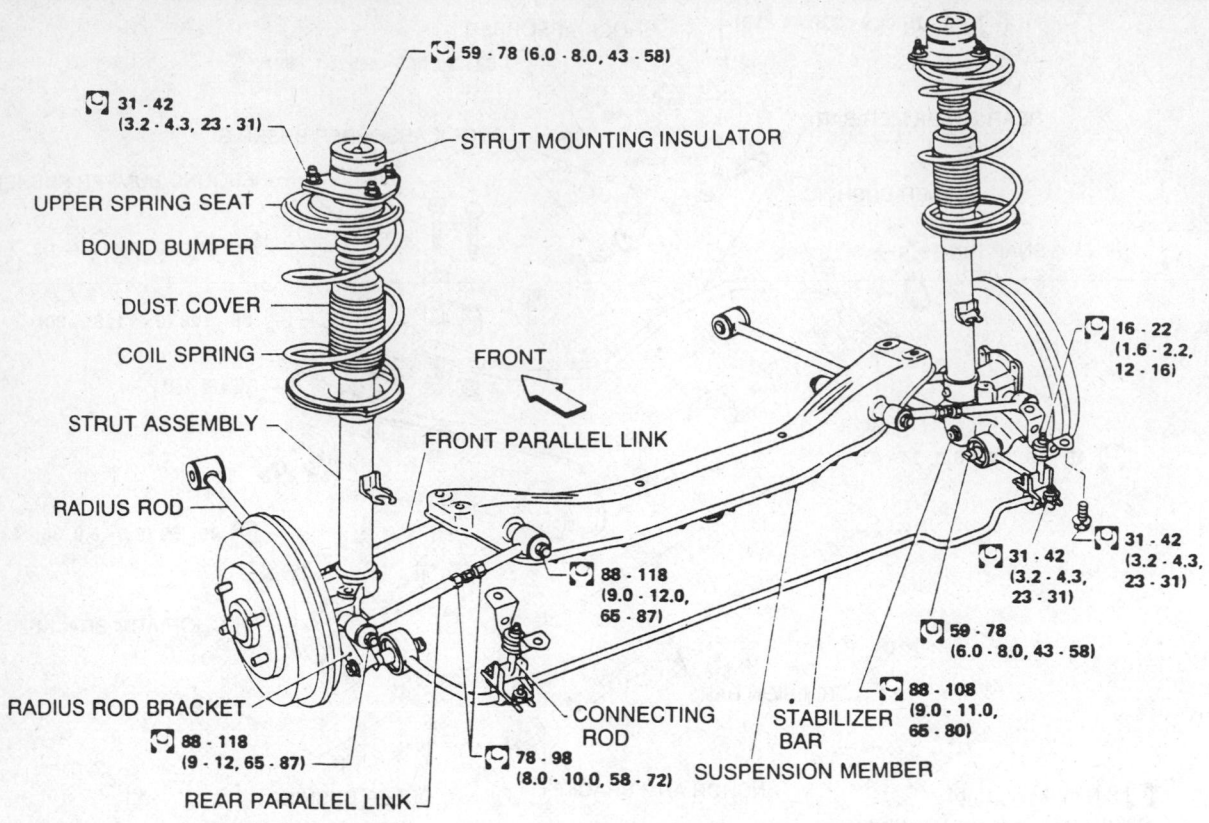

31 - 42 (3.2 - 4.3, 23 - 31)

59 - 78 (6.0 - 8.0, 43 - 58)

STRUT MOUNTING INSULATOR

UPPER SPRING SEAT

BOUND BUMPER

DUST COVER

COIL SPRING

FRONT

STRUT ASSEMBLY

FRONT PARALLEL LINK

RADIUS ROD

16 - 22 (1.6 - 2.2, 12 - 16)

31 - 42 (3.2 - 4.3, 23 - 31)

31 - 42 (3.2 - 4.3, 23 - 31)

88 - 118 (9.0 - 12.0, 65 - 87)

59 - 78 (6.0 - 8.0, 43 - 58)

RADIUS ROD BRACKET

88 - 118 (9 - 12, 65 - 87)

REAR PARALLEL LINK

CONNECTING ROD

78 - 98 (8.0 - 10.0, 58 - 72)

STABILIZER BAR

SUSPENSION MEMBER

88 - 108 (9.0 - 11.0, 65 - 80)

Typical MacPherson strut-type rear suspension—front wheel drive models

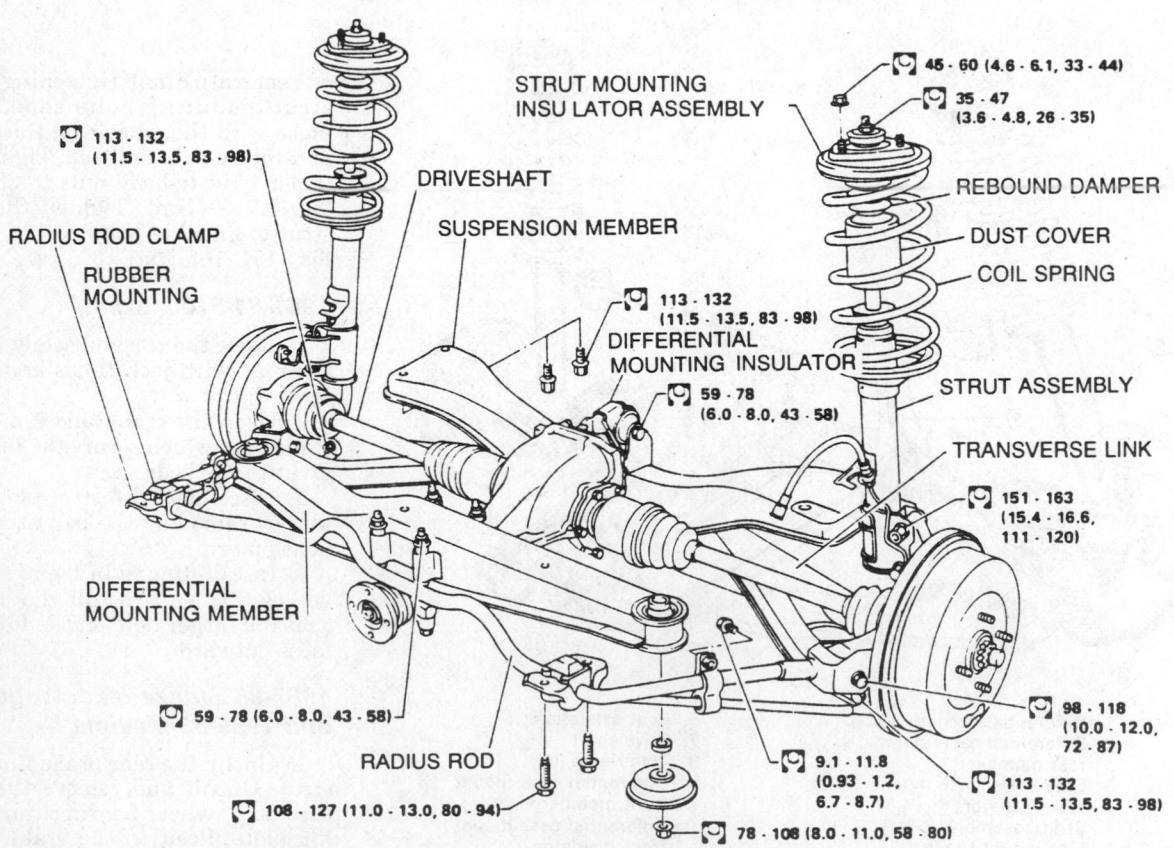

113 - 132 (11.5 - 13.5, 83 - 98)

RADIUS ROD CLAMP

RUBBER MOUNTING

DRIVESHAFT

SUSPENSION MEMBER

STRUT MOUNTING INSULATOR ASSEMBLY

45 - 60 (4.6 - 6.1, 33 - 44)

35 - 47 (3.6 - 4.8, 26 - 35)

REBOUND DAMPER

DUST COVER

COIL SPRING

113 - 132 (11.5 - 13.5, 83 - 98)

DIFFERENTIAL MOUNTING INSULATOR

59 - 78 (6.0 - 8.0, 43 - 58)

STRUT ASSEMBLY

TRANSVERSE LINK

151 - 163 (15.4 - 16.6, 111 - 120)

DIFFERENTIAL MOUNTING MEMBER

59 - 78 (6.0 - 8.0, 43 - 58)

RADIUS ROD

108 - 127 (11.0 - 13.0, 80 - 94)

9.1 - 11.8 (0.93 - 1.2, 6.7 - 8.7)

78 - 106 (8.0 - 11.0, 58 - 80)

98 - 118 (10.0 - 12.0, 72 - 87)

113 - 132 (11.5 - 13.5, 83 - 98)

Typical MacPherson strut-type rear suspension—1986-88 Stanza wagon (4wd)

2. Remove the radius rod mounting bolt, radius rod mounting bracket.

3. Remove the two parallel link mounting bolts.

4. Remove the rear seat and parcel shelf.

5. Position a floor jack under the strut and raise it just enought to support the strut.

6. Remove the three upper strut mounting nuts and then lift out the strut.

7. Installation is in the reverse order of removal. Tightrn all bolts sufficiently to safely support the vehicle and then lower the car to the ground so it rests on its own weight. Tighten the upper strut mounting nuts to 23–31 ft. lbs., the radius rod bracket bolts to 43–58 ft. lbs. and the parallel link mounting bolts to 65–87 ft. lbs.

280ZX and 300ZX

1. Block the front wheels.

2. Raise and support the rear of the vehicle on jackstands.

NOTE: The vehicle should be far enough off the ground so that the rear spring does not support any weight.

3. Working inside the luggage compartment, turn and remove the caps above the strut mounts. Remove the three strut mounting nuts.

4. Remove the mounting bolt for the strut at the lower arm (transverse link) and then lift out the strut.

5. Installation is in the reverse order of removal. Install the upper end first and secure with the nuts snugged down but not fully tightened. Attach the lower end of the strut to the transverse link and the tighten the upper nuts to 22–29 ft. lbs. (30–40 Nm). Tighten the lower mounting bolt to 43–58 ft. lbs. (60–80 Nm).

Springs

REMOVAL & INSTALLATION

Leaf Spring Type

510 AND 1981-82 810 STATION WAGONS

1. Raise the rear of the car and support it with jack stands.

2. Remove the wheels and tires.

3. Disconnect the lower end of the shock absorber and remove the U-bolt nuts.

4. Place a jack under the rear axle.

5. Disconnect the spring shackle bolts at the front and rear of the spring.

6. Lower the jack slowly and remove the spring.

7. Installation is the reverse of removal.

Coil Spring Type

Four types of coil spring suspension are used:

Trailing Arm Type – 310 and 1981-86 Pulsar/Sentra

Four/Five Bar Link Type – 210, 510, 810, Van and 1981-83 200SX

MacPherson Strut Type – 810/Maxima, 280ZX, 300ZX, 1987-88 Pulsar/Sentra, Stanza and Stanza Wagon (4wd)

I.R.S. Coil Spring Type – 1984-88 200SX with independent rear suspension

—————— CAUTION ——————

Coil springs are under considerable tension and can exert enough force to cause bodily injury. Exercise extreme caution when working with them.

TRAILING ARM TYPE

1. Raise the rear of the vehicle and support it on jack stands.

2. Remove the wheels.

3. Disconnect the handbrake linkage and return spring.

4. Unbolt the axle shaft flange at the wheel end.

5. Unbolt the rubber bumper inside the bottom of the coil spring.

6. Jack up the suspension arm and unbolt the shock absorber lower mounting.

7. Lower the jack slowly and cautiously. Remove the coil spring, spring seat, and rubber bumper.

8. Reverse the procedure to install, making sure that the flat face of the spring is at the top.

FOUR/FIVE BAR LINK TYPE

1. Raise the car and support it with jack stands.

2. Support the center of the differential with a jack or other suitable tool.

3. Remove the rear wheels.

4. Remove the bolts securing the lower ends of the shock absorbers.

5. Remove the upper panhard rod mounting bolt on the Van.

6. Lower the jack under the differential slowly and carefully, and remove the coil springs after they are fully extended. Remember the positioning of the upper spring seats.

6. Installation is in the reverse order of removal. Replace the upper spring seats in their correct position and tighten all bolts with the wheels on the ground.

MACPHERSON STRUT TYPE

NOTE: MacPherson strut removal and installation proce- dures are detailed previously in this section.

I.R.S. COIL SPRING TYPE

This suspension is similar to the I.R.S. MacPherson strut type, except this type utilizes separate coil springs and shock absorbers, instead of strut units.

1. Set a suitable spring compressor on the coil spring.

2. Jack up the rear end of the car.

3. Compress the coil spring until it is of sufficient length to be removed. Remove the spring.

4. When installing the spring, be sure the upper and lower spring seat rubbers are not twisted and have not slipped off when installing the coil spring.

Torsion Bar Type

1986-88 STANZA WAGON (2WD)

1. Raise the rear of the vehicle and support it with jack stands.

2. Remove the wheel and tire assembly. Release the parking brake.

3. Remove the inner hub cap, the cotter pin and the wheel bearing lock nut. Remove the brake drum.

4. Disconnect and plug the hydraulic brake line. Disconnect the parking brake cable.

5. Remove the four brake backing plate mounting bolts and then slide the backing plate along with the inner wheel bearing off of the rear axle.

6. Disconnect the rear stabilizer bar.

7. Unbolt the anchor arm bracket and then remove the inner bushing bracket mounting bolts. Remove the torsion bar.

8. Installation is in the reverse order of removal. Tighten the inner bushing and anchor arm mounting bolts to 36–43 ft. lbs. (49–59 Nm). Tighten the stabilizer bar bolts to 65–80 ft. lbs. (88–108 Nm).

Rear Wheel Bearings

NOTE: For wheel bearing procedures on rear wheel drive models, please refer to "Rear Axle Shaft" in the Drive Axle section.

ADJUSTMENT

310

The rear wheel bearings on the 310 are adjusted in the same manner as front wheel bearings. Use this procedure for all 310 models.

1. Raise the rear of the car.

2. Remove the wheel.

3. Remove and discard the cotter pin.

4. Tighten the wheel bearing lock nut to 29–33 ft. lbs.

5. Rotate the drum back and forth a few revolutions to snug down the bearing.

6. After turning the wheel, recheck the torque of the nut then loosen it 90° from its position.

7. Check the drum rotation. If it does not move freely, check for dragging brake shoes, or dirty bearings.

8. Align the cotter pin hole in the spindle with that in the lock nut, and install a new cotter pin.

9. Tighten the nut no more than 15° to align the holes.

Pulsar/Sentra, Stanza and 1985-88 Maxima

1. Apply multi-purpose grease to the following parts:
   a. threaded portion of the wheel spindle.
   b. mating surfaces of the lock washer and outer wheel bearing.
   c. inner hub cap.
   d. grease seal lip.
2. Tighten the wheel bearing nut to 18–25 ft. lbs. (25–34 Nm).
3. Turn the wheel several times in both directions to seat the bearing correctly.
4. Loosen the wheel bearing nut until there is no preload and then tighten it to 6.5–8.7 ft. lbs. (9–12 Nm). Turn the wheel several times again and then retighten it to the same torque again.
5. Install the adjusting cap and align any of its slots with the hole in the spindle.

NOTE: If necessary, tighten the lock nut as much as 15 degrees in order to align the spindle hole with one in the adjusting cap.

6. Rotate the hub in both directions several times while measuring its starting torque and axial play. They should be as follows:
   Axial play: 0
      Starting torque: W/grease seal – 6.9 inch lbs. (0.8 Nm) or less
      When measured at wheel hub bolt – 3.1 lbs. (13.7 N).
7. Correctly measure the rotation from the starting force toward the tangential direction against the hub bolt. The above figures do not allow for any "dragging" resistance. When measuring starting torque, confirm that no "dragging" exists. No wheel bearing axial play can exist at all.
8. Spread the cotter pin and install the inner hub cap.
9. Installation of the remaining components is in the reverse order of removal.

Rear Wheel Alignment

ADJUSTMENT

200SX and 300ZX

Rear toe-in can be adjusted by the use of cams on the inside of rear control arm bushing pins.

NOTE: Always set the cams in the same position on the right and left control arm busing pins.

1987-88 Stanza (exc. 4wd Wagon) and 1985-88 Maxima

Rear toe-in can be adjusted by means of lock nuts and a stud bolt on the rear parallel links. Simply loosen the two lock nuts and then turn the stud bolt to lengthen (decrease toe) or shorten (increase) the link. Be certain that both the left and right links are adjusted to the same length.

NOTE: When tightening the lock nut, or checking its torque, attach a wrench to the "locking" section of the rod in order to prevent the bushing from twisting.

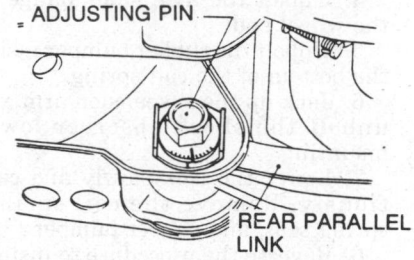

Adjusting the rear wheel toe—1987-88 Pulsar/Sentra (exc. 4wd)

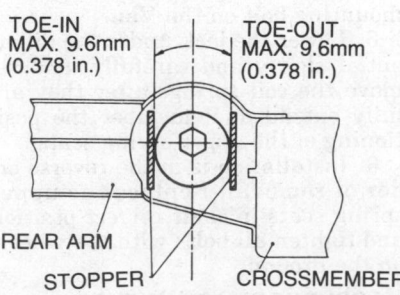

Adjusting the rear wheel toe—200SX shown

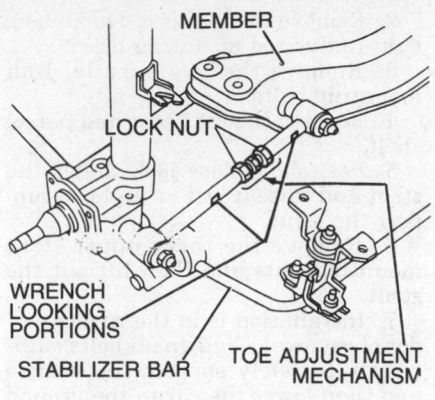

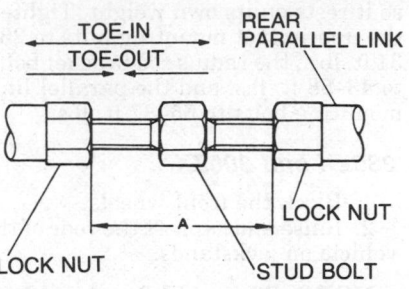

STANDARD LENGTH "A": 49.5mm (1.949 in.)

Adjusting the rear wheel toe—1985-88 Maxima and 1987-88 Stanza

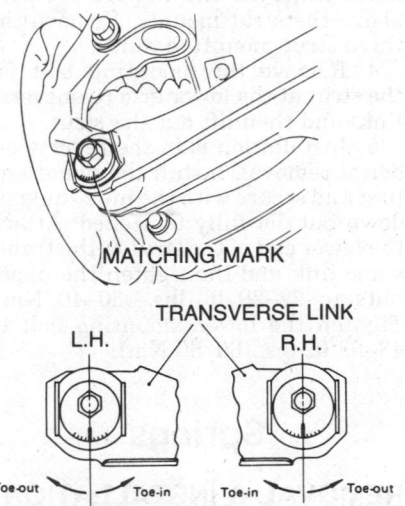

REAR VIEW ON VEHICLE

Adjusting the rear wheel toe—1986-88 Stanza wagon (4wd) and 1987-88 Sentra (4wd)

Sentra (4wd) and Stanza Wagon (4wd)

Rear toe-in can be adjusted by means of a fixing bolt and cam on the outer end of each transverse link.

NOTE: When performing the toe adjustment on the Stanza, be certain that the cams on both the left and right transverse links are set in the same position.

1987-88 Pulsar/Sentra (exc. 4wd)

Rear toe-in can be adjusted by means of adjusting pins on the inner end of each rear parallel link. Toe will change about 2mm (0.08 in.) for each gradation of the pin.

STEERING

Steering Wheel

REMOVAL & INSTALLATION

1. Position the wheels in the straight-ahead direction. The steering wheel should be right-side up and level.
2. Disconnect the battery ground cable.
3. Look at the back of your steering wheel. If there are countersunk screws in the back of the steering wheel spokes, remove the screws and pull off the horn pad. Some models have a horn wire running from the pad to the steering wheel. Disconnect it.

There are three other types of horn buttons or rings on Datsuns and Nissans. The first simply pulls off. The second, which is usually a large, semi-triangular pad, must be pushed up, then pulled off. The third must be pushed in and turned clockwise.

4. Remove the rest of the horn switching mechanism, noting the relative location of the parts. Remove the mechanism only if it hinders subsequent wheel removal procedures.
5. Matchmark the top of the steering column shaft and the steering wheel flange.
6. Remove the attaching nut and remove the steering wheel with a puller.

—————— CAUTION ——————

Do not strike the shaft with a hammer; which may cause the column to collapse.

7. Install the steering wheel in the reverse order of removal, aligning the punch marks. Do not drive or hammer the wheel into place, or you may cause the collapsible steering column to collapse; in which case you'll have to buy a whole new steering column unit.
8. Tighten the steering wheel nut to 22–25 ft. lbs. on the 310 and 22–29 ft. lbs. on the Van. Tighten all other steering wheel nuts to 28–36 ft. lbs.
9. Reinstall the horn button, pad, or ring.

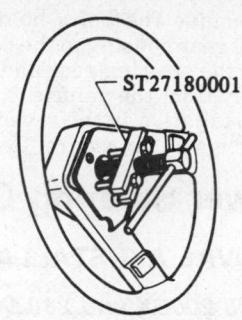

Use a puller to remove the steering wheel

Turn Signal/ Combination Switch

REMOVAL & INSTALLATION

On later models, the turn signal switch is part of a combination switch. The whole unit is removed together.

1. Disconnect the battery ground cable.
2. Remove the steering wheel as previously outlined. Observe the "caution" on the collapsible steering column.
3. Remove the steering column covers.
4. Disconnect the electrical plugs from the switch.
5. Remove the retaining screws and remove the switch.
6. Installation is the reverse of removal. Many models have turn signal switches that have a tab which must fit into a hole in the steering shaft in order for the system to return the switch to the neutral position after the turn has been made. Be sure to align the tab and the hole when installing.

NOTE: On many models (all 1987-88 models), the individual stalk assemblies can be removed without removing the combination switch base assembly. Simply disconnect the electrical lead and remove the two stalk-to-base mounting screws.

Steering Lock

The steering lock/ignition switch/ warning buzzer switch assembly is attached to the steering column by special screws whose heads shear off on installation. The screws must be drilled out to remove the assembly. The ignition switch is on the back of the assembly, and the warning switch on the side. The warning buzzer, which sounds when the driver's door is opened with the steering unlocked,

Steering lock securing screw—typical

is located behind the instrument panel.

Manual Steering Gear

REMOVAL & INSTALLATION

NOTE: The Van, 300ZX and 1985-88 Maxima are available with power steering only.

210

1. Remove the bolts holding the clutch slave cylinder to the transmission housing, and move the slave cylinder aside.
2. Disconnect the front exhaust tube at the manifold and front hanger.
3. Remove the bolt holding the worm shaft to the rubber coupling.
4. Remove the pitman arm from the sector shaft using a suitable puller.
5. Remove the bolts holding the steering gear housing to the body side member and remove the steering gear.
6. Installation is the reverse order of the removal procedure. Check the wheel alignment after the installation.

310

1. Raise and support the front of the vehicle safely and remove the front wheels.
2. Remove the steering joint cover and remove the bolts securing the steering column to the lower joint.
3. Remove the bolt holding the lower joint to the steering gear pinion and disconnect the lower joint from the steering gear.
4. Remove the side rod studs from the steering knuckles and remove the nuts securing the mounting clamps to the body. Remove the mounting clamps.
5. Remove the steering gear and linkage from the vehicle.
6. Installation is the reverse order of the removal procedure.

510

1. Remove the bolt holding the rubber coupling to the worm shaft.
2. Remove the pitman arm from the sector shaft using a suitable puller.
3. Disconnect the front exhaust tube from the exhaust manifold and hanger.
4. Remove the bolts holding the steering gear to the body side member and remove the gear through the engine compartment.
5. Installation is the reverse order of the removal procedure.

1981-86 200SX

1. Disconnect the exhaust pipe from the exhaust manifold, if necessary, and remove the bolt securing the exhaust pipe to the transmission mounting insulator.
2. Remove the bolt holding the worm shaft to the rubber coupling.
3. On 1984-86 models, remove the tie rod ball studs from the knuckle arms using a ball joint removal tool or the equivalent, and disconnect the steering column lower joint.
4. Remove the nut holding the pitman arm to the sector shaft and remove the pitman arm.
5. Remove the steering gear attaching bolts and then remove the steering gear from the vehicle.
6. Installation is the reverse order of the removal procedure. Check the wheel alignment after installation.

280ZX and 1981-84 810/Maxima

1. Raise and support the front of the vehicle safely and remove the front wheels.
2. Remove the lower joint from the steering column at the rubber coupling.
3. Remove the lower joint assembly from the pinion, and remove the splash board (280ZX only).
4. Remove the side rod studs from the steering knuckles.
5. Remove the gear housing-to-crossmember bolts and then remove the steering gear from the vehicle.
6. Installation is the reverse order of the removal procedure.

Pulsar, Sentra and 1982-86 Stanza (Sedan)

1. Raise and support the front of the vehicle safely and remove the wheels.
2. Disconnect the tie rod from the steering knuckle and loosen the steering gear attaching bolts.
3. Remove the bolt securing the lower joint to the steering gear pinion and remove the lower joint from the pinion.

4. Remove the bolts holding the steering gear housing to the body, and remove the steering gear and linkage assembly from the vehicle.
5. Installation is the reverse order of the removal procedure.

Power Steering Gear

REMOVAL & INSTALLATION

1981-83 200SX and 280ZX

1. Remove the air cleaner and remove the bolt securing the U-joint to the worm shaft.
2. Disconnect and plug the hoses from the power steering gear.
3. Remove the pitman arm from the sector shaft, using a suitable puller.
4. Remove the steering gear securing bolts and remove the steering gear from the vehicle.
5. Installation is the reverse order of the removal procedure.

280ZX Turbo

1. Raise and support the front of the vehicle safely and remove the wheels.
2. Remove the bolts holding the power steering hose clamps to the crossmember.
3. Disconnect the power steering hoses at the the steering gear and drain the gear oil into a drain pan. Be sure to plug the lines after draining them.
4. Disconnect the side rod studs from the steering knuckle and remove the lower joint assembly from the pinion shaft.
5. Remove the nuts holding the engine mount insulators to the crossmember.
6. Raise the engine as previously outlined in the engine removal section, and support the crossmember with a floor jack.
7. Loosen the steering gear mounting bolts and remove the bolts holding the crossmember to the body.
8. Lower the floor jack slowly, remove the bolts holding the steering gear to the crossmember, and remove the steering gear and linkage from the vehicle.
9. Installation is the reverse order of the removal procedure.

1984-88 200SX

1. Remove the air cleaner and remove the bolt securing the U-joint to the worm shaft.
2. Disconnect the hoses from the power steering gear and plug the hoses to prevent leakage.
3. Remove the pitman arm from the sector shaft using a suitable tool

and remove the steering gear mounting bolts.
4. Remove the exhaust pipe mounting nut.
5. Disconnect the control cable or linkage for the transmission and position it out of the way.
6. Remove the steering gear from the vehicle.
7. Installation is the reverse order of the removal procedure.

300ZX

1. Block the rear wheels. Raise and support the front of the vehicle on jackstands.
2. Position an oil catch pan under the power steerong gear, remove the hydraulic lines from the gear and drain the oil.
3. Loosen the steering column lower joint shaft bolt.
4. Remove the steering shaft-to-steering pinion gear. Separate the shaft from the steering gear.
5. Remove the tie rod end-to-knuckle arm cotter pins and castle nuts.
6. Separate the tie rods from the knuckle arms using a puller.
7. Remove the steering gear housing-to-suspension crossmember bolts.
8. Position a floor jack under the engine and raise it just enough to support the engine. Loosen the engine mounting bolts and raise the engine about ½ in..
9. Remove the steering gear and linkage from the vehicle.
10. Installation is in the reverse order of removal. Tighten the gear-to-crossmember bolts to 22–29 ft. lbs. and the ball joints to 40–72 ft. lbs.
11. Refill the power steering pump, start the engine and bleed the system.

1981-84 810/Maxima

NOTE: The procedure for these models, is the same as the 280ZX turbo procedures. The only difference is the engine does not have to be raised and the crossmember does not have to be removed from the body.

1981 310

1. Remove the hood as previously outlined, and raise and support the front of the vehicle safely.
2. Remove the upper rod and install a suitable engine lift.
3. Support the engine and remove the following items:
   a. The transmission shift and select rods at the transmission
   b. Lower buffer rod, and front and rear engine mount insulators.
4. Raise the engine and remove the cover from the steering column joint.

5. Remove the lower joint assembly from the steering gear pinion.

6. Remove the side rod studs from the steering knuckles and disconnect the steering hoses from the power steering pump. Plug the hoses to prevent leakage.

7. Remove the steering gear mounting bolts and move the engine forward to remove the steering gear and linkage.

8. Installation is the reverse order of the removal procedure.

1982 310

1. Raise and support the front of the vehicle and remove the wheels.

2. Remove the joint cover and loosen the steering column-to-lower joint attaching bolts.

3. Remove the lower joint assembly from the steering gear pinion.

4. Disconnect the side rod studs at the steering knuckles and disconnect the power steering hoses from the power steering gear. Plug all hoses to prevent leakage.

5. Remove the steering attaching bolts, and remove the steering gear and linkage from the vehicle.

6. Installation is the reverse order of the removal procedure.

Pulsar, Sentra, Stanza and 1985-88 Maxima

1. Raise and support the front of the vehicle safely and remove the wheels.

2. Disconnect the power steering hose from the power steering gear and plug all hoses to prevent leakage.

3. Disconnect the side rod studs from the steering knuckles.

4. On Sentra and Pulsar models, support the transaxle with a suitable transmission jack and remove the exhaust pipe and rear engine mounts.

5. On other models, remove the lower joint assembly from the steering gear pinion.

6. Remove the steering gear and linkage assembly from the vehicle.

7. Installation is the reverse order of the removal procedure.

Power Steering Pump

REMOVAL, INSTALLATION AND BLEEDING

All Models

1. On all 200SX models, remove the air cleaner duct and air cleaner.

2. Loosen the idler pulley lock nut and turn the adjusting nut counterclockwise, in order to remove the power steering belt.

3. Remove the drive belt on the A/C compressor, if so equipped.

4. Loosen the power steering hoses at the pump and remove the bolts holding the power steering pump to the bracket.

5. Disconnect and plug the power steering hoses and remove the pump from the vehicle.

6. Installation is the reverse order of the removal procedure. Bleed the system as follows:

   a. With the engine running, quickly turn the steering wheel all the way to the left and all the way to the right ten times.

   b. Stop the engine and check to see if any more fluid is required in the pump reservoir.

   c. With the steering wheel all the way to the right, open the bleeder screw and let the air flow from the pump.

   d. Tighten the bleeder screw and repeat the procedure until all the air is out of the system.

NOTE: If all the air cannot be bled from the system, then repeat Step c with the engine running.

BELT TENSION ADJUSTMENT

1. Loosen the tension adjustment and mounting bolts.

2. Move the pump toward or away from the engine so that the belt deflects ¼–½ in. midway between the idler pulley and the pump pulley under moderate thumb pressure.

3. Tighten the bolts and recheck the tension adjustment.

Tie Rod Ends (Steering Side Rods)

REMOVAL & INSTALLATION

You will need a ball joint remover for this operation.

1. Jack up the front of the vehicle and support it on jack stands.

2. Locate the faulty tie rod end. It will have a lot of play in it and the dust cover will probably be torn.

3. Remove the cotter key and nut from the tie rod stud. Note the position of the tie rod end in relation to the rest of the steering linkage.

4. Loosen the lock nut holding the tie rod to the rest of the steering linkage.

5. Free the tie rod ball joint from either the relay rod or steering knuckle by using a ball joint remover.

6. Unscrew and remove the tie rod end, counting the number of turns it takes to completely free it.

7. Install the new tie rod end, turning it in exactly as far as you screwed out the old one. Make sure it is correctly positioned in relation to the rest of the steering linkage.

8. Fit the ball joint and nut, tighten them and install a new cotter pin. Before finally tightening the tie rod lock nut or clamp, adjust the toe of the vehicle.

BRAKES

Front disc brakes are used on all models, with drum brakes at the rear; 280ZX, 300ZX, 200SX and later model 810 and Maxima models have rear disc brakes. All models have a vacuum booster system to lessen required pedal pressure. The parking brake operates the rear brakes through a cable system.

For all brake system repair and service procedures not detailed below, please refer to "Brakes" in the Unit Repair Section.

Master Cylinder

REMOVAL & INSTALLATION

NOTE: Please note that the vacuum booster and the brake master cylinder, unlike most vehicles, are located inside the passenger compartment on the Van, under the instrument panel.

Clean the outside of the cylinder thoroughly, particularly around the cap and fluid lines. On ZX models, remove the heatshield plate. Disconnect the fluid lines and cap them to exclude dirt. On models with a fluid level gauge, disconnect the electrical connector. Remove the clevis pin connecting the pushrod to the brake pedal arm inside the vehicle. This pin need not be removed on models with the vacuum booster. Unbolt the master cylinder from the firewall and remove. If the pushrod is not adjustable, there will be shims between the cylinder and the firewall. These shims, or the adjustable pushrod, are used to adjust brake pedal free-play. After installation, bleed the system and check for pedal free-play. The 200SX's pushrod is not adjustable, as the rod between the brake booster and the master cylinder is secured by adhesion. After installation, bleed the system and check the pedal free-play.

PEDAL ADJUSTMENT

NOTE: Ordinary brake fluid will boil and cause brake failure under the high temperatures developed in disc brake systems. Special fluid meeting DOT 3 or 4 specifications for disc brake systems must be used.

Before adjusting the pedal, make sure that the brakes are correctly adjusted.

Adjust the pedal free-play by means of an adjustable pushrod or shims between the master cylinder and the firewall. Adjust the pedal height by means of the pedal arm stop pad. Free-play should be approximately 0.04–0.12 in. on all models.

BRAKE PEDAL SPECIFICATIONS

Model		Pedal Height (in.)
210		6
310		6
510		6
200SX	1981–83	7
	1984–88	MT 7.28–7.68 AT 7.36–7.76
280ZX		8
300ZX		MT 7.17–7.56 AT 7.24–7.64
810/ Maxima	1981–84	7
	1985–88	7.24–7.64
Pulsar	1983–86	MT 7.64–8.03 AT 7.76–8.15
	1987–88	MT 6.18–6.57 AT 6.54–6.93
Sentra	1982–86	MT 7.64–8.03 AT 7.76–8.15
	1987–88	MT 6.10–6.50 AT 6.46–6.85
Stanza Sedan	1982–86	MT 5.85–6.24 AT 5.93–6.32
	1987–88	7.24–7.64
Stanza Wagon	1986 (2wd)	MT 8.86–9.25 AT 8.78–9.17
	1986 (4wd)	MT 8.46–8.86 AT 8.39–8.78
	1987–88	MT 8.46–8.86 AT 8.39–8.78
Van		6.36–6.75

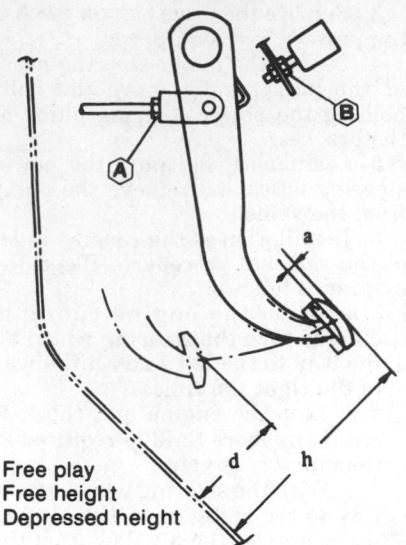

Free play
Free height
Depressed height

Brake pedal adjustment—all models. "B" shows locknut

Brake Proportioning Valve

All models covered in this manual are equipped with brake proportioning valves of several different types. The valves all do the same job, which is to separate the front and rear brake lines, allowing them to function independently, and preventing the rear brakes from locking before the front brakes. Damage, such as brake line leakage, in either the front or rear brake system will not affect the normal operation of the unaffected system. If, in the event of a panic stop, the rear brakes lock up before the front brakes, it could mean the proportioning valve is defective. In that case, replace the entire proportioning valve.

REMOVAL & INSTALLATION

NOTE: On many models, the proportioning valve is incorporated into the master cylinder. Consequently, removal and installation procedures are limited to replacement of the master cylinder unit as a whole.

1. Disconnect and plug the brake lines at the valve.
2. Unscrew the mounting bolt(s) and remove the valve.

NOTE: Do not disassemble the valve

3. Installation is in the reverse order of removal. Bleed the system.

Power Brake Booster

REMOVAL & INSTALLATION

NOTE: Please note that the vacuum booster and the brake master cylinder, unlike most vehicles, are located inside the passenger compartment on the Van, under the instrument panel.

1. Remove the master cylinder.
2. Remove the vacuum hose at the power brake booster.
3. Remove the pushrod from the brake pedal.
4. From under the instrument panel, remove the cowl-to-booster nuts. Remove the brake booster.
5. Installation is in the reverse order of removal.

Wheel Cylinder

REMOVAL, INSTALLATION & OVERHAUL

NOTE: Datsun/Nissan obtains parts from two manufacturers; Nabco and Tokico. Parts are not interchangeable! The manufacturer's name can be found on the wheel cylinder.

1. Disconnect the hydraulic line and remove the wheel cylinder from the brake backing plate.
2. Remove the dust boot and take out the piston. Throw away the piston cup. The dust boot can be reused although it is best to replace it.
3. Wash all of the components in clean brake fluid.
4. Inspect the piston and piston bore. Replace any components that are severely corroded, scored or worn. The piston and piston bore may be polished lightly with crocus cloth; move the cloth around the piston bore, not in and out.
5. Wash the wheel cylinder and piston in clean brake fluid.
6. Coat all new components to be installed with clean brake fluid.
7. Assemble the cylinder and install it on the backing plate. Connect the hydraulic line.
8. Bleed the brake system.

Parking Brake

ADJUSTMENT

Handbrake adjustments are generally not needed, unless the cables have stretched.

All Models

1. Pull up the handbrake lever,

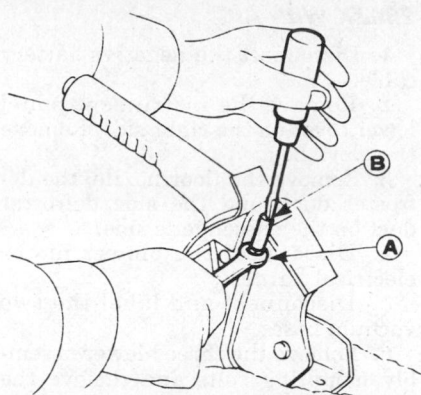

Parking brake adjustment on the 1987-88 Maxima (1987-88 Stanza sedan and Pulsar/Sentra similar)

LOCK NUT

Parking brake adjustment turnbuckle, underneath car

counting the number of ratchet clicks for full engagement. Full engagement should be:

210: 7–8 notches
310: 7–8 notches
510: 7–8 notches
810: 5–6 notches
200SX: 7–8 notches
280ZX: 4–6 notches
300ZX: 8–10 notches
Maxima ('84): 5–6 notches
Maxima ('85-'86): 7–8 notches
Maxima ('87-'88): 11–13 notches
Pulsar ('83-'84): 6–7 notches
Pulsar ('85-'86): 6–8 notches
Pulsar ('87-'88): 7–11 notches
Sentra ('82-'84): 6–7 notches
Sentra ('85-'86): 6–8 notches
Sentra ('87-'88): 11–13 notches
Stanza sedan ('82-'86): 7–8 notches
Stanza sedan ('87-'88): 11–13 notches
Stanza wagon (2wd): 11–17 notches
Stanza wagon (4wd): 8–9 notches
Van: 5–7 notches

2. Release the parking brake.
3. Adjust the lever stroke at the cable equalizer under the car; loosen the lock nut and tighten the adjusting nut to reduce the number of ratchet clicks necessary for engagement. Tighten the lock nut. On the 1987-88 Maxima, 1987-88 Stanza sedan and the 1987-88 Pulsar/Sentra, the locknut and adjuster can be found inside the handbrake assembly, in the passenger compartment.
4. Check the adjustment and repeat as necessary.
5. After adjustment, check to see that the rear brake levers (at the calipers) return to their full off positions

when the lever is released, and that the rear cables are not slack when the lever is released.
6. To adjust the warning lamp, bend the warning lamp switch plate down so that the light comes on when the lever is engaged one notch.

CHASSIS ELECTRICAL

Heater Unit

REMOVAL & INSTALLATION

210 and 510

1. Disconnect the ground cable at the battery. Drain the coolant.
2. Remove the console.
3. Remove the driver's side of the instrument panel.
4. Remove the heater control assembly; remove the defroster ducts, door cables at the doors, harness connector, and control assembly.
5. Remove the radio.
6. Disconnect the heater ducts, side defrosters, and center vent duct.
7. Remove the screws attaching the defroster nozzle to the unit. Disconnect the blower wire, and the heater hoses.
8. Remove the retaining bolts and the heater unit.
9. Installation is the reverse of removal.

310 Without A/C

1. Disconnect the battery ground cable.
2. Set the temperature lever to the HOT position and drain the engine coolant.
3. Remove the instrument panel assembly. See the following section for instructions.
4. Disconnect the control cables and rod from the heater unit. Disconnect the heater motor harness.

310 With A/C

1. Disconnect the battery ground.
2. Set the temperature control lever to HOT and drain the cooling system.
3. Remove the instrument panel.
4. Disconnect the hoses at the core.
5. Disconnect all wiring from the unit.
6. Loosen the band seal at the joint between the cooling and heater units.
7. Unbolt and remove the heater unit.

Pulsar and Sentra

1. Set the "TEMP" lever to the maximum "HOT" position and drain the engine coolant.
2. Disconnect the heater hoses at the engine compartment.
3. Remove the instrument assembly.
4. Remove the heater control assembly.
5. Remove the heater unit assembly.
6. Installation is the reverse of removal.

NOTE: Be sure to bleed the system of air when installing the heater hoses.

1981-86 Stanza

1. Remove the instrument panel.
2. Disconnect the heater hoses and vacuum tube in the engine compartment.
3. Remove the heater control assembly.
4. Unbolt and remove the heater unit.
5. Installation is the reverse of removal.

NOTE: Be sure to bleed the system of air when installing the heater hoses.

200SX

1. Set the TEMP lever to the HOT position and drain the coolant.
2. Disconnect the heater hoses from the driver's side of the heater unit.
3. At this point the manufacturer suggests removing the front seats. To do this, remove the plastic covers over the ends of the seat runners, both front and back, to expose the seat mounting bolts. Remove the bolts and remove the seats.
4. Remove the console box and the floor carpets.
5. Remove the instrument panel lower covers from both the driver's and passenger's sides of the car. Remove the lower cluster lids.
6. Remove the left side ventilator duct.
7. Remove the radio, sound balancer and stereo cassette deck.
8. Remove the instrument panel-to-transmission tunnel stay.
9. Remove the rear heater duct from the floor of the vehicle.
10. Remove the center ventilator duct.
11. Remove the left and right hand side air guides from the lower heater outlets.
12. Disconnect the wiring harness connections.

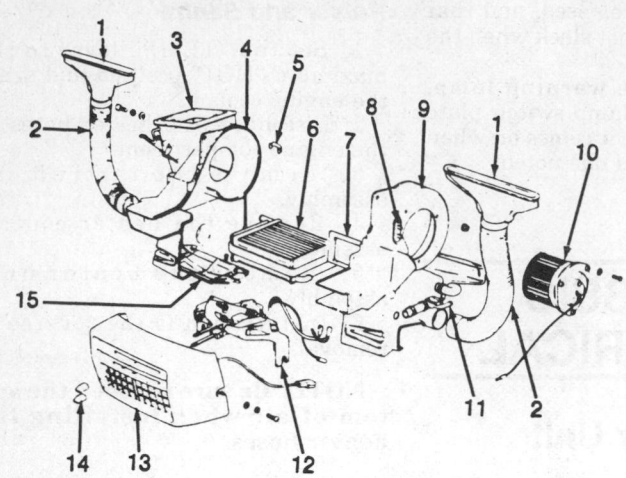

1. Defroster nozzle
2. Defroster hose
3. Air intake box
4. Heater box (L.H.)
5. Clip
6. Heater core
7. Ventilator valve
8. Resistor
9. Heater box (R.H.)
10. Fan and fan motor
11. Heater cock
12. Heater control
13. Center ventilator
14. Knob
15. Heat valve

210 heater

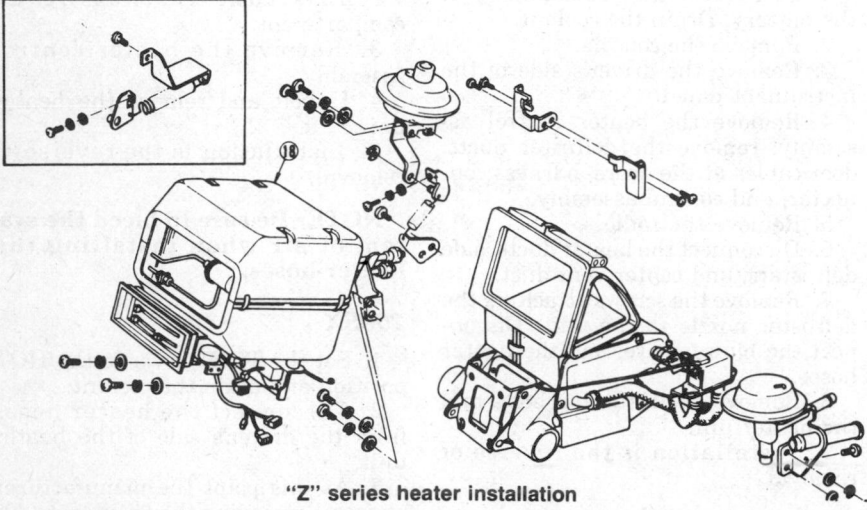

"Z" series heater installation

13. Remove the two screws at the bottom sides of the heater unit and the one screw at the top of the unit and remove the unit together with the heater control assembly.

14. Installation is the reverse of removal.

NOTE: You may be able to skip several of the above steps if only certain components of the heater unit need service.

280ZX Without A/C

1. Disconnect the negative battery cable.

2. Remove the lower instrument panel cover and the glove box.

3. Remove the floor nozzle, defroster duct, and the side defroster duct on the right side.

4. Remove the heater duct.

5. Disconnect the blower motor wiring harness.

6. Disconnect the control cable at the blower assembly by removing the clip.

7. Remove the bolts securing the blower assembly to the firewall and remove the blower assembly.

8. The motor and fan can be removed by removing the three motor retaining screws. The fan simply bolts onto the motor shaft.

9. Installation is in the reverse order of removal.

The motor and fan can also be removed without removing the entire blower housing assembly:

1. Disconnect the negative battery cable.

2. Remove the lower instrument panel cover and the floor nozzle on the right side.

3. Disconnect the blower motor wiring harness.

4. Remove the three motor attaching screws and remove the motor and fan as a unit from the blower housing.

280ZX With A/C

1. Disconnect the negative battery cable.

2. Remove the instrument panel lower cover on the right side. Remove the glove box.

3. Remove the floor nozzle, the defroster duct, and the side defroster duct on the passenger's side.

4. Disconnect the blower motor electrical harness.

5. Disconnect and label the two vacuum hoses.

6. Remove the three blower assembly mounting bolts and remove the assembly.

7. Installation is the reverse order of removal.

The motor can be removed without removing the blower assembly:

1. Disconnect the negative batter cable.

2. Remove the instrument panel lower cover and the floor nozzle on the right side.

3. Disconnect the blower motor electrical harness.

4. Remove the three blower motor attaching screws and remove the motor and fan as an assembly from the blower housing.

5. Installation is the reverse.

300ZX and 1981-86 810/Maxima

NOTE: You may be able to skip several of the following steps if only certain components of the heater assembly need service.

1. Set the TEMP lever to the HOT position and drain the coolant.

2. Disconnect the heater hoses from the driver's side of the heater unit.

3. At this point the manufacturer suggests removing the front seats (810/Maxima only). To do this, remove the plastic covers over the ends of the seat runners, front and back, to expose the seat mounting bolts. Remove the bolts and lift out the seats.

4. Remove the front carpets.

5. Remove the instrument panel lower covers from both the driver's and passenger's sides of the car.

6. Remove the left side ventilator duct.

7. Remove the instrument panel assembly as detailed later in this section.

8. Remove the rear heater duct from the floor of the car (810/Maxima only).

9. Tag and disconnect the wiring harness connectors.

10. Remove the two screws at the bottom sides of the heater unit and the one screw from the top of the unit. Lift out the heater together with the heater control assembly.

11. Installation is the reverse of removal.

Heater Core

REMOVAL & INSTALLATION

210, 510, Pulsar and Sentra

1. Remove the heater unit.
2. Disconnect the inlet and outlet hoses.
3. Remove the case clips and split the case. Remove the core.
4. Installation is the reverse of removal. Always check the operation of the air mix door when re-attaching the heater case halves.

200SX

1. Remove the heater unit as described earlier.
2. Remove the hoses from the heater core and then slide the core from the case.
3. Installation is the reverse of removal.

310

1. Remove the heater unit from the vehicle.
2. Disconnect the inlet and outlet hoses from the core if you have not done so already.
3. Remove the clips securing the case halves and separate the halves.
4. Remove the heater core.
5. Installation is the reverse of removal.

280ZX

1. Remove the heater unit.
2. Remove the water cock.
3. Remove the case clips and split the heater case. Remove the core.

300ZX, 810 and Maxima

1. Remove the heater unit.
2. Remove the center vent cover and heater control assembly, loosening the clips and screws.
3. Remove the screws securing the door shafts.
4. Remove the clips from the case and split the case. Remove the core.
5. Installation is the reverse of removal.

Stanza

1. Remove pedal bracket mounting bolts, steering column mounting bolts, brake and clutch pedal cotter pins.
2. Move the pedal bracket and steering column to the left.
3. Disconnect the air mix door control cable and heater valve control elver, then remove the control lever.

4. Remove the core cover.
5. Disconnect the hoses at the core.
6. Installation is the reverse of removal. Be sure to bleed the system.

Windshield Wiper Motor
REMOVAL & INSTALLATION

Pulsar and Sentra

The wiper motor is on the firewall under the hood The operating linkage is on the firewall inside the car.
1. Detach the motor wiring plug.
2. Inside the car, remove the nut connecting the linkage to the wiper shaft.
3. Unbolt and remove the wiper motor from the firewall.
4. Reverse the procedure for installation.

210, 310, 510, 200SX, 280ZX and Stanza

1. Disconnect the battery ground cable.
2. Disconnect the electrical connector at the motor.
3. Remove the motor attaching bolts. The motor is under the hood, on the firewall.
4. Remove the nut securing the arm to the motor shaft. Remove the motor.
5. Installation is the reverse of removal.

810/Maxima and 300ZX

The wiper motor and operating linkage is on the firewall under the hood.
1. Lift the wiper arms. Remove the securing nuts and detach the arms.
2. Remove the nuts holding the wiper pivots to the body. Remove the air intake grille for access.
3. Open the hood and unscrew the motor from the firewall.
4. Disconnect the wiring connector and remove the wiper motor with the linkage.
5. Reverse the procedure for installation.
NOTE: If the wipers do not park correctly, adjust the position of the automatic stop cover on the wiper motor.

Windshield Wiper Switch—Front

The windshield wiper switch is part of the combination switch which is mounted on the steering column.

REMOVAL & INSTALLATION

Refer to the "Combination Switch,

Removal and Installation" procedures, and replace the windshield wiper switch.

Windshield Wiper Switch—Rear

REMOVAL & INSTALLATION

280ZX

The rear window wiper switch is located on the left-side of the instrument panel.
1. Pull the rear window wiper switch knob from the switch.
2. Using a spanner wrench tool, remove the retaining nut and the washer from the switch.
3. Remove the switch from the back of the instrument panel and disconnect the electrical connector.
4. To install, reverse the removal procedures.

300ZX

The rear window wiper switch is located on the right-side of the instrument panel.
1. Refer to the "Instrument Cluster, Removal and Installation" procedures, in this section and remove the instrument cluster.
2. Remove the nut retaining the instrument combination switch to the dash.
NOTE: The instrument combination switches are secured by hooks and basements.

3. Disconnect the electrical connectors from the rear of the switch, then remove it.
4. To install, reverse the removal procedures.

Fuses
FUSE BOX
LOCATION CHART

Model	Fuse Box Location	Fusible Link Location
210	Under dash at extreme left	Off of battery (+) cable
310	Under dash at extreme right	Right fender area of eng. comp.
510	Under dash at extreme left	Off of battery (+) cable
810	Under dash at extreme right	Right rear of eng. comp. ①

FUSE BOX LOCATION CHART

Model	Fuse Box Location	Fusible Link Location
200SX	Under dash at extreme left	Off of battery (+) cable
280ZX	Under dash at extreme right	Right rear of eng. comp. ①
300ZX	Under dash at extreme left	Off of battery (+) cable
Maxima	Under dash at extreme left	Off of battery (+) cable
Pulsar	Under dash at extreme left	Off of battery (+) cable
Sentra	Under dash at extreme left	Off of battery (+) cable
Stanza (1982–86)	Under dash at extreme right	Off of battery (+) cable
(1987–88)	Under dash at extreme left	Off of battery (+) cable
Van	Under dash at extreme left	Off of battery (+) cable

① A fusible link for the fuel injection system is at the (+) battery cable

Instrument Cluster

REMOVAL & INSTALLATION

210

1. Disconnect the battery ground cable.
2. Remove the steering wheel.
3. Remove the steering column cover.
4. Remove the illuminated control rheostat.
5. Pull off the heater control knob and remove the control panel. Remove the screw attaching the panel to the instrument panel.
6. Pull off the radio knobs; remove the nuts and washers.

7. Remove the ashtray and ashtry holder.
8. Remove the cluster lid screws.
9. Disconnect the electrical connectors.
10. Remove the cluster lid.
11. Remove the cluster gauge screws.
12. Disconnect the speedometer cable by pushing and turning the cap counterclockwise.
13. Disconnect the cluster wires and remove the instrument cluster.

510

1. Disconnect the battery ground cable.
2. Remove the steering column covers. Disconnect the hazard warning switch connector.
3. Remove the wiper switch. Pull out the ashtray, remove the heater control knobs, and remove the heater control plate by inserting a small prybar into the fan lever slit and levering the plate out.
4. Remove the finish plate to the left of the glove compartment.
5. Pull off the radio knobs and remove the nuts and washers.
6. Remove the choke and side defroster knobs.
7. Remove the cluster lid screws.
8. Disconnect the electrical connectors.
9. Remove the cluster lid.
10. Remove the instrument cluster retaining screws. Disconnect the speedometer cable by pushing and turning counterclockwise.
11. Disconnect the instrument cluster wire connectors and remove the cluster.

1981-84 810/Maxima

1. Disconnect the negative battery cable.
2. Remove the instrument panel lower cover.
3. Remove the steering wheel.
4. Disconnect the speedometer cable.
5. Remove the six mounting screws and lift out the cluster lid.
6. Unscrew the mounting bolts and lift off the left side instrument pad (this is the hooded part of the dashboard that the instrument cluster sits in).
7. Loosen the instrument cluster mounting screws, pull it out slightly and disconnect all wiring. Remove the cluster.
8. Installation is in the reverse order of removal.

280ZX

1. Disconnect the negative battery cable.
2. Remove the steering wheel.
3. Remove the steering column cover.
4. Remove the instrument panel lower cover on the left side.
5. Disconnect the speedometer cable at the intermediate connection.
6. Remove the combination switch.
7. Remove the cluster retaining screws, pull out slightly and disconnect the electrical connectors. Remove the instrument cluster.

200SX

1. Disconnect the battery ground terminal.
2. It may be necessary to remove the steering wheel and covers to remove the instrument cluster.
3. Remove the screws holding the cluster lid in place and remove the lid.
4. Remove the five bolts holding the cluster in place and pull the cluster out, then remove all connections from its back. Make sure you mark the wiring to avoid confusion during reassembly.

310, Pulsar, Sentra and Stanza

1. Disconnect the battery terminals.
2. Remove the steering wheel and the steering column covers.
3. Remove the instrument cluster lid by removing its screws.
4. Remove the instrument cluster screws, pull the unit out and disconnect all wiring and cables from its rear. Mark the wires to avoid confusion during assembly. Be careful not to damage the printed circuit.
5. Remove the cluster.
6. Installation is the reverse of removal.

Headlight Switch

REMOVAL & INSTALLATION

Since the headlight switch is part of the combination switch, please refer to "Combination Switch" in this section.

Porsche
911, 924, 928, 944
All Models

SERIAL NUMBER IDENTIFICATION

Vehicle Identification Plate

The chassis number on all models is located on the left (driver) side windshield post and is visible from the outside of the car. On 911 models, the chassis number is also found in the luggage compartment under the rug and on the identification plate near the front hood lock catch. On all other models, the VIN plate is in the engine compartment near the battery.

CHASSIS NUMBER

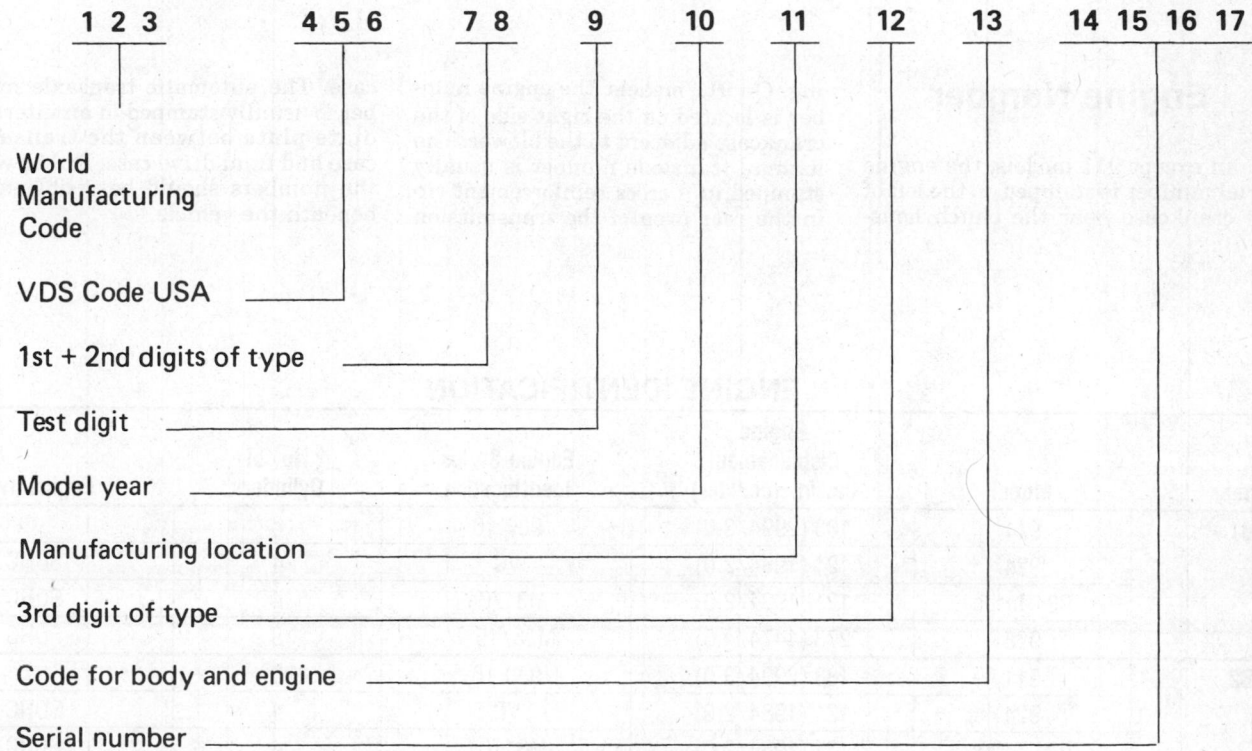

| 1 2 3 | 4 5 6 | 7 8 | 9 | 10 | 11 | 12 | 13 | 14 15 16 17 |

World Manufacturing Code

VDS Code USA

1st + 2nd digits of type

Test digit

Model year

Manufacturing location

3rd digit of type

Code for body and engine

Serial number

911 VIN Identification

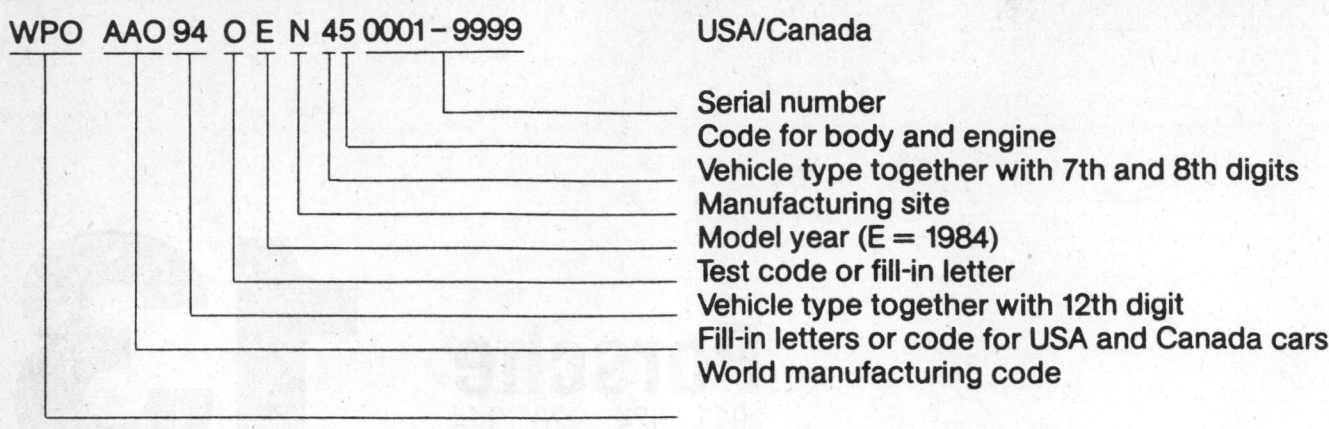

944 VIN Identification

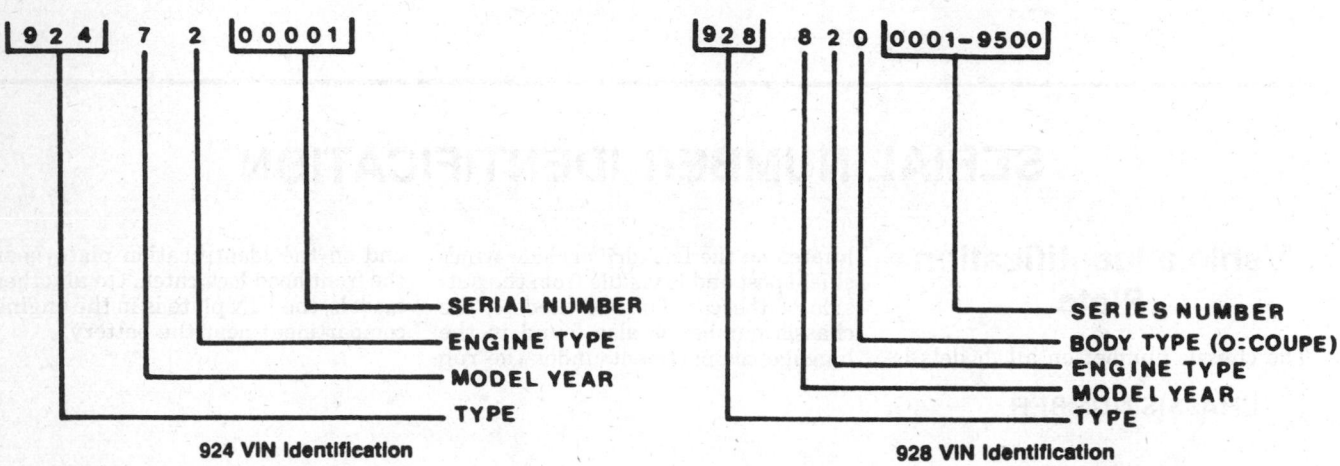

924 VIN Identification   **928 VIN Identification**

Engine Number

On all except 911 models, the engine serial number is stamped on the left of the crankcase near the clutch hous-ing. On 911 models, the engine number is located on the right side of the crankcase adjacent to the blower. The manual transaxle number is usually stamped in a cross reinforcement rib in the rear area of the transmission case. The automatic transaxle num-ber is usually stamped in an interme-diate plate between the transaxle case and final drive case. Either way, the numbers should be visible from beneath the vehicle.

ENGINE IDENTIFICATION

Year	Model	Engine Displacement cu. in. (cc/liter)	Engine Series Identification	No. of Cylinders	Engine Type
1981	911	183 (2994/3.0)	930.16	6	①
	924	121 (1984/2.0)	VC	4	SOHC
	924 Turbo	121 (1984/2.0)	M31/04	4	SOHC
	928	273 (4474/4.5)	M28/15 ②	8	SOHC
1982	911	183 (2994/3.0)	930.16	6	①
	924	121 (1984/2.0)	VC	4	SOHC
	924 Turbo	121 (1984/2.0)	M31/04	4	SOHC
	928	273 (4474/4.5)	M28/15 ②	8	SOHC

ENGINE IDENTIFICATION

Year	Model	Engine Displacement cu. in. (cc/liter)	Engine Series Identification	No. of Cylinders	Engine Type
1983	911	183 (2994/3.0)	930.16	6	①
	928	284 (4664/4.7)	M28/19 ③	8	SOHC
	944	151 (2479/2.5)	M44/02 ④	4	SOHC
1984	911	193 (3164/3.2)	930.21	6	①
	928	284 (4664/4.7)	M28/19 ③	8	SOHC
	944	151 (2479/2.5)	M44/02 ④	4	SOHC
1985	911	193 (3164/3.2)	930.21	6	①
	928S	302 (4957/5.0)	M28/43 ⑤	8	DOHC
	944	151 (2479/2.5)	M44/07 ⑥	4	SOHC
	944 Turbo	151 (2479/2.5)	M44/51	4	SOHC
1986	911	193 (3164/3.2)	930.21	6	①
	911 Turbo	201 (3299/3.3)	930.68	6	①
	928S	302 (4957/5.0)	M28/43 ⑤	8	DOHC
	944	151 (2479/2.5)	M44/07 ⑥	4	SOHC
	944 Turbo	151 (2479/2.5)	M44/51	4	SOHC
1987–88	911	193 (3164/3.2)	930.21	6	①
	911 Turbo	201 (3299/3.3)	930.68	6	①
	924S	151 (2479/2.5)	M44/07 ⑥	4	SOHC
	928S4	302 (4957/5.0)	M28/43 ⑤	8	DOHC
	944	151 (2479/2.5)	M44/07 ⑥	4	SOHC
	944S	151 (2479/2.5)	M44/40 ⑦	4	DOHC
	944 Turbo	151 (2479/2.5)	M44/51	4	SOHC

DOHC—Dual Overhead Camshaft
SOHC—Single Overhead Camshaft
① Air-cooled, 6 cylinder, horizontally opposed, rear-mounted
② M28/16 with automatic transmission
③ M28/20 with automatic transmission
④ M44/04 with automatic transmission
⑤ M28/44 with automatic transmission
⑥ M44/08 with automatic transmission
⑦ 16-valve engine

GENERAL ENGINE SPECIFICATIONS

Year	Model	Engine Displacement cu. in. (cc)	Fuel System Type	Net Horsepower @ rpm	Net Torque @ rpm (ft. lbs.)	Bore × Stroke (in.)	Compression Ratio	Oil Pressure @ rpm
1981	911	183 (2994)	CIS	172 @ 5500	175 @ 4200	3.74 × 2.77	9.3:1	50 @ 5000
	924	121 (1984)	CIS	110 @ 5750	111 @ 3500	3.41 × 3.32	8.0:1	71–100 @ 5000
	924 Turbo	121 (1984)	CIS	154 @ 5750	155 @ 3500	3.41 × 3.32	8.0:1	85 @ 5000
	928	273 (4474)	AFC	220 @ 5500	265 @ 4000	3.74 × 3.11	9.0:1	70 @ 5500
1982	911	183 (2994)	CIS	172 @ 5500	175 @ 4200	3.74 × 2.77	9.3:1	50 @ 5000
	924	121 (1984)	CIS	110 @ 5750	111 @ 3500	3.41 × 3.32	8.0:1	71–100 @ 5000
	924 Turbo	121 (1984)	CIS	154 @ 5750	155 @ 3500	3.41 × 3.32	8.0:1	85 @ 5000
	928	273 (4474)	AFC	220 @ 5500	265 @ 4000	3.74 × 3.11	9.0:1	70 @ 5500
1983	911	183 (2994)	CIS	172 @ 5500	175 @ 4200	3.74 × 2.77	9.3:1	50 @ 5000
	928	284 (4664)	AFC	234 @ 5250	263 @ 5250	3.82 × 3.11	9.3:1	70 @ 5500
	944	151 (2479)	DME	143 @ 5500	137 @ 3000	3.94 × 3.11	9.5:1	50–70 @ 5500

GENERAL ENGINE SPECIFICATIONS

Year	Model	Engine Displacement cu. in. (cc)	Fuel System Type	Net Horsepower @ rpm	Net Torque @ rpm (ft. lbs.)	Bore × Stroke (in.)	Compression Ratio	Oil Pressure @ rpm
1984	911	193 (3164)	DME	200 @ 5900	185 @ 4800	3.74 × 2.93	9.5:1	50 @ 5000
	928	284 (4664)	AFC	234 @ 5250	263 @ 4000	3.82 × 3.11	9.3:1	70 @ 5500
	944	151 (2479)	DME	143 @ 5500	137 @ 3000	3.94 × 3.11	9.5:1	50–70 @ 5500
1985	911	193 (3164)	DME	200 @ 5900	185 @ 4800	3.74 × 2.93	9.5:1	50 @ 5000
	928S	302 (4957)	LH	288 @ 5750	302 @ 2700	3.94 × 3.11	10:1	70 @ 5500
	944	151 (2479)	DME	143 @ 5500	137 @ 3000	3.94 × 3.11	9.5:1	50–70 @ 5500
	944 Turbo	151 (2479)	DME	220 @ 5800	243 @ 3500	3.94 × 3.11	8.0:1	70 @ 5500
1986	911	193 (3164)	KE	200 @ 5900	185 @ 4800	3.74 × 2.93	9.5:1	50 @ 5000
	911 Turbo	201 (3299)	KE	282 @ 5500	278 @ 4000	3.82 × 2.93	7.0:1	60 @ 5500
	928S	302 (4957)	LH	288 @ 5750	302 @ 2700	3.94 × 3.11	10:1	70 @ 5500
	944	151 (2479)	DME	147 @ 5800	144 @ 3000	3.94 × 3.11	9.7:1	50–70 @ 5500
	944 Turbo	151 (2479)	DME	220 @ 5800	243 @ 3500	3.94 × 3.11	8.0:1	70 @ 5500
1987–88	911	193 (3164)	DME	214 @ 5900	195 @ 4800	3.74 × 2.93	9.5:1	50 @ 5000
	911 Turbo	201 (3299)	KE	282 @ 5500	278 @ 4000	3.82 × 2.93	7.0:1	60 @ 5500
	924S	151 (2479)	DME	147 @ 5800	140 @ 3000	3.94 × 3.11	9.7:1	50–70 @ 5500
	928S4	302 (4957)	LH	316 @ 6000	317 @ 3000	3.94 × 3.11	10:1	70 @ 5500
	944	151 (2479)	DME	147 @ 5800	144 @ 3000	3.94 × 3.11	9.7:1	50–70 @ 5500
	944S	151 (2479)	DME	188 @ 6000	170 @ 4300	3.94 × 3.11	10.9:1	50–70 @ 5500
	944 Turbo	151 (2479)	DME	220 @ 5800	243 @ 3500	3.94 × 3.11	8.0:1	50–70 @ 5500

AFC Air Flow Controlled Fuel Injection
CIS Bosch Constant Injection System
DME Digital Motor Electronic Fuel Injection
KE Bosch Electronic CIS Fuel Injection
LH Bosch Air Flow Controlled Fuel Injection

TUNE-UP SPECIFICATIONS

Year	Model	Engine Displacement cu. in. (cc)	Spark Plugs Type	Gap (in.)	Ignition Timing (deg @ rpm)	Compression Pressure (psi)	Fuel Pump (psi)	Idle Speed (rpm)	Valve Clearance In.	Valve Clearance Ex.
1981	911	183 (2994)	W225T30	.028	25B @ 4000	①	66–76	850–1000	0.004	0.004
	924	121 (1984)	W200T30	.030	10B @ 950	①	66–76	850–1000	0.004	0.016
	924 Turbo	121 (1984)	WR7DS	.024	11B @ 900	①	85–95	900–1000	0.004	0.016
	928	273 (4474)	WR8DS	.028	27B @ 3000	①	76–85	700–800	Hyd.	Hyd.
1982	911	183 (2994)	W225T30	.028	25B @ 4000	①	66–76	850–1000	0.004	0.004
	924	121 (1984)	WR6DS	.028	10B @ 950	①	66–76	850–1000	0.004	0.016
	924 Turbo	121 (1984)	WR6DS	.028	11B @ 900	①	85–95	900–1000	0.006	0.016
	928	273 (4474)	WR8DS	.030	27B @ 3000	①	76–85	700–800	Hyd.	Hyd.
1983	911	183 (2994)	W225T30	.030	25B @ 4000	①	66–76	850–1000	0.004	0.016
	928	284 (4664)	WR8DS	.030	26B @ 3000	①	76–85	700–800	Hyd.	Hyd.
	944	151 (2479)	WR8DS	.030	10B @ 850	①	34–40	800–850	Hyd.	Hyd.
1984	911	193 (3164)	WR7DC	.028	25B @ 3800	①	34–40	760–840	0.004	0.004
	928	284 (4664)	WR8DS	.030	26B @ 3000	①	76–85	700–800	Hyd.	Hyd.
	944	151 (2479)	WR8DS	.030	10B @ 850	①	34–40	800–850	Hyd.	Hyd.

TUNE-UP SPECIFICATIONS

Year	Model	Engine Displacement cu. in. (cc)	Spark Plugs Type	Gap (in.)	Ignition Timing (deg @ rpm)	Compression Pressure (psi)	Fuel Pump (psi)	Idle Speed (rpm)	Valve Clearance In.	Valve Clearance Ex.
1985	911	193 (3164)	WR7DC	.028	26B @ 4000	①	34–40	780–820	0.004	0.004
	928S	302 (4957)	WR7DC	.028	10B @ 680	①	34–40	700–750	Hyd.	Hyd.
	944	151 (2479)	WR7DC	.028	10B @ 850	①	34–40	800–850	Hyd.	Hyd.
	944 Turbo	151 (2479)	WR7DC	.028	5B @ 840	①	34–40	800–880	Hyd.	Hyd.
1986	911	193 (3164)	WR7DC	.028	26B @ 4000	①	34–40	780–820	0.004	0.004
	911 Turbo	201 (3299)	W3DP	.028	26B @ 4000	①	34–40	850–950	0.004	0.004
	928S	302 (4957)	WR7DC	.028	10B @ 680	①	28–37	660–700	Hyd.	Hyd.
	944	151 (2479)	WR7DC	.028	10B @ 850	①	34–40	800–880	Hyd.	Hyd.
	944 Turbo	151 (2479)	WR6DC	.028	5B @ 840	①	34–40	800–880	Hyd.	Hyd.
1987	911	193 (3164)	WR7DC	.028	26B @ 4000	①	34–40	780–820	0.004	0.004
	911 Turbo	201 (3299)	W3DP	.028	26B @ 4000	①	34–40	850–950	0.004	0.004
	924S	151 (2479)	WR7DC	.028	5B @ 840	①	34–40	800–880	Hyd.	Hyd.
	928S4	302 (4957)	WR7DC	.028	NA	①	NA	800–880	Hyd.	Hyd.
	944	151 (2479)	WR7DC	.028	10B @ 850	①	34–40	800–880	Hyd.	Hyd.
	944S	151 (2479)	WR7DC	.028	NA	①	34–40	800–880	Hyd.	Hyd.
	944 Turbo	151 (2479)	WR6DC	.028	5B @ 840	①	34–40	800–880	Hyd.	Hyd.
1988	All	SEE UNDERHOOD SPECIFICATIONS STICKER								

NOTE: The Underhood Specifications sticker often reflects tune-up specifications changes made in production. Sticker Figures must be used if they disagree with those in this chart.
B   Before Top Dead Center
A   After Top Dead Center
NA Not available at time of publication
① All cylinders should be within 22 psi of the highest reading.

FIRING ORDERS

NOTE: To avoid confusion, always replace spark plug wires one at a time.

FIRING ORDER: 1-6-2-4-3-5

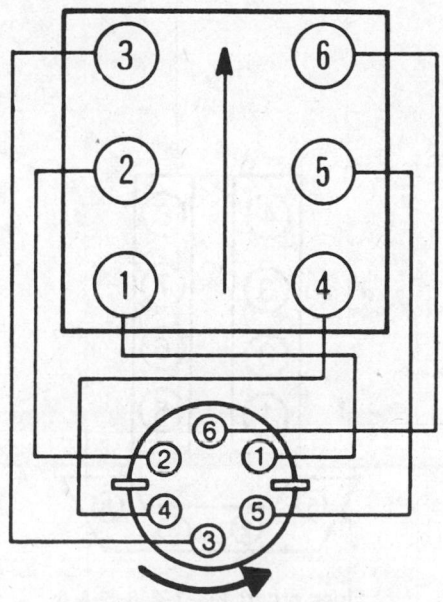

911, 911SC and 911 Turbo Models

FIRING ORDERS

NOTE: To avoid confusion, always replace spark plug wires one at a time.

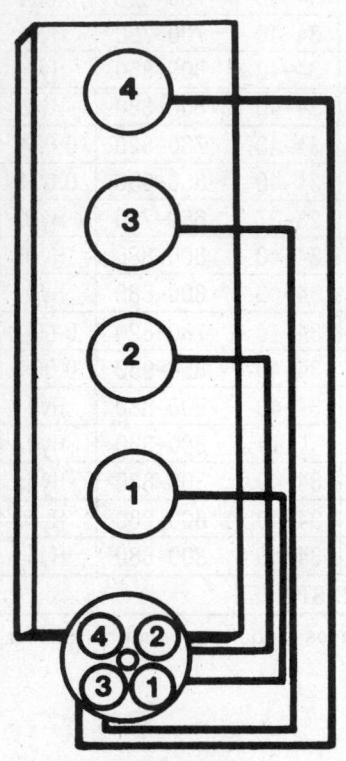

924S and 944 Models

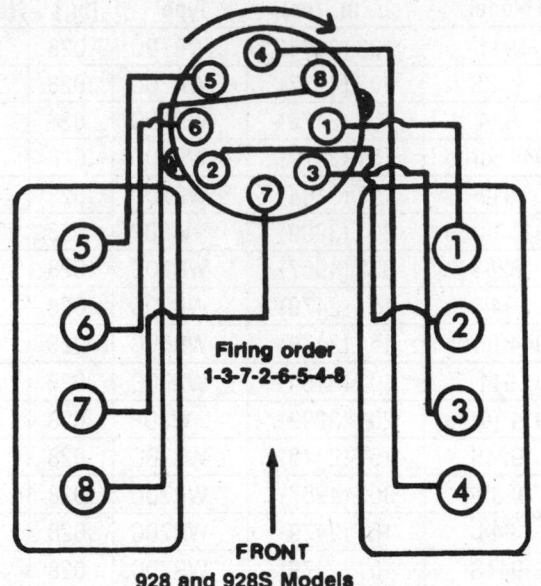

Firing order
1-3-7-2-6-5-4-8

FRONT
928 and 928S Models

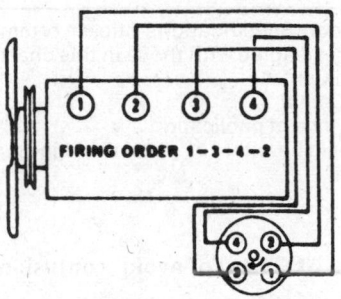

FIRING ORDER 1—3—4—2

924 Models

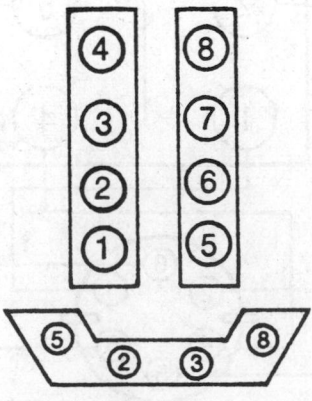

Firing order: 1—3—7—2—6—5—4—8
928S4

CAPACITIES

Year	Model	Engine Displacement cu. in. (cc)	Engine Crankcase with Filter	Engine Crankcase without Filter	Transaxle (pts.) Manual	Transaxle (pts.) Auto.	Drive Axle (pts.)	Fuel Tank (gal.)	Cooling System (qts.)
1981	911	183 (2994)	10.6	—	6.4	—	—	21	—
	924	121 (1984)	5.3	4.7	5.5	6.3	—	16.4	8.5
	924 Turbo	121 (1984)	5.3	4.7	5.2	11.0	—	18.6	8.5
	928	273 (4474)	8.5	8.0	8.0	11.6	—	23	17
1982	911	183 (2994)	10.6	—	6.4	—	—	21	—
	924	121 (1984)	5.3	4.7	5.5	6.3	—	17.4	8.5
	924 Turbo	121 (1984)	5.3	4.7	5.2	11.0	—	17.4	8.5
	928	273 (4474)	8.5	8.0	8.0	11.6	—	23	17
1983	911	183 (2994)	10.6	—	6.4	—	—	21	—
	928	284 (4664)	8.5	8.0	8.0	12.0	—	23	17
	944	151 (2479)	6.4	—	5.5	6.0	—	17.4	8.5
1984	911	193 (3164)	10.6	—	6.6	—	—	22.5	—
	928	284 (4664)	8.5	8.0	8.0	12.0	—	23	17
	944	151 (2479)	6.4	—	5.5	6.0	—	17.4	8.5
1985	911	193 (3164)	10.6	—	6.6	—	—	22.5	—
	928S	302 (4957)	8.5	8.0	8.0	17.0	—	22.7	17
	944	151 (2479)	6.4	—	5.5	6.0	—	21.1	8.5
	944 Turbo	151 (2479)	6.9	—	5.5	—	—	21.1	9.0
1986	911	193 (3164)	10.6	—	6.6	—	—	22.5	—
	911 Turbo	201 (3299)	10.6	—	7.8	—	—	22.5	—
	928S	302 (4957)	8.5	8.0	8.0	17.0	—	22.7	17
	944	151 (2479)	6.4	—	5.5	6.0	—	21.1	8.5
	944 Turbo	151 (2479)	6.9	—	5.5	—	—	21.1	9.0
1987–88	911	193 (3164)	10.6	—	6.6	—	—	22.5	—
	911 Turbo	201 (3299)	10.6	—	7.8	—	—	22.5	—
	924S	151 (2479)	6.4	—	5.5	6.0	—	17.4	9.0
	928S4	302 (4957)	8.5	8.0	8.0	17.0	—	22.7	17
	944	151 (2479)	6.4	—	5.5	6.0	—	21.1	8.5
	944S	151 (2479)	6.4	—	5.5	6.0	—	21.1	8.5
	944 Turbo	151 (2479)	6.9	—	5.5	—	—	21.1	9.0

CRANKSHAFT AND CONNECTING ROD SPECIFICATIONS

All measurements are given in inches

Year	Engine Displacement cu. in. (cc)	Crankshaft Main Brg. Journal Dia.	Crankshaft Main Brg. Oil Clearance	Crankshaft Shaft End-play	Crankshaft Thrust on No.	Connecting Rod Journal Diameter	Connecting Rod Oil Clearance	Connecting Rod Side Clearance
1981	183 (2994)	2.2429–2.2437	0.0004–0.0028	0.0004–0.0077	1	2.0461–2.0468	0.0012–0.0035	0.0079–0.0158
	121 (1984)	2.4000	0.0020–0.0040	0.0040	3	1.9000	0.0008–0.0032	0.0040–0.0092
	121 (1984) Turbo	2.5000	0.0008–0.0030	0.0040	3	1.8900–1.9700	0.0008–0.0030	0.0020–0.0120
	273 (4474)	2.8000	0.0008–0.0039	0.0044–0.0124	3	2.0800	0.0008–0.0028	—

CRANKSHAFT AND CONNECTING ROD SPECIFICATIONS

All measurements are given in inches

| Year | Engine Displacement cu. in. (cc) | Crankshaft | | | | Connecting Rod | | |
		Main Brg. Journal Dia.	Main Brg. Oil Clearance	Shaft End-play	Thrust on No.	Journal Diameter	Oil Clearance	Side Clearance
1982	183 (2994)	2.2429–2.2437	0.0004–0.0028	0.0004–0.0077	1	2.0461–2.0468	0.0012–0.0035	0.0079–0.0158
	121 (1984)	2.4000	0.0020–0.0040	0.0040	3	1.9000	0.0008–0.0032	0.0040–0.0092
	121 (1984) Turbo	2.5000	0.0008–0.0030	0.0040	3	1.8900–1.9700	0.0008–0.0030	0.0020–0.0120
	273 (4474)	2.8000	0.0008–0.0039	0.0044–0.0124	3	2.0800	0.0008–0.0028	—
1983	183 (2994)	2.2429–2.2437	0.0004–0.0028	0.0004–0.0077	1	2.0461–2.0468	0.0012–0.0035	0.0079–0.0158
	284 (4664)	2.8000	0.0008–0.0039	0.0044–0.0124	3	2.0800	0.0008–0.0028	—
	151 (2479)	2.8000	0.0008–0.0039	0.0044–0.0124	3	2.0800	0.0008–0.0028	—
1984	193 (3164)	2.2429–2.2437	0.0004–0.0028	0.0004–0.0077	1	2.0461–2.0468	0.0012–0.0035	0.0079–0.0158
	284 (4664)	2.8000	0.0008–0.0039	0.0044–0.0124	3	2.0800	0.0008–0.0028	—
	151 (2479)	2.8000	0.0008–0.0039	0.0044–0.0124	3	2.0800	0.0008–0.0028	—
1985	193 (3164)	2.2429–2.2437	0.0004–0.0028	0.0004–0.0077	1	2.0461–2.0468	0.0012–0.0035	0.0079–0.0158
	302 (4957)	2.8000	0.0008–0.0039	0.0044–0.0124	3	2.0800	0.0008–0.0028	—
	151 (2479)	2.8000	0.0008–0.0039	0.0044–0.0124	3	2.0800	0.0008–0.0028	—
1986	193 (3164)	2.2429–2.2437	0.0004–0.0028	0.0004–0.0077	1	2.0461–2.0468	0.0012–0.0035	0.0079–0.0158
	201 (3299)	2.2429–2.2437	0.0004–0.0028	0.0004–0.0077	1	2.0461–2.0468	0.0012–0.0035	0.0079–0.0158
	302 (4957)	2.8000	0.0008–0.0039	0.0044–0.0124	3	2.0800	0.0008–0.0028	—
	151 (2479)	2.8000	0.0004–0.0028	0.0044–0.0124	3	2.0800	0.0008–0.0028	—
1987–88	193 (3164)	2.2429–2.2437	0.0004–0.0028	0.0004–0.0077	1	2.0461–2.0468	0.0012–0.0035	0.0079–0.0158
	201 (3299)	2.2429–2.2437	0.0004–0.0028	0.0004–0.0077	1	2.0461–2.0468	0.0012–0.0035	0.0079–0.0158
	302 (4957)	2.8000	0.0008–0.0039	0.0044–0.0124	3	2.0800	0.0008–0.0028	—
	151 (2479)	2.8000	0.0004–0.0028	0.0044–0.0124	3	2.0800	0.0008–0.0028	—

VALVE SPECIFICATIONS

| Year | Engine Displacement cu. in. (cc) | Seat Angle (deg.) | Face Angle (deg.) | Spring Test Pressure (lbs.) | Spring Installed Height (in.) | Stem-to-Guide Clearance (in.) | | Stem Diameter (in.) | |
						Intake	Exhaust	Intake	Exhaust
1981	183 (2994)	45	45	176.4 @ 1.21 ①	1.3779 ②	0.030–0.057	0.050–0.077	0.3531	0.3523
	121 (1984)	45	45¼	—	—	0.0157	0.020	0.353	0.352
	273 (4474)	45	45	—	—	0.0196	0.0196	0.352	0.352

VALVE SPECIFICATIONS

Year	Engine Displacement cu. in. (cc)	Seat Angle (deg.)	Face Angle (deg.)	Spring Test Pressure (lbs.)	Spring Installed Height (in.)	Stem-to-Guide Clearance (in.)		Stem Diameter (in.)	
						Intake	Exhaust	Intake	Exhaust
1982	183 (2994)	45	45	176.4 @ 1.21 ①	1.3779 ②	0.030–0.057	0.050–0.077	0.3531	0.3523
	121 (1984)	45	45¼	—	—	0.0157	0.020	0.353	0.352
	273 (4474)	45	45	—	—	0.0196	0.0196	0.352	0.352
1983	183 (2994)	45	45	176.4 @ 1.21 ①	1.3779 ②	0.030–0.057	0.050–0.077	0.3531	0.3523
	284 (4664)	45	45	—	—	0.0196	0.0196	0.352	0.352
	151 (2479)	45	45	—	—	0.0315	0.0315	0.352	0.352
1984	193 (3164)	45	45	176.4 @ 1.21 ①	1.3779 ②	0.030–0.057	0.050–0.077	0.3531	0.3523
	284 (4664)	45	45	—	—	0.0196	0.0196	0.352	0.352
	151 (2479)	45	45	—	—	0.0315	0.0315	0.352	0.352
1985	193 (3164)	45	45	176.4 @ 1.21 ①	1.3779 ②	0.030–0.057	0.050–0.077	0.3531	0.3523
	302 (4957)	45	45	—	—	0.0196	0.0196	0.352	0.352
	151 (2479)	45	45	—	—	0.0315	0.0315	0.352	0.352
1986	193 (3164)	45	45	176.4 @ 1.21 ①	1.3779 ②	0.030–0.057	0.050–0.077	0.3531	0.3523
	201 (3299)	45	45	176.4 @ 1.21 ①	1.3779 ②	0.030–0.057	0.050–0.077	0.3531	0.3523
	302 (4957)	45	45	—	—	0.0196	0.0196	0.352	0.352
	151 (2479)	45	45	—	—	0.0315	0.0315	0.352	0.352
1987–88	193 (3164)	45	45	176.4 @ 1.21 ①	1.3779 ②	0.030–0.057	0.050–0.077	0.3531	0.3523
	201 (3299)	45	45	176.4 @ 1.21 ①	1.3779	0.030–0.057	0.050–0.077	0.3531	0.3523
	302 (4957)	45	45	—	—	0.0196	0.0196	0.352	0.352
	151 (2479)	45	45	—	—	0.0315	0.0315	0.352	0.352

① 165.3 @ 1.25 for exhaust valve
② 1.3976 in. for exhaust

PISTON AND RING SPECIFICATIONS

All measurements are given in inches.

Year	Engine Displacement cu. in. (cc)	Piston Clearance	Ring Gap			Ring Side Clearance		
			Top Compression	Bottom Compression	Oil Control	Top Compression	Bottom Compression	Oil Control
1981	183 (2994)	0.006	0.004–0.008	0.004–0.008	0.006–0.012	0.003–0.004	0.002–0.003	0.001–0.002
	121 (1984)	0.0011–0.0031	0.0120–0.0200	0.0120–0.0200	0.0120–0.0200	0.0016–0.0028	0.0016–0.0028	0.0016–0.0028
	273 (4474)	0.0031	0.0078–0.0157	0.0078–0.0157	0.0157–0.0551	0.0019–0.0032	0.0019–0.0032	0.0009–0.0053

PISTON AND RING SPECIFICATIONS

All measurements are given in inches.

Year	Engine Displacement cu. in. (cc)	Piston Clearance	Ring Gap			Ring Side Clearance		
			Top Compression	Bottom Compression	Oil Control	Top Compression	Bottom Compression	Oil Control
1982	183 (2994)	0.006	0.004–0.008	0.004–0.008	0.006–0.012	0.003–0.004	0.002–0.003	0.001–0.002
	121 (1984)	0.0011–0.0031	0.0120–0.0200	0.0120–0.0200	0.0120–0.0200	0.0016–0.0028	0.0016–0.0028	0.0016–0.0028
	273 (4474)	0.0031	0.0078–0.0157	0.0078–0.0157	0.0157–0.0551	0.0019–0.0032	0.0019–0.0032	0.0009–0.0053
1983	183 (2994)	0.006	0.004–0.008	0.004–0.008	0.006–0.012	0.003–0.004	0.002–0.003	0.001–0.002
	284 (4664)	0.0031	0.0078–0.0157	0.0078–0.0157	0.0157–0.0551	0.0019–0.0032	0.0019–0.0032	0.0009–0.0053
	151 (2479)	0.0031	0.0078–0.0177	0.0078–0.0177	0.0149–0.0551	0.0019–0.0032	0.0019–0.0032	0.0009–0.0053
1984	193 (3164)	0.006	0.004–0.008	0.004–0.008	0.006–0.012	0.003–0.004	0.002–0.003	0.001–0.002
	284 (4664)	0.0031	0.0078–0.0157	0.0078–0.0157	0.0157–0.0551	0.0019–0.0032	0.0019–0.0032	0.0009–0.0053
	151 (2479)	0.0031	0.0078–0.0177	0.0078–0.0177	0.0149–0.0551	0.0019–0.0032	0.0019–0.0032	0.0009–0.0053
1985	193 (3164)	0.006	0.004–0.008	0.004–0.008	0.006–0.012	0.003–0.004	0.002–0.003	0.001–0.002
	302 (4957)	0.0031	0.0078–0.0177	0.0078–0.0157	0.0157–0.0551	0.0019–0.0032	0.0019–0.0032	0.0009–0.0053
	151 (2479)	0.0031	0.0078–0.0177	0.0078–0.0177	0.0149–0.0551	0.0019–0.0032	0.0019–0.0032	0.0009–0.0053
1986	193 (3164)	0.006	0.004–0.008	0.004–0.008	0.006–0.012	0.003–0.004	0.002–0.003	0.001–0.002
	201 (3299)	0.006	0.004–0.008	0.004–0.008	0.006–0.012	0.003–0.004	0.002–0.003	0.001–0.002
	302 (4957)	0.0031	0.0078–0.0177	0.0078–0.0157	0.0157–0.0551	0.0019–0.0032	0.0019–0.0032	0.0009–0.0053
	151 (2479)	0.0031	0.0078–0.0177	0.0078–0.0177	0.0149–0.0551	0.0019–0.0032	0.0019–0.0032	0.0009–0.0053
1987–88	193 (3164)	0.006	0.004–0.008	0.004–0.008	0.006–0.012	0.003–0.004	0.002–0.003	0.001–0.002
	201 (3299)	0.006	0.004–0.008	0.004–0.008	0.006–0.012	0.003–0.004	0.002–0.003	0.001–0.002
	302 (4957)	0.0031	0.0078–0.0177	0.0078–0.0157	0.0157–0.0551	0.0019–0.0032	0.0019–0.0032	0.0009–0.0053
	151 (2479)	0.0031	0.0078–0.0177	0.0078–0.0177	0.0149–0.0551	0.0019–0.0032	0.0019–0.0032	0.0009–0.0053

TORQUE SPECIFICATIONS

All readings in ft. lbs.

Year	Engine Displacement cu. in. (cc)	Cylinder Head Bolts	Main Bearing Bolts	Rod Bearing Bolts	Crankshaft Pulley Bolts	Flywheel Bolts	Manifold Intake	Manifold Exhaust	Spark Plugs
1981	183 (2994)	24	25	36	58	65	18	14–17	18–22
	121 (1984)	56 ①	58 ②	34–42	181	65	17	14	18–22
	121 (1984) ⑫	72	58 ②	47	181	65	17	14	18–22
	273 (4474)	58 ③	29 ④	42	181	69	17	15	18–22
1982	183 (2994)	24	25	36	58	65	18	14–17	18–22
	121 (1984)	47 ⑤	58 ②	34–42	181	65	17	14	18–22
	121 (1984) ⑫	⑥	58 ②	47	181	72	17	14	18–22
	273 (4474)	⑦	⑧	44.5	181	69	17	15	18–22
1983	183 (2994)	24	25	36	58	65	18	14–17	18–22
	284 (4664)	⑦	⑧	44.5	181	69	17	15	18–22
	151 (2479)	⑦	⑧	55.3	155 ⑪	65	15	15	18–22
1984	193 (3164)	24	25	36	58	65	18	14–17	18–22
	284 (4664)	⑦	⑧	44.5	181	69	17	15	18–22
	151 (2479)	⑦	⑧	55.3	155 ⑪	65	15	15	18–22
1985	193 (3164)	24	25	36	58	65	18	14–17	18–22
	302 (4957)	⑨	⑩	54	213	65	17	15	18–22
	151 (2479)	⑦	⑧	55.3	155 ⑪	65	15	15	18–22
1986	193 (3164)	24	25	36	58	65	18	14–17	18–22
	201 (3299)	24	25	36	58	65	18	14–17	18–22
	302 (4957)	⑨	⑩	54	213	65	17	15	18–22
	151 (2479)	⑦	⑧	55.3	155 ⑪	65	15	15	18–22
1987–88	193 (3164)	24	25	36	58	65	18	14–17	18–22
	201 (3299)	24	25	36	58	65	18	14–17	18–22
	302 (4957)	⑨	⑩	54	213	65	17	15	18–22
	151 (2479)	⑦	⑧	55.3	155 ⑪	65	15	15	18–22

① 63 ft. lbs. warm
② Allen head bolts on cap #5 are torqued to 47 ft. lbs.
③ Tighten in three steps: 1st—14 ft. lbs.; 2nd—36 ft. lbs.; 3rd—61 ft. lbs. Thirty minutes later, loosen each bolt ¼ turn, then retorque each bolt (in order) to 58 ft. lbs.
④ Tighten in two steps: 1st—14 ft. lbs.; 2nd—29 ft. lbs.
⑤ Tighten all head bolts in order to 47 ft. lbs., then (in order) tighten each bolt ½ turn further.
⑥ Tighten in three steps (in order each time): 1st—29 ft. lbs.; 2nd—58 ft. lbs.; 3rd—80 ft. lbs. (engine warm). One hour later, loosen each bolt 30° then repeat tightening sequence. Run the engine to 176°F. (coolant temp.), loosen each bolt 30°, then repeat the tightening sequence again.
⑦ Tighten in three steps (in order each time): 1st—14 ft. lbs.; 2nd—36 ft. lbs.; 3rd—65 ft. lbs. Thirty minutes later, loosen each bolt ¼ turn then repeat the tightening sequence.
⑧ M10 bolts: 1st step—14.5 ft. lbs; 2nd step—33.5 ft. lbs.
　M12 bolts; 1st step—14.5 ft. lbs.; 2nd step—30.0 ft. lbs.; 3rd step—48 ft. lbs.
⑨ 1st step—14 ft. lbs.
　2nd step—turn additional 90°
　3rd step—turn additional 90°
⑩ M12: 1st step—14 ft. lbs.
　　2nd step—29 ft. lbs.
　　3rd step—54 + 3.6 ft. lbs.
　M10: 1st step—14 ft. lbs.
　　2nd step—36 + 3.6 ft. lbs.
⑪ Gear wheel to crankshaft
⑫ Turbocharged

BRAKE SPECIFICATIONS

All measurements in inches unless noted

Year	Model	Lug Nut Torque (ft. lbs.)	Master Cylinder Bore	Brake Disc Minimum Thickness	Brake Disc Maximum Runout	Maximum Brake Drum Diameter	Maximum Lining Thickness Front	Maximum Lining Thickness Rear
1981	911	94	0.813	①	0.004	—	0.080	0.080
	924	80 ②	0.810	0.410	0.004	9.06	0.070	0.090
	924 Turbo	80 ②	0.830	0.480	0.004	9.20	0.070	0.090
	928	80 ②	0.950	0.720 ③④	0.004	—	0.080	0.080
1982	911	94	0.813	①	0.004	—	0.080	0.080
	924	80 ②	0.810	0.472	0.004	9.06	0.070	0.090
	924 Turbo	94	0.830	0.752 ⑤	0.004	—	0.080	0.080
	928	94	0.950	1.228 ⑤	0.004	—	0.080	0.080
1983	911	94	0.813	①	0.004	—	0.080	0.080
	928	94	0.950	1.228	0.004	—	0.080	0.080
	944	94	0.940	0.7283 ③	0.004	—	0.080	0.080
1984	911	94	0.813	0.890	0.004	—	0.080	0.080
	911 Turbo	94	0.937	⑥	0.004	—	0.080	0.080
	928	94	0.950	1.228	0.004	—	0.080	0.080
	944	94	0.940	0.807 ⑦	0.004	—	0.080	0.080
1985	911	94	0.813	0.890	0.004	—	0.080	0.080
	911 Turbo	94	0.937	⑥	0.004	—	0.080	0.080
	928	94	0.950	1.228	0.004	—	0.080	0.080
	944	94	0.940	0.807 ⑦	0.004	—	0.080	0.080
1986	911	94	0.813	0.890	0.004	—	0.080	0.080
	911 Turbo	94	0.937	⑥	0.004	—	0.080	0.080
	928	94	0.950	1.228	0.004	—	0.080	0.080
	944	94	0.940	0.807 ⑦	0.004	—	0.080	0.080
1987-88	911	94	0.813	0.890	0.004	—	0.080	0.080
	911 Turbo	94	0.937	⑥	0.004	—	0.080	0.080
	924S	94	0.940	0.807 ⑦	0.004	—	0.080	0.080
	928	94	0.950	1.228	0.004	—	0.080	0.080
	944	94	0.940	0.807 ⑦	0.004	—	0.080	0.080

① Front: 0.752
　Rear: 0.732
② Alloy wheel: 94 ft. lbs.
③ Rear: 0.7323
④ Floating frame caliper: 0.7323
⑤ Rear: 0.7560
⑥ Front: 1.205
　Rear: 1.047
⑦ Rear: 0.788

WHEEL ALIGNMENT

Year	Model	Caster Range (deg.)	Caster Preferred Setting (deg.)	Camber Range (deg.)	Camber Preferred Setting (deg.)	Toe-in (in.)	Steering Axis Inclination (deg.)
				FRONT			
1981	911	6³/₁₆P–6⁵/₁₆P	6¹/₁₆P	5/₁₆P–11/₁₆P	1/2P	0	—
	924	2¹/₄P–3P	2¹/2P	9/₁₆N–1/₁₆N	5/₁₆N	1/₁₆–1/8	—
	928	3P–3¹/2P	3P	11/₁₆N–5/₁₆N	1/2N	1/₁₆–1/8	—

WHEEL ALIGNMENT

Year	Model	Caster Range (deg.)	Caster Preferred Setting (deg.)	Camber Range (deg.)	Camber Preferred Setting (deg.)	Toe-in (in.)	Steering Axis Inclination (deg.)
1982	911	$6^3/_{16}$P–$6^5/_{16}$P	$6^1/_{16}$P	$^5/_{16}$P–$^{11}/_{16}$P	$^1/_2$P	0	—
	924	$2^1/_4$P–3P	$2^1/_2$P	$^9/_{16}$N–$^1/_{16}$N	$^5/_{16}$N	$^1/_{16}$–$^1/_8$	—
	928	3P–$3^1/_2$P	3P	$^{11}/_{16}$N–$^5/_{16}$N	$^1/_2$N	$^1/_{16}$–$^1/_8$	—
1983	911	$6^3/_{16}$P–$6^5/_{16}$P	$6^1/_{16}$P	$^5/_{16}$P–$^{11}/_{16}$P	$^1/_2$P	0	—
	928	$3^1/_4$P–$3^3/_4$P	$3^1/_2$P	$^{11}/_{16}$N–$^5/_{16}$N	$^1/_2$N	$^3/_{32}$–$^5/_{32}$	—
	944	$2^1/_4$P–3P	$2^1/_2$P	$^1/_{16}$N–$^9/_{16}$N	$^5/_{16}$P	$^1/_{16}$–$^1/_8$	—
1984	911	$6^3/_{16}$P–$6^5/_{16}$P	$6^1/_{16}$P	$^5/_{16}$P–$^{11}/_{16}$P	$^1/_2$P ①	0	—
	928	$3^1/_4$P–$3^3/_4$P	$3^1/_2$P	$^{11}/_{16}$N–$^5/_{16}$N	$^1/_2$N	$^3/_{32}$–$^5/_{32}$	—
	944	$2^1/_4$P–3P	$2^1/_2$P	$^1/_{16}$N–$^9/_{16}$N	$^5/_{16}$P	$^1/_{16}$–$^1/_8$	—
1985	911	$5^{11}/_{16}$P–$6^5/_{16}$P	$6^1/_{16}$P	$^3/_{16}$P–$^5/_{16}$P	$^1/_4$P ①	$^1/_4$	—
	928	3P–4P	$3^1/_2$P	$^{11}/_{16}$N–$^5/_{16}$N	$^1/_2$N	$^3/_{32}$–$^5/_{32}$	—
	944	$2^1/_4$P–3P	$2^1/_2$P	$^1/_{16}$N–$^9/_{16}$N	$^5/_{16}$P	$^1/_{16}$–$^1/_8$	—
1986	911	$5^{11}/_{16}$P–$6^5/_{16}$P	$6^1/_{16}$P	$^3/_{16}$P–$^5/_{16}$P	$^1/_4$P ①	$^1/_4$	—
	928	3P–4P	$3^1/_2$P	$^{11}/_{16}$N–$^5/_{16}$N	$^1/_2$N	$^3/_{32}$–$^5/_{32}$	—
	944	$2^1/_4$P–3P	$2^1/_2$P	$^1/_{16}$N–$^9/_{16}$N	$^5/_{16}$P	$^1/_{16}$–$^1/_8$	—
1987–88	911	$5^{11}/_{16}$P–$6^5/_{16}$P	$6^1/_{16}$P	$^3/_{16}$P–$^5/_{16}$P	$^1/_4$P ①	$^1/_4$	—
	924S	$2^1/_4$P–3P	$2^1/_2$P	$^1/_{16}$N–$^9/_{16}$N	$^5/_{16}$P	$^1/_{16}$–$^1/_8$	—
	928	3P–4P	$3^1/_2$P	$^{11}/_{16}$N–$^5/_{16}$N	$^1/_2$N	$^3/_{32}$–$^5/_{32}$	—
	944	$2^1/_4$P–3P	$2^1/_2$P	$^1/_{16}$N–$^9/_{16}$N	$^5/_{16}$P	$^1/_{16}$–$^1/_8$	—
REAR							
1981	911	—	—	$^3/_{16}$N–$^3/_{16}$P	0	$^3/_{32}$	—
	924	—	—	$1^1/_2$N–$^1/_2$N	1N	0	—
	928	—	—	$^7/_8$N–$^1/_2$N	$^{11}/_{16}$N	$^3/_{32}$–$^5/_{32}$	—
1982	911	—	—	$^3/_{16}$N–$^3/_{16}$P	0	$^3/_{32}$	—
	924	—	—	$1^1/_2$N–$^1/_2$N	1N	0	—
	928	—	—	$^7/_8$N–$^1/_2$N	$^{11}/_{16}$N	$^3/_{32}$–$^5/_{32}$	—
1983	911	—	—	$^3/_{16}$N–$^3/_{16}$P	0	$^3/_{32}$	—
	928	—	—	$^7/_8$N–$^1/_2$N	$^{11}/_{16}$N	$^3/_{32}$–$^5/_{32}$	—
	944	—	—	$^1/_{16}$P–$^{15}/_{16}$N	$^3/_8$N	0	—
1984	911	—	—	$1^3/_{16}$N–$^{13}/_{16}$N	1N	$^3/_{32}$	—
	928	—	—	$^7/_8$N–$^1/_2$N	$^{11}/_{16}$N	$^3/_{32}$–$^5/_{32}$	—
	944	—	—	$^1/_{16}$P–$^{15}/_{16}$N	$^3/_8$N	0	—
1985	911	—	—	$1^3/_{16}$N–$^{13}/_{16}$N	1N	$^3/_{32}$	—
	928	—	—	$^1/_2$N–$^{13}/_{16}$N	$^{11}/_{16}$N	$^3/_{32}$	—
	944	—	—	$^1/_{16}$P–$^{15}/_{16}$N	$^7/_{16}$N	0	—
1986	911	—	—	$1^3/_{16}$N–$^{13}/_{16}$N	1N	$^3/_{32}$	—
	928	—	—	$^1/_2$N–$^{13}/_{16}$N	$^{11}/_{16}$N	$^3/_{32}$	—
	944	—	—	$^1/_{16}$P–$^{15}/_{16}$N	$^7/_{16}$N	0	—
1987–88	911	—	—	$1^3/_{16}$N–$^{13}/_{16}$N	1N	$^3/_{32}$	—
	924S	—	—	$^1/_{16}$P–$^{15}/_{16}$N	$^7/_{16}$N	0	—
	928	—	—	$^1/_2$N–$^{13}/_{16}$N	$^{11}/_{16}$N	$^3/_{32}$	—
	944	—	—	$^1/_{16}$P–$^{15}/_{16}$N	$^7/_{16}$N	0	—

① 911 Turbo: $^1/_2$P

TUNE-UP PROCEDURES

Ignition Timing

ADJUSTMENT

1981–83 911 Models

1. Start the engine and allow it to warm up to normal operating temperature, approximately 194°F (90°C).

2. Turn the ignition switch OFF and connect an inductive timing light according to the manufacturers instructions. Connect an inductive tester/tachometer.

3. Remove the red and blue distributor vacuum hoses. Adjust the engine idle speed to 950 rpm.

4. When the timing light flashes, the 5 degrees BTDC mark on the crankshaft pulley should be aligned with the reference notch on the fan (blower) housing at 950 rpm. If the notches do not align, loosen the retaining nut at the bottom of the distributor mounting flange and slowly rotate the distributor as necessary until the notch and pulley mark are aligned. Timing for the 49 states 911S is TDC at normal idle (Z1 notch on the crank pulley). California 911S models should be set 15 degrees ATDC at idle speed (15 degrees notch to the left of Z1), and the centrifugal advance timing check is no longer performed on these models. Basic timing for the Turbo is 7 degrees ATDC at idle. Full centrifugal advance should be 29 degrees BTDC and it should begin at 4000 rpm.

5. Ignition timing is now correct at idle. Reconnect the vacuum hoses and recheck idle speed. Adjust if necessary.

6. To check the centrifugal advance mechanism, make sure the ignition timing is properly adjusted for the idle rpm (950). Disconnect the distributor vacuum hoses. Check the timing in the normal manner as described in the above procedures. Timing should be 15–20 degrees BTDC at 3000 rpm, and 19–25 degrees BTDC at 6000 rpm.

7. To check the vacuum retard, run the engine at idle speed. Connect the blue (retard) hose at connection 1 of the double vacuum box on the distributor and disconnect the red (advance) hose at connection 2. Check the ignition timing with the timing light; it should be 3–7 degrees ATDC.

8. To check the vacuum advance, connect the blue (retard) hose on connection 2. Adjust engine speed to 950

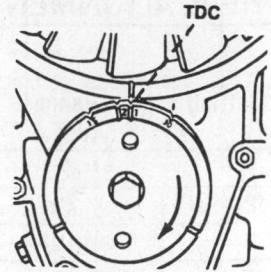

Timing marks on 911 models

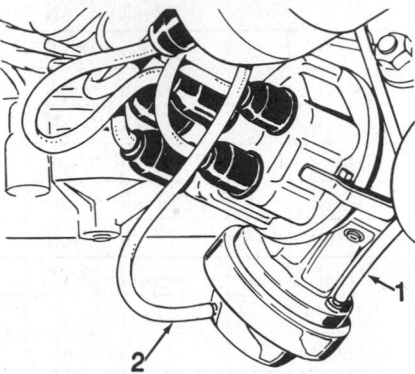

Hose connections for checking vacuum advance/retard on 1981-83 911 models

rpm. Ignition timing should be 8–12 degrees BTDC. Connect all vacuum hoses and check that the engine idle speed is 950 rpm. Adjust if necessary.

NOTE: If the above procedures have been followed and the proper settings cannot be achieved, remove and bench test the distributor with the proper test equipment.

1984–88 911 Models

To check the idle speed, a Porsche special tool (VAG 1367 tester) is required. Terminals **B** and **C** of the test jack (see illustration) located next to the coil must be bridged with a jumper wire in order to bypass the idle regulator. Timing is then checked in the normal manner. At 800 rpm, ignition timing should be 3 degrees ATDC.

Full throttle ignition timing is again checked with the VAG 1367 tester, or with a stroboscopic timing light directed at the 25 degrees timing mark on the crankshaft pulley. Make sure the engine is at normal operating temperature, approximately 194°F (90°C), and that all electrical accessories are OFF. Make sure that the distributor rotor is correctly installed in relation to the mark on the distributor housing.

Bridge terminals **B** and **C** of the test jack; this stimulates full throttle

on the control unit and stops operation of the idle regulator. Full throttle timing should be 25 degrees BTDC at 3800 rpm.

1981–82 924 Models

NOTE: The 924 Turbo uses a Digital Ignition Timing Control (DITC) ignition system. No ignition timing adjustments are necessary or possible.

1. Start the engine and allow it to reach normal operating temperature, then turn the ignition switch OFF.

2. Bypass the idle stabilizer by disconnecting the connector plugs. The plugs are located on the wiring harness on the left (driver side) front wheel well inside the engine compartment. Connect a tachometer according to the manufacturers instructions.

3. Connect a timing light to number one cylinder spark plug lead according to the timing light manufacturers instructions.

4. Start the engine and set the idle speed to 800 rpm.

5. With the engine idling, focus the timing light on the timing port. The timing marks are located on the flywheel.

6. If the ignition timing requires adjustment, loosen the distributor holddown clamp and turn the distributor until the timing is correct. Retighten the holddown bolt.

7. After all adjustments are complete, reconnect the idle stabilizer leads and rev the engine a few times.

8. Check the idle speed after allowing it to stabilize.

1983–88 944 and 924S

The Digital Motor Electronic (DME) ignition system is self-adjusting. No periodic ignition timing adjustments are necessary or possible.

1981–84 928 and 928S

1. Start the engine and allow it to reach normal operating temperature, then turn the ignition switch OFF.

2. Connect a timing light to the engine. A positive (+) terminal for connecting the timing light is located in the engine compartment. Connect a tachometer according to the manufacturers instructions.

—— CAUTION ——
Make sure the ignition switch is OFF when connecting test equipment to the ignition system.

3. With the timing light connected to the ignition cable for No. 1 cylinder, detach both vacuum hoses at the distributor and start the engine.

4. The timing marks are located on the crankshaft pulley and are colored for identification. With the engine at 3000 rpm, focus the timing light on the timing marks. Refer to the Tune-Up Chart for timing specifications.

5. To adjust the timing, loosen the distributor holddown bolt and turn the distributor as necessary. Tighten the holddown bolt when the timing is correct.

6. Once all adjustments are complete, turn the ignition OFF and disconnect all test equipment.

1985–88 928S, 928S4

The EZF ignition system used on 928S models is self-adjusting. The EZK ignition system on 928S4 models uses knock sensors to allow the control unit to constantly adjust the ignition timing according to engine operating conditions. In either case, ignition timing is computer-controlled and not adjustable.

Valve Lash

ADJUSTMENT

911 Models

1. The engine must be cold when adjusting the valves. Remove the rocker arm covers, two per head in the case of the 911.

2. The valves of each cylinder are adjusted with that piston at the top of its compression stroke. Both the intake and exhaust valves will be closed at this point. Turn the engine to align the TDC mark **Z1** with the reference mark.

3. Using the appropriate size feeler gauge (see the Tune-Up Specifications chart), check the clearance between the valve stem and the rocker arm. The feeler gauge should just slip through; if it has to be forced, the clearance will be incorrect.

4. If the clearance is not within specifications, loosen the locknut with a box wrench and use a screwdriver to turn the rocker arm adjusting screw while holding the locknut. A tool to simplify this procedure is available from automotive suppliers; it has a screwdriver bit which can be turned while the locknut is held with a socket.

5. Tighten the locknut while holding the adjusting screw. Recheck the valve clearance to ensure that it wasn't changed when the locknut was tightened. Repeat this procedure on the other valve of No. 1 cylinder.

6. Proceed to adjust the valves of the remaining cylinders in an order of 1–6–2–4–3–5. The piston of the cylinder on which the valves are being ad-

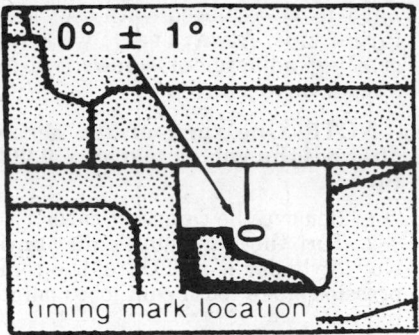

Timing marks on 1981-82 924 models

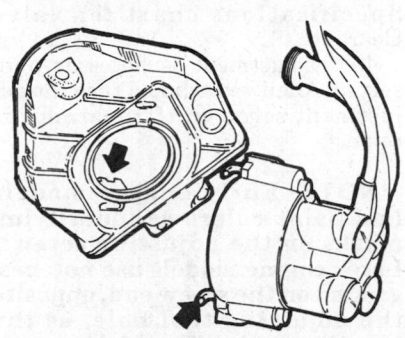

Distributor cap and distributor cap mount of the 944. Note how the distributor cap screw clips are to engage (arrows)

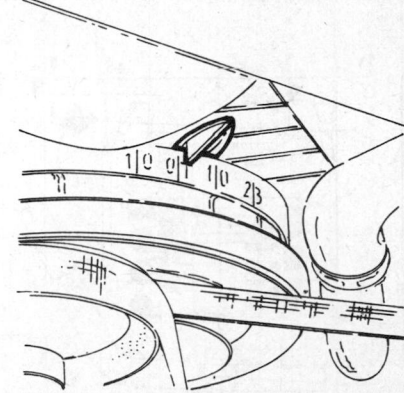

Timing marks on the 928 and 928S are located on the vibration damper at the front of the engine.

justed must be at TDC. Turn the engine until both valves of the cylinder being adjusted are closed. Six cylinder engines have TDC marks for each cylinder on the crankshaft pulley. Adjust the valves in the same manner as detailed for No. 1 cylinder.

7. Install the rocker arm or camshaft housing covers with the new gaskets. Start the engine and check for leaks.

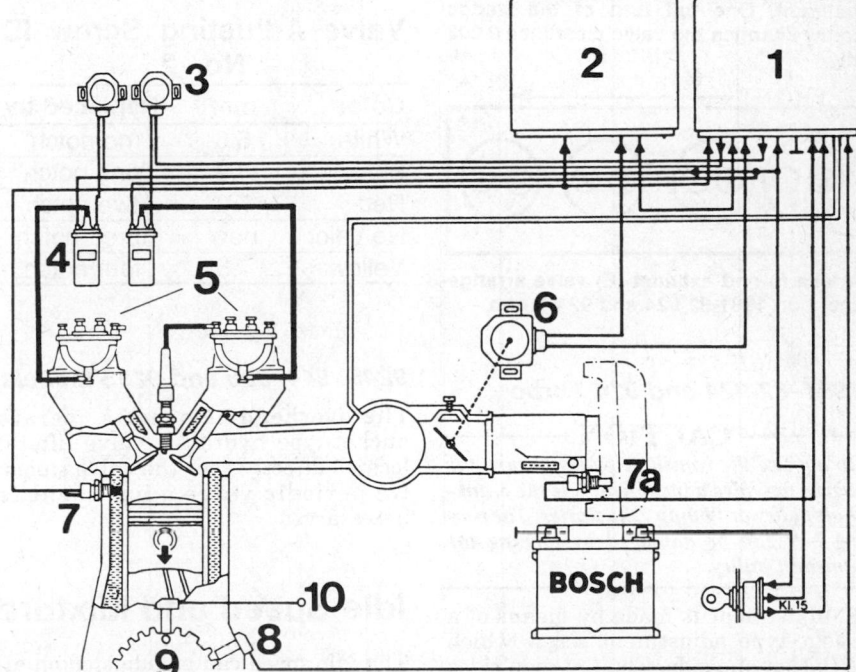

1 — EZF control unit
2 — LH injection control unit
3 — Ignition final stages
4 — Ignition coils
5 — Distributor (2 x 4)
6 — Throttle switches
7 — Temperature sensor II
7a — Temperature sensor I
8 — Ignition timing sensor
9 — Pulse gear ring
10 — TDC sensor

Schematic of EZF ignition system used on 928S models

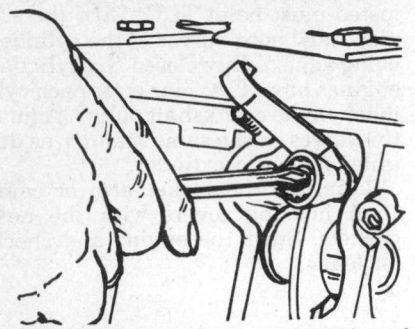

Valve clearance adjustment on 911 models

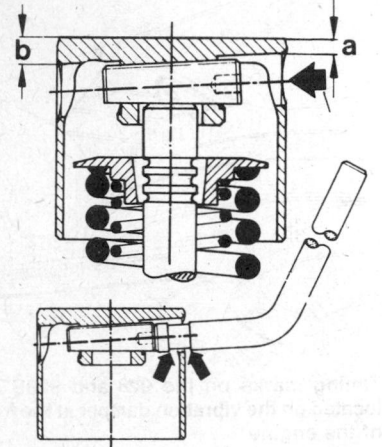

1981-82 924 and 924 Turbo valve lash adjustment. One full turn of the wedge screw changes the valve clearance 0.002 in.

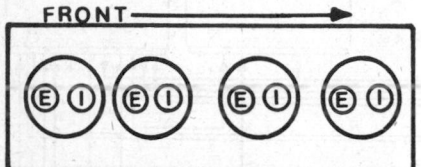

Intake (I) and exhaust (E) valve arrangement on 1981-82 924 and 924 Turbo

1981–82 924 and 924 Turbo

--- CAUTION ---

Do not use the camshaft pulley to turn the engine for valve adjustment. Use the crankshaft pulley or "bump" the starter. The timing belt can be damaged by turning the camshaft pulley.

Adjustment is made by means of a wedge-type adjustment screw which is flat on one side. The flat side rides directly on the valve stem. Five different diameter adjustment screws are available to compensate for wear. Adjustment is made by inserting an Allen wrench through the hole on the cam follower. Adjustment is made in full turns. If more than several turns are necessary to correct the clearance, the adjustment screw will probably

have to be replaced with the next larger size. Always start with the smallest adjustment screws (white) after a valve job.

NOTE: One turn of the screw changes the valve clearance 0.002 in.

1. Remove the camshaft cover.
2. Turn the crankshaft pulley until No. 1 cylinder is at TDC of the compression stoke (both cam lobes pointing up).
3. Insert the correct feeler gauge between the cam follower and the camshaft heel. Refer to the Tune-Up Specifications chart for valve clearance.
4. If adjustment is necessary, insert an Allen wrench and turn the adjustment screw until clearance is correct.

NOTE: Early engine models had paint colors as identifying marks on the adjusting screws. Later engine models use notches, ground on the screw end, opposite the adjusting tool hole, as the identity marks. The higher number of notches indicates the increased thickness of the adjusting screw.

Valve Adjusting Screw ID No. 2

Color	mm	Replaced by
White	6.6	"no notch"
Blue	6.9	"one notch"
Red	7.2	"two notch"
No color	new	"three notch"
Yellow	7.5	"four notch"

924S, 944, 928 and 928S Models

The overhead camshafts operate bucket-type hydraulic valve lifters, located directly over the valve stems. No periodic valve adjustment is necessary.

Idle Speed and Mixture

The idle speed can be adjusted on all 1981 models without the use of emission testing equipment. Idle mixture on all models, and idle speed on 1982–87 models cannot be properly adjusted without the use of an emissions analyzer to read HC and CO. CIS fuel injected engines require the use of a special CO adjusting tool for mixture adjustment.

IDLE SPEED ADJUSTMENT

1981–83 911 and 1986–88 911 Turbo (CIS fuel injection system)

1. Install the exhaust pickup line on to the test connection of the catalytic converter.
2. Connect the CO tester according to the manufacturers instructions.
3. Disconnect the plug for the oxygen sensor, which is located on the left side of the engine compartment.

NOTE: Make sure that the oil tank cap and seal are installed properly before checking or adjusting the idle speed. Air leaks can cause false readings when performing the adjusting procedure.

4. Turn the control screw on the throttle housing until the proper idle rpm is obtained. Refer to the Tune-Up Specifications chart or to the underhood emission sticker for idle rpm specifications.
5. Check the CO level using a suitable emissions analyzer. Correct the CO level as required.
6. If adjustment is necessary, remove the plug from the mixture control unit, which is located between the fuel distributor unit and the venturi, then insert the CO adjusting tool.
7. Do not force the tool down while making the adjustments or the engine will stall. Turn the adjusting screw very slowly, as the slightest turn will change the CO reading radically.
8. Remove the adjusting tool. Accelerate the engine. Allow the engine to return to idle and recheck both the idle speed and the CO level.
9. Once all adjustments are complete, disconnect the test equipment and plug all connections as required.

1984–88 911

NOTE: Idle adjustment on these models can only be performed using a CO analyzer. For accurate adjustments, the procedure must be closely followed.

1. Run the engine up to normal operating temperature. Engine oil temperature must be approximately 194°F (90°C). Intake air temperature must be between 59–95°F.
2. Disconnect the oxygen sensor.
3. Connect the CO analyzer in front of the catalytic converter. Check the CO content percentage at idle. Content in the exhaust gas should be 0.6–1.0%.
4. Reconnect the oxygen sensor.
5. Bridge terminals **B** and **C** on the test connection jack located to the

rear of the coil on the driver's side engine compartment wall to bypass the idle stabilizer.

6. Check the idle speed (rpm) and adjust if necessary. Idle speed should be 800 rpm. Adjustments are made with the throttle housing adjustment screw.

7. Remove the bridge from the test jack. Recheck the CO% content and idle rpm. Remove the CO analyzer probe and close the catalytic converter connection.

1981 924

Idle speed adjustments are performed at the bypass screw located on the throttle housing. The idle stabilizer must be disconnected and bridged before the idle can be adjusted or the stabilizer will attempt to offset any adjustment by advancing or retarding the ignition timing. To bypass the oxygen stabilizer, disconnect its connector, located on the wiring harness on the driver's side front fender well inside the engine compartment. Check the underhood emission sticker for any special instructions on idle speed adjustment and make all adjustments with the engine at normal operating temperature. The ignition timing must be checked and set correctly before adjusting the idle speed.

1981 924 Turbo

The timing control unit stabilizes the idle speed by varying the ignition timing at idle. As a result, basic idle speed adjustment must be made using a timing light.

NOTE: To eliminate the influence of the intake air temperature senor, it must be removed during the idle adjustment procedure.

1. Unscrew the temperature air senor from the intake manifold and place it in the fresh air tray behind the engine firewall, leaving the wire connected (sensor temperature must be below 120°F). A suitable plug (M14 x 1.5) must be screwed in the opening in the intake manifold during adjustment procedures.

2. Run the engine to normal operating temperature.

3. Connect a timing light according to the manufacturers instructions to the ignition wire for No. 1 cylinder.

4. While pointing the timing light at the timing marks, turn the idle control screw (bypass air screw) until the ignition timing mark (dot) is fully visible at the reference edge and jumps partially below the mark.

5. The idle speed should not be below 900 rpm (timing will vary slightly

Idle adjustment screw location on the 924 (arrow)

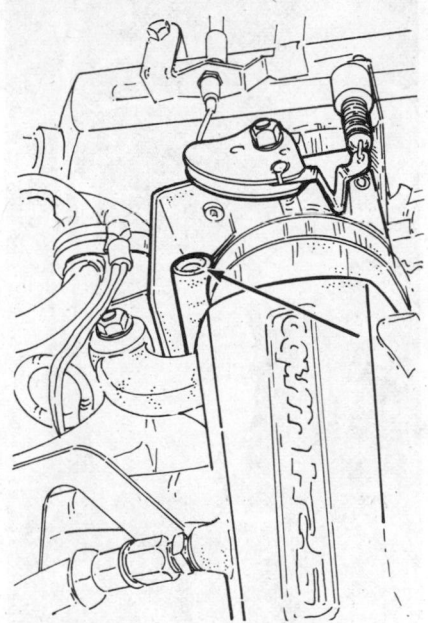

Idle adjustment screw location on the 924 Turbo (arrow)

because ignition timing is being regulated).

1981 928

Idle speed is adjusted at the idle speed screw on the throttle housing. The engine must be at normal operating temperature and in perfect running order. In addition, a separate tachometer must be used; do not adjust the idle speed using the tachometer in the instrument panel. Consult the underhood specifications sticker for

Before adjusting the idle speed on the 1981 924 Turbo, the fresh air sensor (arrow) must be removed and its hole plugged

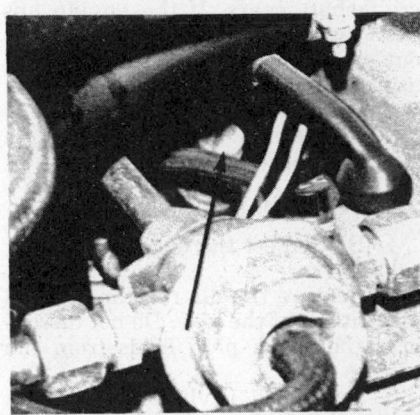

Idle adjustment screw location on the 928 (arrow)

any special information concerning individual engines.

1982–87 924S, 944 and 928 Models

Idle speed is electronically controlled on these models. No adjustment is possible.

ENGINE ELECTRICAL

Distributor
REMOVAL & INSTALLATION

911 Models

1. Remove the heated air intake duct.

2. Unsnap and remove the distributor cap. Position it out of the way.

3. Mark the direction in which the rotor is pointing on the body of the distributor.

NOTE: Some models have a scribe mark indicating the correct rotor position for No. 1 cylinder. On these models it will be more convenient to turn the engine so that the rotor points to this mark before removing the distributor.

4. Detach the distributor leads. Remove the vacuum line.

5. Loosen and remove the retaining nut from the base of the distributor. Pull the distributor straight out of the engine. Check and, if necessary, replace the sealing ring on the distributor housing.

6. Insert the distributor into the engine. Swivel the rotor back and forth to engage the distributor and crankshaft gears. If the engine has been turned while the distributor was out, bring the No. 1 cylinder to TDC as previously described under Ignition Timing.

7. Check and adjust the ignition timing as necessary.

1981–82 924, 924 Turbo

1. Disconnect the negative battery cable.

2. Remove the distributor cap and place it out of the way. Do not disconnect the spark plug leads from the cap.

3. Set the No. 1 cylinder on TDC. In this position, the Z1 mark on the flywheel will align with the timing pointer edge and the mark on the camshaft will be opposite the notch at the top rear of the timing belt cover.

4. Remove the primary wiring from the distributor.

5. Loosen and remove the holddown bolt and clamp, then remove the distributor.

6. If the engine was not turned while the distributor was removed, install the distributor so that the tab for the distributor cap faces the flywheel and the distributor cap mounting clips face in the direction of the car's longitudinal axis. In addition, the distributor rotor must be mounted so that it faces the notch on the distributor body for cylinder No. 1 and aligns with the No. 1 cylinder distributor cap tower.

7. If the engine was moved while the distributor was removed, set the No. 1 cylinder at TDC as described in Step 2 of this procedure, then install the distributor as described in Step 5.

8. When the distributor is installed, reconnect the electrical con-

1. Rotor
2. Stator

Exploded view of 911 distributor

924 and 924 Turbo distributor holddown bolt location (arrow)

nections and install the distributor cap.

1981–84 928 Models

1. Disconnect the negative battery cable.

2. Unsnap the two retaining clips and remove the distributor cap.

3. Set the No. 1 cylinder at top dead center (TDC). The No. 1 cylinder is at top dead center when the TDC mark

on the flywheel or crank pulley aligns with the timing pointer and the distributor cap tower for the No. 1 cylinder spark plug wire. Turn the engine over by hand until these signs are evident.

4. Disconnect the vacuum hose(s) from the distributor, then disconnect the electrical connections at the distributor.

On 1983–84 cars with Hall Effect ignitions, a more positive hold-down clip secures the electrical connector. If earlier cars develop an ignition miss, install clip (Part No. 071 905 252).

5. Loosen and remove the distributor holddown bolt and clamp, then remove the distributor.

6. If the engine has not been turned over since the distributor was removed, align the rotor on the distributor with the No. 1 cylinder distributor cap tower. There is a notch in the distributor body which the rotor will point to when in this position. Install the distributor.

7. If the engine was turned while the distributor was removed, it will be necessary to relocate No. 1 cylinder to TDC on the compression stroke. Remove No. 1 cylinder spark plug, then turn the engine over in the normal direction of rotation while checking for compression with your thumb over the No. 1 cylinder spark plug hole. When this happens, continue turning the engine until the timing mark for TDC on the flywheel or crank pulley aligns with the timing pointer. Install the distributor as described in Step 6.

8. Install the vacuum hoses, electrical connections and distributor cap. Check and adjust the ignition timing.

1983–88 944, 924S and 1985–86 928S

The distributor is not removable. Only the cap is removable. Noise appearing to originate in the vicinity of the distributor of the distributor on 944 models is usually due to a worn Woodruff key on the camshaft sprocket.

NOTE: The distributor rotor is retained by one or three screws accessible after removing the dust cover. If the rotor is removed, new retaining screws must be installed, or the old ones coated with non-hardening sealant.

1987–88 928S4

All 32-valve engines use two distributors, each driven by the exhaust camshaft for the cylinder bank it controls and mounted on the front of the engine. The distributor caps are retained by three screws, as is the rotor.

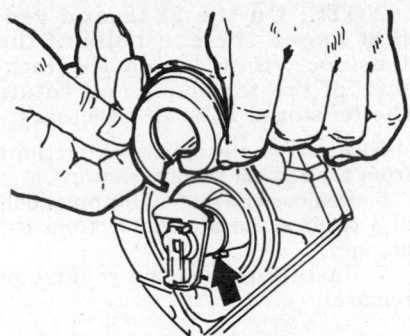

On the 944, the distributor rotor is held to the shaft by a screw (arrow).

The rotor can only be installed one way.

Alternator

PRECAUTIONS

To prevent possibly serious damage to the alternator, regulator and any on-board microprocessor control computers, the following precautions should be taken whenever working with the electrical system.

• Never reverse the battery connections.

• Booster batteries for starting must be connected properly: positive-to-positive and negative-to-negative with the ignition OFF.

• Disconnect the battery cables before using a fast charger; the charger has a tendency to force current through the diodes in the opposite directions for which they were designed. This burns out the diodes.

• Never use a fast charger as a booster for starting the vehicle.

• Never disconnect the voltage regulator while the engine is running.

• Avoid long soldering times when replacing diodes or transistors. Prolonged heat is damaging to AC generators.

• Do not use test lamps of more than 12 volts for checking diode continuity.

• Do not short across or ground any of the terminal on the AC generator.

• The polarity of the battery, generator, and regulator must be matched and considered before making any electrical connections within the system.

• Never operate the alternator on an open circuit and make sure that all connections within the circuit are clean and tight.

• Disconnect the battery terminals when performing any service on the electrical system. This will eliminate the possibility of accidental reversal of polarity.

Alternator pulley nut removal

Alternator removal

Fan belt pulley adjustment spacers

• Disconnect the battery ground cable if arc welding is to be done on any part of the car.

REMOVAL & INSTALLATION

911 Models

The alternator is located in the blower housing.

1. Disconnect the battery ground straps.

2. Remove the air cleaner assembly.

3. Remove the upper shroud retaining bolts.

4. Hold the alternator pulley and remove the pulley nut.

5. Remove the drive belt.

6. Remove the blower housing strap retaining bolts.

7. Pull the blower housing/alternator towards the rear until there is enough clearance to disconnect the wiring.

8. Remove the alternator.

9. Install the alternator in the reverse order of removal. Be sure that the blower housing is seated on the dowel in the crankcase.

10. Tighten the pulley nut to 29 ft. lbs. (39 Nm).

BELT TENSION ADJUSTMENT

911 Models

A correctly tensioned belt can be deflected ½–¾ in. by light hand pressure. If the tension is not within specifications, follow the steps below to adjust or replace the belt.

1. Remove the pulley nut as outlined above in "Alternator Removal and Installation."

2. Remove the outside half of the pulley.

3. Remove the adjustment spacers to increase belt tension. Add spacers to decrease belt tension.

4. When the correct spacer grouping is achieved, install the belt, pulley half, spacers, and nut.

5. Tighten the nut to 29 ft. lbs. (39 Nm).

NOTE: If you have removed spacers, install the extra spacers on the outside of the pulley so they won't become lost or misplaced.

6. Recheck the belt tension after about 60 miles of driving.

1981–82 924 and 924 Turbo

The alternator and voltage regulator are combined in one housing. No voltage adjustment can be made with this until. The regulator can be replaced without removing and disassembling the alternator, just unbolt it from the rear.

1. Disconnect the battery cables.

2. Remove the cooling shroud and scoop from the alternator. The scoop is retained by a snap clip.

3. Remove the oil filter.

4. Disconnect the wire harness multiconnector from the rear of the alternator.

5. Loosen and remove the two allen head retaining bolts.

6. Remove the fan belt, then remove the alternator.

7. Install in the reverse order of removal. Adjust the fan belt tension so that deflection of the belt midway between the pulleys is about ⅜ in.

All Except 911

The voltage regulator is bolted to the

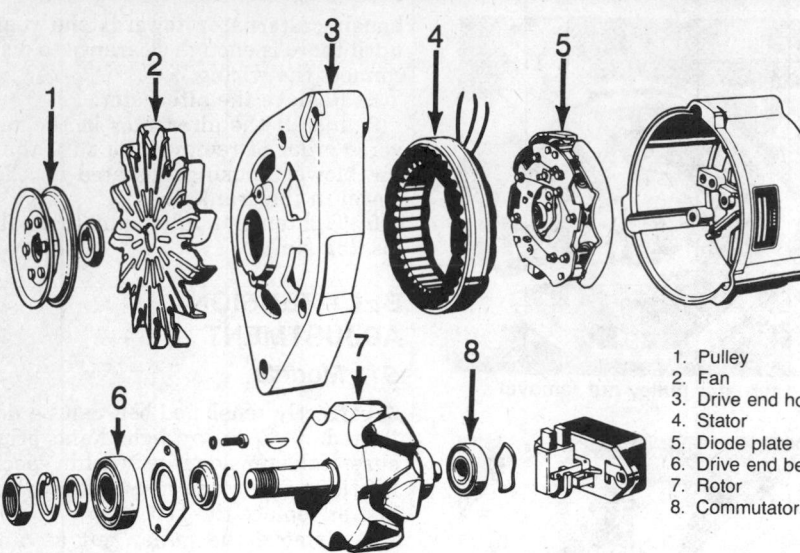

1. Pulley
2. Fan
3. Drive end housing
4. Stator
5. Diode plate
6. Drive end bearing
7. Rotor
8. Commutator bearing

Exploded view of a typical alternator

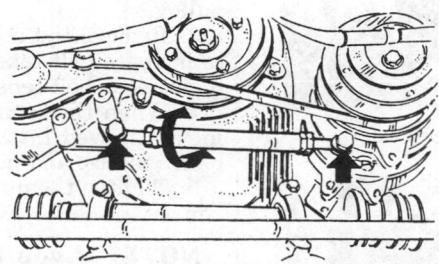

To loosen the alternator and air conditioning compressor drive belt of the 944: Loosen the tensioner end bolts (outer arrow); loosen the locknuts; then turn the tensioner tube (circular arrow) as required. When tightening the belt, the end bolts are to be tightened last

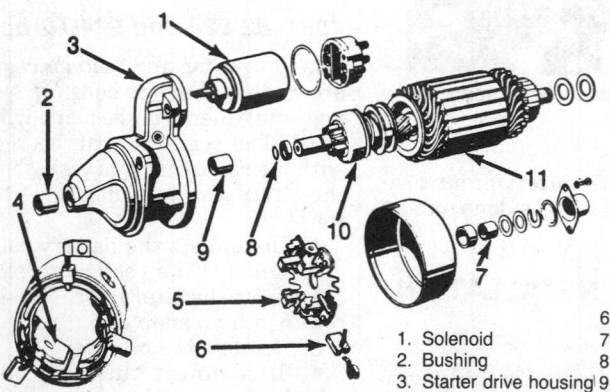

1. Solenoid
2. Bushing
3. Starter drive housing
4. Field coil
5. Brush holder
6. Brush
7. Bushing
8. Lock ring
9. Alternate bushing
10. Starter drive
11. Armature

Exploded view of the starter

rear of the alternator. Remove the alternator before attempting to remove the voltage regulator.

NOTE: The alternator is removed from beneath the vehicle.

1. Remove the battery ground cable.

2. Raise the vehicle and support it safely.

3. Remove the engine splash shield and the alternator cooling vent cover and tube.

4. Loosen the belt tension lock bolt, move the alternator inward and remove the belt from the pulley.

NOTE: On the 924S and 944, first loosen the end bolts of the tensioner, then loosen the locknuts of the tensioner and rotate the tensioner tube as necessary.

5. Remove the wire connections from the rear of the alternator.

6. Remove the alternator pivot bolt and remove the alternator from the engine.

7. Installation is the reverse of removal.

Voltage Regulator

REMOVAL & INSTALLATION

911 Models Only

1. Disconnect the battery ground cable.

2. Disconnect the wiring from the regulator.

3. Remove the mounting screws and remove the regulator.

4. Install the regulator. Do not overtighten the screws.

Starter

REMOVAL & INSTALLATION

911 Models

1. Disconnect the battery ground strap.

2. Raise the rear of the car and support it safely.

3. Tag and then remove the starter electrical connections.

4. Loosen the retaining bolts while supporting the starter, then remove the bolts and pull out the starter.

5. Install the starter in the reverse order of the removal procedure. Make sure that the terminal connections are correctly installed, clean and tight.

6. Lower the car and connect the battery ground strap.

911 STARTER DRIVE REPLACEMENT

1. Remove the starter.

2. Press clutch operating shaft by turning slighty.

3. Pull both off the shaft by turning slightly.

4. Hold the armature in a vise and push the pinion and sleeve onto the shaft until the detent locks.

All Except 911 Models

1. Disconnect the battery ground cable.

2. Raise and support the right front corner of the car.

3. Disconnect the two small wires form the starter solenoid. One wire

connects to the ignition coil and the second to the ignition switch through the wiring harness.

4. Disconnect the large cable, which is the positive battery cable, from the solenoid.

5. Remove the two starter retaining bolts.

6. Pull the starter straight out and to the front, then lower it out of the car.

7. Installation is the reverse of removal.

STARTER DRIVE REPLACEMENT

To replace the brushes or starter drive:

1. Remove the solenoid.
2. Remove the end bearing cap.
3. Loosen both of the long housing screws.
4. Remove the lockwasher and spacer washer.
5. Remove the long housing screws and remove the end cover.
6. Pull the two field coil brushes out of the brush housing.
7. Remove the brush housing assembly.
8. Loosen the nut on the solenoid housing, remove the sealing disc, and remove the solenoid operating lever.
9. Loosen the large screws on the side of the starter body and remove the field coil along with the brushes.

NOTE: If the brushes require replacement, the field coil and brushes and/or the brush housing and its brushes must be replaced as a unit. The armature should be turned on a lathe if it is out-of-round, scored or grooved.

10. If the starter drive is being replaced, push the lock ring down and remove the circlip on the end of the shaft. Remove the lock ring and remove the drive.

11. Assembly is the reverse of disassembly. Use a gear puller to install the lock ring in its groove. Use a new circlip on the shaft.

STARTER SOLENOID REPLACEMENT

1. Remove the starter.
2. Remove the nut which secures the connector strip on the end of the solenoid.
3. Take out the two retaining screws on the mounting bracket and withdraw the solenoid after it has been unhooked from the operating lever.
4. Installation is the reverse of removal. In order to facilitate engage-

ment of the lever, the pinion should be pulled as far as possible when inserting the solenoid.

ENGINE MECHANICAL— 911 MODELS

Engine

REMOVAL & INSTALLATION

911 Models Only

All 911 engines are removed and installed from below the vehicle, with the transaxle attached. The recommended method for removal is to raise the rear of the car high enough for working clearance and then support it on jack stands. A hydraulic transmission/differential jack or service jack of at least 800 lbs. capacity is required for lowering the engine/transaxle and raising it back into the chassis. Have an assistant steady the engine/transaxle during removal. Strap the engine to the jack so that it doesn't slide off. Proceed slowly and carefully as the engine/transaxle combination is both heavy and delicate.

1. Disconnect the battery. Drain the engine and transaxle oil.
2. Open the engine compartment lid and detach the hot air ducts from the air gates and exhaust manifold heat exchangers.
3. Detach the two heater control cables.
4. Remove the hot air ducts from the T-union between the air cleaners and then remove the T-union from the blower housing.
5. Remove the tops of the air cleaners.
6. Tag for identification and then remove the electrical cables from the generator and blower housing.
7. Tag for identification and then remove the wires from the ignition coil.
8. Remove the connections from the oil temperature and pressure sending units.
9. Carefully relieve the fuel system pressure, then remove the fuel line from the fuel pump and detach its clip from the engine shield.
10. Remove the Allen bolts retaining the axle shaft flange to the transaxle. Free the axle shafts from the transaxle and drop them out of the way.

11. Remove the starter electrical leads.
12. Disconnect the clutch cable from the control lever.
13. Remove the ground strap.
14. Detach the back-up light lead.
15. Disconnect the throttle linkage from the cross-shaft at the transaxle.
16. Remove the cover in the center of the rear floor.
17. Detach the rubber shift lever cover from the flange on the body and pull it forward on the control lever.
18. Remove the safety wire from the square-headed joint. Loosen the screw and slide the shift rod off its base.
19. Position the jack, including the flat support plate, under the engine/transaxle. The jack should be under the point of balance of the powertrain.
20. Raise the jack a slight amount.
21. Remove the body mounting bolts on either side of the engine compartment.
22. Remove the body mounting bolts from the short transaxle crossmember. The engine is removed with this crossmember attached.
23. Very carefully lower the engine while your assistants help balance it.
24. Roll the engine/transaxle out from under the car. Remove the starter. Release the throw-out fork tension by disconnecting the return spring if one is used. After releasing throw-out bearing tension, it is necessary to slide the throw-out fork past the bearing. To do this, insert a screwdriver in the opening in the transaxle and turn the bearing 90 degrees. Slide the fork past the bearing. The transaxle may now be separated from the engine.

NOTE: Follow Steps 25–30 for engine and transaxle separation.

25. Remove the engine-to-transaxle bolts and nuts. Carefully pull the transaxle away from the engine. Be sure that the full weight of the transaxle is supported, so as not to damage the pilot bushing, throwout bearing, clutch disc, or pressure plate.
26. Whichever component you are repairing, rebuilding, or replacing may now be moved to a suitable workbench, dolly or engine stand.
27. Before reinstalling the transaxle, fill the pilot bushing in the gland nut with a small amount of graphite grease (no more than 3cc, or $\frac{1}{10}$ oz.).
28. Lightly grease the transmission input shaft splines, starter shaft bushing, and the starter and flywheel gear teeth.
29. Carefully attach the transaxle to the engine. Remember the transmission input shaft will be passing through the throw-out bearing, pressure plate, clutch disc, and pilot bush-

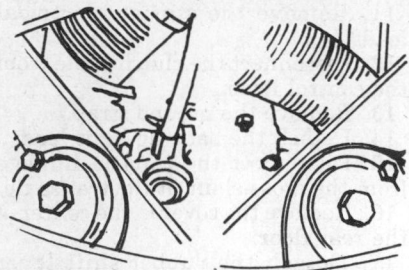

Rear engine-to-body mounts on 911 models

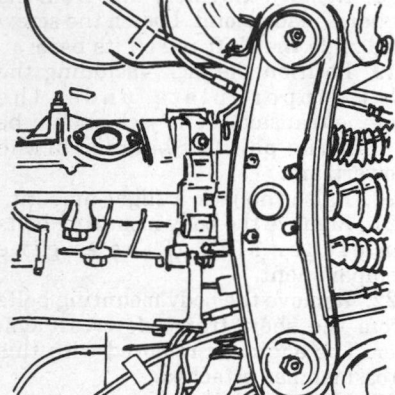

Transaxle crossmember mounting on 911 models

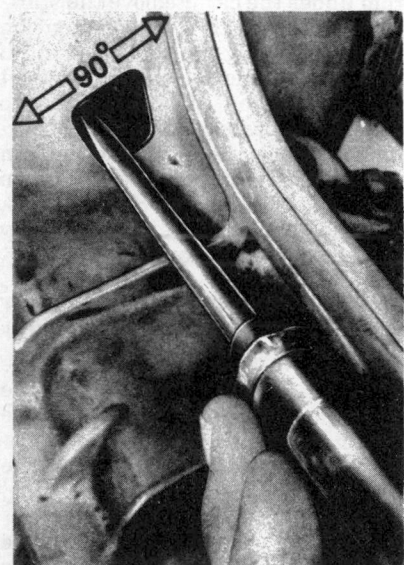

Sliding the fork past the throwout bearing on 911 models

ing, so give ample support during the attachment procedure.

NOTE: If the clutch disc splines and the input shaft splines don't line up, as they so often won't, have an assistant turn the crankshaft pulley until they do.

30. Push the transaxle home so that the mounting flanges are flush. Align the bottom holes and install the bolts.

Releasing throwout bearing tension on 911 models

Install the top bolts, and then tighten all of the remaining bolts evenly.

31. The engine/transaxle is installed by following the removal steps in reverse order.

32. After the engine is installed, check the clutch adjustment.

33. Refill the engine and transaxle with the correct lubricant. Lower the car.

34. Start the engine and check for leaks.

Rocker Shafts

REMOVAL & INSTALLATION

911 Models Only

Each rocker arm has an individual shaft on this single overhead camshaft engine. One or all of the shafts and rocker arms may be removed with the engine in the chassis.

1. Remove the camshaft housing cover nuts and spring washers. Remove the covers.

2. Scribe the rocker arms being removed so that they can be returned to the same position.

3. Unscrew the Allen bolt in the rocker shaft. Push the shaft out of its bore and remove it along with the rocker arm.

NOTE: If the rocker arm is under pressure, you won't be able to push the shaft out. Turn the crankshaft until the rocker rests on the heel of the cam lobe.

4. Check the rocker arm and shaft for excessive wear or damage. Replace any suspect piece.

NOTE: End rockers are installed with the Allen screw heads facing towards cylinders No. 2 and 5 respectively.

5. Place the rocker arm on its shaft.

6. The rocker arm shaft should be centered in its bore so that each groove is recessed 0.059 in. (1.15mm).

   a. Insert a 0.06in. feeler gauge in

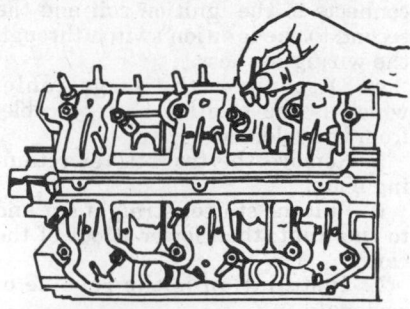

Rocker arm removal on 911 models

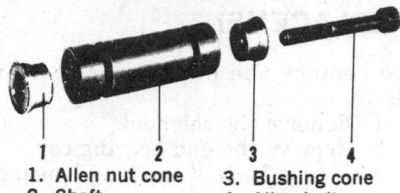

1. Allen nut cone   3. Bushing cone
2. Shaft   4. Allen bolt

Typical 911 rocker arm shaft assembly

the groove on one side of the shaft. Push the shaft in until the feeler gauge is held tight against the edge.

   b. Carefully remove the gauge and push the shaft in approximately 0.06 in. more, using the feeler gauge to judge the distance.

7. Tighten the Allen bolt to 13 ft. lbs. (17.5 Nm).

8. Install the camshaft cover.

Exhaust Manifold/Heat Exchanger

REMOVAL & INSTALLATION

911 Models Only

1. Remove the muffler as previously outlined. Detach and remove the connecting hose from the heat exchanger to the heater valve chamber.

2. Detach the heater hose from the heat exchanger.

3. Remove the three sunken bolts from the bottom of the heat exchanger.

4. Remove the six cylinder head-to-heat exchanger nuts using a universal socket set-up.

5. Remove the heat exchanger.

6. Examine the heat exchanger for damaged flanges or cracks. Replace it, if necessary.

7. Install the heat exchanger in the reverse order of removal. Use new flange gaskets and tighten the retaining nuts and bolts alternately.

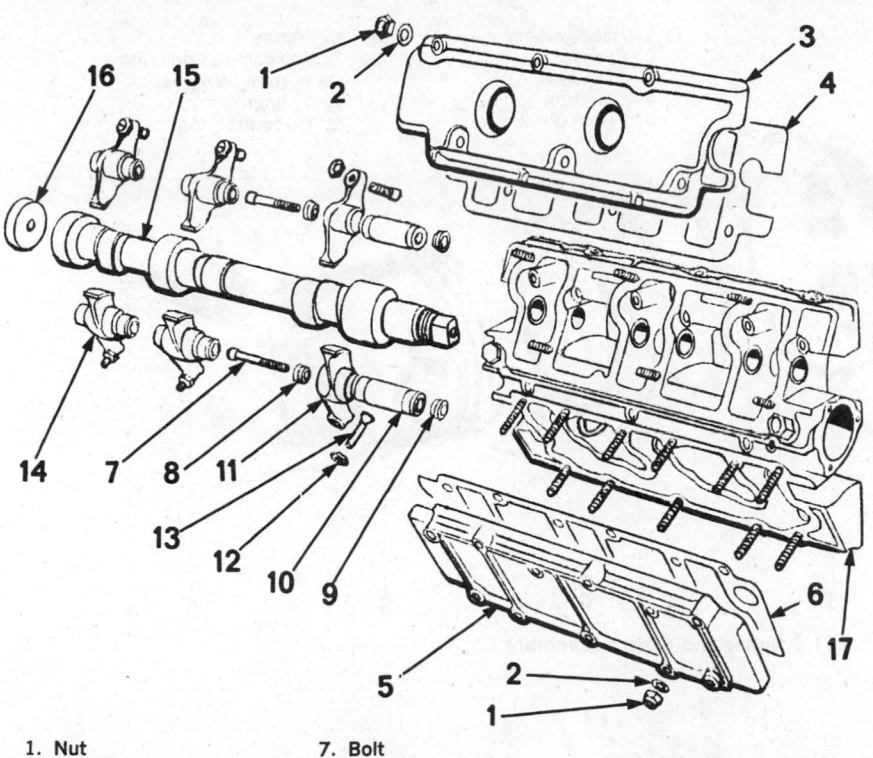

1. Nut
2. Aluminum washer
3. Cover
4. Gasket
5. Cover
6. Gasket
7. Bolt
8. Bushing
9. Nut
10. Rocker arm shaft
11. Rocker arm
12. Nut
13. Adjusting screw
14. Rocker arm assembly
15. Camshaft
16. Cover
17. Housing

Exploded view of 911 camshaft housing assembly

Engine

DISASSEMBLY AND ASSEMBLY

911 Models Only

NOTE: Further component removal and installation requires engine removal and disassembly. Follow steps of engine disassembly and then assembly for the part being replaced. A general engine rebuilding section is included at the end of the book for overhaul procedures not included here.

1. Mount the engine securely on a suitable engine stand.
2. Drain the engine oil and remove the muffler and heat exchanger.
3. Remove the rear engine cover plate.
4. Remove the intake distributor and intake pipe with the injection valves.
5. Remove the distributor and the front engine cover plate.
6. Remove the cooling blower impeller, then remove the cooling blower housing with the alternator attached.
7. Remove the engine mount.

8. Remove the front and rear cylinder jackets with the warm air guides.
9. Remove the oil cooler, oil filter, and oil pump.
10. Remove the rocker arm shafts with the protective tubes, pushrods and tappets.
11. Removal of the cylinder heads on the 911 involves removing the overhead camshafts. All three cylinder heads on each bank can be removed as a unit complete with the camshaft and rockers or each cylinder head can be removed individually. For access to the cylinder heads and valves, the camshaft housing must be disassembled and removed.

Rockers: Scribe a mark on the rockers for later installation. Remove the 5mm Allen retaining screws in the rocker shafts, holding the cone-nut that is released on the other end of the shaft. Push out the shafts and lift away the rockers. Position the camshaft so that the cam lobe does not press against the rocker being removed.

Camshaft: Remove the timing chain cover at each camshaft. Unbolt the chain tensioner and the intermediate wheel, using tools P202 and P203, or equivalent. Withdraw the dowel pin from the camshaft wheel

with tool P212, or equivalent. Remove the sliding wedges and withdraw the wheel and flange. Take the key from the camshaft, then unscrew the three sealing ring screws and remove the sealing ring together with the O-ring and the gasket. Withdraw the camshaft toward the rear. Note that both camshafts turn in the same direction and therefore require that the cam lobes be positioned differently.

Cam Housing: Unscrew the hex nuts and the three Allen screws to lift off the camshaft housing. Each housing fits either cylinder bank.

Cylinder Head: Loosen the cylinder head securing nuts in the reverse of the torque sequence using tool P119, or equivalent, then remove the cylinder head from the engine. Cylinders are numbered from the crankshaft pulley on the left bank as 1, 2 and 3 (left when facing the front of the car), and on the right bank as 4, 5 and 6.

The upper and lower sealing surfaces of the cylinder head (between the head and the camshaft and between the head and the cylinder) should not be machined. Permitted distortion at the cylinder sealing surface must not exceed 0.15mm (0.0059 in.). Examine the mating surfaces to ensure that they are in good condition.

NOTE: If a cylinder head stud is broken above the threads in 911 and Turbo crankcases, a new Dilavar cylinder head stud should be installed. Grind the broken stud flat, then center punch it in the center. Using a ¼ in. carbide-tipped drill bit chucked into a drill press, drill approximately 15mm into the stud. Drive a No. 3 screw extractor approximately 10mm into the bore. Heat the case evenly in an oven or with a torch to 392°F (200°C) to loosen the grip of the Loctite. Turn out the broken stud, re-tap the threads in the crankcase and install a new Dilavar stud (part No. 928 101 921 00).

When installing the cylinder heads, use new cylinder head gaskets with the perforations set towards the cylinder. Carefully position each head, insert the washers and tighten the hex nuts lightly.

The camshaft housing is sealed to the cylinder heads only with sealing compound. Assemble the camshaft housing and oil return pipes on the cylinder heads, but only hand-tighten.

Porsche suggests that at this point in reassembly, the cylinder head be torqued down first and then the cam-

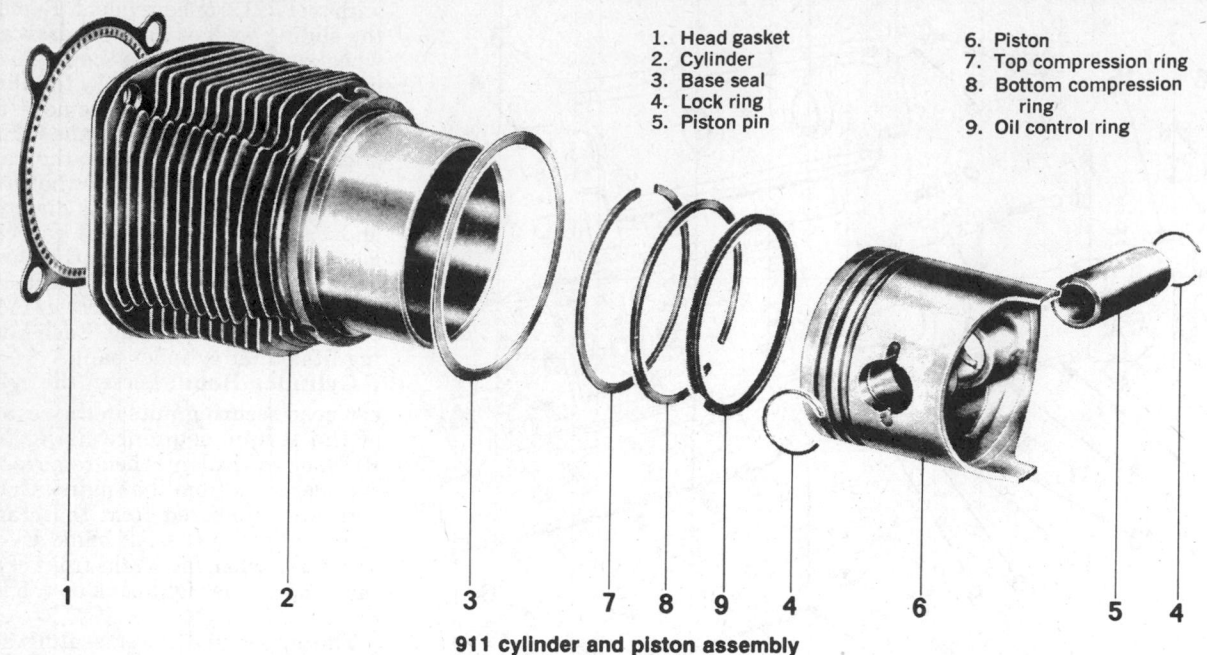

1. Head gasket
2. Cylinder
3. Base seal
4. Lock ring
5. Piston pin
6. Piston
7. Top compression ring
8. Bottom compression ring
9. Oil control ring

911 cylinder and piston assembly

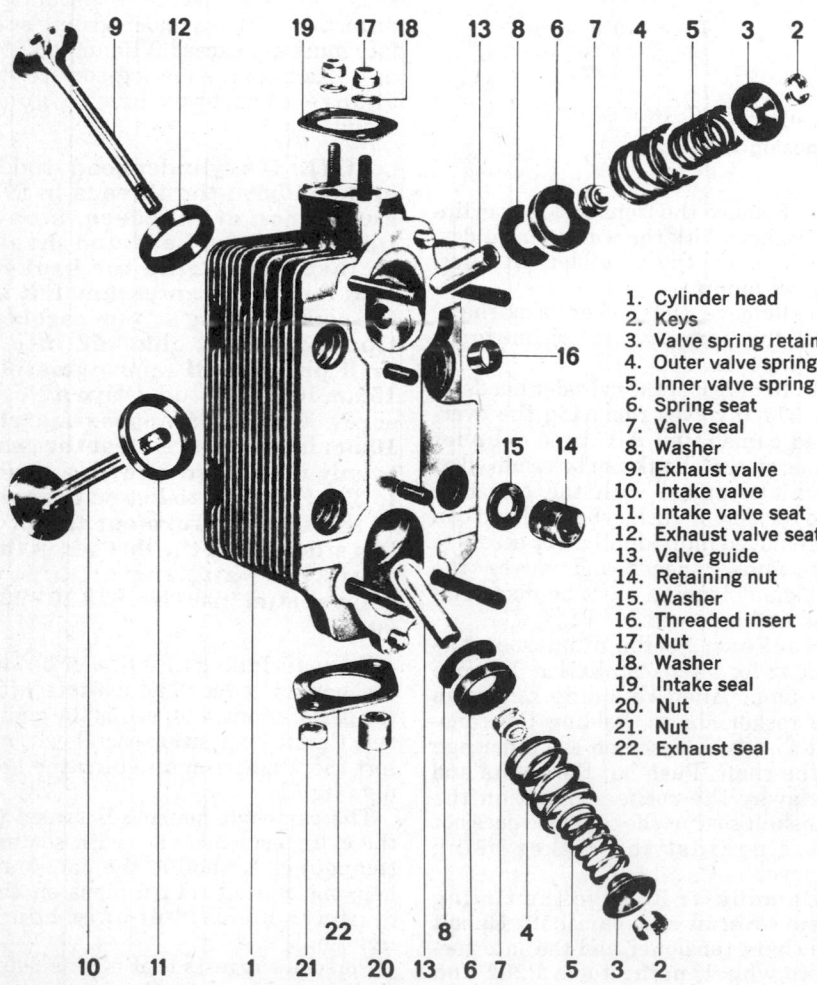

1. Cylinder head
2. Keys
3. Valve spring retainer
4. Outer valve spring
5. Inner valve spring
6. Spring seat
7. Valve seal
8. Washer
9. Exhaust valve
10. Intake valve
11. Intake valve seat
12. Exhaust valve seat
13. Valve guide
14. Retaining nut
15. Washer
16. Threaded insert
17. Nut
18. Washer
19. Intake seal
20. Nut
21. Nut
22. Exhaust seal

911 cylinder head components

Remove the 911 camshaft housing and cylinder heads as a unit

shaft housing. Some mechanics prefer to torque the camshaft housing first for more accurate tensioning. Either way, the camshaft must be checked frequently for free turning. If tightening one side binds the crankshaft, tightening the opposite side must free it again. If not, the housing must be loosened, and tightening steps must be made in a different sequence.

Tighten the cylinder head to 22–24 ft. lbs. (29–32 Nm). Tighten the camshaft housing to 15–18 ft. lbs. (20–24 Nm).

Valve Timing Adjustment: Turn the crankshaft until the mark **Z1** on the crankshaft pulley lines up exactly with the crankcase joint. Taking care that the valves and pistons do not collide with each other, turn both camshafts using tool P202, or equivalent, to bring the punch marks stamped on the face of the camshafts exactly above the vertical center. Back off a

911 valve timing position

little if the slightest resistance is felt during the turn. Then turn the free shaft to bring the valves and pistons into proper harmony before continuing with the first shaft.

With the crankshaft timing marks aligned and the camshaft punch marks exactly on the top, the engine is timed at the firing point in cylinder No. 1 with overlapping in cylinder No. 4. Find which hole in the camshaft sprocket lines up with the corresponding hole in the sprocket flange and insert the alining dowel pin. Slip on the washer and tighten the retaining nut to 101 ft. lbs. (137 Nm).

Adjust cylinder No. 1 intake valve clearance to 0.10mm (0.004 in.) and attach a dial gauge. The gauge sensor must be positioned exactly on the edge of the valve spring retaining collar. Adjust the gauge to a preload of 10mm (0.39 in.) to provide for a sensor travel when the cam lobe depresses the valve. Depress the chain tensioner with a screwdriver to tighten the chain (on the side to be measured) and turn the crankshaft one complete turn until the timing marks are aligned again. The dial gauge should read between 4.2 and 4.6mm (0.165–0.181 in.) A preferred range is 4.25–4.45mm.

If the gauge shows a lower or higher reading, the camshaft has to be readjusted as follows:

1. Remove the sprocket retaining nut, spring washer and aligning dowel pin.

2. Make sure that the crankshaft pulley mark is still aligned with the crankcase joint.

3. Depress the tensioner to tighten the chain and turn the camshaft until the dial gauge indicates 4.4–4.45mm (0.173–0.175 in.)

4. Find the hole in the camshaft sprocket which lines up with the sprocket flange and insert the dowel pin. Replace the spring washer and nut and tighten.

5. Turn the crankshaft two complete turns to the right and read the dial gauge. If the specified value is still not obtained, repeat the steps above.

When the valves overlap in cylinder No. 1, cylinder No. 4 is at firing point (TDC). Repeat the procedure for

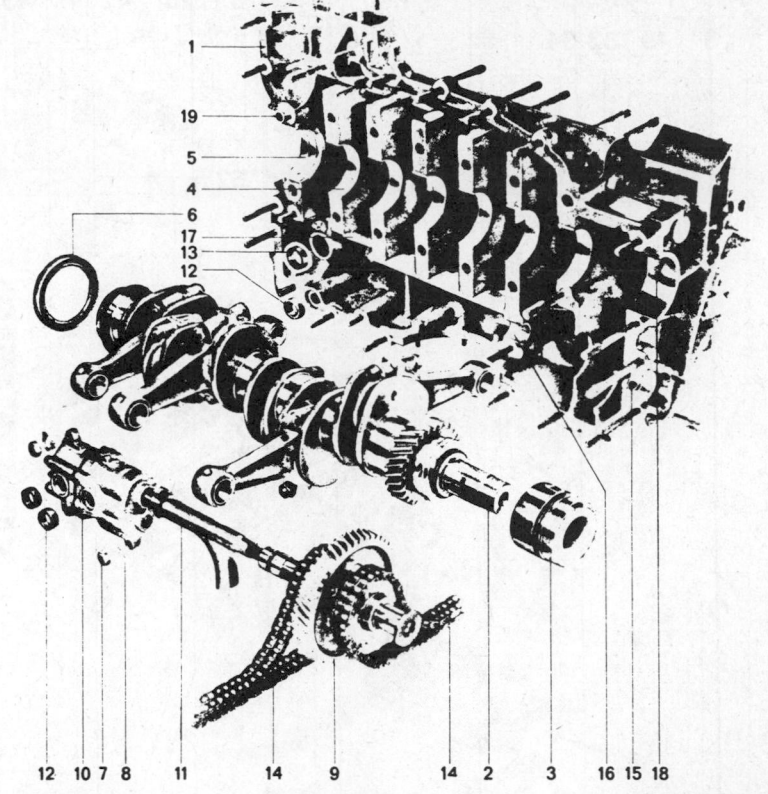

1. Crankcase half
2. Crankshaft assembly
3. No. 8 bearing
4. Bearing shell
5. Thrust bearing shell
6. Seal
7. Nut
8. Lock washer
9. Intermediate shaft
10. Oil pump assembly
11. Connecting shaft
12. Seal
13. Seal
14. Camshaft chain
15. Intermediate shaft thrust bearing
16. Intermediate shaft bearing
17. Oil strainer
18. pin
19. bushing

911 crankcase assembly

cylinder No. 4 valve timing adjustment.

Remove the cylinder heads, cylinders and pistons. Remove the clutch and flywheel. Disassemble the crankcase, being careful not to score any of the mating surfaces by trying to pry the halves apart. Remove the camshaft and crankshaft with the connecting rods.

Assembly is the reverse of disassembly, noting the following procedures:

1. Check the riveting of the camshaft gear and the camshaft. Check the camshaft for out-of-true using V-blocks. The maximum allowable wear is 0.0016 in. Check the end-play of the guide bearing which should be 0.0016–0.0051 in.

2. The oil holes in the crankshaft bearing journals and bearings should have no sharp edges. Carefully remove any metallic, foreign substances before installing the crankshaft and connecting rods.

3. Install the camshaft and gear so that the tooth marked with **0** is located between the two teeth of the crankshaft gear which are identified with a punch mark. Coat the mating surfaces of the housing halves with a thin coat of sealing compound. Be sure that no sealing compound enters the oil ducts.

4. Assemble the crankcase halves and lightly tighten the screw for the oil intake pipe. Screw on the sealing nuts with the sealing ring on the outside and tighten to the specified torque. Rotate the crankshaft to ensure free rotation.

5. Grease the needle bearing in the flywheel with a small amount of multipurpose grease. Moisten the felt ring with engine oil, wiping off any excess.

6. Install the flywheel and adjust the axial play of the crankshaft. Measure the axial play by installing the flywheel with two spacing washers but without the sealing rings. Using a dial gauge, measure the play by rotating the flywheel. The thickness of the third spacer can be computed by subtracting 0.0039 in. from the measured

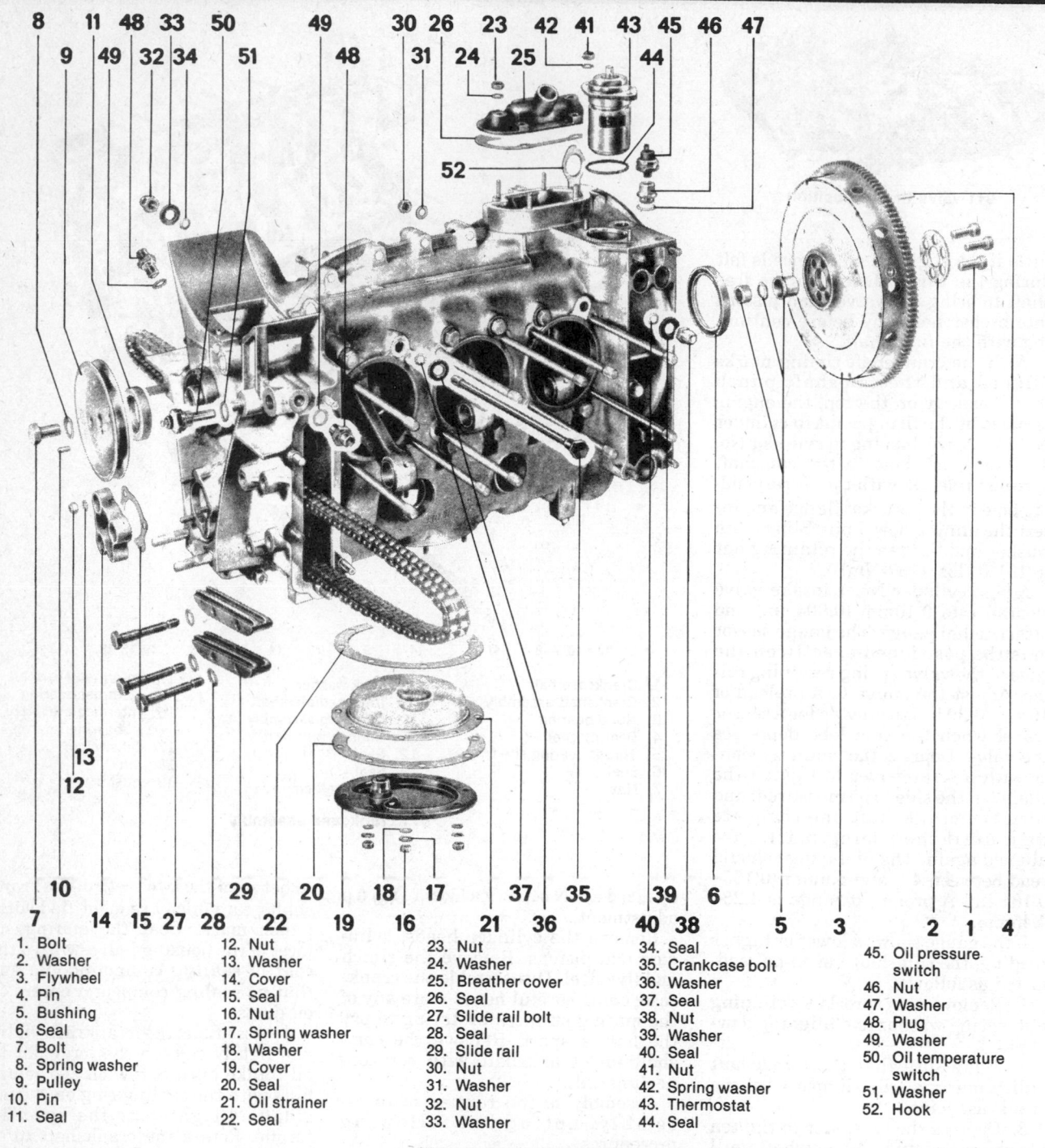

1. Bolt
2. Washer
3. Flywheel
4. Pin
5. Bushing
6. Seal
7. Bolt
8. Spring washer
9. Pulley
10. Pin
11. Seal
12. Nut
13. Washer
14. Cover
15. Seal
16. Nut
17. Spring washer
18. Washer
19. Cover
20. Seal
21. Oil strainer
22. Seal
23. Nut
24. Washer
25. Breather cover
26. Seal
27. Slide rail bolt
28. Seal
29. Slide rail
30. Nut
31. Washer
32. Nut
33. Washer
34. Seal
35. Crankcase bolt
36. Washer
37. Seal
38. Nut
39. Washer
40. Seal
41. Nut
42. Spring washer
43. Thermostat
44. Seal
45. Oil pressure switch
46. Nut
47. Washer
48. Plug
49. Washer
50. Oil temperature switch
51. Washer
52. Hook

911 crankcase assembly

result. Remove the flywheel and install the sealing ring, felt ring and three spacers. Three spacers must always be installed for the required thickness. Spacers are available in the following sizes: 0.0094, 0.0118, 0.0126, 0.0134, 0.0142, and 0.0150 in. Each spacer is marked for proper identification. The axial play of the crankshaft, measured with the engine

assembled and the flywheel screwed on, should be 0.0028–0.0051 in.

7. Clean the contact surface of the clutch disc and flywheel. Check the splining of the input shaft and coat lightly with molybdenum disulphide powder, applied with a brush. The clutch disc should slide easily.

8. Check the clutch throwout bearing. Do not wash in any solvent, but

wipe it clean. Replace bearings which are contaminated or noisy. Grease the guide bushing lightly with molybdenum disulphide paste.

9. Center the clutch disc and clutch flywheel using an input shaft. When a new clutch is installed, the balancing marks should be 180 degrees apart. A white paint stripe on the outside edge of the flywheel indicates the heavy

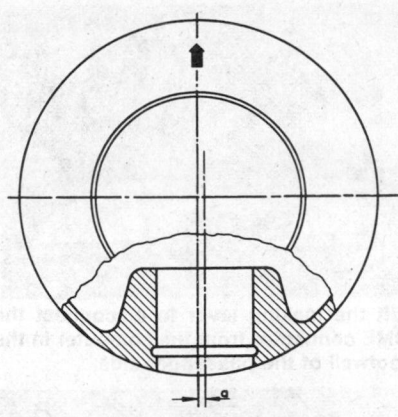

911 piston positioning

end, and a white paint stripe indicates the heavy end of the clutch. Tighten the bolts to 14.5 ft. lbs. (20 Nm).

10. Clean all pistons and check for wear. Check the marking of the pistons according to the following designations:

a. The letter head next to the arrow is the index of the spare parts number.

b. The punched-in arrow indicates that the piston must be installed with the arrow facing the flywheel.

c. The color dot (blue, pink or green) indicates the paired size of the piston.

d. A statement of weight class (+ or –) is punched in or printed. The weight class is indicated by a color dot (brown equals (–) weight and grey equals (+) weight).

e. Number indicates the piston size in mm.

11. Fit the compression and oil scraper rings. The designation TOP should face up.

12. Insert the locking rings of pistons 1 and 2 on the side facing the flywheel. The locking rings of pistons 3 and 4 should be fitted on the impeller side.

13. Fit the piston pin. The piston pin may slide in easily by hand, which is normal. Should the pin not fit easily, heat the piston to approximately 176°F and slide in the piston pin without bottoming the pin on the locking ring. Seat the second locking ring. Lubricate the piston and piston pin.

14. Compress the piston rings using a suitable tool, then lubricate the cylinder bore and fit the cylinder bore to the crankcase with the sealing ring. The studs of the crankcase may not touch the cooling fins of the cylinder.

15. Check the cylinder head for cracks and the spark plug threads for

damage. Replace the sealing ring and the cylinder head. Pre-tighten the cylinder head nuts slightly, then tighten in sequence to the specified torque. Refer to the Torque Specifications Chart at the beginning of this section.

16. Replace the baffle plate. Insert the tappets with engine oil. Slide the protective tubes with the new sealing rings up to the stop, taking care not to damage the sealing rings. Slide the bearing pieces on the rocker arm shafts so that the slots face downward and the broken edges outward when settling on the studs. The clip which secures the protective tubes should enter the slots of the bearing pieces and rest against the bottom edges of the protective tubes.

17. Lubricate the gear wheel and driveshaft and insert into the oil pump housing. Install the oil pump cover with the lubricated rubber sealing ring. Check the gear wheels for proper running. Install the oil pump, with a new seal, into the crankcase. The journal of the driveshaft should be in alignment with the slot in the camshaft gear. Center the oil pump by two crankshaft revolutions and tighten the nuts.

18. Clean the sealing surface on the flange for the oil filter. Lubricate the rubber seal slightly and screw the filter in until the filter is seated. Tighten the oil filter.

19. Install the oil cooler after checking for leaks and tightening all welded seats.

20. Install the front and rear cylinder jackets and warm air guides. Replace the engine mount.

21. Install the cooling blower housing with the alternator and adjust the V-belt tension. Replace the cooling blower impeller and the front engine cover plate.

22. Install the ignition distributor. Bring cylinder No. 1 to TDC/compression. The black notch should be in alignment with the reference mark. The center offset slot in the head of the ignition distributor driveshaft should be at an angle of approximately 12 degrees in relation to the longitudinal axis of the engine. Turn the distributor rotor to the mark for cylinder No. 1 on the distributor housing. Insert the ignition distributor.

23. Replace the oil filler neck with the oil vent.

24. Replace the intake distributor with the intake pipes and injection valves.

25. Mount the rear engine cover plate, then replace the exhaust muffler and heat exchanger. Fill the engine with oil and install it into the vehicle as previously described.

ENGINE MECHANICAL— ALL EXCEPT 911

Engine

REMOVAL & INSTALLATION

1981–82 924, 924 Turbo and 1983–88 924S, 944

NOTE: On turbo equipped models, some turbocharger components may have to be removed during engine removal. Wastegate and turbocharger services can be found following "Exhaust Manifold Removal and Installation."

1. Disconnect the battery cables. Raise the car and support it on jack stands.

2. Support the engine using an overhead hoist. If using a jack under the engine, be careful not to damage the aluminum oil pan. Use a wooden block between the jack and pan.

3. Remove the splash panel. Remove the windshield washer tank and bracket and place it behind the right headlight.

4. On models so equipped, disconnect the clutch cable. Remove the bottom clutch adjustment locknut and detach the cable from the lever.

5. Remove the access plate from the bottom of the clutch housing.

6. Have an assistant turn the engine with the crankshaft pulley. Remove the pressure plate bolts gradually until all pressure is released.

7. Remove the exhaust pipe flange bolts.

8. Remove the bracket at the rear of the transaxle.

9. Remove the entire exhaust system.

10. Remove the backup light switch from the transaxle.

11. Disconnect the axle driveshafts at the transaxle and let them hang down out of the way.

NOTE: If the car is going to be moved around with the engine out of the car, wire the driveshafts up so that they don't become damaged.

12. Remove the clutch housing-to-engine bolts.

13. Place a wooden block under the front tunnel reinforcement to support the transaxle tube.

14. Remove the transaxle mounting

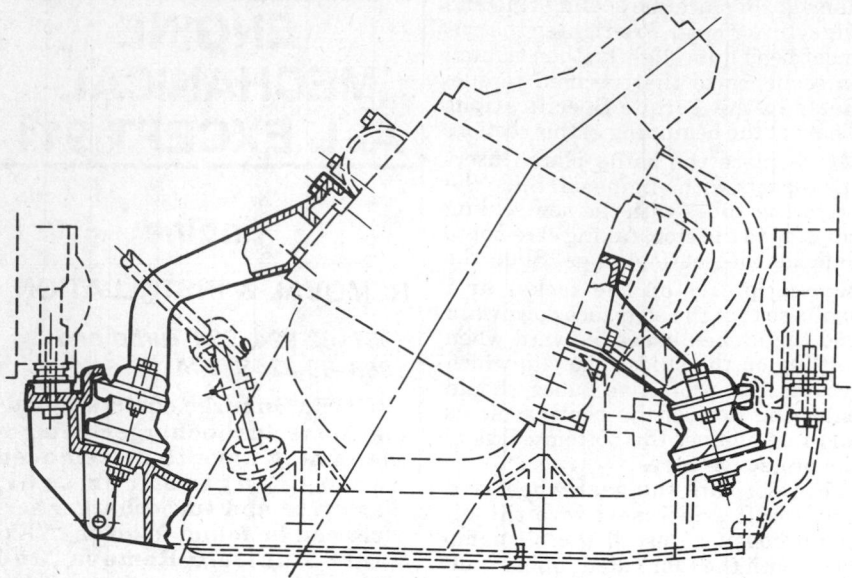

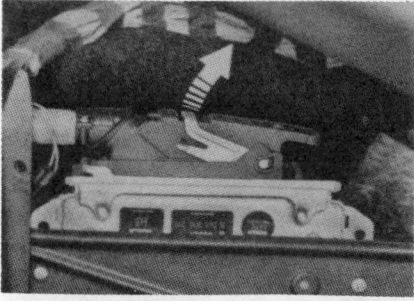

Lift the locking lever to disconnect the DME connector from the computer in the footwell of the passenger side

Disconnect the fuel feed and return lines, cruise control cable and plug connector as shown on 1987-88 944S models

The 944 engine mounts are hydraulically damped. Antifreeze flows through a small hole in a plate between 2 chambers when the mount is under stress, not unlike the action of a hydraulic shock absorber.

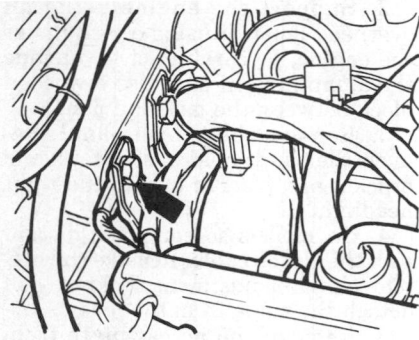

A loose or disconnected engine ground strap on the 944 could cause damage to the DME electronic control unit.

bolts and slide the transaxle toward the rear.

15. Remove the air cleaner. Disconnect the brake booster vacuum line.
16. Relieve the fuel system pressure, then disconnect and plug the fuel line.
17. Disconnect the accelerator cable.
18. Drain the cooling system.
19. Disconnect the radiator hoses. Remove the electric cooling fan.
20. Remove the hood. Detach the air conditioning compressor and place it out of the way. Do not disconnect the refrigerant lines.
21. Remove the radiator and expansion tank. Disconnect the heater hoses from the engine.
22. Disconnect the starter wiring.
23. Attach the engine lift chains to the hoist points on the engine. Disconnect the steering at the rack universal joint.
24. Disconnect the two side mounts

on the engine block. Remove the lift side mount from the car.

NOTE: 924S and 944 models use hydraulically damped engine mounts.

25. Lift the engine from the car.
26. Installation is basically the reverse of removal. Tighten the pressure plate bolts to 24 ft. lbs., the clutch housing bolts to 60 ft. lbs. (12mm bolt), 36 ft. lbs. (10mm bolt) and 20 ft. lbs. (8mm bolt).

NOTE: Make sure the engine-to-frame ground wire is securely connected. Starting the engine with the ground wire disconnected or loose can damage the DME electronic control unit.

1987–88 944S

On 16-valve 944S models, the engine is removed from below the vehicle with the clutch housing attached to the engine.

1. Raise the car and support it safely. Remove the front wheels.
2. Disconnect the ground cable from the battery and body, then disconnect the positive (+) cable from the battery. Take the cables apart and slide both cables with rubber grommets through the firewall. Remove the cable retainers.
3. Remove the cover plate in the footwell on the right (passenger) side. Unscrew the carrier for the DME control unit and disconnect the control unit plugs.
4. Loosen the fuel return hose clamp and pull off the hose. Discon-

nect the fuel feed hose using a backup wrench to hold the fitting while loosening the connection.
5. Disconnect the cable on the cruise control servo motor and disconnect the electrical connectors at the fuel injectors.
6. Loosen the ventilation hose for the toothed belt cover on the air filter lower section at the rear. Loosen and remove the complete filter system.
7. Remove the air flow sensor.
8. Loosen the distributor cap and rotor and remove them. Mark the position of the rotor for installation reference.
9. Remove the oil filter and ATF supply tank.
10. Remove the throttle operating cable with deflection roller and bracket assembly. Disconnect the oxygen sensor plug connector, then loosen and remove the hose clamps on the intake distributor and brake booster.
11. Loosen the cable retainers from the bulkhead, then disconnect the electrical connectors after tagging them for installation. Remove the vacuum hose from the tank ventilation valve.
12. Remove the engine splash guard.
13. Drain the cooling system and disconnect the venting hose for the alternator.
14. Disconnect and remove the coolant hose on the radiator at the bottom right.
15. Disconnect the electrical connec-

tions to the fan motors. Disconnect the fan motor brackets from the radiator and remove from below.

16. Disconnect and remove the coolant and vent hose on the radiator at the top left. Disconnect the harness connector at the temperature switch on the radiator. Disconnect and remove the coolant hose from the expansion tank.

17. Loosen the radiator mounting and remove the radiator from below.

18. Suspend the engine by its front transporting bracket using special tool 10-222-A, or equivalent, to hold the engine in its installed position. Make sure the suspension tool is correctly seated and supporting the engine securely.

19. Loosen the A/C compressor drive belt tensioner and remove the belt. Disconnect the compressor mounting bolts and wire it out of the way with the refrigerant lines connected. Do not let the compressor hang by the refrigerant lines.

20. Disconnect and remove the stabilizer with holders on the body and control arms. Disconnect the right and left tie rods.

21. Disconnect the hose between the ATF cooler and steering.

22. Disconnect the power steering pump, remove the spacer sleeve from the front and wire the pump to the steering gear. Do not let the pump hang by the power steering lines.

23. Disconnect the left and right control arms on the front axle crossmember and rear mount, then remove from the front.

24. Disconnect the universal joint on the steering gear and upper hydraulic engine mounts on the engine supports. Remove the front axle crossmember with steering gear and power steering pump from below.

25. Tag and disconnect the starter wire connectors and remove the starter.

26. Remove the clutch slave cylinder from the clutch housing with the line connected. Loosen and remove the holder for the fluid line on the clutch housisng upper section.

27. Loosen the exhaust assembly at the flange of the exhaust manifold and at the exhaust test line. Disconnect the oxygen sensor.

28. Disconnect the flange behind the catalytic converter and syspension and remove the assembly.

29. Remove the upper transaxle/clutch housing mounting bolts.

30. Disconnect the coolant hoses for the heater above the exhaust manifold and on the cylinder head.

31. Attach a lifting device to the engine and tighten it to support the full

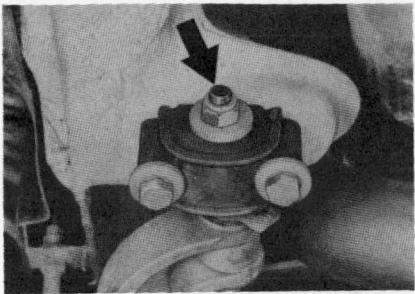

Loosen the through bolt (arrow) when removing the control arms on 1987-88 944S models. Do not remove the bushing bracket bolts.

weight. This is where it gets a little tricky, because the engine is removed from below. That means you have to use some sort of hoist that is tall enough to allow the body to be raised, and will allow the engine to be lowered onto a dolly. A chain hoist positioned directly over the engine compartment works best. Although not mentioned in the manufacturers service manual, it seems likely that this operation is more easily performed with the hood removed. Mark the hinge locations for assembly reference.

—————— **CAUTION** ——————

Make sure the engine is securely supported by the lifting device before proceeding. Serious injury and damage could result.

————————————————————

32. Remove the lower transaxle/clutch housing mounting bolts.

33. Pull the engine forward and press the rubber sleeve out of the firewall and into the engine compartment. Remove the wire harness carefully from the front passenger footwell.

NOTE: Remember that the connector end of the wire harness plugs into a computer which is very sensitive to damage or contamination on the connections. Keep the plug clean and handle it carefully during service.

34. Disconnect the engine from the central tube or shaft and carefully lower the engine onto a dolly. Lower slowly while watching for snags or obstructions and make sure it is securely supported on the dolly before disconnecting the hoist. Roll the engine from beneath the vehicle and continue service as required.

35. Installation is the reverse of removal. When installing the engine, note the following:

a. Guide the DME wire harness connector through the firewall carefully and connect it securely. Make sure the connectors are free

from grease, dirt or damage before installing the connector onto the computer in the front passenger footwell.

b. Install, but don't tighten the transaxle/clutch housing bolts. Tignten the mounting bolts to final torque only after the installation of the hydraulic engine mounts on the front axle crossmember. Torque the mounting bolts to 31 ft. lbs. (42 Nm).

c. When installing control arms, pressing down slightly on the sleeves in the rubber/metal mounts makes installation easier.

d. A steel washer 4mm thick is laid at each of the bolted connections between the right (passenger) side engine support and the hydraulic mount. Make sure they are installed properly.

e. Make sure the radiator fits correctly into its rubber mounts.

36. Torque all bolts to specifications as follows:

a. Stabilizer to aluminum control arm: 18 ft. lbs. (25 Nm)

b. Tie rod to steering knuckle: 15–22 ft. lbs. (20–30 Nm)

c. Steering universal joint: 22 ft. lbs. (30 Nm)

d. Control arm to cross member: 48 ft. lbs. (65 Nm)

e. Crossmember to body: 63 ft. lbs. (85 Nm)

37. Fill and bleed the cooling system and power steering system. Run the engine to normal operating temperature, then check the oil and coolant level and top off if necessary.

928, 928S and 928S4

1. Disconnect the battery ground cable. 1985 and later models are equipped with an engine control computer located on the right (passenger side) kick panel. When removing the engine, carefully disconnect the main harness connector from the computer and feed the wire through the firewall and into the engine compartment. Use care when handling the connector end of the harness to protect it from contamination or damage during service.

2. Remove the engine compartment cross brace.

NOTE: The vehicle must be on its wheels when the cross brace is removed or replaced.

3. Disconnect wiring and hoses to the under side of the hood, loosen hood bolts and supports, and remove the hood.

4. Remove the air intake hoses and the air cleaner assembly.

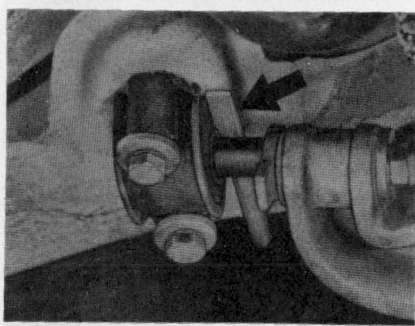

Use a small prybar (arrow) to press down slightly on the sleeves in the control arm bushing mounts to make installation easier

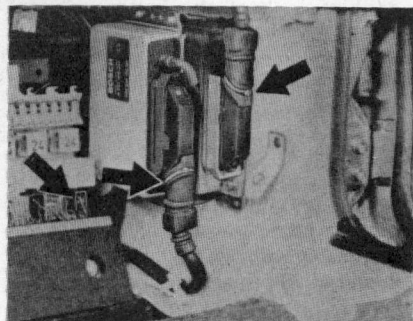

Location of fuel injection and ignition computers on 1985-88 928 models

5. Raise and support the vehicle.

6. Remove the bottom splash pan and drain the coolant from the radiator.

7. Drain the engine block of coolant by removing the drain plugs on the right and left sides of the crankcase.

8. Drain the engine oil.

9. Remove the lower body brace.

10. Disconnect the exhaust pipe flanges at the exhaust manifolds and the right and left side heat shields. Disconnect the secondary air injection lines.

11. Disconnect the body ground cable from the engine.

12. Remove the clutch slave cylinder at the clutch housing. Do not disconnect the hydraulic line.

13. Tag and disconnect the starter wires, then remove the starter along with the clutch housing cover. Remove the starter wires from the clamps on the steering crossmember.

14. Disconnect the clutch release lever at the ball pin by depressing the release lever in the direction of the clutch.

15. On automatic transaxle models, remove both transmission mount bolts. Remove the vacuum hose for the automatic transmission at the cylinder head, along with its clamp.

16. Remove the bolts from the clamping sleeve on the driveshaft and slide the sleeve rearward on the central shaft.

Pins for the TDC sensor must face down as shown when removing the engine on 928 models

CAUTION

On the 928S model, the TDC sensor pins on the flywheel must be at the bottom (facing toward the ground) to prevent damage during engine removal.

17. Unscrew the throwout bearing sleeve mounting bolts and push the sleeve toward the clutch.

18. Disconnect the left and right engine shock absorber at the control arms and remove with the right and left upper shock mounts.

19. On vehicles with air conditioning:

   a. Disconnect the temperature switch wires on the radiator.

   b. Disconnect the power lead to the compressor.

   c. Loosen the compressor, remove the compressor from the mounting brackets. Do not remove the hoses.

   d. Suspend the compressor from the frame with a wire.

20. Remove the air pump filter housing and disconnect the alternator cooling hose.

21. Remove the lower fan shroud from the radiator, remove the cooling hoses and the oil cooler line from the radiator bottom.

22. By lifting the engine one side at a time, remove the engine mounts and carefully set the engine on the front crossmember.

23. On manual transmission models, remove the clutch housing to engine bolts and lower the vehicle to the ground.

24. Remove the upper coolant hose and the vent from the radiator and thermostat housing.

25. Remove the upper oil cooler line form the upper part of the radiator.

26. Loosen the top mounting of the radiator and remove the assembly carefully.

27. Remove the heater hoses and electrical connections from the engine. Tag all electrical connections for identification before removal.

28. On 1981-84 models, remove the electronic control unit and loosen the

ignition coil and set aside. On 1985-88 models, pull off the ignition leads on the left and right sides of the distributor cap. Disconnect both ignition coils and lay them aside. Disconnect the ground wire in front of the right ignition coil on the body.

29. Relieve the fuel system pressure, then disconnect the fuel feed and return lines. Use a backup wrench on the fuel fittings to avoid twisting the line connections.

CAUTION

Fuel pressure must be relieved before attempting to disconnect any fuel lines. Take precautions to avoid the risk of fire.

30. On 1981-84 models, disconnect the hydraulic lines at the power steering pump, then cap them to prevent contamination by dirt or grease. On 1985-88 models, disconnect the oil hoses on the power steering supply tank, drain the oil, then remove the tank.

31. On 1981-84 models, disconnect the vacuum line to the power brake cylinder at the manifold. On 1985-88 models, Disconnect the vacuum hoses to the EZF control unit and brake booster. Remove the hose from the fuel vapor canister to the charging valve.

32. Disconnect the throttle, cruise control and automatic transmission cables by either removing the holder and clamp, or at the ball connectors on the linkage bracket. Tag each cable ball to identify its position for assembly.

NOTE: On air conditioned vehicles, cover the condenser with a wood board to prevent damage during engine removal.

33. On 1985-88 models, remove the central fuse/relay cover and disconnect the plugs for the oxygen sensor, sensor heating and ignition control unit. Disconnect the multipin connectors from the fuel injection and ignition computers at the right kick panel in the passenger compartment. Push the grommet and wire harness through into the engine compartment and carefully remove the connectors.

NOTE: Remember that each multipin connector end of the wire harness plugs into a computer which is very sensitive to damage or contamination on the connections. Keep the plugs clean and handle them carefully during service.

34. Attach a lifting cable to the lifting device and to the engine. Raise the assembly slightly and remove the engine block-to-clutch housing upper

mounting bolts. Disconnect the left and right engine mount bolts at the bottom.

35. Pull the engine forward and remove the short driveshaft with the guide tube.

36. Lift the engine carefully while tilting forward and slowly remove it from the engine compartment. As soon as clearance permits, disconnect and remove the pressure hose from the power steering pump after marking its installed position for installation reference. Remove the engine slowly and watch for snagged wires, linkage, etc. during removal.

37. Installation is the reverse of removal. Refill all fluids, then start the engine and allow it to reach normal operating temperature while checking for leaks.

Cylinder Head

REMOVAL & INSTALLATION

1981–82 924 and 924 Turbo

1. Disconnect the battery cables.
2. Drain the cooling system.
3. Remove the air cleaner.
4. Disconnect the radiator and heater hoses.
5. Tag and disconnect all electrical wires from the cylinder head.
6. Detach the spark plug wires. Remove the distributor.
7. Disconnect the exhaust manifold from the exhaust pipe.
8. Disconnect the EGR line. Remove the exhaust manifold.
9. Relieve the fuel system pressure, then remove the fuel injection lines from the cylinder head.
10. Remove the throttle valve housing and intake manifold as a unit.
11. Disconnect the air pump lines on models so equipped.
12. Remove the timing belt cover. Loosen the tensioner and remove the belt.
13. Loosen the cylinder head bolts in the reverse of the tightening sequence and remove the bolts.
14. Carefully lift off the cylinder head.
15. Installation is the reverse of removal. Be sure to correctly position the new cylinder head gasket. Align the timing marks, then install the timing belt and properly tension it. This procedure is outlined under "Timing Belt Removal and Installation". Tighten the cylinder head bolts in the sequence illustrated to the correct torque value. Refer to the Torque Specifications Chart at the beginning of this section. Follow the information in the chart EXACTLY.

Location of connectors for the oxygen sensor, sensor heating and ignition control unit on 1985-88 928 models

1981–86 928, 928S and 928S4

NOTE: The cylinder heads can be removed with the engine in the vehicle. 1985–88 928S and 928S4 engines are equipped with dual distributors driven off the exhaust camshafts. The cylinder head and camshaft case are one component and the cylinder heads are identical for right and left sides, but the head gaskets are not. The following is a general procedure for both early and late engines.

1. Drain the cooling system; both radiator and engine block.

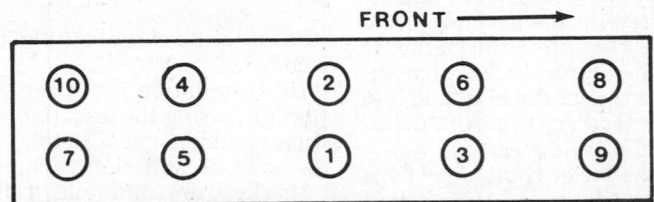

Cylinder head bolt torque sequence for 1981-82 924 models

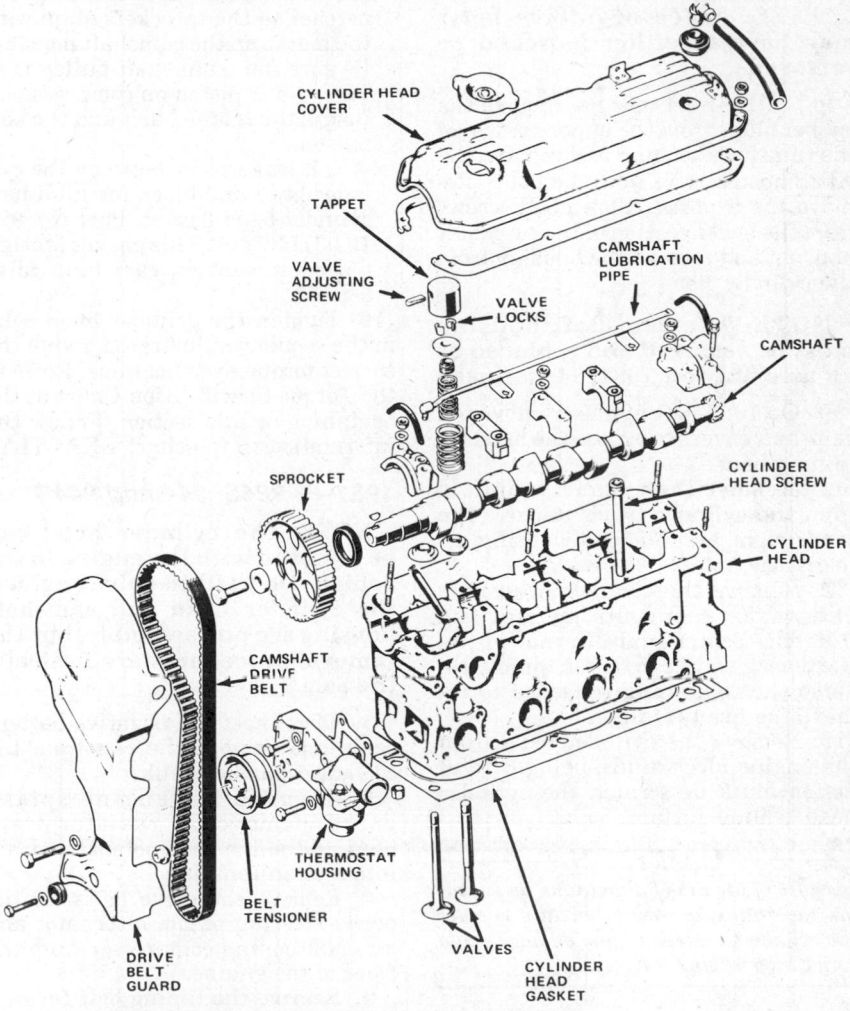

924 cylinder head and related components (924 Turbo similar)

2. Remove the upper timing belt cover assembly. On engines with dual distributors, remove the distributor caps to allow removal of the timing belt cover.

3. Remove the upper coolant hoses and heater hoses from the thermostat housing area.

4. Remove the air intake tube and the air cleaner assembly.

5. Relieve fuel system pressure, then tag and remove all connecting linkages, wires and hoses from the intake manifold and fuel injection system.

6. On 1981–84 models, rotate the engine to bring the crankshaft pulley mark to TDC and, if working with the left cylinder head, matchmark and remove the distributor assembly. On 1985–88 engines, rotate the engine to TDC with all timing marks aligned.

7. Remove the intake manifold and fuel injection system from the cylinder head and engine block.

8. From the lower right side of the engine block, loosen the timing belt tensioner bolt and remove the timing belt from the sprockets.

NOTE: Accessory drive belts may have to either loosened or removed.

9. On 1981–84 models, remove the rubber plugs from the upper portion of the camshaft housing and remove the Allen head screws from the holes. Remove the exposed Allen head screws from the lower portion of the camshaft housing and remove the housing from the cylinder head.

NOTE: The camshaft housing must be removed and replaced as an assembly on 1981–84 engines.

10. On 1985–88 engines, remove the camshaft covers to expose the head retaining bolts.

11. Remove the exhaust manifold from the cylinder head. Remove the inner right and left belt housing, as necessary.

12. Remove the cylinder head nuts and washers, or bolts, by starting from the center and alternating toward each end. If in doubt, simply reverse the tightening sequence to remove the head retainers.

13. Remove the cylinder head from the engine block studs, being careful not to mark or scratch the cylinder head sealing surface.

———— CAUTION ————

Because of the use of aluminum, do not allow the antifreeze coolant mixture to enter the cylinders. Severe engine damage could result after engine start-up.

14. Remove the head gasket from

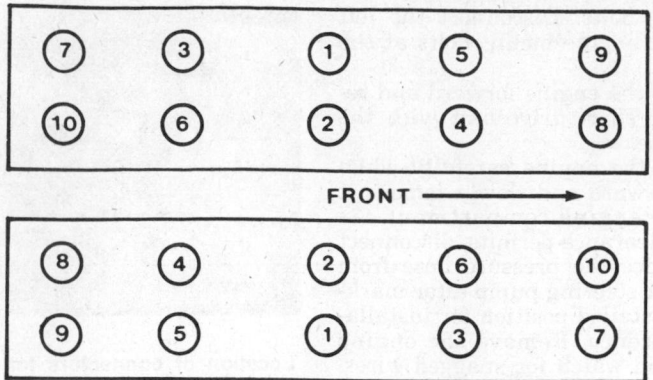

Cylinder head torque sequence for 1981-86 928 models

the studs and clean both the head and the block.

15. Installation is the reverse of removal. During the installation, attention should be given to the following:

a. Left and right cylinder head gaskets are different. TOP/OBEN faces up and the arrow faces forward.

b. Turn both camshafts until the notches on the sprockets align with the marks on the camshaft housing. Be sure the crankshaft pulley is at TDC (No. 1 piston on compression). Install the toothed belt and the belt tensioner.

c. If leaks occur between the cylinder head and block install a new cylinder head gasket, Part No. 928 104 371/372 09. This gasket is original equipment on cars built after 6/15/82.

16. Tighten the cylinder head bolts in the sequence illustrated and to the correct torque specifications. Refer to the Torque Specification Chart at the beginning of this section. Follow the information in the chart EXACTLY.

1983–88 924S, 944 and 944S

NOTE: The cylinder head can be removed with the engine in the vehicle. On 944S 16-valve engines, the cylinder head and camshaft housing are one assembly, but the removal procedures are basically the same.

1. Disconnect the negative battery cable and remove the cap from the coolant expansion tank.

2. Remove the engine splash guard. Remove the radiator drain plug and allow the coolant to drain into a clean container.

3. Remove the drive belts for the power steering pump, alternator and air conditioning compressor from the front of the engine.

4. Remove the timing belt cover.

5. Rotate the engine as necessary

to position the No. 1 piston on TDC-compression. Align the TDC marks of both the camshaft sprocket and the flywheel.

6. Remove the distributor cap. Unscrew the distributor arm and remove the plastic cap.

7. Remove the distributor cap mount.

8. Release the tension of the camshaft drive belt and pull the belt off of the camshaft sprocket.

9. Remove the two rear drive belt cover mounting bolts.

10. Relieve the fuel system pressure, then disconnect and cap the fuel lines.

———— CAUTION ————

Fuel pressure must be relieved before disconnecting any fuel lines. Take precautions to avoid the risk of fire.

11. Remove the plastic cover from the fuel collection tube. Tag and disconnect the wiring connectors from the fuel injectors and lay the wiring harness aside.

12. On all except 944S models, remove the aluminum plugs from the camshaft housing and detach the coolant line from the camshaft housing. Remove the camshaft housing from the cylinder head. On 944S models, remove the camshaft cover.

NOTE: When removing the camshaft housing, use care to keep the hydraulic valve tappets in place.

13. Remove the air cleaner assembly. Remove the bolt of the air intake brace.

14. Remove the intake manifold by disconnecting the following items:

a. Oil dipstick tube bracket
b. Brake booster hose
c. Intake manifold hose
d. Accelerator cable retaining clamp.

15. Remove the intake manifold

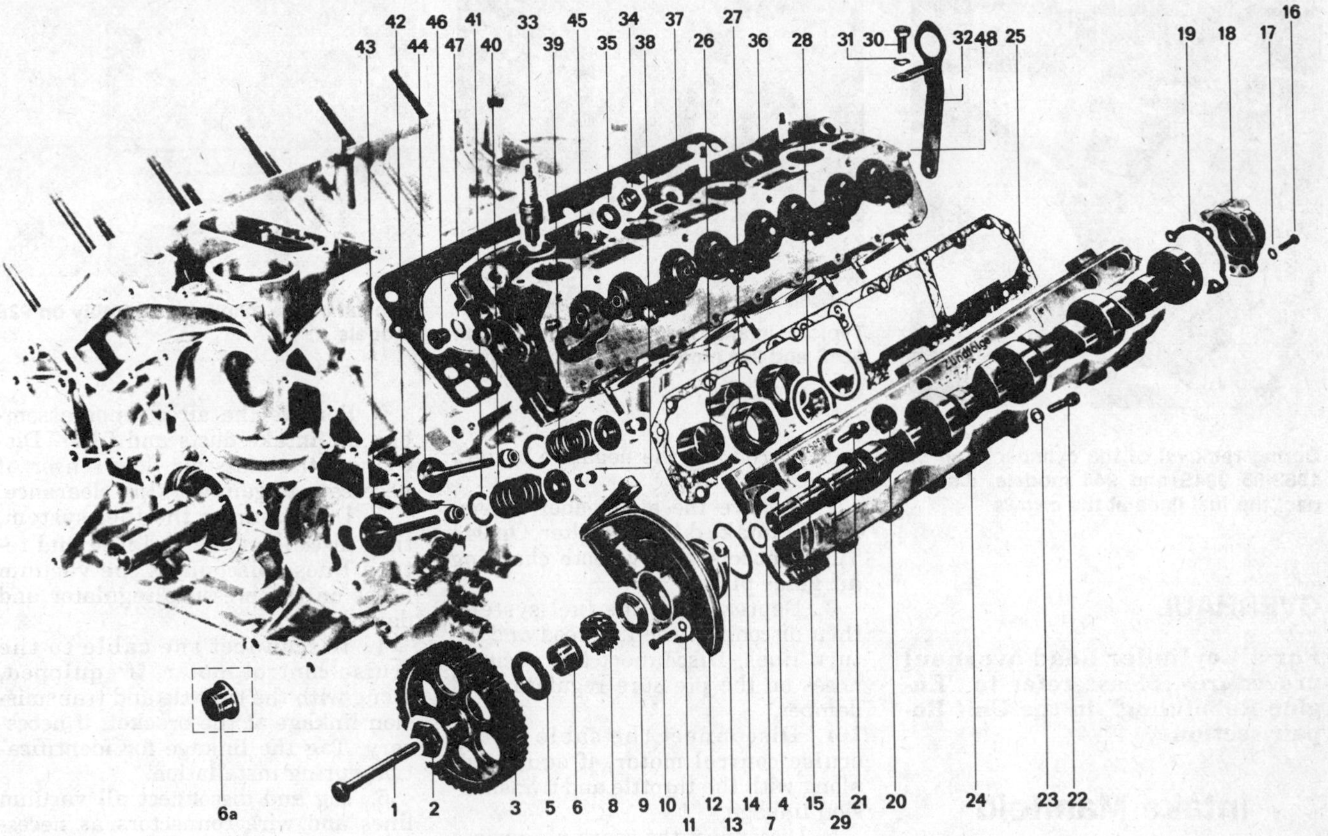

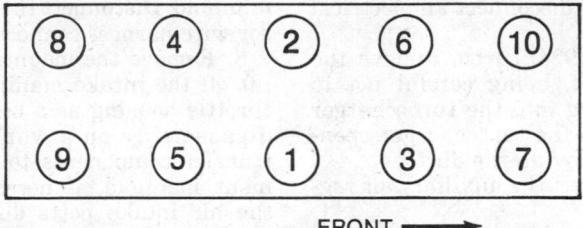

1981-82 928 and 928S cylinder head and related components

1. Bolt	8. Distributor drive gear	16. Bolt	24. Camshaft housing	32. Lifting eye	40. Valve spring
2. Washer	9. Spacer	17. Washer	25. Gasket	33. Spark plug	41. Shim
3. Camshaft sprocket	10. Bolt	18. End cover	26. Hydraulic valve lifter	34. Nut	42. Valve stem seal
4. Woodruff key	11. Washer	19. Gasket	27. Lifter sleeve	35. Washer	43. Intake valve
5. Camshaft oil seal	12. Bearing carrier	20. Plug	28. Gasket	36. Cylinder head	44. Exhaust valve
6. Spacer	13. Seal	21. Bolt with washers	29. Left camshaft	37. Left gasket	45. Valve guide
6a. Spacer	14. O-ring	22. Bolt	30. Bolt	38. Valve keeper	46. Plug
7. O-ring	15. Woodruff key	23. Washer	31. Washer	39. Spring retainer	47. Seal
					48. Dowel pin

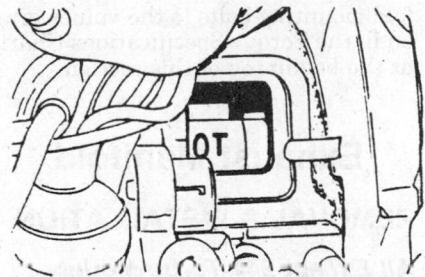

On 1983-88 924S and 944 models, check that the scribe mark on the flywheel is aligned with the TDC mark on the clutch housing

1983-88 924S and 944 cylinder head bolt torque sequence

mounting bolts, then remove the manifold.

16. Remove the bolts from the exhaust manifold/converter pipe flange.

17. Remove the hose clamp from the heater regulating valve and the two screws from the valve neck.

18. Remove the cylinder head

mounting bolts in the reverse order of the installation torque sequence.

19. Remove the cylinder head. Clean all gasket mating surfaces carefully. The cylinder head gasket for the 944 Turbo has a partially recessed silicone bead on both sides and the word "Turbo" stamped in the top surface for identification.

20. Installation is the reverse of the removal procedure. After installing the head, tighten the mounting bolts

in sequence to the correct torque specifications. Refer to the Torque Specifications Chart at the beginning of this section. Torque the camshaft housing mounting bolts to 14 ft. lbs. (19 Nm) and the aluminum plugs to 29 ft. lbs. (39 Nm). Install and adjust the camshaft drive (timing) belt as outlined under "Timing Belt Removal and Installation" procedures. Adjust the power steering pump, alternator and air conditioning compressor drive belt tension.

During removal of the cylinder head on 1983-88 924S and 944 models, disconnect the fuel lines at the arrows

OVERHAUL

For all cylinder head overhaul procedures, please refer to "Engine Rebuilding" in the Unit Repair section.

Intake Manifold

REMOVAL & INSTALLATION

1981–82 924 and 924 Turbo

The intake manifold and throttle valve housing are removed as one unit.

1. Remove the air cleaner on the 924.
2. Disconnect the accelerator cable.
3. Disconnect the EGR connection.
4. Tag and disconnect all electrical leads.
5. On the 924 Turbo, remove the pressure duct, being careful not to drop anything into the turbocharger housing. Cap the turbocharger opening after removing the duct.
6. Disconnect the auxiliary air regulator hose.
7. Remove all vacuum hoses attached to the intake manifold.
8. Remove the eight retaining nuts and remove the throttle valve housing and intake manifold as a unit.
9. Installation is the reverse of removal. Tighten the mounting nuts to 15 ft. lbs. (20 Nm).

1983–88 924S and 944 Models

The intake manifold consists of a cast aluminum assembly with equal length air intake tubes that bolt directly to the cylinder head. The throttle valve assembly bolts to a single flange.

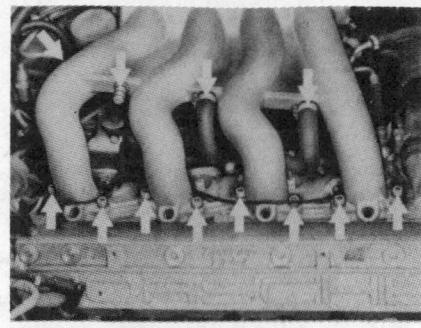

Typical intake manifold mounting on 924S and 944 models (944 Turbo shown)

1. Disconnect the negative battery cable.
2. Remove the air cleaner assembly, air intake ducts and filter. On 944 Turbo models, remove both charging air guide pipes.
3. Depressurize the fuel system, then disconnect the fuel feed and return lines. Disconnect the vacuum hoses on the pressure regulator and damper.
4. Disconnect the cable to the cruise control motor, if equipped, along with the throttle and transmission linkage.
5. Disconnect the spark plug wires and remove the distributor cap. Disconnect the fuel collection pipe with the fuel injectors and ignition leads on the intake manifold and camshaft housing.
6. Remove the fuel collection pipe with fuel injectors and ignition leads from the intake manifold assembly carefully and lay them aside.
7. Tag and disconnect any vacuum lines or hoses attached to the intake manifold. Disconnect the air flow sensor wire harness connector.
8. Remove the mounting nuts and lift off the intake manifold with the throttle housing as a unit. Continue disassembly on a workbench and transfer components to the replacement manifold, if necessary. Cover the air intake ports during service procedures to prevent the entry of dirt or debris.
9. Installation is the reverse of removal. Tighten the mounting bolts to the values given in the Torque Specifications Chart at the beginning of this section.

1981–88 928, 928S and 928S4

The intake manifold assembly consists of a series of equal length pipes, attached by hose clamps and short rubber sleeves to the air cleaner plenum and bolted to the cylinder head.

1. Disconnect the negative battery cable.

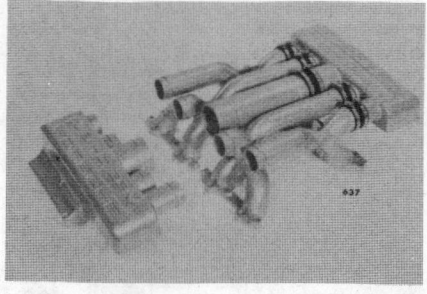

Typical intake manifold assembly on 928 models

2. Remove the air cleaner assembly, air intake ducts and filter. Disconnect the mass air flow sensor, if necessary to gain working clearance.
3. Depressurize the fuel system, then disconnect the fuel feed and return lines. Disconnect the vacuum hoses on the pressure regulator and damper.
4. Disconnect the cable to the cruise control motor, if equipped, along with the throttle and transmission linkage at the bracket, if necessary. Tag the linkage for identification during installation.
5. Tag and disconnect all vacuum lines and wire connectors as necessary to allow removal of the manifold assembly.
6. Remove the mounting bolts from the intake manifold tubes at the cylinder head and remove the manifold with the fuel injectors attached. It may be easier of the early models to remove the injectors before disconnecting the manifold. Use your own discretion.
7. Installation is the reverse of removal procedures. Torque all manifold mounting bolts to the values given in the Torque Specifications Chart at the beginning of this section.

Exhaust Manifold

REMOVAL & INSTALLATION

All Except 944 Turbo Models

NOTE: Always use new gaskets when installing the exhaust manifold.

1. Disconnect the negative battery cable. On the 924 Turbo, remove the turbocharger and wastegate as outlined below.
2. Disconnect the EGR line from the exhaust manifold.
3. On models so equipped, remove the air pump connections.
4. Disconnect the exhaust pipe(s) from the manifold(s) at the flange.

5. Remove the retaining nuts and remove the manifold(s).

6. Clean the cylinder heads(s) and manifold mating surfaces.

7. Using new gaskets, install the exhaust manifold(s). On 928 models, filler seals are placed in grooves on the exhaust ports for sealing between the cylinder head and exhaust manifold.

8. Tighten the nuts to 15 ft. lbs. (20 Nm). Work from the inside out.

9. Install the remaining components in the reverse order of remove. Use a new manifold flange gasket if the old one is deteriorated.

944 Turbo Models

1. Disconnect the negative battery cable.

2. Depressurize the fuel system, then disconnect the fuel hoses from the pressure regulator and the pressure chamber. Tie the fuel hoses back out of the way.

3. Release the pressure from the coolant tank by loosening the radiator cap. Loosen and remove the coolant hoses on the connecting pipe near the water pump. Cap all hoses with a suitable plug to prevent coolant loss during service.

4. Remove the coolant connecting pipe bolts and position the pipe over the cam housing.

5. To remove the exhaust manifolds, it is necessary to remove some of the mounting studs. Both manifolds must be removed together. Remove both exhaust manifold studs from cylinders 1 and 3, and the front stud from cylinders 2 and 4.

6. Working from above, remove the 2–3 manifold first, then remove the 1–4 manifold.

7. Installation is the reverse of removal procedure. Torque all manifold nuts and bolts to 15 ft. lbs. (20 Nm).

Turbocharger

For additional information on turbocharger maintenance, please refer to "Turbocharging" in the Unit Repair Section.

REMOVAL & INSTALLATION

1981–82 924 Turbo

NOTE: When replacing the turbocharger, always replace the oil filter and change the engine oil. Premature turbocharger bearing failure will result if this is not done.

1. Disconnect the negative battery cable.

2. Raise the vehicle and support it

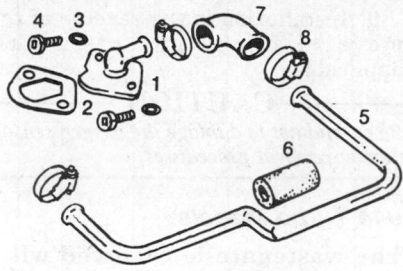

1 & 3. Washer	6. Rubber hose
2 & 4. Bolt	7. Rubber elbow
5. Breather pipe	8. Clamp

On 1981–82 924 Turbos, a metal pipe replaces the breather hose between the turbocharger and crankcase.

safely on jackstands. Remove the engine splash shield.

3. Remove the wastegate as outlined below.

4. Disconnect the oil lines leading to the engine oil cooler, then disconnect the oil feed line for the turbocharger at the oil filter flange. Plug all oil lines.

NOTE: 1981–82 924 Turbos use a metal pipe connecting the oil return hose and turbocharger in place of a breather hose.

5. Disconnect and remove the oil filer flange. Have a pan ready to catch escaping oil.

6. Loosen oil line clamps and pull out the oil lines toward the front.

7. Disconnect the oil return line.

8. Disconnect the pressure duct and remove.

9. Take off the air cleaner duct and remove.

10. Take off the air cleaner upper and lower sections.

11. Remove the three mounting nuts from the bottom of the fuel distributor.

12. Loosen the hose clamps on the dust cover and move the fuel distributor to one side.

13. Unscrew the mounting bolt on the pressure duct and take off the pressure duct.

14. Remove the nuts holding the exhaust manifold/turbocharger. Unscrew the allen head bolts at the base of the unit, then loosen the hose clamp at the bottom of the turbocharger.

15. Disconnect both sides of the stabilizer, then disconnect the steering gear from the control arm.

16. Disconnect the turbocharger base and remove the turbocharger assembly toward the front.

17. Pull off the hose for the wastegate connection.

18. Installation is the reverse of removal with the following notes:

a. When placing the turbocharg-

er on the engine, the allen bolts loosened in Step 13 must still be loose.

b. Push the hose on at the bottom of the turbocharger while installing the unit. There is not enough clearance to install the hose after the turbocharger is installed.

c. First tighten the mounting nuts of the exhaust manifold/turbocharger, then tighten the turbocharger base bolts.

d. Always use new seals on oil lines.

e. Make sure that the round seal fits properly on the pressure duct.

f. First install both pressure ducts, then tighten the bolt(s).

g. Tighten the steering gear bolts to 14 ft. lbs. (19 Nm).

h. Before starting the engine for the first time, lubricating oil for the turbocharger has to be primed for 15 seconds. To do this, pull off the plugs from the manifold pressure limiting switch and operate the starter.

944 Turbo Models

1. Disconnect the negative battery cable.

2. Loosen the air cleaner upper section and remove it together with the air intake duct and filter cartridge.

3. Remove both charging air guide pipes.

4. Depressurize the fuel system, then disconnect the fuel feed and return lines and lay them aside out of the way.

—————— **CAUTION** ——————

Always relieve fuel system pressure before disconnecting any fuel lines. Take precautions to avoid the risk of fire.

5. Tag and disconnect the vacuum hoses from the pressure regulator and damper. Disconnect the cable on the cruise control motor.

6. Disconnect the spark plug cables and remove the distributor cap.

7. Disconnect the fuel collection pipe with the fuel injectors and ignition leads on the intake manifold and camshaft housing.

8. Remove the fuel collection pipe with the fuel injectors attached from the intake manifold carefully and place the assembly aside. Do not allow grease or dirt to contaminate the ends of the injectors during service.

9. Disconnect the throttle cable, then tag and disconnect any remaining vacuum hoses on the intake manifold. Remove the intake manifold assembly with the throttle housing and cover the intake ports on the cylinder head to prevent the entry of dirt or debris during service.

10. Disconnect and remove the guide tube with the oil dipstick and the deflection plate for the master cylinder.

11. Remove the engine splash guard. Drain the cooling system, then loosen and pull off the air hose alternator venting.

12. Disconnect the flange between the turbocharger and the exhaust assembly.

13. Disconnect the exhaust flange on the turbine housing. Disconnect the coolant lines and oil pressure line on the turbocharger.

14. Loosen and remove the intake air cowl between the air flow sensor and turbocharger compressor housing. Disconnect the pressure hose to the charging air cooler (intercooler) and remove the turbocharger assembly from the vehicle.

15. Installation is the reverse of removal. Note the following:

   a. Always use new seals.

   b. Make sure the seal fits correctly on the left engine port.

   c. Insert the seals for the exhaust flanges after coating them with grease to prevent their falling out when installing the turbocharger assembly.

   d. Replace the locknuts for the exhaust flanges and tighten the M8 bolt of the exhaust flange only after installation of all bolts for the exhaust flanges and turbocharger.

Wastegate

REMOVAL & INSTALLATION

1981–82 924 Turbo

1. Raise the vehicle and support it safely with jackstands.

2. Carefully pull off the rubber cap covering the connector for the oxygen sensor.

3. Remove the starter, then remove the bypass line between the exhaust manifold and wastegate.

4. Remove the nuts between the turbine housing and the exhaust pipe.

5. Unscrew the mounting bolts on the flange of the primary muffler/final muffler.

6. Loosen the final muffler bracket and strap, then remove the final muffler.

7. Loosen the heat shields over bypass line II, then loosen the pipe clamp at bypass line II.

8. Detach the holder and control line at the wastegate, them remove the entire line with the wastegate. Some of the early production 924 Turbos have a vent for the wastegate. The vent line connector will be accessible only after lowering the exhaust pipe.

9. Installation is the reverse of removal. Use new gaskets where applicable.

─────── CAUTION ───────
Be careful not to damage the oxygen sensor during removal procedures.

944 Turbo Models

The wastegate is removed with the turbocharger as an assembly. Refer to the turbocharger removal procedures for wastegate service.

Timing Belt Cover

REMOVAL & INSTALLATION

1981–82 924 and 924 Turbo

1. Loosen the alternator mounting bolts, pivot the alternator over, and slip the drive belt off the pulleys.

2. Unscrew the cover retaining bolts and remove the cover. Keep the washer and spacers together.

3. Reposition the spacers and then install the washer and bolts.

4. Install the alternator belt and adjust the tension.

928, 928S and 928S4

The timing cover consists of an outer right upper, and outer left upper and an outer bottom cover. Left and right inner belt guide covers are also used. The outer upper covers can be removed without the removal of the drive belts on 1981–84 models. On 1985–88 engines with dual distributors, the distributor caps and rotors must be removed to remove the upper front covers. The alternator, power steering and air conditioner compressor belts must be removed if the entire timing belt cover is being removed. Disconnect the intake air ducts and air flow sensor, if necessary to gain working clearance.

1983–88 924S and 944 Models

NOTE: On 944 Turbo models, the intercooler assembly and air charge pipes will have to be removed to gain working clearance when removing the timing belt cover.

1. Disconnect the negative battery cable.

2. Loosen the alternator and compressor drive belt tensioner and remove the belt. Remove the power steering drive belt, if equipped.

3. Remove the distributor cap and rotor.

4. Remove the cover retaining bolts and lift off the timing belt cover.

5. Installation is the reverse of the removal procedure.

Timing Belts

CHECKING TENSION

NOTE: A special tension gauge tool (No. 9201) is recommended to check the tension of the camshaft and balance shaft drive belts on all models except the 1981–82 924 and 924 Turbo. See the "Removal, Installation and Tensioning" procedure for 924 and 924 Turbo models. All belt tension checks and adjustments should be performed on a cold engine only.

1981–84 928 and 928S

1. Remove the upper section of the drive belt guard.

2. Rotate the engine in the normal direction of rotation and set the engine to TDC on the compression stroke of No. 1 cylinder. The marks of the camshaft sprockets should be aligned with the marks on the flange bearing.

3. Turn the engine two times by hand in the normal direction of rotation, until the TDC mark is again aligned. Check the condition of the drive belt while turning the engine.

4. Special tool No. 9201 is recommended to check the tension. Pull the lock pin and gauge pin completely out and zero the gauge. Slide the tool onto the belt between the tensioning roller and the lower camshaft sprocket. The measuring pin must rest in the groove of the belt. Push the tester down slowly until the gauge needle engages the belt. Keep the tester horizontal and out of contact with the surrounding objects. Read the value on the gauge. Repeat the process to be sure of an accurate reading.

5. See "Removal, Installation and Tensioning" to tension the drive belt. The gauge should read 9.2 on the scale for a new belt or 7.6–9.0 for a used belt.

1985–88 928S and 928S4

NOTE: These models incorporate a cambelt tension warning light in the instrument cluster. The warning light will illuminate when the belt tension is insufficient.

1. Remove the air guide hoses.

2. Remove the air guide retaining screws and the air guide from the top of the radiator.

3. Remove the distributor caps and the toothed belt cover upper section on the right hand side. Unscrew and

push the toothed belt cover on the left hand side forward.

4. Turn the engine in the normal direction of rotation until No. 1 cylinder is at TDC. Never turn the engine counterclockwise. Marks on the camshaft and flange bearing must be aligned in this position.

5. Turn the engine two more turns until the TDC mark is reached again. Check the bolt, while turning the engine, for wear and damage.

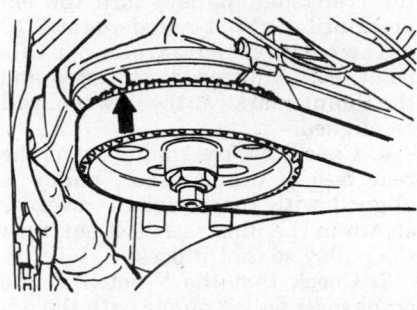

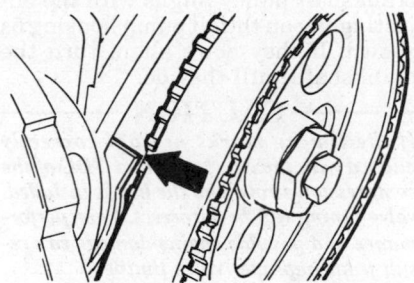

When the 928, 928S engine is at TDC on No. 1 cylinder, the camshaft sprocket marks (arrow) will align with the marks on the housing.

6. Pull the lock pin on tool No. 9201 out and move the test pin opposite the lock pin to the starting position. Place the drag needle the gauge needle.

7. Slide the tool on a released section of the toothed belt. The sliding shoe of the tool on a smooth belt surface and the rolled fitted in a tooth gap.

8. Slowly press down on the tester housing until the gauge tip engages. Read the test gauge without tension, the tester must be kept horizontal to

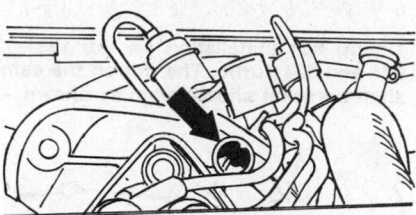

On 1983-88 924S and 944 models, the TDC mark on the camshaft sprocket will align with the cast mark as shown (arrow)

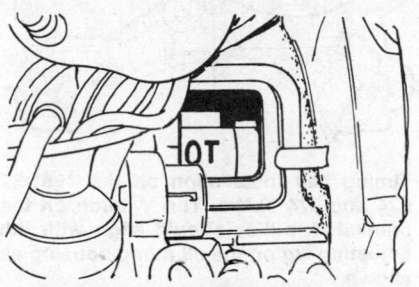

On the 1983-88 924S and 944 models, check that the scribe mark on the flywheel is aligned with the TDC mark on the clutch housing

the toothed belt. The tester must not rest on the plastic cover. The sliding shoes must have their entire surface on the belt. The tool must not be turned or moved on the belt during the testing procedure.

9. The drag needle must always be placed on the gauge needle after the lock pin had engaged. Pull out the lock pin to have the gauge tip disengage.

10. Repeat tension test several times with the engine at TDC. The gauge should read 5.0 ± 0.3. Adjust the belt if necessary.

11. The belt adjusting screw is located on the bottom right side of the engine.

12. Loosen the locknut, tighten the screw to tighten the belt or loosen the screw to loosen the belt. Tighten the locknut.

13. Turn the engine two complete turns and recheck belt tension.

1983–86 924S, 944 and 944 Turbo

BALANCE SHAFTS DRIVE BELT

1. Remove the splash guard under the engine.

2. Remove the alternator compressor belt.

3. Remove the upper and lower belt covers.

4. Release the tension from the belt. There are two methods to release the tension. On older models equipped with guide rollers without a slot, turn the eccentric to release the tension from the belt. On newer models with a locking nut on the guide roller (with

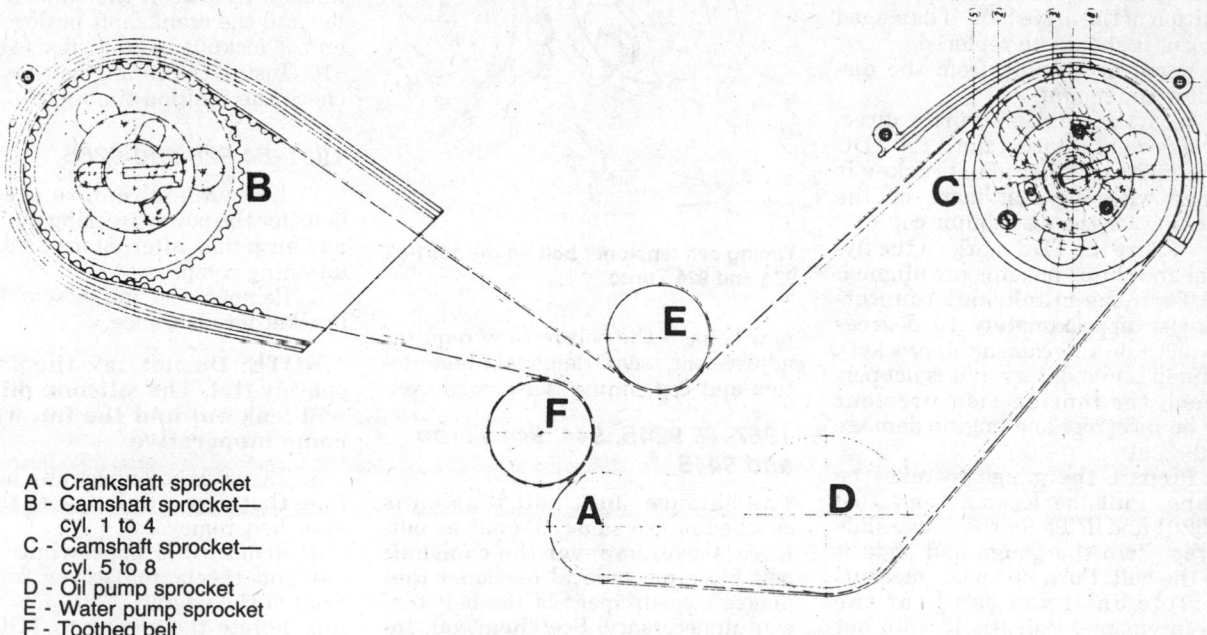

A - Crankshaft sprocket
B - Camshaft sprocket—cyl. 1 to 4
C - Camshaft sprocket—cyl. 5 to 8
D - Oil pump sprocket
E - Water pump sprocket
F - Toothed belt tensioning roller

Camshaft drive belt routing on 928 models

slot), loosen the locknut and slide the roller away from the belt.

5. Remove the plug from the distributor cap mount.

6. Turn the crankshaft in the direction of normal rotation until the TDC mark on the camshaft sprocket aligns with the cast mark.

7. Check to be sure the scribe mark on the flywheel is visible through the clutch housing and opposite the TDC mark.

8. Check that the balance shaft marks are aligned with the marks on the rear belt cover.

9. Special No. 9201 is recommended to check the belt tension. Pull out the lockpin and let the gauge slide drop. Zero the gauge and slide it onto the belt. Push up on the measuring slide until you can hear the lockpin engage. Pull out the lockpin and let the gauge slide drop. Zero the gauge and slide it onto the belt. Push up on the measuring slide until you can hear the lockpin engage. Pull out the lockpin and remove the gauge. Read the measured value. If the guide rollers have no slot, the gauge should read 4.0–4.6 for a new belt, or 3.7–4.3 for a used belt. If the guide roller has a slot, the gauge should read 2.4–3.0 for new and used belts. If necessary, adjust the tension. See "Removal, Installation and Tensioning" for adjustment procedure.

CAMSHAFT BELT

1. Remove the splash guard, belt covers and alternator compressor belt.

2. Turn the crankshaft in the direction of normal rotation and check the condition of the drive belt. If damaged or worn, it should be replaced.

3. Remove the plug from the distributor cap mount.

4. Turn the crankshaft in the direction of normal rotation until the TDC mark on the camshaft sprocket is aligned with the cast mark on the mounting for the distributor cap.

5. Be sure the TDC mark on the flywheel and clutch housing are aligned.

6. Turn the crankshaft counterclockwise approximately 10 degrees (1½ teeth on the camshaft sprocket). This step is mandatory. If it is not performed, the tension measurement may be incorrect and engine damage could result.

7. Prepare the gauge to take the reading. Pull the lockpin from Tool No. 9201 and listen for the gauge slide to drop. Zero the gauge and slide it onto the belt. Push up on the measuring slide until you can hear the lockpin engage. Pull the lockpin out and read the gauge. It should read 2.4–3.0 for used belts, or 3.7–4.3 for

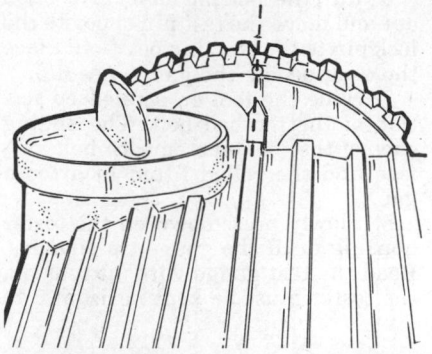

Timing belt installation on the 1981-82 924 and 924 Turbo. The dot on the camshaft sprocket should align as shown

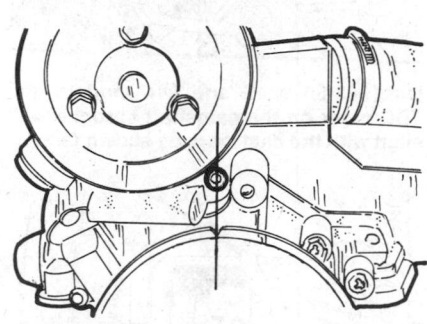

Timing belt installation on the 1981-82 924 and 924 Turbo. The V-notch on the crankshaft pulley should align with the adjusting lug on the oil pump housing as shown

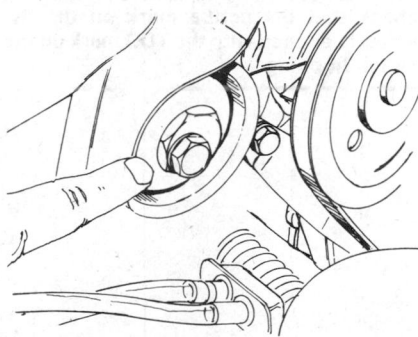

Timing belt tensioner bolt on the 1981-82 924 and 924 Turbo

new belts. If the belt tension requires adjustment, see "Removal, Installation and Tensioning" for procedure.

1987–88 924S, 944, 944 Turbo and 944S

The balance shaft belt tension is checked in the same manner as outlined above, however the camshaft belt has a mechanical tensioner that makes measurement of the belt tension unnecessary. See "Removal, Installation and Tensioning" for mechanical tensioner adjustment.

REMOVAL, INSTALLATION & TENSIONING

1981–82 924 and 924 Turbo

1. Remove the timing belt cover.

2. While holding the larger hex on the tensioner pulley locknut.

3. Release the tensioner from the timing belt.

4. Slide the belt off the two toothed pulleys and remove it.

5. Using the large center bolt on the crankshaft pulley, turn the engine until the No. 1 cylinder is at TDC of the compression stroke. At this point, both valves will be closed and the timing marks at the flywheel will be aligned.

6. Check that the timing dot on the rear face of the camshaft pulley is aligned with the camshaft cover as shown in the illustration. If not, turn the pulley so that it does.

7. Check that the V-notch in the crankshaft pulley aligns with the adjusting lug on the oil pump housing as shown. If they don't align, turn the crankshaft until they do.

--- **CAUTION** ---

If the timing marks are not correctly aligned with the No. 1 piston at TDC of the compression stroke and the belt is installed, valve timing will be incorrect. Poor performance and possible engine damage can result from improper valve timing.

8. Install the belt on the pulleys.

9. Adjust the tensioner by turning the large hex on the pulley to the left until the belt can be twisted 90 degree with the thumb and forefinger at the midpoint between the camshaft pulley and the crankshaft pulley. Tighten the locknut to 30 ft. lbs. (41 Nm).

10. Install the timing belt cover and check the ignition timing.

1981–84 928 and 928S

1. Loosen and remove the drive belts for the power steering pump, fan and air pump, alternator and air conditioning compressor.

2. Remove the fan assembly and bracket for clearance.

NOTE: Do not lay the fan assembly flat. The silicone oil filler will leak out and the fan will become inoperative.

3. Tag and disconnect any hoses or lines that may interfere with the cover or belt removal.

4. Remove the upper right, upper left and the bottom cover from the front of the engine.

5. Rotate the engine to TDC with the No. 1 piston on the compression stroke and the distributor rotor point-

ing to the No. 1 cylinder spark plug wire terminal of distributor cap.

6. Loosen the belt tensioner bolt and remove the belt from the sprockets.

7. Align the camshaft notches with the marks on the cam housings and install a new toothed belt, being sure the crankshaft marks remain aligned at TDC.

NOTE: The water pump pulley is turned by the back of the toothed belt.

8. The drive belt adjusting screw is located on the bottom of the engine at the right front. On 1981 models, tighten the belt tensioner bolt until the belt can be twisted only 90 degrees between the tension roller and the right camshaft sprocket.

On 1982–84 models, loosen the locknut on the adjusting screw and turn it until the correct tension is achieved. Tighten the locknut and turn the engine 2 additional turns, then recheck the tension. Turn the engine in the normal direction of rotation; rotating the engine backwards could damage the belt.

9. Install the covers, hoses or lines, fan and bracket assembly, and the drive belts. Adjust the drive belts to have a deflection of ½ inch between pulleys.

10. Check and adjust the ignition timing as necessary.

1985–88 928S and 928S4

1. Remove the air cleaner intake hoses.

2. Remove the air guide from the top of the radiator.

3. Loosen and remove all drive belts. Tag and disconnect the cables from the throttle, cruise control and automatic transmission.

4. Remove the fan assembly from the engine after disconnecting all wires and cables. If equipped with a viscous fan coupling, do not lay the fan flat or the fluid will leak out. Once the fluid is gone, so is the fan.

5. Remove the distributor caps and wires. Remove the distributor rotors. Disconnect the wiring connectors for the A/C compressor and belt tension indicator.

6. Remove the mounting screws for the upper belt cover on both sides and remove the upper right side cover.

7. Remove and position the power steering pump out of the way with the hoses attached. Wire the power steering pump, if necessary; do not allow it to hang by the fluid hoses.

8. Remove the clutch slave cylinder with the fluid line attached. Take off the clamp on the clutch hose holder

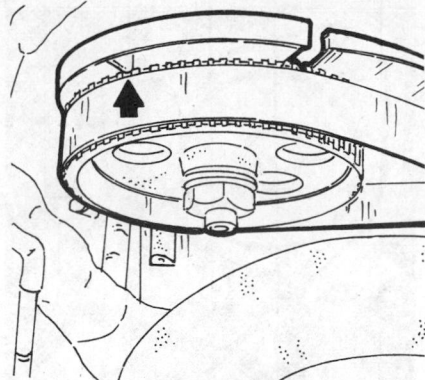

Right-hand camshaft alignment on 928 and 928S

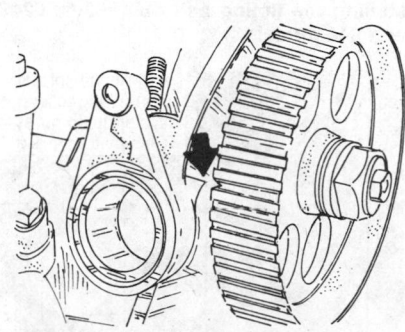

Left hand camshaft alignment of the 928

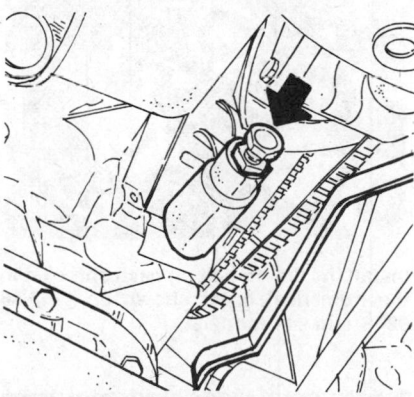

Timing belt tensioner on the 928 and 928S viewed from beneath the car.

and remove the push rod. Allow the cylinder to hang out of the way.

——— **CAUTION** ———
Do not operate the clutch pedal with the slave cylinder disconnected.

9. Align the 45 degrees before TDC mark on the vibration damper with the red needle by turning the crankshaft clockwise. Make sure No. 1 cylinder is on the compression stroke when aligning the 45 BTDC mark.

NOTE: Camshafts may now be turned without damaging the valves after aligning the 45 degree mark.

Loosen the bolts at the arrows to remove the drive belts on 1985-88 928S and 928S4 models

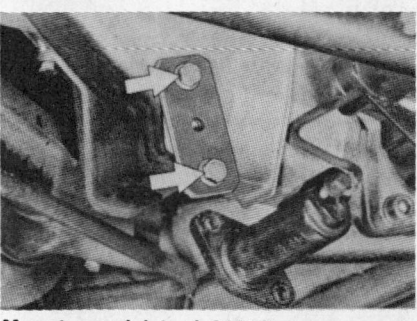

Mount special tool 9161/1 as shown to hold the crankshaft in position on 1985-88 928S and 928S4 models

10. Mount special crankshaft holding tool No. 9161/1 in position. Remove the 27mm crankshaft bolt and remove the pulley, vibration damper and collar.

11. Remove the guide tube for the engine oil dipstick. Remove the alternator and mounting brackets.

12. Remove the center belt cover and left upper cover.

13. Loosen the toothed belt tension with the adjuster screw.

14. Remove the tension roller assembly.

15. Remove the belt from the right side (cylinders 1–4) camshaft sprocket and water pump sprocket, then from the left side (cylinders 5–8) camshaft sprocket, oil pump sprocket and crankshaft sprocket.

16. Install in the reverse order of removal. Turn the engine in the normal direction of rotation carefully to align No. 1 piston at TDC, then rotate the camshafts to the timing marks. Hold the camshafts firmly in this position and install and tension the drivebelt by turning the adjusting screw located on the bottom of the engine on the right front side. A belt tension gauge tool (No. 9201, or equivalent) is necessary for adjustment. Set the belt tension to 4.7–5.3 on the gauge scale.

1983–86 924S, 944 and 944 Turbo

1. Disconnect the negative battery cable.

2. Remove the engine splash guard.

3. Remove the drive belt for the alternator and air conditioning compressor from the front of the engine.

4. Remove the upper and lower timing belt cover.

5. Rotate the engine as necessary to position the No. 1 piston on TDC-compression. Align the marks on both the camshaft pulley and the flywheel.

6. Remove the distributor cap. Unscrew the distributor arm and remove the plastic cap.

7. Remove the distributor cap mount.

8. Release the tension of the camshaft drive (timing) belt and carefully remove the belt from the sprocket.

— **CAUTION** —

DO NOT rotate any of the sprockets while the belt is removed.

9. After making sure that all timing marks are still properly aligned, the new belt may be installed in the following manner:

   a. Install the belt on the crankshaft sprocket first, then to the tensioning roller, water pump pulley, and the camshaft sprocket. Preload the belt slightly by hand each time it is routed around the components, so that it can be pushed onto the camshaft sprocket.

   b. Again, make sure all timing marks have remained aligned.

   c. Carefully turn the crankshaft about 10 crankshaft degrees counterclockwise, which is equal to $1\frac{1}{2}$ teeth from the mark on the camshaft sprocket.

NOTE: A belt tension gauge tool (No. 9201) is needed to complete the remainder of this procedure.

   d. Pull the lockpin out of the special tool. Completely push out the gauge pin which is opposite the lock pin.

   e. Zero the telltale needle of the special tool onto the belt. The slides of the special tool must rest flat with the full surface of the belt.

— **CAUTION** —

DO NOT turn or move the belt while testing the belt tension.

   f. Push the measuring needle of the tool inward slowly until you hear the lockpin engage. Read the value on the dial gauge of the special tool. The value should read as follows:
   New belt—3.7–4.3
   Old belt—2.4–3.0
   g. If necessary, adjust the belt

Align the camshaft sprocket and rear timing belt cover marks as shown before installing the timing belt on 1983-88 924S and 944 models

1. Crankshaft sprocket
2. Tensioning roller
3. Water pump pulley
4. Camshaft sprocket

Install the timing belt on each sprocket in the numerical order shown on 1983-88 924S and 944 models

Timing belt tensioner on 1983-88 924S and 944 models. Turn the large hex as required to tighten or loosen the belt

Special timing belt tension tool shown installed on the 944 timing belt. Note that the tool is installed in the same manner on the balance shaft drive belt. Measuring needle (arrow) is pushed in when setting up the tool

tensions according to the above specifications by turning the tensioning roller clockwise to loosen, or counterclockwise to tighten. Once the correct belt tension is set, tighten the roller mounting nut to 61 ft. lbs. (45 Nm).

   h. Remove the special tool from the belt and install the remaining components in the reverse of Steps 1–8.

1987–88 924S, 944, 944 Turbo and 944S

1. Disconnect the negative battery cable.

2. Remove the engine splash guard.

3. Remove the drive belt for the power steering pump (if equipped), alternator and air conditioning compressor from the front of the engine.

4. Remove the distributor cap. Unscrew the distributor arm and remove the plastic cap.

5. Rotate the engine as necessary to position the No. 1 piston on TDC-compression. Align the marks on both the camshaft pulley and the flywheel.

6. Remove the upper and lower timing belt cover.

7. Remove the distributor cap mount.

8. Release the tension of the camshaft drive (timing) belt by loosening the mechanical adjuster bolts and prying gently with a suitable small prybar. Remove the tensioner assembly from the crankcase upper section and carefully remove the camshaft belt from the sprockets.

9. Install the new belt in reverse sequence. Install the mechanical tensioner and allow it to tension the

Balance shaft idler pulley on 1983-88 924S and 944 models. During removal of the balance shaft drive belt, the pulley should be adjusted so that it does not touch the belt

Balance shaft tensioner nut on 1983-88 924S and 944 models. Turn the nut counterclockwise to loosen the belt; clockwise to tighten

drive belt by spring tension alone. Do not attempt to increase the belt tension by prying on the mechanical adjuster. Tighten the tensioner bolts to 15 ft. lbs. (20 Nm). Rotate the engine two times in the normal direction of rotation and check the timing mark alignment before completing the installation procedure.

Camshaft Coupler Chain Tensioner

REMOVAL & INSTALLATION

1985–88 928S, 928S4 and 944S

NOTE: The intake camshaft is chain-driven off of the exhaust camshaft. This chain is tightened by a hydraulic chain tensioner which maintains the proper chain tension automatically. No adjustment is necessary, but note that the tensioners are different for right and left sides on the 928S and 928S4.

1. With the vehicle on the ground and full weight on the wheels, remove the cross strut.
2. Remove the air intake hoses and complete air cleaner assembly.
3. Loosen the hose clamps on the intake air distributor and vacuum line. Pull off and lay the suction pump aside. Remove the intake air distributor.
4. Remove the lifting bracket from the left rear of the engine.
5. Twist and pull the spark plug wires from the plug. Remove the plug wires form the valve cover clips and remove the valve cover(s).

NOTE: Take note when removing valve cover retaining bolts, some are equipped with a seal.

Loosen bolts A and B on the mechanical tensioner to adjust the timing belt tension on 1987-88 924S, 944, 944Turbo and 944S models

Hydraulic chain tensioner used on 1985-88 928S, 928S4 and 944 models

These bolts must be returned to their original positions.

6. Remove the hollow union bolt and check valve from the cylinder head. A seal is used under the bolt head. Remove the chain tensioner.
7. The chain tensioner piston is under spring pressure. Compress the tensioner piston when removing and secure with suitable binding wire.
8. Install tensioner in reverse order. To apply tensioner to chain on Nos. 1–4 cylinders push tensioner chain up. Nos. 5–8 cylinders, push tensioner chain down. Tighten the

chain tensioner bolts to 6 ft. lbs. (8 Nm) after installation. No further adjustment is necessary.

Balance Shaft Drive Belt

REMOVAL & INSTALLATION

1983–88 924S, 944, 944 Turbo and 944S

1. Disconnect the negative (ground) battery cable.
2. Remove the engine splash guard.
3. Remove the alternator and air conditioning drive belt.
4. Remove the camshaft drive (timing) belt cover.
5. Loosen the balance shaft idler pulley so that the pulley does not touch the balance shaft drive belt.
6. Rotate the crankshaft clockwise as necessary to position the No. 1 cylinder at TDC on the compression stroke.

NOTE: At this point, the marks on the balance shaft sprockets should be aligned with the marks on the rear belt cover.

7. Turn the tensioner nut counterclockwise to loosen the balance shaft drive belt. Carefully remove the old belt from the sprocket.

NOTE: There are two types of tensioners used. The older type (without a slot) is an eccentric that is turned to adjust tension. The newer type (with a slot) is held in place by a locknut and slides away from the belt to release tension.

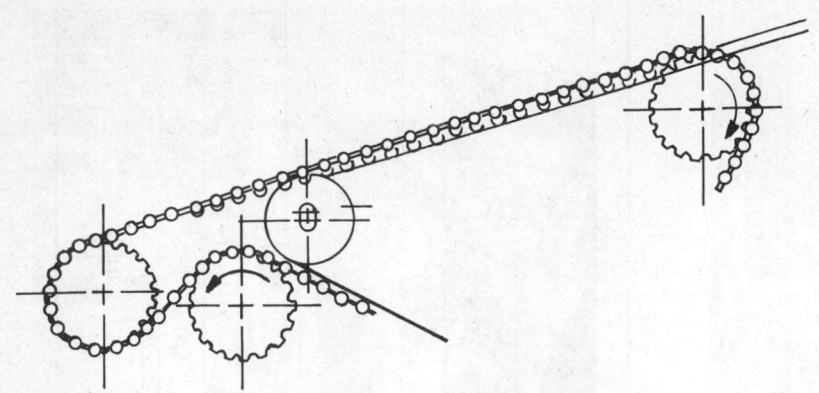

Maintain 0.002-0.004 in. clearance between the guide roller and the lower balance shaft on the 1983-88 924S and 944

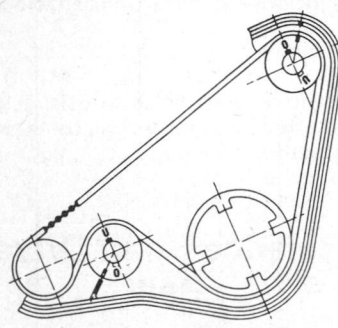

Prior to removing or installing the balance shaft drive belt, the balance shaft sprocket marks should be aligned with the marks on the rear cover as shown

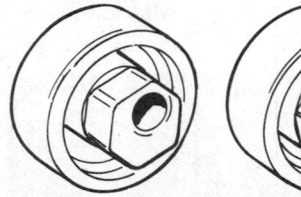

Old style eccentric tensioner (without slot) is on the left; newer style eccentric tensioner (with slot) is on the right

—————— CAUTION ——————
DO NOT move any sprocket while the belt is removed, or while installing the new belt.

8. Carefully route the new belt around the sprocket, making sure that the color coded tooth of the belt faces away from the sprockets.

9. Adjust the belt tension in the same manner as the camshaft drive (timing) belt, according to the appropriate steps of the "Timing Belt Removal and Installation" procedure. Turn the tensioner nut (same one used during Step 7) to tighten the belt to the proper value (2.4–3.0 dial reading).

On guide rollers with no slot, loosen the locknut and turn the eccentric clockwise to tighten or counterclockwise to loosen. Tighten the locknut to 33 ft. lbs. (44 Nm).

10. On rollers with a slot, adjust the idler pulley so that there is 0.5mm clearance between the pulley and the portion of the belt below the pulley. Tighten the pulley nut in this position. The remaining components are installed in the reverse order of removal.

NOTE: If the correct clearance cannot be obtained, rotate the

pulley 180 degrees and repeat Step 10. A special clearance gauge (tool No. 9207) is available to aid in the adjustment.

Timing Sprockets

REMOVAL & INSTALLATION

On all models, the camshaft and crankshaft sprockets are located by keys on their respective shafts and each is retained by a single bolt. To remove either or both of the sprockets, first remove the timing belt cover and belt and then use the following general procedure.

NOTE: When removing the crankshaft sprocket on the 924, don't remove the four bolts which retain the outer belt pulley to the timing belt sprocket.

1. Remove the center bolt.
2. Gently pry the sprocket off the shaft. If the sprocket is stubborn, use a gear puller. Don't hammer on the sprocket.
3. Remove the sprocket and the key.
4. Install the sprocket in the reverse order of removal.
5. Tighten the center bolt on the crankshaft sprocket to 58 ft. lbs. (79 Nm); tighten the camshaft sprocket retaining bolt to 33 ft. lbs. (45 Nm).

NOTE: 944 models equipped with polygon head bolts instead of the Allen head bolts should be torqued to 48 ft. lbs. (65 Nm).

6. Install the timing belt. Check valve timing and belt tension, then install the cover.

Camshaft

REMOVAL & INSTALLATION

1981–82 924 and 924 Turbo

1. Remove the timing belt.
2. Remove the camshaft sprocket.
3. Remove the air cleaner.
4. Remove the camshaft cover.
5. Remove the distributor and mounting housing.
6. Remove the oil injection tube and then reinstall the retaining nuts hand tight.
7. Unscrew and remove the No. 1, 3 and 5 bearing caps (No. 1 is at the front of the engine).
8. Unscrew the No. 2 and 4 bearing caps, diagonally and in increments.
9. Lift the camshaft out of the cylinder head.
10. Lubricate the camshaft journals and lobes with assembly lube or gear oil before installing it in the cylinder head. Bolts are tightend to 8 ft. lbs. (11 Nm) and nuts to 20 ft. lbs. (27 Nm).
11. Tighten bearing caps No. 2 and 4 carefully in a diagonal pattern.
12. Install bearing caps No. 1, 3 and 5.
13. Install the oil injection tube. You will have to loosen the nuts on No. 2 and 4 again.
14. Install the camshaft cover using new gaskets and seals.
15. Install the camshaft pulley and the timing belt.
16. Check the valve clearance.

1981–84 928, 1983–88 924S, 944 and 944 Turbo

Refer to the "Cylinder Head Removal and Installation" section for the removal of the cam housing as a unit.

1. Remove the hydraulic lifters, lifter sleeves and gaskets from the cam housing.
2. Remove the rear housing end plate and gasket.
3. On the 928, remove the camshaft sprocket, the front bearing carrier on the right head an the distributor and bearing carrier on the left cam housing. On the 944, remove the camshaft sprocket and the bearing carriers.
4. Pull the camshaft to the rear and out of the cam housing.
5. The distributor gear and spacer

can be removed from the camshaft at this time.

6. Installation is the reverse of removal.

NOTE: The front camshaft seals can be replaced while the front bearing carriers are off the cam housing or when the timing sprocket is removed from the camshaft.

1985–88 928S, 928S4 and 944S

The camshaft housing and cylinder head are one unit on these models. Refer to the "Cylinder Head Removal and Installation" procedures and remove the camshaft housing covers, timing belt and camshaft sprocket. Remove the hydraulic chain tensioner as previously described, then remove the camshaft bearing caps and lift out both camshafts together with the timing chain.

Camshaft bearing caps are numbered from 1–8. Check that the bearing cap positions and cylinder head numbers are correct when installing. Bearing caps are installed so that the numbers are on the outside. The camshafts themselves have identification numbers located on the face of the camshaft and the timing chain sprockets have marks to help when adjusting the timing. The drive chain has two copper-plated links which are used for the basic adjustment of the exhaust camshaft to the intake camshaft.

CAMSHAFT TIMING ADJUSTMENT

1985–88 928S and 928S4

1. Set the No. 1 cylinder at TDC on the compression stroke and make sure the camshaft drive belt tension is adjusted properly.

2. Check that the marks on the camshaft sprockets and flange bearings are aligned properly.

3. Check that the marks (early version) or cast tabs (late version) on the camshafts are aligned properly. The marks should face the exhaust side of the cylinder head, while the cast tabs should align with the bright links on the camshaft chain.

4. Install a dial gauge holder (such as VW 387) with a dial gauge on the cylinder head. Set the dial gauge with a 5mm preload to Zero on the hydraulic lifter of No. 6 cylinder intake valve. The dial gauge must be perpendicular to the intake valve.

5. Slowly move the crankshaft in the normal direction of rotation (clockwise) past TDC while observing the reading on the dial gauge. Contin-

Correct alignment of early version camshaft marks. The marks should face the exhaust side of the cylinder head as shown

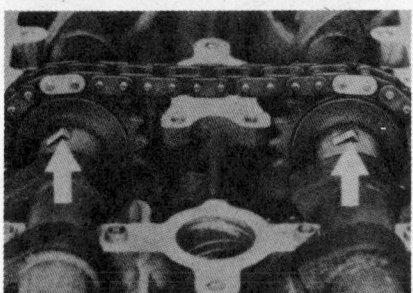

Correct alignment of late version camshaft marks with the bright links on the camshaft chain

Dial gauge installed on the hydraulic lifter. Set the gauge with a 5mm preload to 0 when adjusting the camshaft timing on 1985–88 928S, 928S4 and 944S models

ue turning until the dial indicates 2.0 ± 0.1mm lift. The 20 degrees ATDC mark should now be lined up with the pointer on the drive belt cover. If it is, then the valve timing is correct and no adjustment is necessary.

NOTE: Make all measurements using metric specifications when checking or adjusting valve timing, and make all steps and adjustments as smoothly and accurately as possible. If the engine is rotated a little past 2mm lift when setting up the measurement, continue around in the normal direction of rotation and begin at Step 1 again. Never rotate the engine counterclockwise to align any timing marks; always rotate the engine clockwise. All timing degree specifications and timing

mark alignments are on the No. 1 cylinder compression stroke, either approaching or leaving Top Dead Center.

6. If the alignment of the pointer and the 20 degrees ATDC mark is not correct, remove the ignition rotor and install three additional M5 x 15 bolts into the camshaft sprocket to prevent the camshaft and sprocket from turning while loosening the sprocket bolts.

7. Turn the crankshaft clockwise until the dial gauge reads 2.0 ± .01mm, then loosen the sprocket bolts.

8. Turn the crankshaft to 20 degrees ATDC (on cylinder No. 1 compression stroke), then retorque the camshaft mounting bolt to 47 ft. lbs. (65 Nm). Hold the sprocket securely with the bolts as before.

9. Remove the M5 x 15 bolts from the sprocket and recheck the camshaft timing on cylinder bank 1–4 by rotating the engine clockwise to TDC on cylinder No. **6** (NOT No. 1).

10. Install the dial gauge on the hydraulic lifter for the intake valve of No. 1 cylinder. The dial gauge must be perpendicular to the intake valve.

11. Slowly rotate the crankshaft clockwise away from TDC/No. 6 and observe the reading on the dial gauge. Continue turning until the dial indicates 1.6 ± 0.1mm lift. The 20 degrees ATDC mark should now be aligned with the pointer on the drive belt cover.

12. If the alignment of the pointer and the 20 degrees ATDC mark is not correct, repeat the timing procedure from Step 1.

13. When installing the cylinder head cover, additional sealing is required. Apply a small bead of silicone Silastic 730 RTV sealer (or equivalent) in the area whereend camshaft bearing caps meet the head cover mating surface. Avoid using excessive amounts of the sealer and torque the head cover bolts to 7 ft. lbs. (10 Nm). On 928S4 engines, 12 spacers are used between the guide washers and the mounting bolt heads. These spacers should only be added to the four mounting bolts along the bottom (exhaust side) of the cover and the two mounting bolts, one centered at each end of the cover.

1987–88 944S

1. Rotate the engine in the normal direction of rotation to set No. 1 cylinder at TDC/compression. Check the cambelt tension adjustment as previously described.

2. Remove the distributor cap and make sure the rotor is pointing

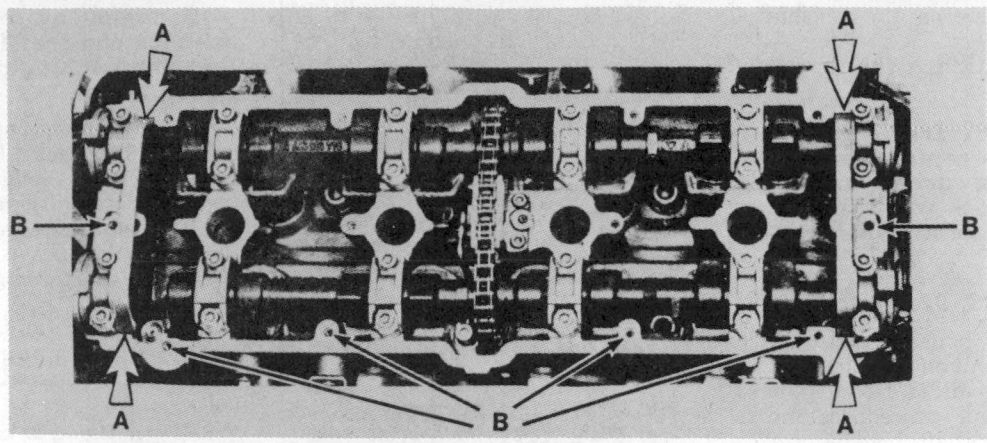

On 928S4 models, apply silicone sealer at the arrows (A) and the spacers at the cover bolt holes indicated (B)

Correct cam lobe alignment for No. 1 cylinder at TDC/compression on 944S models

Install dial gauges as shown to set camshaft timing on 944S models

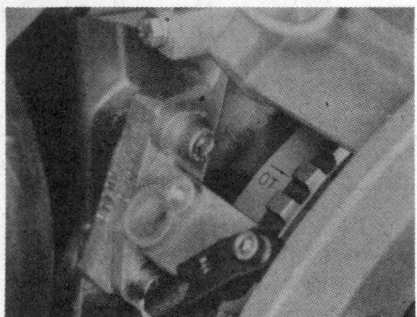

TDC mark alignment on the crankshaft pulley for 944S models.

Install three M5 x 15 bolts as shown to hold the sprocket in place

straight up. Check that the cam lobes for No. 1 cylinder are leaning in toward one another with the noses at approximately 10 and 2 o'clock. The notch on the flywheel should also be aligned with the TDC notch in the bellhousing, visible from beneath the vehicle. If the engine is out of the vehicle, align the OT marks on the crankshaft pulley with the mark on the engine case, just under the magnetic timing probe bracket.

3. Install a dial gauge holder and indicator on the piston crown of No. 1 cylinder and preload to 3mm. Install a second dial indicator to the hydraulic tappet of No. 1 intake valve and again

preload to 3mm. The second dial indicator must be perpendicular to the intake valve.

4. Remove the rotor and install three M5 x 15 bolts to secure the camshaft sprocket while loosening the sprocket center bolt. Loosen the center bolt while counterholding to prevent engine rotation, then loosen the M5 x 15 bolts.

5. Turn the engine against its normal direction of rotation slowly, until the camshaft gear comes up against the stop withing the feather key groove. Tighten the M5 x 15 bolts to 4 ft. lbs. (6 Nm) and the sprocket center bolt to 29 ft. lbs. (40 Nm).

6. Rotate the engine in the normal direction of rotation slowly, until the highest piston stroke position is indicated by the dial gauge.

NOTE: Do not rotate the engine against the normal direction of rotation in an attempt to correct for overshoot. If you pass the indicated timing mark positions, keep rotating the engine around and start all over again.

7. Set the dial indicator on the hydraulic tappet of No. 1 intake valve to 0, then slowly rotate past TDC (No. 1/compression) while observing the dial indicator reading. Rotate until the dial gauge indicates 1.4 ± 0.1mm.

8. Loosen the central and auxiliary bolts, while making sure the dial gauge reading doesn't change, then rotate the engine slowly until the highest piston stroke is indicated on the gauge. In this position, No. 4 cylinder is at TDC/compression.

9. Tighten the auxiliary bolts and the sprocket center bolt. Torque the center bolt to 48–52 ft. lbs. (65–70 Nm). Rotate the crankshaft two more times in the normal direction of rotation, then recheck the adjustment. If correct, remove the M5 x 15 bolts from the sprocket and install the rotor and distributor cap.

Piston and Connecting Rod

POSITIONING

1981–82 924 and 924 Turbo

Pistons and connecting rods are removed after the cylinder head and oil pan have been removed. Connecting rod and piston assemblies must be marked on disassembly. The projections on the connecting rods must face

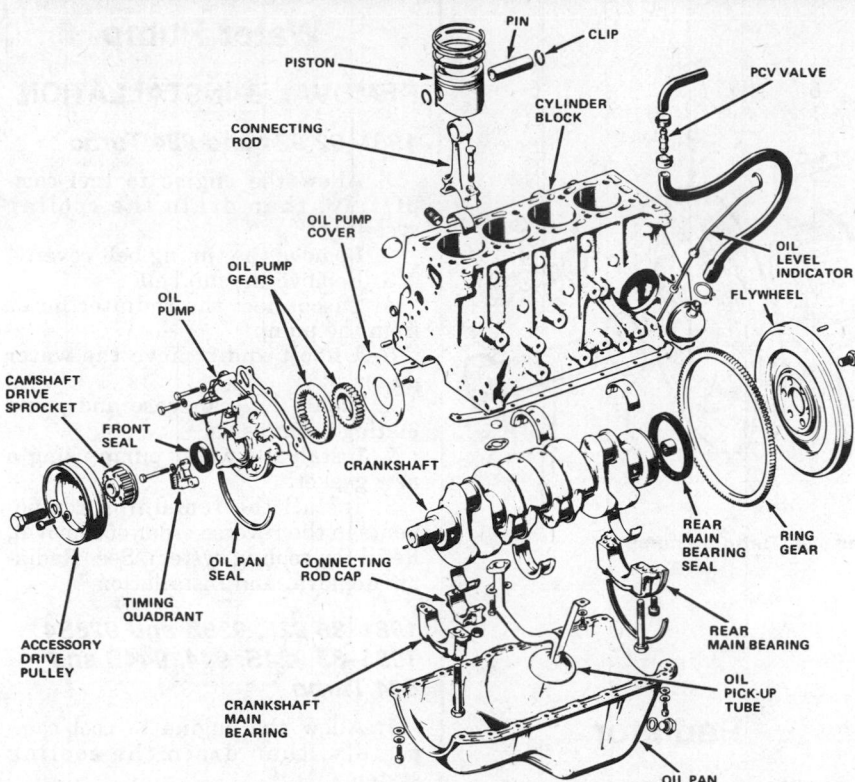

Exploded view of cylinder block and related components on 1981-82 924 and 924 Turbo

toward the front of the engine when installed. The arrow or notch in the piston crown must face toward the front of the engine.

1981–88 928, 928S and 928S4
1983–88 924S, 944, 944S and 944 Turbo

The pistons and connecting rods may be removed after the cylinder head and the pan have been removed. The connecting rod ends are offset. On the 928, make sure that the narrow side with the small chamfer faces the neighboring connecting rod, while the wide side with the large chamfer faces the crankshaft web. The pistons must be installed with the valve pockets facing toward the exhaust manifold. The wrist pin is pressed out of the piston after the snaprings are removed.

ENGINE LUBRICATION

NOTE: For all 911 service procedures, see "Engine Disassembly" in the 911 Engine Mechanical section.

Oil Pan

REMOVAL & INSTALLATION

1981–82 924 and 924 Turbo

1. Drain the oil. Remove the engine splash shield.
2. Disconnect the temperature sending unit wire connector.
3. Disconnect the side engine mounts and raise the engine with a hydraulic jack for pan removal clearance.
4. Remove the pan retaining bolts and lower the pan from the car.
5. Install the pan using the reverse of the removal procedure. Use new gaskets and seals and clean all gasket mating surfaces carefully. Remove the oil dipstick for additional venting when refilling the engine with oil. This will prevent blue exhaust smoke following any oil change due to oil entering the intake system through the breather.

1981–88 928, 928S and 928S4
1983–88 924S, 944, 944S and 944 Turbo

1. Raise the vehicle and support it safely with jackstands.
2. Remove the bottom protective engine plate.

3. Drain the engine oil and unscrew the oil fill pipe from the pan. Disconnect the oil level indicator wire.
4. Remove the oil pan retaining bolts and maneuver the oil pan downward so that the oil pump suction tube is not twisted or damaged.
5. Clean all gasket mating surfaces carefully. Using a new gasket, install the oil pan in the reverse order of removal.

Rear Main Bearing Oil Seal

REPLACEMENT

1981–82 924 and 924 Turbo

The rear main oil seal is located in the back of the cylinder block. Replacement involves first disconnecting the torque tube and pulling the transaxle back, removing the clutch housing and then removing the flywheel to gain access to the seal.
1. Carefully pry the seal out.
2. Lightly oil the replacement seal with engine oil and carefully tap it into place. Do not damage the seal or score the flywheel.
3. Install the flywheel, clutch housing and torque tube and transaxle. Tighten the flywheel-to-crankshaft bolts to 65 ft. lbs. (88 Nm).

1981–88 928, 928S and 928S4
1983–88 924S, 944, 944S and 944 Turbo

The rear main oil seal can be replaced by separating the clutch housing from the engine and removing the flywheel. Remove the seal from the engine block with a sharp edged tool, being careful not to mark the crankshaft surface. Using a special centering tool, install the seal into the engine block with the lubricated lip towards the crankshaft. Reassemble in the reverse order of disassembly.

Oil Pump

REMOVAL & INSTALLATION

1981–82 924 and 924 Turbo

The oil pump is driven directly from the crankshaft.
1. Remove the oil pan.
2. Remove the timing belt cover.
3. Remove the timing belt.
4. Remove the crankshaft pulley.
5. Unbolt and remove the oil pump. Remove the oil pickup.
6. Clean and then install the oil pickup to the replacement oil pump.

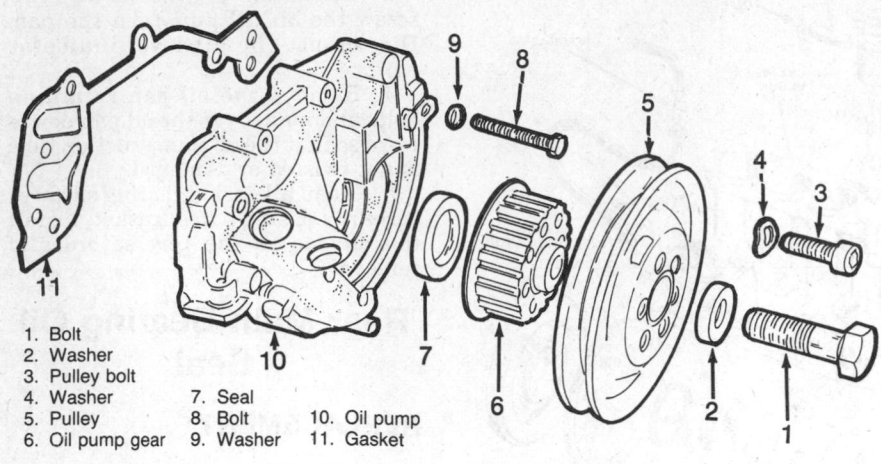

1. Bolt
2. Washer
3. Pulley bolt
4. Washer
5. Pulley
6. Oil pump gear
7. Seal
8. Bolt
9. Washer
10. Oil pump
11. Gasket

Exploded view of the 1981-82 924 and 924 Turbo oil pump

7. Install the oil pump. Tighten the pump-to-crankcase bolts to 8 ft. lbs. (11 Nm).

8. Install the remaining components in reverse order of removal.

1981-88 928, 928S and 928S4
1983-88 924S, 944, 944S and 944 Turbo

The oil pump is located on the front of the engine block and is driven by the toothed timing belt.

1. Remove the timing belt as described under "Timing Belt Removal and Installation."

2. Remove the oil pump sprocket and the oil pump retaining bolts.

3. Remove the oil pump from the engine block.

4. Installation is the reverse of removal. Install a new O-ring seal on the pump body.

NOTE: An oil pump shaft seal is used and can be replaced after removal of the sprocket and woodruff key.

ENGINE COOLING

NOTE: Porsche recommends using only a phosphate-free coolant/antifreeze in the cooling system. Use of other types of coolant may cause corrosion of the cooling system, and subsequent overheating and damage to aluminum parts.

Radiator

REMOVAL & INSTALLATION

All Models

1. Drain the cooling system into a suitable clean container. If not contaminated, the coolant may be reused.

2. Remove the fan and radiator shroud.

3. Remove the radiator hoses. Disconnect any fluid cooler lines attached to the radiator.

4. Disconnect the expansion tank, if necessary for clearance and move it out of the way.

5. Unbolt the radiator and remove it by lifting straight up.

6. Installation is the reverse of removal. Refill the cooling system as follows:

   a. Set the heater to the FULL HOT position

   b. Remove the vent plug on the radiator hose

   c. Fill the cooling system with the recommended amount of coolant

   d. Start the engine and run it for one minute at fast idle

   e. Replace the vent plug when no more air bubbles appear at the plug opening.

The coolant hose from the radiator to the expansion tank has been known to rub the headlight linkage on some 944 models. Tie the hose away from the linkage and secure the front hood cable to the coolant hose. A new preformed top coolant hose is installed on later models.

Water Pump

REMOVAL & INSTALLATION

1981-82 924 and 924 Turbo

1. Allow the engine to cool completely, then drain the cooling system.

2. Remove the timing belt cover.

3. Remove the fan belt.

4. Disconnect the radiator hoses from the pump.

5. Unbolt and remove the water pump.

6. Clean the crankcase and pump mating surfaces.

7. Install the water pump using a new gasket.

8. Install the remaining components in the reverse order of removal. Refill the cooling system. See "Radiator Removal and Installation."

1981-88 928, 928S and 928S4
1983-88 924S, 944, 944S and 944 Turbo

1. Allow the engine to cool completely, then drain the cooling system.

2. Rotate the engine to TDC, with the Number one piston on the firing stroke and the distributor rotor pointing to the No. 1 terminal of the distributor cap.

3. On the 924S and 944, remove the timing belt cover assembly as previously outlined. On the 928, remove the upper right and left timing belt covers and remove the fan and bracket.

NOTE: Maintain upright position of the fan assembly so that the silicone fluid does not drain out on 928 models equipped with a viscous coupling cooling fan.

4. Loosen and remove the toothed drive belt from the water pump pulley (refer to the "Timing Belt Removal and Installation" section).

5. Remove the bolts and water pump from the engine block.

6. Using a new gasket, install the water pump in the reverse order of removal.

Thermostat

REMOVAL & INSTALLATION

All Models

The thermostat is located in the upper radiator hose neck on the engine. What follows is a general procedure for all engines.

1. Allow the engine to cool com-

pletely, then drain the cooling system.

2. Don't disconnect the radiator hose, just unbolt the neck and lift out the thermostat.

3. Clean the mating surfaces and install the new thermostat (spring down) using a new gasket.

4. Refill the cooling system. See "Radiator Removal and Installation."

Fuel filter on the 944. Loosen the line fittings first (outer arrows) then the filter mounting clamp (inner arrow) to remove the filter

EMISSION CONTROLS

NOTE: Please refer to "Emission Control" in the Unit Repair section for system maintenance procedures. Due to the complex nature of modern electronic engine control systems, comprehensive diagnosis and testing procedures fall outside the confines of this repair manual. For complete information on diagnosis, testing and repair procedures concerning all modern engine and emission control systems, please refer to *"Chilton's Guide To Electronic Engine Controls."*

FUEL SYSTEM

Fuel Filter

REMOVAL & INSTALLATION

1981–88 911 and 911 Turbo Models

The fuel filter is located in the fuel line, mounted near the tank. Replacement involves depressurizing the fuel system and disconnecting the line fittings from the filter canister. Install a new fuel filter and tighten the fittings using a backup wrench on the nuts to avoid twisting the fuel line.

1981–82 924 and 924 Turbo 1983–88 924S, 944, 944S and 944 Turbo

On the 1981–82 924 and 924 Turbo, the fuel filter is located in the fuel line on the driver's side of the engine compartment. On the 1983–88 924S and 944, the fuel filter is located at the right rear of the vehicle above the axle halfshaft.

1. Place a shop rag under the filter.
2. Using a line wrench, unscrew both line connections from the filter.

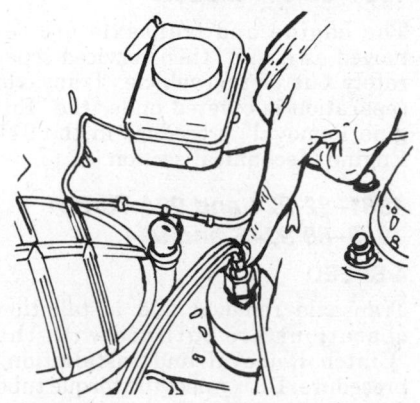

Fuel filter location on 1981-82 924 models

3. Loosen the filter clamp and remove the filter.

4. Install the replacement filter in the line and tighten both fittings. Tighten the filter clamp, if so equipped.

1981–86 928 and 928S

The fuel filter and fuel accumulator on 928 models are located behind a cover, in front of the right rear wheel well. On 928S models, remove the shield underneath the gas tank. Disconnect the fuel lines, remove the filter and install in reverse order.

Fuel Pump

TESTING & ADJUSTMENT

No adjustments may be made to the fuel pump. If the pump is not functioning properly, it must be discarded and replaced. To check the function of the fuel pump, the pump should be connected to a pressure gauge. Be careful not to switch the electrical leads. If the pump fails to pump its normal capacity, or it cannot pump that capacity at its specified rate of current consumption, it must be replaced.

A pressure tester such as P 378, or equivalent is necessary to check the fuel pressure on all models. The pressure gauge is attached the fuel distributor test connection after first relieving the fuel system pressure. Make sure the sealing ball does not fall out when taking off the capped nut. Start the engine and measure the fuel pressure at idle. On all models, the fuel pressure should be approximately 28 psi (2 bar) at idle.

——— CAUTION ———

Relieve fuel system pressure before attempting to disconnect any fuel lines. Take precautions to avoid the risk of fire while working on the fuel system and cap all line openings to prevent contamination of the fuel system by dirt.

REMOVAL & INSTALLATION

1981–88 911 Models

The Turbo is equipped with two electric pumps. One is mounted at the front crossmember, near the fuel tank; the second at the rear, near the engine. All 911 fuel pumps are located at the front near the tank.

1. Remove the cap nuts.
2. Withdraw the pump with its mounting bracket.
3. Loosen the hose clamp and remove the pump from its bracket.
4. Loosen the hose clamps and remove the three fuel lines from the pump.
5. Install the pump using a reverse of the removal procedure. Coat both electrical terminals with grease and make sure that the rubber boot is firmly seated.

1981–82 924 and 924 Turbo

Two fuel pumps are used. One is located in the fuel tank and the second is located in the right rear wheel well.

IN-TANK PUMP

1. Disconnect the negative battery cable.

2. Raise the rear of the vehicle.

3. Drain the fuel tank.

4. Disconnect the electrical connections from the fuel pump.

5. Disconnect the fuel line. Have a container ready to catch any residual fuel left in the system.

6. Unscrew the pump from the bottom of the fuel tank.

7. When installing a new pump, make sure the gasket for the pump is in place. After installation, fill the tank with a few gallons of fuel and check for leaks.

EXTERNAL PUMP

1. Disconnect the negative battery cable. Drain the fuel tank.

2. Raise the rear of the vehicle and support it with jack stands.

3. Locate the fuel pump. Quickly remove and plug the fuel lines form the pump.

4. Loosen the strap and remove the fuel pump.

5. Install a new pump in the reverse order of the removal procedure.

1983–88 924S, 944, 944S and 944 Turbo

924S and 944 models are equipped with one fuel pump located near the fuel tank behind the right rear wheel. Replacement involves simply depressurizing the fuel system and disconnecting the fuel lines and electrical connector from the pump. Remove the fuel pump and its mounting bracket as an assembly and separate the two on a workbench.

1981–88 928, 928S and 928S4

A single fuel pump is located with the fuel filter on a mutual mounting bracket, underneath a plastic hood on top of the fuel tank.

1. Disconnect the negative battery cable.

2. Raise the rear of the vehicle and support it on jack stands. Expose the fuel pump.

3. Pinch shut the hose running from the fuel tank to the fuel pump with a suitable clamp.

4. Disconnect the pump wiring, disconnect both fittings from the pump, loosen its retaining strap and remove the pump. Some fuel will be present in the lines. Have a container ready to catch it.

5. Install a new pump in the reverse order of pump removal.

Fuel Injection

Due to the complex nature of modern fuel injection systems, comprehensive diagnosis and testing procedures fall outside the confines of this repair manual. **For complete information on fuel injection diagnosis, testing and repair procedures, please refer to** Chilton's Guide To Fuel Injection And Feedback Carburetors.

MANUAL TRANSAXLE

REMOVAL & INSTALLATION

1981–88 911 Models

The engine and transaxle are removed as a unit, then serviced separately out of the vehicle. Transaxle separation is covered under the "Engine Removal" procedure in the 911 Engine Mechanical section.

1981–82 924 and 924 Turbo
1983–88 924S and 944

4 SPEED

Transaxle removal and installation operations are outlined with the "Clutch Removal and Installation" procedure. Disconnect the torque tube from the transaxle for servicing.

5 SPEED

1. Raise the vehicle and support it safely on jackstands.

2. Remove the entire exhaust system from behind the catalytic converter.

3. Disconnect the wires from the backup light switch.

4. Remove the reinforcement strut at the front of the transaxle to facilitate work procedures.

5. Engage 5th gear. Remove the rubber cap from the front transmission cover. Position the socket head screw for removal by turning a rear wheel (hold the other wheel). Unscrew the screw from the coupling using a long reach extension and a 6 mm socket. Keep the transaxle in 5th gear.

6. Detach the axle half-shafts from the transaxle and suspend them on wire to prevent damage.

7. Remove the self-locking nuts from the transmission mounts (the rubber/metal mounts).

8. Position a jack underneath the transmission and secure the transaxle to it using a strap.

9. Unscrew the bolts from the rubber/metal mounts, lift the transaxle slightly with he jack and remove the mounts. Do not lift the unit too far, as the brake line for the left rear wheel may be damaged.

10. Disconnect the shift linkage.

11. Remove the bolts between the drive shaft tube and the transaxle. Remove or disconnect any other interfering components, then carefully remove the transaxle unit, moving rearward and down.

12. Installation is the reverse of removal.

1981–88 928, 928S and 928S4

1. Remove the nuts from the spring strut bolts extending into the trunk compartment.

2. Remove the battery and loosen the rear wheels.

3. Place the transmission in fifth gear.

4. Raise the vehicle and remove the rubber plug from underneath the front of the transmission. Looking into the hole, position the coupling bolt head between the drive and input shafts, so that it can be removed.

NOTE: During removal of the bolt, do not allow the shaft to turn and jam the socket or bolt in the transmission housing.

5. Place the transmission in neutral, remove the rear wheels and remove the brake calipers. Wire the calipers to the frame; do not allow them to hang from their brake hoses.

6. Remove the exhaust system from the catalytic converter rearward.

7. Remove the exhaust heat shield and the battery box.

8. Disconnect the backup light switch wires and loosen the pulse transmitter for the speedometer. Remove the wires form the clip.

9. Move the dust cover from the shift rod coupling and remove the locking set screw. Remove the shift rod from the main rod.

10. Disconnect the axle shafts at the transmission end. Suspend the axles from the cross member.

11. disconnect the stabilizer bar at the lower control arm.

12. Support the transaxle assembly from the stabilizer bar with the use of a strap, chain or heavy wire.

13. Remove the transmission-to-rear axle cross member bolts and the bolts between the rear axle cross member and frame.

14. Mark the position of the rear axle cross member and place a jack under member. Remove the bolts and tilt the rear axle so that the spring struts and control arms do not twist. Support the rear axle in the tilted position to keep the weight off the lower control arm link pins.

15. Place under the transmission assembly and remove the bolts between the drive shaft tube and the transmis-

sion. Remove the holding strap, pull the unit rearward and lower.

16. Installation is the reverse of removal.

LINKAGE ADJUSTMENT

Linkage adjustments are not normally required and should be attempted only if familiar with direct-distant shift mechanisms.

1981–88 911 Models

1. Position the shift lever in Neutral. Remove the rear tunnel cover in front of the rear seat.
2. Pull the rubber dust cover forward on the shift rod.
3. Loosen the clamp bolt on the shift rod.
4. Move the transmission selector shaft all the way to its left stop, keeping it in Neutral.
5. With the transmission still in Neutral, move the gearshift rod to the right to its stop.
6. Tighten the clamp bolt to 18 ft. lbs. (24 Nm).
7. Test the shift lever. Play should be the same in all gears in all directions.

1981–82 924 4 Speed

1. Place the transaxle in Neutral.
2. Raise the rear of the vehicle, support it safely on jackstands and block the front wheels.
3. Make sure the intermediate lever on the selector shaft leans toward the back of the car approximately 5 degrees. If not, loosen the lever's pinch bolt and adjust it to this position.
4. Move the intermediate lever to the middle of the neutral travel.
5. Loosen the link piece retaining bolt at the rear of the selector shaft and move the bolt in its slot until the link piece is vertical. Tighten the bolt.
6. Adjust the shift plate at the bottom of the shift lever in the passenger compartment until the lever is at an 82 degree angle (rearward) with the propeller shaft tunnel.

All 5–Speeds

These transaxles usually require adjustment only when the unit has been overhauled. Shift fork and shifter adjustments are covered in the overhaul procedures.

OVERHAUL

For all manual transaxle overhaul procedures, please refer to "Manual Transaxle Overhaul" in the Unit Repair section.

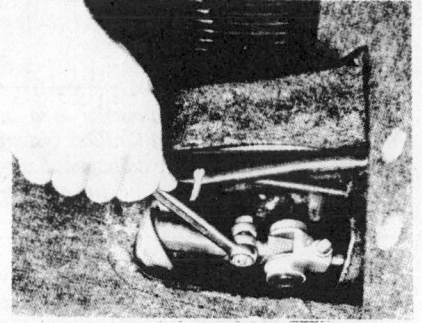
Shift linkage adjustment on 911 models

CLUTCH

REMOVAL & INSTALLATION

1981–88 911 Models

1. Remove the engine and transaxle as a unit from the vehicle. Separate the engine/transaxle assembly as described under "Engine Removal" in the 911 Engine Mechanical section.
2. Gradually loosen the pressure plate bolts one or two turns at a time in a criss-cross pattern to prevent distortion.
3. Remove the pressure plate and clutch disc.
4. Check the clutch disc for uneven or excessive lining wear. Examine the pressure plate for cracking, scorching, or scoring. Replace any questionable components.

5. Check the clutch release bearing for wear, and replace if necessary. Measure the clutch disc for wear; new thickness is 8.1mm, and the maximum wear limit is 6.3mm. Clutch disc run-out (maximum) is 0.6mm.
6. Fill the pilot bearing with about 2cc of grease.
7. Install the clutch disc and pressure plate. Use a pilot shaft or an old transaxle input shaft to keep the disc centered.
8. Gradually tighten the pressure plate-to-flywheel bolts in a criss-cross pattern. Torque the bolts to 18 ft. lbs. (24 Nm).
9. Install the throwout bearing.
10. Install the transaxle on the engine and install the engine/transaxle assembly as previously described.

1981–82 924 Non-Turbo

To gain access to the clutch disc and

Centering the clutch disc with a pilot shaft

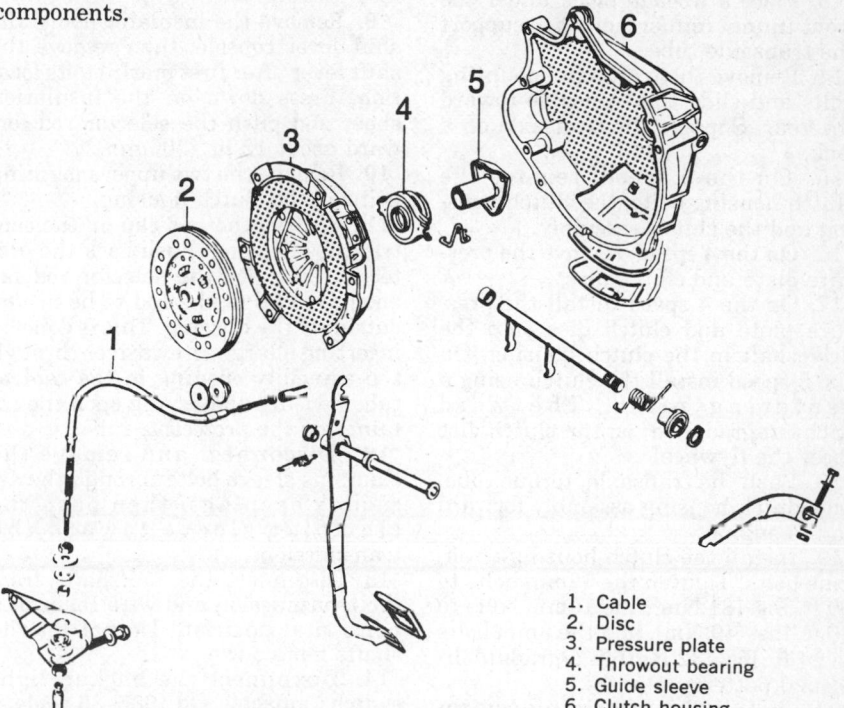

1. Cable
2. Disc
3. Pressure plate
4. Throwout bearing
5. Guide sleeve
6. Clutch housing

Exploded view of the clutch assembly on 1981-82 924 non-turbo

pressure plate assembly, the transaxle, torque tube and clutch housing must be unbolted and pulled back out of the way.

1. Disconnect the battery ground cable. Raise and support the car safely with jackstands.
2. Support the engine with an overhead hoist or a jack and cradle under the engine.
3. Remove the engine splash shield.
4. Disconnect the clutch cable.
5. Remove the bottom clutch adjustment lock nut and detach the cable from the lever.
6. On the 4 speed, remove the access plate from the bottom of the clutch housing. Have an assistant turn the engine with the crankshaft pulley. Remove the pressure plate bolts gradually until all pressure is released.
7. Remove the exhaust pipe flange bolts.
8. Remove the bracket at the rear of the transaxle and any other attachment which will hinder the transaxle's rearward movement.
9. Remove the entire exhaust system.
10. Remove the backup light switch from the transaxle.
11. Disconnect the axle driveshafts at the transaxle and let them hang down out of the way.
12. On the 4 speed, remove the clutch housing-to-engine bolts. On the 5 speed, disconnect the center tube from the clutch housing.
13. Place a wooden block under the front tunnel reinforcement to support the transaxle tube.
14. Remove the transaxle mounting bolts and slide the transaxle toward the rear. Support the transaxle on a jack.
15. On the 5 speed, remove the clutch housing bolts, the clutch housing and the clutch assembly.
16. On the 4 speed, remove the pressure plate and clutch disc.
17. On the 4 speed install the pressure plate and clutch disc onto the driveshaft in the clutch housing. On the 5 speed install the clutch using a centering pilot. The word "Schwungradseite" on the clutch disc faces the flywheel.
18. Push the transaxle, torque tube, and clutch housing assembly forward to the engine.
19. Install the clutch housing-to-engine bolts. Tighten the 12mm bolts to 60 ft. lbs. (81 Nm), the 10mm bolts to 36 ft. lbs. (49 Nm), and the 8mm bolts to 24 ft. lbs. (32 Nm) in a gradual diagonal pattern.
20. Install the remaining components in the reverse order of removal. Adjust the clutch.

1981–82 924 Turbo
1983–88 924S and 944

CAUTION
The flywheel sensing components used in these models for the digital ignition system are very delicate and easily damaged. Exercise care when handling, removing and installing these components.

1. Disconnect the negative battery cable and the ground wire from the body to the clutch housing.
2. Remove the socket head bolts and remove the reference mark sensor and speed sensor from the bracket.
3. Disconnect the wire harness for the starter at the upper mounting point. It may be necessary to remove the air cleaner to gain access.
4. Disconnect the oxygen sensor wire and remove the exhaust assembly at the manifold.
5. Remove the heat shield above the catalytic converter and the splash shield. Remove the rear exhaust pipe bracket together with the bracket bolted on the central tube.
6. Pull back the dust cover, then remove the lockwire on the clamp bolt of the selector linkage and remove the bolt.
7. Lift and fold down the dust cover and sleeve on the shift lever. Remove the shift lever boot retainer and remove the shift knob.
8. Remove the circlip on the shift lever, then pull off the selector rod and washer on the bolt of the shift lever.
9. Remove the insulator above the shift lever console, then remove the shift lever after first marking its location. Press down on the insulation sheet and push the selector rod forward about 12 in. (300mm).
10. Remove the two upper mounting bolts on the clutch housing.
11. Remove the end cap on the central tube housing. Push back the protective tube for the selector rod far enough to allow the rod to be moved outside of the housing. This is done by inserting a large screwdriver through the assembly opening in the central tube housing and prying open the retainer on the protective tube.
12. Disconnect and remove the clamping sleeve bolts through the assembly openings, then push the clamping sleeve toward the transmission.
13. Disconnect the halfshafts from the transmission and wire them in a horizontal position. Do not let the shafts hang down.
14. Disconnect the backup light switch connector. On 1985–88 models, pull off the plug on the speedometer drive.

15. Place a suitable transmission jack under the transaxle and secure the transaxle to the jack. Raise the jack slightly to take the pressure off the transaxle mounts.
16. Remove the transaxle mounting bolts, then lower the transaxle with the central tube until the tube rests on the crossmember. Remove the transaxle/central tube flange bolts, then remove the transaxle from the rear.
17. Remove the starter, then unscrew the clutch line mounting clamps.
18. Detach the clutch slave cylinder from the clutch housing, but do not disconnect the hydraulic line from the cylinder.
19. Disconnect the starter wire harness from the clutch housing. Pull out the release lever shaft mounting bolt, then remove the four central tube/clutch housing mounting bolts.
20. Pull back the selector rod (which had been moved forward for transaxle removal), to avoid damage when moving the central tube.
21. Move the central tube back until the housing rests on the transaxle carrier. Make sure the brake lines are not damaged by the tube.

NOTE: If the central tube cannot be moved out of the clutch housing without applying force, hold the engine tight with the transport eye mounted on the camshaft housing with special tool VW 10–222. If this is the case, the engine has excessive inclination at the rear. Check the engine mounts.

22. Remove the guard on the clutch housing and the right support.
23. Remove the two lower mounting bolts on the clutch housing after removing the engine mount nuts and pushing the engine to the right. Move out the guard and clutch housing with the release lever as an assembly.
24. Disconnect the clutch assembly from the flywheel and remove it.
25. Check the flywheel, starter ring gear, pilot bearing in the flywheel, crankshaft seal, release bearing, guide sleeve, release lever, pressure plate and clutch disc for wear or damage. Replace parts as necessary.
26. Coat the guide sleeve with multipurpose grease, then apply a light coat to the spline of the drive shaft and the area of the pilot bearing/flywheel. Lubricate the release lever pivot, ball socket and needle bearings with white grease.
27. Make sure the clutch disc and flywheel are clean and free from grease, then install the clutch disc. Use a suitable clutch alignment tool

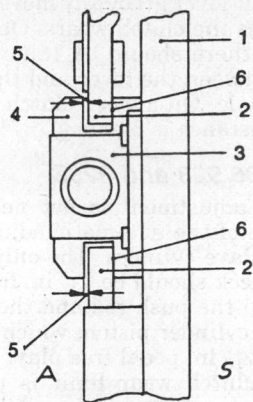

1. Intermediate ring
2. Intermediate plate
3. Stop bracket
4. Stop
5. Distance 0.7 to 1.0 mm
6. Position of intermediate plate
A. Release bearing side
S. Flywheel side

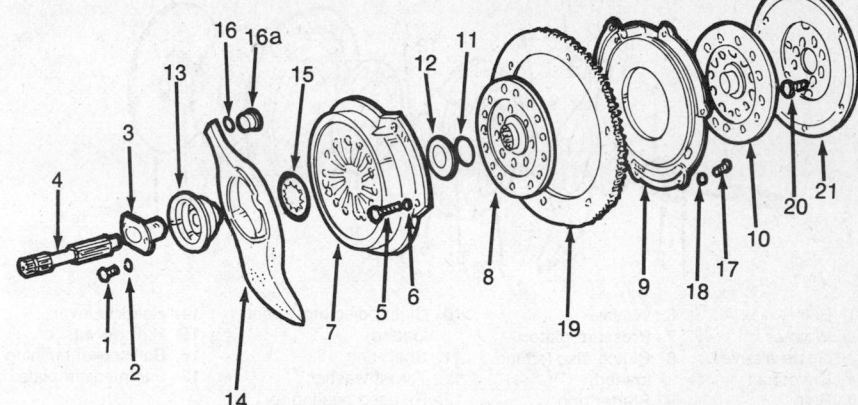

1. Bolt	7. Pressure plate	11. Snap-ring	16A. Ball socket bushing
2. Washer	8. Clutch disc (spring	12. Thrust washer	17. Bolt
3. Guide sleeve	loaded)	13. Release bearing	18. Washer
4. Driveshaft	9. Intermediate plate	14. Release lever	19. Starter ring
5. Bolt	10. Clutch disc (not spring	15. Preload washer	20. Bolt
6. Washer	loaded)	16. Snap-ring	21. Flywheel with centering
			collar

Diameter centered clutch assembly on 928 and 928S

To prevent clutch drag on the 928, move the three clutch stop brackets toward the pressure plate until the correct gap (5) exists

to center the clutch disc and install the mounting bolts. Tighten the clutch disc bolts in a crisscross pattern evenly to 18 ft. lbs. (25 Nm).

28. Continue installation in reverse of the removal procedures. When installing the clutch housing assembly, make sure the flywheel reference bolts are facing down to avoid damage during installation. Tighten the central tube mounting bolts AFTER the engine and transaxle mounting bolts have been tightened. Torque the clutch housing-to-engine bolts to 54 ft. lbs (75 Nm), the central tube flange-to-clutch housing bolts to 30 ft. lbs. (42 Nm), and the driveshaft-to-transmission input shaft clamp bolt to 58 ft. lbs. (80 Nm).

1981–88 928, 928S and 928S4

1. Disconnect the negative battery cable.
2. Raise the vehicle and support it safely with jackstands.
3. Remove the lower body brace.
4. Remove the clutch slave cylinder and keep hydraulic lines attached.
5. Remove the starter and clutch housing cover as a unit and attach to the stabilizer bar with a wire. Remove the catalytic converter.
6. Remove the coupling screws and push the coupler rearward on the driveshaft.
7. Remove the release bearing sleeve bolts and move the sleeve towards the flywheel.
8. Matchmark the clutch components and loosen all pressure plate

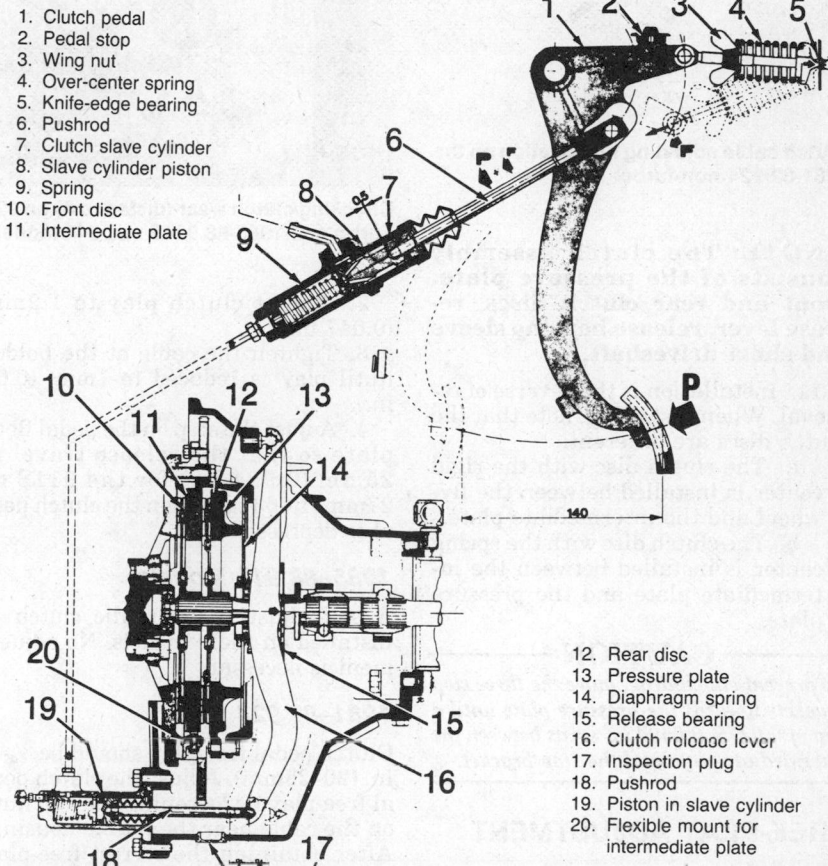

1. Clutch pedal
2. Pedal stop
3. Wing nut
4. Over-center spring
5. Knife-edge bearing
6. Pushrod
7. Clutch slave cylinder
8. Slave cylinder piston
9. Spring
10. Front disc
11. Intermediate plate

12. Rear disc
13. Pressure plate
14. Diaphragm spring
15. Release bearing
16. Clutch release lever
17. Inspection plug
18. Pushrod
19. Piston in slave cylinder
20. Flexible mount for intermediate plate

Hydraulic clutch actuation system on the 928 and 928S. Clutch wear can be checked after removing the rubber plug (17).

mounting bolts evenly until all the pressure is removed from the plate.

9. Remove the mounting bolts and press down on the release lever (towards the flywheel) and disconnect

the release lever at the ball stud.

10. Push the complete clutch assembly rearward and move the assembly downward and out of the clutch housing.

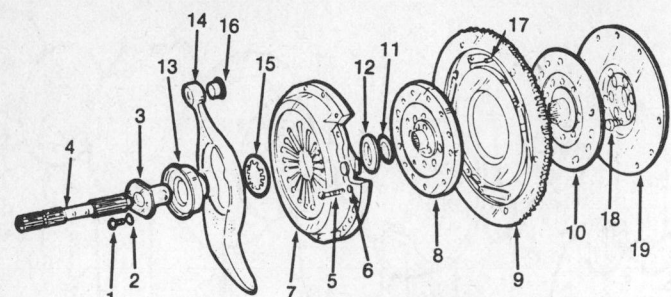

1. Bolt
2. Washer
3. Guide sleeve
4. Driveshaft
5. Bolt
6. Washer
7. Pressure plate
8. Clutch disc (spring loaded)
9. Starter ring
10. Clutch disc (not spring loaded)
11. Snap-ring
12. Thrust washer
13. Release bearing
14. Release lever
15. Preload washer
16. Ball socket bushing
17. Intermediate plate

Dowel pin centered clutch assembly on 928 and 928S

Clutch cable adjusting nut location on the 1981-82 924 non-turbo

NOTE: The clutch assembly consists of the pressure plate, front and rear clutch discs, release lever, release bearing sleeve and short driveshaft.

11. Installation is the reverse of removal. When installing, note that the clutch discs are different:

   a. The clutch disc with the rigid center is installed between the flywheel and the intermediate plate.

   b. The clutch disc with the spring center is installed between the intermediate plate and the pressure plate.

—————— CAUTION ——————

To prevent clutch drag, move the three stop brackets towards the pressure plate until a gap of 0.0275–0.0394 in. exists between the intermediate plate and the stop bracket.

FREE-PLAY ADJUSTMENT

1981–84 911 Models

These models are equipped with an auxiliary spring to reduce pedal effort. Free-play is no longer checked at the pedal. Play is checked by measuring the distance between the adjusting belt and the positioning lever. The distance should be 1mm (0.04 in.).

1. Release the cable.

Checking clutch wear (distance A) on 924 Turbo and 1983-88 924S and 944 models

2. Adjust clutch play to 1.2mm (0.047 in.).

3. Tighten the cable at the holder until play is reduced to 1mm. (0.04 in.).

4. Adjust the stop on the pedal floor plate so that the release travel is 25mm (0.984 in.) for the 911S or 27mm (1.063 in.) when the clutch pedal is depressed.

1985–88 911 Models

A self-adjusting hydraulic clutch is installed on these models. No adjustment is necessary.

1981–82 924

Clutch pedal free-play should be $\frac{3}{4}$–1 in. (20–25mm). Adjust the clutch pedal free-play by loosening the two nuts on the cable near the intake housing. After obtaining the correct free-play at the pedal, tighten the adjusting nuts.

1981–82 924 Turbo
1983–88 924S and 944

The clutch linkage is self-adjusting. Clutch wear can be checked by removing the rubber plug located on the starter side of the bell housing. The throwout lever gradually moves backwards as the clutch wears. On a new clutch, there should be 18mm clearance between the lever and the front of the hole. On a worn clutch the replace distance is 34mm.

1981–86 928 and 928S

Clutch adjustment is not necessary because of the automatic adjustment of the slave cylinder. The only clearance check should be $\frac{3}{32}$ in. free play between the push rod and the clutch master cylinder piston, which should give a $\frac{3}{16}$ in. pedal free play.

The clutch wear limit is reached when, upon removal of a rubber plug on the slave cylinder side of the clutch housing, the front edge of the release lever can just be seen.

PEDAL TRAVEL ADJUSTMENT

1981–84 911 Models Only

1. Pull the front carpeting back.
2. Loosen the two retaining bolts on the pedal stop.
3. Move the pedal up or down until reverse can be engaged with only a slight amount of gear clash.
4. Tighten the pedal stop bolts.
5. Double check the adjustment by shifting into reverse several times. Reinstall the floor carpeting.

Clutch Cable

REMOVAL & INSTALLATION

1981–84 911 Models

1. Fold back the front tunnel carpeting.
2. Disconnect the clutch cable from the pedal by removing the clevis retaining pin.
3. Pull up the clutch cable and remove the clevis and locknut from the threaded portion of the clutch cable.
4. Remove the cable from the clutch release lever at the transmission.
5. Pull the clutch cable out of the vehicle to the rear.
6. Lubricate the new clutch cable and install it from the rear. Check the clutch play at the adjustment bolt with a feeler gauge. If necessary, adjust to 1.0 ± 0.1mm with the adjusting bolt.

Clutch Master Cylinder

REMOVAL & INSTALLATION

1985–88 911 Models

The hydraulic clutch receives its fluid

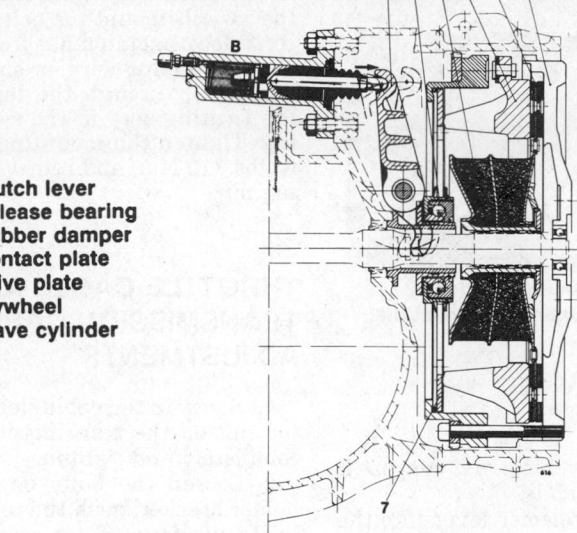

1. Clutch lever
2. Release bearing
3. Rubber damper
4. Contact plate
5. Drive plate
6. Flywheel
B. Slave cylinder

Hydraulic clutch slave cylinder mounting on 1985-88 911 models

from the brake fluid tank to master cylinder, where it passes through the line to the slave cylinder mounted on the transmission case. The master cylinder is attached to the pedal bracket assembly.

All Except 911 Models

The clutch master cylinder is located beside the brake master cylinder in the engine compartment and shares the brake master cylinder's fluid reservoir. Access is limited and, depending on model year and options, several other components may have to be relocated before the clutch master cylinder can be removed.

1. Drain the clutch section of the fluid reservoir. Remove and plug the line leading to the clutch master cylinder from the brake master cylinder fluid reservoir.

CAUTION

Be very careful not to let any brake fluid drip onto painted surfaces, as it will permanently discolor them.

---

2. From inside the car, disconnect the clutch master cylinder pushrod.
3. Disconnect the fluid tube which runs to the clutch slave cylinder from the master cylinder and plug it. Before loosening the tube's fitting, wrap a rag around it so that brake fluid is not spilled.
4. Disconnect and remove the master cylinder from the vehicle.
5. Installation is the reverse of removal. Bleed the system at the slave cylinder. For information, see the pro-

cedures outlined under "Slave Cylinder Removal".

Clutch Slave Cylinder

REMOVAL & INSTALLATION

1985–88 911 Models

The slave cylinder is removed by disconnecting the fluid line and removing the mounting bolts, then pulling the slave cylinder out with the pushrod. When installing, lubricate the pushrod and make sure the end en-

gages the clutch lever. Bleed the cylinder by loosening the bleeder screw above the hydraulic line connection, as described below.

All Except 911 Models

1. Drain the clutch section of the brake fluid reservoir.
2. Jack up the vehicle and support it on stands. Locate the slave cylinder—it is at the bottom of the bell housing.
3. Disconnect the clutch fluid line form the slave cylinder.
4. Remove the retaining bolts and remove the slave cylinder.
5. Installation is the reverse of removal. Prime the cylinder with clean brake fluid before installing.

BLEEDING THE HYDRAULIC CLUTCH SYSTEM

When the slave cylinder is installed, the system must be bled. To bleed the system, fill the clutch portion of the fluid reservoir with clean brake fluid, then attach a hose to the bleed nipple on the slave cylinder and position the other end of the hose so that it is submerged in a partially filled container of brake fluid. Have an assistant pump up the clutch pedal several times, then open the bleed nipple with a wrench. Air bubbles will appear at the side of the hose submerged in the brake fluid. When the bubbles stop (with your assistant's foot still pressing on the clutch pedal), close the bleed nipple. Have your assistant pump up the pedal again and repeat the process until no bubbles

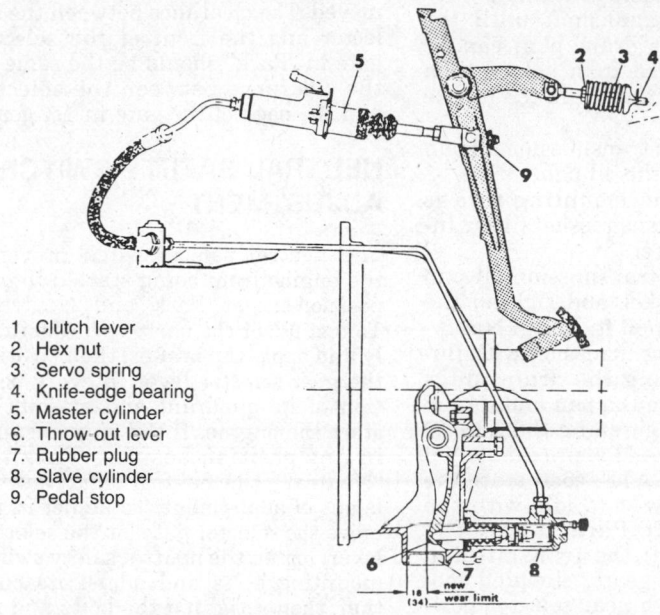

1. Clutch lever
2. Hex nut
3. Servo spring
4. Knife-edge bearing
5. Master cylinder
6. Throw-out lever
7. Rubber plug
8. Slave cylinder
9. Pedal stop

Hydraulic clutch assembly used on the 924 Turbo, 924S and 944 models

appear in the container, then close the bleed nipple and test the pedal. If the pedal feels spongy, there is probably still some air in the system. Repeat the bleeding procedure.

NOTE: During the bleeding process, make sure the fluid in the clutch section of the reservoir does not completely disappear or you'll be pumping the system up with air rather than liquid.

AUTOMATIC TRANSAXLE

REMOVAL & INSTALLATION

Removal and installation of the automatic transaxle is performed in the same manner as the previous "Manual Transmission Removal and Installation". Be sure to mark all linkage, etc. to facilitate the installation of the unit.

PAN REMOVAL AND FILTER SERVICE

The vehicle must be on a level surface when draining or refilling the transmission. Operate the vehicle until the transmission reaches normal operating temperature before servicing the pan and filter. Be careful, the fluid will be hot.

1. Remove the oil drain plug in the transmission oil pan and let the ATF drain into a suitable container.
2. Turn the crankshaft until the torque converter drain plug can be seen and removed from below, then remove the plug and drain the torque converter.
3. Remove the transmission oil pan bolts and lower the oil pan.
4. Remove the mounting screws and lower the transmission filter. Install the new filter.
5. Install the transmission oil pan with a new gasket and tighten the mounting bolts to 6 ft. lbs. (8 Nm).
6. Refill the transmission with fluid after installing the drain plugs with new seals in the pan and torque converter and tightening them to 10 ft. lbs. (14 Nm). Add approximately 6 qts. (5 liters) of ATF, then start the engine and allow it to idle with the shift selector in Park. Apply the brakes and shift the transmission through all the gears, stopping momentarily at each gear selector position. Recheck the fluid level and top off if necessary.

Replace the transmission filter by removing the mounting screws at the arrows

SHIFT LINKAGE ADJUSTMENT

1. Raise the vehicle and support it safely on jackstands.
2. Move the selector lever into the Park position.
3. Loosen the clamping bolt at the transmission lever.
4. Pull the transmission lever against the stop.
5. Tighten the clamping bolt with the lever in this position.

NOTE: When tightening the clamping bolt, make sure that the cable does not twist and that the transmission lever does not bend. The in-car selector lever must not touch the selector gate in either the "Park" or the "1" positions.

6. Apply the brakes while running the engine at idle and move the selector lever form "Park" to "Reverse", then from "Neutral" to "Drive". In each case the gear should engage within one second after the selector is moved. The clearance between the selector and the front of the selector gate in "Park" should be the same as the clearance between the selector and the back of the gate in 1st gear.

NEUTRAL SAFETY SWITCH ADJUSTMENT

The neutral safety switch prevents the engine from being started in any position except "Park" and "Neutral". To test it, set the parking brake firmly and apply the brakes, then position the gear selector lever in every position of its quadrant and attempt to start the engine. If the engine starts in any position besides "Park" or "Neutral", the neutral safety switch is out of adjustment. To adjust it, remove the selector gate for the selector lever, loosen the neutral safety switch mounting bolts and adjust its position, then retighten the bolts and repeat the test.

On 928 models, the neutral safety switch is mounted on the side of the transmission. To adjust it, first loosen the switch mounting bolts, then insert a locating pin made from 4mm diameter welding wire, or similar 4mm bar stock, through the lug and into the locating bore in the switch housing. Tighten the mounting bolts to 7 ft. lbs. (10 Nm) and remove the locating pin.

THROTTLE CABLE AND TRANSMISSION CABLE ADJUSTMENTS

1. Screw in the cable sleeve mounting nut on the transmission bracket completely and tighten.
2. Loosen the bolts on the roller holder bracket, push the roller holder in its slot forward (as seen from the driving direction) as far as possible and tighten the bolts.

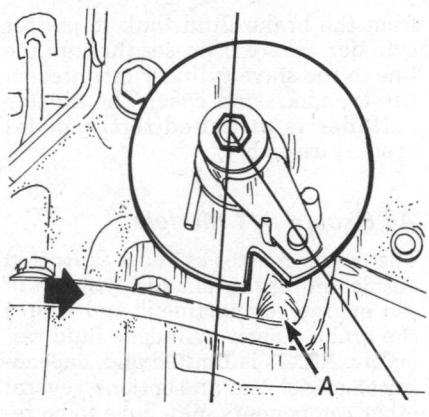

A. Reinforcement rib

On the 924, turn the roller so that the operating lever faces forward at an angle of 29°

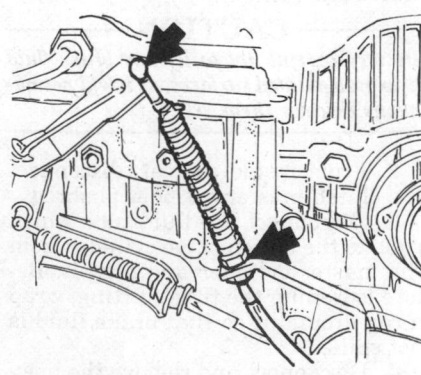

To adjust the throttle cable of the 924, screw in the cable sleeve mounting nut as far as possible on the bracket then tighten (lower arrow)

3. Completely loosen the short cable at the firewall and the long cable on the roller holder.

4. Turn the roller so that the operating lever faces forward at an angle of 29 degrees; in this position the opening for the cable locator will face the reinforcement rib of the holder.

5. Hold the roller in this position and mount the throttle valve push rod without tension on the rod.

6. Place the cable around the roller in the correct position and adjust the long cable sleeve until the cable locator just rests in the opening without tension.

7. Adjust the cable going to the accelerator pedal so that it does not have tension at the adjuster.

When the cable has been adjusted correctly, the accelerator peal will be in its neutral position (11 degrees 30 minutes inclination from the pedal stop), the throttle valve will be closed and the lever on the transmission will be on its bottom stop.

8. To check the full throttle position adjustment, depress the accelerator pedal to the first noticable pressure point and check whether the throttle valve is fully open.

9. To check the kickdown adjustment, depress the pedal past the full throttle pressure point until it comes against its stop and check to make sure the roller has lifted off the operating lever by about ¼ in. In this position the lever on the transmission should be resting on the final stop or at most about 1 degree away.

BAND ADJUSTMENTS

1981–82 924

NOTE: Adjust the band with the transmission positioned horizontally, or the band could jam. Only the second gear band is adjustable.

1. Locate the second gear band adjuster. It is on the driver's side of the case next to the selector levers.

2. Loosen the locknut and tighten the adjusting screw to 7 ft. lbs. (9.5 Nm).

3. Loosen the screw and tighten it to 4 ft. lbs. (5.5 Nm).

4. From this position, loosen the screw exactly 2½ turns and secure with the locknut.

All 1983–88 Models

Band adjustments are not required on the automatic transmission. No procedure is given by the manufacturer.

DRIVE AXLE

Halfshaft

REMOVAL & INSTALLATION

1981–88 911 Models

1. Raise the rear of the car and support it safely on jackstands.

2. Remove the wheels. Remove the brake caliper and disc.

3. Raise the trailing arm with a hydraulic jack.

4. Remove the lower shock absorber mounting.

5. Install a fixture similar to Porsche tool P36b to hold the hub.

6. Remove the cotter pin and, using a long ratchet handle extension, remove the hub nut.

7. Remove the Allen bolts at the axle driveshaft/transaxle flange.

8. Use a flat chisel to pry the flanges apart.

——— CAUTION ———
Don't damage the flanges when separating them.

9. Check the axle driveshaft joints for excessive play and replace them if necessary.

10. Use a new gasket on the transaxle flange. Ensure that the flanges are clean and free from burrs.

11. Pack the joints with a moly grease.

12. Install the axle driveshaft using a reverse of the removal procedure.

13. Tighten the flange bolts to 60 ft. lbs. (81.5 Nm). The hollow side of the lock washer should face the spacer slate.

14. Using a long extension handle wrench, tighten the castellated nut to 217–253 ft. lbs. (295–344 Nm) and install a new cotter pin.

NOTE: Be prepared to apply considerable force on this unit.

15. Tighten the shock absorber bolt to 54 ft. lbs. (73 Nm).

16. Install the brake caliper and disc.

17. Install the wheels and lower the car.

All Except 911 Models

1. Raise the rear of the car and support it safely on jackstands.

2. Remove the six star bolts on the inside joint at the transaxle.

3. Remove the six bolts at the stub axle. Use a wide, flat bladed prybar to pry the flanges apart.

4. Drop the axle driveshaft down and out on 924 and 944 models. On

Hub nut removal (Porsche tool P36b shown)

928 models, remove the axle from the upper left side of the hub assembly.

5. Pack the constant velocity joints with grease before installation.

6. Installation is the reverse of removal. Tighten the bolts to 30 ft. lbs. (41 Nm).

CV JOINT OVERHAUL

For all CV-joint overhaul procedures, please refer to "CV-Joint Overhaul" in the Unit Repair section.

FRONT SUSPENSION

Shock Absorbers

REMOVAL & INSTALLATION

1981–88 911 Models

1. Raise the front of the car and support it safely on jackstands. Remove the wheels.

2. Remove the brake line from the clip on the suspension strut. A small amount of brake fluid will run out of the line, plug it so that dirt cannot enter the system.

3. Unscrew the retaining bolts and remove the caliper.

4. Using a soft mallet, tap the hub cap to loosen it.

5. Pry the hubcap off with a small prybar.

6. Loosen the Allen screw in the wheel bearing clamp. Unscrew the clamp nut and remove the nut and washer.

7. Remove the wheel hub along with the brake disc and wheel bearing.

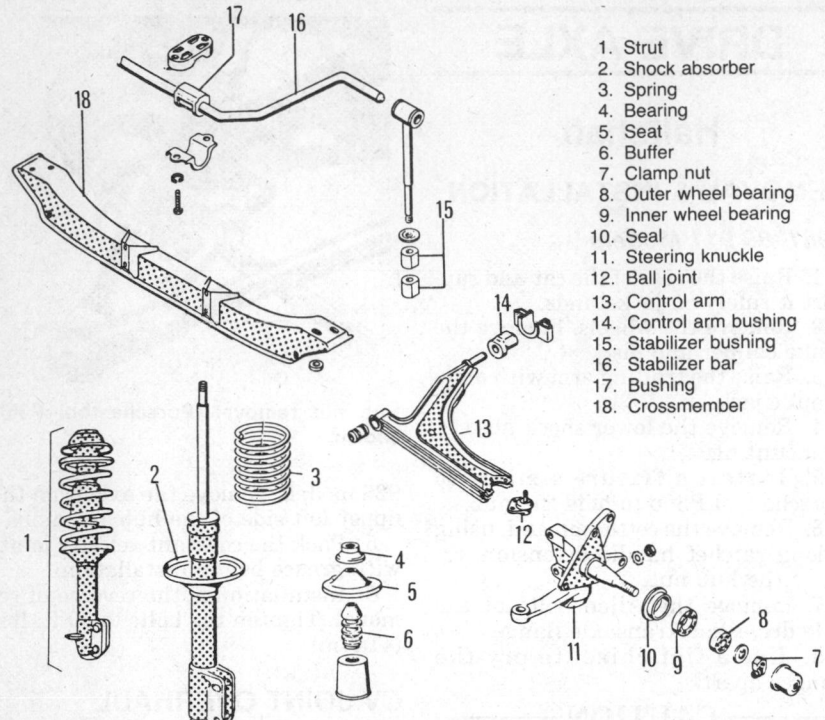

1. Strut
2. Shock absorber
3. Spring
4. Bearing
5. Seat
6. Buffer
7. Clamp nut
8. Outer wheel bearing
9. Inner wheel bearing
10. Seal
11. Steering knuckle
12. Ball joint
13. Control arm
14. Control arm bushing
15. Stabilizer bushing
16. Stabilizer bar
17. Bushing
18. Crossmember

Front suspension of the 924, 924 Turbo, and 944

8. Remove the backing plate retaining bolts and remove the plate.

9. Withdraw the cotter pin from the castellated nut on the tie rod end and remove the nut. Using a suitable puller, remove the tie rod joint from the strut.

10. Remove the control arm-to-strut ball joint retaining bolt and pull the ball joint out of the strut by pulling down on the lower control arm.

NOTE: The torsion bar adjusting screw will have to be loosened and the adjusting arm removed.

11. Remove the keeper for the nut on the top of the strut. Unscrew the nut and remove it, the keeper plate, and washer.

12. Remove the strut from the bottom. It will be necessary to loosen and pull the side of the luggage compartment out for clearance.

13. Check the shock absorber strut for excessive free travel and leaking. Replace the shock absorber if it is at all suspect.

14. Install the strut in a reverse order of the removal.

15. Tighten the top nut to 58 ft. lbs. (79 Nm). Use a new keeper plate and ensure that the peg on the plate is pointing up.

16. Tighten the ball joint nut to 47 ft. lbs. (64 Nm).

NOTE: Remember to install the washer between the ball joint seal and strut.

17. Install the torsion bar adjusting lever as described under "Torsion Bar Removal and Installation."

18. Tighten the tie rod nut to 33 ft. lbs. (45 Nm) and install a new cotter pin.

19. Torque the backing plate bolts to 18 ft. lbs. (24 Nm).

20. Install and adjust the wheel bearings.

21. Tighten the caliper retaining bolts to 50 ft. lbs. (68 Nm).

22. Bleed the brakes.

23. Install the wheels and lower the car.

24. Check the front wheel alignment.

MacPherson Strut

REMOVAL & INSTALLATION

1981–88 924, 924S and 944 Models

Front wheel alignment must be reset after a strut is removed.

1. Raise the front of the car and support it safely on jackstands.

2. Remove the brake line from the bracket on the strut.

3. Remove the two through bolts that retain the strut to the steering knuckle.

4. Remove the four retaining nuts from the inner fender in the engine compartment.

5. Pry the lower control arm down and remove the strut from the car.

6. To replace either the spring or shock absorber, place the strut in a spring compressor and remove the large retaining nut at the top.

7. Installation is the reverse of removal.

—————— **CAUTION** ——————

Any attempt to remove the retaining nut without a suitable spring compressor can result in serious injury.

1981–88 928, 928S and 928S4

1. Remove the self-locking nuts on the upper strut mount, located on the inner fender panel.

2. Remove the front wheel. Remove the flange locknut and press the upper ball joint from the spindle carrier.

3. Remove the inner pivot shaft nuts from the upper control arm.

4. Remove the shock absorber mounting bolts and remove the shock and upper arm as an assembly.

OVERHAUL

For all spring and shock absorber removal and installation procedures, and all strut overhaul procedures, please refer to "Strut Overhaul" in the Unit Repair section.

Torsion Bars

REMOVAL & INSTALLATION

1981–88 911 Models

1. Raise the front of the car and support it safely with jackstands.

2. Remove the torsion bar adjusting screw.

3. Take the adjusting lever off the torsion bar and withdraw the seal.

4. Unscrew the retaining bolts from the front mount cover bracket and remove the bracket.

5. Using a drift, carefully drive the torsion bar out of the front of the arm.

6. Check the torsion bar for spline damage and rust. If necessary, replace the bar.

7. Give the torsion bar a light coating of grease before installing it.

NOTE: Torsion bars are marked "L" and "R" to identify them and are not interchangeable.

8. Insert the end cap of the torsion bar, protruding side out, into the control arm. Drive the torsion bar into position with a drift. Carefully.

9. Tighten the retaining bolts on the front mount to 34 ft. lbs. (46 Nm).

Ball Joint

INSPECTION

With the front wheels in the straight-ahead position, insert a suitable prybar between the control arm and wheel rim. Insert a vernier caliper between the upper edge of the control arm and lower edge of the steering knuckle mounting bolt and measure the distance. Press down on the prybar to lever out the play, then check the distance again with the caliper. The wear limit is 1.5mm.

REMOVAL & INSTALLATION

1981–88 911 Models

See the procedure under "Front Shock Absorber Removal & Installation" for ball joint removal and replacement.

1981–82 924 and 924 Turbo
1983–88 924S and 944 Models

1. Remove the lower control arm.
2. Drill out the the rivets retaining the ball joint to the control arm.
3. Install the replacement ball joint using the bolts and nuts supplied in the kit.
4. Reinstall the control arm and align the front wheels.

1981–88 928, 928S and 928S4

NOTE: The front wheels must be realigned after the suspension work is done.

The upper ball joint is replaced as a unit with the upper arm assembly. Refer to the "Strut Removal and Installation" procedure. The lower ball joint may be replaced by removing the nut from the ball joint stud and pressing the stud from the spindle. The alignment eccentric bolts are removable and the ball joint can be removed from the lower arm assembly.

Upper Control Arm

REMOVAL & INSTALLATION

1981–88 928, 928S and 928S4

The upper control arm can be removed after first removing the MacPherson Strut assembly and disconnecting the ball joint from the steering knuckle. See the "MacPherson Strut Removal & Installation" procedures. When installing, tighten the upper control arm-to-body nuts to 101 ft. lbs. (140 Nm) and the upper control arm-to-steering knuckle nut to 47 ft. lbs. (65 Nm).

1. Upper control arm
2. Lower control arm support
3. Lower control arm
4. Lower shock mount
5. Lower ball joint
6. Caster eccentric (outer), camber eccentric (inner)
7. Stabilizer bar
8. Bushing
9. Link
10. Steering knuckle
11. Inner front wheel seal
12. Inner front wheel bearing
13. Outer front wheel bearing
14. Upper shock mount
15. Upper spring seat
16. Spring
17. Suspension stop
18. Lower spring seat
19. Shock absorber

Exploded view of the 928 and 928S front suspension

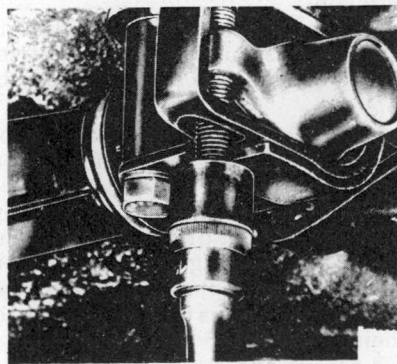

Torsion bar adjusting screw on 911 models

10. Slide the seal onto the torsion bar from the open side of the crossmember.
11. Using a tire iron, or other suitable lever, pry the control arm down as far as possible. While holding the control arm, slide the adjusting lever onto the splines of the torsion bar. There should only be a slight amount of clearance at the lever adjusting point.
12. Grease the adjusting screw threads with a moly grease and hand tighten the screw.
13. Check that the end cap is properly seated in the control arm.

14. Install the rubber mount cover bracket. Tighten the retaining bolts to 34 ft. lbs. (46 Nm).
15. Lower the car.
16. Check the front wheel alignment.

Stabilizer Bar

REMOVAL & INSTALLATION

1981–88 911 Models

1. Raise the front of the car and support it safely on jackstands.
2. Loosen the stabilizer clamp bolts and pry the lever ends off their mounts.
3. Remove the stabilizer bar along with the levers.
4. Check the rubber bushings for deterioration and, if necessary, replace them. Lubricate the bushings with glycerine or some other rubber preservative. Do not use oil or grease for lubrication.
5. Install the stabilizer bar in a reverse order of the removal.
6. The square end of the stabilizer should protrude slightly above the clamp. Tighten the clamp nuts to 18 ft. lbs. (24 Nm).

Lower Control Arm

REMOVAL & INSTALLATION

1981–82 924 and 924 Turbo
1983–88 924S and 944 Models

1. Raise the front of the car and support it safely on jackstands.
2. Remove the thru-bolts at the front that retain the control arm to the suspension crossmember.
3. Detach the stabilizer bar from the control arm.
4. Remove the two bolts that retain the control arm bracket at the rear.
5. Remove the ball joint pinch bolt at the steering knuckle.
6. Pry the control arm down and remove it from the car.
7. Installation is the reverse of removal. Caster must be reset after the control arm has been removed.

1981–88 928, 928S and 928S4

NOTE: The front wheels must be aligned upon completion of the installation.

1. Raise and support the vehicle safely, then remove the wheel.
2. Mark the alignment eccentrics on the lower arm for approximate installation location, if the ball joint is to be removed.
3. Remove the strut bottom link bracket and stabilizer link bolt.
4. Remove the lower ball joint stud nut and press the stud from the spindle. Move the spindle and upper arm upward and block it to gain working clearance.
5. Remove the bolts from the tie-down bracket and control arm bracket. Lower the control arm from the vehicle.
6. The lower ball joint can be replaced, if necessary, while the lower arm is out of the vehicle.
7. Installation is the reverse of removal.

Front Wheel Bearings

ADJUSTMENT

1981–88 911 Models

Check and adjust the front wheel bearings after the car has not been run for a few hours. The bearings will be cold then.

1. The front wheel bearings are correctly adjusted when the thrust washer can be moved slightly sideways under light pressure from a small prybar, but no bearing play is evident when the wheel hub is shaken axially.
2. Raise the front of the car, sup-

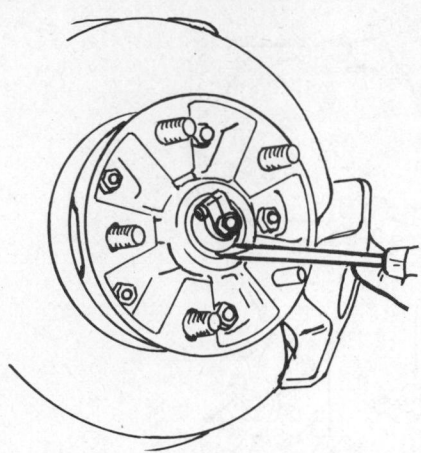

Checking wheel bearing play on 911 models

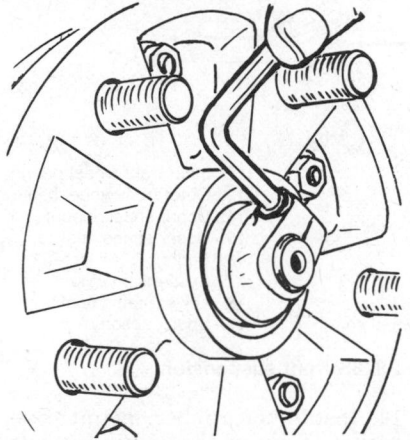

Final tightening of the wheel clamp nut on 911 models. Check the play again before installing the hub cap

port it on jackstands, and remove the wheels. Turn the hub several times to seat the bearings.

3. Pry the hub cap off and perform the check described in Step 1.

NOTE: Don't press the prybar against the hub. Hold it lightly in your hand so you get a better feel.

4. If the bearings require an adjustment, loosen the Allen screw and turn the clamp nut in or out as necessary.
5. Tighten the clamp nut Allen screw to 11 ft. lbs. (15 Nm) without altering the adjusted position of the clamp nut.
6. Double check the adjustment and readjust, if necessary.
7. Give the clamp nut and thrust washer a light coating of lithium grease. Tap the hub cap into place with a plastic or rubber mallet.
8. Install the wheels and lower the car.

All Except 911 Models

The front wheel bearings are correct-ly adjusted when the thrust washer can be moved slightly sideways under light pressure, but no bearing play is evident when the wheel hub is shaken axially.

1. Raise the front of the vehicle and remove the wheels.
2. Pry the hub cap off and perform the check as described above. Don't press against the hub.
3. If the bearings require an adjustment, loosen the Allen screw and turn the clamp nut. Proper adjustment is achieved when the flat washer can just be moved by finger pressure on a screwdriver.
4. Tighten the clamp nut Allen screw to 11 ft. lbs. (15 Nm) without altering the adjusted position of the clamp nut.

REMOVAL & INSTALLATION

1981–88 911 Models

NOTE: The inner bearing, seal, and outer bearing may be removed and lubricated once the hub/disc assembly is off the car. If after cleaning, the bearings are noticeably worn or damaged they should be replaced along with their races. If the bearings are satisfactory, skip the race removal steps.

1. Remove the brake disc/hub assembly.
2. Match mark the hub and disc for correct reassembly, remove the five assembly bolts, and separate the hub and disc.
3. Pry the inner seal out of the hub. Remove the inner bearing and outer bearing.
4. Wash the bearings in solvent and blow them dry. Examine the bearings for pitting, scoring, or other damage. Replace the bearing and race as a unit if there is any question as to their condition.
5. Heat the wheel hub to 250–300°F.
6. Press the inner bearing race out of the hub on a press table, using suitable spacers to prevent damaging the hub.
7. Press out the outer bearing race, using suitable spacers and a support fabricated from the accompanying drawing.
8. Press a new inner bearing race into the hub and then press in a new outer bearing race.
9. Pack the bearings with a lithium multipurpose grease.
10. Align the match marks and install the hub in the disc. Insert the assembly bolts from the inside out and tighten them to 17 ft. lbs. (23 Nm).
11. Lightly coat the spindle with

grease. Fill the hub with about 2 oz of grease. Lubricate and install the bearings.

12. Grease the sealing edges of a new inner oil seal and carefully tap it into place. The oil seal must be flush with the hub.

13. Install the hub/disc assembly on the car.

14. Adjust the wheel bearings as previously described.

All Except 911 Models

1. Raise the front of the vehicle and support it safely with jackstands.

2. Remove the front wheels.

3. Remove the bearing hub cap.

4. Pry out the seal with a suitable prybar, being careful not to damage the sealing surface in the process.

5. Match mark the hub and disc for correct reassembly, remove the five assembly bolts, and separate the hub and disc. Pry the inner seal out of the hub. Remove the inner bearing and outer bearing.

6. Wash the bearings in solvent and blow them dry. Examine the bearings for pitting, scoring, or other damage. Replace the bearing and race as a unit if there is any question as to their condition.

7. Heat the wheel hub to 250–300°F.

8. Press the inner bearing race out of the hub on a press table, using suitable spacers to prevent damaging the hub.

10. Press out the outer bearing race, using suitable spacers and a support.

11. Press a new inner bearing race into the hub and then press in a new outer bearing race.

12. Pack the bearings with a lithium multipurpose grease.

13. Align the match marks and install the hub in the disc. Insert the assembly bolts from the inside out and tighten them to 7 ft. lbs. (10 Nm).

14. Lightly coat the spindle with grease. Fill the hub with about 2 oz of grease. Lubricate and install the bearings.

15. Grease the sealing edges of a new inner oil seal and carefully tap it into place. The oil seal must be flush with the hub.

16. Install the hub/disc assembly on the car.

17. Adjust the wheel bearings as previously described.

Front Wheel Alignment

CAMBER ADJUSTMENT

911 Models

Camber is adjusted at the top of the

Caster and camber adjustment locations on 911 models

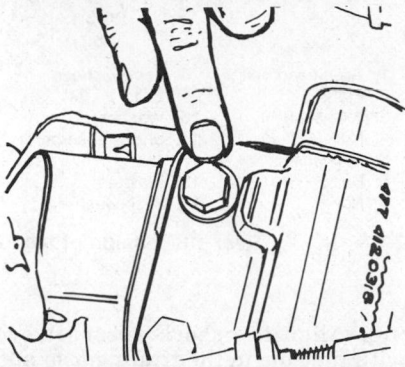

Camber is adjusted at the upper strut eccentric on the 924, 924 Turbo, and 944

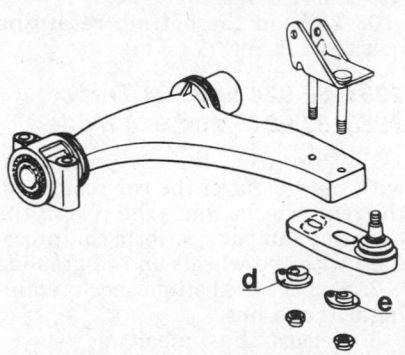

Front suspension caster (e) and camber (d) adjustment eccentrics on the 928 and 928S

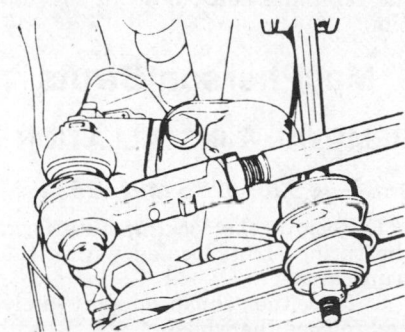

Tie rod ends are adjustable for toe (924 shown, others similar)

strut. Pull back the luggage compartment rug to expose the three mounting bolts. Scrape the undercoating from the bolts and plates. Scribe the positions of the two plates under the

Caster is adjusted at the lower control arm mounting on the 924, 924 Turbo, and 944

bolts. Loosen the bolts and move the strut in or out as necessary to correct the camber angle.

924, 924 Turbo, 924S and 944 Models

Camber is adjusted at the upper strut-to steering knuckle retaining bolt.

928, 928S and 928S4 Models

Camber is adjusted by turning the cam bolts on the inner arm bushings.

CASTER ADJUSTMENT

911 Models

Caster is adjusted in the same manner as camber, except that the strut is moved forward or backward to change the caster angle.

All Except 911 Models

Caster is adjusted by loosening the two control arm-to-crossmember bolts and moving the control arm laterally. 1983–88 928 models have the slots for adjusting the caster eccentrics sealed with an elastic sealing compound. This compound must be removed to make camber adjustment, then replace after adjustment to prevent the entry of dirt which could make adjusting difficult.

TOE-IN ADJUSTMENT

911 Models

Toe-in is set with the front wheels straight ahead. Tie rod length is adjusted by loosening the tie rod clamps and moving them an equal amount in or out to obtain the correct toe-in.

924, 924 Turbo, 924S and 944

Toe-in is set by loosening the locknuts on the tie rod ends and turning them in or out as necessary.

928 and 928S

Toe-in adjustments are made by turning cam bolts, located at the rear of the front control arms.

REAR SUSPENSION

Shock Absorbers

REMOVAL & INSTALLATION

1981–88 911 Models

1. Leave the car standing on the ground, or back it onto low ramps, so that the shock absorber is not tensioned.
2. Open the engine compartment

Bottom rear shock absorber mount on 911 models

Top rear shock absorber mount on 911 models

lid and remove the rubber cover from the top of the shock absorber.
3. Hold the shock absorber shaft and remove the nut.
4. On the bottom, remove the retaining nut and bolt.
5. Remove the shock absorber.
6. If the shock exhibits excessive free travel or is leaking, replace it.
7. Install the shock up through the body and screw the nut on hand-tight.

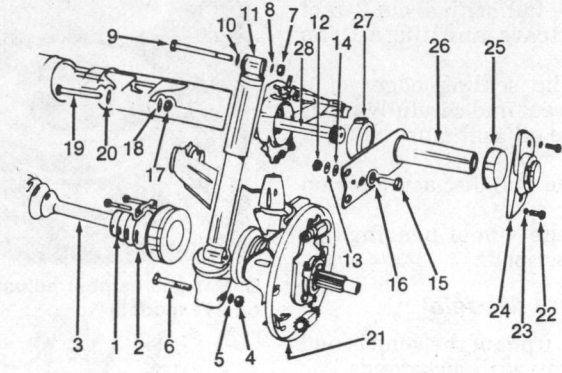

1. Allen head bolt	8. Lockwasher	15. Bolt	22. Bolt
2. Plate	9. Bolt	16. Plain washer	23. Lockwasher
3. Axle shaft	10. Washer	17. Nut, self-locking	24. Cover
4. Nut	11. Shock absorber	18. Plain washer	25. Rubber mount, outer
5. Lockwasher	12. Nut	19. Bolt	26. Torsion plate
6. Bolt	13. Washer	20. Plain washer	27. Rubber mount, inner
7. Nut	14. Plain washer	21. Trailing arm	28. Torsion bar

Rear suspension of the 924 and 924 Turbo (944 similar)

8. Align the shock absorber eye with the hole in the trailing arm and install the nut and bolt.
9. Tighten the top nut and install the rubber cover.
10. Tighten the bottom retaining bolt to 54 ft. lbs. (73 Nm).

1981–82 924 and 924 Turbo 1983–88 924S and 944 Models

1. This procedure is performed with the weight of the car resting on the rear wheels. Raise the rear of the car using ramps or perform this procedure with the wheels on the ground.
2. Remove the bottom shock retaining bolt and nut.
3. Remove the top bolt.
4. Remove the shock absorber.
5. Install the replacement shock in the reverse order of removal. Tighten the retaining bolts to 50 ft. lbs. (68 Nm).

MacPherson Struts

REMOVAL & INSTALLATION

1981–88 928, 928S and 928S4

1. Remove the locking nuts form the spring strut, located within the trunk area.
2. Raise the vehicle, support safely and remove the wheel.
3. Remove the front nut on the outer pivot pin rod and remove the pivot rod from the rubber bushings.
4. Disconnect the stabilizer bar link from the lower control arm.
5. Remove the spring strut form the vehicle.
6. Installation is the reverse of removal.

NOTE: The spring can be removed from the shock unit with the use of a spring clamping tool. An adjusting nut and sleeve is used to control the vehicle rear height.

OVERHAUL

For all spring and shock absorber removal and installation procedures, and all strut overhaul procedures, please refer to "Strut Overhaul" in the Unit Repair section.

Torsion Bars

REMOVAL & INSTALLATION

1981–88 911 Models

1. Raise the rear of the car and support it safely with jackstands.
2. Remove the wheel on the side where the torsion bar is being removed.
3. Fabricate a fixture similar to the one shown. The fixture is necessary to hold the trailing arm while it is raised and lowered. The special Porsche tool for this purpose is number P 289.
4. Using a hydraulic jack under the holding fixture, raise the trailing arm.
5. Remove the lower shock absorber bolt.
6. Remove the trailing arm retaining bolts. Remove the toe and chamber adjusting bolts.
7. Remove the four retaining bolts from the trailing arm cover. Withdraw the spacer.

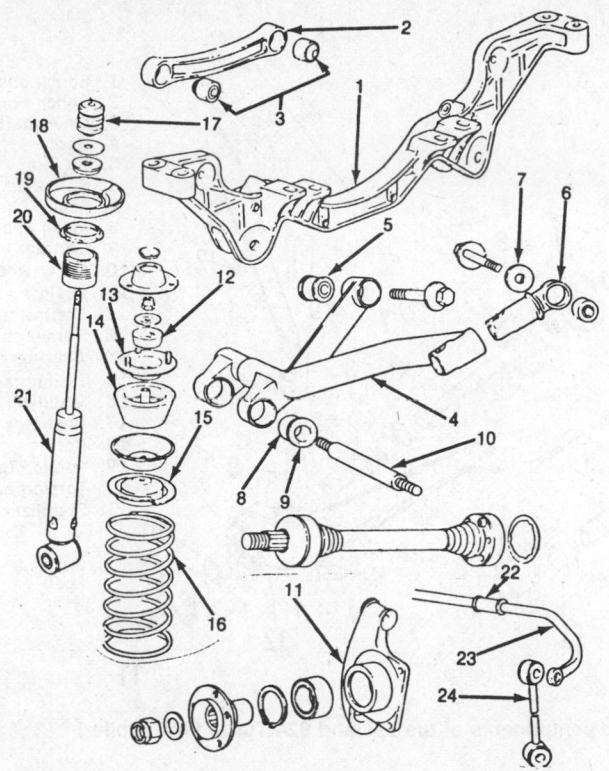

Installing the trailing arm cover on 911 models

1. Rear axle crossmember
2. Upper strut
3. Upper strut bushings
4. Lower control arm
5. Lower control arm inner bushing
6. Lower control arm rocker mount
7. Lower control eccentric
8. Lower control arm outer bushing
9. Cone washer
10. Pivot pin
11. Wheel bearing carrier
12. Upper shock mount
13. Shock mount retainer
14. Lower shock mount
15. Upper spring mount
16. Coil spring
17. Shock bumper
18. Lower spring seat
19. Suspension height adjuster
20. Flange
21. Shock absorber
22. Stabilizer bar mount
23. Stabilizer bar
24. Link

Exploded view of the 928 and 928S rear suspension

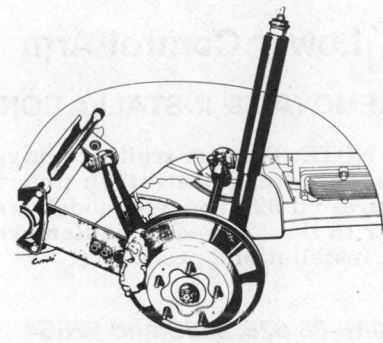

Typical rear suspension on 911 models

Raising the trailing arm on 911 models

8. Using two small prybars, pry off the trailing arm cover.

9. Remove the holding fixture.

10. Knock out the round body plug and remove the trailing arm.

11. Paint a reference mark on the torsion bar support, matching the location of the "L" or "R" side identification letter, so that the torsion bar may be installed in the same position.

NOTE: The torsion bars are splined to allow adjustment of the rear riding height.

12. Remove the torsion bar. Do not scratch the protective paint on the torsion bar, or it will corrode and possible develop fatigue cracks.

NOTE: If you are removing a broken torsion bar, the inner end can be knocked from its seat by removing the opposite torsion bar

and tapping through with a steel rod. Torsion bars are not interchangeable from side-to-side and are marked "L" and "R" for identification.

13. Check the torsion bar splines for damage and replace if necessary. If any corrosion is present on the bar, replace it.

14. Coat the torsion bar lightly with a multipurpose grease. Carefully grease the splines.

15. Apply glycerine or another rubber preservative to the torsion bar support.

16. Install the torsion bar, matching the "L" or "R" with the paint mark you made before removal.

17. Install the trailing arm cover into position and start the three accessible bolts.

18. Raise the trailing arm into place with the holding fixture (or special tool P 289) until the spacer and the fourth bolt can be installed.

19. Assemble the remaining components in a reverse order of their removal.

20. Tighten the trailing arm cover bolts to 34 ft. lbs. (46 Nm). Tighten the trailing arm retaining bolts to 65 ft. lbs. (88 Nm).

21. Tighten the camber adjusting bolt to 43 ft. lbs. (58 Nm) and the toe-in adjusting bolt to 36 ft. lbs. (49 Nm). Tighten the shock absorber bolt to 45 ft. lbs. (61 Nm).

22. Adjust the rear wheel camber and toe-in.

1981–82 924 and 924 Turbo 1983–88 924S and 944 Models

NOTE: This procedure requires that the rear wheel camber and toe-in be checked and adjusted as the final step.

1. Raise the rear of the car and support it safely on jackstands.

2. Remove the wheel on the side

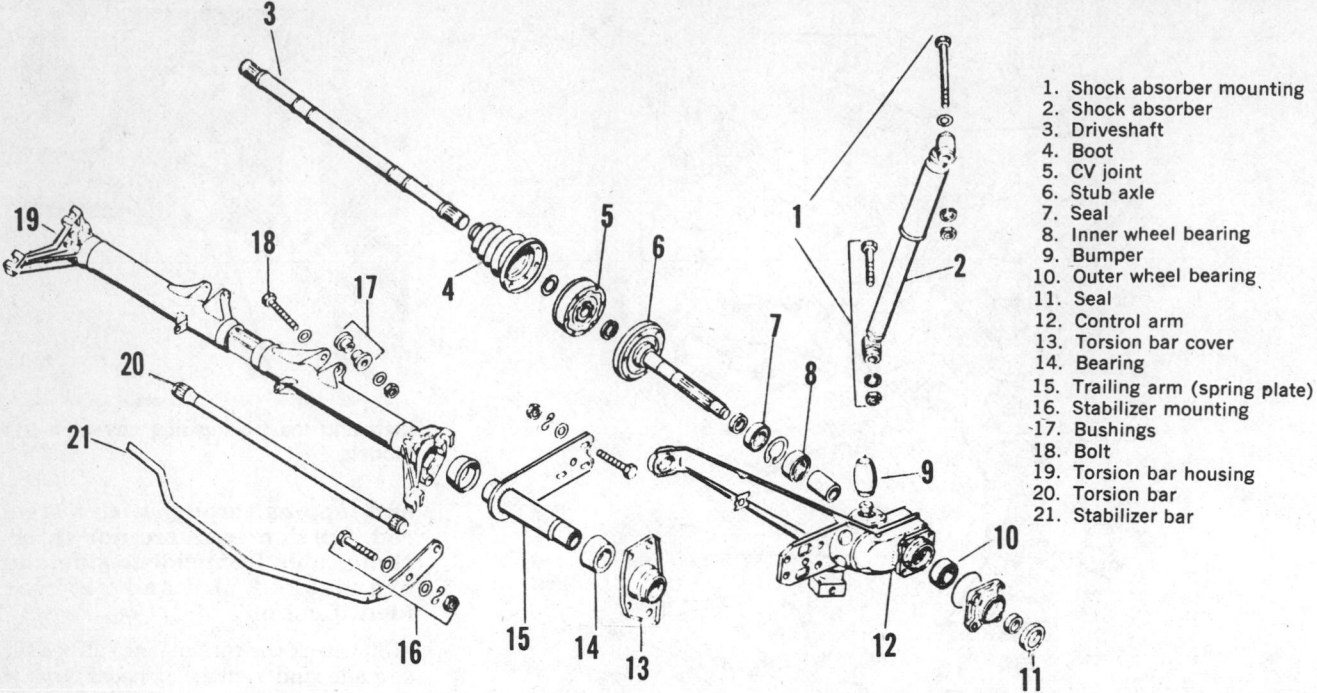

1. Shock absorber mounting
2. Shock absorber
3. Driveshaft
4. Boot
5. CV joint
6. Stub axle
7. Seal
8. Inner wheel bearing
9. Bumper
10. Outer wheel bearing
11. Seal
12. Control arm
13. Torsion bar cover
14. Bearing
15. Trailing arm (spring plate)
16. Stabilizer mounting
17. Bushings
18. Bolt
19. Torsion bar housing
20. Torsion bar
21. Stabilizer bar

Rear control arm and related components of the 924 and 924 Turbo (944 similar)

where the torsion bar is being removed.

3. Using a hydraulic jack and a block of wood with a slot cut in it, raise the trailing arm.

4. Remove the lower shock absorber bolt.

5. Remove the trailing arm retaining bolts, then remove the toe and camber adjusting bolts.

6. Remove the four retaining bolts from the trailing arm cover.

7. Pry off the trailing arm cover.

8. Lower the jack.

9. Remove the round body plug and remove the trailing arm.

10. Paint a reference mark on the torsion bar support, matching the location of the "L" or "R" side identification letter, so that the torsion bar may be installed in the same position.

NOTE: The torsion bars are splined to allow adjustment of the rear riding height.

11. Remove the torsion bar. Do not scratch the protective paint on the torsion bar, or it will corrode and possibly develop fatigue cracks.

NOTE: If you are removing a broken torsion bar, the inner end can be knocked from its seat by removing the opposite torsion bar and tapping it through with a steel bar. Torsion bars are not interchangeable from side to side and are marked "L" and "R" for identification.

12. Check the torsion bar splines for damage and replace the bar if necessary. If there is any corrosion on the bar, replace it.

13. Coat the torsion bar lightly with grease. Carefully grease the splines.

14. apply glycerine or another rubber preservative to the torsion bar support.

15. Install the torsion bar, matching the L or R with the paint mark you made before removal.

16. Install the trailing arm cover into position and start the three accessible bolts.

17. Raise the trailing arm into place with a jack and wooden block until the spacer and the fourth bolt can be installed.

18. Assemble the remaining components in the reverse order of their removal.

19. tighten the trailing arm cover bolts to 25 ft. lbs. (34 Nm). Tighten the shock absorber bolt to 50 ft. lbs. (68 Nm).

20. Adjust rear wheel camber and toe in.

Upper Control Arm

REMOVAL & INSTALLATION

1981–88 928, 928S and 928S4

1. Raise the vehicle and support it safely on jackstands. Remove the rear

wheels and support the lower arm assembly with a jack.

2. Loosen and remove the inner and outer bolts from the upper arm ends.

3. Remove the upper arm from the rear crossmember and from the rear flexible mount. The bushings are replaceable.

4. Installation is the reverse of removal.

Lower Control Arm

REMOVAL & INSTALLATION

NOTE: For rear trailing arm removal and installation procedures on 924 and 944 models, refer to the "Torsion Bar Removal & Installation" procedure.

1981–88 928, 928S and 928S4

1. Raise the vehicle and support it safely on jackstands. Remove the rear wheels.

2. Support the hub assembly and the spring strut with a hydraulic jack.

3. Remove the outer pivot pins nuts and washers. Disconnect the stabilizer bar link.

4. Remove the inner pivot bolts from the hub assembly and the spring strut. The bushings are replaceable.

5. Installation is the reverse of removal.

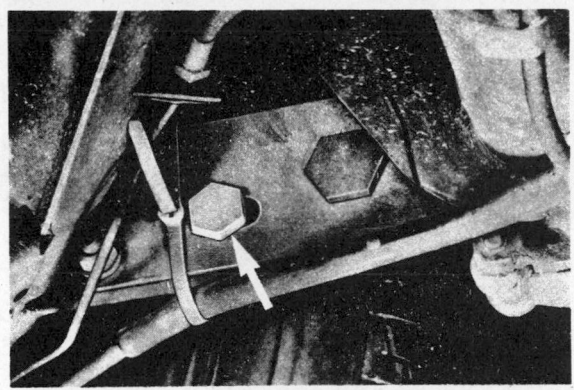

Rear camber adjustment on the 944

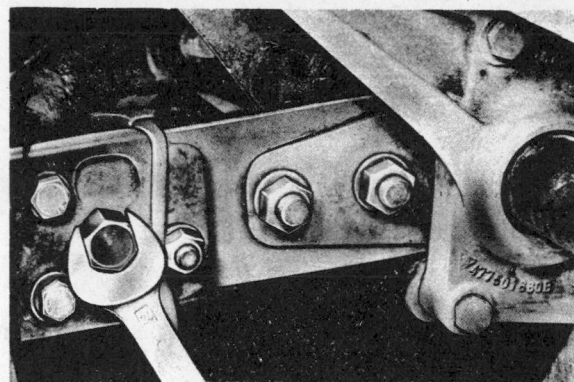

Rear toe-in adjustment on the 944

Rear wheel alignment points of the 924 and 924 Turbo. Loosen the fasteners (arrows) to alter the camber and toe-in

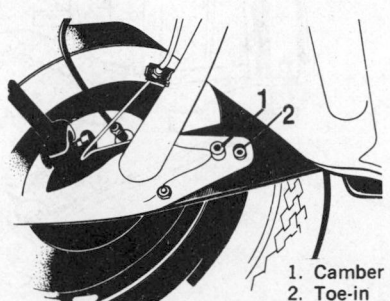

1. Camber
2. Toe-in

Rear wheel alignment adjustment points on 911 models

Steering wheel center cover removal on 911 models

Stabilizer

REMOVAL & INSTALLATION

1981–88 911 Models

1. Raise the rear of the car and safely support it with stands.
2. Using a large prybar, pry the upper eyes of the stabilizer bar off the studs in the trailing arm.
3. Remove the body mounting brackets.
4. Remove the stabilizer.
5. Check the rubber bushings for wear or damage and, if necessary, replace them.
6. Installation is the reverse of removal.

Rear Wheel Alignment

CAMBER ADJUSTMENT

911 Models

The rear-most of the two Allen bolts on the trailing arm provides camber adjustment. Tighten the bolt to 43 ft. lbs. (58 Nm) after the camber is adjusted to specifications.

All Except 911 Models

Rear wheel camber is adjusted by changing the trailing arm spring plate setting. To increase positive camber, loosen the spring plate-to-trailing arm bolts (with the wheels on the ground). To increase negative camber, do so with car on a hoist. Tighten bolts after adjustment to 66 ft. lbs. (90 Nm).

TOE-IN ADJUSTMENT

911 Models

The front Allen bolt on the trailing arm adjusts the toe-in. Tighten the bolt to 36 ft. lbs. (49 Nm) after toe-in is adjusted to specification.

All Except 911 Models

Rear wheel toe-in is adjusted by moving the control arm in the slots of the spring plates.

STEERING

Steering Wheel

REMOVAL & INSTALLATION

911 Models

1. Disconnect the battery(ies). Place the wheels in a straight ahead position.
2. Twist the center cover to the left and remove it.

3. Remove the horn contact pin.
4. Remove the steering wheel nut.
5. Mark the steering wheel and the shaft so that it can be reinstalled in the same position.
6. Remove the steering wheel. Catch the bearing support ring and spring.
7. Install the spring and bearing support ring on the wheel hub.
8. Lightly grease the horn contact ring.
9. Install the wheel. Make sure that you align the match marks before removal.
10. Tighten the steering wheel nut to 58 ft. lbs. (79 Nm).
11. Twist the center cover back on to the right to snap it into place.

All Except 911 Models

1. Disconnect the negative battery cable.
2. Remove horn pad and straighten the front wheels.
3. If necessary, disconnect the horn wiring. Matchmark the steering wheel to the steering shaft.
4. Remove retaining nut and washer.
5. Use a suitable steering wheel puller to remove the wheel.

— **CAUTION** —
Do NOT strike the steering wheel!

6. Installation is the reverse of removal. Align the matchmarks on the wheel and shaft made in Step 3. Make sure the wheels are straight ahead and steering wheel is centered, then torque steering wheel nut to 33–36 ft. lbs. (45–49 Nm).

Turn Signal Switch

REMOVAL & INSTALLATION

911 Models

The combination turn signal, headlight dimmer, and flasher switch is located in the steering column housing. The wiper/washer switch removal and installation procedure is identical.

1. Remove the steering wheel as outlined above.
2. Reach under the instrument panel and disconnect all wiring to the switch.
3. Remove the two horn contact ring screws, disconnect the wire, and remove the ring.
4. Remove the two upper housing retaining nuts. Pull the entire assembly off the column, leading the switch wires through the hole in the housing.
5. Remove the three retaining screws and remove the switch.
6. Reverse the removal steps to reinstall the switch.

All Except 911 Models

1. Disconnect the negative battery cable.
2. Remove the steering wheel as previously described.
3. Disconnect the wire harness connector at the switch.
4. Remove the four screws holding the switch to the steering column and remove the switch.
5. Install in reverse of the removal procedure. Do not overtighten the mounting screws.

Ignition Lock and Switch

REMOVAL & INSTALLATION

911 Models

1. Disconnect the negative battery cable and remove the ignition switch cover.
2. Drill out the two shear bolts which retain the switch.
3. Remove the steering lock and spacer.
4. Disconnect the wire harness connector and remove the switch.
5. Install the new ignition switch/steering lock into position on the steering column.
6. Insert the protective plate.

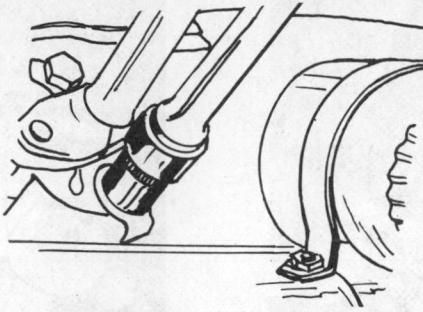

Disconnecting the steering coupling on 911 models

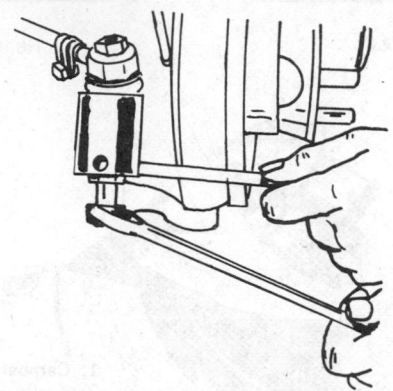

Removing the tie-rod ends on 911 models

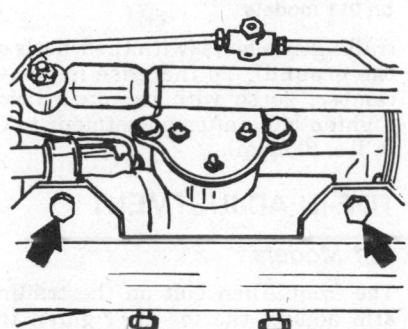

Rack and pinion retaining bolts on 911 models

7. Install and evenly tighten the new shear bolts until the heads break off.
8. Install the ignition switch cover and reconnect the negative battery cable.

All Except 911 Models

1. Disconnect the negative battery cable.
2. Remove steering wheel as previously described.
3. Drill out the casing tube shear bolts, then disconnect the wire harness connectors and pull the column and casing out of the car.
4. Remove the pinch bolt holding the switch housing to the column.
6. Remove the retaining screw and pull the ignition switch from the rear of the casing.

7. Depress the lock cylinder retainer with an ice pick or similar tool and remove the lock cylinder.
8. Installation is the reverse of removal. Make sure the wheels are straight ahead and steering wheel is centered when installing. Tighten the shear bolts until the heads break off.

Steering Gear

REMOVAL & INSTALLATION

911 Models

1. Remove the front luggage compartment carpeting. Raise the front of the car and support it safely with jackstands.
2. Remove the auxiliary heater duct from the steering post and position it to one side.
3. Open the access door and the intermediate steering shaft cover by prying the spring clips off with a small prybar.
4. Remove the three heater/fuel pump retaining bolts and position the pump to one side.
5. Remove the cotter pin from the lower universal joint bolt and loosen the castellated nut. Pull the universal joint off the steering shaft.
6. Remove the Allen bolts from the steering shaft bushing bracket. Remove the bracket and pull the bushing and dust cover.
7. Loosen and remove the steering coupling bolts.
8. Remove the retaining bolts and remove the bottom shield.
9. Remove the cotter pins and nuts, and then pull the tie rod ends out of the suspension struts with a suitable puller.
10. Remove the two rack and pinion housing retaining bolts.
11. Remove the right side crossmember brace.
12. Pull the steering assembly out the right side of the car.
13. Remove the retaining bolts from the tie rod yokes.
14. Installation is the reverse of the removal procedure.
15. Tighten the yoke bolts to 34 ft. lbs. (46 Nm).
16. Make sure that the crossmember brace mounts without binding. Tighten the nuts to 47 ft. lbs. (64 Nm) and the bolts to 34 ft. lbs. (46 Nm).
17. Install the steering housing bolts with new lockwashers and tighten to 34 ft. lbs. (46 Nm).
18. Tighten the tie rod end nuts to 33 ft. lbs. (45 Nm) and install new cotter pins.
19. Tighten the steering bushing bracket Allen bolts to 18 ft. lbs. (24 Nm).

20. Install new washers on the steering coupling bolts and tighten them to 18 ft. lbs. (24 Nm).
21. Lower the car.

All Except 911 Models

1. Raise the front of the car and support it safely. Remove the front wheels and splash shield.
2. Remove the stabilizer by disconnecting the stabilizer mounts on the control arms and stabilizer suspension on the side members.
3. Disconnect the ground wire on the front axle crossmember. Remove the bolt connecting gear box to steering column driveshaft.
2. Disconnect and press out the tie rod ends from the steering knuckles. Disconnect the power steering fluid lines at the pump, if equipped, and cap the ends to prevent contamination by dirt during service.
3. Remove the four mounting bolts and remove the steering gear and tie rods from the car.
4. Remove the tie rods from the steering gear on a workbench, if necessary.
5. To install, reverse the above. Center steering gear with Porsche special tool No. 9116 or its equivalent. Be sure that both tie rod lengths are equal (68–68.5mm). Tighten tie rod counter nuts to 29 ft. lbs. (39 Nm) and gear box to driveshaft bolt to 23 ft. lbs. (31 Nm). If equipped with power steering, tighten the fluid line connections to 14 ft. lbs. (20 Nm) and bleed the system as described below.

ADJUSTMENT

Tighten adjusting screw (on front of gear box) until it just touches the washer. Hold adjusting screw tightly and tighten locknut.

Power Steering Pump

REMOVAL & INSTALLATION

924 and 944 Models

1. Remove the lower engine splash shield.
2. Disconnect the fluid lines on the power steering pump. Catch the escaping fluid in a suitable container and discard. Do not reuse power steering fluid.
3. Unscrew the connecting rod on the power steering pump and nut, then turn the connecting rod down.
4. Remove the mounting bolts from the pump housing and remove the drive belt.
5. Raise the power steering pump in its bracket and remove the spacer from below.

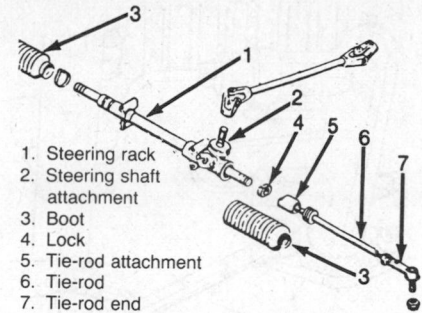

1. Steering rack
2. Steering shaft attachment
3. Boot
4. Lock
5. Tie-rod attachment
6. Tie-rod
7. Tie-rod end

Steering rack of the 924, 924 Turbo, and 944

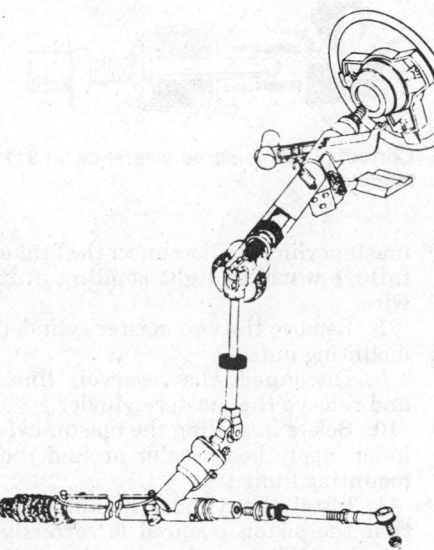

Steering column and gear used on the 928 and 928S

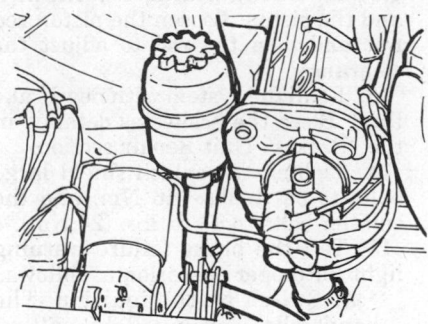

The 944 power steering reservoir is located on the inner wheel well under the hood.

6. Lower the power steering pump from the vehicle.
7. Installation is the reverse of removal. Tighten the power steering pressure hose fitting at the pump to 22 ft. lbs. (30 Nm). Adjust the pump drive belt tension and bleed the power steering system as described below.

928 Models

1. Disconnect the intake hose to the air cleaner on the left side, then drain the hydraulic fluid from the reservoir into a suitable container and discard. Do not reuse power steering fluid.
2. Remove the engine splash shield.
3. Loosen the front mounting bolts on the power steering pump slightly, then remove the rear bolt from the pump.
4. Remove the drive belt from the power steering pump pulley.
5. Remove the left upper section of the drive belt cover to facilitate removal procedures.
6. Disconnect the pressure and suction hoses from the pump. Cap the hose ends to prevent contamination by dirt during service procedure.
7. Remove the front mounting bolts and lower the power steering pump from the vehicle.
8. Installation is the reverse of removal. Make sure the power steering hoses are not routed close to the exhaust manifold, or hose failure will occur. Tighten the pump hose connections to 43 ft. lbs. (60 Nm). Adjust the drive belt tension and bleed the power steering system as described below.

BELT ADJUSTMENT

The power steering pump drive belt is properly adjusted if the belt can be moved about 10mm at a point midway between the pulleys.

BLEEDING POWER STEERING SYSTEM

1. Fill the power steering reservoir with fluid, then start and immediately stop the engine several times to allow the system to fill with fluid. The level in the reservoir will drop very quickly, so fluid must be added frequently during this step to keep the fluid at the maximum level mark on the reservoir. Do not let the reservoir run dry.
2. When the reservoir fluid level stops dropping, start the engine and allow it to idle.
3. Turn the steering wheel from lock-to-lock quickly to bleed the air from the system. Do not apply pressure on the wheel at each lock or hold the wheel in the lock position to avoid building up unnecessary pressure.
4. Watch the oil level during this procedure and keep adding oil until the level stops dropping. The fluid level should remain constant at the full mark on the reservoir tank and no air bubbles should rise in the hydraulic

fluid while turning the steering wheel.

5. Stop the engine and observe the fluid level in the reservoir. It should not rise more than 10mm. If the fluid level between a running and stopped engine deviates more than 10mm, there is still air trapped in the hydraulic system. Repeat the procedure. After all air is bled from the system, recheck the fluid level in the reservoir and top off as necessary.

Tie Rod Ends

REMOVAL & INSTALLATION

1. Loosen the self-locking nut which connects the tie rod to the steering knuckle. Mark the tie rod position on the threads of the steering rack rod, then loosen the jam nut.

2. Remove the self-locking nut and discard. Using a ball joint separator, remove the tie rod end from the steering knuckle. Unscrew the tie rod end from the steering rack, counting how many complete turns it takes to remove it.

3. Install a new tie rod end in reverse order of removal, threading the new tie rod end the same number of turns as counted in Step 2, then tighten the jam nut. Tighten the new tie rod self-locking nut to 47 ft. lbs. (65 Nm). Check the front wheel alignment.

BRAKES

For all brake system repair and service procedures not detailed below, please refer to "Brakes" in the Unit Repair section.

Master Cylinder

REMOVAL & INSTALLATION

1981–88 911 Models

1. Pull the accelerator back and out of its pushrod. Pull back the driver's side carpeting.

2. Unscrew the floorboard retainer(s) under the brake and clutch pedals.

3. Remove the master cylinder dust cover.

4. Raise the front of the car up and support it safely with jackstands.

5. Siphon the brake fluid out of the reservoir. Discard the fluid, don't save it for reuse.

6. Unbolt the front splash shield.

7. Remove the brake lines from the

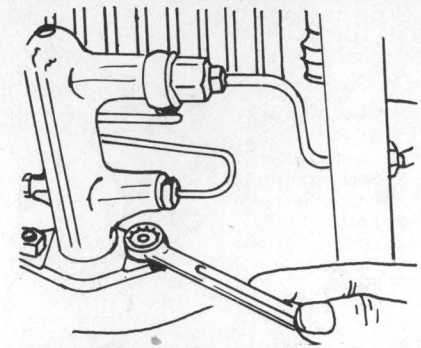

Master cylinder removal on 911 models

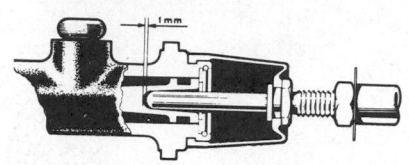

Correct piston pushrod clearance on 911 models

master cylinder. Disconnect the brake failure warning light sending unit wire.

8. Remove the two master cylinder mounting nuts.

9. Disconnect the reservoir lines and remove the master cylinder.

10. Before installing the master cylinder, apply body sealer around the mounting flange.

11. Install the cylinder, making sure that the piston pushrod is correctly positioned. Torque the mounting nuts to 18 ft. lbs. (24 Nm).

12. The piston pushrod should have 0.04 in. (1mm) clearance between it and the piston. Loosen the piston rod nut and turn the rod to adjust the clearance.

13. Refill the system with new brake fluid. Bleed the brakes as detailed in the "Brakes" Unit Repair section.

14. Tighten the splash shield large bolts to 34 ft. lbs. (46 Nm) and the smaller bolts to 18 ft. lbs. (24 Nm).

15. Test the brake failure warning light for proper operation as follows:

   a. Switch on the ignition. The handbrake warning light will go on. If it doesn't, replace the bulb.

   b. Start the engine. While you depress the brake pedal, have an assistant open a bleeder valve on one of the wheels to simulate a brake failure. The light should go on.

   c. When your assistant closes the valve, the light should go out.

   d. Repeat the test on the other brake circuit.

If the light fails to light during one of the tests, check the circuit failure sender which screws into the master cylinder.

All Except 911 Models

1. To prevent brake fluid from spilling out and damaging the paint, place a protective cover over the fender.

2. Disconnect and plug the brake lines.

3. Disconnect the electrical plug from the sending unit for the brake failure switch.

4. Remove the tow master cylinder mounting nuts.

5. Lift the master cylinder and reservoir out of the engine compartment being careful not to spill any fluid on the fender. Discard the brake fluid.

CAUTION
Do not depress the brake pedal while the master cylinder is removed.

---

6. Position the master cylinder and reservoir assembly onto the studs for the booster and tighten the nuts to no more than 10 ft. lbs. (13 Nm).

7. Remove the plugs and connect the brake lines.

8. Bleed the brake system.

Power Brake Booster

REMOVAL & INSTALLATION

1981–88 911 Models

1. Remove the lock pin for the master cylinder operating rod.

2. Remove the mounting bolts for the brake master cylinder, located inside the luggage compartment floor plate.

3. Siphon the fluid from the brake reservoir, being careful not to spill any brake fluid on painted surfaces. Discard the fluid.

4. Disconnect the stop light switch, vacuum hose and remove the brake fluid lines.

5. Remove the upper bolt for the brace and the nuts for the booster base.

6. Remove the brake booster and master cylinder as an assembly. The brace and operating rod do not have to be disconnected at the pedal assembly to remove the brake booster.

7. Installation is the reverse of removal. Torque the booster base nuts and master cylinder bolt to 18 ft. lbs. (25 Nm). Torque the support rod bolt to 25 ft. lbs. (35 Nm). Bleed the brake system.

1981–82 924 and 924 Turbo 1983–88 924S and 944 Models

1. Pull the brake fluid reservoir out of the master cylinder and drain the brake fluid into a suitable container. Discard the fluid and do not allow it to spill on any painted surfaces.

2. Disconnect the brake lines from the master cylinder, then remove the master cylinder as previously described.

3. Disconnect the vacuum hose to the check valve on the booster and remove the oil dipstick.

4. Carefully pry off the fuel line holding clip on the mounting bolt.

5. Remove the lockpin for the pushrod on the brake pedal.

6. Remove the mounting nuts for the brake booster/adapter assembly. The mounting nuts are accessible after disconnecting the throttle cable and pulling down the insulation sheet in the footwell.

7. Remove the brake booster from above in the engine compartment.

8. Installation is the reverse of removal. Tighten the booster and master cylinder mounting nuts to 15 ft. lbs (21 Nm). Bleed the brake system.

1981–88 928, 928S and 928S4

1. Remove the brake master cylinder as previously described.

2. On 1981–83 models, remove the pressure regulator on the wheel housing.

3. Depress the brake pedal and secure the pushrod for the master cylinder with a suitable hose clamp.

4. Adjust the connector to limit the amount of protrusion of the pushrod from the booster, then depress the brake pedal again and adjust the position of the hose clamp. Remove the connector.

5. Remove the cover, then remove the brake booster mounting nuts. If applicable, remove the right front brake line from the holder and push it toward the engine carefully.

6. Route the hose for the clutch master cylinder and the wire harness connectors so they will not interfere with removal.

7. Remove the brake booster. The air cleaner lower section may have to be removed to allow clearance for the booster assembly.

8. Installation is the reverse of removal. Replace the gasket between the booster and firewall. Tighten the booster and master cylinder mounting nuts to 17 ft. lbs. (23 Nm). Bleed the brake system.

Parking Brake Cable

ADJUSTMENT

1981–88 911 Models

1. Raise the rear of the car and support it safely on jackstands. Remove the wheels.

2. Release the handbrake lever.

3. Push the brake pads away from the disc so that it can be turned by hand.

4. Loosen the cable adjusting nuts to release tension.

5. Insert a screwdriver into the disc access hole and rotate the handbrake star wheel until the disc can no longer be turned by hand.

6. Repeat this operation on the other side.

7. Readjust the cable nuts to take up the slack.

8. Pull up the center tunnel cover and handbrake lever boot at the rear. By looking through the two inspection holes, see if the cable equalizer is exactly perpendicular to the car's centerline.

9. If the equalizer positioning is off, correct it by loosening or tightening the cable adjusting nuts. Tighten the locknuts after the adjustment is correct.

10. Back off each brake star wheel by four or five teeth until the disc can be turned by hand.

11. Check the handbrake lever clearance. There should be a slight clearance at the lever. The handbrake should be set when the lever is pulled up.

12. After completing the handbrake adjustment, depress the brake pedal several times to reposition the rear caliper pistons. Check the fluid level in the reservoir and top it up, if necessary.

1981–82 924 and 924 Turbo

1. Raise the rear wheel and support on stands. Adjust the rear brakes.

2. Remove the parking brake handle boot.

3. Pull the lever up two teeth.

4. tighten the parking brake adjusting nut until both wheels can just barely be turned by hand.

1981–88 928, 928S and 928S4
1983–88 924S and 944 Models

1. Raise the vehicle and remove the rear wheels.

2. Release the parking brake lever and move the disc brake pads so that the rotor can be easily moved.

3. Loosen the cable adjusting nuts so that no tension exists on the cable.

4. Insert a screwdriver through the hole in the brake rotor and turn the brake adjuster until the rotor cannot be moved.

5. Turn the adjuster in the opposite direction just until the rotor is free to rotate.

6. Pull the brake lever up two notches and adjust the cable so that the rotors can just be turned.

NOTE: At four notches of the lever, the rotors should be tight and unable to turn.

7. Release the handbrake and make sure the rotors turn freely. Install the wheels and lower the vehicle.

REMOVAL & INSTALLATION

1981–88 911 Models

1. Raise the rear of the car and support it safely on jackstands. Remove the wheels.

2. Remove the center tunnel cover and handbrake lever boot.

3. Remove the heater control knob.

4. Remove the handbrake support housing bolts.

5. Unscrew the heater control lever nut. Remove the cup spring, discs, and the lever.

6. Slightly raise the handbrake support housing. Snap off the retaining clip and pull out the cable equalizing stud.

7. Disconnect the handbrake light switch wire.

8. Remove the handbrake support housing.

9. Detach the cables from the cable equalizer.

10. Remove the rear brake calipers.

11. Remove the rear brake discs and spacer rings.

12. Remove the cotter pin, castellated nut and disc from each cable. Pull the cable toward the center of the car.

13. Pull the cables out from the center tunnel in the passenger compartment.

14. Lubricate the replacement cables with multipurpose grease and then feed them into the tube.

15. Place a washer between the spacer sleeve and the brake expander. Place another washer under the castellated nut.

16. Tighten the nut until a new cotter pin can be inserted. Make sure that the brake expander is correctly seated.

17. Install the brake disc and calipers.

18. Connect the handbrake light wire to the switch.

19. Insert the heater control lever into the handbrake support housing.

20. Install and clip the equalizer stud. Ensure that the handbrake cables are correctly seated.

21. Torque the handbrake support housing bolts to 18 ft. lbs. (24 Nm).

22. Install a friction disc, the heater control lever, another friction disc, pressure disc, cup spring, and the nut.

23. Tighten the nut so that the lever doesn't slip back when the heater is on full, and yet isn't too tight to operate.

24. Bleed the brakes.

25. Check the handbrake adjustment.

26. Install the wheels and lower the car.

All Except 911 Models

The parking brake cable is attached to the handbrake lever by two nuts, one of which serves as a locknut for the adjusting nut. To remove the cable, remove both the locknut and adjusting nut and feed the cable rearward. Disconnect the parking brake cable at the rear wheels, then install the new cable and feed it back forward to the handbrake lever. Adjust the parking brake cable as previously described.

CHASSIS ELECTRICAL

Heater Core and Blower Assembly

REMOVAL & INSTALLATION

911 Models

1. Disconnect the battery cables.

2. Remove the front luggage compartment carpeting.

3. Open the blower compartment lid. Remove the steering shaft cover.

4. Disconnect the electrical wiring.

5. Loosen the hose clamps and disconnect the hoses from the blower.

6. Pull the blower off the air intake stack and remove it from the car.

7. Install the blower on the intake stack. Make sure that the sealing ring is correctly seated.

8. Fasten the hoses on the blower and tighten the hose clamps.

9. Connect the electrical wiring.

10. Install the steering shaft cover and close the blower compartment lid.

11. Cement the carpeting to the right front side panel.

12. Connect the battery cables.

All Except 911 Models

The heater core and blower are contained in the heater assembly which is removed and disassembled to ser-

vice either component. The heater assembly is located under the center of the instrument panel. What follows is a general procedure.

1. Disconnect the battery ground cable.

2. Drain the cooling system.

3. Disconnect the two hoses from the heater core connections at the firewall.

4. Unplug the heater electrical connector.

5. Detach the center console and the right side of the instrument panel.

6. Remove the heater control knobs from the instrument pane.

7. Remove the two retaining screws and remove the controls from the instrument panel.

8. Disconnect the heater control cables.

9. Using a screwdriver, pry the retaining clip off the heater housing. Detach the left and right hoses.

10. Remove the heater-to-instrument panel mounting screws and lower the heater.

11. Pull out the two pins and remove the heater top cover. Pry the retaining clips off and separate the two heater halves.

12. Remove the heater core and/or blower.

13. Installation is the reverse of removal. Refill the cooling system.

Windshield Wiper Motor

REMOVAL & INSTALLATION

911 Models

The windshield wiper motor and linkage are located in front of the instrument panel.

1. Pull back the front luggage compartment carpeting. Disconnect the battery cable.

2. Remove the retaining clip and air duct. Remove the fresh air box.

3. Disconnect the blower motor wires.

4. Remove the wiper arms. Remove the rubber bushings under the arms and unscrew the shaft retaining nuts.

5. Pull the motor and linkage down as a unit. Separate the motor and linkage.

6. Installation is the reverse of the removal procedure.

REAR WIPER MOTOR REMOVAL

1. Pull the wiper arm from the rear window.

2. Open the engine compartment lid.

3. Disconnect the wiper motor electrical wiring.

4. Disconnect the wiper arm linkage at the bellcrank.

5. Remove the three wiper motor bracket bolts and remove the motor/linkage assembly.

6. Install the wiper motor/linkage assembly in a reverse order of removal.

7. Adjust the linkage at the bellcrank for correct wiper operation.

All Except 911 Models

The windsheild wiper motor is located on the driver's side of the cowl under a plastic cover.

1. Remove the cover.

2. Disconnect the battery ground cable.

3. Unscrew the wiper linkage, disconnect the electrical plugs, unscrew the motor, remove the mounting screw on the frame, lift frame slightly, and remove motor.

4. Installation is the reverse of removal. Note the following during installation:

    a. Connect the plug and turn on the ignition before fastening the linkage.

    b. Move the wiper arms to the off position and mount the linkage.

Fuse and Relay Panel

LOCATION

On 911 models, the fuse box is located in the left front of the luggage compartment.

The fuse panel on the 924, 924 Turbo, 924S and 944 is located underneath the dashboard on the driver's side of the vehicle. The relays are arranged above the fuses. On some models, and additional line of fuses is located above the main fuse/relay panel.

The fuse panel on the 928, 928S and 928S4 is located beneath a hinged wooden panel at the front of the passenger's floor area. Pull back the carpet to expose the cover. The relays are arranged below the fuse line.

On all models, fuse amperage ratings and applications are given in the owner's manual.

SAAB
900, 9000

SERIAL NUMBER IDENTIFICATION

Vehicle Identification Plate

900 Series

The vehicle serial number is located in two places on all vehicles. The serial number is stamped on a plate at the lower left hand corner of the windshield, and the serial number is punched in the vehicle body under the left side of the rear seat cushion.

The vehicle serial number is located on the right side of the rear cross beam in the luggage compartment.

9000 Series

These vehicles have the chassis number plate located on the inner right fender panel and the left fire wall area of the engine compartment. The chassis number is also punched in the vehicle body, left of the right rear light, behind the panel in the luggage compartment.

Engine Number

The engine identification number is stamped on a plate which is secured to the upper portion of the engine directly forward of the fuel injection unit. To avoid confusion, always replace spark plug wires one at a time

ENGINE IDENTIFICATION

Year	Model	Engine Displacement cu. in. (cc/liter)	Engine Series Identification	No. of Cylinders	Engine Type
1981	900	121 (1985)	B201	4	SOHC 8-Valve
	900	121 (1985)	B201 (Turbo)	4	SOHC 8-Valve
1982	900	121 (1985)	B201	4	SOHC 8-Valve
	900	121 (1985)	B201 (Turbo)	4	SOHC 8-Valve
1983	900	121 (1985)	B201	4	SOHC 8-Valve
	900	121 (1985)	B201 (Turbo)	4	SOHC 8-Valve
1984	900	121 (1985)	B201	4	SOHC 8-Valve
	900	121 (1985)	B201 (Turbo)	4	SOHC 8-Valve
1985	900	121 (1985)	B201	4	SOHC 8-Valve
	900	121 (1985)	B202 (Turbo)	4	DOHC 16-Valve
	9000	121 (1985)	B202 (Turbo)	4	DOHC 16-Valve
1986	900	121 (1985)	B201	4	SOHC 8-Valve
	900	121 (1985)	B202 (Turbo)	4	DOHC 16-Valve
	900	121 (1985)	B202	4	DOHC 16-Valve
	9000	121 (1985)	B202 (Turbo)	4	DOHC 16-Valve

ENGINE IDENTIFICATION

Year	Model	Engine Displacement cu. in. (cc/liter)	Engine Series Identification	No. of Cylinders	Engine Type
1987-88	900	121 (1985)	B201	4	SOHC 8-Valve
	900	121 (1985)	B202 (Turbo)	4	DOHC 16-Valve
	900	121 (1985)	B202	4	DOHC 16-Valve
	9000	121 (1985)	B202 (Turbo)	4	DOHC 16-Valve

SOHC—Single Overhead Camshaft
DOHC—Double Overhead Camshaft

GENERAL ENGINE SPECIFICATIONS

Year	Model	Engine Displacement cu. in. (cc)	Fuel System Type	Net Horsepower @ rpm	Net Torque @ rpm (ft. lbs.)	Bore × Stroke (in.)	Compression Ratio	Oil Pressure @ rpm
1981	900	121 (1985)	Fuel Injection	110 @ 5500 ②	119 @ 3500 ③	3.543 × 3.071	9.25:1	64–71 ④
	900 Turbo	121 (1985)	Fuel Injection	135 @ 4800	160 @ 3500	3.543 × 3.071	7.2:1	64–71 ④
1982	900	121 (1985)	Fuel Injection	110 @ 5500 ②	119 @ 3500 ③	3.543 × 3.071	9.25:1	64–71 ④
	900 Turbo	121 (1985)	Fuel Injection	135 @ 4800	160 @ 3500	3.543 × 3.071	8.5:1	64–71 ④
1983	900	121 (1985)	Fuel Injection	110 @ 5500 ②	119 @ 3500 ③	3.543 × 3.071	9.25:1	64–71 ④
	900 Turbo	121 (1985)	Fuel Injection	135 @ 4800	160 @ 3500	3.543 × 3.071	8.5:1	64–71 ④
1984	900	121 (1985)	Fuel Injection	110 @ 5500 ②	119 @ 3500 ③	3.543 × 3.071	9.25:1	64–71 ④
	900 Turbo	121 (1985)	Fuel Injection	135 @ 4800	160 @ 3500	3.543 × 3.071	8.5:1	64–71 ④
1985	900	121 (1985)	Fuel Injection	110 @ 5500 ②	119 @ 3500 ③	3.543 × 3.071	9.25:1	64–71 ④
	900 Turbo	121 (1985)	Fuel Injection	160 @ 5500	188 @ 3000	3.543 × 3.071	9.0:1	64–71 ④
	9000	121 (1985)	Fuel Injection	175 @ 5300	201 @ 3000	3.543 × 3.071	9.0:1	64–71 ④
1986	900	121 (1985)	Fuel Injection	110 @ 5500 ②	119 @ 3500 ③	3.543 × 3.071	9.25:1	64–71 ④
	900 Turbo	121 (1985)	Fuel Injection	160 @ 5500	188 @ 3000	3.543 × 3.071	9.0:1	64–71 ④
	900 ①	121 (1985)	Fuel Injection	160 @ 5500	188 @ 3000	3.543 × 3.071	9.0:1	51–74 ④
	9000	121 (1985)	Fuel Injection	175 @ 5300	201 @ 3000	3.543 × 3.071	9.0:1	51–74 ④
1987	900	121 (1985)	Fuel Injection	110 @ 5500 ②	119 @ 3500 ③	3.543 × 3.071	9.25:1	64–71 ④
	900 Turbo	121 (1985)	Fuel Injection	160 @ 5500	188 @ 3000	3.543 × 3.071	9.0:1	64–71 ④
	900 ①	121 (1985)	Fuel Injection	160 @ 5500	188 @ 3000	3.543 × 3.071	9.0:1	51–74 ④
	9000	121 (1985)	Fuel Injection	175 @ 5300	201 @ 3000	3.543 × 3.071	9.0:1	51–74 ④

GENERAL ENGINE SPECIFICATIONS

Year	Model	Engine Displacement cu. in. (cc)	Fuel System Type	Net Horsepower @ rpm	Net Torque @ rpm (ft. lbs.)	Bore × Stroke (in.)	Compression Ratio	Oil Pressure @ rpm
1988	900	121 (1985)	Fuel Injection	110 @ 5500 ②	119 @ 3500 ③	3.543 × 3.071	9.25:1	64–71 ④
	900 Turbo	121 (1985)	Fuel Injection	160 @ 5500	188 @ 3000	3.543 × 3.071	9.0:1	64–71 ④
	900 ①	121 (1985)	Fuel Injection	160 @ 5500	188 @ 3000	3.543 × 3.071	9.0:1	51–74 ④
	9000	121 (1985)	Fuel Injection	175 @ 5300	201 @ 3000	3.543 × 3.071	9.0:1	51–74 ④

① DOHC—Double Overhead Camshaft
② 115 @ 5500 w/o Catalytic Converter
  118 @ 4800 Canada
③ 123 @ 3500 w/o Catalytic Converter or Canada
④ at 2000 rpm

ENGINE TUNE-UP SPECIFICATIONS

Year	Model	Engine Displacement cu. in. (cc)	Spark Plugs Type	Gap (in.)	Ignition Timing (deg.) MT	AT	Compression Pressure (psi)	Fuel Pump (psi)	Idle Speed (rpm) MT	AT	Valve Clearance In.	Ex.
1981	900	121 (1985)	①	.024–.028	⑤	⑤	N/A	⑧	875	875	.008–.010	.016–.018
	900 Turbo	121 (1985)	②	.024–.028	⑤	⑤	N/A	⑧	875	875	.008–.010	.018–.020
1982	900	121 (1985)	①	.024–.028	⑤	⑤	N/A	⑧	875	875	.008–.010	.016–.018
	900 Turbo	121 (1985)	②	.024–.028	⑤	⑤	N/A	⑧	875	875	.008–.010	.018–.020
1983	900	121 (1985)	①	.024–.028	⑤	⑤	N/A	⑧	875	875	.008–.010	.016–.018
	900 Turbo	121 (1985)	②	.024–.028	⑤	⑤	N/A	⑧	875	875	.008–.010	.018–.020
1984	900	121 (1985)	①	.024–.028	⑤	⑤	N/A	⑧	875	875	.008–.010	.016–.018
	900 Turbo	121 (1985)	②	.024–.028	⑤	⑤	N/A	⑧	875	875	.008–.010	.018–.020
1985	900	121 (1985)	①	.024–.028	⑤	⑤	N/A	⑧	875	875	.008–.010	.016–.018
	900 Turbo	121 (1985)	③	.024–.028	⑥	⑥	N/A	⑧	875	875	HYD	HYD
	9000	121 (1985)	③	.024–.028	⑥	⑥	N/A	⑧	875	875	HYD	HYD
1986	900	121 (1985)	①	.024–.028	⑤	⑤	N/A	⑧	875	875	.008–.010	.016–.018
	900 ⑨	121 (1985)	④	.024–.028	⑦	⑦	N/A	⑧	875	875	HYD	HYD
	900 Turbo	121 (1985)	③	.024–.028	⑥	⑥	N/A	⑧	875	875	HYD	HYD
	9000	121 (1985)	③	.024–.028	⑥	⑥	N/A	⑧	875	875	HYD	HYD

ENGINE TUNE-UP SPECIFICATIONS

Year	Model	Engine Displacement cu. in. (cc)	Spark Plugs Type	Spark Plugs Gap (in.)	Ignition Timing (deg.) MT	Ignition Timing (deg.) AT	Compression Pressure (psi)	Fuel Pump (psi)	Idle Speed (rpm) MT	Idle Speed (rpm) AT	Valve Clearance In.	Valve Clearance Ex.
1987	900	121 (1985)	①	.024–.028	⑤	⑤	N/A	⑧	875	875	.008–.010	.016–.018
	900 ⑨	121 (1985)	④	.024–.028	⑦	⑦	N/A	⑧	875	875	HYD	HYD
	900 Turbo	121 (1985)	③	.024–.028	⑥	⑥	N/A	⑧	875	875	HYD	HYD
	9000	121 (1985)	③	.024–.028	⑥	⑥	N/A	⑧	875	875	HYD	HYD
1988				SEE UNDERHOOD SPECIFICATION STICKER								

① BP6ES, W7DC, N9Y, N9YC
② BP6ES, W7DC, N9YC, BP7ES
③ BCPES, F7DC, C9GY, C9YC, C7GY
④ BCP6ES, C9YC, F7DC

⑤ 20° @ 2000 RPM
  18° @ 2000 RPM Canada with MT
  23° @ 2000 RPM Canada with AT

⑥ 16° BTDC @ 850 RPM
DOHC—Double Overhead Camshaft
⑦ 14° @ 850 RPM

⑧ Fuel injected engines: Fuel line pressure before the control pressure regulator is 66.9–69.7 (setting valve), and 48.5–54.0 psi (warm engine) after the control pressure regulator (located in fuel distributor).
⑨ DOHC—Double Overhead Camshaft

FIRING ORDERS

NOTE: To avoid confusion, always replace spark plug wires one at a time.

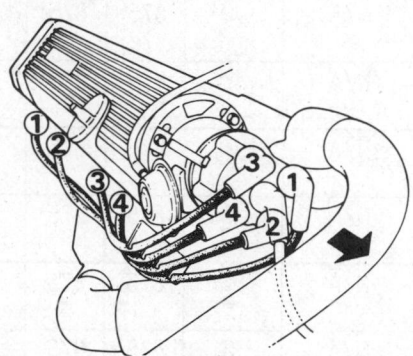

Firing order and ignition cable positioning eight valve engine

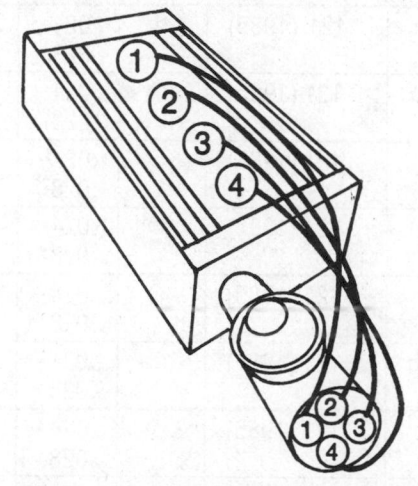

Firing order and ignition cable positioning sixteen valve engine

CAPACITIES

Year	Model	Engine Displacement cu. in. (cc)	Engine Crankcase with Filter	Engine Crankcase without Filter	Transmission (pts.) 4-Spd	Transmission (pts.) 5-Spd	Transmission (pts.) Auto.	Drive Axle (pts.)	Fuel Tank (gal.)	Cooling System (qts.)
1981	900	121 (1985)	4.0	3.5	5.2	6.4	17	2.6 ②	16.5	10.5
	900 Turbo	121 (1985)	4.5	4.0	5.2	6.4	17	2.6 ②	16.5	10.5
1982	900	121 (1985)	4.0	3.5	5.2	6.4	17	2.6 ②	16.5	10.5
	900 Turbo	121 (1985)	4.5	4.0	5.2	6.4	17	2.6 ②	16.5	10.5
1983	900	121 (1985)	4.0	3.5	5.2	6.4	17	2.6 ②	16.5	10.5
	900 Turbo	121 (1985)	4.5	4.0	5.2	6.4	17	2.6 ②	16.5	10.5

CAPACITIES

Year	Model	Engine Displacement cu. in. (cc)	Engine Crankcase with Filter	Engine Crankcase without Filter	Transmission (pts.) 4-Spd	Transmission (pts.) 5-Spd	Transmission (pts.) Auto.	Drive Axle (pts.)	Fuel Tank (gal.)	Cooling System (qts.)
1984	900	121 (1985)	4.0	3.5	5.2	6.4	17	2.6 ②	16.5	10.5
	900 Turbo	121 (1985)	4.5	4.0	5.2	6.4	17	2.6 ②	16.5	10.5
1985	900	121 (1985)	4.0	3.5	5.2	6.4	17	2.6 ②	16.5	10.5
	900 Turbo	121 (1985)	4.5	4.0	5.2	6.4	17	2.6 ②	16.5	10.5
	9000	121 (1985)	4.5	4.0	5.2	6.4	17	2.6 ②	16.5	10.5
1986	900	121 (1985)	4.0	3.5	5.2	6.4	17	2.6 ②	18.0	10.5
	900 Turbo	121 (1985)	4.5	4.0	5.2	6.4	17	2.6 ②	18.0	10.5
	900 ①	121 (1985)	4.0	3.5	5.2	6.4	17	2.6 ②	18.0	10.5
	9000	121 (1985)	4.5	4.0	5.2	6.4	17	2.6 ②	18.0	10.5
1987	900	121 (1985)	4.0	3.5	5.2	6.4	17	2.6 ②	18.0	10.5
	900 Turbo	121 (1985)	4.5	4.0	5.2	6.4	17	2.6 ②	18.0	10.5
	900 ①	121 (1985)	4.0	3.5	5.2	6.4	17	2.6 ②	18.0	10.5
	9000	121 (1985)	4.5	4.0	5.2	6.4	17	2.6 ②	18.0	10.5
1988	900	121 (1985)	4.0	3.5	5.2	6.4	17	2.6 ②	18.0	10.5
	900 Turbo	121 (1985)	4.5	4.0	5.2	6.4	17	2.6 ②	18.0	10.5
	900 ①	121 (1985)	4.0	3.5	5.2	6.4	17	2.6 ②	18.0	10.5
	9000	121 (1985)	4.5	4.0	5.2	6.4	17	2.6 ②	18.0	10.5

① DOHC—Double Overhead Camshaft
② 3.0 for Borg Warner Type 37

CAMSHAFT SPECIFICATIONS

Year	Engine Displacement cu. in. (cc)	Journal Diameter 1	Journal Diameter 2	Journal Diameter 3	Journal Diameter 4	Journal Diameter 5	Lobe Lift In.	Lobe Lift Ex.	Bearing Clearance	Camshaft End Play
1981	121 (1985)	1.1394	1.1394	1.1394	1.1394	1.1394	①	②	N/A	.0031–.0098
1982	121 (1985)	1.1394	1.1394	1.1394	1.1394	1.1394	①	②	N/A	.0031–.0098
1983	121 (1985)	1.1394	1.1394	1.1394	1.1394	1.1394	①	②	N/A	.0031–.0098
1984	121 (1985)	1.1394	1.1394	1.1394	1.1394	1.1394	①	②	N/A	.0031–.0098
1985	121 (1985)	1.1394	1.1394	1.1394	1.1394	1.1394	①	②	N/A	.0031–.0098
	121 (1985) ③	1.1387–1.1392	1.1387–1.1392	1.1387–1.1392	1.1387–1.1392	1.1387–1.1392	①④	②⑤	N/A	.0031–.0138
1986	121 (1985)	1.1394	1.1394	1.1394	1.1394	1.1394	①	②	N/A	.0031–.0098
	121 (1985) ③	1.1387–1.1392	1.1387–1.1392	1.1387–1.1392	1.1387–1.1392	1.1387–1.1392	①④	②⑤	N/A	.0031–.0138
1987	121 (1985)	1.1394	1.1394	1.1394	1.1394	1.1394	①	②	N/A	.0031–.0098
	121 (1985) ③	1.1387–1.1392	1.1387–1.1392	1.1387–1.1392	1.1387–1.1392	1.1387–1.1392	①④	②⑤	N/A	.0031–.0138

CAMSHAFT SPECIFICATIONS

Year	Engine Displacement cu. in. (cc)	Journal Diameter 1	2	3	4	5	Lobe Lift In.	Ex.	Bearing Clearance	Camshaft End Play
1988	121 (1985)	1.1394	1.1394	1.1394	1.1394	1.1394	①	②	N/A	.0031–.0098
	121 (1985) ③	1.1387–1.1392	1.1387–1.1392	1.1387–1.1392	1.1387–1.1392	1.1387–1.1392	①④	②⑤	N/A	.0031–.0138

① Injection Engine 0.425 in. Turbo, not APC 0.358 in. Turbo with APC 0.425 in.
② Injectino Engine 0.433 in. Turbo, not APC 0.413 in. Turbo with APC 0.433 in.
APC = Automatic Performance Control
③ DOHC—Double Overhead Camshaft
④ .3406–.2618 9000 Series Vehicle
⑤ .3406 9000 Series Vehicle

CRANKSHAFT AND CONNECTING ROD SPECIFICATIONS

All measurements are given in inches.

Year	Engine Displacement cu. in. (cc)	Crankshaft Main Brg. Journal Dia.	Main Brg. Oil Clearance	Shaft End-play	Thrust on No.	Connecting Rod Journal Diameter	Oil Clearance	Side Clearance
1981	121 (1985)	2.283–2.284	.0008–.0024	.003–.011	3	2.2047–2.2054	.0010–.0024	NA
1982	121 (1985)	2.283–2.284	.0008–.0024	.003–.011	3	2.2047–2.2054	.0010–.0024	NA
1983	121 (1985)	2.283–2.284	.0008–.0024	.003–.011	3	2.2047–2.2054	.0010–.0024	NA
1984	121 (1985)	2.283–2.284	.0008–.0024	.003–.011	3	2.2047–2.2054	.0010–.0024	NA
1985	121 (1985)	2.283–2.284	.0008–.0024	.003–.011	3	2.2047–2.2054	.0010–.0024	NA
1986	121 (1985)	2.283–2.284	.0008–.0024	.003–.011	3	2.2047–2.2054	.0010–.0024	NA
1987	121 (1985)	2.283–2.284	.0008–.0024	.003–.011	3	2.2047–2.2054	.0010–.0024	NA
1988	121 (1985)	2.283–2.284	.0008–.0024	.003–.011	3	2.2047–2.2054	.0010–.0024	NA

NA—Not available at time of publication

VALVE SPECIFICATIONS

Year	Engine Displacement cu. in. (cc)	Seat Angle (deg.)	Face Angle (deg.)	Spring Test Pressure (lbs.)	Spring Installed Height (in.)	Stem-to-Guide Clearance (in.) Intake	Exhaust	Stem Diameter (in.) Intake	Exhaust
1981	121 (1985)	45	44.5	178–198 @ 1.16	1.56	.020	.020	.3134–.3139	.3132–.3142
1982	121 (1985)	45	44.5	178–198 @ 1.16	1.56	.020	.020	.3134–.3139	.3132–.3142
1983	121 (1985)	45	44.5	178–198 @ 1.16	1.56	.020	.020	.3134–.3139	.3132–.3142
1984	121 (1985)	45	44.5	178–198 @ 1.16	1.56	.020	.020	.3134–.3139	.3132–.3142
1985	121 (1985)	45	44.5	178–198 @ 1.16	1.56	.020	.020	.3134–.3139	.3132–.3142
	121 (1985) ①	45	44.5	133–145 @ 1.18	1.45	.020	.020	.2740–.2746	.2738–.2748
1986	121 (1985)	45	44.5	178–198 @ 1.16	1.56	.020	.020	.3134–.3139	.3132–.3142
	121 (1985) ①	45	44.5	133–145 @ 1.18	1.45	.020	.020	.2740–.2746	.2738–.2748

VALVE SPECIFICATIONS

Year	Engine Displacement cu. in. (cc)	Seat Angle (deg.)	Face Angle (deg.)	Spring Test Pressure (lbs.)	Spring Installed Height (in.)	Stem-to-Guide Clearance (in.)		Stem Diameter (in.)	
						Intake	Exhaust	Intake	Exhaust
1987	121 (1985)	45	44.5	178–198 @ 1.16	1.56	.020	.020	.3134–.3139	.3132–.3142
	121 (1985) ①	45	44.5	133–145 @ 1.18	1.45	.020	.020	.2740–.2746	.2738–.2748
1988	121 (1985)	45	44.5	178–198 @ 1.16	1.56	.020	.020	.3134–.3139	.3132–.3142
	121 (1985) ①	45	44.5	133–145 @ 1.18	1.45	.020	.020	.2740–.2746	.2738–.2748

① DOHC—Double Overhead Camshaft

PISTON AND RING SPECIFICATIONS

All measurements are given in inches.

Year	Engine Displacement cu. in. (cc)	Piston Clearance	Ring Gap			Ring Side Clearance		
			Top Compression	Bottom Compression	Oil Control	Top Compression	Bottom Compression	Oil Control
1981	121 (1985)	.0009–.0020	.014–.022	.012–.018	.015–.055	.002–.003	.002–.003	NA NA
1982	121 (1985)	.0009–.0020	.014–.022	.012–.018	.015–.055	.002–.003	.002–.003	NA NA
1983	121 (1985)	.0009–.0020	.014–.022	.012–.018	.015–.055	.002–.003	.002–.003	NA NA
1984	121 (1985)	.0009–.0020	.014–.022	.012–.018	.015–.055	.002–.003	.002–.003	NA NA
1985	121 (1985)	.0009–.0020	.014–.022	.012–.018	.015–.055	.002–.003	.002–.003	NA NA
	121 (1985) ①	.0009–.0020	.013–.021	.011–.017	.014–.055	.002–.003	.002–.003	NA NA
1986	121 (1985)	.0009–.0020	.014–.022	.012–.018	.015–.055	.002–.003	.002–.003	NA NA
	121 (1985) ①	.0009–.0020	.013–.021	.011–.017	.014–.055	.002–.003	.002–.003	NA NA
1987	121 (1985)	.0009–.0020	.014–.022	.012–.018	.015–.055	.002–.003	.002–.003	NA NA
	121 (1985) ①	.0009–.0020	.013–.021	.011–.017	.014–.055	.002–.003	.002–.003	NA NA
1988	121 (1985)	.0009–.0020	.014–.022	.012–.018	.015–.055	.002–.003	.002–.003	NA NA
	121 (1985) ①	.0009–.0020	.013–.021	.011–.017	.014–.055	.002–.003	.002–.003	NA NA

① DOHC—Double Overhead Camshaft   NA—Not available at time of publication

TORQUE SPECIFICATIONS

All readings in ft. lbs.

Year	Engine Displacement cu. in. (cc)	Cylinder Head Bolts	Main Bearing Bolts	Rod Bearing Bolts	Crankshaft Pulley Bolts	Flywheel Bolts	Manifold		Spark Plugs
							Intake	Exhaust	
1981	121 (1985)	①	40	80	140	43	13	18	18–21
1982	121 (1985)	②	40	80	140	43	13	18	18–21

TORQUE SPECIFICATIONS

All readings in ft. lbs.

Year	Engine Displacement cu. in. (cc)	Cylinder Head Bolts	Main Bearing Bolts	Rod Bearing Bolts	Crankshaft Pulley Bolts	Flywheel Bolts	Manifold		Spark Plugs
							Intake	Exhaust	
1983	121 (1985)	②	40	80	140	43	13	18	18–21
1984	121 (1985)	②	40	80	140	43	13	18	18–21
1985	121 (1985)	②③	40	80	140	43	13	18	18–21
1986	121 (1985)	②③	40	80	140	43	13	18	18–21
1987-88	121 (1985)	②③	40	80	140	43	13	18	18–21

① 1981—with 17mm screw head: 69 ft. lbs.
  with 15mm screw head: 1st stage—44 ft. lbs.
  2nd stage—65 ft. lbs.—Run engine to warm.
  Allow 30 minute cool time—Retighten to 65 ft. lbs.
② 1982–88—1st stage—43 ft. lbs.
  2nd stage—72 ft. lbs.—run engine to warm.
  Allow 30 minutes cool time—Retighten to 72 ft. lbs.
  1984–88: Tighten each bolt another 1¾ (90°) of a turn.
③ Turbo 16-Valve—1st stage—45 ft. lbs.
  2nd stage—67 ft. lbs.
  Engine to normal operating temp.
  Allow to cool for 30 minutes.
  3rd stage—Tighten another 90° turn (quarter turn).
  Retorque after 1200 miles or after engine reaches normal operating temperature.

BRAKE SPECIFICATIONS

All measurements in inches unless noted.

Year	Model	Lug Nut Torque (ft. lbs.)	Master Cylinder Bore	Brake Disc		Standard Brake Drum Diameter	Minimum Lining Thickness	
				Minimum Thickness	Maximum Runout		Front	Rear
1981	900	65–80	NA	.461 ①	—	—	.040	.040
1982	900	65–80	NA	.461 ①	—	—	.040	.040
1983	900	65–80	NA	.461 ①	—	—	.040	.040
1984	900	65–80	NA	.461 ①	—	—	.040	.040
1985	900	65–80	NA	.461 ①	—	—	.040	.040
	9000	76–90	NA	.787 ②	.768 ③	—	.039	.039
1986	900	65–80	NA	.461 ①	—	—	—	—
	9000	76–90	NA	.787 ②	.768 ③	—	.039	.039
1987	900	65–80	NA	.461 ①	—	—	—	—
	9000	76–90	NA	.787 ②	.768 ③	—	.039	.039
1988	900	65–80	NA	.461 ①	—	—	—	—
	9000	76–90	NA	.787 ②	.768 ③	—	.039	.039

NA—Not available at time of publication
① .374 Rear
② .295 Rear
③ .276 Rear

WHEEL ALIGNMENT

Year	Model	Caster		Camber		Toe-in (in.)	Steering Axis Inclination (deg.)
		Range (deg.)	Preferred Setting (deg.)	Range (deg.)	Preferred Setting (deg.)		
1981	900	1½–2½ ①	2 ①	0–1	½	5/64	NA
1982	900	1½–2½ ①	2 ①	0–1	½	5/64	NA
1983	900	1½–2½ ①	2 ①	0–1	½	5/64	NA
1984	900	1½–2½ ①	2 ①	0–1	½	5/64	NA

WHEEL ALIGNMENT

| Year | Model | Caster | | Camber | | Toe-in (in.) | Steering Axis Inclination (deg.) |
		Range (deg.)	Preferred Setting (deg.)	Range (deg.)	Preferred Setting (deg.)		
1985	900	$1^1/_2$–$2^1/_2$ ①	2 ①	0–1	$^1/_2$	$^5/_{64}$	NA
	9000	$1^1/_8$–$2^1/_8$	$1^5/_8$	$1^1/_8$N–$^1/_8$N	$^5/_8$N	$^1/_{16}$	NA
1986	900	$1^1/_2$–$2^1/_2$ ①	2 ①	0–1	$^1/_2$	$^5/_{64}$	NA
	9000	$1^1/_8$–$2^1/_8$	$1^5/_8$	$1^1/_8$N–$^1/_8$N	$^5/_8$N	$^1/_{16}$	NA
1987	900	$1^1/_2$–$2^1/_2$ ①	2 ①	0–1	$^1/_2$	$^5/_{64}$	NA
	9000	$1^1/_8$–$2^1/_8$	$1^5/_8$	$1^1/_8$N–$^1/_8$N	$^5/_8$N	$^1/_{16}$	NA
1988	900	$1^1/_2$–$2^1/_2$ ①	2 ①	0–1	$^1/_2$	$^5/_{64}$	NA
	9000	$1^1/_8$–$2^1/_8$	$1^5/_8$	$1^1/_8$N–$^1/_8$N	$^5/_8$N	$^1/_{16}$	NA

NA—Not available at time of publication
① Manual Steering $^1/_2$–$1^1/_2$
N = Negative

TUNE UP PROCEDURES

Ignition Timing

ADJUSTMENT

Ignition timing is set in the conventional manner, using the marks that are located on the flywheel. However, the engine is also equipped for checking the timing using an ignition service (TSI) instrument.

The equipment in the vehicle comprises a pin in the engine flywheel and a service socket in the clutch cover. The ignition service instrument is connected to the clutch cover by means of a special connector and t the plug lead No. 1 cylinder by means of a terminal. The ignition service instrument is also connected to the ignition service socket at the fuse box and by means of an impulse transmitter at the plug lead for No. 1 cylinder.

The Saab ignition service instrument consists of a tachometer, cam angle meter, stroboscope lamp and switch for operating the starter.

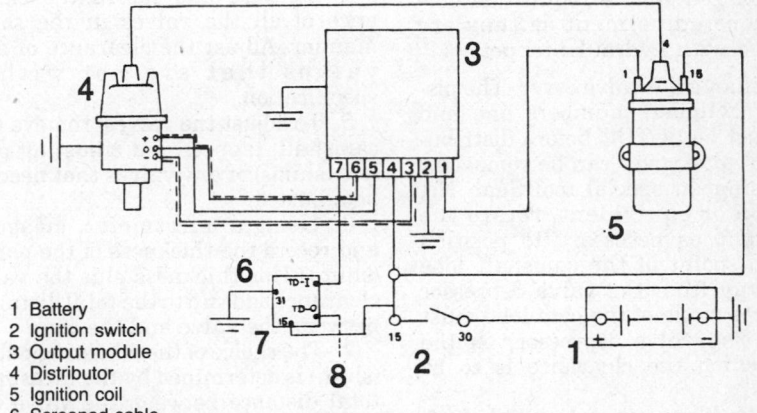

1 Battery
2 Ignition switch
3 Output module
4 Distributor
5 Ignition coil
6 Screened cable
7 Ignition pulse amplifier
8 Ignition pulse socket

Electronic ignition system components—9000 Series

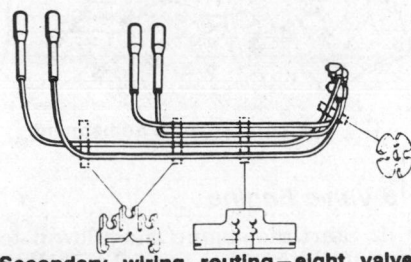

Secondary wiring routing—eight valve engine

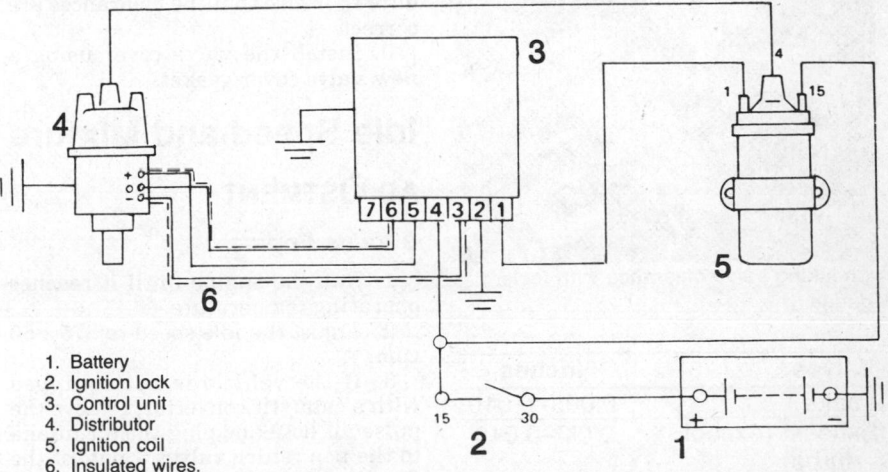

1. Battery
2. Ignition lock
3. Control unit
4. Distributor
5. Ignition coil
6. Insulated wires.

Electronic ignition system schematic—eight valve engine

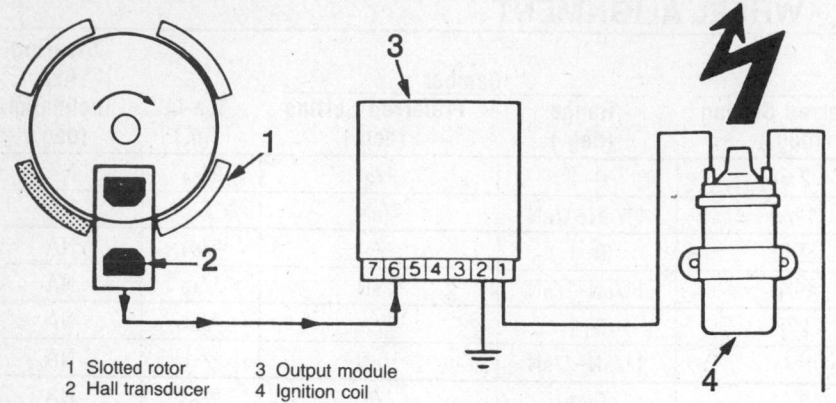

1 Slotted rotor   3 Output module
2 Hall transducer   4 Ignition coil

Output module—sixteen valve engine

Valve Lash

ADJUSTMENT

All 1985–88 vehicles equipped with a turbocharged engine require no normal valve adjustment as they are equipped with hydraulic tappets.

1. Remove the valve cover. The pistons of cylinders numbers one and four must be at TDC before distributor and valve cover can be removed.

2. Using an special tool Saab No. 8392185 or equivalent, rotate the crankshaft as necessary to position the high point of the camshaft lobe 180° away from the valve depressor face, base circle of the cam lobe must contact the valve depressor, on the valve which the clearance is to be checked.

NOTE: The special crankshaft turning wrench fits the center screw of the crankshaft belt pulley at the dash panel.

Checking valve clearance with feeler gauge

Valves	inches
Intake	0.008–0.010
Exhaust (except turbo)	0.016–0.018
Exhaust (turbo)	0.018–0.020

3. Check the maximum and minimum clearances using a feeler gauge. The minimum feeler gauge should slip in, but the maximum feeler gauge should not.

4. Measure and record the clearance of all the valves in the same manner. Adjust the clearance of any valves that are not within specification.

5. To adjust the valves, remove the camshaft, tappets and adjusting pallets (shims) of any valves that need to be adjusted.

6. Using a micrometer, measure and record the thickness of the pallet (shim). This thickness plus the valve clearance adds up to the total distance between the valve and the cam.

7. The choice of the adjusting pallet (shim) is determined by the measured total distance between the valve depressor (tappet) and the cam, less the specified valve clearance for an intake or exhaust valve as the case may be.

8. Insert the new adjusting pallet (shim) an the valve depressor (tappet) and reinstall the camshaft.

9. Repeat the measurement procedure to insure that the clearances are correct.

10. Install the valve cover using a new valve cover gasket.

Idle Speed and Mixture

ADJUSTMENT

8 Valve Engine

1. Run the engine until it reaches operating temperature.

2. Adjust the idle speed to 875 ± 50 rpm.

3. If the vehicle is not equipped with a catalytic converter, remove the pulse/air hose and plug the air intake to the non return valves. Connect the CO meter sensor to the exhaust pipe.

4. Remove the oxygen sensor wire.

5. On vehicles equipped with a catalytic converter, remove and plug the front exhaust pipe and connect the CO meter sensor to the pipe with the aid of a connecting piece. Remove the oxygen sensor wire.

6. Read and adjust the idle speed and CO valve as required. Before each reading, increase the engine speed and allow it to return to idle. Wait 30 seconds before taking the next CO reading.

7. Adjust the idle speed by turning the idle adjusting screw on the throttle valve housing.

8. Adjust the CO by turning the adjusting screw located on the fuel distributor clockwise for a richer mixture and counterclockwise for a leaner mixture. These adjustments affect each other, therefore these adjustments should be carried out in steps.

9. On catalyst equipped vehicles, connect the oxygen sensor wire and remove the CO meter probe from the front exhaust pipe connection. Install the plug in the front exhaust pipe. Insert the probe at the rear of the tailpipe. The CO meter reading should be less than 0.4% on 1981 vehicles and less 0.3% on 1982–88 vehicles with the engine at idle, and the engine and converter at normal operating temperature.

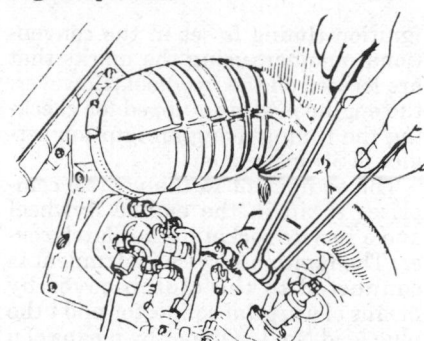

CIS injection idle speed adjustment

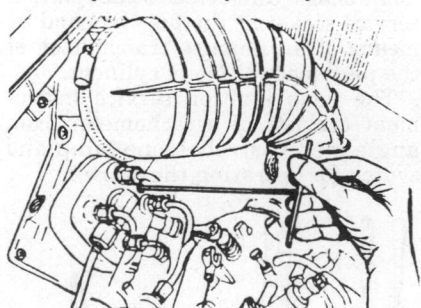

CIS injection Co value adjustment

16 Valve Engine

1. Start the engine and allow it to run until it reaches normal operating temperature.

2. Connect a tachometer to the engine.

3. Ground the green/red lead of the single pole test socket on the right hand wheel housing to close the idling control valve. Use a jumper lead to do the grounding.

4. Set the idling speed to 800 ± 25 rpm.

5. Disconnect the jumper lead from the test socket. Check that the engine speed changes and then settles down at 850 ± 75 rpm.

6. CO value at simulated full load conditions should be 4.0–6.0%. Refer to underhood specifications label.

NOTE: Be careful not to confuse the connector for the throttle switch with that of the idling control valve, as this will destroy the electronic control unit!

ENGINE ELECTRICAL

Distributor
REMOVAL & INSTALLATION

1. Disconnect the negative battery cable. Remove the distributor cap after marking the location of the No. 1 spark plug wire on the distributor housing. Number one cylinder is at the rear of the engine.

Distributor assemvly location

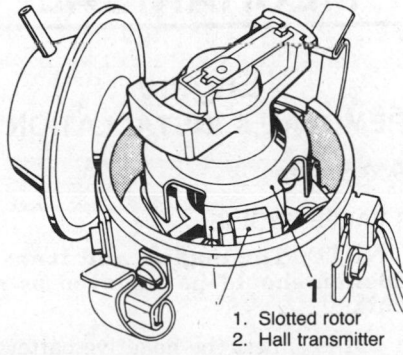

1. Slotted rotor
2. Hall transmitter

Distributor assembly with Hall effect pick up

2. Disconnect the primary wire and Hall transducer connector from the distributor and hose from the vacuum advance unit.

3. Crank the engine until the flywheel marking is at TDC (0°) and the distributor rotor is pointing to the indicating or reference mark on the distributor housing for the number one cylinder.

4. Match mark the distributor housing to the valve cover housing. Remove the distributor retaining bolts and pull the distributor forward from the end of the valve cover housing. Note the position of the distributor drive lugs. Do not rotate the engine crankshaft when the distributor is removed from the engine.

5. Installation is the reverse of the removal procedure. Be sure to align the distributor rotor to the number one spark plug wire reference mark on the distributor housing, while aligning the match marks on the valve cover housing and distributor housing.

Alternator
PRECAUTIONS

Several precautions must be observed with alternator equipped vehicles to avoid damage to the unit.

• If the battery is removed for any reason, make sure it is reconnected with the correct polarity. Reversing the battery connections may result in damage to the one-way rectifiers.

• When utilizing a booster battery as a starting aid, always connect the positive to positive terminals, and the negative terminal from the booster battery to a good engine ground on the car being started.

• Never use a fast charger as a booster to start vehicles with alternating-current (AC) circuits.

• Disconnect the battery cables when charging the battery with a fast charger.

• Never attempt to polarize an alternator.

• Avoid long soldering times when making alternator repairs. Prolonged head will damage the alternator.

• Do not use test lamps of more than 12 volts when checking diode continuity.

• Do not short across or ground any of the alternator terminals.

• The polarity of the battery, alternator and regulator must be matched and considered before making any electrical connections within the system.

• Never separate the alternator on an open circuit. Make sure all connections within the circuit are clean and tight.

• Disconnect the battery ground terminal when performing any service on electrical components.

• Disconnect the battery if arc welding is to be done on the vehicle.

BELT TENSION ADJUSTMENT

Adjust the alternator belt tension so that the belt can be depressed about ½ inch at the midpoint of its longest straight run.

REMOVAL & INSTALLATION
1981–84

1. Disconnect the negative battery cable.

2. Remove the alternator wiring connections, retaining screw and the adjusting screw.

NOTE: A new alternator mounting using a thrubolt and nut, was introduced during the 1983 model year. The thrubolt

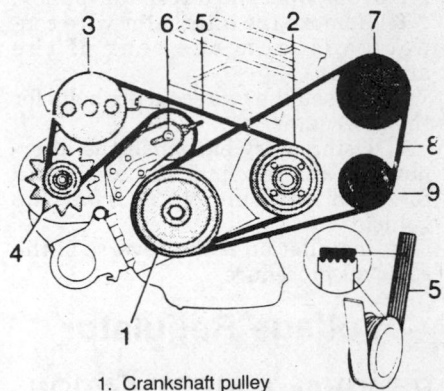

1. Crankshaft pulley
2. Water pump pulley
3. Steering servo pump pulley
4. Alternator pulley
5. Multi-groove belt
6. Belt tensioner
7. Compressor
8. Compressor belt
9. Adjusting device

Serpentine drive belt routing

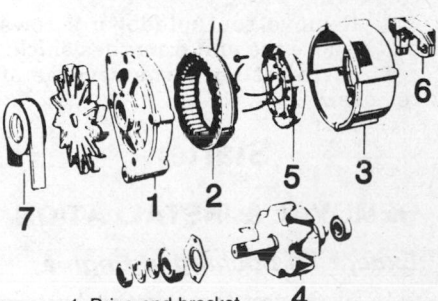

1. Drive end bracket
2. Stator
3. Slip-ring end bracket
4. Rotor
5. Rectifier unit
6. Voltage regulator and brush holder
7. Pulley

Exploded view of Bosch 80A alternator

and nut cannot be removed with the alternator mounted in the vehicle. The alternator mounting must be unbolted from the engine before the alternator can be separated from the mounting. Use the same precautions concerning the battery cable and alternator wiring as exercised with the earlier unit.

3. Remove the alternator belt.

4. Remove the alternator from the vehicle.

5. Installation is the reverse of removal.

1985–88

1. Disconnect the negative battery cable.

2. Raise and support the vehicle safely.

3. Remove the right front wheel assembly.

4. Remove the inner fender panel from the right fender.

5. Loosen the alternator belt and remove it from the alternator pulley.

6. Remove the alternator wire connections from the rear of the alternator.

7. Loosen the two securing bolts for the alternator.

8. Using a pry bar, push the alternator to the left, pull the alternator forward and remove it from the vehicle.

9. Installation is the reverse of the removal procedure.

Voltage Regulator

REMOVAL & INSTALLATION

NOTE: The voltage regulator is incorporated into the back of the alternator.

1. Disconnect the negative battery cable.

2. Remove the voltage regulator connecting wires.

3. Remove the holddown screws and remove the unit from the vehicle.

4. Installation is the reverse of removal.

Starter

REMOVAL & INSTALLATION

Except Turbocharged Engine

1. Disconnect the negative battery cable.

2. Remove the flywheel cover. Remove the gearbox dipstick if the vehicle is equipped with manual transmission.

3. Remove the starter motor heat shield and the rear mounting bolts.

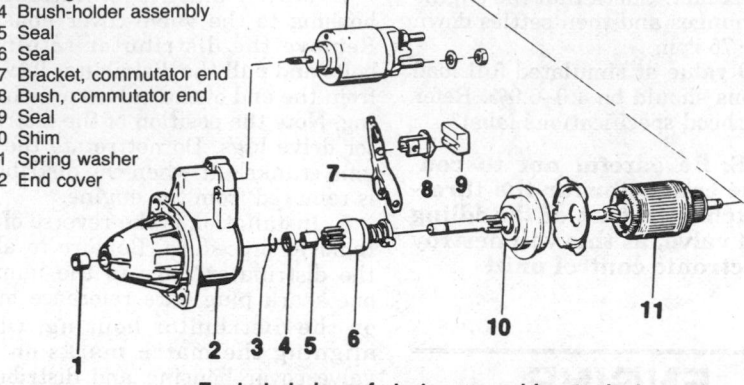

1 Drive end bush
2 Pinion bracket assembly
3 Circlip
4 Stop ring
5 Pinion-end bush
6 Starter pinion
7 Pinion-engaging lever
8 Bearing bracket
9 Seal
10 Epicyclic gear set
11 Armature
12 Solenoid
13 Casing
14 Brush-holder assembly
15 Seal
16 Seal
17 Bracket, commutator end
18 Bush, commutator end
19 Seal
20 Shim
21 Spring washer
22 End cover

Exploded view of starter assembly—typical

4. Disconnect the starter motor wires. Remove the front mounting bolts.

5. Remove the starter from the vehicle.

6. Installation is the reverse of removal.

Turbocharged Engine

1. Disconnect the negative battery cable. Remove the battery and the battery tray.

2. Remove the turbocharger suction pipe, preheater hose and the flywheel cover.

3. Remove the gearbox dipstick if equipped with manual transmission. Remove the bracket and bolts between the turbocharger and the gearbox.

4. Disconnect the starter motor wires.

5. Loosen the oil return pipe on the turbocharger enough to allow it to be bent slightly.

6. Remove the starter motor heat shield and the rear mounting bolts.

7. Remove the front starter mounting bolts.

8. Remove the starter from the vehicle. The starter will have to be tilted downward and then lifted out forward.

9. Installation is the reverse the removal procedure. Be sur to use a new gasket on the oil return pipe connecting flange on the turbocharger.

STARTER DRIVE REPLACEMENT

1. Have the starter armature out of the starter case and locked in a vise with the starter drive unit upward.

2. Remove the circlip on the end of the armature shaft, limiting the movement of the drive unit.

3. Remove the washer and the drive gear assembly from the armature shaft. A planetary gear set is located between the starter drive gear and the armature coils.

4. Install the drive gear, the limiting washer, and the circlip. Complete the starter assembly.

STARTER SOLENOID REPLACEMENT

1. Disconnect the negative battery cable.

2. Remove the starter assembly from the vehicle.

3. Separate the solenoid assembly from the starter assembly.

4. Installation is the reverse of the removal procedure.

ENGINE MECHANICAL

Engine
REMOVAL & INSTALLATION

900 Series

8 VALVE ENGINE

NOTE: The engine and transmission should be removed as a unit.

1. Disconnect the negative battery cable. Drain the radiator.

2. Disconnect the windshield wash-

er hose, unbolt the hood hinge links and remove the hood from the vehicle.

3. If the vehicle is equipped with power steering, disconnect the lines at the servo pump.

4. Disconnect the positive battery lead at the starter. Remove the radiator hoses. Remove the engine ground wire. Disconnect the temperature transmitter cable. Remove the coil.

5. Disconnect the cable harness from the clutch cover. If the vehicle is equipped with manual transmission, disconnect the hydraulic line from the clutch slave cylinder and plug the lines.

6. Disconnect the CI system electrical connections from the warm up regulator, thermotime switch cold start valve and the auxiliary air valve. On catalytic converter equipped vehicles, also disconnect the oxygen sensor and the throttle switch cables.

7. Disconnect the oil pressure transmitter cable. Loosen the fuel line connections at the fuel distributor. Remove the air filter along with the mixture control unit.

8. Disconnect the throttle cable. Disconnect the hose at the expansion tank. Disconnect the heater hoses at the heater. Disconnect the brake vacuum hose.

9. Remove the clips and remove the bellows from the inner drivers.

10. Place the spacer (Saab tool No. 83–93–209) or equivalent between the upper control arm underside and the vehicle body.

NOTE: Insert the tool from the engine compartment side. The spacer makes the front suspension unloaded when the vehicle is raised.

11. Lift the front end of the vehicle and support it safely.

12. Remove the lower end piece from the control arm. Pull out the steering knuckle assembly and support the end piece against the control arm outer end.

13. If the vehicle is equipped with manual transmission put the gear lever in neutral. Remove the nut and tap out the taper pin in the gear shift rod joint. Separate the joint from the gear shift rod.

14. If the vehicle is equipped with automatic transmission, remove the retaining screw from the gear selector cable at the transmission. Withdraw the cable with the gear selector rod in its extreme forward position "P". Slide back the spring loaded sleeve on the gear shift rod and unhook the end of the cable.

15. Separate the exhaust pipe from the exhaust manifold. Disconnect the speedometer cable from the transmission.

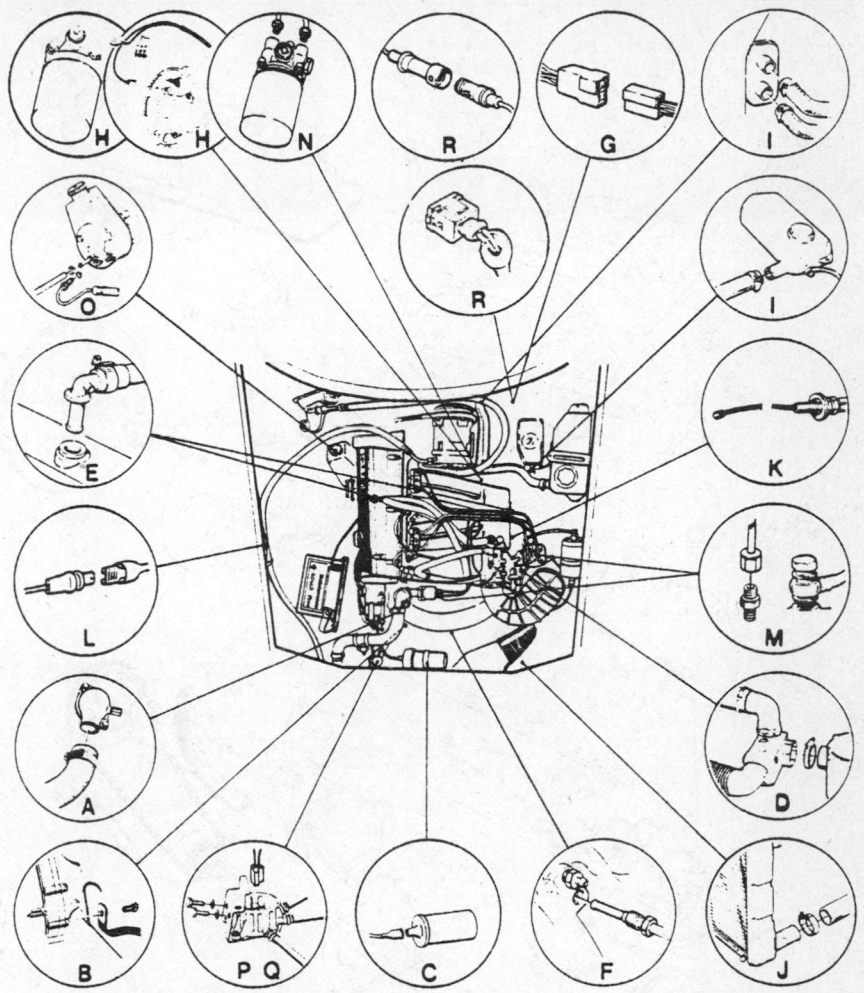

Disconnect these points before removing the engine—8 valve engines

16. Remove the rear engine mounting bolts. Slacken the front engine mounting nut so that the mounting can be lifted out of the bracket.

17. Attach the hoist to the two lugs on the engine and raise the assembly slightly. Move the assembly to one side and free the two universal joints.

18. Carefully remove the unit from the vehicle.

19. Installation is the reverse of removal. Upon installation properly seal the transaxle to engine assembly.

16 VALVE ENGINE

NOTE: The engine and transaxle assembly are removed together.

1. Remove the hood, after scribing lines around the mounting bolt positions to aid later refitting.

2. Install Saab special tool No 83–93–209 under the upper control arm on the right hand side.

3. Disconnect and remove the battery.

4. Drain the engine coolant.

5. Slacken the wheel nuts on the right hand front wheel.

6. Raise the front of the vehicle and place jack stands underneath the front jacking points.

7. Put the transmission selector into reverse.

8. Underneath the vehicle, remove the taper pin from the gearshift rod joint.

9. Disconnect the speedometer cable.

10. Remove the bolt securing the exhaust pipe to the clamp bracket on the transaxle.

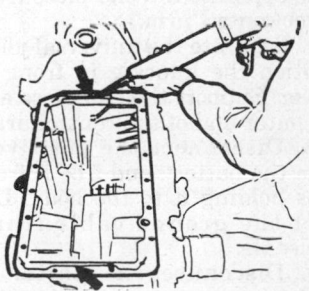

Sealer should only be applied to the grooves at each end of the steel engine to transaxle gasket on 1984–88 vehicles

connector (ground lead). Disconnect the lead at the alternator and the green/white cable to the positive terminal on the regulator. Disconnect the ground (black) cable. Disconnect the black cable from the oil pressure switch. Disconnect the cable for the A.I.C. actuator. Disconnect the yellow/white cable from the temperature transmitter. Disconnect the gray cable from the knock detector. Release the cable harness from the clip on the fuel injection manifold, from the rear of the engine and from the coolant hose between the engine and the expansion tank.

22. Withdraw the loose cables and guide the harness unit out of the engine compartment. Place it on top of the power distribution unit.

23. Remove the adjusting bolt in the alternator bracket, remove the drive belts and lift off the alternator.

24. Disconnect the brake servo hose from the intake manifold. Disconnect the throttle cable and sheath.

25. Remove the air conditioner compressor and bracket from the block. Place them on the filter housing for the heater system. Secure the alternator so it will not drop or become damaged.

26. Disconnect the fuel lines at their connections at the front of the fuel injection manifold and on the fuel pressure regulator.

27. Remove the coil.

28. Disconnect the turbo pressure line from the turbo compressor and the intercooler/throttle housing.

29. Remove the auxiliary fan.

30. Remove the air mass meter together with the suction pipe for the turbo unit. Disconnect the hoses at the solenoid valve and the crankcase ventilation at the suction pipe.

31. Disconnect the cables from the Hall transmitter and coil in the distributor. Free the Hall transmitter cable from the clips on the clutch cover.

32. Disconnect the solenoid valve hoses from the connections on the turbo unit and charging pressure regulator.

33. Disconnect the hydraulic hose from the clutch slave cylinder. Plug the hose to stop fluid from escaping.

34. Remove the engine mounting bolts.

35. Attach suitable lifting equipment to the engine lifting hooks. Raise the engine until the left hand, inner CV-joint can be separated.

36. Raise the engine to enable the hoses on the oil cooler to be disconnected.

37. Disconnect the hose to the power steering pump and drain the oil in the system.

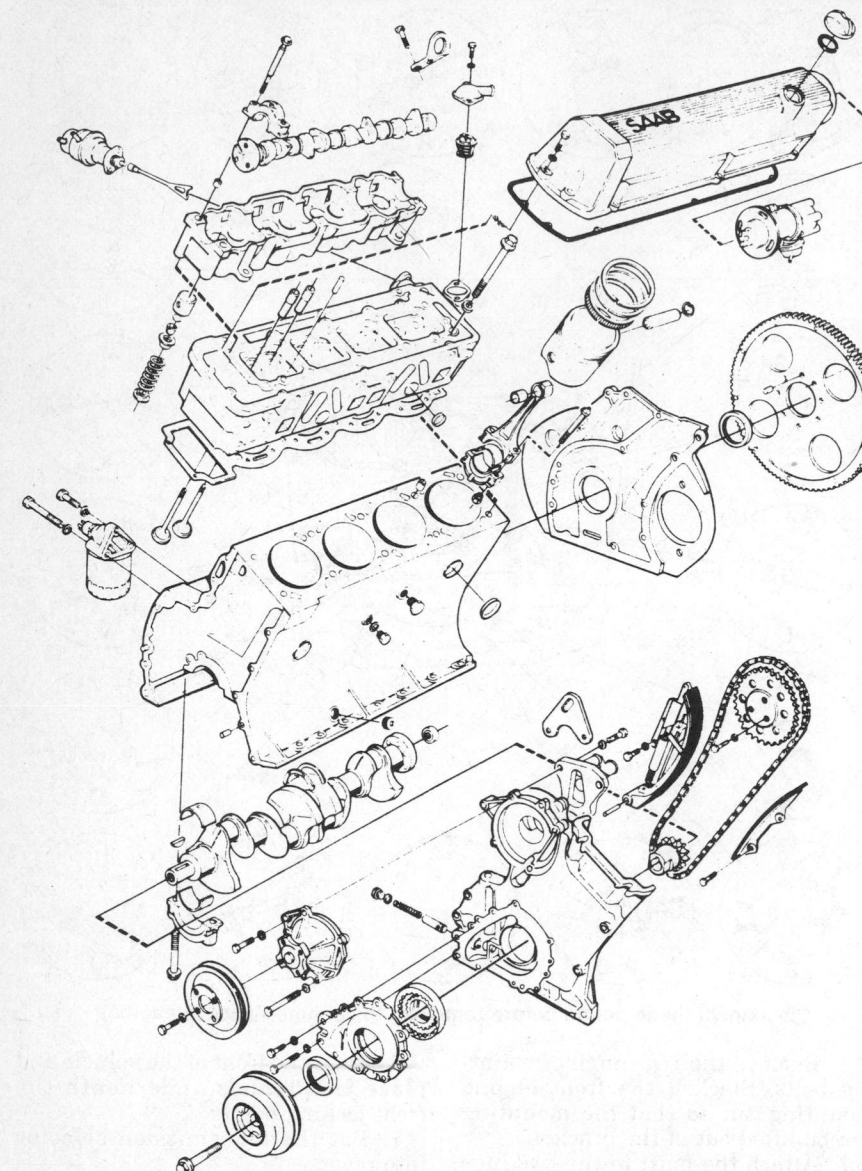

Eight valve engine and related components

11. Loosen the clips around the rubber boots on the CV-joints and slide the boots clear (this operation can also be done from above).

12. On the right hand side of the vehicle, remove the front wheel.

13. Separate the end piece from the lower control arm.

14. Separate the universal joint and position the knuckle in front of the driver. Support the end piece against the outer end of the control arm.

15. Disconnect the positive lead from the battery and free it from the clips holding it to the body. Disconnect the ground cable from the transaxle.

16. Disconnect the starter motor leads.

17. Unbolt the exhaust pipe from the exhaust manifold.

18. Disconnect the pressure pipe from the steering servo pump and have a plug handy to prevent oil escaping from the pipe. Take care not to drip oil onto the engine mounting and control arm rubbers.

19. From the left hand side of the vehicle, disconnect the cooling system hoses at the following connections, the heat exchanger valve, the expansion tank, the bottom of the radiator and the thermostat housing.

20. Disconnect the left hand fuel injection system cable harness as follows, at the air mass meter sensor, at the throttle switch, at the A.I.C. actuator, at the injectors, at the the NTC resistor (thermostatic switch) and at the ground points on the front lifting lug. Use the proper tool to release the tension in the springs on the terminal blocks.

21. Disconnect the block and plug

NOTE: **When lifting the engine out of the vehicle, keep it close to the fire wall to prevent the radiator and solenoid valve from being damaged by the front engine mounting.**

38. Before installation, check that the inner CV-joint boots are packed with the correct grease.

39. Suspend the engine from the lifting gear. Adjust the lifting gear so that the front engine mounting is slightly lower than the rear mounting.

40. Lower the engine into the engine compartment until the hoses to the oil cooler and servo pump can be connected.

41. Guide the engine into position, attending to the following items in order, the front engine mounting, left hand inner CV-joint and right hand inner CV-joint. Lower the engine until it rests on the rear engine mountings and install the mounting bolts. Unhook the lifting gear and unbolt the lifting lug from the water pump.

42. Reverse the remaining removal steps for installation.

9000 Series

NOTE: **The engine and transaxle assembly are removed together.**

1. Raise the vehicle and support it safely.

2. Drain the cooling system. Remove the battery.

3. Remove the thrubolt for the expansion tank, disconnect the tank from the suction and remove the overflow hoses from the radiator.

4. Disconnect the upper radiator hose.

5. Loosen the drive belt for the compressor by loosening the lock nut, and loosening the adjusting nut under the lock nut.

6. Disconnect the upper connection on the oil cooler, loosen the pipe clip on the radiator and slide the pipe down behind the radiator.

7. Unplug the connector to the electromagnetic clutch on the compressor and loosen the compressor mounting complete with the belt tensioner.

8. Place a protective cloth over the radiator member and rest the compressor on the radiator member. Secure the compressor to the radiator member.

9. Remove the turbo pressure pipe, situated between the turbo unit and the intercooler.

10. Disconnect the Lambda probe connector leads and disconnect them from the clips.

11. From the engine compartment, unbolt the flange joint between the exhaust pipe and the exhaust manifold. Push the exhaust pipe to one side and unhook the rubber hangers from the exhaust system. Disconnect the bottom coolant hose from the water pump.

12. From underneath the vehicle, remove the bottom retaining bolt for the radiator fan.

13. Disconnect the speedometer drive from the gearbox.

14. Select the fourth gear and separate the rubber joint in the gear selector linkage.

15. Remove the clips on the rubber gaiters over the inboard universal joints and slide the gaiters off the drive axles.

16. Disconnect the electrical leads from the alternator and the starter motor. Unplug the connector for the oil pressure switch.

17. Remove the clips and remove the top radiator hose.

18. Disconnect the top radiator at the cylinder head.

19. Unscrew the junction block from the battery shelf. Remove the clamp for the fuel filter.

20. Remove the battery shelf from the compartment.

21. Disconnect the high tension lead from the ignition coil at the distributor cap.

22. Remove the solenoid valve from the bracket on the radiator and unplug the electrical connections.

23. Remove the bolts from the top of the radiator fan. Disconnect the wiring loam and lift out the fan.

24. Pull the connector off the air mass meter. Disconnect the air mass meter from the air intake duct socket connector and the air cleaner. Leave the rubber socket connector attached to the turbo unit.

25. Remove the air intake duct by pulling it out of the aperture in the wing and twisting the ends inwards.

26. Remove the air cleaner top section first, then the remaining section.

27. Disconnect the relief valve hose from the turbo pressure pipe and remove the pipe.

28. Disconnect the Hall Effect transducer, the earth lead from the gear box and the electrical connector for the back up lights.

29. Disconnect the end of the throttle cable and disconnect the throttle linkage.

30. Install a clamp to the hydraulic line to the slave cylinder and pinch the line tightly. With proper wrenches, open the line to the clutch slave cylinder.

31. Remove the front wheels.

32. From both sides of the vehicle, slacken the lower bolts retaining the steering swivel member to the strut assembly. Remove the two upper bolts.

33. Pivot the steering swivel member outwards to pull the inboard universal joint out of the drive shaft. Position dust covers over the exposed drive shaft cups.

34. Remove the engine stay bolt.

35. Remove the steering reservoir for the servo and position it within the engine compartment. Drain the fluid from the container.

36. Disconnect the large bore hose and the delivery hose from the steering servo pump and plug the open ends.

37. Disconnect the fuel return lie from the pressure regulator.

38. Remove the nut from the rear engine mounting and back off the front mount bolts a few turns.

39. Attach the lifting sling (SAAB No. 83–92–409) to the rear lifting lug.

40. Lift the engine sufficiently to provide access for the removal of the components located between the engine and the fire wall.

41. Disconnect the vacuum hoses from the inlet manifold.

42. Remove the coolant hoses running between the heat exchanger and the water pump pipe.

43. Separate the cooling between the fuel pipe and the fuel injection manifold. Do not allow the fuel to spill or collect.

44. Cut the clips securing the wiring looms to the oil pipe, water pipe, inlet manifold steady bar and the oil supply pipe.

45. Unclip the wiring loom to the fuel injection manifold.

46. Disconnect the grounding connections and the electrical connectors from the wiring harness.

47. Unbolt the air cooled oil cooler and place it on top of the engine. The two lower bolts need only be loosened.

48. Carefully remove the engine from the vehicle, taking care not to damage the radiator.

49. Installation is the reverse of the removal procedure. Fill the engine with coolant, oil and power steering fluid. Test engine operation.

Cylinder Head

REMOVAL & INSTALLATION

900 Series

8 VALVE ENGINE

1. Disconnect the negative battery cable. Drain the radiator.

2. Remove the rubber bellows from between the air flow sensor and the throttle valve housing and disconnect the throttle cable from the throttle valve housing.

3. Disconnect the cable from the temperature transmitter. Remove the vacuum hose of the power brake booster from the intake manifold.

4. Disconnect the fuel lines from the fuel distributor to the injection valves. Tape the ends of the lines to prevent dirt from entering the system. Remove the bracket from the throttle valve housing mounting.

5. Remove the hose clamps at the connections to the thermostat housing, water pump and intake manifold.

6. Unbolt the exhaust pipe from the exhaust manifold.

7. Remove the distributor cap and ignition wires. Rotate the engine until cylinder No. 1 and No. 4 are at TDC. This must be done due to the design of the distributor driving dog which only allows the valve cover/distributor assembly to be removed with the engine in this position. Remove the valve cover.

8. Remove the camshaft sprocket bolts. Keep the chain on the sprocket and place sprocket/chain assembly between chain guide and tensioner. A center bolt is not used on the sprocket.

9. Remove the two bolts from the timing cover under the front of the head.

10. Remove the cylinder head bolts. On 1981 vehicles mount two guide pins in two of the cylinder head bolt holes.

11. Raise the vehicle and support it safely. Place a support under the rear end of the engine. Remove the engine mounting bolt in the cylinder head.

12. Remove the screws in the transmission cover. Remove the cylinder head from the vehicle.

13. Installation is the reverse of the removal procedure. Be sure to use a new cylinder head gasket. Torque the bolts first to 44 ft. lbs. and then to 70 ft. lbs.

14. Make sure that the markings on the camshaft and the bearing cap are in line with one another.

15. Check that the flywheel mark is in line with the mark on the cylinder block and that the engine is set on No. 1 cylinder.

16. Install the two screws in the timing cover on the front of the cylinder head. Install the timing chain and sprocket as follows remove the tension from the chain tensioner with special tool No. 83–93–357 or equivalent. Hook the tool into the catch of the tensioner and pull upwards. Place the timing sprocket on the camshaft so that the mark on the sprocket and the screw holes coincide. If necessary, move the chain to position. Install the three retaining bolts in the sprocket and camshaft. If the distributor is mounted to the valve cover, the rotor should be facing the line on the edge

of the distributor housing.

16 VALVE ENGINE

1. Remove the hood after scribing reference marks next to the mounting bolts, to aid later installation.

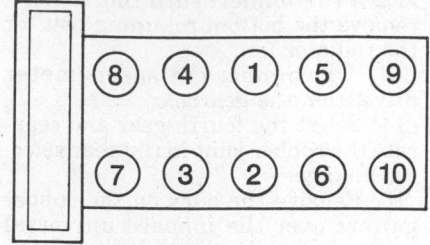

Cylinder head bolt torque sequence

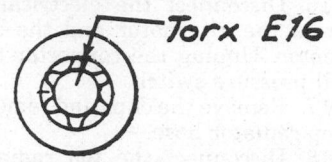

Top view of Torx head cylinder head bolts

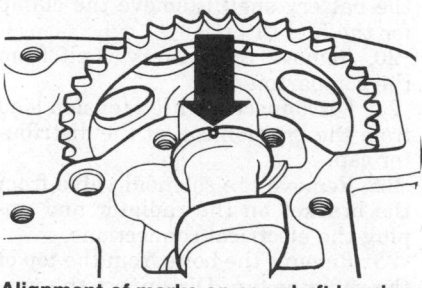

Alignment of marks on camshaft bearing caps

Alignment of cam gear to camshaft

2. Remove the battery.

3. Drain the coolant from the radiator and cylinder block.

4. Remove the exhaust manifold and turbo unit.

5. Remove the tensioning pulley and drive belt for the air conditioner compressor.

6. Slacken the securing bolts for the steering pump bracket, remove the drive belt and push the pump out of the way.

7. Undo the wiring harness clips on the cylinder head.

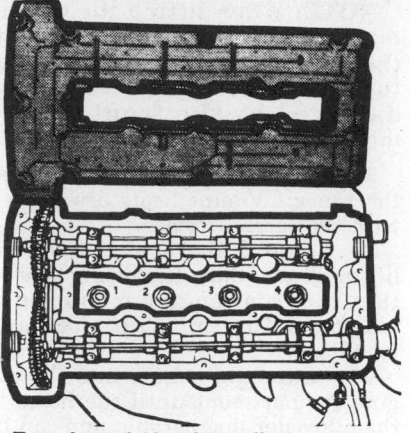

Top view of 16 valve cylinder head

8. Remove the two bolts in the timing cover, which are screwed into the cylinder head from underneath.

9. Remove the bolts in the right-hand engine mounting which are screwed into the cylinder head, together with the spacer sleeves.

10. Disconnect the hose between the thermostat housing and the radiator at the thermostat housing.

11. Remove the fuel pressure regulator and disconnect the ground leads for the fuel injection system.

12. Remove the A.I.C. actuator. Remove the bracket for the A/C compressor from the cylinder head.

13. Remove the intake manifold complete with injectors and injection manifold.

14. Disconnect the lead from the temperature transmitter.

15. Remove the lid on the valve cover and the ignition cables together with the distributor cap.

16. Remove the valve cover. Disconnect the crankcase ventilation hose and remove the semi circular rubber plug halves from the cylinder head.

17. Remove the A/C compressor and put it on the air intake for the heating system.

18. Line up the timing marks on the crankshaft and camshafts. To do this, remove the cover on the transaxle bell housing which reveals the timing marks on the flywheel. Turn the engine so that the "0" mark on the flywheel is lined up with the mark on the housing, or the end plate if the clutch cover has been removed. This makes certain that the pistons for No. 1 and 4 cylinders are at TDC.

19. Remove the cam chain tensioner.

20. Block up the engine to lift the cylinder head off the block. Remove the cylinder head bolts and siphon off the oil from the cylinder head.

21. Install a guide pin in one of the bolt holes and lift off the cylinder head, making sure the pivoting guide for the cam chain is not damaged.

22. To install, align the "0" mark on the flywheel with the timing mark on the housing. Line up the marks on the camshafts with their respective timing marks.

23. Install the cylinder head gasket, making sure that it is held in position by the guide sleeves in the cylinder head flange.

24. Install the guide pin (Saab special tool No. 83–92–128 or equivalent) and position the timing chain and pivoting guide.

25. Carefully install the cylinder head. Use the guide pin as a pivot for the head, which must be turned slightly to enable it to pass the pivoting guide. Thereafter, alignment will be determined by the guide sleeves.

26. Install the cylinder head bolts and tighten them in three stages. Stage 1, torque to 45 ft. lbs. evenly. Stage 2, torque to 63 ft. lbs. evenly. Stage 3, another 90° (¼ turn). Retighten the bolts after the engine has reached normal operating temperature. Remember to install the two M8 sized bolts in the underside of the cylinder head.

27. Install the camshaft sprockets, fitting the sprocket for the exhaust cam first. Make sure that the chain between the crankshaft sprocket and the camshaft sprocket is kept tight. Next install the intake cam sprocket. Keep the chain tight between the sprockets.

28. Lightly tighten the center bolts securing the camshaft sprockets. Adjust the chain tensioner and install it under tension. Tighten the bolt.

29. Release the tensioner by pressing the pivoting guide firmly against it. Thereafter, press the pivoting guide against the chain to put a basic tension on the chain.

30. Depress the pivoting guide to check that the tensioner is working. Rotate the crankshaft two complete turns clockwise, viewed from the transmission end. Check that the earlier settings of the crankshaft and camshaft timings have not changed. Tighten the cam sprocket bolts to 49 ft. lbs.

31. Continue the installation in the reverse order of the removal procedure.

9000 Series

1. Disconnect the negative battery cable. Raise and support the vehicle safely.

2. Remove the right front wheel assembly and the inner fender panel.

3. Drain the coolant. Remove the radiator expansion tank. Disconnect the steering servo reservoir and set aside. Leave the hoses attached.

4. Loosen the compressor drive belt and remove the belt.

5. Disconnect the electrical leads from the air compressor.

6. Unbolt the compressor from its mounting bracket. Disconnect the top pipe connecting on the air cooled oil cooler and push the pipe to one side. Rest the compressor on the radiator crossmember. Unbolt the compressor mounting bracket and remove it.

7. Unbolt the front exhaust pipe flange and unhook the rubber hangers.

8. Remove the steady bar for the turbo unit and the oil return pipe.

9. Disconnect the hose from the intercooler at the turbo unit. Disconnect the oil supply pipe from the turbo.

10. Disconnect the hose between the air mass meter and the turbo unit. Disconnect the coolant hose from the thermostat housing and the hose from the cylinder head.

11. Disconnect the oil supply hose or pipe so as not to obstruct the removal of the exhaust manifold. If necessary, remove the clip holding the pipe to the cylinder head and slave cylinder.

12. Unbolt and lift off the exhaust manifold complete with the turbo unit, pushing the oil supply pipe out of the way at the same time.

13. Disconnect the lead to the temperature transducer.

14. Remove the engine stay bracket from its attachment point on the wing.

15. Remove and remove the bolt securing the engine stay bracket to the cylinder head. Remove the intake manifold from the cylinder head.

16. Disconnect the breather hose for the crankcase ventilation from the camshaft cover.

17. Disconnect the vacuum hose and the Hall Effect transducer lead from the distributor and remove the distributor cap complete with the high tension leads.

18. Unscrew and remove the spark plug inspection plate and the clips for the high tension leads.

19. Remove the camshaft cover.

20. Line up the crankshaft with the "0" timing mark and check that the camshaft timing marks also coincide. Remove the camshaft sprockets.

21. Remove the camshaft tensioner. Remove the two cylinder head bolts adjacent to the timing cover, which is accessible from below.

22. Disconnect the starter motor lead from the clip on the thermostat housing.

23. Remove the ten Torx® type cylinder head bolts.

24. Install a guide pin in the drilled hole in the right hand top corner of the cylinder head. Make sure that the timing chain is positioned such that the pivoting chain guide will not obstruct the cylinder head and carefully

lift the cylinder head from the engine block.

25. Before installation, clean both the cylinder head and the engine block surfaces. Install a new gasket. Be sure the crankshaft is lined up in the "0" position and that the camshafts are in line with their respective timing marks.

NOTE: When the pistons of the number one and four cylinders are at top dead center, the crankshaft "0" mark on the fly wheel must be in line with the mark on the clutch cover or the end plate, if the clutch cover has been removed. The marks on the camshafts must be in line with those on the cam bearing caps. This indicates the exhaust valves for number one and four cylinders are closed.

26. Install a guide pin in the drilled hole in the top of the right hand corner of the cylinder head and lower the cylinder head carefully into position on the engine block. Locate the cylinder head on the guide sleeves.

27. Install the cylinder head bolts, tightening them in the correct sequence to the specified torque. Stage 1, torque to 44 ft. lbs. Stage 2, torque to 67 ft. lbs. Stage 3, run the engine to normal operating temperature and allow the engine to cool for 30 minutes. Stage 4, slacken the bolts and retighten each bolt to 66 ft. lbs. Stage 5, tighten by turning the bolts through a further 90° (¼ turn).

28. Position the inlet valve camshaft sprocket, followed by the exhaust valve camshaft sprocket. Be sure that the chain is correctly positioned between the guides. Tighten the sprocket center bolts to the specified torque, 48 ft. lbs.

29. Install the timing chain tensioner. Advance the tensioner before installing it. Release the tensioner and rotate the crankshaft two revolutions. Make sure the camshaft and flywheel timing marks are correctly aligned.

30. Install the two halves of the split seal and the camshaft cover. Install the bolt at the distributor end and the middle bolt at the other end first. Tighten the bolts to 16 ft. lbs.

31. Check that the timing marks for the distributor rotor are lined up. Install the distributor cap and connect the lead for the Hall Effect transducer. Connect all vacuum hoses.

32. Connect the high tension leads to the spark plugs. Secure the leads in the clips. Install the inspection plate and tighten the retaining screws.

33. Install the clip securing the starter motor lead to the thermostat housing.

34. Install a new gasket on the inlet manifold and install the manifold in place. Install the top securing bolts first and then install the lower bolts, using an extension bar.

35. Install the bolt for the engine stay bracket to the cylinder head and position the stay bracket in place. Install a new gasket onto the exhaust manifold and position the exhaust manifold to the cylinder head.

36. Install the oil supply pipe. Install the clip and the slave cylinder bolt. Install the oil return line and the steady bar for the turbo unit.

37. Connect the hose between the turbo unit and the intercooler. Connect the cooler hose to the thermostat housing and the hose to the cylinder head.

38. Install the air mass meter socket connector into the turbo unit and tighten the clip. Connect the hose between the intercooler and the turbo unit.

39. Install and tighten the nuts securing the front section of the exhaust pipe to the turbo compressor. Bolt the A/C compressor mounting bracket onto the cylinder head and engine block.

40. Install the A/C compressor. Leave the coolant hose in the bracket when installting the compressor. Tighten the securing bolts to the specified torque.

41. Connect the electrical leads and make sure the lead is clear of the compressor pulley. Install the steering servo reservoir. Install the coolant expansion tank and tighten the hose clip.

42. Connect the top pipe to the air cooled oil cooler and secure the cooler to the radiator. Install the overflow line between the expansion tank and the radiator.

43. Install the compressor belt, adjust the tension and tighten the belt tensioner bolt. Install the inner right wheel arch, and install the wheel.

44. Lower the vehicle and tighten the wheel. Connect the negative battery cable and fill the cooling system with coolant. Start the engine and test the engine operation.

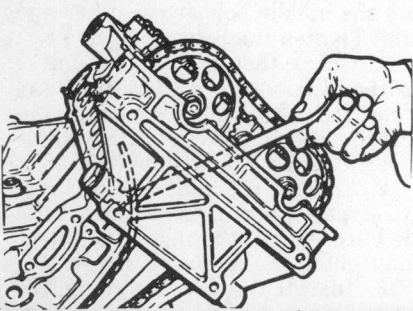

Releasing chain tensioner – sixteen valve engine

OVERHAUL

For all cylinder head overhaul procedures, please refer to the "Engine Rebuilding" in the Unit Repair section.

Intake Manifold

REMOVAL & INSTALLATION

8 Valve Engine

1. Disconnect the negative battey cable. Disconnect all hoses, wires and connectors that would inhibit the intake manifold from being removed.

2. It may be necessary to remove the distributor cap and the ignition wires to gain clearance. Remove the throttle valve housing.

3. Remove the intake manifold retaining bolts. Remove the intake manifold from the engine.

4. Installation is the reverse of the removal procedure. Be sure the proper gasket is used. A coolant leakage could occur if the wrong one is used.

16 Valve Engine

1. Disconnect the negative battery cable. Disconnect all hoses, wires and connectors that would inhibit the intake manifold being removed.

2. Remove the turbo pressure pipe, the lubricating oil pressure pipe and the return oil pipe.

3. Remove the intake manifold re-

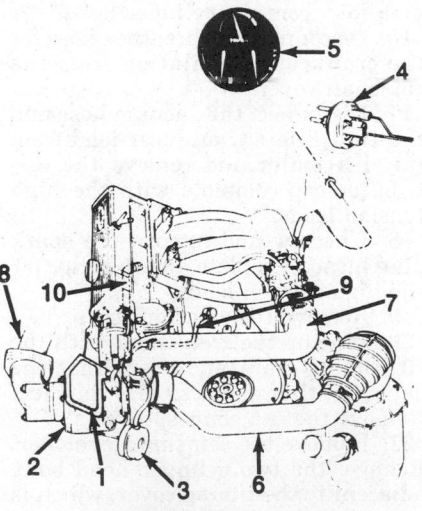

1. Turbocharger
2. Wastegate boost control
3. Diaphragm capsule
4. Over-pressure guard
5. Turbo gauge
6. Hose, air cleaner to turbocharger
7. Hose, turbocharger to inlet manifold
8. Exhaust outlet pipe
9. Oil supply line
10. Oil return line

Eight valve engine turbocharger assembly

taining bolts. Remove the intake manifold along with the injection manifold, injectors and the A.I.C. regulator.

4. Installation is the reverse of the removal procedure. Be sure the proper gasket is used. A coolant leak could occur if the wrong one is used.

Exhaust Manifold

REMOVAL & INSTALLATION

1. Disconnect the negative battery cable. Disconnect all necessary hoses, wires, and connectors that would inhibit the exhaust manifold from being removed.

2. Unbolt the exhaust pipe at the connecting flange.

3. If the vehicle is equipped with a heat shield, remove it.

4. Remove the exhaust manifold bolts. Remove the exhaust manifold from the vehicle.

5. Installation is the reverse of removal.

Turbocharger
REMOVAL & INSTALLATION

900 Series

1. Disconnect the negative battery cable. Remove the charge pressure regulator and block off the exhaust pipe. Remove the battery as required. Remove the tension on compressor belt.

2. Disconnect the hose between the compressor and the throttle housing.

3. Disconnect the oil supply line and the oil return line at the turbo unit.

4. Remove the retaining bolts securing the turbo to the exhaust manifold. Remove the turbo unit from the vehicle. Plug the holes in the turbo unit to prevent dirt from entering.

5. Installation is the reverse of the removal procedure.

6. Fill the lubricating inflow of the turbo unit with engine oil before connecting the oil return line at the turbo.

7. Crank the engine for about 30 seconds with terminal 15 on the ignition coil disconnected. This will fill the lubricating system of the turbo before the engine is started.

9000 Series

1. Disconnect the negative battery cable. Release the tension on the compressor belt by slackening the belt tensioner.

2. Disconnect the top pipe coupling on the air cooled oil cooler and disconnect the clips securing the pipe to the radiator.

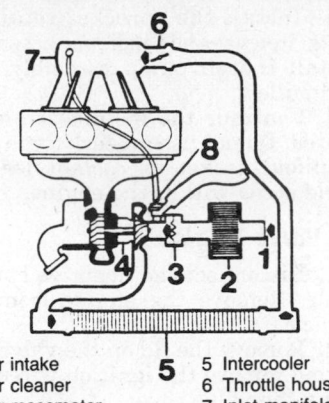

1 Air intake
2 Air cleaner
3 Air massmeter
4 Turbo unit
5
5 Intercooler
6 Throttle housing
7 Inlet manifold
8 Relief valve

Sixteen valve engine turbocharger assembly

3. Remove the compressor mounting bolts. Insert a sheet of metal to protect the oil cooler and lift the compressor towards the expansion tank.

4. Remove the solenoid valve from its mounting on the radiator and disconnect the electrical leads.

5. Disconnect the electrical leads at the radiator fan. Unbolt and remove the fan.

6. Unplug the electrical connectors for the air mass meter. Disconnect the toggle fasteners securing the air mass meter to the air cleaner cover and pull the rubber socket connector off the turbo unit.

7. Disconnect the turbo pressure pipe from the compressor.

8. Remove the retaining bolts of the oil pipe to the turbo unit. Unbolt the clutch slave cylinder and remove the clip securing the oil pipe to the cylinder head. Disconnect the oil pipe banjo coupling from the block and undo the clip on the inlet manifold.

9. Disconnect the exhaust pipe from the turbo compressor.

10. Disconnect the front rubber hangers for the exhaust pipe.

11. Remove the steady bar bracket between the sump and the compressor. Remove the securing bolts and loosen the oil return lines. Cap the aperture to prevent washers or nuts from the exhaust manifold dropping inside during the removal.

12. Remove the nuts securing the exhaust manifold to the cylinder head.

13. Lift the exhaust manifold from the cylinder head, along with the turbo unit.

14. Should further disassembly be necessary, complete as required.

15. To install, position the turbo unit to the exhaust manifold and tighten the retaining nuts. Install the new lock nuts with the locking flange turned inwards.

16. Install a new gasket over the studs for the exhaust manifold and install the manifold/turbo unit to the cylinder head assembly. Tighten the nuts to 30 ft. lbs.

17. Install the clip holding the turbo oil supply pipe to the inlet manifold. Connect and tighten the banjo coupling to the engine block. Make sure that the copper washers are in good condition. Secure the pipe to the turbo unit.

18. Install the return oil pipe and the steady bar bracket between the turbo unit and the crankcase. Connect the rubber hangers for the front exhaust hanger.

19. Bolt the exhaust pipe to the turbo compressor. Use new locking nuts with the locking flanges turned outward. Tighten to 19 ft. lbs.

20. Install the turbo pressure pipe to the compressor and assemble the air mass meter and rubber socket connector between the air cleaner body and the inlet side of the turbo compressor.

21. Assemble the fan and solenoid valve, securing the electrical leads into their clips. Connect the return hose to the solenoid valve. Insert a piece of metal to protect the oil cooler and install the A/C compressor.

22. Reconnect the oil pipe to the oil cooler and secure the pipe clip to the radiator. Install the compressor belt and tighten it to specification.

TROUBLESHOOTING

For more information on turbocharging, please refer to "Turbocharging" in the Unit Repair section.

Front Cover

OIL SEAL REPLACEMENT

8 Valve Engine

1. Disconnect the negative battery cable. Remove the alternator belt. If the vehicle is equipped with power steering or air conditioning, remove the required belts.

2. Remove the clutch cover (torque converter cover) and lock the crankshaft using Saab tool No. 83–92–987 or equivalent by locking the tool to the ring gear.

3. From under the vehicle, remove

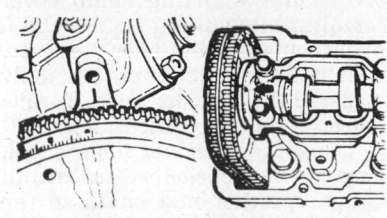

Timing mark location—eight valve engine

the pulley retaining bolt using Saab tool No. 83–92–961 or equivalent. Remove the pulley from the vehicle.

4. Pull off the old seal ring using a suitable tool.

5. Installation is the reverse of removal. Torque the retaining bolt to 137 ft. lbs.

16 Valve Engine

1. Disconnect the negative battery cable. Raise and support the vehicle safely.

2. Remove the right front wheeland tire assembly. remove the inner front fender panel.

3. Loosen and remove the drive belts.

4. Remove the retaining bolt for the crankshaft pulley.

5. Remove the crankshaft pulley.

6. Using a pry bar, carefully remove the oil seal without marring the crankshaft stub end.

7. Install a new, oiled seal, using an appropriate seal installer.

8. Install the pulley and tighten the retaining bolt to 134 ft. lbs. (180 Nm).

9. Tighten the drive belts, using a belt tension gauge. (New belt—180 lbs.; Used belt—120 lbs.)

10. Install the forward section of the inner fender panel.

11. Replace the front wheel and lower the vehicle.

Timing Chain and Sprockets
REMOVAL & INSTALLATION

8 Valve Engine

1. Disconnect the negative battery cable. Remove the engine from the vehicle.

2. Remove the distributor cap and ignition wires. Rotate the engine un-

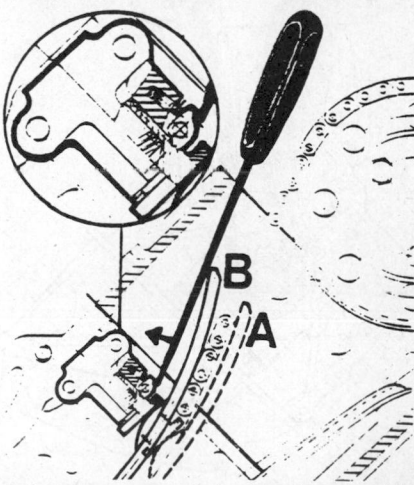

Releasing cam chain tensioner—eight valve engine

til cylinder No. 1 and No. 4 are at TDC. This must be done due to the design of the distributor driving dog which only allows the valve cover/distributor assembly to be removed with the engine in this position.

3. Remove the valve cover assembly. Remove the sprocket from the camshaft and rest it on the chain tensioner and the chain guide.

4. Remove the cylinder head. Remove the crankshaft pulley and oil pump assembly. Remove the water pump and pulley assembly.

5. Remove the timing chain cover.

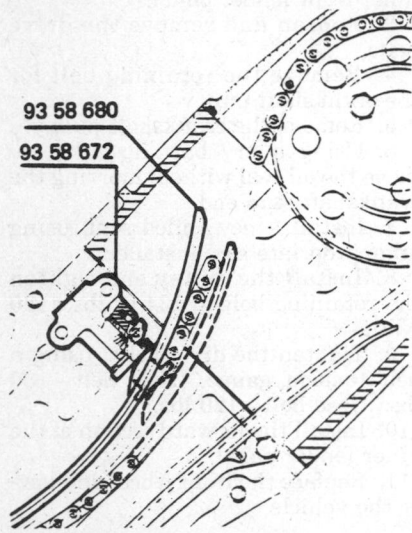

Chain tensioner and related components—eight valve engine

93 58 680
93 58 672

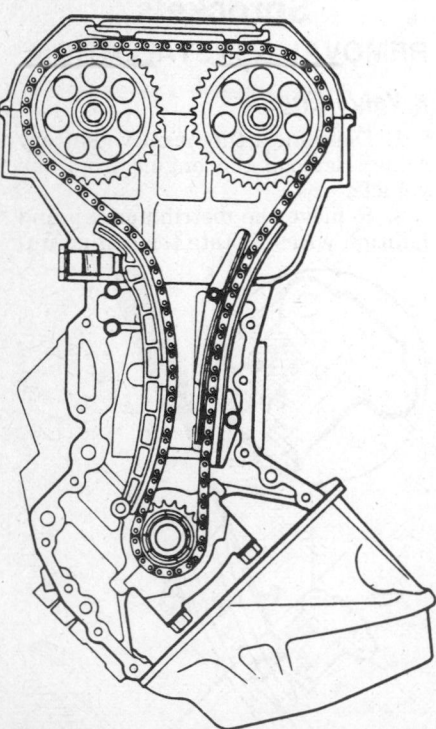

Timing mark location—sixteen valve engine

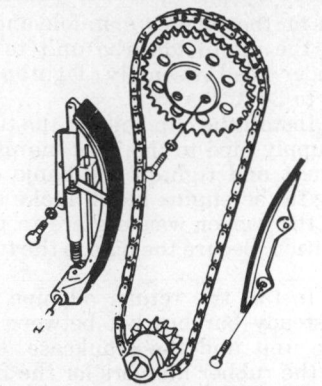

Timing chain assembly—eight valve engine

Remove the timing chain and chain wheel from the engine. Remove the chain tensioner, if required.

NOTE: 1984–88 engines beginning with engine No. E57340, are equipped with a new cam chain tensioner that requires a different release procedure. The new tensioner is also a direct replacement for the old style unit and may be used in all engines. A complete tensioner kit, consisting of the tensioner body and guide, must be used. To release the pressure on the cam chain, pivot the reverse latch on the tensioner body with a screwdriver or small pry bar. This will allow movement of the chain guide from point A to point B. When reinstalling the cam sprocket to the camshaft, the reverse latch must again be pivoted to release pressure on the chain guide.

6. To install the chain assembly, have the No. 1 piston at TDC and the camshaft in position for No. 1 cylinder firing position to be in its firing mode, before the cylinder head is installed.

7. Do not rotate either the camshaft or the crankshaft without the chain in place. Damage to the valves or pistons can occur, after the cylinder head is installed.

8. Replace the chain tensioner, if removed.

9. Place the camshaft sprocket to the chain and suspend it from the crankshaft sprocket. Position the chain between the chain guide and the tensioner.

10. Install the timing chain cover assembly while pulling up the chain to avoid being caught under the cover.

11. Install the water pump assembly and install the cylinder head. Torque the head bolts to specification.

12. Using the tensioner release tool, disengage the tensioner and install the cam sprocket and chain to the camshaft. Align the marks on the sprocket and the camshaft bearing.

13. Install the sprocket retaining bolts. Release the tensioner assembly. Install the oil pump assembly, seal and pulley.

14. Continue the installation as required. Do not use an early type inlet manifold gasket as coolant leakage could occur within the engine.

16 Valve Engine

1. Disconnect the negative battery cable. Remove the engine from the vehicle.

2. Remove the lid on the valve cover and remove the ignition wires. Remove the valve cover.

3. Position the crankshaft for TDC, with the "0" mark on the flywheel in line with the timing mark on the transaxle end plate. These marks must be aligned before the timing chain is removed.

SPECIAL TOOL

Crankshaft locking procedure

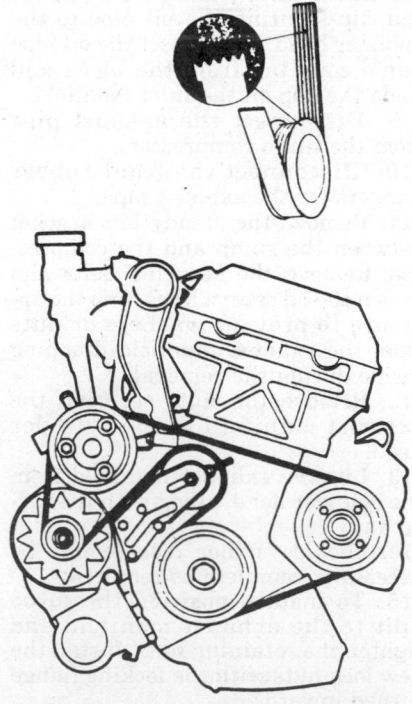

Serpentine drive belt adjustment

4. Remove the crankshaft pulley using a puller. Remove the water pump, located behind the crankshaft pulley. Remove the timing cover, two bolts of which are screwed into the underside of the cylinder head.

5. The cam chain and crankshaft timing sprocket should now both be visible. From above, release the timing chain tensioner by pressing the pivoting guide firmly against it. Remove the chain tensioner.

6. Using a special tool to hold the camshafts, remove the center bolts securing the camshaft sprockets. Throughout this procedure, keep the camshafts in their basic correct setting. If they are rotated out of position at any stage, especially without their sprockets and chain, the valves can be damaged.

7. Disconnect the timing chain from the sprockets and remove the chain, clearing it from the crankshaft sprockets.

8. To install the timing chain, place the chain around the crankshaft sprocket. Run the chain up through the opening in the cylinder head if not already done. Install the chain and sprocket on the exhaust cam first. Make sure the chain is taut between the crankshaft and camshaft sprockets. Install the bolts but do not tighten.

9. Install the chain and sprocket to the intake cam. Keep the chain taut between the cam sprockets while it is being installed. Install the bolts but do not tighten. Make sure the chain is seated in the guide tensioner grooves.

10. Tension the chain tensioner by fully depressing the piston and then rotating it to the locked position.

11. Install the chain tensioner with the piston under tension. Make sure that the copper gasket is in good condition and that the sealing surface is clean and free from burrs.

12. Trigger the chain tensioner by pressing the pivoting chain guide against it, thereafter, press the pivoting guide against the chain to give the chain its basic tension. Check that the chain tensioner maintains tension on the chain when the pressure on the chain guide is released and that the basic setting stop for the tensioner holds the chain guide tight against the chain. A limited amount of play will be present until the hydraulic pressure takes over once the engine is running.

13. Check the setting by rotating the crankshaft two complete turns in its normal direction of rotation around to the timing mark. The basic setting of the cams should remain unaltered.

14. Lock the exhaust cam by using a wrench on the cast hex bolt and torque the sprocket bolt to 48 ft. lbs. Repeat this on the intake cam.

15. Complete the procedure on the intake cam sprocket. When loosening or torquing the sprocket center bolts, hold the cam still using a wrench installed over the flats on the camshaft. The accuracy of the timing chain adjustment will depend on the condition of the chain.

Camshaft

REMOVAL & INSTALLATION
8 Valve Engine

1. Disconnect the negative battery cable. Remove the distributor cap and ignition wires. Rotate the engine until cylinder No. 1 and No. 4 are at TDC. This must be done due to the design of the distributor driving dog which only allows the valve cover/distributor assembly to be removed with the engine in this position.

2. Remove the valve cover assembly.

3. Be sure both the crankshaft and camshaft are at the No. 1 cylinder firing mode and the indexing lines still are aligned.

4. Remove the camshaft sprocket, keeping the chain on the sprocket. Place the sprocket between the chain guide and tensioner.

5. Remove the camshaft bearing caps and lift the camshaft from the bearing assembly housing. The bearing assembly housing can then be removed, if necessary.

6. Installation is the reverse of the removal procedure. Be sure that the timing marks are properly aligned.

16 Valve Engine

1. Disconnect the negative battery cable. Remove the engine from the vehicle.

2. Remove the lid on the valve cover. Disconnect the spark plug wires and vacuum hose from the distributor and remove the distributor cap.

3. Remove the valve cover and position the crankshaft for TDC. The "0" mark on the flywheel should be in line with the timing mark on the bell housing end plate.

4. Remove the distributor. Remove the oil pipe.

5. Remove the center bolts securing the camshaft sprockets. Use a proper holding tool to hold the camshafts from rotating. Always keep the camshafts in their correct basic setting. If the setting of the crankshaft or camshafts is altered at this stage the valves can be damaged.

6. Remove the camshaft timing chain tensioner. Remove the camshaft sprockets.

7. Remove the camshaft bearing caps. Keep them in correct order for later reassembly. Lift out the camshafts.

8. Installation is the reverse the removal procedure. When installing, the bearing caps marked 1–5 belong to the intake cam, while those marked 6–10 go with the exhaust cam. Torque the bearing cap bolts to 11 ft. lbs.

Pistons and Connecting Rod
POSITIONING

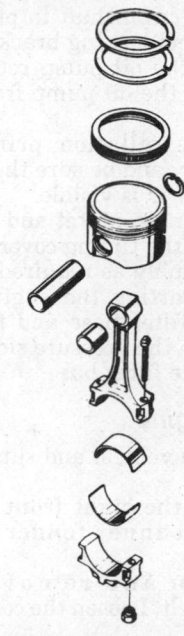

Piston and connecting rod assembly

ENGINE LUBRICATION

Rear Main Bearing Oil Seal

REMOVAL & INSTALLATION

8 Valve Engine

This seal is otherwise known as the crankshaft seal at the flywheel end. The seal can be changed with the engine in the vehicle, but the clutch and flywheel must first be removed.

1. Remove the clutch and the flywheel from the vehicle.

2. Remove the old seal ring using the proper tool.

3. Install the new seal with the spring ring turned inwards toward the crankshaft using the proper seal installation tool.

4. Continue the installation in the reverse order of the removal.

Oil Pump
REMOVAL & INSTALLATION

8 Valve Engine

The oil pump is a gear type pump and is driven by the crankshaft. It is positioned between the timing cover and crankshaft pulley. The pump assembly can be removed with the engine in the vehicle.

1. Disconnect the negative battery cable. Remove the crankshaft pulley.
2. Lock the crankshaft in place by using a flywheel locking bracket.
3. Remove the oil pump retaining bolts. Remove the oil pump from the timing cover.
4. Before installation, prime the pump assembly and be sure the mark on the outer gear is visible.
5. Install a new gasket and install the pump and the timing cover. Complete the assembly as required.
6. Before starting the engine, remove the oil filter base and fill the passageway on the pressure side with oil. Replace the filter base.

16 Valve Engine

1. Raise the vehicle and support it safely.
2. Remove the right front wheel and the front inner fender panel section.
3. Loosen and remove the multigroove belt. Loosen the compressor drive belt.
4. Remove the crankshaft pulley. It may be necessary to hold the crankshaft while removing the pulley bolt.
5. Remove the oil pump cover retaining bolts. Remove the oil pump.
6. Before installing the pump, install a new O-ring seal.
7. Install the pump to the engine and install the retaining bolts.
8. Install the pulley and drive belts. Tighten the pulley bolt to 140 ft. lbs. torque. Tighten the new drive belt to 180 lbs. strand tension or a used belt to 120 lbs. strand tension.
9. Install the inner fender panel and the right front wheel. Lower the vehicle and check oil pump operation.

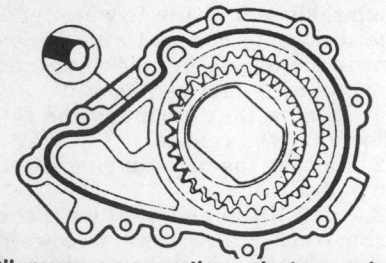

Oil pump crosssection—sixteen valve engine

ENGINE COOLING

Radiator
REMOVAL & INSTALLATION

1. Disconnect the negative battery cable. Drain the radiator. As required, remove the radiator grille. As required disconnect and plug the transmission lines.
2. Disconnect the hoses from the radiator. Disconnect the electrical leads to the radiator fan and the auxiliary fan, if equipped.
3. Disconnect the electrical lead to the thermal switch and solenoid valve. Remove the ignition coil and solenoid valve from the bracket. Remove the oil cooler.
4. Remove the two bolts from the upper radiator support Lift the radiator out of the vehicle by pulling the top of the radiator slightly backwards.
5. Installation is the reverse of the removal procedure.

Water Pump
REMOVAL & INSTALLATION

8 Valve Engine

1. Disconnect the negative battery cable. Drain the cooling system.
2. Remove the necessary components in order to gain access to the water pump assembly.
3. Remove the drive belts. Remove the water pump pulley.
4. Remove the water pump retaining bolts. Remove the water pump from the engine.
5. Installation is the reverse of the removal procedure.

16 Valve Engine

1. Disconnect the negative battery cable. Raise and support the vehicle safely.
2. Remove the right front wheel assembly. Remove the front section of the inner fender panel.
3. Drain the engine coolant. Loosen the drive belts. Remove the water pump pulley and the belt tensioning pulley.
4. Remove the clips holding the oil lines at the oil cooler. Remove the clips securing the water pipe to the engine block. Disconnect the coolant hoses from the water pump.
5. Remove the bolt securing the water pump to the bracket. Remove the water pump.

6. Installation is the reverse of the removal procedure.

Thermostat
REMOVAL & INSTALLATION

Thermostats on both the 8 valve and 16 valve engines are located in housings on the fronts of the cylinder heads, facing their respective radiators. The housings are cast elbows, which are unbolted from the heads in order to gain access to the thermostats. When installing the new thermostat, always install with the spring facing down. Use sealing compound on the joining surfaces of the elbow and head.

EMISSION CONTROLS

Please refer to "Emission Control" in the Unit Repair section for system maintenance procedures. Due to the complex nature of modern electronic engine control systems, comprehensive diagnosis and testing procedures fall outside the confines of this repair manual. For complete information on diagnosis, testing and repair procedures concerning all modern engine and emission control systems, please refer to *"Chilton's Guide to Electronic Engine Controls".*

EGR MAINTENANCE REMINDER SYSTEM

EGR Indicator Light

1. Reset the counter unit by pressing the push button on the counter unit.
2. The counter is located at the flasher relay bracket under the instrument panel.
3. The push button is accessible by inserting one hand under the guard panel, near to the wire connector to the counter unit.

Oxygen Sensor Indicator Light

1. Remove the padding from under the instrument panel.
2. Locate the counter on the flasher relay bracket.
3. Depress the button on the inner side, towards the fire wall, with one finger.
4. Install the padding under the instrument panel.

FUEL SYSTEM

Fuel Filter
REMOVAL & INSTALLATION

1. Disconnect the electrical connectors at the fuel pump. Remove the fuel pump fuse.
2. Crank the engine until fuel is exhausted from the system. Disconnect the negative battery cable.
3. Carefully remove the fuel filter fittings, using the proper wrench and covering it with a shop towel.
4. Remove the fuel filter assembly from the vehicle.
5. Installation is the reverse of the removal procedure. The filter is installed with arrows pointing in direction of flow.

Fuel Pump
PRESSURE TESTING

Voltage Check

1. Remove the round cover plate from the top of the fuel pump.
2. Measure the voltage between the positive and negative terminals when the fuel pump is operating.
3. The lowest permissible voltage is 11.5 volts.

Capacity Check

NOTE: **Be sure that the fuel filter is not clogged and that the battery is fully charged.**

1. Disconnect the return fuel pipe from the fuel distributor.
2. Connect the test pipe to the fuel distributor and place the other end in a suitable container.
3. On vehicles with the safety switch on the air flow sensor, remove the switch connector from the air flow sensor.
4. On vehicles with the fuel pump relay and the pulse sensor, remove the pump relay. Connect a jumper lead between terminals 30 and 87 on 900 series vehicles.
5. Switch on the ignition and allow the pump to run for 30 seconds. Measure the quantity of fuel. The proper specification should be 900cc/30 seconds. This should be measured in the return line.

REMOVAL & INSTALLATION

NOTE: **All vehicles are equipped with a plastic gas tank. Care should be exercised when removing the fuel pump from the plastic gas tank.**

1. Disconnect the electrical connectors at the fuel pump. Remove the fuel pump fuse.
2. Crank the engine until fuel is exhausted from the system. Disconnect the negative battery cable.
3. Remove the rear floor panel in the luggage compartment. Remove the valve cover from above the fuel pump.
4. Disconnect the electrical connections from the fuel pump.
5. Carefully disconnect the fuel lines from the fuel pump. Be sure to use the proper wrench and cover it with a shop towel while removing the connections.
6. Remove the fuel pump mounting clamp. Lift the fuel pump from the tank assembly.
7. Installation is the reverse of the removal.

Fuel Injection

Due to complex nature of modern fuel injection systems, comprehensive diagnosis and testing procedures fall outside the confines of this repair manual. For complete information on fuel injection diagnosis, testing and repair procedures please refer to *"Chilton's Guide to Fuel Injection And Feedback Carburetors".*

MANUAL TRANSAXLE

REMOVAL & INSTALLATION
900 Series

1. Remove the engine and transaxle from the vehicle as an assembly.
2. Position the engine and transaxle assembly in a suitable holding fixture. Drain the engine oil.
3. Remove the clutch shaft using a slide hammer and special tool 87–90–529.
4. Remove the slave cylinder retaining bolts. Remove the bolts retaining the transaxle assembly to the engine.
5. Carefully separate the engine from the transaxle.

9000 Series

1. Disconnect the negative battery cable. Remove the battery. Raise and support the vehciel safely.
2. Remove the air intake duct for the air cleaner from the fender. Remove the washer fluid reservoir and disconnect the positive lead from the washer terminal block.
3. Remove the fuel filter, the terminal block and the battery tray.
4. Remove the electrical connector from the air mass meter and remove the air mass meter carefully.
5. Remove the intake dust cover for the air cleaner.
6. Disconnect the Hall transmitter lead at the distributor.
7. Remove the cover and the filter element from the air cleaner.
8. Remove the air cleaner body.
9. Remove the turbo pressure pipe.
10. Disconnect the battery ground cable and the back-up light switch leads from the gear box assembly.
11. Install a clamp onto the hose in the slave cylinder line and pinch the hose together. Separate the pressure line between the pipe and the hose.
12. Remove the left engine mount and attach the engine to an engine lifting beam, or its equivalent.
13. Be sure the lifting beam or its equivalent is properly secured and seated.
14. Remove the left front wheel assembly and the inner fender panel.
15. Separate the suspension arm from the ball joint on the left side.
16. Disconnect the speedometer cable. Do not allow the drive gear to fall into the gear box.
17. Separate the two halves of the selector rod joint and remove the clip from the dust cover on the intermediate drive shaft.
18. Unbolt the support bar from the inlet manifold. Unbolt the starter motor from the gear box and push the support bar out of the way. Allow the starter motor to hang, but support it to prevent undue strain on the electrical wires.
19. Leave one of the bolts in position in the top of the flange between the engine and the gear box. Remove the other bolts and install the locating dowels, if available.
20. Loosen the two subframe pivot mountings and remove the four securing bolts.
21. Unbolt the front attachment point for the subframe. Unbolt the four subframe mounting bolts.
22. Remove the bolts securing the lower attaching point for the wheel arch bracket and let the subframe hang from the antiroll bar.
23. Remove the clip securing the rubber boot on the inboard universal joint. Withdraw the drive shaft and install protective covers to the open ends of the boot and drive cup.
24. Attach a lifting sling to the transaxle and remove the remaining bolt. Carefully remove the transaxle assembly from the vehicle.
25. Installation is the reverse of the removal procedure.

OVERHAUL

For all transaxle overhaul procedure, please refer to "Manual Transaxle Overhaul" in the Unit Repair Section.

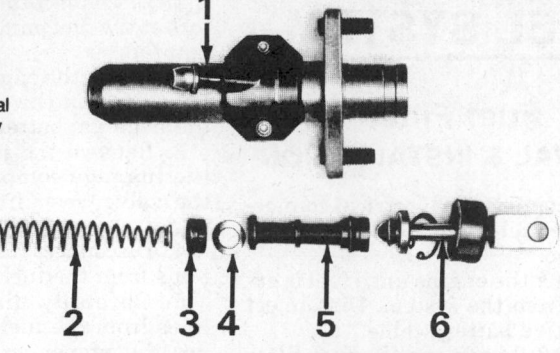

1. Housing
2. Spring with seat
3. Sealing
4. Washer
5. Piston and rear seal
6. Push rod assembly

Exploded view of clutch master cylinder

CLUTCH

REMOVAL & INSTALLATION

900 Series

1. Disconnect the negative battery cable. Remove the clutch housing cover.

2. Install the spacer (SAAB part No. 83–90–023) between the clutch fork and the diaphragm spring. Keep the clutch pedal depressed when the ring is being installed.

3. Unhook the spring clip and remove the cover located in front of the clutch shaft. Remove the clutch shaft plastic propeller.

4. Remove the clutch shaft by means of an M8 bolt installed in the shaft end and Saab tool No. 83–93–175. Withdraw the shaft as far as possible.

5. Remove the clutch slave cylinder retaining bolts.

6. Remove the clutch retaining bolts and remove the clutch, clutch disc and the slave cylinder complete with the clutch release bearing. Be sure that the slave cylinder sleeve is not damaged by the clutch during the removal procedure.

7. Installation is the reverse of the removal procedure.

Pressure plate and related components

9000 Series

1. Disconnect the negative battery cable. Remove the transaxle assembly.

2. Install a flywheel locking tool, if available and remove the clutch assembly from the flywheel.

3 To install the clutch assembly, use a centering arbor type tool or an appropriate input shaft to center the clutch plate to the flywheel.

4. Tighten the pressure plate bolts to 10.4–19.4 ft. lbs. Remove the flywheel lock, if used.

5. Slide the transaxle assembly over the locating dowels, engaging the transaxle input shaft into the clutch plate splines.

6. Secure the transaxle to the engine with the necessary attaching bolts. Remove the lifting sling from the transaxle.

7. Continue the installation in the reverse order of the removal procedure.

CLUTCH HEIGHT/FREE PLAY ADJUSTMENT

1. Remove the inspection hole cover and look through the inspection hole.

2. When the distance between the plastic sleeve front edge and the front edge of the turned surface is less than 2.0 mm the clutch disc must be replaced.

Clutch Master Cylinder

REMOVAL & INSTALLATION

1. Disconnect the negative battery cable. Remove the clamp holding the pipe from the cylinder at the body and remove the pipe at the cylinder.

2. Remove the left hand screen under the instrument panel.

3. Remove the pin holding the push rod to the clutch pedal.

4. Remove the bolts inside the dash panel. Remove the clutch cylinder from inside the engine compartment.

5. Remove the hose from the fluid container and hang it out of the way so that the fluid does not come out.

6. Installation is the reverse of the removal procedure.

Clutch Slave Cylinder

REMOVAL & INSTALLATION

900 Series

1. Disconnect the negative battery cable.

2. Remove the clutch assembly.

3. Remove the clutch release bearing together with the clutch slave cylinder.

4. Installation is the reverse of the removal procedure.

9000 Series

1. Disconnect the negative battery cable.

2. Remove the transaxle from the vehicle.

3. Remove the clutch release bearing. Disconnect the pressure pipe. Remove the bleed nipple.

4. Remove the retasining bolts that hold the slave cylinder in place.

5. Remove the clutch slave cylinder.

6. Installation is the reverse of the removal procedure.

BLEEDING THE HYDRAULIC CLUTCH SYSTEM

1. Connect a hose to the slave cylinder bleeder valve. Place the other end of the hose in a suitable jar partially filled with brake fluid.

2. Fill the master cylinder with brake fluid.

3. Open the bleeder valve on the slave cylinder a half turn.

4. Place a cooling system tester gauge over the opening of the master cylinder.

5. Pump the tester until all air has been expelled from the system.

6. Close the slave cylinder bleeder valve.

7. Check that all air has been removed from the system by depressing the clutch pedal.

AUTOMATIC TRANSAXLE

REMOVAL & INSTALLATION

1. Disconnect the negative battery cable. Remove the engine and transmission as a unit from the vehicle.
2. Remove the flywheel cover. Remove the starter.
3. Disconnect the throttle wire from the throttle valve housing.
4. Remove all bolts from the mating surfaces of the engine and transmission.
5. Remove the four bolts securing the flywheel ring gear to the torque converter. These bolts can be reached from above the oil pump mounting.
6. Turn the flywheel so that the two place angles will be horizontal. Carefully lift the engine off of the transmission.
7. Installation is the reverse of the removal procedure. When installing the engine and transmission together, make sure that the mating surfaces are clean. Check that the two guide sleeves are installed into the transmission.

PAN REMOVAL

1. Disconnect the negative battery cable. Raise and support the vehicle safely.
2. Properly support the transaxle assembly. Remove the transaxle crossmember.
3. Drain the automatic transaxle fluid. Remove the pan retaining bolts. Remove the transaxle pan from the vehicle.
4. Installation is the reverse of the removal procedure.

FILTER SERVICE

1. Disconnect the negative battery cable. Remove the transaxle fluid pan.
2. Remove the fluid lines for the front servo brake band that are connected to the drain valve. Remove the level lines. Note the position of the O-ring.
3. Remove the filter assembly.
4. Installation is the reverse of the removal procedure.

LINKAGE ADJUSTMENT

1. Remove the gear selector lever cover.
2. Slack off the gear selector lever housing nuts with tool No. 83–91–23 or equivalent.

3. Lift the gear selector lever housing and turn it so that the adjustment nuts of the cable will be reachable.
4. Adjust the cable longer or shorter to bring the "N" and "D" clearance to specification.
5. Assemble the gear selector housing and check the clearance in "N" and "D".
6. The proper setting of the selector cable can be accomplished by adding or removing shims at the transmission case end of the cable. A maximum of 3 shims may be used.

NEUTRAL SAFETY SWITCH ADJUSTMENT

1. Disconnect the wires from the switch. The wide terminals are for back-up lights and the narrow ones are for the starter motor.
2. Loosen the lock nut and unscrew the switch two turns.
3. With the selector in Drive, connect a test light between the narrow terminals. The light should light up.
4. Screw in the switch until the light goes out. Mark that position on both the transmission and the switch.
5. Move the test light, the wide terminals and screw switch in until the light goes out again. Count the number between the two lights going out.
6. Turn the switch to a point halfway between the two lights out points.
7. Secure the lock nut to 4–6 ft. lbs. torque. If the safety switch is locked too tight, it may be damaged.

BAND ADJUSTMENT

Type 35 Transmission

FRONT BAND (INSIDE TRANSMISSION)

1. Place tool No. 87–90–73 or equivalent, ¼ inch thickness gauge between the adjusting screw and the boss on the piston.
2. Loosen the lock nut.
3. Tighten the adjusting screw to two inch lbs. of torque and tighten the lock nut. On transmissions with self adjusting mechanism, check the gap

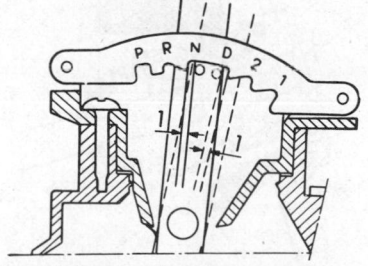

Manual linkage clearance, equal in "N" and "D"

between the self adjusting spring and the lever. It should be 1.5 to 2.0 thread flights.

REAR BAND

The rear band adjusting screw is located outside the transmission case on the drivers side of the vehicle.

1. Loosen the lock nut a few turns.
2. Tighten the adjusting screw to 20 ft. lbs. and then back off ¾ turn.
3. Hold the adjusting screw and torque the lock nut to 30–40 ft. lbs.

Type 37 Transmission

FRONT BAND (INSIDE TRANSMISSION)

Type 001 to 007 A/T

Up to serial numbers 001–1700, 002–2800

1. Loosen the lock nut and position tool number 87–90–073 or equivalent ¼ in. thick, between the adjusting screw and the piston pin.
2. Tighten the adjusting screw to 9 ft. lbs. and then loosen 1 turn.
3. Hold the adjusting screw and tighten the lock nut to 24–28 ft. lbs.

After serial numbers 001–1710, 002–2801

1. Loosen the lock nut and position tool number 87–90–030 or equivalent, $^{11}/_{32}$ in. thick, between the screw and the piston pin.
2. Tighten the adjusting screw to 9 ft. lbs. 'Do not' loosen the adjusting screw.
3. Hold the adjusting screw and tighten the lock nut to 24–28 ft. lbs.

Type 008, 009 A/T.

1. Adjustment of the front band is accomplished after the removal of the rear oil pan.
2. Loosen the lock nut and place a spacer tool number 87–91–329, which measures 0.310 in., between the adjusting screw and the piston rod.
3. Tighten the adjusting screw to a torque of 11 inch lbs. The adjusting screw must not be moved following the adjustment.
4. Hold the adjusting screw in this position and tighten the lock nut to 15–20 ft. lbs.

REAR BAND

The rear band adjusting screw is located on the outside of the transmission on the left side.

1. Loosen the lock nut a few turns.
2. Tighten the adjusting screw to 10 ft. lbs. with tool number 87–90–115 or equivalent. Back off the adjusting screw ¾ turn.
3. Hold the adjusting screw and tighten the lock nut to 24–28 ft. lbs.

DRIVE AXLE

Halfshaft
REMOVAL & INSTALLATION

900 Series

NOTE: The entire front axle assembly must be removed in order to remove the halfshaft from the vehicle.

1. Disconnect the negative battery cable. Remove the upper shock absorber bolt.
2. Raise the vehicle and support it safely. Remove the wheel and tire assembly.
3. Remove the brake housing and position it on the wheel housing to avoid damage to the brake hose. Remove the brake disc and parking brake assembly along with the cable.
4. Remove the large clamp from the rubber bellows on the inner universal joint. To separate the inner universal joint, install the cover (SAAB part No. 7323736) in the rubber bellows to stop the needle bearings from falling out and to keep dirt from entering. Install the protective cap (SAAB part No. 7838469) on the inner driver.
5. Disconnect the tie rod from the steering arm using the proper tool. Remove the nut on the upper ball joint. Remove the bolts from the lower control arm bracket.
6. Remove the halfshaft through the wheel housing and remove the entire front axle assembly.
7. If the differential bearing cap is to be removed, remove the retaining bolts and remove the cap and the inner drive using the proper removal tools.
8. Installation is the reverse of the removal procedure.

9000 Series

1. Disconnect the negative battery cable. Remove the hubcap and loosen the center axle nut. Raise and support the vehicle safely.
2. Remove the inner fender panel for working access.
3. Unbolt the MacPherson strut from the steering swivel member and detach the flexible brake hose from the clip on the strut.
4. Loosen the clip on the rubber boot on the inboard universal joint.
5. Separate the two halves of the joint. Install protective covers over the rubber boot and the drive axle.
6. Remove the hub center nut and withdraw the drive shaft from the steering swivel member.

7. Installation is the reverse of the removal procedure.
8. Torque the bolts securing the strut to the steering swivel to 56–75 ft. lbs.
9. Tighten the hub center nut to 195–208 ft. lbs.

CV JOINT OVERHAUL

For all CV-Joint overhaul procedures, please refer to "CV-Joint Overhaul" in the Unit Repair section.

Front Wheel Drive Hub Knuckle and Bearings

REMOVAL & INSTALLATION
900 Series

NOTE: The entire front axle assembly must be removed from the vehicle when removing the wheel bearings.

1. Disconnect the negative battery cable. Remove the upper bolt of the shock absorber.
2. Raise the vehicle and support it safely. Remove the tire and wheel assembly.
3. Remove the brake housing and position it by the wheel housing to avoid damage to the brake hose. Remove the brake disc and parking brake assembly with the cable.
4. Remove the large clamp from the rubber bellows on the inner universal joint. To separate the inner universal joint, install the cover (SAAB part No. 7323736) in the rubber bellows to stop the needle bearing from falling out and to keep dirt from entering. Install the protective cap (SAAB part No. 7838469) on the inner drive.
5. Disconnect the tie rod from the steering arm using the proper tool. Remove the nut on the upper ball joint. Remove the bolts from the lower control arm bracket.

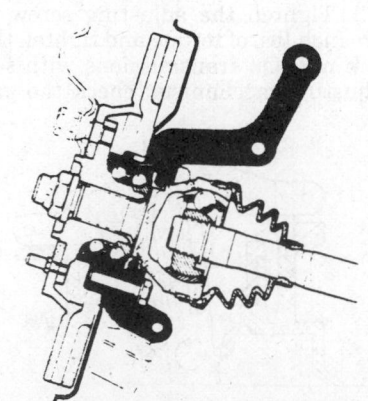

Front axle assembly—9000 Series

6. Remove the drive shaft through the wheel housing and remove the entire front axle assembly.
7. Place the steering knuckle housing in a press and press out the drive shaft.
8. remove the lockring and press out the bearing using a suitable drift.
9. Installation is the reverse of the removal procedure.

9000 Series

The front wheel bearing are double row angular contact bearings which are permanently lubricated and maintenance free. The bearings cannot be replaced individually. To remove the hub proceed as follows.

1. Loosen the hub center nut and the wheel bolts.
2. Raise the vehicle and support it safely.
3. Remove the tire and wheel assembly. Remove the hub center nut and thrust washer.
4. Remove the flexible brake hose from its support clip.
5. Unbolt the caliper and rest it upon the suspension arm.
6. Unscrew the locating stud for the disc and remove it from the hub.
7. Push in on the drive shaft. Remove the four bolts securing the hub to the steering swivel member.
8. Lift the hub and disc back plate from the suspension assembly. Renew the bearings or replace the hub.
9. The installation of the hub is in the reverse of the removal procedure.
10. Tighten the four hub securing bolts to 40–43 ft. lbs., and the center hub nut to 195–208 ft. lbs.

FRONT SUSPENSION

Shock Absorbers

REMOVAL & INSTALLATION
900 Series

1. Disconnect the negative battery cable. Remove the upper shock absorber nut.
2. Raise the vehicle and support it safely. Remove the tire and wheel assembl.
3. Remove the shock absorber retaining bolts. Remove the shock from the vehicle. Save all washers and rubber parts.
4. Installation is the reverse of removal.

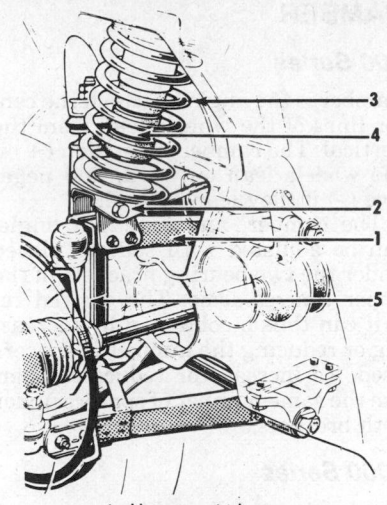

1. Upper control arm
2. Lower spring support
3. Coil spring
4. Rubber buffer
5. Shock absorber

Front suspension assembly

MacPherson Struts

REMOVAL & INSTALLATION

9000 Series

1. Disconnect the negative battery cable. Raise and support the vehicle safely. Remove the front tire and wheel assembly.
2. Remove the front brake hose from the retaining clip on the strut assembly.
3. Unbolt the strut from the steering swivel arm.
4. Remove the three retaining bolts from the top of the strut.
5. Remove the strut from the vehicle..
6. Installation is the reverse of the removal procedure.

OVERHAUL

For all spring and shock absorber removal and installation procedures, and all strut overhaul procedures, please refer to "Strut Overhaul" in the Unit Repair Section.

Springs
REMOVAL & INSTALLATION

900 Series

1. Disconnect the negative battery cable. Remove the upper shock absorber retaining nuts.
2. Raise and support the vehicle safely. Remove the tire and wheel assembly.
3. Install a spring compression tool or equivalent, engaging the upper shanks directly in the spring at the

second free turn from the top of the lower shanks around the spring caps. These alignment shanks are located on the last turn of the spring with the color coded cup right beside the end of the coil.
4. Compress the spring at the top end, approximately 1½ in. If the upper spring attachment of the steel cone is left behind in the wheel housing, remove it.
5. Remove the spring and the steel cone from the vehicle.
6. Installation is the reverse of removal.

Ball Joints

REMOVAL & INSTALLATION

1. Disconnect the negative battery cable. Raise and support the vehicle safely. Remove the tire and wheel assembly.
2. Remove the brake housing and position it out of the way so that the brake hose will not be damaged.
3. Remove the nut that holds the ball joint ball bolt to the steering knuckle housing. Remove the bolt using the proper removal tool.
4. Remove the ball joint from the control arm assembly.
5. Installation is the reverse of removal.

Upper Control Arm

REMOVAL & INSTALLATION

900 Series

NOTE: To remove the left upper control arm, the engine must first be removed from the vehicle.

1. Raise the vehicle and support it safely.

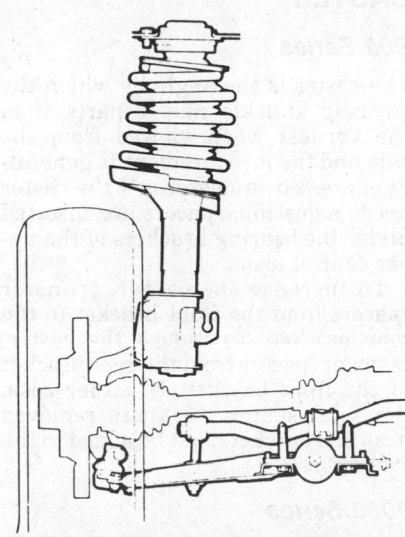

Front suspension assembly – 9000 Series

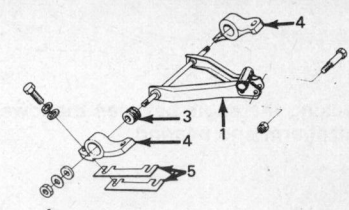

1. Upper control arm
3. Rubber bushing
4. Bearing
5. Spacers

Upper control arm assembly

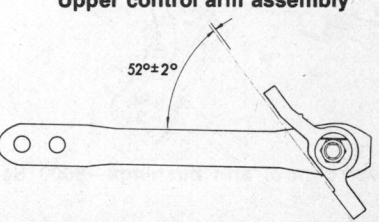

$52° \pm 2°$

Checking the angle between the upper control arm and bearing

2. Remove the tire and wheel assembly. Remove the shock absorber. Compress the coil spring, using a spring compression tool.
3. Remove the two bolts attaching the upper ball joint and lower spring seat to the upper control arm.
4. Remove the bolts from both upper control arm bearing brackets.
5. Remove the coil spring from the vehicle.
6. Remove the control arm and bearings from the vehicle. Save the spacers under the bearings and record the number of spacers used under each bearing.
7. Remove both of the bearing nuts. Now the bearings and bushings can be removed from the control arm.
8. Installation is the reverse of the removal procedure. When installing the bearings to the control arm, the angle between the control arm and the bearing should be $52 \pm 2°$ when both nuts are tightened.

Lower Control Arm

REMOVAL & INSTALLATION

900 Series

1. Disconnect the negative battery cable. Raise the vehicle and support it safely. Remove the tire and wheel assembly.

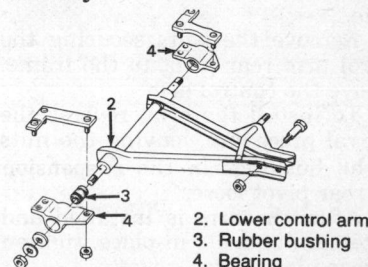

2. Lower control arm
3. Rubber bushing
4. Bearing

Lower control arm bushings – 900 Series

Checking the angle between the lower control arm and bearing

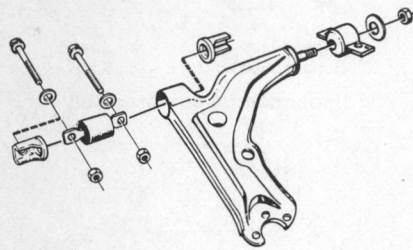

Lower control arm bushings—9000 Series

2. Disconnect the lower end of the shock absorber.

3. Remove the two bolts that attach the ball joint to the control arm.

4. Remove the lower control arm attaching bolts from under the engine compartment floor.

5. Remove the control arm and its attaching brackets from the vehicle.

6. Remove the control arm bearing nuts and remove the bearings from the control arm.

7. Installation is the reverse of the removal procedure. When installing the bearings to the control arm., the angle between the control arm and the bearing should be $18 \pm 2°$ when both nuts are tightened.

9000 Series

1. Disconnect the negative battery cable. Raise the vehicle and support it safely. Remove the tire and wheel assembly.

2. Remove the bolts securing the suspension arm to the ball joint.

3. Remove the nut from the bolt securing the suspension arm to the antiroll bar link. Remove the upper securing bolt for the link.

4. Press down on the suspension arm and withdraw the antiroll bar link.

5. Remove the nuts at the front of the suspension arm from the bolts securing the arm to the frame.

6. Remove the rear bolts securing the reinforcement member to the frame.

7. Remove the bolts securing the control arm rear pivot to the frame. Remove the control arm.

8. To install the arm, reverse the removal procedure, leaving the nuts for the bushings in the suspension arm rear pivot loose.

9. After the arm is installed and the remaining bolts in place, tighten the rear pivot bolts.

10. Check the wheel alignment and

adjust as required, after the vehicle has been allowed to settle by bouncing or driving.

Front Wheel Alignment
TOE-IN

1. Roll the vehicle straight forward on a level floor and stop it without using brakes. It must not be moved backward after this.

2. Take a reading of measurement A with the toe-in gauge between the front wheel rims level with the axles. Mark the measurement points with chalk. Roll the vehicle forward until the chalk marks are level with but behind the axles, and take a reading of B. Any necessary adjustment is made by altering the length of the tie rod.

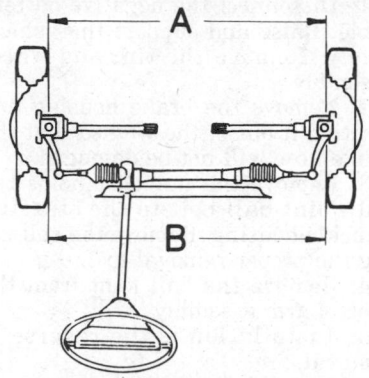

Toe-in adjustment

3. Remove the nut on the outer end of the tie rod and the outer clip on the steering gear rubber bellow.

4. Using the proper tool rotate the tie rod right or left and adjust it until the toe-in is within specification. Hold the bellows during the twisting.

5. Lock the locking nut when adjustment is complete.

CASTER

900 Series

The caster is the angle by which the steering knuckle axis departs from the vertical when viewed from the side and the measurement is generally expressed in degrees. If the caster needs adjusting, spacers are inserted under the bearing brackets of the upper control arms.

To increase the caster, transfer spacers from the front bracket to the rear bracket. To reduce the caster, transfer spacers from the rear bracket to the front bracket. In either case, the total spacer thickness removed from one bracket must be added to the other one.

9000 Series

Caster is not adjustable.

CAMBER

900 Series

Camber is the angle by which the center lines of the wheels lean from the vertical. The camber is position (+) if the wheels lean outward, and negative (–) if they lean inward.

The camber, and king pin angle, can be adjusted with spacers placed under the two bearing brackets of the upper control arms. The desired result can thus be obtained by increasing or reducing the number of spacers used. To increase or reduce camber, use the same number of spacers under both brackets.

9000 Series

Camber is not adjustable.

REAR SUSPENSION

Shock Absorbers

REMOVAL & INSTALLATION

1. Disconnect the negative battery cable. Raise the vehicle and support it safely.

2. Place a suitable jackstand under the rear axle to prevent it from dropping and stretching the brake lines.

3. Position a jack at the rear of the springlink. Remove the shock absorber retaining nuts.

4. Remove the bolts in the springlink mounting on the rear axle (antiroll bar on the 9000 series).

5. Lower the springlink so that the shock absorber can be removed from the vehicle.

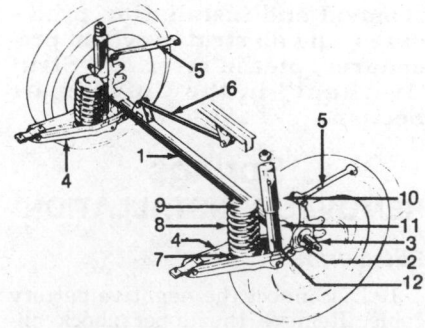

1. Rear axle	7. Spring seat
2. End piece	8. Coil spring
3. Stub axle	9. Spring insulator
4. Spring links	10. Rubber buffer
5. Rear links	11. Stop
6. Cross bar	12. Shock absorber

Rear suspension assembly

6. Installation is the reverse of removal.

Springs

REMOVAL & INSTALLATION

1. Disconnect the negative battery cable. Raise and support the vehicle safely.

2. Remove the tire and wheel assembly. Position a jack under the springlink and disconnect the lower end of the shock absorber.

3. From underneath of the vehicle, remove the two lock nuts that secure the front springlink bearing to the body of the vehicle.

4. Position a jackstand under the rear axle to prevent the brake lines from being damaged by the weight of the rear axle.

5. Lower the springlink so that the spring can be removed from the vehicle together with the upper spring support and the rubber spacer at the lower spring seating which is retained by the spring tension.

6. Installation is the reverse of the removal procedure.

Rear Wheel Bearings

REMOVAL & INSTALLATION

900 Series

UP TO AND INCLUDING CHASSIS NOS. AC1021263, AC2007508, AC3006827 AND AC6001805

NOTE: Each rear wheel hub has two tapered roller bearings. The inner bearing as a larger diameter than the outer bearing.

1. Raise the vehicle and support it safely.

2. Remove the tire and wheel assembly. Remove the brake housing and the brake disc. Support the brake housing to avoid damage to the brake pipe.

3. Remove the dust cap. Remove the locknut and the washer. Pull off the hub, if necessary, use a suitable puller.

4. Remove the seal ring using a suitable tool. Remove the inner rings of both bearings.

5. Place a suitable drift in the milled recesses of the hub and drive out the outer bearing rings. It is advisable to place wooden board under the hub to avoid deforming the end faces.

6. Installation is the reverse of the removal procedure. Torque the lock nut to 36 ft. lbs., than slacken the nut completely and torque it to 2.9 ft. lbs.

INSTALLATION FROM CHASSIS NOS. AC1021264, AC2007509, AC3006828 AND AC6001806

1. Slide the hub onto the stub axle and install the washer lock nut.

2. Tighten the lock nut to a torque of 210 ft. lbs. (300 Nm). If the part of the nut collar that had previously been staked comes in line with the locking groove, install a new nut.

3. Stake the nut collar into the locking groove.

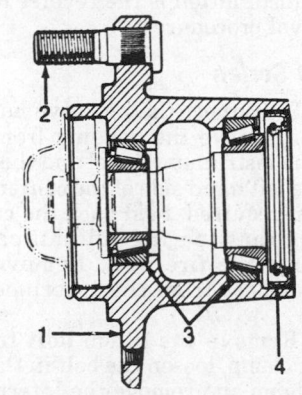

Rear wheel hub and bearings—typical

4. Complete the assembly by installing the dust cap and install the brake disc, brake housing, wheel and wheel nuts.

9000 Series

The wheel bearings are not press fitted on the outboard drive shaft or stub axle, but are incorporated in the hub. The wheel bearings are double row, angular contact bearings which are permanently lubricated and maintenance free. The bearings cannot be replaced individually.

1. Disconnect the negative battery cable. Raise the vehicle and support it safely.

2. Remove the tire and wheel assembly.

3. Remove the brake caliper and disc back plate. Support the disc caliper on the rear axle. Remove the brake disc.

4. Remove the dust cap from the hub center nut. Remove the center nut and thrust washer. Pull the hub from the axle.

5. Upon installation of the hub, install the thrust washer and the nut.

6. Tighten the center nut to a torque of 195–208 ft. lbs..

7. Lock the nut by using drift to punch the flange of the nut in the stub axle thread. Install the dust cap, the disc brake components, the wheel, and then lower the vehicle.

STEERING

Steering Wheel

REMOVAL & INSTALLATION

1. Disconnect the negative battery cable.

2. On some vehicles it will be necessary to remove the bottom cover of the steering wheel bearing.

3. Remove the steering wheel safety pad. Remove the steering wheel emblem. Remove the horn contact. Remove the steering wheel holding nut and washer.

4. Remove the steering wheel using the proper steering wheel removal tool.

5. Installation is the reverse of removal.

Combination Switch

REMOVAL & INSTALLATION

1. Disconnect the negative battery cable.

2. Remove the steering wheel.

3. Remove the cover beneath the bearing support.

4. Remove the combination switch retaining bolts and electrical connections.

5. Remove the switch from the vehicle.

6. Installation is the reverse of the removal procedure.

Manual Steering Gear

REMOVAL & INSTALLATION

900 Series

1. Disconnect the negative battery cable. Remove the left screen under the instrument panel and loosen the rubber bellows at the body lead through for the steering gear intermediate shaft, if required.

2. Raise and support the vehicle safely. Remove the bolt holding the joint to the steering gear pinion or intermediate shaft.

3. Loosen the steering column tube from the body and separate the steering column joint from the pinion. Position the steering column so that the wiring harness is not damaged.

4. Remove both tire and wheel assemblies. Remove the tie rod ends at the steering arms with the proper removal tool. Remove the two steering gear clamps.

5. Move the rack to the right as far as possible. Lift the steering gear to

the right so that the tie rod can be bent down in the opening of the engine compartment floor.

6. Pull the rack to the left and lift the steering gear down through the opening in the engine compartment floor.

7. Installation is the reverse of the removal procedure.

ADJUSTMENT

Radial Play

1. Install the plunger without the spring and screw on the cap without the gasket by hand until it butts against the plunger. Do not use a wrench, as you will damage the cap.

2. Measure the clearance between the cap and the housing with a feeler gauge.

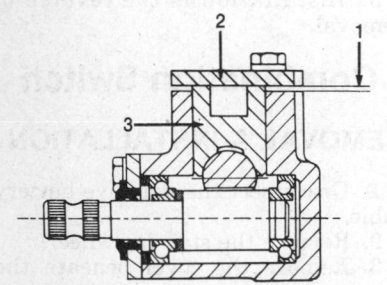

1. Clearance to be measured with feeler gauge
2. Cap
3. Plunger

Radial-play adjustment

3. Add 0.002–0.006 in. to the measured clearance to allow for the play to be left between the plunger and cap after assembly. Measure the thickness of the gasket and shims with a micrometer. Shims are available in thickness of 0.005 in., 0.0075 in., 0.010 in., 0.015 in. and 0.020 in.

Power Steering Gear

REMOVAL & INSTALLATION

900 Series

1. Disconnect the negative battery cable. Remove the left screen under the instrument panel and loosen the rubber bellows at the body lead through for the steering gear intermediate shaft, if required. Disconnect and plug the power steering fluid lines.

2. Raise and support the vehicle safely. Remove the bolt holding the joint to the steering gear pinion or intermediate shaft.

3. Loosen the steering column tube from the body and separate the steering column joint from the pinion. Position the steering column so that the wiring harness is not damaged.

4. Remove both tire and wheel assemblies. Remove the tie rod ends at the steering arms with the proper removal tool. Remove the two steering gear clamps.

5. Move the rack to the right as far as possible. Lift the steering gear to the right so that the tie rod can be bent down in the opening of the engine compartment floor.

6. Pull the rack to the left and lift the steering gear down through the opening in the engine compartment floor.

7. Installation is the reverse of the removal procedure.

9000 Series

1. Disconnect the negative battery cable. Remove the padding from under the instrument panel and the trim on the left hand side of the center tunnel, as required. Fold back the carpet where the steering column passes through the fire wall. Remove the rubber boot from the intermediate shaft.

2. Remove the pinch bolt in the lower clamp, loosen the bolt in the upper clamp and remove the intermediate shaft.

3. Remove the cover panel from the fire wall. Take care not to damage the gasket, seal and plastic bushing.

4. Raise and support the vehicle safely. Remove both tire and wheel assemblies.

5. Remove the rear section of the inner fender panel under the left fender.

6. Separate the left and right tie rod ends from the steering arms.

7. Drain the power steering fluid from the pump reservoir.

8. Disconnect the hoses from the pump and reservoir. Plug the openings to prevent fluid from leaking out and dirt from entering.

9. Remove the retaining bolts from the rack and pinion assembly.

10. Remove the vertical brace between the engine subframe and the body.

11. Lift out the rack and pinion unit through the left fender inner panel

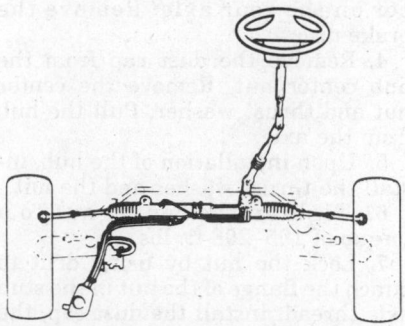

Power steering assembly – 9000 Series

opening. Do not damage the rubber boots or brake hose.

12. Installation is the reverse of the removal procedure. Fill the reservoir and bleed the system by allowing the engine to run at idle.

ADJUSTMENT

Radial Play

900 SERIES

1. Screw in the adjusting screw all the way until the resistance of the twisting steering gear is felt.

2. Back off the adjusting screw ½ turn.

3. Check that the steering gear can be turned from lock to lock in both directions without jamming.

4. Tighten the lock nut with a torque of 50–60 ft. lbs.

9000 SERIES

1. Turn the adjusting screw completely in.

2. Back off the adjusting screw approximately 40–60 ft. lbs.

3. Tighten the lock nut to 47–54 ft. lbs. (65–75 Nm).

Power Steering Pump

REMOVAL & INSTALLATION

900 Series

1. Disconnect the negative battery cable. Drain the fluid from the power steering pump.

2. Drain the coolant from the drain cock on the engine block and disconnect the hose from between the expansion tank and the water pump.

3. Disconnect the power steering pump hoses. Grip the hexagonal nipple on the pump when removing the delivery line.

4. Unbolt the pump unit from the bracket and the engine mounting. Remove the power steering belt. Remove the pump complete with its mounting.

5. Installation is the reverse of the removal procedure.

9000 Series

1. Disconnect the negative battery cable. Remove the fluid from the pump reservoir.

2. Raise and support the vehicle safely. Remove the right front wheel and the right inner fender panel.

3. Remove the drive belt. Remove the bracket for the engine oil filler pipe. Remove the engine stay bracket. Disconnect the hoses from the pump. Plug the openings.

4. Remove the pump retaining bolts. Remove the pump. Note that one bolt is located behind the pump

pulley and is accessible only through the aperature in the pulley.

5. Installation is the reverse of the removal procedure.

BELT ADJUSTMENT

900 Series

Tighten the belt so that when pressure is applied to the belt at a given point the distance between both belt pulleys is 5–10mm.

9000 Series

1. After the belt has been installed, a strand tension gauge must be used to tighten the belt properly.
2. A new belt must be tightened to 185 ± 15 lbs. or 800 ± 65 N.
3. A used belt must be tightened to 120 ± 10 lbs. or 535 ± 45 N.

SYSTEM BLEEDING

1. Fill the power steering pump with the proper fluid.
2. Start the engine and top off the level of fluid to 0.4 in. above the bottom of the filter.
3. Turn the steering wheel from left to right several times to expel air from the system.
4. Refill the pump as needed.
5. Allow the engine to operate at idle.

Tie Rod Ends

REMOVAL & INSTALLATION

1. Disconnect the negative battery cable. Raise and support the vehicle safely.
2. Remove the tire and wheelassembly. Remove the nut.
3. Disconnect the ball joint bolt from the steering arm using the proper removal tool. Do not knock the ball joint bolt out, as this could cause damage to the ball joint and other related parts.
4. Back off the nut that locks the end assembly to the tie rod.
5. Unscrew the end assembly from the tie rod.
6. Installation is the reverse of the removal procedure. Check and adjust the toe-in as required.

BRAKES

For all service and adjustment procedures not detailed below, please refer to "Brakes" in the Unit Repair Section.

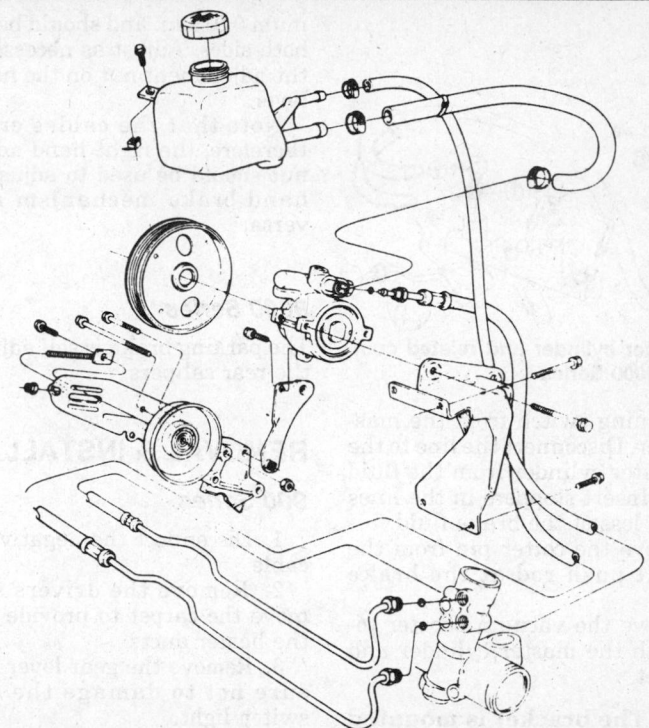

Power steering system and related components – 9000 Series

Master Cylinder

REMOVAL & INSTALLATION

1. Disconnect the negative battery cable. Disconnect the electrical connection to the brake warning switch.
2. Disconnect the hose from the clutch master cylinder to the fluid reservoir. Insert a plastic stopper in the nipple of the reservoir.
3. Disconnect the brake lines to the master cylinder.
4. Remove the nuts that hold the master cylinder to the power brake booster. Remove the master cylinder from the vehicle.
5. Installation is the reverse of removal. Bleed the system as required.

Power Brake Booster

REMOVAL & INSTALLATION

1. Disconnect the negative battery cable. Remove the steering column bearing cover, ash tray and safety padding screw. Remove the upper circlip on the brake pedal push rod, if equipped.
2. Remove the two electrical connections on the brake light switch. Remove the safety padding screws in the engine compartment.
3. Remove the vacuum hose from the non return valve which is located on the vacuum booster.
4. Disconnect the brake lines and the electrical connections for the

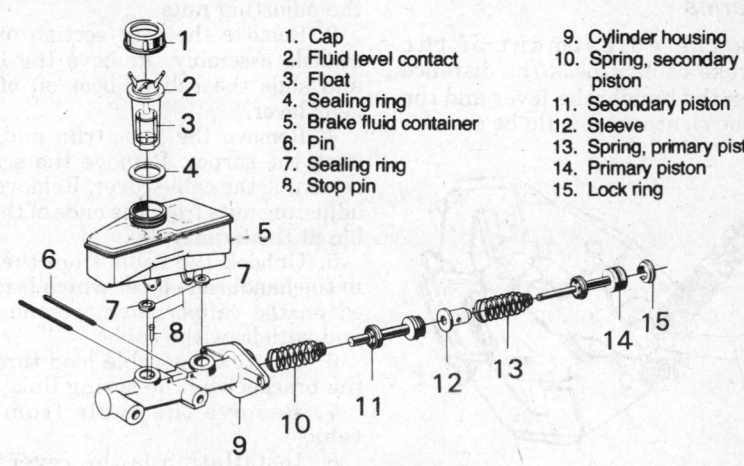

1. Cap	9. Cylinder housing
2. Fluid level contact	10. Spring, secondary piston
3. Float	
4. Sealing ring	11. Secondary piston
5. Brake fluid container	12. Sleeve
6. Pin	13. Spring, primary piston
7. Sealing ring	14. Primary piston
8. Stop pin	15. Lock ring

Typical brake master cylinder

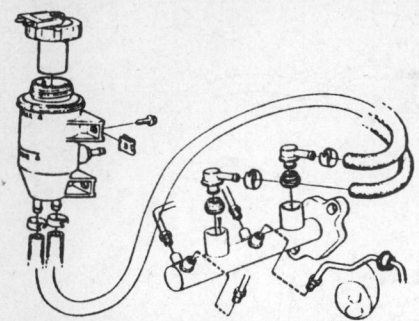

Brake master cylinder and related components—9000 Series

brake warning switch from the master cylinder. Disconnect the line to the clutch master cylinder from the fluid reservoir. Insert stoppers in the lines to prevent loss of the brake fluid.

5. Remove the cotter pin from the servo unit push rod at the brake pedal.

6. Remove the vacuum booster together with the master cylinder and the bracket.

NOTE: The bracket is mounted on the dash panel with 4 bolts and nuts. Three of these bolts are accessible from underneath in the passenger compartment after removal of the screen section and parts of the dash panel insulation felt below the instrument panel. The fourth nut is accessible from the engine compartment by the bracket.

7. Separate the master cylinder and the bracket from the vacuum booster.

8. Installation is the reverse of removal. Bleed the system as required.

Parking Brake Cable

ADJUSTMENT

900 Series

Check the adjustment of the handbrake cable. Check the distance between the handbrake lever and the yoke: the clearance should be a maxi-

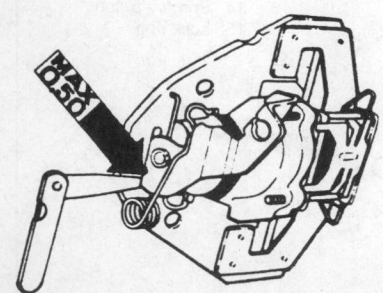

Parking brake adjustment procedure

mum 0.019 in. and should be equal on both sides. Adjust as necessary using the adjustment nut on the handbrake lever.

Note that the cables cross over therefore, the right hand adjustment nut should be used to adjust the left hand brake mechanism and vice versa.

9000 Series

The parking brake is self adjusting on the rear calipers.

REMOVAL & INSTALLATION

900 Series

1. Disconnect the negative battery cable.

2. Remove the drivers seat. Remove the carpet to provide access to the heater ducts.

3. Remove the gear lever cover. Be sure not to damage the ignition switch light.

4. Remove the air ducts and cover plates. Disconnect the cable from the adjustment nut on the handbrake lever. Remove the clip holding the two cables to the floor.

5. Remove the rubber bushing in the side of the wheel housing. Disconnect the cable from the handbrake lever at the brake cylinder housing.

6. Remove the cable from underneath inside the engine compartment.

7. Installation is the reverse of the removal procedure.

9000 Series

1. Disconnect the negative battery cable. Remove the passenger seat.

2. Slide the bush seal off the handbrake lever from inside the vehicle. Lift the plastic locking plate off the adjusting nuts.

3. Remove the rear section of the console assembly. Remove the bezel and slide the rubber boot off of the gear lever.

4. Remove the floor trim and fold back the carpet. Remove the screws retaining the cable cover. Remove the adjusting nuts from the ends of the cable at the handbrake.

5. Unhook the cable from the slot in the handbrake lever which is located on the caliper. Remove the boot and withdraw the cable.

6. Unscrew the cable lead through the bracket and the spring link.

7. Remove the cable from the vehicle.

8. Installation is the reverse of the removal procedure.

CHASSIS ELECTRICAL

Heater Blower
REMOVAL & INSTALLATION

900 Series

1. Disconnect the negative battery cable.

2. Remove the switch panel and the upper section of the instrument panel.

3. Disconnect the electrical leads to the fan motor.

4. Remove the retaining screws for the right hand defroster valve housing.

5. Remove the fan retaining screws. Remove the fan from its housing.

6. The installation is in the reverse of the removal procedure.

9000 Series
WITH AIR CONDITION

1. Disconnect the negative battery cable. Remove the hood assembly.

2. Disconnect the wiper arms. Remove the covers on the evaporator and wiper motor. Unplug the connector for the fan control unit on vehicles with automatic climate control.

3. Remove the false fire wall panel.

4. Remove the plastic drainage tube moulding below the windshield moulding.

5. Remove the securing bolts the electronic ignition control unit and position it out of the way.

6. Remove the clip and unplug the connectors. Remove the complete wiper assembly.

7. Remove the rubber lead through panel for the coolant hoses. Drain cooling system. Disconnect the quick release couplings for the coolant hoses at the heat exchanger.

8. Remove the throttle dash pot assembly.

9. Remove the vacuum pump retaining screws. Position the pump out of the way.

10. Remove the evaporator body retaining screws and the clips for the refrigerant hoses.

11. Remove the lock washer and disconnect the cable for the temperature valve.

12. Carefully lift the evaporator and remove the clips on either side of the fan. Remove the complete fan assembly by twisting the fan diagonally upwards.

13. Remove the screw in the center of the casing. Release the clips and the grille at the discharge duct.

14. Separate the fan housing and undo the securing screw for the fan motor.

15. Lift the cover upward and withdraw the motor complete with the impeller.

16. To install the fan motor assembly, reverse the removal procedure. Be careful not to separate the connector for the radiator fan control when installing the false fire wall panel.

WITHOUT AIR CONDITION

1. Disconnect the negative battery cable.

2. Remove the cover from the windshield wipers.

3. Remove the fresh air filter assembly.

4. Unplug the connectors for the fan motor and fan resistors.

5. Disconnect the temperature control cable.

6. Release the clips on either side of the fan body and turn the body diagonally upwards.

7. Remove the screws in the center of the casing, release the clips and remove the grille from the discharge duct.

8. Separate the fan casing. Remove the screw securing the fan motor.

9. Lift the cover for the lead and withdraw the motor complete with impeller.

10. Installation is the reverse of the removal procedure.

Heater Core

REMOVAL & INSTALLATION

900 Series

1. Disconnect the negative battery cable. Remove the dash panel under the switches on the steering column and the lower section of the instrument panel.

2. Remove the air diffuser and retaining screws.

3. Remove the left defroster and speaker grill.

4. Remove the control rod from between the coolant shut off valve and the control rod by sliding the rod as far forward as it will go to free it from the knob, then pull it rearward to free it from the shut off valve.

NOTE: The plastic joint at the control knob is accessible from underneath once the switches below the heater controls have been moved backward.

5. Remove the lower section of the heater housing.

6. Drain the coolant and disconnect the hoses. Plug the ends of the hoses to prevent coolant from leaking into the compartment.

7. Separate the heater core from the housing and guide it backward and downward. It will be necessary to disconnect the brake pedal return spring and depress the brake pedal slightly.

8. The water valve and the heater core can be separated after their removal. Do not kink or break the capillary tube.

9. Installation is the reverse of the removal procedure.

9000 Series

1. Disconnect the negative battery cable. Remove the hood assembly.

2. Disconnect the wiper arms. Remove the covers on the evaporator and wiper motor. Unplug the connector for the fan control unit on vehicles with automatic climate control.

3. Remove the false fire wall panel. Drain the radiator.

4. Remove the plastic drainage tube moulding below the windshield moulding.

5. Remove the securing bolts the electronic ignition control unit and position it out of the way.

6. Remove the clip and unplug the connectors. Remove the complete wiper assembly.

7. Remove the rubber lead through panel for the coolant hoses. Drain cooling system. Disconnect the quick release couplings for the coolant hoses at the heat exchanger.

8. Remove the throttle dash pot assembly.

9. Remove the vacuum pump retaining screws. Position the pump out of the way.

10. Remove the evaporator body retaining screws and the clips for the refrigerant hoses.

11. Remove the lock washer and disconnect the cable for the temperature valve.

12. Carefully lift the evaporator and remove the clips on either side of the fan. Remove the complete fan assembly by twisting the fan diagonally upwards.

13. Remove the screw in the center of the casing. Release the clips and the grille at the discharge duct.

14. Separate the fan housing and undo the securing screw for the fan motor.

15. Lift the cover upward and withdraw the motor complete with impeller.

16. Release the retaining clips and disconnect the hoses from the heater core.

17. Pull the heater core from the engine side of the fire wall.

18. To install, position new O-rings and connect the heater hoses. Complete the assembly in the reverse order of the removal procedure.

Radio

Most radios used in Saab vehicles are dealer installed or aftermarket units. It is therefore impossible to give specific procedures for removal and installation of these units. Care should be exercised when servicing a vehicle that has a radio problem. Late model vehicles, with factory installed radios, are equipped with a theft proof mechanism that renders the radio non functionable unless the owner knows the six digit combination.

Windshield Wiper Switch

REMOVAL & INSTALLATION

1. Disconnect the negative battery cable.

2. Pull the steering wheel as far forward as it will go. Remove the cover from under the steering column assembly.

3. Disconnect the electrical connector from the switch assembly.

4. Remove the switch retaining screws. Remove the switch from the vehcile.

5. Installation is the reverse of the removal procedure.

Windshield Wiper Motor

REMOVAL & INSTALLATION

900 Series

1. Disconnect the negative battery cable. Remove the wiper arms from the vehicle. Remove the rubber grommets.

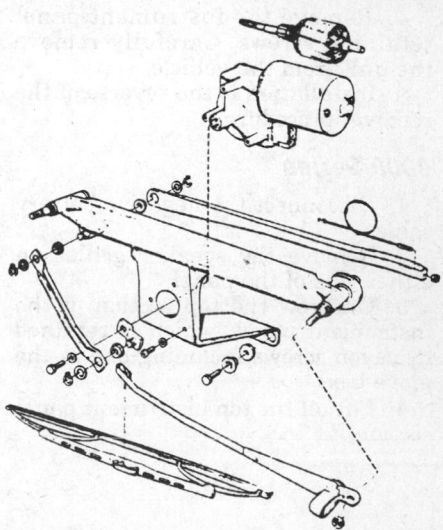

Windshield wiper and motor assembly

2. Remove the four mounting screws. Disconnect the electrical lead. Remove the wiper unit from the vehicle.

3. Separate the wiper motor from the wiper assembly.

4. Installation is the reverse of the removal procedure.

9000 Series

1. Disconnect the negative battery cable.

2. Raise the covers on the wiper arms, remove the retaining nuts and lift the arms off.

3. Remove the rubber grommets from the spindles and remove the four bulkhead panel bolts.

4. Lift the bulkhead panel from the vehicle.

5. Disconnect the electrical connector from the wiper motor.

6. Remove the spindle nuts and remove the four retaining bolts for the wiper motor bracket.

7. Push downward and pull forward on the push rod for the left hand wiper.

8. Lift out the wiper motor assembly complete with the bracket and the push rod linkage.

9. Installation is the reverse of the removal procedure.

Instrument Cluster

REMOVAL & INSTALLATION

900 Series

1. Disconnect the negative battery cable. Remove the steering wheel.

2. Remove the four screws in the switch panel and tilt the panel back.

3. Remove the left speaker/defroster grille. Pull apart the instrument panel connectors. Disconnect the speedometer cable.

4. Remove the instrument panel retaining screws. Carefully remove the unit from the vehicle.

5. Installation is the reverse of the removal procedure.

9000 Series

1. Disconnect the negative battery cable.

2. Remove the speaker grilles on either side of the panel.

3. Unscrew the top section of the instrument panel, which is retained by seven screws including one in the glove box.

4. Lift off the top instrument panel section.

5. Remove the air duct from the opening in the top.

6. Disconnect the speedometer cable, the vacuum hoses to the turbo pressure gauge and unplug all connectors to the display panel.

7. Remove the two screws of the instrument display panel.

8. Withdraw the instrument cluster through the top of the instrument panel.

9. Installation is the reverse of removal procedure. Be sure the air duct fitting is tight when reassembling the duct tubing.

Ignition Switch

REMOVAL & INSTALLATION

900 Series

1. Disconnect the negative battery cable.

2. Remove the center console.

3. Disconnect the electrical connections from the switch.

4. Remove the assembly from the vehicle.

5. Installation is the reverse of removal.

9000 Series

1. Disconnect the negative battery cable.

2. Remove the steering wheel assembly.

3. Remove the cover panels from the wiper/washer and direction indicator switches.

4. Remove the upper section of the instrument panel. Remove the instrument cluster assembly.

5. Remove the instrument unit in the following order:

    a. Unplug the connectors on the right hand side of the unit.

    b. Disconnect the pressure gauge hose.

    c. Disconnect the speedometer cable.

6. Remove the clip securing the wiring loom and flexible ducts to the steering column.

7. Unplug the connector for the wipers, direction signals and leads for the horn switch and ignition switch.

8. Remove the pinch bolt in the upper joint, loosen the other bolts and withdraw the universal joint from the splines on the steering column shaft.

9. Remove the steering column wheel adjustment assembly by tapping out the roll pin and removing the nut and washer. Withdraw the shaft from the clamp and lift the upper section of the steering wheel adjustment assembly. Remove three socket headed bolts and lift off the holder for the directional indicator unit.

10. Remove the upper section of the steering column, removing the rubber bushing completely from the housing.

11. Remove the shake proof washer. Remove the column bearing.

12. With the switch support out remove the socket headed screws and remove the ignition switch.

13. To remove the cylinder, turn the ignition key to position number one, press in on the locking tab and withdraw the cylinder.

14. Installation is the reverse of the removal procedure.

Headlight Switch

REMOVAL & INSTALLATION

1. Disconnect the negative battery cable.

2. Pull the switch from its mounting on the instrument panel assembly.

3. Disconnect the electrical connectors from the switch.

4. Remove the switch from the vehicle.

5. Installation is the reverse of the removal procedure.

Stoplight Switch

REMOVAL & INSTALLATION

1. Disconnect the negative battery cable.

2. Remove the necessary trim and padding to gain access to the switch assembly.

3. Disconnect the electrical connections from the switch assembly.

4. Remove the switch from its mounting.

5. Installation is the reverse of the removal procedure.

Fuses and Circuit Breakers

LOCATION

The fuse panel is located under the hood of the vehicle. It is on the left hand side for the 900 series vehicles. The fuse panel for the 9000 series vehicles is located and accessed through an access panel in the glove compartment.

Subaru 15
1600, 1800, Justy,
XT Coupe—All Models

SERIAL NUMBER IDENTIFICATION

Vehicle Identification Plate

The Vehicle Identification Plate is on the bulkhead in the engine compartment.

Engine Number

The engine number is stamped on the front right-side of the crankcase (except 1200 engines) or at the rear-side of the engine below the cylinder head (1200 engines).

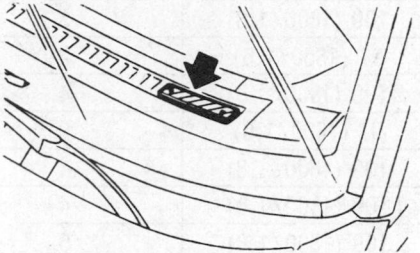

Vehicle Identification Number is located on the left-side of the dash

Vehicle Identification Number

The Vehicle Identification Number (VIN) is stamped on a plate located on the top of the dashboard on the driver's-side, visible through the windshield.

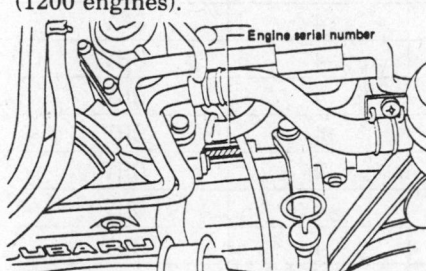

The engine number is stamped on the front right-side of the crankcase—except 1200 (OHC) engines

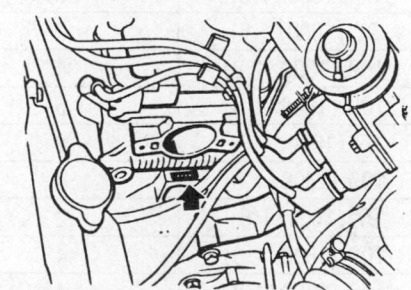

The engine number is stamped on the rear-side of the engine, below the cylinder head—1200 (OHC) engines

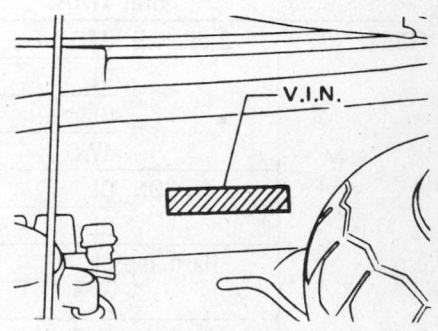

Vehicle Identification Plate is located on a plate attached to the bulkhead panel in the engine compartment

ENGINE IDENTIFICATION

Year	Model		Engine Displacement cu. in. (cc/liter)	Engine Series Identification	No. of Cylinders	Engine Type Type
1981	2 dr. H.B.	STD	97 (1600/1.6)	1	4	OHV
		DL	97 (1600/1.6)	2	4	OHV
		GL	109 (1800/1.8)	4	4	OHV
		4WD	109 (1800/1.8)	5	4	OHV
	4 dr. SDN.	DL	97 (1600/1.6)	2	4	OHV
		GL	109 (1800/1.8)	4	4	OHV

ENGINE IDENTIFICATION

Year	Model	Engine Displacement cu. in. (cc/liter)	Engine Series Identification ①	No. of Cylinders	Engine Type Type
1981	2 dr. H.B. STD	97 (1600/1.6)	1	4	OHV
	DL	97 (1600/1.6)	2	4	OHV
	GL	109 (1800/1.8)	4	4	OHV
	4WD	109 (1800/1.8)	5	4	OHV
	4 dr. SDN. DL	97 (1600/1.6)	2	4	OHV
	GL	109 (1800/1.8)	4	4	OHV
	Hard Top DL	97 (1600/1.6)	2	4	OHV
	GLF	109 (1800/1.8)	4	4	OHV
	S. W. 2WD	97 (1600/1.6)	2	4	OHV
	4WD	97 (1600/1.6)	3	4	OHV
	Brat 4WD	109 (1800/1.8)	5	4	OHV
1982	2 dr. H.B. STD	97 (1600/1.6)	2	4	OHV
	DL	97 (1600/1.6)	2	4	OHV
	GL	109 (1800/1.8)	4	4	OHV
	4WD	109 (1800/1.8)	5	4	OHV
	4 dr. SDN. DL	97 (1600/1.6)	2	4	OHV
	GL	109 (1800/1.8)	4	4	OHV
	Hard Top DL	97 (1600/1.6)	2	4	OHV
	GLF	109 (1800/1.8)	4	4	OHV
	S. W. 2WD	109 (1800/1.8)	4	4	OHV
	4WD	109 (1800/1.8)	5	4	OHV
	Brat 4WD	109 (1800/1.8)	5	4	OHV
1983	2 dr. H.B. STD	97 (1600/1.6)	2	4	OHV
	DL	97 (1600/1.6)	2	4	OHV
	GL	109 (1800/1.8)	4	4	OHV
	4WD	109 (1800/1.8)	5	4	OHV
	4 dr. SDN. DL	97 (1600/1.6)	2	4	OHV
	GL	109 (1800/1.8)	4	4	OHV
	Hard Top DL	97 (1600/1.6)	2	4	OHV
	GL	109 (1800/1.8)	4	4	OHV
	S. W. 2WD	109 (1800/1.8)	4	4	OHV
	4WD	109 (1800/1.8)	5	4	OHV
	Brat 2WD	109 (1800/1.8)	5	4	OHV
1984	2 dr. H.B. STD	97 (1600/1.6)	2	4	OHV
	GL	109 (1800/1.8)	4	4	OHV
	4WD	109 (1800/1.8)	5	4	OHV
	4 dr. SDN DL	97 (1600/1.6)	2	4	OHV
	GL	109 (1800/1.8)	4	4	OHV
	4WD	109 (1800/1.8)	5	4	OHV
	Hard Top DL	97 (1600/1.6)	2	4	OHV
	GL	109 (1800/1.8)	4	4	OHV
	4WD	109 (1800/1.8)	5	4	OHV
	S. W. 2WD	109 (1800/1.8)	4	4	OHV
	4WD	109 (1800/1.8)	5	4	OHV
	Brat 4WD	109 (1800/1.8)	5	4	OHV

ENGINE IDENTIFICATION

Year	Model		Engine Displacement cu. in. (cc/liter)	Engine Series Identification ①	No. of Cylinders	Engine Type Type
1985	2 dr. H.B.	STD	97 (1600/1.6)	2	4	OHV
		2WD	109 (1800/1.8)	4	4	OHV
		4WD	109 (1800/1.8)	5	4	OHV
	Brat	4WD	109 (1800/1.8)	5	4	OHV
	4 dr. SDN.	2WD	109 (1800/1.8)	4	4	OHC
		4WD	109 (1800/1.8)	5	4	OHC
		4WD ②	109 (1800/1.8)	7	4	OHC
	S. W.	2WD	109 (1800/1.8)	4	4	OHC
		4WD	109 (1800/1.8)	5	4	OHC
	XT Coupe	2WD	109 (1800/1.8)	4	4	OHC
		4WD	109 (1800/1.8)	7	4	OHC
1986	2 dr. H.B.	STD	97 (1600/1.6)	2	4	OHV
		2WD	109 (1800/1.8)	4	4	OHC
		4WD	109 (1800/1.8)	5	4	OHC
	Brat	4WD	109 (1800/1.8)	5	4	OHC
	4 dr. SDN.	2WD	109 (1800/1.8)	4	4	OHC
		4WD	109 (1800/1.8)	5	4	OHC
		4WD ②	109 (1800/1.8)	7	4	OHC
	3 dr.	2WD	109 (1800/1.8)	4	4	OHC
		4WD	109 (1800/1.8)	5	4	OHC
	S. W.	2WD	109 (1800/1.8)	4	4	OHC
		4WD	109 (1800/1.8)	5	4	OHC
		4WD ②	109 (1800/1.8)	7	4	OHC
	XT Coupe	2WD	109 (1800/1.8)	4	4	OHC
		4WD	109 (1800/1.8)	7	4	OHC
1987-88	Brat	4WD	109 (1800/1.8)	5	4	OHC
	4 dr. SDN.	2WD	109 (1800/1.8)	4	4	OHC
		4WD	109 (1800/1.8)	5	4	OHC
		4WD ②	109 (1800/1.8)	7	4	OHC
	3 dr.	2WD	109 (1800/1.8)	4	4	OHC
		4WD	109 (1800/1.8)	5	4	OHC
	S. W.	2WD	109 (1800/1.8)	4	4	OHC
		4WD	109 (1800/1.8)	5	4	OHC
		4WD ②	109 (1800/1.8)	7	4	OHC
	XT Coupe	2WD	109 (1800/1.8)	4	4	OHC
		4WD	109 (1800/1.8)	7	4	OHC
	Justy	2WD	73 (1200/1.2)	7	3	OHC
		4WD	73 (1200/1.2)	8	3	OHC

OHC—Overhead Cam
OHV—Overhead Valve
HB—Hatchback
SDN—Sedan
S. W.—Station Wagon
2WD—Two Wheel Drive
4WD—Four Wheel Drive
① The engine code is the 6th digit of the VIN identification number.
② Equipped with air suspension.

GENERAL ENGINE SPECIFICATIONS

Year	Model	Engine Displacement cu. in. (cc)	Fuel System Type	Net Horsepower @ rpm	Net Torque @ rmp (ft. lbs.)	Bore × Stroke (in.)	Compression Ratio	Oil Pressure @ 2000 rpm
1981	4-cyl (OHV)	97 (1600)	2 bbl	67 @ 5200	81 @ 2400	3.62 × 2.36	8.5:1	36–57
	4-cyl (OHV)	109 (1800)	2 bbl	72 @ 4800	92 @ 2400	3.62 × 2.64	8.7:1	50–57
1982	4-cyl (OHV)	97 (1600)	2 bbl	67 @ 5200	81 @ 2400	3.62 × 2.36	8.5:1	36–57
	4-cyl (OHV)	109 (1800)	2 bbl	72 @ 4800	92 @ 2400	3.62 × 2.64	8.7:1	50–57
1983	4-cyl (OHV)	97 (1600)	2 bbl	67 @ 5200	81 @ 2400	3.62 × 2.36	9.0:1	36–57
	4-cyl (OHV)	109 (1800)	2 bbl	72 @ 4800	92 @ 2400	3.62 × 2.64	8.7:1	50–57
	4-cyl (OHV)	109 (1800)	EGI Turbo	111 @ 4800	123 @ 2000	3.62 × 2.64	7.7:1	57–64
1984	4-cyl (OHV)	97 (1600)	2 bbl	67 @ 5200	81 @ 2400	3.62 × 2.36	9.0:1	36–57
	4-cyl (OHV)	109 (1800)	2 bbl	72 @ 4800	92 @ 2400	3.62 × 2.64	8.7:1	50–57
	4-cyl (OHV)	109 (1800)	EGI Turbo	111 @ 4800	123 @ 2000	3.62 × 2.64	7.7:1	57–64
1985	4-cyl (OHV)	97 (1600)	2 bbl	67 @ 5200	81 @ 2400	3.62 × 2.36	8.5:1	57–64
	4-cyl (OHV)	109 (1800)	2 bbl	73 @ 4400	94 @ 2400	3.62 × 2.64	8.7:1	57–64
	4-cyl (OHC)	109 (1800)	2 bbl	82 @ 4800	101 @ 2800	3.62 × 2.64	9.0:1	57–64
			MFI	94 @ 5200	101 @ 2800	3.62 × 2.64	9.0:1	57–64
			MFI Turbo	111 @ 4800	134 @ 2800	3.62 × 2.64	7.7:1	57–64
1986	4-cyl (OHV)	97 (1600)	2 bbl	67 @ 5200	81 @ 2400	3.62 × 2.36	8.5:1	57–64
	4-cyl (OHV)	109 (1800)	2 bbl	73 @ 4400	94 @ 2400	3.62 × 2.64	8.7:1	57–64
	4-cyl (OHC)	109 (1800)	2 bbl	82 @ 4800	101 @ 2800	3.62 × 2.64	9.0:1	57–64
			SPFI	90 @ 5600	101 @ 2800	3.62 × 2.64	9.5:1	57–64
			MFI Turbo	110 @ 4800	134 @ 2800	3.62 × 2.64	7.7:1	57–64
1987–88	4-cyl (OHV)	97 (1600)	2 bbl	67 @ 5200	81 @ 2400	3.62 × 2.36	9.0:1	57–64
	4-cyl (OHV)	109 (1800)	2 bbl	73 @ 4400	94 @ 2400	3.62 × 2.64	8.7:1	57–64
	4-cyl (OHC)	109 (1800)	2 bbl	82 @ 4800	92 @ 2400	3.62 × 2.64	9.0:1	57–64
			SPFI	90 @ 5600	101 @ 2800	3.62 × 2.64	9.5:1	57–64
			MPFI	94 @ 5200	101 @ 2800	3.62 × 2.64	9.0:1	57–64
			MPFI Turbo	110 @ 4800	134 @ 2800	3.62 × 2.64	7.7:1	57–64
	3-cyl (OHC)	73 (1200)	2 bbl	66 @ 5200	70 @ 3200	3.07 × 3.27	9.0:1	35–40

EGI—Electronic Fuel Gasoline Injection (Turbo charged)
MFI—Multi Point Fuel Injection
MPFI—Multi Point Fuel Injection
SPFI—Single Point Fuel Injection

ENGINE TUNE-UP SPECIFICATIONS

Year	Model	Engine Displacement cu. in. (cc)	Spark Plugs type	Gap (in.)	Ignition Timing (deg.) MT	AT	Compression Pressure (psi)	Fuel Pump (psi)	Idle Speed (rpm) [2] MT	AT	Valve Clearance In.	Ex.
1981	Brat HB	97 (1600)	BPES-11	0.040	8B @ 700	—	175	1.3–2.0	700	—	0.010	0.014
	Carburetor	109 (1800)	BPES-11	0.040	8B @ 700	8B @ 800	175	1.3–2.0	700	800	0.010	0.014
1982	Brat HB	97 (1600)	BPES-11	0.040	8B @ 700	—	175	1.3–2.0	700	—	0.010	0.014
	Carburetor	109 (1800)	BPES-11	0.040	8B @ 700	8B @ 800	175	1.3–2.0	700	800	0.010	0.014

ENGINE TUNE-UP SPECIFICATIONS

Year	Model	Engine Displacement cu. in. (cc)	Spark Plugs type	Gap (in.)	Ignition Timing (deg.) MT	AT	Compression Pressure (psi)	Fuel Pump (psi)	Idle Speed (rpm) ② MT	AT	Valve Clearance In.	Ex.
1983	Brat HB	97 (1600)	BPR6ES-11	0.040	8B @ 700	—	175	1.3–2.0	700	800	0.010	0.014
	Carburetor	109 (1800)	BPR6ES-11	0.040	8B @ 700	8B @ 800	175	1.3–2.0	700	800	0.010 ①	0.014 ①
	Turbo	109 (1800)	BPR6ES-11	0.040	15B @ 800	—	156	43.4	800	—	0	0
1984	Brat HB	97 (1600)	BPR6ES-11	0.040	8B @ 700	—	175	1.3–2.0	700	—	0.010	0.014
	Carburetor	109 (1800)	BPR6ES-11	0.040	8B @ 700	8B @ 800	175	1.3–2.0	700	800	0.010 ①	0.014 ①
	Turbo	109 (1800)	BPR6ES-11	0.040	15B @ 800	—	156	43.4	800	—	0	0
1985	Brat HB	97 (1600)	BPR6ES-11	0.040	8B @ 700	—	168	1.3–2.0	700	—	0	0
	Carburetor	109 (1800)	BPR6ES-11	0.040	8B @ 700	8B @ 800	168	2.6–3.3	650	800	0	0
	MPFI	109 (1800)	BPR6ES-11	0.040	6B @ 700	6B @ 800	161	61–71	700	800	0	0
	Turbo	109 (1800)	BPR6ES-11	0.040	20B @ 700	20B @ 800	145	61–71	700	800	0	0
	XT Coupe	109 (1800)	BPR6ES-11	0.040	6B @ 700	6B @ 800	161	61–71	700	800	0	0
	XT Coupe Turbo	109 (1800)	BPR6ES-11	0.040	25B @ 700	25B @ 800	145	61–71	700	800	0	0
1986	Brat HB	97 (1600)	BPR6ES-11	0.040	8B @ 700	—	168	2.6–3.3	700	—	0	0
	Carburetor	109 (1800)	BPR6ES-11	0.040	8B @ 700	8B @ 800	161	2.6–3.3	700	800	0	0
	SPFI	109 (1800)	BPR6ES-11	0.040	—	20B @ 700	168	28–43	—	700	0	0
	MPFI	109 (1800)	BPR6ES-11	0.040	6B @ 700	6B @ 700	161	61–71	700	800	0	0
	MPFI Turbo	109 (1800)	BPR6ES-11	0.040	25B @ 700	25B @ 800	145	61–71	700	800	0	0
1987	Brat	97 (1600)	BPR6ES-11	0.040	8B @ 700	—	168	2.6–3.3	700	—	0	0
	Carburetor	109 (1800)	BPR6ES-11	0.040	8B @ 700	8B @ 800	161	2.6–3.3	700	800	0	0
	SPFI	109 (1800)	BPR6ES-11	0.040	20B @ 700	20B @ 700	168	36–50	700	700	0	0
	MPFI Turbo	109 (1800)	BPR6ES-11	0.040	20B @ 700	20B @ 800	145	61–71	700	800	0	0
	Justy	73 (1200)	BPR6ES-11	0.040	5B @ 800	—	160	1.3–2.0	800 ③	—	0.0051–0.0067 ④	0.0090–0.0106 ④
1988					SEE UNDERHOOD SPECIFICATION STICKER							

NOTE: The underhood specifications sticker often reflects tune-up specification changes made in production. Sticker figures must be used if they disagree with those in this chart.

B—Before Top Dead Center
M—Manual transmission
A—Automatic transmission

① 0 if equipped with hydraulic lifters
② ± 100 rpm
③ ± 50 rpm
④ Adjust cold

FIRING ORDERS

NOTE: To avoid confusion, always replace spark plug wires one at a time.

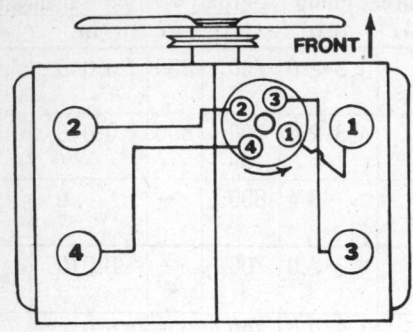

Firing order is 1-3-2-4

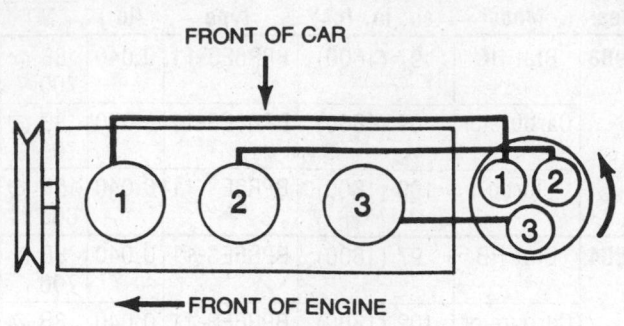

Firing order is 1-3-2

CAPACITIES

Year	Model	Engine Displacement cu. in. (cc)	Engine Crankcase with Filter	Engine Crankcase without Filter	Transmission (pts.) 4-Spd	Transmission (pts.) 5-Spd	Transmission (pts.) Auto.	Drive Axle (pts.)	Fuel Tank (gal.)	Cooling System (qts.)
1981	1600 Series	97 (1600)	3.8	3.5	5.8	5.8	12.5 ③	6.34 ①	13.2 ②	5.6
	1800 Series	109 (1800)	3.8	3.5	5.8	5.8	12.5 ③	6.34 ①	13.2 ②	5.8
1982	1600 Series	97 (1600)	3.8	3.5	5.8	5.8	12.5 ③	6.34 ①	13.2 ②	5.6
	1800 Series	109 (1800)	3.8	3.5	5.8	5.8	12.5 ③	6.34 ①	13.2 ②	5.8
1983	1600 Series	97 (1600)	4.2	3.2	5.8	5.8	10.8–12.6 ④	1.6	15.9 ⑤	5.6
	1800 Series	109 (1800)	4.2	3.2	5.8	5.8	10.8–12.6 ④	1.6	15.9 ⑤	5.8
1984	1600 Series	97 (1600)	4.2	3.2	5.8	5.8	10.8–12.6 ④	1.6	15.9 ⑤	5.6
	1800 Series	109 (1800)	4.2	3.2	5.8	5.8	10.8–12.6 ④	1.6	15.9 ⑤	5.8
1985	1600 Series	97 (1600)	4.2	3.2	5.8	5.8	10.8–12.6 ④	1.6	15.9	5.6
	1800 Series	109 (1800)	4.2	3.2	5.8	5.8	10.8–12.6 ④	1.6	15.9	5.8
	XT	109 (1800)	4.2	3.2	—	5.4	12.6–13.6 ⑥	1.6	15.9	6.1
1986	1600 Series	97 (1600)	4.2	3.2	—	5.4	12.6–13.6 ⑥	1.6	15.9	5.8
	1800 Series	109 (1800)	4.2	3.2	—	5.4	12.6–13.6 ⑥	1.6	15.9	5.8
	XT	109 (1800)	4.2	3.2	—	5.4	12.6–13.6 ⑥	1.6	15.9	6.1
1987–88	1800 Series	109 (1800)	4.2	3.2	—	5.4	12.6–13.6 ⑥	1.6	15.9	5.8
	XT	109 (1800)	4.2	3.2	—	5.4	12.6–13.6 ⑥	1.6	15.9	6.1
	Justy	73 (1200)	3.0	1.9	—	2.1	—	—	9.2	4.5

OHV—Overhead Valve
OHC—Overhead Cam
① 4WD rear differential: 1.7 pts.
② 4WD vehicles: 11.9 gal.
③ Automatic transmission differential: 2.5 pts.
④ 4WD Automatic: 12.6–13.6 pts.
   Automatic differential: 2.6 pts.
⑤ 4WD: 14.5 gal.
   Regular Hatchback: 13.2 gal.
   4WD Hatchback: 11.9 gal.
⑥ 4WD Models: 14.4–15.2 pts.

CAMSHAFT SPECIFICATIONS

All measurements given in inches.

Year	Engine Displacement cu. in. (cc)	Journal Diameter 1	2	3	4	5	Lobe Lift In.	Ex.	Bearing Clearance	Camshaft End Play
1981	97 (1600)	1.0220–1.0226	1.0220–1.0226	1.4157–1.4163	—	—	0.2093–0.2132	0.2093–0.2132	0.0010–0.0023	0.0008–0.0035
	109 (1800)	1.2582–1.2589	1.2582–1.2589	1.4157–1.4163	—	—	0.2093–0.2132	0.2093–0.2132	0.0010–0.0023	0.0008–0.0035
1982	97 (1600)	1.0220–1.0226	1.0220–1.0226	1.4157–1.4163	—	—	0.2093–0.2132	0.2093–0.2132	0.0010–0.0023	0.0008–0.0035
	109 (1800)	1.2582–1.2589	1.2582–1.2589	1.4157–1.4163	—	—	0.2093–0.2132	0.2093–0.2132	0.0010–0.0023	0.0008–0.0035
1983	97 (1600)	1.0220–1.0226	1.0220–1.0226	1.4157–1.4163	—	—	0.2093–0.2132	0.2093–0.2132	0.0010–0.0023	0.0008–0.0035
	109 (1800)	1.2582–1.2589	1.2582–1.2589	1.4157–1.4163	—	—	0.2093–① 0.2132	0.2093–① 0.2132	0.0010–0.0023	0.0008–0.0035
1984	97 (1600)	1.0220–1.0226	1.0220–1.0226	1.4157–1.4163	—	—	0.2093–0.2132	0.2093–0.2132	0.0010–0.0023	0.0008–0.0035
	109 (1800)	1.2582–1.2589	1.2582–1.2589	1.4157–1.4163	—	—	0.2093–① 0.2132	0.2093–① 0.2132	0.0010–0.0023	0.0008–0.0035
1985	97 (1600)	1.0220–1.0226	1.0220–1.0226	1.4157–1.4163	—	—	0.2093–0.2132	0.2093–0.2132	0.0010–0.0023	0.0008–0.0035
	109 (1800)	1.4946–1.4953	1.9080–1.9087	1.9671–1.9677	③	—	②	②	0.0008–0.0021	0.0012–0.0102
1986	97 (1600)	1.0220–1.0226	1.0220–1.0226	1.4157–1.4163	—	—	0.2093–0.2132	0.2093–0.2132	0.0010–0.0023	0.0008–0.0035
	109 (1800)	1.4946–1.4953	1.9080–1.9087	1.9671–1.9677	③	—	② ④	② ④	0.0008–0.0021	0.0012–0.0102
1987-88	109 (1800)	1.4946–1.4953	1.9080–1.9087	1.8883–1.8890	③	—	⑤	⑤	0.0008–0.0021	0.0012–0.0102
	73 (1200)	—	—	—	—	—	0.1920–0.1928	0.1920–0.1928	—	0.0012–0.0150

① If equipped with Hydraulic lifters: 0.1934–0.1973 in.
② Cam Lobe Height: Carburetor (standard): 1.5394–1.5433 in.
    Carburetor (undersize): 1.5606–1.5646 in.
    MPFI (non-turbo): 1.5650–1.5689 in.
    MPFI (turbo): 1.5606–1.5646 in.
③ Camshaft distributor LH journal: 1.5340–1.5346 in.
④ Cam Lobe Height: SPFI 1.5650–1.5689 in.
⑤ Cam Lobe Height: 1.5650–1.5689 in.

CRANKSHAFT AND CONNECTING ROD SPECIFICATIONS

All measurements are given in inches.

Year	Engine Displacement cu. in. (cc)	Crankshaft Main Brg. Journal Dia.	Main Brg. Oil Clearance	Shaft End-play	Thrust on No.	Connecting Rod Journal Diameter	Oil Clearance	Side Clearance
1981	97 (1600)	1.9667–① 1.9673	0.0004–② 0.0016	0.0016–0.0054	2	1.7715–1.7720	0.0008–0.0028	0.0028–0.0130
	109 (1800)	2.1636–2.1642	0.0004–② 0.0012	0.0016–0.0054	2	1.7715–1.7720	0.0008–0.0028	0.0028–0.0130
1982	97 (1600)	1.9667–① 1.9673	0.0004–② 0.0016	0.0016–0.0054	2	1.7715–1.7720	0.0008–0.0028	0.0028–0.0130
	109 (1800)	2.1636–2.1642	0.0004–② 0.0016	0.0016–0.0054	2	1.7715–1.7720	0.0008–0.0028	0.0028–0.0130

CRANKSHAFT AND CONNECTING ROD SPECIFICATIONS

All measurements are given in inches.

Year	Engine Displacement cu. in. (cc)	Crankshaft				Connecting Rod		
		Main Brg. Journal Dia.	Main Brg. Oil Clearance	Shaft End-play	Thrust on No.	Journal Diameter	Oil Clearance	Side Clearance
1983	97 (1600)	1.9668– ① 1.9673	0.0004– ② 0.0016	0.0004– 0.0037	2	1.7715– 1.7720	0.0008– 0.0028	0.0028– 0.0130
	109 (1800)	2.1636– 2.1642	0.0004– ② 0.0012	0.0004– 0.0037	2	1.7715– 1.7720	0.0008– 0.0028	0.0028– 0.0130
1984	97 (1600)	1.9668– ① 1.9673	0.0004– ⑤ 0.0014	0.0004– 0.0037	2	1.7715– 1.7720	0.0008– 0.0028	0.0028– 0.0130
	109 (1800)	2.1636– 2.1642	0.0004– ② 0.0012	0.0004– 0.0037	2	1.7715– 1.7720	0.0008– 0.0028	0.0028– 0.0130
1985	97 (1600)	1.9668– ① 1.9673	0.0004– ⑤ 0.0014	0.0004– 0.0037	2	1.7715– 1.7720	0.0008– 0.0028	0.0028– 0.0130
	109 (1800)	③	④	0.0004– 0.0037	2	1.7715– 1.7720	0.0004– 0.0021	0.0028– 0.0130
1986	97 (1600)	1.9668– ① 1.9673	0.0004– ⑤ 0.0014	0.0004– 0.0037	2	1.7715– 1.7720	0.0004– 0.0028	0.0028– 0.0130
	109 (1800)	③	④	0.0004– 0.0037	2	1.7715– 1.7720	0.0004– 0.0021	0.0028– 0.0130
1987–88	109 (1800)	③	④	0.0004– 0.0037	2	1.7715– 1.7720	0.0004– 0.0021	0.0028– 0.0130
	73 (1200)	1.6525– 1.6529	0.0006– 0.0018	0.0031– 0.0070	4	1.6531– 1.6535	0.0008– 0.0021	0.0028– 0.0118

OHV—Overhead Valve
OHC—Overhead Cam
① Center: 1.9673–1.9633
② Center: 0.0004–0.0010

③ Front: 2.1637–2.1642
   Center: 2.1635–2.1642
   Rear: 2.1636–2.1642

④ Front & Rear: 0.0001–0.0014
   Center: 0.0003–0.0011
⑤ Center: 0.0004–0.0012

VALVE SPECIFICATIONS

Year	Engine Displacement cu. in. (cc)	Seat Angle (deg)	Face Angle (deg)	Spring Test Pressure (lbs.) ③	Spring Height (in.) ③	Stem-to-Guide Clearance (in.) ▲		Stem Diameter (in.)	
						Intake	Exhaust	Intake	Exhaust
1981	97 (1600)	45	45	42–48 @1.22 ④	1.18 ⑨	0.0014– 0.0026	0.0016– 0.0028	0.3130– 0.3136	0.3128– 0.3134
	109 (1800)	45	45	42–48 @1.22 ④	1.18 ⑨	0.0014– 0.0026	0.0016– 0.0028	0.3130– 0.3136	0.3128– 0.3134
1982	97 (1600)	45	45	42–48 @1.22 ④	1.18 ⑨	0.0014– 0.0026	0.0016– 0.0028	0.3130– 0.3136	0.3128– 0.3134
	109 (1800)	45	45	42–48 @1.22 ④	1.18 ⑨	0.0014– 0.0026	0.0016– 0.0028	0.3130– 0.3136	0.3128– 0.3134
1983	97 (1600) ①	45	45–45.5	41.7–48.3 @1.122 ④	1.48 ⑩	0.0014– 0.0026	0.0016– 0.0028	0.3130– 0.3136	0.3128– 0.3134
	109 (1800) ①	45	45–45.5	41.7–48.3 @1.122 ④	1.48 ⑩	0.0014– 0.0026	0.0016– 0.0028	0.3130– 0.3136	0.3128– 0.3134
	109 (1800) ②	45	45–45.5	45.2–51.8 @1.181 ④	1.48 ⑩	0.0014– 0.0026	0.0016– 0.0028	0.3130– 0.3136	0.3128– 0.3134
1984	97 (1600) ①	45	45–45.5	41.7–48.3 @1.122 ④	1.48 ⑩	0.0014– 0.0026	0.0016– 0.0028	0.3130– 0.3136	0.3128– 0.3134
	109 (1800) ①	45	45–45.5	41.7–48.3 @1.122 ④	1.48 ⑩	0.0014– 0.0026	0.0016– 0.0028	0.3130– 0.3136	0.3128– 0.3134
	109 (1800) ②	45	45–45.5	45.2–51.8 @1.181 ④	1.48 ⑩	0.0014– 0.0026	0.0016– 0.0028	0.3130– 0.3136	0.3128– 0.3134

VALVE SPECIFICATIONS

Year	Engine Displacement cu. in. (cc)	Seat Angle (deg)	Face Angle (deg)	Spring Test Pressure (lbs.) ③	Spring Height (in.) ③	Stem-to-Guide Clearance (in.) Intake	Exhaust	Stem Diameter (in.) Intake	Exhaust
1985	97 (1600)	45	45–45.5	41.7–48.3 @1.122 ④	1.48 ⑩	0.0014–0.0026	0.0016–0.0028	0.3130–0.3136	0.3128–0.3134
	109 (1800)	45	45	45.2–51.8 @1.121 ④	1.12 ⑪	0.0014–0.0026	0.0016–0.0028	0.2736–0.2742	0.2734–0.2740
1986	97 (1600)	45	45–45.5	41.7–48.3 @1.122 ④	1.48 ⑩	0.0014–0.0026	0.0016–0.0028	0.3130–0.3136	0.3128–0.3134
	109 (1800)	45	45	45.2–51.8 @1.121 ④	1.12 ⑪	0.0014–0.0026	0.0016–0.0028	0.2736–0.2742	0.2734–0.2740
1987-88	109 (1800)	45	45	45.2–51.8 @1.121 ④	1.12 ⑪	0.0014–0.0026	0.0016–0.0028	0.2736–0.2742	0.2734–0.2740
	73 (1200)	45	45	⑧	1.25	0.0008–0.0020	0.0016–0.0028	0.2742–0.2748	0.2734–0.2740

OHV—Overhead Valve
OHC—Overhead Cam
① With manual trans.
② With auto. trans.
③ All values are for the inner spring

④ Outer spring: 112–127 @ 1.201
⑤ Outer spring: 116.6–134.7 @ 1.260
⑥ Outer spring: 100.5–115.5 @ 1.240
⑦ Outer spring: 112.9–129.7 @ 1.240

⑧ Spring: 112.8–129.8 @ 1.248
⑨ Outer spring: 1.20
⑩ Outer spring: 1.56
⑪ Outer spring: 1.24

PISTON AND RING SPECIFICATIONS
All measurements are given in inches.

Year	Engine Displacement cu. in. (cc)	Piston Clearance	Ring Gap Top Compression	Bottom Compression	Oil Control	Ring Side Clearance Top Compression	Bottom Compression	Oil Control
1981	97 (1600)	0.001–0.002	0.0080–0.0130	0.0080–0.0130	0.0080–0.0350	0.001–0.003	0.001–0.003	—
	109 (1800)	0.001–0.002	0.0080–0.0130	0.0080–0.0130	0.0080–0.0350	0.001–0.003	0.001–0.003	—
1982	97 (1600)	0.001–0.002	0.0080–0.0130	0.0080–0.0130	0.0080–0.0350	0.001–0.003	0.001–0.003	—
	109 (1800)	0.001–0.002	0.0080–0.0130	0.0080–0.0130	0.0080–0.0350	0.001–0.003	0.001–0.003	—
1983	97 (1600)	0.0004–0.0016	0.0079–0.0138	0.0079–0.0138	0.0079–0.0354	0.0016–0.0031	0.0012–0.0028	—
	109 (1800)	0.0004–0.0016	0.0079–0.0138	0.0079–0.0138	0.0079–0.0354	0.0016–0.0031	0.0012–0.0028	—
1984	97 (1600)	0.0004–0.0016	0.0079–0.0138	0.0079–0.0138	0.0079–0.0354	0.0016–0.0031	0.0012–0.0028	—
	109 (1800)	0.0004–0.0016	0.0079–0.0138	0.0079–0.0138	0.0079–0.0354	0.0016–0.0031	0.0012–0.0028	—
1985	97 (1600)	0.0004–0.0016	0.0079–0.0138	0.0079–0.0138	0.0079–0.0354	0.0016–0.0031	0.0012–0.0028	—
	109 (1800)	0.0004–0.0016	0.0079–0.0138	0.0079–0.0138	0.0120–0.0350	0.0016–0.0031	0.0012–0.0028	—
1986	97 (1600)	0.0004–0.0016	0.0079–0.0138	0.0079–0.0138	0.0790–0.0354	0.0016–0.0031	0.0012–0.0028	—
	109 (1800)	0.0004–0.0016	0.0079–0.0138	0.0079–0.0138	0.0120–0.0350	0.0016–0.0031	0.0012–0.0028	—
1987-88	109 (1800)	0.0004–0.0016	0.0079–0.0138	0.0079–0.0138	0.0120–0.0350	0.0016–0.0031	0.0012–0.0028	—
	73 (1200)	0.0015–0.0024	0.0079–0.0138	0.0079–0.0138	0.0120–0.0350	0.0014–0.0030	0.0010–0.0026	—

OHV—Overhead Valve   OHC—Overhead Cam

TORQUE SPECIFICATIONS
All readings in ft. lbs.

Year	Engine Displacement cu. in. (cc)	Cylinder Head Bolts	Rod Bearing Bolts	Crankcase Halves	Crankshaft Pulley Bolt	Flywheel To Crankshaft Bolt	Manifold Intake	Manifold Exhaust	Spark Plugs
1981	97 (1600)	37–43 ①	29–31	④	39–42	30–33 ③	13–16	12–15	14–22
	109 (1800)	47 ②	29–31	④	39–42	30–33 ③	13–16	12–15	14–22
1982	97 (1600)	37–43 ①	29–31	④	39–42	30–33 ③	13–16	12–15	14–22
	109 (1800)	47 ②	29–31	④	39–42	30–33 ③	13–16	12–15	14–22
1983	97 (1600)	37–43 ①	29–31	④	47–54	30–33 ③	13–16	19–22	14–22
	109 (1800)	47 ②	29–31	④	47–54	30–33 ③	13–16	19–22	14–22
1984	97 (1600)	37–43 ①	29–31	④	47–54	30–33 ③	13–16	19–22	14–22
	109 (1800)	47 ②	29–31	④	47–54	30–33 ③	13–16	19–22	14–22
1985	97 (1600)	37–43 ①	29–31	④	47–54	30–33 ③	13–16	19–22	14–22
	109 (1800)	44–50	29–31	⑤	66–79	51–55	13–16	19–22	14–22
1986	97 (1600)	37–43 ①	29–31	④	47–54	30–33 ③	13–16	19–22	14–22
	109 (1800)	44–50	29–31	⑤	66–79	51–55	13–16	19–22	14–22
1987–88	109 (1800)	44–50	29–31	⑤	66–79	51–55	13–16	19–22	14–22
	73 (1200)	48–54	29–35	30–35 ⑥	47–54	65–71	18–22	14–22	13–17

OHV—Overhead Valve
OHC—Overhead Cam

① First step: 22 ft. lbs.
② First step: 22 ft. lbs.
   Second step: 43 ft. lbs.
   Third step: 47 ft. lbs.
③ Driveplate (A/T): 36–39 ft. lbs.
④ 10 mm bolts: 29–35 ft. lbs.
   8 mm bolts: 17–19 ft. lbs.
   6 mm bolts: 3–4 ft. lbs.
⑤ 10 mm bolts: 29–35 ft. lbs.
   8 mm bolts: 17–20 ft. lbs.
⑥ Main bearing bolts

BRAKE SPECIFICATIONS
All measurements in inches unless noted

Year	Model	Lug Nut Torque (ft. lbs.)	Master Cylinder Bore	Brake Disc Minimum Thickness	Brake Disc Maximum Runout	Standard Brake Drum Diameter	Minimum Lining Thickness Front	Minimum Lining Thickness Rear
1981	All	58–72	0.8125	0.394	0.0039	7.09	0.295 ①	0.059
1982	All	58–72	0.8125	0.394	0.0039	7.09	0.295 ①	0.059
1983	All	58–72	0.8125	0.394	0.0039	7.09	0.295 ①	0.059
1984	All	58–72	0.8125	0.610	0.0039	7.09	0.295 ①	0.059
1985	All	58–72	0.8125	0.630 ③	0.0039	7.09	0.295 ①	0.059 ②
1986	All	58–72	0.8125	0.630 ③	0.0039	7.09	0.295 ①	0.059 ②
1987–88	All except Justy	58–72	0.8125	0.630 ③	0.0039	7.09	0.295 ①	0.059 ②
	Justy	58–72	0.8125	0.610	0.0059	7.09	0.295 ①	0.067

① Includes metal backing
② 0.256 in.: Rear disc brake. Includes metal backing
③ 0.335 in.: Rear disc brake.

WHEEL ALIGNMENT

Year	Model	Caster Range (deg.)	Caster Preferred Setting (deg.)	Camber Range (deg.)	Camber Preferred Setting (deg.)	Toe-in (in.)
1981	2 WD Exc. Station Wagon	1³/₁₆N–⁵/₁₆P	⁷/₁₆N	³/₄P–2¹/₄P	1¹/₂P	¹/₁₆–⁵/₁₆
	2 WD Station Wagon	1³/₁₆N–1¹/₁₆P	¹/₁₆N	1P–2¹/₂P	1³/₄P	¹/₁₆–⁵/₁₆

WHEEL ALIGNMENT

Year	Model	Caster Range (deg.)	Caster Preferred Setting (deg.)	Camber Range (deg.)	Camber Preferred Setting (deg.)	Toe-in (in.)
1981	4 WD Exc. Station Wagon	$1^1/_4$N–$^1/_4$P	$^1/_2$N	$1^{13}/_{16}$P–$3^5/_{16}$P	$2^9/_{16}$P	$^1/_4$–$^{15}/_{16}$
	4 WD Station Wagon	$1^7/_{16}$N–$^1/_{16}$P	$^{11}/_{16}$N	$1^{13}/_{16}$P–$3^5/_{16}$P	$2^9/_{16}$P	$^1/_4$–$^{15}/_{16}$
1982	2 WD Exc. Station Wagon	$1^3/_{16}$N–$^5/_{16}$P	$^7/_{16}$N	$^3/_4$P–$2^1/_4$P	$1^1/_2$P	0–$^5/_{64}$
	2 WD Station Wagon	$^{13}/_{16}$N–$^{11}/_{16}$P	$^1/_{16}$N	1P–$2^1/_2$P	$1^3/_4$P	0–$^5/_{64}$
	4 WD Exc. Station Wagon	$1^1/_4$N–$^1/_4$P	$^1/_2$N	$1^{13}/_{16}$P–$3^5/_{16}$P	$2^9/_{16}$P	$^3/_{64}$–$^1/_8$
	4 WD Station Wagon	$1^7/_{16}$N–$^1/_{16}$P	$^{11}/_{16}$N	$1^{13}/_{16}$P–$3^5/_{16}$P	$2^9/_{16}$P	$^3/_{64}$–$^1/_8$
1983	2 WD Exc. Station Wagon	$1^1/_4$N–$^1/_4$P	$^1/_2$N	$1^7/_{16}$P–$2^{15}/_{16}$P	$2^3/_{16}$P	$^1/_4$–$^5/_{32}$
	2 WD Station Wagon	$^{13}/_{16}$N–$^{11}/_{16}$P	$^1/_{16}$N	1P–$2^1/_2$P	$1^3/_4$P	0–$^5/_{64}$
	4 WD Exc. Station Wagon	$1^1/_4$N–$^1/_4$P	$^1/_2$N	$1^{11}/_{16}$P–$3^3/_{16}$P	$2^7/_{16}$P	$^{15}/_{64}$–$^5/_{32}$ ①
	4 WD Station Wagon	$1^7/_{16}$N–$^1/_{16}$P	$^{11}/_{16}$N	$1^{11}/_{16}$P–$3^3/_{16}$P	$2^7/_{16}$P	$^{15}/_{64}$–$^5/_{32}$ ①
1984	2 WD Exc. Station Wagon	$1^1/_4$N–$^1/_4$P	$^1/_2$N	$1^7/_{16}$P–$2^{15}/_{16}$P	$2^3/_{16}$P	$^1/_4$–$^5/_{32}$
	2 WD Station Wagon	$^{13}/_{16}$N–$^{11}/_{16}$P	$^1/_{16}$N	1P–$2^1/_2$P	$1^3/_4$P	0–$^5/_{64}$
	4 WD Exc. Station Wagon	$1^1/_4$N–$^1/_4$P	$^1/_2$N	$1^{11}/_{16}$P–$3^3/_{16}$P	$2^7/_{16}$P	$^{15}/_{64}$–$^5/_{32}$ ①
	4 WD Station Wagon	$1^7/_{16}$N–$^1/_{16}$P	$^{11}/_{16}$N	$1^{11}/_{16}$P–$3^3/_{16}$P	$2^7/_{16}$P	$^{15}/_{64}$–$^5/_{32}$ ①
1985	2 WD XT Coupe	$3^5/_{16}$P–$4^{13}/_{16}$P	$4^1/_{16}$P	$^3/_4$N–$^3/_4$P	0	$^1/_8$–$^1/_8$
	4 WD XT Coupe	$2^5/_8$P–$4^1/_8$P	$3^3/_8$P	$^1/_{16}$N–$1^3/_8$P	$^5/_8$P	$^3/_{64}$–$^1/_8$
	2 WD Sedan	$1^3/_4$P–$3^1/_4$P	$2^1/_2$P	0–$1^1/_2$P	$^3/_4$P	$^{13}/_{64}$–$^3/_{64}$ ①
	4 WD Sedan w/ Air Sup.	$1^7/_{16}$P–$2^{15}/_{16}$P	$2^3/_{16}$P	$^7/_{16}$P–$1^{15}/_{16}$P	$1^{13}/_{16}$P	$^{13}/_{64}$–$^3/_{64}$ ①
	4 WD Sedan wo/ Air Sup.	$1^1/_{16}$P–$2^9/_{16}$P	$1^{13}/_{16}$P	$^{15}/_{16}$P–$2^7/_{16}$P	$1^{11}/_{16}$P	$^{13}/_{64}$–$^3/_{64}$ ①
	2 WD Station Wagon	$1^5/_{16}$P–$2^{13}/_{16}$P	$2^1/_{16}$P	$^1/_4$P–$1^3/_4$P	1P	$^{13}/_{64}$–$^3/_{64}$ ①
	4 WD Station Wagon w/ Air Sup.	$1^7/_{16}$P–$2^{15}/_{16}$P	$2^3/_{16}$P	$^7/_{16}$P–$1^{15}/_{16}$P	$1^{13}/_{16}$P	$^{13}/_{64}$–$^3/_{64}$ ①
	4 WD Station Wagon wo/ Air Sup.	$^{13}/_{16}$P–$2^5/_{16}$P	$1^9/_{16}$P	$^{15}/_{16}$P–$2^7/_{16}$P	$1^3/_4$P	$^{13}/_{64}$–$^3/_{64}$ ①
	2 WD Hatchback	$1^1/_4$N–$^1/_4$P	$^1/_2$N	$1^7/_{16}$P–$2^{15}/_{16}$P	$2^3/_{16}$P	$^1/_4$–$^5/_{32}$
	Brat	$1^7/_{16}$N–$^1/_{16}$P	$^{11}/_{16}$N	$1^{11}/_{16}$P–$3^3/_{16}$P	$2^7/_{16}$P	$^{15}/_{64}$–$^5/_{32}$ ①

WHEEL ALIGNMENT

Year	Model	Caster Range (deg.)	Caster Preferred Setting (deg.)	Camber Range (deg.)	Camber Preferred Setting (deg.)	Toe-in (in.)
1986	2 WD XT Coupe	$3^5/_{16}$P–$4^{13}/_{16}$P	$4^1/_{16}$P	$^3/_4$N–$^3/_4$P	0	$^1/_8$–$^1/_8$
	4 WD XT Coupe	$2^5/_8$P–$4^1/_8$P	$3^3/_8$P	$^1/_{16}$N–$1^3/_8$P	$^5/_8$P	$^3/_{64}$–$^1/_8$
	2 WD Sedan	$1^3/_4$P–$3^1/_4$P	$2^1/_2$P	0–$1^1/_2$P	$^3/_4$P	$^{13}/_{64}$–$^3/_{64}$ ①
	4 WD Sedan w/ Air Sup.	$1^7/_{16}$P–$2^{15}/_{16}$P	$2^3/_{16}$P	$^7/_{16}$P–$1^{15}/_{16}$P	$1^{13}/_{16}$P	$^{13}/_{64}$–$^3/_{64}$ ①
	4 WD Sedan wo/ Air Sup.	$1^1/_{16}$P–$2^9/_{16}$P	$1^{13}/_{16}$P	$^{15}/_{16}$P–$2^7/_{16}$P	$1^{11}/_{16}$P	$^{13}/_{64}$–$^3/_{64}$ ①
	2 WD Station Wagon	$1^5/_{16}$P–$2^{13}/_{16}$P	$2^1/_{16}$P	$^1/_4$P–$1^3/_4$P	1P	$^{13}/_{64}$–$^3/_{64}$ ①
	4 WD Station Wagon w/ Air Sup.	$1^7/_{16}$P–$2^{15}/_{16}$P	$2^3/_{16}$P	$^7/_{16}$P–$1^{15}/_{16}$P	$1^{13}/_{16}$P	$^{13}/_{64}$–$^3/_{64}$ ①
	4 WD Station Wagon wo/ Air Sup.	$1^{13}/_{16}$P–$2^5/_{16}$P	$1^9/_{16}$P	$^{15}/_{16}$P–$2^7/_{16}$P	$1^3/_4$P	$^{13}/_{64}$–$^3/_{64}$ ①
	2 WD Hatchback	$1^1/_4$N–$^1/_4$P	$^1/_2$N	$1^7/_{16}$P–$2^{15}/_{16}$P	$2^3/_{16}$P	$^1/_4$–$^5/_{32}$
	Brat	$1^7/_{16}$N–$^1/_{16}$P	$^{11}/_{16}$N	$1^{11}/_{16}$P–$3^3/_{16}$P	$2^7/_{16}$P	$^{15}/_{64}$–$^5/_{32}$ ①
1987–88	2 WD XT Coupe	$3^5/_{16}$P–$4^{13}/_{16}$P	$4^1/_{16}$P	$^3/_4$N–$^3/_4$P	0	$^1/_8$–$^1/_8$
	4 WD XT Coupe	$2^5/_8$P–$4^1/_8$P	$3^3/_8$P	$^1/_{16}$N–$1^3/_8$P	$^5/_8$P	$^3/_{64}$–$^1/_8$
	2 WD Sedan	$1^3/_4$P–$3^1/_4$P	$2^1/_2$P	0–$1^1/_2$P	$^3/_4$P	$^{13}/_{64}$–$^3/_{64}$ ①
	4 WD Sedan w/ Air Sup.	$1^7/_{16}$P–$2^{15}/_{16}$P	$2^3/_{16}$P	$^7/_{16}$P–$1^{15}/_{16}$P	$1^{13}/_{16}$P	$^5/_{64}$–$^5/_{16}$ ①
	4 WD Sedan wo/ Air Sup.	$1^1/_{16}$P–$2^9/_{16}$P	$1^{13}/_{16}$P	$^{15}/_{16}$P–$2^7/_{16}$P	$1^{11}/_{16}$P	$^5/_{64}$–$^5/_{16}$ ①
	2 WD Station Wagon	$1^5/_{16}$P–$2^{13}/_{16}$P	$2^1/_{16}$P	$^1/_4$P–$1^3/_4$P	1P	$^{13}/_{64}$–$^3/_{64}$ ①
	4 WD Station Wagon w/ Air Sup.	$1^7/_{16}$P–$2^{15}/_{16}$P	$2^3/_{16}$P	$^7/_{16}$P–$1^{15}/_{16}$P	$1^{13}/_{16}$P	$^5/_{64}$–$^5/_{16}$ ①
	4 WD Station Wagon wo/ Air Sup.	$1^{13}/_{16}$P–$2^5/_{16}$P	$1^9/_{16}$P	$^{15}/_{16}$P–$2^7/_{16}$P	$1^3/_4$P	$^5/_{64}$–$^5/_{16}$ ①
	Brat	$1^7/_{16}$N–$^1/_{16}$P	$^{11}/_{16}$N	$1^{11}/_{16}$P–$3^3/_{16}$P	$2^7/_{16}$P	$^{15}/_{64}$–$^5/_{32}$ ①
	Justy	$1^1/_2$P–$3^1/_2$P	$2^1/_2$P	$^{21}/_{64}$N–$1^{21}/_{33}$P	$^{21}/_{32}$P	$^{15}/_{64}$–$^3/_{64}$ ①

P—Positive   N—Negative   ① Toe out

TUNE-UP PROCEDURES

Electronic Ignition

AIR GAP ADJUSTMENT

1. The distributor cap is held on by two clips. Release them with a screwdriver and lift the cap straight up and off, with the wires attached. Inspect the cap for cracking, carbon tracks or a worn center contact. Replace it (if necessary) by transferring the wires one at a time from the old cap to the new one.

2. To remove the rotor, pull it straight. Replace it if its contacts are worn, burned or pitted. DO NOT file the contacts. To replace, press it firmly onto the shaft.

3. Before replacing the ignition rotor, check the reluctor air gap. Using a non-magnetic feeler gauge, rotate the engine until a reluctor spoke is aligned with the pick-up coil (either bump the engine around with the starter or turn it with a wrench on the crankshaft pulley bolt).

4. Adjustment, if necessary, made by loosening the pick-up coil mounting screws (1600 and 1800—2WD) or the stator screw (1600 and 1800—4WD; 1200) and shifting its position, on the "breaker plate", either closer or far-

ther from the reluctor. Tighten the screws and recheck the gap. The air gap specifications are: 0.008–0.016 in. (1600 and 1800—2WD; carburetor), 0.012–0.020 in. (1600 and 1800—4WD; EFI models) or 0.012–0.016 (1200).

5. Inspect the ignition wires for cracks or brittleness. Replace them one at a time to prevent cross-wiring, carefully press the replacement wires into place. The cores of wires used with electronic ignition are more susceptible to breakage than those of standard wires, so treat them gently.

Ignition Timing

On the Carbureted, the SPFI and the MPFI (1600 and 1800) engines, the ignition timing marks are located on the edge of the flywheel, at the rear of the engine. The marks mounted on the flywheel and are visible through a port in the flywheel housing located just behind the dipstick. A plastic cover protects the port through which the flywheel-mounted marks are visible.

The ignition timing marks, on the turbocharged (1800) engine, are located on the front right-side near the crankshaft pulley.

The ignition timing marks, on the carbureted (1200—1987-88) engine, are located on the crankshaft pulley at the front of the engine.

ADJUSTMENT

NOTE: An inductive timing light is recommended because it is not susceptible to cross-firing or false triggering due to the greater voltage of the electronic ignition.

1. After cleaning the timing marks, connect a timing light to the ignition following the manufacturer's instruction.
2. If equipped with a carburetor, disconnect and plug the distributor vacuum advance line. If equipped with a turbocharger, disconnect the black (8-pole) electrical connector between the distributor and the knock control unit.

NOTE: On the 1200 (1987-88 engine), the sub-hose used for the distributor vacuum advance angle is indicated with a red mark.

3. Start the engine, allow it to reach normal operating temperature and aim the timing light at the timing marks on the flywheel or the crankshaft pulley.
4. If necessary to adjust the ignition timing, loosen the distributor hold down bolt, then rotate the dis-

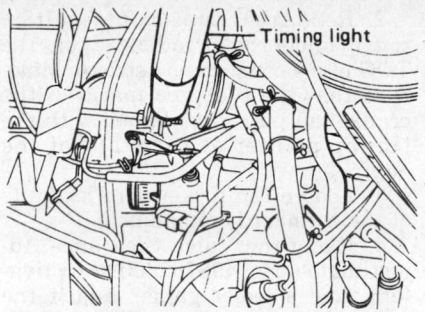

View of the timing mark located on the flywheel, looking through the slot in the flywheel housing at the top rear of the engine—non-turbo.

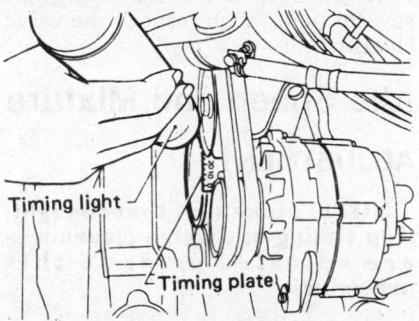

View of the timing marks on the turbo engines—1800 (OHC) 1983 and later

tributor clockwise to advance or counterclockwise to retard the timing.

5. After adjustment, tighten the distributor bolt and recheck the ignition timing.

NOTE: If equipped with a carburetor, reconnect the distributor vacuum advance line. If equipped with a turbocharger, reconnect the black (8-pole) electrical connector between the distributor and the knock control unit.

Valve Lash

ADJUSTMENT

1600 (1981-87) and 1800 (1981-84)

NOTE: The 1983-84 (OHV) 1800 engine with automatic transmission and all 1985-88 (OHC) 1800 engines use hydraulic lash adjusters; no periodic adjustment is necessary.

1. Before adjusting the valves, make sure the cylinder head nuts/bolts are torqued (tightened) to the proper specifications. To torque the head and intake manifold nuts/bolts, use the following procedure:
  a. Make sure the engine is Cold.
  b. Remove the valve covers from both sides of the engine.

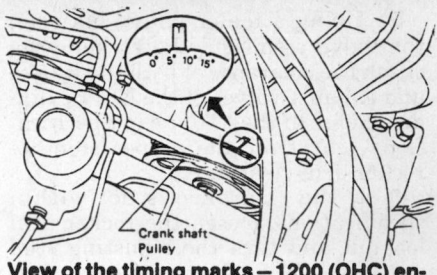

View of the timing marks—1200 (OHC) engine

c. On the right-side of the engine (driver's side), loosen the three intake manifold-to-cylinder head bolts no more than 60 degrees.

NOTE: DO NOT loosen the left-side intake manifold-to-cylinder head bolts.

d. Refer to the "Cylinder Head, Removal and Installation" section for the correct pattern to use while checking and retorquing the cylinder head.

NOTE: It is important to follow the proper tightening sequence when checking the head nuts/bolts. Warpage of the cylinder or water leaks could occur if the proper tightening pattern is not followed.

e. Loosen the center cylinder head nut/bolt no more than 60 degrees.

NOTE: If the bolts are loosened to 90 degrees, coolant leaks may occur.

f. Lubricate the nut/bolt with engine oil, torque and loosen the bolts 4–5 times. Retighten the nut/bolt to the specified torque.
g. Move on to the next nut/bolt and perform the same steps as before, proceed until all of the nuts/bolts have been tightened.
h. Go back to No. 1 nut/bolt and recheck the torque, tighten if necessary. Recheck the rest of the nuts/bolts following the specified order.
i. After rechecking all the head nuts/bolts tighten the intake manifold bolts on the right-side, cylinder head.
j. Rotate the engine so that the No. 1 piston is at top dead center (TDC) of its compression stroke. To determine the TDC, remove the distributor cap and the plastic flywheel housing dust cover (if equipped). The No. 1 piston is at TDC when the distributor rotor is pointing to the No. 1 spark plug lead terminal and the O degree mark on the flywheel or the crankshaft pulley is opposite the pointer on the housing or front cover.

2. Using a feeler gauge between the valve stem and the rocker arm, check the clearance of both the intake and exhaust valves of the No. 1 cylinder. Refer to the "Tune-Up Specifications" chart for the proper stem-to-rocker arm clearance.

3. If the clearance is not within specifications, loosen the rocker arm locknut and turn the adjusting stud until the valve clearance is correct. The stud should just touch the gauge; don't clamp the gauge tightly between the stud and head of the valve.

4. Tighten the locknut and recheck the valve stem-to-rocker clearance.

5. The other valves are adjusted in the same way; position each piston to TDC of its compression stroke, then check and adjust the valves for that cylinder. The proper valve adjustment sequence is 1–3–2–4, which is the firing order.

6. To bring the No. 3 piston to TDC of its compression stroke, rotate the crankshaft 180 degrees and make sure that the distributor rotor is pointing to the No. 3 spark plug terminal. Rotate the crankshaft 180 degrees after each valve adjustment before going on to the next adjustment.

7. Using the Valve Clearance Adjusting tool No. 498767000 or equivalent, and a feeler gauge, adjust the valve clearance of the cylinder which on TDC.

8. After adjusting the valve clearance, torque the rocker arm locknuts to 10–13 ft. lbs. Rotate the crankshaft several times, then recheck the valve clearance.

9. When the valve adjustment is complete, install the distributor cap, the valve covers and the dust cover (if equipped) on the flywheel housing port.

1200 (1987-88)

NOTE: The valve clearance should be checked every 15 months or 15,000 miles, whichever occurs first.

1. With the engine Cold, remove the valve cover.

NOTE: Before adjusting the valve clearance, check the cylinder head torque.

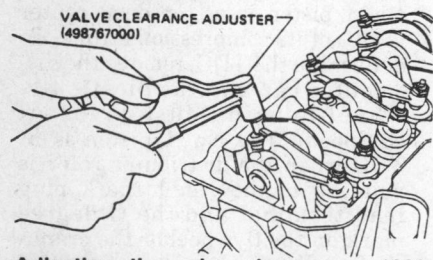

Adjusting the valve clearance— 1200 (OHC) engine

2. Rotate the crankshaft to position the cylinder being adjusted on the TDC of it's compression stroke. Make sure that the 0 degree mark on the crankshaft pulley is aligned with the timing pointer at the front of the engine.

3. Loosen the rocker arm locknuts of the cylinder being adjusted.

4. Using the Valve Clearance Adjusting tool No. 498767000 or equivalent, and a feeler gauge, adjust the valve clearance of the cylinder which on TDC.

5. After adjusting the valve clearance, torque the rocker arm locknuts to 12–17 ft. lbs. Rotate the crankshaft several times, then recheck the valve clearance.

Idle Speed and Mixture

ADJUSTMENT

NOTE: Make sure that the ignition timing and valve clearances are adjusted prior to this procedure.

Carburetor Models

IDLE SPEED

1. Operate the engine and allow it to reach normal operating temperature.

2. Stop the engine and connect a tachometer in accordance with the manufacturer's instructions.

3. Perform one of the following procedures:

   a. If equipped with air injection (air pump), disconnect the air hoses from the air distribution manifolds; plug the hoses and the manifold openings.

   b. If equipped with a distributor vacuum retard unit, disconnect and plug the hose that runs to the distributor.

   c. If equipped with a secondary air cleaner or purge valve/hose, disconnect and plug the hose to the engine.

4. Remove the air cleaner.

5. Check proper idle speed in the "Tune-Up Specifications" chart and adjust to that setting by turning the throttle adjusting screw.

NOTE: On all vehicles, the idle mixture MUST BE adjusted with a CO meter, ONLY

6. Disconnect the tachometer. Reconnect the hoses to the air injection manifold (if equipped). Install the air cleaner.

IDLE MIXTURE

NOTE: This procedure is not to be performed unless the carbure-

Idle speed adjustment

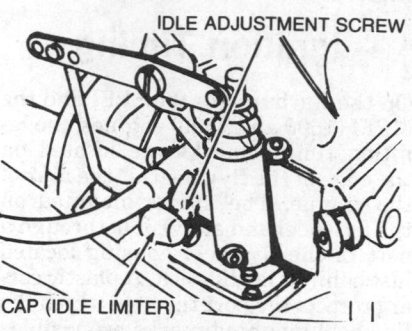

Idle mixture adjustment

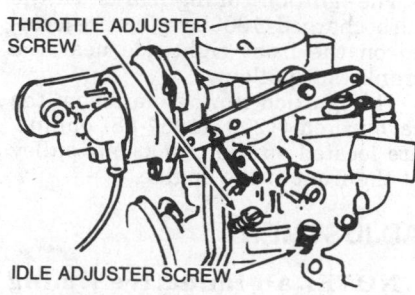

Throttle adjuster and idle adjuster screw locations

tor is removed from the engine or disassembled.

1. Using a drill, make a hole through the idle mixture screw plug, then pry the plug from the carburetor.

2. Start the engine and allow it to reach normal operating temperatures.

3. Disconnect and plug the air suction valve-to-air cleaner hose.

4. Disconnect and plug the idle compensator-to-intake manifold hose; plug both openings.

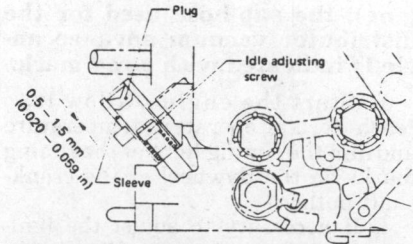

View of the idle mixture screw and plug— carburetor models

5. Without the secondary air, inspect the idle speed and the CO%. Using the throttle adjusting screw and the idle mixture adjusting screw, adjust the idle speed and the CO%. The idle speed is 600–800 rpm (M/T) or 700–900 rpm (A/T) and the CO% is 1.0–2.0% (without secondary air) or 0–0.4% (with secondary air).

6. After adjustment, unplug and replace the disconnected hoses. Using a new plug, install it into the idle mixture housing.

Turbo Models

1. Operate the engine and allow it to reach normal operating temperature.

2. Set the gear indicator to **P** or **N** for automatic transmissions and/or "Neutral" for manual transmissions.

3. Before inspecting the engine idle speed, check for:

   a. The engine has reached normal operating temperature and the O_2 sensor had warmed up at an engine speed of 2,500 rpm for one minute after the engine has warmed-up.

   b. Disconnect the purge hose from the intake manifold; plug the openings.

   c. Inspect all of the vacuum hoses, the rocker cover and the oil filter cap; make sure that they are properly connected to the intake system properly.

   d. Check the auxiliary air valve to make sure that it is completely Closed.

4. Adjust the idle speed by using the idle adjusting screw found on the throttle body.

   CO content (%) 800 ± 100
   HC contents (ppm) 200 max.

5. After adjusting the ignition timing and idle speed, check the idle CO and HC contents in the exhaust gas.

NOTE: The CO content adjusting screw of the air flow meter need not be adjusted as the air/fuel ratio is feedback controlled.

6. If the CO and HC contents are out of specification, correct the problem by performing the following procedures:

   a. Check the EGI system.

   b. Connect a jumper wire and check to see if the ECS lamp flashes with the engine at idle speed. If it does, the EGI system is working properly.

   c. Check the fuel injectors.

   d. Check the fuel pressure.

   e. Remove the fuel injector and direct air pressure into the nozzle to see if air leaks at the nozzle tip. If air leaks, replace the injectors.

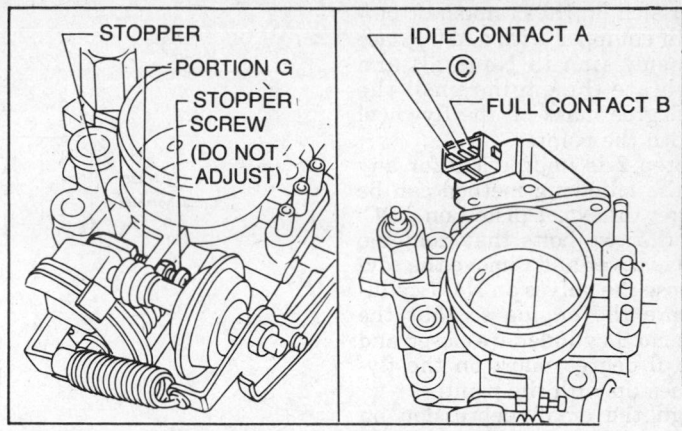

Fuel injection adjustment terminals

Fuel Injection Models

NOTE: Adjustment of the SPFI and the MPFI systems are not recommended.

1. Using a feeler gauge, between the stopper screws and the stopper (g) check for continuity between terminals **A** and **C**.

2. Make sure that the terminals **A** and **C** are conducting when the throttle is Closed.

3. Make sure that terminals **A** and **C** when the thickness of the gauge is 0.55 in.; this will relate to a throttle opening of 1.5 degrees.

4. Make sure that **A** and **C** are not conducting when the thickness is 0.92 in.; this indicates a throttle opening of 2.5 degrees.

5. If the above measurements are not met, loosen the throttle switch-to-throttle body screws.

6. Turn the throttle switch main body until the adjustment is correct.

ENGINE ELECTRICAL

Distributor
REMOVAL & INSTALLATION

Undisturbed Engine

1. Remove the air cleaner assembly. If equipped, label and disconnect the hose(s) from the distributor.

2. Disconnect the primary wire from the coil. On models equipped with a breakerless ignition, disconnect the distributor electrical wiring connector from the vehicle wiring harness.

3. Disconnect the distributor cap retaining clamps or remove the screws and the cap from the distributor. Position the cap and ignition wires aside.

NOTE: If necessary to remove the ignition wires from the cap to provide room to remove the distributor, be sure to label the wires and the cap terminals for easy and accurate reinstallation.

4. Using chalk or paint, mark the distributor rotor-to-distributor housing and the distributor housing-to-engine relationships.

NOTE: Marking of the distributor is important if installation is to be performed easily and accurately.

5. Remove the distributor-to-engine hold-down bolt.

6. Remove the distributor from the engine, taking care not to damage or lose the O-ring.

NOTE: DO NOT disturb the engine while the distributor is removed. If you crank or rotate the engine while the distributor is removed you will have to retime the engine.

7. If the engine was not disturbed while the distributor was removed, position the distributor in the block (make sure the O-ring is in place), align the distributor rotor-to-housing marks and the distributor housing-to-engine marks.

NOTE: If equipped with an octane selector, install and tighten the hold-down bolt finger tight.

8. To complete the installation, reverse the removal procedures. Recheck the ignition timing.

Disturbed Engine

If the engine has been cranked, disassembled or the timing otherwise lost, proceed as follows:

1. If equipped, remove the plastic dust cover from the timing port on the flywheel housing.

2. Remove the No. 1 spark plug.

Use a wrench on the crankshaft pulley bolt (if equipped with a M/T, place the transmission in Neutral) and slowly rotate the engine until the TDC O degree mark on the flywheel aligns with the pointer.

3. If Step 2 is impractical for any reason, the following method can be used to get the No. 1 piston on TDC. Remove the two bolts that hold the right valve cover and remove the cover to expose the valves on No. 1 cylinder. Rotate the engine so that the valves in No. 1 cylinder are closed and the TDC 0 degree mark on the flywheel lines up with the pointer.

4. Align the small depression on the distributor drive pinion with the mark on the distributor housing; this will align the rotor with the No. 1 spark plug terminal on the distributor cap.

NOTE: If equipped with an octane selector, set the pointer midway between the A and R. Make sure the O-ring is located in the proper position.

5. Align the distributor housing-to-engine matchmarks and install the distributor into the engine. Make sure the drive is engaged. Install the hold-down bolt fingertight. Using a timing light, perform the ignition timing procedures.

6. To complete the installation, remove the timing light and reverse the removal procedures.

Alternator

PRECAUTIONS

Observing these precautions will ensure safe handling of the electrical system components and will avoid damage to the vehicle's electrical system:

1. Be absolutely sure of the polarity of a booster battery before making connections. Connect the cables positive-to-positive and negative-to-negative. If jump starting, connect the positive cables first and the last connection to a ground on the body of the booster vehicle, so that arcing cannot ignite the hydrogen gas that may have accumulated near the battery. Even a momentary connection of a booster battery with polarity reserved may damage the alternator diodes.

2. Disconnect both vehicle battery cables before attempting to charge the battery.

3. Never ground the alternator output or battery terminal. Be cautious when using metal tools around a battery to avoid creating a short circuit between the terminals.

4. Never run an alternator without

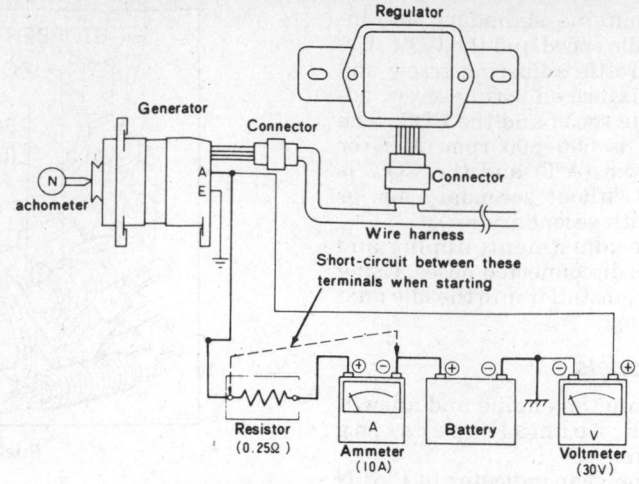

Voltage adjustment test schematic

a load unless the field circuit is disconnected.

5. Never attempt to polarize an alternator.

6. Never disconnect any electrical components with the ignition switch turned On.

BELT TENSION ADJUSTMENT

1. To adjust the belt tension, first loosen the alternator-to-bracket adjusting bolt.

2. Lift up on the alternator to increase the tension on the belt. When it takes moderate thumb pressure to move the longest span of belt ½ in., the tension adjustment is correct.

3. Tighten the adjusting bolt so that the alternator will not move in the adjusting bracket.

REMOVAL & INSTALLATION

1. Disconnect the negative battery terminal from the battery.

2. Label and disconnect the wiring from the alternator.

3. Remove the alternator-to-engine nuts and bolts.

4. Remove the drive belt and the alternator.

5. To install, reverse the removal procedures.

Voltage Regulator

NOTE: The 1983-88 models have a solid state regulator built into the alternator. This regulator is non-adjustable and is serviced, when necessary, by replacement ONLY.

ADJUSTMENTS

On Vehicle

This test should be made after the engine compartment and the regulator

have had a chance to cool down. The test should never be done on a "hot" engine.

1. Make sure all electrical equipment on the vehicle is turned Off or disconnected.

2. Using a 10A ammeter, a 30V voltmeter, and a ¼Ω resistor, connect a test circuit as shown in the illustration.

3. BEFORE STARTING THE ENGINE, connect a jumper wire from the far terminal of the ¼Ω resister to the negative terminal of the ammeter. After the engine is started, disconnect the jumper but be sure to reconnect it each time the engine is restarted.

4. Start the engine and gradually increase the speed from idle to about 2000 rpm.; 2000 engine rpm is equal to about 1200 alternator rpm.

5. The voltage reading will change due to the temperature around the regulator.

NOTE: The ammeter reading should be below 5 amps. Recharge or substitute the battery with a charged one if the reading is not below 5 amps.

6. If the voltage is not within the specified range, adjust as follows.

   a. Remove the screws and the regulator cover. Loosen the locknut and turn the adjusting screw until the voltage falls to within the specifications.

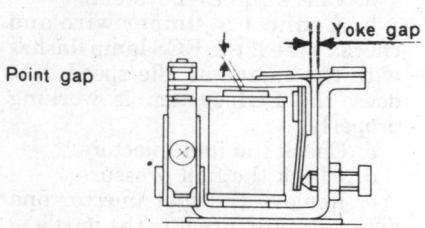

Adjustment points of the voltage regulator

b. If the voltage cannot be brought within specs, proceed with a mechanical adjustment.

c. If the voltage is now within the required specs: shut off the engine, remove the test equipment, replace the regulator cover and reconnect any electrical system components or accessories that were disconnected.

Charge Relay Adjustment—Off Vehicle

NOTE: The opening voltage of the charge relay is 8–10V at alternator terminal A. However, the coil on the charge relay operates at ½ of this voltage (i.e. 4–5V).

1. Remove the regulator from the vehicle.
2. Connect a the test circuit illustrated with a vehicle battery, a 0–150Ω rheostat, a voltmeter, a heavy-duty switch and a test light.
3. Close the switch with a rheostat set at 150Ω (maximum).
4. Gradually decrease the resistance.
5. When the test light turns Off, the voltmeter should read 4–5V.
6. If the light doesn't turn Off at the specified setting, remove the regulator cover and make the following adjustments. Loosen the locknut on the charge relay and turn the adjusting screw until the voltage falls within specifications. Tighten the locknut.
7. If the charge relay voltage cannot be brought within specifications, perform the "Mechanical Adjustments" outlined next.
8. If the charge relay is working properly, replace the cover and install it in the vehicle.

Mechanical Adjustments

—————— **CAUTION** ——————

All mechanical adjustments must be performed with the regulator removed from the vehicle to prevent to the battery and/or the charging system.

1. Remove the voltage regulator from the vehicle and cover from the regulator.

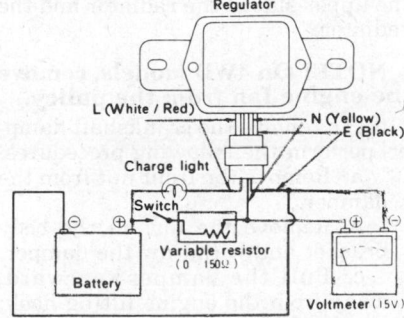

Charge relay test circuit

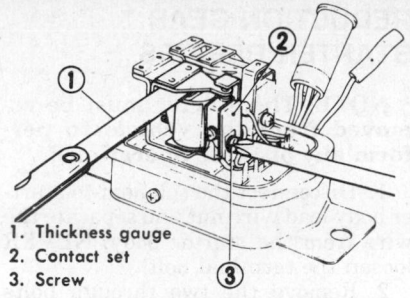

1. Thickness gauge
2. Contact set
3. Screw

Adjusting the core gap

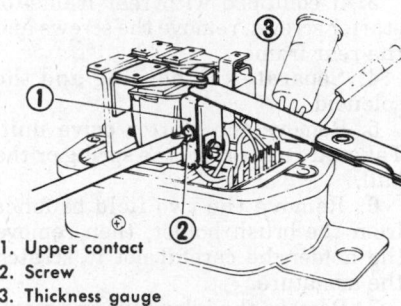

1. Upper contact
2. Screw
3. Thickness gauge

Adjusting the point gap

2. Inspect both sets of points. If they are rough or dirty, polish them with an ignition point file.

NOTE: If the points are so badly damaged that polishing them doesn't help, replace the regulator.

3. Measure and adjust the gaps of both the voltage regulator and the charge relay in the same manner. To adjust both sets of gaps, perform the following procedures:

NOTE: It is not necessary to adjust the yoke gap.

a. CORE GAP—measure the clearance for both the regulator and charge relay between their armatures and coil cores. To adjust each point set, loosen the contact set-to-yoke screw and move the set up or down, then tighten the screw.

b. POINT GAP—measure the distances between the points for both the voltage regulator and charge relay. To adjust each point set, loosen the upper contact screw and move the contact up or down, then tighten the screw.

4. Reinstall the regulator and test its operation. If the voltage still cannot be brought within specifications, replace the regulator. If the voltage is still incorrect, the fault probably lies in the alternator.

REMOVAL & INSTALLATION

1. Disconnect the negative battery terminal from the battery.

2. Disconnect the multi-wire connector and automatic choke lead from the regulator.
3. Remove the two regulator-to-fender screws and the regulator from the vehicle.
4. To install, reverse the removal procedures.

Starter

Two types of starter motors are used, the direct-drive motor and the reduction-gear motor.

The direct-drive motor uses a drive mounted on the end of the armature to engage the engine flywheel.

The reduction-gear motor uses an idler gear driven by the end of the armature to turn the starter drive. The rotation speed of the starter drive is reduced to approximately ⅓ of the armature speed.

REMOVAL & INSTALLATION

1. Remove the spare tire from the engine compartment.
2. Disconnect the negative battery terminal from the battery.
3. Disconnect the wiring harness from the starter.
4. Remove the starter-to-transaxle nuts and the starter.
5. To install, reverse the removal procedures.

DIRECT DRIVE STARTER— OVERHAUL

Starter Drive Replacement

1. Refer to the "Solenoid, Replacement" procedures in this section and remove the solenoid from the starter.
2. Remove the end frame cap, the lock plate, the spring and the rubber seal.
3. Remove the through-bolts, then pull the end frame rearward and remove it. Remove the brushes from their holders by first pushing the holder spring aside.
4. Remove the brush holder plate and pull the yoke from the main housing (which surrounds the stator coils). Remove the plate and seal from the rear of the yoke.
5. Unscrew and remove the solenoid lever set bolt, then, pull the armature, the overrunning clutch and the lever from the yoke.
6. Using a length of pipe, the same diameter as the armature shaft, tap the pinion stop collar toward the starter drive to expose the snaping. Using a pair of snaping pliers, remove the snaping from the armature shaft, then slide off the pinion stop collar.

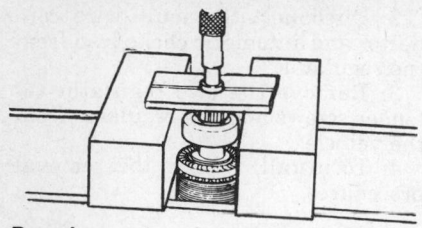

Pressing snap ring collar back into position

7. Remove the starter drive from the threaded spline; be careful not to damage the spline.

8. To install the starter drive, slip the starter drive onto the armature shaft and drive the pinion stop collar past the snapring groove. Gently push the snapring over the end of the armature shaft; work it down until it slips in to the snapring groove.

9. Supporting the stop collar (the armature must hang below, unsupported) press the end of the armature shaft downward until the collar rests against the ring and the ring is in the groove of the collar.

10. To complete the reassembly, reverse the disassembly procedures.

Solenoid Replacement

1. With the starter removed from the vehicle, remove the nut from underneath the solenoid terminal and disconnect the wires.

2. Remove the solenoid-to-starter screws.

3. Lift the solenoid and pull it rearward to separate it from the starter.

4. To install, reverse the removal procedures. Be sure to engage the hook on the end of the solenoid with the starter drive lever before installing the solenoid-to-starter screws.

Brush Replacement

1. Remove the starter from the engine. Remove the two thru-bolts.

2. Remove the end frame cap screws, the cap, the lock plate, the spring and the rubber seal.

3. Slide the end frame from the starter assembly.

4. Move each brush holder spring aside and remove the starter brushes from their holders.

5. Lift off the brush holder plate. The yoke may now be separated from the housing by sliding them apart.

6. If the brushes are worn to less than 0.043 in., they should be replaced by soldering in new ones.

———— **CAUTION** ————

When soldering in new positive brushes (those attached to the field coil) be careful not to get excess solder or dirt on the field coil.

7. To complete the reassembly, reverse the disassembly procedures.

REDUCTION GEAR STARTER REPAIRS

NOTE: The starter must be removed from the vehicle to perform any of these operations.

1. Disconnect the solenoid-to-starter body lead wire nut and separate the wire from the starter body; NEVER loosen the terminal bolt.

2. Remove the two through bolts and the solenoid-to-housing screws.

3. If equipped with rear frame-to-starter screws, remove the screws and the rear frame.

4. Separate the housing and the solenoid.

5. Remove the starter drive unit. Take care not to lose the spring or the ball.

6. Remove the two field brushes from the brush holder, then remove the holder; be careful not to scratch the armature.

7. Remove the idler gear and starter drive from the solenoid; be careful not to lose the rollers.

8. Inspect the component parts for wear. If the solenoid is faulty, replace it as a unit. Check the gears for chips or worn teeth. If the brushes are worn, replace the assembly.

NOTE: Take care when soldering in the field brushes, DO NOT get excessive solder or dirt on the field coils.

9. To ressemble the starter motor, reverse the disassembly procedures. Using high temperature grease, grease the ball, rollers and gears. If you have removed the armature be sure to reinstall the felt washer.

10. Reinstall the starter motor onto the engine; make sure all connections are tight.

ENGINE MECHANICAL

Engine
REMOVAL & INSTALLATION

1600 and 1800 — Carburetor

NOTE: On all models, the engine is removed separately from the transaxle.

1. Open the hood as far as possible and secure it with the stay. Disconnect the negative battery terminal from the battery.

2. Remove the ground cable-to-intake manifold bolt and disconnect the cable. It is unnecessary to remove the cable fully: leave it routed along the side of the body.

3. Remove the spare tire from the engine compartment.

4. Remove the emission control system hoses from the air cleaner. Remove the air cleaner brackets and the wing nut, then lift the air cleaner assembly off the carburetor.

5. Position a drain pan (to catch the gasoline) under the fuel line union. At the union, remove the hose clamp, then pull the hose(s) to disconnect them.

6. Position a drain pan under the engine, remove the drain plug and drain the oil from the crankcase.

7. To drain the engine coolant, perform the following procedures:

 a. Position a clean container, large enough to hold the contents of the cooling system, under the radiator drain plug.

 b. Open the drain plug on the radiator; turn it so that it's slot faces downward.

 c. Disconnect both the hoses from the radiator.

 d. Disconnect the heater hoses from the pipe on the side of the engine.

 e. If equipped with an automatic transmission, disconnect the oil cooler lines from the radiator.

8. Disconnect the following electrical wiring connectors:

 a. Alternator multi-connector

 b. Oil pressure sender connector

 c. Engine cooling fan connectors

 d. Temperature sender connector

 e. Primary distributor lead

 f. Secondary ignition leads (ignition-side)

 g. Starter wiring harness

 h. Anti-dieseling solenoid lead

 i. Automatic choke lead

 j. EGR vacuum solenoid

 k. EGR coolant temperature switch

 l. If equipped with an automatic transmission, disconnect the neutral safety switch harness and downshift solenoid harness.

9. Loosen the radiator-to-chassis bolts, remove the ground lead from the upper-side of the radiator and the radiator.

NOTE: On 4WD models, remove the engine fan from the pulley.

10. To remove the crankshaft damper, perform the following procedures:

 a. Remove the front nut from the damper.

 b. Remove the nut on the body bracket and withdraw the damper.

 c. Pull the damper rearward, away from the engine lifting hook; be careful not to lose any of the damper parts.

11. Remove the starter-to-engine bolts and the starter from the vehicle.

12. Disconnect the following cables, hoses and linkages, by performing the following procedure:

   a. Loosen the screw on the carburetor throttle lever. Remove the outer end of the accelerator cable and withdraw it.

   b. Remove the vacuum hose and the purge hose from the vapor canister.

   c. If equipped with a manual transmission, remove the clutch return spring from the release lever/intake manifold and the clutch cable from the lever.

   d. If equipped with an automatic transmission, disconnect the vacuum hose from the transmission.

   e. Disconnect the vacuum hose from the power brake unit (if equipped).

13. On 4WD models, remove the skid plate-to-chassis bolts and the plate.

14. To remove the Y-shaped exhaust pipe, perform the following procedures:

   a. Remove the exhaust pipe-to-cylinder head nuts.

   b. Remove the exhaust pipe-to-pre-muffler nuts/bolts.

   c. While supporting the exhaust pipe by hand, remove the exhaust pipe-to-transmission bracket bolts, then lower the exhaust pipe.

15. If equipped with an automatic transmission, remove the torque converter bolts by performing the following procedures:

   a. Remove the timing hole cover from the torque converter housing.

   b. Through the timing hole, remove the torque converter-to-drive plate bolts.

NOTE: Be careful that the bolts DO NOT fall into the torque converter housing.

16. Connect a chain hoist and a cable to the engine, with hooks at the front and rear engine hangers. Adjust the hoist so that the weight of the engine is supported but DO NOT raise the engine.

17. Using a floor jack, position it under the transaxle to support it's weight when the engine is removed.

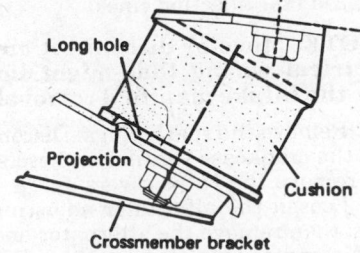

Engine mount alignment

18. Remove the engine-to-transmission nuts (four each on top and bottom).

19. Remove the front engine mount-to-crossmember nuts.

20. Using the hoist, raise the engine slightly (about 1 in.). Keeping it level, move the engine forward, off the transaxle input shaft.

CAUTION

DO NOT raise the engine more than 1.0 in. prior to removing it from the input shaft or damage may occur to the driveshaft double offset joints. If equipped with a manual transmission, be sure that the input shaft does not interfere with the clutch spring assembly; if equipped with an automatic transmissions, leave the torque converter on the transaxle input shaft.

21. Hoist the engine carefully until it is completely out of the vehicle, then secure it onto a workstand.

22. To install the engine, use new gaskets and reverse the removal procedures. Torque the transmission-to-engine bolts to 34–40 ft. lbs., the torque converter-to-drive plate bolts to 17–20 ft. lbs., the engine mount-to-crossmember bolts to 14–24 ft. lbs., the crankshaft damper nut to 7–10 ft. lbs., the exhaust pipe-to-engine bolt to 19–22 ft. lbs., the exhaust pipe-to-premuffler nuts to 31–38 ft. lbs. and the radiator-to-chassis bolts to 6–10 ft. lbs. Adjust of the clutch and accelerator linkage. Refill the crankcase and cooling system.

NOTE: Use care not to damage the input shaft splines or the clutch spring when lowering the engine in place.

23. When installing the crankshaft damper, perform the following adjustments:

   a. Tighten the body bracket nut.

   b. Turn the front nut until the clearance between the front washer and rubber cushion is 0.

   c. Insert the bushing and tighten the front nut.

1800 — Turbo, MPFI and SPFI

1. Open the hood and prop it, securely. Remove the spare tire and the spare tire bracket.

2. If equipped with Turbo or MPFI, perform the following procedures to reduce the fuel pressure:

   a. From under the vehicle, disconnect the fuel pump electrical harness connector.

   b. Crank the engine for at least 5 seconds. If the engine starts, allow it to run until it stalls.

   c. Reconnect the fuel pump connector.

3. Remove the negative battery terminal from the battery.

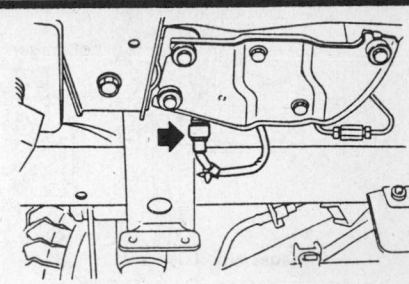

Disconnect the fuel pump's electrical harness connector — 1800 (OHC) — MPFI and Turbo

4. Disconnect the air temperature sensor plug from the engine compartment.

5. Label and disconnect the fuel system hoses and the evaporative emissions system hoses.

6. Label and disconnect the vacuum hoses from the cruise control, the Master-Vac, the air intake shutter and the heater air intake door.

7. Disconnect the electrical wiring connectors from the the alternator, the EGI, the thermoswitch, the electric fan, the A/C condenser and the ignition coil, then disconnect the main engine harness.

8. Label and disconnect the spark plug wires, the engine ground strap and the fusible link assembly.

9. Disconnect the accelerator linkage. Remove the windshield washer reservoir and position it behind the right-strut tower.

10. To remove the power steering pump, perform the following procedures:

   a. Loosen the alternator pivot and mounting bolts, then shift the alternator to loosen the drive belt and remove the belt.

   b. Remove the pulley from the power steering pump.

   c. Remove the power steering pump-to-engine bolts and clamp.

   d. Remove the engine oil filler pipe brace.

   e. Remove the power steering pump and secure it to the bulkhead without disturbing the pressure lines.

11. Loosen the air intake duct hose clamps and remove the duct; seal the openings to keep dirt out of the air intake passages. Remove the upper cover.

12. Remove the air intake-to-flow meter line and cover the openings.

13. Remove the horizontal damper and clip.

14. To remove the center section of the exhaust pipe, perform the following procedures:

   a. Disconnect the temperature sensor connector.

   b. If equipped, disconnect the exhaust pipe-to-turbocharger bolts.

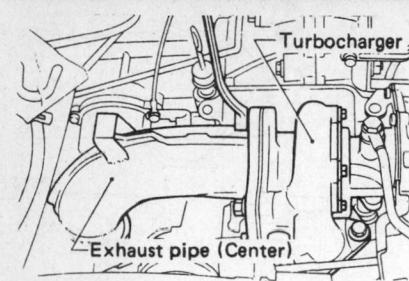

Disconnecting the exhaust pipe at the turbocharger

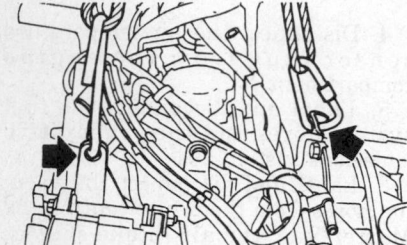

Hooks for lifting the turbo engine out of the vehicle

c. Remove the rear cover.

d. Remove the center exhaust section-to-transmission bolt.

e. Remove the hanger bolts, then carefully remove the exhaust pipe (clearance is tight) to avoid damage.

f. Slightly loosen the attaching bolts, then remove the torque converter cover.

15. If equipped, disconnect the turbocharger oil supply and drain lines. Remove the turbo-to-exhaust bolts, the turbo assembly, the lower cover and the gasket.

16. Disconnect the electrical connector from the O₂ sensor. Remove the torque converter-to-drive plate bolts.

17. Using a chain hoist, connect it to the crankshaft damper bracket and support the engine. Remove the upper engine-to-transmission bolts; leave the starter in place.

18. Drain the engine coolant, using a hose to lead coolant to a clean container. Disconnect the upper/lower radiator hoses, the oil cooler lines, the ground wire and the radiator.

19. Disconnect the oil cooler lines from the engine and drain the oil into a clean container. Disconnect the heater hoses from the side of the engine.

20. Remove the front engine mount, then the lower engine-to-transmission nuts.

21. Position a floor jack under the transmission, then raise the engine/transmission slightly. Pull the engine forward until the transmission shaft clears the clutch, then carefully raise the engine out of the engine compartment.

22. To install, use new gaskets and keep the following points in mind:

a. After installing all major mounting nuts and bolts finger tight, tighten the upper transmission-to-engine bolts just snug, then, remove the engine/transmission support. Tighten the lower transmission-to-engine bolts, then tighten the engine-to-mount nuts.

b. When torquing the turbocharger (if equipped) and the exhaust system bolts, be sure to go back and forth, tighten the bolts evenly.

23. To complete the installation, reverse the removal procedures. Torque the upper transmission-to-engine bolts to 14–17 ft. lbs., the torque converter-to-drive plate bolts to 17–20 ft. lbs., the turbocharger-to-exhaust system (if equipped) bolts to 31–38 ft. lbs., the exhaust system-to-transmission bolt to 18–25 ft. lbs., the exhaust system hanger bolts to 7–13 ft. lbs., the rear exhaust pipe joint nuts to 7–13 ft. lbs., the power steering pump pulley bolts to 25–30 ft. lbs., the power steering pump mounting bolts to 18–25 ft. lbs. Adjust the crankshaft damper by tightening the nuts on the body-side of the damper until the clearance is 0.08 in.; torque the locknuts to 6.5–9.4 ft. lbs. Adjust the accelerator pedal so there is 0.04–1.2 in. between the pin and stop. Adjust the cable for an end play of 0–0.08 in. on the actuator side. Replenish all of the fluids. Run the engine to normal operating temperatures and check for leaks in oil cooler and lines.

1200 Engine – 1987-88

1. Disconnect the negative battery terminal from the battery.

2. Raise and support the front of the vehicle on jackstands.

3. Raise and support the hood with the stay so that it opens wider than usual.

4. Position a drain pan under the radiator, remove the drain plug and the radiator cap, then drain the cooling system.

5. Remove the bumper and the grille.

6. Disconnect the electrical connectors and the hoses from the radiator and remove the radiator.

7. Disconnect the hood release cable and remove the radiator upper member.

8. Label, then disconnect the hoses and cables from the air cleaner, the carburetor, the heater unit the brake booster, the clutch, the accelerator cable from the carburetor, the speedometer cable from the transmission and the electrical wiring harness from the distributor.

9. Disconnect the pitching stopper from the bracket.

10. Remove the engine splash covers and the exhaust pipes.

11. Disconnect the gearshift rod and stay from the transmission.

12. Remove the transverse link. Using a rod, remove the spring pin and separate the front axle shaft.

13. Remove the engine/transmission mounting brackets.

14. Using an engine hoist and a cable, attach it to the engine and lift it slightly.

15. Remove the center member and crossmember from the vehicle.

16. Lift the engine/transmission assembly carefully and remove it from the vehicle.

17. Remove the engine from the transmission, then secure the engine to a workstand.

18. To install, reverse the removal procedures. Refill the cooling system.

Cylinder Head

REMOVAL & INSTALLATION

Overhead Valve (OHV) Engines

Although it is physically possible (on some models) to remove the cylinder heads with the engine installed, head gasket failure will result upon installation, due to misalignment of the cylinder head. The cylinder heads should be removed with the engine Cold to prevent warpage.

1. Refer to the "Engine, Removal and Installation" procedures in this section and remove the engine and secure it onto a workstand.

2. Remove the intake manifold together with the carburetor and the various pollution control devices.

NOTE: The exhaust manifolds should have been separated from the cylinder heads before the engine was removed.

3. Remove the EGR pipe from the intake manifold and cylinder head. On the 1982-84 models, remove the thermostatic rater valve, the hose and the oil filter pipe bracket. On the turbo models, remove the turbocharger and exhaust manifold, then disconnect the fuel injection lines.

NOTE: Move or disconnect any electrical wiring that might impair the intake manifold removal.

4. Remove the spark plugs. Disconnect the crankcase ventilation hose(s) and remove the valve covers.

5. Loosen the alternator adjusting bolts, then remove the alternator and the alternator bracket from the cylinder head.

6. If equipped with air injection, remove the distribution tubes from the cylinder heads; be careful NOT to distort the injection tubes.

NOTE: In the following step, it is necessary to loosen the valve rocker locknuts and adjusting screws; this applies to solid lifter engines ONLY. The 1983-84 engines, with automatic transmissions, are equipped with hydraulic lifters; the adjustment of the lifter screws and locknuts must not be disturbed!

7. If equipped with an 1800 Turbo, remove the knock sensor with a 27mm deep well socket ONLY! (A standard socket will damage the electrical terminals). Using a Phillips screwdriver, remove the fuel injector(s).

8. If equipped with solid lifters, loosen the valve rocker locknuts and adjusting screws. Loosen the rocker shaft mounting nuts, then remove the rocker arm assembly and pushrods.

NOTE: If the pushrods are to be reused, keep them in order so that they are installed in the original positions. The pushrods for all engines are identified by knurling (or the absence of knurling). If you are replacing the pushrods, make sure the knurled patterns are similar or that the unmarked pushrods are replaced by unmarked rods; the markings vary from year-to-year. For example, the 1981-82, 1800 engine, uses pushrods with 2 knurled marks, while the 1983-87, 1600 engines have 2 knurled marks, a single mark for solid lifter, 1800 engines and no markings for hydraulic lifter engines.

9. Loosen the cylinder head nuts in sequence, then remove the cylinder heads and gaskets.

10. Using a putty knife, clean the gasket mounting surfaces.

11. To install, use new gaskets, sealant (on both sides of the new cylinder head gasket) and reverse the removal procedures. Torque the cylinder head-to-engine bolts in sequence. After the cylinder head is torqued to specifications (see "Torque Specifications" chart), remove the rocker arm shaft bolts/nuts and the spacers, then install the rocker arm shafts. On later models, torque the cylinder head with the rocker arm shaft in place, in the sequence shown for the model year. Recheck the torque of the No. 1 bolt after torque is correct on the others. On models which use studs and nuts, lightly oil the threads before install the nuts.

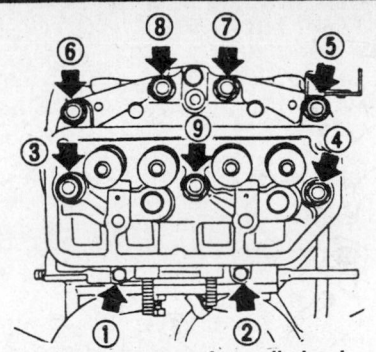

Loosening sequence for cylinder head bolts—1981

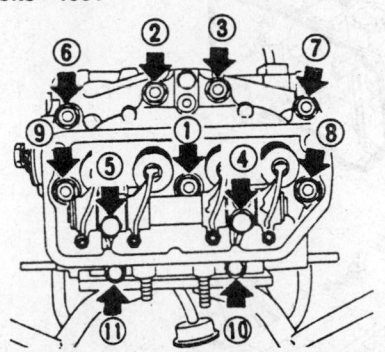

Tightening sequence for cylinder head bolts—1981

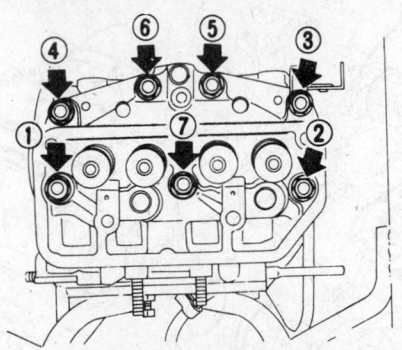

Loosening sequence for cylinder head bolts—1982 and later

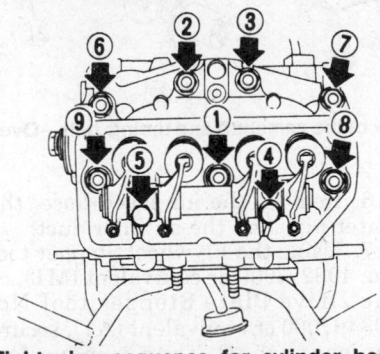

Tightening sequence for cylinder head bolts—1982 and later

NOTE: The cylinder heads must be installed with the cylinders in the vertical position to avoid misalignment and to permit the head gasket to settle evenly around the cylinder.

Overhead Cam (OHC) Engines

1800 ENGINE — 1984-88

1. Refer to the "Engine, Removal and Installation" procedures in this section and remove the engine from the vehicle, then secure it to a workstand.

2. If equipped with MPFI or Turbo, separate the fuel pump's electrical connector, located under the vehicle, start the engine and allow it to run out of fuel, then reconnect the electrical connector.

3. Label and disconnect the spark plug wires and vacuum hoses, remove the spark plugs.

4. Using chalk, mark the distributor-to-engine position, then remove the distributor-to-engine bolt and the distributor from the engine.

5. Loosen the water pump-to-pulley nut and the alternator-to-engine bolts, then remove the drive belt.

6. Remove the alternator-to-engine bolts and the alternator from the vehicle.

NOTE: If equipped with air conditioning, the compressor will have to be moved out of the way (WITHOUT DISCONNECTING THE HOSES) in order to remove the alternator.

7. If equipped, remove the silencer hoses and the silencers.

8. If equipped, remove the ASV(s) and the ASV pipe together with brackets.

9. Remove the EGR pipe cover and the EGR pipe.

10. Remove the PCV hose and blow-by hoses.

11. Remove the air bleed hose from the thermostat case.

12. Disconnect each electrical wiring harnesses. Remove the intake manifold-to-cylinder head bolts and the intake manifolds from the cylinder heads.

13. For MPFI, SPFI and turbocharged models, perform the following procedures:

   a. Remove the air intake boot.

   b. Disconnect the electrical connector from the oil pressure switch.

   c. Disconnect the air bleed hose from the intake manifold.

   d. Remove the air flow meter-to-turbocharger duct (Turbo Models).

   e. Remove the air intake duct.

   f. If equipped with a turbocharger, disconnect the cooling inlet hose from the cooling pipe side and the outlet hose from the turbocharger side.

   g. Remove the front exhaust pipe from the cylinder head (Turbo Models).

   h. Remove the clips, the ground

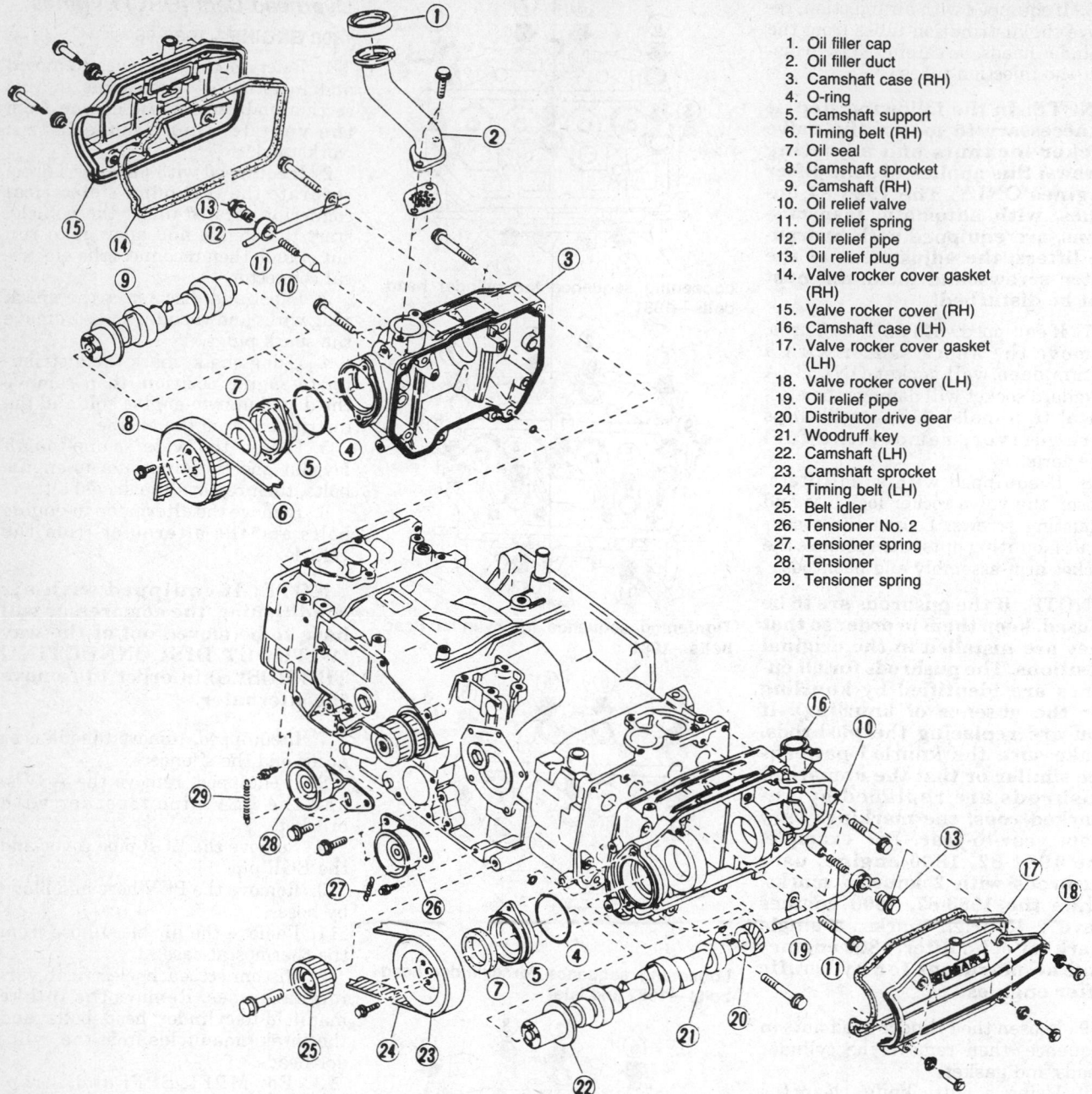

1. Oil filler cap
2. Oil filler duct
3. Camshaft case (RH)
4. O-ring
5. Camshaft support
6. Timing belt (RH)
7. Oil seal
8. Camshaft sprocket
9. Camshaft (RH)
10. Oil relief valve
11. Oil relief spring
12. Oil relief pipe
13. Oil relief plug
14. Valve rocker cover gasket (RH)
15. Valve rocker cover (RH)
16. Camshaft case (LH)
17. Valve rocker cover gasket (LH)
18. Valve rocker cover (LH)
19. Oil relief pipe
20. Distributor drive gear
21. Woodruff key
22. Camshaft (LH)
23. Camshaft sprocket
24. Timing belt (LH)
25. Belt idler
26. Tensioner No. 2
27. Tensioner spring
28. Tensioner
29. Tensioner spring

Exploded view of the camshaft and timing belt—Overhead cam engine

terminal and the knock sensor terminal, then remove the wiring harness.

NOTE: If equipped with air conditioning, the compressor will have to be moved aside (WITHOUT DISCONNECTING THE HOSES) in order to remove the alternator.

14. If equipped with power steering, remove the power steering oil pump bracket-to-engine bolts and the pump bracket.

15. Remove the alternator brackets and the adjusting bar.

16. Remove the air bleed hose, the water pipe and the oil filler duct.

17. Using the Flywheel Stopper tool No. 498277000 or equivalent (MT), or the Drive Plate Stopper tool No. 498497000 or equivalent (AT), secure the crankshaft, then remove the crankshaft pulley bolt and the pulley.

18. Remove the water pump pulley and the pulley cover.

19. Remove the oil level gauge guide along with the gauge.

20. Remove the timing belt cover plate (Turbo Models).

21. Remove the left, right and front belt covers.

22. Loosen the tensioner mounting bolts on the #1 cylinder by ½ turn.

23. With the tensioner fully turned to slacken the belt, tighten the mounting bolts.

24. Using a piece of chalk, mark the rotating direction of the timing belt.

25. Loosen the tensioner No. 2 mounting bolts on #2 cylinder by ½ turn.

26. Using the Tensioner Wrench tool No. 499007000 or equivalent, fully rotate the tensioner to slacken the belt, then tighten the tensioner mounting bolts.

NOTE: Cover the Tensioner Wrench clamping tips with a rubber hose or waste cloth to prevent crankshaft or pulley from being damaged.

27. Remove the timing belt after marking the rotating direction of the belt.

28. Using the Camshaft Sprocket Wrench tool No. 499207000 or equivalent, remove the camshaft sprocket.

29. Remove the right-hand belt cover No. 2, the left-hand belt cover No. 2 and belt cover.

30. Remove the valve rocker covers and gaskets. Then remove the camshaft cases, the camshaft support and the camshaft as a unit.

NOTE: When removing the camshaft case, the valve rockers may come off. To prevent them from being damaged, be sure to place a cloth or rubber mat under the cylinder heads.

31. Remove the valve lash adjusters from the cylinder heads.

NOTE: DO NOT lay down the removed adjusters; keep them upright. Store the removed valve rockers and adjusters in the order of their removal so that they can be reinstalled correctly.

32. If equipped with a turbocharger, remove the turbocharger coolers together with the union screws and gaskets from the cylinder heads.

33. Remove the cylinder heads and gaskets.

34. Using a putty knife, clean the gasket mounting surfaces.

35. To install, use new gaskets, sealant (if necessary) and reverse the removal procedures. Torque the cylinder head-to-engine bolts (in 3 Steps) to 47 ft. lbs.

1200 ENGINE — 1987-88

1. Refer to the "Engine, Removal and Installation" procedures in this section and remove the engine from the vehicle.

2. Using the Engine Stand tool No. 499815500 or equivalent, attach them to the engine.

3. Remove the suction and the air cleaner hoses from the air cleaner.

4. Remove the carburetor-to-distributor vacuum hoses.

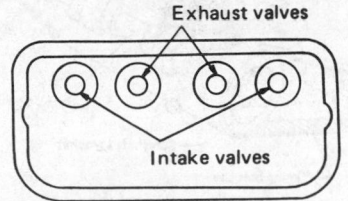

Valve arrangement in cylinder head

5. Loosen the alternator-to-engine bolts, reduce the drive belt tension and remove the drive belt.

6. Label and disconnect the spark plug wires from the spark plug.

NOTE: When removing the spark plug wires, be sure to pull the wires by using the caps.

7. Using the Crank and Camshaft Pulley Wrench tool No. 499205500 or equivalent, secure the crankshaft pulley and remove the pulley bolt.

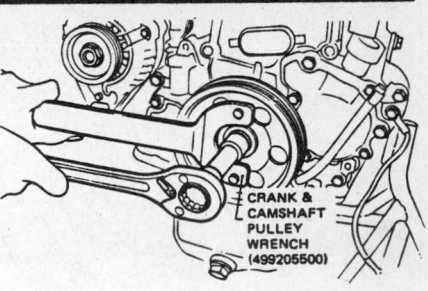

Removing the crankshaft pulley bolt—1200 (OHC) engine

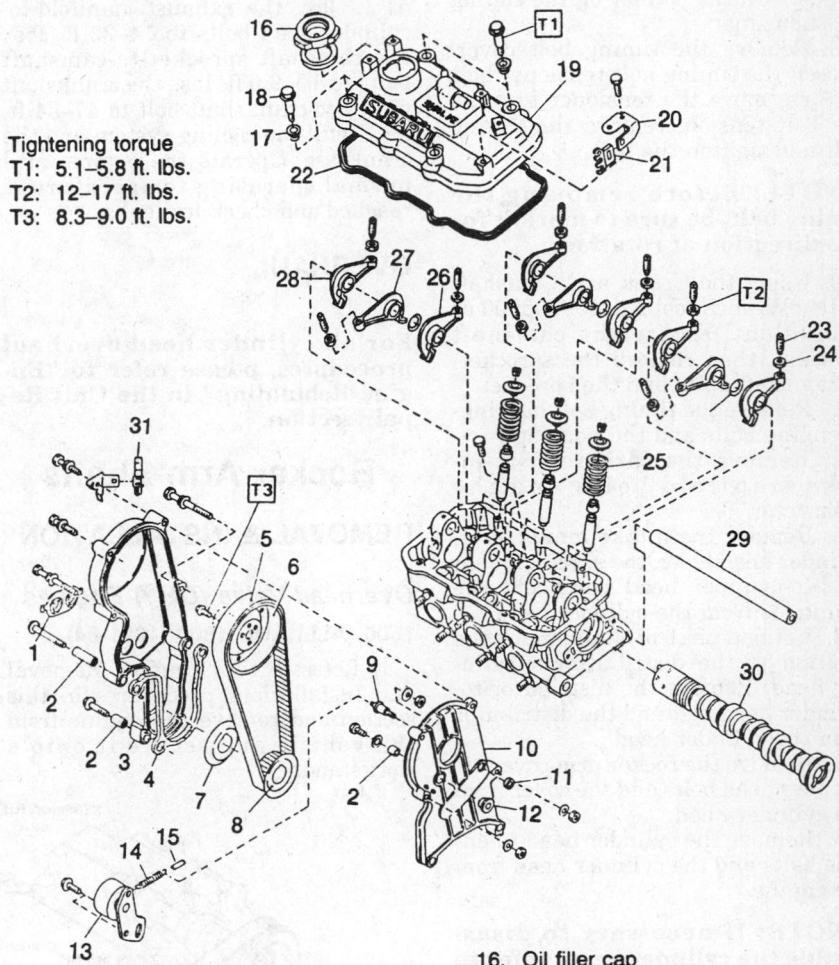

Tightening torque
T1: 5.1–5.8 ft. lbs.
T2: 12–17 ft. lbs.
T3: 8.3–9.0 ft. lbs.

1. Timing belt cover plug	16. Oil filler cap
2. Spacer	17. Seal washer
3. Cam-belt cover 2	18. Rocket cover bolt
4. Belt cover sealing 2	19. Valve rocker cover CP
5. Timing belt	20. High-tension cable stay
6. Camshaft sprocket	21. Vacuum hose supporter
7. Camshaft drive plate	22. Rocker cover gasket
8. Crankshaft sprocket	23. Valve rocker screw
9. Tensioner spring bolt	24. Nut
10. Belt cover	25. Valve spring
11. Cam-belt cover	26. Valve rocker arm No. 2
12. Belt cover mount CP	27. Valve rocker arm No. 3
13. Tensioner CP	28. Valve rocker arm
14. Cam-belt tensioner spring	29. Valve rocker shaft
15. Tensioner spring damper	30. Camshaft
	31. Stay

Exploded view of the cylinder head assembly—1200 (OHC) engine

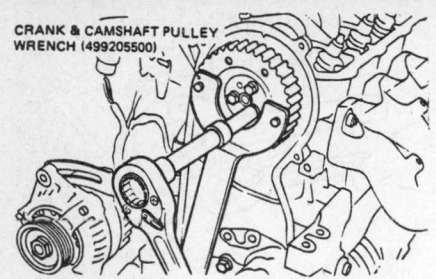

CRANK & CAMSHAFT PULLEY WRENCH (499205500)

Removing the camshaft sprocket bolts – 1200 (OHC) engine

8. Remove the timing belt cover. Rotate the crankshaft until the alignment mark on the camshaft sprocket aligns with the pointer on the timing belt housing.

9. Remove the timing belt cover. Loosen the timing belt tensioner bolt ½ turn, move the tensioner to relax the belt tension, remove the timing belt and tighten the bolt.

NOTE: Before removing the timing belt, be sure to mark it for the direction of rotation.

10. Using the Crank and Camshaft Pulley Wrench tool No. 499205500 or equivalent, secure the camshaft sprocket, then remove the sprocket-to-camshaft bolts and the sprocket.

11. Remove the timing belt housing-to-engine bolts and the housing.

12. Remove the carburetor-to-intake manifold bolts and the carburetor.

13. Remove the intake manifold-to-cylinder head bolts, the exhaust manifold-to-cylinder head bolts and the manifolds from the cylinder head.

14. Using a piece of chalk, mark the position of the distributor-to-cylinder head. Remove the distributor-to-cylinder head bolt and the distributor from the cylinder head.

15. Remove the rocker arm cover-to-cylinder head bolts and the cover from the cylinder head.

16. Remove the cylinder head-to-engine bolts and the cylinder head from the engine.

NOTE: If necessary to disassemble the cylinder head, refer to the "Valve, Removal and Installation" procedures in this section

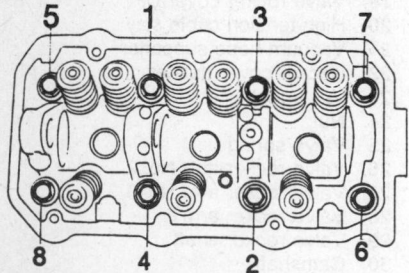

View of the cylinder head torquing sequence – 1200 (OHC) engine

and remove the valves from the cylinder head.

17. Using a putty knife, clean the gasket mounting surfaces. Inspect the cylinder head for cracks, distortion and/or damage, if necessary, replace the cylinder head.

NOTE: Using a straight edge and the feeler gauge, inspect the cylinder head for flatness; the distortion must not exceed 0.020 in.

18. To install, use new gaskets, sealant (where necessary) and reverse the removal procedures. Torque the cylinder head-to-engine bolts (3 Steps) to 51 ft. lbs., the exhaust manifold-to-cylinder head bolts to 14–22 ft. lbs., the camshaft sprocket-to-camshaft bolts to 8.3–9.0 ft. lbs., the crankshaft pulley-to-crankshaft bolt to 47–54 ft. lbs. Refill the cooling system and the crankcase. Operate the engine until normal operating temperature is reached and check for leaks.

OVERHAUL

For all cylinder head overhaul procedures, please refer to "Engine Rebuilding" in the Unit Repair section.

Rocker Arm Shafts

REMOVAL & INSTALLATION

Overhead Valve (OHV) Engines

1600 (ALL) AND 1800 (1981-84)

1. Refer to the "Engine, Removal and Installation" procedures in this section and remove the engine from the vehicle and secure it onto a workstand.

2. Remove the valve cover-to-cylinder head bolts and the valve covers, then discard the gaskets.

3. Remove the rocker arm assemblies-to-cylinder heads bolts and the rocker arm assemblies from the engine.

4. Withdraw the pushrods from their bores, being sure to keep them in the same order in which they were removed.

NOTE: It is a good idea to tag each pushrod as it is removed from its bore, to aid in correct installation.

5. Using a putty knife, clean the gasket mounting surfaces.

6. To install, use new gaskets, sealant (if necessary) and reverse the removal procedures. Tighten the valve rocker assembly-to-cylinder head nuts to 47 ft. lbs. Adjust the valve clearance.

Overhead Cam (OHC) Engines

1800 – 1984-88

The OHC engines DO NOT use a rocker arm shaft, the valve rocker simply floats between the valve stem and the hydraulic lifter, the center of the valve rocker rides against the camshaft.

To replace the valve rockers, please refer to the "Cylinder Head, Removal and Installation" procedures in this section and replace the valve rocker.

1200 – 1987-88

1. Refer to the "Engine, Removal and Installation" procedures in this section and remove the engine from the vehicle.

2. Using the Engine Stand tool No. 499815500 or equivalent, attach them to the engine.

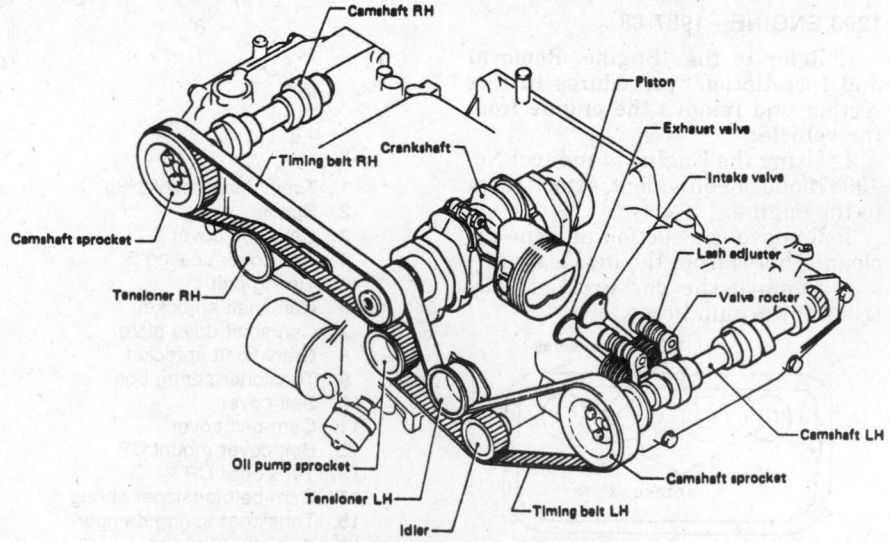

View of the internal components – 1800 (OHC) engine

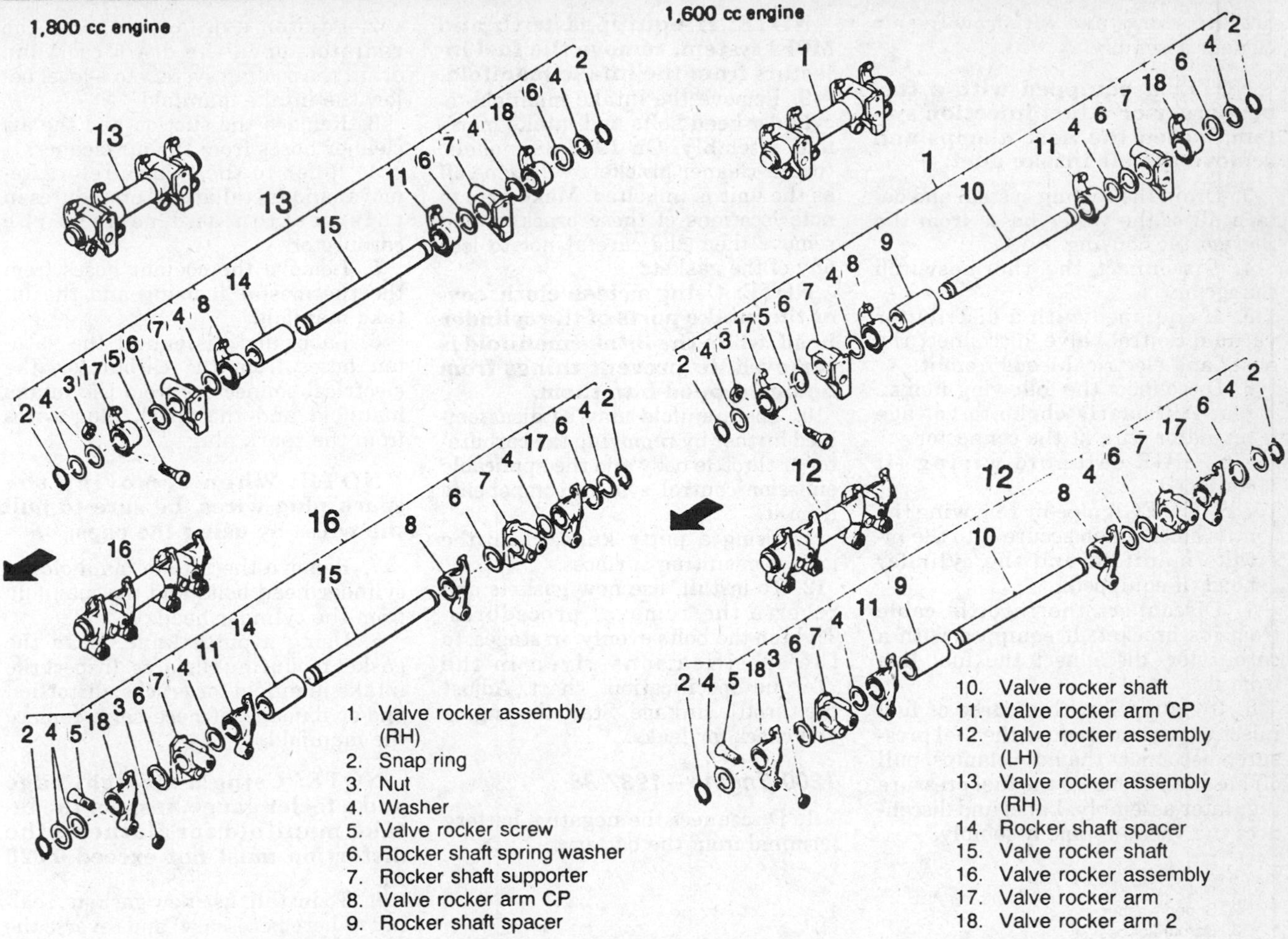

1,800 cc engine   1,600 cc engine

1. Valve rocker assembly (RH)
2. Snap ring
3. Nut
4. Washer
5. Valve rocker screw
6. Rocker shaft spring washer
7. Rocker shaft supporter
8. Valve rocker arm CP
9. Rocker shaft spacer
10. Valve rocker shaft
11. Valve rocker arm CP
12. Valve rocker assembly (LH)
13. Valve rocker assembly (RH)
14. Rocker shaft spacer
15. Valve rocker shaft
16. Valve rocker assembly
17. Valve rocker arm
18. Valve rocker arm 2

Exploded view of the rocker arm assemblies—1600 (OHV) and 1800 (OHV) engines

3. Remove the suction and the air cleaner hoses from the air cleaner.

4. Loosen the alternator-to-engine bolts, reduce the drive belt tension and remove the drive belt.

5. Using the Crank and Camshaft Pulley Wrench tool No. 499205500 or equivalent, secure the crankshaft pulley and remove the pulley bolt.

6. Remove the timing belt cover. Rotate the crankshaft until the alignment mark on the camshaft sprocket aligns with the pointer on the timing belt housing.

7. Remove the timing belt cover. Loosen the timing belt tensioner bolt ½ turn, move the tensioner to relax the belt tension, remove the timing belt and tighten the bolt.

NOTE: Before removing the timing belt, be sure to mark it for the direction of rotation.

8. Using the Crank and Camshaft Pulley Wrench tool No. 499205500 or equivalent, secure the camshaft sprocket, then remove the sprocket-to-camshaft bolts and the sprocket.

9. Remove the timing belt housing-to-engine bolts and the housing.

10. Remove the carburetor-to-intake manifold bolts and the carburetor.

11. Remove the rocker arm cover-to-cylinder head bolts and the cover from the cylinder head.

12. Using the Valve Clearance Adjuster tool No. 498767000 or equivalent, loosen the valve adjuster locknuts and back-off the adjusting screw.

13. Remove the valve rocker arm shaft-to-journal bolt, pull out the rocker arm shaft, then remove the spring washers, the valve rocker arms. Keep the rocker arms and the spring washers in order to make the installation easier.

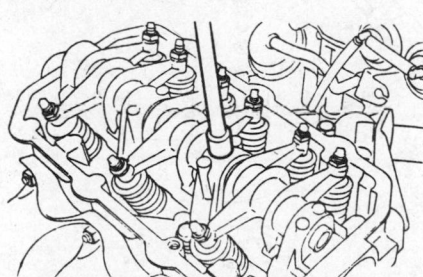

Removing the rocker arm shaft-to-journal bolt—1200 (OHC) engine

14. Using a putty knife, clean the gasket mounting surfaces. Inspect the rocker arm for wear; the clearance between the rocker arm and the shaft is between 0.0006–0.0022 in.

15. To install, use new gaskets, sealant (where necessary) and reverse the removal procedures. Torque the camshaft sprocket-to-camshaft bolts to 8.3–9.0 ft. lbs., the crankshaft pulley-to-crankshaft bolt to 47–54 ft. lbs. Refill the cooling system and the crankcase. Operate the engine until normal operating temperature is reached and check for leaks.

Intake Manifold

REMOVAL & INSTALLATION

1600 and 1800 Engines

——— CAUTION ———
DO NOT perform this operation on a Warm engine; wait until the engine is Cold.

1. Remove the spare tire from the engine compartment.

2. Disconnect the emission control system hoses, remove the mounting

bracket screws and withdraw the air cleaner assembly.

NOTE: If equipped with a turbocharger or a fuel injection system, loosen the hose clamps and remove the air intake duct.

3. Drain the cooling system and detach all of the water hoses from the thermostat housing.

4. Disconnect the thermoswitch connector.

5. If equipped with a distributor vacuum control valve, disconnect the hoses and electrical leads from it.

6. Disconnect the following items:
   a. Automatic choke-to-voltage regulator wire at the connector.
   b. EGR solenoid wiring (if equipped).
   c. The EGR pipe by removing the nuts/bolts which secure it to the intake manifold and the cylinder head (if equipped).

7. Disconnect the throttle cable from it's bracket. If equipped with a carburetor, disconnect the fuel line from it.

8. If equipped with a turbo or fuel injection system, reduce the fuel pressure, disconnect the hose clamps, pull off hoses and remove the fuel pressure regulator assembly. Label and disconnect the vacuum pipe assembly.

NOTE: If equipped with and MPFI system, remove the fuel injectors from the intake manifold.

9. Remove the intake manifold-to-cylinder head bolts and intake manifold assembly. On 1982-88 models, the air cleaner brackets will come off as the unit is unbolted. Make sure to note locations of these brackets and remove them; be careful not to lose any of the gaskets.

NOTE: Using a clean cloth, cover the intake ports of the cylinder head, while the intake manifold is removed, to prevent things from being dropped into them.

10. The manifold may be disassembled further by removing the carburetor or throttle body and the applicable emission control system components from it.

11. Using a putty knife, clean the gasket mounting surfaces.

12. To install, use new gaskets and reverse the removal procedures. Tighten the bolts evenly, in stages, to the specifications given in the "Torque Specification" chart. Adjust the throttle linkage. Start the engine and check for leaks.

1200 Engine — 1987-88

1. Disconnect the negative battery terminal from the battery.

2. Position a drain pan under the radiator, open the drain cock and drain the cooling system to a level below the intake manifold.

3. Remove the suction and the air cleaner hoses from the air cleaner.

4. Refer to the "Carburetor, Removal and Installation" procedures in this section and remove the carburetor.

5. Remove the coolant hoses from the thermostat housing and the intake manifold.

6. Label and disconnect the vacuum hoses from the carburetor, the electrical connectors from the intake manifold and the spark plug wires from the spark plug.

NOTE: When removing the spark plug wires, be sure to pull the wires by using the caps.

7. Remove the intake manifold-to-cylinder head bolts and the manifold from the cylinder head.

8. Using a putty knife, clean the gasket mounting surfaces. Inspect the intake manifold for cracks, distortion and/or damage, if necessary, replace the manifold.

NOTE: Using a straight edge and a feeler gauge, inspect the intake manifold for flatness; the distortion must not exceed 0.020 in.

9. To install, use new gaskets, sealant (where necessary) and reverse the removal procedures. Torque the intake manifold-to-cylinder head nuts/bolts to 14–22 ft. lbs. and the carburetor-to-intake manifold nuts to 14–22 ft. lbs. Refill the cooling system. Operate the engine until normal operating temperature is reached and check for leaks.

Exhaust Manifold
REMOVAL & INSTALLATION
1600 and 1800 Engines
NON-TURBO

An exhaust manifold, as a separate item, is not found on these models. Instead, the Y-shaped exhaust pipe bolts directly to a flange on each cylinder head. Removal procedures for this exhaust pipe can be found in the "Engine, Removal and Installation" section.

1. Raise and support the vehicle on jackstands.

2. Disconnect the electrical connector from the O2 sensor.

3. From the upper shell cover, remove the air duct.

4. Loosen the front exhaust pipe-to-cylinder head nuts.

5. Remove the front exhaust pipe-to-rear exhaust pipe nuts, then sepa-

1. Nut
2. Spring washer
3. Carburetor gasket
4. Washer
5. Bolt (8 x 26 x 23)
6. Bolt
7. Thermostat case cover
8. Thermostat case cover gasket
9. Thermostat
10. Thermometer
11. Bolt
12. Bolt
13. Spring washer

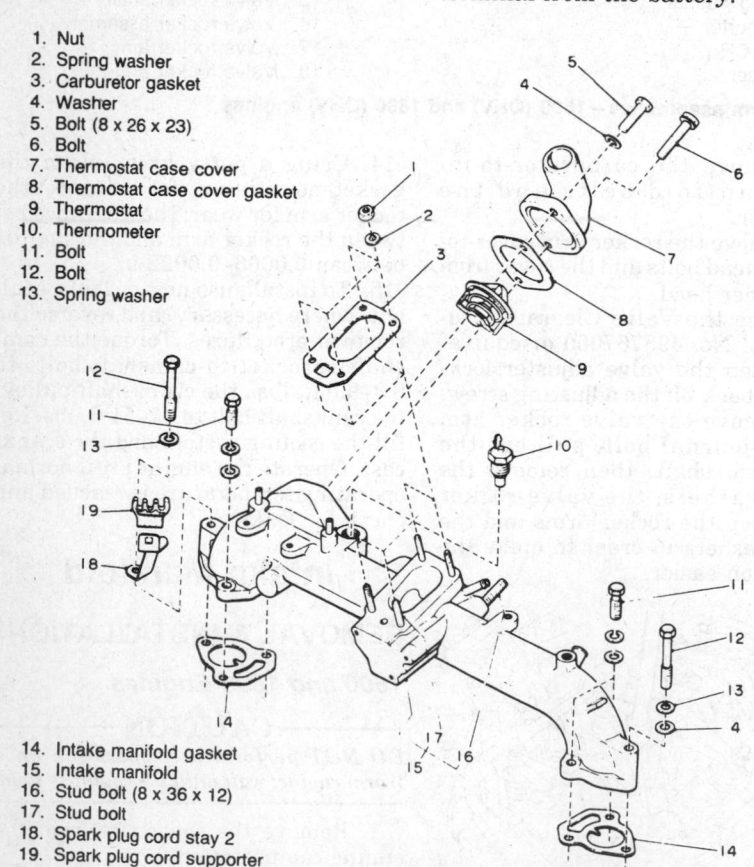

14. Intake manifold gasket
15. Intake manifold
16. Stud bolt (8 x 36 x 12)
17. Stud bolt
18. Spark plug cord stay 2
19. Spark plug cord supporter

Exploded view of a typical 1600 intake manifold (1800 similar)

rate the pipes; discard the gasket.

6. Remove the front exhaust pipe-to-bracket bolt. While supporting the front exhaust pipe, remove the pipe-to-cylinder head nuts and front exhaust pipe from the vehicle; discard the gaskets.

7. Using a putty knife, clean the gasket mounting surfaces.

8. To install, use new gaskets and reverse the removal procedures. Torque the front exhaust pipe-to-cylinder head nuts to 19–22 ft. lbs., the front exhaust pipe-to-rear exhaust pipe nuts to 9–17 ft. lbs. and the front exhaust pipe-to-bracket 18–25 ft. lbs. Start the engine and check for exhaust leaks.

TURBO

This model is unique in having a crossover pipe that links both exhaust ports at the cylinder heads and the exhaust inlet at the turbocharger so as to feed all the exhaust through the turbo.

1. Raise and support the vehicle on jackstands.

2. If equipped, remove the left/right sheetmetal covers from the turbocharger. Remove the turbocharger-to-exhaust pipe bolts and separate the turbocharger from the pipe.

3. Remove the turbo bracket-to-front exhaust pipe nuts and the right-side splash pan.

4. If equipped with a 4WD unit, skid plate-to-chassis bolts and the plate from the vehicle.

5. Loosen the engine-to-mount bracket bolts and the engine-to-pitching stopper bolts. Using a floor jack, raise the engine slightly until the bolts protrude above the surface of the crossmember.

6. Disconnect the front exhaust pipe-to-cylinder head bolts and separate the exhaust pipe between the crossmember-to-cylinder head clearance.

NOTE: If equipped with a power steering unit, be careful not to damage the power steering hoses.

7. Using a putty knife, clean the gasket mounting surfaces.

8. To install, use new gaskets (flat surface facing the cylinder head) and reverse the removal procedures. Torque the exhaust pipe-to-cylinder head nuts to 19–22 ft. lbs., the front exhaust pipe-to-turbocharger nuts to 18–25 ft. lbs. and the turbocharger-to-center exhaust pipe nuts to 18–25 ft. lbs. Start the engine and check for exhaust leaks.

1200 Engine

1. Raise and support the front of the vehicle on jackstands.

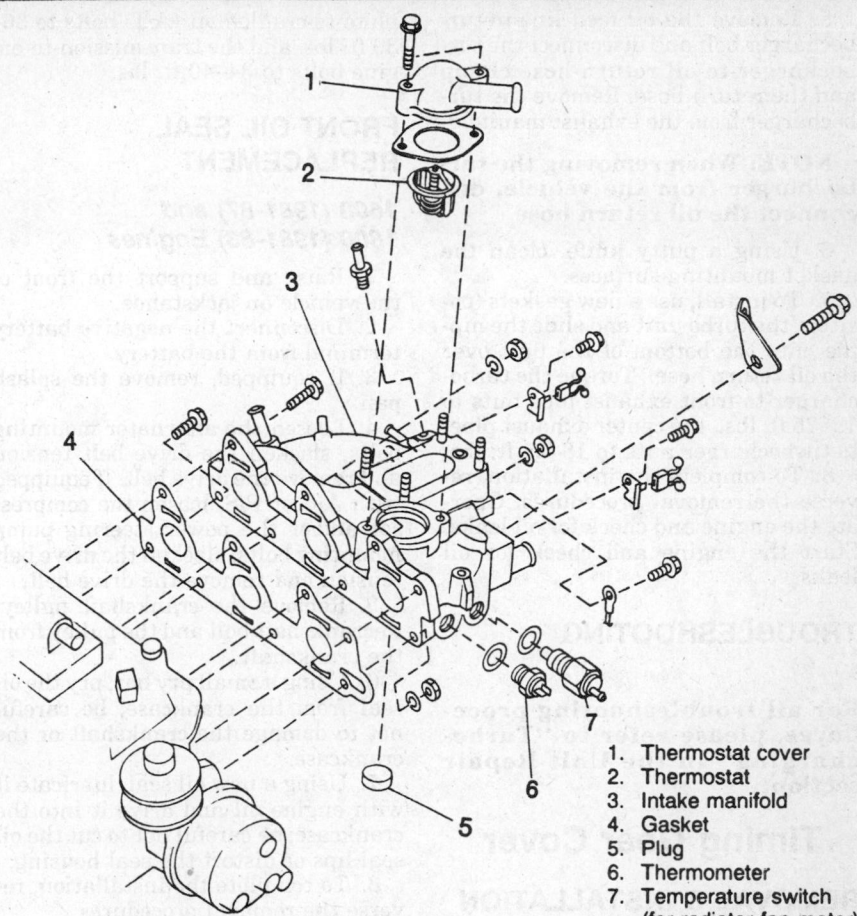

Exploded view of the intake manifold—1200 (OHC) engine

1. Thermostat cover
2. Thermostat
3. Intake manifold
4. Gasket
5. Plug
6. Thermometer
7. Temperature switch (for radiator fan motor)

2. Remove the exhaust manifold cover-to-exhaust manifold bolts and the cover from the manifold.

3. Disconnect the electrical connector from the O₂ sensor.

4. Remove the exhaust manifold-to-front exhaust pipe nuts/bolts, then separate the pipe from the manifold and discard the gasket.

5. Remove the exhaust manifold-to-cylinder head nuts and the manifold from the vehicle; discard the gasket.

6. Using a putty knife, clean the gasket mounting surfaces.

7. To install, use new gaskets and reverse the removal procedures. Torque the exhaust manifold-to-cylinder head nuts to 14–22 ft. lbs. and the exhaust pipe-to-exhaust manifold nuts/bolts to 17–31 ft. lbs. Start the engine and check for exhaust leaks.

Turbocharger—1800 Engine
REMOVAL & INSTALLATION

NOTE: DO NOT allow dirt to enter either the intake or outlet openings or the unit may be destroyed at startup.

1. Remove the air cleaner.

2. Disconnect the airflow meter-to-turbocharger inlet clamp, then remove the air intake duct. Cover the airflow meter and turbocharger openings.

3. Loosen the turbocharger-to-air outlet hose clamp and the throttle body inlet-to-air inlet hose clamp. Remove the turbocharger-to-throttle body hose. Plug all of the openings.

4. Remove the turbocharger-to-center exhaust pipe nuts and the front exhaust pipe-to-turbocharger nuts.

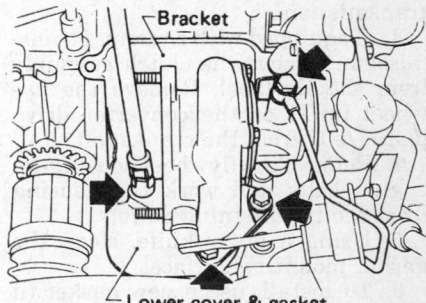

When removing the turbo, disconnect the oil supply line at upper right, and then remove the three bolts from the lower flange, the turbo assembly, and, finally, the gasket

5. Remove the oil feed line-to-turbocharger bolt and disconnect the turbocharger-to-oil return hose clamp and the return hose. Remove the turbocharger from the exhaust manifold.

NOTE: When removing the turbocharger from the vehicle, disconnect the oil return hose.

6. Using a putty knife, clean the gasket mounting surfaces.

7. To install, use a new gaskets (position the turbo unit and slide the nipple onto the bottom of the unit over the oil return hose). Torque the turbocharger-to-front exhaust pipe nuts to 18–25 ft. lbs., the center exhaust pipe-to-turbocharger nuts to 18–25 ft. lbs.

8. To complete the installation, reverse the removal procedures. Operate the engine and check for oil leaks. Start the engine and check for oil leaks.

TROUBLESHOOTING

For all troubleshooting procedures, please refer to "Turbocharging" in the Unit Repair section.

Timing Gear Cover

REMOVAL & INSTALLATION

Overhead Valve (OHV) Engines

**1600 (1981-87) and
1800 (1981-83) Engines**

The flywheel housing covers the timing gears and acts as the timing gear cover. In order to remove it, the engine MUST BE removed from the vehicle.

1. Refer to the "Engine, Removal and Installation" procedures in this section and remove the engine from the vehicle.

2. Separate the engine from the transmission. If equipped with an automatic transmission, remove the torque converter with the transmission.

3. If equipped with a manual transmission, remove the clutch assembly from the flywheel. Remove the flywheel (M/T) or the converter drive plate (A/T) from the crankshaft.

4. Remove the flywheel housing-to-engine bolts and work the housing from the two aligning dowels.

5. Using a putty knife, clean the gasket mounting surfaces.

6. To install, use a new gasket (if equipped) and reverse the removal procedures. Torque the flywheel housing-to-engine bolts to 14–20 ft. lbs., the flywheel-to-crankshaft (M/T) bolts to 30–33 ft. lbs. or the drive

plate-to-crankshaft (A/T) bolts to 36–39 ft. lbs. and the transmission-to-engine bolts to 34–40 ft. lbs.

FRONT OIL SEAL REPLACEMENT

*1600 (1981-87) and
1800 (1981-83) Engines*

1. Raise and support the front of the vehicle on jackstands.

2. Disconnect the negative battery terminal from the battery.

3. If equipped, remove the splash pan.

4. Loosen the alternator mounting bolts, slacken the drive belt tension and remove the drive belt. If equipped with A/C or P/S, loosen the compressor and/or the power steering pump mounting bolts, slacken the drive belt tension and remove the drive belt.

5. Remove the crankshaft pulley-to-crankshaft bolt and the pulley from the crankshaft.

6. Using a small pry bar, pry the oil seal from the crankcase; be careful not to damage the crankshaft or the crankcase.

7. Using a new oil seal, lubricate it with engine oil and drive it into the crankcase; be careful not to cut the oil seal lips or distort the seal housing.

8. To complete the installation, reverse the removal procedures.

Timing Belt Cover

REMOVAL & INSTALLATION

Overhead Cam (OHC) Engines

1800 (1984-88)

1. Loosen the water pump pulley nut/bolts and the alternator-to-engine bolts, the remove the drive belt.

2. Disconnect the electrical connector from the oil pressure switch.

3. Remove the oil level gauge guide with the gauge.

4. Remove the timing hole cover from the top of the flywheel housing.

5. Using the Flywheel Stopper tool No. 498277000 or equivalent (M/T), or the Drive Plate Stopper tool No. 498407000 or equivalent (A/T), insert it through the timing hole (in the flywheel housing) and lock the flywheel.

6. If equipped with a turbocharger, remove the belt cover plate.

7. Remove the left-side, the right-side and the front timing belt cover.

8. To install, reverse the removal procedures. Torque the timing belt covers to 3.3–4 ft. lbs.

1200 (1987-88)

1. Loosen the alternator-to-engine bolts, relax the drive belt tension and

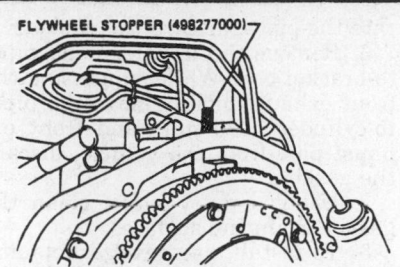

FLYWHEEL STOPPER (498277000)

Using the flywheel stopper tool (for M/T) to lock the flywheel; the drive plate locking tool (for A/T) is similar

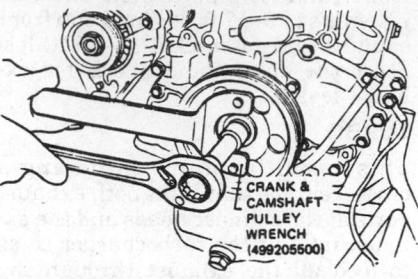

CRANK & CAMSHAFT PULLEY WRENCH (499205500)

Removing the crankshaft pulley bolt—1200 (OHC) engine

remove the drive belt from the front of the engine.

2. Using a socket wrench (through the hole in the right fender) and the Crank/Crankshaft Pulley Wrench tool No. 499205500 or equivalent (to hold the crankshaft pulley), remove the crankshaft pulley-to-crankshaft bolt and the pulley from the crankshaft.

3. Remove the timing belt cover-to-engine bolts and the cover from the engine.

4. Using a putty knife, clean the gasket mounting surfaces.

5. To install, reverse the removal procedures.

Timing Belt and Tensioner

ADJUSTMENT

Overhead Cam (OHC) Engines

1800 ENGINE

1. Refer to the "Timing Belt Cover, Removal and Installation" procedures in this section and remove the timing belt cover.

2. Loosen the timing belt tensioner bolts ½ turn so that the tensioners will move.

3. Allow the spring pressure to adjust the pressure on the timing belt.

4. Using a Timing Belt Tension Wrench tool No. 499437000 or equivalent, apply 17–19 ft. lbs. (new timing belt and head gasket) or 10–12 ft. lbs. (original timing belt and head gasket) to the left-side camshaft sprocket in the counterclockwise direction.

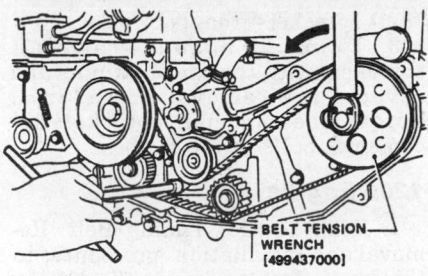

Torquing the timing belt tensioner bolts – 1800 (OHC) engine

5. While applying tension to the left-side camshaft sprocket, torque the timing belt tensioner-to-engine bolts to 12.7–14.8 ft. lbs.

NOTE: When tightening the timing belt tensioner bolts, torque the lower bolt, first, then the upper bolt, second.

6. Using a Timing Belt Tension Wrench tool No. 499437000 or equivalent, apply 17–19 ft. lbs. (new timing belt and head gasket) or 10–12 ft. lbs. (original timing belt and head gasket) to the right-side camshaft sprocket in the counterclockwise direction.

7. While applying tension to the right-side camshaft sprocket, torque the timing belt tensioner-to-engine bolts to 12.7–14.8 ft. lbs.

NOTE: When tightening the timing belt tensioner bolts, torque the lower bolt, first, then the upper bolt, second.

8. To complete the installation, reverse the removal procedures.

1200 ENGINE

No periodic adjustment of the timing belt is necessary; the tensioner spring controls the pressure on the timing belt. If necessary to adjust the timing belt perform the following procedures.

1. Refer to the "Timing Belt Cover, Removal and Installation" procedures in this section and remove the timing belt cover.

2. Loosen the timing belt tensioner bolts ½ turn so that the tensioner will move.

3. Allow the spring pressure to adjust the pressure on the timing belt.

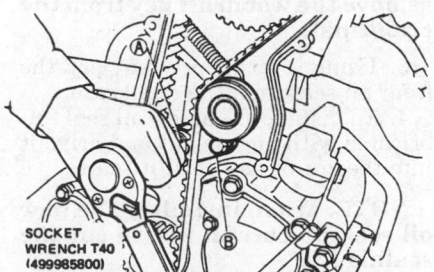

Torquing the timing belt tensioner bolts – 1200 (OHC) engine

4. Tighten the timing belt tensioner; tighten bolt (A) first and (B) second.

5. To complete the installation, reverse the removal procedures.

REMOVAL & INSTALLATION

Overhead Cam (OHC) Engines

1800 ENGINE

1. Refer the "Timing Belt Cover, Removal and Installation" procedures in this section and remove the timing belt covers.

2. At the No. 1 cylinder-side, loosen the tensioner-to-engine bolts by ½ turn.

3. Turn the tensioner fully to slacken the timing belt, the tighten the tensioner-to-engine bolts.

4. Using a piece of chalk, mark the rotating direction of the timing belt, then remove it.

5. At the No. 2 cylinder-side, loosen the tensioner-to-engine bolts by ½ turn.

6. Using the Tensioner Wrench tool No. 499007000 or equivalent, fully rotate the tensioner to slacken the belt, then tighten the tensioner mounting bolts.

NOTE: Cover the tensioner wrench clamping tips with a rubber hose or cloth to prevent the crankshaft or pulley from being damaged.

7. Using a piece of chalk, mark the rotating direction of the timing belt, then remove it.

8. To remove the belt tensioners, perform the following procedures:

   a. Loosen the tensioner-to-engine bolts and relax the spring pressure.

   b. Remove the tensioner bolts and the springs from the tensioners.

9. To install the belt tensioners, perform the following procedures:

   a. Connect the spring to the tensioner and the engine.

   b. Using the bolts, attach the tensioner/spring assembly to the engine.

   c. If installing the right-side tensioner, push down on the tensioner and secure the bolts.

   d. If installing the left-side tensioner, use the Tensioner Wrench tool No. 499007000 or equivalent, to raise the tensioner/spring assembly all the way, then tighten the bolts.

10. Install the crankshaft pulley and tighten the pulley bolt temporarily.

11. Through the timing hole (on top of the flywheel housing), align the center of the three lines (scribed on the flywheel) with the timing mark on the flywheel housing.

12. Align the timing mark on the left-side camshaft sprocket with the notch on the belt cover. Then install the left-side timing belt onto the crankshaft sprocket, the oil pump sprocket, the belt idler and the camshaft sprocket; install the belt in this order to prevent downward slackening of the belt.

13. Loosen the left-side timing belt tensioner bolts ½ turn so that the tensioners will move. Allow the spring pressure to adjust the pressure on the timing belt.

14. Using a Timing Belt Tension Wrench tool No. 499437000 or equivalent, apply 17–19 ft. lbs. (new timing belt and head gasket) or 10–12 ft. lbs. (original timing belt and head gasket) to the left-side camshaft sprocket in the counterclockwise direction.

15. While applying tension to the left-side camshaft sprocket, torque the timing belt tensioner-to-engine bolts to 12.7–14.8 ft. lbs.

NOTE: When tightening the timing belt tensioner bolts, torque the lower bolt, first, then the upper bolt, second.

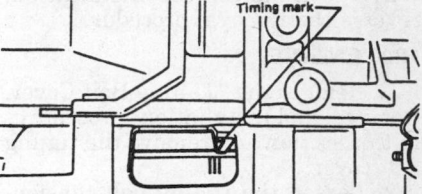

Aligning the flywheel marks with the flywheel housing indicator – 1800 (OHC) engine

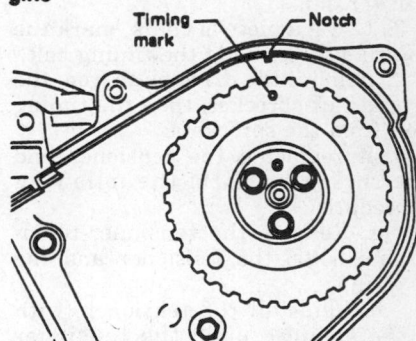

Aligning the left-side camshaft sprocket timing mark with the notch on the belt cover – 1800 (OHC) engine – right-side is similar

Using the tensioner wrench when moving the belt tensioner – 1800 (OHC) engine

16. Realign the flywheel with the timing marks on the flywheel housing.

17. Align the right-side camshaft sprocket timing mark with the notch in the belt cover. Install the right-side timing belt to the crankshaft sprocket and the camshaft sprocket to prevent slackening on the belt on the upper side.

18. Loosen the tensioner-to-engine bolts and allow the spring pressure to adjust the belt pressure.

19. Using a Timing Belt Tension Wrench tool No. 499437000 or equivalent, apply 17–19 ft. lbs. (new timing belt and head gasket) or 10–12 ft. lbs. (original timing belt and head gasket) to the right-side camshaft sprocket in the counterclockwise direction.

20. While applying tension to the right-side camshaft sprocket, torque the timing belt tensioner-to-engine bolts to 12.7–14.8 ft. lbs.

NOTE: When tightening the timing belt tensioner bolts, torque the lower bolt, first, then the upper bolt, second.

21. To complete the installation, reverse the removal procedures.

1200 ENGINE

1. Refer to the "Timing Belt Cover, Removal and Installation" procedures in this section and remove the timing belt cover.

2. Loosen the timing belt tensioner-to-engine bolts ½ turn so that the tensioner will move; relax the timing belt tension.

3. Using a piece of chalk, mark the rotating direction of the timing belt.

4. Remove the drive plate from the crankshaft sprocket, then the timing belt from the sprockets.

5. If replacing the tensioner and the spring, perform the following procedures:

   a. Remove the tensioner-to-engine bolts, the tensioner and the spring.

   b. Reinstall the tensioner (with the spring), push the tensioner away from the tension direction and secure the bolts.

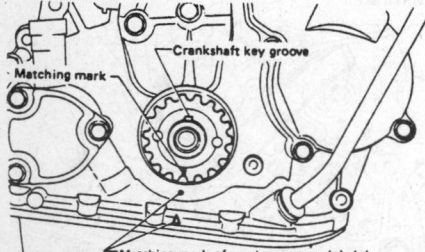

Aligning the timing marks of the crankshaft sprocket with the crankcase cover — 1200 (OHC) engine

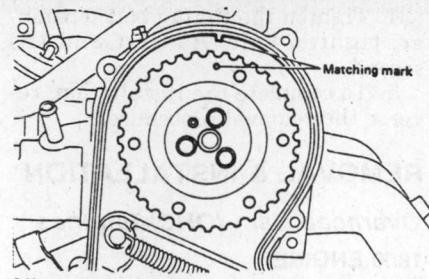

Aligning the timing marks of the camshaft sprocket with the crankcase cover — 1200 (OHC) engine

6. Align the timing mark on the crankshaft sprocket with the timing mark on the crankcase cover. Install the drive plate onto the crankshaft sprocket.

7. Align the timing mark on the camshaft sprocket with the timing mark on the crankcase cover.

8. Install the timing belt onto the sprockets.

NOTE: When installing the used timing belt, be sure that it is installed in the direction of rotation.

9. Loosen the tensioner bolts and allow the spring pressure to adjust the pressure on the timing belt. Tighten the timing belt tensioner; tighten bolt (A) first and (B) second.

10. To complete the installation, reverse the removal procedures. Torque the crankshaft pulley-to-crankshaft bolt to 47–54 ft. lbs.

Timing Sprockets—OHC Engines

REMOVAL & INSTALLATION

1800 Engine

1. Refer to the "Timing Belt, Removal and Installation" procedures in this section and remove the timing belt.

2. Using a socket wrench and the Camshaft Sprocket Wrench tool No. 499207000 or equivalent, remove the camshaft sprocket-to-camshaft bolts and the sprockets; remove the cam-

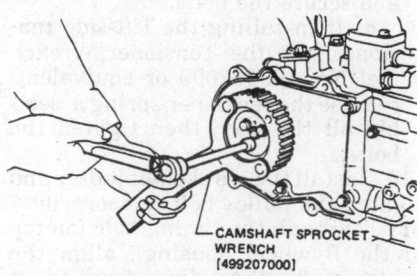

Replacing the camshaft sprockets — 1800 (OHC) engine

shaft sprockets from both sides.

3. To install, align the camshaft sprockets with the camshaft pins and reverse the removal procedures. Torque the camshaft sprockets-to-camshaft bolts to 7–8 ft. lbs.

1200 Engine

1. Refer to the "Timing Belt, Removal and Installation" procedures in this section and remove the timing belt.

2. Using a socket wrench and the Camshaft Sprocket Wrench tool No. 499205500 or equivalent, remove the camshaft sprocket-to-camshaft bolts and the sprockets; remove the camshaft sprockets from both sides.

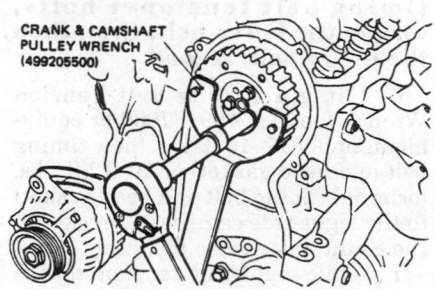

Replacing the camshaft sprockets — 1200 (OHC) engine

3. To install, align the camshaft sprockets with the camshaft pins and reverse the removal procedures. Torque the camshaft sprockets-to-camshaft bolts to 8–9 ft. lbs.

OIL SEAL REPLACEMENT

1800 (OHC) and 1200 (OHC) Engines

1. Refer to the "Timing Belt, Removal and Installation" procedures in this section and remove the timing belt.

2. On the 1800 engine, slide both the No. 1 and No. 2 crankshaft sprockets from the crankshaft. On the 1200 engine, slide crankshaft sprocket from the crankshaft.

NOTE: When removing the crankshaft sprockets, be sure to remove the woodruff key from the crankshaft.

3. Using a small pry bar, pry the front oil seal from the crankcase.

4. To install, use a new oil seal (lubricated with engine oil) and drive it into the crankcase until it seats.

NOTE: When installing the new oil seal, be careful not to cut the sealing lips.

5. To complete the installation, reverse the removal procedures.

Camshaft

REMOVAL & INSTALLATION

Overhead Valve (OHV) Engines

1600 (1981-87)
and 1800 (1981-83)

The camshaft turns on journals that are machined directly into the crankcase.

1. Refer the the "Engine, Removal and Installation" procedures in this section and remove the engine from the vehicle, then separate the transmission from the engine.

2. Remove the clutch assembly/flywheel (M/T) or the torque converter drive plate (A/T).

3. Remove the flywheel housing-to-engine bolts and the housing from the engine.

4. Remove the crankshaft gear from the crankshaft.

5. Straighten the lockwashers and remove the camshaft thrust plate-to-engine bolts.

NOTE: The lockwashers are straightened and the bolts removed through the access holes in the camshaft gear.

6. Remove the rocker arm-to-cylinder head covers, the rocker arm-to-cylinder head assemblies, the push rods and valve lifters.

NOTE: When removing the push rods and valve lifters, be sure to the items in order for reassembly purposes.

7. Pull the camshaft toward the rear of the engine and remove it from the engine; be careful not to damage the bearing journals and/or the camshaft lobes.

NOTE: Remove the oil seal; be sure to replace it with a new one when reassembling the engine.

8. Inspect the camshaft for wear and/or damage; if necessary, replace it.

9. Using a dial micrometer and a set of **V** blocks, measure the camshaft bearing wear and the camshaft bend; the bend limit is 0.002 in.

10. Using a putty knife, clean the gasket mounting surfaces.

11. Install the camshaft and torque the thrust plate bolts. Using a feeler gauge or a dial indicator, move the camshaft (fore and aft), then measure the end-play, it should be 0.008 in. or less.

12. To complete the installation, use new gaskets, sealant (where necessary), assemble the engine and reverse the removal procedures. Refill the cooling system and the crankcase.

Start the engine, allow it to reach normal operating temperatures and check for leaks.

Overhead Cam (OHC) Engines

1800 (1984-88)

1. Refer to the "Cylinder Head, Removal and Installation" procedures in this section and remove the camshaft case (with the camshaft).

2. Remove the camshaft support-to-camshaft case bolts and the support from the case.

3. Remove the camshaft from the camshaft case, be careful not to damage the camshaft journals or the lobes.

4. Inspect the camshaft for wear and/or damage; if necessary, replace it.

5. Using a dial micrometer and a set of **V** blocks, measure the camshaft bearing wear and the camshaft bend; the bend limit is 0.0010 in.

6. Using a putty knife, clean the gasket mounting surfaces.

7. Install the camshaft and torque the thrust plate bolts. Using a feeler gauge or a dial indicator, move the camshaft (fore and aft), then measure the end-play, it should be 0.001–0.010 in.

8. To complete the installation, use new gaskets, sealant (where necessary), assemble the engine and reverse the removal procedures. Start the engine, allow it to reach normal operating temperatures and check for leaks. Check and adjust the ignition timing.

1200 (1987-88)

1. Refer to the "Camshaft Sprocket, Removal and Installation" and to the "Rocker Arm Shaft, Removal and Installation" procedures in this section, then remove the camshaft sprocket and the rocker arm shaft assembly.

2. Remove the electrical connectors and the distributor cap from the distributor. Remove the distributor-to-engine bolt and the distributor from the engine.

3. Remove the camshaft thrust plate-to-engine bolts, then pull the camshaft from the rear of the engine; be careful not to damage the camshaft journals or the camshaft lobes.

4. Inspect the camshaft for wear and/or damage; if necessary, replace it.

5. Using a dial micrometer and a set of **V** blocks, measure the camshaft bearing wear and the camshaft bend; the bend limit is 0.002 in.

6. Using a putty knife, clean the gasket mounting surfaces.

7. Install the camshaft and torque the thrust plate bolts. Using a feeler gauge or a dial indicator, move the

camshaft (fore and aft), then measure the end-play, it should be 0.0012–0.0150 in.

8. To complete the installation, use new gaskets, sealant (where necessary), assemble the engine and reverse the removal procedures. Check and adjust the ignition timing.

Pistons and Connecting Rods

REMOVAL & INSTALLATION

Overhead Valve (OHV) Engine

1. Refer to the "Engine, Removal and Installation" procedures in this section and remove the engine from the vehicle. Separate the engine from the transmission.

2. Remove the intake manifold, the oil pan, the clutch assembly (M/T), the flywheel (M/T) or drive plate (A/T) and the flywheel housing.

3. Remove the rocker arm covers, the rocker arm-to-cylinder head assemblies, the push rods and the valve lifters.

NOTE: When removing the push rods and the valve lifters, be sure to keep them in order for reinstallation purposes. If equipped with a hydraulic lifter engine, tilt the crankcase and remove the lifters; it is not necessary to loosen the valve rocker adjusting screws.

4. Remove the cylinder head-to-engine bolts, in the reverse order of the torquing sequence and gaskets. Remove the oil strainer retainer nut/bolt; use a chisel to remove the oil strainer.

5. Using the holes in the camshaft gear, remove the camshaft thrust plate-to-engine lockwashers and bolts.

6. Using a 0.55 in. Allen wrench, remove the crankcase plugs (of No. 3 and No. 4 piston-side) from the rear of the crankcase.

7. Using a wrench on the crankshaft pulley bolt, rotate the crankshaft so that the No. 3 and No. 4 pistons are at the Bottom Dead Center

USE THIS SHAPE OF WRENCH

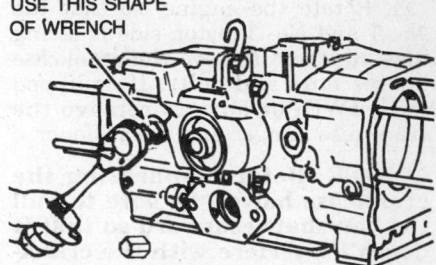

Removing or installing crankcase plugs

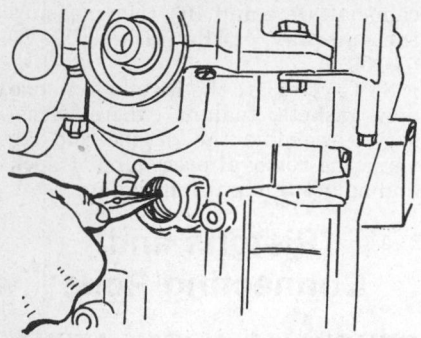

Removing or installing the piston pin circlip through the crankcase holes

(BDC) of the their compression stroke.

8. Using the piston circlip (needle-nose) pliers, insert them through the crankcase plug holes and remove the wrist pin-to-pistons circlips.

9. Using a Wrist Pin Removal tool No. 399094310 or equivalent, through the rear service holes, remove the wrist pins through the crankcase plug holes.

NOTE: Keep the circlips and the wrist pins together for each cylinder so that they DO NOT become mixed.

10. Using a 0.55 in. Allen wrench, remove the crankcase plugs (of No. 1 and No. 2 piston-side) from the front of the crankcase.

11. Using a wrench on the crankshaft pulley bolt, rotate the crankshaft so that the No. 1 and No. 2 pistons are at the Bottom Dead Center (BDC) of the their compression stroke.

12. Using the piston circlip (needle-nose) pliers, insert them through the crankcase plug holes and remove the wrist pin-to-pistons circlips.

13. Using a Wrist Pin Removal tool No. 399094310 or equivalent, through the front service holes, remove the wrist pins through the crankcase plug holes.

NOTE: Keep the circlips and the wrist pins together for each cylinder so that they do not become mixed.

14. Rotate the engine, so that the No. 1 and No. 3 piston-side is facing upward, them remove the crankcase halves nuts and bolts. If equipped with 4WD, be sure to remove the crankcase hanger and the stiffener.

NOTE: Before separating the crankcase halves, be sure to pull the camshaft rearward so that it doesn't interfere with the crankcase. If equipped with solid lifters, install the Valve Lifter Re-

taining Clips tool No. 899804100 or equivalent, to keep the lifters from dropping out of the upper crankcase.

15. Separate the crankcase halves. Remove the front oil seal, the O-ring and the back-up ring; be sure to replace them with new ones when reassembling the engine.

NOTE: Keep the pistons and the wrist pins together for each cylinder so that they DO NOT become mixed. Mark the pistons and the connecting rods so that the direction is not changed when they are installed.

16. Remove the crankshaft together with the connecting rods, the distributor gear and the crankshaft gear as an assembly. Remove the camshaft, the camshaft gear and the thrust plate as an assembly.

17. Using a Ridge Reamer tool, remove the ridge from the top of the cylinder (unworn area) to facilitate the removal of the pistons by performing the following procedures:

　a. Place the piston at the bottom of its bore and cover it with a rag.

　b. Cut the ridge away using a ridge reamer, exercising extreme care to avoid cutting too deeply.

　c. Remove the rag and remove the cuttings that remain on the piston.

NOTE: If the ridge is not removed and new rings are installed, damage to the new rings will result!

18. If the piston rings are to be replaced, remove them with a ring expander. Keep the rings in removal sequence and with the piston from which they were removed. Check all clearances. Refer to "Engine Rebuilding" in the Unit Repair section and the appropriate specification charts. Install the pistons with a ring compressor.

19. To assemble the engine, use new gaskets, Fuji® Bond C sealant or

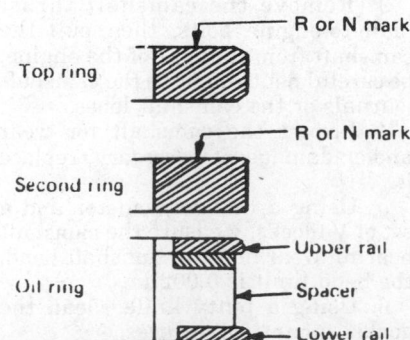

Cross-sectional view of the Riken piston rings—1600 (OHV) and 1800 (OHV) engines

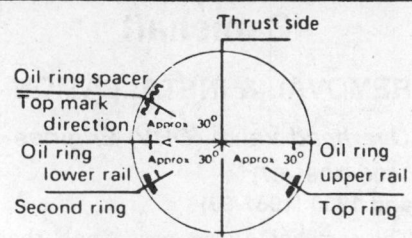

Piston ring gap position

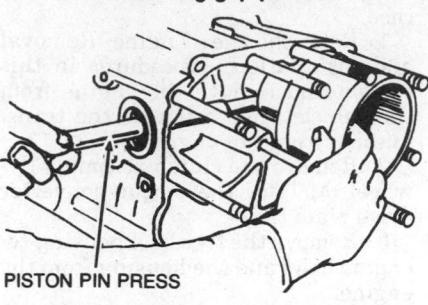

PISTON PIN PRESS

Installation of piston and pin when cylinder liners are used

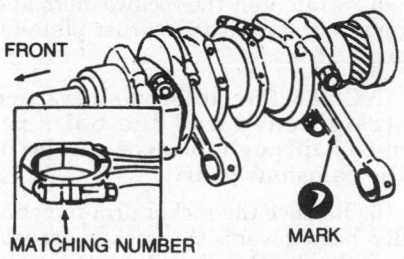

Position each connecting rod with the side mark facing forward. Each connecting rod has its own mating cap with a matching number

equivalent (on the crankcase halves) and reverse the disassembly procedures, paying particular attention to all torque figures and sequences.

Overhead Cam (OHC) Engine

1800 ENGINE

1. Refer to the "Cylinder Head, Removal and Installation" procedures in this section and remove the cylinder heads from the vehicle.

NOTE: If equipped with a turbocharger, remove the cooling pipe with the union screws and gaskets from the cylinder head.

2. Turn the oil pump pulley to align the notch with the pulley notch with the bolt position, then remove the pump outer rotor from the cylinder block.

3. If equipped with a M/T, remove the clutch cover, the clutch disc and the flywheel; if equipped with an A/T, remove the drive plate. Remove the flywheel housing with the housing cover from the crankcase.

4. Remove the oil pan-to-engine bolts and the oil pan from the engine.

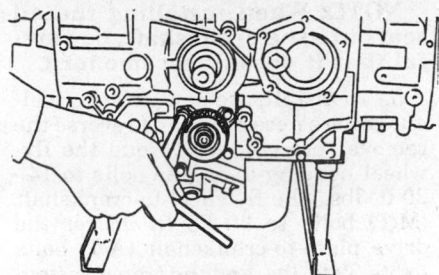

Removing the oil pump rotor from the cylinder block—1800 (OHC) engine

Remove the oil strainer and the strainer stays.

5. Remove the separator cover.

6. Using a 14mm hexagon wrench, remove the service hole plugs from the front of the crankcase. Turn the crankshaft to position the No. 1 and No. 2 pistons to their TDC positions.

7. Using a pair of needle-nose pliers, remove the piston pin circlip from the piston.

8. Using the Piston Pin Remover tool No. 399094310 or equivalent, remove the piston pin from the No. 1 and No. 2 pistons.

NOTE: When removing the piston pins, circlips and pistons, be sure keep the items in order for reinstallation purposes.

9. Using a 14mm hexagon wrench, remove the service hole plugs from the rear of the crankcase. Turn the crankshaft to position the No. 3 and No. 4 pistons to their TDC positions.

7. Using a pair of needle-nose pliers, remove the piston pin circlip from the piston.

8. Using the Piston Pin Remover tool No. 399094310 or equivalent, remove the piston pin from the No. 3 and No. 4 pistons.

9. Remove the cylinder block connecting bolts, except the one under the center journal; loosen the remaining bolt until it can be turned by hand.

10. Turn the cylinder block so that the No. 1/No. 3 cylinders are on the upper side, then separate the cylinder blocks from one another.

NOTE: When separating the cylinder blocks, DO NOT allow the connecting rod(s) to fall and damage the cylinder block.

11. From the crankshaft, remove the front and rear oil seal.

12. Remove the crankshaft (with the connecting rods) from the crankcase.

13. Using a Ridge Reamer tool, remove the ridge from the top of the cylinder (unworn area) to facilitate the removal of the pistons by performing the following procedures:

  a. Place the piston at the bottom of its bore and cover it with a rag.

b. Cut the ridge away using a ridge reamer, exercising extreme care to avoid cutting too deeply.

c. Remove the rag and remove the cuttings that remain on the piston.

NOTE: If the ridge is not removed and new rings are installed, damage to the new rings will result!

14. Using a hammer handle or a wooden bar, force the pistons out through the top of the cylinder block(s), the crankshaft bearings from the cylinder block.

15. Using a putty knife, clean the gasket mounting surfaces.

16. Inspect the cylinder block, the piston and the crankshaft for damage, wear, warpage and/or clogging of the oil passages; if necessary, replace the damaged parts.

17. Install new crankshaft bearings into the cylinder blocks and the crankshaft assembly into the left-hand cylinder block.

18. Using Three-bond® 1215 sealant or equivalent, apply it along the mating surface of the cylinder block. Install the right-hand cylinder block onto the assembly. Torque the cylinder block bolts to 17–20 ft. lbs. (8mm) or 29–35 ft. lbs. (10mm).

19. Using a dial micrometer, check the crankshaft thrust clearance; it should be 0.0004–0.0037 in.

20. Using a piston ring expander tool, install new rings onto the pistons.

21. Using engine oil, lubricate the piston assembly. Turn the crankshaft so that the No. 1 and No. 2 connecting rods are positioned at BTD.

22. Using the Piston Ring Compression tool No. 398744300 or equivalent, compress the piston rings into the piston assembly. Then, using a hammer handle, drive the piston assembly into the cylinder block.

23. Using the Piston Pin Guide tool No. 399284300 or equivalent, install the piston pin and the circlip through the service hole.

24. Turn the crankshaft until the No. 3 and No. 4 connecting rods are

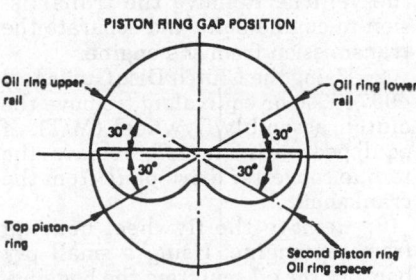

Positioning of the piston rings—1800 (OHC) engine

Apply liquid packing along this line.
Applying sealant to the cylinder block halves—1800 (OHC) engine

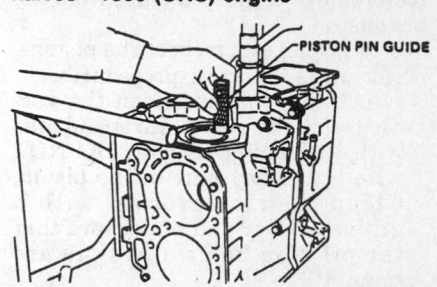

Installing the piston pin and circlip into the cylinder block—1800 (OHV) engine

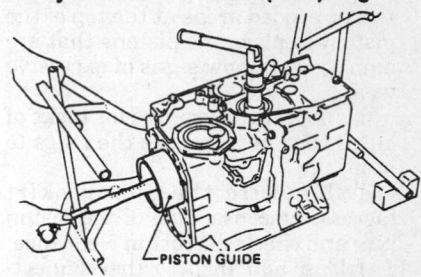

Installing the piston assembly into the cylinder block—1800 (OHC) engine

positioned at BDC, then install the piston pin and circlip.

25. To complete the installation, use new gaskets, sealant (where necessary) and reverse the removal procedures.

1200 ENGINE

1. Refer to the "Engine, Removal and Installation" procedures in this section and remove the engine from the vehicle.

2. Refer to the "Cylinder Head, Removal and Installation" procedures in this section and remove the cylinder head.

3. Remove the oil pan and the oil strainer assembly.

4. Stamp the cylinder number on the machined surfaces of the bolt bosses of the connecting rod and cap for identification when reinstalling. If the pistons are to be removed from the connecting rod, mark the cylinder number on the piston with a silver pencil or quick drying paint for proper cylinder identification and cap to rod location.

5. Examine the cylinder bore above

the ring travel. If a ridge exists, remove it with a ridge reamer before attempting to remove the piston and rod assembly.

6. Remove the rod bearing cap and bearing.

7. Install a guide hose over the rod bolt threads; this will prevent damage to the bearing journal and rod bolt threads.

8. Using a hammer handle, remove the rod/piston assemblies through the top of the cylinder bore

9. Using a piston ring expanding tool, remove the piston rings from the pistons.

10. To clean and inspect the pistons, perform the following procedures:

a. Using solvent, clean the varnish from the piston skirts and pins with a cleaning solvent; DO NOT wire brush any part of the piston. Clean the ring grooves with a groove cleaner and make sure that the oil ring holes and slots are clean.

b. Inspect the piston for cracked ring lands, scuffed or damaged skirts, eroded areas at the top of the piston. Replace the pistons that are damaged or show signs of excessive wear.

c. Inspect the grooves for nicks of burrs that might cause the rings to hang up.

d. Measure the piston skirt (across the center line of the piston pin) and check the piston clearance.

11. Clean and inspect the connecting rods; check for twisted or bent rods and inspect for nicks or cracks. Replace the connecting rods that are damaged.

12. Install the rings on the piston, bottom ring first, using a piston ring expander. There is a high risk of breaking or distorting the rings and/or scratching the piston, if the rings are installed by hand or other means.

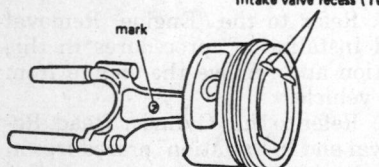

View of the connecting rod mark and the piston head notches — 1200 (OHC) engine

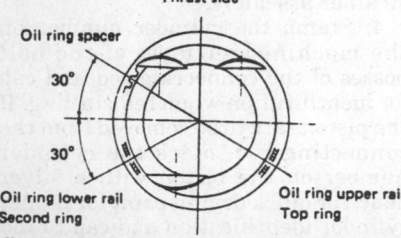

View of the piston ring positioning — 1200 (OHC) engine

13. Position the rings on the piston; spacing of the various piston ring gaps is crucial to the proper oil retention and cylinder wear.

14. The pistons and connecting rods are notched and/or marked to indicate which way they should be installed. If the pistons are not marked, mark them before removal. Then reinstall them in the proper position.

ENGINE LUBRICATION

Oil Pan
REMOVAL & INSTALLATION

1. Raise and support the front of the vehicle on jackstands.

2. Position a drain pan under the engine, remove the drain plug and drain the oil from the crankcase.

3. Remove the oil pan-to-crankcase bolts and the oil pan.

4. Using a putty knife, clean the gasket mounting surfaces. Wash the engine sludge from the oil pan.

5. To install, use a new gasket, sealant (if necessary) and reverse the removal procedures. Torque the oil pan-to-crankcase bolts to 3.3–4.0 ft. lbs.

Rear Main Oil Seal

REPLACEMENT

1600 (OHV) — 1981-87 and 1800 (OHV) — 1981-83 Engines

The rear main oil seal is located in the flywheel housing (timing gear cover). The flywheel housing covers the timing gears and acts as the timing gear cover. In order to remove it, the engine MUST BE removed from the vehicle. The oil seal is pressed into the housing.

1. Refer to the "Engine, Removal and Installation" procedures in this section and remove the engine from the vehicle. Remove the transmission-to-engine bolts and separate the transmission from the engine.

2. Using the Clutch Disc Guide tool 499747000 or equivalent, remove the clutch assembly/flywheel (M/T). If equipped with an A/T, remove the torque converter drive plate from the crankshaft.

3. Remove the flywheel housing from the engine. Using a small pry bar, pry the oil seal from the housing.

4. To install, use a new oil seal and press it into the flywheel housing.

NOTE: When installing the oil seal onto the crankshaft, be careful that it doesn't become torn.

5. To install, use new gaskets, sealant (where necessary) and reverse the removal procedures. Torque the flywheel housing-to-engine bolts to 14–20 ft. lbs., the flywheel-to-crankshaft (M/T) bolts to 30–33 ft. lbs. or the drive plate-to-crankshaft (A/T) bolts to 36–39 ft. lbs. and the transmission-to-engine bolts to 34–40 ft. lbs.

1800 (OHC) Engine

1. Refer to the "Engine, Removal and Installation" procedures in this section and remove the engine from the vehicle. Remove the transmission-to-engine bolts and separate the transmission from the engine.

2. Using the Clutch Disc Guide tool 499747000 or equivalent, remove the clutch assembly/flywheel (M/T). If equipped with an A/T, remove the

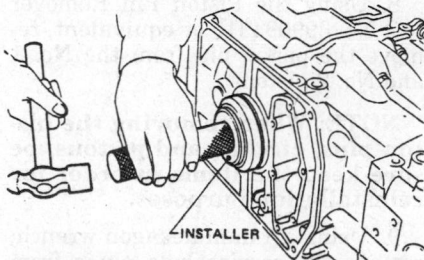

Installing the rear oil seal — 1800 (OHC) engine

torque converter drive plate from the crankshaft.

3. Using a small pry bar, pry the oil seal from the crankcase; be careful not to damage the crankshaft or the crankcase housing.

4. Using a new rear oil seal, coat the seal lips with grease and the housing with engine oil.

5. Using the Rear Oil Seal Installation tool No. 499587000 or equivalent, drive the new oil seal into the crankcase until it seats.

6. To complete the installation, reverse the removal procedures.

1200 (OHC) Engine

1. Refer to the "Engine, Removal and Installation" procedures in this section and remove the engine from the vehicle

2. Remove the clutch assembly and the flywheel from the crankshaft.

3. Using a small pry bar, pry the rear oil seal from the crankcase; be careful not to damage the crankshaft or the crankcase housing.

4. To install, use a new oil seal, lubricate the seal with engine oil.

5. Using the Crankshaft Rear Oil Seal Guide tool No. 498725600 or equivalent, and the Rear Oil Seal

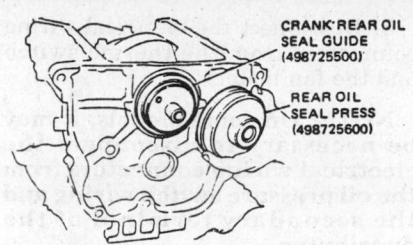

CRANK REAR OIL
SEAL GUIDE
(498725500)

REAR OIL
SEAL PRESS
(498725600)

**Installing the rear oil seal—1200 (OHC)
engine**

Press tool No. 498725500 or equivalent, drive the new oil seal into the housing until it seats.

6. To complete the installation, reverse the removal procedures.

Oil Pump

REMOVAL & INSTALLATION

1600 (OHV) and 1800 (OHV)— Non-Turbo Engine

The oil pump can be removed with the engine in the vehicle. The oil pump and the oil filter can be removed as a unit.

1. Remove the oil pump-to-engine bolts, the oil pump with the gasket.

NOTE: The oil pump is driven directly by the camshaft.

2. Using a putty knife, clean the gasket mounting surfaces.

3. To install, use a new gasket, sealant (if necessary) and reverse the removal procedures. Check and/or refill the crankcase.

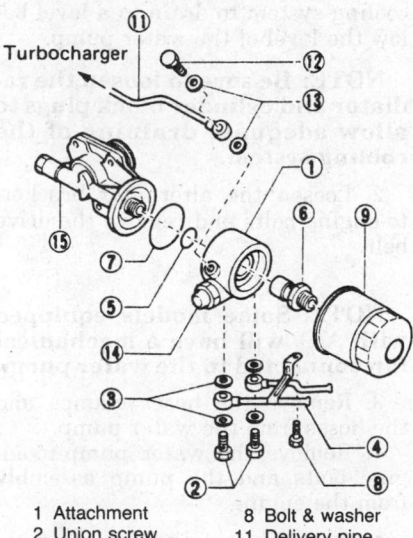

Turbocharger

1 Attachment	8 Bolt & washer
2 Union screw	11 Delivery pipe
3 Gasket	12 Union screw
4 Pipe	13 Gasket
5 O-ring	14 Thermo valve
6 Connector	15 Oil pump
7 O-ring	

Modified oil pump used with the overhead valve turbo engine

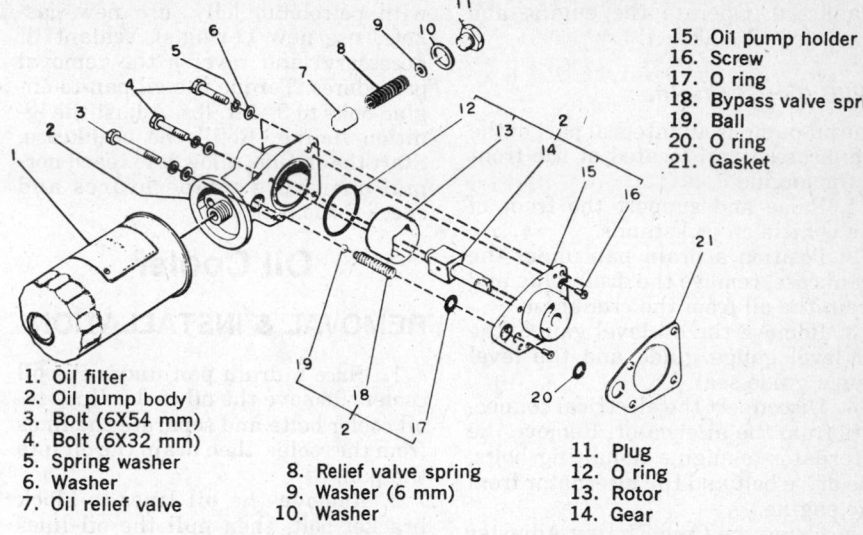

	11
1. Oil filter	15. Oil pump holder
2. Oil pump body	16. Screw
3. Bolt (6X54 mm)	17. O ring
4. Bolt (6X32 mm)	18. Bypass valve spring
5. Spring washer	19. Ball
6. Washer	20. O ring
7. Oil relief valve	21. Gasket
8. Relief valve spring	11. Plug
9. Washer (6 mm)	12. O ring
10. Washer	13. Rotor
	14. Gear

Exploded view of the oil pump—overhead valve engines

NOTE: Be sure that the oil pump shaft fits into the slotted end of the camshaft and that the mating surfaces are flush.

1800 (OHV)—Turbo Engine

1. Position a catch pan under oil filter and pump assembly. Using a strap wrench, remove the oil filter.

2. Remove the three bolts which fasten the two oil cooler lines (bottom) and the turbocharger supply line (side) of the attachment. Remove the oil cooler pipes brace-to-engine bolt.

3. Using one hand to support the attachment, unscrew the connector which retains it to the other. Gently pull the attachment free of the O-rings which seal it.

4. Remove the oil pump-to-engine bolts and the pump from the vehicle.

5. Using a putty knife, clean the gasket mounting surfaces.

6. To install, use new washers (over the bolts), new O-rings and reverse the removal procedures. Torque the piping-to-attachment bolts to 25 ft. lbs., the attachment connector to

22 ft. lbs., the piping brace-to-block bolt to 20 ft. lbs.

1800 (OHC) Engine

1. Disconnect the negative battery terminal from the battery.

2. Place an oil pan under the crankcase, remove the drain plug and drain the oil from the crankcase.

3. Remove the left and right-front timing belt covers.

4. Loosen the tensioner mounting bolts on the #1 cylinder.

5. Turn the tensioner to fully loosen the belt, then tighten the mounting bolts.

6. Using a piece of chalk, mark the rotating direction of the timing belt, then remove the belt from the vehicle.

7. Remove the oil pump-to-engine bolts and the oil pump along with the oil filter from the cylinder block.

8. Remove the oil pump's outer rotor from the cylinder block.

9. Using a putty knife, clean the gasket mounting surfaces.

10. To install, reverse the removal procedures. Check and/or refill the

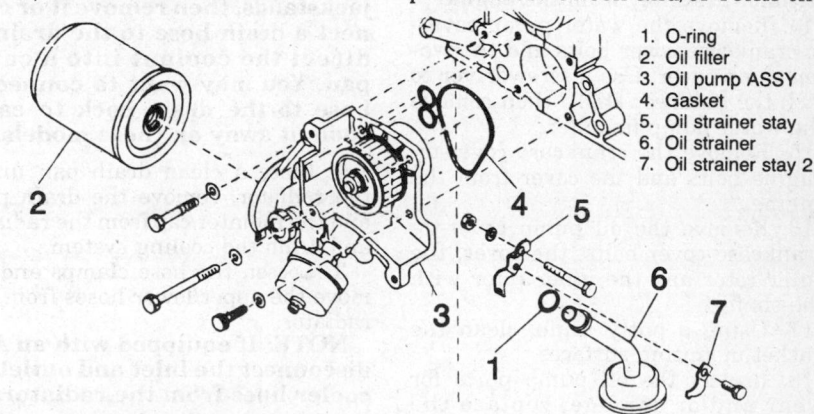

| 1. O-ring |
| 2. Oil filter |
| 3. Oil pump ASSY |
| 4. Gasket |
| 5. Oil strainer stay |
| 6. Oil strainer |
| 7. Oil strainer stay 2 |

Exploded view of the oil pump—Overhead cam engine

crankcase. Operate the engine and check for oil leaks.

1200 (OHC) Engine

The oil pump is an integral part of the crankcase cover, located at the front of the engine.

1. Raise and support the front of the vehicle on jackstands.

2. Position a drain pan under the crankcase, remove the drain plug and drain the oil from the crankcase.

3. Remove the oil level gauge, the oil level gauge guide and the level gauge guide seal.

4. Disconnect the electrical connectors from the alternator. Remove the alternator-to-engine mounting bolts, the drive belt and the alternator from the engine.

5. Using the Cam Timing Adjuster Plate tool No. 498715410 or equivalent, and the Puller tool No. 899521421 or equivalent, remove the crankshaft pulley bolt and the crankshaft pulley.

6. Remove the timing belt cover-to-engine bolts and the cover from the engine.

7. Remove the timing belt tensioner-to-engine bolts, the spring and the tensioner.

8. Using a piece of chalk, mark the rotating direction of the timing belt.

9. Remove the crankshaft drive plate and the timing belt.

10. Using the Cam Timing Adjuster tool No. 498715410 or equivalent, remove the camshaft sprocket-to-camshaft bolts and the sprocket from the camshaft.

11. Remove the inner timing belt cover-to-engine bolts and the cover from the engine.

12. From under the engine, remove the flywheel housing cover-to-engine bolts and the cover from the engine.

13. Remove the oil pan-to-engine bolts and the pan from the engine; discard the gasket. Remove the oil strainer-to-engine bolts and the strainer assembly from the engine.

14. Remove the water pump cover-to-crankcase cover bolts and the water pump cover. Use a screwdriver to lock the balancer shaft, then remove the water pump impeller.

15. Remove the crankcase cover-to-engine bolts and the cover from the engine.

16. Remove the oil pump cover-to-crankcase cover bolts, the cover, the outer rotor and the inner rotor with the shaft.

17. Using a putty knife, clean the gasket mounting surfaces.

18. Inspect the oil pump parts for wear and/or damage; replace the parts if necessary.

19. To install, pack the oil pump with petroleum jelly, use new gaskets, use new O-ring(s), sealant (if necessary) and reverse the removal procedures. Torque the oil pan-to-engine bolts to 3–4 ft. lbs. Adjust the ignition timing. Refill the crankcase. Start the engine, allow it to reach normal operating temperatures and check for leaks.

Oil Cooler

REMOVAL & INSTALLATION

1. Place a drain pan under the oil cooler. Remove the oil cooler lines-to-oil cooler bolts and separate the lines from the cooler, then drain the oil into the pan.

2. Remove the oil lines-to-block bracket bolt, then pull the oil lines away from the block and drain them into the pan.

3. Remove the oil cooler mounting bolts and remove it.

4. To install, use new sealing gaskets (on the cooler lines) and reverse the removal procedures. Torque the piping bracket-to-block bolt to 20 ft. lbs. and the piping-to-attachment bolts to 25 ft. lbs. Check and/or refill the crankcase.

ENGINE COOLING

Radiator

REMOVAL & INSTALLATION

1. Disconnect the negative battery terminal from the battery.

NOTE: If equipped with an undercover, either raise and support the front of the vehicle on jackstands, then remove it or connect a drain hose to the drain to direct the coolant into a catch pan. You may want to connect a hose to the drain cock to carry coolant away on these models.

2. Place a clean drain pan under the radiator, remove the drain plug and the radiator cap from the radiator and drain the cooling system.

3. Loosen the hose clamps and remove the upper/lower hoses from the radiator.

NOTE: If equipped with an A/T, disconnect the inlet and outlet oil cooler lines from the radiator.

4. Remove the radiator-to-chassis bolts.

5. Disconnect the electrical wiring connectors from the thermo switch and the fan motor.

NOTE: On some models, it may be necessary to disconnect the electrical wiring connectors from the oil pressure switch wiring and the secondary terminal of the distributor.

6. Remove the cooling fan/motor assembly-to-radiator bolts and the assembly from the radiator. Remove the radiator-to-chassis bolts and lift the radiator up and away from the vehicle.

NOTE: The 4WD models also have an engine driven fan.

7. To install, use new hoses (if necessary) and reverse the removal procedures. Refill the cooling system. Start the engine, allow it to reach normal operating temperatures and inspect for leaks.

Water Pump

REMOVAL & INSTALLATION

──────── CAUTION ────────
DO NOT preform this operation on a hot engine. Depress the button on the radiator cap to relieve the pressure in the cooling system.

All Engines—Except 1200 (OHC)

1. Position a clean drain pan under the radiator, remove the drain plug and the radiator cap, then allow the cooling system to drain to a level below the level of the water pump.

NOTE: Be sure to loosen the radiator and cylinder block plugs to allow adequate draining of the cooling system.

2. Loosen the alternator bracket-to-engine bolts and remove the drive belt.

NOTE: Some models equipped with A/C, will have a mechanical fan connected to the water pump.

3. Remove the hoses clamps and the hoses from the water pump.

4. Remove the water pump-to-engine bolts and the pump assembly from the engine

NOTE: On the 1800 Turbo, the timing scale plate will come off along with the top/left bolts. Note the location of the scale and then remove it with the two bolts.

5. Using a putty knife, clean the gasket mounting surfaces.

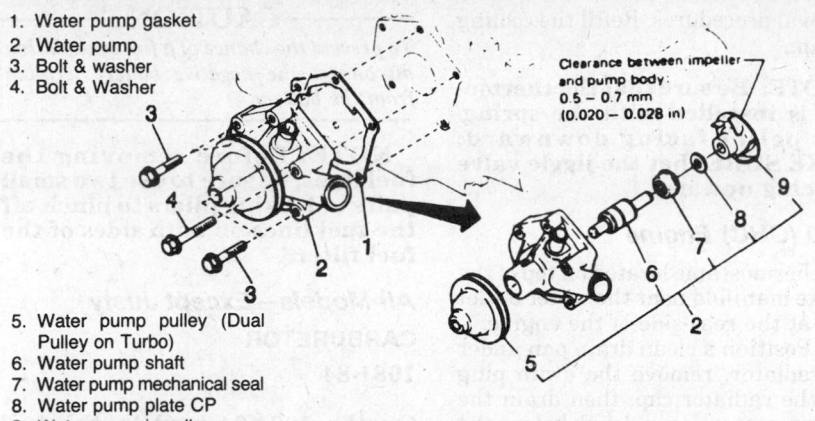

1. Water pump gasket
2. Water pump
3. Bolt & washer
4. Bolt & Washer

Clearance between impeller and pump body:
0.5 – 0.7 mm
(0.020 – 0.028 in)

5. Water pump pulley (Dual Pulley on Turbo)
6. Water pump shaft
7. Water pump mechanical seal
8. Water pump plate CP
9. Water pump impeller

Water pump installation—Overhead valve engine, typical

6. To install, use a new gasket, sealant (if necessary) and reverse the removal procedures. Adjust the drive belt tension and refill the cooling system to the proper level. Operate the engine until it reaches normal operating temperatures and check for leaks or abnormal noise.

1200 (OHC) Engines

1. Raise and support the front of the vehicle on jackstands.
2. Position a clean drain pan under the radiator, remove the drain plug and drain the coolant system.
3. Position a drain pan under the crankcase, remove the drain plug and drain the crankcase.
4. Remove the oil level gauge, the oil level gauge guide and the seal.
5. Disconnect the electrical wiring connector from the alternator. Loosen the alternator-to-engine bolts, relax and remove the drive belt from the alternator.

NOTE: If equipped with A/C or P/S, remove the drive belt from the A/C compressor and/or the power steering pump.

6. Remove the crankshaft pulley-to-crankshaft bolt. Using the Cam Timing Adjuster Plate tool No. 498715410 or equivalent, and the Puller tool No. 899521421 or equivalent, remove the crankshaft pulley from the front of the crankshaft.
7. Remove the outer timing belt cover-to-engine bolts and the cover.
8. Remove the timing belt tensioner spring and the tensioner.
9. Using a piece of chalk, mark the rotating direction of the timing belt. From the crankshaft, remove the drive plate and the timing belt.
10. Remove the camshaft sprocket-to-camshaft bolts. Using the Cam Timing Adjuster Plate tool No. 498715410 or equivalent, remove the camshaft sprocket from the camshaft.

Remove the inner timing belt cover-to-engine bolts, the cover and the bracket from the engine.

11. From under the engine, remove the flywheel housing, the oil pan and the gasket; discard the gasket.
12. Remove the water pump-to-crankcase cover and the water pump impeller.

1. Gasket
2. Pulley cover
3. Water pump pulley
4. Seal
5. Water by-pass hose
6. Water pump ASSY
7. O-ring
8. Water pipe

9. Water pump hub
10. Water pump case
11. Water pump shaft
12. Water pump mechanical seal
13. Ceramic plate
14. Water pump plate
15. Water pump impeller

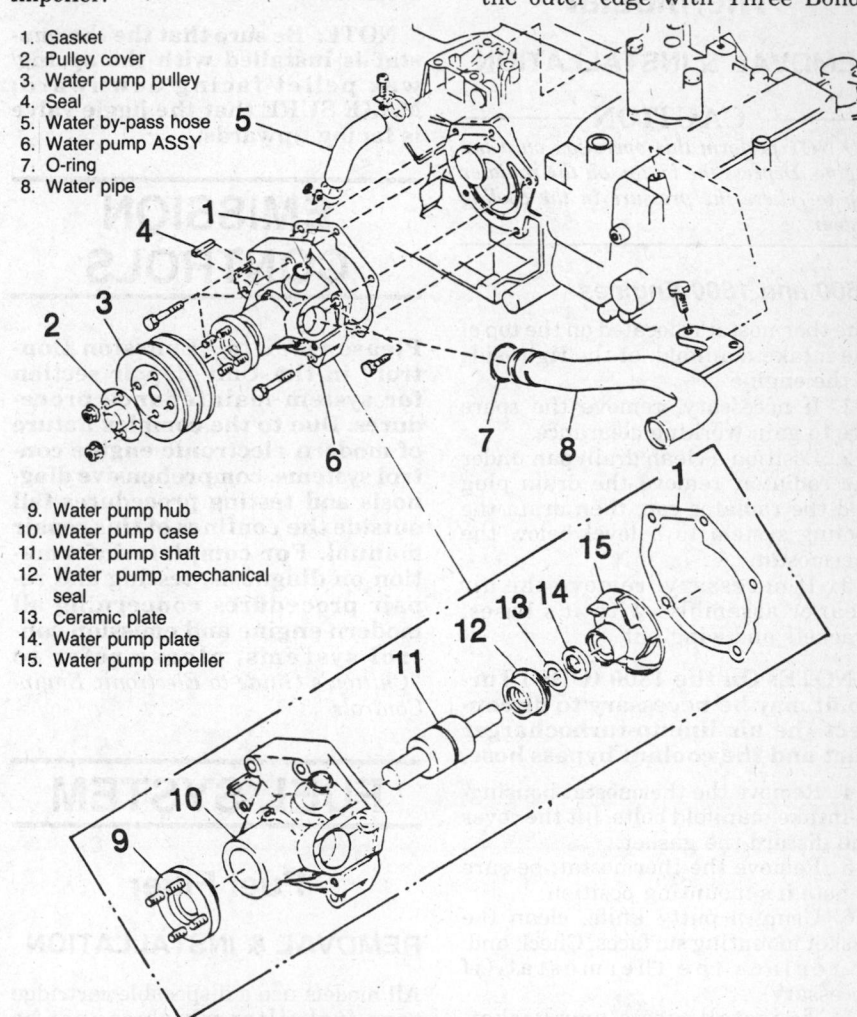

Water pump installation—Overhead cam engine

NOTE: When removing the impeller, insert a screwdriver into the balancer shaft to lock it.

13. Remove the crankcase cover-to-engine bolts and the cover from the engine.
14. Using a putty knife, clean the gasket mounting surfaces.
15. If water is being noticed in the crankcase, replace the water pump gasket by performing the following procedures:

   a. Using the Mechanical Seal Press tool No. 498835400 or equivalent, press the seal from the crankcase cover.

NOTE: The water pump seal can also be removed by using the Mechanical Seal Removal tool No. 499715400 or equivalent, and the Mechanical Seal Remover Plate tool No. 499685510 or equivalent.

   b. Inspect the ceramic seat for cracks and the pump for wear, corrosion or damage.
   c. Before installing the seal, coat the outer edge with Three Bond®

No. 1303 or equivalent, locking agent.

d. Using the Mechanical Seal Press tool No. 498835400 or equivalent, or the Mechanical Seal Installer tool No. 499795400 or equivalent, press the new water pump seal into the crankcase cover until it seat against the balancer shaft; the tip clearance should be 0.012–0.035 in.

NOTE: When installing a new water pump impeller, add 1 or 2 spacers before measuring the tip clearance.

16. To complete the installation, use new gaskets, sealant (where necessary) and reverse the removal procedures. Torque the impeller to balancer shaft to 7–8 ft. lbs. Refill the cooling system and the crankcase. Adjust the timing belt and the drive belt. Adjust the ignition timing. Operate the engine until normal operating temperatures are reached and check for leaks.

Thermostat

REMOVAL & INSTALLATION

---CAUTION---

DO NOT perform this operation on a hot engine. Depress the button on the radiator cap to relieve the pressure in the cooling system.

1600 and 1800 Engines

The thermostat is located on the top of the intake manifold, at the right-side of the engine.

1. If necessary, remove the spare tire to gain working clearance.
2. Position a clean drain pan under the radiator, remove the drain plug and the radiator cap, then drain the cooling system to a level below the thermostat.
3. If necessary, remove the air cleaner assembly, with it's hoses, brackets and wing nut.

NOTE: On the 1800 (OHC) Turbo, it may be necessary to disconnect the air line-to-turbocharger duct and the coolant bypass hose.

4. Remove the thermostat housing-to-intake manifold bolts, lift the cover and discard the gasket.
5. Remove the thermostat; be sure to note it's mounting position.
6. Using a putty knife, clean the gasket mounting surfaces. Check and/or replace the thermostat (if necessary).
7. To install, use a new gasket, sealant (if necessary) and reverse the

removal procedures. Refill the cooling system.

NOTE: Be sure that the thermostat is installed with the spring/wax pellet facing downward; MAKE SURE that the jiggle valve is facing upwards.

1200 (OHC) Engine

The thermostat is located on top of the intake manifold near the water outlet hose at the rear-side of the engine.

1. Position a clean drain pan under the radiator, remove the drain plug and the radiator cap, then drain the cooling system to a level below the thermostat.
2. Remove the thermostat housing-to-intake manifold bolts, lift the housing and remove the thermostat.
3. Using a putty knife, clean the gasket mounting surfaces. Check and/or replace the thermostat (if necessary).
4. To install, use a new gasket, sealant (if necessary) and reverse the removal procedures. Refill the cooling system.

NOTE: Be sure that the thermostat is installed with the spring/wax pellet facing downward; MAKE SURE that the jiggle valve is facing upwards.

EMISSION CONTROLS

Please refer to "Emission Control" in the Unit Repair section for system maintenance procedures. Due to the complex nature of modern electronic engine control systems, comprehensive diagnosis and testing procedures fall outside the confines of this repair manual. For complete information on diagnosis, testing and repair procedures concerning all modern engine and emission control systems, please refer to "Chilton's Guide to Electronic Engine Controls".

FUEL SYSTEM

Fuel Filter

REMOVAL & INSTALLATION

All models use a disposable cartridge type fuel filter which cannot be cleaned.

---CAUTION---

To prevent the chance of a fire or explosion, disconnect the negative battery terminal from the battery.

NOTE: Before removing the fuel lines, be sure to use two small pairs of locking pliers to pinch off the fuel lines on both sides of the fuel filter.

All Models—Except Justy

CARBURETOR

1981-84

On the 1981-84 models, the fuel filter is located in the engine compartment.

1. Loosen, but DO NOT remove, the two hose clamp nuts, located at either end of the filter.
2. Work the hoses from the filter necks.
3. Snap the filter out of it's mounting bracket.
4. Discard the old filter.

NOTE: When removing the old filter, be careful not to allow any fuel to drop onto hot engine components.

5. To install, reverse the removal procedures. Be sure that the hose clamps are tightened securely.

1985-88

On the 1985-88 models, the fuel filter is located on a bracket under the center of the vehicle.

1. Raise and support the vehicle on jackstands.
2. Place a catch pan under fuel filter, to catch the excess fuel.
3. Disconnect the hose clamps and the fuel hoses from the fuel filter.
4. Pull the fuel filter from the bracket and remove it from the vehicle.
5. To install, use a new filter and reverse the removal procedures. Start the engine and check for leaks.

Fuel Injected Models

The fuel filter is located on a bracket

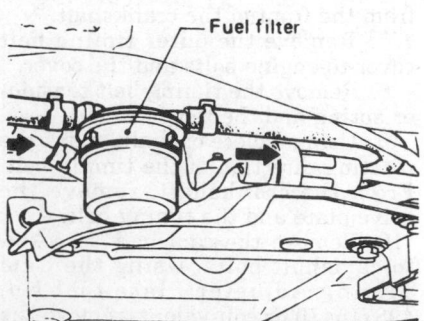

Fuel filter location—carburetor models

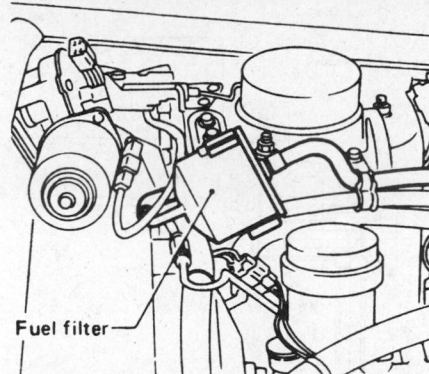

Fuel filter location—fuel injected models

in the engine compartment on the front-left fender.

1. Relieve the fuel pressure by performing the following procedures:

a. Disconnect the electrical wiring connector from the fuel pump.

b. Crank the engine for more than five seconds. If the engine starts, let the engine run until it stops.

c. Turn the ignition switch Off and reconnect the electrical wiring connector of the fuel pump.

2. Loosen the hose clamp screws and pull the filter from the bracket.

3. To install, reverse the removal procedures. Start the engine and check for leaks.

Justy

The fuel filter is located on a crossmember under the center floor. It is a non-disassembling cartridge type.

1. Raise and support the vehicle on jackstands.

2. Remove the fuel pump bracket-to-chassis bolts and lower the bracket.

3. Disconnect the electrical wiring harness from the fuel pump.

4. Place a catch pan under fuel filter, to catch the excess fuel.

5. Disconnect the hose clamps and the fuel hoses from the fuel filter.

6. Remove the fuel filter-to-bracket nut/bolt and the filter from the bracket.

7. To install, use a new filter and reverse the removal procedures. Start the engine and check for leaks.

Electric Fuel Pump

The electric fuel pump is located in the engine compartment (1981-83 models) or under the center of the vehicle, in front of the fuel tank (1984–88 models); if found to be defective, replace it.

PRESSURE TESTING

1. Raise and support the vehicle on jackstands.

2. Using a fuel pressure gauge, connect into the fuel line.

3. Turn the ignition switch On and observe the fuel pressure; it should be 2.6–3.3 psi (carbureted), 61–71 psi (MPFI) or 36–50 psi (SPFI). If the fuel pump does not meet specifications, replace the pump.

4. After testing, disconnect the pressure gauge and reconnect the fuel line.

REMOVAL & INSTALLATION

——— CAUTION ———

To prevent the chance of a fire or explosion, disconnect the negative battery terminal from the battery.

NOTE: Before removing the fuel lines, be sure to use two small pairs of locking pliers to pinch off the fuel lines on both sides of the fuel filter.

Carburetor Models

1. Remove the fuel delivery hoses from the fuel pump.

2. Disconnect the electrical harness connector from the fuel pump.

3. Loosen the fuel pump bracket-to-chassis nuts or bolts and the pump from the vehicle; be careful not to lose any washers or cushions.

4. Inspect the fuel pump; if found to be defective, replace it.

5. To install, reverse the removal procedures. Be sure the ground wire does not contact the pump body or the unit may vibrate. Start the engine and check for leaks.

Fuel Injected Models

1. Disconnect the electrical wiring connector to the fuel pump. Crank the engine for at least five seconds. If the engine starts, let it run until it stalls. Then, turn Off the ignition.

2. Raise and support the front of the vehicle on jackstands. Devise a clamp for the thicker hose leading to the pump and clamp it off a few inches from the nipple on the pump. This will prevent the fuel from running out of the tank while the pump is disconnected.

3. Being careful not to bend the hose sharply, loosen the hose clamp and disconnect the large hose leading into the pump; do the same with the outlet from the damper.

4. Remove the pump bracket-to-chassis bolts and the pump.

5. Inspect the pump operation; if defective, replace.

NOTE: If you want to check whether or not the pump operates, connect a 12V power supply via the harness connector.

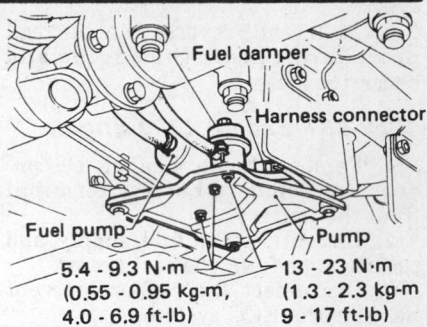

5.4 - 9.3 N·m
(0.55 - 0.95 kg-m, 4.0 - 6.9 ft-lb)

13 - 23 N·m
(1.3 - 2.3 kg-m 9 - 17 ft-lb)

Fuel pump and damper on the 1800 Turbo wagon

——— CAUTION ———

When connecting a power supply to the pump, be sure to make the connections well away from the pump in case spilled fuel is present or fuel comes out when the pump starts up. Don't run the pump for more than a few seconds.

6. To install, reverse the removal procedures. Make sure all hoses are in good condition (no cracks) or replace them.

NOTE: If the connector for the hose between the tank and pump has a thicker portion to limit the position of the hose, make sure to install the hose until it rests against the limit. Otherwise, make sure the hose is at least 1 in. past the end of the connector. Make sure the clamp is installed behind the end of the hose but well past the first bulge on the connector. Be careful not to lose the rubber mount.

Carburetor

REMOVAL & INSTALLATION

1981

1. Remove the air cleaner emission control system hoses, mounting bracket screws, wing nut and lift the air cleaner assembly from the carburetor.

2. Disconnect the negative battery terminal from the battery and the fuel lines from the carburetor.

3. Disconnect the vacuum hoses from the servo diaphragm, the automatic choke diaphragms, the distributor and the EGR port (if equipped).

4. Disconnect the anti-dieseling switch and automatic choke heater electrical leads.

5. Remove the accelerator cable from the throttle lever.

6. Remove the carburetor-to-intake manifold nuts and the carburetor; cover the hole in the intake manifold, to prevent anything from falling in.

7. To install, reverse the removal procedures. Start the engine and check for leaks.

1982-88 — Except 1200 Engine

1. Remove the air cleaner. Disconnect the negative battery terminal from the battery.

2. Disconnect the fuel supply and return lines from the carburetor.

3. Disconnect the carburetor vent hose for the ECC system.

4. Disconnect the remaining vacuum hoses to distributor and etc.

5. Disconnect the EGR tube (if equipped).

6. If equipped with an Hitachi carburetor, perform the following procedures:

   a. Disconnect the ignition retard, if applicable.

   b. Disconnect the vacuum hoses from the solenoid valves, the main diaphragm on high-altitude carburetors and the secondary main air bleed.

   c. Disconnect the duty solenoid valve connector on those models, if equipped.

7. On both types of carburetor, disconnect the electrical harness connectors and the accelerator cable from the throttle lever.

8. Drain some coolant out of the radiator, to a level below the water-heated throttle bore.

9. Remove the carburetor-to-intake manifold nuts and remove the carburetor from the vehicle.

NOTE: If equipped with a Carter-Weber carburetor, disconnect the vent hose and remove the connector with the spacer and gasket, then cover the intake manifold opening.

10. To install, reverse the removal procedures. Make sure to adjust the throttle linkage. Refill the cooling system. Start the engine and check for leaks.

1200 Engine — 1987-88

1. Disconnect the negative battery terminal from the battery.

2. Remove the air cleaner by performing the following procedures:

   a. Label and disconnect these hoses from the air cleaner: The Blow-by hose, the ASV hose, the vacuum hose, the air duct and the boot.

   b. Remove the brake booster vacuum-to-air cleaner hose.

   c. Remove the distributor-to-ignition coil from the clamp.

   d. Remove the air cleaner mounting bolts and the wing nut, then remove the air cleaner from the carburetor.

3. Disconnect and remove the accelerator cable, the vacuum hoses, the fuel hose(s) and the electrical connectors.

4. Remove the carburetor-to-intake manifold bolts, the carburetor and the gasket.

5. To install, use new gasket and reverse the removal procedures. Start the engine and check for leaks.

OVERHAUL

For all carburetor overhaul procedures, please refer to "Carburetor Overhaul" in the Unit Repair section.

PRIMARY/SECONDARY THROTTLE LINKAGE ADJUSTMENT

Hitachi

1. With the carburetor removed from the engine, operate the linkage so that the connecting rod contacts the groove on the end of the secondary actuating lever.

2. Measure the clearance between the lower end of the primary throttle valve and it's bore. It should be about 0.24 in. (1981-84), 0.27 in. (except 1200 engine — 1985-88) or 0.263 in. (1200 engine — 1987-88) models.

3. Adjust the clearance by bending the connecting rod.

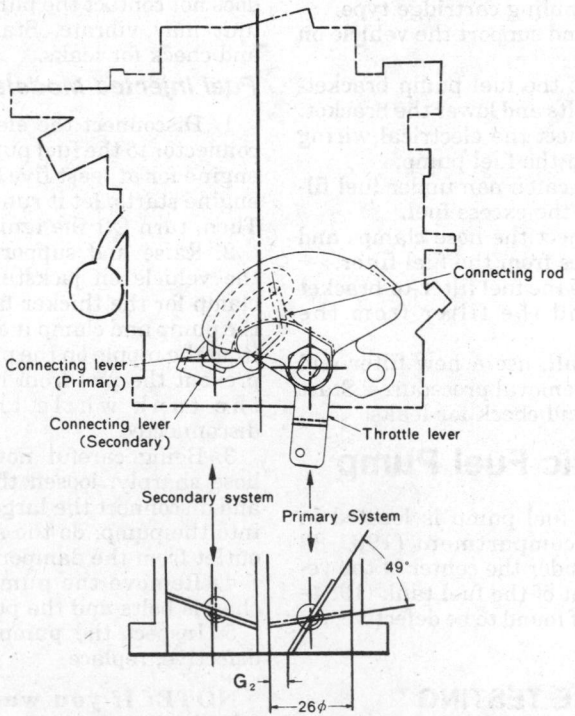

Float adjustment—Hitachi

4. Check that the linkage operates smoothly.

FLOAT AND FUEL LEVEL ADJUSTMENT

Hitachi

On models with a sight glass on the carburetor float bowl, the fuel should be level (within $\frac{1}{16}$ in.) with the dot on the glass when the engine is running. The float level may be adjusted with the carburetor installed on the engine:

1. Disconnect the accelerator pump actuating rod from the pump lever.

2. Remove the throttle return spring.

3. Disconnect the choke cable from the choke lever, and remove it from the spring hanger.

$G_2 = 6.0$mm when primary throttle valve opening is 49° from full close. (EA63A)

Throttle linkage adjustment—Hitachi

4. Remove the spring hanger, the choke bellcrank and the remaining air horn retaining screws.

5. Lift the air horn slightly, disconnect the choke connecting rod and remove the air horn.

6. Invert the air horn (float up), and measure the distance between the surface of the air horn and the float.

7. Bend the float arm until the clearance is approximately 0.41 in. (1981-83), 0.433–0.453 in. (1984), 0.709–0.724 in. (1985), 0.453–0.492 in. (except 1200 engine – 1986-88) or 0.437 in. (1200 engine – 1987-88).

8. Invert the air horn to it's installed position and measure the distance between the float arm and the needle valve stem. This dimension should be 0.050–0.065 in. (1981-85) or 0.059–0.075 in. (1986-88), it is adjusted by bending the float stops.

Carter-Weber (1981-84)

1. Remove the air horn gasket, then position the float at the air horn.

FAST IDLE

Model	Primary Throttle-to-bore Clearance (in.)
1981–82	
All AT	0.060
MT (exc. C-W)	0.050①
1983	
DCP306–17	0.0386
DCP306–18	0.0386
DCP306–19	0.0480
DCP306–20	0.0480
DCP306–21	0.0480
1984	
DCP306–23	0.0386
DCP306–24	0.0480
DCP306–25	0.0520
DCP306–26	0.0551
DCP306–27	0.0563
1985	
DCZ328–502	0.0453
DCZ328–503	0.0484
DCZ328–504	0.0524
DCZ328–505	0.0571
1986	
DCZ328–502A	0.0472
DCZ328–503A	0.0587
DCZ328–504A	0.0524
DCZ328–505A	0.0571
1987–88	
DCZ328–504C	0.0524
DCZ328–505C	0.0571
DFC328	0.0303

① HB-STD, HB-DL, SD-DL and HT-DL use 0.041 in.

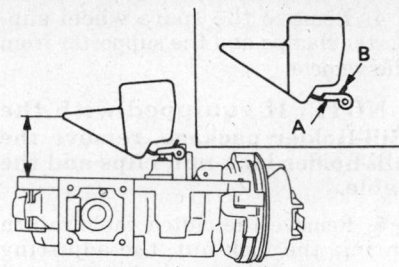
Float setting—Carter/Weber

2. Turn the air horn upside down to free the float.

3. Measure the distance between the surface of the air horn and the float; bend portion (A) to adjust.

4. Turn the air horn right side up to lower the float. Measure the distance from the lower surface of the air horn to the tip end of the float and make sure it is not less than 1.50 in.; bend portion (B) to adjust.

NOTE: The needle must be free while adjusting the distance.

FAST IDLE ADJUSTMENT

Hitachi

1. Refer to the "Carburetor, Removal and Installation" procedures in this section and remove the carburetor from the intake manifold.

2. With the choke plate fully Closed, operate the fast idle cam and the linkage to position the primary throttle valve at that it's slightly Open position.

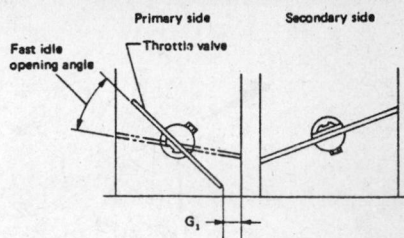
Adjusting the choke valve—1200 (OHC) engine

NOTE: In this position, the top of the cam adjusting lever rests on the highest (first) step of the fast idle cam; this angle is called the fast idle opening angle (suitable for Cold weather starting).

3. Using a carburetor Plug Gauge Set or drill bit, measure the G₁ clearance (the clearance between the lower edge of the primary throttle valve and its bore). To adjust the valve opening, adjust the fast idle screw.

4. To install, reverse the removal procedures. Start the engine and check the carburetor performance.

Carter-Weber (1981-84)

NOTE: Before adjusting the fast idle make sure the idle speed and mixture have been adjusted properly.

1. With the engine at operating temperature and the choke fully Open, place the fast idle lever on the 3rd step of the cam.

2. Turn the fast idle adjusting screw until the speed is 2000 rpm.

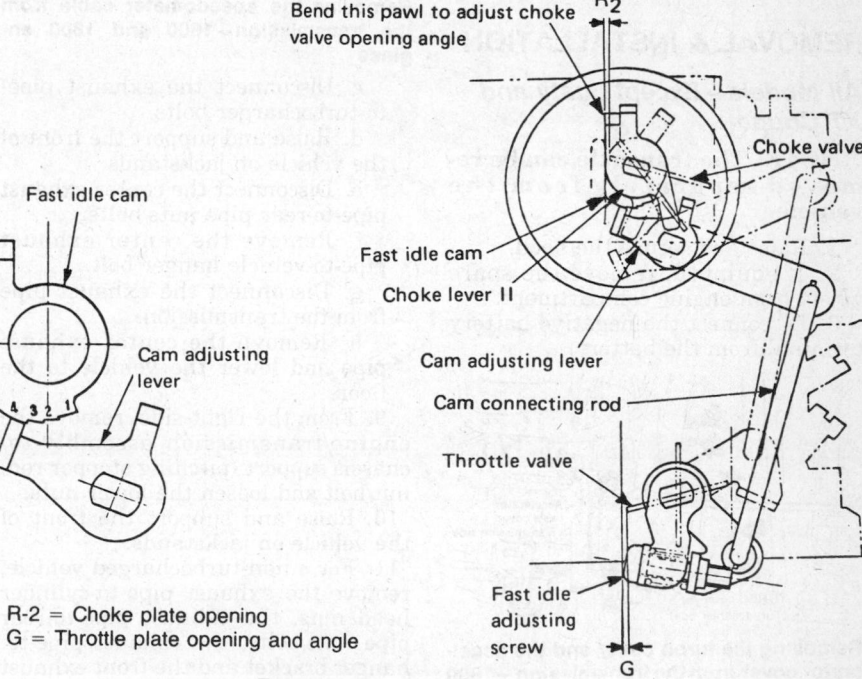
R-2 = Choke plate opening
G = Throttle plate opening and angle

Fast idle adjustment—Hitachi

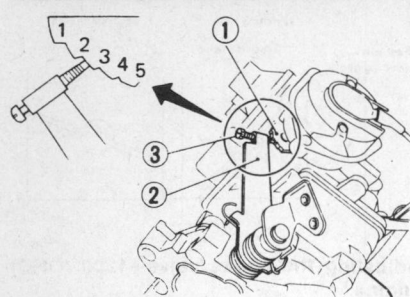

1. Cam
2. Fast idle lever
3. Fast idle adjusting screw

Fast idle adjustment—Carter/Weber

OVERHAUL

NOTE: For all carburetor overhaul procedures, please refer to "Carburetor Service" in the Unit Repair section.

Fuel Injection

Due to the complex nature of modern fuel injection systems, comprehensive diagnosis and testing procedures fall outside the confines of this repair manual. For complete information on fuel injection diagnosis, testing and repair procedures please refer to *Chilton's Guide To Fuel Injection And Feedback Carburetors.*

MANUAL TRANSAXLE

REMOVAL & INSTALLATION

All Models—Except Justy and XT Coupe

NOTE: The transaxle can be removed separately from the vehicle.

1. Raise and secure the hood.
2. If equipped, remove the spare wheel from engine compartment.
3. Disconnect the negative battery terminal from the battery.

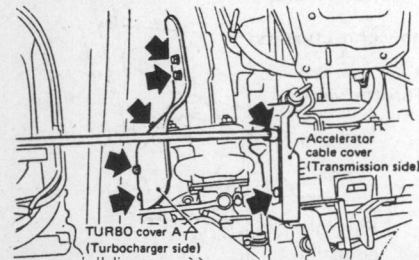

Removing the turbo cover and the accelerator cover from the transmission—1800 (OHC) turbo

4. Remove the spare wheel supporter clamps and the supporter from the vehicle.

NOTE: If equipped with the Hill-Holder package, remove the hill-holder lock-nut, clips and the cable.

5. Remove the clutch cable return spring, the lock-nut, the adjusting nut, the cable clip and the clutch cable.

NOTE: If equipped with a carburetor, remove the air duct.

6. From the transmission, disconnect and remove the speedometer cable and the speedometer cable clip.
7. Disconnect the electrical wiring connectors from the back-up lamp switch, the O_2 sensor (exhaust pipe), the transmission-to-chassis ground strap and starter. Remove the starter and move it aside.
8. If equipped with a turbocharger, perform the following procedures:
   a. Remove the accelerator cable cover from the transmission.
   b. Remove the turbo covers from the turbocharger and the center exhaust pipe.

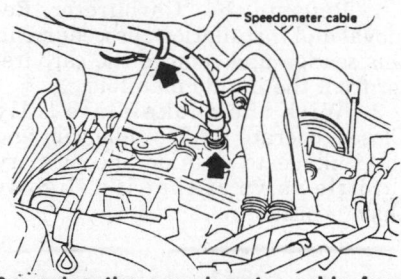

Removing the speedometer cable from the transmission—1600 and 1800 engines

   c. Disconnect the exhaust pipe-to-turbocharger bolts.
   d. Raise and support the front of the vehicle on jackstands.
   e. Disconnect the center exhaust pipe-to-rear pipe nuts/bolts.
   f. Remove the center exhaust pipe-to-vehicle hanger bolt.
   g. Disconnect the exhaust pipe from the transmission.
   h. Remove the center exhaust pipe and lower the vehicle to the floor.
9. From the right-side, remove the engine/transmission assembly-to-chassis support (pitching stopper rod) nut/bolt and loosen the lower nuts.
10. Raise and support the front of the vehicle on jackstands.
11. For a non-turbocharged vehicle, remove the exhaust pipe-to-cylinder head nuts, the exhaust pipe-to-rear pipe nuts/bolts, the exhaust pipe-to-hanger bracket and the front exhaust pipe from the vehicle.

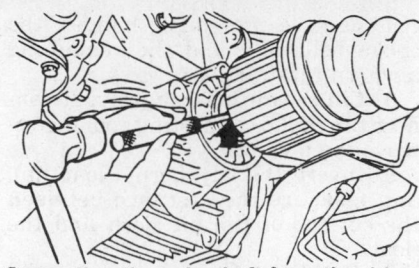

Separating the axle shaft from the driveshaft

NOTE: If equipped with a (4WD), disconnect the rear exhaust pipe from the muffler.

12. If equipped with 4WD, disconnect the driveshaft from the rear of the transmission and plug the opening to prevent oil from draining from the opening.
13. Remove the retaining spring, the CP (clevis pin) rod and stay from the transmission.
14. Loosen the stabilizer-to-transverse link nuts and bolts, on the lower side of the plate.

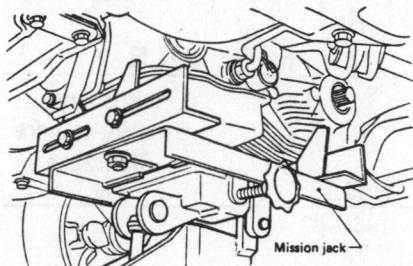

Installing a transmission jack to the transmission

15. Remove the transverse link by performing the following procedures:
   a. Remove the hand brake cable bracket from the transverse link.
   b. Remove the transverse link-to-crossmember nut/bolt and the link from the vehicle.
16. Using a hammer and the pin punch, drive the spring pin (discard it) from the axle shaft/drive shaft assembly, then push the tire outward to separate the axle shaft from the driveshaft; perform this procedures on each side.
17. Remove the engine-to-transmission nuts.
18. Position a transmission jack under the transmission and secure the jack to the transmission. Remove the rear rubber cushion mounting nuts.
19. Remove the rear and the rigid crossmember-to-chassis bolts and crossmembers from the vehicle.
20. Moving the floor jack rearward and downward, remove the transmission from the vehicle.
21. To install, align the chamfered holes of the axle shaft with the driveshaft (install a new spring pin) and re-

verse the removal procedures. Torque the crossmember-to-chassis bolts to 27–49 ft. lbs., the rigid crossmember-to-chassis bolts to 65–87 ft. lbs., the rubber cushion-to-crossmember bolts to 20–35 ft. lbs., the lower engine-to-transmission bolts to 34–40 ft. lbs., the transverse link-to-front crossmember nuts/bolts (use new self-locking nuts) to 43–51 ft. lbs., the transverse link-to-stabilizer bolts to 14–22 ft. lbs., the pitching stopper rod-to-engine/transmission assembly nut/bolt to 34–40 ft. lbs.

XT Coupe

1. Raise and support the hood securely.
2. Disconnect the negative battery terminal from the battery.
3. If equipped with a turbocharger, perform the following procedures:

    a. Remove the turbo covers from the turbocharger and the center exhaust pipe.

    b. Disconnect the center exhaust pipe-to-turbocharger bolts.

    c. Raise and support the front of the vehicle on jackstands.

    d. Disconnect the center exhaust pipe-to-rear pipe nuts/bolts.

    e. Remove the center exhaust pipe-to-vehicle hanger bolt.

    f. Disconnect the center exhaust pipe from the transmission.

NOTE: Disconnect the rear exhaust pipe from the muffler.

    g. Remove the center exhaust pipe from the vehicle.

4. If NOT equipped with a turbocharger, perform the following procedures:

    a. Raise and support the front of the vehicle on jackstands.

    b. Disconnect the front exhaust pipe from the engine.

NOTE: When disconnecting the exhaust pipe from the engine, remove all of the nuts except one.

    c. Disconnect the front exhaust pipe-to-rear exhaust pipe nuts/bolts and the front exhaust pipe-to-transmission hanger nut/bolt.

    d. Remove the single front exhaust pipe-to-engine nut and the exhaust pipe from the vehicle.

NOTE: If equipped with 4WD, disconnect the rear exhaust pipe from the muffler.

5. Remove the clutch cable and the Hill-Holder cable (if equipped).
6. Disconnect the speedometer cable from the transmission.
7. Disconnect the electrical harness connectors from the neutral start switch, the back-up light switch and the transmission cord (4WD).

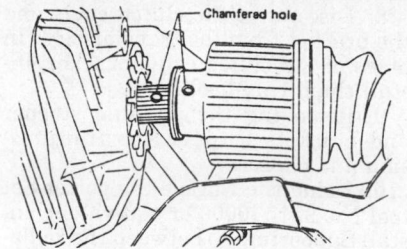

Aligning the chamfered holes of the axle shaft with the driveshaft

NOTE: On the 4WD vehicle, the transmission cord connector consists of the back-up light switch and the indicator light (Selective 4WD) or the indicator light switch (Full-Time 4WD).

8. If equipped with 4WD, disconnect the 4WD vacuum hose (Selective 4WD) or the differential lock vacuum hose (Full-Time 4WD).
9. Remove the starter-to-transmission bolts and the starter from the transmission.
10. Remove the air intake duct (Turbo) or the air intake boot (Non-Turbo).
11. Remove the pitching stopper rod-to-engine bracket nut/bolt, the rod and the engine bracket from the engine. Using the Engine Support Bracket tool No. 927010000 or equivalent, install it to the engine hanger. Using the Engine Support Assembly tool No. 927000000 or equivalent, install it to the support bracket.
12. On the right-side of the vehicle, remove the engine-to-transmission bolt.
13. Raise and support the vehicle on jackstands.
14. Remove the rigid crossmember-to-chassis bolts and the crossmember from the vehicle.

TORQUE SPECIFICATIONS
(ft. lbs.)

Transverse link to front crossmember	50
Stabilizer to leading rod and rear crossmember	15
Rear crossmember to vehicle body	60
Front crossmember to vehicle body	40
Front engine mount to crossmember	20
Rear engine mount to crossmember	20
Propeller shaft to rear differential (4WD)	15

15. If equipped with 4WD, remove the rear driveshaft center bearing assembly-to-chassis bolts and the driveshaft-to-rear differential flange bolts, then remove the driveshaft from the vehicle.

NOTE: When removing the driveshaft from the transmission, be sure to plug the opening to prevent oil from flowing out.

16. Remove the CP stay-to-transmission nut/bolt, the spring and the CP rod-to-transmission nut/bolt.
17. To disconnect the front driveshafts from the axle shafts (on each side), perform the following procedures:

    a. On the lower-side of the plate, loosen the stabilizer-to-transverse link nut/bolt.

    b. Remove the handbrake cable bracket-to-transverse link.

    c. Remove the transverse link-to-crossmember bolt on each side and lower the transverse link.

    d. Using a pin punch and a hammer, drive out the axle shaft-to-driveshaft spring pin; discard the spring pin.

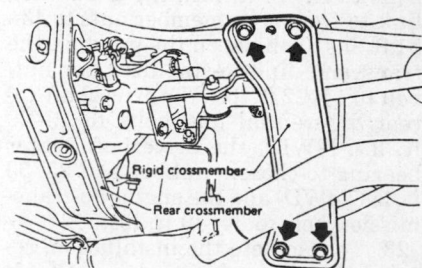

View of the rigid and rear crossmembers—XT Coupe

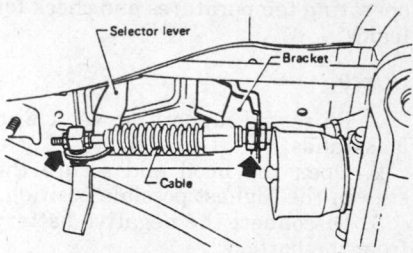

View of the the selector cable and the selector cable bracket—XT Coupe.

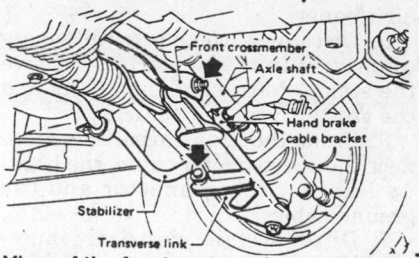

View of the front-suspension assembly—XT Coupe

e. Push outward on the wheel assembly to separate the axle shaft from the driveshaft.

18. Remove the engine-to-transmission bolts.

19. Using a transmission jack, position it under and secure it to the transmission.

NOTE: When using a transmission jack, always support the transmission case; NEVER place it under the oil pan.

20. Remove the rear crossmember-to-transmission bolts, the rear crossmember-to-chassis bolts and the rear crossmember from the vehicle.

21. Lower the transmission jack and remove the transmission from the vehicle.

NOTE: Move the transmission jack rearward until the mainshaft clears the clutch cover, then lower the transmission from the vehicle.

22. To install, use new spring pins and gaskets. Torque the transmission rubber cushion-to-rear crossmember nuts to 20–35 ft. lbs., the rear crossmember-to-chassis bolts to 65–87 ft. lbs., the lower transmission-to-engine bolts to 34–40 ft. lbs., the transverse link-to-front crossmember nuts to 43–51 ft. lbs. (vehicle on the ground), the transverse link-to-stabilizer bar nut/bolt to 14–22 ft. lbs., the driveshaft-to-rear differential nuts/bolts to 13–20 ft. lbs. (4WD), the driveshaft center bearing-to-chassis nut/bolts to 25–33 ft. lbs. (4WD) and the engine-to-transmission bolt to 34–40 ft. lbs.

23. To complete the installation, reverse the removal procedures. Check and/or refill the transmission. Start the engine, allow it to reach normal operating temperatures and check for leaks.

Justy

1. Raise and support the vehicle on jackstands.

2. Open the hood and secure the stay in the highest possible position.

3. Disconnect the negative battery from the battery.

4. Disconnect the hoses and cables from the air cleaner, then remove the air cleaner.

5. Disconnect the electrical wiring connectors from the starter. Remove the starter-to-transmission bolts and the starter from the vehicle.

6. From the transmission, disconnect the speedometer cable, the backup light switch connector and the ground cable.

7. Disconnect the electrical connector between the ignition coil and the distributor.

8. Disconnect the clutch cable and the bracket from the transmission. In place of the clutch cable bracket, install the lifting hook.

9. Removing the pitching stopper and brackets between the transmission and chassis.

10. Using the Engine Supporter Set tool No. 921540000 or equivalent, install Supporter (A) between the radiator and the engine, then Supporter (B) in place of the pitching stopper.

11. Install the vertical hoist to the transmission lifting hook and raise the transmission slightly.

12. From under the vehicle, remove the under covers.

13. Disconnect the rear exhaust pipe from the front exhaust pipe and the vehicle.

14. Remove the center crossmember-to-engine/transmission assembly bolts.

15. Using a pin punch and a hammer, drive out the axle shaft-to-driveshaft spring pin; discard the spring pin; separate the axle shaft.

16. Remove the transmission mounting bracket.

17. Disconnect the gearshift rod and stay from the transmission.

18. Remove the transmission-to-engine bolts and separate the transmission from the engine.

19. Using the vertical hoist, lift the transmission from the vehicle.

20. To install, use new spring pins and reverse the removal procedures. Start the engine, allow it to reach normal operating temperatures and check for leaks.

OVERHAUL

For all overhaul procedures, please refer to "Manual Transaxle/Transmission Overhaul" or the "Automatic Transaxle/Transmission Overhaul" in the Unit Repair section.

CLUTCH

REMOVAL & INSTALLATION

1. Refer to the "Transaxle, Removal and Installation" procedures in this section and remove the transaxle from the vehicle.

2. Gradually loosen the pressure plate-to-flywheel assembly bolts; loosen the bolts one turn at a time, working around the pressure plate. DO NOT unscrew all the bolts on one side at one time.

3. Remove the clutch plate and the disc.

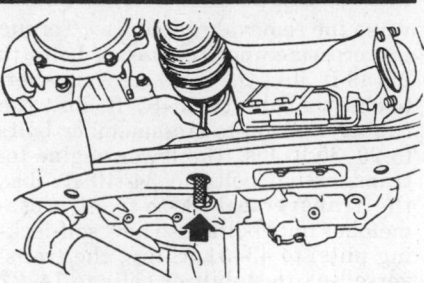

Removing the spring pin from the axle shaft – Justy

NOTE: DO NOT allow oil or grease to get on the clutch disc.

4. Inspect the parts for wear or damage and replace any parts as necessary.

NOTE: Replace the clutch disc if there is any oil or grease on the facing. DO NOT wash or attempt to lubricate the throw-out bearing. If it requires replacement, the bearing may be pressed out and a new one pressed into the holder.

5. To install the clutch assembly, perform the following procedures:

a. Using Clutch Disc Guide tool No. 499747000 or equivalent (Non-Turbo – 1600 and 1800 engines), No. 499747100 or equivalent (Turbo – 1800 engine), or No. 499745500 or equivalent (1200 engine), insert it through the clutch assembly and into the pilot needle bearing.

b. Gradually tighten the pressure plate-to-flywheel bolts one turn at a time, working around the cover. Torque pressure plate-to-flywheel bolts to 11–12 ft. lbs. (1600 and 1800 engines) or 7–8 ft. lbs. (1200 engine).

NOTE: When installing the clutch pressure plate assembly, make sure that the 0 marks on the flywheel and the clutch pressure plate assembly are at least 120 degrees apart. This is for purposes of balance. Also, make sure that the clutch disc is installed properly, noting the FRONT and REAR markings.

6. To complete the installation, reverse the removal procedures. Adjust the pedal free-play and height.

FREE-PLAY ADJUSTMENT

1. Remove the clutch release fork return spring.

2. Loosen the cable locknut, then adjust the spherical nut so that there is 0.08–0.12 in. on the 1981-84 models, 0.08–0.12 in. on the 1985-88 (2WD – Non-Turbo, 1600 and 1800 engines), 0.12–0.16 in. on the 1985-88

(2WD/4WD – Turbo, 1800 engines), or 0.08–0.16 in. on the 1987-88 (1200 engine) play between the spherical nut and the release fork seat.

3. Tighten the locknut and reconnect the release spring.

Clutch Cable

REMOVAL & INSTALLATION

The clutch cable is connected to the clutch pedal at one end and to the clutch release lever on the other end.

The cable conduit is retained by a bolt and clamp on the clutch pedal bracket and by a clip type clamp on a bracket mounted on the flywheel housing.

1. If necessary, raise and support the front of the vehicle on jackstands.
2. Disconnect both ends of the cable and the conduit, then remove the assembly from under the vehicle.
3. Using engine oil, lubricate the clutch cable; if the cable is defective, replace it.
4. To install the cable and conduit, reverse the removal procedures.

CABLE ADJUSTMENT

The clutch cable can be adjusted at the cable bracket where the cable is attached to the side of the transmission housing.

1. Remove the circlip and clamp.
2. Slide the cable end in the direction desired and then replace the circlip and clamp into the nearest gutters on the cable end.

NOTE: The cable should not be stretched out straight nor should it have right angle kinks in it. Any cures should be gradual.

3. Operate the clutch to check it's operation.

AUTOMATIC TRANSAXLE

REMOVAL & INSTALLATION

All Models – Except XT Coupe

NOTE: The transaxle can be removed separately from the vehicle.

1. Raise and secure the hood.
2. If equipped, remove the spare wheel from engine compartment.
3. Disconnect the negative battery terminal from the battery.
4. Remove the spare wheel sup-

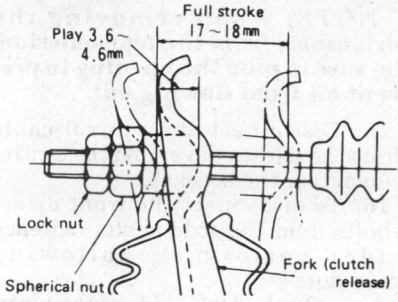
Clutch linkage free-play adjustment at the release fork

porter clamps and the supporter from the vehicle.

5. If equipped with a carburetor, remove the air duct.
6. Disconnect the diaphragm vacuum hose (2WD) and/or the air breather hose (4WD).
7. From the transmission, disconnect and remove the speedometer cable and the speedometer cable clip.
8. Disconnect the electrical wiring connectors from the back-up lamp switch, the O_2 sensor (exhaust pipe), the transmission-to-chassis ground strap and starter. Remove the starter and move it aside.
9. If equipped with a turbocharger, perform the following procedures:
    a. Remove the accelerator cable cover from the transmission.
    b. Remove the turbo covers from the turbocharger and the center exhaust pipe.
    c. Disconnect the exhaust pipe-to-turbocharger bolts.
    d. Raise and support the front of the vehicle on jackstands.
    e. Disconnect the center exhaust pipe-to-rear pipe nuts/bolts.
    f. Remove the center exhaust pipe-to-vehicle hanger bolt.
    g. Disconnect the exhaust pipe from the transmission.
    h. Remove the center exhaust pipe and lower the vehicle to the floor.
10. Remove the timing hole from the flywheel housing. Working through the timing plug hole, remove the torque converter-to-drive plate bolts.

NOTE: Be careful that the bolts do not fall into the converter housing.

11. Disconnect and plug the oil cooler hose from the transmission; be careful not to damage the O-ring.
12. From the right-side, remove the engine/transmission assembly-to-chassis support (pitching stopper rod) nut/bolt and loosen the lower nuts.
13. Raise and support the front of the vehicle on jackstands.
14. For a non-turbocharged vehicle, remove the exhaust pipe-to-cylinder head nuts, the exhaust pipe-to-rear

pipe nuts/bolts, the exhaust pipe-to-hanger bracket and the front exhaust pipe from the vehicle.

15. If equipped with 4WD, disconnect the driveshaft from the rear of the transmission and plug the opening to prevent oil from draining from the opening.
16. Disconnect the linkage rod from the shift lever.
17. Loosen the stabilizer-to-transverse link nuts and bolts, on the lower side of the plate.
18. Remove the transverse link by performing the following procedures:
    a. Remove the hand brake cable bracket from the transverse link.
    b. Remove the transverse link-to-crossmember nut/bolt and the link from the vehicle.
19. Using a hammer and the pin punch, drive the spring pin (discard it) from the axle shaft/drive shaft assembly, then push the tire outward to separate the axle shaft from the driveshaft; perform this procedures on each side.
20. Remove the engine-to-transmission nuts.
21. Position a transmission jack under the transmission and secure the jack to the transmission. Remove the rear rubber cushion mounting nuts.
22. Remove the rear crossmember-to-chassis bolts and the crossmember from the vehicle.
23. Moving the floor jack rearward and downward, remove the transmission from the vehicle.
24. To install, align the chamfered holes of the axle shaft with the driveshaft (install a new spring pin) and reverse the removal procedures. Torque the crossmember-to-chassis bolts to 27–49 ft. lbs., the rubber cushion-to-crossmember bolts to 20–35 ft. lbs., the lower engine-to-transmission bolts to 34–40 ft. lbs., the transverse link-to-front crossmember nuts/bolts (use new self-locking nuts) to 43–51 ft. lbs., the transverse link-to-stabilizer bolts to 14–22 ft. lbs., the pitching stopper rod-to-engine/transmission assembly nut/bolt to 34–40 ft. lbs.

XT Coupe

1. Raise and support the hood securely.
2. Disconnect the negative battery terminal from the battery.
3. If equipped with a turbocharger, perform the following procedures:
    a. Remove the turbo covers from the turbocharger and the center exhaust pipe.
    b. Disconnect the center exhaust pipe-to-turbocharger bolts.
    c. Raise and support the front of the vehicle on jackstands.

d. Disconnect the center exhaust pipe-to-rear pipe nuts/bolts.

e. Remove the center exhaust pipe-to-vehicle hanger bolt.

f. Disconnect the center exhaust pipe from the transmission.

g. Remove the center exhaust pipe from the vehicle.

4. If NOT equipped with non-turbocharger vehicles, perform the following procedures:

a. Raise and support the front of the vehicle on jackstands.

b. Disconnect the front exhaust pipe from the engine.

NOTE: When disconnecting the exhaust pipe from the engine, remove all of the nuts except one.

c. Disconnect the front exhaust pipe-to-rear exhaust pipe nuts/bolts and the front exhaust pipe-to-transmission hanger nut/bolt.

d. Remove the single front exhaust pipe-to-engine nut and the exhaust pipe from the vehicle.

5. Disconnect the speedometer cable from the transmission.

6. Disconnect the electrical harness connectors from the O_2 sensor, the transmission harness connector, the inhibitor switch and the revolution sensor (4WD).

NOTE: On the 4WD vehicle, the transmission cord connector consists of the back-up light switch and the indicator light (Selective 4WD) or the indicator light switch (Full-Time 4WD).

7. If equipped with 4WD, disconnect the 4WD vacuum hose. Remove the air breather-to-pitching stopper clip band.

8. Remove the starter-to-transmission bolts and the starter from the transmission.

9. Remove the air intake duct (Turbo) or the air intake boot (Non-Turbo).

10. Remove the timing hole plug (on top of the flywheel housing) and the torque converter-to-drive plate bolts.

11. Remove the pitching stopper rod-to-engine bracket nut/bolt, the rod and the engine bracket from the engine. Using the Engine Support Bracket tool No. 927010000 or equivalent, install it to the engine hanger. Using the Engine Support Assembly tool No. 927000000 or equivalent, install it to the support bracket.

12. On the right-side of the vehicle, remove the engine-to-transmission bolt.

13. Raise and support the vehicle on jackstands.

14. Remove the rear driveshaft center bearing assembly-to-chassis bolts and the driveshaft-to-rear differential flange bolts, then remove the driveshaft from the vehicle.

NOTE: When removing the driveshaft from the transmission, be sure to plug the opening to prevent oil from flowing out.

15. Disconnect the control cable from the selector lever and the control cable from the bracket.

16. To disconnect the front driveshafts from the axle shafts (on each side), perform the following procedures:

a. On the lower-side of the plate, loosen the stabilizer-to-transverse link nut/bolt.

b. Remove the handbrake cable bracket-to-transverse link.

c. Remove the transverse link-to-crossmember bolt on each side and lower the transverse link.

d. Using a pin punch and a hammer, drive out the axle shaft-to-driveshaft spring pin; discard the spring pin.

e. Push outward on the wheel assembly to separate the axle shaft from the driveshaft.

17. Remove the engine-to-transmission bolts.

18. Disconnect and plug the oil cooler lines at the transmission.

19. Using a transmission jack, position it under and secure it to the transmission.

NOTE: When using a transmission jack, always support the transmission case; NEVER place it under the oil pan.

20. Remove the rear crossmember-to-transmission bolts, the rear crossmember-to-chassis bolts and the rear crossmember from the vehicle.

21. Lower the transmission jack and remove the transmission from the vehicle.

22. To install, use new spring pins and gaskets. Torque the transmission rubber cushion-to-rear crossmember nuts to 9–17 ft. lbs. (2WD) or 20–35 ft. lbs. (4WD), the rear crossmember-to-chassis bolts to 39–49 ft. lbs., the lower transmission-to-engine bolts to 34–40 ft. lbs., the transverse link-to-front crossmember nuts to 43–51 ft. lbs. (vehicle on the ground), the transverse link-to-stabilizer bar nut/bolt to 14–22 ft. lbs., the driveshaft-to-rear differential nuts/bolts to 13–20 ft. lbs. (4WD), the driveshaft center bearing-to-chassis nut/bolts to 25–33 ft. lbs. (4WD), the engine-to-transmission bolt to 34–40 ft. lbs., the torque converter-to-drive plate bolts to 17–20 ft. lbs.

23. To complete the installation, reverse the removal procedures. Check and/or refill the transmission. Start the engine, allow it to reach normal operating temperatures and check for leaks.

PAN REMOVAL

1. Raise and support the vehicle on a level surface on jackstands.

2. Position a drain pan under the transmission, remove the drain plug and drain the transmission.

3. Remove the oil pan-to-transmission bolts and lower the oil pan from the transmission.

4. Using a putty knife, clean the gasket mounting surfaces.

5. Using solvent, wash the oil pan and inspect the pan for pieces of metal (indicating wear).

6. To install, use a new gasket, sealant (if necessary) and reverse the removal procedures.

FILTER SERVICE

1. Refer to the "Oil Pan, Removal and Installation" procedures in this section and remove the oil pan.

2. Remove the oil stainer-to-transmission bolt and the oil strainer from the transmission.

3. Using solvent, wash the oil strainer and the oil pan, then inspect the pan for pieces of metal (indicating wear).

4. Using a putty knife, clean the gasket mounting surfaces.

5. To install, use a new gasket, sealant (if necessary) and reverse the removal procedures.

SHIFT LINKAGE ADJUSTMENT

1. Loosen the clamp nuts on the shifting rod at the bottom of the shift lever on the transmission.

2. Place the selector lever in Neutral and hold it forward against the detent.

3. Check that the transmission shift lever is in the Neutral position (pull it all the way back into Park and push it forward two positions).

4. Tighten the clamp nuts.

KICKDOWN SOLENOID ADJUSTMENT

An audible click should be heard from the solenoid on the right-side of the transmission, when the accelerator pedal is pushed down all the way with the engine off and the ignition switch On. The switch is operated by the upper part of the accelerator lever inside the vehicle. The position of the switch can be varied to give quicker or slower kickdown response.

NEUTRAL SAFETY SWITCH ADJUSTMENT

This switch is mounted on the transmission shift lever shaft, bolted to the transmission. It also operates the back-up lights.

1. Remove the shift lever shaft nut.
2. Remove the shift lever from the shaft.
3. Make sure that the slot in the shaft is vertical (Neutral position).
4. Remove the switch mounting bolts but leave the switch in place.
5. Remove the setscrew from the lower face of the switch.
6. Insert a 0.059 in. drill bit through the set screw hole. Turn the switch slightly so that the bit passes through into the back part of the switch.
7. Bolt the switch down.
8. Remove the drill bit and replace the set screw.
9. Install the lever and tighten the shaft nut.
10. Make sure that the engine can start only in Park or Neutral and that the back-up lights turn On in Reverse; adjust the shift linkage, if necessary.

BRAKE BAND ADJUSTMENT

This adjustment can be performed on the outside of the transmission.

1. Raise and support the vehicle on jackstands (on a level surface).
2. Locate the adjusting screw above the pan on the left-side of the transmission.
3. Loosen the locknut.
4. Torque the adjusting screw to 6.5 ft. lbs., then turn it back exactly two full turns.
5. Tighten the lock nut.

NOTE: Following the above procedure will adjust the transmission brake band to the factory specified setting.

6. If any of the following conditions are detected, the adjusting screw can be moved ¼ turn in either direction after Step 4. Turn the screw ¼ turn clockwise, if transmission:
• Jolts when shifting from 1st to 2nd.
• Engine speed abruptly rises from 2nd to 3rd.
• Shift delays in kickdown from 3rd to 2nd.
Turn the screw ¼ turn counter-clockwise if:
• The vehicle slips from 1st to 2nd.
• There is braking action at shift from 2nd to 3rd.

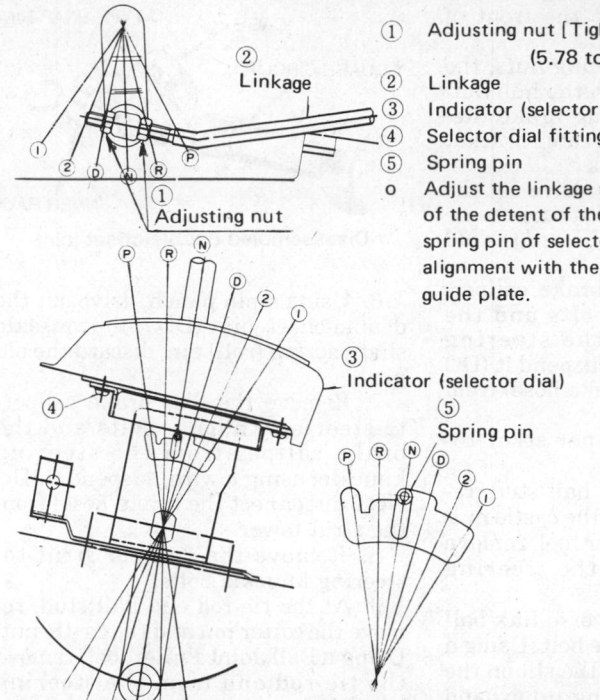

① Adjusting nut [Tightening torque: (5.78 to 8.68 ft-lb)
② Linkage
③ Indicator (selector dial)
④ Selector dial fitting screw
⑤ Spring pin
o Adjust the linkage so that the position "N" of the detent of the manual valve and the spring pin of selector lever will come in alignment with the position "N" of the guide plate.

Details for automatic shift linkage adjustment

TRANSFER CASE

DRIVE SELECTOR ADJUSTMENT

There are no adjustments available for the drive selector. If you notice looseness or too much shifting play, it is a sign of worn parts which must be replaced.

REMOVAL & INSTALLATION

Please refer to the "Transaxle, Removal and Installation" procedures in this section and remove the transaxle, then disassemble the transfer case from the transxle.

DRIVE AXLE

The drive axle consists of a double-offset joint (DOJ) at the inner end, an axle shaft, a constant velocity (CV) joint at the outer end and a stub axle.

Front Halfshaft
REMOVAL & INSTALLATION

All Models—Except Justy

1. Disconnect the negative battery terminal from the battery.
2. Engage the parking brake. Remove the front wheel grease cap and the cotter pin. Loosen the wheel hub nuts and the halfshaft castle nut.

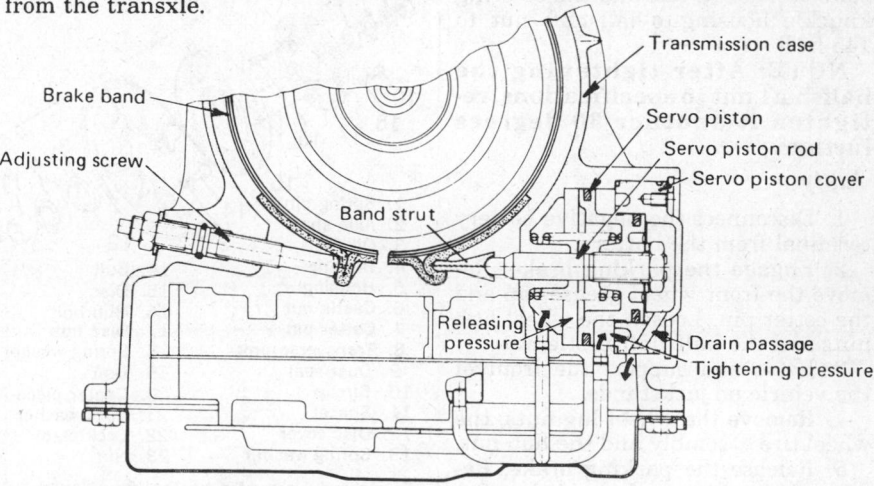

Second gear band adjustment mechanism

3. Raise and support the front of the vehicle on jackstands.

4. Remove the wheel lug nuts, the wheel/tire assembly and the hub nut.

5. Release the parking brake. Remove the parking brake cable bracket from the transverse link.

6. Using a pin punch, drive out the double-offset joint (DOJ)-to-transaxle shaft, spring (roll) pin; discard the old pin.

7. Remove the disc brake caliper-to-steering knuckle bolts and the brake caliper from the steering knuckle; using a wire, suspend it (DO NOT disconnect the brake hose) from the strut tower.

8. Remove the damper strut-to-steering knuckle bolts.

9. At the tie-rod end ball stud, remove the cotter pin and the castle nut. Using a Ball Joint Puller tool, remove the tie-rod end from the steering knuckle.

10. Remove the transverse link ball stud-to-steering knuckle bolt. Using a cold chisel, drive it into the slit on the steering knuckle housing (to expand the joint), then lower the transverse link from the steering knuckle.

11. Using the Puller tool No. 926470000 or equivalent, press the halfshaft from the steering knuckle housing.

12. Clean and inspect the parts for wear and/or damage.

13. Install the halfshaft into the steering knuckle housing and attach the Installation Spacer tool No. 925130000 or 922430000 or equivalent, onto the outer bearing inner race; be careful not to damage the oil seal lip.

14. To install, use a new spring pin and reverse the removal procedures. Torque the transverse link ball joint-to-housing bolts to 22–29 ft. lbs., the damper strut-to-housing bolts to 22–29 ft. lbs., the disc cover-to-housing bolts to 4–19 ft. lbs. and the steering knuckle housing-to-halfshaft nut to 145 ft. lbs.

NOTE: After tightening the halfshaft nut to specifications, retighten it another 30 degrees further.

Justy

1. Disconnect the negative battery terminal from the battery.

2. Engage the parking brake. Remove the front wheel grease cap and the cotter pin. Loosen the wheel hub nuts and the halfshaft castle nut.

3. Raise and support the front of the vehicle on jackstands.

4. Remove the wheel lug nuts, the wheel/tire assembly and the hub nut.

5. Release the parking brake. Remove the parking brake cable bracket from the transverse link.

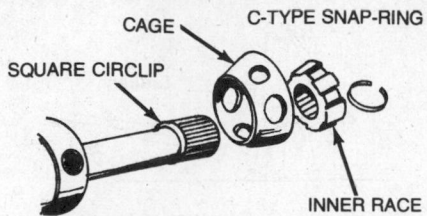

Disassembled double-offset joint

6. Using a pin punch, drive out the double-offset joint (DOJ)-to-transaxle shaft, spring (roll) pin; discard the old pin.

7. Remove the disc brake caliper-to-steering knuckle bolts and the brake caliper from the steering knuckle; using a wire, suspend it (DO NOT disconnect the brake hose) from the strut tower.

8. Remove the damper strut-to-steering knuckle bolts.

9. At the tie-rod end ball stud, remove the cotter pin and the castle nut. Using a Ball Joint Puller tool, remove the tie-rod end from the steering knuckle.

10. Remove the transverse link ball stud-to-steering knuckle bolt. Using a cold chisel, drive it into the slit on the steering knuckle housing (to expand the joint), then lower the transverse link from the steering knuckle.

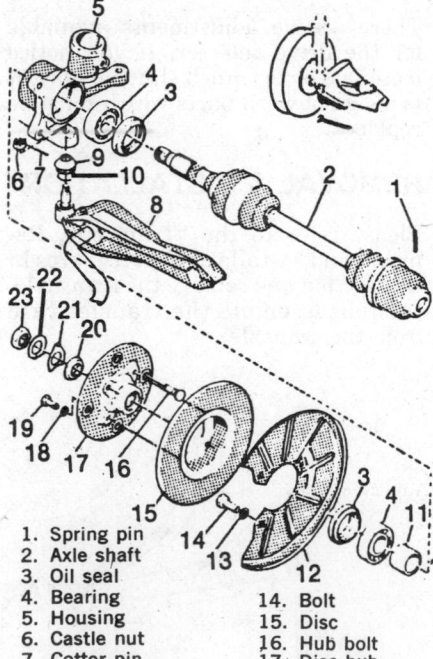

1. Spring pin
2. Axle shaft
3. Oil seal
4. Bearing
5. Housing
6. Castle nut
7. Cotter pin
8. Transverse link
9. Dust seal
10. Circlip
11. Spacer
12. Disc cover
13. Spring washer
14. Bolt
15. Disc
16. Hub bolt
17. Disc hub
18. Spring washer
19. Bolt
20. Center piece
21. Lock washer
22. Lock plate
23. Nut

Exploded view of a typical front axle assembly

11. Using the Removal tools No. 922493000 and No. 921122000 or equivalent, press the halfshaft from the housing.

12. Clean, inspect and/or replace the necessary parts.

13. Using the Installation tool No. 922430000 or equivalent, press the halfshaft into the housing.

14. To complete the installation, use a new spring pin and reverse the removal procedures. Torque the transverse link ball joint-to-housing bolt to 25–33 ft. lbs., the steering knuckle arm-to-tie rod end ball joint nut to 18–22 ft. lbs. (after tightening, turn the nut 60 degrees further), the housing-to-strut bolts to 25–33 ft. lbs., the brake disc cover to 13–23 ft. lbs., the caliper-to-steering knuckle bolts to 31–46 ft. lbs. and the halfshaft-to-housing nut to 130 ft. lbs.

NOTE: After tightening the halfshaft nut, turn the nut 30 degrees further, to align the slot in the nut with a hole in the shaft.

CV-JOINT OVERHAUL

For all overhaul procedures, please refer to "CV-Joint Overhaul" in the Unit Repair section.

Driveshaft—4WD

REMOVAL & INSTALLATION

1. Raise and support the vehicle on jackstands.

2. Position a drain pan under the rear of the transaxle, the catch the excess oil from the transaxle; plug the transaxle opening (if necessary).

3. Remove the driveshaft flange-to-rear differential flange bolts and separate the driveshaft from the differential flange.

NOTE: If equipped with a center bearing, remove the center bearing-to-chassis bolts and lower the center bearing from the vehicle.

4. While supporting the rear of the driveshaft, gently pull the it rearward to remove it from the vehicle.

5. To install, reverse the removal procedures. Torque the center bearing-to-chassis bolts to 25–33 ft. lbs. and the driveshaft-to-rear differential flange bolts to 13–20 ft. lbs. Check and/or refill the transaxle.

OVERHAUL

Selective snap-rings are used to provide proper clearance of the gearing cap to yoke. The clearance should be 0.0008 in. and the opposing snap-rings must be of the same thickness.

1. Using chalk, matchmark the flange yoke, the sleeve yoke and the U-joint so the parts can be reassembled in the exact same relationship.

2. Using a flat-blade pry bar, pry off the bearing race snap rings.

3. Using a brass hammer, tap on the other side of the yoke to remove the bearing race.

NOTE: Make sure you don't lose any roller bearings.

4. To install, grease the roller bearings and reverse the removal procedures.

Rear Halfshaft—4WD

REMOVAL & INSTALLATION

1981-82 Models

1. Raise and support the rear of the vehicle on jackstands.

2. Rotate the rear wheel to position the halfshaft. Using a pin punch, drive the spring pins from the halfshaft-to-axle spindle and the halfshaft-to-rear differential connection.

3. Remove the halfshaft assembly.

4. To disassemble the ball spline, position the driveshaft in a vise, then remove the rubber band, the snapring and the stopper.

5. To disassemble the U-joint, remove the snap-ring and the needle bearing.

6. To reassemble and install, reverse the removal procedures.

NOTE: Selective snap-rings are used to obtain a clearance of 0.0008 in. between the bearing cap and driveshaft yoke.

The snap-ring thicknesses are as follow:

    0.0587 in.
    0.0598 in.
    0.0610 in.
    0.0622 in.
    0.0457 in.
    0.0646 in.
    0.0657 in.

Thickness	Paint Color
0.0795 in.	Yellow
0.0803 in.	Red
0.0811 in.	Green
0.0819 in.	Blue
0.0827 in.	Light Brown
0.0835 in.	No paint
0.0843 in.	Pink

7. To install, use new spring pins and reverse the removal procedures.

1983-88 Models

1. Firmly apply the parking brake.

2. Remove the rear wheel cap and the cotter pin, then loosen the castle nut.

3. Disconnect the shock absorber from the inner arm.

4. Loosen the crossmember outer bushing lock bolts. Remove the inner trailing arm-to-chassis bolt and the inner arm.

5. Raise and support the rear of the vehicle on jackstands. Remove the rear wheel assemblies.

6. Using a 0.24 in. (6mm) dia. steel rod or a pin punch, drive the inner/outer spring pins from the DOJ's (Double Offset Joint).

7. With the trailing arm fully lowered, remove the ball joint from the trailing arm spindle and the inner DOJ from the differential spindle.

8. Remove the castle nut and the brake drum (drum brakes) or rear wheel caliper (disc brakes).

NOTE: If equipped with rear disc brakes, remove the brake caliper and suspend it on a wire; DO NOT disconnect the brake hose from the caliper.

9. Disconnect and plug the brake hose from the inner arm bracket.

10. If equipped with rear brake drums, remove the brake assembly from the trailing arm.

11. Disconnect the inner arm from the outer arm and remove the inner arm from the vehicle.

12. Secure the inner arm in a vise, then using a hammer and a punch, straighten the staked portion of the ring nut. Using the Wrench tool No. 925550000 or equivalent, remove the ring nut.

13. Using a plastic hammer on the outside of the spindle, drive it inward to remove it.

14. Clean, inspect and/or replace the necessary parts.

15. Using an abor press and a piece of 1.38 in. dia. (35mm) pipe, insert the spindle from the inside and press the outer bearing's inner race from outside.

16. Using the Wrench tool No. 925550000 or equivalent, torque the axle shaft ring nut to 127–163 ft. lbs. Using a punch and a hammer, stake the ring nut, facing the ring nut groove.

17. To complete the installation, use new spring pins and reverse the removal procedures. Torque the backing plate-to-axle housing bolts to 34–43 ft. lbs. (if equipped), the axle spindle-to-axle housing nut to 145 ft. lbs. and the shock absorber-to-inner arm

bolt to 65–87 ft. lbs. Bleed the brake system.

NOTE: After tightening the rear axle halfshaft-to-axle housing nut, tighten the axle shaft nut 30 degrees further. Be careful not to install the DOJ and the CVJ oppositely.

Rear Halfshaft, Bearing And Seals— 4WD

REMOVAL & INSTALLATION

1. Refer to the "Rear Halfshaft, Removal and Installation" procedures in this section and remove the halfshaft.

2. From the inner arm housing, remove the oil seal.

3. From outside the housing, insert the spindle and extract the inner bearing's outer race and the spacer. Using an arbor press and the spindle, push the outer bearing's inner race from the housing.

4. Using an arbor press, press the inner bearing's inner race from the spindle.

5. Clean, inspect and/or replace the necessary parts.

6. Using an arbor press, install the inner bearing's inner race onto the spindle and the outer races (inner and outer bearings) into the housing.

7. Inside the housing, grease the bearing outer race.

8. Using an abor press and a piece of 1.38 in. dia. (35mm) pipe, insert the spindle from the inside and press the outer bearing's inner race from outside.

9. Using the Wrench tool No. 925550000 or equivalent, torque the axle shaft ring nut to 127–163 ft. lbs. Using a punch and a hammer, stake the ring nut, facing the ring nut groove.

10. Using the Oil Seal Installation tool No. 925530000 or equivalent, and a new oil seal, install a new oil seal into the housing.

11. To complete the installation, use new spring pins and reverse the removal procedures. Torque the backing plate-to-axle housing bolts to 34–43 ft. lbs. (if equipped), the axle spindle-to-axle housing nut to 145 ft. lbs. and the shock absorber-to-inner arm bolt to 65–87 ft. lbs. Bleed the brake system.

NOTE: After tightening the rear axle halfshaft-to-axle housing nut, tighten the axle shaft nut 30 degrees further. Be careful not to install the DOJ and the CVJ oppositely.

FRONT SUSPENSION

MacPherson Strut Assembly

REMOVAL & INSTALLATION

1. Raise and support the front of the vehicle on jackstands.
2. Remove the negative battery terminal from the battery.
3. Remove the wheel/tire assembly.
4. Disconnect and plug the brake union bolt/hose from the brake caliper.

NOTE: If necessary, disconnect the handbrake cable from the brake caliper lever and the handbrake cable hanger from the transverse link and the tie-rod end. Remove the handbrake cable end.

5. Remove the brake hose bracket-to-strut chose clip and the brake hose from the strut.
6. Remove the strut-to-steering knuckle housing bolts and separate the strut from the steering knuckle housing.

NOTE: If the strut is rusted into the steering knuckle housing, use Liquid Wrench® to dissolve the rust.

7. Remove the strut-to-body nuts and the strut from the body.
8. To install, reverse the removal procedures. Torque the strut-to-body nuts to 22–29 ft. lbs. (all models — except Justy) or 25–40 ft. lbs. (Justy) and the strut-to-steering knuckle housing bolts to 22–29 ft. lbs. (all models — except Justy) or 25–40 ft. lbs. (Justy).

OVERHAUL

NOTE: For all spring and shock absorber Removal and Installation procedures, and all strut overhaul procedures, please refer to "Strut Overhaul" in the Unit Repair Section.

Ball Joints

INSPECTION

1. Raise and support the front of the vehicle on jackstands.
2. Using a pry bar, position it under the wheel, then pry upward on the wheel several times; if more than 0.012 in. (3mm) of movement is noticed at the ball joint, replace it.
3. Inspect the ball joint's dust seal, if it is broken, replace it.

REMOVAL & INSTALLATION

All Models

1. Raise and support the front of the vehicle on jackstands. Remove the wheels.
2. Remove the cotter pin and the castellated nut from the ball joint. Remove the steering knuckle-to-ball joint bolt and the ball joint from the vehicle.
3. Inspect the ball joint for damage to the boot that retains grease or stress cracks.
4. To install, use a new the ball joint and reverse the removal procedures. Torque the ball joint stud-to-steering knuckle housing bolt to 22–29 ft. lbs. (1981-84) or 28–37 ft. lbs. (1985–88).
5. Connect the ball joint to the transverse link and install the castellated nut. Torque the ball joint-to-lower control arm nut to 29 ft. lbs. Then, torque the nut further, just until the castellations are aligned with the hole in the end of the ball stud. Install a new cotter pin and bend it around the nut.

Lower Control Arm

REMOVAL & INSTALLATION

1. Raise and support the front of the vehicle on jackstands; block the rear wheels.
2. Remove the parking brake cable clamp nut and clamp from the control arm.
3. Remove the lower control arm-to-crossmember self-locking nut; be sure to note the installation sequence of the spacers.

NOTE: If equipped with a stabilizer bar, remove the stabilizer bar-to-control arm self-locking nuts/bolts; note the installation sequence of the spacers.

4. Remove the leading rod-to-lower control arm nuts/bolts and separate the leading rod from the lower control arm.
5. From the steering knuckle-to-ball joint connection, remove the steering knuckle-to-ball joint nut/bolt.
6. Using a medium prybar, separate the lower control arm from the steering knuckle and the lower control arm from the crossmember.
7. To install, reverse the removal procedures. DO NOT grease the upper

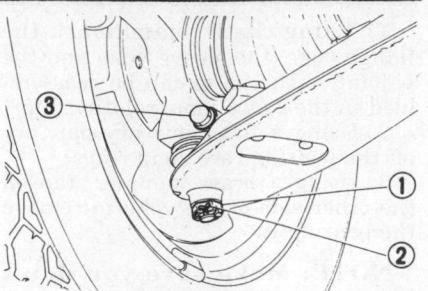

To remove the ball joints, remove the cotter ping (2), castellated nut (1) and bolt (3)

ball joint stud which fits into the steering knuckle housing. Torque the ball joint-to-steering knuckle housing nut/bolt to 22–29 ft. lbs. (1981–84) or 28–37 ft. lbs. (1985–88), the stabilizer-to-lower control arm nuts/bolts to 51–58 ft. lbs. (1981–84) or 54–69 ft. lbs. (1985–88) and the lower control arm-to-crossmember nuts/bolts to 40–47 ft. lbs. or 43–51 ft. lbs. (1985–88).

NOTE: Use new self-locking nuts on the crossmember and stabilizer bar mounts. Be sure to tighten the stabilizer fasteners with the weight of the vehicle on the ground.

Front Wheel Bearings

ADJUSTMENT

There is no bearing preload adjustment, other than tightening the axle shaft nut to the proper specifications. See the char below.

REMOVAL & INSTALLATION

All Models — Except Justy

1. Refer to the "Front Halfshaft, Removal and Installation" procedures in this section and remove the halfshaft from the vehicle; be sure to remove the steering knuckle from the vehicle.
2. Using your finger, move the spacer (inside the steering knuckle) in the radial direction.
3. Using a brass bar, insert it through the inner race of the outer bearing, then tap the bar with a hammer to drive out the bearing (with the oil seal); discard the bearing and the oil seal.

ITEM	TORQUE (ft.lbs.)
Backing plate bolts	22–35
Lower control arm nut	25–29
Tie rod end nut	18–22
Shock to axle housing	22–29
Axle shaft nut	170

4. Remove the spacer and the inner bearing.

5. Position the brass bar through the outer race of the inner bearing, then using a hammer, drive the out the bearing (with the oil seal); discard the bearing and the oil seal.

6. Clean and inspect the parts for wear, cracks and/or damage; if necessary, replace the damaged parts.

7. Using new bearings, pack them with wheel bearing grease.

8. Using the Die tool No. 925140000 (1981-84) or 926490000 (1985-88) or equivalent, install the steering knuckle onto the die.

9. Using a press and the Punch tool No. 925140000 (1981-84) or 926490000 (1985-88) or equivalent, press the outer bearing into the housing until it contacts the housing stopper.

10. Using ⅓ oz. of wheel bearing grease, pack the inside of the housing.

11. Invert the housing on the Die tool No. 925140000 (1981-84) or 926490000 (1985-88) or equivalent, and install the spacer.

12. Using a press and the Punch tool No. 925140000 (1981-84) or 926490000 (1985-88) or equivalent, press the inner bearing into the housing until it contacts the housing stopper.

13. Using a press and the Punch tool No. 925140000 (1981-84) or 926490000 (1985-88) or equivalent, position the new outer oil seal in the punch tool so that the lip faces the groove, then press it into the steering knuckle housing, until it comes in contact with the bearing end face.

14. Invert the steering knuckle housing onto the Punch tool No. 925140000 (1981-84) or 926490000 (1985-88) or equivalent, so that the seal lip faces the groove.

15. Using a press and the Die tool No. 925140000 (1981-84) or 926490000 (1985-88) or equivalent, press the new inner oil seal into the steering knuckle housing, until it comes in contact with the bearing end face.

16. To installation the steering knuckle, fit the housing onto the axle shaft and attach a spacer of the Installation tool No. 925130000 or 922430000 or equivalent, on the outer bearing inner race; be careful not to damage the oil seal. Thread the axle shaft onto the installation tool, then turn the handle to draw the axle into the housing, until it is seated.

17. To complete the installation, reverse the removal procedures.

Justy

1. Refer to the "Front Halfshaft, Removal and Installation" procedures in this section and remove the halfshaft from the vehicle; be sure to remove the steering knuckle from the vehicle.

2. Using your finger, move the spacer (inside the steering knuckle) in the radial direction.

3. Using a brass bar, insert it through the inner race of the outer bearing, then tap the bar with a hammer to drive out the bearing (with the oil seal); discard the bearing and the oil seal.

4. Remove the spacer and the inner bearing.

5. Position the brass bar through the outer race of the inner bearing, then using a hammer, drive the out the bearing (with the oil seal); discard the bearing and the oil seal.

6. Clean and inspect the parts for wear, cracks and/or damage; if necessary, replace the damaged parts.

7. Using new bearings, pack them with grease.

8. Using the Stand tool No. 922441000 or equivalent, install the steering knuckle onto the stand.

9. Using the Bearing Installer tool No. 922470000 or equivalent, and the Handle tool No. 498477000 or equivalent, press the inner bearing into the housing until it contacts the housing stopper.

10. Using ¼ oz. of wheel bearing grease, pack the inside of the housing.

11. Invert the housing on the Stand tool No. 922441000 or equivalent, and install the spacer.

12. Using the Bearing Installer tool No. 922470000 or equivalent, and the Handle tool No. 498477000 or equivalent, press the outer bearing into the housing until it contacts the housing stopper.

13. Using a press and the Oil Seal Installer tool No. 922450000 or equivalent, press the new outer oil seal into the steering knuckle housing, until it comes in contact with the bearing end face.

14. Invert the steering knuckle housing.

15. Using a press and the Oil Seal Installer tool No. 922460000 or equivalent, press the new inner oil seal into the steering knuckle housing, until it comes in contact with the bearing end face.

16. To complete the installation, reverse the removal procedures.

Front End Alignment
ADJUSTMENT

Caster and Camber

Caster and camber are not adjustable on these models. If either of these specifications is not within the factory recommended range, this would indicate bent or damaged parts that must be replaced.

Toe-In

Toe-in is adjusted by loosening the locknuts on the tie rods and turning the tie rods.

NOTE: Before performing the toe-in adjustment, park the vehicle on a level, solid surface, check and/or inflate the tires to the specified pressure, be sure that the steering gear is centered by aligning the marks on it and that the wheels are straight-ahead.

Tighten the locknuts after the toe-in adjustment is completed.

REAR SUSPENSION

Shock Absorbers
REMOVAL & INSTALLATION

All Models (1981-84) — Except Justy

Semi-trailing arms mounted to torque tubes, which act on an internal torsion bar, are used. Shock absorbers are mounted to the trailing arm, close to the stub axle.

1. Raise and support the rear of the vehicle on jackstands.

2. Remove the wheel cover and loosen the lug nuts. Set the parking brake and blocking the front wheels.

3. Remove the lug nuts and the rear wheels.

4. Loosen the upper shock absorber-to-chassis nuts.

5. Remove the washer and the bushing, being sure to note their correct assembly sequence for installation.

6. Remove the shock absorber-to-trailing arm pin nut (nut and bolt on later models) and the shock absorber. Note the installation positions of the washers.

7. To install, reverse the removal procedures. Torque the shock absorber-to-chassis nuts to 22–32 ft. lbs. Adjust the ride height bolts, if equipped.

NOTE: DO NOT fully tighten the upper mounting nuts until the lower shock nut has been installed with the washer and the pin shoulder contracting each other.

Justy (1987-88)

An independent strut type rear suspension, consisting of a double-acting cylindrical oil damper with strut mount separately mounted coil spring, lower arm and trailing link.

1. Pull the parking brake lever and set the parking brake.
2. Loosen the wheel lug nuts.
3. Raise and support the rear of the vehicle on jackstands. Remove the wheel assemblies.
4. From the upper portion of the strut mount, remove the trim cover.
5. Remove the shock absorber-to-body nut.
6. Remove the shock absorber-to-axle housing nuts/bolts and the shock absorber from the vehicle.
7. To install, use a new shock absorber (if necessary) and reverse the removal procedures. Torque the shock absorber-to-housing nuts/bolts to 54–61 ft. lbs. and the shock absorber-to-body nuts to 29–43 ft. lbs.

MacPherson Strut

REMOVAL & INSTALLATION

All Models (1985-88)—Except Justy

NOTE: Before performing this procedure, unload the vehicle.

1. Remove the upper strut-to-body bolts.
2. Set the parking brakes.
3. Loosen the rear wheel lug nuts.
4. Raise and support the rear of the vehicle on jackstands. Remove the rear wheel assemblies.
5. Remove the strut-to-inner arm bolts and the shock absorber from the inner arm.
6. To install, use a new strut and reverse the removal procedures. Torque the strut-to-inner arm bolts to 65–87 ft. lbs. and the strut-to-body bolts to 65–94 ft. lbs.

OVERHAUL

NOTE: For all spring and shock absorber removal and installa-tion procedures, and all strut overhaul procedures, please refer to "Strut Overhaul" in the Unit Repair section.

Coil Springs

REMOVAL & INSTALLATION

Justy

1. Pull the parking brake lever and set the parking brake.
2. Loosen the wheel lug nuts.
3. Raise and support the rear of the vehicle on jackstands. Remove the rear wheel assemblies.
4. From the upper portion of the strut mount, remove the trim cover.
5. Remove the shock absorber-to-body nut.
6. Push the lower arm downward and pull out the coil spring.
7. To install, reverse the removal procedures. Torque the shock absorber-to-body nuts to 29–43 ft. lbs.

Torsion Bar

REMOVAL & INSTALLATION

All Models (1981-84)

NOTE: Only on the 4WD models, the center arm is used.

1. Raise and support the rear of the vehicle on jackstands. Remove the rear wheels.
2. Support the rear axles in a position eliminating load from the torsion bar.
3. Remove the lockbolt for the outer bushing and the outer arm-to-inner arm bolts. Pull the outer arm and torsion bar out of the crossmember. The torsion bar may not be removed from the outer arm.

NOTE: If equipped with 4WD, remove the center arm after the torsion bars are removed from both sides.

4. Inspect the center arm and torsion bars for cracks and/or corrosion; if necesary, replace it.
5. To install, reverse the removal procedure, keeping the following points in mind:
   a. The torsion bar's splines MUST BE aligned with those in the outer arm and the crossmember so that the outer arm align with the inner arm, as it did during removal or the ride height will be effected.
   b. If removing both torsion bars, make sure the markings(**R** or **L**) correspond with the side of the vehicle the bar is being installed.
6. To complete the installation, reverse the removal procedures. Torque the inner arm-to-outer arm to 87–101 ft. lbs. and the outer bushing lockbolt to 23–29 ft. lbs.

Rear Control (Inner) Arms

REMOVAL & INSTALLATION

All Models—Except Justy

NOTE: The vehicle must be in the unloaded condition.

1. Loosen the rear wheel lug nuts.
2. Raise and support the rear of the vehicle on jackstands; position the jackstands under the crossmember.
3. Remove the wheel/tire assemblies.
4. Remove the shock absorber/strut-to-inner arm nut/bolt and separate the shock absorber/strut from the inner arm.

R.H.　　　　L.H.

View of the torsion bar directional markings—rear suspension (1981-84)

5. If equipped with 4WD, perform the following procedures:
   a. Using a 0.24 in. (6mm) pin punch, drive the spring pins from the halfshaft-to-axle shaft and the halfshaft-to-differential assembly.
   b. While pushing downward on the inner arm, separate the halfshaft from the axle shaft.
   c. Pull the halfshaft from the differential and position it out of the way.
6. Disconnect and plug the brake hose from the brake pipe on each inner arm.
7. Remove the outer arm-to-inner arm nuts/bolts, then separate the in-

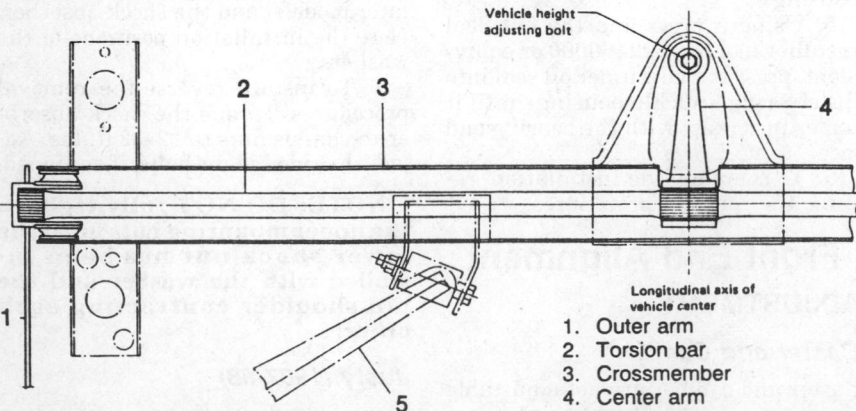

Cross-sectional view of the torsion bar and center arm.

1. Outer arm
2. Torsion bar
3. Crossmember
4. Center arm
5. Inner arm

ner arm from the outer arm and support the inner arm with a jackstand.

8. Remove the inner arm-to-crossmember nut/bolt and the inner arm from the vehicle.

9. To install, use new spring pins (4WD) and reverse the removal procedures. Torque the inner arm-to-crossmember nuts/bolts to 54–69 ft. lbs. (1981-84) or 80–101 ft. lbs. (1985-88), the inner arm-to-outer arm bolts to 87–108 ft. lbs. (1981-84) or 108–130 ft. lbs. (1985–88) and the shock absorber-to-inner arm nut/bolt to 65–87 ft. lbs. Bleed the brake system. Check and/or adjust the rear vehicle height and the rear wheel alignment.

Justy

1. Refer to the "Coil Spring, Removal and Installation" procedures in this section and remove the coil spring.

NOTE: Position the jackstands so that they will not interfere with the control arm.

2. Remove the control arm-to-crossmember nut/bolt and separate the control arm from the crossmember.

3. Remove the control arm-to-axle housing nut/bolt, then separate the control arm from the axle housing and the vehicle.

4. To install, reverse the removal procedures. Torque the control arm-to-axle housing nut/bolt to 54–69 ft. lbs. and the control arm-to-crossmember nut/bolt to 43–58 ft. lbs.

Rear Wheel Bearings—2WD Only

NOTE: If removing the wheel bearing on a 4WD model, refer to the "Rear Axle, Removal and Installation" procedures in this section and replace the rear axle bearings.

REMOVAL & INSTALLATION

1. Apply the hand brake and loosen the rear wheel lug nuts.

NOTE: If performing this procedure on the Justy model, be sure to release the parking brake.

2. Raise and support the rear of the vehicle on jackstands. Remove the rear wheel assemblies.

3. If equipped with rear disc brakes, remove the caliper and support it on a wire.

4. Using a small prybar, remove the rear wheel grease cap.

5. Using a hammer and a punch, flatten the lock washer and loosen the

axle nut. Remove the lock washer and the thrust plate. When removing the drum or disc, be careful not to drop the inner race from the outer bearing.

NOTE: If the brake drum, on the Justy model, is difficult to remove, use the Wheel Puller tool No. 9224930000 or equivalent, to remove the brake drum.

6. Using a gear puller, remove the spacer and the inner race of the inner bearing.

7. Using a brass drift and a hammer, drive the outer race of the inner bearing (with the oil seal) from the drum or disc.

8. Using a brass drift and a hammer, drive the outer race of the outer bearing from the drum or disc.

9. Clean and inspect the parts for damage, wear and/or corrosion; replace the parts, if necessary.

10. Using the Bearing Installation tool No. 925220000 (all models, except Justy) or 922111000 (Justy) or equivalent, press the outer race of the inner bearing into the drum or disc until it seats against the shoulder.

NOTE: When pressing the bearing, be sure not to exceed the load to the bearing, so as not to damage it.

11. Apply a small amount of grease to the oil seal lips, then install the oil seal until it is flush with the drum or disc.

12. Using the Bearing Installation tool No. 921130000 (all models, except Justy) or 922111000 (Justy) or equivalent, press the outer race of the outer bearing into the drum or disc until it seats against the shoulder.

13. Apply approximately ⅛ oz. of wheel bearing grease to the inner and the outer bearings. Fill the disc or drum hub with 1 oz. of wheel bearing grease.

14. Install a new spacer O-ring, the spacer and the inner race of the inner bearing onto the trailing arm spindle.

NOTE: When installing the spacer, be sure to face the stepped surface toward the bearing. Use a new thrust plate and lock washer.

15. To complete the installation, reverse the removal procedures. Adjust the wheel bearing.

ADJUSTMENT

1. Temporarily tighten the axle nut to 36 ft. lbs. (all models, except Justy) or 29 ft. lbs. (Justy); turn the drum or disc (back and forth) several times to ensure that the bearings are properly seated.

2. Turn the nut backwards ⅛–¹⁄₁₀

turn in order to obtain the correct starting force.

3. Using a spring gauge, at a 90 degrees to the wheel lug, check the rotating force; the force should be 1.9–3.2 lbs. (all models, except Justy) or 3.1–4.4 lbs. (Justy)

4. After adjustment is complete, bend the lock washer.

5. After installing a new O-ring to the grease cap, install the cap with a plastic hammer.

6. To compete the installation, reverse the removal procedures.

STEERING

Steering Wheel

REMOVAL & INSTALLATION

1. Disconnect the negative battery terminal from the battery.

2. Disconnect the horn lead from the wiring harness, located beneath the instrument panel.

NOTE: On the XT Coupe, use a small prybar to remove the horn pad.

3. Working behind the steering wheel, remove the steering wheel cover-to-steering wheel screws. It may be necessary to lower the column from the dash by removing the screws.

4. Lift the crash pad assembly from the front of the wheel.

5. Matchmark the steering wheel and the column for installation.

6. Remove the steering wheel retaining nut. Using a Steering Wheel Puller tool, pull the steering wheel from the column.

7. To install, reverse the removal procedures. Align the matchmarks and tighten the steering wheel-to-steering column nut to 22–29 ft. lbs. (all models, except Justy) or 36–43 ft. lbs. (Justy).

NOTE: DO NOT hammer on the steering wheel or the steering column; damage to the collapsible column could result.

Combination Switch

REMOVAL & INSTALLATION

All Models (1981-86)—Except XT Coupe

The combination switch is fitted onto the steering switch, the turn signal switch and the hazard warning light switch.

1. Remove the lower cover-to-instrument panel screws and detach the lower cover.

2. Remove the covers-to-steering column screws and detach the column covers (upper and lower).

3. Remove the steering wheel cover and the nut. Using a Steering Wheel Puller tool, pull the steering wheel from the steering column.

4. Remove the harness-to-steering column clip and band, then disconnect the electrical connectors. Remove the combination switch.

5. To install, reverse the removal procedures. Align the matchmarks and tighten the steering wheel-to-steering column nut to 22–29 ft. lbs.

All Models (1987-88)

The combination switch is located on the steering column and is combined with the head light flasher switch, the turn signal switch, the hazard warning light switch and the parking light switch. A transistorized turn and hazard unit is incorporated in the combination switch.

1. Remove the lower cover-to-instrument panel screws and the lower cover.

2. Remove the covers-to-steering column screws and the column covers (upper and lower).

3. Remove the steering wheel cover and the nut. Using the Steering Wheel Puller tool, pull the steering wheel from the steering column.

4. Remove the electrical harness-to-steering column clip and band fitting, then disconnect the electrical connectors.

5. Remove the combination switch-to-control wing bracket screws and the combination switch.

6. To install, reverse the removal procedures. Align the matchmarks and tighten the steering wheel-to-steering column nut to 22–29 ft. lbs. (all models, except Justy) or 36–43 ft. lbs. (Justy).

Ignition Switch

REMOVAL & INSTALLATION

The ignition switch is mounted to the steering column using shear bolts. These bolts are constructed so that the heads shear off when the bolt is torqued.

1. Refer to the "Steering Wheel, Removal & Installation" procedures in this section and remove the steering wheel.

2. Remove the upper/lower column covers from the steering column.

3. Remove the hazard knob.

4. Using a drill, drill a pilot hole into the shear bolts, then using a

screw extractor, remove the screws from the steering column.

5. Remove the ignition switch from the steering column.

6. To install, reverse the removal procedures. Be sure to use new shear bolts to install the ignition switch.

Manual Steering Gear

All Subaru models are equipped with rack and pinion steering. No maintenance is required.

REMOVAL & INSTALLATION

1. Disconnect the negative battery terminal from the battery.

2. Raise and support the front of the vehicle on jackstands, then remove the front wheels.

3. Remove the tie-rod end cotter pin and loosen the castle nut. Using a Ball Joint Puller tool, separate the tie-rod ends from the housing knuckle arm.

4. If necessary, disconnect the handbrake cable hanger from the tie rod.

5. On the 1981–84 models, remove the rubber coupling nuts/bolts; On the

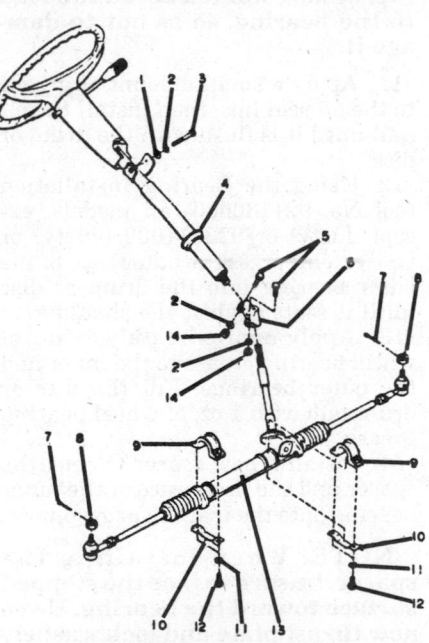

1. Washer
2. Spring washer
3. Bolt
4. Bushing (steering column)
5. Bolt
6. Universal joint
7. Cotter pin
8. Castle nut
9. Gearbox bracket
10. Lock plate
11. Washer
12. Bolt
13. Steering gearbox
14. Nut

Typical steering system

1985–88 models, remove the pinch bolt from the torque rod universal joint. Disconnect the pinion with the gearbox from the steering column.

6. If equipped with an air stove pipe, disconnect it.

7. Disconnect the exhaust manifold-to-engine bolts, pull downward on the exhaust manifold.

8. Remove the boot from the steering gear.

9. Remove the steering gear box-to-crossmember bolts, pull downward on the steering gear to disconnect the pinion flange. Turn the gearbox rearward and remove it toward the left-side.

NOTE: When removing the gearbox, be careful not to damage the gearbox boot.

10. Inspect the removed parts for wear and/or damage; if necessary, replace the parts.

11. To install, reverse the removal procedures. Torque the steering gearbox-to-crossmember bolts to 33–40 ft. lbs. (1981–84) or 35–52 ft. lbs. (1985–88), the pinch bolt-to-universal joint to 15–20 ft. lbs. (1985–88), the exhaust manifold-to-engine bolts to 19–22 ft. lbs., the rubber coupling-to-steering gear bolts to 10–14.5 ft. lbs. (1981–85) and the tie-rod end-to-steering knuckle nut to 18–22 ft. lbs. Adjust the toe-in and the turning angles.

NOTE: When torquing the tie-rod end-to-steering knuckle nuts, torque the nut 60 degrees turn (all models, except Justy) or 45 degrees turn (Justy) further, after torquing to specifications.

ADJUSTMENT

Tighten the backlash adjuster until it bottoms, back off the screw 15 degrees (all 1981-84 and Justy) or 25 degrees (all 1985-88 models, except Justy) and torque the locknut to 22–36 ft. lbs. (all 1981-84 models, XT Coupe and Justy) or 36–47 ft. lbs. (all 1985-88 models, except XT Coupe and Justy); a clearance of 0.0025 in. (all 1981-84 models and Justy) or 0.004 in. (all 1985-88 models, except Justy) is provided between the screw tip and the sleeve plate.

Power Steering Gear

The power steering gearbox is a rack and pinion type integral system. The power cylinder is built in the gearbox, using the rack shaft as a piston. The control valve is arranged around the pinion shaft.

REMOVAL & INSTALLATION

All Models – Except Justy

1. Disconnect the negative battery terminal from the battery.
2. Remove the spare tire. On the XT Coupe turbo, remove the spare tire support.
3. If necessary, disconnect the thermo sensor connector.
4. Raise and support the front of the vehicle on jackstands.
5. Remove the front wheel/tire assemblies.
6. Disconnect the electrical connector from the O_2 sensor, the remove the front exhaust pipe assembly.

NOTE: If equipped with an air stove, remove it.

7. Remove the tie-rod end cotter pin and loosen the castle nut. Using a Ball Joint Puller tool, separate the tie-rod ends from the steering knuckle arm.
8. Remove the jack-up plate and the clamp.
9. From the power steering gear, remove the center pressure pipe, connect a vinyl hose to the pipe and joint, then turn the steering wheel to discharge the fluid into a container.

NOTE: When discharging the power steering fluid, turn the steering wheel fully, left and right. Be sure to disconnect the other pipe and drain the fluid in the same manner.

10. Make alignment marks on the steering shaft universal joint assembly-to-power steering unit and the steering shaft-to-universal joint assembly. Remove the lower/upper universal joint-to-shaft bolts. Lift the universal joint assembly upward and secure it out of the way.
11. From the control valve of the gearbox assembly, remove the power steering 'C' and 'D' pressure pipes; remove pipe 'D' 1st and pipe 'C' 2nd.
12. From the control valve of the gearbox assembly, remove the power steering 'A' and 'B' pressure pipes; remove pipe 'A' 1st and pipe 'B' 2nd.
13. Remove the power steering gearbox-to-crossmember assembly bolts and the gearbox assembly from the vehicle.

NOTE: When installing the universal joint assembly, be sure to align the matchmarks.

14. To install, reverse the removal procedures. Torque the power steer-

ing gearbox-to-crossmember bolts to 33–40 ft. lbs. (1981-84) or 35–52 ft. lbs. (1985-88), the power steering pressure pipes to 7–12 ft. lbs., the universal joint assembly-to-power steering gearbox bolts to 16–19 ft. lbs., the universal joint assembly-to-steering shaft bolts to 16–19 ft. lbs., the tie-rod end-to-steering knuckle nut to 18–22 ft. lbs. (after torquing, turn it 60 degrees further) and the wheel lug nuts to 58–72 ft. lbs. Refill and bleed the power steering system. Check and/or adjust the toe-in and the steering angle.

ADJUSTMENT

Tighten the backlash adjuster until it bottoms, back off the screw 30 degrees (all models, except Justy) and torque the locknut to 22–36 ft. lbs. (all models, except Justy); 0.0049 in. (all models, except Justy) should be provided between the screw tip and the sleeve plate.

Power Steering Pump
REMOVAL & INSTALLATION

Non Turbo (1981–84)

1. Disconnect the negative battery terminal from the battery.
2. Remove the spare tire from the engine compartment.

NOTE: If equipped with a carburetor, remove the carburetor shield.

3. Raise and support the front of the vehicle on jackstands. Remove the jack-up plate.
4. Position a drain pan (to catch the fluid) under the power steering gear box. Remove the fluid line flare nuts from the center of the power steering gearbox, then turn the steering wheel from left to right to drain the gearbox.
5. Loosen the idler pulley adjustment bolts and remove the drive belt; it may be necessary to hit the idler pulley with a plastic hammer, to loosen it.
6. Disconnect the electrical connectors and remove the air cleaner hoses.

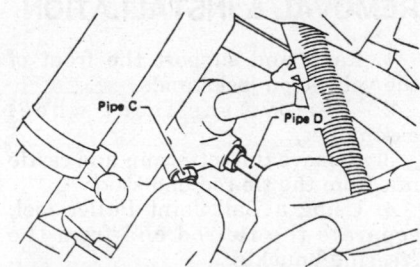

View of the power steering gear box pressure pipes – all 1985-88 models – except Justy

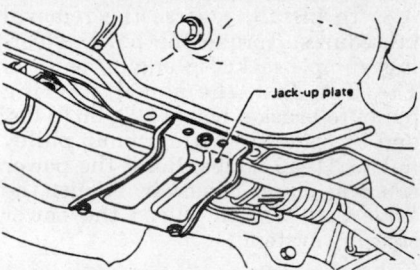

View of the jack-up plate – all 1985-88 models – except Justy

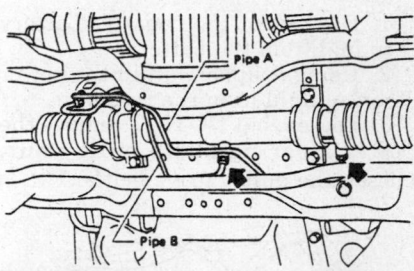

Remove the pressure pipes to drain the power steering fluid – all 1985-88 models – except Justy

Remove the air cleaner assembly, the engine oil dipstick and any other items that will prevent the pump removal.

7. Disconnect the fluid hoses from the back of the pump.
8. Remove the power steering pump-to-vehicle bolts/nuts and the pump from the vehicle.
9. To install, reverse the removal procedures. Torque the power steering pump bracket-to-engine bolts to 18–25 ft. lbs., power steering pump-to-engine bracket bolts to 33–44 ft. lbs. and the belt tensioner-to-engine bolt to 14–22 ft. lbs. Adjust the drive belt tension. Refill and bleed the power steering system.

Turbo (1982–84)

1. Disconnect the negative battery terminal from the battery. If necessary, remove the spare tire from the engine compartment.
2. Drain the power steering fluid from the oil reservoir located on the pump by syphoning the oil out.
3. Loosen but DO NOT remove the power steering pump pulley nut.
4. Loosen the idler pulley-to-engine bolts, move the idler pulley toward the power steering pump and remove the drive belt(s).
5. Remove the power steering pump pulley nut and the pulley.
6. Using two wrenchs, disconnect the power steering pump line at the pipe. Loosen the oil line clamp and disconnect it from the reservoir; keep the oil off the belts.
7. Remove the power steering pump-to-bracket bolts and remove it from the engine.

8. To install, reverse the removal procedures. Torque the power steering pump bracket-to-engine bolts to 13–16 ft. lbs., the power steering pump-to-bracket bolts to 22–36 ft. lbs. and the power steering pump pulley nut to 31–46 ft. lbs. Refill the power steering pump reservoir. Adjust the drive belt tension. Bleed the power steering system.

All Models (1985-88) — Except Justy

1. Disconnect the negative battery terminal from the battery.

2. Using a siphon, drain the power steering fluid from the reservoir.

3. Loosen, but DO NOT remove the power steering pump pulley nut. Loosen the pulley drive belt(s).

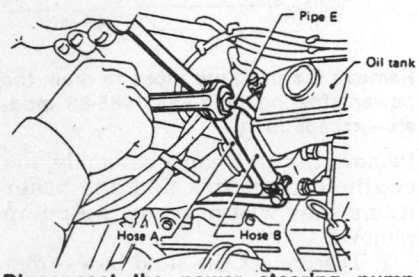

Disconnect the power steering pump hose(s) from the pressure pipe(s) — all 1985-88 models — except Justy

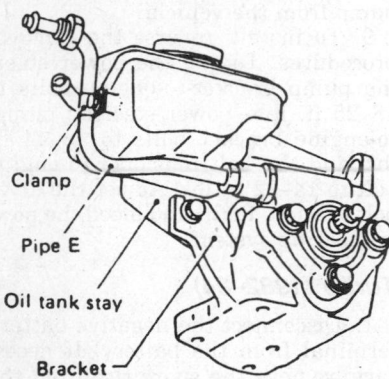

View of the power steering pump with reservoir — all 1985-88 models — except Justy

4. Remove the power steering pump pulley nut and the pulley.

5. Disconnect and plug the **A** pressure hose from the **E** pipe. Disconnect the **B** pressure hose from the oil tank.

NOTE: When disconnecting the A hose, use two wrenches to prevent the E pipe from twisting.

6. Remove the **E** hose-to-reservoir clamp.

7. Loosen the reservoir-to-bracket bolt, then the **A** and **B** bolts on the upper part of the reservoir; to remove the bolts on the reservoir will allow the fluid to run out.

NOTE: To minimize the fluid loss from the reservoir, remove both bolts while the reservoir is pressed against the oil pump, then quickly remove the reservoir. It is a good idea to remove the pump and the reservoir as a unit, then separate the reservoir from the pump on a bench.

8. Remove the power steering pump-to-bracket bolts and the pump from the vehicle.

9. To install, use new O-rings and reverse the removal procedures. Torque the power steering pump-to-bracket bolts to 22–36 ft. lbs., the reservoir stay-to-bracket bolts to 14–17 ft. lbs., the reservoir-to-pump bolts to 14–22 ft. lbs. and the pulley nut-to-pump nut to 31–46 ft. lbs. Refill the power steering reservoir. Bleed the power steering system.

DRIVE BELT ADJUSTMENT

1. Using a pair of adjustable jawed pliers (with a piece of rag between the jaws), remove the idler cover cap by turning and pulling.

2. Turn the adjusting bolt until the correct belt tension is obtained. If removing the belt, loosen the adjusting bolt until the drive belt can be removed.

3. After a new belt is installed and the correct tension obtained, replace the idler cap cover by pushing in and turning.

SYSTEM BLEEDING

1. Raise and support the front of the vehicle on jackstands.

2. Refill the reservoir with power steering fluid.

3. With the engine running, turn the steering wheel (back and forth), from lock to lock, until the air is removed from the fluid.

4. Lower the vehicle, recheck the reservoir fluid level and replace the reservoir cap.

Tie Rod Ends

REMOVAL & INSTALLATION

1. Raise and support the front of the vehicle on jackstands.

2. Remove the front wheel assemblies.

3. Remove the cotter pin and castle nut from the tie rod end stud.

4. Using a Ball Joint Puller tool, separate the tie rod end from the steering knuckle.

5. If the ball joints have excessive play, replace them.

6. To install, reverse the removal procedures. Torque the castle nut to 18–22 ft. lbs.

BRAKES

For all brake system repair and service not detailed below, please refer to "Brakes" in the Unit Repair section.

Master Cylinder

REMOVAL & INSTALLATION

—————— CAUTION ——————
Avoid spilling brake fluid on painted surfaces, it will lift the paint.

1. Disconnect and plug the brake lines at the master cylinder.

NOTE: It is advised to throughly drain the fluid from the master cylinder before performing any removal procedures.

2. If equipped with fluid level indicator, disconnect the electrical harness connector from the master cylinder.

3. Remove the master cylinder-to-power booster nuts and the master cylinder from the vehicle.

4. To install, reverse the removal procedures. Torque the master cylinder-to-power booster nuts to 7–13 ft. lbs. Refill the brake reservoir(s). Bleed the brake system.

Proportioning Valve

The proportioning valve is attached to a bracket and is located directly under the master cylinder. It's purpose it provide even braking pressure to all of the wheels.

REMOVAL & INSTALLATION

All Models — Except Justy

The Justy uses a Dual Proportioning Valve (DPV)

1. Disconnect and plug the four brake tubes from the proportioning valve.

2. Remove the proportioning valve-to-bracket bolts and the valve from the vehicle.

NOTE: If equipped with an electrical connector, disconnect it.

3. To install, reverse the removal procedures. Torque the proportioning valve-to-bracket bolts to 15–21 ft. lbs. Bleed the brake system.

Justy

1. Disconnect and plug the six brake tubes from the proportioning valve.

2. Remove the proportioning valve-to-bracket bolts and the valve from the vehicle.

NOTE: If equipped with an electrical connector, disconnect it.

3. To install, reverse the removal procedures. Torque the proportioning valve-to-bracket bolts to 3–5 ft. lbs. Bleed the brake system.

Power Brake Booster

The power brake booster uses engine manifold vacuum against a diaphragm to assist in the application of the brakes. The vacuum is regulated to be proportional to the pressure placed on the pedal.

REMOVAL & INSTALLATON

1. Refer to the "Master Cylinder, Removal and Installation" procedures in this section and remove the master cylinder.

2. Disconnect the vacuum hose from the power brake booster.

3. Remove the brake pedal push rod-to-power booster spring pin/clevis pin, then disconnect the push rod from the brake pedal.

4. From under the dash, remove the power booster-to-firewall nuts and the booster from the vehicle.

5. To install, reverse the removal procedures. Torque the power brake booster-to-firewall nuts to 9–17 ft. lbs. and the master cylinder-to-power brake booster nuts to 9–13 ft. lbs. Refill the master cylinder reservoir. Bleed the braking system.

Wheel Cylinder

REMOVAL & INSTALLATION

1. Raise and support the rear of the vehicle on jackstands. Remove the wheel/tire assemblies.

2. Remove the brake drum and the brake shoes from the backing plate.

3. Disconnect and plug the brake line at the back of the wheel cylinder.

4. Remove the wheel cylinder-to-backing plate bolts and the wheel cylinders from the backing plates.

NOTE: If the wheel cylinder sticks to the backing plate, use a plastic mallet to dislodge it.

5. Remove the rubber boots from both ends of the wheel cylinder and push out the inner pistons and spring together with the rubber cups.

6. Inspect the inside of the wheel cylinder bore. If it is worn or scratched in any way, it should be honed with a wheel cylinder hone or a piece or crocus cloth until the scratches are removed.

NOTE: For safety reasons, Chilton recommends to replace the wheel cylinders instead of overhauling them.

7. Replace the rubber cups with new ones. The internal replacement parts are usually supplied in a wheel cylinder rebuilding kit.

8. Reassemble the wheel cylinder.

9. To install, reverse the removal procedures. Bleed the rear brake system.

Parking Brake Cable
ADJUSTMENT

1: Pull the parking brake lever up forcefully. Release it and repeat several times.

2. It should take the specified number of notches to apply the parking brake:
1981-82 – 6–9 notches – all models
1983-88 – 3–5 notches – all models, except Justy
1987-88 – 6 notches – Justy

3. Loosen the locknut on the turnbuckle and adjust the length of the cable, so that the parking brake is applied within specifications.

4. Tighten the locknut and recheck operation of the parking brake lever.

REMOVAL & INSTALLATION

All Models – Except Justy

1. Loosen the wheel nuts, then raise and support the front of the vehicle on jackstands. Remove the front wheels.

2. Remove the parking brake cover and loosen the locknut. Loosen the parking brake adjuster until the tension is almost released, then, disconnect the inner cable ends from the equalizer.

3. Remove the clips that fasten the cable grommets in place where the cable passes through the body.

4. Pull the parking brake cable clamp from the caliper and disconnect the end of the cable.

NOTE: On 1981 vehicles, remove the front-most exhaust system cover.

5. Remove the cable-to-transverse link bracket bolts and the bracket.

6. Remove the cable-to-crossmember bracket bolt and the bracket.

7. Detach the cable rear crossmember guide and pull the cable from the passenger compartment.

8. To install, reverse the removal procedures. Make sure the cable passes through the guide inside the driveshaft tunnel. Adjust the parking brakes.

Justy

1. Set the parking brake lever.

2. Remove the hub cap, the cotter pin, the castle nut and the wheel lug nuts.

3. Raise and support the rear of vehicle on jackstands. Release the brake lever.

4. Remove the wheel assemblies and the brake drums.

5. Disassemble the equalizer joint to separate the parking brake cable from the rod.

6. Remove the exhaust cover-to-vehicle bolts and the cover.

7. Remove the cable clamps and the hangers.

8. Disconnect the parking brake cable from the parking brake lever.

9. Disconnect the parking brake cable from the backing plate of the rear brake assemblies.

10. To install, reverse the removal procedures. Torque the mounting clamps and hanger bolts to 9–17 ft. lbs. and the exhaust cover-to-body bolts to 4–7 ft. lbs. Adjust the parking brakes.

CHASSIS ELECTRICAL
Heater Unit

Most 1981 Subaru's use dealer-installed air conditioning units which work separately from the vehicle's heating system. Therefore, heater service should be unaffected by the addition of air conditioning, save only that some of the A/C components may get in the way during heater removal and installation. In this case DO NOT attempt to service any of the A/C system components; if accidentally discharge, refrigerant could cause severe burns or damage could result to the air conditioning system.

Blower Motor

REMOVAL & INSTALLATION

With A/C
EXCEPT XT COUPE AND JUSTY

1. Disconnect the negative battery terminal from the battery.

2. Remove the luggage shelf and glovebox.

3. Remove the heater duct-to-blower case screws and the heater duct from the case.

4. Set the mode lever to CIRC for access, then disconnect the vacuum hose from the actuator.

5. Disconnect the blower electrical connector. Remove the actuator-to-blower case screws and a clip, then separate the actuator from the blower case.

6. Remove the blower case assembly from the body of the heater unit. Remove the blower/motor assembly bolts, the blower/motor assembly and seal from the case.

7. If replacing the motor, remove the attaching nut, washers and pull the blower from the motor shaft. Transfer these parts to the new motor.

8. To install, reverse the removal procedures. Make sure the seal is in good condition, if necessary, replace it.

XT COUPE ONLY

1. Remove the lower cover from the passenger-side of the instrument panel.

2. Remove the glove box.

3. Remove the heater duct (or separate evaporator from the blower assembly for air conditioner equipped vehicles).

4. Disconnect the motor harness and the resistor harness.

5. Remove the blower assembly.

6. To install, reverse the removal procedures. Torque the blower assembly mounting bolts 4.0–6.9 ft. lbs.

With A/C
ALL MODELS—EXCEPT JUSTY

1. Disconnect the vacuum hose and the electrical connector from the air conditioning unit.

2. Remove the blower cage-to-chassis bolts.

3. Remove the motor-to-blower case bolts and separate the motor from the case.

4. If replacing the motor, transfer the blower wheel to the new motor by removing the attaching nut, the washers and install these parts on the new motor.

5. To install, reverse the removal procedures.

JUSTY

1. Disconnect the negative battery terminal from the battery.

2. Remove the instrument panel-to-blower motor electrical harness connector from the blower motor.

3. Remove the resistor-to-instrument panel electrical connector.

4. Remove the blower assembly from the vehicle.

5. Remove the blower motor-to-

blower assembly screws and the motor from the assembly.

6. Remove the fan-to-motor nut and the fan from the motor.

NOTE: When installing the blower assembly, BE SURE that the electrical harness is not caught in the motor flange.

7. To install, reverse the removal procedures.

Heater Core
REMOVAL & INSTALLATION

NOTE: The heater unit must be removed from the vehicle to service the heater core.

All Models—Except Justy

1. Remove the water valve cover and disconnect the water valve.

2. Disconnect the control rod from the defroster doors.

3. Separate the heater case by removing the twelve retaining springs.

4. Disconnect the air intake shutter return spring. Remove the heater core.

5. To replace the blower motor, remove three screws that hold it in place. The blower wheel is mounted on the motor shaft and may be removed by taking off the large nut that secures it.

6. To install, reverse the removal procedures. Be sure to check the operation of intake shutter spring.

Justy

1. Refer to the "Heater Unit, Removal and Installation" procedures in this section and remove the heater unit from the vehicle.

2. Remove the heater core cushion.

3. Loosen the heater core holder and remove the holder.

4. Pull the heater core from the heater unit.

5. To install, replace the urethane seal and reverse the removal procedures. Refill the cooling system.

Heater Unit
REMOVAL & INSTALLATION

All Models—Except XT Coupe and Justy

The heater unit contains the core and blower. The entire assembly must be removed from the vehicle before either the blower or core can be serviced.

1. Disconnect the negative battery terminal from the battery.

2. Position a drain pan under the radiator, remove the drain plug and

drain the engine coolant to a level below the heater unit.

3. Disconnect the heater hoses from the heater unit.

4. Remove the rubber grommet the heater hoses run through on the kick panel inside the vehicle. The location is slightly above and to the right of the accelerator pedal.

5. Remove the radio box or console and the instrument panel.

6. If equipped with a luggage shelf, remove it.

7. Disconnect the heater control cables and the fan motor electrical harness.

8. Disconnect the heater unit-to-blower assembly duct. Remove the ducts from the right and left defroster nozzles.

9. Remove the heater unit-to-chassis bolts, lift the unit and remove it from the vehicle.

10. To install, reverse the removal procedures. Refill the cooling system. Start the engine, allow it to reach normal operating temperatures and check for leaks.

XT Coupe

1. Position a drain pan under the radiator, remove the drain plug and drain the engine coolant to a level below the heater unit.

2. From the engine compartment, remove inlet/outlet heater hoses from the heater unit.

3. Remove the instrument panel-to-dash screws and the instrument panel from the vehicle.

4. Disconnect the electrical harness coming from motor and the temperature control cable.

5. Remove the heater unit; be careful not to spill the residual coolant in the heater core.

6. To install, reverse the removal procedures. Torque the heater unit-to-chassis bolts to 4.0–6.9 ft. lbs. Refill the cooling system. Start the engine, allow it to reach normal operating temperatures and check for leaks.

Justy

1. Disconnect the negative battery terminal from the battery.

2. Place a catch pan under the radiator, remove the drain plug and drain the cooling system to a level below the heater unit.

3. From the engine compartment, remove the inlet/outlet hoses from the heater unit.

4. From under the instrument panel, pull the right/left defroster ducts from the defroster nozzles, then, pull the ducts from the heater unit.

5. Disconnect the fan switch-to-blower motor electrical wiring connector(s).

6. From behind the right-side of the center instrument panel, disconnect the air mix control cable from the heater unit. From behind the left-side of the center instrument panel, disconnect the mode control cable from the heater unit.

7. Remove the heater unit-to-center instrument panel bolts.

8. Remove the glove box (pocket)-to-instrument panel screws and the glove box.

9. From the blower assembly, disconnect the inside/outside air control cable.

10. Remove the instrument panel assembly.

11. Remove the heater unit-to-chassis bolts and the blower assembly-to-chassis bolts, then the heater unit; be careful not to spill the residual coolant in the heater core.

NOTE: When removing the heater unit assembly through body hole, be careful not to damage the heater pipe.

12. To install the mode cable, perform the following procedures:

a. Place the mode lever in the VENT position.

b. Turn the mode lever downward so that the link boss (which connects the cable ring) is positioned farthest from the clamp (flush mounted) to heat case.

c. Position the mode cable ring in the link boss, pull it fully toward the clamp and clamp it securely; make sure that the mode link does not move from its lowest position.

d. Push the cable ring into the link boss, then ensure proper connection.

13. To install the inside/outside air cable, perform the following procedures:

a. Manually set the inside/outside air shutter to allow the inside blower air inlet to Open.

b. On the control panel, position the inside/outside air control lever on CIRC. Position the inside/outside air cable ring in the blower link boss, pull it fully toward the clamp flush-mounted to the heater case and clamp it securely; make sure that the blower link does not move away from its position.

c. Push the cable connecting ring into the link boss, to ensure that it is properly connected.

14. To install the air mix cable, perform the following procedures:

a. On the control panel, position the temperature control lever to the HOT position.

b. Turn the air mix link downward so that the air mix link boss is positioned farthest from the clamp

(flush-mounted) to the heater case.

c. Position the air mix cable ring in the link boss, pull it fully toward the clamp and clamp it; be sure that the link does not move away from its lowest position.

d. Push the cable connecting ring into the link boss to ensure proper connection.

15. To complete the installation, reverse the removal procedures. Refill the cooling system. Start the engine, allow it to reach normal operating temperatures and check for leaks.

Windshield Wiper Motor

REMOVAL & INSTALLATION

All Models—Except Justy

1. Disconnect the negative battery terminal from the battery.

2. Remove the wiper blades from the wiper arms by pulling the retaining lever up and sliding the blade away from the arm.

3. Slide the covering boot up the wiper arm.

4. Remove the wiper arms-to-linkage nuts and the arms.

5. Disconnect the electrical wiring connectors from the wiper motor.

6. Remove the cowl-to-body screws and the cowl from the vehicle.

7. Find or fabricate a ring which has the same diameter as the outer diameter of the plastic joint that retains the linkage to the wiper motor. Force the ring down over the joint to force the four plastic retaining jaws inward, then disconnect and remove the linkage.

8. Remove the wiper motor-to-firewall bolts and the motor.

9. To install, reverse the removal procedures. Install the wiper arms after the ignition switch has been On for a few seconds to put the linkage in Park position.

Justy

FRONT

1. Disconnect the negative battery terminal from the battery.

2. At the wiper motor, disconnect the electrical connector.

3. Remove the wiper motor-to-cowl bolts.

4. Separate the wiper link from the motor.

5. Remove the wiper motor-to-cawl panel screws and the wiper motor-to-link bolts, then separate the motor from the panel.

6. If necessary, replace the wiper motor.

7. To install, reverse the removal procedures. Check the wiper operation.

REAR

1. At the rear window, pull the wiper blade outward from the arm and press down on the clip, then remove the blade from the arm.

2. Remove the wiper arm cover.

3. Loosen the wiper arm-to-wiper assembly nut, then remove the nut and the arm from the assembly.

4. Remove the wiper assembly-to-rear gate cap, nut and cushion.

5. From inside of the rear gate, remove the wiper motor assembly trim panel.

6. Disconnect the electrical connector from the wiper motor assembly.

7. Remove the wiper motor assemby-to-rear gate bolts and the motor assembly from the rear gate.

8. If necessary, replace the wiper motor.

9. To install, reverse the removal procedures. With the rear wiper motor switch in the Off position, install the wiper arm blade so that it is positioned 0.98 in. above the rear glass molding.

Instrument Cluster

REMOVAL & INSTALLATION

All Models—Except XT Coupe

1. Disconnect the negative battery terminal from the battery.

2. Remove the bolts securing the steering column and pull it down.

3. Disconnect the electrical wiring connectors, then remove the meter visor screws and the visor—except on GL and GLF models.

4. On the GL and GLF models, remove the center ventilator control lever by pulling it. Remove the three screws accessible through the ventilator grill to the right of the cluster and the one screw accessible through the grill on the left; remove the visor.

5. On the station wagon 4WD GL, remove the turn signal lamp switch.

6. Remove the combination meter screws, then pull the meter out far enough to disconnect the speedometer cable and electrical connectors from behind, then remove the combination meter.

7. To install, reverse the removal procedures.

XT Coupe

1. Remove the lower cover on the driver's-side.

2. Remove the side ventilation duct.

3. Open the fuse box lid. Remove

the fuse box-to-instrument panel screws and the fuse box.

4. Remove the lower cover on the passengers-side.

5. Using a medium prybar, pry the upper cover (at three points) from the instrument panel (both sides and middle section).

6. Remove the console.

7. Remove the steering column assembly, the combination meter and the control wing as a unit.

8. Disconnect the electrical harness connectors from the radio and other parts.

9. Remove the instrument panel-to-chassis bolts and the instrument panel from the vehicle.

10. To install, reverse the removal procedures.

NOTE: Two persons are needed to install the instrument panel in the vehicle, being careful not to strike it against adjacent parts during installation.

While setting the instrument panel in position, be careful not to obstruct the air outlets of the heater and blower with harness connectors. Also do not allow them to be caught between the bracket and the instrument panel.

Justy

1. Disconnect the negative battery terminal from the battery.

2. At the instrument cluster, remove the clips, the tapping screw, the choke knob/nut and the trim panel.

3. Remove the instrument cluster glass-to-dash screws, two clips and the glass from the instrument cluster.

4. Remove the instrument cluster-to-dash screws and pull the cluster forward.

5. Remove the speedometer cable and the electrical connectors from the rear of the instrument cluster, the remove the instrument cluster from the vehicle.

6. To install, reverse the removal procedures.

Headlight Switch

REMOVAL & INSTALLATION

All (1981-84) Models

The switch is located at the left-side of the instrument panel and is combined with the illumination intensity control switch.

1. Disconnect the negative battery terminal from the battery.

2. Remove the steering column-to-dash screws and pull downward on the steering column.

3. Remove the instrument cluster visor-to-dash screws and the visor from the instrument cluster.

4. Disconnect the electrical harness connector from the headlight switch assembly.

5. Pull the headlight knob out, then remove the headlight switch-to-visor nut and the switch from the visor.

6. To install, reverse the removal procedures. Check the operation of the headlights.

All (1985-88) Models—Except Justy

The headlight switch is a part of a lighting switch assembly, installed on a control wing at the left-side of the steering wheel.

1. Disconnect the negative battery terminal from the battery.

2. Remove the lower steering column (upper/lower) cover screws and the upper/lower covers from the column.

3. Remove the steering wheel center cover, the steering wheel-to-shaft nut and the steering wheel from the steering column.

4. Disconnect the electrical harness-to-steering column clip and band.

5. Remove the combination switch-to-steering column screws and the switch assembly from the steering wheel.

6. Remove the left-control wing-to-steering column bolts and the left-control wing from the steering column.

7. Remove the control wing case screws and separate the cases from each other; this will provide access to the headlight switch.

8. To replace the headlight switch knob, perform the following procedures:

a. Using a pin rod, lightly push the pawl (inside the switch knob) inward and pull the knob outward.

NOTE: When removing the switch knob, be careful not to damage the switch brush.

b. To install the knob onto the switch, place the knob on the switch, place your finger on the back side of the switch and squeeze the knob onto the switch.

9. If necessary, replace the headlight switch.

10. To install, reverse the removal procedures.

NOTE: When reassembling the control wing cases; be careful get the electrical harness caught between the cases.

Justy

The headlight switch is a part of a gang switch located on the left side of the instrument panel

1. Disconnect the negative battery terminal from the battery.

2. Remove the lower instrument panel cover and disconnect the electrical connectors.

3. Remove the upper instrument cluster glass screw and pull outward on the glass.

4. From the rear of the instrument panel cover, remove the lighting switch-to-panel screw and the lighting switch assembly from the cover.

5. To install, reverse the removal procedures.

Fuse Box

LOCATION

The fuse box is located under the left-side of the instrument panel. The amperage for each fuse is stamped on the fuse box cover.

If equipped with 4WD, a fuse holder is located near the ignition coil. For servicing purposes, to change 4WD to FWD, insert a 15A fuse into the FWD fuse holder. The FWD pilot lamp (on the instrument panel) will turn On to indicate the the vehicle is set in the FWD mode.

On the Justy model, a main fuse is located in the engine compartment, next to the brake master cylinder; all current (except for the starter) will flow through this fuse. When replacing the main fuse(s), be aware of the amperage rating; a 30A (pink) or a 60A (yellow).

Fusible Link

LOCATION

All Models—Except Justy

Fusible links are located next to the positive battery terminal. All current except for the starter motor flows through it. If excessive current flows through it, the fusible metal melts, which will in turn open the circuit. This action will protect the electrical equipment from damage.

Toyota

Camry, Celica, Corona, Corolla, Cressida, MR2, Starlet, Supra, Tercel, Van

SERIAL NUMBER IDENTIFICATION

Vehicle Identification Plate

All models have the vehicle identification number (VIN) stamped on a plate which is attached to the left side of the instrument panel. This plate is visible through the windshield.

The serial number consists of a series identification number followed by a six digit production number.

Engine Number

Basically, 1981-88 Toyota vehicles have used eight types of engines: The "A"series (1A-C, 3A, 3A-C, 4A-C, 4A-CL, 4A-GE, 4A-GEC, 4A-GELC); "M" series (4M-E, 5M-E, 5M-GE, 7M-GE, 7M-GTE);"R" series (20R, 22R, 22R-E);"S" series (2S-E, 3S-GE, 3S-FE); "T" series (3T-C); "E" series (3E); "C" series diesel (1C-L, 1C-TL, 2C-L) and the "Y" series (3Y-EC, 4Y-EC). Engines within each series are similar, as the cylinder block designs are the same. Variances within each series may be due to ignition types (point of electronic), displacements (bore X stroke), cylinder head design (single or double overhead camshafts and fuel injection). Refer to the accompanying engine I.D. chart.

When ordering engine parts, it may be necessary to obtain the engine serial number. Serial numbers of the engines may be found on the following locations:

"A" and "E" series engines—stamped vertically on the left side rear of the engine block.

"K" series engines—stamped on the right side of the engine, below the spark plugs.

"M" series engines—stamped horizontally on the passengers side of the engine block, behind the alternator.

"R" series engine—stamped horizontally on the driver's side of the engine, behind the alternator.

"T" series engines—stamped horizontally on the driver's side of the engine, just above the alternator.

"S" and "C" engines—stamped horizontally on the right side of the block.

ENGINE IDENTIFICATION

Year	Model	Engine Displacement cu. in. (cc/liter)	Engine Series Identification	No. of Cylinders	Engine Type
1981	Tercel	88.6 (1452/1.4)	1A-C, 3A, 3A-C	4	SOHC
	Corolla	108.0 (1770/1.8)	3T-C	4	OHV
	Starlet	78.7 (1290/1.3)	4K-C	4	OHV
	Corona	144.4 (2367/2.4)	22R	4	SOHC
	Celica	144.4 (2367/2.4)	22R	4	SOHC
	Supra	168.4 (2759/2.8)	5M-E	6	SOHC
	Cressida	168.4 (2759/2.8)	5M-E	6	SOHC

ENGINE IDENTIFICATION

Year	Model	Engine Displacement cu. in. (cc/liter)	Engine Series Identification	No. of Cylinders	Engine Type
1982	Tercel	88.6 (1452/1.4)	1A-C, 3A, 3A-C	4	SOHC
	Corolla	108.0 (1770/1.8)	3T-C	4	OHV
	Starlet	78.7 (1290/1.3)	4K-C	4	OHV
	Corona	144.4 (2367/2.4)	22R	4	SOHC
	Celica	144.4 (2367/2.4)	22R	4	SOHC
	Supra	168.4 (2759/2.8)	5M-GE	6	DOHC
	Cressida	168.4 (2759/2.8)	5M-E	6	SOHC
1983	Tercel	88.6 (1452/1.4)	3A, 3A-C	4	SOHC
	Corolla	97.0 (1587/1.6)	4A-C, 4A-LC	4	SOHC
	Starlet	78.7 (1290/1.3)	4K-E	4	OHV
	Camry	121.7 (1995/2.0)	2S-E	4	SOHC
	Celica	144.4 (2367/2.4)	22R, 22R-E	4	SOHC
	Supra	168.4 (2759/2.8)	5M-GE	6	DOHC
	Cressida	168.4 (2759/2.8)	5M-GE	6	DOHC
1984	Tercel	88.6 (1452/1.4)	3A, 3A-C	4	SOHC
	Corolla	97.0 (1587/1.6)	4A-C, 4A-LC	4	SOHC
		112.2 (1839/1.8)	1C-L, 1C-LC (Diesel)	4	SOHC
	Starlet	78.7 (1290/1.3)	4K-E	4	OHV
	Camry	121.7 (1995/2.0)	2S-E	4	SOHC
		112.2 (1839/1.8)	1C-TL (Diesel)	4	SOHC, TURBO
	Celica	144.4 (2367/2.4)	22R, 22R-E	4	SOHC
	Supra	168.4 (2759/2.8)	5M-GE	6	DOHC
	Van	122.0 (1998/2.0)	3Y-EC	4	OHV
	Cressida	168.4 (2759/2.8)	5M-GE	6	DOHC
1985	Tercel	88.6 (1452/1.4)	3A, 3A-C	4	SOHC
	Corolla	97.0 (1587/1.6)	4A-C, 4A-LC	4	SOHC
		97.0 (1587/1.6)	4A-GE	4	DOHC
		112.2 (1839/1.8)	1C-L, 1C-LC (Diesel)	4	SOHC
	Camry	121.7 (1995/2.0)	2S-E	4	SOHC
		112.2 (1839/1.8)	1C-TL (Diesel)	4	SOHC, TURBO
	Celica	144.4 (2367/2.4)	22R, 22R-E	4	SOHC
	Supra	168.4 (2759/2.8)	5M-GE	6	DOHC
	MR2	97.0 (1587/1.6)	4A-GE	4	DOHC
	Van	122.0 (1998/2.0)	3Y-EC	4	OHV
	Cressida	168.4 (2759/2.8)	5M-GE	6	DOHC
1986	Tercel	88.6 (1452/1.4)	3A, 3A-C	4	SOHC
	Corolla	97.0 (1587/1.6)	4A-C, 4A-LC	4	SOHC
		97.0 (1587/1.6)	4A-GE	4	DOHC
	Camry	121.7 (1995/2.0)	2S-E	4	SOHC
		120.4 (1974/2.0)	2C-T (Diesel)	4	SOHC, TURBO

ENGINE IDENTIFICATION

Year	Model	Engine Displacement cu. in. (cc/liter)	Engine Series Identification	No. of Cylinders	Engine Type
1986	Celica	121.7 (1995/2.0)	2S-E	4	SOHC
		121.9 (1998/2.0)	3S-GE	4	DOHC
	Supra	168.4 (2759/2.8)	5M-GE	6	DOHC
		180.3 (2954/3.0)	7M-GE	6	DOHC
	MR2	97.0 (1587/1.6)	4A-GE	4	DOHC
	Van	136.5 (2237/2.2)	4Y-EC	4	OHV
	Cressida	168.4 (2759/2.8)	5M-GE	6	DOHC
1987-88	Tercel	88.6 (1452/1.4)	3A-C	4	SOHC
		88.9 (1456/1.4)	3E	4	SOHC
	Corolla	97.0 (1587/1.6)	4A-LC	4	SOHC
		97.0 (1587/1.6)	4A-GEC, 4A-GELC	4	DOHC
	Camry	121.9 (1998/2.0)	3S-FE	4	DOHC
	Celica	121.9 (1998/2.0)	3S-FE, 3S-GE	4	DOHC
	Supra	180.3 (2954/3.0)	7M-GE	6	DOHC
		180.3 (2954/3.0)	7M-GTE	6	DOHC, TURBO
	MR2	97.0 (1587/1.6)	4A-GELC	4	DOHC
	Van	136.5 (2237/2.2)	4Y-EC	4	OHV
	Cressida	168.4 (2759/2.8)	5M-GE	6	DOHC

OHV Overhead Valves
SOHC Single Overhead Camshaft
DOHC Double Overhead Camshaft

GENERAL ENGINE SPECIFICATIONS

Year	Model	Engine Displacement cu. in. (cc)	Fuel System Type	Net Horsepower @ rpm	Net Torque @ rpm (ft. lbs.)	Bore × Stroke (in.)	Compression Ratio	Oil Pressure ④
1981	Tercel	88.6 (1452)①	2 bbl	60 @ 4800	72 @ 2800	3.05 × 3.03	8.7:1	4.3
		88.6 (1452)	2 bbl	62 @ 4800	75 @ 4800	3.05 × 3.03	9.0:1	4.3
	Corolla	108.0 (1770)	2 bbl	75 @ 5000	95 @ 2600	3.35 × 3.07	9.0:1	4.3
	Starlet	78.7 (1290)	2 bbl	58 @ 5200	67 @ 3600	2.95 × 2.87	9.0:1	4.3
	Corona	144.4 (2367)	2 bbl	96 @ 4800	129 @ 2800	3.62 × 3.50	9.0:1	4.3
	Celica	144.4 (2367)	2 bbl	96 @ 4800	129 @ 2800	3.62 × 3.50	9.0:1	4.3
	Supra	168.4 (2759)	EFI	116 @ 4800	145 @ 3600	3.27 × 3.35	8.8:1	4.3
	Cressida	168.4 (2759)	EFI	116 @ 4800	145 @ 3600	3.27 × 3.35	8.8:1	4.3
1982	Tercel	88.6 (1452)①	2 bbl	60 @ 4800	72 @ 2800	3.05 × 3.03	8.7:1	4.3
		88.6 (1452)	2 bbl	62 @ 5200	75 @ 4800	3.05 × 3.03	9.0:1	4.3
	Corolla	108.0 (1770)	2 bbl	70 @ 4600	93 @ 2400	3.35 × 3.07	9.0:1	4.3
	Starlet	78.7 (1290)	2 bbl	58 @ 5200	67 @ 3600	2.95 × 2.87	9.0:1	4.3
	Corona	144.4 (2367)	2 bbl	96 @ 4800	129 @ 2800	3.62 × 3.50	9.0:1	4.3
	Celica	144.4 (2367)	2 bbl	96 @ 4800	129 @ 2800	3.62 × 3.50	9.0:1	4.3
	Supra	168.4 (2759)	EFI	145 @ 5200	155 @ 4800	3.27 × 3.35	8.8:1	4.3
	Cressida	168.4 (2759)	EFI	116 @ 4800	145 @ 3600	3.27 × 3.35	8.8:1	4.3

GENERAL ENGINE SPECIFICATIONS

Year	Model	Engine Displacement cu. in. (cc)	Fuel System Type	Net Horsepower @ rpm	Net Torque @ rpm (ft. lbs.)	Bore × Stroke (in.)	Compression Ratio	Oil Pressure ④
1983	Tercel	88.6 (1452)	2 bbl	62 @ 5200	75 @ 2800	3.05 × 3.03	9.0:1	4.3
	Corolla	97.0 (1587)	2 bbl	70 @ 4800	85 @ 2800	3.19 × 3.03	9.0:1	4.3
	Starlet	78.7 (1290)	EFI	58 @ 4200	74 @ 3400	2.95 × 2.87	9.5:1	4.3
	Camry	121.7 (1995)	EFI	93 @ 4200	113 @ 2400	3.31 × 3.54	8.7:1	4.3
	Celica	144.4 (2367)	2 bbl	96 @ 4800	129 @ 2800	3.62 × 3.50	9.0:1	4.3
		144.4 (2367)	EFI	105 @ 4800	137 @ 2800	3.62 × 3.50	9.0:1	4.3
	Supra	168.4 (2759)	EFI	150 @ 5200	159 @ 4400	3.27 × 3.35	8.8:1	4.3
	Cressida	168.4 (2759)	EFI	143 @ 5200	154 @ 4400	3.27 × 3.35	8.8:1	4.3
1984	Tercel	88.6 (1452)	2 bbl	62 @ 5200	75 @ 2800	3.05 × 3.03	9.0:1	4.3
	Corolla	97.0 (1587)	2 bbl	70 @ 4800	85 @ 2800	3.19 × 3.03	9.0:1	4.3
		112.2 (1839)	DFI	56 @ 4500	76 @ 3000	3.27 × 3.35	22.5:1	4.3
	Starlet	78.7 (1290)	EFI	58 @ 4200	74 @ 3400	2.95 × 2.87	9.5:1	4.3
	Camry	121.7 (1995)	EFI	93 @ 4200	113 @ 2400	3.31 × 3.54	8.7:1	4.3
		112.2 (1839)	TDFI	73 @ 4500	104 @ 3000	3.27 × 3.35	22.5:1	4.3
	Celica	144.4 (2367)	2 bbl	96 @ 4800	129 @ 2800	3.62 × 3.50	9.0:1	4.3
		144.4 (2367)	EFI	105 @ 4800	137 @ 2800	3.62 × 3.50	9.0:1	4.3
	Supra	168.4 (2759)	EFI	150 @ 5200	159 @ 4400	3.27 × 3.35	8.8:1	4.3
	Van	122.0 (1998)	EFI	90 @ 4400	120 @ 3000	3.39 × 3.39	8.8:1	4.3
	Cressida	168.4 (2759)	EFI	143 @ 5200	154 @ 4400	3.27 × 3.35	8.8:1	4.3
1985	Tercel	88.6 (1452)	2 bbl	62 @ 4800	76 @ 2800	3.05 × 3.03	9.0:1	4.3
	Corolla	97.0 (1587)	2 bbl	70 @ 4800	85 @ 2800	3.19 × 3.03	9.0:1	4.3
		97.0 (1587)	EFI	112 @ 6600	97 @ 4800	3.19 × 3.03	9.4:1	4.3
		112.2 (1839)	DFI	56 @ 4500	76 @ 3000	3.27 × 3.35	22.5:1	4.3
	Camry	121.7 (1995)	EFI	93 @ 4200	113 @ 2400	3.31 × 3.54	8.7:1	4.3
		112.2 (1839)	TDFI	73 @ 4500	104 @ 3000	3.27 × 3.35	22.5:1	4.3
	Celica	144.4 (2367)	2 bbl	96 @ 4800	129 @ 2800	3.62 × 3.50	9.0:1	4.3
		144.4 (2367)	EFI	116 @ 4800	140 @ 2800	3.62 × 3.50	9.0:1	4.3
	Supra	168.4 (2759)	EFI	161 @ 5600	169 @ 4400	3.27 × 3.35	8.8:1	4.3
	MR2	97.0 (1587)	EFI	112 @ 6600	97 @ 4800	3.19 × 3.03	9.4:1	4.3
	Van	122.0 (1998)	EFI	90 @ 4400	120 @ 3000	3.39 × 3.39	8.8:1	4.3
	Cressida	168.4 (2759)	EFI	156 @ 5200	165 @ 4400	3.27 × 3.35	8.8:1	4.3
1986	Tercel	88.6 (1452)	2 bbl	62 @ 4800	76 @ 2800	3.05 × 3.03	9.0:1	4.3
	Corolla	97.0 (1587)	2 bbl	74 @ 5200	85 @ 2800	3.19 × 3.03	9.0:1	4.3
		97.0 (1587)	EFI	112 @ 6600	97 @ 4800	3.19 × 3.03	9.4:1	4.3
	Camry	121.7 (1995)	EFI	95 @ 4400	116 @ 4000	3.31 × 3.54	8.7:1	4.3
		120.4 (1974)	TDFI	79 @ 4500	117 @ 3000	3.39 × 3.39	23.0:1	4.3
	Celica	121.7 (1995)	EFI	97 @ 4400	118 @ 4000	3.31 × 3.54	8.7:1	4.3
		121.9 (1998)	EFI	135 @ 6000	125 @ 4800	3.39 × 3.39	9.2:1	4.3
	Supra	168.4 (2759)	EFI	161 @ 5600	169 @ 4400	3.27 × 3.35	9.2:1	4.3
		180.3 (2954)	EFI	200 @ 6000	185 @ 4800	3.27 × 3.58	9.2:1	4.3
	MR2	97.0 (1587)	EFI	112 @ 6600	97 @ 4800	3.19 × 3.03	9.4:1	4.3

GENERAL ENGINE SPECIFICATIONS

Year	Model	Engine Displacement cu. in. (cc)	Fuel System Type	Net Horsepower @ rpm	Net Torque @ rpm (ft. lbs.)	Bore × Stroke (in.)	Compression Ratio	Oil Pressure ④
1986	Van	136.5 (2237)	EFI	101 @ 4400	132 @ 3000	3.58 × 3.40	8.8:1	4.3
	Cressida	168.4 (2759)	EFI	156 @ 5200	165 @ 4400	3.27 × 3.35	9.2:1	4.3
1987-88	Tercel	88.6 (1452)	2 bbl	62 @ 4800	76 @ 2800	3.05 × 3.03	9.0:1	4.3
		88.9 (1456)	2 bbl	78 @ 6000	87 @ 4000	2.87 × 3.54	9.3:1	4.3
	Corolla	97.0 (1587)	2 bbl	74 @ 5200	86 @ 2800	3.19 × 3.03	9.0:1	4.3
		97.0 (1587)	EFI	112 @ 6600②	97 @ 4800	3.19 × 3.03	9.4:1	4.3
	Camry	121.9 (1998)	EFI	115 @ 5200	124 @ 4400	3.39 × 3.39	9.3:1	4.3
	Celica	121.9 (1998)	EFI	115 @ 5200	124 @ 4400	3.39 × 3.39	9.3:1	4.3
		121.9 (1998)	EFI	135 @ 6000	125 @ 4800	3.39 × 3.39	9.2:1	4.3
	Supra	180.3 (2954)	EFI	200 @ 6000	185 @ 4800	3.27 × 3.58	9.2:1	4.3
		180.3 (2954)	EFI③	230 @ 5600	246 @ 4000	3.27 × 3.58	8.4:1	4.3
	MR2	97.0 (1587)	EFI	112 @ 6600	97 @ 4800	3.19 × 3.03	9.4:1	4.3
	Van	136.5 (2237)	EFI	101 @ 4400	132 @ 3000	3.58 × 3.40	8.8:1	4.3
	Cressida	168.4 (2759)	EFI	156 @ 5200	165 @ 4400	3.27 × 3.35	9.2:1	4.3

EFI Electronic Fuel Injection
DFI Diesel Fuel Injection
TDFI Turbodiesel Fuel Injection
① 1A-C
② FX-16: 108 @ 6600
③ Turbocharged
④ At idle

GASOLINE ENGINE TUNE-UP SPECIFICATIONS

Year	Model	Engine Displacement cu. in. (cc)	Spark Plugs Type	Gap (in.)	Ignition Timing (deg.) MT	AT	Compression Pressure (psi)	Fuel Pump (psi)	Idle Speed (rpm) MT	AT	Valve Clearance In.	Ex.
1981	Tercel	88.6 (1452)①	BP6EK-A	0.039	5B	—	177	2.6–3.5	650	—	0.008	0.012
		88.6 (1452)②	BPR5EA-L	0.031	5B	5B	177	2.6–3.5	650	800	0.008	0.012
		88.6 (1452)③	BPR5EA-11	0.043	5B	5B	177	2.6–3.5	550	800	0.008	0.012
	Corolla	108.0 (1770)	BPR5EA	0.043	7B	7B	163	2.6–3.5	850	850	0.008	0.013
	Starlet	78.7 (1290)	BPR5EA-11 ④	0.043	8B	—	156	2.8–4.2	650	—	0.008	0.012
	Corona	144.4 (2367)	BPR5EA-L	0.031	8B	8B	171	2.2–4.3	800	850	0.008	0.012
	Celica	144.4 (2367)	BPR5EA-L	0.031	8B	8B	171	2.2–4.3	800	850	0.008	0.012
	Supra	168.4 (2759)	BPR5EA-L	0.031	8B	8B	156	33–38	800	800	0.011	0.014
	Cressida	168.4 (2759)	BPR5EA-L	0.031	—	8B	156	33–38	—	800	0.011	0.014
1982	Tercel	88.6 (1452)①	BP6EK-A	0.039	5B	—	177	2.6–3.5	650	—	0.008	0.012
		88.6 (1452)②	BPR5EA-L	0.031	5B	5B	177	2.6–3.5	650	800	0.008	0.012
		88.6 (1452)③	BPR5EA-11	0.043	5B	5B	177	2.6–3.5	550	800	0.008	0.012

GASOLINE ENGINE TUNE-UP SPECIFICATIONS

Year	Model	Engine Displacement cu. in. (cc)	Spark Plugs Type	Gap (in.)	Ignition Timing (deg.) MT	AT	Compression Pressure (psi)	Fuel Pump (psi)	Idle Speed (rpm) MT	AT	Valve Clearance In.	Ex.
1982	Corolla	108.0 (1770)	BPR5EA-11 ⑤	0.043	7B	7B	163	2.6–3.5	⑥	⑥	0.008	0.013
	Starlet	78.7 (1290)	BPR5EA-11 ④	0.043	12B	—	156	2.8–4.2	650	—	0.008	0.012
	Corona	144.4 (2367)	BPR5EA-L	0.031	8B	8B	171	2.2–4.3	700⑦	750⑦	0.008	0.012
	Celica	144.4 (2367)	BPR5EA-L	0.031	8B	8B	171	2.2–4.3	700⑦	750⑦	0.008	0.012
	Supra	168.4 (2759)	BPR5EY	0.031	8B	8B	164	35–38	650	650	Hyd.	Hyd.
	Cressida	168.4 (2759)	BPR5EA-L	0.031	—	8B	156	33–38	—	800	0.011	0.014
1983	Tercel	88.6 (1452)②	BPR5EA-L	0.031	5B	5B	178	2.6–3.5	⑧	⑧	0.008	0.012
		88.6 (1452)③	BPR5EA-11	0.043	5B	5B	178	2.6–3.5	⑨	⑨	0.008	0.012
	Corolla	97.0 (1587)	BPR5EA-L11 ④	0.043	5B	5B	178	2.5–3.5	⑩	⑩	0.008	0.012
	Starlet	78.7 (1290)	BPR5EP-11	0.043	5B	—	185	36–38	700	—	Hyd.	Hyd.
	Camry	121.7 (1995)	BPR5EA-L11	0.043	5B	5B	171	28–36	700	700	Hyd.	Hyd.
	Celica	144.4 (2367)	BPR5EY	0.031	8B	8B	171	2.5–3.8	700	700	0.008	0.012
		144.4 (2367)	BPR5EY	0.031	5B	5B	171	35–38	750	750	0.008	0.012
	Supra	168.4 (2759)	BPR5EP-11	0.043	10B	10B	164	35–38	650	650	Hyd.	Hyd.
	Cressida	168.4 (2759)	BPR5EP-11	0.043	—	10B	164	35–38	—	650	Hyd.	Hyd.
1984	Tercel	88.6 (1452)②	BPR5EA-L	0.031	5B	5B	178	2.6–3.5	⑧	⑧	0.008	0.012
		88.6 (1452)③	BPR5EA-11 ⑪	0.043	5B	5B	178	2.6–3.5	⑨	⑨	0.008	0.012
	Corolla	97.0 (1587)	BPR5EL-L11 ⑫	0.043	5B	5B	178	2.5–3.5	⑬	⑬	0.008	0.012
	Starlet	78.7 (1290)	BPR5EP-11	0.043	5B	—	185	36–38	700	—	Hyd.	Hyd.
	Camry	121.7 (1995)	BPR5EA-L11	0.043	5B	5B	171	28–36	700	750	Hyd.	Hyd.
	Celica	144.4 (2367)	BPR5EY	0.031	8B	8B	171	2.5–3.8	700	700	0.008	0.012
		144.4 (2367)	BPR5EY	0.031	5B	5B	171	35–38	750	750	0.008	0.012
	Supra	168.4 (2759)	BPR5EP-11	0.043	10B	10B	164	35–38	650	650	Hyd.	Hyd.
	Van	122.0 (1998)	BPR5EP-11	0.043	8B	8B	171	33–38	700	750	Hyd.	Hyd.
	Cressida	168.4 (2759)	BPR5EP-11	0.043	—	10B	164	35–38	—	650	Hyd.	Hyd.
1985	Tercel	88.6 (1452)②	BPR5EY	0.031	5B	5B	178	2.6–3.5	⑧	⑧	0.008	0.012
		88.6 (1452)③	BPR5EY-11 ⑭	0.043	5B	5B	178	2.6–3.5	⑨	⑨	0.008	0.012
	Corolla	97.0 (1587)	BPR5EY-11 ⑱	0.043	5B	5B	178	2.5–3.5	⑬	⑬	0.008	0.012
		97.0 (1597)	BCPR5EP-11	0.043	10B	—	179	33–39	800	—	0.008	0.012
	Camry	121.7 (1995)	BPR5EA-L11	0.043	5B	5B	171	28–36	700	750	Hyd.	Hyd.
	Celica	144.4 (2367)	BPR5EY	0.031	8B	8B	171	2.5–3.8	700	700	0.008	0.012
		144.4 (2367)	BPR5EY	0.031	5B	5B	171	35–38	750	750	0.008	0.012
	Supra	168.4 (2759)	BPR5EP-11	0.043	10B	10B	164	35–38	650	650	Hyd.	Hyd.
	MR2	97.0 (1597)	BCPR5EP-11	0.043	10B	10B	179	33–39	800	800	0.008	0.012
	Van	122.0 (1998)	BPR5EP-11	0.043	8B	8B	171	33–38	700	750	Hyd.	Hyd.

GASOLINE ENGINE TUNE-UP SPECIFICATIONS

Year	Model	Engine Displacement cu. in. (cc)	Spark Plugs Type	Gap (in.)	Ignition Timing (deg.) MT	AT	Compression Pressure (psi)	Fuel Pump (psi)	Idle Speed (rpm) MT	AT	Valve Clearance In.	Ex.
1985	Cressida	168.4 (2759)	BPR5EP-11	0.043	—	10B	164	35–38	—	650	Hyd.	Hyd.
1986	Tercel	88.6 (1452)②	BPR5EY	0.031	5B	5B	178	2.6–3.5	⑧	⑧	0.008	0.012
		88.6 (1452)③	BPR5EY-11 ⑭	0.043	5B	5B	178	2.6–3.5	⑨	⑨	0.008	0.012
	Corolla	97.0 (1587)	BPR5EY-11	0.043	5B	5B	178	2.5–3.5	⑬	⑬	0.008	0.012
		97.0 (1597)	BCPR5EP-11	0.043	10B	10B	179	33–38	800	800	0.008	0.012
	Camry	121.7 (1995)	BPR5EY-11	0.043	10B	10B	171	28–36	700	700	Hyd.	Hyd.
	Celica	121.7 (1995)	BPR5EY-11	0.043	10B	10B	171	35–38	700	700	Hyd.	Hyd.
		121.9 (1998)	BCPR5EP-11	0.043	10B	10B	171	35–38	750	750	0.008	0.012
	Supra	168.4 (2759)	BPR5EP-11	0.043	10B	10B	164	35–38	650	650	Hyd.	Hyd.
		180.3 (2954)	BCPR5EP-11	0.043	10B	10B	156	33–40	700	700	0.008	0.010
	MR2	97.0 (1597)	BCPR5EP-11	0.043	10B	10B	179	33–38	800	800	0.008	0.012
	Van	136.5 (2237)	BPR5EP-11	0.043	12B	12B	178	33–38	700	750	Hyd.	Hyd.
	Cressida	168.4 (2759)	BPR5EP-11	0.043	—	10B	164	35–38	--	650	Hyd.	Hyd.
1987	Tercel	88.6 (1452)	BPR5EY-11 ⑭	0.043	5B	5B	178	2.6–3.5	650	900	0.008	0.012
		88.9 (1456)	BPR5EY-11	0.043	3B	3B	184	2.6–3.5	650	900	0.008	0.008
	Corolla	97.0 (1587)	BPR5EY-11	0.043	5B	5B	163	2.5–3.5	700	850	0.008	0.012
		97.0 (1597)	BCPR5EP-11	0.043	10B	10B	179	33–38	800	800	0.008	0.010
	Camry	121.9 (1998)	BCPR5EY-11	0.043	10B	10B	178	38–44	700	750	0.009	0.013
	Celica	121.9 (1999) ⑯	BCPR5EY-11	0.043	10B	10B	178	38–44	700	700	0.009	0.013
		121.9 (1998)	BCPR5EP-11	0.043	10B	10B	178	33–38	750	750	0.008	0.010
	Supra	180.3 (2954)	BCPR5EP-11	0.043	10B	10B	156	33–40	700	700	0.008	0.010
		180.3 (2954) ⑰	BCPR6EP-N8	0.031	10B	10B	142	33–40	650	650	0.008	0.010
	MR2	97.0 (1597)	BCPR5EP-11	0.043	10B	10B	179	33–38	800	—	0.008	0.010
	Van	136.5 (2237)	BPR5EP-11	0.043	8B	8B	171	33–38	700	750	Hyd.	Hyd.
	Cressida	168.4 (2759)	BPR5EP-11	0.043	—	10B	164	35–38	--	650	Hyd.	Hyd.

1988   SEE UNDERHOOD SPECIFICATIONS STICKER

NOTE: The Underhood Specifications sticker often reflects tune-up specification changes made in production. Sticker figures must be used if they disagree with those in this chart.

MT Manual transmission
AT Automatic transmission
NA Not adjustable
A After Top Dead Center
B Before Top Dead Center
Hyd. Hydraulic valve lash adjusters
① 1A-C
② 3A
③ 3A-C
④ Calif.: BPR5EA-L; 0.031 in.
⑤ Canada: BPR5ES; 0.031 in.
⑥ Without power steering:
   U.S MT—650 rpm
   U.S. AT—750 rpm
   Can. MT—700 rpm
   Can. AT—750 rpm

With power steering: 850 rpm
⑦ Canada: 850 rpm
⑧ W/PS: MT—800 rpm
   AT—900 rpm
   W/O PS: MT—650 rpm
   AT—800 rpm
⑨ W/PS: MT—800 rpm
   AT: 900 rpm
   W/O PS: 4 spd—550 rpm
   5 spd—650 rpm
   AT—800 rpm
⑩ W/PS: MT—650 rpm
   AT—800 rpm
   W/O PS: MT—800 rpm
   AT—900 rpm

⑪ Calif.:BPR5EA-L11
   Can. wagon w/3A-C: BPR5EA-L
⑫ Canada: BPR5EA-L; 0.031 in.
⑬ W/PS: MT—800 rpm (1986—750 rpm)
   AT—900 rpm (1986—850 rpm)
   W/O PS: MT—700 rpm
   AT—800 rpm
⑭ Can. wagon w/MT: BPR5EY; 0.031 in.
⑮ Canada: BPR5EY; 0.031 in.
⑯ 3S-FE
⑰ Turbocharged

DIESEL ENGINE TUNE-UP SPECIFICATIONS

Year	Engine Displacement cu. in. (cc)	Valve Clearance		Intake Valve Opens (deg.)	Injection Pump Setting (deg.)	Injection Nozzle Pressure (psi)		Idle Speed (rpm)	Cranking Compression Pressure (psi)
		Intake (in.)	Exhaust (in.)			New	Used		
1984	112.2 (1839)	0.008–0.012	0.010–0.014	11B	25–30B	2062–2205	1920–2205	700	427
	112.2 (1839)①	0.008–0.012	0.010–0.014	11B	25–30B	2062–2205	1920–2205	750	427
1985	112.2 (1839)	0.008–0.012	0.010–0.014	11B	25–30B	2062–2205	1920–2205	700	427
	112.2 (1839)①	0.008–0.012	0.010–0.014	11B	25–30B	2062–2205	1920–2205	750	427
1986	120.4 (1974)	0.008–0.012	0.010–0.014	11B	25–30B	2062–2205	1920–2205	750	427

① 1C-TL turbodiesel

FIRING ORDERS

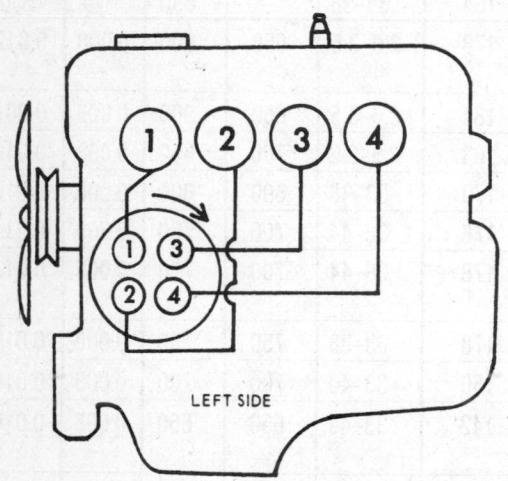

Firing order—R–series engines

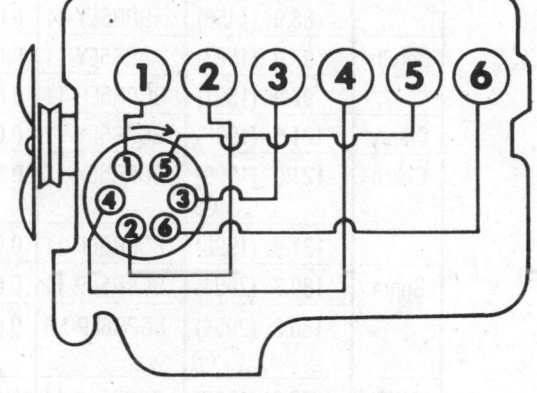

Firing order—5M-GE engines

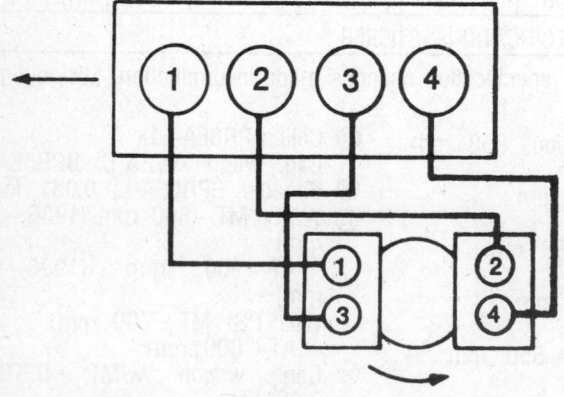

Firing order—A-series engines (1983 shown; others similar)

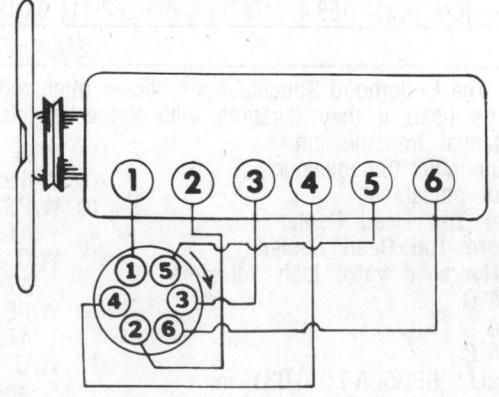

Firing order—4M-E, 5M-E engines

FIRING ORDER

NOTE: To avoid confusion, always replace spark plug wires one at a time.

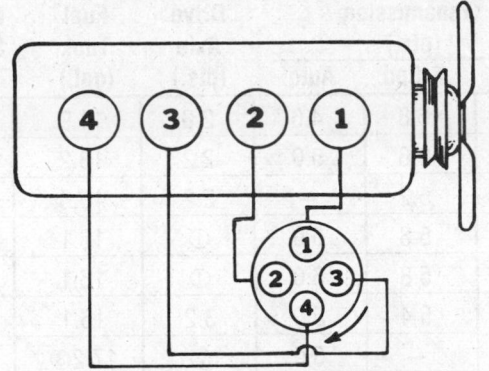

Firing order—all T— and K–series engines

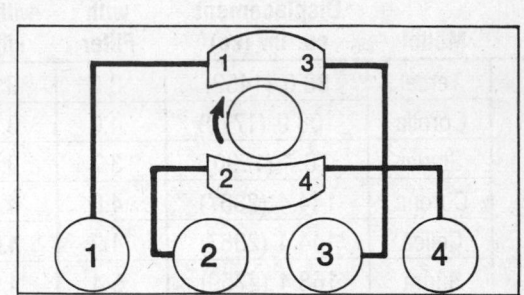

Firing order—2-SE engine

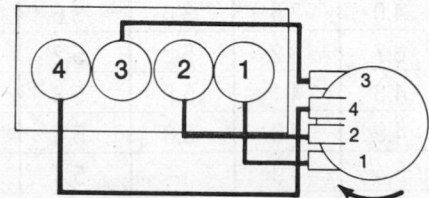

Firing order—3Y-EC, 4Y-EC, 3S-GE, 3S-FE and 4A-GE (MR2)

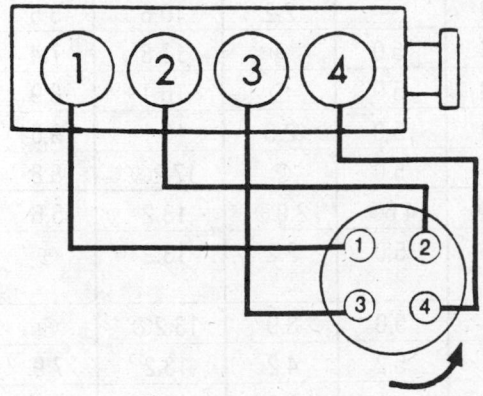

Firing order—3E

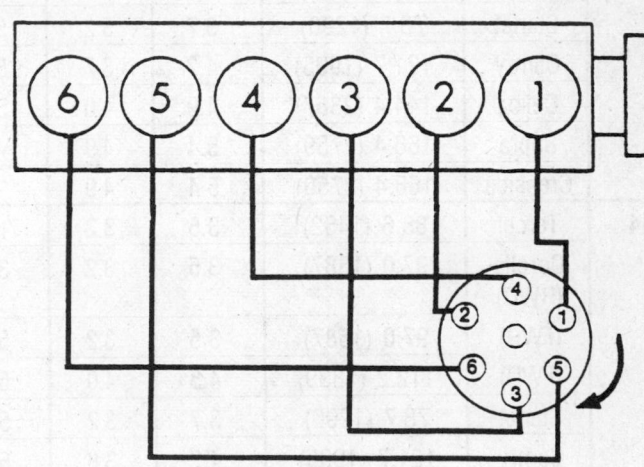

Firing order—7M-GE

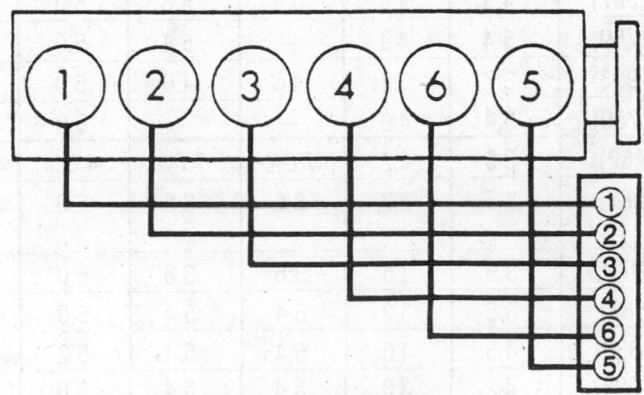

Firing order—7M-GTE

CAPACITIES

Year	Model	Engine Displacement cu. in. (cc)	Engine Crankcase with Filter	Engine Crankcase without Filter	Transmission (pts.) 4-Spd	Transmission (pts.) 5-Spd	Transmission (pts.) Auto.	Drive Axle (pts.)	Fuel Tank (gal.)	Cooling System (qts.)
1981	Tercel	88.6 (1452)	3.5	3.2	6.8	6.8	4.6	2.0	11.9	5.4
	Corolla	108.0 (1770)	4.0	3.5	3.6	3.6	5.0	2.2	13.2	8.8
	Starlet	78.7 (1290)	3.7	3.2	5.2	5.2	—	2.2	10.6	5.5
	Corona	144.4 (2367)	4.8	4.1	5.8	5.8	5.0	①	16.1	8.5
	Celica	144.4 (2367)	4.9	4.0	5.8	5.8	5.0	①	16.1	8.9
	Supra	168.4 (2759)	5.4	4.9	—	5.4	5.0	3.2	16.1	9.5
	Cressida	168.4 (2759)	5.4	4.9	—	—	5.0	②	17.2③	8.8
1982	Tercel	88.6 (1452)	3.5	3.2	6.8	6.8	4.6	2.0	11.9	5.4
	Corolla	108.0 (1770)	4.0	3.5	3.6	3.6	5.0	2.2	13.2	8.8
	Starlet	78.7 (1290)	3.7	3.2	5.2	5.2	—	2.2	10.6	5.5
	Corona	144.4 (2367)	4.8	4.1	5.8	5.8	5.0	①	16.1	8.5
	Celica	144.4 (2367)	4.9	4.0	5.8	5.8	5.0	①	16.1	8.9
	Supra	168.4 (2759)	5.4	4.9	—	5.4	5.0	2.6	16.1	8.5
	Cressida	168.4 (2759)	5.4	4.9	—	—	5.0	②	17.2③	8.8
1983	Tercel	88.6 (1452)	3.5	3.2	6.8④	6.8④	4.6⑤	2.0⑥	11.9	5.4
	Corolla	97.0 (1587)	3.5	3.2	3.6	3.6	5.0	2.2	13.2⑦	⑧
	Starlet	78.7 (1290)	3.7	3.2	5.2	5.2	—	2.2	10.6	5.5
	Camry	121.7 (1995)	4.2	3.7	5.4	5.4	5.0	⑨	13.8	7.4
	Celica	144.4 (2367)	4.9	4.0	5.8	5.8	5.0	①	16.1	8.9
	Supra	168.4 (2759)	5.4	4.9	—	5.4	5.0	2.6	16.1	9.5
	Cressida	168.4 (2759)	5.4	4.9	—	—	5.0	②	17.2③	8.8
1984	Tercel	88.6 (1452)	3.5	3.2	7.0④	7.0④	4.6⑤	2.0⑥	13.2	5.6
	Corolla (RWD)	97.0 (1587)	3.5	3.2	3.6	3.6	5.0	2.2	13.2	⑧
	(FWD)	97.0 (1587)	3.5	3.2	5.4	5.4	5.0	3.0	13.2⑦	⑧
	(FWD)	112.2 (1839)	4.5	4.0	5.4	5.4	5.2	4.2	13.2	7.9
	Starlet	78.7 (1290)	3.7	3.2	5.2	5.2	—	2.2	10.6	5.5
	Camry	121.7 (1995)	4.2	3.8	5.4	5.4	5.0	4.2	14.5	7.4
		112.2 (1839)	4.5	4.0	5.4	5.4	5.0	4.2	14.5	8.9
	Celica	144.4 (2367)	4.9	4.0	5.8	5.8	5.0	⑪	16.1	8.9
	Supra	168.4 (2759)	5.4	4.9	—	5.4	5.0	2.6	16.1	7.8
	Van	122.0 (1998)	3.7	3.2	4.6	4.6	5.0	2.6	15.9	7.5
	Cressida	168.4 (2759)	5.4	4.9	—	—	5.0	2.6⑫	18.2③	9.2
1985	Tercel	88.6 (1452)	3.5	3.2	7.0④	7.0④	4.6⑤	2.0⑥	13.2	5.6
	Corolla (RWD)	97.0 (1587)	3.5	3.2	3.6	3.6	5.0	2.2	13.2	⑧
	(FWD)	97.0 (1587)❸	3.9	3.5	3.6	3.6	5.0	2.8	13.2	⑧
	(FWD)	97.0 (1587)	3.5	3.2	5.4	5.4	5.0	3.0	13.2⑦	⑧
	(FWD)	112.2 (1839)	4.5	4.0	5.4	5.4	5.2	4.2	13.2	7.9
	Camry	121.7 (1995)	4.2	3.8	5.4	5.4	5.0	4.2	14.5	7.4
		112.2 (1839)	4.5	4.0	5.4	5.4	5.0	4.2	14.5	8.9

CAPACITIES

Year	Model	Engine Displacement cu. in. (cc)	Engine Crankcase with Filter	Engine Crankcase without Filter	Transmission (pts.) 4-Spd	Transmission (pts.) 5-Spd	Transmission (pts.) Auto.	Drive Axle (pts.)	Fuel Tank (gal.)	Cooling System (qts.)
1985	Celica	144.4 (2367)	4.9	4.0	5.8	5.8	5.0	(11)	16.1	8.9
	Supra	168.4 (2759)	5.4	4.9	—	5.4	5.0	2.6	16.1	7.8
	MR2	97.0 (1587)	3.9	3.5	—	4.8	—	—	10.8	13.6
	Van	122.0 (1998)	3.7	3.2	4.6	4.6	5.0	2.6	15.9	7.5
	Cressida	168.4 (2759)	5.4	4.9	—	—	5.0	2.6⑫	18.2③	9.2
1986	Tercel	88.6 (1452)	3.5	3.2	7.0④	7.0④	4.6⑤	2.0⑥	13.2	5.6
	Corolla (RWD)	97.0 (1587)	3.5	3.2	3.6	3.6	5.0	2.2	13.2	⑧
	(RWD)	97.0 (1587)⑬	3.9	3.5	3.6	3.6	5.0	2.8	13.2	⑧
	(FWD)	97.0 (1587)	3.5	3.2	5.4	5.4	5.0	3.0	13.2⑦	⑧
	Camry	121.7 (1995)	4.2	3.8	5.4	5.4	5.0	4.2	14.5	7.4
		112.2 (1839)	4.5	4.0	5.4	5.4	5.0	4.2	14.5	8.9
	Celica	121.7 (1995)	4.2	3.8	5.4	5.4	5.0	4.2	15.9	7.4
		121.9 (1998)	4.1	3.8	5.4	5.4	5.0	4.2	15.9	7.4
	Supra	168.4 (2759)	5.4	4.9	—	5.4	5.0	2.6	16.1	7.8
		180.3 (2954)	4.7	3.9	—	5.0	3.4	2.8	18.5	8.6
	MR2	97.0 (1587)	3.9	3.5	—	4.8	—	—	10.8	13.6
	Van	122.0 (1998)	3.7	3.2	4.6	4.6	5.0	2.6	15.9	8.9
	Cressida	168.4 (2759)	5.4	4.9	—	—	5.0	2.6⑫	18.2③	9.2
1987-88	Tercel	88.6 (1452)	3.5	3.2	7.2④	7.2④	4.6⑤	2.0	13.2	5.6
		88.9 (1456)	3.4	3.1	5.0	5.0	5.2	3.0	11.9	4.9
	Corolla (RWD)	97.0 (1587)	3.5	3.2	3.6	3.6	5.0	2.2	13.2	⑧
	(RWD)	97.0 (1587)⑬	3.9	3.5	3.6	3.6	5.0	2.8	13.2	⑧
	(FWD)	97.0 (1587)	3.5	3.2	5.4	5.4	5.0	3.0	13.2⑦	6.3
	Camry	121.9 (1998)	4.3	3.9	5.4	5.4	5.2	3.4	15.9	6.8
	Celica	121.9 (1998)	4.3	3.9	5.4	5.4	4.2	3.4	15.9	6.8
		121.9 (1998)⑭	4.1	3.8	5.4	5.4	5.0	3.4	15.9	7.4
	Supra	180.3 (2954)	4.7	3.9	—	5.0	3.4	2.8	18.5	8.6
		180.3 (2954)⑮	4.7	3.9	—	6.4	3.4	2.8	18.5	8.7
	MR2	97.0 (1587)	3.9	3.5	—	4.8	—	—	10.8	13.6
	Van (2wd)	122.0 (1998)	3.7	3.2	4.6	4.6	5.2	3.0	15.9	8.9
	(4wd)	122.0 (1998)	3.7	3.2	5.4	5.4	—	⑯	15.9	7.9
	Cressida	168.4 (2759)	5.4	4.9	—	5.0	3.4	2.6⑫	18.5	8.7

① Unitized: 2.6
   Banjo: 2.8
② 7.5 in.: 1.3
   8.0 in.: 1.9
③ Station wagon: 16.2
④ 4wd: 4.1
⑤ 4wd: 4.4
⑥ 4wd: 2.2
⑦ Station wagon: 12.4

⑧ 1983-84: MT—5.7, AT—6.6
   1985-87: FWD—6.3; RWD MT—5.9, AT—5.8
⑨ MT: 5.4
   AT: 4.2
⑩ FWD: 5.4
⑪ IRS W/MT: 2.6; W/AT: 2.2

⑫ Station wagon: 3.0
⑬ 4A-GE
⑭ 3S-GE
⑮ 7M-GTE
⑯ Front: 2.6
   Rear: 3.8

CAMSHAFT SPECIFICATIONS
All measurements given in inches.

Year	Engine Displacement cu. in. (cc)	Journal Diameter 1	2	3	4	5	6	7	Bearing Clearance	Camshaft End Play
1981	1A-C,3A, 3A-C 88.6 (1452)	1.1015– 1.1022	1.1015– 1.1022	1.1015– 1.1022	1.1015– 1.1022	—	—	—	0.0015– 0.0029	0.0031– 0.0071
	3T-C 108.0 (1770)	1.8291– 1.8297	1.8292– 1.8199	1.8094– 1.8100	1.7996– 1.8002	1.7897– 1.7904	—	—	0.0010– 0.0026	0.0030– 0.0060
	4K-C 78.7 (1290)	1.7011– 1.7018	1.6911– 1.6917	1.6813– 1.6819	1.6716– 1.6722	—	—	—	①	0.0030– 0.0060
	22R 144.4 (2367)	1.2984– 1.2992	1.2984– 1.2992	1.2984– 1.2992	1.2984– 1.2992	—	—	—	0.0004– 0.0020	0.0031– 0.0071
	5M-E 168.4 (2759)	1.3378– 1.3384	1.3378– 1.3384	1.3378– 1.3384	1.3378– 1.3384	1.3378– 1.3384	1.3378– 1.3384	1.3378– 1.3384	0.0007– 0.0022	0.0031– 0.0071
1982	1A-C,3A, 3A-C 88.6 (1452)	1.1015– 1.1022	1.1015– 1.1022	1.1015– 1.1022	1.1015– 1.1022	—	—	—	0.0015– 0.0029	0.0031– 0.0071
	3T-C 108.0 (1770)	1.8291– 1.8297	1.8292– 1.8199	1.8094– 1.8100	1.7996– 1.8002	1.7897– 1.7904	—	—	0.0010– 0.0026	0.0030– 0.0060
	4K-C 78.7 (1290)	1.7011– 1.7018	1.6911– 1.6917	1.6813– 1.6819	1.6716– 1.6722	—	—	—	①	0.0030– 0.0060
	22R 144.4 (2367)	1.2984– 1.2992	1.2984– 1.2992	1.2984– 1.2992	1.2984– 1.2992	—	—	—	0.0004– 0.0020	0.0031– 0.0071
	5M-E 168.4 (2759)	1.3378– 1.3384	1.3378– 1.3384	1.3378– 1.3384	1.3378– 1.3384	1.3378– 1.3384	1.3378– 1.3384	1.3378– 1.3384	0.0007– 0.0022	0.0031– 0.0071
	5M-GE 168.4 (2759)	1.4944– 1.4951	1.6913– 1.6919	1.7110– 1.7116	1.7307– 1.7313	1.7504– 1.7510	1.7700– 1.7707	1.7897– 1.7904	0.0010– 0.0026	0.0028– 0.0098
1983	3A, 3A-C 88.6 (1452)	1.1015– 1.1022	1.1015– 1.1022	1.1015– 1.1022	1.1015– 1.1022	—	—	—	0.0015– 0.0029	0.0031– 0.0071
	4A-C, 4A-LC 97.0 (1587)	1.1015– 1.1022	1.1015– 1.1022	1.1015– 1.1022	1.1015– 1.1022	—	—	—	0.0015– 0.0029	0.0031– 0.0071
	4K-E 78.7 (1290)	1.7011– 1.7018	1.6911– 1.6917	1.6813– 1.6819	1.6716– 1.6722	—	—	—	②	0.0030– 0.0060
	2S-E 121.7 (1995)	1.8291– 1.8297	1.8192– 1.8199	1.8094– 1.8100	1.7996– 1.8002	1.7897– 1.7904	1.7799– 1.7805	—	0.0010– 0.0026	0.0031– 0.0091
	22R, 22RE 144.4 (2367)	1.2984– 1.2992	1.2984– 1.2992	1.2984– 1.2992	1.2984– 1.2992	—	—	—	0.0004– 0.0020	0.0031– 0.0071
	5M-GE 168.4 (2759)	1.4944– 1.4951	1.6913– 1.6919	1.7110– 1.7116	1.7307– 1.7313	1.7504– 1.7510	1.7700– 1.7707	1.7897– 1.7904	0.0010– 0.0026	0.0028– 0.0098
1984	3A, 3A-C 88.6 (1452)	1.1015– 1.1022	1.1015– 1.1022	1.1015– 1.1022	1.1015– 1.1022	—	—	—	0.0015– 0.0029	0.0031– 0.0071
	4A-C, 4A-LC 97.0 (1587)	1.1015– 1.1022	1.1015– 1.1022	1.1015– 1.1022	1.1015– 1.1022	—	—	—	0.0015– 0.0029	0.0031– 0.0071
	4K-E 78.7 (1290)	1.7011– 1.7018	1.6911– 1.6917	1.6813– 1.6819	1.6716– 1.6722	—	—	—	②	0.0030– 0.0060
	2S-E 121.7 (1995)	1.8291– 1.8297	1.8192– 1.8199	1.8094– 1.8100	1.7996– 1.8002	1.7897– 1.7904	1.7799– 1.7805	—	0.0010– 0.0026	0.0031– 0.0091
	22R, 22RE 144.4 (2367)	1.2984– 1.2992	1.2984– 1.2992	1.2984– 1.2992	1.2984– 1.2992	—	—	—	0.0004– 0.0020	0.0031– 0.0071

CAMSHAFT SPECIFICATIONS
All measurements given in inches.

Year	Engine Displacement cu. in. (cc)	Journal Diameter 1	2	3	4	5	6	7	Bearing Clearance	Camshaft End Play
1984	1C-L,1C-LC,1C-TL 112.2 (1839)	1.1014–1.1022	1.1014–1.1022	1.1014–1.1022	1.1014–1.1022	—	—	—	0.0015–0.0029	0.0031–0.0071
	3Y-EC 122.0 (1998)	1.8291–1.8297	1.8192–1.8199	1.8094–1.8100	1.7996–1.8002	1.7897–1.7904	—	—	0.0010–0.0032	0.0028–0.0087
	5M-GE 168.4 (2759)	1.4944–1.4951	1.6913–1.6919	1.7110–1.7116	1.7307–1.7313	1.7504–1.7510	1.7700–1.7707	1.7897–1.7904	0.0010–0.0026	0.0028–0.0098
1985	3A, 3A-C 88.6 (1452)	1.1015–1.1022	1.1015–1.1022	1.1015–1.1022	1.1015–1.1022	—	—	—	0.0015–0.0029	0.0031–0.0071
	4A-C, 4A-LC 97.0 (1587)	1.1015–1.1022	1.1015–1.1022	1.1015–1.1022	1.1015–1.1022	—	—	—	0.0015–0.0029	0.0031–0.0071
	4A-GE 97.0 (1587)	1.3768–1.3791	1.3768–1.3791	1.3768–1.3791	1.3768–1.3791	—	—	—	0.0014–0.0028	0.0031–0.0075
	2S-E 121.7 (1995)	1.8291–1.8297	1.8192–1.8199	1.8094–1.8100	1.7996–1.8002	1.7897–1.7904	1.7799–1.7805	—	0.0010–0.0026	0.0031–0.0091
	22R, 22RE 144.4 (2367)	1.2984–1.2992	1.2984–1.2992	1.2984–1.2992	1.2984–1.2992	—	—	—	0.0004–0.0020	0.0031–0.0071
	1C-L,1C-LC,1C-TL 112.2 (1839)	1.1014–1.1022	1.1014–1.1022	1.1014–1.1022	1.1014–1.1022	—	—	—	0.0015–0.0029	0.0031–0.0071
	3Y-EC 122.0 (1998)	1.8291–1.8297	1.8192–1.8199	1.8094–1.8100	1.7996–1.8002	1.7897–1.7904	—	—	0.0010–0.0032	0.0028–0.0087
	5M-GE 168.4 (2759)	1.4944–1.4951	1.6913–1.6919	1.7110–1.7116	1.7307–1.7313	1.7504–1.7510	1.7700–1.7707	1.7897–1.7904	0.0010–0.0026	0.0028–0.0098
1986	3A, 3A-C 88.6 (1452)	1.1015–1.1022	1.1015–1.1022	1.1015–1.1022	1.1015–1.1022	—	—	—	0.0015–0.0029	0.0031–0.0071
	4A-C, 4A-LC 97.0 (1587)	1.1015–1.1022	1.1015–1.1022	1.1015–1.1022	1.1015–1.1022	—	—	—	0.0015–0.0029	0.0031–0.0071
	4A-GE 97.0 (1587)	1.0610–1.0616	1.0610–1.0616	1.0610–1.0616	1.0610–1.0616	—	—	—	0.0014–0.0028	0.0031–0.0075
	2S-E 121.7 (1995)	1.8291–1.8297	1.8192–1.8199	1.8094–1.8100	1.7996–1.8002	1.7897–1.7904	1.7799–1.7805	—	0.0010–0.0026	0.0031–0.0091
	3S-GE 121.9 (1998)	1.0614–1.0620	1.0614–1.0620	1.0614–1.0620	1.0614–1.0620	—	—	—	0.0010–0.0024	0.0039–0.0094
	2C-T 120.4 (1974)	1.1014–1.1022	1.1014–1.1022	1.1014–1.1022	1.1014–1.1022	—	—	—	0.0015–0.0029	0.0031–0.0071
	4Y-EC 136.5 (2237)	1.8291–1.8297	1.8192–1.8199	1.8094–1.8100	1.7996–1.8002	1.7897–1.7904	—	—	0.0010–0.0032	0.0028–0.0087
	5M-GE 168.4 (2759)	1.4944–1.4951	1.6913–1.6919	1.7110–1.7116	1.7307–1.7313	1.7504–1.7510	1.7700–1.7707	1.7897–1.7904	0.0010–0.0026	0.0028–0.0098
	7M-GE 180.3 (2954)	1.0610–1.4951	1.0586–1.6919	1.0586–1.7116	1.0586–1.7313	1.0586–1.7510	1.0586–1.7707	1.0586–1.7904	0.0010–0.0037③	0.0031–0.0075
1987-88	3A-C 88.6 (1452)	1.1015–1.1022	1.1015–1.1022	1.1015–1.1022	1.1015–1.1022	—	—	—	0.0015–0.0029	0.0031–0.0071
	3E 88.9 (1456)	1.0622–1.0628	1.0622–1.0628	1.0622–1.0628	1.0622–1.0628	—	—	—	0.0015–0.0029	0.0031–0.0071

CAMSHAFT SPECIFICATIONS
All measurements given in inches.

Year	Engine Displacement cu. in. (cc)	Journal Diameter 1	2	3	4	5	6	7	Bearing Clearance	Camshaft End Play
1987-88	4A-LC 97.0 (1587)	1.1015–1.1022	1.1015–1.1022	1.1015–1.1022	1.1015–1.1022	–	–	–	0.0015–0.0029	0.0031–0.0071
	4A-GEC, 4A-GELC 97.0 (1587)	1.0610–1.0616	1.0610–1.0616	1.0610–1.0616	1.0610–1.0616	–	–	–	0.0014–0.0028	0.0031–0.0075
	3S-FE 121.9 (1998)	1.0614–1.0620	1.0614–1.0620	1.0614–1.0620	1.0614–1.0620	–	–	–	0.0010–0.0024	0.0018–0.0039
	3S-GE 121.9 (1998)	1.0614–1.0620	1.0614–1.0620	1.0614–1.0620	1.0614–1.0620	–	–	–	0.0010–0.0024	0.0047–0.0079
	4Y-EC 136.5 (2237)	1.8291–1.8297	1.8192–1.8199	1.8094–1.8100	1.7996–1.8002	1.7897–1.7904	–	–	0.0010–0.0032	0.0028–0.0087
	5M-GE 168.4 (2759)	1.4944–1.4951	1.6913–1.6919	1.7110–1.7116	1.7307–1.7313	1.7504–1.7510	1.7700–1.7707	1.7897–1.7904	0.0010–0.0026	0.0028–0.0098
	7M-GE, 7M-GTE 180.3 (2954)	1.0610–1.4951	1.0586–1.6919	1.0586–1.7116	1.0586–1.7313	1.0586–1.7510	1.0586–1.7707	1.0586–1.7904	0.0010–0.0037③	0.0031–0.0075

① Nos. 1 & 4: 0.0010–0.0026
  Nos. 2 & 3: 0.0014–0.0028
② Nos. 1 & 4: 0.0010–0.0026
  Nos. 2 & 3: 0.0016–0.0030
③ No. 1: 0.0014–0.0028

CRANKSHAFT AND CONNECTING ROD SPECIFICATIONS
All measurements are given in inches.

Year	Engine Displacement cu. in. (cc)	Crankshaft Main Brg. Journal Dia.	Main Brg. Oil Clearance	Shaft End-play	Thrust on No.	Connecting Rod Journal Diameter	Oil Clearance	Side Clearance
1981	1A-C, 3A, 3A-C 88.6 (1452)	1.8892–1.8898	0.0012–0.0026	0.0008–0.0073	3	1.5742–1.5748	0.0008–0.0020	0.0059–0.0098
	3T-C 108.0 (1770)	2.2825–2.2835	0.0009–0.0019	0.0008–0.0087	3	1.8889–1.8897	0.0009–0.0019	0.0063–0.0012
	4K-C 78.7 (1290)	1.9676–1.9685	0.0006–0.0016	0.0016–0.0095	3	1.6526–1.6535	0.0006–0.0016	0.0079–0.0150
	22R 144.4 (2367)	2.3614–2.3622	0.0006–0.0020	0.0008–0.0087	3	2.0862–2.0866	0.0010–0.0022	0.0063–0.0102
	5M-E 168.4 (2759)	2.3617–2.3627	0.0013–0.0023	0.0020–0.0098	4	2.0463–2.0472	0.0008–0.0021	0.0063–0.0117
1982	1A-C, 3A, 3A-C 88.6 (1452)	1.8892–1.8898	0.0012–0.0026	0.0008–0.0073	3	1.5742–1.5748	0.0008–0.0020	0.0059–0.0098
	3T-C 108.0 (1770)	2.2825–2.2835	0.0009–0.0019	0.0008–0.0087	3	1.8889–1.8897	0.0009–0.0019	0.0063–0.0012
	4K-C 78.7 (1290)	1.9676–1.9685	0.0006–0.0016	0.0016–0.0095	3	1.6526–1.6535	0.0006–0.0016	0.0079–0.0150
	22R 144.4 (2367)	2.3614–2.3622	0.0006–0.0020	0.0008–0.0087	3	2.0862–2.0866	0.0010–0.0022	0.0063–0.0102
	5M-E, 5M-GE 168.4 (2759)	2.3617–2.3627	0.0013–0.0023	0.0020–0.0098	4	2.0463–2.0472	0.0008–0.0021	0.0063–0.0117

CRANKSHAFT AND CONNECTING ROD SPECIFICATIONS

All measurements are given in inches.

Year	Engine Displacement cu. in. (cc)	Crankshaft				Connecting Rod		
		Main Brg. Journal Dia.	Main Brg. Oil Clearance	Shaft End-play	Thrust on No.	Journal Diameter	Oil Clearance	Side Clearance
1983	3A, 3A-C 88.6 (1452)	1.8892–1.8898	0.0012–0.0026	0.0008–0.0073	3	1.5742–1.5748	0.0008–0.0020	0.0059–0.0098
	4A-C, 4A-LC 97.0 (1587)	1.8892–1.8898	0.0005–0.0019	0.0008–0.0073	3	1.5742–1.5748	0.0008–0.0020	0.0059–0.0098
	4K-E 78.7 (1290)	1.9676–1.9685	0.0006–0.0016	0.0016–0.0095	3	1.6526–1.6535	0.0006–0.0016	0.0079–0.0150
	2S-E 121.7 (1995)	2.1648–2.1654	0.0008–0.0019①	0.0008–0.0087	3	1.8892–1.8898	0.0009–0.0022	0.0063–0.0083
	22R, 22R-E 144.4 (2367)	2.3614–2.3622	0.0006–0.0020	0.0008–0.0087	3	2.0862–2.0866	0.0010–0.0022	0.0063–0.0102
	5M-GE 168.4 (2759)	2.3617–2.3627	0.0013–0.0023	0.0020–0.0098	4	2.0463–2.0472	0.0008–0.0021	0.0063–0.0117
1984	3A, 3A-C 88.6 (1452)	1.8892–1.8898	0.0012–0.0026	0.0008–0.0073	3	1.5742–1.5748	0.0008–0.0020	0.0059–0.0098
	4A-C, 4A-LC 97.0 (1587)	1.8892–1.8898	0.0005–0.0019	0.0008–0.0073	3	1.5742–1.5748	0.0008–0.0020	0.0059–0.0098
	4K-E 78.7 (1290)	1.9676–1.9685	0.0006–0.0016	0.0016–0.0095	3	1.6526–1.6535	0.0006–0.0016	0.0079–0.0150
	2S-E 121.7 (1995)	2.1648–2.1654	0.0008–0.0019①	0.0008–0.0087	3	1.8892–1.8898	0.0009–0.0022	0.0063–0.0083
	22R, 22R-E 144.4 (2367)	2.3614–2.3622	0.0010–0.0022	0.0008–0.0087	3	2.0862–2.0866	0.0010–0.0022	0.0063–0.0102
	3Y-EC 122.0 (1998)	2.2829–2.2835	0.0008–0.0020	0.0008–0.0087	3	1.8892–1.8898	0.0008–0.0020	0.0063–0.0123
	1C-L,1C-LC,1C-TL 112.2 (1839)	2.2435–2.2441	0.0013–0.0026	0.0016–0.0094②	3	1.9877–1.9882	0.0014–0.0025	0.0031–0.0118
	5M-GE 168.4 (2759)	2.3617–2.3627	0.0013–0.0023	0.0020–0.0098	4	2.0463–2.0472	0.0008–0.0021	0.0063–0.0117
1985	3A, 3A-C 88.6 (1452)	1.8892–1.8898	0.0012–0.0026	0.0008–0.0073	3	1.5742–1.5748	0.0008–0.0020	0.0059–0.0098
	4A-C, 4A-LC 97.0 (1587)	1.8892–1.8898	0.0005–0.0019	0.0008–0.0073	3	1.5742–1.5748	0.0008–0.0020	0.0059–0.0098
	4A-GE 97.0 (1587)	1.8892–1.8898	0.0005–0.0019	0.0008–0.0087	3	1.5742–1.5748	0.0008–0.0020	0.0059–0.0098
	2S-E 121.7 (1995)	2.1648–2.1654	0.0008–0.0019①	0.0008–0.0087	3	1.8892–1.8898	0.0009–0.0022	0.0063–0.0083
	22R, 22R-E 144.4 (2367)	2.3614–2.3622	0.0010–0.0022	0.0008–0.0087	3	2.0862–2.0866	0.0010–0.0022	0.0063–0.0102
	3Y-EC 122.0 (1998)	2.2829–2.2835	0.0008–0.0020	0.0008–0.0087	3	1.8892–1.8898	0.0008–0.0020	0.0063–0.0123
	1C-L,1C-LC,1C-TL 112.2 (1839)	2.2435–2.2441	0.0013–0.0026	0.0016–0.0094②	3	1.9877–1.9882	0.0014–0.0025	0.0031–0.0118
	5M-GE 168.4 (2759)	2.3617–2.3627	0.0013–0.0023	0.0020–0.0098	4	2.0463–2.0472	0.0008–0.0021	0.0063–0.0117

CRANKSHAFT AND CONNECTING ROD SPECIFICATIONS

All measurements are given in inches.

| Year | Engine Displacement cu. in. (cc) | Crankshaft | | | | Connecting Rod | | |
		Main Brg. Journal Dia.	Main Brg. Oil Clearance	Shaft End-play	Thrust on No.	Journal Diameter	Oil Clearance	Side Clearance
1986	3A, 3A-C 88.6 (1452)	1.8892–1.8898	0.0005–0.0015	0.0008–0.0073	3	1.5742–1.5748	0.0008–0.0020	0.0059–0.0098
	4A-C, 4A-LC 97.0 (1587)	1.8892–1.8898	0.0005–0.0015	0.0008–0.0073	3	1.5742–1.5748	0.0008–0.0020	0.0059–0.0098
	4A-GE 97.0 (1587)	1.8892–1.8898	0.0005–0.0015	0.0008–0.0087	3	1.5742–1.5748	0.0008–0.0020	0.0059–0.0098
	2S-E 121.7 (1995)	2.1648–2.1654	0.0008–0.0019①	0.0008–0.0087	3	1.8892–1.8898	0.0009–0.0022	0.0063–0.0083
	3S-GE 121.9 (1998)	2.1648–2.1654	0.0008–0.0019①	0.0008–0.0087	3	1.8892–1.8898	0.0009–0.0022	0.0063–0.0124
	4Y-EC 136.5 (2237)	2.2829–2.2835	0.0008–0.0020	0.0008–0.0087	3	1.8892–1.8898	0.0008–0.0020	0.0063–0.0123
	2C-T 120.4 (1974)	2.2435–2.2441	0.0013–0.0026	0.0016–0.0094②	3	1.9877–1.9882	0.0014–0.0025	0.0031–0.0118
	5M-GE 168.4 (2759)	2.3617–2.3627	0.0013–0.0023	0.0020–0.0098	4	2.0463–2.0472	0.0008–0.0021	0.0063–0.0117
	7M-GE 180.3 (2954)	2.3625–2.3627	0.0012–0.0022	0.0020–0.0098	4	2.1659–2.1663	0.0012–0.0019	0.0063–0.0117
1987-88	3A-C 88.6 (1452)	1.8891–1.8898	0.0006–0.0013	0.0008–0.0087	3	1.5742–1.5748	0.0008–0.0020	0.0059–0.0098
	3E 88.9 (1456)	1.9683–1.9685	0.0006–0.0014	0.0008–0.0087	3	1.8110–1.8113	0.0006–0.0019	0.0059–0.0138
	4A-LC 97.0 (1587)	1.8891–1.8898	0.0006–0.0013	0.0008–0.0087	3	1.5742–1.5748	0.0008–0.0020	0.0059–0.0098
	4A-GEC, 4A-GELC 97.0 (1587)	1.8891–1.8898	0.0005–0.0015	0.0008–0.0087	3	1.5742–1.5748	0.0008–0.0020	0.0059–0.0098
	3S-FE, 3S-GE 121.9 (1998)	2.1648–2.1653	0.0007–0.0015①	0.0008–0.0087	3	1.8892–1.8898	0.0009–0.0022	0.0063–0.0123
	4Y-EC 136.5 (2237)	2.2829–2.2835	0.0008–0.0020	0.0008–0.0087	3	1.8892–1.8898	0.0008–0.0020	0.0063–0.0123
	5M-GE 168.4 (2759)	2.3625–2.3627	0.0012–0.0048	0.0020–0.0098	4	2.1659–2.1663	0.0008–0.0021	0.0063–0.0117
	7M-GE, 7M-GTE 180.3 (2954)	2.3625–2.3627	0.0012–0.0022	0.0020–0.0098	4	2.1659–2.1663	0.0012–0.0019	0.0063–0.0117

① No. 3: 0.0012–0.0022
② 1C-L: 0.0008–0.0047

VALVE SPECIFICATIONS

| Year | Engine Displacement cu. in. (cc) | Seat Angle (deg.) | Face Angle (deg.) | Spring Test Pressure (lbs.) | Spring Installed Height (in.) | Stem-to-Guide Clearance (in.) | | Stem Diameter (in.) | |
						Intake	Exhaust	Intake	Exhaust
1981	1A-C, 3A, 3A-C 88.6 (1452)	45	44.5	52.0	1.520	0.0010–0.0024	0.0012–0.0026	0.2744–0.2750	0.2742–0.2748

VALVE SPECIFICATIONS

Year	Engine Displacement cu. in. (cc)	Seat Angle (deg.)	Face Angle (deg.)	Spring Test Pressure (lbs.)	Spring Installed Height (in.)	Stem-to-Guide Clearance (in.) Intake	Exhaust	Stem Diameter (in.) Intake	Exhaust
1981	3T-C 108.0 (1770)	45	44.5	57.9	1.484	0.0010– 0.0024	0.0012– 0.0026	0.3139	0.3139
	4K-C 78.7 (1290)	45	44.5	70.1	1.512	0.0012– 0.0026	0.0014– 0.0028	0.3136– 0.3142	0.3134– 0.3140
	22R 144.4 (2367)	45	44.5	55.1	1.594	0.0008– 0.0024	0.0012– 0.0028	0.3138– 0.3145	0.3136– 0.3142
	5M-E 168.4 (2759)	45	44.5	37.3– 46.5	1.630	0.0010– 0.0024	0.0014– 0.0028	0.3138– 0.3144	0.3134– 0.3140
1982	1A-C, 3A, 3A-C 88.6 (1452)	45	44.5	52.0	1.520	0.0010– 0.0024	0.0012– 0.0026	0.2744– 0.2750	0.2742– 0.2748
	3T-C 108.0 (1770)	45	44.5	57.9	1.484	0.0010– 0.0024	0.0012– 0.0026	0.3139	0.3139
	4K-C 78.7 (1290)	45	44.5	70.1	1.512	0.0012– 0.0026	0.0014– 0.0028	0.3136– 0.3142	0.3134– 0.3140
	22R 144.4 (2367)	45	44.5	55.1	1.594	0.0008– 0.0024	0.0012– 0.0028	0.3138– 0.3145	0.3136– 0.3142
	5M-E 168.4 (2759)	45	44.5	37.3– 46.5	1.630	0.0010– 0.0024	0.0014– 0.0028	0.3138– 0.3144	0.3134– 0.3140
	5M-GE 168.4 (2759)	45	44.5	①	②	0.0010– 0.0024	0.0012– 0.0026	0.3138– 0.3144	0.3134– 0.3140
1983	3A, 3A-C 88.6 (1452)	45	44.5	52.0	1.520	0.0010– 0.0024	0.0012– 0.0026	0.2744– 0.2750	0.2742– 0.2748
	4A-C, 4A-LC 97.0 (1587)	45	44.5	52.0	1.520	0.0010– 0.0024	0.0012– 0.0026	0.2744– 0.2750	0.2742– 0.2748
	4K-E 78.7 (1290)	45	44.5	77.2	1.512	0.0012– 0.0026	0.0014– 0.0028	0.3136– 0.3142	0.3134– 0.3140
	2S-E 121.7 (1995)	45.5	45.5	68.0	1.555	0.0010– 0.0024	0.0012– 0.0026	0.3138– 0.3144	0.3136– 0.3142
	22R, 22-RE 144.4 (2367)	45	44.5	55.1	1.594	0.0008– 0.0024	0.0012– 0.0028	0.3138– 0.3145	0.3136– 0.3142
	5M-GE 168.4 (2759)	45	44.5	①	②	0.0010– 0.0024	0.0012– 0.0026	0.3138– 0.3144	0.3134– 0.3140
1984	3A, 3A-C 88.6 (1452)	45	44.5	52.0	1.520	0.0010– 0.0024	0.0012– 0.0026	0.2744– 0.2750	0.2742– 0.2748
	4A-C, 4A-LC 97.0 (1587)	45	44.5	52.0	1.520	0.0010– 0.0024	0.0012– 0.0026	0.2744– 0.2750	0.2742– 0.2748
	4K-E 78.7 (1290)	45	44.5	77.2	1.512	0.0012– 0.0026	0.0014– 0.0028	0.3136– 0.3142	0.3134– 0.3140
	2S-E 121.7 (1995)	45.5	45.5	68.0	1.555	0.0010– 0.0024	0.0012– 0.0026	0.3138– 0.3144	0.3136– 0.3142
	22R, 22-RE 144.4 (2367)	45	44.5	55.1	1.594	0.0008– 0.0024	0.0012– 0.0028	0.3138– 0.3145	0.3136– 0.3142

VALVE SPECIFICATIONS

Year	Engine Displacement cu. in. (cc)	Seat Angle (deg.)	Face Angle (deg.)	Spring Test Pressure (lbs.)	Spring Installed Height (in.)	Stem-to-Guide Clearance (in.)		Stem Diameter (in.)	
						Intake	Exhaust	Intake	Exhaust
1984	3Y-EC 122.0 (1998)	45	45.5	63.0	1.589	0.0010–0.0024	0.0012–0.0026	0.3138–0.3144	0.3136–0.3142
	1C-L,1C-LC,1C-TL 112.2 (1839)	45	44.5	53.0	1.587	0.0008–0.0022	0.0014–0.0028	0.3140–0.3146	0.3134–0.3142
	5M-GE 168.4 (2759)	45	44.5	①	②	0.0010–0.0024	0.0012–0.0026	0.3138–0.3144	0.3134–0.3140
1985	3A, 3A-C 88.6 (1452)	45	44.5	52.0	1.520	0.0010–0.0024	0.0012–0.0026	0.2744–0.2750	0.2742–0.2748
	4A-C, 4A-LC 97.0 (1587)	45	44.5	52.0	1.520	0.0010–0.0024	0.0012–0.0026	0.2744–0.2750	0.2742–0.2748
	4A-GE 97.0 (1587)	45	44.5	34.8	1.366	0.0010–0.0024	0.0012–0.0026	0.2350–0.2356	0.2348–0.2354
	2S-E 121.7 (1995)	45.5	45.5	71.4	1.555	0.0010–0.0024	0.0012–0.0026	0.3138–0.3144	0.3136–0.3142
	22R, 22-RE 144.4 (2367)	45	44.5	55.1	1.594	0.0008–0.0024	0.0012–0.0028	0.3138–0.3145	0.3136–0.3142
	3Y-EC 122.0 (1998)	45	44.5	63.0	1.589	0.0010–0.0024	0.0012–0.0026	0.3138–0.3144	0.3136–0.3142
	1C-L,1C-LC,1C-TL 112.2 (1839)	45	44.5	53.0	1.587	0.0008–0.0022	0.0014–0.0028	0.3140–0.3146	0.3134–0.3142
	5M-GE 168.4 (2759)	45	44.5	①	②	0.0010–0.0024	0.0015–0.0027	0.3138–0.3144	0.3134–0.3140
1986	3A, 3A-C 88.6 (1452)	45	44.5	52.0	1.520	0.0010–0.0024	0.0012–0.0026	0.2744–0.2750	0.2742–0.2748
	4A-C, 4A-LC 97.0 (1587)	45	44.5	52.0	1.520	0.0010–0.0024	0.0012–0.0026	0.2744–0.2750	0.2742–0.2748
	4A-GE 97.0 (1587)	45	44.5	34.8	1.366	0.0010–0.0024	0.0012–0.0026	0.2350–0.2356	0.2348–0.2354
	2S-E 121.7 (1995)	45.5	45.5	71.4	1.555	0.0010–0.0024	0.0012–0.0026	0.3138–0.3144	0.3136–0.3142
	3S-GE 121.9 (1998)	45.5	44.5	38.6	1.366	0.0010–0.0023	0.0012–0.0025	0.2346–0.2352	0.2344–0.2350
	4Y-EC 136.5 (2237)	45	44.5	63.0	1.589	0.0010–0.0024	0.0012–0.0026	0.3138–0.3144	0.3136–0.3142
	2C-T 120.4 (1974)	45	44.5	53.0	1.587	0.0008–0.0022	0.0014–0.0028	0.3140–0.3146	0.3134–0.3142
	5M-GE 168.4 (2759)	45	44.5	①	②	0.0010–0.0024	0.0015–0.0027	0.3138–0.3144	0.3134–0.3140
	7M-GE 180.3 (2954)	45	44.5	35.0	1.639	0.0010–0.0024	0.0012–0.0026	0.2350–0.2356	0.2348–0.2354
1987-88	3A-C 88.6 (1452)	45	44.5	52.0	1.520	0.0010–0.0024	0.0012–0.0026	0.2744–0.2750	0.2742–0.2748
	3E 88.9 (1456)	45	44.5	35.1	1.384	0.0010–0.0024	0.0012–0.0026	0.2350–0.2356	0.2348–0.2354

VALVE SPECIFICATIONS

Year	Engine Displacement cu. in. (cc)	Seat Angle (deg.)	Face Angle (deg.)	Spring Test Pressure (lbs.)	Spring Installed Height (in.)	Stem-to-Guide Clearance (in.) Intake	Exhaust	Stem Diameter (in.) Intake	Exhaust
1987-88	4A-LC 97.0 (1587)	45	44.5	52.0	1.520	0.0010–0.0024	0.0012–0.0026	0.2744–0.2750	0.2742–0.2748
	4A-GEC, 4A-GELC 97.0 (1587)	45	44.5	35.9	1.366	0.0010–0.0024	0.0012–0.0026	0.2350–0.2356	0.2348–0.2354
	3S-FE 121.9 (1998)	45.5	44.5	39.6	1.366	0.0010–0.0024	0.0030–0.0026	0.2350–0.2356	0.2348–0.2354
	3S-GE 121.9 (1998)	45.5	44.5	38.6	1.366	0.0010–0.0023	0.0012–0.0025	0.2346–0.2352	0.2344–0.2350
	4Y-EC 136.5 (2237)	45	44.5	63.0	1.589	0.0010–0.0024	0.0012–0.0026	0.3138–0.3144	0.3136–0.3142
	5M-GE 168.4 (2759)	45	44.5	①	②	0.0010–0.0024	0.0012–0.0026	0.3138–0.3144	0.3136–0.3142
	7M-GE 180.3 (2954)	45	44.5	35.0	1.639	0.0010–0.0024	0.0012–0.0026	0.2350–0.2356	0.2348–0.2354

① Intake: 76.5–84.4; Exhaust: 73.4–80.9
② Intake: 1.575; Exhaust: 1.693

PISTON AND RING SPECIFICATIONS
All measurments are given in inches.

Year	Engine Displacement cu. in. (cc)	Piston Clearance	Ring Gap Top Compression	Bottom Compression	Oil Control	Ring Side Clearance Top Compression	Bottom Compression	Oil Control
1981	1A-C, 3A, 3A-C 88.6 (1452)	0.0039–0.0047	0.0079–0.0157	0.0059–0.0138	0.0039–0.0236	0.0016–0.0031	0.0012–0.0028	Snug
	3T-C 108.0 (1770)	0.0020–0.0028	0.0039–0.0098	0.0059–0.0118	0.0079–0.0276	0.0008–0.0024	0.0006–0.0022	Snug
	4K-C 78.7 (1290)	0.0012–0.0020	0.0039–0.0110	0.0039–0.0118	0.0080–0.0350	0.0012–0.0028	0.0008–0.0024	Snug
	22R 144.4 (2367)	0.0020–0.0028	0.0094–0.0142	0.0071–0.0154	Snug	0.0080 max.	0.0080 max.	Snug
	5M-E 168.4 (2759)	0.0020–0.0028	0.0039–0.0110	0.0039–0.0110	0.0079–0.0200	0.0012–0.0028	0.0008–0.0024	Snug
1982	1A-C, 3A, 3A-C 88.6 (1452)	0.0039–0.0047	0.0079–0.0157	0.0059–0.0138	0.0039–0.0236	0.0016–0.0031	0.0012–0.0028	Snug
	3T-C 108.0 (1770)	0.0020–0.0028	0.0039–0.0098	0.0059–0.0118	0.0079–0.0276	0.0008–0.0024	0.0006–0.0022	Snug
	4K-C 78.7 (1290)	0.0012–0.0020	0.0039–0.0110	0.0039–0.0118	0.0080–0.0350	0.0012–0.0028	0.0008–0.0024	Snug
	22R 144.4 (2367)	0.0020–0.0028	0.0094–0.0142	0.0071–0.0154	Snug	0.0080 max.	0.0080 max.	Snug
	5M-E 168.4 (2759)	0.0020–0.0028	0.0039–0.0110	0.0039–0.0110	0.0079–0.0200	0.0012–0.0028	0.0008–0.0024	Snug
	5M-GE 168.4 (2759)	0.0020–0.0028	0.0083–0.0146	0.0067–0.0209	0.0079–0.0276	0.0012–0.0028	0.0008–0.0024	Snug

PISTON AND RING SPECIFICATIONS
All measurments are given in inches.

Year	Engine Displacement cu. in. (cc)	Piston Clearance	Ring Gap			Ring Side Clearance		
			Top Compression	Bottom Compression	Oil Control	Top Compression	Bottom Compression	Oil Control
1983	3A, 3A-C 88.6 (1452)	0.0039–0.0047	0.0079–0.0157	0.0059–0.0138	0.0039–0.0236	0.0016–0.0031	0.0012–0.0028	Snug
	4A-C, 4A-LC 97.0 (1587)	0.0039–0.0047	①	②	③	0.0016–0.0031	0.0012–0.0028	Snug
	4K-E 78.7 (1290)	0.0012–0.0020	0.0063–0.0118	0.0059–0.0118	④	0.0012–0.0028	0.0008–0.0024	Snug
	2S-E 121.7 (1995)	0.0006–0.0014	0.0110–0.0197	0.0079–0.0177	0.0079–0.0311	0.0012–0.0028	0.0012–0.0028	Snug
	22R, 22R-E 144.4 (2367)	0.0020–0.0028	0.0094–0.0142	0.0071–0.0154	Snug	0.0080 max.	0.0080 max.	Snug
	5M-GE 168.4 (2759)	0.0020–0.0028	0.0083–0.0146	0.0067–0.0209	0.0079–0.0276	0.0012–0.0028	0.0008–0.0024	Snug
1984	3A, 3A-C 88.6 (1452)	0.0039–0.0047	0.0079–0.0157	0.0059–0.0138	0.0039–0.0236	0.0016–0.0031	0.0012–0.0028	Snug
	4A-C, 4A-LC 97.0 (1587)	0.0039–0.0047	①	②	③	0.0016–0.0031	0.0012–0.0028	Snug
	4K-E 78.7 (1290)	0.0012–0.0020	0.0063–0.0118	0.0059–0.0118	④	0.0012–0.0028	0.0008–0.0024	Snug
	2S-E 121.7 (1995)	0.0006–0.0014	0.0110–0.0197	0.0079–0.0177	0.0079–0.0311	0.0012–0.0028	0.0012–0.0028	Snug
	22R, 22R-E 144.4 (2367)	0.0020–0.0028	0.0094–0.0142	0.0071–0.0154	Snug	0.0080 max.	0.0080 max.	Snug
	3Y-EC 122.0 (1998)	0.0030–0.0037	0.0087–0.0185	0.0059–0.0165	0.0079–0.0323	0.0012–0.0028	0.0012–0.0028	Snug
	1C-L,1C-LC,1C-TL 112.2 (1839)	0.0016–0.0024	0.0098–0.0193	0.0079–0.0173	0.0079–0.0193	0.0079–0.0081	0.0079–0.0081	Snug
	5M-GE 168.4 (2759)	0.0020–0.0028	0.0083–0.0146	0.0067–0.0209	0.0079–0.0276	0.0012–0.0028	0.0008–0.0024	Snug
1985	3A, 3A-C 88.6 (1452)	0.0039–0.0047	0.0079–0.0157	0.0059–0.0138	0.0039–0.0236	0.0016–0.0031	0.0012–0.0028	Snug
	4A-C, 4A-LC 97.0 (1587)	0.0039–0.0047	0.0098–0.0185	0.0059–0.0165	0.0118–0.0401	0.0016–0.0031	0.0012–0.0028	Snug
	4A-GE 97.0 (1587)	0.0039–0.0047	0.0098–0.0185	0.0059–0.0165	0.0118–0.0401	0.0012–0.0028	0.0008–0.0024	Snug
	2S-E 121.7 (1995)	0.0006–0.0014	0.0110–0.0209	0.0083–0.0189	0.0079–0.0323	0.0012–0.0028	0.0008–0.0024	Snug
	22R, 22R-E 144.4 (2367)	0.0012–0.0020	0.0094–0.0142	0.0071–0.0154	Snug	0.0080 max.	0.0080 max.	Snug
	3Y-EC 122.0 (1998)	0.0030–0.0037	0.0087–0.0185	0.0059–0.0165	0.0079–0.0323	0.0012–0.0028	0.0012–0.0028	Snug
	1C-L,1C-LC,1C-TL 112.2 (1839)	0.0016–0.0024	0.0106–0.0213	0.0098–0.0205	0.0079–0.0205	0.0080	0.0080	Snug
	5M-GE 168.4 (2759)	0.0020–0.0028	0.0091–0.0161	0.0098–0.0217	0.0067–0.0335	0.0012–0.0028	0.0008–0.0024	Snug

PISTON AND RING SPECIFICATIONS
All measurments are given in inches.

Year	Engine Displacement cu. in. (cc)	Piston Clearance	Ring Gap			Ring Side Clearance		
			Top Compression	Bottom Compression	Oil Control	Top Compression	Bottom Compression	Oil Control
1986	3A, 3A-C 88.6 (1452)	0.0039–0.0047	0.0079–0.0185	0.0059–0.0204	0.0118–0.0402	0.0016–0.0031	0.0012–0.0028	Snug
	4A-C, 4A-LC 97.0 (1587)	0.0035–0.0043	0.0098–0.0185	0.0059–0.0165	0.0118–0.0401	0.0016–0.0031	0.0012–0.0028	Snug
	4A-GE 97.0 (1587)	0.0039–0.0047	0.0098–0.0185	0.0078–0.0165	0.0118–0.0401	0.0012–0.0028	0.0008–0.0024	Snug
	2S-E 121.7 (1995)	0.0006–0.0014	0.0110–0.0209	0.0083–0.0189	0.0079–0.0323	0.0012–0.0028	0.0008–0.0024	Snug
	3S-GE 121.9 (1998)	0.0012–0.0020	0.0130–0.0213	0.0079–0.0173	0.0079–0.0354	0.0008–0.0024	0.0006–0.0022	Snug
	4Y-EC 136.5 (2237)	0.0026–0.0033	0.0091–0.0189	0.0063–0.0173	0.0051–0.0185	0.0012–0.0028	0.0012–0.0028	Snug
	2C-T 120.4 (1974)	0.0018–0.0026	0.0106–0.0213	0.0098–0.0205	0.0079–0.0323	0.0080	0.0080	Snug
	5M-GE 168.4 (2759)	0.0024–0.0031	0.0114–0.0185	0.0098–0.0217	0.0067–0.0335	0.0012–0.0028	0.0008–0.0024	Snug
	7M-GE 180.3 (2954)	0.0024–0.0031	0.0091–0.0150	0.0098–0.0209	0.0039–0.0201	0.0012–0.0028	0.0008–0.0024	Snug
1987-88	3A-C 88.6 (1452)	0.0039–0.0047	0.0079–0.0185	0.0079–0.0204	0.0118–0.0402	0.0016–0.0031	0.0012–0.0028	Snug
	3E 88.9 (1456)	0.0028–0.0035	0.0102–0.0142	0.0118–0.0177	0.0059–0.0157	0.0016–0.0031	0.0012–0.0028	Snug
	4A-LC 97.0 (1587)	0.0035–0.0043	0.0098–0.0138	0.0059–0.0165	0.0078–0.0276	0.0016–0.0031	0.0012–0.0028	Snug
	4A-GEC, 4A-GELC 97.0 (1587)	0.0039–0.0047	0.0098–0.0138	0.0078–0.0118	0.0078–0.0276	0.0016–0.0031	0.0012–0.0028	Snug
	3S-FE 121.9 (1998)	0.0018–0.0026	0.0106–0.0193	0.0106–0.0197	0.0079–0.0311	0.0012–0.0028	0.0012–0.0028	Snug
	3S-GE 121.9 (1998)	0.0012–0.0020	0.0130–0.0213	0.0079–0.0173	0.0079–0.0350	0.0012–0.0028	0.0008–0.0024	Snug
	4Y-EC 136.5 (2237)	0.0026–0.0033	0.0091–0.0189	0.0063–0.0173	0.0051–0.0185	0.0012–0.0028	0.0012–0.0028	Snug
	5M-GE 168.4 (2759)	0.0024–0.0031	0.0091–0.0150	0.0098–0.0209	0.0040–0.0201	0.0012–0.0028	0.0008–0.0024	Snug
	7M-GE 180.3 (2954)	0.0024–0.0031	0.0091–0.0150	0.0098–0.0209	0.0039–0.0201	0.0012–0.0028	0.0008–0.0024	Snug
	7M-GTE 180.3 (2954)	0.0028–0.0035	0.0114–0.0173	0.0098–0.0209	0.0039–0.0220	0.0012–0.0028	0.0008–0.0024	Snug

① 4A-C: TP—0.0098–0.0138
   Riken—0.0079–0.0138
② 4A-C: 0.0059–0.0118
③ 4A-C: TP—0.0079–0.0276
   Riken—0.0118–0.0354
④ 4K-E: T—0.0080–0.0280
   R—0.0120–0.0350

TORQUE SPECIFICATIONS
All readings in ft. lbs.

Year	Engine Displacement cu. in. (cc)	Cylinder Head Bolts	Main Bearing Bolts	Rod Bearing Bolts	Crankshaft Pulley Bolts	Flywheel Bolts	Manifold Intake	Manifold Exhaust	Spark Plugs
1981	1A-C, 3A, 3A-C 88.6 (1452)	40–47	40–47	26–32	80–94	55–61	15–21	15–21	11–15
	3T-C 108.0 (1770)	62–68	53–63	29–36	55–75	42–47	14–18	22–32	11–15
	4K-C 78.7 (1290)	40–47	40–47	29–37	55–75	40–47	15–21 ①	15–21 ①	11–15
	22R 144.4 (2367)	53–63	69–83	40–47	102–130	73–86	13–19	29–36	11–15
	5M-E 168.4 (2759)	55–61	72–78	31–34	98–119	51–57	10–15	13–16	11–15
1982	1A-C, 3A, 3A-C 88.6 (1452)	40–47	40–47	26–32	80–94	55–61	15–21	15–21	11–15
	3T-C 108.0 (1770)	62–68	53–63	29–36	55–75	42–47	14–18	22–32	11–15
	4K-C 78.7 (1290)	40–47	40–47	29–37	55–75	40–47	15–21 ①	15–21 ①	11–15
	22R 144.4 (2367)	53–63	69–83	40–47	102–130	73–86	13–19	29–36	11–15
	5M-E 168.4 (2759)	55–61	72–78	31–34	98–119	51–57	10–15	13–16	11–15
	5M-GE 168.4 (2759)	55–61	72–78	31–34	98–119	51–57	15–17	26–32	11–15
1983	3A, 3A-C 88.6 (1452)	40–47	40–47	26–32	80–94	55–61	15–21	15–21	11–15
	4A-C, 4A-LC 97.0 (1587)	40–47	40–47	26–32	80–94	55–61	15–21	15–21	11–15
	4K-E 78.7 (1290)	40–47	40–47	29–37	55–75	40–47	15–21 ①	15–21 ①	11–15
	2S-E 121.7 (1995)	45–50	40–45	33–38	78–82	70–75	30–33	30–33	11–15
	22R, 22R-E 144.4 (2367)	53–63	69–83	40–47	102–130	73–86	13–19	29–36	11–15
	5M-GE 168.4 (2759)	55–61	72–78	31–34	98–119	51–57	15–17	26–32	11–15
1984	3A, 3A-C 88.6 (1452)	40–47	40–47	34–39	80–94	55–61	15–21	15–21	11–15
	4A-C, 4A-LC 97.0 (1587)	40–47	40–47	26–32	80–94	55–61	15–21	15–21	11–15
	4K-E 78.7 (1290)	40–47	40–47	29–37	55–75	40–47	15–21 ①	15–21 ①	11–15
	2S-E 121.7 (1995)	45–50	40–45	33–38	78–82	70–75	30–33	30–33	11–15
	22R, 22R-E 144.4 (2367)	53–63	69–83	40–47	102–130	73–86	13–19	29–36	11–15

TORQUE SPECIFICATIONS
All readings in ft. lbs.

Year	Engine Displacement cu. in. (cc)	Cylinder Head Bolts	Main Bearing Bolts	Rod Bearing Bolts	Crankshaft Pulley Bolts	Flywheel Bolts	Manifold Intake	Manifold Exhaust	Spark Plugs
1984	3Y-EC 122.0 (1998)	②	55–60	33–38	78–82	60–63	7–11	33–38	11–15
	1C-L,1C-LC, 1C-TL 112.2 (1839)	60–65	75–78	45–50	70–75	63–68	10–15	32–36	11–15
	5M-GE 168.4 (2759)	55–61	72–78	31–34	98–119	51–57	15–17	26–32	11–15
1985	3A, 3A-C 88.6 (1452)	40–47	40–47	34–39	80–94	55–61	15–21	15–21	11–15
	4A-C, 4A-LC 97.0 (1587)	40–47	40–47	26–32	80–94	55–61	15–21	15–21	11–15
	4A-GE 97.0 (1587)	40–47	40–47	26–32	80–94	55–61	15–21	15–21	11–15
	2S-E 121.7 (1995)	45–50	40–45	33–38	78–82	70–75	30–33	30–33	11–15
	22R, 22R-E 144.4 (2367)	53–63	69–83	40–47	102–130	73–86	13–19	29–36	11–15
	3Y-EC 122.0 (1998)	②	55–60	33–38	78–82	60–63	7–11	33–38	11–15
	1C-L,1C-LC, 1C-TL 112.2 (1839)	60–65	75–78	45–50	70–75	63–68	10–15	32–36	11–15
	5M-GE 168.4 (2759)	55–61	72–78	31–34	155–163	51–57	15–17	26–32	11–15
1986	3A, 3A-C 88.6 (1452)	40–47	40–47	34–39	80–94	55–61	15–21	15–21	11–15
	4A-C, 4A-LC 97.0 (1587)	40–47	40–47	26–32	80–94	55–61	15–21	15–21	11–15
	4A-GE 97.0 (1587)	40–47	40–47	26–32	80–94	55–61	15–21	15–21	11–15
	2S-E 121.7 (1995)	45–50	40–45	33–38	78–82	70–75	30–33	30–33	11–15
	3S-GE 121.9 (1998)	38–42	40–45	40–45	78–82	③	12–16	30–34	11–15
	4Y-EC 136.5 (2237)	②	55–60	33–38	116	60–63	7–11	33–38	11–15
	2C-T 120.4 (1974)	④	75–78	45–50	70–75	63–68	10–15	32–36	11–15
	5M-GE 168.4 (2759)	55–61	72–78	31–34	155–163	51–57	15–17	26–32	11–15
	7M-GE 180.2 (2954)	55–61	72–78	45–49	185–205	51–57	11–15	26–32	11–15
1987-88	3A-C 88.6 (1452)	40–47	40–47	34–39	80–94	55–61	15–21	15–21	11–15
	3E 88.9 (1456)	④	40–47	27–31	105–117	60–70	11–17	33–42	11–15

TORQUE SPECIFICATIONS
All readings in ft. lbs.

Year	Engine Displacement cu. in. (cc)	Cylinder Head Bolts	Main Bearing Bolts	Rod Bearing Bolts	Crankshaft Pulley Bolts	Flywheel Bolts	Manifold Intake	Manifold Exhaust	Spark Plugs
1987-88	4A-LC 97.0 (1587)	40–47	40–47	32–40	80–94	55–61	15–21	15–21	11–15
	4A-GE 97.0 (1587)	40–47	40–47	32–40	100–110	50–58	15–21	15–21	11–15
	3S-FE 121.9 (1998)	45–50	40–45	33–38	78–82	70–75	11–17	27–33	11–15
	3S-GE 121.9 (1998)	38–42	40–45	44–50	78–82	③	12–16	30–34	11–15
	4Y-EC 136.5 (2237)	②	55–60	33–38	116	60–63	7–11	33–38	11–15
	5M-GE 168.4 (2759)	55–61	72–78	31–34	185–205	51–57	11–15	26–32	11–15
	7M-GE, 7M-GTE 180.2 (2954)	55–61	72–78	45–49	185–205	51–57	11–15	26–32	11–15

① Intake and exhaust manifolds combined
② 12mm bolt: 12–16; 14mm bolt: 63–68
③ New: 65; Used: 63
④ See text

BRAKE SPECIFICATIONS
All measurements in inches unless noted

Year	Model	Lug Nut Torque (ft. lbs.)	Master Cylinder Bore	Brake Disc Minimum Thickness	Brake Disc Maximum Runout	Standard Brake Drum Diameter	Minimum Lining Thickness Front	Minimum Lining Thickness Rear
1981	Tercel	65–86	①	0.354	0.006	7.126②	0.040	0.040
	Corolla	65–86	①	0.453	0.006	9.079	0.040	0.040
	Starlet	65–86	0.813	0.350	0.006	7.950	0.040	0.040
	Corona	65–86	0.876	0.453	0.006	9.079	0.040	0.040
	Celica	65–86	0.813	0.453	0.006	9.079	0.118	0.040
	Supra	65–86	0.813	0.453③	0.006	—	0.118	0.040
	Cressida	65–86	①	0.669	0.006	9.079	0.040	0.040
1982	Tercel	65–86	①	0.354	0.006	7.126②	0.040	0.040
	Corolla	65–86	①	0.453	0.006	9.079	0.040	0.040
	Starlet	65–86	0.813	0.350	0.006	7.950	0.040	0.040
	Corona	65–86	0.876	0.453	0.006	9.079	0.040	0.040
	Celica	65–86	①	0.750	0.006	9.079	0.118	0.040
	Supra	65–86	①	0.750④	0.006	—	0.118	0.040
	Cressida	65–86	①	0.669	0.006	9.079	0.040	0.040
1983	Tercel	65–86	①	0.394	0.006	7.126②	0.040	0.040
	Corolla	65–86	①	0.453	0.006	9.079	0.040	0.040
	Starlet	65–86	0.813	0.350	0.006	7.950	0.040	0.040
	Camry	65–86	①	0.827	0.006	7.913	0.040	0.040
	Celica	65–86	①	0.750	0.006	9.079	0.118	0.040

BRAKE SPECIFICATIONS
All measurements in inches unless noted

Year	Model	Lug Nut Torque (ft. lbs.)	Master Cylinder Bore	Brake Disc Minimum Thickness	Brake Disc Maximum Runout	Standard Brake Drum Diameter	Minimum Lining Thickness Front	Rear
1983	Supra	65–86	①	0.750④	0.006	—	0.118	0.040
	Cressida	65–86	①	0.669	0.006	9.079	0.040	0.040
1984	Tercel	65–86	①	0.394	0.006	7.126②	0.040	0.040
	Corolla	65–86	①	0.453	0.006	9.079⑤	0.040	0.040
	Starlet	65–86	0.813	0.350	0.006	7.950	0.040	0.040
	Camry	65–86	①	0.827	0.006	7.913	0.040	0.040
	Celica	65–86	①	0.750	0.006	9.079	0.118	0.040
	Supra	65–86	①	0.750④	0.006	—	0.118	0.040
	Van	65–86	①	0.748	0.006	10.079	0.040	0.040
	Cressida	65–86	①	0.669	0.006	9.079	0.040	0.040
1985	Tercel	65–86	①	0.394	0.006	7.126②	0.040	0.040
	Corolla	65–86	①	⑥	0.006	9.079⑤	0.040	0.040
	Camry	65–86	①	0.827	0.006	7.913	0.040	0.040
	Celica	65–86	①	0.750	0.006	9.079	0.118	0.040
	Supra	65–86	①	0.750④	0.006	—	0.118	0.040
	MR2	65–86	①	0.669⑧	0.006	—	0.040	0.040
	Van	65–86	①	0.748	0.006	10.079	0.040	0.040
	Cressida	65–86	①	⑦	0.006	9.079	0.040	0.040
1986	Tercel	65–86	①	0.394	0.006	7.126②	0.040	0.040
	Corolla	65–86	①	⑥	0.006	9.079⑤	0.040	0.040
	Camry	65–86	①	0.827	0.006	7.913	0.040	0.040
	Celica	65–86	①	0.827⑧	0.006	7.913	0.040	0.040
	Supra	65–86	①	0.750④	0.006	—	0.118	0.040
	MR2	65–86	①	0.669⑧	0.006	—	0.040	0.040
	Van	65–86	①	0.748	0.006	10.079	0.040	0.040
	Cressida	65–86	①	⑦	0.006	9.079	0.040	0.040
1987-88	Tercel	65–86	①	0.394	0.006	7.126②	0.040	0.040
	Corolla	65–86	①	⑥	0.006	9.079⑤	0.040	0.040
	Camry	65–86	①	0.827	0.006	9.079	0.040	0.040
	Celica	65–86	①	0.827⑧	0.006	7.913	0.040	0.040
	Supra	65–86	①	0.827④	0.006	—	0.040	0.040
	MR2	65–86	①	0.827⑧	0.006	—	0.040	0.040
	Van	65–86	①	0.748⑨	0.006	10.079	0.040	0.040
	Cressida	65–86	①	⑦	0.006	9.079	0.040	0.040

① Not specified by the manufacturer
② Wagon & 4wd: 7.913
③ Rear disc: 0.354
④ Rear disc: 0.669
⑤ FWD: 7.874
⑥ FWD: 0.492
  RWD & FX16: 0.669
  Rear disc: 0.315
⑦ Rear disc: 0.354
⑧ 4wd: 0.945

WHEEL ALIGNMENT

Year	Model	Caster Range (deg.)	Caster Preferred Setting (deg.)	Camber Range (deg.)	Camber Preferred Setting (deg.)	Toe-in (in.)	Steering Axis Inclination (deg.)
1981	Tercel	$1\frac{2}{3}$P–$2\frac{2}{3}$P	$2\frac{1}{16}$P	0–1P	$\frac{1}{2}$P	0.04–0.12	$11\frac{1}{3}$
	Corolla (Sedan)	$\frac{3}{4}$P–$2\frac{1}{4}$P	$1\frac{3}{4}$P	$\frac{1}{2}$P–$1\frac{1}{2}$P	1P	0.04–0.16	$8\frac{1}{2}$P
	(Wagon)	$1\frac{1}{16}$P–$2\frac{1}{4}$P	$1\frac{17}{32}$P	$\frac{1}{2}$P–$1\frac{1}{2}$P	1P	0.04–0.16	$8\frac{1}{3}$
	Starlet	$1\frac{2}{3}$P–$2\frac{1}{3}$P	2P	$\frac{1}{3}$P–1P	$\frac{2}{3}$P	0.04–0.12	$9\frac{3}{4}$
	Corona	$1\frac{1}{4}$P–$2\frac{1}{4}$P	$1\frac{3}{4}$P	$\frac{1}{2}$P–$1\frac{1}{2}$P	1P	0–0.08	$7\frac{2}{3}$
	Celica	$1\frac{1}{6}$P–$2\frac{1}{6}$P	$1\frac{2}{3}$P	$\frac{1}{2}$P–$1\frac{1}{2}$P	1P	[1]	$7\frac{1}{2}$
	Supra	$1\frac{1}{4}$P–$2\frac{1}{4}$P	$1\frac{3}{4}$P	$\frac{1}{3}$P–$1\frac{1}{3}$P	$\frac{5}{6}$P	0.04 out–0.04 in	$7\frac{2}{3}$
	Cressida	1P–2P	$1\frac{1}{2}$	$\frac{1}{3}$P–$1\frac{1}{3}$P	$\frac{5}{6}$P	0.08–0.16 out	9
1982	Tercel	$1\frac{2}{3}$P–$2\frac{2}{3}$P	$2\frac{1}{16}$P	0–1P	$\frac{1}{2}$P	0.04–0.12	$11\frac{1}{3}$
	Corolla (Sedan)	$\frac{3}{4}$P–$2\frac{1}{4}$P	$1\frac{3}{4}$P	$\frac{1}{2}$P–$1\frac{1}{2}$P	1P	0.04–0.16	$8\frac{1}{2}$P
	(Wagon)	$1\frac{1}{16}$P–$2\frac{1}{4}$P	$1\frac{17}{32}$P	$\frac{1}{2}$P–$1\frac{1}{2}$P	1P	0.04–0.16	$8\frac{1}{3}$
	Starlet	$1\frac{2}{3}$P–$2\frac{1}{3}$P	2P	$\frac{1}{3}$P–1P	$\frac{2}{3}$P	0.04–0.12	$9\frac{3}{4}$
	Corona	$1\frac{1}{4}$P–$2\frac{1}{4}$P	$1\frac{3}{4}$P	$\frac{1}{2}$P–$1\frac{1}{2}$P	1P	0–0.08	$7\frac{2}{3}$
	Celica	$2\frac{5}{6}$P–$3\frac{5}{6}$P	$3\frac{1}{3}$P	$\frac{1}{2}$P–$1\frac{1}{2}$P	1P	[2]	$9\frac{1}{3}$
	Supra	$3\frac{2}{3}$P–$4\frac{2}{3}$P	$4\frac{1}{6}$P	$\frac{1}{3}$P–$1\frac{1}{3}$P	$\frac{5}{6}$P	0.08–0.16 in	$10\frac{1}{2}$
	Cressida	1P–2P	$1\frac{1}{2}$	$\frac{1}{3}$P–$1\frac{1}{3}$P	$\frac{5}{6}$P	0.08–0.16 out	9
1983	Tercel (2wd)	[3]	[4]	$\frac{1}{6}$N–$\frac{5}{6}$P	$\frac{1}{3}$P	0.06 out–0.04 in	$12\frac{1}{2}$
	(4wd)	$1\frac{5}{6}$P–$2\frac{5}{6}$P	$2\frac{1}{2}$P	$\frac{1}{3}$P–$1\frac{1}{3}$P	$\frac{5}{6}$P	0	$11\frac{2}{3}$
	Corolla (Sedan)	$\frac{3}{4}$P–$2\frac{1}{4}$P	$1\frac{3}{4}$P	$\frac{1}{2}$P–$1\frac{1}{2}$P	1P	0.04–0.16	$8\frac{1}{2}$P
	(Wagon)	$1\frac{1}{16}$P–$2\frac{1}{4}$P	$1\frac{17}{32}$P	$\frac{1}{2}$P–$1\frac{1}{2}$P	1P	0.04–0.16	$8\frac{1}{3}$
	Starlet	$1\frac{1}{3}$P–$2\frac{1}{3}$P	$1\frac{5}{6}$P	$\frac{1}{6}$P–$1\frac{1}{6}$P	$\frac{2}{3}$P	0.04–0.12	$9\frac{3}{4}$
	Camry	[5]	[6]	0–1P	$\frac{1}{2}$P	[7]	$12\frac{1}{2}$
	Celica	$2\frac{5}{6}$P–$3\frac{5}{6}$P	$3\frac{1}{3}$P	$\frac{1}{2}$P–$1\frac{1}{2}$P	1P	[2]	$9\frac{1}{3}$
	Supra	$3\frac{2}{3}$P–$4\frac{2}{3}$P	$4\frac{1}{6}$P	$\frac{1}{3}$P–$1\frac{1}{3}$P	$\frac{5}{6}$P	0.08–0.16 in	$10\frac{1}{2}$
	Cressida	1P–2P	$1\frac{1}{2}$	$\frac{1}{3}$P–$1\frac{1}{3}$P	$\frac{5}{6}$P	0.08–0.16 out	9
1984	Tercel (Sedan)	[3]	[4]	$\frac{1}{6}$N–$\frac{5}{6}$P	$\frac{1}{3}$P	0.06 out–0.04 in	$12\frac{1}{2}$
	(Wagon)	[8]	[9]	$\frac{1}{4}$N–$\frac{3}{4}$P	$\frac{1}{4}$P	0.04 out–0.04 in	13
	(4wd)	2P–3P	$2\frac{1}{2}$P	$\frac{1}{3}$P–$2\frac{1}{3}$P	$1\frac{1}{3}$P	0.04 out–0.04 in	$11\frac{2}{3}$
	Corolla (exc. SR5)	$\frac{1}{3}$P–$1\frac{1}{3}$P	$\frac{5}{6}$P	1N–0	$\frac{1}{2}$N	0–0.04	—
	(SR5)	[10]	[11]	$\frac{1}{4}$N–$\frac{3}{4}$P	$\frac{1}{4}$P	0–0.08	—
	Starlet	$1\frac{1}{3}$P–$2\frac{1}{3}$P	$1\frac{5}{6}$P	$\frac{1}{6}$P–$1\frac{1}{6}$P	$\frac{2}{3}$P	0.04–0.12	$9\frac{3}{4}$
	Camry	[5]	[6]	0–1P	$\frac{1}{2}$P	[7]	$12\frac{1}{2}$
	Celica	$2\frac{5}{6}$P–$3\frac{5}{6}$P	$3\frac{1}{3}$P	$\frac{1}{2}$P–$1\frac{1}{2}$P	1P	[2]	$9\frac{1}{3}$
	Supra	$3\frac{2}{3}$P–$4\frac{2}{3}$P	$4\frac{1}{6}$P	$\frac{1}{3}$P–$1\frac{1}{3}$P	$\frac{5}{6}$P	0.08–0.16 in	$10\frac{1}{2}$
	Van	$1\frac{1}{2}$P–$2\frac{1}{2}$P	2P	0–1P	$\frac{1}{2}$P	0.04 out–0.04 in	10P

WHEEL ALIGNMENT

Year	Model	Caster Range (deg.)	Caster Preferred Setting (deg.)	Camber Range (deg.)	Camber Preferred Setting (deg.)	Toe-in (in.)	Steering Axis Inclination (deg.)
1984	Cressida (Sedan)	2P–3P	$2\frac{1}{2}$P	$\frac{1}{4}$P–$1\frac{1}{4}$P	$\frac{3}{4}$P	0.08–0.16	9
	(Wagon)	$1\frac{2}{3}$P–$2\frac{2}{3}$P	$2\frac{1}{6}$P	$\frac{2}{3}$P–$1\frac{1}{3}$P	$\frac{5}{6}$P	0.08–0.16	9
1985	Tercel (Sedan)	③	④	$\frac{1}{6}$N–$\frac{5}{6}$P	$\frac{1}{3}$P	0.06 out–0.04 in	$12\frac{1}{2}$
	(Wagon)	⑧	⑨	$\frac{1}{4}$N–$\frac{3}{4}$P	$\frac{1}{4}$P	0.04 out–0.04 in	13
	(4wd)	2P–3P	$2\frac{1}{2}$P	$\frac{1}{3}$P–$2\frac{1}{3}$P	$1\frac{1}{3}$P	0.04 out–0.04 in	$11\frac{2}{3}$
	Corolla (exc. SR5)	$\frac{1}{3}$P–$1\frac{1}{3}$P	$\frac{5}{6}$P	1N–0	$\frac{1}{2}$N	0–0.04	—
	(SR5)	⑩	⑪	$\frac{1}{4}$N–$\frac{3}{4}$P	$\frac{1}{4}$P	0–0.08	—
	Camry	⑤	⑥	0–1P	$\frac{1}{2}$P	⑦	$12\frac{1}{2}$
	Celica	$2\frac{5}{6}$P–$3\frac{5}{6}$P	$3\frac{1}{3}$P	$\frac{1}{2}$P–$1\frac{1}{2}$P	1P	②	$9\frac{1}{3}$
	Supra	$3\frac{2}{3}$P–$4\frac{2}{3}$P	$4\frac{1}{6}$P	$\frac{1}{3}$P–$1\frac{1}{3}$P	$\frac{5}{6}$P	0.08–0.16 in	$10\frac{1}{2}$
	Van	$1\frac{1}{2}$P–$2\frac{1}{2}$P	2P	0–1P	$\frac{1}{2}$P	0.04 out–0.04 in	10P
	MR2	$4\frac{3}{4}$P–$5\frac{3}{4}$P	$5\frac{1}{4}$P	$\frac{1}{4}$N–$\frac{3}{4}$P	$\frac{1}{4}$P	0–0.08	12P
	Cressida (Sedan)	2P–3P	$2\frac{1}{2}$P	$\frac{1}{4}$P–$1\frac{1}{4}$P	$\frac{3}{4}$P	0.08–0.16	9
	(Wagon)	$1\frac{2}{3}$P–$2\frac{2}{3}$P	$2\frac{1}{6}$P	$\frac{2}{3}$P–$1\frac{1}{3}$P	$\frac{5}{6}$P	0.08–0.16	9
1986	Tercel (Sedan)	③	④	$\frac{1}{6}$N–$\frac{5}{6}$P	$\frac{1}{3}$P	0.06 out–0.04 in	$12\frac{1}{2}$
	(Wagon)	⑧	⑨	$\frac{1}{4}$N–$\frac{3}{4}$P	$\frac{1}{4}$P	0.04 out–0.04 in	13
	(4wd)	$1\frac{15}{16}$P–$2\frac{15}{16}$P	$2\frac{7}{16}$P	$\frac{1}{16}$P–$1\frac{1}{16}$P	$\frac{9}{16}$P	0.08 out–0	$11\frac{13}{16}$
	Corolla (RWD)	⑫	⑬	$\frac{1}{2}$N–1P	$\frac{1}{4}$P	0.04 out–0.12 in	9
	(FWD)	$\frac{3}{16}$P–$1\frac{11}{16}$P	$\frac{15}{16}$P	1N–$\frac{1}{2}$P	$\frac{1}{4}$N	0.04 out–0.12 in	$12\frac{1}{2}$
	Camry	$\frac{7}{16}$P–$1\frac{3}{4}$P	1P	$\frac{3}{16}$N–$1\frac{1}{4}$P	$\frac{9}{16}$P	0–0.16	$12\frac{1}{2}$
	Celica	$\frac{7}{16}$P–$1\frac{15}{16}$P	$1\frac{3}{16}$P	$\frac{15}{16}$N–$\frac{9}{16}$P	$\frac{3}{16}$N	0.08 out–0.08 in	$13\frac{1}{2}$
	Supra	$3\frac{7}{16}$P–$4\frac{15}{16}$P	$4\frac{3}{16}$P	$\frac{1}{16}$P–$1\frac{9}{16}$P	$\frac{13}{16}$P	0.04–0.20	$10\frac{1}{4}$
	Van	$1\frac{3}{4}$P–$3\frac{1}{4}$P	$2\frac{1}{2}$P	$\frac{3}{4}$N–$\frac{1}{2}$P	0	0.08 out–0.08 in	$10\frac{1}{2}$
	MR2	$4\frac{3}{4}$P–$5\frac{3}{4}$P	$5\frac{1}{4}$P	$\frac{1}{4}$N–$\frac{3}{4}$P	$\frac{1}{4}$P	0–0.08	12
	Cressida (Sedan)	$4\frac{1}{16}$P–$5\frac{9}{16}$P	$4\frac{13}{16}$P	$\frac{5}{16}$N–$1\frac{3}{16}$P	$\frac{7}{16}$P	0–0.16	$10\frac{1}{2}$
	(Wagon)	$3\frac{1}{2}$P–5P	$4\frac{1}{4}$P	$\frac{5}{16}$N–$1\frac{3}{16}$P	$\frac{7}{16}$P	0–0.16	$10\frac{1}{2}$
1987-88	Tercel (Sedan)	⑭	⑮	$\frac{3}{4}$N–$\frac{3}{4}$P	0	0.08 out–0.08 in	$12\frac{1}{2}$
	(Wagon)	⑧	⑨	$\frac{3}{4}$N–$\frac{3}{4}$P	0P	0.12 out–0.04 in	$12\frac{1}{2}$
	(4wd)	$1\frac{11}{16}$P–$3\frac{3}{16}$P	$2\frac{1}{4}$P	$\frac{3}{16}$N–$1\frac{5}{16}$P	$\frac{9}{16}$P	0.12 out–0.04 in	12
	Corolla (RWD)	⑫	⑬	$\frac{1}{2}$N–1P	$\frac{1}{4}$P	0.04 out–0.12 in	9
	(FWD)	$\frac{1}{8}$P–$1\frac{5}{8}$P	$\frac{7}{8}$P	1N–$\frac{1}{2}$P	$\frac{1}{4}$N	0.04 out–0.12 in	$12\frac{1}{2}$
	Camry (Sedan)	$\frac{15}{16}$P–$2\frac{7}{16}$P	$1\frac{11}{16}$P	$\frac{3}{16}$N–$1\frac{5}{16}$P	$\frac{9}{16}$P	0.04 out–0.12 in	$12\frac{3}{4}$

WHEEL ALIGNMENT

Year	Model	Caster Range (deg.)	Caster Preferred Setting (deg.)	Camber Range (deg.)	Camber Preferred Setting (deg.)	Toe-in (in.)	Steering Axis Inclination (deg.)
	(Wagon)	$\frac{1}{4}$P–$1\frac{3}{4}$P	1P	$\frac{1}{4}$N–$1\frac{1}{4}$P	$\frac{1}{2}$P	0.04 out–0.12 in	13
	Celica	$\frac{7}{16}$P–$1\frac{15}{16}$P	$1\frac{3}{16}$P	$\frac{15}{16}$N–$\frac{9}{16}$P	$\frac{3}{16}$N	0.08 out–0.08 in	$13\frac{1}{2}$
	Supra	$6\frac{3}{4}$P–$8\frac{1}{4}$P	$7\frac{1}{2}$P	$\frac{13}{16}$N–$\frac{11}{16}$P	$\frac{1}{16}$N	0.08 out–0.08 in	11
	Van (2wd)	$1\frac{3}{4}$P–$3\frac{1}{4}$P	$2\frac{1}{2}$P	$\frac{13}{16}$N–$\frac{11}{16}$P	$\frac{1}{16}$N	0.08 out–0.08 in	$10\frac{1}{2}$
	(4wd)	$1\frac{1}{16}$P–$3\frac{9}{16}$P	$2\frac{13}{16}$P	$\frac{9}{16}$N–$\frac{15}{16}$P	$\frac{3}{16}$P	0.08 out–0.08 in	$12\frac{1}{2}$
	MR2	$4\frac{5}{16}$P–$5\frac{13}{16}$P	$5\frac{1}{16}$P	$\frac{1}{2}$N–1P	$\frac{1}{4}$P	0–0.08	12
	Cressida (Sedan)	$4\frac{1}{16}$P–$5\frac{9}{16}$P	$4\frac{13}{16}$P	$\frac{5}{16}$N–$1\frac{3}{16}$P	$\frac{7}{16}$P	0–0.16	$10\frac{1}{2}$
	(Wagon)	$3\frac{1}{2}$P–5P	$4\frac{1}{4}$P	$\frac{5}{16}$N–$1\frac{3}{16}$P	$\frac{7}{16}$P	0–0.16	$10\frac{1}{2}$

① Man. Str.: 0–0.08
Pwr. Str.: 0.12–0.20
② Man. Str.: 0.12–0.20
Pwr. Str.:0.16–0.24
③ Man. Str.: $\frac{2}{3}$P–$1\frac{2}{3}$P
Pwr. Str.: $2\frac{1}{6}$P–$3\frac{1}{6}$P
④ Man. Str.: $1\frac{1}{6}$P
Pwr. Str.: $2\frac{2}{3}$P
⑤ Man. Str.: $\frac{1}{2}$P–$1\frac{1}{2}$P
Pwr. Str.: 2P–3P
⑥ Man. Str.: 1P
Pwr. Str.: $2\frac{1}{2}$P
⑦ Man. Str.: 0
Pwr. Str.: 0.08
⑧ Man. Str.: $\frac{1}{6}$N–$1\frac{1}{3}$P
Pwr. Str.: $1\frac{1}{4}$P–3P
⑨ Man. Str.: $\frac{2}{3}$P
Pwr. Str.: $2\frac{1}{4}$P
⑩ Man. Str.: $2\frac{1}{4}$P–$3\frac{1}{4}$P
Pwr. Str.: $3\frac{1}{6}$P–$4\frac{1}{6}$P
⑪ Man. Str.: $2\frac{3}{4}$P
Pwr. Str.: $3\frac{2}{3}$P
⑫ Man. Str.: 2P–$3\frac{1}{2}$P
Pwr. Str.: 3P–$3\frac{1}{2}$P
⑬ Man. Str.: $2\frac{3}{4}$P
Pwr. Str.: $3\frac{3}{4}$P
⑭ Man. Str.: $\frac{1}{4}$P–$1\frac{3}{4}$P
Pwr. Str.: $1\frac{3}{4}$P–$3\frac{1}{4}$P
⑯ Man. Str.: 1P
Pwr. Str.: $2\frac{1}{2}$P

TUNE-UP PROCEDURES

Breaker Points and Condenser

ADJUSTMENTS

1981-82 Tercel with 3A Engine

NOTE: All but the Tercel with the 3A engine are equipped with transistorized, electronic ignition systems, no breaker point adjustments is necessary or possible.

Loosen the clips which attach the distributor cap to the distributor body and lift the cap straight up. Leave the leads connected to the cap. Remove the rotor and dust cover.

Clean the distributor cap and rotor with alcohol. Inspect them for cracks and other signs of wear or damage. Polish the points with a point file.

NOTE: Do not use emery cloth or sandpaper; these may leave particles on the points, causing them to arc.

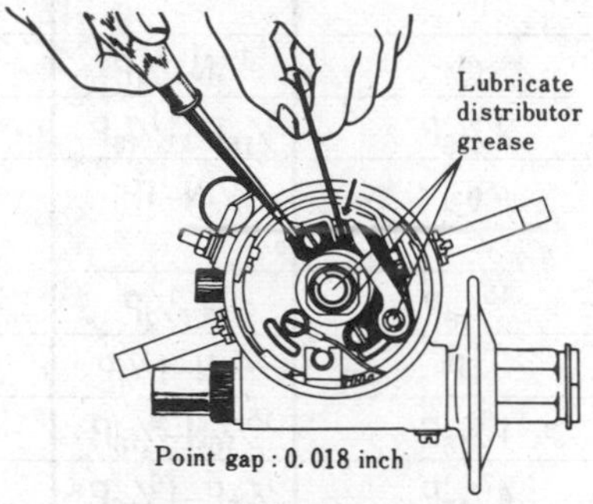

Adjusting breaker point gap

If the points are badly pitted or worn replace them as follows:

1. Unfasten the point lead connector.
2. Remove the point retaining clip and remove the point holddown screw.
3. Remove the point set.
4. Installation is the reverse for removal.

After replacing the points, or as a routine maintenance, adjust the the points to the specification.

1. Rotate the engine by hand or by using a remote starter switch, so that the rubbing block is on the high point of the cam lobe.
2. Insert a feeler gauge of the proper thickness between the points, a slight drag should be felt.
3. If no drag is felt or if the feeler gauge cannot be inserted at all, loosen, but do not remove, the point holddown screw.
4. Insert a suitable tool into the adjustment slot. Rotate the tool until the proper point gap is attained.
5. Tighten the point holddown screw. Lubricate the cam lobes, breaker arm, rubbing block, arm pivot, and distributor shaft with a small amount of special high-temperature distributor grease.

Check the operation of the centrifugal advance mechanism by moving the rotor clockwise. Release the rotor, it should return to its original position. If it does not, check it for binding.

Check the vacuum advance unit by removing the cap and pressing in on the octane selector. Release the octane selector. It should snap back to its original position. Check for binding if it fails to do so.

Replace the condenser if it is suspect or as routine maintenance during the point replacement operation, in the following manner:

1. Remove the nut and washer from the condenser lead terminal.
2. Remove the condenser mounting screw and withdraw the condenser.
3. Installation is the reversal of re-

moval. The condenser is mounted on the outside of the distributor body on all models.

4. Install the dust cover, rotor, and the distributor cap on the distributor. Adjust the dwell and timing.

Dwell Angle

ADJUSTMENT

1981–82 Tercel with 3A Engine

Connect a dwell/tachometer, in accordance with the manufacturers instructions, between the distributor primary lead and a ground.

―――― **CAUTION** ――――

On vehicles with electronic ignition, hook the dwell meter or tachometer to the negative (–) side of the coil, not to the distributor primary lead; damage to the ignition control unit will result.

With the engine warmed up and running at the specified idle speed, take a dwell reading.

If the point dwell is not within specifications, shut the engine off and adjust the point gap. Increasing the point gap decreases the dwell angle and vice versa. Install the dust cover, rotor, and cap. Check the dwell reading again.

Electronic Ignition

All gasoline engine vehicles are equipped with electronic ignition except the Tercel with the 3A engine. The 3A engine uses a breaker point type ignition. The electronic ignition system uses an ignition signal generating system in place of the breaker points. It consist of a rotor, a magnetic element and a pick up coil all mounted inside the distributor. The system needs no routine maintenance. Repair is limited to replacement of defective parts and adjustments of the air gap.

NOTE: Air gap adjustment and checking is not possible on the 4A-GE, 7M-GE and 5M-GE. Air gap adjustments are not possible on the 2S-E, 3E, 3S-GE, 3S-FE, 3Y-EC, 3A-C (1983-87), 4A-L, 4A-CL, 4A-GEC, 4A-GELC, 7M-GELC, 4Y-EC and 5M-GE. The air gap on these engines may be checked, but if out of specification, adjustment is made by component replacement.

AIR GAP ADJUSTMENT

1. Remove the distributor cap, rotor, and the dust shield.
2. Turn the crankshaft until a

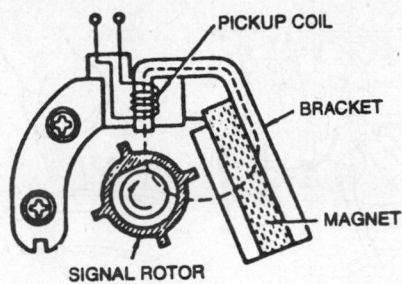

Components of the electronic ignition signal generator

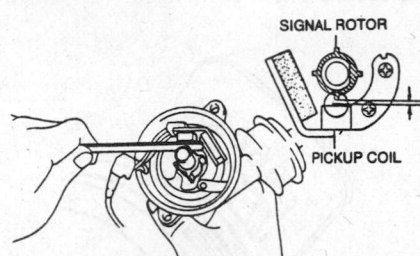

Checking the air gap on the electronic ignition system—all engines except 1983 and later 3A-C and 4A-C

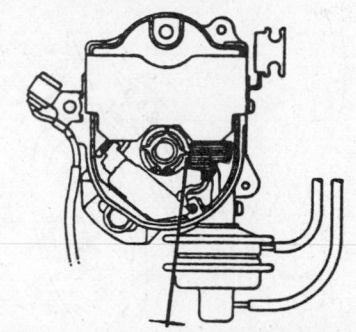

Checking the air gap on the electronic ignition system—1983 and later 3A-C and 4A-C

tooth on the signal rotor aligns with the projection on the pickup coil.

3. Using a nonmagnetic feeler gauge, measure the distance between the signal rotor tooth and the pickup coil projection. The gap should be 0.008–0.016 in.
4. If the gap is incorrect, loosen the two pickup coil to distributor mounting screws. Using a suitable tool in the notch of the pickup coil mounting, turn the pickup coil until the gap is correct.
5. Tighten the pickup coil mounting screws and recheck the gap.
6. Install the distributor cap and the rotor.

Ignition Timing

ADJUSTMENTS

All Except 5M-GE, 4A-GE, 3S-GE, 2SE (1986) and 1985 22R-E Engines

1. Warm up the engine and set the

parking brake. Connect a tachometer and check the engine speed to see that it is within specifications. Adjust as required.

2. On vehicles with electronic ignition, hook the dwell meter or tachometer to the negative (–) side of the coil, not to the distributor primary lead, damage to the ignition control until will result.
3. 1983–87 A-series engines and all 1984–88 engines require a special type of tachometer which hooks up to the service connector wire coming out of the distributor. As many tachometers are not compatible with this hookup, we recommend that you consult with the manufacturer before purchasing a certain type.
4. Connect a timing light to the engine, as outlined in the instructions supplied by the manufacturer of the light.
5. Disconnect the vacuum line from the distributor vacuum unit and plug the line. If a vacuum advance/retard distributor is used, disconnect and plug both vacuum lines from the distributor.
6. Allow the engine to run at the specified idle speed with the gear shift in neutral for vehicles with manual transmissions, and in Drive for vehicles with automatic transmissions. Be sure that the parking brake is firmly set and that the wheels are chocked.
7. Point the timing light at the timing marks. With the engine at idle, timing should be at the specification. If it is not, loosen the pinch bolt at the base and rotate the distributor to advance or retard the timing, as required.
8. Stop the engine and tighten the pinch bolt. Start the engine and recheck the timing. Stop the engine and disconnect the timing light and the tachometer. Connect the vacuum line(s) to the vacuum and advance unit.

5M-GE, 7M–GE, 4Y-EC, 4A-GE, 4A-GEC, 4A-GELC, 3S-FE, 3S-GE, 2S-E (1986-87) and 22R-E (1985)

1. Connect a timing light to the engine following the manufacturer's instructions.
2. These engines require a special type of tachometer which hooks up to the service connector wire coming out of the distributor. As many tachometers are not compatible with this hookup, we recommend that you consult with the manufacturer before purchasing a certain type.
3. Start the engine and run it at idle. Remove the rubber cap from the check connector and short the connector at terminals (T-E).

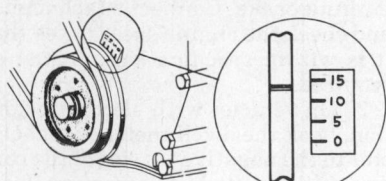

Timing marks—5M-E engine

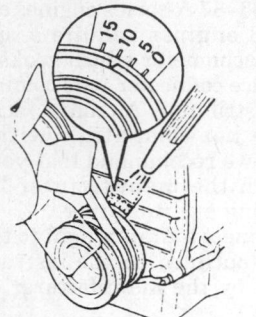

Timing marks—2S-E, 3S-GE and 5M-GE

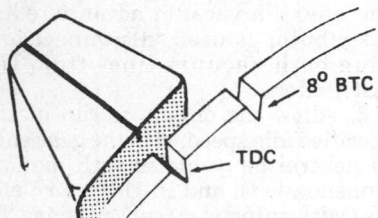

Timing marks—20R engines

Timing marks—22R and 22R-E engines

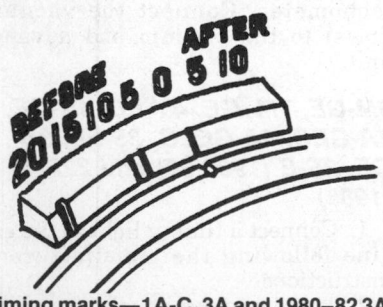

Timing marks—1A-C, 3A and 1980–82 3A-C engines

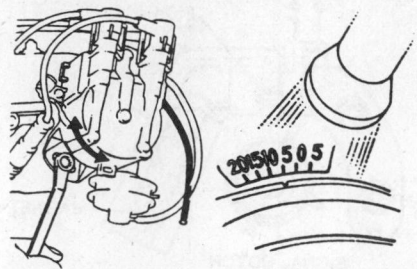

Timing marks—4A-C, 4A-GE (Corolla GTS only) and 1983 and later 3A-C engines (note disconnected vacuum hose

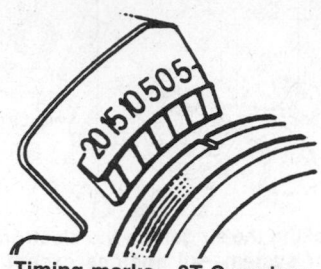

Timing marks—3T-C engines

Timing marks—3Y-EC, and 4Y-EC

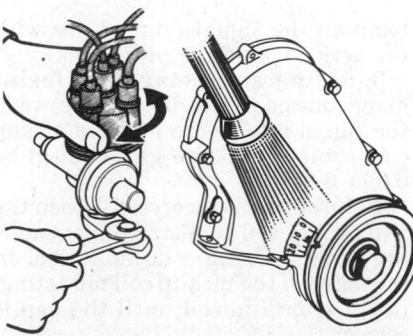

Timing marks—4K–C and 4K–E engines

3E

1. Remove the cap. Using the proper tachometer, connect the test probe of the tachometer to the service probe connector at the integrated ignition assembly (IIA).

2. Disconnect the vacuum hose from the IIA sub diaphragm and plug it.

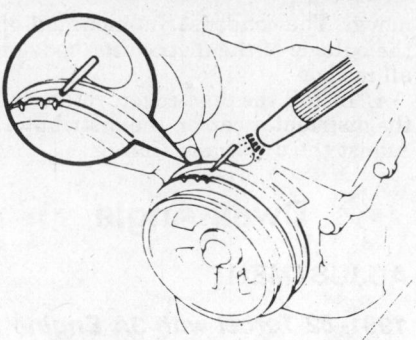

Timing marks—4A-GE (MR2)

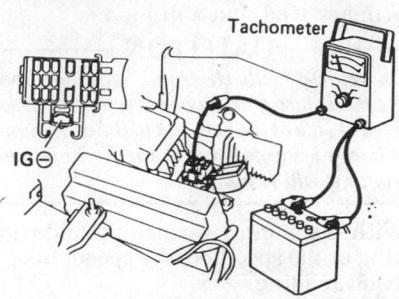

Tachometer hook-up—5M-GE (Cressida only); 1983–85 Camry similar

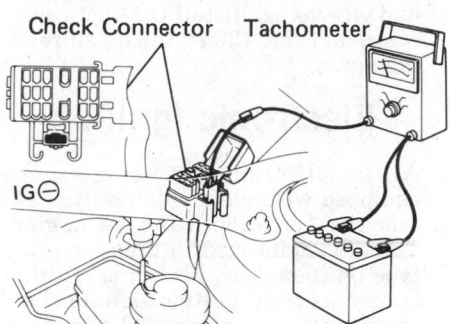

Tachometer hook-up—3S-GE

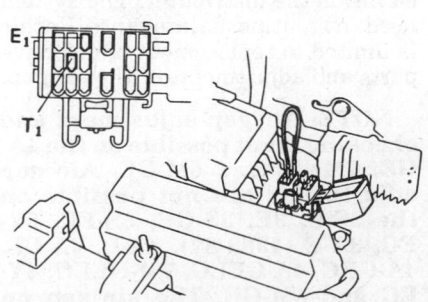

Shorting the test connector—Cressidas with 5M-GE engines

4. Loosen the distributor pinch bolt just enough so that the distributor can be turned. Aim the timing light at the marks on the crankshaft pulley and slowly turn the distributor until the timing mark is aligned. Tighten the distributor pinch bolt. Unshort the connector.

3. With the engine idling and the electric fan off, check the timing.

4. Loosen the holddown bolt. Adjust the timing as required.

5. Retighten the holddown bolt. Recheck the ignition timing.

TACHOMETER HOOK-UP

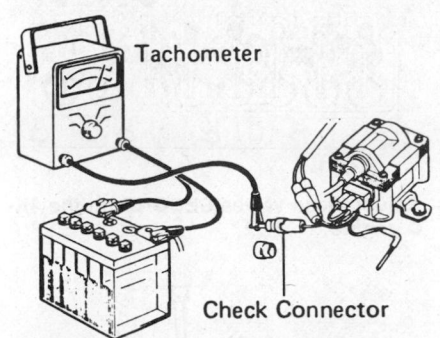

Tachometer hook-up—Supras with 5M-GE engines

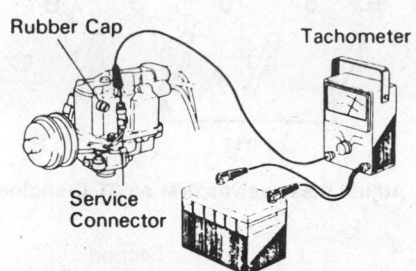

Tachometer hook-up—3Y-EC and 4Y-EC engines

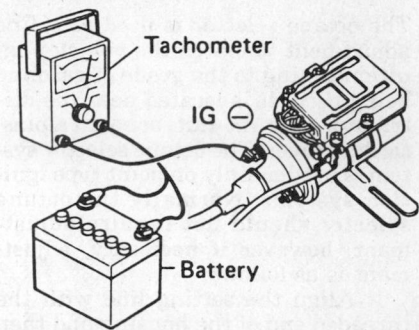

Tachometer hook-up—1985 and later 22R-E and 4A-GE engines

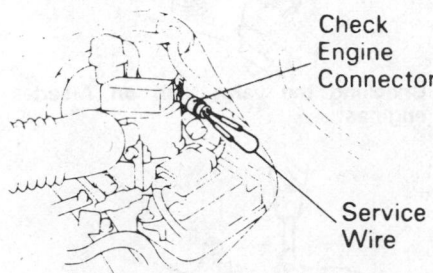

Shorting the check connector—4Y-EC

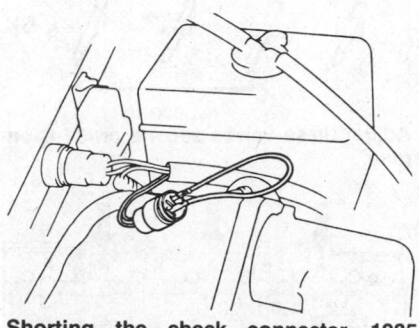

Shorting the check connector—1985 22R-E

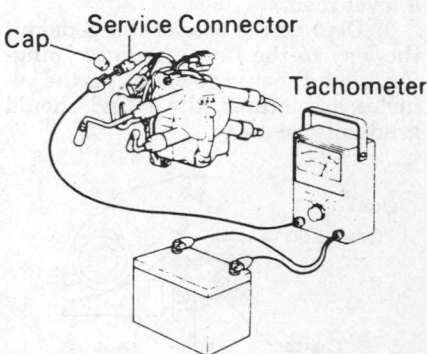

Tachometer hook-up—1986 and later 2S-E

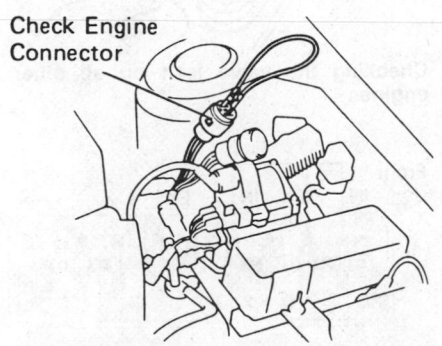

Shorting the test connector—Supras with 5M-GE engines

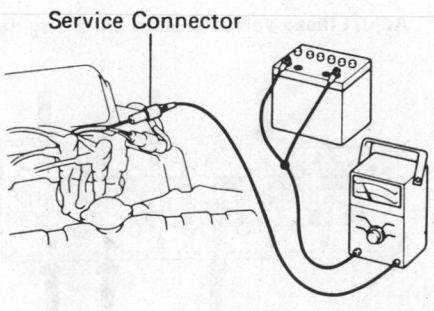

Tachometer hook-up—4A-C engines (1983 and later 3A-C similar)

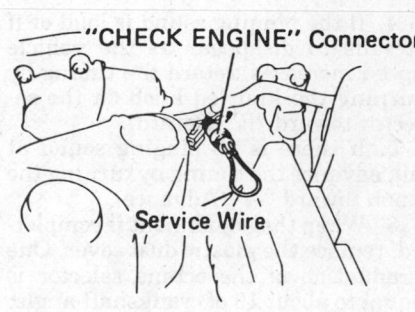

Shorting the check connector—1983–85 4A-GE engines

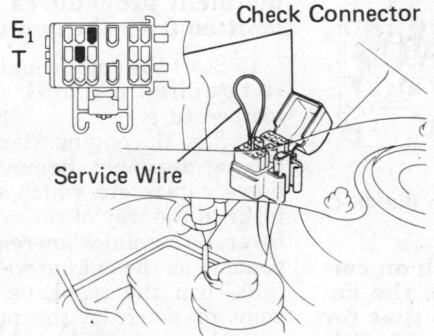

Shorting the test connector—3S-GE and 1986 and later 2S-E

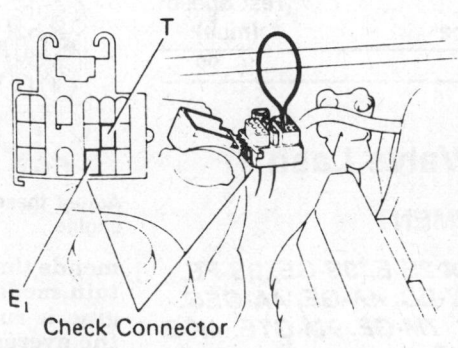

Shorting the check connector—1986 and later 4A-GE

Octane Selector

The octane selector is used as a fine adjustment to match the vehicle's ignition timing to the grade of gasoline being used. It is located near the distributor vacuum unit, beneath a plastic dust cover. The octane selector system is used mainly on point type ignition systems. Normally the octane selector should not require adjustment, however if necessary, adjustment is as follows:

1. Align the setting line with the threaded end of the housing and then align the center line with the setting mark on the housing.

2. Drive the vehicle to the speed specified in the chart, in high gear, on a level road.

3. Depress the accelerator pedal all the way to the floor. A slight "pinging" sound should be heard. As the vehicles accelerates, the sound should gradually go away.

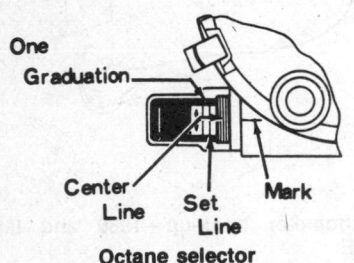

Octane selector

4. If the pinging sound is loud or if it fails to disappear as the vehicle speed increases, retard the timing by turning the knurled knob on the selector toward "R" (Retard).

5. If there is no pinging sound at all, advance the timing by turning the knob toward "A" (Advance).

6. When the adjustment is completed, replace the plastic dust cover. One graduation of the octane selector is equal to about 10 of crankshaft angle.

OCTANE SELECTOR TEST SPEEDS

Engine Type	Test Speed (mph)
20 R	16–22

Valve Lash

ADJUSTMENT

All Except 2S-E, 3S-GE, 3S-FE, 3Y-EC, 4Y-EC, 4A-GE, 4A-GEC, 4A-GELC, 7M-GE, 7M-GTE, 4K-E and 5M-GE

NOTE: Although Toyota recom-

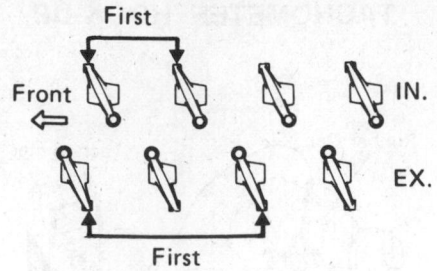

Adjust these valves first on 3T-C engine

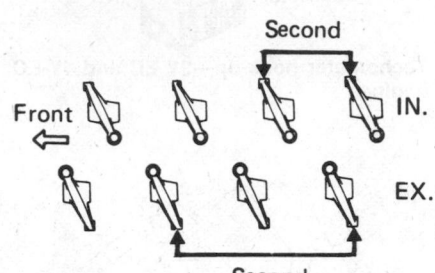

Adjust these valves second on 3T-C engine

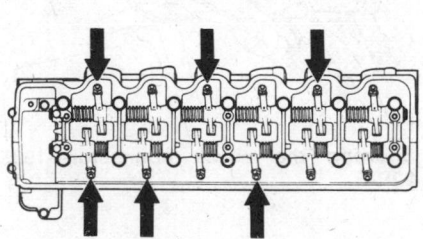

Adjust these valves first on 5M-E engine

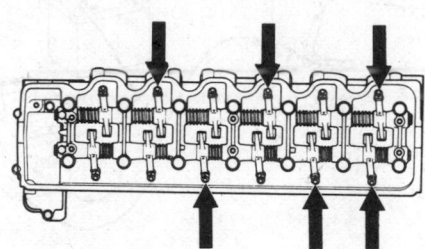

Adjust these velves second on 5M-E engine

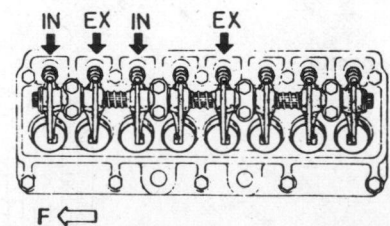

Adjust these valves FIRST on the 4K-C engine

mends that the valve lash on certain models be set while the engine is running, we feel that for the average owner/mechanic it is more convenient to adjust the valves statically (engine off).

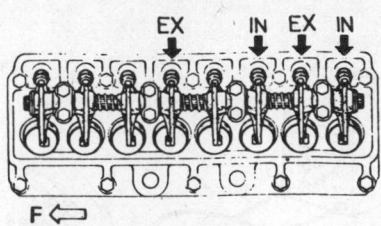

Adjust these valves SECOND on the 4K-C engine

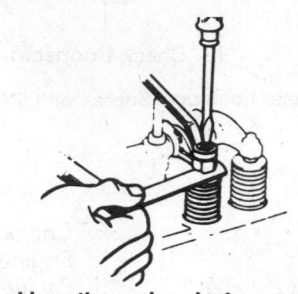

Checking the valve lash on A-series engines

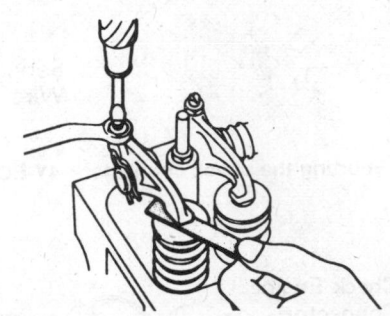

Checking the valve lash on all other engines

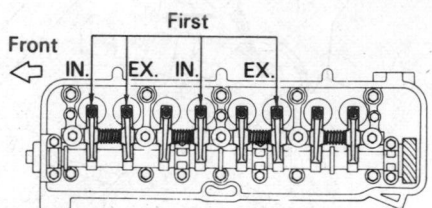

Adjust these valves 1st on A–series engines

Thus, running valve lash and adjustment procedures have been omitted from the manual.

1. Start the engine and run it until it reaches normal operating temperature.

2. Stop the engine. Remove the air cleaner assembly. Remove any other hoses, cables, etc. which are attached to, or in the way of the cylinder head cover. Be careful when removing components as the engine will be hot.

3. Turn the crankshaft until the point or notch on the pulley aligns with the "0" or "T" mark on the timing scale. This will insure that the engine is at TDC.

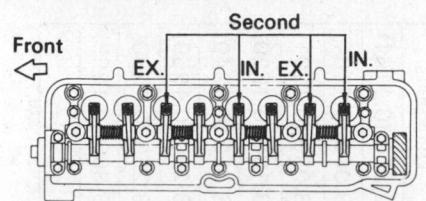

Adjust these valves 2nd on A—series engines

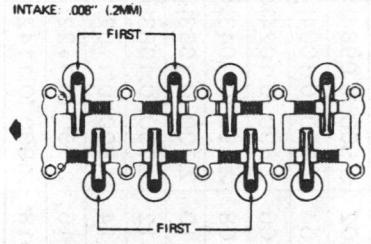

INTAKE .008" (.2MM)
FIRST
FIRST
EXHAUST .012" (.3MM)

Adjust these valves 1st on R—series engines

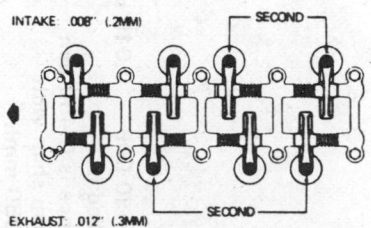

INTAKE .008" (.2MM)
SECOND
SECOND
EXHAUST .012" (.3MM)

Adjust these valves 2nd on R—series engines

NOTE: Check that the rocker arms on the No.1 cylinder are loose. If not, turn the crankshaft one complete revolution (360°).

4. Retighten the cylinder head bolts on all engines to the proper torque specifications. Also, retighten the valve rocker support bolts to the proper specifications.

5. Using a flat feeler gauge, check the clearance between the bottom of the rocker arm and the top of the valve stem. This measurement should correspond to specification.

6. If the clearance is not within specification, the valves will require adjustment. Loosen the locknut on the end of the rocker arm and, still holding the nut with an open end wrench, turn the adjustments screw to achieve the correct clearance.

7. Once the correct valve clearance is achieved, keep the adjustment screw from turning with a suitable tool and then tighten the locknut. Recheck the valve clearances.

8. Turn the engine one complete revolution (360°) and adjust the remaining valves. Follow Steps 5–7 and use the valve arrangement illustration marked SECOND.

9. Use a new gasket and then install the cylinder head cover. Install

any other components which were removed.

2S-E, 3Y-EC, 4Y-EC, 4K-E and 5M-GE

These engines are equipped with hydraulic lash adjusters in the valve train. These adjusters maintain a zero clearance between the rocker arm and valve stem, no adjustment is possible or necessary.

4A-GE, 4A-GEC, 4A-GELC and Diesel

1. Start the engine and run it until it reaches normal operating temperature.

2. Stop the engine. Remove the air cleaner assembly. Remove any other hoses, cables, etc. which are attached to, or in the way of the cylinder head cover. Be careful when removing components as the engine will be hot.

3. Use a wrench and turn the crankshaft until the notch in the pulley aligns with the timing pointer in the front cover. This will insure that engine is at TDC.

NOTE: Check that the valve lifters on the No 1 cylinder are loose and those on No 4 cylinder are tight. If not, turn the crankshaft one complete revolution (360) and then realign the marks.

4. Using a flat feeler gauge measure the clearance between the camshaft lobe and the valve lifter. Check only the valves listed under FIRST in the accompanying valve arrangement illustrations for your particular engine.

NOTE: If the measurement is within specifications, go on to the next step. If not, record the measurement taken for each individual valve.

5. Turn the crankshaft one complete revolution and realign the timing marks. Measure the clearance of the valves shown in the valve arrangement illustration marked SECOND.

NOTE: If the measurement for this set of valves (and also the previous one) is within specification, you need go no further, the procedure is finished. If not, record the measurements and then proceed to Step 6.

6. Turn the crankshaft to position the intake camshaft lobe of the cylinder to be adjusted, upward. Both intake and exhaust valve clearance may be adjusted at the same time if so required.

7. Using a suitable tool, turn the

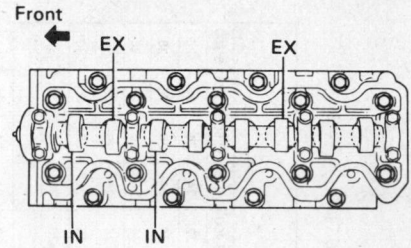

Adjust these valves FIRST on diesel engines

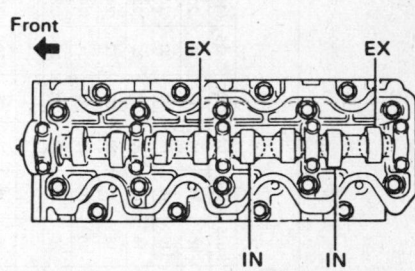

Adjust these valves SECOND on diesel engines

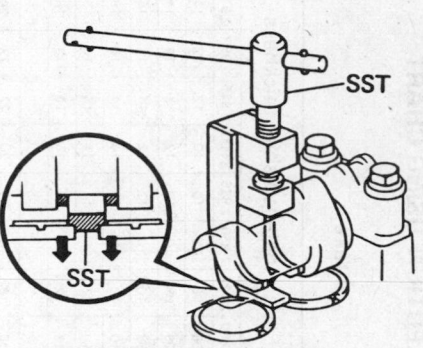

Using the special tool to depress the valve lifter on the diesel engine

Removing the valve and adjusting shim— diesel engines

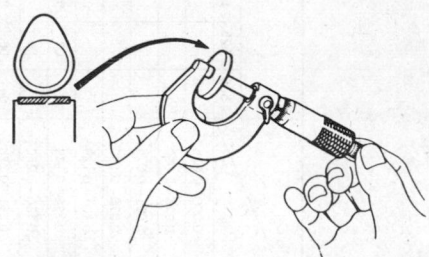

Measuring the shim size (thickness)—3S-GE and 4A-GE engines

SHIM SELECTION USING CHART

Intake

Intake valve clearance (cold):
0.15 – 0.25 mm (0.006 – 0.010 in.)

Example:
2.800 mm Installed is
Measured clearance is 0.450 mm
Replace 2.800 mm shim with
shim No. 24 (3.050 mm).

Shim Selection Chart—4A-GE

Shim thickness mm (in.)

Shim No.	Thickness	Shim No.	Thickness
02	2.500 (0.0984)	20	2.950 (0.1161)
04	2.550 (0.1004)	22	3.000 (0.1181)
06	2.600 (0.1024)	24	3.050 (0.1201)
08	2.650 (0.1043)	26	3.100 (0.1220)
10	2.700 (0.1063)	28	3.150 (0.1240)
12	2.750 (0.1083)	30	3.200 (0.1260)
14	2.800 (0.1102)	32	3.250 (0.1280)
16	2.850 (0.1122)	34	3.300 (0.1299)
18	2.900 (0.1142)		

Installed shim thickness (mm) / Measured clearance (mm)

Measured clearance (mm)	2.500	2.525	2.550	2.575	2.600	2.625	2.650	2.675	2.700	2.725	2.750	2.775	2.800	2.825	2.850	2.875	2.900	2.925	2.950	2.975	3.000	3.025	3.050	3.075	3.100	3.125	3.150	3.175	3.200	3.225	3.250	3.275	3.300
0.000–0.025								02	02	04	04	06	06	08	08	10	10	12	12	14	14	16	16	18	18	20	20	22	22	24	24	26	26
0.026–0.050							02	02	04	04	06	06	08	08	10	10	12	12	14	14	16	16	18	18	20	20	22	22	24	24	26	26	28
0.051–0.075						02	02	04	04	06	06	08	08	10	10	12	12	14	14	16	16	18	18	20	20	22	22	24	24	26	26	28	28
0.076–0.100					02	02	04	04	06	06	08	08	10	10	12	12	14	14	16	16	18	18	20	20	22	22	24	24	26	26	28	28	30
0.101–0.125				02	02	04	04	06	06	08	08	10	10	12	12	14	14	16	16	18	18	20	20	22	22	24	24	26	26	28	28	30	30
0.126–0.149			02	02	04	04	06	06	08	08	10	10	12	12	14	14	16	16	18	18	20	20	22	22	24	24	26	26	28	28	30	30	32
0.150–0.250																																	
0.251–0.275	04	06	06	08	08	10	10	12	12	14	14	16	16	18	18	20	20	22	22	24	24	26	26	28	28	30	30	32	32	34	34	34	34
0.276–0.300	06	06	08	08	10	10	12	12	14	14	16	16	18	18	20	20	22	22	24	24	26	26	28	28	30	30	32	32	34	34	34	34	34
0.301–0.325	06	08	08	10	10	12	12	14	14	16	16	18	18	20	20	22	22	24	24	26	26	28	28	30	30	32	32	34	34	34	34	34	34
0.326–0.350	08	08	10	10	12	12	14	14	16	16	18	18	20	20	22	22	24	24	26	26	28	28	30	30	32	32	34	34	34	34	34	34	34
0.351–0.375	08	10	10	12	12	14	14	16	16	18	18	20	20	22	22	24	24	26	26	28	28	30	30	32	32	34	34	34	34	34	34	34	34
0.376–0.400	10	10	12	12	14	14	16	16	18	18	20	20	22	22	24	24	26	26	28	28	30	30	32	32	34	34	34	34	34	34	34	34	34
0.401–0.425	10	12	12	14	14	16	16	18	18	20	20	22	22	24	24	26	26	28	28	30	30	32	32	34	34	34	34	34	34	34	34	34	34
0.426–0.450	12	12	14	14	16	16	18	18	20	20	22	22	24	24	26	26	28	28	30	30	32	32	34	34	34	34	34	34	34	34	34	34	34
0.451–0.475	12	14	14	16	16	18	18	20	20	22	22	24	24	26	26	28	28	30	30	32	32	34	34	34	34	34	34	34	34	34	34	34	34
0.476–0.500	14	14	16	16	18	18	20	20	22	22	24	24	26	26	28	28	30	30	32	32	34	34	34	34	34	34	34	34	34	34	34	34	34
0.501–0.525	14	16	16	18	18	20	20	22	22	24	24	26	26	28	28	30	30	32	32	34	34	34	34	34	34	34	34	34	34	34	34	34	34
0.526–0.550	16	16	18	18	20	20	22	22	24	24	26	26	28	28	30	30	32	32	34	34	34	34	34	34	34	34	34	34	34	34	34	34	34
0.551–0.575	16	18	18	20	20	22	22	24	24	26	26	28	28	30	30	32	32	34	34	34	34	34	34	34	34	34	34	34	34	34	34	34	34
0.576–0.600	18	18	20	20	22	22	24	24	26	26	28	28	30	30	32	32	34	34	34	34	34	34	34	34	34	34	34	34	34	34	34	34	34
0.601–0.625	18	20	20	22	22	24	24	26	26	28	28	30	30	32	32	34	34	34	34	34	34	34	34	34	34	34	34	34	34	34	34	34	34
0.626–0.650	20	20	22	22	24	24	26	26	28	28	30	30	32	32	34	34	34	34	34	34	34	34	34	34	34	34	34	34	34	34	34	34	34
0.651–0.675	20	22	22	24	24	26	26	28	28	30	30	32	32	34	34	34	34	34	34	34	34	34	34	34	34	34	34	34	34	34	34	34	34
0.676–0.700	22	22	24	24	26	26	28	28	30	30	32	32	34	34	34	34	34	34	34	34	34	34	34	34	34	34	34	34	34	34	34	34	34
0.701–0.725	22	24	24	26	26	28	28	30	30	32	32	34	34	34	34	34	34	34	34	34	34	34	34	34	34	34	34	34	34	34	34	34	34
0.726–0.750	24	24	26	26	28	28	30	30	32	32	34	34	34	34	34	34	34	34	34	34	34	34	34	34	34	34	34	34	34	34	34	34	34
0.751–0.775	24	26	26	28	28	30	30	32	32	34	34	34	34	34	34	34	34	34	34	34	34	34	34	34	34	34	34	34	34	34	34	34	34
0.776–0.800	26	26	28	28	30	30	32	32	34	34	34	34	34	34	34	34	34	34	34	34	34	34	34	34	34	34	34	34	34	34	34	34	34
0.801–0.825	26	28	28	30	30	32	32	34	34	34	34	34	34	34	34	34	34	34	34	34	34	34	34	34	34	34	34	34	34	34	34	34	34
0.826–0.850	28	28	30	30	32	32	34	34	34	34	34	34	34	34	34	34	34	34	34	34	34	34	34	34	34	34	34	34	34	34	34	34	34
0.851–0.875	28	30	30	32	32	34	34	34	34	34	34	34	34	34	34	34	34	34	34	34	34	34	34	34	34	34	34	34	34	34	34	34	34
0.876–0.900	30	30	32	32	34	34	34	34	34	34	34	34	34	34	34	34	34	34	34	34	34	34	34	34	34	34	34	34	34	34	34	34	34
0.901–0.925	30	32	32	34	34	34	34	34	34	34	34	34	34	34	34	34	34	34	34	34	34	34	34	34	34	34	34	34	34	34	34	34	34
0.926–0.950	32	32	34	34	34	34	34	34	34	34	34	34	34	34	34	34	34	34	34	34	34	34	34	34	34	34	34	34	34	34	34	34	34
0.951–0.975	32	34	34	34	34	34	34	34	34	34	34	34	34	34	34	34	34	34	34	34	34	34	34	34	34	34	34	34	34	34	34	34	34
0.976–1.000	34	34	34	34	34	34	34	34	34	34	34	34	34	34	34	34	34	34	34	34	34	34	34	34	34	34	34	34	34	34	34	34	34
1.001–1.025	34	34	34	34	34	34	34	34	34	34	34	34	34	34	34	34	34	34	34	34	34	34	34	34	34	34	34	34	34	34	34	34	34
1.026–1.050	34	34	34	34	34	34	34	34	34	34	34	34	34	34	34	34	34	34	34	34	34	34	34	34	34	34	34	34	34	34	34	34	34

SHIM SELECTION USING CHART

Exhaust

Shim thickness — mm (in.)

Shim No.	Thickness	Shim No.	Thickness
02	2.500 (0.0984)	20	2.950 (0.1161)
04	2.550 (0.1004)	22	3.000 (0.1181)
06	2.600 (0.1024)	24	3.050 (0.1201)
08	2.650 (0.1043)	26	3.100 (0.1220)
10	2.700 (0.1063)	28	3.150 (0.1240)
12	2.750 (0.1083)	30	3.200 (0.1260)
14	2.800 (0.1102)	32	3.250 (0.1280)
16	2.850 (0.1122)	34	3.300 (0.1299)
18	2.900 (0.1142)		

Exhaust valve clearance (cold):
0.20 — 0.30 mm (0.008 — 0.012 in.)

Example: Measured clearance is 0.450 mm
2.800 mm Installed is
Replace 2.800 mm shim with
shim No. 22 (3.000 mm).

Shim Selection Chart—4A-GE

Installed shim thickness (mm) vs. Measured clearance (mm)

Measured clearance (mm)	2.500	2.525	2.550	2.575	2.600	2.625	2.650	2.675	2.700	2.725	2.750	2.775	2.800	2.825	2.850	2.875	2.900	2.925	2.950	2.975	3.000	3.025	3.050	3.075	3.100	3.125	3.150	3.175	3.200	3.225	3.250	3.275	3.300
0.000—0.025										02	02	04	04	06	06	08	08	10	10	12	12	14	14	16	16	18	18	20	20	22	22	24	24
0.026—0.050									02	02	04	04	06	06	08	08	10	10	12	12	14	14	16	16	18	18	20	20	22	22	24	24	26
0.051—0.075								02	02	04	04	06	06	08	08	10	10	12	12	14	14	16	16	18	18	20	20	22	22	24	24	26	26
0.076—0.100							02	02	04	04	06	06	08	08	10	10	12	12	14	14	16	16	18	18	20	20	22	22	24	24	26	26	28
0.101—0.125						02	02	04	04	06	06	08	08	10	10	12	12	14	14	16	16	18	18	20	20	22	22	24	24	26	26	28	28
0.126—0.150					02	02	04	04	06	06	08	08	10	10	12	12	14	14	16	16	18	18	20	20	22	22	24	24	26	26	28	28	30
0.151—0.175				02	02	04	04	06	06	08	08	10	10	12	12	14	14	16	16	18	18	20	20	22	22	24	24	26	26	28	28	30	30
0.176—0.199			02	02	04	04	06	06	08	08	10	10	12	12	14	14	16	16	18	18	20	20	22	22	24	24	26	26	28	28	30	30	32
0.200—0.300																																	
0.301—0.325	04	06	06	08	08	10	10	12	12	14	14	16	16	18	18	20	20	22	22	24	24	26	26	28	28	30	30	32	32	34	34	34	34
0.326—0.350	06	06	08	08	10	10	12	12	14	14	16	16	18	18	20	20	22	22	24	24	26	26	28	28	30	30	32	32	34	34	34	34	34
0.351—0.375	06	08	08	10	10	12	12	14	14	16	16	18	18	20	20	22	22	24	24	26	26	28	28	30	30	32	32	34	34	34	34	34	34
0.376—0.400	08	08	10	10	12	12	14	14	16	16	18	18	20	20	22	22	24	24	26	26	28	28	30	30	32	32	34	34	34	34	34	34	34
0.401—0.425	08	10	10	12	12	14	14	16	16	18	18	20	20	22	22	24	24	26	26	28	28	30	30	32	32	34	34	34	34	34	34	34	34
0.426—0.450	10	10	12	12	14	14	16	16	18	18	20	20	22	22	24	24	26	26	28	28	30	30	32	32	34	34	34	34	34	34	34	34	34
0.451—0.475	10	12	12	14	14	16	16	18	18	20	20	22	22	24	24	26	26	28	28	30	30	32	32	34	34	34	34	34	34	34	34	34	34
0.476—0.500	12	12	14	14	16	16	18	18	20	20	22	22	24	24	26	26	28	28	30	30	32	32	34	34	34	34	34	34	34	34	34	34	34
0.501—0.525	12	14	14	16	16	18	18	20	20	22	22	24	24	26	26	28	28	30	30	32	32	34	34	34	34	34	34	34	34	34	34	34	34
0.526—0.550	14	14	16	16	18	18	20	20	22	22	24	24	26	26	28	28	30	30	32	32	34	34	34	34	34	34	34	34	34	34	34	34	34
0.551—0.575	14	16	16	18	18	20	20	22	22	24	24	26	26	28	28	30	30	32	32	34	34	34	34	34	34	34	34	34	34	34	34	34	34
0.576—0.600	16	16	18	18	20	20	22	22	24	24	26	26	28	28	30	30	32	32	34	34	34	34	34	34	34	34	34	34	34	34	34	34	34
0.601—0.625	16	18	18	20	20	22	22	24	24	26	26	28	28	30	30	32	32	34	34	34	34	34	34	34	34	34	34	34	34	34	34	34	34
0.626—0.650	18	18	20	20	22	22	24	24	26	26	28	28	30	30	32	32	34	34	34	34	34	34	34	34	34	34	34	34	34	34	34	34	34
0.651—0.675	18	20	20	22	22	24	24	26	26	28	28	30	30	32	32	34	34	34	34	34	34	34	34	34	34	34	34	34	34	34	34	34	34
0.676—0.700	20	20	22	22	24	24	26	26	28	28	30	30	32	32	34	34	34	34	34	34	34	34	34	34	34	34	34	34	34	34	34	34	34
0.701—0.725	20	22	22	24	24	26	26	28	28	30	30	32	32	34	34	34	34	34	34	34	34	34	34	34	34	34	34	34	34	34	34	34	34
0.726—0.750	22	22	24	24	26	26	28	28	30	30	32	32	34	34	34	34	34	34	34	34	34	34	34	34	34	34	34	34	34	34	34	34	34
0.751—0.775	22	24	24	26	26	28	28	30	30	32	32	34	34	34	34	34	34	34	34	34	34	34	34	34	34	34	34	34	34	34	34	34	34
0.776—0.800	24	24	26	26	28	28	30	30	32	32	34	34	34	34	34	34	34	34	34	34	34	34	34	34	34	34	34	34	34	34	34	34	34
0.801—0.825	24	26	26	28	28	30	30	32	32	34	34	34	34	34	34	34	34	34	34	34	34	34	34	34	34	34	34	34	34	34	34	34	34
0.826—0.850	26	26	28	28	30	30	32	32	34	34	34	34	34	34	34	34	34	34	34	34	34	34	34	34	34	34	34	34	34	34	34	34	34
0.851—0.875	26	28	28	30	30	32	32	34	34	34	34	34	34	34	34	34	34	34	34	34	34	34	34	34	34	34	34	34	34	34	34	34	34
0.876—0.900	28	28	30	30	32	32	34	34	34	34	34	34	34	34	34	34	34	34	34	34	34	34	34	34	34	34	34	34	34	34	34	34	34
0.901—0.925	28	30	30	32	32	34	34	34	34	34	34	34	34	34	34	34	34	34	34	34	34	34	34	34	34	34	34	34	34	34	34	34	34
0.926—0.950	30	30	32	32	34	34	34	34	34	34	34	34	34	34	34	34	34	34	34	34	34	34	34	34	34	34	34	34	34	34	34	34	34
0.951—0.975	30	32	32	34	34	34	34	34	34	34	34	34	34	34	34	34	34	34	34	34	34	34	34	34	34	34	34	34	34	34	34	34	34
0.976—1.000	32	32	34	34	34	34	34	34	34	34	34	34	34	34	34	34	34	34	34	34	34	34	34	34	34	34	34	34	34	34	34	34	34
1.001—1.025	32	34	34	34	34	34	34	34	34	34	34	34	34	34	34	34	34	34	34	34	34	34	34	34	34	34	34	34	34	34	34	34	34
1.026—1.050	34	34	34	34	34	34	34	34	34	34	34	34	34	34	34	34	34	34	34	34	34	34	34	34	34	34	34	34	34	34	34	34	34
1.051—1.075	34	34	34	34	34	34	34	34	34	34	34	34	34	34	34	34	34	34	34	34	34	34	34	34	34	34	34	34	34	34	34	34	34
1.076—1.100	34	34	34	34	34	34	34	34	34	34	34	34	34	34	34	34	34	34	34	34	34	34	34	34	34	34	34	34	34	34	34	34	34

SHIM SELECTION CHART

Exhaust

Measured Clearance (mm) / Installed Shim Thickness (mm)

The chart is a shim selection matrix. Installed Shim Thickness columns (mm): 2.200, 2.225, 2.250, 2.275, 2.300, 2.325, 2.350, 2.375, 2.400, 2.425, 2.450, 2.475, 2.500, 2.525, 2.550, 2.575, 2.600, 2.625, 2.650, 2.675, 2.700, 2.725, 2.750, 2.775, 2.800, 2.825, 2.850, 2.875, 2.900, 2.925, 2.950, 2.975, 3.000, 3.025, 3.050, 3.075, 3.100, 3.125, 3.150, 3.175, 3.200, 3.225, 3.250, 3.275, 3.300, 3.325, 3.350, 3.375, 3.400.

Measured Clearance rows (mm): 0.000–0.025, 0.026–0.050, 0.051–0.075, 0.076–0.100, 0.101–0.125, 0.126–0.150, 0.151–0.175, 0.176–0.200, 0.201–0.225, 0.226–0.249, 0.250–0.350, 0.351–0.375, 0.376–0.400, 0.401–0.425, 0.426–0.450, 0.451–0.475, 0.476–0.500, 0.501–0.525, 0.526–0.550, 0.551–0.575, 0.576–0.600, 0.601–0.625, 0.626–0.650, 0.651–0.675, 0.676–0.701, 0.701–0.725, 0.726–0.750, 0.751–0.775, 0.776–0.800, 0.801–0.825, 0.826–0.850, 0.851–0.875, 0.876–0.900, 0.901–0.925, 0.926–0.950, 0.951–0.975, 0.976–1.000, 1.001–1.025, 1.026–1.050, 1.051–1.075, 1.076–1.100, 1.101–1.125, 1.126–1.150, 1.151–1.175, 1.176–1.200, 1.201–1.225, 1.226–1.250, 1.251–1.275, 1.276–1.300, 1.301–1.325, 1.326–1.350, 1.351–1.375, 1.376–1.400, 1.401–1.425, 1.426–1.450, 1.451–1.475, 1.476–1.500, 1.501–1.525, 1.526–1.550.

Shim Thickness

Shim No.	Thickness mm (in.)	Shim No.	Thickness mm (in.)
01	2.20 (0.0866)	27	2.85 (0.1122)
03	2.25 (0.0886)	29	2.90 (0.1142)
05	2.30 (0.0906)	31	2.95 (0.1161)
07	2.35 (0.0925)	33	3.00 (0.1181)
09	2.40 (0.0945)	35	3.05 (0.1201)
11	2.45 (0.0965)	37	3.10 (0.1220)
13	2.50 (0.0984)	39	3.15 (0.1240)
15	2.55 (0.1004)	41	3.20 (0.1260)
17	2.60 (0.1024)	43	3.25 (0.1280)
19	2.65 (0.1043)	45	3.30 (0.1299)
21	2.70 (0.1063)	47	3.35 (0.1319)
23	2.75 (0.1083)	49	3.40 (0.1339)
25	2.80 (0.1102)		

Exhaust Valve Clearance (cold): 0.25 – 0.35 mm (0.0010 – 0.014 in.)

Example: 2.700 mm (0.1063 in.) shim installed
Measured clearance is 0.450 mm (0.0177 in.).
Replace 2.700 mm (0.1063 in.) shim with shim No. 27.

Shim Selection Chart—Diesel

SHIM SELECTION CHART

Intake

Shim Thickness

Shim No.	Thickness mm (in.)	Shim No.	Thickness mm (in.)
01	2.20 (0.0866)	27	2.85 (0.1122)
03	2.25 (0.0886)	29	2.90 (0.1142)
05	2.30 (0.0906)	31	2.95 (0.1161)
07	2.35 (0.0925)	33	3.00 (0.1181)
09	2.40 (0.0945)	35	3.05 (0.1201)
11	2.45 (0.0965)	37	3.10 (0.1220)
13	2.50 (0.0984)	39	3.15 (0.1240)
15	2.55 (0.1004)	41	3.20 (0.1260)
17	2.60 (0.1024)	43	3.25 (0.1280)
19	2.65 (0.1043)	45	3.30 (0.1299)
21	2.70 (0.1063)	47	3.35 (0.1319)
23	2.75 (0.1083)	49	3.40 (0.1339)
25	2.80 (0.1102)		

Intake Valve Clearance (cold): 0.20 – 0.30 mm
(0.008 – 0.012 in.)

Example: 2.700 mm (0.1063 in.) shim installed
Measured clearance is 0.350 mm (0.0138 in.).
Replace 2.700 mm (0.1063 in.) shim with
shim No. 25.

Shim Selection Chart—Diesel

The chart below is a shim selection matrix. The left column lists the Measured Clearance (mm) ranges; the top row lists the Installed Shim Thickness (mm) from 2.200 to 3.400. The intersecting cells give the replacement shim number (01–49).

Installed Shim Thickness (mm): 2.200, 2.225, 2.250, 2.275, 2.300, 2.325, 2.350, 2.375, 2.400, 2.425, 2.450, 2.475, 2.500, 2.525, 2.550, 2.575, 2.600, 2.625, 2.650, 2.675, 2.700, 2.725, 2.750, 2.775, 2.800, 2.825, 2.850, 2.875, 2.900, 2.925, 2.950, 2.975, 3.000, 3.025, 3.050, 3.075, 3.100, 3.125, 3.150, 3.175, 3.200, 3.225, 3.250, 3.275, 3.300, 3.325, 3.350, 3.375, 3.400

Measured Clearance (mm) ranges (left column):
0.000–0.025, 0.026–0.050, 0.051–0.075, 0.076–0.100, 0.101–0.125, 0.126–0.150, 0.151–0.175, 0.176–0.199, 0.200–0.300, 0.301–0.325, 0.326–0.350, 0.351–0.375, 0.376–0.400, 0.401–0.425, 0.426–0.450, 0.451–0.475, 0.476–0.500, 0.501–0.525, 0.526–0.550, 0.551–0.575, 0.576–0.600, 0.601–0.625, 0.626–0.650, 0.651–0.675, 0.676–0.700, 0.701–0.725, 0.726–0.750, 0.751–0.775, 0.776–0.800, 0.801–0.825, 0.826–0.850, 0.851–0.875, 0.876–0.900, 0.901–0.925, 0.926–0.950, 0.951–0.975, 0.976–1.000, 1.001–1.025, 1.026–1.050, 1.051–1.075, 1.076–1.100, 1.101–1.125, 1.126–1.150, 1.151–1.175, 1.176–1.200, 1.201–1.225, 1.226–1.250, 1.251–1.275, 1.276–1.300, 1.301–1.325, 1.326–1.350, 1.351–1.375, 1.376–1.400, 1.401–1.425, 1.426–1.450, 1.451–1.475, 1.476–1.500

SHIM SELECTION USING CHART

Intake

Intake valve clearance chart — Installed shim thickness (mm) columns run from 2.000 to 3.300 in 0.025 mm increments. Cell values are shim numbers.

Measured clearance (mm)	Shim numbers (reading left to right)
0.000–0.025	02 02 02 04 04 06 06 08 08 10 10 12 12 14 14 16 16 18 18 20 20 22 22 24 24 26 26 28 28 30 30 32 32 34 34 36 36 38 38 40 40 42 42 44 44 46 46
0.026–0.050	02 02 02 04 04 06 06 08 08 10 10 12 12 14 14 16 16 18 18 20 20 22 22 24 24 26 26 28 28 30 30 32 32 34 34 36 36 38 38 40 40 42 42 44 44 46 46 48
0.051–0.075	02 02 04 04 06 06 08 08 10 10 12 12 14 14 16 16 18 18 20 20 22 22 24 24 26 26 28 28 30 30 32 32 34 34 36 36 38 38 40 40 42 42 44 44 46 46 48
0.076–0.100	02 02 02 04 04 06 06 08 08 10 10 12 12 14 14 16 16 18 18 20 20 22 22 24 24 26 26 28 28 30 30 32 32 34 34 36 36 38 38 40 40 42 42 44 44 46 46 48 48 50
0.101–0.125	02 02 02 04 04 06 06 08 08 10 10 12 12 14 14 16 16 18 18 20 20 22 22 24 24 26 26 28 28 30 30 32 32 34 34 36 36 38 38 40 40 42 42 44 44 46 46 48 48 50 50
0.126–0.149	02 02 02 04 04 06 06 08 08 10 10 12 12 14 14 16 16 18 18 20 20 22 22 24 24 26 26 28 28 30 30 32 32 34 34 36 36 38 38 40 40 42 42 44 44 46 46 48 48 50 50 52
0.150–0.250	(no replacement required)
0.251–0.275	04 06 06 08 08 10 10 12 12 14 14 16 16 18 18 20 20 22 22 24 24 26 26 28 28 30 30 32 32 34 34 36 36 38 38 40 40 42 42 44 44 46 46 48 48 50 50 52 52 54 54 54
0.276–0.300	06 06 08 08 10 10 12 12 14 14 16 16 18 18 20 20 22 22 24 24 26 26 28 28 30 30 32 32 34 34 36 36 38 38 40 40 42 42 44 44 46 46 48 48 50 50 52 52 54 54 54
0.301–0.325	06 08 08 10 10 12 12 14 14 16 16 18 18 20 20 22 22 24 24 26 26 28 28 30 30 32 32 34 34 36 36 38 38 40 40 42 42 44 44 46 46 48 48 50 50 52 52 54 54 54
0.326–0.350	08 08 10 10 12 12 14 14 16 16 18 18 20 20 22 22 24 24 26 26 28 28 30 30 32 32 34 34 36 36 38 38 40 40 42 42 44 44 46 46 48 48 50 50 52 52 54 54 54
0.351–0.375	08 10 10 12 12 14 14 16 16 18 18 20 20 22 22 24 24 26 26 28 28 30 30 32 32 34 34 36 36 38 38 40 40 42 42 44 44 46 46 48 48 50 50 52 52 54 54 54
0.376–0.400	10 10 12 12 14 14 16 16 18 18 20 20 22 22 24 24 26 26 28 28 30 30 32 32 34 34 36 36 38 38 40 40 42 42 44 44 46 46 48 48 50 50 52 52 54 54 54
0.401–0.425	10 12 12 14 14 16 16 18 18 20 20 22 22 24 24 26 26 28 28 30 30 32 32 34 34 36 36 38 38 40 40 42 42 44 44 46 46 48 48 50 50 52 52 54 54 54
0.426–0.450	12 12 14 14 16 16 18 18 20 20 22 22 24 24 26 26 28 28 30 30 32 32 34 34 36 36 38 38 40 40 42 42 44 44 46 46 48 48 50 50 52 52 54 54 54
0.451–0.475	12 14 14 16 16 18 18 20 20 22 22 24 24 26 26 28 28 30 30 32 32 34 34 36 36 38 38 40 40 42 42 44 44 46 46 48 48 50 50 52 52 54 54 54
0.476–0.500	14 14 16 16 18 18 20 20 22 22 24 24 26 26 28 28 30 30 32 32 34 34 36 36 38 38 40 40 42 42 44 44 46 46 48 48 50 50 52 52 54 54 54
0.501–0.525	14 16 16 18 18 20 20 22 22 24 24 26 26 28 28 30 30 32 32 34 34 36 36 38 38 40 40 42 42 44 44 46 46 48 48 50 50 52 52 54 54 54
0.526–0.550	16 16 18 18 20 20 22 22 24 24 26 26 28 28 30 30 32 32 34 34 36 36 38 38 40 40 42 42 44 44 46 46 48 48 50 50 52 52 54 54 54
0.551–0.575	16 18 18 20 20 22 22 24 24 26 26 28 28 30 30 32 32 34 34 36 36 38 38 40 40 42 42 44 44 46 46 48 48 50 50 52 52 54 54 54
0.576–0.600	18 18 20 20 22 22 24 24 26 26 28 28 30 30 32 32 34 34 36 36 38 38 40 40 42 42 44 44 46 46 48 48 50 50 52 52 54 54 54
0.601–0.625	18 20 20 22 22 24 24 26 26 28 28 30 30 32 32 34 34 36 36 38 38 40 40 42 42 44 44 46 46 48 48 50 50 52 52 54 54 54
0.626–0.650	20 20 22 22 24 24 26 26 28 28 30 30 32 32 34 34 36 36 38 38 40 40 42 42 44 44 46 46 48 48 50 50 52 52 54 54 54
0.651–0.675	20 22 22 24 24 26 26 28 28 30 30 32 32 34 34 36 36 38 38 40 40 42 42 44 44 46 46 48 48 50 50 52 52 54 54 54
0.676–0.700	22 22 24 24 26 26 28 28 30 30 32 32 34 34 36 36 38 38 40 40 42 42 44 44 46 46 48 48 50 50 52 52 54 54 54
0.701–0.725	22 24 24 26 26 28 28 30 30 32 32 34 34 36 36 38 38 40 40 42 42 44 44 46 46 48 48 50 50 52 52 54 54 54
0.726–0.750	24 24 26 26 28 28 30 30 32 32 34 34 36 36 38 38 40 40 42 42 44 44 46 46 48 48 50 50 52 52 54 54 54
0.751–0.775	24 26 26 28 28 30 30 32 32 34 34 36 36 38 38 40 40 42 42 44 44 46 46 48 48 50 50 52 52 54 54 54
0.776–0.800	26 26 28 28 30 30 32 32 34 34 36 36 38 38 40 40 42 42 44 44 46 46 48 48 50 50 52 52 54 54 54
0.801–0.825	26 28 28 30 30 32 32 34 34 36 36 38 38 40 40 42 42 44 44 46 46 48 48 50 50 52 52 54 54 54
0.826–0.850	28 28 30 30 32 32 34 34 36 36 38 38 40 40 42 42 44 44 46 46 48 48 50 50 52 52 54 54 54
0.851–0.875	28 30 30 32 32 34 34 36 36 38 38 40 40 42 42 44 44 46 46 48 48 50 50 52 52 54 54 54
0.876–0.900	30 30 32 32 34 34 36 36 38 38 40 40 42 42 44 44 46 46 48 48 50 50 52 52 54 54 54
0.901–0.925	30 32 32 34 34 36 36 38 38 40 40 42 42 44 44 46 46 48 48 50 50 52 52 54 54 54
0.926–0.950	32 32 34 34 36 36 38 38 40 40 42 42 44 44 46 46 48 48 50 50 52 52 54 54 54
0.951–0.975	32 34 34 36 36 38 38 40 40 42 42 44 44 46 46 48 48 50 50 52 52 54 54 54
0.976–1.000	34 34 36 36 38 38 40 40 42 42 44 44 46 46 48 48 50 50 52 52 54 54 54
1.001–1.025	34 36 36 38 38 40 40 42 42 44 44 46 46 48 48 50 50 52 52 54 54 54
1.026–1.050	36 36 38 38 40 40 42 42 44 44 46 46 48 48 50 50 52 52 54 54 54
1.051–1.075	36 38 38 40 40 42 42 44 44 46 46 48 48 50 50 52 52 54 54 54
1.076–1.100	38 38 40 40 42 42 44 44 46 46 48 48 50 50 52 52 54 54 54
1.101–1.125	38 40 40 42 42 44 44 46 46 48 48 50 50 52 52 54 54 54
1.126–1.150	40 40 42 42 44 44 46 46 48 48 50 50 52 52 54 54 54
1.151–1.175	40 42 42 44 44 46 46 48 48 50 50 52 52 54 54 54
1.176–1.200	42 42 44 44 46 46 48 48 50 50 52 52 54 54 54
1.201–1.225	42 44 44 46 46 48 48 50 50 52 52 54 54 54
1.226–1.250	44 44 46 46 48 48 50 50 52 52 54 54 54
1.251–1.275	44 46 46 48 48 50 50 52 52 54 54 54
1.276–1.300	46 46 48 48 50 50 52 52 54 54 54
1.301–1.325	46 48 48 50 50 52 52 54 54 54
1.326–1.350	48 48 50 50 52 52 54 54 54
1.351–1.375	48 50 50 52 52 54 54 54
1.376–1.400	50 50 52 52 54 54 54
1.401–1.425	50 52 52 54 54 54
1.426–1.450	52 52 54 54 54
1.451–1.475	52 54 54 54
1.476–1.500	54 54 54
1.501–1.525	54 54
1.526–1.550	54

Shim thickness mm (in.)

Shim No.	Thickness	Shim No.	Thickness
02	2.000 (0.0787)	30	2.700 (0.1063)
04	2.050 (0.0807)	32	2.750 (0.1083)
06	2.100 (0.0827)	34	2.800 (0.1102)
08	2.150 (0.0846)	36	2.850 (0.1122)
10	2.200 (0.0866)	38	2.900 (0.1142)
12	2.250 (0.0886)	40	2.950 (0.1161)
14	2.300 (0.0906)	42	3.000 (0.1181)
16	2.350 (0.0925)	33	3.050 (0.1201)
18	2.400 (0.0945)	46	3.100 (0.1220)
20	2.450 (0.0965)	48	3.150 (0.1240)
22	2.500 (0.0984)	50	3.200 (0.1260)
24	2.550 (0.1004)	52	3.250 (0.1280)
26	2.600 (0.1024)	54	3.300 (0.1299)
28	2.650 (0.1043)		

Intake valve clearance (cold):
0.15 - 0.25 mm (0.006 - 0.010 in.)

Example: A 2.800 mm shim is installed and measured clearance is 0.450 mm (0.0177 in.).
Replace the 2.800 mm shim with shim No. 44 (3.050 mm).

Shim selection chart—3S-GE

SHIM SELECTION USING CHART

Exhaust

Installed shim thickness (mm)

Column headers (left to right): 2.000, 2.025, 2.050, 2.075, 2.100, 2.125, 2.150, 2.175, 2.200, 2.225, 2.250, 2.275, 2.300, 2.325, 2.350, 2.375, 2.400, 2.425, 2.450, 2.475, 2.500, 2.525, 2.550, 2.575, 2.600, 2.625, 2.650, 2.675, 2.700, 2.725, 2.750, 2.775, 2.800, 2.825, 2.850, 2.875, 2.900, 2.925, 2.950, 2.975, 3.000, 3.025, 3.050, 3.075, 3.100, 3.125, 3.150, 3.175, 3.200, 3.225, 3.250, 3.275, 3.300

Measured clearance (mm)	Shim No. sequence (reading along the installed-shim-thickness columns)
0.000-0.025	02 02 02 04 04 06 06 08 08 10 10 12 12 14 14 16 16 18 18 20 20 22 22 24 24 26 26 28 28 30 30 32 32 34 34 36 36 38 38 40 40 42 42 44 44
0.026-0.050	02 02 02 04 04 06 06 08 08 10 10 12 12 14 14 16 16 18 18 20 20 22 22 24 24 26 26 28 28 30 30 32 32 34 34 36 36 38 38 40 40 42 42 44 44 46
0.051-0.075	02 02 02 04 04 06 06 08 08 10 10 12 12 14 14 16 16 18 18 20 20 22 22 24 24 26 26 28 28 30 30 32 32 34 34 36 36 38 38 40 40 42 42 44 44 46 46
0.076-0.100	02 02 02 04 04 06 06 08 08 10 10 12 12 14 14 16 16 18 18 20 20 22 22 24 24 26 26 28 28 30 30 32 32 34 34 36 36 38 38 40 40 42 42 44 44 46 46 48
0.101-0.125	02 02 02 04 04 06 06 08 08 10 10 12 12 14 14 16 16 18 18 20 20 22 22 24 24 26 26 28 28 30 30 32 32 34 34 36 36 38 38 40 40 42 42 44 44 46 46 48 48
0.126-0.150	02 02 04 04 06 06 08 08 10 10 12 12 14 14 16 16 18 18 20 20 22 22 24 24 26 26 28 28 30 30 32 32 34 34 36 36 38 38 40 40 42 42 44 44 46 46 48 48 50
0.151-0.175	02 02 02 04 04 06 06 08 08 10 10 12 12 14 14 16 16 18 18 20 20 22 22 24 24 26 26 28 28 30 30 32 32 34 34 36 36 38 38 40 40 42 42 44 44 46 46 48 48 50 50
0.176-0.199	02 02 02 04 04 06 06 08 08 10 10 12 12 14 14 16 16 18 18 20 20 22 22 24 24 26 26 28 28 30 30 32 32 34 34 36 36 38 38 40 40 42 42 44 44 46 46 48 48 50 50 52
0.200-0.300	
0.301-0.325	04 06 06 08 08 10 10 12 12 14 14 16 16 18 18 20 20 22 22 24 24 26 26 28 28 30 30 32 32 34 34 36 36 38 38 40 40 42 42 44 44 46 46 48 48 50 50 52 52 54 54 54
0.326-0.350	06 06 08 08 10 10 12 12 14 14 16 16 18 18 20 20 22 22 24 24 26 26 28 28 30 30 32 32 34 34 36 36 38 38 40 40 42 42 44 44 46 46 48 48 50 50 52 52 54 54 54
0.351-0.375	06 08 08 10 10 12 12 14 14 16 16 18 18 20 20 22 22 24 24 26 26 28 28 30 30 32 32 34 34 36 36 38 38 40 40 42 42 44 44 46 46 48 48 50 50 52 52 54 54 54
0.376-0.400	08 08 10 10 12 12 14 14 16 16 18 18 20 20 22 22 24 24 26 26 28 28 30 30 32 32 34 34 36 36 38 38 40 40 42 42 44 44 46 46 48 48 50 50 52 52 54 54 54
0.401-0.425	08 10 10 12 12 14 14 16 16 18 18 20 20 22 22 24 24 26 26 28 28 30 30 32 32 34 34 36 36 38 38 40 40 42 42 44 44 46 46 48 48 50 50 52 52 54 54 54
0.426-0.450	10 10 12 12 14 14 16 16 18 18 20 20 22 22 24 24 26 26 28 28 30 30 32 32 34 34 36 36 38 38 40 40 42 42 44 44 46 46 48 48 50 50 52 52 54 54 54
0.451-0.475	10 12 12 14 14 16 16 18 18 20 20 22 22 24 24 26 26 28 28 30 30 32 32 34 34 36 36 38 38 40 40 42 42 44 44 46 46 48 48 50 50 52 52 54 54 54
0.476-0.500	12 12 14 14 16 16 18 18 20 20 22 22 24 24 26 26 28 28 30 30 32 32 34 34 36 36 38 38 40 40 42 42 44 44 46 46 48 48 50 50 52 52 54 54 54
0.501-0.525	12 14 14 16 16 18 18 20 20 22 22 24 24 26 26 28 28 30 30 32 32 34 34 36 36 38 38 40 40 42 42 44 44 46 46 48 48 50 50 52 52 54 54 54
0.526-0.550	14 14 16 16 18 18 20 20 22 22 24 24 26 26 28 28 30 30 32 32 34 34 36 36 38 38 40 40 42 42 44 44 46 46 48 48 50 50 52 52 54 54 54
0.551-0.575	14 16 16 18 18 20 20 22 22 24 24 26 26 28 28 30 30 32 32 34 34 36 36 38 38 40 40 42 42 44 44 46 46 48 48 50 50 52 52 54 54 54
0.576-0.600	16 16 18 18 20 20 22 22 24 24 26 26 28 28 30 30 32 32 34 34 36 36 38 38 40 40 42 42 44 44 46 46 48 48 50 50 52 52 54 54 54
0.601-0.625	16 18 18 20 20 22 22 24 24 26 26 28 28 30 30 32 32 34 34 36 36 38 38 40 40 42 42 44 44 46 46 48 48 50 50 52 52 54 54 54
0.626-0.650	18 18 20 20 22 22 24 24 26 26 28 28 30 30 32 32 34 34 36 36 38 38 40 40 42 42 44 44 46 46 48 48 50 50 52 52 54 54 54
0.651-0.675	18 20 20 22 22 24 24 26 26 28 28 30 30 32 32 34 34 36 36 38 38 40 40 42 42 44 44 46 46 48 48 50 50 52 52 54 54 54
0.676-0.700	20 20 22 22 24 24 26 26 28 28 30 30 32 32 34 34 36 36 38 38 40 40 42 42 44 44 46 46 48 48 50 50 52 52 54 54 54
0.701-0.725	20 22 22 24 24 26 26 28 28 30 30 32 32 34 34 36 36 38 38 40 40 42 42 44 44 46 46 48 48 50 50 52 52 54 54 54
0.726-0.750	22 22 24 24 26 26 28 28 30 30 32 32 34 34 36 36 38 38 40 40 42 42 44 44 46 46 48 48 50 50 52 52 54 54 54
0.751-0.775	22 24 24 26 26 28 28 30 30 32 32 34 34 36 36 38 38 40 40 42 42 44 44 46 46 48 48 50 50 52 52 54 54 54
0.776-0.800	24 24 26 26 28 28 30 30 32 32 34 34 36 36 38 38 40 40 42 42 44 44 46 46 48 48 50 50 52 52 54 54 54
0.801-0.825	24 26 26 28 28 30 30 32 32 34 34 36 36 38 38 40 40 42 42 44 44 46 46 48 48 50 50 52 52 52 52
0.826-0.850	26 26 28 28 30 30 32 32 34 34 36 36 38 38 40 40 42 42 44 44 46 46 48 48 50 50 52 52 54 54 54
0.851-0.875	26 28 28 30 30 32 32 34 34 36 36 38 38 40 40 42 42 44 44 46 46 48 48 50 50 52 52 54 54 54
0.876-0.900	28 28 30 30 32 32 34 34 36 36 38 38 40 40 42 42 44 44 46 46 48 48 50 50 52 52 54 54 54
0.901-0.925	28 30 30 32 32 34 34 36 36 38 38 40 40 42 42 44 44 46 46 48 48 50 50 52 52 54 54 54
0.926-0.950	30 30 32 32 34 34 36 36 38 38 40 40 42 42 44 44 46 46 48 48 50 50 52 52 54 54 54
0.951-0.975	30 32 32 34 34 36 36 38 38 40 40 42 42 44 44 46 46 48 48 50 50 52 52 54 54 54
0.976-1.000	32 32 34 34 36 36 38 38 40 40 42 42 44 44 46 46 48 48 50 50 52 52 54 54 54
1.001-1.025	32 34 34 36 36 38 38 40 40 42 42 44 44 46 46 48 48 50 50 52 52 54 54 54
1.026-1.050	34 34 36 36 38 38 40 40 42 42 44 44 46 46 48 48 50 50 52 52 54 54 54
1.051-1.075	34 36 36 38 38 40 40 42 42 44 44 46 46 48 48 50 50 52 52 54 54 54
1.076-1.100	36 36 38 38 40 40 42 42 44 44 46 46 48 48 50 50 52 52 54 54 54
1.101-1.125	36 38 38 40 40 42 42 44 44 46 46 48 48 50 50 52 52 54 54 54
1.126-1.150	38 38 40 40 42 42 44 44 46 46 48 48 50 50 52 52 54 54 54
1.151-1.175	38 40 40 42 42 44 44 46 46 48 48 50 50 52 52 54 54 54
1.176-1.200	40 40 42 42 44 44 46 46 48 48 50 50 52 52 54 54 54
1.201-1.225	40 42 42 44 44 46 46 48 48 50 50 52 52 54 54 54
1.226-1.250	42 42 44 44 46 46 48 48 50 50 52 52 54 54 54
1.251-1.275	42 44 44 46 46 48 48 50 50 52 52 54 54 54
1.276-1.300	44 44 46 46 48 48 50 50 52 52 54 54 54
1.301-1.325	44 46 46 48 48 50 50 52 52 54 54 54
1.326-1.350	46 46 48 48 50 50 52 52 54 54 54
1.351-1.375	46 48 48 50 50 52 52 54 54 54
1.376-1.400	48 48 50 50 52 52 54 54 54
1.401-1.425	48 50 50 52 52 54 54 54
1.426-1.450	50 50 52 52 54 54 54
1.451-1.475	50 52 52 54 54 54
1.476-1.500	52 52 54 54 54
1.501-1.525	52 54 54 54
1.526-1.550	54 54 54
1.551-1.575	54 54
1.576-1.600	54

Shim thickness mm (in.)

Shim No.	Thickness	Shim No.	Thickness
02	2.000 (0.0787)	30	2.700 (0.1063)
04	2.050 (0.0807)	32	2.750 (0.1083)
06	2.100 (0.0827)	34	2.800 (0.1102)
08	2.150 (0.0846)	36	2.850 (0.1122)
10	2.200 (0.0866)	38	2.900 (0.1142)
12	2.250 (0.0886)	40	2.950 (0.1161)
14	2.300 (0.0906)	42	3.000 (0.1181)
16	2.350 (0.0925)	33	3.050 (0.1201)
18	2.400 (0.0945)	46	3.100 (0.1220)
20	2.450 (0.0965)	48	3.150 (0.1240)
22	2.500 (0.0984)	50	3.200 (0.1260)
24	2.550 (0.1004)	52	3.250 (0.1280)
26	2.600 (0.1024)	54	3.300 (0.1299)
28	2.650 (0.1043)		

Exhaust valve clearance (cold):
0.20 - 0.30 mm (0.008 - 0.012 in.)

Example: A 2.800 mm shim is installed and measured clearance is 0.450 mm (0.0177 in.).
Replace the 2.800 mm shim with shim No. 42 (3.000 mm).

Shim selection chart—3S-GE

Adjusting Shim Selection Using Chart

INTAKE

Measured clearance (mm)	2.500	2.550	2.600	2.620	2.640	2.650	2.660	2.680	2.700	2.720	2.740	2.750	2.760	2.780	2.800	2.820	2.840	2.850	2.860	2.880	2.900	2.920	2.940	2.950	2.960	2.980	3.000	3.020	3.040	3.050	3.060	3.080	3.100	3.120	3.140	3.150	3.160	3.180	3.200	3.250	3.300
0.000–0.025							02	02	02	02	02	04	04	04	06	06	06	08	08	08	10	10	10	12	12	12	14	14	14	16	16	16	18	18	18	20	20	20	22	24	
0.026–0.050					02	02	02	02	02	02	04	04	04	06	06	06	08	08	08	10	10	10	12	12	12	14	14	14	16	16	16	18	18	18	20	20	20	22	22	24	26
0.051–0.075				02	02	02	02	02	02	04	04	04	06	06	06	08	08	08	10	10	10	12	12	12	14	14	14	16	16	16	18	18	18	20	20	20	22	22	22	24	26
0.076–0.100			02	02	02	02	02	02	04	04	04	06	06	06	08	08	08	10	10	10	12	12	12	14	14	14	16	16	16	18	18	18	20	20	20	22	22	22	24	24	26	28
0.101–0.125			02	02	02	02	04	04	04	06	06	06	08	08	08	10	10	10	12	12	12	14	14	14	16	16	16	18	18	18	20	20	20	22	22	22	24	24	24	26	28
0.126–0.150		02	02	02	04	04	04	06	06	06	08	08	08	10	10	10	12	12	12	14	14	14	16	16	16	18	18	18	20	20	20	22	22	22	24	24	24	26	26	28	30
0.151–0.175		02	02	04	04	04	06	06	06	08	08	08	10	10	10	12	12	12	14	14	14	16	16	16	18	18	18	20	20	20	22	22	22	24	24	24	26	26	26	28	30
0.176–0.189		02	04	04	06	06	06	06	08	08	10	10	10	10	12	12	14	14	14	16	16	18	18	18	20	20	22	22	22	22	24	24	26	26	26	26	28	30	32		
0.190–0.290																																									
0.291–0.300	04	06	08	10	10	10	10	12	12	14	14	14	14	16	16	18	18	18	18	20	20	22	22	22	22	24	24	26	26	26	26	28	28	30	30	30	30	32	32	34	
0.301–0.325	04	06	08	10	10	10	12	12	12	14	14	16	16	16	18	18	18	20	20	20	22	22	22	24	24	24	26	26	26	28	28	28	30	30	30	32	32	32	34		
0.326–0.350	06	08	10	10	12	12	12	14	14	14	16	16	16	18	18	18	20	20	20	22	22	22	24	24	24	26	26	26	28	28	28	30	30	30	32	32	32	34	34		
0.351–0.375	06	08	10	12	12	12	14	14	14	16	16	16	18	18	18	20	20	20	22	22	22	24	24	24	26	26	26	28	28	28	30	30	30	32	32	32	34	34	34		
0.376–0.400	08	10	12	12	14	14	14	16	16	16	18	18	18	20	20	20	22	22	22	24	24	24	26	26	26	28	28	28	30	30	30	32	32	32	34	34	34	34			
0.401–0.425	08	10	12	14	14	14	16	16	16	18	18	18	20	20	20	22	22	22	24	24	24	26	26	26	28	28	28	30	30	30	32	32	32	34	34	34	34				
0.426–0.450	10	12	14	14	16	16	16	18	18	18	20	20	20	22	22	22	24	24	24	26	26	26	28	28	28	30	30	30	32	32	32	34	34	34	34						
0.451–0.475	10	12	14	16	16	16	18	18	18	20	20	20	22	22	22	24	24	24	26	26	26	28	28	28	30	30	30	32	32	32	34	34	34	34							
0.476–0.500	12	14	16	16	18	18	18	20	20	20	22	22	22	24	24	24	26	26	26	28	28	28	30	30	30	32	32	32	34	34	34	34									
0.501–0.525	12	14	16	18	18	18	20	20	20	22	22	22	24	24	24	26	26	26	28	28	28	30	30	30	32	32	32	34	34	34	34										
0.526–0.550	14	16	18	18	20	20	20	22	22	22	24	24	24	26	26	26	28	28	28	30	30	30	32	32	32	34	34	34	34												
0.551–0.575	14	16	18	20	20	20	22	22	22	24	24	24	26	26	26	28	28	28	30	30	30	32	32	32	34	34	34														
0.576–0.600	16	18	20	20	22	22	22	24	24	24	26	26	26	28	28	28	30	30	30	32	32	32	34	34	34	34															
0.601–0.625	16	18	20	22	22	22	24	24	24	26	26	26	28	28	28	30	30	30	32	32	32	34	34	34	34																
0.626–0.650	18	20	22	22	24	24	24	26	26	26	28	28	28	30	30	30	32	32	32	34	34	34	34																		
0.651–0.675	18	20	22	24	24	24	26	26	26	28	28	28	30	30	30	32	32	32	34	34	34	34																			
0.676–0.700	20	22	24	24	26	26	26	28	28	28	30	30	30	32	32	32	34	34	34	34																					
0.701–0.725	20	22	24	26	26	26	28	28	28	30	30	30	32	32	32	34	34	34	34																						
0.726–0.750	22	24	26	26	28	28	28	30	30	30	32	32	32	34	34	34	34																								
0.751–0.775	22	24	26	28	28	28	30	30	30	32	32	32	34	34	34	34																									
0.776–0.800	24	26	28	28	30	30	30	32	32	32	34	34	34	34																											
0.801–0.825	24	26	28	30	30	30	32	32	32	34	34	34	34																												
0.826–0.850	26	28	30	30	32	32	32	34	34	34	34																														
0.851–0.875	26	28	30	32	32	32	34	34	34																																
0.876–0.900	28	30	32	32	34	34	34	34																																	
0.901–0.925	28	30	32	34	34	34	34																																		
0.926–0.950	30	32	34	34	34																																				
0.951–0.975	30	32	34																																						
0.976–1.000	32	34																																							
1.001–1.025	34	34																																							
1.026–1.090	34																																								

	Shim thickness		mm (in.)
Shim No.	Thickness	Shim No.	Thickness
02	2.50 (0.0984)	20	2.95 (0.1161)
04	2.55 (0.1004)	22	3.00 (0.1181)
06	2.60 (0.1024)	24	3.05 (0.1201)
08	2.65 (0.1043)	26	3.10 (0.1220)
10	2.70 (0.1063)	28	3.15 (0.1240)
12	2.75 (0.1083)	30	3.20 (0.1260)
14	2.80 (0.1102)	32	3.25 (0.1280)
16	2.85 (0.1122)	34	3.30 (0.1299)
18	2.90 (0.1142)		

Intake valve clearance (Cold):
   0.19 — 0.29 mm (0.007 — 0.011 in.)

EXAMPLE: The 2.800 mm (0.1102 in.) shim is installed and measured clearance is 0.450 mm (0.0177 in.). Replace the 2.800 mm (0.1102 in.) shim with No. 22 shim.

Shim selection chart—3S-FE

Adjusting Shim Selection Using Chart
EXHAUST

Measured clearance (mm)	Installed shim thickness (mm)
	2.500 2.550 2.600 2.620 2.640 2.650 2.660 2.680 2.700 2.720 2.740 2.750 2.760 2.780 2.800 2.820 2.840 2.850 2.860 2.880 2.900 2.920 2.940 2.950 2.960 2.980 3.000 3.020 3.040 3.050 3.060 3.080 3.100 3.120 3.140 3.150 3.160 3.180 3.200 3.250 3.300
0.000–0.025	02 02 02 02 02 04 04 04 06 06 06 08 08 08 10 10 10 12 12 12 14 14 14 16 16 16 18 20 22
0.026–0.050	02 02 02 02 02 04 04 04 04 06 08 08 08 08 10 10 12 12 12 12 14 14 16 16 16 16 18 20 22
0.051–0.075	02 02 02 02 02 04 04 04 06 06 06 08 08 10 10 10 12 12 12 14 14 14 16 16 16 18 18 18 20 22 24
0.076–0.100	02 02 02 02 02 04 04 06 06 06 08 08 10 10 10 10 12 12 14 14 14 14 16 16 18 18 18 18 20 20 22 24
0.101–0.125	02 02 02 02 02 04 04 04 06 06 06 08 08 08 10 10 10 12 12 12 14 14 14 16 16 16 18 18 18 20 20 20 22 24 26
0.126–0.150	02 02 02 02 02 04 04 04 04 06 06 08 08 08 08 10 10 12 12 12 12 14 14 16 16 16 16 18 18 20 20 20 20 22 22 24 26
0.150–0.175	02 02 02 02 02 04 04 04 06 06 06 08 08 10 10 10 12 12 12 14 14 14 16 16 18 18 18 20 20 20 22 22 22 24 26 28
0.176–0.200	02 02 02 02 02 04 04 06 06 06 08 08 10 10 10 10 12 12 14 14 14 16 16 18 18 18 18 20 20 22 22 22 22 24 26 28
0.201–0.225	02 02 02 02 04 04 04 06 06 06 08 08 08 10 10 12 12 12 14 14 16 16 18 18 18 20 20 20 22 22 22 24 24 24 26 28 30
0.226–0.250	02 02 04 04 04 06 06 08 08 08 08 10 10 12 12 14 14 16 16 18 18 20 20 20 20 22 22 24 24 24 26 26 28 30
0.251–0.275	02 04 04 04 06 06 08 08 08 08 10 10 10 12 12 14 14 14 16 16 18 18 20 20 20 22 22 22 24 24 26 26 26 28 30 32
0.275–0.279	02 04 04 06 06 06 08 08 08 10 10 12 12 12 14 14 14 16 16 18 18 20 20 20 22 22 24 24 26 26 26 28 30 32
0.280–0.380	
0.381–0.400	04 06 08 10 10 10 10 12 12 14 14 14 14 16 16 18 18 18 20 20 22 22 22 24 24 26 26 26 28 28 30 30 30 30 32 32 34
0.401–0.425	06 08 10 10 10 12 12 12 14 14 14 16 16 16 18 18 20 20 20 22 24 24 26 26 26 28 28 30 30 32 32 32 34 34
0.426–0.450	06 08 10 12 12 12 12 14 14 16 16 16 16 18 18 20 20 20 22 22 24 24 26 26 28 28 28 30 30 32 32 32 34 34
0.451–0.475	08 10 12 12 12 14 14 14 16 16 16 18 18 18 20 20 22 22 22 24 24 26 26 26 28 28 30 30 30 32 32 34 34 34 34
0.476–0.500	08 10 12 14 14 14 14 16 16 18 18 18 20 20 22 22 22 24 24 26 26 26 28 28 30 30 30 32 32 34 34 34 34
0.501–0.525	10 12 14 14 14 16 16 16 18 18 18 20 20 22 22 22 24 24 24 26 26 28 28 30 30 30 32 32 32 34 34 34
0.526–0.550	10 12 14 16 16 16 16 18 18 20 20 20 20 22 22 24 24 24 26 26 28 28 30 30 32 32 32 32 34 34 34
0.551–0.575	12 14 16 16 16 18 18 18 20 20 20 22 22 22 24 24 24 26 26 26 28 28 30 30 30 32 32 32 34 34 34 34
0.576–0.600	12 14 16 18 18 18 18 20 20 22 22 22 22 24 24 26 26 26 26 28 28 30 30 30 32 32 34 34 34 34 34
0.601–0.625	14 16 18 18 18 20 20 20 22 22 22 24 24 24 26 26 26 28 28 28 30 30 32 32 32 34 34 34 34
0.626–0.650	14 16 18 20 20 20 20 22 22 24 24 24 24 26 26 28 28 28 30 30 32 32 32 32 34 34 34
0.651–0.675	16 18 20 20 20 22 22 22 24 24 24 26 26 26 28 28 28 30 30 30 32 32 32 34 34 34 34
0.676–0.700	16 18 20 22 22 22 22 24 24 26 26 26 26 28 28 30 30 30 30 32 32 34 34 34 34 34
0.701–0.725	18 20 22 22 22 24 24 24 26 26 26 28 28 28 30 30 30 32 32 32 34 34 34 34
0.726–0.750	18 20 22 24 24 24 24 26 26 28 28 28 28 30 30 32 32 32 32 34 34 34
0.751–0.775	20 22 24 24 24 26 26 26 28 28 28 30 30 30 32 32 32 34 34 34 34
0.776–0.800	20 22 24 26 26 26 26 28 28 30 30 30 30 32 32 34 34 34 34 34
0.801–0.825	22 24 26 26 26 28 28 28 30 30 30 32 32 32 34 34 34 34
0.826–0.850	22 24 26 28 28 28 28 30 30 32 32 32 32 34 34 34 34
0.851–0.875	24 26 28 28 28 30 30 30 32 32 32 34 34 34 34
0.876–0.900	24 26 28 30 30 30 30 32 32 34 34 34 34 34
0.901–0.925	26 28 30 30 30 32 32 32 34 34 34 34
0.926–0.950	26 28 30 32 32 32 32 34 34 34
0.951–0.975	28 30 32 32 32 34 34 34 34
0.976–1.000	28 30 32 34 34 34 34 34
1.001–1.025	30 32 34 34 34 34
1.026–1.050	30 32 34 34
1.051–1.075	32 34 34
1.076–1.100	32 34
1.101–1.125	34 34
1.126–1.180	34

Shim thickness			mm (in.)
Shim No.	Thickness	Shim No.	Thickness
02	2.50 (0.0984)	20	2.95 (0.1161)
04	2.55 (0.1004)	22	3.00 (0.1181)
06	2.60 (0.1024)	24	3.05 (0.1201)
08	2.65 (0.1043)	26	3.10 (0.1220)
10	2.70 (0.1063)	28	3.15 (0.1240)
12	2.75 (0.1083)	30	3.20 (0.1260)
14	2.80 (0.1102)	32	3.25 (0.1280)
16	2.85 (0.1122)	34	3.30 (0.1299)
18	2.90 (0.1142)		

Exhaust valve clearance:
0.28 — 0.38 mm (0.011 — 0.015 in.)

EXAMPLE: The 2.800 mm (0.1102 in.) shim is installed and measured clearance is 0.450 mm (0.0177 in.). Replace the 2.800 mm (0.1102 in.) shim with No. 18 shim.

Shim selection chart — 3S-FE

Exhaust

Installed Shim Thickness (mm)

Measured Clearance (mm) column headers across the top (shim thickness in mm):
2.500, 2.525, 2.550, 2.575, 2.600, 2.620, 2.625, 2.640, 2.650, 2.660, 2.675, 2.680, 2.700, 2.720, 2.725, 2.740, 2.750, 2.760, 2.775, 2.780, 2.800, 2.820, 2.825, 2.840, 2.850, 2.860, 2.875, 2.880, 2.900, 2.920, 2.925, 2.940, 2.950, 2.960, 2.975, 2.980, 3.000, 3.020, 3.025, 3.040, 3.050, 3.060, 3.075, 3.080, 3.100, 3.120, 3.125, 3.140, 3.150, 3.175, 3.180, 3.200, 3.225, 3.250, 3.275, 3.300

Measured Clearance (mm) ranges (rows):

Measured Clearance (mm)
0.000 – 0.009
0.010 – 0.025
0.026 – 0.040
0.041 – 0.050
0.051 – 0.070
0.071 – 0.090
0.091 – 0.100
0.101 – 0.120
0.121 – 0.140
0.141 – 0.150
0.151 – 0.170
0.171 – 0.190
0.191 – 0.199
0.200 – 0.300
0.301 – 0.320
0.321 – 0.325
0.326 – 0.340
0.341 – 0.350
0.351 – 0.370
0.371 – 0.375
0.376 – 0.390
0.391 – 0.400
0.401 – 0.420
0.421 – 0.425
0.426 – 0.440
0.441 – 0.450
0.451 – 0.470
0.471 – 0.475
0.476 – 0.490
0.491 – 0.500
0.501 – 0.520
0.521 – 0.525
0.526 – 0.540
0.541 – 0.550
0.551 – 0.570
0.571 – 0.575
0.576 – 0.590
0.591 – 0.600
0.601 – 0.620
0.621 – 0.625
0.626 – 0.640
0.641 – 0.650
0.651 – 0.670
0.671 – 0.675
0.676 – 0.690
0.691 – 0.700
0.701 – 0.720
0.721 – 0.725
0.726 – 0.740
0.741 – 0.750
0.751 – 0.770
0.771 – 0.775
0.776 – 0.790
0.791 – 0.800
0.801 – 0.820
0.821 – 0.825
0.826 – 0.840
0.841 – 0.850
0.851 – 0.870
0.871 – 0.875
0.876 – 0.890
0.891 – 0.900
0.901 – 0.925
0.926 – 0.950
0.951 – 0.975
0.976 – 1.000
1.001 – 1.025
1.026 – 1.050
1.051 – 1.075

The body of the chart lists shim numbers (02, 04, 06, 08, 10, 12, 14, 16, 18, 20, 22, 24, 26, 28, 30, 32, 34) at the intersection of each measured clearance row and installed shim thickness column.

Shim thicknesses mm (in.)

Shim No.	Thickness	Shim No.	Thickness
02	2.500 (0.0984)	20	2.950 (0.1161)
04	2.550 (0.1004)	22	3.000 (0.1181)
06	2.600 (0.1024)	24	3.050 (0.1201)
08	2.650 (0.1043)	26	3.100 (0.1220)
10	2.700 (0.1063)	28	3.150 (0.1240)
12	2.750 (0.1083)	30	3.200 (0.1260)
14	2.800 (0.1102)	32	3.250 (0.1280)
16	2.850 (0.1122)	34	3.300 (0.1299)
18	2.900 (0.1142)		

Exhaust valve clearance (cold):
0.20 – 0.30 mm (0.008 – 0.012 in.)

Example: A 2.800 mm shim is installed and the measured clearance is 0.450 mm. Replace the 2.800 mm shim with shim No. 22 (3.000 mm).

Shim selection chart—4A-GELC and 4A-GEC

Intake

Installed Shim Thickness (mm)

Column headers (mm): 2.500, 2.525, 2.550, 2.575, 2.600, 2.620, 2.625, 2.640, 2.650, 2.660, 2.675, 2.680, 2.700, 2.720, 2.725, 2.740, 2.750, 2.760, 2.775, 2.780, 2.800, 2.820, 2.825, 2.840, 2.850, 2.860, 2.875, 2.880, 2.900, 2.920, 2.925, 2.940, 2.950, 2.960, 2.975, 2.980, 3.000, 3.020, 3.025, 3.040, 3.050, 3.060, 3.075, 3.080, 3.100, 3.120, 3.125, 3.140, 3.150, 3.160, 3.175, 3.180, 3.200, 3.225, 3.250, 3.275, 3.300

Measured Clearance (mm) ranges (left column):

Measured Clearance (mm)
0.000 – 0.009
0.010 – 0.025
0.026 – 0.029
0.030 – 0.040
0.041 – 0.050
0.051 – 0.070
0.071 – 0.075
0.076 – 0.090
0.091 – 0.100
0.101 – 0.120
0.121 – 0.125
0.126 – 0.140
0.141 – 0.149
0.150 – 0.250
0.251 – 0.270
0.271 – 0.275
0.276 – 0.290
0.291 – 0.300
0.301 – 0.320
0.321 – 0.325
0.326 – 0.340
0.341 – 0.350
0.351 – 0.370
0.371 – 0.375
0.376 – 0.390
0.391 – 0.400
0.401 – 0.420
0.421 – 0.425
0.426 – 0.440
0.441 – 0.450
0.451 – 0.470
0.471 – 0.475
0.476 – 0.490
0.491 – 0.500
0.501 – 0.520
0.521 – 0.525
0.526 – 0.540
0.541 – 0.550
0.551 – 0.570
0.571 – 0.575
0.576 – 0.590
0.591 – 0.600
0.601 – 0.620
0.621 – 0.625
0.626 – 0.640
0.641 – 0.650
0.651 – 0.670
0.671 – 0.675
0.676 – 0.690
0.691 – 0.700
0.701 – 0.720
0.721 – 0.725
0.726 – 0.740
0.741 – 0.750
0.751 – 0.770
0.771 – 0.775
0.776 – 0.790
0.791 – 0.800
0.801 – 0.820
0.821 – 0.825
0.826 – 0.840
0.841 – 0.850
0.851 – 0.870
0.871 – 0.875
0.876 – 0.890
0.891 – 0.900
0.901 – 0.925
0.926 – 0.950
0.951 – 0.975
0.976 – 1.000
1.001 – 1.025

(The body of the chart is a matrix of shim numbers 02–34 corresponding to each measured clearance row and installed shim thickness column.)

Shim thicknesses — mm (in.)

Shim No.	Thickness	Shim No.	Thickness
02	2.500 (0.0984)	20	2.950 (0.1161)
04	2.550 (0.1004)	22	3.000 (0.1181)
06	2.600 (0.1024)	24	3.050 (0.1201)
08	2.650 (0.1043)	26	3.100 (0.1220)
10	2.700 (0.1063)	28	3.150 (0.1240)
12	2.750 (0.1083)	30	3.200 (0.1260)
14	2.800 (0.1102)	32	3.250 (0.1280)
16	2.850 (0.1122)	34	3.300 (0.1299)
18	2.900 (0.1142)		

Intake valve clearance (cold):
0.15 – 0.25 mm (0.006 – 0.010 in.)

Example: A 2.800 mm shim is installed and the measured clearance is 0.450 mm. Replace the 2.800 mm shim with shim No. 24 (3.050 mm).

Shim selection chart — 4A-GELC and 4A-GEC

Exhaust

Shim selection chart — Installed Shim Thickness (mm)

The chart lists Measured Clearance (mm) ranges against Installed Shim Thickness values (2.500 through 3.300 mm) to determine the replacement shim number.

Measured Clearance (mm) ranges:

0.000 – 0.009
0.010 – 0.025
0.026 – 0.040
0.041 – 0.050
0.051 – 0.070
0.071 – 0.090
0.091 – 0.100
0.101 – 0.120
0.121 – 0.140
0.141 – 0.150
0.151 – 0.170
0.171 – 0.190
0.191 – 0.199
0.200 – 0.300
0.301 – 0.320
0.321 – 0.325
0.326 – 0.340
0.341 – 0.350
0.351 – 0.370
0.371 – 0.375
0.376 – 0.390
0.391 – 0.400
0.401 – 0.420
0.421 – 0.425
0.426 – 0.440
0.441 – 0.450
0.451 – 0.470
0.471 – 0.475
0.476 – 0.490
0.491 – 0.500
0.501 – 0.520
0.521 – 0.525
0.526 – 0.540
0.541 – 0.550
0.551 – 0.570
0.571 – 0.575
0.576 – 0.590
0.591 – 0.600
0.601 – 0.620
0.621 – 0.625
0.626 – 0.640
0.641 – 0.650
0.651 – 0.670
0.671 – 0.675
0.676 – 0.690
0.691 – 0.700
0.701 – 0.720
0.721 – 0.725
0.726 – 0.740
0.741 – 0.750
0.751 – 0.770
0.771 – 0.775
0.776 – 0.790
0.791 – 0.800
0.801 – 0.820
0.821 – 0.825
0.826 – 0.840
0.841 – 0.850
0.851 – 0.870
0.871 – 0.875
0.876 – 0.890
0.891 – 0.900
0.901 – 0.925
0.926 – 0.950
0.951 – 0.975
0.976 – 1.000
1.001 – 1.025
1.026 – 1.050
1.051 – 1.075

Shim thicknesses			mm (in.)
Shim No.	Thickness	Shim No.	Thickness
02	2.500 (0.0984)	20	2.950 (0.1161)
04	2.550 (0.1004)	22	3.000 (0.1181)
06	2.600 (0.1024)	24	3.050 (0.1201)
08	2.650 (0.1043)	26	3.100 (0.1220)
10	2.700 (0.1063)	28	3.150 (0.1240)
12	2.750 (0.1083)	30	3.200 (0.1260)
14	2.800 (0.1102)	32	3.250 (0.1280)
16	2.850 (0.1122)	34	3.300 (0.1299)
18	2.900 (0.1142)		

Exhaust valve clearance (cold):
0.20 — 0.30 mm (0.008 — 0.012 in.)

Example: A 2.800 mm shim is installed and the measured clearance is 0.450 mm. Replace the 2.800 mm shim with shim No. 22 (3.000 mm).

Shim selection chart — 7M-GE and 7M-GTE

Intake

Installed Shim Thickness (mm)

Measured Clearance (mm) — column headers (installed shim thickness, mm):
2.500 · 2.525 · 2.550 · 2.575 · 2.600 · 2.620 · 2.640 · 2.650 · 2.660 · 2.675 · 2.680 · 2.700 · 2.720 · 2.725 · 2.740 · 2.750 · 2.760 · 2.775 · 2.780 · 2.800 · 2.820 · 2.825 · 2.840 · 2.850 · 2.860 · 2.875 · 2.880 · 2.900 · 2.920 · 2.925 · 2.940 · 2.950 · 2.960 · 2.975 · 2.980 · 3.000 · 3.020 · 3.025 · 3.040 · 3.050 · 3.060 · 3.075 · 3.080 · 3.100 · 3.120 · 3.125 · 3.140 · 3.150 · 3.160 · 3.175 · 3.180 · 3.200 · 3.225 · 3.250 · 3.275 · 3.300

Measured Clearance (mm) rows:

0.000 – 0.009
0.010 – 0.025
0.026 – 0.029
0.030 – 0.040
0.041 – 0.050
0.051 – 0.070
0.071 – 0.075
0.076 – 0.090
0.091 – 0.100
0.101 – 0.120
0.121 – 0.125
0.126 – 0.140
0.141 – 0.149
0.150 – 0.250
0.251 – 0.270
0.271 – 0.275
0.276 – 0.290
0.291 – 0.300
0.301 – 0.320
0.321 – 0.325
0.326 – 0.340
0.341 – 0.350
0.351 – 0.370
0.371 – 0.375
0.376 – 0.390
0.391 – 0.400
0.401 – 0.420
0.421 – 0.425
0.426 – 0.440
0.441 – 0.450
0.451 – 0.470
0.471 – 0.475
0.476 – 0.490
0.491 – 0.500
0.501 – 0.520
0.521 – 0.525
0.526 – 0.540
0.541 – 0.550
0.551 – 0.570
0.571 – 0.575
0.576 – 0.590
0.591 – 0.600
0.601 – 0.620
0.621 – 0.625
0.626 – 0.640
0.641 – 0.650
0.651 – 0.670
0.671 – 0.675
0.676 – 0.690
0.691 – 0.700
0.701 – 0.720
0.721 – 0.725
0.726 – 0.740
0.741 – 0.750
0.751 – 0.770
0.771 – 0.775
0.776 – 0.790
0.791 – 0.800
0.801 – 0.820
0.821 – 0.825
0.826 – 0.840
0.841 – 0.850
0.851 – 0.870
0.871 – 0.875
0.876 – 0.890
0.891 – 0.900
0.901 – 0.920
0.928 – 0.950
0.951 – 0.975
0.978 – 1.000
1.001 – 1.025

Shim thicknesses mm (in.)

Shim No.	Thickness	Shim No.	Thickness
02	2.500 (0.0984)	20	2.950 (0.1161)
04	2.550 (0.1004)	22	3.000 (0.1181)
06	2.600 (0.1024)	24	3.050 (0.1201)
08	2.650 (0.1043)	26	3.100 (0.1220)
10	2.700 (0.1063)	28	3.150 (0.1240)
12	2.750 (0.1083)	30	3.200 (0.1260)
14	2.800 (0.1102)	32	3.250 (0.1280)
16	2.850 (0.1122)	34	3.300 (0.1299)
18	2.900 (0.1142)		

Intake valve clearance (cold):
0.15 – 0.25 mm (0.006 – 0.010 in.)

Example: A 2.800 mm shim is installed and the measured clearance is 0.450 mm. Replace the 2.800 mm shim with shim No. 24 (3.050 mm).

Shim selection chart – 7M-GE and 7M-GTE

valve lifter so that the notch is easily accessible.

8. Install SST No. 09248–64010 (diesels), 09248–70011 (4A-GE) between the two camshafts lobes and then turn the handle so that the tool presses down both (intake and exhaust) valve lifters evenly. On the 4A-GE, the tool will work on only one valve lifter at a time.

9. Using a suitable tool and a magnet, remove the valve shims.

10. Measure the thickness of the old shim with a micrometer. Locate that particular measurement in the "Installed Shim Thickness" column of the accompanying charts, then locate the previously recorded measurement (from Step 3 or 5) for that valve in the "Measured Clearance " column of the charts. Index the two columns to arrive at the proper replacement shim thickness.

11. Install the new shim, remove the special tool and then recheck the valve clearance.Installation of the remaining components is in the reverse order of removal.

7M–GE and 7M–GTE

1. Remove the cylinder head covers.
2. Use a wrench and turn the crankshaft until the notch in the pulley aligns with the timing mark 0 of the No. 1 timing belt cover. This will insure that engine is at TDC.

NOTE: Check that the valve lifters on the No 1 cylinder are loose and those on No 6 cylinder are tight. If not, turn the crankshaft one complete revolution (360) and then realign the marks.

3. Using a flat feeler gauge measure the clearance between the camshaft lobe and the valve lifter. This measurement should correspond to specification. Check only the valves listed under FIRST in the accompanying valve arrangement illustrations for your particular engine.

NOTE: If the measurement is within specifications, go on to the next step. If not, record the measurement taken for each individual valve.

4. Turn the crankshaft ⅔ revolution (240°).
5. Measure the clearance of the valves shown in the valve arrangement illustration marked SECOND.

NOTE: If the measurement is within specifications, go on to the next step. If not, record the measurement taken for each individual valve.

6. Turn the crankshaft ⅔ revolution (240°).

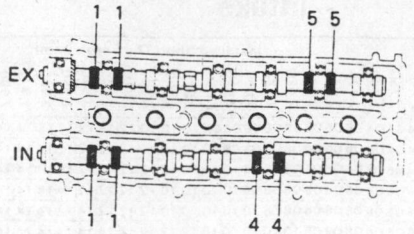

Adjust these valves first 7M-GE and 7M-GTE

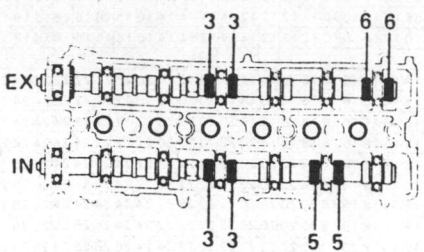

Adjust these valves second 7M-GE and 7M-GTE

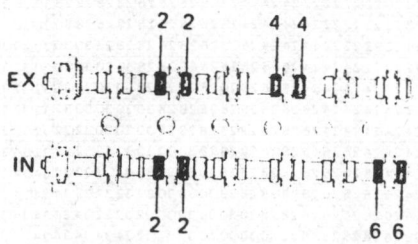

Adjust these valves third 7M-GE and 7M-GTE

7. Measure the clearance of the valves shown in the valve arrangement illustration marked THIRD.

NOTE: If the measurement for this set of valves (and also the previous ones) is within specifications, you need go no further, the procedure is finished. If not, record the measurements and then proceed to Step 6.

8. Turn the crankshaft to position the intake camshaft lobe of the cylinder to be adjusted, upward.

NOTE: Both intake and exhaust valve clearance may be adjusted at the same time if so required.

7. Using a suitable tool, turn the valve lifter so that the notch is easily accessible.

8. Install SST No. 09248–55010 between the two camshafts lobes and then turn the handle so that the tool presses down both (intake and exhaust) valve lifters evenly.

9. Using a suitable tool and a magnet, remove the valve shims.

10. Measure the thickness of the old shim with a micrometer. Locate that particular measurement in the "Installed Shim Thickness" column of the accompanying charts, then locate the previously recorded measurement (from Step 3 or 5) for that valve in the "Measured Clearance " column of the charts. Index the two columns to arrive at the proper replacement shim thickness.

NOTE: Replacement shims are available in 17 sizes, in increments of 0.05mm (0.0020 in.), from 2.00mm (0.0787 in.) to 3.300mm (0.1299 in.)

11. Install the new shim, remove the special tool and then recheck the valve clearance.

12. Installation of the remaining components is in the reverse order of removal.

3S-GE and 3S-FE

1. Remove the cylinder head covers.
2. Use a wrench and turn the crankshaft until the notch in the pulley aligns with the timing mark 0 of the No. 1 timing belt cover. This will insure that engine is at TDC.

NOTE: Check that the valve lifters on the No 1 cylinder are loose and those on No 4 cylinder are tight. If not, turn the crankshaft one complete revolution (360) and then realign the marks.

3. Using a flat feeler gauge measure the clearance between the camshaft lobe and the valve lifter. This measurement should correspond to specification. Check only the valves listed under FIRST in the accompanying valve arrangement illustrations for your particular engine.

NOTE: If the measurement is within specifications, go on to the next step. If not, record the measurement taken for each individual valve.

4. Turn the crankshaft one complete revolution and realign the timing marks as previously described.
5. Measure the clearance of the valves shown in the valve arrangement illustration marked SECOND.

NOTE: If the measurement for this set of valves (and also the previous one) is within specifications, you need go no further, the procedure is finished. If not, record the measurements and then proceed to Step 6.

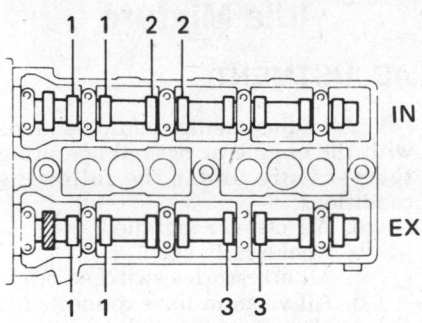

Adjust these valves FIRST on 3S-GE and 4A-GE engines

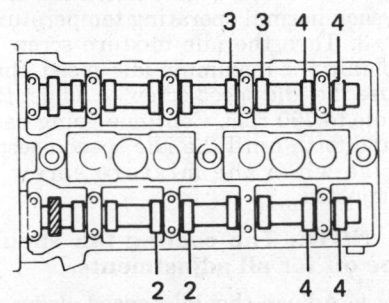

Adjust these valves SECOND on 3S-GE and 4A-GE engines

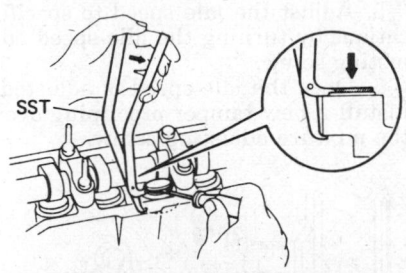

Depressing the valve lifter to remove the shim—3S-GE and 4A-GE engines

6. Turn the crankshaft to position the intake camshaft lobe of the cylinder to be adjusted, upward.

NOTE: Both intake and exhaust valve clearance may be adjusted at the same time if so required.

7. Using a suitable tool, turn the valve lifter so that the notch is easily accessible.

8. Install SST No. 09248–70012 (3S-GE), No. 09248–55010 (3S-FE) between the two camshafts lobes and then turn the handle so that the tool presses down both (intake and exhaust) valve lifters evenly.

9. Using a suitable tool and a magnet, remove the valve shims.

10. Measure the thickness of the old shim with a micrometer. Locate that particular measurement in the "Installed Shim Thickness" column of the accompanying charts, then locate

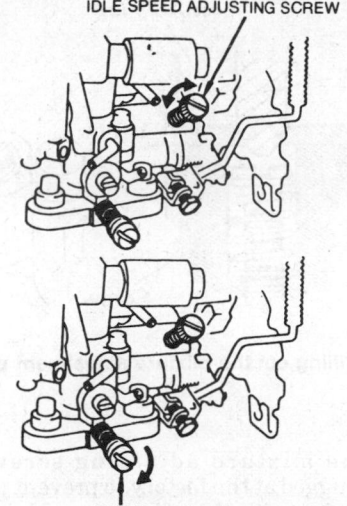

Carbuertor adjustment points for the 4K-C engine

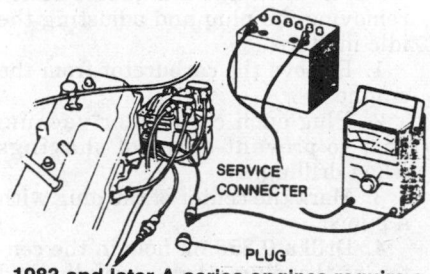

1983 and later A-series engines require a special tachometer hook-up

the previously recorded measurement (from Step 3 or 5) for that valve in the "Measured Clearance " column of the charts. Index the two columns to arrive at the proper replacement shim thickness.

NOTE: Replacement shims are available in 27 sizes, in increments of 0.05mm (0.0020 in.), from 2.00mm (0.0787 in.) to 3.300mm (0.1299 in.)

11. Install the new shim, remove the special tool and then recheck the valve clearance.

12. Installation of the remaining components is in the reverse order of removal.

Idle Speed

ADJUSTMENT
Carbureted Engines

The idle speed and mixture should be adjusted under the following conditions: the air cleaner must be installed, the choke fully opened, the transmission should be in Neutral (N), all accessories (incl. the electric engine cooling fan, if so equipped) should be turned off, all vacuum lines should be set to specification.

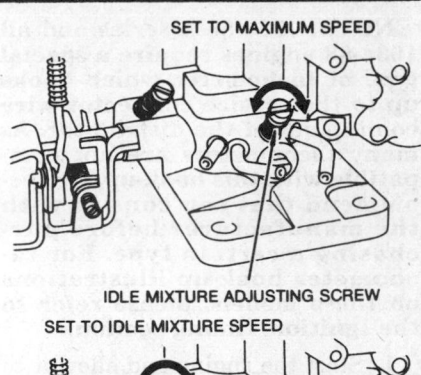

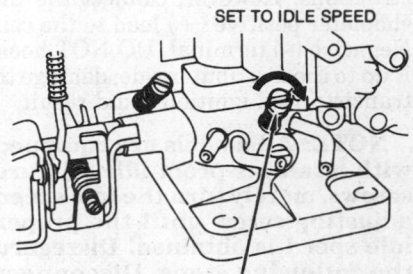

Carburetor adjustment points for the "A" series engines—typical

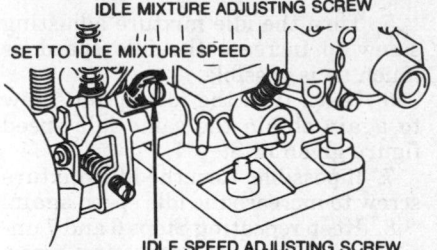

Carburetor adjustment points for the 3T-C engine

NOTE: 1983-88 A-series and all 1984-88 engines require a special type of tachometer which hooks up to the service connector wire coming out of the distributor. As many tachometers are not compatible with this hook-up, we recommend that you consult with the manufacturer before purchasing a certain type. For tachometer hook-up illustrations on these models, please refer to the Ignition Timing section.

1. Start the engine and allow it to reach normal operating temperature.
2. Check the float setting; the fuel level should be just about even with the spot on the sight glass. If the fuel level is too high or low, adjust the float level as outlined in "Fuel System" section.
3. Connect a tachometer in accordance with it's manufacturer's instructions. However, connect the tachometer positive (+) lead to the coil Negative (–) terminal. DO NOT hook it up to the distributor side; damage to transistorized ignition could result.

NOTE: All models are equipped with a tamper-proof idle mixture screws, merely turn the idle speed adjusting screw until the proper idle speed is obtained. Disregard the following steps. Disconnect the tachometer after the adjustment is complete.

4. Turn the idle speed adjusting screw to obtain one of the following initial idle speeds:
20R—900 rpm
1A-C, 2A-3A—750 rpm

NOTE: On the 1983 Starlet, race the engine at 2500 rpm for 2 min. before adjusting the idle speed.

5. Turn the idle mixture adjusting screw to increase the idle speed as much as is possible.
6. Next, turn the idle speed screw to again obtain the same idle speed figure given in Step 4.
7. If possible, turn the idle mixture screw to increase the idle speed again.
8. Keep repeating Steps 6 and 7 until the idle mixture adjusting screw will no longer increase the idle speed above the figure specified in Step 4.
9. Slowly turn the idle mixture screw clockwise, until the idle speed specified in the "Tune-Up Specifications" chart is reached (this makes the mixture leaner).
10. Disconnect the tachometer.

MIXTURE ADJUSTING SCREW PLUG REMOVAL

To conform with Federal regulations,

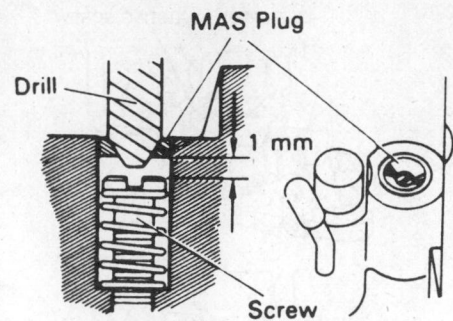

Drilling out the mixture adjustment plug

the mixture adjusting screw is plugged at the factory to prevent tampering with the adjustment. Normally, this plug should not be removed. When troubleshooting a rough idle, check all other possible causes before removing the plug and adjusting the idle mixture.

1. Remove the carburetor from the engine.
2. Plug each carburetor vacuum port to prevent entry of shavings when drilling.
3. Mark the center of the plug with a punch.
4. Drill a 0.256 in. hole in the center of the plug. Drill carefully and slowly to avoid drilling into the screw, since there is only 0.04 in. clearance between the plug and the screw. The drill may force the plug off.
5. Lightly seat the mixture screw by inserting a screwdriver into the drilled hole and turning the screw clockwise. Be careful not to tighten the screw or damage to the needle tip may result.
6. If the plug is still in place, use a 0.295 in. drill bit to force the plug out of the hole.
7. Remove the mixture adjusting screw and inspect it for damage. If the tapered needle portion is damaged or scored, replace the mixture adjusting screw.
8. Fully seat the mixture adjusting screw lightly once again, then back it out the following number of turns:
    a. Tercel (except Canada 4WD wagon)—3 ½ turns counterclockwise.
    b. Tercel Canada 4WD wagon—2 ½ turns counterclockwise.
    c. Corolla (USA models)—3 ¼ turns counterclockwise.
    d. Corolla (Canada models)—2 ½ turns counterclockwise.
    e. All other models—3 ½ turns counterclockwise.
9. Install the carburetor and continue the idle speed and mixture adjustments as outlined below.

Idle Mixture

ADJUSTMENT

1. All adjustments should be made with the engine at normal operating temperature under the following conditions:
    a. Air cleaner installed.
    b. Choke fully open.
    c. All accessories switched off.
    d. All vacuum lines connected.
    e. Ignition timing set to specifications.
    f. Transmission in Neutral.
2. Start the engine and allow it to reach normal operating temperature.
3. Turn the idle mixture screw to obtain the maximum idle speed, then use the idle speed screw to adjust the idle to 700 rpm. Continue going back and forth until the idle speed doesn't rise when the mixture screw is adjusted.

NOTE: The cooling fan should be off for all adjustments.

4. Adjust the idle speed down to 650 rpm by turning in the idle mixture screw (lean drop method of adjustment).
5. Adjust the idle speed to specifications by turning the idle speed adjusting screw.
6. Once the idle speed is adjusted, install a new tamper-proof plug over the mixture adjusting screw.

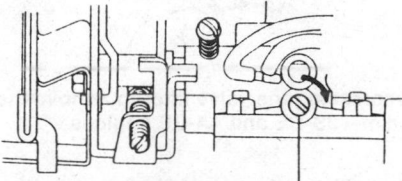

Idle Mixture Adjusting Screw

Location of the idle mixture adjusting screw—carbureted engines

Fuel Injected Engines

4M-E, 5M-E, 5M-GE, 7M-GE AND 7M-GTE

NOTE: In order to complete this procedure you will need a voltmeter and a EFI idle adjusting wire harness (Special Service Tool No. 09842–14010) which is available at your Toyota dealer.

1. Behind the battery on the left front fender apron is a service connector. Remove the rubber caps from the connector and connect the EFI idle adjusting wire harness.
2. Connect the positive lead of the voltmeter to red wire of the wiring harness and then connect the negative lead to the black wire.

3. Hook up a tachometer as per manufacture's instruction's.

NOTE: Please refer to "Ignition Timing" for tachometer hook-up illustrations.

4. Warm up to the oxygen sensor by running the engine at 2,500 rpm for about two minutes. The needle of the voltmeter should be fluctuating at this time, if not, turn the idle mixture adjusting screw until it does.

5. Set the idle speed to specifications (see "Tune-Up Specifications" chart) by turning the idle speed adjusting screw.

NOTE: The idle speed should be set immediately after warm-up while the needle of the voltmeter is fluctuating.

6. The idle adjustment procedure for 5M-GE engine is now complete. Follow the remaining steps for the 4M-E and 5M-E engines.

7. Remove the rubber cap from the idle adjusting connector and short both terminals of the connector with a wire.

8. While the connector is still shorted, run the engine at 2,500 rpm for two more minutes.

9. With the engine at idle and the connector still shorted, read and remember the voltage shown on the voltmeter.

10. Remove the short circuit wire from the connector and then race the engine to 2,500 rpm once.

11. Adjust the idle mixture adjusting screw until the median of the indicated voltage range is the same as the reading taken in Step 8.

12. Replug the idle mixture adjusting screw hole. Disconnect the tachometer, the voltmeter and the special wiring harness. Replace the rubber cap to the service connector and the idle adjusting connector.

22R-E, 2S-E, 3S-GE, 3E, 3S-FE, 3Y-EC, 4Y-EC, 4K-E 4A-GE, 4A-GEC AND 4A-GELC

1. Run the engine until it reaches normal operating temperature.

2. The air cleaner should be in place and all wires and vacuum hoses connected. All accessories should be off and transmission in neutral.

3. Connect a tachometer to the engine.

NOTE: Please refer to "Ignition Timing" for tachometer hook-up illustrations.

— CAUTION —
Never allow the tachometer or coil terminals to be grounded. This will damage the injection system.

4. Run the engine at 2500 rpm for 2 minutes.

5. Let the engine return to idle. Pinch the No.1 air intake chamber vacuum hose on the 3S-GE. On the 2S-E, disconnect the vacuum switching valve (VCV) from the idle speed control (ISC) motor. Set the idle speed by turning the idle adjusting screw to obtain the proper idle speed.

6. Remove the tachometer.

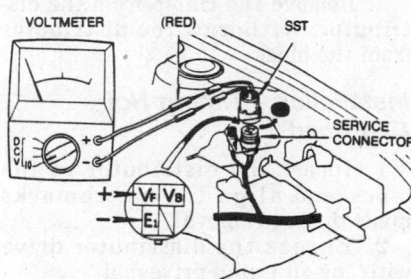

The service connector is found on the left front fender apron; right front apron on 1982 and later Supra

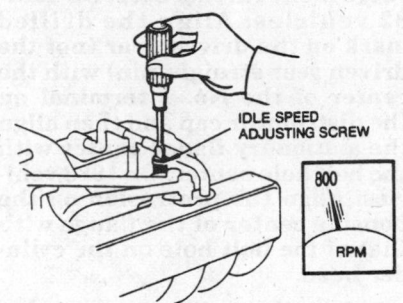

Idle speed adjustment—22R-E, 4M-E and 5M-E engines

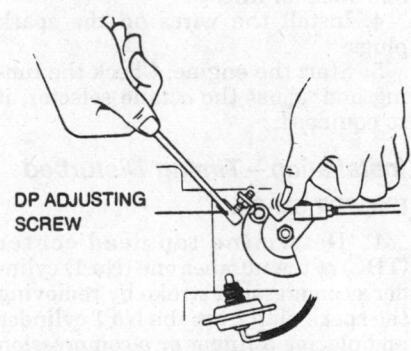

Loosen the locknut and turn the adjusting screw to set the dashpot

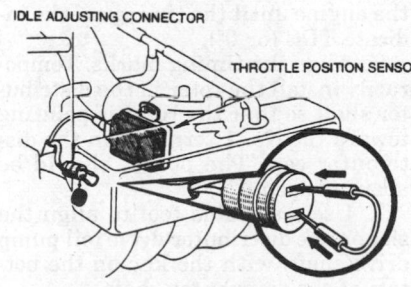

Short the idle adjustment connector

Idle adjusting harness Special Service Tool

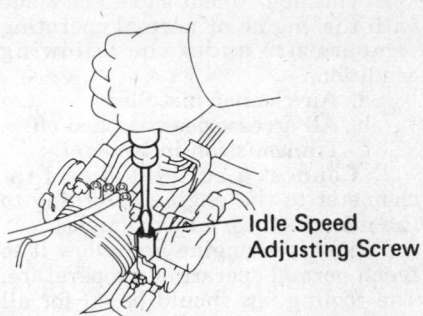

Adjusting the idle speed—4A-GE (4K-E and 22R-E similar)

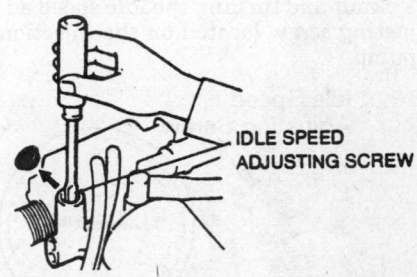

Idle speed adjustment on the 4K-E engines

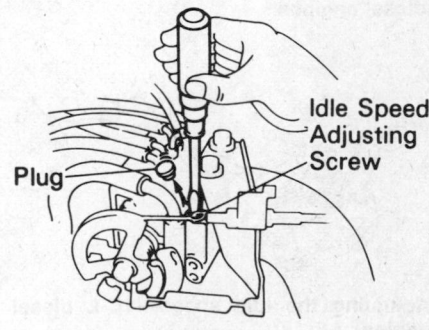

Adjusting the idle speed—2S-E

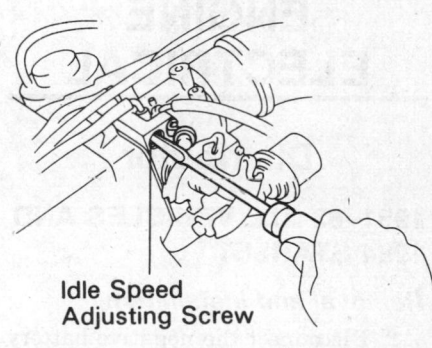

Idle speed adjustment—3Y-EC and 4Y-EC engines

Idle Speed Diesel Engine

ADJUSTMENT

1. This adjustment should be made with the engine at normal operating temperature under the following conditions:
   a. Air cleaner installed.
   b. All accessories switched off.
   c. Transmission in Neutral.
2. Connect a suitable diesel tachometer to the engine according to the manufacturer's instructions.
3. Start the engine and allow it to reach normal operating temperature. The cooling fan should be off for all adjustments.
4. Check the idle speed with the tachometer. It should be 700 rpm. If not, adjust the idle speed by loosening the locknut and turning the idle speed adjusting screw located on the injection pump.

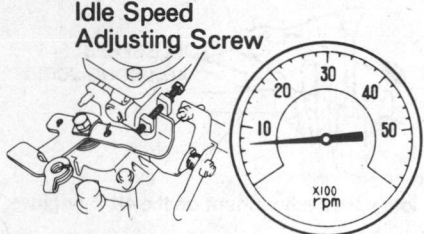

Idle speed adjustment—1C-TC and 2C-T diesel engines

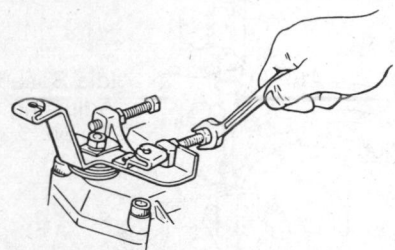

Adjusting the idle speed—1C-L diesel engines

ENGINE ELECTRICAL

Distributor

1981–83 ALL VEHICLES AND 1984 STARLET

Removal and Installation

1. Disconnect the negative battery cable. Unfasten the cables from the spark plugs, after marking the wiring

order. Remove the high tension cable from the coil.
2. Remove the primary wire and the vacuum line from the distributor. Remove the distributor cap.
3. Matchmark the distributor housing and the engine block. Mark the rotor position in the distributor as well. This will aid in correct positioning of the distributor during installation.
4. Remove the clamp from the distributor. Withdraw the distributor from the block.

Installation—Timing Not Disturbed

1. Insert the distributor in the block and align the matchmarks made during removal.
2. Engage the distributor drive with the oil pump driveshaft.

NOTE: Before installing the distributor on A-series engines, there is one further step. On 1981-82 vehicles: Align the drilled mark on the driven gear (not the driven gear straight pin) with the center of the No. 1 terminal on the distributor cap and then align the stationary flange center with the bolt hole center. On 1983 vehicles: Align the protrusion on the housing center of the flange with that of the bolt hole on the cylinder head.

3. Install the distributor clamp, cap, high tension wire, primary wire, and vacuum line.
4. Install the wires on the spark plugs.
5. Start the engine. Check the timing and adjust the octane selector, if so equipped.

Installation—Timing Disturbed
EXCEPT 5M-GE

1. Determine top dead center (TDC) of the number one (No.1) cylinder's compression stroke by removing the spark plug from the No.1 cylinder and placing a finger or a compression gauge over the spark plug hole. Crank the engine until compression pressure starts to build up. Continue cranking the engine until the timing marks indicate TDC (or 0°).
2. Align the timing marks. Temporarily install the rotor in the distributor shaft so that the rotor is pointing toward the No. 1 terminal in the distributor cap. The points should be about to open.
3. Use a suitable tool to align the slot on the distributor drive (oil pump drive shaft) with the key on the bottom of the distributor shaft.
4. Install the distributor in the

block by rotating it slightly (no more than one gear tooth in either direction) until the driven gear meshes with the drive. Oil the distributor spiral gear and the oil pump driveshaft end before distributor installation.
5. Rotate the distributor, once it is installed, so that the points are just

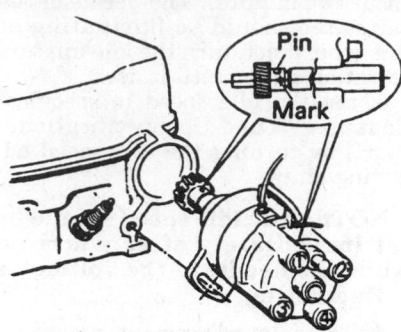

1980–82 A-series distributor alignment

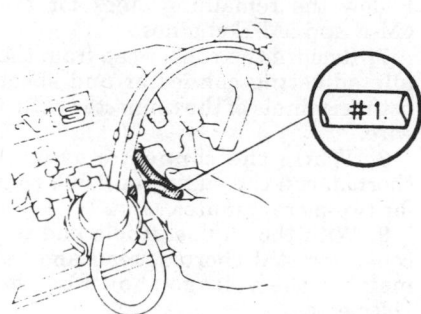

Pinch the No. 1 vacuum hose—3S-GE

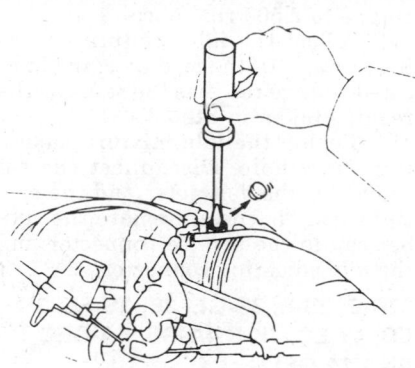

Idle speed adjustment—3S-GE

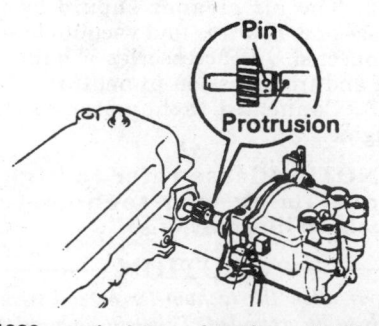

1983 and later A-series distributor alignment

about to open. Temporarily tighten the pinch bolt.

6. Remove the rotor and install the dust cover. Replace the rotor and the distributor cap. Install the primary wire and the vacuum line.

7. Install the No. 1 cylinder spark plug. Connect the cables to the spark plugs in the proper order by using the marks made during removal. Install the high tension wire on the coil.

8. Start the engine. Adjust the ignition timing and the octane selector, if so equipped.

5M-GE

1. Determine top dead center (TDC) of the number one (No.1) cylinder's compression stroke by removing the spark plug from the No.1 cylinder and placing a finger or a compression gauge over the spark plug hole. Crank the engine until compression pressure starts to build up. Continue cranking the engine until the timing marks indicate TDC (or 0°).

2. Remove the oil filler cap. Looking into the camshaft housing with the aid of a flashlight, check to make sure that the match hole on the second (No. 2) journal of the camshaft housing is aligned with the hole in the No. 2 journal of the camshaft. If the holes are not aligned, rotate the camshaft one full turn.

3. Install a new O-ring on the distributor cap shaft. Make sure the distributor cap is still removed at this time. Align the matchmark on the distributor spiral gear with that of the distributor housing.

4. Insert the distributor into the camshaft housing, aligning the center of the mounting flange with that of the bolt hole in the side of the housing.

5. Align the rotor tooth in the distributor with the pickup coil. Temporarily install the distributor pinch bolt. Install the distributor cap, and install the oil filler cap.

6. Install the No. 1 cylinder spark plug. Connect the cables to the spark plugs in the proper order by using the marks made during removal. Install the high tension wire on the coil.

7. Start the engine. Adjust the ignition timing and the octane selector, if so equipped.

1984-88 VEHICLES EXCEPT STARLET

NOTE: Procedures for the 5M-GE are the same as those in the "1981-83" procedures.

Removal and Installation

1. On the Van, remove the right

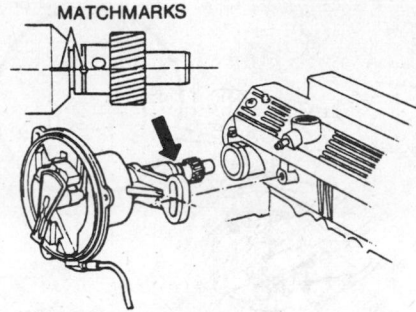
Align the matchmarks on the distributor gear and housing—5M-GE

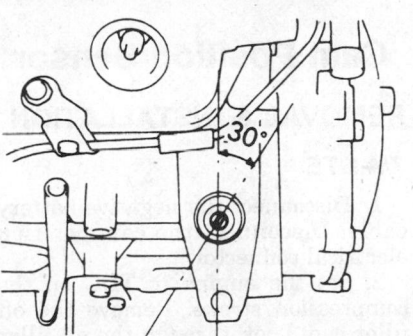
Drive rotor slot alignment—3Y-EC and 4Y-EC

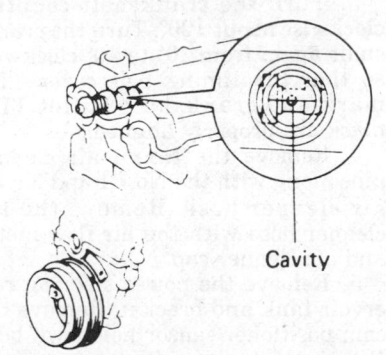
Setting the No. 1 cylinder to TDC of the compression stroke—4A-GE

front seat and engine service hole cover.

2. On all engines, disconnect the battery ground, disconnect the electrical leads, vacuum hoses, and spark plug wires from the distributor.

3. Remove the hold down bolts, and pull the distributor from the engine.

4. Set the engine at TDC of the No. 1 cylinder's firing stroke. This can be accomplished by removing the No. 1 spark plug and turn the engine by hand with your thumb over the spark plug hole. As No.1 is coming up on its firing stroke, you'll feel pressure against your thumb. Make sure the timing marks are set at 0.

NOTE: On the 4A-GE, 4A-GEC and 4A-GELC align the groove on the crankshaft pulley with the

"0" mark on the No.#1 timing cover. Remove the oil filler cap and check that you can see the cavity in the camshaft.

5. On all except the Van, MR2 and Corolla GTS, and Camry, coat the spiral gear and governor shaft tip with clean engine oil. Align the protrusion on the distributor housing with the pin on the spiral gear drill mark side. Insert the distributor, aligning the center of the flange with the bolt hole on the cylinder head. Tighten the bolts.

6. On the Van, locate the top end of the drive rotor in the distributor hole and position the slot 30° off of the center axis. Align the drilled mark on the driven gear with the groove on the distributor housing. Insert the distributor, aligning the stationary flange center with bolt hole in the head. Tighten the bolts.

7. On the Camry, remove the right front wheel and fender apron seal, remove the hole plug of the No.#2 timing belt cover, and, using a mirror, align the mark on the oil seal retainer with the center of the small hole on the camshaft pulley clockwise. Install the plug, fender apron and seal, and the wheel. Coat the spiral gear with clean engine oil, align the protrusion on the housing with the mark on the spiral gear and insert the distributor, aligning the center of the flange with the bolt hole on the head. Tighten the bolts.

8. On the 1984-85 Celica, rotate the crankshaft until the timing mark is aligned with the 5° BTDC mark; make sure the rocker arms on the No.#1 cylinder are loose. Install the rotor and then begin to install the distributor with the rotor pointing upward and the distributor mounting hole at about center position on the bolt hole; When fully installed, the rotor will rotate to the position shown. Remove the rotor and align the signal rotor tooth with the pickup coil projection. Tighten the mounting bolts.

On the 1986-88 Celica with the 2S-E engine, refer to Step 4 and the Camry procedures.

On the 1986-88 Celica GTS with the 3S-GE engine, turn the crankshaft clockwise until the slot in the forward end of the No.#1 camshaft (front of car) is positioned in the vertical position. Lightly coat a new O-ring with the engine oil and slide it into position. Align the drilled mark on the coupling with the notch of the shaft housing. Insert the distributor into the cylinder head so that the center of the flange is aligned with center of the mounting bolt hole.

9. On the MR2 and the Corolla GTS, install a new O-ring. Align the

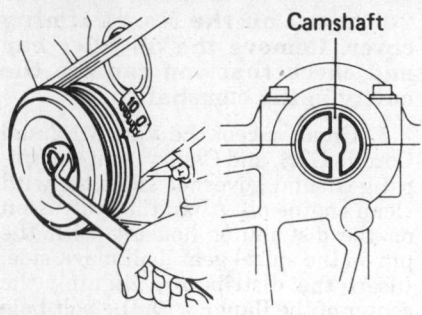

Positioning the No. 1 camshaft on the 3S-GE

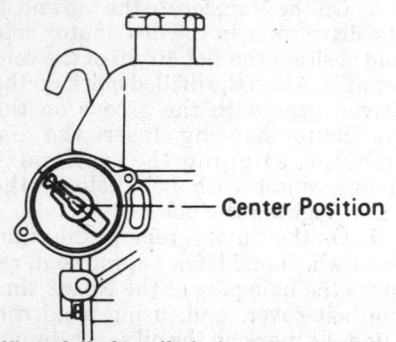

When fully installed, the rotor will rotate to the position shown—22R-E

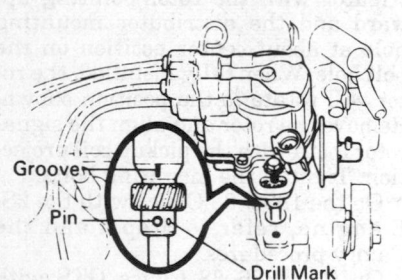

Align the drilled mark on the drive gear with the cavity of the housing—4A-GE

Align the groove on the housing with the pin on the driven gear drill mark side—3Y-EC and 4Y-EC engines

drilled mark on the distributor driven gear with the cavity of the housing. Insert the distributor, aligning the center of the flange with that of the bolt hole on the cylinder head. Tighten the holddown bolts.

10. On all vehicles, connect the spark plug wires and then check the ignition timing.

Align the drilled mark on the coupling with the notch on the housing—3S-GE

Cam Position Sensor

REMOVAL & INSTALLATION

7M-GTE

1. Disconnect the negative battery cable. Disconnect the cam position electrical connector.

2. Set the engine to TDC on the compression stroke. Remove the oil filler cap. Look through the oil filler cap and turn the crankshaft clockwise until the cam nose can be seen.

3. Turn the crankshaft counterclockwise about 120°. Turn the crankshaft again from 10° to 40° clockwise so that the timing belt cover TDC mark and crankshaft pullet TDC mark are properly aligned.

4. Remove the No.#4 air cleaner pipe along with the No.#1 and No.#2 air cleaner hose. Remove the air cleaner hose with the air flow meter and air cleaner cap.

5. Remove the power steering reservoir tank and bracket. Remove the cam positioner sensor holddown bolt. Remove the cam position sensor from the cylinder head. Remove the O-ring.

6. Installation is the reverse of the removal procedure. Align the drilled mark on the driven gear with the groove of the housing. Insert the cam position sensor, aligning the center of the flange with that of the bolt hole on the cylinder head.

Alternator

PRECAUTIONS

• Always observe proper polarity of the battery connections; be especially careful when jump starting the car.

• Never ground or short out any alternator or regulator terminals.

• Never operate the the alternator with any of its or the battery's leads disconnected.

• Always remove the battery or disconnect its output lead while charging it.

• Always disconnect the ground cable when replacing any electrical components.

• Never subject the alternator to excessive heat or dampness if the engine is being steamcleaned.

• Never use arc welding equipment with the alternator connected.

REMOVAL & INSTALLATION

NOTE: On some vehicles, the alternator is mounted very low on the engine. On these vehicles it may be necessary to remove the gravel shield and work from underneath the vehicle in order to gain access to the alternator.

1. Disconnect the negative battery cable.

2. Remove the air cleaner, if necessary, to gain access to the alternator.

3. Unfasten the bolts which attach the adjusting link to the alternator. Remove the alternator drive belt.

4. Unfasten and tag the alternator attaching bolt and then withdraw the alternator from its bracket.

5. Installation is the reverse of the removal procedure. After installing the alternator, adjust the belt tension.

BELT TENSION ADJUSTMENT

Inspection and adjustment to the alternator drive belt should be performed every 3000 miles or if the alternator has been removed.

1. Inspect the drive belt to see that it is not cracked or worn. Be sure that its surfaces are free of grease or oil.

2. Push down on the belt halfway between the fan and the alternator pulleys (or crankshaft pulley) with thumb pressure. Belt deflection should be ⅜–½ in.

3. If the belt tension requires adjustment, loosen the adjusting link bolt and move the alternator until the proper belt tension is obtained.

4. Do not over tighten the belt, as damage to the alternator bearings could result. Tighten the adjusting link bolt.

Voltage Regulator

REMOVAL & INSTALLATION

1. Disconnect the negative battery cable.

2. Disconnect the wiring harness connector from the regulator.

3. Remove the regulator securing bolts. Remove the regulator, complete with its condenser.

4. Installation is the reverse of the removal procedure.

VOLTAGE ADJUSTMENT

1. Connect a voltmeter to the battery terminals.
2. Start the engine and gradually increase its speed to about 1500 rpm.
3. At this speed, voltage reading should fall within specification.
4. If the voltage does not fall within the specifications, remove the cover from the regulator and adjust it by bending the adjusting arm.
5. Repeat Steps 2 and 3. If the voltage cannot be brought to specifications, proceed with the mechanical adjustments.

MECHANICAL ADJUSTMENTS

NOTE: Perform the proceeding voltage adjustment before beginning the mechanical adjustments.

Field Relay

1. Remove the cover from the regulator assembly.
2. Use a feeler gauge to check the amount that the contact spring is deflected while the armature is being depressed.
3. If the measurement is not within specifications, adjust the regulator by bending point holder P.
4. Check the point gap with a feeler gauge against specifications.
5. Adjust the point gap, as required, by bending the point holder P1.
6. Clean off the points with emery cloth if they are dirty and wash them with solvent.

Voltage Regulator

1. Use a feeler gauge to measure the air (armature) gap. If it is not within the specifications, adjust it by bending the low speed point holder.
2. Check the point gap with a feeler gauge. If it is not within specifications, adjust it by bending the high speed point holder. Clean the points with emery cloth and wash them off with solvent.
3. Check the amount of contact spring deflection while depressing the armature. The specification should be the same as that for the contact spring on the field relay. If the amount of deflection is not within specification, replace, do not adjust, the voltage regulator.

Go back and perform the steps outlined under "Voltage Adjustment," above. If the voltage cannot be brought within specifications after regulator replacement, the alternator is probably defective and should be replaced.

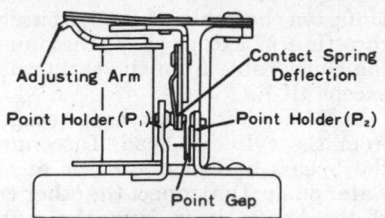

Field relay components

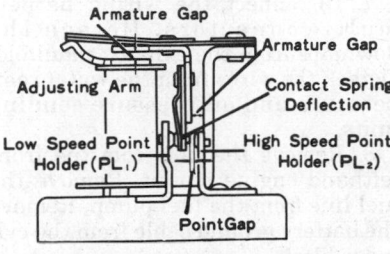

Voltage regulator components

NOTE: On all vehicles with the "IC" type regulator there are no adjustments necessary. If found to be defective, it must be replaced.

Internal (IC) Regulator

The IC regulator is mounted on the alternator housing, is transistorized, and is nonadjustable.

REMOVAL & INSTALLATION

1. Disconnect the negative battery cable.
2. Remove the end cover of the regulator.
3. Remove the three screws that go through the terminals.
4. Remove the (two) top mounting screws that mount the regulator to the alternator. Remove the regulator.
5. To install the new IC regulator. Place the regulator in position on the alternator. Install and secure the (two) top mounting screws. Install the (three) terminal screws. Install the end cover.
6. Reconnect the battery ground cable.

Starter

REMOVAL & INSTALLATION

1. Disconnect the negative battery cable. Disconnect the cable which runs from the starter to the battery, at the battery end.
2. Remove the air cleaner assembly, if necessary, to gain access to the starter.
3. On some vehicles with automatic transmissions, it may be necessary

to disconnect the throttle linkage connecting rod.
4. Disconnect all of the wiring at the starter. Remove the starter retaining bolts. Remove the starter from the vehicle..
5. Installation is the reverse of the removal procedure.

STARTER DRIVE REPLACEMENT

Direct Drive Starter

1. Remove the starter from the engine.
2. Remove the solenoid from the starter.
3. Remove the through bolts and take off the end plate.
4. Slide the armature shaft far enough out to disengage the clutch forks.
5. Remove the retaining clip and washer from the shaft.
6. Slide the starter drive assembly from the shaft.
7. Install in reverse of removal. Always use a new retaining clip.

Reduction Gear Starter

Remove the starter, then follow Steps 1–4 of the starter solenoid procedure for the reduction gear starter.

STARTER SOLENOID & BRUSH REPLACEMENT

Direct Drive Starter

1. Remove the starter from the vehicle. Remove the field coil lead from the solenoid terminal.
2. Unfasten the solenoid retaining screws. Remove the solenoid by tilting it upward and withdrawing it.
3. Remove the end frame bearing cover screws and remove the cover. Remove the thrubolts. Remove the commutator endframe.
4. Withdraw the brushes from their holder if they are to be replaced. Minimum brush length should be 0.40 in. Replace the brushes with new ones if required.
5. Dress the new brushes with emery cloth so that they will make proper contact.
6. Use a spring scale to check the brush spring tension. Replace the springs if they do not meet specifications.
7. Assembly is the reverse of disassembly. Pack the end bearing cover with multipurpose grease before installing it.

Reduction Gear Starter

1. Remove the starter from the vehicle. Disconnect the solenoid lead.

2. Loosen the two bolts on the starter housing and separate the field frame from the solenoid. Remove the O-ring and felt dust seal.

3. Remove the two screws and separate the starter drive from the solenoid. Withdraw the clutch and gears. Remove the ball from the clutch shaft bore or solenoid.

4. Using the proper tool, separate the brush and brush spring and remove the brush from the brush holder.

5. Minimum brush length should be 0.04 in. Replace the brushes if they are too short. Check the gears for wear or damage. Replace as required.

6. Assembly is the reverse of disassembly. Lubricate all bearings and gears with high temperature grease. Grease the ball before inserting in the clutch shaft bore. Align the tab on the brush holder with the notch on the field frame. Check the positive (+) brush leads to see that they are not grounded. Align the mark on the solenoid with the bolt anchors on the field frame.

ENGINE MECHANICAL

Engine

REMOVAL & INSTALLATION

1981–83 4K-C and 4K-E

1. Drain the cooling system. Unfasten the cable which runs from the battery to the starter at the battery terminal. Scribe marks on the hood and hinges. Remove the hood.

2. Unfasten the headlight bezel retaining screws and remove the bezels. Remove the five radiator grille attachment screws and remove the grille.

3. Remove the hood lock assembly after detaching the release cable. Unfasten the nuts from the horn retainers and disconnect the wiring. Remove the horn assembly.

4. Remove the air cleaner from its bracket. Remove the windshield washer tank from its bracket. Remove both the upper and lower radiator hoses from the engine. On vehicles with automatic transmission, disconnect the oil lines from the oil cooler. Remove the radiator mounting bolts and remove the radiator.

5. Remove the accelerator cable from its support on the valve cover.

Unfasten the cable at the carburetor throttle arm, except 4K-E. Disconnect the choke cable from the carburetor, except 4K-E.

6. Detach the water hose retainer from the cylinder head. Disconnect the bypass and heater hoses at the water pump. Disconnect the other end of the heater hose from the water valve. Remove the heater control cable from the water valve.

7. Disconnect the wiring harness multi connectors. Detach the downpipe from the exhaust manifold. Detach the wires from the water temperature and oil pressure sending units.

8. Remove the nut from the front lefthand engine mount. Remove the fuel line from the fuel pump. Remove the battery ground cable from the cylinder block.

9. Remove the nut from the front righthand engine mount. Remove the clip and detach the cable from the clutch release lever. Remove the primary and high tension wires from the coil.

10. Detach the back-up light switch wire at its connector on the right side of the extension housing. Remove the carpet from the transmission tunnel. Remove the boots from the shift lever.

11. Remove the snapring from the gearshift selector lever base. Withdraw the selector lever assembly.

12. Raise and support the vehicle safely. Disconnect the driveshaft from the transmission. Drain the oil from the manual transmission. Detach the exhaust pipe support bracket from the extension housing.

13. Remove the insulator bolt from the rear engine mount. Place a jack under the transmission and remove the four bolts from the rear crossmember.

13. Install lifting hooks on the engine lifting brackets. Attach a suitable hoist. Lift the engine slightly then move it toward the front of the vehicle. Bring the engine the rest of the way out at an angle.

14. Installation is the reverse of the removal procedure.

1981–82 3T-C, 1981–86 4A-C and 1983–88 4A-LC

1. Drain the cooling system, transmission, and engine oil.

2. Disconnect the battery to starter cable at the positive battery terminal.

3. Scribe marks on the hood and its hinges. Remove the hood supports from the body. Remove the hood. Do not remove the supports from the hood.

4. Unfasten the headlight bezel retaining screws and remove the bezels. Remove the five radiator grille at-

tachment screws and remove the grille.

5. Remove the hood lock assembly after detaching the release cable. Unfasten the nuts from the horn retainers and disconnect the wiring. Remove the horn assembly.

6. Detach both the upper and lower hoses from the radiator. On vehicles equipped with automatic transmission, disconnect the lines from the oil cooler. Remove the radiator.

7. Unfasten the clamps and remove the heater and bypass hoses from the engine. Remove the heater control cable from the water valve.

8. Remove the wiring from the coolant temperature and oil pressure sending units. Remove the air cleaner assembly.

9. Unfasten the accelerator torque rod from the carburetor. On vehicles equipped with automatic transmissions remove the transmission linkage.

10. Remove the emission control system hoses and wiring, as necessary. Remove the clutch hydraulic line support bracket. Unfasten the high tension and primary wires from the coil.

11. Mark the spark plug cables and remove them from the distributor. Detach the righthand front engine mount. Remove the fuel line at the pump.

12. Detach the downpipe from the exhaust manifold. Detach the left hand front engine mount. Disconnect all of the wiring harness multiconnectors.

13. On vehicles equipped with manual transmission remove the shift lever boot and the shift lever cap boot.

14. Unfasten the four gear selector cap retaining screws and remove the gasket and withdraw the gear selector lever assembly from the top of the transmission. On five speed transmission, the floor console must be removed first.

15. Raise and support the vehicle safely. On vehicles equipped with automatic transmission, disconnect the gear selector control rod.

16. Detach the exhaust pipe support bracket. Disconnect the driveshaft from the rear of the transmission.

17. Unfasten the speedometer cable from the transmission. Disconnect the wiring from the back-up light switch and the neutral safety switch, if equipped.

18. Detach the clutch release cylinder assembly, complete with hydraulic lines. Do not disconnect the lines. Unbolt the rear support member mounting insulators.

19. Support the transmission and detach the rear support member re-

taining bolts. Remove the support member.

20. Install lifting hooks on the engine lifting brackets. Attach a suitable hoist to the engine. Remove the jack from under the transmission.

21. Raise the engine and move it toward the front of the vehicle. Use care to avoid damaging the components which remain on the vehicle.

22. Installation is the reverse of the removal procedure.

1981, 1984–85 22R

1. Drain the cooling system, transmission, and engine oil.

2. Disconnect the battery to starter cable at the positive battery terminal.

3. Scribe marks on the hood and its hinges. Remove the hood supports from the body. Remove the hood. Do not remove the supports from the hood.

4. Unfasten the headlight bezel retaining screws and remove the bezels. Remove the radiator grille attachment screws and remove the grille.

5. Remove the fan shroud, the hood lock base and the base support. Remove the wiring from the coolant temperature and oil pressure sending units. Remove the air cleaner assembly.

6. Unfasten the accelerator torque rod from the carburetor. On vehicles equipped with automatic transmissions remove the transmission linkage.

7. Remove the emission control system hoses and wiring, as necessary. Remove the clutch hydraulic line support bracket. Unfasten the high tension and primary wires from the coil.

8. Mark the spark plug cables and remove them from the distributor. Detach the righthand front engine mount. Remove the fuel line at the pump.

9. Detach the downpipe from the exhaust manifold. Detach the left hand front engine mount. Disconnect all of the wiring harness multiconnectors.

10. If the vehicle is equipped with manual transmission remove the center console if so equipped. Remove the shift lever boot.

11. Unfasten the four shift lever cap retaining screws. Remove the cap and withdraw the shift lever assembly.

12. If equipped with automatic transmission remove the transmission selector linkages. On vehicles equipped with a floor mounted selector, disconnect the control rod from the transmission. On vehicles equipped with column mounted gear selector, remove the shifter rod.

13. Disconnect the neutral safety switch wiring connector. Raise and support the vehicle safely.

14. Remove the retaining screws and remove the parking brake equalizer support bracket. Disconnect the cable which runs between the lever and the equalizer.

15. Remove the speedometer cable from the transmission. Disconnect the back-up light wiring. Remove the driveshaft.

16. Detach the clutch release cylinder assembly, complete with hydraulic lines. Do not disconnect the lines. Unbolt the rear support member mounting insulators.

17. Support the transmission and detach the rear support member retaining bolts. Remove the support member.

18. Install lifting hooks on the engine lifting brackets. Attach a suitable hoist to the engine. Remove the jack from under the transmission.

19. Raise the engine and move it toward the front of the vehicle. Use care to avoid damaging the components which remain on the vehicle.

20. Installation is the reverse of the removal procedure.

1982–83 22R

1. Disconnect the battery cables. Matchmark and remove the hood. Drain the coolant. Remove the air cleaner assembly.

2. Disconnect the accelerator linkage from the carburetor. Disconnect the transmission cable from the carburetor if equipped with automatic transmission.

3. Mark and disconnect all wiring and hoses from the engine. Label each item so that it may be reattached correctly during assembly.

4. Remove the radiator grille. Remove the hood lock brace, radiator upper baffle, and the hood lock. Remove the radiator and the fan shroud.

5. If the vehicle is equipped with air condition, properly discharge the refrigerant. Remove the air conditioning condenser from the vehicle.

6. Loosen the air conditioning compressor mounting bolts, remove the drive belt, remove the mounting bolts, and lay the compressor aside.

7. If the vehicle is equipped with power steering, loosen the idler pulley bolts. Remove the power steering pump drive belt. Remove the power steering pump mounting bolts. Move the pump out of the way. It is not necessary to disconnect the hydraulic lines from the pump.

8. Disconnect the upper side of the engine shock absorber from the left engine mount. Remove the engine mount bolts from each side of the engine.

9. Remove the console to gain access to the shift lever on vehicles with manual transmissions. Remove the shift lever.

10. Raise and support the vehicle safely. Remove the engine undercover. Drain the engine oil.

11. Remove the exhaust pipe clamp from the transmission housing, disconnect the exhaust pipe from the manifold.

12. On vehicles equipped with manual transmission, remove the clutch release cylinder. Disconnect the speedometer cable from the transmission.

13. On vehicles equipped with automatic transmission, disconnect the shift linkage from the shift lever.

14. Disconnect the wiring from the back-up light switch, neutral start switch, overdrive solenoid, oil pressure sending unit and starter assembly.

15. Place a jack under the transmission, with a block of wood between the jack and the transmission. Raise the jack just enough to support the transmission. Remove the transmission crossmember. Remove the driveshaft.

17. Attach the engine lifting equipment to the engine. Carefully lift the engine and the transmission assembly out of the vehicle.

18. Installation is the reverse of the removal procedure.

1983–85 22R-E

1. Disconnect the battery cables. Matck mark and remove the hood. Drain the coolant. Remove the air cleaner assembly.

2. Disconnect the accelerator linkage from the carburetor. Disconnect the transmission cable from the carburetor if equipped with automatic transmission.

3. Mark and disconnect all wiring and hoses from the engine. Label each item so that it may be reattached correctly during assembly.

4. Remove the radiator grille. Remove the hood lock brace, radiator upper baffle, and the hood lock. Remove the radiator and the fan shroud.

5. Disconnect the automatic transmission actuator cable, accelerator cable and throttle cable from the bracket on the side of the EFI intake chamber.

6. Tag and disconnect the PCV hoses, the brake booster hose, the cruise control actuator hose, the air control valve hose and the air control valve. Remove the EGR vacuum modulator and bracket.

7. Tag and disconnect the remaining emission control hoses as necessary, including the air valve hoses from the intake chamber and throttle

body, the water bypass hoses from the throttle body, the air control valve hose to the actuator and the pressure regulator hose from the intake chamber.

8. Tag and disconnect the cold start injector pipe and the cold start injector, the throttle position sensor wire and the air valve wire.

9. Remove the bolt holding the EGR valve to the intake chamber. Disconnect the chamber from the stay, then remove the chamber from the intake manifold with the throttle body attached.

10. Tag and disconnect the water temperature sender, overdrive thermoswitch, start injection time, temperature sensor and injection wires..

11. Remove the two bolts from the top and bottom of the steering universal, and remover the sliding yoke.

12. Disconnect the tie rod ends. Disconnect the pressure line mounting bolts from the front crossmember.

13. Without disconnecting the oil pipe, remove the mounting bolts to the rack and pinion assembly and carefully suspend it from the front crossmember without stretching the fluid hoses.

14. If the vehicle is equipped with power steering, loosen the idler pulley bolts. Remove the power steering pump drive belt. Remove the power steering pump mounting bolts. Move the pump out of the way. It is not necessary to disconnect the hydraulic lines from the pump.

15. Disconnect the upper side of the engine shock absorber from the left engine mount. Remove the engine mount bolts from each side of the engine.

16. Remove the console to gain access to the shift lever. Remove the shift lever.

17. Raise and support the vehicle safely. Remove the engine undercover. Drain the engine oil.

18. Remove the exhaust pipe clamp from the transmission housing, disconnect the exhaust pipe from the manifold, and allow the pipe to hang downward.

19. On vehicles equipped with manual transmission, remove the clutch release cylinder. Disconnect the speedometer cable from the transmission.

20. On vehicles equipped with automatic transmission, disconnect the shift linkage from the shift lever.

21. Disconnect the wiring from the back-up light switch, neutral start switch, overdrive solenoid, oil pressure sending unit and starter assembly.

22. Place a jack under the transmis-sion, with a block of wood between the jack and the transmission. Raise the jack just enough to support the transmission. Remove the transmission crossmember. Remove the driveshaft.

23. Attach the engine lifting equipment to the engine. Carefully lift the engine and the transmission assembly out of the vehicle.

24. Installation is the reverse of the removal procedure.

1981–82 5M-E

1. Disconnect the battery cables and remove the battery. Match mark the hood remove it.

2. Remove the fan shroud. Drain the cooling system. Disconnect both the upper and lower radiator hoses. Disconnect and plug the oil lines from the oil cooler on vehicles equipped with automatic transmission.

3. Detach the hose which runs to the thermal expansion tank and remove the expansion tank from its mounting bracket. Remove the radiator. Disconnect the heater and bypass hoses from the engine.

4. Disconnect the oil pressure light sender wiring, the alternator electrical connector, and the back-up light switch wiring. Disconnect the power brake unit vacuum lines.

5. Disconnect the engine cooler hoses at the oil filter, if so equipped. Disconnect the power steering fluid cooler hose, if so equipped.

6. Remove the air cleaner assembly. Detach the emission control system wires and hoses, as required. Unfasten the distributor primary wire and the high tension wire from the coil.

7. Disconnect the wiring from the starter and temperature gauge sender. Remove the fuel line from the fuel pump. Disconnect the heater control cable from the water valve. Unfasten the heater control vacuum hose.

8. Remove the accelerator linkage from the carburetor. On fuel injected vehicles, disconnect the accelerator linkage from the throttle body. Tag and disconnect any remaining hoses, lines, or wires which may still be attached to the engine.

9. If equipped with manual transmission detach the clutch hydraulic line from its master cylinder connections. Install a cap on the master cylinder fitting to keep the hydraulic fluid from running out.

10. Detach the pressure feed lines from the steering gear housing as required. Raise and support the vehicle safely.

11. Detach the exhaust pipe from the downpipe and remove the exhaust pipe hangers. Disconnect the speedometer cable from the transmission.

12. On vehicles equipped manual transmission, remove the center console securing screws, the gearshift knob, the gearshift boot, and then unfasten the console wiring multiconnector. Lift the console over the gearshift lever. Remove the screws that retain the shift lever retainer to the shift tower and withdraw the shift lever assembly.

13. On vehicles equipped with automatic transmission, unfasten the connecting rod swivel nut and detach the control rod from the gear selector lever.

14. Disconnect the parking brake lever rod, return spring, intermediate rod, and the cable from the equalizer. Remove the driveshaft.

15. Remove the left hand gravel shield. Remove the front engine mounts. Properly support the transmission. Remove the rear engine mounts and the rear crossmember.

16. Attach a hoist to the engine and carefully remove the engine from the vehicle.

17. Installation is the reverse of the removal procedure.

1982–88 5M-GE

1. Disconnect the battery cables and remove the battery. Match mark the hood remove it. Remove the air cleaner assembly.

2. Remove the fan shroud. Drain the cooling system. Disconnect both the upper and lower radiator hoses. Disconnect and plug the oil lines from the oil cooler on vehicles equipped with automatic transmission.

3. Detach the hose which runs to the thermal expansion tank and remove the expansion tank from its mounting bracket. Remove the radiator.

4. On vehicles equipped with automatic transmission, remove the throttle cable bracket from the cylinder head. Remove the accelerator and actuator cable bracket from the cylinder head.

5. Tag and disconnect the cylinder head ground cable, the oxygen sensor wire, the oil pressure sending unit, alternator wires, the high tension coil wire, the water temperature sending, the thermo switch wires, the starter wires, and the ECT connectors for the solenoid resistor wire connector.

6. Tag and disconnect the brake booster vacuum hose from the air intake chamber, along with the EGR valve vacuum hose. Disconmnect the actuator vacuum hose from the air intake chamber, if equipped with cruise control. Disconnect the heater bypass hoses from the engine.

7. Remove the glove box, and remove the ECU computer module. Dis-

connect the three connectors, and pull out the EFI wiring harness from the engine compartment side of the firewall.

8. Remove the four shroud and four fluid coupling screws, and the shroud and coupling as a unit. Remove the engine undercover protector.

9. Disconnect the coolant reservoir hose. Remove the radiator. Remove the coolant expansion tank.

10. Remove the air condition compressor drive belt, and remove the compressor mounting bolts. Without disconnecting the refrigerant hoses, lay the compressor to one side and secure it.

NOTE: The air condition system is charged with the refrigerant R-12, which is dangerous when released. Do not disconnect the hoses when removing the engine, unless absolutely necessary.

11. Disconnect the power steering pump drive belt and remove the pump stay. Unbolt the pump and lay it aside without disconnecting the fluid hoses.

12. Remove the engine mounting bolts from each side of the engine. Remove the engine ground cable.

13. On vehicles equipped with manual transmission, remove the shift lever from the inside of the vehicle.

14. Raise and support the vehicle safely. Drain the engine oil.

15. Disconnect the exhaust pipe from the exhaust manifold. Remove the exhaust pipe clamp from the transmission housing.

16. On vehicles equipped with manual transmission, remove the clutch slave cylinder. Disconnect the speedometer cable at the transmission.

17. On vehicles equipped with automatic transmission, disconnect the shift linkage from the shift lever. On vehicles equipped with manual transmission, disconnect the wire from the back-up light switch. Remove the stiffener plate from the ground cable.

18. Disconnect and plug the fuel line from the fuel filter and the return hose from the fuel hose support.

19. Remove the two bolts from the top and bottom of the steering universal, and remover the sliding yoke.

20. Disconnect the tie rod ends. Disconnect the pressure line mounting bolts from the front crossmember.

21. Remove the intermediate shaft from the driveshaft.

22. Position a jack under the transmission, with a wooden block between the two to prevent damage to the transmission case. Place a wooden block between the cowl panel and the cylinder head rear end to prevent damage to the heater hoses.

23. Unbolt the engine rear support member from the frame, along with the ground cable.

24. Make sure all wiring is disconnected, all hoses disconnected, and everything clear of the engine and transmission. Attach an engine lift hoist chain to the lift brackets on the engine, and carefully lift the engine and transmission up and out of the vehicle.

25. Installation is the rverse of the removal procedure.

1981–82 1A-C, 1981–86 3A and 1981–88 3A-C

1. Disconnect the negative battery cable. Remove the hood. Remove the air cleaner asssembly. Drain the radiator.

2. Cover both driveshaft boots with a shop towel. Remove the solenoid valve connector, water temperature switch connector, and the electric fan connector.

3. Remove the exhaust support plate bolts, and the exhaust pipe.

4. Remove the top radiator support. Remove the top and bottom radiator hoses. Disconnect and plug the transmission fluid lines, as required. Remove the radiator with the fan assembly.

5. Remove the windshield washer tank. Remove the heater hoses. Remove and plug the lines to the fuel pump.

6. Remove the accelerator cable, choke cable, and ground strap. Remove the brake booster vacuum line. Remove the coil wire and unplug the alternator.

7. Remove the clutch release cable. Remove the wires on the starter. Remove the temperature sending and oil pressure switch connectors. Remove the battery ground strap from the block.

8. Raise and support the vehicle safely. Remove the engine mounting bolts. Remove the engine shock absorbers. As required, remove the starter assembly.

9. Support the differential assembly with a jack. Remove the transaxle mounting bolts.

10. On vehicles equipped with automatic transmission it will be necessary to remove the torque converter retaining bolts.

11. The grille may be removed if necessary to give better leverage when removing the engine.

12. Using the proper engine lifting equipment carefully remove the engine from the vehicle. If equipped with automatic transaxle, while the engine is suspended from the hoist, pull it forward about two inches. Insert a pry bar in this opening and gently separate the torque converter from the engine.

13. Tie the transaxle housing to the cowl to keep support on the transaxle.

14. Installation is the reverse of the removal procedure.

1986–88 3S-GE

1. Disconnect and remove the battery. Match mark and remove the hood. Drain the cooling system.

2. Tag and disconnect the connector high tension lead at the ignition coil. Remove the four nuts and two bolts securing the upper suspension brace. Remove the brace.

3. On vehicles equipped with automatic transmission, disconnect the throttle cable and its bracket at the throttle body.

4. Disconnect the throttle cable from the throttle body on vehicles equipped with manual transmission.

5. Remove the overflow tank. Remove the cruise control actuator and its bracket. Remove the oxygen sensor.

6. Tag and disconnect the cooling fan leads at the radiator. Disconnect the heater hoses. Disconnect the automatic transmission fluid cooler lines, if equipped. Remove the radiator and the two supports.

7. Remove the air cleaner assembly and bracket. Remove the igniter.

8. Tag, disconnect and plug the fuel hoses at the filter and fuel return pipe. Disconnect the speedometer cable.

9. Disconnect the transaxle control cable at the shift and selector levers on vehicles equipped with manual transaxle and then remove it from the bracket. On vehicles equipped with automatic transaxle, disconnect the cable at the swivel and at the bracket and then remove it.

10. Unbolt the air conditioning compressor and position it out of the way with the refrigerant lines still attached.

11. Tag and disconnect any remaining wires or electrical leads. Tag and disconnect any remaining vacuum hoses.

12. Raise and support the vehicle safely. Drain the engine oil.

13. Remove the right side engine under cover. Remove the lower suspension crossmember. Remove both halfshaft assemblies.

14. Unbolt the power steering pump. Disconnect the two vacuum hoses and remove the drive belt. Position the pump out of the way with the hydraulic lines still connected to it.

15. Disconnect the exhaust pipe at the manifold. Remove the rear engine mount bolt. Lower the vehicle and then remove the front engine mount

bolts. Remove the power steering pump reservoir and position it out of the way.

16. Attach an engine hoist to the lifting hooks. Take up the engine's weight with the hoist and remove the right and left engine mounts.

17. Slowly and carefully, remove the engine and transaxle assembly. Be careful not to hit the power steering gear housing or the neutral safety switch.

18. Installation is the reverse of the removal procedure.

1983–86 2S-E

1. Disconnect and remove the battery. Drain the coolant system. Remove the hood.

2. Disconnect and tags all cables, electrical wires and vacuum lines attached to various engine parts.

3. Remove the cruise control actuator and bracket. Disconnect the radiator and heater hoses. Disconnect the automatic transmission cooler lines. Remove the radiator.

4. Remove the air cleaner assembly and air flow meter. Disconnect all wiring and linkage at the transmission.

5. Pull out the fuel injection system wiring harness. Secure the assembly to the right side of fender apron.

6. Disconnect and plug the fuel lines at the fuel filter and return pipes. Unbolt the air condition compressor and position it out of the way.

7. Disconnect the speedometer cable at the transmission. Remove the clutch release cylinder without disconnecting the fluid line.

8. Raise and support the vehicle safely. Drain the engine oil. Drain the transaxle fluid. Unbolt both halfshafts.

9. Unbolt the power steering pump and position it out of the way. Disconnect the exhaust pipe from the manifold. Disconnect the front and rear engine mounts at the frame member.

10. Attach an engine crane at the lifting eyes. Take up the engine weight with the crane and remove the right and left side engine mounts.

11. Carefully, remove the engine and transaxle assembly from the vehicle.

12. Installation is the reverse of the removal procedure.

1984–85 3Y-EC and 1986–88 4Y-EC

1. Disconnect the negative battery cable. Remove the front seat. Remove the engine cover. Drain the coolant. Disconnect the radiator and heater hoses.

2. Disconnect and tag all vacuum hoses, electrical wires and cables attached to various engine parts that may inhibit engine removal.

3. Remove the air cleaner assembly. Unbolt the power steering pump and secure it out of the way.

4. Remove the fan shroud. Remove the fan and fan clutch. Do not lay the fan on its side, as damage may result. Unbolt the air condition compressor and secure it out of the way.

5. Raise and support the vehicle safely. Drain the engine oil. Remove the driveshaft.

6. Disconnect and remove the exhaust system. Remove the transmission control cable. Remove the clutch release cylinder.

7. Remove the starter. Remove the speedometer cable. Disconnect all remaining hoses and cables from the transmission.

8. Remove the engine tensioner cable. Remove the engine underpan. Remove the strut bar.

9. Place an engine jack under the engine and take up the weight. Unbolt and remove the engine mounts. Carefully lower the engine from the vehicle.

10. Installation is the reverse of the removal procedure.

1984–85 1C-L, 1C-LT, 1C-LC and 1986 2C-T

1. Disconnect and remove the battery. Drain the coolant. Matchmark and remove the hood.

2. Remove the relay block bracket and position the assembly out of the way without disconnecting any electrical leads. Remove the cruise control actuator.

3. If the vehicle is not equipped with cruise control, disconnect the accelerator cable at the injection pump. Disconnect the throttle cable at the injection pump. Remove the air cleaner assembly.

4. Disconnect and remove the heater hoses. Remove the radiator.

5. Tag, disconnect and plug the fuel inlet and outlet hoses, the vacuum pump vacuum hoses, the pressure hose for the turbocharger warning switch, the idle up vacuum hoses and the HAC vacuum hose.

6. Tag and disconnect all electrical wires, vacuum hoses and cables which may interfere with engine removal.

7. Disconnect the speedometer cable. Remove the transaxle case protection shield. Disconnect the transaxle control cable at the swivel and bracket and lift it out.

8. Remove the windshield washer and radiator reservoir tanks.

9. Unbolt the power steering pump, remove the drive belt and then position the pump out of the way with the hydraulic lines still connected. Unbolt and position the air condition compressor out of the way.

10. Raise and support the vehicle safely. Drain the engine oil. Drain the transaxle fluid.

11. Unbolt both halfshafts. Unbolt the left side steering knuckle for halfshaft removal.

12. Disconnect the exhaust pipe at the turbocharger elbow manifold on the 1C-L engine.

13. Remove the rear engine insulator. Lower the vehicle and remove the front engine mount bolts.

14. Attach an engine lifting hoist at the hooks. Take up the weight of the engine with the hoist and then remove the right and left engine mounts.

15. Slowly and carefully, remove the engine/transaxle assembly from the vehicle.

16. Installation is the reverse of the removal procedure.

1984–86 4A-GE

COROLLA

1. Disconnect the battery cables. Remove the battery. Remove the hood and the engine cover.

2. Remove the No. 2 air cleaner hose. Disconnect the actuator and accelerator cables from their bracket on the cylinder head.

3. Remove the center console; lift up the shift boot and then remove the shifter.

4. Remove the air cleaner assembly. Drain the engine oil Drain the transmission fluid.

5. Drain the radiator. Remove the radiator hoses. Remove the radiator and shroud.

6. Remove the power steering pump along with its bracket. Loosen the water pump pulley retaining nuts, remove the drive belt adjusting bolt. Remove the drive belt.

7. Remove the retaining nuts and then remove the fluid coupling with the fan and the water pump pulley.

8. Remove the air condition compressor and bracket. Position the assembly out of the way. Do not disconnect the two air condition hoses.

9. Remove the distributor assembly. Tag and disconnect the electrical wires at the starter assembly.

10. Remove the exhaust pipe bracket from the pipe and the clutch housing. Disconnect the exhaust manifold from the exhaust pipe. Disconnect the oxygen sensor, remove the heat insulator from the manifold. Remove the manifold.

11. Remove the pulsation damper at the fuel delivery pipe. Disconnect the fuel hose with the two washers and then disconnect the fuel return hose from the pressure regulator.

12. Remove the cold start injector pipe. Remove the PCV hose at the intake manifold. Tag and disconnect all related vacuum hoses.

13. Remove the wiring harness and the vacuum pipe from the No.3 timing cover. Tag and disconnect all related wires and then position the harness out of the way.

14. Raise the vehicle and support it safely. Remove the engine mounting bolts on either side of the engine.

15. Unbolt the clutch release cylinder without disconnecting the hydraulic line and then position it out of the way.

16. Disconnect the driveshaft. Tag and disconnect the speedometer cable and the back-up switch connector. Remove the O-ring.

17. Disconnect the bond cables from the clutch and extension housings. Lower the vehicle.

18. Attach an engine hoist to the lift bracket on the engine. Support the rear engine mounting with a jack to prevent damage. Remove the rear engine mounting bolts. Remove the engine from the vehicle.

19. Remove the starter, the two stiffener plates and then separate the transmission from the engine.

20. Installation is in the reverse of the removal procedure.

MR-2

1. Disconnect and remove the battery. Remove the air cleaner assembly. Drain the coolant. Drain the engine oil.

2. Remove the fuel tank protectors and the engine undercover.

3. Disconnect the accelerator cable. Disconnect the cruise control at the cable actuator, if equipped. On vehicles with automatic transmission, disconnect the throttle cable.

4. Disconnect the heater hoses at the water inlet housing on the rear of the cylinder head cover. Disconnect the radiator hose and the air bleeder hose at the water inlet housing.

5. Disconnect and plug the fuel line at the fuel filter. Disconnect the fuel return hose. Tag and disconnect the vacuum hose at the charcoal canister.

6. Tag and disconnect the engine ground strap and the main wiring harness connector at the engine. Disconnect the back-up light switch connector as required.

7. Disconnect the speedometer cable. Remove the transaxle gravel shield. Remove the ground strap from the water inlet housing.

8. Remove the radiator overflow tank. Remove the air conditioner drive belt. Remove the alternator drive belt. Remove the alternator. Disconnect the radiator hose at the water outlet housing.

9. Tag and disconnect the two connectors at the igniter, the noise filter connector, the cooling fan electrical connector, the cylinder head ground strap, the air condition compressor connector and the high tension leads at the ignition coil.

10. Remove the rear luggage compartment trim. Tag and disconnect the circuit opening relay connector, the ball connections at the electronic control unit and the electrical lead for the cooling fan computer.

11. Pull the main wiring harness out and through the engine compartment.

12. Remove the mounting bolts and remove the air conditioning compressor. Position it out of the way without disconnecting the refrigerant lines.

13. On vehicles equipped with a manual transmission, disconnect the control cables from the outer shift lever and gear shift selector lever. On vehicles equipped with automatic transmission, disconnect the control cable at the gear shift lever.

14. On vehicles equipped with a manual transmission, remove the control cable bracket on the transaxle. Remove the clutch release cylinder.

15. Disconnect the engine oil cooler lines, if equipped. Disconnect the automatic transmission fluid lines if equipped.

16. Remove the exhaust pipe assembly. Remove the oxygen sensor at the exhaust manifold.

17. On vehicles equipped with automatic transmsssion, remove the mounting bolts and remove the stiffener plate at the transaxle. Remove the flywheel shield.

18. Remove the right halfshaft. Disconnect the left halfshaft from the side gear shaft and position it out of the way.

19. Remove the front and rear engine mount bolts. Place a block of wood on an hydraulic floor jack and carefully position the jack under the engine. Raise the jack just enough to ease the engine's weight on the mounts. Remove the right and left engine mounts.

20. Make sure there are no remaining wires or hoses connected to the engine and then slowly and carefully raise the vehicle while lowering the jack supporting the engine/transaxle assembly.

21. Installation is the reverse of the removal procedure.

1987–88 3E
TERCEL SEDAN

1. Disconnect and remove the battery. Remove the hood. Remove the engine under covers.

2. Drain the coolant. Disconnect and plug the transaxle fluid lines, if equipped. Remove the radiator. Remove the washer tank. Disconnect the heater hoses.

3. If the vehicle is equipped with cruise control disconnect and remove the actuator assembly. Disconnect the accelerator cable. If the vehicle is equipped with automatic transaxle disconnect the accelerator cable.

4. Disconnect and plug the fuel line hoses. Remove the charcoal canister assembly. Disconnect the brake booster hose.

5. Disconnect the speedometer cable from the transaxle. Disconnect the transaxle control cables from their mounting.

6. Remove the clutch release cylinder. Remove the selecting bell crank.

7. Disconnect the engine ground strap, the oxygen sensor wire, the oil pressure switch wire, the coolant fan wire, the water temperature gauge wire, the back up light switch and neutral safety switch wires.

8. Disconnect the wiring harness from the intake manifold. Remove the intake manifold ground strap. Disconnect the CMH connector, the alternator electrical connector and the starter electrical wires. Remove the VSV.

9. Remove the power steering pump and position it to the side. Remove the air condition compressor and position it to the side.

10. Disconnect the exhaust pipe at the manifold. Remove the halfshafts.

11. Properly support the engine/transaxle assembly. Attach the engine chain hoist to the engine lifting hooks.

12. Remove the rear mounting through bolt. Remove the rear mounting assembly. Remove the front mounting through bolt. Remove the front mounting assembly.

13. Remove the right and left side mounting bolts and brackets. Carefully lift the engine assembly out of the vehicle.

14. Installation is the reverse of the removal procedure.

TERCEL WAGON

1. Disconnect and remove the battery. Remove the battery carrier. Remove the hood.

2. Drain the coolant. Disconnect and plug the transaxle fluid lines, if equipped. Remove the radiator. Remove the washer tank. Disconnect the heater hoses. If equipped with air condition remove the condenser fan assembly.

3. Remove the power steering pump and position it to the side. Remove the air condition compressor and position it to the side.

4. Disconnect the engine ground strap, the oxygen sensor wire, the distributor connector, the ground strap from the dash panel, the oil pressure switch wire, the coolant fan wire, the water temperature gauge wire, the back up light switch and neutral safety switch wires.

5. Disconnect the accelerator cable. If the vehicle is equipped with automatic transaxle disconnect the accelerator cable.

6. Disconnect and plug the fuel line hoses. Disconnect the vacuum hose for the VSV idle-up. Disconnect the brake booster hose.

7. Disconnect the air suction filter from the cylinder block. Remove the transaxle upper mount bolts.

8. Raise and support the vehicle safely. Remove the front exhaust pipe. Remove the oil cooler lines, if equipped.

9. If equipped, disconnect the clutch release cable. Remove the stiffner plates. Disconnect the engine mounting absorber.

10. Remove the engine mount bolts. Remove the torque converter cover. Remove the torque converter bolts.

11. Properly position a lifting device under the transaxle assembly. Remove the lower transaxle retaining bolts. As required, remove the starter.

12. Properly support the engine/transaxle assembly. Attach the engine chain hoist to the engine lifting hooks. Carefully remove the engine from the vehicle.

14. Installation is the reverse of the removal procedure.

1987–88 4A-GEC and 4A-GELC

1. Disconnect and remove the battery. Remove the air cleaner assembly. Drain the coolant. Drain the engine oil.

2. Remove the fuel tank protectors and the engine undercover.

3. Disconnect the accelerator cable. Disconnect the cruise control at the cable actuator, if equipped. On vehicles with automatic transmission, disconnect the throttle cable.

4. Disconnect the heater hoses at the water inlet housing on the rear of the cylinder head cover. Disconnect the radiator hose and the air bleeder hose at the water inlet housing.

5. Disconnect and plug the fuel line at the fuel filter. Disconnect the fuel return hose. Tag and disconnect the vacuum hose at the charcoal canister.

6. Tag and disconnect the engine ground strap and the main wiring harness connector at the engine. Disconnect the back-up light switch connector as required.

7. Disconnect the speedometer cable. Remove the transaxle gravel

shield. Remove the ground strap from the water inlet housing.

8. Remove the radiator overflow tank. Remove the air conditioner drive belt. Remove the alternator drive belt. Remove the alternator. Disconnect the radiator hose at the water outlet housing.

9. Tag and disconnect the two connectors at the igniter, the noise filter connector, the cooling fan electrical connector, the cylinder head ground strap, the air condition compressor connector and the high tension leads at the ignition coil.

10. Remove the rear luggage compartment trim. Tag and disconnect the circuit opening relay connector, the ball connections at the electronic control unit and the electrical lead for the cooling fan computer.

11. Pull the main wiring harness out and through the engine compartment.

12. Remove the mounting bolts and remove the air conditioning compressor. Position it out of the way without disconnecting the refrigerant lines.

13. On vehicles equipped with a manual transmission, disconnect the control cables from the outer shift lever and gear shift selector lever. On vehicles equipped with automatic transmission, disconnect the control cable at the gear shift lever.

14. On vehicles equipped with a manual transmission, remove the control cable bracket on the transaxle. Remove the clutch release cylinder.

15. Disconnect the engine oil cooler lines, if equipped. Disconnect the automatic transmission fluid lines if equipped.

16. Remove the exhaust pipe assembly. Remove the oxygen sensor at the exhaust manifold.

17. On vehicles equipped with automatic transmssion, remove the mounting bolts and remove the stiffener plate at the transaxle. Remove the flywheel shield.

18. Remove the right halfshaft. Disconnect the left halfshaft from the side gear shaft and position it out of the way.

19. Remove the front and rear engine mount bolts. Place a block of wood on an hydraulic floor jack and carefully position the jack under the engine. Raise the jack just enough to ease the engine's weight on the mounts. Remove the right and left engine mounts.

20. Make sure there are no remaining wires or hoses connected to the engine and then slowly and carefully raise the vehicle while lowering the jack supporting the engine/transaxle assembly.

21. Installation is the reverse of the removal procedure.

1986 7M-GE

1. Disconnect the battery cables and remove the battery. Drain the cooling system. Remove the hood.

2. Remove the washer tank. Remove the air cleaner assembly. If equipped with automatic transmission remove the throttle cable bracket from the valve cover.

3. Remove the accelerator cable and the cruise control actuator bracket from the valve cover.

4. Tag and disconnect the engine ground strap, the oxygen sensor wire, the oil pressure switch wire, the alternator wires, the high tension wire from the distributor, the distributor electrical connector, the water temperature sender switch electrical connector, the ECT wires, the starter wires, the solenoid resistor wire connector and the knock sensor electical connector.

5. Disconnect the brake booster hose, the actuator vacuum hose, if equipped with cruise control. Disconnect the EGR vacuum hose. Disconnect the heater hoses.

6. Remove the glove box. Remove the computer. Disconnect the three electrical wires and pull out the EFI wire harness from the cowl panel.

7. Remove the radiator fan shroud and fan assembly. Remove the radiator. Remove the coolant reserve tank.

8. If equipped with air condition remove the air compressor assembly and position it to the side. If equipped with power steering remove the power steering pump and position it to the side.

9. Remove the engine mounting bolts. From inside the vehicle remove the shift lever, if equipped with manual transmission.

10. Raise and support the vehicle safely. Drain the engine oil.

11. Disconnect the exhaust pipe from the exhaust manifold. Remove the exhaust pipe clamp from the transmission housing.

12. If equipped with manual transmission remove the clutch master cylinder.

13. Remove the speedometer cable. If equipped with automatic transmission disconnect the shift linkage from the shift lever.

14. Disconnect the electrical wire from the back-up light switch. Remove the stiffener plate along with the ground strap.

15. Disconnect and plug the fuel line at the pump. Remove the power steering gear housing.

16. Remove the intermediate shaft from the driveshaft. Properly support

the engine and transmission. Remove the engine mounts. Remove the transmission mount and crossmember.

17. Position a piece of wood between the engine firewall and the rear of the cylinder head to prevent damage to the heater hose.

18. Make sure there are no remaining wires or hoses connected to the engine and then slowly and carefully remove the engine and transmission from the vehicle.

19. Installation is the reverse of the removal procedure.

1987–88 7M-GE and 7-MGTE

1. Disconnect the negative battery cable. Remove the hood. Remove the engine under cover.

2. Drain the cooling system. Remove the radiator. Drain the engine oil. On 7M-GE remove the air cleaner assembly. On 7M-GTE remove the No. 4 air cleaner pipe along with the No. 1 and 2 air cleaner hose.

3. Remove the No. 7 air cleaner hose with the air flow meter and air cleaner cap.

4. Remove the air condition belt. Remove the alternator drive belt, water pump pulley and fan assembly. Remove the power steering belt.

5. Disconnect the brake booster hose, the heater valve hose, the cruise control hose and the charcoal canister hose. Remove the heater hoses.

6. Disconnect the engine ground strap, the noise filter connector, the therft deterrent horn connector, the check connector, the solenoid resistor connector, if equipped, the ignition coil connector on the 7M-GT, the igniter connectors on the 7M-GTE, the main relay connector, the alternator electrical connectors, the oxygen sensor connector on the 7M-GE, the heater valve connector, the ECU connector and the ECT connector.

7. Disconnect the cruise control cable, if equipped. Disconnect the accelerator cable. Disconnect the throttle cable, if equipped with automatic transmission.

8. Remove the air condition compressor. It may be possible to position the unit to the side without completely removing it from the vehicle.

9. On the 7M-GTE engine remove the No.6 air cleaner hose and the upper radiator outlet hose.

10. Remove the power steering pump. It may be possible to position the unit to the side without completely removing it from the vehicle.

11. If equipped with manual transmission remove the shift lever. Disconnect the ground strap from the fuel hose clamp. On the 7M-GTE engine remove the engine mounting absorber.

12. Disconnect and plug the fuel lines.

13. Raise and support the vehicle safely. Remove the exhaust pipe. Remove the driveshaft.

14. Disconnect the speedometer cable. If equipped with automatic transmission remove the shift linkage. If equipped with manual transmission remove the clutch release cylinder.

15. Properly support the engine and transmission assembly. Remove the No. 1 front crossmember. Remove the engine retaining mounts.

16. Position a piece of wood between the engine firewall and the rear of the cylinder head to prevent damage to the heater hose.

17. Make sure there are no remaining wires or hoses connected to the engine and then slowly and carefully remove the engine and transmission from the vehicle.

18. Installation is the reverse of the removal procedure.

1987–88 3S-FE

CAMRY

1. Disconnect the negative battery cable. Remove the hood. Drain the engine coolant. Tag and disconnect all vacuum hoses, electrical wires and cables that are necessary to remove the engine.

2. Remove the radiator. If the vehicle is equipped with automatic transaxle, disconnect the throttle cable and bracket from the throttle body.

3. Disconnect the accelerator cable from the throttle body. Disconnect the cruise control actuator and bracket, if equipped.

4. Disconnect the ground wire from the alternator upper bracket. Remove the air cleaner assembly, air flow meter and air cleaner hose.

5. Remove the igniter. Remove the heater hoses. Disconnect and plug the fuel lines. Disconnect the speedometer cable.

6. If equipped with manual transaxle, remove the clutch release cylinder and tube bracket. Do not disconnect the tube from the bracket. Disconnect the transaxle control cable.

7. Remove the air condition compressor and position it to the side. Do not disconnect the lines. Remove the power steering pump and position it to the side. Do not disconnect the lines.

8. Raise and support the vehicle safely. Drain the engine oil. Remove the engine under covers.

9. Remove the suspension lower crossmember. Remove the halfshafts.

10. Disconnect the exhaust pipe from the catalytic converter. Disconnect the engine mounting center crossmember member.

11. Lower the vehicle. Disconnect the TCCS and the ECU electrical connectors.

12. Properly attach the lifting device to the engine. Raise the engine slightly and remove the engine retaining brackets and bolts.

13. Carefully remove the engine/transaxle assembly from the vehicle. Be carefull not to hit the power steering gear housing or the neutral safety switch.

14. Installation is the reverse of the removal procedure.

CELICA

1. Disconnect the battery cables. Remove the battery. Remove the hood. Drain the engine coolant. Tag and disconnect all vacuum hoses, electrical wires and cables that are necessary to remove the engine.

2. Disconnect the ignition coil connector and high tension wire from the coil. Remove the suspension upper brace.

3. Remove the radiator. Remove the reservoir tank. If the vehicle is equipped with automatic transaxle, disconnect the throttle cable and bracket from the throttle body.

4. Disconnect the accelerator cable from the throttle body. Remove the cruise control actuator and bracket, if equipped. Remove the oxygen sensor.

5. Remove the air cleaner assembly, air flow meter and air cleaner hose. Remove the air cleaner bracket.

6. Remove the igniter. Remove the heater hoses. Disconnect and plug the fuel lines. Disconnect the speedometer cable.

7. If equipped with manual transaxle, remove the clutch release cylinder and tube bracket. Do not disconnect the tube from the bracket. Disconnect the transaxle control cable.

8. Remove the air condition compressor and position it to the side. Do not disconnect the lines.

9. Raise and support the vehicle safely. Drain the engine oil. Drain the transaxle fluid. Remove the right under cover.

10. Remove the power steering pump and position it to the side. Do not disconnect the lines. Remove the suspension lower crossmember. Remove the halfshafts.

11. Disconnect the exhaust pipe from the catalytic converter. Remove the engine rear mounting bolt. Lower the vehicle. Disconnect the TCCS and the ECU electrical connectors. Remove the power steering pump reservoir mounting bolts.

12. Properly attach the lifting device to the engine. Raise the engine slightly and remove the engine retaining brackets and bolts.

13. Carefully remove the engine/transaxle assembly from the vehicle. Be carefull not to hit the power steering gear housing or the neutral safety switch.

14. Installation is the reverse of the removal procedure.

Cylinder Head

NOTE: Do not perform this operation on a warm engine. Remove the head bolts in sequence and in several steps. Loosen the head bolts evenly. Keep the pushrods in their original order. Do not attempt to slide the cylinder head off the block, as it is located with dowel pins. Lift the head straight up and off the block.

REMOVAL & INSTALLATION
4K-C

1. Disconnect the negative battery cable. Drain the cooling system.

2. Remove the air cleaner assembly from its bracket, complete with its attendant hoses.

3. Disconnect the hoses from the air injection system or the vacuum switching valve lines.

4. Detach the accelerator cable from its support on the cylinder head cover and also from the carburetor throttle arm.

5. Remove the choke cable and fuel lines from the carburetor. Remove the water hose bracket from the cylinder head cover.

6. Unfasten the water hose clamps and remove the hoses from the water pump and the water valve. Detach the heater temperature control cable from the water valve.

7. Disconnect the PCV line from the cylinder head cover. Unbolt and remove the valve cover.

8. Remove the valve rocker support securing bolts and nuts. Lift out the valve rocker assembly. Remove the pushrods from their bores.

9. Unfasten the hose clamps and remove the upper radiator hose from the water outlet. Remove the wires from the spark plugs.

10. Disconnect the wiring and the fluid line from the windshield washer assembly. Remove the assembly. Unfasten the exhaust pipe flange from the exhaust manifold.

11. Remove the head assembly retaining bolts. Remove the head from the engine. Place the cylinder head on wooden blocks to prevent damage to it.

12. Installation is the reverse of the removal procedure. Clean both the cylinder head and block gasket mounting surfaces. Always use a new

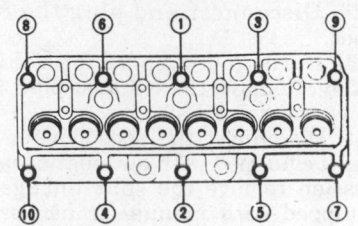

Cylinder head tightening sequence—K-series engines

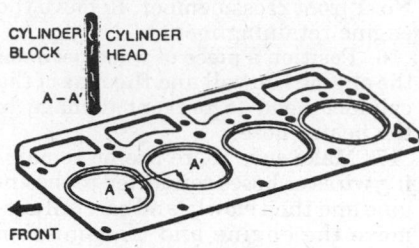

Gasket installation—4K-E

head gasket. Be sure that the top side of the gasket is facing upward.

13. When installing the head on the block, be sure to tighten the bolts in the proper sequence and in several stages, to the specified torque.

14. Adjust the valve clearance to specification with each piston at top dead center (TDC) of its compression stroke.

4K-E

1. Disconnect the negative battery cable. Drain the engine coolant Loosen the two hose clamps and remove the air cleaner hose.

2. Disconnect the throttle cable from the two places it attaches to the air intake chamber and the throttle body.

3. Tag and disconnect the four vacuum hoses connected to the air intake chamber. Do the same for the spark plug wires, the temperature detect switch wire and the water temperature sender gauge wire.

4. Tag and disconnect all remaining wires, hoses and leads attached to the cylinder head or which might interfere with its removal. Remove the spark plugs and tube. Remove the intake and exhaust manifold.

5. Remove the cylinder head cover. Remove the rocker shaft assembly. Remove the pushrods. Make sure that the pushrods remain in the correct order.

6. Loosen the cylinder head bolts in the proper sequence. Cylinder head warpage or cracking could result from removing the bolts in the wrong order.

7. Lift the cylinder head from the dowels on the block and place it on wooden blocks. If the head is difficult

to remove, carefully pry with a small prybar between the head and the block. Be very careful not to damage the cylinder head and/or block surfaces.

8. Installation is the reverse of the removal procedure. Clean the cylinder head and block gasket mounting surfaces. Be sure to properly install the head gasket. The cylinder head bolts should be torqued in the proper sequence and to the proper specification. Adjust the valves.

3T-C

1. Disconnect the negative battery cable. Drain the cooling system.

2. Remove the air cleaner assembly from its bracket, complete with its attendant hoses.

3. Disconnect the vacuum lines which run from the vacuum switching valve to the various emission control devices mounted on the cylinder head.

4. Disconnect the mixture control valve hose which runs to the intake manifold and remove the valve from its mounting bracket.

5. Unfasten the water hose clamps and remove the hoses from the water pump and the water valve. Detach the heater temperature control cable from the water valve.

6. Detach the water temperature sender wiring. Remove the choke stove pipe and its intake pipe. Remove the PCV hose from the intake manifold.

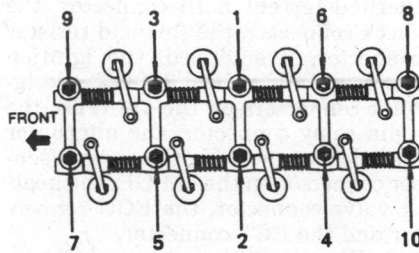

Cylinder head tightening sequence—T-series engines

7. Disconnect the fuel and vacuum lines from the carburetor. Remove the clutch hydraulic line bracket from the cylinder head.

8. Raise the vehicle and support it safely. Unfasten the exhaust pipe clamp. Remove the exhaust manifold from the cylinder head.

9. Remove the valve cover. Remove the valve train assembly. Remove the pushrods.

10. Remove the cylinder head bolts in the reverse of the tightening sequence. Remove the cylinder head along with the intake manifold from the engine.

11. Separate the intake manifold from the cylinder head.

12. Installation is the reverse of the removal procedure.

13. Clean both the cylinder head and block gasket mounting surfaces. Always use a new head gasket. Be sure that the top side of the gasket is facing upward.

14. Properly torque the cylinder head bolts to specification.

22R

1. Disconnect the negative battery cable. Remove the three exhaust pipe flange nuts and separate the pipe from the manifold.

3. Drain the engine oil. Drain the cooling system both radiator and block. Remove the air cleaner assembly.

4. Mark all vacuum hoses to aid installation, and disconnect them. Remove all linkages, fuel lines, etc., from the carburetor, cylinder head, and manifolds. Remove the wire supports.

5. Mark the spark plug leads and disconnect them from the plugs.

6. If equipped, disconnect and move the air injection system hoses. Mark the hose locations so that they may be properly reinstalled.

7. If equipped with air conditioning, remove the upper compressor mounting bracket.

8. If equipped with power steering, remove the power steering pump and position it out of the way without disconnecting the hydraulic lines.

9. Matchmark the distributor housing and block. Remove the distributor. Remove the valve cover.

10. Using a wrench on the crankshaft pulley, rotate the crankshaft until the No. 1 cylinder is at TDC on its compression stroke (both valves of the No. 1 cylinder closed).

11. Place matchmarks on both the camshaft sprocket and the timing chain to indicate the relationship between these items.

12. Remove the rubber camshaft seals. Use a 19mm wrench to remove the cam sprocket bolt. Slide the distributor drive gear off of the cam and wire the cam sprocket in place.

13. Remove the timing chain cover 14mm bolt at the front end of the head. This must be done before the head bolts are removed.

14. Remove the cylinder head bolts in the proper order. Improper removal could cause head damage.

15. Using pry bars applied evenly at the front and the rear of the valve rocker assembly, pry the assembly off of its mounting dowels.

16. Lift the head off of its dowels. Do not pry it off. Support the head on a workbench.

17. Installation is the reverse of the

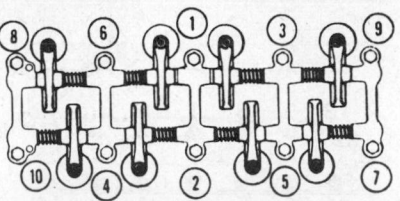

Cylinder head tightening sequence—R-series engines

removal procedure. Torque the cylinder head to specification and in proper sequence.

22R-E

1. Disconnect the negative battery cable. Drain the engine coolant. Drain the engine oil. Remove the air cleaner assembly.

2. Disconnect the oxygen sensor wire and then disconnect the exhaust pipe from the manifold. Disconnect the upper radiator hose from the heater hose.

3. Disconnect the actuator, accelerator and throttle cables from the bracket on the side of the cylinder head.

4. Tag and disconnect all hoses from the head. Remove the EGR vacuum modulator and its bracket.

5. Tag and disconnect the throttle position sensor wire, the cold start injector pipe and wire.

6. Remove the EGR valve. Disconnect the air intake chamber and its mounting, unscrew the mounting bolts and remove the chamber along with the throttle body.

7. Tag and disconnect all remaining wires. Remove the fuel line, the pulsation damper and the air valve.

8. Remove the spark plugs. Remove the power steering pump, if equipped and position it to one side with the hoses still attached.

9. Remove the cylinder head cover. After removing the cylinder head cover, cover the oil return hole in the head with a rag to prevent objects from falling in.

10. Matchmark the distributor housing and block. Remove the distributor. Remove the valve cover.

11. Using a wrench on the crankshaft pulley, rotate the crankshaft until the No. 1 cylinder is at TDC on its compression stroke (both valves of the No. 1 cylinder closed).

12. Place matchmarks on both the camshaft sprocket and the timing chain to indicate the relationship between these items.

13. Remove the rubber camshaft seals. Use a 19mm wrench to remove the cam sprocket bolt. Slide the distributor drive gear off of the cam and wire the cam sprocket in place.

14. Remove the timing chain cover

14mm bolt at the front end of the head. This must be done before the head bolts are removed.

15. Remove the cylinder head bolts in the proper order. Improper removal could cause head damage.

16. Using pry bars applied evenly at the front and the rear of the valve rocker assembly, pry the assembly off of its mounting dowels.

17. Lift the head off of its dowels. Do not pry it off. Support the head on a workbench.

18. Installation is the reverse of the removal procedure. Torque the cylinder head to specification and in proper sequence.

5M-E

1. Disconnect the negative battery cable. Drain the cooling system.

2. Remove the water hose bracket from the cylinder head cover.

3. Unfasten the hose clamps and remove the hoses from the water pump and the water valve.

4. Disconnect the heater temperature control cable from the water valve. Disconnect the PCV hoses from the cylinder head cover and the intake air connector.

5. Disconnect the air valve and the air control valve hoses from the intake air connector.

6. Disconnect the intake air connector from the air intake chamber and the air flow meter and remove it.

7. Tag and disconnect all hoses, lines and wires leading from the air intake chamber and the throttle body. Unscrew the seven mounting bolts and remove the air intake chamber and the throttle body as one unit.

8. Tag and disconnect the wiring connectors at the fuel injectors. Unscrew the four mounting bolts and remove the fuel delivery pipe with the injectors. When removing the injectors and the delivery pipe, be sure to have a container underneath, to catch the large quantity of fuel.

9. Remove the intake manifold retaining bolts. Remove the intake manifold.

10. Remove the spark plug wires. Remove the spark plugs. Remove the distributor assembly. Remove the exhaust manifold and the oil pressure light sender.

11. Remove the valve cover retaining bolts. Remove the valve cover assembly. Place a cloth over the timing gear to prevent anything from falling into the timing gear cover.

12. Turn the engine so that No. 1 piston is at TDC on its compression stroke (both valves closed). Remove the timing chain tensioner. The matchmarks on the timing chain and gear should now be aligned.

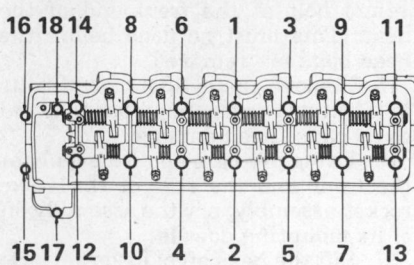

Cylinder head tightening sequence—4M–E engines

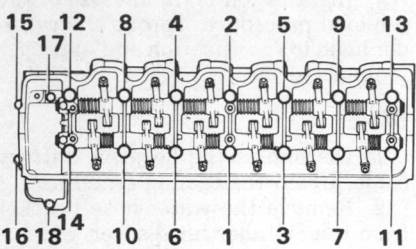

Cylinder head tightening sequence—5M–E engines

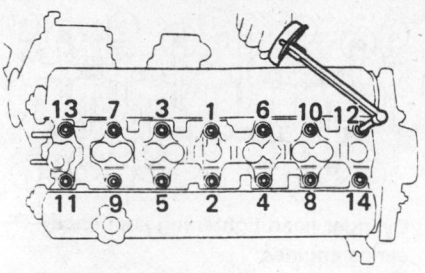

Cylinder head tightening sequence—5M–GE engines

13. Straighten out the lockplate and unfasten the timing gear retaining bolt (left hand thread). Withdraw the timing gear from the camshaft.

14. Loosen and remove the rocker arm shaft mounting bolts. Loosen the bolt in two or three stages. Remove the rocker arm shaft assembly.

15. Remove the camshaft bearing caps, be sure to keep them in order. Lift the camshaft off the head.

16. In two or three stages, loosen then remove the cylinder head bolts in the reverse order of the installation torque sequence. Lift the cylinder head off the engine block.

17. Installation is the reverse of the removal procedure.

18. Prior to installation, thoroughly clean the cylinder block and head mating surfaces.

19. Be sure to torque the cylinder head to specification and in the proper sequence.

20. Adjust the valves to specification.

5M-GE

1. Disconnect the battery cables. Drain the cooling system.

2. Disconnect the exhaust pipe from the exhaust manifold.

3. Remove the throttle cable bracket from the cylinder head if equipped with automatic transmission, and remove the accelerator and actuator cable bracket.

4. Tag and disconnect the ground cable, oxygen sensor wire, high tension coil wire, distributor connector, solenoid resistor wire connector and thermo- switch wire, if equipped with automatic transmission.

5. Tag and disconnect the brake booster vacuum hose, EGR valve vacuum hose, fuel hose from the intake manifold and actuator vacuum hose, if equipped with cruise control.

6. Disconnect the radiator upper hose from the thermostat housing, and disconnect the two heater hoses.

7. Disconnect the No. 1 air hose from the air intake connector. Remove the two clamp bolts, loosen the throttle body hose clamp and remove the air intake connector and the connector pipe.

8. Tag and disconnect all emission control hoses from the throttle body and air intake chamber, the two PCV hoses from the cam cover and the fuel hose from the fuel support.

9. Remove the air intake chamber stay and the vacuum pipe and ground cable. Remove the bolt that attaches the spark plug wire clip, leaving the wires attached to the clip. Remove the distributor from the cylinder head with the cap and wires attached, by removing the distributor holding bolt.

10. Tag and disconnect the cold start injector wire and disconnect the cold start injector fuel hose from the delivery pipe.

11. Loosen the nut of the EGR pipe, remove the five bolts and two nuts and remove the air intake chamber and gasket.

12. Remove the glove box and remove the ECU module. Disconnect the three connectors and pull the EFI (fuel injection) wire harness out through the engine side of the firewall.

13. Remove the pulsation damper and the No. 1 fuel pipe. Remove the water outlet housing by first loosening the clamp and disconnecting the water by pass hose.

14. Remove the intake manifold.

15. Disconnect the power steering pump drive belt and remove the power steering pump without disconnecting the fluid hoses. Position the pump out of the way.

16. Disconnect the oxygen sensor connector and remove the exhaust manifold.

17. Remove the timing belt and camshaft timing gears. Remove the timing belt cover stay, and remove the oil pressure regulator and gasket. Remove the No. 2 timing belt cover and gasket.

18. Tag and disconnect any other wires, linkage and/or hoses still attached to the cylinder head.

19. Carefully remove the fourteen head bolts gradually in two or three passes and in numerical order. Head warpage or cracking could result from removing the head bolts in incorrect order.

20. Carefully lift the cylinder head from the dowels on the cylinder block, resting the mating surface on wooden blocks on the work bench. If the head is difficult to remove, tap around the mating surface gently with a rubber hammer. Keep in mind the head is aluminum and is easily damaged.

21. Installation is the reverse of the removal procedure.

22. Prior to installation, thoroughly clean the cylinder block and head mating surfaces.

23. Be sure to torque the cylinder head to specification and in the proper sequence.

24. Adjust the valves to specification, as required.

1A-C, 3A, 3A-C, 4A-C and 4A-LC

1. Disconnect the negative battery cable. Remove the exhaust pipe from the manifold. Drain the cooling system.

2. Remove the air cleaner and all necessary hoses. Mark all the necessary vacuum lines for easy installation and then remove them.

3. Remove all linkage from the carburetor. Disconnect and plug the fuel lines at the cylinder head and manifold.

4. Remove the fuel pump. Remove the carburetor. Remove the manifold.

5. Remove the valve cover. Note the position of the spark plug wires and remove them. Remove the spark plugs.

6. Set the engine on No. 1 cylinder to top dead center. This is accomplished by removing the No. 1 spark plug, placing your finger over the hole and then turning the crankshaft pulley until you feel pressure exerted against your finger.

7. Remove the crankshaft pulley with the proper tool. Remove the water pump pulley. Remove the top and bottom timing chain cover.

8. Matchmark the camshaft pulley and timing belt for reassembly. Loosen the belt tensioner. Remove the water pump.

9. Remove the timing belt. Do not bend, twist, or turn the belt inside out.

10. Remove the rocker arm bolts and

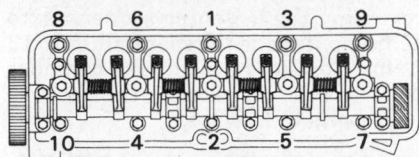

Cylinder head tightening sequence—A–series engines

remove the rocker arms. Remove the camshaft pulley by holding the camshaft with a suitable tool and removing the belt in the pulley end of the shaft. Do not hold the cam on the lobes, as damage will result.

11. Remove the camshaft seal. Remove the camshaft bearing caps and set them down in the order they appear on the engine. Remove the camshaft.

12. Loosen the head bolts in the reverse order of the torque sequence. Lift the head directly up. Do not attempt to slide it off.

13. Installation is the reverse of the removal procedure

14. When replacing the head always use a new gasket. Also replace the camshaft seal, making sure to grease the lip before installation.

15. The following torques are needed for installation: cam bearing caps 8–10 ft. lbs., cam sprocket 29–39 ft. lbs., crankshaft pulley 55–61 ft. lbs., manifold bolts 15–21 ft. lbs., rocker arm bolts 17–19 ft. lbs., timing gear idler bolt 22–32 ft. lbs., belt tension 0.24–0.28 in. Adjust the valves to the proper clearances.

2S-E

1. Disconnect the negative battery cable. Drain the coolant. Disconnect the throttle cable.

2. Remove the air cleaner assembly. Disconnect and tag all wires connected to or running across the head. Disconnect and tag all vacuum hoses connected to or running across the head.

3. Remove the vacuum pipe from the valve cover cover. Disconnect and tag any remaining cables. Remove the alternator. Remove the distributor.

4. Remove the upper radiator hose and bypass hose. Unbolt and remove the water outlet housing. Disconnect the heater hoses.

5. Disconnect the two air hoses from the fuel injection air valve. Unbolt and remove the rear end housing. Remove the heater pipe.

6. Disconnect the fuel line at the filter and the fuel return line at the return pipe.

7. Raise and support the vehicle safely. Drain the oil.

8. Disconnect the exhaust pipe at

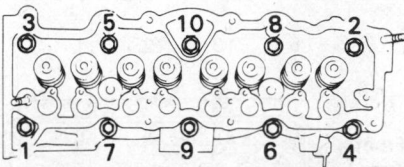

2SE cam housing removal sequence

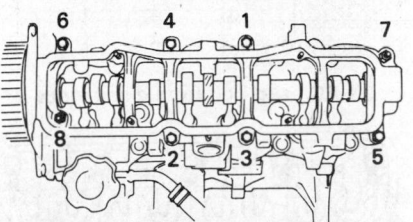

2SE head bolt loosening sequence

2SE cam housing torque sequence

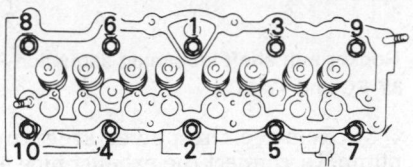

2SE head bolt torque sequence

the manifold. Disconnect the power steering pump hoses.

9. Remove the intake manifold stay. Lower the vehicle.

10. Remove the timing belt. Remove the No. 1 idler pulley and tension spring.

11. Remove the throttle body. Remove the valve cover.

12. Unbolt and remove the camshaft housing. Loosen the bolts gradually in the proper order. Remove the rocker arms and the lash adjusters.

13. Loosen and remove the head bolts., in three passes and in the reverse of the installation torque sequence. Remove the cylinder head from the vehicle. Place it on wood blocks in a clean work area.

14. Installation is the reverse of the removal procedure.

15. Always use a new head gasket. Tighten the head bolts, in three passes, according to specification.

16. When installing the camshaft housing, note that RTV silicone gasket compound is used in place of a gasket. Run a 2mm bead of compound around the sealing surface of the housing. Torque the housing bolts, in three passes, according to specification, to 11 ft. lbs.

1C-L, 1C-TL, 1C-LC and 2C-T

1. Disconnect the negative battery cable. Drain the coolant.

2. If equipped, remove the cruise control actuator.

3. Disconnect and tag all wires connected to or running across the head. Disconnect and tag all vacuum hoses connected to or running across the head.

4. Disconnect and tag all cables and linkage rods connected to or running across the head.

5. Raise and support the vehicle safely. Drain the oil. Disconnect the exhaust pipe from the turbocharger or manifold.

6. Lower the vehicle. Remove the turbocharger assembly. Remove the water outlet and pipe.

7. Remove the heater hoses. Remove the heater pipe. Remove the bypass hoses. Remove the glow plugs. Remove the injector nozzles.

8. Remove the level gauge guide support mounting bolt. Remove the number 2 timing cover.

9. Turn the engine so that No. 1 cylinder is at TDC of the firing stroke. Make sure that the line mark on the camshaft pulley is aligned with the top surface of the head.

10. Remove the timing belt and camshaft pulley. Remove the belt tension spring. Remove the No. 1 idler pulley. Remove the camshaft No. 3 pulley.

11. Remove the valve cover. Remove the front head lifting eye.

12. Loosen the head bolts gradually, in three passes, in the proper sequence. Remove the cylinder head. If the head is difficult to break loose, there is a recess at the front end which you may pry with a suitable tool.

13. Installation is the reverse of the removal procedure.

14. Always use a new head gasket. Make sure that all sealing surfaces are absolutely clean. Lightly coat all bolt threads with clean engine oil.

15. On the 1C-T and 1C-LT, tighten the head bolts, in three stages, in the proper sequence to 62 ft. lbs.

16. On the 2C-T, tighten the head bolts, in three stages, in the proper sequence, to 33 ft. lbs. Mark the front side of the top of each head bolt with a dab of paint. Tighten the bolts, in the properorder, an additional 90°. When all the bolts are through, tighten them once more, in the proper order, another 90°. The paint mark should now be facing rearward, directly opposite of where it was originally.

17. When installing the valve cover, note that RTV silicone gasket compound is used in place of a gasket.

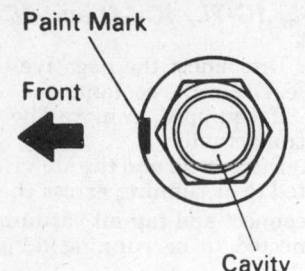

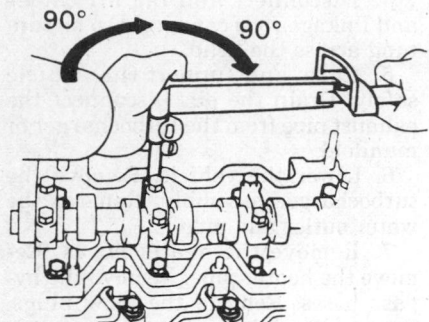

Mark each cylinder head bolt with a dab of paint prior to angle-torqueing—2C-T

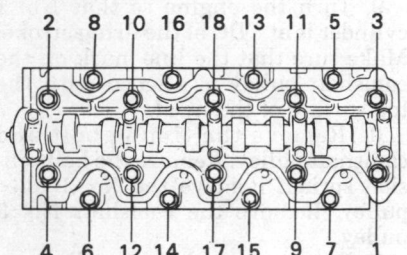

Diesel engine head bolt removal sequence

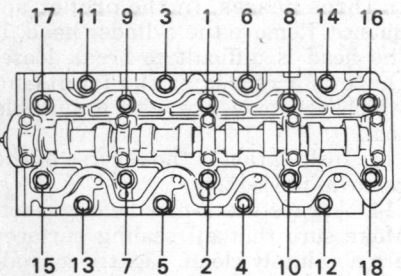

Diesel engine head bolt torque sequence

Torque the valve cover bolts to 65 inch lbs.

18. Torque the camshaft pulley bolt to 72 ft. lbs. (65 ft. lbs. on 2C-T). Make sure that the timing marks align by rotating the engine 2 full revolutions and rechecking the alignment. Torque the No. 1 idler pulley bolt to 27 ft. lbs.

3Y-EC and 4Y-EC

1. Disconnect the negative battery cable. Remove the right front seat.
2. Remove the engine cover. Drain the coolant. Drain the oil.

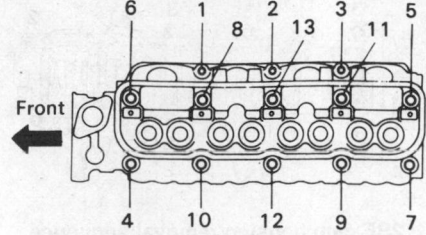

3Y-EC head bolt loosening sequence

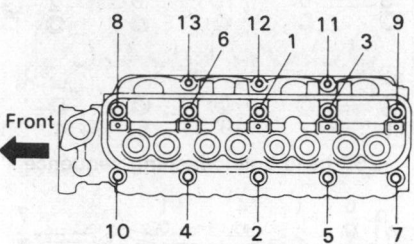

3Y-EC head bolt torque sequence

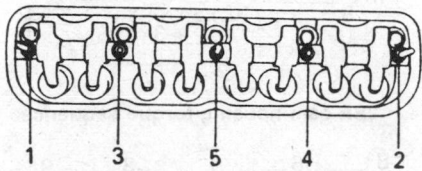

Rocker arm shaft loosening sequence—
3Y-EC and 4Y-EC

3. Remove the power steering pump. Disconnect the exhaust pipe at the manifold.
4. Disconnect and tag all wires, vacuum hoses and cables attached to or running across the head.
5. Remove the throttle body. Remove the EGR valve. Disconnect the coolant bypass hoses.
6. Remove the air intake chamber. Remove the fuel lines from the injectors. Disconnect the fuel line and fuel return line. Remove the spark plugs and tubes.
7. Remove the valve cover. Remove the rocker arm shaft assembly, loosening the bolts in the proper order. Remove the pushrods and keep them in order for installation.
8. Loosen the head bolts, in three passes, in the proper sequence. Remove the cylinder head from the engine. If the head is difficult to break loose, there is a recess at the front end of the head which you may pry with a suitable tool.
9. Installation is the reverse of the removal procedure.
10. Always use a new head gasket. Make sure that all sealing surfaces are clean.
11. Tighten the head bolts gradually, in three passes, in the proper sequence, to 65 ft. lbs. for 14mm bolts and 14 ft. lbs. for 12mm bolts.
12. Tighten the rocker shaft bolts,

reversing the loosening sequences, to 17 ft. lbs. Torque the spark plugs to 13 ft. lbs. Torque the air intake chamber bolts to 9 ft. lbs. Torque the throttle body bolts to 9 ft. lbs.

4A-GE, 4A-GEC and 4A-GELC

1. Disconnect the negative battery cable. Remove the engine undercover. Drain the coolant. Drain the engine oil.
2. Loosen the clamp and then disconnect the No. 1 air cleaner hose from the throttle body. Disconnect the actuator and accelerator cables from the bracket on the throttle body.
3. If equipped with power steering, Remove the power steering pump and its bracket. Position the pump to one side.
4. Loosen the water pump pulley set nuts. Remove the drive belt adjusting bolt and then remove the belt. Remove the set nuts and then remove the fluid coupling along with the fan and the water pump pulley.
5. Disconnect the upper radiator hose at the water outlet on the cylinder head. Disconnect the two heater hoses at the water bypass pipe and the cylinder head rear plate.
6. Remove the distributor. Remove the cold start injector pipe and the PCV hose from the cylinder head.
7. Remove the pulsation damper from the delivery pipe. Disconnect the fuel return hose from the pressure regulator.
8. Tag and disconnect all vacuum hoses which may interfere with cylinder head removal. Remove the wiring harness and the vacuum pipe from the No. 3 timing cover. Tag and disconnect all wires which might interfere with cylinder head removal Position the wiring harness to one side.
9. Disconnect the exhaust bracket from the exhaust pipe. Disconnect the exhaust manifold from the exhaust pipe.
10. Remove the vacuum tank and the VCV valve. Remove the exhaust manifold.
11. Remove the two mounting bolts and remove the water outlet housing from the cylinder head with the No. 1 bypass pipe and gasket. Pull the No. 1 bypass pipe out of the housing.
12. Remove the fuel delivery pipe along with the fuel injectors. When removing the delivery pipe, be very careful not to drop or bump the fuel injector nozzles. Do not remove the injector cover.
13. Unscrew the two mounting bolts and remove the intake manifold stay. Remove the intake manifold along with the air control valve.
14. Remove the cylinder head covers and their gaskets. Remove the spark

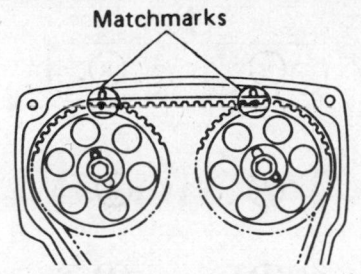

Place matchmarks on the camshaft timing pulleys and belt—4A-GE

plugs. Check the valve clearance. Remove the No. 1 and No. 2 timing belt covers and their gaskets.

15. Rotate the crankshaft pulley until its groove is in alignment with the "0" mark on the No. 1 timing belt cover. Check that the valve lifters on the No. 1 cylinder are loose. If not, rotate the crankshaft one complete revolution (360°).

16. Place matchmarks on the timing belt and two timing pulleys. Loosen the idler pulley bolts and move the pulley to the left as far as it will go and then retighten the bolt.

17. Remove the timing belt from the camshaft pulleys. When removing the timing belt, support the belt so that the meshing of the crankshaft timing pulley and the timing belt does not shift. Never drop anything inside the timing case cover. Be sure that the timing belt does not come in contact with dust or oil.

18. Lock the camshafts and remove the timing pulleys. Remove the No. 4 timing belt cover.

19. Using an indicator, measure the end play of each camshaft. If not within specification, replace the thrust bearing.

20. Loosen each camshaft bearing cap bolt a little at a time and in the sequence shown. Remove the bearing caps, camshaft and oil seal.

21. Using SST No. 09205-16010, loosen the cylinder head bolts gradually in three stages, and in the proper order.

22. Remove the cylinder head from the vehicle.

23. To install position the cylinder head on the block with a new gasket. Lightly coat the cylinder head bolts with engine oil and then install the short head bolts on the intake side and the long ones on the exhaust side. Tighten the bolts in three stages, in the proper sequence. On the final pass, torque the bolt to 43 ft. lbs.

24. Position the camshafts into the cylinder head. Position the bearing caps over each journal with the arrows pointing forward.

25. Tighten each bearing cap a little at a time and in the reverse of the re-

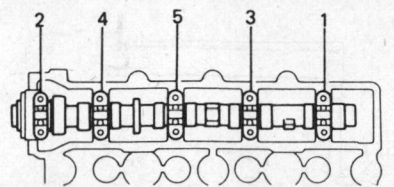

Loosen the camshaft bearing caps in this order—4A-GE

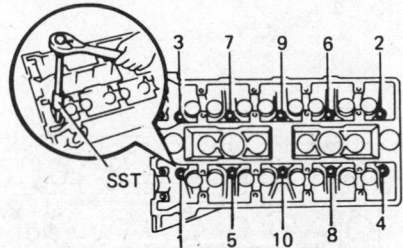

Cylinder head bolt removal sequence—4A-GE

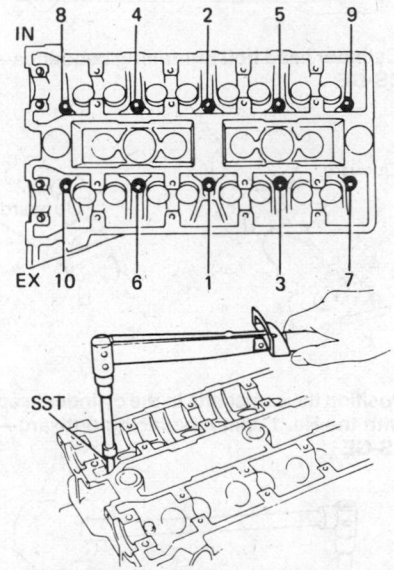

Cylinder head bolt tightening sequence—4A-GE

moval sequence. Tighten to 9 ft. lbs. Recheck the camshaft end play.

26. Using SST No. 09223-50010, drive the camshaft oil seals onto the end of the camshafts. Be careful not to install the oil seals crooked. Install the No. 4 timing belt cover.

27. Install the camshaft timing pulleys making sure that the camshaft knock pins and the matchmarks are in alignment. Lock each camshaft and tighten the pulley bolts to 34 ft. lbs.

28. Align the matchmarks made during removal and then install the timing belt on the camshaft pulley. Loosen the idler pulley set bolt. Make sure the timing belt meshing at the crankshaft pulley does not shift.

29. Rotate the crankshaft clockwise two revolutions from TDC to TDC. Make sure that each pulley aligns

Position the camshafts into the cylinder head as shown—4A-GE

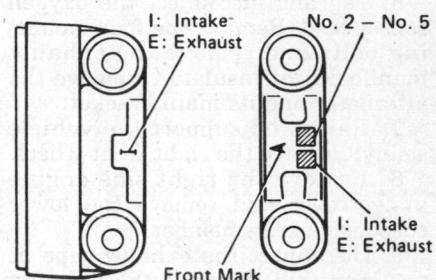

Camshaft bearing cap positioning on the 4A-GE (the arrows must always point forward)

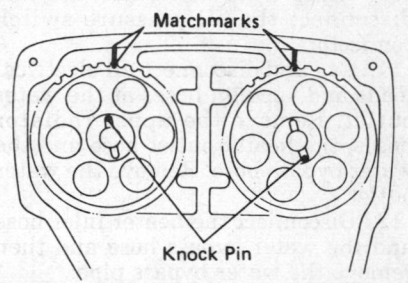

Align the camshaft knockpin with the camshaft timing pulley—4A-GE

with the marks made previously. If the marks are not in alignment, the valve timing is wrong. Shift the timing belt meshing slightly and then repeat Steps 27-29.

30. Tighten the set bolt on the timing belt idler pulley to 27 ft. lbs. Measure the timing belt deflection at the top span between the two camshaft pulleys. It should deflect no more than 0.16 in. at 4.4 lbs. of pressure. If deflection is greater, readjust by using the idler pulley.

31. Installation of the remaining components is in the reverse order of removal.

3S-GE

1. Disconnect the negative battery cable. Drain the coolant.

2. Tag and disconnect the ignition coil connector and the spark plug wire at the ignition coil. Remove the four nuts and two bolts and lift out the upper suspension brace.

3. On vehicles equipped with automatic transmission, disconnect the throttle cable with its bracket from

the throttle body. Disconnect the accelerator cable from the throttle body. Remove the radiator overflow tank.

4. If equipped, remove the cruise control actuator and its bracket.

5. Disconnect the air flow meter connector. Remove the air cleaner cap clips. Loosen the hose clamp and remove the air cleaner hose and the air flow meter along with the air cleaner top. Lift out the filter element and then remove the air cleaner case.

6. Tag and disconnect the oxygen sensor lead. Remove the four mounting bolts and remove the exhaust manifold heat insulator. Remove the alternator and its main bracket.

7. Raise and support the vehicle safely. Remove the right front wheel.

8. Remove the right side engine under cover and remove the lower suspension crossmember.

9. Disconnect the exhaust pipe at the manifold. Remove the exhaust manifold stay and the EGR pipe. Unbolt the manifold and remove it along with the lower heat insulator.

10. Remove the distributor. Tag and disconnect the oil pressure switch connector.

11. Tag and disconnect all electrical leads and vacuum hoses at the water outlet. Remove the upper radiator hoses, the heater outlet hose and the water bypass hose. Remove the water outlet.

12. Disconnect the heater inlet hose and the water bypass hose and then remove the water bypass pipe.

13. Disconnect the throttle position sensor lead, the ventilation hose, the air valve hose and any emission control vacuum hoses at the throttle body. Remove the four bolts and lift out the throttle body.

14. Remove the forward engine hanger and the No. 2 intake manifold stay. Remove the EGR vacuum modulator.

15. Tag and disconnect any remaining vacuum hoses which may interfere with cylinder head removal. Tag and disconnect the fuel injector electrical leads at the injector.

16. Disconnect the fuel inlet hose at the fuel filter. Disconnect the fuel return hose at the return pipe.

17. Remove the No. 1 and No. 3 intake manifold stays. Tag and disconnect the two VSV connectors. Disconnect the two power steering vacuum hoses. Remove the intake manifold and the air control valve.

18. Remove the fuel delivery pipe with the injectors attached. Pull the four injector insulators out of the injector holes in the cylinder head.

19. Remove the cylinder head cover. Remove the spark plugs. Remove the No. 1 engine hanger.

20. Remove the power steering res-

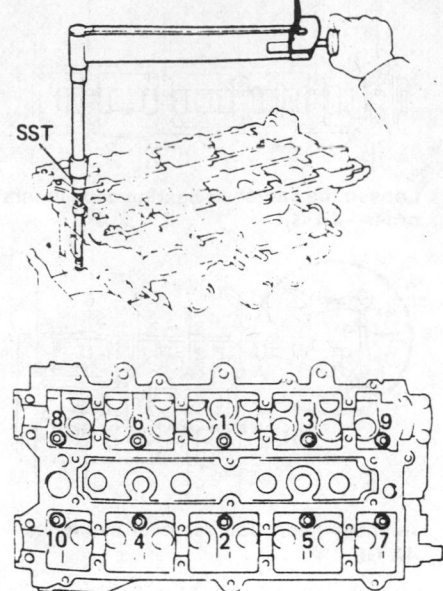

Cylinder head bolt tightening sequence—3S-GE

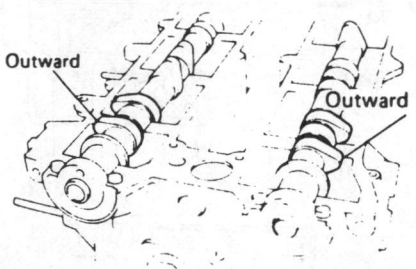

Position the camshafts in the cylinder head with the No. 1 cam lobe facing outward—3S-GE

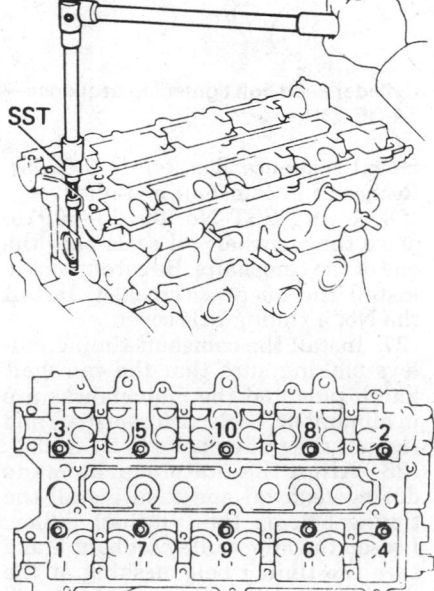

Cylinder head bolt loosening sequence—3S-GE

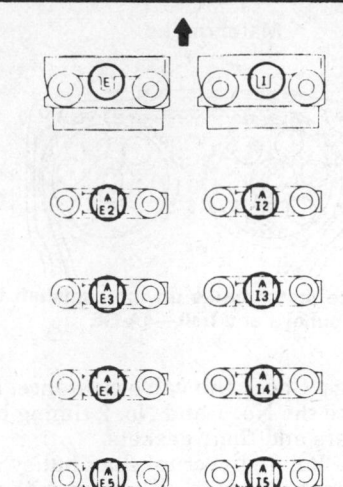

Camshaft bearing cap positioning on the 3S-GE. The arrows should point forward and they must be in numerical order

ervoir and position it out of the way with the hydraulic lines still attached.

21. Remove the camshaft timing pulleys. Remove the No. 1 idler pulley and tension spring.

22. Remove the bolt holding the No. 2 and No. 3 timing covers. Remove the four mounting bolts and remove the No. 3 timing cover.

23. Loosen and remove the camshaft bearing caps, in several stages, and in the proper sequence. Lift out the camshafts and the oil seal. When removing the camshaft bearing caps, keep them in the proper order.

24. Loosen and remove the cylinder head bolts, in several stages, and in the proper sequence. Remove the cylinder head.

25. To install position the cylinder head onto the cylinder block with a new gasket. Lightly coat the cylinder head bolts with engine oil, install them into the head and tighten them in several passes, in the proper sequence, to 40 ft. lbs.

26. Position the camshafts into the cylinder head so that the No. 1 cam lobes are facing outward.

27. Apply silicone sealant to the outer edge of the mating surface on the No. 1 bearing cap only. Position the bearing caps over each journal with the arrows pointing forward and in numerical order from the front to the rear.

28. Lightly coat the cap bolt threads with engine oil. Tighten them in several stages, and in the proper sequence, to 14 ft. lbs.

29. Check the camshaft thrust clearance. Coat the inside of a new oil seal with grease and carefully tap it onto the camshaft with a drift (SST No. 09223–50010). Install the No. 3 timing belt cover.

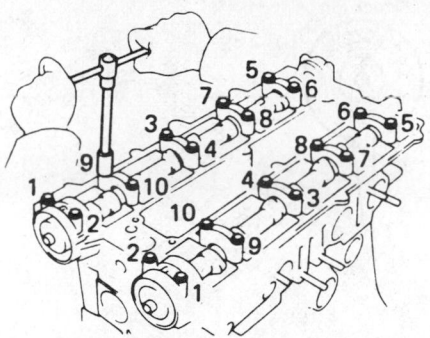

Remove the camshaft bearing caps in the order shown on the 3S-GE

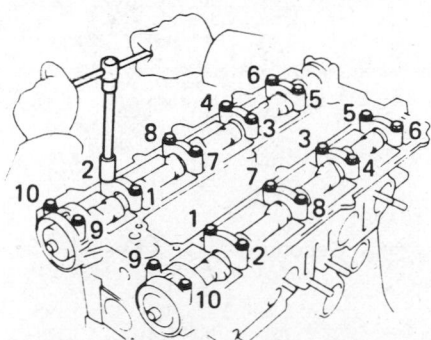

Tighten the camshaft bearing caps in this order on the 3S-GE

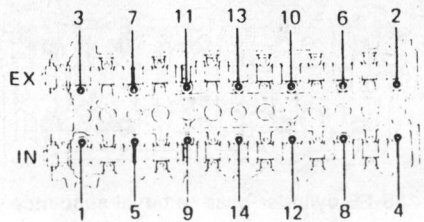

7M-GE and 7M-GTE cylinder head removal sequence

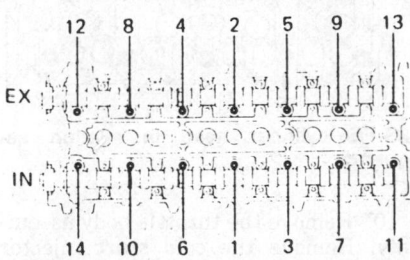

7M-GE and 7M-GTE cylinder head installation sequence

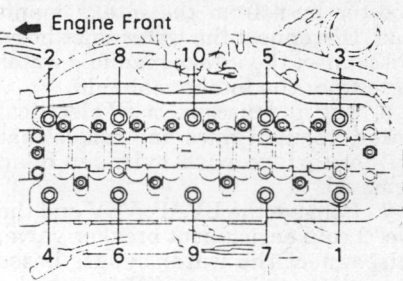

3E cylinder head removal sequence

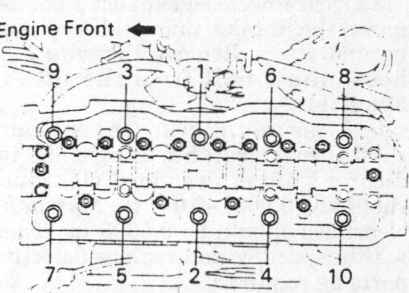

3E cylinder head installation sequence

30. Connect the idler pulley tension spring to the pulley and the pin on the cylinder head. Install the idler pulley onto the pivot pin, force it to the left as far as it will go and tighten it. Make sure that the tension spring is not out of groove in the pin. Install the camshaft timing pulleys and the timing belt.

31. Installation of the remaining components is in the reverse order of removal. Tighten the lower suspension crossmember end bolts to 154 ft. lbs. and the center bolt to 29 ft. lbs. Tighten the upper suspension brace bolts to 15 ft. lbs. and the nuts to 47 ft. lbs. Refill the engine with coolant. Check the idle speed and ignition timing.

7M-GE and 7M-GTE

1. Disconnect the negative battery cable. Drain the coolant.

2. Disconnect the exhaust pipe from the exhaust manifold. Disconnect the cruise control cable, if equipped.

3. Disconnect the accelerator cable. Disconnect the throttle cable, if equipped with automatic transmission. Disconnect the engine ground strap.

4. On the 7M-GE remove the No. 1 air cleaner hose along with the intake air pipe assembly. On the 7M-GTE remove the No. 4 air cleaner pipe along with the No. 1 and No. 2 air cleaner hose.

5. Disconnect the cruise control vacuum hose, the charcoal canister hose and the brake booster hose.

6. Remove the radiator inlet hose. Disconnect the heater inlet hose. Remove the alternator assembly.

7. On the 7M-GTE remove the power steering reservoir tank. On the 7M-GTE remove the cam position sensor.

8. Remove the air intake chamber with the connector. Remove the PCV pipe. Disconnect and tag all required hoses and vacuum connections that are required to remove the cylinder head from the vehicle.

9. Remove the EGR pipe mounting bolts. Remove the manifold retaining bolts. On the 7M-GE remove the throttle body bracket. On the 7M-GTE remove the ISC pipe.

10. Remove the air intake connector mounting bolt. On the 7M-GE remove the cold start injector tube. On the 7M-GTE disconnect the cold start injector. Disconnect the EGR vacuum modulator from the bracket.

11. Disconnect the engine wire from the clamps of the intake chamber. Remove the nuts and bolts, vacuum pipes and intake chamber with the connector and gasket.

12. On the 7M-GTE remove the ignition coil and bracket. Disconnect all electrical connections that are required to remove the cylinder head from the engine.

13. Remove the pulsation damper, the VSV and the No. 1 fuel pipe. Remove the No. 3 fuel pipe. On the 7M-GTE remove the auxiliary air pipe.

14. On the 7M-GE remove the high tension wires and the distributor. Remove the oil dipstick. On the 7M-GTE remove the turbocharger assembly.

15. Remove the exhaust manifold. Remove the water outlet housing. Remove the valve covers. Remove the spark plugs.

16. Remove the timing belt and the camshaft timing pulleys. Remove the cylinder head retaining bolts gradually and in the proper sequence. Carefully remove the cylinder head from the engine.

17. Installation is the reverse of the removal procedure.

18. Be sure to use a new gasket and install if in the proper direction. Torque the cylinder head bolts to specification and in the proper sequence.

3E

1. Disconnect the negative battery cable. Drain the coolant. remove the engine under cover.

2. If equipped with power steering, remove the power steering pump and bracket. If equipped with air condition and without powersteering remove the idler pulley bracket.

3. Disconnect the radiator hoses. Disconnect the accelerator cable. If equipped with automatic transmission, disconnect the throttle cable from the bracket.

4. Remove the timing belt and the camshaft timing pulley. Disconnect the heater inlet hose. Disconnect and plug the fuel lines.

5. Remove the air suction hose and valve assembly. Disconnect the brake

booster hose from the intake manifold. Disconnect the water inlet hose. Disconnect the intake manifold water hose from the intake manifold.

6. Tag and disconnect all electrical wires, vacuum lines and cables that will interfere with cylinder head removal.

7. Remove the EVAP, VSV and the No. 2 cold enrichment breaker valve. Disconnect the water bypass hoses from the carburetor. Remove the valve cover.

8. Disconnect the exhaust pipe. Remove the intake manifold stay and ground strap. Remove the wire harness clamp bolt from the intake manifold.

9. Measure the cylinder head camshaft thrust clearance using a dial indicator gauge. Standard clearance should be 0.0031–0.071 in. Maximum clearance should be 0.0098 in. If not within specification replace defective parts as required.

10. Loosen then remove the cylinder head bolts in three phases and in the proper sequence. Remove the cylinder head from the engine.

11. Installation is the reverse of the removal procedure.

12. Be sure to use a new head gasket. Torque the cylinder head to specification and in three phases.

3S-FE

1. Disconnect the negative battery cable. Drain the coolant.

2. If equipped with automatic transmission, disconnect the throttle cable and bracket from the throttle body.

3. Disconnect the accelerator cable and bracket from the throttle body and intake chamber.

4. If equipped with cruise control, remove the actuator and bracket. Remove the air cleaner hose. Remove the alternator.

5. Remove the oil pressure gauge, engine hangers and alternator upper bracket.

6. Raise and support the vehicle safely. Remove the right tire and wheel assembly.

7. Remove the right under cover. Remove the suspension lower crossmember. Disconnect the exhaust pipe from the catalytic converter. Separate the exhaust pipe from the catalytic converter.

8. Disconnect the water temperature sender gauge connector, water temperature sensor connector, cold start injector time switch connector, upper radiator hose, water hoses, and the emission control vacuum hoses.

9. Remove the water outlet and gaskets. Remove the distributor. Remove the water bypass pipe. Remove the EGR valve tond modulator.

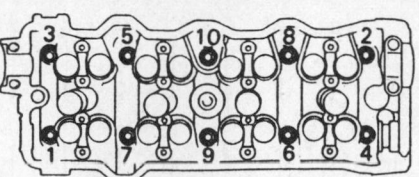

3S-FE cylinder head removal sequence

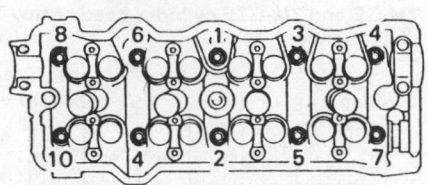

3S-FE cylinder head installation sequence

10. Remove the throttle body assembly. Remove the cold start injector pipe. Remove the air intake chamber air hose, the throttle body air hose, and the power steering pump hoses, if equipped. Remove the air tube.

11. Remove the intake manifold retaining bolts. Remove the intake manifold. Remove the fuel delivery pipe and the injectors. Remove the spark plugs.

12. Remove the camshaft timing pulley. Remove the No. 1 idler pulley and tension spring. Remove the No. 3 timing belt cover. Properly support the timing belt so that meshing of the crankshaft timing pulley does not occur and the timing belt does not shift.

13. Remove the valve cover. Arragne the grommets in order so that they can be reinstalled in the correct order.

14. To remove the exhaust camshaft, set the knock pin of the exhaust camshaft at 10–45° BTDC of camshaft angle. This angle will help to lift the exhaust camshaft level and evenly by pushing No. 2 and No. 4 cylinder camshaft lobes of the exhaust camshaft toward their valve lifters.

15. Secure the exhaust camshaft sub gear to the main gear using a service bolt. When removing the exhaust camshaft be sure that the torsional spring force of the sub gear has been eliminated.

16. Remove the No. 1 and No. 2 rear bearing cap bolts and remove the cap. Uniformly loosen and remove bearing cap bolts No. 3 to No. 8 in several phases and in the proper sequence. Do not remove bearing cap bolts No. 9 and 10 at this time. Remove No. 1, 2, and 4 bearing caps.

17. Alternately loosen and remove bearing cap bolts No. 9 and 10. As these bolts are loosened check to see that the camshaft is being lifted out straight and level.

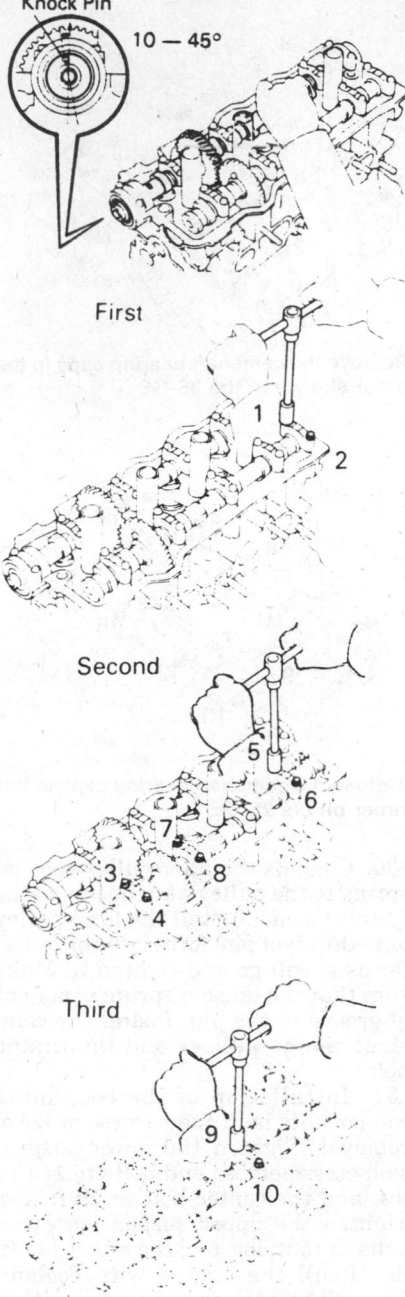

3S-FE exhaust camshaft removal procedure

NOTE: If the camshaft is not lifting out straight and level retighten No. 9 and 10 bearing cap bolts. Reverse Steps 16 through 14, than start over from Step 14. Do not attempt to pry the camshaft from its mounting.

18. Remove the exhaust camshaft from the engine.

19. To remove the intake camshaft, set the knock pin of the intake camshaft at 80–115° BTDC of camshaft angle. This angle will help to lift the intake camshaft level and evenly by pushing No. 1 and No. 3 cylinder cam-

Rocker Arm Shafts

shaft lobes of the intake camshaft toward their valve lifters.

20. Remove the No. 1 and No. 2 rear bearing cap bolts and remove the front bearing cap and oil seal. If the cap will not come apart easily, leave it in place without the bolts.

21. Uniformly loosen and remove bearing cap bolts No. 3 to No. 8 in several phases and in the proper sequence. Do not remove bearing cap bolts No. 9 and 10 at this time. Remove No. 1, 3, and 4 bearing caps.

22. Alternately loosen and remove bearing cap bolts No. 9 and 10. As these bolts are loosened and after breaking the adhesion on the front bearing cap, check to see that the camshaft is being lifted out straight and level.

NOTE: If the camshaft is not lifting out straight and level retighten No. 9 and 10 bearing cap bolts. Reverse Steps 22 through 19, than start over from Step 19. Do not attempt to pry the camshaft from its mounting.

23. Remove the intake camshaft from the engine.

24. Loosen then remove the cylinder head bolts in three phases and in the proper sequence. Remove the cylinder head from the engine.

25. Installation is the reverse of the removal procedure.

26. Be sure to use a new head gasket. Apply a light coat of clean engine oil to the threads of the head bolts before installation. Torque the cylinder head to specification and in three phases.

27. Before installing the intake camshaft, apply multi purpose grease to the thrust portion of the camshaft. Position the camshaft at 80° BTDC of camshaft angle on the cylinder head. Apply seal packing kit 08826—00080 or equivalent and apply it to the front bearing cap. Coat the bearing cap bolts with clean engine oil. Uniformly and in several phases tighten the camshaft bearing caps to 14 ft. lbs.

28. To install the exhaust camshaft, set the knock pin of the camshaft at 10° BTDC of camshaft angle. Apply multipurpose grease to the thrust portion of the camshaft. Position the exhaust camshaft gear with the intake camshaft gear so that the timing marks are in alignment with one another. Be sure to use the proper alignment marks on the gears. Do not use the assembly reference marks.

29. Turn the intake camshaft clockwise or counterclockwise little by little until the exhaust camshaft sits in the bearing journals evenly without rocking the camshaft on the bearing journals.

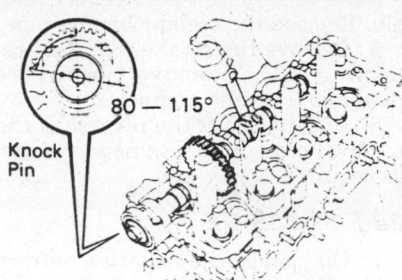

80 — 115°

Knock Pin

First

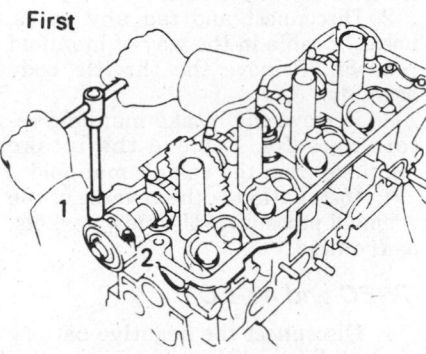

Second

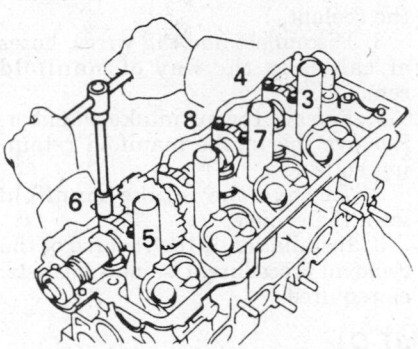

Third

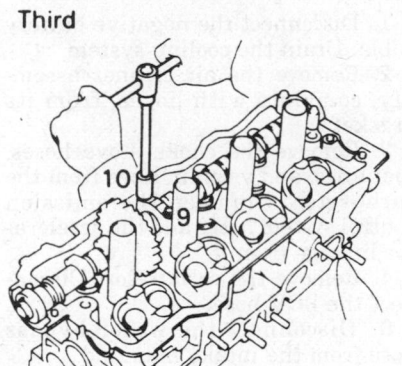

3S-FE intake camshaft removal procedure

30. Coat the bearing cap bolts with clean engine oil. Uniformly and inseveral phases tighten the camshaft bearing caps to 14 ft. lbs. Remove the service bolt from the assembly.

For all cylinder head procedures, please refer to "Engine Rebuilding" in the Unit Repair section.

REMOVAL & INSTALLATION

4K-C and 4K-E

1. Disconnect the negative battery cable. Remove the air cleaner.
2. Remove the PCV valve. Remove the spark plug wires.
3. Remove the valve cover. Loosen the rocker shaft bolts, alternating front to rear.
4. Remove the shaft assembly and oil tube.
5. Installation is the reverse of the removal procedure. Torque bolts in alternating, front to rear sequence, to 14—16 ft. lbs. Torque the oil pipe bolts to 14 ft. lbs. Check the valve clearance.

3T-C

1. Disconnect the negative battery cable. Remove the air cleaner.
2. Remove the PCV valve. Remove the spark plug wires.
3. Disconnect the fuel inlet from the carburetor.
4. Remove the valve cover. The cylinder head bolts also serve as the rocker arm shaft bolts. Remove in circular rotation from the ends towards the center.
5. Lift off the shaft assemblies.
6. Installation is the reverse of the removal procedure. Install and tighten the cylinder head bolts in circular rotation from the center toward the ends. Torque to 63 ft. lbs. Check the valve clearance.

22R and 22R-E

1. Disconnect the negative battery cable. Remove the air cleaner.
2. Disconnect all hoses and linkage clipped to the valve cover.
3. Remove the spark plug wires. Remove the carburetor. Remove the valve cover.
4. Remove the distributor. Set the No. 1 piston at TDC of the compression stroke.
5. Paint mating marks on the timing chain and sprocket, and drive gear.
6. Remove the distributor drive gear, leaving the chain and sprocket in position.
7. Remove the one 14mm chain cover bolt in the front of the head. This must be done before the head bolts, which also serve as rocker shaft bolts, are removed.
8. Remove the head bolts in diagonal pattern. Start at the front carburetor side. This must be done to prevent head warpage.
9. Remove the shaft assemblies

from the head. It may be necessary to use a pry bar to evenly lift the assemblies from the dowels.

10. Installation is the reverse of the removal procedure. Torque the head bolts in a diagonal pattern, starting at the center. Tighten in three equal stages to 64 ft. lbs. Torque the chain cover bolt to 12 ft. lbs. Torque the drive gear bolt to 65 ft. lbs.

5M-E

1. Disconnect the negative battery cable. Remove the air cleaner assembly.
2. Remove the choke stove outlet and inlet hose. Remove the valve cover.
3. Remove the two front clamp bolts. Loosen the rocker arm shaft bolts in a rotating order starting at the ends and working towards the center.
4. Remove the bolts and lift off the rocker shaft assemblies.
5. Installation is the reverse of the removal procedure. Tighten the rocker arm shafts bolts, in a rotating order from the center to the ends, to 25 ft. lbs. Torque the front end clamp bolts to 9 ft. lbs. Check the valve clearance.

1A-C, 3A, 3A-C, 4A-C, 4A-LC, 3Y-EC and 4Y-EC

1. Disconnect the negative battery terminal.
2. Remove the air cleaner and all necessary hoses.
3. Remove all linkage from the carburetor.
4. Remove the valve cover and gasket.
5. Remove the rocker arm bolts.
6. Installation is the reverse of the removal procedure. Install a new valve cover gasket before replacing the valve cover. Tighten the rocker arm bolt to 17–19 ft. lbs.

2S-E, 3S-GE, 4A-GE, 5M-GE, 3S-FE, 3E, 7M-GE, 7M-GTE, 4A-GELC, 4A-GEC and Diesel

These engines do not utilize rocker arms shafts. The valves are activated directly by the camshaft.

Intake Manifold

REMOVAL & INSTALLATION

1C-L, 1C-TL and 2C-T

1. Disconnect the negative battery cable. Drain the coolant. Remove the air cleaner.
2. Disconnect and tag any wire, hose or cable in the way of manifold removal.
3. Remove the turbocharger assem-

bly. Remove the coolant bypass pipe.
4. Remove the intake manifold retaining bolts. Remove the intake manifold from the engine.
5. Installation is the reverse of the removal procedure. Use new gaskets, as required.

2S-E and 3S-GE

1. Disconnect the negative battery cable. Drain the coolant.
2. Disconnect and tag any wires, hoses or cable in the way of manifold removal. Remove the throttle body assembly.
3. Remove the intake manifold retaining bolts. Remove the intake manifold from the vehicle.manifold.
4. Installation is the reverse of the removal procedure. Use new gaskets, as required.

3Y-EC and 4Y-EC

1. Disconnect the negative battery ground. Remove the right front seat.
2. Remove the engine cover. Drain the coolant.
3. Disconnect and tag wires, hoses or cables in the way of manifold removal.
4. Remove the air intake chamber. Remove the intake manifold retaining bolts.
5. Remove the intake manifold from the vehicle.
6. Installation is the reverse of the removal procedure. Use new gaskets, as required.

3T-C

1. Disconnect the negative battery cable. Drain the cooling system.
2. Remove the air cleaner assembly, complete with hoses, from its bracket.
3. Remove the choke stove hoses, fuel lines, and vacuum lines from the carburetor. Unfasten the emission control system hoses and the accelerator linkage from it.
4. Remove the carburetor. Disconnect the PCV hose.
5. Disconnect the water bypass hose from the intake manifold.
6. Remove the intake manifold retaining bolts. Remove the intake manifold from the engine.
7. Installation is the reverse of the removal procedure. Use new gaskets, as required. Tighten the bolts, in several stages, working from the inside out.

22R

1. Disconnect the negative battery cable.
2. Drain the cooling system.
3. Remove the air cleaner, complete with hoses, from the carburetor.

Disconnect and mark the vacuum lines from the EGR valve and carburetor.
4. Remove the fuel lines, electrical leads, accelerator linkage, and water hose from the carburetor.
5. Remove the water bypass hose from the manifold. Remove the intake manifold retaining bolts.
6. Remove the intake manifold, complete with carburetor and EGR valve.
7. Installation is the reverse of the removal procedure. Be sure to use a new gasket, as required. Tighten the bolts in several stages working from the inside bolts outward.

22R-E

1. Disconnect the negative battery cable. Drain the cooling system.
2. Disconnect the air intake hose from both the air cleaner assembly on one end and the air intake chamber on the other.
3. Tag and disconnect all vacuum lines attached to the intake chamber and manifold.
4. Tag and disconnect the wires to the cold start injector, throttle position sensor, and the water hoses from the throttle body. Remove the EGR valve from the intake chamber.
5. Tag and disconnect the actuator cable, accelerator cable and automatic transmission throttle cable, if equipped from the cable bracket on the intake chamber.

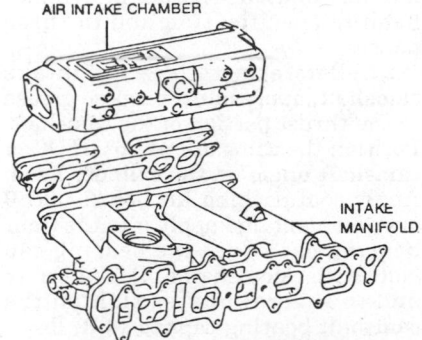

Intake manifold assembly—22R-E

6. Unbolt the air intake chamber from the intake manifold and remove the chamber with the throttle body attached. Disconnect the fuel hose from the delivery pipe.
7. Tag and disconnect the air valve hose from the intake manifold. Make sure all hoses, lines and wires are tagged for later installation and disconnected from the intake manifold.
8. Remove the intake manifold retaining bolts. Remove the manifold from the cylinder head, removing the delivery pipe and injection nozzle in unit with the manifold.

9. Installation is the reverse of the removal procedure. Use new gaskets, as required.

5M-E and 5M-GE

1. Disconnect the negative battery cable. Drain the engine coolant.

2. Disconnect and tag wires, hoses or cables in the way of manifold removal.

3. Remove the air intake chamber. Disconnect and move the wiring away from the fuel delivery and injector pipe. Remove the fuel injector and delivery pipe.

4. Remove the fuel pressure regulator, which is mounted on the center of the intake manifold.

5. Remove the EGR valve from the rear of the manifold. Mark and disconnect the radiator hoses, heater hoses, and vacuum lines from the intake manifold.

6. Remove the distributor cap and position it out of the way.

7. Remove ther intake manifold retaining bolts. Remove the intake manifold and gasket from the engine.

8. Installation is the reverse of the removal procedure. Use new gaskets, as required. Torque the manifold fasteners to 10–15 ft. lbs.

4A-GE, 4A-GEC and 4A-GELC

1. Disconnect the negative battery cable. Drain the coolant. Remove the air cleaner assembly.

2. Disconnect and tag wires, hoses or cables in the way of manifold removal.

3. Remove the necessary components in order to gain access to the intake manifold retaining bolts.

4. Remove the intake manifold retaining bolts. Remove the intake manifold from the vehicle.

5. Installation is ther reverse of the removal procedure. Use new gaskets, as required.

3S-GE

1. Disconnect the negative battery cable. Drain the coolant. Remove the air cleaner assembly.

2. Disconnect and tag wires, hoses or cables in the way of manifold removal.

3. Remove the necessary components in order to gain access to the intake manifold retaining bolts.

4. Remove the intake manifold retaining bolts. Remove the intake manifold from the vehicle.

5. Installation is ther reverse of the removal procedure. Use new gaskets, as required.

3S-FE

1. Disconnect the negative battery

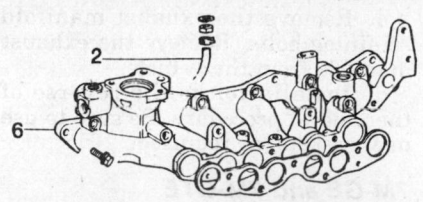

1. Fuel hose
2. Fuel return hose
3. Fuel pipe
4. Delivery pipe and injector
5. Pressure regulator
6. Intake manifold
7. Throttle body
8. Cold start injector
9. Air intake chamber

Intake manifold assembly—4M-E, 5M-E and 5M-GE

cable. drain the coolant. Remove the air cleaner assembly.

2. Disconnect and tag wires, hoses or cables in the way of manifold removal.

3. Remove the necessary components in order to gain access to the intake manifold retaining bolts.

4. Remove the throttle body assembly. Remove the cold start injector pipe.

5. Remove the air tube assembly. If equipped with power steering remove the hoses before removing the air tube assembly.

6. Remove the intake manifold retaining bolts. Remove the intake manifold from the vehicle.

5. Installation is the reverse of the removal procedure. Use new gaskets, as required.

3E

1. Disconnect the negative battery cable. Drain the coolant. Remove the air cleaner assembly.

2. Disconnect and tag wires, hoses or cables in the way of manifold removal.

3. Remove the necessary components in order to gain access to the intake manifold retaining bolts.

4. Remove the carburetor assembly. Remove the intake manifold water hose.

5. Remove the intake manifold retaining bolts. Remove the intake manifold from the vehicle.

6. Installation is the reverse of the removal procedure. Use new gaskets, as required.

7M-GE and 7M-GTE

1. Disconnect the negative battery cable. Drain the coolant. Remove the air cleaner assembly.

2. Disconnect and tag wires, hoses or cables in the way of manifold removal.

3. Remove the necessary components in order to gain access to the intake manifold retaining bolts.

4. Remove the air intake connector

along with the air intake chamber assembly.

5. Remove the intake manifold retaining bolts. Remove the intake manifold from the vehicle.

6. Installation is the reverse of the removal procedure. Use new gaskets, as required.

Exhaust Manifold

REMOVAL & INSTALLATION

3T-C

1. Disconnect the negative battery cable. Detach the manifold heat stove intake pipe.

2. Unfasten the nut on the stove outlet pipe union. Remove the wiring from the emission control system thermosensor.

3. Unfasten the U-bolt from the downpipe bracket. Unfasten the downpipe flange from the manifold.

4. Remove the manifold retaining bolts. Remove the bolts in two or three stages, working from the inside out.

5. Remove the exhaust manifold from the vehicle.

6. Installation is the reverse of the removal procedure. Use a new gasket, as required.

22R and 22R-E

1. Disconnect the negative battery cable. Remove the three exhaust pipe flange bolts and disconnect the exhaust pipe from the manifold.

2. Disconnect the spark plug leads. Matchmark the distributor rotor, housing and the engine block. Remove the distributor.

3. Remove the air cleaner tube from the heat stove. Remove the outer part of the heat stove.

4. Remove the manifold complete with air injection tubes and the inner portion of the heat stove. Separate the inner portion of the heat stove from the manifold.

5. Installation is the reverse of the removal procedure. Tighten the retaining nuts to 29–36 ft. lbs. working from the inside out. Install the distributor and set the timing. Tighten the exhaust pipe flange nuts to 25–32 ft. lbs.

5M-E, 3Y-EC, 4Y-EC, 2S-E, 1C-L, 1C-LT and 2C-T

1. Disconnect the negative battery cable. Raise the vehicle and support it safely. Remove the right hand gravel shield from beneath the engine.

2. Remove the downpipe support bracket. Unfasten the bolts from the flange and detach the downpipe from the manifold.

3. Remove the automatic choke and air cleaner stove hoses from the exhaust manifold, if so equipped. Remove the EGR valve, if so equipped.

4. Remove, or move aside, any of the air injection system components which may be in the way when removing the manifold.

5. Remove the exhaust manifold retaining bolts, in two or three stages, starting from the inside, working out. Remove the exhaust manifold from the vehicle.

6. Installation is the reverse of the removal procedure. Use a new gasket, as required. Tighten the retaining bolts to specifications.

3S-GE, 4A-GE, 4A-GEC, 4A-GELC and 5M-GE

1. Disconnect the negative battery cable. Raise and support the vehicle safely. Remove the right hand gravel shield from underneath the car.

2. Remove the exhaust pipe support stay. Unbolt the exhaust pipe from the exhaust manifold flange.

3. Disconnect the oxygen sensor connector. On the 3S-GE, remove the upper heat insulator.

4. Remove the manifold retaining bolts. Remove the exhaust manifold from the vehicle.

5. Installation is the reverse of the removal procedure. Use a new gasket, as required. Torque all nuts evenly to 25–33 ft. lbs.

3S-FE

1. Disconnect the negative battery cable. Remove the exhaust manifold heat insulator shield assembly.

2. Remove the necessary components in order to gain access to the exhaust manifold retaining bolts.

3. Disconnect the exhaust manifold bolts at the exhaust pipe. It may be necessary to raise and support the vehicle safely before removing these bolts.

4. Remove the exhaust manifold retaining bolts. Remove the exhaust manifold from the vehicle.

5. Installation is the reverse of the removal procedure. Be sure to use new gaskets, as required.

3E

1. Disconnect the negative battery cable. Remove the exhaust manifold heat insulator shield assembly.

2. Remove the necessary components in order to gain access to the exhaust manifold retaining bolts.

3. Disconnect the exhaust manifold bolts at the exhaust pipe. Disconnect the oxygen sensor electrical wire. It may be necessary to raise and support the vehicle safely before removing these bolts.

4. Remove the exhaust manifold retaining bolts. Remove the exhaust manifold from the vehicle.

5. Installation is the reverse of the removal procedure. Be sure to use new gaskets, as required.

7M-GE and 7M-GTE

1. Disconnect the negative battery cable. Remove the exhaust manifold heat insulator shield assembly, if equipped.

2. Remove the necessary components in order to gain access to the exhaust manifold retaining bolts.

3. Disconnect the exhaust manifold bolts at the exhaust pipe. It may be necessary to raise and support the vehicle safely before removing these bolts.

4. If equipped with turbocharger, remove it.

5. Remove the exhaust manifold retaining bolts. Remove the exhaust manifold from the vehicle.

6. Installation is the reverse of the removal procedure. Be sure to use new gaskets, as required.

Combination Manifold

REMOVAL & INSTALLATION

4K-C

1. Disconnect the negative battery cable. Remove the air cleaner assembly, complete with hoses.

2. Disconnect the accelerator and choke linkages from the carburetor, as well as the fuel and vacuum lines.

3. Remove, or move aside, any of the emission control system components which are in the way.

4. Unfasten the retaining bolts and remove the carburetor from the manifold.

5. Loosen the manifold retaining nuts, working from the inside out.

6. Remove the intake/exhaust manifold assembly from the cylinder head as a complete unit.

7. Installation is the reverse of the removal procedure. Use new gaskets. Tighten the bolts, working from the inside out and in two or three stages.

4K-E

1. Disconnect the negative battery cable. Loosen the two hose clamps and remove the air cleaner hose.

2. Disconnect the throttle cable from its two attachment points on the air intake chamber and the throttle body. Position the cable out of the way.

3. Tag and disconnect all vacuum hoses leading from the air intake chamber.

4. Tag and disconnect the three electrical leads attached to the air intake chamber.

5. Unscrew and remove the two air intake chamber support brackets. Remove the air intake pipe to manifold retaining bolts and lift off the air intake chamber and pipes as an assembly. The air intake assembly must be supported while removing the pipe retaining bolts.

6. Tag and disconnect the four injector wires. Remove the two wire harness clamps and then remove the EFI solenoid wiring harness from the delivery pipe.

7. Disconnect the heater outlet hoses. Disconnect the exhaust pipe from the exhaust manifold. Remove the six mounting bolts and then remove the combination manifold.

8. Installation is the reverse of the removal procedure. Use new gaskets, as required.

1A-C, 3A, 3A-C, 4A-C and 4A-LC

1. Disconnect the negative battery cable.

2. Remove the air cleaner and all necessary hoses.

3. Remove all the carburetor linkages.

4. Remove the carburetor.

5. Remove the intake/exhaust manifold pipe.

6. Remove the intake/exhaust manifold.

7. Installation is the reverse of the removal procedure. Tighten the manifold bolts to 15–21 ft. lbs.

Turbocharger

REMOVAL & INSTALLATION

1. Disconnect the negative battery cable. Remove the air cleaner.

2. Disconnect and tag all wiring and hoses in the way of turbocharger removal.

3. Remove the compressor elbow and relief hose.

4. Remove the heat shields.

5. Disconnect the exhaust pipe from the turbo elbow.

6. Disconnect the turbocharger oil pipes.

7. Remove the turbocharger retaining bolts. Remove the turbocharger from the vehicle.

8. Installation is the reverse of the removal procedure. Torque the turbocharger mounting bolts to 38 ft. lbs.

TROUBLESHOOTING

For more information on turbocharging, please refer to "Turbocharging" in the Unit Repair section.

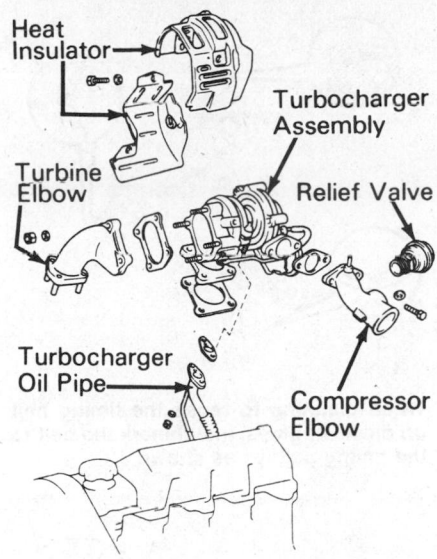

Turbocharger assembly

Front Cover

REMOVAL & INSTALLATION

4K-C, 4K-E and 3T-C

1. Disconnect the negative battery cable. Drain the cooling system. Drain the oil.
2. Remove the air cleaner assembly, complete with hoses, from its bracket.
3. Remove the hood latch as well as its brace and support.
4. Remove the headlight bezels. Remove the grille assembly.
5. Remove the hoses from the engine. If equipped, remove the radiator shroud. Remove the radiator retaining bolts. Remove the radiator from the vehicle.
6. Loosen the drive belt adjusting link. Remove the drive belt. Remove the alternator retaining bolts. Remove the alternator from the vehicle.
7. If equipped, disconnect the hoses from the air pump and remove it.
8. Remove the fan and water pump as an assembly.
9. Unfasten the crankshaft pulley retaining bolt. Remove the crankshaft pulley with a gear puller. Remove the gravel shield from underneath the engine.
10. On 4K-C and 4K-E engines, remove the nuts and washers from both the right and left front engine mounts. Detach the exhaust pipe flange from the exhaust manifold. Slightly raise the front of the engine.
11. On 3T-C engine, remove the rght hand brace plate.
12. Remove the front oil pan bolts, to gain access to the bottom of the timing chain cover. It may be necessary

to insert a thin suitable tool between the pan and the gasket in order to break the pan loose. Use care not to damage the gasket.
13. Remove the cover from the engine.
14. Installation is the reverse of the removal procedure. On the 3T-C engine apply sealer to the two front corners of the oil pan gasket.

22R, 22R-E and 5M-E

1. Disconnect the negative battery cable. Remove the cylinder head from the engine.
2. Remove the radiator. Remove the alternator.
3. If equipped with an air pumps, remove the pump and bracket from the engine. If equipped with power steering, remove the pump.
4. Remove the fan and water pump as a complete assembly. To prevent the fluid from running out from the fan coupling, do not tip the assembly over on its side.
5. Unfasten the crankshaft pulley securing bolts and remove the pulley with a gear puller. Do not remove the 10mm bolt from its hole, if installed, as it is used for balancing.
6. Drain the engine oil. Loosen the bolts which secure the front of the oil pan. Lower the front of the oil pan.
7. Remove the bolts which secure the timing chain cover. Remove the cover from the engine.
8. Installation is the reverse of the removal procedure. Apply sealer to the gaskets for both the timing chain cover and the oil pan. Some engines use two gaskets on the timing chain cover.

1A-C, 3A, 3A-C, 4A-LC and 4A-C

1. Disconnect the negative battery cable.
2. Remove all drive belts.
3. Bring the No. 1 cylinder to TDC on the compression stroke.

4. Remove the crankshaft pulley with a suitable puller.
5. Remove the water pump pulley.
6. Remove the upper and lower timing case covers.
7. Installation is the reverse of removal. Tighten the timing belt cover to 61–99 inch lbs.

2S-E, 3S-GE, 3Y-EC, 4A-GE, 4A-GEC, 4A-GELC, 4Y-EC, 5M-GE and Diesels

For front cover removal procedures on these engines, please refer to the "Timing Belt Removal and Installation" procedure.

3E and 3S-FE

1. Disconnect the negative battery cable. On 3E engine, remove the air cleaner assembly. Remove all drive belts.
2. On the 3S-FE engine remove the alternator and bracket. If equipped with cruise control remove the actuator and bracket assembly.
3. Raise and support the vehicle safely. Remove the right tire and wheel asssembly. Remove the right side engine under cover. Remove the right side engine mount insulator.
4. On the 3E engine, remove the valve cover.
5. Remove the crankshaft pulley. Remove the engine front cover retaining bolts. Remove both front covers from the engine.
6. Installation is the reverse of the removal procedure.

7M-GE and 7M-GTE

1. Disconnect the negative battery cable. It may be necessary to remove the radiator for clearance.
2. Remove the drive belts. Remove the crankshaft pulley.
3. Remove the front cover retaining bolts. Remove the front covers from the engine.

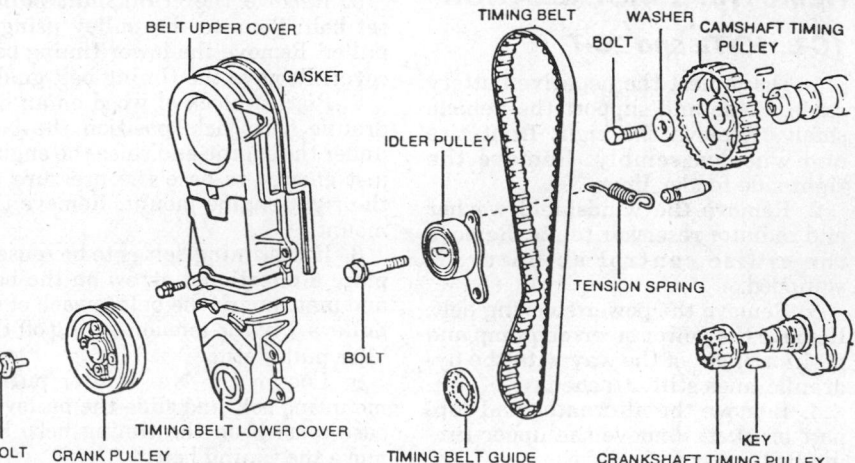

Front cover and related components—A-series engines

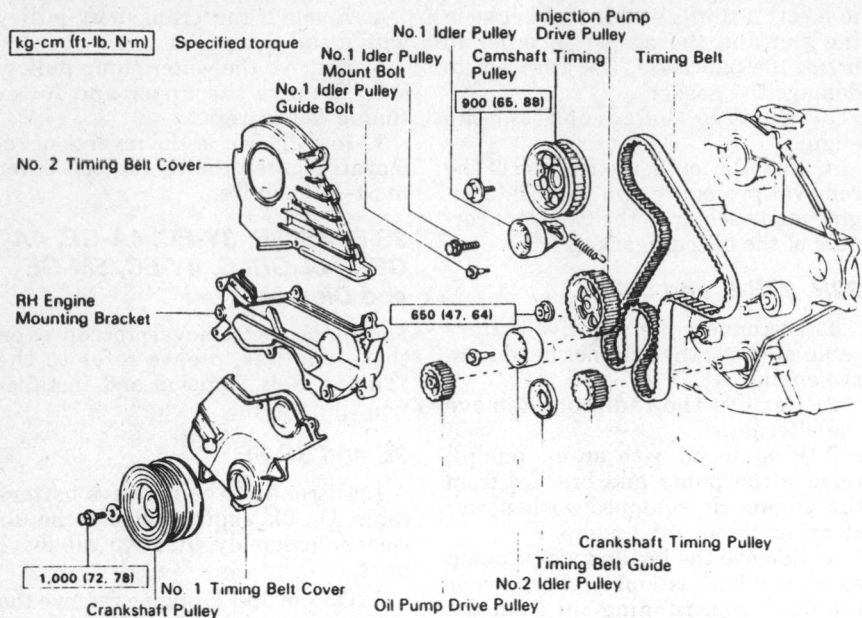

kg-cm (ft-lb, N·m)	Specified torque

Labels: No. 2 Timing Belt Cover, No.1 Idler Pulley Guide Bolt, No.1 Idler Pulley Mount Bolt, No.1 Idler Pulley, Camshaft Timing Pulley, Injection Pump Drive Pulley, Timing Belt, 900 (65, 88), RH Engine Mounting Bracket, 650 (47, 64), 1,000 (72, 78), No. 1 Timing Belt Cover, Crankshaft Pulley, Crankshaft Timing Pulley, Timing Belt Guide, No.2 Idler Pulley, Oil Pump Drive Pulley

Front cover and related components—diesel engines

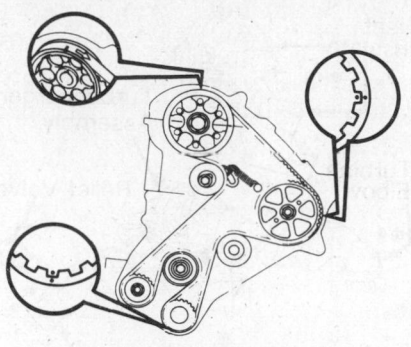

When planning to reuse the timing belt on diesel engines, matchmark the belt to the timing pulleys as shown

4. Installation is the reverse of the removal procedure.

OIL SEAL REPLACEMENT

1. Remove the front cover.
2. Inspect the oil seal for signs of wear, leakage, or damage.
3. If worn, pry the old seal out. Remove it toward the front of the cover. Once the seal has been removed, it must be replaced.
4. Use a socket, pipe, or block of wood and a hammer to drive the oil seal into place. Work from the front of the cover. Be extremely careful not to damage the seal.
5. Install the front cover.

Timing Chain (or Belt) And Tensioner

REMOVAL & INSTALLATION

1C-L, 1C-TL and 2C-T

1. Disconnect the negative battery cable. Raise and support the vehicle safely. Remove the right front tire and wheel assembly. Remove the right side fender liner.
2. Remove the windshield washer and radiator reservoir tanks. Remove the cruise control actuator, if equipped.
3. Remove the power steering belt. Remove the power steering pump and position it out of the way with the hydraulic lines still attached.
4. Remove the alternator and support bracket. Remove the upper timing belt cover.
5. Turn the crankshaft pulley

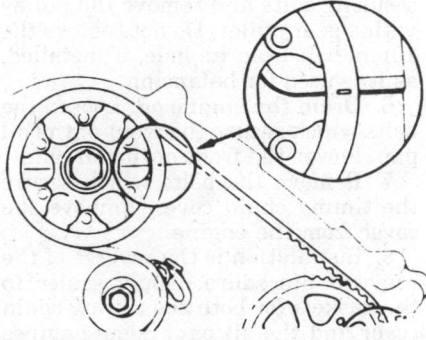

Aligning the timing pulley marks with the top end of the cylinder head—diesel engines

clockwise until the line on the camshaft timing pulley is in alignment with the top end of the cylinder head, this will put the engine at TDC of the compression stroke.
6. Remove the crankshaft pulley set bolt. Remove the pulley using a puller. Remove the lower timing belt cover. Remove the timing belt guide.
7. Place a block of wood on an hydraulic floor jack, position the jack under the engine and raise the engine just enough to ease the pressure on the right engine mount. Remove the mount.
8. If the timing belt is to be reused, place a directional arrow on the belt and matchmark the belt to each of its pulleys. Pry the tension spring off the idler pulley stud.
9. Loosen the No. 1 idler pulley mounting bolt and slide the pulley to ease tension on the timing belt. Remove the timing belt.
10. When installing the timing belt,

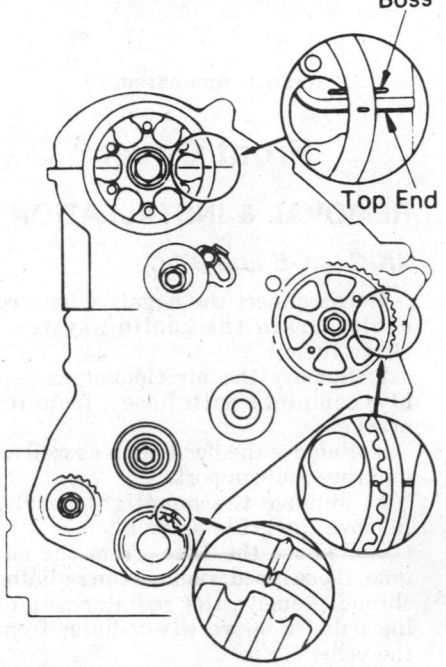

Timing pulley alignment on the diesel engine

align the mark on the camshaft timing pulley with the top end of the cylinder head. Do not align the cylinder head cover with the boss.
11. Align the grooves of the crankshaft timing pulley and the oil pump. Align the cavity in the injection pump drive pulley with the line on the water pump pulley.
12. Secure the injection pump pulley in place until the timing belt has been installed because the drive pulley will not come to rest by itself at the matchmark position.
13. Install the timing belt. If using the old one, install it as removed. If using a new timing belt, install it so that the numbers and letters may be read from the rear side of the engine.
14. Stretch he tension spring over the stud on the No. 1 idler pulley.

15. Using the crankshaft pulley mounting bolt, turn the engine two complete revolutions, from TDC to TDC. Check that all pulley to belt matchmarks are still in alignment, if not, remove the belt and start again.

16. Tighten the No. 1 idler pulley set bolt to 27 ft.lbs. Be sure not to move the pulley bracket while tightening the bolt.

17. Install the right side engine mount bracket and tighten the 10mm bolts to 17 ft. lbs. and the 12mm bolts to 47 ft. lbs.

18. If the vehicle is equipped with power steering or air condition, do not tighten the 12mm bolts at this time.

19. Install the right side engine mount and then lower the engine. Install the timing belt guide with the cup side facing out.

20. Install the lower timing belt cover. Install the crankshaft pulley and tighten the set bolt to 72 ft. lbs.

21. Installation of the remaining components is in the reverse order of the removal procedure.

2S-E

1. Disconnect the negative battery cable. Raise and support the vehicle safely. Remove the right front tire and wheel assembly. Remove the right side fender liner.

2. Remove the windshield washer and radiator reservoir tanks. Remove the cruise control actuator, if equipped.

3. Remove the power steering belt. Remove the power steering pump and position it out of the way with the hydraulic lines still attached.

4. Remove the alternator and support bracket. Remove the upper timing belt cover. Set the No. 1 cylinder to TDC of the compression stroke.

5. On USA vehicles, align the oil seal retainer mark with the center of the small "E" mark on the camshaft timing pulley by turning the crankshaft pulley clockwise.

6. On Canada vehicles, align the oil seal retainer mark with the center of the small hole on the camshaft timing pulley by turning the crankshaft pulley clockwise.

7. If the timing belt is to be reused, place a directional arrow on the belt and matchmark the camshaft timing pulley to the belt. Loosen the No. 1 idler pulley set bolt and shift the pulley to the left as far as it will go. Tighten the set bolt. Remove the timing belt from the camshaft pulley.

8. Remove the camshaft timing pulley. Remove the camshaft pulley. Remove the lower timing belt cover.

9. Remove the timing belt and guide. If the belt is to be reused, matchmark it to the remaining pul-

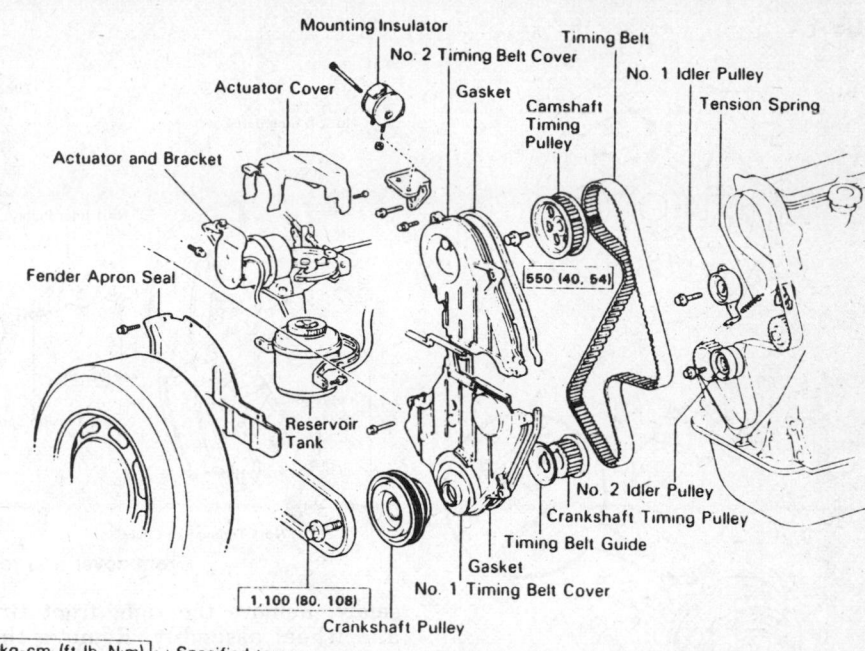

Front cover and related components—2S-E

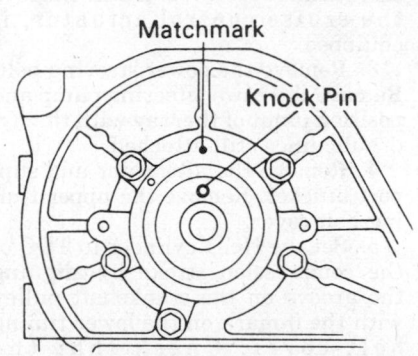

Align the camshaft knock pin with the matchmark on the camshaft oil seal retainer—2S-E

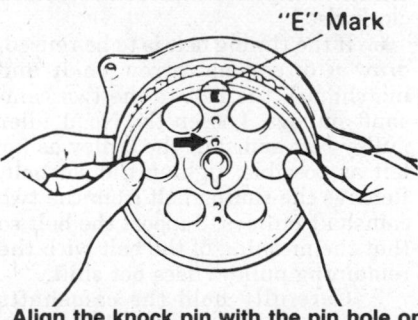

Align the knock pin with the pin hole on the timing pulley "E" mark slide—U.S. 2S-E

leys. Remove the No. 1 idler pulley. Remove the No. 2 idler pulley. Remove the crankshaft timing pulley and the oil pump pulley.

10. Install the oil pump pulley and tighten to 20 ft. lbs. Install the crankshaft timing pulley by sliding it over the crankshaft key.

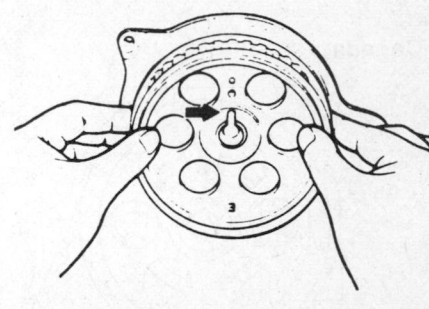

Align the knock pin with the pin hole on the timing pulley—Canada 2S-E

11. Install the No. 2 idler pulley and tighten it to 31 ft. lbs. Install the No. 1 idler pulley and tension spring. Pry the pulley to the left as far as it will go and tighten the set bolt.

12. Install the timing belt cover over all but the camshaft timing pulley. If reusing the old belt, be sure to align all the matchmarks made earlier. Install the timing belt guide with the cup side facing outward.

13. Install the lower timing belt cover and then install the crankshaft pulley. Tighten the set bolt to 80 ft. lbs.

14. Check that the No. 1 cylinder is at TDC by turning the crankshaft pulley clockwise until the groove on the pulley is aligned with the 0 mark on the timing cover.

15. When installing the camshaft timing pulley, align the camshaft knock pin with the matchmark on the camshaft oil seal retainer. On USA vehicles, align the knock pin with the pin hole on the timing pulley "E" mark side. On Canada vehicles, align

USA

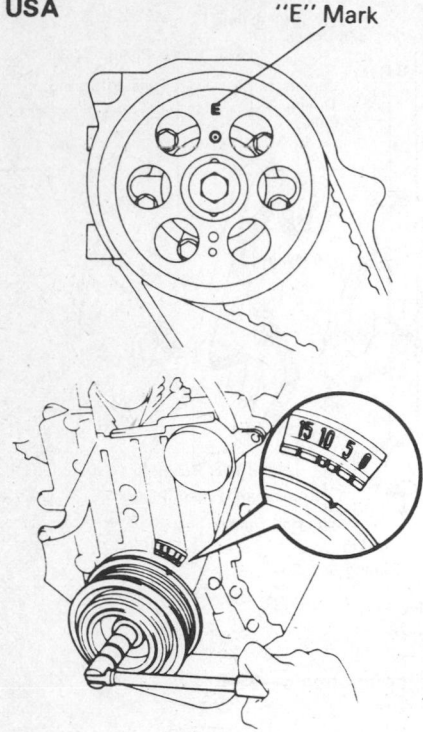

"E" Mark

Canada

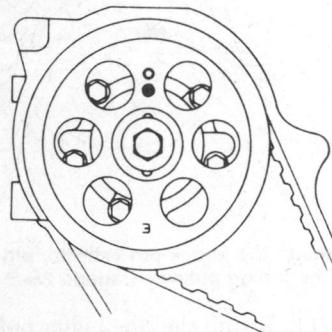

Setting the No. 1 cylinder to TDC of the compression stroke—2S-E

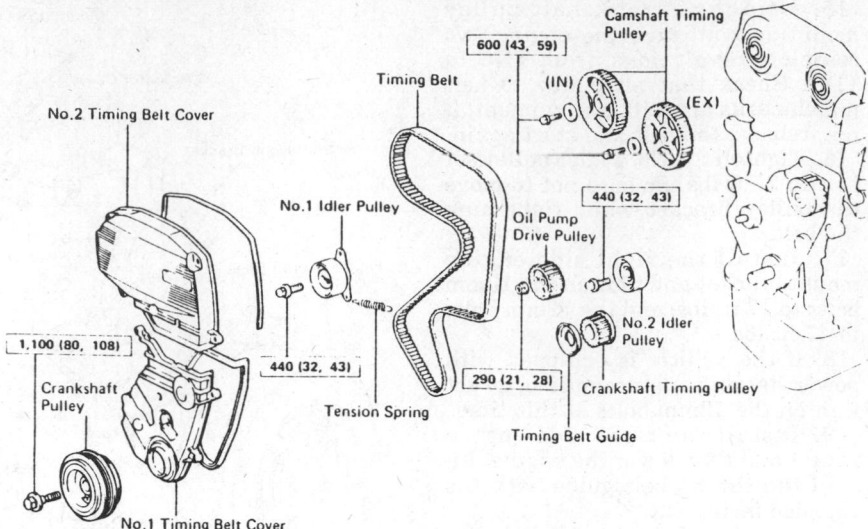

Front cover and related components—3S-GE

the knock pin with the pin hole on the timing pulley.

16. Check that the matchmark on the oil seal retainer and the center of the small hole on the camshaft timing pulley are in alignment. Tighten the pulley set bolt to 40 ft. lbs.

17. Install the timing belt around the camshaft pulley. Loosen the idler pulley set bolt ½ turn. Turn the crankshaft pulley two complete revolutions clockwise and then tighten the No. 1 idler pulley set bolt to 31 ft. lbs.

18. Installation of the remaining components is in the reverse order of removal. Tighten the right engine mount to 38 ft. lbs.

3S-GE

1. Disconnect the negative battery cable. Raise and support the vehicle

safely. Remove the right front tire and wheel assembly. Remove the right side fender liner.

2. Remove the windshield washer and radiator reservoir tanks. Remove the cruise control actuator, if equipped.

3. Remove the power steering belt. Remove the power steering pump and position it out of the way with the hydraulic lines still attached.

4. Remove the alternator and support bracket. Remove the upper timing belt cover.

5. Set the No. 1 cylinder to TDC of the compression stroke by aligning the groove on the crankshaft pulley with the 0 mark on the lower timing belt cover. Check that the matchmarks on the two camshaft timing pulleys and the rear timing belt cover are aligned, if not, turn the crankshaft one complete revolution clockwise.

6. If the timing belt is to be reused, draw a directional arrow on it and matchmark the belt to the two camshaft pulleys. Loosen the No. 1 idler pulley bolt and shift the pulley as far left as possible; tighten the set bolt. Remove the timing belt from the two camshaft pulleys. Support the belt so that the meshing of the belt with the remaining pulleys does not shift.

7. Carefully hold the camshafts with an adjustable wrench and remove the camshaft pulley set bolts. Remove the pulleys and their set pins.

8. Remove the crankshaft pulley. Remove the lower timing belt.

9. Remove the timing belt guide and then remove the timing belt from the remaining pulleys. Be sure to matchmark the belt to the pulleys if it is to be reused.

10. Remove the No. 1 idler pulley and the tension spring. Remove the

No. 2 idler pulley, the crankshaft timing pulley and the oil pump pulley.

11. Install the oil pump pulley and tighten it to 21 ft. lbs. Install the crankshaft timing pulley by sliding it onto the crankshaft over the woodruff key. Install the No. 2 idler pulley and tighten it to 32 ft. lbs.

12. Install the No. 1 idler pulley and the tension spring. Move the pulley as far to the left as it will go and then tighten it.

13. Install the timing belt on all pulleys except the two camshaft pulleys. Make sure the matchmarks made earlier are in alignment.

14. Install the timing belt guide with the cup side out. Install the lower timing belt cover and then install the crankshaft pulley. Tighten it to 80 ft. lbs.

15. Check that the No. 1 cylinder is at TDC of the compression stroke for the crankshaft. The crankshaft pulley groove should be aligned with the 0 mark on the lower timing belt cover.

16. Check that the No. 1 cylinder is at TDC of the compression stroke for the camshaft.

NOTE: There are two types of camshafts, one with two holes on the timing pulley contact surface and one with five holes on the timing pulley contact surface. All replacement camshaft have five holes.

TWO HOLE: Using a wrench, turn the camshafts so that the camshaft knock pin aligns with the matchmark on the rear timing belt cover. And the No. 1 cam lobe is pointing outward as shown.

FIVE HOLE: Using a wrench, turn the camshaft so that the knock pin aligns with the notch in the No. 1 camshaft bearing cap.

17. Hang the timing belt on the two camshaft timing pulleys. Align all matchmarks made during removal. The "S" mark on the pulley should face outward.

NOTE: There are two types of camshaft pulleys. One has five holes on the camshaft contact surface and one has one hole on the contact surface. All replacement pulleys have, you guessed it, five holes.

Align the timing pulley matchmark with the rear timing belt cover matchmark and install the pulleys with the belt.

NOTE: On one hole pulleys, match the camshaft knock pin with the camshaft pulley hole. On five hole pulleys, insert the knock pin into whichever pulley and camshaft holes are aligned.

Hold the camshaft with an adjustable wrench and tighten the pulley set bolt to 43 ft. lbs.

18. Loosen the No. 1 idler pulley set bolt just enough to move the pulley so it tensions the timing belt. Turn the crankshaft two complete revolutions clockwise and then tighten the idler pulley set bolt to 32 ft. lbs. Check for proper timing belt tension.

19. Installation of the remaining components is in the reverse order of removal. Tighten the engine mount bracket bolts to 38 ft. lbs.. Tighten the engine mount bolts to 58 ft. lbs. and the nuts to 38 ft. lbs.

3Y-EC and 4Y-EC

1. Disconnect the negative battery cable. Drain the engine coolant. Remove the radiator.

2. Remove all drive belts. Remove the fan and the water pump pulley.

3. Remove the distributor. Remove the cold start injector.

4. Remove the rocker shaft assembly and the pushrods. Remove the valve lifters with a magnet and keep them in order when you set them down.

5. Remove the crankshaft pulley and then remove the timing chain cover.

6. Check the slack in the timing chain with a tension gauge. Maximum slack should be no more than 0.531 in at 22 lbs. (98 N). Anything greater than this will require timing chain and sprocket replacement.

7. Reinstall the crankshaft pulley to the crankshaft. Hold the crank pulley while loosening the camshaft pulley bolt. Remove both pulley at the same time with the timing chain still attached.

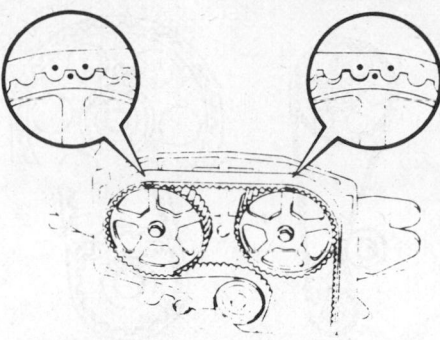

If the timing belt is to be reused on the 3S-GE, place matchmarks on the belt and pulleys

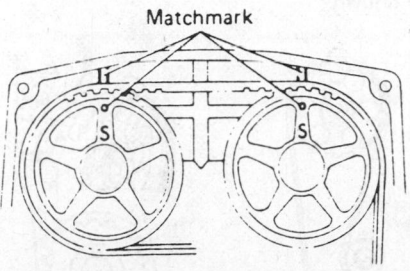

Align the matchmarks on the camshaft timing pulleys with those on the rear timing belt cover—3S-GE

Hold the camshaft with an adjustable wrench when removing the camshaft timing pulleys on the 3S-GF

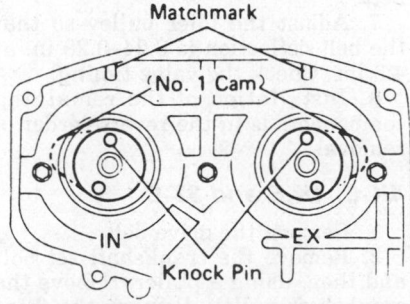

Turn the camshafts so that the knock pins align with the matchmark on the rear timing cover and the No. 1 lobes are facing outward—3S-GE (two hole type)

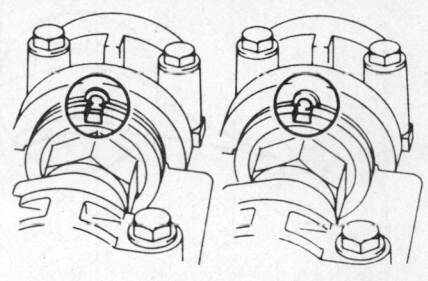

Align the knock pin and the No. 1 bearing cap mark—3S-GE (five hole type)

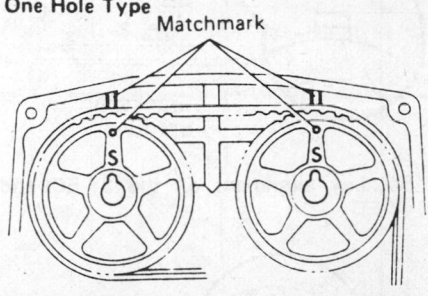

Align the camshaft knock pin with the hole in the camshaft timing pulley—3S-GE (one hole type pulley only)

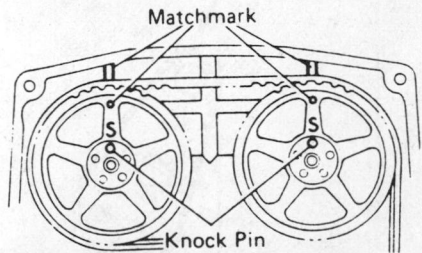

Insert the knock pin into whichever camshaft timing pulley and camshaft holes are aligned—3S-GE (five hole type pulley only)

8. Remove the vibration damper. Remove the camshaft thrust plate and carefully slide the camshaft out of the block.

9. Carefully insert the camshaft into the cylinder block and then install the thrust plate with the beveled side facing out. Tighten the mounting bolts to 13 ft. lbs. Install the vibration damper and tighten it to 13 ft. lbs.

10. Rotate the crankshaft so that the set key is facing upward. Rotate the camshaft so that the key is aligned with the mark on the thrust plate.

11. Install the timing chain around the two sprockets so that the timing link is aligned with with the marks on the sprockets. Install the timing chain/sprocket assembly onto the cylinder block.

12. Install the crankshaft pulley, lightly coat the camshaft sprocket

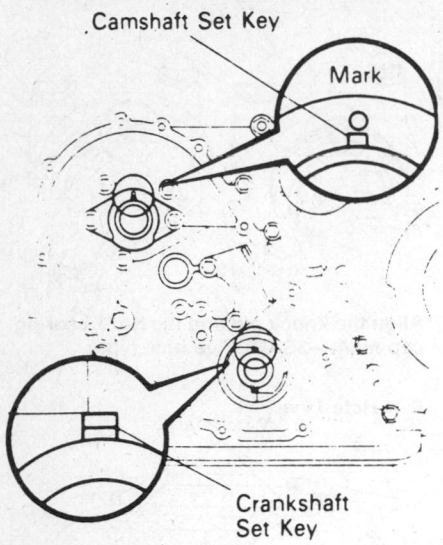

Set key alignment on the 3Y-EC and 4Y-EC

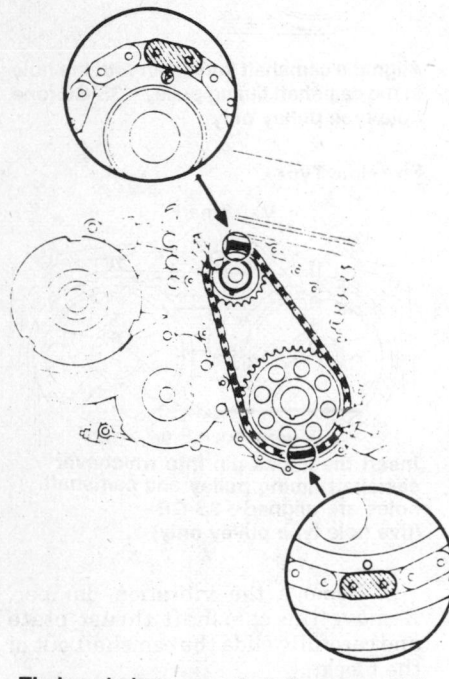

Timing chain-to-sprocket alignment—3Y-EC and 4Y-EC

bolt with engine oil an then tighten it to 67 ft. lbs. Remove the crankshaft pulley.

13. Install the chain tensioner and tighten it to 13 ft. lbs. Install the timing chain cover. Tighten the bolts to 52 inch lbs.

14. Installation of the remaining components is in the reverse order of removal.

1A-C, 3A, 3A-C, 4A-LC and 4A-C

1. Remove the timing belt upper and lower covers.

2. If the timing belt is to be reused, mark an arrow in the direction of en-

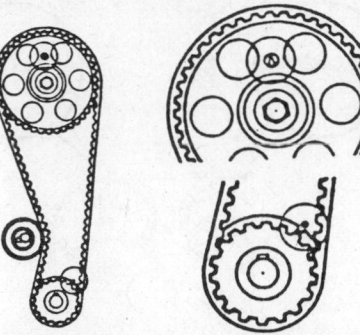

When checking the valve timing, turn the crankshaft two (2) complete revolutions clockwise from TDC to TDC and make sure that each pulley aligns with the marks shown

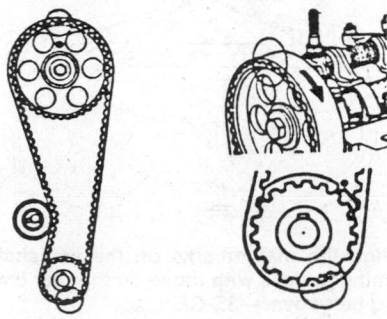

Mark the timing belt before removal

gine revolution on its surface. Matchmark the belt to the pulleys as shown in the illustration.

3. Loosen the idler pulley bolt, push it to the left as far as it will go and then temporarily tighten it.

4. Remove the timing belt, idler pulley bolt, idler pulley and the return spring Do not bend, twist, or turn the belt inside out. Do not allow grease or water to come in contact with it.

5. Inspect the timing belt for cracks, missing teeth or overall wear. Replace as necessary. Install the return spring and idler pulley.

6. Install the timing belt. Align the marks made earlier if reusing the old belt.

7. Adjust the idler pulley so that the belt deflection is 0.24–0.28 in. at 4.5 lbs. Check the valve timing.

8. Installation of the remaining components is in the reverse order of removal.

4K-C, 4K-E and 3T-C

1. Remove the drive belts.

2. Remove the crankshaft set bolt and then, using a puller, remove the crankshaft pulley. Remove the front cover.

3. Using a spring scale, measure the timing chain slack. If the slack is more than 0.531 in. at 22 lbs. of ten-

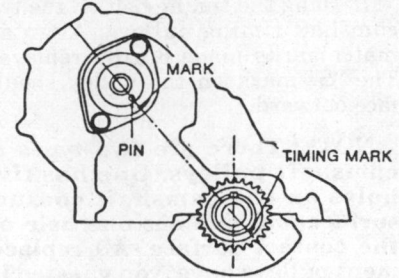

Align the camshaft dowel pin and mark on the thrust plate

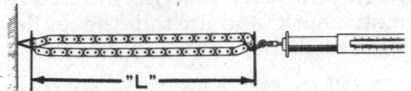

"K" and "T" series engines—measure the timing chain stretch between the arrows as indicated

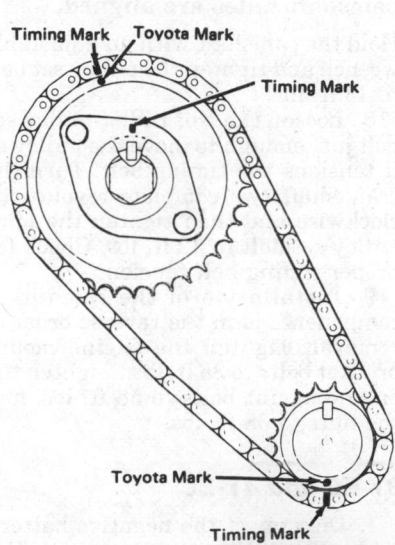

Proper alignment of the "T" series engine timing marks

sion, replace the chain and sprockets on the 4K-C and 4K-E engines.

4. Remove the timing chain tensioner and vibration damper.

5. On 4K-C and 4K-E engines, remove the camshaft sprocket set bolt and then remove the timing chain and sprocket together. Use a gear puller to remove the crankshaft sprocket. Remove the chain and both sprockets at the same time.

6. Measure the timing chain length with the chain fully stretched. It should be no more than 10.7 in. for 4K-C and 4K-E engines and 11.472 in. for the 3T-C engine in any three positions. Wrap the chain around a sprocket. Using a vernier caliper, measure the outer sides of the chain rollers. If the measurement is less than 2.339 in. on the crankshaft sprocket or 4.480 in. around the cam-

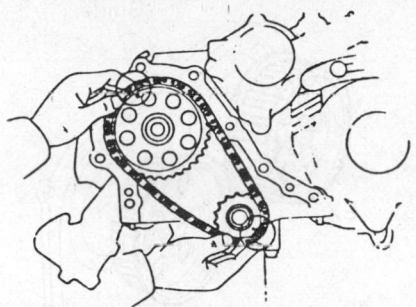

Align the marks on the two sprockets with the bright links on the timing chain

shaft sprocket, replace the chain and sprocket.

Installation for the 4K-E and 4K-C engines is performed in the following order:

1. Install the crankshaft sprocket.

2. Set the No. 1 piston to TDC and align the camshaft dowel pin with the mark on the thrust plate.

3. Install the timing chain around the two sprockets, make sure that the marks on the two sprockets are aligned with the marks (usually bright links) on the timing chain.

4. Install the timing chain and the two sprockets on to the shafts. Make sure the timing marks are aligned with the camshaft dowel pin and the mark on the thrust plate.

5. Install the timing chain tensioner and the vibration damper.

6. Installation of the remaining components is in the reverse order of removal.

Installation for the 3T-C engine is performed in the following order:

1. Align the key in the camshaft with the mark on the thrust plate. Face the key in the crankshaft straight up.

2. Install the timing chain around the two sprockets so that the bright links line up with the timing marks on the sprockets.

3. Install the chain and the gears on to the shafts.

4. Squirt oil into the cylinder in the chain tensioner and then install it to the cylinder block.

5. Install the chain damper parallel to the chain so that there is 0.020 in. space in between.

6. Installation of the remaining components is in the reverse order of removal.

22R and 22R-E

1. Remove the cylinder head. Remove the front cover.

2. Seperate the chain from the damper. Remove the chain along with the camshaft sprocket.

3. Remove the crankshaft sprocket and the oil pump drive with a puller.

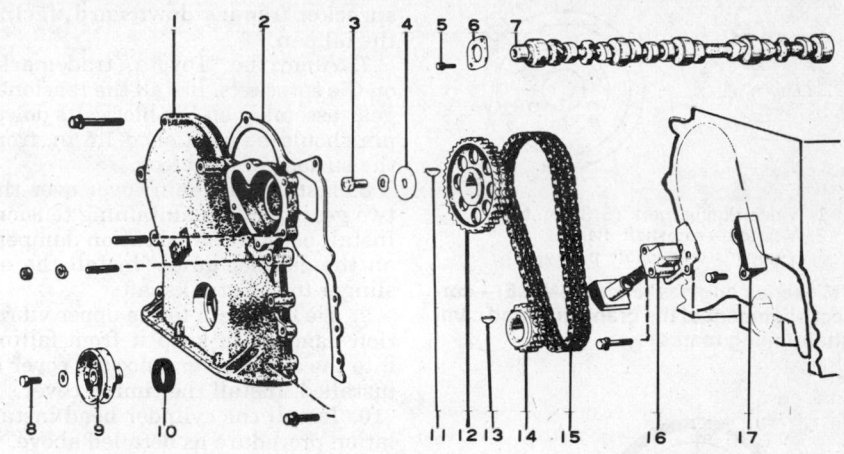

1. Timing chain cover
2. Timing chain cover gasket
3. Bolt
4. Plate washer
5. Bolt
6. Plate
7. Camshaft
8. Bolt
9. Crankshaft pulley
10. Front oil seal
11. Woodruff key
12. Camshaft sprocket
13. Woodruff key
14. Crankshaft sprocket
15. Timing chain
16. Chain tensioner
17. Chain vibration damper

Timing chain and related components—"T" series engines

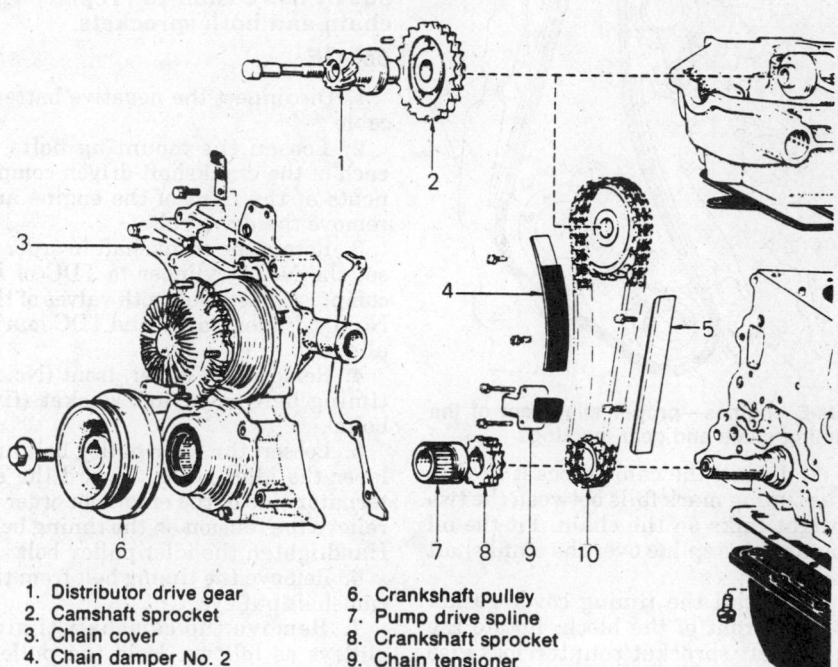

1. Distributor drive gear
2. Camshaft sprocket
3. Chain cover
4. Chain damper No. 2
5. Chain damper No. 1
6. Crankshaft pulley
7. Pump drive spline
8. Crankshaft sprocket
9. Chain tensioner
10. Chain

Front cover and timing chain components—R-series engines

Inspect the chain for wear or damage. Replace it, if necessary.

4. Inspect the chain tensioner for wear. If it measures less than 0.43 in., replace it.

5. Check the dampers for wear. If they are below specification replace them. Upper damper should be 0.20 in. Lower damper should be 0.18 in.

6. To install rotate the crankshaft pulley until its key is at TDC. Slide the sprocket in place over the key.

7. Place the chain cover over the sprocket so that its single bright link aligns with the mark on the crank sprocket.

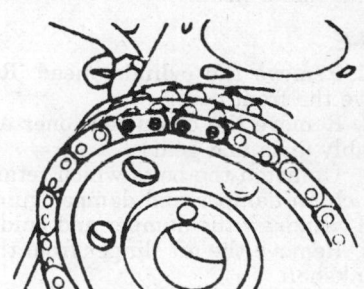

"R" series engines—align the timing marks between the two bright links of the timing chain

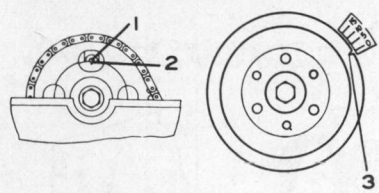

1. Valve timing mark (5/32 in. hole)
2. V-notch—camshaft flange
3. V-notch—crankshaft pulley

"M" series engines (except 5M-GE)—correct alignment of the crankshaft and camshaft timing marks

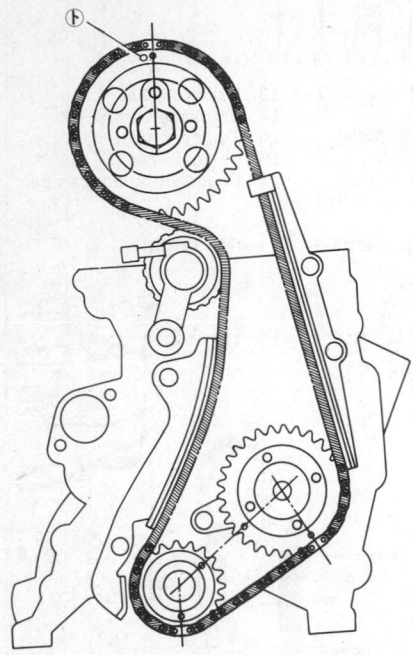

5M-E engines—proper alignment of the timing chain and gear markings

8. Install the cam sprocket so that the timing mark falls between the two bright links on the chain. Fit the oil pump drive spline over the crankshaft key.

9. Install the timing cover gasket on the front of the block. Rotate the camshaft sprocket counterclockwise to remove the slack from the chain.

10. Install the timing chain cover and cylinder head.

5M-E

1. Remove the cylinder head. Remove the front cover.

2. Remove the chain tensioner assembly (arm and gear).

3. Unfasten the bolts which retain the chain damper and damper guide and withdraw the damper and guide.

4. Remove the oil slinger from the crankshaft.

5. Remove the timing chain. Inspect the chain for wear or damage. Replace it if necessary.

6. To install, position the No. 1 cylinder at TDC. Position the crankshaft

sprocket 0-mark downward, facing the oil pan.

7. Align the "Toyota" trademarks on the sprockets. Install the tensioner gear assembly on the block. Its dowel pin should be positioned 1.5 in. from the surface of the block.

8. Install the chain cover over the two gears while maintaining tension. Install both of the vibration dampers an the damper guide. Install the oil slinger to the crankshaft.

9. Tie the chain to the upper vibration damper, to keep it from falling into the chain cover, once the cover is installed. Install the timing cover.

10. Install the cylinder head installation procedure as detailed above.

NOTE: If proper valve timing cannot be obtained, it is possible to adjust it by placing the camshaft slotted pin in the second or third hole on the camshaft timing gear, as required. If the timing is out by more than 15°, replace the chain and both sprockets.

5M-GE

1. Disconnect the negative battery cable.

2. Loosen the mounting bolts of each of the crankshaft-driven components at the front of the engine and remove the drive belts.

3. Rotate the crankshaft in order to set the No. 1 cylinder to TDC of its compression stroke (both valves of the No. 1 cylinder closed, and TDC marks aligned).

4. Remove the upper, front (No. 3) timing belt cover and gasket (five bolts).

5. Loosen the idler pulley bolt and lever the idler pulley toward the alternator side of the engine in order to relieve the tension on the timing belt. Handtighten the idler pulley bolt.

6. Remove the timing belt from the camshaft pulleys.

7. Remove the camshaft timing pulleys as follows. Hold the pulleys stationary with a spanner wrench. Remove the center pulley bolt. Do not attempt to use timing belt tension as a tool to remove the center pulley bolts, as the belt could become damaged.

NOTE: Do not interchange the intake and exhaust timing pulleys, as they differ for use with each camshaft.

8. Remove the center crankshaft pulley bolt. Using a puller, remove the crankshaft pulley.

9. Using chalk or crayon, mark the timing belt to indicate its direction of rotation. This mark must face the same direction during installation of the belt.

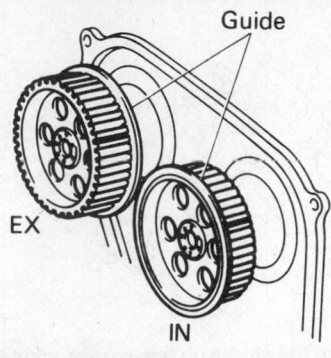

5M-GE engines—When installing the camshaft sprockets, be sure that the guides are positioned as shown. (IN—intake camshaft sprocket; EX—exhaust camshaft sprocket)

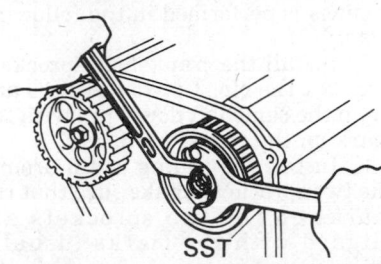

5M-GE engines—Use a spanner wrench (SST) as shown, to hold the camshaft sprocket while loosening the camshaft sprocket bolt. DO NOT attempt to use belt tension to hold the sprocket in place while removing the camshaft sprocket bolt

10. Remove the lower timing belt cover, then the belt.

11. If damaged, the crankshaft pulley can be removed using a puller; the oil pump drive shaft pulley can be removed in the same manner as the camshaft pulleys.

12. Inspect the timing belt for damage, such as cuts, cracks, missing teeth, abrasions, nicks, etc. If the belt teeth are damaged, check that the camshafts rotate freely and correct as necessary.

13. Should damage be evident on the belt face, check the idler pulley belt surface for damage. If damage is present on one side of the belt only, check the belt guide and the alignment of each pulley. If the belt teeth are excessively worn, check the timing belt cover gasket for damage and/or proper installation.

14. Check the idler pulley for damage and smoothness of rotation. Also check the free length of the tension spring, which should be 2.776 in., measured between the inside of each end "clip". Replace the spring if the length exceeds this limit.

15. Install the timing belt as follows. Install the crankshaft and oil pump drive shaft if these items were removed previously. Torque the oil

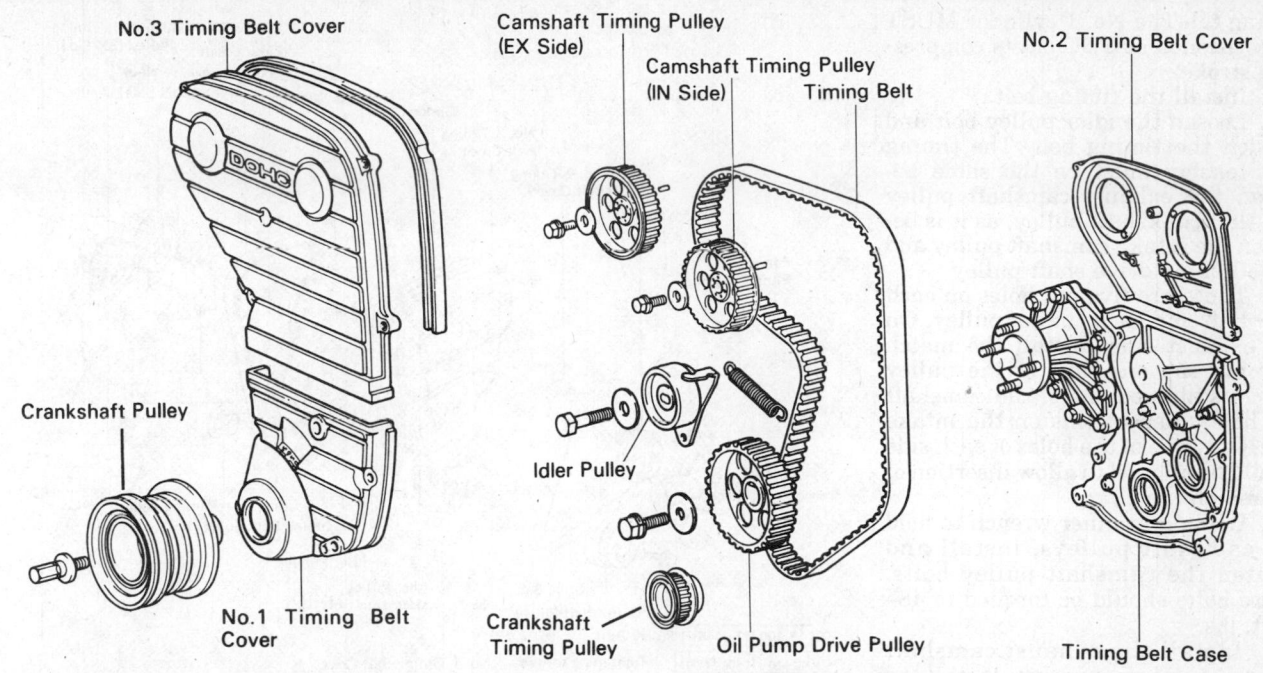

No.3 Timing Belt Cover

Camshaft Timing Pulley
(EX Side)

Camshaft Timing Pulley
(IN Side)

Timing Belt

No.2 Timing Belt Cover

Crankshaft Pulley

No.1 Timing Belt
Cover

Idler Pulley

Crankshaft
Timing Pulley

Oil Pump Drive Pulley

Timing Belt Case

Timing chain, covers and related components—5M-GE engines

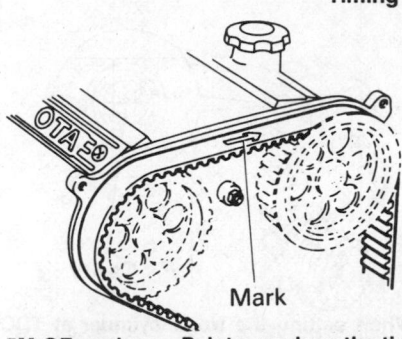

Mark

5M-GE engines—Paint a mark on the timing belt prior to belt removal to indicate the belts direction of normal rotation. Point the mark in the same direction if the belt is to be reinstalled

pump drive shaft center pulley bolt to 14–18 ft. lbs. The crankshaft pulley must be evenly driven into place.

16. Install the idler pulley and the tension spring. Lever the pulley towards the alternator side of the engine and tighten the bolt.

17. Check the mark made during Step 9 of removal and temporarily install the timing belt on the crankshaft pulley. The mark must face in the same direction as it did originally.

18. Install the lower timing belt cover. Install the crankshaft pulley and torque the center pulley bolt to 98–119 ft.lbs.

19. Remove the oil filter cap of the intake camshaft cover, and the complete camshaft cover on the exhaust side.

20. Check that the match holes of both No. 2 camshaft journals are visible through the camshaft housing

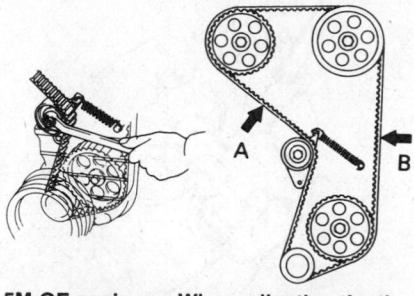

5M-GE engines—When adjusting the timing belt tension, be sure the tension at "A" is the same as that at "B"

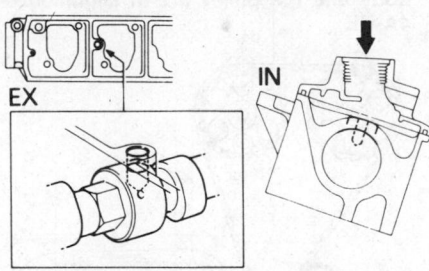

EX   IN

5M-GE engines—Proper alignment of the camshaft matchmarks with the match holes of the camshaft housings (IN—intake; EX—exhaust)

match holes. If necessary, temporarily install the camshaft pulley and guide pin, and rotate the camshaft(s) until the holes are aligned.

21. Install the timing pulleys. Note that the belt guide of the exhaust camshaft pulley should be positioned towards the engine; the belt guide of the intake camshaft pulley should be positioned away from the engine. Do

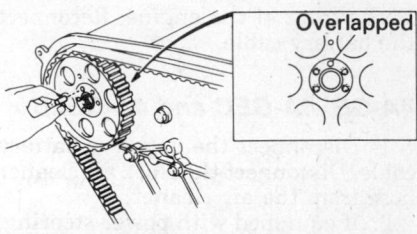

Overlapped

5M-GE engines—Locating the overlapped holes of the camshaft and the camshaft sprocket. Install the match pin into the aligned set of holes (typical of either the intake or exhaust camshaft)

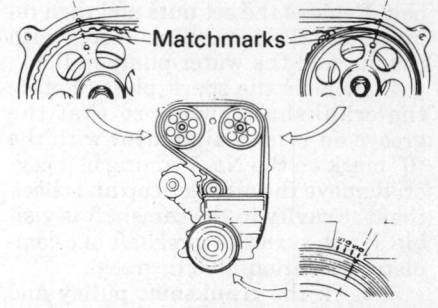

Matchmarks

5M-GE engines—Alignment of the camshaft sprocket marks with the no. 2 timing cover marks. Note the position of the crankshaft pulley (TDC)

not yet install the pulley retaining bolts.

22. Align the following marks. Each camshaft pulley mark must be aligned with its respective mark on the rear, upper (No. 2) timing belt cover. Align the crankshaft pulley notch on with the TDC (0) mark of the

timing tab. The No. 1 cylinder MUST be positioned at TDC on its compression stroke.

23. Install the timing belt.

24. Loosen the idler pulley bolt and tension the timing belt. The timing belt tension must be the same between the exhaust camshaft pulley and the crankshaft pulley, as it is between the intake camshaft pulley and the oil pump drive shaft pulley.

25. There are five pin holes on each camshaft and each timing pulley. On the exhaust side: Install the match pin into the one hole of the pulley which is aligned one of the camshaft pin holes. Repeat this on the intake side. Only one of the holes of each side should be aligned to allow insertion of the match pins.

26. Using a spanner wrench to hold the camshaft pulleys, install and tighten the camshaft pulley bolts. These bolts should be torqued to 48—54 ft. lbs.

27. Install the exhaust camshaft cover, using a new gasket. Install the oil filler cap. Install the timing belt cover and gasket.

28. Install and adjust the drive belts at the front of the engine. Reconnect the battery cable.

4A-GE, 4A-GEC and 4A-GELC

1. Disconnect the negative battery cable. Disconnect the No. 2 air cleaner hose from the air cleaner.

2. If equipped with power steering, remove the power steering pump and position it out of the way. Do not disconnect the pump hydraulic lines.

3. Loosen the water pump pulley set nuts, remove the drive belt adjusting bolt and then remove the drive belt. Remove the set nuts and then remove the fluid coupling along with the fan and the water pump pulley.

4. Remove the spark plugs. Rotate the crankshaft pulley so that the groove on it is in alignment with the "0" mark on the No. 1 timing belt cover. Remove the oil filler cap and check that the cavity in the camshaft is visible. If not, turn the camshaft one complete revolution (360 degrees).

5. Lock the crankshaft pulley and remove the pulley bolt. Using a gear puller, remove the crankshaft pulley. Remove the three timing belt covers and their gaskets. Remove the timing belt guide.

6. Loosen the bolt on the idler pulley, push it to the left as far as it will go and then retighten it. If reusing the timing belt, draw an arrow on it in the direction of engine revolution (clockwise) and then matchmark the belt to the pulleys as indicated.

7. Remove the timing belt. Remove

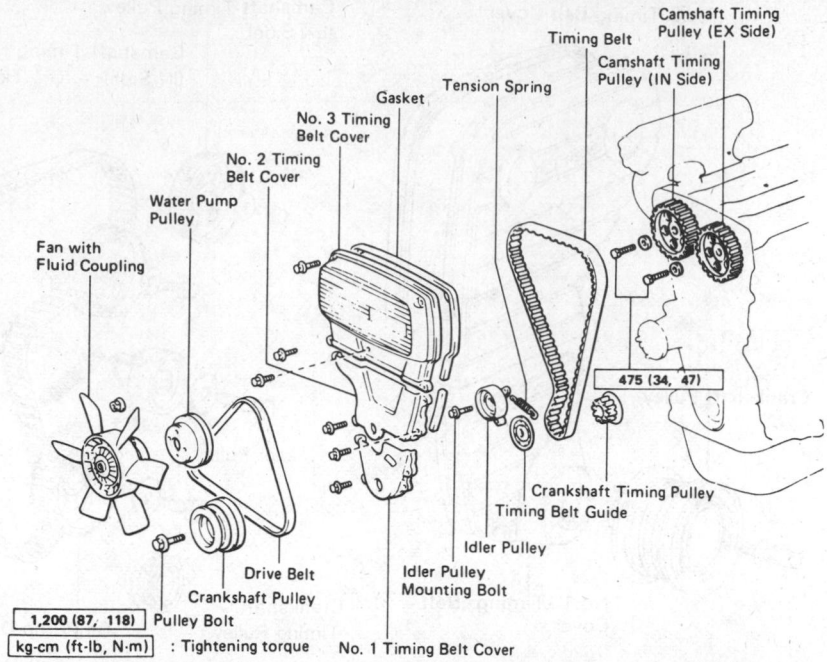

Exploded view of the 4A-GE timing belt and its components

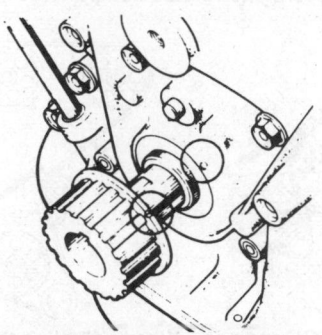

When installing the crankshaft pulley, make sure the TDC marks on the oil pump body and the pulley are in alignment—4A-GE

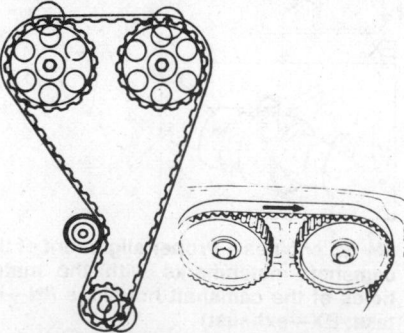

If the timing belt is to be reused, draw a directional arrow and matchmark the belt to the pulleys as shown—4A-GE

the idler pulley bolt, the pulley and the tension spring.

8. Remove the cylinder head covers, lock the camshaft and remove the camshaft timing pulleys.

9. Install the camshaft timing pulleys and cylinder head covers.

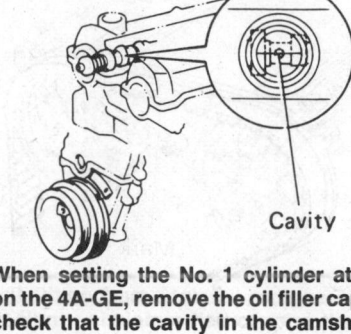

When setting the No. 1 cylinder at TDC on the 4A-GE, remove the oil filler cap and check that the cavity in the camshaft is visible

10. Install the crankshaft timing pulley so that the marks on the pulley and the oil pump body are in alignment.

11. Install the idler pulley and its tension spring, move it to the left as far as it will go and tighten it temporarily.

12. Install the timing belt. If the old one is being used, align all the marks made during removal.

13. Installation of the remaining components is in the reverse order of removal.

3S-FE

1. Disconnect the negative battery cable. Raise and support the vehicle safely. Remove the right tire and wheel assembly.

2. If equipped remove the cruise control actuator and bracket. Remove the drive belts.

3. Remove the alternator and alter-

nator bracket. Raise the engine enough to remove the right side engine mounting assembly.

4. Remove the spark plugs. Remove the number two timing cover. Position the number one cylinder to TDC on the compression stroke.

5. If reusing the belt place matchmarks on the timing belt and the camshaft pulley. Loosen the mount bolt of the NO. 1 idler pulley and position the pulley toward the left as far as it will go. Tighten the bolt. Remove the belt from the camshaft pulley.

6. Remove the camshaft pulley. Remove the crankshaft pulley using the proper removal tool. Remove the No. 2 timing cover.

7. Remove the timing belt and the belt guide. If reusing the belt mark the belt and the crankshaft pulley in the direction of engine rotation.

8. Remove the No. 1 idler pulley and the tension spring. Remove the No. 2 idler pulley. Remove the crankshaft timing pulley. Remove the oil pump pulley.

9. Inspect the belt for defects. Replace as required. Inspect the idler pulleys and springs. Replace defective components as required.

10. Align the cuttouts of the oil pump pulley and shaft. Install the oil pump pulley and torque the retaining nut to 21 ft. lbs.

11. To install the crankshaft pulley, align the pulley set key with the key groove of the pulley and slide it in position. Install the No. 2 idler pulley and torque the bolt to 31 ft. lbs. Be sure that the pulley moves freely.

12. Temporarily install the No. 1 idler pulley and tension spring. Pry the pulley toward the left as far as it will go. Tighten the bolt.

13. Temporarily install the timing belt. If reusing the old belt align the marks made during removal. Install the timing belt guide.

14. Install the No. 1 timing belt cover. Install the crankshaft pulley and torque the bolt to 80 ft. lbs.

15. Install the camshaft pulley by aligning the camshaft knock pin with the knock pin groove. Install the washer and torque the retaining bolt to 40 ft. lbs.

16. With the engine set at TDC on the compression stroke install the timing belt. If reusing the belt align with the marks made during the removal procedure.

17. Once the belt is installed be sure that there is tension between the crankshaft pulley, water pump pulley and camshaft pulley. Loosen the NO. 1 idler pulley mount bolt ½ turn. Turn the crankshaft pulley two revolutions from TDC in the clockwise direction. Torque the No. 1 idler pulley mount bolt to 31 ft. lbs.

18. Continue the installation in the reverse order of the removal procedure.

3E

1. Disconnect the negative battery cable. Remove the right side engine under cover.

2. Remove the drive belts. Remove the alternator and alternator bracket. Remove the air cleaner assembly. Remove the spark plugs.

3. Raise the engine and remove the right side engine mounting insulator assembly.

4. Remove the valve cover. Set the engine to TDC on the compression stroke. Remove the crankshaft pulley using the proper removal tool.

5. Remove both timing belt covers. Remove the timing belt guide. Remove the timing belt and the No. 1 idler pulley. If using the old belt matchmark it in the direction of engine rotation. Matchmark the pulleys.

6. Remove the tension spring. Remove the No. 2 idler pulley. Remove the crankshaft pulley. Remove the camshaft pulley. Remove the oil pump pulley.

7. Inspect the belt for defects. Replace as required. Inspect the idler pulleys and springs. Replace defective components as required.

8. Align and install the oil pump pulley. Torque the retaining bolt to 20 ft. lbs.

9. To install the camshaft timing pulley, align the camshaft knock pin with the No. 1 bearing cap mark. Align the knock pin hole on the 3E mark side with the camshaft knock pin hole. Torque the retaining bolt to 37 ft. lbs.

10. Install the crankshaft timing pulley and align the TDC marks on the oil pump body and the crankshaft timing pulley. Install the No. 1 idler pulley. Pry the idler pulley toward the left as far as it will go and tempororarily tighten the retaining bolt.

11. Install the No. 2 idle pulley and torque the retaining bolt to 20 ft. lbs. Install the timing belt. If reusing the old belt align it with the marks made during the removal procedure.

12. Inspect the valve timing and the belt tension by loosening the No 1 idler pulley set bolt. Temporarily install the crankshaft pulley bolt and turn the crankshaft two complete revcolutions in the clockwise direction.

13. Check that each pulley aligns with the proper markings. Torque the No. 1 idler pulley bolt to 13 ft. lbs.

Check for proper belt tension. Install the belt guide.

14. Install the timing belt covers. Align and install the crankshaft pulley. Torque the retaining bolt to 112 ft. lbs.

15. Continue the installation in the reverse order of the removal procedure.

7M-GE and 7M-GTE

1. Disconnect the negative battery cable. Drain the cooling system. Remove the radiator. Remove the water outlet.

2. Remove the spark plugs. Remove the drive belts. Remove the No. 3 timing belt cover.

3. Position the engine at TDC on the compression stroke. Remove the timing belt from the camshaft sprockets. If reusing the belt matchmark the belt and the sprockets in the direction of engine rotation.

4. Remove the camshaft pulleys. Remove the crankshaft pulley using the proper removal tools. Remove the power steering air pipe, if equipped.

5. If equipped with air condition remove the compressor and position it out of the way. Do not disconnect the refrigerant lines.

6. Remove the No. 1 timing belt cover. Remove the timing belt. Remove the idler pulley and the tension spring. Remove the oil pump drive pulley.

7. Inspect the belt for defects. Replace as required. Inspect the idler pulleys and springs. Replace defective components as required.

8. Install the oil pump drive pulley and retaining bolt. Torque the bolt to 16 ft. lbs.

9. Install the crankshaft timing pulley. Temporarily install the idler pulley and tension spring. Torque the assembly to 36 ft. lbs. Pry the idler pulley toward the left as far as it will go and temporarily tighten the bolt.

10. Temporarily install the timing belt. If reusing the old belt install it using the marks made during the removal procedure. Install the No. 1 timing belt cover.

11. If equipped with air condition, install the compressor assembly. If equipped, install the power steering air pipe.

12. Align the set key with the key groove and install the crankshaft pulley and torque the retaining bolt to 195 ft. lbs.

13. Install the camshaft timing pulleys. Torque the retaining bolts to 36 ft. lbs.

14. Loosen the idler pulley bolt. Install the timing belt to the INTAKE side and the EXHAUST side. Torque the idler pulley bolt to 36 ft. lbs.

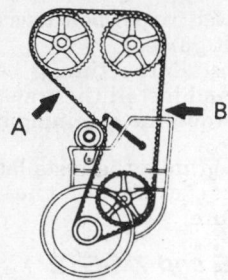

7M-GE and 7M-GTE timing belt tension check

15. Make sure that the timing belt tension A is equal to the timing belt tension B. If not adjust the idler pulley. Turn the engine two complete revolutions in the clockwise direction and check to see that everything is aligned properly.

16. Turn both the intake and exhaust camshaft pulleys inward at the same time to slaken the timing belt between the two sprockets. Belt defelection should be 4.4–6.6 lbs. If not adjust the idler pulley.

17. Continue the installation in the reverse order of the removal procedure.

Camshaft

REMOVAL & INSTALLATION

2S-E

1. Remove the timing belt. Remove the cylinder head cover.
2. Remove the camshaft pulley. Remove the camshaft bearing caps.
3. Turning the camshaft slowly, slide it from the housing.
4. Installation is the reverse of the removal procedure. Always use new oil seals.

1C-L, 1C-TL and 2C-T

1. Remove the cylinder head.
2. Remove the camshaft pulley.
3. Remove the thrust plate.
4. Unbolt and remove the camshaft bearing caps.
5. Turning the camshaft slowly, slide the camshaft from the head.
6. Installation is the reverse of the removal procedure.

3Y-EC and 4Y-EC

1. Remove the timing chain.
2. Remove the camshaft thrust plate.
3. Turning the camshaft slowly, slide it from the block.
4. Installation is the reverse of the removal procedure. Coat the camshaft with clean engine oil prior to insertion.

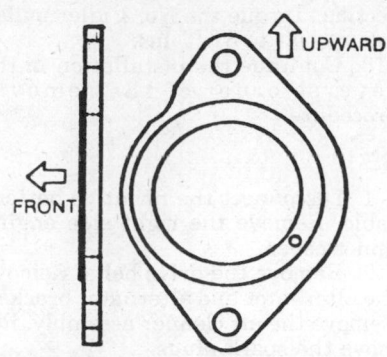

Proper positioning of the thrust plate—K-series engines

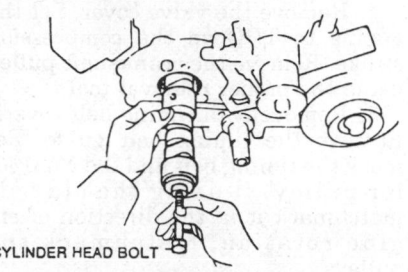

Use a cylinder head bolt to remove and install the camshaft

4K-C, 4K-E and 3T-C

1. Remove the cylinder head.
2. Remove the distributor. Remove the radiator.
3. Remove the timing chain.
4. Remove the valve lifters in the proper sequence. Be sure to keep them in order.
5. Remove the fuel pump on carbureted engines.
6. Remove the two thrust plate set bolts and pull off the thrust plate.
7. Screw a cylinder head bolt into the end of the camshaft. Slowly turn the camshaft and pull it out being careful not to damage the bearing.
8. Inspect the camshaft and bearings.
9. Coat the camshaft bearings and journals lightly with oil and then carefully install it into the cylinder block.
10. Install the thrust plate in the proper position and torque the two bolts to 4–6 ft. lbs. on the 4K-C and 4K-E engines and 7–11 ft. lbs. on the 3T-C engine.
11. Installation of the remaining components is in the reverse order of removal procedure.

5M-GE

1. Remove the two camshaft covers.
2. Remove the timing belt assembly.
3. Following the sequence shown, loosen the camshaft housing nuts and

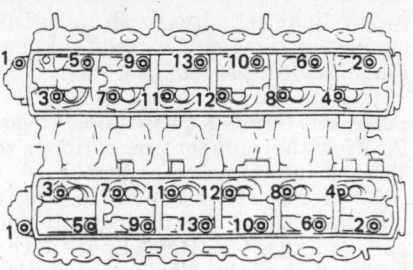

5M-GE camshaft housing bolt removal sequence. Loosen bolts gradually on three passes

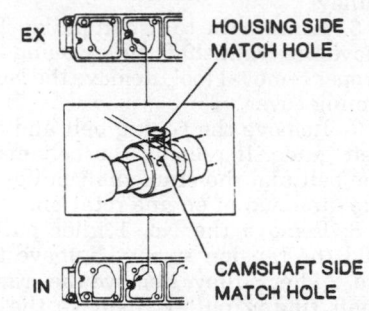

5M-GE camshaft housing torque sequence

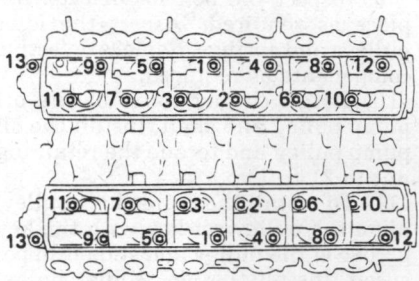

Before installing the camshaft housings, align the match hole on each No. 2 cam journal with the hole in the housing

bolts in three passes. Remove the housings (with camshafts) from the cylinder head.

4. Remove the camshaft housing rear covers. Squirt clean oil down around the cam journals in the housing, to lubricate the lobes, oil seals and bearings as the cam is removed. Begin to pull the camshaft out of the back of the housing slowly, turning it as you pull. Remove the cam completely.

5. To install, lubricate the entire camshaft with clean oil. Insert the cam into the housing from the back, and slowly turn it as you push it into the housing. Install new O-rings and the housing end covers.

6. Installation of the remaining components is in the reverse order of removal. Tighten camshaft housing bolts to 15–17 ft. lbs. in the proper sequence.

All Other Engines

All of these engines utilize an over-

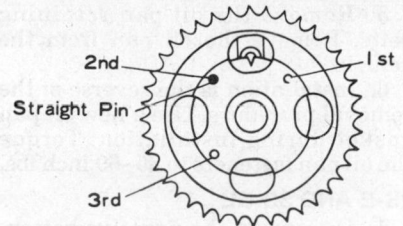

"M" series engines (except 5M-GE)—camshaft sprocket installation for 3–9° valve timing retard

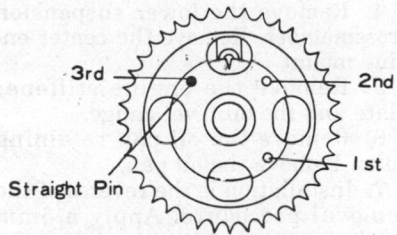

"M" series engines (except 5M-GE)—camshaft sprocket installation for 9–15° valve timing retard

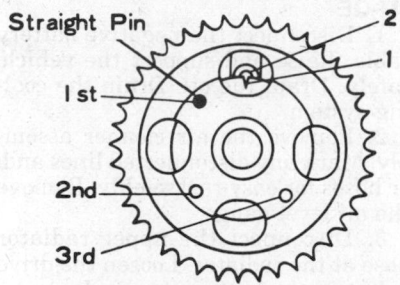

"M" series engines (except 5M-GE)—camshaft sprocket installation for normal valve timing

head camshaft (OHC). Therefore, the procedure for removing the camshaft is given as part of the cylinder head removal procedure.

NOTE: It will not be necessary to completely remove the cylinder head in order to remove the camshaft. Therefore, proceed only as far as necessary, to remove the camshaft, with the cylinder head removal procedure.

Piston and Connecting Rod

POSITIONING

For all piston and connecting rod overhaul procedures, please refer to "Engine Rebuilding" in the Unit Repair section.

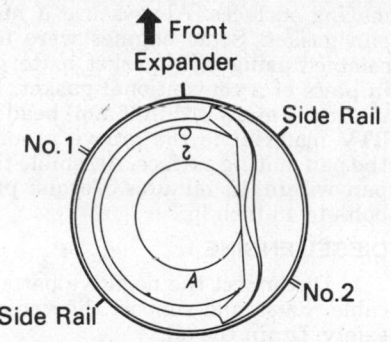

Piston ring gap positioning—"A" series engines

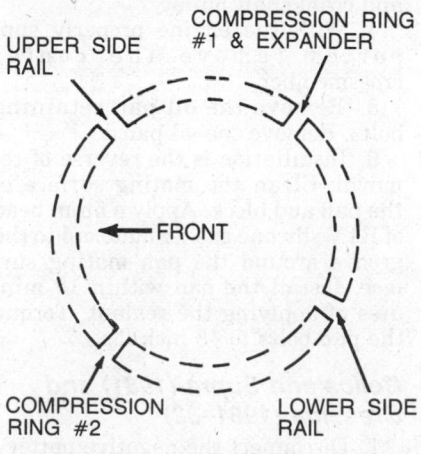

Piston ring gap positioning—"M" series engines

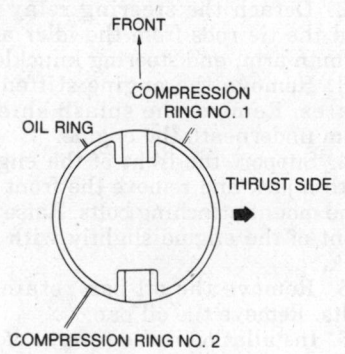

Piston ring gap positioning—"K" series engines

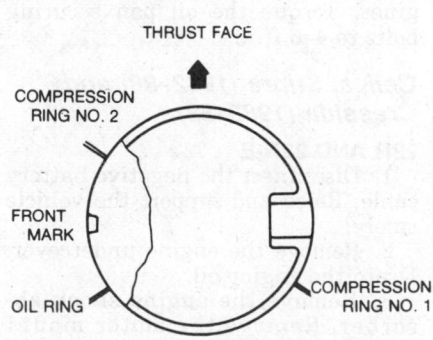

Piston ring gap positioning—"R" series engines

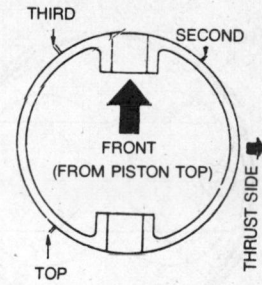

Piston ring gap positioning—"T" series engines

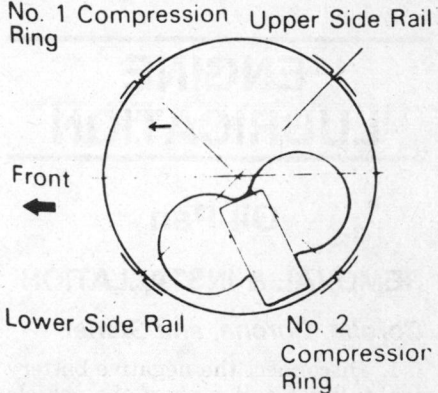

Piston ring gap positioning—diesel engines

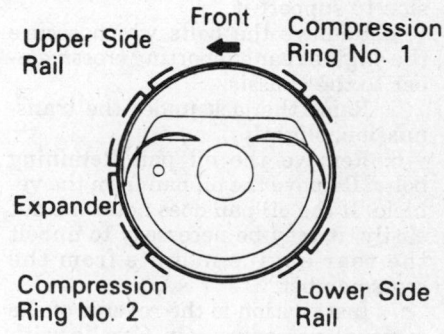

Piston ring gap positioning—2S-E

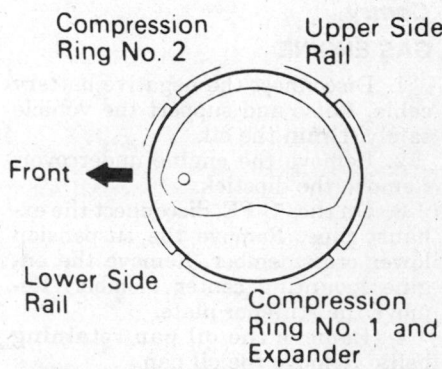

Piston ring gap positioning—3Y-EC and 4Y-EC

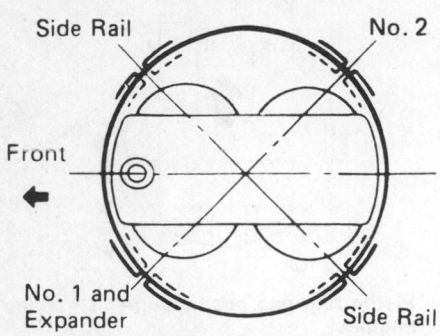

Piston ring gap positioning—4A-GE

ENGINE LUBRICATION

Oil Pan

REMOVAL & INSTALLATION

Corolla, Corona, and Starlet

1. Disconnect the negative battery cable. Raise and support the vehicle safely. Drain the oil.
2. Remove the splash shield from underneath the engine.
3. Place a jack under the transmission to support it.
4. Remove the bolts which secure the engine rear supporting crossmember to the chassis.
5. Raise the jack under the transmission, slightly.
6. Remove the oil pan Retaining bolts. Remove the oil pan from the vehicle. If the oil pan does not come out easily, it may be necessary to unbolt the rear engine mounts from the crossmember.
7. Installation is the reverse of the removal procedure. On Corolla with 3T-C engine and Corona, apply liquid sealer to the four corners of the oil pan.

Camry

GAS ENGINE

1. Disconnect the negative battery cable. Raise and support the vehicle safely. Drain the oil.
2. Remove the engine undercover. Remove the dipstick.
3. On the 3S-FE, disconnect the exhaust pipe. Remove the suspension lower crossmember. Remove the engine mounting center member. Remove the stiffener plate.
4. Remove the oil pan retaining bolts. Remove the oil pan.
5. Installation is the reverse of the removal procedure. Clean the gasket

mating surfaces. Always use a new pan gasket. Some engines were assembled using RTV gasket material in place of a conventional gasket. In that case, apply a thin (5mm) bead of RTV material to the groove around the pan mating surface. Assemble the pan within 15 minutes. Torque pan bolts to 48 inch lb.

DIESEL ENGINE

1. Disconnect the negative battery cable. Raise and support the vehicle safely. Drain the oil.
2. Remove the engine undercovers. Remove the timing belt.
3. Remove the lower idler pulley and crankshaft pulley.
4. With the engine properly supported remove the center crossmember.
5. Remove the oil pan retaining bolts. Remove the oil pan.
6. Installation is the reverse of removal. Clean the mating surface of the pan and block. Apply a 5mm bead of RTV silicone gasket material to the groove around the pan mating surface. Install the pan within 15 minutes of applying the sealant. Torque the pan bolts to 48 inch lbs.

Celica and Supra (1981) and Cressida (1981–82)

1. Disconnect the negative battery cable. Raise and support the vehicle safely. Drain the oil.
2. Detach the steering relay rod and the tie rods from the idler arm, pitman arm, and steering knuckles.
3. Remove the engine stiffening plates. Remove the splash shields from underneath the engine.
4. Support the front of the engine with a jack and remove the front engine mount attaching bolts. Raise the front of the engine slightly with the jack.
5. Remove the oil pan retaining bolts. Remove the oil pan.
6. Installation is the reverse of the removal procedure. Apply liquid sealer to the four corners of the oil pan gasket used on 2T-C and 3T-C engines. Torque the oil pan securing bolts to 4–6 ft. lbs.

Celica, Supra (1982–88) and Cressida (1983–88)

22R AND 22R-E

1. Disconnect the negative battery cable. Raise and support the vehicle safely.
2. Remove the engine undercover. Drain the engine oil.
3. Remove the engine shock absorber. Remove the motor mount bolts.
4. Place a jack under the transmission and raise the engine slightly.

5. Remove the oil pan retaining bolts. Remove the oil pan from the vehicle.
6. Installation is the reverse of the removal procedure. Use a new oil pan gasket during installation. Torque the oil pan fasteners to 35–69 inch lbs.

2S-E AND 3S-GE

1. Disconnect the negative battery cable. Raise the vehicle and support it safely. Drain the engine oil.
2. Remove the engine undercovers.
3. On the 3S-GE, disconnect the exhaust pipe from the exhaust manifold.
4. Remove the lower suspension crossmember. Remove the center engine mount.
5. Remove the engine stiffener plate and the oil level gauge.
6. Remove the oil pan retaining bolts. Remove the oil pan.
7. Installation is the reverse of the removal procedure. Apply a 5mm bead of RTV gasket material to the groove around the pan flange. Apply the oil within 3 minutes of application and tighten the mounting bolts and nuts to 48 inch lbs.

5M-GE

1. Disconnect the negative battery cable. Raise and support the vehicle safely. Drain the oil. Drain the cooling system.
2. Remove the air cleaner assembly. Mark any disconnected lines and/or hoses for easy reassembly. Remove the oil level gauge.
3. Disconnect the upper radiator hose at the radiator. Loosen the drive belts.
4. Remove the fan shroud bolts. Remove the four fluid coupling flange attaching nuts, then remove the fluid coupling along with the fan and the fan shroud.
5. Remove the engine undercover. Remove the exhaust pipe clamp bolt from the exhaust pipe stay.
6. Remove the two stiffener plates from the exhaust pipe. If equipped with manual transmission, remove the clutch housing undercover.
7. Remove the four engine mount bolts from each side of the engine.
8. Place a jack under the transmission and raise the engine about 1¾ in.
9. Remove the oil pan retaining bolts. Remove the oil pan from the engine.
10. Installation is the reverse of the removal procedure. Use a new oil pan gasket during installation. Apply a small amount of sealer to the oil pan gasket at each of the four corners of the oil pan. Torque the oil pan fasteners to 57–82 inch lbs.

7M-GE and 7M-GTE

1. Disconnect the negative battery cable. Remove the hood.

2. Raise and support the vehicle safely. Remove the engine under cover. Drain the engine oil.

3. If equipped with automatic transmission, remove the fluid cooler hose clamp.

4. Remove the No. 1 front suspension crossmember. Remove the front exhaust pipe bracket and stiffener plates.

5. On the 7M-GTE disconnect the engine oil cooler hose from the engine oil pan.

6. Remove the brake hose brackets and clips. Disconnect the intermediate shaft. Disconnect the stabilizer bar links from the lower control arms.

7. Properly support the engine assembly. Remove the engine mounting bolts. Remove the Tems actuator assembly.

8. Remove the shock absorbers from the body. Disconnect the front suspension member.

9. Remove the oil pan retaining bolts. Remove the oil pan from the engine.

10. Installation is the reverse of the removal procedure.

Tercel

1A-C, 3A and 3A-C

1. Disconnect the negative battery cable. Drain the cooling system. Remove the radiator.

2. Raise and support the vehicle safely. Drain the engine oil.

3. Remove the engine under cover. Remove the stabilizer bracket bolts and lower the stabilizer assembly. Remove the right and left stiffener plates.

4. Remove the oil pan retaining bolts. Remove the oil pan from the vehicle.

5. Installation is the reverse of the removal procedure.

3E

1. Disconnect the negative battery terminal. Raise and support the vehicle safely. Drain the oil.

2. Remove the right hand engine under cover. Remove the sway bar and any other necessary steering linkage parts.

3. Disconnect the exhaust pipe from the manifold. Raise the engine enough to take the weight off of it.

4. Remove the timing belt.

5. Continue to raise the engine enough to remove the oil pan. Remove the oil pan retaining bolts. Remove the oil pan.

6. Installation is the reverse of the removal procedure.

MR2

1. Disconnect the negative battery

cable. Raise and support the vehicle safely. Drain the engine oil.

2. Remove the exhaust manifold pipe. Remove the timing belt. Remove the crankshaft timing pulley.

3. Support the weight of the engine with a floor jack and then remove the right side engine mount.

4. Remove the oil pan retaining bolts. remove the oil pan..

5. Installation is in the reverse order of removal. Apply a 3mm bead of RTV gasket material to the groove around the pan flange. Apply the oil pan within 5 minutes of application and tighten the mounting bolts and nuts to 43 inch lbs.

Van

1. Disconnect the negative battery cable. raise and support the vehicle safely. Drain the oil.

2. Remove the left and right stiffener plates.

3. Remove the oil pan retaining bolts. remove the oil pan from the vehicle.

4. Installation is the reverse of the removal procedure. Clean the pan and block mating surfaces. Apply a 5mm bead of RTV gasket material to the groove around the pan flange. Install the pan within 15 minutes of applying the sealant. Torque the pan bolts to 9 ft. lbs.

Rear Main Oil Seal
REMOVAL & INSTALLATION

NOTE: The 1A-C, 3A and 3A-C engines must be removed from the vehicle before this procedure can be attempted.

1. Remove the transmission.
2. Remove the clutch cover assembly and flywheel.
3. Remove the oil seal retaining plate, complete with the oil seal.
4. Using a suitable tool pry the old seal from the retaining plate. Be careful not to damage the plate.
5. Install the new seal, carefully, by using a block of wood to drift into place. Do not damage the seal as a leak will result.
6. Lubricate the lips of the seal with multipurpose grease. Installation is the reverse of removal.

Oil Pump
REMOVAL & INSTALLATION
All Others

1. Remove the oil pan.
2. Unbolt the oil pump retaining bolts. Remove the oil pump from the engine.

3. Installation is the reverse of the removal procedure.

1A-C, 3A, 3A-C, 2S-E, 3S-GE, 4A-C RWD and 4A-GE

1. Remove the fan shroud. Raise and support the vehicle safely.

2. Drain the oil. On the Tercel, drain the coolant and remove the radiator.

3. Remove the oil pan and the oil strainer. Remove the crankshaft pulley and the timing belt. Remove the oil lever gauge guide and then the gauge.

4. Remove the mounting bolts and then use a rubber mallet to carefully tap the oil pump body from the cylinder block.

5. To install, position a new gasket on the cylinder block.

6. Position the oil pump on the block so that the teeth on the pump drive gear are engaged with the teeth of the crankshaft gear.

7. Installation of the remaining components is in the reverse order of removal.

4A-C FWD and 1C-L Diesel

1. Disconnect the negative battery cable. Remove the hood.

2. Raise and support the vehicle safely. Remove the engine cover under. Drain the oil.

3. Disconnect the center engine mount. Remove the oil pan and oil strainer.

4. Attach an engine hoist to the two engine lifting brackets and suspend the engine.

5. Remove the drive belts. Remove the water pump pulley, air condition idler pulley and the crankshaft pulley.

6. Remove the timing belt. Remove the oil lever gauge guide and then the gauge.

7. Remove the mounting bolts and then use a rubber mallet to carefully tap the oil pump body from the cylinder block.

8. To install, position a new gasket on the cylinder block.

9. Position the oil pump on the block so that the teeth on the pump drive gear are engaged with the teeth of the crankshaft gear.

10. Installation of the remaining components is in the reverse order of removal.

22R and 22R-E Series

1. Remove the oil pan.
2. Remove the three bolts which secure the oil strainer.
3. Remove the drive belts, the pulley bolt, and the crankshaft pulley.
4. Unfasten the bolts which secure

the oil pump housing and remove the pump assembly.

5. Remove the oil pump drive spline and the rubber O-ring.

6. Installation is the reverse of removal. Apply a sealer to the top oil pump housing bolts. Use a new oil strainer gasket.

3S-FE and 3E

1. Remove the oil pan. Remove the oil strainer. On 3E remove the dipstick.

2. Raise the engine using a chain hoist. Remove the timing belt and Pulleys.

3. Remove the oil pump from the engine.

4. Installation is the reverse of the removal procedure.

ENGINE COOLING

Radiator

REMOVAL & INSTALLATION

1. Disconnect the negative battery cable. Drain the cooling system.

2. Remove the radiator hoses. If equipped with an automatic transmission, Disconnect and plug the oil cooler lines.

3. Remove the hood lock from the radiator upper support, as required. It may be necessary to remove the grille in order to gain access to the hood lock/radiator support assembly.

4. Remove the fan shroud, as required. If equipped with electric fan, disconnect the wiring harness and thermoswitch connector.

5. Disconnect the hose from the thermal expansion tank and remove the tank from its bracket.

6. Unbolt and remove the radiator upper support.

7. Remove the radiator retaining bolts. Remove the radiator from the vehicle.

8. Installation is the reverse of the removal procedure.

Water Pump

REMOVAL & INSTALLATION

1. Disconnect the negative battery cable. Drain the cooling system.

2. Remove the fan shroud retaining bolts and remove the fan shroud, if equipped. Loosen and remove all drive belts.

3. Remove all necessary components in order to gain access to the water pump retaining bolts.

4. On some vehicles it will be necessary to remove the timing covers. On Camry equipped with a diesel engine, remove the timing covers and injection pump pulley.

5. As required remove the complete air cleaner assembly.

6. Remove all hoses from the water pump assembly.

7. Remove the water pump retaining bolts. Remove the water pump and fan assembly.

NOTE: If the fan is equipped with a fluid coupling, do not tip the fan/pump assembly on its side, as the fluid will run out.

8. Installation is the reverse of the removal procedure. Always use a new gasket between the pump body and its mounting. Check for leaks after installation is completed.

Thermostat

REMOVAL & INSTALLATION

1. Disconnect the negative battery cable. Drain the cooling system.

2. Remove the upper radiator hose from the thermostat housing.

3. Remove the thermostat housing retaining bolts. Remove the thermostat housing from the engine.

4. Remove the thermostat.

5. Installation is the reverse of the removal procedure. Be sure to use a new thermostat gasket. Be sure that the thermostat is installed with the spring pointing down.

EMISSION CONTROLS

Please refer to "Emission Control" in the Unit Repair section for system maintenance procedures. Due to the complex nature of modern electronic engine control systems, comprehensive diagnosis and testing procedures fall outside the confines of this repair manual. For complete information on diagnosis, testing and repair procedures concerning all modern engine and emission control systems, please refer to *"Chilton's Guide to Electronic Engine Controls".*

MAINTENANCE REMINDER STYTEM

The warning light comes on while the engine is being cranked, to test its operation, just like any of the other warning lights.

1. If the warning light comes on and stays on, check the components of the air injection system. If these are not defective, check the ignition system for faulty leads, plugs, points, or control box.

2. If no problems can be found check the wiring for the light or shorts or opened circuits.

3. If nothing else can be found wrong check the operation of the emission control system computer.

OXYGEN SENSOR WARNING LIGHT

Many vehicles are equipped with an oxygen sensor warning light on the instrument panel. The light may go on when the vehicle is started, then it should go out. If the light stays on, check your odometer. The light is hooked up to an elapsed mileage counter which goes off every 30,000 miles. This is your signal that it is time to replace the oxygen sensor and have the entire system checked out. After replacement of the sensor, the elapsed mileage counter must be reset.

Reset Procedure

MILEAGE COUNTER

1. Locate the counter. It can be found under the left side of the instrument panel, on the brake pedal bracket.

2. Unscrew the mounting bolt, disconnect the wiring connector and remove the counter.

3. Remove the bolt on top of the counter.

4. Lift off the counter cover and push the reset switch. The warning light on the instrument panel must go out at this time.

5. Installation is in the reverse order of removal.

CANCEL SWITCH

To reset the warning light remove the canel switch. Pry open the tab and move the switch to the opposite position. On all vehicles except Cressida the switch is usuall located behind or above the left kick panel. On Cressida the switch is located on a small panel next to the steering column.

GASOLINE ENGINE FUEL SYSTEM

Fuel Filter

REPLACEMENT

Carbureted Engines

All engines employ a disposable, in line filter; when dirty, or at recommended intervals, remove from line and replace.

Fuel Injected Engines

IN-LINE FILTERS

1. Unbolt the retaining screws and remove the protective shield for the fuel filter.
2. Place a pan under the delivery pipe (large connection) to catch the dripping fuel and SLOWLY loosen the union bolt to bleed off the fuel pressure.
3. Remove the union bolt and drain the remaining fuel.
4. Disconnect and plug the inlet line.
5. Unbolt and remove the fuel filter.

NOTE: When tightening the fuel line bolts to the fuel filter, you must use a torque wrench. The tightening torque is very important, as under or over tightening may cause fuel leakage. Insure that there is no fuel line interference and that there is sufficient clearance between it and any other parts.

6. Coat the flare nut, union nut and bolt threads with engine oil.
7. Hand tighten the inlet line to the fuel filter.
8. Install the fuel filter and then tighten the inlet bolt to 23–33 ft. lbs.
9. Reconnect the delivery pipe using new gaskets and then tighten the union bolt to 18–25 ft. lbs.
10. Run the engine for a few minutes and check for any fuel leaks.
11. Install the protective shield.

IN-TANK FILTERS

1. Disconnect the negative battery cable. Drain the gasoline from the fuel tank.
2. Remove the fuel tank from the vehicle as outlined in this section.
3. Remove the fuel pump bracket retaining bolts and remove the fuel pump bracket.
4. Remove the retaining clip from the fuel filter hose and remove the fuel filter.
5. Install a new fuel filter and reverse the removal procedure to complete the installation procedure.

Mechanical Fuel Pump

All 1A-C, 3A, 3A-C, 3T-C and 4A-C engines use a mechanical type fuel pump. It is located on the right rear of the cylinder head. 20R and 22R engines also use a mechanical type fuel pump. It is located on the right front of the cylinder head.

REMOVAL & INSTALLATION

1. Disconnect and plug the fuel lines to the pump.
2. Remove the bolts which hold the pump to the cylinder head.
3. Remove the pump assembly.
4. Installation is the reverse of removal. Always use a new gasket when installing a fuel pump.

TESTING

1. Remove the line which runs from the fuel pump to the carburetor.
2. Attach a pressure gauge to the outlet side of the pump.
3. Run the engine and check the pressure.
4. Check the pressure against the specifications.
5. If the pressure is below the specifications replace the pump.
6. Reconnect the carburetor line.

Electric Fuel Pump

All models (except those mentioned previously) use an electric fuel pump.

On models with carbureted engines, and all late model engines with fuel injection, the electric fuel pump is located inside of the fuel tank. On certain early fuel injected engines, the fuel pump is mounted at the rear of the vehicle, outside of the fuel tank.

Either type of fuel pump cannot be repaired if defective—it must be replaced.

REMOVAL & INSTALLATION

In-Tank Models

1. Disconnect the negative (–) cable from the battery.

NOTE: On most models, removal of the fuel tank is necessary.

2. On sedans and hardtops, remove the trim panel from inside the trunk.
3. On station wagons, raise the rear of the vehicle, in order to gain access to the pump.

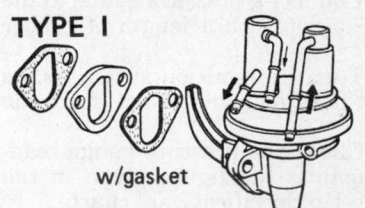

TYPE I

w/gasket

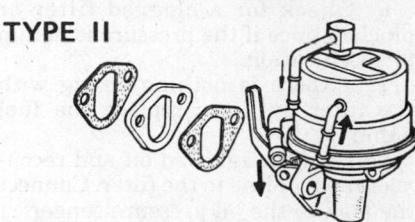

TYPE II

Typical mechanical fuel pump styles

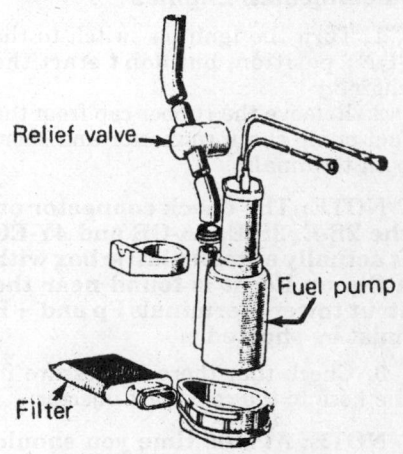

Relief valve

Fuel pump

Filter

Typical electric fuel pump

4. Remove the screws which secure the pump access plate to the tank. Withdraw the plate, gasket, and pump assembly.
5. Disconnect the leads and hoses from the pump.
6. Installation is performed in the reverse order of removal. Use a new gasket on the pump access plate.

In-Line Models

The pump used on these models is removed by simply disconnecting the fuel lines and electrical connector from the pump and dismounting the pump.

TESTING

— **CAUTION** —

Do not operate the fuel pump unless it is immersed in gasoline and connected to its resistor.

Carbureted Engines

1. Disconnect the lead from the oil pressure warning light sender.
2. Unfasten the line from the outlet side of the fuel filter.

3. Connect a pressure gauge to the filter outlet with a length of rubber hose.

4. Turn the ignition switch to the "ON" position, but do not start the engine.

5. Check the pressure gauge reading against the figure given in the "Tune-Up Specifications" chart.

6. Check for a clogged filter or pinched lines if the pressure is not up to specification.

7. If there is nothing wrong with the filter or lines, replace the fuel pump.

8. Turn the ignition off and reconnect the fuel line to the filter. Connect the lead to the oil pressure sender.

Fuel Injected Engines

1. Turn the ignition switch to the "ON" position, but don't start the engine.

2. Remove the rubber cap from the fuel pump check connector and short both terminals.

NOTE: The check connector on the 2S-E, 3S-E, 4A-GE and 4Y-EC is actually a small plastic box with a flip-up lid; it is found near the strut tower. Terminals Fp and +B must be shorted.

3. Check that there is pressure in the hose to the cold start injector.

NOTE: At this time you should be able to hear the fuel return noise from the pressure regulator.

4. If no pressure can be felt in the line, check the fuses and all other related electrical connections. If everything is alright, the fuel pump will probably require replacement.

5. Remove the service wire, reinstall the rubber cap and turn off the ignition switch.

Fuel Return Cut Valve

Carbureted Engines Only

The fuel return cut valve controls the amount of fuel returned to the gas tank according to the engine load. This prevents percolation when the engine is hot and the load light.

INSPECTION

Attach a long tube to the return pipe of the valve. Put a container under it to catch the fuel. With the engine at idle, fuel should go into the container. Pinch off the vacuum line. If the valve is operating correctly, the fuel flow should stop.

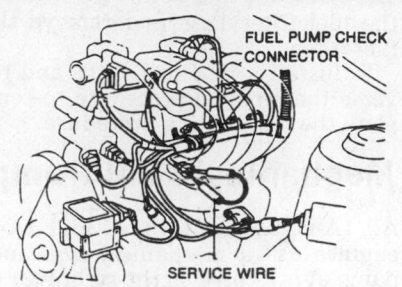

Shorting the fuel pump check connector—typical

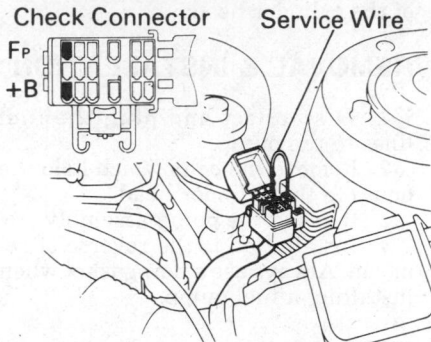

Shorting the fuel pump check connector—box-type (3S-GE shown)

Carburetors

The carburetors used on Toyota models are conventional two barrel, downdraft types similar to domestic carburetors.

REMOVAL & INSTALLATION

NOTE: During carburetor removal, be sure to mark all hoses, lines and electrical connectors, etc., so that these items may be properly reconnected during installation.

1. Remove the air cleaner housing, disconnect all air hoses from the air cleaner base, and disconnect the battery ground cable.

NOTE: On 20R and 22R engines, drain the coolant to prevent it from running into the intake manifold when the carburetor is removed.

2. Disconnect the fuel line, choke pipe, and distributor vacuum line. On 20R and 22R engines disconnect the choke coolant hose.

3. Remove the accelerator linkage. (With an automatic transmission, also remove the throttle rod to the transmission.)

4. Disconnect any remaining hoses, etc., from the carburetor.

5. Remove the four nuts that secure the carburetor to the manifold

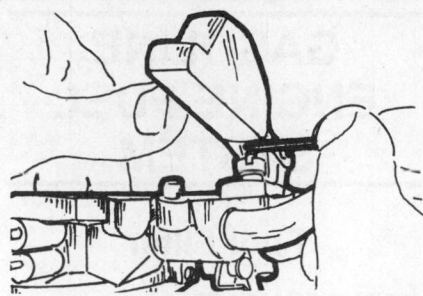

"A" and "T" series engines—measure the lowered float level as shown

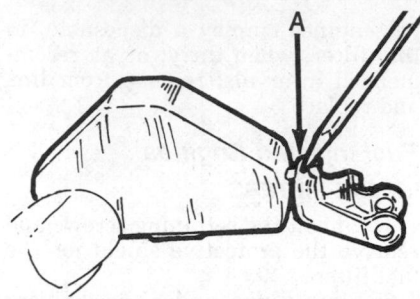

"A" and "T" series engines—adjust the raised float level at (A)

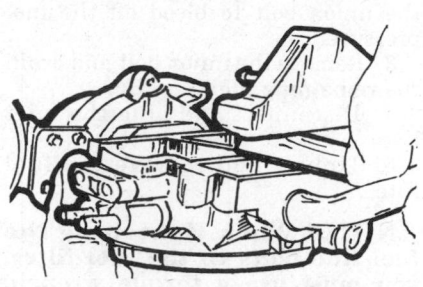

"A" and "T" series engines—measure the raised float level as shown

and lift off the carburetor and gasket.

6. Cover the open manifold with a clean rag to prevent small objects from dropping into the engine.

7. Installation is performed in the reverse order of removal. After the engine is started, check for fuel leaks and float level settings.

OVERHAUL

For all carburetor overhaul procedures, please refer to "Carburetor Service" in the Unit Repair section.

FLOAT LEVEL ADJUSTMENT

Float level adjustments are unnecessary on models equipped with a carburetor sight glass, if the fuel level falls within the lines or aligns with the dot when the engine is running.

There are two float level adjustments which may be made on Toyota carburetors. One is with the air horn inverted, so that the float is in a fully

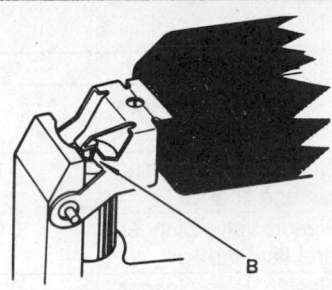

"K" series engines—adjust the lowered float level at (B)

"K" series engines—adjust the raised float level at (A)

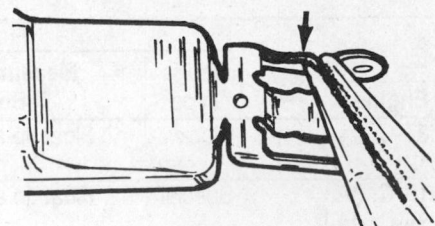

"A" and "T" series engines—adjust the lowered float level at (B)

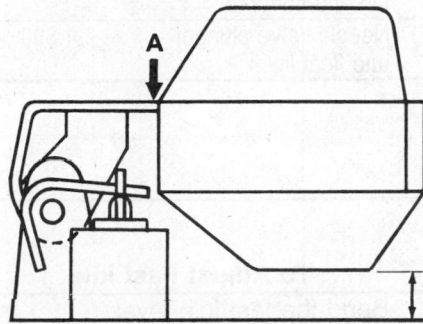

"R" series engines—measure as indicated and bend at (A) to adjust

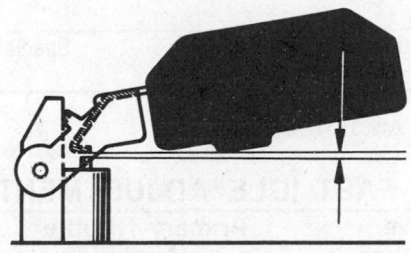

"K" series engines—measure the lowered float level as indicated

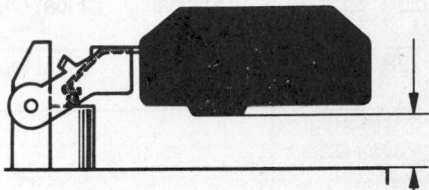

"K" series engines—measure the raised float level as indicated

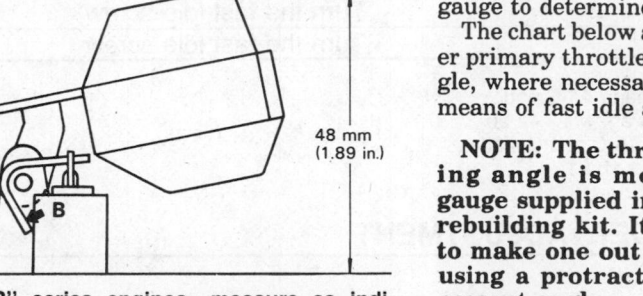

48 mm (1.89 in.)

"R" series engines—measure as indicated and bend at (B) to adjust

raised position; the other is with the air horn in an upright position, so that the float falls to the bottom of its travel.

The float level is either measured with a special carburetor float level gauge, which comes with a rebuilding kit, or with a standard wire gauge.

NOTE: Gap specifications are also given so that a float level gauge may be fabricated.

Adjust the float level by bending the tabs on the float levers, either upper or lower, as required.

FAST IDLE ADJUSTMENT

Off Vehicle

The fast idle adjustment is performed with the choke valve fully closed, except on the 2C-T and 3T-C engines which should have the choke valve fully open.

Adjust the gap between the throttle valve edge and bore to the specifications, where given, in the "Fast Idle Specifications" chart. Use a wire gauge to determine the gap.

The chart below also gives the proper primary throttle valve opening angle, where necessary, and the proper means of fast idle adjustment.

NOTE: The throttle valve opening angle is measured with a gauge supplied in the carburetor rebuilding kit. It is also possible to make one out of cardboard by using a protractor to obtain the correct angle.

On Vehicle

NOTE: Disconnect the EGR valve vacuum line on 20R and 22R engines.

1. Apply the emergency brake and block the wheels. Start the engine and let it run until it reaches normal operating temperature. Connect a suitable tachometer to the engine and check the idle speed and adjust as necessary.

2. Stop the engine and remove the air cleaner. Plug the air suction hose (on California and Canada models) to prevent leakage of the exhaust gas and plug the air suction valve hose (California models) and plug the hot idle compensator hose to prevent rough idling.

3. Disconnect the hose from the Thermostatic Vacuum Switching Valve (TVSV) M port (second from the top) and plug the M port. This will shut off the choke opener and the EGR system.

4. Set the fast idle cam, by holding the throttle slightly open and pushing the choke valve closed as you release the throttle valve.

5. Start the engine, but do not depress the accelerator pedal. set the fast idle speed by turning the fast idle adjustment screw. The fast idle speed should be 3000 rpm.

6. After setting the fast idle speed check the curb idle speed and throttle position speed and adjust as necessary.

AUTOMATIC CHOKE ADJUSTMENT

NOTE: The automatic choke should be adjusted with the carburetor installed and the engine running. On 20R and 22R engines, do not loosen the center bolt; the coolant will leak out.

1. Check to see that the choke valve will close from fully opened when the coil housing is turned counterclockwise (4M engines—clockwise).

2. Align the mark on the coil housing with the center line on the thermostat case. In this position, the choke valve should be fully closed when the ambient temperature is 77°F.

3. If necessary, adjust the mixture by turning the coil housing. If the mixture is too rich, rotate the housing clockwise; of too lean, rotate the housing counterclockwise. On models equipped with the 4M engine, rotate the housing in exactly the reverse direction of the above.

NOTE: Each graduation on the thermostat case is equivalent to 9°F.

FLOAT LEVEL ADJUSTMENTS

Engine	Float Raised			Float Lowered		
	Gauge Type	Measure Distance Between	Gap (in.)	Gauge Type	Measure Distance Between	Gap (in.)
3T-C	Block	Float tip and air horn	0.138①	Wire	Needle valve bushing pin and float lip	0.047
1A-C, 3A, 3A-C, 4A-C	Special	Float tip and air horn	0.158③	Special	Needle valve plunger and float tab	0.047④
4K-C	Special	Float tip and air horn	0.030	Special	Needle valve plunger and float tip	0.02
20R '80	Special	Float end and air horn	0.197②	Special	Needle valve bushing pin and float tab	0.039
22R '81–'83	Special	Float top and air horn	0.386	Special	Needle valve plunger and float lip	1.890

①1980–81—0.236
②1980—0.276
③1983 and later: 0.283
④1983 and later: 0.0657–0.0783

FAST IDLE ADJUSTMENT

Engine	Throttle Valve to Bore Clearance (in.)	Primary Throttle Angle (deg.)	To Adjust Fast Idle
4K-C	0.040①	9②	Bend the fast idle lever
3T-C	0.032	7	Turn the fast idle adjusting screw
20R, 22R	0.047	24	Turn the fast idle screw
1A-C	—	22	Turn the fast idle screw
3A	—	21	Turn the fast idle screw
3A-C, 4A-C	—	③	Turn the fast idle screw

—Not applicable
①0.037 in 1980–83
②20° open
③1980–82: 22°
1983–86 (exc. Canada 4A-C and Canada wag. w/4×4): 20°
(Canada 4A-C and Canada wag. w/4×4): 21°

CHOKE UNLOADER ADJUSTMENT

Engine	Choke Valve Angle (deg.)			Bend to Adjust
	Throttle Valve Fully Closed (deg.)	From Closed to Fully Open (deg.)	Throttle Valve Open (Total) (deg.)	
4K-C	9	20	90	Fast idle cam follower or choke shaft tab
20R, 22R	—	50①	90	Fast idle lever, follower or choke shaft tab
3T-C, 1A, 3A, 3A-C, 4A-C	20	—	47②	Fast idle lever

—Not applicable
①45° for 22R engines
②1983 and later: U.S.—41
Canada—47

MANUAL CHOKE ADJUSTMENT

1. Close the choke by turning the choke shaft lever.
2. Check the 1st throttle valve opening angle with the tool supplied in the rebuild kit.
3. Adjust by turning the fast idle adjusting screw.

CHOKE BREAK ADJUSTMENT

20R and 22R

1. Push the rod which come out of the upper (choke break) diaphragm so that the choke valve opens.
2. Measure the choke valve opening angle. It should be 38°.
3. Adjust the angle, if necessary, by bending the relief lever link.

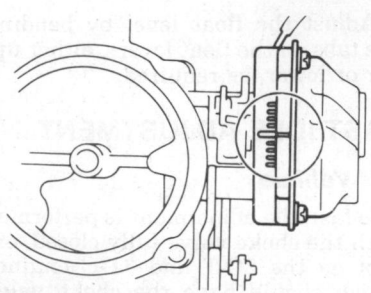

Align the marks on the choke housing

INITIAL IDLE MIXTURE SCREW ADJUSTMENT

When assembling the carburetor, turn the idle mixture screw the number of turns specified below. After the carburetor is installed, perform the appropriate idle/speed mixture adjustment as outlined above.

4K-C—1½ turns from seating
1A-C—2¼ turns from seating
3A, 3A-C, 4A-C—2¾ turns from seating (1981-83); 3¼ turns from seating (1984-87, U.S.); 2½ turns from seating (1984-87, Canada)
20R, 22R—1¾ turns from seating

—————— CAUTION ——————
Seat the idle mixture screw lightly; overtightening will damage its tips.
——————————————————————

UNLOADER ADJUSTMENT

Make the unloader adjustment with the primary valve fully opened. The total angle of choke valve opening, in the chart, is measured with either a special gauge, supplied in the carburetor rebuilding kit, or a gauge of the proper angle fabricated from cardboard.

Fuel Injection

Due to the complex nature of modern fuel injection systems, comprehensive diagnosis and testing procedures fall outside the confined of this repair manual. For complete information on fuel injection diagnosis, testing and repair procedures please refer to *Chilton's Guide To Fuel Injection and Feedback Carburetors.*

DIESEL ENGINE FUEL SYSTEM

For further information on the diesel fuel system, please refer to the "Diesel Service" in the Unit Repair section.

Fuel Filter

REMOVAL & INSTALLATION

1. Disconnect the negative battery cable.
2. Unplug the fuel filter warning switch at the connector.
3. Loosen the fuel filter clamp bolt. Place a suitable container under-

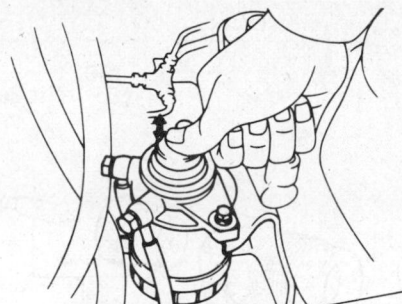
Priming the diesel fuel filter

neath the filter and drain any fuel remaining in the filter body.
4. Using a strap-wrench, remove the filter and the warning switch.
5. Remove the warning switch and its O-ring.
6. Use a new O-ring when installing the warning switch and lightly coat t with fuel.
7. Use a new gasket when installing the filter; coat it with fuel also. On the 1C-L and 1C-TL screw the filter in HANDTIGHT only. On the 2C-T, screw the filter in by hand and then tighten it a further ¾ of a turn with the strap-wrench.
8. Tighten the fuel filter clamp bolt and reconnect the warning switch lead.
9. Depress the priming pump on top of the filter a few times, start the engine and check for leaks.

Diesel Injection Pump

REMOVAL & INSTALLATION

1. Drain the cooling system.
2. Disconnect the accelerator and cruise control cables from the pump.
3. Disconnect the fuel cut off wire at the pump.
4. Disconnect the fuel inlet and outlet hoses, the water by-pass hoses, the boost compensator hoses, the A/C or heater idle-up vacuum hoses and the heater hose.
5. Remove the injector pipes at the pump.
6. Remove the pump pulley.
7. Matchmark the raised timing mark on the pump flange with the block. Unbolt and remove the pump.
8. Installation is the reverse of removal. There must be no clearance between the pump bracket and stay. The diesel injection timing can be found below and by refering to 'Timing Belt' in the Engine Mechanical section.

DIESEL INJECTION TIMING

All Engine Models

NOTE: This procedure requires

the use of a plunger stroke measuring tool and dial indicator.

1. Remove the injection pump head bolt and install stroke measuring tool 09275-54010 or equivalent, along with the dial indicator.
2. Rotate the engine in the normal direction of rotation to set No. 1 cylinder to approximately 25-30° BTDC on the compression stroke.
3. Use a screwdriver to turn the

Timing mark alignment at 25-30° BTDC

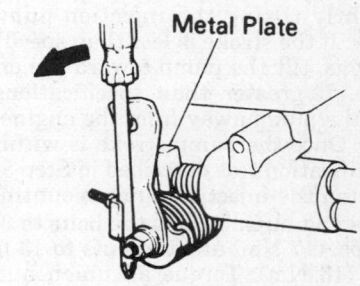
Install plate on cold start lever as shown

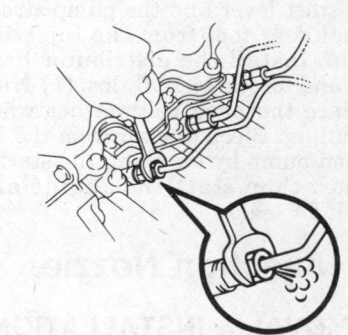
Bleeding the fuel lines on a diesel engine

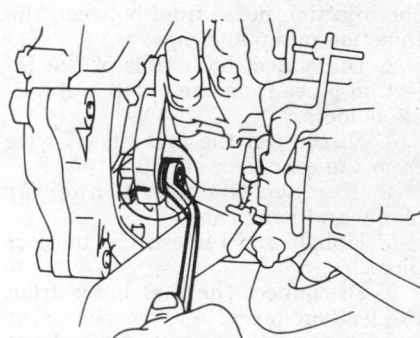
Matchmark the index mark on the injection pump flange to the cylinder block—diesel engines

cold start lever 20° counterclockwise, then place a metal plate 0.335–0.394 in. (8.5–10mm) thick between the cold start lever and thermo wax plunger.

4. Zero the dial indicator, then check to make sure the indicator remains at zero while rotating the crankshaft pulley slightly to the left and right.

5. Slowly rotate the crankshaft pulley until the No. 1 cylinder comes to TDC/compression, then measure the plunger stroke. It should read as follows on the dial indicator.

    a. 0.032 in. (0.80 mm) at TDC on the 1C-L, 1C-LC and the 1C-TL engines.

    b. 0.028 in. (0.70 mm) at TDC on the 2C-T engine.

6. To adjust the injection timing, loosen the four injection lines and the union bolt of the fuel inlet line. Loosen the injection pump mounting bolts and nuts.

7. Adjust the plunger stroke by slightly tilting the injection pump body. If the stroke is less than specifications, tilt the pump toward the engine. If greater than specifications, tilt the pump away from the engine.

8. Once the pump stroke is within specifications (as described in Step 5), tighten the injection pump mounting bolts and nuts. Torque the bolts to 34 ft. lbs. (47 Nm) and the nuts to 13 ft. lbs. (18 Nm). Torque all union nuts and bolts to 22 ft. lbs. (29 Nm).

9. Remove the metal plate from the cold start lever and the pump stroke measuring tool from the injection pump. Install the distributor head bolt and torque to 12 ft. lbs. (17 Nm). Replace the head bolt washer when installing. Bleed any air from the injection pump by cranking the starter motor, then start the engine and check for leaks.

Injection Nozzle

REMOVAL & INSTALLATION

1. Loosen the clamps and remove the injection hoses from between the injection pump and pipe.

2. Disconnect both ends of the injection pipes from the pump and nozzle holders.

3. Disconnect the fuel cut off wire from the connector clamp.

4. Remove the nut, connector clamp and bond cable.

5. Unbolt and remove the injector pipes.

6. Disconnect the fuel hoses from the leakage pipes.

7. Remove the four nuts, leakage pipe and four washers.

8. Unscrew and remove the nozzles.

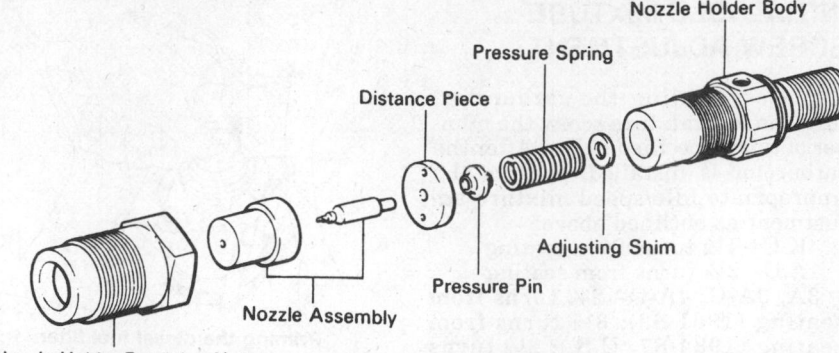

Diesel injection nozzle

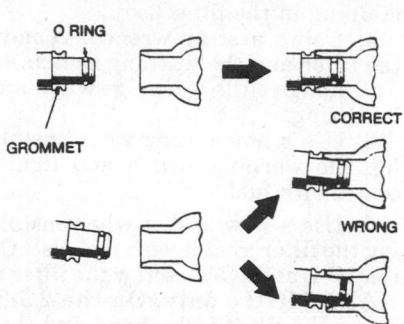

Make sure that you insert the injector into the fuel delivery pipe properly

9. Installation is the reverse of removal. Torque the nozzles to 47 ft. lbs. Always use new nozzle seat gaskets and seats. Bleed the system by loosening the pipes at the nozzles and cranking the engine until all air is expelled and fuel sprays.

MANUAL TRANSMISSION

REMOVAL & INSTALLATION

Van

1. Disconnect the negative battery cable. Raise and support the vehicle safely.

2. Drain the transmission. Matchmark and remove the driveshaft from the vehicle. On 4WD remove both driveshafts.

3. Remove the transmission control cables. On 4wd remove the transfer indicator switch electrical connector. Remove the clutch release cylinder.

4. Remove the starter. Disconnect the speedometer cable. Disconnect the back-up light switch.

5. Remove the exhaust clamp and bracket from the transmission case. Disconnecxt the front exhaust pipe. As required, remove the stiffener plate.

6. Support the engine and the transmission using the proper equipment.

7. On 2WD remove the rear engine mount and bracket. Remove the engine to transmission attaching bolts. Remove the transmission assembly from the vehicle.

8. On 4WD remove the engine rear mounting bolt. Remove the transmission mounting bolts. Pull the assembly down and toward the rear. Remove the transmission along with the transfer case. Seperate the assembly.

9. Installation is the reverse of the removal procedure. Coat the input shaft splines with chassis lube prior to installation.

Starlet

1. Disconnect the negative battery cable. Drain the radiator and remove the upper radiator hose. Remove the shift lever.

2. Raise and support the vehicle safely. Remove the driveshaft. Disconnect the exhaust system at the catalytic converter.

3. Disconnect the speedometer cable. Disconnect the clutch release cable at the clutch fork. Disconnect the back-up light switch electrical connector.

4. Support the engine and the transmission using the proper equipment. Unbolt the engine rear mounts. Remove the rear crossmember.

5. Remove the exhaust pipe bracket. Remove the starter assembly.

6. Remove the transmission to engine retaining bolts. Carefully remove the transmission from the vehicle.

7. Installation is the reverse of the removal procedure.

Corolla RWD

1981–83

1. Disconnect the negative battery cable. Drain the radiator and remove the upper radiator hose. Remove the shift lever.

2. Raise and support the vehicle

safely. Drain the transmission fluid. Remove the driveshaft.

3. Disconnect the speedometer cable. Disconnect the back-up light switch electrical connectors.

4. Disconnect the exhaust pipe clamp. Remove the clutch release cylinder. Remove the starter.

5. Support the engine and transmission using the proper equipment. Remove the rear crossmember assembly.

6. Remove the transmission to engine retaining bolts. Remove the transmission from the vehicle.

7. Installation is the reverse of thremoval procedure.

1984–87

1. Disconnect the negative battery cable. Turn the distributor to gain working clearance.

2. Remove the console. Remove the shift lever.

3. Raise and support the vehicle safely. Drain the transmission fluid. Remove the front exhaust pipe.

4. Disconnect the driveshaft flange from the flange on the differential. Remove the center support bearing and the heat insulator assembly. Remove the driveshaft.

5. Disconnect the speedometer cable. Disconnect the back-up light switch electrical connector.

6. Remove the clutch release cylinder. Remove the starter.

7. Support the engine and the transmission using the proper equipment. Remove the rear crossmember.

8. Remove the stiffener plate. Remove the transmission to engine retaining bolts. Carefully remove the transmission from the vehicle.

9. Installation is the reverse of the removal procedure.

Cressida

1. Disconnect the negative battery cable. Drain the radiator and remove the upper radiator hose.

2. Remove the console. Remove the shift lever assembly.

3. Raise and support the vehicle safely. Drain the transmission fluid.

4. If the vehicle is equipped with power steering remove the steering gear housing. It may be possible to remove the gear and properly suspend it out of the way without disconnecting the fluid lines.

5. Remove the driveshaft. Disconnect the exhaust pipe from the tailpipe. Remove the clamp from the transmission case.

6. Disconnect the speedometer cable. Disconnect the back-up light switch electrical connector.

7. Remove the clutch release cylinder. Remove the starter.

8. Support the engine and the transmission using the proper equipment. remove the rear crossmember assembly.

9. Remove the transmission to engine retaining bolts. Carefully lower the transmission to the floor.

10. Installation is the reverse of removal procedure.

Supra

1981–86

1. Disconnect the negative battery cable. Drain the radiator and remove the upper radiator hose. Remove the console and the shift lever.

3. Raise the vehicle and support it safely. Drain the transmission fluid. Matchmark and remove the driveshaft from the vehicle.

4. If the vehicle is equipped with power steering remove the steering gear housing. It may be possible to remove the gear and properly suspend it out of the way without disconnecting the fluid lines.

5. Remove the bolt from the exhaust pipe stiffener plate. Disconnect the speedometer cable and the back-up light switch connector from the transmission.

6. Unbolt the clutch release cylinder. It may not be necessary to disconnect the hydraulic line from the clutch cylinder. Remove the starter assembly.

7. Support the engine and the transmission using the proper equippment. Remove the transmission support crossmember.

8. Remove the transmission mounting bolts. Carefully, move the transmission rearward, down, and out of the vehicle.

9. Installation is the reverse of the removal procedure.

1987–88

1. Disconnect the negative battery cable. Remove the center console trim panel. Remove the shift lever.

2. Raise and support the vehicle safely. Drain the transmission fluid. Remove the driveshaft.

3. Disconnect the exhaust front pipe from the tailpipe. On some vehicles it will be necessary to remove the front exhaust pipe.

4. Disconnect the speedometer cable. Disconnect the back-up light switch electrical connector. If the vehicle is equipped with ABS disconnect the rear speed sensor electrical connector.

5. Remove the clutch release cylinder. Remove the starter assembly.

6. Support the engine and the transmission using the proper equippment. Remove the transmission support crossmember.

7. Remove the transmission mounting bolts. Remove the flywheel housing bolts. Carefully, move the transmission rearward, down, and out of the vehicle.

NOTE: On Some vehicles it will be necessary to remove the transmission with the clutch cover and disc. To do this pull the release fork through the left clutch housing hole and then remove the assembly.

9. Installation is the reverse of the removal procedure.

Celica RWD

1. Disconnect the negative battery cable. Drain the radiator and remove the upper radiator hose. Remove the console and the shift lever.

2. Raise the vehicle and support it safely. Drain the transmission fluid.

3. Matchmark and remove the driveshaft from the vehicle. Remove the bolt from the exhaust pipe stiffener plate.

4. If the vehicle is equipped with power steering remove the steering gear housing. It may be possible to remove the gear and properly suspend it out of the way without disconnecting the fluid lines.

5. Disconnect the speedometer cable and the back-up light switch connector from the transmission. Remove the exhaust pipe clamp bolt.

5. Unbolt the clutch release cylinder. It may not be necessary to disconnect the hydraulic line from the clutch cylinder. Remove the starter assembly.

6. Support the engine and the transmission using the proper equippment. Remove the transmission support crossmember.

7. Remove the transmission mounting bolts. Carefully, move the transmission rearward, down, and out of the vehicle.

8. Installation is the reverse of removal procedure.

Corona

1. Disconnect the negative battery cable. Disconnect the positive battery to starter cable, complete with fusible link.

2. Drain the radiator and remove the upper radiator hose. Detach the accelerator rod and link at the firewall side.

3. Raise and support the vehicle safely. Remove the exhaust pipe clamp. Remove the clutch master cylinder, but do not disconnect the fluid lines.

4. Disconnect the back-up light switch lead and the speedometer ca-

ble. Matchmark and remove the driveshaft.

5. Support the engine and the transmission using the proper equipment

6. Cover the back end of the valve cover with cloths and remove the rear crossmember.

7. Remove the bolts which secure the shift lever. Remove the shift lever. Remove the starter assembly.

8. Remove the bolts which secure the transmission to the engine block. Carefully remove the transmission from the vehicle.

9. Installation is the reverse of the removal procedure.

LINKAGE ADJUSTMENT

Van

1. Disconnect the negative battery cable. Position the selector lever in the neutral position.

2. Remove the console assembly. With the shift lever in the neutral position check that the guide pin (.024 in. rod) inserts smoothly into the shift lever retainer hole.

3. If necessary adjust the lever in the neutral position by loosening the locknuts and inserting the guide pin through the holes.

4. After adjustment, tighten the locknut.

OVERHAUL

For all manual transmission overhaul procedures, please refer to "Manual Transmission" in the Unit Repair section.

MANUAL TRANSAXLE

REMOVAL & INSTALLATION

Tercel

1981–84

1. Disconnect the negative battery cable. Drain the radiator and remove the top radiator hose.

2. Remove the air cleaner assembly. Disconnect the clutch cable. Remove the upper transaxle to engine bolts. Remove both driveshafts.

3. Raise and support the vehicle safely. Drain the transaxle fluid. Remove the front exhaust pipe.

4. Remove the right side stiffener plate bolts. Remove the No. one gear shift rod. Remove the lever housing rod.

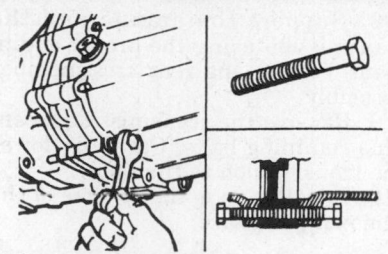

Split the transmission from the transaxle like this on the Tercel

5. Disconnect the back-up light switch electrical connector. Disconnect the speedometer cable. Disconnect the ground strap.

6. Support the engine and the transaxle using the proper equipment. Remove the remaining transaxle to engine retaining bolts. Remove the rear crossmember assembly.

7. Carefully remove the transaxle from the vehicle.

8. Installation is the reverse of the removal procedure.

1985–86 EXCEPT 4WD

1. Disconnect the negative battery cable. Remove the air cleaner assembly.

2. Raise and support the vehicle safely. Drain the transaxle fluid.

3. On some vehicles it will be necessary to remove the catalytic converter air inlet pipe. Remove the front exhaust pipe.

4. Disconnect the gear shift rod. Disconnect the shift lever housing rod. Disconnect the back-up light switch electrical connector. Disconnect the speedometer cable.

5. Support the engine and the transaxle using the proper equipment. Remove the transaxle to engine retaining bolts. Remove the rear crossmember assembly.

6. Remove the ten retaining bolts and two nuts from the assembly. From the transaxle side of the assembly install four bolts of equal length and equally spaced into the assembly. Seperate the transaxle from the transaxle case by turning these bolts a little at a time. Carefully remove the transaxle from the vehicle.

8. Installation is the reverse of the removal procedure.

1986 4WD

1. Disconnect the negative battery cable. Remove the air cleaner assembly.

2. Remove the console. Remove the shift lever assembly.

3. Raise and support the vehicle safely. Drain the transaxle fluid.

4. On some vehicles it will be necessary to remove the catalytic converter air inlet pipe. Remove the front exhaust pipe.

5. Disconnect the selector rod from the rear drive shift link lever. Disconnect the speedometer cable.

6. Disconnect the back-up light switch electrical connector. Disconnect the 4WD and the low gear indicator switch electrical connectors.

7. Support the engine and the transaxle using the proper equipment. Remove the transaxle to engine retaining bolts. Remove the rear crossmember assembly.

8. Remove the ten retaining bolts and two nuts from the assembly. From the transaxle side of the assembly install four bolts of equal length and equally spaced into the assembly. Seperate the transaxle from the transaxle case by turning these bolts a little at a time. Carefully remove the transaxle from the vehicle.

9. Installation is the reverse of the removal procedure.

1987–88 SEDAN

1. Disconnect the negative battery cable. If the vehicle is equipped with cruise control remove the battery. Remove the cruise control actuator and retaining bracket.

2. Remove the clutch release cylinder and tube clamp. Disconnect the back-up light switch electrical connector.

3. Disconnect the transaxle shift control cables. Remove the selecting bellcrank along with the bracket from the transaxle case. Remove the upper transaxle to engine retaining bolts.

4. Raise and support the vehicle safely. Remove the under covers. Drain the transaxle fluid. Disconnect the speedometer cable.

5. Disconnect both driveshafts. Remove the engine rear mounting brackets. Remove the starter assembly.

6. Support the engine and transaxle assembly using the proper equipment. Disconnect the left engine mounting.

7. Remove the remaining engine to transaxle retaining bolts. Carefully remove the transaxle assembly from the vehicle.

8. Installation is the reverse of the removal procedure.

1987–88 2WD WAGON

1. Disconnect the negative battery cable. Remove the air cleaner assembly. Remove the upper transaxle to engine retaining bolts.

2. Remove both driveshaft assemblies.

3. Raise and support the vehicle safely. Drain the transaxle fluid. Disconnect the clutch cable.

4. On some vehicles it will be necessary to remove the catalytic con-

verter air inlet pipe. Remove the front exhaust pipe.

5. Disconnect the selector rod. Disconnect the shift lever housing rod. Disconnect the speedometer cable.

6. Disconnect the back-up light switch electrical connector. Remove the right side stiffener plate.

7. Support the engine and transaxle assembly using the proper equipment. Remove the rear crossmember. Remove the remaining engine to transaxle retaining bolts.

8. Carefully remove the transaxle from the vehicle.

9. Installation is the reverse of the removal procedure.

1987–88 4WD WAGON

1. Disconnect the negative battery cable. Remove the air cleaner assembly.

2. Remove the console. Remove the shift lever assembly. Remove the upper engine to transaxle retaining bolts.

3. Raise and support the vehicle safely. Drain the transaxle fluid. Remove both driveshafts.

4. On some vehicles it will be necessary to remove the catalytic converter air inlet pipe. Remove the front exhaust pipe.

5. Disconnect the selector rod from the rear drive shift link lever. Disconnect the speedometer cable. Remove the right stiffener plate.

6. Disconnect the back-up light switch electrical connector. Disconnect the 4WD and the low gear indicator switch electrical connectors.

7. Support the engine and the transaxle using the proper equipment. Remove the remaining transaxle to engine retaining bolts. Remove the rear crossmember assembly.

NOTE: Properly position a piece of wood between the engine and the firewall so that the assembly will not make contact with the power brake booster when it is removed.

8. Carefully remove the transaxle assembly from the vehicle.

9. Installation is the reverse of the removal procedure.

Corolla FWD

1984–85

1. Disconnect the negative battery cable. Drain the radiator.

2. Remove the air cleaner. Disconnect the back-up light switch.

3. Remove the speedometer cable. Disconnect the control cable at the transaxle.

4. Unbolt the coolant inlet line from the transaxle. Remove the clutch release cylinder.

5. Raise and support the vehicle safely. Remove the undercover.

6. Remove the front and rear support members. Remove the engine center support member.

7. Unbolt the right driveshaft from the transaxle. Disconnect the steering knuckle from the lower arm.

8. Pull the steering knuckle outward and remove the left driveshaft.

9. Remove the starter. Remove the flywheel cover plate.

10. Properly support the engine and disconnect the left engine mount.

11. Properly support the transaxle assembly. Remove the transaxle to engine attaching bolts. Lower the left side of the engine and pull the transaxle free.

12. Installation is the reverse of the removal procedure. Coat the input shaft splines with chassis lube prior to installation.

1986–88 EXCEPT C52 TRANSAXLE

1. Disconnect the negative battery cable. Remove the air cleaner assembly.

2. Disconnect the back-up light switch electrical connector. Remove the speedometer cable. Disconnect the transmission control cables.

3. Raise and support the vehicle safely. Remove the water inlet from the transaxle. Remove the clutch release cylinder.

4. Remove the under cover. Remove the front and rear mounting. Remove the engine mounting center member.

5. Disconnect the driveshaft from the transaxle. Disconnect the steering knuckle from the lower control arm. Pull the steering knuckle outward and remove the left driveshaft.

6. Remove the starter. Disconnect the ground strap. Remove the NO. two engine rear plate.

7. Support the engine and the transaxle using the proper equipment. Remove the left engine mounting.

8. Remove the engine to transaxle retaining bolts. Carefully remove the transaxle assembly from the vehicle.

9. Installation is the reverse of thremoval procedure.

1987–88 C52 TRANSAXLE

1. Disconnect the negative battery cable. Drain the radiator. Remove the air cleaner assembly. Remove the engine cooling fan assembly.

2. Disconnect the oxygen sensor electrical connector and the back-up light switch connector.

3. Remove the clutch release cylinder. It may be possible to leave the fluid lines attached to the cylinder.

4. Disconnect the water inlet from the transaxle. Disconnect the trans-

axle control cables. Disconnect the speedometer cable. Disconnect the ground cable.

5. Remove the starter. Remove the engine under covers. Remove the front exhaust pipe.

6. Disconnect the front and rear mountings. Remove the engine mounting center member.

7. Remove the left front wheel. Loosen the six nuts while depressing the brake pedal. Disconnect the driveshaft from the side gear shaft. Disconnect the lower ball joint from the lower control arm. Pull the shock absorber outward. Remove the driveshaft.

8. Support the engine and the transaxle assembly using the proper equipment. Remove the No. two engine rear plate. Remove the left hand engine mounting.

9. Remove the transaxle retaining bolts. Carefully remove the transaxle assembly from the vehicle.

10. Installation is the reverse of the removal procedure.

Camry

1983–86

1. Disconnect the negative battery cable. Remove the engine and the transaxle as an assembly from the vehicle.

2. Position the assembly in a suitable holding fixture.

3. Seperate the engine from the transaxle.

4. Installation is the reverse of the removal procedure.

1987–88

1. Disconnect the negative battery cable. Remove the clutch release cylinder and tube clamp. Remove the clutch tube bracket.

2. Disconnect the control cables. Disconnect the back-up light switch electrical connector. Remove the ground strap.

3. Remove the starter assembly. Remove the transaxle upper mounting bolts.

4. Raise and support the vehicle safely. Remove the under covers. Drain the transaxle fluid. Disconnect the speedometer cable.

5. Remove the suspension lower crossmember. Remove the engine mounting center member.

6. Disconnect both driveshafts. Remove the center driveshaft. Disconnect the left steering knuckle from the lower control arm. Remove the stabilizer bar.

7. Properly support the engine and remove the left engine mount.

8. Properly support the transaxle assembly. Remove the engine to transaxle bolts, lower the left side of the engine and carefully ease the

transaxle out of the engine compartment.

9. Installation is the reverse of the removal procedure.

MR2

1. Disconnect the negative battery cable. Drain the radiator. Raise and suport the vehicle safely. Drain the transaxle fluid.

2. Disconnect the back-up light switch and the speedometer cable at the transaxle.

3. Loosen the mounting bolts and remove the water inlet from the transaxle.

4. Remove the engine undercover. Remove the fuel tank protector.

5. Disconnect the transaxle control cables at the transaxle and position them out of the way.

6. Remove the water hose clamp from the control cable bracket and then remove the No. two control cable bracket.

7. Remove the main control cable bracket and the clutch release cylinder. Position these components out of the way.

8. Disconnect the exhaust pipe from the manifold, remove the pipe bracket from the chassis and then remove the exhaust pipe assembly from the bracket.

9. Remove the transaxle protector. Disconnect the halfshaft from the side gear shaft. Remove the starter assembly.

10. Remove the No. two engine rear plate. Remove the front and rear engine mounts from the body.

11. Properly support the engine and remove the left engine mount.

12. Properly support the transaxle assembly. Remove the engine to transaxle bolts, lower the left side of the engine and carefully ease the transaxle out of the engine compartment.

13. Remove the side gear shaft from the transaxle.

14. Installation is the reverse of the removal procedure.

Celica FWD

1. Disconnect the negative battery cable. On some 1987–88 vehicles it may be necessary to remove the battery. Remove the air cleaner assembly.

2. On 1987 vehicles remove the clutch tube bracket. Disconnect the back-up light switch at the transaxle. Disconnect the speedometer and the engine ground strap.

3. Disconnect the transaxle control cable and position them out of the way.

4. Unbolt the clutch release cylinder. It may be possible to position it

out of the way with the hydraulic line still attached.

5. Remove the upper transaxle retaining bolts. Raise and support the vehicle safdely. Remove the engine undercover. Drain the transaxle fluid.

6. Disconnect the exhaust pipe from the manifold. Remove the lower suspension crossmember. Remove the starter assembly.

7. Properly support the engine and transaxle assembly. Remove the front and rear transaxle mounts. Remove the center engine mount.

8. Disconnect both halfshafts at the transaxle. Unbolt the steering knuckle from the suspension arm and pull it outward. Remove the left halfshaft.

9. On some vehicles remove the No. two rear engine plate. With the engine properly supported remove the left engine mount.

10. Remove the engine to transaxle bolts, lower the left side of the engine and carefully ease the transaxle out of the engine compartment.

11. Installation is the reverse of the removal procedure.

LINKAGE ADJUSTMENT

Camry

1983-85

1. Disconnect the negative battery cable. Remove the console.

2. Insert a guide pin (.020 in. rod) into the shift lever hole. Turn the buckle to align the shift lever hole and the shift support hole.

3. If adjustment is required loosen the locknut, make the adjustment and retighten the locknut.

OVERHAUL

For all transaxle overhaul procedures, please refer to "Manual Transaxle Overhaul" in the Unit Repair section.

CLUTCH

REMOVAL & INSTALLATION

1. Disconnect the negative battery cable. Remove the transmission assembly from the vehicle.

Note: On some 1987–88 Supra's the clutch assembly is removed along with the transmission. On 1983–86 Camry the engine and transaxle are removed from the vehicle as an assembly.

2. Remove the clutch pressure plate retaining bolts. Remove the pressure plate assembly.

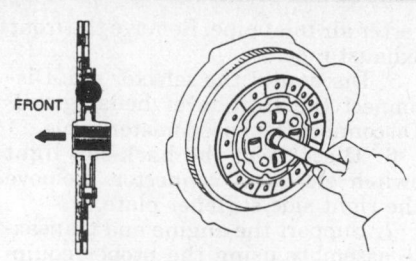

Use a clutch pilot tool to center the clutch disc on the flywheel

3. Remove the clutch disc.

4. Installation is the revewrse of the removal procedure.

FREE-PLAY ADJUSTMENT

All Except Tercel and Starlet

1. Adjust the clearance between the master cylinder piston and the pushrod to specification by loosening the pushrod locknut and rotating the pushrod while depressing the clutch pedal lightly.

2. Tighten the locknut when finished the adjustment.

3. Adjust the release cylinder freeplay by loosening the release cylinder pushrod locknut and rotating the pushrod until proper specification is obtained.

4. Measure the clutch pedal freeplay after performing the adjustments. If it fails to fall within specification, repeat the procedure.

Tercel and Starlet

1. Depress the clutch pedal several times.

2. Depress the clutch pedal until resistance is felt. Freeplay should be within specification.

3. Check the clutch release sector pawl. Six notches should remain between the pawl and the end of the sector. If less than six notches, replace the clutch disc. If the clutch disc has been replaced, the pawl should be between three and ten notches.

4. To obtain either the used or new position on the 1981–82 Starlet, change the position of the E-ring.

Clutch Cable

REMOVAL & INSTALLATION

Starlet

1. Disconnect the negative battery cable.

2. Remove and record the E-ring position on the clutch pedal.

3. Disconnect the sector tension spring from the clutch pedal.

4. Disconnect the clutch release cable from the release fork lever.

CLUTCH PEDAL FREE-PLAY ADJUSTMENTS

Model	Master Cylinder piston-to-pushrod clearance (in.)	Release cylinder-to-release fork free-play (in.)	Pedal free-play (in.)
Corolla 1200	0.02	1.00–1.40	0.8–1.4
(RWD) 1600	0.02	Not adj.	0.79–1.58
1800, 1600 ('83–'86)	Not adj.	Not adj.	0.51–0.91 ④
Corolla (FWD)	Not adj.	Not adj.	0.51–0.91 (gas) ⑤ 0.20–0.59 (diesel) ⑤
Corona '79–'82	Not adj.	Not adj.	0.51–0.91
Celica	Not adj.	Not adj.	0.51–0.91 ①
Supra	Not adj.	Not adj.	0.20–0.59
Starlet	Not adj.	Not adj.	0.08–1.18 ②
Tercel	Not adj.	Not adj.	0.08–1.10 ③
Van	Not adj.	Not adj.	0.20–0.59
Camry	Not adj.	Not adj.	0.20–0.59
Cressida	Not adj.	Not adj.	0.20–0.59
MR2	Not adj.	Not adj.	0.197–0.59

FWD Front Wheel Drive
RWD Rear Wheel Drive
① For turn-over type: 0.20–0.50
② '83–'84: 0.08–1.38
③ '86–'87: 0.08–0.98
④ '86–'87: 4A-GE: 0.20–0.59
⑤ '86–'87: 0.28–0.67

5. Disconnect the clutch release cable from the release sector.

6. Remove the glove box door. Remove the clips and the cable from the groove of the pulley. Remove the release cable.

7. Installation is the reverse of the removal procedure.

Tercel

1981–86 AND 1987–88 WAGON

1. Disconnect the negative battery cable.

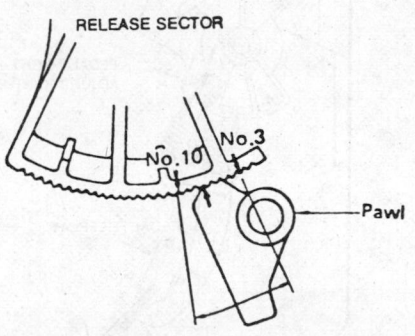

Pawl and sector position for a new clutch—Tercel and Starlet

2. Disconnect the sector tension spring from the clutch pedal.

3. Disconnect the clutch release cable from the release fork lever.

4. Turn the release sector toward the front side and disconnect the release cable from the release sector. Remove the release cable.

5. Installation is the reverse of the removal procedure.

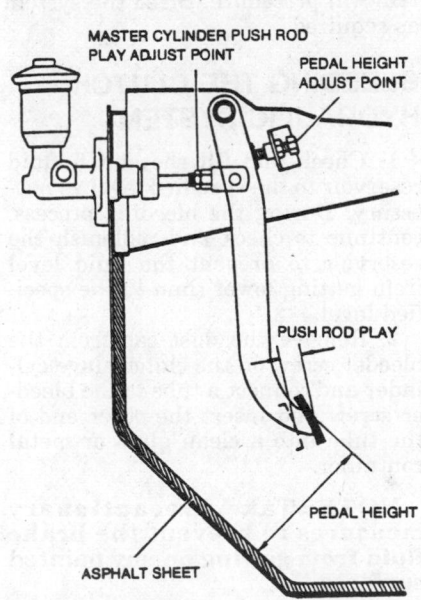

Clutch pedal adjusting points—all except the Tercel, Starlet and Corolla 1200

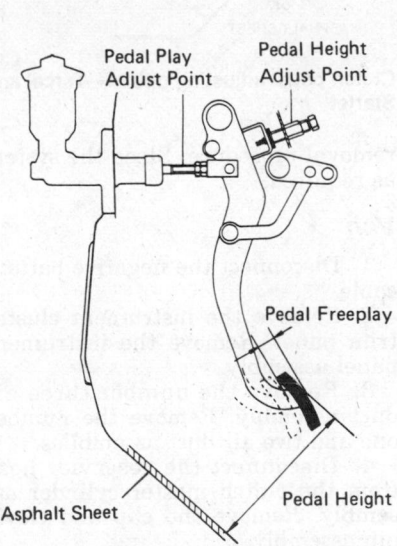

Camry clutch pedal adjustment

Push Rod Play and Freeplay Adjust Point

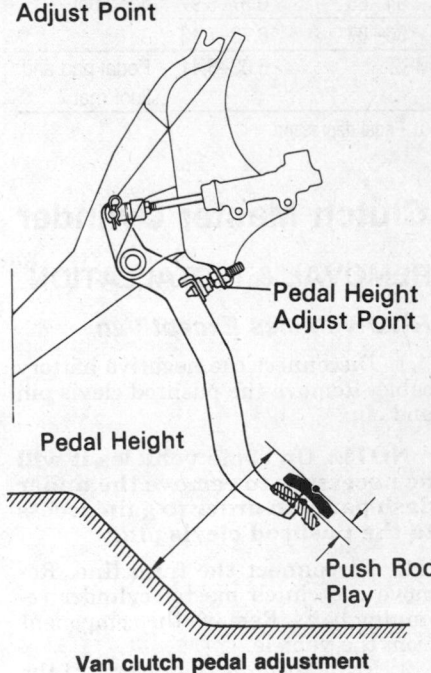

Van clutch pedal adjustment

PEDAL HEIGHT SPECIFICATIONS

Model/Year	Height (in.)	Measure Between
Tercel		Pedal pad and floor mat
'80–'83	6.65	
'84–'85	6.97–7.36	
'86–'87	7.15–7.44	
Corolla 1800	6.89–7.28	Pedal pad and floormat
Corolla 1600 (RWD)		Pedal pad and floormat
'83–'85	6.34–6.72	
'86–'87	6.44–6.83	
Corolla (FWD)		Pedal pad and floor mat
'83–'85	5.650–6.043	
'86–'87	5.827–6.220	
Corona		Pedal pad and floor mat
'80–'82	6.5–6.9	
Celica		Pedal pad and floor mat
'80–'81	6.48–6.87	
'82–'85	6.06–6.46	
'86–'87	6.02–6.42	
Supra		Pedal and floor mat
'80	6.48–6.87	
'81–'86	6.06–6.46	
Cressida	6.10–6.50	From floor mat
Station Wagon (all)	9.6	Pedal pad and firewall
Starlet	6.93	Pedal pad and floor mat
Camry		Pedal pad and kick panel
'83–'85	7.539–7.933	
'86–'87	7.99–8.39	
Van		Pedal pad and floor mat
'84–'85	6.57–6.97	
'86–'87	6.73–7.13	
MR2	6.03–6.41	Pedal pad and floor mat

① Pedal depressed

Clutch Master Cylinder

REMOVAL & INSTALLATION

RWD Vehicles Except Van

1. Disconnect the negative battery cable. Remove the pushrod clevis pin and clip.

NOTE: On some vehicles it will be necessary to remove the under dash panel in order to gain access to the pushrod clevis pin.

2. Disconnect the fluid line. Remove the clutch master cylinder retaining bolts. Remove the component from the vehicle.

3. Installation is the reverse of the

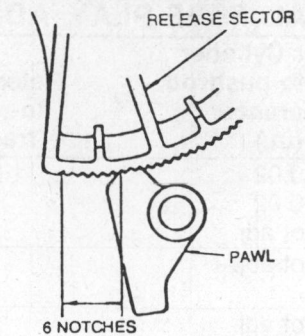

Minimum pawl and sector position for a used clutch—Tercel and Starlet

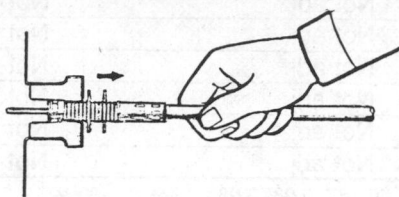

E-ring adjustment—1981–82 Starlet

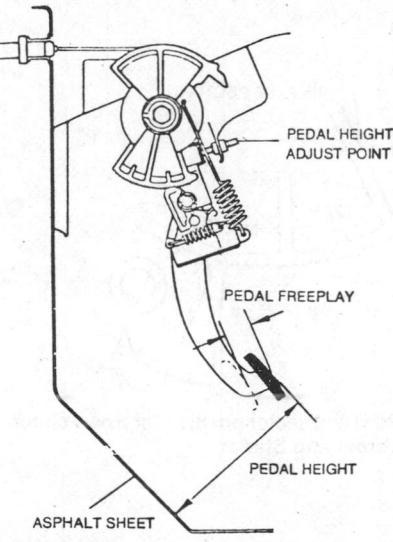

Clutch pedal adjusting points—Tercel and Starlet

removal procedure. Bleed the system as required.

Van

1. Disconnect the negative battery cable.
2. Remove the instrument cluster trim panel. Remove the instrument panel assembly.
3. Remove the number three air duct assembly. Remove the number one and two air duct assemblies.
4. Disconnect the reservior hose from the clutch master cylinder assembly. Remove the clip and clevis pin assembly.
5. Disconnect the fluid line. Remove the clutch master cylinder re-

taining bolts. Remove the component from the vehicle.

6. Installation is the reverse of the removal procedure. Bleed the system as required.

FWD Vehicles

1. Disconnect the negative battery cable. On MR2 remove the luggage compartment cover to gain access to the assembly. On Tercel, remove the reservoir tank from the clutch master clyinder.

2. Remove the pushrod clevis pin and clip.

NOTE: On some vehicles it will be necessary to remove the under dash panel in order to gain access to the pushrod clevis pin.

3. Disconnect the fluid line. Remove the clutch master cylinder retaining bolts. Remove the component from the vehicle.

4. Installation is the reverse of the removal procedure. Bleed the system as required.

Clutch Slave Cylinder

REMOVAL & INSTALLATION

1. Disconnect the negative battery cable. Raise and support the vehicle safely.

2. Remove the gravel shield, if equipped. Disconnect the fluid line from the assembly.

3. Remove the slave cylinder retaining bolts. Remove the clutch slave cylinder from the vehicle.

4. Installation is the reverse of the removal procedure. Bleed the system as required.

BLEEDING THE CLUTCH HYDRAULIC SYSTEM

1. Check and fill the clutch fluid reservoir to the specified level as necessary. During the bleeding process, continue to check and replenish the reservoir to prevent the fluid level from getting lower than ½ the specified level.

2. Remove the dust cap from the bleeder screw on the clutch slave cylinder and connect a tube to the bleeder screw and insert the other end of the tube into a clean glass or metal container.

NOTE: Take precautionary measures to prevent the brake fluid from getting on any painted surfaces.

3. Pump the clutch pedal several times, hold it down and loosen the bleeder screw slowly.

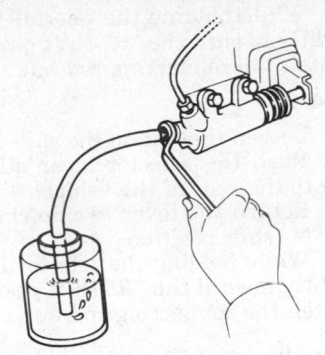

Bleeding the clutch hydraulic system

4. Tighten the bleeder screw and release the clutch pedal gradually. Repeat this operation until air bubbles disappear from the brake fluid being expelled out through the bleeder screw.

5. Repeat until all evidence of air bubbles completely disappears from the fluid being pumped out of the tube.

6. When the air is completely removed tighten the bleeder screw and replace the dust cap.

7. Check and refill the master cylinder reservoir as necessary.

8. Depress the clutch pedal several times to check the operation of the clutch and check for leaks.

AUTOMATIC TRANSMISSION

REMOVAL & INSTALLATION

Van

2 WHEEL DRIVE

1. Disconnect the negative battery cable. Disconnect the throttle cable. Disconnect all wires attached to the transmission assembly.

2. Raise and support the vehicle safely.

3. Drain the transmission fluid. Matchmark and remove the driveshaft.

4. Disconnect the exhaust pipe from the transmission case. Disconnect the shift cable. Disconnect the speedometer cable.

5. Disconnect the fluid lines. Remove the starter.

6. Support the engine and transmission using the proper equipment. Remove the transmission mounting through bolt.

7. Properly support the fuel tank. Remove the fuel tank mounting bolts. Remove the rear transmission support bolt.

8. Remove the two stiffener plates from the transmission.

9. Pry out the service hole cover at the torque converter housing. Remove the torque converter bolts.

10. Remove the transmission to engine bolts. Slowly and carefully guide the transmission away from the engine. Lower the assembly to the floor.

11. Installation is the reverse of the removal procedure.

4 WHEEL DRIVE

1. Disconnect the negative battery cable. Disconnect the transmission throttle cable. Disconnect the three wiring connectors at the starter.

2. Raise and support the vehicle safely. Drain the fluid from the transmission and the transfer case.

3. Disconnect the ATF thermo sensor electrical connector. Remove the front and rear driveshafts.

4. Disconnect the exhaust pipe from the exhaust manifold. Remove the exhaust pipe clamp from the transmission housing.

5. Disconnect the transmission shift cable from the transmission outer lever. Disconnect the vacuum hoses from the vacuum actuator. Disconnect the speed sensor and the four wheel drive indicator connectors.

6. Disconnect the speedometer cable, ground strap and transfer case indicator switch electrical connector.

7. Disconnect the oil cooler lines from the transmission case. Remove the control cable bracket from the transmission case.

8. Remove the starter. Support the engine and transmission assembly using the proper equipment.

9. Remove the transmission mounting through bolt. Remove both stiffner plates from the transmission case.

10. Remove the torque converter access cover. Remove the torque converter bolts. Remove the bolts that retain the transmission to the engine.

11. Carefully remove the transmission assembly from the vehicle.

12. Installation is the reverse of the removal procedure.

Corolla RWD

1. Disconnect the negative battery cable. On 1981–83 vehicles drain the radiator and remove the upper radiator hose.

2. Remove the air cleaner assembly. Disconnect the transmission throttle cable. Disconnect the starter assembly electrical connections.

3. Raise and support the vehicle safely. Drain the transmission fluid. Remove the driveshaft.

4. Remove the exhaust pipe clamp. Disconnect the exhaust pipe from the exhaust manifold.

5. Disconnect the manual shift linkage. Disconnect the oil cooler lines. Remove the starter.

6. Support the engine and transmission using the proper equipment. Remove the rear crossmember.

7. Disconnect the speedometer cable. Disconnect all necessary electrical wiring from the transmission.

8. Remove the torque converter cover. Remove the torque converter to engine retaining bolts.

9. Remove the bolts retaining the transmission to the engine. Carefully remove the transmission from the vehicle.

10. Installation is the reverse of the removal procedure.

Cressida

1. Disconnect the negative battery cable. Drain the radiator and remove the upper radiator hose. Remove the air cleaner assembly. Disconnect the transmission throttle cable.

2. Raise and support the vehicle safely. Drain the transmission fluid. Remove the driveshaft along with the center bearing.

3. Remove the exhaust pipe together with the catalytic converter. Disconnect the manual shift linkage. Remove the speedometer cable.

4. Disconnect the oil cooler lines. As necessary remove the transmission oil filler tube. As required, remove the starter assembly.

5. Remove both stiffener plates and the catalytic converter cover from the transmission housing and cylinder block.

6. Support the engine and transmission using the proper equipment. Remove the rear crossmember.

7. Remove the torque converter cover. Remove the torque converter to engine retaining bolts.

9. Remove the bolts retaining the transmission to the engine. Carefully remove the transmission from the vehicle.

10. Installation is the reverse of the removal procedure.

Supra

1. Disconnect the negative battery cable. On 1981–86 vehicles drain the radiator and remove the upper radiator hose. Remove the air cleaner assembly. Disconnect the transmission throttle cable.

2. Raise and support the vehicle safely. Drain the transmission fluid. Disconnect the electrical connectors for the neutral safety switch and back up lights.

3. Remove the intermediate driveshaft along with the center bearing. Disconnect the exhaust pipe from the tail pipe.

4. Disconnect the transmission oil cooler lines. Disconnect the manual shift linkage. Disconnect the speedometer cable.

5. Remove the exhaust pipe bracket and torque converter cover. Remove both stiffener brackets.

6. On 1981–86 vehicles remove the power steering gear housing from the crossmember. Be sure to plug the fluid lines, as required.

7. Support the engine and transmission using the proper equipment. Remove the rear crossmember.

8. Remove the engine under cover. Remove the torque converter to engine retaining bolts. Remove the starter.

9. Remove the bolts retaining the transmission to the engine. Carefully remove the transmission from the vehicle.

10. Installation is the reverse of the removal procedure.

Celica RWD

1. Disconnect the negative battery cable. Drain the radiator and remove the upper radiator hose. Remove the air cleaner assembly. Disconnect the transmission throttle cable.

2. Raise and support the vehicle safely. Drain the transmission fluid. Remove the driveshaft along with the center bearing. Disconnect the necessary electical connectors in order to remove the transmission.

3. Disconnect the manual shift linkage. Remove the speedometer cable. Remove the sliding yoke from the gear housing and shift mechanism.

4. Disconnect the oil cooler lines. Remove the front exhaust pipe.

5. Remove the power steering gear housing from the crossmember. Be sure to plug the fluid lines, as required.

6. Support the engine and transmission using the proper equipment. Remove the rear crossmember.

7. Remove the engine under cover. Remove the torque converter cover. Remove the torque converter to engine retaining bolts. Remove the starter.

8. Remove the bolts retaining the transmission to the engine. Carefully remove the transmission from the vehicle.

9. Installation is the reverse of the removal procedure.

Corona

1. Disconnect the negative battery cable. Remove the air cleaner. Disconnect the accelerator cable.

2. Disconnect the throttle link rod at the carburetor side, then disconnect the back-up light wiring. Remove the upper starter bolts.

3. Raise and support the vehicle safdely. Drain the transmission fluid.

4. Remove the lower starter mounting bolt. Remove the starter from the vehicle.

5. Unbolt the parking brake equalizer support. Remove the bolts securing the driveshaft to the companion flange. Remove the driveshaft.

6. Remove the bolts from the crossshaft body, the cotter pin from the manual lever, and the crossshaft socket from the transmission.

7. Remove the exhaust pipe bracket from the torque converter housing. Disconnect the oil cooler lines from the transmission. Remove the line bracket from the bell housing.

8. Disconnect the speedometer cable from the transmission. Unbolt both support braces from the transmission housing.

9. Support the engine and transmission using the proper equipment. Remove the rear crossmember.

7. Remove the torque converter cover. Remove the torque converter to engine retaining bolts. Remove the starter.

8. Remove the bolts retaining the transmission to the engine. Carefully remove the transmission from the vehicle.

9. Installation is the reverse of the removal procedure.

PAN REMOVAL

1. Raise and support the vehicle safely. Remove the drain plug. Drain the fluid in a suitable container.

2. Remove the drain pan retaining bolts.

3. Remove the pan. Discard the gasket.

4. Remove th filter, as required.

5. Installation is the reverse of the removal procedure. Refill the unit with the proper grade and type transmission fluid.

LINKAGE ADJUSTMENT

Van

1. Loosen the nut on the shift linkage. Push the selector lever all the way to the rear of the vehicle.

2. Return the lever two notches to the "N" shift position.

3. While holding the selector lever slightly toward the "R" shift position tighten the connecting rod nut.

Corolla RWD

1981–83

1. Push the selector lever all the way to the front of the vehicle.

2. Return the lever three notches to the "N" shift position.

3. While holding the selector lever slightly toward the "R" shift position tighten the connecting rod nut.

1984–88

1. Loosen the nut on the shift linkage. Push the selector lever all the way to the rear of the vehicle.

2. Return the lever two notches to the "N" shift position.

3. While holding the selector lever slightly toward the "R" shift position tighten the connecting rod nut.

Cressida and Supra

1981–84

1. Push the selector lever all the way to the front of the vehicle.

2. Return the lever three notches to the "N" shift position.

3. While holding the selector lever slightly toward the "R" shift position tighten the connecting rod nut.

1985–88

1. Loosen the nut on the shift linkage. Push the selector lever all the way to the rear of the vehicle.

2. Return the lever two notches to the "N" shift position.

3. While holding the selector lever slightly toward the "R" shift position tighten the connecting rod nut.

Celica RWD

1981–84

1. Push the selector lever all the way to the front of the vehicle.

2. Return the lever three notches to the "N" shift position.

3. While holding the selector lever slightly toward the "R" shift position tighten the connecting rod nut.

1985

1. Loosen the nut on the shift linkage. Push the selector lever all the way to the rear of the vehicle.

2. Return the lever two notches to the "N" shift position.

3. While holding the selector lever slightly toward the "R" shift position tighten the connecting rod nut.

NEUTRAL SAFETY SWITCH

Van

1. Loosen the neutral start switch bolt. Position the selector in the "N" position.

2. Align the switch shaft groove with the neutral base line which is located on the switch.

3. Tighten the bolt.

Corolla RWD

1981–83

1. Loosen the neutral start switch

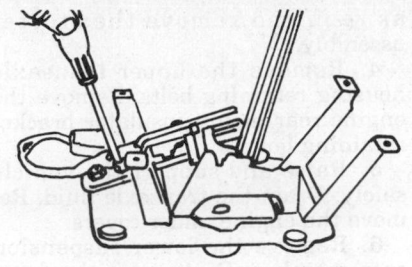

Adjusting the neutral safety switch on models with the three speed Toyoglide and floor mounted shift

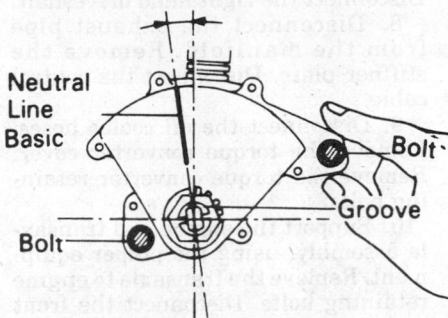

Neutral safety switch adjustment—most late models similar

bolt. Position the selector in the "N" position.

2. Align the switch shaft groove with the neutral base line which is located on the switch.

3. Tighten the bolt.

1984–88

1. Loosen the neutral start switch retaining bolts. Disconnect the switch electrical connector.

2. Position the selector lever in the "N" position.

3. Connect an ohmmeter between the terminals.

4. Adjust the switch to the point where there is continuity between terminals "N" and "B".

5. Connect the switch electrical connector.

Cressida and Supra

1981–84 AND 1987–88

1. Loosen the neutral start switch bolt. Position the selector in the "N" position.

2. Align the switch shaft groove with the neutral base line which is located on the switch.

3. Tighten the bolt.

1985–86

1. Loosen the neutral start switch retaining bolts. Disconnect the switch electrical connector.

2. Position the selector lever in the "N" position.

3. Connect an ohmmeter between the terminals.

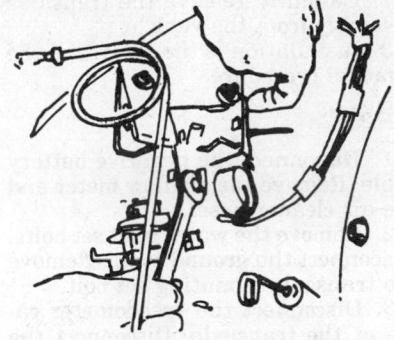

Adjusting the neutral safety switch on models with the three speed Toyoglide and a column-mounted shift

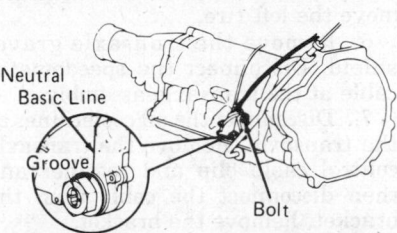

Neutral safety switch adjustment—early models

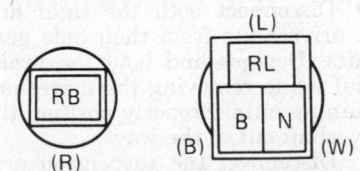

Checking the neutral safety switch for continuity between the connectors

4. Adjust the switch to the point where there is continuity between terminals "N" and "B".

5. Connect the switch electrical connector.

Celica RWD

1981–83

1. Loosen the neutral start switch bolt. Position the selector in the "N" position.

2. Align the switch shaft groove with the neutral base line which is located on the switch.

3. Tighten the bolt.

1984–85

1. Loosen the neutral start switch retaining bolts. Disconnect the switch electrical connector.

2. Position the selector lever in the "N" position.

3. Connect an ohmmeter between the terminals.

4. Adjust the switch to the point where there is continuity between terminals "N" and "B".

5. Connect the switch electrical connector.

AUTOMATIC TRANSAXLE

REMOVAL & INSTALLATION

Tercel

1. Disconnect the negative battery cable. On some vehicles it will be necessary to drain the radiator and remove the upper radiator hose. Remove the air cleaner assembly.

2. Raise and support the vehicle safely. Remove both driveshafts. Drain the fluid from the transaxle. On some vehicles it may be necessary to drain the differential fluid.

3. Remove the torque converter cover. Remove the bolts that retain the torque converter to the crankshaft. Remove the exhaust pipe. Remove the shift lever rod.

4. Remove the speedometer cable, back-up light connector. If equipped with four wheel drive remove the electrical solenoid connector. Disconnect and remove all throttle linkage.

5. Remove the fluid lines from the transaxle. On some vehicles it may be necessary to remove the starter assembly. On four wheel drive vehicles remove the rear driveshaft.

6. Support the engine and transaxle using a suitable jack. Remove the rear crossmember.

7. Remove the transaxle to engine retaining bolts. Seperate the transaxle from the engine and carefully remove it from the vehicle.

8. Installation is the reverse of the removal procedure.

Corolla FWD

1. Disconnect the negative battery cable. Remove the air cleaner.

2. Disconnect the neutral start switch. Disconnect the speedometer cable.

3. Remove the shift control cable. Disconnect the throttle linkage.

4. Disconnect the oil cooler hose.

5. Drain the radiator. Remove the water inlet pipe.

6. Raise and support the vehicle safely. Drain the transaxle fluid. As required remove the exhaust front pipe.

7. Remove the engine undercover. Remove the front and rear transaxle mounts.

8. Support the engine and transaxle using the proper equipment. Remove the engine center support member.

9. Remove the halfshafts. Remove the starter assembly. As required remove the steering knuckles.

10. Remove the flywheel cover plate. Remove the torque converter bolts.

11. Remove the left engine mount. Remove the transaxle to engine bolts. Slowly and carefully back the transaxle away from the engine. Lower the assembly to the floor.

12. Installation is the reverse of the removal procedure.

Camry

1983–86

1. Disconnect the negative battery cable.

2. Remove the engine and transaxle assembly from the vehicle as one component.

3. Position the engine/transaxle assembly in a suitable holding fixture. Seperate the engine from the transaxle assembly.

4. Installation is the reverse of the removal procedure.

1987–88

1. Disconnect the negative battery cable. Remove the air flow meter and the air cleaner assembly.

2. Disconnect the transaxle wire connector. Disconnect the neutral safety switch electrical connector.

3. Disconnect the transaxle ground strap. Disconnect the throttle cable from the throttle linkage.

4. Remove the transaxle case protector. Disconnect the speedometer cable. Disconnect the control cable.

5. Disconnect the oil cooler hoses. Remove the upper starter retaining bolts, as required remove the starter assembly. Remove the upper transaxle housing bolts. Remove the engine rear mount insulator bracket set bolt.

6. Raise and support the vehicle safely. Drain the transaxle fluid.

7. Remove the left front fender apron seal. Disconnect both driveshafts.

8. Remove the suspension lower crossmember assembly. Remove the center driveshaft.

9. Remove the engine mounting center crossmember. Remove the stabilizer bar. Remove the left steering knuckle from the lower control arm.

10. Remove the torque converter cover. Remove the torque converter retaining bolts.

11. Properly support the engine and transaxle assembly. Remove the rear engine mounting bolts. Remove the remaining transaxle to engine retaining bolts.

12. Carefully remove the transaxle assembly from the vehicle.

13. Installation is the reverse of the removal procedure.

MR2

1. Disconnect the negative battery cable. Remove the air flow meter and the air cleaner hose.

2. Remove the water inlet set bolts. Disconnect the ground strap. Remove the transaxle mounting set bolt.

3. Disconnect the speedometer cable at the transaxle. Disconnect the throttle cable from the throttle linkage and the bracket.

4. Raise and support the vehicle safely. Drain the transaxle fluid. Remove the left tire.

5. Remove the transaxle gravel shield. Disconnect the speedometer cable at the transaxle assembly.

6. Remove the transaxle gravel shield. Disconnect the speedometer cable at the transaxle assembly.

7.. Disconnect the oil cooler lines at the transaxle. Remove the transaxle control cable clip and retainer and then disconnect the cable from the bracket. Remove the bracket.

8. Remove the starter assembly. Disconnect the exhaust pipe at the manifold. Remove the pipe.

9. Remove the stiffner plate. Remove the rear engine end plate. Remove the torque converter cover. Remove the torque converter retaining bolts.

10. Disconnect both the right and left driveshafts from their side gear shafts. Depress and hold the brake pedal while removing the driveshaft retaining nuts. Properly position the driveshaft out of the way.

11. Disconnect the suspension arm from the rear axle carrier, using the proper tools. Disconnect the rear axle carrier from the lower control arm.

12. Disconnect the driveshaft from the side gear shaft. Properly position the driveshaft out of the way.

13. Support the engine and transaxle assembly, using the proper equipment. Remove the transaxle to engine retaining bolts. Disconnect the front and rear transmission mount bolts.

14. Carefully lower the transaxle assembly to the floor.

15. Installation is the reverse of the removal procedure.

Celica FWD

1. Disconnect the negative battery cable. Remove the air flow meter and the air cleaner hose.

2. Disconnect the speedometer cable. Remove the starter assembly electrical connections. Disconnect the throttle cable from the throttle linkage and bracket.

3. Disconnect the ground strap. Remove the starter retaining bolts and

as required remove the starter assembly.

4. Remove the upper transaxle housing retaining bolts. Remove the engine rear mount insulator bracket retaining bolt.

5. Raise and support the vehicle safely. Drain the transaxle fluid. Remove the engine under covers.

6. Remove the lower suspension crossmember. Disconnect the front and rear mounting. Remove the engine mounting center member.

7. Remove the left hand driveshaft. Disconnect the right hand driveshaft.

8. Disconnect the exhaust pipe from the manifold. Remove the stiffner plate. Disconnect the control cable.

9. Disconnect the oil cooler hoses. Remove the torque converter cover. Remove the torque converter retaining bolts.

10. Support the engine and transaxle assembly, using the proper equipment. Remove the transaxle to engine retaining bolts. Disconnect the front and rear transmission mount bolts.

11. Carefully lower the transaxle assembly to the floor.

12. Installation is the reverse of the removal procedure.

PAN REMOVAL

1. Raise and support the vehicle safely. Remove the drain plug. Drain the fluid in a suitable container.

2. Remove the drain pan retaining bolts.

3. Remove the pan. Discard the gasket.

4. Remove th filter, as required.

5. Installation is the reverse of the removal procedure. Refill the unit with the proper grade and type transmission fluid.

LINKAGE ADJUSTMENT

Tercel

1981–86

1. Push the selector lever all the way to the front of the vehicle.

2. Return the lever three notches to the "N" shift position.

3. While holding the selector lever slightly toward the "R" shift position tighten the connecting rod nut.

1987–88

1. Loosen the swivel nut on the selector lever.

2. Push the lever fully toward the right side of the vehicle.

3. Return the lever two notches to the "N" position.

4. While holding the selector lever slightly toward the "R" shift position tighten the swivel nut.

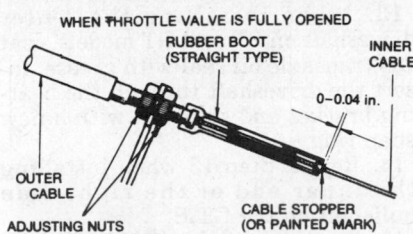

WHEN THROTTLE VALVE IS FULLY OPENED
RUBBER BOOT (STRAIGHT TYPE) · INNER CABLE · OUTER CABLE · ADJUSTING NUTS · CABLE STOPPER (OR PAINTED MARK) · 0–0.04 in.

Throttle linkage adjustment—1980 and later models

WAGON

1. Push the selector lever all the way to the rear of the vehicle.
2. Return the lever two notches to the "N" shift position.
3. While holding the selector lever slightly toward the "R" shift position tighten the connecting rod nut.

Corolla FWD, Camary, MR2 and Celica FWD

1. Loosen the swivel nut on the selector lever.
2. Push the lever fully toward the right side of the vehicle.
3. Return the lever two notches to the "N" position.
4. While holding the selector lever slightly toward the "R" shift position tighten the swivel nut.

NEUTRAL SAFETY SWITCH

Tercel, MR2 and Celica FWD

1. Loosen the neutral start switch bolt. Position the selector in the "N" position.
2. Align the switch shaft groove with the neutral base line which is located on the switch.
3. Tighten the bolt.

Corolla FWD

1984–85

1. Loosen the neutral start switch retaining bolts.
2. Connect an ohmmeter between the terminals.
3. Adjust the switch to the point where there is continunity between the terminals.

1986–88

1. Loosen the neutral start switch bolt. Position the selector in the "N" position.
2. As required disconnect the switch electrical connector. Align the switch shaft groove with the neutral base line which is located on the switch.
3. Tighten the bolt.

Camry

1983–85

1. Loosen the neutral start switch retaining bolts.

2. Connect an ohmmeter between the terminals.
3. Adjust the switch to the point where there is continunity between the terminals.

1986–88

1. Loosen the neutral start switch bolt. Position the selector in the "N" position.
2. Align the switch shaft groove with the neutral base line which is located on the switch.
3. Tighten the bolt.

TRANSFER CASE

REMOVAL & INSTALLATION

1987-88 4WD Van

1. Disconnect the negative battery cable and raise and support the vehicle safely.
2. Remove the transfer case protector and drain the transfer case oil into a suitable drain pan.
3. Matchmark and remove the front and rear drive (propeller) shafts. Disconnect the transfer indicator switch connector.
4. Disconnect the speed sensor connector, If so equipped.
5. Disconnect the speedometer cable and ground strap. On vehicles equipped with an automatic transaxle, diaconnect the vacuum hoses from the vacuum actuator.
6. On vehicles equipped with a manual transaxle, disconnect the transfer control cable by removing the retaining clip and washer. Then remove the retainer from the bracket.
7. Disconnect the front exhaust pipe by removing the exhaust front pipe clamp from the bracket and then disconnect the exhaust front pipe from the exhaust manifold.
8. Using a suitable transmission jack or equivalent, raise the transmission enough to remove the weight from the rear mounting.
9. Remove the rear engine mounting bolt(s). Remove the transfer case mounting bolts and remove the transfer case by pulling the transfer case toward the rear of the vehicle. Remove the rear engine mounting bracket and place the transfer case in a suitable holding fixture.
10. Installation is the reverse order of the removal procedure. When installing the transfer case, place a new gasket to the transfer case adaptor and align the input shaft with the transmission output shaft, then push the transfer case fully into position.
11. Be sure to apply a suitable

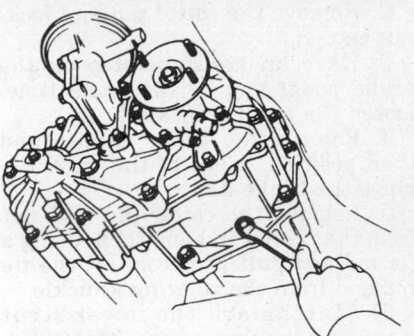

Removing the transfer case assembly from the vehicle

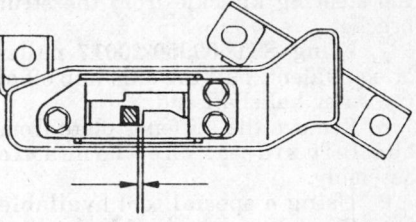

1 mm or less

Proper transfer case shifter adjustment clearance

thread sealer to the two front bolt threads. Install and torque the retaining bolts to 27 ft. lbs. Torque the following bolts as follows:
 a. Rear engine mounting bracket bolts — 21 ft. lbs.
 b. Rear engine mounting bolt — 36 ft. lbs.
 c. Front exhaust pipe clamp bolts — 46 ft. lbs.
12. After installation is complete, fill the transfer case with 1.3 quarts of a suitable 75W-90 gear oil.
13. Shift the transfer shift lever into the H4 position. Loosen the three detent plate installation bolts. Pull the top of the shift lever using a little force (4.4–8.8 lbs.).
14. With the shift lever now in the proper position, adjust the clearance between the detent plate H4 stopper surface and the shift lever so that it is 0.04 in. (1 mm) or less. Then tighten the detent plate installation bolts. Road test the vehicle and check it for proper operation.

DRIVE AXLE

Halfshafts

REMOVAL & INSTALLATION

Tercel

1. Raise the front of the vehicle and support it with jacks stands.

2. Remove the cotter pin and lock-nut cap.

3. Have an assistant step on the brake pedal and at the same time, loosen the gearing locknut.

4. Remove the brake caliper and then position it out of the way. Remove the brake disc.

5. Remove the cotter pin and nut from the tie rod end and then, using a tie rod end puller, disconnect the tie rod end from the steering knuckle.

6. Matchmark the lower strut mounting bracket where it attaches to the steering knuckle, remove the mounting bolts and then disconnect the steering knuckle from the strut bracket.

7. Using SST 09950-20017 puller or equivalent, pull the axle hub off of the outer halfshaft end.

8. Remove the stiffener plate from the left side of the transaxle assembly.

9. Using a special tool available from Toyota, tap the halfshaft out of the transaxle casing.

NOTE: Be sure to cover the halfshaft input hole.

10. Installation is in the reverse order of removal. Please note the following:

a. Coat the oil seal in the transaxle input hole with MP grease before inserting the halfshaft.

b. Tighten the steering knuckle-to-strut bolts to 105 ft. lbs.

c. Tighten the tie rod end nut to 29–43 ft. lbs.

d. Tighten the bearing locknut to 137 ft. lbs.

e. Tighten the stiffner plate bolts to 29 ft. lbs.

f. The length between the left and right halfshafts should be less than 7.626 in.

g. Check the front wheel alignment.

Corolla FWD

1. Raise and support the front end on jackstands.

2. Remove the cotter pin, locknut cap and locknut from the hub.

3. Remove the engine under cover. Remove the six nuts attaching the halfshaft (front drive shaft) to transaxle (differential side gear).

4. Remove the brake caliper from the steering knuckle and support it out of the way with a wire. Remove the rotor disc.

5. Disconnect the steering knuckle from the lower arm by removing the bolt and two nuts, then disconnect the lower arm from the steering knuckle.

6. Using SST 09950-20017 puller or equivalent, pull the axle hub from the halfshaft. Be sure to cover the

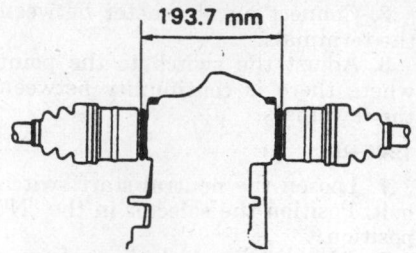

193.7 mm

The left and right halfshafts should be 7.626 in. apart

dust boot with a shop rag to prevent damage to the the bolt.

7. Installation is the reverse of removal. Torque the steering knuckle to 47 ft. lbs.; the caliper bolts to 65 ft. lbs.; the bearing nut to 137 ft. lbs. and the halfshaft nuts to 27 ft. lbs.

Celica FWD (1986-88)

1. Raise and support the front of the vehicle on jackstands.

2. Remove the wheels.

3. Remove the cotter pin, cap and locknut from the hub.

4. Remove the engine under covers (Celica).

5. Drain the transmission fluid or the differential fluid on the GT-S.

6. Remove the transaxle gravel shield on the GT-S.

7. Loosen the six nuts attaching the inner end of the halfshaft to transaxle (all except Celica GT-S). It's a good idea to have a friend sit in the car and depress the brake pedal while removing the nuts.

NOTE: Wrap the exposed end of the halfshaft in an old shop cloth to prevent damage to it.

Remove the cotter pin from the tie end rod and then press the tie rod out of the steering knuckle.

8. Remove the bolt and two nuts and disconnect the steering knuckle from the lower arm control.

9. On all but the GT-S, use a two-armed gear puller or the like and press the halfshaft out of the steering knuckle.

10. On the GT-S, mark a spot somewhere on the left-side halfshaft and measure the distance between the spot and the transaxle case. Using SST 09520–32060, pull the halfshaft out of the transaxle.

11. On the GT-S, use a two-armed puller and press the outer end of the right-side shaft out of the steering knuckle. Use a pair of pliers to remove the snap ring at the inner end and pull the halfshaft out of the center driveshaft.

12. On all but the GT-S, remove the snap ring on the center driveshaft with a pair of pliers and then pull the center shaft out of the transaxle case.

13. When installing the center driveshaft on ST and GT models, coat the transaxle oil seal with grease, insert the driveshaft through the bearing bracket and secure it with a new snap ring.

14. Repeat Step 13 when installing the inner end of the right-side halfshaft on the GT-S.

15. On the right-side halfshaft of the GT-S, use a new snap ring, coat the transaxle oil seal with grease and then press the inner end of the shaft into the differential housing. Check that the measurement made in Step 10 is the same. Check that there is 0.08–0.11 in. (2–3mm) of axial play. Check also that the halfshaft will not come out by trying to pull it with your hand.

16. Press the outer end of each halfshaft into the steering knuckle on the GTS.

17. On the ST and GT, press the outer end of the halfshafts into the steering knuckle and then fingertighten the nuts on the inner end.

18. Connect the steering knuckle to the lower control arm and tighten the bolts to 94 ft. lbs. (127 Nm).

19. Connect the tie rod end to the steering knuckle and tighten the nut to 36 ft. lbs. (49 Nm). Install a new cotter pin.

20. Tighten the hub locknut to 137 ft. lbs. (186 Nm) while depressing the brake pedal. Install the cap and use a new cotter pin.

21. On the ST and GT, tighten the six nuts on the inner halfshaft ends to 27 ft. lbs. (36 Nm) while depressing the brake pedal.

22. Install the transaxle gravel shield on the GT-S.

23. Fill the transaxle with gear oil or fluid.

24 Install the engine under cover.

Camry

1. Raise and support the front of the vehicle on jackstands.

2. Remove the wheels.

3. Remove the cotter pin, cap and locknut from the hub.

4. Remove the transaxle gravel shield on models with w/MT. Remove the engine under cover and front fender apron seal.

5. Loosen the six nuts attaching the inner end of the halfshaft to transaxle. It's a good idea to have a friend sit in the car and depress the brake pedal while removing the nuts.

NOTE: Wrap the exposed end of the halfshaft in an old shop cloth to prevent damage to it.

6. Remove the brake caliper with the hydraulic line still attached, position it out of the way and suspend it with a wire. Remove the rotor.

7. On all diesel models and on the left side of gas engine w/AT, remove the two bolts attaching the ball joint to the steering knuckle. Pull the lower control arm down while pulling the strut outward; this will disconnect the inner end of the halfshaft from the transaxle.

8. Using a two-armed puller, or the like, press the outer end of the halfshaft from the steering knuckle and then remove the halfshaft.

9. On gasoline engined models, it is also possible to remove the right-side center driveshaft. Drain the transaxle fluid, remove the snap ring with pliers and pull the driveshaft out of the transaxle case.

To install:

10. When installing the center driveshaft, coat the transaxle oil seal with grease, insert the driveshaft through the bearing bracket and secure it with a new snap ring.

11. Press the outer end of the halfshaft into the steering knuckle, position the inner end and install the six nuts fingertight.

12. Reconnect the ball joint to the steering knuckle on models that it was disconnected and tighten the bolts to 83 ft. lbs. (113 Nm).

13. Install the rotor and brake caliper. Tighten the caliper-to-knuckle bolts to 65 ft. lbs. (88 Nm).

14. Tighten the wheel bearing locknut to 137 ft. lbs. (186 Nm) while depressing the brake pedal. Install the locknut cap and use a new cotter pin.

15. Tighten the six inner end nuts to 27 ft. lbs. (36 Nm) while depressing the brake pedal.

16. Install the transaxle gravel shield on models so equipped.

17. Fill the transaxle with fluid (ATF Dexron® 11 on models with a gasoline engine).

MR2

1. Raise and support the front of the vehicle on jackstands.

2. Remove the wheels.

3. Remove the cotter pin, cap and locknut from the hub.

4. Remove the transaxle gravel shield.

5. Loosen the six nuts attaching the inner end of the halfshaft to transaxle. It's a good idea to have a friend sit in the car and depress the brake pedal while removing the nuts.

NOTE: Wrap the exposed end of the halfshaft in an old shop cloth to prevent damage to it.

6. On models equipped with a automatic transaxle, Remove the two bolts holding the ball joint to the rear axle carrier and discoonect the lower arm from the rear axle carrier.

7. Also on models equipped with a automatic transaxle, remove the cotter pin and nut and using SST 09610-20012 or equivalent, disconnect the suspension arm from the rear axle carrier.

8. While holding the halfshaft, use a plastic mallet and carefully knock the outer end of the wheel hub assembly. Remove the halfshaft.

To install:

1. Press the outer end of the halfshaft into the wheel hub assembly.

2. Position the inner end of the halfshaft and install the six nuts fingertight.

3. Install the transaxle gravel shield.

4. Tighten the wheel bearing locknut to 137 ft. lbs. (186 Nm) while depressing the brake pedal. Install the locknut cap and use a new cotter pin.

5. Tighten the six inner end nuts to 27 ft. lbs. (36 Nm) while depressing the brake pedal. Torque the suspension arm nut to 36 ft. lbs. and the lower arm to rear axle carrier to 83 ft. lbs.

6. Fill the transaxle with fluid.

1983-88 Cressida, 1982-86 Supra and 1983-85 Celica GTS

1. Raise and support the rear of the vehicle on jackstands.

2. Place matchmarks on the halfshaft and flanges.

3. Remove the four nuts retaining the halfshaft to the differential and disconnect the halfshaft from the differential.

4. Remove the four nuts retaining the halfshaft to the axle shaft and disconnect the halfshaft from the axleshaft. Remove the halfshaft from the under the vehicle.

5. Installation is the reverse order of the removal procedure. Be sure to line up the matchmarks on the halfshaft and torque the retaining nuts to 51 ft. lbs.

1987-88 Supra

1. Raise and support the rear of the vehicle safely. Remove the rear wheels.

2. Using a suitable jack, raise the number two suspension arm until it is horizontal. Place matchmarks to the rear halfshaft and side gear shaft flange.

3. Remove the six retaining nuts (while and assistant is depressing the brake pedal) and disconnect the rear halfshaft from the differential.

4. Remove the cotter pin and lock nut cap. Loosen and remove the bearing lock nut.

5. Using a suitable plastic hammer, tap out the rear halfshaft.

6. Installation is the reverse order of the removal procedure. Torque the bearing lock nut to 203 ft. lbs. and the six halfshaft retaining bolts to 51 ft. lbs.

1987 4WD Van

1. Raise and support the vehicle safely. Remove the six retaining nuts holding the halfshaft to the differential side gear shaft.

2. Remove the flange as follows:
   a. Remove the hub grease cap from the flange.
   b. Remove the bolt with it's washer.
   c. Remove the mounting nuts.
   d. Using a brass drift and a hammer, tap the bolt heads and remove the cone washers.
   e. Install and tighten the two bolts to the flange and remove the flange.

3. Remove the free locking hub as follows:
   a. Set the control handle to free.
   b. Remove the cover mounting bolts and pull off the cover. Remove the bolt and washer.
   c. Remove the free wheeling hub body mounting nuts and washers. Using a brass drift and a hammer, tap on the bolt heads and remove the cone washers. Pull off the free wheeling hub body.

4. Remove the automatic locking hub as follows:
   a. Remove the hub cover using a suitable torx® socket. Remove the axle bolt and washer.
   b. Remove the automatic locking hub body mounting nuts and washers. Using a brass drift and a hammer, tap on the bolt heads and remove the cone washers. Pull off the free wheeling hub body.

NOTE: Do not tap on the hub body when removing the cone washer. If the stud bolt is damaged or deformed, replace it with a new one.

c. Pull off the hub body. Remove the snap ring from the brake subassembly and pry off the brake subassembly.

NOTE: Never strike the brake shoe with any pry tools, apply the pry bar to the brake drum to remove the snap ring. Do not drop the brake shoe subassembly.

d. Using a suitable torx® socket, remove the brake drum. If necessary, remove the adjusting nut using tool SST 09607-60020 or equivalent.

5. Using a suitable pair of snap ring pliers, remove the snap ring from the drive shaft.

6. Jack up the lower suspension

arm and remove the front drive shaft. To prevent damage to the boot, place a shop rag between the lower suspension arm and the front drive shaft.

7. Apply molybdenum disulphide lithium base grease to the outboard joint shaft.

8. Insert the front drive shaft into the steering knuckle and temporarily connect the front drive shaft to the side differential gear shaft with the six bolts and nuts.

9. Install the spacer to the front drive shaft and install the snap ring.

10. Install the flange, free wheeling hub and automatic locking hub, by reversing the removal procedure. Use the following torque specification:

   a. Install the six nuts with cone washers on the flange and torque them to 23 ft. lbs.

   b. Install the flange bolt with washer in the drive shaft and torque it to 13 ft. lbs.

   c. Install the six nuts with cone washers on the free wheeling hub body and torque them to 23 ft. lbs.

   d. Torque the free wheeling hub cover mounting bolts to 7 ft. lbs.

   e. Adjust the preload on the automatic locking hub adjusting nut to 43 ft. lbs. Then turn the hub right and left two or three times (loosen the adjusting nut so it can be turned by hand). Retighten the adjusting nut to 11 ft. lbs. Using a spring tension gauge, check the preload, it should be 5 to 8 lbs.

11. Torque the front drive shaft mounting bolts and nuts to 50 ft.

CV JOINT OVERHAUL

For all CV-joint overhaul procedures, please refer to "CV-Joint Overhaul" in the Unit Repair section.

Driveshaft and U-Joints

REMOVAL & INSTALLATION

Rear Wheel Drive and 4 X 4 Only

1. Raise the rear of the car with jacks and support the rear axle housing with jackstands.

2. Matchmark the driveshaft and companion flange. Unfasten the bolts which attach the driveshaft universal joint yoke flange to the mounting flange on the differential drive pinion.

3. On models equipped with three universal joints, perform the following:

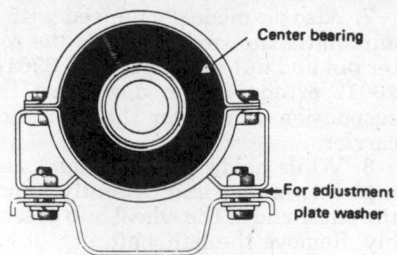

Center bearing adjustment

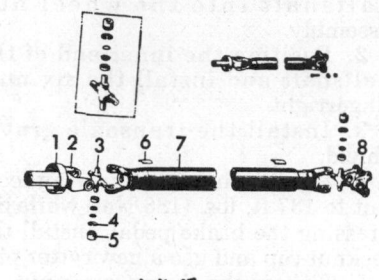

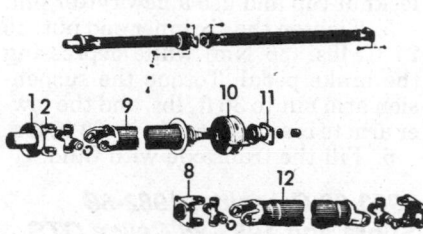

1. Transmission end of driveshaft
2. U-joint yoke and sleeve
3. U-joint spider
4. Snap ring
5. U-joint spider bearing
6. Balancing weight
7. Driveshaft
8. U-joint yoke flange
9. Intermediate driveshaft assembly
10. Center bearing support
11. U-joint flange assembly
12. Driveshaft
   Two-piece driveshaft only

Driveshaft components—the upper illustration shows a single piece driveshaft

   a. Remove the driveshaft sub-assembly from the U-joint sleeve yoke.

   b. Remove the center support bearing from its bracket.

4. Remove the driveshaft end from the transmission.

5. Install an old U-joint yoke in the transmission or, if none is available, use a plastic bag secured with a rubber band over the hole to keep the transmission oil from running out.

NOTE: On 1982-87 Supra models, the exhaust pipe assembly must be removed in order to remove the driveshaft assembly.

6. Remove the driveshaft from beneath the vehicle.

Installation is performed in the following order:

1. Apply multipurpose grease on the section of the U-joint sleeve which is to be inserted into the transmission.

2. Insert the driveshaft sleeve into the transmission.

—————— **CAUTION** ——————
Be careful not to damage any of the seals.

3. For models equipped with three U-joints and center bearings, perform the following:

   a. Adjust the center bearing clearance with no load placed on the driveline components; the top of the rubber center cushion should be 0.04 in. behind the center of the elongated bolt hole.

   b. Install the center bearing assembly.

NOTE: Use the same number of washers on the center bearing brackets as were removed.

   c. Matchmark the arrow marks on the driveshaft and grease fittings.

4. Align the matchmarks. Secure he U-joint flange to the differential pinion flange with the mounting bolts.

—————— **CAUTION** ——————
Be sure that the bolts are of the same type as those removed and that they are tightened securely.

5. Remove the jack stands and lower the vehicle.

U-JOINT OVERHAUL

NOTE: As the U-joints on many late model vehicles are non-serviceable, the entire driveshaft must be replaced in the vent of U-joint problems.

Rear Axle Shafts

NOTE: For rear axle shaft removal on FWD models, please refer to "Rear Axle Hub, Carrier and Bearing"

REMOVAL & INSTALLATION

Rear Wheel Drive Models

ALL EXCEPT 1982-86 SUPRA AND 1983-85 CELICA GTS AND 1983-88 CRESSIDA

1. Raise the rear of the car and support it securely by using jack stands.

2. Drain the oil from the axle housing.

3. Remove the wheel disc, unfasten the lug nuts, and remove the wheel.

4. Punch matchmarks on the brake drum and the axle shaft to maintain rotational balance.

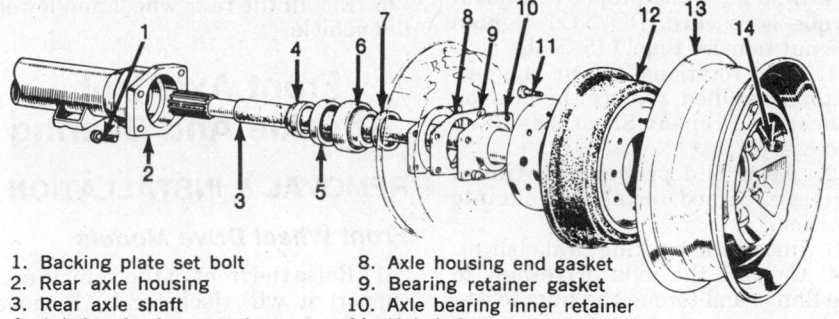

1. Backing plate set bolt
2. Rear axle housing
3. Rear axle shaft
4. Axle bearing inner retainer
5. Oil seal
6. Bearing
7. Spacer
8. Axle housing end gasket
9. Bearing retainer gasket
10. Axle bearing inner retainer
11. Hub bolt
12. Brake drum assembly
13. Wheel
14. Hub nut

Typical solid rear axle components

5. Remove the brake drum and related components, as detailed above.
6. Remove the rear bearing retaining nut.
7. Remove the backing plate attachment nuts through the access holes in the rear axle shaft flange.
8. Use a slide hammer with a suitable adapter to withdraw the axle shaft from its housing.

— CAUTION —

Use care not to damage the oil seal when removing the axle shaft.

9. Repeat the procedure for the axle shaft on the opposite side.

— CAUTION —

Be careful not to mix the components of the two sides.

10. Installation is performed in the reverse order of removal. Coat the lips of the rear housing oil seal with multipurpose grease prior to installation of the rear axle shaft. Torque the bearing retaining nut to specifications.

NOTE: Always use new nuts, as they are the self-locking type.

AXLE BEARING RETAINING NUT SPECIFICATIONS

Model	Torque range (ft. lbs.)
Corolla 1600	26–38
Corolla 1800	19–23
Corona	29–36
Tercel	22
Celica②	19–23
Supra①	19–23
Cressida	22
Van	48

① Except 1982 and later—See text
② Except 1983 and later GTS—See text.

SUPRA (1982-87), CELICA GTS (1983-85) AND CRESSIDA (1983-87)

Remove the axle shaft in the following manner:

1. Raise the rear of the vehicle and support it safely with jackstands.
2. Disconnect the axle driveshaft from the axle flange and lower the axle drive shaft out of the way.
3. Apply the parking brake completely (pulled up as far as possible).
4. Remove the axle flange nut.

NOTE: The axle flange nut is staked in place. It will be necessary to loosen the staked part of the nut with a hammer and chisel, prior to loosening the nut.

5. Using Toyota special service tool No. SST 09557–22022 (or its equivalent), disconnect the axle flange from the axle shaft. Be careful not to lose the plate washer from the nearing side of the flange.
6. Remove the parking brake shoes.
7. Using Toyota special service tool No. SST 09520–00031 (or its equivalent), pull out the rear axle shaft, along with the oil seal and outer bearing.
Inspect the components:
8. Clean and inspect the bearings, races, and seal. If these parts are in good condition, repack the bearings with MP grease No. 2 and proceed to Step 15 to install the axle shaft.

To replace the bearings and seals:

9. Using a hammer and chisel, increase the clearance between the axle shaft hub and the outer bearing.
10. Using a puller installed with the jaws in the gap made in Step 9, pull

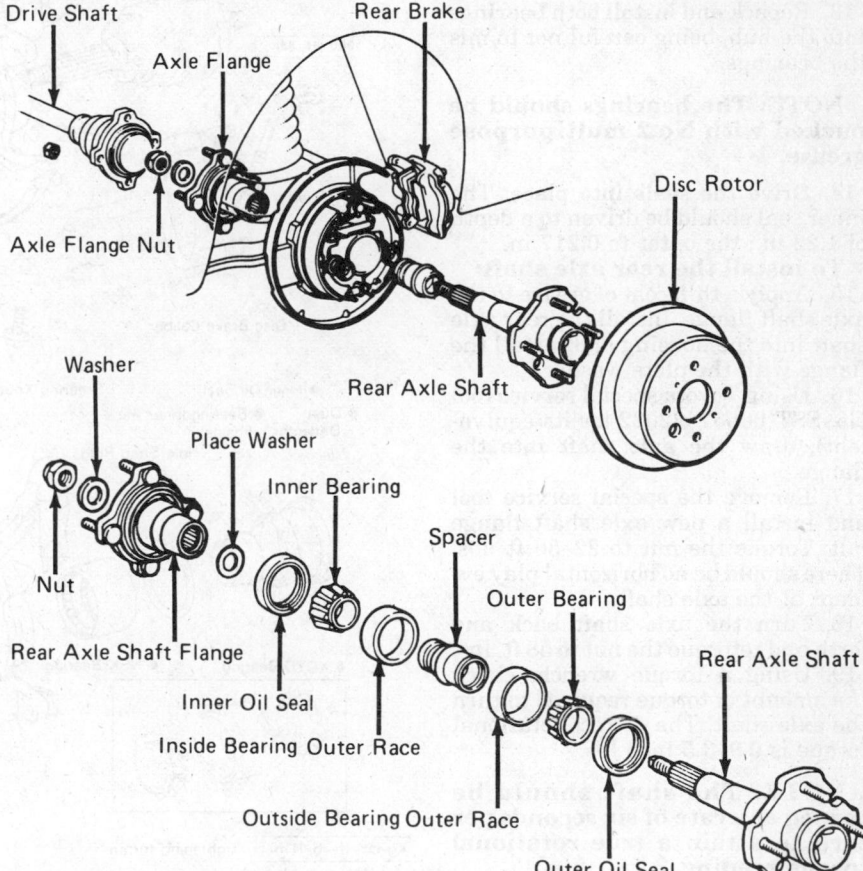

Rear axle shafts—Supra (1982 and later), Celica GTS (1983–85) and Cressida (1983 and later)

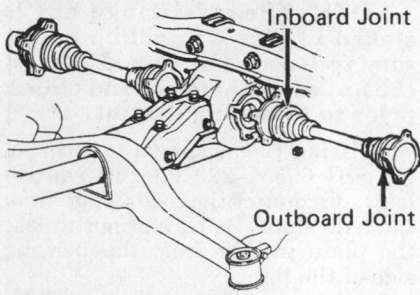

Rear axle halfshafts—Supra (1982 and later), Celica GTS (1983–85) and Cressida (1983 and later)

the outer bearing from the axle shaft and remove the oil seal.

11. Drive the outer bearing race out of the hub with a brass drift and a hammer.

NOTE: Bearing and races must be replaced in matched sets. NEVER use a new bearing with an old race, or vice-versa.

12. Drive the new outer bearing race into the axle shaft hub until it is completely seated.

NOTE: The inner bearing race is replaced in the same manner as Steps 11 and 12.

13. Repack and install both bearings into the hub, being careful not to mix the bearings.

NOTE: The bearings should be packed with No.2 multipurpose grease.

14. Drive the seals into place. The inner seal should be driven to a depth of 1.22 in.; the outer to 0.217 in.

To install the rear axle shaft:

15. Apply a thin coat of grease to the axle shaft flange. Install the rear axle shaft into the housing and install the flange with the plate washer.

16. Using Toyota special service tool No. SST 09557-22022 (or its equivalent), draw the axle shaft into the flange.

17. Remove the special service tool and install a new axle shaft flange nut. Torque the nut to 22–36 ft. lbs. There should be no horizontal play evident at the axle shaft.

18. Turn the axle shaft back and forth and retorque the nut to 58 ft. lbs.

19. Using a torque wrench, check the amount of torque required to turn the axle shaft. The correct rotational torque is 0.9–3.5 inch lbs.

NOTE: The shaft should be turned at a rate of six seconds per turn to attain a true rotational torque reading.

20. If the rotational torque is less than specified, tighten the nut 5–10°

at a time until the proper rotational torque is reached. DO NOT tighten the nut to more than 145 ft. lbs.

21. If the rotational torque is greater than specified, replace the bearing spacer and repeat Steps 18–20 (if necessary).

22. After the proper rotational torque is reached, restake the nut into position.

23. Install the parking brake shoes.

24. Connect the axle driveshaft to the flange and torque the nuts to 44–57 ft. lbs.

—————— **CAUTION** ——————

If the maximum torque is exceeded while retightening the nut, replace the bearing spacer and repeat Steps 18–20. DO NOT back off the axle shaft nut to reduce the rotational torque.

25. Install the rear wheel and lower the vehicle.

Front Axle Hub, Knuckle And Bearing

REMOVAL & INSTALLATION

Front Wheel Drive Models

1. Raise the front of the vehicle and support it with jackstands. Remove the wheel.

2. Remove the cotter pin from the bearing locknut cap and then remove the cap.

3. Have a friend depress the brake pedal and loosen the bearing locknut.

4. Remove the brake caliper mounting nuts, position the caliper

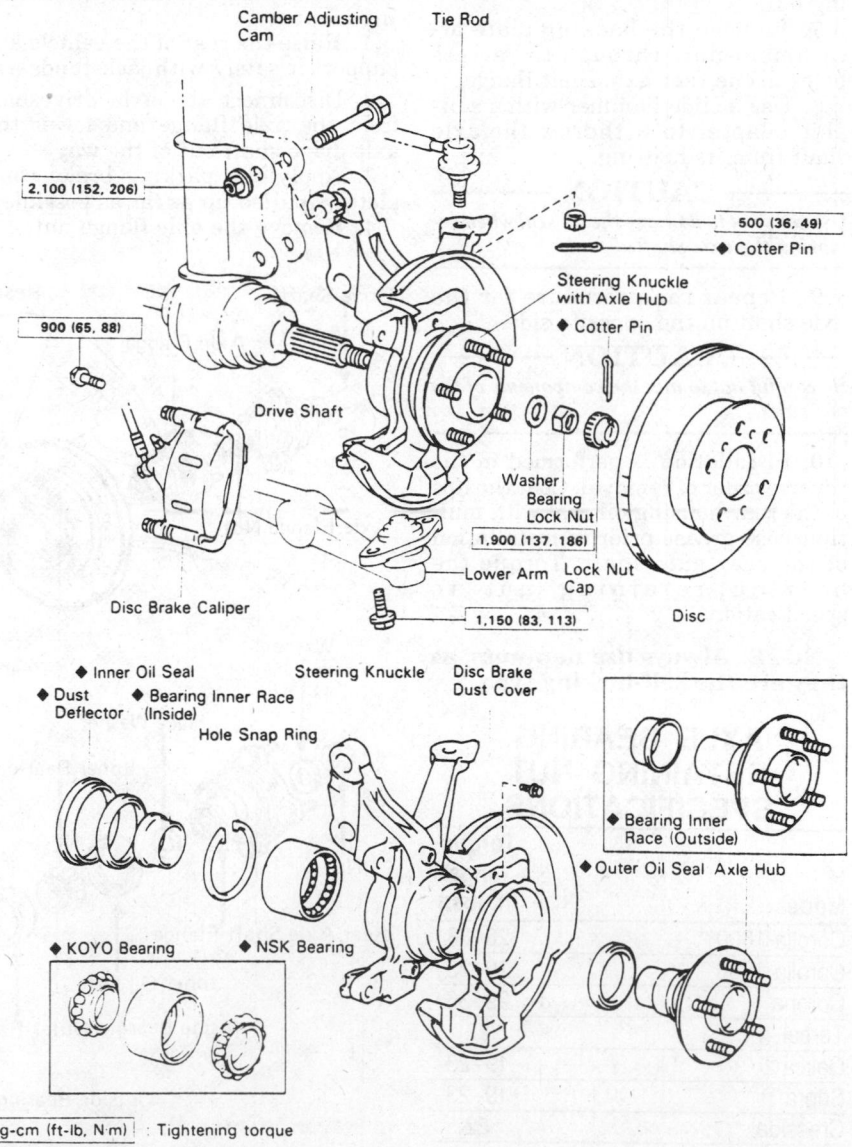

Front axle hub and steering knuckle assembly—front wheel drive models

out of the way with the hydraulic line still attached and suspend it with a wire.

5. Remove the disc brake.

6. Remove the cotter pin and nut from the tie rod end and then, using a tie rod end removal tool, remove the tie rod.

7. Place matchmarks on the shock absorber lower mounting bracket and the camber adjustment cam, remove the bolts and separate the steering knuckle from the strut.

8. Remove the two ball joint attaching nuts and disconnect the lower control arm from the steering knuckle.

9. Carefully grasp the axle hub and pull it out from the halfshaft. This may require a two-armed puller or the like.

NOTE: Be sure to cover the halfshaft boot with a shop rag to protect it from any damage.

10. Clamp the steering knuckle in a vise. Remove the dust deflector, remove the nut holding the steering knuckle to the ball joint. Press the ball joint out of the steering knuckle.

11. Remove the dust deflector from the hub.

12. Use a slide hammer to remove the bearing inner oil seal and then remove the hole snap ring with needle-nose pliers.

13. Remove the three bolts attaching the steering knuckle to the disc brake dust cover.

14. Use a two-armed puller to remove the axle hub from the steering knuckle.

15. Remove the bearing inner race (inside).

16. Remove the bearing inner race (outside).

17. Remove the oil seal from the knuckle.

18. Position an old bearing inner race (outside) on the bearing and then use a hammer and a drift to carefully knock the bearing out of the knuckle.

To install:

1. Press a new bearing into the steering knuckle.

2. Using an oil seal installation tool, drive a new oil seal into the knuckle.

3. Install the disc brake dust cover onto the knuckle using liquid sealant.

4. Apply grease between the oil seal lip, oil seal and the bearing and then press the axle hub into the steering knuckle.

5. Install a new hole snap ring into the knuckle with pliers.

6. Press a new oil seal onto the knuckle and coat the contact surface of the seal and the halfshaft with grease. Press a new duct deflector into the knuckle.

7. Position the ball joint on the steering knuckle and tighten the nut to 14 ft. lbs. (20 Nm). Remove the nut, install a new one and tighten it to 82 ft. lbs. (111 Nm).

8. Connect the knuckle assembly to the lower strut bracket. Insert the mounting bolts from the rear and make sure the matchmarks made earlier are in alignment. Tighten the nuts to 105 ft. lbs. (142 Nm); Camry/Celica—152 ft. lbs. (206 Nm).

9. Connect the tie rod end to the knuckle, tighten the nut to 36 ft. lbs. (49 Nm) and install a new cotter pin.

10. Connect the ball joint to the lower control arm and tighten the bolt to 47 ft. lbs. (64 Nm).

11. Install the brake disc and the caliper. Tighten the caliper mounting bolts to 65 ft. lbs. (88 Nm).

12. Install the bearing locknut while having someone depress the brake pedal. Tighten it to 137 ft. lbs. (186 Nm). Install the adjusting nut cap and insert a new cotter pin.

13. Check the alignment.

4WD Van

1. Raise the front of the vehicle and support it with jackstands. Remove the wheel.

2. Remove the brake caliper mounting nuts, position the caliper out of the way with the hydraulic line still attached and suspend it with a wire.

3. Remove the flange as follows:

a. Remove the hub grease cap from the flange.

b. Remove the bolt with it's washer.

c. Remove the mounting nuts.

d. Using a brass drift and a hammer, tap the bolt heads and remove the cone washers.

e. Install and tighten the two bolts to the flange and remove the flange.

4. Remove the free locking hub as follows:

a. Set the control handle to free.

b. Remove the cover mounting bolts and pull off the cover. Remove the bolt and washer.

c. Remove the free wheeling hub body mounting nuts and washers. Using a brass drift and a hammer, tap on the bolt heads and remove the cone washers. Pull off the free wheeling hub body.

5. Remove the automatic locking hub as follows:

a. Remove the hub cover using a suitable torx® socket. Remove the axle bolt and washer.

b. Remove the automatic locking hub body mounting nuts and washers. Using a brass drift and a hammer, tap on the bolt heads and remove the cone washers. Pull off the free wheeling hub body.

NOTE: Do not tap on the hub body when removing the cone washer. If the stud bolt is damaged or deformed, replace it with a new one.

c. Pull off the hub body. Remove the snap ring from the brake subassembly and pry off the brake subassembly.

NOTE: Never strike the brake shoe with any pry tools, apply the pry bar to the brake drum to remove the snap ring. Do not drop the brake shoe subassembly.

d. Using a suitable torx® socket, remove the brake drum. If necessary, remove the adjusting nut using tool SST 09607-60020 or equivalent.

6. Remove the axle hub with disc as follows:

a. Without automatic locking hub - use a suitable tool and release the lock washer.

b. Without automatic locking hub - using a suitable lock nut wrench, remove the lock nut and lock washer.

c. Using a suitable lock nut wrench, remove the adjusting nut.

d. Remove the axle hub with the disc together with the bearings.

7. Using a suitable tool, pry out the oil seal and remove the inner bearing from the hub.

8. Remove the hub dust cover.

9. Disconnect the cotter pin and nut from the tie rod connected to the steering knuckle. Using a suitable tie rod puller, disconnect the tie rod from the steering knuckle.

10. Remove the two bolts and disconnect the stabilizer bar from the lower suspension arm.

11. Check the steering knuckle bushing thrust clearance as follows:

a. Install a bolt in the drive shaft.

b. Using a feeler gauge, measure the front drive shaft thrust clearance between the steering knuckle outside bushing and spacer, by pulling the bolt and applying 22 lbs. of pressure.

c. Standard front drive shaft thrust clearance - 0.0030 - 0.0272 in.

d. Maximum front drive shaft clearance - 0.039 in.

12. Using a suitable pair of snap ring pliers, remove the snap ring and spacer.

13. Remove the steering knuckle as follows:

a. Remove the cotter pin and nut from the upper ball joint.

b. Using a suitable puller (SST-

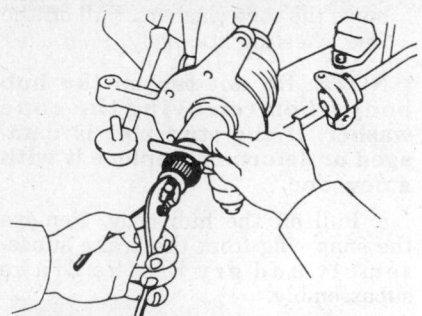

Checking the front drive shaft thrust clearance

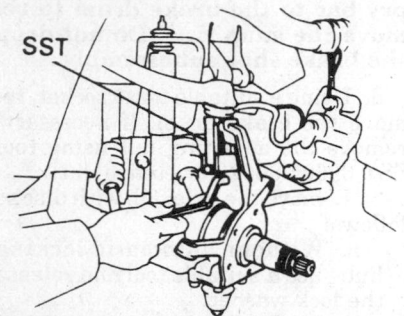

Separating the ball joint from the steering knuckle

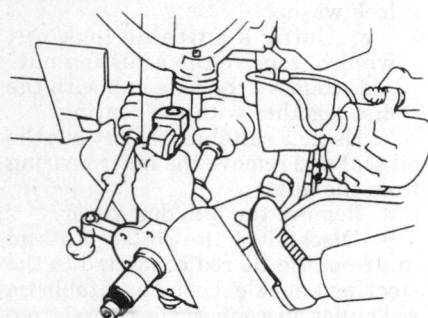

Removing the steering knuckle

09628-62011), disconnect the steering knuckle from the upper suspension arm.

c. Remove the four bolts holding the lower ball joint to the steering knuckle.

d. Push the lower suspension arm down and remove the steering knuckle.

To install:

1. Apply molybednum disulphide lithium base grease to the drive shaft.

2. Push the lower suspension arm down and install the steering knuckle. Connect the lower ball joint the steering knuckle, install and torque the four bolts with washers. Torque to 43 ft. lbs.

3. Connect the upper suspension arm to the steering knuckle, install the nut and torque it to 83 ft. lbs.

4. Install a new cotter pin. If the cotter pin holes do not line up, correct

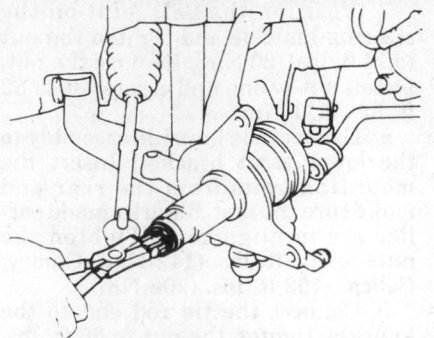

Installing the spacer and snap ring

by tightening the nut by the smallest amounts possible.

5. Install the spacer and snap ring to the front drive shaft.

6. If replacing the steering knuckle bushing, recheck the front drive shaft thrust clearance:

a. Install a bolt in the drive shaft.

b. Using a feeler gauge, measure the front drive shaft thrust clearance between the steering knuckle outside bushing and spacer, by pulling the bolt and applying 22 lbs. of pressure.

c. Standard front drive shaft thrust clearance — 0.0030–0.0272 in.

d. Maximum front drive shaft clearance — 0.039 in.

7. If the clearance is not within specifications, replace the spacer. The spacer thickness is 0.0709 in. to 0.0886 in.

8. Connect the stabilizer to the lower suspension arm. Torque it to 14 ft. lbs.

9. Connect the tie rod to the steering knuckle and torque the nut to 67 ft. lbs. Install a new cotter pin. If the cotter pin holes do not line up, correct by tightening the nut by the smallest amounts possible.

10. Install the hub dust cover.

11. Install the flange, free wheeling hub and automatic locking hub, by reversing the removal procedure. Use the following torque specification:

a. Install the six nuts with cone washers on the flange and torque them to 23 ft. lbs.

b. Install the flange bolt with washer in the drive shaft and torque it to 13 ft. lbs.

c. Install the six nuts with cone washers on the free wheeling hub body and torque them to 23 ft. lbs.

d. Torque the free wheeling hub cover mounting bolts to 7 ft. lbs.

e. Torque the front drive shaft mounting bolts and nuts to 50 ft.

f. Adjust the preload on the automatic locking hub adjusting nut to 43 ft. lbs. Then turn the hub right

and left two or three times (loosen the adjusting nut so it can be turned by hand). Retighten the adjusting nut to 11 ft. lbs. Using a spring tension gauge, check the preload, it should be 5 to 8 lbs.

12. Install the brake caliper and caliper mounting nuts. Install the wheels and lower the vehicle. Check the wheel alignment and road test the vehicle.

FRONT SUSPENSION

Shock Absorbers

REMOVAL & INSTALLATION

Van

1. Remove the hubcap and loosen the lug nuts.

2. Raise the front of the car and support it on the chassis jacking plates provided, with jack stands.

—— **CAUTION** ——

Do not support the weight of the car on the suspension arm; the arm will deform under its weight.

3. Unfasten the lug nuts and remove the wheel.

4. Remove the lock nut and nut. Remove the retainers and cushion.

5. Remove the bolt, spring washer and nut.

6. Remove the shock absorber.

7. Installation is the reverse order of the removal procedure.

MacPherson Struts

REMOVAL & INSTALLATION

All Except Van

1. Remove the hubcap and loosen the lug nuts.

2. Raise the front of the car and support it on the chassis jacking plates provided, with jack stands.

—— **CAUTION** ——

Do not support the weight of the car on the suspension arm; the arm will deform under its weight.

3. Unfasten the lug nuts and remove the wheel.

4. Remove the union bolt and two washers and disconnect the front brake line from the disc brake caliper. Remove the clip from the brake hose and pull off the brake hose from the brake hose bracket.

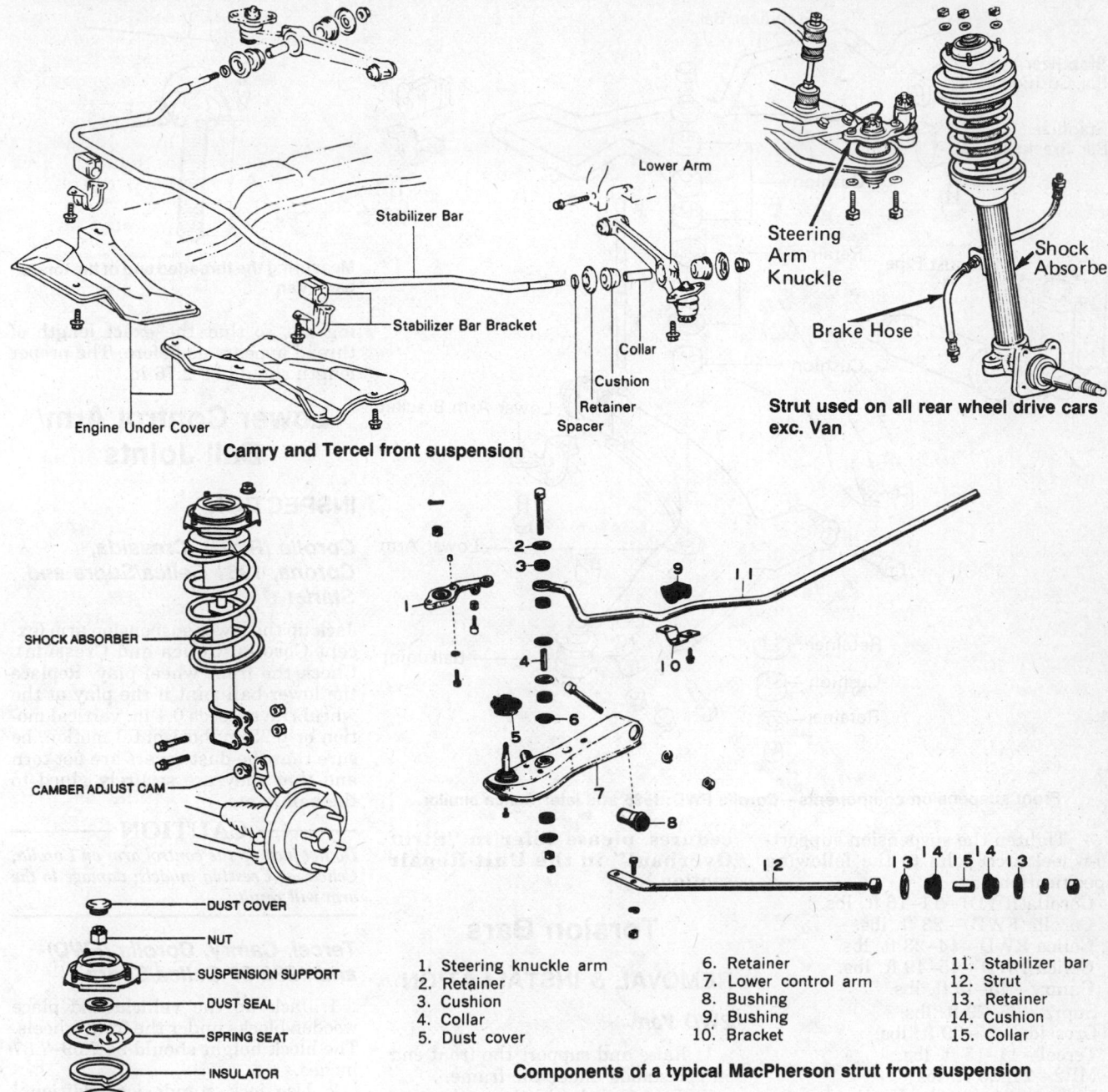

Camry and Tercel front suspension

Strut used on all rear wheel drive cars exc. Van

Steering Arm Knuckle

Shock Absorber

Brake Hose

Lower Arm

Stabilizer Bar

Stabilizer Bar Bracket

Engine Under Cover

Collar

Cushion

Retainer

Spacer

SHOCK ABSORBER

CAMBER ADJUST CAM

DUST COVER

NUT

SUSPENSION SUPPORT

DUST SEAL

SPRING SEAT

INSULATOR

COIL SPRING

BUMPER

Strut used on all front wheel drive cars

1. Steering knuckle arm
2. Retainer
3. Cushion
4. Collar
5. Dust cover
6. Retainer
7. Lower control arm
8. Bushing
9. Bushing
10. Bracket
11. Stabilizer bar
12. Strut
13. Retainer
14. Cushion
15. Collar

Components of a typical MacPherson strut front suspension

5. Remove the caliper and wire it out of the way. Match mark on the strut lower bracket and camber adjust cam. Remove the two bolts and nuts which attach the strut lower end to the steering knuckle lower arm.

6. Remove the three nuts (four nuts on the FX models) which secure the upper strut mounting plate to the top of the wheel arch.

NOTE: Press down on the suspension lower arm, in order to remove the strut assembly. This must be done to clear the collars on the steering knuckle arm bolt holes when removing the shock/spring assembly.

Installation is performed in the reverse order of removal. Be sure to note the following, however:

1. Align the hole in the upper suspension support with the shock ab-

sorber piston or end, so that they fit properly.

2. Always use a new nut and nylon washer on the shock absorber piston rod end when securing it to the upper suspension support. Torque the nut to 29–40 ft. lbs.

— CAUTION —
Do not use an impact wrench to tighten the nut.

3. Coat the suspension support bearing with multipurpose grease prior to installation. Pack the space in the upper support with multipurpose grease, also, after installation.

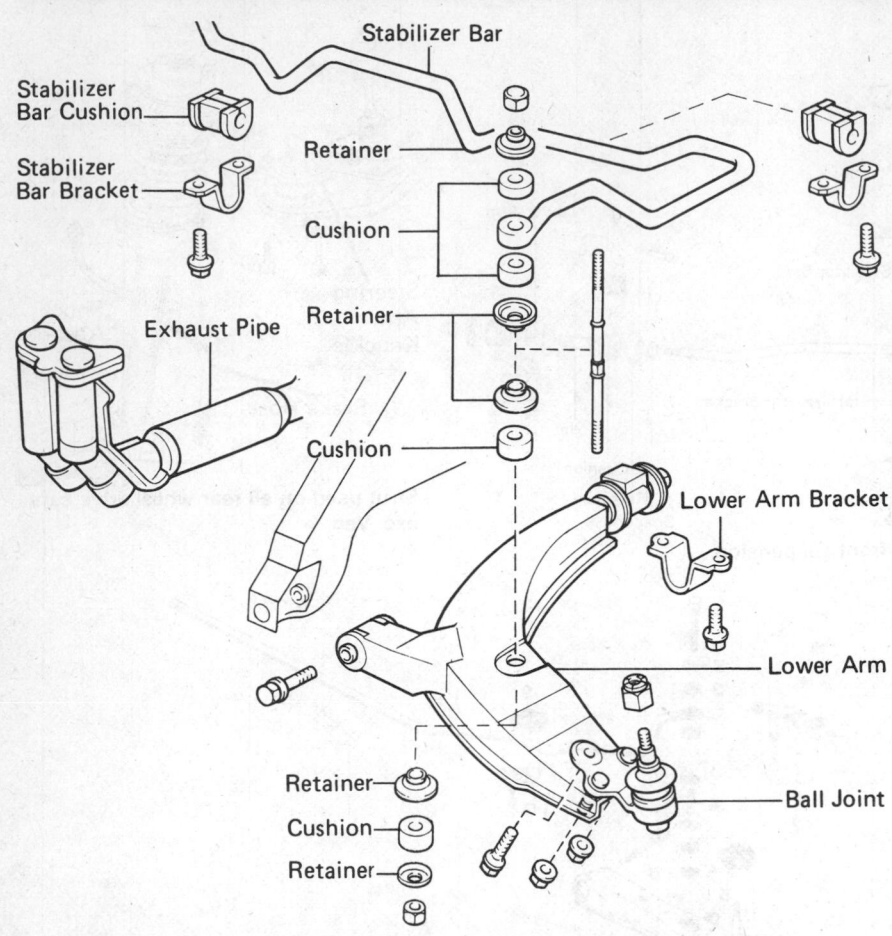

Front suspension components—Corolla FWD: 1986 and later Celica similar

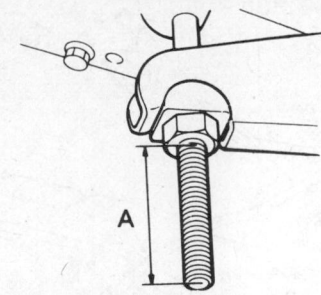

Measuring the threaded end of the torsion bar—Van

4. Tighten the suspension support-to-wheel arch bolts to the following specifications:
   Corolla(RWD) – 11–16 ft. lbs.
   Corolla(FWD) – 23 ft. lbs.
   Celica RWD – 14–23 ft. lbs.
   Celica FWD – 45–49 ft. lbs.
   Camry – 45–49 ft. lbs.
   Supra – 25–29 ft. lbs.
   Cressida – 25–29 ft. lbs.
   Tercel – 11–15 ft. lbs.
   MR2 – 21–25 ft. lbs.
5. Tighten the shock absorber-to-steering knuckle arm bolts to the following specifications:
   Corolla (RWD): 50–65 ft. lbs.
   Corolla (FWD): Gas 105 ft. lbs.; Diesel 152 ft. lbs.
   MR2 and Tercel: 105 ft. lbs.
   Celica RWD and Supra: 72 ft. lbs.
   Cressida: 80 ft. lbs.
   All others: 65 ft. lbs.
6. Adjust the front wheel bearing preload as outlined below.
7. Bleed the brake system.

OVERHAUL

For all spring and shock absorber removal and installation procedures, and all strut overhaul pro- cedures, please refer to "Strut Overhaul" in the Unit Repair section.

Torsion Bars

REMOVAL & INSTALLATION

2WD Van

1. Raise and support the front end on jackstands under the frame.
2. Remove the boots and place paint matchmarks on the torsion bar, anchor arm and torque arm.
3. Remove the locknut and measure the threaded end "A" as shown. Use this figure for an installation reference.
4. Remove the adjusting nut. Remove the anchor arm and torsion bar and spring.
5. Installation is the reverse of removal. There are left and right identification marks on the rear end of the torsion bar springs. Be careful not to interchange the torsion bar springs. Apply a light coating of molybdenum disulphide lithium grease to the splined end of the torsion bar. Align all matchmarks. Tighten the adjust-

ing nut so that the exact length of thread appears as before. The proper length should be 2.76 in.

Lower Control Arm/ Ball Joints

INSPECTION

Corolla (RWD), Cressida, Corona, 1981 Celica/Supra and Starlet

Jack up the lower suspension arm (except Corolla, Celica and Cressida). Check the front wheel play. Replace the lower ball joint if the play at the wheel rim exceeds 0.1 in. vertical motion or 0.25 in. horizontal motion. be sure that the dust covers are not torn and that they are securely glued to the ball joints.

─────── CAUTION ───────
Do not jack up the control arm on Corolla, Celica, or Cressida models; damage to the arm will result.

Tercel, Camry, Corolla (FWD) and 1982-87 Celica/Supra

1. Jack up the vehicle and place wooden blocks under the front wheels. The block height should be 7.09–7.87 inches.
2. Use jack stands for additional safety.
3. Make sure the front wheels are in a straight forward position.
4. Check the wheels.
5. Lower the jack until there is approximately half a load on the front springs.
6. Move the lower control arm up and down to check that there is no ball joint play.

Van

1. Raise and support the front end with jackstands under the frame.
2. Have someone apply the brakes while you move the lower arm up and down.

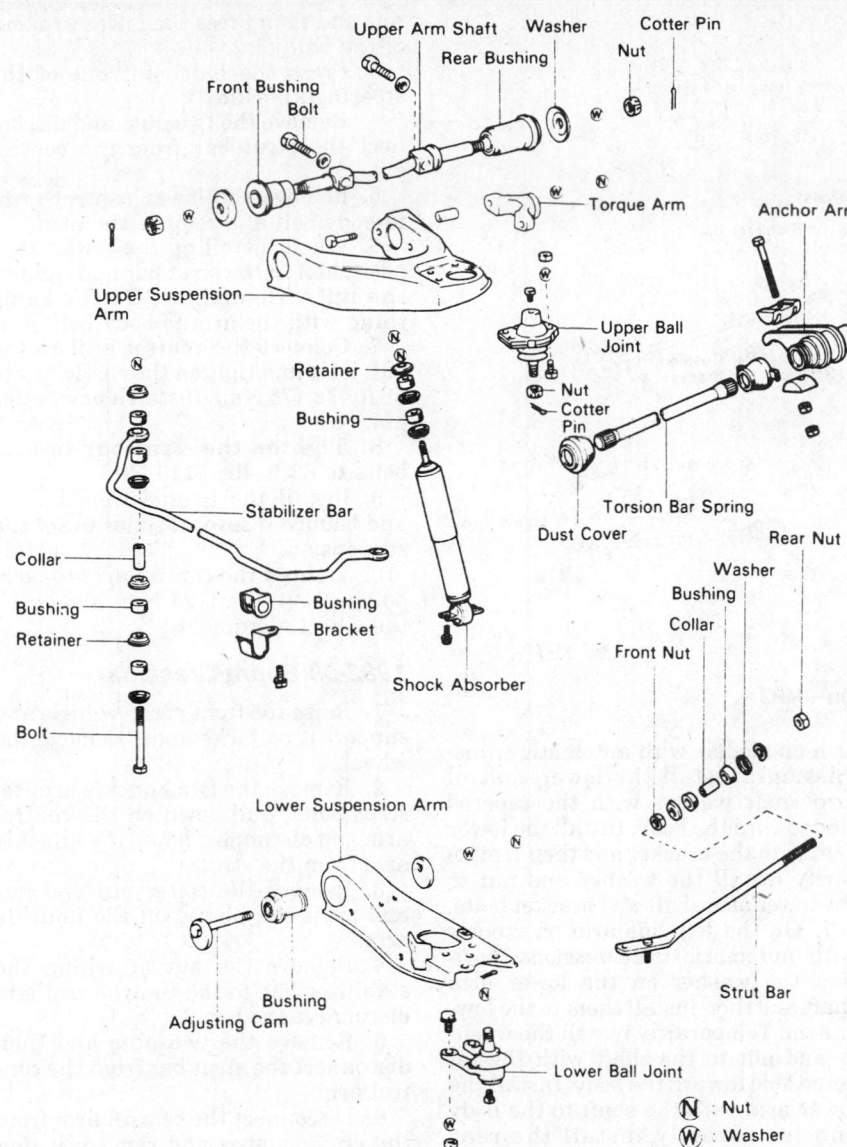

Upper Arm Shaft Washer Cotter Pin
Rear Bushing Nut
Front Bushing
Bolt
Torque Arm
Anchor Arm
Upper Suspension Arm
Upper Ball Joint
Retainer
Nut
Bushing
Cotter Pin
Stabilizer Bar
Torsion Bar Spring
Dust Cover
Collar
Rear Nut
Bushing
Washer
Retainer
Bushing
Bushing
Bracket
Collar
Front Nut
Bolt
Shock Absorber
Lower Suspension Arm
Adjusting Cam
Bushing
Strut Bar
Lower Ball Joint
N : Nut
W : Washer

Van front suspension

3. Vertical play should not exceed 0.09 in.

REMOVAL & INSTALLATION

NOTE: On models equipped with both upper and lower ball joints – if both ball joints are to be removed, always remove the lower and then the upper ball joint.

Corolla (RWD), 1981 Celica/ Supra/Cressida and Starlet

The ball joint and control arm cannot be separated from each other. If one fails, then both must be replaced as an assembly, in the following manner:
1. Peform Steps 1–7 of the first "Front Spring Removal and Installation" procedure. Skip Step 6.
2. Remove the stabilizer bar securing bolts.

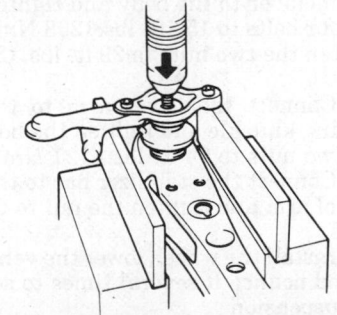

Ball joint removal, with a press, on the Celica, RWD Corolla, Cressida and Starlet

3. Unfasten the torque strut mounting bolts.
4. Remove the control arm mounting bolt and detach the arm from the front suspension member.
5. Remove the steering knuckle

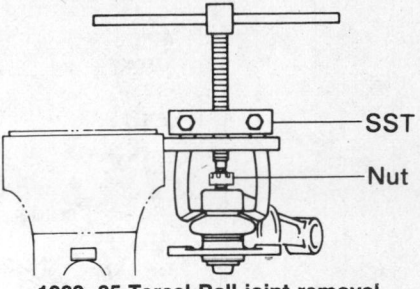

1983–85 Tercel Ball joint removal

arm from the control arm with a ball joint puller.

Inspect the suspension components, which were removed for wear or damage. Replace any parts, as required.

Installation is the reverse of removal. Note the following, however:
1. When installing the control arm on the suspension member, tighten the bolts partially at first.
2. Complete the assembly procedure and lower the car to the ground.
3. Bounce the front of the car several times. Allow the suspension to settle, then tighten the lower control arm bolts to 51–65 ft. lbs.

— CAUTION —
Use only the bolt which was designed to fit the lower control arm. If a replacement is necessary, see an authorized dealer for the proper part.

4. Remember to lubricate the ball joint.
Check the front end alignment.

1981-82 Tercel and 1982-85 Celica

1. Jack up your vehicle and support it with jack stands.

— CAUTION —
Do not jack up your car on the lower control arms.

2. Remove the front wheels.
3. Remove the tie rod end.
4. Remove the stabilizer bar end.
5. Remove the strut bar end.
6. Place a jack under the lower control arm for support.
7. Remove the bolt from the bottom of the steering knuckle.
8. Remove the bolt from the lower control arm.
9. Remove the control arm.

NOTE: The lower ball joint cannot be separated from the lower control arm. It must be replaced as a complete unit.

10. The following torques are required:
Bottom steering knuckle nut 40–52 ft. lbs.; stabilizer bar 11–15 ft. lbs.; tie rod end 37–50 ft. lbs.; strut bar 29–39

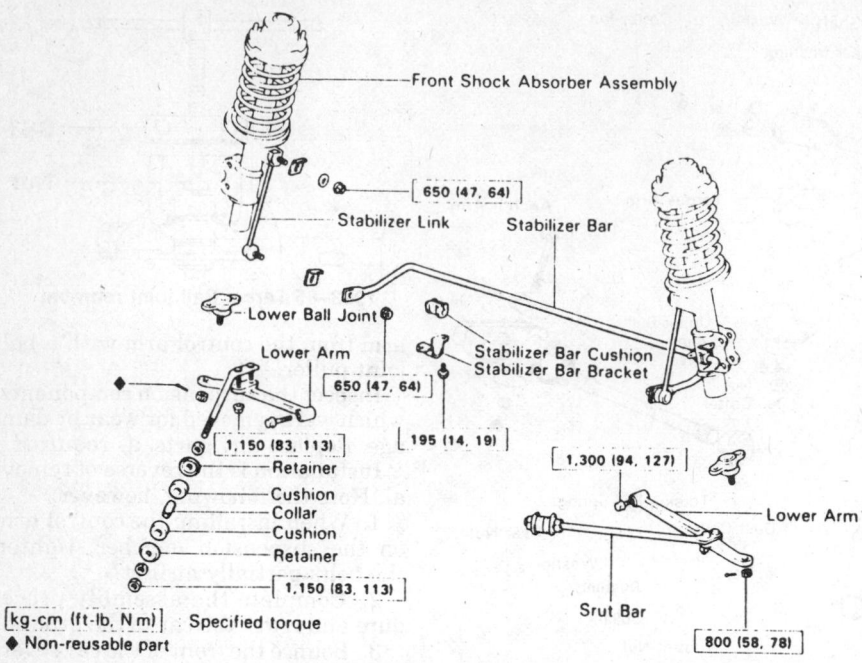

Front suspension—MR2

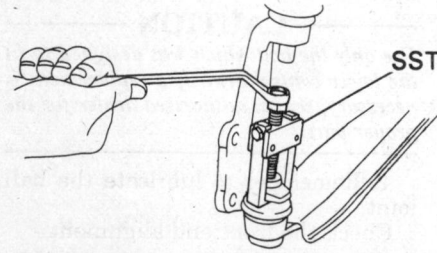

Typical ball joint separation without a press

ft. lbs.; lower control arm 51–65 ft. lbs.

1986-88 Celica (FWD)

1. Raise the front of the vehicle and support it with jack stands. Remove the wheel.

2. Remove the bolt and two nuts and disconnect the lower control arm from the steering knuckle.

3. Remove the nut and disconnect the stabilizer bar from the control arm.

4. On all but the left-side control arm on models with automatic transmissions, remove the control arm front set nut and washer. Remove the rear bracket bolts and then remove the arm.

5. On the left-side arm on models with automatic transmissions, remove the control arm front set nut and washer. Remove the four bolts and two nuts that attach the lower suspension crossmember to the frame and remove the crossmember. Remove the bolt and nut and lift out the lower arm with the lower arm shaft.

6. On all but the left-side control

arm on models with automatic transmissions, install the lower control arm shaft washer with the tapered side toward the body. Install the lower arm with the bracket and then temporarily install the washer and nut to the lower arm shaft and bracket bolts.

7. On the left-side arm on models with automatic transmissions, position the washer on the lower arm shaft and then install them to the lower arm shaft and then install the washer and nut to the shaft with the tapered side toward the body. Install the lower arm with the shaft to the body and temporarily install the rear brackets. Install the bolt and nut to the lower arm shaft and tighten them to 154 ft. lbs. (208 Nm). Install the crossmember to the body and tighten the four bolts to 154 ft. lbs. (208 Nm). Tighten the two nuts to 29 ft. lbs. (39 Nm).

8. Connect the lower arm to the steering knuckle and tighten the bolt and two nuts to 94 ft. lbs. (127 Nm).

9. Connect the stabilizer bar to the control arm and tighten the nut to 26 ft. lbs.

10. Install the wheel, lower the vehicle and bounce it several times to set the suspension.

11. Tighten the front set nut to 156 ft. lbs. (212 Nm). Tighten the rear bracket bolts to 72 ft. lbs. (98 Nm).

MR2

1. Raise the front of the vehicle and support it with jackstands. Remove the wheel.

2. Remove the cotter pin and castle

nut and then press the lower arm out of the ball joint.

3. Press the ball joint out of the steering knuckle.

4. Remove the two nuts and disconnect the strut bar from the control arm.

5. Remove the lower control arm-to-body bolt and remove the arm.

6. When installing the lower arm, position it in the strut bar and tighten the nuts fingertight. Do the same thing with the arm-to-body bolt.

7. Connect the control arm to the ball joint and tighten the castle nut to 58 ft. lbs. (78 Nm). Install a new cotter pin.

8. Tighten the strut bar-to-arm bolts to 83 ft. lbs. (113 Nm).

9. Install the tires, lower the car and bounce it several times to set the suspension.

10. Tighten the control arm-to-body bolt to 94 ft. lbs. (127 Nm) and check the wheel alignment.

1982-88 Supra/Cressida

1. Raise the front of the vehicle and support it on jackstands. Remove the wheel.

2. Remove the two knuckle arm-to-strut bolts, pull down on the control arm and disconnect it and the knuckle arm from the strut.

3. Remove the cotter pin and nut and press the tie rod off the knuckle arm.

4. Remove the nut attaching the stabilizer bar to the control arm and disconnect the bar.

5. Remove the two nuts and then disconnect the strut bar from the control arm.

6. Disconnect the control arm from the crossmember and remove it and the rack boot protector as an assembly.

7. Remove the cotter pin and nut and then press the knuckle arm off the control arm.

To install:

1. Press the knuckle arm into the control arm and then install the assembly into the crossmember.

2. Connect the stabilizer bar to the control arm and tighten the nut to 13 ft. lbs. (18 Nm).

3. Connect the strut bar to the control arm and tighten the nuts to 48 ft. lbs. (60 Nm).

4. Connect the knuckle arm to the strut housing and tighten the bolts to 72 ft. lbs. (98 Nm).

5. Install the wheel and lower the vehicle. Bounce the car several times to set the suspension and then tighten the control arm-to-body bolt to 80 ft. lbs. (108 Nm).

6. Check the front wheel alignment.

Camry, Corolla (FWD) and 1983-88 Tercel

1. Raise the front of the vehicle and support it with jackstands. Remove the wheel.
2. Remove the two bolts attaching the ball joint to the steering knuckle.
3. Remove the stabilizer bar nut, retainer and cushion.
4. Jack up the opposite wheel until the body of the car just lifts off the jackstand.
5. Loosen the lower control arm mounting bolt, wiggle the arm back and forth and then remove the bolt. Disconnect the lower control arm from the stabilizer bar.

NOTE: When removing the lower control arm (on the Tercel), be careful not to lose the caster adjustment spacer.

6. On the Tercel and Camry, carefully mount the lower control arm in a vise and then, using a ball joint removal tool, disconnect the ball joint from the arm.
7. Installation is in the reverse order of removal. Please note the following:
   a. Tighten the ball joint-to-control arm nut to 51–65 ft. lbs. and use a new cotter pin (Tercel) and 67 ft. lbs. (Camry).
   b. Tighten the steering knuckle-to-control arm bolts to 59 ft. lbs. on the Tercel; 47 ft. lbs. on the Corolla and 83 ft. lbs. on the Camry.
   c. Tighten the stabilizer bar bolt to 13 ft. lbs. on the Corolla.
   d. Before tightening the stabilizer bar nuts, on the Tercel and Camry, or the control arm bracket bolts on the Corolla, mount the wheels and lower the car. Bounce the car several times to settle the suspension and then tighten the stabilizer bolts on the Tercel and Camry to 66–90 ft. lbs.
   e. Tighten the arm-to-body bolts on the Tercel and Camry to 83 ft. lbs. On the Corolla, tighten the front arm bolts to 83 ft. lbs. and the rear bolts to 64 ft. lbs.
   f. Check the front end alignment.

2WD VAN

1. Raise and support the front end on jackstands under the frame.
2. Remove the hub and caliper.
3. Remove the steering knuckle dust coverand steering knuckle as previously outlined..
4. Support the lower arm with a floor jack.
5. Remove the two cotter pins and nuts and disconnect the steering knuckle from the lower ball joint.
6. Disconnect the upper ball joint from the knuckle.

7. Using a ball joint removal tool, remove the ball joint from the arm.
8. Installation is the reverse of removal. Torque the top ball joint nut to 22 ft. lbs., and the bottom ball joint nut to 50 ft. lbs.

4WD VAN

1. Raise and support the front end on jackstands under the frame.
2. Remove the steering knuckle as outlined in this section.
3. Remove the lower ball joint retaining bolts and nuts and remove the lower ball joint from the lower suspension arm.
4. Remove the upper ball joint retaining bolts and nuts and remove the upper ball joint from the upper suspension arm.
5. Installation is the reverse order of the removal procedure. Torque the upper ball joint bolts and nuts to 22 ft. lbs. Torque the lower ball joint bolts and nuts to 49 ft. lbs.

Corona

1. Remove the hubcap and loosen the lug nuts.
2. Jack up your vehicle and support it with jackstands.
3. Remove the lug nuts and the wheel.
4. Compress the coil spring by placing a jack underneath the control arm and raising it.
5. Remove the cotter pin and the castellated nut from the ball joint.
6. Use a ball joint puller to detach the lower ball joint from the steering knuckle.
7. Wire the steering knuckle out of the way.
8. Remove the bolt and remove the ball joint.

Installation is the reverse of removal. Tighten the stud nut to 51–65 ft. lbs.

Upper Ball Joint

INSPECTION

Disconnect the ball joint from the steering knuckle and check free-play by hand. Replace the ball joint, if it is noticeably loose.

REMOVAL & INSTALLATION

NOTE: On models equipped with both upper and lower ball joints—if both are to be removed, always remove the lower one first.

Corona and Van

1. Remove the steering knuckle as detailed in "Lower Ball Joint Removal & Installation".

2. Suspend the steering knuckle with a wire.
3. Use an open end wrench to remove the upper ball joint.

Installation is performed in the reverse order from removal. Note the following:

1. Install the upper ball joint dust cover with the escape valve toward the rear.
2. Use sealer on the dust cover before installing it.
3. Tighten the upper ball joint-to-steering knuckle bolt to 4–50 ft. lbs. on the Corona and 22 ft. lbs. on the Van.

Lower Control Arm
REMOVAL & INSTALLATION

Corolla (RWD), 1981 Celica/ Supra/Cressida and Starlet

1. Raise and support the front end.
2. Remove the wheel.
3. Disconnect the steering knuckle from the control arm.
4. Disconnect the tie rod, stabilizer bar and strut bar from the control arm.
5. Remove the control arm mounting bolts, and remove the arm.
6. Install in reverse of above. Tighten, but do not torque fasteners until car is on the ground.
7. Lower car to ground, rock it from side-to-side several times and torque control arm mounting bolts to 51–65 ft. lbs., stabilizer bar to 16 ft. lbs., strut bar to 40 ft. lbs., and shock absorber to 65 ft. lbs.

Corona

1. Raise and support the vehicle.
2. Remove the front wheel.
3. Remove the shock absorber and disconnect the stabilizer from the lower arm.
4. Install a spring compressor and fully tighten it.
5. Place a jack under the lower arm seat.
6. Disconnect the lower ball joint from the knuckle and lower the jack.
7. Remove the ball joint from the arm, remove the cam plates and bolts and take off the arm.
8. Install in reverse of above. Tighten all fasteners, but do not torque them to specification until vehicle is on the ground.
9. Lower the vehicle and rock it from side-to-side several times.
10. With no load in vehicle, torque the lower arm mounting bolts to 94–130 ft. lbs.

2WD Van

1. Raise and support the front end on jackstands under the frame.

2. Remove the wheel assembly. Remove the shock absorber.

3. Remove the cotter pin and nut and using a suitable tie rod puller, remove the tie rod. Disconnect the stabilizer bar from the lower arm.

4. Disconnect the strut bar from the lower arm.

5. Remove the two bolts and nuts holding the ball joint to the lower suspension arm. Disconnect the ball joint from the knuckle. A ball joint separator is necessary.

6. Place a matchmark on the adjusting cam.

7. Remove the adjusting cam and nut and remove the lower arm.

8. Installation is the reverse of removal. Observe the following torques:
   a. Lower ball joint and strut bar — 49 ft. lbs.
   b. Tie rod nut — 43 ft. lbs.

4WD VAN

1. Raise and support the front end on jackstands under the frame.

2. Remove the wheel assembly. Disconnect the shock absorber from the lower suspension arm.

3. Remove the cotter pin and nut from the lower ball joint and disconnect the lower suspension arm from the lower ball joint.

4. Place matchmarks on the front and rear adjusting cams. Remove the nuts and adjusting cam and remove the lower suspension arm.

5. Installation is the reverse of the removal procedure. Observe the following torques:
   a. Lower suspension arm to lower ball joint — 83 ft. lbs.
   b. Stabilizer bar to the lower suspension arm — 14 ft. lbs.
   c. Shock absorber to lower suspension arm — 70 ft. lbs.
   d. Adjusting cam nuts — 152 ft. lbs.

All Others

Please refer to "Lower Control Arm/Ball Joints."

Upper Control Arm

REMOVAL & INSTALLATION

Corona

1. Remove the upper arm mounting nuts from inside the engine compartment, but do not remove the bolts.

2. Raise the vehicle, support the lower arm and remove the wheel.

3. On vehicles equipped with a ball joint wear sensor, remove the wiring from the clamp on the arm.

4. Remove the upper ball joint.

5. Remove the control arm mounting bolts.

6. Pry out the arm with a pry bar.

7. Install in reverse of removal. Do not tighten fasteners until vehicle is on ground.

8. Lower vehicle and torque the control arm mounting bolts to 95–130 ft. lbs.

2WD Van

1. Raise and support the front end with jackstands under the frame.

2. Remove the torsion bar.

3. Remove the cool air intake duct.

4. Remove the four bolts, spring washers and nust and disconnect the upper arm from the upper ball joint.

5. Unbolt and remove the upper suspension arm.

6. Installation is the reverse of removal.

4WD Van

1. Raise and support the front end with jackstands under the frame. Remove the wheel assembly.

2. Remove the torsion bar. Remove the right hand side front seat. Remove the console box.

3. Remove the transmission and transfer shit levers with retainers. Disconnect the control and shift cables from the shift levers.

4. Disconnect the brake cable from the brake lever and remove the brake lever assembly.

5. Disconnect the parking brake cable from the intermidiate lever and remove it. Disconnect the shift cable from the transmision and remove it.

6. Remove the seat floor panel. Remove the fan shroud. Remove the radiator mounting bolts and nuts (do not drain the radiator).

7. Remove the shock absorber nuts, cushion and retainers and disconnect the shock absorber from the frame. Do not disconnect the shock absorber from the lower suspension arm.

8. Remove the cotter pin and nut and disconnect the upper ball joint from the steering knuckle.

9. Remove the two upper suspension arm retaining bolts and remove the upper suspension arm from the frame.

10. Installation is the reverse of removal procedure. Observe the following torques:
   a. Upper suspension arm retaining bolts — 112 ft. lbs.
   b. Upper suspension arm to steering knuckle nut — 83 ft. lbs.

Front Wheel Bearings

NOTE: For information concerning rear wheel bearings/adjustments on 1982-88 Supra and 1983-88 Celica GTS and Cressida models, refer to "Axle Shaft Removal and Installation" procedure for that model.

REMOVAL & INSTALLATION

Rear Wheel Drive

1. Remove the disc/hub assembly, as detailed above.

2. If either the disc or the entire hub assembly is to be replaced, unbolt the hub from the disc.

NOTE: If only the bearings are to be replaced, do not separate the disc and hub.

3. Using a brass rod as a drift, tap the inner bearings cone out. Remove the oil seal and the inner bearings.

NOTE: Throw the old oil seal away.

Measuring wheel bearing pre-load with a spring scale

4. Drive out the inner bearing cup.

5. Drive out the outer bearing cup.

Inspect the bearings and the hub for signs of wear or damage. Replace components, as necessary.

Installation is performed in the following order:

1. Install the inner bearing cup an then the outer bearing cup, by driving them into place.

———— CAUTION ————
Use care not to cock the bearing cups in the hub.

2. Pack the bearings, hub inner well and grease cap with multipurpose grease.

3. Install the inner bearing into the hub.

4. Carefully install a new oil seal with a soft drift.

5. Install the hub on the spindle. Be sure to install all of the washers and nuts which were removed.

6. Adjust the bearing preload.

7. Install the caliper assembly.

PRELOAD ADJUSTMENT

1. With the front hub/disc assembly installed, tighten the castellated nut to the torque figure specified.

2. Rotate the disc back and forth, two or three times, to allow the bearing to seat properly.

3. Loosen the castellated nut until it is only fingertight.

4. Tighten the nut firmly, using a box wrench.

5. Measure the bearing preload with a spring scale attached to a wheel mounting stud. Check it against the specifications.

6. Install the cotter pin.

NOTE: If the hole does not align with the nut (or cap) holes, tighten the nut slightly until it does.

7. Finish installing the brake components and the wheel.

PRELOAD SPECIFICATIONS

Model/Year	Initial Torque Setting (ft. lbs.)	Preload (oz.)
Tercel '80–'83	22	13–30
Corolla ①	19–23	11–25
Celica	19–26	11–25
Corona	19–26	12–31
Supra ①	19–23	11–24
Cressida ①	22	37–56
Starlet		
'81–'82	22	1–1.5
'83–'84	22	0.8–1.9

① Except models w/IRS

Front Wheel Drive Models

Please refer to "Front Axle Hub and Bearings."

Front Wheel Alignment

ADJUSTMENT

Front end alignment measurements require the use of special equipment. Before measuring alignment or attempting to adjust it, always check the following points:

1. Be sure that the tires are properly inflated.

2. See that the wheels are properly balanced.

3. Check the ball joints to determine worn or loose.

4. Check front wheel bearing adjustment.

5. Be sure that the car is on a level surface.

6. Check all suspension parts for tightness.

CASTER

Corolla (RWD), Cressida (1981-84), Celica (RWD), Supra and 1981-82 Tercel

Caster is the tilt of the front steering axis either forward or backward away from the front of the vehicle.

If the caster is found to be out of tolerance with the specifications, it may be adjusted by turning the nuts on the rear end of the strut bar (where it attaches to the body) on all models but the Starlet and the 1983-87 Tercel. The caster is decreased by lengthening the strut bar and increased by shortening it. One turn of the adjusting nut is equal to 8' of tilt on the Corolla (RWD), 9' on the Celica/Supra and Cressida and 7' on the 1981-82 Tercel, 1' is 1/60 of a degree.

NOTE: If the caster still cannot be adjusted within the limits, inspect or replace any damaged or worn suspension parts.

Camry and Cressida (1985-88)

Increase or decrease the number of spacers on the stabilizer bar. Each spacer changes caster by 30'.

2WD Van

Caster is changed by turning the adjusting cam or strut bar nut. Each graduation of the cam gives 12' of change; each turn of the nut gives 25' change.

Corolla (FWD) and Celica (FWD)

Caster is not adjustable.

MR2

Caster is changed by turning the adjusting nut on the strut bar. Each revolution of the nut changes the caster by 18'.

CAMBER

Except Corona

Camber is the slope of the front wheels from the vertical when viewed from the front of the vehicle. When the wheels tilt outward at the top, the camber is positive (+). When the wheels tilt inward at the top, the camber is negative (). The amount of positive and negative camber is measured in degrees from the vertical and the measurement is called camber angle. Camber is preset at the factory, therefore, it is not adjustable on any model but the 1983-87 Tercel, Camry, Van, MR2, FWD Celica, and FWD Corolla. If the camber angle is out of tolerance, inspect or replace worn or damaged suspension parts.

Camber on these models is adjustable by means of a camber adjustment bolt on the lower strut mounting bracket. Loosen the shock absorber set nut and then turn the adjusting bolt until the camber is within specifications. Camber will change about 20'

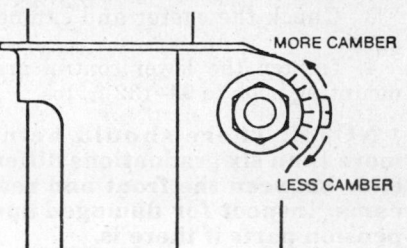

Camber adjusting bolt on the 1983 and later Tercel, front wheel drive Corolla and Camry

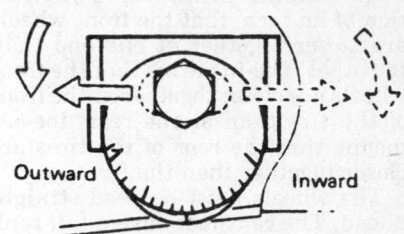

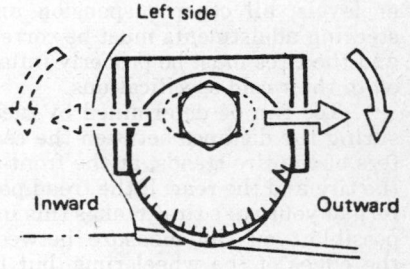

Corona front end alignment adjusting cams

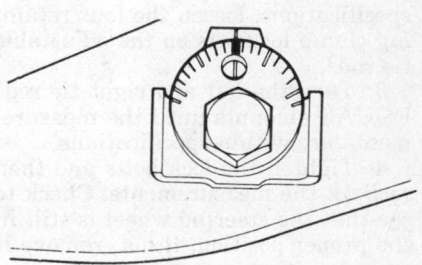

Van caster and camber adjustment cam

(MR2: 18') for each graduation on the cam. One minute (1') is equal to 1/60 of a degree.

CASTER AND CAMBER

Corona

Caster and camber angles are measured in the same way and with the same equipment as all the other models above.

However, the method of adjustment is different:

1. Measure the camber and adjust it with the rear adjusting cam.

2. Measure the caster and adjust it with the front adjusting cam.

3. Check the caster and camber again.

4. Tighten the lower control arm mounting bolts to 94–132 ft. lbs.

NOTE: There should be no more than six graduations difference between the front and rear cams; inspect for damaged suspension parts if there is.

TOE

Toe is the amount, measured in a fraction of an inch, that the front wheels are closer together at one end than the other. Toe-in means that the front wheels are closer together at the front of the tire than at the rear; toe-out means that the rear of the tires are closer together than the front.

The wheels must be dead straight ahead. The car must have a full tank of gas, all fluids must be at their proper levels, all other suspension and steering adjustments must be correct and the tires must be properly inflated to their cold specifications.

1. Toe can be determined by measuring the distance between the centers of the tire treads, at the front of the tire and the rear. If the tread pattern of your car's tires makes this impossible, you can measure between the edges of the wheel rims, but be sure to move the car and measure in a few places to avoid errors caused by bent rims or wheel run-out.

2. If the measurement is not within specifications, loosen the four retaining clamp locknuts on the adjustable tie rods.

3. Turn the left and right tie rods EQUAL amounts until the measurements are within specifications.

4. Tighten the lock bolts and then recheck the measurements. Check to see that the steering wheel is still in the proper position. If not, remove it and reposition it.

REAR SUSPENSION

Shock Absorbers

REMOVAL & INSTALLATION

All Exc. Supra (1982-86), Cressida (1983-88) and Celica GTS (1983-85)

1. Raise the rear of the car and support it with jackstands. Position an hydraulic jack under the rear axle.

2. Unfasten the upper shock absorber retaining nuts. It may be necessary to hold the shock absorber shaft with a suitable tool while removing the top retaining nut.

NOTE: Always remove and install the shock absorbers one at a time. Do not allow the rear axle to hang in place as this may cause undue damage.

3. Remove the lower shock retaining nut where it attaches to the rear axle housing.

4. Remove the shock absorber.

5. Inspect the shock for wear, leaks or other signs of damage.

6. Installation is in the reverse order of removal. Please note the following:
—tighten the upper retaining nuts to 16–24 ft. lbs.
—tighten the lower retaining nuts to 22–32 ft. lbs.

Supra (1982-86), Cressida (1983-88) and Celica GTS (1983-85)

1. Jack up the rear end of the car, keeping the pad of the hydraulic floor jack underneath the differential housing. Support the suspension control arms with safety stands.

2. Remove the brake hose clips. Disconnect the stabilizer bar end.

3. Disconnect the drive halfshaft at the CV-joint on the wheel side.

4. With a jackstand underneath the suspension control arm, unbolt the shock absorber at its lower end. Using a screwdriver to keep the shaft from turning, remove the nut holding the shock absorber to its upper mounting. Remove the shock.

5. Installation is in the reverse order of removal. Torque the halfshaft nuts to 44–57 ft. lbs.; torque the upper shock mounting nut to 14–22 ft. lbs., and the lower shock mounting nut to 22–32 ft. lbs.

MacPherson Struts

REMOVAL & INSTALLATION

Tercel

1. Working inside the car, remove the shock absorber cover and package tray bracket.

2. Raise the rear of the vehicle and support it with jackstands. Remove the wheel.

3. Disconnect the brake line from the wheel cylinder (if necessary). Disconnect the brake line from the flexible hose at the mounting bracket on the strut tube. Disconnect the flexible hose from the strut.

4. Loosen the nut holding the suspension support to the shock absorber.

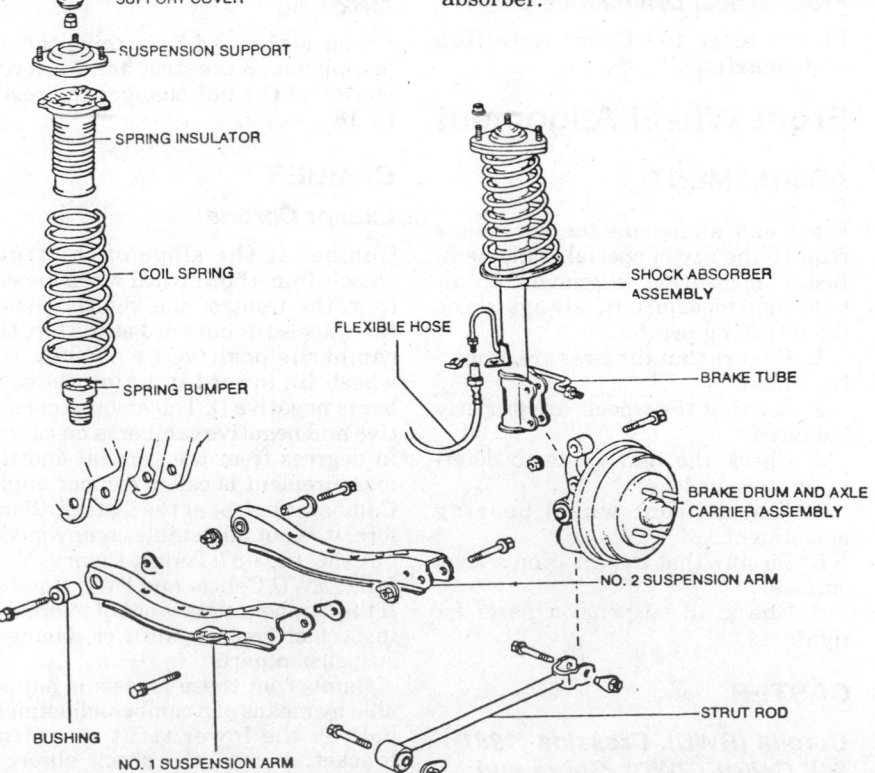

Rear suspension components—1983 and later Tercel (exc 4 × 4), Camry and front wheel drive Corolla

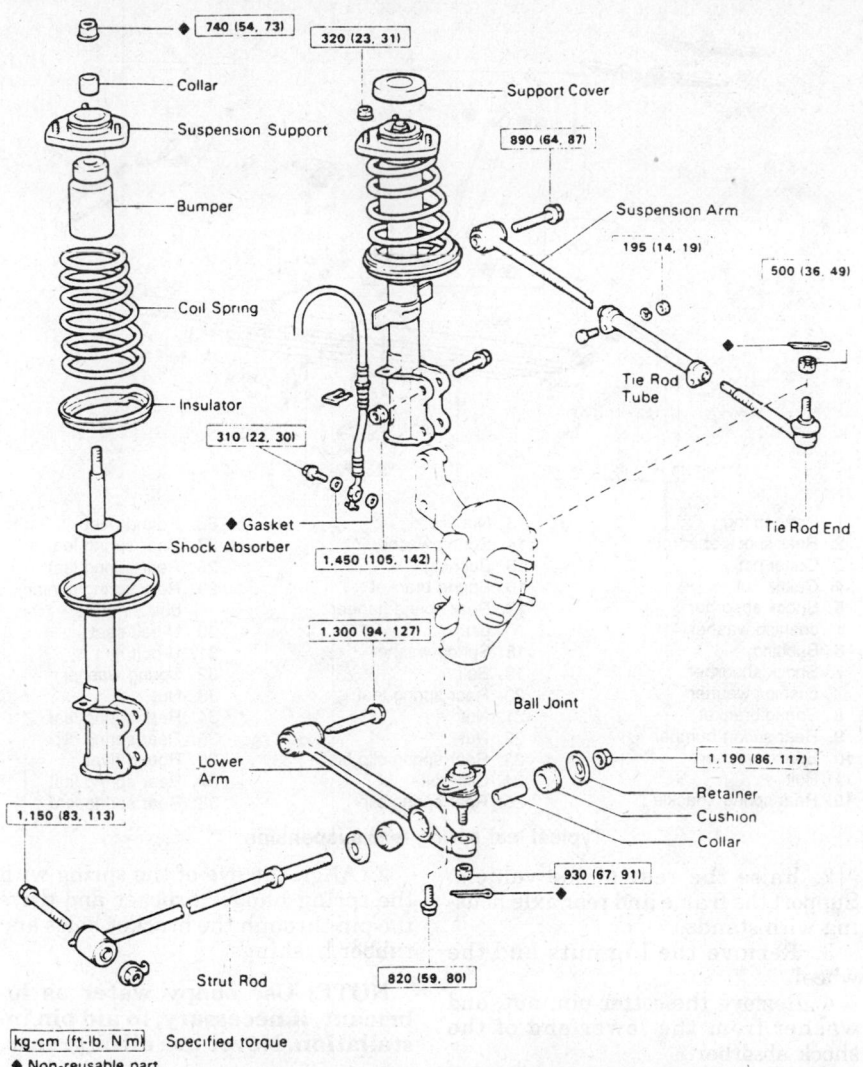

740 (54, 73) ◆
320 (23, 31)

— Collar
— Suspension Support
— Bumper
— Coil Spring
— Insulator
Support Cover
890 (64, 87)

Suspension Arm
195 (14, 19)
500 (36, 49)
Tie Rod Tube

310 (22, 30)
◆ Gasket
Shock Absorber
1.450 (105, 142)
Tie Rod End

1.300 (94, 127)
Ball Joint
Lower Arm
1.190 (86, 117)
Retainer
Cushion
Collar
1.150 (83, 113)
930 (67, 91)
820 (59, 80)
Strut Rod

kg-cm (ft-lb, N m) Specified torque
◆ Non-reusable part

Rear suspension components—MR2

——— CAUTION ———
Do not remove the nut.

5. Remove the bolts and nuts mounting on the strut on the axle carrier and then disconnect the strut.

6. Remove the three upper strut mounting nuts and carefully remove the strut assembly.

7. Installation is in the reverse order of removal. Please note the following:

a. Tighten the upper strut retaining nuts to 17 ft. lbs.

b. Tighten the lower strut-to-axle carrier bolts to 105 ft. lbs.

c. Tighten the nut holding the suspension support to the shock absorber to 36 ft. lbs.

d. Bleed the brakes.

Corolla FWD and Camry

1. On the 4-door sedan, remove the package tray and vent duct.

2. On the hatchback, remove the speaker grilles.

3. Disconnect the brake line from the wheel cylinder.

4. Remove the brake line from the brake hose.

5. Disconnect the brake hose from its bracket on the strut.

6. Remove the strut suspension support cover. Loosen, but do not remove, the nut holding the suspension support to the strut.

7. Unbolt the strut from the rear arm and or axle carrier.

8. Unbolt the strut from the body.

9. Installation is the reverse of removal. Torque the strut-to-body bolts to 17 ft. lbs.; the strut-to-rear arm bolts to 105 ft. lbs. and the suspension support-to-strut nut to 36 ft. lbs.

10. Refill and bleed the brake system.

Celica FWD (1986-88)

1. Raise the rear of the vehicle and

support it with jackstands. Position an hydraulic jack underneath the rear hub assembly; raise it just enough to support the assembly.

2. On the liftback, remove the rear speaker grilles.

3. On the coupe, remove the suspension service hole cover.

4. On the ST and GT models, disconnect and plug the brake line at the backing plate. Remove the clip and E-ring and then disconnect the brake hose and tube from the strut housing.

5. On the GT-S, remove the union bolts and gaskets and disconnect the brake line from the brake cylinder. Remove the clip and E-ring from the strut and then disconnect the brake hose from the strut housing.

6. Loosen, but do not remove, the nut attaching the suspension support to the strut.

7. Disconnect the stabilizer bar at the lower end of the strut housing.

8. Disconnect the strut at the axle carrier.

9. Remove the three strut-to-body bolts and then remove the strut.

To install:

1. Tighten the upper strut-to-body nuts to 23 ft. lbs. (31 Nm).

2. Tighten the lower strut-to-carrier bolts to 119 ft. lbs. (162 Nm).

3. Connect the stabilizer bar to the strut and tighten the bolts to 26 ft. lbs. (35 Nm).

4. Tighten the strut holding nut to 36 ft. lbs. (49 Nm). Install the dust cover onto the suspension support.

5. Reconnect the brake line and hose. Bleed the system, lower the car and check the rear wheel alignment.

MR2

1. Raise the rear of the vehicle and support it with jackstands. Position an hydraulic floor jack underneath the rear hub assembly; raise it just enough to support the assembly.

2. Remove the union bolts and gaskets and disconnect the brake line from the brake cylinder. Remove the clip and E-ring from the strut and then disconnect the brake hose from the strut housing.

3. Matchmark the lower strut bracket and the camber adjusting cam, remove the two axle carrier bolts and the adjusting cam and disconnect the strut from the carrier.

4. Remove the engine hood side panel.

5. Remove the three upper strut-to-body nuts and then remove the strut.

To install:

1. Position the strut and tighten the upper mounting nuts to 23 ft. lbs. (31 Nm).

2. Install the engine hood side panel.

3. Connect the axle carrier to the lower strut bracket. Insert the mounting bolts from the rear and align the matchmarks made in Step 3. Tighten the nuts to 105 ft. lbs. (142 Nm).

4. Connect the brake line, bleed the system and check rear wheel alignment.

1987-88 Supra

1. Raise and support the rear of the vehicle safely. Remove the wheel assemblies.

2. Remove the speaker grill and interior quarter panel trim.

3. Disconnect the strut from the axle carrier.

4. Remove the strut cap. Remove the TEMS (Toyota electronic modulated suspension) actuator.

5. Remove the three strut mounting nuts from the body and remove the strut assembly.

6. Mount the strut assembly in a suitable vise. Using a suitable spring compressor, compress the coil spring.

7. Remove the strut suspension support nut. Remove the strut suspension support, remove the coil spring and bumper.

To install:

1. Mount the strut in a suitable vise. Using a suitable spring compressor, compress the coil spring.

2. Install the bumper to the strut, align the coil spring end with the lower seat hollow and install the coil spring.

3. Align the strut suspension support hole and piston rod and install it. Align the suspension support with the strut lower bushing.

4. Install the strut suspension support nut and torque it to 20 ft. lbs. Connect the strut assembly with the three retaining nuts and torque them to 10 ft. lbs.

5. Connect the strut assembly to the axle carrier and torque it to 101 ft. lbs.

6. Install the TEMS actuator and strut cap. Install the quarter panel trim panel and speaker grille.

OVERHAUL

For all spring and shock absorber removal and installtion procedures, and all strut overhaul procedure, please refer to "STRUT OVERHAUL" in the Unit Repair section.

Springs

REMOVAL & INSTALLATION

Leaf Springs

1. Loosen the rear wheel lub nuts.

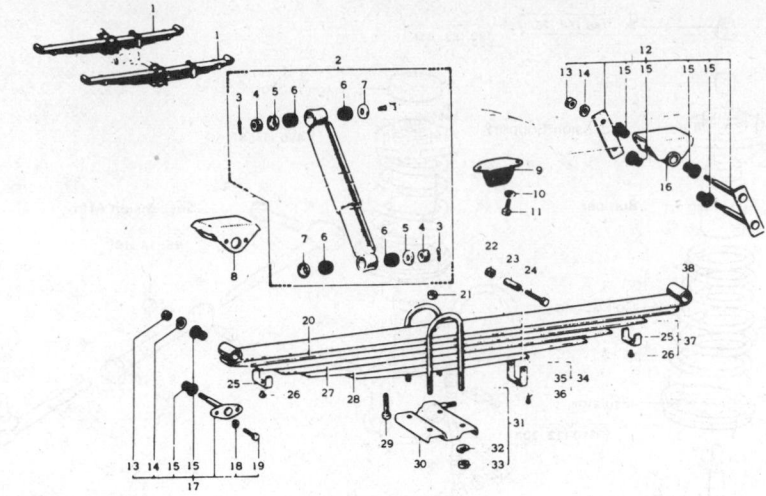

1. Rear spring	13. Nut	26. Round rivet
2. Rear shock absorber	14. Spring washer	27. Rear spring leaf
3. Cotter pin	15. Bushing	28. Rear spring leaf
4. Castle nut	16. Spring bracket	29. Rear spring center
5. Shock absorber	17. Rear spring hanger	bolt
cushion washer	pin	30. U-bolt seat
6. Bushing	18. Spring washer	31. U-bolt
7. Shock absorber	19. Bolt	32. Spring washer
cushion washer	20. Rear spring leaf	33. Nut
8. Spring bracket	21. Nut	34. Rear spring leaf
9. Rear spring bumper	22. Nut	35. Rear spring clip
10. Spring washer	23. Rear spring clip bolt	36. Round rivet
11. Bolt	24. Clip bolt	37. Rear spring leaf
12. Rear spring shackle	25. Rear spring clip	38. Rear spring leaf

Typical leaf spring rear suspension

2. Raise the rear of the vehicle. Support the frame and rear axle housing with stands.

3. Remove the lug nuts and the wheel.

4. Remove the cotter pin, nut, and washer from the lower end of the shock absorber.

5. Detach the shock absorber from the spring seat pivot pin.

6. Remove the parking brake cable clamp.

NOTE: Remove the parking brake equalizer, if necessary.

7. Unfasten the U-bolt nuts and remove the spring seat assemblies.

8. Adjust the height of the rear axle housing so that the weight of the rear axle is removed from the rear springs.

9. Unfasten the spring shackle retaining nuts. Withdraw the spring shackle inner plate. Carefully pry out the spring shackle with a bar.

10. Remove the spring bracket pin from the front end of the spring hanger and remove the rubber bushings.

11. Remove the spring.

CAUTION

Use care not to damage the hydraulic brake line or the parking brake cable.

Installation is performed in the following order:

1. Install the rubber bushings in the eye of the spring.

2. Align the eye of the spring with the spring hanger bracket and drive the pin through the bracket holes and rubber bushings.

NOTE: Use soapy water as lubricant, if necessary, to aid pin installation. Never use oil or grease.

3. Fingertighten the spring hanger nuts and/or bolts.

4. Install the rubber bushings in the spring eye at the opposite end of the spring.

5. Raise the free end of the spring. Install the spring shackle through the bushings and the bracket.

6. Install the shackle inner plate and fingertighten the retaining nuts.

7. Center the bolt head in the hole which is provided in the spring seat on the axle housing.

8. Fit the U-bolts over the axle housing. Install the lower spring seat.

9. Tighten the U-bolt nuts.

NOTE: Some models have two sets of nuts, while others have a nut and lockwasher.

10. Install the parking brake cable clamp. Install the equalizer, if it was removed.

11. On passenger cars:
   a. Install the shock absorber end at the spring seat. Tighten the nuts.
   b. Install the wheel and lug nuts. Lower the car to the ground.

c. Bounce the car several times.

d. Tighten the spring bracket pins and shackles.

Coil Springs

1. Loosen the rear wheel lug nuts.
2. Jack up the rear axle housing and support the frame with jack stands. Leave the jack in place under the rear axle housing.
3. Remove the lug nuts and wheel.
4. If so equipped, disconnect the rear stabilizer bar from the axle housing (or suspension arm, on Supra (1982-88), Celica GTS (1983-85) and Cressida (1983-85) models. Remove the bolt holding the stabilizer bar bushing to the rear axle housing.
5. Unfasten the lower shock absorber end. On the Van, Corolla RWD and Tercel 4X4, disconnect the lateral control rod from the axle.

NOTE: On Supra (1982-86), Cressida (1983-88) and Celica GTS (1983-88) models with IRS suspension, remove the rear halfshafts.

6. Slowly lower the jack under the rear axle housing until the axle is at the bottom of its travel.
7. Withdraw the coil spring, complete with its insulator.
8. Inspect the coil spring and insulator for wear, cracks, or weakness; replace either or both, as necessary.
9. Installation is performed in the reverse order of removal.

Rear Axle Hub, Carrier and Bearing

REMOVAL & INSTALLATION

Tercel (Except Wagon)

1. Raise the rear of the vehicle and support it with jackstands.
2. Remove the rear wheel and tire assembly.
3. Remove the brake drum.
4. Remove the locknut cap and cotter pin. Pry off the locknut and then remove the locknut itself.
5. Pull of the axle hub along with the outer wheel bearing and thrust washer.
6. Disconnect and plug the brake line where it connects to the brake backing plate.
7. Unbolt the rear axle shaft from the carrier and remove it along with the brake backing plate.
8. Remove the bolt and nut attaching the carrier to the strut rod.
9. Remove the bolt and nut attaching the carrier to the No. 1 suspension arm.
10. Remove the bolt and nut

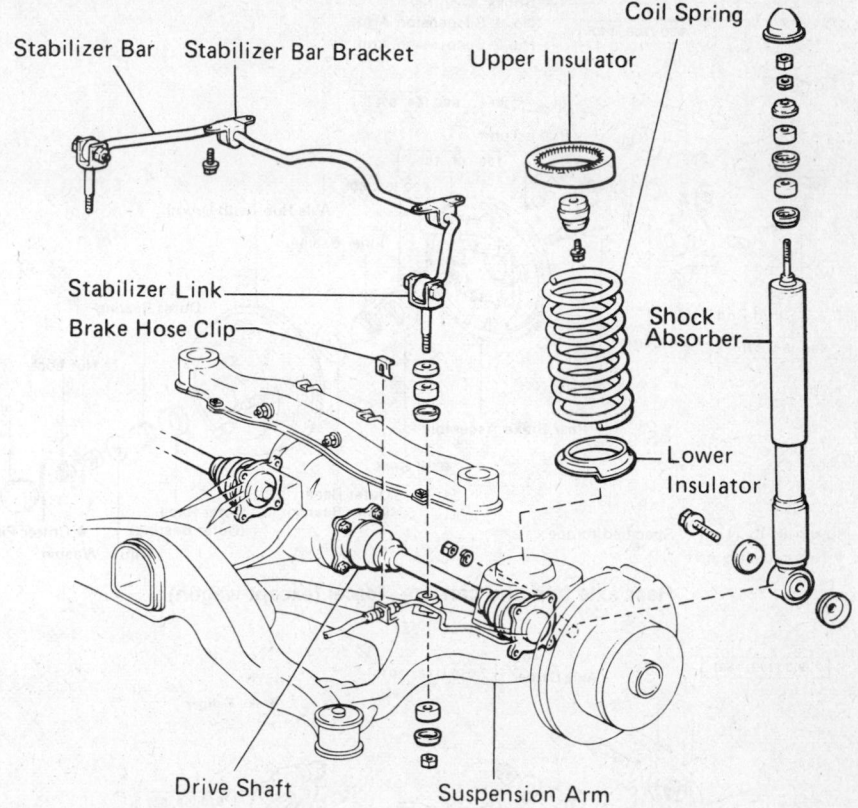

Rear suspension—Supra (1982 and later), Celica GTS (1983 and later) and Cressida (1985 and later)

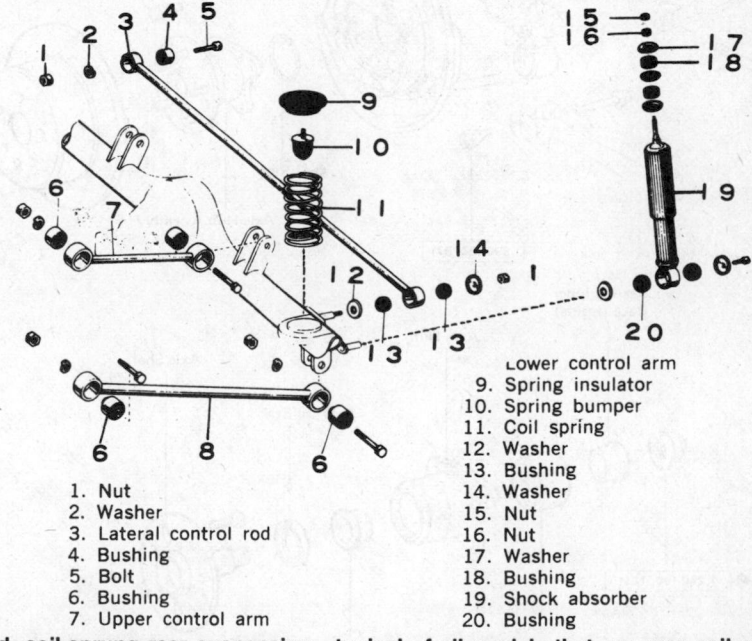

1. Nut
2. Washer
3. Lateral control rod
4. Bushing
5. Bolt
6. Bushing
7. Upper control arm

8. Lower control arm
9. Spring insulator
10. Spring bumper
11. Coil spring
12. Washer
13. Bushing
14. Washer
15. Nut
16. Nut
17. Washer
18. Bushing
19. Shock absorber
20. Bushing

Solid, coil-sprung rear suspension—typical of all models that use rear coil springs (except those with IRS)

attaching the carrier to the No. 2 suspension arm.

11. Unbolt the carrier from the rear strut tube and remove the carrier.
12. Pry the inner bearing oil seal out of the brake drum and then remove the inner bearing.

13. Using a brass drift and hammer, drive out the bearing races.

To install:

1. Press new outer bearing races into the axle hub and fill it and the bearing cap with grease.
2. Coat your palm with grease and

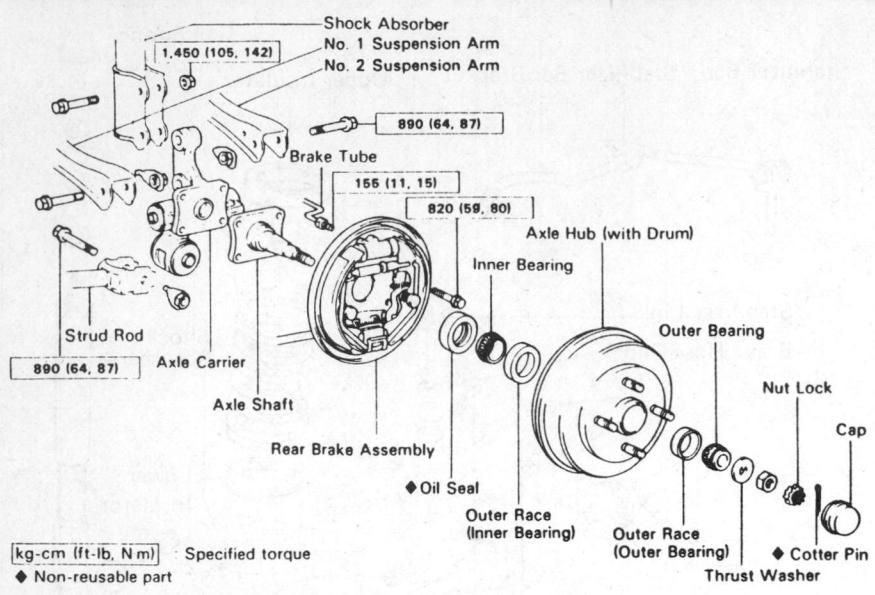

Rear axle hub and carrier—Tercel (except wagon)

kg-cm (ft-lb, N m) : Specified torque
◆ Non-reusable part

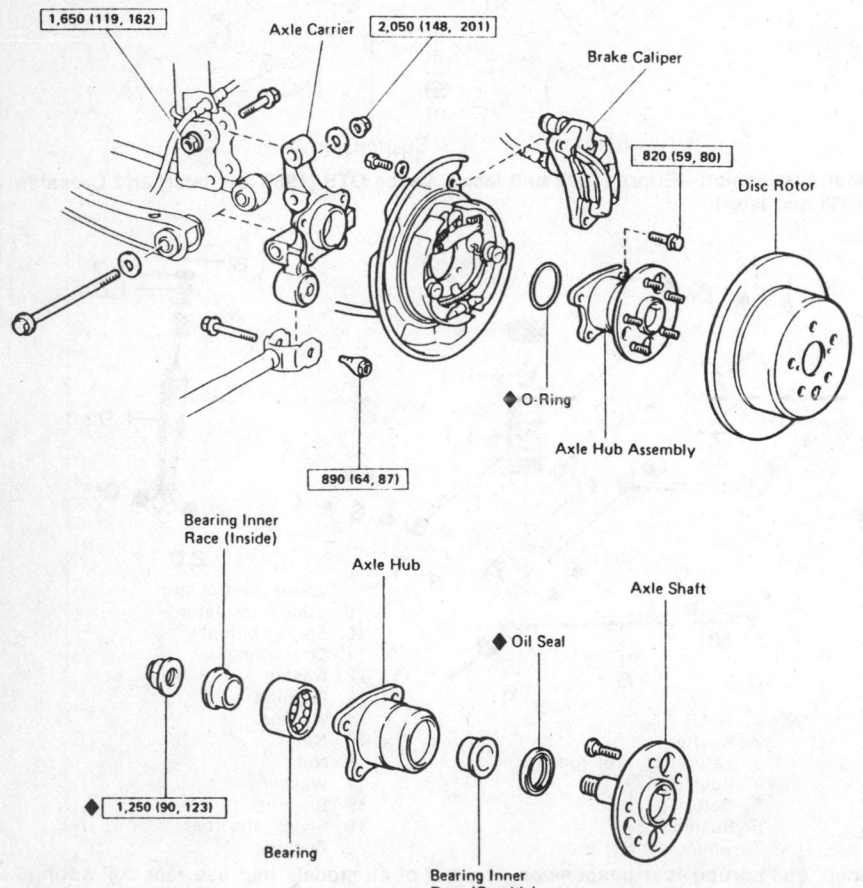

Rear axle hub and carrier—Camry, Celica (1986 and later) and Tercel wagon (except 4 × 4)

press the bearing into your palm until the grease oozes out the other side.

3. Position the inner bearing into the hub and then drive in a new oil seal. Coat the seal with grease.

4. Position the axle carrier onto the strut tube and tighten the bolts to 105 ft. lbs. (142 Nm).

5. Install the bolt and nut attatching the carrier to the No. 2 sus-

pension arm; fingertighten it only.

NOTE: Make sure that the lip of the nut is on the flange of the arm, not over it.

6. Repeat Step 5 for the No. 1 suspension arm.

NOTE: Make sure that the lip of the nut is in the hole on the arm.

7. Install the strut rod-to-carrier bolt so that the lip of the nut is in the groove on the bracket.

8. Install the axle shaft and brake backing plate. Tighten the four bolts to 59 ft. lbs. (80 Nm).

9. Reconnect the brake line and then slide the axle hub/brake drum onto the axle shaft. Install the outer bearing, fill the hole with grease and position the thrust washer. Install the bearing locknut and tighten it to 22 ft. lbs. (29 Nm).

10. Spin the axle hub several times to snug down the bearing and then loosen the bearing locknut until it can be turned by hand.

NOTE: There must be absolutely NO brake drag at this time.

11. Retighten the bearing locknut until there is a bearing preload of 0.9–2.2 lbs.(3.2–9.8 N) while turning the wheel.

12. Install the locknut lock, a new cotter pin and the cap. If the cotter pin hole does not line up properly, align the holes by tightening the nut.

13. Bleed the brakes.

14. Lower the vehicle and bounce it a few times to set the rear suspension.

15. Tighten the suspension arm bolts and the strut rod bolt to 64 ft. lbs. (87 Nm).

Camry, Corolla, Celica and Tercel Wagon (Except 4 X 4)

1. Raise the rear of the vehicle and support it with jackstands.

2. Remove the rear wheel and tire assembly.

3. Remove the brake drum. On the Corolla FX, remove the disc brake caliper from the axle carrier and suspend it with a wire.

4. Disconnect and plug the brake line at the backing plate.

5. Remove the four axle hub-to-carrier bolts and slide off the hub and brake assembly. Remove the O-ring.

6. Remove the bolt and nut attaching the carrier to the strut rod.

7. Remove the bolt and nut attaching the carrier to the No. 1 suspension arm.

8. Remove the bolt and nut attatching the carrier to the No. 2 suspension arm.

9. Unbolt the carrier from the rear strut tube and remove the carrier.

10. Using a hammer and cold chisel, loosen the staked part of the hub nut and remove the nut.

11. Using a two-armed puller or the like, press the axle shaft from the hub.

12. Remove the bearing inner race (inside).

13. Using a two-armed puller again, pull off the bearing inner race (outside) over the bearing and then press it out of the hub.

To install:

1. Position a new bearing inner race (outside) on the bearing and then press a new oil seal into the hub. Coat the lip of the seal with grease.

2. Position a new bearing inner race (inside) on the bearing and then press the inner race with the hub onto the axle shaft.

3. Install the nut and tighten it to 90 ft. lbs. (123 Nm). Stake the nut with a brass drift.

4. Position the axle carrier on the strut tube and tighten the nuts to 119 ft. lbs. (162 Nm).

5. Install the bolt and nut attaching the carrier to the No. 2 suspension arm; fingertighten it only.

NOTE: Make sure that the lip of the nut is in the hole on the arm.

6. Repeat Step 5 for the No. 1 suspension arm.

NOTE: Make sure that the lip of the nut is in the hole on the arm.

7. Install the strut rod-to-carrier bolt so that the lip of the nut is in the groove on the bracket.

8. Install a new O-ring onto the axle carrier. Install the axle hub and brake backing plate. Tighten the four bolts to 59 ft. lbs. (80 Nm).

9. Reconnect the brake line, install the brake drum and then bleed the brakes.

10. Lower the vehicle and bounce it a few times to set the rear suspension.

11. Tighten the suspension arm bolts and the strut rod bolt to 64 ft. lbs. (87 Nm).

MR2

1. Raise the rear of the vehicle and support it with jackstands.

2. Remove the rear wheel and tire assembly. Remove the cotter pin, bearing lock nut cap and bearing lock nut.

3. Disconnect the parking brake cable. Remove the disc brake caliper from the rear axle carrier and suspend it with wire. Remove the rotor disc (check the bearing play in axial direction - 0.0020 in. or less.

4. Disconnect the rear axle carrier from the lower arm. Remove the cot-

ter pin and nut from the suspension arm.

5. Using a suitable tool separate the suspension arm from the rear axle carrier.

6. Place matchmarks on the strut lower bracket and camber adjusting cam.

7. Remove the two axle carrier set nuts and two bolts with the camber adjusting cam. Remove the rear axle carrier and axle hub.

8. Remove the dust deflector from the axle hub. Using a suitable puller remove the inner oil seal. Remove the hole snap ring.

9. Remove the three bolts holding the disc brake dust cover to the rear axle carrier. Using a suitable puller remove the axle hub from the rear axle carrier.

10. Remove the bearing inner (inside) race. Using a suitable puller remove the bearing inner race (outside) from the rear axle hub.

11. Using a suitable puller remove the outer oil seal.

12. Remove the hub bearing by first placing the removed inner race (oustide) in the bearing and using a suitable press, press out the bearing. Be sure to always replace the bearing as an assembly.

13. Installation is the reverse order of the removal procedure. Observe the following torques:

    a. Two camber adjusting cam set bolts — 166 ft. lbs.

    b. Suspension arm nut — 36 ft. lbs.

    c. Rear axle carrier to the lower arm — 59 ft. lbs.

    d. Brake caliper — 43 ft. lbs.

    e. Bearing lock nut — 137 ft. lbs.

1987-88 Supra

1. Raise the rear of the vehicle and support it with jackstands.

2. Remove the rear wheel and tire assembly. Remove the disc brake caliper from the rear axle carrier and suspend it with wire. Remove the rotor disc (check the axle shaft flange runout - 0.0020 in.

3. Remove the rear drive shaft. Disconnect the parking brake cable assembly.

4. Remove the bolt and nut attaching the carrier to the No. 1 suspension arm. Using a suitable tool, disconnect gthe No.1 suspension arm from the axle carrier.

5. Remove the bolt and nut attatching the carrier to the No. 2 suspension arm.

6. Disconnect the strut rod from the axle carrier. Disconnect the strut assembly from the axle carrier.

7. Disconnect the upper arm from the body and remove the axle hub as-

sembly. Remove the upper arm mounting nut and remove the upper arm from the axle carrier.

8. Separate the backing plate and axle carrier. Using a suitable puller, remove the upper arm from the axle carrier.

9. Remove the dust deflector from the axle hub. Using a suitable puller remove the inner oil seal. Remove the hole snap ring.

10. Using a suitable press, press out the bearing outer race from the axle carrier.Be sure to always replace the bearing as an assembly.

11. Remove the bearing inner race (inside) and two bearings from the bearing outer race.

13. Installation is the reverse order of the removal procedure. Observe the following torques:

    a. Backing plate to axle carrier nuts — 43 ft. lbs.

    b. Backing plate to axle carrier bolts — 19 ft. lbs.

    c. No. 1 suspension arm nut — 43 ft. lbs.

    d. Upper arm mounting nut — 80 ft. lbs.

    e. Strut assembly nut — 101 ft. lbs.

    f. Upper arm to body bolt — 121 ft. lbs.

    g. No. 2 suspension arm to axle carrier — 121 ft. lbs.

    h. Strut rod to axle carrier — 121 ft. lbs.

    i. Disc brake caliper bolts — 34 ft. lbs.

STEERING

Steering Wheel

REMOVAL & INSTALLATION

Three Spoke

———— **CAUTION** ————

Do not attempt to remove or install the steering wheel by hammering on it. Damage to the energy-absorbing steering column could result.

1. Unfasten the horn and turn signal multi-connector(s) at the base of the steering column shroud.

2. Loosen the trim pad retaining screws from the back side of the steering wheel.

3. Lift the trim pad and horn button assembly(ies) from the wheel.

4. Remove the steering wheel hub retaining nut.

5. Scratch matchmarks on the hub and shaft to aid in correct installation.

6. Use a steering wheel puller to remove the steering wheel.

Installation is the reverse of removal. Tighten the wheel retaining nut to 15–22 ft. lbs., on 1981-82 models; 25 ft. lbs. on 1983-87 models.

Two Spoke

The two spoke steering wheel is removed on the same manner as the three spoke, except that the trim pad should be pried off with a small prybar. Remove the pad by lifting it toward the top of the wheel.

Four Spoke

-------- **CAUTION** --------

Do not attempt to remove or install the steering wheel by hammering on it. Damage to the energy absorbing steering column could result.

1. Unfasten the horn and turn signal connectors at the base of the steering column shroud, underneath the instrument panel.
2. Gently pry the center emblem off of the steering wheel.
3. Insert a wrench through the hole and remove the steering wheel retaining nut.
4. Scratch matchmarks on the hub and shaft to aid installation.
5. Use a steering wheel puller to remove the steering wheel.

Installation is the reverse of removal. Tighten the steering wheel retaining nut to 15–22 ft. lbs., except on the Celica/Supra which is tightened to 22–28 ft. lbs.

Combination Switch

REMOVAL & INSTALLATION

1. Disconnect the negative battery cable.
2. Unscrew the two retaining bolts and remove the steering column garnish.
3. Remove the upper and lower steering column covers.
4. Remove the steering wheel as detailed previously.
5. Trace the switch wiring harness to the multi-connector. Push in the lock levers and pull apart the connectors.
6. On models equipped with electronic modulated suspension, remove the steering sensor. Unscrew the four mounting screws and remove the switch.
7. Installation is in the reverse order of removal.

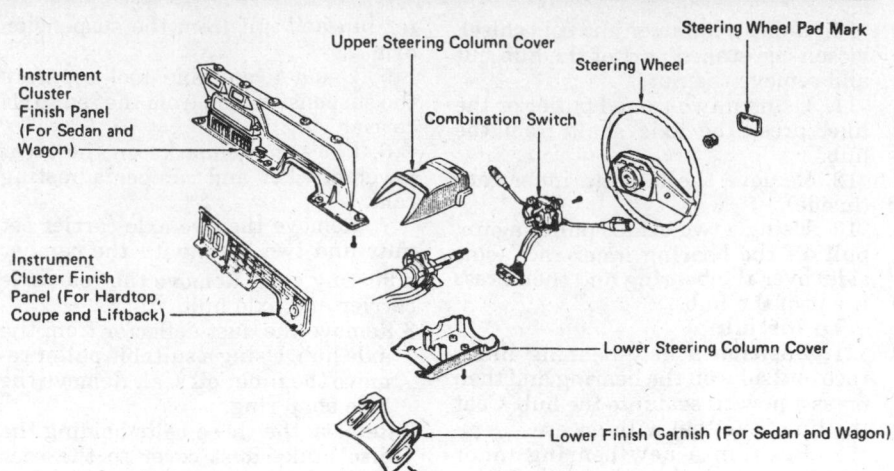

Typical combination switch mounting

Ignition Lock/ Switch

REMOVAL & INSTALLATION

1. Disconnect the negative (–) battery cable.
2. Unfasten the ignition switch connector underneath the instrument panel.
3. Remove the screws which secure the upper and lower halves of the steering column cover. Remove the lower instrument panel garnish on Corona models first.
4. Turn the lock cylinder to the "ACC" position with the ignition key.
5. Push the lock cylinder stop in with a small, round object (cotter pin, punch, etc.).

NOTE: On some models it may be necessary to remove the steering wheel and turn signal switch first.

6. Withdraw the lock cylinder from the lock housing while depressing the stop tab.
7. To remove the ignition switch, unfasten its securing screws and withdraw the switch from the lock housing.

Installation is performed in the following order:

1. Align the locking cam with the hole in the ignition switch and insert the switch into the lock housing.
2. Secure the switch with its screw(s).
3. Make sure that both the lock cylinder and column lock are in the "ACC" position. Slide the cylinder into the lock housing until the stop tab engages the hole in the lock.
4. The rest of the installation in the reverse order of removal.

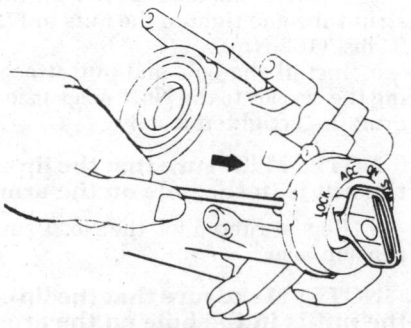

Ignition lock/switch removal

Steering Gear

REMOVAL & INSTALLATION

Corolla (RWD) and Corona

1. Raise and support the vehicle safely. Remove the front wheels. Remove the bolt attaching the coupling yoke (u-joint) to the steering worm.
2. Disconnect the relay rod from the pitman arm. Disconnect the cotter pin and nut holding the knuckle arm to the tie rod.
3. On 1983-87 Corollas with power steering, remove the front exhaust pipe, disconnect and plug the hydraulic lines and then wire them out of the way.
4. Remove the gear housing bracket set bolts and remove the steering gear housing down and to the left.
5. Install in reverse of removal. Torque the housing-to-frame bolts to 25–36 ft. lbs.; the coupling yoke bolt to 15–20 ft. lbs. (26 ft. lbs. – 1983-87); the relay rod to 36–50 ft. lbs.

Cressida and 1981 Celica/Supra

1. Raise and support the vehicle

safely and remove the front wheels. Open the hood, and find the steering gearbox. Place matchmarks on the coupling and steering column shaft. Disconnect the solenoid connectors.

2. Disconnect the Pitman arm from the relay rod using a tie rod puller on the Pitman arm set nut. Disconnect the tie rod ends from the steering knuckles.

3. Remove the steering damper on models so equipped.

4. Disconnect the steering gearbox at the coupling. Unbolt the gearbox from the chassis and remove. Remove the grommets from the gear housing.

5. Installation is in the reverse order of removal, with the exception of first aligning the matchmarks and connecting the steering shaft to the coupling before you bolt the gearbox into the car permanently. Tighten the steering damper bolts to 20 ft. lbs. Tighten the tir rod ends to 43 ft. lbs. Tighten the mounting bracket bolts to 50–60 ft. lbs.

Corolla (FWD), Camry, 1982-85 Celica and 1982-88 Supra

1. Raise and support the vehicle safely. Remove the front wheels. Open the hood. Remove the two set bolts, and remove the sliding yoke from between the steering rack housing and the steering column shaft. On Supras, unbolt and remove the intermediate shaft (rack housing side first).

2. Remove the cotter pin and nut holding the knuckle arm to the tie rod end. Using a tie rod puller, disconnect the tie rod end from the knuckle arm.

3. On Corollas and Camrys with power steering, remove the lower cross member, remove the engine under cover, center engine mount member and the rear engine mount.

4. On 1987-88 Supra models, remove the No. 1 air intake connector with No. 2 air hose (7M-GTE only).

5. Tag and disconnect the power steering lines if equipped. Remove the steering gear housing brackets. Slide the gear housing to the right hand side and then to the left hand side to remove the housing.

6. Installation is the reverse of removal. Torque the rack housing mounting bolts to 29–39 ft. lbs., on the Celica and Supra; 43 ft. lbs. on the Corolla and Camry, and the tie rod set nuts to 37–50 ft. lbs. on the Celica and Supra; 36 ft. lbs. on the the Corolla and Camry. Use a new cotter pin. On Supras, install the intermediate shaft column side first, then rack side. On Corollas w/power steering, tighten the rear engine mount bolts to 29 ft. lbs. (38 ft. lbs. on Camry). Tighten the center mounting member to 29 ft. lbs.

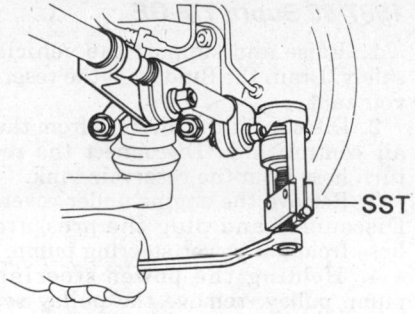

Typical tie rod end removal

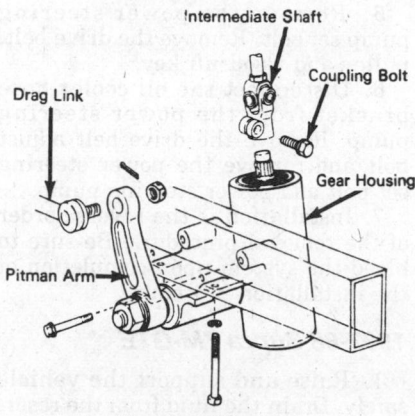

Van steering gear

On power steering-equipped cars, bleed the power steering system and check for fluid leaks. Adjust toe-in on all models.

1986-87 Celica (FWD)

1. Raise and support the vehicle safely. Remove the front wheels.

2. Remove the both engine under covers.

3. Remove the two bolts that connect the steering column U-joint to the rack and then disconnect the column from the rack.

4. Remove the cotter pin and nut and then using a tie rod end removal tool, disconnect the tie rod end from the steering knuckle.

5. Remove the lower suspension crossmember.

6. Remove the mounting bolts and remove the center engine mount member.

7. Disconnect the exhaust pipe from the manifold. Position it out of the way.

8. Tag and disconnect the two hydraulic lines. Position them out of the way and suspend them with a wire.

9. Remove the rear engine mount bracket.

10. Remove the mounting bolts and brackets and lower steering rack from the vehicle.

To install:

1. Position the rack assembly, install the grommets and brackets and

then tighten the two bolts and two nuts to 43 ft. lbs. (59 Nm).

2. Install the rear engine mount bracket and tighten the two bolts to 38 ft. lbs. (52 Nm).

3. Connect the hydraulic lines and tighten the union nuts to 29 ft. lbs. (39 Nm).

4. Connect the exhaust pipe to the manifold.

5. Install the center engine mount member and tighten the bolts to 29 ft. lbs. (39 Nm).

6. Install the lower crossmember and tighten the five outer bolts to 154 ft. lbs. (208 Nm). Tighten the center bolts to 29 ft. lbs.

7. Installation of the remaining components is in the reverse order of removal. Tighten the tie rod end nuts to 36 ft. lbs. (49 Nm) and use a new cotter pin. Tighten the steering column U-joint bolts to 26 ft. lbs. (35 Nm). Fill the power steering pump with DEXRON® 11, bleed the system and check the wheel alignment.

MR2, Tercel and Starlet

1. Jack up the vehicle and support it with jack stands.

2. Remove both front wheels.

3. Place matchmark on the main shaft, joint yoke and pinion shaft. Remove the intermediate shaft from the worm gear shaft.

4. Remove both tie rod ends.

5. Remove the lower suspension crossmember.Remove the center floor crossmember.

6. Remove the rack housing bracket mounting bolts and brackets.

NOTE: Be careful not to damage the rubber boots.

7. Remove the steering linkage.

8. Installation is the reverse of removal.

Van

1. Raise and support the front of the vehicle safely and remove the front wheels.

2. Remove the cotter pin and set nut and disconnect the tie rod ends from the steering knuckle arm. Remove the steering shaft coupling bolt. Disconnect the fluid lines.

3. Remove the Pitman arm nut; loosen the drag link set nut.

4. Using a puller, remove the Pitman arm.

5. Remove the three bolts and bevell gear. Disconnect the torque shaft from the pinion shaft. Unbolt and remove the gear housing.

6. Installation is the reverse of removal. Torque the gear housing bolts to 56 ft. lbs.; the Pitman arm nut to 90 ft. lbs. and the coupling bolt to 18 ft. lbs.

ADJUSTMENTS

Adjustments to the manual steering gear are not necessary during normal service. Adjustments are performed only as part of overhaul.

Power Steering Pump

REMOVAL & INSTALLATION

All Models Except The 1987-88 Supra

1. Raise and support the front of the vehcile safely. Remove the fan shroud.
2. On Camry Celica (FWD), remove the right front wheel and the engine under cover. Remove the lower suspension crossmember.
3. Unfasten the nut from the center of the pump pulley. Disconnect the vacuum hose from the air control valve, if so equipped.

NOTE: Use the drive belt as a brake to keep the pulley from rotating.

4. Withdraw the drive belt. On some models it may be necessary to remove the pulley in order to remove the drive belt.
5. On models equipped with an idler pulley and on the Corolla FX, push on the drive belt to hold the pulley in place and remove the pulley set nut. Loosen the idler pulley set nut and adjusting bolt. Remove the drive belt and loosen the drive pulley to remove the woodruff key.
6. Remove the pulley and the Woodruff key from the pump shaft.
7. Detach and plug the intake and outlet hoses from the pump reservoir.

NOTE: Tie the hose ends up high so the fluid cannot flow out of them. Drain or plug the pump to prevent fluid leakage.

8. Remove the bolt from the rear mounting brace.
9. Remove the front bracket bolts and withdraw the pump.

Installation is performed in the reverse order of removal. Note the following, however:

1. Tighten the pump pulley mounting bolt to 25–39 ft. lbs.
2. Tighten the five outer mounting bolts on the lower crossmember to 154 ft. lbs. Tighten the center bolt to 29 ft. lbs. (Celica FWD).
3. Adjust the pump drive belt tension. The belt should deflect 0.13–0.93 in. under thumb pressure applied midway between the air pump and the power steering pump.
4. Fill the reservoir with DEXRON® automatic transmission fluid. Bleed the air from the system.

1987-88 Supra 7M-GE

1. Raise and support the vehicle safely. Drain the fluid from the reservoir tank.
2. Disconnect the air hose from the air control tank. Disconnect the return hose from the reservoir tank.
3. Remove the engine under cover. Disconnect and plug the pressure hose from the power steering pump.
4. Holding the power steering pump pulley, remove the pulley set nut. Remove the drive belt adjusting nut.
5. Remove the power steering pump set bolt. Remove the drive belt, pulley and woodruff key.
6. Disconnect the oil cooler hose bracket from the power steering pump. Remove the drive belt adjust bolt and remove the power steering set bolt and power steering pump.
7. Installation is the reverse order of the removal procedure. Be sure to bleed the system upon completion of the installation procedure.

1987-88 Supra 7M-GTE

1. Raise and support the vehicle safely. Drain the fluid from the reservoir tank.
2. Remove the number one and number two air hoses with the number four air cleaner pipe.
3. Disconnect the connector from the air flow meter. Remove the air flow meter installation bolt. Loosen the five clamps and disconnect the air hoses, release the three clips on the air cleaner case. Loosen the number seven air hose clamp and remove the number seven air cleaner hose with the air flow meter.
4. Remove the oil reservoir tank with bracket. Disconnect the two air hoses from the air control valve on the power steering pump.
5. Remove the adjusting strut. Remove the engine under cover.
6. Holding the power steering pump pulley, remove the pulley set nut. Remove the drive belt adjusting nut.
7. Remove the power steering pump set bolt. Remove the drive belt, pulley and woodruff key.
8. Disconnect and plug the pressure hose from the power steering pump.
9. Remove the power steering set bolt and power steering pump.
10. Installation is the reverse order of the removal procedure. Be sure to bleed the system upon completion of the installation procedure.

BLEEDING

1. Raise the front of the car and support it securely with jack stands.
2. Fill the pump reservoir with DEXRON® automatic transmission fluid.
3. Rotate the steering wheel from lock to lock several times. Add fluid if necessary.
4. With the steering wheel turned fully to one lock, crank the starter while watching the fluid level in the reservoir.

NOTE: Do not start the engine. Operate the starter with a remote starter switch or have an assistant do it from inside the car. Do not run the starter for prolonged periods.

5. Repeat Step 4 with the steering wheel turned to the opposite lock.
6. Start the engine. With the engine idling, turn the steering wheel from lock to lock two or three times.
7. Lower the front of the car and repeat Step 6.
8. Center the wheel at the midpoint of its travel. Stop the engine.
9. The fluid level should not have risen more than 0.2 in. If it does, repeat Step 7.
10. Check for fluid leakage.

Tie Rod Ends

REMOVAL & INSTALLATION

1. Scribe alignment marks on the tie rod and rack end (rack and pinion cars only).
2. Working at the steering knuckle arm, pull out the cotter pin and then remove the castellated nut.
3. Using a tie rod end puller, disconnect the tie rod from the steering knuckle arm.
4. Repeat the first two steps on the other end of the tie rod (where it attaches to the relay rod).

To install (non-rack and pinion cars):

1. Turn the tie rods in their adjusting tubes until they are of equal lengths.
2. Turn the tie rod do that they cross at 90°. Tighten the adjusting tube clamps so that they lock the ends in position.
3. Connect the tie rods and tighten the nuts to 37–50 ft. lbs.
4. Check the toe. Adjust if necessary.

Rack and pinion cars:

1. Align the alignment marks on the tie rod and rack end.
2. Install the tie rod end.
3. Tighten the nuts to 11–14 ft. lbs. on 1981-83 models; 19 ft. lbs. on 1984-88 models.

BRAKES

For all brake system repair and service procedures not detailed below, please refer to "Brakes" in the Unit Repair section.

Master Cylinder

REMOVAL & INSTALLATION

All Except Van

— CAUTION —

Be careful not to spill brake fluid on the painted surfaces of the vehicle; it will damage the paint.

1. Disconnect the level warning switch connector. Remove the fluid in the master cyclinder with a suitable syringe or the like. Unfasten the hydraulic lines from the master cylinder.
2. Detach the hydraulic fluid pressure differential switch wiring connectors.
3. Loosen the master cylinder reservoir mounting nuts.
4. Then do one of the following:
   a. On models with manual brakes, remove the master cylinder securing bolts and the clevis pin from the brake pedal. Remove the master cylinder.
   b. On other models with power brakes, unfasten the nuts and remove the master cylinder assembly from the power brake unit.

Installation is performed in the reverse order of removal. Note the following, however:
1. Before tightening the master cylinder mounting nuts or bolts, screw the hydraulic line into the cylinder body a few turns.
2. After installation is completed, bleed the master cylinder and the brake system.

Van

1. Disconnect the negative battery cable.
2. Remove the instrument cluster face panel, comination meter, cluster, lower cluster panel, air duct number three and air duct number one and two.
3. Remove the defroster ducts.
4. Syphon off the fluid from the master cylinder with a syringe.
5. Disconnect the brakes lines from the master cylinder. Disconnect the two reservoir hose from the master cyclinder.
6. Unbolt and remove the master cylinder. Installation is the reverse of removal. Torque the nuts to 9 ft. lbs.

Proportioning Valve

A proportioning valve is used on all models to reduce the hydraulic pressure to the rear brakes because of weight transfer during high speed stops. This helps to keep the rear brakes from locking up by improving front to rear brake balance.

REMOVAL & INSTALLATION

1. Disconnect the brake lines from the valve unions.
2. Remove the valve mounting bolt, if used, and remove the valve.

NOTE: If the proportioning valve is defective, it must be replaced as an assembly; it cannot be rebuilt.

3. Installation is the reverse of removal. Bleed the brake system after it is completed.

Load Sensing Proportioning and By-Pass Valve (LSP/BV)

VAN

1. Disconnect the number two shackle from the bracket by , removing the cotterpin, then remove the nut to disconnect the number two shackle from the bracket. Remove the reatianer, two bushings and the collar.
2. Using a suitable line wrench, disconnect the brake tubes from the valve body.
3. Remove the valve bracket mounting bolts and remove the load sensing proportioning and by-pass valve.
4. Installtion is the reverse order of the removal procedure. Bleed brake system after it is completed.

Power Brake Booster

REMOVAL & INSTALLATION

All Models Except The Van

1. Remove the master cyclinder. Disconnect the vacuum hose from the brake booster.
2. Remove the instrument lower finish panel (not necessary on all models). On the MR2 models, remove the wheel guard, instrument lower finish panel and air duct.
3. Remove the brake pedal return spring. Remove clip and clevis pin.
4. Remove the four brake booster nuts and clevis pin. Pull out the brake booster and gasket.
5. Installtion is the reverse order of the removal procedure. Bleed the brake system after it is completed.

Van

1. Remove the master cylinder assembly. Disconnect the vacuum hose from the brake booster.
2. Remove the instrument cluster lower finish panel. Remove the steering column assembly and disconnect the four connectors.
3. Loosen the clutch pedal retaining nut and bolt. Remove the nut and pull out the bolt until the bolt head goes in.
4. Loosen the two clutch master cyclinder retaining bolts and pull them out until the brake pedal bracket is free from the clutch master cylinder. Pull out the throttle cable from the cable hook.
5. Remove the three mounting bolts of the brake and clutch pedal bracket lower side.
6. Remove the two mounting bolts of the pedal bracket upper side. Pull out the brake booster with the bracket to the underside. Remove the cotter pin and clevis. Remove the four nuts and remove the brake booster from the bracket.
7. Installtion is the reverse order of the removal procedure. Bleed the brake system after it is completed.

Wheel Cylinder

REMOVAL & INSTALLATION

1. Plug the master cylinder inlet to prevent hydraulic fluid from leaking.
2. Remove the brake drums and shoes.
3. Working from behind the backing plate, disconnect the hydraulic line from the wheel cylinder.
4. Unfasten the screws retaining the wheel cylinder and withdraw the cylinder.

Installation is performed in the reverse order of removal. However, once the hydraulic line has been disconnected from the wheel cylinder, the union seat must be replaced. To replace the seat, proceed in the following manner:
1. Use a screw extractor with a diameter of 0.1 in. and having reverse threads, to remove the union seat from the wheel cylinder.
2. Drive in the new union seat with a $5/16$ in. bar, used as a drift.

Remember to bleed the brake system after completing wheel cylinder, brake shoe and drum installation.

Parking Brake Cable

ADJUSTMENT

NOTE: The rear brake compo-

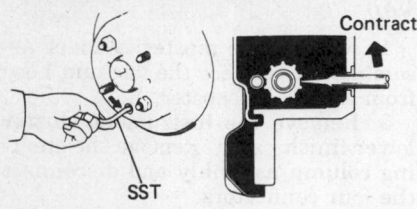

Parking brake adjustment—models with rear disc brakes; the arrow indicates the direction for loosening the parking brake shoes

nents should be in good condition and properly adjusted before performing this adjustment.

1. Slowly pull the parking brake lever upward, without depressing the button on the end of it, and while counting the number of notches required until the parking brake is applied.

NOTE: Two "clicks" are equal to one notch.

2. Check the number of notches against specifications.

3. If the brake system requires adjustment, loosen the cable adjusting nut cap which is located at the rear of the parking brake lever.

NOTE: On some models, the adjustment and lock nuts are located under the vehicle, beneath the lever assembly.

4. Take up the slack in the parking brake cable by rotating the adjusting nut with another open end wrench.
  a. If the number of notches is less than specified, turn the nut counterclockwise.
  b. If the number of notches is more than specified, turn the nut clockwise.
5. Tighten the adjusting cap, using care not to disturb the setting of the adjusting nut.
6. Check the rotation of the rear wheels to be sure that the brakes are not dragging.
7. The following is a list of parking brake adjustment specifications:
  a. 1981-82 Corolla — 4–7 notches.
  b. 1981-82 Tercell — 2–5 notches.
  c. 1983-88 Tercell 2WD — 5–8 notches.
  e. 1983-88 Tercell 4WD — 6–8 notches.
  f. 1981-82 Celica — 3–7 notches.
  g. 1983-88 Celica rear disc brakes — 5–8 notches.
  h. 1983-88 Corolla RWD -rear drum brakes — 5–8 notches.
  i. 1983-88 Corolla RWD -rear disc brakes — 6–9 notches.

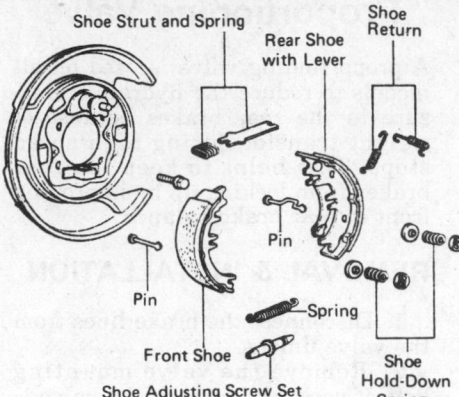

Shoe Strut and Spring
Rear Shoe with Lever
Shoe Return
Pin
Pin
Spring
Front Shoe
Shoe Adjusting Screw Set
Shoe Hold-Down Spring

Exploded view of the parking brake on models with rear disc brakes

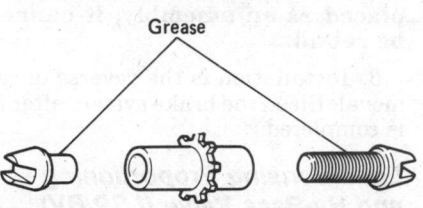

Grease

Before assembly, lubricate the adjuster parts as indicated—models with rear disc brakes

  j. 1983-88 Corolla FWD — 4–7 notches.
  k. 1986-88 MR2 — 5–8 notches.
  l. 1981-88 Cressida — 5–8 notches.
  m. 1983-88 Camry — 5–8 notches.
  n. 1982-83 Supra — 4–7 notches.
  o. 1984-88 Supra — 5–8 notches.
  p. 1981-82 Corona - console — 3–6 notches.
  q. 1981-82 Corona - pedal — 4–8 notches.
  r. 1981-84 Starlet — 4–7 notches.
  s. 1984-88 Van all series except the YR29 series — 7–9 notches.
  t. 1984-88 Van YR29 series — 6–8 notches.

CHASSIS ELECTRICAL

Heater Blower

NOTE: On most of the later Toyota models, the air conditioner assembly is integral with the heater assembly (including the blower motor) and therefore the blower motor removal may differ from the procedures detailed below. In some case it may be necessary to remove the A/C-Heater housing and assembly to remove the blower motor.

REMOVAL & INSTALLATION

Corona

1. Disconnect the negative battery cable. Remove the package tray.
2. Remove the trim panel and disconnect the heater blower motor wiring harness.
3. Loosen the three screws which secure the motor to the housing and remove the blower motor assembly.
4. Installation is the reverse order of the removal procedure.

Celica and Supra

1. Disconnect the negative battery cable. Working from under the instrument panel, unfasten the defroster hoses from the heater box.
2. Unplug the multi-connector. Loosen the mounting screws and withdraw the blower assembly.
3. Installation is the reverse order of the removal procedure.

Cressida

1. Disconnect the negative battery cable. Remove the instrument panel undercover and cowl side trim panel.
2. Remove the air duct and the glove box. Disconnect the heater control cable from the blower motor and remove the blower duct.
3. Disconnect the heater relay from the heater relay electrical connector.
4. Remove the retaining screws from the blower motor assembly. Remove the assembly from the vehicle.
5. Remove the blower motor from the blower motor assembly.
6. Installation is the reverse order of the removal procedure.

Corolla (RWD) and Starlet

1. Disconnect the negative battery cable and disconnect the blower motor wiring harness.
2. Remove the right hand defroster hose.
3. Remove the three retaining screws which secure the blower motor and lift out the blower motor. Separate the fan from the motor.
4. Installation is the reverse order of the removal procedure.

Corolla (FWD) and Tercel

1. Disconnect the negative battery cable. Remove the under tray, if so equipped.
2. Remove the blower duct and air duct. Before removing the air duct, remember to remove the two attaching clamps.
3. Remove the glove box and the heater control cable.

4. Disconnect the electrical connector on the blower motor.

5. Remove the blower motor retaining bolts and remove the blower motor.

6. Installation is the reverse order of the removal procedure.

NOTE: Due to the lack of information available at the time of this publication, a general blower motor removal and installation procedure is outlined for the later Toyota models. The removal steps can be altered as required by the technician.

All Other Models

1. Disconnect the negative battery cable. Remove the three screws attaching the retainer.

2. Remove the glove box. Remove the duct between the blower motor assembly and the heater assembly.

3. Disconnect the blower motor wire connector at the blower motor case.

4. Disconnect the air source selector control cable at the blower motor assembly.

5. Loosen the nuts and bolts attaching the blower motor to the blower case, remove the blower motor from the vehicle.

6. Installation is the reverse order of the removal procedure.

Heater Core

NOTE: On some of the later Toyota models, the air conditioner assembly is integral with the heater assembly (including the heater core) and therefore the heater core removal may differ from the procedures detailed below. In some case it may be necessary to remove the A/C-Heater housing and assembly to remove the heater core.

REMOVAL & INSTALLATION

Corona

1. Disconnect the negative battery cable.

2. Drain the cooling system.

3. Disconnect the heater hoses from the engine.

4. Remove the center console, if so equipped.

5. Remove the package tray and disconnect the heater air duct.

6. Unfasten the screws and take the glove compartment out of the dash.

7. Working through the glove compartment opening, remove the rear duct.

8. Detach the ventilation duct.

9. Remove the instrument cluster.

10. Remove the radio, if installed.

11. Remove the heater control assembly.

12. Take the defroster duct assembly out.

13. Tilt the heater assembly to the right and withdraw it from the package tray side.

14. Remove the water valve and outlet hose from the heater assembly.

15. Take off the retaining band and remove the bolt.

16. Take out the core.

17. Installation is the reverse of the removal procedure.

Celica, Supra and Camry

1. Drain the cooling system.

2. Remove the console, if so equipped, by removing the shift knob (manual), wiring connector, and console attaching screws.

3. Remove the carpeting from the tunnel.

4. If necessary, remove the cigarette lighter and ash tray.

5. Remove the package tray, if it makes access to the heater core difficult.

6. Remove the securing screws and remove the center air outlet on the MarkII/.

7. Remove the bottom cover/intake assembly screws and withdraw the assembly.

8. Remove the cover from the water valve.

9. Remove the water valve.

10. Remove the hose clamps and remove the hoses from the core.

11. Remove the core.

12. Installation is the reverse of the removal procedure.

Cressida

1. Disconnect the negative battery cable. Drain the coolant system into a suitable drain pan. Remove the hood release and the fuel lid release levers.

2. Remove the left hand instrument panel undercover and lower center pad. Remove the finish plate, then remove the radio assembly.

3. Remove the heater control knobs, heater control panel and ashtray.

4. Remove the right side instrument panel undercover, glove box door and glove box.

5. Remove the front pillar garnish, cluster finish panel and instrument cluster gauge assembly.

6. Remove the safety pad and side defroster hose. Remove the heater assembly air ducts.

7. Remove the lower pad reinforcement and remove the front seats. Remove the center console assembly and the cowl side trim panel.

8. Remove the scuff plate, then position the floor carpeting aside. Remove the rear heater duct, if so equipped and heater control assembly.

9. Disconnect the heater hoses from the heater core assembly, remove the heater core grommet.

10. Remove the blower motor duct, center duct and instrument panel brace. Remove the heater core assembly from the vehicle.

12. Remove the nuts securing the heater core to the heater core assembly and remove the heater core.

13. Installation is the reverse order of the removal procedure. Refill the coolant system, start the vehicle and check for coolant leaks.

Corolla (FWD)

1. Disconnect the negative battery cable. Drain the coolant system into a suitable drain pan.

2. Remove the center console, scarf plate and front seats.

3. Position the floor carpet out of the way and remove the heater duct, if so equipped.

4. Remove the under tray, glove box and blower duct.

5. On the Corolla station wagon and sedan models, remove the following components:

   a. Remove the heater control knobs and lens. Remove the cluster lower center panel finish, ashtray and heater control assembly.

   b. Remove the instrument cluster finish panel, radio and air ducts.

6. On the Corolla coupe and liftback models, remove the following components:

   a. The instrument cluster finish panel, instrument cluster, radio trim panel and radio.

   b. Ashtray, heater control knobs, heater control panel, heater control assembly and air duct.

7. Disconnect the heater hoses from the heater core assembly and remove the heater hose grommet.

8. Remove the heater core assembly retaining screws and remove the heater core assembly from the vehicle.

9. Remove the heater core from the heater core assembly.

10. Installation is the reverse order of the removal procedure. Refill the coolant system, start the vehicle and check for coolant leaks.

Corolla (RWD)

1. Disconnect the negative battery cable and drain the cooling system.

2. Disconnect the heater hose from the engine compartment side.

3. Remove the knobs from the heater and fan controls.

4. Remove the two securing screws, and take the heater control panel off.

5. Remove the heater control, complete with cables.

6. Disconnect the wiring harness.

7. Remove the three heater assembly securing bolts and remove the assembly.

8. Separate the core from the heater assembly.

9. Installation is the reverse of the removal procedure.

Starlet

1. Disconnect the negative battery cable. Drain the coolant system into a suitable drain pan.

2. Remove the rear heater duct, if so equipped. Remove the under tray if so equipped.

3. Remove the cowl side trim, glove box and air damper assembly. Remove the air duct, defroster hoses and the inside air duct.

4. Remove the radio finish plate, clock and radio. Remove the ashtray, heater control knobs and heater control front panel.

5. Remove the heater blower switch and heater control assembly. Remove the ignition coil, then disconnect the heater hoses from the heater core assembly.

6. Remove the heater hose grommet. Remove the screws securing the heater core assembly and remove the heater core assembly from the vehicle.

7. Remove the heater core from the heater core assembly.

8. Installation is the reverse order of the removal procedure. Refill the coolant system, start the vehicle and check for coolant leaks.

Tercel

1. Disconnect the negative battery terminal.

2. Drain the radiator.

3. Remove the ash tray and retainer.

4. Remove the rear heater duct (optional).

5. Remove the left and right side defroster ducts.

6. Remove the under tray (optional).

7. Remove the glove box.

8. Remove the main air duct.

9. Disconnect the radio and remove it.

10. Disconnect the heater control cables and remove them.

11. Disconnect the heater hoses.

12. Remove the front and rear air ducts.

13. Remove the electrical connector.

14. Remove the heater bolts and remove the heater.

NOTE: Slide the heater to the right side of car to remove it.

15. Remove the heater core.

16. Installation is the reverse of removal.

NOTE: Due to the lack of information available at the time of this publication, a general heater core removal and installation procedure is outlined for the later Toyota models. The removal steps can be altered as required by the technician.

All Other Models

1. Disconnect the negative battery cable. Drain the coolant system into a suitable drain pan. Disconnect the heater hose at the engine compartment.

2. Remove the six clips retaining the lower part of the heater unit case, then remove the lower part of the case.

3. Using a suitable tool, carefully pry open the lower part of the heater unit case.

4. Remove the heater core assembly from the heater unit case.

5. Installation is the reverse order of the removal procedure. Reconnect the heater hose and refill the coolant system. Start the engine and check for coolant leaks.

Radio

REMOVAL & INSTALLATION

Celica, Supra, Camry and Cressida

1. Remove the knobs from the radio.

2. Remove the nuts from the radio control shafts.

3. Detach the antenna lead from the jack on the radio case.

4. Remove the cowl air intake duct.

5. Detach the power and speaker leads.

6. Remove the radio support nuts and bolts.

7. Remove the radio from beneath the dashboard.

8. Remove the nuts which secure the speaker through the service hole in the top of the glove box.

9. Remove remainder of the speaker securing nuts from above the radio mounting location.

10. Remove the speaker.

11. Installation is the reverse of removal.

Corolla, Tercel and Starlet

1. Remove the two screws from the top of the dashboard center trim panel.

2. Lift the center panel out far enough to gain access to the cigarette lighter wiring and disconnect the wiring. Remove the trim panel.

3. Unfasten the screws which secure the radio to the instrument panel braces.

4. Lift out the radio and disconnect the leads from it. Remove the radio.

5. Installation is the reverse of removal.

Corona
INSTRUMENT PANEL-MOUNTED

1. Remove the two screws securing the instrument cluster surround and remove the surround.

2. Remove the knobs from the heater controls and remove the heater control face.

3. Remove the four screws which secure the center trim panel (two are behind the heater control opening).

4. Remove the radio knobs and remove the center trim panel.

5. Remove the four screws which secure the radio bracket.

6. Pull the radio far enough out to remove the antenna, power, and speaker leads.

7. Remove the radio.

8. Installation is the reverse of removal.

CONSOLE-MOUNTED

1. Remove the screws which secure the console and remove the console, by lowering the armrest rearward and lifting up on the center of the console.

2. Unplug the radio and disconnect the antenna lead.

3. Remove the radio knobs.

4. Remove the radio bracket and then remove the radio.

5. Installation is the reverse of removal.

Windshield Wiper Switch

REMOVAL & INSTALLATION

The windshield wiper switch is incorporated with the cobination switch, therefore it is necessary to refer to the comination switch removal procedure in order to remove the windshield wiper switch.

Front Windshield Wiper Motor

REMOVAL & INSTALLATION

Tercel and Corolla (FWD)

1. Disconnect the negative battery terminal.

2. Insert a small prybar between the linkage and the motor.

3. Pry up to separate the linkage from the motor.

4. Disconnect the electrical connector from the motor.

5. Remove the mounting bolts and remove the motor.

6. Installation is the reverse of removal.

Corolla (RWD), Corona, and Starlet

1. Disconnect the wiper motor connector.

2. Remove the service cover and loosen the wiper motor bolts.

3. Use a small prybar to separate the wiper link-to-motor connection.

— CAUTION —
Be careful not to bend the linkage.

4. Withdraw the wiper motor assembly.

5. Installation is in the reverse order of removal.

Celica, Supra, Camry and Cressida

1. Remove the access hole cover.

2. Separate the wiper and motor by prying gently with a small prybar.

3. Remove the left and right cowl ventilators.

4. Remove the wiper arms and the linkage mounting nuts. Push the linkage pivot ports into the ventilators.

5. Loosen the wiper link connectors at their ends and with the linkage from the cowl ventilator.

6. Start the wiper motor and turn the ignition key off when the crank is at the position illustrated.

NOTE: The wiper motor is difficult to remove when it is in the parked position. If the motor is turned off at the wiper switch, it will automatically return to this position.

7. Unplug the connector.

8. Loosen the motor bolts and withdraw the motor.

9. Installation is the reverse of removal. Be sure to install the wiper motor with it in the park position by connecting the multi-connector and operating the wiper control switch. Assemble the crank.

MR2

1. With the wiper arms in the UP position and the wiper switch on LOW, turn the ignition switch OFF.

2. Disconnect the negative battery cable. Disconnect the wiper motor electrical connector, then remove the light retractor relay from the wiper bracket.

3. Remove the wiper motor set bolts. Manually lower thr wiper arms, then hook the wiper link hook to the dash panel service hole.

4. Disconnect the wiper motor link. Remove the wiper motor attaching bolts then remove the wiper motor.

5. Installation is the reverse order of the removal procedure.

Rear Windshield Wiper Motor

REMOVAL & INSTALLATION

All Models

1. Disconnect the negative battery terminal.

2. Remove the wiper arm and rear door trim cover. Disconnect the wiper motor wire connector.

3. Remove the wiper motor bracket attaching bolts and the wiper motor along with the bracket.

4. Installation is the reverse order of the removal procedure.

Instrument Cluster

REMOVAL & INSTALLATION

Corolla (RWD) and Starlet

1. Disconnect the negative battery cable.

2. Remove the instrument cluster surround.

3. Remove the center trim panel. Disconnect the cigarette lighter wiring before completely removing the panel.

4. Remove the speedometer cable and disconnect it.

5. Pull the instrument cluster out just far enough so that its wiring harness may be disconnected.

6. Remove the cluster.

7. Installation is the reverse of removal.

Corona

1. Disconnect the negative (–) battery cable.

2. Remove the two instrument cluster surround.

3. Remove the side air outlet control knob and the clock setting knob.

4. Lift out the panel.

5. Unfasten the five screws which secure the cluster to the instrument panel support.

6. Disconnect the speedometer cable and the instrument cluster wiring harness.

7. Lift out the cluster assembly.

8. Installation is the reverse of removal.

Cressida

1. Disconnect the battery.

2. Detach the heater control cables at the heater box.

3. Loosen the steering column clamping nuts and lower the column.

— CAUTION —
Be careful when handling the column; it is the collapsible type. Cover the column shroud with a cloth to protect it.

4. Loosen the instrument panel screws and tilt the panel forward.

5. Detach the speedometer cable and wiring connectors. Remove the entire panel assembly.

6. Remove the instruments from the panel as required.

7. Installation is the reverse of removal.

Tercel and Corolla (FWD)

1. Disconnect the negative battery terminal.

2. Remove the steering column cover.

NOTE: Be careful not to damage the collapsible steering column mechanism.

3. Remove the screws from the instrument panel.

4. Gently pull the panel out approximately half way.

5. Disconnect the speedometer and any other electrical connections that are necessary.

6. Remove the panel at this time.

7. Installation is the reverse of removal.

Camry, Celica and Supra

1. Disconnect the negative battery cable at the battery.

2. Remove the fuse box cover from under the left side of the instrument panel.

3. Remove the heater control knobs.

4. Using a screwdriver, carefully pry off the heater control panel.

5. Unscrew the cluster finish panel retaining screws and pull out the bottom of the panel.

6. Unplug the two electrical connectors and unhook the speedometer cable.

7. Remove the instrument cluster.

8. Installation is performed in the reverse of the previous steps.

Headlight Switch

REMOVAL & INSTALLATION

1. Disconnect the negative battery cable. Scribe alignment lines on the steering wheel and steering shaft.

2. Using a steering wheel puller, remove the steering wheel.

3. Remove the headlight and dimmer switch assembly.

4. Installation is the reverse order of the removal procedure.

Stoplight Switch

REMOVAL & INSTALLATION

1. Disconnect the negative battery cable. Remove the brake pedal tension spring.

2. Disconnect the stoplight switch connector.

3. Remove the switch mounting nut, then slide the switch from the mounting bracket.

4. Installation is the reverse order of the removal procedure.

Fuses and Fusible Links

All models have one fusible link and it is usually located in the main battery feed wire need the battery. This link will protect all the circuits except for the starter motor.

FUSE BLOCK LOCATION

All Except Corona, MR2, Starlet and Van

There are three fuse blocks, one is located in the engine compartment on the driver's side wheel weel. One on the right side kick panel under the instrument panel and the other on the left side kick panel under the instrument panel. The main fuse block being the one located on the left (driver's) side kick panel. Some of the earlier models have only one fuse block which is usually located on the left kick panel.

Corona and MR2

The fuse block is located on the left (driver's) side kick panel.

Starlet

The fuse block is located behind a flip-down door on the cowl of the instrument panel on the left hand side.

Van

The fuse box is located on the right side of the dash, behind the glove box.

Volkswagen

Cabriolet, Dasher, Fox, Golf, Jetta, Rabbit, Quantum, Scirocco, Vanagon

SERIAL NUMBER IDENTIFICATION

Vehicle Identification Plate

All models also have an identification plate bearing the chassis number on the top of the instrument panel at the driver's side. This plate is easily visible through the windshield and aids in rapid identification.

The Vanagon has an additional vehicle identification number on the right engine cover plate in the engine compartment and behind the front passengers seat.

On the 1981–88 front wheel drive models the fifth position of the VIN code indicates engine and the tenth, the year. The year code will be a letter. "B"–1981; "C"–1982; etc.

On the Vanagon the first two numbers are the first two digits of the car's model number and the third digit stands for the car's model year. For example a 1 as the third digit means that the car was produced during the 1981 model year, a 2 would signifies 1982, and so forth.

Engine number location – Vanagon diesel engine

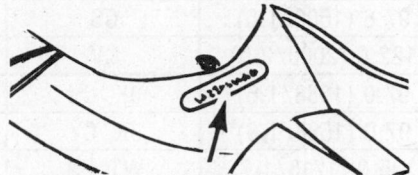

Chassis number location under rear seat

Engine Number

On Vanagon models with both the suitcase air-cooled engine and the Waterboxer (1984–88) engine, the number is stamped on the crankcase near the ignition coil and below the crankcase breather. The diesel engine number is stamped on the block between the injection pump and the vacuum pump.

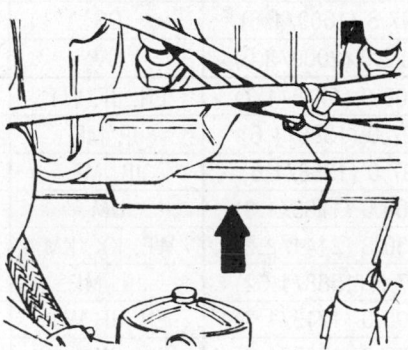

Engine number location

Chassis number

On all front wheel drive models, except the Fox, the engine number is stamped on the engine block between the fuel pump and the distributor. The Fox's engine number is located on the left side of the engine bolck just below the cylinder head, and on the vehicle data plate.

Vehicle Identification Label

This label is located in the luggage compartment beside the spare wheel on the Rabbit, Golf and GTI, at the rear panel on the Jetta, Fox and Scirocco, under the floor covering on the Quantum, on the left side of the cross panel behind the rear bench seat on the Rabbit Convertible (Cabriolet) and and behind the front passenger's seat on the Vanagon.

The label is marked with the Vehicle Identification Number, Vehicle Code, Engine and Transmission Code, Paint and Interior code (needed for matching paint colors) and Option codes.

17 VOLKSWAGEN

ENGINE IDENTIFICATION

Year	Model	Engine Displacement cu. in. (cc/liter)	Engine Series Identification	No. of Cylinders	Engine Type Type
1981	Dasher (Diesel)	97.0 (1588/1.6)	WT, EN	4	Water cooled in-line Diesel
	Jetta	97.0 (1588/1.6)	EJ	4	SOHC
	Jetta	105.0 (1715/1.7)	WT, EN	4	SOHC
	Rabbit (Diesel)	97.0 (1588/1.6)	CR	4	Water cooled in-line Diesel
	Rabbit	105.0 (1715/1.7)	WT, EN	4	SOHC
	Scirocco	105.0 (1715/1.7)	WT, EN	4	SOHC
	Vanagon	120.0 (1970/1.9)	CV	4	Air cooled flat four
1982	Jetta (Diesel)	97.0 (1588/1.6)	CR	4	Water cooled in-line Diesel
	Jetta (Turbo Diesel)	97.0 (1588/1.6)	CR	4	Water cooled in-line Diesel
	Jetta	105.0 (1715/1.7)	WT, EN	4	SOHC
	Quantum (Turbo Diesel)	97.0 (1588/1.6)	CR	4	Water cooled in-line Diesel
	Quantum	105.0 (1715/1.7)	WT, EN	4	SOHC
	Quantum	130.8 (2144/2.2)	WE, KX, KM	5	SOHC
	Rabbit	105.0 (1715/1.7)	WT, EN	4	SOHC
	Scirocco	105.0 (1715/1.7)	WT, EN	4	SOHC
	Vanagon (Diesel)	97.6 (1600/1.6)	CS	4	Water cooled in-line Diesel
	Vanagon	122.0 (2000/2.0)	CV	4	Air cooled flat four
1983	Jetta (Diesel)	97.0 (1588/1.6)	JK, CY	4	Water cooled in-line Diesel
	Jetta (Turbo Diesel)	97.0 (1588/1.6)	JK, CY	4	Water cooled in-line Diesel
	Jetta	105.0 (1715/1.7)	WT, EN	4	SOHC
	Quantum (Turbo Diesel)	97.0 (1588/1.6)	JR, MF	4	SOHC
	Quantum	130.8 (2144/2.2)	WE, KX, KM	5	SOHC
	Quantum	105.0 (1715/1.7)	EN, JF, WT	4	SOHC
	Quantum	109.0 (1780/1.8)	JH	4	SOHC
	Rabbit (Diesel)	97.0 (1588/1.6)	JK, CY	4	Water cooled in-line Diesel
	Rabbit	105.0 (1715/1.7)	WT, EN	4	SOHC
	Rabbit (Conv.)	109.0 (1780/1.8)	JH	4	SOHC
	Rabbit (GTI)	109.0 (1780/1.8)	JH	4	SOHC
	Scirocco	109.0 (1780/1.8)	JH	4	SOHC
	GTI	109.0 (1780/1.8)	JH	4	SOHC
	GLI	109.0 (1780/1.8)	JH	4	SOHC
	Vanagon (Diesel)	97.6 (1600/1.6)	CS	4	Water cooled in-line Diesel
	Vanagon	122.0 (2000/2.0)	CV	4	Air cooled flat four
1984	Jetta	105.0 (1715/1.7)	EN, JF, WT	4	SOHC
	Jetta (Diesel)	97.0 (1588/1.6)	JP, ME	4	SOHC
	Jetta (Turbo Diesel)	97.0 (1588/1.6)	JR, MF	4	Water cooled in-line Diesel
	Quantum	109.0 (1780/1.8)	UM	4	SOHC
	Quantum	130.8 (2144/2.2)	WE, KX, KM	5	SOHC
	Quantum (Turbo Diesel)	97.0 (1588/1.62)	JR, MF	4	Water cooled in-line Diesel
	Rabbit	105.0 (1715/1.7)	EN, JF, WT	4	SOHC
	Rabbit (Conv.)	109.0 (1780/1.8)	GX	4	SOHC
	Rabbit (GTI)	109.0 (1780/1.8)	HT	4	SOHC
	Rabbit (Diesel)	97.0 (1588/1.6)	JP, ME	4	Water cooled in-line Diesel
	Scirocco	109.0 (1780/1.8)	GX	4	SOHC

ENGINE IDENTIFICATION

Year	Model	Engine Displacement cu. in. (cc/liter)	Engine Series Identification	No. of Cylinders	Engine Type Type
1984	GTI	109.0 (1780/1.8)	HT	4	SOHC
	GLI	109.0 (1780/1.8)	—	4	SOHC
	Vanagon (Diesel)	97.6 (1600/1.6)	CS	4	Water cooled in-line Diesel
	Vanagon	122.0 (2000/2.0)	DH	4	Water cooled flat four
1985	Jetta	109.0 (1780/1.8)	GX	4	SOHC
	Jetta (Diesel)	97.0 (1588/1.6)	ME	4	Water cooled in-line Diesel
	Jetta (Turbo Diesel)	97.0 (1588/1.6)	MF	4	Water cooled in-line Diesel
	Quantum	109.0 (1780/1.8)	GX	4	SOHC
	Quantum (Turbo Diesel)	97.0 (1588/1.6)	MF	4	Water cooled in-line Diesel
	Quantum	136.0 (2226/2.2)	WE, KX, KM	5	SOHC
	Scirocco	109.0 (1780/1.8)	GX	4	SOHC
	Cabriolet	109.0 (1780/1.8)	GX	4	SOHC
	GTI	109.0 (1780/1.8)	HT	4	SOHC
	GLI	109.0 (1780/1.8)	HT	4	SOHC
	Golf	109.0 (1780/1.8)	GX	4	SOHC
	Golf (Diesel)	97.0 (1588/1.6)	ME	4	Water cooled in-line Diesel
	Vanagon	115.9 (1900/1.9)	DH	4	Water cooled flat four
1986	Jetta	109.0 (1780/1.8)	GX	4	SOHC
	Jetta (Diesel)	97.0 (1588/1.6)	ME	4	Water cooled in-line Diesel
	Jetta (Turbo Diesel)	97.0 (1588/1.6)	MF	4	Water cooled in-line Diesel
	Quantum	109.0 (1780/1.8)	GX	4	SOHC
	Quantum (Turbo Diesel)	97.0 (1588/1.6)	MF	4	Water cooled in-line Diesel
	Quantum	136.0 (2226/2.2)	WE, KX, KM	5	SOHC
	Cabriolet	109.0 (1780/1.8)	GX	4	SOHC
	Scirocco	109.0 (1780/1.8)	GX	4	SOHC
	GTI	109.0 (1780/1.8)	RD	4	SOHC
	GLI	109.0 (1780/1.8)	RD	4	SOHC
	Golf	109.0 (1780/1.8)	GX	4	SOHC
	Golf (Diesel)	97.0 (1588/1.6)	ME	4	Water cooled in-line Diesel
	Vanagon	128.1 (2100/2.1)	MV	4	Water cooled flat four
1987-88	Jetta	109.0 (1780/1.8)	GX	4	SOHC
	Jetta (Diesel)	97.0 (1588/1.6)	ME	4	Water cooled in-line Diesel
	Jetta (Turbo Diesel)	97.0 (1588/1.6)	MF	4	Water cooled in-line Diesel
	Jetta 16V	109.0 (1780/1.8)	PL	4	DOHC
	Quantum	109.0 (1780/1.8)	GX	4	SOHC
	Quantum (Turbo Diesel)	97.0 (1588/1.6)	MF	4	Water cooled in-line Diesel
	Quantum	136.0 (2226/2.2)	WE, KX, KM	5	SOHC
	Cabriolet	109.0 (1780/1.8)	GX	4	SOHC
	Scirocco	109.0 (1780/1.8)	GX	4	SOHC
	Scirocco 16V	109.0 (1780/1.8)	PL	4	DOHC
	GTI	109.0 (1780/1.8)	RD	4	SOHC
	GTI 16V	109.0 (1780/1.8)	PL	4	DOHC
	GLI	109.0 (1780/1.8)	RD	4	SOHC
	GLI 16V	109.0 (1780/1.8)	PL	4	DOHC

ENGINE IDENTIFICATION

Year	Model	Engine Displacement cu. in. (cc/liter)	Engine Series Identification	No. of Cylinders	Engine Type Type
1987–88	Golf	109.0 (1780/1.8)	GX	4	SOHC
	Golf (Diesel)	97.0 (1588/1.6)	ME	4	Water cooled in-line Diesel
	Fox	109.0 (1780/1.8)	UM	4	SOHC
	Vanagon	128.1 (2100/2.1)	MV	4	Water cooled flat four

GENERAL ENGINE SPECIFICATIONS

Year	Model	Engine Displacement cu. in. (cc)	Fuel System Type	Net Horsepower @ rpm	Net Torque @ rpm (ft. lbs.)	Bore × Stroke (in.)	Compression Ratio	Oil Pressure @ rpm
1981	Dasher (Diesel)	97.0 (1588)	Fuel Inj.	52 @ 4800	72 @ 3000	3.01×3.40	23.0:1	28 @ 2000
	Jetta	97.0 (1588)	Fuel Inj.	78 @ 5500	84 @ 3200	3.13×3.15	8.0:1	28 @ 2000
	Jetta	105.0 (1715)	Fuel Inj.	74 @ 5000	90 @ 3000 ②	3.13×3.40	8.2:1	28 @ 2000
	Rabbit	105.0 (1715)	Fuel Inj.	74 @ 5000	90 @ 3000 ②	3.13×3.40	8.2:1	28 @ 2000
	Rabbit	105.0 (1715)	1 bbl.	65 @ 5000	88 @ 2800	3.13×3.40	8.2:1	28 @ 2000
	Rabbit (Diesel)	97.0 (1588)	Fuel Inj.	52 @ 4800	72 @ 3000	3.01×3.40	23.0:1	28 @ 2000
	Scirocco	105.0 (1715)	Fuel Inj.	74 @ 5000	90 @ 3000 ②	3.13×3.40	8.2:1	28 @ 2000
	Vanagon	120.0 (1970)	Fuel Inj.	67 @ 4200	101 @ 3000	3.70×2.80	7.3:1	42
1982	Jetta	105.0 (1715)	CIS Fuel Inj.	74 @ 5000 ①	90 @ 3000	3.13×3.40	8.2:1	28 @ 2000
	Jetta (Diesel)	97.0 (1588)	Fuel Inj.	52 @ 4800	72 @ 2000	3.01×3.40	23.0:1	28 @ 2000
	Jetta (Turbo Diesel)	97.0 (1588)	Fuel Inj.	68 @ 4500	98 @ 2800	3.01×3.40	23.0:1	74 @ 5000
	Quantum	105.0 (1715)	CIS Fuel Inj.	74 @ 5000 ①	90 @ 3000	3.13×3.40	8.2:1	28 @ 2000
	Quantum (Turbo Diesel)	97.0 (1588)	Fuel Inj.	68 @ 4500	98 @ 2800	3.01×3.40	23.0:1	74 @ 5000
	Quantum	130.8 (2144)	CIS Fuel Inj.	100 @ 5100	112 @ 3000	3.12×3.40	8.2:1	28 @ 2000
	Rabbit	105.0 (1715)	CIS Fuel Inj.	74 @ 5000 ①	90 @ 3000	3.13×3.40	8.2:1	28 @ 2000
	Rabbit	105.0 (1715)	1 bbl.	65 @ 5000	88 @ 2800	3.13×3.40	8.2:1	28 @ 2000
	Rabbit (Diesel)	97.0 (1588)	Fuel Inj.	52 @ 4800	72 @ 3000	3.01×3.40	21.0:1	74 @ 5000
	Scirocco	105.0 (1715)	CIS Fuel Inj.	74 @ 5000 ①	90 @ 3000	3.13×3.40	8.2:1	28 @ 2000
	Vanagon	122.0 (2000)	Fuel Inj.	67 @ 4200	101 @ 3000	3.70×2.80	7.3:1	42
	Vanagon (Diesel)	97.6 (1600)	Fuel Inj.	49 @ 4200	72 @ 2000	3.01×3.40	23.0:1	28 @ 2000
1983	Jetta	105.0 (1715)	CIS Fuel Inj.	74 @ 5000 ①	90 @ 3000	3.13×3.40	8.2:1	28 @ 2000
	Jetta (Diesel)	97.0 (1588)	Fuel Inj.	52 @ 4800	72 @ 2000	3.01×3.40	23.0:1	28 @ 2000
	Jetta (Turbo Diesel)	97.0 (1588)	Fuel Inj.	68 @ 4500	98 @ 2800	3.01×3.40	23.0:1	74 @ 5000
	Quantum	105.0 (1715)	CIS Fuel Inj.	74 @ 5000 ①	90 @ 3000	3.13×3.40	8.2:1	28 @ 2000
	Quantum	109.0 (1780)	CIS Fuel Inj.	88 @ 5500	96 @ 3250	3.19×3.40	9.0:1	28 @ 2000
	Quantum	130.8 (2144)	CIS Fuel Inj.	100 @ 5100	112 @ 3000	3.12×3.40	8.2:1	28 @ 2000
	Quantum (Turbo Diesel)	97.0 (1588)	Fuel Inj.	68 @ 4500	98 @ 2800	3.01×3.40	23.0:1	74 @ 5000
	Rabbit	105.0 (1715)	CIS Fuel Inj.	74 @ 5000 ①	90 @ 3000	3.13×3.40	8.2:1	28 @ 2000
	Rabbit	105.0 (1715)	1 bbl.	65 @ 5000	88 @ 2800	3.13×3.40	8.2:1	28 @ 2000
	Rabbit (Conv.)	109.0 (1780)	CIS Fuel Inj.	74 @ 5000	90 @ 3000	3.13×3.40	8.2:1	28 @ 2000
	Rabbit (GTI)	109.0 (1780)	CIS Fuel Inj.	90 @ 5500	100 @ 3000	3.19×3.40	8.5:1	28 @ 2000
	Rabbit (Diesel)	97.0 (1588)	Fuel Inj.	52 @ 4800	97 @ 2800	3.01×3.40	23.0:1	74 @ 5000
	Scirocco	105.0 (1715)	CIS Fuel Inj.	74 @ 5000 ①	90 @ 3000	3.13×3.40	8.2:1	28 @ 2000
	Scirocco	109.0 (1780)	CIS Fuel Inj.	90 @ 5500	100 @ 3000	3.19×3.40	8.5:1	28 @ 2000
	GTI	109.0 (1780)	CIS Fuel Inj.	90 @ 5500	100 @ 3000	3.19×3.40	8.5:1	28 @ 2000
	GLI	109.0 (1780)	CIS Fuel Inj.	90 @ 5500	100 @ 3000	3.19×3.40	8.5:1	28 @ 2000

GENERAL ENGINE SPECIFICATIONS

Year	Model	Engine Displacement cu. in. (cc)	Fuel System Type	Net Horsepower @ rpm	Net Torque @ rpm (ft. lbs.)	Bore × Stroke (in.)	Compression Ratio	Oil Pressure @ rpm
1983	GTI (Diesel)	97.0 (1588)	Fuel Inj.	52 @ 4800	72 @ 3000	3.01×3.40	23.0:1	74 @ 5000
	Vanagon	122.0 (2000)	Fuel Inj.	67 @ 4200	101 @ 3000	3.70×2.80	7.3:1	42
	Vanagon (Diesel)	97.6 (1600)	Fuel Inj.	49 @ 4200	72 @ 2000	3.01×3.40	23.0:1	28 @ 2000
1984	Jetta	105.0 (1715)	CIS Fuel Inj.	74 @ 5000	90 @ 3000 ②	3.13×3.40	8.2:1	28 @ 2000
	Jetta (Diesel)	97.0 (1588)	Fuel Inj.	52 @ 4800	72 @ 2000	3.01×3.40	23.0:1	28 @ 2000
	Jetta (Turbo Diesel)	97.0 (1588)	Fuel Inj.	68 @ 4500	98 @ 2800	3.01×3.40	23.0:1	74 @ 5000
	Quantum	109.0 (1780)	CIS Fuel Inj.	88 @ 5500	96 @ 3250	3.19×3.40	9.0:1	28 @ 2000
	Quantum	130.0 (2144)	CIS Fuel Inj.	100 @ 3000	112 @ 3000	3.12×3.40	8.2:1	28 @ 2000
	Quantum (Turbo Diesel)	97.0 (1588)	Fuel Inj.	68 @ 4500	98 @ 2800	3.01×3.40	23.0:1	74 @ 5000
	Rabbit	105.0 (1715)	1 bbl.	65 @ 5000	88 @ 2800	3.13×3.40	8.2:1	28 @ 2000
	Rabbit (Conv.)	109.0 (1780)	CIS Fuel Inj.	90 @ 5500	100 @ 3000	3.19×3.40	8.5:1	28 @ 2000
	Rabbit (GTI)	109.0 (1780)	CIS Fuel Inj.	90 @ 5500	100 @ 3000	3.19×3.40	8.5:1	28 @ 2000
	Rabbit (Diesel)	97.0 (1588)	Fuel Inj.	52 @ 4800	97 @ 2800	3.01×3.40	23.0:1	74 @ 5000
	Rabbit	105.0 (1715)	CIS Fuel Inj.	74 @ 5000	90 @ 3000 ②	3.13×3.40	8.2:1	28 @ 2000
	Scirocco	109.0 (1780)	CIS Fuel Inj.	90 @ 5500	100 @ 3000	3.19×3.40	8.5:1	28 @ 2000
	GTI (Diesel)	97.0 (1588)	Fuel Inj.	52 @ 4800	72 @ 3000	3.01×3.40	23.0:1	74 @ 5000
	GTI	109.0 (1780)	CIS Fuel Inj.	90 @ 5500	100 @ 3000	3.19×3.40	8.5:1	28 @ 2000
	GLI	109.0 (1780)	CIS Fuel Inj.	90 @ 5500	100 @ 3000	3.19×3.40	8.5:1	28 @ 2000
	Vanagon (Diesel)	97.6 (1600)	Fuel Inj.	49 @ 4200	72 @ 2000	3.01×3.40	23.0:1	28 @ 2000
	Vanagon	115.9 (1900)	Fuel Inj.	82 @ 4800	106 @ 2600	3.70×2.72	8.6:1	29 @ 2000
1985	Jetta	109.0 (1780)	CIS Fuel Inj.	85 @ 5250	98 @ 3000	3.19×3.40	8.5:1	28 @ 2000
	Jetta (Diesel)	97.0 (1588)	Fuel Inj.	52 @ 4800	72 @ 2000	3.01×3.40	23.0:1	28 @ 2000
	Jetta (Tubo Diesel)	97.0 (1588)	Fuel Inj.	68 @ 4500	48 @ 2800	3.01×3.40	23.0:1	74 @ 5000
	Quantum	109.0 (1780)	CIS Fuel Inj.	88 @ 5500	96 @ 3250	3.19×3.40	9.0:1	28 @ 2000
	Quantum (Turbo Diesel)	97.0 (1588)	Fuel Inj.	68 @ 4500	98 @ 2800	3.01×3.40	23.0:1	74 @ 5000
	Quantum	136.0 (2226)	Fuel Inj.	110 @ 5500	122 @ 2500	3.19×3.40	8.5:1	28 @ 2000
	Cabriolet	109.0 (1780)	CIS Fuel Inj.	90 @ 5500	100 @ 3000	3.19×3.40	8.5:1	28 @ 2000
	Scirocco	109.0 (1780)	CIS Fuel Inj.	90 @ 5500	100 @ 3000	3.19×3.40	8.5:1	28 @ 2000
	GTI	109.0 (1780)	CIS Fuel Inj.	100 @ 5500	107 @ 3000	3.20×3.40	10.0:1	28 @ 2000
	GLI	109.0 (1780)	CIS Fuel Inj.	100 @ 5500	107 @ 3000	3.20×3.40	10.0:1	28 @ 2000
	Golf	109.0 (1780)	CIS Fuel Inj.	85 @ 5250	98 @ 3000	3.19×3.40	8.5:1	28 @ 2000
	Golf (Diesel)	97.0 (1588)	Fuel Inj.	52 @ 4800	70 @ 2000	3.01×3.40	23.0:1	74 @ 5000
	Vanagon	115.9 (1900)	Fuel Inj.	82 @ 4800	106 @ 2600	3.70×2.72	8.6:1	29 @ 2000
1986	Jetta	109.0 (1780)	CIS Fuel Inj.	88 @ 5500	110 @ 3250	3.19×3.40	9.0:1	28 @ 2000
	Jetta (Diesel)	97.0 (1588)	Fuel Inj.	52 @ 4800	72 @ 2000	3.01×3.40	23.0:1	28 @ 2000
	Jetta (Turbo Diesel)	97.0 (1588)	Fuel Inj.	68 @ 4500	98 @ 2800	3.01×3.40	23.0:1	74 @ 5000
	Quantum	109.0 (1780)	CIS Fuel Inj.	88 @ 5500	96 @ 3250	3.19×3.40	9.0:1	28 @ 2000
	Quantum (Turbo Diesel)	97.0 (1588)	Fuel Inj.	68 @ 4500	98 @ 2800	3.01×3.40	23.0:1	74 @ 5000
	Quantum	136.0 (2226)	Fuel Inj.	110 @ 5500	122 @ 2500	3.19×3.40	8.5:1	28 @ 2000
	Cabriolet	109.0 (1780)	CIS Fuel Inj.	90 @ 5500	100 @ 3000	3.19×3.40	8.5:1	28 @ 2000
	Scirocco	109.0 (1780)	CIS Fuel Inj.	90 @ 5500	100 @ 3000	3.19×3.40	8.5:1	28 @ 2000
	GTI	109.0 (1780)	CIS Fuel Inj.	100 @ 5500	110 @ 3250	3.20×3.40	10.0:1	28 @ 2000
	GLI	109.0 (1780)	CIS Fuel Inj.	100 @ 5500	110 @ 3250	3.20×3.40	10.0:1	28 @ 2000
	Golf	109.0 (1780)	CIS Fuel Inj.	85 @ 5250	98 @ 3000	3.19×3.40	9.0:1	28 @ 2000

GENERAL ENGINE SPECIFICATIONS

Year	Model	Engine Displacement cu. in. (cc)	Fuel System Type	Net Horsepower @ rpm	Net Torque @ rpm (ft. lbs.)	Bore × Stroke (in.)	Compression Ratio	Oil Pressure @ rpm
1986	Golf (Diesel)	97.0 (1588)	Fuel Inj.	52 @ 4800	70 @ 2000	3.01×3.40	23.0:1	74 @ 5000
	Vanagon	128.1 (2100)	Fuel Inj.	90 @ 4800	117 @ 3200	3.70×2.99	9.0:1	29 @ 2000
1987–88	Jetta	109.0 (1780)	CIS Fuel Inj.	85 @ 5250	110 @ 3250	3.19×3.40	8.5:1	28 @ 2000
	Jetta (Diesel)	97.0 (1588)	Fuel Inj.	52 @ 4800	72 @ 2000	3.01×3.40	23.0:1	28 @ 2000
	Jetta (Turbo Diesel)	97.0 (1588)	Fuel Inj.	68 @ 4500	98 @ 2800	3.01×3.40	23.0:1	74 @ 5000
	Jetta 16V	109.0 (1780)	CIS Fuel Inj.	123 @ 5800	120 @ 4200	3.20×3.40	10.0:1	28 @ 2000
	Quantum	109.0 (1780)	CIS Fuel Inj.	88 @ 5500	96 @ 3250	3.19×3.40	9.0:1	28 @ 2000
	Quantum (Turbo Diesel)	97.0 (1588)	Fuel Inj.	68 @ 4500	98 @ 2800	3.01×3.40	23.0:1	74 @ 5000
	Quantum	136.0 (2226)	Fuel Inj.	110 @ 5500	122 @ 2500	3.19×3.40	8.5:1	28 @ 2000
	Cabriolet	109.0 (1780)	CIS Fuel Inj.	90 @ 5500	100 @ 3000	3.19×3.40	8.5:1	28 @ 2000
	Scirocco	109.0 (1780)	CIS Fuel Inj.	90 @ 5500	100 @ 3000	3.19×3.40	8.5:1	28 @ 2000
	Scirocco 16V	109.0 (1780)	CIS Fuel Inj.	123 @ 5800	120 @ 4200	3.20×3.40	10.0:1	28 @ 2000
	GTI	109.0 (1780)	CIS Fuel Inj.	100 @ 5500	110 @ 3250	3.20×3.40	10.0:1	28 @ 2000
	GTI 16V	109.0 (1780)	CIS Fuel Inj.	123 @ 5800	120 @ 4200	3.20×3.40	10.0:1	28 @ 2000
	GLI	109.0 (1780)	CIS Fuel Inj.	100 @ 5500	110 @ 3250	3.20×3.40	10.0:1	28 @ 2000
	GLI 16V	109.0 (1780)	CIS Fuel Inj.	123 @ 5800	120 @ 4200	3.20×3.40	10.0:1	28 @ 2000
	Golf	109.0 (1780)	CIS Fuel Inj.	85 @ 5250	98 @ 2000	3.19×3.40	4.0:1	28 @ 2000
	Golf (Diesel)	97.0 (1588)	Fuel Inj.	52 @ 4800	70 @ 2000	3.01×3.40	23.0:1	74 @ 5000
	Golf 16V	109.0 (1780)	CIS Fuel Inj.	123 @ 5800	120 @ 4200	3.20×3.40	10.0:1	28 @ 2000
	Fox	109.0 (1780)	CIS Fuel Inj.	81 @ 5500	93 @ 3250	3.20×3.40	9.0:1	28 @ 2000
	Vanagon	128.1 (2100)	Fuel Inj.	90 @ 4800	117 @ 3200	3.70×2.99	9.0:1	29 @ 2000

GASOLINE ENGINE TUNE-UP SPECIFICATIONS

Year	Model	Engine Displacement cu. in. (cc)	Spark Plugs Type	Gap (in.)	Ignition Timing (deg.) MT	AT	Compression Pressure (psi)	Fuel Pump (psi)	Idle Speed (rpm) MT	AT	Valve Clearance In. ③	Ex. ③
1981	Dasher (49 states)	97.0 (1588)	W175T30 N8Y	0.024–0.032	3 ATDC @ Idle	3 ATDC @ Idle	142–184	NA	850–1000	850–1000 ②	0.008–0.012	0.016–0.020
	Dasher (California)	97.0 (1588)	WR7DS N8GY	0.024–0.028	3 ATDC @ Idle	3 ATDC @ Idle	142–184	NA	880–1000	880–1000	0.008–0.012	0.016–0.020
	Jetta (49 states)	105.0 (1715)	W175T30 N8Y	0.024–0.032	3 ATDC @ Idle	3 ATDC @ Idle	142–184	NA	850–1000	850–1000 ②	0.008–0.012	0.016–0.020
	Jetta (California)	105.0 (1715)	WR7DS N8GY	0.024–0.028	3 ATDC @ Idle	3 ATDC @ Idle	142–184	NA	880–1000	880–1000	0.008–0.012	0.016–0.020
	Rabbit (49 states)	105.0 (1715)	W175T30 N8Y	0.024–0.032	3 ATDC @ Idle	3 ATDC @ Idle	142–184	NA	850–1000	850–1000 ②	0.008–0.012	0.016–0.020
	Rabbit (California)	105.0 (1715)	WR7DS N8GY	0.024–0.028	3 ATDC @ Idle	3 ATDC @ Idle	142–184	NA	880–1000	880–1000	0.008–0.012	0.016–0.020
	Scirocco (49 states)	105.0 (1715)	W175T30 N8Y	0.024–0.032	3 ATDC @ Idle	3 ATDC @ Idle	142–184	NA	850–1000	850–1000 ②	0.008–0.012	0.016–0.020
	Scirocco (California)	105.0 (1715)	WR7DS N8GY	0.024–0.028	3 ATDC @ Idle	3 ATDC @ Idle	142–148	NA	880–1000	880–1000	0.008–0.012	0.016–0.020
	Vanagon (49 states)	120.0 (1970)	W145M2 N288	0.028	7.5 BTDC	7.5 BTDC	85–136	28 @ 4000 rpm	800–950	850–1000	Hyd	Hyd ⑦
	Vanagon (California)	120.0 (1970)	W145M2 N288	0.028	5 ATDC ④	5 ATDC ④	85–136	28 @ 4000 rpm	850–900	850–900	Hyd	Hyd ⑦

GASOLINE ENGINE TUNE-UP SPECIFICATIONS

Year	Model	Engine Displacement cu. in. (cc)	Spark Plugs Type	Gap (in.)	Ignition Timing (deg.) MT	Ignition Timing (deg.) AT	Compression Pressure (psi)	Fuel Pump (psi)	Idle Speed (rpm) MT	Idle Speed (rpm) AT	Valve Clearance In. ③	Valve Clearance Ex. ③
1982	Jetta (49 states)	105.0 (1715)	W175T30 N8Y	0.024–0.032	3 ATDC @ Idle	3 ATDC @ Idle	131–174	NA	850–1000	850–1000 ②	0.008–0.012	0.016–0.020
	Jetta (California)	105.0 (1715)	WR7DS N8GY	0.024–0.028	3 ATDC @ Idle	3 ATDC @ Idle	131–174	NA	880–1000	880–1000	0.008–0.012	0.016–0.020
	Quantum (49 states)	105.0 (1715)	W175T30 N8Y	0.024–0.032	3 ATDC @ Idle	3 ATDC @ Idle	131–174	NA	850–1000	850–1000 ②	0.008–0.012	0.016–0.020
	Quantum (California)	105.0 (1715)	WR7DS N8GY	0.024–0.028	3 ATDC @ Idle	3 ATDC @ Idle	131–174	NA	880–1000	880–1000	0.008–0.012	0.016–0.020
	Rabbit (49 states)	105.0 (1715)	W175T30 N8Y	0.024–0.032	3 ATDC @ Idle	3 ATDC @ Idle	131–174	NA	850–1000	850–1000 ②	0.008–0.012	0.016–0.020
	Rabbit (California)	105.0 (1715)	WR7DS N8GY	0.024–0.028	3 ATDC @ Idle	3 ATDC @ Idle	131–174	NA	880–1000	880–1000	0.008–0.012	0.016–0.020
	Scirocco (49 states)	105.0 (1715)	W175T30 N8Y	0.024–0.032	3 ATDC @ Idle	3 ATDC @ Idle	131–174	NA	850–1000	850–1000 ②	0.008–0.012	0.016–0.020
	Scirocco (California)	105.0 (1715)	WR7DS N8GY	0.024–0.028	3 ATDC @ Idle	3 ATDC @ Idle	131–174	NA	880–1000	880–1000	0.008–0.012	0.016–0.020
	Vanagon (49 states)	120.0 (1970)	W145M2 N288	0.028	7.5 BTDC	7.5 BTDC	85–135	28 @ 4000 rpm	800–950	850–1000	Hyd	Hyd ⑦
	Vanagon (California)	120.0 (1970)	W145M2 N288	0.028	5 ATDC ④	5 ATDC ④	85–136	28 @ 4000 rpm	850–900	850–900	Hyd	Hyd ⑦
1983	Jetta (49 states)	105.0 (1715)	W175T30 N8Y	0.024–0.032	3 ATDC @ Idle	3 ATDC @ Idle	131–174	NA	850–1000	850–1000 ②	0.008–0.012	0.016–0.020
	Jetta (California)	105.0 (1715)	WR7DS N8GY	0.024–0.028	3 ATDC @ Idle	3 ATDC @ Idle	131–174	NA	880–1000	880–1000	0.008–0.012	0.016–0.020
	Quantum (49 states)	105.0 (1715)	W175T30 N8Y	0.024–0.032	3 ATDC @ Idle	3 ATDC @ Idle	131–174	NA	850–1000	850–1000 ②	0.008–0.012	0.016–0.020
	Quantum (California)	105.0 (1715)	WR7DS N8GY	0.024–0.028	3 ATDC @ Idle	3 ATDC @ Idle	131–174	NA	880–1000	880–1000	0.008–0.012	0.016–0.020
	Quantum (49 states)	130.8 (2144)	W7D N8Y	0.024–0.028	6 BTDC @ Idle	3 ATDC @ Idle	131–174	NA	850–1000	850–1000	0.008–0.012	0.016–0.020
	Quantum (California)	130.8 (2144)	WR7DS N8GY	0.024–0.028	6 BTDC @ Idle	3 ATDC @ Idle	131–174	NA	850–1000	850–1000	0.008–0.012	0.016–0.020
	Rabbit (49 states)	105.0 (1715)	W175T30 N8Y	0.024–0.032	3 ATDC @ Idle	3 ATDC @ Idle	131–174	NA	850–1000	850–1000 ②	0.008–0.012	0.016–0.020
	Rabbit (California)	105.0 (1715)	WR7DS N8GY	0.024–0.028	3 ATDC @ Idle	3 ATDC @ Idle	131–174	NA	880–1000	880–1000	0.008–0.012	0.016–0.020
	Scirocco (49 states)	105.0 (1715)	W175T30 N8Y	0.024–0.032	3 ATDC @ Idle	3 ATDC @ Idle	131–174	NA	850–1000	850–1000 ②	0.008–0.012	0.016–0.020
	Scirocco (California)	105.0 (1715)	WR7DS N8GY	0.024–0.028	3 ATDC @ Idle	3 ATDC @ Idle	131–174	NA	880–1000	880–1000	0.008–0.012	0.016–0.020
	Scirocco (49 states)	109.0 (1780)	WR7DS N8YGY	0.024–0.028	6 BTDC @ Idle	6 BTDC @ Idle	131–174	NA	880–1000	880–1000	0.008–0.012	0.016–0.020
	Scirocco (California)	109.0 (1780)	WR7DS N8YGY	0.024–0.028	6 BTDC @ Idle	6 BTDC @ Idle	131–174	NA	880–1000	880–1000	0.008–0.012	0.016–0.020
	Cabriolet (49 states)	109.0 (1780)	WR7DS N8YGY	0.024–0.028	6 BTDC @ Idle	6 BTDC @ Idle	131–174	NA	880–1000	880–1000	0.008–0.012	0.016–0.020
	Cabriolet (California)	109.0 (1780)	WR7DS N8YGY	0.024–0.028	6 BTDC @ Idle	6 BTDC @ Idle	131–174	NA	880–1000	880–1000	0.008–0.012	0.016–0.020

GASOLINE ENGINE TUNE-UP SPECIFICATIONS

Year	Model	Engine Displacement cu. in. (cc)	Spark Plugs Type	Gap (in.)	Ignition Timing (deg.) MT	AT	Compression Pressure (psi)	Fuel Pump (psi)	Idle Speed (rpm) MT	AT	Valve Clearance In. ③	Ex. ③
1983	GTI (49 states)	109.0 (1780)	WR7DS N8YGY	0.024–0.028	6 BTDC @ Idle	6 BTDC @ Idle	131–174	NA	880–1000	880–1000	0.008–0.012	0.016–0.020
	GTI (California)	109.0 (1780)	WR7DS N8YGY	0.024–0.028	6 BTDC @ Idle	6 BTDC @ Idle	131–174	NA	880–1000	880–1000	0.008–0.012	0.016–0.020
	GLI (49 states)	109.0 (1780)	WR7DS N8YGY	0.024–0.028	6 BTDC @ Idle	6 BTDC @ Idle	131–174	NA	880–1000	880–1000	0.008–0.012	0.016–0.020
	GLI (California)	109.0 (1780)	WR7DS N8YGY	0.024–0.028	6 BTDC @ Idle	6 BTDC @ Idle	131–174	NA	880–1000	880–1000	0.008–0.012	0.016–0.020
	Vanagon (49 states)	120.0 (1970)	W145M2 N288	0.028	7.5 BTDC	7.5 BTDC	85–135	28 @ 4000 rpm	800–950	850–1000	Hyd	Hyd ⑦
	Vanagon (California)	120.0 (1970)	W145M2 N288	0.028	5 ATDC ④	5 ATDC ④	85–135	28 @ 4000 rpm	850–950	850–950	Hyd	Hyd ⑦
1984	Jetta (49 states)	105.0 (1715)	W175T30 N8Y	0.024–0.032	3 ATDC @ Idle	3 ATDC @ Idle	131–174	NA	850–1000	850–1000 ②	0.008–0.012	0.016–0.020
	Jetta (California)	105.0 (1715)	WR7DS N8GY	0.024–0.028	3 ATDC @ Idle	3 ATDC @ Idle	131–174	NA	880–1000	880–1000	0.008–0.012	0.016–0.020
	Quantum (49 states)	105.0 (1715)	W175T30 N8Y	0.024–0.032	3 ATDC @ Idle	3 ATDC @ Idle	131–174	NA	850–1000	850–1000 ②	0.008–0.012	0.016–0.020
	Quantum (California)	105.0 (1715)	WR7DS N8GY	0.024–0.028	3 ATDC @ Idle	3 ATDC @ Idle	131–174	NA	880–1000	880–1000	0.008–0.012	0.016–0.020
	Quantum (49 states)	130.8 (2144)	W7D N8Y	0.024–0.028	6 BTDC @ Idle	3 ATDC @ Idle	142–184	NA	850–1000	850–1000	0.008–0.012	0.016–0.020
	Quantum (California)	130.8 (2144)	WR7DS N8GY	0.024–0.028	6 BTDC @ Idle	3 ATDC @ Idle	142–184	NA	850–1000	850–1000	0.008–0.012	0.016–0.020
	Rabbit (49 states)	105.0 (1715)	W175T30 N8Y	0.024–0.032	3 ATDC @ Idle	3 ATDC @ Idle	131–174	NA	850–1000	850–1000 ②	0.008–0.012	0.016–0.020
	Rabbit (California)	105.0 (1715)	WR7DS N8GY	0.024–0.028	3 ATDC @ Idle	3 ATDC @ Idle	131–174	NA	880–1000	880–1000	0.008–0.012	0.016–0.020
	Cabriolet (49 states)	109.0 (1780)	WR7DS N8YGY	0.024–0.028	6 BTDC @ Idle	6 BTDC @ Idle	131–174	NA	880–1000	880–1000	0.008–0.012	0.016–0.020
	Cabriolet (California)	109.0 (1780)	WR7DS N8YGY	0.024–0.028	6 BTDC @ Idle	6 BTDC @ Idle	131–174	NA	880–1000	880–1000	0.008–0.012	0.016–0.020
	Scirocco (49 states)	105.0 (1715)	W175T30 N8Y	0.024–0.032	3 ATDC @ Idle	3 ATDC @ Idle	131–174	NA	850–1000	850–1000 ②	0.008–0.012	0.016–0.020
	Scirocco (California)	105.0 (1715)	WR7DS N8GY	0.024–0.028	3 ATDC @ Idle	3 ATDC @ Idle	131–174	NA	880–1000	880–1000	0.008–0.012	0.016–0.020
	Scirocco (49 states)	109.0 (1780)	W175T30 N8YGY	0.024–0.028	6 BTDC @ Idle	6 BTDC @ Idle	131–174	NA	880–1000	880–1000	0.008–0.012	0.016–0.020
	Scirocco (California)	109.0 (1780)	WR7DS N8YGY	0.024–0.028	6 BTDC @ Idle	6 BTDC @ Idle	131–174	NA	880–1000	880–1000	0.008–0.012	0.016–0.020
	GTI (49 states)	109.0 (1780)	WR7DS N8YGY	0.024–0.028	6 BTDC @ Idle	6 BTDC @ Idle	131–174	NA	880–1000	880–1000	0.008–0.012	0.016–0.020
	GTI (California)	109.0 (1780)	WR7DS N8YGY	0.024–0.028	6 BTDC @ Idle	6 BTDC @ Idle	131–174	NA	880–1000	880–1000	0.008–0.012	0.016–0.020
	GLI (49 states)	109.0 (1780)	WR7DS N8YGY	0.024–0.028	6 BTDC @ Idle	6 BTDC @ Idle	131–174	NA	880–1000	880–1000	0.008–0.012	0.016–0.020
	GLI (California)	109.0 (1780)	WR7DS N8YGY	0.024–0.028	6 BTDC @ Idle	6 BTDC @ Idle	131–174	NA	880–1000	880–1000	0.008–0.012	0.016–0.020

GASOLINE ENGINE TUNE-UP SPECIFICATIONS

Year	Model	Engine Displacement cu. in. (cc)	Spark Plugs Type	Gap (in.)	Ignition Timing (deg.) MT	AT	Compression Pressure (psi)	Fuel Pump (psi)	Idle Speed (rpm) MT	AT	Valve Clearance In. ③	Ex. ③
1984	Vanagon (49 states)	115.9 (1915)	W7CO N288 14L-7C	0.028	5 ATDC @ Idle	5 ATDC @ Idle	116– 189	⑥	800– 900 ⑤	800– 900 ⑤	Hyd	Hyd ⑦
	Vanagon (California)	115.9 (1915)	W7CO N288 14L-7C	0.028	5 ATDC @ Idle	5 ATDC @ Idle	116– 189	⑥	800– 900 ⑤	800– 900 ⑤	Hyd	Hyd ⑦
1985	Jetta	109.0 (1780)	WR7DS N8GY	0.024– 0.032	6 BTDC @ Idle	6 BTDC @ Idle	123– 174	NA	850– 1000	850– 1000	Hyd	Hyd
	Quantum	109.0 (1780)	WR7DS N8GY	0.028– 0.032	6 BTDC @ Idle	6 BTDC @ Idle	123– 174	NA	850– 1000	850– 1000	Hyd	Hyd
	Quantum	136.0 (2226)	WR7DS N8GY	0.028– 0.032	6 BTDC @ Idle	3 ATDC @ Idle	123– 174	NA	850– 1000	850– 1000	0.008– 0.012	0.016– 0.020
	Cabriolet	109.0 (1780)	WR7DS N8GY	0.024– 0.032	6 BTDC @ Idle	6 BTDC @ Idle	123– 174	NA	850– 1000	850– 1000	Hyd	Hyd
	Scirocco	109.0 (1780)	WR7DS N8GY	0.024– 0.032	6 BTDC @ Idle	6 BTDC @ Idle	123– 174	NA	850– 1000	850– 1000	Hyd	Hyd
	GTI	109.0 (1780)	WR7DS N8GY	0.024– 0.032	6 BTDC @ Idle	6 BTDC @ Idle	123– 174	NA	850– 1000	850– 1000	Hyd	Hyd
	GLI	109.0 (1780)	WR7DS N8GY	0.024– 0.032	6 BTDC @ Idle	6 BTDC @ Idle	123– 174	NA	850– 1000	850– 1000	Hyd	Hyd
	Golf	109.0 (1780)	WR7DS N8GY	0.024– 0.032	6 BTDC @ Idle	6 BTDC @ Idle	123– 174	NA	850– 1000	850– 1000	Hyd	Hyd
	Vanagon	115.9 (1915)	W7CO N288 14L-7C	0.028	5 ATDC @ Idle	5 ATDC @ Idle	116– 189	⑥	800– 900 ⑤	800– 900 ⑤	Hyd	Hyd ⑦
1986	Jetta	109.0 (1780)	W7DTC N8GY	0.028– 0.032	6 BTDC @ Idle	6 BTDC @ Idle	123– 174	NA	800– 900	800– 900	Hyd	Hyd
	Quantum	109.0 (1780)	W7DTC	0.028– 0.035	6 BTDC @ Idle	6 BTDC @ Idle	123– 174	NA	800– 900	800– 900	Hyd	Hyd
	Quantum	136.0 (2226)	W7DTC	0.024– 0.031	6 BTDC @ Idle	3 ATDC @ Idle	123– 174	NA	800– 900	800– 900	Hyd	Hyd
	Cabriolet	109.0 (1780)	WR7DS N8GY	0.024– 0.032	6 BTDC @ Idle	6 BTDC @ Idle	123– 174	NA	850– 1000	850– 1000	Hyd	Hyd
	Scirocco	109.8 (1799)	F6 DTC	0.027– 0.035	6 BTDC @ Idle	6 BTDC @ Idle	123– 174	NA	800– 900	800– 900	Hyd	Hyd
	GTI	109.0 (1780)	W7DTC N8GY	0.028– 0.032	6 BTDC @ Idle	6 BTDC @ Idle	123– 174	NA	800– 900	800– 900	Hyd	Hyd
	GLI	109.0 (1780)	W7DTC N8GY	0.028– 0.032	6 BTDC @ Idle	6 BTDC @ Idle	123– 174	NA	800– 900	800– 900	Hyd	Hyd
	Golf	109.0 (1780)	WR7DS N8GY	0.028– 0.032	6 BTDC @ Idle	6 BTDC @ Idle	123– 174	NA	800– 900	800– 900	Hyd	Hyd
	Vanagon	128.1 (2109)	W7CCO N288 14L-7C	0.028	5 BTDC @ Idle	5 BTDC @ Idle	142– 185	⑥	800– 900 ⑧	800– 900 ⑧	Hyd	Hyd ⑦
1987	Jetta	109.0 (1780)	W7DTC N8GY	0.028– 0.034	6 BTDC @ Idle	6 BTDC @ Idle	123– 174	NA	800– 900	800– 900	Hyd	Hyd
	Jetta 16V	109.0 (1780)	F6DTC	0.027– 0.035	6 BTDC @ Idle	6 BTDC @ Idle	123– 174	NA	800– 900	800– 900	Hyd	Hyd

GASOLINE ENGINE TUNE-UP SPECIFICATIONS

Year	Model	Engine Displacement cu. in. (cc)	Spark Plugs Type	Spark Plugs Gap (in.)	Ignition Timing (deg.) MT	Ignition Timing (deg.) AT	Compression Pressure (psi)	Fuel Pump (psi)	Idle Speed (rpm) MT	Idle Speed (rpm) AT	Valve Clearance In. ③	Valve Clearance Ex. ③
1987	Quantum	109.0 (1780)	W7DTC	0.028–0.035	6 BTDC @ Idle	6 BTDC @ Idle	123–174	NA	800–900	800–900	Hyd	Hyd
	Quantum	136.0 (2226)	W7DTC	0.024–0.031	6 BTDC @ Idle	3 ATDC @ Idle	123–174	NA	800–900	800–900	Hyd	Hyd
	Cabriolet	109.0 (1780)	WR7DS N8GY	0.024–0.032	6 BTDC @ Idle	6 BTDC @ Idle	123–174	NA	850–1000	850–1000	Hyd	Hyd
	Scirocco	109.0 (1780)	WR7DS N8GY	0.024–0.032	6 BTDC @ Idle	6 BTDC @ Idle	123–174	NA	850–1000	850–1000	Hyd	Hyd
	Scirocco 16V	109.0 (1780)	F6DTC	0.027–0.035	6 BTDC @ Idle	6 BTDC @ Idle	123–174	NA	800–900	800–900	Hyd	Hyd
	GTI	109.0 (1780)	W7DTC N8GY	0.028–0.034	6 BTDC @ Idle	6 BTDC @ Idle	123–174	NA	800–900	800–900	Hyd	Hyd
	GTI 16V	109.0 (1780)	F6DTC	0.027–0.035	6 BTDC @ Idle	6 BTDC @ Idle	123–174	NA	800–900	800–900	Hyd	Hyd
	GLI	109.0 (1780)	W7DTC N8GY	0.028–0.034	6 BTDC @ Idle	6 BTDC @ Idle	123–174	NA	800–900	800–900	Hyd	Hyd
	GLI 16V	109.0 (1780)	F6DTC	0.027–0.035	6 BTDC @ Idle	6 BTDC @ Idle	123–174	NA	800–900	800–900	Hyd	Hyd
	Golf	109.0 (1780)	WR7DS N8GY	0.024–0.032	6 BTDC @ Idle	6 BTDC @ Idle	123–174	NA	850–1000	850–1000	Hyd	Hyd
	Golf 16V	109.0 (1780)	F6DTC	0.027–0.035	6 BTDC @ Idle	6 BTDC @ Idle	123–174	NA	800–900	800–900	Hyd	Hyd
	Fox	109.0 (1780)	W7DTC	0.027–0.035	6 BTDC @ Idle	6 BTDC @ Idle	123–174	NA	840–880	840–880	Hyd	Hyd
	Vanagon	128.1 (2109)	W7C00 N288 14L-7C	0.028	5 BTDC @ Idle	5 BTDC @ Idle	142–185	⑥	800–900 ⑧	800–900 ⑧	Hyd	Hyd ⑦
1988	All				SEE UNDERHOOD SPECIFICATION STICKER							

NOTE: The underhood specifications sticker often reflects tune-up specification changes made in production. Sticker figures must be used if they disagree with those in this chart.

① Non-California Rabbit w/1 barrel carburetor; timing 7½ BTDC @ Idle
② W/o idle stabilizer
③ Valve clearance need not be adjusted unless it varies more than 0.002 in. from specifications.
④ Idle stabilizer must be bypassed (plugs connected together).
⑤ W/vacuum hoses connected
⑥ 29 psi @ Idle speed @ approx. 2.0 bar w/vacuum hoses connected.
⑦ Valves must still be adjusted when cylinder heads have been removed; see "Valve Lash" in text.
⑧ Disconnect the No. 1 input terminal to the idle stabilization control unit.

FIRING ORDERS

NOTE: To avoid confusion, always replace spark plug wires one at a time.

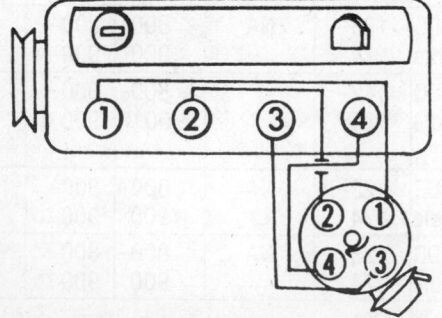

Firing order: 4 cylinder engines; 1–3–4–2

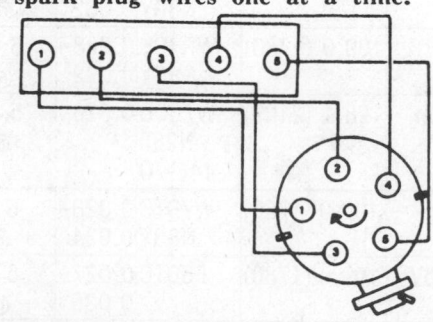

Firing order: 5 cylinder engine: 1–2–4–5–3

DIESEL ENGINE TUNE-UP SPECIFICATIONS

Year	Engine Displacement cu. in. (cc)	Valve Clearance ① Intake (in.)	Valve Clearance ① Exhaust (in.)	Intake Valve Opens (deg.)	Injection Pump Setting (deg.)	Injection Nozzle Pressure (psi) New	Injection Nozzle Pressure (psi) Used	Idle Speed (rpm)	Cranking Compression Pressure (psi)
1981	97.0 (1588)	0.008–① 0.012	0.016–① 0.020	N.A.	Align Marks	1885 ③	1706 ③	800–850 ②④	406 minimum
1982	97.0 (1588)	0.008–① 0.012	0.016–① 0.020	N.A.	Align Marks	1885 ③	1706 ③	800–850 ②④	406 minimum
1983	97.0 (1588)	0.008–① 0.012	0.016–① 0.020	N.A.	Align Marks	1885 ③	1706 ③	800–850 ②④	406 minimum
1984	97.0 (1588)	0.008–① 0.012	0.016–① 0.020	N.A.	Align Marks	1885 ③	1706 ③	800–850 ②④	406 minimum
1985	97.0 (1588)	0.008–① 0.012	0.016–① 0.020	N.A.	Align Marks	1885 ③	1706 ③	800–850 ②④	406 minimum
1986	97.0 (1588)	0.008–① 0.012	0.016–① 0.020	N.A.	Align Marks	1885 ③	1706 ③	800–850 ②④	406 minimum
1987	97.0 (1588)	0.008–① 0.012	0.016–① 0.020	N.A.	Align Marks	1885 ③	1706 ③	800–850 ②④	406 minimum
1988	SEE UNDERHOOD STICKER								

N.A. Not Available
① Warm clearance given—Cold clearance:
Intake   0.006–0.010
Exhaust   0.014–0.018
② Volkswagen has lowered the idle speed on early models to this specification.
   Valve clearance need not be adjusted unless it varies more than 0.002 in. from specification.
③ Turbo diesel: New—2306; Used—2139
④ Turbo diesel: 900–1000

CAPACITIES

Year	Model	Engine Displacement cu. in. (cc)	Engine Crankcase with Filter	Engine Crankcase without Filter	Transmission (pts.) 4-Spd	Transmission (pts.) 5-Spd	Transmission (pts.) Auto.	Drive Axle (pts.)	Fuel Tank (gal.)	Cooling System (qts.)
1981	Dasher (Diesel)	97.0 (1588)	3.7	3.2	3.2	4.2	NA	1.6	12.0	12.2
	Jetta	97.0 (1588)	4.5	4.0	3.2	4.2	12.8 ⑥	1.6	10.0	9.8
	Jetta	105.0 (1715)	4.5	4.0	3.2	4.2	12.8	1.6	10.0	9.8
	Rabbit	105.0 (1715)	4.5	4.0	3.2	4.2	12.8 ⑥	1.6	10.0	9.8
	Rabbit (Diesel)	97.0 (1588)	3.7	3.2	3.2	4.2	NA	1.6	10.0	14.3
	Scirocco	105.0 (1715)	4.5	4.0	3.2	4.2	12.8 ⑥	1.6	10.0	9.8
	Vanagon	120.0 (1970)	3.7	3.2	NA	7.4	5.3	—	15.9	NA
1982	Jetta (Diesel)	97.0 (1588)	4.8	4.3	NA	4.2	6.4	1.6	10.5	13.8
	Jetta	105.0 (1715)	4.8	4.3	NA	4.2	6.4	1.6	10.5	10.2
	Quantum	105.0 (1715)	3.6	3.2	NA	4.2	6.4	1.6	16.0	11.0
	Quantum	130.8 (2144)	3.6	3.2	NA	4.2	6.4	1.6	16.0	11.0
	Quantum (Diesel)	97.0 (1588)	4.0	3.5	NA	4.2	6.4	1.6	16.0	13.0
	Rabbit	105.0 (1715)	4.7	4.2	3.2	4.2	6.4	1.6	10.0	9.8
	Rabbit (Diesel)	97.0 (1588)	4.7	4.2	3.2	4.2	6.4	1.6	10.0	9.8
	Scirocco	105.0 (1715)	4.8	4.3	NA	4.2	6.4	1.6	10.5	10.2
	Vanagon	122.0 (2000)	3.7	3.2	NA	7.4	5.3	—	15.9	—
	Vanagon (Diesel)	97.6 (1600)	4.7	4.2	NA	7.4	5.3	—	15.9	—

CAPACITIES

Year	Model	Engine Displacement cu. in. (cc)	Engine Crankcase with Filter	without Filter	Transmission (pts.) 4-Spd	5-Spd	Auto.	Drive Axle (pts.)	Fuel Tank (gal.)	Cooling System (qts.)
1983	Jetta	105.0 (1715)	4.8	4.3	—	4.2	6.4	1.6	10.5	10.2
	Jetta (Diesel)	97.0 (1588)	4.8	4.3	—	4.2	6.4	1.6	10.5	13.8
	Jetta (Turbo-Diesel)	97.0 (1588)	4.8	4.3	—	4.2	6.4	1.6	10.5	13.8
	Quantum	105.0 (1715)	3.6	3.2	—	4.2	6.4	1.6	16.0	13.0
	Quantum	109.0 (1780)	4.0	3.5	—	4.2	6.4	1.6	16.0	10.0
	Quantum	130.8 (2144)	4.0	3.5	—	4.2	6.4	1.6	16.0	13.0
	Quantum (Turbo-Diesel)	97.0 (1588)	4.0	3.5	—	4.2	6.4	1.6	16.0	13.0
	Rabbit	105.0 (1715)	4.7	4.2	3.2	4.2	6.4	1.6	10.0	13.8
	Rabbit	109.0 (1780)	4.7	4.2	3.2	4.2	6.4	1.6	10.0	13.8
	Rabbit (Conv.)	109.0 (1780)	4.8	4.3	—	4.2	6.2	1.6	10.5	10.2
	Rabbit (Diesel)	97.0 (1588)	4.7	4.2	3.2	4.2	6.4	1.6	10.0	13.8
	Scirocco	105.0 (1715)	4.8	4.3	NA	4.2	6.4	1.6	10.5	10.2
	Scirocco	109.0 (1780)	4.8	4.3	NA	4.2	6.4	1.6	10.5	10.2
	GTI	109.0 (1780)	4.7	4.2	3.2	4.2	6.4	1.6	10.0	13.8
	GTI (Diesel)	97.0 (1588)	4.7	4.2	3.2	4.2	6.4	1.6	11.0	13.8
	GLI	109.0 (1780)	4.3	3.7	3.2	4.2	—	1.6	14.5	14.5
	Vanagon (Diesel)	97.6 (1600)	3.7 ③	3.2 ④	—	7.4	5.3	—	15.9	—
	Vanagon	122.0 (2000)	3.7 ③	3.2 ④	—	7.4	5.3	—	15.9	—
1984	Jetta	105.0 (1715)	4.8	4.3	—	4.2	6.4	1.6	10.5	10.2
	Jetta (Diesel)	97.0 (1588)	4.8	4.3	—	4.2	6.4	1.6	10.5	13.8
	Quantum (4 cyl.)	109.0 (1780)	3.6	3.2	—	4.2	6.4	1.6	16.0	13.0
	Quantum (5 cyl.)	130.0 (2144)	4.0	3.5	—	4.2	6.4	1.6	16.0	12.0
	Quantum (Diesel)	97.0 (1588)	4.0	3.5	—	4.2	6.4	1.6	16.0	14.0
	Rabbit	105.0 (1715)	4.7	4.2	3.2	4.2	6.4	1.6	10.0	13.8
	Rabbit (Conv.)	109.0 (1780)	4.8	4.3	—	4.2	6.2	1.6	10.5	10.2
	Rabbit (Diesel)	97.0 (1588)	4.7	4.2	3.2	4.2	6.4	1.6	10.0	13.8
	Scirocco	109.0 (1780)	4.8	4.3	—	4.2	6.4	1.6	10.5	10.2
1984	GTI	109.0 (1780)	4.7	4.2	3.2	4.2	6.4	1.6	10.0	13.8
	GTI (Diesel)	97.0 (1588)	4.7	4.2	3.2	4.2	6.4	1.6	11.0	13.8
	GLI	109.0 (1780)	4.3	3.7	3.2	4.2	—	1.6	14.5	14.5
	Vanagon	97.0 (1588)	3.7 ③	3.2 ④	—	7.4	5.3	—	15.9	—
	Vanagon	115.9 (1915)	4.7	3.7	—	⑤	5.3	—	15.9	—
1985	Jetta	105.0 (1715)	4.8	4.3	—	4.2	6.4	1.6	13.7	13.6
	Jetta (Diesel)	97.0 (1588)	4.8	4.3	—	4.2	6.4	1.6	13.7	13.6
	Jetta (Turbo-Diesel)	97.0 (1588)	4.8	4.3	—	4.2	6.4	1.6	13.7	13.6
	Quantum (4 cyl.)	109.0 (1780)	3.6	3.2	—	4.2	6.4	1.6	16.0	13.0
	Quantum (5 cyl.)	136.0 (2226)	4.0	3.5	—	4.2	6.4	1.6	16.0	17.8
	Quantum (Diesel)	97.0 (1588)	4.0	3.5	—	4.2	6.4	1.6	16.0	14.8
	Cabriolet	109.0 (1780)	4.8	4.3	3.2	4.2	6.4	1.6	13.7	10.2
	Scirocco	109.0 (1780)	4.8	4.3	3.2	4.2	6.4	1.6	13.7	10.2
	GTI	109.0 (1780)	4.3	3.7	3.2	4.2	—	1.6	14.5	14.5
	GLI	109.0 (1780)	4.3	3.7	3.2	4.2	—	1.6	14.5	14.5
	Golf	109.0 (1780)	4.3	3.7	3.2	4.2	6.4	1.6	14.5	14.5
	Golf	97.0 (1588)	4.3	3.7	3.2	4.2	6.4	1.6	14.5	14.5

CAPACITIES

Year	Model	Engine Displacement cu. in. (cc)	Engine Crankcase with Filter	Engine Crankcase without Filter	Transmission (pts.) 4-Spd	Transmission (pts.) 5-Spd	Transmission (pts.) Auto.	Drive Axle (pts.)	Fuel Tank (gal.)	Cooling System (qts.)
1985	Vanagon	115.9 (1915)	4.3	3.7	3.2	4.2	6.4	1.6	14.5	14.5
1986	Jetta	109.0 (1780)	4.8	4.3	—	4.2	6.4	1.6	13.7	13.6
	Jetta (Diesel)	97.0 (1588)	4.8	4.3	—	4.2	6.4	1.6	13.7	13.6
	Jetta (Turbo-Diesel)	97.0 (1588)	4.8	4.3	—	4.2	6.4	1.6	13.7	13.6
	Quantum (4 cyl.)	109.0 (1780)	3.6	3.2	—	4.2	6.4	1.6	16.0	13.0
	Quantum (5 cyl.)	136.0 (2226)	4.0	3.5	—	4.2	6.4	1.6	16.0	17.8
	Quantum (Diesel)	97.0 (1588)	4.0	3.5	—	4.2	6.4	1.6	16.0	14.8
	Cabriolet	109.0 (1780)	4.8	4.3	3.2	4.2	6.4	1.6	13.7	10.2
	Scirocco	109.0 (1780)	4.8	4.3	3.2	4.2	6.4	1.6	13.7	10.2
	GTI	109.0 (1780)	4.3	3.7	3.2	4.2	—	1.6	14.5	14.5
	GLI	109.0 (1780)	4.3	3.7	3.2	4.2	—	1.6	14.5	14.5
	Golf	109.0 (1780)	4.3	3.7	3.2	4.2	6.4	1.6	14.5	14.5
	Golf (Diesel)	97.0 (1588)	4.3	3.7	3.2	4.2	6.4	1.6	14.5	14.5
	Vanagon	128.1 (2109)	4.8	4.2	—	⑤	5.3	—	18.5	—
1987-88	Jetta	109.0 (1780)	4.8	4.3	—	4.2	6.4	1.6	13.7	13.6
	Jetta (Diesel)	97.0 (1588)	4.8	4.3	—	4.2	6.4	1.6	13.7	13.6
	Jetta (Turbo-Diesel)	97.0 (1588)	4.8	4.3	—	4.2	6.4	1.6	13.7	13.6
	Jetta 16V	109.0 (1780)	4.8	4.3	—	4.2	6.4	1.6	13.7	13.6
	Quantum (4 cyl.)	109.0 (1780)	3.6	3.2	—	4.2	6.4	1.6	16.0	13.0
	Quantum (5 cyl.)	136.0 (2226)	4.0	3.5	—	4.2	6.4	1.6	16.0	17.8
	Quantum (Diesel)	97.0 (1588)	4.0	3.5	—	4.2	6.4	1.6	16.0	14.8
	Cabriolet	109.0 (1780)	4.8	4.3	3.2	4.2	6.4	1.6	13.7	10.2
	Scirocco	109.0 (1780)	4.8	4.3	3.2	4.2	6.4	1.6	13.7	10.2
	GTI	109.0 (1780)	4.3	3.7	3.2	4.2	—	1.6	14.5	14.5
	GLI	109.0 (1780)	4.3	3.7	3.2	4.2	—	1.6	14.5	14.5
	Golf	109.0 (1780)	4.3	3.7	3.2	4.2	6.4	1.6	14.5	14.5
	Golf (Diesel)	97.0 (1588)	4.3	3.7	3.2	4.2	6.4	1.6	14.5	14.5
	Golf 16V	97.0 (1588)	4.3	3.7	3.2	4.2	6.4	1.6	14.5	14.5
	Vanagon	128.1 (2109)	4.8	4.2	—	⑤	5.3	—	18.5	—

Conv. = torque converter
① 5.3 when changed
② 6.4 refill; 12.8 when changed
③ Diesel: 4.7
④ Diesel: 4.2

⑤ Type 091: 3.7 qt.
Type 091/1: 3.2 qt. w/gasoline engine; 4.2 qt. with diesel
Type 094: 4.0 qt.
⑥ Dry refill; normal refill is 6.4 pts.
NA: Not available

CRANKSHAFT AND CONNECTING ROD SPECIFICATIONS

All measurements are given in inches.

Year	Engine Displacement cu. in. (cc)	Crankshaft Main Brg. Journal Dia.	Crankshaft Main Brg. Oil Clearance	Crankshaft Shaft End-play	Crankshaft Thrust on No.	Connecting Rod Journal Diameter	Connecting Rod Oil Clearance	Connecting Rod Side Clearance
1981	97.0 (1588)	2.126	0.001–0.003	0.003–0.007	3	1.811	0.001–0.003	0.015 ①
	105.0 (1715)	2.126	0.001–0.003	0.003–0.007	3	1.811	0.001–0.003	0.015
	120.0 (1970)	2.3609–2.3617 ③	0.002–0.004	0.0027–0.005	1 at flywheel	2.1644 2.1653	0.0008–0.0027	0.004–0.016

CRANKSHAFT AND CONNECTING ROD SPECIFICATIONS
All measurements are given in inches.

| Year | Engine Displacement cu. in. (cc) | Crankshaft | | | | Connecting Rod | | |
		Main Brg. Journal Dia.	Main Brg. Oil Clearance	Shaft End-play	Thrust on No.	Journal Diameter	Oil Clearance	Side Clearance
1982	97.0 (1588)	2.126	0.001–0.003	0.003–0.007	3	1.811	0.001–0.003	0.015 ①
	97.6 (1600)	2.126	0.001–0.003	0.003–0.007	3	1.811	0.001–0.003	0.015
	105.0 (1715)	2.126	0.001–0.003	0.003–0.007	3	1.811	0.001–0.003	0.015
	120.0 (1970)	2.3609–2.3617 ③	0.002–0.004	0.0027–0.005	1 at flywheel	2.1644 2.1653	0.0008–0.0027	0.004–0.016
	122.0 (2000)	2.126	0.001–0.003	0.003–0.007	3	1.811	0.001–0.003	0.015
	130.8 (2144)	2.2822	0.0006–0.003	0.003–0.007	4	1.811	0.0006–0.002	0.016
1983	97.0 (1588)	2.126	0.001–0.003	0.003–0.007	3	1.811	0.001–0.003	0.015 ①
	97.6 (1600)	2.126	0.001–0.003	0.003–0.007	3	1.811	0.001–0.003	0.015
	105.0 (1715)	2.126	0.001–0.003	0.003–0.007	3	1.811	0.001–0.003	0.015
	109.0 (1780)	2.126	0.001–0.003	0.003–0.007	3	1.881	0.001–0.003	0.015
	120.0 (1970)	2.3609–2.3617 ③	0.002–0.004	0.0027–0.005	1 at flywheel	2.1644 2.1653	0.0008–0.0027	0.004–0.016
	122.0 (2000)	2.126	0.001–0.003	0.003–0.007	3	1.811	0.001–0.003	0.015
	130.8 (2144)	2.2822	0.0006–0.003	0.003–0.007	4	1.811	0.0006–0.002	0.016
1984	97.0 (1588)	2.126	0.001–0.003	0.003–0.007	3	1.811	0.001–0.003	0.015 ①
	97.6 (1600)	2.126	0.001–0.003	0.003–0.007	3	1.811	0.001–0.003	0.015
	105.0 (1715)	2.126	0.001–0.003	0.003–0.007	3	1.811	0.001–0.003	0.015
	109.0 (1780)	2.126	0.001–0.003	0.003–0.007	3	1.881	0.001–0.003	0.015
	115.9 (1900)	2.126	0.001–0.003	0.003–0.007	3	1.811	0.001–0.003	0.015
	115.9 (1915)	2.3992–2.3996 ④ ②	NA	0.003–0.005	1 at flywheel	2.1993–2.1998	NA	0.028
	130.8 (2144)	2.2822	0.0006–0.003	0.003–0.007	4	1.811	0.0006–0.002	0.016
1985	97.0 (1588)	2.126	0.001–0.003	0.003–0.007	3	1.811	0.001–0.003	0.015 ①
	109.0 (1780)	2.126	0.001–0.003	0.003–0.007	3	1.881	0.001–0.003	0.015
	115.9 (1900)	2.126	0.001–0.003	0.003–0.007	3	1.811	0.001–0.003	0.015
	115.9 (1915)	2.3992–2.3996 ④ ②	NA	0.003–0.005	1 at flywheel	2.1993 2.1998	NA	0.028–
	136.0 (2226)	2.126	0.001–0.003	0.003–0.007	3	1.811	0.001–0.003	0.015

CRANKSHAFT AND CONNECTING ROD SPECIFICATIONS

All measurements are given in inches.

Year	Engine Displacement cu. in. (cc)	Crankshaft Main Brg. Journal Dia.	Crankshaft Main Brg. Oil Clearance	Crankshaft Shaft End-play	Crankshaft Thrust on No.	Connecting Rod Journal Diameter	Connecting Rod Oil Clearance	Connecting Rod Side Clearance
1986	97.0 (1588)	2.126	0.001–0.003	0.003–0.007	3	1.811	0.001–0.003	0.015 ①
	109.0 (1780)	2.126	0.001–0.003	0.003–0.007	3	1.881	0.001–0.003	0.015
	128.1 (2100)	2.126	0.001–0.003	0.003–0.007	3	1.811	0.001–0.003	0.015
	128.1 (2109)	2.3992– ② 2.3996 ④	NA	0.003–0.005	1 at flywheel	2.1993 2.1998	NA	0.028
	136.0 (2226)	2.2822	0.0006–0.003	0.003–0.007	4	1.811	0.0006–0.002	0.016
1987–88	97.0 (1588)	2.126	0.001–0.003	0.003–0.007	3	1.811	0.001–0.003	0.015 ①
	109.0 (1780)	2.126	0.001–0.003	0.003–0.007	3	1.881	0.001–0.003	0.015
	128.1 (2100)	2.126	0.001–0.003	0.003–0.007	3	1.811	0.001–0.003	0.015
	128.1 (2109)	2.3992– ② 2.3996 ④	NA	0.003–0.005	1 at flywheel	2.1993 2.1998	NA	0.028
	136.0 (2226)	2.2822	0.0006–0.003	0.003–0.007	4	1.811	0.0006–0.002	0.016

N.A. Not Available
① Wear limit
② Bearings marked with blue dot. Bearings marked with red dot 2.3988–2.3991. Both specs for journals 1 and 3 only. No. 2 journal diameter 2.1988–2.1996 in.
③ Journals No. 1, 2, 3. Journal No. 4: 1.5739–1.5748
④ Journals No. 1, 2, 3. Journal No. 4: 1.5993–1.6000
NOTE: Main and connecting rod bearings are available in 3 under sizes.

VALVE SPECIFICATIONS
Front Wheel Drive Models

Year	Engine Displacement cu. in. (cc)	Seat Angle (deg.)	Face Angle (deg.)	Spring Test Pressure (lbs.)	Spring Installed Height (in.)	Stem-to-Guide Clearance (in.) Intake	Stem-to-Guide Clearance (in.) Exhaust	Stem Diameter (in.) Intake	Stem Diameter (in.) Exhaust
1981	97.0 (1588)	45	45	NA	NA	0.039 max	0.051 max	0.3140	0.3130
	97.0 Diesel (1588)	45	45	96–106 @ 0.92	NA	0.051 max	0.051 max	0.3140	0.3130
	105.0 (1715)	45	45	NA	NA	0.039	0.051 max	0.3140 max	0.3130
1982	97.0 (1588)	45	45	NA	NA	0.039 max	0.051 max	0.3140	0.3130
	97.0 Diesel (1588)	45	45	96–106 @ 0.92	NA	0.051 max	0.051 max	0.3140	0.3130
	97.6 (1600)	45	45	NA	NA	0.039 max	0.051 max	0.3140	0.3130
	105.0 (1715)	45	45	NA	NA	0.039 max	0.051 max	0.3140	0.3130
	130.8 (2111)	45	45	NA	NA	0.039 max	0.051 max	0.3140	0.3130

VALVE SPECIFICATIONS
Front Wheel Drive Models

Year	Engine Displacement cu. in. (cc)	Seat Angle (deg.)	Face Angle (deg.)	Spring Test Pressure (lbs.)	Spring Installed Height (in.)	Stem-to-Guide Clearance (in.)		Stem Diameter (in.)	
						Intake	Exhaust	Intake	Exhaust
1983	97.0 (1588)	45	45	NA	NA	0.039 max	0.051 max	0.3140	0.3130
	97.0 Diesel (1588)	45	45	96–106 @ 0.92	NA	0.051 max	0.051 max	0.3140	0.3130
	105.0 (1715)	45	45	NA	NA	0.039 max	0.051 max	0.3140	0.3130
	109.0 (1780)	45	45	NA	NA	0.039 max	0.051 max	0.3140	0.3130
	130.8 (2144)	45	45	NA	NA	0.039 max	0.051 max	0.3140	0.3130
1984	97.0 Diesel (1588)	45	45	96–106 @ 0.92	NA	0.051 max	0.051 max	0.3140	0.3130
	105.9 (1715)	45	45	NA	NA	0.039 max	0.051 max	0.3140	0.3130
	109.0 (1780)	45	45	NA	NA	0.039 max	0.051 max	0.3140	0.3130
	130.8 (2144)	45	45	NA	NA	0.039 max	0.051 max	0.3140	0.3130
1985	97.0 Diesel (1588)	45	45	96–106 @ 0.92	NA	0.051 max	0.051 max	0.3140	0.3130
	109.0 (1780)	45	45	NA	NA	0.039 max	0.051 max	0.3140	0.3130
	136.0 (2226)	45	45	NA	NA	0.039 max	0.051 max	0.3140	0.3130
1986	97.0 Diesel (1588)	45	45	96–106 @ 0.92	NA	0.051 max	0.051 max	0.3140	0.3130
	109.0 (1780)	45	45	NA	NA	0.039 max	0.051 max	0.3140	0.3130
	136.0 (2226)	45	45	NA	NA	0.039 max	0.051 max	0.3140	0.3130
1987–88	97.0 Diesel (1588)	45	45	96–106 @ 0.92	NA	0.051 max	0.051 max	0.3140	0.3130
	109.0 (1780)	45	45	NA	NA	0.039 max	0.051 max	0.3140	0.3130
	136.0 (2226)	45	45	NA	NA	0.039 max	0.051 max	0.3140	0.3130

NOTE: Exhaust valves must be ground by hand.

VALVE SPECIFICATIONS
Rear Wheel Drive Vanagon

Year	Engine Displacement cu. in. (cc)	Seat Angle (deg.)		Face Angle (deg.)		Valve Seat Width (in.)		Spring Test Pressure (lbs. @ in.)	Valve Guide Inside Dia. (in.)		Stem to Guide Clearance (in.)		Stem Diameter (in.)	
		Intake	Exhaust	Intake	Exhaust	Intake	Exhaust		Intake	Exhaust	Intake	Exhaust	Intake	Exhaust
1981	120.0 (1970)	30	45	30	45	0.07–0.08	0.078–0.098	168–186 @ 1.14	0.3150–0.3157	0.3534–0.3538	0.018	0.014	0.3125–0.3129	0.3507–0.3511

VALVE SPECIFICATIONS
Rear Wheel Drive Vanagon

Year	Engine Displacement cu. in. (cc)	Seat Angle (deg.) Intake	Seat Angle (deg.) Exhaust	Face Angle (deg.) Intake	Face Angle (deg.) Exhaust	Valve Seat Width (in.) Intake	Valve Seat Width (in.) Exhaust	Spring Test Pressure (lbs. @ in.)	Valve Guide Inside Dia. (in.) Intake	Valve Guide Inside Dia. (in.) Exhaust	Stem to Guide Clearance (in.) Intake	Stem to Guide Clearance (in.) Exhaust	Stem Diameter (In.) Intake	Stem Diameter (In.) Exhaust
1982	120.0 (1970)	30	45	30	45	0.07–0.08	0.078–0.098	168–186 @ 1.14	0.3150–0.3157	0.3534–0.3538	0.018	0.014	0.3125–0.3129	0.3507–0.3511
	97.0 (1588)	45	45	45	45	0.078	0.096	96–106 @ 0.92	NA	NA	0.039 max	0.051 max	0.314	0.313
1983	120.0 (1970)	30	45	30	45	0.07–0.08	0.078–0.098	168–186 @ 1.14	0.3150–0.3157	0.3534–0.3538	0.018	0.014	0.3125–0.3129	0.3507–0.3511
	97.0 (1588)	45	45	45	45	0.078	0.096	96–106 @ 0.92	NA	NA	0.039 max	0.051 max	0.314	0.313
1984	97.0 (1588)	45	45	45	45	0.078	0.096	96–106 @ 0.92	NA	NA	0.039 max	0.051 max	0.314	0.313
	115.9 (1915)	45	45	45	45	0.055–0.098	0.055–0.098	NA	NA	NA	0.047 max	0.047 max	0.313–0.314	0.3508–0.3512
1985	115.9 (1915)	45	45	45	45	0.055–0.098	0.055–0.098	NA	NA	NA	0.047 max	0.047 max	0.313–0.314	0.3508–0.3512
1986	128.1 (2109)	45	45	45	45	0.055–0.098	0.055–0.098	NA	NA	NA	0.047 max	0.047 max	0.313–0.314	0.3508–0.3512
1987–88	128.1 (2109)	45	45	45	45	0.055–0.098	0.055–0.098	NA	NA	NA	0.047 max	0.047 max	0.313–0.314	0.3508–0.3512

N.A.: Not available

PISTON AND RING SPECIFICATIONS
All measurements are given in inches.

Year	Engine Displacement cu. in. (cc)	Piston Clearance	Ring Gap Top Compression	Ring Gap Bottom Compression	Ring Gap Oil Control	Ring Side Clearance Top Compression	Ring Side Clearance Bottom Compression	Ring Side Clearance Oil Control
1981	97.0 (1588)	0.001–0.003	0.0120–0.0180	0.0120–0.0180	0.0120–0.0180	0.0008–0.0020	0.0008–0.0020	0.0008–0.0020
	97.0 (1588) Diesel	0.001–0.003	0.0120–0.0200	0.0120–0.0200	0.0100–0.0160	0.0020–0.0040	0.0020–0.0030	0.0010–0.0020
	105.0 (1715)	0.001–0.003	0.0120–0.0180	0.0120–0.0180	0.0120–0.0180	0.0008–0.0020	0.0008–0.0020	0.0008–0.0020
	120.0 (1970)	0.0016–0.0023	0.0160–0.0210	0.0160–0.0210	0.0100–0.0160	0.0020–0.0030	0.0020–0.0030	0.0010–0.0020
1982	97.0 (1588)	0.001–0.003	0.0120–0.0180	0.0120–0.0180	0.0120–0.0180	0.0008–0.0020	0.0008–0.0020	0.0008–0.0020
	97.0 (1588) Diesel	0.001–0.003	0.0120–0.0200	0.0120–0.0200	0.0100–0.0160	0.0020–0.0040	0.0020–0.0030	0.0010–0.0020
	97.6 (1600)	0.001–0.003	0.0120–0.0180	0.0120–0.0180	0.0120–0.0180	0.0008–0.0020	0.0008–0.0020	0.0008–0.0020
	105.0 (1715)	0.001–0.003	0.0120–0.0180	0.0120–0.0180	0.0120–0.0180	0.0008–0.0020	0.0008–0.0020	0.0008–0.0020
	120.0 (1970)	0.0016–0.0023	0.0160–0.0210	0.0160–0.0210	0.0100–0.0160	0.0020–0.0030	0.0020–0.0030	0.0010–0.0020
	130.8 (2144) 5 cyl.	0.0011	0.0100–0.0200	0.0100–0.0200	0.0100–0.0200	0.0008–0.0030	0.0008–0.0030	0.0008–0.0030

PISTON AND RING SPECIFICATIONS

All measurements are given in inches.

Year	Engine Displacement cu. in. (cc)	Piston Clearance	Ring Gap			Ring Side Clearance		
			Top Compression	Bottom Compression	Oil Control	Top Compression	Bottom Compression	Oil Control
1983	97.0 (1588)	0.001–0.003	0.0120–0.0180	0.0120–0.0180	0.0120–0.0180	0.0008–0.0020	0.0008–0.0020	0.0008–0.0020
	97.0 (1588) Diesel	0.001–0.003	0.0120–0.0200	0.0120–0.0200	0.0100–0.0160	0.0020–0.0040	0.0020–0.0030	0.0010–0.0020
	105.0 (1715)	0.001–0.003	0.0120–0.0180	0.0120–0.0180	0.0120–0.0180	0.0008–0.0020	0.0008–0.0020	0.0008–0.0020
	109.0 (1780)	0.001–0.003	0.0120–0.0180	0.0120–0.0180	0.0120–0.0180	0.0008–0.0020	0.0008–0.0020	0.0008–0.0020
	120.0 (1970)	0.0016–0.0023	0.0160–0.0210	0.0160–0.0210	0.0100–0.0160	0.0020–0.0030	0.0020–0.0030	0.0010–0.0020
	130.8 (2144) 5 cyl.	0.0011	0.0100–0.0200	0.0100–0.0200	0.0100–0.0200	0.0008–0.0030	0.0008–0.0030	0.0008–0.0030
1984	97.0 (1588) Diesel	0.001–0.003	0.0120–0.0200	0.0120–0.0200	0.0100–0.0160	0.0020–0.0040	0.0020–0.0030	0.0010–0.0020
	105.9 (1715)	0.001–0.003	0.0120–0.0180	0.0120–0.0180	0.0120–0.0180	0.0008–0.0020	0.0008–0.0020	0.0008–0.0020
	109.0 (1780)	0.001–0.003	0.0120–0.0180	0.0120–0.0180	0.0120–0.0180	0.0008–0.0020	0.0008–0.0020	0.0008–0.0020
	115.9 (1915)	0.001–0.008	0.0120–0.0180	0.0120–0.0200	0.0100–0.0160	0.0020–0.0030	0.0020–0.0030	0.0010–0.0020
	120.0 (1970)	0.0016–0.0023	0.0160–0.0210	0.0160–0.0210	0.0100–0.0160	0.0020–0.0030	0.0020–0.0030	0.0010–0.0020
1985	97.0 (1588) Diesel	0.001–0.003	0.0120–0.0200	0.0120–0.0200	0.0100–0.0180	0.0020–0.0040	0.0020–0.0030	0.0010–0.0020
	109.0 (1780)	0.001–0.003	0.0120–0.0180	0.0120–0.0180	0.0120–0.0180	0.0008–0.0020	0.0008–0.0020	0.0008–0.0020
	115.9 (1915)	0.001–0.008	0.0120–0.0180	0.0120–0.0200	0.0100–0.0160	0.0020–0.0030	0.0020–0.0030	0.0010–0.0020
	120.0 (1970)	0.0016–0.0023	0.0160–0.0210	0.0160–0.0210	0.0100–0.0160	0.0020–0.0030	0.0020–0.0030	0.0010–0.0020
	130.8 (2144) 5 cyl.	0.0011	0.0100–0.0200	0.0100–0.0200	0.0100–0.0200	0.0008–0.0030	0.0008–0.0030	0.0008–0.0030
1986	97.0 (1588) Diesel	0.001–0.003	0.0120–0.0200	0.0120–0.0200	0.0100–0.0180	0.0020–0.0040	0.0020–0.0030	0.0010–0.0020
	109.0 (1780)	0.001–0.003	0.0120–0.0180	0.0120–0.0180	0.0120–0.0180	0.0008–0.0020	0.0008–0.0020	0.0008–0.0020
	128.1 (2109)	0.001–0.008	0.0120–0.0180	0.0120–0.0200	0.0100–0.0160	0.0020–0.0030	0.0020–0.0030	0.0010–0.0020
	136.0 (2226) 5 cyl.	0.0011	0.0100–0.0200	0.0100–0.0200	0.0100–0.0200	0.0008–0.0030	0.0008–0.0030	0.0008–0.0030
1987–88	97.0 (1588) Diesel	0.001–0.003	0.0120–0.0200	0.0120–0.0200	0.0100–0.0180	0.0020–0.0040	0.0020–0.0030	0.0010–0.0020
	109.0 (1780)	0.001–0.003	0.0120–0.0180	0.0120–0.0180	0.0120–0.0180	0.0008–0.0020	0.0008–0.0020	0.0008–0.0020
	128.1 (2109)	0.001–0.008	0.0120–0.0180	0.0120–0.0200	0.0100–0.0160	0.0020–0.0030	0.0020–0.0030	0.0010–0.0020
	136.0 (2226) 5 cyl.	0.0011	0.0100–0.0200	0.0100–0.0200	0.0100–0.0200	0.0008–0.0030	0.0008–0.0030	0.0008–0.0030

TORQUE SPECIFICATIONS
Front Wheel Drive Models
All readings in ft. lbs.

Year	Engine Displacement cu. in. (cc)	Clyinder Head Bolts	Main Bearing Bolts	Rod Bearing Bolts ①	Crankshaft Pulley Bolts	Flywheel Bolts	Manifold Intake	Manifold Exhaust	Spark Plugs
1981	97.0 (1588)	③	47	33 ⑧	58 ⑦	54 ②	18	18	22
	97.0 Diesel (1588)	⑤	47	33 ⑧	56 ⑦	54 ②	18	18	22
	105.0 (1715)	③	47	33 ⑧	58 ⑦	54 ②	18	18	22
1982	97.0 Diesel (1588)	⑤	47	33 ⑧	56 ⑦	54 ②	18	18	22
	97.6 (1600)	③	47	33 ⑧	58 ⑦	54 ②	18	18	22
	105.0 (1715)	③	47	33 ⑧	58 ⑦	54 ②	18	18	22
	130.8 (2144)	③	47	36 ⑧	58 ⑦	54 ②	18	18	22
1983	97.0 Diesel (1588)	⑤	47	33 ⑧	56 ⑦	54 ②	18	18	22
	105.0 (1715)	③	47	33 ⑧	58 ⑦	54 ②	18	18	22
	109.0 (1780)	③	47	33 ⑧	58 ⑦	54 ②	18	18	22
	130.8 (2144)	③	47	36 ⑧	58 ⑦	54 ②	18	18	22
1984	97.0 Diesel (1588)	⑤	47	33 ⑧	56 ⑦	54 ②	18	18	14
	105.9 (1715)	③	47	33 ⑧	58 ⑦	54 ②	18	18	14
	109.0 (1780)	③	47	33 ⑧	58 ⑦	54 ②	18	18	14
	120.0 (1970)	③	47	33 ⑧	58 ⑦	54 ②	18	18	14
1985	97.0 Diesel (1588)	⑤	47	33 ⑧	130	54 ②	18	18	14
	109.0 (1780)	③	47	33 ⑧	145 ⑦	54 ②	18	18	14
	120.0 (1970)	③	47	33 ⑧	145 ⑦	54 ②	18	18	14
	130.8 (2144)	③	47	33 ⑧	145 ⑦	54 ②	18	18	14
1986	97.0 Diesel (1588)	⑤	47	33 ⑧	130	54 ②	18	18	14
	109.0 (1780)	③	47	33 ⑧	145 ⑦	54 ②	18	18	14
	136.0 (2226)	③	47	33 ⑧	145 ⑦	54 ②	18	18	14
1987-88	97.0 Diesel (1588)	⑤	47	33 ⑧	130	54 ②	18	18	14
	109.0 (1780)	③	47	33 ⑧	145 ⑦	54 ②	18	18	14
	136.0 (2226)	③	47	33 ⑧	145 ⑦	54 ②	18	18	14

① Always use new bolts.
② Pressure plate to crankshaft bolts
③ With 12 points (polygon) head bolts
    Torque in 4 steps:
    1st step—29 ft/lbs.
    2nd step—43 ft/lbs.
    3rd step—additional ½ turn (180°) further in one movement (two 90° turns are permissible)
    Note tightening sequence
    Do not retorque at 1,000 miles

   With 6 point (hex) head bolts
    Torque in steps to 54 ft/lbs. with engine cold, when engine is warmed up, torque to 61 ft/lbs.
    Head bolts must be retorqued after 1,000 miles.
④ Always use new bolts
⑤ Rabbit/Jetta/Quantum
    Torque in 6 steps
    1st step—29 ft/lbs.
    2nd step—43 ft/lbs.
    3rd step—additional ½ turn (180°) further in one movement (two 90° turns are permissible)
    Note tightening sequence
    4th step—run engine until oil temp is 50°C.
    5th step—tighten bolts ¼ turn more.
    Head bolts must be retorqued after 1,000 miles.
⑥ 5 cylinder—36 ft. lbs.
⑦ '83-'88 w/14mm bolt; 145 ft. lbs. 5 cylinder—253 ft. lbs.
⑧ Stretch bolts: 22 ft. lbs. plus ¼ (90°) turn.

GASOLINE ENGINE TORQUE SPECIFICATIONS
Rear Wheel Drive Vanagon
All readings in ft. lbs.

Year	Engine Displacement (cc)	Cylinder Head Nuts	Rod Bearing Bolts	Generator Pulley	Crankshaft Pulley Bolt	Flywheel to Crankshaft Bolts	Fan to Hub	Hub to Crankshaft	Crankcase Half Nuts Sealing Nuts	Crankcase Half Nuts Non-Sealing Nuts	Drive Plate to Crankshaft ④	Spark Plugs	Oil Strainer Cover
1981	120.0 (1970)	23	24	—	—	80 ①	14	23	23	14	61	22	7–9
1982	120.0 (1970)	23	24	—	—	80 ①	14	23	23	14	61	22	7–9
1983	120.0 (1970)	23	24	—	—	80 ①	14	23	23	14	61	22	7–9
1984	115.9 (1915)	②	33	—	253 ③	80	—	—	⑤	⑤	65	14	—
1985	115.9 (1915)	②	33	—	253 ③	80	—	—	⑤	⑤	65	14	—
1986	128.1 (2109)	②	33	—	253 ③	80	—	—	⑤	⑤	65	14	—
1987–88	128.1 (2109)	②	33	—	253 ③	80	—	—	⑤	⑤	65	14	—

① Automatic transmission drive plate—65 ft. lbs.
② Coat surface of cap nuts with D3 sealing compound, torque all bolts in sequence to 7 ft. lbs., then torque all bolts in sequence to 33 ft. lbs.
③ Triple V-belt pulley on cars with air conditioning or power steering only. Single V-belt pulley bolt 43 ft. lbs.
④ Torque converter plate
⑤ Crankcase top (small) nuts 14 ft. lbs. after coating both sides of washer with D3 compound; lower nuts (large) 25 ft. lbs. after coating with D3.

BRAKE SPECIFICATIONS
All measurements in inches unless noted

Year	Model	Lug Nut Torque (ft. lbs.)	Master Cylinder Bore	Brake Disc Minimum Thickness	Brake Disc Maximum Runout	Maximim Brake Drum Diameter	Minimum Lining Thickness Front	Minimum Lining Thickness Rear
1981	Dasher	80	0.820	0.410 ②	0.002	7.080	0.250	0.098
	Jetta	80	0.820	0.410 ②	0.002	7.080	0.250	0.098
	Rabbit	80	0.820	0.410 ②	0.002	7.080	0.250	0.098
	Scirocco	80	0.820	0.410 ②	0.002	7.080	0.250	0.098
	Vanagon	87–94	0.938	0.453	0.004	9.920	0.079	0.100
1982	Jetta	80	0.820	0.410 ②	0.002	7.080	0.250	0.098
	Quantum	80	0.820	0.410 ②	0.002	7.080	0.250	0.098
	Rabbit	80	0.820	0.410 ②	0.002	7.080	0.250	0.098
	Scirocco	80	0.820	0.410 ②	0.002	7.080	0.250	0.098
	Vanagon	87–94	0.938	0.453	0.004	9.920	0.079	0.100
1983	Jetta	80	0.820	0.410 ②	0.002	7.080	0.250	0.098
	Quantum	80	0.820	0.410 ②	0.002	7.080	0.250	0.098
	Rabbit	80	0.820	0.410 ②	0.002	7.080	0.250	0.098
	Scirocco	80	0.820	0.410 ②	0.002	7.080	0.250	0.098
	Vanagon	87–94	0.938	0.453	0.004	9.920	0.079	0.100
1984	Jetta	80	0.820	0.410 ②	0.002	7.080	0.250	0.098
	Quantum	80	0.820	0.410 ②	0.002	7.080	0.250	0.098
	Rabbit	80	0.820	0.410 ②	0.002	7.080	0.250	0.098
	Scirocco	80	0.820	0.410 ②	0.002	7.080	0.250	0.098
	Vanagon	87–94	0.938	0.453	0.004	9.920	0.079	0.098

BRAKE SPECIFICATIONS

All measurements in inches unless noted

Year	Model	Lug Nut Torque (ft. lbs.)	Master Cylinder Bore	Brake Disc Minimum Thickness	Brake Disc Maximum Runout	Maximim Brake Drum Diameter	Minimum Lining Thickness Front	Minimum Lining Thickness Rear
1985	Jetta	80	0.820	0.393 ③ ⑤	0.002	7.087	0.276	0.098 ④
	Quantum	80	0.820	0.410 ②	0.002	7.080	0.250	0.098
	Rabbit	80	0.820	0.410 ②	0.002	7.080	0.250	0.098
	Scirocco	80	0.820	0.410 ②	0.002	7.080	0.250	0.098
	GTI	80	0.820	0.393 ③ ⑤	0.002	7.087	0.276	0.098 ④
	GLI	80	0.820	0.393 ③ ⑤	0.002	7.087	0.276	0.098 ④
	Golf	80	0.820	0.393 ③ ⑤	0.002	7.087	0.276	0.098 ④
	Vanagon	87–94	0.938	0.453	0.004	9.920	0.079	0.098
1986	Jetta	80	0.820	0.393 ③ ⑤	0.002	7.087	0.276	0.098 ④
	Quantum	80	0.820	0.410 ②	0.002	7.080	0.250	0.098
	Scirocco	80	0.820	0.410 ②	0.002	7.080	0.250	0.098
	GTI	80	0.820	0.393 ③ ⑤	0.002	7.087	0.276	0.098 ④
	GLI	80	0.820	0.393 ③ ⑤	0.002	7.087	0.276	0.098 ④
	Golf	80	0.820	0.393 ③ ⑤	0.002	7.087	0.276	0.098 ④
	Vanagon	87–94	0.938	0.453	0.004	9.920	0.079	0.098
1987–88	Jetta	80	0.820	0.393 ③ ⑤	0.002	7.087	0.276	0.098 ④
	Quantum	80	0.820	0.410 ②	0.002	7.080	0.250	0.098
	Scirocco	80	0.820	0.410 ②	0.002	7.080	0.250	0.098
	GTI	80	0.820	0.393 ③ ⑤	0.002	7.087	0.276	0.098 ④
	GLI	80	0.820	0.393 ③ ⑤	0.002	7.087	0.276	0.098 ④
	Golf	80	0.820	0.393 ③ ⑤	0.002	7.087	0.276	0.098 ④
	Fox	80	0.820	0.393 ③ ⑤	0.002	7.087	0.276	0.098 ④
	Vanagon	87–94	0.938	0.453	0.004	9.920	0.079	0.098

NOTE: Minimum lining thickness is as recommended by manufacturer. Due to variations in state inspection regulations, the minimum thickness may be different than that recommended by the manufacturer.

① 7.91 in Quantum
② Vented discs: 0.728
③ Vented discs; 0.708
④ Disc brake: 0.276
⑤ Rear disc brake: 0.315

FRONT WHEEL ALIGNMENT

Year	Model	③Caster Range (deg.)	③Caster Preferred Setting (deg.)	③Camber Range (deg.)	③Camber Preferred Setting (deg.)	Toe-in (in.)	Steering Axis Inclination (deg.)
1981	Dasher	0–1P	1/2P	0–1P	1/2P	3/32	10 1/2P
	Rabbit	1 5/16P–2 5/16P	1 3/16P	3/16N–13/16P	15/16P	5/16	10 1/2P
	Jetta	1 5/16P–2 5/16P	1 3/16P	3/16N–13/16P	15/16P	5/16	10 1/2P
	Scirocco	1 5/16P–2 5/16P	1 13/16P	3/16N–13/16P	5/16P	5/16	10 1/2P
	Quantum ①	0–1P	1/2P	15/32N–5/32N	21/32N	5/32	NA
	Quantum ②	15/16P–1 15/16P	1 7/16P	15/32N–5/32N	21/32N	5/32	NA
	Vanagon	7P–7 1/2P	7 1/4P	1/2N–1/2P	0	5/64	NA
1982	Rabbit	1 5/16P–2 5/16P	1 13/16P	3/16N–13/16P	5/16P	5/16	10 1/2P
	Jetta	1 5/16P–2 5/16P	1 13/16P	3/16N–13/16P	5/16P	5/16	10 1/2P
	Scirocco	1 5/16P–2 5/16P	1 13/16P	3/16N–13/16P	5/16P	5/16	10 1/2P
	Quantum ①	0–1P	1/2P	15/32N–5/32N	21/32N	5/32	NA

FRONT WHEEL ALIGNMENT

Year	Model	③Caster Range (deg.)	Preferred Setting (deg.)	③Camber Range (deg.)	Preferred Setting (deg.)	Toe-in (in.)	Steering Axis Inclination (deg.)
1982	Quantum ②	$15/16$P–$1^{15}/16$P	$1^7/16$P	$15/32$N–$5/32$N	$21/32$N	$5/32$	NA
	Vanagon	7P–$7^1/2$P	$7^1/4$P	$1/2$N–$1/2$P	0	$5/64$	NA
1983	Rabbit	$15/16$P–$2^5/16$P	$1^{13}/16$P	$3/16$N–$13/16$P	$5/16$P	$5/16$	$10^1/2$P
	Jetta	$15/16$P–$2^5/16$P	$1^{13}/16$P	$3/16$N–$13/16$P	$5/16$P	$5/16$	$10^1/2$P
	Scirocco	$15/16$P–$2^5/16$P	$1^{13}/16$P	$3/16$N–$13/16$P	$5/16$P	$5/16$	$10^1/2$P
	Quantum ①	0–1P	$1/2$P	$15/32$N–$5/32$N	$21/32$N	$5/32$	NA
	Quantum ②	$15/16$P–$1^{15}/16$P	$1^7/16$P	$15/32$N–$5/32$N	$21/32$N	$5/32$	NA
	Vanagon	7P–$7^1/2$P	$7^1/4$P	$1/2$N–$1/2$P	0	$5/64$	NA
1984	Rabbit	$15/16$P–$2^5/16$P	$1^{13}/16$P	$3/16$N–$13/16$P	$5/16$P	$5/16$	$10^1/2$P
	Jetta	$15/16$P–$2^5/16$P	$1^{13}/16$P	$3/16$N–$13/16$P	$5/16$P	$5/16$	$10^1/2$P
	Scirocco	$15/16$P–$2^5/16$P	$1^{13}/16$P	$3/16$N–$13/16$P	$5/16$P	$5/16$	$10^1/2$P
	Quantum ①	0–1P	$1/2$P	$15/32$N–$5/32$N	$21/32$N	$5/32$	NA
	Quantum ②	$15/16$P–$1^{15}/16$P	$1^7/16$P	$15/32$N–$5/32$N	$21/32$N	$5/32$	NA
	Vanagon	7P–$7^1/2$P	$7^1/4$P	$1/2$N–$1/2$P	0	$5/64$	NA
1985	Rabbit	$15/16$P–$2^5/16$P	$1^{13}/16$P	$3/16$N–$13/16$P	$5/16$P	$5/16$	$10^1/2$P
	Jetta	1P–2P	1P	$13/16$N–$5/32$N	$1/2$N	0	NA
	Scirocco	$15/16$P–$2^5/16$P	$1^{13}/16$P	$3/16$N–$13/16$P	$5/16$P	$5/16$	$10^1/2$P
	Quantum ①	0–1P	$1/2$P	$15/32$N–$5/32$N	$21/32$N	$5/32$	NA
	Quantum ②	$15/16$P–$1^{15}/16$P	$1^7/16$P	$15/32$N–$5/32$N	$21/32$N	$5/32$	NA
	Golf	1P–2P	1P	$3/4$N–$1/16$N	$3/8$N	0	NA
	GTI	$1^1/16$P–$2^1/16$P	$1^9/16$P	$15/16$N–$1/4$N	$9/16$N	0	NA
	GLI	$1^1/16$P–$2^1/16$P	$1^9/16$P	$15/16$N–$1/4$N	$9/16$N	0	NA
	Vanagon	7P–$7^1/2$P	$7^1/4$P	$1/2$N–$1/2$P	0	$5/64$	NA
1986	Scirocco	$15/16$P–$2^5/16$P	$1^{13}/16$P	$3/16$N–$13/16$P	$5/16$P	$5/16$	$10^1/2$P
	Quantum ①	0–1P	$1/2$P	$15/32$N–$5/32$N	$21/32$N	$5/32$	NA
	Quantum ②	$15/16$P–$1^{15}/16$P	$1^7/16$P	$15/32$N–$5/32$N	$21/32$N	$5/32$	NA
	Golf	1P–2P	1P	$3/4$N–$1/16$N	$3/8$N	0	NA
	GTI	$1^1/16$P–$2^1/16$P	$1^9/16$P	$15/16$N–$1/4$N	$9/16$N	0	NA
	Jetta	1P–2P	1P	$13/16$N–$5/32$N	$1/2$N	0	NA
	GLI	$1^1/16$P–$2^1/16$P	$1^9/16$P	$15/16$N–$1/4$N	$9/16$N	0	NA
	Vanagon	7P–$7^1/2$P	$7^1/4$P	$1/2$N–$1/2$P	0	$5/64$	NA
1987–88	Quantum ①	0–1P	$1/2$P	$15/32$N–$5/32$N	$21/32$N	$5/32$	NA
	Quantum ②	$15/16$P–$1^{15}/16$P	$1^7/16$P	$15/32$N–$5/32$N	$21/32$N	$5/32$	NA
	Golf	1P–2P	1P	$3/4$N–$1/16$N	$3/8$N	0	NA
	GTI	$1^1/16$P–$2^1/16$P	$1^9/16$P	$15/16$N–$1/4$N	$9/16$N	0	NA
	Jetta	1P–2P	1P	$13/16$N–$5/32$N	$1/2$N	0	NA
	GLI	$1^1/16$P–$2^1/16$P	$1^9/16$P	$15/16$N–$1/4$N	$9/16$N	0	NA
	Fox	1P–2P	1P	$13/16$N–$5/32$N	$1/2$N	0	NA
	Scirocco	$15/16$P–$2^5/16$P	$1^{13}/16$P	$3/16$N–$13/16$P	$5/16$P	$5/16$	$10^1/2$P
	Vanagon	7P–$7^1/2$P	$7^1/4$P	$1/2$N–$1/2$P	0	$5/64$	NA

① W/o link rod
② W/link rod
③ Not adjustable
N—Negative, P—Positive

REAR WHEEL ALIGNMENT

Year	Model	Caster Range (deg.)	Caster Preferred Setting (deg.)	Camber Range (deg.)	Camber Preferred Setting (deg.)	Toe-in (in.)	Steering Axis Inclination (deg.)
1981	Dasher	NA	NA	$1\frac{5}{16}$N–0	$\frac{21}{32}$N	0	NA
	Rabbit	NA	NA	$1\frac{13}{16}$N–$1\frac{1}{16}$N	$1\frac{1}{4}$N	$\frac{5}{16}$	NA
	Jetta	NA	NA	$1\frac{13}{16}$N–$1\frac{1}{16}$N	$1\frac{1}{4}$N	$\frac{5}{16}$	NA
	Scirocco	NA	NA	$1\frac{13}{16}$N–$1\frac{1}{16}$N	$1\frac{1}{4}$N	$\frac{5}{16}$	NA
	Quantum	NA	NA	2N–$1\frac{21}{64}$N	$1\frac{11}{16}$N	$\frac{13}{32}$	NA
	Vanagon	NA	NA	$1\frac{5}{16}$N–$\frac{5}{16}$N	$\frac{13}{16}$N	0	NA
1982	Rabbit	NA	NA	$1\frac{13}{16}$N–$1\frac{1}{16}$N	$1\frac{1}{4}$N	$\frac{5}{16}$	NA
	Jetta	NA	NA	$1\frac{13}{16}$N–$1\frac{1}{16}$N	$1\frac{1}{4}$N	$\frac{5}{16}$	NA
	Scirocco	NA	NA	$1\frac{13}{16}$N–$1\frac{1}{16}$N	$1\frac{1}{4}$N	$\frac{5}{16}$	NA
	Quantum	NA	NA	2N–$1\frac{21}{64}$N	$1\frac{11}{16}$N	$\frac{13}{32}$	NA
	Vanagon	NA	NA	$1\frac{5}{16}$N–$\frac{5}{16}$N	$\frac{13}{16}$N	0	NA
1983	Rabbit	NA	NA	$1\frac{13}{16}$N–$1\frac{1}{16}$N	$1\frac{1}{4}$N	$\frac{5}{16}$	NA
	Jetta	NA	NA	$1\frac{13}{16}$N–$1\frac{1}{16}$N	$1\frac{1}{4}$N	$\frac{5}{16}$	NA
	Scirocco	NA	NA	$1\frac{13}{16}$N–$1\frac{1}{16}$N	$1\frac{1}{4}$N	$\frac{5}{16}$	NA
	Quantum	NA	NA	2N–$1\frac{21}{64}$N	$1\frac{11}{16}$N	$\frac{13}{32}$	NA
	Vanagon	NA	NA	$1\frac{5}{16}$N–$\frac{5}{16}$N	$\frac{13}{16}$N	0	NA
1984	Rabbit	NA	NA	$1\frac{13}{16}$N–$1\frac{1}{16}$N	$1\frac{1}{4}$N	$\frac{5}{16}$	NA
	Jetta	NA	NA	$1\frac{13}{16}$N–$1\frac{1}{16}$N	$1\frac{1}{4}$N	$\frac{5}{16}$	NA
	Scirocco	NA	NA	$1\frac{13}{16}$N–$1\frac{1}{16}$N	$1\frac{1}{4}$N	$\frac{5}{16}$	NA
	Quantum	NA	NA	2N–$1\frac{21}{64}$N	$1\frac{11}{16}$N	$\frac{13}{32}$	NA
	Vanagon	NA	NA	$1\frac{5}{16}$N–$\frac{5}{16}$N	$\frac{13}{16}$N	0	NA
1985	Rabbit	NA	NA	$1\frac{13}{16}$N–$1\frac{1}{16}$N	$1\frac{1}{4}$N	$\frac{5}{16}$	NA
	Jetta	NA	NA	2N–$1\frac{11}{32}$N	$1\frac{11}{16}$N	$\frac{3}{8}$	NA
	Scirocco	NA	NA	$1\frac{13}{16}$N–$1\frac{1}{16}$N	$1\frac{1}{4}$N	$\frac{5}{16}$	NA
	Quantum	NA	NA	2N–$1\frac{21}{64}$N	$1\frac{11}{16}$N	$\frac{13}{32}$	NA
	Golf	NA	NA	2N–$1\frac{11}{32}$N	$1\frac{11}{16}$N	$\frac{3}{8}$	NA
	GTI	NA	NA	2N–$1\frac{11}{32}$N	$1\frac{11}{16}$N	$\frac{3}{8}$	NA
	GLI	NA	NA	2N–$1\frac{11}{32}$N	$1\frac{11}{16}$N	$\frac{3}{8}$	NA
	Vanagon	NA	NA	$1\frac{5}{16}$N–$\frac{5}{16}$N	$\frac{13}{16}$N	0	NA
1986	Scirocco	NA	NA	$1\frac{13}{16}$N–$1\frac{1}{16}$N	$1\frac{1}{4}$N	$\frac{5}{16}$	NA
	Quantum	NA	NA	2N–$1\frac{21}{64}$N	$1\frac{11}{16}$N	$\frac{13}{32}$	NA
	Golf	NA	NA	2N–$1\frac{11}{32}$N	$1\frac{11}{16}$N	$\frac{3}{8}$	NA
	GTI	NA	NA	2N–$1\frac{11}{32}$N	$1\frac{11}{16}$N	$\frac{3}{8}$	NA
	Jetta	NA	NA	2N–$1\frac{11}{32}$N	$1\frac{11}{16}$N	$\frac{3}{8}$	NA
	GLI	NA	NA	2N–$1\frac{11}{32}$N	$1\frac{11}{16}$N	$\frac{3}{8}$	NA
	Vanagon	NA	NA	$1\frac{5}{16}$N–$\frac{5}{16}$N	$\frac{13}{16}$N	0	NA
1987–88	Quantum	NA	NA	2N–$1\frac{21}{64}$N	$1\frac{11}{16}$N	$\frac{13}{32}$	NA
	Golf	NA	NA	2N–$1\frac{11}{32}$N	$1\frac{11}{16}$N	$\frac{3}{8}$	NA
	GTI	NA	NA	2N–$1\frac{11}{32}$N	$1\frac{11}{16}$N	$\frac{3}{8}$	NA
	Jetta	NA	NA	2N–$1\frac{11}{32}$N	$1\frac{11}{16}$N	$\frac{3}{8}$	NA
	GLI	NA	NA	2N–$1\frac{11}{32}$N	$1\frac{11}{16}$N	$\frac{3}{8}$	NA
	Fox	NA	NA	$1\frac{13}{16}$N–$1\frac{1}{16}$N	$1\frac{1}{4}$N	$\frac{5}{16}$	NA
	Scirocco	NA	NA	$1\frac{13}{16}$N–$1\frac{1}{16}$N	$1\frac{1}{4}$N	$\frac{5}{16}$	NA
	Vanagon	NA	NA	$1\frac{5}{16}$N–$\frac{5}{16}$N	$\frac{13}{16}$N	0	NA

N—Negative, P—Positive   NA: Not adjustable

TUNE-UP PROCEDURES

Breaker Points and Condenser

REMOVAL, INSTALATION & ADJUSTMENT

NOTE: 1981–83 California Vanagon vehicles, all 1984–88 Vanagons, and all 1981–88 front wheel drive models are equipped with a breakerless, electronic ignition system.

Snap off the two retaining clips on the distributor cap. Unfasten the ground strap at the suppressor leads. Remove the cap and examine it for cracks, deterioration, or carbon tracking. Replace the cap, if necessary, by transferring one wire at a time from the old cap. Replace the rotor at every other tune-up. Remove the dust shield.

NOTE: Vehicles with a radio may be equipped with a static shield. Unscrew the ground strap and remove the shield before removing the cap.

Check the points for pitting and burning. Slight imperfections on the contact surface may be filed off with a point file. It is best to replace the breaker point set. Always replace the condenser when you replace the point set.

To replace the breaker points:
1. Remove the distributor cap.
2. Remove the rotor.
3. Unsnap the point connector from the terminal at the side of the distributor. Remove the retaining screw and lift out the point set.
4. Install the new point set, making sure that the pin on the bottom engages the hole in the breaker plate.
5. Install the wire connector and the retaining screws (hand-tight).
6. Turn the engine with a wrench on the crankshaft pulley until the breaker arm rubbing block on the points set is on the high point of one of the cam lobes. Turn the engine only in the direction of normal rotation to avoid damage to the timing belt.
7. The proper size feeler gauge should just slip through the points with a slight drag. If the gap is incorrect, pivot a screwdriver in the point set notch and the two projections on the breaker plate to bring it within specifications.
8. When the gap is correct, tighten the retaining screw. Recheck the adjustment.
9. Lubricate the distributor cam with silicone grease (some point sets come with a grease capsule).
10. Install the dust cover, rotor and distributor cap.
11. Check the dwell angle and the ignition timing.
12. The condenser is mounted on the the outside of the distributor. Undo the mounting screw and the terminal block to replace.

Dwell Angle

The dwell angle or cam angle is the number of degrees that the distributor cam rotates while the points are closed. There is an inverse relationship between dwell angle and point gap. Increasing the point gap will decrease the dwell angle and vice versa. Checking the dwell angle with a meter is a far more accurate method of measuring point opening than the feeler gauge method.

ADJUSTMENT

NOTE: The dwell angle on all cars with the electronic ignition system is set at the factory and not adjustable.

1. Setting the dwell angle with a dwell meter achieves the same effect as setting the point gap but offers better accuracy.

NOTE: The dwell must be set before setting the timing. Setting the dwell will alter the timing, but when the timing is set, the dwell will not change.

2. Attach the positive lead of the dwell meter to the coil terminal which has a wire leading to the distributor. The negative lead should be attached to a good ground.
3. Remove the distributor cap and rotor. Turn the ignition ON and turn the engine over using a starter or a starter button. Read the dwell from the meter and open or close the points to adjust the dwell.

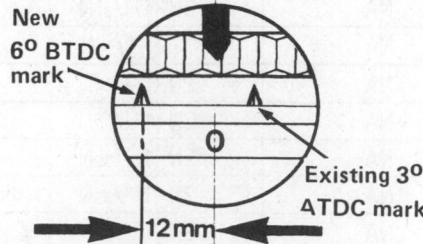

Timing mark conversion—1.7 liter Rabbit with 5-speed transmission and fuel injection

New 6° BTDC mark

Existing 3° ATDC mark

12mm

NOTE: Dwell specifications are listed in the "Tune-Up Sepcifications" chart.

4. Reinstall the cap and rotor and start the engine. Check the dwell and reset it if necessary.

Ignition Timing

ADJUSTMENT

Breaker Point Ignition Systems

FWD MODELS

NOTE: On 1984 Rabbit models with 5 speed trans. and fuel injection, the flywheel must be marked at 6° BTDC to allow the use of a standard (strobe) timing light. The 3° ATDC timing mark does not apply to these models.

The following procedure should be used to locate and mark the flywheel:
1. Unscrew the plastic plug in the timing hole. This can be found on top of the transaxle, near the engine block.

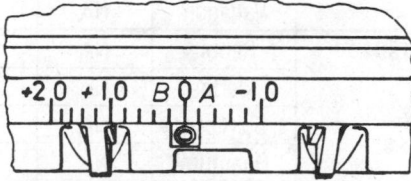

Westmoreland Rabbits with a 200mm clutch may have a "universal" flywheel installed. Each timing mark is equal to 2°. Marks to the left of the O are BTDC, to the right ATDC

2. Turn the engine to TDC on the No. 1 cylinder.
3. Spray the flywheel in this area with blue engineering dye or the equivalent.
4. Use a compass to scribe the flywheel 12mm (0.47 in.) to the left of the "0" TDC mark.
5. Use a chisel to mark the measured spot permanently on the flywheel.
6. Check and adjust the timing, and reinstall the plastic plug.
Dwell or point gap must be set before the timing is set. Also, the idle speed must be set to specifications.
1. Attach the timing light as outlined above or according to the manufacturer's instructions. Hook up a dwell/tachometer since you'll need an rpm indication for correct timing.
2. Locate the timing mark opening in the clutch or torque converter housing at the rear of the engine directly behind the distributor. The OT mark stands for TDC or 0° advance. The other mark designates the correct timing position. Mark them with

chalk so that they will be more visible. Don't disconnect the vacuum line.

NOTE: Some models do not have an OT mark.

3. Start the engine and allow it to reach the normal idle speed.

4. Shine the timing light at the marks.

5. The light should now be flashing when the timing mark and the V-shaped pointer are aligned.

6. If not, loosen the distributor hold-down bolt and rotate the distributor very slowly to align the marks.

7. Tighten the mounting nut when the ignition timing is correct.

8. Recheck the timing when the distributor is secured. With ignition timing correctly adjusted, the spark plugs will fire just before the piston hits the top of the compression stroke, thus providing maximum power and economy.

RWD Vanagon

NOTE: The engine must be warmed up before the timing is set (oil temperature of 122–158°F).

1. Remove the No. 1 spark plug wire from the distributor cap and attach the timing light lead. Disconnect the vacuum hose if so advised by the "Tune-Up Specifications" chart (and readjust the idle speed if necessary).

2. Start the engine and run it at the specified rpm. Aim the timing light at the crankshaft pulley on upright fan engines and at the engine cooling fan on the suitcase engines. The rubber plug in the fan housing will have to be removed before the timing marks on the suitcase engine can be seen.

3. Read the timing and rotate the distributor accordingly.

NOTE: Rotate the distributor in the opposite direction of normal rotor rotation to advance the timing. Retard the timing by turning the distributor in the normal direction of rotor rotation.

4. It is necessary to loosen the clamp at the base of the distributor before the distributor can be rotated. It may also be necessary to put a small amount of white paint or chalk on the timing marks to make them more visible.

ELECTRONIC IGNITION

FWD Models

1. Run the engine to normal operating temperature. Connect tachometer.

2. Stop the engine. Disconnect the plugs on the idle stabilizer at the con-

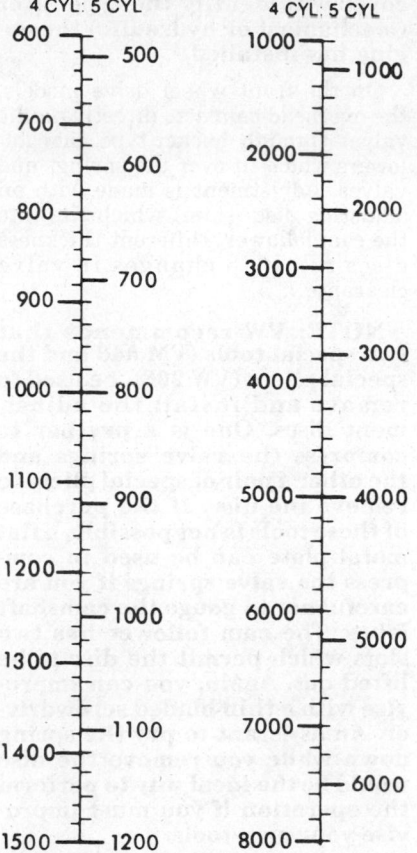

Tach. Conv. Chart.

4 CYL	5 CYL		4 CYL	5 CYL
600	500		1000	
				1000
700	600		2000	
800				2000
	700		3000	
900				3000
	800		4000	
1000				
	900		5000	4000
1100				
1200	1000		6000	5000
1300				
	1100		7000	6000
1400				
1500	1200		8000	

Conversion chart—to convert 4 cylinder tachometer reading to 5 cylinder applications

trol unit and plug them together (see illustration). On the carbureted Rabbit except models with the Carter TYF feedback model, disconnect the vacuum retard hose and plug it. Disconnect and plug both vacuum lines on models with the Carter TYF carburetor.

3. Check the idle speed. It should be between 800 and 1000 rpm.

4. With your timing light attached according to manufacturer's instructions, shine the light on the timing hole. The pointer in the hole must line up with the notch in the flywheel. To adjust the timing, loosen the distribution at its base and turn it until the timing marks line up.

5. On the carbureted Rabbit, rein-

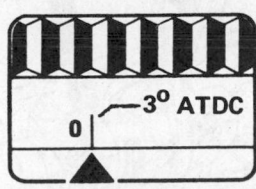

Timing mark—Quantum with A/T and Dasher. Early Dashers had two marks on the flywheel, when timing early models use the 3° mark to the right of the OT mark

stall the vacuum hoses. Idle speed should drop to 600–750 rpm.

6. Stop the engine and reconnect the plugs at the control unit. On the carbureted Rabbit, start the engine and rev it a few times to activate the idle stabilizer. On the carbureted Rabbit, the idle speed should now be 850–950 rpm.

RWD Vanagon

1981–85

1. Run the engine until it reaches normal operating temperature and then turn it off.

2. Bypass the idle stabilizer by pulling the two leads from the unit and connecting them together.

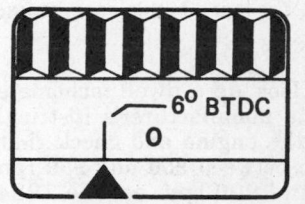

Timing mark—Quantum with M/T

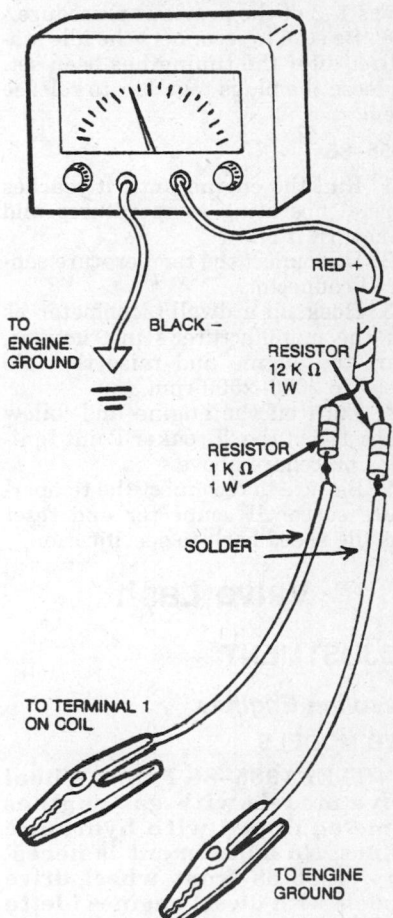

Adapter for attaching a tachometer to 1981–88 carbureted Rabbit with electronic ignition

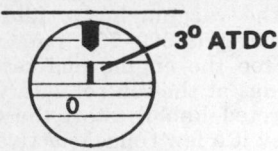

Timing mark—Rabbit, Jetta and Scirocco models with CIS, except 1.8 liter and carbureted engines

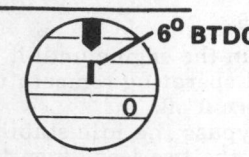

1.8 liter, manual transmission timing mark. Carbureted engines are also timed at BTDC. The mark, in this case, represents 7½°

3. Hook up a dwell/tachometer as per the manufacturer's instructions, start the engine and check that the idle is between 850 and 950 rpm, or 800 and 900 rpm on the 1984–85 models.

4. Turn off the engine and follow Steps 1–3 of the previous procedure.

5. Be sure to reconnect the idle stabilizer after the timing has been set. Squeeze the plugs together to release them.

1986–88

1. Run the engine until it reaches normal operating temperatures and then turn it off.

2. Disconnect the temperature sensor II connector.

3. Hook up a dwell/tachometer as per the manufacturer's instructions, start the engine and raise the idle speed to 2000–2500 rpm.

4. Turn off the engine and follow Steps 1–3 of the "Breaker Point Ignition" procedure above.

5. Be sure to reconnect the temperature sensor II connector and reset the idle speed back to specification.

Valve Lash

ADJUSTMENT

Gasoline Engines

FWD MODELS

NOTE: 1985–88 Front wheel drive models with gas engines come equipped with hydraulic lifters; No adjustment is necessary. 1986–88 front wheel drive models with diesel engines (Jetta and Golf), except for early production Golfs, are equipped with hydraulic valve lifters; as with the gasoline engines—No adjustment

is required. A label on the valve cover will identify the type lifter (mechanical or hydraulic) the engine has installed.

On the front wheel drive models, the overhead cam acts directly on the valves through bucket-type cam followers which fit over the springs and valves. Adjustment is made with an adjusting disc (shim) which fits into the cam follower. Different thickness discs result in changes in valve clearance.

NOTE: VW recommends that two special tools (VM 546 and the special pliers (VW 208), be used to remove and install the adjustment discs. One is a pry bar to compress the valve springs and the other a pair of special pliers to remove the disc. If the purchase of these tools is not possible, a flat metal plate can be used to compress the valve springs if you are careful not to gouge the camshaft lobes. The cam follower has two slots which permit the disc to be lifted out. Again, you can improvise with a thin bladed screwdriver. An assistant to pry the spring down while you remove the disc would be the ideal way to perform the operation if you must improvise your own tools.

Valve clearance is checked with the engine moderately warm (coolant temperature should be about 95°F (35°C).

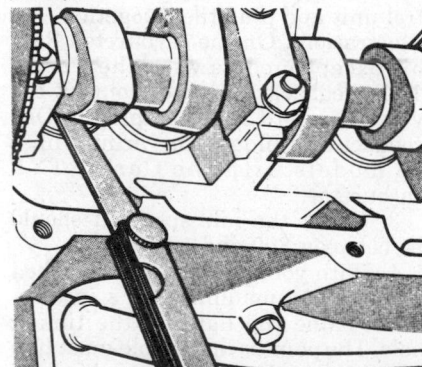

Check the valve clearance with a feeler gauge. The camshaft lobe should not be putting pressure on the valve shim

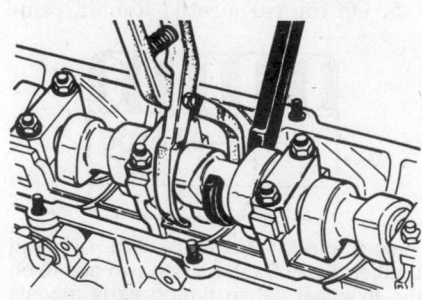

Tools used for valve adjustment

1. Remove the accelerator linkage (if necessary), the upper drive belt cover (if necessary), the air cleaner and any hoses or lines which may be in the way.

2. Remove the cylinder head cover. Valve clearance is checked in the firing order 1–3–4–2 for the 4 cylinder and 1–2–4–5–3 for the 5 cylinder engines, with the piston of the cylinder being checked at TDC of the compression stroke. Both valves will be closed at this position and the cam lobes will be pointing straight up.

3. Turn the crankshaft pulley bolt with a socket wrench to position the camshaft for checking.

NOTE: There is a hole behind the front license plate, on Dasher models, through which a wrench can be inserted.

CAUTION
Do not turn the camshaft by the camshaft mounting bolt, this will stretch the drive belt. When turning the crankshaft pulley bolt, turn it CLOCKWISE ONLY.

4. With the No. 1 piston at TDC (¼ turn past for the diesel) of the compression stroke, determine the clearance with a feeler gauge. Intake clearance should be 0.008–0.012 in; exhaust clearance should be 0.016–0.020 in.

NOTE: When adjusting the clearances on the diesel engine, the pistons must not be at TDC. Turn the crankshaft ¼ turn past TDC so that the valves do not contact the pistons when the tappets are depressed.

5. Continue on to check the other cylinders in the firing order, turning the crankshaft to bring each particular piston to the top of the compression stroke (¼ turn for the diesel). Record the individual clearances as you go along.

6. If measured clearance is within tolerance levels (0.002 in.), it is not necessary to replace the adjusting discs.

7. If adjustment is necessary, the discs will have to be removed and replaced with thicker or thinner ones which will yield the correct clearance. Discs are available in 0.002 in. increments from 0.12 in. to 0.17 in.

NOTE: The thickness of the adjusting discs are etched on one side. When installing, the marks must face the cam followers. Discs can be reused if they are not worn or damaged.

8. To remove the discs, turn the cam followers so that the grooves are

accessible when the pry bar is depressed.

9. Press the cam follower down with the pry bar and remove the adjusting discs with the special pliers or the screwdriver.

10. Replace the adjustment discs as necessary to bring the clearance within the 0.002 in. tolerance level. If the measured clearance is larger than the given tolerance, remove the existing disc and insert a thicker one to bring the clearance up to specification. If it is smaller, insert a thinner one.

11. Recheck all valve clearances after adjustment.

12. To install, reverse the removal procedures.

RWD VANAGON

All Vanagon engines, come equipped with hydraulic lifters; No routine valve adjustment is necessary, as the lifter constantly adjusts to take up clearance in the valve train. However, the valves must still be adjusted whenever the cylinder heads have been removed.

The rocker arms in the Vanagon engines are equipped with conventional locknut-type adjusters. The rockers must be adjusted only when the head(s) have been removed.

1. Remove the rocker arm covers, Then back out the adjusting screws on the rocker arms so that the ball-shaped end is flush with the surface of the rocker arm.

2. Turn the crankshaft until No. 1 cylinder is at TDC on compression. Both valves should be closed, and the mark on the distributor rotor should be in line with the mark on the distributor housing.

3. Turn the adjusting screws in so that they just touch the valve stems.

4. Turn the adjusting screws 2 turns clockwise and tighten the locknuts.

5. Rotate the crankshaft 180° and adjust cylinder No. 2. Repeat the procedure on cylinders 3 and 4 until all valves are adjusted.

MODELS WITH DIESEL ENGINES

Check the valve clearance every 20,000 miles in firing order, with the engine at normal operating temperature.

1. Remove the camshaft cover.

2. Set the engine at TDC on No. 1 cylinder by aligning the 0°T mark on the flywheel with the pointer.

NOTE: When adjusting clearances on a diesel, the pistons must not be at TDC. Turn the crakshaft ¼ turn past TDC, so that the valves do not contact the pistons when the tappets are depressed.

3. The valve clearances of cylinder No. 1 should be checked when the valves of No. 4 cylinder overlap, i.e., when both No. 4 cylinder valves move in opposite directions simultaneously. It may be necessary to turn the crankshaft slightly to find this position. When this happens, the exhaust valve is closing and the intake opening. Check and note the clearance of both the intake and exhaust valves for No. 1 cylinder.

4. Turn the crankshaft 180° in the normal direction of rotation. Check and note the valve clearances of cylinder No. 3 at the overlap position of cylinder No. 2.

5. Turn the crankshaft 180°. Check and note the valve clearances of cylinder No. 1.

6. Turn the crankshaft 180°. Check and note the valve clearances of cylinder No. 2 at the overlap position of cylinder No. 3.

7. Compare the noted clearances with those listed in the "Tune-Up Specifications" chart. Adjustment is made by replacing the tappet clearance shim in the top of each tappet. These are available in 26 sizes ranging from 3.0mm (0.119 in.) to 4.25mm (0.166 in.) in increments of 0.05mm (0.002 in.). The thickness of each shim is marked on the bottom (these shims are available from VW dealers).

NOTE: If a valve clearance deviates 0.002 in. or less from the specified clearance, it need not be adjusted.

8. To remove a tappet clearance shim turn the cylinder to TDC and press down the tappet so that the shim can be lifted out. A special tool is available from VW for this operation. Once the shim is removed, check its size and determine what size will be needed to produce the required adjustment.

9. Install the required shim. When all the clearances have been corrected, recheck valve clerances.

Idle Speed and Mixture Gasoline Engines (Carbureted Models)

IDLE SPEED ADJUSTMENT

1982–84 Rabbit With Carter TYF

1. Run the engine to normal operating temperatures. Make sure that the choke is fully OPEN and not sticking. Remove the PCV valve from the valve cover. Turn OFF all of the electrical equipment.

2. Connect a tachometer, a timing light and a dwell meter to the engine.

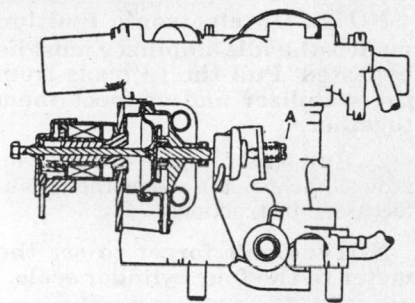

Idle speed adjustment screw (A)—Carter TYF carburetor

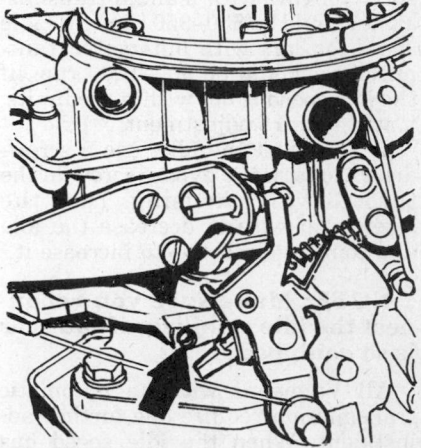

Idle mixture adjustment screw—1981–88 carbureted Rabbit

Connect the dwell meter to the test receptacle on the lower strut tower.

3. Start the engine and run it at 2000 rpm for 5 seconds. Check the idle speed (850–1000 rpm) and the dwell (it will fluctuate between 18–45 degrees).

4. If the idle is incorrect, disconnect the idle stabilizer plugs and connect them together.

5. Disconnect and plug the vacuum advance and the retard hoses at the distributor.

6. To adjust the idle speed, turn the idle speed screw, located near the solenoid plunger. Adjust the idle speed to 820–900 rpm with the solenoid energized.

NOTE: On vehicles equipped with A/C, turn the A/C "ON", set the control to "COLD", the fan to "FAST", disengage the A/C compressor clutch and adjust the idle speed to 820–900 rpm.

7. When the idle speed is adjusted, remove the test equipment and reinstall the hoses and electrical connectors.

1981–83 RWD Vanagon

1. Thoroughly warm up the engine so that the oil will be hot and the auxiliary air regulator will be fully closed.

NOTE: On electronic ignition models the idle stabilizer must be bypassed. Pull the to leads from the stabilizer and connect them together.

2. Turn off the engine and hook up a dwell/tachometer as per the manufacturer's instructions.

NOTE: Don't forget to set the meter to the four cylinder scale.

3. Start the engine, speed it up and then allow it to return to idle. The idle speed for cars with manual transmissions should be 850–950 rpm. The idle speed for cars with automatic transmissions should be 900–1000 rpm. If the idle speed is not within the limits, it will require adjustment.

4. To adjust the idle, use a screwdriver to turn the bypass screw in the throttle valve housing. Turn the screw clockwise to decrease the idle and counter clockwise to increase it.

NOTE: Make sure you reconnect the idle stabilizer if your car is so equipped.

All Vanagons with an automatic transmission require one further adjustment. When the idle speed has been set properly, set the parking brake, block the front wheels and then put the car in "Drive." The idle should drop between 150–200 rpm. If it drops more than this you will have to adjust the idle speed regulator. To adjust:

1. With the engine idling, place the transmission in "Park" and use a feeler gauge to check the clearance between the end of the plunger and the lever on the throttle valve shaft. It should be between 0.020–0.040 in.

2. If the gap is not within specifications, loosen the locknut on the plunger and screw the plunger in or out until the clearance is correct.

1984–85 RWD Vanagon

1. Make sure the engine has been run up to operating temperature, all electrical accessories are OFF (including the radiator fan), and the throttle valve switch is ON at idle. Always make sure the ignition switch is OFF when the tester is connected.

2. Connect the tester (VW part No. VAG 1367 or equivalent) as shown in the accompanying illustration: "A" to the alternator or terminal box, and "B" to the TDC sender.

3. Connect the CO meter to the receptacle in the left exhaust pipe.

4. Check the ignition timing, and adjust if necessary.

5. Disconnect the idle stabilizer electrical plugs, and connect them together. Start the engine and again

check ignition timing. Timing should be 5° ATDC with rpm below 1000. Adjust if necessary.

6. Run the engine at idle speed. Check engine speed after two minutes and adjust if necessry. Adjust by turning the screw on the throttle valve housing.

7. Stop the engine. Check the CO and adjust if necessary. Connect the idle stabilizer. Disconnect the electrical connection at the oxygen sensor. Start the engine and check the CO content—it should be 0.3–1.1%.

8. If the CO value is above 1.1%, pinch the crankcase hose. The CO should drop below 1.1%. If it does, a CO adjustment is not necessary. If it does NOT, continue.

9. Stop the engine. To adjust the CO, punch the plug in the CO adjusting hole. Drill a $\frac{3}{32}$ in. hole in the center of the plug, $\frac{9}{64}$–$\frac{5}{32}$ in. deep, NO MORE. Keep the area clean of metal shavings.

10. Screw a $\frac{1}{8}$ in. sheet metal screw into the plug and remove the plug, using pliers.

11. Reinstall the air intake sensor, and with the oxygen sensor disconnected, start the engine.

12. Adjust the CO content to 0.7% using the CO adjusting screw (underneath the plug).

13. Stop the engine. Drive in a new plug until it is flush with the intake air sensor. Reconnect the electrical connection at the oxygen sensor. CO content should be 0.3–1.1% with both the oxygen sensor and the idle stabilizer connected.

Idle Speed and Mixture (Fuel Injected Models)

IDLE AND CO ADJUSTMENT

CIS-E 1981–88 – All Models

NOTE: On 1.8 liter CIS engines equipped with a manual preheat valve on the air cleaner housing. The valve is marked S (summer) and W (winter). When servicing, position the valve to S (unless work area is below freezing). After servicing, return valve to the position that matches climate conditions.

NOTE: On Golf and Jetta models, starting in 1985, two versions of the 1.8L "GX" engine are offered. One with CIS-E, the other with CIS and emission controls. If the vehicle is equipped with CIS and emission controls refer to the next following procedure sequence.

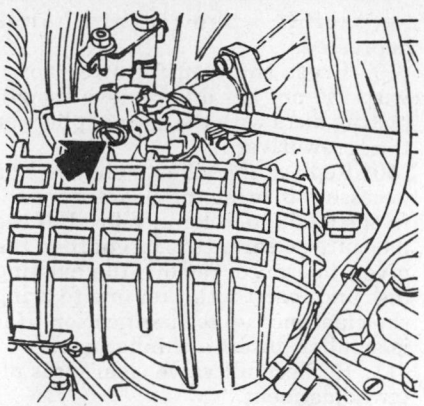

Idle speed adjustment screw—fuel injected Dasher

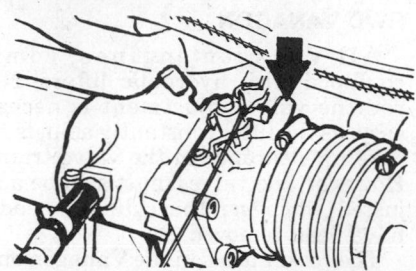

Idle speed adjustment screw—fuel injected Rabbit, Jetta, Scirocco

1. The engine must be at operating temperature.

2. Disconnect the crankcase breather hose at the cylinder head cover and plug the hose on models thru 82. On 1983–88 models, except the 5 cylinder, leave the hose open. Plug the hose on 5 cylinder models.

3. Disconnect the two plugs on the idle stabilizer at the control unit and plug them together.

4. Turn "OFF" the electrical accessories.

NOTE: Only adjust the idle when the radiator fan is not on.

NOTE: On the Quantum, remove the cap from the "T" piece in the charcoal canister vent hose near the right fender. On all others, remove the charcoal canister vent hose at the elbow below the intake boot.

5. Connect a tachometer and timing light. Check the timing. Adjust if necessary.

6. Using adapter hose US-4492, connect a CO meter to the CO test point on the engine.

7. Start the engine, accelerate briefly, check and/or adjust the idle speed and the timing.

8. Remove the air sensor housing plug, insert adjusting tool P377 and adjust the dwell to 38–52 degrees, by turning the mixture adjust screw.

9. Check the CO reading. If it is too high, check for leaks in the intake or

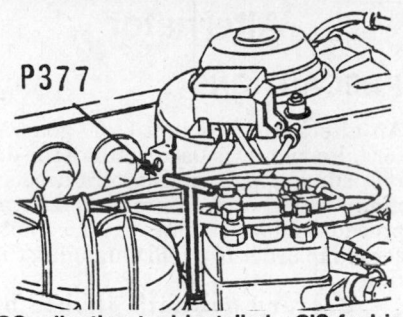

CO adjusting tool installed—CIS fuel injection (Rabbit, Jetta, Scirocco shown)

exhaust systems and malfunctions in the fuel system.

10. Check the idle speed against the specifications chart or your underhood sticker. Adjust the idle at the idle adjustment screw on the throttle chamber (850–1000 rpm).

11. When adjustment is completed, reinstall the removed items and remove the test equipment.

1985–88 — CIS and Emission Controls

1. The following must be checked prior to adjustment: engine oil temperature at normal operating 176° F, radiator fan and A/C off, no exhaust system leaks and oxygen regulation operating.

2. Clamp the idle speed boost hose tightly to prevent flow.

3. Pull the breather hoses from the cylinder head to allow fresh air circulation—hose at intake manifold, hose from air cleaner.

4. Remove the "T" connector from the carbon canister at the intake air boot. Turn the "T" connector 90° and insert blank side with 0.059 in. restrictor into the hole in the intake boot.

5. Connect a suitable duty meter to measure ignition timing and rpm.

6. Start and run engine at idle. Check timing (4–8 ATDC) and idle rpm (under 1000).

7. Adjust as necessary. Timing 6° ATDC. Idle rpm—900.

8. Stop engine and remove the test equipment. Connect all hoses removed.

1986–88 RWD Vanagon

1. Make sure the engine has been run up to operating temperature, all electrical accessories are OFF (including the radiator fan), and the throttle valve switch is in the CLOSED position at idle. The crankcase breather hose should be removed from the oil vent and plugged. Check to see that the idle stabilizer is operating properly; with the ignition turned ON, the valve should vibrate and hum.

2. Connect the tester (VW part No.

VAG 1367 or equivalent) as shown in the accompanying illustartion; using adapter VW 1473, connect the tester VW 1473 or equivalent to the No. 1 terminal of the ignition coil.

3. Connect the CO meter to the left hand exhaust pipe using Sun tool No. 120.239 or equivalent.

4. With the ignition switched OFF, disconnect the oxygen sensor connector and the idle stabilizer control valve connector.

5. Run the engine at idle speed after two minutes and adjust if necessry. Adjust if necessary by turning the adjusting screw (1) on the throttle valve housing. The idle speed should be 880 ± 50 rpm.

6. Check the CO and adjust as necessary. The CO should be 0.3–1.1% If the CO % is above this level use the following procedures.

7. Stop the engine. To adjust the CO, first remove the screw caps. Center punch the plug in the CO adjusting hole. Drill a $\frac{3}{32}$ in. hole in the center of the plug, $\frac{9}{64}$–$\frac{5}{32}$ in. deep, NO MORE. Keep the area clean of metal shavings.

8. Screw a sheet metal screw into the plug and remove the plug using pliers.

9. Start the engine and set the idle speed to 880 ± 50 rpm, and the CO content to 0.7% by alternately turning the adjusting screws to obtain the correct specifications.

10. Reconnect the oxygen sensor connector and the idle stabilizer connector. Let the engine idle for approx. 2 minutes. Check the CO content and correct if necessry by repeating the above procedure.

11. Stop the engine. Drive a new plug until it is flush with the intake air sensor.

Idle Speed Diesel Engine

IDLE SPEED/MAXIMUM SPEED ADJUSTMENTS

All Models

Volkswagen diesel engines have both an idle speed and a maximum speed adjustment. The maximum engine speed adjustment prevents the engine from over-revving and self-destructing. The adjusters are located side by side on top of the injection pump. The screw closest to the engine is the idle speed adjuster, while the outer screw is the maximum speed adjuster.

1. The idle and maximum speed must be adjusted with the engine warm (normal operating temperature).

NOTE: Because the diesel engine has no conventional ignition, you will need a special adaptor (US 1324) to connect your tachometer, or use the tachometer in the instrument panel, if equipped. You should check with the manufacturer of your tachometer to see if it will work with diesel engines.

2. Adjust all engines to the specified idle speed.

3. When adjustment is correct, lock the locknut on the screw and apply non-hardening thread sealer (Loctite or similar) to prevent the screw from vibrating loose.

4. The maximum speed for all engines is between 5300–5400 rpm (1981–88) or 5050–5150 (turbo). If it is not in this range, loosen the screw and correct the speed (turning the screw clockwise decreases rpm).

5. Lock the nut on the adjusting screw and apply a dab of thread sealer in the same manner as you did on the idle screw.

--- CAUTION ---
Do not attempt to squeeze more power out of your engine by raising the maximum speed (rpm). If you do, you'll probably be in for a major overhaul in the not too distant future.

Special adapter VW 1324 is necessary to use an external tachometer on diesel engines

ENGINE ELECTRICAL

Distributor

REMOVAL & INSTALLATION

All Models

1. Take off the vacuum hose(s) at the distributor. Then, disconnect the coil high tension wire.

2. Detach the primary wire. Late

models use a connector plug retained by a spring clip. Unfasten the clip and disconnect the plug. Remove the distributor cap and shield (if equipped).

3. Tag and disconnect any additional wires leading from the distributor. Bring the No. 1 cylinder to top dead center (TDC) on the compression stroke by rotating the engine so that the rotor points to the No. 1 spark plug wire tower on the distributor cap and the timing marks are aligned at 0°. Mark the rotor-to-distributor relationship. Also, matchmark the distributor housing-to-crankcase relationship.

4. Remove the bolt and lift off the retaining flange. Lift the distributor straight out of the engine.

NOTE: If the engine has not been disturbed while the distributor was out i.e., the crankshaft was not turned, then reinstall the distributor in the reverse order of removal. Carefully align the marks.

If the engine has been rotated while the distributor was out, then proceed as follows:

1. Bring the No. 1 cylinder to TDC on the compression stroke and align the timing marks on 0°. Align the matchmarks and insert the distributor into the crankcase. If the matchmarks are gone, have the rotor pointing to the No. 1 spark plug wire tower upon insertion.

2. If the oil pump drive doesn't engage, remove the distributor and using a long screwdriver, turn the pump shaft so that it is parallel to the centerline of the crankshaft.

3. Install the distributor, aligning the marks, and reconnect the condenser and coil wires. Reinstall the distributor cap and tighten the retaining nut.

4. Install the cap. Retime the engine.

Distributor Driveshaft
REMOVAL & INSTALLATION

Vanagon Only

1. Bring the engine to TDC on the compression stroke of No. 1 cylinder. Align the timing marks at 0°.
2. Remove the distributor.
3. Remove the spacer spring from the driveshaft.
4. Grasp the shaft and turn it slowly to the left while withdrawing it from its bore.

On the 1984–88 Vanagon Waterboxer, an extractor with a 0.583–0.782 in. diameter must be screwed ino the driveshaft, in order to remove the shaft.

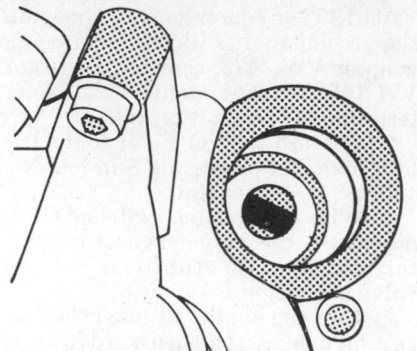
The oil pump drive should be parallel to the crankshaft

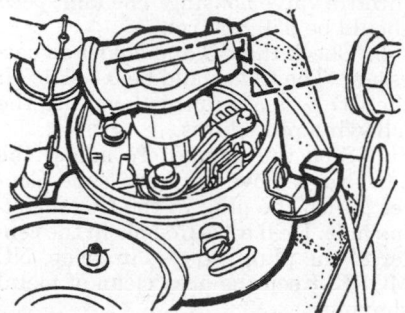
Rotor alignment with the notch for No. 1 cylinder

5. Remove the washer found under the shaft.

— **CAUTION** —
Make sure that this washer does not fall down into the engine.

6. To install, make sure that the engine is at TDC on the compression stroke for No. 1 cylinder with the timing marks aligned at 0°. Make sure the rotor is pointing to the No. 1 cylinder mark on the edge of the distributor housing. If not, turn it until it is.

7. Replace the washer and insert the shaft into its bore.

NOTE: Due to the slant of the teeth on the drive gears, the shaft must be rotated slightly to the left when it is inserted into the crankcase.

8. When the shaft is properly inserted on the air cooled Vanagon 2000 engines, the slot should be about 12° out of parallel with the center line of the engine and the slot offset should be facing outside the engine.

On the 1984–88 Waterboxer, insert the shaft so that the offset slot in the top of the driveshaft is pointing toward the tapped hole in the crankcase. The small-segment points toward the water pump.

9. Reinstall the spacer spring.
10. Reinstall the distributor and fuel pump, if removed.
11. Retime the engine.

Alternator

PRECAUTIONS

An alternating current (AC) generator (alternator) is used. Unlike the direct current (DC) generators used in many older cars, there are several precautions which must be strictly observed in order to avoid damaging the unit.

• Battery polarity should be checked before any connection, such as jumper cables or battery charge leads, are made. Reversing the battery connections will result in damage to the diodes.

• The battery must never be disconnected while the alternator is running.

• Booster batteries should be connected positive to positive and negative to the booster battery and a good ground on the disabled vehicle's engine.

• Never use a fast charger as a booster to start cars with AC circuits; use a "trickle charger."

• When servicing the battery with a charger, always disconnect the car battery cables.

• Never attempt to polarize an AC generator.

• Avoid long soldering times when replacing diodes or transistors. Prolonged heat is damaging to alternators.

• Do not use test lamps of more than 12 volts (V) for checking diode continuity.

• Do not short across or ground any of the terminals on the alternator.

• The polarity of the battery, alternator, and regulator must be matched and considered before making any electrical connections within the system.

• Never operate the alternator on an open circuit. Make sure that all connections within the circuit are clean and tight.

• Disconnect the battery terminals when performing any service on the electrical system. This will eliminate the possibility of accidental reversal of polarity.

• Disconnect the battery ground cable if arc welding is to be done on any part of the car.

REMOVAL & INSTALLATION
FWD Models

The alternator and voltage regulator are combined in one housing. No voltage adjustment can be made with this unit. The regulator can be replaced without removing the alternator. Unbolt the regulator and remove from the rear.

Removing the lower alternator bolt through the timing cover

1. Disconnect the battery cables.
2. Remove the multi-connector retaining bracket and unplug the connector from the rear of the alternator.
3. Loosen and remove the top mounting nut and bolt.
4. Using a socket inserted through the timing belt cover (it is not necessary to remove the cover), loosen the lower mounting bolt.
5. Swing the alternator over and remove the alternator belt.
6. Remove the lower nut and bolt.
7. Remove the alternator.
8. Install the alternator with the lower bolt. Do not tighten it at this point.
9. Install the alternator belt over the pulleys.
10. Loosely install the top mounting bolt and pivot the alternator until the belt is correctly tensioned.
11. Tighten the top and bottom bolts to 14 ft. lbs.
12. Connect the alternator and battery wires.

RWD Vanagon

1. Disconnect the negative battery cable.
2. Disconnect the alternator wiring harness at the voltage regulator (non-integral voltage regulator models) and starter.
3. Pull out the dipstick and remove the oil filler neck.
4. Loosen the alternator adjusting bolt and remove the drive belt.
5. Remove the right rear engine cover plate and the alternator cover plate.
6. Disconnect the warm air duct at the right side, and remove the heat exchanger bracket and connecting pipe from the blower.
7. Disconnect the cool air intake elbow at the alternator. Remove the attaching bolt and lift out the alternator from above.
8. Reverse the above procedure to install, taking care to ensure that the rubber grommet on the intake cover for the wiring harness is installed correctly. After installation, adjust the drive belt so that moderate thumb pressure midway on the belt depresses the belt about ½ in.

Voltage Regulator

REMOVAL & INSTALLATION

NOTE: The voltage regulator is attached to the rear of the alternator. Since no adjustment can be performed on the regulator, it is serviced by replacement ONLY.

FWD Models

1. Remove the 2 mounting screws.
2. Disconnect the electrical connectors and remove the regulator.
3. To install, reverse the removal procedures.

RWD Vanagon

WITH SEPERATE REGULATOR

Disconnect the battery. The regulator is located in the engine compartment and is secured in place by two screws. Take careful note of the wiring connections before removing the wiring from the regulator.

WITH INTERNAL REGULATOR

Later Vanagon models, both air and water-cooled, are equipped with voltage regulators which are built into the alternator. These regulators can be replaced without removing the alternator. To replace the regulator, remove the alternator drive belt and remove the front half of the alternator case. The regulator is the six-sided black component inside.

NOTE: If the voltage regulator is replaced, a supressor condenser must be added (if not already installed) in the alternator. This condenser is noticeable as a rectangular black component mounted above the voltage regualtor in the alternator.

VOLTAGE ADJUSTMENT

Volkswagen voltage regulators are sealed and cannot be adjusted. A malfunctioning regulator must be replaced as a unit.

Starter

REMOVAL & INSTALLATION

FWD Models

WITH BOSCH STARTERS

1. Disconnect the battery ground cable.
2. Raise the front of the vehicle.

NOTE: If equipped with a diesel engine, it may be necessary to install on engine support and remove the right engine mount.

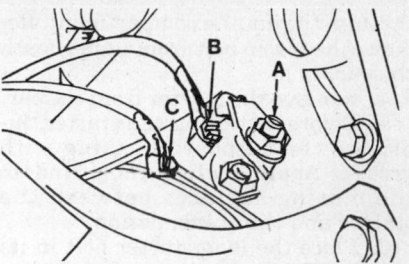

Dasher starter electrical connections: (A) solenoid, (B) coil, (C) positive battery cable

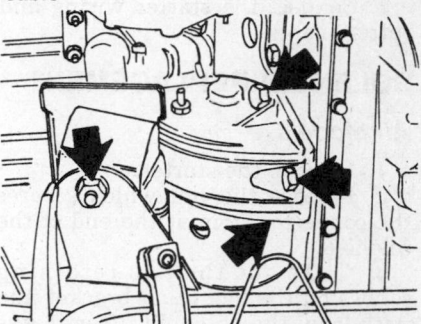

Quantum and Dasher starter removal—remove the engine mount and carrier on the starter side (arrows)

3. Mark with tape and then disconnect the wires from the starter solenoid.
4. Disconnect the large cable.
5. Remove the starter retaining nuts.
6. Unscrew the bolt. Remove the starter.
7. To install, reverse the removal procedures.

WITH MITSUBISHI STARTERS

1. Disconnect the battery ground cable.
2. Support the weight of the engine with either Volkswagen Special Tool 10–222 or use a jack with a block of wood under the oil pan. Don't jack the engine too high, just take the weight off the motor mounts. Be careful not to bend the oil pan.
3. Remove the engine/transmission cover plate.
4. Unbolt and remove the starter side motor mount and carrier.
5. Disconnect and mark the starter wiring.
6. Remove the bolts holding the starter and the starter.
7. To install, reverse the removal procedures. Torque the starter bolts and nuts to 14 ft. lbs.

RWD Vanagon

1. Disconnect the battery.
2. Disconnect the wiring from the starter.
3. The starter is held in place by two bolts. Remove the upper bolt

through the engine compartment. Remove the lower bolt from underneath the car.

4. Remove the starter from the car.

5. Before installing the starter, lubricate the outboard bushing with grease. Apply sealing compound to the mating surfaces between the starter and the transmission.

6. Place the long starter bolt in its hole in the starter and locate the starter on the transmission housing. Install the other bolt.

7. Connect the starter wiring and battery cables.

SOLENOID REPLACEMENT

All Models

1. Remove the starter.

2. Remove the nut which secures the connector strip at the end of the solenoid.

3. Take out the two retaining screws on the mounting bracket and withdraw the solenoid after it has been unhooked from its actuating lever.

4. When replacing a defective solenoid with a new one, care should be taken to see that the distance (a) in the accompanying diagram is 19mm when the magnet is drawn inside the solenoid.

5. Installation is the reverse of removal. In order to facilitate engagement of the actuating rod, the pinion should be pulled out as far as possible when inserting the solenoid.

Diesel Glow Plugs

GLOW PLUG SYSTEM CHECK

All Models

NOTE: The 1982–88 diesels, except turbocharged models, have a new type quick-glow system. Nominal glow time is seven seconds. Although the wiring for this system is the same as the earlier system, the glow plugs and relay cannot be paired or interchanged with earlier parts or vice versa.

1. Connect a test light between, No.4 cylinder glow plug and ground. The glow plugs are connected by a flat, coated busbar (located near the bottom of the cylinder head).

2. Turn the ignition key to the heating (pre-glow) position. The test light should light.

3. If not, possible problems include the glow plug relay, the ignition switch and the fuse box relay plate and the glow plug fuse or a break in the wire to the relay terminal.

INDIVIDUAL GLOW PLUG TEST

1. Remove the wire and busbar from the glow plugs.

2. Connect a test light to the battery positive terminal.

3. Touch the test light probe to each glow plug in turn. If the test light lights, the plug is good. If the light does not light, replace the glow plug(s).

GASOLINE ENGINE MECHANICAL

Engine

REMOVAL & INSTALLATION

1981–84 FWD Models—Except Dasher and Quantum

The engine and transmission assembly is to be lowered from the vehicle. If the vehicle is carbureted, simply remove any hoses or wiring from the carburetor, which will interfere with the engine removal procedures; ignore any procedures relating to the fuel injection system.

NOTE: If equipped with A/C, turn "ON" the ignition and the A/C control (engine stopped), remove the compressor clutch bolt, press the clutch from the A/C compressor shaft (using a ⅝ in. × 18 UNF bolt), turn "OFF" the ignition and the A/C, then disconnect the compressor clutch wire.

1. Disconnect the negative battery cable.

2. Remove the fuel tank cap to relieve the pressure on the fuel system.

NOTE: If equipped with an automatic transmission, place the selector lever in the "PARK" position and disconnect the positive battery cable.

3. Remove the air intake duct between the fuel distributor and the throttle housing.

4. Remove the radiator cap. Turn the heater temperature control valve to fully OPEN. Place a container under the thermostat housing, remove the thermostat flange and drain the coolant.

5. Remove the upper radiator and heater hoses from the engine. Remove

the electrical connector from the radiator fan motor, the radiator mounting nuts, the upper radiator clamp clip, the clamp and the radiator.

6. Remove the electrical connectors from the alternator, the thermoswitch, the oil pressure switch, the warm-up regulator and the distributor condenser wire.

NOTE: If equipped with A/C, turn the drive belt tensioner with an open end wrench until a 10mm Allen wrench can be inserted into the socket head bolts. Remove the tensioner bolts and the tensioner. Remove the alternator, the timing belt cover and the compressor mounting bracket bolts (under the timing cover) and the preheat hose. Remove the diagonal braces, the support brace, the compressor and the bracket, then move the compressor aside; DO NOT disconnect the refrigerant hoses.

7. Remove the pre-heat tube from the rear of the engine.

8. Remove the distributor vacuum hoses and the EGR temperature valve.

9. Remove the coil and the coolant temperature sensor wires.

—— CAUTION ——

Be careful when disconnecting the fuel system, for the fuel may still be under pressure.

10. Place a container (to catch the fuel) under the cold start valve, then remove the fuel line and the warm-up regulator.

11. Remove the electrical connectors from the cold start valve and the auxiliary air regulator.

12. At the throttle body, remove the vacuum lines of the brake booster and the vacuum amplifier (if equipped).

13. Remove the PCV hose from the cylinder head cover.

14. At the throttle body. pull back the accelerator cable clip and discon-

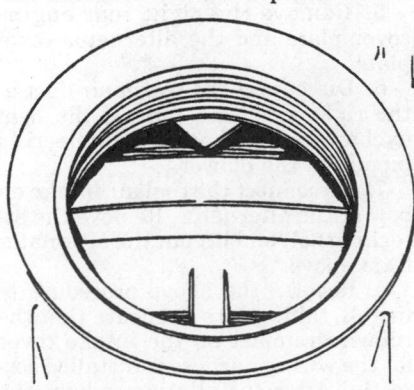

Aligning flywheel for manual transmission and engine separation—Rabbit, Jetta, Scirocco

nect the cable from the ball. Loosen the accelerator cable locknut and remove the cable from the cylinder head cover.

15. Remove the fuel injectors, then position the entire assembly aside.

16. Disconnect the electrical connectors from the starter, the back-up light switch and the ground cable from the transmission.

17. If equipped with a manual transmission, at the clutch cable, loosen the locknut, remove the clip from under the clutch lever and the cable. If equipped with an automatic transmission, disconnect the selector cable from the transmission and the bracket.

18. Remove the speedometer cable clamp and the cable.

19. Remove the upper starter bolts and the starter.

20. Remove the nuts from the exhaust flex-pipe and the relay shaft. Disconnect the lever from the relay shaft.

21. Remove the driveshafts from the mounting flanges.

22. Remove the horn (move aside), the front mounts cup bolts, the cup and the front mount.

23. At both front wheels, remove the axle nuts.

24. At both steering knuckles, remove the ball joint lock bolts. Using a large pry bar, pry the ball joints from the bearing housings.

25. Swing the wheel and strut assembly away from the vehicle, then remove the drive axles from the wheel hubs.

NOTE: With the driveshafts removed, reconnect the ball joints and lock bolts so that the vehicle may be lowered on its wheels.

26. Remove the transmission-to-crossmember mounting nuts and the right front wheel and tire assembly.

27. Attach an engine sling tool US–1105 to the engine and using an overhead crane, lift the engine slightly.

28. Remove the clip from the gearshift lever rod, the rod from the selector shaft lever and the relay shaft with the gearshift lever rod. Open the clip on the front of the selector rod and remove the rod from the relay lever.

29. Remove the right and left side engine mount-to-body bolts.

30. Lower the engine and transmission assembly onto a dolly.

31. Raise the vehicle and slide the engine and transmission assembly clear of the vehicle.

32. To install, reverse the removal procedures. Torque the ball joint-to-steering knuckle to 36 ft. lbs. (49 Nm), the drive axle nut to 174 ft. lbs. (236 Nm), the driveshaft flange-to-transmission to 30 ft. lbs. (41 Nm), the

starter bolts to 33 ft. lbs. (45 Nm) for 10mm or 54 ft. lbs. (73 Nm) for 12mm and the thermostat flange to 7 ft. lbs. (9 Nm). Refill the cooling system.

1985–88 – Except Dasher, Fox and Quantum

NOTE: The engine and transmission assembly is lifted out of the vehicle.

1. Disconnect the battery cables and remove the battery.

2. Remove the fuel tank cap to relieve the pressure on the fuel system.

NOTE: If equipped with an automatic transmission, place the selector lever in the "PARK" position.

3. Remove the air intake duct between the fuel distributor and the throttle housing.

4. Remove the radiator cap. Turn the heater temperature control valve to fully OPEN. Place a container under the thermostat housing, remove the thermostat flange and drain the coolant.

5. Remove the upper radiator and heater hoses from the engine. Remove the electrical connector from the radiator fan motor, the radiator mounting nuts, the upper radiator clamp clip, the clamp, the shroud and the radiator.

6. At the front of the vehicle, remove the apron, the trim and the grille. Disconnect the headlight electrical connectors and the hood release cable from the hood latch.

NOTE: If equipped with power steering, remove the drive belt, the mounting bolts, the pump and the fluid reservoir, then suspend it from the crossmember with a wire.

7. Remove the electrical connectors from the alternator, the thermoswitch, the oil pressure switch, the warm-up regulator and the distributor condenser wire.

NOTE: If equipped with A/C, remove the trim panel, the lower apron, the condenser and duct work from the crossmember and radiator, the idle boost valve vacuum hose, the air filter assembly, the air flow assembly and the compressor, then move it aside.

8. Remove the pre-heat tube from the rear of the engine.

9. Remove the distributor vacuum hoses and the EGR temperature valve.

10. Remove the coil (secondary), the coolant temperature sensor, the Lambda sensor and the knock sensor (if equipped) wires.

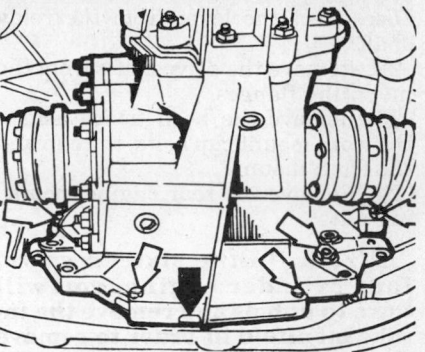

Remove the lower engine/transmission bolts and flywheel cover (arrows)

— **CAUTION** —

Be careful when disconnecting the fuel system, for the fuel may still be under pressure.

11. Place a container (to catch the fuel) under the cold start valve, then remove the fuel line and the warm-up regulator.

12. Remove the electrical connectors from the cold start valve and the auxiliary air regulator.

13. At the throttle body, remove the vacuum lines of the brake booster, the vacuum amplifier and the vacuum amplifier (if equipped).

14. Remove the PCV hose from the cylinder head cover.

15. At the throttle body, pull back the accelerator cable clip and disconnect the cable from the ball. Loosen the accelerator cable locknut and remove the cable from the cylinder head cover.

16. Remove the fuel injectors, then position the entire assembly aside.

17. Disconnect the electrical connectors from the starter, the back-up light switch and the ground cable from the transmission.

18. If equipped with a manual transmission, at the clutch cable, loosen the locknut, remove the clip from under the clutch lever and the cable. If equipped with an automatic transmission, disconnect the selector cable from the transmission and the bracket.

19. Remove the speedometer cable clamp and the cable. Remove the upper starter bolts and the starter.

20. If equipped with a manual transmission, remove the transmission and upshift indicator vacuum switches. If equipped with an automatic transmission, remove the CIS-E wiring harness.

NOTE: On the GTI/GLI models, remove the idle stabilizer control valve, the throttle plate switch and the knock sensor.

21. Remove the nuts from the exhaust flex-pipe and the relay shaft.

Disconnect the lever from the relay shaft.

22. Remove the driveshafts from the mounting flanges.

23. Remove the horn (move aside), the front mount cup bolts, the cup and the front mount.

24. Remove the rear engine mounting nuts.

NOTE: On the sixteen valve, four cylinder engine, you will have to unbolt and remove the intake manifold in order to remove the engine.

25. Attach an engine sling tool US–1105 to the engine. Then, using an overhead crane, lift the engine slightly.

26. Remove the clip from the gearshift lever rod, the rod from the selector shaft lever and the relay shaft with the gearshift lever rod. Open the

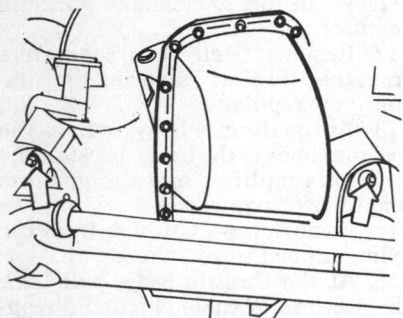

Quantum, Dasher engine side mounts

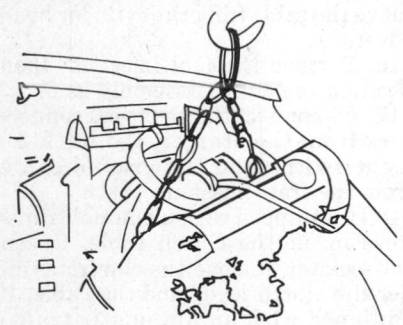

Lifting the Quantum and Dasher engine out of the car. Note that it must be turned for removal

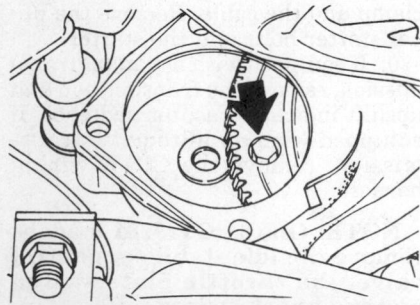

On automatic transmissions, remove three torque converter-to-flywheel bolts through the starter hole (Quantum and Dasher)

clip on the front of the selector rod and remove the rod from the relay lever.

27. Remove the right and left side engine mount-to-body bolts.

28. Slightly lower and tilt the engine and transmission, then lift the engine/transmission assembly, turning slightly at the same time, carefully out of the car.

29. To install, reverse the removal procedures. Torque the ball joint-to-steering knuckle to 36 ft. lbs. (49 Nm), the drive axle nut to 174 ft. lbs. (236 Nm), the driveshaft flange-to-transmission to 30 ft. lbs. (41 Nm), the starter bolts to 33 ft. lbs. (45 Nm), the transmission-to-body mount to 33 ft. lbs. (41 Nm) for 10mm or 54 ft. lbs. (73 Nm) for 12mm, the power steering bolts to 14 ft. lbs. (19 Nm) and the thermostat flange to 7 ft. lbs. (9 Nm). Refill the cooling system.

4 Cylinder—Dasher and Quantum

1. Disconnect the negative battery cable.

2. Set the heater control to full OPEN, remove the radiator cap and drain the cooling system. Remove the radiator hoses from the engine.

3. Remove the power steering mounting bolts, the drive belt and move the pump aside, leaving the hoses attached.

4. Disconnect the electrical connectors from the thermo-time switch, the alternator and the control pressure regulator.

5. Disconnect the distributor vacuum hoses from the distributor.

6. Remove the control pressure regulator bolts and move the regulator aside, with the fuel lines attached.

7. Disconnect the radiator fan wires. Remove the radiator bolts and the radiator assembly with the air duct.

8. Remove the clip on the clutch cable and disconnect the cable.

9. Remove the left engine mount nut.

10. Disconnect the coolant temperature sender wire from the engine, oxygen sensor thermo-switch, the Hall sending unit wire and the coil wire from the distributor.

11. Disconnect the electrical connectors from the auxiliary air regulator, the cold start and the frequency valves.

12. Remove the emissions canister hose from the air duct.

13. Remove the preheater hose and the cold start valve (leave the fuel line attached).

14. Disconnect the distributor vacuum hose from the intake manifold. Remove the accelerator cable, the crankcase breather hose and the brake booster hose.

CAUTION

BE CAREFUL when disconnecting the fuel system, for the system may be under pressure.

15. Remove the fuel injectors (protect them with caps), the fuel distributor (leave the lines attached) and move them aside.

NOTE: If equipped with A/C, remove the throttle body housing, the auxiliary air regulator, the horn bracket, the crankcase pulley nuts, the drive belt, the compressor bracket bolts, the compressor and the condenser. Place and tie the compressor and the condenser aside, so that the hoses are not under pressure.

16. Remove the right engine mount nuts.

17. Remove the exhaust pipe at the manifold.

18. Remove the starter wiring and the starter. Remove the lower engine-to-transmission bolts and the flywheel cover plate.

19. If equipped with an automatic transmission, remove the torque converter-to-drive plate bolts. Attach the engine support tool VW 785/1B or equivalent to the transmission and support it.

20. Loosen the nuts on the outer half of the damper pulley and remove the drive belt.

21. Remove the A/C compressor bracket mounting bolts and move the compressor aside (with the lines attached).

22. Attach the engine sling US-1105 or equivalent to the engine, support it with a vertical hoist and lift the engine slightly, then remove the right engine mount.

23. Remove the upper engine-to-transmission bolts, separate the engine from the transmission, lift and turn the engine to remove it from the vehicle.

NOTE: If equipped with an automatic transmission, secure the torque converter to the transmission to keep it from falling out.

24. To install, reverse the removal procedures. Torque the transmission-to-engine bolts to 40 ft. lbs. (54 Nm), the engine mount bolts to 25 ft. lbs. (34 Nm), the exhaust pipe-to-exhaust manifold to 18 ft. lbs. (24 Nm), the starter bolts to 14 ft. lbs. (19 Nm), the torque converter-to-drive plate bolts to 22 ft. lbs. (30 Nm), the torque support bolts to 18 ft. lbs. (24 Nm), the power steering pump bolts to 14 ft. lbs. (19 Nm) and the A/C compressor lower bolts to 18 ft. lbs. (24 Nm) or the upper bolts 22 ft. lbs. (30 Nm). Adjust

the belt tension to ⅜ in. deflection and refill the cooling system.

5 Cylinder—Quantum

1. Disconnect the negative battery cable.
2. Move the heater control valve to fully "OPEN" and remove the radiator cap.
3. At the power steering pump, remove the drive belt cover, the drive belt, the mounting bolts and the pump; move the pump aside with the hoses connected.
4. Remove the grille and the radiator cover.
5. Remove the lower radiator hose and drain the coolant.
6. Remove the front bumper with the energy absorber.
7. Remove the vacuum hoses from the intake manifold, the upper radiator hose, the radiator hose from the thermostat housing and the heater hose (drain the remaining coolant).
8. Disconnect the electrical connectors from the oil pressure switch, the control pressure regulator and the thermo-time switches, then move aside.
9. Remove the cylinder head cover ground wire.
10. Remove the control pressure regulator (leave the lines attached) and the ball joint circlip (disconnect it at the push rod).
11. Remove the alternator drive belt, the bracket bolts and the alternator assembly, then hang with a wire (leave the wires attached).
12. Remove the air duct and the front engine stop.
13. Disconnect the electrical connectors from the cold start valve, the frequency valve, the throttle switch, the idle stabilizer valve, the Hall sender at the distributor and the oxygen sensor.
14. Remove the accelerator cable circlip and disconnect the cable rod from the throttle body.
15. Remove the distributor cap, the cold start valve and the vacuum hose from the thermopneumatic valve.
16. Remove the fuel injection cooling hose.
17. Remove the fuel injectors from the intake manifold; leave the fuel lines connected.

NOTE: When removing the fuel injectors and the cold start valve, place caps on the ends to protect them from damage.

18. Remove the air filter housing bolts and the filter.

NOTE: If equipped with an automatic transmission, disconnect the oil cooler hoses.

19. Remove the heater hoses. Remove the exhaust pipe bracket from the engine and transmission assembly.

NOTE: If equipped with A/C, remove the drive belt, the electrical connector at the compressor, the compressor bracket-to-engine bolts and the compressor assembly, then move it aside and support it on a wire. DO NOT support the compressor with the hoses under tension.

20. Attach the supporting tool 2084 to the crankshaft pulley and remove the crankshaft bolt.
21. Of the 4 crankshaft pulley bolts, remove 2 and loosen 2. To loosen the pulley, tap lightly on the remaining bolts. Remove the bolts and the pulley

NOTE: When removing the pulley from the crankshaft, leave the drive belt sprocket attached to the crankshaft.

22. Remove the front engine mount and the subframe-to-body bolts. Remove the exhaust pipe from the exhaust manifold and the support bracket.
23. Disconnect the starter cables and the starter.
24. Remove the torque converter-to-drive plate bolts and the lower engine-to transmission bolts. Unhook the shift rod clip and disconnect the rod.
25. Remove the rubber plugs from the left side frame member. Using the support tool VW 785/1, connect it to the transmission and to the frame member, then adjust to make contact with the transmission.
26. Remove both engine mount nuts and the upper engine-to-transmission bolts (leave 1 bolt in place).
27. Attach the engine support tool US 1105 and the lift tool 9019 to the engine.

NOTE: If equipped with an auto. trans., secure the torque converter before removing the engine from the transmission.

28. Remove the last engine-to-transmisssion bolt and lift the engine, while prying the engine apart from the transmission. Remove the engine from the vehicle.
29. To install, reverse the removal procedures. Torque the transmission-to-engine bolts to 22 ft. lbs. (30 Nm) for 8mm, 32 ft. lbs. (43 Nm) for 10mm or 43 ft. lbs. (58 Nm) for 12mm, the engine mount bolts to 32 ft. lbs. (43 Nm), the exhaust pipe-to-manifold bolts to 22 ft. lbs. (30 Nm), the subframe-to-body bolts 51 ft. lbs. (69

Nm), the torque converter-to-drive plate bolts to 22 ft. lbs. (30 Nm), the front engine stop bolts to 32 ft. lbs. (43 Nm), the damper pulley center bolt to 253 ft. lbs. (343 Nm), the crankshaft pulley bolts to 14 ft. lbs. (19 Nm), the power steering pump bolts to 14 ft. lbs. (19 Nm) and the A/C compressor bolts to 29 ft. lbs. (39 Nm). Adjust the belt tension and refill the cooling system.

NOTE: When installing the crankshaft pulley, align the match mark on the sprocket with the mark on the pulley. When installing the crankshaft bolt, lubricate the threads with Loctite® 573 or equivalent. When installing the engine, shake the engine into position (this will allow the engine to seat properly).

Fox

NOTE: The engine is lifted out of the vehicle after seperation from the transmission.

1. Disconnect the battery ground cable and remove the battery.
2. Open the heating valve and the cap on the coolant expansion tank. Drain the coolant by removing the hoses. Then seperate the electrical connector from the radiator fan.

——— **CAUTION** ———

CAUTION: Do not disconnect or loosen any refrigerant hose connections during engine removal on cars equipped with air conditioning.

3. On cars equipped with air conditioning:
   a. Loosen the compressor support bolts and remove the compressor.
   b. Remove the radiator cooling fan, air ducts and radiator.
   c. Remove the condenser.
   d. Place the air conditioning compressor and condenser out of the way without disconnecting any refrigerant lines.
4. Disconnect the radiator thermo switch and remove the radiator cover. Disconnect the motor mount and remove the rubber bushing. Remove the radiator with the air ducts and fan.
5. Detach and label all the electrical wires connecting the engine to the body.
6. Disconnect and plug the fuel line at the fuel pump. Detach the coolant hoses at the left end of the engine. Disconnect the accelerator cable and remove the air cleaner.
7. Disconnect the speedometer cable from the transmission. Detach the clutch cable.
8. Remove the vacuum hoses. Remove the wire from the ignition coil, the vacuum unit hose, and the plug

for the Hall system from the distributor.

9. Remove the fuel injectors and install protective caps and plugs.

10. Remove the cold start valve leaving the fuel line connected.

11. Loosen the charcoal filter clamp and move the filter to the rear of the engine compartment.

12. Remove the upper engine to transmission bolts.

13. Remove the left and right engine mounting bolts.

14. Remove the engine stop and the air duct from the intake manifold.

15. Disconnect and lable the starter cables. Then remove the starter mounting bolts and the starter.

16. Remove the two lower engine to transmission bolts. Then remove the cover plate bolts and the cover plate.

17. Disconnect the exhaust pipe from the manifold at the flange. Then remove the bolt from the exhaust pipe support and remove the exhaust pipe from the manifold.

18. Install transmission support bar (VW 758/1) with slight preload.

19. Install chain (US 1105) on the engine lifting eyes, located on the left side of the cylinder head.

20. Lift the engine until its weight is taken off the engine mounts.

21. Adjust the support bar to contact the transmission.

22. Seperate the engine and transmission.

23. Carefully lift the engine out of the engine compartment so as not to damage the transmission main shaft, clutch and body.

To install: Proceed in the reverse order of removal and note the following.

24. Lubricate the clutch release bearing and transmission main shaft splines with MoS_2 grease or an equvalent. Do Not lubricate the guide sleeve for the clutch release bearing.

25. Carefully guide the engine into the vehicle and attach to the transmission while keeping weight off of the motor mounts.

26. Install and tighten the upper engine to transmission bolts.

27. Remove the transmission support bar and lower the engine onto the engine mounts.

28. Reconnect and tighten the starter cables, being carefull not to let the cables touch the engine, causing a short circuit and possibly a fire.

29. The remainder of the engines installation is the reverse of the removal procedure.

NOTE: Tighten the engine mounts and subframe bolts with the engine running at idle speed.

30. Torque the cold start valve, the radiator mount bolts, and the engine to transmission cover plate bolts to 7 ft. lbs.

31. Torque the engine to transmission bolts to 42 ft. lbs., the engine mount bolts to 26 ft. lbs., the engine stop to body bolck and exhaust pipe support bolts to 18 ft. lbs., the exhaust pipe to manifold bolts to 22 ft. lbs. and the starter bolts to 15 ft. lbs.

Air-Cooled RWD Vanagon

The Volkswagen engine is mounted on the transmission, which in turn is attached to the frame. There are two bolts and two studs attaching the engine to the transmission.

When removing the engine from the car, it is recommended that the rear of the car be about 3 ft. off the ground. Remove the engine by bringing it out from underneath the car. Proceed with the following steps to remove the engine.

1. Disconnect the battery ground cable.

2. Disconnect the generator wiring.

3. Remove the air cleaner.

4. Disconnect the throttle cable and remove the electrical connections to the automatic choke, coil, electromagnetic cutoff jet, and the oil pressure sending unit.

5. Disconnect the fuel hose at the front engine cover plate and seal it to prevent leakage.

6. Raise the car and support it with jack stands.

7. Remove the flexible air hoses between the engine and heat exchangers, disconnect the heater flap cables, unscrew the two lower engine mounting nuts, and slide a jack under the engine. Remove the two bolts from the rubber engine mounts located next to the muffler.

8. On all automatic models, remove the four bolts from the converter drive plate through the holes in the transmission case. After the engine is removed, hold the torque converter on the transmission input shaft by using a strap bolted to the bellhousing.

9. Raise the jack until it just contacts the engine and have an assistnat hold the two upper mounting bolts so that the nuts can be removed from the bottom.

10. When the engine mounts are disconnected and there are no remaining cables or wires left to be disconnected, move the engine toward the back of the car so that the clutch or converter plate disengages from the transmission.

11. Lower the engine out of the car.

12. Installation is the reverse of the above. When the engine is lifted into position, it should be rotated using the generator pulley so that the clutch plate hub will engage the transmission shaft splines. Tighten the upper mounting bolts first. Check the clutch, pressure plate, throwout bearing, and pilot bearing for wear.

1984–88 RWD Vanagon Waterboxer

1. Disconnect the battery ground cable.

2. Remove the air cleaner from the air flow sensor and the air intake duct.

3. Tag and disconnect the alterntor wire at the alternator.

4. Tag and disconnect the plugs at the fuel injectors, the plug at the throttle valve switch, and the plug at the auxiliary air regulator.

5. Disconnect the hoses at the charcoal filter valve.

6. Tag and disconnect the fuel hoses near the distributor. Remove the accelerator cable from the throttle valve lever. On automatic transmission models, remove the circlip and spring from the accelerator rod.

7. Tag and disconnect the plug at the oxygen sensor, the plugs at the distributor, oil pressure switch, temperature sensor, temperature sender, and coolant level warning switch (located at the coolant expsansion tank).

8. Block the coolant hoses with clamps and open the coolant expansion tank cap. Remove the drain plugs at the cylinder heads and drain the coolant.

NOTE: Always replace the sealing rings underneath the drain plugs during installation.

9. Disconnect the brake booster line, and disconnect all coolant hoses. Remove the coolant expansion tank.

10. Remove the engine-to-transaxle bolts and nuts on the left and right sides.

11. On automatic transmission models, remove the three bolts which attach the torque converter to the drive plate through the hole on the top of the transaxle housing.

12. Disconnect the starter wiring.

13. On automatic transmission models, disconnect the accelerator rod.

14. Jack up the vehicle (if not already done) and safely support it with jackstands, raising the vehicle high enough that the engine can be lowered out from underneath.

——— CAUTION ———

The safe support of the rear end of the vehicle in this procedure is crucial.

15. Remove the engine plates from underneath.

16. Loosen the transmission mounting bolt.

17. Support the underside of the engine with a transmission jack, making sure there is a wooden block or pad between the jack and engine.

18. Remove the engine carrier bolts. Carefully lower the engine/transaxle assembly slightly. Keep the wiring harness aside so that it can pass the oil filler tube. Lower the assembly more so that you have access to the lower engine mounting bolts. Remove the engine from the transaxle and lower it out of the vehicle. Mount the engine on an engine stand for service.

19. To install, reverse the above procedure and note the following:

a. Replace all self-locking nuts on the engine mounts during reassembly.

b. Check the clutch release bearing for wear and replace if necessary.

c. Lube the clutch release bearing and main shaft splines lightly with a molybdenum disulfide grease. DO NOT lube the guide sleeve for the release bearing.

d. Check and adjust the accelerator cable and throttle controls.

e. Use the following torque specifications for installation: Engine-to-transmission, 22 ft. lbs.; engine carrier-to-body, 18 ft. lbs., transmission mounts 22 ft. lbs.; torque converter-to-drive plate 14 ft. lbs.

f. Refill the cooling system, following the "Cooling System Refill" later in this section.

Cylinder Head

REMOVAL & INSTALLATION

FWD Models

NOTE: The engine should be cold before the cylinder head can be removed. The 4 cyl. engine head is retained by 10 head bolts and the 5 cyl. engine uses 12 head bolts.

─────── CAUTION ───────

Do not disconnect or loosen any refrigerant hose connections during cylinder head removal.

────────────────────

CARBURETED ENGINES

1. Disconnect the battery ground cable.
2. Drain the cooling system.
3. Remove the air cleaner. Disconnect the fuel line.
4. Disconnect the radiator, heater, and choke hoses.
5. Disconnect all electrical wires. Remove the spark plug wires.
6. Separate the exhaust manifold from the exhaust pipe.
7. Disconnect the EGR line from

the exhaust manifold. Remove the EGR valve and filter from the intake manifold.

8. Remove the carburetor.
9. Disconnect the air pump fittings.
10. Remove the timing belt cover and belt.
11. Loosen the cylinder head bolts in the reverse of the tightening sequence.
12. Remove the bolts and lift the head straight off.
13. Install the new cylinder head gasket with the word TOP or OBEN up.
14. Install bolts No. 10 and 8 first; these holes are smaller and will properly locate the gasket and cylinder head.
15. Install the remaining bolts. Tighten them in stages in the sequence shown in the illustration. Refer to the "Torque Specifications" chart for specific tightening instructions.
16. To complete the installation, reverse the removal procedures.

FUEL INJECTED ENGINES

1. Disconnect the battery ground cable.
2. Drain the cooling system.
3. Disconnect the air duct from the throttle valve assembly.
4. Disconnect the throttle valve assembly.
5. Remove the injectors and disconnect the line from the cold start valve.
6. Disconnect the radiator and heater hoses.
7. Disconnect the vacuum and PCV lines (label lines for installation).
8. Remove the auxiliary air regulator from the intake manifold.
9. Disconnect all electrical lines and remove the spark plugs (label all lines and wires for installation).
10. Separate the exhaust manifold from the exhaust pipe.
11. Remove the EGR line from the exhaust manifold.
12. Remove the intake manifold.
13. Remove the timing belt cover and belt.
14. Loosen the cylinder head bolts in the reverse of the tightening sequence.
15. Remove the bolts and lift the head straight off.

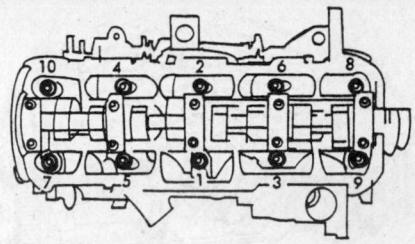

Cylinder head tightening sequence—4 cylinder engines

16. Check the flatness of the cylinder block in both width and length, then diagonally from each corner.
17. Install the new cylinder head gasket with the word TOP or OBEN facing upward.
18. Install bolts No. 10 and 8 first. These holes are smaller and will properly locate the gasket and cylinder head.
19. Install the remaining bolts. Torque the bolts in sequence in 3 steps: 29 ft. lbs., (39 Nm) 44 ft. lbs. (60 Nm) and an additional ½ turn.

NOTE: Polygon (12 point) head bolts are torqued cold. Torque in sequence to 54 ft. lbs. (73 Nm) and an additional ¼ turn.

20. To complete the installation, reverse the removal procedures.

Cylinder head gaskets for the 1.8 liter engine have two breather holes and larger bore dimension

RWD Vanagon

AIR-COOLED ENGINE

In order to remove the cylinder head from either pair of cylinders, it is necessary to lower the engine.

1. Remove the valve cover and gasket. Remove the rocker arm assembly. Unbolt the intake manifold from the cylinder head. The cylinder head is held in place by eight studs. Since the cylinder head also holds the cylinders in place in the VW engine, and the cylinders are not going to be re-

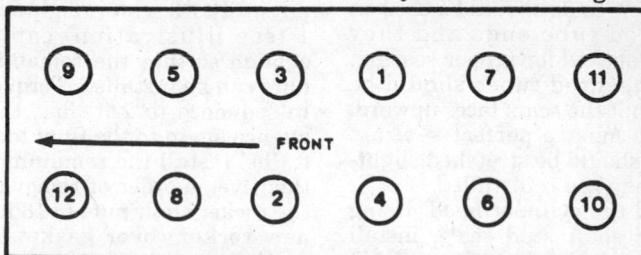

Cylinder head tightening sequence—5 cylinder engines

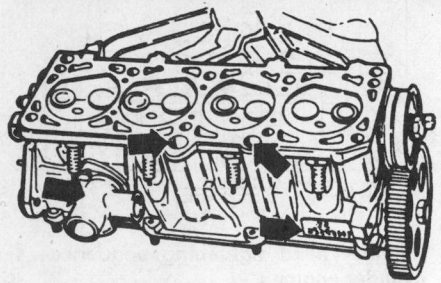

Cylinder heads for 1.8 liter engines can be identified by two breather holes on the gasket surface, the hose connection between Nos. 3 and 4 cylinder and a casting number above No.1 plug location

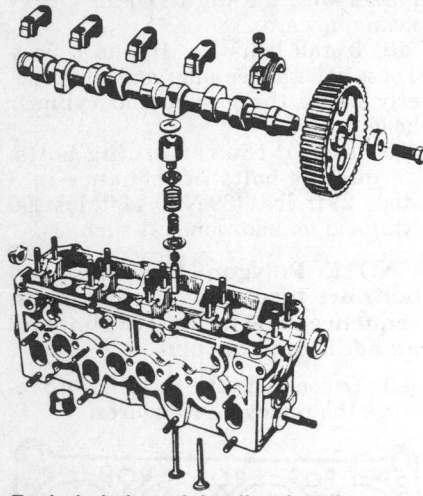

Exploded view of the diesel engine cylinder head. Note tapered camshaft nose. Gasoline engine has a blunt camshaft nose and key– located drive sprocket

moved it will be necessary to hold the cylinders in place after the head is removed.

2. After the rocker arm cover, rocker arm retaining nuts, and rocker arm assembly have been removed, the cylinder head nuts can be removed and the cylinder head lifted off.

3. When reinstalling the cylinder head, the head should be checked for cracks both in the combustion chamber and in the intake and exhaust ports. Cracked heads must be replaced.

4. Spark plug threads should be checked. New seals should be used on the pushrod tube ends and they should be checked for proper seating.

5. The pushrod tubes should be turned so that the seam faces upward. In order to ensure perfect sealing, used tubes should be stretched slightly before they are reinstalled.

6. Install the cylinder head. Using new rocker shaft stud seals, install the pushrods and rocker shaft assembly.

NOTE: Pay careful attention to the orientation of the shaft as described in the "Rocker Shaft" section.

7. Torque the cylinder head in three stages. Adjust the valve clearance. Using a new gasket, install the rocker cover. It may be necessry to readjust the valves after the engine has been run a few minutes and allowed to cool.

WATERBOXER ENGINE

On the Waterboxer, it is not necessary to remove or lower the engine to remove the cylinder heads. Either head can be removed and installed while the engine is in place in the vehicle.

1. Drain the coolant from the cooling system using the coolant drain plugs on the bottom of each cylinder head.

NOTE: When installing the drain plugs, always use new sealing rings underneath the plugs.

2. Follow Steps 1 and 2 of "Air Cooled Cylinder Head" removal and installation.

3. Before installing the head, make sure all gasket contact areas are completely clean and free of any damage. Always replace the head gasket, applying a thin bead (1–2mm) of sealing compound D 000 400 (VW part No. or equivalent) to the gasket surface facing the cylinder head. Do not use too much, as excess sealant could plug cylinder head coolant passages.

4. The pushrod tubes should be installed so that the small end faces the cylinder head, and so that the seam on the tube is facing upward. Guide the tubes into the hydraulic lifter holes carefully. Always replace the sealing rings.

NOTE: If the pushrod tube rests on the edge of the valve lifter, the basic valve setting will be incorrect and the lifter(s) will be damaged when the engine is started.

5. Install the cylinder head, using a new gasket and sealer as mentioned above. Coat the cyulinder head cap nuts with D3 sealer. Tighten Stud No. 1 (see illustration) cap nut just enough so that the remaining 7 cap nuts can be installed. Torque all nuts in sequence to 7 ft. lbs., then in sequence again to the final torque of 25 ft. lbs. Install the remaining parts in the reverse order of removal. Torque the rocker shaft nuts to 18 ft. lbs. Use new rocker cover gaskets. Fill the cooling system, following "Cooling System Filling" later in this section.

OVERHAUL

For all cylinder head overhaul procedures, please refer to "Engine Rebuilding" in the Unit Repair section.

Rocker Shafts
REMOVAL & INSTALLATION

Vanagon Only

1. Before the valve rocker assembly can be reached, it is necessary to lever off the clip that retains the valve cover and then remove the valve cover.

2. Remove the rocker arm retaining nuts, the rocker arm shaft, and the rocker arms. Remove the stud seals.

3. Before installing the rocker arm mechanism, be sure that the parts are as clean as possible.

4. Install new stud seals. On the air-cooled Vanagon models, the chamfered edges must point outward and the slots must face downward and the pushrod tube retaining wire must engage the slots in the rocker arm shaft supports as well as the grooves in the pushrod tubes. On the Vanagon Waterboxer, the slot on the rocker shaft support faces upward.

5. Tighten the retaining nuts to the proper torque. Use only the copper colored nuts that were supplied with the engine.

6. Make sure that the ball ends of the pushrods are centered in the sockets of the rocker arms.

7. Adjust the valve clearance. Install the valve cover using a new gasket.

Intake Manifold
REMOVAL & INSTALLATION

FWD Models
CARBURETED ENGINES

1. Remove the air cleaner. Drain the cooling system.

2. Disconnect the accelerator cable.

3. Disconnect the EGR valve connections.

4. Detach all electrical leads.

5. Disconnect the coolant hoses.

6. Disconnect the fuel line from the carburetor.

7. Remove the vacuum hoses from the carburetor.

8. Loosen and remove the retaining bolts and lift off the manifold.

9. Install a new gasket. Install the manifold and tighten the bolts from the inside out. Tightening torque is 18 ft. lbs. (24 Nm).

10. Install the remaining components in the reverse order of removal. Refill the cooling system.

FUEL INJECTED ENGINES

1. Disconnect the air duct from the throttle valve body. Drain the cooling system.

2. Disconnect the accelerator cable.

3. Remove the injectors and disconnect the line from the cold start valve.

4. Disconnect the coolant hoses.

5. Disconnect the vacuum and the emission control hoses (label all wires for installation).

6. Remove the auxiliary air regulator.

7. Disconnect all electrical lines (label all wires for installation).

8. Disconnect the EGR line from the exhaust manifold.

9. Loosen and remove the retaining bolts and lift off the manifold.

10. Install a new gasket(s). Install the manifold and tighten the bolts to 18 ft. lbs. (24 Nm).

11. Install the remaining components in the reverse order of removal.

RWD Vanagon

1. Remove the air cleaner.

2. Remove the pressure switch which is mounted under the right pair of intake manifold pipes. Disconnect the injector wiring.

3. Remove the fuel injectors by removing the two nuts which secure them in place. See Step 7 for proper injector installation.

4. After removing the intake manifold outer cover plate, remove the two screws which secure the manifold inner cover plate.

5. The manifold may be removed by removing the two nuts and washers which hold the manifold flange to the cylinder head.

6. Installation is the reverse of the above. The inner manifold cover should be installed first, but leave the cover loose until the outer cover and manifold are in place. Always use new gaskets.

7. Connect the fuel hoses to the injectors, if removed, after assembling the injector retainer plate in place. Make sure that the sleeves are in place on the injector securing studs. Carefully slip the injectors into the manifold and install the securing nuts. Never force the injectors in or out of the manifold. Reconnect the injector wiring.

Intake Air Distributor
REMOVAL & INSTALLATION

The intake air distributor is located at the center of the engine at the junction of the intake manifold pipes.

NOTE: It is not necessary to remove the distributor if only the manifold pipes are to be removed.

---

1. Remove the air cleaner and pressure switch which are located under the right pair of manifold pipes.

2. Push the four rubber hoses onto the intake manifold pipes.

3. Remove the accelerator cable and the throttle valve switch.

4. Disconnect the accelerator cable.

5. Disconnect the vacuum hoses leading to the ignition distributor and the pressure sensor and disconnect the hose running to the auxiliary air regulator.

6. Remove those bolts under the air distributor which secure the air distributor to the crankcase and remove the air distributor.

7. Installation is the reverse of removal.

Exhaust Manifold
REMOVAL & INSTALLATION
FWD Models Only

1. Disconnect the EGR tube from the exhaust manifold.

2. Remove the interfering air pump components, if equipped.

3. Remove the air cleaner hose from the exhaust manifold.

4. Disconnect the intake manifold support.

5. Separate the exhaust pipe from the manifold or turbocharger.

6. Remove the turbocharger (if equipped). Remove the retaining nuts and remove the manifold.

7. Clean the cylinder head and manifold mating surfaces.

8. Install the exhaust manifold using a new gasket.

9. Tighten the nuts to 18 ft. lbs. (24 Nm). Work from the center to the outer edges.

10. Install the remaining components in the reverse order of removal. Use a new manifold flange gasket.

Heat Exchangers
REMOVAL & INSTALLATION
Vanagon Only
AIR-COOLED

1. Disconnect the air hose at the outlet of each exchanger.

2. Disconnect the warm air tube at the outside end of the exchanger.

3. Disconnect the three bolts which secure each exchanger to the muffler.

4. Remove the four nuts, two at each exhaust port, which secure the exchanger to the cylinder head.

Installation is the reverse of the above. Always use new gaskets.

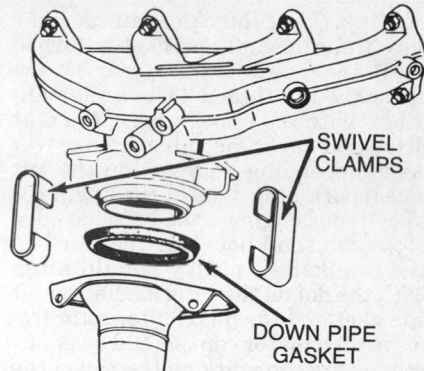

Swivel type exhaust pipe mounting used on various models from 1983

Front Cover
REMOVAL & INSTALLATION
FWD Only

1. Loosen the alternator mounting bolts and if equipped, the power steering pump and air conditioner compressor bolts, if their drive belts will interfere with cover removal.

2. Pivot the alternator or driven component and slip the drive belt from the pulleys.

3. Unscrew the belt cover retaining nuts and remove the cover. On some models with two piece covers, it may be necessary to remove the crankshaft pulley.

4. Reposition the spacers and nuts on the mounting studs so they will not get lost.

5. Service vehicle as necessary and reinstall the belt cover in the reverse order of removal.

Timing Belt

NOTE: The timing belt is designed to last for more than 60,000 miles and normally does not require tension adjustment. If the belt is removed, breaks or is replaced, the basic timing must be checked and the belt retensioned.

REMOVAL & INSTALLATION
FWD Models Only

NOTE: Timing belt installation will be less confusing if the engine is set for No. 1 cylinder at TDC (top dead center) prior to belt removal or replacement.

1. Refer to the "Timing Belt Cover, Removal and Installation" procedures and remove the timing belt cover(s).

2. Turn the engine until the 0° mark on the flywheel is aligned with the stationary pointer on the bell

housing. Turn the camshaft or make sure the camshaft sprocket is turned until the mark on the rear of the sprocket is aligned (4 cylinder engines) with the upper edge of the rear drive belt cover (or valve (cam) cover edge, depending on year) on the left side (spark plug side) of the engine or (5 cylinder engines) the left side edge of the camshaft housing. The notch on the crankshaft pulley should align with the dot on the intermediate shaft sprocket and the distributor rotor (remove distributor cap) should be pointing toward the mark on the rim of the distributor housing.

3. Remove the crankshaft drive pulley(s).

4. On 4 cylinder engines, hold the large nut on the tensioner pulley and loosen the smaller pulley lock nut. Turn the tensioner counterclockwise to relieve the tension on the timing belt.

5. On 5 cylinder engines, loosen the

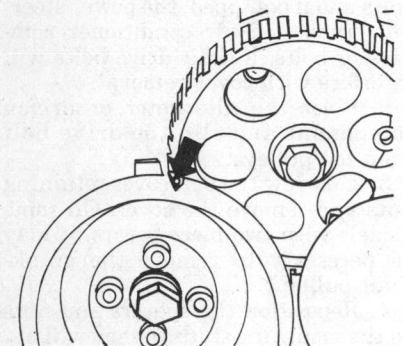

Crankshaft pulley and intermediate shaft sprocket alignment

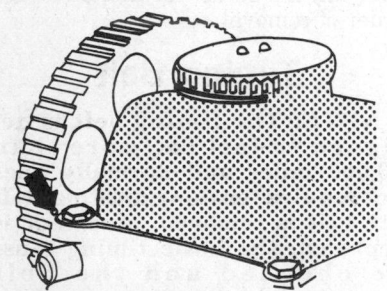

Camshaft sprocket timing marks aligned with cover flange (shown) or inner-upper timing cover bracket

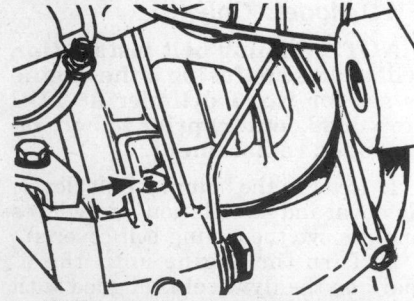

0° T or TDC mark on the flywheel

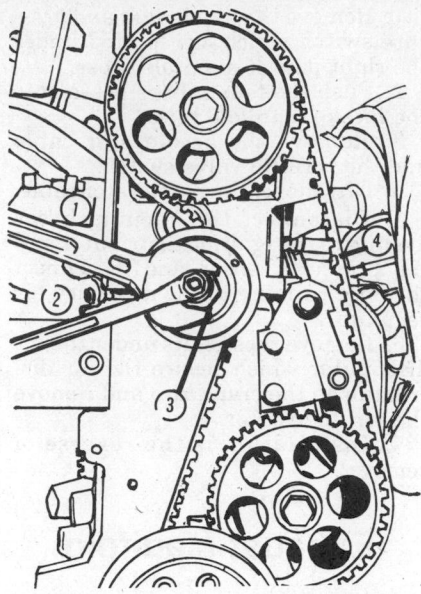

Turn the tensioner (3) toward (1) to tighten belt and toward (2) to loosen. Check tension at (4)

water pump bolts and turn the pump clockwise to relieve timing belt tension.

6. Slide the timing belt from the pulleys.

7. Install the timing belt and retension with pulley or water pump. Reinstall the crankshaft pulley(s). Recheck alignment of timing marks.

— CAUTION —

If the timing marks are not correctly aligned with the No. 1 piston at TDC of the compression stroke and the belt is installed, valve timing will be incorrect. Poor performance and possible engine damage can result from improper valve timing.

8. Check the timing belt tension. The tension is correct when the belt can be twisted 90° with the thumb and the index finger along the straight run between the camshaft sprocket and the water pump.

9. Turn the engine two complete revolutions (clockwise rotation) and align the flywheel mark at TDC. Recheck belt tension and timing marks. Readjust as required.

10. Reinstall the timing belt cover and drive belts in the reverse order of removal.

TIMING INSPECTION

1. Refer to the "Timing Belt Cover, Removal & Installation" procedures and remove the timing belt covers. Remove the cylinder head cover.

NOTE: The drive belt must be checked for proper tension and must be centered in the sprockets before checking the timing.

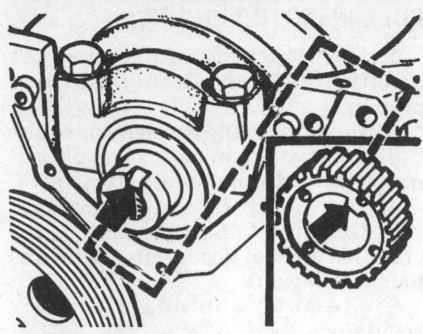

Late models have a locating lug contained by the crankshaft sprocket

2. Turn the engine so that the No. 1 cylinder is at TDC. The No. 1 cylinder camshaft lobes should be pointing upward and the TDC mark on the flywheel should be aligned with the bellhousing mark.

3. Fix the camshaft in position with tool VW 2065 or 2065A. Align the tool as follows:

a. Turn the crankshaft until one end of the tool touches the cylinder head.

b. Measure the gap at the other end of the tool with a feeler gauge.

c. Take half of the measurement and insert a feeler gauge of that thickness between the tool and the cylinder head; turn the camshaft so the tool rests on the feeler gauge.

d. Insert a second feeler gauge of the same thickness on the other side, between the tool and the cylinder head.

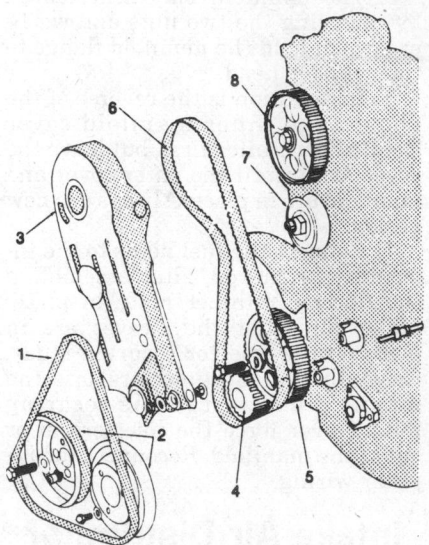

1. Alternator belt
2. Belt pulleys
3. Timing gear cover
4. Crankshaft sprocket
5. Intermediate sprocket
6. Drive belt
7. Tensioner
8. Camshaft sprocket

Exploded view of camshaft drive arrangement

4. Lock the injector pump sprocket in position with pin 2064.

5. Check that the marks on the sprocket, pump and mounting plate are aligned. Check that the TDC mark on the flywheel is aligned with the bellhousing mark.

ADJUSTMENT

1. Refer to Steps 1–4 of the above procedure.

2. After the camshaft is set in position and the timing is at TDC, loosen the camshaft sprocket mounting bolt ½ turn.

3. Tap the back of sprocket with a rubber hammer to loosen. Hand tighten the bolt to remove endplay.

4. Loosen the belt tensioner and remove the belt from the injector pump sprocket.

5. Turn the injector pump sprocket until the marks on the sprocket, pump and mounting bracket align. Insert pin 2064 through the hole in the sprocket and mounting bracket to lock in position.

6. Reinstall the camshaft drive belt. Tighten the camshaft mounting bolt to 33 ft. lbs. Remove the camshaft setting bar and the lock pin from the injector pump sprocket. Install VW tool VW210 (Belt tension gauge).

7. Adjust tension by turning the tensioner clockwise, reading on the tension gauge should be 12–13. Lock tensioner in position.

8. Turn the crankshaft 2 complete turns (clockwise rotation) and recheck belt tension. Strike the drive belt once with a rubber hammer between the camshaft and injector pump sprockets to eliminate play.

9. Recheck the timing and re-adjust if necessary.

Timing Sprockets

REMOVAL & INSTALLATION

FWD Models, All Engines

Depending on the year and model, the timing sprockets are located on the shaft by a key, a self-contained drive lug or in the case of the diesel engine camshaft—a tapered fit. All sprockets are retained by a bolt. To remove any or all sprockets, removal of the timing belt cover(s) and belt is required.

NOTE: When removing the crankshaft pulley, it is necessary to remove the four bolts which hold the outer component drive pulley to the timing belt sprocket. Remove the component drive belt, center retaining bolt and crankshaft pulley.

1. Remove the center retaining bolt.

2. Gently pry the sprocket off the shaft.

3. If the sprocket is stubborn in coming off, use a gear puller. Don't hammer on the sprocket. On diesel engines, loosen the camshaft center bolt 1 turn and tap the rear of the sprocket with a rubber hammer. When the sprocket loosens, remove the bolt and gear.

4. Remove the sprocket and key (if equipped).

5. Install the sprocket in the reverse order of removal.

6. Tighten the center bolt to 58 ft. lbs. (78 Nm). Models having a crankshaft sprocket with a self-contained index lug require 145 ft. lbs. (196 Nm) of torque on the center bolt.

7. Install the timing belt, check valve timing, tension belt, and install the cover.

OIL SEAL REPLACEMENT

FWD Gasoline Engines

4 CYLINDER

1. Refer to the "Timing Belt, Removal and Installation" procedures and remove the timing belt.

2. Remove the crankshaft sprocket bolt and sprocket.

3. Use a small pry bar to pry the oil seal or the seal removal tool 10–219 to pull the seal from the carrier.

NOTE: When removing the oil seal, BE CAREFUL not to damage the carrier.

4. To install, use installation tool 10–203 to press the seal flush with the carrier, then remove the tool. Install the aluminum installation ring and tool 10–203 to the seal, then press the seal 0.08 in. (2.0mm) into the carrier.

5. To complete the installation, reverse the removal procedures. Torque the crankshaft pulley bolt to 58 ft. lbs. (80 Nm) for 12mm or 145 ft. lbs. (200 Nm) for 14mm. Check and/or adjust the timing.

5 CYLINDER

1. Refer to the "Timing Belt, Removal and Installation" procedures and remove the timing belt.

2. Remove the damper pulley-to-crankshaft bolt and the damper pulley and sprocket assembly.

3. Using the seal removal tool 2086, pull the oil seal from the seal carrier.

4. To install, attach guide sleeve tool 2080A to the crankshaft, lubricate the oil seal lips and slide it over the guide tool. Slide the outer sleeve over the guide sleeve. Using the

sprocket bolt, press the seal in the oil pump housing until the seal is seated. Remove the installation tools.

5. To complete the installation, reverse the removal procedures. Torque the damper pulley-to-crankshaft bolt to 252 ft. lbs. (350 Nm). Check and/or adjust the timing.

Camshaft

REMOVAL & INSTALLATION

FWD Models

1. Remove the timing belt cover(s), the timing belt, camshaft sprocket and camshaft (valve) cover.

NOTE: Number the bearing caps from front to back. Scribe an arrow facing front. The caps are offset and must be installed correctly. Factory numbers on the caps are not always on the same side.

2. Remove the front and rear bearing caps. Loosen the remaining bearing cap nuts diagonally in several steps, starting from the outside caps near the ends of the head and working toward the center.

3. Remove the bearing caps and the camshaft.

4. Install a new oil seal and end plug in the cylinder head. Lightly coat the camshaft bearing journals and lobes with a film of assembly lube or heavy engine oil. Install the bearing caps in the reverse order of removal. Tighten the cap nuts diagonally and

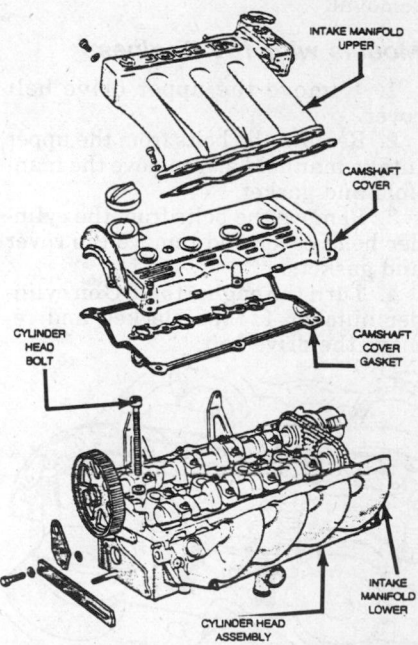

Exploded view, 16V DOHC camshaft assembly

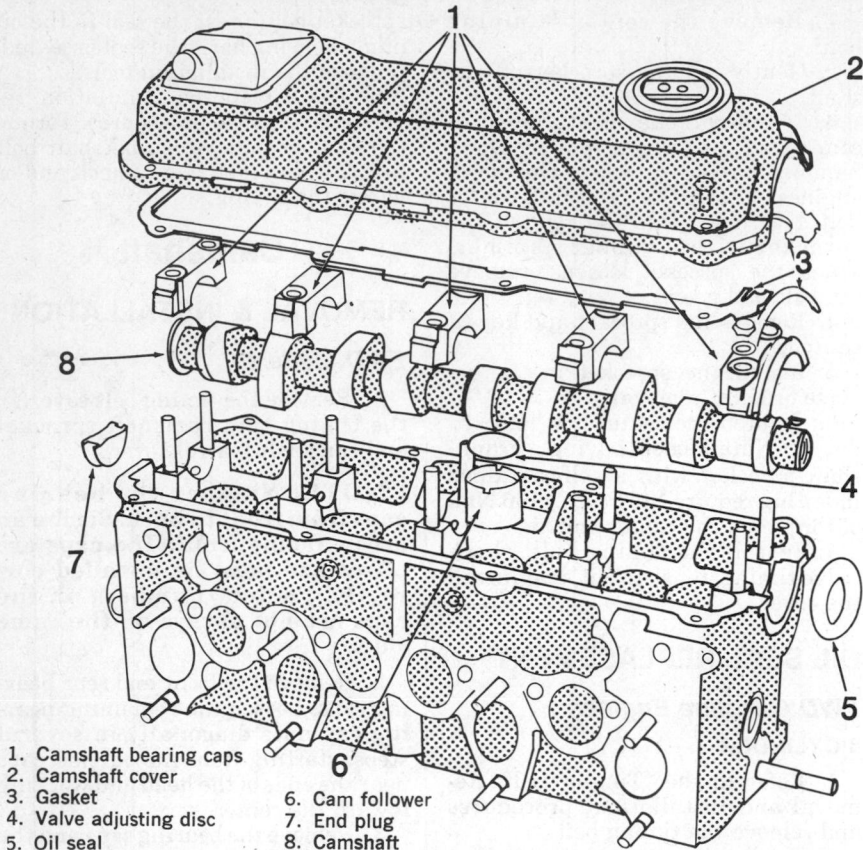

1. Camshaft bearing caps
2. Camshaft cover
3. Gasket
4. Valve adjusting disc
5. Oil seal
6. Cam follower
7. End plug
8. Camshaft

Exploded view of the camshaft assembly—gasoline engines (diesel similar)

in several steps until they are torqued to 14 ft. lbs.

5. Install the drive sprocket and timing belt. Check valve clearance and adjust if necessary. Install remaining parts in reverse order of removal.

Models with 16V Engines

1. Remove the upper drive belt cover.

2. Remove the bolts from the upper intake manifold and remove the manifold and gasket.

3. Remove the bolts from the cylinder head cover and remove the cover and gaskets.

4. Turn the engine to TDC on cylinder number 1, then slacken and remove the drive belt.

Camshaft sprocket timing marks at TDC

16V DOHC, roller chain and sproket

5. Remove the camshaft sprocket.

6. On the intake camshaft, remove bearing caps 5 and 7 as well as the last bearing caps. Then loosen bearing caps 6 and 8 alternately and diagonally.

7. On the exhaust camshaft, remove bearing caps 1 and 3 as well as the first and last bearing caps. Then loosen bearing caps 2 and 4 alternately and diagonally.

NOTE: First and last bearing caps are located either at the front and/or rear of the camshafts and are not numbered.

8. Remove the remaining bearing cap bolts and remove the cam shafts.

9. Install the camshaft drive chain so that the marks on the chain sprockets are matched at the base of the cylinder head, directly across from each other.

10. On the intake camshaft, install

and tighten bearing caps 6 and 8 alternately and diagonally to 11 ft. lbs.

11. Install and tighten the remaining bearing caps to 11 ft. lbs.

12. On the exhaust camshaft, tighten bearing caps 2 and 4 alternately and diagonally to 11 ft. lbs.

13. Install and tighten the remaining bearing caps to 11 ft. lbs.

14. Position the camshaft sprocket and torque to 47.9 ft. lbs.

15. Install the drive belt and adjust the timing.

16. Install the remaining components in the reverse order of their removal.

RWD Vanagon

1. Removal of the camshaft requires splitting the crankcase. See "Crankcase Disassembly". The camshaft and its bearing shells are then removed from the crankcase halves.

2. Before reinstalling the camshaft, it should be checked for wear on the lobe surfaces and on the bearing surfaces. In addition, the riveted joint between the camshaft timing gear and the camshaft should be checked for tightness.

3. The camshaft should be checked for a maximum run-out of 0.0008 in (0.0015 in. on Waterboxer).

4. The timing gear should be checked for the correct tooth contact and for wear.

5. If the camshaft bearing shells are worn or damaged, new shells should be fitted. The camshaft bearing shells should be installed with the tabs engaging the notches in the crankcase. It is usually a good idea to replace the bearing shells under any circumstances. Before installing the camshaft, the bearing journals and cam lobes should be generously coated with oil.

6. When the camshaft is installed, care should be taken to ensure that the timing gear tooth marked (0) is located between the two teeth of the crankshaft timing gear marked with a center punch. Coat the camshaft end cap with sealant, and make sure it is installed in its original position.

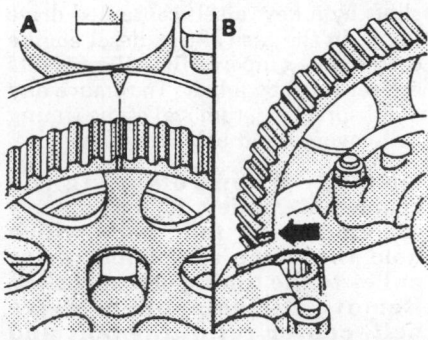

Exhaust cam pulley timing mark at TDC

7. The camshaft end-play is measured at the No. 3 bearing on all engines including Waterboxer. End-play is 0.0015–0.005 in. (0.04–0.12mm) and the wear limit is 0.006 in. (0.16mm).

Pistons and Connecting Rods

NOTE: 1.8L engines using rod bolts with a smooth surface between threads and short knurled shank and having a round head containing six notches are stretch type bolts and cannot be reused. Always use new bolts when servicing.

POSITIONING

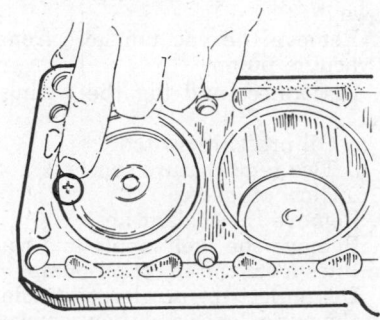

The arrow on the piston must face the camshaft drive belt

For all piston and connecting rod overhaul procedures, please refer to "Engine Rebuilding" in the unit repair section.

DIESEL ENGINE MECHANICAL

Diesel Engine

REMOVAL & INSTALLATION

All Models Except Dasher, Quantum and Vanagon

1. Disconnect the negative battery cable.
2. Turn the heater control to fully "Open." Remove the radiator cap, the radiator hose at the thermostat housing and drain the cooling system.
3. Remove the radiator fan, the alternator and the fuel fitter.

——— CAUTION ———
BE CAREFUL when disconnecting the fuel system, for the system may be under pressure.

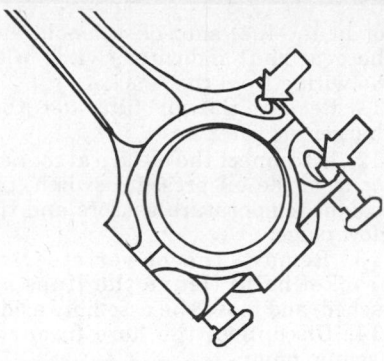

The connecting rod and cap alignment casting grooves must face the intermediate shaft

4. Disconnect the electrical connects of the fuel shut-off solenoid, the glow plugs, the oil pressure switch and the coolant temperature sensor.

NOTE: If equipped with power steering, remove the drive belt, the bracket bolts (leave the lines attached) and move the assembly aside.

5. Remove the heater and the radiator hoses.
6. At the injection pump, disconnect the accelerator cable with the bracket and remove the fuel supply and the return hoses.
7. Disconnect the cold start cable.

NOTE: If equipped with A/C, remove the drive belt, the electrical connector at the compressor, the compressor bracket-to-engine bolts and the compressor assembly, then move it aside and support it on a wire. DO NOT support the compressor with the hoses under tension.

8. Disconnect the electrical connectors from the starter, the back-up switch and the transmission mount ground wire.

NOTE: If equipped with man. trans., disconnect the clutch cable and remove the relay shaft lever.

9. Remove the exhaust pipe nuts or spring clips.

NOTE: If equipped with a turbocharger, disconnect the turbocharger-to exhaust manifold bolts, the turbocharger-to-transmission bracket, the air intake ducts and the oil line. Remove the turbocharger from the engine.

10. Disconnect the drive shafts from the drive flanges. Lower the vehicle to the ground, then remove the axle hub nuts and disconnect the lower ball joints from the steering knuckles.
11. Raise the vehicle, swing the

strut assemblies away from the vehicle and pull out the drive shafts.
12. Remove the starter, the horn, the oil filter and the front engine mount.
13. Reconnect the ball joints so that the vehicle may be lowered to the ground.
14. Remove the rear engine mount and the right front wheel.
15. Attack the engine support tool US 1105 and a vertical lift to the engine, then lift it slightly.

NOTE: If equipped with a man. trans., remove the relay shaft and the gearshift lever rods.

16. Remove both side engine mount-to-body bolts.
17. Lower the engine and transmission assembly onto a dolly. Raise the vehicle and slide the dolly from under the vehicle.
18. To install, reverse the removal procedures. Torque the transmission-to-engine bolts to 33 ft. lbs. (45 Nm) for 10mm or 54 ft. lbs. (73 Nm) for 12mm, the engine mount bolts to 25 ft. lbs. (34 Nm), the turbocharger-to-exhaust manifold bolts to 18 ft. lbs. (24 Nm), the starter bolts to 14 ft. lbs. (19 Nm), the torque converter-to-drive plate bolts to 22 ft. lbs. (30 Nm), the front engine stop bolts to 18 ft. lbs. (24 Nm), the power steering pump bolts to 14 ft. lbs. (19 Nm) and the A/C compressor bolts to 18 ft. lbs. (24 Nm) for 8mm or 58 ft. lbs. (78 Nm) for 12mm. Adjust the belt tension and refill the cooling system.

1981–83 Dasher and Quantum

——— CAUTION ———
Do not disconnect the refrigerant lines on cars equipped with air conditioning.

1. Remove the negative battery cable.
2. Set the heat control to hot. Remove the lower radiator hose and remove the thermostat to drain the coolant. Remove the thermoswitch electrical connector and the radiator brace at the bottom of the radiator, remove the top radiator shroud, upper hose, radiator mounting bolts, and remove the radiator and fan.
3. Remove the supply and return lines from the injection pump. Disconnect the throttle cable from the pump and remove the cable mounting bracket. Disconnect the cold start cable at the pin, and remove the electrical connector from the fuel shut-off solenoid.
4. Disconnect the electrical connectors from the oil pressure switch, coolant temperature sensor and glow plugs. Remove the radiator hose from

the head and the vacuum hose from the vacuum pump.

5. Loosen the adjusting nuts and unhook the clutch cable from the lever.

6. Remove the hose from the water pump.

7. On the Quantum, unbolt the rear of the turbocharger (if equipped) from the exhaust system.

8. Loosen the right engine mount.

9. Remove the alternator after tagging the wires for installation.

10. Remove the front engine mounts.

11. Disconnect the exhaust pipe from the manifold, and the pump bracket from the transmission.

12. Loosen the left engine mount.

13. Remove the starter.

14. Remove the engine-to-transmission bolts, and the flywheel cover bolts.

15. Attach a lifting chain to the engine and raise the engine until the transmission touches the steering rack. Remove the left engine mount.

16. Support the transmission with a jack and raise and turn the engine at the same time to remove.

17. Installation is the reverse. Tighten the engine-to-transmission bolts to 40 ft. lbs. (54 Nm), and the engine mount bolts to 29 ft. lbs. (39 Nm). After installation adjust the throttle and cold starting cables.

1984–88 Quantum

1. Disconnect the negative battery cable.

2. Remove the horn and the cover plates of the engine and the transmission.

3. Move the heater control valve to fully "Open" and remove the radiator cap.

4. Remove the 2 lower hoses of the thermostat housing and drain the coolant.

5. Disconnect the electrical connections from the fan, the thermoswitch and the series resistor near the alternator.

6. Remove the radiator-to-engine coolant hose, the radiator bolts, the right fan connector and the radiator.

7. Remove the fuel supply and the return lines from the fuel injector.

——— CAUTION ———

BE CAREFUL when disconnecting the fuel system, for the system may be under pressure.

8. Remove the accelerator cable from the fuel injection pump and from the support bracket.

9. Disconnect the cold start cable at the electrical connector and the mounting washer from the support.

10. Disconnect the electrical connec-

tor at the fuel shut-off solenoid and the gear shift indicator switch with the wiring from the bracket.

11. Remove the air filter-to-turbocharger air filter hose.

12. Disconnect the electrical connector from the oil pressure switch, the coolant temperature sensors and the glow plugs.

13. Remove the power steering bracket bolts (leave the lines attached) and move the assembly aside.

14. Disconnect the hose from the vacuum pump.

15. Remove the clutch cable lock plate and unhook the cable.

16. Remove the 2 nuts from both engine mounts and the engine torque support bolts at the front of the engine.

17. Remove the alternator and the front engine stop.

NOTE: If equipped with A/C, remove the pulley nuts from the compressor, the drive belt, the compressor bracket bolts and the compressor. Place and tie the compressor aside so that the hoses are not under pressure.

18. Remove the turbocharger from the exhaust manifold and the turbocharger-to-transmission bracket.

19. Disconnect the electrical connectors and remove the starter; set the starter on the engine subframe.

20. Remove the 2 bottom engine-to-transmission bolts and the flywheel cover plate bolts.

NOTE: If equipped with an auto. trans., remove the cover plate and the torque converter mounting bolts.

21. Install the engine support bar VW 785/1B under the front of the transmission and support it.

22. Attach the engine lifting tool US 1105 and a vertical lift to the engine and lift the engine and transmission assembly free of the engine mounts.

23. Adjust the support bar under the transmission.

24. Remove the 3 upper transmission-to-engine bolts and pry the engine from the transmission.

NOTE: If equipped with an automatic transmission, secure the torque converter to the transmission to keep it from falling out.

25. Lift the engine from the engine compartment.

26. To install, reverse the removal procedures. Torque the transmission-to-engine bolts to 40 ft. lbs. (54 Nm), the engine mount bolts to 25 ft. lbs. (34 Nm), the turbocharger-to-exhaust manifold bolts to 18 ft. lbs. (24 Nm), the starter bolts to 14 ft. lbs. (19 Nm), the torque converter-to-drive plate

bolts to 22 ft. lbs. (30 Nm), the front engine stop bolts to 18 ft. lbs. (24 Nm), the power steering pump bolts to 14 ft. lbs. (19 Nm) and the A/C compressor bolts to 18 ft. lbs. (24 Nm) for 8mm or 58 ft. lbs. (78 Nm) for 12mm. Adjust the belt tension and refill the cooling system.

RWD Vanagon

1. Disconnect the negative battery cable.

2. Remove the top of the air cleaner.

3. Open the coolant expansion tank. Disconnect the lower hose from the water pump at the connecting pipe to the radiator. Disconnect the center hose from the water pump. Disconnect the hose from the cylinder head and oil cooler and move it out of the way.

4. Remove the vacuum hose from the vacuum pump.

5. Disconnect and tag the wiring from:

   a. Oil pressure switch

   b. Two temperature sensors

   c. Glow plugs

6. Remove the coolant hose.

7. Remove the fuel supply and return lines from the injection pump.

8. Disconnect the accelerator cable from the pump lever and then remove the retaining clip at the bracket and position it to one side.

9. Disconnect the cold start cable at the lockscrew.

10. Disconnect the fuel shut-off solenoid.

11. Remove the coolant reservoir and the oil filler cap and dipstick.

12. Remove the nuts from the rear engine mounts but leave the bolts in place.

13. Remove all (7) engine/transmission mounting bolts.

14. Remove the bolts and remove the support member.

15. Support the engine.

16. Remove the nuts from the front engine mounts and then remove the front and rear engine mount bolts.

17. Lower the engine/transmission assembly until the engine can be separated from the transmission.

18. Support the transmission, remove the engine from the transmission and then lower it from the vehicle.

To install:

1. Installation is in the reverse order of removal, please note the following:

   a. Do not interchange the fuel supply and fuel return pipe union screws. For identification, the return pipe union screw is marked with OUT on the hex. The return line also has a smaller diameter than the supply line.

b. Adjust the cold start cable and refill the cooling system.

c. Pertinent tightening torques are:

engine-to-transmission – (M10 bolts) 33 ft. lbs.; (M12 bolts) 58 ft. lbs.

engine mounts – 61 ft. lbs.
support member – 33 ft. lbs.
fuel line union screws – 18 ft. lbs.

Cylinder Head
REMOVAL & INSTALLATION

Diesel and Turbo Diesel
ALL MODELS

NOTE: The cylinder head is retained by Allen bolts. The engine should be cold when the head is removed to avoid chances of warpage. The word TOP or OBEN on the new gasket should face up.

1. Disconnect the negative battery cable.
2. Drain the cooling system.
3. Remove the air cleaner and duct.
4. Clean and disconnect the fuel (injector) lines.
5. Tag and disconnect all electrical wires and leads.
6. If equipped, disconnect and plug all lines coming from the brake booster vacuum pump and remove the pump.
7. Disconnect the air supply tubes (Turbo Diesels only) and then unbolt and remove the intake manifold.
8. Disconnect and plug all lines coming from the power steering pump and remove the pump and V-belt (if equipped).
9. Disconnect and remove the oil supply and return lines from the Turbocharger (if applicable).
10. Remove the exhaust manifold heat shields (if equipped). Remove the glow plugs and the fuel injectors.
11. Separate the exhaust pipe from the exhaust manifold or turbocharger and then remove the manifold.

NOTE: On turbo diesels, the exhaust manifold is removed with the turbocharger and wastegate still attached.

12. Disconnect all radiator and heater hoses where they are attached to the cylinder head and position them out of the way.
13. Remove the drive belt cover and the drive belt.
14. Remove the PCV hose.
15. Remove the cylinder head cover.
16. Loosen the cylinder head bolts in the reverse order of the tightening sequence shown in the illustration.
17. Remove the bolts and lift the cylinder head straight off.

CAUTION

If the head sticks, loosen it by compression or rap it upward with a soft rubber mallet. Do not force anything between the head and the engine block to pry it upward; this may result in serious damage.

---

18. Clean the cylinder head and engine block mating surfaces thoroughly and then install the new gasket without any sealing compound. Make sure the words TOP or OBEN are facing up when the gasket is installed.

NOTE: Depending upon piston height above the top surface of the engine block, there are three gaskets of different thicknesses which can be used. Be sure that the new gasket has the same identifying number as the one being replaced.

19. Place the cylinder head on the engine block and install bolts No. 8 and 10 first. These holes are smaller and will properly locate the head on the engine block.
20. Install the remaining bolts. Torque the bolts in sequence using 3 steps: (6 points) 35 ft. lbs. (47 Nm), 50 ft. lbs. (60 Nm), 65 ft. lbs. (88 Nm) and retorque to 65 ft. lbs. (88 Nm), after warming the engine; (12 point) 29 ft. lbs. (39 Nm), 43 ft. lbs. (58 Nm), an additional ½ turn and retorque an additional ¼ turn, after warming the engine.
21. Installation of all other components is in the reverse order of removal.
22. After about 1000 miles, remove the cylinder head cover and retighten the cylinder head bolts, turning the bolts in sequence ¼ turn (90°) WITHOUT loosening them first. This is done one bolt at a time, in the proper sequence, without interruption.

OVERHAUL

For all cylinder head overhaul procedures, please refer to "Engine Rebuilding" in the unit repair section.

Intake Manifold
REMOVAL & INSTALLATION

Diesel and Turbo Diesel
All Models

1. Disconnect the negative battery cable.
2. Disconnect the air duct from the throttle valve body. Drain the cooling system.
3. Disconnect the accelerator cable. Disconnect the hose that runs between the air duct and the turbocharger (turbo diesel only).

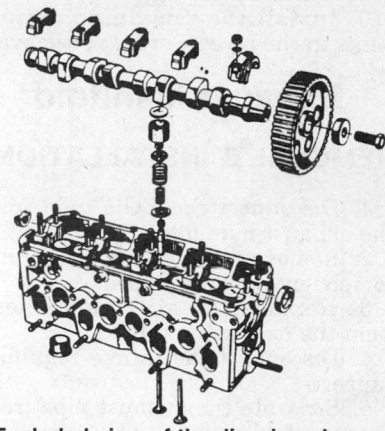

Exploded view of the diesel engine cylinder head

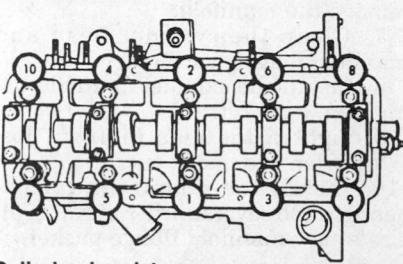

Cylinder head torque sequence—diesel engine

4. Remove the air cleaner. Remove the injectors and disconnect the line from the cold start valve.
5. Disconnect all coolant valves. Disconnect and plug all lines coming from the brake booster vacuum pump and remove the pump.
6. Disconnect all vacuum and emission control hoses (label all hoses for installation). Disconnect the PCV line.
7. Disconnect the EGR line from the exhaust manifold. Disconnect and remove the blow-off valve and then disconnect the hose which runs from the intake manifold to the turbocharger (turbo diesel only).
8. Loosen and remove the retaining bolts and lift off the manifold.
9. Install a new gasket. Install the manifold and tighten the bolts to 18 ft. lbs.

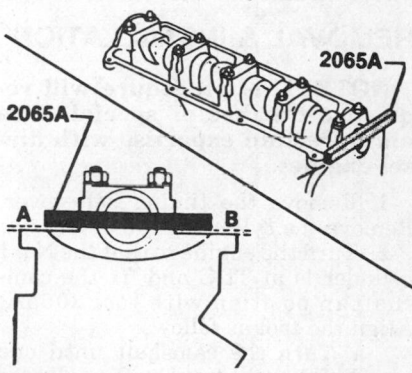

Use the special tool to fix the camshaft in position

10. Install the remaining components in the reverse order of removal.

Exhaust Manifold

REMOVAL & INSTALLATION

1. Disconnect the EGR tube from the exhaust manifold.
2. Remove the interfering air pump components if so equipped.
3. Remove the air cleaner hose from the exhaust manifold.
4. Disconnect the intake manifold support.
5. Separate the exhaust pipe from the manifold.
6. Remove the retaining nuts and remove the manifold.
7. Clean the cylinder head and manifold mating surfaces.
8. Install the exhaust manifold using a new gasket.
9. Tighten the nuts to 18 ft. lbs. Work from the inside out.
10. Install the remaining components in the reverse order of removal. Use a new manifold flange gasket.

Front Cover
REMOVAL & INSTALLATION

1. Loosen the alternator mounting bolts.
2. Pivot the alternator and slip the drive belt off the sprockets.
3. Unscrew the cover retaining nuts and remove the cover.
4. Reposition the spacers on the studs and then install the washers and nuts.
5. Install the alternator belt and adjust its tension.

Timing Belt

NOTE: The timing belt is designed to last for more than 60,000 miles and does not normally require tension adjustments. If the belt is removed or replaced, the basic valve timing must be checked and the belt retensioned.

REMOVAL & INSTALLATION

NOTE: This procedure will require a number of special tools and a certain expertise with diesel engines.

1. Remove the timing belt cover. Remove the cylinder head cover.
2. Turn the engine so that the No. 1 cylinder is at TDC and fix the camshaft in position with tool 2065A. Align the tool as follows:
   a. Turn the camshaft until one end of the tool touches the cylinder head.

b. Measure the gap at the other end of the tool with a feeler gauge.
   c. Take half of the measurement and insert a feeler gauge of this thickness between the tool and the cylinder head; turn the camshaft so that the tool rests on the feeler gauge.
   d. Insert a second feeler gauge of the same thickness between the other end of the tool and the cylinder head.
3. Lock the injection pump sprocket in position with pin 2064.
4. Check that the marks on the sprocket, bracket and pump body are in alignment (engine at TDC).
5. Loosen the timing belt tensioner. Remove the V-belt from the crankshaft.
6. Remove the timing belt.
To install:
7. Check that the TDC mark on the flywheel is aligned with the reference marks.
8. Loosen the camshaft sprocket bolt ½ turn and then loosen the gear from the camshaft end by tapping it with a rubber mallet.
9. Install the timing belt and remove pin 2064 from the injection pump sprocket.
10. Tension the belt by turning the tensioner to the right. Check the belt tension as detailed later, in the section.
11. Tighten the camshaft sprocket bolt to 33 ft. lbs.
12. Remove the tool from the camshaft.

13. Turn the crankshaft two turns in the direction of engine rotation (clockwise) and then strike the belt once with a rubber mallet between the camshaft sprocket and the injection pump sprocket.
14. Check the belt tension again. Check the injection pump timing.

TENSION ADJUSTMENT

NOTE: Special tool VW210 will be required for this procedure.

Tension adjustment on the front timing belt is performed in the same manner as with the other engines. Deflection is also checked in the same position, but with the special tool VW210 rather than your fingers. Proper tension is achieved when the scale reads 12–13.

Timing Sprockets

REMOVAL & INSTALLATION

The intermediate shaft and crankshaft sprockets are located by keys on their respective shafts and each is retained by a bolt. The camshaft sprocket is taper-fit and has no key. To remove any or all of the pulleys, first remove the timing belt cover and belt.

NOTE: When removing the crankshaft pulley, don't remove the four Allen head bolts which hold the outer belt pulley to the timing belt sprocket.

1. Remove the center bolt or nut.
2. Gently pry the sprocket off the shaft. If the gear does not come off easily, use a gear puller. Don't hammer on the sprocket.
3. Remove the sprocket and key (if used).

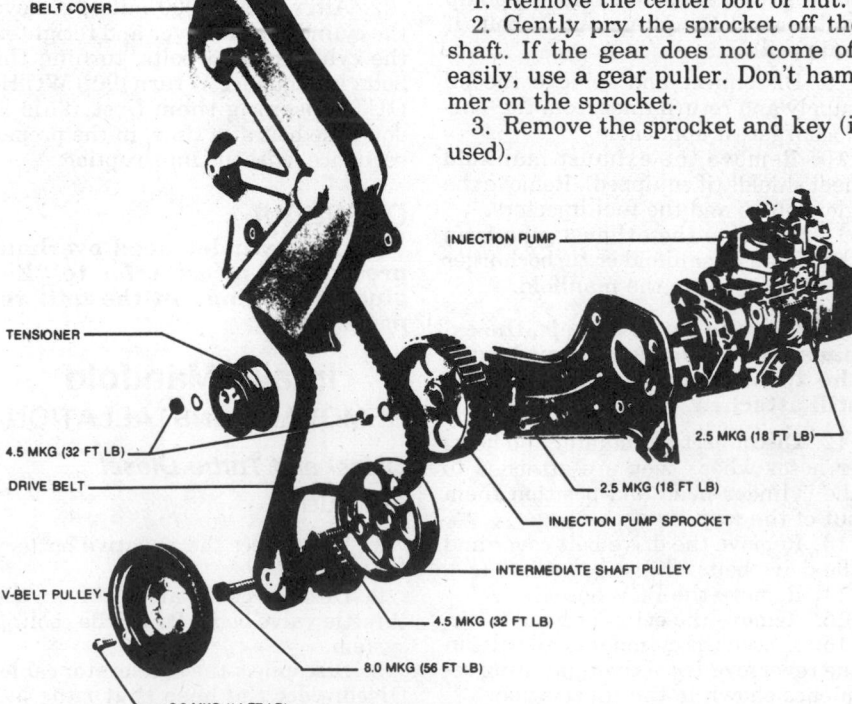

Timing belt installation—diesel engine

4. Install in the reverse order of removal.

5. Coat the center bolt with Loctite or similar locking compound, and tighten to 33 ft. lbs. on the top sprockets and 108 ft. lbs. on the crankshaft sprocket.

6. Install the timing belt, check the valve timing, tension the belt, and install the cover.

OIL SEAL REPLACEMENT

Exept Quantum

1. Refer to the "Timing Belt, Removal and Installation" procedures and remove the timing belt.
2. Remove the crankshaft sprocket.
3. Using a small pry bar, pry the seal from the carrier or use the seal extractor tool 10–219 to pull out the seal.

NOTE: When removing the seal, be careful not to damage the carrier.

4. To install, lubricate the new seal lips, use the seal installation tool 10–203 to press the new seal into the carrier and reverse the removal procedures. Torque the crankshaft pulley bolt to 58 ft. lbs. (80 Nm) for 12mm or 145 ft. lbs. (200 Nm) for 14mm. Check and/or adjust the timing.

Quantum

1. Refer to the "Timing Belt, Removal and Installation" procedures and remove the timing belt.
2. Remove the crankshaft sprocket.
3. Install the hex head bolt of the seal removal tool 3083 into the seal extractor guide 2085.
4. Attach the tools to the oil seal and pull the seal from the carrier.
5. To install, slide the sleeve of the installation tool 3083 onto the crankshaft journal, lubricate the seal and slide it over the sleeve. Install the thrust sleeve against the oil seal and press it in until seated.
6. To complete the installation procedures, reverse the removal procedures. Torque the crankshaft pulley bolt to 58 ft. lbs. (80 Nm) for 12mm or 145 ft. lbs. (200 Nm) for 14mm. Check and/or adjust the timing.

Camshaft
REMOVAL & INSTALLATION

1. Remove the timing belt (refer to proper section for correct details).
2. Remove the camshaft sprocket.
3. Remove the air cleaner.
4. Remove the camshaft cover.
5. Unscrew and remove the No. 1, 3, and 5 bearing caps (No. 1 is at the front).

6. Unscrew the No. 2 and 4 bearing caps, diagonally and in increments.
7. Lift the camshaft out of the cylinder head.
8. Lubricate the camshaft journals and lobes with assembly lube or gear oil before installing it in the cylinder head.
9. Replace the camshaft oil seal with a new one whenever the cam is removed.
10. Install the No. 1, 3 and 5 bearing caps and tighten the nuts to 14 ft. lbs. Note that the bores are offset, and the numbers are not always on the same side.
11. Install the No. 2 and 4 bearing caps and diagonally tighten the nuts to 14 ft. lbs.

NOTE: If checking end play, install a dial indicator so that the feeler touches the camshaft snout. End-play should be no more than 0.006 i. (0.15mm).

Piston and Connecting Rods

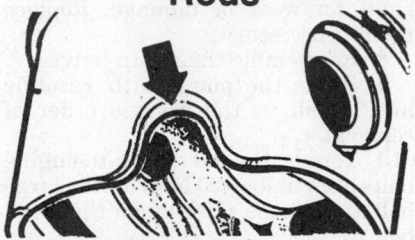

Turbo diesel pistons are equipped with a cut–out to provide clearance for a block mounted oil spray valve

POSITIONING

For all piston and connecting rod overhaul procedures, please refer to "Engine Rebuilding" in the unit repair section.

ENGINE LUBRICATION

The lubrication system is a conventional wet-sump design. The gear-type oil pump is driven by the intermediate shaft for all (except the 5 cyl engine). The 5 cyl. engine has the oil pump mounted at the lower front of the engine. The pump is connected to and operated by the crankshaft. A pressure relief valve limits pressure and prevents extreme pressure from developing in the system. All oil is filtered by a full flow replaceable filter.

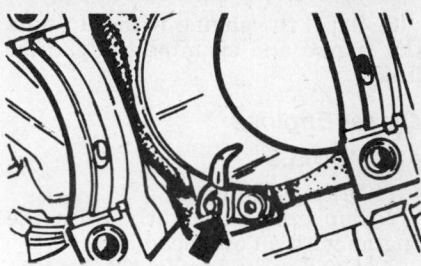

Oil jet used in turbo diesel engine to provide a spray of oil to the piston which helps cooling and lubrication

A bypass valve assures lubrication in the event the filter becomes plugged. The oil pressure switch is located at the end of the cylinder head gallery (the end of the system) to assure accurate pressure readings.

NOTE: Turbocharged diesel engines use an oil cooler mounted between the oil filter and engine. Always check tightness of the cooler retaining nut when changing the oil filter. Nut should be torqued to 18 ft. lbs.

Oil Pan
REMOVAL & INSTALLATION

Gasoline Engines

DASHER and QUANTUM

1. Drain the oil pan.
2. Support and slightly raise the engine with an overhead hoist.
3. Gradually loosen the engine crossmember mounting bolts. Remove the left and right side engine mounts.
4. Lower the crossmember very carefully.
5. Loosen and remove the oil pan retaining bolts.
6. Lower the pan from the vehicle.
7. Install the pan using a new gasket and sealer.
8. Tighten the retaining bolts in a crosswise pattern. Tighten 4 cyl pan bolts to 14 ft. lbs. (20 Nm), or 5 cyl pan bolts to 7 ft. lbs. (10 Nm).
9. Raise the crossmember. Tighten the crossmember bolts to 42 ft. lbs. (57 Nm) and the engine mounting bolts to 32 ft. lbs. (43 Nm).
10. Refill the engine with oil. Start the engine and check for leaks.

ALL MODELS—EXCEPT DASHER and QUANTUM

1. Drain the engine oil.
2. Loosen and remove the bolts retaining the oil pan.
3. Lower the pan from the car.
4. Install the pan using a new oil pan gasket.
5. Tighten the retaining bolts in a criss-cross pattern. Tighten hex head bolts to 14 ft. lbs. (20 Nm).

6. Refill the engine with oil. Start the engine and examine the pan for leaks.

Diesel Engines
ALL MODELS

1. Drain the oil pan.
2. Support and slightly raise the engine with an overhead hoist.
3. Gradually loosen the engine crossmember mounting bolts. Remove the front and rear side engine mounts.
4. Lower the crossmember very carefully.
5. Loosen and remove the oil pan retaining bolts.
6. Lower the pan from the car.
7. Install the pan using a new gasket and sealer.
8. Tighten the retaining bolts in a crosswise pattern. Tighten hex head bolts to 14 ft. lbs., or Allen head bolts to 7 ft. lbs.
9. Raise the crossmember. Tighten the crossmember bolts to 42 ft. lbs. and the engine mounting bolts to 32 ft. lbs.
10. Refill the engine with oil. Start the engine and check for leaks.

Rear Main Oil Seal
REPLACEMENT

All Models

The rear main oil seal is located in a housing on the rear of the cylinder block. To replace the seal on the Dasher and Quantum, it is necessary to remove the transmission and perform the work on an engine stand or work bench. See "Transmission Removal and Installation."

On the Golf, Rabbit, Fox, Jetta and Scirocco, the engine should be removed from the car.

1. Remove the transmission and flywheel.
2. Using a small pry bar tool 2086 (5 cyl.) or 10–221 (4 cyl.), very carefully pry the old seal out of the support ring.
3. Remove the seal.
4. Lightly oil the new seal and press it into place using tool 2003/2A, to start the seal and tool 2003/1, to seat the seal. Be careful not to dam-

age the seal or score the crankshaft.
5. Install the flywheel and transmission. Torque pressure plate-to-crankshaft bolts to 54 ft. lbs. (73 Nm) for 1981–82 models or 72 ft. lbs. (100 Nm) for 1983–88 models and the flywheel-to-pressure plate to 14 ft. lbs. (20 Nm). Torque the flywheel to engine bolts, on all diesel engines, to 36 ft. lbs.

Oil Pump
REMOVAL & INSTALLATION

Gasoline Engines
4 CYLINDER FWD MODELS

1. Remove the oil pan.
2. Remove the two mounting bolts.
3. Pull the oil pump down and out of the engine.
4. Unscrew the mounting bolts and separate the pump halves.
5. Remove the driveshaft and gear from the upper body.
6. Clean the bottom half in solvent. Pry up the metal edges to remove the filter screen for cleaning.
7. Examine the gears and driveshaft for wear or damage. Replace them if necessary.
8. Reassemble the pump halves.
9. Prime the pump with vasoline and install in the reverse order of removal.
10. Torque the oil pump-to-engine bolts to 14 ft. lbs. (20 Nm) for the large bolt and 7 ft. lbs. (10 Nm) for the small bolt.

5 CYLINDER FWD MODELS

1. Refer to the "Timing Belt, Removal and Installation" procedures in this section and remove the timing belt.
2. Remove the drive belt sprocket from the crankshaft.
3. Remove the oil dip stick and drain the crankcase.
4. Remove the engine-to-subframe bolts, raise the engine slightly and remove the oil pan.
5. Remove the oil pickup tube bolts and the tube.
6. Remove the oil pump-to-engine bolts and the oil pump.
7. Remove the gasket and clean the gasket mounting surfaces.
8. At the rear of the oil pump, remove the end cover bolts and the cover.
9. Check the pump for wear and/or damage, replace the parts if necessary.
10. Pack the pump with petroleum jelly and reassemble the pump.
11. To install, reverse the removal procedures. Torque the pump-to-engine bolts to 14 ft. lbs. (20 Nm). Refill the engine with oil. Start the engine and check for leaks.

RWD VANAGON

1. The oil pump can be taken out only after the engine is removed from the car and the air intake housing, the belt pulley fan housing, and fan are dismantled.
2. Remove the four pump securing nuts and, prying on either side of the pump, pry the pump assembly out of the crankcase.
3. To dissasemble the pump, the pump cover must be pressed apart.
4. Prior to assembly, check the oil pump body for wear, especially the gear seating surfce. If the pump body is worn, the result will be loss of oil pressure. Check the driven gear shaft for tightness and, if necessary, peen it tightly into place or replace the pump housing. The gears should be checked for excessive wear, backlash, and end-play. Maximum end-play without a gasket is 1mm (0.004 in.). The end-play can be checked using a T-square and a feeler gauge. Check the mating surface of the pump body and the crankcase for damage and cleanliness. Install the pump into the crankcase with a new gasket. Do not use any sealing compound.
5. Turn the camshaft several revolutions in order to center the pump body opposite the slot in the camshaft.
6. On air-cooled Vanagon models, the pump was installed complete.
7. Tighten the securing nuts.

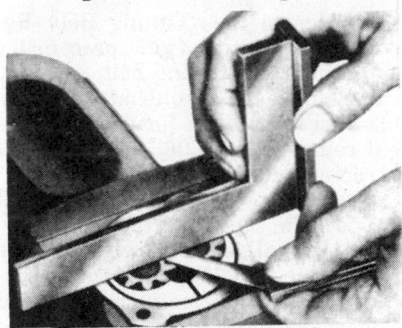
Checking oil pump end play

Diesel Engines
ALL MODELS

1. Remove the oil pan.
2. Remove the two mounting bolts.
3. Pull the oil pump down and out of the engine.
4. Unscrew the two bolts and separate the pump halves.
5. Remove the driveshaft and gear from the upper body.
6. Clean the bottom half in solvent. Pry up the metal edges to remove the filter screen for cleaning.
7. Examine the gear and driveshaft for wear or damage. Replace them if necessary.
8. Reassemble the pump halves.
9. Prime the pump with oil and install in the reverse order of removal.

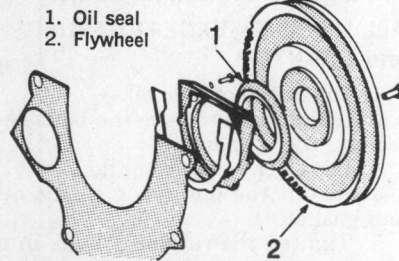
1. Oil seal
2. Flywheel

Rear main oil seal assembly

Oil Strainer

REMOVAL & INSTALLATION

Vanagon

AIR-COOLED ENGINE

The strainer is secured by a single bolt at the center of the strainer. Once taken out, the strainer must be thoroughly cleaned and all traces of oil gaskets removed prior to installing new ones. The suction pipe should be checked for tightness and proper position. When the strainer is installed, be sure that the suction pipe is correctly seated in the strainer. If necessray, the strainer may be bent slightly. The measurement from the strainer flange to the tip of the suction pipe should be 10mm. The measurement from the flange to the bottom of the strainer should be 6mm. The Vanagon has a spin-off replaceable oil filter as well as the strainer in the crankcase. The oil filter is located at the left rear corner of the engine.

WATERBOXER

The water-cooled engine does not employ an oil strainer. Instead, it relies solely on a spin-on oil filter.

Oil Cooler

REMOVAL & INSTALLATION

Vanagon

AIR-COOLED ENGINE ONLY

NOTE: The Waterboxer does not employ an oil cooler.

The Vanagon coolers are mounted near the oil filter, at the left corner of the engine.

The oil cooler may be removed without taking the engine out of the car. The Vanagon cooler is accessible through the left side engine cowling, working either in the engine compartment or from underneath the car.

The oil cooler can be removed after the three retaining nuts have been taken off. The gaskets should be removed along with the cooler and replaced with new gaskets. If the cooler is leaking, check the oil pressure relief valve. The studs and bracket on the cooler should be checked for tightness. Make certain that the hollow ribs of the cooler do not touch one another. The cooler must not be clogged with dirt. Clean the contact surfaces on the crankcase, install new gaskets, and attach the oil cooler. The air-cooled Vanagon has a spacer ring between the crankcase and the cooler at each securing screw. If these rings are omitted, the seals may be squeezed

too tightly, resulting in oil stoppage and resultant engine damage. Use double retaining nuts and locking compound on the cooler studs.

ENGINE COOLING

NOTE: When replacing coolant/antifreeze in all models, only a phosphate-free product must be used to help prevent damage to the water jacket sealing surfaces of the cylinder head. Other types of coolant may cause corrosion of the cooling system thus leading to engine overheating and damage.

Radiator and Fan

REMOVAL & INSTALLATION

Gasoline Engines

FWD MODELS

4 Cylinder Engine
1. Drain the cooling system.

NOTE: Various late models have the radiator retained by locating tabs at the bottom and two mounting brackets at the top. Disconnect hoses, wiring connectors and top brackets. Remove the radiator and fan assembly.

2. Remove the inner shroud mounting bolts.
3. Disconnect the lower radiator hose.
4. Disconnect the thermostatic switch lead.

NOTE: The 1984–88 diesel Quantum may have 2 fans on the radiator.

5. Remove the lower radiator shroud.
6. Remove the lower radiator mounting units.
7. Disconnect the upper radiator hose.
8. Detach the upper radiator shroud.
9. Remove the side mounting bolts and top clip and lift the radiator and fan out as an assembly.
10. To install, reverse the removal procedures. Torque the mounting bolts to 7 ft. lbs. (10 Nm).

5 Cylinder Engine
1. Drain the cooling system.
2. Remove the three pieces of the radiator cowl and the fan motor assembly. Take care in removing the fan motor connectors to avoid bending them.

3. Remove the upper and lower radiator hoses and the coolant tank supply hose.
4. Disconnect the coolant temperature switch located on the lower right side of the radiator.
5. Remove the radiator mounting bolts and lift out the radiator.
6. Installation is the reverse of removal. Torque radiator mounting bolts to 7 ft. lbs. (10 Nm).

RWD VANAGON

Waterboxer Engine Only
1. Remove the spare tire, the spare tire bracket and the radiator grille.
2. Drain the cooling system.
3. Disconnect the coolant hoses.
4. Unbolt and remove the radiator.
5. Unbolt the fan motor from its mounting shroud.
6. Disconnect the electrical connection.
7. Remove the fan/motor assembly.
8. Reverse the above procedure to install. Follow the procedure below for filling the cooling system.

Diesel Engine

ALL MODELS

1. Drain the cooling system.
2. Remove the inner shroud mounting bolts.
3. Disconnect the lower radiator hose.
4. Disconnect the thermostatic switch lead, if equipped.
5. Remove the lower radiator shroud.
6. Remove the lower radiator mounting units.
7. Disconnect the upper radiator hose.
8. Detach the upper radiator shroud.
9. Remove the side mounting bolts and lift the radiator and fan out as an assembly.
10. Installation is the reverse of removal.

FILLING THE COOLING SYSTEM

RWD Vanagon

WATERBOXER ENGINE ONLY

NOTE: Volkswagen specifies the use of a specially-formulated coolant, part No. ZVW 237 102 in the Waterboxer engine. Antifreeze other than this may cause corrosion of the cooling system, leading to engine damage.

1. Set the heater control to maximum heat.
2. Open the control valve for the auxiliary heater under the rear seat.
3. Remove the radiator grille.

4. Jack up the vehicle approximately 15¾ in. at the front, under the crossmember using a floor jack. Support the front end with jackstands.

5. Open the bleeder screw on the radiator.

6. Open the bleeder valve in the engine compartment.

7. Fill the coolant expansion tank until the tank is full (approximately 4.25–5.3 qts.).

8. Start the engine. Run it up to 2000 rpm, and top up the tank until coolant flows from the bleeder screw on the radiator. Wait until the coolant flowing is free of bubbles.

9. Add more coolant until the tank is full. Close the tank cap.

10. Shut off the engine. Restart the engine after 20 seconds.

11. At 2000 rpm, open the expansion cap.

12. Close the bleeder screw on the radiator when coolant flows out. Add coolant if necessary and close the tank cap.

13. Close the bleeder screw in the engine compartment, and switch off the engine. If necessary, top up the expansion tank.

Fan
REMOVAL & INSTALLATION

RWD Vanagon
AIR-COOLED ENGINE ONLY

1. Pry out the alternator cover insert, and, using a 12 point Allen wrench, loosen the alternator adjusting belt, the ignition timing scale and the grille over the fan. Remove the three socket head screws attaching the fan and crankshaft assembly to the crankshaft and remove the fan and pulley.

2. Disconnect the cooling air control cable at the flap control shaft.

3. On models so equipped, pull out the rubber elbow for the alternator from the front half of the fan housing.

4. Remove the four nuts retaining the fan housing to the engine crankcase. The assembled fan housing may then be removed by pulling it to the rear and off the engine. It is not necessary to separate the fan housing halves or remove the alternator to remove the fan housing.

5. Reverse the above procedure to install.

Water Pump
REMOVAL & INSTALLATION

Gasoline Engines
FWD MODELS

4 Cylinder Engine
1. Drain the cooling system.

2. Remove the alternator and drive belt. Remove the air injection pump belt, if equipped.

3. Disconnect the lower radiator hose, engine hose and heater hose from the water pump. Remove the timing belt cover-to-water pump bolt.

4. Remove the four pump retaining bolts. Notice where the different length bolts are located.

5. Turn the pump slightly and lift it out of the engine block.

6. Installation is the reverse of removal. Use a new seal on the mating surface of the engine. Torque the pump-to-engine bolts to 15 ft. lbs. (20 Nm).

NOTE: On 1985–88 Golf models with power steering use the same V-belt pulley. The pulley is marked with the word Klima. When installing the pulley on models with A/C – Klima faces out. On non-A/C models – Klima must face inward toward the engine.

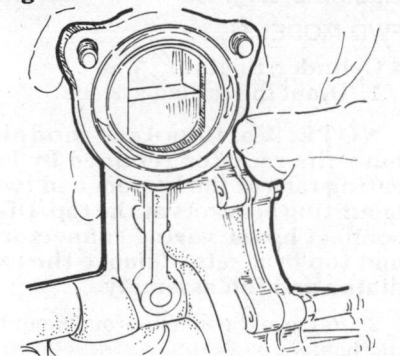

Check the condition of the O-ring before installing the water pump

5 Cylinder Engine
1. Drain the cooling system.

2. Remove the timing belt cover.

3. Turn the crankshaft to place the engine on TDC; align the flywheel with the mark on the clutch housing.

4. Loosen the water pump to relieve the tension on the timing belt.

5. Remove the timing belt.

6. Remove the water pump mounting bolts and the pump.

7. Clean the water pump mounting surfaces.

8. To install, use a new O-ring and reverse the removal procedures. Torque the water pump-to-engine bolts to 14 ft. lbs. (20 Nm).

RWD VANAGON
Waterboxer Engine
1. Drain the cooling system.

2. Remove the alternator, drive belt and V belt pulley. Remove the air injection pump belt, if equipped.

3. Without disconnecting any A/C refrigerant lines, disconnect the air conditioning compressor and secure it safely out of the way. Then remove the compressor bracket and crossover pipe.

4. Disconnect the lower radiator hose, engine hose and heater hose from the water pump.

5. Remove the water pump mounting bolts.

6. Turn the pump on an angle and remove it from the vehicle.

7. Clean the water pump mounting surfaces.

8. To install, use a new O-ring and reverse the removal procedures. Torque the water pump-to-engine bolts to 14 ft. lbs. (20 Nm).

Diesel Engine
ALL MODELS

1. Drain the cooling system.

2. Remove the alternator and drive belt.

3. Remove the timing belt cover.

4. Disconnect the lower radiator hoses, engine hose, and heater hose from the water pump.

5. Remove the pump retaining bolts. Notice where the different length bolts are located.

6. Turn the pump slightly and lift it out of the engine block.

7. Installation is the reverse of removal. Use a new seal on the mating surface with the engine. Check O-ring condition and replace if necessary.

Thermostat
REMOVAL & INSTALLATION

4 Cylinder Gas and Diesel Engines
FRONT AND REAR WHEEL DRIVE MODELS

The thermostat is located in the bottom radiator hose neck on the water pump.

1. Drain the cooling system.

2. Remove the two retaining bolts from the lower water pump neck.

NOTE: It's not necessary to disconnect the hose.

3. Move the neck, with the hoses attached, out of the way.

4. Remove the thermostat.

5. Install a new seal on the water pump neck.

6. Install the thermostat with the spring end up.

7. Replace the water pump neck and tighten the two retaining bolts. Torque the bolts to 7 ft. lbs. (10 Nm).

FWD Models
5 CYLINDER ENGINE

The thermostat is located on the lower radiator hose neck, on the left side of the engine block, behind the water pump housing.

Follow Steps 1–3 of the "4 Cylinder" procedure.

1. Carefully pry the thermostat out of the engine block.
2. Install a new O-ring on the water pump neck.
3. Install the thermostat.

NOTE: When installing the thermostat, the spring end should be pointing toward the engine block.

4. Reposition the water pump neck and tighten the retaining bolts. Torque the mounting bolts to 7 ft. lbs. (10 Nm).

RWD Vanagon
WATERBOXER ENGINE

The thermostat is mounted inside a coolant elbow on the driver's side cylinder head (the left side, as you face the rear of the vehicle). Unbolt the elbow and remove the thermostat. Make sure the O-ring is in good condition and properly seated during installation.

EMISSION CONTROLS

Please refer to "Emission Control" in the Unit Repair section for system maintenance procedures. Due to the complex nature of the modern electronic engine control systems, comprehensive diagnosis and testing procedures fall outside the confines of this repair manual. For complete information on diagnosis, testing and repair procedures concerning all modern engine and emission control systems, please refer to *"Chilton's Guide to Electronic Engine Controls"*.

EGR MAINTENANCE REMINDER SYSTEM

The EGR reminder light in the speedometer should light up every 15,000 miles as a reminder for maintenance.

To reset the light switch, press the white button. The speedometer light should go out.

GASOLINE FUEL SYSTEM

For service information, refer to the "Carburetor" or the Fuel Injection" sections in the Unit Repair section.

Fuel Filter

REMOVAL & INSTALLATION

Carburetor

NOTE: The fuel filter is installed between the fuel pump and the carburetor.

1. Wrap a towel around the filter and remove the fuel lines.
2. Remove the filter from the mounting bracket.

NOTE: When installing a new fuel filter, place it with the 2 tubes facing UP.

3. To install, reverse the removal procedures.

CIS System

ALL FWD MODELS EXCEPT 1985–88 CABRIOLET, GOLF, GTI AND JETTA

NOTE: The filter is located in the engine compartment.

1. Disconnect the negative battery cable.
2. Remove the fuel filter mounting nuts and lift the filter from the mount.
3. Loosen the filter cap and the fuel lines to relieve the pressure in the system.

— **CAUTION** —

When relieving the pressure in the fuel system, place a container under the filter to catch the excess fuel.

4. Disconnect the fuel lines and remove the filter.

NOTE: When installing the fuel lines, use 4 new sealing rings.

5. To install, reverse the removal procedures. Torque the fuel lines-to-new filter to 14 ft. lbs. (20 Nm).

1985–88 CABRIOLET, GOLF, GTI AND JETTA

NOTE: The fuel filter is located in the fuel pump assembly, mounted under the vehicle, in front of the fuel tank.

1. Disconnect the negative battery cable.

2. Raise and support the rear of the vehicle on jackstands.
3. Loosen the fuel lines to relieve the pressure in the system.

— **CAUTION** —

When relieving the pressure in the fuel system, place a container under the filter to catch the excess fuel.

4. Remove the fuel lines, the mounting bracket nut and the filter.

NOTE: When installing the fuel lines, use 4 new sealing rings.

5. To install, reverse the removal procedures. Torque the fuel lines-to-new filter to 14 ft. lbs. (20 Nm).

RWD VANAGON

NOTE: The fuel filter is located near the front axle, next to the fuel pump.

1. Disconnect the negative battery cable.
2. Raise the front of the vehicle and support it safely on jack stands.
3. Loosen the fuel lines to relieve the pressure in the system.

— **CAUTION** —

When relieving the pressure in the fuel system, place a container under the filter to catch the excess fuel.

4. Remove the fuel lines, the mounting bracket nut and the filter.
5. Installation is the reverse of the removal procedure.

Mechanical Fuel Pump

NOTE: The mechanical fuel pump found on carbureted Rabbits is mounted on the side of the engine block.

CLEANING

The filter screen can be removed from the pump and cleaned.

1. Remove the center cover screw.
2. Remove the screen and gasket. Clean the screen in solvent.
3. Replace the screen.
4. Install a new gasket and replace the cover.

NOTE: Make sure the depression in the pump cover engages the projection on the body of the pump.

REMOVAL & INSTALLATION

The pump cannot be repaired and must be replaced when defective.

1. Disconnect and plug both fuel lines.
2. Remove the two Allen head retaining bolts.

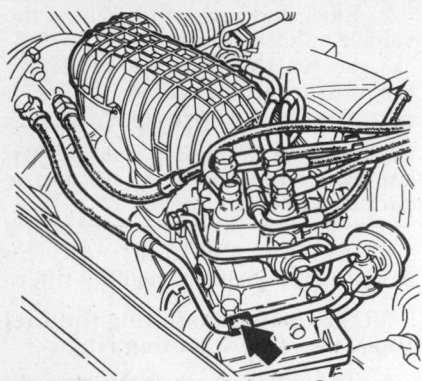

Excessive fuel pump noise on Quantum models can be eliminated with the installation of a fuel damper. Consult the dealer for necessary parts

3. Remove the fuel pump and its plastic flange.

4. Replace the pump in the reverse order of removal. Use a new flange seal.

Electric Fuel Pump

TESTING—ELECTRICAL

NOTE: Volkswagen uses a continuous injection system (CIS) in its fuel injected gasoline engines. The system includes an electric fuel pump mounted in front of the right rear axle on Fox's, Rabbits and Sciroccos, near the front axle on the Vanagon, and mounted below the fuel accumulator near the rear wheel on Dashers. The Jetta fuel pump is on the passenger's side in front of the rear wheel (accessible through a cover plate). The Quantum fuel pump is mounted inside the top of the car's plastic fuel tank (accessible through the rear cargo area, underneath the carpet).

1. Have an assistant operate the starter. Listen at the rear wheel on all the front wheel drive models, and at the front axle on Vanagons to determine if the pump is running.

2. If the pump is not running, check the fuse on the front of the fuel pump relay.

1985 and later gas engine fuel pump assembly

3. If the fuse is good, replace the fuel pump relay.

4. If the fuel pump still does not operate, the fuel pump is faulty and must be replaced.

TESTING—FUEL PUMP DELIVERY

1. Check the condition of the fuel filter, make sure it is clean.

2. Connect a jumper wire between the No. 1 terminal on the ignition coil and ground.

3. Disconnect the return fuel line and hold it in a measuring container with a capacity of 1 quart or 1000cc.

4. Have an assistant run the starter for 30 seconds while watching the quantity of fuel delivered.

The minimum allowable flow is 900cc ($\frac{9}{10}$ of a quart) in 30 seconds.

For Dashers with the type A fuel pump, identified by the fuel inlet and outlet ports being at opposite ends of the pump, the pump must deliver 1000cc (1 quart) of fuel in 32 seconds. For Dashers with the type B fuel pump, identified by the inlet and outlet ports forming a 90° angle through the center of the pump, the pump must deliver 1000cc (1 quart) of fuel in 40 seconds. Quantum fuel pump must deliver 700cc of fuel in 30 seconds.

NOTE: For the above test, the battery must be fully charged. Also, make sure you have plenty of fuel in the tank.

If the pump fails its specific test, check for a dirty fuel filter, blocked lines or blocked fuel tank strainer (if so equipped). If all of these are in good condition, replace the pump.

REMOVAL & INSTALLATION

All FWD Models Except— 1985–88 Cabriolet, Golf, GTI, Jetta And All Quantum Models

NOTE: The fuel pump is located under the vehicle in front of the rear axle on the right side.

1. Disconnect the negative battery cable.

2. Raise and support the rear of the vehicle on jackstands.

3. Disconnect the electrical connector.

4. Loosen the fuel lines to relieve the pressure in the system.

———— CAUTION ————

When relieving the pressure in the fuel system, place a container under the fuel pump to catch the excess fuel.

5. Remove the mounting bolts and the fuel pump.

NOTE: When installing the fuel lines, use 4 new sealing rings.

6. To install, reverse the removal procedures.

1985–88 Cabriolet, Golf, GTI, Jetta and All Quantum Models

NOTE: The fuel pump assembly is located under the vehicle in front of the fuel tank.

1. Disconnect the negative battery cable.

2. Raise and support the vehicle on jackstands.

3. Disconnect the electrical connector.

4. Loosen the fuel lines to relieve the pressure in the system.

———— CAUTION ————

When relieving the pressure in the fuel system, place a container under the filter to catch the excess fuel.

5. Remove the adapter and the mounting ring from the fuel pump, then pull the pump from the assembly

———— CAUTION ————

BE CAREFUL when removing the fuel pump, for excess fuel will drain from the reservoir.

6. To install, use a new O-ring and reverse the removal procedures.

RWD Vanagon

1. Disconnect the fuel pump wiring. Pull the plug from the pump but do not pull on the wiring.

2. Disconnect the fuel hoses and plug them to prevent any leakage.

3. Remove the two nuts which secure the pump and then remove the pump.

4. Reconnect the fuel pump hoses and wiring and install the pump on the vehicle.

ADJUSTMENTS
Vanagon Only

Electric fuel pump pressure is 28 psi (29 psi on the Waterboxer). Fuel pump pressure is determined by a pressure regulator which diverts part of the fuel pump output to the gas tank when 28 psi is reached. The regulator, located on the engine firewall, has a screw and locknut on its end. Loosen the locknut and adjust the screw to adjust the pressure. Do not force the screw in or out if it does not turn.

Transfer Pump

NOTE: The transfer is a new feature on the 1985–88 Cabriolet, Golf, GTI and Jetta, it is located

in the fuel tank and attached to the end of the sending unit.

REMOVAL & INSTALLATION

1. Disconnect the negative cable.
2. Open the rear of the vehicle, pull back the carpet and remove the cover plate from the floor.
3. Disconnect the electrical connector from the sending unit.
4. Remove the fuel hoses from the sending unit.
5. Unscrew the plastic cap and lift the sending unit from the fuel tank.
6. Remove the transfer pump from the sending unit.
7. To install, reverse the removal procedures.

Carburetor
REMOVAL & INSTALLATION

1. Remove the air cleaner.
2. Disconnect the fuel line.
3. Drain some of the coolant and then disconnect the choke hoses.
4. Disconnect the distributor and EGR valve vacuum lines.
5. Disconnect the electrical lead for the idle cut-off valve. For 1982–88 models, also disconnect the feedback solenoid, anti-diesel connector and the bowl vent connector.
6. Remove the clip which secures the throttle linkage to the carburetor. Detach the linkage, being careful not to lose any washers or bushings.
7. Unbolt the carburetor from the manifold and remove it.
8. Use a new gasket when replacing the carburetor. Don't overtighten the nuts.

AUTOMATIC CHOKE ADJUSTMENT

The standard adjustment on all versions of the automatic choke is with the two notches aligned with the notch on the housing. To adjust, loosen the three clamping screws and move the outer part of the choke unit.

THROTTLE GAP ADJUSTMENT
1982–84 Rabbit

Throttle gap is set at the factory and should not be tampered with.

FAST IDLE ADJUSTMENT
1982–84 Rabbit

1. Run the engine until it reaches normal operating temperature. Make sure that the timing and idle speed are set to specifications.

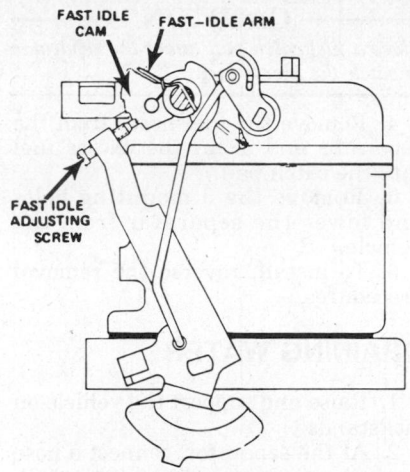

Adjusting the fast idle—1982 Rabbit

2. Run the engine at idle and set the fast idle adjustment screw to the second step of the fast idle cam.
3. Disconnect the purge valve. Disconnect and plug the vacuum hose at the EGR valve.
4. Connect a tachometer as per the manufacturer's instructions and check that the engine speed is 2800–3200 rpm. If not, turn the fast idle screw until it is.
5. Reconnect the purge valve and the vacuum hose at the EGR valve.

CHOKE GAP ADJUSTMENT
1982–84 Rabbit

1. Set the cold idle speed adjuster screw in its upper notch.
2. Connect a manually operated vacuum pump to the connection on the pulldown unit and build up vacuum.
3. Close the choke valve by hand with the lever and check the choke valve gap with a drill. The gap should be 3.3–3.7mm. (3.9mm for 1982–88).
4. Adjust the gap using the adjusting screw in the end of the vacuum unit at the side of the choke unit. After adjusting, lock the screw with sealant.

THROTTLE LINKAGE ADJUSTMENT
All Models (Carburetor Equipped)

Throttle linkage adjustments are not normally required. However, it is a good idea to make sure that the throttle(s) in the carburetor open all the way when the accelerator pedal is held on the wide-open position. Only the primary (first stage) throttle valve will open when the pedal is pushed with the engine off: the secondary throttle on Volkswagen two-barrel carburetors is vacuum-operated.

Make note of the following:
  a. Always be careful not to kink or twist the cables during installation or adjustment—this can cause rapid wear and binding.
  b. The accelerator cable will only bend one way—make sure you install it with the bends in the right positions.

NOTE: When installing new cables, all bends should be as wide as possible, and fittings between which the inner cable is exposed must be aligned.

OVERHAUL

For all carburetor overhaul procedures, please refer to "Carburetor Service" in the Unit Repair Section.

Fuel Injection

Due to the complex nature of modern fuel injection systems, comprehensive diagnosis and testing procedures fall outside the confines of this repair manual. For complete information on fuel injection diagnosis, testing and repair procedures please refer to *Chilton's Guide To Fuel Injection And Feedback Carburetors.*

DIESEL FUEL SYSTEM

Fuel Filter

REMOVAL & INSTALLATION

NOTE: The fuel filter is located in the engine compartment near the fuel injection pump.

Except 1985–88 Golf/Jetta

1. Disconnect the negative battery cable.
2. Using tool US–4462, loosen the fuel filter clamp.
3. Remove the top 2 filter assembly nuts.
4. Lift the filter assembly straight up and remove the old filter.

NOTE: When installing a new filter, coat the outside and partly fill it with diesel fuel.

5. To install, reverse the removal procedures. Torque the filter assembly-to-mount nuts to 18 ft. lbs. (25 Nm). Start the engine, accelerate it a few times (to clear the air bubbles) and check for fuel leaks.

1985–88 Golf And Jetta

1. Using clamps, pinch off the fuel lines at the fuel filter.
2. Remove the fuel lines from the filter.
3. Loosen the mounting clamp or screws and lift the filter assembly straight up. Remove the old filter.

NOTE: When installing a new filter, coat the outside and partly fill it with diesel fuel.

4. To install, reverse the removal procedures. Torque the filter assembly-to-mount nuts to 18 ft. lbs. (25 Nm). Start the engine, accelerate it a few times (to clear the air bubbles) and check for fuel leaks.

DRAINING WATER

1. Disconnect the negative battery cable.
2. Remove the fuel return line from the injection pump to provide room to open the vent screw on the fuel filter flange.
3. Remove the 2 filter assembly mounting nuts and lift the filter from the mount.

NOTE: When draining the water from the fuel filter, place container under the filter to catch the water and the excess fuel.

4. Loosen the drain plug on the bottom of the filter and drain the fuel into a container, until it runs free of water.
5. Tighten the drain plug.
6. To install, reverse the removal procedures. Torque the filter assembly mounting nuts to 18 ft. lbs. (25 Nm). Start the engine, accelerate it a few times (to clear the air bubbles) and check for leaks.

Water Separator

1985–88

NOTE: The water separator is located in front of the fuel tank under the right side of the vehicle; it's purpose is to filter the water from the fuel. When the water level in the separator reaches a certain point, a sensor turns on the glow plug indicator light, causing it to blink continuously.

REMOVAL & INSTALLATION

1. Disconnect the negative battery cable.
2. Raise and support the vehicle on jackstands.
3. At the separator, disconnect the electrical connector and clamp both fuel hoses.

CAUTION

Place a fuel catch pan under the separator to catch the excess fuel.

---

4. Remove the fuel hoses from the separator and drain the excess fuel into the catch pan.
5. Remove the 3 mounting bolts and lower the separator from the vehicle.
6. To install, reverse the removal procedures.

DRAINING WATER

1. Raise and support the vehicle on jackstands.
2. At the separator, connect a hose from the separator drain to a catch pan.

CAUTION

Place a fuel catch pan under the separator to catch the excess fuel.

---

3. Open the drain valve (3 turns) and remove the water until a steady stream of fuel flows from the separator, then close the valve.

Diesel Injection Pump
REMOVAL & INSTALLATION

1. Refer to the "Diesel Timing Cover, Removal and Installation" procedures in this section and remove the timing belt cover(s).
2. Remove the cylinder head cover and the plug cover on top of the bell housing.
3. Turn the crankshaft to place the No. 1 cyl on TDC of the compression stroke (the TDC mark on the flywheel must align with the pointer).
4. Loosen the camshaft nut and tap the back of the camshaft sprocket with a rubber mallet until it is loose, then remove the sprocket.
5. Fasten the setting bar tool 2065A to the end of the camshaft. Turn the camshaft until one end of the bar touches the cylinder head. Using a feeler gauge, measure the clearance at the other end. Using 2 feeler gauges of half of the acquired measurement, insert them between each end of the bar and the cylinder head.

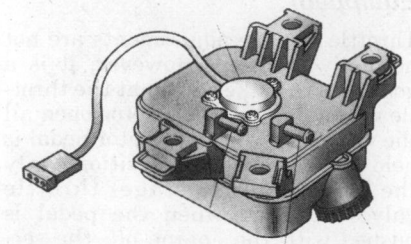

Water separator for 1985 and later diesel engine

6. Loosen the tensioner pulley and remove the timing belt from the engine.
7. Loosen the shaft nut from the injection pump sprocket.
8. Install the sprocket puller tool 3032 and apply tension to the injection pump sprocket.
9. Using a light hammer, strike the puller spindle head with a few light blows to loosen the sprocket from the tapered shaft.
10. Remove the injection pump shaft nut and the sprocket.
11. Using a box wrench tool 3035, disconnect the fuel lines from the injection pump and cover the openings with a clean cloth.

CAUTION

To avoid damaging the injection pump plunger, DO NOT loosen the bolts on the fuel distributor head.

---

12. Disconnect the fuel cut-off valve, the accelerator and the cold start cables from the injection pump.
13. Remove the injection pump-to-mounting bracket bolts and the injection pump from the engine.

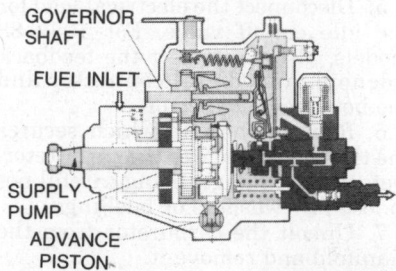

Fuel injection pump for 1985 and later diesel engine

14. To install, set the injection timing (align the mark on top of the injection pump with the mark on the mounting plate) and reverse the removal procedures. Torque the injection pump mounting bolts to 18 ft. lbs. (25 Nm), the injection pump sprocket nut to 33 ft. lbs. (45 Nm) and the fuel injection lines-to-pump to 18 ft. lbs. (25 Nm).

NOTE: When installing the fuel supply and the return pipe union screws, DO NOT interchange them; the return pipe union screw is marked with OUT on the head.

INJECTION TIMING

1. Refer to the "Diesel Timing Belt, Removal and Installation" procedures in this section and remove the timing belt.
2. Turn the crankshaft to place the No. 1 cyl on TDC of the compression stroke (the TDC mark on the flywheel must align with the pointer).

NOTE: The cold start cable MUST NOT be pulled in (the actuation lever on the injection pump must be in Neutral).

3. Turn the injection pump sprocket so that the mark on the sprocket is aligned with the mark on the mounting plate.

4. Using the pin tool 2064, insert it through the sprocket hole, locking the sprocket to the injection pump.

5. Loosen the camshaft nut and tap the back of the camshaft sprocket with a rubber mallet until it is loose, then remove the sprocket.

6. Fasten the setting bar tool 2065A to the end of the camshaft. Turn the camshaft until the end of the bar touches the cylinder head. Using a feeler gauge, measure the clearance at the other end. Using 2 feeler gauges of half of the acquired measurement, insert them between each end of the bar and the cylinder head.

7. Install the camshaft sprocket, torque the sprocket nut to 33 ft. lbs. (45 Nm) and remove the setting bar tool.

8. Install the timing belt and remove the lock pin tool from the injection pump sprocket.

9. Tension the drive belt by turning the tensioner pulley clockwise until belt flex of ½ in. (13mm) is established between the camshaft and the pump sprockets.

10. Turn the crankshaft 2 complete revolutions and check the belt tension.

NOTE: It may be necessary to strike the timing belt between the camshaft and the pump sprockets with a rubber mallet to eliminate the play in the drive belt.

11. Remove the sealing plug on the injection pump head, then install the adapter tool 2066 and a dial micrometer (preload the micrometer to 2.5mm).

12. Slowly turn the engine counterclockwise until the dial gauge stops moving, then zero the micrometer.

13. Turn the engine clockwise until the TDC mark on the flywheel aligns with the pointer on the bell housing.

NOTE: The adjusting value is 0.036–0.038 in. (0.93–0.97mm) for the diesel engine or 0.038–0.040 in. (0.98–1.02mm) for the turbo diesel.

14. If adjustment of the pump is necessary, loosen the 2 upper mounting bolts, the rear support bolt and the lower front bolt through the sprocket, then turn the pump until the correct value is reached.

15. To complete the installation, reverse the removal procedures. Torque

the pump cover plug to 11 ft. lbs. (15 Nm). Check the delivery rate, the idle and the maximum speeds.

Fuel Injectors
REMOVAL & INSTALLATION

1. Using the wrench tool 3035, remove the fuel lines from the injectors.

2. Using the sprocket wrench tool SW–27, remove the fuel injectors from the engine.

— CAUTION —
Always remove the fuel injector lines as a complete set and DO NOT bend the formed pipes.

NOTE: When installing the injectors, always use new heat shields. Install them with the wide sides facing up.

3. To install, reverse the removal procedures. Torque the fuel injectors to 51 ft. lbs. (70 Nm) and the fuel lines-to-injectors to 18 ft. lbs. (25 Nm).

MANUAL TRANSAXLE

REMOVAL & INSTALLATION

All FWD Models Except Dasher, Fox and Quantum

1. Disconnect the negative battery cable.

2. Disconnect the back-up light switch connector and the speedometer cable from the transaxle (plug the speedometer cable hole).

3. Connect the engine sling tool 10–222A to the engine and support slightly.

4. Remove the upper transaxle-to-engine bolts.

5. At the transaxle housing, disconnect the clutch cable from the clutch release lever.

6. Remove the 3 mounting bolts from the right engine support.

7. At the gear selector lever shaft, disconnect the short rod and the connecting rod from the lever. Remove the long selector rod from the relay lever.

8. Remove the mounting bolt and the 2 upper bolts from the left transaxle housing-to-mount.

9. Remove the left wheel housing liner.

10. Detach the axle shafts from the transaxle and support on a wire.

11. Remove the large and the small cover plates from behind the right drive flange.

NOTE: On models thru 1984, DO NOT remove the large cover plate.

12. Remove the starter and the front mount assembly.

13. Remove the 3rd mounting bolt from the left transaxle mount.

14. Lower the transaxle slightly and remove the left transaxle mounting bolts.

15. Push the engine-to-transaxle assembly to the right as far as possible ¹⁄₁₆ in. (4mm).

16. Place a transaxle support jack under the transaxle, remove the lower transaxle-to-engine bolts and lower the transaxle from the vehicle.

17. To install, coat the input shaft lightly with Moly lube and reverse the removal procedures. Torque the engine-to-transaxle bolts to 55 ft. lbs. (75 Nm), the starter bolts to 44 ft. lbs. (60 Nm), the axle shaft-to-flange to 33 ft. lbs. (45 Nm) and the transaxle-to-housing mount to 44 ft. lbs. (60 Nm). Adjust the clutch free play.

Dasher and Fox

1. Disconnect the battery ground cable.

2. Disconnect the exhaust pipe from the manifold and its bracket on the transaxle.

3. Remove the square-headed bolt on the shift linkage. Later models have a hex head bolt.

4. Press the shift linkage coupling off.

5. Disconnect the clutch cable.

6. Disconnect the speedometer cable.

7. Detach the halfshafts from the transaxle.

8. Remove the starter.

9. Remove the inspection plate.

10. Remove the engine-to-transaxle bolts.

11. Remove the transaxle crossmember.

12. Support the transaxle with a jack.

13. Pry the transaxle out from engine.

14. Lift the transaxle out of the car with an assistant.

15. Installation is the reverse of removal. Observe the following when installing the transaxle.

a. When installing the transaxle crossmember, do not fully tighten the bolts until the transaxle is aligned and fully installed in the vehicle.

b. Tighten the engine-to-transaxle bolts to 40 ft. lbs.

c. Tighten the axle shaft bolts to 33 ft. lbs. (45 Nm).

d. On models with the rubber core rear transaxle mount, the rubber core must be centered in its housing.

e. Make sure there is a ⅜ in. clearance between the header pipe and the floor of the vehicle.

f. Adjust the clutch (see below).

Quantum

1. Disconnect the battery ground strap.
2. Disconnect the exhaust pipe from the manifold and its bracket.
3. Unhook the clutch cable.
4. Detach the speedometer cable.
5. Remove the upper engine-to-transaxle bolts.
6. Remove the engine support bolts on both sides of the engine block (front).
7. Remove the front muffler and exhaust pipe.
8. Unbolt both axle shafts at the transaxle.
9. Disconnect the back-up light wiring.
10. Remove the inspection plate on the bottom of transaxle case.
11. Remove the starter bolt.
12. Remove the shift rod coupling bolt; pry off the shift rod coupling ball with a prybar.
13. Pull off the shift rod coupling from the shift rod.
14. Place a jack under the transaxle and lift slightly.
15. Remove the transaxle support bolts and transaxle rubber mounts.
16. Remove the front transaxle support bolts and lower the transaxle-to-engine support bolts.
17. Slowly pry the transaxle from the engine.
18. Lower the transaxle out of the car.

NOTE: Lubricate the main shaft splines with molybdenum-disulfide grease.

19. To install, reverse the removal procedures and finger tighten the bolts. When the mounting bolts are aligned and free of tension, tighten them. Torque the transaxle-to-engine bolts to 40 ft. lbs. (54 Nm), the axleshaft-to-drive flange bolts to 33

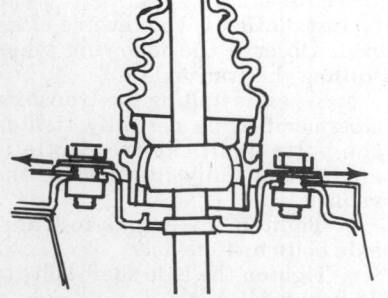

Quantum and Dasher manual transmission second gear shift lever adjustment

ft. lbs. (45 Nm), the transaxle-to-mount bolts to 18 ft. lbs. (24 Nm), and the transaxle mount-to-body bolts to 80 ft. lbs. (108 Nm).

RWD Vanagon

1. Disconnect the negative battery cable.
2. Remove the engine.
3. Remove the socket head screws which secure the driveshafts to the transmission. Remove the bolts from the transmission end first and then remove the shafts.

NOTE: It is not necessary to remove the driveshafts entirely from the car if the car does not have to be moved while the transaxle is out.

4. Disconnect the clutch slave cylinder from the clutch lever and remove the clutch cable and its guide tube from the transaxle. Loosen the square head bolt at the shift linkage coupling located near the rear of the transaxle. Slide the coupling off the inner shaft lever. It is necessary to work under the car to reach the coupling.
5. Disconnect the starter wiring.
6. Disconnect the back-up light switch wiring.
7. Remove the front transaxle mounting bolts.
8. Support the transaxle with a jack and remove the transaxle from the car.
9. Carefully lower the jack and remove the transaxle from the car.
10. To install, jack the transaxle into position and loosely install the bolts.
11. Tighten the transmission carrier bolts first, then tighten the front mounting nuts.
12. Install the driveshaft bolts with new lockwashers. The lockwashers should be positioned on the bolt with the convex side toward the screw head.
13. Reconnect the wiring, the clutch slave cylinder linkage and bleed the clutch system.

NOTE: It may be necessary to align the transmission so that the driveshaft joints do not rub the frame.

14. Install the engine.

SHIFT LINKAGE ADJUSTMENT

Dasher and Quantum

An adjusting tool, VW 3014, (VW 3057 for Quantum) must be used on these models.

1. Place the lever in Neutral.

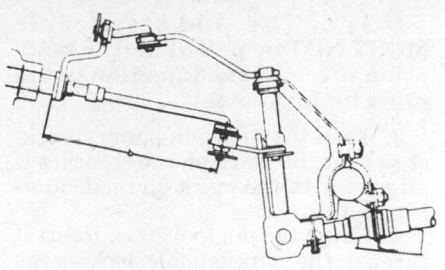

The long rod on the Rabbit and Scirocco shift linkage is to be adjusted to a length (b) of 6.42-6.50 in.

2. Working under the car, loosen the clamp nut.
3. Inside the car, remove the gear lever knob and the shift boot. It is not necessary to remove the console. Align the centering holes of the lever housing and the lever bearing housing.
4. Install the tool with the locating pin toward the front. Push the lever to the left side of the tool cut-out. Tighten the lower knurled knob to secure the tool.
5. Move the top slide of the tool to the left stop and tighten the upper knurled knob.
6. Push the shift lever to the right side of the cutout. Align the shift rod and shift finger under the car, and tighten the clamp nut. Remove the tool.
7. Place the lever in first. Press the lever to the left side against the stop. Release the lever; it should spring back ¼-½ in. If not, move the lever housing slightly sideways to correct. Check that all gears can be engaged easily, particularly reverse.

Rabbit, Scirocco and 1981–84 Jetta

1. Align the holes of the lever housing plate with the holes of the lever bearing plate.
2. Loosen the shift rod clamp. Pull the boot off the lever housing and push it out of the way. It may be necessary to loosen the screws in the cover plate to free the boot.
3. Check that the shift finger is in the center of the stopping plate.

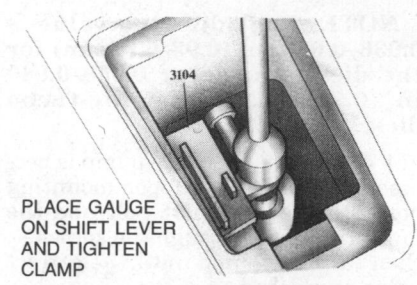

PLACE GAUGE ON SHIFT LEVER AND TIGHTEN CLAMP

Adjusting the shift linkage on the 1985 and later manual transaxle

4. Adjust the shift rod end so that it is ¾ in. (⁹⁄₃₂ in. for five speed transmissions) from the right side of the lever housing. Tighten the shift rod clamp and check the shifter operation.

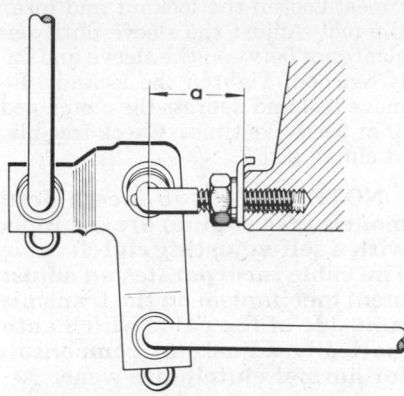

The short angled rod on the Rabbit and Scirocco shift linkage is to be adjusted to a length (a) of 1.18—1.25 in.

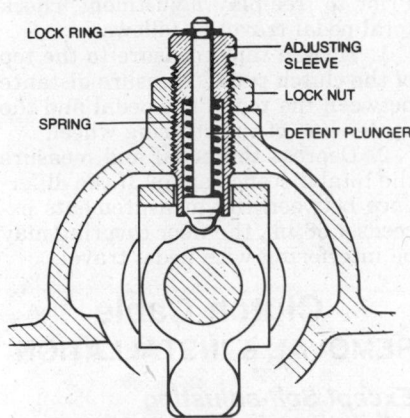

On Rabbit, Jetta and Scirocco, loosen the locknut and turn the adjusting sleeve

1985–88 Golf And Jetta

1. Place the shifter lever into the Neutral position.
2. Under the vehicle, loosen the clamp on the shifter rod.

NOTE: The shifter lever MUST move freely on the shifter rod.

3. Remove the shifter knob and the boot.
4. Position the gauge alignment tool 3104 on the shifting mechanism (lock it in place).
5. Place the transaxle selector lever in the Neutral position.
6. Align the shift rod with the selector lever and torque the clamp to 19 ft. lbs. (26 Nm).

NOTE: The shifter linkage MUST NOT be under load during the adjustment.

7. To complete the installation, reverse the removal procedures. Check the shifting of the gears.

Fox

1. Shift into Neutral.
2. Remove the gear shift lever knob and shift boot.
3. Loosen the clamp nuts and check that shift finger slides freely on the shift rod.
4. Move the gear shift lever to the right side, between third and fourth gear position. The gear shift lever should remain perpendicular to the ball housing.
5. With the inner shift lever in neutral and the gear shift lever bewtween second and third gear, tighten the clamp nut.
6. Check the engagement of all gears, including reverse, and make sure that the gear shift lever moves freely.

RWD Vanagon

1. The Volkswagen shift linkage is not adjustable. When shifting becomes difficult or there is an excessive amount of play in the linkage, check the shifting mechanism for worn parts. Make sure the shift linkage coupling is tightly connected to the inner shaft lever located at the rear of the transaxle under the rear seat. Worn parts may be found in the shift lever mechanism and the suports for the linkage rod sometimes wear out.
2. The gear shift lever can be removed after the front floor mat has been lifted.
3. After the two retaining screws have been removed from the gear shift lever ball housing, the gear shift lever, ball housing, ruber boot, and spring are removed as a unit.

———— **CAUTION** ————
Carefully mark the position of the stop plate and note the position of the turned up ramp at the side of the stop plate. Normally the ramp is turned up and on the right hand side of the hole.

4. Installation is the reverse of removal.
5. Lubricate all moving parts with grease.
6. Test the gear shift pattern. If there is difficulty in shifting, adjust the stop plate back and forth in its slotted holes.

OVERHAUL

For all transaxle overhaul procedures, please refer to "Manual Transaxle Overhaul" in the Unit Repair section.

CLUTCH

NOTE: 1985–88 Quantum 5 cyl models are equipped with hydraulic clutch linkage, the slave cylinder is equipped with a bleeder screw to purge air from the system. The clutch pedal linkage rod is adjustable to maintain proper pedal height (10mm above brake pedal).

Clutch Assembly
REMOVAL & INSTALLATION

Dasher, Fox and Quantum

1. Remove the transaxle.
2. Matchmark the flywheel and pressure plate if the pressure plate is being reused.
3. Gradually loosen the pressure plate bolts one or two turns at a time in a crisscross pattern to prevent distortion.
4. Remove the pressure plate and disc.
5. Check the clutch disc for uneven or excessive lining wear. Examine the pressure plate for cracking, scorching or scoring. Replace any questionable components.
6. Install the clutch disc and pressure plate. Use a dummy shaft to keep the disc centered.
7. Gradually tighten the pressure plate-to-flywheel bolts in a crisscross pattern. Tighten the bolts to 18 ft. lbs. (24 Nm).
8. Install the throwout bearing.
9. Install the transaxle on the engine.
10. Replace the transaxle.

Golf, Rabbit, Jetta, GTI, GLI and Scirocco

1. Remove the transaxle.
2. Attach a toothed flywheel holder tool VW-558 to the flywheel and gradually loosen the flywheel-to-pressure plate bolts one or two turns at a time in a crisscross pattern to prevent distortion.
3. Remove the flywheel and the clutch disc.
4. Use a small prybar to remove the release plate retaining ring. Remove the release plate.
5. Lock the pressure plate in place with tool VW-558 and unbolt it from the crankshaft. Loosen the bolts one or two turns at a time in a crisscross pattern to prevent distortion.
6. On installation, use new bolts to attach the pressure plate to the crankshaft. Use a thread locking compound and torque the bolts in a diagonal pattern to 54 ft. lbs. (73 Nm).

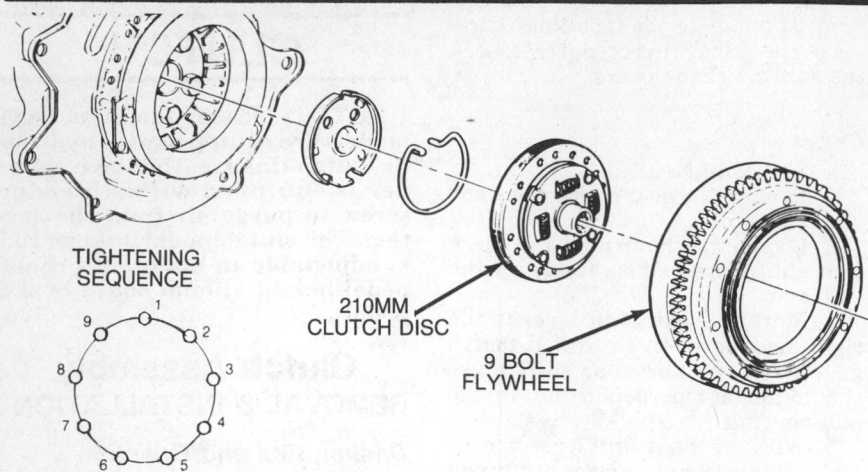

TIGHTENING SEQUENCE

210MM CLUTCH DISC

9 BOLT FLYWHEEL

Clutch assembly on transverse mounted engines. 210mm late model shown

7. Lubricate the clutch disc splines with multi-purpose grease. Lubricate the release plate contact surface and pushrod socket with multi-purpose grease. Install the release plate, retaining ring, and clutch disc.

8. Install a centering tool VW–547 to align the clutch disc.

9. Install the flywheel, tightening the bolts one or two turns at a time in a crisscross pattern to prevent distortion. Torque the bolts to 14 ft. lbs. (19 Nm).

10. Replace the transmission.

RWD Vanagon

The clutch used in all models is a single dry disc mounted on the flywheel with a diaphragm spring type pressure plate. The release bearing is the ball bearing type and does not require lubrication. The Vanagon utilizes a hydraulically engaged clutch. It features a clutch pedal operated master cylinder and a bell housing mounted slave cylinder.

1. Remove the engine.

2. Remove the pressure plate securing bolts one turn at a time until all spring pressure is released.

3. Remove the bolts and remove the clutch assembly.

NOTE: Notice which side of the clutch disc faces the flywheel and install the new disc in the same direction.

4. Before installing the new clutch, check the condition of the flywheel. It should not have excessive heat cracks and the friction surface should not be scored or warped. Check the condition of the throw out bearing. If the bearing is worn, replace it.

5. Lubricate the pilot bearing in the end of the cankshaft with grease.

6. Insert a pilot shaft, used for centering the clutch disc, through the clutch disc and place the disc against the flywheel. The pilot shaft will hold the disc in place.

NOTE: Make sure the correct side of the clutch disc is facing outward. The disc will rub the flywheel if it is incorrectly positioned.

8. After making sure that the pressure plate aligning dowels will fit into the pressure plate, gradually tighten the bolts.

9. Remove the pilot shaft and reinstall the engine.

10. Adjust the clutch pedal freeplay.

11. Bleed the clutch.

PEDAL HEIGHT/FREEPLAY ADJUSTMENT

Clutch pedal free-play should be ⅝ in. for all Dashers. All other models should have $^{27}/_{32}$ to 1 in. free-play.

Clutch pedal-free play is the distance the pedal can be depressed before the linkage starts to act on the throwout bearing. Clutch free-play insures that the clutch plate is fully engaged and not slipping. Clutches with no, or insufficient, free-play often wear out quickly and give marginal power performance.

1. Adjust the clutch pedal free-play by loosening or tightening the two nuts (or locknut and threaded sleeve) on the cable near the oil filter on the Dasher, Fox and Quantum. On the Golf, Rabbit, Jetta and Scirocco, the left side (driver's) at the front of the transaxle.

NOTE: Correct free-play cannot be measured correctly if the floor covering interferes with clutch pedal travel. See the following section for instruction on late model adjustment.

2. Loosen the locknut and loosen or tighten the adjusting nut or sleeve until desired play is present. Depress the clutch pedal several times and recheck free-play. Readjust if necessary.

Tighten the locknut.

3. On late models, VW recommends that a special tool (US5043) be used to determine proper adjustment. The procedure for adjustment follows; depress the clutch pedal several times. Loosen the locknut and insert the tool. Adjust the sleeve until zero clearance between the sleeve and tool is reached. Tighten the locknut. Remove tool and depress the clutch pedal at least five times. Check free-play at clutch pedal.

NOTE: 1986–88 (5 speed) Jetta models (gas engine) are equipped with a self-adjusting clutch cable. The cable incorporates an adjustment mechanism on the transmission side of the cable which automatically adjusts to compensate for normal clutch disc wear.

Checking Total Clutch Pedal Travel

Prior to free-play adjustment, check total pedal travel as follows:

1. Hook a tape measure to the top of the clutch pedal. Measure distance between the top of the pedal and the center-line of the steering wheel.

2. Depress the pedal and measure the total distance again. If the difference between the measurements exceeds 4.68 in., the floor covering may be interfering with pedal travel.

Clutch Cable
REMOVAL & INSTALLATION

Except Self-adjusting

1. Loosen the adjustment.

2. Disengage the cable from the clutch arm.

3. Unhook the cable from the pedal. Remove the threaded eye from the end of the cable. Remove the adjustment nut(s).

4. Remove the C-clip which holds the outer cable at the adjustment point. Remove all the washers and bushings, first noting their locations.

5. Pull the cable out of the firewall toward the engine compartment side.

6. Install and connect the new cable. Adjust the pedal free-play.

Self-adjusting

1. Depress the pedal and release several times.

2. Compress the spring located under the boot at the top of the adjuster mechanism and remove the cable at the release lever.

3. Unhook the eye from the clutch pedal and remove the cable.

4. Install the new cable onto the pedal. Compress the spring and have a helper pull the cable down and install to the release lever.

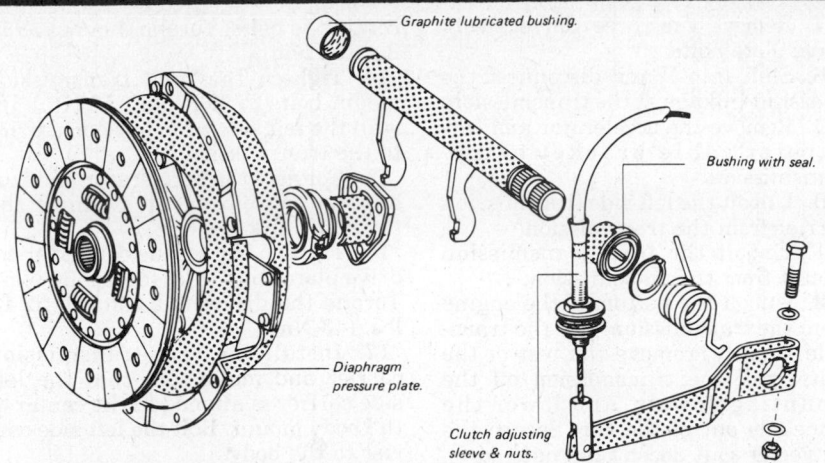

Graphite lubricated bushing.

Bushing with seal.

Diaphragm pressure plate.

Clutch adjusting sleeve & nuts.

Quantum and Dasher clutch components; the adjusting sleeve and nuts are adjacent to the oil filter in the engine compartment

5. If the adjuster spring is retained by a strap, remove the strap after cable installation.

6. Depress the clutch pedal several times to adjust the cable.

Clutch Master Cylinder
REMOVAL & INSTALLATION

RWD Vanagon

1. Siphon the hydraulic fluid from the master cylinder (clutch) reservoir.

2. Pull back the carpeting from the pedal area and lay down some absorbent rags.

3. Pull the elbow connection from the top of the master cylinder.

4. Disconnect and plug the pressure line from the rear of the master cylinder.

5. Remove the master cylinder mounting bolts and remove the cylinder to the rear.

6. Reverse the above procedure to install, taking care to bleed the system and adjust pedal free-play.

Clutch Slave Cylinder
REMOVAL & INSTALLATION
RWD Vanagon

1. Locate the slave cylinder on the bell housing.

2. Disconnect and plug the pressure line from the slave cylinder.

3. Disconnect the return spring from the pushrod.

4. Remove the retaining circlip from the boot and remove the boot.

5. Remove the circlip and slide the slave cylinder rearwards from its mount.

6. Remove the spring clip from the mount.

7. Reverse the above procedure to install, taking care to bleed the system and adjust pedal free-play.

CLUTCH SYSTEM BLEEDING AND ADJUSTMENT

Whenever air enters the clutch hydraulic system due to leakage, or if any part of the system is removed for service, the system must be bled. The hydraulic system uses high quality brake fluid meeting SAEJ1703 or DOT3 or DOT4 specifications. Brake fluid is highly corrosive to paint finishes and care should be exercised that no spillage occurs. The procedure is as follows:

1. Top up the clutch fluid reservoir and make sure the cap vent is open.

2. Locate the slave cylinder bleed nipple and remove all dirt and grease from the valve. Attach a hose to the nipple and submerge the other end of the hose in a jar containing a few inches of clean brake fluid.

3. Find a friend to operate the clutch pedal. When your friend depresses the clutch pedal slowly to the floor, open the bleeder valve about one turn. Have your friend keep the pedal on the floor until you close the bleeder valve. Repeat this operation several times until no air bubbles are emitted from the tube.

NOTE: Keep a close check on the fluid level in the fluid reservoir. Never let the level fall below the ½ full mark.

4. After bleeding discard the old fluid and top up the reservoir.

5. The clutch pedal should have a free-play of 0.20–0.28 in., and a 7 in. total travel. If either of the above are not to specifications, adjust the master cylinder as follows.

6. Loosen the master cylinder pushrod locknut and shorten the pushrod length slightly.

7. Loosen the master cylinder bolts and push the cylinder as far forward as it will go. Retighten the bolts.

8. Remove the rubber cap from the

clutch pedal stop screw and adjust distance to 0.89 in. Install the rubber cap.

9. Then lengthen the pushrod as necessary to obtain a pedal free-play of 0.20–0.28 in. Tighten the pushrod locknut.

10. Road-test the car.

AUTOMATIC TRANSAXLE

REMOVAL & INSTALLATION

Dasher and Quantum

The following procedures are for both types of Dasher automatic transmissions, the 003 and the 089. The type numbers are visible on the top of the automatic transmission unit (as opposed to the differential unit) of the transaxle. Another way to tell the type 003 transmission from the 089 is the type 003 has a vacuum modulator hose coming from the driver's side front of the transmission above the pan. The type 089 does not. Don't confuse the ATF filler pipe with the above mentioned hose. Quantum transmission is the 089 model.

1. Disconnect the battery ground strap.

2. Raise the car and place the support stands so that you will have free access to the transaxle and axle shafts.

3. Disconnect the speedometer cable.

4. On the 089, remove the accelerator cable from the throttle valve housing.

5. Remove two of the upper engine/transaxle bolts. On the 089 transmission support the engine with either special tool 10–222 or an appropriate jack.

6. Disconnect the exhaust pipe.

7. Remove the torque converter cover plate. On the 003 transmission, remove the vacuum modulator hose.

8. Remove the circlip holding the selector lever cable to the lever and remove the cable.

9. Remove the starter.

10. On the 003, disconnect the kickdown switch wires.

11. The torque converter is mounted to the flywheel by three bolts. The bolts are accesible through the starter hole. You'll have to turn the engine over by hand to remove all three.

12. Remove the axle shaft-to-transaxle socket head bolts.

13. Matchmark the position of the ball joint on the left control arm and

remove the ball joint from the arm. Hold the wheel assembly out away from the arm to provide clearance between the axle shaft and the transmission.

14. Remove the exhaust pipe from the transaxle bracket.

15. Disconnect the remaining transmission controls. Those you cannot reach can be removed when the transaxle is lowered a little.

16. Unbolt the transaxle crossmember and remove it from the transaxle.

17. Support the transaxle on a jack and loosen the lower engine/transaxle bolts.

18. On the 089 transmission, remove all engine/transaxle bolts. Have an assistant pull the left wheel out as far as it will go and slowly lower the transmission, making sure the torque converter does not fall off.

19. On the 003 transmission, loosen the union nut on the ATF filler pipe so that the pipe can be swivelled. Remove the engine/transaxle bolts and lower the unit. You may have to pull the left wheel out a little so that the axle shaft clears the transaxle case. Make sure the torque converter does not fall off.

20. Installation is the reverse of removal with the following notes.

   a. On both transaxles, the torque converter nipple must be about $^{13}/_{16}$ in. from the bell housing face surface. If it sticks out further than this, the oil pump shaft has probably pulled out. You'll have to manipulate the converter and shaft until it goes in again.

   b. Tighten the engine/transaxle bolts to 40 ft. lbs. (30 Nm) and the torque converter bolts to 20–23 ft. lbs. (27–31 Nm). New torque converter bolts should be used. Torque the axleshaft bolts to 33 ft. lbs. (45 Nm) and the ball joint-to-control arm bolts to 45 ft. lbs. (61 Nm). Check the shift linkage adjustment.

1981–84 Rabbit, Scirocco, Jetta

The engine and transaxle may be removed together as explained under "Engine Removal & Installation" or the transaxle may be removed alone, as explained here.

1. Disconnect both battery cables.

2. Disconnect the speedometer cable at the transmission.

3. Support the left end of the engine at the lifting eye. Attach a hoist to the transaxle.

4. Unbolt the rear transmission carrier from the body then from the transaxle. Unbolt the left side carrier from the body.

5. Unbolt the halfshafts and wire them up.

6. Remove the starter.

7. Remove the three converter-to-drive plate bolts.

8. Shift into P and disconnect the floorshift linkage at the transmission.

9. Remove the accelerator and carburetor cable bracket at the transmission.

10. Unbolt the left side transmission carrier from the transmission.

11. Unbolt the front transmission mount from the transmission.

12. Unbolt the bottom of the engine from the transmission. Lift the transaxle slightly, remove the rest of the bolts, pull the transmission off the mounting dowels, and lower the transaxle out of the car. Secure the converter so it doesn't fall out.

— CAUTION —
Don't tilt the torque converter.

To install:

13. Be sure the torque converter is fully seated on the one-way clutch support. Push the transmission onto the mounting dowels and install two bolts. Lift the unit until the left driveshaft can be installed and install the

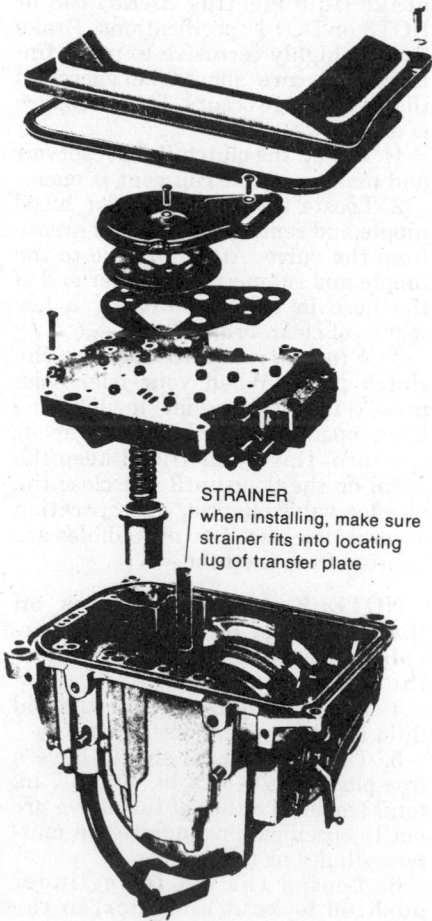

STRANER
when installing, make sure strainer fits into locating lug of transfer plate

Beginning with transaxle 13 03 8, an additional strainer is used beneath the valve body. It cannot be installed on earlier models

rest of the bolts. Torque them to 39 ft. lbs. (53 Nm).

14. Tighten the front transmission mount bolts to 39 ft. lbs. (53 Nm). Install the left side transmission carrier to the transmission.

15. Connect the accelerator and carburetor cable bracket. Connect the floorshift linkage.

16. Tighten the torque converter-to-drive plate bolts to 22 ft. lbs. (30 Nm). Torque the driveshaft bolts to 32 ft. lbs. (43 Nm).

17. Install the rear transmission carrier and make sure that the left side carrier is aligned in the center of the body mount. Bolt the left side carrier to the body.

18. Connect the speedometer cable and the battery cables.

1985–88 Golf, Jetta And Scirocco

1. Disconnect the negative battery cable.

2. Remove the speedometer cable from the transaxle and the upper starter mounting bolts.

3. Connect the engine support tool 10–222A to the engine and lift it slightly.

4. Remove the 3 bolts from the right engine mount. Remove the left transaxle mount complete with the support.

5. Push the engine to the rear and remove the front engine mount.

6. Remove the left axle shaft, the lower starter bolts and the starter.

7. Remove the transaxle oil pan protective plate.

8. Place the shift selector lever in the Park position, then remove the selector cable and bracket from the transaxle.

9. Remove the accelerator cable and the accelerator pedal cable.

NOTE: When removing the accelerator cable, BE CAREFUL not to change the adjustment.

10. Remove the 3 torque converter bolts from the drive plate.

11. Remove the right ball joint from the control arm and the right axle shaft from the transaxle.

NOTE: When removing the ball joint from the control arm, be careful not to damage the boot.

12. Push the engine to the right as far as possible, remove the left axle shaft and support on a wire.

13. Place a transmission jack under the transaxle and support it.

14. Remove the lower transaxle-to-engine bolts and push the transaxle from the centering pins.

15. Pull the transaxle back and lower it from the vehicle.

CAUTION

Keep the torque converter from falling off of the transaxle.

16. To install, reverse the removal procedures. Torque the transaxle-to-engine bolts to 55 ft. lbs. (75 Nm), the torque converter-to-drive plate to 26 ft. lbs. (35 Nm) and the axle shaft-to-flange to 33 ft. lbs. (45 Nm). Adjust the accelerator cable and the shift selector lever.

RWD Vanagon

NOTE: The engine and transaxle must be removed as an assembly.

1. Remove the battery ground cable.
2. Remove the warm air hoses and air cleaner. Remove the boot between the dipstick tube and the body and the boot between the oil filler neck and the body.
3. Disconnect the cooling air bellows at the body.
4. Disconnect the wires at the regulator and the alternator wires at the snap connector located by the regulator. Disconnect the auxiliary air regulator and the oil pressure switch at the snap connectors located by the distributor.
5. Disconnect the accelerator cable.
6. Disconnect the right fuel return line.
7. Raise the car.
8. Disconnect the hoses from the heat exchangers.
9. Disconnect the starter wires and push the engine wiring harness through the engine cover plate.
10. Disconnect the fuel supply line and plug it.
11. Remove the heater booster exhaust pipe.
12. Remove the rear axles and cover the ends to protect them from dirt.
13. Remove the selector cable by unscrewing the cable sleeve.
14. Remove the wire from the kickdown switch.
15. Remove the bolts from the rubber transmission mountings, taking careful note of the position, number, and thickness of the spacers that are present.

CAUTION

These spacers must be reinstalled exactly as they were removed. Do not detach the transmission carrier from the body.

16. Support the engine and transmission assembly in such a way that it may be lowered and moved rearward at the same time.
17. Remove the engine carrier bolts and the engine and transmission assembly from the car.

18. Matchmark the flywheel and the torque converter and remove the three attaching bolts.
19. Remove the engine-to-transmission bolts and separate the engine and transmission.

CAUTION

Exercise care when separating the engine and transmission as the torque converter will easily slip off the input shaft if the transmission is tilted downward.

20. Installation is as follows. Install and tighten the engine-to-transmission bolts after aligning the match marks on the flywheel and converter.
21. Making sure the matchmarks are aligned, install the converter-to-flywheel bolts.
22. Make sure the rubber buffer is in place and the two securing studs do not project more than 0.7 in. from the transmission case.
23. Tie a cord to the slot in the engine compartment seal. This will make positioning the seal easier.
24. Lift the assembly far enough to allow the accelerator cable to be pushed through the front engine cover.
25. Continue lifting the assembly into place. Slide the rubber buffer into the locating tube in the rear axle carrier.
26. Insert the engine carrier bolts and raise the engine until the bolts are at the top of their elongated slots. Tighten the bolts.

NOTE: A set of three gauges must be obtained to check the alignment of the rubber buffer in its locating tube. The dimensions are given in the illustration as is the measuring technique. The rubber buffer is centered horizontally where the 11mm gauge can be inserted on both sides. The buffer is located vertically when the 10mm gauge can be inserted on the bottom side and the 12mm gauge can be inserted on the top side. See Steps 27 and 28 for adjustment.

27. Install the rubber transmission mount bolts with spacers of the correct thickness. The purpose of the spacers is to center the rubber buffer vertically in its support tube. The buffer is not supposed to carry any weight; it absorbs torsional forces only.
28. To locate the buffer horizontally in its locating tube, the engine carrier must be vertical and parallel to the fan housing. It is adjusted by moving the engine carrier bolts in elongated slots. Further travel may be obtained by moving the brackets attached to the body. It may be necessary to ad-

just the two rear suspension wishbones with the center of the transmission after the rubber buffer is horizontally centered. Take the car to a dealer or alignment specialist to align the rear suspension.
29. Adjust the selector level cable.
30. Connect the wire to the kickdown switch.
31. Install the rear axles. Make sure the lockwashers are placed with the convex side out.
32. Reconnect the fuel hoses and heat exchanger hoses. Install the pipe for the heater booster.
33. Lower the car and pull the engine compartment seal into place with the cord.
34. Reconnect the fuel injection and engine wiring. Push the starter wires through the engine cover plate and connect the wires to the starter.
35. Install the intake duct with the fan and hoses, also the cooling air intake.

PAN REMOVAL/ INSTALLATION AND FILTER SERVICE
Dasher and Quantum

VW recommends that the automatic transmission fluid be replace every 30,000 miles or 20,000 miles if used for trailer towing, mountain driving, or other severe service.

1. Four (4) quarts of automatic transmission fluid (Dexron®) and a pan gasket are required.
2. Slide a drain pan under the transmission. Jack up the front of the car and support it.
3. Remove the drain plug and allow all the fluid to drain.

NOTE: Some models are not equipped with pan drain plugs. In this case, empty the pan by loosening the pan bolts and allowing the fluid to drain out.

4. Remove the pan retaining bolts and drop the pan.
5. Discard the old gasket and clean the pan with solvent.
6. Unscrew and clean the circular strainer. If it is dirty, it should be replaced.
7. Install the strainer, but don't tighten the bolt too much—specified torque is only 4 ft. lbs. (5 Nm).
8. Refill the transmission with about 2¾ qts of fluid. Check the level with the dipstick. Run the car for a few minutes and check again.

Golf, Rabbit, Scirocco GTI, GLI And Jetta

NOTE: As of transmission No. 09096 a new, cleanable oil filter is used which requires a deeper oil

pan. Also beginning with transmission number EQ–15 106, the drain plug was no longer installed in the oil pan.

1. Remove the drain plug and let the fluid drain into a pan. If the pan has no drain plug, loosen the pan bolts until a corner of the pan can be lowered to drain the fluid.

2. Remove the pan bolts and take off the pan.

3. Discard the old gasket and clean the pan out. Be careful not to get any threads or lint from rags into the pan.

4. The filter needn't be replaced unless the fluid is dirty or smells burnt. The specified torque for the strainer screws is 2 ft. lbs. (3 Nm).

NOTE: Beginning with Transmission number 13 03 8, there is an additional strainer under the valve body. When installing it, be sure if fits into the locating lug of the transfer plate.

5. Replace the pan with a new gasket and tighten the bolts, in a crisscross pattern, to 14 ft. lbs.

6. Using a long-necked funnel, pour in 2½ qts. of Dexron® automatic transmission fluid through the dipstick tube. Start the engine and shift through all the transmission ranges with the car stationary. Check the level on the dipstick with the lever in Neutral. It should be up to the lower end of the dipstick. Drive the car until it is warmed up and recheck the level.

RWD Vanagon

1. Some models have a drain plug in the pan. Remove the plug and drain the transmission. On models without the plug, loosen the pan bolts 2–3 turns and lower one corner of the pan to drain.

2. Remove the pan bolts and remove the pan from the transmission.

NOTE: It may be necessary to tap the pan with a rubber hammer to loosen it.

3. Use a new gasket and install the pan. Tighten the bolts loosely until the pan is properly in place, then tighten the bolts fully, moving in a diagonal pattern.

NOTE: Do not overtighten the bolts.

4. Refill the transmission with ATF.

5. At 5 minute intervals, retighten the pan bolts two or three times. The Volkswagen automatic transmission has a filter screen secured by a screw to the bottom of the valve body. Remove the pan and remove the filter screen from the valve body.

CAUTION

Never use a cloth that will leave the slightest bit of lint in the transmission when cleaning transmission parts. The lint will expand when exposed to transmission fluid and clog the valve body and filter.

Clean the filter screen with compressed air.

LINKAGE ADJUSTMENT

FWD Models

Check the cable adjustment as follows:

1. Run the engine at 1000–1200 rpm with the parking brake on.

2. Select Reverse—a drop in engine speed should be noticed.

3. Select Park—engine speed should increase. Pull the shift lever against Reverse, the engine speed shouldn't drop (because reverse gear has not been engaged).

4. Move the shift lever to engage Reverse—engine speed should drop as the gear engages.

5. Move the shift lever to Neutral—an increase in engine speed should be noticed.

6. Shift the lever into Drive—a noticeable drop in engine speed should result.

7. Shift into 1—the lever must engage without having to overcome any resistance.

8. To adjust the cable—shift into Park.

On Dashers (from chassis no. 3–5 2 044957 and later) and Quantum, the shift cable clamp is loosened from inside the passenger's compartment. Have an assistant under the car press the transmission lever toward the Park position and tighten the clamp.

On all other models, shift into Park, loosen the cable clamp at the transmission end of the cable, press the transmission lever all the way to the left and tighten the cable clamp.

RWD Vanagon

Make sure the shifting cable is not kinked or bent and that the linkage and cable are properly lubricated.

1. Move the gear shift lever to the Park position.

2. Loosen the clamp which holds the front and rear halves of the shifting rod together. Loosen the clamping bolts on the transmission lever.

3. Press the lever on the transmission rearward as far as possible. Spring pressure will be felt. The manual valve must be on the stop in the valve body.

4. Holding the transmission lever against its stop, tighten the clamping bolt.

5. Holding the rear shifting rod half, push the front half forward to take up any clearance and tighten the clamp bolt.

6. Test the shift pattern.

TRANSMISSION CABLE ADJUSTMENT

FWD Models Only

NOTE: Early Dashers with the type 003 automatic transmission (identified by the modulator hose attached to the driver's side front of the transmission above the pan) have a kickdown switch rather than a throttle cable. See below for switch test.

Make sure the throttle is closed, and the choke and fast idle cam are off (carbureted models).

1. Detach the cable end at the transmission.

2. Press the lever at the transmission into its closed throttle position.

3. You should be able to attach the cable end onto the transmission lever without moving the lever.

4. Adjust the cable length to the correct setting.

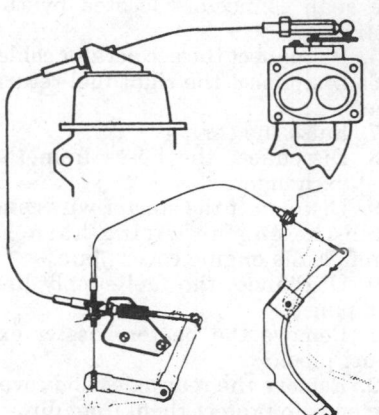

Rabbit, Jetta, Scirocco automatic transmission cable arrangement—fuel injected

KICKDOWN SWITCH CHECK

Dasher Only

NOTE: Early Dashers with the type 003 automatic transmission (identified by the modulator hose attached to the driver's side front of the transmission above the pan) are the only VWs equipped with kickdown switches. All other models have throttle cable kickdowns (see above).

1. Turn the ignition switch ON.

2. Floor the accelerator—you should hear a click from the solenoid on the transmission.

3. Replace the solenoid if no sound

is heard. The solenoid is housed in the valve body and is accessible only by removing this unit from the transmission: a job you should depend on a qualified mechanic to perform.

NEUTRAL START/BACK-UP LIGHT SWITCH

The combination neutral start and back-up light switch is mounted inside the shifter housing. The starter should operate in Park or Neutral only. Adjust the switch by moving it on its mounts. The back-up lights should only come on when the switch selector is in the Reverse position.

FIRST AND SECOND GEAR (FRONT AND REAR) BAND ADJUSTMENTS
Dasher W/Type 003 Transmission Only

The type 003 transmission is identified by the modulator hose attached to the driver's side front of the transmission above the pan.

NOTE: The transmission must be horizontal when the band adjustments are performed.

The adjustment screws are located at the top of the transmission housing with the first gear band being closest to the front of the unit on the passenger's side of the car. The second gear band adjustment screw is located toward the rear of the unit on the driver's side of the vehicle.

1. To adjust the first gear band, loosen the locknut and tighten the adjusting screw to 7 ft. lbs.
2. Loosen the screw and retighten it to 3.5 ft. lbs. (4. 5 Nm).
3. Turn the screw out 3¼–3½ turns and then tighten the locknut.
4. To adjust the second gear band, repeat Steps 1 and 2 on the second

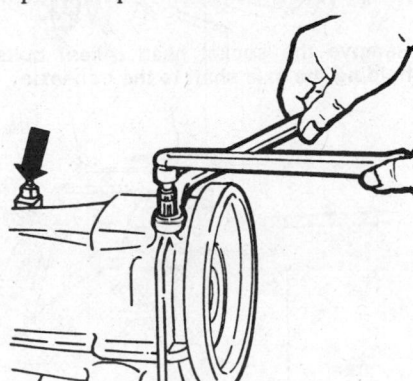

Dasher type 003 transaxle band adjustment—front band (first gear) being adjusted, arrow locates second gear band adjustment screw

gear band adjusting screw, then turn the screw out exactly 2½ turns and tighten the locknut.

FRONT (SECOND) BAND ADJUSTMENT
RWD Vanagon

1. Tighten the front band adjusting screw to 7 ft. lbs.
2. Loosen the screw and tighten it to 3.5 ft. lbs.
3. From this position, loosen the screw exactly 1¾–2 turns and tighten the locknut.

SECOND GEAR (REAR) BAND ADJUSTMENT
Dasher and Quantum W/Type 089 Transmission and All Other Models W/Type 010

NOTE: The transmission must be horizontal when band adjustments are performed.

1. Loosen the locknut on the adjusting screw, which is located on the front of the Rabbit and Scirocco transmission and the driver's side on the Dasher.
2. Tighten the adjusting screw to 7 ft. lbs. (10 Nm).
3. Loosen the screw and tighten it again to 4 ft. lbs. (5 Nm).
4. Turn the screw out exactly 2½ turns and then tighten the locknut.

REAR (FIRST) BAND ADJUSTMENT
Vanagon

1.Tighten the rear band adjusting screw to 7 ft. lbs.
2.Then loosen the screw and retighten it to 3.5 ft. lbs.
3.From this position, loosen the screw exactly 3¼–3½ turns and tighten the locknut.

DRIVE AXLE

Halfshaft

REMOVAL & INSTALLATION
Dasher, Fox and Quantum

NOTE: When removing the right side halfshaft, you must detach the exhaust pipe from the manifold and the transaxle bracket. Be sure to buy a new exhaust flange gasket.

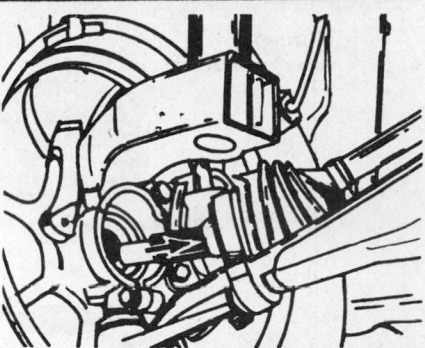

Pulling the Dasher halfshaft from the steering knuckle—Quantum and Fox similar

1. With the car on the ground, remove the front axle nut.

NOTE: Use a longer breaker bar with an extension (length of pipe).

2. Raise and support the front of the vehicle.
3. Remove the socket head bolts retaining the halfshaft to the transaxle flange.

NOTE: When removing the left side halfshaft on automatic transmission models, matchmark the ball joint (left side) mounting position in relation to the lower control arm. Remove the 2 ball joint retaining nuts and separate the ball joint from the control arm to create room to remove the halfshaft.

4. Pull the transaxle side of the halfshaft out and up and place it on top of the transaxle.
5. Pull the axle shaft from the steering knuckle.
6. Installation is the reverse of removal. Tighten the transaxle bolts to 25–33 ft. lbs. (34–45 Nm). The axle nut should be tightened to 145 ft. lbs. (196 Nm) (M 18 nut), or 175 ft. lbs. (237 Nm) (M 20 nut).

NOTE: Be aware that the halfshafts are 2 different lengths on automatic transmission models, with the left side shaft being slightly longer than the right. Manual transmission and automatic transmission shafts are of different lengths and should not be interchanged.

Golf, Rabbit, Scirocco, GTI, GLI and Jetta

1. Complete Steps 1–3 under "Dasher and Quantum". Disregard the first NOTE.
2. Remove the bolt holding the ball joint to the steering knuckle and separate the knuckle from the ball joint.
3. Removing the ball joint from the

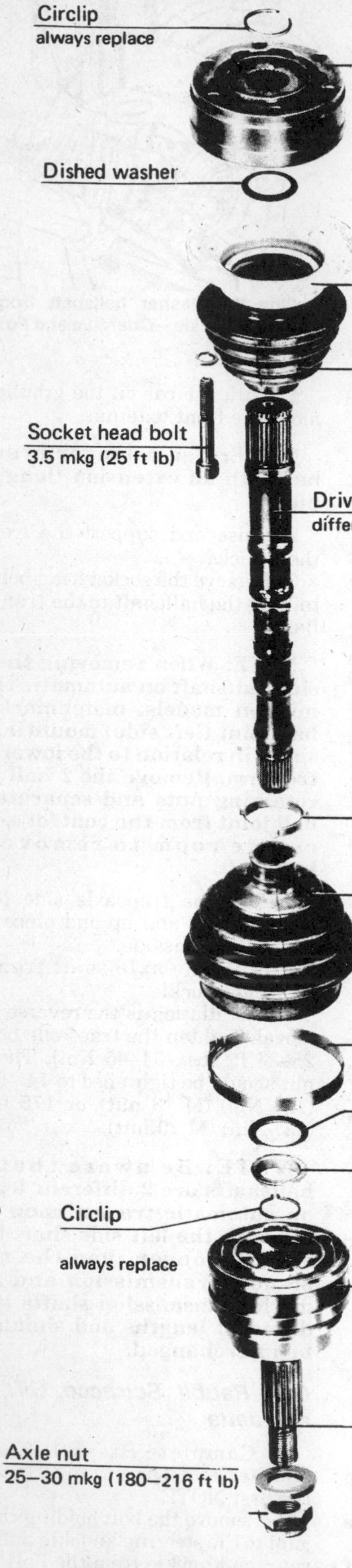

Circlip
always replace

Constant velocity joint, inner

Dished washer

Cap
**check for wear,
replace if replace if necessary**

Boot
**check for wear,
replace if necessary**

Socket head bolt
3.5 mkg (25 ft lb)

Drive shaft
differ in length,

Clamp
always replace

Boot
**check for wear,
replace if necessary**

Clamp
always replace

Dished washer

Thrust washer

Circlip

always replace

Constant velocity joint, outer

Axle shaft

Axle nut
25–30 mkg (180–216 ft lb)

Exploded view of the Dasher halfshaft—Quantum similar

knuckle should give enough clearance to remove the shaft. It pulls right out of the steering hub.

4. Installation is the reverse of removal. Tighten the axle shaft-to-transaxle bolts to 33 ft. lbs. (44 Nm), the ball joint bolt to 21 ft. lbs. (28 Nm) and the axle nut to 173 ft. lbs. (234 Nm). Be sure to check the alignment after work is completed.

RWD Vanagon

1. Raise the rear of the vehicle and support it safely.
2. Remove the wheel, grease cap, cotter pin and the axle nut.
3. Remove the brake drum and wheel hub.
4. Disconnect the brake line hose. Remove the brake assembly and backing plate.
5. Remove the 4 retaining bolts and remove the wheel bearing housing.
6. Slide the drive axle out of the axle housing.
7. Press the drive axle from the bearing housing using special tool VW411.
8. Pry the inner and outer grease seals from the bearing housing using a small pry bar.
9. Remove the spacer sleeve, then remove the outter bearing using a brass drift and hammer.

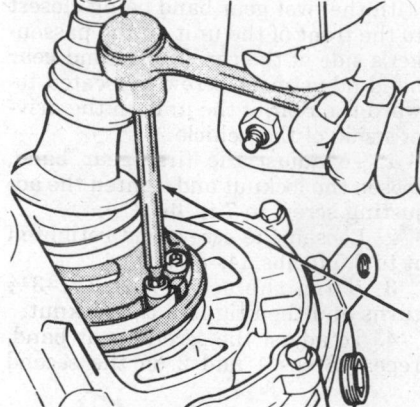

Remove the socket head (Allen) bolts holding the axle shaft to the transaxle

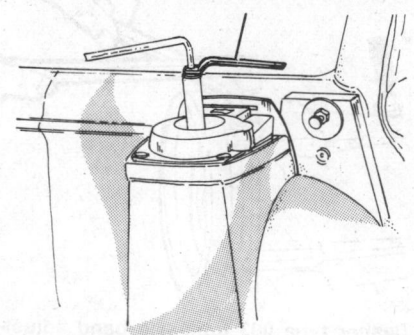

Strut self-locking nut, removal/installation

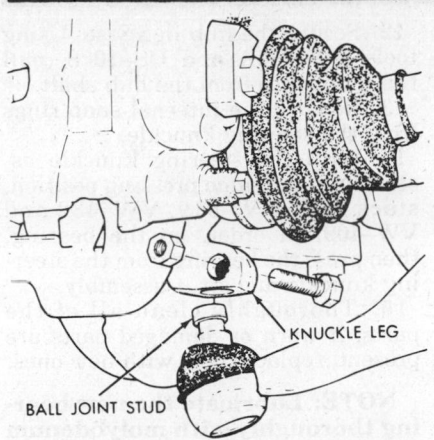

KNUCKLE LEG

BALL JOINT STUD

Remove ball joint from knuckle to remove axle shaft—Rabbit, Jetta, Scirocco

10. Remove the inner grease seal and sir clip. Press out the inner wheel bearing using special tools VW412 and 244b. Then, remove the spacer sleeve.

11. Pack new wheel bearings with fresh grease.

12. Install a new spacer sleeve in the inner wheel bearing housing. Press the inner wheel bearing in using special tools VW407, VW472 and VW401, until it is seated in the bearing housing. Fill the space between the inner and outer bearing with multi-purpose grease. Press the outer bearing into position using the same tools used to place the inner bearing. Install new spacer sleeves, sir clip and grease seals.

13. Press the drive axle into the bearing housing using special tools VW412 and 402.

14. Installation of the drive axle is the reverse of the removal procedure.

15. Torque the wheel bearing housing to axle housing retaining bolts to 14 ft. lbs.

16. Install the remaining components in the reverse order of their removal.

17. Torque the brake line hose snug. Torque the axle nut to 360 ft.lbs. Torque the lug nuts to 102 ft. lbs.

18. Bleed the brake system and check for leaks.

CV-Joints

OVERHAUL

The constant velocity joints (CV) can be disassembled. However, VW states that the components are machined to a matched tolerance and that the entire CV-joint must be replaced.

For all CV-joint overhaul procedures, please refer to "CV-Joint Overhaul" in the Unit Repair section.

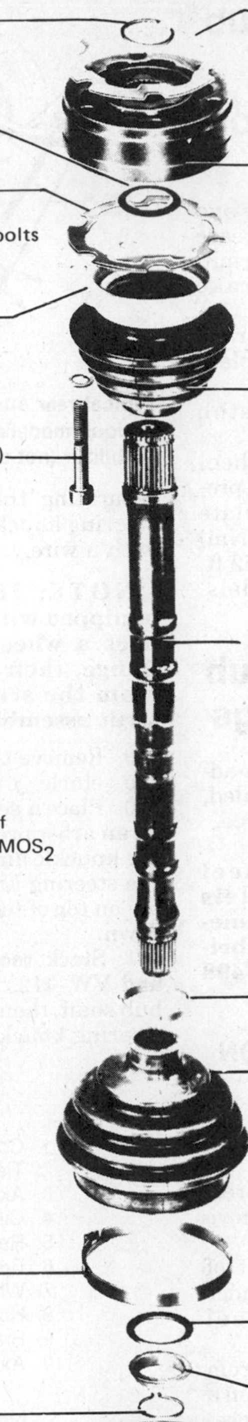

Circlip
always replace

Dished washer

Gasket
note correct position otherwise socket head bolts become loose.

Protective cap

Gasket
Insert in joint flange before installing axle shaft. note correct position otherwise socket head bolts become loose.

Constant velocity joint, inner

4.5 mkg (32 ft lb)

Boot
check for wear replace if necessary

Drive shaft
differ in length and material

Note
If velocity joint was disassembled for checking of wear, pump 45 grams of MOS_2 grease into each side of joint when assembling.

Clamp
always replace

Boot
check for wear replace if necessary

Clamp
always replace

Dished washer

Thrust washer

Circlip
always replace

Constant velocity joint, outer

installing: drive onto shaft until circlip engages in shaft groove.

Axle nut
24 mkg (173 ft lb)

Exploded view of the Rabbit, Jetta and Scirocco halfshaft

Rear Axle Shafts/Stub Axles

REMOVAL & INSTALLATION

FWD Models Only

1. Raise the rear of the vehicle and support it safely. Remove the grease cap, cotter pin, locknut, adjusting nut, spacer, wheel bearing and brake drum.
2. Disconnect and plug the brake line. Remove the brake backing plate with the brakes attached.
3. Unbolt and remove the stub axle.
4. To install, repack the wheel bearings and reverse the removal procedures. Torque the backing plate mounting bolts to 44 ft. lbs. (60 Nm) on the Dasher and Quantum or 52 ft. lbs. (70 Nm) for all other models. Bleed the brake system.

Front Wheel Drive Hub Knuckle and Bearings

The front wheel bearings are non-adjustable on all models and are sealed, so they should be maintenance-free.

NOTE: Replacement wheel bearings for Quantum models with an enlarged outside diameter require NO moly paste lubrication (Bearing number 321 498 625D).

REMOVAL & INSTALLATION

Dasher, Fox And Quantum

1. Remove the grease cup from the wheel spindle.
2. Have an assistant apply pressure to the brake pedal and remove the wheel spindle.
3. Raise and support the front of the vehicle on jackstands (place under the frame). Remove the wheel assembly.
4. Remove the brake caliper from the steering knuckle and suspend on a wire, DO NOT remove the brake hose.
5. Remove the brake disc from the hub assembly.
6. Loosen the ball joint-to-steering knuckle bolt and separate the ball joint from the steering knuckle by prying down on it with a large pry bar.
7. Remove the tie rod end-to-steering knuckle nut and use a ball joint puller to separate the tie rod from the steering knuckle.
8. While supporting the axle shaft, pull the steering knuckle and hub assembly out from the vehicle. After

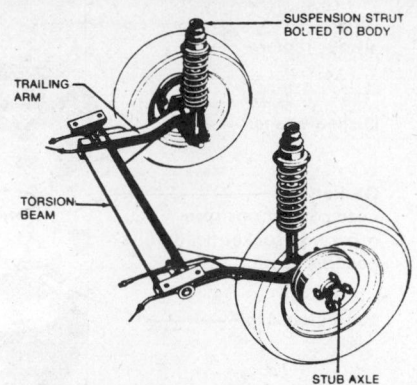

Typical rear suspension (except Dasher) Various models are equipped with a rear stabilizer (not shown)

separating the axle shaft from the steering knuckle assembly, support it with a wire.

NOTE: If the Quantum is equipped with a 5 cyl engine, connect a wheel puller to the hub flange, then push the axle shaft from the steering knuckle and strut assembly.

9. Remove the strut assembly from the vehicle.
10. Place a set of parallel rail blocks on an arbor press to support the steering knuckle and strut assembly. Place the steering knuckle and hub assembly on top of tools with the hub facing down.
11. Stack tool VW–295A. VW–420 and VW–412, in order, on top of the hub shaft, then press the hub from the steering knuckle and strut assembly.

12. Secure the hub in a vise. Using tools VW–295A and US–1078, pull the inner race from the hub shaft.
13. Remove the internal snap rings from the steering knuckle.
14. With the steering knuckle assembly in the same pressing position, stack tools VW–519, VW–432 and VW–409, in order, on the bearing, then press the bearing from the steering knuckle and strut assembly.
15. Thoroughly clean all of the parts. If worn or damaged parts are present, replace them with new ones.

NOTE: Lubricate the new bearing thoroughly with molybdenum grease. Install the outside internal snap ring in the steering knuckle.

16. To install the new bearing, place a flat plate on the arbor press, then the steering knuckle and strut assembly (in the same position for extracting the bearing). On top of the steering knuckle assembly, stack the new bearing, then tools 40–20 and VW–411, in order and press the bearing into the steering knuckle, until it seats against the bottom retaining ring. Install the other retaining ring.
17. Lift the steering knuckle assembly and place the hub on a flat surface followed by the steering knuckle (it must be facing the same direction).
18. Stack tools VW–519, VW–432 and VW–412, in order, on top the bearing, then press the hub into the steering knuckle assembly.

1. Cotter pin
2. Tie rod
3. Axle driveshaft
4. Circlip
5. Retainer nut
6. Brake caliper
7. Wheel bearing
8. Hub
9. Brake disc
10. Axle nut

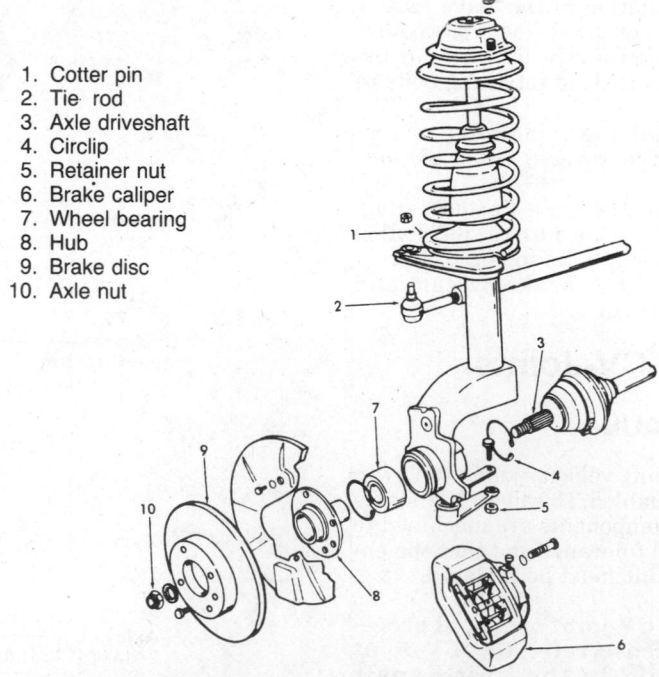

Dasher front suspension components—Quantum similar

NOTE: When pressing the hub into the steering knuckle, support the inner race of the bearing with tool VW-519.

19. To complete the installation, reverse the removal procedures. Torque the control arm-to-steering knuckle to 37 ft. lbs. (50 Nm), the tie rod to the steering knuckle to 22 ft. lbs. (30 Nm) and the axle shaft hub nut to 170 ft. lbs. (230 Nm) and the brake caliper-to-steering knuckle to 52 ft. lbs. (50 Nm).

1981–84 Rabbit, Jetta And Scirocco

1. Remove the grease cup from the wheel spindle.
2. Have an assistant apply pressure to the brake pedal and remove the wheel spindle lock nut.
3. Raise and support the front of the vehicle on jackstands (place under the frame). Remove the wheel assembly.
4. Remove the brake caliper from the steering knuckle and suspend on a wire, DO NOT remove the brake hose.
5. Remove the brake disc from the hub assembly.
6. Loosen the ball joint-to-steering knuckle bolt and separate the ball joint from the steering knuckle by prying down on it with a large pry bar.
7. Remove the tie rod end-to-steering knuckle nut and use a ball joint puller to separate the tie rod from the steering knuckle.
8. While supporting the axle shaft, pull the steering knuckle and hub assembly out from the vehicle. After separating the axle shaft from the steering knuckle assembly, support it with a wire.
9. Remove the strut-to-steering knuckle bolts and the steering knuckle assembly from the vehicle.
10. Place tools VW-401 and VW-402 on top of parallel rail blocks on an arbor press to support the steering knuckle assembly. Place the steering knuckle and hub assembly on top of tools with the hub facing down.
11. Stack tool VW-418A, VW-421 and VW-409, in order, on top of the hub shaft, then press the hub from the steering knuckle.

NOTE: To press out the hub, if equipped with a drum brake, substitute tools VW-421 and VW-409 with tools VW-431 and VW-411.

12. Secure the hub in a vise. Using tools VW-431 and US-1078, pull the inner race from the hub shaft.
13. Remove the internal snap rings from the steering knuckle.
14. With the steering knuckle assembly in the same pressing position, stack tools VW-433, VW-420 and VW-412, in order, on the bearing and press the bearing from the steering knuckle.

NOTE: To press out the wheel bearing, if equipped with a drum brake, substitute tools VW-433, VW-420 and VW-412 with tools VW-415A, VW-433 and VW-411.

15. Thoroughly clean all of the parts. If worn or damaged parts are present, replace them with new ones.

NOTE: Lubricate the new bearing thoroughly with molybdenum grease.

16. To install the new bearing, use the same set up used to extract the bearing, place the new bearing on the steering knuckle and press it into the steering knuckle, until it seats against the bottom retaining ring. Install the other retaining ring.
17. Lift the steering knuckle assembly and place the hub on a flat surface followed by the steering knuckle (it must be facing the same direction).
18. Stack tools VW-519, VW-432 and VW-412, on order, on top of the bearing, then press the hub into the steering knuckle assembly.

NOTE: When pressing the hub into the steering knuckle, support the bearing with tool VW-519.

19. To complete the installation, reverse the removal procedures. Torque the steering knuckle-to-strut to 59 ft. lbs. (80 Nm), the control arm-to-steering knuckle to 37 ft. lbs. (50 Nm), the tie rod to the steering knuckle to 22 ft. lbs. (30 Nm) and the axle shaft hub nut to 174 ft. lbs. (240 Nm).

1985–88 Golf, Jetta, GTI, GLI And Scirocco

1. Remove the grease cup from the wheel spindle.
2. Have an assistant apply pressure to the brake pedal and remove the wheel spindle lock nut.
3. Raise and support the front of the vehicle on jackstands (place under the frame). Remove the wheel assembly.
4. Remove the brake caliper from the steering knuckle and suspend on a wire, DO NOT remove the brake hose.
5. Remove the brake disc and the backing plate from the hub assembly.
6. Loosen the ball joint-to-steering knuckle bolt and separate the ball joint from the steering knuckle by prying down on it with a large pry bar.
7. Remove the tie rod end-to-steering knuckle nut and use a ball joint puller to separate the tie rod from the steering knuckle.
8. While supporting the axle shaft, pull the steering knuckle and hub assembly out from the vehicle. After separating the axle shaft from the steering knuckle assembly, support it with a wire.
9. Remove the strut-to-steering knuckle bolts and the steering knuckle from the vehicle.
10. Place tools VW-401 and 3110 on an arbor press. Place the steering knuckle and hub assembly on top of tool 3110 with the hub facing down inside of the tool.
11. Place tools VW-295 and VW-408A on top of the hub shaft, then press the hub from the steering knuckle.
12. Secure the hub in a vise. Using tool 30–11, pull the inner race from the hub shaft.

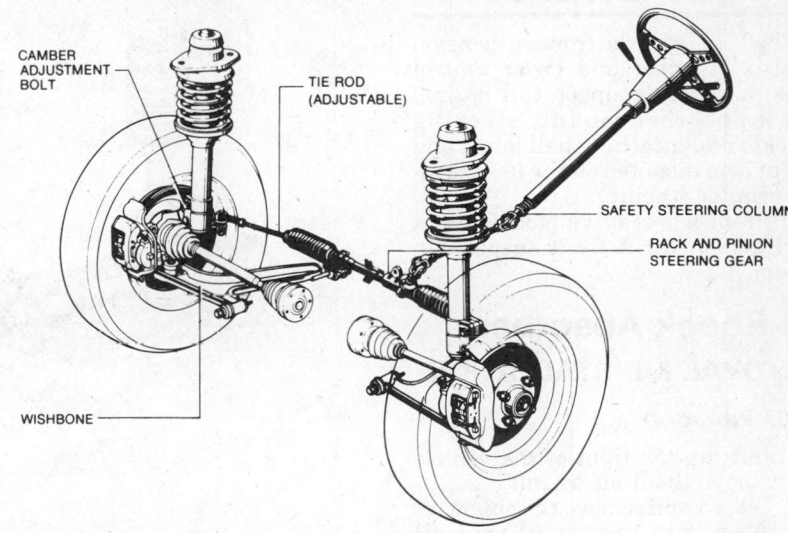

Typical Rabbit, Jetta, Scirocco steering and front suspension components

CAMBER ADJUSTMENT BOLT

TIE ROD (ADJUSTABLE)

SAFETY STEERING COLUMN

RACK AND PINION STEERING GEAR

WISHBONE

13. Remove the internal snap ring from the steering knuckle.

14. With the steering knuckle in the same position on tool 3110, place tools VW–433 and VW–407 on the bearing and press the bearing from the steering knuckle.

15. Thoroughly clean all of the parts. If worn or damaged parts are present, replace them with new ones.

NOTE: Lubricate the new bearing thoroughly with molybdenum grease.

16. To install the new bearing, place tools VW–401, VW–402 and VW–459/2 on the arbor press. Place the steering knuckle on tool VW–459/2 with large opening facing upward.

17. Place the new bearing on the steering knuckle and tools VW–472/1 and VW–412 on top of the bearing, then press the bearing into the steering knuckle until it seats. Install the internal locking ring and the inner race.

18. Replace tool VW–459/2 with tool VW–519, place the hub on top of bearing and press the hub into the steering knuckle.

NOTE: When pressing the hub into the steering knuckle, support the bearing.

19. To complete the installation, reverse the removal procedures. Torque the steering knuckle-to-strut to 59 ft. lbs. (80 Nm), the control arm-to-steering knuckle to 37 ft. lbs. (50 Nm), the tie rod to the steering knuckle to 26 ft. lbs. (35 Nm) and the axle shaft hub nut to 170 ft. lbs. (230 Nm).

FRONT SUSPENSION

On the Vanagon, the front suspension consists of upper and lower control arms, a separate upper coil spring/shock absorber mount, steering knuckle and attaching ball joints and a strut arm mounted on the lower control arm for stability.

All front wheel drive models use a MacPherson Strut front suspension system.

Shock Absorber

REMOVAL & INSTALLATION

RWD Vanagon

1. Jack up the front of the vehicle and remove the front wheel.

2. Loosen and remove the single retaining nut at the top of the coil spring/shock absorber upper mount.

3. Remove the through bolt which retains the bottom of the shock absorber to the lower control arm and pull the shock abosrber out through the bottom of the lower control arm.

4. Reverse the procedure to install.

MacPherson Strut

REMOVAL & INSTALLATION

Dasher, Fox and Quantum

1. With the car on the ground, remove the front axle nut. Loosen the wheel bolts.

2. Raise and support the front of the car. Remove the wheels.

3. Remove the brake caliper from the strut and hang it with wire. Detach the brake line clips from the strut.

4. At the tie rod end, remove the cotter pin, back off the castellated nut, and pull the end off the strut with a puller.

5. Loosen the stabilizer bar bushings and detach the end from the strut being removed.

6. Remove the ball joint from the strut.

7. Pull the axle driveshaft from the strut.

8. Remove the upper strut-to-fender retaining nuts.

9. Pull the strut assembly down and out of the car.

10. Installation is the reverse of removal. The axle nut is tightened to 145 ft. lbs. (196 Nm) (M 18 nut) or 175 ft. lbs. (237 Nm) (M 20 nut). Tighten the ball joint-to-strut nut to 25 ft. lbs. (34 Nm) (M8 nut) or 36 ft. lbs. (49 Nm) (M10 nut), the caliper-to-strut bolts to 44 ft. lbs. (60 Nm) and the stabilizer-to-control arm bolts to 7 ft. lbs. (9 Nm).

1981–84 Rabbit, Jetta and Scirocco

1. Remove the brake hose from the strut clip.

2. Mark the position of the camber adjustment bolts before removing them from the hub (wheel bearing housing). These bolts also serve as the lower strut mounting bolts.

3. Remove the upper mounting nuts and remove the strut from the car.

4. Installation is the reverse of removal. The upper nuts are tightened to 14 ft. lbs. (19 Nm) and the adjusting bolt (upper) to hub to 58 ft. lbs. (80 Nm). Tighten the lower adjusting bolt-to-hub to 43 ft. lbs. (58 Nm). Use new washers on the lower bolts. If the shock absorber was replaced, camber will have to be adjusted.

1985–88 Golf, Jetta, GTI, GLI And Scirocco

1. Raise and support the front of the vehicle. Remove the wheel if necessary.

2. Mark the position of the lower strut bolts before removing them from the steering knuckle.

3. Remove the upper mounting nut and the strut from the vehicle.

4. To install, reverse the removal procedures. Torque the strut-to-body nut to 44 ft. lbs. (60 Nm) and the strut-to-steering knuckle bolts to 59 ft. lbs. (80 Nm).

OVERHAUL

For all spring and shock absorber removal and installation procedures, and all overhaul procedures, please refer to "Strut Overhaul" in the Unit Repair section.

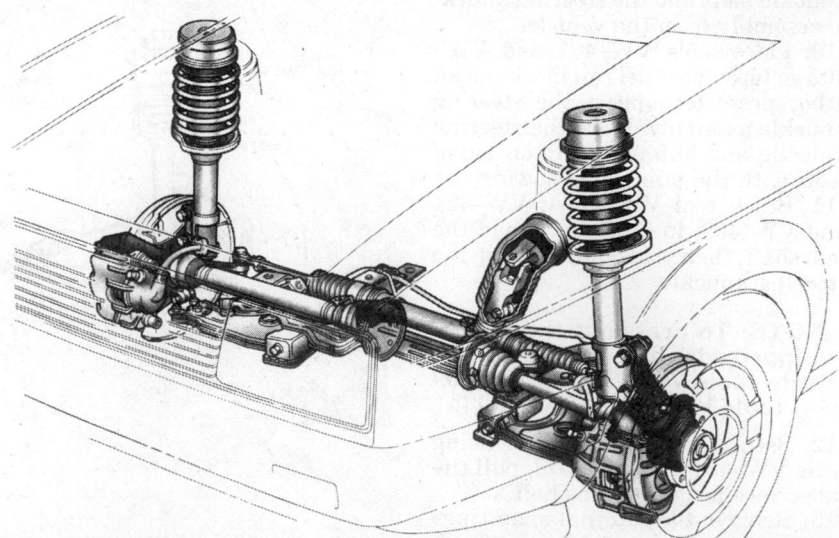

View of the front suspension system for 1985 and later models—except Quantum

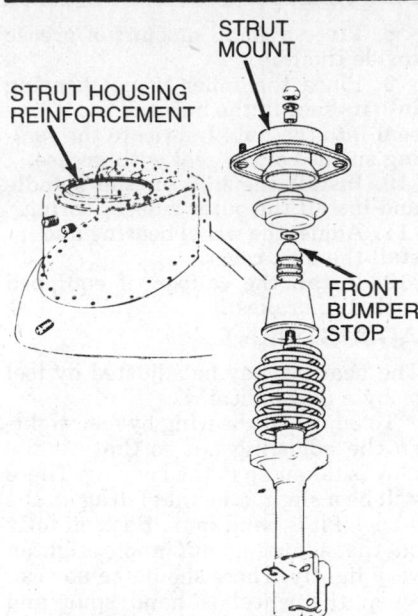

STRUT MOUNT

STRUT HOUSING REINFORCEMENT

FRONT BUMPER STOP

Front strut and mounting—GTI

Ball Joints

INSPECTION

1. A quick initial inspection can be made with the vehicle on the ground.

2. To test the upper ball joint on the Vanagon, grasp the top of the tire and vigorously pull the top of the tire in and out. Test both sides in this manner.

3. If the ball joints are excessively worn, there will be an audible tap as the ball moves around in its socket. Excess play can sometimes be felt through the tire.

4. On all models, a more rigorous test may be performed by jacking the car under the lower torsion arm and inserting a lever under the tire.

5. Lift up gently on the lever so as to pry the tire upward.

6. If the ball joints are worn, the tire will move upward ⅛–¼ in. or more.

7. On the Vanagon, if the tire displays excessive movement, have an assistant inspect each joint, as the tire is pried upward, to determine which ball joint is defective.

REMOVAL & INSTALLATION

FWD Models

1. Jack up the front of the car and support it on stands.

2. Matchmark the ball joint-to-control arm position on the Dasher, Fox and Quantum.

3. Remove the retaining bolt and nut from the hub (wheel bearing housing).

4. Pry the lower control arm and ball joint down and out of the strut.

5. Remove the 2 ball joint-to-lower control arm retaining nuts and bolts on the Dasher, Fox and Quantum. Drill out the rivets on 1981–84 Rabbit, Jetta and Scirocco; enlarge the holes to $^{21}/_{64}$ in.

6. Remove the ball joint assembly.

7. Install the Dasher, Fox or Quantum ball joint in the reverse order of removal. If no parts were installed other than the ball joint, align the matchmarks made in Step 2. No camber adjustment is necessary if this is done. Pull the ball joint into alignment with pliers. Tighten the two control arm-to-ball joint bolts to 47 ft. lbs. (64 Nm) and the strut-to-ball joint bolt to 25 ft. lbs. (34 Nm) (M8 bolt) or 36 ft. lbs. (49 Nm) (M10 bolt).

8. On all other models bolt the new ball joint in place. Torque the bolts to 18 ft. lbs. (25 Nm). Tighten the retaining bolt for the ball joint stud to 37 ft. lbs. (50 Nm).

RWD Vanagon

UPPER BALL JOINT

1. Raise the vehicle and support it on jack stands, then remove the wheel.

2. Place a jack under the lower control arm as close to the steering knuckle as possible and jack up just enough to put a slight load on the coil spring.

3. Loosen the steering knuckle-to-ball joint nut but do not remove completely.

4. Free the ball joint from the steering knuckle using a ball joint removal tool. Then remove the nut.

5. Remove the two upper ball joint to upper control arm bolts and remove the ball joint.

6. Reverse procedure to install. Check wheel alignment.

LOWER BALL JOINT

1. Jack up the front of the vehicle

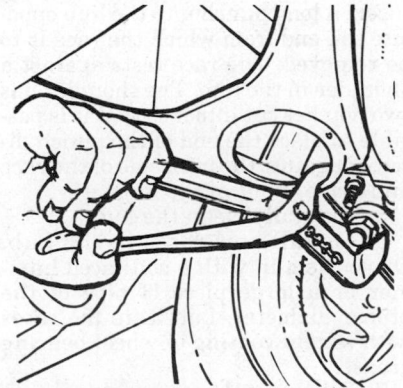

Pulling the Dasher ball joint into alignment on installation

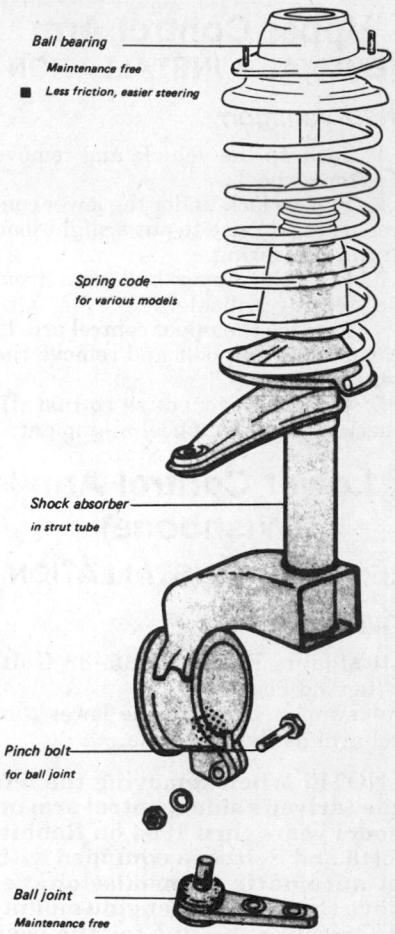

Ball bearing

Maintenance free

■ Less friction, easier steering

Spring code
for various models

Shock absorber
in strut tube

Pinch bolt
for ball joint

Ball joint
Maintenance free

A pinch bolt holds the ball joint to the combination strut and steering knuckle

and support it on stands, then remove the wheel.

2. Place a jack under the lower control arm as close to steering knuckle as possible and put a slight load on the coil spring by jacking up the jack.

3. Disconnect the brake caliper hose from the caliper, and remove the brake caliper and rotor if they are in the way.

4. Loosen the upper ball joint to steering knuckle to ball joint nut, but do not remove it. Free the upper ball joint from the steering knuckle and remove the nut.

5. Remove the lower ball joint to lower control arm nut and free the ball joint from the control arm using a ball joint removal tool. Remove the steering knuckle.

6. Press the ball joint off the steering knuckle.

7. Press a new ball joint in place on knuckle, observing any alignment marks on the ball joint and the knuckle.

8. Reverse the procedure to install. Bleed the brakes.

Upper Control Arm
REMOVAL & INSTALLATION

RWD Vanagon

1. Jack up the vehicle and remove the front wheel.
2. Place a jack under the lower control arm and raise to put a slight load on the coil spring.
3. Free the upper ball joint from the steering knuckle.
4. Remove the upper control arm to frame mounting bolt and remove the control arm.
5. Reverse procedure to install. Check and adjust wheel alignment.

Lower Control Arm (Wishbone)
REMOVAL & INSTALLATION

FWD Models

All Models Except 1985–88 Golf, Jetta And Scirocco
Volkswagen refers to the lower control arm as the wishbone.

NOTE: When removing the left side (driver's side) control arm on model years thru 1984 on Rabbit, Jetta and Scirocco equipped with an automatic transmission, remove the front left engine mounting, remove the nut for the rear mounting, remove the engine mounting support and raise the engine to expose the front control arm bolt.

1. Raise the vehicle and support it on jack stands. Remove the wheel.
2. Remove the nut and bolt attaching the ball joint to the hub (wheel bearing housing) and pry the joint down and out of the hub.
3. Unfasten the stabilizer bar on models so equipped.
4. Unbolt and remove the control arm-to-subframe (crossmember) mounting bolts on the Dasher, Fox or Quantum. On the 1981–84 Rabbit, Jetta and Scirocco, remove the control arm mounting bolts from the frame.
5. Remove the control arm. See procedures above for ball joint removal and installation.
6. Installation is the reverse of removal. Tighten the Dasher, Fox or Quantum control arm-to-subframe bolts to 44 ft. lbs. (60 Nm), and the 1981–84 Rabbit, Jetta and Scirocco control arm-to-frame front bolt to 50 ft. lbs. (68 Nm), bushing clamp bolts to 32 ft. lbs. (43 Nm). Tighten the ball joint to hub bolt to 21 ft. lbs. (28 Nm) on the Rabbit, Jetta and Scirocco, and to 25 ft. lbs. (34 Nm) (M 8 nut) or 36 ft. lbs. (48 Nm) (M 10 nut).

1985–88 Golf, Jetta And Scirocco

1. Refer to the "Ball Joint, Removal and Installation" procedures in this section and separate the ball joint from the steering knuckle.

NOTE: If replacing the lower control arm, separate the ball joint from the control arm.

2. If equipped, remove the stabilizer bar from the control arm.
3. Remove the control arm-to-subframe bolts and the control arm from the vehicle.
4. To install, reverse the removal procedures. Torque the control arm-to-subframe to 96 ft. lbs. (130 Nm), the stabilizer-to-control arm to 18 ft. lbs. (25 Nm) or the ball joint-to-steering knuckle to 37 ft. lbs. (50 Nm).

RWD Vanagon

1. Jack up the vehicle and remove the wheel.
2. Remove the coil spring.
3. Remove the lower control arm to frame mounting bolt and remove the control arm.
4. Reverse the procedure to install.

Front Wheel Bearings
REMOVAL & INSTALLATION

Vanagon

For front wheel bearing removal and installation procedures on all front wheel drive models please refer to the Drive Axle section.

1. Jack up the car and remove the wheel and tire.
2. Remove the caliper and disc (if equipped with disc brakes) or brake drum.
3. To remove the inside wheel bearing, pry the dust seal out of the hub with a screwdriver. Lift out the bearing and its inner race.
4. To remove the outer race for either the inner or outer wheel bearing, insert a long punch into the hub opposite the end from which the race is to be removed. The race rests against a shoulder in the hub. The shoulder has two notches cut into it so that it is possible to place the end of the punch directly against the back side of the race and drive it out of the hub.
5. Carefully clean the hub.
6. Install new races in the hub. Drive them in with a soft faced hammer or a large piece of pipe of the proper diameter. Lubricate the races with a light coating of wheel bearing grease.
7. Force wheel bearing grease into the sides of the tapered roller bearings so that all spaces are filled.

8. Place a small amount of grease inside the hub.
9. Place the inner wheel bearing into its race in the hub and tap a new seal into the hub. Lubricate the sealing surface of the seal with grease.
10. Install the hub on the spindle and install the outer wheel bearing.
11. Adjust the wheel bearing and install the dust cover.
12. Install the caliper (if equipped with disc brakes).

ADJUSTMENT

The bearing may be adjusted by feel or by a dial indicator.

To adjust the bearing by feel, tighten the adjusting nut so that all the play is taken up in the bearing. There will be a slight amount of drag on the wheel if it is hand spun. Back off fully on the adjusting nut and retighten very lightly. There should be no drag when the wheel is hand spun and there should be no perceptible play in the bearing when the wheel is grasped and wiggled from side to side.

To use a dial indicator, remove the dust cover and mount a dial indicator against the hub. Grasp the wheel at the side and pull the wheel in and out along the axis of the spindle. Read the axial play on the dial indicator. Screw the adjusting nut in or out to obtain 0.001–0.005 in. of axial play. Secure the adjusting nut and recheck the axial play.

Front Wheel Alignment
CASTER ADJUSTMENT

FWD Models

Other than the replacement of damaged suspension components, caster is not adjustable on any model.

Vanagon

Caster on the coil spring suspension is adjusted by moving the strut bar. Loosen the locknut and then turn the adjusting nut clockwise to increase the caster and counterclockwise to decrease the caster.

CAMBER ADJUSTMENT
Dasher, Fox and Quantum

Camber is adjusted by loosening the two ball joint-to-lower control arm bolts, and moving the ball joint in or out as necessary.

Golf, Rabbit, Scirocco, Jetta

Camber is adjusted by loosening the nuts of the two bolts holding the top of the wheel bearing housing to the bottom of the strut, and turnng the top eccentric bolt. The range of adjustment is 2°.

On models from 1985 the original top bolt can be replaced with a long shank bolt (N903334.01) and adjusted after new bolt is installed—if more adjustment is necessary the lower bolt can also be replaced with a new style.

Vanagon

Camber is the tilt of the top of the wheel, inward or outward, from true vertical. Outward tilt is positive, inward tilt is negative.

The upper control arm pivots on an eccentric bolt. To adjust the camber, loosen the retaining nut and rotate the bolt.

TOE-IN ADJUSTMENT
Dasher and Quantum

Toe-in is checked with the wheels straight ahead. The left tie rod is adjustable. Loosen the nuts and clamps and adjust the length of the tie rod for correct toe-out. If the steering wheel is crooked, remove and align it.

Fox

NOTE: Steering gear tool 3075 must be used to adjust toe on vehicles with two adjustable tie rods.

1. Turn the steering gear to the center position.
2. Remove front bolt A from the steering gear cover.
3. Attach centering tool 3075 with bracket B over mounting nut on the left tie rod.
4. Remove the bolt from the spacer on the chain of the centering tool.
5. Put the spacer under the hole marked with an L and insert a bolt through this hole and the hole in the spacer, then tighten to the steering gear.
6. Measure and divide the total toe in half.
7. Loosen the clamps and outer lock nut on both sides.
8. Turn both tie rods until the specified setting for Toe is reached.
9. Tighten the clamps and lock nuts on the tie rods.
10. Check and reposition steering wheel in center position if necessary.
11. Remove the centering tool and tighten bolt A to 15 ft. lbs. (20 Nm).
12. If the steering wheel is crooked after the toe adjustment has been made, remove, straighten and reinstall the wheel.

Golf, Rabbit, Scirocco, Jetta

Toe-in is checked with the wheels straight ahead. Only the right tie rod is adjustable, but replacement left tie rods are adjustable. Replacement left tie rods should be set to the same length as the original. Toe-in should be adjusted only with the right tie rod. If the steering wheel is crooked, remove and align it.

Vanagon

Toe-in is the adjustment made to make the front wheels point slightly into the front. Toe-in is adjusted on all types of front suspensions by adjusting the length of the tierod sleeves.

REAR SUSPENSION

Shock Absorbers

REMOVAL & INSTALLATION

Dasher Only

NOTE: Only remove one shock absorber at a time. Do not allow the rear axle to hang by its body mounts only, as it may damage the brake lines.

This operation requires the use of either special tool VW 655/3 or a suitable spring compressor and floor jack.
1. Raise the car and support it on jackstands. Do not place the jackstands under the axle beam.
2. Remove the wheel.
3. Attach special tool VW 655/3 between the axle beam and a prefabricated hook hung on the body frame above the beam. Jack the tool until you can see the shock absorber compressing. If you are using a spring compressor and a floor jack, compress the spring a little and, placing the floor jack under the beam below the spring, jack it up until you see the shock absorber compress.
4. Unbolt and remove the shock absorber.
5. Installation is the reverse of removal. Tighten the shock absorber bolts to 43 ft. lbs. (58 Nm).

NOTE: There are two types of shock absorbers for the Dasher and they have different mounts. Make sure you get the correct type for your vehicle.

Vanagon

Procedures for removing the shock absorbers are detailed in the "Trailing Arm Removal and Installation" section.

MacPherson Strut
REMOVAL & INSTALLATION

Golf, Fox, Rabbit, Jetta, GTI And Scirocco

1. Raise and support the rear of the vehicle.
2. Support the axle, but do not put any load on the springs.
3. Remove the rubber guard from inside the car.
4. Remove the nut, washer and mounting disc.
5. Unbolt the strut assembly from the rear axle and remove it.
6. To install reverse the removal procedures. Torque the strut-to-body nut to 44 ft. lbs. (60 Nm) and strut-to-axle body to 59 ft. lbs. (80 Nm).

Quantum

1. Remove the shock strut cover inside car.
2. Unscrew the strut from the body.
3. Slowly lift the vehicle until the wheels are slightly off the ground.
4. Unscrew the strut from the axle.
5. Take the strut out of the lower mounting. Press the wheel down slightly when removing the strut.

———— CAUTION ————
Do not remove both suspension struts at the same time as this will overload the axle beam bushings.

6. Guide the strut out carefully between the wheel and the wheel housing. Do not damage the paint on the spring and wheel housing.
7. To install reverse the removal procedures. Torque the strut-to-body to 26 ft. lbs. (35 Nm) and the strut-to-axle to 52 ft. lbs. (70 Nm).

OVERHAUL

For all spring and shock absorber removal and installation procedures, and all overhaul procedures, please refer to "Strut Overhaul" in the Unit Repair section.

Coil Springs
REMOVAL & INSTALLATION

Dasher Only

1. Raise the car on a lift.
2. Support the axle.
3. Install a spring compressor on the coil spring, and remove.
4. Installation is the reverse of removal.

NOTE: It is not necessary to replace both springs if only one is damaged.

RWD Vanagon

Procedures for removing the coil spring are detailed in the "Trailing Arm Removal and Installation" section.

Trailing Arm
REMOVAL & INSTALLATION

RWD Vanagon Only

1. Raise the rear of the car and support it with jack stands.
2. Remove the wheel and then disconnect the brake line from the wheel cylinder.
3. Unbolt the driveshaft at the transaxle side.
4. Unscrew the four wheel hub mounting bolts and remove it along with the driveshaft.
NOTE: Removal of the brake drum may provide better access to the wheel hub mounting bolts.
5. Place a floor jack under the trailing arm to hold its position and then remove the upper and lower shock absorber retaining bolts and remove the shock absorber.
6. Lower the trailing arm until you can remove the coil spring. Note the positioning of the upper spring plate and the lower spring seat.
7. Unscrew the two trailing arm mounting bolts and then remove the trailing arm.
8. Installation is in the reverse order of removal. When installing the coil spring, be sure that the contours for the end of the spring in the seat and the trailing arm are aligned. Also, turn the spring plate so that the end of the spring fits into the depression on the plate.
9. Adjust the camber and toe.

Rear Suspension Adjustments
RWD Vanagon Only

It is possible to adjust the camber and the toe. To adjust the toe, loosen the INSIDE mounting bolt on the trailing arm and slide it forward or backward in the horizontal slot until the proper toe is achieved. To adjust the camber, loosen the OUTSIDE mounting bolt on the trailing arm and slide it up or down until the proper camber is achieved. Being careful not to move the bolts, tighten them both to 65 ft. lbs. after adjustment.

Rear Wheel Bearings (FWD Models Only)

For wheel bearing adjustment, removal and installation procedures on Rear wheel drive models refer to the Drive Axle section.

ADJUSTMENT

Before attempting to adjust the wheel bearings, tighten the adjustment nut while turning the wheel to seat the bearings. Wheel bearing clearance is correctly adjusted when the thrust washer under the adjusting nut can be moved slightly with a screwdriver. Do not twist or pry with the screwdriver. Install a new cotter pin.

REMOVAL & INSTALLATION

1. Raise the rear of the vehicle and support it safely.
2. Remove the grease cap, cotter pin, locknut, adjusting nut, spacer and wheel bearing.
3. Remove the brake drum, pry out the grease seal and remove the inner bearing.
4. Pack the bearings, and install in the reverse order of removal.

STEERING

Steering Wheel
REMOVAL & INSTALLATION

All Models

1. Disconnect the negative battery cable.
2. The center cover pad may be pulled from the wheel on most models (cover varies depending on model), or is attached by screws from the back of the steering wheel.
3. Disconnect the horn wire.
4. Loosen and remove the steering shaft nut.
NOTE: Mark the steering shaft and steering wheel so that the wheel may be installed in the same position on the shaft.
4. Using a steering wheel puller, remove the wheel from the splined steering shaft. Do not strike the end of the steering shaft.
5. Replace the wheel in the reverse order of removal. Make sure to align the matchmarks made on the steering wheel and steering shaft. On the Golf, Rabbit, Jetta, GTI, GLI and Scirocco, install the steering wheel with the road wheels straight ahead and the cancelling lug pointing to the left. On the Dasher, Fox and Quantum, with the road wheels straight ahead, the cancelling lug on the steering wheel must point to the right and the turn signal lever must be in the neutral position. On the Vanagon install the steering wheel with the road wheels straight ahead. The gap between the turn signal switch housing and the back of the wheel is 0.08–0.159 in. In-

stall the switch with the lever in the neutral position. Tighten the steering shaft nut to 30 ft. lbs. (40 Nm) for 1985–88, Golf, Jetta and Scirocco or 36 ft. lbs. (49 Nm) for all other models.

Combination Switch
REMOVAL & INSTALLATION

All Models

1. Disconnect the negative battery cable.
2. Remove the steering wheel.
3. Remove the four turn signal switch securing screws.
4. Disconnect the turn signal switch wiring plug under the steering column.
5. Pull the switch and wiring guide rail up and out of the steering column.
6. Reverse the above steps to install. Make sure the spacers located behind the switch, if installed originally, are in position. The distance between the steering wheel and the steering column housing is 0.08–0.159. Install the switch with the lever on the central position.

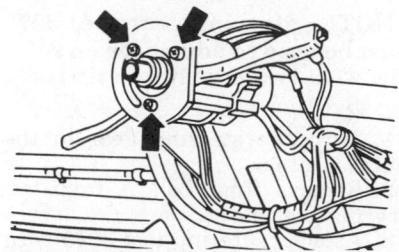

Removing the steering column switches on the 1985 and later Quantum

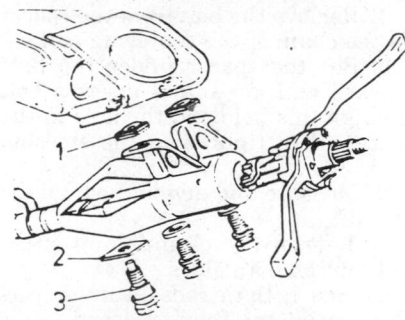

Removing the steering column mounting parts for 1985 and later Jetta

Ignition Switch
REMOVAL & INSTALLATION

FWD Models

The ignition switch is located at the bottom of the ignition key cylinder body. To remove the ignition switch, remove the steering lock body, see below for procedures. On all models, remove the switch by removing the screw at the bottom of the switch and pulling the switch out.

NOTE: On the 1985–88 models, remove the upper and lower steering column covers.

Installation is the reverse of removal.

RWD Vanagon

1. Disconnect the negative battery terminal.
2. Remove the steering wheel.
3. Loosen the mounting screws and then remove the upper and lower steering column trim.
4. Unscrew the four retaining bolts and then pull off the steering column switch.
5. Loosen the steering lock housing clamp bolt and pull the assembly up and out slightly.
6. Disconnect the wiring and remove the steering lock housing.
7. Unscrew the ignition switch screw and pull out the switch.
8. Installation is in the reverse order of removal.

Steering Lock

REMOVAL & INSTALLATION

FWD Models

On some models, the hole in the lock body for removing the steering lock cylinder was not drilled by Volkswagen. To make the hole, use the following measurements in conjunction with the illustrations. Drill the hole where "a" and "b" intersect on the lock body. The hole should be drilled ⅛ in. deep.

    a = 12mm (0.472 in.)
    b = 10mm (0.393 in.)

NOTE: Measurements are given in metric form first because this unit of measurement will be easier to make.

Remove the lock cylinder by pushing a small drill bit or piece of wire into the hole and pulling the cylinder out. It might be easier to insert the ignition key, turn it to the right a little and pull on it.

To remove the lock body, proceed as follows:

1. Remove the steering wheel and turn signal switch. See above for procedures. Remove the steering column shaft covers.
2. The lock is clamped to the steering column with special bolts whose heads shear off on installation. These must be drilled out in order to remove the switch.
3. On replacement, make sure that the lock tang is aligned with the slot in the steering column.

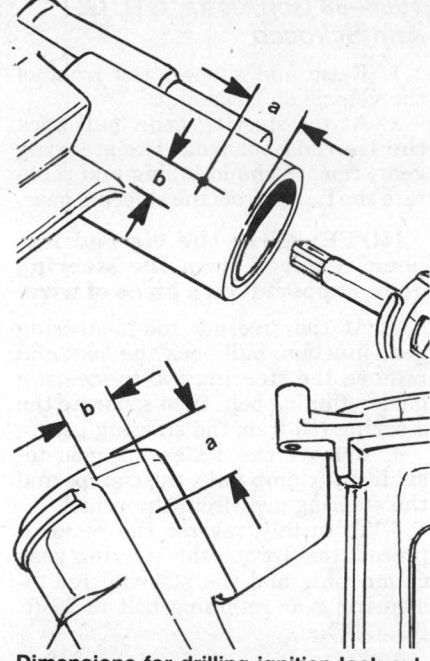

Dimensions for drilling ignition lock cylinder hole (if not equipped)

RWD Vanagon

1. Remove the ignition switch.
2. With the key in the cylinder and turned to the On position, pull the lock cylinder out far enough so the securing pin can be depressed through a hole in the side of the lock cylinder housing.
3. As the pin is depressed, gently push the cylinder into its housig. Make sure the pin engages correctly and that the retainer fits easily in place. Do not force any parts together; when they are correctly aligned, they will fit easily together.

Manual Steering Gear

REMOVAL & INSTALLATION

Dasher, Fox and Quantum

1. Pry off the lock plate and remove both tie rod mounting bolts from the steering rack, inside the engine compartment. Pry the tie rods out of the mounting pivot.
2. Remove the lower instrument panel trim.
3. Remove the shaft clamp bolt, pry off the clip, and drive the shaft toward the inside of the car with a brass drift.
4. Remove the steering gear mounting bolts.
5. Turn the wheels all the way to the right and remove the steering gear through the opening in the right wheelhousing.
6. For installation, temporarily install the tie rod mounting pivot to the rack with both mounting bolts. Remove one bolt, install the tie rod, and replace the bolt. Do the same on the other tie rod. Make sure to install a new lockplate. Torque the tie rod bolts to 39 ft. lbs. (53 Nm), the mounting pivot bolt to 15 ft. lbs. (20 Nm), and the steering gear to body mounting bolts to 15 ft. lbs.

1981–84 Rabbit, Jetta and Scirocco

1. Disconnect the steering shaft

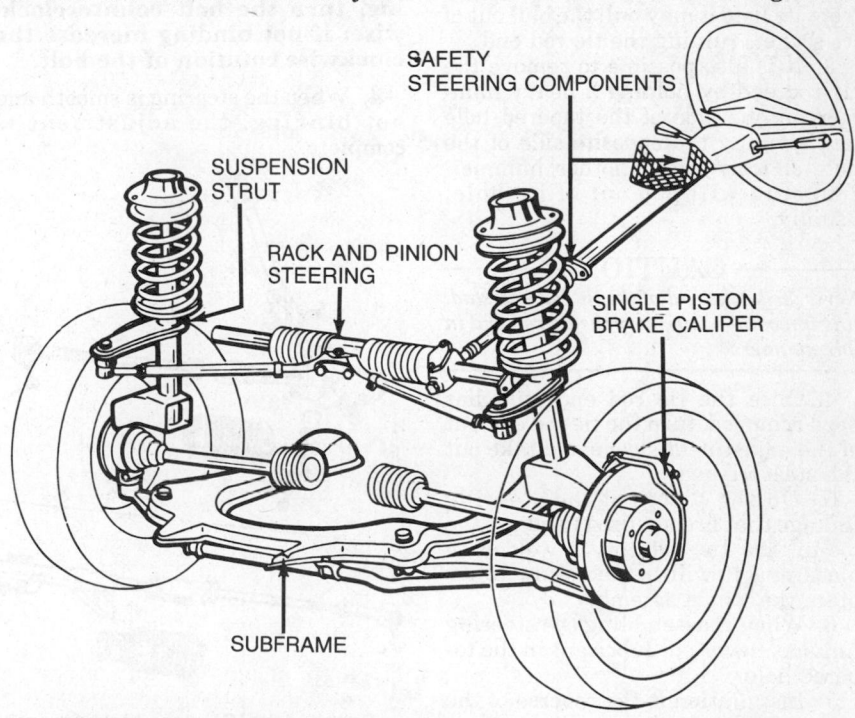

Dasher front suspension and steering components—Quantum similar

universal joint and wire up out of the way.

2. Disconnect the tie rods at the steering rack and wire up and out of the way.

3. Remove the steering rack and drive.

4. Install the steering rack and drive and torque the attaching hardware to 14 ft. lbs. (19 Nm).

5. Set the steering rack with equal distances between the housing on the right side and left side.

6. Install the tie rods and screw both sides to the measurements shown in the illustration.

7. Tighten the steering gear adjusting screw until it touches the thrust washer. Tighten the locknut.

8. Install the steering shaft.

9. Check the front end alignment.

RWD Vanagon

1. Detach the connecting shaft from the coupling disc and remove the tie rods from the steering knuckle. All tie ends are secured by a nut which holds the tapered tie rod end stud into a matching tapered hole. There are several ways to remove the tapered stud from its hole after the nut has been removed.

2. First, there are several types of removal tools available from auto parts stores. These tools include directions for their use. One of the most commonly available tools is the fork shaped tool which is a wedge that is forced under the tie rod end. This tool should be used with caution because instead of removing the tie rod end from its hole it may pull the ball out of its socket, ruining the tie rod end.

3. It is also possible to remove the tie rod end by holding a heavy hammer on one side of the tapered hole and striking the opposite side of the hole sharply with another hammer. The stud will pop out of its hole, usually.

― CAUTION ―

Never strike the end of the tie rod end stud. It is impossible to remove the tie rod end in this manner.

4. Once the tie rod end stud has been removed, turn the tie rod end out of the adjustment sleeve and take out the steering gear.

5. On the pieces of the steering linkage that are not used to adjust the toe-in, the tie rod end is welded in place and it will be necessary to replace the whole assembly.

6. When reassembling the steering linkage, never put lubricant in the tapered hole.

7. Installation is the reverse of the removal procedure.

1985–88 Golf, Jetta, GTI, GLI And Scirocco

1. Raise and support the front of the vehicle on jackstands.

2. At the steering gear, pull back the tie rod boot from the steering gear, remove the lock ring and separate the tie rod from the steering gear.

NOTE: After the tie rod has been removed from the steering gear, support it on a piece of wire.

3. At the steering rod-to-steering gear junction, pull back the boot and remove the steering rod-to-steering gear retaining bolt, then separate the steering rod from the steering gear.

4. Remove the 4 steering gear-to-subframe clamp nuts, the clamps and the steering gear from the vehicle.

5. To install, reverse the removal procedures. Torque the steering gear clamp nuts and the steering rod-to-steering gear retaining bolt to 22 ft. lbs. (30 Nm).

ADJUSTMENT
FWD Models

1. Raise and support the vehicle on jackstands, then turn the wheels to the straight ahead position.

2. On the side of the steering gear, turn the adjusting nut 20 degrees clockwise.

3. Road test to see of the steering is binding.

NOTE: If the steering is binding, turn the bolt counterclockwise; if not binding increase the clockwise rotation of the bolt.

4. When the steering is smooth and not binding, the adjustment is complete.

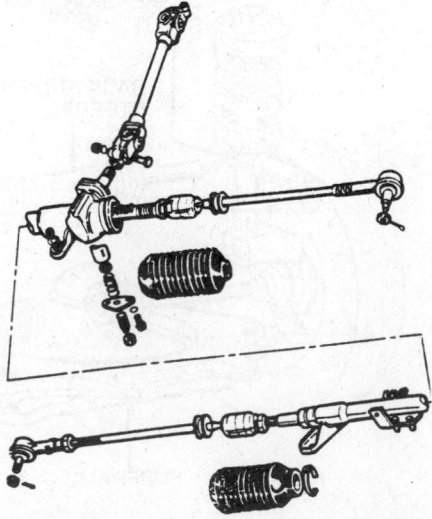

Rabbit, Jetta, Scirocco steering gear

RWD Vanagon

The steering gear on the Vanagon is not adjustable. If problems develop, the gear must be replaced.

Power Steering Gear

REMOVAL & INSTALLATION

Dasher, Fox and Quantum

1. Pry off the lock plate and remove both tie rod mounting bolts from the steering rack, inside the engine compartment. Pry the tie rods out of the mounting pivot.

2. Remove the lower instrument panel trim.

3. Remove the shaft clamp bolt, pry off the clip, and drive the shaft toward the inside of the car with a brass drift.

4. Disconnect the power steering lines. Remove the steering gear mounting bolts.

5. Turn the wheels all the way to the right and remove the steering gear through the opening in the right wheelhousing.

6. For installation, temporarily install the tie rod mounting pivot to the rack with both mounting bolts. Remove one bolt, install the tie rod, and replace the bolt. Do the same on the other tie rod. Make sure to install a new lockplate. Torque the tie rod bolts to 39 ft. lbs. (53 Nm), the mounting pivot bolt to 15 ft. lbs. (20 Nm), and the steering gear to body mounting bolts to 15 ft. lbs.

1985–88 Golf, Jetta, GTI, GLI And Scirocco

1. Raise and support the vehicle on jackstands.

2. Remove the suction hose at the power steering pump and the pressure lines from the steering gear.

NOTE: Place a catch pan under the power steering pump suction hose to catch the fluid when removing the power steering lines, then discard the fluid.

3. At the tie rod ends, loosen the tie rod lock nuts, mark the position of the tie rod to the tie rod end. Unscrew the tie rod from the tie rod ends, BE SURE to count and record the number of turns necessary to remove the rods (for installation purposes).

4. At the steering rod-to-steering gear junction, pull back the boot and remove the clamping bolts, then separate the steering rod from the steering gear.

5. Remove the steering gear-to-subframe clamp nuts, the clamps and the steering gear assembly from the vehicle.

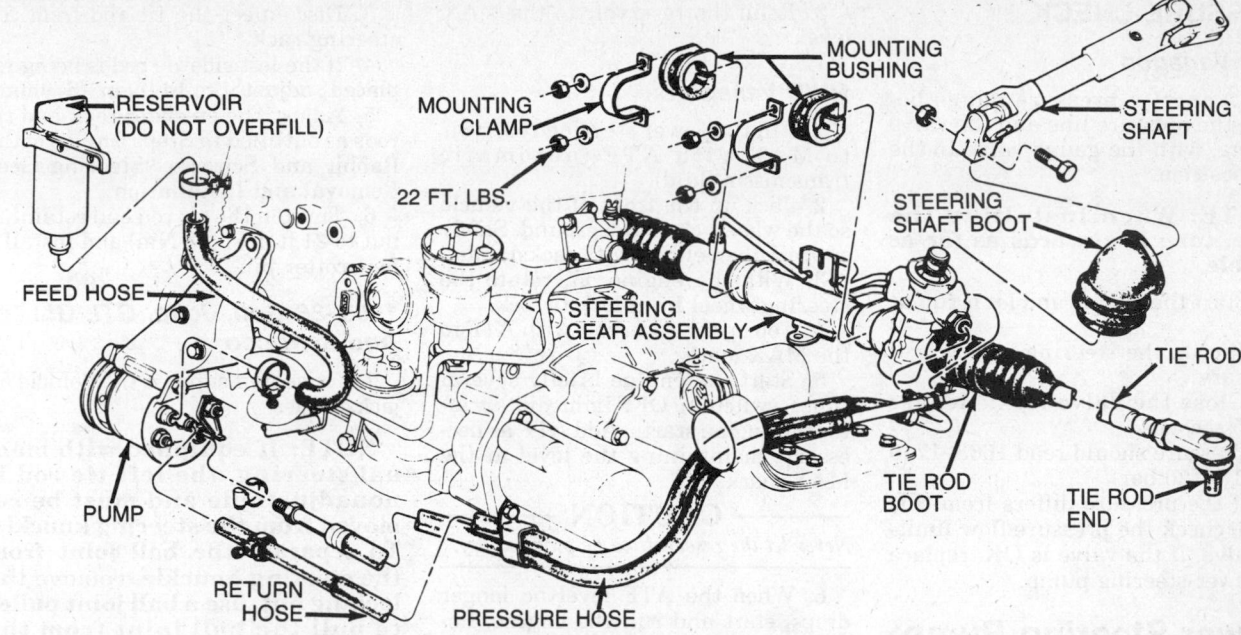

RESERVOIR (DO NOT OVERFILL)

MOUNTING CLAMP

MOUNTING BUSHING

STEERING SHAFT

22 FT. LBS.

FEED HOSE

STEERING SHAFT BOOT

STEERING GEAR ASSEMBLY

TIE ROD

PUMP

TIE ROD BOOT

TIE ROD END

RETURN HOSE

PRESSURE HOSE

Typical rack and pinion power steering

NOTE: If it is necessary to remove the tie rods from the steering gear, place the assembly in a vise, pull back the boot and separate the tie rod from the steering gear.

6. Connect the engine support tool 10–222A to the engine and transaxle assembly, remove the engine and transaxle mount bolts, then raise the engine-to-transaxale assembly to remove the steering gear assembly.

NOTE: To remove the steering gear assembly, the left wheel may have to be removed.

7. To install, use new O-rings at the pressure hose connections and reverse the removal procedures. Torque the pressure hose-to-steering gear fittings to 15 ft. lbs. (20 Nm), the steering gear clamp nuts and the steering rod-to-steering gear retaining bolt to 22 ft. lbs. (30 Nm). Fill the reservoir with approved power fluid and bleed the system.

RWD Vanagon

1. Detach the connecting shaft from the coupling disc.
2. Remove the tie rod retaining nut from the end stud.
3. Using a forked shaped tie rod removal tool and hammer, remove the tie rod end from the steering knuckle, being careful not to pull the ball out of its socket.

—— **CAUTION** ——

Never strike the end of the tie rod end stud. It is impossible to remove the tie rod end in this manner.

4. Disconnect the power steering lines from the steering gear housing.

NOTE: Place a catch pan under the power steering pump suction hose to catch the fluid when removing the power steering lines, then discard the fluid.

5. Unscrew the tie rod from the tie rod ends, BE SURE to count and record the number of turns necessary to remove the rods (for installation purposes).
6. At the steering rod-to-steering gear junction, pull back the boot and remove the clamping bolts, then separate the steering rod from the steering gear.
7. Remove the steering gear-to-subframe clamp nuts, the clamps and the steering gear assembly from the vehicle.
8. To install, use new O-rings at the pressure hose connections and reverse the removal procedures.

NOTE: When reassembling the steering linkage, never put lubricant in the tapered hole.

9. Torque the pressure hose-to-steering gear fittings to 15 ft. lbs. (20 Nm), the steering gear clamp nuts and the steering rod-to-steering gear retaining bolt to 22 ft. lbs. (30 Nm). Fill the reservoir with approved power fluid and bleed the system.

ADJUSTMENTS
FWD Models

1. Refer to the "Power Steering Gear, Removal and Installation" procedures in this section and remove the steering gear.

2. Loosen the crown nut at the adjusting bolt on the side of the steering gear.
3. Using tool VW–524, turn the adjusting nut until the rack can be moved by hand without binding.
4. Hold the adjusting nut securely and tighten the crown nut.
5. To install, use new O-rings at the pressure hose connections and reverse the removal procedures. Torque the pressure hose-to-steering gear fittings to 15 ft. lbs. (20 Nm), the steering gear clamp nuts and the steering rod-to-steering gear retaining bolt to 22 ft. lbs. (30 Nm). Fill the reservoir with approved power fluid and bleed the system.

RWD Vanagon
CHECKING FOR LEAKS

1. With the engine running, rotate the steering wheel lock-to-lock and hold it in position no longer than 5 seconds.
2. Check all line connections and tighten them if necessary.
3. If the steering pinion is leaking, replace the valve housing seal, the pinion housing seal, and the O-ring between the valve housing and pinion housing.
4. If the steering rack seals are leaking (check by pulling the boot off the steering gear), disassemble the steering gear and replace all sealing components.
5. Check the power steering pump for leaks.
NOTE: Always change the reservoir filter whenever the fluid is changed.

PRESSURE CHECK

RWD Vanagon

1. Connect a pressure gauge between the pressure line and the valve housing, with the gauge valve in the open position.

NOTE: When installing the gauge, turn it upwards as far as possible.

2. Start the engine and let it run at idle.
3. Top up the steering reservoir if necessary.
4. Close the valve for no longer than 5 seconds.
5. Pressure should read 1668–1740 psi (115–120 bar).
6. If the pressure differs from this figure, check the pressure/flow limiting valve. If the valve is OK, replace the power steering pump.

Power Steering Pump
REMOVAL & INSTALLATION

All Models

1. Place a catch pan under the power steering pump to catch the fluid.
2. Remove the suction hose and the pressure line from the pump, then drain the fluid into the catch pan (discard the fluid).
3. Loosen the tensioning bolt at the front of the tensioning bracket and remove the drive belt from the pump's drive pulley.
4. Remove the pump's mounting bolts and lift the pump from the vehicle.
5. To install, reverse the removal procedures. Torque the mounting bolts to 15 ft. lbs. (20 Nm). Tension the drive belt. Fill the reservoir with approved power steering fluid and bleed the system.

BELT ADJUSTMENT

NOTE: To tension the drive belt, adjust the tensioner bolt, so that the belt will flex ½ in. under light thumb pressure.

SYSTEM BLEEDING

FWD Models

1. Fill the reservoir to the MAX level mark with approved power steering fluid.
2. With engine idling, turn the wheels from the right to the left side as far as possible, several times.

NOTE: Continue bleeding the system until NO air bubbles are present in the fluid.

3. Refill the reservoir to the MAX level.

RWD Vanagon

1. Fill the power steering reservoir to MAX with ATF (automatic transmissin fluid).
2. Jack up the front of the vehicle so the wheels clear the ground. Safely support the vehicle with jackstands.
3. With the engine off, rotate the steering wheel from lock to lock.
4. Top up the reservoir with ATF to the MAX mark.
5. Start the engine briefly several times, switching OFF immediately after the engine starts. Add ATF as necessary, maintaining the level at the MAX mark.

— CAUTION —
Never let the reservoir to be pumped dry.

6. When the ATF level no longer drops, start and run the engine. Rotate the steering wheel lock to lock several times. Check that no bubbles appear in the reservoir, and that the level remains steady.

Tie Rod Ends

REMOVAL & INSTALLATION

Dasher, Fox and Quantum

1. Raise the car and remove the front wheels.
2. Disconnect the outer end of the steering tie rod from the steering knuckle by removing the cotter pin and nut and pressing out the tie rod end. A small puller or press is required to free the tie rod end.
3. Under the hood, pry off the lockplate and remove the mounting bolts from both tie rod inner ends. Pry the tie rod out of the mounting pivot.
4. First install the mounting pivot to the rack with both mounting bolts. Remove one bolt, install the tie rod, and replace the bolt. Do the same on the other tie rod. Be sure to install a new lockplate. The inner tie rod end bolts should be torqued to 40 ft. lbs. (54 Nm).
5. If you are replacing, both tie rods on the Fox, or the adjustable left tie rod on the Dasher or Quantum, adjust it to the same length as the old one(s). Check the toe in when the job is done.
6. Use new cotter pins when installing the outer tie rod ends. Torque the nut to 22 ft. lbs. (30 Nm).

1981–84 Rabbit, Jetta and Scirocco

1. Center the steering rack.
2. Remove the cotter pin and nut from the tie rod end.

3. Disconnect the tie rod from the steering rack.
4. If the left side tie rod is being replaced, adjust it to 14.92 in. (379mm).
5. Adjust the steering rack and tie rods as outlined in Steps 5 and 6 of the Rabbit and Scirocco "Steering Gear Removal and Installation."
6. Tighten the tie rod end retaining nut to 21 ft. lbs. (28 Nm) and install a new cotter pin.

1985–88 Golf, Jetta, GTI, GLI And Scirocco

1. Raise and support the vehicle on jackstands.

NOTE: If equipped with manual steering, the left tie rod is nonadjustable and must be removed from the steering knuckle. To separate the ball joint from the steering knuckle, remove the locking nut, use a ball joint puller to pull the ball joint from the steering knuckle.

2. At the tie rod ends, loosen the tie rod lock nuts, mark the position of the tie rod to the tie rod end. Unscrew the tie rod from the tie rod ends, BE SURE to count and record the number of turns necessary to remove the rods (for installation purposes).
3. At the steering rod-to-steering gear junction, pull back the boot and remove the clamping bolts, then separate the steering rod from the steering gear.
4. To install, reverse the removal procedures. Torque the ball joint-to-steering knuckle to 26 ft. lbs. (35 Nm).

RWD Vanagon

For tie rod end removal and installation please refer to Steering Gear removal and installation section.

BRAKES

For all brake system repair and service procedures not detailed below, please refer to "Brakes" in the Unit Repair section.

Master Cylinder

REMOVAL & INSTALLATION

FWD Models

1. Disconnect and plug the brake lines.
2. Disconnect the electrical plug from the sending unit for the brake failure switch.
3. Remove the 2 master cylinder mounting nuts.

4. Lift the master cylinder and reservoir out of the engine compartment being careful not to spill any fluid on the fender. Empty out and discard the brake fluid.

CAUTION
Do not depress the brake pedal while the master cylinder, front brake discs or drum brake shoes are removed.

5. Position the master cylinder and reservoir assembly onto the studs for the booster and install the washers and nuts. Tighten the nuts to 15 ft. lbs. (20 Nm).
6. Remove the plugs and connect the brake lines.
7. Bleed the entire brake system.

RWD Vanagon

NOTE: The reservoirs on the Vanagon is underneath the raised portion of the instrument panel.

1. Grasp the two recesses provided on the back of the instrument cluster frame and pull it forward.
2. Tag and disconnect any wiring leading to the back of the instrument cluster and then remove it.

Brake Pressure Regulator (Proportioning Valve)

NOTE: The Dasher has two different kinds of brake pressure regulators: two pressure sensitive regulators mounted at the master cylinder and one load sensitive regulator mounted at the rear axle. Other models have only load sensitive regulator.

The brake pressure regulator is located on the left rear side of the car near the rear axle (except on the Fox and Dasher). The Dasher and Fox regulator is on the right rear side near the axle. The pressure ratio of the regulator can be adjusted by your Volkswagen dealer with special pressure gauges and alignment tools.

NOTE: Not all Rabbits and Sciroccos are equipped with brake proportioning valves.

REMOVAL & INSTALLATION

1. Raise the rear of the vehicle and support it safely.
2. Using a brake line wrench, loosen the lines to the proportioning valve. Have a suitable container handy to catch the brake fluid.
3. Remove the retaining nuts that secure the proportioning valve to the frame.

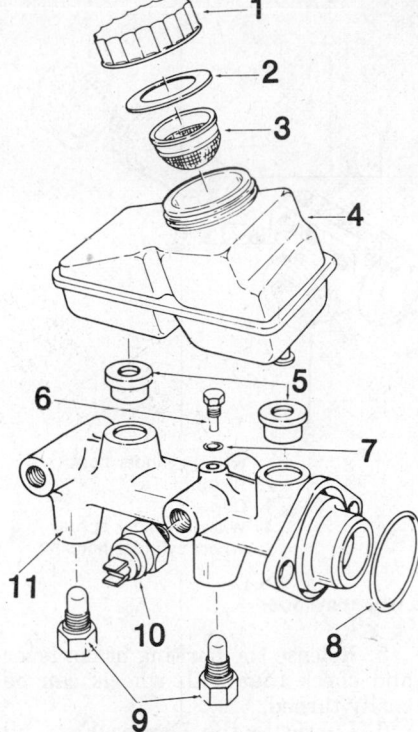

1. Reservoir cap
2. Washer
3. Filter screen
4. Reservoir
5. Master cylinder plugs
6. Stop screw
7. Stop screw seal
8. Master cylinder seal
9. Residual pressure valves
10. Warning light sender unit
11. Brake master cylinder housing

Master cylinder assembly for Rabbit, Jetta and Scirocco (typical)—Dasher and Quantum similar

4. Install in the reverse of removal.
5. Bleed the brake system.

Power Brake Booster

REMOVAL & INSTALLATION

1. Remove the master cylinder from in front of the booster.
2. In the driver's compartment, remove the clevis pin on the end of the booster pushrod by unclipping it and pulling it out of the clevis.
3. On the gasoline engine models, remove the vacuum line running from the booster to intake manifold. On diesel engines, the line connects to a special vacuum pump located where the distributor on a gasoline engine would be. Remove the line.
4. On the Rabbit, Jetta and Scirocco, unbolt the booster bracket where it connects to the firewall. On the Dasher, Fox and Quantum remove the two nuts from inside the driver's compartment, or the four nuts holding the

booster to its bracket. Remove the booster.
5. The brake booster cannot be repaired and must be replaced if its diaphragm leaks or it fails to operate.
6. Installation is the reverse of removal.
7. Bleed the brakes after installing the master cylinder. See above for procedures.
8. After the system is installed, check to make sure that the rear brake lights work. If not, you have misaligned the light switch at the brake pedal.

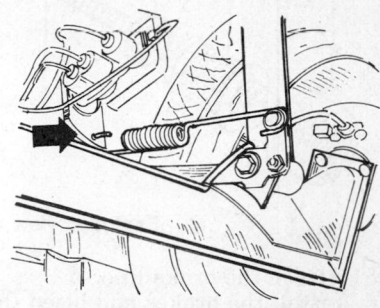

Relieving pressure at the proportioning valve. Push lever (arrow) toward rear axle

Vacuum Pump

REMOVAL & INSTALLATION

Diesel Engines with Power Brakes Only

One line of the vacuum pump runs to the power brake booster and the other line runs to the engine. Unclamp and remove both lines. Unbolt and remove the pump. The diaphragm inside the pump is replaceable. Remove the screws holding the vacuum hose inlet cover to the pump body and remove the cover. Unscrew the retaining nut and remove the diaphragm. Install the new diaphragm with the molded center toward the top. Don't overtighten the retaining nut.

Wheel Cylinder

REMOVAL & INSTALLATION

FWD Models

1. Remove the brake shoes.
2. Loosen the brake line on the rear of the cylinder, but do not pull the line away from the cylinder or it may bend.
3. Remove the bolts and lockwashers that attach the wheel cylinder to the backing plate and remove the cylinder.
4. Position the new wheel cylinder on the backing plate and install the cylinder attaching bolts and lockwashers.

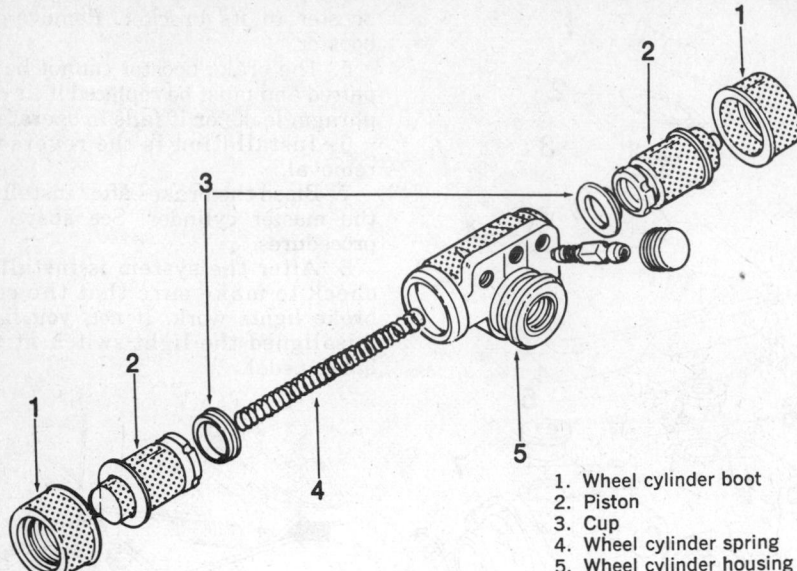

1. Wheel cylinder boot
2. Piston
3. Cup
4. Wheel cylinder spring
5. Wheel cylinder housing

Exploded view of the wheel cylinder

5. Attach the brake line.
6. Install the brakes and bleed the system.

RWD Vanagon

1. Remove the brake drum and brake shoes.
2. Disconnect the brake line from the cylinder and remove the bolts which secure the cylinder to the backing plate.
3. Remove the cylinder from the vehicle.
4. Installation is the reverse of the removal procedure.

Parking Brake Cable

ADJUSTMENT

FWD Models

Dasher, Fox and Quantum parking brake adjustment is made at the cable compensator, which is attached to the lever pushrod underneath the car. On all other vehicles, the position of the cable end nuts are below the front of the hand brake lever. Adjustment is performed at the cable end nuts.

Drum Type

1. Block the front wheels. Raise the rear of the car.
2. Apply the parking brake so that the lever is on the second notch.
3. The Dasher and Quantum adjustment is made directly under the passenger compartment.
4. Tighten the compensator nut or adjusting nuts until both rear wheels can just be turned by hand. On models with self-adjusting rear brakes, you shouldn't be able to turn them at all.

5. Release the parking brake lever and check that both wheels can be easily turned.
6. Lubricate the Dasher Fox and Quantum compensator with chassis grease.

Disc Type

— **CAUTION** —

After installing new rear brake pads, push the brake pedal FIRMLY several times to permit the pistons and the brake pads to adjust to the brake disc. ALWAYS adjust the rear disc brakes before adjusting the parking brake.

1. Block the front wheels, then raise and support the rear of the vehicle.
2. Disengage the parking brake.
3. Tighten the adjusting nuts of the parking brake cables until the parking brake levers (on top of each rear wheel caliper) rise off the stops.

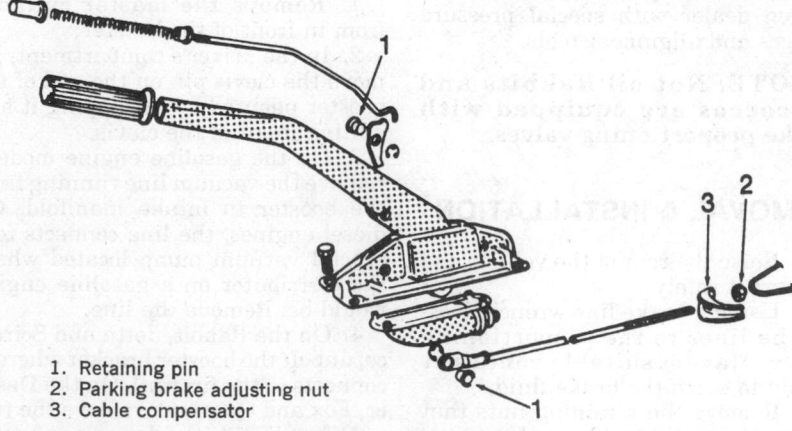

1. Retaining pin
2. Parking brake adjusting nut
3. Cable compensator

Dasher parking brake linkage and adjusting point (Quantum similar)

NOTE: The maximum distance the lever can rise off the stop is 0.039 in. (1mm).

4. Reconnect the parking brake cable.

RWD Vanagon

Brake cable adjustment is performed at the handbrake lever in the passenger compartment. There is a cable for each rear wheel and there are two adjusting nuts at the lever.
1. Loosen the locknut.
2. Jack up the rear wheel to be adjusted so that it can be hand spun.
3. Turn the adjusting nut until a very slight drag is felt as the wheel is spun.
4. Back off on the adjusting nut until the lever can be pulled up three notches.

— **CAUTION** —

Never pull up on the handbrake lever with the cables disconnected.

5. Tighten the locknut

REMOVAL & INSTALLATION

Drum Type

ALL MODELS EXCEPT DASHER, FOX, QUANTUM AND VANAGON

1. Jack up the rear of the vehicle.
2. Block the front wheels and release the handbrake.
3. Remove the rear brake shoes.
4. Remove the cable adjusting nut(s) and detach the cable guides from the floor pan.
5. Replace the cable and brake shoes. Check the parking brake adjustment.

DASHER, FOX AND QUANTUM

1. Raise and support the rear of the car. Release the parking brake.
2. Remove the rear brake drums.

3. Disconnect the cable from the shoe asssembly by pushing the spring forward and removing the cable from the adjusting arm.

4. Remove the cable compensating spring.

5. Back off the equalizer nut and guide the cable through the trailing arms and supports.

6. Installation is the reverse of removal.

7. Adjust if necessary.

RWD VANAGON

1. Disconnect the cables at the handbrake lever by removing the two nuts which secure the cables to the lever. Pull the cables rearward to remove that end from the lever bracket.

2. Remove the brake drum and detach the cable end from the lever attached to the rear brake shoe.

3. Remove the brake cable bracket from the backing plate and remove the cable from the vehicle.

4. Reverse the above steps to install and adjust the cable.

Disc Type

1. Raise and support the rear of the vehicle on jackstands.

2. Release the parking brake.

NOTE: It may be necessary to unscrew the adjusting nuts to provide slack in the brake cable.

3. At each rear wheel brake caliper, remove the spring clip retaining the parking brake cable to the caliper.

4. Lift the cable from the caliper mount and disengage it from the parking brake lever.

5. To install, reverse the removal procedures and adjust the parking brake cables.

CHASSIS ELECTRICAL

Heater

The heater core and blower on all models are contained in the heater box (fresh air housing located in the center of the passenger compartment under the dashboard). On air conditioned Fox's, Rabbits, Jettas and Sciroccos, the evaporator is located in the heater box. On air conditioned Dashers and Quantums, the evaporator is located under the hood separate from the heater box.

REMOVAL & INSTALLATION

Without Console

1. Disconnect the battery ground cable.

2. Drain the cooling system.

3. Remove the windshield washer container from its mounts and remove the ignition coil only if they restrict your access to the heater components under the hood.

4. Disconnect the two hoses from the heater core connections at the firewall.

5. Unplug the blower fan electrical connections. Some models are equipped with an external series resistor mounted on the heater box. Do not try to remove the wires from the resistor.

6. Remove the heater control knobs on the dash.

7. Remove the two retaining screws and remove the controls from the dash complete with brackets.

8. Some models have a cable attached to a lever which is operated by a round knob on the dashboard. Remove the cable from the lever.

9. Remove either the clips or the screws holding the heater box in place and remove the heater box with the heater controls.

10. To install, reverse the removal procedures. Be sure to refill the cooling system.

With Center Console

1. Disconnect the negative battery cable.

2. Drain the engine coolant.

NOTE: Save the coolant for reuse.

3. Trace the heater hoses coming from the firewall and disconnect them. One leads to the back of the cylinder head and the other leads to the heater valve located above and behind the oil filter.

4. Detach the cable for the heater valve.

5. Remove the center console.

6. Remove the left and right covers below the instrument panel.

7. Pull off the fresh air/heater control knobs.

8. Pull off the trim plate.

9. Remove the screws for the controls.

10. Remove the center cover mounting screws and remove the cover.

11. Detach the right, left and center air ducts.

12. Remove the heater housing retaining spring.

13. Remove the cowl for the air plenum which is located under the hood and in front of the windshield.

14. Remove the heater housing mounting screws and remove the heater housing. The mounting screws are under the hood where the air plenum was.

15. Installation is in the reverse order of removal. Be sure to replace all sealing material.

Heater Blower
REMOVAL & INSTALLATION

All Except 1985–88 Golf And Jetta

1. Remove the heater unit from the vehicle. See above for procedures.

2. Remove the screws holding the cover on the heater box and remove the cover. Remove the blower motor cover, if equipped.

3. Remove the electrical connections from the blower motor after matchmarking them to insure that you assemble them in the correct order.

4. Remove the clamp or screws holding the motor in place and remove the motor.

5. Installation is the reverse of removal.

1985–88 Golf And Jetta

NOTE: The blower motor is located behind the glove box and it may be necessary to remove the glove box to gain access to the motor.

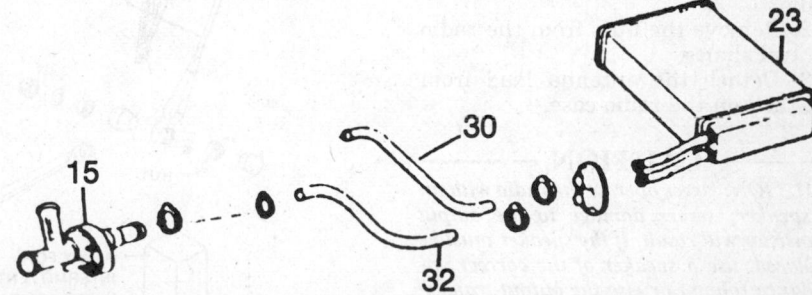

Rabbit, Scirocco and Jetta heater core (23), hoses (30 and 32), and heater control valve (15)

WITHOUT A/C

1. Disconnect the wires at the blower motor.
2. At the blower motor flange near the cowl, disengage the retaining lug (pull down on the lug).
3. Turn the motor in the clockwise direction, to release it from it's mount, then lower it from the plenum.
4. To install, reverse the removal procedures.

WITH A/C

1. Disconnect the wires from the blower motor.
2. Remove the 3 mounting screws and pull the motor from the plenum.
3. To install, reverse the removal procedures.

Heater Core

REMOVAL & INSTALLATION

NOTE: On some models, it is possible to remove the heater core without removing the heater box. Proceed as follows:
  a. Drain the cooling system.
  b. Locate and remove the heater core cover in the side of the heater box.
  c. Disconnect the heater hoses from the core and pull the core out.

1. Remove the heater box from the vehicle.
2. If the unit has a core cover in its side, remove the screws or unclip the cover and remove it. The core should pull out.
3. On other models, remove the heater box clips that hold the two halves of the heater box together, separate the halves after removing any components that are in the way and remove the heater core.

Radio

REMOVAL & INSTALLATION

1. Remove the knobs from the radio.
2. Remove the nuts from the radio control shafts.
3. Detach the antenna lead from the jack on the radio case.

CAUTION

CAUTION: Never operate the radio without a speaker; severe damage to the output transistor will result. If the speaker must be replaced, use a speaker of the correct impedance (ohms) or else the output transistors will be damaged and require replacement.

---

4. Detach the power and speaker leads.
5. Remove the radio support nuts and bolts.
6. Withdraw the radio from beneath the dashboard.
7. Installation is performed in the reverse order of removal.

Windshield Wiper/ Washer Switch

REMOVAL & INSTALLATION

1. Using your hands, pull off the steering wheel cover.
2. Remove the steering wheel lock nut and spacer.
3. Using a wheel puller, remove the steering wheel.
4. Remove the three retaining screws and remove the combination turn signal, headlight switch.
5. Remove the windshield wiper/washer switch.
6. Installation is the reverse of the removal procedure.

Windshield Wiper Motor

REMOVAL & INSTALLATION

Dasher and Quantum

1. Unplug the multi-connector from the wiper motor.
2. Remove the three motor-to-linkage bracket retaining screws.

3. Carefully pry the motor crank out of the two linkage arms.
4. Remove the motor from the car.
5. Install the motor in the reverse order of removal. The crank arm should be at a right angle to the motor.

1981–84 Rabbit, Scirocco, Jetta

When removing the wiper motor, leave the mounting frame in place. On all models with two front wiper arms, do not remove the wiper drive crank from the motor shaft.

On Sciroccos with one front wiper arm, matchmark the drive crank and motor arm and then remove the arm.

NOTE: If, for any reason you must remove the wiper drive crank from the motor shaft on two wiper arm models, matchmark both parts for reassembly.

1. Access is with the hood open. Disconnect the battery ground cable.
2. Detach the connecting rods from the motor crank arm.
3. Pull off the wiring plug.
4. Remove the 4 mounting bolts. You may have to energize the motor for access to the top bolt.
5. Remove the motor. Reverse the procedure for installation.

1985–88 Golf, Fox, Rabbit, GTI, Jetta And Scirocco

1. Disconnect the electrical connector to the wiper motor.

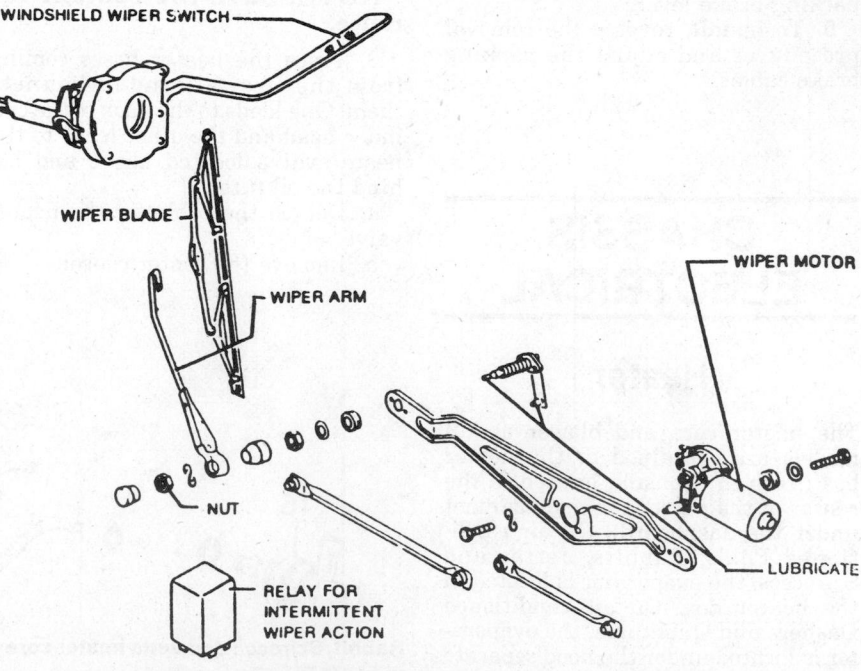

Rabbit, Jetta, Scirocco front wiper motor and linkage

2. Disconnect the crank arm from the wiper arm assembly.

3. Remove the retaining nut and the crank arm from the wiper motor shaft.

4. Remove the motor mounting bolts and the motor from the vehicle.

5. To install, run the motor and turn it off (it will stop in the Park position).

6. Install the motor to the vehicle.

7. To install the crank arm, raise it 4 degrees from horizontal on the right side and connect it to the motor shaft.

8. To complete the installation, connect the crank arm to the wiper assembly and reverse the removal procedures.

RWD Vanagon

1. Disconnect the ground wire from the battery.

2. Remove both wiper arms.

3. Remove the bearing cover and nut.

4. Remove the heater branch connections under the instrument panel.

5. Disconnect the wiper motor wiring.

6. Remove the wiper motor securing screw and remove the motor.

7. Reverse the above steps to install.

Instrument Cluster
REMOVAL & INSTALLATION

Dasher

1. Remove the radio or shelf.

2. Pull the knobs off the fresh air control and fan switch.

3. Remove the six instrument cluster to dashboard retaining screws.

4. Snap out the light, emergency flasher and rear window defogger switches.

5. Disconnect the air fan switch electrical connector.

6. Remove the instrument cluster and disconnect the speedometer cable and the multi-point connector from the back of the cluster.

7. To install, reverse the removal procedures.

Scirocco, 1981 Rabbit and Jetta

1. Disaconnect the battery ground cable.

2. Remove the fresh air controls trim plate.

3. Remove the radio or glove box.

4. Unscrew the speedometer drive cable from the back of the speedometer. Detach the electrical plug.

5. Remove the attaching screw inside the radio/glove box opening.

6. Remove the instrument cluster. Reverse the procedure for installation.

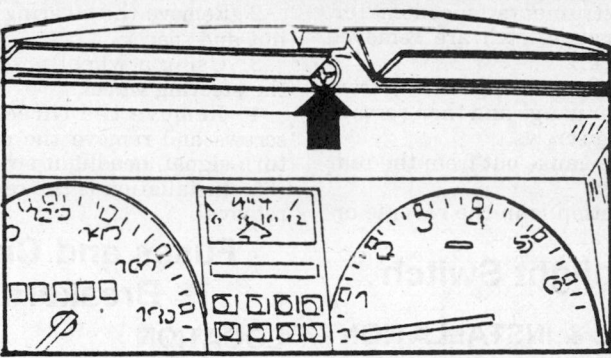

Tip down cluster panel, revealing inside Phillips screw

1982–84 Scirocco

1. Disconnect battery ground cable.

2. Remove the two Phillips head screws on the inner top surface of the instrument compartment (see illustration).

3. Start to pull down on the instrument compartment. Inside the top center of the compartment you will see another Phillips screw (as you pull the compartment out). Remove the screws.

4. Tip out the top of the instrument cluster.

5. Remove the speedometer cable by twisting the tabs of the plastic fixture around the end of the cable.

6. Disconnect the multi-point connector and remove instrument cluster.

7. To install, reverse the removal procedures.

1982–88 Quantum

1. Disconnect battery ground strap.

2. Carefully pry off switch trim below instruments.

3. Pull heater control knobs off and press out heater control trim.

4. Remove two Phillips head screws holding heater control trim to panel.

5. Remove the 7 Phillips screws around perimeter of instrument cluster.

6. Disconnect all wiring to switches and warning lamps. Remove all trim panels.

7. The remainder of the procedure can be completed by following the Scirocco procedure beginning at Step 3.

1985–88 Golf, Fox, GTI, Jetta And Scirocco

1. Pull off all of the temperature control knobs and levers.

2. Unclip the control lever trim plate, separate the electrical connectors and remove the plate.

NOTE: Remove any switches from the trim which is necessary.

3. Remove the retaining screws and the instrument panel trim plate.

4. Remove the retaining screws and pull out the instrument panel.

5. Squeeze the clips on the speedometer cable head and remove the cable from the instrument cluster.

6. Disconnect all of the vacuum hose and the electrical connections.

7. To install, reverse the removal procedures.

RWD Vanagon

1. To remove the instrument cluster on the Vanagon, grasp the two recesses provided at the back of the cluster and pull it forward.

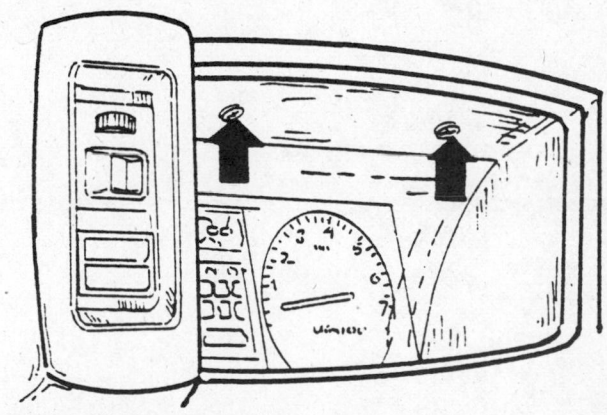

Instrument cluster removal—Scirocco (Quantum similar)

2. All instruments (speedometer, clock, fuel gauge, etc.) are removed from the back.

3. Unhook any wiring leading from the particular gauge and then remove the retaining screws.

4. Pull the gauge out from the rear of the cluster.

5. Installation is in the reverse order of removal.

Headlight Switch

REMOVAL & INSTALLATION

1. Using your hands, pull off the steering wheel cover.

2. Remove the steering wheel lock nut and spacer.

3. Using a wheel puller, remove the steering wheel.

4. Remove the three retaining screws and remove the combination turn signal, headlight switch.

5. Installation is the reverse of the removal.

Fuses and Circuit Breakers

LOCATION

All major circuits are protected from overloading or short circuiting by fuses. A 12 position fusebox is located beneath the dashboard near the steering column, or located in the luggage compartment on some air conditioned models.

When a fuse blows, the cause should be investigated. Never install a fuse of a larger capacity than specified and never use foil or a bolt or nail in place of a fuse. However, always carry a few spares in case of emergency. There are ten 8 amp (white) fuses and two 16 amp (red) fuses in the VW fusebox. Circuits number 9 and 10 use the 16 amp fuses. To replace a fuse, pry off the clear plasic cover at either end of the subject fuse.

Volvo 18
240, 260, 740, 760, 780 Series
All Models

SERIAL NUMBER IDENTIFICATION

Vehicle Identification Plate

The VIN plate on these cars is located on the top left surface of the dash, and is also stamped on the right hand door pillar. Emission control information is on a label located on the left hand shock tower under the hood. There is also a model plate on the right hand shock tower that includes the VIN number, engine type, emission equipment, vehicle weights and color codes.

Last three digits of Engine Identification Number printed on label on timing belt cover.

B21 series engine number locations

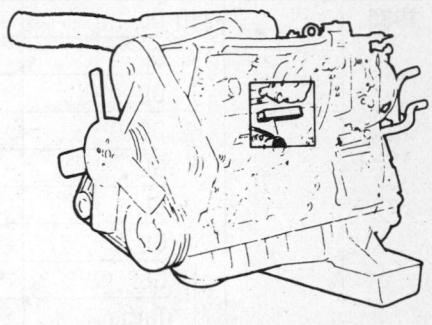

D24 and D24T engine number location

Engine Number

The engine type designation, part number, and serial number are given on the left side of the block (4). The last figures of the part number are stamped on a tab and are followed by the serial number stamped on the block.

Transmission Number

The transmission type designation, serial number, and part number appear on a metal plate (5) riveted to the underside of the transmission. The final drive reduction ratio, part number, and serial number are found on a metal plate (6) riveted to the left-hand side of the differential.

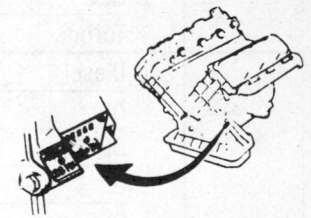

B28F engine number locations

ENGINE IDENTIFICATION

Year	Model		Engine Displacement cu. in. (cc/liter)	Engine Series Identification	No. of Cylinders	Engine Type
1981	240	DL	130 (2127/2.2)	B21F	4	OHC
		DL	130 (2127/2.2)	B21F-MPG	4	OHC
		DL ①	130 (2127/2.2)	B21A	4	OHC
		GL	130 (2127/2.2)	B21F	4	OHC
		GL ①	140 (2320/2.3)	B23E	4	OHC

ENGINE IDENTIFICATION

Year		Model	Engine Displacement cu. in. (cc/liter)	Engine Series Identification	No. of Cylinders	Engine Type
1981		GLT	130 (2127/2.2)	B21F-Turbo	4	OHC
		GLT ②	130 (2127/2.2)	B21F	4	OHC
		GLT ①	140 (2320/2.3)	B23E	4	OHC
	260	Coupe	174 (2849/2.9)	B28F	6	OHC
		GL	130 (2127/2.2)	B21F	4	OHC
		GL	145 (2383/2.4)	D24	6	OHC
		GLE	174 (2849/2.9)	B28F	6	OHC
1982	240	DL	130 (2127/2.2)	B21F	4	OHC
		DL ①	130 (2127/2.2)	B21A	4	OHC
		GL	130 (2127/2.2)	B21F	4	OHC
		GL	145 (2383/2.4)	D24	6	OHC
		GL ①	140 (2320/2.3)	B23E	4	OHC
		GLT	130 (2127/2.2)	B21F-Turbo	4	OHC
		GLT	130 (2127/2.2)	B21F	4	OHC
		GLT ①	140 (2320/2.3)	B23E	4	OHC
	260	GLE	174 (2849/2.9)	B28F	6	OHC
1983	240	DL	140 (2320/2.3)	B23F	4	OHC
		DL	130 (2127/2.2)	B21F-Turbo	4	OHC
		DL	145 (2383/2.4)	D24	6	OHC
		DL ①	130 (2127/2.2)	B21A	4	OHC
		GL	140 (2320/2.3)	B23F	4	OHC
		GL	145 (2383/2.4)	D24	6	OHC
		GL ①	140 (2320/2.3)	B23E	4	OHC
		GLT ①	140 (2320/2.3)	B23E	4	OHC
		Turbo	130 (2127/2.2)	B21F-Turbo	4	OHC
	760	GLE	174 (2849/2.9)	B28F	6	OHC
		GLE	145 (2383/2.4)	D24-Turbo	6	OHC
		Turbo	140 (2320/2.3)	B23F-Turbo	4	OHC
1984	240	Diesel	145 (2383/2.4)	D24	6	OHC
		DL	140 (2320/2.3)	B23F	4	OHC
		DL ①	130 (2127/2.2)	B21A	4	OHC
		GL	140 (2320/2.3)	B23F	4	OHC
		GLE ①	140 (2320/2.3)	B23F	4	OHC
		Turbo	130 (2127/2.2)	B21F-Turbo	4	OHC
	760	GLE	174 (2849/2.9)	B28F	6	OHC
		GLE	145 (2383/2.4)	D24-Turbo	6	OHC
		Turbo	140 (2320/2.3)	B23F-Turbo	4	OHC
1985	240	Diesel	145 (2383/2.4)	D24	6	OHC
		DL	140 (2320/2.3)	B230F	4	OHC
		GL	140 (2320/2.3)	B230F	4	OHC
		Turbo	130 (2127/2.2)	B21F-Turbo	4	OHC
	740	GLE	140 (2320/2.3)	B230F	4	OHC
		TD ②	145 (2383/2.4)	D24-Turbo	6	OHC
		Turbo	140 (2320/2.3)	B230F-Turbo	4	OHC

ENGINE IDENTIFICATION

Year	Model		Engine Displacement cu. in. (cc/liter)	Engine Series Identification	No. of Cylinders	Engine Type
1985	760	GLE	174 (2849/2.9)	B28F	6	OHC
		GLE TD	145 (2383/2.4)	D24-Turbo	6	OHC
		Turbo	140 (2320/2.3)	B230F-Turbo	4	OHC
1986	240	DL	140 (2320/2.3)	B230F	4	OHC
		GL	140 (2320/2.3)	B230F	4	OHC
	740	GL	140 (2320/2.3)	B230F	4	OHC
		GLE	140 (2320/2.3)	B230F	4	OHC
		GLE TD	145 (2383/2.4)	D24-Turbo	6	OHC
		Turbo	140 (2320/2.3)	B230F-Turbo	4	OHC
	760	GLE	174 (2849/2.9)	B28F	6	OHC
		Turbo	140 (2320/2.3)	B230F-Turbo	4	OHC
1987-88	240	DL	140 (2320/2.3)	B230F	4	OHC
		GL	140 (2320/2.3)	B230F	4	OHC
	740	GL	140 (2320/2.3)	B230F	4	OHC
		GLE	140 (2320/2.3)	B230F	4	OHC
		Turbo	140 (2320/2.3)	B230F-Turbo	4	OHC
	760	GLE	174 (2849/2.9)	B280F	6	OHC
		Turbo	140 (2320/2.3)	B230F-Turbo	4	OHC
	780		174 (2849/2.9)	B280F	6	OHC

① Canada only
② Station Wagon

GENERAL ENGINE SPECIFICATIONS

Year	Model		Engine Displacement cu. in. (cc)	Fuel System Type	Net Horsepower @ rpm	Net Torque @ rpm (ft. lbs.)	Bore × Stroke (in.)	Compression Ratio	Oil Pressure @ rpm
1981	240	DL	130 (2127) B21F	CIS	107 @ 5500	114 @ 2500	3.62 × 3.15	9.3:1	35-85 @ 2000
		DL	130 (2127) B21F-MPG	CIS	99 @ 5000	114 @ 3000	3.62 × 3.15	9.3:1	35-85 @ 2000
		DL ①	130 (2127) B21A	1-bbl SU	96 @ 5250	121 @ 2500	3.62 × 3.15	9.3:1	35-85 @ 2000
		GL	130 (2127) B21F	CIS	107 @ 5500	114 @ 2500	3.62 × 3.15	9.3:1	35-85 @ 2000
		GL ①	140 (2320) B23E	CIS	129 @ 5500	135 @ 4500	3.78 × 3.15	10.0:1	35-85 @ 2000
		GLT	130 (2127) B21F-Turbo	CIS	126 @ 5400	150 @ 3750	3.62 × 3.15	7.5:1	35-85 @ 2000
		GLT ②	130 (2127) B21F	CIS	107 @ 5500	114 @ 2500	3.62 × 3.15	9.3:1	35-85 @ 2000
		GLT ①	140 (2320) B23E	CIS	129 @ 5500	135 @ 4500	3.78 × 3.15	10.0:1	35-85 @ 2000
	260	Coupe	174 (2849) B28F	CIS	130 @ 5500	153 @ 2750	3.58 × 2.86	8.8:1	60 @ 3000
		GL	130 (2127) B21F	CIS	107 @ 5500	114 @ 2500	3.62 × 3.15	9.3:1	35-85 @ 2000

GENERAL ENGINE SPECIFICATIONS

Year	Model	Engine Displacement cu. in. (cc)	Fuel System Type	Net Horsepower @ rpm	Net Torque @ rpm (ft. lbs.)	Bore × Stroke (in.)	Compression Ratio	Oil Pressure @ rpm
1981	GL	145 (2383) D24	DFI	78 @ 4800	102 @ 3000	3.01 × 3.40	23.5:1	28 @ 2000
	GLE	174 (2849) B28F	CIS	130 @ 5500	153 @ 2750	3.58 × 2.86	8.8:1	60 @ 3000
1982	240 DL	130 (2127) B21F	CIS	98 @ 5000	112 @ 3000	3.62 × 3.15	9.3:1	35–85 @ 2000
	DL ③	130 (2127) B21F	LH	105 @ 5400	119 @ 3000	3.62 × 3.15	9.3:1	35–85 @ 2000
	DL ①	130 (2127) B21A	1-bbl Zenith	100 @ 5250	122 @ 2500	3.62 × 3.15	9.3:1	35–85 @ 2000
	GL	130 (2127) B21F	CIS	98 @ 5000	112 @ 3000	3.62 × 3.15	9.3:1	35–85 @ 2000
	GL	145 (2383) D24	DFI	76 @ 4800	98 @ 2800	3.01 × 3.40	23.0:1	28 @ 2000
	GL ①	140 (2320) B23E	CIS	127 @ 5500	133 @ 4500	3.78 × 3.15	10.0:1	35–85 @ 2000
	GLT	130 (2127) B21F-Turbo	CIS	127 @ 5400	150 @ 3750	3.62 × 3.15	7.5:1	35–85 @ 2000
	GLT	130 (2127) B21F	CIS	98 @ 5000	112 @ 3000	3.62 × 3.15	9.3:1	35–85 @ 2000
	GLT ①	140 (2320) B23E	CIS	127 @ 5500	133 @ 4500	3.78 × 3.15	10.0:1	35–85 @ 2000
	260 GLE	174 (2849) B28F	CIS	130 @ 5500	153 @ 2750	3.58 × 2.86	8.8:1	60 @ 3000
1983	240 DL	140 (2320) B23F	LH	107 @ 5400	127 @ 3500	3.78 × 3.15	10.3:1	35–85 @ 2000
	DL	130 (2127) B21F-Turbo	CIS	127 @ 5400	150 @ 3750	3.62 × 3.15	7.5:1	35–85 @ 2000
	DL	145 (2383) D24	DFI	78 @ 4800	102 @ 3000	3.01 × 3.40	23.5:1	28 @ 2000
	DL ①	130 (2127) B21A	1-bbl Zenith	100 @ 5250	122 @ 2500	3.62 × 3.15	9.3:1	35–85 @ 2000
	GL	140 (2320) B23F	LH	107 @ 5400	127 @ 3500	3.78 × 3.15	10.3:1	35–85 @ 2000
	GL	145 (2383) D24	DFI	78 @ 4800	102 @ 3000	3.01 × 3.40	23.5:1	28 @ 2000
	GL ①	140 (2320) B23E	CIS	115 @ 5000	133 @ 3000	3.62 × 3.15	10.3:1	35–85 @ 2000
	GLT ①	140 (2320) B23E	CIS	115 @ 5000	133 @ 3000	3.62 × 3.15	10.3:1	35–85 @ 2000
	Turbo	130 (2127) B21F-Turbo	CIS	127 @ 5400	150 @ 3750	3.62 × 3.15	7.5:1	35–85 @ 2000
	760 GLE	174 (2849) B28F	CIS	134 @ 5500	159 @ 2700	3.58 × 2.86	8.8:1	60 @ 3000
	GLE	145 (2383) D24-Turbo	DFI	106 @ 4800	140 @ 2400	3.01 × 3.40	23.0:1	28 @ 2000
	Turbo	140 (2320) B23F-Turbo	LH	157 @ 5300	184 @ 2900	3.78 × 3.15	8.7:1	35–85 @ 2000

GENERAL ENGINE SPECIFICATIONS

Year	Model	Engine Displacement cu. in. (cc)	Fuel System Type	Net Horsepower @ rpm	Net Torque @ rpm (ft. lbs.)	Bore × Stroke (in.)	Compression Ratio	Oil Pressure @ rpm
1984	240 Diesel	145 (2383) D24	DFI	78 @ 4800	102 @ 3000	3.01 × 3.40	23.5:1	28 @ 2000
	DL	140 (2320) B23F ④	LH	113 @ 5400	136 @ 2750	3.78 × 3.15	9.5:1	35–85 @ 2000
	DL	140 (2320) B23F ⑤	LH	114 @ 5400	133 @ 3500	3.78 × 3.15	10.3:1	35–85 @ 2000
	DL ①	130 (2127) B21A	1-bbl Zenith	100 @ 5250	122 @ 2500	3.62 × 3.15	9.3:1	35–85 @ 2000
	GL	140 (2320) B23F ④	LH	113 @ 5400	136 @ 2750	3.78 × 3.15	9.5:1	35–85 @ 2000
	GL	140 (2320) B23F ⑤	LH	114 @ 5400	133 @ 3500	3.78 × 3.15	10.3:1	35–85 @ 2000
	GLE ①	140 (2320) B23F ④	LH	113 @ 5400	136 @ 2750	3.78 × 3.15	9.5:1	35–85 @ 2000
	GLE ①	140 (2320) B23F ⑤	LH	114 @ 5400	133 @ 3500	3.78 × 3.15	10.3:1	35–85 @ 2000
	Turbo	130 (2127) B21F-Turbo	CIS	131 @ 5400	155 @ 3750	3.62 × 3.15	7.5:1	35–85 @ 2000
	760 GLE	174 (2849) B28F	CIS	134 @ 5500	159 @ 2700	3.58 × 2.86	8.8:1	60 @ 3000
	GLE	145 (2383) D24-Turbo	DFI	106 @ 4800	140 @ 2400	3.01 × 3.40	23.0:1	28 @ 2000
	Turbo	140 (2320) B23F-Turbo	LH	157 @ 5300	184 @ 2900	3.78 × 3.15	8.7:1	35–85 @ 2000
1985	240 Diesel	145 (2383) D24	DFI	80 @ 4800	103 @ 2800	3.01 × 3.40	23.0:1	28 @ 2000
	DL	140 (2320) B230F	LH	114 @ 5400	136 @ 2750	3.78 × 3.15	9.8:1	35–85 @ 2000
	GL	140 (2320) B230F	LH	114 @ 5400	136 @ 2750	3.78 × 3.15	9.8:1	35–85 @ 2000
	Turbo	130 (2127) B21F-Turbo	CIS	162 @ 5100	181 @ 3900	3.62 × 3.15	7.5:1	35–85 @ 2000
	740 GLE	140 (2320) B230F	LH	114 @ 5400	136 @ 2750	3.78 × 3.15	9.8:1	35–85 @ 2000
	TD	145 (2383) D24-Turbo	DFI	106 @ 4800	140 @ 2400	3.01 × 3.40	23.0:1	28 @ 2000
	Turbo	140 (2320) B230F-Turbo	LH	160 @ 5300	187 @ 2900	3.78 × 3.15	8.7:1	35–85 @ 2000
	760 GLE	174 (2849) B28F	CIS	134 @ 5500	159 @ 2700	3.58 × 2.86	8.8:1	60 @ 3000
	GLE TD	145 (2383) D24-Turbo	DFI	106 @ 4800	140 @ 2400	3.01 × 3.40	23.0:1	28 @ 2000
	Turbo	140 (2320) B230F-Turbo	LH	160 @ 5300	187 @ 2900	3.78 × 3.15	8.7:1	35–85 @ 2000
1986	240 DL	140 (2320) B230F	LH	114 @ 5400	136 @ 2750	3.78 × 3.15	9.8:1	35–85 @ 2000
	GL	140 (2320) B230F	LH	114 @ 5400	136 @ 2750	3.78 × 3.15	9.8:1	35–85 @ 2000

GENERAL ENGINE SPECIFICATIONS

Year	Model	Engine Displacement cu. in. (cc)	Fuel System Type	Net Horsepower @ rpm	Net Torque @ rpm (ft. lbs.)	Bore × Stroke (in.)	Compression Ratio	Oil Pressure @ rpm
1986	740 GL	140 (2320) B230F	LH	114 @ 5400	136 @ 2750	3.78 × 3.15	9.8:1	35–85 @ 2000
	GLE	140 (2320) B230F	LH	114 @ 5400	136 @ 2750	3.78 × 3.15	9.8:1	35–85 @ 2000
	GLE TD	145 (2383) D24-Turbo	DFI	106 @ 4800	140 @ 2400	3.01 × 3.40	23.0:1	28 @ 2000
	Turbo	140 (2320) B230F-Turbo	LH	160 @ 5300	187 @ 2900	3.78 × 3.15	8.7:1	35–85 @ 2000
	760 GLE	174 (2849) B28F	CIS	136 @ 5500	159 @ 2700	3.58 × 2.86	8.8:1	60 @ 3000
	Turbo	140 (2320) B230F-Turbo	LH	160 @ 5300	187 @ 2900	3.78 × 3.15	8.7:1	35–85 @ 2000
1987–88	240 DL	140 (2320) B230F	LH	111 @ 5400	136 @ 2750	3.78 × 3.15	9.8:1	35–85 @ 2000
	GL	140 (2320) B230F	LH	111 @ 5400	136 @ 2750	3.78 × 3.15	9.8:1	35–85 @ 2000
	740 GL	140 (2320) B230F	LH	114 @ 5400	136 @ 2750	3.78 × 3.15	9.8:1	35–85 @ 2000
	GLE	140 (2320) B230F	LH	114 @ 5400	136 @ 2750	3.78 × 3.15	9.8:1	35–85 @ 2000
	Turbo	140 (2320) B230F-Turbo	LH	160 @ 5300	187 @ 2900	3.78 × 3.15	8.7:1	35–85 @ 2000
	760 GLE	174 (2849) B280F	LH	146 @ 5100	173 @ 3750	3.58 × 2.86	9.5:1	57 @ 3000
	Turbo	140 (2320) B230F-Turbo	LH	160 @ 5300	187 @ 2900	3.78 × 3.15	8.7:1	35–85 @ 2000
	780	174 (2849) B280F	LH	146 @ 5100	173 @ 3750	3.58 × 2.86	9.5:1	57 @ 3000

CIS—Continuous Injection System
DFI—Diesel Fuel Injection
LH—LH-Jetronic Injection

① Canada only
② Station Wagon
③ California only
④ With manual transmission
⑤ With automatic transmission

GASOLINE ENGINE TUNE-UP SPECIFICATIONS

Year	Model	Engine Displacement cu. in. (cc)	Spark Plugs Type	Spark Plugs Gap (in.)	Ignition Timing ③ (deg.) MT	Ignition Timing ③ (deg.) AT	Compression Pressure (psi)	Fuel Pump (psi)	Idle Speed (rpm) MT	Idle Speed (rpm) AT	Valve Clearance In.	Valve Clearance Ex.
1981	240 DL	130 (2127) B21F	WR7DS	0.030	8B ④	8B ④	NA	64–75	900	900	0.014–0.016	0.014–0.016
	DL	130 (2127) B21F-MPG	WR7DS	0.030	8B ④	8B ④	NA	64–75	900	900	0.014–0.016	0.014–0.016
	DL	130 (2127) B21A ①	W7DC	0.030	12B ④	12B ④	NA	64–75	900	900	0.014–0.016	0.014–0.016
	GL	130 (2127) B21F	WR7DS	0.030	8B ④	8B ④	NA	64–75	900	900	0.014–0.016	0.014–0.016

GASOLINE ENGINE TUNE-UP SPECIFICATIONS

Year	Model	Engine Displacement cu. in. (cc)	Spark Plugs Type	Gap (in.)	Ignition Timing [3] (deg.) MT	AT	Compression Pressure (psi)	Fuel Pump (psi)	Idle Speed (rpm) MT	AT	Valve Clearance In.	Ex.
1981	GL	140 (2320) B23E [1]	W6DC	0.030	10B [4]	10B [4]	NA	64–75	900	900	0.014–0.016	0.014–0.016
	GLT	130 (2127) B21F-Turbo	WR7DS	0.030	12B [5]	12B [5]	NA	64–75	900	900	0.014–0.016	0.014–0.016
	GLT	130 (2127) B21F [2]	WR7DS	0.030	8B [4]	8B [4]	NA	64–75	900	900	0.014–0.016	0.014–0.016
	GLT	140 (2320) B23E [1]	W6DC	0.030	10B [4]	10B [4]	NA	64–75	900	900	0.014–0.016	0.014–0.016
	260 Coupe	174 (2849) B28F	WR6DS	0.030	10B [6]	10B [6]	NA	64–75	900	900	0.008–0.010	0.008–0.010
	GL	130 (2127) B21F	WR7DS	0.030	8B [4]	8B [4]	NA	64–75	900	900	0.014–0.016	0.014–0.016
	GLE	174 (2849) B28F	WR6DS	0.030	10B [6]	10B [6]	NA	64–75	900	900	0.008–0.010	0.008–0.010
1982	240 DL	130 (2127) B21F	WR7DS	0.030	12B [4]	12B [4]	NA	64–75	900	900	0.014–0.016	0.014–0.016
	DL	130 (2127) B21A [1]	W7DC	0.030	12B [4]	12B [4]	NA	64–75	900	900	0.014–0.016	0.014–0.016
	GL	130 (2127) B21F	WR7DS	0.030	12B [4]	12B [4]	NA	64–75	900	900	0.014–0.016	0.014–0.016
	GL	140 (2320) B23E [1]	W6DC	0.030	10B [4]	10B [4]	NA	64–75	900	900	0.014–0.016	0.014–0.016
	GLT	130 (2127) B21F-Turbo	WR7DS	0.030	12B	12B	NA	64–75	900	900	0.014–0.016	0.014–0.016
	GLT	130 (2127) B21F	WR7DS	0.030	12B [4]	12B [4]	NA	64–75	900	900	0.014–0.016	0.014–0.016
	GLT	140 (2320) B23E [1]	W6DC	0.030	10B [4]	10B [4]	NA	64–75	900	900	0.014–0.016	0.014–0.016
	260 GLE	174 (2849) B28F	WR6DS	0.030	10B [6]	10B [6]	NA	64–75	900	900	0.008–0.010	0.008–0.010
1983	240 DL	140 (2320) B23F	WR7DS	0.030	12B [4]	12B [4]	NA	64–75	750	750	0.014–0.016	0.014–0.016
	DL	130 (2127) B21F-Turbo	WR7DS	0.030	12B	12B	NA	64–75	900	900	0.014–0.016	0.014–0.016
	DL	130 (2127) B21A [1]	W7DC	0.030	7B [4]	7B [4]	NA	64–75	900	900	0.014–0.016	0.014–0.016
	GL	140 (2320) B23F	WR7DS	0.030	12B [4]	12B [4]	NA	64–75	750	750	0.014–0.016	0.014–0.016
	GL	140 (2320) B23E [1]	W6DC	0.030	10B [4]	10B [4]	NA	64–75	900	900	0.014–0.016	0.014–0.016
	GLT	140 (2320) B23E [1]	W6DC	0.030	10B [4]	10B [4]	NA	64–75	900	900	0.014–0.016	0.014–0.016
	Turbo	130 (2127) B21F-Turbo	WR7DS	0.030	12B [4]	12B [4]	NA	64–75	900	900	0.014–0.016	0.014–0.016
	760 GLE	174 (2849) B28F	WR6DS	0.026	23B [7]	23B [7]	NA	64–75	750	750	0.004–0.006	0.010–0.012
	Turbo	140 (2320) B23F-Turbo	WR7DC	0.026	12B [4]	12B [4]	NA	64–75	750	750	0.014–0.016	0.014–0.016

GASOLINE ENGINE TUNE-UP SPECIFICATIONS

Year	Model	Engine Displacement cu. in. (cc)	Spark Plugs Type	Gap (in.)	Ignition Timing ③ (deg.) MT	AT	Compression Pressure (psi)	Fuel Pump (psi)	Idle Speed (rpm) MT	AT	Valve Clearance In.	Ex.
1984	240 DL	140 (2320) B23F	WR7DS	0.030	12B ④	12B ④	NA	64–75	750	750	0.014–0.016	0.014–0.016
	DL	130 (2127) B21A ①	W7DC	0.030	12B ④	12B ④	NA	64–75	900	900	0.014–0.016	0.014–0.016
	GL	140 (2320) B23F	WR7DS	0.030	12B ④	12B ④	NA	64–75	750	750	0.014–0.016	0.014–0.016
	GLE	140 (2320) B23F ①	WR7DS	0.030	12B ④	12B ④	NA	64–75	750	750	0.014–0.016	0.014–0.016
	Turbo	130 (2127) B21F-Turbo	WR7DS	0.030	12B ⑤	12B ⑤	NA	64–75	900	900	0.014–0.016	0.014–0.016
	760 GLE	174 (2849) B28F	WR6DS	0.026	23B ⑦	23B ⑦	NA	64–75	750	750	0.004–0.006	0.010–0.012
	Turbo	140 (2320) B23F-Turbo	WR7DC	0.026	12B ④	12B ④	NA	64–75	750	750	0.014–0.016	0.014–0.016
1985	240 DL	140 (2320) B230F	WR7DC	0.030	12B ④	12B ④	NA	64–75	750	750	0.014–0.016	0.014–0.016
	GL	140 (2320) B230F	WR7DC	0.030	12B ④	12B ④	NA	64–75	750	750	0.014–0.016	0.014–0.016
	Turbo	130 (2127) B21F-Turbo	WR7DS	0.030	12B ④	12B ④	NA	64–75	900	900	0.014–0.016	0.014–0.016
	740 GLE	140 (2320) B230F	WR7DC	0.030	12B ④	12B ④	NA	64–75	750	750	0.014–0.016	0.014–0.016
	Turbo	140 (2320) B230F-Turbo	WR7DC	0.026	12B ④	12B ④	NA	64–75	750	750	0.014–0.016	0.014–0.016
	760 GLE	174 (2849) B28F	HR6DC	0.026	23B ⑦	23B ⑦	NA	64–75	750	750	0.004–0.006	0.010–0.012
	Turbo	140 (2320) B230F-Turbo	WR7DC	0.026	12B ④	12B ④	NA	64–75	750	750	0.014–0.016	0.014–0.016
1986	240 DL	140 (2320) B230F	WR7DC	0.030	12B ④	12B ④	NA	64–75	750	750	0.014–0.016	0.014–0.016
	GL	140 (2320) B230F	WR7DC	0.030	12B ④	12B ④	NA	64–75	750	750	0.014–0.016	0.014–0.016
	740 GL	140 (2320) B230F	WR7DC	0.030	12B ④	12B ④	NA	64–75	750	750	0.014–0.016	0.014–0.016
	GLE	140 (2320) B230F	WR7DC	0.030	12B ④	12B ④	NA	64–75	750	750	0.014–0.016	0.014–0.016
	Turbo	140 (2320) B230F-Turbo	WR7DC	0.026	12B ④	12B ④	NA	64–75	750	750	0.014–0.016	0.014–0.016
	760 GLE	174 (2849) B28F	HR6DC	0.026	23B ⑦	23B ⑦	NA	64–75	750	750	0.004–0.006	0.010–0.012
	Turbo	140 (2320) B230F-Turbo	WR7DC	0.026	12B ④	12B ④	NA	64–75	750	750	0.014–0.016	0.014–0.016
1987	240 DL	140 (2320) B230F	WR7DC	0.030	12B ④	12B ④	NA	64–75	750	750	0.014–0.016	0.014–0.016
	GL	140 (2320) B230F	WR7DC	0.030	12B ④	12B ④	NA	64–75	750	750	0.014–0.016	0.014–0.016
	740 GL	140 (2320) B230F	WR7DC	0.030	12B ④	12B ④	NA	64–75	750	750	0.014–0.016	0.014–0.016

GASOLINE ENGINE TUNE-UP SPECIFICATIONS

Year	Model	Engine Displacement cu. in. (cc)	Spark Plugs Type	Gap (in.)	Ignition Timing ③ (deg.) MT	AT	Compression Pressure (psi)	Fuel Pump (psi)	Idle Speed (rpm) MT	AT	Valve Clearance In.	Ex.
1987	GLE	140 (2320) B230F	WR7DC	0.030	12B ④	12B ④	NA	64–75	750	750	0.014–0.016	0.014–0.016
	Turbo	140 (2320) B230F-Turbo	WR7DC	0.026	12B ④	12B ④	NA	64–75	750	750	0.014–0.016	0.014–0.016
	760 GLE	174 (2849) B280F	HR6DC	0.026	16B ④	16B ④	NA	64–75	750	750	0.004–0.006	0.010–0.012
	Turbo	140 (2320) B230F-Turbo	WR7DC	0.026	12B ④	12B ④	NA	64–75	750	750	0.014–0.016	0.014–0.016
	780 780	174 (2849) B280F	HR6DC	0.026	16B ④	16B ④	NA	64–75	750	750	0.004–0.006	0.010–0.012
1988	ALL	SEE UNDERHOOD SPECIFICATIONS STICKER										

NOTE: Some models are equipped with the Constant Idle Speed system (CIS) and cannot be adjusted.
① Canada only
② Station Wagon

③ Vacuum advance disconnected, A/C turned off
④ @ 750 rpm
⑤ @ 900 rpm
⑥ @ 800 rpm
⑦ @ 2500 rpm

DIESEL ENGINE TUNE-UP SPECIFICATIONS

Year	Model	Engine Displacement cu. in. (cc)	Valve Clearance ① Intake (in.)	Exhaust (in.)	Intake Valve Opens (deg.)	Injection Pump Setting ⑧ (deg.)	Injection Nozzle Pressure (psi) New	Used	Idle Speed (rpm)	Cranking Compression Pressure (psi) ⑤
1981	260 GL	145 (2383) D24	0.006–0.010	0.014 0.018	NA	0.0265–0.0295 ②	1845–1700 ③		720–880 ④	340–455
1982	240 GL	145 (2383) D24	0.006–0.010	0.014–0.018	NA	0.0265–0.0295 ②	1845–1700 ③		720–880 ④	340–455
1983	240 DL	145 (2383) D24	0.006–0.010	0.014–0.018	NA	0.0265–0.0295 ②	1845–1700 ③		720–880 ④	340
	GL	145 (2383) D24	0.006–0.010	0.014–0.018	NA	0.0265–0.0295 ②	1845–1700 ③		720–880 ④	340–455
	760 GLE	145 (2383) D24-Turbo ⑥	0.006–0.010	0.014–0.018	NA	0.0283–0.0315	2318–2062 ⑦		750	313–455
1984	240 Diesel	145 (2383) D24	0.006–0.010	0.014–0.018	NA	0.0265–0.0295 ②	1845–1700 ③		720–880 ④	340–455
	760 GLE	145 (2383) D24-Turbo	0.006–0.010	0.014–0.018	NA	0.0283–0.0315	2318–2062 ⑦		750	313–455
1985	240 Diesel	145 (2383) D24	0.006–0.010	0.014–0.018		0.0265–0.0295 ②	1845–1700 ③		720–880 ④	340–455
	740 TD (S)	145 (2383) D24-Turbo ⑥	0.006–0.010	0.014–0.018	NA	0.0283–0.0315	2318–2062 ⑦		830	313 455
	760 GLE TD	145 (2383) D24-Turbo ⑥	0.006–0.010	0.014–0.018	NA	0.0283–0.0315	2318–2062 ⑦		830	313–455

DIESEL ENGINE TUNE-UP SPECIFICATIONS

Year	Model	Engine Displacement cu. in. (cc)	Valve Clearance ① Intake (in.)	Exhaust (in.)	Intake Valve Opens (deg.)	Injection Pump Setting ⑧ (deg.)	Injection Nozzle Pressure (psi) New	Used	Idle Speed (rpm)	Cranking Compression Pressure (psi) ⑤
1986	740 GLE TD	145 (2383) D24-Turbo ⑥	0.006–0.010	0.014–0.018	NA	0.0283–0.0315	2318–2062 ⑦		830	313–455

NOTE: When setting injection timing, distributor plunger stroke must be at Top Dead Center
① Cold
② See text. Acceptable range when checking 0.0287–0.0315 in.
③ Acceptable range. When servicing set to 1775–1920 psi
④ Maximum safe speed: 5100–5200 rpm (high idle)
⑤ Maximum difference between cylinders 115 lbs. psi
⑥ Turbo-Diesel
⑦ Acceptable range. When servicing set to 2205–2318 psi.
⑧ Plunger stroke

FIRING ORDERS

NOTE: To avoid confusion, always replace spark plug wires one at a time.

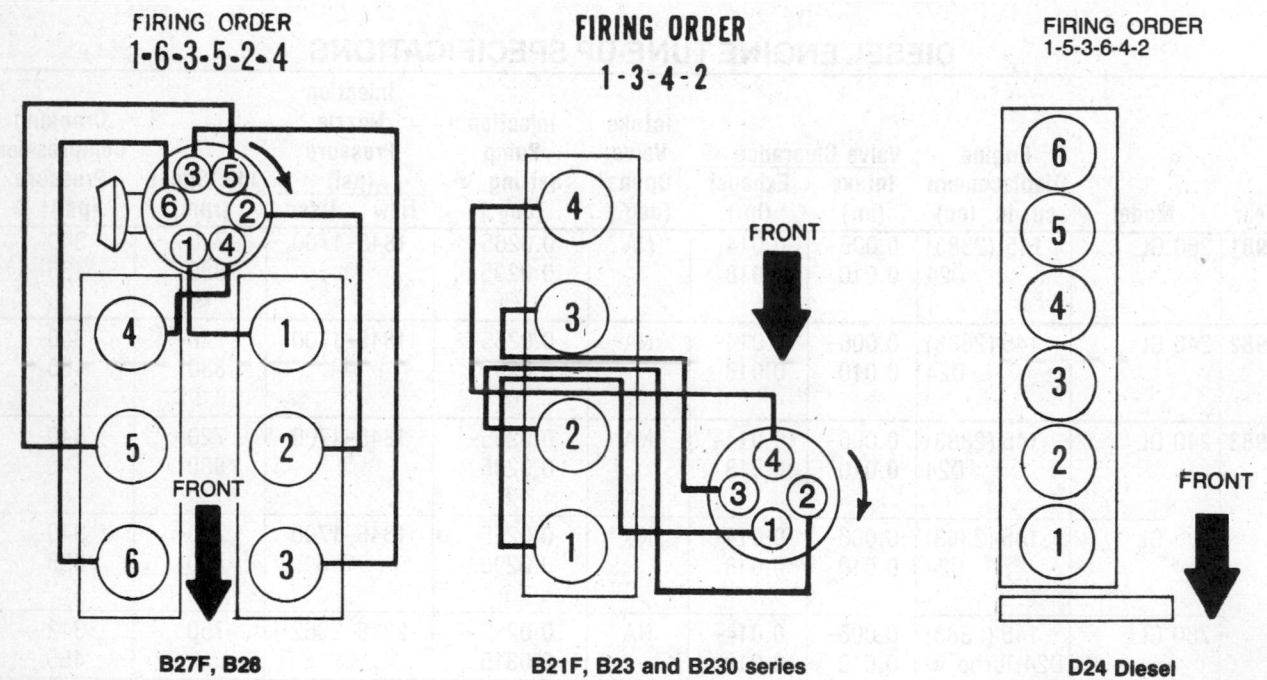

FIRING ORDER
1-6-3-5-2-4

B27F, B28

FIRING ORDER
1-3-4-2

B21F, B23 and B230 series

FIRING ORDER
1-5-3-6-4-2

D24 Diesel

CAPACITIES

Year	Model	Engine Displacement cu. in. (cc)	Engine Crankcase ③ with Filter	without Filter	Transmission (pts) 4-Spd	5-Spd	Auto.	Drive Axle (pts.)	Fuel Tank (gal.)	Cooling System (qts.)
1981	240 DL	130 (2127) B21F	4.0	3.5	4.8	—	14.6	④	15.8	10.0
	DL	130 (2127) B21F-MPG	4.0	3.5	4.8	—	14.6	④	15.8	10.0

CAPACITIES

Year	Model	Engine Displacement cu. in. (cc)	Engine Crankcase ③ with Filter	without Filter	Transmission (pts) 4-Spd	5-Spd	Auto.	Drive Axle (pts.)	Fuel Tank (gal.)	Cooling System (qts.)
1981	DL	130 (2127) B21A	4.0	3.5	4.8	—	14.6	④	15.8	10.0
	GL	130 (2127) B21F	4.0	3.5	4.8	—	14.6	④	15.8	10.0
	GL	140 (2320) B23E ①	4.0	3.5	4.8	—	14.6	④	15.8	10.0
	GLT	130 (2127) B21F-Turbo	4.0	3.5	4.8	—	14.6	④	15.8	10.0
	GLT	130 (2127) B21F ②	4.0	3.5	4.8	—	14.6	④	15.8	10.0
	GLT	140 (2320) B23E ①	4.0	3.5	4.8	—	14.6	④	15.8	10.0
	260 Coupe	174 (2849) B28F	6.8	6.3	4.8	—	14.6	④	15.8	11.5
	GL	130 (2127) B21F	4.0	3.5	4.8	—	14.6	④	15.8	10.0
	GL	145 (2383) D24	7.4	6.6	4.8	—	14.6	④	15.8	10.0
	GLE	174 (2849) B28F	6.8	6.3	4.8	—	14.6	④	15.8	11.5
1982	240 DL	130 (2127) B21F	4.0	3.5	4.8	—	15.6	④	15.8	10.0
	DL	130 (2127) B21A ①	4.0	3.5	4.8	—	15.6	④	15.8	10.0
	GL	130 (2127) B21F	4.0	3.5	4.8	—	15.6	④	15.8	10.0
	GL	145 (2383) D24	7.4	6.6	4.8	—	15.6	④	15.8	10.0
	GL	140 (2320) B23E ①	4.0	3.5	4.8	—	15.6	④	15.8	10.0
	GLT	130 (2127) B21F-Turbo	4.0	3.5	4.8	—	15.6	④	15.8	10.0
	GLT	130 (2127) B21F	4.0	3.5	4.8	—	15.6	④	15.8	10.0
	GLT	140 (2320) B23E ①	4.0	3.5	4.8	—	15.6	④	15.8	10.0
	260 GLE	174 (2849) B28F	6.8	6.3	4.8	—	15.6	④	15.8	11.5
1983	240 DL	140 (2320) B23F	4.0	3.5	4.8	—	15.6	④	15.8	10.0
	DL	130 (2127) B21F-Turbo	4.0	3.5	4.8	—	15.6	④	15.8	10.0
	DL	145 (2383) D24	7.4	6.6	4.8	—	15.6	④	15.8	10.0
	DL	130 (2127) B21A ①	4.0	3.5	4.8	—	15.6	④	15.8	10.0
	GL	140 (2320) B23F	4.0	3.5	4.8	—	15.6	④	15.8	10.0

CAPACITIES

Year	Model	Engine Displacement cu. in. (cc)	Engine Crankcase ③ with Filter	without Filter	Transmission (pts) 4-Spd	5-Spd	Auto.	Drive Axle (pts.)	Fuel Tank (gal.)	Cooling System (qts.)
1983	GL	145 (2383) D24	7.4	6.6	4.8	—	15.6	④	15.8	10.0
	GL	140 (2320) B23E ①	4.0	3.5	4.8	—	15.6	④	15.8	10.0
	GLT	140 (2320) B23E ①	4.0	3.5	4.8	—	15.6	④	15.8	10.0
	Turbo	130 (2127) B21F-Turbo	4.0	3.5	4.8	—	15.6	④	15.8	10.0
	760 GLE	174 (2849) B28F	6.9	6.3	4.8	—	15.6	④	15.8	10.5
	GLE	145 (2383) D24-Turbo	6.3	5.2	4.8	—	15.6	④	15.8	11.5
	Turbo	140 (2320) B23F-Turbo	4.1	3.6	4.8	—	15.6	④	15.8	10.0
1984	240 Diesel	145 (2383) D24	7.4	6.6	4.8	—	15.6	④	15.8	10.0
	DL	140 (2320) B23F	4.0	3.5	4.8	—	15.6	④	15.8	10.0
	DL	130 (2127) B21A ①	4.0	3.5	4.8	—	15.6	④	15.8	10.0
	GL	140 (2320) B23F	4.0	3.5	4.8	—	15.6	④	15.8	10.0
	GLE	140 (2320) B23F ①	4.0	3.5	4.8	—	15.6	④	15.8	10.0
	Turbo	130 (2127) B21F-Turbo	4.0	3.5	4.8	—	15.6	④	15.8	10.0
	760 GLE	174 (2849) B28F	6.9	6.3	4.8	—	15.6	④	15.8	10.5
	GLE	145 (2383) D24-Turbo	6.3	5.2	4.8	—	15.6	④	15.8	11.5
	Turbo	140 (2320) B23F-Turbo	4.1	3.6	4.8	—	15.6	④	15.8	10.0
1985	240 Diesel	145 (2383) D24	7.4	6.6	4.8	—	15.6	④	15.8	10.0
	DL	140 (2320) B230F	4.0	3.5	4.8	—	15.6	④	15.8	10.0
	GL	140 (2320) B230F	4.0	3.5	4.8	—	15.6	④	15.8	10.0
	Turbo	130 (2127) B21F-Turbo	4.0	3.5	4.8	—	15.6	④	15.8	10.0
	740 GLE	140 (2320) B230F	4.1	3.6	4.8	—	15.6	④	15.8	10.0
	TD ②	145 (2383) D24-Turbo	6.3	5.2	4.8	—	15.6	④	15.8	11.5
	Turbo	140 (2320) B230F-Turbo	4.1	3.6	4.8	—	15.6	④	15.8	10.0
	760 GLE	174 (2849) B28F	6.9	6.3	4.8	—	15.6	④	15.8	10.5

CAPACITIES

Year	Model	Engine Displacement cu. in. (cc)	Engine Crankcase ③ with Filter	without Filter	Transmission (pts) 4-Spd	5-Spd	Auto.	Drive Axle (pts.)	Fuel Tank (gal.)	Cooling System (qts.)
1985	GLE TD	145 (2383) D24-Turbo	6.3	5.2	4.8	—	15.6	④	15.8	11.5
	Turbo	140 (2320) B230F-Turbo	4.1	3.6	4.8	—	15.6	④	15.8	10.0
1986	240 DL	140 (2320) B230F	4.0	3.5	4.8	—	15.6	④	15.8	10.0
	GL	140 (2320) B230F	4.0	3.5	4.8	—	15.6	④	15.8	10.0
	740 GL	140 (2320) B230F	4.1	3.6	4.8	—	15.6	④	15.8	10.0
	GLE	140 (2320) B230F	4.1	3.6	4.8	—	15.6	④	15.8	10.0
	GLE TD	145 (2383) D24-Turbo	6.3	5.2	4.8	—	15.6	④	15.8	11.5
	Turbo	140 (2320) B230F-Turbo	4.1	3.6	4.8	—	15.6	④	15.8	10.0
	760 GLE	174 (2849) B28F	6.9	6.3	4.8	—	15.6	④	15.8	10.5
	Turbo	140 (2320) B230F-Turbo	4.1	3.6	4.8	—	15.6	④	15.8	10.0
1987–88	240 DL	140 (2320) B230F	4.0	3.5	—	2.8	15.6	④	15.8	10.0
	GL	140 (2320) B230F	4.0	3.5	—	2.8	15.6	④	15.8	10.0
	740 GL	140 (2320) B230F	4.1	3.6	4.8	—	15.6	④	15.8	10.0
	GLE	140 (2320) B230F	4.1	3.6	4.8	—	15.6	④	15.8	10.0
	Turbo	140 (2320) B230F-Turbo	4.1	3.6	4.8	—	15.6	④	15.8	10.0
	760 GLE	174 (2849) B28F	6.3	5.8	4.8	—	15.8	④	15.8	10.5
	Turbo	140 (2320) B230F-Turbo	4.1	3.6	4.8	—	15.8	④	15.8	10.0
	780	174 (2849) B280F	6.3	5.8	4.8	—	15.8	④	15.8	10.5

① Canada only
② Station Wagon
③ Models w/turbo: add 0.7 qt. if oil cooler has been drained
④ 1030 axle: 2.8 pts.
   1031 axle: 3.4 pts.

CRANKSHAFT AND CONNECTING ROD SPECIFICATIONS

All measurements are given in inches.

Year	Engine Displacement cu. in. (cc)	Crankshaft				Connecting Rod		
		Main Brg. Journal Dia.	Main Brg. Oil Clearance	Shaft End-play	Thrust on No.	Journal Diameter	Oil Clearance	Side Clearance
1981	130 (2127) B21F	2.4981–2.4986	0.0011–0.0033	0.0015–0.0058	5	2.1255–2.1260	0.0009–0.0028	0.006–0.014
	130 (2127) B21A ①	2.4981–2.4986	0.0011–0.0033	0.0015–0.0058	5	2.1255–2.1260	0.0009–0.0028	0.006–0.014
	130 (2127) B21F-Turbo	2.4981–2.4986	0.0011–0.0033	0.0015–0.0058	5	2.1255–2.1260	0.0009–0.0028	0.006–0.014
	140 (2320) B23E ①	2.4981–2.4986	0.0011–0.0033	0.0015–0.0058	5	2.1255–2.1260	0.0009–0.0028	0.006–0.014
	145 (2383) D24	2.2833–2.2825	0.0006–0.0030	0.0028–0.0071	4	1.8802–1.8810	0.0047 ②	0.0158
	174 (2849) B28F	2.7583	0.0035	0.0106	4	2.0585	0.0031	0.015
1982	130 (2127) B21F	2.4981–2.4986	0.0011–0.0033	0.0015–0.0058	5	2.1255–2.1260	0.0009–0.0028	0.006–0.014
	130 (2127) B21A ①	2.4981–2.4986	0.0011–0.0033	0.0015–0.0058	5	2.1255–2.1260	0.0009–0.0028	0.006–0.014
	130 (2127) B21F-Turbo	2.4981–2.4986	0.0011–0.0033	0.0015–0.0058	5	2.1255–2.1260	0.0009–0.0028	0.006–0.014
	140 (2320) B23E ①	2.4981–2.4986	0.0011–0.0033	0.0015–0.0058	5	2.1255–2.1260	0.0009–0.0028	0.006–0.014
	145 (2383) D24	2.2833–2.2825	0.0006–0.0030	0.0028–0.0071	4	1.8802–1.8810	0.0047 ②	0.0158
	174 (2849) B28F	2.7583	0.0035	0.0106	4	2.0585	0.0031	0.015
1983	130 (2127) B21A ①	2.4981–2.4986	0.0011–0.0033	0.0015–0.0058	5	2.1255–2.1260	0.0009–0.0028	0.006–0.014
	130 (2127) B21F-Turbo	2.4981–2.4986	0.0011–0.0033	0.0015–0.0058	5	2.1255–2.1260	0.0009–0.0028	0.006–0.014
	140 (2320) B23F	2.4981–2.4986	0.0011–0.0033	0.0015–0.0058	5	2.1255–2.1260	0.0009–0.0028	0.006–0.014
	140 (2320) B23E ①	2.4981–2.4986	0.0011–0.0033	0.0015–0.0058	5	2.1255–2.1260	0.0009–0.0028	0.006–0.014
	140 (2320) B23F-Turbo	2.4981–2.4986	0.0011–0.0033	0.0015–0.0058	5	2.1255–2.1260	0.0009–0.0028	0.006–0.014
	145 (2383) D24	2.2833–2.2825	0.0006–0.0030	0.0028–0.0071	4	1.8802–1.8810	0.0047 ②	0.0158
	145 (2383) D24-Turbo	2.2833–2.2825	0.0006–0.0030	0.0028–0.0071	4	1.8802–1.8810	0.0047 ②	0.0158
	174 (2849) B28F	2.7583	0.0035	0.0106	4	2.0585	0.0031	0.015
1984	130 (2127) B21A ①	2.4981–2.4986	0.0011–0.0033	0.0015–0.0058	5	2.1255–2.1260	0.0009–0.0028	0.006–0.014
	130 (2127) B23F	2.4981–2.4986	0.0011–0.0033	0.0015–0.0058	5	2.1255–2.1260	0.0009–0.0028	0.006–0.014
	140 (2320) B23F-Turbo	2.4981–2.4986	0.0011–0.0033	0.0015–0.0058	5	2.1255–2.1260	0.0009–0.0028	0.006–0.014
	140 (2320) B23F-Turbo	2.4981–2.4986	0.0011–0.0033	0.0015–0.0058	5	2.1255–2.1260	0.0009–0.0028	0.006–0.014

CRANKSHAFT AND CONNECTING ROD SPECIFICATIONS

All measurements are given in inches.

Year	Engine Displacement cu. in. (cc)	Crankshaft				Connecting Rod		
		Main Brg. Journal Dia.	Main Brg. Oil Clearance	Shaft End-play	Thrust on No.	Journal Diameter	Oil Clearance	Side Clearance
1984	145 (2383) D24	2.2833–2.2825	0.0006–0.0030	0.0028–0.0071	4	1.8802–1.8810	0.0047 ②	0.0158
	145 (2383) D24-Turbo	2.2833–2.2825	0.0006–0.0030	0.0028–0.0071	4	1.8802–1.8810	0.0047 ②	0.0158
	174 (2849) B28F	2.7583	0.0035	0.0106	4	2.0585	0.0031	0.015
1985	130 (2127) B21F-Turbo	2.4981–2.4986	0.0011–0.0033	0.0015–0.0058	5	2.1255–2.1260	0.0009–0.0028	0.006–0.014
	140 (2320) B230F	2.4981–2.4986	0.0011–0.0033	0.0015–0.0058	5	2.1255–2.1260	0.0009–0.0028	0.006–0.014
	140 (2320) B230F-Turbo	2.4981–2.4986	0.0011–0.0033	0.0015–0.0058	5	2.1255–2.1260	0.0009–0.0028	0.006–0.014
	145 (2383) D24	2.2833–2.2825	0.0006–0.0030	0.0028–0.0071	4	1.8802–1.8810	0.0047 ②	0.0158
	145 (2383) D24-Turbo	2.2833–2.2825	0.0006–0.0030	0.0028–0.0071	4	1.8802–1.8810	0.0047 ②	0.0158
	174 (2849) B28F	2.7583	0.0035	0.0106	4	2.0585	0.0031	0.015
1986	140 (2320) B230F	2.4981–2.4986	0.0011–0.0033	0.0015–0.0058	5	2.1255–2.1260	0.0009–0.0028	0.006–0.014
	140 (2320) B230F-Turbo	2.4981–2.4986	0.0011–0.0033	0.0015–0.0058	5	2.1255–2.1260	0.0009–0.0028	0.006–0.014
	145 (2383) D24-Turbo	2.2833–2.2825	0.0006–0.0030	0.0028–0.0071	4	1.8802–1.8810	0.0047 ②	0.0158
	174 (2849) B28F	2.7583	0.0035	0.0106	4	2.0585	0.0031	0.015
1987-88	140 (2320) B230F	2.4981–2.4986	0.0011–0.0033	0.0015–0.0058	5	2.1255–2.1260	0.0009–0.0028	0.006–0.014
	140 (2320) B230F-Turbo	2.4981–2.4986	0.0011–0.0033	0.0015–0.0058	5	2.1255–2.1260	0.0009–0.0028	0.006–0.014
	174 (2849) B280F	2.7583	0.0035	0.0106	4	2.0585	0.0031	0.015

① Canada only
② New clearance: 0.0005–0.0024 in.

VALVE SPECIFICATIONS

Year	Engine Displacement cu. in. (cc)	Seat Angle (deg.)	Face Angle (deg.)	Spring Test Pressure (lbs. @ in.)	Spring Installed Height (in.)	Stem-to-Guide Clearance (in.)		Stem Diameter (in.)	
						Intake	Exhaust	Intake	Exhaust
1981	130 (2127) B21F	44.75	45.5	170 @ 1.06	1.77	0.0012–0.0024	0.0024–0.0035	0.3132–0.3135	0.3128–0.3126
	130 (2127) B21A ①	44.75	45.5	170 @ 1.06	1.77	0.0012–0.0024	0.0024–0.0035	0.3132–0.3135	0.3128–0.3126
	130 (2127) B21F-Turbo	44.75	45.5	170 @ 1.06	1.77	0.0012–0.0024	0.0024–0.0035	0.3132–0.3135	0.3128–0.3126

VALVE SPECIFICATIONS

Year	Engine Displacement cu. in. (cc)	Seat Angle (deg.)	Face Angle (deg.)	Spring Test Pressure (lbs. @ in.)	Spring Installed Height (in.)	Stem-to-Guide Clearance (in.) Intake	Stem-to-Guide Clearance (in.) Exhaust	Stem Diameter (in.) Intake	Stem Diameter (in.) Exhaust
1981	140 (2320) B23E ①	45	44.5	165 @ 1.06	1.77	0.0012–0.0024	0.0024–0.0035	0.3132–0.3138	0.3128–0.3124
	145 (2383) D24	45	⑤	⑥	⑦	⑧	⑧	0.3140	0.3130
	174 (2849) B28F	②	②	143 @ 1.18	1.85	③	③	④	④
1982	130 (2127) B21F	44.75	45.5	170 @ 1.06	1.77	0.0012–0.0024	0.0024–0.0035	0.3132–0.3135	0.3128–0.3126
	130 (2127) B21A ①	44.75	45.5	170 @ 1.06	1.77	0.0012–0.0024	0.0024–0.0035	0.3132–0.3135	0.3128–0.3126
	130 (2127) B21F-Turbo	44.75	45.5	170 @ 1.06	1.77	0.0012–0.0024	0.0024–0.0035	0.3132–0.3135	0.3128–0.3126
	140 (2320) B23E ①	45	44.5	165 @ 1.06	1.77	0.0012–0.0024	0.0024–0.0035	0.3132–0.3138	0.3128–0.3124
	145 (2383) D24	45	⑤	⑥	⑦	⑧	⑧	0.3140	0.3130
	174 (2849) B28F	②	②	143 @ 1.18	1.85	③	③	④	④
1983	130 (2127) B21A ①	44.75	45.5	170 @ 1.06	1.77	0.0012–0.0024	0.0024–0.0035	0.3132–0.3135	0.3128–0.3126
	130 (2127) B21F-Turbo	44.75	45.5	170 @ 1.06	1.77	0.0012–0.0024	0.0024–0.0035	0.3132–0.3135	0.3128–0.3126
	140 (2320) B23F	45	44.5	165 @ 1.06	1.77	0.0012–0.0024	0.0024–0.0035	0.3132–0.3138	0.3128–0.3124
	140 (2320) B23E ①	45	44.5	165 @ 1.06	1.77	0.0012–0.0024	0.0024–0.0035	0.3132–0.3138	0.3128–0.3124
	140 (2320) B23F-Turbo	45	44.5	165 @ 1.06	1.77	0.0012–0.0024	0.0024–0.0035	0.3132–0.3138	0.3128–0.3124
	145 (2383) D24	45	⑤	⑥	⑦	⑧	⑧	0.3140	0.3130
	145 (2383) D24-Turbo	45	⑤	⑥	⑦	⑧	⑧	0.3140	0.3130
	174 (2849) B28F	②	②	143 @ 1.18	1.85	③	③	④	④
1984	130 (2127) B21A ①	44.75	45.5	170 @ 1.06	1.77	0.0012–0.0024	0.0024–0.0035	0.3132–0.3135	0.3128–0.3126
	130 (2127) B21F-Turbo	44.75	45.5	170 @ 1.06	1.77	0.0012–0.0024	0.0024–0.0035	0.3132–0.3135	0.3128–0.3126
	140 (2320) B23F	45	44.5	165 @ 1.06	1.77	0.0012–0.0024	0.0024–0.0035	0.3132–0.3138	0.3128–0.3124
	140 (2320) B23F-Turbo	45	44.5	165 @ 1.06	1.77	0.0012–0.0024	0.0024–0.0035	0.3132–0.3138	0.3128–0.3124
	145 (2383) D24	45	⑤	⑥	⑦	⑧	⑧	0.3140	0.3130
	145 (2383) D24-Turbo	45	⑤	⑥	⑦	⑧	⑧	0.3140	0.3130
	174 (2849) B28F	②	②	143 @ 1.18	1.85	③	③	④	④

VALVE SPECIFICATIONS

Year	Engine Displacement cu. in. (cc)	Seat Angle (deg.)	Face Angle (deg.)	Spring Test Pressure (lbs. @ in.)	Spring Installed Height (in.)	Stem-to-Guide Clearance (in.) Intake	Stem-to-Guide Clearance (in.) Exhaust	Stem Diameter (in.) Intake	Stem Diameter (in.) Exhaust
1985	130 (2127) B21F-Turbo	44.75	45.5	170 @ 1.06	1.77	0.0012–0.0024	0.0024–0.0035	0.3132–0.3135	0.3128–0.3126
	140 (2320) B230F	44.75	45.5	170 @ 1.06	1.77	0.0012–0.0024	0.0024–0.0035	0.3132–0.3135	0.3128–0.3126
	140 (2320) B230F-Turbo	44.75	45.5	170 @ 1.06	1.77	0.0012–0.0024	0.0024–0.0035	0.3132–0.3135	0.3128–0.3126
	145 (2383) D24	45	⑤	⑥	⑦	⑧	⑧	0.3140	0.3130
	145 (2383) D24-Turbo	45	⑤	⑥	⑦	⑧	⑧	0.3140	0.3130
	174 (2849) B28F	②	②	143 @ 1.18	1.85	③	③	④	④
1986	140 (2320) B230F	44.75	45.5	170 @ 1.06	1.77	0.0012–0.0024	0.0024–0.0035	0.3132–0.3135	0.3128–0.3126
	140 (2320) B230F-Turbo	44.75	45.5	170 @ 1.06	1.77	0.0012–0.0024	0.0024–0.0035	0.3132–0.3135	0.3128–0.3126
	145 (2383) D24-Turbo	45	⑤	⑥	⑦	⑧	⑧	0.3140	0.3130
	174 (2849) B28F	②	②	143 @ 1.18	1.85	③	③	④	④
1987–88	140 (2320) B230F	44.75	45.5	170 @ 1.06	1.77	0.0012–0.0024	0.0024–0.0035	0.3132–0.3135	0.3128–0.3126
	140 (2320) B230F-Turbo	44.75	45.5	170 @ 1.06	1.77	0.0012–0.0024	0.0024–0.0035	0.3132–0.3135	0.3128–0.3126
	174 (2849) B280F	②	②	143 @ 1.18	1.85	③	③	④	④

NOTE: Exhaust valves for turbo engines (including turbo diesel) are stellite coated and must not be machined. They may be ground against the valve seat.

① Canada only
② Intake: 29.5 degrees
Exhaust: 30 degrees
③ Tapered valve guide ID: 0.3150–0.3158
④ Tapered valve stem;
Intake: Base = 0.3135–0.3141 Top = 3139–0.3145
Exhaust: Base = 0.3127–0.3133 Top = 3136–0.3141
⑤ Intake: 44.5 degrees
Exhaust: 45 degrees
⑥ Two springs per valve; inner spring 49 lbs. @ 0.72 in.; outer spring 100 lbs. @ 0.878 in.
⑦ Inner 1.335 in.; outer 1.583 in.
⑧ Clearance measured w/new valve guide and w/valve stem edge to edge w/valve guide upper end. Max. clearance 0.051 in.; new clearance 0.012 in.

PISTON AND RING SPECIFICATIONS

All measurements are given in inches.

Year	Engine Displacement cu. in. (cc)	Piston Clearance	Ring Gap Top Compression	Ring Gap Bottom Compression	Ring Gap Oil Control	Ring Side Clearance Top Compression	Ring Side Clearance Bottom Compression	Ring Side Clearance Oil Control
1981	130 (2127) B21F	0.0004–0.0012	0.0138–0.0217	0.0138–0.0217	0.010–0.016	0.0016–0.0028	0.0016–0.0028	0.0016–0.0028
	130 (2127) B21A ①	0.0004–0.0012	0.0138–0.0217	0.0138–0.0217	0.010–0.016	0.0016–0.0028	0.0016–0.0028	0.0016–0.0028

PISTON AND RING SPECIFICATIONS

All measurements are given in inches.

Year	Engine Displacement cu. in. (cc)	Piston Clearance	Ring Gap			Ring Side Clearance		
			Top Compression	Bottom Compression	Oil Control	Top Compression	Bottom Compression	Oil Control
1981	130 (2127) B21F-Turbo	0.0004–0.0012	0.0138–0.0217	0.0138–0.0217	0.010–0.016	0.0016–0.0028	0.0016–0.0028	0.0016–0.0028
	140 (2320) B23E ① ②	0.0020–0.0028	0.0014–0.026	0.0014–0.022	0.010–0.024	0.0015–0.0028	0.0015–0.0028	0.0012–0.0024
	145 (2383) D24	0.0012–0.0020	0.0012–0.0020	0.0012–0.0020	0.010–0.019	0.0043–0.0055	0.0028–0.0039	0.0012–0.0028
	174 (2849) B28F	0.0008–0.0016	0.0016–0.0022	0.0016–0.0022	0.015–0.055	0.0018–0.0029	0.0010–0.0021	0.0004–0.0092
1982	130 (2127) B21F	0.0004–0.0012	0.0138–0.0217	0.0138–0.0217	0.010–0.016	0.0016–0.0028	0.0016–0.0028	0.0016–0.0028
	130 (2127) B21A ①	0.0004–0.0012	0.0138–0.0217	0.0138–0.0217	0.010–0.016	0.0016–0.0028	0.0016–0.0028	0.0016–0.0028
	130 (2127) B21F-Turbo	0.0004–0.0012	0.0138–0.0217	0.0138–0.0217	0.010–0.016	0.0016–0.0028	0.0016–0.0028	0.0016–0.0028
	140 (2320) B23E ① ②	0.0020–0.0028	0.0014–0.0026	0.0014–0.0022	0.010–0.024	0.0015–0.0028	0.0015–0.0028	0.0012–0.0024
	145 (2383) D24	0.0012–0.0020	0.0012–0.0020	0.0012–0.0020	0.010–0.019	0.0043–0.0055	0.0028–0.0039	0.0012–0.0028
	174 (2849) B28F	0.0008–0.0016	0.0016–0.0022	0.0016–0.0022	0.015–0.055	0.0018–0.0029	0.0010–0.0021	0.0004–0.0092
1983	130 (2127) B21A ①	0.0004–0.0016	0.0140–0.0260	0.0140–0.0220	0.010–0.024	0.0016–0.0028	0.0016–0.0028	0.0012–0.0024
	130 (2127) B21F-Turbo	0.0008–0.0016	0.0140–0.0260	0.0140–0.0220	0.010–0.024	0.0016–0.0028	0.0016–0.0028	0.0012–0.0024
	140 (2320) B23F ②	0.0020–0.0028	0.0014–0.0026	0.0014–0.0022	0.010–0.024	0.0015–0.0028	0.0015–0.0028	0.0012–0.0024
	140 (2320) B23E ① ②	0.0020–0.0028	0.0014–0.0026	0.0014–0.0022	0.010–0.024	0.0015–0.0028	0.0015–0.0028	0.0012–0.0024
	140 (2320) B23F-Turbo ②	0.0020–0.0028	0.0014–0.0026	0.0014–0.0022	0.010–0.024	0.0015–0.0028	0.0015–0.0028	0.0012–0.0024
	145 (2383) D24	0.0012–0.0020	0.0012–0.0020	0.0012–0.0020	0.010–0.019	0.0043–0.0055	0.0028–0.0039	0.0012–0.0028
	145 (2383) D24-Turbo	0.0012–0.0020	0.0012–0.0020	0.0012–0.0020	0.010–0.019	0.0043–0.0055	0.0028–0.0039	0.0012–0.0028
	174 (2849) B28F	0.0007–0.0015	0.0157–0.0236	0.0157–0.0236	0.0157–0.0570	0.0017–0.0029	0.0009–0.0212	0.0003–0.0091
1984	130 (2127) B21A ①	0.0004–0.0016	0.0140–0.0260	0.0140–0.0220	0.010–0.024	0.0016–0.0028	0.0016–0.0028	0.0012–0.0024
	130 (2127) B21F-Turbo	0.0008–0.0016	0.0140–0.0260	0.0140–0.0220	0.010–0.024	0.0016–0.0028	0.0016–0.0028	0.0012–0.0024
	140 (2320) B23F ②	0.0020–0.0028	0.0014–0.0026	0.0014–0.0022	0.010–0.024	0.0015–0.0028	0.0015–0.0028	0.0012–0.0024

PISTON AND RING SPECIFICATIONS
All measurements are given in inches.

Year	Engine Displacement cu. in. (cc)	Piston Clearance	Ring Gap			Ring Side Clearance		
			Top Compression	Bottom Compression	Oil Control	Top Compression	Bottom Compression	Oil Control
1984	140 (2320) B23F-Turbo	0.0020–0.0028 ②	0.0014–0.0026	0.0014–0.0022	0.010–0.024	0.0015–0.0028	0.0015–0.0028	0.0012–0.0024
	145 (2383) D24	0.0012–0.0020	0.0012–0.0020	0.0012–0.0020	0.010–0.019	0.0043–0.0055	0.0028–0.0039	0.0012–0.0028
	145 (2383) D24-Turbo	0.0012–0.0020	0.0012–0.0020	0.0012–0.0020	0.010–0.019	0.0043–0.0055	0.0028–0.0039	0.0012–0.0028
	174 (2849) B28F	0.0007–0.0015	0.0157–0.0236	0.0157–0.0236	0.0157–0.0570	0.0017–0.0029	0.0009–0.0212	0.0003–0.0091
1985	130 (2127) B21F-Turbo	0.0008–0.0016	0.0140–0.0260	0.0140–0.0220	0.010–0.024	0.0016–0.0028	0.0016–0.0028	0.0012–0.0024
	140 (2320) B230F	0.0004–0.0012	0.0118–0.0217	0.0118–0.0217	0.0118–0.0236	0.0024–0.0036	0.0016–0.0028	0.0012–0.0026
	140 (2320) B230F-Turbo	0.0004–0.0012	0.0118–0.0217	0.0118–0.0217	0.0118–0.0236	0.0024–0.0036	0.0016–0.0028	0.0012–0.0026
	145 (2383) D24	0.0012–0.0020	0.0012–0.0020	0.0012–0.0020	0.010–0.019	0.0043–0.0055	0.0028–0.0039	0.0012–0.0028
	145 (2383) D24-Turbo	0.0012–0.0020	0.0012–0.0020	0.0012–0.0020	0.010–0.019	0.0043–0.0055	0.0028–0.0039	0.0012–0.0028
	174 (2849) B28F	0.0007–0.0015	0.0157–0.0236	0.0157–0.0236	0.0157–0.0570	0.0017–0.0029	0.0009–0.0212	0.0003–0.0091
1986	140 (2320) B230F	0.0004–0.0012	0.0118–0.0217	0.0118–0.0217	0.0118–0.0236	0.0024–0.0036	0.0016–0.0028	0.0012–0.0026
	140 (2320) B230F-Turbo	0.0004–0.0012	0.0118–0.0217	0.0118–0.0217	0.0118–0.0236	0.0024–0.0036	0.0016–0.0028	0.0012–0.0026
	145 (2383) D24-Turbo	0.0012–0.0020	0.0012–0.0020	0.0012–0.0020	0.010–0.019	0.0043–0.0055	0.0028–0.0039	0.0012–0.0028
	174 (2849) B28F	0.0007–0.0015	0.0157–0.0236	0.0157–0.0236	0.0157–0.0570	0.0017–0.0029	0.0009–0.0212	0.0003–0.0091
1987-88	140 (2320) B230F	0.0004–0.0012	0.0118–0.0217	0.0118–0.0217	0.0118–0.0236	0.0024–0.0036	0.0016–0.0028	0.0012–0.0026
	140 (2320) B230F-Turbo	0.0004–0.0012	0.0118–0.0217	0.0118–0.0217	0.0118–0.0236	0.0024–0.0036	0.0016–0.0028	0.0012–0.0026
	174 (2849) B280F	0.0007–0.0015	0.0157–0.0236	0.0157–0.0236	0.0157–0.0570	0.0017–0.0029	0.0009–0.0212	0.0003–0.0091

① Canada only
② Pistons with two different heights have been fitted to B23E engines. Piston clearance on version 1 (3.1654 in piston height) listed above; clearance on version 2 pistons (3.0079 in.) is 0.004–0.0016 in.

TORQUE SPECIFICATIONS
All readings in ft. lbs.

Year	Engine Displacement cu. in. (cc)	Cylinder Head Bolts	Main Bearing Bolts	Rod Bearing Bolts	Crankshaft Pulley Bolts	Flywheel Bolts	Manifold		Spark Plugs
							Intake	Exhaust	
1981	130 (2127) B21F	76–83 ②	85–91	43–48	107–128	47–54	15	15	25–29
	130 (2127) B21A ①	⑧	85–91	43–48	107–128	47–54	15	15	15–18
	130 (2127) B21F-Turbo	⑧	85–91	43–48	107–128	47–54	15	15	15–18
	140 (2320) B23E ①	⑧	85–91	43–48	107–128	47–54	15	15	15–18
	145 (2383) D24	⑤	48	33	332 ⑥	55	18	18	⑦
	174 (2849) B28F	③	④	33–37	175–200	33–37	7–11	7–11	8–11
1982	130 (2127) B21F	76–83 ②	85–91	43–48	107–128	47–54	15	15	25–29
	130 (2127) B21A ①	⑧	85–91	43–48	107–128	47–54	15	15	15–18
	130 (2127) B21F-Turbo	⑧	85–91	43–48	107–128	47–54	15	15	15–18
	140 (2320) B23E ①	⑧	85–91	43–48	107–128	47–54	15	15	15–18
	145 (2383) D24	⑤	48	33	332 ⑥	55	18	18	⑦
	174 (2849) B28F	③	④	33–37	118–132	33–37	7–11	7–11	8–11
1983	130 (2127) B21A ①	⑧	85–91	43–48	107–128	47–54	15	15	15–18
	130 (2127) B21F-Turbo	⑧	85–91	43–48	107–128	47–54	15	15	15–18
	140 (2320) B23F	⑧	85–91	43–48	107–128	47–54	15	15	15–18
	140 (2320) B23E ①	⑧	85–91	43–48	107–128	47–54	15	15	15–18
	140 (2320) B23F-Turbo	⑧	85–91	43–48	107–128	47–54	15	15	15–18
	145 (2383) D24	⑤	48	33	332 ⑥	55	18	18	⑦
	145 (2383) D24-Turbo	⑤	48	33	332 ⑥	55	18	18	⑦
	174 (2849) B28F	③	④	33–37	177–206	33–37	7–11	7–11	8–11
1984	130 (2127) B21A ①	⑧	85–91	43–48	107–128	47–54	15	15	15–18
	130 (2127) B21F-Turbo	⑧	85–91	43–48	107–128	47–54	15	15	15–18
	140 (2320) B21F	⑧	85–91	43–48	107–128	47–54	15	15	15–18
	140 (2320) B23F-Turbo	⑧	85–91	43–48	107–128	47–54	15	15	15–18

TORQUE SPECIFICATIONS
All readings in ft. lbs.

Year	Engine Displacement cu. In. (cc)	Cylinder Head Bolts	Main Bearing Bolts	Rod Bearing Bolts	Crankshaft Pulley Bolts	Flywheel Bolts	Manifold Intake	Manifold Exhaust	Spark Plugs
1984	145 (2383) D24	⑤	48	33	332 ⑥	55	18	18	⑦
	145 (2383) D24-Turbo	⑤	48	33	332 ⑥	55	18	18	⑦
	174 (2849) B28F	③	④	33–37	177–206	33–37	7–11	7–11	8–11
1985	130 (2127) B21F-Turbo	⑧	85–91	43–48	107–128	47–54	15	15	15–18
	140 (2320) B230F	⑧	80	14	43	47–54	12	12	15–18
	140 (2320) B230F-Turbo	⑧	80	14	43	47–54	12	12	15–18
	145 (2383) D24	⑤	48	33	332 ⑥	55	18	18	⑦
	145 (2383) D24-Turbo	⑤	48	33	332 ⑥	55	18	18	⑦
	174 (2849) B28F	③	④	33–37	177–206	33–37	7–11	7–11	8–11
1986	140 (2320) B230F	⑧	80	14	43	47–54	12	12	15–18
	140 (2320) B230F-Turbo	⑧	80	14	43	47–54	12	12	15–18
	145 (2383) D24-Turbo	⑤	48	33	332 ⑥	55	18	18	⑦
	174 (2849) B28F	③	④	33–37	177–206	33–37	7–11	7–11	8–11
1987–88	140 (2320) B230F	⑧	80	14	43	47–54	12	12	15–18
	140 (2320) B230F-Turbo	⑧	80	14	43	47–54	12	12	15–18
	174 (2849) B280F	③	④	33–37	177–206	33–37	7–11	7–11	8–11

① Canada only
② Torque head bolts in two stages; first, tighten in sequence to 43 ft. lbs., then to 76–83 ft. lbs.
③ Torque heads bolts in sequence to 7 ft. lbs., then 22 ft. lbs., then 44 ft. lbs. Wait 10–15 minutes and slacken the bolts ½ turn. Then torque to 11–14 ft. lbs. and then protractor torque to 116–120° (⅓ of a turn). Finally run to operating temperature, shut off and allow to cool for 30 min. Following the sequence, slacken, torque to 11–14 ft. lbs., and protractor torque to 113–117° each bolt.
④ Torque main bearing nuts to 22 ft. lbs., in sequence. Then slacken 1st nut ½ turn, tighten to 22–26 ft. lbs., and protractor torque to 73–77°. Repeat for remaining nuts following the sequence.
⑤ Torquing these bolts is a six-step procedure:
  A. Torque to 30 ft. lbs.
  B. Torque to 44 ft. lbs.
  C. Torque to 55 ft. lbs.
  D. Tighten 180°, in one movement, without stopping.
  E. Run engine until oil temperature is minimum 50°C–120°F.
  F. Tighten 90°, in one movement, without stopping. After driving 600–1,000 miles., retorque bolts w/engine cold. DO NOT slacken first.
⑥ Using regular torque wrench. If Volvo tool 5188 is used, torque to 255 ft. lbs.
⑦ Injector: 50 ft. lbs.
⑧ Torque head bolts in three stages; first, tighten in sequence to 15 ft. lbs., then to 44 ft. lbs. Protractor (angle) tighten 90° more.

BRAKE SPECIFICATIONS

All measurements in inches unless noted.

Year	Model	Lug Nut Torque (ft. lbs.)	Master Cylinder Bore	Brake Disc Minimum Thickness	Brake Disc Maximum Runout	Standard Brake Drum Diameter	Minimum Lining Thickness Front	Minimum Lining Thickness Rear
1981	240 DL	88	0.878	② (F) 0.330 (R)	0.004 (F) 0.004 (R)	—	0.060	0.060
	GL	88	0.878	② (F) 0.330 (R)	0.004 (F) 0.004 (R)	—	0.060	0.060
	GLT	88	0.878	② (F) 0.330 (R)	0.004 (F) 0.004 (R)	—	0.060	0.060
	260 Coupe	88	0.878	② (F) 0.330 (R)	0.004 (F) 0.004 (R)	—	0.060	0.060
	GL	88	0.878	② (F) 0.330 (R)	0.004 (F) 0.004 (R)	—	0.060	0.060
	GLE	88	0.878	② (F) 0.330 (R)	0.004 (F) 0.004 (R)	—	0.060	0.060
1982	240 DL	88	0.878	② (F) 0.330 (R)	0.004 (F) 0.004 (R)	—	0.060	0.060
	GL	88	0.878	② (F) 0.330 (R)	0.004 (F) 0.004 (R)	—	0.060	0.060
	GLT	88	0.878	② (F) 0.330 (R)	0.004 (F) 0.004 (R)	—	0.060	0.060
	260 GLE	88	0.878	② (F) 0.330 (R)	0.004 (F) 0.004 (R)	—	0.060	0.060
1983	240 DL	88	0.878	② (F) 0.330 (R)	0.004 (F) 0.004 (R)	—	0.060	0.060
	GL	88	0.878	② (F) 0.330 (R)	0.004 (F) 0.004 (R)	—	0.060	0.060
	GLT	88	0.878	② (F) 0.330 (R)	0.004 (F) 0.004 (R)	—	0.060	0.060
	Turbo	88	0.878	② (F) 0.330 (R)	0.004 (F) 0.004 (R)	—	0.060	0.060
	760 GLE	63	③	④ (F) 0.330 (R)	0.004 (F) 0.004 (R)	—	0.118	0.078
	Turbo	63	③	④ (F) 0.330 (R)	0.004 (F) 0.004 (R)	—	0.118	0.078
1984	240 Diesel	88	0.878	② (F) 0.330 (R)	0.004 (F) 0.004 (R)	—	0.060	0.060
	DL	88	0.878	② (F) 0.330 (R)	0.004 (F) 0.004 (R)	—	0.060	0.060
	GL	88	0.878	② (F) 0.330 (R)	0.004 (F) 0.004 (R)	—	0.060	0.060
	GLE	88	0.878	② (F) 0.330 (R)	0.004 (F) 0.004 (R)	—	0.060	0.060
	Turbo	88	0.878	② (F) 0.330 (R)	0.004 (F) 0.004 (R)	—	0.060	0.060
	760 GLE	63	③	④ (F) 0.330 (R)	0.003 (F) 0.004 (R)	—	0.118	0.078
	Turbo	63	③	④ (F) 0.330 (R)	0.003 (F) 0.004 (R)	—	0.118	0.078

BRAKE SPECIFICATIONS
All measurements in inches unless noted.

Year	Model		Lug Nut Torque (ft. lbs.)	Master Cylinder Bore	Brake Disc Minimum Thickness	Brake Disc Maximum Runout	Standard Brake Drum Diameter	Minimum Lining Thickness Front	Minimum Lining Thickness Rear
1985	240	Diesel	88	0.878	② (F) 0.330 (R)	0.004 (F) 0.004 (R)	—	0.060	0.060
		DL	88	0.878	② (F) 0.330 (R)	0.004 (F) 0.004 (R)	—	0.060	0.060
		GL	88	0.878	② (F) 0.330 (R)	0.004 (F) 0.004 (R)	—	0.060	0.060
		Turbo	88	0.878	② (F) 0.330 (R)	0.004 (F) 0.004 (R)	—	0.060	0.060
	740	GLE	63	③	④ (F) 0.330 (R)	0.003 (F) 0.004 (R)	—	0.118	0.078
		TD ①	63	③	④ (F) 0.330 (R)	0.003 (F) 0.004 (R)	—	0.118	0.078
		Turbo	63	③	④ (F) 0.330 (R)	0.003 (F) 0.004 (R)	—	0.118	0.078
	760	GLE	63	③	④ (F) 0.330 (R)	0.003 (F) 0.004 (R)	—	0.118	0.078
		GLE TD	63	③	④ (F) 0.330 (R)	0.003 (F) 0.004 (R)	—	0.118	0.078
		Turbo	63	③	④ (F) 0.330 (R)	0.003 (F) 0.004 (R)	—	0.118	0.078
1986	240	DL	88	0.878	② (F) 0.330 (R)	0.004 (F) 0.004 (R)	—	0.060	0.060
		GL	88	0.878	② (F) 0.330 (R)	0.004 (F) 0.004 (R)	—	0.060	0.060
	740	GL	63	③	④ (F) 0.330 (R)	0.003 (F) 0.004 (R)	—	0.118	0.078
		GLE	63	③	④ (F) 0.330 (R)	0.003 (F) 0.004 (R)	—	0.118	0.078
		GLE TD	63	③	④ (F) 0.330 (R)	0.003 (F) 0.004 (R)	—	0.118	0.078
		Turbo	63	③	④ (F) 0.330 (R)	0.003 (F) 0.004 (R)	—	0.118	0.078
	760	GLE	63	③	④ (F) 0.330 (R)	0.003 (F) 0.004 (R)	—	0.118	0.078
		Turbo	63	③	④ (F) 0.330 (R)	0.003 (F) 0.004 (R)	—	0.118	0.078
1987–88	240	DL	88	0.878	② (F) 0.330 (R)	0.004 (F) 0.004 (R)	—	0.060	0.060
		GL	88	0.878	② (F) 0.330 (R)	0.003 (F) 0.004 (R)	—	0.060	0.060
	740	GL	63	③	④ (F) 0.330 (R)	0.003 (F) 0.004 (R)	—	0.118	0.078
		GLE	63	③	④ (F) 0.330 (R)	0.003 (F) 0.004 (R)	—	0.118	0.078
		Turbo	63	③	④ (F) 0.330 (R)	0.003 (F) 0.004 (R)	—	0.118	0.078

BRAKE SPECIFICATIONS

All measurements in inches unless noted.

Year	Model		Lug Nut Torque (ft. lbs.)	Master Cylinder Bore	Brake Disc		Standard Brake Drum Diameter	Minimum Lining Thickness	
					Minimum Thickness	Maximum Runout		Front	Rear
1987-88	760	GLE	63	③	④ (F) 0.330 (R)	0.003 (F) 0.004 (R)	—	0.118	0.078
		Turbo	63	③	④ (F) 0.330 (R)	0.003 (F) 0.004 (R)	—	0.118	0.078
	780	780	63	③	④ (F) 0.330 (R)	0.003 (F) 0.004 (R)	—	0.118	0.078

① Station Wagon
② Ventilated: 0.820
   Non-ventilated: 0.536
③ Early type: 0.878
   Late type: 0.938
④ Ventilated: 0.788
   Non-ventilated: 0.433

WHEEL ALIGNMENT

Year	Model		Caster		Camber		Toe-in (in.)	Steering Axis Inclination (deg.)
			Range (deg.)	Preferred Setting (deg.)	Range (deg.)	Preferred Setting (deg.)		
1981	240	DL	3P–4P ②	–	1P–1$\frac{1}{2}$P	–	$\frac{1}{8}$ ③	12
		GL	3P–4P ②	–	1P–1$\frac{1}{2}$P	–	$\frac{1}{8}$ ③	12
		GLT	3P–4P ②	–	$\frac{1}{4}$P–$\frac{3}{4}$P	–	$\frac{1}{8}$ ③	12
	260	Coupe	3P–4P ②	–	1P–1$\frac{1}{2}$P	–	$\frac{1}{8}$ ③	12
		GL	3P–4P ②	–	1P–1$\frac{1}{2}$P	–	$\frac{1}{8}$ ③	12
		GLE	3P–4P ②	–	$\frac{1}{4}$P–1$\frac{3}{4}$P	–	$\frac{1}{8}$ ③	12
1982	240	DL	3P–4P ②	–	1P–1$\frac{1}{2}$P	–	$\frac{1}{8}$ ③	12
		GL	3P–4P ②	–	1P–1$\frac{1}{2}$P	–	$\frac{1}{8}$ ③	12
		GLT	3P–4P ②	–	$\frac{1}{4}$P–$\frac{3}{4}$P	–	$\frac{1}{8}$ ③	12
	260	GLE	3P–4P ②	–	$\frac{1}{4}$P–$\frac{3}{4}$P	–	$\frac{1}{8}$ ③	12
1983	240	DL	3P–4P ②	–	1P–1$\frac{1}{2}$P	–	$\frac{1}{8}$ ③	12
		GL	3P–4P ②	–	1P–1$\frac{1}{2}$P	–	$\frac{1}{8}$ ③	12
		GLT	3P–4P ②	–	$\frac{1}{4}$P–$\frac{3}{4}$P	–	$\frac{1}{8}$ ③	12
		Turbo	3P–4P ②	–	1P–1$\frac{1}{2}$P	–	$\frac{1}{8}$ ③	12
	760	GLE	4$\frac{1}{2}$P–5$\frac{1}{2}$P	–	$\frac{3}{16}$N–$\frac{13}{16}$P	–	$\frac{9}{64}$	NA
		Turbo	4$\frac{1}{2}$P–5$\frac{1}{2}$P	–	$\frac{3}{16}$N–$\frac{13}{16}$P	–	$\frac{9}{64}$	NA
1984	240	Diesel	3P–4P ②	–	1P–1$\frac{1}{2}$P	–	$\frac{1}{8}$ ③	12
		DL	3P–4P ②	–	1P–1$\frac{1}{2}$P	–	$\frac{1}{8}$ ③	12
		GL	3P–4P ②	–	1P–1$\frac{1}{2}$P	–	$\frac{1}{8}$ ③	12
		GLE	3P–4P ②	–	$\frac{1}{4}$P–$\frac{3}{4}$P	–	$\frac{1}{8}$ ③	12
		Turbo	3P–4P ②	–	1P–1$\frac{1}{2}$P	–	$\frac{1}{8}$ ③	12
	760	GLE	4$\frac{1}{2}$P–5$\frac{1}{2}$P	–	$\frac{3}{16}$N–$\frac{13}{16}$P	–	$\frac{9}{64}$	NA
		Turbo	4$\frac{1}{2}$P–5$\frac{1}{2}$P	–	$\frac{3}{16}$N–$\frac{13}{16}$P	–	$\frac{9}{64}$	NA

WHEEL ALIGNMENT

Year	Model		Caster Range (deg.)	Caster Preferred Setting (deg.)	Camber Range (deg.)	Camber Preferred Setting (deg.)	Toe-in (in.)	Steering Axis Inclination (deg.)
1985	240	Diesel	3P–4P	–	$1/4$P–$3/4$P	$1/2$P	$1/8$	12
		DL	3P–4P	–	$1/4$P–$3/4$P	$1/2$P	$1/8$	12
		GL	3P–4P	–	$1/4$P–$3/4$P	$1/2$P	$1/8$	12
		Turbo	3P–4P	–	$1/4$P–$3/4$P	$1/2$P	$1/8$	12
	740	GLE	$4^1/2$P–$5^1/2$P	–	$3/16$N–$13/16$P	–	$9/64$	NA
		TD ①	$4^1/2$P–$5^1/2$P	–	$3/16$N–$13/16$P	–	$9/64$	NA
		Turbo	$4^1/2$P–$5^1/2$P	–	$3/16$N–$13/16$P	–	$9/64$	NA
	760	GLE	$4^1/2$P–$5^1/2$P	–	$3/16$N–$13/16$P	–	$9/64$	NA
		GLE TD	$4^1/2$P–$5^1/2$P	–	$3/16$N–$13/16$P	–	$9/64$	NA
		Turbo	$4^1/2$P–$5^1/2$P	–	$3/16$N–$13/16$P	–	$9/64$	NA
1986	240	DL	3P–4P	–	$1/4$P–$3/4$P	$1/2$P	$1/8$	12
		GL	3P–4P	–	$1/4$P–$3/4$P	$1/2$P	$1/8$	12
	740	GL	$4^1/2$P–$5^1/2$P	–	$3/16$N–$13/16$P	–	$9/64$	NA
		GLE	$4^1/2$P–$5^1/2$P	–	$3/16$N–$13/16$P	–	$9/64$	NA
		GLE TD	$4^1/2$P–$5^1/2$P	–	$3/16$N–$13/16$P	–	$9/64$	NA
		Turbo	$4^1/2$P–$5^1/2$P	–	$3/16$N–$13/16$P	–	$9/64$	NA
	760	GLE	$4^1/2$P–$5^1/2$P	–	$3/16$N–$13/16$P	–	$9/64$	NA
		Turbo	$4^1/2$P–$5^1/2$P	–	$3/16$N–$13/16$P	–	$9/64$	NA
1987–88	240	DL	3P–4P	–	$1/4$P–$3/4$P	$1/2$P	$1/8$	12
		GL	3P–4P	–	$1/4$P–$3/4$P	$1/2$P	$1/8$	12
	740	GL	$4^1/2$P–$5^1/2$P	–	$3/16$N–$13/16$P	–	$9/64$	NA
		GLE	$4^1/2$P–$5^1/2$P	–	$3/16$N–$13/16$P	–	$9/64$	NA
		Turbo	$4^1/2$P–$5^1/2$P	–	$3/16$N–$13/16$P	–	$9/64$	NA
	760	GLE	$4^1/2$P–$5^1/2$P	–	$3/16$N–$13/16$P	–	$9/64$	NA
		Turbo	$4^1/2$P–$5^1/2$P	–	$3/16$N–$13/16$P	–	$9/64$	NA
	780	780	$4^1/2$P–$5^1/2$P	–	$3/16$N–$13/16$P	–	$9/64$	NA

N – Negative
P – Positive

① Station Wagon
② Manual steering: 2P–3P
③ Manual steering: $13/64$

TUNE-UP PROCEDURES

Breaker Points

ADJUSTING BREAKER POINTS WITH A DWELL METER

Adjusting the B21A breaker points with a dwell meter (if available) is a more precise method of adjustment than the feeler gauge method. Calibrate the dwell meter to the four-cylinder position, and connect it between the distributor primary terminal and a ground. Remove the distributor cap and rotor. Loosen the breaker point set screw about ⅛ of a turn. Observing the dwell meter, reset the screw of the stationary contact to obtain the proper (62°) dwell angle. Tighten the set screw and recheck the dwell. Install the rotor and cap, start the engine, and make a final dwell check.

ADJUSTING BREAKER POINTS WITH A FEELER GAUGE

The Canadian B21A models (carburetor-equipped) are also equipped with a conventional breaker points type ignition system.

To replace and adjust a new set of points, remove the distributor cap and rotor. Disconnect the wire leads from both points and condenser. Remove the points hold-down screw, condenser attaching screw, and remove the points assembly and condenser. Lightly grease the distributor cam lobe on the surface that makes contact with the points set. Install the new points assembly and condenser, attach the wire leads of both and tighten the condenser attaching screw. Do not fully tighten the points hold-down screw.

Turn the crankshaft bottom pulley (by placing a socket on the pulley bolt) until the cam lobe on the distributor shaft has fully raised the breaker arm. The points should now be up on the peak of the shaft eccentric, and should be at their most wide open point. Insert a 0.017 in. feeler gauge in between both contacts, and loosen the breaker plate hold-down screw. There will be a slight drag on the feeler gauge when the gap is properly set. Tighten the hold-down screw when you are satisfied, rotate the engine once and recheck the gap. Make sure all leads are securely attached, replace the rotor and distributor cap.

Ignition Timing

ADJUSTMENT

All Except Diesel

Volvo recommends that the ignition timing be checked at 15,000 mile intervals.

Clean the crankshaft damper and pointer on the water pump housing with a solvent-soaked rag so that the marks can be seen. Connect a timing light according to the manufacturer's instructions. Scribe a mark on the crankshaft damper and on the marker with chalk or luminescent (day-glo) paint to highlight the correct timing setting. Disconnect and plug the distributor vacuum line and also disconnect the hose between the air cleaner and the inlet duct at the duct. Disconnect and plug the vacuum hose at the EGR valve.

Attach a tachometer to the engine and set the idle speed to specifications. With the engine running, aim the timing light at the pointer and the marks on the damper. If the marks do not coincide, stop the engine, loosen the distributor pinch bolt, and start the engine again. While observing the timing light flashes on the markers, grasp the distributor vacuum regulator and rotate the distributor until the marks do coincide. Stop the engine and tighten the distributor pinch bolt, taking care not to disturb the setting.

Reconnect all disconnected hoses and remove the timing light and tachometer from the engine.

Diesel

1. Remove the rear timing gear

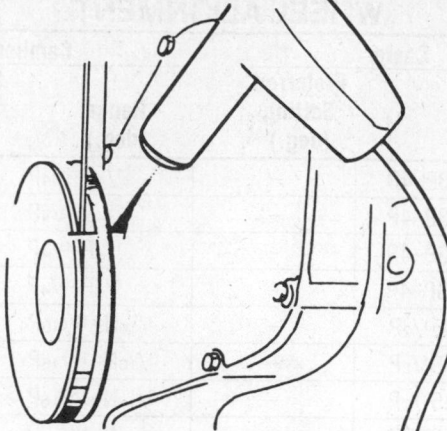

Aim timing light at the pointer and marks on the damper

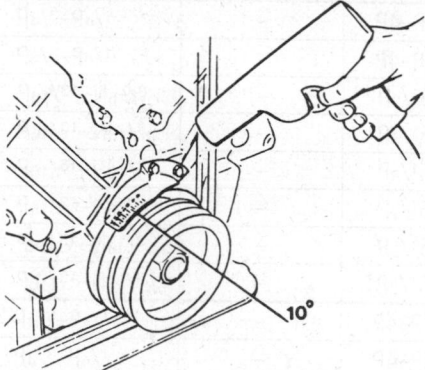

Engine timing marks—B27F and B28F engines

cover and disconnect the cold-start device. Loosen the forward screw on the cold-start device control lever, press the lever back toward the stop.

NOTE: Do not loosen the screw closest to the timing belt.

2. Rotate the engine to align the mark on the injection gear with the mark on the pump bracket. The '0' mark on the flywheel should be centered at the timing mark window and with No. 1 cylinder at top dead center.

3. Remove the plug from the rear of the pump and install the Volvo dial indicator adapter No. 5194 or equivalent, with a measuring range of 0-0.1 in. (0-3mm). Set the indicator gauge at approximately 0.08 in. (2mm).

4. Rotate the engine slowly counterclockwise until the lowest reading on the dial indicator is observed, then re-set the dial indicator to zero.

5. Rotate the engine slowly in the clockwise direction until the '0' mark on the flywheel is centered at the timing mark window. The dial indicator should read within the specified range.

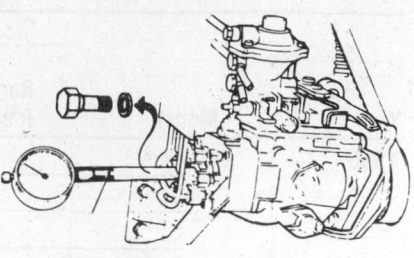

Installing the dial indicator

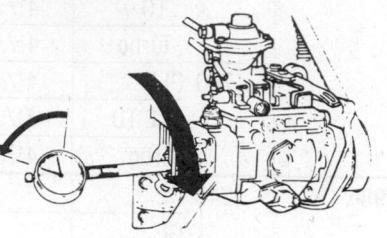

Setting the injection pump

NOTE: When the engine is turned past the timing mark, turn the engine back a ¼ of a turn. Rotate the engine in the clockwise direction until the 'O' mark on the flywheel is centered in the timing mark window.

6. If the dial indicator setting is outside the specified range, loosen the pump bolts and turn the pump until the dial indicator shows the correct setting. Then re-tighten the pump bolts.

7. Crank the engine over by hand two revolutions and re-check the injection pump timing. If it is still out of specifications readjust as necessary.

8. Remove the dial indicator and adapter, reinstall the rear plug and rear timing gear cover, then reconnect the cold start device.

Valve Lash

ADJUSTMENT

B21, B23 and B230

Valve clearance is checked every 15,000 miles. If it is necessary to adjust valve clearance, you will need three special tools: first, a valve tappet depressor tool used to push down the tappet sufficiently to remove the adjusting disc (shim) (Volvo tool No.999 5022); second, a specially shaped pliers to actually remove and install the valve adjusting disc (Volvo tool No. 999 5026); and third, a set of varying thickness valve adjusting discs to make the necessary adjustments.

1. Remove the valve cover. Scribe

DIESEL INJECTION TIMING

All Models	Dial Indicator Reading In. (mm)
Checking Specifications	0.0283–0.0315 (0.72–0.80)
Adjusting Specifications	0.0295 (0.75)

chalk marks on the distributor body indicating each of the four spark plug wire leads in the cap. Remove the distributor cap.

2. Crank over the engine with a remote starter switch, or with a wrench on the crankshaft pulley center bolt (22mm hex) until the engine is in the firing position for No. 1 cylinder. At this point, the 0 degree or TDC mark on the crankshaft pulley is aligned with the timing pointer, the rotor is pointing at the No. 1 spark plug wire cap position, and the camshaft lobes for No. 1 cylinder are pointing at the 10 o'clock and 2 o'clock positions. At this point, the clearance between the cam lobe and valve depressor (tappet) may be checked for the intake and exhaust valve of cylinder No. 1, using a feeler gauge. When checking clearance, the wear limit is 0.012-0.018 in. for a cold engine, and 0.012-0.020 in. for a hot one (176°F).

3. Repeat Step 2 for cylinders 3, 4, and 2 (in that order). Each time, rotate the crankshaft pulley 180° so that the rotor is pointing to the spark plug wire cap position for that cylinder, and the cam lobes are pointing at the 10 and 2 o'clock positions for the valves of that cylinder.

4. If any of the valve clearance measurements are outside the wear limit, you will have to remove the old valve adjusting disc and install a new one to bring the clearance within specifications. First, rotate the valve depressors (tappets) until their notches are at a right angle to the engine center line. Attach valve depressor tool No. 999 5022 or equivalent to the camshaft and screw down the tool spindle until the depressor (tappet) groove is just above the edge of its bore and still accessible with the special pliers (tool No. 999 5026).

5. Remove the valve adjusting disc and measure with a micrometer. The valve clearance should be set to these tolerances: 0.014-0.016 in. for a cold engine, and 0.016-0.018 for a hot one. So, if the measured clearance had been 0.019 in. and the desired clearance 0.016 in. (for a net difference of 0.003 in.), then the new valve adjusting disc should be 0.003 in. thicker than the old one to take up the clearance. Valve adjusting discs are available from Volvo in sizes from 0.130 to

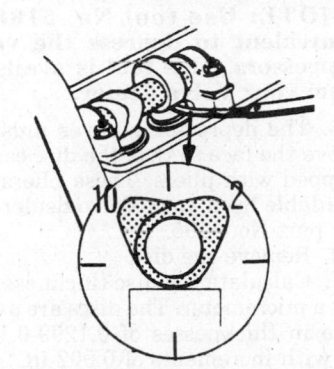

B21, B23, and B230 series camshaft lobes at "10 and 2 O'clock" positions, indicating that subject cylinder is in the firing position and the valves can be adjusted

Positioning a new valve adjustment shim in the head. Shim must be oiled

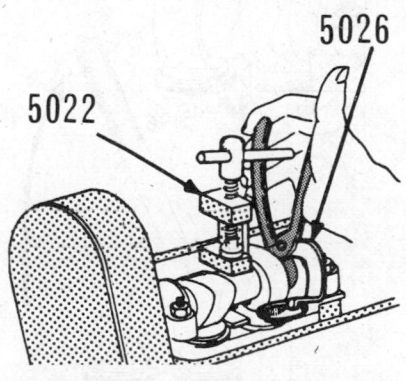

B21, B23, and B230 series valve adjustment tools—tappet depressor is on left, shim pliers on right

0.180 in. (in 0.002 in. increments). Always oil the new disc and install it with the marks facing down.

6. Remove the valve tappet depressor tool. Rotate the engine a few times and recheck clearance. Install the valve cover with a new gasket.

B28F and B280F

Valve clearance is checked every 15,000 miles. No special tools are required.

1. In order to gain access to the valve covers, disconnect or remove the following:

    a. Air conditioning compressor from bracket (do not disconnect refrigerant hoses)

    b. EGR valve and hoses

    c. A/C compressor bracket

    d. Fuel injection control pressure regulator

    e. Air pump

    f. Vacuum pump

    g. Hoses and wires from solenoid valve (Calif. only)

2. Using a 36mm hex socket on the crankshaft pulley bolt, rotate the crankshaft to the No. 1 cylinder TDC position. At this point the '0' mark on the timing plate aligns with the crankshaft pulley notch, the distributor rotor is pointing to the No. 1 cylinder spark plug wire cap position, and both valves for No. 1 cylinder have clearance. At this position, adjust the intake valves of cylinders No. 1, 2 and 4, and the exhaust valves of cylinders No. 1, 3, and 6. Insert a feeler gauge between the rocker arm and valve stem. Loosen the locknut and turn the adjusting screw in the required direction. Tighten the locknut and recheck clearance. Clearance is 0.004-0.006 in. intake and 0.010-0.012 in. exhaust for a cold engine and 0.006-0.008 in. intake and 0.012-0.014 in. exhaust for a hot engine. The B28F cold intake valve adjustment 0.008-0.010 in.; cold exhaust valve adjustment 0.012-0.014 in.

3. Rotate the crankshaft pulley one full 360° turn to adjust the remaining valves. At this point, the '0' mark will again align with the pulley notch, the rotor is pointing 180 degrees opposite its former position, and the No. 1 cylinder rockers contact the ramps of the camshaft. At this position (see illustration), adjust the intake valves of cylinders No. 3, 5, and 6, and the exhaust valves of cylinders No. 2, 4, and 5.

4. Install the valve covers with new gaskets. Connect all disconnected equipment.

D24 and D24T Diesel Engines

NOTE: Always check valve clearances with the cylinder at

TDC; turn the engine ¼ turn past TDC to set valves.

1. Remove the valve cover.
2. Use a $^{11}/_{16}$ in. socket on the crankshaft pulley. Turn the pulley until the engine is ready to fire on the

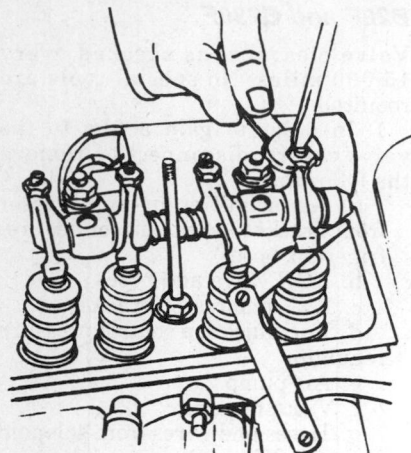

Adjusting valve clearance on the B27 and B28 V6

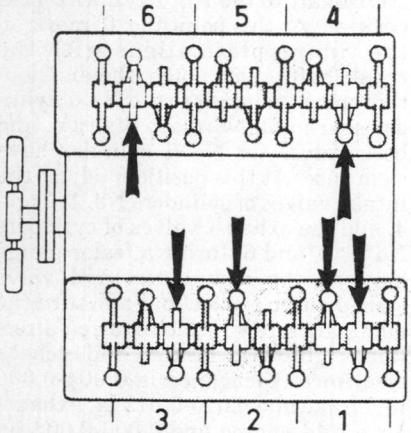

On B27 and 28 with no. 1 cylinder at TDC, adjust these valves (arrows)

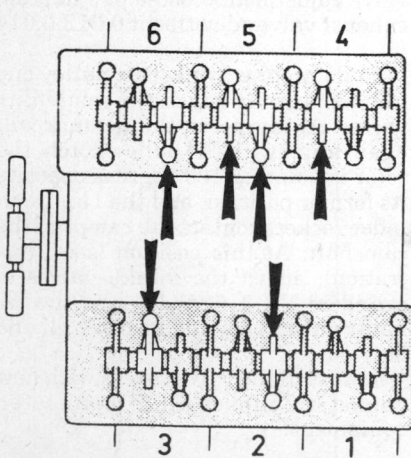

On B27 and 28, rotate the crankshaft 360 degrees and adjust the remaining valves (arrow)

No. 1 cylinder. The flywheel timing mark should be at zero.

NOTE: The piston should be at ¼ turn past top dead center when setting the valve clearance.

3. Line up the valve depressors.
4. Turn them so that the notches point slightly upward.

NOTE: Use tool No. 5196 or equivalent to depress the valve depressors, This tool is available from your Volvo dealer.

5. The depressor grooves must be above the face so that the disc can be gripped with pliers. These pliers are available from your Volvo dealer under part No. 5195.
6. Remove the disc.
7. Calculate the disc thickness, using a micrometer. The discs are available in thicknesses of 0.1299-0.1673 in. with increments of 0.002 in.
8. Cold engine: 0.008 – intake, 0.0016 – exhaust. Warm engine: 0.0010 – intake, 0.0018 – exhaust.

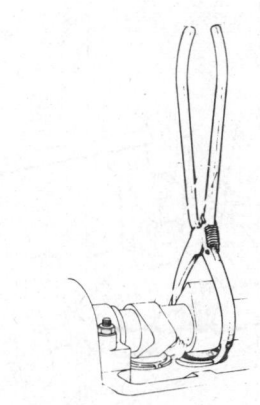

Removing valve adjusting disc (shim)— D24 engines

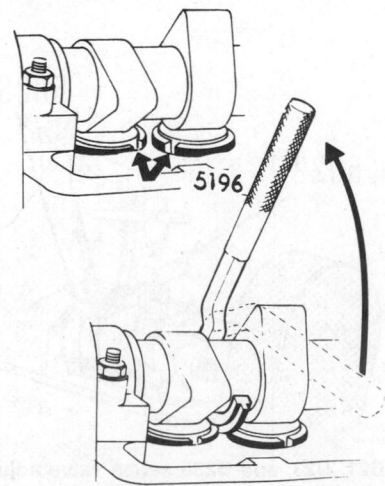

Cam disc removal D24 engine

NOTE: Always use new discs when performing this procedure.

9. Oil the new disc and install it with the marked side down.
10. Check the remaining valve clearances.
11. Use the following sequence 1, 5, 3, 6, 2, 4.
12. Recheck the valve clearance for all cylinders.
13. Rotate the engine several times, and recheck the clearance.
14. Install the valve cover with a new gasket.

Idle Speed and Mixture Gasoline Engines

ADJUSTMENT

Adjustment of idle mixture on both of these systems requires the use of a CO meter. However, the idle speed adjustment may be set using a tachometer (follow the manufacturer's instructions for hook-up).

Mechanical Injection (K-Jetronic) CIS

1981 B21F

1. Run the engine to normal operating temperature. Disconnect the throttle control rod at the lever. Make sure the cable and pulley run smoothly and do not bind in any position.
2. Remove the ECU cover panel. Deactivate the ECU by disconnecting the white-red wire from terminal 12 of the blue connector plug at the ECU. Reinstall the connector plug.

NOTE: The same wire ends at the ignition coil but cannot be disconnected there.

3. Connect a tachometer to the engine according to the manufacturer's instructions. Connect a test light across the battery positive terminal and the terminal on the throttle micro switch with the yellow wire connected. Start the engine. The test light must NOT light up. If it does, adjust the micro switch position by slackening the switch retaining screws. Move the switch down until the light goes out, then retighten the screws. This adjustment is temporary; final adjustment will follow later on.
4. Idle speed should be 850-900 rpm. If outside these limits, adjust idle speed by proceeding to Step 5. If idle speed is within these limits, continue to Step 6.
5. If the idle speed is outside the stated limits, use the throttle position adjustment screw to adjust the speed to 850-900 rpm. The test light must NOT light up; if it does, readjust the

micro switch position. Reconnect the white-red wire in terminal 12 of the blue connector plug at the ECU to reactivate the ECU. The idle speed should have changed to 900 rpm (850-950 rpm is permitted). Stop the engine.

6. Reconnect the throttle control rod at the lever, making sure the cable pulley is completely retracted. If the control rod length must be adjusted, disconnect the throttle cable and automatic transmission kickdown cable (if equipped). Loosen the locknuts on either end of the rod and adjust the rod as necessary by turning it, then tighten the locknuts. Attach the throttle cable and adjust it if necessary by turning the nut on the end of the cable as shown. Automatic transmission kickdown cable length should be checked at closed and open throttle with the engine OFF. Open throttle cable measurement should be checked with the throttle pedal in the car depressed, NOT by actuating the linkage by hand. The cable should be pulled out 50mm, or 1.9 in.

7. Adjust the micro switch by moving the switch UP, with the engine not running and the throttle closed. Slacken the switch retaining screws, and move the switch UP until the test light lights up. Set the switch position by moving the switch DOWN 2-5.5mm or 0.08-0.10 in. The test light must not light up, or the adjustment will have to be preformed again.

8. Remove the test light, reinstall the ECU panel.

1981 B21F MPG, 1982-83 B21F and B23E

The procedures for these engine models are the same as those for the 1981 B21F above, EXCEPT that the ECU from the 1982-83 has two extra terminals, 7 and 10. To deactivate the ECU, Ground terminal 10 with the connector in place by inserting a copper wire along the terminal wire. Also, the idle speed should be 700 rpm with the ECU deactivated, and 750 rpm, (700-800 rpm permitted) with the ECU activated. On Step 2, DO NOT reinstall the connector plug.

1981-85 B21F Turbo

1. Follow the procedures in Step 1 and 2 of the 1981 B21F procedure EXCEPT do not reinstall the connect plug. Note the procedure above for deactivating 1982 and later ECUs.

2. Connect a test light across the battery positive terminal and the orange wire terminal on the micro (throttle) switch. The test light must NOT light up while adjusting the idle speed (the electric circuit through the micro switch is open). If the test light

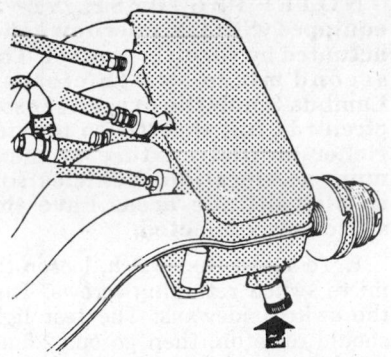

Mechanical (K-Jetronic) injection idle speed adjustment

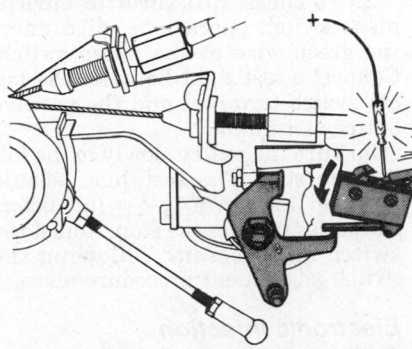

Adjusting throttle micro switch—B21F with K-Jetronic injection. Adjust idle if test light lights up at idle speed

illuminates, adjust the micro switch position by slackening the switch retaining screws and moving the switch down until the test light goes out. Tighten the screws. This is a temporary adjustment; the final adjustment will follow later on.

3. Run the engine to normal operating temperature if not already done. Connect a tachometer to the engine and check idle speed; idle speed should be 850 rpm. If idle speed is outside these limits, follow the procedure below.

4. Using the throttle position adjustment screw, adjust throttle position until the idle speed reaches 850 rpm. The test light must NOT light up. If necessary adjust the micro switch position DOWN.

5. Activate the ECU by reconnecting the white-red wire in terminal 12 of the blue connector on 1981 models, and by disconnecting the ground wire that was inserted at terminal 10 of the blue connector on 1982 and later models.

6. After activating the ECU, the idle speed should change to 900 rpm on (850-900 permitted) on 1981 models, and to 900 rpm (880-920 rpm permitted) on 1982 and later models. Stop the engine and install the ECU panel.

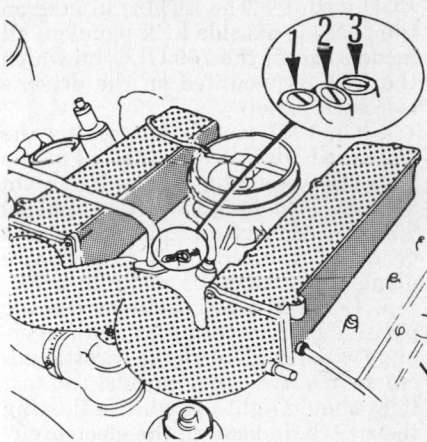

B27, 28 idle balance (nos. 1 and 2), and air adjusting screws (no. 3)

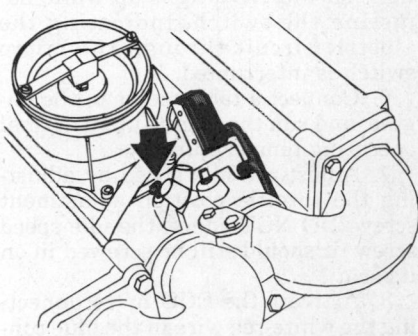

On 1981 and later B28F, make sure the idle speed adjustment screw is bottomed on its seat; this screw is used to adjust idle speed on non-CIS engines

7. Reconnect and adjust the throttle control rod and cable, and the automatic transmission kickdown cable (if equipped) by following Step 6 of the '1981 B21F' procedure.

8. Adjust the B21F Turbo throttle switch by inserting a 0.3mm feeler gauge between the throttle adjustment screw and the throttle control lever. Move the switch UP until the test light lights up. Set the switch by moving it DOWN until the test light just goes out. Disconnect all test instruments, install the ECU panel.

1981-86 B28F

1. Disconnect the throttle rod at the cable pulley. Check the cable assembly, making sure the cable and pulley run smoothly and do not bind in any position. Check the throttle, make sure the throttle shaft and plate do not bind during operation.

2. Screw in the idle speed adjustment screw all the way until it just seats.

NOTE: This screw is used to adjust the idle speed on engines without the CIS system.

3. Remove the access panel to the

ECU module. (The ECU is located on the passenger's side kick panel on all models except the 760 GLE, on which the ECU is mounted on the driver's side kick panel).

4. On 1981 models, disconnect the white-red wire at terminal 12 of the blue connector plug at the ECU. On 1982-86 models, ground terminal 10 with the connector in place. This can be done by inserting a copper wire along the number 10 terminal wire.

5. Connect a test light across the positive battery terminal and the orange wire terminal on the throttle micro switch. On 1981 models, the test light should light up, while adjusting the switch, indicating the electric circuit through the micro switch is closed. On 1982-86 models, the test light should NOT light up while adjusting the switch, indicating the electric circuit through the micro switch is interrupted.

6. Connect a tachometer to the engine, and run the engine up to normal operating temperature.

7. Adjust the idle speed by adjusting the throttle position adjustment screw. DO NOT adjust the idle speed screw (it should still be screwed in on its seat).

8. Activate the ECU by reconnecting the white-red wire in the blue connector at the ECU. With the ECU activated, the idle speed should change to 900 rpm on 1981 and 1982 models (850-950 permitted on 1981, 880-920 permitted on 1982) and 750 rpm on 1983-86. Shut off the engine and install the ECU panel.

9. Reconnect the throttle control rod at the cable pulley. Disconnect the throttle cable and automatic transmission kickdown cable. The cable pulley should be completely retracted. Adjust the control rod length as necessary. Attach and adjust the throttle cable.

10. Check automatic transmission kickdown cable length at closed and open throttle with the engine off. Open throttle measurement should be checked with the throttle pedal in the car depressed, NOT by actuating the linkage by hand. Cable movement should be 50mm or about 1.9 in. Cable length with closed throttle should be 1mm with open throttle 51mm.

11. To adjust the throttle micro switch, insert 0.12 in. feeler gauge between the throttle position adjustment screw and the throttle stop. On 1981 models, adjust the switch by turning the adjustment screw until the test light goes out. On 1982 and later models, turn the adjustment screw until the test light lights up.

Full Throttle Enrichment Switch

NOTE: The B28F V6 is equipped with two micro switches actuated by throttle control. This second micro switch closes a Lambda-Sond (the oxygen sensor) circuit at full throttle to provide richer air/fuel mixture at maximum acceleration. Vehicles sold in high-altitude areas have this switch disconnected.

1. To adjust the switch, loosen the micro switch retaining screws. Turn the switch sideways. The test light should come on, then go out 2.5mm ($^3/_{32}$ in.) before the pulley touches the full throttle stop. Tighten the retaining screws.

2. To check full throttle enrichment switch operations, disconnect the green wire at the micro switch. Connect a test light between the micro switch terminal and the positive battery terminal.

3. Turn the pulley slowly to the full throttle stop. The test light should light up 1-4mm ($^1/_{32}$–$^5/_{32}$ in.) before the pulley touches the stop. Adjust the switch as necessary, following the switch adjustment procedure above.

Electronic Injection (LH-Jetronic)

1982 B21F and 1983-88 B23F and B230F

1. Seat the throttle butterfly valve by loosening the stop nut on the adjuster screw. Unscrew the adjuster a couple of turns. Set the adjuster screw by screwing it in until it just touches the lever, then screw it in an additional ¼ turn. Tighten the lock nut.

2. Disconnect the CIS connector on the firewall. This is the connector that is directly behind the engine.

3. Connect a test light across the battery positive terminal and the orange wire terminal in the connector. Start the engine. The test light should light up at idle speed. If it does not, readjust the adjuster screw for the throttle butterfly valve position.

4. Open the throttle slightly by hand at the throttle control lever, with the engine running. The test light should go out. If it does not, run through the procedure again and try a new throttle switch.

1987-88 B280F

1. Ground the CIS test point. The CIS test point is the Red/White wire in the two wire connector which is located in the engine compartment across from the air conditioning compressor.

2. The Green/White wire is the test point location for the oxygen sensor test.

3. Grounding the Red/White wire

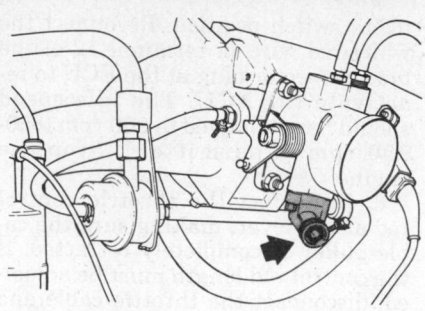

L-Jetronic idle adjustment location

will set the air valve in the wide open position.

4. Adjust the basic idle speed to 700 rpm. Disconnect the ground wire from the CIS test point. The idle speed should increase to 750 rpm.

Diesel Fuel Injection

SETTING THE IDLE SPEED

NOTE: To correctly set the idle speed you will need either the Volvo Monotester and adapter 9950 or a suitable photoelectric tachometer, since a gasoline engine tachometer by itself cannot be used on a diesel engine owing to the fact that a diesel engine does not have an electric ignition system.

1. Connect a suitable tachometer to the engine and run the engine to normal operating temperature.

2. Idle speed should be 720-880 rpm.

3. If not, adjust the idle speed by loosening the locknut and turning the idle speed screw on the fuel injection pump.

4. Tighten the locknut and apply a dab of paint or thread sealer to the adjusting screw to prevent it from vibration loose.

5. After adjusting idle speed and maximum engine speed, adjust the engine throttle linkage.

SETTING THE MAXIMUM ENGINE SPEED

The diesel engine is governed by the fuel injection pump so that engine rpm will not exceed 5100-5300 rpm. Because of the extremely high compression ratio (23.5:1) and the great stored energy diesel oil contains, the diesel engine cannot be run at the high rpm levels of modern gasoline engines, as it would place a tremendous strain on the pistons, wrist pins, connecting rods and bearing of the engine.

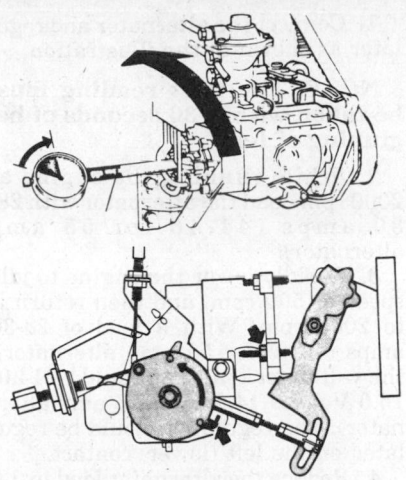

Diesel engine maximum speed stop. Turn the pulley to bring the engine to maximum speed.

To adjust the maximum idle speed you will need a special tachometer which will work on the diesel engine. See the 'NOTE' under 'Setting The Idle Speed', above.

1. Connect the tachometer and run the engine to normal operating temperature.
2. Run the engine to maximum speed by turning the cable pulley counterclockwise.

—————— **CAUTION** ——————

Do not race the engine longer than absolutely necessary.

3. Maximum speed should be between 5100-5300 rpm.
4. If not, loosen the locknut and adjust using the maximum speed screw.
5. Tighten the locknut and apply a dab of paint or thread sealer to the adjusting screw to prevent it from vibrating loose.

—————— **CAUTION** ——————

Do not attempt to squeeze more power out of your diesel by extending the maximum speed.

6. After adjusting the maximum speed, adjust the engine throttle linkage.

ENGINE ELECTRICAL

Distributor
REMOVAL & INSTALLATION

1. Unsnap the distributor cap clasps and remove the cap.
2. Crank the engine until No. 1 cylinder is at Top Dead Center (TDC). At

this point, the rotor should point to the spark plug wire socket for No. 1 cylinder, and the 0° timing mark on the crankshaft damper should be aligned with the pointer. For ease of assembly, scribe a chalkmark on the distributor housing to note the position of the rotor.

3. Disconnect the negative battery terminal. Disconnect the primary lead from the coil at its terminal on the distributor housing. On electronic fuel-injected models, disconnect the plug for the triggering contacts. On all models except Canadian B21A, remove the retaining screw for the primary voltage wire connector and pull it from the distributor housing.
4. Remove the vacuum hose(s) from the regulator. Take care not to damage the bakelite connection during removal.
5. Remove the distributor attaching screw and lift out the distributor.
6. When ready to install the distributor, if the engine has been disturbed (cranked), find TDC for No. 1 cylinder as outlined under 'Valve Lash Adjustment'. If the engine has not been disturbed, install the distributor with the rotor pointing to the No. 1 cylinder spark plug wire socket, or the chalkmark made prior to removal. On B21, B27 and B28F engines, the distributor drive gear teeth are beveled, which will cause the rotor to turn counterclockwise as the distributor is installed. For this reason, it is necessary to back off the rotor clockwise (about 60° and on the B21, and 40° on the B27 and B28F) to compensate for this. What is necessary is that the rotor aligns with the mark made prior to removal after the distributor is bolted down.
7. Connect the primary lead to its terminal on the distributor housing. On electronic fuel injected models, connect the plug for the triggering contacts. Push the primary voltage wire connector into its slot in the distributor housing and tighten the retaining screw.
8. Connect the vacuum hose(s) to the bakelite connection(s) on the vacuum regulator, (if so equipped).
9. If the distributor was disassembled, or if the contact point setting was disturbed, proceed to set the point gap and/or dwell angle on B21A (Canadian) engines.
10. Install the distributor cap and secure the clasps. Proceed to set the ignition timing. Tighten the distributor attaching screw.

Alternator
PRECAUTIONS

Several precautions must be observed

when performing work on alternator equipment.

If the battery is removed for any reason, make sure that it is reconnected with the correct polarity. Reversing the battery connections may result in damage to the one-way rectifiers.

Never operate the alternator with the main circuit broken. Make sure that the battery, alternator, and regulator leads are not disconnected while the engine is running.

Never attempt to polarize an alternator.

When charging a battery that is installed in the vehicle, disconnect the negative battery cable. This is very important.

When utilizing a booster battery as a starting aid, always connect it in parallel; negative to negative, and positive to positive.

When arc welding is to be performed on any part of the vehicle, disconnect the negative battery cable, disconnect the alternator leads, and unplug the voltage regulator.

DRIVE BELT ADJUSTMENT

Accessory drive belt tension is correct when the deflection made with light finger pressure on the at a midway point is about ½ in. Any belt that is glazed, frayed, or stretched so that it cannot be tightened sufficiently must be replaced.

Incorrect belt tension is corrected by moving the driven accessory (alternator, air pump, power steering pump or air conditioning compressor) away from or toward the driving pulley. Loosen the mounting and adjusting bolts on the respective accessory and tighten them, once the belt tension is correct. Never position a metal pry bar on the rear end of the alternator air pump or power steering pump housing, they can be deformed easily.

REMOVAL & INSTALLATION

1. Disconnect the negative battery cable.
2. Disconnect the electrical leads to the alternator. Remove all necessary components in order to gain access to the alternator retaining bolts.
3. Remove the adjusting arm-to-alternator bolt and the adjusting arm-to-engine bolt.
4. Remove the alternator mounting bolt.
5. Remove the fan belt and lift the alternator forward and out.
6. Reverse the above procedure to install, taking care to properly tension the fan (drive) belt.

Voltage Regulator

REMOVAL & INSTALLATION

1. Disconnect the negative battery cable.
2. Disconnect the leads or plug socket from the old regulator taking note of their location.
3. Remove the hold-down screws from the old regulator and install the new one.
4. Connect the leads or plug socket and reconnect the negative battery cable.

VOLTAGE ADJUSTMENT

Motorola (S.E.V. Marchal) Regulator

If the Motorola A.C. regulator is found to be defective, it must be replaced. No adjustments can be made on this unit.

The following test may be performed on the Motorola regulator to see if it is functioning properly. An ammeter, tachometer, and voltmeter are required.

1. Connect the testing equipment at the alternator.
2. Run the engine at 2500 rpm (5000 alternator rpm) for 15 seconds. With no load on the alternator, and the regulator ambient temperature at 77°F, the reading n the voltmeter should be 13.1-14.4 V.
3. Load the alternator with 10-15 amps (high-beam headlights) while the engine is running at 2500 rpm. The voltmeter reading should again be 13.1-14.4 V. Replace the regulator if it does not fall within these limits.
4. For a more accurate indication of the regulator's performance, drive the vehicle for about 45 minutes at a minimum speed of 30 mph. The regulator will be at the correct working temperature immediately after this drive.
5. With the engine running at 2500 rpm, and the regulator ambient temperature at 77°F, the voltmeter reading should be 13.85-14.25 V.

Bosch A.C. Regulator (35, 55 and 70 Amp)

The Bosch A.C. regulator is fully adjustable. To determine which adjustments are necessary — if any — perform the following test. (An ammeter, 12 V control lamp, tachometer, and voltmeter are required for this test)

NOTE: Where the numerical values differ for the 35 amp voltage regulator and the 55 amp unit, the figures for the 55 amp regulator will be given in parentheses.

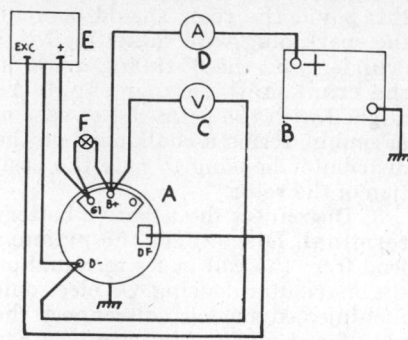

A. Alternator
B. Battery 60 Ah
C. Voltmeter 0—20 amps.
D. Ammeter 0—50 amps.
E. Voltage regulator
F. Warning lamp 12 volts. 2 watts

Wiring diagram for testing Motorola regulator

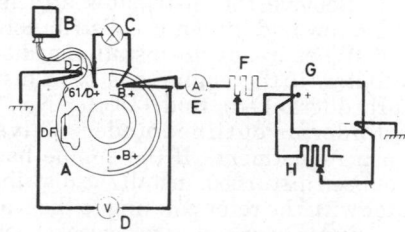

A. Alternator
B. Voltage lamp 12 volts
C. Control lamp 12 volts, 2 watts
D. Voltmeter 0-20 volts
F. Regulator resistance
G. Battery 60 amperehours
H. Load resistance
E. Ammeter 0-50 amps

Wiring diagram for testing Bosch A.C. regulator

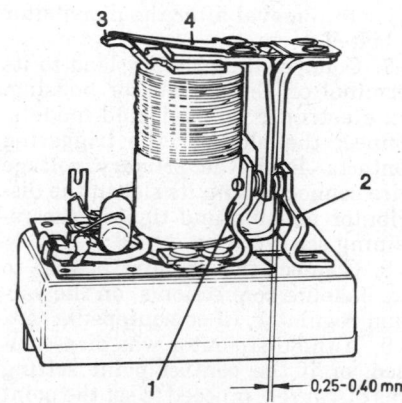

1. Regulator contact for lower control range (lower contact)
2. Regulator contact for upper control range (upper contact)
3. Spring tensioner
4. Spring upper section: Steel spring Lower section: Bimetal spring

Bosch A.C. voltage adjustments

1. Connect the alternator and regulator as shown in the illustration.

NOTE: The first reading must be taken within 30 seconds of beginning of test.

2. While running the engine at 2000 rpm, load the alternator with 28-30 amps (44-46 for 55 amp alternator).
3. Rapidly lower the engine to idle speed or 500 rpm, and then return it to 2000 rpm. With a load of 28-30 amps (44-46 for 55 amp alternator), the voltmeter reading should be 14.0-15.0 V (13.9-14.8 V for 55 amp alternator). The regulator should be regulated on the left (lower) contact.
4. Reduce the alternator load to 3-8 amps. The voltmeter reading should not decrease more than 0.3 (0.4 for 44 amp, alternator) V. The regulator should be regulated on the right (upper) contact.
5. Adjustment is made by bending the stop bracket for the bi-metal spring. Bending the stop bracket down lowers the regulating voltage; bending it up raises the voltage. If the voltmeter reading for the low amp alternator load decreased more than 0.3 (0.4 for 55 amp alternator), V, compared to the reading for the high amp alternator load, adjust the regulator by bending the holder for the left (lower) contact and simultaneously adjust the gap between the right (upper) contact and the movable contact. The gap should be adjusted to 0.010-0.015 in. (0.25-0.40mm). If the holder is bent toward the right (upper) contact, the regulating voltage under high amp alternator load will be lowered.

To avoid faulty adjustments due to residual magnetism in the regulator core, it may be necessary to rapidly lower the engine rpm to idle after each adjustment, then raise it to 2000 rpm to take a new reading.

NOTE: Warm regulators may be cooled to ambient temperature by directing a stream of compressed air on them. Final readings should be make with the regulator at ambient temperature.

Starter

REMOVAL & INSTALLATION

1. Disconnect the negative battery cable at the battery.
2. Disconnect the leads from the starter motor. Remove the necessary components in order to gain access to the starter retaining bolts. Raise and support the vehicle, as required.
3. Remove the bolts retaining the starter motor brace to the cylinder

block (B21 only) and the bolts retaining the starter motor to the flywheel housing and lift it off.

4. To install, position the starter motor to the flywheel housing and install the retaining bolts finger-tight. Torque the bolts to approximately 25 ft. lbs., and apply locking compound to the threads.

5. Connect the starter motor leads and the negative battery cable.

STARTER DRIVE REPLACEMENT

In order to remove the starter pinion drive, it is necessary to disassemble the starter. The procedure for disassembling the starter is as follows:

1. Remove the starter from the vehicle.

2. Unscrew the two screws and remove the small cover from the front end of the starter shaft.

3. Unsnap the lockwasher and remove the adjusting washers from the front end of the shaft.

4. Unscrew the two screws retaining the commutator bearing shield and remove the shield.

5. Lift up the brushes and retainers and remove the brush bridge from the rotor shaft. The negative brushes are removed with the bridge while the positive brushes remain in the field winding. Do no remove the steel washer and the fiber washer at this time.

6. Unscrew the nut retaining the field terminal connection to the control solenoid.

7. Unscrew the two solenoid-to-starter housing retaining screws and remove the solenoid.

8. Remove the drive end shield and rotor from the stator.

9. Remove the rubber and metal sealing washers from the housing.

10. Unscrew the nut and remove the screw on which the engaging arm pivots.

11. Remove the rotor, with the pinion and engaging arm attached, from the drive end shield.

12. Push back the stop washer and remove the snap-ring from the rotor shaft.

13. Remove the stop washer and pull off the starter pinion with a gear puller.

While the starter is disassembled, a few quick checks may be performed. Check the rotor shaft, commutator, and windings. If the rotor shaft is bent or worn, it must be replaced. Maximum rotor shaft radial throw is 0.003 in. If the commutator is scored or worn unevenly, it should be turned. Minimum commutator diameter is 1.3 in. Check the end shield which

houses the brushes, for excessive wear. Maximum bearing clearance is 0.005 in.

14. Lubricate the starter.

15. Press the starter pinion onto the rotor shaft. Install the stop washer and secure it with a new snap-ring.

16. Position the engaging arm on the pinion. Install the rotor into the drive end frame.

17. Install the screw and nut for the engaging arm pivot.

18. Install the rubber and metal sealing washers into the drive end housing.

19. Install the stator onto the rotor and drive end shield.

20. Position the solenoid so that the eyelet on the end of the solenoid plunger fits onto the engaging arm (shift lever). Tighten the solenoid retaining screws.

21. Place the metal and fiber washers on the rotor shaft.

22. Install the brush bridge on the rotor shaft and replace the brushes.

23. Fit the commutator bearing shield into position and install the retaining screws.

24. Install the adjusting washers and snap a new lockwasher into position on the end of the shaft. Make sure that the rotor axial clearance does not exceed 0.12 in. If necessary, adjust the clearance with washers, maintaining a minimum clearance of 0.002 in.

25. Replace the small cover over the front end of the shaft and install the two retaining screws.

26. Install the starter.

SOLENOID REPLACEMENT

1. Remove the starter from the vehicle.

2. Unscrew the two solenoid-to-starter housing retaining screws and remove the solenoid.

3. As a final test, wipe the solenoid clean and press in the armature. Test its operation by connecting it to a battery. If the solenoid still does not function, replace it with a new unit.

4. Position the new solenoid so that the eyelet on the end of the plunger fits into the engaging arm. Tighten the retaining screws.

5. Replace the starter.

Diesel Glow Plug

REMOVAL & INSTALLATION

1. Disconnect the negative battery cable.

2. Remove all necessary components in order to gain access to the glow plug.

3. Remove the electrical connector from the glow plug.

4. Carefully remove the glow plug from its mounting on the engine, using the proper tools.

5. Installation is the reverse of the removal procedure.

ENGINE MECHANICAL

Engine

REMOVAL & INSTALLATION

B21F, B23E and B230F Models

1. On cars equipped with manual transmission, remove the four retaining clips and lift up the shifter boot. Then, remove the snap-ring from the shifter.

2. Remove the battery.

3. Disconnect the windshield washer hose and engine compartment light wire. Scribe marks around the hood mount brackets on the underside of the hood for later alignment. Remove the hood.

4. Remove the overflow tank cap. Drain the cooling system.

5. Remove the upper and lower radiator hoses. Disconnect the overflow hoses at the radiator. Disconnect the PCV hose at the cylinder head.

6. On cars equipped with automatic transmission disconnect the oil cooler lines at the radiator.

7. Remove the radiator and fan shroud.

8. Remove the air cleaner assembly and hoses.

9. Disconnect the hoses at the air pump. Remove the air pump and drive belt, if equipped.

10. Disconnect the vacuum pump hoses and remove the vacuum pump. disconnect the power brake booster vacuum hose.

11. Remove the power steering pump, drive belt and bracket. Position to one side.

12. On cars equipped with air conditioning, remove the crankshaft pulley and compressor drive belt. Then, install the pulley again for reference. Remove the A/C wire connector and the compressor from its bracket and position to one side. Remove the bracket.

13. disconnect the vacuum hoses from the engine. Disconnect the carbon canister hoses.

14. Disconnect the distributor wire connector, high tension lead, starter cables, and the clutch cable clamp.

15. Disconnect the wiring harness at

the voltage regulator. Disconnect the throttle cable at the pulley and the wire for the A/C at the intake manifold solenoid.

16. Remove the gas cap. Disconnect the fuel lines at the filter and return pipe.

17. At the firewall, disconnect the electrical connectors for the ballast resistor, and relays. Disconnect the heater hoses.

18. Disconnect the micro switch connectors at the intake manifold, and all remaining harness connectors to the engine.

19. Drain the crankcase.

20. Remove the exhaust manifold flange retaining nuts. Loosen the exhaust pipe clamp bolts and remove the bracket for the front exhaust pipe mount. On B21FT (Turbo) models, disconnect the turbo from the intake hose, disconnect the other hoses from the turbo unit, and disconnect the turbocharger from the exhaust system.

21. From underneath, remove the front motor mount bolts.

22. On cars equipped with automatic transmission, place the gear selector lever in Park and disconnect the gear shift control rod from the transmission.

23. On manual transmission cars, disconnect the clutch cable. Then, loosen the set screw, drive out the pivot pin, and remove the shifter from the control rod.

24. Disconnect the speedometer and the driveshaft from the transmission.

25. On overdrive equipped models, disconnect the control wire from the shifter.

26. Raise and support the vehicle safely. Then, using a floor jack and a wooden block, support the weight of the engine beneath the transmission.

27. Remove the bolts for the rear transmission mount. Remove the transmission support crossmember.

28. Lift out the engine using the proper lifting equipment.

29. Reverse the above procedure to install. Adjust gear selector linkage, check and adjust throttle linkage.

B28F and B280F

1. On cars equipped with manual transmission, remove the shifter assembly. From underneath, loosen the set screw and drive out the pivot pin. Then, pull up the boot, remove the reverse pawl bracket, and snap-ring for the shifter, and lift out the shifter.

2. Remove the battery.

3. Disconnect the windshield washer hose and engine compartment light wire. Scribe marks around the hood mount brackets on the underside of the hood for later hood alignment. Remove the hood.

4. Remove the air cleaner assembly.

5. Remove the splash guard under the engine.

6. Drain the cooling system.

7. Remove the overflow tank cap. Remove the upper and lower radiator hoses, and disconnect the overflow hoses at the radiator.

8. On cars equipped with automatic transmission, disconnect the transmission cooler lines at the radiator.

9. Remove the radiator and fan shroud.

10. Disconnect the heater hoses, power brake hose at the intake manifold and the vacuum pump hose at the pump. Remove the vacuum pump and O-ring in the valve cover. Remove the gas cap.

11. At the firewall disconnect the fuel lines (CAUTION: High pressue) at the filter and return pipe, disconnect the relay connectors and all other wire connectors. Disconnect the distributor wires.

12. Disconnect the evaporative control carbon canister hoses and the vacuum hose at the EGR valve.

13. Disconnect the voltage regulator wire connector.

14. Disconnect the throttle cable (and kickdown cable on automatic transmission cars), the vacuum amplifer hose at the T-pipe, and the hoses at the thermostat.

15. Disconnect the air pump hose at the backfire valve, the solenoid valve wire, and the micro switch wire.

16. Remove the exhaust manifold flange retaining nuts (both sides).

17. On cars equipped with air conditioning, remove the compressor and drive belt, and place it to one side. Do not disconnect the refrigerant hoses.

18. Drain the crankcase.

19. Remove the power steering pump, drive belt, and bracket. Position to one side.

20. From underneath, remove the retaining nuts for the front motor mounts.

21. Remove, as required, the front exhaust pipe.

22. On 49 states models, remove the front exhaust pipe hangers and clamps and allow the system to hang.

23. On cars equipped with automatic transmission, place the shift lever in 'Park'. Disconnect the shift control lever at the transmission.

24. On manual transmission cars, disconnect the clutch cylinder from the bell housing. Leave the cylinder connected (secure it to the car).

25. Disconnect the speedometer cable and driveshaft at the transmission.

26. Jack up the front of the car and place jack stands beneath the rein-forced box member area to the rear of each front jacking attachment. Then, using a floor jack and a thick, wide wooden block, support the weight of the engine beneath the oil pan.

27. Remove the bolts for the rear transmission mount. Remove the transmission support crossmember.

28. Lift out the engine and transmission as a unit.

29. Reverse the above procedure to install. Adjust gear selector linkage, check and adjust throttle linkage.

D24 and D24T

1. Matchmark and remove the hood.

2. Disconnect the negative battery terminal.

3. Drain the radiator coolant.

4. Remove the four clips and pull up the rubber boot on the shift lever.

5. Disconnect the back-up light and overdrive connector if so equipped.

6. Remove the bracket for the reverse inhibitor.

7. Release the lock ring on the shift lever.

8. Move the lock ring, rubber ring, and plastic journal up on the lever.

NOTE: On cars with automatic transmissions place the shift lever in Park before disconnecting.

9. Disconnect the top and bottom radiator hoses.

10. Disconnect the lower hose at the cold start device, and drain the coolant into a suitable container.

11. On vehicles with automatic transmissions remove the cooling lines from the radiator.

12. Disconnect the expansion tank hose.

13. Unbolt and remove the radiator.

14. Disconnect the electrical connection at the firewall.

15. Remove the heater hoses at the control valve.

16. Disconnect the hose from the vacuum pump.

17. Disconnect the accelerator cable from the pulley and bracket.

18. Disconnect the vacuum line to the brake booster.

19. Disconnect the fuel lines.

NOTE: Thoroughly clean all connections prior to disconnecting them.

20. Plug all fuel lines to prevent dirt from entering them.

21. Disconnect the wires at the main terminal.

22. Disconnect the glow plug relay.

23. Remove the relay retaining screws and hang the relay and the wire bundle on the engine.

24. Remove the power steering

pump and brackets, and tie it out of the way.

25. Remove the starter wires and the battery ground strap.

26. Remove the fan, spacer, pulley and drive belts.

27. Remove the air cleaner and all necessary hoses.

28. Disconnect the alternator wires.

29. Disconnect the exhaust pipe at the front exhaust manifold.

30. Drain the engine oil.

31. Disconnect the exhaust pipe at the rear exhaust manifold.

32. On D24T models, remove the inlet hose from the turbo pipe, and the snap-ring from the turbo intake pipe. Remove the compressor intake pipe and plug the hole immediately with a clean rag. Disconnect the oil return pipe bolts, and move the return pipe aside. Plug the holes. Remove the oil delivery pipe from the turbo unit, and plug the holes. Remove the compressor and exhaust pipes from the turbo unit, and remove the turbocharger.

33. Disconnect the clutch cable, return spring, vibration damper, and rubber buffer.

34. Pull out the clutch cable from the clutch lever and housing.

35. Disconnect the speedometer from the transmission.

NOTE: On cars with automatic transmissions disconnect the shift lever.

36. Disconnect the shift lever and push it up into the car.

37. Remove the driveshaft from the transmission.

38. Support the transmission with a jack and remove the rear crossmember.

39. Remove the engine mounts.

　a. Left side: Remove the nuts from the front axle member.

　b. Right side: Remove the lower nut from the rubber pad.

40. Gently put tension on your engine removal hoist.

41. Remove the left engine mount assembly.

42. Remove the engine using the proper lifting device.

43. Installation is the reverse of removal. Adjust gear selector linkage, and check and adjust throttle linkage. Use new gaskets on the turbocharger if equipped.

Cylinder Head

REMOVAL & INSTALLATION

NOTE: To prevent warpage of the head, removal should be attempted only on a cold engine.

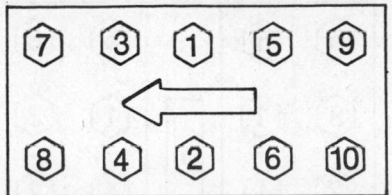

Cylinder head bolt tightening sequence—B21 and B23 series

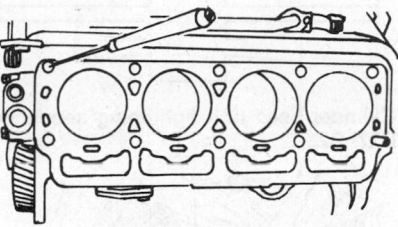

Guide stud installation

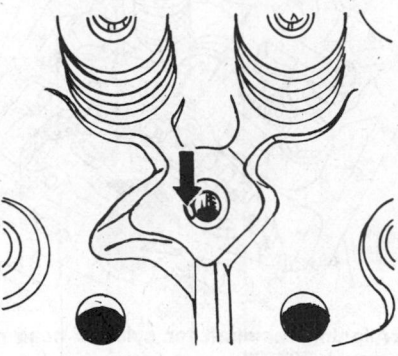

Oil feed hole in head

B21F, B23 and B230 Models

1. Disconnect the battery.

2. Remove the overflow tank cap and drain the coolant. Disconnect the upper radiator hose.

3. Remove the distributor cap and wires.

4. Remove the PCV hoses.

5. Remove the EGR valve and vacuum pump.

6. Remove the air pump, if equipped, and air injection manifold. Disconnect and remove all hoses to the turbocharger if equipped. Plug all open hoses and holes immediately.

7. Remove the exhaust manifold and header pipe bracket.

8. Remove the intake manifold. Disconnect the manifold brace and the hose clamp to the bellows for the fuel injection air/flow unit. Disconnect the throttle cable, and all vacuum hoses and electrical connectors to the fuel injection unit.

9. Remove the fuel injectors.

10. Remove the valve cover.

11. Loosen the fan shroud and remove the fan. Remove the shroud. Remove the upper belts and pulleys.

12. Remove the timing belt cover. Remove the timing belt.

13. Remove the camshaft (if so desired).

14. Remove the cylinder head 10mm Allen head bolts, and remove the cylinder head from the vehicle.

15. To install, reverse the removal procedure. Oil the head bolts. Tighten the head bolts in the prescribed torque sequence first to 44 ft. lbs., then to 81 ft. lbs. After the engine has been run 30 minutes, slacken the bolts to relieve any pretension, and then retorque to 81 ft. lbs. To set the valve timing, follow the steps for timing belt installation later in this section.

B28F and B280F

1. Disconnect the battery. Drain the coolant.

2. Remove the air cleaner assembly and all attaching hoses.

3. Disconnect the throttle cable. On automatic transmission equipped cars, disconnect the kick-down cable.

4. Disconnect the EGR vacuum hose and remove the pie between the EGR valve and manifold.

5. Remove the oil filler cap, and cover the hole with a rag. Disconnect the PCV pipe(s) from the intake manifold.

6. Remove the front section of the intake manifold.

7. Disconnect the electrical connector and fuel line at the cold start injector. Disconnect the vacuum hose, both fuel lines. and the electrical connector from the control pressure regulator.

8. Disconnect the hose, pipe, and electrical connector from the auxiliary air valve. Remove the auxiliary air valve.

9. Disconnect the electrical connector from the fuel distributor. Remove the wire loom from the intake manifolds. Disconnect the spark plug wires.

10. Disconnect the fuel injectors from their holders.

11. Disconnect the distributor vacuum hose, carbon filter hose, and diverter valve hose from the intake manifold. Also, disconnect the power brake hose and heater hose at the intake manifold.

12. Disconnect the throttle control link from it pulley.

13. On cars equipped with an EGR vacuum amplifier, disconnect the wires from the throttle micro switch and solenoid valve.

14. At the firewall, disconnect the fuel lines from the fuel filter and return line.

15. Remove the two attaching screws and lift out the fuel distributor and throttle housing assembly.

16. On cars not equipped with an EGR vacuum amplifier, disconnect the EGR valve hose from underneath the throttle housing.

17. Remove the cold start injector, rubber ring, and pipe.

18. Remove the four retaining bolts and lift off the intake manifold. Remove the rubber rings.

19. Remove the splash guard beneath the engine.

20. If removing the left cylinder head, remove the air pump from its bracket.

21. Remove the vacuum pump and O-ring in the valve cover. Remove the vacuum hose from the wax thermostat.

22. If removing the right cylinder head, disconnect the upper radiator hose.

23. On air conditioned models, remove the AC compressor and secure it to on side. Do not disconnect the refrigerant lines.

24. Disconnect the distributor leads and remove the distributor. Remove the EGR valve, bracket and pipe. At the firewall, disconnect the electrical connectors at the relays.

25. On air conditioned models, remove the rear compressor bracket.

26. Disconnect the coolant hose(s) from the water pump to the cylinder head(s). If removing the left cylinder head disconnect the lower radiator hose at the water pump.

27. Disconnect the air injection system supply hose from the applicable cylinder head. Separate the air manifold at the rear of the engine. If removing the left cylinder head, remove the backfire valve and air hose.

28. Remove the valve cover(s).

29. On the left cylinder head, remove the Allen head screw and four upper bolts to the timing gear cover. On the right cylinder head, remove the four upper bolts to the timing gear cover and the front cover plate.

30. From beneath the car, remove the exhaust pipe clamps for both header pipes.

31. If removing the right cylinder head, remove the retainer bracket bolts and pull the dipstick tube out of the crankcase.

32. Remove the applicable exhaust manifold(s).

33. Remove the cover plate at the rear of the cylinder head.

34. Rotate the camshaft sprocket (for the applicable cylinder head) into position so that the large sprocket hole aligns with the rocker arm shaft. With the camshaft in this position, loosen the cylinder head bolts in sequence (same sequence as tightening), and remove the rocker arm and shaft assembly.

35. Loosen the camshaft retaining

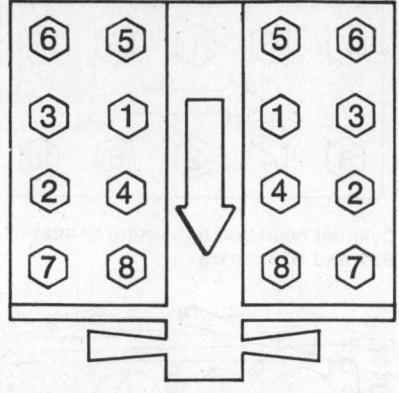

Cylinder head bolt tightening sequence, B27, B28

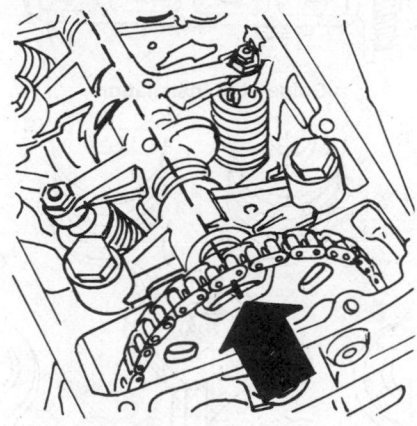

Aligning camshaft for cylinder head removal, B27, 28

fork bolt (directly in back of sprocket) and slide the fork away from the camshaft.

36. Next, it is necessary to hold the cam chain stretched during camshaft removal. Otherwise, the chain tensioner will automatically take up the slack, making it impossible to reinstall the sprocket on the cam without removing the timing chain cover to loosen the tensioner device. To accomplish this, a special sprocket retainer tool (Volvo No. 999 5104) is installed over the sprocket with two bolts in the top of the timing chain cover. A bolt is then screwed into the sprocket to hold it in place.

37. Remove the camshaft sprocket center bolt and push the camshaft to the rear, so it clears the sprocket.

38. Remove the cylinder head.

NOTE: Do not remove the cylinder head by pulling straight up. Instead, lever the head off by inserting two spare head bolts into the front and rear inboard cylinder head bolt holes, and pulling toward the applicable wheel housing. Otherwise, the cylinder liners may be pulled up, breaking the lower liner seal and leaking

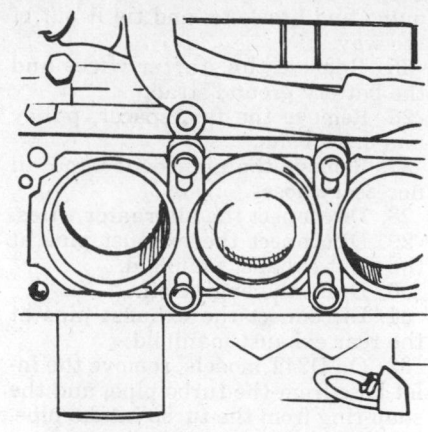

Cylinder liner holders installed

coolant into the crankcase. If any do pull up, new liner seals must be used, and the crankcase completely drained. If the head(s) seem stuck, gently tap around the edges of the head(s) with a rubber mallet, to break the joint.

39. Remove the head gasket. Clean the contact surfaces with a plastic scraper and lacquer thinner.

40. If the head is going to be off for any length of time , install liner holders (Volvo special tool No. 999 5093) or two strips of thick stock steel with holes for the head bolts, so that the liner stay pressed down against their seals. Install the holders widthwise between the middle four head bolt holes.

Reverse the above procedure to install, using the following installation notes:

a. There are a pair of guide dowels at both outboard corners of the head. If they fell down during removal, pull them back out with a puller hammer. They can be propped up with a ⅛ in. drill shank.

b. Remove the liner holders.

c. The right and left head gaskets are different.

d. Check the timing chain cover gasket. If damaged, replace only the upper section.

e. Oil the head bolt threads. Position the head on the dowels and install (hand tight) one center head bolt. Then, slide the camshaft forward into position against the sprocket and install the sprocket center bolts, and remove the retainer tool.

f. Before installing the head bolts, remove the guide dowel shanks, if used.

g. Using the correct tightening sequence, tighten the head bolts to 7 ft. lbs., then 22 ft. lbs., and then 44 ft. lbs. Next slacken the head bolts (in the tightening sequence) to relieve any pre-tension. Now, tighten

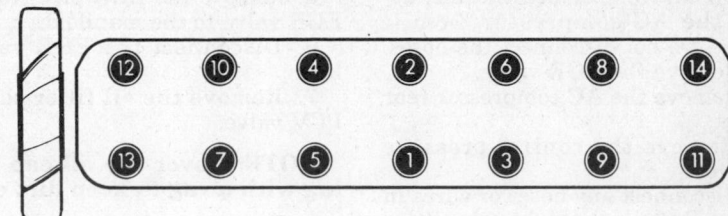

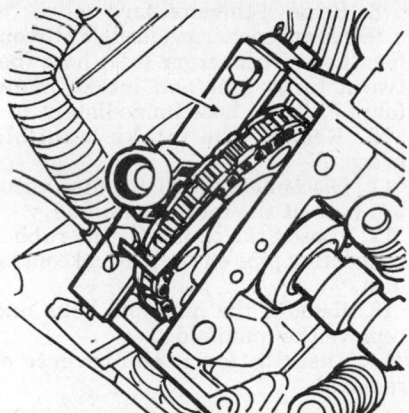

B27, 28 camshaft sprocket retainer tool

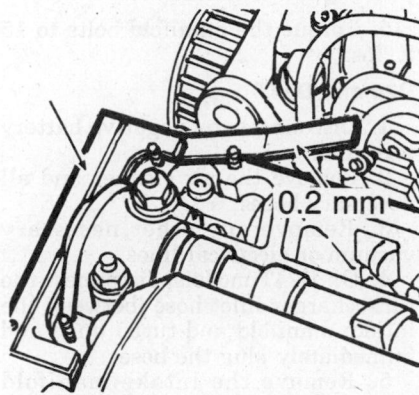

0.2 mm

Camshaft position gauge

Diesel head bolt torque sequence. Loosen bolts in reverse order starting at 14

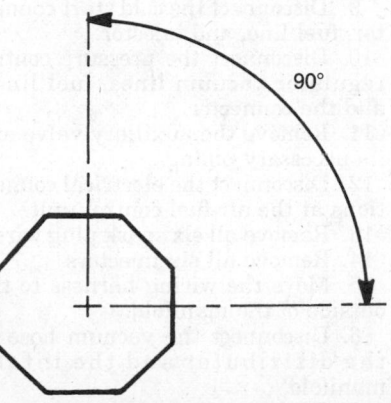

90°

Protractor (angle) torquing, 90° shown. Do not exceed specified degrees

the bolts to 11-14 ft. lbs. Finally, tighten the head bolts exactly one-third of a full 360° turn (116-120°) in the tightening sequence. This is critical for proper piston liner O-ring sealing. If necessary, use a protractor to ensure accuracy.

h. Adjust the valves after completing assembly.

i. After running the engine to operating temperature, allow to cool for 30 minutes, and retorquing the head bolts. Following the tightening sequence slacken the bolts to relieve any pre-tension, then tighten to 11-14 ft. lbs. and finally protractor torque them to 113-117° (one-third of a full turn).

D24 and D24T

1. Disconnect the negative battery terminal.
2. Remove the engine splash guard.
3. Disconnect the exhaust pipe from the transmission bracket. On D24T models, disconnect all hoses to the turbocharger, and plug any open holes.
4. Disconnect the exhaust pipe from the rear exhaust manifold.
5. Disconnect the exhaust pipe from the front exhaust manifold.

6. Remove the air cleaner and all necessary hoses.
7. Drain the radiator.
8. Remove the bottom and top radiator hoses.
9. Remove the bottom hose from the cold start device and drain it into a suitable container.
10. Remove the top cold start hose.
11. Remove the vacuum pump and the plunger.
12. Remove all the fuel lines and plug the fuel line connections.

NOTE: Carefully remove all dirt from the fuel line connections to prevent dirt from entering the system.

13. Remove the glow plug wires and temperature sender wire.
14. Remove the rear injector return line hose.
15. Remove the valve cover.
16. Remove the front and rear timing belt covers.
17. Set the engine at top dead center and the fuel pump to the injection position for the Number one cylinder.
18. Remove the timing belt shield from the head.

NOTE: Be careful not to drop the washers or bolts into the lower cover.

19. Loosen the bolts on the water pump and the belt idler pulley.
20. Remove the belt from the camshaft.

21. Use special tool No. 5199 or a suitable replacement to hold the cam gear steady while removing it.
22. Loosen the fuel pump bracket retaining screws to loosen the belt tension.
23. Remove the belt.
24. Remove the rear camshaft gear; see Step 21 for this procedure.
25. Remove the head bolts, and remove the head.
26. Installation is the reverse of removal.

NOTE: From late 1980, new type cylinder head bolts are used on the D24 diesel. They are longer and 1mm wide. Torquing these bolts is a six-step procedure:
1. Torque to 30 ft. lbs.
2. Torque to 44 ft. lbs.
3. Torque to 55 ft. lbs.
4. Tighten 180°, in one movement, without stopping.
5. Run engine until oil temperature is minimum 120°F.
6. Tighten 90°, in one movement, without stopping.

NOTE: Always use a new gasket when replacing the head.

The following special tools are needed for reinstallation of the head: Belt tension gauge no 5197, camshaft position gauge No. 5190.

OVERHAUL

For all overhaul procedures, please refer to 'Engine Rebuilding' in the Unit Repair section.

Rocker Shafts

REMOVAL & INSTALLATION
B28F and B280F

1. Disconnect the battery.
2. Remove the air cleaner assembly.
3. Disconnect the air pump bracket.
4. Remove the left valve cover (if so desired).
5. Tie the upper radiator hose out of the way and remove the oil filler cap and carbon canister hose.

6. On air conditioned models, remove the AC compressor from it bracket. Do not disconnect the hoses.

7. Remove the EGR valve.

8. Remove the AC compressor rear bracket.

9. Remove the control pressure regulator.

10. Disconnect any hoses or wires in the way. Remove the right valve cover (if so desired).

11. The rocker arm bolts double as cylinder head bolts. When loosening, follow the cylinder head bolt tightening sequence diagram. If removing both rocker shafts, mark them left and right.

NOTE: Do not jar or strike head while rockers and bolts are out, as cylinder liner O-ring seals may break, necessitating teardown of engine to clean coolant out of crankcase and installation of new seals.

12. To install, reverse removal procedure. Follow cylinder head installation procedure for proper torque sequence.

Intake Manifold

REMOVAL & INSTALLATION

Inlet Duct

1. Disconnect the negative battery cable.

2. disconnect the throttle and downshift linkage. Remove from the inlet duct, the positive crankcase ventilation, distributor advance, pressure sensor (electronic fuel injection models only) and power brake hoses.

3. On electronic fuel injected models (B21FLH, B23F), disconnect the contact for the throttle valve switch, and remove the ground cable for the inlet duct.

4. Remove the bolts for the inlet duct stay. Remove the inlet duct-to-cylinder head retaining nuts and slide the inlet duct off the studs. Discard the old gasket.

5. To install, reverse the above procedure. Use a new inlet duct gasket. Torque the nuts to 13-16 ft. lbs.

Intake Manifold

B28F and B280F

1. Disconnect the negative battery cable. Remove the air cleaner and all necessary hoses.

2. Drain the radiator coolant.

3. Remove the throttle cable from the pulley and bracket.

4. On automatic transmission cars remove the throttle cable that is connected to the transmission.

5. Remove the EGR pipe from the EGR valve to the manifold.

6. Disconnect the EGR vacuum line.

7. Remove the oil filler cap and PCV valve.

NOTE: Cover the oil cap opening with a rag to keep dirt out.

8. Remove the front manifold bolts and remove the front section of the manifold.

9. Disconnect the cold start connector, fuel line, and injector.

10. Disconnect the pressure control regulator vacuum lines, fuel lines, and the connector.

11. Remove the auxiliary valve and its necessary piping.

12. Disconnect the electrical connections at the air fuel control unit.

13. Remove all six spark plug wires.

14. Remove all six injectors.

15. Move the wiring harness to the outside of the manifold.

16. Disconnect the vacuum hose at the distributor and the intake manifold.

17. Disconnect the heater hose at the intake manifold.

18. Disconnect the hose to the diverter valve.

19. Disconnect the vacuum hose to the power brake booster.

20. Disconnect the throttle cable link.

21. Disconnect the wires to the micro switch.

22. Pull the wires away from the intake manifold.

23. Remove the fuel filter line and the return line.

24. Remove the air control unit.

25. Disconnect the vacuum hose from the throttle valve housing.

26. Remove the pipe and cold start injector assembly.

27. Remove the intake manifold from the vehicle.

28. Installation is the reverse of removal.

NOTE: Always use new gaskets when reinstalling the manifold.

29. Torque the manifold bolts to 7-11 ft. lbs.

B21, B23 and B230 Engines

1. Disconnect the negative battery cable. Remove the air cleaner and all necessary hoses.

2. Remove the PCV valve.

3. Remove the connector at the cold start injector.

4. Remove the fuel hose from the cold start injector.

5. Remove the cold start injector.

6. Remove the connector on the auxiliary valve.

7. Disconnect the hoses at the auxiliary valve.

8. Remove the auxiliary valve.

9. On turbocharged models, disconnect the turbocharger inlet hose (between turbo unit and intake manifold). Plug the hose immediately.

10. Remove the intake manifold brace.

11. Disconnect the distributor vacuum hose at the intake manifold.

12. Loosen the clamp for the rubber connecting pipe on the air-fuel control unit.

13. Remove the manifold bolts and remove the manifold.

14. Installation is the reverse of removal.

NOTE: Remember to install new manifold gaskets before replacing the manifold.

15. Torque the manifold bolts to 15 ft. lbs.

D24 and D24T

1. Disconnect the negative battery terminal.

2. Remove the air cleaner and all necessary hoses.

3. Remove any other necessary vacuum or electrical lines.

4. On D24T models, disconnect the turbocharger inlet hose (between the intake manifold and turbo unit) and immediately plug the hose.

5. Remove the intake manifold bolts and remove the manifold.

6. Installation is the reverse of removal.

NOTE: Always use a new gasket when reinstalling the intake manifold.

7. Torque the intake bolts to 18 ft. lbs.

Exhaust Manifold

REMOVAL & INSTALLATION

B28F AND B280F

Depending upon the type of optional equipment your particular vehicle has the exhaust manifolds may be removed from underneath the car.

1. Raise and support the vehicle safely.

2. Unbolt the crossover pipe from the left and right side of the exhaust manifolds, (if so equipped).

NOTE: If your car has the 'Y' type exhaust pipe disconnect this pipe at the left and right manifolds.

3. Remove any other necessary hardware.

4. Remove the left and right side manifolds.

5. Installation is the reverse of removal.

NOTE: Always use new gaskets when reinstalling the manifolds.

6. Torque the manifold bolts to 7-11 ft. lbs.

B21, B23 and B230 Engines

1. Disconnect the negative battery cable. Remove the air cleaner and all necessary hoses.
2. Remove the EGR valve pipe from the manifold.
3. Remove the exhaust pipe from the exhaust manifold. On B21FT, remove the exhaust pipe from the turbocharger.
4. Remove the manifold bolts and remove the manifold.

NOTE: Remember to install new manifold gaskets before installing the manifold.

5. Installation is the reverse of removal.
6. Torque the manifold bolts to 10-20 ft. lbs.

D24 and D24T

1. Disconnect the negative battery terminal.
2. Remove the air cleaner and all necessary hoses.
3. Remove the exhaust pipes from the manifolds. On D24T models, remove the exhaust pipe from the turbocharger.

NOTE: The exhaust manifold is made in two separate sections.

4. Remove any other necessary hardware.
5. Remove the intake manifold.
6. Remove the exhaust manifold in two sections.
7. Installation is the reverse of removal.

NOTE: Always use new gaskets when reinstalling the exhaust manifold.

8. Torque the bolts to 18 ft. lbs.

Turbocharger

For further information on turbocharging, please refer to 'Turbocharging' in the Unit Repair section.

REMOVAL & INSTALLATION

B21FT, B23FT and B230FT

1. Disconnect the battery ground cable.
2. Disconnect expansion tank from retainer. Remove expansion tank retainer.
3. Remove preheater hose to the air cleaner. Remove the pipe and rubber bellows between the air/fuel control

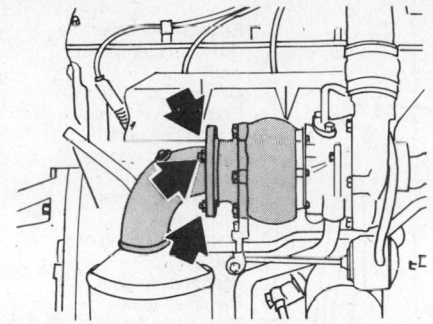
Disconnect the turbocharger unit from the exhaust system

unit and the turbocharger unit. Pull out the crankcase ventilation hose from the pipe.
4. Remove the pipe and pipe connector between the turbocharger unit and the intake manifold.

NOTE: Cover the turbocharger intake and outlet ports to keep dirt out of the system.

5. Disconnect the exhaust pipe and secure it aside.
6. Disconnect the spark plug wires at the plugs.
7. Remove the upper heat shield. Remove the brace between the turbocharger unit and the manifold.
8. Remove the lower heat shield by removing the one retaining screw underneath the manifold.
9. Remove the oil pipe clamp, retaining screws on the turbo unit and the pipe connection screw in the cylinder block under the manifold. DO NOT allow any dirt to enter the oilways.
10. Remove the manifold retaining screws and washers. Let one nut remain in position to keep the manifold in position.
11. Remove the oil delivery pipe. Cover the opening on the turbo unit.
12. Disconnect the air/fuel control unit by loosening the clamps. Move the unit with the lower section of the air cleaner up to the right side wheel housing. Place a cover over the wheel housing as protection.
13. Remove the air cleaner filter.
14. Remove the remaining nut and washer on the manifold. Lift the assembly forward and up. Remove the manifold gaskets. Disconnect the return oil pipe O-ring from the cylinder block.
15. Disconnect the turbocharger unit from the manifold.
16. Installation is the reverse of removal. Be sure to use a new gasket for the exhaust manifold and a new O-ring to the return oil pipe. Keep everything clean during assembly, and use extreme care in keeping dirt out

of the various turbo inlet and outlet pipes and hoses.

D24T

1. Remove the negative battery cable.
2. Remove the inlet hose from the turbo pipe.
3. Remove the complete air cleaner assembly, and the preheater hoses.
4. Remove the snap-ring form the turbocharger intake pipe, and remove the compressor intake pipe. Plug the hose immediately.
5. Disconnect the bolts securing the oil return pipe to the turbo unit. Move the pipe aside, and plug the holes immediately.
6. Remove the oil delivery pipe from the turbocharger and plug the holes.
7. Press the compressor pipe into the intake pipe. Remove the exhaust pipe from the turbocharger.
8. Raise and support the vehicle safely. Remove the exhaust pipe from the transmission support bracket and from the joint. Remove the exhaust pipe.
9. Remove the turbocharger securing nuts, and lower the front end of the turbo unit. Remove the turbocharger. Remove the compressor pipe.
10. If the turbocharger is replaced complete, transfer the necessary parts to the new unit. Always use new gaskets.
11. Installation is the reverse of removal. Make sure all hoses are connected without the addition of any dirt into the system. This is crucial to the life of the turbocharger and the engine.

Timing Belt Cover

REMOVAL & INSTALLATION

B21, B23 and B230 Engines

1. Disconnect the negative battery cable. Loosen the fan shroud and remove the fan. Remove the shroud.
2. Loosen the alternator, air pump, power steering pump (if so equipped), and A/C compressor (if so equipped), and remove their drive belts.
3. Remove the water pump pulley.
4. Remove the four retaining bolts and lift off the timing belt cover.
5. Reverse the above procedure to install.

D24 and D24T

1. Disconnect the negative battery cable. Drain the engine coolant.
2. Remove the splash guard under the engine. Disconnect the lower hose at the radiator. Remove the expansion tank cap.

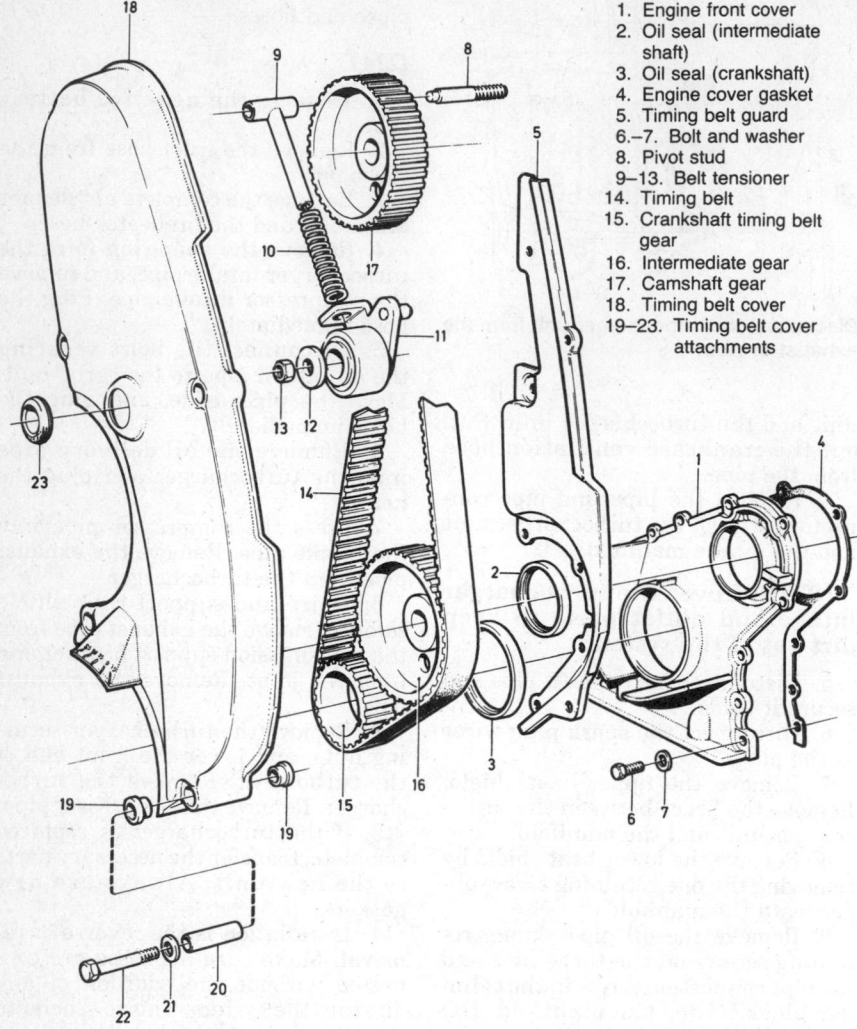

1. Engine front cover
2. Oil seal (intermediate shaft)
3. Oil seal (crankshaft)
4. Engine cover gasket
5. Timing belt guard
6.–7. Bolt and washer
8. Pivot stud
9–13. Belt tensioner
14. Timing belt
15. Crankshaft timing belt gear
16. Intermediate gear
17. Camshaft gear
18. Timing belt cover
19–23. Timing belt cover attachments

Timing belt assembly—all four cylinder engines similar

tension spring can be locked in this position by inserting the shank end of a 3mm drill through the pusher rod.

3. Remove the six retaining bolts and the crankshaft pulley.

4. Remove the belt, taking care not to bend it at any sharp angles. The belt should be replaced at 45,000 mile intervals, if it becomes oil soaked or frayed, or if it is on a car that has been sitting idle for any length of time.

5. If the crankshaft, idler shaft, or camshaft were disturbed while the belt was out, align each shaft with is corresponding index mark to assure proper valve timing and ignition timing, as follows:

   a. Rotate the crankshaft so that the notch in the convex crankshaft gear belt guide aligns with the embossed mark on the front cover (12 o'clock position).

   b. Rotate the idler shaft so that the dot on the idler shaft drive sprocket aligns with the notch on the timing belt rear cover (four o'clock position).

   c. Rotate the camshaft so that the notch in the camshaft sprocket inner belt guide aligns with the notch in the forward edge of the valve cover (12 o'clock position).

6. Install the timing belt (don't use any sharp tools) over the sprockets, and then over the tensioner roller. New belts have yellow marks. The two lines on the drive belt should fit toward the crankshaft marks. The next mark should then fit toward the intermediate shaft marks, etc. Loosen the tensioner nut and let the spring tension automatically take up the slack. Tighten the tensioner nut to 37 ft. lbs.

7. Rotate the crankshaft one full revolution clockwise, and make sure the timing marks still align.

8. Reverse Step 1-3 to install.

D24 and D24T

1. Remove the timing belt cover.
2. Set cylinder No. 1 to TDC and injection, using a 27mm ($^{11}/_{16}$ in.) socket on the vibration damper bolt to turn the engine to position for No. 1 cylinder injection. Both cam lobes should point up at equally large angles. The flywheel timing mark should be set a '0'.
3. Remove the vibration damper center bolt. It may be necessary to use Volvo special wrenches 5187 (to hold) and 5188 (to remove). The engine may have to be turned slightly to allow the holding wrench to rest temporarily on the cooling fan.
4. Check to make sure No. 1 cylinder is at TDC. If necessary, adjust the flywheel to the 0 mark.

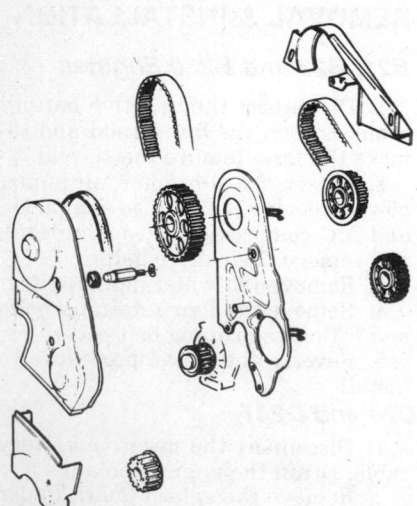

D24 Diesel timing belt cover and assembly

3. Remove the radiator.
4. Remove the cooling fan with spacer and pulley.
5. Remove the fan belt. Remove the drive belt for the power steering pump.
6. Remove the valve cover.
7. Remove the front and rear timing gear covers.
8. Installation is the reverse of removal.

Timing Belt

REMOVAL & INSTALLATION

B21, B23 and B230 Engines

1. Remove the timing belt cover.
2. To remove the tension from the belt, loosen the nut for the tensioner and press the idler roller back. The

Locking the tensioner spring with drill bit shank

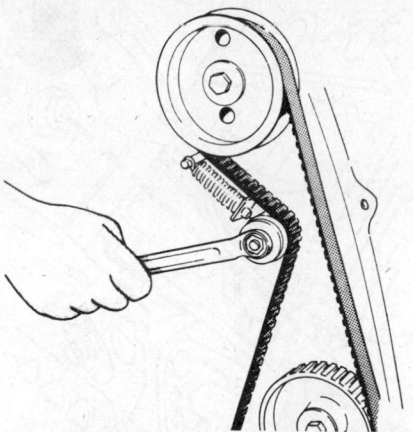

Timing belt tensioner—four cylinder engines

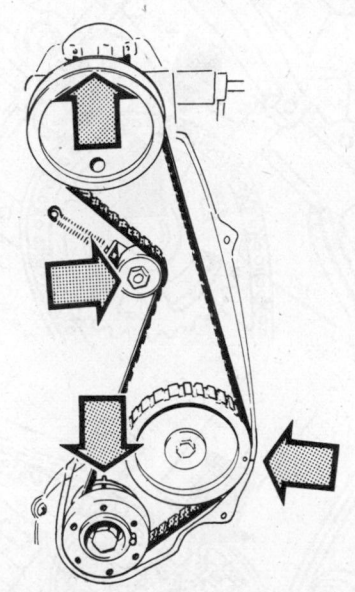

Make sure all timing marks are lined up including marks on the new belt—B21, B23 and B230 series

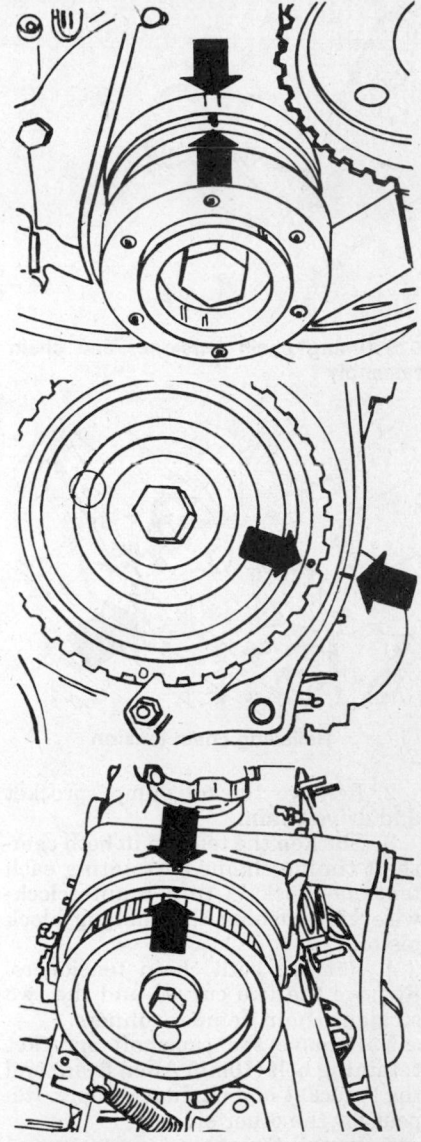

Aligning (top to bottom) crankshaft sprocket, idler shaft sprocket, and camshaft sprocket with their respective timing index marks prior to installing timing belt

5. Remove the vibration damper by removing the four 6mm Allen bolts.

NOTE: The vibration damper and the crankshaft gear may be stuck together. You may have to tap them apart.

6. Remove the camshaft gear belt by removing the lower belt shield, and releasing the retaining bolts for coolant pump.

7. Pull the gear belt straight out and off of the gears.

8. Installation is the reverse of removal.

NOTE: The idler pulley MUST be replaced when replacing the timing gear belt. Remove the center bolt using a puller. Tap the new idler pulley into position, and install the center bolt.

Timing Chain Cover

REMOVAL & INSTALLATION

B28F and B280F

1. Disconnect the negative battery cable. Remove the air cleaner and valve covers.

2. Loosen the fan shroud and remove the fan. Remove the shroud.

3. Loosen the alternator, air pump, power steering pump, and A/C compressor (if so equipped) and remove their drive belts.

4. Block the flywheel from turning, remove the crankshaft pulley nut (36mm) and the pulley.

NOTE: Do not drop the pulley key into the crankcase.

5. Remove the power steering pump and place to one side. Remove the pump bracket.

6. Remove the timing chain cover retaining bolts (25 11mm hex bolts), tap and remove the cover.

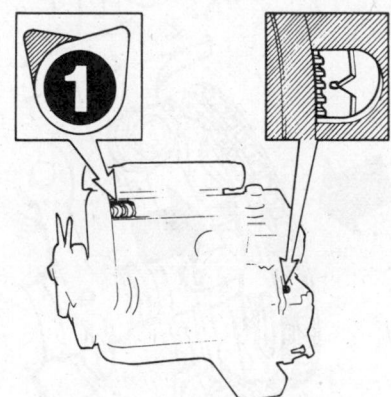

Setting No. 1 cylinder to TDC and injection position—D24. Cam lobes are "up", flywheel on 0

7. Clean the gasket contact surfaces. Place the upper gasket on the cover and the lower gasket on the block. Install the cover and tighten to 7-11 ft lbs. Trim the gaskets flush with the valve cover.

8. Install a new crankshaft seal.

9. Block the flywheel, install the pulley, (and key) and tighten the 36mm nut to 118-132 ft lbs.

10. Reverse Steps 1-5 to install.

Timing Chain

REMOVAL & INSTALLATION

B28F and B280F

1. Remove the timing chain cover.

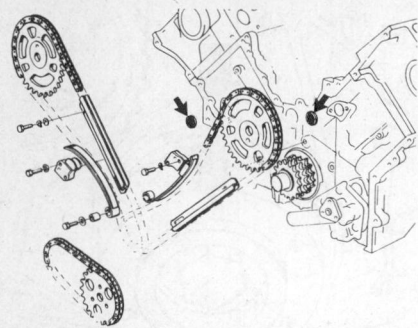

B28 timing chain tensioner and chain assembly

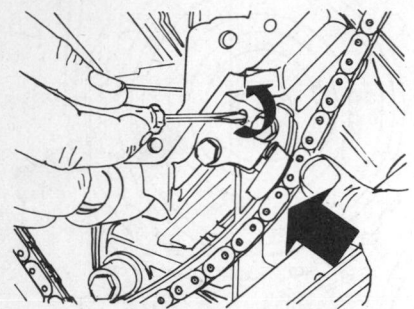

Relieving chain tension

2. Remove the oil pump sprocket and drive chain.

3. Slacken the tension in both camshaft timing chains by rotating each tensioner lock ¼ turn counterclockwise and pushing the rubbing block piston.

4. Remove both chain tensioners. Remove the two curved and the two straight chain damper/runners.

5. Remove the camshaft sprocket retaining bolt (10mm Allen head) and the sprocket and chain assembly. Repeat for the other side.

6. Install the chain tensioners and tighten to 5 ft. lbs. Install the curved chain damper/runners and tighten to 7-11 ft. lbs. Install the straight chain damper/runners and torque to 5 ft. lbs.

7. First install the left (driver) side camshaft sprocket and chain. Rotate the crankshaft (use crankshaft nut, if necessary) until No. 1 cylinder is at TDC. At this point, the crankshaft key is pointing directly to the left side camshaft, and the left side camshaft key groove is pointing straight up (12 o'clock). Place the chain on the left side sprocket so that the sprocket notchmark is centered precisely between the two white lines on the chain. Position the chain on the crankshaft sprocket (inner), making sure that the other white line on the chain aligns with the crankshaft sprocket notch. While holding the left side chain and sprockets in this position, install the sprocket and chain on the left side camshaft (chain stretched

Left side camshaft timing chain installation sequence—V6 engines

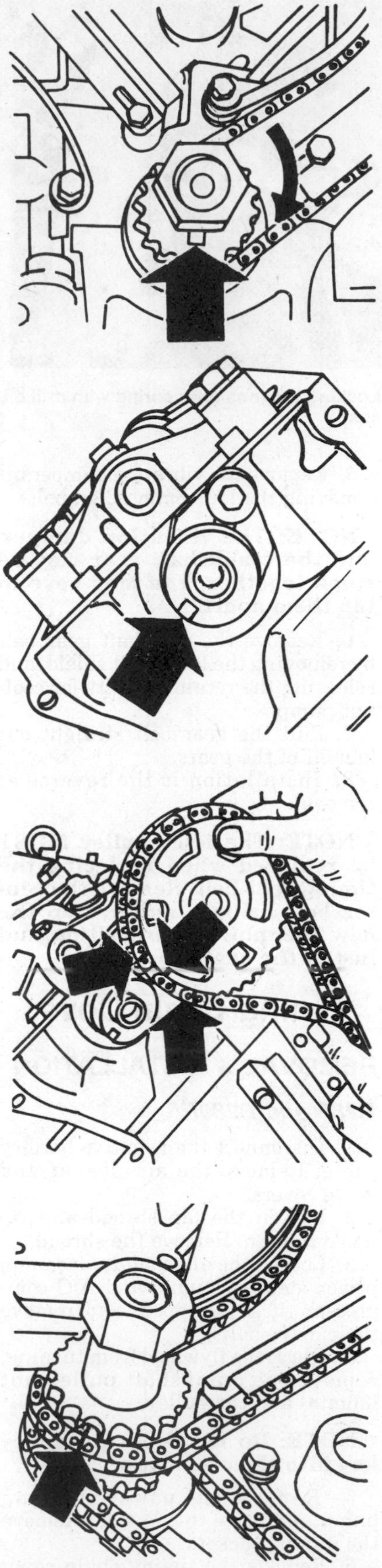

Right side camshaft timing chain installation sequence

on tension side) so that the sprocket pin fits into the camshaft recess. Tighten the sprocket center bolt to 51-59 ft. lbs. (use screwdriver to keep cam from turning).

8. To install the right side camshaft sprocket and chain, rotate the crankshaft clockwise until the crankshaft key points staight down (6 o'clock). Align the camshaft key groove so that it is pointing halfway between the 8 and 9 o'clock positions (at this position, the No. 6 cylinder rocker arms will rock). Place the chain on the right side sprocket so that the sprocket notchmark is centered precisely between the two white lines on the chain. Then, position the chain on the middle crankshaft sprocket, making sure that the other white line aligns with the crankshaft sprocket notch. Install the sprocket and chain on the camshaft so that the sprocket notch fits into the camshaft recess. Tighten the sprocket nut to 51-59 ft. lbs.

9. Rotate the chain tensioners ¼ turn clockwise each. The chains are tensioned by rotating the crankshaft two full turns clockwise. Recheck to make sure the alignment marks coincide.

10. Install the oil pump sprocket and chain.

11. Install the timing chain cover.

Camshaft

REMOVAL & INSTALLATION

B21, B23 and B230 Engines

1. Remove the timing belt cover.
2. Remove the valve cover.
3. Remove the camshaft center bearing cap. Install special camshaft press tool (Volvo No. 5021) over the center bearing journal to hold the camshaft in place while removing the other bearing caps.
4. Remove the four remaining bearing caps.
5. Remove the seal from the forward edge of the camshaft.
6. Release camshaft press tool, and lift out the camshaft.
7. Reverse the above procedure to install. Make sure the camshaft and followers are well oiled before installation.

B28F and B280F

1. Remove the cylinder head.
2. Remove the camshaft rear cover plate.
3. Remove the camshaft retaining fork at the front of the cylinder head.
4. Pull the camshaft out the rear of the head.
5. Reverse the above to install. Oil

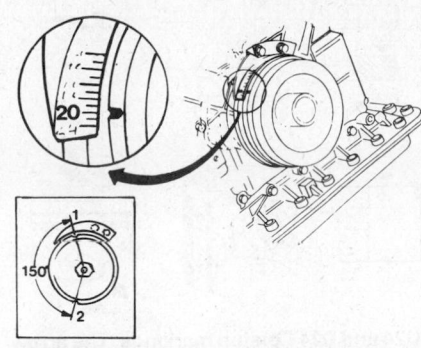

B28F static timing. Rotate the crankshaft until the engine is approximately 20° B.T.D.C. on cylinder 1. The pulley has two marks: "1" is T.D.C. for cylinder No. 1; "2" is T.D.C. for cylinder No. 6. The marks are 150° apart.

Four cylinder camshaft press tool installed

the camshaft and followers before installation.

D24 and D24T
TIMING GEAR

NOTE: This is the timing gear removal procedure. Camshaft removal follows.

1. disconnect the negative battery terminal.
2. Drain the radiator.
3. Remove the expansion tank hose.
4. Remove the top and bottom radiator hoses.
5. Remove the fan with the spacer and pulley.
6. Remove all the drive belts.
7. Remove the valve cover.
8. Remove the timing gear belt cover.
9. Set the No. 1 cylinder to TDC.

NOTE: This is accomplished by turning the crankshaft pulley with an ¹¹/₁₆ in. socket. The flywheel timing mark should be set at '0'.

10. Remove the crankshaft pulley bolt.

11. Remove the four Allen head bolts in the center of the pulley and remove the pulley.

NOTE: The pulley and the crankshaft gear may be stuck together. Gently tap them apart with a rubber hammer.

12. Remove the lower belt shield.
13. Loosen and remove the timing belt.
14. Remove the front camshaft gear.

NOTE: Use Volvo tool No. 5199 or another suitable tool to prevent the camshaft from turning.

15. Remove the rear timing belt cover.
16. Loosen the injection pump bracket to release tension from the injection pump drive belt.
17. Remove the timing belt.
18. Remove the rear camshaft gear.

NOTE: See Step 14 for this procedure.

19. Installation is the reverse of removal.

The following torque specifications are needed: Front camshaft gear 33 ft. lbs., rear camshaft gear 73 ft. lbs., crankshaft pulley 330 ft. lbs., crankshaft pulley Allen bolts 15 ft. lbs.

CAMSHAFT

1. Follow the procedure for the camshaft gear removal.
2. Remove the first and fourth bearing caps.
3. Remove the second and third bearing caps.

NOTE: Loosen the bearing cap nuts on an alternating basis to prevent cam distortion.

4. Remove the camshaft and discard the seals.
5. Installation is the reverse of removal, with the following suggestions.

   a. When reinstalling the cam you must use special tool No. 5190 available from your Volvo dealer.

   b. Place grease on the oil seal lips before installation. The seals must be driven into place with Volvo tool No. 5200 or a suitable substitute.

   c. Torque the cam bearing caps to 15 ft. lbs.

   d. The second and third bearing caps should be installed first.

Pistons and Connecting Rods

For all piston and connecting rod overhaul procedures, please refer to 'Engine Rebuilding' in the Unit Repair section.

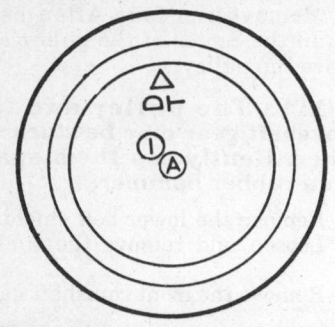

B27, 28 piston positioning. Arrowhead faces forward

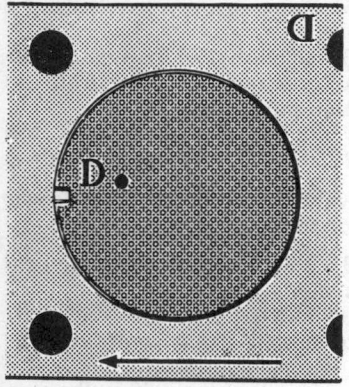

B21F series piston positioning. Notch faces forward

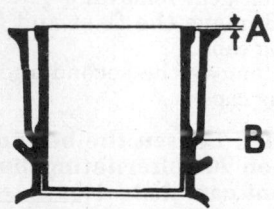

Correct B27, 28 piston liner height "A" above block face is 0.0091 in. Shims are available for installation at point "B" and should be uniform for all cylinders

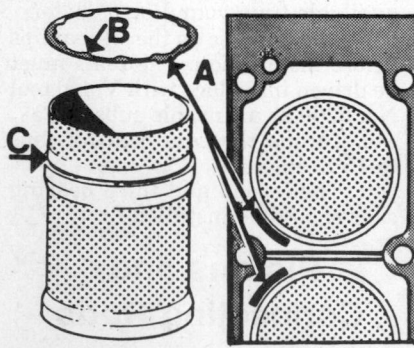

When installing B27 and B28 liner shims, color marking "A" must face up and be positioned where shown. Inside tabs "B" fit into liner groove

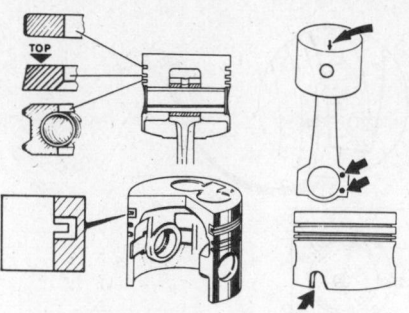

D24 and D24T piston markings. The arrow on the piston crown and marks on the con rod big-end denote the front of the engine (must be facing front). The lower compression ring is marked with the word "TOP" to indicate this side must face up.

POSITIONING

On all engines, the notch or arrow stamped on top of the piston must face the front of the engine. On the B21 the connecting rod marking must face the front of the engine.

ENGINE LUBRICATION

Oil Pan

REMOVAL & INSTALLATION

B21, B23 and B230 Engines

1. Disconnect the negative battery cable. Raise and support the vehicle safely.
2. Drain the engine oil.
3. Remove the splash guard.
4. Remove the engine mount retaining nuts.
5. Remove the lower bolt and loosen the top bolt on the steering column yoke.
6. Slide the yoke assembly up on the steering shaft.
7. Jack up the front of the engine.
8. Remove the retaining bolts for the front axle crossmember.
9. Remove the crossmember.
10. Remove the left engine mount.
11. Remove the pan support bracket.
12. Remove the pan bolts and remove the pan.
13. Installation is the reverse of removal.

NOTE: Always use a new pan gasket when reinstalling the pan.

The following torque specifications are needed: Pan bolts 8 ft. lbs. Steering yoke lower bolt, 18 ft. lbs.

B28F and B280F

1. Disconnect the negative battery cable. Remove the splash guard.
2. Drain the crankcase.
3. Remove the oil pan retaining bolts. Swivel the pan past the stabilizer bar and remove.
4. Reverse the above to install.

D24 and D24T

In order to remove the oil pan from the vehicle the engine must be remove first. After engine removal be sure that the engine is positioned in a suitable holding fixture.

Rear Main Oil Seal

REMOVAL & INSTALLATION

D24 and D24T

1. Disconnect the negative battery terminal.
2. Remove the transmission.
3. Remove all but one starter bolt to keep it from falling out.
4. Remove the clutch and pressure plate assembly (if so equipped).
5. Remove the pilot bearing.
6. Remove the flywheel.

NOTE: Use special tool No. 5112 or a suitable replacement to keep the flywheel from turning while removing the bolts.

7. Remove the oil seal with a suitable tool.
8. Check the contact surfaces on the seal holder and crankshaft.
9. Installation is the reverse of removal. When reinstalling a new seal use special tool No. 5208 available from Volvo or a suitable replacement. Coat the seal with oil before installation. Torque the flywheel bolts to 55 ft. lbs. Use a liquid sealer (Loctitek or similar product) on the bolts prior to installing them.

B28F and B280F

1. Disconnect the negative battery terminal.
2. Remove the transmission.
3. Remove the clutch and pressure plate (if so equipped).
4. Remove the flywheel (drive plate on automatic transmissions).

Pan support bracket—B21 and B23 series engines (view from under car)

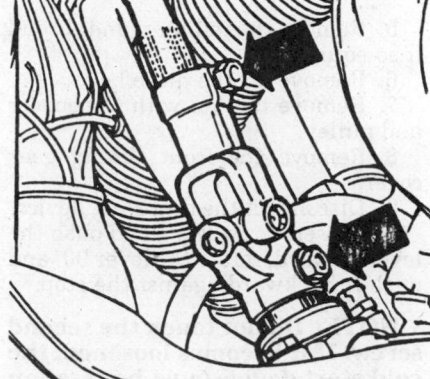

Steering yoke removal; arrows indicate retaining nuts

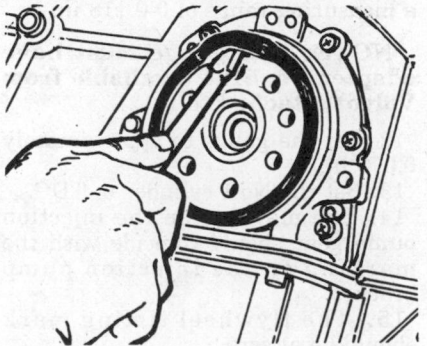

Removing diesel crankshaft rear oil seal

NOTE: On automatic transmissions remove the crankshaft spacer.

5. Remove the two rear pan bolts.
6. Remove the bolts in the seal housing and then the housing.

NOTE: Gently remove the housing so as not to damage the oil pan gasket.

7. Use special tool No. 5107 to remove the old seal and install the new one. This tool is available from Volvo or use a suitable replacement.
8. Installation is the reverse of removal. The following torque specifica-

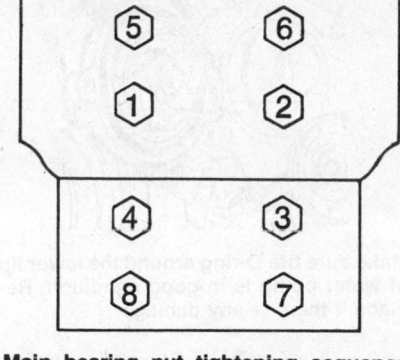

Main bearing nut tightening sequence, B27, B28

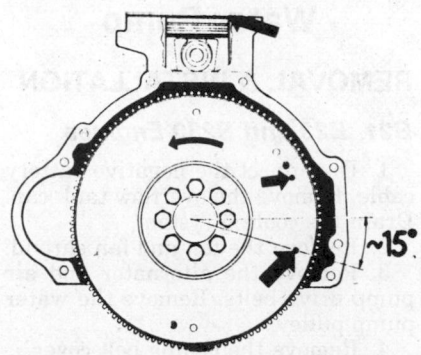

Flywheel installation—B21, B23 and B230 series

tions are needed: Flywheel 33-37 ft. lbs., Seal housing 7-11 ft. lbs.

B21, B23 and B230 Engines

1. Disconnect the negative battery terminal.
2. Remove the transmission.
3. Remove the clutch and pressure plate (if so equipped).
4. Remove the pilot bearing snapring and remove the bearing.
5. Remove the flywheel or driveplate which ever is applicable.

NOTE: Be careful not to press in the activator pins for the timing device.

6. Remove the rear oil pan brace.
7. Remove the two center bolts from the pan that bolt into the seal housing.
8. Loosen two bolts on either side of the two in the seal housing.
9. Remove the six seal housing bolts, and remove the seal housing.

NOTE: Be careful not to damage the oil pan gasket when removing the seal housing.

10. Remove the seal using special tool No. 2817 or a suitable replacement.
11. Installation is the reverse of removal.

NOTE: Use a new gasket on the seal housing and coat the seal with oil prior to installation.

Torque the flywheel to 47-54 ft. lbs. When installing the flywheel turn the crankshaft to bring the No. 1 piston to TDC. The lower flywheel pin should be installed approximately 15° from the horizontal and opposite the starter. Install the bolts.

Oil Pump

REMOVAL & INSTALLATION

B21, B23 and B230 Engines

1. Remove the oil pan.
2. Remove the two oil pump retaining bolts, and pull the delivery tube from the block.
3. When installing, use new sealing rings at either end of the delivery tube. Also, make sure you 'prime' the pump (remove all air) by filing it with clean engine oil and operating the pump by hand, before installaton.

B28F and B280F

The oil pump body is cast integrally with the cylinder block. It is chain driven by a separate sprocket on the crankshaft and is located behind the timing chain cover. The pick-up screen and tube are serviced by removing the oil pan. To check the pump gears or remove the oil pump cover:

1. Disconnect the negative battery cable. Remove the air cleaner and valve covers.
2. Loosen the fan shroud and remove the fan. Remove the shroud.
3. Loosen the alternator, air pump, power steering pump, and AC compressor (if so equipped) and remove their drive belts.
4. Block the flywheel from turning, and remove the 36mm bolt and the crankshaft pulley.

NOTE: Do not drop key into crankcase.

5. Remove the timing gear cover (25 bolts).
6. Remove the oil pump drive sprocket and chain.
7. Remove the oil pump cover, and gears.
8. Reverse the removal procedure to install. Prime the pump (remove all air) by filling it with clean engine oil and operating the pump by hands, before installation.

D24 and D24T

1. Remove the engine from the car.
2. Remove the oil pan and the oil suction pipe.

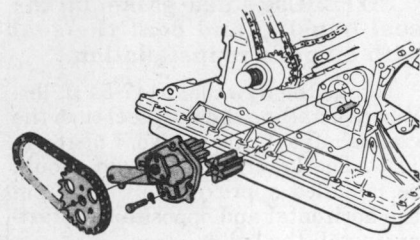

B28F oil pump installation—B27 similar

3. Remove the front timing belt cover, timing belt, vibration damper, and lower timing belt cover.

NOTE: Do not allow the crankshaft to turn when disconnected from the camshaft. If this should happen the fuel injection timing must be reset.

4. Remove the crankshaft gear and seal with a puller.
5. Remove the timing belt inner shield.
6. Remove the oil pump bolts and remove the pump.

NOTE: The oil pump can not be repaired. It must be replaced as a unit.

7. When installing the oil pump the triangular mark on the pump outer gear must face the oil pump rear cover.
8. Installation is the reverse of removal. Fill the oil pump with clean engine oil and 'prime' the pump by operating it by hand prior to installation.

ENGINE COOLING

Radiator

REMOVAL & INSTALLATION

1. Disconnect the negative battery cable. Remove the radiator and expansion tank caps, disconnect the lower radiator hose, and drain the cooling system.
2. Remove the expansion tank and hose, and drain the coolant. Remove the upper radiator hose. On cars with automatic transmission, disconnect and plug the transmission oil cooler lines at the radiator.
3. Remove the retaining bolts for the radiator and fan shroud, if so equipped, and lift out the radiator.
4. Installation is the reverse of the

Make sure the O-ring around the lower lip of water pump is in good condition. Replace if there is any damage

removal procedure. Start the engine and check for leaks.

Water Pump

REMOVAL & INSTALLATION

B21, B23 and B230 Engines

1. Disconnect the negative battery cable. Remove the overflow tank cap. Drain the cooling system.
2. Remove the fan and fan shroud.
3. Remove the alternator and air pump drive belts. Remove the water pump pulley.
4. Remove the timing belt cover.
5. Remove the lower radiator hose.
6. Remove the retaining bolt for the coolant pipe (beneath exhaust manifold) and pull the pipe rearward.
7. Remove the six retaining bolts and lift off the water pump.
8. Clean the gasket contact surfaces thoroughly, and use a new gasket and O-rings (especially between the cylinder head and top of water pump).
9. Installation is the reverse of the removal procedure.

B28F and B280F

1. Disconnect the negative battery cable. Remove the front and main sections of the intake manifold.
2. Remove the overflow tank cap and drain the cooling system.
3. disconnect both radiator hoses. On automatic transmission cars, disconnect the transmission cooler lines at the radiator. Disconnect the fan shroud. Remove the radiator and fan shroud.
4. Remove the fan.
5. Remove the hoses from the water pump to each cylinder head.
6. Remove the fan belts. Remove the water pump pulley.
7. Loosen the hose clamps at the rear of the water pump.
8. Remove the water pump from the block (three bolts).
9. Transfer the thermal time lender and temperature sensor to the new water pump.

10. Transfer the thermostat cover, thermostat, and rear pump cover to the new pump.
11. Reverse the removal procedure to install.

D24 and D24T

1. Disconnect the negative battery cable. Drain the radiator.
2. Remove the splash guard shield from under the engine.
3. Remove the expansion tank.
4. Remove the top and bottom radiator hoses.

NOTE: On cars with automatic transmissions remove the cooler lines from the radiator.

5. Remove the radiator (and shroud if so equipped).
6. Remove all the drive belts.
7. Remove the fan with the spacer and pulley.
8. Remove the front timing gear cover.
9. Disconnect the cold start device.
10. Loosen screw No. 1 and push the lever forward, rotate the lever 90° and push it backward against the stop.

NOTE: Do not touch the second screw. If it becomes loosened, the cold start device must be reset on a test bench.

11. Remove the injection pump plug and install a dial indicator gauge with a measuring range of 0-0.118 in.

NOTE: This gauge must have adapter No. 5194 (available from Volvo) attached to it.

12. Set the gauge to approximately 0.078 in.
13. Set the No.1 cylinder to TDC.
14. The marking on the injection pump gear should coincide with the marking on the injection pump bracket.
15. The flywheel timing mark should be at zero.
16. Turn the engine ¼ turn past zero and then back to zero again. This is done in order to place slack in the timing belt on the drive side. Otherwise the engine setting would be incorrect.

NOTE: The gauge must not move during the remainder of the work. If it does the engine must be completely retimed.

17. Loosen the water pump bolts to release the belt tension.
18. Remove the timing bolt from the camshaft gear.
19. Remove the camshaft gear.
20. Remove the vibration damper.
21. Remove the lower belt guard.
22. Loosen the bracket for the fan and alternator.

23. Remove the lower retaining bolt and move the bracket away from the engine.
24. Remove the inner belt shield and water pump.
25. Installation is the reverse of removal.

NOTE: Grease the O-ring before installing it in the water pump.

The following torque specifications are needed. Vibration damper screws 15 ft. lbs., crankshaft center bolt 255 ft. lbs., camshaft gear 33 ft. lbs., pump setting 0.0256-0.0287 in.

Thermostat

REMOVAL & INSTALLATION

1. Disconnect the lower radiator hose and drain the cooling system.
2. Remove the two bolts securing the thermostat housing to the cylinder head and carefully lift the housing free.

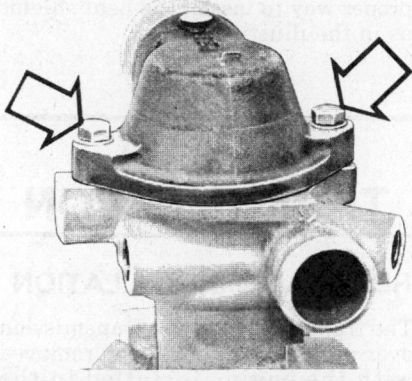

Remove the two top water pump bolts for access to the V6 thermostat

3. Remove all old gasket material from the mating surfaces and remove the thermostat.
4. Test the operation of the thermostat by immersing it in a container of heated water. Replace any thermostat that does not open at the correct temperature.
5. Place the thermostat, with a new gasket, in the cylinder head. Fit the thermostat housing to the head and hand-tighten the two bolts until snug. Do not tighten the bolts more than ¼ turn past snug.
6. Connect the lower radiator hose and replace the coolant.

COOLING SYSTEM BLEEDING

1. Fill the radiator with the proper type of coolant.
2. With the radiator cap off, start

the engine and allow it to run and reach normal operating temperature.
3. Run the heater at full force and with the temperature lever in the hot position. Be sure that the heater control valve is functioning.
4. Shut the engine off and recheck the coolant level, refill as necessary.

EMISSION CONTROLS

Please refer to "Emission Control" in the Unit Repair section for system maintenance procedures. Due to the complex nature of modern electronic engine control system, comprehensive diagnosis and testing procedures fall outside the confines of this repair manual. For complete information on diagnosis, testing and repair procedures concerning all modern engine and emission control systems, please refer to *"Chilton's Guide to Electronic Engine Controls".*

GASOLINE FUEL SYSTEM

NOTE: All Volvos manufactured for sale in the U.S. are equipped with fuel injection. One Canadian engine, the B21A, is equipped with a one-barrel carburetor.

Fuel Filter

REMOVAL & INSTALLATION

1. Loosen the fuel cap.
2. Clean the filter connections carefully before removing.
3. Disconnect the nipples and remove the seals.
4. Remove the filter and clamp.
5. Transfer the nipples and clamp to the new filter.

NOTE: Fuel flow direction arrow is marked on the new (and old) filter. Arrow follows direction from fuel tank to engine.

Fuel Pump

REMOVAL & INSTALLATION

1. Disconnect the negative battery cable. Remove the filler cap. Remove the electrical lead from the pump as well as the template to which the pump is mounted.
2. Clean around the hose connections. Pinch shut the fuel lines, loosen the hose clamps, and disconnect the lines.
3. Loosen the retaining nuts and remove the pump from its rubber mounts.
4. Install the new pump on its rubber mounts and tighten the retaining nuts.
5. Reconnect the fuel lines, tighten the hose clamps, and remove the pinchers.
6. Mount the template beneath the car and connect the electrical lead.
7. Start the engine and check for leaks.

Carburetor

REMOVAL & INSTALLATION

1. Disconnect the negative battery cable.
2. Remove the air cleaner. Remove all necessary components in order to gain access to the carburetor retaining bolts.
3. Remove all linkages, as required.
4. Disconnect the fuel line using the proper tools.
5. Remove the carburetor retaining bolts. Remove the carburetor from the vehicle.
6. Installation is the reverse of the removal procedure.

OVERHAUL

For all carburetor overhaul procedures, please refer to 'Carburetor Service' in the Unit Repair section.

Fuel Injection

Due to the complex nature of modern fuel injection systems, comprehensive diagnosis and testing procedures fall outside the confines of this repair manual. For complete information on fuel injection diagnosis, testing and repair procedures please refer to *Chilton's Guide To Fuel Injection And Feedback Carburetors.*

DIESEL FUEL SYSTEM

Fuel Filter

REPLACEMENT

The fuel filter must be drained every 7,500 miles. Place a drain pan under the drain screw to collect the condensate. Loosen the bleeder screw several turns. Loosen the drain screw and drain until clean fuel flows out. Tighten the drain screw and the bleeder screw.

Diesel Injection Pump

REMOVAL & INSTALLATION

NOTE: Several special tools are needed to remove and install the pump and to set its timing. If these tools are not available, do not attempt to remove the pump. The tool numbers (Volvo part numbers) are given in the procedure.

1. Pinch off and remove the two coolant hoses running to the cold-start device on the fuel pump.
2. Disconnect the accelerator linkage at the pump and disconnect the wire from the stop valve on the top of the pump.
3. Remove the rear timing belt cover and thoroughly clean the fuel lines, and their connections at the injection pump.
4. Disconnect the fuel lines at the pump and plug the open connections to prevent dirt from entering the fuel system.
5. Remove the vacuum pump and its plunger.
6. Clean and remove the delivery lines at the fuel injectors. Plug all connections.
7. Set cylinder No. 1 to TDC on the injection stroke. At this position, the O mark on the flywheel aligns with the pointer and the notch on the injection pump pulley aligns with the notch on the pump housing. Both valves on No. 1 cylinder are closed and their camshaft lobes are pointing up at equally large angles.
8. Loosen the retaining bolts for the injection pump and push the pump up, then remove the pump drive belt. Tighten one bolt to hold the pump in the upper position.
9. Loosen the center bolt in the rear camshaft gear while using wrench No. 5199 to the gear. The bolts will be

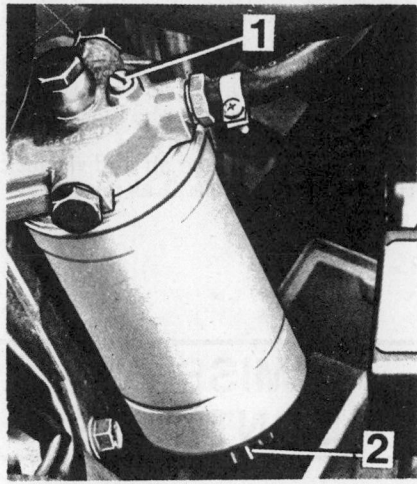

Diesel fuel filter service location. #1 is bleeder screw, #2 is drain

easily accessible if wrench No. 5201 is used.

NOTE: The camshaft must not rotate. Loosen the bolt only enough to rotate the gear on the camshaft.

10. Insert pin No. 5193 into the injection pump gear to lock it in position and remove the injection pump gear nut.
11. With the pin still in position, use a puller to remove the pump gear.
12. Remove the bolts retaining the front injection pump bracket to the engine, then remove the hex screws retaining the pump and remove the pump from the engine.
13. Install the pump on the engine and tighten the bolts only finger-tight so that pump position can be adjusted.
14. Set the injection pump so that the mark on pump and the pump bracket align, then tighten the retaining bolts.
15. Make sure the shaft key is correctly installed and install the injection pump gear, washer and nut. Use pin No. 5193 to hold the gear while tightening the nut.
16. Proceed to 'Setting the Injection Pump Timing', below.
17. After the injection pump timing is set, fill the pump with clean diesel fuel through the fuel line connection only if a new fuel pump is being installed or if the old pump was drained and rebuilt.
18. Install the rear timing gear cover. Connect the fuel lines and fuel delivery pipes. Tighten the fuel delivery line cap nuts and the fuel line banjo bolts to 18 ft. lbs. When installing the fuel line on the pump, do not mix the banjo bolts; the bolt for the fuel return line has a small hole in it and is marked OUT.

19. Install the vacuum pump and all remaining components in the reverse order of removal. Adjust the accelerator linkage.

Diesel Fuel Injectors

REMOVAL & INSTALLATION

1. Thoroughly clean the fuel delivery line connections around each fitting before removing.
2. Unscrew each fitting from its injector. Plug or tape the end of each fitting to prevent any dirt or grit from entering the fuel system.
3. Using a box-end wrench, unscrew the injector form the cylinder head. Remove the small heat shield and discard. Use care not to damage any part of the injector (especially the nozzle tip) while it is out of the engine. Plug each injector hole in the head with a piece of clean rag to prevent dirt from entering.
4. Installation is the reverse of removal. Be sure to use new heat shields with each injector. Note the proper way to install the heat shields as in the illustration.

MANUAL TRANSMISSION

REMOVAL & INSTALLATION

The transmission or the transmission over-drive assembly may be removed with the engine installed in the vehicle.

240 and 260 Models

1. Disconnect the battery. At the firewall, disconnect the back-up light connector.
2. Jack up the front of the car and install jack stands. Loosen the set screw and drive out the pin for the shifter rod. Disconnect the shift lever from the rod.
3. Inside the car, pull up the shift boot. Remove the fork for the reverse gear detent. Remove the snap-ring and lift up the shifter. If overdrive-equipped, disconnect the engaging switch wire.
4. On 240 series models, disconnect the clutch cable and return spring at the throw-out fork and flywheel housing. On 260 series models, remove the bolts retaining the slave cylinder to the flywheel housing the tie the cylinder back out of the way (do not disconnect).
5. Disconnect the exhaust pipe

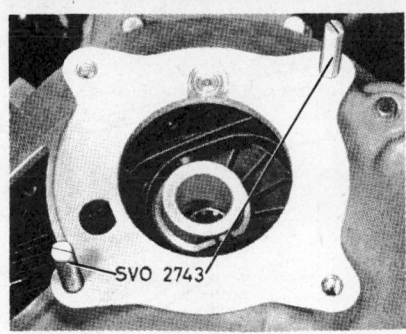

Transmission guide pins installed

bracket(s) from the flywheel cover. Remove the oil pan splash guard.

6. Using a floor jack and a block of wood, support the engine beneath the oil pan. Remove the transmission support crossmember.

7. Disconnect the driveshaft. Disconnect the speedometer cable. If so equipped, disconnect the overdrive wire.

8. Remove the starter retaining bolts and pull free of the flywheel housing.

9. Support the transmission using another floor jack. Remove the flywheel (bell) housing-to-engine bolts and remove the transmission.

10. Reverse Steps 1-9 to install. Tighten the flywheel housing-to-engine bolts to 25-35 ft. lbs.

740, 760 and 780 Models

1981-85

1. Disconnect the battery ground cable.

2. Remove the ash tray and holder assembly. Remove the trim box around the gear shift lever.

3. Disconnect the shift lever cover from the floor. Remove the snap-ring at the base of the shift lever.

4. Jack up the car and safely support it with jackstands. From underneath the car, disconnect the gear shift rod at the gear shift lever. Remove the lock screw, and press out the pivot pin. Push up on the shift lever, and pull it up and out of the car.

5. Matchmark the driveshaft and transmission flanges for later assembly. Disconnect the driveshaft from the transmission.

6. Separate the exhaust pipe at the joint under the car. Detach the bracket from the front end of the exhaust pipe (near the bend).

7. Unbolt the transmission crossmember; at the same time, detach it from the rear support (rubber bushing).

8. Remove the rear support from the transmission.

9. Tag and disconnect the electrical connectors from the overdrive, back-up light connector and the solenoid.

10. Cut the plastic clamp at the gear shift assembly for the wiring harness.

11. Remove the starter motor retaining bolts. On models with the B28F V6, remove the cover plate under the bellhousing and the cover plate for the other starter motor opening.

12. On B28F models (hydraulic clutch), remove the slave cylinder from the bellhousing and upper bolts holding the bellhousing. On D24T models, (mechanical clutch), detach the clutch cable from the release fork and the bellhousing.

13. Place a transmission jack or a standard hydraulic floor jack underneath the gearbox (center section) of the transmission so that the transmission is resting on the jack pad. Remove the lower bolts holding the bellhousing, and carefully lower the transmission a few inches as you roll it back so the input shaft will clear. Stop the jack and make sure all wires and linkage are disconnected, then lower the transmission the rest of the way.

14. Reverse the above procedure for removal, making note of the following: use a plastic cable tie to secure the wiring harness to the gear shift assembly where the original plastic clamp was cut. Adjust clutch clearance on D24T models to 1-3mm (0.004-0.012 in.) between the release fork and bearing. When sliding the transmission into place make sure the release bearing is correctly positioned in the shift fork, and that the input shaft is aligned in the clutch disc. Adjust the shifter.

1986-88

1. Disconnect the negative battery cable.

2. Attach a lifting beam, Volvo tool No. 5006, to the rear of the engine. This will support the engine once the transmission is removed.

3. Raise and support the vehicle safely.

4. disconnect the driveshaft at the transmission flange.

5. Disconnect the support bearing for the driveshaft at the crossmember.

6. Remove the driveshaft from the vehicle.

7. disconnect the exhaust system at the muffler.

8. Loosen the lock screw at the shifter assembly. Remove the pin through the gear shift lever. Remove the lock pin ring. Push the gear shift lever up.

9. Remove the transmission crossmember and bracket. Cut the wire straps and disconnect the wires at the transmission.

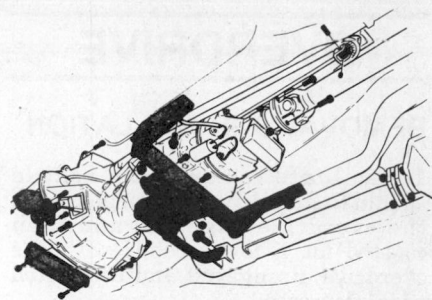

760 GLE manual transmission mounting—740 series similar

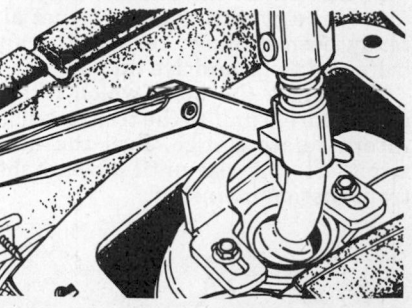

Reverse gear detent clearance adjustment—manual transmission models

10. Disconnect the clutch cable at the clutch slave cylinder.

11. Disconnect the exhaust system attachment at the transmission cover.

12. Position a transmission jack under the transmission assembly. Remove the transmission to engine retaining bolts. Remove the transmission from the vehicle.

13. Installation is the reverse of the removal procedure.

14. Be sure to fill the unit with the proper type fluid. Adjust the clutch as required.

LINKAGE ADJUSTMENT

Reverse gear detent clearance is the only adjustment that can be made to the shift linkage. Remove the shift lever cover, trim frame and ash tray assembly. Engage first gear and adjust the clearance between the detent plate and the gear shift lever. Also check clearance should be 0.004-0.06 in.

TRANSMISSION LUBRICATION

The Volvo manual transmissions use Automatic Transmission Fluid type F or G. The oil level should be up to the filler plug hole.

OVERHAUL

For all overhaul procedures, please refer to 'Manual Transmission Overhaul' in the Unit Repair Section.

OVERDRIVE

REMOVAL & INSTALLATION

To facilitate removal, the vehicle should first be driven in 4th gear with the overdrive engaged, and then coasted for a few seconds with the overdrive disengaged and the clutch pedal depressed.

1. Remove the transmission from the vehicle.
2. Disconnect the solenoid cables.
3. If the overdrive unit has not already been drained, remove the six bolts and the overdrive oil pan.
4. Remove the bolts which retain the overdrive unit to the transmission intermediate flange. Pull the unit straight to the rear until it clears the transmission mainshaft.

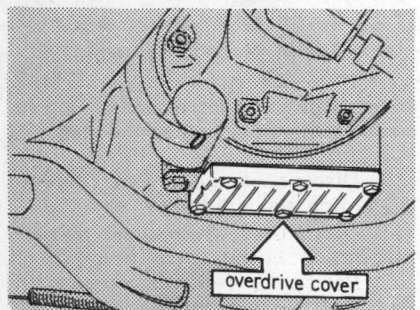

M46 overdrive bottom cover

5. Reverse the above procedure to install. Install the overdrive oil pan with a new gasket. After installation of the transmission (which automatically fills the overdrive) to the proper level with Automatic Transmission Fluid type F or G. Check the lubricant level in the transmission after driving 6-9 miles. The oil level should be up to the filter plug hole.

CLUTCH

REMOVAL & INSTALLATION

1. Remove the transmission.
2. Scribe alignment marks on the clutch and flywheel. In order to prevent warpage, slowly loosen the bolts which retain the clutch to the flywheel diagonally in rotation. Remove the bolts and lift off the clutch and pressure plate.
3. Inspect the clutch assembly.
4. When ready to install, wash the pressure plate and flywheel with solvent to remove any traces of oil, and wipe them clean with a cloth.

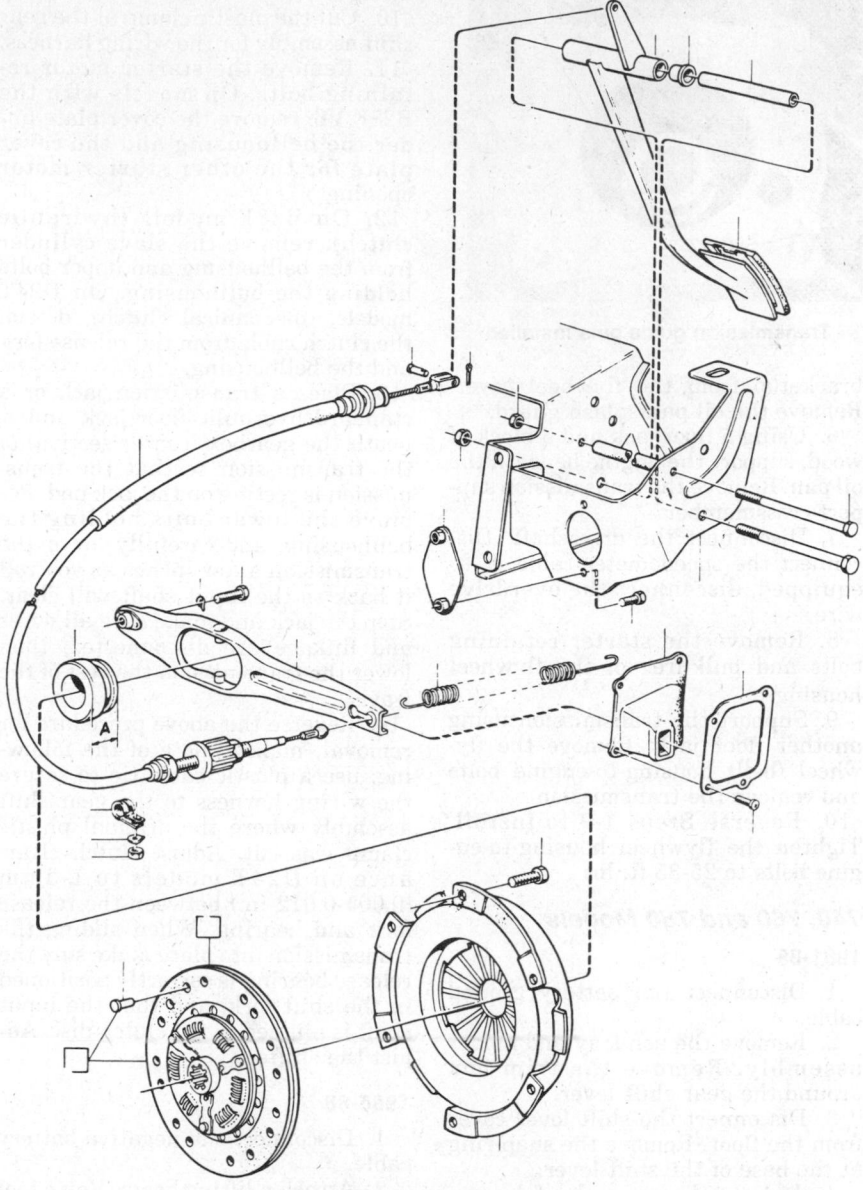

240 series—clutch linkage

5. Position the clutch assembly (the longest side of the hub facing backwards) to the flywheel and align the bolt holes. Insert a pilot shaft (centering mandrel or drift), or an input shaft from an old transmission of the same type, through the clutch assembly and flywheel so that the flywheel pilot bearing is centered.
6. Install the six bolts which retain the clutch assembly to the flywheel and tighten them diagonally in rotation, a few turns at a time. After all the bolts are tightened, remove the pilot shaft (centering mandrel).
7. Install the transmission.
8. On the 260 (GLE, 760 GLE etc.) bleed the clutch hydraulic system, if necessary.

CLUTCH ADJUSTMENT

240, DL, GL, GLT and 760 GLE with D24T Turbodiesel

The play in the manually-operated clutches in these four cylinder Volvos can be adjusted. Clutch play is adjusted underneath the at the clutch fork. Loosen the lock nut on the fork side of the cable bracket, then turn the adjust nut until the proper play is achieved. Tighten the lock nut. Clutch play for all 4 cylinder engines except Turbo is 3-5mm (about $\frac{3}{16}$ in.) Turbo clutch play (free movement rearward) is 1-3mm (about $\frac{5}{64}$ in. or 0.04-0.12 in.). D24T clutch play is the same as the gasoline turbo above.

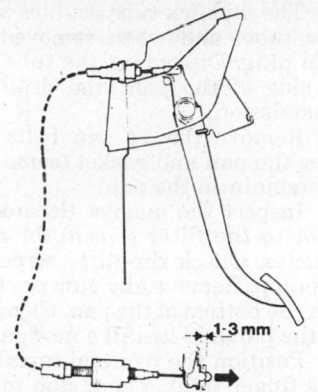

Clutch free-play clearance—B21F Turbo

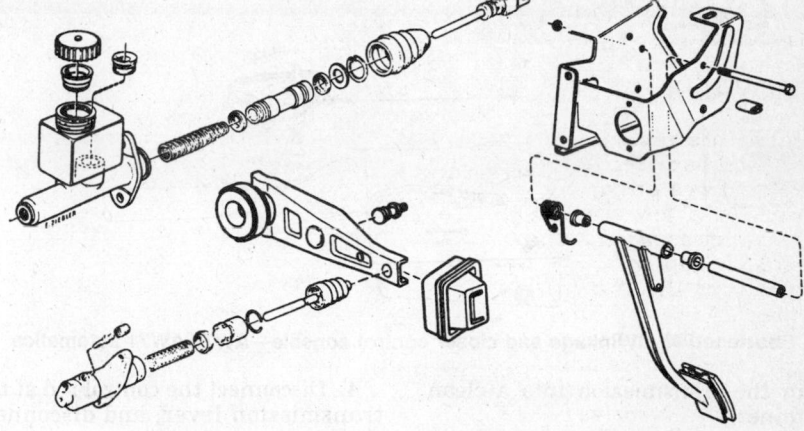

260 series clutch linkage—GLE and Coupe (all V6) similar

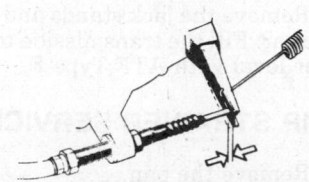

Clutch fork play adjustment, manual (non-hydraulic) clutches. Locknut at center, adjusting nut at left

Clutch Master Cylinder

REMOVAL & INSTALLATION

260 GLE and Coupe

1. Disconnect the negative battery cable. Drain the clutch reservoir with a bulb syringe.
2. Remove the fluid pipe from the master cylinder.
3. Remove the two retaining bolts and remove the master cylinder.
4. Install in the reverse order. Fill the reservoir with fluid and bleed the at the slave cylinder on the flywheel housing.

760 with B28F and B280F V6

1. Remove the panel under the instrument panel. Remove the locking spring and pin from the clutch pedal assembly.
2. Disconnect the hose from the clutch fluid reservoir.
3. Unscrew the nipple from the cylinder housing. Place a container underneath the cylinder to catch the fluid that will spill out. Unbolt and remove the cylinder housing.
4. Reverse the above procedure to install. Make sure there is 1mm (0.04 in.) clearance between the pushrod and the pistons, and adjust if necessary. Fill the reservoir with DOT 4 brake fluid and bleed the system.

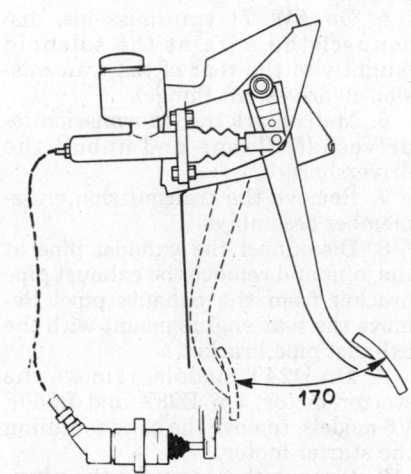

Clutch master cylinder and slave cylinder location—V6 models. Clutch travel is about 6.7 in. (170 mm)

Clutch Slave Cylinder

REMOVAL & INSTALLATION

260, GLE 1981-82, Coupe and 760 with B28 and B280 V6

The slave cylinder is unbolted from the flywheel housing after its fluid tube is disconnected and plugged. Be sure to bleed the system after installation.

AUTOMATIC TRANSMISSION

REMOVAL & INSTALLATION

240 Models

1. Disconnect the negative battery cable. Remove the dipstick and filler pipe clamp.

2. Remove the bracket and throttle cable from the dashboard and throttle control, respectively.
3. Disconnect the exhaust pipe at the manifold.
4. Raise the car and support it on jack stands at the front and rear axles.
5. Drain the fluid into a clean container.
6. Disconnect the driveshaft from the transmission flange.
7. Disconnect the selector lever controls and remove the reinforcing bracket from the pan.
8. Remove the torque converter attaching bolts.
9. Support the transmission with a jack equipped with a holding fixture.
10. Remove the crossmember.
11. Disconnect the exhaust pipe brackets and remove the speedometer cable form the case.
12. Remove the filler pipe.
13. Place a wooden block between the engine and firewall and lower the jack until the engine is against the block.

NOTE: If the battery cable appears to stretch to much, remove it.

14. Disconnect the starter wires, remove the converter housing bolts and pull the transmission backwards to clear the guide pins.
15. Install in the reverse of removal. Torque all 14mm bolts to 35 ft. lbs.

260 Models

1. Disconnect the negative battery cable. Remove air cleaner.
2. Disconnect throttle cable.
3. Remove the two upper converter housing bolts.
4. Remove the filler pipe.
5. Raise the vehicle, support it front and rear with jack stands and

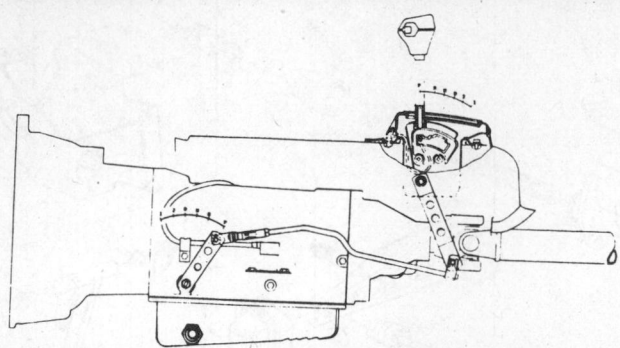

Shortened shaft linkage and closer control console—AW70/AW71 automatics

drain the transmission into a clean container.

6. Remove the splash shield (8 bolts).

7. Disconnect the front muffler from the rubber suspender.

8. Disconnect the driveshaft from the transmission flange.

9. Remove the exhaust pipe brackets at the rear of the transmission.

10. Remove the rear crossmember.

11. Remove the rear engine support and exhaust pipe bracket.

12. Remove the speedometer cable.

13. Disconnect the cooler lines at the transmission.

14. Remove the electrical connections from transmission.

15. Remove neutral start switch.

16. Remove shift control rod.

17. Remove the engine-to-transmission cover plate.

18. Remove starter motor and cover.

19. Remove converter-to-drive plate bolts.

20. Position jack, with holding fixture, under transmission.

21. Remove the two lower converter housing bolts.

22. Pull the transmission back and down to clear the guide pins.

23. Installation is the reverse of removal. Torque the converter housing bolts to 35 ft. lbs. Torque filler pipe nut to 70 ft. lbs. Torque converter-to-drive plate bolts to 35 ft. lbs. Adjust control rod so that ⅛ in. of thread is visible. Torque crossmember bolts to 35 ft. lbs.

740, 760 and 780 Models

1. Disconnect the negative battery cable. Place the gear selector in the Park position.

2. Disconnect the kickdown cable at the throttle pulley on the engine. Disconnect the battery ground cable.

3. Disconnect the oil filler tube at the oil pan, and drain the transmission oil.

——— **CAUTION** ———
The oil will be scalding hot if the car was recently driven.

4. Disconnect the control rod at the transmission lever, and disconnect the reaction rod at the transmission housing.

5. On AW 71 transmissions, disconnect the wire at the solenoid (slightly to the rear of the transmission-to-driveshaft flange).

6. Matchmark the transmission-to-driveshaft flange and unbolt the driveshaft.

7. Remove the transmission crossmember assembly.

8. Disconnect the exhaust pipe at the joint and remove the exhaust pipe bracket from the exhaust pipe. Remove the rear engine mount with the exhaust pipe bracket.

9. On D24T models, remove the starter motor. On B28F and B280F V6 models, remove the bolts retaining the starter motor.

10. Remove the cover for the alternate starter motor location on B28F and B280F models. Remove the cover plate at the torque converter housing bottom on B28F and B280F models.

11. Disconnect the oil cooler lines at the transmission.

12. Remove the two upper screws at the torque converter cover. Remove the oil filler tube.

13. Place a transmission jack or a standard hydraulic floor jack underneath the transmission.

14. Remove the screws retaining the torque converter to the drive plate. Pry the torque converter back from the drive plate with a small pry bar.

15. Slowly lower the transmission as you pull it back to clear the input shaft. Do not tilt the transmission forward or the torque converter may slide off.

16. Reverse the above procedure for installation. Move the gear selector to the 'P' position before attaching the control rod. Adjust the gear shift linkage and connect and adjust the kickdown cable.

PAN REMOVAL

1. Raise the car and place jack stands underneath.

2. The dipstick tube doubles as the filler tube, and when removed, the drain plug. Disconnect the tube from the side of the pan, and drain the transmission.

3. Remove the 14 pan bolts, and lower the pan and gasket (some fluid will remain in the pan).

4. Inspect the magnet (located adjacent to the filter screen) for metal particles. Check the filter screen for the pump. Remove any gum or sludge from the bottom of the pan. Clean and dry the pan and install a new gasket.

5. Position the pan and install the bolts finger-tight. Then, stop torque, diagonally in rotation, to 4.4-7.4 ft. lbs.

6. Connect the dipstick tube and tighten to 59-74 ft. lbs.

7. Remove the jack stands and lower the car. Fill the transmission to the proper level with ATF Type F.

PUMP STRAINER SERVICE

1. Remove the pan.

2. Remove the bolts which retain the front pump wire-mesh strainer to the valve body, and lower the strainer.

3. Clean the strainers in an alcohol based solvent solution.

4. Position the strainer to the valve body and install the retaining screws and bolts. Torque the bolts to 3.7-4.4 ft. lbs.

5. Install the pan with a new gasket.

BAND ADJUSTMENTS—ALL TRANSMISSIONS

The BW55 and AW55, AW70 and AW71 transmissions are equipped with a multi-disc brake (band) system which does not require any adjustment. No provision is made for band adjustment, even at overhaul.

NEUTRAL START SWITCH ADJUSTMENT

All models have an adjustable switch, located beneath the shifter quadrant on the tunnel. To adjust:

1. Remove the shifter quadrant cover.

2. Place the shifter lever in Park. Check that the round switch contact centers over the indicating line for 'P' (park). If not, loosen the two switch mounting screws and align the switch.

3. Place the shifter lever in Neutral. Repeat the check and adjust as necessary.

4. Finally check that the engine starts only in Park or Neutral, and

check that the back-up lights work only in Reverse.

GEAR SELECTOR LINKAGE ADJUSTMENT

240, 260 Models Except BW55 Transmission

NOTE: The gear selector shift console has been moved forward on cars equipped with the AW70/AW71 transmissions. The shift linkage is also shortened on these cars.

1. Disconnect the shift rod from the transmission lever. Place both the transmission lever and the gear selector lever in the '2' position.

2. Adjust the length of the shift control rod so that a small clearance of 0.04 in. is obtained between the gear selector lever inhibitor and the inhibitor plate, when the shift control rod is connected to the transmission lever.

3. Position the gear selector lever in Drive and make sure that a similar small clearance of 0.04 in. exists between the lever inhibitor and the inhibitor plate. Disconnect the shift control rod from the transmission lever and adjust, if necessary.

4. Lock the control rod bolt with its safety clasp and tighten the locknut. Make sure that the control rod lug follows with the transmission lever.

5. After moving the transmission lever to the Park and '1' positions, make sure that the clearances remain the same. In addition, make sure that the output shaft is locked with the selector lever in the Park position.

BW55 Transmission

1. With the engine off, check that the distance between the 'D' position and its forward stop is equal to the distance between the '2' position and its rearward stop, when the gear selector is moved. If you are not sure, remove the gear quadrant cover, and measure.

2. If adjustment is necessary, a rough setting is made by loosening the locknut and rotating the clevis on the control rod to the transmission. A fine adjustment can be made by rotating the knurled sleeve between the control rod locknut and the pivot for the gear selector lever. Increasing the rod length will decrease clearance between the Drive position and its forward stop, and vice versa. Maximum permissible length of exposed thread between the locknut and the control rod is 1.1 in.

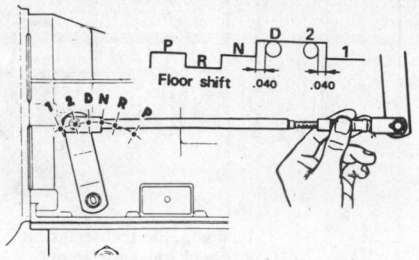

Adjusting automatic transmission gear selector. Clearance in position D toward position N is the same as the clearance in position 2 toward position 1. Adjust at the bottom end of the gear selector.

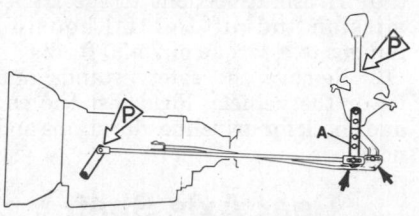

740 and 760 automatic transmission gear linkage. "A" is adjusting rod arm; arrows point to locknuts on adjustment (left) and reaction rod (right) arms

740, 760 and 780 Models

NOTE: Before adjusting the shift linkage, make sure the starter motor operates only in Park or Neutral positions; that the back-up lights light up only in Reverse; that the shift lever is vertical in Park with the car level; that the clearance between Drive and Neutral is the same or less than the clearance between 2 and 1.

BASIC ADJUSTMENT

1. Place the shift lever in Park.
2. Loosen the locknuts on the adjustment and reaction rods (on the linkage under the car).
3. Make sure the shift lever is in 'P'. Turn the driveshaft until it enters a locked position.
4. Position the adjusting rod arm (A) vertically and tighten the locknut. The gear shift lever may contact the dashboard if the adjusting rod arm is positioned too far backwards.
5. Press the reaction rod arm backwards until a slight resistance is felt. Tighten the locknut to 3.5 ft. lbs.

ADJUSTING CLEARANCE

1. Check that the clearance between Drive and Neutral is the same or less than the clearance between 2 and 1 on the shift lever. If clearance is correct, tighten the locknut to 12-17 ft. lbs. If clearance is not correct, adjust as follows:

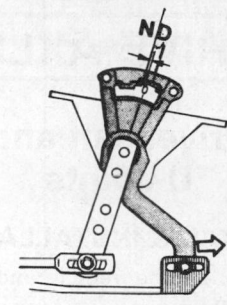

Checking clearance between D and N, and 1 and 2

2. If no clearance is felt in Drive, move the reaction rod arm rearwards about 2mm or 0.08 in.
3. If no clearance is felt in position 2, move the reaction rod arm forwards about 3mm or 0.12 in. Tighten the locknut.
4. After adjustment, check that the car starts only in Park or Neutral, and that the back-up light does NOT light up in Reverse, reduce clearance in Drive by moving the rod arm forward slighty.

THROTTLE AND DOWNSHIFT CABLE ADJUSTMENT

1. First, adjust the throttle plate angle and throttle cable. Disconnect the cable at the control pulley and the linkage rod at the throttle shaft. Set the throttle plate angle by loosening the adjusting screw locknut and backing off the screw. Then, turn in the screw until it just makes contact and then one additional turn. Tighten the locknut. Adjust the linkage rod so that it fits onto the throttle shaft pulley ball without moving the cable pulley. Attach the throttle cable to the pulley and adjust the cable sheath so that the cable is stretched but does not move the cable pulley. Finally, fully depress the gas pedal and check that the pulley contacts the full throttle abutment.

2. With the transmission cable hooked up, check that there is 0.010-0.040 in. clearance between the cable clip and the adjusting sheath. The cable should be stretched at idle. Pull out the cable about ½ in. and release. A distinct click should be heard from the transmission as the throttle can returns to its initial position. Depress the gas pedal again to wide open throttle. Check that the transmission cable moves about 2 in. Adjust as necessary at the adjusting sheath.

DRIVE AXLE

Driveshaft and U-Joints

REMOVAL & INSTALLATION

1. Jack up the vehicle and install safety stands.

2. Mark the relative positions of the driveshaft yokes and transmission and differential housing flanges for purposes of assembly. Remove the nuts and bolts which retain the front and rear driveshaft sections to the transmission and differential housing flanges, respectively. Remove the support bearing housing from the driveshaft tunnel, and lower the driveshaft and universal joint assembly as a unit.

3. Pry up the lock washer and remove the support bearing retaining nut. Pull off the rear section of the driveshaft with the intermediate universal joint and splined shaft of the front section. The support bearing may now be pressed off the driveshaft.

4. Remove the support from it housing.

5. For removal of the universal joints from the driveshaft, consult 'Universal Joint Overhaul'.

6. Inspect the driveshaft sections for straightness. Using a dial indicator, or rolling the shafts along a flat surface, make sure that the driveshaft out-of-round does not exceed 0.010 in. Do not attempt to straighten a damaged shaft. Any shaft exceeding 0.010 in. out-of-round will cause substantial vibration, and must be replaces. Also, inspect the support bearing by pressing the races against each other by hand, and turning them in opposite directions. If the bearing binds at any point, it must be discarded and replaced.

7. Install the support bearing into its housing.

8. Press the support bearing and housing onto the front driveshaft section. Push the splined shaft of the front section, with the intermediate universal joint and rear driveshaft section, into the splined sleeve of the front section. Install the retaining nut and lock washer for the support bearing.

9. Taking note of the alignment marks made prior to removal, position the driveshaft and universal joint assembly to its flange connections and install but do not tighten its retaining nuts and bolts. Postition the support bearing housing to the driveshaft tunnel and install the retaining

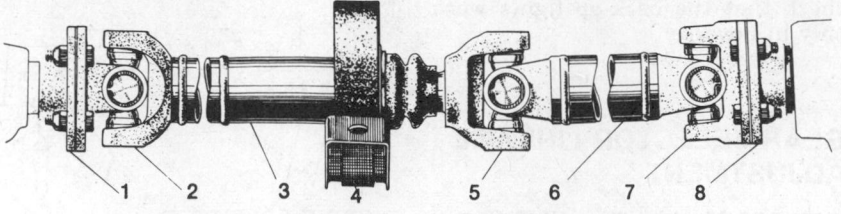

1. Flange on transmission
2. Front universal joint
3. Front section of driveshaft
4. Support bearing
5. Intermediate universal joint
6. Rear section of driveshaft
7. Rear universal joint
8. Flange on rear axle

Driveshaft with support bearing

nut. Tighten the nuts which retain the driveshaft sections to the transmission and differential housing flanges to a torque of 25-30 ft. lbs.

10. Remove the safety stands and lower the vehicle. Road test the car and check for driveline vibrations and noise.

Rear Axle Shaft

REMOVAL & INSTALLATION BEARING AND OIL SEAL REPLACEMENT

1. Raise the vehicle and install safety stands.

2. Remove the applicable wheel and tire assembly.

3. Place a wooden block beneath the brake pedal, plug the master cylinder reservoir vent hole, and remove and plug the brake line from the caliper. Be careful not to allow any brake fluid to spill onto the disc or pads. Remove the two bolts which retain brake caliper to the axle housing, and lift off the caliper. Lift off the brake disc.

4. Remove the thrust washer bolts through the holes in the axle shaft flange. Using a slide hammer, remove the axle shaft, bearing and oil seal assembly. You may be able to pull out the shaft by temporarily reinstalling the brake disc and using this to grab on to while pulling out the axle shaft.

5. Using an arbor press, remove the axle shaft bearing and its locking ring from the axle shaft. Remove and discard the old oil seal.

6. Fill the space between the lips of the new oil seal with wheel bearing grease. Position the new seal on the axle shaft. Using an arbor press, install the bearing with a new locking ring, onto the axle shaft.

7. Thoroughly pack the bearing with wheel bearing grease. Install the axle shaft into the housing, rotating it so that it indexes with the differential. Install the bolts for the thrust washer and tighten to 36 ft. lbs.

8. Install the brake disc. Position the brake caliper to its retainer on the

axle housing and install the two retaining bolts. Torque the caliper retaining bolts to 45-50 ft. lbs.

9. Unplug the brake line and connect it to the caliper. Bleed the caliper of all air trapped in the system.

10. Position the wheel and tire assembly on its lugs and hand-tighten the lug nuts. Remove the jack stands and lower the vehicle. Torque the lug nuts to 70-100 ft. lbs.

FRONT SUSPENSION

MacPherson Strut

REMOVAL & INSTALLATION

1. Remove the hub cap and loosen the lug nuts a few turns.

2. Firmly apply the parking brake and place blocks in back of the rear wheels.

3. Jack up the front of the car with a hoist or using a floor jack at the center of the front crossmember. When the wheels are 2-3 in. off the ground, the car is high enough. Place jack stands beneath the front jacking points. Then, remove the floor jack from the crossmember (if used), and reposition it beneath the applicable lower control arm to provide support at the outer end. Remove the wheel and tire assembly.

4. Using a boll joint puller, disconnect the steering rod from the steering arm.

5. Disconnect the stabilizer bar at the link upper attachment.

6. Remove the bolt retaining the brake line bracket to the fender well.

7. Open the hood and remove the cover for the strut assembly upper attachment.

8. While keeping the strut from turning, loosen and remove the nut for the upper attachment.

9. Before lowering the strut assembly, wire or tie the strut to some stationary component, or use a holding fixture such as SVO 5045, to prevent the strut from traveling down too far and damaging the hydraulic brake lines. Then lower the jack supporting the lower arm and allow the strut to tilt out to about a 60 degree angle. At this angle, the top of the strut assembly should just protrude past the wheel well, allowing removal of the strut from the top.

10. Carefully lift and guide the strut assembly into its upper attachment in the spring tower. Connect the stabilizer bar to the stabilizer link. Guide the shock absorber spindle into the upper attachment and raise the jack beneath the lower control are. Install the washer and nut on top of the shock absorber spindle. While holding the spindle from turning, tighten the nut to 15-25 ft. lbs. Install the cover.

11. Attach the brake line bracket to its mount. Tighten the nut retaining the stabilizer bar to the link. Connect the steering rod at the steering arm.

12. Install the wheel and tire assembly. Remove the jack stands and lower the car. Jounce the suspension a few times and then road test.

OVERHAUL

For all spring and shock absorber removal and installation procedures and any other strut overhaul procedures, please refer to 'Strut Overhaul' in the Unit Repair Section.

Lower Control Arm

REPLACEMENT

1. Jack up car, support on stands and remove wheels.
2. Remove stabilizer bar.
3. Remove ball joint from control arm.
4. Remove control arm front retaining bolt.
5. Remove control arm rear attachment plate.
6. Remove attachment plate from control arm.
7. Remove stabilizer link from control arm.
8. Install in reverse of removal.

NOTE: Right and left bushings are not interchangeable. The right side bushing should be turned so that the small slots point horizontally when installed. Torque the retaining bolt to 55 ft. lbs., the rear bushing to 4 ft. lbs. and the rear attachment bolts to 30 ft. lbs.

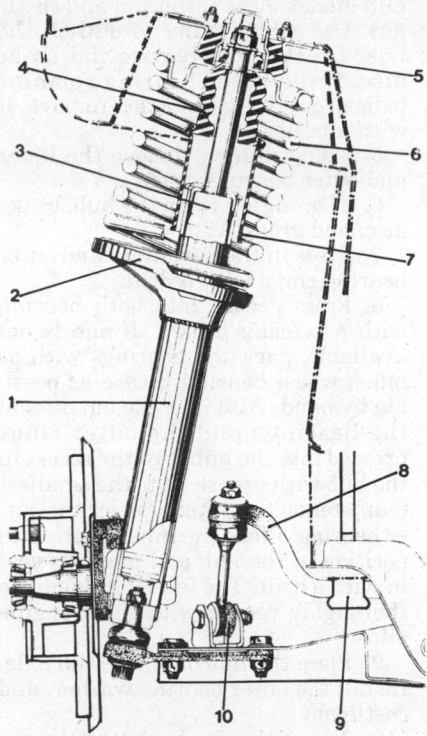

1. Strut assembly
2. Lower spring support
3. Shock absorber
4. Rubber bumper
5. Upper attachment
6. Coil spring
7. Ruber sleeve, protecting the shock absorber
8. Stabilizer bar
9. Stabilizer bar attachment
10. Stabilizer link

Front suspension—240, 260 (DL, GL) series

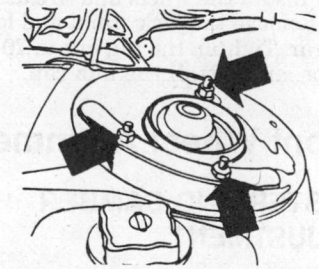

Loosen the upper strut nuts to adjust the camber on 240, 260 (DL, GL) series

Lower Ball Joint

REMOVAL & INSTALLATION

240 and 260 Models

1. Jack up the front of the car and install jack stands beneath the front jacking attachments.
2. Remove the tire and wheel assembly.
3. Reach in between the spring

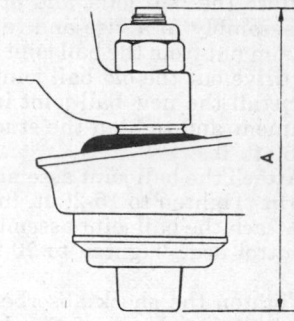

Spring–type lower ball joint maximum allowable length

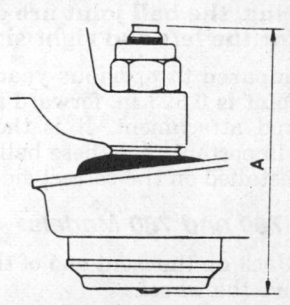

Non-spring type lower ball joint maximum allowable length

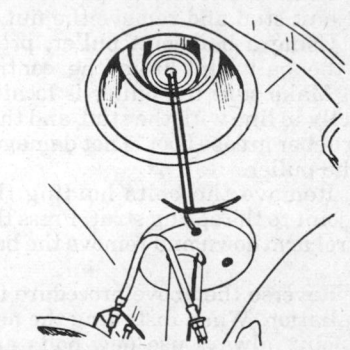

Suspending the top of the strut from the body with a wire while removing the lower ball joint

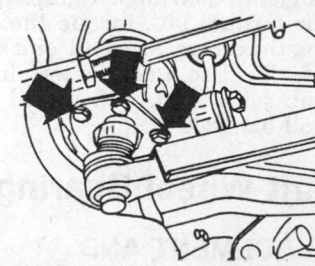

Late type lower ball joint-to-strut retaining bolts

coils and loosen the shock absorber cap nut a few turns.

4. Remove the four bolts (12mm) retaining the ball joint seat to the bottom of the strut.

5. Remove the three nuts (19mm) retaining the ball joint to the lower control arm.

6. Place the ball joint and attachment assembly in a vise and remove the 19mm nut from the ball joint stud. Then, drive out the old ball joint.

7. Install the new ball joint in the attachment and tighten the stud nut to 35-50 ft. lbs.

8. Attach the ball joint assembly to the strut. Tighten to 15-20 ft. lbs.

9. Attach the ball joint assembly to the control arm. Tighten to 70-95 ft. lbs.

10. Tighten the shock absorber cap nut. Install the wheel and tire. Lower the car and road-test.

NOTE: On models with power steering, the ball joint are different for the left and right side.

Compared to previous years, the ball joint is 0.393 in. forward in control rod attachment. It is therefore most important that these ball joints are installed on the correct side.

740, 760 and 780 Models

1. Jack up the front end of the car. Remove the wheel.

2. Remove the bolt connecting the anti-roll bar link to the control arm.

3. Remove the cotter pin for the ball joint stud and remove the nut.

4. Using a ball joint puller, press out the ball joint from the control arm. Make sure the puller is located directly in line with the stud, and that the rubber grease boot is not damaged by the puller.

5. Remove the bolts holding the ball joint to the spring strut. Press the control arm down and remove the ball joint.

6. Reverse the above procedure for installation. When installing the new ball joint, always use new bolts and coat all threads with a liquid thread sealer. Torque bolts to 22 ft. lbs., checking that the bolt heads sit flat on the ball joint, then angle-tighten (protractor-torque) 90°. torque the nut holding the control arm ball joint stud to 44 ft. lbs. Use a new cotter pin on the ball joint stud, and install the anti-roll bar link.

Front Wheel Bearings

REPLACEMENT AND ADJUSTMENT

1. Remove the hub cap, and loosen the lug nuts a few turns.

2. Firmly apply the parking brake. Jack up the front of the car and place jack stands beneath the lower control arms. Remove the wheel and tire assembly.

3. Remove the front caliper.

4. Pry off the grease cap from the hub. Remove the cotter pin and castle nut. Use a hub puller to pull off the hub. On the 760, remove the brake disc. If the inner bearing remains lodged on the stub axle, remove it with a puller.

5. Using a drift, remove the inner and outer bearing rings.

6. Thoroughly clean the hub, brake disc, and grease cap.

7. Press in the new inner and outer bearing rings with a drift.

8. Press grease into both bearing with a bearing packer. If one is not available, pack the bearings with as much wheel bearing grease as possible by hand. Also coat the outsides of the bearings and the outer rings pressed into the hub. Fill the recess in the hub with grease up to the smallest diameter on the outer ring for the outer bearing. Place the inner bearing in position in the hub and press its seal in with a drift. The felt ring should be thoroughly coated with light engine oil.

9. Place the hub onto the stub axle. Install the outer bearing washer, and castle nut.

10. Adjust the front wheel bearings by tightening the castle nut to 45 ft. lbs. to seat the bearings. Then, back off the nut 1/3 of a turn counterclockwise. Torque the nut to 1 ft. lb. If the nut slot does not align with the hole in the stub axle, tighten the nut until the cotter pin may be installed. Make sure that the wheel spins freely without any side play.

11. Fill the grease cap halfway with wheel bearing grease, and install it on the hub.

12. Install the front caliper.

13. Install the wheel and tire assembly. Remove the jack stand and lower the car. Tighten the lug nut to 70-100 ft. lbs. and install the hub cap.

Front Wheel Alignment

CASTER AND CAMBER ADJUSTMENT

Caster angle is fixed by suspension design and cannot be adjusted. If caster is not within specifications, check front end parts for damage and replace as necessary.

Camber angle, however, may be adjusted. At the strut upper attachment to the body, two of the three bolts holes are eccentric, allowing the upper end of the strut to tilt out or in as necessary. A special pivot lever tool SVO No. 5038, which attaches to the tops of the strut upper attachment retaining bolt threads is recommended for this job. To adjust, loosen the three retaining nuts, install the pivot lever tool, and adjust to specifications. After adjusting, torque the nuts to 15-25 ft. lbs.

TOE-IN ADJUSTMENT

Toe in may be adjusted after performing the caster and camber adjustments. With a wheel spreader, measure the distance (X) between the rear of the right and left front tires, at spindle (hub) height, and then measure the distance (Y) between the front of the right and left front tires, also at spindle (hub) height. Subtract the front distance (Y) from the rear distance (X), and compare that to the specifications table. $X - Y = $ toe-in. If the adjustment is not correct, loosen the locknuts on both sides of the tie rod, and rotate the tie rod itself. Toe-in is increased by turning the tie rod in the normal forward rotation of the wheels, and reduced by turning it in the opposite direction. After the final adjustment is make, torque the locknuts to 55-65 ft. lbs., being careful not the disturb the adjustment.

REAR SUSPENSION

Shock Absorbers

REMOVAL & INSTALLATION

1. Remove the hub cap and loosen the lug nuts a few turns. Place blocks in front of the front wheels. Jack up the rear of the car to unload the shock absorbers and place jack stands in front of the rear jacking points. Remove the wheel and tire assembly.

2. Remove the nuts and bolts which retain the shock absorber to its upper and lower attachments and remove the shock absorber. Make sure that the spacing sleeve, inside the axle support arm for the lower attachment, is not misplaced.

3. The damping effect of the shock absorber may be tested by securing the lower attachment in a vise and extending and compressing it. A properly operating shock absorber should off approximately three times as much resistance to extending the unit as compressing it. Replace the shock absorber if it does not function as above, or if it fixed rubber bushings are damaged. Replace any leaking shock absorber.

4. To install, position the shock absorber to its upper and lower attachments. Make sure that the spacing sleeve is installed inside the axle support (trailing) arm and is aligned with the lower attachment bolt hole. Install the retaining nuts and bolts, and torque to 63 ft. lbs. On 240 and 760 series models, the shock fits inside the support arm. On all 260 models, the shock attaches on the outboard side of the support arm.

5. Install the wheel and tire assembly. Remove the jack stands and lower the car. Tighten the lug nuts to 70-100 ft. lbs., and install the hub cap.

Springs

REMOVAL & INSTALLATION

1. Remove the hub cap and loosen the lug nuts a few turns. Jack up the car and place jack stands in front of the rear jacking points. Remove the wheel and tire assembly.

2. Place a hydraulic jack beneath the rear axle housing and raise the housing sufficiently to compress the spring. Loosen the nuts for the upper and lower spring attachments.

————— CAUTION —————

Due to the fact that the spring is compressed under several hundred pounds of pressure, when it is freed from its lower attachment, it will attempt to suddenly spring back to its extended position. It is therefore imperative that the axle housing be lowered with extreme care until the spring is fully extended. As an added safety measure, a chain may be attached to the lower spring coil and secured to the axle housing.

3. Disconnect the shock absorber at its upper attachment. Carefully lower the jack and axle housing until the spring is fully extended. Remove the spring.

4. To install, position the retaining bolt and inner washer, for the upper attachment, inside the spring and then, while holding the outer washer and rubber spacer to the upper body attachment, install the spring and inner washer to the upper attachment (sandwiching the rubber spacer), and tighten the retaining bolt.

5. Raise the jack and secure the bottom of the spring to its lower attachment with the washer and retaining bolt.

6. Connect the shock absorber to its upper attachment. Install the wheel and tire assembly.

7. Remove the jack stands and lower the car. Tighten the lug nuts to 70-100 ft. lbs. and install the hub cap.

═══ STEERING ═══

Steering Wheel

REMOVAL & INSTALLATION

NOTE: The use of a knock-off type steering wheel puller, or the use of a hammer may damage the collapsible column and is not recommended.

240 and 260 Models

1. Disconnect the negative battery cable.

2. Remove the retaining screws for the upper half of the molded turn signal housing and lift off the housing.

3. Pry off the steering wheel impact pad.

4. Disconnect the horn plug contact.

5. Remove the steering wheel nut.

6. With the front wheels pointing straight ahead, and the steering wheel centered, install a steering wheel puller. On 240 and 260 models, use a universal type puller, such as SVO 2263.

7. To install, make sure that the front wheels are pointing straight ahead, then place the centered steering wheel on the column with the plug contact to the left. Install the nut and tighten to 20-30 ft. lbs.

8. Connect the horn plug contact and install the impact pad.

9. Install the upper turn signal housing half.

10. Connect the negative battery cable and test the operation of the horn.

740, 760 and 780 Models

1. Disconnect the negative battery cable.

2. Gently pry up the lower edge of the steering wheel center pad and remove it.

3. Unscrew the steering wheel center nut, and pull off the wheel.

4. When installing, torque the center nut to 26 ft. lbs.

Turn Signal Switch

REMOVAL & INSTALLATION

1. Disconnect the negative battery cable.

2. Remove the steering wheel.

3. Remove the upper and lower steering column casings.

4. Unscrew the turn signal switch/lever assembly.

5. Disconnect the wires from the switch.

6. Installation is the reverse of the removal procedure.

Ignition Lock/Switch

REPLACEMENT

240 and 260 Models

1. Remove noise insulation panel and center side panel.

2. Disconnect the wires from the switch.

3. Pry out the switch with a suitable tool.

4. Install in reverse of removal.

740, 760 and 780 Models

1. Remove the sound proofing under the instrument panel.

2. Disconnect the connector from the ignition switch.

3. Remove the upper steering column casing and the panel around the ignition switch.

4. Loosen the mounting screw for the switch.

5. Insert the key and turn it to the start position. Through the hole beneath the holder, press in the catch and remove the ignition switch.

6. To install, insert the key and turn and depress the locking tab. Remove the key. Position the switch and release the locking tab by inserting the key. Tighten the mounting screw and reverse the rest of the removal procedure. Test the switch.

Manual Steering Gear

REMOVAL & INSTALLATION

1. Disconnect the negative battery cable. Remove the lock bolt and nut from the column flange (at the steering gear). Bend apart the flange slightly with a suitable tool.

2. Jack up the front end. The stands should be positioned at the jack supports. Remove the front wheels.

3. Disconnect the steering rods from the steering arms, using a ball joint puller.

4. Remove the splash guard.

5. Disconnect the steering gear from the front axle member.

6. Disconnect the steering gear from the steering gear flange. Remove steering gear.

7. Install rubber spacers and plates for the steering gear attachment points.

8. Position the steering gear, and guide the pinion shaft into the steering shaft flange. The recess on the pinion shaft should be aligned towards the lock bolt opening in the flange.

9. Attach the steering gear to the front axle member. Check that the U-bolts are aligned in the plate slots. Install flat washers and nuts.

10. Install the splash guard.

11. Connect the steering rods to the steering arms.

12. Install the front wheels and lower the vehicle.

13. Install the lock bolt for the steering shaft flange.

PITMAN ARM ADJUSTMENT

On a steering gear with a marked pitman arm and pitman arm shaft (on the steering gear), make sure that the marks align.

On a steering gear without the marks, lift up the front of the vehicle so that the front wheels are free. Turn the steering wheel to its center position (count the number of turns). Lower the vehicle. If the vehicle is correctly loaded, the wheels should now point straight forward. If the wheels do not, remove the pitman arm from the shaft with a puller. Then set the left wheel straight ahead should be in it center position. Tighten the pitman arm nut to 100-120 ft. lbs.

Power Steering Gear

REMOVAL & INSTALLATION

1. Disconnect the negative battery cable. Loosen the steering column shaft flange from the pinion shaft. Remove the lock bolt and bend apart the flange slightly.

2. Jack up the front end. Position jack stands at the front jack supports. Remove the front wheels.

3. Disconnect the steering rods from the steering arms, with a ball joint puller.

4. Remove the splash guard.

5. Disconnect the hoses at the steering gear. Install protective plugs in the hose connections.

6. Remove the steering gear from the front axle member.

7. Remove the steering gear by pulling down until it is free from the steering shaft flange. On the 740 and 760 GLE, disconnect the lower steering shaft from the steering gear by removing the snap rings from the clamps. Loosen the upper clamp bolt, remove the lower clamp bolt and slide the joint up on the shaft. Then remove the unit on the left side of the vehicle.

8. Position the steering gear and attach the pinion shaft to the steering shaft flange.

9. Install right side U-bolt and bracket, but do NOT tighten the nuts.

10. Install left side retaining bolts, and tighten. Tighten the U-bolt nuts.

11. Connect the steering rods to the steering arms.

12. Install the lock bolt on the steering column flange.

13. Connect the return and pressure hoses to the steering gear.

Power Steering Pump

REMOVAL & INSTALLATION

1. Disconnect the negative battery cable. Remove all dirt and grease from around the suction line connections and from around the delivery line of the pump housing.

2. Using a container to catch any power steering fluid that might run out, disconnect the lines, and plug them to prevent dirt from entering the system.

3. Remove the tensioning bolt and the attaching bolts.

4. Clear the pump free of the fan belt and lift it out.

5. If a new pump is to be used, the old brackets, fitting, and pulley must be transferred from the old unit. The pulley may be removed with a puller, and pressed on the pump shaft with a press tool. Under no circumstances should the pulley be hammered on, as this will damage the pump bearings.

6. To install, place the pump in position and loosely fit the attaching bolts. Connect the lines to the pump with new seals.

7. Place the fan belt onto the pulley and adjust the fan belt tension as outlined in Chapter one.

8. Tighten the tensioning bolt and the attaching bolts.

9. Fill the reservoir with Type 'A' automatic transmission fluid and bleed the system.

POWER STEERING SYSTEM BLEEDING

1. Fill the reservoir up to the edge with Automatic Transmission Fluid Type 'A'. Raise the front wheels off the ground, and install safety stands. Place the transmission in neutral and apply the parking brake.

2. Keeping a can of ATF Type 'A' within easy reach, start the engine and fill the reservoir as the level drops.

3. When the reservoir level has stopped dropping, slowly turn the steering wheel from lock to lock several reservoir if necessary.

4. Locate the bleeder screw on the power steering gear. Open the bleeder screw ½-1 turn, and close it when oil starts flowing out.

5. Continue to turn the steering wheel slowly until the fluid in the reservoir is free of air bubbles.

6. Stop the engine and observe the oil level in the reservoir. If the oil level rises more than ¼ in. past the level mark, air still remains the system. Continue bleeding until the level rise is correct.

7. Remove the safety stands and lower the car.

Tie Rod Ends

REPLACEMENT

The ball joints of the tie rod may be replaced individually. After the ball joint is disconnected, the locknut on the tie rod is loosened and the clamp bolt released. The ball joint is then screwed out of the tie rod, taking note of the number of turns. The new ball joint is screwed in the same number of turns, and the clamp bolt and locknut tightened. The ball joint is locked to the rod with 55-65 ft. lbs. of torque. The new ball joint is pressed into its connection and the ball stud not tightened to 23-27 ft. lbs.

After reconditioning of the rods and joints, the wheel alignment must be adjusted.

BRAKES

For all brake system repair and adjustment procedures not detailed below, please refer to 'Brakes' in the Unit Repair Section.

Master Cylinder

REMOVAL & INSTALLATION

1. Disconnect the negative battery cable. To prevent brake fluid form spilling onto and damaging the paint, place a protective cover over the fender apron, and rags beneath the master cylinder.

2. Disconnect and plug the brake lines from the master cylinder.

3. Remove the nuts which retain the master cylinder and reservoir assembly to the vacuum booster, and lift the assembly forward, being careful not to spill any fluid on the fender. Empty out and discard the brake fluid.

--- CAUTION ---
Do not depress the brake pedal while the master cylinder is removed.

4. In order for the master cylinder to function properly when installed to the vacuum booster, the adjusting nut

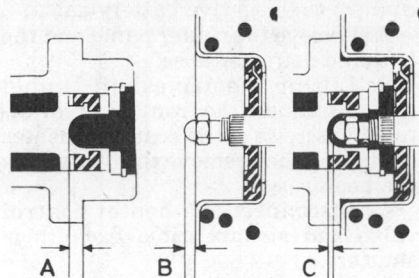

Adjusting thrust rod

for the thrust rod of the booster must not prevent the primary piston of the master cylinder from returning to its resting position. A clearance (C) of 0.004-0.04 in. is required between the thrust rod and primary piston with the master cylinder installed. The clearance may be adjusted by rotating the adjusting nut for the booster thrust rod in the required direction. To determine what the clearance (C) will be when the master cylinder and booster are connected, first measure the distance (A) between the face of the attaching flange and the center of the primary piston on the master cylinder, then measure the distance (B) that the thrust rod protrudes from the fixed surface of the booster (making sure that the thrust rod is depressed fully with a partial vacuum existing in the booster). When measurement is subtracted from measurement (A), clearance (C) should be obtained. If not, adjust the length of the thrust rod by turning the adjusting screw to suit. After the final adjustment is obtained apply a few drops of locking compound, such as Loctitek, to the adjusting nut.

5. Position the master cylinder and reservoir assembly onto the studs for the booster, and install the washers and nuts. Tighten the nuts to 17 ft. lbs.

6. Remove the plugs and connect the brake lines.

7. Bleed the entire brake system.

Brake System Warning Valve

VALVE RESETTING

1. Disconnect the plug contact and screw out the warning switch so that the pistons inside the valve may return to their normal position.

2. Repair and bleed the faulty hydraulic circuit.

3. Screw in the warning switch and tighten it to a torque of 10-14 ft. lbs. Connect the plug contact.

REPLACEMENT

1. Placing a rag beneath the valve to catch the brake fluid, loosen the pipe connections, and disconnect the brake lines. Disconnect the electrical plug contact, and lift out the valve.

2. connect the new warning valve in the reverse order of removal, and connect the plug contact.

3. Bleed the entire brake system.

Proportioning Valves

REPLACEMENT

Sophisticated pressure testing equipment is required to troubleshoot the dual hydraulic system in order to determine if the proportioning valve(s) are in need of replacement. However, if the car is demonstration signs of rear wheel lock-up under moderate to heavy braking pressure, and other variables such as tire pressure, tread depth, etc., have been ruled out, the valve(s) may be at fault. The valves are not rebuildable, and must be replaced as a unit.

1. Unscrew, disconnect and plug the brake pipe from the master cylinder, at the valve connection.

2. Slacken the connection for the flexible brake hose to the rear wheel a maximum of ¼ turn.

3. Remove the bolt(s) which retain the valve to the underbody, and unscrew the valve from the rear brake hose.

4. To install the valve, place a new seal on it, and screw the valve onto the rear brake hose and hand tighten. Secure the valve to the underbody with the retaining bolt(s).

5. Connect the brake pipe and tighten both connections, making sure that there is no tension on the flexible rear hose.

6. Bleed the brake system.

Power Brake Booster

REMOVAL & INSTALLATION

1. Disconnect the negative battery cable.

2. Remove the master cylinder to power booster retaining bolts and position the master cylinder to one side. Be careful not to damage the brake lines.

3. Disconnect the vacuum assist hose, from the booster.

4. From inside the vehicle, disconnect the brake pedal rod.

5. Remove the power booster retaining bolts. Remove the power booster from the vehicle.

6. Installation is the reverse of the removal procedure.

Parking Brake Cable

ADJUSTMENT

1. Remove the rear ashtray (between the front seat backs) or the rear of the center console on the 740 and 760.

2. Tighten the parking brake cable adjusting screw so that the brake is fully applied when pulled up 2-3 notches.

3. If one cable is stretched more than the other, they can be individually adjusted by removing the parking brake cover (2 screws) and turning the individual cable adjusting nut at the front of each yoke pivot.

4. Install the ashtray, and parking brake cover (if equipped).

REMOVAL AND INSTALLATION

240 AND 260 Models

1. Apply the parking brake. Remove the hub caps for the rear wheels and loosen the lug nuts a few turns.

2. Place blocks in front of the front wheels. Jack up the rearend and place jackstands beneath the rear axle. Remove the wheel and tire assembly. Release the parking brake.

3. Remove the bolt and the wheel from the pulley.

4. Remove the rubber cover for the front attachment of the cable sleeve and nut, as well as the attachment for the rubber suspension ring on the frame. Remove the cable from the other side of the attachment in the same manner.

5. Hold the return spring in position. Pry up the lock and remove the lock pin so that the cable releases form the lever.

6. Remove the return spring with washers. Loosen the nut for the rear attachment of the cable sleeve. Lift the cable forward after loosening both side of the attachments, and remove it.

7. To install, first adjust the rear brake shoes of the parking brake as outlined in Step 3, 4 and 5 under 'Parking Brake Adjustment'.

8. Install new rubber cable guides for the cable suspension. Place the cable in position in the rear attachment and tighten the nut. Install the washers and return spring. Oil the lock pin and install it, together with the cable, on the lever. Install the attachment and rubber cable guide on the frame.

9. Install the cable in the same manner on the side of the vehicle.

10. Place the cable sleeve in position in the front attachments and install the rubber covers.

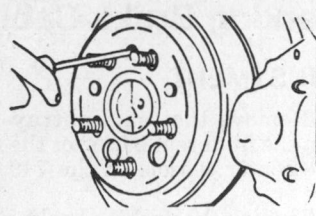

Adjusting the parking brake through the access hole in the rear hub

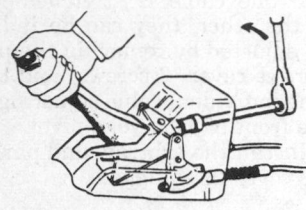

Adjust the 1981 and later parking brake if it is not fully applied after pulling the lever 10–11 notches. After adjusting, good braking power should be obtained after pulling the lever 2–3 notches

11. Lubricate and install the pulley on the pull rod. Adjust the pulley so that the parking brake is fully engaged with the lever at the third or fourth notch.

12. Install the wheel and tire assemblies. Remove the jack stands and lower the vehicle. Tighten the lug nut to 70-100 ft. lbs. and install the hub caps.

740, 760 and 780

The 700 serie parking brake system employs two cable, a short one on the right hand side and long one on the left.

SHORT CABLE, RIGHT SIDE

1. Jack up the rear of the car and safely support it with jackstands.

2. Remove the right brake caliper rear wheel. Remove the right brake caliper and hang it from the coil spring with a wire. Remove the brake disc. Unhook the rear return spring and remove the brake shoes.

3. Push out the pin holding the cable to the brake lever. Remove the rubber bellows (boot) from the backing plate, and remove the bellows from the cable.

4. Remove the spring clip, pin and cable from the back of the differential housing. Remove the cable guide on the differential by removing the top bolt from the housing cover. Remove the cable.

5. Install the cable guide on the new cable. Check the rubber bellows for wear or damage and replace if necessary. Install the bellows and position it through the hole in the backing

plate. Make sure the bellows sits correctly on the backing plate.

6. Smear the contact surfaces of the brake levers with a thin layer of heat resistant graphite grease. Connect the cable to the lever and install the pin.

NOTE: The arrow stamped on the lever should point upward and outwards.

7. Push the cable through and place the lever in position behind the rear axle flange.

8. Install the cable guide on the axle. Connect the cable to the equalizer using the pin and spring clip.

9. Install the brake shoes and rear return spring. Install the brake disc and caliper. Use new bolts. and torque to 43 ft. lbs. Make sure the disc rotates freely. Adjust the parking brake. Install the wheel and lower the car.

LONG CABLE, LEFT SIDE

1. Remove the center console.

2. Slacken the parking brake adjusting screw. Remove the cable lock ring and remove the cable. Pull out the cable from the spring sleeve.

3. Jack up the rear end of the car and safely support it with jackstands. Remove the left rear wheel.

4. Remove the left rear brake caliper and hang it from the coil spring with a piece of wire. Remove the brake disc and rear return spring. Remove the brake shoes.

5. Push out the pin holding the cable to the lever. Remove the rubber bellows from the backing plate and remove the bellows from the cable.

6. Pull out the cable from the backing plate and the equalizer on top of the rear axle.

7. Remove the cable clamp on the sub-frame (above the driveshaft) and the cable.

8. Install the new cable through the grommet in the floor; check that the grommet sits correctly. Clamp the cable to the sub-frame.

9. Follow Step 6-9 of the 'Short Cable' procedure above to finish installation. Adjust the cable and install the console.

CHASSIS ELECTRICAL

Heater

REMOVAL & INSTALLATION
240 and 260 Models
STANDARD HEATING SYSTEM

1. Drain the cooling system. Dis-

connect the negative battery cable.

2. Remove the center panel and the lefthand defroster hose.

3. Lift up the driveshaft tunnel mat, disconnect the front and rear attaching screws of the rear seat heater ducts, and then remove the ducts from the heater.

4. Disconnect the heater control valve and air-mix cable from their shutters.

5. Disconnect and plug the pressure hose at the heater. Also plug the heater pipes to prevent residual coolant from spilling onto the carpet.

6. Remove the attaching screws which secure the left-hand upper bracket to the dashboard and the left-hand lower bracket to the transmission tunnel.

7. Remove the glovebox by unscrewing the four attaching screws, removing the glovebox door stop, and disconnecting the wires from the glovebox courtesy light.

8. Disconnect the defroster and floor heating cables from their levers.

9. Disconnect the fan motor wires at the switch contact plate.

10. Remove the attaching screws which secure the right-hand upper bracket to the dashboard and the right-hand lower bracket to the transmission tunnel.

11. Remove the right-hand defroster hose. Disconnect the hose between the heater and the dashboard circular vents. Lift the heater unit to the right, and then out of the vehicle.

12. Reverse the above procedure to install, taking care to ensure that the air vent rubber seal is properly located, and that the fan motor ground cable is attached to the upper righthand bracket attaching screw.

COMBINATION HEATER—AIR CONDITIONER SYSTEM

——— CAUTION ———

When working on this system, DO NOT disconnect any refrigerant lines. The refrigerant, R-12, is dangerous when released and can burn your skin.

1. Drain the radiator. Disconnect the negative battery cable.

2. Remove the heater hoses from the heater pipes at the engine side of the firewall. Plug the heater pipes.

3. Remove the evaporator hose brackets from their body mounts and disconnect the dryer from its bracket. Position the dryer as close to the firewall as the evaporator hose permits.

4. Remove the instrument cluster by removing the steering column molded casings, removing the bracket retaining screw and lowering it toward the steering column, removing

the four instruments cluster retaining screws, disconnecting the speedometer cable, tilting the speedometer out of its snap fitting, moving the electrical plug contacts, then lifting the cluster out of the vehicle.

5. Remove the air hose between the central unit and the left inner air vent. Remove the hose from the vacuum motor for the left defroster nozzle.

6. Remove the left-side panel from the central unit.

7. Lift up the driveshaft tunnel mat and disconnect the rear seat heater duct from the central unit.

8. Remove the heater pipe from the passenger side of the firewall.

9. Remove the upper and lower attaching screws for the left support leg. Remove the attaching screws which secure the upper bracket to the dashboard and the lower bracket to the transmission tunnel.

NOTE: If the upper bracket screw holes are slotted, the screws need only be slackened a few turns.

10. Remove the right-side panel from the central unit.

11. Remove the glovebox by unscrewing the four attaching screws, removing the glovebox door stop, and disconnecting the glovebox courtesy light wires.

12. Remove the right defroster nozzle, and also the air hose between the central unit and the right inner air vent.

13. Lift up the driveshaft tunnel mat and disconnect the rear seat heater duct from the central unit.

14. Remove the upper and lower attaching screws for the right support leg. Remove the lower attaching screws for the control panel.

15. Disconnect the fan motor wires and the ground wires from the control panel.

16. Disconnect the yellow lead cable form its plug contact.

17. Separate the halves of the vacuum hose connector and disconnect the vacuum tank hose at the connector.

18. Position the control panel as far back on the transmission tunnel as the cables permit.

19. Remove the screws which attach the upper brackets to the firewall and the lower brackets to the transmission tunnel.

20. Remove the thermostat clamp from the central unit, and the two evaporator cover retaining clamps.

21. Without disconnecting any of the refrigerant lines, remove the evaporator from the central unit, placing it on the right-hand side of the firewall.

22. Remove the molded dashboard padding from beneath the glovebox.

23. Remove the retaining clamps for the right outer vent duct, and remove the duct. Pry off the locking retainer for the blower, and remove the turbine. Remove the clamps which retain the blower housing (inner end) to the central unit and remove the housing.

24. Remove the passenger's front seat cushion and lift the central unit forward and onto the floor of the vehicle. Be careful not to lace undue stress on the connected refrigerant lines.

25. Reverse the above procedure to install, taking care to ensure that the evaporator pipes and thermostat capillary are enclosed in sealing compound, that the drainage tubes are inserted in the respective transmission tunnel holes, and that the ground cable are connected.

740, 760 and 780 Models

This model is equipped with a climate unit which incorporates a heating and air conditioning system. The steering wheel, passenger's seat and dashboard must be removed entirely for the climate unit to be removed. Heater core and blower motor removal and replacement are covered below.

Blower

REMOVAL & INSTALLATION
240 and 260 Models
STANDARD HEATING SYSTEM

1. Disconnect the negative battery cable. Remove the heater unit.

2. Place the unit on its side with the control valve facing upward. Remove the spring clips and separate the housing halves.

3. Lift out the old fan motor and replace it with a new unit, making sure that the support leg without the 'foot' points to the output for the defroster channel.

4. Assemble the heater housing halves with new spring clips, and seal the joint without clips with soft sealing compound.

5. Install the heater unit.

COMBINATION HEATER–AIR CONDITIONER SYSTEM

In order to remove the blower motor, both the right and left blower wheels must first be removed. The heater unit does not have to be removed.

1. Disconnect the negative battery cable.

2. Lift the carpet and remove the central unit side panels.

3. Remove the retaining screws for the control panel and move the panel as for back on the transmission tunnel as the electrical cables will permit.

4. Remove the attaching screws for

the rear seat heater ducts and disconnect the ducts from the central unit.

5. Remove the instrument cluster.

6. Remove the glovebox by unscrewing the four attaching screws, removing the glovebox door stop, and disconnecting the wires from the glovebox courtesy light. Remove the molded dashboard padding from beneath the glovebox.

7. Disconnect the vacuum hoses to the left and right defroster nozzle vacuum motors, then remove the nozzles and the left and right air ducts.

8. Remove the air hoses between the left and right inside air vents.

9. Remove the clamps on the central unit outer ends, and remove the ends.

10. Pry off the locking retainer for the turbines (blower wheels), and remove both left and right blower wheels.

11. Position the heater control valve capillary tube to one side.

12. Remove the left inner end (blower housing) from the central unit.

13. Unscrew the three retaining screws and remove the fan motor retainer.

14. Disconnect the plug contact from the fan motor control panel. Release the tabs of electric cables from the plug contact, and, removing the rubber grommet, pull the electrical cables down through the central unit right opening.

15. Remove the fan motor from the left opening.

16. Reverse the above procedure to install.

740, 760 and 780 Models

1. Disconnect the negative battery cable. Remove the panel beneath the glove compartment.

2. Unfasten the screws securing the fan motor, and lower the motor. Disconnect the hose for air cooling on the motor, and disconnect the wiring.

3. Remove the motor and fan.

4. To install, reconnect the wiring to the fan motor. Spread a sealer around the mounting face of the fan mounting flange, and install the fan motor. Reconnect the hose for cooling, and check fan operation. Reinstall the panel beneath the glove compartment.

Heater Core

REMOVAL & INSTALLATION

240 and 260 Models
STANDARD HEATING SYSTEM

1. Disconnect the negative battery cable. Remove the heater unit.

2. Place the unit on its side with the control valve facing upward. Remove the spring clips and separate the housing halves.

3. Disconnect the capillary tube from the heater core and then lift out the core.

4. Reverse the above procedure to install, being careful to transfer the foam plastic packing to the new heater core, and to install the fragile capillary tube carefully on the core.

COMBINATION HEATER—AIR CONDITIONER SYSTEM

—————— CAUTION ——————

Do not disconnect the refrigerant lines from the air conditioning system. These lines carry a dangerous refrigerant, the gas R-12.

1. Disconnect the negative battery cable. Remove the combination heater-air conditioner unit.

2. Remove the left outer end of the central unit. Remove the locking retainer and the turbine (blower wheel).

3. Remove the two retaining screws for the left transmission tunnel bracket.

4. Remove the lockring for the left intake shutter shaft.

5. Remove the three retaining screws and lift off the inner end.

6. Remove the three retaining screws for the fan motor retainer.

7. Disconnect the heater hoses at the heater core.

8. Remove the clamps which retain the central unit halves together, lift off the left half, and remove the heater core.

9. Reverse the above procedure to install, taking care to transfer the foam plastic packing to the new heater core.

740, 760 and 780 Models

1. Disconnect the negative battery cable.

2. Pinch the hoses to the heater core near the firewall in the engine compartment. Use locking pliers. Make sure the hoses are pinched sufficiently so that the hose is completely blocked off. Remove the hose clamps on the engine compartment side of the hoses (close to the firewall).

3. Press down the clip under the ashtray and pull the tray out. Remove the cigarette lighter and the storage compartment.

4. Remove the engine console around the shift lever and parking brake. Unplug the connector.

5. Remove the panel beneath the driver's side dashboard, and remove the air duct to the steering column outlet.

6. Pull down the driver's side floor

mat and remove the front and rear edge side panel screws. Remove the panels.

7. On the passenger's side, remove the 3 clips that fasten the panel beneath the glove compartment and remove the panel. Remove the glove compartment and its lighting.

8. Pull down the floor mat on the right side and remove the front and rear edge side panel screws.

9. Remove the radio compartment by pressing forward on the inner wall and removing the screw.

10. Remove the screws inside the center console and remove the side panel screws and the panels.

11. Remove the panel around the heater control. Remove the radio compartment console and remove the control panel. Free the central electrical unit and remove the mounting.

12. Remove the center panel vent, and the screw holding the distribution unit. Mark all air ducts to the panel vents and to the distribution unit with tape for later installation, and remove the ducts.

13. Remove the vacuum hoses from the vacuum motors.

14. Remove the distribution unit. Remove the heater core retaining clips and remove the heater core.

15. To reinstall, reverse the above procedure taking note of the following vacuum hose connections: On climate unit-equipped cars, connect the red hose to the upper shutter for the panel vents, and the light brown hose to the lower shutter. Connect the yellow and blue hoses to the floor/defrost shutter, the yellow to the lower one. On automatic climate control-equipped cars, connect the red hose to the upper shutter for the panel vent, and the blue hose to the defrost vent. Connect the light brown hose to the lower shutter for the panel unit.

Windshield Wiper Motor

REMOVAL & INSTALLATION

240 and 260 Models

1. Disconnect the negative battery cable.

2. Disconnect the drive link from the wiper motor lever by unsnapping the locking tab underneath the dashboard.

3. Open the hood and disconnect the plug contact from the motor, located on the firewall.

4. Remove the three attaching screws and lift out the motor.

5. Reverse the above procedure to install, taking care to transfer the rubber seal, rubber damper, and spacer sleeves to the new motor.

740, 760 and 780 Models

1. Disconnect the negative battery cable. Remove the wiper arms.

2. Lift up the hood to its uppermost position by pushing the catch on the hood hinges.

3. Remove the plastic clips and screw securing the wiper mechanism cover plate. Remove the cover plate by lifting it upwards and forwards. Close the hood.

4. Remove the cover below the windshield.

5. Unbolt the motor from its mount. Disconnect the motor wires at the connectors.

6. Installation is the reverse of removal.

screws.

5. Disconnect the speedometer cable.

6. Tilt the cluster out of its snap fitting and disconnect the plug contact. On vehicles equipped with a tachometer, disconnect the tachometer sending wire.

7. Lift the cluster out of the dashboard.

8. Reverse the above procedure to install.

1986-88 240 Models and 740, 760 and 780 Models

1. Disconnect the negative battery cable. Remove the soundproofing above the foot pedals.

2. Remove the two catches and screws holding the panel.

3. Press the instrument panel forwards. Remove the panel from the dash.

4. Disconnect the connectors, and remove the instrument panel completely.

Fuses

LOCATION

On 240, 260 series the fuse box is located beneath a protective cover, below the dashboard, in front of the driver's door. On the 740, 760 and 780 the fuses are located under a plastic panel in the center console, behind the ashtray.

On electronic fuel injected models, an additional fuse box is located in the engine compartment on the left wheel well. It houses a single fuse protecting the electrical fuel pump.

Yugo
GV

19

SERIAL NUMBER IDENTIFICATION

Vehicle Identification Plate

An identification plate is riveted to the radiator housing under the hood. It contains information on the body type and serial number, as well as a listing of the engine type used in the model. In addition, the body number is stamped into the right front shock tower in the engine compartment.

The chassis VIN number is stamped on a small plate that is affixed to the dash and is visible through the windshield.

Engine Number

The engine number is stamped on a pad located on the side of the engine block, near the thermostat housing.

Vehicle Identification Label

A vehicle identification label is affixed to the underside of the hood or to a panel in the engine compartment and contains information on emission control devices, specifications for tune-up and ignition timing and the recommended idle speed settings. Some models may also have a vacuum circuit diagram on the underhood sticker.

ENGINE IDENTIFICATION

Year	Model	Engine Displacement cu. in. (cc/liter)	Engine Series Identification	No. of Cylinders	Engine Type
1986	GV	68 (1116/1.1)	128A064	4	SOHC
1987	GV	68 (1116/1.1)	128A064	4	SOHC
1988	GV	68 (1116/1.1)	128A064	4	SOHC

GENERAL ENGINE SPECIFICATIONS

Year	Model	Engine Displacement cu. in. (cc)	Fuel System Type	Net Horsepower @ rpm	Net Torque @ rpm (ft. lbs.)	Bore × Stroke (in.)	Compression Ratio	Oil Pressure @ rpm
1986	128A	68 (1116)	2 bbl	55 @ 6000	52 @ 4600	3.150 × 2.185	9.2:1	60@3000
1987	128A	68 (1116)	2 bbl	55 @ 6000	52 @ 4600	3.150 × 2.185	9.2:1	60@3000
1988	128A	68 (1116)	2 bbl	55 @ 6000	52 @ 4600	3.150 × 2.185	9.2:1	60@3000

GASOLINE ENGINE TUNE-UP SPECIFICATIONS

Year	Model	Engine Displacement cu. in. (cc)	Spark Plugs Type	Gap (in.)	Ignition Timing (deg.) MT	AT	Compression Pressure (psi)	Fuel Pump (psi)	Idle Speed (rpm) MT	AT	Valve Clearance In.	Ex.
1986	128A	68 (1116)	RN9Y	0.030	12B	—	185	2.5	800	—	0.016	0.018
1987–88	128A	68 (1116)	RN9Y	0.030	12B	—	185	2.5	800	—	0.016	0.018

CAPACITIES

Year	Model	Engine Displacement cu. in. (cc)	Engine Crankcase with Filter	without Filter	Transmission (pts.) 4-Spd	5-Spd	Auto.	Drive Axle (pts.)	Fuel Tank (gal.)	Cooling System (qts.)
1986	128A	68 (1116)	4.5	4.0	6.8	—	—	—	8.4	7.0
1987–88	128A	68 (1116)	4.5	4.0	6.8	—	—	—	8.4	7.0

FIRING ORDERS

NOTE: To avoid confusion, always replace spark plug wires one at a time.

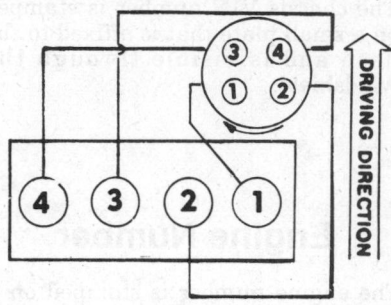

68 cu. in. (1116cc) engine Firing order
1–3–4–2 Distributor rotation: clockwise

CAMSHAFT SPECIFICATIONS
All measurements given in inches.

Year	Engine Displacement cu. in. (cc)	Journal Diameter 1	2	3	4	5	Lobe Lift In.	Ex.	Bearing Clearance	Camshaft End Play
1986	68 (1116)	1.1789–1.1795	1.8872–1.8878	1.8951–1.8957	1.9030–1.9035	1.9108–1.9114	NA	NA	0.0012–0.0028	NA
1987–88	68 (1116)	1.1789–1.1795	1.8872–1.8878	1.8951–1.8957	1.9030–1.9035	1.9108–1.9114	NA	NA	0.0012–0.0028	NA

NA—Not available at time of publication

CRANKSHAFT AND CONNECTING ROD SPECIFICATIONS
All measurements are given in inches.

Year	Engine Displacement cu. in. (cc)	Crankshaft				Connecting Rod		
		Main Brg. Journal Dia.	Main Brg. Oil Clearance	Shaft End-play	Thrust on No.	Journal Diameter	Oil Clearance	Side Clearance
1986	68 (1116)	1.9994–2.0002	0.0016–0.0033	0.002–0.010	5	1.7913–1.7920	0.0014–0.0034	NA
1987–88	68 (1116)	1.9994–2.0002	0.0016–0.0033	0.002–0.010	5	1.7913–1.7920	0.0014–0.0034	NA

NA—Not available at time of publication

VALVE SPECIFICATIONS

Year	Engine Displacement cu. in. (cc)	Seat Angle (deg.)	Face Angle (deg.)	Spring Test Pressure (in. @ lb.)	Spring Installed Height (in.)	Stem-to-Guide Clearance (in.)		Stem Diameter (in.)	
						Intake	Exhaust	Intake	Exhaust
1986	68 (1116)	45	45	①	②	0.006 max	0.006 max	0.3139–0.3146	0.3139–0.3146
1987–88	68 (1116)	45	45	①	②	0.006 max	0.006 max	0.3139–0.3146	0.3139–0.3146

① Inner: 33 @ 1.22
Outer: 86 @ 1.42
② Inner: 1.22
Outer: 1.42

PISTON AND RING SPECIFICATIONS
All measurments are given in inches.

Year	Engine Displacement cu. in. (cc)	Piston Clearance	Ring Gap			Ring Side Clearance		
			Top Compression	Bottom Compression	Oil Control	Top Compression	Bottom Compression	Oil Control
1986	68 (1116)	0.001–0.002	0.0118–0.0177	0.0079–0.0140	0.0079–0.0140	0.0018–0.0030	0.0001–0.0022	0.0008–0.0019
1987–88	68 (1116)	0.001–0.002	0.0118–0.0177	0.0079–0.0140	0.0079–0.0140	0.0018–0.0030	0.0001–0.0022	0.0008–0.0019

TORQUE SPECIFICATIONS
All readings in ft. lbs.

Year	Engine Displacement cu. in. (cc)	Cylinder Head Bolts	Main Bearing Bolts	Rod Bearing Bolts	Crankshaft Pulley Bolts	Flywheel Bolts	Manifold		Spark Plugs
							Intake	Exhaust	
1986	68 (1116)	①	59	38	101	61	20	20	27
1987–88	68 (1116)	①	59	38	101	61	20	20	27

① M12 bolts: 69
M10 bolts: 28

BRAKE SPECIFICATIONS
All measurements in inches unless noted

| Year | Model | Lug Nut Torque (ft. lbs.) | Master Cylinder Bore | Brake Disc | | Standard Brake Drum Diameter | Minimum Lining Thickness | |
				Minimum Thickness	Maximum Runout		Front	Rear
1986	GV	64	0.750	0.354	0.08	7.298	0.059	0.059
1987–88	GV	64	0.750	0.354	0.08	7.298	0.059	0.059

WHEEL ALIGNMENT

| Year | Model | Caster | | Camber | | Toe-in (in.) | Steering Axis Inclination (deg.) |
		Range (deg.)	Preferred Setting (deg.)	Range (deg.)	Preferred Setting (deg.)		
1986	GV	1¾P-2¾P	2¼P	1-2P	1½P	0	NA
1987–88	GV	1¾P-2¾P	2¼P	1-2P	1½P	0	NA

NA—Not available at time of publication

TUNE-UP PROCEDURES

Ignition Timing

ADJUSTMENT

1. Connect a tachometer and a timing light to the engine according to the manufacturer's instructions.

2. Start the engine and allow it to reach normal operation temperature.

3. Stop the engine and locate and clean the timing marks on the engine.

4. Start the engine and check the idle speed. Adjust to specifications if necessary.

5. Check the timing with the timing light. If not within specifications, loosen the distributor holddown bolt and rotate the distributor to advance or retard the timing as necessary.

6. Once the timing is set to specifications, check and readjust the idle speed if necessary.

Valve Lash

ADJUSTMENT

Valve clearance is adjusted by replacing the valve tappet discs. A tapped depressing tool is necessary for this procedure.

1. Rotate the engine in the normal direction of rotation to set No. 1 cylinder at TDC on the compression stroke.

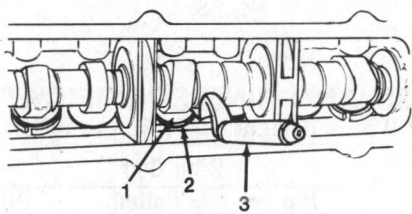

1. Shim to be removed
2. Tappets depressed by tool
3. Tappet depressor A60421

Replace the adjusting disc to adjust valve clearance

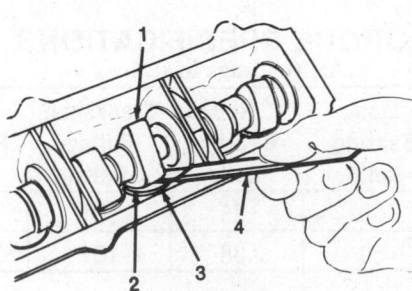

1. Camshaft lobe
2. Tappet plate
3. Tappet
4. Feeler gauge

Checking valve clearance

2. Remove the camshaft cover.

3. Use a feeler gauge between the heel of the camshaft lobe and the tappet disc to measure the valve clearance with the engine cold. Check the clearances of cylinders No. 1 & 4.

4. Rotate the engine one full revolution and check the remaining valve tappet clearances. If both intake and exhaust valve clearance is within specifications, no adjustment is necessary.

5. If valve clearance is excessive, use a syringe to remove oil from around the tappets to simplify disc removal. Insert the tappet depressor tool A–60421, or equivalent, and release the spring pressure from the adjusting disc. Remove the adjusting disc with needle nose pliers or a short burst of compressed air.

6. Use a micrometer to measure the disc thickness upon removal and record this figure, noting the cylinder number and intake or exhaust valve shim.

7. Add the difference between actual and specified valve clearance to the thickness of the adjusting disc to determine which size disc to install in order to bring the clearance within specifications. Tappet discs are available for service in a range of thicknesses 3.25-4.70mm. The thickness of the shim is stamped on one of its flat surfaces and this side should be assembled toward the tappet.

8. Once the proper size disc is installed, recheck the valve clearance and install the camshaft cover with a new gasket.

Idle Speed and Mixture

ADJUSTMENT

1. Start the engine and allow it to reach normal operating temperature.
2. Check and adjust the idle speed and ignition timing, if necessary.
3. Insert a suitable exhaust gas analyzer probe into the tailpipe and read the CO% and HC level on the analyzer meter.
4. Check the underhood emission control sticker for CO and HC specifications. If adjustment is necessary, turn the idle mixture screw on the carburetor in or out to bring the emission levels into compliance with specifications.
5. Re-adjust the idle speed, if necessary. Do not reset the ignition timing.

ENGINE ELECTRICAL

Distributor

REMOVAL & INSTALLATION

1. Disconnect the spark plug wires from the spark plugs, then remove the distributor cap from the distributor with the wires attached. Number the spark plug leads with tape to ease installation.
2. Disconnect the vacuum line from the distributor vacuum advance diaphragm.
3. Rotate the engine in the normal direction of rotation to set No. 1 cylinder at TDC on the compression stroke.
4. Scribe a mark from the distributor body to the block, then again in line with the rotor. These two matchmarks will allow you to check that the distributor is installed correctly and the timing is close enough to allow the engine to start and idle.
5. Loosen the distributor holddown screw and disconnect any remaining wiring connectors from the distributors.
6. Remove the holddown screw and lift the distributor straight up to remove it. Do not rotate the engine with the distributor removed. Check rotor, pickup assembly and stator for cracks or damage and replace components as necessary.
7. Installation is the reverse of removal. Align the matchmarks made earlier and check the timing.

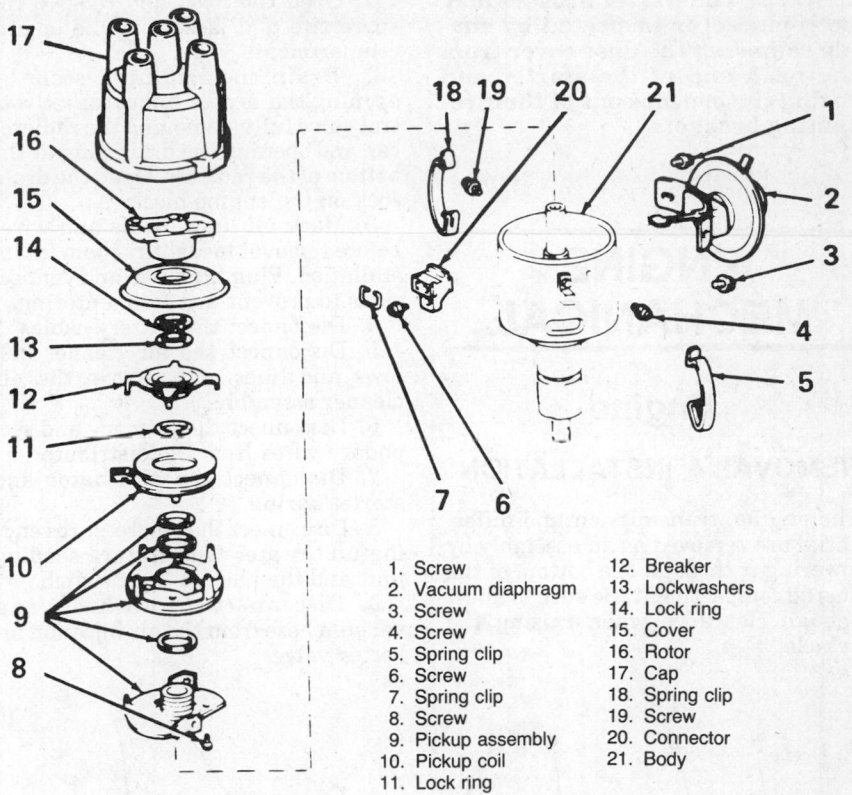

1. Screw		12. Breaker
2. Vacuum diaphragm		13. Lockwashers
3. Screw		14. Lock ring
4. Screw		15. Cover
5. Spring clip		16. Rotor
6. Screw		17. Cap
7. Spring clip		18. Spring clip
8. Screw		19. Screw
9. Pickup assembly		20. Connector
10. Pickup coil		21. Body
11. Lock ring		

Exploded view of Bosch distributor

Alternator

REMOVAL & INSTALLATION

1. Disconnect the battery cables.
2. Tag and disconnect the alternator wiring.
3. Loose the adjusting bolt and remove the drive belt.
4. Remove the mounting bolts and lift the alternator from the engine.
5. Installation is the reverse of removal. Make sure all connections are clean and tight. Adjust the alternator drive belt tension.

Voltage Regulator

REMOVAL & INSTALLATION

The voltage regulator is integral with the alternator and can only be removed during alternator overhaul. All models use an electronic, non-adjustable regulator that can be damaged if the battery cables are removed while the engine is running.

Starter

REMOVAL & INSTALLATION

1. Disconnect the battery cables.
2. Remove the spare tire and jack.
3. Remove any splash shields that may be in the way to gain access to the starter.
4. Tag and disconnect the starter wiring.
5. Remove the three mounting bolts and lift the starter from the engine compartment.
6. Installation is the reverse of removal.

STARTER DRIVE REPLACEMENT

The starter drive can be replaced once the starter has been removed by removing the mounting bolts and separating the drive housing from the starter housing. The end bushing in the drive housing need only be replaced if worn or damaged.

STARTER SOLENOID REPLACEMENT

The starter solenoid can be replaced without disassembling the starter. Remove the solenoid mounting screws and remove the solenoid from the starter assembly. The solenoid is replaced as a unit.

NOTE: The starter brushes may be replaced or inspected by simply removing the dust cover from the back end of the starter and lifting the brushes out of their retaining brackets.

ENGINE MECHANICAL

Engine

REMOVAL & INSTALLATION

The engine, transmission and differential are removed as an assembly by lowering it through the bottom of the engine compartment. Be sure to allow enough clearance when raising the vehicle.

1. Open the hood and remove the spare tire and jack from the engine compartment.
2. Drain the cooling system by opening the heater temperature control valve fully, removing the radiator cap and opening the drain plug at the bottom of the radiator. Open the drain cock on the engine block.
3. Mark all lines, hoses and wires before removal to identify them for installation. Plug all hoses and connections to prevent dirt from entering.
4. Disconnect the battery cables.
5. Disconnect the air cleaner bellows and lines and remove the air cleaner assembly.
6. Disconnect the primary and secondary wires from the distributor.
7. Disconnect the alternator and starter wiring.
8. Disconnect the oil pressure sending unit, water temperature sending unit and the backup light switch.
9. Disconnect the air hoses and vacuum hose from the air injection diverter valve.

10. Disconnect the accelerator cable from the carburetor.
11. Disconnect the vacuum and fuel evaporative hoses from the carburetor and intake manifold.
12. Disconnect the wiring connectors from the carburetor choke and anti-dieseling solenoid.
13. Disconnect the fuel supply and return hoses.
14. Disconnect the exhaust pipe from the manifold.
15. Disconnect the two radiator hoses from the thermostat housing.
16. Disconnect the heater hoses from the engine.
17. Disconnect the speedometer cable from the transmission by unscrewing the securing ring.
18. Remove the clutch cable from the clutch release lever after loosening the locknut.
19. Attach a lifting fixture to the engine and place the hoist under light tension.
20. Raise the car and support it safely. Remove both front wheels.

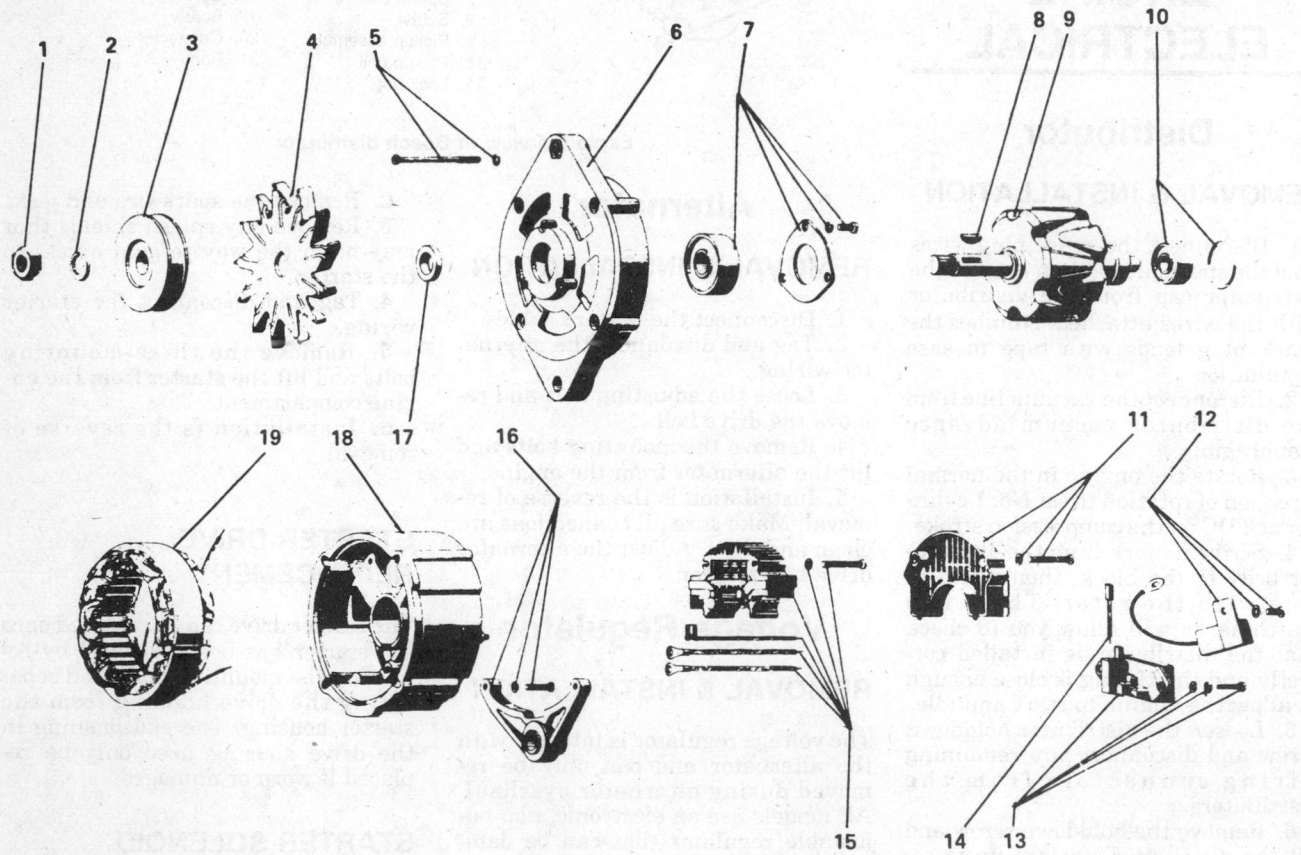

1. Nut	6. Frame
2. Spring washer	7. Bearing and retainer plate
3. Pulley	8. Key
4. Fan	9. Rotor
5. Through bolt	10. Bearing and backing washer
11. Rectifier plate	16. Support
12. Condenser	17. Thrust ring
13. Voltage regulator	18. Rear frame
14. Brush	19. Stator
15. Rectifier	

Exploded view of Iskra alternator

21. Unscrew the left tie rod end nut and disconnect the tie rod joint using a suitable tie rod fork. Do not hammer on the tie rod stud.

22. Remove the sway bar bracket bolts and the nut securing the sway bar to the control rod. Remove the sway bar.

23. Remove the mounting bolts and nuts and remove the shock absorber and strut assembly from the steering knuckle.

24. Remove th CV-joint nuts from both front wheels, Work the shaft of each CV joint out of its seat in the knuckles. Secure the axle shafts with wire to retain them in their seats in the differential.

25. Remove the exhaust pipe support bracket from the transmission housing. Disconnect the ground strap from the transmission housing.

26. Disconnect the gearshift linkage by removing the pinch bolt and nut at the shifter rod.

27. Disconnect the crossmember from the underbody. Make sure the engine hoist is supporting the weight before attempting to remove the crossmember.

28. Working in the engine compartment from above, disconnect the reaction strut from the engine.

29. Remove the front right engine mount bolt.

30. Using the hoist, lower the engine and transaxle assembly through the bottom of the engine compartment. Set the assembly on a dolly and roll it out from beneath the car. Continue disassembly on a workbench or engine stand.

31. Installation is the reverse of removal procedures. Refill the cooling system and check all fluid levels before attempting to start the engine.

NOTE: Replace any self-locking nuts removed in the course of service.

Cylinder Head

REMOVAL & INSTALLATION

1. Disconnect the positive (+) battery cable.
2. Drain the cooling system and remove the spare tire from the engine compartment.
3. Mark all lines, hoses and wires before removal to identify them for installation. Plug all hoses and lines to prevent the entry of dirt.
4. Disconnect the air cleaner assembly and remove it from the engine.
5. Disconnect the accelerator cable from the carburetor. Disconnect the

wires from the choke and anti-dieseling solenoid.
6. Disconnect the fuel supply and return hoses from the carburetor.
7. Disconnect the vacuum fuel evaporative hoses from the intake manifold and carburetor.
8. Remove the carburetor.
9. Remove the thermostat housing from the cylinder head. Coolant hoses may remain attached to the housing.
10. Remove the timing belt cover.
11. Remove the air pump and support bracket.
12. Disconnect the coolant hose from the cylinder head outlet.
13. Remove the alternator without disconnecting the wires and lay it aside.
14. Loosen the tension pulley and remove the timing belt from the cam sprocket.
15. Remove the upper belt shield.
16. Disconnect the exhaust pipe from the exhaust manifold.
17. Disconnect the EGR lines from the EGR valve and from the manifold.
18. Disconnect the spark plug wires.
19. Disconnect the wiring to all cylinder head sensors.
20. Loosen the cylinder head bolts in reverse of the torque sequence, then remove the bolts.

NOTE: The nuts on the carburetor side will require the use of a special wrench A–50131/1/2, or equivalent.

21. Remove the cylinder head with the intake and exhaust manifolds attached. Continue disassembly on a clean workbench.
22. Installation is the reverse of removal. Clean all gasket mating surfaces and install new gaskets. Torque all cylinder head bolt in sequence to specifications in two steps.

OVERHAUL

For all cylinder head overhaul procedures, please refer to Engine Rebuilding in the Unit Repair Section.

Intake Manifold

REMOVAL & INSTALLATION

1. Disconnect the positive (+) battery cable.
2. Remove the spare tire from the engine compartment.
3. Disconnect and remove the air cleaner assembly.
4. Disconnect the accelerator cable and the choke and anti-dieseling solenoid wired from the carburetor.

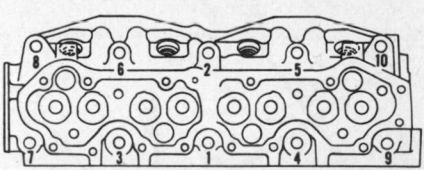

Cylinder head bolt torque sequence

5. Disconnect the fuel supply and return hoses from the carburetor and intake manifold.
6. Disconnect the vacuum fuel evaporative hoses from the carburetor and intake manifold.
7. Remove the carburetor.
8. Disconnect the EGR lines from the EGR valve and from the manifold.
9. Disconnect any brackets or braces that may be in the way, then loosen the intake manifold mounting bolts in sequence, working from the center outward in a spiral pattern.
10. Installation is the reverse of removal. Clean all gasket mating surfaces and use new gaskets. Torque intake manifold mounting bolts in sequence to specification.

Exhaust Manifold

REMOVAL & INSTALLATION

1. Remove the intake manifold as described above.
2. Disconnect the exhaust pipe from the manifold.
3. Disconnect the EGR valve from the exhaust manifold.
4. Loosen the exhaust manifold mounting bolts and remove the manifold.
5. Installation is the reverse of removal. Torque all exhaust manifold bolts in sequence to specifications.

Timing Belt and Tensioner

REMOVAL & INSTALLATION

1. Remove the timing belt cover. The lower retaining screw of the cover must be removed from under the vehicle after removing the right splash guard.
2. Align the timing mark on the back of the camshaft sprocket with the timing mark on the shield. The timing mark on the crankshaft pulley should coincide with the timing mark on the cover.
3. Apply the hand brake firmly and shift the transmission into first gear to prevent the crankshaft from rotating.

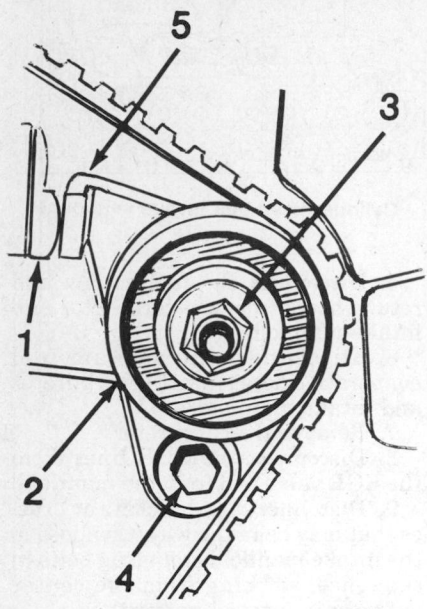

1. Tensioner
2. Tensioner pulley
3. Pulley nut
4. Support bolt
5. Support

Timing belt tensioner

4. Loosen the upper nut and the alternator-to-bracket bolt and remove the drive belt.

5. Loosen the timing belt tensioner retaining nut and move the tensioner toward the engine mount, then tighten the nut to hold it there. Remove the timing belt with the slack on the tensioner side.

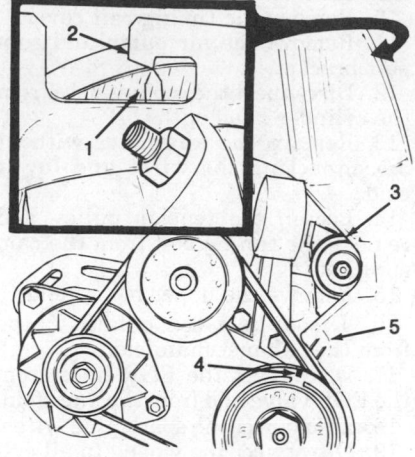

1. Sprocket index mark
2. Belt shield index mark
3. Belt tensioner
4. Timing mark
5. Belt cover timing mark

Timing mark alignment

6. Install a new timing belt. Make sure the belt teeth are properly seated in the sprockets.

7. Loosen the nut holding the tensioner and allow the tensioner to tighten the belt. Torque the tensioner nut in this position to 33 ft. lbs.

8. Check that the timing marks are still correctly aligned, then install the alternator drive belt and adjust the tension to obtain ½ in. deflection with moderate thumb pressure.

9. Install the timing belt cover and check the ignition timing.

NOTE: Timing belts cannot be reused once removed from the engine. Do not attempt to adjust the timing belt tension after the initial installation.

Camshaft

REMOVAL & INSTALLATION

1. Remove the cylinder head from the engine.

2. Remove the camshaft housing cover.

3. Loosen the center bolt and remove the camshaft sprocket.

4. Loosen the camshaft housing bolts in stages to allow the gradual release of valve spring pressure.

NOTE: When lifting the camshaft housing from the head, be careful that the tappets stay in position in their bores and do not fall out and become mixed up or damaged.

5. Remove the camshaft housing bolts and lift off the camshaft housing. Continue disassembly on a clean workbench.

6. Check that the camshaft bores in the housing are not out-of-round, scored, worn or show any signs of seizure. If any defects are noted, replace the housing. Make sure the camshaft journals and lobe surfaces are absolutely smooth in perfect condition. If

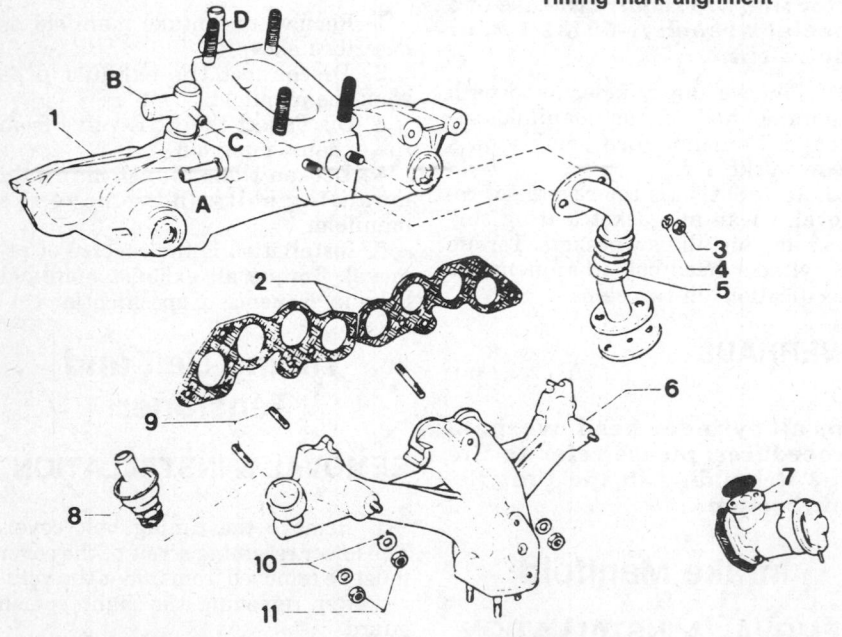

A. Coolant line connection
B. Power brake booster connection
C. Temperature vacuum valve connection
D. Oil separator connection
1. Intake manifold
2. Gasket
3. Nut
4. Lockwasher
5. EGR pipe
6. Exhaust manifold
7. EGR valve
8. Check valve
9. Manifold studs
10. Washers
11. Nuts

Exploded view of the intake and exhaust manifold

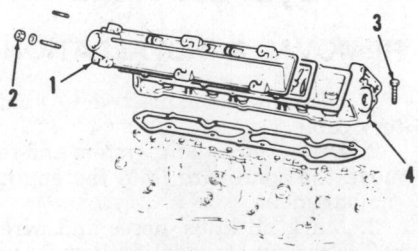

1. Camshaft housing cover
2. Nut
3. Bolt
4. Nut
5. Camshaft housing

Exploded view of the camshaft housing and cylinder head

any traces of seizure or scoring are noted, the camshaft should be replaced.

7. Install the camshaft in reverse of the removal procedures. Torque the camshaft housing nuts to 14 ft. lbs. and replace the camshaft drive end seal. Torque the camshaft sprocket bolt to 61 ft. lbs.

Piston and Connecting Rods

POSITIONING

For all piston and connecting rod overhaul procedures, please refer to Engine Rebuilding in the Unit Repair Section.

ENGINE LUBRICATION

Oil Pan

REMOVAL & INSTALLATION

1. Raise the vehicle and support it safely.

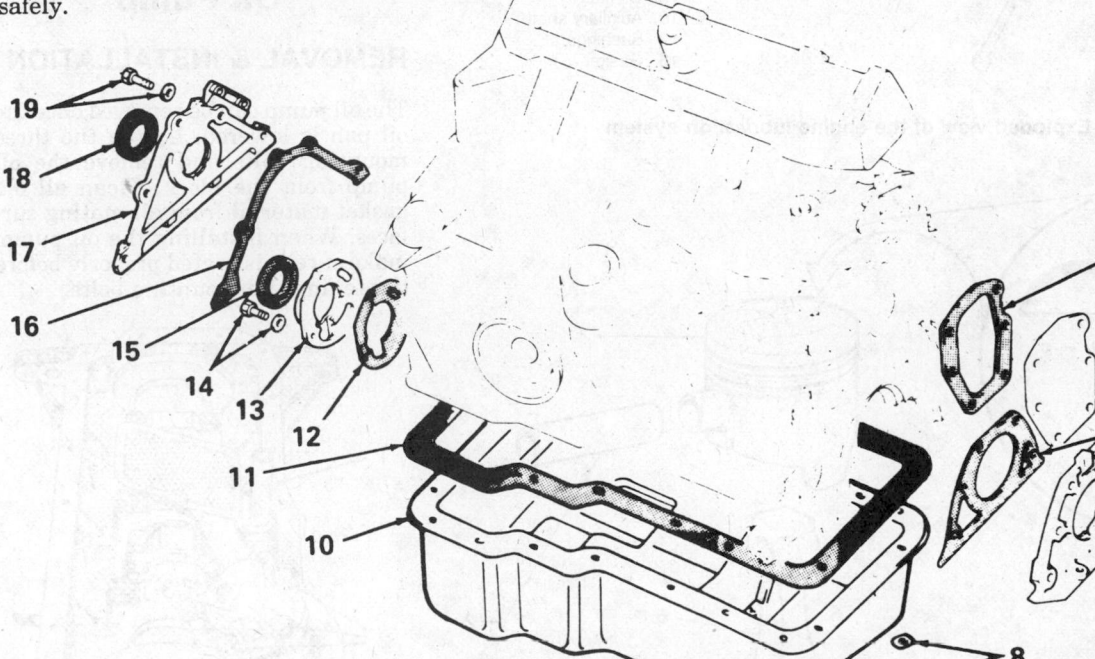

1. Seal
2. Dowel
3. Adjusting disc
4. Tappet
5. Locks
6. Upper cups
7. Inner springs
8. Outer springs
9. Lower cups
10. Exhaust valve guide
11. Exhaust valve
12. Flat washers
13. Intake valve
14. Intake valve guide
15. Oil seal
16. Camshaft
17. Welch plug

Exploded view of the valve mechanism

1. Gasket
2. Bolt and lockwsher
3. Water jacket cover plate
4. Gasket
5. Flywheel end cover plate
6. Oil seal
7. Bolt and lockwasher
8. Bolt and lockwasher
9. Oil drain plug
10. Oil pan
11. Gasket
12. Gasket
13. Auxiliary shaft lockplate
14. Bolt and lockwasher
15. Oil seal
16. Gasket
17. Timing gear end cover plate
18. Oil seal
19. Bolt and lockwasher

Engine gaskets and seals

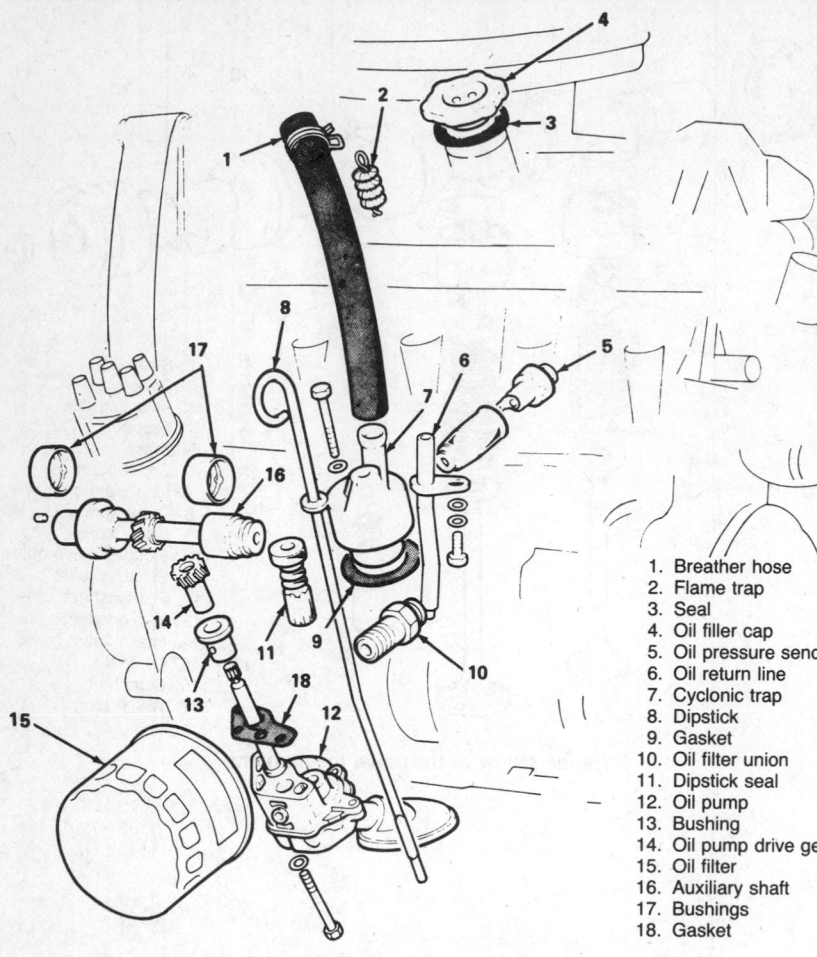

1. Breather hose
2. Flame trap
3. Seal
4. Oil filler cap
5. Oil pressure sender
6. Oil return line
7. Cyclonic trap
8. Dipstick
9. Gasket
10. Oil filter union
11. Dipstick seal
12. Oil pump
13. Bushing
14. Oil pump drive gear
15. Oil filter
16. Auxiliary shaft
17. Bushings
18. Gasket

Exploded view of the engine lubrication system

2. Remove the engine splash shield, if equipped.

3. Drain the engine oil and remove the oil filter.

4. Remove the bolts and washers mounting the oil pan to the engine block and lower the oil pan.

5. Clean all gasket mating surfaces and flush the oil pan with solvent to remove any deposits.

6. Installation is the reverse of removal. Use a new oil pan gasket and tighten the pan mounting bolts. Do not overtighten the pan bolts or oil leakage may occur.

Rear Main Bearing Oil Seal

REMOVAL & INSTALLATION

The rear main bearing seal is installed in the flywheel end cover plate. The transaxle and flywheel must be removed to gain access to the cover plate mounting bolts. With the cover installed, the distance between the cover seal and crankshaft should be equal all around the circumference. Torque the flywheel bolts to 61 ft. lbs. when installing.

Oil Pump

REMOVAL & INSTALLATION

The oil pump can be removed once the oil pan is lowered. Loosen the three mounting bolts and remove the oil pump from the block. Clean all old gasket material from all mating surfaces. When installing the oil pump, make sure it is seated properly before tightening the mounting bolts.

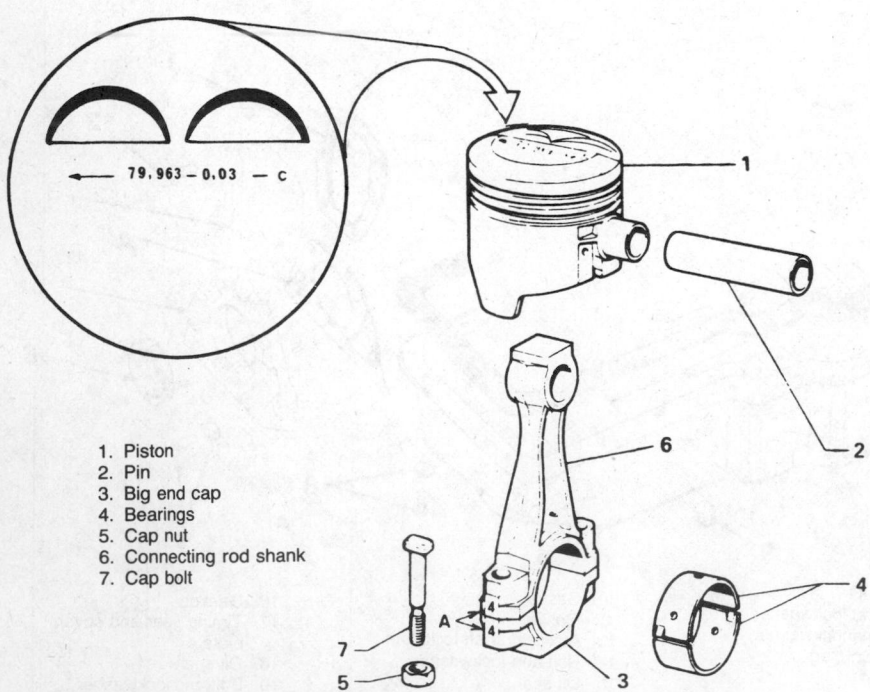

1. Piston
2. Pin
3. Big end cap
4. Bearings
5. Cap nut
6. Connecting rod shank
7. Cap bolt

Piston and connecting rod markings

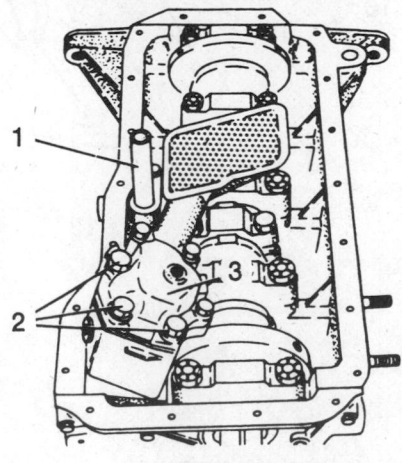

1. Oil return pipe
2. Bolt
3. Oil pump

Location of oil pump mounting bolts

ENGINE COOLING

Radiator

REMOVAL & INSTALLATION

1. Allow the engine to cool completely, then drain the cooling system.
2. Disconnect the negative battery cable.
3. Disconnect the upper and lower radiator hoses from the radiator. Disconnect the overflow hose.
4. Disconnect the temperature senor connectors and the cooling fan connector.
5. Remove the cooling fan assembly by loosening the four mounting nuts, then removing the nuts and washers and lifting the fan and motor shroud away from the radiator.
6. Remove the radiator bracket mounting bolts and lift the radiator out of the engine compartment.
7. Installation is the reverse of removal. Refill the cooling system and check for leaks.

NOTE: When pressure testing the cooling system, the radiator should hold 12–13 psi with a pressure tester attached to the filler neck. The cap vent valve should open at 11–12 psi.

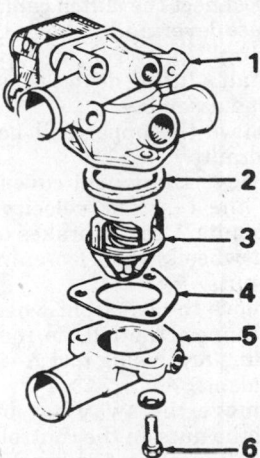

1. Thermostat housing
2. Seal
3. Thermostat
4. Gasket
5. Housing cover
6. Bolt

Exploded view of the thermostat assembly

Water Pump

REMOVAL & INSTALLATION

1. Allow the engine to cool and remove the timing belt cover.
2. Remove the air pump and drive belt.
3. Loosen the alternator and remove the drive belt.
4. Drain off enough coolant to bring the level below that of the water pump.
5. Remove the two bolts holding the intake pipe to the water pump and disconnect the pipe.
6. Remove the four bolts and lockwashers holding the pump to the engine block, then remove the pump and gasket.
7. Installation is the reverse of removal. Clean all gasket mating surfaces and use new gaskets. Refill the cooling system and check for leaks.

Thermostat

REMOVAL & INSTALLATION

1. Allow the engine to cool, then drain off enough coolant to bring the level below that of the thermostat housing.
2. Remove the spare tire from the engine compartment.
3. Disconnect the coolant hoses from the housing outlets.
4. Remove the three mounting bolts and lift off the thermostat housing and gasket. Remove the thermostat.
5. Installation is the reverse of removal. Clean all gasket mating surfaces and use new gaskets. Make sure the thermostat is installed correctly into the housing. The thermostat seal should be replaced with the thermostat.

1. Gasket
2. Water pump
3. Gasket
4. Pipe
5. Vacuum switch connection (4 port)
6. Vacuum switch connection (3 port)
7. Thermostat
8. Hose

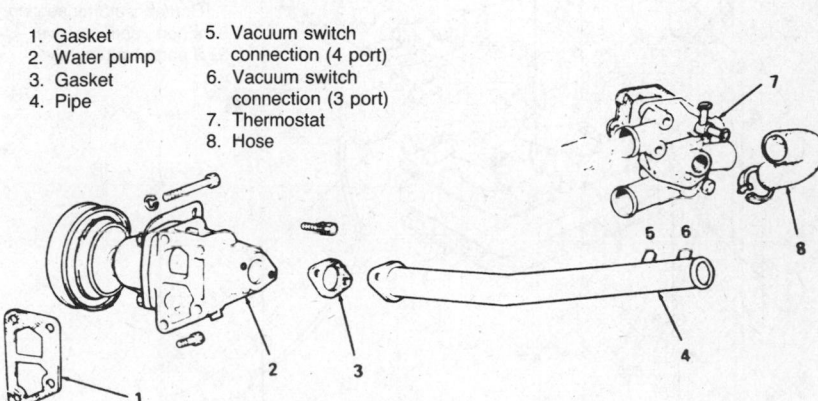

Exploded view of the water pump assembly

COOLING SYSTEM BLEEDING

When the cooling system is filled with coolant, a small amount of air will inevitably be trapped in the pipe connecting the radiator and the union containing the thermostat. Allowance is made for this by adding an extra 3–5 oz. of coolant to the expansion tank, which will be drawn into the system as soon as the bottom thermostat valve open. No other bleeding procedures are necessary.

EMISSION CONTROLS

Please refer to Emission Controls in the Unit Repair Section for system maintenance procedures. Due to the complex nature of modern electronic engine control systems, comprehensive diagnosis and testing procedures fall outside the confines of this repair manual. For complete information on diagnosis, testing and repair of engine and emission control systems, please refer to *"Chilton's Guide to Electronic Engine Controls"*.

FUEL SYSTEM

Fuel Filter

REPLACEMENT

An inline fuel filter is mounted near the fuel pump on all models. To replace the filter, simply remove the mounting clamps and disconnect the filter from the fuel line. When installing a new filter, make sure the arrow on the filter points toward the carburetor. Check all hoses and clamps for signs of wear, deterioration or leakage and replace components as necessary.

Fuel Pump

PRESSURE TESTING AND ADJUSTMENT

The normal fuel pump pressure is 2–3 psi @ 400 rpm. Tee a pressure gauge between the fuel pump and filter when checking system pressure. If fuel pressure is not within specifications, it may be adjusted by removing the fuel pump and replacing the gasket behind the pump insulator. Replacement gaskets come in three different sized to adjust the pump stroke and raise or lower the fuel pressure.

REMOVAL & INSTALLATION

1. Locate the fuel pump on the side of the engine block near the distributor and clean any grease or dirt from the pump area.
2. Loosen the hose clamps and disconnect the fuel lines from the pump.
3. Remove the two nuts and washers holding the fuel pump to the engine block studs.
4. Carefully remove the fuel pump, insulator, pushrod and gaskets from the engine block.

5. Clean all gasket mating surfaces.
6. Installation is the reverse of removal. Make sure the pump actuating rod is installed correctly and use new gaskets.

Carburetor

REMOVAL & INSTALLATION

1. Allow the engine to cool, then remove the air cleaner assembly.
2. Remove the spare tire from the engine compartment.

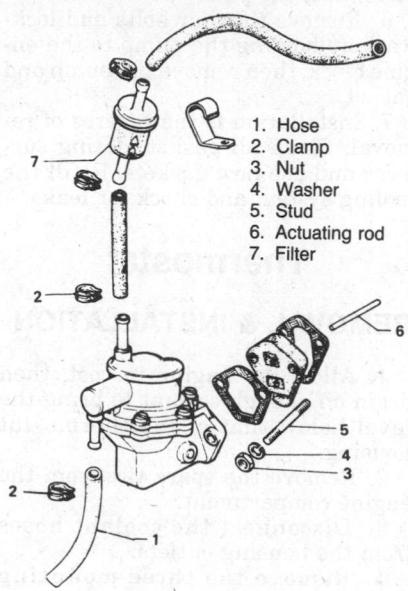

1. Hose
2. Clamp
3. Nut
4. Washer
5. Stud
6. Actuating rod
7. Filter

Fuel pump assembly

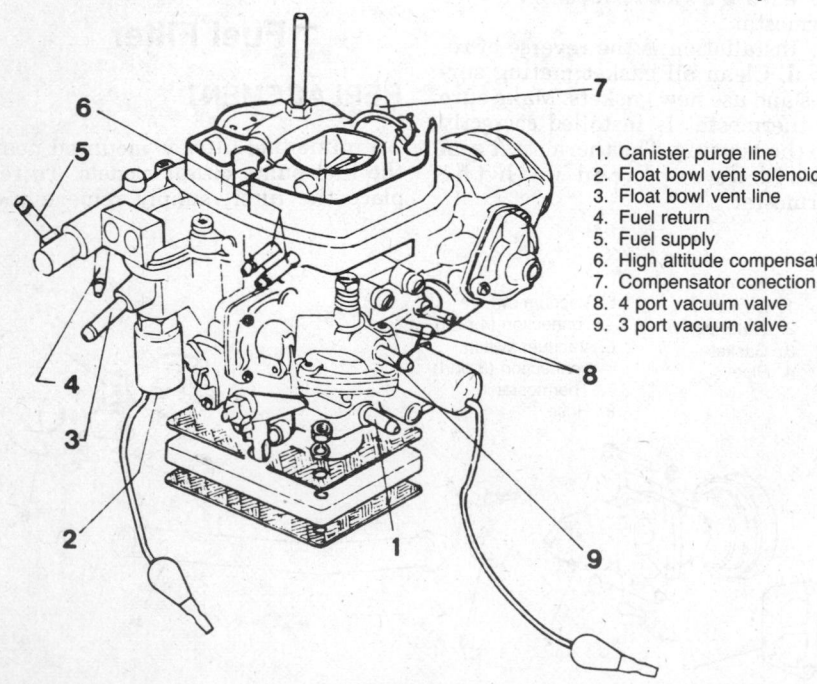

1. Canister purge line
2. Float bowl vent solenoid
3. Float bowl vent line
4. Fuel return
5. Fuel supply
6. High altitude compensator
7. Compensator conection
8. 4 port vacuum valve
9. 3 port vacuum valve

Carter-Weber 740 carburetor

3. Tag and disconnect all vacuum lines to the carburetor.
4. Disconnect the accelerator linkage and electrical connector from the solenoid valves. Tag the solenoid valve connectors to avoid confusion.
5. Disconnect the fuel line.
6. Remove the mounting nuts and washers, then lift the carburetor off the intake manifold.
7. Installation is the reverse of removal. Clean all gasket mating surfaces and use new plate gaskets.

OVERHAUL

For all carburetor overhaul procedures, please refer to Carburetor Service in the Unit Repair Section.

MANUAL TRANSAXLE

REMOVAL & INSTALLATION

1. Disconnect the positive (+) battery cable.
2. Remove the spare tire from the engine compartment.
3. Raise the vehicle and support it safely on jackstands. Make sure there is enough clearance to remove the transaxle from beneath the vehicle.
4. Remove the speedometer cable from the transaxle housing by unscrewing the ring nut.
5. Disconnect the clutch cable from the release lever and unhook the return spring.
6. Install a lifting device to support the engine assembly.
7. Remove the upper bell housing bolts and nuts.
8. Remove the wheel covers and unscrew the constant velocity (CV) joint hub nuts. Use the brakes to hold the front wheels when loosening the CV hub nuts.
9. Remove the left front wheel.
10. Disconnect the left tie rod from the steering arm using tool A–47035, or equivalent.
11. Remove the sway bar by unscrewing the nuts on the control arms and the bolts for the tow brackets on the body.
12. Remove the bolt holding the control arm to the body.
13. Disconnect the backup light switch connector.
14. Disconnect the exhaust pipe bracket.
15. Disconnect the shifter linkage at the transaxle.

16. Remove the starter.
17. Remove the flywheel cover.
18. Remove the lower support crossmember.
19. Remove the remaining bell housing bolts.
20. Disconnect the ground cable from the transaxle housing.
21. Disconnect the axle boot flange nuts and screws. Remove the outer clamps on the CV-joint boots and pull the boots back along the axle shaft to uncover the joints. Using snapring pliers, open the snapring on the joints and remove the axle shaft ends from their seats in the joints. Turn the front wheels, if necessary for working clearance and remove the axle shafts from the differential.
22. Separate the transaxle assembly from the engine and carefully lower it down and out of the vehicle.
23. Installation is the reverse of removal. Make sure the axle shaft snapring is properly installed in its groove by moving the axle shafts in and out a few times after installation into the hubs.

LINKAGE ADJUSTMENT

In cases of faulty gear engagement or slipping out of gear, adjust the shifter by loosening the two rod mounting bolts at the transaxle and shifing the shifter rod forward or back in the elongated holes of the flexible link. Tighten the bolts and check shifter operation.

OVERHAUL

For all manual transaxle overhaul procedures, please refer to Manual Transaxle Overhaul in the Unit Repair Section.

CLUTCH

REMOVAL & INSTALLATION

1. Remove the transaxle as described above.
2. If the same clutch assembly is to be installed, mark the position between the pressure plate and the flywheel so that the assembly can be installed in its original location and correct balance is maintained.
3. Remove the pressure plate by gradually loosening the attaching bolts to the flywheel a little at a time in a crisscross pattern until all spring pressure is relieved.
4. Remove the pressure plate and clutch disc.

CAUTION

The clutch disc contains asbestos, a substance considered carcinogenic (cancer-causing) if inhaled. Avoid breathing any dust during clutch removal procedures and wear a particle mask. Do not allow grease or oil to contaminate the clutch disc during service.

---

5. Check that the surface of friction material on the clutch disc is not less than $\frac{1}{16}$ in. from the rivet heads and is not cracked or glazed. If any problems are noted, replace the disc.
6. Check that the fingers of the diaphragm spring on the pressure plate are not broken, cracked or misaligned. Check the facing for heat cracks scoring or burns. Minor imperfections may be removed by dressing the pressure plate with medium grit emery cloth. Replace the pressure plate if any scoring is noted.
7. Check the throwout bearing for wear and replace if questionable. Check the throwout bearing fork and linkage.
8. Inspect the flywheel surface for heat cracks, scoring or burns. Minor surface imperfections may be machined, but deep scoring will require the replacement of the flywheel.
9. Installation is the reverse of removal. Make sure the clutch and flywheel surfaces are clean. If the old clutch is being installed, align the matchmarks made earlier. With the protruding part of the clutch disc facing away from the flywheel, loosely

install the pressure plate mounting bolts to the flywheel. Use a clutch centering tool (A–70210 or equivalent) to center the clutch disc in the pressure plate, then gradually torque the mounting bolts to 12 ft. lbs.

FREE-PLAY ADJUSTMENT

Adjust the clutch cable to allow 1 in. of pedal free play by loosening the locknut on the threaded end of the clutch cable at the release lever near the transaxle. Tighten the locknut when adjustment is complete and lubricate the cable pivot with a small dab of lithium grease. If free-play adjustment cannot be obtained, either the clutch is worn or the cable has stretched to the point where replacement is required.

Clutch Cable

REMOVAL & INSTALLATION

1. Remove the clip from the pin on the clutch pedal, then remove the cable eyelet from the pin.
2. Remove the spare tire from the engine compartment.
3. Remove the locknut and pivot nut from the clutch cable at the release lever near the transaxle.
4. Remove the threaded end of the cable from the lever and remove the ring.

1. Plug	12. Release fork
2. Washer	13. Bolt
3. Lockwasher	14. Lockwasher
4. Nut	15. Bushing
5. Support bracket	16. Throwout bearing
6. Clip	17. Flange
7. Bolt and lockwasher	18. Return spring
8. Clutch pedal	19. Spring clip
9. Pad	20. Clutch cable
10. Nuts	21. Ring
11. Seal	22. Lever

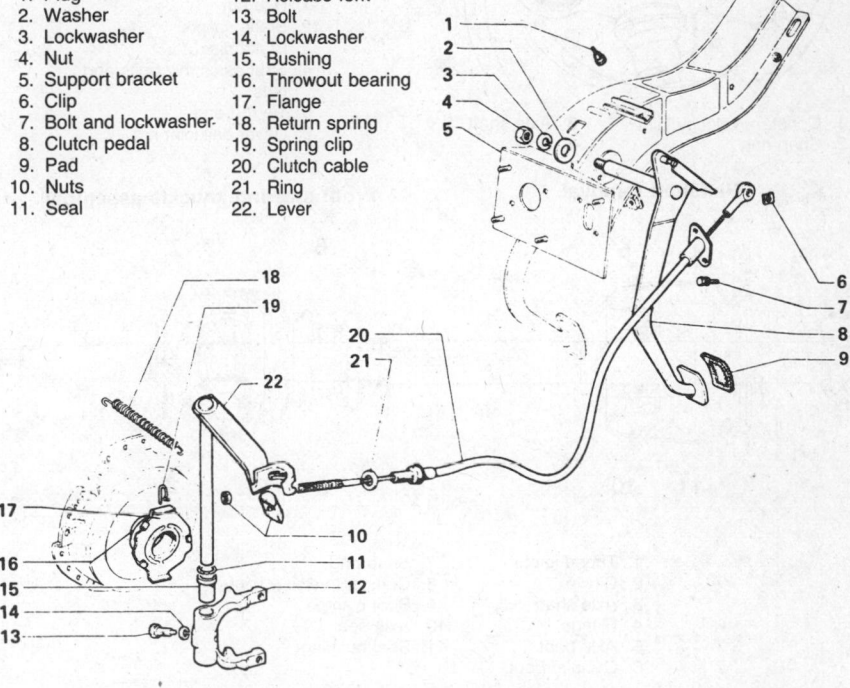

Clutch cable and release mechanism

5. Remove the two bolts mounting the cable flange to the firewall, then remove the cable from the engine compartment side.

6. Installation is the reverse of removal. Lubricate the clutch cable pivot points and adjust the pedal free play as previously described.

DRIVE AXLE

Halfshafts

REMOVAL & INSTALLATION

1. Drain some oil from the transaxle.
2. Unscrew the axle boot flange nuts and screws.
3. Remove the outer clamps on the CV-joint boots and pull the boots back along the axle shaft so as to completely uncover the joints.

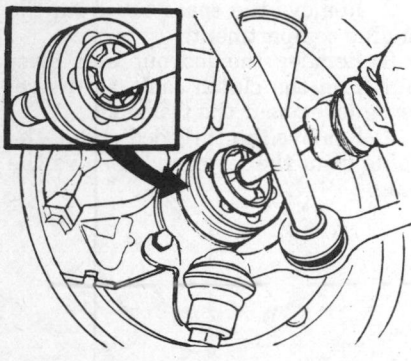

1. Constant velocity joint
2. Snap ring
3. Axle shaft
4. Boot

Halfshaft removal

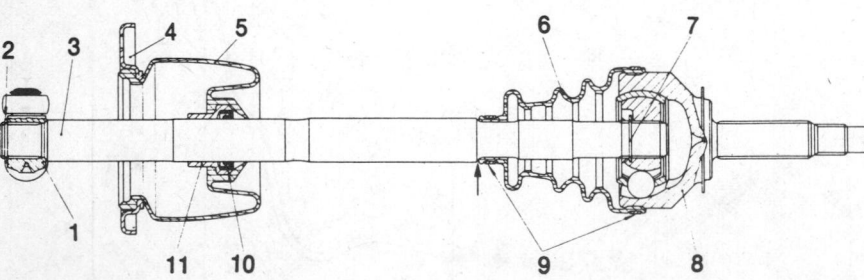

1. Tripod joint
2. Circlip
3. Axle shaft
4. Flange
5. Axle boot
6. CV joint boot
7. Snap ring
8. Constant velocity joint
9. Boot clamps
10. Axle seal
11. Seal bushing

Typical halfshaft assembly

4. Clean the grease off the joints with a clean rag. Remove the axle hub nuts.

5. Using suitable snapring pliers, open the snapring on the joints and pull the shafts out of their seats in the joint.

6. Turn the wheels to enable the shafts to be fully removed from their seats in the differential.

7. To replace the axle boot and seal, remove the snapring from the inner end of the axle and slide the tripod joint off its spline. Remove the boot, bushing and seal together. When replacing, use tool A–70375–J over the end of the axle to avoid damage to the seal lip when sliding the boot onto the axle shaft.

8. Installation is the reverse of removal. Make sure the axle shaft snapring is installed properly in its groove by moving the axle shaft in and out a few times. It is extremely important that the snapring be seated properly or damage to the halfshaft could occur.

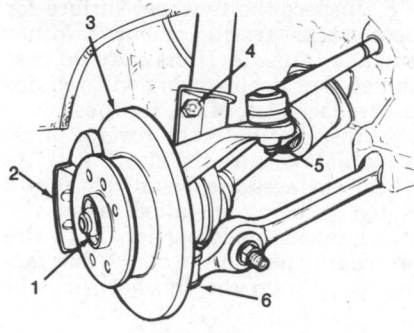

1. Hub nut
2. Brake caliper
3. Brake disc
4. Strut assembly bolts and nuts
5. Tie rod end
6. Lower ball joint nut

Front steering knuckle assembly

CV-JOINT OVERHAUL

For all CV-joint overhaul procedures, please refer to CV-Joint Overhaul in the Unit Repair Section.

Front Axle Hub and Bearing

REMOVAL & INSTALLATION

1. Raise the front of the vehicle and support it under the frame with jackstands.
2. Remove the front axle nut and tire.
3. Remove the brake caliper assembly and wire it up out of the way. Do not allow the caliper to hang by its brake hose.
4. Remove the brake rotor.
5. Remove the two bolts and nuts attaching the strut assembly to the knuckle.
6. Remove the nut holding the control arm to the knuckle.
7. Using tool A–47038m or equivalent, separate the ball joint from the knuckle.
8. Remove the nut attaching the tie rod ball joint to the steering arm, then separate the tie rod from the arm using tool A–47035 or equivalent.
9. Slide the knuckle and hub off the CV joint shaft. Bearing replacement requires the use of a bench press to remove the install the bearing assembly.
10. Installation is the reverse of removal. Torque the hub nut to 159 ft lbs., then stake the nut in place. Torque the control arm nut to 58 ft. lbs. and the tie rod nut to 25 ft lbs.

NOTE: All suspension nuts and bolts should be torqued to specifications with the suspension under a load. Lower the vehicle to the ground and remove all jackstands when making final torque adjustments.

FRONT SUSPENSION

MacPherson Strut

REMOVAL & INSTALLATION

1. Raise the front of the vehicle and support it safely on jackstands. Allow the front suspension to hang down.

2. Remove the front tire.

3. Remove the two bolts and nuts holding the strut assembly to the steering knuckle.

4. Open the hood and remove the nuts mounting the strut assembly to the body at the strut tower.

5. Lower the strut assembly down and out of the wheel well.

6. Installation is the reverse of removal. The strut assembly must be disassembled to replace the shock absorber cartridge.

OVERHAUL

For all spring and shock absorber insert removal & installation procedures, and all strut overhaul procedures, please refer to Strut Overhaul in the Unit Repair Section.

Ball Joints

REPLACEMENT

The front ball joints are integral with the control arm and cannot be replaced separately. If excessive play is noted, replace the front control arm as outlined below.

Lower Control Arm

REMOVAL & INSTALLATION

1. Raise the front of the vehicle and support it safely with jackstands. Allow the front suspension to hang.

2. Remove the front tire.

3. Remove the brake caliper from the steering knuckle and wire it up out of the way. Do not allow the brake caliper to hang by its brake hose.

4. Remove the nut and adjustment shims securing the sway bar to the control arm.

NOTE: When removing the sway bar, note the number of adjustment shims between the end of the bar and the control arm bushing.

5. Remove the ball joint nut and use a separator tool to break the ball joint loose from the steering knuckle. It may be necessary to remove the halfshaft axle nut and slide the halfshaft back out of the front hub to gain working clearance to remove the ball joint and control arm from the knuckle.

6. Remove the bolt and nut securing the control arm to the body bracket.

7. Remove the control arm and ball joint as an assembly.

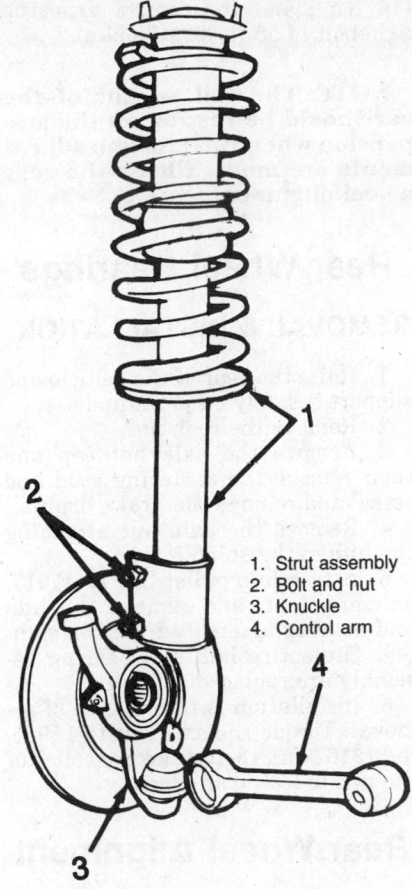

1. Strut assembly
2. Bolt and nut
3. Knuckle
4. Control arm

Front strut and knuckle assembly

8. Installation is the reverse of removal. Control arm bushings must be pressed in and out. Torque the sway bar nut to 43 ft. lbs. (59 Nm); control arm-to-body bolt to 29 ft. lbs. (39 Nm); and the lower ball joint nut to 58 ft. lbs. (78 Nm).

Front Wheel Bearing

REPLACEMENT

The front wheel bearing is pressed out of the front steering knuckle with a bench press when replacement is necessary. See Drive Axle for steering knuckle removal procedures.

Front Wheel Alignment

ADJUSTMENT

Camber and caster are adjusted by installing or removing shims from the sway bar mounting at the control arm. Toe-in is adjusted by turning the tie rod sleeve after loosening the pinch bolts.

REAR SUSPENSION

Shock Absorbers

REMOVAL & INSTALLATION

1. Raise the rear of the vehicle and support it safely on jackstands. Place a jack under the rear control arm to relieve spring pressure and remove the tire.

2. Open the trunk and disconnect the top shock absorber mounting nut. Remove the nut, washer and rubber grommet.

3. Working in the wheel well, disconnect the lower shock absorber mounting bolt.

4. Remove the shock absorber.

5. Installation is the reverse of removal. Open and compress the new shock once or twice to bleed any air from the shock absorber before installing. Torque the lower shock mounting bolt to 43 ft. lbs. (59 Nm).

NOTE: Shims must be inserted between the bushings and shock absorber mounting bracket. Take note of the number and location of the shims during removal and replace them upon installation.

Leaf Spring

REMOVAL & INSTALLATION

1. Raise the vehicle and support it under the frame with jackstands.

2. Remove both rear tires.

3. Place a floor jack under the left end of the spring and apply pressure while freeing the anchor pad on the control arm.

4. Remove the anchor pad mounting bolts, then slowly release the pressure on the control arm and allow the spring to hang down.

5. Repeat Steps 3 & 4 for the right side control arm.

6. Remove the two spring guides holding the leaf spring to the body, then lower the spring down and out from under the vehicle.

7. Installation is the reverse of removal. Make sure that the spring leaves are neither cracked, nor broken and that the contact surfaces of the spring are clean and perfectly smooth. Replace any worn rubber isolator pads. Torque the spring anchor pad nuts to 22 ft. lbs. (29 Nm) with the full weight of the vehicle resting on the suspension.

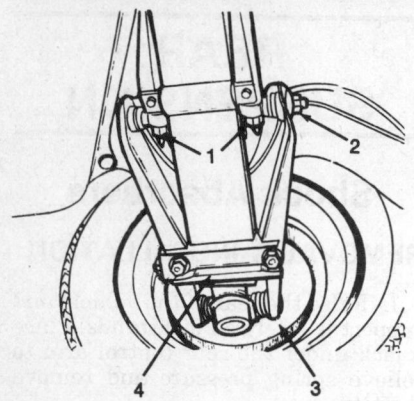

1. Control arm mount nuts
2. Control arm pivot pin nuts
3. Control arm/stub axle bolt
4. Spring anchor

Rear control arm assembly

Control Arm

REMOVAL & INSTALLATION

1. Raise the rear of the vehicle and support it safely on jackstands, with the weight resting on the frame and the rear suspension hanging.
2. Remove the rear tires.
3. Disconnect and plug the rear brake hose at the metal line connection. Cap the metal brake line to prevent the entry of dirt or moisture into the brake system.
4. Release the hand brake and detach the cable from the levers on the rear brake backing plate.
5. Disconnect the brake compensator bar from the right control arm, if necessary.
6. Place a floor jack under the control arm and apply pressure upward to compress the leaf spring.
7. Open the trunk and remove the upper shock absorber mounting nut, washer and rubber grommet. The shock is removed with the control arm as an assembly.
8. Detach the rubber pads attaching the leaf spring to the control arm(s).
9. Remove the nuts attaching the swivels of the control arms to the body.
10. Remove the control arm as an assembly with the shock absorber by sliding it out and off the leaf spring. Continue disassembly on a clean workbench. Control arm bushings must be pressed in and out using a variety of special mandrel tools.
11. Installation is the reverse of removal. Torque the control arm mounting nuts to 36 ft lbs (49 Nm); control arm pivot pin nuts to 36 ft lbs

(49 Nm); and the control arm/stub axle bolt to 58 ft. lbs. (78 Nm).

NOTE: The full weight of the car should be resting on the suspension when final torque adjustments are made. Check the rear wheel alignment.

Rear Wheel Bearings

REMOVAL & INSTALLATION

1. Raise the rear of the vehicle and support it safely on jackstands.
2. Remove the rear tire.
3. Remove the axle nut cap and then remove the centering stud and screw and remove the brake drum.
4. Remove the axle nut attaching the hub to the spindle.
5. Attach hub puller tool A-47017, or equivalent, and remove the hub and bearing assembly from the spindle. The entire hub and bearing assembly are replaced as a unit.
6. Installation is the reverse of removal. Torque the axle nut to 159 ft. lbs. (216 Nm), then stake the collar of the nut to lock it in place.

Rear Wheel Alignment

The camber and toe-in of the rear wheels can be adjusted by the use of shims inserted between the control arm pin and the body. See the Alignment Specifications Chart for settings and service limits.

STEERING

Steering Wheel

REMOVAL & INSTALLATION

1. Center the steering wheel and the front tires.
2. Disconnect the battery ground (–) cable.
3. Pry the horn button off the steering wheel using a suitable tool.
4. Remove the horn button sprint.
5. Remove the steering wheel mounting nut and mark the relationship between the steering wheel and the shaft.
6. Remove the steering wheel from the shaft using a suitable wheel puller.
7. Installation is the reverse of removal. Torque the steering wheel mounting nut to 36 ft. lbs. (49 Nm).

Combination Switch

REMOVAL & INSTALLATION

The combination switch controls the turn signals, high beams and windshield wiper/washer functions.
1. Disconnect the negative (–) battery cable.
2. Remove the steering wheel and horn assembly.
3. Remove the steering column shrouds to gain access to the combination switch wiring harness.
4. Disconnect the combination switch connector at the base of the steering column. Remove any harness retaining clips that may be present.
5. Remove the combination switch mounting screws to the steering column, then feed the wiring harness up and remove the switch assembly from the steering column.
6. Installation is the reverse of removal. Torque the steering wheel center nut to 36 ft. lbs. (49 Nm).

Ignition Lock/Switch

REMOVAL & INSTALLATION

The ignition lock and switch assembly is clamped around the steering column and held in place by breakaway-head bolts. Remove the steering column shrouds to gain access to the ignition switch, then drill out the two mounting bolts and use a bolt extractor tool to remove them. It is not necessary to remove the steering wheel. Replacement ignition switch/lock assemblies come with new breakaway bolts for mounting.

Manual Steering Gear

REMOVAL & INSTALLATION

1. Center the steering wheel and front wheels, then mark the universal joint and the steering box shaft for reference at installation.
2. Remove the pinch bolt and disconnect the steering box.
3. Raise the front of the vehicle and support it safely.
4. Remove the tie rod ball joint nut at the steering knuckle and disconnect the tie rod from the knuckle using A-47035 or equivalent. Disconnect both tie rods.
5. Remove the mounting bolts holding the steering rack to the body and remove the rack assembly from the vehicle.
6. Installation is the reverse of removal. Torque the tie rod castle nuts to 25 ft. lbs. (34 Nm) with the weight of the car on the suspension and check

the front end alignment. Adjust the toe-in if necessary.

ADJUSTMENT

Steering rack pinion and travel adjustments are possible only during a complete overhaul. Adjustments are made by adding shims at the pinion bearing and rack thrust block. Pinion bearing shims are available in 0.12mm, 0.20mm, 0.25mm, and 0.45mm sizes; thrust block shims are available in 0.10mm and 0.15mm.

Tie Rod Ends

REMOVAL & INSTALLATION

Make sure the tie rod ball is not loose in its socket. If it shows signs of play, or if the boot is damaged, replace the tie rod end.

1. Raise the front of the vehicle and support if safely.
2. Remove the nut attaching the tie rod joint to the steering knuckle.
3. Install puller tool A–47035, or equivalent, and separate the tie rod and steering knuckle.
4. Loosen the locknuts on the tie rod sleeve, if equipped, and remove the tie rod end from the sleeve. Count the number of turns and install the new tie rod the same number of turns to bring the alignment approximately to specifications.
5. If the sleeve and tie rod are one piece, loosen the locknut and rotate the tie rod and sleeve to remove it from the steering rack. Again, count the number of turns to install the replacement part in about the same position.
6. Installation is the reverse of removal. Adjust the toe-in and check the front end alignment.

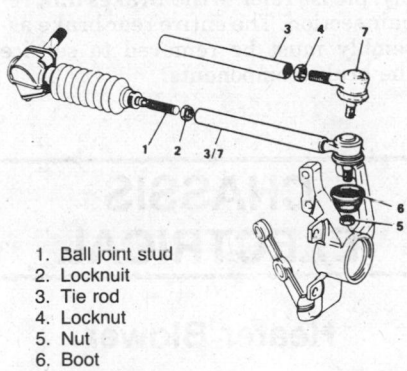

1. Ball joint stud
2. Locknut
3. Tie rod
4. Locknut
5. Nut
6. Boot
7. Tie rod end
3/7 Tie rod with end

Tie rods could have either configuration

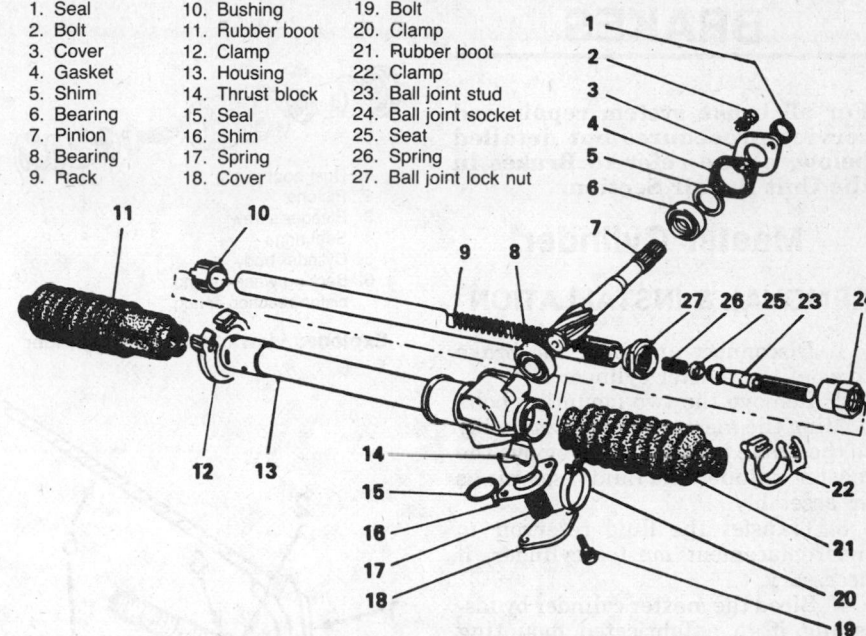

1. Seal
2. Bolt
3. Cover
4. Gasket
5. Shim
6. Bearing
7. Pinion
8. Bearing
9. Rack
10. Bushing
11. Rubber boot
12. Clamp
13. Housing
14. Thrust block
15. Seal
16. Shim
17. Spring
18. Cover
19. Bolt
20. Clamp
21. Rubber boot
22. Clamp
23. Ball joint stud
24. Ball joint socket
25. Seat
26. Spring
27. Ball joint lock nut

Exploded view of the steering rack assembly

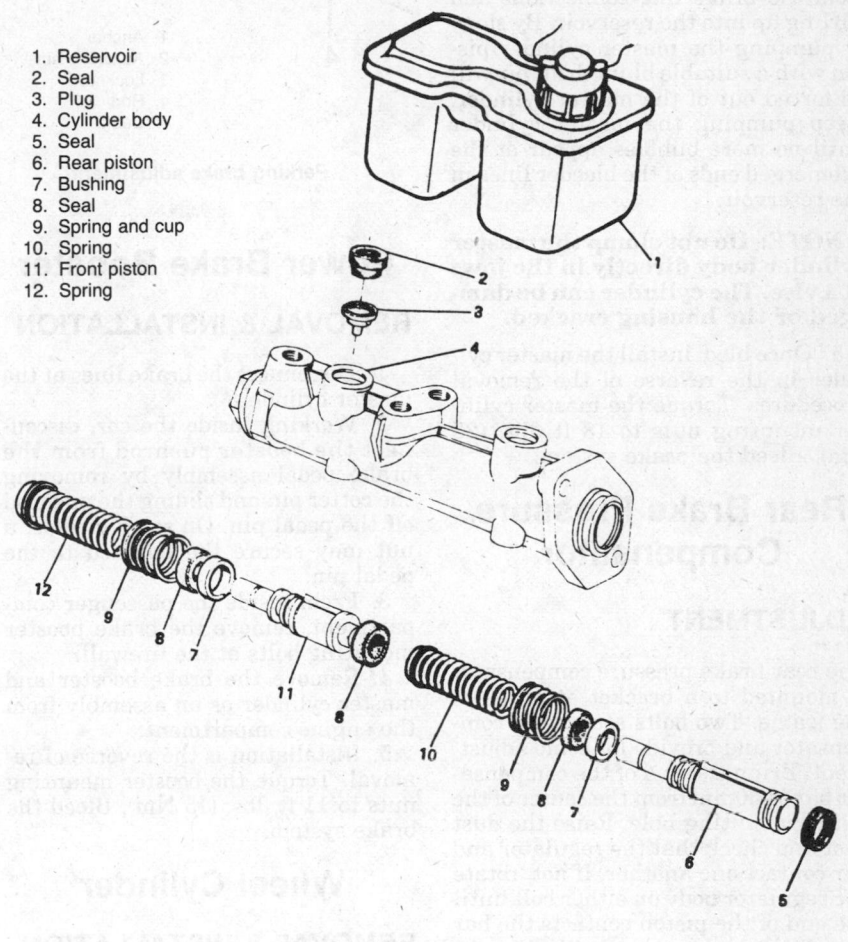

1. Reservoir
2. Seal
3. Plug
4. Cylinder body
5. Seal
6. Rear piston
7. Bushing
8. Seal
9. Spring and cup
10. Spring
11. Front piston
12. Spring

Exploded view of the master cylinder

BRAKES

For all brake system repair and service procedures not detailed below, please refer to Brakes in the Unit Repair Section.

Master Cylinder

REMOVAL & INSTALLATION

1. Disconnect and plug the brake lines at the master cylinder.
2. Remove the two mounting bolts holding the master cylinder assembly to the brake booster, then remove the master cylinder and fluid reservoir as an assembly.
3. Transfer the fluid reservoir to the replacement master cylinder, if necessary.
4. Bleed the master cylinder by fastening it to a fabricated mounting plate clamped in a vise, filling the reservoir with clean brake fluid, then attaching two bleeder lines running from the brake line connections and curling up into the reservoir. By slowly pumping the master cylinder piston with a suitable blunt drift, air will be forced out of the master cylinder. Keep pumping the master cylinder until no more bubbles appear at the submerged ends of the bleeder lines in the reservoir.

NOTE: Do not clamp the master cylinder body directly in the jaws of a vise. The cylinder can be damaged or the housing cracked.

5. Once bled, install the master cylinder in the reverse of the removal procedures. Torque the master cylinder mounting nuts to 18 ft. lbs. (25 Nm). Bleed the brake system.

Rear Brake Pressure Compensator

ADJUSTMENT

The rear brake pressure compensator is mounted to a bracket attached to the frame. Two bolts secure the compensator and provide for some adjustment. Bring the end of the compensator bar to 60mm from the center of the buffer mounting hole. Raise the dust boot and check that the regulator and bar contact one another. If not, rotate the regulator body on either bolt until the end of the piston contacts the bar end. Tighten the mounting bolts to 18 ft. lbs. (25 Nm) when adjustment is complete, starting with the lower bolt first.

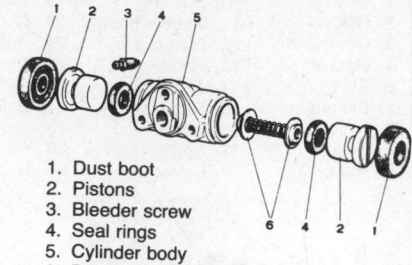

1. Dust boot
2. Pistons
3. Bleeder screw
4. Seal rings
5. Cylinder body
6. Backing washers and piston reaction spring

Exploded view of the wheel cylinder

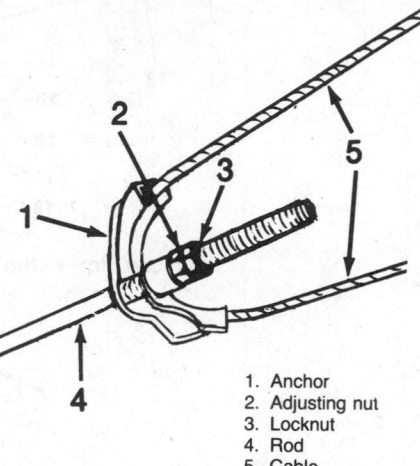

1. Anchor
2. Adjusting nut
3. Locknut
4. Rod
5. Cable

Parking brake adjustment

Power Brake Booster

REMOVAL & INSTALLATION

1. Disconnect the brake lines at the master cylinder.
2. Working inside the car, disconnect the booster pushrod from the brake pedal assembly by removing the cotter pin and sliding the pushrod off the pedal pin. On some models, a nut may secure the pushrod to the pedal pin.
3. From inside the passenger compartment, remove the brake booster mounting bolts at the firewall.
4. Remove the brake booster and master cylinder as an assembly from the engine compartment.
5. Installation is the reverse of removal. Torque the booster mounting nuts to 11 ft. lbs. (15 Nm). Bleed the brake system.

Wheel Cylinder

REMOVAL & INSTALLATION

1. Raise the rear of the vehicle and support it safely.

2. Remove the rear tire.
3. Remove the centering stud and mounting bolt and remove the rear brake drum.
4. Disconnect the brake hydraulic line at the wheel cylinder.
5. Disassemble the brake shoes to gain access to the wheel cylinder assembly. Remove the mounting bolts holding the wheel cylinder to the backing plate and remove the wheel cylinder from the vehicle.
6. Further wheel cylinder disassembly should be done on a clean workbench. See the Brakes unit repair section for more details.
7. Installation is the reverse of removal. Torque the wheel cylinder mounting bolts to 7.5 ft. lbs. (10 Nm) with washers. Bleed the brake system.

Parking Brake Cable

ADJUSTMENT

1. Fully depress the brake pedal a few times to make sure the brake pistons are in the correct position.
2. Raise the car and support it safely.
3. Starting from the released position (full down), pull up the handbrake three or four clicks. The rear wheel should not turn manually.
4. If the wheels can be turned by hand, loosen the lock nut on the adjuster and turn the adjusting nut until the rear wheels are locked.
5. Check that the handbrake releases fully with no brake drag, then tighten the adjuster locknut.

REMOVAL & INSTALLATION

The parking brake cables can be disconnected at each rear wheel cylinder lever and at the handbrake lever to replace the assembly. For more information on parking brake disassembly, please refer to the Brakes unit repair section. The entire rear brake assembly must be removed to service the brake components.

CHASSIS ELECTRICAL

Heater Blower

REMOVAL & INSTALLATION

1. Drain the coolant from both the engine radiator and the heater core by

opening the radiator drain petcock and moving the heater controls to full warm.

2. Loosen the clamps and remove the heater core hoses from the core connections.

3. Remove the attaching screw and nut from the air shutter control rod.

4. Remove the air duct after removing the screw and washer from inside and slide out the radiator housing spring clips.

5. Remove the outside air vent control rod.

6. Disconnect the heater valve control cable.

7. Remove the heater core, then back out the fan housing attaching nuts from the body.

8. Disconnect the yellow and blue-black wires at the fan switch.

NOTE: The fan ground cable is located on the left side of the radiator and is released by removing one of the nuts attaching the fan assembly to the body.

9. Remove the fan assembly from the vehicle.

10. Installation is the reverse of removal. Make sure the gasket between the fan housing and the body is installed correctly.

Heater Core

REMOVAL & INSTALLATION

Follow Steps 1–6 under Heater Blower Removal and remove the heater core. Reverse the procedure to install the heater core. Make sure all hose

connections are tight and run the engine until it reaches normal operating temperature with the heater controls set to full heat to make sure the heater core fills with coolant.

Radio

REMOVAL & INSTALLATION

The radio is mounted in the center console and is removed with the console as an assembly. Remove the console mounting screws, disconnect all wiring from the radio and console, then lift out the radio and center console. Continue disassembly on a workbench. Install in reverse order. Make sure all electrical connections are tight.

Windshield Wiper Switch

REMOVAL & INSTALLATION

See the procedures under Combination Switch Removal to replace the windshield wiper switch.

Windshield Wiper Motor

REMOVAL & INSTALLATION

1. Remove the wiper arm and blade assembly.

2. Remove the cowl nuts on the wiper transmission just below the wiper arm.

3. Raise the hood and remove the two bolts holding the wiper transmission and motor assembly to the cowling.

4. Lift the wiper motor and transmission out as a unit and continue disassembly on a workbench.

5. Installation is the reverse of removal.

Rear Wiper Motor

REMOVAL & INSTALLATION

1. Remove the wiper blade and arm.

2. Remove the cowl nut located just below the wiper arm.

3. Open the rear hatch and remove the wiper motor cover plate.

4. Remove the wiper motor mounting bolt and remove the wiper motor. Disconnect the wiring connector.

5. Installation is the reverse of removal.

Instrument Cluster

REMOVAL & INSTALLATION

The instrument cluster containing the speedometer, temperature and fuel gauges and the warning lights is removed as an assembly by removing the mounting screw, then gently pulling the cluster outward. Reach behind the cluster and disconnect the speedometer cable and electrical connectors. Label all connectors with tape to identify them when reconnecting the cluster. The cluster is usually replaced as an assembly. Disconnect the

1. Water shield
2. Housing
3. Water drain plug
4. Nut
5. Spring washer
6. Valve
7. Gasket
8. Gasket
9. Radiator
10 Gasket
11. Spring clips
12. Impeller attaching nut
13. Impeller
14. Rubber pad
15. Motor
16. Fan housing
17. Switch

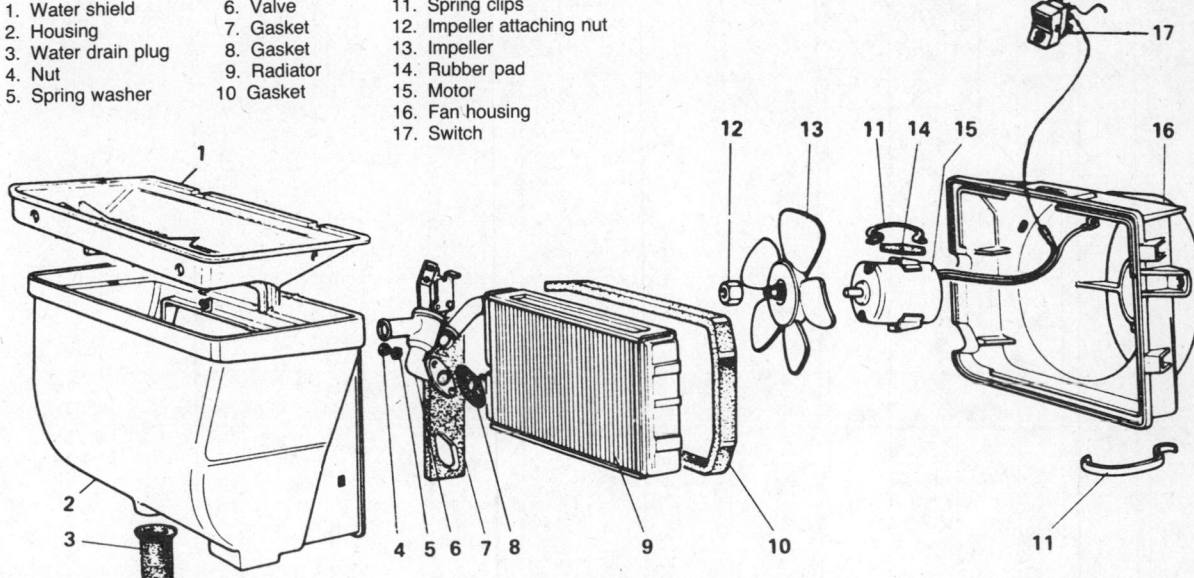

Heater assembly components

positive (+) battery cable before attempting to remove any electrical component or the instrument cluster.

Fuses and Fusible Links

LOCATION

The fuse box is located under the right side of the hood and has a plastic cover with the fuse numbers clearly marked. The fuse box contains eight 8 amp fuses and two 16 amp fuses protecting all exterior lighting on separate right or left circuits, all accessories and gauges, carburetor electric choke circuit, stoplight switch and hazard warning switch. When troubleshooting any electrical problem, or if diagnosing carburetor choke or radiator cooling fan problems, always check the fuse box first.

NOTE: The alternator, ignition and charging systems are unprotected by any fuses or fusible links. There are three relays for horn, defroster and high-beams located under the hood next to the fuse box.

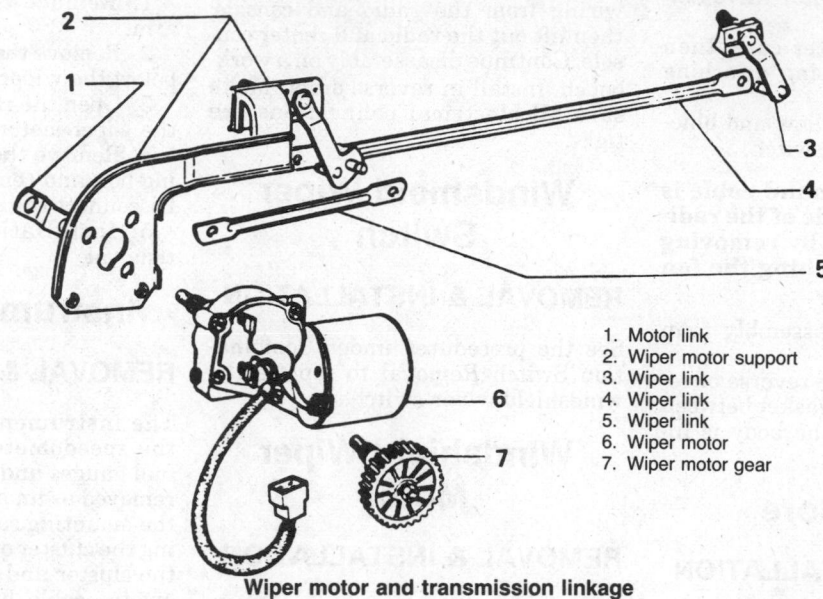

1. Motor link
2. Wiper motor support
3. Wiper link
4. Wiper link
5. Wiper link
6. Wiper motor
7. Wiper motor gear

Wiper motor and transmission linkage

Basic Maintenance 20

INTRODUCTION

Routine maintenance is probably the most important part of automobile care and the easiest to neglect. A regular program aimed at monitoring essential systems ensures that all components are in good and safe working order, and can prevent small problems from developing into major headaches. Routine maintenance also pays big dividends in keeping major repair costs at a minimum and extending the life of the car.

The owner's manual that came with your car includes a maintenance schedule, indicating service intervals in numbers of months or thousand of miles. This schedule should always be followed. We have provided, in each section, a guide to service intervals based on an averaging of manufacturer's recommendations. In most cases, the suggested interval offered here will be close to that given by the manufacturer of your car, but the manufacturer's schedule should always take precedence.

We have divided the maintenance work to be done into three categories: Under Hood, Under Car, and Exterior. The checks in each section require only a few minutes of attention every few weeks; the services to be performed can be easily accomplished in a morning. The most important part of any maintenance program is regularity. The few minutes or occasional morning spent on these seemingly trivial tasks will forestall or eliminate major problems later.

UNDER HOOD
Automatic Transmission, Automatic Transaxle

The fluid level in the automatic transmission or transaxle should be checked every three months or 6000 miles. All automatic transmissions have a dipstick for fluid level checks.

1. Drive the car until it is at normal operating temperature. The level should not be checked immediately after the car has been driven for a long time at high speed, or in city traffic in hot weather; in those cases, the transmission should be given a half hour to cool down.

2. Stop the car, apply the parking brake, then shift slowly through all gear positions, ending in Park. Leave the engine running.

3. Remove the dipstick, wipe it clean, then reinsert it, pushing it fully home.

4. Pull the dipstick again and, holding it horizontally, read the fluid level.

5. Cautiously feel the end of the dipstick to determine the temperature. Most dipsticks are marked with both cool and hot levels. If the fluid is not up to the correct level, more will have to be added.

6. Fluid is added through the dipstick tube. You will probably need the aid of a spout or a long-necked funnel. Be sure that whatever you pour through is perfectly clean and dry. Fluid recommendations can be found in the owner's manual.

Add fluid slowly, and in small amounts, checking the level frequently between additions. Do not overfill, which will cause foaming, fluid loss, slippage, and possible transmission damage.

Fill the automatic transmission through the dipstick tube

Battery

FLUID LEVEL (EXCEPT "MAINTENANCE FREE" BATTERIES)

Check the battery electrolyte level at least once a month, or more often in hot weather or during periods of extended car operation. The level can be checked through the case on translucent polypropylene batteries; the cell caps must be removed on other models. The electrolyte level in each cell should be kept filled to the split ring inside, or the line marked on the outside of the case.

If the level is low, add only distilled water, or colorless, odorless drinking water, through

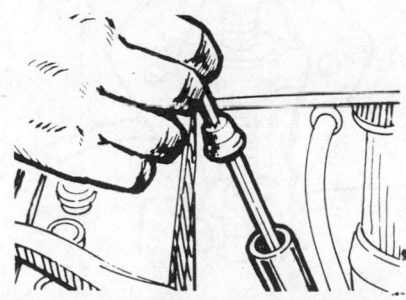
Check the automatic transmission fluid level with the dipstick provided

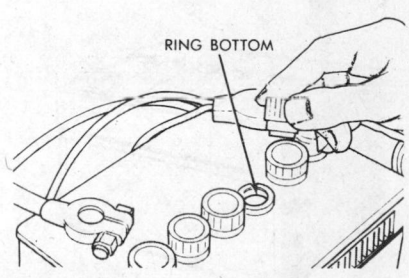
Fill the battery cell to the bottom of the split ring

the opening until the level is correct. Each cell is completely separate from the others, so each must be checked and filled individually.

If water is added in freezing weather, the car should be driven several miles to allow the water to mix with the electrolyte. Otherwise, the battery could freeze.

SPECIFIC GRAVITY (EXCEPT "MAINTENANCE FREE" BATTERIES)

While not technically exact, a practical measurement of the chemical condition of the battery is indicated by measuring the specific gravity of the acid (electrolyte) contained in each cell. The electrolyte in a fully charged battery is usually between 1.260 and 1.280 times as heavy as pure water at the same temperature (80°F). Variations in the specific gravity readings for a fully charged battery may differ. Therefore, it is most important that all battery cells produce an equal reading.

As a battery discharges, a chemical change takes place within each cell. The sulfate factor of the electrolyte combines chemically with the battery plates, reducing the weight of the electrolyte. A reading of the specific gravity of the acid, or electrolyte, of any partially charged battery, will therefore be less than that taken in a fully charged one.

The hydrometer is the instrument used for determining the specific gravity of liquids. The battery hydrometer is readily available from many sources, including local auto replacement parts stores. The following chart gives an indication of specific gravity value, related to battery charge condition. If, after charging, the specific gravity between any two cells varies more than 50 points (.050), the battery is probably bad.

Specific Gravity Reading	Charged Condition
1.260–1.280	Fully charged
1.230–1.250	Three-quarter charged
1.200–1.220	One-half charged
1.170–1.190	One-quarter charged
1.140–1.160	Just about flat
1.110–1.130	All the way down

CABLES AND CLAMPS

Once a year, the battery terminals and the cable clamps should be cleaned. Loosen the clamps and remove the cables, negative cable first. On batteries with posts on top, the use of a puller specially made for the purpose is recommended. These are inexpensive, and available in auto parts stores. Side terminal battery cables are secured with a bolt.

Clean the cable clamps and the battery terminal with a wire brush until all corrosion, grease, etc. is removed and the metal is shiny. It is especially important to clean the inside of the clamp thoroughly, since a small deposit of foreign material or oxidation there will prevent a sound electrical connection and inhibit either starting or charging. Special tools are available for cleaning these parts, one type for conventional batteries and another type for side terminal batteries.

Before installing the cables, loosen the battery hold-down clamp or strap, remove the battery and check the battery tray. Clear it of any debris, and check it for soundness. Rust should be wire brushed away, and the metal given a coat of anti-rust paint. Replace the battery and tighten the hold-down clamp or strap securely, but be careful not to overtighten, which will crack the battery case.

Clean the clamp with a wire brush

After the clamps and terminals are clean, reinstall the cables, negative cable last; do not hammer on the clamps to install. Tighten the clamps securely, but do not distort them. Give the clamps and terminals a thin external coat of grease after installation, to retard corrosion.

Check the cables at the same time that the terminals are cleaned. If the cable insulation is cracked or broken, or if the ends are frayed, the cable should be replaced with a new cable of the same length and gauge.

NOTE: Keep flame or sparks away from the battery; it gives off explosive hydrogen gas. Battery electrolyte contains sulphuric acid. If you should splash any on your skin or in your eyes, flush the affected area with plenty of clear water; if it lands in your eyes, get medical help immediately.

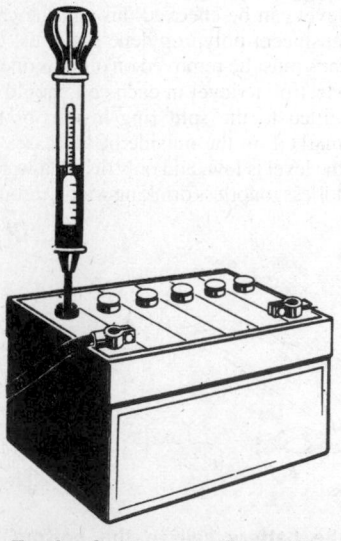

Testing battery specific gravity

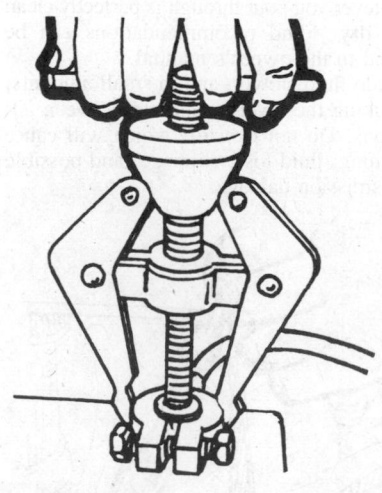

Use a puller to remove the clamp on post-type batteries

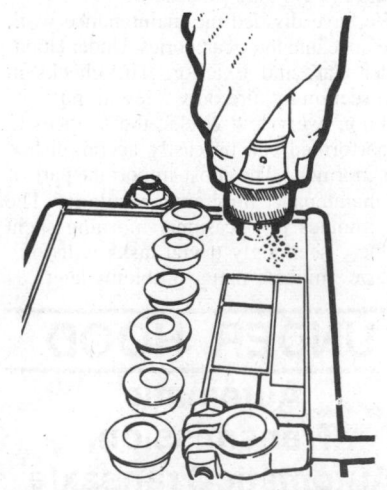

The posts are easily cleaned with a wire brush, or the battery post tool shown

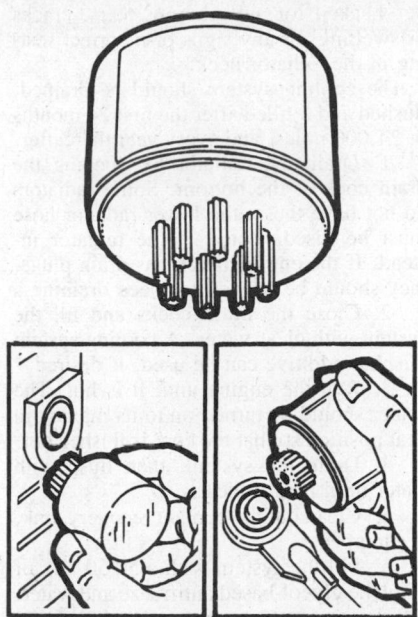

A special tool is required to clean the terminals and clamps on side terminal batteries

Brake Fluid

Once a month, the fluid level in the brake master cylinder should be checked.

1. Park the car on a level surface.

2. Clean off the master cylinder cover before removal. Some covers are retained by a bolt. Some of the newer master cylinders with plastic reservoirs have screw caps. Remove the cover, being careful not to drop or tear the rubber diaphragm which will probably be underneath. Be careful also not to drip any brake fluid on painted surfaces, as it eats paint.

NOTE: Brake fluid absorbs moisture from the air, which reduces effectiveness and will corrode brake parts once in the system. Never leave the master cylinder or the brake fluid container uncovered for any longer than necessary.

3. The fluid level should be about ¼ inch below the lip of the master cylinder well.

4. If fluid addition is necessary, use only extra heavy duty disc brake fluid meeting DOT 3 or DOT 4 specifications. The fluid should be reasonably fresh, because brake fluid deteriorates with age.

5. Replace the cover, making sure that the diaphragm is correctly seated.

If the brake fluid is constantly low, the system should be checked for leaks. However, it is normal for the fluid level to fall gradually as the disc brake pads wear; expect the fluid level to drop about ⅛ inch for every 10,000 miles of wear.

Belt Tension

Every six months or 12,000 miles, check

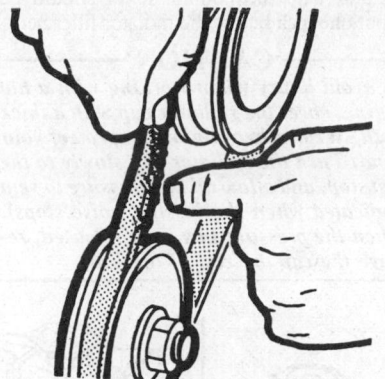

Check the belts for wear

the water pump, alternator, power steering pump, air pump, and air conditioning compressor drive belts for proper tension. Also look for signs of wear, fraying, separation, glazing and so on, and replace the belts as required.

Belt tension should be checked with a gauge made for the purpose. If a gauge is not available, tension can be checked with moderate thumb pressure applied to the belt at its longest span midway between pulleys. If the belt has a free span less than twelve inches, it should deflect approximately ⅛–¼ inch. If the span is longer than twelve inches, deflection can range between ⅛ and ⅜ inches.

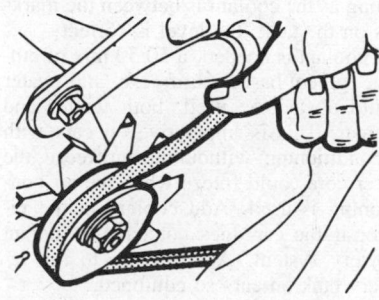

Check the belt tension at the middle of the longest span between pulleys

To adjust or replace belts:

1. Loosen the driven accessory's pivot and mounting bolts. Some air conditioning compressor belts are tensioned by an idler pulley; in this case, loosen the idler pulley and use a ½ in. drive ratchet in the square hole provided to lever the idler pulley up or down.

2. Move the accessory toward or away from the engine until the tension is correct. You can use a wooden hammer handle or broomstick as a lever, but do not use anything metallic.

3. Tighten the bolts and recheck the tension. If new bolts have been installed, run the engine for a few minutes, then recheck and readjust as necessary.

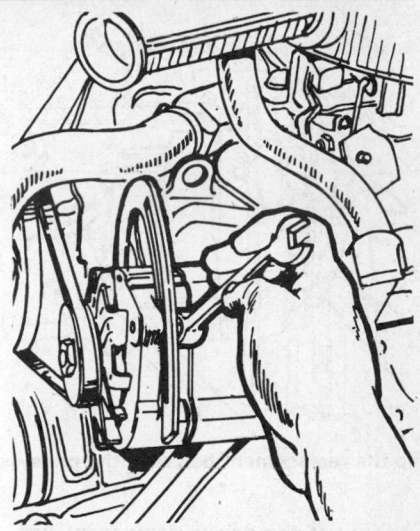

To either adjust or remove a belt, loosen the driven component's adjusting bolt

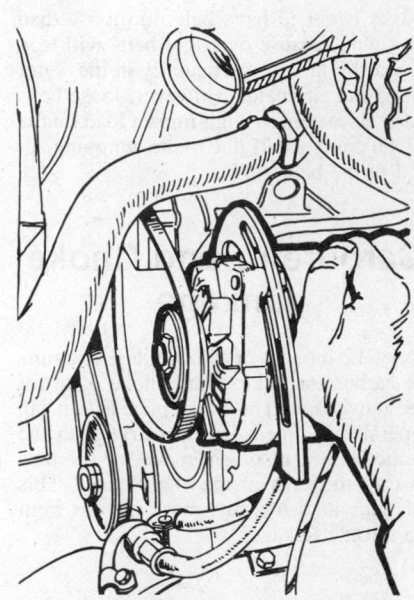

Push the component toward the engine to remove the belt

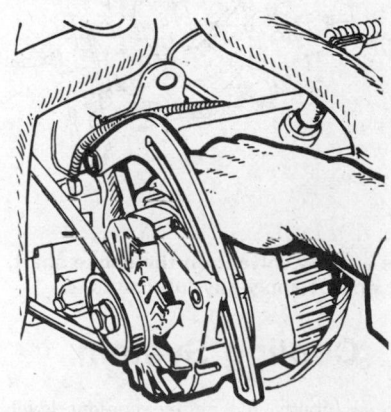

Pull outwards on the component to tension the belt, then tighten the bolts; recheck the belt tension after tightening

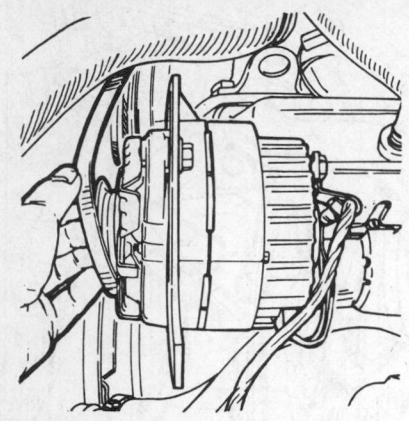

Slip the replacement belt over the pulley

NOTE: If the driven component has two drive belts, the belts should be replaced in pairs to maintain proper tension.

It is better to have belts too loose than too tight, because overtight belts will lead to bearing failure, particularly in the water pump and alternator. However, loose belts place an extremely high impact load on the driven components due to the whipping action of the belt.

Carburetor and Choke Linkage

Every 12 months or 6000 miles, examine the carburetor linkage and choke plate for free movement. The choke plate action can generally be freed, if necessary, with the application of a solvent made for the purpose to the ends of the choke shaft. This solvent will also clean grease and dirt from the throttle linkage.

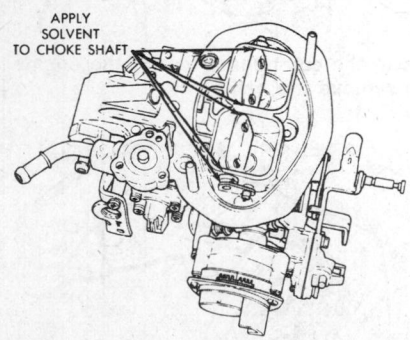

Use a spray solvent on the choke shaft, but do not apply any lubricants

Cooling System

Once a month, the engine coolant level should be checked. On cars without a coolant recovery system, this should only be done when the engine is cold. Remove the radiator cap; the coolant level should be about one inch below the radiator filler neck.

— **CAUTION** —

To avoid injury when working with a hot engine, cover the radiator cap with a thick cloth. Wear a heavy glove to protect your hand. Turn the radiator cap slowly to the first stop, and allow all the pressure to vent (indicated when the hissing noise stops). When the pressure has been released, remove the cap the rest of the way.

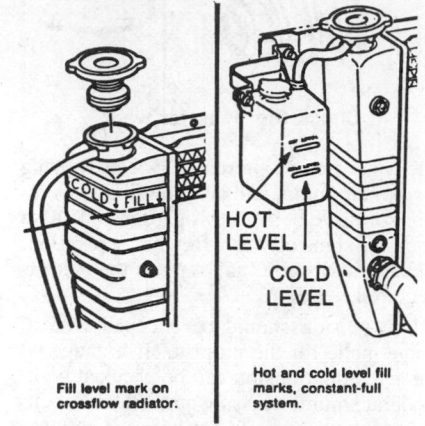

Fill level mark on crossflow radiator.

Hot and cold level fill marks, constant-full system.

Proper coolant level is about one inch below the radiator neck, or between the lines on the recovery tank

On cars with a coolant recovery tank, coolant should be visible within the tank; as long as the coolant is between the markings on the tank, the level is correct.

If coolant is needed, a 50/50 mix of ethylene glycol-based antifreeze and water should always be used, both winter and summer. This is imperative on cars with air conditioning; without the antifreeze, the heater core could freeze when the air conditioning is used. Add coolant to the radiator if the car does not have a coolant recovery system. Add coolant to the recovery tank on cars so equipped.

The radiator hoses and clamps and the radiator cap should be checked at the same time as the coolant level. Hoses which are brittle, cracked, or swollen should be replaced. Clamps should be checked for tightness (screwdriver tight only—do not allow the clamp to cut into the hose or crush the fitting). The radiator cap gasket should

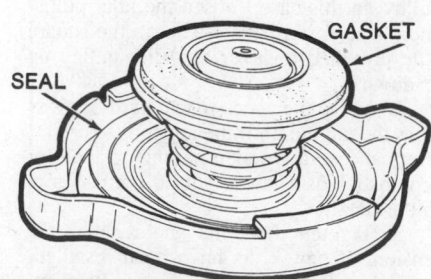

Check the radiator cap gasket and sealing surface

be checked for any obvious tears, cracks or swelling, or any signs of incorrect seating in the radiator neck.

The cooling system should be drained, flushed and refilled after the first 24 months or 24,000 miles, and every year thereafter.

1. Drain the radiator by opening the drain cock at the bottom. Some radiators do not have these; the lower radiator hose must be disconnected at the radiator instead. If the engine block has drain plugs, they should be opened to speed draining.

2. Close the drain cocks and fill the system with clear water. A cooling system flushing additive can be used, if desired.

3. Run the engine until it is hot. The heater should be turned on to its maximum heat position so that the core is flushed out.

4. Drain the system, then flush with water until it runs clear.

5. Clean out the coolant recovery tank, if equipped.

6. Fill the system with a 50/50 mix of ethylene glycol-based antifreeze and water. Fill the coolant recovery tank midway between the marks with this mixture also.

7. Run the engine until it is hot, then let it cool and top up the radiator or coolant recovery tank as necessary with the antifreeze/water mixture.

Heat Riser

The heat riser is a thermostatically or vacuum operated valve in the exhaust manifold (not all cars have one). It closes when the engine is warming up, in order to preheat the incoming fuel/air mixture. If it sticks open, the result will be frequent stalling during warmup, especially in cold and damp weather. If it sticks shut, the result will be a rough idle after the engine is warm.

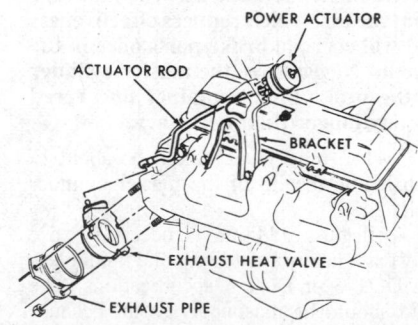

Exploded view of a vacuum-operated heat riser

The heat riser should move freely. It can be checked easily when the engine is cold by giving the counterweight on the valve shaft a twirl, or pulling the vacuum rod to open and shut the valve. If the valve is sticking or binding, a quick shot of solvent made for the purpose will free it up. This solvent should be applied every six months or 6000 miles to keep the valve free. If the valve is still stuck after application of the solvent, sometimes rapping the end of the

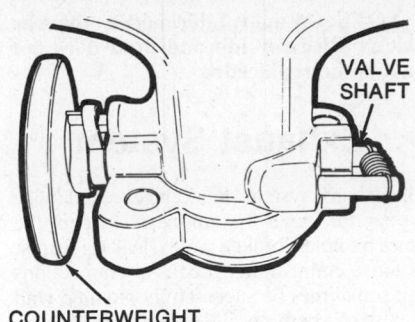

Thermostatically-operated heat control valve

shaft lightly with a hammer will break it loose. Otherwise, the components will have to be removed for further repairs.

Ignition Cables

The ignition system (points, condenser, rotor, spark plugs, etc.) receives regular attention in the form of a tune-up, and thus is not covered here. But one of the most commonly overlooked components is the ignition cable, or spark plug wire.

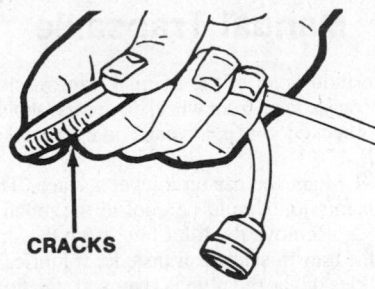

Inspect the ignition cables for cracks or breaks in the insulation

Although they rarely show any visible signs of deterioration, the ignition cables should be checked at every tune-up, and replaced at least every 50,000 miles. Cracking and embrittlement are of course obvious signs of wear, but most newer ca-

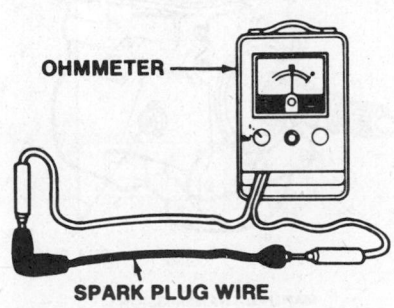

Test the ignition cables with an ohmmeter. Conventional ignition cables should be removed from the distributor cap, but electronic ignition wires should first be tested through the cap

bles have silicone insulation and thus are not prone to display these conditions.

The most reliable way to check the cables is with an ohmmeter. On conventional ignitions, the resistance should be less than 7,000 ohms per foot (wire removed). On cars with electronic ignitions, it is generally recommended to leave the wire attached to the distributor cap; test with one lead from the ohmmeter connected to the corresponding terminal in the distributor cap, the other lead touched to the disconnected end of the cable at the spark plug. Then, if resistance seems close to the limit, remove the wire from the cap and retest. In general, the spark plug wires on electronic ignitions should be replaced if the total resistance is over 36,000 ohms.

Always replace the cables with new ones of the same type. Replace the wires one at a time, working from the longest to the shortest.

Oil Level

The engine oil should be checked on a regular basis, ideally at each fuel stop, or once a week. It is best to check when the engine is at operating temperature, but checking the level immediately after shutting off the engine will give a false reading, because all of the oil will not yet have drained back into the crankcase. The car should be parked on a level surface to obtain an accurate reading.

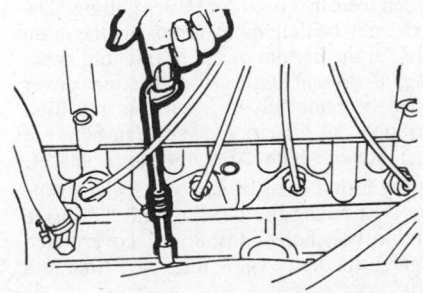

Check the engine oil level with the dipstick

1. Remove the oil dipstick. Wipe it clean, then replace it, seating it firmly.

2. Remove the dipstick again and hold it horizontally to prevent the oil from running. The level should be between the "Add" and "Full" marks on the dipstick. The dipstick may be marked "Add" and "Full," "Add" and "Safe," or may have lines scribed on it; in any case, the oil level should be above the lower marking.

3. If the oil is below the lower mark, enough oil should be added to the engine to raise the level to the upper mark. The markings are usually spaced so that one quart of oil will raise the level from the "Add" mark to the "Full" mark. Oil is added through the capped opening in the valve cover. Only oils labeled SF (gasoline engines) or CC (diesel engines) should be

Add oil through the valve cover

used; select a viscosity that will be compatible with the temperatures expected until the next drain interval.

4. Replace the dipstick, then check the level again after any additions of oil. Be careful not to overfill, which will lead to leakage and seal damage.

Power Steering

The power steering fluid level is usually checked with a dipstick inserted into the pump reservoir. The dipstick may be attached to the reservoir cap, or inserted into a tube on the pump body. The level should be checked at every oil change. On some models, the power steering reservoir is translucent, allowing the level to be checked through the sides of the container without removing the cap. On others, the reservoir is a metal canister with a wingnut-attached

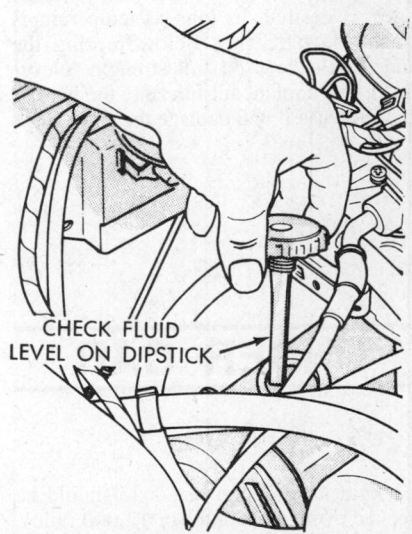

The power steering fluid level on many models is checked by means of a dipstick installed in the reservoir

cap. After the cap is removed, the level is checked with the scribed lines on the inside of the container.

On most models, the fluid level may be checked with the fluid either warm or cold. If checked with the fluid cold, the level will be slightly lower than with the fluid warm. If doubts arise about the specific procedures

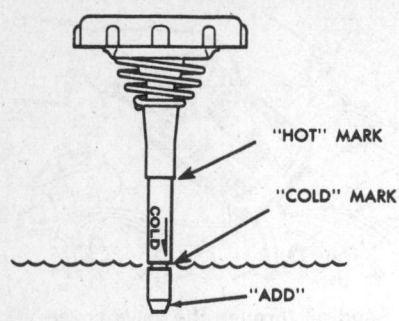

Typical power steering dipstick markings

for the car being checked, consult the owner's manual.

1. On all models, with the engine off, remove the dipstick, remove the cap or check the level through the side of the reservoir. If warm, the level should be between the "Hot" and "Cold" marks or even with the scribed line in the reservoir. If the fluid is cold, the level should be slightly lower.

2. If the level is low, add power steering fluid until the correct level is reached. Do not overfill the reservoir.

Windshield Washer Fluid

Check the fluid level in the windshield washer tank at every oil level check. The fluid can be mixed in a 50% solution with water, if desired, as long as temperatures remain above freezing. Below freezing, the fluid should be used full strength. Never add engine coolant antifreeze to the washer fluid, because it will damage the car's paint.

UNDER CAR

Axle

The fluid level in the rear axle should be checked every 12 months or 12,000 miles.

1. With the car parked on a level surface, remove the filler plug. The plug can be found either in the rear cover of the differential, or on the front of the pinion housing.

2. If lubricant trickles out when the plug is removed, the level is correct. If not, stick your finger in the hole (watch out for sharp threads); the fluid level should be even with edge of the filler hole.

3. If lubricant is needed, use SAE 80W-90 GL-5 gear oil (SAE 80W GL-5 in very cold climates) to fill standard axles. Limited

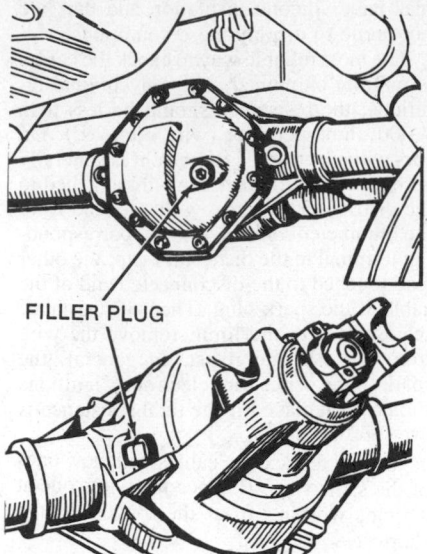

Rear axle filler plug locations

slip axles require a special lubricant, available in auto parts stores.

4. When the level is correct, install the plug and tighten until snug. Do not over-tighten.

Standard axles should be drained and re-filled with fresh lubricant every 15,000 miles when the car is used to pull a trailer. Limited slip axles should be drained and refilled at the first 7500 miles; the limited slip lubricant should be changed every 7500 miles when the car is used for trailer pulling. The axle may be drained by removing the drain plug at the bottom of the differential housing, if present. Otherwise, the rear cover must be removed, or a suction gun used through the filler hole. When installing a rear cover which does not use a gasket, apply a thin bead of silicone sealer to the cover, running the bead around the inside of the bolt holes. Install the cover, then tighten the bolts a few turns at a time in a crisscross pattern.

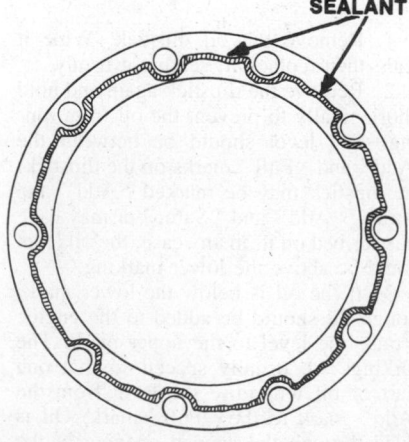

Apply a bead of silicone sealer to the rear cover if no gasket is used

NOTE: On many later models, the rear axle is filled for life and fluid does not have to be replaced.

Exhaust System

The exhaust system should be checked twice a year for general soundness. Inspect the pipes for holes, broken welds, leaking seams, or loose connections. Leaks at connections can sometimes be successfully repaired with the use of a commercial exhaust pipe sealer, but holes or breaks warrant replacement of the part. The exhaust pipe hangers and straps should be examined for any breaks or cracks; replace these as necessary. Some slight cracking of rubber hangers is normal, but deep cracks or cuts are cause for replacement.

——— CAUTION ———
Check the exhaust system only when it is cold. The temperature on an exhaust system using a catalytic converter can reach 1000°F after only a short period of engine operation.

Manual Transmission, Manual Transaxle

The fluid level in the manual transmission (or transaxle on front wheel drive cars) should be checked twice a year, or every 6000 miles.

1. Park the car on a level surface. The transmission should be cool to the touch.

2. Remove the filler plug from the side of the transmission or transaxle. If lubricant trickles out as the plug is removed, the fluid level is correct. If not, stick your finger into the hole (watch out for sharp threads); the lubricant should be right up to the edge of the filler hole.

3. If lubricant is needed, consult the owner's manual for the correct weight and type of fluid.

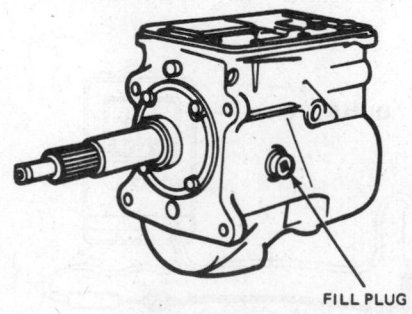

MANUAL TRANSMISSION
FILL TO BOTTOM OF FILLER HOLE WITH VEHICLE ON LEVEL GROUND.

Typical manual transmission filler plug location

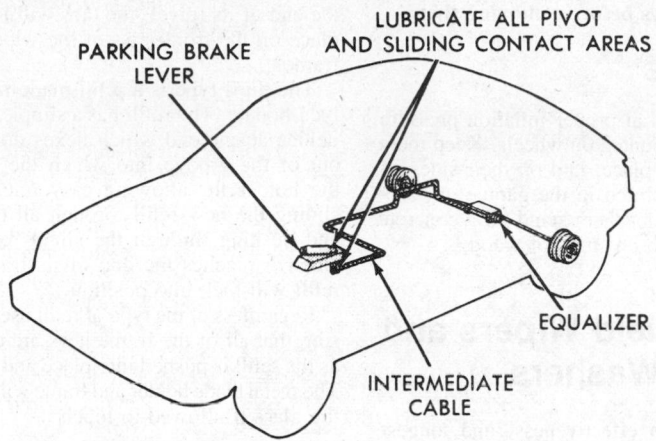

Lubricate the parking brake cable with white waterproof grease

NOTE: Some manual transmission/transaxle assemblies are filled with automatic transmission fluid rather than gear oil. Consult the owner's manual for lubricant information.

4. When the level is correct, install the filler plug and tighten until snug.

Parking Brake Linkage

The parking brake cable assembly should be inspected twice a year for fraying, kinks, and binding. A smooth white waterproof lubricant should be applied at the same time to all pivot points and areas in sliding contact.

Suspension Lubrication

Depending on the year of manufacture, there may be as many as twelve grease fittings on the suspension parts, or as few as two. Typical locations for grease nipples are on the ball joints, control arm pivot points, steering linkage, and the tie rod ends.

Lubricate these fittings with a small hand operated grease gun filled with EP chassis lubricant. Pump grease into the fitting slowly, until it begins to ooze out around the joint, or until the grease begins to expand the rubber boot around the fitting. Be extremely careful not to rupture any seals or boots, as this will lead to lubricant loss and contamination of the parts involved.

Occasionally, the grease nipples may become clogged with dirt or hardened grease. If so, unscrew them with a wrench of the proper size and clean them out with solvent. When reinstalled, they may be covered with plastic caps made for the purpose, or a piece of aluminum foil.

The chassis and suspension parts should be lubricated once a year, or every 7500 miles, whichever comes first.

Transfer Case

The transfer case on the four wheel drive Subaru shares a common lubricant supply with the transmission, therefore the transfer case lubricant supply does not have to be checked separately.

EXTERIOR

Drain Holes and Underbody

Most cars have drain holes spaced along the lower edge of the rocker panels and doors. These holes should be cleared of any debris or rust twice a year. A small screwdriver can be used to open plugged drain holes.

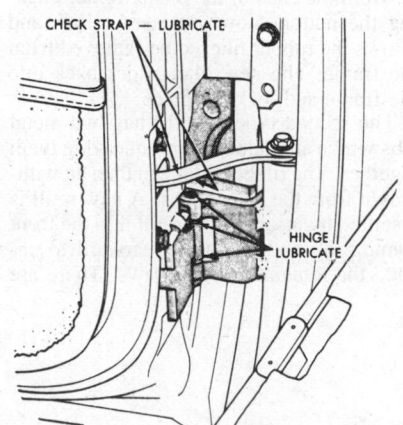

Use engine oil to lubricate the door, hood, and trunk hinges

Every spring, the underbody should be flushed with clear water to remove deposits of mud, road salt, and debris. It is advisable to loosen any packed-in sediment before flushing to assure a more thorough cleaning.

Hinges and Locks

Once a year, the door, hood, and trunk hinges, and all locks should be lubricated to ensure smooth operation. The hinge points should be lightly oiled. Lock cylinders may be easily lubricated with a shot of silicone spray directed into the keyhole. Silicone lubricant also works well on the door latch mechanisms, and keeps the door, trunk, and window weatherseals pliable when applied in a light film.

Tires

Tires should be checked weekly for proper air pressure. A chart, located either in the glove compartment or on the driver's or passenger's door, gives the recommended inflation pressures. Maximum fuel economy and tire life will result if the pressure is maintained at the highest figure given on the chart. Pressures should be checked before driving since pressure can increase as

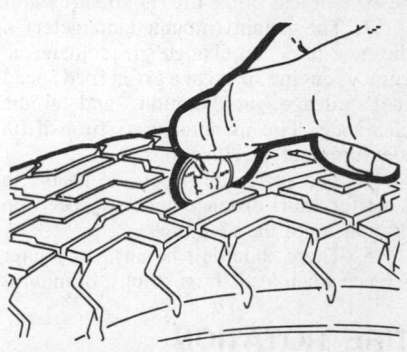

Tire tread depth can be checked with a penny. If the top of Lincoln's head is visible, the tires are due for replacement

much as six pounds per square inch (psi) due to heat buildup. It is a good idea to have your own accurate pressure gauge, because not all gauges on service station air pumps can be trusted. When checking pressures, do not neglect the spare tire. Note that some spare tires require pressures considerably higher than those used in the other tires.

While you are about the task of checking air pressure, inspect the tire treads for cuts, bruises and other damage. Check the air valves to be sure that they are tight. Replace any missing valve caps.

Check the tires for uneven wear that might indicate the need for front end alignment or tire rotation. Tires should be replaced when a tread wear indicator appears as a solid band across the tread.

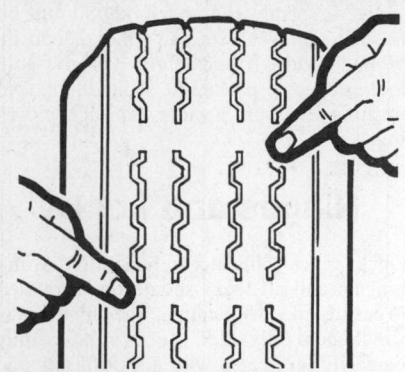

Tread wear indicators will appear as a band across the tire when the tread has worn out.

When buying new tires, give some thought to the following points, especially if you are considering a switch to larger tires or a different profile series:

1. All four tires must be of the same construction type. This rule cannot be violated. Radial, bias, and bias-belted tires must not be mixed.

2. The wheels should be the correct width for the tire. Tire dealers have charts of tire and rim compatibility. A mismatch will cause sloppy handling and rapid tire wear. The tread width should match the rim width (inside bead to inside bead) within an inch. For radial tires, the rim width should be 80% or less of the tire (not tread) width.

3. The height (mounted diameter) of the new tires can change speedometer accuracy, engine speed at a given road speed, fuel mileage, acceleration, and ground clearance. Tire manufacturers furnish full measurement specifications.

4. The spare tire should be usable, at least for short distance and low speed operation, with the new tires.

5. There shouldn't be any body interference when loaded, on bumps, or in turns.

TIRE ROTATION

Tire rotation is recommended every 6000 miles or so, to obtain maximum tire wear. The pattern you use depends on whether or not your car has a usable spare. Radial tires should not be cross-switched (from one side of the car to the other); they last longer if their direction of rotation is not changed. Snow tires sometimes have directional arrows molded onto the side of their carcass; the arrow shows the direction of rotation. They will wear very rapidly if the rotation is reversed. Studded tires will lose their studs if their rotational direction is reversed.

NOTE: Mark the wheel position or direction of rotation on radial tires or studded snow tires before removing them.

STORAGE

Store the tires at proper inflation pressure if they are mounted on wheels. Keep them in a cool dry place, laid on their sides. If the tires are stored in the garage or basement, do not let them stand on a concrete floor; set them on strips of wood.

Windshield Wipers and Washers

For maximum effectiveness, and longest element life, the windshield and wiper blades should be kept clean. Dirt, tree sap, road tar and so on will cause streaking, smearing and blade deterioration if left on the glass. It is advisable to wash the windshield carefully with a commercial glass cleaner at least once a month. Wipe off the rubber blades with the wet rag afterwards. For access to the blades on wiper systems which park below the hood line, turn the ignition key to "On" and run the wipers to the center of the windshield. Shut the wipers off with the ignition key, not the wiper switch. Do not attempt to move the wipers by hand; damage to the motor and drive mechanism will result.

If the blades are found to be cracked, broken or torn, they should be replaced immediately. Replacement intervals will vary with usage, although ozone deterioration usually limits blade life to about one year. If the wiper pattern is smeared or streaked, or if the blade chatters across the glass, the elements should be replaced. It is easiest and most sensible to replace the elements in pairs.

There are basically three different types of refills, which differ in their method of replacement. One type has two release buttons, approximately one-third of the way up from the ends of the blade frame. Pushing the buttons down releases a lock and allows the rubber filler to be removed from the frame. The new filler slides back into the frame and locks in place.

The second type of refill has two metal tabs which are unlocked by squeezing them together. The rubber filler can then be withdrawn from the frame jaws. A new refill is installed by inserting the refill into the front frame jaws and sliding it rearward to engage the remaining frame jaws. There are

usually four jaws; be certain when installing that the refill is engaged in all of them. At the end of its travel, the tabs will lock into place on the front jaws of the wiper blade frame.

The third type is a refill made from polycarbonate. The refill has a simple locking device at one end which flexes downward out of the groove into which the jaws of the holder fit, allowing easy release. By sliding the new refill through all the jaws and pushing through the slight resistance when it reaches the end of its travel, the refill will lock into position.

Regardless of the type of refill used, make sure that all of the frame jaws are engaged as the refill is pushed into place and locked. The metal blade holder and frame will scratch the glass if allowed to touch it.

WASHER NOZZLE ADJUSTMENT

Centered Single Post–Non-Adjustable Nozzles

This type is usually located on the rear center of the hood panel, directly in front of the windshield. By loosening the body retaining nut from under the hood, the nozzle body can be turned to provide the best spray discharge to cover the windshield. Tighten the retaining nut while holding the nozzle in position.

Centered Single Post–Adjustable Nozzles

This nozzle is adjusted with a wrench, screwdriver, or pliers. If the nozzle has no gripping area, the adjustment is made by inserting a stiff wire into the nozzle opening and moving the nozzle in the direction desired. When using the wire as an adjuster tool, do not force the nozzle; the wire can be broken within the nozzle opening.

Individual Nozzles

A tab is usually fastened to the nozzle stem to assist in turning the nozzle in the desired direction. If a tab is not present, use a pair of pliers to gently move the nozzle.

Wiper Arm Nozzles

No adjustment is necessary on this type of nozzle, because the opening is centered on the wiper arm and moves along with the arm.

Air Conditioning Service 21

AIR CONDITIONING SYSTEMS

Automotive air conditioning systems are basic in design and operation, but many different components are used by the vehicle manufacturers to operate and control the systems to their specifications.

Basic System

The basic air conditioning system utilizes the compressor, condenser, evaporator, receiver-drier, expansion valve and a thermostatic or ambient type switch to control evaporator freeze-up. The controls are manually operated and the unit is basic in design. This system is usually installed as an add-on or after-market unit. A sight glass may be used in the system.

P.O.A. System

The P.O.A. (pilot operated absolute) suction throttling valve system contains the compressor condenser, evaporator, receiver-drier, expansion valve and a suction throttling valve. The suction throttling valve is used to keep the refrigerant gas in the evaporator at a pressure which will not allow the temperature of the evaporator core surface to go below 32 degrees F., thus preventing evaporator freeze-up. For the system to operate effectively, an equalizer line is connected between the suction side of the suction throttling valve and the ex-

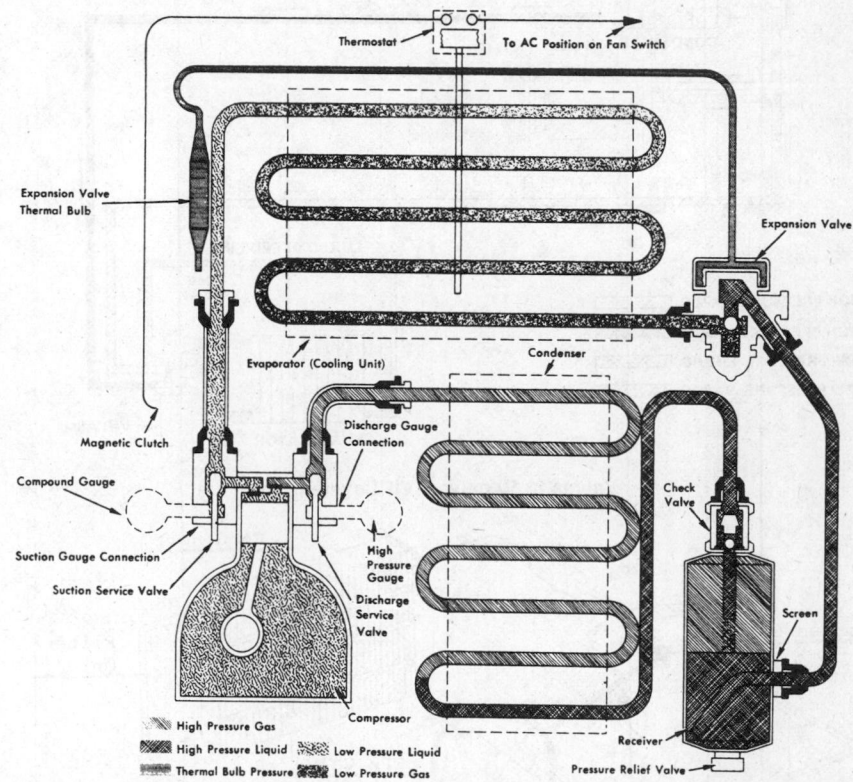

Basic air conditioning system

pansion valve diaphragm. This modifies the operation of the expansion valve which now is controlled by the evaporator outlet temperature and compression suction pressure.

When a crank type compressor is used with the P.O.A. system, an accumulator is placed between the evaporator and the com-

pressor. The accumulator operates as its name implies, accumulating any liquid refrigerant that may have passed from the evaporator and to prevent its moving to the compressor as a liquid, which may, in its form, cause internal compressor damage. A sight glass is normally used in this system.

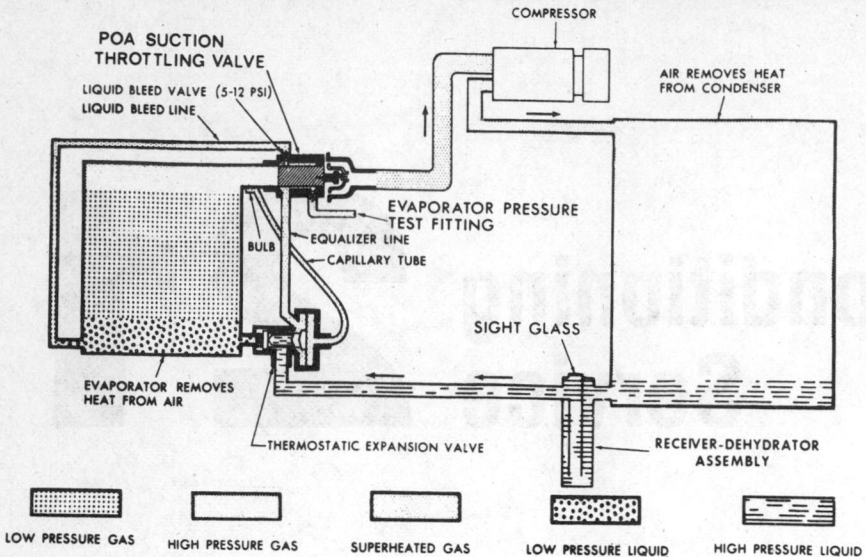

Pilot Operated Absolute (POA) system

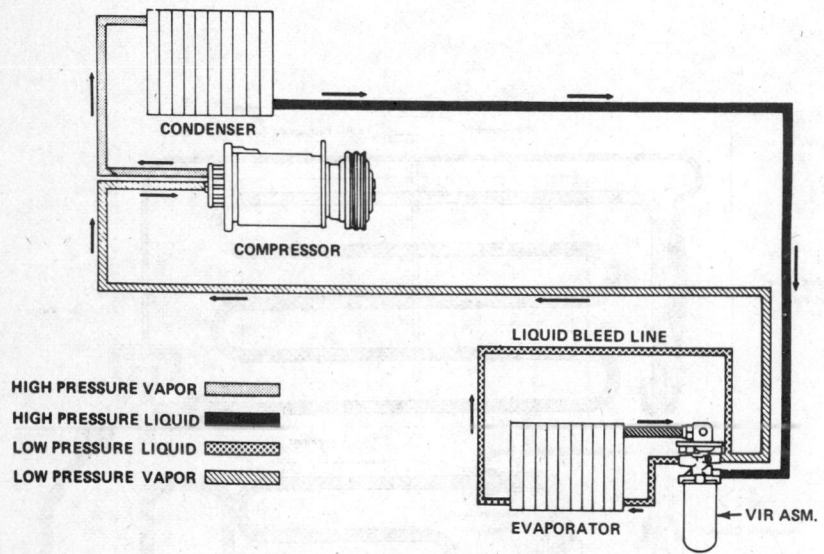

Valves In Receiver (VIR) system

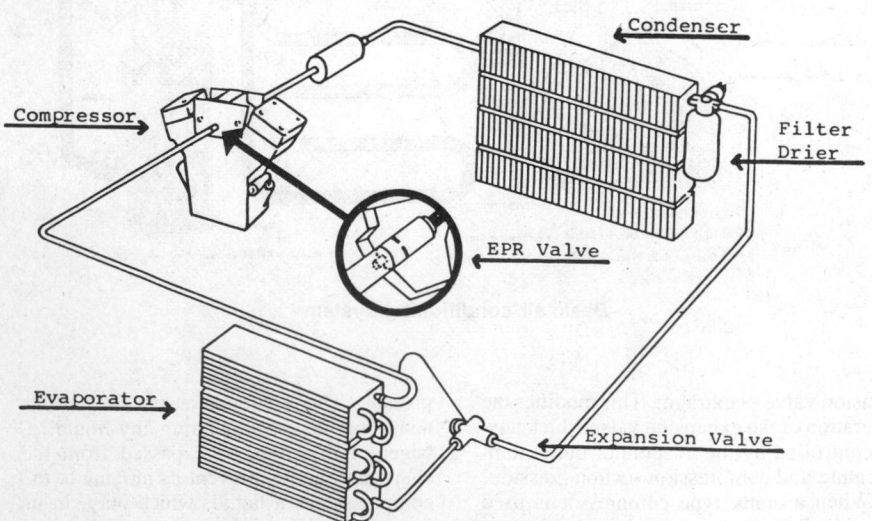

Evaporator Pressure Regulator (EPR) system

V.I.R. System

The V.I.R. system contains the compressor evaporator, condenser, muffler and a unit containing the P.O.A. valve, expansion valve and the receiver-drier. This unit is called the V.I.R. (valves in receiver) assembly. A muffler is normally used with this system and is located between the compressor and the condenser to absorb the compressor pulsations.

The V.I.R. assembly eliminates the outside equalizer line between the outlet of the P.O.A. valve and the expansion valve. The equalizer is now a drilled orfice in the wall between the P.O.A. valve and the expansion valve cavities of the V.I.R. housing. Should the valve prove defective during tests, the unit should be replaced, as it is not repairable or adjustable. A sight glass is normally used with this system.

E.P.R. System

The E.P.R. (evaporator pressure regulator) system includes the condenser, muffler, low pressure shut off valve receiver-drier, expansion valve, evaporator and a V-block, reciprocating crank type compressor. The E.P.R. valve is mounted on the suction side of the compressor and operates in conjunction with the expansion valve assembly, to regulate the flow of refrigerant from the evaporator to the compressor, under light air conditioning loads. By regulating the refrigerant flow, the evaporator temperature is controlled and freezing of the evaporator is prevented.

In contrast to other systems, the E.P.R. system uses the reheat procedure to control the temperature of the air, after it is cooled by passing through the evaporator fins. A manually controlled operating lever is connected to the heater water flow control valve and to a blend air door and the opening of the blend door proportions the amount of air around and through the heater core to control the mix of the cool and hot air for the desired inside temperature. A sight glass is used with this system.

Two types of expansion valves are used with this system. The first type has a capillary tube, mounted in a well on the suction line. The second type has no capillary tube, but senses the need to meter refrigerant into the evaporator by an internal sensing tube. This type of expansion valve is called the "H" type.

"H" Valve System

As was described in the E.P.R. system, the "H" expansion valve can be used with the E.P.R. valve, located in the V-block, reciprocating crank type compressor, to control the amount of refrigerant metered into the evaporator and to control the temperature of the evaporator coils to prevent freeze-up of the condensed moisture. However, when the "H" valve is used with the three piston, axial compressor, a cycling switch is used to control the temperature of the evaporator to prevent freeze-up, rather than the E.P.R. valve, as used with the reciprocating crank type compressor. This can be called the "H" valve system for explanation purposes only and should be recognized as such. The "H" system uses the same components as the other systems, basically the compressor (axial type), condenser, evaporator, expansion valve without a capillary tube ("H" type), receiver-drier, muffler and a low pressure shut off valve. The cycling clutch switch uses a capillary tube, attached to the surface of the suction line, to sense the need for refrigerant movement and compressor operation, therefore causing the electrical clutch pulley and coil to operate the compressor on demand from the cycling switch and to open the circuit to the coil when the demand is not needed. A sight glass is used with this system.

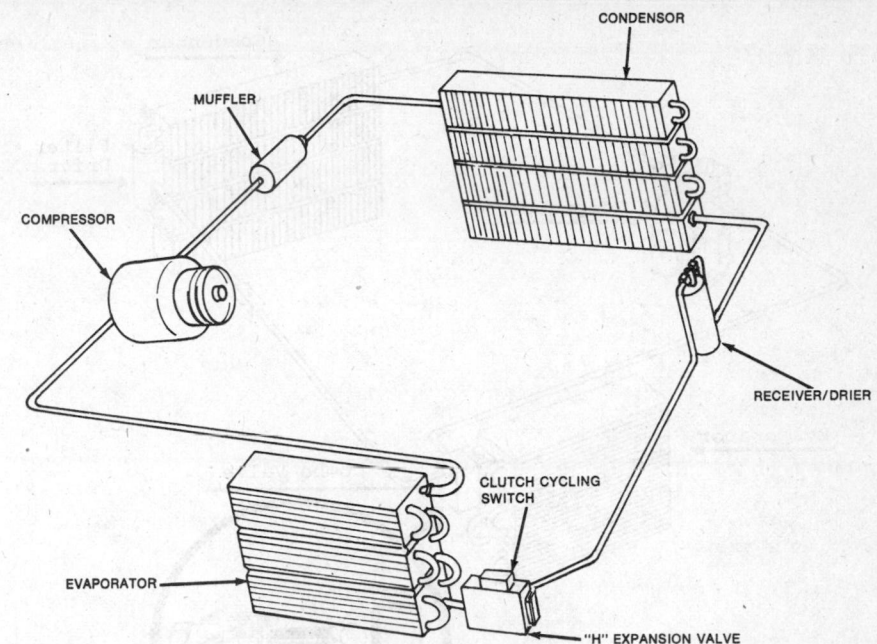

H type expansion valve system

CCOT System

The CCOT (cycling clutch orifice tube) system includes the compressor, condensor, evaporator, an accumulator-drier, a clutch cycling switch with a capillary tube, and a fixed orifce tube, mounted to the evaporator, replacing the expansion valve.

The clutch cycling switch with a temperature probing capillary tube, cycles the compressor clutch off and on as required to maintain a selected comfortable temperature within the vehicle, while preventing evaporator freeze-up. Full control of the system is maintained through the use of a selector control, mounted in the dash assembly. The selector control makes use of a vacuum supply and electrical switches to operate mode doors and the blower motor. A sight glass is not used in this system and one should not be installed. When charging the system, the correct quantity of refrigerant must be installed by measurement.

STV/BPO System

The STV/BPO (suction throttling valve/by-pass orifice) system uses either two types of external expansion valves or a mini-combination valve assembly contains an expansion valve, suction throttling valve and a service port. The expansion valve is of the "H" block design and is used to regulate the flow of refrigerant into the evaporator core. It is also the dividing point for the high and low pressure within the system. The suction throttling valve is used to control the evaporator pressure and to prevent coil freeze-up. The suction throttling starts when the compressor suction pressure decreases below the valve setting. The compressor suction pressure can continue to drop, but the evaporator pressure is held steady by the controlling or throttling action

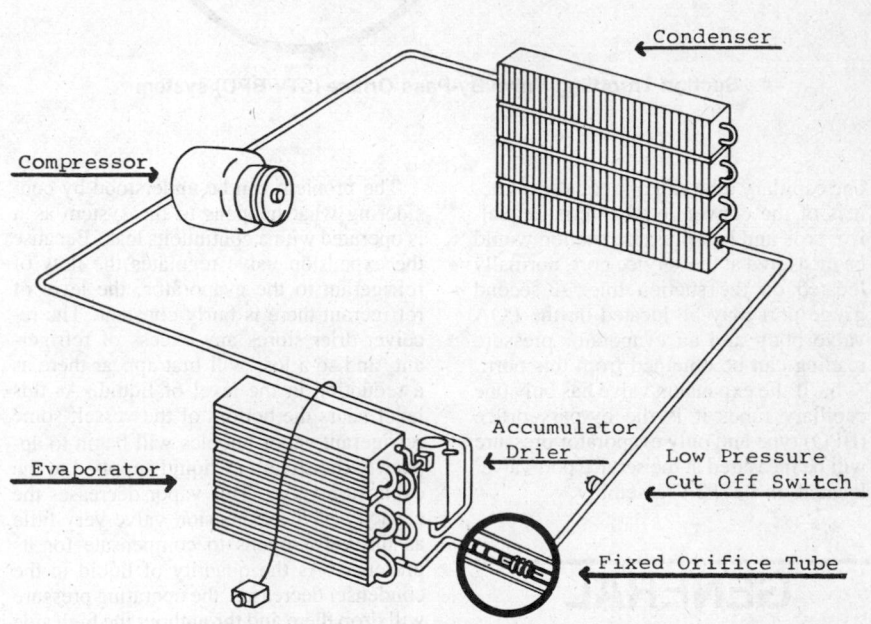

Cycling Clutch Orifice Tube (CCOT) system

of the STV. A pressure differential valve is used within the combination valve assembly, to allow oil–laden refrigerant to by-pass the restriction formed when the STV assembly is closed, to assure oil return to the compressor during times of reduced heat loads on the system. The by-pass valve remains closed under high heat loads since ample oil is moving through the system and compressor.

Evaporator pressure can only be measured on this system and a special type connector must be used to attach the high pressure gauge line to the service gauge port.

When either of the external type expansion valves are used, separate suction throttling valves are used. The operation of each is basically the same as the components of the combination valve assembly.

The type of external expansion valve used with the system will dictate either low suction or evaporator pressure measurements from the gauge service ports. To determine the pressure measurement that may be obtained from the system, examine the external expansion valve for one of the following conditions:

a. Should the expansion valve have

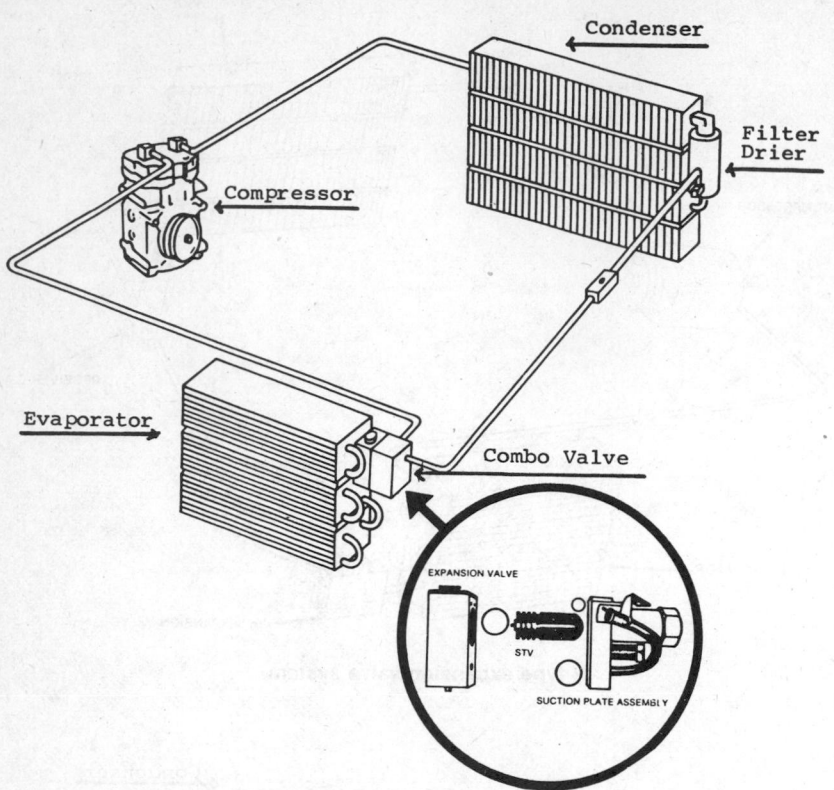

Condenser

Filter Drier

Compressor

Evaporator

Combo Valve

EXPANSION VALVE

STV

SUCTION PLATE ASSEMBLY

Suction Throttling Valve/By-Pass Orifice (STV/BPO) system

one capillary tube and one equalizer line, it is of the conventional external equalizer type and low pressure suction would be measured at the service port, normally located on the suction line. A second gauge port may be located on the POA valve body and an evaporator pressure reading can be obtained from this port.

b. If the expansion valve has only one capillary tube, it is the by-pass orfice (BPO) type and only evaporator pressure will be measured at the service port valve, located on the STV assembly.

GENERAL SERVICING PROCEDURES

The most important aspect of air conditioning service is the maintenance of a pure and adequate charge of refrigerant in the system. A refrigeration system cannot function properly if a significant percentage of the charge is lost. Leaks are common because the severe vibration encountered in an automobile can easily cause a sufficient cracking or loosening of the air conditioning fittings; as a result, the extreme operating pressures of the system force refrigerant out.

The problem can be understood by considering what happens to the system as it is operated with a continuous leak. Because the expansion valve regulates the flow of refrigerant to the evaporator, the level of refrigerant there is fairly constant. The receiver-drier stores any excess of refrigerant, and so a loss will first appear there as a reduction in the level of liquid. As this level nears the bottom of the vessel, some refrigerant vapor bubbles will begin to appear in the stream of liquid supplied to the expansion valve. This vapor decreases the capacity of the expansion valve very little as the valve opens to compensate for its presence. As the quantity of liquid in the condenser decreases, the operating pressure will drop there and throughout the high side of the system. As the R-12 continues to be expelled, the pressure available to force the liquid through the expansion valve will continue to decrease, and, eventually, the valve's orifice will prove to be too much of a restriction for adquate flow even with the needle fully withdrawn.

At this point, low side pressure will start to drop, and severe reduction in cooling capacity, marked by freeze-up of the evaporator coil, will result. Eventually, the operating pressure of the evaporator will be lower than the pressure of the atmosphere surrounding it, and air will be drawn into the system wherever there are leaks in the low side.

Because all atmospheric air contains at least some moisture, water will enter the system and mix with the R-12 and the oil. Trace amounts of moisture will cause sludging of the oil, and corrosion of the system. Saturation and clogging of the filter-drier, and freezing of the expansion valve orifice will eventually result. As air fills the system to a greater and greater extent, it will interfere more and more with the normal flows of refrigerant and heat.

From this description, it should be obvious that much of the repairman's time will be spent detecting leaks, repairing them, and then restoring the purity and quantity of the refrigerant charge. A list of general precautions that should be observed while doing this follows:

1. Keep all tools as clean and dry as possible.

2. Thoroughly purge the service gauges and hoses of air and moisture before connecting them to the system. Keep them capped when not in use.

3. Thoroughly clean any refrigerant fitting before disconnecting it in order to minimize the entrance of dirt into the system.

4. Plan any operation that requires opening the system beforehand, in order to minimize the length of time it will be exposed to open air. Cap or seal the open ends to minimize the entrance of foreign material.

5. When adding oil, pour it through an extremely clean and dry tube or funnel. Keep the oil capped whenever possible. Do not use oil that has not been kept tightly sealed.

6. Use only refrigerant 12. Purchase refrigerant intended for use in only automatic air conditioning systems. Avoid the use of refrigerant-12 that may be packaged for another use, such as cleaning, or powering a horn, as it is impure.

7. Completely evacuate any system that has been opened to replace a component, or that has leaked sufficiently to draw in moisture and air. This requires evacuating air and moisture with a good vacuum pump for at least one hour.

If a system has been open for a considerable length of time it may be advisable to evacuate the system for up to 12 hours (overnight).

8. Use a wrench on both halves of a fitting that is to be disconnected, so as to avoid placing torque on any of the refrigerant lines.

9. When overhauling a compressor, pour some of the oil into a clean glass and inspect it. If there is evidence of dirt or metal particles, or both, flush all refrigerant components with clean refrigerant before evacuating and recharging the system. In addition, if metal particles are present, the compressor should be replaced.

10. Schrader valves may leak only when under full operating pressure. Therefore, if leakage is suspected but cannot be located, operate the system with a full charge of refrigerant and look for leaks from all Schrader valves. Replace any faulty valves.

Additional Preventive Maintenance Checks

ANTIFREEZE

In order to prevent heater core freeze-up during A/C operation, it is necessary to maintain permanent type antifreeze protection of +15 degrees F. or lower. A reading of −15 degrees F. is ideal since this protection also supplies sufficient corrosion inhibitors for the protection of the engine cooling system.

NOTE: The same antifreeze should not be used longer than the manufacturer specifies.

RADIATOR CAP

For efficient operation of an air conditioned car's cooling system, the radiator cap should have a holding pressure which meets manufacturer's specifications. A cap which fails to hold these pressures should be replaced.

CONDENSER

Any obstruction of, or damage to, the condenser configuration will restrict the air flow which is essential to its efficient operation. It is therefore a good rule to keep this unit clean and in proper physical shape.

NOTE: Bug screens are regarded as obstructions.

CONDENSATION DRAIN TUBE

This single molded drain tube expels the condensation, which accumulates on the bottom of the evaporator housing, into the engine compartment.

If this tube is obstructed, the air conditioning performance can be restricted and condensation buildup can spill over onto the vehicle's floor.

Safety Precautions

Because of the importance of the necessary safety precautions that must be exercised when working with air conditioning systems and R-12 refrigerant, a recap of the safety precautions are outlined.

1. Avoid contact with a charged refrigeration system, even when working on another part of the air conditioning system or vehicle. If a heavy tool comes into contact with a section of copper tubing or a heat exchanger, it can easily cause the relatively soft material to rupture.

2. When it is necessary to apply force to a fitting which contains refrigerant, as when checking that all system couplings are securely tightened, use a wrench on both parts of the fitting involved, if possible. This will avoid putting torque on refrigerant tubing.

(It is advisable, when possible, to use tube or line wrenches when tightening these flare nut fittings.

3. Do not attempt to discharge the system by merely loosening a fitting, or removing the service valve caps and cracking these valves. Precise control is possible only when using the service gauges. Place a rag under the open end of the center charging hose while discharging the system to catch any drops of liquid that might escape. Wear protective gloves when connecting or disconnecting service gauge hoses.

4. Discharge the system only in a well ventilated area, as high concentrations of the gas can exclude oxygen and act as an anesthetic. When leak testing or soldering, this is particularly important, as toxic gas is formed when R-12 contacts any flame.

5. Never start a system without first verifying that both service valves are backseated, if equipped, and that all fittings

throughout the system are snugly connected.

6. Avoid applying heat to any refrigerant line or storage vessel. Charging may be aided by using water heated to less than 125° to warm the refrigerant container. Never allow a refrigerant storage container to sit out in the sun, or near any other source of heat, such as a radiator.

7. Always wear goggles when working on a system to protect the eyes. If refrigerant contacts the eyes, it is advisable in all cases to see a physician as soon as possible.

8. Frostbite from liquid refrigerant should be treated by first gradually warming the area with cool water, and then gently applying petroleum jelly. *A physician should be consulted.*

9. Always keep refrigerant drum fittings capped when not in use. Avoid sudden shock to the drum, which might occur from dropping it, or from banging a heavy tool against it. *Never carry a drum in the passenger compartment of a car.*

10. Always completely discharge the system before painting the vehicle (if the paint is to be baked on), or before welding anywhere near refrigerant lines.

AIR CONDITIONING TOOLS AND GAUGES

Test Gauges

Most of the service work performed on any air conditioning system requires the use of a set of two gauges, one for the high (head) pressure side of the system, the other for the low (suction) side.

The low side gauge records both pressure and vacuum. Vacuum readings are calibrated from 0–30 inches and the pressure graduations read from 0 to no less than 60 psi.

The high side guage measures pressure from 0 to at least 600 psi.

Both gauges are threaded into a manifold that contains two hand shut-off valves. Proper manipulation of these valves and the use of the attached-test hoses allow the user to perform the following services:

1. Test high and low side pressures.
2. Remove air, moisture, and contaminated refrigerant.
3. Purge the system of (refrigerant).
4. Charge the system (with refrigerant).

The manifold valves are designed so they have no direct effect on gauge readings, but serve only to provide for, or cut off, flow of refrigerant through the manifold. During all testing and hook-up operations, the valves are kept in a closed position to

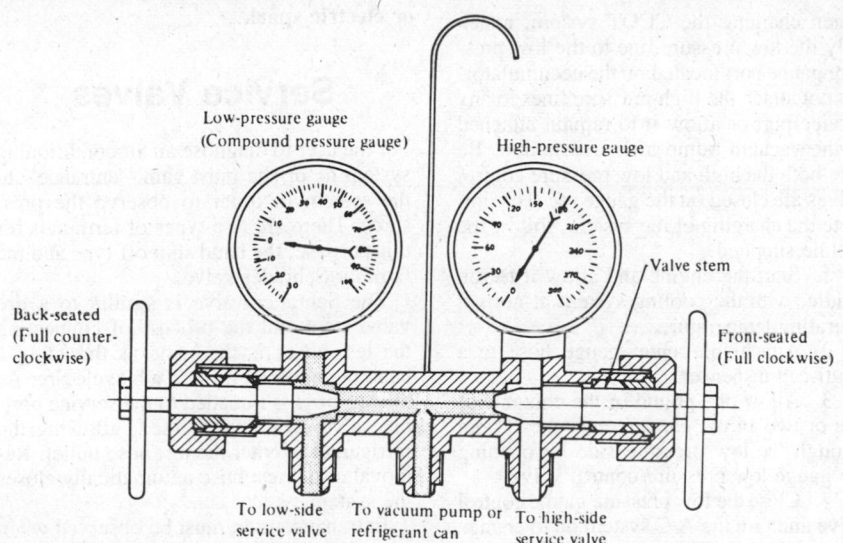

Low-pressure gauge
(Compound pressure gauge)

High-pressure gauge

Valve stem

Back-seated
(Full counter-clockwise)

Front-seated
(Full clockwise)

To low-side service valve   To vacuum pump or refrigerant can   To high-side service valve

Typical manifold gauge set

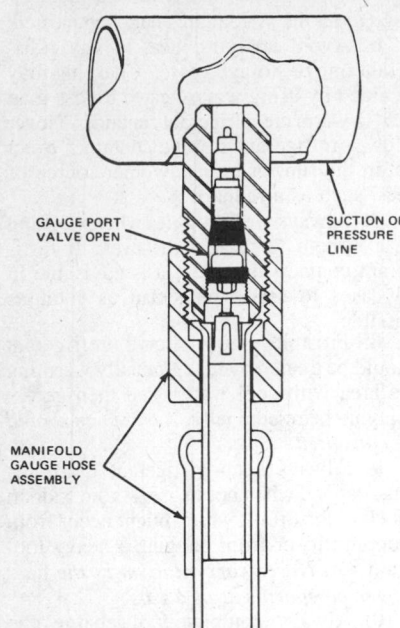

GAUGE PORT VALVE OPEN

SUCTION OR PRESSURE LINE

MANIFOLD GAUGE HOSE ASSEMBLY

Manifold gauge hose connected to a Schraeder type service port

avoid disturbing the refrigeration system. The valves are opened only to purge the system of refrigerant or to charge it.

When purging the system, the center hose is uncapped at the lower end, and both valves are cracked open slightly. This allows refrigerant pressure to force the entire contents of the system out through the center hose. During charging, the valve on the high side of the manifold is closed, and the valve on the low side is cracked open. Under these conditions, the low pressure in the evaporator will draw refrigerant from the relatively warm refrigerant storage container into the system.

SYSTEMS WITH A SIGHT GLASS

Air conditioning systems that use a sight glass as a means to check the refrigerant level should be carefully checked to avoid under or over charging. The gauge set should be attached to the system for verification of pressures.

To check the system with the sight glass, clean the glass and start the vehicle engine. Operate the air conditioning controls on maximum for approximately five minutes to stabilize the system. The room temperature should be above 70 degrees. Check the sight glass for one of the following conditions:

1. If the sight glass is clear, the compressor clutch is engaged, the compressor discharge line is warm and the compressor inlet line is cool, the system has a full charge of refrigerant.

2. If the sight glass is clear, the compressor clutch is engaged and there is no significant temperature difference between

the compressor inlet and discharge lines, the system is empty or nearly empty. By having the gauge set attached to the system, a measurement can be taken. If the gauge reads less than 25 psi, the low pressure cut-off protection switch has failed.

3. If the sight glass is clear and the compressor clutch is disengaged, the clutch is defective, or the clutch circuit is open, or the system is out of refrigerant. Bypass the low pressure cut-off switch momentarily to determine the cause.

4. If the sight glass shows foam or bubbles, the system can be low on refrigerant. Occasional foam or bubbles is normal when the room temperature is above 110 degrees or below 70 degrees. To verify, increase the engine speed to approximately 1500 rpm and block the airflow through the condensor in order to increase the compressor discharge pressure to 225–250 psi. If the sight glass still shows bubbles or foam, the refrigerant level is low.

--- **CAUTION** ---

Do not operate the vehicle engine any longer than necessary with the condensor airflow blocked. This blocking action also blocks the cooling system radiator and will cause the system to overheat rapidly.

When the system is low on refrigerant, a leak is present or the system was not properly charged. Use a leak detector and locate the problem area and repair. If no leakage is found, charge the system to its capacity.

--- **CAUTION** ---

It is not advisable to add refrigerant to a system utilizing the suction throttling valve and a sight glass, because the amount of refrigerant required to remove the foam or bubbles will result in an overcharge and potentially damage system components.

CCOT SYSTEM

When charging the CCOT system, attach only the low pressure line to the low pressure gauge port located on the accumulator. Do not attach the high pressure lines to any service port or allow it to remain attached to the vacuum pump after evacuation. Be sure both the high and low pressure control valves are closed on the gauge set. To complete the charging of the system, follow the outline supplied.

1. Start the engine and allow it to run at idle, with the cooling system at normal operating temperature.

2. Attach the center gauge hose to a multi-can dispenser.

3. Allow one pound or the contents of one or two 14 oz. cans to enter the system through the low pressure side by opening the gauge low pressure control valve.

4. Close the low pressure gauge control valve and turn the A/C system on to engage the compressor. Place the blower motor in its high mode.

5. Open the low pressure gauge control valve and draw the remaining charge into the system.

6. Close the low pressure gauge control valve and the refrigerant source valve on the multi-can dispenser. Remove the low pressure hose from the accumulator quickly to avoid loss of refrigerant through the Schrader valve.

7. Install the protective cap on the gauge port and check the system for leakage.

8. Test the system for proper operation.

Leak Testing the System

There are several methods of detecting leaks in an air conditioning system; among them, the two most popular are (1) halide leak-detection or the "open flame method," and (2) electronic leak-detection.

The halide leak detection is a torch like device which produces a yellow-green color when refrigerant is introduced into the flame at the burner. A brilliant blue or violet color indicates the presence of large amounts of refrigerant at the burner. A small leak will cause the flame to turn a yellow-green color.

An electronic leak detector is a small portable electronic device with an extended probe. With the unit activated, the probe is passed along those components of the system which contain refrigerant. If a leak is detected, the unit will sound an alarm signal or activate a display signal depending on the manufacturer's design. It is advisable to follow the manufacturer's instructions as the design and function of the detection may vary significantly.

NOTE: Caution should be taken to operate either type of detector in well ventilated areas, so as to reduce the chance of personal injury, which may result from coming in contact with poisonous gases produced when R-12 is exposed to flame or electric spark.

Service Valves

For the user to diagnose an air conditioning system he or she must gain "entrance" to the system in order to observe the pressures. There are two types of terminals for this purpose, the hand shut off type and the familiar Schrader valve.

The Schrader valve is similar to a tire valve stem and the process of connecting the test hoses is the same as threading a hand pump outlet hose to a bicycle tire. As the test hose is threaded to the service port, the valve core is depressed, allowing the refrigerant to enter the test hose outlet. Removal of the test hose automatically closes the system.

Extreme caution must be observed when removing test hoses from the Schrader valves as some refrigerant will normally escape,

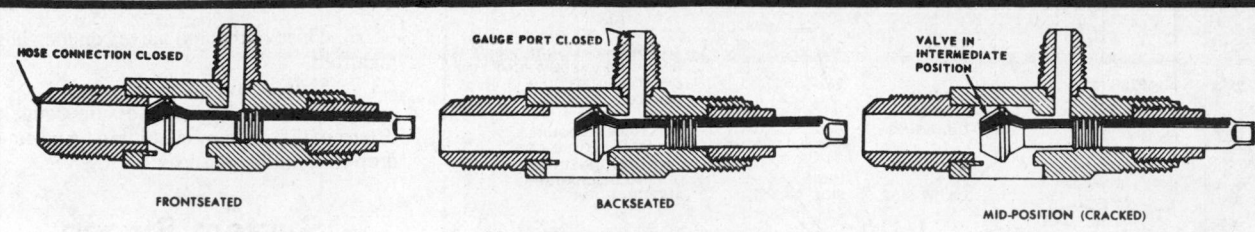

Manual service valve positions

usually under high pressure (observe safety precautions).

Some systems have hand shut-off valves (the stem can be rotated with a special racheting box wrench) that can be positioned in the following three ways:

1. FRONT SEATED—Rotated to full clockwise position.

   a. Refrigerant will not flow to the compressor, but will reach the test gauge port. COMPRESSOR WILL BE DAMAGED IF SYSTEM IS TURNED ON IN THIS POSITION.

   b. The compressor is now isolated and ready for service. However, care must be exercised when removing service valves from the compressor as a residue of refrigerant may still be present within the compressor. Therefore, remove service valves slowly, observing all safety precautions.

2. BACK SEATED—Rotated to full counterclockwise position. Normal position for system while in operation. Refrigerant flows to compressor but not to test gauge.

3. MID-POSITION (CRACKED)—Refrigerant flows to entire system. Gauge port (with hose connected) open for testing.

USING THE MANIFOLD GAUGES

The following are step-by-step procedures to guide the user to correct gauge usage.

1. WEAR GOGGLES OR FACE SHIELD DURING ALL TESTING OPERATIONS. BACKSEAT HAND SHUTOFF TYPE SERVICE VALVES.

2. Remove caps from the high and low side of the service ports. Make sure both gauge valves are closed.

3. Connect the low side test hose to the service valve that leads to the evaporator (located between the evaporator outlet and the compressor).

4. Attach the high side test hose to the service valve that leads to the condenser.

5. Mid-position hand shutoff type service valves.

6. Start the engine and allow for warmup. All testing and charging of the system should be done after the engine and system have reached normal operation temperatures (except when using certain charging stations).

7. Adjust the air conditioner controls to maximum cold.

8. Observe the gauge readings. When

BAR GAUGE MANIFOLD AND COMPRESSOR SERVICE VALVE SETTINGS

Condition	Manifold Valves	Compressor Valves
Testing System	Both fully closed	Both cracked off backseat
Depressurizing System	Both cracked open	Both at mid position
Evacuating the system	Both wide open	Both at mid position
Charging in gas form with compressor running	High pressure valve closed Low pressure valve cracked	High pressure valve cracked off backseat Low pressure valve at mid position
Charging in liquid form with compressor off	Low pressure valve closed High pressure valve wide open	Both valves mid positioned

Note: A very small leak, causing system discharge about every two weeks, can be caused by a leaky Schrader type service valve. Check these valves with extra care when testing for a small leak.

the gauges are not being used it is a good idea to:

   a. Keep both hand valves in the closed position.

   b. Attach both ends of the high and low service hoses to the manifold if extra outlets are present on the manifold, or plug them if not. Also, keep the center charging hose attached to an empty refrigerant can. This extra precaution will reduce the possibility of moisture entering the gauges. If air and moisture have gotten into the gauges, purge the hoses by supplying refrigerant under pressure to the center hose with both gauge valves open and all openings unplugged.

DISCHARGING, EVACUATING AND CHARGING

Discharging the System

CAUTION
Perform this operation in a well-ventilated area.

When it is necessary to remove (purge)

the refrigerant pressurized in the system, follow this procedure:

1. Operate the air conditioner for at least 10 minutes.

2. Attach the gauges, shut off the engine and air conditioner.

3. Place a container or rag at the outlet of the center charging hose on the gauge. The refrigerant will be discharged there and this precaution will avoid its uncontrolled exposure.

4. Open the low side hand valve on the gauge slightly.

5. Open the high side hand valve slightly.

NOTE: Too rapid a purging process will be identified by the appearance of an oil foam. If this occurs, close the hand valves a little more until this condition stops.

6. Close both hand valves on the gauge set when the pressures read 0 and all the refrigerant has left the system.

Evacuating the System

Before charging any system it is necessary to purge the refrigerant and draw out the trapped moisture with a suitable vacuum pump. Failure to do so will result in ineffective charging and possible damage to the system.

Use this hook-up for the proper evacuation procedure:

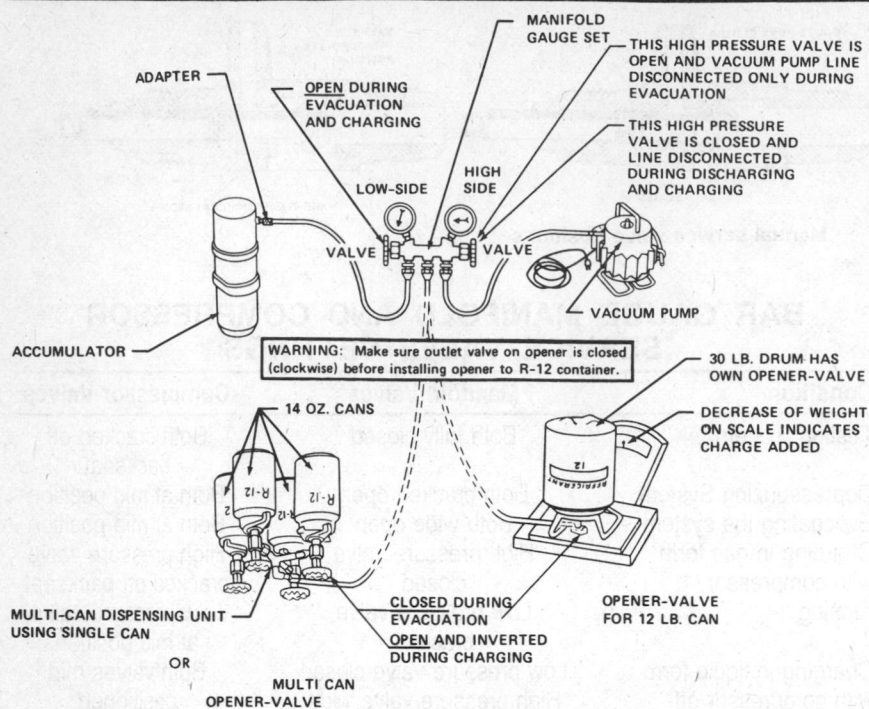

Typical gauge connections for discharge, evacuation and charging the system

1. Connect both service gauge hoses to the high and low service outlets.

2. Open both high and low side hand valves on the gauge manifold.

3. Open both service valves a slight amount (from back seated position), allow the refrigerant to discharge from the system.

4. Install the center charging hose of the gauge set to the vacuum pump.

5. Operate the vacuum pump for at least one hour (if the system has been subjected to open conditions for a prolonged period of time, it may be necessary to "pump the system down" overnight. Refer to the "System Sweep" procedure).

NOTE: If the low pressure gauge does not show at least 28" hg. within 5 minutes, check the system for a leak or loose gauge connectors.

6. Close both hand valves on the gauge manifold.

7. Shut off the pump.

8. Observe the low pressure gauge to determine if vacuum is holding. A vacuum drop may indicate a leak.

System Sweep

An efficient vacuum pump can remove all the air contained in a contaminated air conditioning system very quickly because of its vapor state. Moisture, however, is far more difficult to remove because the vacuum must force the liquid to evaporate before it will be able to remove it from the system. If a system has become severely contaminated, as, for example, it might become after all the charge was lost in conjunction with vehicle accident damage, moisture removal is extremely time consuming. A vacuum pump could remove all of the moisture only if it were operated for 12 hours or more.

Under these conditions, sweeping the system with refrigerant will speed the process of moisture removal considerably. To sweep, follow the following procedure:

1. Connect a vacuum pump to the gauges, operate it until vacuum ceases to increase, then continue operation for ten more minutes.

2. Charge the system with 50% of its rated refrigerant capacity.

3. Operate the system at fast idle for ten minutes.

4. Discharge the system.

5. Repeat twice the process of charging to 50% capacity, running the system for ten minutes, and discharging it, for a total of three sweeps.

6. Replace the drier.

7. Pump the system down as detailed in Step 1.

8. Charge the system.

Charging the System

CAUTION
Never attempt to charge the system by opening the high pressure gauge control while the compressor is operating. The compressor accumulating pressure can burst the refrigerant container, causing severe personal injuries.

BASIC SYSTEM

In this procedure the refrigerant enters the suction side of the system as a vapor while the compressor is running. Before proceeding, the system should be in a partial vacuum after adequate evacuation. Both hand valves on the gauge manifold should be closed.

1. Attach both test hoses to their respective service valve ports. Mid-position manually operated service valves, if present.

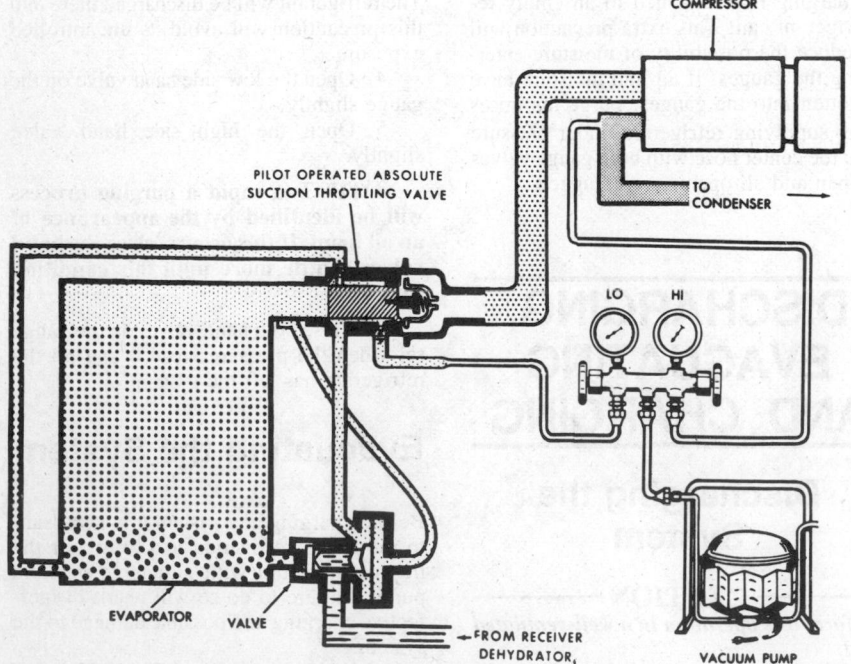

Schematic for evacuating the system

2. Install a dispensing valve (closed position) on the refrigerant container (single and multiple refrigerant manifolds are available to accommodate one to four 15 oz. cans).

3. Attach the center charging hose to the refrigerant container valve.

4. Open the dispensing valve on the refrigerant can.

5. Loosen the center charging hose coupler where it connects to the gauge manifold to allow the escaping refrigerant to purge the hose of contaminants.

6. Tighten the center charging hose connection.

7. Purge the low pressure test hose at the gauge manifold.

8. Start the engine, roll down the windows and adjust the air conditioner to maximum cooling. The engine should be at normal operating temperature before proceeding. The heated environment helps the liquid vaporize more efficiently.

9. Crack open the low side hand valve on the manifold. Manipulate the valve so that the refrigerant that enters the system does not cause the low side pressure to exceed 40 psi. Too sudden a surge may permit the entrance of unwanted liquid to the compressor. Since liquids cannot be compressed, the compressor will suffer damage if compelled to attempt it. If the suction side of the system remains in a vacuum, the system is blocked. Locate and correct the condition before proceeding any further.

NOTE: Placing the refrigerant can in a container of warm water (no hotter than 125° F) will speed the charging process. Slight agitation of the can is helpful too, but be careful not to turn the can upside down.

Some manufacturers allow for a partial charging of the A/C system in the form of a liquid (can inverted and compressor off) by opening the high side gauge valve only, and putting the high side compressor service valve in the middle position (if so equipped). The remainder of the refrigerant is then added in the form of a gas in the normal manner, through the suction side only.

SYSTEMS WITHOUT SIGHT GLASS, EXCEPT CCOT SYSTEM

The following procedure can be used to quickly determine whether or not an air conditioning system has the proper charge of refrigerant (providing ambient temperature is above 70° F. or 21° C.). This check can be made in a manner of minutes, thus facilitating system diagnosis by pinpointing the problem to the amount of charge in the system or by eliminating this possibility from the overall checkout.

1. Engine must be warm (thermostat open).

2. Hood and body doors open.

3. Selector lever set at NORM.

4. Temperature lever at COLD.

5. Blower on HI.

6. Normal engine idle.

7. Hand-feel the temperature of the evaporator inlet and outlet pipes with the compressor engaged.

   a. Both same temperature or some degree cooler than ambient—proper condition: check for other problems.

   b. Inlet pipe cooler than outlet pipe—low refrigerant charge.

• Add a slight amount of refrigerant until both pipes feel the same.

• Then add 15 oz. (1 can) additional refrigerant.

   c. Inlet pipe has front accumulation—outlet pipe warmer: proceed as in Step b above.

If during the charging process the head pressure exceeds 200 psi, place an electric fan in front of the car and direct the turbulent air to the condenser. If no fan is available, repeatedly pour cool water over the top of the condenser. These cooling actions may be necessary on an extremely warm day to help dissipate the heat emitted by the engine during idle.

If this fails and pressure on the discharge side continues to rise, the system may be overcharged or the engine might be overheating. *Never* allow head pressure to go beyond 240 psi. during charging. If this condition occurs, stop the engine, find and correct the problem.

8. Continue dispensing refrigerant until the container is no longer cool to the touch. On a humid day, the outside of the container will frost. When the frost disappears the can is usually empty. To detach the dispensing can:

   a. close the low pressure test gauge hand valve.

   b. crack open the low pressure test hose at the manifold until the remaining pressure escapes.

   c. tighten the hose coupler.

   d. loosen the hose coupler connected to the refrigerant can.

   e. discard the empty can and repeat Steps 2–8.

9. Continue to add refrigerant to the required capacity of the system. (Usually marked on the compressor).

CAUTION

DO NOT OVERCHARGE. This condition is usually indicated by an abnormally high side pressure reading and a noisy compressor resulting in ineffective cooling and damage to the system.

SYSTEMS WITH A SIGHT GLASS

Air conditioning systems that use a sight glass as a means to check the refrigerant level should be carefully checked to avoid under or over charging. The gauge set should be attached to the system for verification of pressures.

To check the system with the sight glass, clean the glass and start the vehicle engine. Operate the air conditioning controls on maximum for approximately five minutes

Amount of refrigerant / Check item	Almost no refrigerant	Insufficient	Suitable	Too much refrigerant
Temperature of high pressure and low pressure lines.	Almost no difference between high pressure and low pressure side temperature.	High pressure side is warm and low pressure side is fairly cold.	High pressure side is hot and low pressure side is cold.	High pressure side is abnormally hot.
State in sight glass.	Bubbles flow continuously. **Bubbles will disappear and something like mist will flow when refrigerant is nearly gone.**	The bubbles are seen at intervals of 1 - 2 seconds.	Almost transparent. Bubbles may appear when engine speed is raised and lowered. **No clear difference exists between these two conditions.**	No bubbles can be seen.
Pressure of system.	High pressure side is abnormally low.	Both pressure on high and low pressure sides are slightly low.	Both pressures on high and low pressure sides are normal.	Both pressures on high and low pressure sides are abnormally high.
Repair.	**Stop compressor immediately** and conduct an overall check.	Check for gas leakage, repair as required, replenish and charge system.		Discharge refrigerant from service valve of low pressure side.

Using a sight glass to determine the relative refrigerant charge

to stabilize the system. The room temperature should be above 70 degrees. Check the sight glass for one of the following conditions:

1. If the sight glass is clear, the compressor clutch is engaged, the compressor discharge line is warm and the compressor inlet line is cool, the system has a full charge of refrigerant.

2. If the sight glass is clear, the compressor clutch is engaged and there is no significant temperature difference between the compressor inlet and discharge lines, the system is empty or nearly empty. By having the gauge set attached to the system, a measurement can be taken. If the gauge reads less than 25 psi, the low pressure cut-off protection switch has failed.

3. If the sight glass is clear and the compressor clutch is disengaged, the clutch is defective, or the clutch circuit is open, or the system is out of refrigerant. By-pass the low pressure cut-off switch momentarily to determine the cause.

4. If the sight glass shows foam or bubbles, the system can be low on refrigerant. Occasional foam or bubbles is normal when the room temperature is above 110 degrees or below 70 degrees. To verify, increase the engine speed to approximately 1500 rpm and block the airflow through the condenser in order to increase the compressor discharge pressure to 225–250 psi. If the sight glass still shows bubbles or foam, the refrigerant level is low.

—————— CAUTION ——————
Do not operate the vehicle engine any longer than necessary with the condenser airflow blocked. This blocking action also blocks the cooling system radiator and will cause the system to overheat rapidly.

When the system is low on refrigerant, a leak is present or the system was not properly charged. Use a leak detector and locate the problem area and repair. If no leakage is found, charge the system to its capacity.

—————— CAUTION ——————
It is not advisable to add refrigerant to a system utilizing the suction throttling valve and a sight glass, because the amount of refrigerant required to remove the foam or bubbles will result in an overcharge and potentially damaged system components.

CCOT SYSTEM

When charging the CCOT system, attach only the low pressure line to the low pressure gauge port located on the accumulator. Do not attach the high pressure line to any service port or allow it to remain attached to the vacuum pump after evacuation. Be sure both the high and the low pressure control valves are closed on the gauge set. To complete the charging of the system, follow the outline supplied.

1. Start the engine and allow it to run at idle, with the cooling system at normal operating temperature.

2. Attach the center gauge hose to a single or multi-can dispenser.

3. With the multi-can dispenser inverted, allow one pound or the contents of one or two 14 oz. cans to enter the system through the low pressure side by opening the gauge low pressure control valve.

4. Close the low pressure gauge control valve and turn the A/C system on to engage the compressor. Place the blower motor in its high mode.

5. Open the low pressure gauge control valve and draw the remaining charge into the system.

6. Close the low pressure gauge control valve and the refrigerant source valve, on the multi-can dispenser. Remove the low pressure hose from the accumulator quickly to avoid loss of refrigerant through the Schrader valve.

7. Install the protective cap on the gauge port and check the system for leakage.

8. Test the system for proper operation.

Leak Testing the System

There are several methods of detecting leaks in an air conditioning system; among them, the two most popular are (1) halide leak-detection or the "open flame method," and (2) electronic leak-detection.

The halide leak detection is a torch like device which produces a yellow-green color when refrigerant is introduced into the flame at the burner. A purple or violet color indicates the presence of large amounts of refrigerant at the burner.

An electronic leak detector is a small portable electronic device with an extended probe. With the unit activated, the probe is passed along those components of the system which contain refrigerant. If a leak is detected, the unit will sound an alarm signal or activate a display signal depending on the manufacturer's design. It is advisable to follow the manufacturer's instructions as the design and function of the detection may vary significantly.

—————— CAUTION ——————
Caution should be taken to operate either type of detector in well ventilated areas, so as to reduce the chance of personal injury, which may result from coming in contact with poisonous gases produced when R-12 is exposed to flame or electric spark.

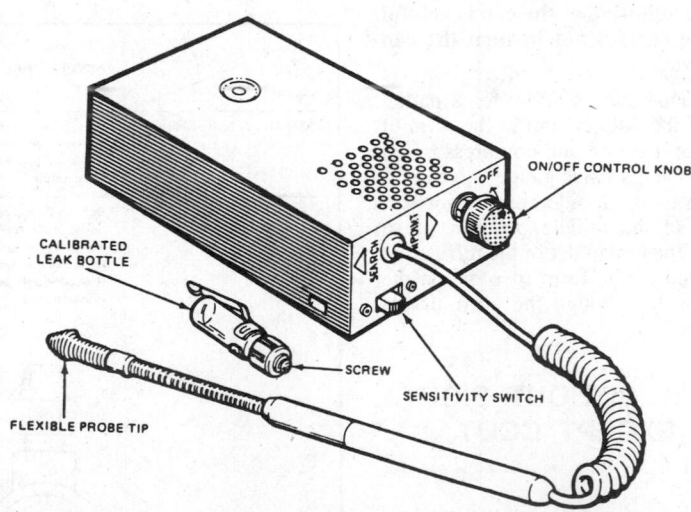

Electronic leak detector

Diesel Service 22

NOTE: Most procedures associated with diesel engined cars are similar to gas engined cars, although many parts of the diesel engine are unique compared to their gas engine counterparts. Standard maintenance and service procedures are given here while component removal, installation and adjustment procedures unique to diesel engines can be found in the appropriate section.

HOW THE DIESEL ENGINE WORKS

Four-stroke diesels require four piston strokes for the complete cycle of actions, exactly like a gasoline engine. The difference lies in how the fuel mixture is ignited. A diesel engine does not rely on a conventional spark ignition to ignite the fuel mixture for the power stroke. Instead, a diesel relies on the heat produced by compressing air in the combustion chamber to ignite the fuel and produce a power stroke. This is known as a compression-ignition engine. No fuel enters the cylinder on the intake stroke, only air. At the end of the compression stroke, fuel is sprayed into the precombustion chamber (prechamber). The mixture ignites and spreads out into the main combustion chamber, forcing the piston downward (power stroke). The fuel/air mixture ignites because of the very high combustion chamber temperatures generated by the extraordinarily high compression ratios used in diesel engines. Typically, the compression ratios used in automotive diesels run any-

where from 16:1 to 23:1. A typical spark-ignition engine has a ratio of about 8:1. This is why a spark-ignition engine which continues to run after you have shut off the engine is said to be "dieseling". It is running on combustion chamber heat alone.

Designing an engine to ignite on its own combustion chamber heat poses certain problems. For instance, although a diesel engine has no need for a coil, spark plugs, or a distributor, it does need what are known as "glow plugs". These superficially resemble spark plugs, but are only used to warm the combustion chambers when the engine is cold. Without these plugs, cold starting would be impossible, due to the enormously high compression ratios and the characteristics of the diesel fuel itself.

All diesel engines use fuel injection, be-

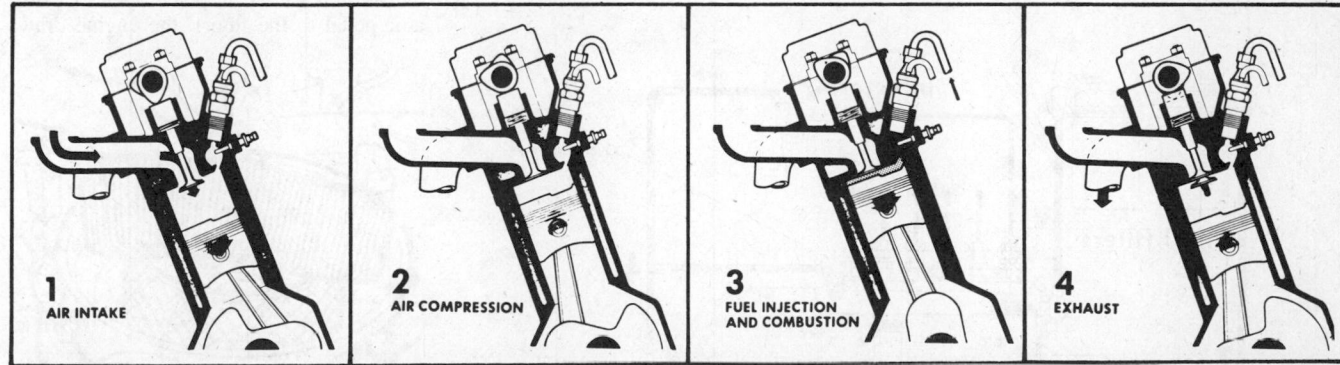

4-stroke diesel engine cycle. At *air intake* (1), rotation of the crankshaft drives a toothed belt that turns the camshaft, opening the intake valve. As the piston moves down, a vacuum is created, sucking fresh air into the cylinder, past the open intake valve. *Air compression* (2): As the piston moves up, both valves are closed, and the air is compressed about 23 times smaller than its original volume. The compressed air reaches a temperature of about 1,650°F., far above the temperature needed to ignite diesel fuel. *Fuel injection and compression* (3): As the piston reaches the top of the stroke, the air temperature is at its maximum. A fine mist of fuel is sprayed into the prechamber, where it ignites, and the flame front spreads rapidly into the combustion chamber. The piston is forced downward by the pressure (about 500 psi) of expanding gases. *Exhaust* (4): As the energy of combustion is spent and the piston begins to move upward again, the exhaust valve opens, and burnt gases are forced out past the open valve. As the piston starts down, the exhaust valve closes, the intake valve opens, and the air intake stroke begins again.

Increasingly, modern diesel engines are being equipped with turbochargers, exhaust gas—driven devices that force more air into the engine to increase power output

Maintenance and Service Procedures

Maintenance procedures for the diesel engine generally fall into three categories:
1. Fuel system
2. Starting system
3. Engine mechanical systems

Of these, the fuel system is usually the most likely source of engine troubles, and should be high on the list for regular maintenance attention.

FUEL SYSTEM

The typical diesel engine fuel system consists of fuel tank, fuel feed and return lines, mechanical fuel injection pump, fuel injectors and lines, and a large capacity fuel filter. On some models, the engine may also be equipped with a small, low pressure fuel pump which feeds the injection pump.

In addition to these, the air intake system (air cleaner, inlet manifold) should be checked over regularly to insure unrestricted air flow into the cylinders.

In operation, fuel is sucked out of the fuel tank by the injection pump (or its feed pump) and fed by the injection pump to the injectors in the cylinder head at a very high pressure. Before the fuel is allowed to enter the main injection pump, it passes through a specially built fuel filter which traps solid particles (and water on some models) in the fuel. Fuel that is not used is pumped back to the fuel tank through the fuel return lines. This recirculated fuel helps cool the injection pump.

Air Cleaner

On a gasoline engine, the volume of air taken in by the engine is controlled by throttle valves. When the throttle valves are closed (engine idling), air intake is restricted. When the throttle valves are wide open (accelerator pedal to the floor), the engine draws

cause unlike spark-ignited engines, the fuel cannot be drawn through the intake tract

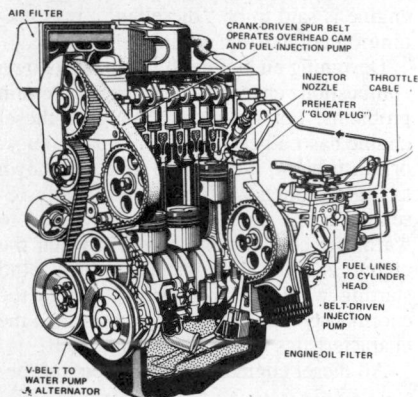

Cutaway view of typical 4-cylinder diesel engine.

and into the cylinders. The introduction of fuel into a diesel engine must be precisely timed so that each cylinder "fires" at the proper moment. Also, the fuel injection pressure (at the cylinder) must be great enough to overcome the high compression pressures, and properly atomize the fuel without the aid of a moving air mass (as in a carbureted gas engine). It is not uncommon for diesel engine fuel injection pressures to be set at 1500–1700 psi.

Diesel engines share many of their basic mechanical components with gasoline engines, though the cylinder block, head(s), crankshaft, connecting rods, pistons, etc., are manufactured to be much stronger for use in diesel engines. The additional strength of the components is necessary due to the very high cylinder pressure generated within the diesel engine.

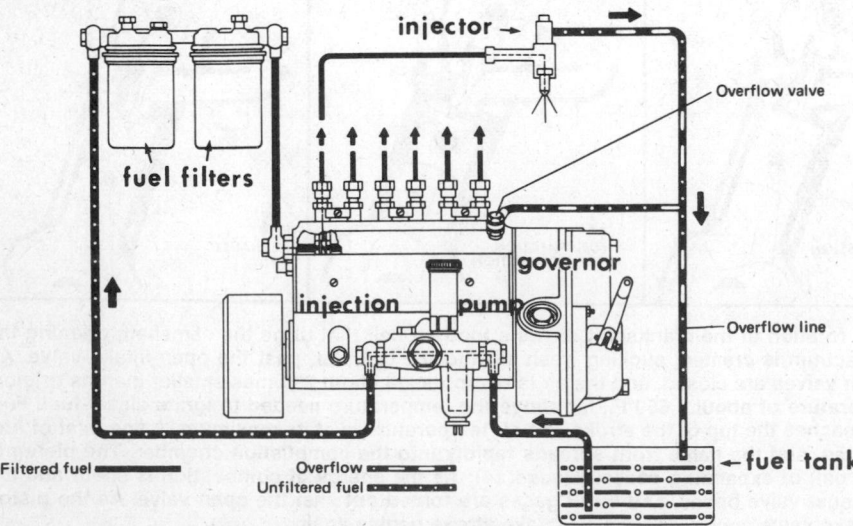

Typical diesel engine fuel system schematic

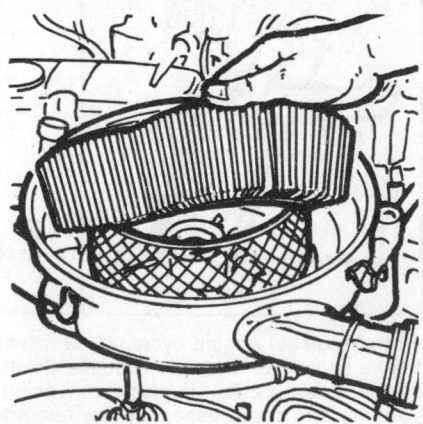

Because a greater quantity of air passes through the diesel engine, air filter maintenance is particularly important. Most diesel air filters on passenger cars are similar to their counterparts on gasoline engines.

in the maximum amount of air it possibly can. This applies to both carbureted and fuel injected gasoline engines.

The speed (rpm) of a diesel engine is controlled by the quantity of fuel which is injected into the engine; no air metering restrictions (throttle valves) are used. Because of this, diesel engines ingest as much air as they possibly can under all conditions. A much greater volume of air passes through the air cleaner of a diesel per mile, therefore, diesel air filters must either be larger or the filter replacement intervals more frequent than those of a similarly sized gasoline engine.

One word of caution: never remove the air cleaner on a diesel with the engine running, and never run the engine with the air cleaner removed. The volume of air drawn through the inlet manifold is very great, and, because the inlet manifold is unobstructed, anything drawn into the inlet manifold (air cleaner wing nut, etc.) goes straight to the combustion chambers, where it can cause major engine damage.

Fuel Filter

The diesel engine fuel filter is usually larger than the filter used on gasoline engines. The extra capacity is needed to trap the suspended particles in diesel fuel, which is generally "dirtier" than gasoline.

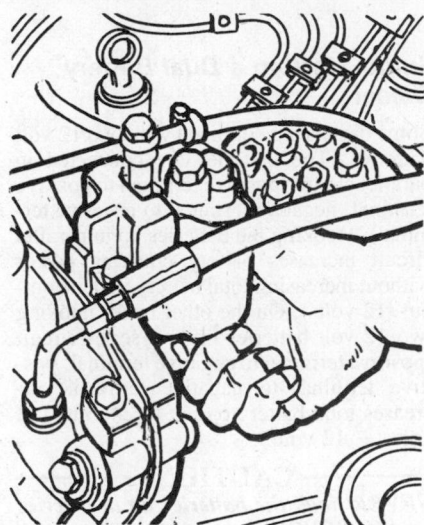

Many diesel engines use a spin-on type primary fuel filter.

On some engines, the fuel filter looks like a second engine oil filter, and is removed and installed in the same manner as the canister-type oil filter.

The fuel filter must be changed according to the manufacturer's suggested interval. See the owner's manual for information.

After installing the fuel filter start the engine and check for leaks. Run the engine for about two minutes, then stop the engine for the same amount of time to allow any air trapped in the injection system to bleed off.

Many diesels also have a small, in-tank filter which is usually maintenance-free.

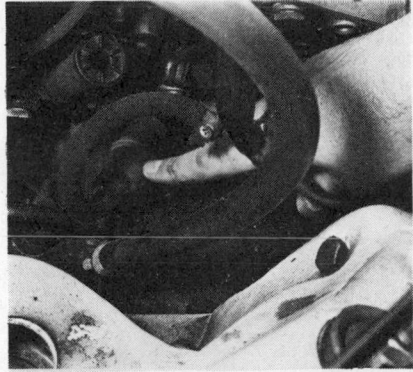

A smaller, in-line secondary filter is used on many engines.

Check the tightness of the clamps securing the injector lines. Note that the injector lines are all the same length.

Mercedes-Benz diesel engines use this stop switch, which shuts off fuel delivery

Water In Fuel

Diesel fuel is a hydrophilic fluid, that is, it naturally attracts water. Since diesel fuel and water do not mix, the water remains floating beneath the fuel at the bottom of the tank. This water must be removed every now and then, or it will be sucked into the fuel circuit and pass through the injection system, causing corrosion and possible component failure (injection pumps can cost up to $1,000). Water in the fuel system will also cause the engine to run poorly, if at all.

Most diesel fuel tanks are equipped with

a separator which can isolate from 1 to 3 gallons of water from the fuel.

Many diesels are also equipped with "Water in Fuel" lights in the dashboard which warn of the presence of water in the fuel tank. These warning systems can be installed on models not so equipped.

On some diesels, there is a water catcher in the bottom of the fuel filter which can easily be bled off. In addition, there are several bolt-on water filters on the market which attach to the fuel line under the hood and separate water from the fuel. Depending on which kind you buy, draining water from the system is simply a matter of opening the petcock at the bottom of the filter and letting the water drain out, or, if money is no object, a separator is available on which water is drained from the filter simply by activating a switch on the dashboard.

Removing Water from the Fuel Tank

Treat diesel fuel with the same respect you would gasoline, and after the procedure, properly dispose of the fuel.

1. Remove the fuel tank cap.
2. Connect a pump or siphon hose to the ¼ in. fuel return hose (smaller of the two fuel hoses) above the rear axle, or under the hood near the fuel pump (on the passenger's side of the engine, near the front).
3. Siphon until all water is removed from the tank. Do not use your mouth to create siphon vacuum, EVER! The best method is to siphon the water into a large capacity see-through container. The water will collect at the bottom of the container.
4. When all water has been removed from the tank, be sure to reinstall the fuel return hose and fuel cap.

NOTE: If the entire fuel system (not just the tank) is contaminated by water, the vehicle must be stopped immediately and the fuel system must be purged. This includes draining and removing the fuel tank, blowing low pressure compressed air backwards through the fuel feed and return lines, and bleeding the water out of all injection components. This job should be referred to a qualified technician.

Cold Weather Fuel System Maintenance

—————— CAUTION ——————
NEVER use "starting aids" (e.g.—ether) to help start a diesel engine—serious engine damage will result.

As will be explained later under "Fuel Recommendations", diesel fuel tends to become "cloudy", or thicker, as the temperature drops. The thicker the diesel fuel becomes, the slower it flows through the fuel system, until finally it stops flowing altogether somewhere near the bottom of the thermometer.

One way to fight sluggish fuel flow is to use winterized blends of diesel fuel, straight No. 1 diesel fuel or add cold weather additives to the fuel to improve flow in cold weather.

NOTE: Consult your owners manual for recommendations and be sure to use a fuel conditioner compatible with water separators.

Another way is to install an aftermarket fuel system pre-heater. These are generally canisters which connect into the fuel line and use coolant from the engine cooling system to heat the fuel before it reaches the injection pump. The one drawback with this system is the engine must be started before the pre-heater begins to work. Also available are electric fuel warmers. These pre-heat the fuel going into the filter and can be used in conjunction with the coolant-type fuel heater.

Cold weather additives and fuel conditioners can help improve cold weather flow of diesel fuel.

Some manufacturers offer an optional electric diesel fuel heater and engine block heaters. The fuel heater is thermostatically controlled to heat the fuel before it enters the fuel filter when fuel temperature is 20°F or lower. The fuel heater works only when the ignition key is in the RUN position. On these models, the fuel tank filter has a by-pass valve which allows fuel to flow to the heater when the tank filter is covered with fuel wax. The engine block heater is equipped with an electrical cord wrapped up in the engine compartment. The cord

Some diesel engines come equipped with a built-in heating system to keep the engine warm in cold temperatures.
Most OEM heaters work from 110-volt house current.

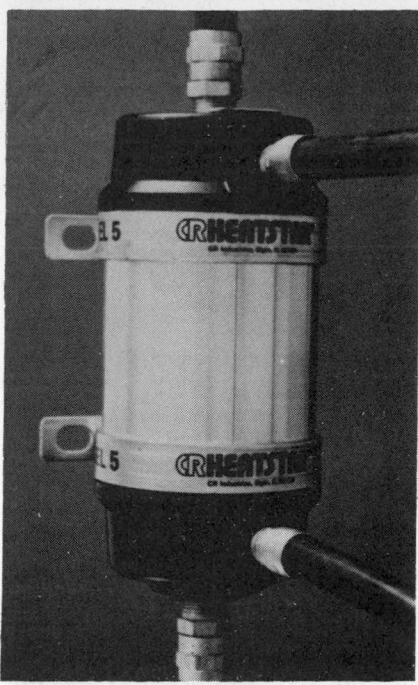

Some aftermarket diesel fuel warmers are thermostatically controlled heat exchangers that use engine coolant to keep diesel fuel above its "cloud point," the temperature at which it gels and forms wax that can clog a fuel system.

plugs into regular 110 volt household current. The block heater can be used, according to the type of oil in the crankcase, up to eight hours or overnight to warm up the block.

STARTING SYSTEM

The diesel starting system includes one (sometimes two) heavy duty batteries, the starter, and the glow plug circuit. In addition to the heavy duty battery(ies), the majority of diesel engines also have starters and battery cables designed specifically as heavy duty items for diesel usage only. Because of the high compression of any diesel, the torque required to turn the engine is much greater than a gasoline engine. The starter must be powerful enough to handle the increased load; the battery cables must be thick enough to withstand the heat generated by the starter load.

For battery maintenance, see the regular "Maintenance" section. Jump starting procedures for a dual battery car are given below. Starter maintenance is included in the appropriate car section.

The glow plug circuit is used on the diesel to initially start the engine. When the ignition switch is turned to the ON position, a light will come on in the instrument panel signalling that the glow plugs are preheating the combustion chambers. After a certain interval (depending on how cold the engine is), the light will go off. This signals that the starter may be engaged and the engine started. If the glow plug circuit mal-

functions, especially in cold weather, the engine will be almost impossible to start.

---------- **CAUTION** ----------
NEVER use "starting aids" (e.g.—ether) to help start a diesel engine—serious engine damage will result.

Glow Plug Testing

To test each individual glow plug, disconnect the busbar and/or wire connector from the glow plug and connect a test light between the glow plug terminal and the positive battery terminal. If the test light lights, the glow plug is working. Replace individual glow plugs which do not work.

NOTE: Some diesel engines are equipped with either "slow glow" or "fast glow" glow plugs. Do not attempt to interchange any parts of these two glow plug systems.

To test the glow plug circuit, connect a test light to the terminal of one of the glow plugs (glow plug wiring still attached) and turn the ignition to the heating position. The test light should light for a short while. If not, the glow plug circuit is malfunctioning and must be diagnosed and repaired.

NOTE: Perform this operation on a cold engine only.

Jump-Starting a Dual Battery Diesel

Some diesels are equipped with two 12 volt batteries. The batteries are connected in parallel circuit (positive terminal to positive terminal, negative terminal to negative terminal). Hooking the batteries up in parallel circuit increases battery cranking power without increasing total battery voltage output (12 volts). On the other hand, hooking two 12 volt batteries up in a series circuit (positive terminal to negative terminal, positive terminal to negative terminal) increases total battery output to 24 volts (12 volts + 12 volts).

---------- **CAUTION** ----------
NEVER hook the batteries up in a series circuit; SEVERE electrical system damage will result.

In the event that a dual battery diesel must be jumped started, use the following procedure.

1. Open the hood and locate the batteries.

2. Position the donor car so that the jumper cables will reach from its battery (must be 12 volt, negative ground) to the appropriate battery in the diesel. Do not allow the cars to touch.

3. Shut off all electrical equipment on both vehicles. Turn off the engine of the donor car, set the parking brakes on both vehicles and block the wheels. Also, make sure both vehicles are in Neutral (manual

transmission models) or Park (automatic transmission models).

4. Using the jumper cables, connect the positive (+) terminal of the donor car battery to the positive terminal of one (not both) of the diesel batteries.

5. Using the second jumper cable, connect the negative (−) terminal of the donor battery to a solid, stationary, metallic point on the diesel (alternator bracket, engine block, etc.). Be very careful to keep the jumper cables away from moving parts (cooling fan, alternator belt, etc.) on both vehicles.

6. Start the engine of the donor car and run it at moderate speed.

7. Start the engine of the diesel.

8. When the diesel starts, disconnect the battery cables in the reverse order of attachment.

ENGINE MECHANICAL SYSTEMS

Included are engine lubrication and engine compression.

Although diesel engines are very low in carbon monoxide (CO) and hydrocarbon (HC) emissions, "particulate" emission output is very high from diesel engines. This is evident from the black smoke emitted by diesels, which is most noticeable during hard acceleration or high engine loads. The particulates are made up of mostly soot (carbon) and sulpher particles. The majority of these particulates are released into the atmosphere. However, some of the particulate matter, because it is produced within the engines cylinders, is left inside the engine and gradually contaminates the engine oil. This contamination makes the oil corrosive, due to the sulpher, and abrasive, due to the carbon. Serious engine damage will result if these contaminants continue to accumulate in the oil. Engine oil and filters of diesel engines must be changed more frequently than those of gasoline engines, due to the increased rate at which the contaminants form in the diesel. Consult the "Maintenance" section for oil and filter change procedures. The manufacturer's recommended oil change interval will be given in the owner's manual. An explanation of diesel engine oils is given at the end of this section.

As explained earlier, very high cylinder compression is the key to the operation of the diesel engine. The normal compression of most gasoline engines will rarely exceed 180 psi; whereas with diesel engines, compression pressures of 350–400 psi are commonplace.

── CAUTION ──

DO NOT attempt to check the compression of a diesel engine with a standard compression gauge—personal injury could result. A special, high pressure compression gauge is needed to safely check the compression of any diesel.

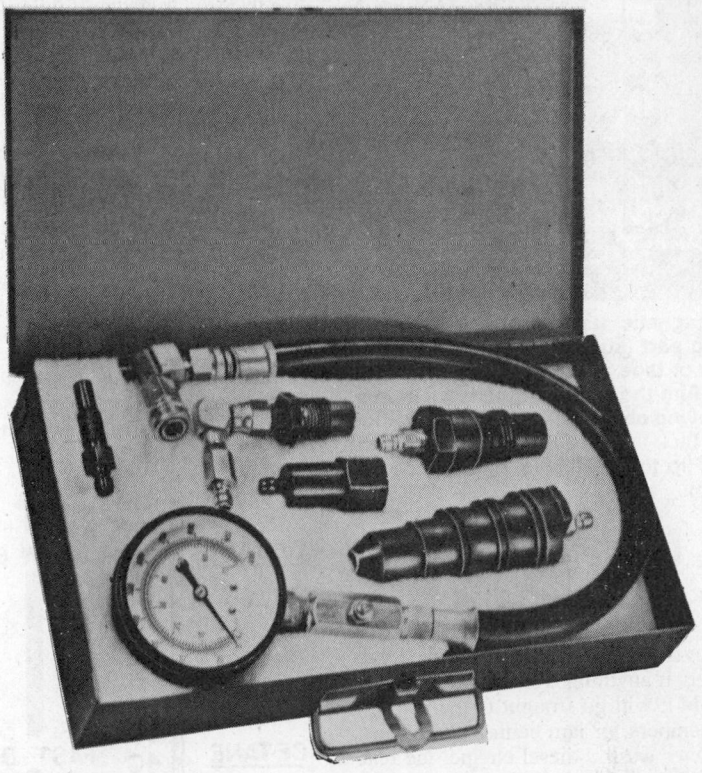

A diesel compression tester kit with adaptors (Courtesy S & G Tools).

Compression Test

1. Remove the air cleaner.
2. Disconnect the wire from the fuel shutoff solenoid terminal of the injection pump.
3. Disconnect the wires from the glow plugs and remove all glow plugs.
4. Screw compression gauge into the glow plug hole in the cylinder being checked.
5. Crank the engine, allowing six "puffs" for each cylinder.

The lowest reading cylinder should not be less than 70% of the highest, and no cylinder should be less than 275 pounds.

Idle Speed Adjustments

Idle speed adjustment procedures for individual diesel engines are given in the car section. Consult the following section for procedures to measure idle speed

Connecting a Tachometer to a Diesel Engine

As mentioned earlier, the diesel engine does not require an electrical ignition system. Because of this, problems arise when attempts are made to connect a tachometer to the engine for the purpose of idle adjustments, etc. The average gasoline engine tachometer senses the ignition spark pulses and converts them into a readable engine rpm signal. This type of tachometer is use-

less on the diesel engine, because of the diesel's compression ignition system.

There are several magnetic and photoelectric tachometers available from various tool manufacturers which were designed specifically for use with the diesel engine. These units can run into a little more money than the average do-it-yourselfer may be willing to spend, in which case any adjustments requiring the monitoring of engine rpm should be performed by a competent service technician.

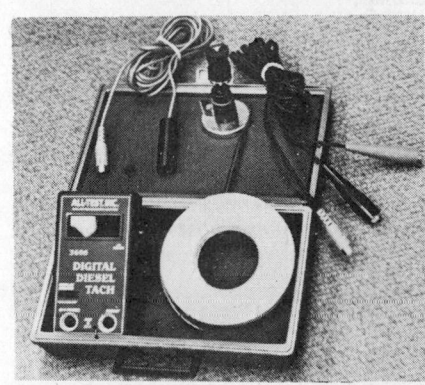

The newest equipment for measuring idle speed on a diesel engine includes (clockwise from lower left) a digital diesel tach display, photomagnetic pick-up with display input, magnetic swivel base (holder), DC power source for the display unit and a roll of magnetic tape.

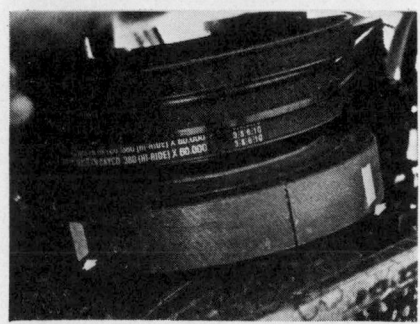

The magnetic tape is attached to any moving part (such as the balancer). The pieces of tape must be at least 6 inches apart. Aim the photomagnetic pick-up at the moving object and adjust the position of the pick-up until the "on-target" light is lit. Flip the switch to TACH and read the rpm.

Diesel Engine Precautions

- Never run the engine with the air cleaner removed: if anything is sucked into the inlet manifold it will go straight to the combustion chambers, or jam behind a valve.
- Never wash a diesel engine: the reaction of a warm fuel injection pump to cold (or even warm) water can ruin the pump.
- Never operate a diesel engine with one or more fuel injectors removed unless fully familiar with injector testing procedures: some diesel injection pumps spray fuel at up to 1400 psi—enough pressure to allow the fuel to penetrate your skin.
- Do not skip engine oil and filter changes.
- Strictly follow the manufacturer's oil and fuel recommendations as given in the owner's manual.
- Do not use home heating oil as fuel for your diesel.
- Do not use "starting aids" (e.g.—ether) in the automotive diesel engine, as these "aids" can cause severe internal engine damage.
- Do not run a diesel engine with the "Water in Fuel" warning light on in the dashboard.
- If removing water from the fuel tank yourself, use the same caution you would use when working around gasoline engine fuel components.
- Do not allow diesel fuel to come in contact with rubber hoses or components on the engine, as it can damage them.

Fuel and Oil Recommendations

FUEL

Fuel makers produce two grades of diesel fuel, No. 1 and No. 2, for use in automotive diesel engines. Generally speaking, No. 2 fuel is recommended over No. 1 for driving in temperatures above 20°F. In fact, in many areas, No. 2 diesel is the only fuel available. By comparison, No. 2 diesel fuel is less volatile than No. 1 fuel, and gives better fuel economy. No. 2 fuel is also a better injection pump lubricant.

Two important characteristics of diesel fuel are its cetane number and its viscosity.

The cetane number of a diesel fuel refers to the ease with which a diesel fuel ignites. High cetane numbers mean that the fuel will ignite with relative ease or that it ignites well at low temperatures. Naturally, the lower the cetane number, the higher the temperature must be to ignite the fuel. Most commercial fuels have cetane numbers that range from 35 to 65. No. 1 diesel fuel generally has a higher cetane rating than No. 2 fuel.

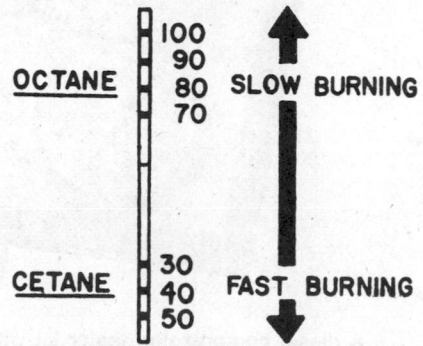

Cetane (diesel engine) versus octane (gasoline engine) ratings. The higher the cetane number, the faster the fuel burns

Viscosity is the ability of a liquid, in this case diesel fuel, to flow. Using straight No. 2 diesel fuel below 20°F can cause problems, because this fuel tends to become cloudy, meaning wax crystals begin forming in the fuel. In extreme cold weather, No. 2 fuel can stop flowing altogether. In either case, fuel flow is restricted, which can result in a "no start" condition or poor engine performance. Fuel manufacturers often "winterize" No. 2 diesel fuel by using various fuel additives and blends (No. 1 diesel fuel, kerosene, etc.) to lower its winter-time viscosity. Generally speaking, though, No. 1 diesel fuel is more satisfactory in extremely cold weather.

NOTE: No. 1 and No. 2 diesel fuels will mix and burn with no ill effects, although the engine manufacturer will undoubtedly recommend one or the other. Consult the owner's manual for information.

Depending on local climate, most fuel manufacturers make winterized No. 2 fuel available seasonally.

Many automobile manufacturers publish pamphlets giving the locations of diesel fuel stations nationwide. Contact the local dealer for information.

Do not substitute home heating oil for automotive diesel fuel. While in some cases, home heating oil refinement levels equal those of diesel fuel, many times they are far below diesel engine requirements. The result of using "dirty" home heating oil will be a clogged fuel system, in which case the entire system may have to be dismantled and cleaned.

One more word on diesel fuels. Don't thin diesel fuel with gasoline in cold weather. The lighter gasoline, which is more explosive, will cause rough running at the very least, and may cause extensive engine damage if enough is used.

OIL

Diesel engines require different engine oil from those used in gasoline engines. Besides doing the things gasoline engine oil does, diesel oil must also deal with increased engine heat and the diesel blow-by gases, which create sulphuric acid, a high corrosive.

Under the American Petroleum Institute (API) classifications, gasoline engine oil codes begin with an "S", and diesel engine oil codes begin with a "C". This first letter designation is followed by a second letter code which explains what type of service (heavy, moderate, light) the oil is meant for. For example, the top of a typical oil can will include: "API SERVICES SC, SD, SE, CA, CB, CC". This means the oil in the can is a good, moderate duty engine oil when used in a diesel engine.

It should be noted here that the further

COMPARISON OF #1 AND #2 DIESEL FUEL

Requirement	1-D	2-D
Flash Point, °F minimum	100	125
Cetane Number, minimum	40	40
Viscosity at 100°F, Centistokes		
Minimum	1.4	2.0
Maximum	2.5	4.3
Water and Sediment, % by volume maximum	Trace	0.05
Sulfur, % by weight maximum	0.5	0.5
Ash, % by weight maximum	0.01	0.01

Flash Point: The temperature at which diesel fuel ignites when exposed to a flame *in the open air*.
Cetane Number: See text

down the alphabet the second letter of the API classification is, the greater the oil's protective qualities are (CD is the severest duty diesel engine oil, CA is the lightest duty oil, etc.). The same is true for gasoline engine oil classifications (SF is the severest duty gasoline engine oil, SA is the lightest duty oil, etc.).

Many diesel manufacturers recommend an oil with both gasoline and diesel engine API classifications. Consult the owner's manual for specifications.

The top of the oil can will also contain an SAE (Society of Automotive Engineers) designation, which gives the oil's viscosity. A typical designation will be: SAE 10W-30, which means the oil is a "winter" viscosity oil, meaning it will flow and give protection at low temperatures.

On the diesel engine, oil viscosity is critical, because the diesel is much harder to start (due to its higher compression) than a gasoline engine. Obviously, if you fill the crankcase with a very heavy oil during winter (SAE 20W-50, for example), the starter is going to require a lot of current from the battery to turn the engine. And, since batteries don't function well in cold weather in the first place, you may find yourself stranded some morning. Consult the owner's manual for recommended oil specifications for the climate you live in.

LUBE OIL ANALYSIS

From an oil sample a laboratory can diagnose many potential engine problems—from piston wear to impending bearing failure. What's more, the laboratory can spot them quicker, and with greater accuracy. Just as easily, the lab can give the diesel a clean bill of health, saving the car owner unnecessary servicing and other routine preventive maintenance, costly in time and money.

There's nothing new about engine lube oil analysis. Thousands of the nation's trucks and buses regularly have their engine's lube oil analyzed by laboratories specializing in this type of work. What is new is the availability of lube oil analysis to individual vehicle owners rather than, as before, almost exclusively to companies operating fleets of diesel equipment.

Lube oil analysis can be a valuable indicator of internal engine condition.

Here's how lube oil analysis works. You write one of the several laboratories that offer individual diesel vehicle owners lube analysis service. By return mail you'll receive an oil sampling kit. It will probably contain a two-ounce plastic oil sampling container with a screw-on plastic top. Instructions tell you how to take the sample. Usually, a lab-bound sample of diesel lube oil may be taken in any of three ways, but always right after the engine has been shut off, so that the sampled oil is as close as possible to normal engine operating temperature. That's important to assure that the lab's test will be accurate. Oil samples can be taken during normal oil changes, when lube oil is drained anyway. Between oil changes, a sample can be drawn from the engine through the dipstick tube (where you normally check the oil's level). In drawing an oil sample from the dipstick tube, a small suction bulb fitted with a length of disposable tubing is used. The tubing is merely inserted into the dipstick tube, the suction bulb depressed, and the oil sample drawn. The third method of sampling is by loosening the drain plug on the engine's by-pass oil filter (if your diesel has one). A little oil is caught in the lube sampling container. In all cases, extreme cleanliness is a must, so as not to contaminate the sample with dirt, grease, or other substances not actually found inside the engine. For example, using a rag that contains solvents, metal filings, or other impurities can contaminate the oil sample, leading to false and even alarming lab reports. A bit of technique is required: In taking a sample of lube oil during a routine oil drain, about half of the crankcase's lube oil should be allowed to drain out before the sample is taken. The sample taken, the date, make and model of the engine, its mileage, mileage since last oil change, and sometimes oil type are noted on the container's label, and the container is mailed to the laboratory.

Shortly, you'll receive the lab's report, which, based on a number of tests, including spectrochemical analysis (using a spectrometer, which can detect the presence of virtually all basic elements and contaminants), tells what's in the oil in what quantities and analyzes both the probable source of what was found and whether it indicates trouble. For one example, the finding of more than trace amounts of copper in an oil sample may strongly point to excessive bearing wear in a particular diesel whose bearings contain copper. Some analyses report on as many as eighteen basic elements that may be found in a diesel's lube oil sample, and in the report's "recommendation" may pinpoint their probable source—as, "indicates piston ring wear." Also indicated is the presence of such contaminants as water, solids (the products of oxidation and engine blow-by), and fuel dilution. Noted, too, is the lubricity of the sample—whether, or not, in the lab's opinion, it is still doing its internal engine lubricating job.

NOTE: Never use lube analysis and a lab's report of "good oil" to extend, beyond the manufacturer's recommendation, the mileage period between oil changes. Follow the manufacturers recommendations.

The more frequently an engine is lube-sampled, the more accurate and meaningful the lab's reports. Infrequent samplings, although they can spot sudden, unusual changes in internal engine condition, may fail to show the gradual deterioration of engine parts. Ideally, you should have the laboratory analyze a lube sample every other oil change. For most automobile diesels, that's every 6,000 miles. Analysis costs from $7 to $11 per sample. Drive an average 18,000 miles a year and you'd change your diesel's oil three times. In that time, you'd submit three samples to the lab at an annual lube analysis cost of $21 to $33.

Aftermarket Fuel System Accessories

Due to reasons described previously, most diesel engine problems can be attributed to either fuel contamination or cold weather fuel performance characteristics. Diesel-engined vehicle manufacturers have designed and installed various systems to combat these problems, but ultimately, their best efforts are limited by cost.

Inconvenience is a major concern to diesel owners. If water accumulates (in substantial quantities) in the diesel fuel system, the fuel and water must be siphoned from the fuel tank and purged from the remainder of the fuel system. It goes without saying that this operation is a messy, time-consuming process. Even if the vehicle is equipped with a water/fuel separator having a drain valve, the owner must manually open the valve from either under the hood or beneath the vehicle.

Although the fuel filter installed by the manufacturer offers adequate performance when maintained properly, the addition of another, separate diesel fuel filter is a wise improvement.

If you live in an extremely cold climate, you've probably experienced cold starting problems due to fuel "waxing", plugged filters, "gelled" fuel, etc. If your vehicle is not factory-equipped with the optional fuel line or cylinder block heaters, these

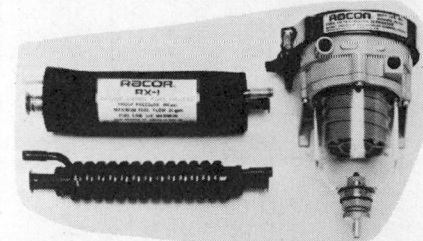

Aftermarket fuel filter/water separator and fuel line heater

heaters can be purchased from the after-market (retail auto parts manufacturers). The installation of either of these items can improve cold-starting dramatically.

WATER/FUEL SEPARATORS

Centrifugal Action

Sometimes referred to as a "cyclonic" water/fuel separator, this device uses baffles which spin the fuel as it comes through the separator inlet. Since water is heavier than diesel fuel, the water will spin away from the fuel, sink to the bottom of the separator, and collect in the sediment bowl.

This type of separator is most efficient in dealing with large water droplets. If the water is in emulsion with the fuel, that is, if the water is equally dispersed through the fuel in very small droplets, some of the water will remain with the fuel to travel through the fuel system.

Coalescing Action

In this type of separator, the fuel must pass through a coalescent filtering media before proceeding through the fuel system. The idea behind the coalescent media is to trap even the smallest droplets of water on the media. As the small droplets combine into larger, heavier droplets, gravity acts on the droplets to pull them downward, off of the media and into the sediment bowl.

FUEL FILTER/SEPARATOR COMBINATION UNITS

Most separators of either the centrifugal or coalescent types are available with disposeable fuel filtering elements which are built into the separator unit. If your car already has a large, disposeable filter, it would probably be more cost-effective to stay with a separator only, and to change the factory-equipped filter at the recommended intervals. Should your vehicle have a fairly small filter, and/or an inconveniently located water drain (or none at all), choose the filter/separator combination. The filter/separator offers both increased fuel filtering ability and efficient water separation.

Convenience Add-Ons

Available with many separators and filter/separators are items such as dash-mounted water-in-fuel indicator lamps, audible water-in-fuel alarms, and dash-controlled water ejection systems. A properly chosen system would warn you of water in the fuel, and allow you to eject the water by simply "flipping" a dash-mounted switch.

Installing a Separator

Clear installation instructions and the necessary installation parts will be provided with the separator kit. Follow those instructions exactly. A general list of suggestions follows:

1. Fuel additives should not be used unless approved by the separator manufacturer.

2. Do not install a separator within 4″ of any exhaust system component.

3. If plastic fittings are supplied with the kit, do not replace them with metal fittings. Also, use extreme caution when tightening the fittings, especially those made of plastic.

4. Use a fuel-proof sealer on all fitting threads, only if the threads are not factory-coated with sealer.

5. Use only fuel-proof hoses for the installation.

6. Do not eliminate the original equipment fuel filter, even if a filter/separator is installed.

7. For new car warranty purposes, a filter/separator should be located BEFORE the original equipment filter. The fuel must pass through the original filter last, before entering the fuel injection pump.

8. If any type of fuel line heater is installed, it is best to position the heater between the fuel tank and the separator inlet.

9. To ease the job of the separator, the separator should be installed between the fuel transfer pump and the tank (unless the separator manufacturer specifies otherwise). Fuel and water which have been churned through the fuel transfer pump will be more difficult to separate.

10. Be sure that any wiring (for warning lamps, water ejection, etc.) is routed and connected properly. If the wiring must pass through a drilled hole, be sure to use a rubber grommet between the drilled component(s) and the wire to prevent damage to the wire.

FUEL LINE HEATERS

Two popular types of fuel line heaters are available for diesel passenger cars. Both types raise the temperature of the fuel to prevent "waxing" and "gelling" of the fuel in the lines during cold weather operation. One type uses engine coolant as a heating source. In order for this type to heat the fuel, the engine must first be started and allowed to run until the coolant temperature increases. Though this type of heater will usually increase fuel mileage, it offers no aid in starting ability.

The other type of heater uses a 12V DC electric heating element. This type is recommended, due to its ability to warm the fuel BEFORE the engine is started. This type of heater will also usually increase the overall fuel mileage.

Installation

Follow the manufacturer's instructions exactly. Also, see suggestions 5, 8, and 9 under "Separator Installation".

CYLINDER BLOCK HEATERS

A cylinder block heater electrically (usually 110V house current) heats the engine coolant, which in turn warms the cylinder block, heads, and engine oil. In this case, the warmth is not used to alter the characteristics of the fuel. Block heaters offer two main advantages when starting a diesel in cold weather:

1. The reduced viscosity (thinning) of the engine oil from the warmth allows the engine to be "turned over" easier (and faster) by the starter. Less strain is imposed on the starting system.

2. Because the diesel relies on the heat of compression to ignite the fuel, the increase in the base combustion chamber temperature results in a higher tempearture during compression. This allows the fuel to ignite easier than if just the glow plugs were used.

Installation

Most cylinder block heaters replace one of the existing freeze (or expansion) plugs of the cylinder block. Follow the manufacturers installation instructions exactly. Also, refer to the manufacturers recommendations for usage.

Carburetor Service 23

Functions

Gasoline is the source of fuel for power in the automobile engine and the carburetor is the mechanism which automatically mixes liquid fuel with air in the correct proportions to provide the desired power output from the engine. The carburetor performs this function by metering, atomizing, and mixing fuel with air flowing through the engine.

A carburetor also regulates the volume of air-to-fuel mixture which enters the engine. It is the carburetor's regulation of the mixture flow which gives the operator control of the engine speed.

METERING

The automotive internal conbustion engine operates efficiently within a relatively small range of air-to-fuel ratios. It is the function of the carburetor to meter the fuel in exact proportions to the air flowing into the engine, so that the optimum ratio of air-to-fuel is maintained under all operating conditions. Regulations governing exhaust gas emissions have made the proper metering of fuel by the carburetor an increasingly important factor. Too rich a mixture will result in poor fuel economy and increased emissions, while too lean a mixture will result in loss of power and generally poor performance.

Carburetors are matched to engines so that metering can be accomplished by using carefully calibrated metering jets which allow fuel to enter the engine at a rate proportional to the engine's ability to draw air.

ATOMIZATION

The liquid fuel must be broken up into small particles so that it will more readily mix with air and vaporize. The more contact the fuel has with the air, the better the vapor-

ization. Atomization can be accomplished in two ways: air may be drawn into a stream of fuel which will cause a turbulence and break the solid stream of fuel into smaller particles; or a nozzle can be positioned at the point of highest air velocity in the carburetor and the fuel will be torn into a fine spray as it enters the air stream.

DISTRIBUTION

The carburetor is the primary device involved in the distribution of fuel to the engine. The more efficiently fuel and air are combined in the carburetor, the smoother the flow of vaporized mixture through the intake manifold to each combustion chamber. Hence, the importance of the carburetor in fuel distribution.

Principles

VACUUM

All carburetors operate on the basic principle of pressure difference. Any pressure less than atmospheric pressure is considered vacuum or a low pressure area. In the engine, as the piston moves down on the intake stroke with the intake valve open, a partial vacuum is created in the intake manifold. The farther the piston travels downward, the greater the vacuum created in the manifold. As vacuum increases in the manifold, a difference in pressure occurs between the carburetor and cylinder. The carburetor is positioned in such a way that the high pressure above it, and the vacuum or low pressure beneath it, causes air to be drawn through it. Fuel and air always move from high to low pressure areas.

VENTURI PRINCIPLE

To obtain greater pressure drop at the tip

of the fuel nozzle so that fuel will flow, the principle of increasing the air velocity to create a low pressure area is used. The device used to increase the velocity of the air flowing through the carburetor is called a venturi. A venturi is a specially designed restriction placed on the air flow. In order for the air to pass through the restriction, it must accelerate, causing a pressure drop or vacuum as it passes.

Circuits

FLOAT CIRCUIT

The float circuit includes the float, float bowl, and a needle valve and seat. This circuit controls the amount of gas allowed to flow into the carburetor.

As the fuel level rises, it causes the float to rise which pushes the needle valve into its seat. As soon as the valve and seat make contact, the flow of gas is cut off from the fuel inlet. When the level of fuel drops, the float sinks and releases the needle valve from its seat which allows the gas to flow in. In actual operation, the fuel is maintained at practically a constant level. The float tends to hold the needle valve partly closed so that the incoming fuel just balances the fuel being withdrawn.

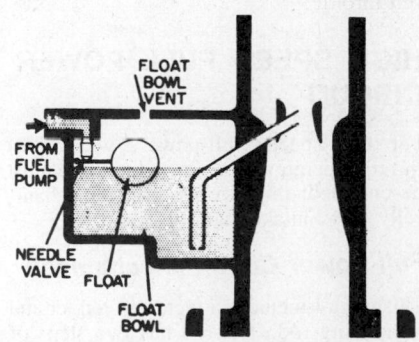

Typical float circuit

IDLE AND LOW SPEED CIRCUIT

When the throttle is closed or only slightly opened, the air speed is low and practically no vacuum develops in the venturi. This means that the fuel nozzle will not feed. Thus, the carburetor must have another circuit to supply fuel during operation with a closed or slightly opened throttle.

This circuit is called the idle and low speed circuit. It consists of passages in which air and gas can flow beneath the throttle plate. With the throttle plate closed, there is high vacuum from the intake manifold. Atmospheric pressure pushes the air/fuel mixture through the passages of the idle and low speed circuit and past the tapered point of the idle adjustment screw, which regulates engine idle mixture volume.

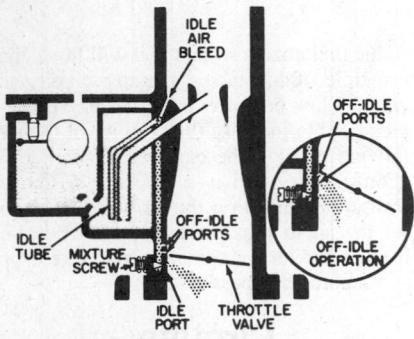

Typical idle and low speed circuit

HIGH SPEED PARTIAL LOAD CIRCUIT

When the throttle plate is opened sufficiently, there is little difference in vacuum between the upper and lower part of the air horn. Thus, little air/fuel mixture will discharge from the low speed and idle circuit. However, under this condition enough air is moving through the air horn to produce vacuum in the venturi to cause the main nozzle or high speed nozzle to discharge fuel. The circuit from the float bowl to the main nozzle is called the high speed partial load circuit. A nearly constant air/fuel ratio is maintained by this circuit from part to full-throttle.

HIGH SPEED FULL POWER CIRCUIT

For high-speed, full-power, wide open throttle operation, the air/fuel mixture must be enriched; this is done either mechanically or by intake manifold vacuum.

Full Power Circuit (Mechanical)

This circuit includes a metering rod jet and a metering rod. The rod has two steps of different diameters and is attached to the throttle linkage.

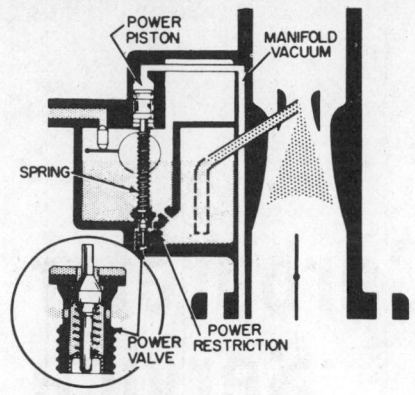

Typical power circuit

When the throttle is wide open, the metering rod is lifted, bringing the smaller diameter of the rod into the jet. When the throttle is partly closed, the larger diameter of the metering rod is in the jet. This restricts fuel flow to the main nozzle but adequate amounts of fuel do flow for part-throttle operation.

Full Power Circuit (Vacuum)

This circuit is operated by intake manifold vacuum. It includes a vacuum diaphragm or piston linked to a valve.

When the throttle is opened so that intake manifold vacuum is reduced, the spring raises the diaphragm or piston. This allows more fuel to flow in, either by lifting a metering rod or by opening a power valve.

ACCELERATOR PUMP CIRCUIT

For acceleration, the carburetor must deliver additional fuel. A sudden inrush of air is caused by rapid acceleration or applying full throttle.

When the throttle is opened, the pump lever pushes the plunger down and this forces fuel to flow through the accelerator pump circuit and out the pump jet. This fuel enters the air passage through the carburetor to supply additional fuel demands.

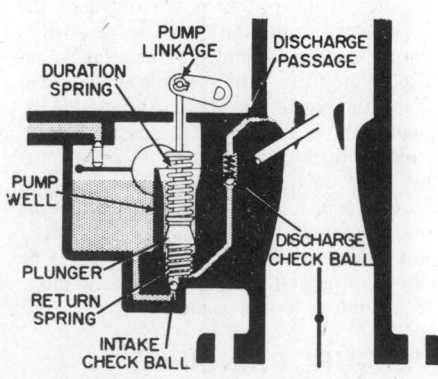

Typical accelerator pump circuit

CHOKE

When starting an engine, it is necessary to increase the amount of fuel delivered to the intake manifold. This increase is controlled by the choke.

The choke consists of a valve in the top of the air horn controlled mechanically by an automatic device. When the choke valve is closed, only a small amount of air can get past it. When the engine is cranked, a fairly high vacuum develops in the air horn. This vacuum causes the main nozzle to discharge a heavy stream of fuel. The quantity delivered is sufficient to produce the correct air/fuel mixture needed for starting the engine. The choke is released either manually or by heat from the engine.

OVERHAUL

Generally, when a carburetor requires major service, a rebuilt one is purchased on an exchange basis, or a kit may be bought for overhauling the carburetor.

The kit contains the necessary parts and some form of instructions for carburetor rebuilding. The instructions may vary between a simple exploded view and detailed step-by-step rebuilding instructions. Unless you are familiar with carburetor overhaul, the latter should be used.

There are some general overhaul procedures which should always be observed:

Efficient carburetion depends greatly on careful cleaning and inspection during overhaul since dirt, gum, water, or varnish in or on the carburetor parts are often responsible for poor performance.

Overhaul your carburetor in a clean, dust-free area. Carefully disassemble the carburetor, referring often to the exploded views. Keep all similar and lookalike parts segregated during disassembly and cleaning to avoid accidental interchange during assembly. Make a note of all jet sizes.

When the carburetor is disassembled, wash all parts except diaphragms, electric choke units, pump plunger, and any other plastic, leather, fiber, or rubber parts in clean carburetor solvent. Do not leave parts in the solvent any longer than is necessary to sufficiently loosen the deposits. Excessive cleaning may remove the special finish from the float bowl and choke valve bodies, leaving these parts unfit for service. Rinse all parts in clean solvent and blow them dry with compressed air or allow them to air dry. Wipe clean all cork, plastic, leather, and fiber parts with a clean, lint-free cloth.

Blow out all passages and jets with compressed air and be sure that there are no restrictions or blockages. Never use wire or similar tools to clean jets, fuel passages, or air bleeds. Clean all jets and valves separately to avoid accidental interchange.

Chcck all parts for wear or damage. If wear or damage is found, replace the defective parts. Especially check the following:

1. Check the float needle and seat for wear. If wear is found, replace the complete assembly.

2. Check the float hinge pin for wear and the float(s) for dents or distortion. Replace the float if fuel has leaked into it.

3. Check the throttle and choke shaft bores for wear or an out-of-round condition. Damage or wear to the throttle arm, shaft, or shaft bore will often require replacement of the throttle body. These parts require a close tolerance of fit; wear may allow air leakage, which could affect starting and idling.

NOTE: Throttle shafts and bushings are not included in overhaul kits. They can be purchased separately.

4. Inspect the idle mixture adjusting needles for burrs or grooves. Any such condition requires replacement of the needle, since you will not be able to obtain a satisfactory idle.

5. Test the accelerator pump check valves. They should pass air one way but not the other. Test for proper seating by blowing and sucking on the valve. Replace the valve if necessary. If the valve is satisfactory, wash the valve again to remove breath moisture.

6. Check the bowl cover for warped surfaces with a straightedge.

7. Closely inspect the valves and seats for wear and damage, replacing as necessary.

8. After the carburetor is assembled, check the choke valve for freedom of operation.

Carburetor overhaul kits are recommended for each overhaul. These kits contain all gaskets and new parts to replace those that deteriorate most rapidly. Failure to replace all parts supplied with the kit (especially gaskets) can result in poor performance later.

Some carburetor manufacturers supply overhaul kits of three basic types: minor repair; major repair; and gasket kits. Basically, they contain the following:

Minor Repair Kits:
    All gaskets
    Float needle valve
    Volume control screw
    All diaphragms
    Spring for the pump diaphragm
Major Repair Kits:
    All jets and gaskets
    All diaphragms
    Float needle valve
    Volume control screw
    Pump ball valve
    Main jet carrier
    Float
    Complete intermediate rod
    Intermediate pump lever
    Complete injector tube
    Some cover hold-down screws and washers
Gasket Kits:
    All gaskets

After cleaning and checking all components, reassemble the carburetor, using new parts and referring to the exploded view. When reassembling, make sure that all screws and jets are tight in their seats, but do not overtighten, as the tips will be distorted. Tighten all screws gradually, in rotation. Do not tighten needle valves into their seats; uneven jetting will result. Always use new gaskets. Be sure to adjust the float level when reassembling.

Stromberg Carburetors Only

The preceding information applies to Stromberg carburetors also, but the following, additional suggestions should be followed.

1. Soak the small cork gaskets (jet gland washers) in penetrating oil or hot water for at least a half hour prior to assembly, or they will invariably split.

2. When the jet is fully assembled, the jet tube should be a close fit without any lateral play, but it should be free to move smoothly. A few drops of oil, or polishing of the tube may be necessary to achieve this.

3. If the jet sealing ring washer is made of cork, soak it in hot water for a minute or two prior to installation.

4. Adjust the float height.

5. Center the jet so that the piston will fall freely (when raised) and seat with a distinct click. If the jet is not centered properly, it will hang up in the tube.

TROUBLESHOOTING

NOTE: Carburetor problems cannot be isolated effectively unless all other engine systems are functioning correctly and the engine is properly tuned.

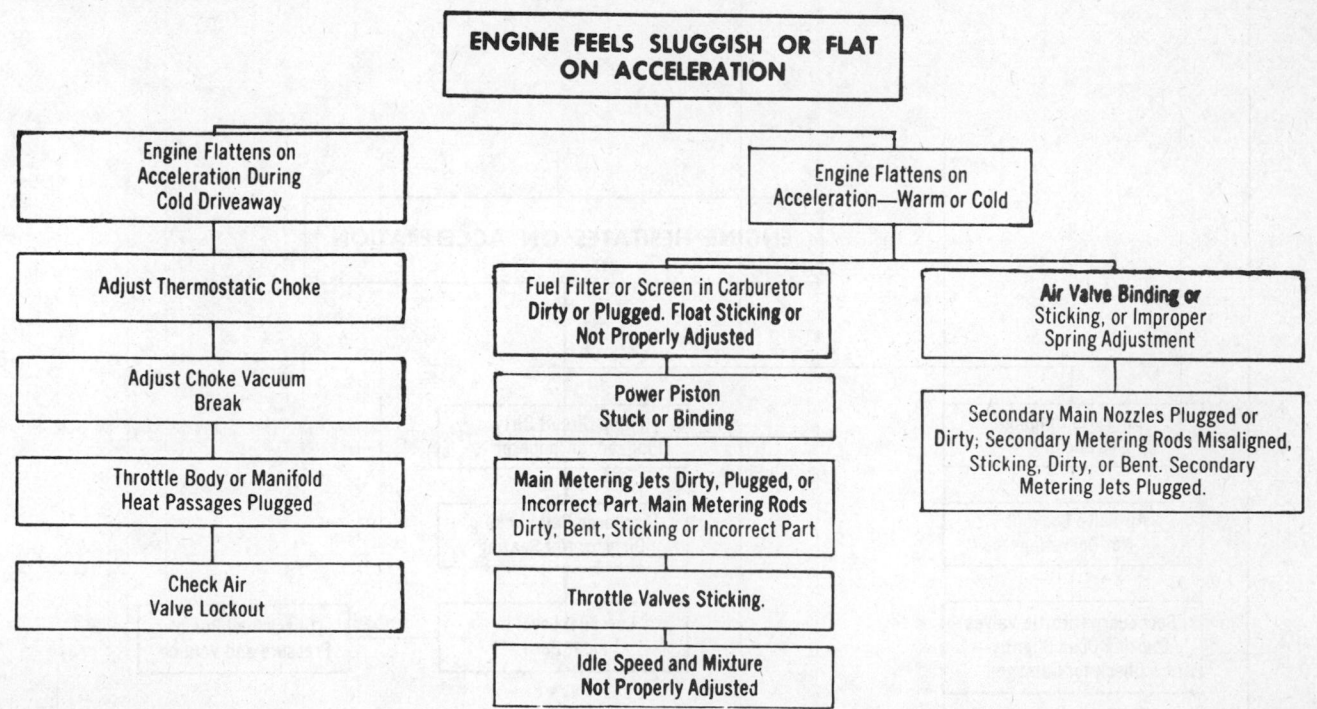

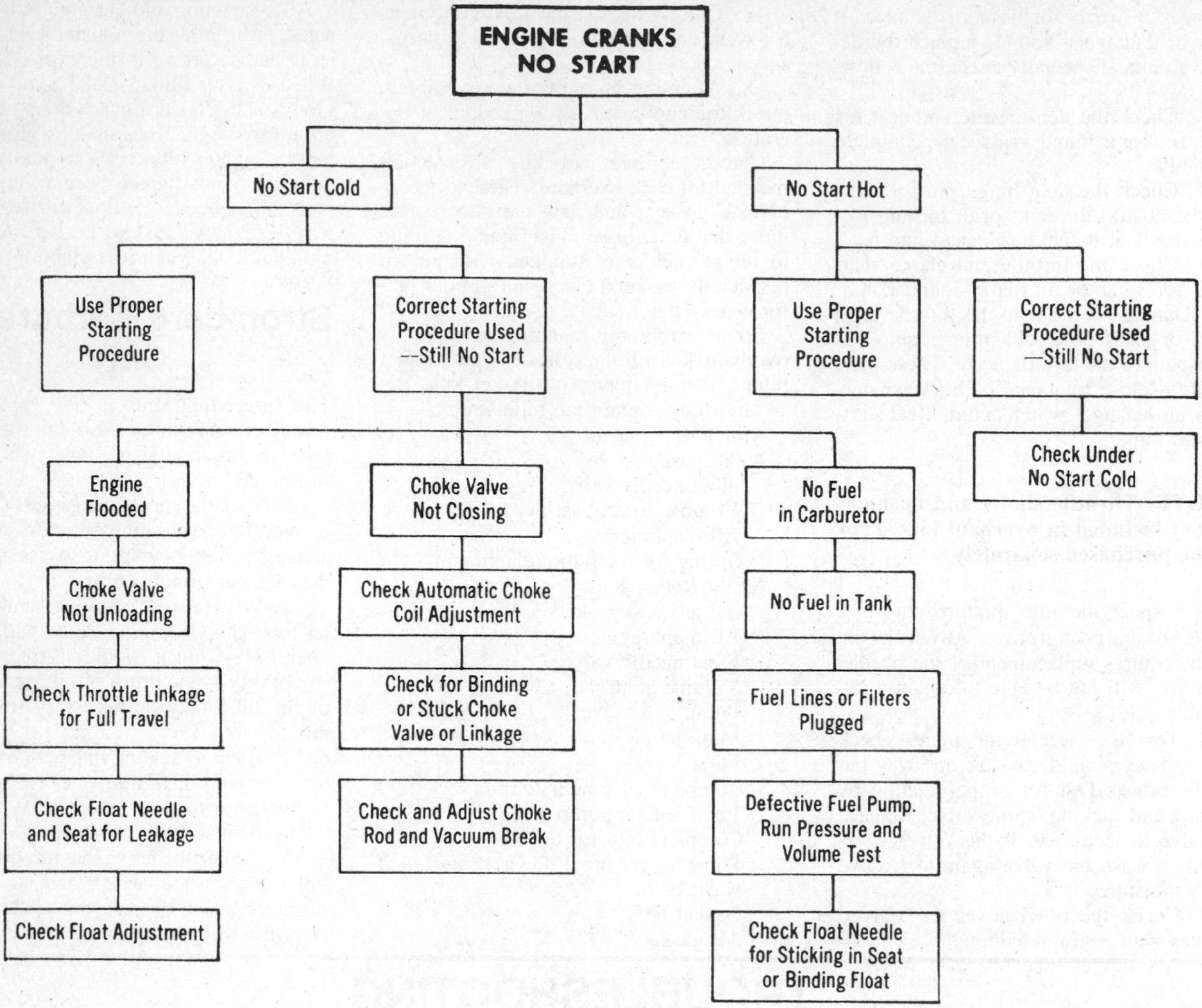

ENGINE CRANKS NO START

- No Start Cold
  - Use Proper Starting Procedure
  - Correct Starting Procedure Used —Still No Start
    - Engine Flooded
      - Choke Valve Not Unloading
      - Check Throttle Linkage for Full Travel
      - Check Float Needle and Seat for Leakage
      - Check Float Adjustment
    - Choke Valve Not Closing
      - Check Automatic Choke Coil Adjustment
      - Check for Binding or Stuck Choke Valve or Linkage
      - Check and Adjust Choke Rod and Vacuum Break
    - No Fuel in Carburetor
      - No Fuel in Tank
      - Fuel Lines or Filters Plugged
      - Defective Fuel Pump. Run Pressure and Volume Test
      - Check Float Needle for Sticking in Seat or Binding Float
- No Start Hot
  - Use Proper Starting Procedure
  - Correct Starting Procedure Used —Still No Start
    - Check Under No Start Cold

ENGINE HESITATES ON ACCELERATION

- Air Valve Binding or Sticking
  - Air Valve Lockout Not Operating
  - Secondary Throttle Valves Sticking Open Slightly— Check for Damage
- Pump Circuit Dirty, Plugged, or Inoperative
  - Discharge Ball Sticking, Dirty, or Not Seating
  - Low Fuel Level in Float Bowl — Check Fuel Pump Pressure and Volume

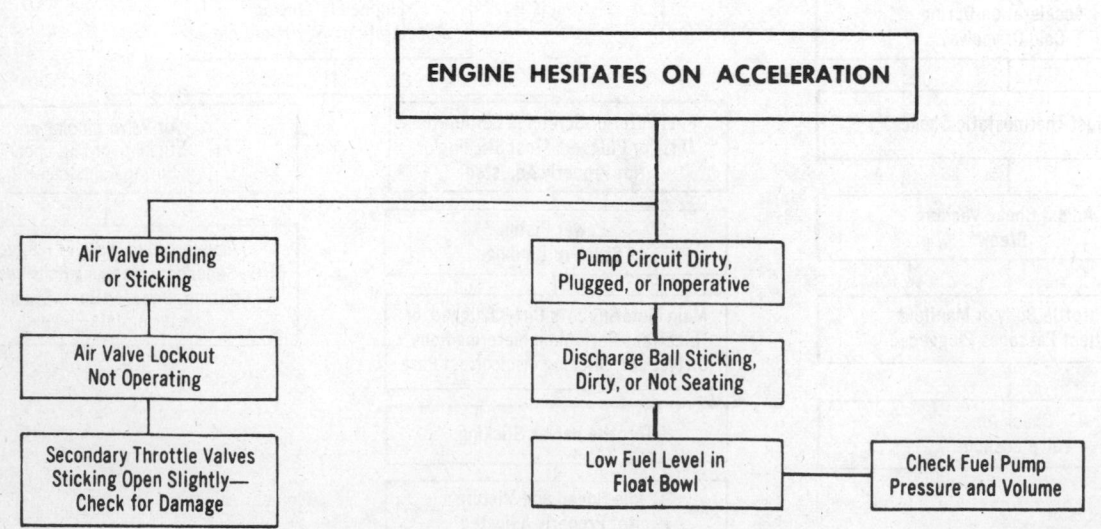

Emission Controls 24

EMISSION CONTROLS

History

The first state to recognize the automobile pollution problem was California in 1959 and enacted the first standards for automobile emissions through the newly formed California Air Resources Board. The emission standards became effective in 1961.

In 1968, the United States Congress enacted the Clean Air Act, recognizing the work of the California Air Resources Board, by adopting California's test procedures and emissions standards as a beginning point. However, the federal regulations preempted those of any state enacting emission standards and legislation, meaning that federal regulations would override any state or state laws that may be in conflict with the federal act.

Waivers of federal preemption could be petitioned by a state or vehicle manufacturer for the purpose of advocating early establishment of emission standards, to delay the start of emission programs where the need is deemed necessary for the good of the people of the state or to further explore the development of emission control devices to be placed on the vehicles to control harmful emissions.

Federal approval of state applications for the waivers of federal preemption concerning stricter emission standards over the federal standards, forced the manufacturers to construct vehicles with emission components necessary to control emission in three areas, California, 49 State and High Altitude (over 4000 ft. in elevation).

Since the enactment of the first clean air legislation by California and the Federal Government, to date, thirty-one states have enacted automobile emission standards, either state wide or confined to heavily populated city areas within the state. The remaining states either rely on the federally mandated emission standards for clean air or have no regulations to date.

Emission Types

Most pollution produced by an automobile comes from gasoline or gasoline by-products. The three main sources of pollutants are the fuel tank and carburetor, crankcase and exhaust. The exhaust is the major contributor of hydrocarbon pollutant, about 60%. The other sources account for the remaining 40% of the pollutants.

CRANKCASE EMISSIONS

The crankcase emissions are comprised of water, acids, unburned fuel, oil fumes and particulates. The emissions are classified as hydrocarbons (HC) and are formed by the small amount of unburned, compressed air/fuel mixture entering the crankcase from the combustion area during the compression and power strokes, between the cylinder walls and piston rings. The heat of the compression and combustion help to form the remaining crankcase emissions.

Since the conception of the internal combustion engine, these crankcase emissions are expelled into the atmosphere through a road draft tube, mounted on the lower side of the engine block. Fresh air was directed into the crankcase through an open oil filler cap or breather, with the air passing through the crankcase cavity and expelling part of the blow-by gases out the road draft tube by the movement of air as the vehicle was in motion and by the movement of engine fan air when the vehicle was stationary with the engine in the idle mode.

To control the crankcase emission, the road draft tube was deleted and in its place, a hose and/or tubing was routed from the crankcase to the intake manifold so that the blow-by emission could be burned with the air/fuel mixture. However, it was found that intake manifold vacuum would

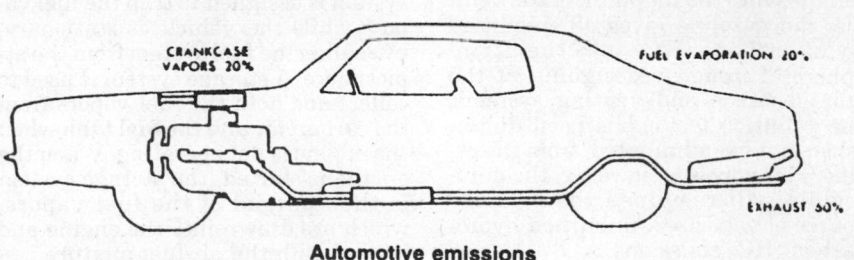

CRANKCASE VAPORS 20% FUEL EVAPORATION 20% EXHAUST 50%

Automotive emissions

vary in strength at the wrong time and not allow the proper emission flow. A regulating type valve was needed to control the flow of air through the crankcase to relieve the volume of blow-by gases generated by the engine operation.

It was determined through testing, that the removal of the blow-by gases from the crankcase, as quickly as possible, was most important to the longevity of the engine. Should large accumulations of blow-by gases remain and condense, dilution of the engine oil would occur to form water, soots, resins, acids and lead salts, resulting in the formation of sludge and varnishes. This condensation of the blow-by gases occur more frequently on vehicles used in numerous starting and stopping conditions, excessive idling and when the engine is not allowed to attain normal operating temperature through short runs.

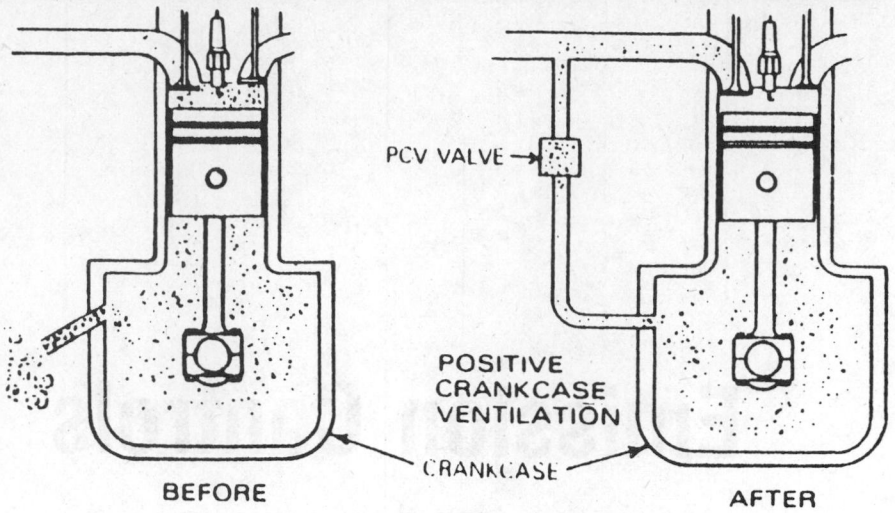

Positive crankcase ventilation (PCV) systems

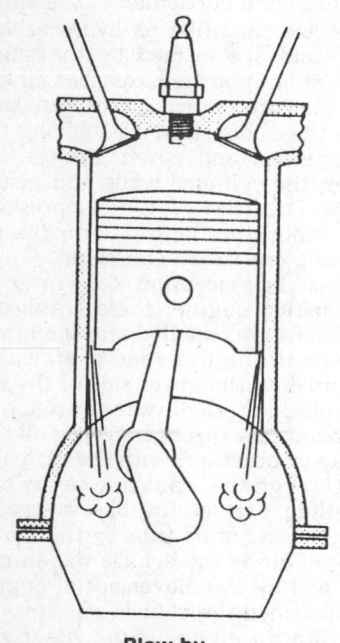

Blow-by

EVAPORATIVE EMISSIONS

Gasoline fuel is a major source of pollution, before and after it is burned in the automobile engine. From the time the fuel is refined, stored, pumped and transported, again stored until it is pumped into the fuel tank of the vehicle, the gasoline gives off unburned hydrocarbons (HC) into the atmosphere. Through redesigning of the storage areas and venting systems, the pollution factor has been diminished, but not eliminated, from the refinery standpoint. However, the automobile still remained the primary source of vaporized, unburned hydrocarbon (HC) emissions.

Fuel pumped from an underground storage tank is cool, but when exposed to a warmer ambient temperature, will expand. Before controls were mandated, an owner would fill the fuel tank with fuel from an underground storage tank and park the vehicle for some time in warm area, such as a parking lot. As the fuel would warm, it would expand and should no provisions or area be provided for the expansion, the fuel would spill out the filler neck and onto the ground, causing hydrocarbon (HC) pollution and creating a severe fire hazard. To correct this condition, the vehicle manufacturers added overflow plumbing and/or gasoline tanks with built in expansion areas or domes.

However, this did not control the fuel vapor emission from the fuel tank and the carburetor bowl. It was determined that most of the fuel evaporation occurred when the vehicle was stationary and the engine not operating. Most vehicle will carry 5 to 25 gallons of gasoline and should a large concentration of vehicles be parked in one area, such as a large parking lot, excessive fuel vapor emissions would take place, increasing as the temperature would.

To prevent the vapor emission from escaping into the atmosphere, the fuel system is designed to trap the fuel vapors while the vehicle is stationary, by sealing the fuel system from the atmosphere. A storage system is used to collect and hold the fuel vapors from the carburetor and the fuel tank when the engine is not operating. When the engine is started, the storage system is then purged of the fuel vapors, which are drawn into the engine and burned with the air/fuel mixture.

EXHAUST EMISSIONS

The exhaust gases emitted into the atmosphere are a combination of burned and unburned fuel. To understand the exhaust emission and its composition, we must recall basic chemistry.

When we introduce the air/fuel mixture into the engine, we are mixing air, composed of nitrogen (78%), oxygen (21%) and other gases (1%) with the fuel, which is 100% hydrocarbons (HC), in a semi-controlled ratio. As the combustion process is accomplished, power is produced to move the vehicle while the heat of combustion is transferred to the cooling system. The exhaust gases are then composed of nitrogen, a diatomic gas (N_2) the same as was introduced in the engine, carbon dioxide (CO_2), the same gas that is used in beverage carbonation and water vapor (H_2O). The nitrogen (N_2), for the most part passes through the engine unchanged, while the oxygen (O_2) reacts (burns) with the hydrocarbons (HC) and produces the carbon dioxide (CO_2) and the water vapors (H_2O). If this chemical process would be the only process to take place, the exhaust emissions would be harmless. However, during the combustion process, other pollutants are formed and are considered dangerous. These pollutants are carbon monoxide (CO), hydrocarbons (HC), oxides of nitrogen (NOx), oxides of sulfer (SOx) and engine particulates.

Hydrocarbons

Hydrocarbons (HC) are essentially unburned fuel that has not been successfully burned during the combustion process or has escaped into the atmosphere through fuel evaporation. The prime sources of incomplete combustion are rich air/fuel mixtures, low engine temperatures and improper spark timing, while the prime sources of the hydrocarbon emission through fuel evaporation comes from the vehicle's fuel tank and carburetor bowl.

To accomplish the reduction of combustion hydrocarbon emission, engine modification were made to minimize dead space and surface area in the combustion chamber, leaning to the air/fuel mixture through improved carburetion, fuel injection and by the addition of external controls to aid in further combustion of the hydrocarbons outside the engine. Two such methods were the addition of an air injection system, to inject fresh air into the exhaust manifold(s) and the installation of a catalytic converter, a unit that is able to burn traces of hydrocarbons without affecting the internal combustion process or fuel economy.

To control hydrocarbon emissions through fuel evaporation, modifications were made to the fuel tank and carburetor bowl to allow storage of the fuel vapors during periods of engine shut-down, and at specific times during engine operation, to purge and burn these same vapors by blending them with the air/fuel mixture.

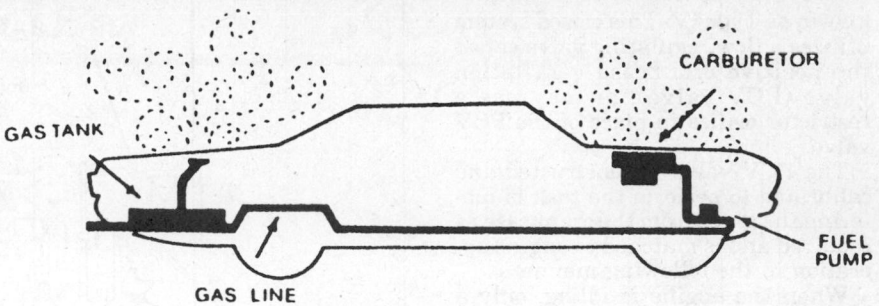

Evaporative emissions

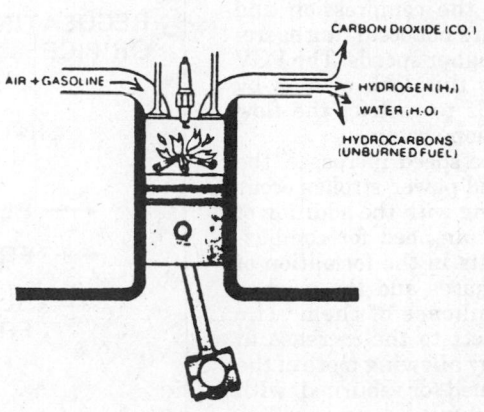

Combustion products

Carbon Monoxide

Carbon monoxide (CO) is formed when not enough oxygen is present during the combustion process to convert carbon to carbon dioxide (CO_2). An increase in the carbon monoxide (CO) emission is normally accompanied by an increase in the hydrocarbon (HC) emission because of the lack of oxygen (O) to completely burn all of the fuel mixture.

Carbon monoxide (CO) also increases the rate at which the photochemical smog is formed by speeding up the conversion of nitric oxide (NO) to nitrogen (NO_2). To accomplish this, carbon monoxide (CO) combines with oxygen (O_2) and nitrogen dioxide (NO_2) to produce carbon dioxide (CO_2) and nitrogen dioxide (NO_2).

The dangers of carbon monoxide, which is an odorless, colorless toxic gas, are many. When carbon monoxide is inhaled into the lungs and passed into the blood stream, oxygen is replaced by the carbon monoxide (CO) in the red blood cells, causing a reduction in the amount of oxygen being supplied to the many parts of the body. This lack of oxygen causes headaches, lack of coordination, reduced mental alertness and should the carbon monoxide concentration be high enough, death could result.

Oxides of Nitrogen

Normally, nitrogen is a diatomic, inert gas, but when heated to approximately 2500°F through the combustion process, this gas becomes active and causes an increase in the nitric oxide (NO) emission.

Oxides of nitrogen (NOx) are composed of approximately 97–98% nitric oxide (NO). Nitric oxide is colorless gas, but when it is passed into the atmosphere, it combines with oxygen (O) and forms nitrogen dioxide (NO_2). The nitrogen dioxide then combines with chemically active hydrocarbons (HC) and when in the presence of sunlight, causes the formation of photochemical smog.

Emission Control Systems

CRANKCASE EMISSION CONTROL SYSTEM

The crankcase emissions were responsible for approximately 20% of all harmful automotive pollutants before any emission controls were installed on the vehicles. The crankcase emissions are the result of compressed gases being forced past the piston rings on both the compression and power strokes, resulting in an accumulation of gases (known as blow-by gases), in the crankcase. These blow-by gases become mixed with vapors from the agitated lubricating oil and must be relieved from the crankcase area to prevent damaging pressures from building up.

Prior to the early 60's, a road draft tube was used to ventilate the crankcase, which allowed the pollutants to be emitted into the atmosphere. With the installation of a regulating valve and necessary plumbing, the road draft tube was eliminated and the gases routed to the air intake area, to be drawn into the engine vacuum was used as the controlling factor to draw the crankcase gases into the engine, but was found that the vacuum source varied at the wrong times.

Different systems were experimented with, some with flow control valves while others merely direct the gases to the air cleaner assembly. Other systems had open breather caps with the fresh air supply being tapped from the air cleaner snorkel.

By 1968, all vehicle manufactured in the United States were equipped with a closed crankcase ventilation system, which did not allow any of the blow-by gases and oil vapors to escape into the atmosphere. This system is known as Type IV. This closed system utilizes a flow regulating valve called the positive crankcase ventilation valve (PCV valve), or may use a restrictor orifice in place of the PCV valve.

The PCV valve is constructed and calibrated to perform the task of metering the gases from the crankcase as required and is matched to engine operation in the following manner.

When the engine is idling, only a small amount of air and fuel is needed for combustion, resulting in a small amount of blow-by gases being produced because the compression and power strokes are not occurring as frequently as at higher speeds. The PCV valve reacts to this lack of blow-by gases and tends to restrict the flow into the induction system.

As the engine speed increases, the compression and power strokes occur more often, along with the addition of more fuel and air need for combustion. This results in the formation of more blow-by gases and the need to purge the crankcase of them. The PCV valve reacts to the increase in blow-by gases by allowing more of the gases to be burned (or reburned) with the air/fuel mixture.

It should be noted that the PCV valve is constructed and calibrated in such a manner as to prevent engine backfires from entering the crankcase to avoid detonation of the accumulated blow-by gases.

In the closed crankcase ventilation system, the fresh air intake, located in the air cleaner or snorkel, has a dual role. Not only is it a source of fresh air for the crankcase ventilation system, but doubles as an overload release of blow-by gases into the carburetor air stream should the PCV valve fail to control the build up of blow-by gases, rather than allowing the excess gases to escape into the atmosphere. With the use of this closed system, the hydrocarbon (HC) emissions produced in the crankcase, are prevented from entering the atmosphere.

FUEL EVAPORATIVE EMISSION CONTROL SYSTEM

Fuel evaporation vapors were found to account for approximately 20% of the total automotive emission problem and was more severe with ambient temperature increases. The sources of the hydrocarbon vapor emissions were the fuel tank and carburetor bowl, both of which were vented to the atmosphere. Another problem was the overfilling of the fuel tank, which under changes of temper-

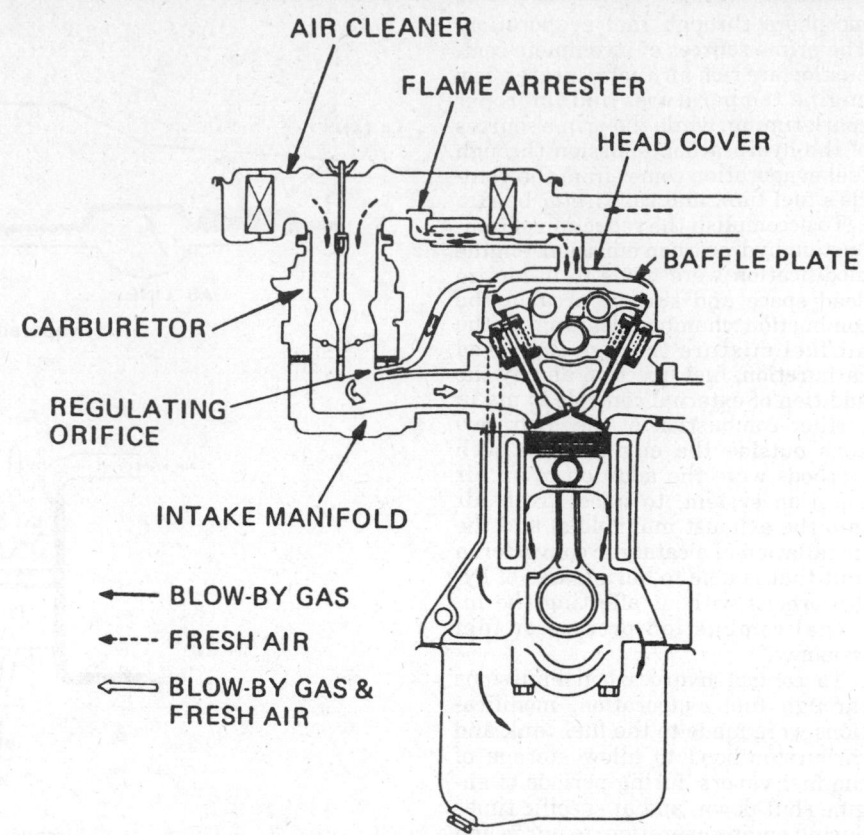

AIR CLEANER
FLAME ARRESTER
HEAD COVER
BAFFLE PLATE
CARBURETOR
REGULATING ORIFICE
INTAKE MANIFOLD

← BLOW-BY GAS

←---- FRESH AIR

⇐ BLOW-BY GAS & FRESH AIR

Positive crankcase ventilation (PCV) system air flow

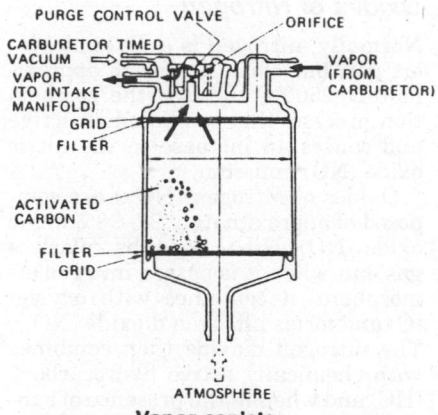

PURGE CONTROL VALVE
ORIFICE
CARBURETOR TIMED VACUUM
VAPOR (TO INTAKE MANIFOLD)
VAPOR (FROM CARBURETOR)
GRID
FILTER
ACTIVATED CARBON
FILTER GRID
ATMOSPHERE

Vapor canister

ature or by having the vehicle parked on an incline, would spill gasoline from the tank. A means of trapping the vapor emission and preventing gasoline leakage was a major undertaking.

One of the early systems used, was the engine crankcase to store the fuel vapors when the engine was not running. When the engine was started, the vapors were purged from the crankcase by the positive crankcase ventilation system. Certain drawbacks were noted in this system, some of which were the dilution of engine lubricating oils with gasoline, an overrich air/fuel mixture during the

purge cycle and danger of gasoline vapor detonation within the crankcase during engine start up.

To prevent fuel loss from the tank due to expansion, an expansion dome has been manufactured into the top to the fuel tanks and the fillpipes have been redesigned to prevent filling the fuel tank above a desired level. Certain vehicles use added plumbing to increase the area volume need, should the fuel expand. This added plumbing is normally part of the vapor control system with necessary valves to control both vapors and liquids included.

After much experimenting and testing, a general system was designed that could control both vapor and liquid emissions by sealing the fuel system from the atmosphere. Although each manufacture of vehicles has designed their own vapor control system, similar components are used, resulting in systems that are basically the same in the manner or vapor collection and storage. However, the manner in which the vapors are purged may vary greatly.

EXHAUST EMISSION CONTROL SYSTEM

The exhaust emission control system encompasses the automotive engine

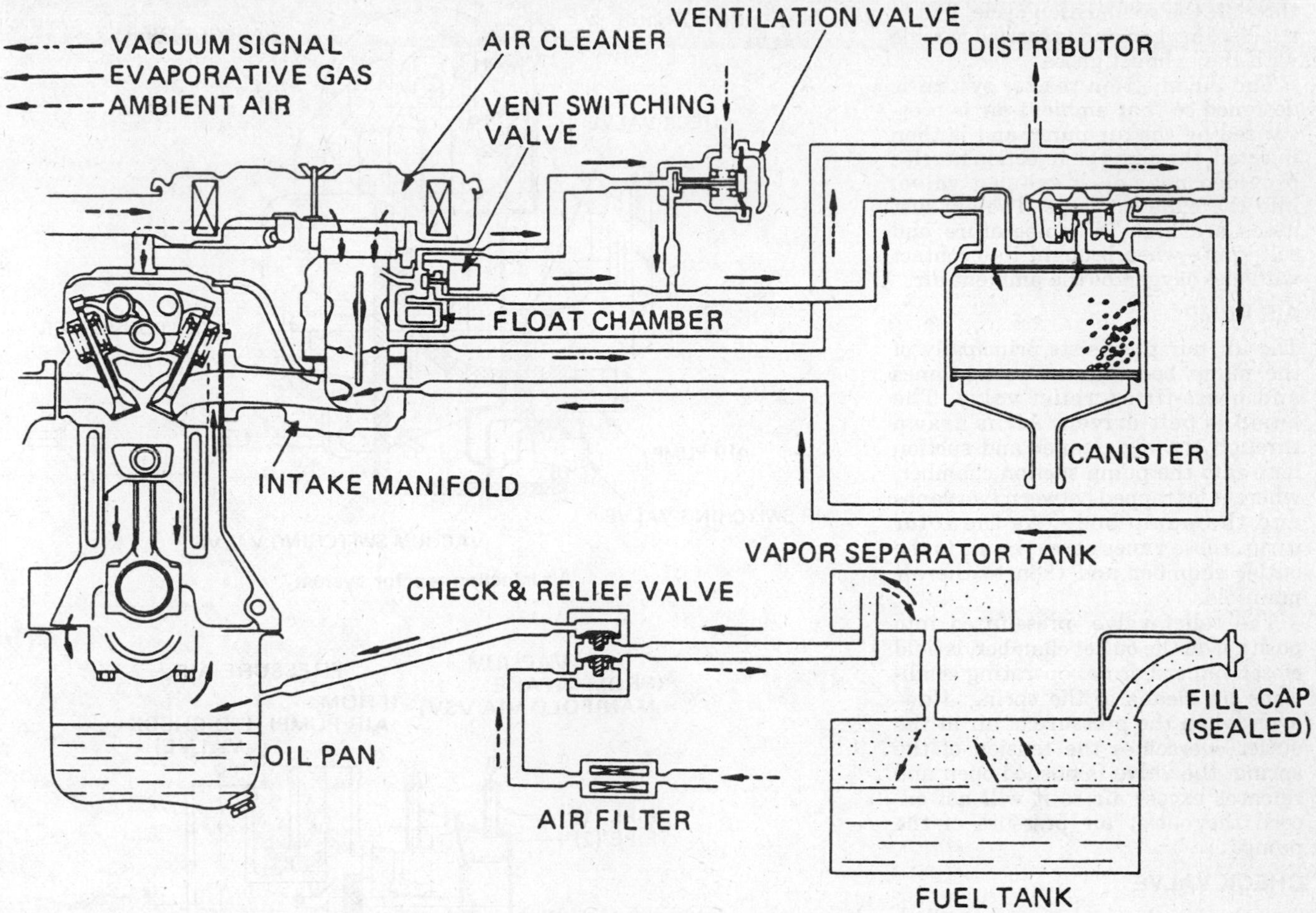

→ ‑·‑ VACUUM SIGNAL
→ ‑‑ EVAPORATIVE GAS
→ ‑‑‑ AMBIENT AIR

VENTILATION VALVE

AIR CLEANER

TO DISTRIBUTOR

VENT SWITCHING VALVE

FLOAT CHAMBER

CANISTER

INTAKE MANIFOLD

VAPOR SEPARATOR TANK

CHECK & RELIEF VALVE

FILL CAP (SEALED)

OIL PAN

AIR FILTER

FUEL TANK

Fuel evaporative emission control—early system

from the entrance of air into the engine's induction system until the exhaust by-product of the combustion process emerges from the tail pipe.

The engine exhaust was found to be responsible for approximately 60% of all automobile emissions before any pollution controls were installed on the engines. Through the trail and error period of the late 60's and early 70's, many different systems were used, some separately and others in conjunction with other systems. While a number of the controls were dropped, others were refined and improved, resulting in greater emission control and driveability.

Air Injection Reactor System (AIR)

In gasoline engines, it is difficult to burn the air/fuel mixture completely through combustion that takes place within the combustion chambers. Under certain operating conditions, more unburned gas is produced

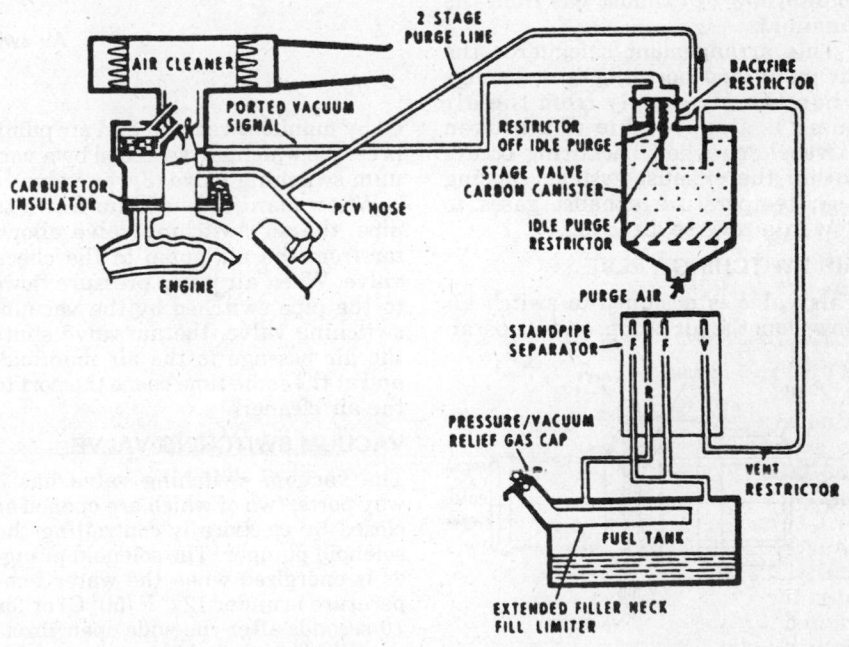

AIR CLEANER

2 STAGE PURGE LINE

PORTED VACUUM SIGNAL

BACKFIRE RESTRICTOR

RESTRICTOR OFF IDLE PURGE

STAGE VALVE CARBON CANISTER

CARBURETOR INSULATOR

IDLE PURGE RESTRICTOR

PCV HOSE

ENGINE

PURGE AIR

STANDPIPE SEPARATOR

PRESSURE/VACUUM RELIEF GAS CAP

VENT RESTRICTOR

FUEL TANK

EXTENDED FILLER NECK FILL LIMITER

Typical fuel evaporative emission control system

through the combustion cycle, due to a lack of oxygen and is carried outside with the exhaust gases.

The air injection reactor system is designed so that ambient air is pressurized by the air pump and is then injected, through the injection nozzles provided near each exhaust valve, into the exhaust gases. The exhaust gases are high in temperature and self-ignite when brought into contact with the oxygen of the ambient air.

AIR PUMP

The air pump consists principally of the pump body, cover, rotor, vanes and press-fitted relief valve. The pump is belt-driven. Air is drawn through the air cleaner and suction hose into the pump suction chamber, where it is trapped between two vanes and the pump body. As the rotor turns, these vanes carry the air to the outlet chamber and then to the air manifold.

The relief valve, press-fitted into position on the outlet chamber, is held closed under normal operating conditions by means of the spring. However, when the pressure of air at the outlet overcomes the tension of the spring, the valve is pushed open and releases excess air so it will not exceed the outlet air pressure of the pump.

CHECK VALVE

The check valve is designed to allow air to pass through in only one direction. The valve is pushed open when the pressure of air supplied from the air pump overcomes the valve spring tension, but closes with the counterflow of exhaust gas from the manifold.

This arrangement safeguards the air pump and hoses against damage when the air supply from the air pump is stopped, due to a broken drivebelt or when backfiring occurs within the exhaust system, causing high temperature exhaust gases to flow in a reverse direction.

AIR SWITCHING VALVE

This valve is designed to switch air flow from the air pump, and is operat-

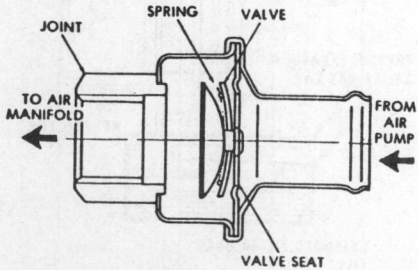

Check valve

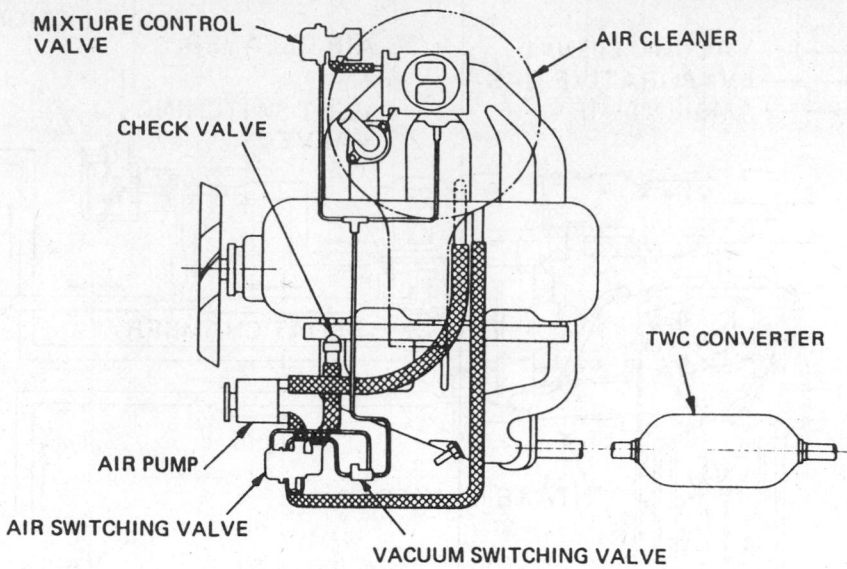

Air injection reactor system

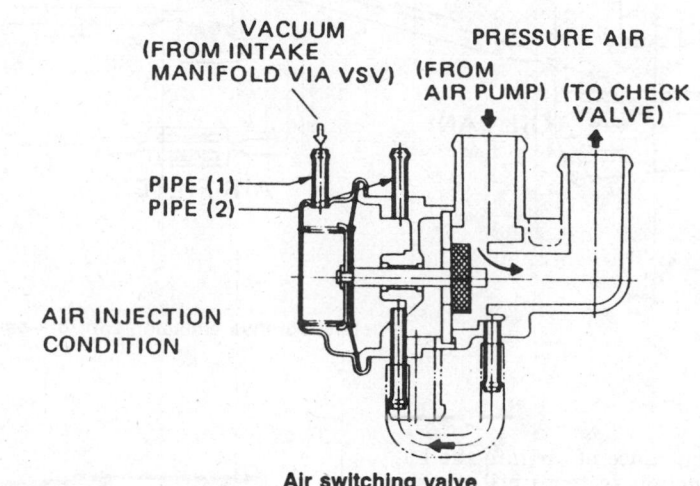

Air switching valve

ed by manifold vacuum and air pump pressure which are switched by a vacuum switching valve (3 way valve).

When manifold vacuum flows to pipe, the air switching valve allows air from the air pump to the check valve. When air pump pressure flows to the pipe switched by the vacuum switching valve, the air valve shuts the air passage to the air manifold, and at the same time opens the port to the air cleaner.

VACUUM SWITCHING VALVE

The vacuum switching valve has 3 way ports, two of which are opened or closed by electrically controlling the solenoid plunger. The solenoid plunger is energized when the water temperature is under 122° F (50° C) or for 10 seconds after the wide open throttle (WOT) switch is turned on with the condition that the water tempera-

ture is over 122° F (50° C). (However, the solenoid plunger is de-energized immediately when WOT switch is turned off within this 10 seconds). When energized, the vacuum switching valve connects the diaphragm chamber of the air switching valve to the intake manifold, permitting the manifold vacuum to be applied to the diaphragm chamber. When the solenoid plunger is de-energized, it plugs the ports, so the two inner diaphragm chambers of the air switching valve are connected.

AIR MANIFOLD AND AIR INJECTION NOZZLES

Pressured air from the air pump is fed through the check valve, into the air manifold, where it is distributed to the nozzles. The nozzles are installed in position near the exhaust valves

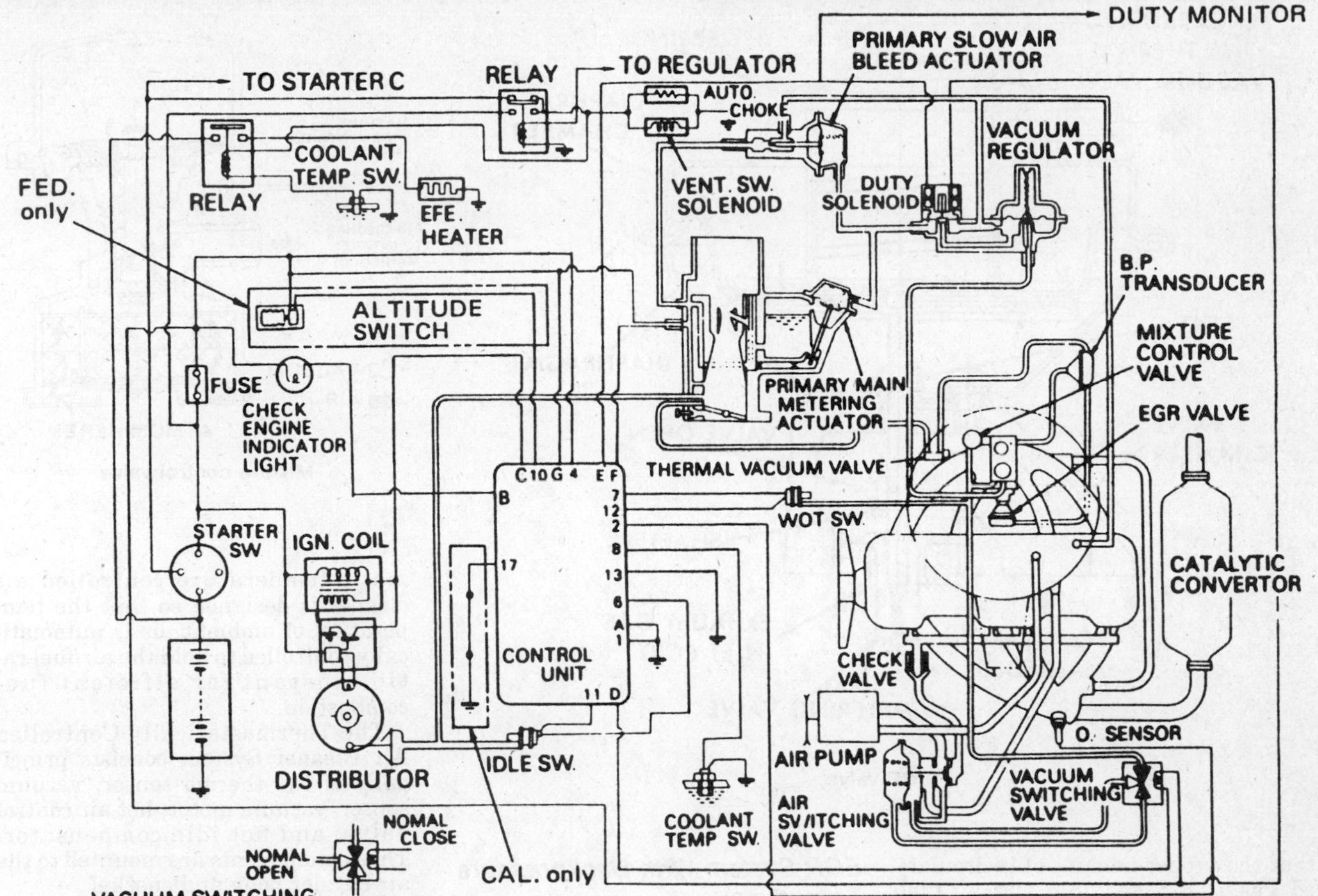

→ DUTY MONITOR

Emission control system

(diagram labels)

TO STARTER C — RELAY — TO REGULATOR — PRIMARY SLOW AIR BLEED ACTUATOR

AUTO. CHOKE — VACUUM REGULATOR

FED. only — RELAY — COOLANT TEMP. SW. — EFE. HEATER — VENT. SW. SOLENOID — DUTY SOLENOID

B.P. TRANSDUCER

ALTITUDE SWITCH — PRIMARY MAIN METERING ACTUATOR — THERMAL VACUUM VALVE — MIXTURE CONTROL VALVE — EGR VALVE

FUSE — CHECK ENGINE INDICATOR LIGHT

STARTER SW. — IGN. COIL — CONTROL UNIT (C 10 G 4 E F / B / 7 / 12 / 2 / 8 / 17 / 13 / 6 / A / 11 D) — WOT SW. — CATALYTIC CONVERTOR

DISTRIBUTOR — IDLE SW. — CAL. only — CHECK VALVE — O. SENSOR

AIR PUMP — AIR SWITCHING VALVE — VACUUM SWITCHING VALVE

COOLANT TEMP. SW.

NOMAL CLOSE / NOMAL OPEN / COMMON
VACUUM SWITCHING VALVE OPERATION

---

and pointed toward the valve. Thus, air is continuously injected into the exhaust manifold while the engine is running.

Mixture Control Valve

The purpose of the mixture control valve is to prevent the backfiring in the exhaust system during deceleration. The mixture control valve is designed to supply air into the intake manifold to prevent over-enrichment of the air/fuel mixture, when the throttle valve in the carburetor is suddenly closed.

The mixture control valve is held closed under normal operating conditions. When the vacuum in the intake manifold increases rapidly, the valve opens, allowing the air into the intake manifold.

Exhaust Gas Recirculation System (EGR)

Varied types of EGR valves are used with different control components, so

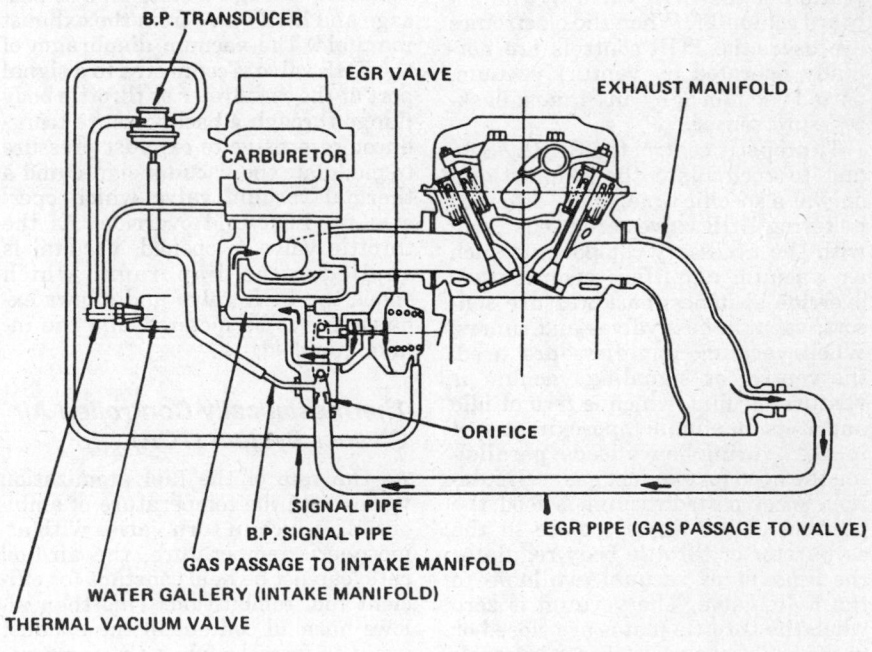

Exhaust gas recirculation (EGR) system

(diagram labels)

B.P. TRANSDUCER — EGR VALVE — EXHAUST MANIFOLD — CARBURETOR — ORIFICE — SIGNAL PIPE — B.P. SIGNAL PIPE — GAS PASSAGE TO INTAKE MANIFOLD — WATER GALLERY (INTAKE MANIFOLD) — THERMAL VACUUM VALVE — EGR PIPE (GAS PASSAGE TO VALVE)

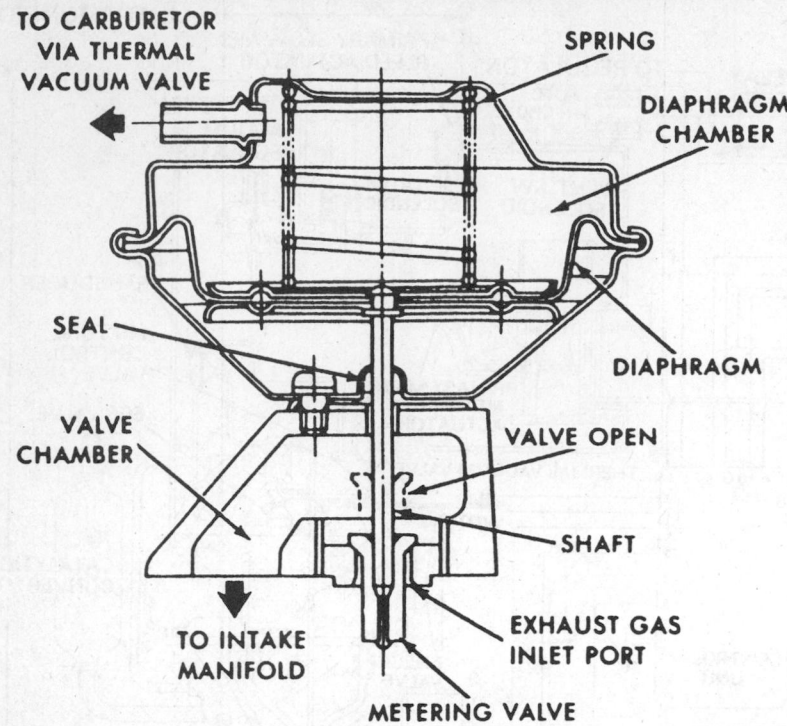

TO CARBURETOR VIA THERMAL VACUUM VALVE

SPRING

DIAPHRAGM CHAMBER

SEAL

DIAPHRAGM

VALVE CHAMBER

VALVE OPEN

SHAFT

TO INTAKE MANIFOLD

EXHAUST GAS INLET PORT

METERING VALVE

EGR valve

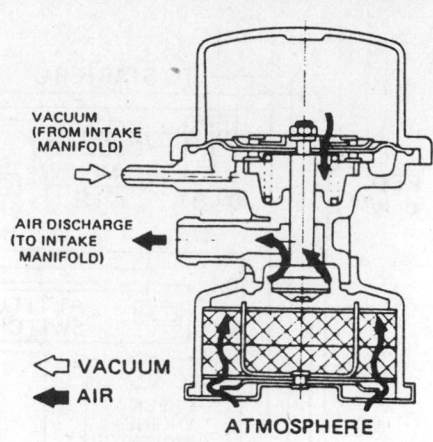

VACUUM (FROM INTAKE MANIFOLD)

AIR DISCHARGE (TO INTAKE MANIFOLD)

◁ VACUUM
◀ AIR

ATMOSPHERE

Mixture control valve

that the proper amount of recirculated gas is directed into the air/fuel mixture at a specific time. The EGR valves are vacuum operated, either by intake manifold vacuum or by ported vacuum. With the increased use of electronics, sensors and controlling solenoids are used to regulate the operation of the EGR valve by the on-board computer. When the electronics are used, the EGR controls are normally operated by venturi vacuum, ported vacuum or by an exhaust backpressure sensor.

To properly control the EGR system and to recirculate the exhaust gas only at a specific time, many different metering EGR valves are used, along with the necessary components such as; vacuum amplifier, temperature override switches, backpressure sensors, vacuum bias valves and timers. When vacuum amplifiers are used, the control or signaling vacuum is venturi vacuum, which is zero at idle and at its maximum (approximately 4 in. Hg.) during heavy loads, paralleling the need for exhaust gas recirculation. When ported vacuum is used, the position of the throttle plate in the carburetor or throttle body regulates the amount of vacuum available to the EGR valve. The vacuum is zero when the throttle plates are closed or in the wide open position, again paralleling the need for exhaust gas recirculation.

EGR System With Backpressure Transducer

The EGR system is used to reduce combustion temperature in the combustion chamber, thereby reducing oxides of nitrogen emissions. The exhaust gas is drawn into the intake manifold through a steel pipe or passage and EGR valve from the exhaust manifold. The vacuum diaphragm of the EGR valve is connected to a signal port at the carburetor or throttle body flange through a backpressure transducer responsive to exhaust pressure to modulate the vacuum signal and a thermal vacuum valve which operates for EGR cold override. As the throttle valve is opened, vacuum is applied to the diaphragm, which opens the EGR valve and allows exhaust gas to be metered into the intake manifold.

Thermostatically Controlled Air Cleaner System (TCA)

As the rate of the fuel atomization varies with the temperature of ambient air, which in turn varies with atmospheric temperature, the air/fuel ratio can not be held constant for efficient fuel combustion. This then allows harmful content in the exhaust gases to increase when the temperature of ambient air is inadequate for efficient fuel atomization. The auto-

matic temperature controlled air cleaner is designed so that the temperature of ambient air is automatically controlled to hold the air/fuel ratio constant for efficient fuel combustion.

The Thermostatically Controlled Air Cleaner System consists principally of the thermo sensor, vacuum sensor, vacuum motor, hot air control valve, and hot idle compensator. These components are mounted to the air cleaner body and snorkel.

When the engine is off, no vacuum is present at the sensor unit or at the vacuum motor. The force of the vacuum motor spring closes off the heated air passage from the exhaust manifold heat stove (snorkel passage open).

When the engine is started cold, the thermo sensor is cool allowing maximum vacuum to the vacuum motor. Maximum vacuum at the vacuum motor completely opens the hot air control valve, closing off the ambient passage through the snorkel and opening the air passage from the manifold heat stove. Should the engine be heavily accelerated while in this mode, the vacuum level in the system will drop to a low enough level so that the diaphragm spring will overcome the vacuum an open the snorkel passage.

As the engine heats up and the air past the thermo sensor reaches between 100°–111° F (38°–44° C), the thermo sensor comes into operation and begins to bleed off the supply of vacuum from the intake manifold.

At approximately 111° F (44° C), the thermo sensor completely bleeds off all vacuum to the vacuum motor so that the diaphragm spring closes the hot air control valve to the heat stove passage and opens the ambient air passage through the snorkel.

Extended idling, climbing a slope or continuous high speed driving is immediately followed by a considerable increase in engine and engine compartment temperature.

With this heat build-up, excessive fuel vapors enter the intake manifold causing an over rich mixture that results in rough idle and increased carbon monoxide emission. To prevent this, the air cleaner is equipped with a hot idle compensator. As the engine heats up and air past the hot idle compensator reaches a specified temperature, the compensator opens to feed ambient air into the intake manifold to lean out the temporarily rich mixture.

High Altitude Emission Control System

Altitude compensating system consists of altitude switch, solenoid valve and electronic control unit. The altitude switch senses from the atmospheric pressure and energizes the solenoid valve and ECU at high altitude. The solenoid valve opens and leans the air/fuel mixture by adding air to the carburetor altitude compensation passage. The ECU changes open duty cycle, also leaning the air/fuel ratio at high altitude and reducing hydrocarbon and carbon monoxide emissions. At low altitude, electric current from the altitude switch is shut off and altitude compensating system does not operate.

Closed Loop Emission Control System

Closed loop emission control is a system that precisely controls the air/fuel mixture near the 14.7:1 ratio, allowing the use of a three-way catalyst to reduce oxides of nitrogen, oxidize hydrocarbons and carbon monoxide. The essential components are an exhaust gas oxygen sensor, an electronic controller, a vacuum controller with duty solenoid, a controlled air/fuel ratio carburetor and a three way catalytic converter.

The oxygen sensor used in the closed loop control system consists of a closed end zirconia sensor placed in the engine exhaust gas stream. This sensor is mounted in the exhaust manifold. The sensor generates a voltage which varies with the oxygen content in the exhaust gas stream. As oxygen content rises, (lean mixture) voltage falls, and as oxygen content falls, (rich mixture) voltage rises.

Early Fuel Evaporation System (EFE)

The electric EFE system utilizes a ceramic heater grid located underneath

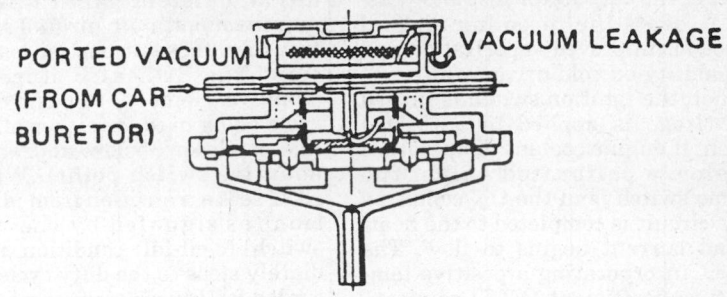

NORMAL OPERATING CONDITION

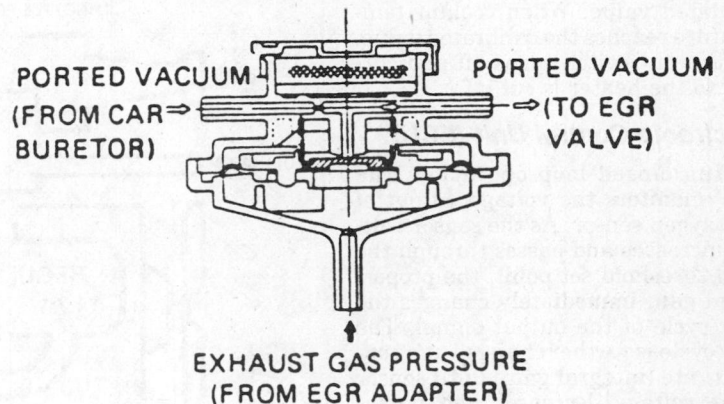

HIGH EXHAUST PRESSURE CONDITION

Backpressure transducer

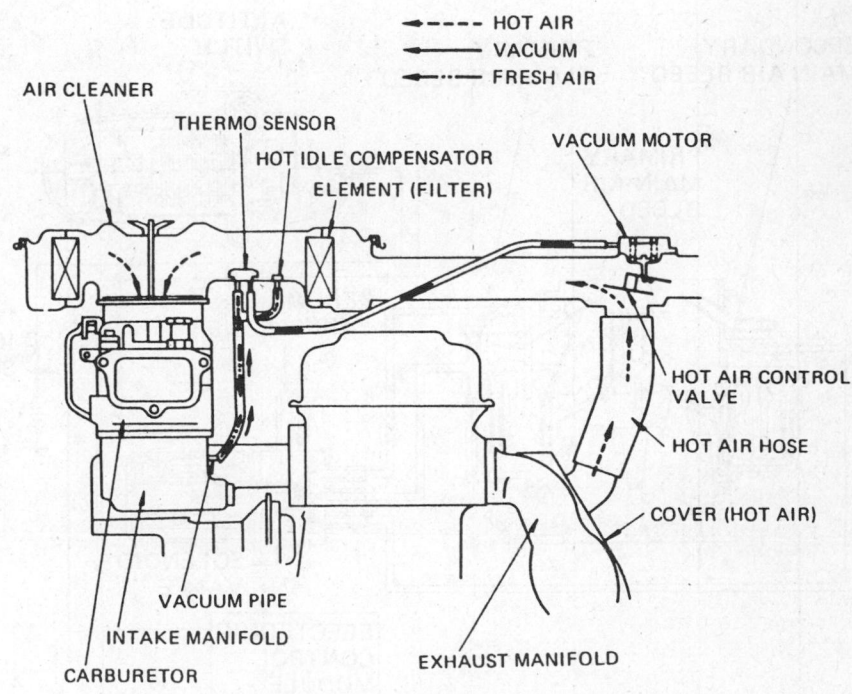

Thermostatically control air cleaner system

the primary bore of the carburetor as a part of the carburetor insulator gasket. It heats the incoming air/fuel charge for improved vaporization and driveability on cold drive-away.

When the ignition switch is turned on, voltage is applied to a thermo switch. If engine coolant temperature is below a calibrated value, the thermo switch is in the ON condition and a circuit is completed to the heater and current begins to flow. The heater, incorporating a positive temperature coefficient (PTC) semiconductor element, increases in temperature and then self-regulates at a calibrated temperature, except at high engine speeds when the air/fuel flow will reduce the temperature below the regulated value. When coolant temperature reaches the calibrated value, the thermo switch turns off and current to the heater is cut off.

Electronic Control Unit (ECU)

During closed loop operation, the ECU monitors the voltage output of the oxygen sensor. As the sensor voltage increases and passes through the ECU threshold set point, the proportional gain immediately changes the duty cycle of the output signal. The duty cycle is further changed at a constant rate (integral gain) until sensor input voltage decreases and passes through the ECU threshold set point.

The selection of integral and proportional gain rates by the ECU is based on engine operating conditions

(idle or off-idle condition). At idle condition, different gain rates are required for optimum air/fuel ratio control than those at partial load condition. The ECU also stores in an adaptive memory, the current duty cycle being used for either idle or off-idle condition (below and above the adaptive switch point). When the ECU sees a transition from idle condition (as signaled by the vacuum switch) to off-idle condition, it immediately steps to the duty cycle last recorded for desired air/fuel mixture operation. From then on, while at that

engine operating condition, the system uses the basic proportional and integral gain controls as previously described.

Catalytic Converter

The catalytic converters are mounted in the engine exhaust stream and works as a gas reactor in which its major function is to speed up the heat producing chemical reaction between the exhaust gas components, in order to reduce the carbon monoxide, hydrocarbon and oxides of nitrogen in the

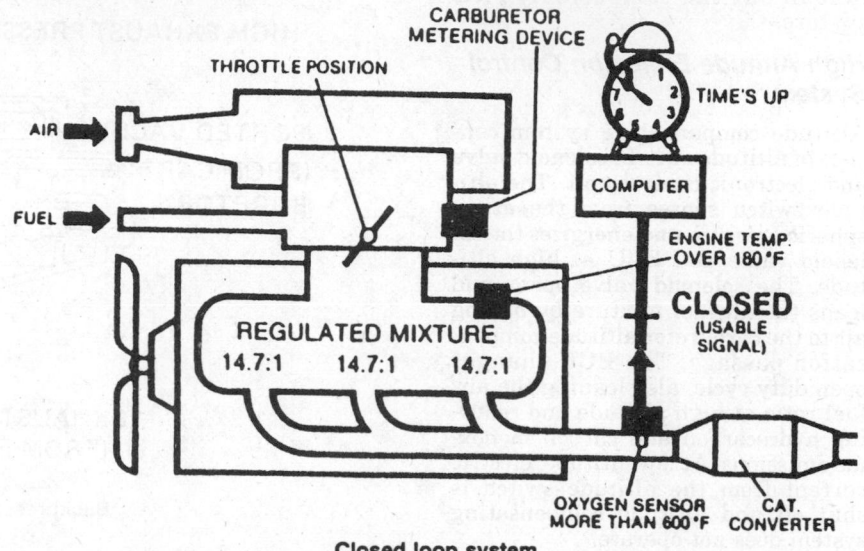

Closed loop system

High altitude emission control system

engine exhaust. Unleaded fuel must be used in vehicles equipped with catalytic converters.

The catalyst material is either a ceramic substrate or pellets that are coated with a base of alumina and then impregnated with catalytically active, precious (noble) metals. It is the surface of the catalyst material that controls the heat producing chemical reaction.

Two main types of converters containing two precious (noble) metals, platinum and palladium to effectively catalyze the oxidation of the hydrocarbons and carbon monoxide. The second type converter used is considered a three-way catalyst, containing a small percentage of platinum and a greater percentage of rhodium in the front part of the converters to reduce the oxides of nitrogen, while platinum and palladium are used in the rear section to oxidize the hydrocarbons and carbon monoxide, as was done in the two way converters.

Three-Way Catalytic Converter

The three-way catalytic converters use a combination of catalyst which produce two different chemical reactions, oxidation and reduction. By adding fresh air to the unburned hydrocarbons and carbon monoxide within the converter, the oxidizing of combustion process takes place.

Just the reverse process is required to lower the oxides of nitrogen emissions. The oxides of nitrogen already contains excessive oxygen and the process of separating the excess oxygen from the nitrogen is called a reducing reaction.

This reducing or reducing process is done in the front section of the converter while the oxidizing process is accomplished in the rear section. A fresh air connector is located on the center of the converter shell, to add fresh air from the air system as required.

To enable the three-way converter to operate properly, the engine's air/fuel ratio must be held within a tight range (the desired 14.7:1 air/fuel ratio). This is accomplished with the use of the latest computer controlled electronic engine components.

Different control components are used by the vehicle manufacturers to prevent converter damage and/or burnout. Unleaded fuels must be used in the vehicles equipped with the catalytic converters to prevent contamination failure.

Thermal Reactor System

The thermal reactor is installed in place of the exhaust manifold. It is much heavier and heat resistant. Its purpose is to collect the exhaust gases in a common area, to keep their temperature higher for a longer period of time, thus allowing further oxidation or burning of the exhaust gas and secondary air mix burned emissions.

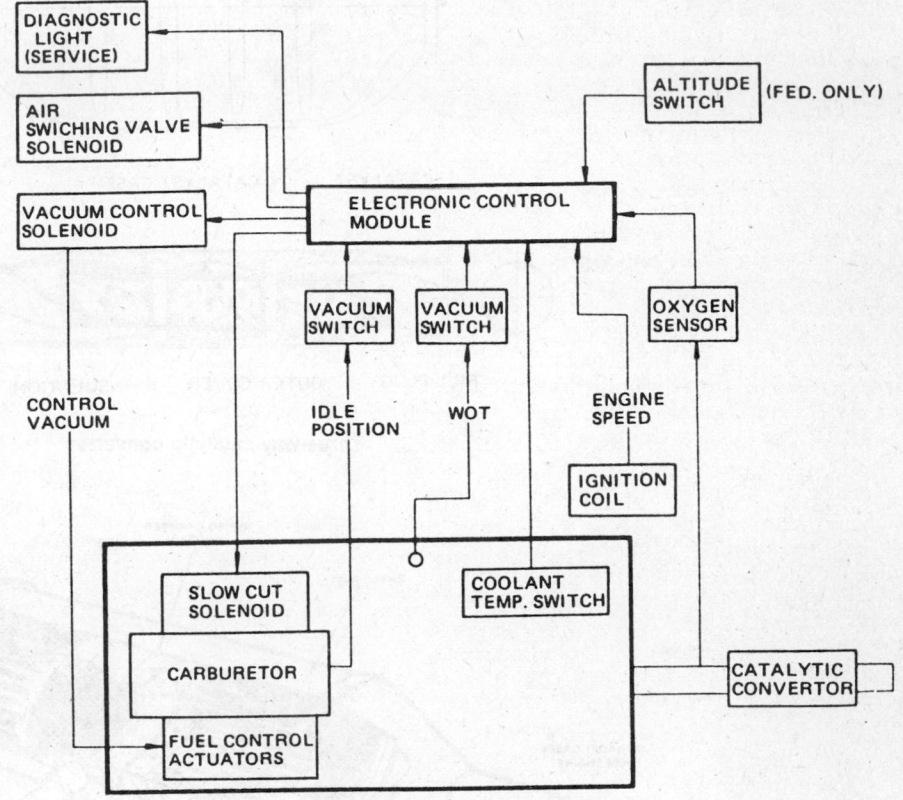

Closed loop control system

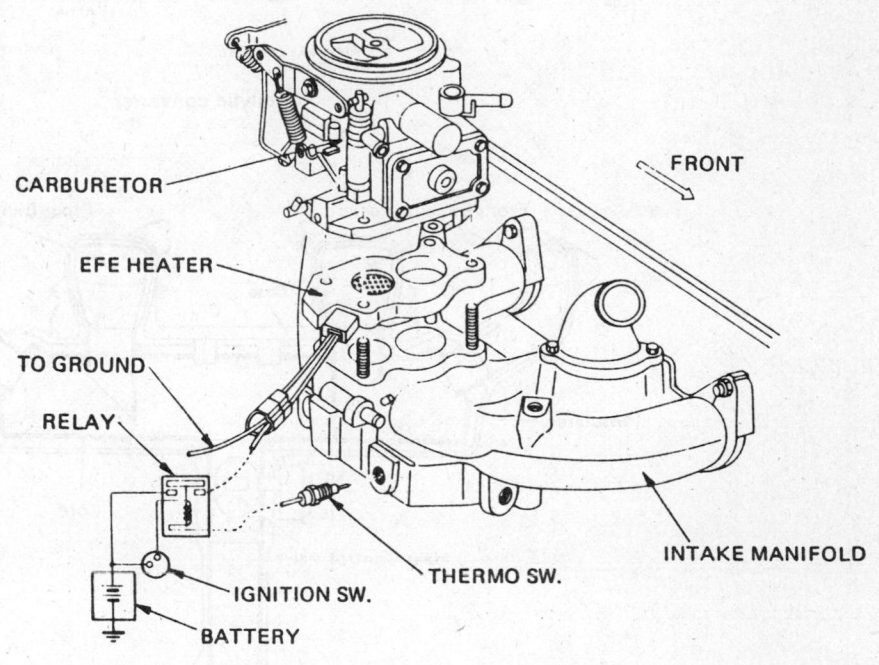

Early fuel evaporation (EFE) system

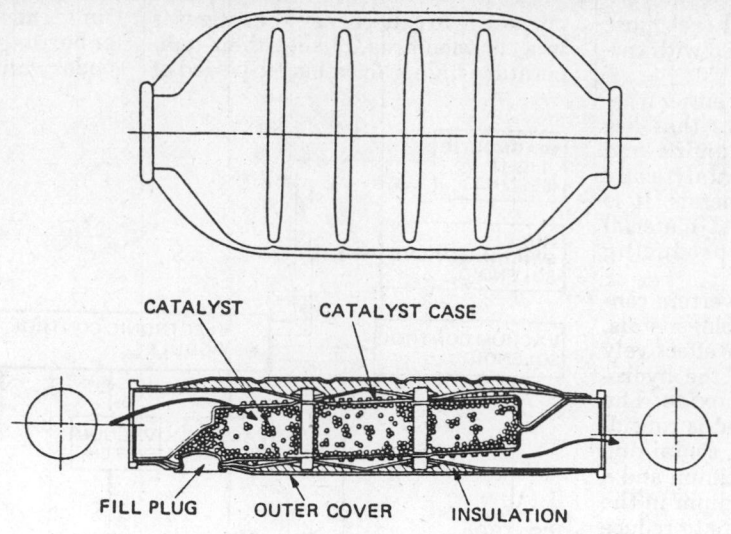

Three-way catalytic converter

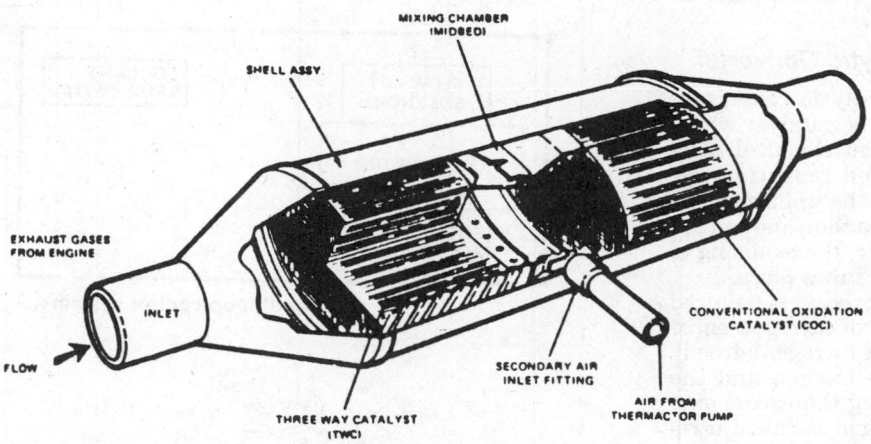

Catalytic converter

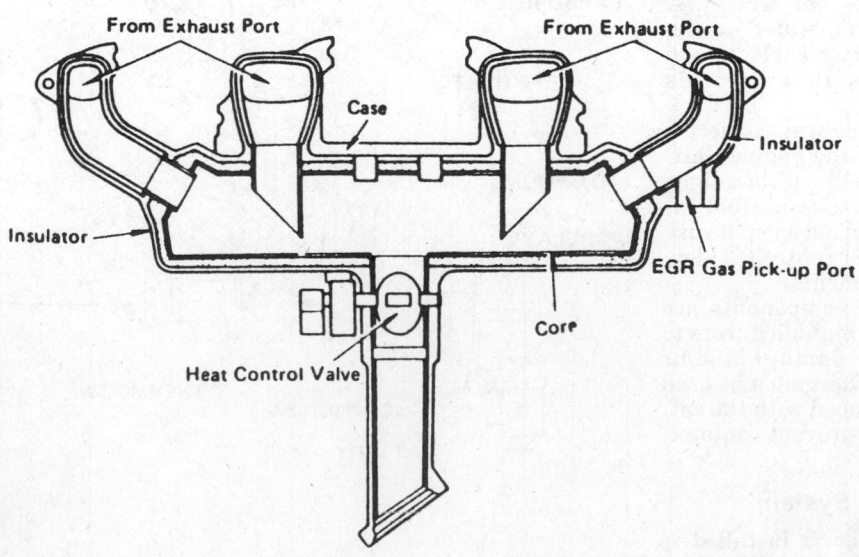

Thermal reactor system

Electronic Engine Controls 25

ENGINE ELECTRONICS

History

In the latter part of the 1960's, Robert Bosch introduced the first true electronically controlled engine with an on-board computer. Today, almost every car produced has some kind electronic engine control. The once mechanically controlled engine functions of early model cars are all but extinct.

The first system, Bosch D-Jetronic, is comprised of electrically energized fuel injectors in which the injection time is controlled by an electronic control unit (ECU). The early system delivered a basic quantity of fuel and varied from this point depending upon engine load, engine speed and engine temperature.

Since the early days of the ECU, the controls have become more complex, with a much greater amount of computer memory and even the ability to learn.

In this section, the topics will include different types of electronically controlled fuel induction, spark control, the sensors and switches that provide the ECU with information, other non-engine related controls that the ECU might supply and some ECU self-diagnostics.

The most common fuel induction system with an ECU is electronic fuel injection. In this system, fuel can be delivered many different ways. One of which is the single point injection

(SPI) were one or two injectors are mounted on a throttle body assembly. Fuel is delivered constantly through the injector(s), but in varying quantities. The SPI system very much resembles a carbureted system. SPI is more commonly known as throttle body injection (TBI). Another fuel injection system is multi-point injection (MPI). This system supplies one injector for each cylinder, usually positioned in the intake manifold, just above the intake valve. In MPI, fuel can be injected in two ways. One is to energize a group of injectors, thus atomizing fuel in the intake manifold and storing it for a short time until the intake valve opens. The second way is to sequentially energize each cylinder's injector as the intake valve is opened. This injection is the more efficient, effective and more complex system.

Another fuel induction system utilizing an ECU is the feedback carburetor (FBC). A conventional carburetor is still used, but it has a more precise air/fuel mixture control which is achieved through an integral mixture control solenoid. The solenoid is energized on and off by the ECU to maintain mixture demand. The ECU calculates air/fuel mixture demand changes by the data it receives through remote sensors. The most important sensor (and makes the system possible) is an oxygen (O_2) sensor (which will be discussed later in this section). The ECU monitors the exhaust gases for rich/lean conditions by way of the O_2 sensor and, in turn, controls the air/fuel mixture by increasing or decreasing the duty cycles (on and off) to the mixture control solenoid for an optimum 14.7:1 air/fuel ratio.

ECU Self-Diagnostics

The ECU can detect a malfunction or abnormality in the sensors or in the ECU itself and display a warning light on the instrument panel when it does. When this occurs, the ECU stores a trouble code for future system diagnosis. If the problem is sever enough to where it inhibits closed loop operation, the ECU will assume a backup system. This fail-safe circuit is pre-programmed into the ECU for minimal driveability operation so the vehicle can be driven to a nearby service facility. The trouble codes are usually a two digit numbers identified by the number of diagnostic LED or check engine light flashes. The trouble codes assist the service technician in isolating a faulty circuit or component within the system.

Electronic Data Sensors

The engine control system consists of various data sensors. Although data sensor names and applications vary from system to system, the most common input sensors/switches are:

- oxygen (O_2) sensor
- coolant temperature sensor
- manifold air pressure (MAP) sensor
- vehicle speed sensor (VSS)
- throttle position sensor (TPS)
- engine speed reference or distributor reference (rpm)
- air flow sensor
- air intake temperature sensor
- crankshaft sensor
- detonation (knock) sensor
- throttle body temperature sensor

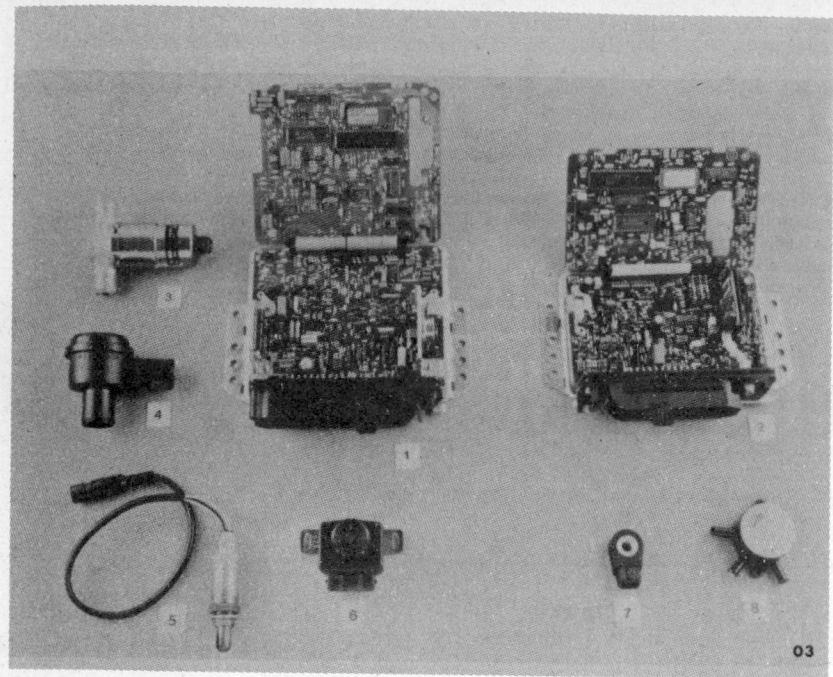

Engine electronic components

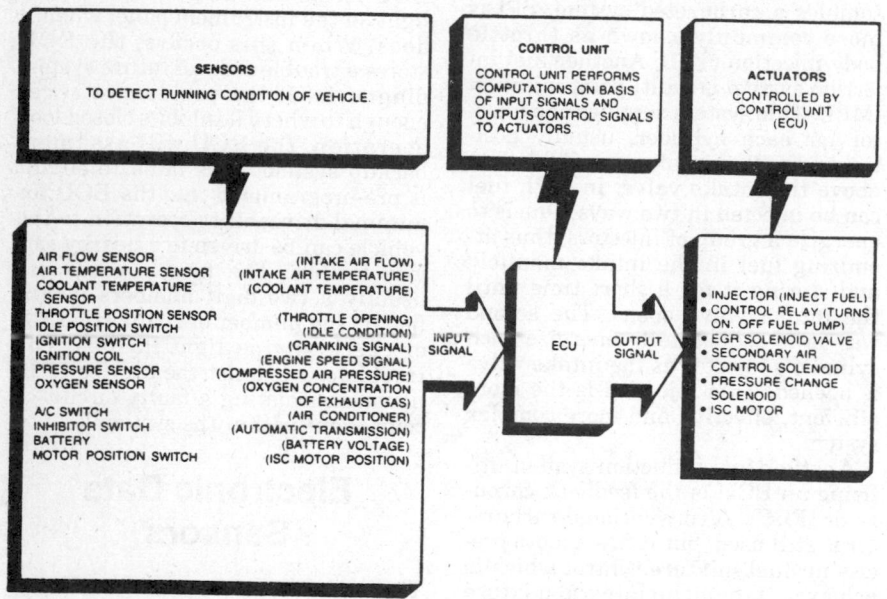

Typical fuel control system with ECU

- throtle idle switch
- transmission or drive switch
- a/c compressor clutch switch
- power steering pump switch
- altitude or barometric pressure sensor
- wide open throttle switch

Electronically Controlled Devices

Some of the output devices that the

ECU may control vary from system to system, but the most common output or ECU controlled devices are:

- fuel injector(s)
- air/fuel mixture solenoid
- fuel pump relay
- a/c compressor clutch relay
- idle air control (IAC) valve
- idle speed control (ISC) motor
- ignition spark/timing
- canister purge solenoid

- torque converter clutch solenoid (automatic transmission)
- air management system (air induction)
- idle-up or throttle kicker solenoid
- alternator field control (charging system)
- turbocharger boost wastegate
- cooling fan relay

Component Description

THROTTLE BODY

The throttle body, in most fuel injected systems, is usually an alumunum housing that consists of one or two throttle blades which are attached to a throttle shaft. The housing has a throttle position sensor (TPS) sensor, idle air control motor and, in some cases, throttle body temperature sensor. On SPI systems, the housing also has an injector(s) and (in some cases) a fuel pressure regulator. The throttle body throttle blade controls the amount of air that enters the engine as well as the amount of vacuum.

ELECTRONIC CONTROL UNIT (ECU)

The ECU monitors and controls all engine control functions. The ECU consists of input and output devices, a central processing unit, a power supply and various memory banks. The input and output devices of the ECU convert electrical signals received by the data sensors and switches to the digital signal that are used by the central processing unit. The central processing unit receives digital signals that are used to perform all mathematical computations and logic functions necessary to deliver proper air/fuel mixture. The central processing unit is also responsible for calculating spark timing information. The main source of power that allows the ECU to function is generated from the battery of the vehicle and transported through the ignition system. The memory bank of the ECU is programmed with exact information that is used by the ECU during the open loop mode. This data is also used when a sensor of other component fails, allowing the vehicle to be driven to a repair facility.

CALIBRATION ASSSEMBLY OR PROM (PROGRAMMABLE READ ONLY MEMORY)

Some vehicle manufactures use one

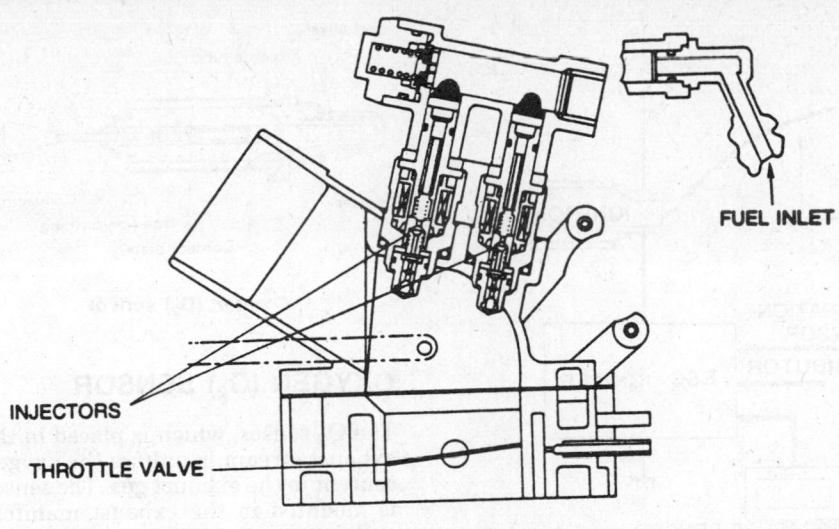

FUEL INLET

INJECTORS

THROTTLE VALVE

Throttle body—TBI type

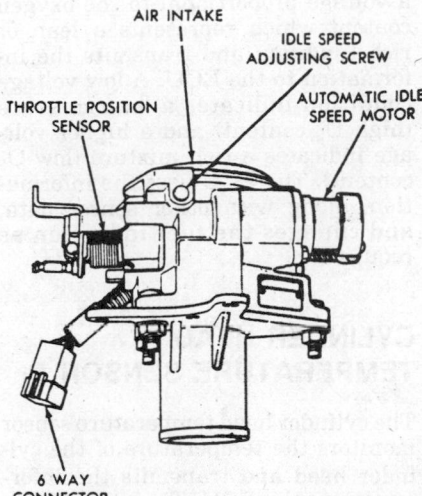

AIR INTAKE

IDLE SPEED
ADJUSTING SCREW

THROTTLE POSITION
SENSOR

AUTOMATIC IDLE
SPEED MOTOR

6 WAY
CONNECTOR

Throttle body—MFI type

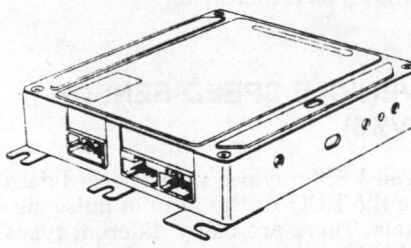

Electronic control unit (ECU)

ECU for several different model vehicles. This interchangeable ECU is possible through the use of a calibration assembly or prom. Information about the vehicle's engine, transmission, body and drive axle ratio are programmed and permanently stored into the assembly. If the battery supply should become disconnected from the ECU, the data stored into the assembly is not lost.

ELECTRONIC SPARK CONTROL (ESC)

The vehicles equipped with an ESC have the ability to change the ignition timing under any and all operating conditions. Data from various remote sensors (coolant temperature, throttle position, rpm, etc.) is transmitted to the ESC. The ESC computes the information and triggers the ignition spark at precisely the right instant. Some ESC systems (ie.,turbocharged engines) use a detonation (knock) sensor which senses pre-ignition and transmits the information to the ESC. The ESC modifies spark advance and boost pressure in order to eliminate knock.

MASS AIR FLOW SENSOR

The mass air flow (MAF) sensor is only incorporated in some Multi-point fuel injection systems. The MAF sensor is a very complex device which measures the air mass of the engine intake. Because the air mass is always changing with temperature, humidity and altitude, the fuel delivery rate must be adjusted to compensate for these changes so that a precise fuel mixture can be maintained.

AIR TEMPERATURE SENSOR

The air temperature sensor is located in the air stream of the air flow meter. The sensor supplies incoming air temperature information to the ECU. The ECU uses this data, along with other data, to regulate fuel injection rate.

THROTTLE POSITION SENSOR (TPS)

The TPS can be either a switch (or a combination of switches) or a variable resistor which is much more accurate in throttle position. The switch type TPS consists of switches that open and close at different throttle positions (usually at idle and wide open throttle) and sends the information to the ECU. The variable resistor type receives a reference voltage from the ECU and responds back to the ECU with a proportional voltage directly related to the position of the throttle plate.

ENGINE COOLANT TEMPERATURE SENSOR

The coolant temperature sensor is located in the engine coolant passage, usually located in the intake manifold. The sensor is resistor based and changes resistance as coolant temper-

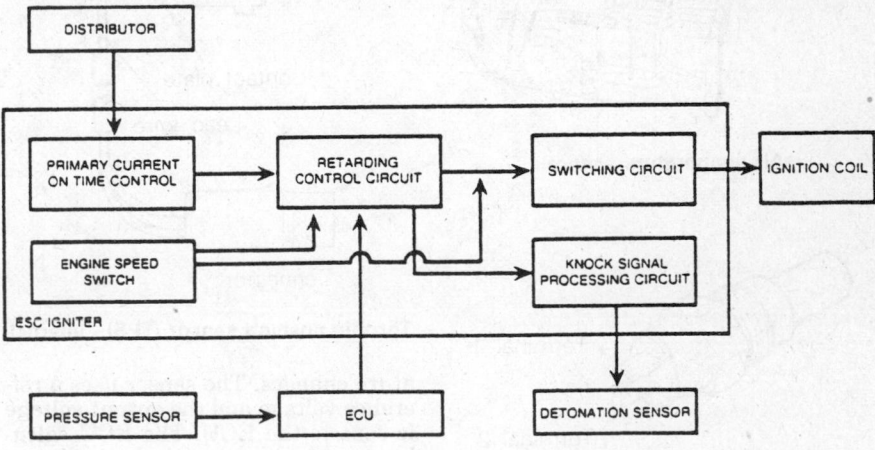

Electronic spark control (ESC) ignition with detonation sensor

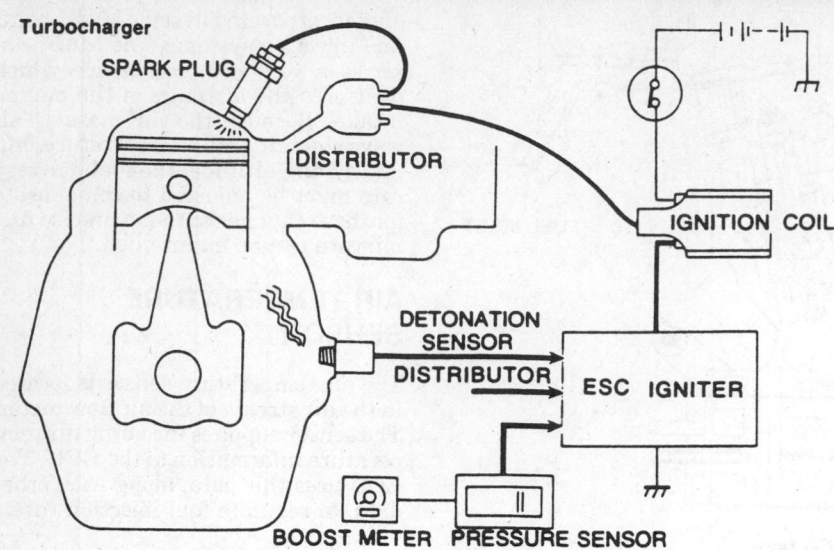

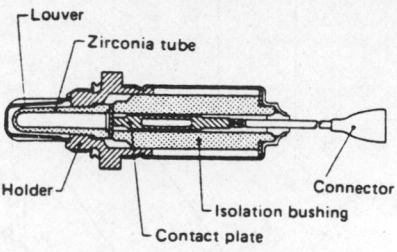

Oxygen (O₂) sensor

Electronic spark control (ESC) ignition system

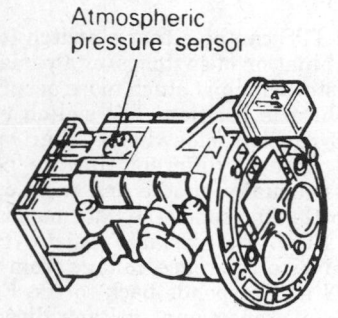

Mass air flow (MAF) sensor

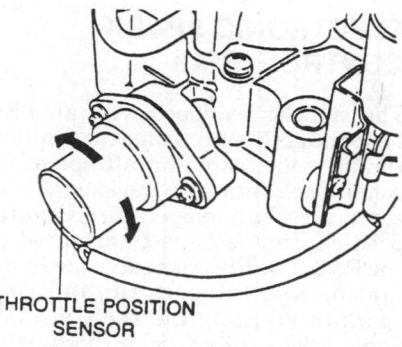

Throttle position sensor (TPS)

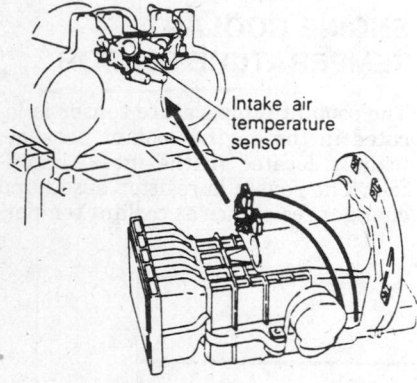

Air temperature sensor

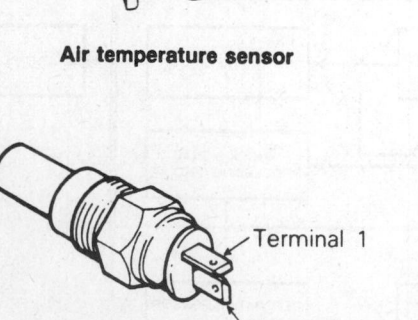

Coolant temperature sensor

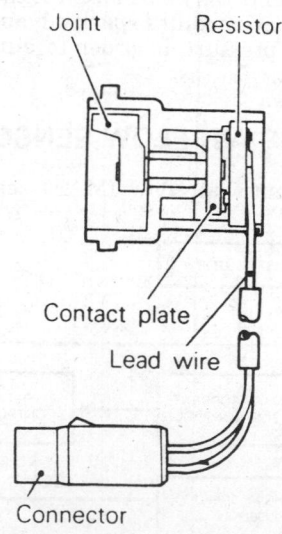

Throttle position sensor (TPS) — Internal

OXYGEN (O₂) SENSOR

The O₂ sensor, which is placed in the exhaust stream, monitors the oxygen content in the exhaust gas. The sensor is mounted in the exhaust manifold and is sometimes internally heated electrically for faster switching to the closed loop mode. The sensor produces a voltage proportional to the oxygen content which represents a lean or rich condition and transmits the information to the ECU. A low voltage condition indicates a lean mixture (high O₂ content) and a higher voltage indicates a rich mixture (low O₂ content). The ECU uses the information, along with other sensor data, and changes the fuel induction as required.

CYLINDER HEAD TEMPERATURE SENSOR

The cylinder head temperature sensor monitors the temperature of the cylinder head and transmits the information to the ECU. The sensor is located in the cylinder head and is a temperature sensitive resistive unit known as a thermistor.

VEHICLE SPEED SENSOR (VSS)

The VSS provides vehicle speed data to the ECU in the form of pulse signals. There are many different types of VSS, some using a reed switch installed in the speedometer unit and others using a optical type. In the optical type a light emitting diode (LED) is used to transmit light and photo diode receives the light. A shutter device, which is usually in-line with the speedometer cable, allows the LED light to reach the photo diode in vehicle speed related pulses. The reed switch type relies on a reed switch that opens and closes by way of a rotating magnet. The magnet rotates proportionally with the vehicle speed.

ature changes. The sensor uses a reference voltage and the output voltage is sent to the ECU. The ECU calculates engine warm up and provides an optimum fuel enrichment when the engine is cold.

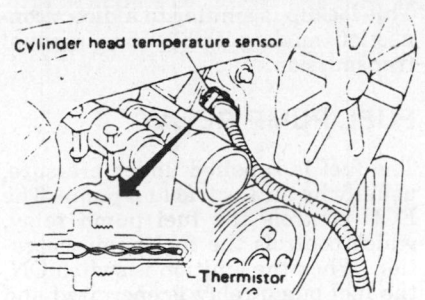

Cylinder head temperature sensor

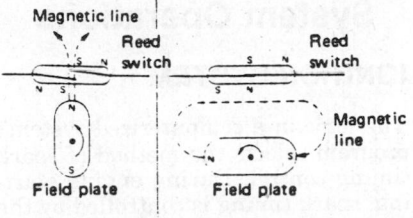

Vehicle speed sensor (VSS) — reed switch type

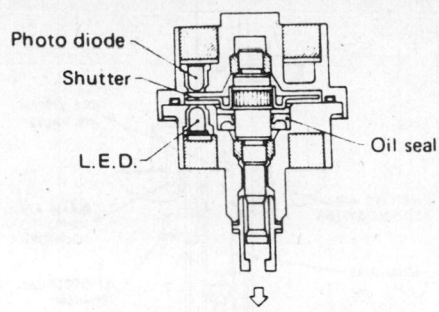

Vehicle speed sensor (VSS) — photo type

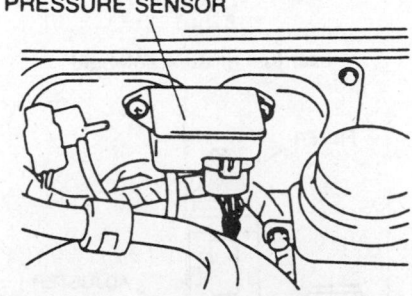

Manifold air pressure (MAP) sensor

Detonation (knock) sensor

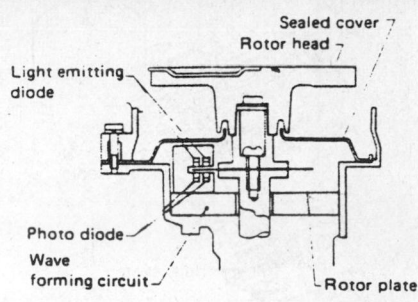

Crankshaft position sensor — distributor mounted

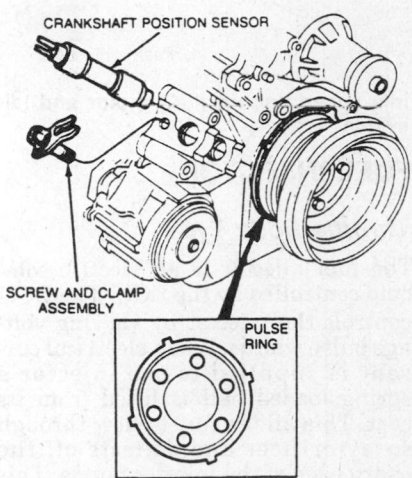

Crankshaft position sensor — near crankshaft pulley

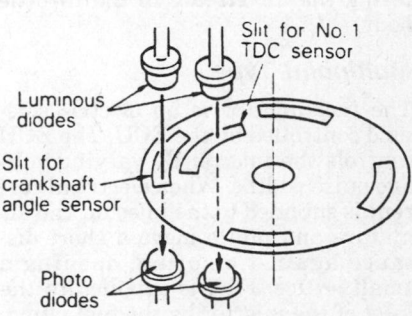

Crankshaft position sensor — optical type

MANIFOLD AIR PRESSURE (MAP) SENSOR

The MAP sensor is a device that monitors manifold absolute pressure. The sensor is mounted remotely and senses vacuum through a connecting hose. The MAP sensor has a reference voltage from the ECU and transmits remaining voltage to the ECU to calculate engine load. The ECU uses this data along with other data to determine fuel demands.

DETONATION (KNOCK) SENSOR

The detonation sensor generates a signal when pre-ignition (knock) occurs in one or more combustion chambers. The sensor is made of a material that is sensitive to oscillation that the engine knock produces and sends signals to the ECU. The ECU, in turn, delays the ignition signal which retards the ignition timing and continues to do this until the engine knock ceases.

CRANKSHAFT (REFERENCE MARK) SENSOR

The crankshaft sensor may be located at either the rear of the engine, at the flywheel, at the front of the engine, near the crankshaft pulley or mounted in the distributor. The sensor detects crankshaft position in relation to top dead center and transmits the signals to ECU.

IDLE SPEED CONTROL (ISC) MOTOR

The ISC is sometimes included on a feedback carburetor system and mounted to the side of the carburetor. The motor driven ISC maintains a steady idle by way of the ECU. When an added load is put on the engine (air conditioning or when the vehicle is in drive) the ECU can increase the idle via the ISC by extending a plunger which opens the throttle valve.

AIR/FUEL MIXTURE SOLENOID

The air/fuel mixture solenoid on a feedback carburetor operates in conjuntion with the fixed metering jets end/or the manually adjustable idle speed mixture screw. The ECU energizes and de-energizes the solenoid in the closed loop mode. The solenoid usually controls a fixed air bleed and/or fuel discharge port.

IDLE AIR CONTROL (IAC)

The IAC in a fuel injection system controls the air flow around the throttle plate by extending and retracting a bypass valve in the bypass port. The ECU controls the valve by sending voltage pulses called counts or steps to increase or decrease the bypass air flow, thus increasing and decreasing the idle speed.

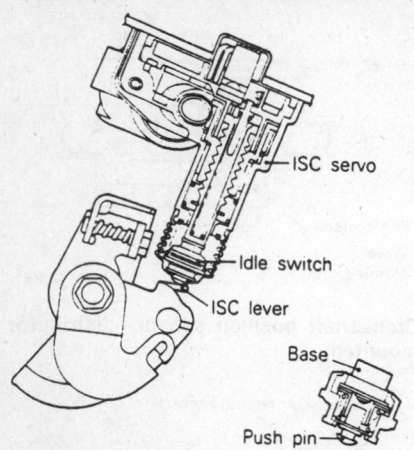

Idle speed control (ISC) motor and idle switch

FUEL INJECTOR

Throttle Body Type

The fuel injector is an electric solenoid controlled by the ECU. The ECU controls the injector by varying voltage pulse widths. When electrical current is supplied to the injector a spring loaded ball is lifted from its seat. This allows fuel to flow through spray orifices and deflects off the sharp edge of the injector nozzle. This action causes the fuel to form a 45° cone shaped spray pattern before entering the air stream in the throttle body.

Multipoint Type

The fuel injector is an electric solenoid controlled by the ECU. The ECU controls the injector by varying voltage pulse widths. When electrical current is supplied to the injector, the armature and pintle move a short distance against a spring, opening a small orifice. Fuel is supplied to the inlet of the injector by the fuel pump, then passes through the injector, around the pintle and out the orifice. Since the fuel is under high pressure, a fine spray is developed in the shape of a hollow cone. The injector, through this spraying action, atomizes the fuel and distributes it into the air entering the combustion chamber.

TORQUE CONVERTER CLUTCH (TCC) SOLENOID

The TCC solenoid is used on some automatic transmission, which allows for better fuel economy. When certain engine and vehicle speeds have been met, the ECU energizes the solenoid. This allows transmission fluid to flow into passages in the torque converter, which causes the converter to lock up.

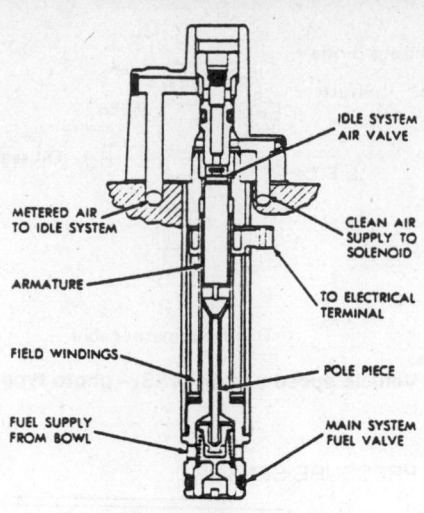

Air/fuel mixture solenoid

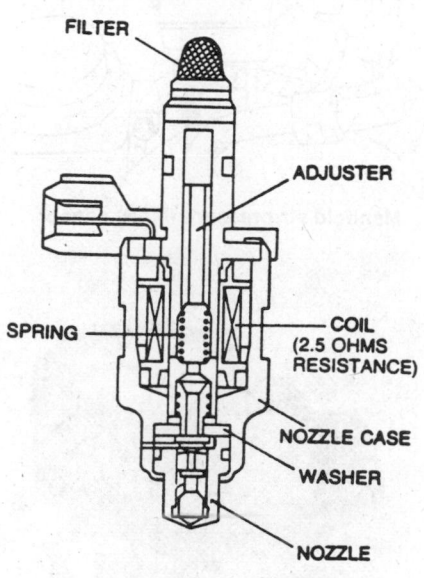

Fuel Injector – TBI type

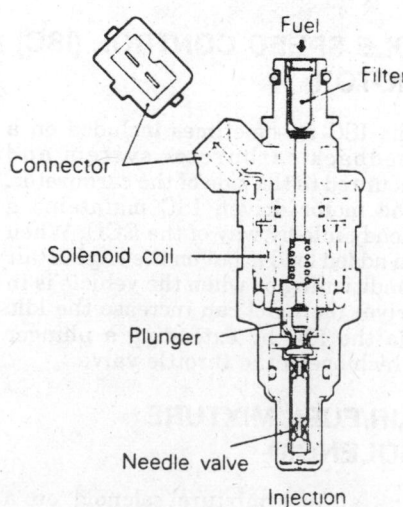

Fuel Injector – MFI type

This lockup is similar to a direct connection made possible in a manual transmission.

FUEL PUMP RELAY

The fuel is supplied under pressure, usually by an electric fuel pump. The ECU controls the fuel pump relay, which controls the fuel pump operation. When the ignition is switch ON, the fuel pump relay is energized and the fuel pump is activated. The pump primes the fuel system with fuel to a pre-determined pressure.

System Operations

IGNITION SYSTEM

The logic in a computerized system's program selects the method of spark timing control. During engine starting, spark timing is controlled by the mechanical setting of the distributor. Once the engine is running, spark timing is turned over to the ECU. This scheme ensures that the car will start regardless of whether the electronic control system is working or not.

The goal of electronic spark timing is to produce maximum engine power by adjustment the advance of the ignition firing in relationship to top dead center (TDC). The spark timing can be chosen to produce the best engine power with input variables of engine rpm, engine coolant temperature, initial and operating manifold or barometric pressure.

The total spark advance is determined by computing the information received from the various engine sensors which affect spark timing. The processor will then adjust the timing according to information that has been calibrated in it. The processor has programmed into it specific information on:

Warm-Up Spark Advance – this is used when the engine is cold, since a greater amount of advance is required while the engine warms up.

Special Spark Advance – to improve fuel economy during steady driving conditions.

Spark Advance Due to Barometric Pressure – this is used when barometric pressure exceeds a preset calibrated amount.

All of this information is then added together and the initial mechanical advance is subtracted to determine the final spark advance.

The processor receives a timing pulse from a sensor which indicates crankshaft position for top dead center and engines rpm. The processor makes a decision based upon this information and the information that was calibrated into it. At that time, the computer sends a pulse to the ignition actuator circuit, which opens the ignition coil primary circuit to generate a secondary voltage pulse to fire the spark plugs. In some cases, the circuitry to open the primary of the coil may be in the computerized controller. The spark selection is performed mechanically by the distributor and rotor contacts as it is done in a non-electronic controlled system.

The ignition timing works along with electronic fuel control to control emissions and provide for optimum fuel economy and driveability because engine power, fuel economy and emissions are dependent on spark advance of the engine timing.

The system just described is considered to operate in open-loop. There are some electronically controlled ignition systems which receive an input from a knock sensor. These systems operate in a closed-loop mode which allows the ignition system to monitor the engine for mechanical changes, such as engine knock.

Engine knock is a condition where the air/fuel mixture in the cylinder does not burn normally. The pressure rise during this burning is so rapid compared to normal combustion that it is accompanied by an audible "knock".

Through some low level knock is acceptable, it is important to avoid excessive knock. To control engine knock, a knock sensor is installed in the engine or intake manifold. This helps to detect excessive engine knock.

The knock sensor is a tuned accelerometer and produces an output voltage depending on the amount of engine vibration occurring in a certain frequency band. When the processor receives a signal from the knock sensor, it retards the spark advance until the knocking stops and then starts increasing it again. This cycle is repeated as long as engine knock occurs.

FUEL CONTROL

In order for the processor to control fuel, it requires a sensor or sensors to monitor the state of the engine, and one or more actuators to do the actual controlling. The sensors measure: exhaust gas oxygen, manifold or barometric absolute pressure, engine rpm and speed, inlet air and coolant temperatures. Actuators are energized to control the air/fuel ratio.

The primary purpose of this control system is to maintain air/fuel ratio at or near 14.7:1 ratio. This is accomplished in two modes (during normal

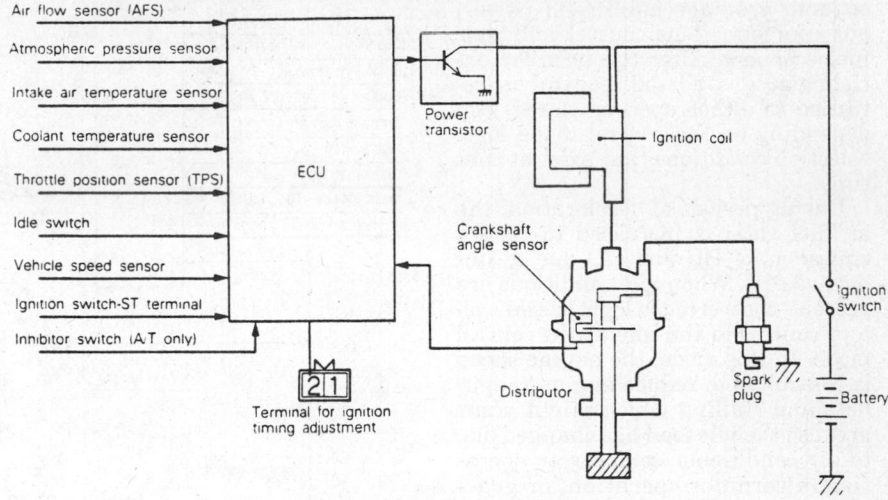

Ignition system with ECU

Electronic distributor assembly

engine operation) open and closed loop. The electronic fuel control system can operate in closed loop only when certain conditions are satisfied. Open loop mode is employed whenever these conditions are not satisfied. However, for either mode, the exhaust emissions will satisfy federal requirements if the average air/fuel ratio is held within the tolerance limits.

In addition to open and closed loop control modes, a practical fuel control system has other operating modes depending on engine conditions. These handle such conditions as starting, rapid acceleration or heavy load, sudden deceleration, idling, etc.

An automotive engine has various operating modes as the operating conditions change. Preprogrammed into the processor, control logic determines the operating mode from the engine conditions that exist. From these engine conditions, the system determines which operating modes are to be performed.

There are seven different engine operating modes which affect fuel control: engine crank, engine warmup, open loop, closed loop control, hard acceleration, deceleration and idle. The program for mode control logic determines the engine operating mode by reading various sensors.

When the ignition switch is initially switched on, the mode control logic automatically selects an engine-start control scheme which provides the low air/fuel ratio required for starting the engine. Once the engine rpm rises above the cranking value, the controller identifies the engine-started mode and passes control to the program for the engine warm-up mode. This operating mode keeps the air/fuel ratio low to prevent engine stall during cool weather until engine coolant temperature rises above a preset value.

When the coolant temperature rises, the mode control logic directs the system to operate in the open loop control mode until a certain time has elapsed and the exhaust gas sensor warms up enough to provide accurate readings. This condition is detected by monitoring the exhaust gas sensor's output for voltage readings above a certain minimum air/fuel mixture voltage set point. When the sensor has indicated a rich mixture a certain number of times (depending on calibration) and after the engine has been in open loop for a specific time, the control mode logic selects the closed loop mode for the system. The engine remains in the closed loop mode until either the exhaust gas sensor cools and fails to switch (from rich to lean) for a certain length of time, or a hard acceleration or deceleration occurs. If the sensor cools, the control mode logic selects the open loop mode again.

During hard acceleration of heavy engine loads, the control mode logic chooses a scheme which provides a rich air/fuel mixture for the duration of the acceleration or heavy load. This scheme provides maximum power, but poor emissions control and poor fuel economy. After the need for enrichment has passed, control is returned to either open or closed loop depending on the control mode logic selection conditions that exist at that time.

During periods of deceleration, the air/fuel ratio is increased to reduce emissions of HC and CO due to unburned fuel. When idle conditions are present, control mode logic passes system control to the idle speed control mode. In this mode, the engine speed is controlled to reduce engine roughness and stalling which might occur because the idle load has changed due to air conditioner compressor operation, alternator operation, or gearshift positioning from PARK or NEUTRAL to DRIVE.

Engine Crank

While the engine is being cranked, the fuel control system must provide an intake air/fuel ratio anywhere from 2:1 to 12:1, depending on engine temperature. Low temperatures affect the carburetor's ability to atomize or mix the incoming air and fuel. At low temperature, the fuel tends to form into large droplets. The larger fuel droplets tend to increase the apparent air/fuel ratio because the amount of usable fuel in the air is reduced, therefore, the system must provide a decreased air/fuel ratio to provide the engine with a more combustible air/fuel mixture. The engine temperature is read by the processor through an analog to digital converter from a temperature sensor in the engine water coolant passage. The processor's calibration determines what the proper air/fuel ratio must be at that temperature. The air/fuel is determined and controlled as in the open loop mode.

Engine Warm-up

While the engine is warming up, an enriched air/fuel ratio is still needed to keep it running smoothly, but the required air/fuel ratio changes as the temperature increases. Therefore, the fuel control system will stay in the open loop mode, but the air/fuel ratio commands continue to be altered due to the temperature changes. The emphasis in this control mode is on rapid and smooth engine warm-up. Fuel economy and emission control are still a secondary concern. The controller determines the warm-up time period based on the coolant temperature when the warm-up mode was selected. Naturally, an initially cold engine requires a longer warm-up time than a warm engine. The time allowed by

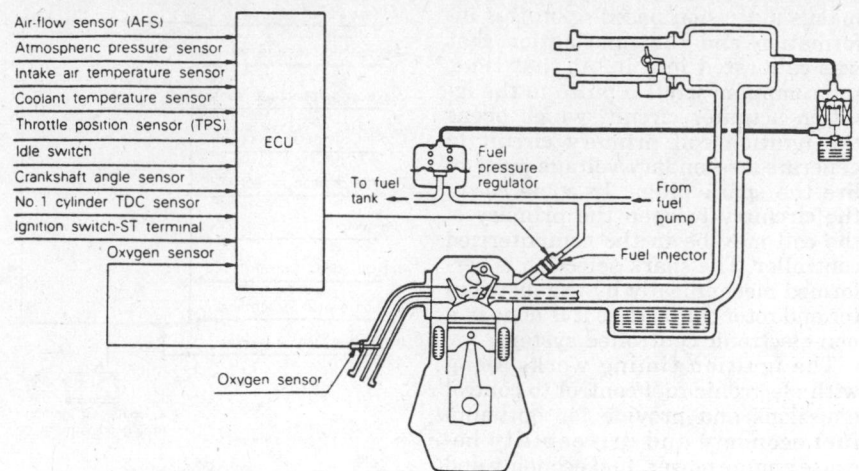

Fuel Injection system with ECU

the controller timer is chosen according to the calibration of the processor.

OPEN LOOP CONTROL

Open loop fuel control is used when the engine has not reached a preset operating condition. This condition is sensed by various sensors located in and around the engine, and include engine coolant temperature, air charge temperature, engine time on, etc. After all these preset conditions are met, the system will go into closed loop. During certain operating conditions, such as a wide open throttle condition the system will go back into open loop.

CLOSED LOOP CONTROL

Closed loop fuel control is selected when the engine is warm and the exhaust gas oxygen sensor exceeds its minimum operating temperature. The intake air/fuel ratio is controlled in a closed loop by measuring the exhaust gas at the exhaust manifold and altering the input fuel flow rate or the air entering the main metering systems (depending on the type of fuel system used).

ACCELERATION ENRICHMENT (OPEN LOOP)

During periods of heavy engine load, such as wide open acceleration, fuel control is adjusted to provide an enriched ratio to maximize engine power while neglecting fuel economy and emission.

The computer detects this condition by reading the throttle position sensor voltage or the MAP sensor. Low intake manifold vacuum or throttle position corresponds to heavy engine loads. The fuel control system controller responds by increasing the amount of fuel to enter the intake manifold or to decrease the amount of air in the main metering system. This

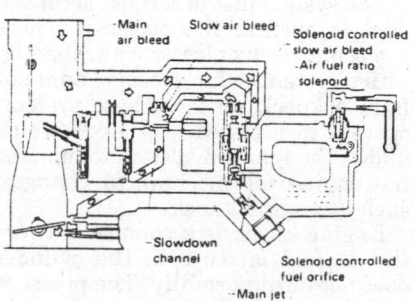

Feedback carburetor air flow

enrichment allows the engine to operate with a power greater than that allowed when emissions and fuel economy are controlled within specifications.

DECELERATION AND IDLE SPEED CONTROL (OPEN LOOP)

During periods of light engine load and high rpm, such as during closed throttle deceleration, coasting or engine idle, the engine requires a very lean air/fuel ratio to reduce excess emissions of HC and CO. Deceleration is indicated by a sudden increase in manifold vacuum and throttle position, indicating a closed throttle. When these conditions are detected by the processor, it computes a change in the amount of fuel required or amount of air entering the main or idle speed passages (depending on type of fuel system used). On certain engine applications with electronic fuel injection, the fuel may even be turned completely off during closed throttle deceleration.

Idle speed control is used to prevent engine stall during idle. The goal is to allow the engine to idle at as low an rpm as possible, yet keeping the engine from running rough and stalling when power takeoff accessories such as air conditioning compressor is turned on.

Turbocharging 26

DESCRIPTION

A turbocharger is an exhaust-driven turbine which drives a centrifugal compressor wheel. The compressor is usually located between the air cleaner and the engine's intake man-ifold, while the turbine is located between the exhaust manifold and the muffler. Primarily, the turbocharger compresses the air entering the engine, forcing more air into the cylinders. This allows the engine to efficiently burn more fuel, thereby producing more horsepower.

All of the exhaust gases pass through the turbine housing. The expansion of these gases, acting on the turbine wheel, causes it to turn. After passing through the turbine the exhaust gases are routed to the atmosphere through the exhaust system. On some non-automotive applications, the turbocharger provides sufficient muffling of the exhaust noises to eliminate the need for a muffler.

1. V-band coupling
2. Compressor housing
3. Bolt, turbine
4. Lockplate, turbine
5. Clamp, turbine
6. Turbine housing
7. Nut, shaft
8. Turbine shaft wheel
9. Compressor wheel
10. Lockplate, backplate
11. Bolt, backplate
12. Backplate (vaneless on some models)
13. O-ring (used on vaned backplate)
14. Seal ring
15. Seal spacer
16. Piston ring
17. Thrust collar
18. Inboard thrust washer
19. Bearing retainer
20. Bearing washer
21. Bearing
22. Center housing
23. Shroud, turbine
24. Drive screw
25. Nameplate
26. Piston ring, turbine
27. Pin

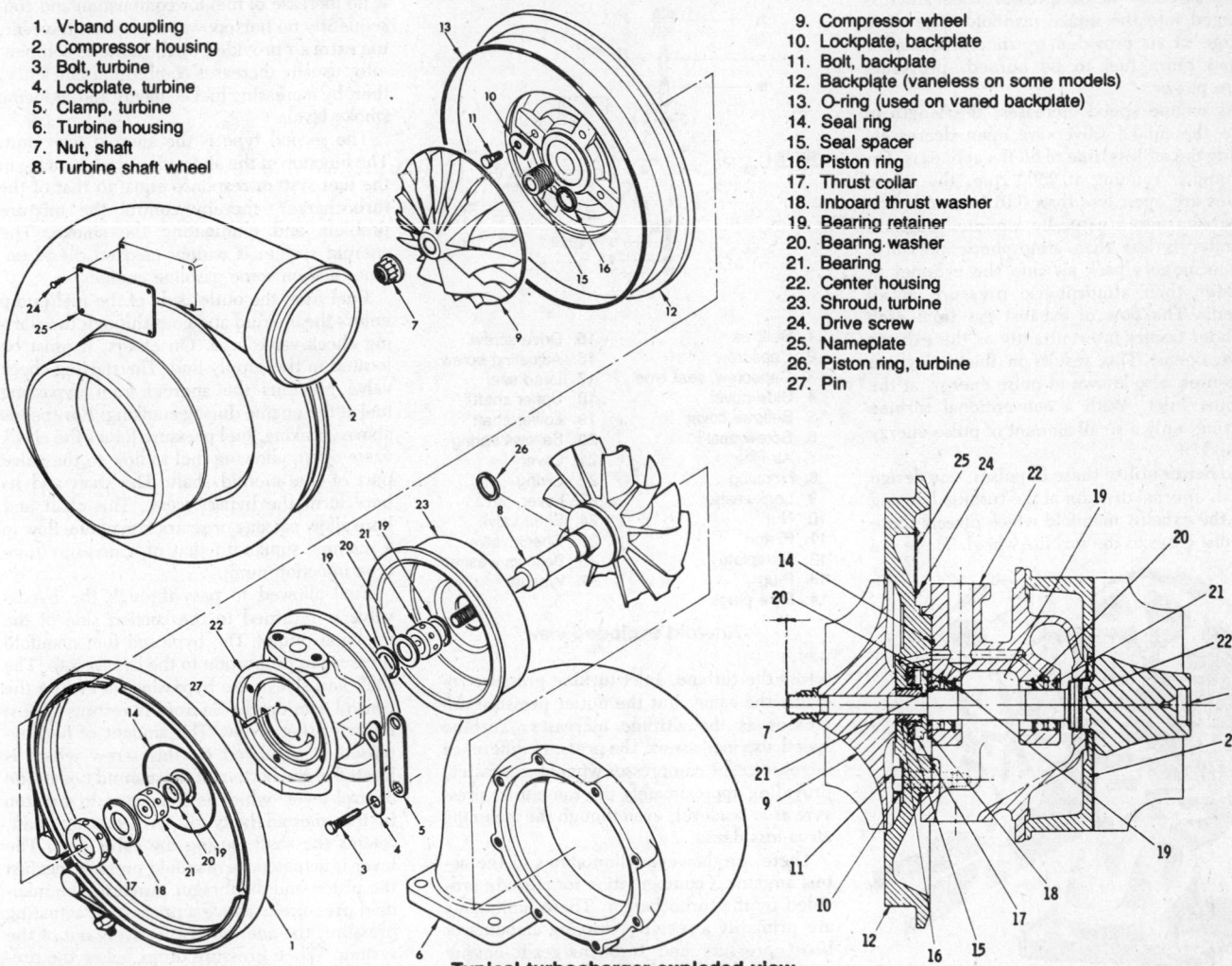

Typical turbocharger exploded view

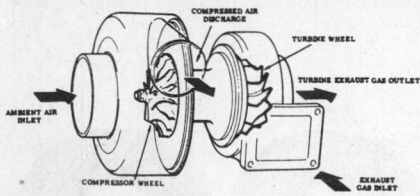

Typical turbocharger air flow schematic

The turbine also functions as a spark arrester. For example, the US Department of Agriculture recognizes the turbocharger as an adequate spark arrester for forestry operations.

OPERATION

The compressor and turbine are each enclosed in their own housings and are directly connected by a shaft. The housings are constructed of light alloy and are designed for maximum heat dissipation. The only power loss from the turbine to the compressor is the slight friction of the shaft journal bearings. Air is drawn in through the filtered intake system, compressed by the compressor wheel and discharged into the intake manifold. The extra charge of air provided by the turbocharger allows more fuel to be burned, providing more power.

As engine speed increases, the length of time the intake valves are open decreases, giving the air less time to fill the cylinders. On an engine running at 2500 rpm, the intake valves are open less than 0.017 second. The air drawn into a naturally aspirated engine's cylinder is less than atmospheric pressure. Turbochargers pack air into the cylinder at greater than atmospheric pressure at all speeds. The flow of exhaust gas from each cylinder occurs intermittantly as the exhaust valve opens. This results in fluctuating gas pressures, also known as pulse energy, at the turbine inlet. With a conventional turbine housing, only a small amount of pulse energy is used.

To better utilize these impulses, one design has an internal division in the turbine housing and the exhaust manifold which directs these exhaust gases to the turbine wheel. There is a

Altitude compensator

separate passage for each half of the engine cylinder exhaust.

On some four and six cylinder engines built to accommodate turbochargers, there is a separate passage for the front two or three cylinders and another for the rear half.

By using a fully divided exhaust system combined with a dual scroll turbine housing, the result is a highly effective nozzle velocity. This produces higher turbine speeds and manifold pressures than can be obtained with an undivided system.

At high altitudes, a naturally aspirated engine drops 3% in horsepower per 1000 feet elevation due to a 3% decrease in air density per 1000 feet.

With a turbocharged engine, an increase in altitude also increases the pressure drop

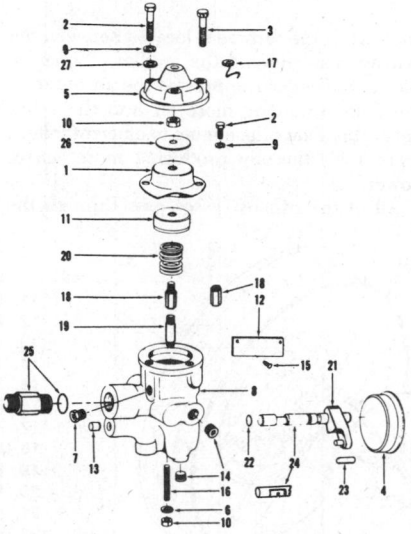

1. Bellows
2. Capscrew
3. Capscrew, seal type
4. Side cover
5. Bellows cover
6. Screw seal
7. Air filter
8. Housing
9. Lockwasher
10. Nut
11. Piston
12. Dataplate
13. Plug
14. Pipe plugs
15. Drive screw
16. Adjusting screw
17. Lead seal
18. Upper shaft
19. Lower shaft
20. Bellows spring
21. Lever
22. O-ring
23. Lever, pin
24. Shaft valve
25. Check valve
26. Bellows washer
27. Washer

Aneroid exploded view

across the turbine. Inlet turbine pressure remains the same, but the outlet pressure decreases as the altitude increases. Turbine speed also increases as the pressure difference increases. The compressor wheel turns faster, providing approximately the same inlet pressure as at sea level, even though the incoming air is less dense.

There are, however, limitations to the actual amount of compensation for altitude provided by the turbocharger. These limitations are primarily a result of varying amounts of boost pressure and turbocharger-to-engine match. To make up for the difference in altitude compensation, an altitude compensator

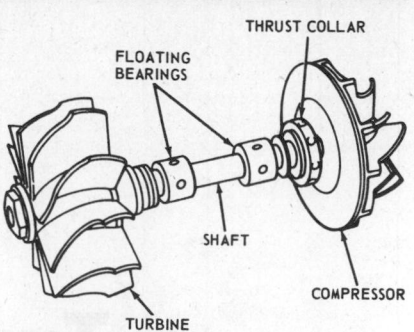

Basic parts of the turbocharger

is added to the system. During rapid acceleration or rapid engine load changes, the turbocharger speed, reflected in manifold pressure, inherently lags behind the power or fuel demand exercised by the opening of the throttle. This lag does not exist in the fuel system, so an overly rich mixture accompanied by heavy smoke occurs until the turbocharger catches up.

On diesel engines, two types of altitude compensators are used. One is a compressed air type which is very similar in appearance to the turbocharger. This type supplies compressed air to the intake manifold at a pressure about equal to sea level pressure. There is no increase of fuel for combustion and consequently no horsepower increase. However, the extra air provided by the altitude compensator usually increases combustion efficiency, thereby increasing fuel economy and reducing smoke levels.

The second type is the aneroid type unit. The function of the aneroid is to create a lag in the fuel system response equal to that of the turbocharger, thereby control the mixture problem and eliminating the smoke. The aneroid system is widely used on diesel engines and on some gasoline engines.

Fuel from the outlet side of the fuel pump enters the aneroid and goes through the starting check valve area. On others, it must be located in the supply line. The starting check valve prevents the aneroid from bypassing fuel at the engine during cranking. For speeds above cranking, fuel pressure forces the check valve open, allowing fuel to flow to the valve port of the aneroid shaft. The shaft and its bore form the bypass valve. This shaft and bore allow passage or restriction of fuel flow in a manner similar to that of a pressure/time type injection pump.

Fuel allowed to pass through the bypass valve is returned to the suction side of the injection pump. The bypassed fuel manifold pressure in proportion to the bypass rate. The shaft and sleeve are bypassing fuel when the control arm on the aneroid is resting against the adjusting screw. The amount of fuel bypassed is regulated by this screw which is located at the bottom of the aneroid body. The control lever, which is connected to a piston in the aneroid body by an actuating shaft, rotates the shaft closing the valve port. The lever is actuated by manifold pressure against the piston and diaphragm. Anytime the manifold pressure is above a present air actuating pressure, the aneroid is effectively out of the system. When pressure drops below the preset figure, the aneroid comes into the system.

In modern automotive gasoline engine applications with their stricter emission control standards, turbocharger lag is compensated for by means of modified spark control and/or an enrichment vacuum regulator system. The spark control system changes the ignition timing on demand and the vacuum regulator system regulates vacuum flow at the carburetor through a remote power enrichment port.

Some engines, particularly passenger car applications, in which boost pressure must be held at low levels, utilize a wastegate unit. Since turbocharger operation is self-perpetuating, unchecked operation will increase boost pressure beyond the operating capabilities of these engines. Some method of limiting this boost increases must be used. The principle means is by the inclusion of a wastegate in the system. The wastegate, usually located in the outlet elbow assembly, is activated when boost pressure reaches a predetermined level (usually 3-7 psi depending on application). The wastegate opens and bypasses exhaust flow around the turbine.

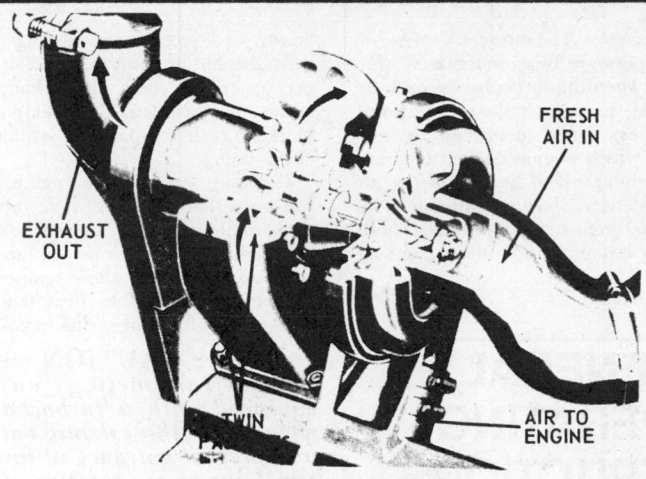

Twin passage turbine

LUBRICATION

Since turbine speeds routinely reach 140,000 rpm, adequate lubrication is vitally important. Turbochargers are lubricated by engine oil. Depending on the application, the lubrication may be either pressure-fed or gravity-fed. In areas of very heavy load or when shut-down after peak operation is routine, pressure feeding, sometimes with a separate oil pump, is used. In cases where a separate oil pump is used, the pump continues operating during spin-down. Since all parts of the rotating assemblies are protected by a film of oil, no metal-to-metal contact occurs. Consequently, no appreciable wear should occur. If a constant supply of clean engine oil is maintained, bearing life should be indefinite. If the unit has floating sleeve type bearings, they provide oil clearance between the bearing and housing as well as between the bearing and shaft. When the turbocharger is operating, this allows the bearing

to turn as the shaft turns. All clearances in the turbocharger are closely controlled and carefully machined. Any dirt in the oil will adversely affect service life of the working parts. Oil and filter changes should occur regularly. Some manufacturers recommend more frequent oil changes for turbocharged engines. In any case, on turbocharged engines, the oil filter(s) should ALWAYS be changed with the engine oil. ALWAYS use oil of the recommended viscosity for that particular engine application. Check the owner's manual for your engine or vehicle for recommended intervals and proper viscosity.

TWO-CYCLE APPLICATIONS

Turbochargers may be used in addition to the regular scavenging process. In these cases, the air is drawn into the blower or scavenging pump and then transferred to the turbocharger where it is compressed and forced into the engine.

At light loads, there is little energy available to drive the turbocharger. The mechanically driven blower alone supplies scavenging air to cylinders. At increased loads, the turbocharger speeds up and takes in a sufficient amount of additional air to allow the inlet

pressure to drop to atmospheric levels, causing the blower check valve to open. At this engine speed, the blower becomes unloaded, saving engine power, and the turbocharger enters the load range where it alone can provide scavenging and turbocharging. Under ideal conditions, the engine starting air contains enough energy to start the turbocharger and also supply enough air for combustion. In some applications, however, turbochargers can be equipped with additional methods for supplying necessary scavenging air while the engine is being started. This can be accomplished either mechanically by coupling the turbocharger to the crankshaft in such a manner that it is mechanically driven during starting and automatically disconnects when exhaust pressure is high enough or by jet air starting, where air is blown through jets into the turbocharger turbine or compressor. The air passing through the compressor also aids in scavenging during starting.

INTERCOOLERS

When the air passing through the compressor is compressed it becomes heated and expands. Expanding air is less dense, therefore less air is forced into the engine. This helps defeat the turbocharging process. To overcome this condition, some engine applications use a heat exchanger, also known as an inter-

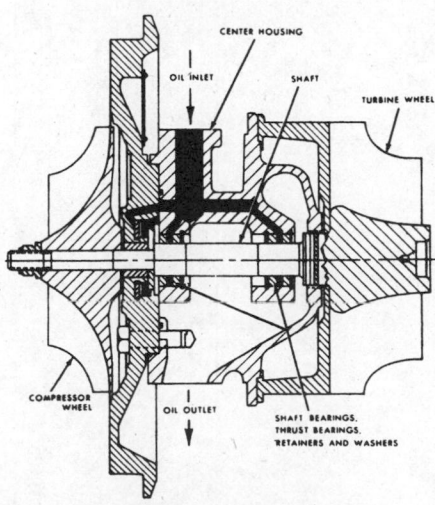

Turbocharger oil flow

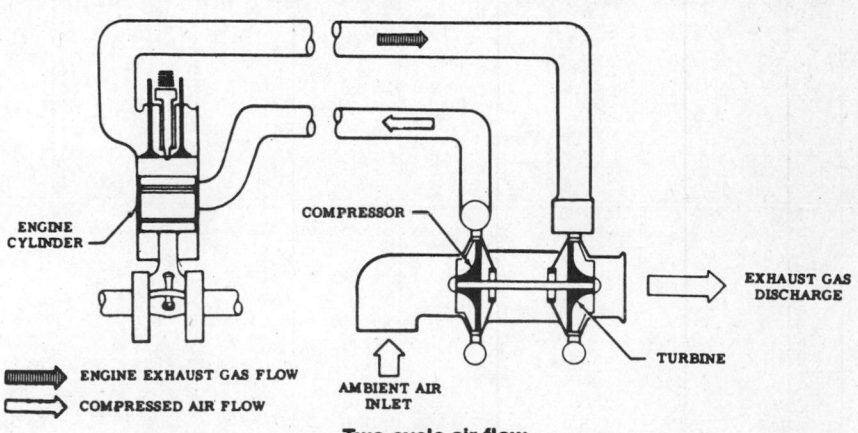

Two cycle air flow

cooler or after cooler. The intercooler reduces intake air temperature by as much as 90° F.

Located between the turbocharger and the intake manifold, the intercooler is a series of connected tubes, finned to provide dissipation, through which engine coolant is circulated. The carrying off of heat from the air makes the air denser, allowing more air to be forced into the engine. This provides more power, greater economy and quieter combustion.

GENERAL OPERATING INSTRUCTIONS FOR TURBOCHARGED ENGINES

1. After starting the engine, make sure there is sufficient oil pressure before accelerating or applying load.
2. When starting in cold weather, allow the engine to run a sufficient length of time (up to five minutes for diesel engines in extreme cold) before applying load or accelerating. This will insure adequate lubrication.
3. Should the engine stall at normal operating temperature, restart it immediately. This will prevent a rapid rise in the turbocharger

known as "temperature soaking". Also, the turbocharger, running hot during operation, may experience coking due to hot oil build-up in the center section. This coking will cause a blockage of the oil passages leading to failure of the unit.

4. Before stopping the engine, allow it to run for a short length of time (up to two or three minutes for some diesels) to allow internal engine temperatures to normalize or equalize. Failure to allow temperature normalization can lead to heat fatigue and/or blockage of oil passages due to coking.

CAUTION

When transporting an engine equipped with a turbocharger, always cover the exhaust outlet. This will prevent entrance of foreign material and/or the rotation of the turbine. Turbine rotation on a stopped engine could lead to bearing failure since no lubricating oil will be provided.

PREVENTIVE MAINTENANCE

1. Inspect all mountings and connections regularly to make sure they are secure and no leakage is present.
2. Make certain that there is no restriction in air flow at the crankcase ventilation system.

3. Run the engine at various, normal operating speeds and listen for unusual noises at the turbocharger.

Turbochargers normally emit a shrill whistle or whine. Bearings about to fail also emit a shrill whine, somewhat different from normal turbocharger noise. Try to distinguish between the two.

NOTE: After engine shut-off, the turbocharger will whine during rundown. Don't confuse this with bearing failure noise. Grating or scraping noises could indicate improper turbine or compressor wheel-to-housing clearances. If any such noises are heard, the unit should be removed for inspection.

4. Check the unit for unusual vibrations during operation.
5. Check for unusual smoking under load conditions. Excessive smoke means an incorrect air/fuel ratio.
6. Inspect and replace the air filter according to your owner's manual recommendations.

TROUBLE-SHOOTING

The turbocharger is a relatively simple unit. Most problems occur in other parts of the engine such as the lubrication system or the fuel system. With proper routine maintenance, the unit should give troublefree operation.

Engine Rebuilding 27

This section describes, in detail, the procedures involved in rebuilding a typical engine. The procedures are basically identical to those used in rebuilding engines of nearly all design and configurations.

The section is divided into two parts. The first, Cylinder Head Reconditioning, assumes that the cylinder head is removed from the engine, all manifolds are removed, and the cylinder head is on a workbench. The camshaft should be removed from overhead cam cylinder heads. The second section, Cylinder Block Reconditioning, covers the block, pistons, connecting rods and crankshaft. It is assumed that the engine is mounted on a work stand, and the cylinder head and all accessories are removed.

Procedures are identified as follows:

Unmarked—Basic procedures that must be performed in order to successfully complete the rebuilding process.

Starred (*)—Procedures that should be performed to ensure maximum performance and engine life.

Double starred (**)—Procedures that may be performed to increase engine performance and reliability.

In many cases, a choice of methods is also provided. Methods are identified in the same manner as procedures. The choice of method for a procedure is at the discretion of the user.

The tools required for the basic rebuilding procedure should, with minor exceptions, be those included in a mechanic's tool kit. An accurate torque wrench, and a dial indicator (reading in thousandths) mounted on a universal base should be available. Special tools, where required, all are readily available from the major tool suppliers. The services of a competent automotive machine shop must also be readily available.

When assembling the engine, any parts that will be in frictional contact must be prelubricated, to provide protection on initial start-up. Any product specifically formulated for this purpose may be used. NOTE: *Do not use engine oil*. Where semi-permanent (locked but removable) installation of bolts or nuts is desired, threads should be cleaned and coated with Loctite® or a similar product (non-hardening).

Aluminum has become increasingly popular for use in engines, due to its low weight and excellent heat transfer characteristics. The following precautions must be observed when handling aluminum engine parts:

—Never hot-tank aluminum parts.

—Remove all aluminum parts (identification tags, etc.) from engine parts before hot-tanking (otherwise they will be removed during the process).

—Always coat threads lightly with engine oil or anti-seize compounds before installation, to prevent seizure.

—Never over-torque bolts or spark plugs in aluminum threads. Should stripping occur, threads can be restored using any of a number of thread repair kits available (see next section).

Magnaflux and Zyglo are inspection techniques used to locate material flaws, such as stress cracks. Magnafluxing coats the part with fine magnetic particles, and subjects the part to a magnetic field. Cracks cause breaks in the magnetic field, which are outlined by the particles. Since Magnaflux is a magnetic process, it is applicable only to ferrous materials. The Zyglo process coats the material with a fluorescent dye penetrant, and then subjects it to blacklight inspection, under which cracks glow brightly. Parts made of any material may be tested using Zyglo. While Magnaflux and Zyglo are excellent for general inspection, and locating hidden defects, specific checks of suspected cracks may be made at lower cost and more readily using spot check dye. The dye is sprayed onto the suspected area, wiped off, and the area is then sprayed with a developer. Cracks then will show up brightly. Spot check dyes will only indicate surface cracks; therefore, structural cracks below the surface may escape detection. When questionable, the part should be tested using Magnaflux or Zyglo.

REPAIRING DAMAGED THREADS

Several methods of repairing damaged threads are available. Heli-Coil® (shown here), Keenserts® and Microdot® are among the most widely used. All involve basically the same principle—drilling out stripped threads, tapping the hole and installing a prewound insert— making welding, plugging and oversize fasteners unnecessary.

Two types of thread repair inserts are usually supplied—a standard type for most Inch Coarse, Inch Fine, Metric Coarse and Metric Fine thread sizes and a spark plug type to fit most spark plug port sizes. Consult the individual manufacturer's catalog to determine exact applications. Typical thread repair kits will contain a selection of prewound threaded inserts, a tap (corresponding to the outside diameter threads of the insert) and an installation tool. Most manufacturers also supply blister-packed thread repair inserts separately and a master kit with a variety of taps and inserts plus installation tools.

Before effecting a repair to a threaded hole, remove any snapped, broken or damaged bolts or studs. Penetrating oil can be used to free frozen threads; the offending item can be removed with locking pliers or with a screw or stud extractor. After the hole is clear, the thread can be repaired as follows.

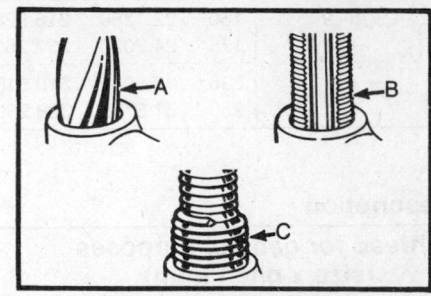

A. Drill out the damaged threads with the specified drill. Drill completely through the hole or to the bottom of a blind hole.

B. With the tap supplied tap the hole to receive the threaded insert. Keep the tap well oiled and back it out frequently to avoid clogging the threads.

C. Screw the threaded insert onto the installation tool until the tang engages the slot. Screw the insert into the tapped hole until it is ¼–½ turn below the top surface. After installation, break the tang off with a hammer and punch.

STANDARD TORQUE SPECIFICATIONS AND CAPSCREW MARKINGS

Newton-Meter has been designated as the world standard for measuring torque and will gradually replace the foot-pound and kilogram-meter torque measuring standard. Torquing tools are still being manufactured with foot-pounds and kilogram-meter scales, along with the new Newton-Meter standard. To assist the repairman, foot-pounds, kilogram-meter and Newton-Meter are listed in the following charts, and should be followed as applicable.

U.S. BOLTS

SAE Grade Number	1 or 2			5			6 or 7			8		
Capscrew Head Markings Manufacturer's marks may vary. Three-line markings on heads below indicate SAE Grade 5. 	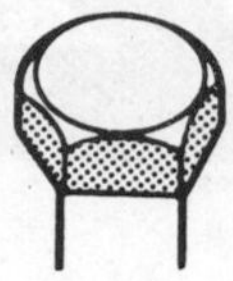						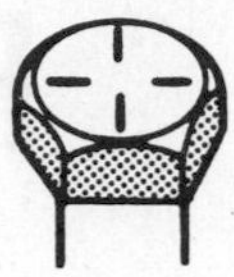					
Usage	Used Frequently			Used Frequently			Used at Times			Used at Times		
Quality of Material	Indeterminate			Minimum Commercial			Medium Commercial			Best Commercial		
Capacity Body Size	Torque			Torque			Torque			Torque		
(inches)–(thread)	Ft-Lb	kgm	Nm	Ft-Lb	kgm	Nm	Ft-Lb	kgm	Nm	Ft-Lb	kgm	Nm
1/4–20	5	0.6915	6.7791	8	1.1064	10.8465	10	1.3630	13.5582	12	1.6596	16.2698
–28	6	0.8298	8.1349	10	1.3830	13.5582				14	1.9362	18.9815
5/16–18	11	1.5213	14.9140	17	2.3511	23.0489	19	2.6277	25.7605	24	3.3192	32.5396
–24	13	1.7979	17.6256	19	2.6277	25.7605				27	3.7341	36.6071
3/8–16	18	2.4894	24.4047	31	4.2873	42.0304	34	4.7022	46.0978	44	6.0852	59.6560
–24	20	2.7660	27.1164	35	4.8405	47.4536				49	6.7767	66.4351
7/16–14	28	3.8132	37.9629	49	6.7767	66.4351	55	7.6065	74.5700	70	9.6810	94.9073
–20	30	4.1490	40.6745	55	7.6065	74.5700				78	10.7874	105.7538
1/2–13	39	5.3937	52.8769	75	10.3725	101.6863	85	11.7555	115.2445	105	14.5215	142.3609
–20	41	5.6703	55.5885	85	11.7555	115.2445				120	16.5860	162.6960
9/16–12	51	7.0533	69.1467	110	15.2130	149.1380	120	16.5960	162.6960	155	21.4365	210.1490
–18	55	7.6065	74.5700	120	16.5960	162.6960				170	23.5110	230.4860
5/8–11	83	11.4789	112.5329	150	20.7450	203.3700	167	23.0961	226.4186	210	29.0430	284.7180
–18	95	13.1385	128.8027	170	23.5110	230.4860				240	33.1920	325.3920
3/4–10	105	14.5215	142.3609	270	37.3410	366.0660	280	38.7240	379.6240	375	51.8625	508.4250
–16	115	15.9045	155.9170	295	40.7985	399.9610				420	58.0860	568.4360
7/8–9	160	22.1280	216.9280	395	54.6285	535.5410	440	60.8520	596.5520	605	83.6715	820.2590
–14	175	24.2025	237.2650	435	60.1605	589.7730				675	93.3525	915.1650
1–8	236	32.5005	318.6130	590	81.5970	799.9220	660	91.2780	894.8280	910	125.8530	1233.7780
–14	250	34.5750	338.9500	660	91.2780	849.8280				990	136.9170	1342.2420

METRIC BOLTS

Description — Torque ft-lbs. (Nm)

Thread for general purposes (size x pitch (mm))	Head Mark 4		Head Mark 7	
6 x 1.0	2.2 to 2.9	(3.0 to 3.9)	3.6 to 5.8	(4.9 to 7.8)
8 x 1.25	5.8 to 8.7	(7.9 to 12)	9.4 to 14	(13 to 19)
10 x 1.25	12 to 17	(16 to 23)	20 to 29	(27 to 39)
12 x 1.25	21 to 32	(29 to 43)	35 to 53	(47 to 72)
14 x 1.5	35 to 52	(48 to 70)	57 to 85	(77 to 110)
16 x 1.5	51 to 77	(67 to 100)	90 to 120	(130 to 160)
18 x 1.5	74 tc 110	(100 to 150)	130 to 170	(180 to 230)
20 x 1.5	110 to 140	(150 to 190)	190 to 240	(160 to 320)
22 x 1.5	150 to 190	(200 to 260)	250 to 320	(340 to 430)
24 x 1.5	190 to 240	(260 to 320)	310 to 410	(420 to 550)

CAUTION: Bolts threaded into aluminum require much less torque

NOTE: This engine rebuilding section is a guide to accepted rebuilding procedures. Typical examples of standard rebuilding procedures are illustrated.

CYLINDER HEAD RECONDITIONING

Procedure	Method
Identify the valves:	Invert the cylinder head, and number the valve faces front to rear, using a permanent felt-tip marker.
Remove the rocker arms (OHV engines only):	Remove the rocker arms with shaft(s) or balls and nuts. Wire the sets of rockers, balls and nuts together, and identify according to the corresponding valve.
Remove the camshaft (OHC engines only):	See the engine service procedures earlier in this book for details concerning specific engines.
Remove the valves and springs:	Using an appropriate valve spring compressor (depending on the configuration of the cylinder head), compress the valve springs. Lift out the keepers with needlenose pliers, release the compressor, and remove the valve, spring, and spring retainer.
Remove glow plugs and fuel injectors (Diesel engines only):	Label and remove all fuel injectors and glow plugs from the head. Glow plugs unscrew. See the appropriate car section for injector removal. Inspect glow plugs for bulges, cracks or signs of melting. Clean injector tips with a steel brush, then inspect for evidence of melting.
Remove pre-combustion chamber inserts (Diesel engines only): 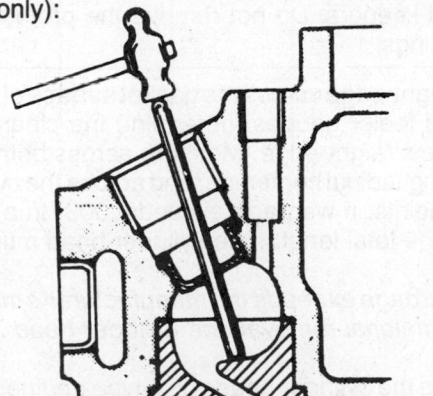 Removing pre-combustion chamber with a drift (© G.M. Corp.)	**Remove the pre-combustion chambers using a hammer and a thin, blunt brass drift, inserted through the injector hole (or glow plug hole, whichever is more convenient). If chamber is to be reused, carefully remove all carbon from it. NOTE: *Remove chamber only if being replaced, if a glow plug tip has broken off and must be removed, or if chamber is obviously damaged or loose.*
Check the valve stem-to-guide clearance: 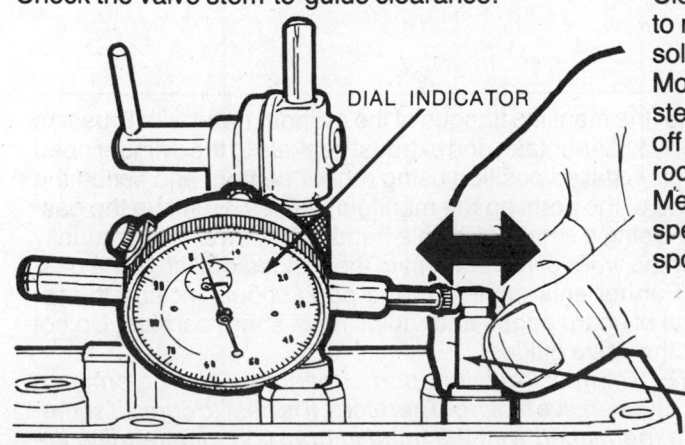 DIAL INDICATOR — VALVE STEM — Checking the valve stem-to-guide clearance	Clean the valve stem with lacquer thinner or a similar solvent to remove all gum and varnish. Clean the valve guides using solvent and an expanding wire-type valve guide cleaner. Mount a dial indicator so that the stem is at 90° to the valve stem, as close to the valve guide as possible. Move the valve off its seat, and measure the valve guide-to-stem clearance by rocking the stem back and forth to actuate the dial indicator. Measure the valve stems using a micrometer, and compare to specifications, to determine whether stem or guide wear is responsible for excessive clearance.

CYLINDER HEAD RECONDITIONING

Procedure	Method
De-carbon the cylinder head and valves:	Chip carbon away from the valve heads, combustion chambers, and ports, using a chisel made of hardwood. Remove the remaining deposits with a stiff wire brush. NOTE: *Ensure that the deposits are actually removed, rather than burnished.*

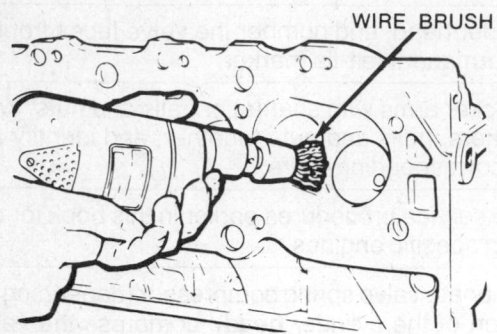

WIRE BRUSH

Removing carbon from the cylinder head

Procedure	Method
Hot-tank the cylinder head (cast iron heads only): CAUTION: *Do not hot-tank aluminum parts.*	Have the cylinder head hot-tanked to remove grease, corrosion, and scale from the water passages. NOTE: *In the case of overhead cam cylinder heads, consult the operator to determine whether the camshaft bearings will be damaged by the caustic solution.*
Degrease the remaining cylinder head parts:	Using solvent (i.e., Gunk), clean the rockers, rocker shaft(s) (where applicable), rocker balls and nuts, springs, spring retainers, and keepers. Do not remove the protective coating from the springs.
Check the cylinder head for warpage:	Place a straight-edge across the gasket surface of the cylinder head. Using feeler gauges, determine the clearance at the center of the straight-edge. Measure across both diagonals, along the longitudinal centerline, and across the cylinder head at several points. If warpage exceeds .003′ in a 6′ span, or .006′ over the total length, the cylinder head must be resurfaced. NOTE: *If warpage exceeds the manufacturer's maximum tolerance for material removal, the cylinder head must be replaced.* When milling the cylinder heads of V-type engines, the intake manifold mounting position is altered, and must be corrected by milling the manifold flange a proportionate amount.

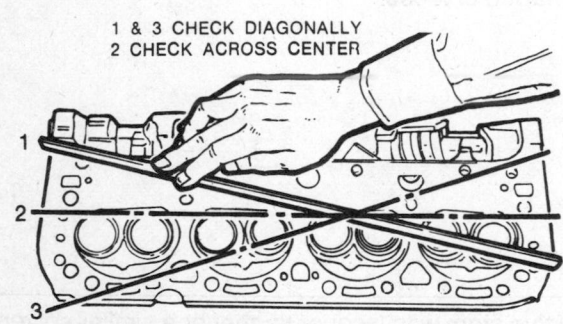

1 & 3 CHECK DIAGONALLY
2 CHECK ACROSS CENTER

Checking cylinder head for warpage

Procedure	Method
**Porting and gasket matching:	**Coat the manifold flanges of the cylinder head with Prussian blue dye. Glue intake and exhaust gaskets to the cylinder head in their installed position using rubber cement and scribe the outline of the ports on the manifold flanges. Remove the gaskets. Using a small cutter in a hand-held power tool gradually taper the walls of the port out to the scribed outline of the gasket. Further enlargement of the ports should include the removal of sharp edges and radiusing of sharp corners. Do not alter the valve guides. NOTE: *The most efficient port configuration is determined only by extensive testing. Therefore, it is best to consult someone experienced with the head in question to determine the optimum alterations.*

CYLINDER HEAD RECONDITIONING

Procedure / **Method**

*Knurling the valve guides:

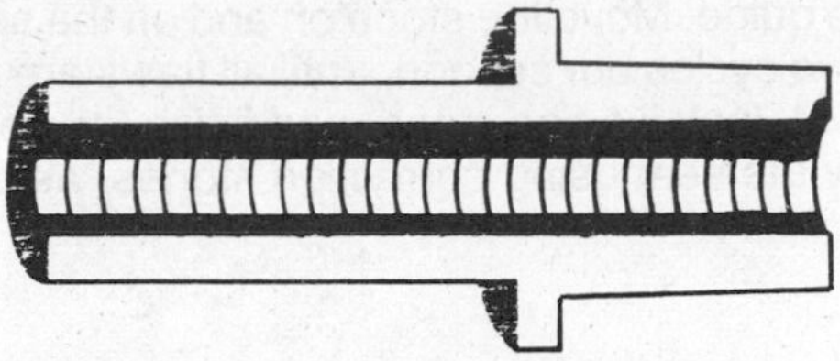

Cut-away view of a knurled valve guide

*Valve guides which are not excessively worn or distorted may, in some cases, be knurled rather than replaced. Knurling is a process in which metal is displaced and raised, thereby reducing clearance. Knurling also provides excellent oil control. The possibility of knurling rather than replacing valve guides should be discussed with a machinist.

Replacing the valve guides:

NOTE: *Valve guides should only be replaced if damaged or if an oversize valve stem is not available.*

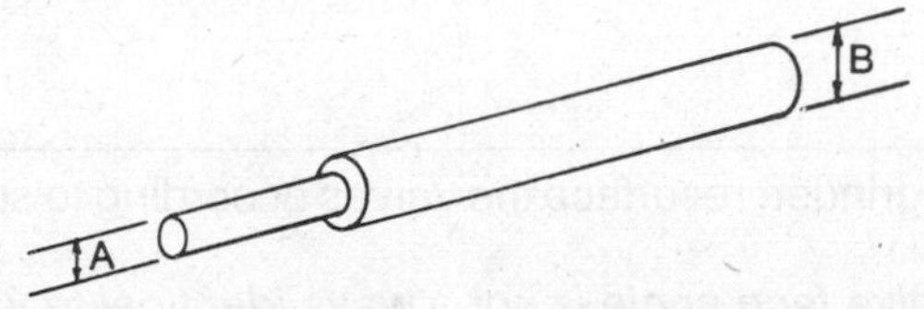
B
A
A—VALVE GUIDE I.D.
B—LARGER THAN THE VALVE GUIDE O.D.

Valve guide removal tool

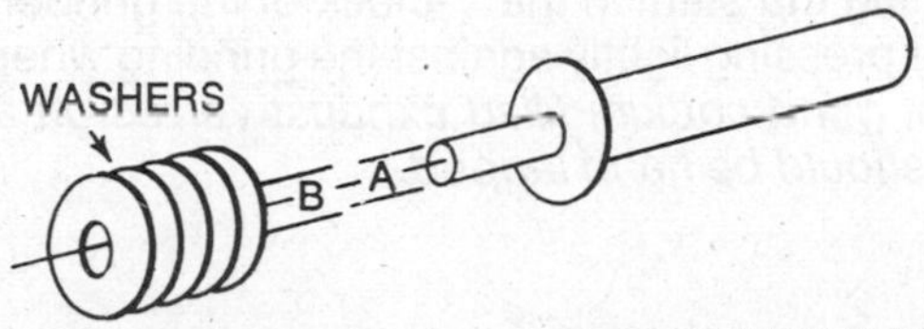
WASHERS
B
A
A—VALVE GUIDE I.D.
B—LARGER THAN THE VALVE GUIDE O.D.

Valve guide installation tool (with washers used for installation)

Depending on the type of cylinder head, valve guides may be pressed, hammered, or shrunk in. In cases where the guides are shrunk into the head, replacement should be left to an equipped machine shop. In other cases, the guides are replaced as follows: Press or tap the valve guides out of the head using a stepped drift (see illustration). Determine the height above the boss that the guide must extend, and obtain a stack of washers, their I.D. similar to the guide's O.D., of that height. Place the stack of washers on the guide, and insert the guide into the boss.

NOTE: *Valve guides are often tapered or beveled for installation.*

Using the stepped installation tool (see illustration), press or tap the guides into position. Ream the guides according to the size of the valve stem.

Replacing valve seat inserts:

Replacement of valve seat inserts which are worn beyond resurfacing or broken, if feasible, must be done by a machine shop.

Resurfacing the valve seats using reamers:

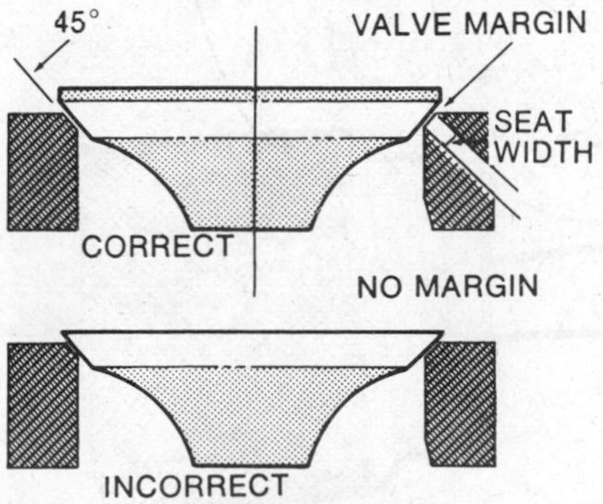
45°
VALVE MARGIN
SEAT WIDTH
CORRECT
NO MARGIN
INCORRECT

Valve seat width and centering

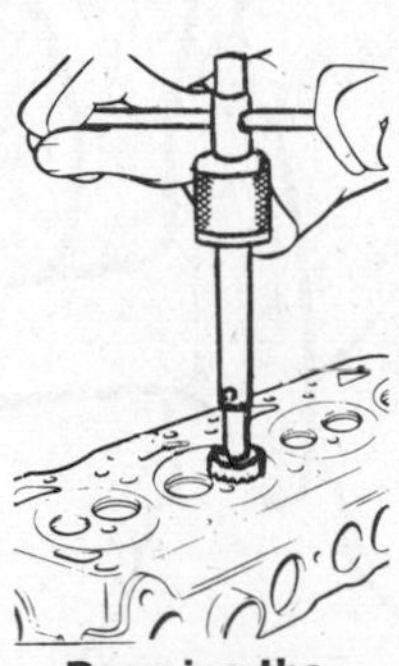

Reaming the valve seat

Select a reamer of the correct seat angle, slightly larger than the diameter of the valve seat, and assemble it with a pilot of the correct size. Install the pilot into the valve guide, and using steady pressure, turn the reamer clockwise.

CAUTION: *Do not turn the reamer counterclockwise.*

Remove only as much material as necessary to clean the seat. Check the concentricity of the seat (see below). If the dye method is not used, coat the valve face with Prussian blue dye, install and rotate it on the valve seat. Using the dye marked area as a centering guide, center and narrow the valve seat to specifications with correction cutters.

NOTE: *When no specifications are available, minimum seat width for exhaust valves should be 5/64", intake valves 1/16".*

After making correction cuts, check the position of the valve seat on the valve face using Prussian blue dye.

NOTE: *Do not cut induction hardened seats; they must be ground.*

CYLINDER HEAD RECONDITIONING

Procedure	Method

*Resurfacing the valve seats using a grinder:

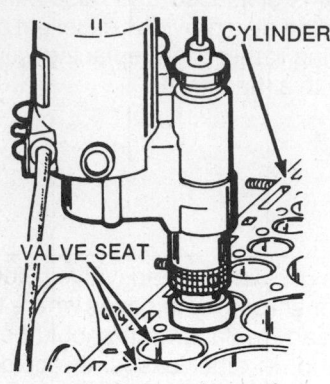

Grinding a valve seat

*Select a pilot of the correct size, and a coarse stone of the correct seat angle. Lubricate the pilot if necessary, and install the tool in the valve guide. Move the stone on and off the seat at approximately two cycles per second, until all flaws are removed from the seat. Install a fine stone, and finish the seat. Center and narrow the seat using correction stones, as described above.

Resurfacing (grinding) the valve face:

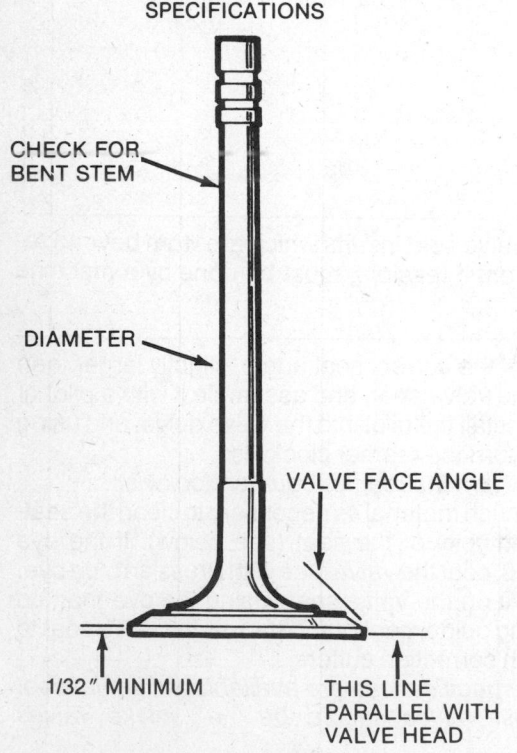

FOR DIMENSIONS, REFER TO SPECIFICATIONS

CHECK FOR BENT STEM

DIAMETER

VALVE FACE ANGLE

1/32" MINIMUM

THIS LINE PARALLEL WITH VALVE HEAD

Critical valve dimensions

Using a valve grinder, resurface the valves according to specifications.
CAUTION: *Valve face angle is not always identical to valve seat angle.*
A minimum margin of 1/32" should remain after grinding the valve. The valve stem top should also be squared and resurfaced, by placing the stem in the V-block of the grinder, and turning it while pressing lightly against the grinding wheel.
NOTE: *Do not grind sodium filled exhaust valves on a machine. These should be hand lapped.*

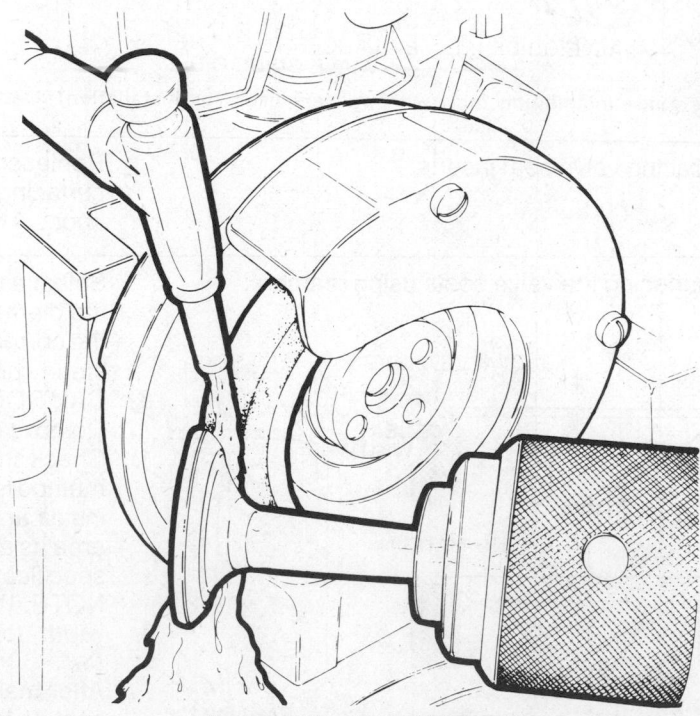

Valve grinding by machine

CYLINDER HEAD RECONDITIONING

Procedure	Method

Checking the valve seat concentricity:

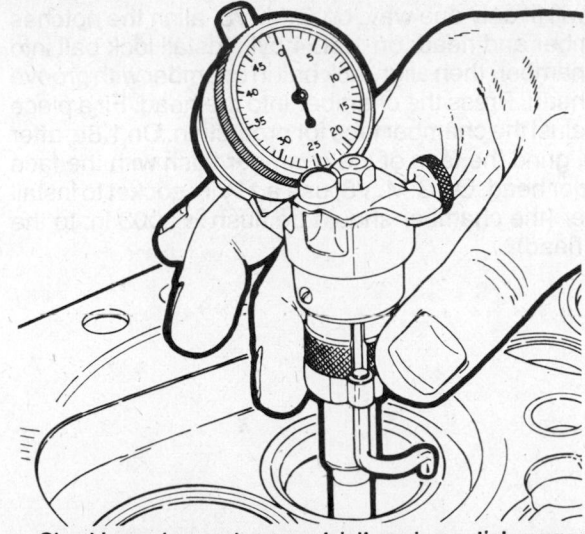

Checking valve seat concentricity using a dial gauge

Coat the valve face with Prussian blue dye, install the valve, and rotate it on the valve seat. If the entire seat becomes coated, and the valve is known to be concentric, the seat is concentric.

*Install the dial gauge pilot into the guide, and rest the arm on the valve seat. Zero the gauge, and rotate the arm around the seat. Run-out should not exceed .002″.

---

*Lapping the valves:
NOTE: *Valve lapping is done to ensure efficient sealing of resurfaced valves and seats.*

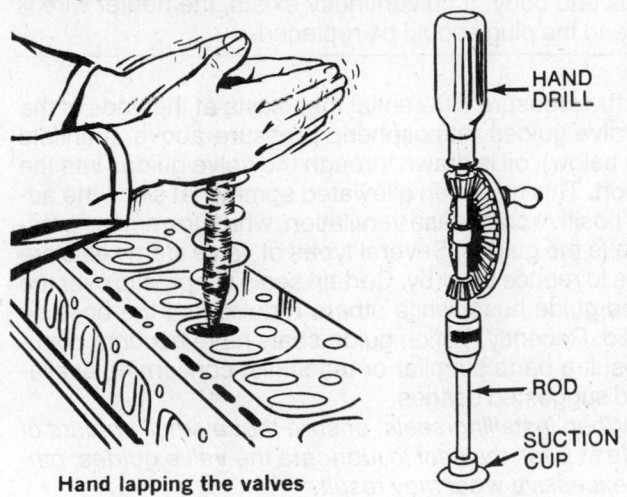

HAND DRILL

ROD

SUCTION CUP

Hand lapping the valves

Home made mechanical valve lapping tool

*Invert the cylinder head, lightly lubricate the valve stems, and install the valves in the head as numbered. Coat valve seats with fine grinding compound, and attach the lapping tool suction cup to a valve head.
NOTE: *Moisten the suction cup.*
Rotate the tool between the palms, changing position and lifting the tool often to prevent grooving. Lap the valve until a smooth, polished seat is evident. Remove the valve and tool, and rinse away all traces of grinding compound.
**Fasten a suction cup to a piece of drill rod, and mount the rod in a hand drill. Proceed as above, using the hand drill as a lapping tool.
CAUTION: *Due to the higher speeds involved when using the hand drill, care must be exercised to avoid grooving the seat.* Lift the tool and change direction of rotation often.

Check the valve springs:

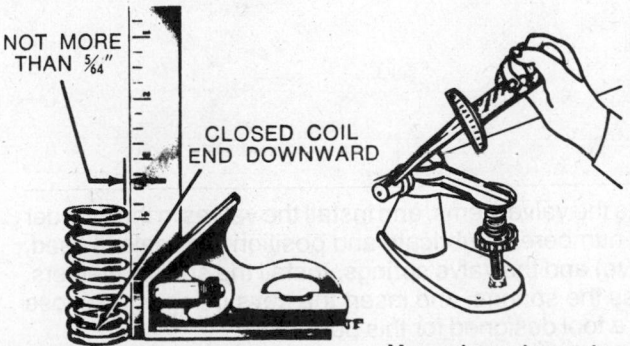

NOT MORE THAN 5/64″

CLOSED COIL END DOWNWARD

Checking valve spring free length and squareness

Measuring valve spring test pressure

Place the spring on a flat surface next to a square. Measure the height of the spring, and rotate it against the edge of the square to measure distortion. If spring height varies (by comparison) by more than 1/16″ or if distortion exceeds 1/16″, replace the spring.
**In addition to evaluating the spring as above, test the spring pressure at the installed and compressed (installed height minus valve lift) height using a valve spring tester. Springs used on small displacement engines (up to 3 liters) should be ∓ 1 lb. of all other springs in either position. A tolerance of ∓ 5 lbs. is permissible on larger engines.

CYLINDER HEAD RECONDITIONING

Procedure	Method
Install pre-combustion chambers (Diesel engines only)	Pre-combustion chambers are press-fit into the head. The chambers will fit only one way: on G.M. V8, align the notches in the chamber and head; on 1.8L 4 cyl., install lock ball into groove in chamber, then align lock ball in chamber with groove in cylinder head. Press the chamber into the head. Fit a piece of metal against the chamber face for protection. On 1.8L, after installation, grind the face of the chamber flush with the face of the cylinder head. On G.M. V8, use a 1¼ in. socket to install the chamber (the chamber should be flush ± .003 in. to the face of the head).

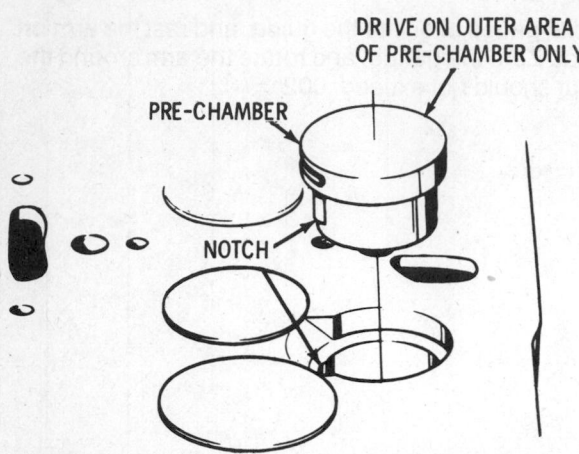

DRIVE ON OUTER AREA OF PRE-CHAMBER ONLY

PRE-CHAMBER

NOTCH

Align the notches to install the pre-combustion chamber (© G.M. Corp.)

Install fuel injectors and glow plugs (Diesel engines)	Before installing glow plugs, check for continuity across plug terminals and body. If no continuity exists, the heater wire is broken and the plug should be replaced.
*Install valve stem seals:	*Due to the pressure differential that exists at the ends of the intake valve guides (atmospheric pressure above, manifold vacuum below), oil is drawn through the valve guides into the intake port. This has been alleviated somewhat since the addition of positive crankcase ventilation, which lowers the pressure above the guides. Several types of valve stem seals are available to reduce blow-by. Certain seals simply slip over the stem and guide boss, while others require that the boss be machined. Recently, Teflon guide seals have become popular. Consult a parts supplier or machinist concerning availability and suggested usages. NOTE: *When installing seals, ensure that a small amount of oil is able to pass the seal to lubricate the valve guides; otherwise, excessive wear may result.*

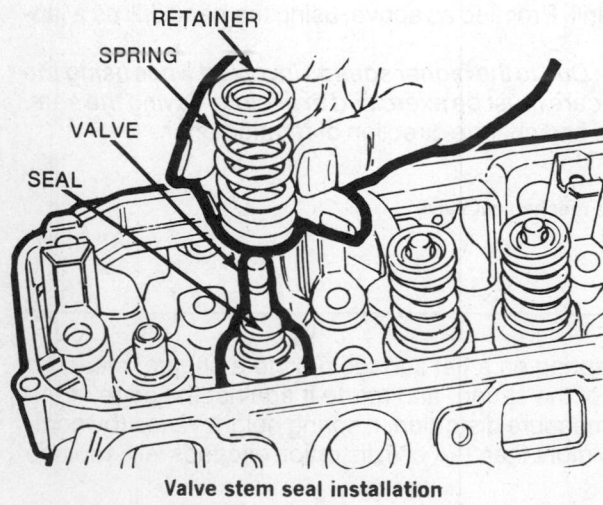

RETAINER

SPRING

VALVE

SEAL

Valve stem seal installation

Install the valves:	Lubricate the valve stems, and install the valves in the cylinder head as numbered. Lubricate and position the seals (if used, see above) and the valve springs. Install the spring retainers, compress the springs, and insert the keys using needlenose pliers or a tool designed for this purpose. NOTE: *Retain the keys with wheel bearing grease during installation.*

CYLINDER HEAD RECONDITIONING

Procedure	Method

Check valve spring installed height:

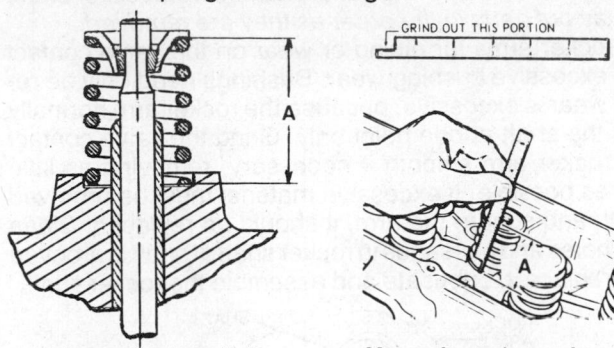

Valve spring installed height dimension

Measuring valve spring installed height

Measure the distance between the spring pad and the lower edge of the spring retainer, and compare to specifications. If the installed height is incorrect, add shim washers between the spring pad and the spring.
CAUTION: *Use only washers designed for this purpose.*

Install the camshaft (OHC engines only) and check end play:

See the engine service procedures earlier in this book for details concerning specific engines.

Inspect the rocker arms, balls, studs, and nuts (OHV engines only):

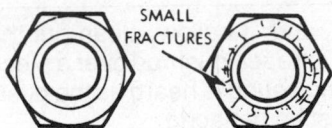

Stress cracks in the rocker nuts

Visually inspect the rocker arms, balls, studs, and nuts for cracks, galling, burning, scoring or wear. If all parts are intact, liberally lubricate the rocker arms and balls, and install them on the cylinder head. If wear is noted on a rocker arm at the point of valve contact, grind it smooth and square, removing as little material as possible. Replace the rocker arm if excessively worn. If a rocker stud shows signs of wear, it must be replaced (see below). If a rocker nut shows stress cracks, replace it. If an exhaust ball is galled or burned, substitute the intake ball from the same cylinder (if it is intact), and install a new intake ball.
NOTE: *Avoid using new rocker balls on exhaust valves.*

Replacing rocker studs (OHV engines only):

AS STUB BEGINS TO PULL UP, IT WILL BE NECESSARY TO REMOVE THE NUT AND ADD MORE WASHERS

3/8" NUT

FLAT WASHERS

Extracting a pressed-in rocker stud

In order to remove a threaded stud, lock two nuts on the stud, and unscrew the stud using the lower nut. Coat the lower threads of the new stud with Loctite®, and install.

Two alternative methods are available for replacing pressed in studs. Remove the damaged stud using a stack of washers and a nut (see illustration). In the first, the boss is reamed .005–.006" oversize, and an oversize stud pressed in. Control the stud extension over the boss using washers, in the same manner as valve guides. Before installing the stud, coat it with white lead and grease. To retain the stud more positively drill a hole through the stud and boss, and install a roll pin. In the second method, the boss is tapped, and a threaded stud installed. Retain the stud using Loctite® Stud and Bearing Mount.

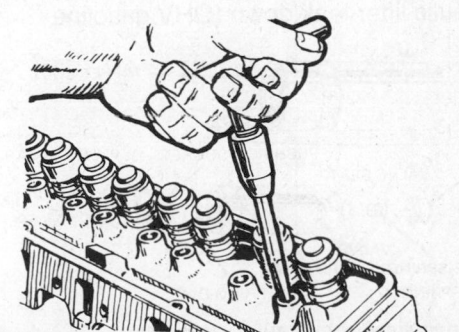

Reaming the stud bore for oversize rocker studs

CYLINDER HEAD RECONDITIONING

Procedure	Method

Inspect the rocker shaft(s) and rocker arms (OHV engines only):

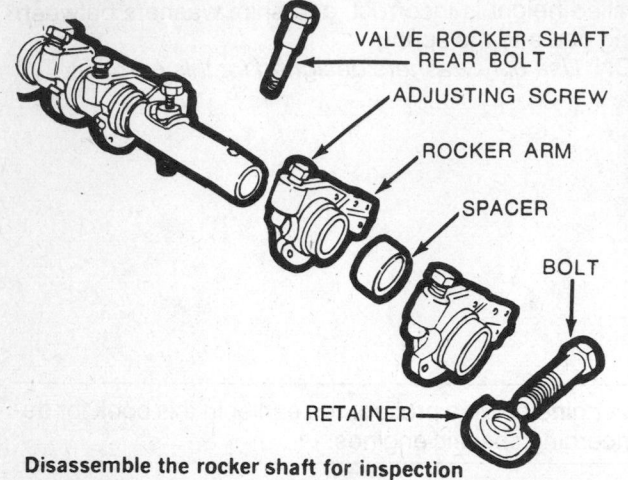

VALVE ROCKER SHAFT REAR BOLT

ADJUSTING SCREW

ROCKER ARM

SPACER

BOLT

RETAINER

Disassemble the rocker shaft for inspection

Remove rocker arms, springs and washers from rocker shaft. NOTE: *Lay out parts in the order as they are removed.* Inspect rocker arms for pitting or wear on the valve contact point, or excessive bushing wear. Bushings need only be replaced if wear is excessive, because the rocker arm normally contacts the shaft at one point only. Grind the valve contact point of rocker arm smooth if necessary, removing as little material as possible. If excessive material must be removed to smooth and square the arm, it should be replaced. Clean out all oil holes and passages in rocker shaft. If shaft is grooved or worn, replace it. Lubricate and assemble the rocker shaft.

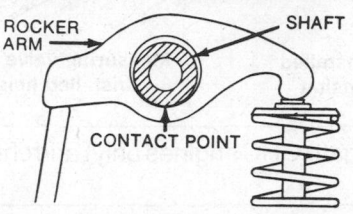

ROCKER ARM — SHAFT

CONTACT POINT

Rocker arm-to-rocker shaft contact area

Inspect the camshaft bushings and the camshaft (OHC engines):

See next section.

Inspect the pushrods (OHV engines only):

Remove the pushrods, and, if hollow, clean out the oil passages using fine wire. Roll each pushrod over a piece of clean glass. If a distinct clicking sound is heard as the pushrod rolls, the rod is bent, and must be replaced.

*The length of all pushrods must be equal. Measure the length of the pushrods, compare to specifications, and replace as necessary.

Inspect the valve lifters (OHV engines only):

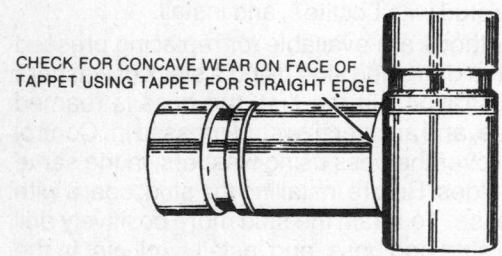

CHECK FOR CONCAVE WEAR ON FACE OF TAPPET USING TAPPET FOR STRAIGHT EDGE

Checking the lifter face

Remove lifters from their bores, and remove gum and varnish, using solvent. Clean walls of lifter bores. Check lifters for concave wear as illustrated. If face is worn concave, replace lifter, and carefully inspect the camshaft. Lightly lubricate lifter and insert it into its bore. If play is excessive, an oversize lifter must be installed (where possible). Consult a machinist concerning feasibility. If play is satisfactory, remove, lubricate, and reinstall the lifter.
NOTE: *1981 and later G.M. diesel V8 valve lifters have roller cam followers. Check these for smooth operation and wear. The roller should rotate freely, but without excessive play. Check the rollers for missing or broken needle bearings. If the roller is pitted or rough, check the camshaft lobe for wear.*

*Testing hydraulic lifter leak down (OHV gasoline engines only):

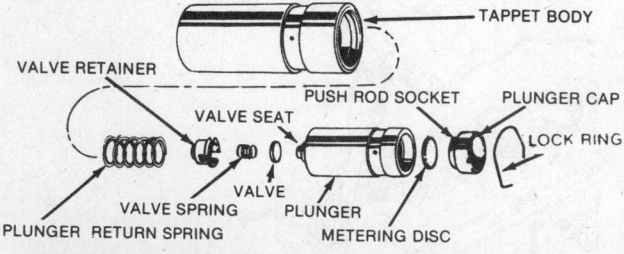

TAPPET BODY

VALVE RETAINER

PUSH ROD SOCKET

PLUNGER CAP

LOCK RING

VALVE SEAT

VALVE

VALVE SPRING

PLUNGER

PLUNGER RETURN SPRING

METERING DISC

Typical exploded view of hydraulic valve lifter

Submerge lifter in a container of kerosene. Chuck a used pushrod or its equivalent into a drill press. Position container of kerosene so pushrod acts on the lifter plunger. Pump lifter with the drill press, until resistance increases. Pump several more times to bleed any air out of lifter. Apply very firm, constant pressure to the lifter, and observe rate at which fluid bleeds out of lifter. If the fluid bleeds very quickly (less than 15 seconds), lifter is defective. If the time exceeds 60 seconds, lifter is sticking. In either case, recondition or replace lifter. If lifter is operating properly (leak down time 15–60 seconds), lubricate and install it.

CYLINDER HEAD RECONDITIONING

Procedure	Method
Bleed the hydraulic lifters (diesel engines only):	After the cylinder heads are installed on G.M. V8 diesels, the valve lifters must be bled down before the crankshaft is turned. Failure to bleed down the lifters will cause damage to the valve train. See diesel engine rocker arm replacement procedure in Oldsmobile 88, 98, etc. car section for procedures. NOTE: *When installing new lifters, prime by working the lifter plunger while submerged in clean kerosene or diesel fuel.*

CYLINDER BLOCK RECONDITIONING

Procedure	Method
Checking the main bearing clearance: 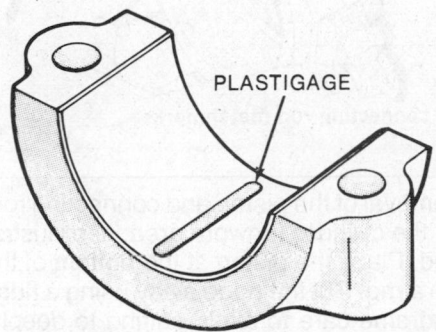 **Plastigage® installed on the lower bearing shell** 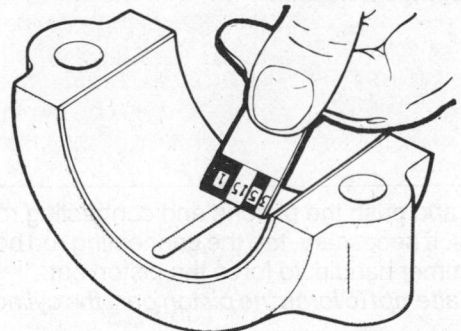 **Measuring Plastigage® to determine bearing clearance**	Invert engine, and remove cap from the bearing to be checked. Using a clean, dry rag, thoroughly clean all oil from crankshaft journal and bearing insert. NOTE: *Plastigage is soluble in oil; therefore, oil on the journal or bearing could result in erroneous readings.* Place a piece of Plastigage along the full length of journal, reinstall cap, and torque to specifications. Remove bearing cap, and determine bearing clearance by comparing width of Plastigage to the scale on Plastigage envelope. Journal taper is determined by comparing width of the Plastigage strip near its ends. Rotate crankshaft 90° and retest, to determine journal eccentricity. NOTE: *Do not rotate crankshaft with Plastigage installed.* If bearing insert and journal appear intact, and are within tolerances, no further main bearing service is required. If bearing or journal appear defective, cause of failure should be determined before replacement. *Remove crankshaft from block (see below). Measure the main bearing journals at each end twice (90° apart) using a micrometer, to determine diameter, journal taper and eccentricity. If journals are within tolerances, reinstall bearing caps at their specified torque. Using a telescope gauge and micrometer, measure bearing I.D. parallel to piston axis and at 30° on each side of piston axis. Subtract journal O.D. from bearing I.D. to determine oil clearance. If crankshaft journals appear defective, or do no meet tolerances, there is no need to measure bearings; for the crankshaft will require grinding and/or undersize bearings will be required. If bearing appears defective, cause for failure should be determined prior to replacement.
Checking the connecting rod bearing clearance:	Connecting rod bearing clearance is checked in the same manner as main bearing clearance, using Plastigage. Before removing the crankshaft, connecting rod side clearance also should be measured and recorded. *Checking connecting rod bearing clearance, using a micrometer, is identical to checking main bearing clearance. If no other service is required, the piston and rod assemblies need not be removed.

CYLINDER BLOCK RECONDITIONING

Procedure	Method

Removing the crankshaft:

Using a punch, mark the corresponding main bearing caps and saddles according to position (i.e., one punch on the front main cap and saddle, two on the second, three on the third, etc.). Using number stamps, identify the corresponding connecting rods and caps, according to cylinder (if no numbers are present). Remove the main and connecting rod caps, and place sleeves of plastic tubing over the connecting rod bolts, to protect the journals as the crankshaft is removed. Lift the crankshaft out of the block.

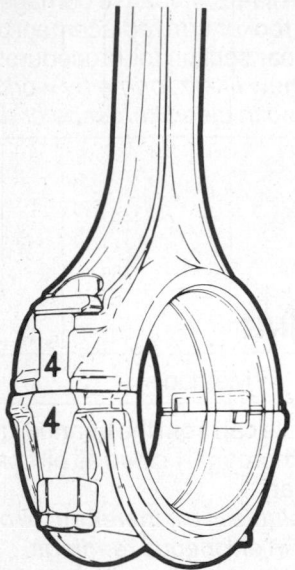

Connecting rod matched to cylinder with a number stamp

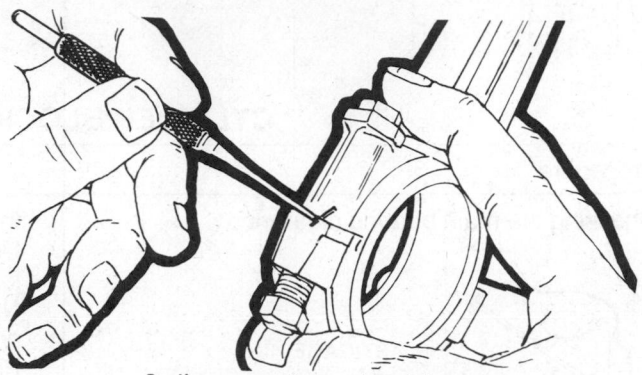

Scribe connecting rod matchmarks

Remove the ridge from the top of the cylinder:

In order to facilitate removal of the piston and connecting rod, the ridge at the top of the cylinder (unworn area; see illustration) must be removed. Place the piston at the bottom of the bore, and cover it with a rag. Cut the ridge away using a ridge reamer, exercising extreme care to avoid cutting to deeply. Remove the rag, and remove cuttings that remain on the piston.

CAUTION: *If the ridge is not removed, and new rings are installed, damage to rings will result.*

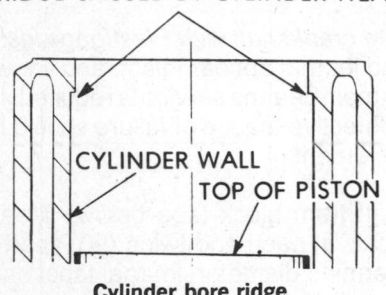

RIDGE CAUSED BY CYLINDER WEAR

CYLINDER WALL
TOP OF PISTON

Cylinder bore ridge

Removing the piston and connecting rod:

Invert the engine, and push the pistons and connecting rods out of the cylinders. If necessary, tap the connecting rod boss with a wooden hammer handle, to force the piston out.

CAUTION: *Do not attempt to force the piston past the cylinder ridge* (see above).

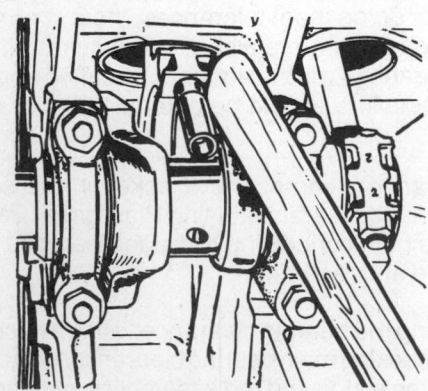

Removing the piston

CYLINDER BLOCK RECONDITIONING

Procedure	Method
Service the crankshaft:	Ensure that all oil holes and passages in the crankshaft are open and free of sludge. If necessary, have the crankshaft ground to the largest possible undersize. **Have the crankshaft Magnafluxed, to locate stress cracks. Consult a machinist concerning additional service procedures, such as surface hardening (e.g., nitriding, Tuftriding) to improve wear characteristics, cross drilling and chamfering the oil holes to improve lubrication, and balancing.
Removing freeze plugs:	Drill a small hole in the middle of the freeze plugs. Thread a large sheet metal screw into the hole and remove the plug with a slide hammer.
Remove the oil gallery plugs:	Threaded plugs should be removed using an appropriate (usually square) wrench. To remove soft, pressed in plugs, drill a hole in the plug, and thread in a sheet metal screw. Pull the plug out by the screw using pliers.
Hot-tank the block: NOTE: *Do not hot-tank aluminum parts.*	Have the block hot-tanked to remove grease, corrosion, and scale from the water jackets. NOTE: *Consult the operator to determine whether the camshaft bearings will be damaged during the hot-tank process.*

Check the block for cracks:	Visually inspect the block for cracks or chips. The most common locations are as follows:
	    Adjacent to freeze plugs.
	    Between the cylinders and water jackets.
	    Adjacent to the main bearing saddles.
	    At the extreme bottom of the cylinders.
	Check only suspected cracks using spot check dye (see introduction). If a crack is located, consult a machinist concerning possible repairs.
	
	**Magnaflux the block to locate hidden cracks. If cracks are located, consult a machinist about feasibility of repair.

Install the oil gallery plugs and freeze plugs:	Coat freeze plugs with sealer and tap into position using a piece of pipe, slightly smaller than the plug, as a driver. To ensure retention, stake the edges of the plugs. Coat threaded oil gallery plugs with sealer and install. Drive replacement soft plugs into block using a large drift as a driver. *Rather than reinstalling lead plugs, drill and tap the holes, and install threaded plugs.
*Check the deck height:	*The deck height is the distance from the crankshaft centerline to the block deck. To measure, invert the engine, and install the crankshaft, retaining it with the center main cap. Measure the distance from the crankshaft journal to the block deck, parallel to the cylinder centerline. Measure the diameter of the end (front and rear) main journals, parallel to the centerline of the cylinders, divide the diameter in half, and subtract it from the previous measurement. The results of the front and rear measurements should be identical. If the difference exceeds .005″, the deck height should be corrected. NOTE: *Block deck height and warpage should be corrected at the same time.*

CYLINDER BLOCK RECONDITIONING

Procedure	Method
Check the block deck for warpage:	Using a straightedge and feeler gauges, check the block deck for warpage in the same manner that the cylinder head is checked (see Cylinder Head Reconditioning). If warpage exceeds specifications, have the deck resurfaced. NOTE: *In certain cases a specification for total material removal (Cylinder head and block deck) is provided. This specification must not be exceeded.*

Check the bore diameter and surface:

Measuring the cylinder bore with a dial gauge

Visually inspect the cylinder bores for roughness, scoring, or scuffing. If evident, the cylinder bore must be bored or honed oversize to eliminate imperfections, and the smallest possible oversize piston used. The new pistons should be given to the machinist with the block, so that the cylinders can be bored or honed exactly to the piston size (plus clearance). If no flaws are evident, measure the bore diameter using a telescope gauge and micrometer, or dial guage, parallel and perpendicular to the engine centerline, at the top (below the ridge) and bottom of the bore. Subtract the bottom measurements from the top to determine taper, and the parallel to the centerline measurements from the perpendicular measurements to determine eccentricity. If the measurements are not within specifications, the cylinder must be bored or honed, and an oversize piston installed. If the measurements are within specifications the cylinder may be used as is, with only finish honing (see below).

NOTE: *Prior to boring, check the block deck warpage, height and bearing alignment.*

CAUTION: *The 4 cyl. 140 G.M. engine cylinder walls are impregnated with silicone. Boring or honing can be done only by a shop with the proper equipment.*

TELESCOPE GAUGE 90° FROM PISTON PIN

Measuring cylinder bore with a telescope gauge

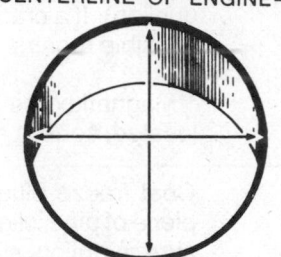

← CENTERLINE OF ENGINE →

A—AT RIGHT ANGLE TO CENTERLINE OF ENGINE
B—PARALLEL TO CENTERLINE OF ENGINE

Cylinder bore measuring points

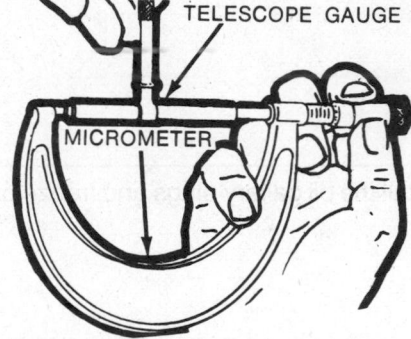

TELESCOPE GAUGE

MICROMETER

Determining cylinder bore by measuring telescope gauge with a micrometer

Check the cylinder block bearing alignment:	Remove the upper bearing inserts. Place a straightedge in the bearing saddles along the centerline of the crankshaft. If clearance exists between the straightedge and the center saddle, the block must be alignbored.

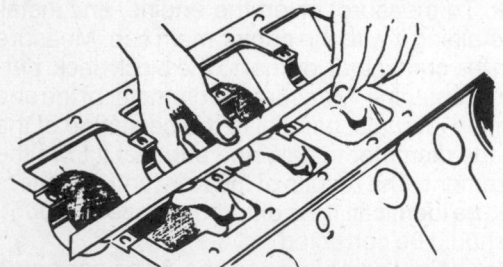

Checking main bearing saddle alignment

CYLINDER BLOCK RECONDITIONING

Procedure	Method

Clean and inspect the pistons and connecting rods:

Using a ring expander, remove the rings from the piston. Remove the retaining rings (if so equipped) and remove piston pin.

NOTE: *If the piston pin must be pressed out, determine the proper method and use the proper tools; otherwise the piston will distort.*

Clean the ring grooves using an appropriate tool, exercising care to avoid cutting too deeply. Thoroughly clean all carbon and varnish from the piston with solvent.

CAUTION: *Do not use a wire brush or caustic solvent on pistons.*

Inspect the pistons for scuffing, scoring, cracks, pitting, or excessive ring groove wear. If wear is evident, the piston must be replaced. Check the connecting rod length by measuring the rod from the inside of the large end to the inside of the small end using calipers (see illustration). All connecting rods should be equal length. Replace any rod that differs from the others in the engine.

*Have the connecting rod alignment checked in an alignment fixture by a machinist. Replace any twisted or bent rods.

*Magnaflux the connecting rods to locate stress cracks. If cracks are found, replace the connecting rod.

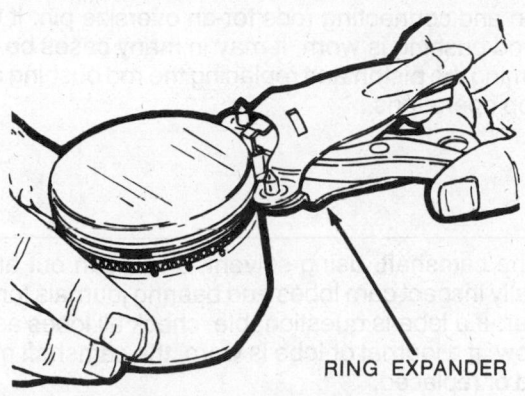

RING EXPANDER

Removing the piston rings

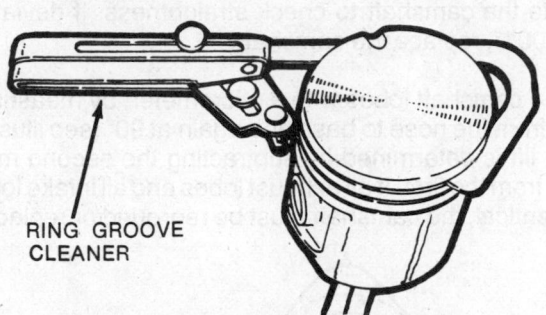

RING GROOVE CLEANER

Cleaning the piston ring grooves

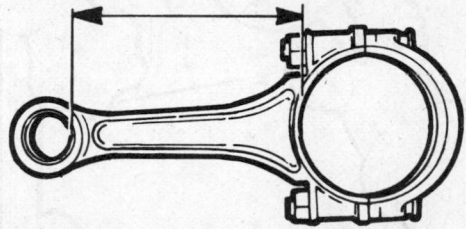

Check the connecting rod length (arrow)

Fit the pistons to the cylinders:

Using a telescope gauge and micrometer, or a dial gauge, measure the cylinder bore diameter perpendicular to the piston pin, 2½° below the deck. Measure the piston perpendicular to its pin on the skirt. The difference between the two measurements is the piston clearance. If the clearance is within specifications or slightly below (after boring or honing), finish honing is all that is required. If the clearance is excessive, try to obtain a slightly larger piston to bring clearance within specifications. Where this is not possible, obtain the first oversize piston, and hone (or if necessary, bore) the cylinder to size.

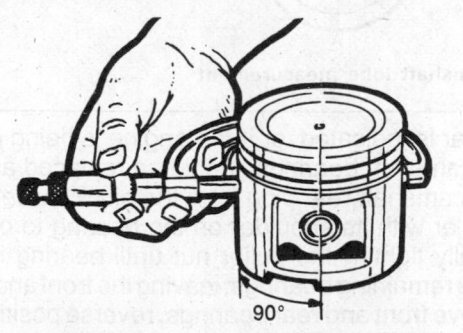

90°

Measuring the piston prior to fitting

Assemble the pistons and connecting rods:

Inspect piston pin, connecting rod small end bushing, and piston bore for galling, scoring, or excessive wear. If evident, replace defective part(s). Measure the I.D. of the piston boss and connecting rod small end, and the O.D. of the piston pin. If within specifications, assemble piston pin and rod.

CAUTION: *If piston pin must be pressed in, determine the proper method and use the proper tools; otherwise the piston will distort.*

CYLINDER BLOCK RECONDITIONING

Procedure	Method

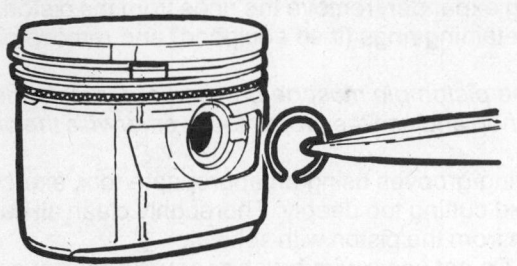

Installing piston pin lock rings

Install the lock rings; ensure that they seat properly. If the parts are not within specifications, determine the service method for the type of engine. In some cases, piston and pin are serviced as an assembly when either is defective. Others specify reaming the piston and connecting rods for an oversize pin. If the connecting rod bushing is worn, it may in many cases be replaced. Reaming the piston and replacing the rod bushing are machine shop operations.

Clean and inspect the camshaft:

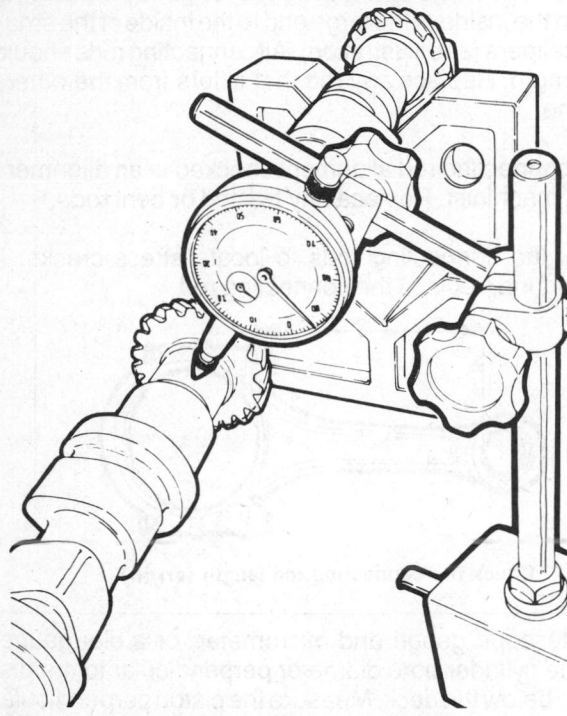

Checking the camshaft for straightness

Degrease the camshaft, using solvent, and clean out all oil holes. Visually inspect cam lobes and bearing journals for excessive wear. If a lobe is questionable, check all lobes as indicated below. If a journal or lobe is worn, the camshaft must be reground or replaced.

NOTE: *If a journal is worn, there is a good chance that the bushings are worn.*

If lobes and journals appear intact, place the front and rear journals in V-blocks, and rest a dial indicator on the center journal. Rotate the camshaft to check straightness. If deviation exceeds .001°, replace the camshaft.

*Check the camshaft lobes with a micrometer, by measuring the lobes from the nose to base and again at 90° (see illustration). The lift is determined by subtracting the second measurement from the first. If all exhaust lobes and all intake lobes are not identical, the camshaft must be reground or replaced.

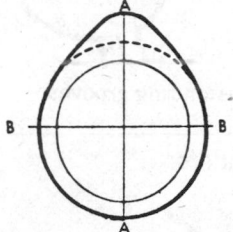

Camshaft lobe measurement

Replace the camshaft bearings (OHV engines only):

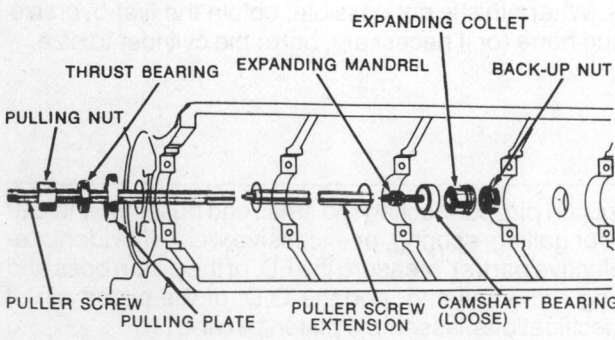

Camshaft removal and installation tool (typical)

If excessive wear is indicated, or if the engine is being completely rebuilt, camshaft bearings should be replaced as follows: Drive the camshaft rear plug from the block. Assemble the removal puller with its shoulder on the bearing to be removed. Gradually tighten the puller nut until bearing is removed. Remove remaining bearings, leaving the front and rear for last. To remove front and rear bearings, reverse position of the tool, so as to pull the bearings in toward the center of the block. Leave the tool in this position, pilot the new front and rear bearings on the installer, and pull them into position: Return the tool to its original position and pull remaining bearings into postion.

NOTE: *Ensure that oil holes align when installing bearings.*

Replace camshaft rear plug, and stake it into position to aid retention.

CYLINDER BLOCK RECONDITIONING

Procedure	Method

Finish hone the cylinders:

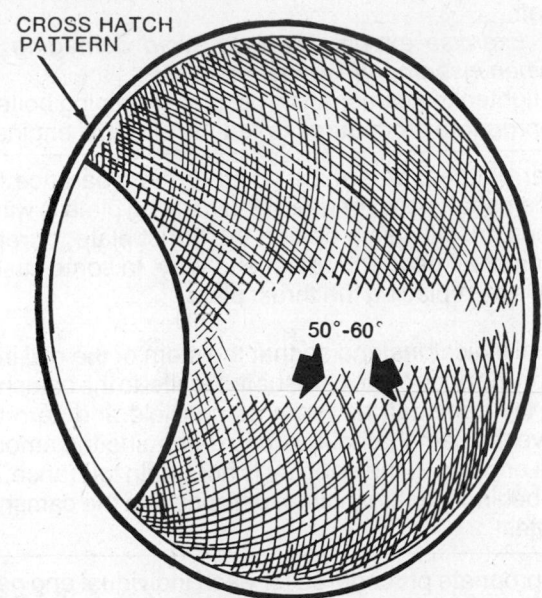

CROSS HATCH PATTERN

50°-60°

Chuck a flexible drive hone into a power drill, and insert it into the cylinder. Start the hone, and move it up and down the cylinder at a rate which will produce approximately a 60° cross-hatch pattern (see illustration).
NOTE: *Do not extend the hone below the cylinder bore.*
After developing the pattern, remove the hone and recheck piston fit. Wash the cylinders with a detergent and water solution to remove abrasive dust, dry, and wipe several times with a rag soaked in engine oil.

Check piston ring end-gap:

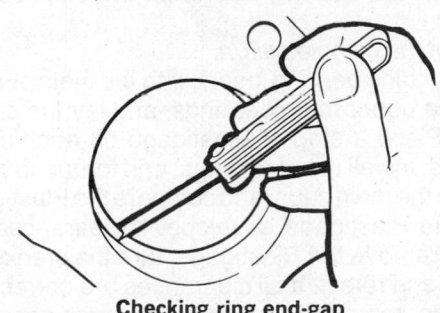

Checking ring end-gap

Compress the piston rings to be used in a cylinder, one at a time, into that cylinder, and press them approximately 1″ below the deck with an inverted piston. Using feeler gauges, measure the ring end-gap, and compare to specifications. Pull the ring out of the cylinder and file the ends with a fine file to obtain proper clearance.
CAUTION: *If inadequate ring end-gap is utilized, ring breakage will result.*

Install the piston rings:

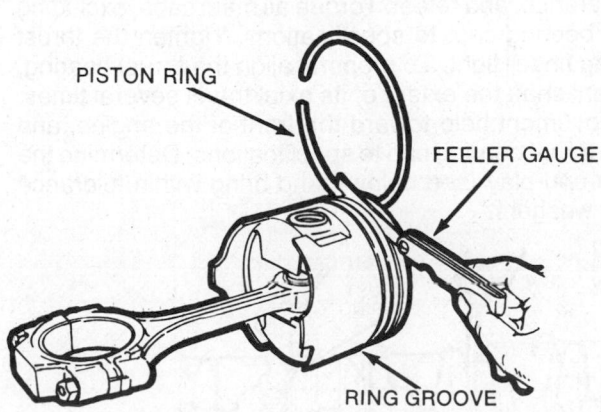

PISTON RING

FEELER GAUGE

RING GROOVE

Checking ring side clearance

Inspect the ring grooves in the piston for excessive wear or taper. If necessary, recut the groove(s) for use with an over-width ring or a standard ring and spacer. If the groove is worn uniformly, overwidth rings, or standard rings and spacers may be installed without recutting. Roll the outside of the ring around the groove to check for burrs or deposits. If any are found, remove with a fine file. Hold the ring in the groove, and measure side clearance. If necessary, correct as indicated above.
NOTE: *Always install any additional spacers above the piston ring.*
The ring groove must be deep enough to allow the ring to seat below the lands (see illustration). In many cases, a "go-no-go" depth gauge will be provided with the piston rings. Shallow grooves may be corrected by recutting, while deep grooves require some type of filler or expander behind the piston. Consult the piston ring supplier concerning the suggested method. Install the rings on the piston, lowest ring first, using a ring expander.
NOTE: *Position the ring markings as specified by the manufacturer (see car section).*

CYLINDER BLOCK RECONDITIONING

Procedure	Method
Install the camshaft (OHV engines only):	Liberally lubricate the camshaft lobes and journals, and install the camshaft. CAUTION: *Exercise extreme care to avoid damaging the bearings when inserting the camshaft.* Install and tighten the camshaft thrust plate retaining bolts. See the appropriate procedures for each individual engine.

Check camshaft end-play (OHV engines only):

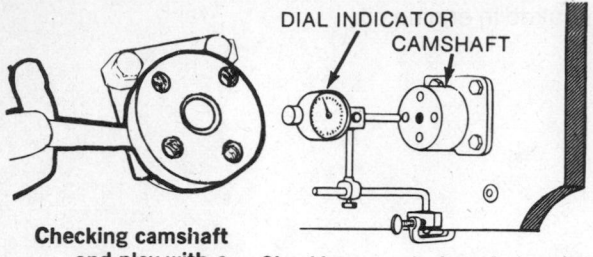

Checking camshaft end-play with a feeler gauge

Checking camshaft end-play with a dial indicator

Using feeler gauges, determine whether the clearance between the camshaft boss (or gear) and backing plate is within specifications. Install shims behind the thrust plate, or reposition the camshaft gear and retest end-play. In some cases, adjustment is by replacing the thrust plate.

*Mount a dial indicator stand so that the stem of the dial indicator rests on the nose of the camshaft, parallel to the camshaft axis. Push the camshaft as far in as possible and zero the gauge. Move the camshaft outward to determine the amount of camshaft endplay. If the endplay is not within tolerance, install shims behind the thrust plate, or reposition the camshaft gear and retest.

Install the rear main seal (where applicable):	See the appropriate procedures for each individual engine.

Install the crankshaft:

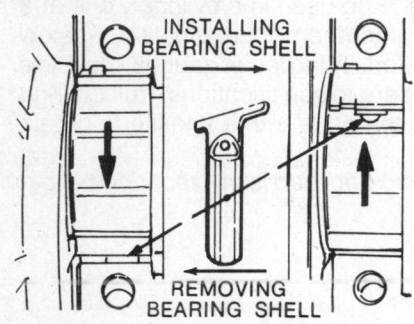

Removal and installation of upper bearing insert using a roll-out pin

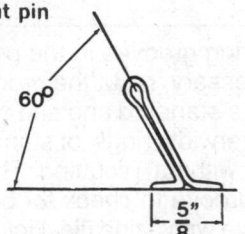

Home-made bearing roll-out pin

Thoroughly clean the main bearing saddles and caps. Place the upper halves of the bearing inserts on the saddles and press into position.
NOTE: *Ensure that the oil holes align.*
Press the corresponding bearing inserts into the main bearing caps. Lubricate the upper main bearings, and lay the crankshaft in position. Place a strip of Plastigage on each of the crankshaft journals, install the main caps, and torque to specifications. Remove the main caps, and compare the Plastigage to the scale on the Plastigage envelope. If clearances are within tolerances, remove the Plastigage, turn the crankshaft 90°, wipe off all oil and retest. If all clearances are correct, remove all Plastigage, thoroughly lubricate the main caps and bearing journals, and install the main caps. If clearances are not within tolerance, the upper bearing inserts may be removed, without removing the crankshaft, using a bearing roll out pin (see illustration). Roll in a bearing that will provide proper clearance, and retest. Torque all main caps, excluding the thrust bearing cap, to specifications. Tighten the thrust bearing cap finger tight. To properly align the thrust bearing, pry the crankshaft the extent of its axial travel several times, the last movement held toward the front of the engine, and torque the thrust bearing cap to specifications. Determine the crankshaft end-play (see below), and bring within tolerance with thrust washers.

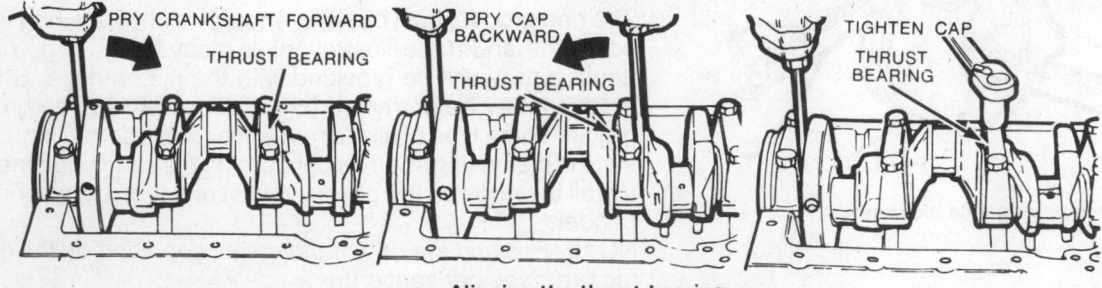

Aligning the thrust bearing

CYLINDER BLOCK RECONDITIONING

Procedure	Method

Measure crankshaft end-play:

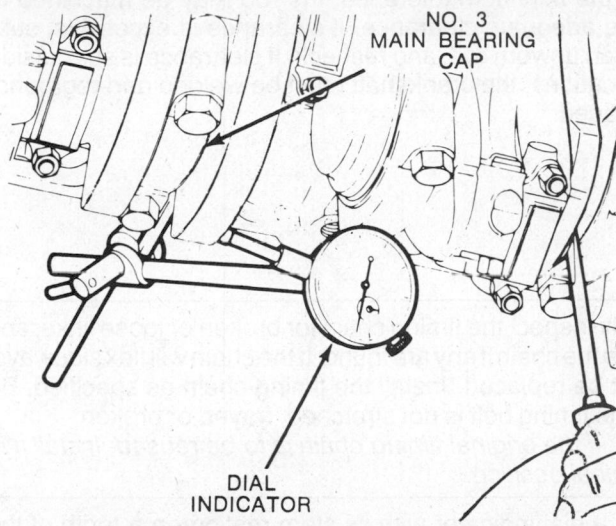

Checking crankshaft end-play with a dial indicator

Mount a dial indicator stand on the front of the block, with the dial indicator stem resting on the nose of the crankshaft, parallel to the crankshaft axis. Pry the crankshaft the extent of its travel rearward, and zero the indicator. Pry the crankshaft forward and record crankshaft end-play.

NOTE: *Crankshaft end-play also may be measured at the thrust bearing, using feeler gauges* (see illustration).

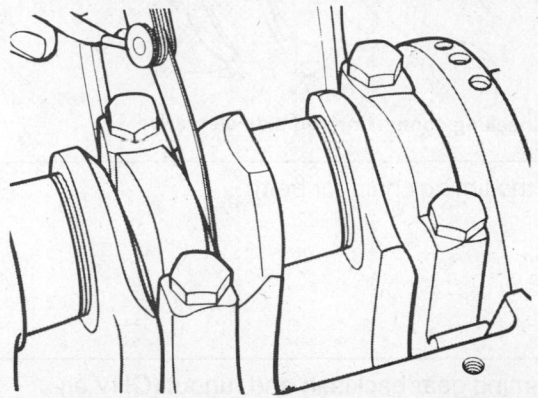

Checking crankshaft end-play with a feeler gauge

Install the pistons:

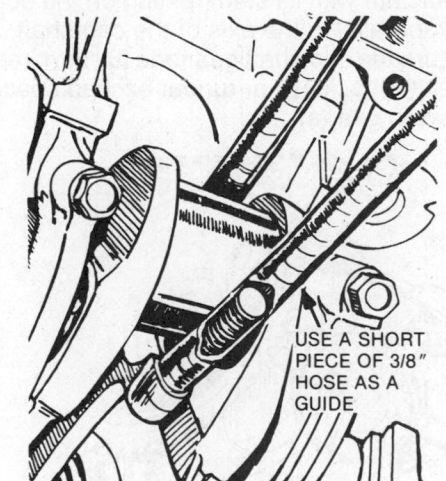

Tubing used to protect crankshaft journals and cylinder walls during piston installation

Press the upper connecting rod bearing halves into the connecting rods, and the lower halves into the connecting rod caps. Position the piston ring gaps according to specifications (see car section), and lubricate the pistons. Install a ring compressor on a piston, and press two long (8″) pieces of plastic tubing over the rod bolts. Using the tubes as a guide, press the pistons into the bores and onto the crankshaft with a wooden hammer handle. After seating the rod on the crankshaft journal, remove the tubes and install the cap finger tight. Install the remaining pistons in the same manner. Invert the engine and check the bearing clearance at two points (90° apart) on each journal with Plastigage.

NOTE: *Do not turn the crankshaft with Plastigage installed.* If clearance is within tolerances, remove *all* Plastigage, thoroughly lubricate the journals, and torque the rod caps to specifications. If clearance is not within specifications, install different thickness bearing inserts and recheck.

CAUTION: *Never shim or file the connecting rods or caps.* Always install plastic tube sleeves over the rod bolts when the caps are not installed, to protect the crankshaft journals.

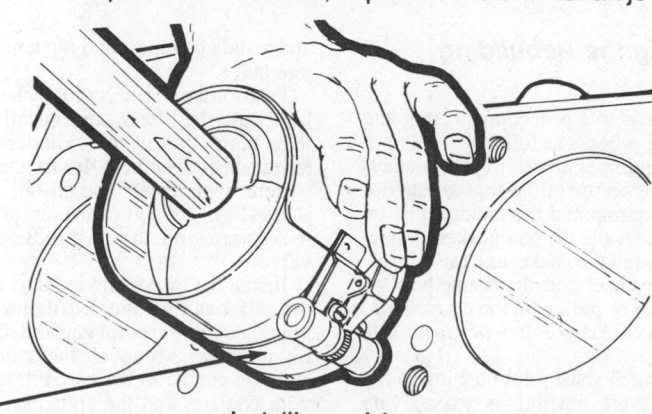

Installing a piston

CYLINDER BLOCK RECONDITIONING

Procedure	Method
Check connecting rod side clearance:	Determine the clearance between the sides of the connecting rods and the crankshaft, using feeler gauges. If clearance is below the minimum tolerance, the rod may be machined to provide adequate clearance. If clearance is excessive, substitute an unworn rod, and recheck. If clearance is still outside specifications, the crankshaft must be welded and reground, or replaced.

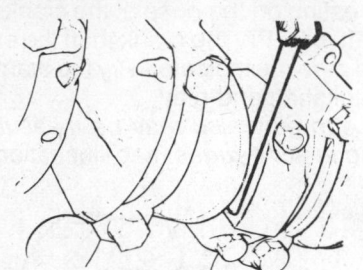

Checking connecting rod side clearance

Procedure	Method
Inspect the timing chain (or belt):	Visually inspect the timing chain for broken or loose links, and replace the chain if any are found. If the chain will flex sideways, it must be replaced. Install the timing chain as specified. Be sure the timing belt is not stretched, frayed or broken. NOTE: *If the original timing chain is to be reused, install it in its original position.*
Check timing gear backlash and runout (OHV engines):	Mount a dial indicator with its stem resting on a tooth of the camshaft gear (as illustrated). Rotate the gear until all slack is removed, and zero the indicator. Rotate the gear in the opposite direction until slack is removed, and record gear backlash. Mount the indicator with its stem resting on the edge of the camshaft gear, parallel to the axis of the camshaft. Zero the indicator, and turn the camshaft gear one full turn, recording the runout. If either backlash or runout exceed specifications, replace the worn gear(s).

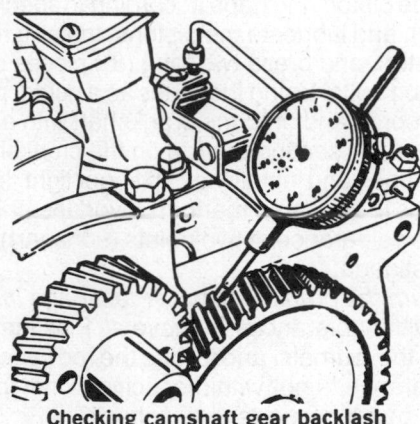

Checking camshaft gear backlash

Checking camshaft gear runout

Completing the Rebuilding Process

Following the above procedures, complete the rebuilding process as follows:

Fill the oil pump with oil, to prevent cavitating (sucking air) on initial engine start up. Install the oil pump and the pickup tube on the engine. Coat the oil pan gasket as necessary, and install the gasket and the oil pan. Mount the flywheel and the crankshaft vibration damper or pulley on the crankshaft. NOTE: *Always use new bolts when installing the flywheel.*

Inspect the clutch shaft pilot bushing in the crankshaft. If the bushing is excessively worn, remove it with an expanding puller and a slide hammer, and tap a new bushing into place.

Position the engine, cylinder head side up. Lubricate the lifters, and install them into their bores. Install the cylinder head, and torque it as specified. Insert the pushrods (where applicable), and install the rocker shaft(s) (if so equipped) or position the rocker arms on the pushrods. Adjust the valves.

Install the intake and exhaust manifolds, the carburetor(s), the distributor and spark plugs. Adjust the point gap and the static ignition timing. Mount all accessories and install the engine in the car. Fill the radiator with coolant, and the crankcase with high quality engine oil.

Break-in Procedure

Start the engine, and allow it to run at low speed for a few minutes, while checking for leaks. Stop the engine, check the oil level, and fill as necessary. Restart the engine, and fill the cooling system to capacity. Check the point dwell angle and adjust the ignition timing and the valves. Run the engine at low to medium speed (800–2500 rpm) for approximately ½ hour, and retorque the cylinder head bolts. Road test the car, and check again for leaks.

Follow the manufacturer's recommended engine break-in procedure and maintenance schedule for new engines.

CV-Joint Overhaul 28

CONSTANT VELOCITY JOINTS

Front wheel drive vehicles present several unique problems to engineers because the driveshaft must do three things, simultaneously. It must allow the wheels to turn for steering, telescope to compensate for road surface vibrations, and it must transmit torque continuously without vibration.

To compensate for these three factors a two-joint driveshaft allows the front wheels to perform these functions. This driveshaft mates disc type straight groove ball joint design with the bell type Rzeppa CV universal joint.

The Rzeppa joint on the outboard end of each driveshaft provides steering ability by allowing drive wheels to steer up to 43° while transmitting all available torque to the wheels. The inboard joint allows telescoping (up to 1½″) through the rolling action of balls in straight grooves and operates at angles up to 20°. The combined action of these two ball type u-joints eliminates vibration.

The typical front wheel drive vehicle uses two driveshaft assemblies—one to each driving wheel. Each assembly has a CV-joint at the wheel end called the outboard joint. A second joint on each shaft located at the transaxle end is called the inboard joint. This joint may be either the ball or tripode type. It allows the slip motion required when the driveshaft must shorten or lengthen in response to suspension action when traveling over an irregular surface.

Constant velocity joints are precision machined parts that have difficult jobs to perform in a hostile environment. They are exposed to heat, shock, torque, and many thousands of miles of service. For this reason, the lubricants used are specially formulated to be compatible with the rubber boot and give proper lubrication. Most CV-joint repair kits have this special lubricant included.

NOTE: Wear pattern in a used ball or tripode CV-joint are impossible to match during reassembly. If there are any signs of wear, abnormal operating noise, corrosion, heat discoloration, the joint must be replaced.

TROUBLESHOOTING

Noises from the engine, drive axles, suspension and steering in the front drive cars can be misleading to the untrained ear. Ideally a smooth road serves best for detecting operating condition(s) that cause noise.

• A humming noise could indicate that early stage of insufficient or incorrect lubricant.

• Worn driveshaft joints will cause a continuous knock at low speeds.

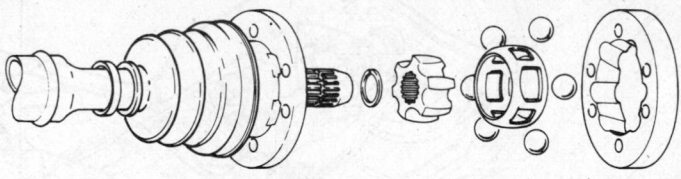

Ball style (Rzeppa) plunging CV joint

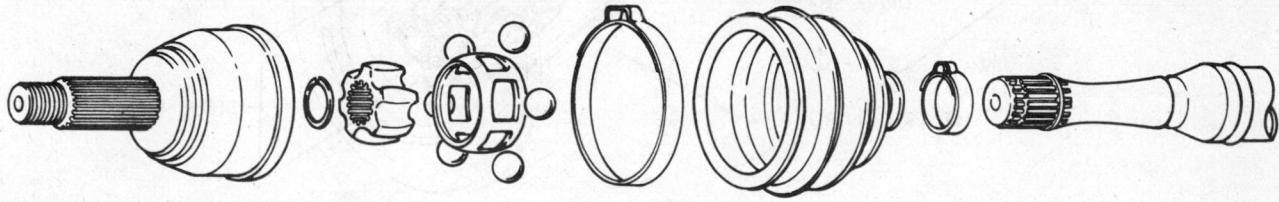

Fixed CV joint

• A popping or clicking sound on sharp turns indicates trouble in the outer or wheel end joint.

• The clunk noise at acceleration from coasting or deceleration from a load pull indicates two possibilities—damaged inner or transaxle joint or differential problem(s).

• An inner joint will create a vibration during acceleration due to plunging action hanging up and releasing repeatedly. Probable cause would be foreign particles or lack of lubrication, or improper assembly.

• Remember that tires, suspension, engine, and exhaust system are all up front to add their noises.

• Make a check with front wheels elevated off ground. Spin the wheels by hand to determine if wheel bearing could be noisy or if out of round tires are causing vibration. Many wheel bearings are prelubed and sealed at the factory.

— CAUTION —

Personal injury can occur from spinning wheels by engine power. Spinning a wheel at excess speed may cause damage to CV-joints that could be operating at angles too steep when wheels are allowed to hang. Over speeding might also cause damage to tires and the differential.

SHAFT REMOVAL

1. Remove the hub nut and discard it.
2. Drain the lubricant from the transaxle.

— CAUTION —

The lubricant may be hot.

3. The speedometer pinion gear assembly must be removed before the right drive shaft can be removed. (Automatic transaxles only).
4. Rotate the driveshaft to view the circlip.
5. Compress the circlip tangs with needle nose pliers as you pry into the side gear. This compresses the circlip in position for shaft removal later. Keep an awl between the differential pinion shaft and the end face of the shaft to prevent circlip reentry to the groove.
6. Remove the ball joint clamp bolt. Drop the lower arm too allow clearance. This will permit the front wheel to swing free.
7. Pull the outer splined shaft from the wheel hub, when swinging wheel hub away. Do not pull on the shaft. Grasp the joint housing.

8. Remove the inner joint by pulling outward on the inner joint housing. Do not pull the shaft.

NOTE: Do not allow the assembly to hang at either end. This can jam the CV-joint and cause vibration during operation. If necessary, support the shaft at either end by rope or wire.

INNER JOINT/BOOT

9. Place the assembly in a vise. Care must be taken not the crush the tubular shafts. Some shafts are solid steel.
10. If the inner joint needs replacement, cut the small rubber clamp, large metal clamp, and remove the rubber boot. These items must be discarded.
11. Inspect for internal wear and/or damage.
12. Clean the grease by hand from inside the joint housing and around the 3 ball trunnion assembly to inspect. Mark the tripod and housing for proper reassembly, if it is to be reinstalled.
13. To replace the boot, CV-joint, or both, remove the snap ring from the groove and tap the trunnion lightly with a brass drift pin. Leave the tripode bearings on the

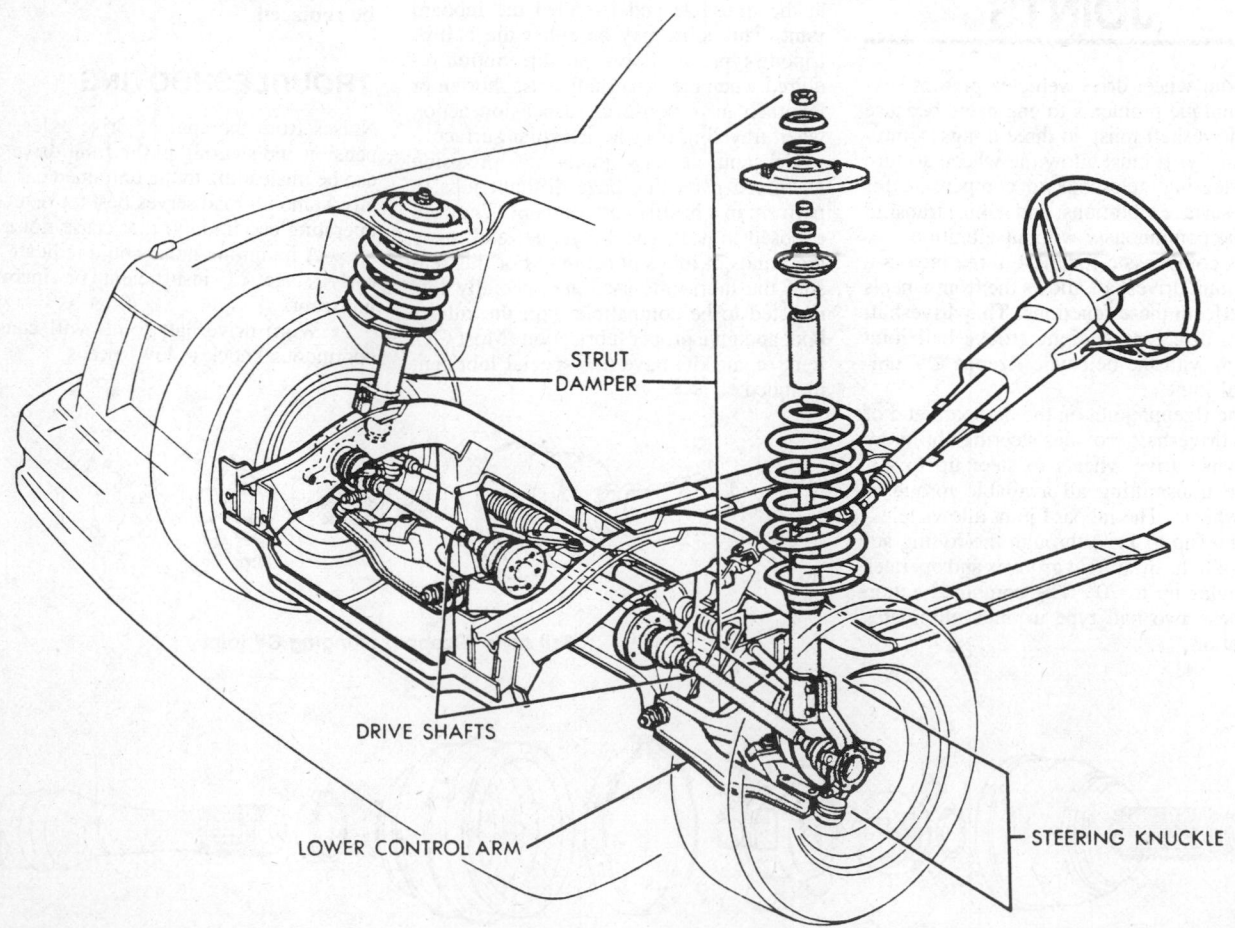

Typical CV driveshaft assembly

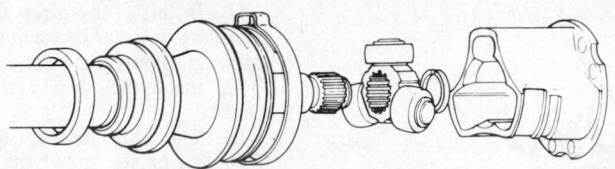

Closed tulip plunging CV joint

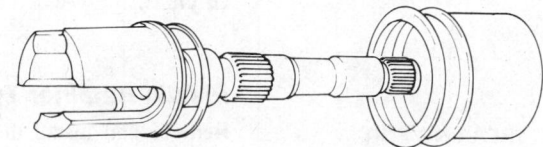

Open tulip plunging CV joint

movement as the driveshaft rotates. The bearings used are needle bearings.

A conventional universal joint will cause the driveshaft to speed up and slow down through each revolution and cause a corresponding change in the velocity of the driven shaft. This change in speed causes natural vibrations to occur through the driveline, necessitating a third type of universal joint: the constant velocity joint. A rolling ball moves in a curved groove, located between two yoke-and-cross universal joints, connected to each other by a coupling yoke. The result is a uniform motion as the driveshaft rotates, avoiding the fluctuations in driveshaft speed. This type of joint is found in cars with sharp driveline angles, or where the extra measure of isolation is desirable.

trunnion. Care must be taken to support the bearings as they may fall off.

14. Installation is the reverse of removal with the following recommendations: When reinstalling the tripode on the shaft place the chamfer face toward the retainer groove. The grease provided with the repair kit must be used. It can not be substituted with any other type grease.

OUTER JOINT/BOOT

1. Place the shaft in a vise. Be careful not to over tighten the vise thereby damaging the shaft.

2. Remove the boot and clamps. Discard these parts.

3. Using a soft hammer rap sharply on the housing. This forces the inner race over the internal circlip. Never remove the slinger from the housing.

4. Remove and discard the circlip. A new one is included with the boot kit. Leave the lock ring in place.

NOTE: Never disassemble the cage and balls from the housing. Reuse the joint assembly with a new boot kit, unless the grease is contaminated and prior diagnosis indicated trouble. In that case replace the joint and boot.

5. Installation is the reverse of removal.

UNIVERSAL JOINTS

U-joint is mechanic's jargon for universal joint. U-joints should not be confused with U-bolts, which are U-shaped bolts used to connect U-joints to the differential pinion flange.

Universal joints provide flexibility between the driveshaft and axle housing to accommodate changes in the angle between

them (changes of length are accommodated by the sliding splined yoke between the driveshaft and transmission). The engine and transmission are mounted rigidly on the car frame, while the driving wheels are free to move up and down in relation to the frame. The angles between the transmission, driveshaft and axle change constantly as the car responds to various road conditions.

To give flexibility and still transmit power as smoothly as possible, several types of universal joints are used.

The most common type of universal joint is the cross and yoke type. Yokes are used on the ends of the driveshaft with the yoke arms opposite each other. Another yoke is used opposite the driveshaft and when placed together, both yokes engage a center member, or cross, with four arms spaced 90° apart (the U-joint cross is alternately referred to as a spider, and the arms are called trunnions). A bearing cup (or cap) is used on each arm of the cross to accommodate

CROSS AND YOKE U-JOINT OVERHAUL

There are two types of cross and yoke U-joints. One type retains the cross within the yoke with C-shaped snap rings. The second type of joint is held together by injection molded plastic retainer rings. The second type cannot be reassembled with the same parts, once disassembled. However, repair kits are available.

Snap-Ring Type

1. Remove the driveshaft. For the correct procedure, see the car section for the model you are working on.

2. If the front yoke is to be disassembled, matchmark the driveshaft and sliding splined yoke (transmission yoke) so that driveline balance is preserved upon reassembly. Remove the snap rings which retain the bearing caps.

3. Select two sockets, one small enough

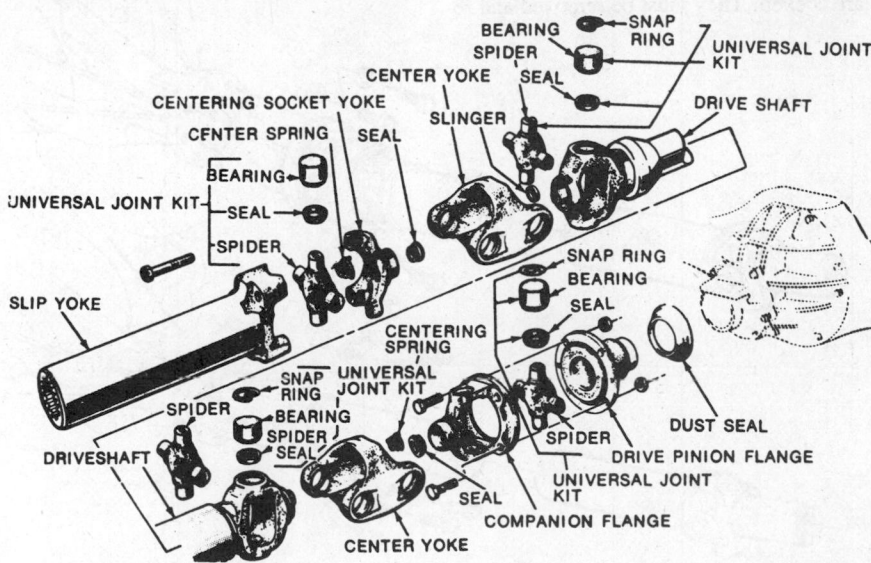

Typical driveshaft with cardan type U-joints

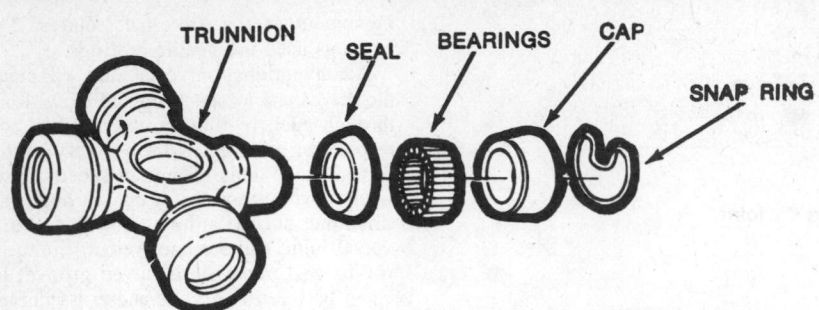

TRUNNION SEAL BEARINGS CAP SNAP RING

Snap ring type universal joint

to pass through the yoke holes for the bearing caps, the other large enough to receive the bearing cap.

4. Using a vise or a press, position the small and large sockets on either side of the U-joint. Press in on the smaller socket so that it presses the opposite bearing cap out of the yoke and into the larger socket. If the cap does not come all the way out, grasp it with a pair of pliers and work it out.

5. Reverse the position of the sockets so that the smaller socket presses on the cross. Press the other bearing cap out of the yoke.

6. Repeat the procedure on the other bearings.

7. To install, grease the bearing caps and needles thoroughly if they are not pre-greased. Start a new bearing cap into one side of the yoke. Position the cross in the yoke.

8. Select two sockets small enough to pass through the yoke holes. Put the sockets against the cross and the cap, and press the bearing cap ¼ inch below the surface of the yoke. If there is a sudden increase in the force needed to press the cap into place, or if the cross starts to bind, the bearings are cocked. They must be removed and re-

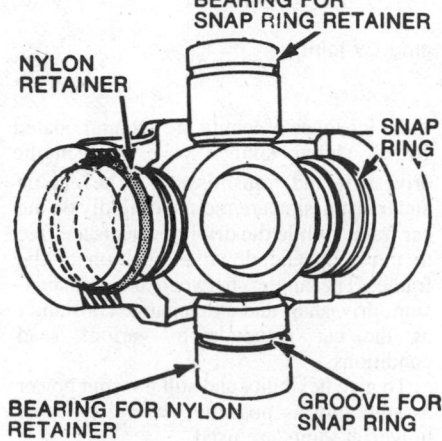

BEARING FOR SNAP RING RETAINER

NYLON RETAINER

SNAP RING

BEARING FOR NYLON RETAINER

GROOVE FOR SNAP RING

U-joint locking methods

started in the yoke. Failure to do so will greatly reduce the life of the bearing.

9. Install a new snap ring.

10. Start a new bearing into the opposite side. Place a socket on it and press in until the opposite bearing contacts the snap ring.

11. Install a new snap ring. It may be necessary to grind the facing surface of the snap ring slightly to permit easier installation.

12. Install the other bearings in the same manner.

13. Check the joint for free movement. If binding exists, smack the yoke ears with a brass or plastic faced hammer to seat the bearing needles. Do not strike the bearings, and support the shaft firmly. Do not install the driveshaft until free movement exists at all joints.

Plastic Retainer Type

Remove and install the bearing caps and trunnion (cross) as described for the snap-ring type universal joints. On an original universal joint, however, the bearing caps will be secured in the yokes with injected plastic. The plastic will shear when the bearing caps are pressed. Service snap-rings are installed in the groove on the inside (of yoke) of the installed caps.

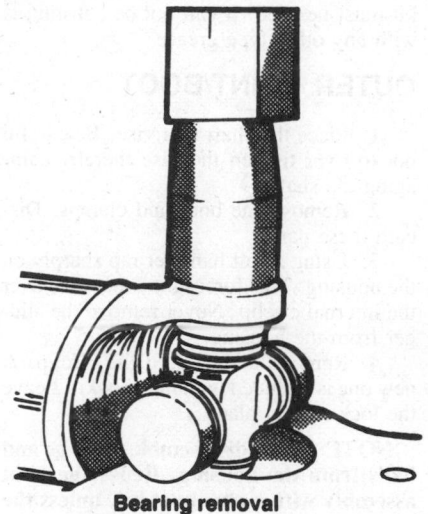

Bearing removal

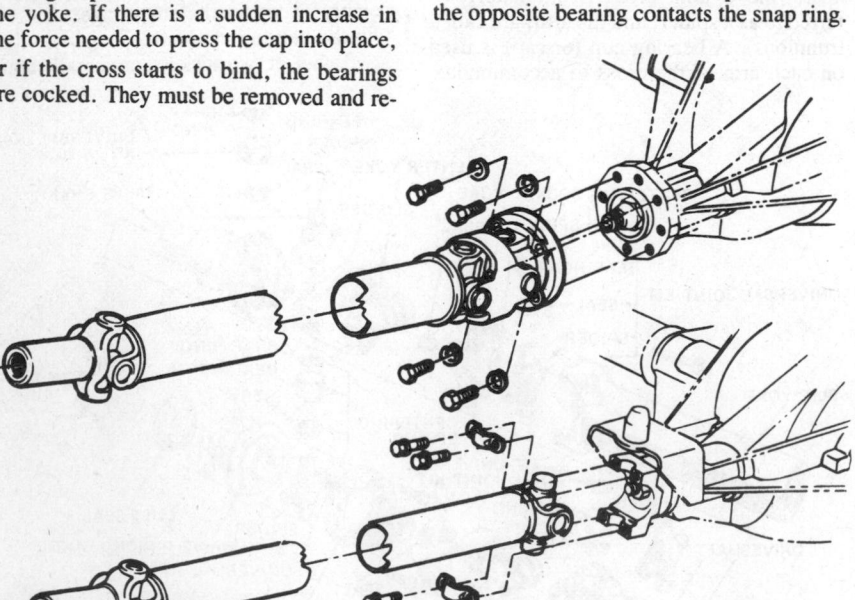

The driveshaft may be retained to the differential pinion by a flange (top) or by U-bolts or straps (bottom)

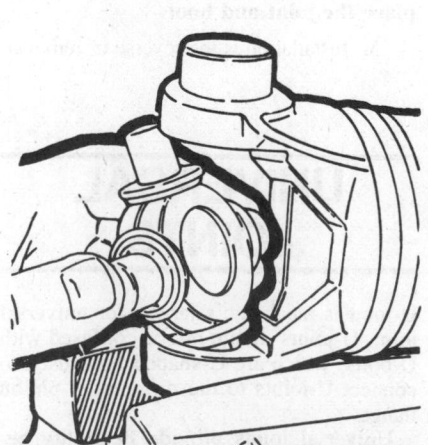

Press a bearing cap into the yoke, then install the cross

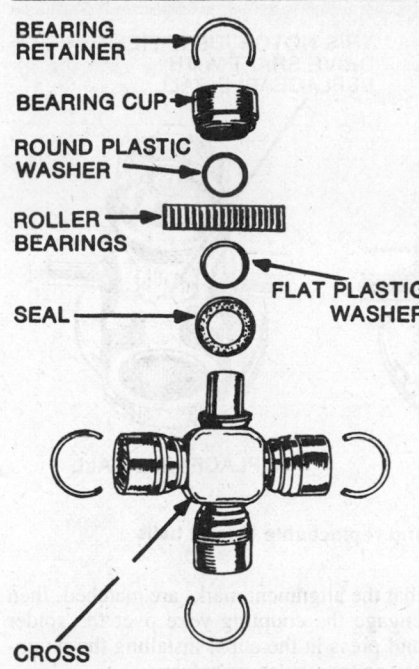

BEARING RETAINER
BEARING CUP
ROUND PLASTIC WASHER
ROLLER BEARINGS
SEAL
FLAT PLASTIC WASHER
CROSS

Plastic retainer U-joint repair kit components

NOTE: The plastic which retains the bearing will be sheared when the bearing cup is pressed out. Be sure to remove the remains of the plastic retainer from the ears of the yoke. It is easier to remove the remains if a small pin or punch is first driven through the injection holes in the yoke. Failure to remove all of the plastic remains may prevent the bearing cups from being pressed into place and the bearing retainers from being properly seated.

CARDAN TYPE U-JOINT OVERHAUL

Some with Cardan type U-joints use snap rings to retain the bearing cups in the yokes. Other cars have plastic retainers. Be sure to obtain the correct rebuilding kit.

1. Use a punch to mark the coupling yoke and the adjoining yokes before disassembly, to ensure proper reassembly and driveline balance.

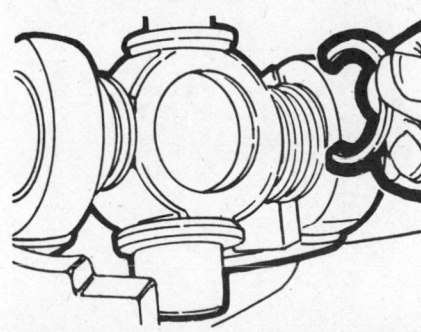

Service snap rings are installed inside the yoke

2. It is easiest to remove the bearings from the coupling yoke first. Follow the order indicated in the illustration.

3. Support the driveshaft horizontally on a press stand, or on the workbench if a vise is being used.

4. If snap rings are used to retain the bearing cups, remove them. Place the rear ear of the coupling yoke over a socket large enough to receive the cup. Place a smaller socket, or a cross press made for the purpose, over the opposite cup. Press the bearing cup out of the coupling yoke ear. If the cup is not completely removed, insert a spacer and complete the operation, or grasp the cup with a pair of slip joint pliers and work it out. If the cups are retained by plastic, this will shear the retainers. Remove any bits of plastic.

5. Rotate the driveshaft and repeat the operation on the opposite cup.

6. Disengage the trunnions of the spider, still attached to the flanged yoke, from the coupling yoke, and pull the flanged yoke and spider from the center ball on the ball support tube yoke.

NOTE: The joint between the shaft and coupling yoke can be serviced without disassembly of the joint between the coupling yoke and flanged yoke.

7. Pry the seal from the ball cavity, remove the washers, spring and three seats. Examine the ball stud seat and the ball stud for scores or wear. Worn parts can be replaced with a kit. Clean the ball seat cavity and fill it with grease. Install the spring, washer, ball seats, and spacer (washer) over the ball.

8. To assemble, insert one bearing cup

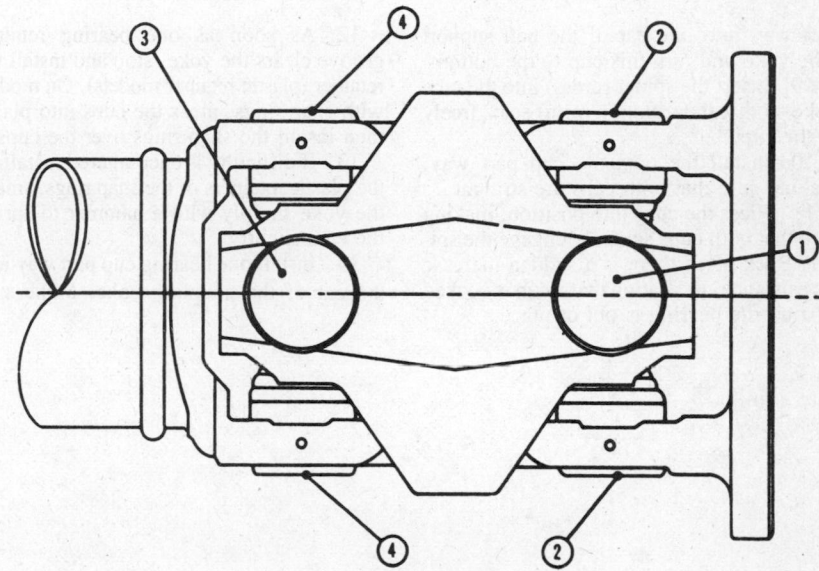

Cardan joint disassembly sequence

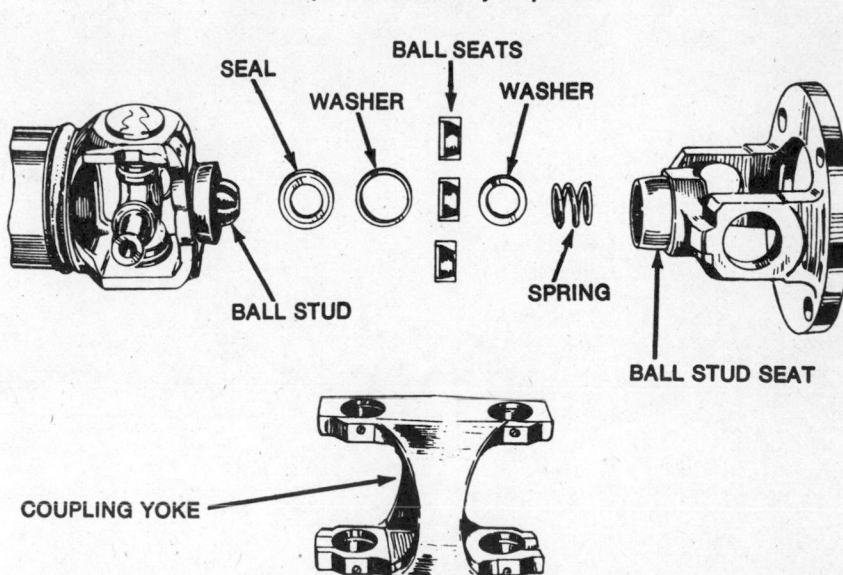

SEAL
WASHER
BALL SEATS
WASHER
BALL STUD
SPRING
BALL STUD SEAT
COUPLING YOKE

Cardan type joint

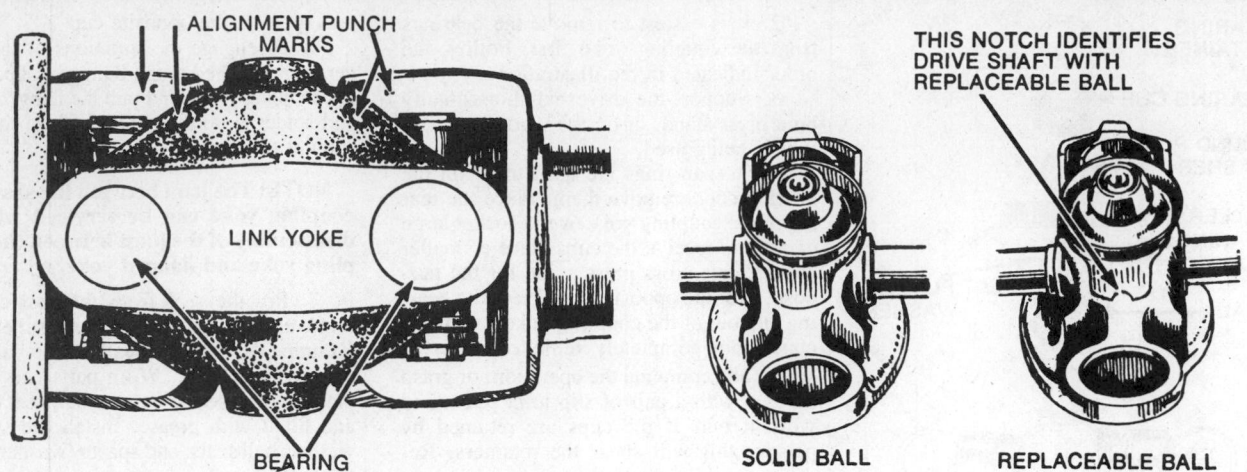

Match marks for double cardan joint

Solid and replaceable U-joint balls

part way into one ear of the ball support tube yoke and turn this cup to the bottom.

9. Insert the spider (cross) into the tube yoke so that the trunnion (arm) seats freely in the cup.

10. Install the opposite cup part way, making sure that both cups are straight.

11. Press the cups into position, making sure that both cups squarely engage the spider. Back off if there is a sudden increase in resistance, indicating that a cup is cocked or a needle bearing is out of place.

12. As soon as one bearing retainer groove clears the yoke, stop and install the retainer (plastic retainer models). On models with snap rings, press the cups into place, then install the snap rings over the cups.

13. If difficulty is encountered installing the plastic retainers or the snap rings, smack the yoke sharply with a hammer to spring the ears slightly.

14. Install one bearing cup part way into the ear of the coupling yoke. Make sure

that the alignment marks are matched, then engage the coupling yoke over the spider and press in the cups, installing the retainers or snap rings as before.

15. Install the cups and spider into the flanged yoke as with the previous yoke.

NOTE: The flange yoke should snap over center to the right or left and up or down by the pressure of the ball seat spring.

Manual Transmission Overhaul **29**

MANUAL TRANSMISSION APPLICATION CHART

Make	Vehicle		Transmission		Reference Type No.	Page
	Year	Model	Model	Speeds		
BMW	81-83	320i	242/9, 18, 18.50	4	4	29-12
			265/6	5	5	29-15
	81-88	528i, 633, 635CSI	262/9.20, 9.90①	4	3	29-9
		733, 735i	262/9.10	4	3	29-9
			262/9.30, 9.35	4	3	29-9
			265/6	5	5	29-15
	82-88	528e, 318i, 325e, 533i, 535i	265/6, 265/OD, 260/5, 260/OD, 240(ZF-S5-16)	5	5	29-15
Chrysler Corp.	81-83	Challenger, Sapporo, Conquest	KM132, B, G	5	2	29-7
Hyundai	87-88	Stellar	KM-132	5	2	29-7
	86-88	Pony	KM-110, KM-119	4	1	29-4
Isuzu	81-88	I-Mark (RWD)	–	4	17	29-40
		Impulse	–	5	18	29-43
Mazda	81-88	RX-7	–	5	15	29-37
	81-82	626	–	4 & 5	14	29-35
Mercedes-Benz	81-88	All	–	4 & 5	16	29-40
Merkur	85-88	XR4Ti	–	5	23	29-56
Mitsubishi	83-88	Starion	KM132, B, G	5	2	29-7

MANUAL TRANSMISSION APPLICATION CHART

Make	Vehicle		Transmission		Reference Type No.	Page
	Year	Model	Model	Speeds		
Nissan/Datsun	81-82	210	F4W56A	4	10	29-24
			FS5W60A	5	13	29-31
	87-88	210	F4W60L	4	8	29-21
	81	510	F4W63L	4	7, 12②	29-19
			FS5W63A	5	11	29-25
	81-84	810, Maxima	FS5W71B	5	9	29-23
	81-88	200SX	FS5W71B, C	5	9	29-23
	81-83	280Z, ZX, Turbo	FS5W71B	5	9	29-23
			FS5R90A	5	6	29-17
	84-88	300ZX, Turbo	FS5W71C	5	9	29-23
			FS5R30A	5	27	29-66
			FS5R90	5	6	29-17
	87-88	Van	RS5W71C	5	24	29-60
Toyota	81-88	Celica (RWD), Supra, Cressida	W50, W55, W58③	5	21	29-51
	81-88	Corolla	T40, T41, T50	4 & 5	20	29-49
	81-82	Corona	W50	5	21	29-51
	81-84	Starlet	K40, K50	4 & 5	19	29-45
	87-88	Supra	R154	5	25	29-62
	87-88	4WD Van	G53	5	26	29-64
Volvo	81-88	All	M45, M46	4	22	29-54

NOTE: Although certain late model transmissions may differ slightly from earlier models, certain basic similarities will usually exist, thus enabling overhaul of the newest models with the guidlines given in the text.

① 262/9.90 is the model designation for 1982-83 California transmissions

② Two different versions of the same model were imported; see the illustration to identify the transmission be overhauled

③ The W55 and W58 transmissions used in 1981 and later models are similar to the W50 and P51

TYPE 1

4 & 5 Speed Transmission Model KM 110, KM 119 Mitsubishi

DISASSEMBLY

1. Remove the clutch assembly.
2. Remove the under cover.
3. Remove the back-up lamp switch. Remove the steel ball from the extension housing.
4. Remove the extension housing assembly, with the gearshift lever placed in the reverse and overtop position.
5. Remove the snap-ring. Remove the speedometer drive gear and the steel ball. Also remove the gear front snap-ring.
6. Remove the mainshaft rear bearing. Remove the bearing front snap-ring.
7. Remove the reverse idler gear and related parts.
8. Loosen and remove the mainshaft intermediate locknut and the countershaft gear rear end locknut. The mainshaft intermediate locknut cannot be removed and therefore is to be loosened only.
9. Remove the three poppet springs from the right-hand side of the transmission case, and then remove three poppet springs and three balls.
10. Remove the cotter pin retaining the 1-2 and 3-4 speed shift forks.
11. Pull the 1-2 speed shift rail toward the rear of the case. Remove the counter overdrive gear and the ball bearing simultaneously with the rail.
12. Pull the 3-4 speed shift rail out toward the rear of the case.
13. Remove the mainshaft nut.
14. Remove the overdrive-reverse synchronizer assembly, the overdrive gear, and the overdrive-reverse shift rail and shift fork at the same time. Pull off the spacer also.
15. Remove two interlock plungers.
16. Remove the spacer and the counter reverse gear.
17. Remove the rear retainer.
18. Remove the front bearing retainer and spacer.
19. Insert rear stopper plate special tool between the clutch gear and synchronizer ring of the 3rd speed gear, and the front stopper plate between the clutch gear and the synchronizer ring of the main drive gear.

NOTE: The front and rear stopper plates inserted are special tools used to prevent the 3-4 speed synchronizer from damage by the main drive gear bearing when these bearings are removed or installed.

20. Remove the mainshaft bearing snapring. Remove the ball bearing. After removal of the bearing, slide special tool Mainshaft Support in place of the bearing over the mainshaft to support the mainshaft.
21. Remove the main drive gear

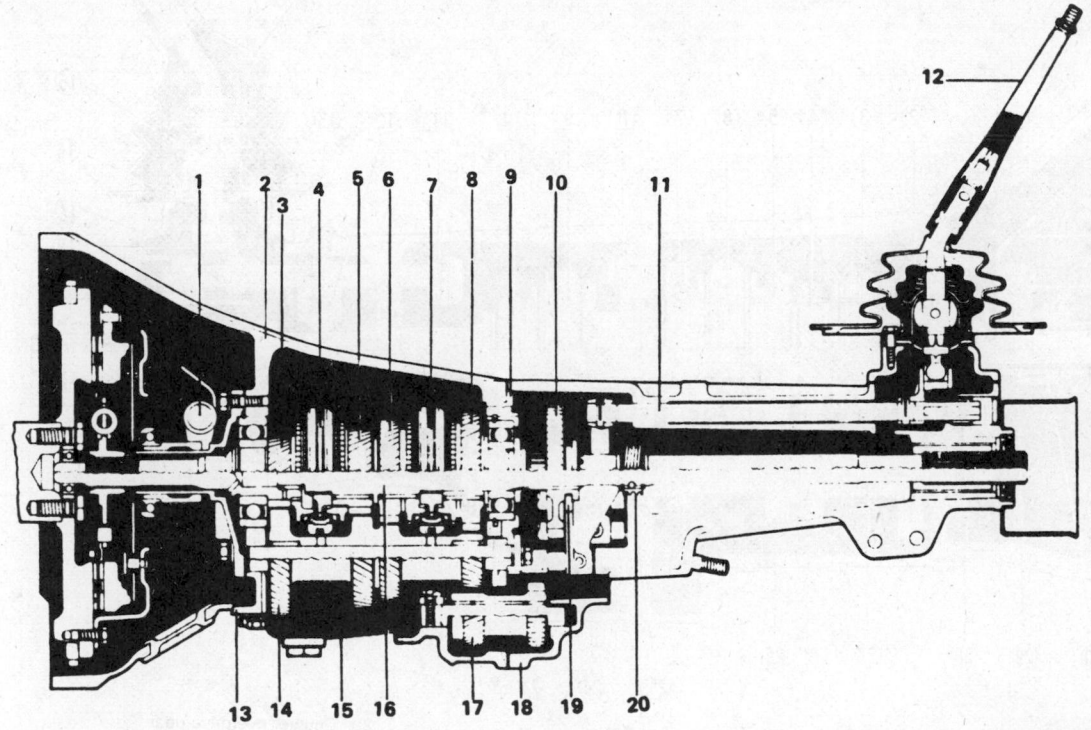

1. Clutch control shaft	7. Synchronizer sleeve (for first-second speeds)
2. Transmission case	8. First-speed gear
3. Main drive gear	9. Rear bearing retainer
4. Synchronizer sleeve (for third-fourth speeds)	10. Reverse gear
5. Third-speed gear	11. Control shaft
6. Second-speed gear	12. Transmission control lever assembly

13. Front gear bearing retainer
14. Counter gear
15. Under cover
16. Mainshaft
17. Reverse idler gear, front
18. Extension housing
19. Shift fork
20. Speedometer drive gear

Cross section of the 4-speed transmission, model KM 110

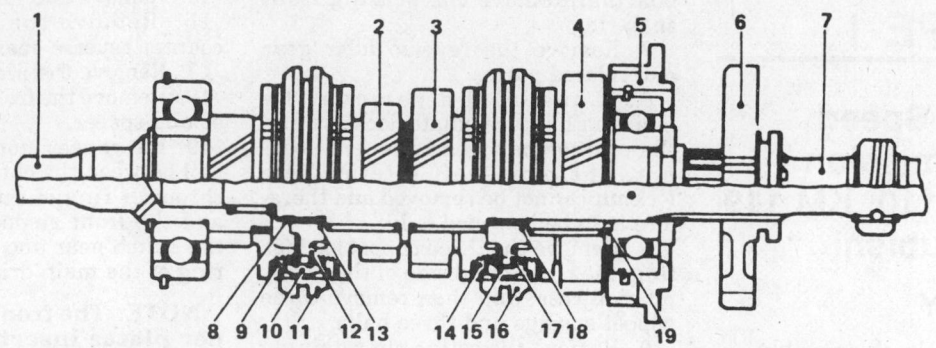

1. Main drive gear
2. Third speed gear
3. Second speed gear
4. First speed gear
5. Rear bearing retainer
6. Reverse gear
7. Mainshaft
8. Snap ring
9. Synchronizer ring
10. Synchronizer piece
11. Synchronizer sleeve
12. Synchronizer spring
13. Synchronizer hub (third-fourth)
14. Synchronizer ring
15. Synchronizer piece
16. Synchronizer sleeve
17. Synchronizer spring
18. Synchronizer hub (first-second)
19. Spacer

Assembled view of the KM110 mainshaft assembly

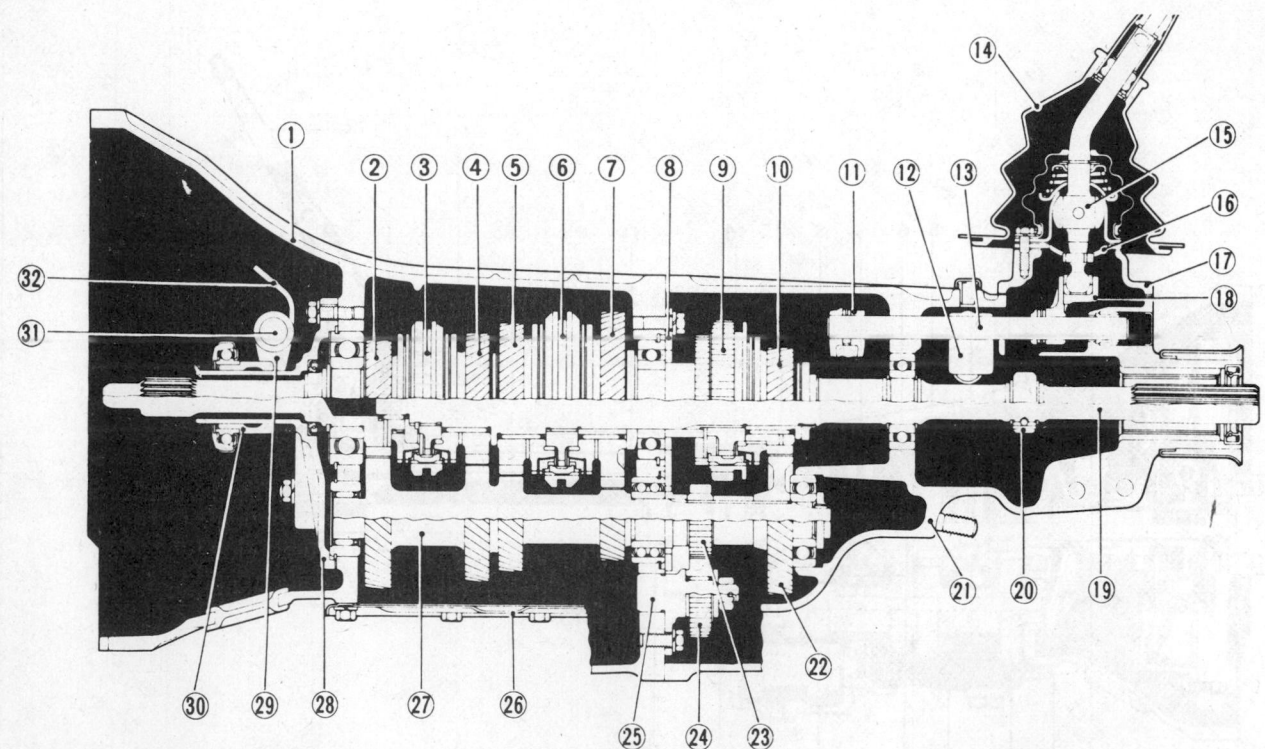

1. Transmission case
2. Main drive pinion
3. Synchronizer assy (3-4 speed)
4. 3rd speed gear
5. 2nd speed gear
6. Synchronizer assy (1-2 speed)
7. 1st speed gear
8. Rear bearing retainer
9. Synchronizer assy (overdrive)
10. Overdrive gear
11. Control finger
12. Neutral return finger
13. Control shaft
14. Control level cover
15. Control lever assy
16. Stopper plate
17. Control housing
18. Change shifter
19. Mainshaft
20. Speedometer drive gear
21. Extension housing
22. Counter overdrive gear
23. Counter reverse gear
24. Reverse idler gear
25. Reverse idler gear shaft
26. Under cover
27. Counter gear
28. Front bearing retainer
29. Clutch shift arm
30. Release bearing carrier
31. Clutch control shaft
32. Return spring

Cross section of 5-speed transmission, model KM 119

bearing snap-rings. Pull off the bearing.

22. Remove special tools.

23. Remove the countershaft gear front bearing snap-ring, of the countershaft gear front bearing.

24. Remove the countershaft gear front bearing snap-ring, of the countershaft gear front bearing.

25. Remove mainshaft adapter special tool. Lower the mainshaft assembly and at the same time take the 1st speed gear rear bearing spacer out of the case. Shift the 3-4 speed synchronizer sleeve to the 3rd speed side to permit easy removal of the countershaft gear without interference with the sleeve.

26. Remove the countershaft gear.

27. Remove the 1-2 speed and 3-4 speed shift forks.

28. Remove the main drive gear.

29. Remove the mainshaft. Disassemble the mainshaft related parts. The synchronizer hub, sleeve, piece and spring, and the bearings for the 3-4 speed should be so laid as to prevent confusion with the 1-2 speed parts.

ASSEMBLY

1. Slide the 3rd speed gear and the needle bearing over the mainshaft from the front.

2. Install the synchronizer ring.

3. Assemble the 3-4 speed synchronizer hub and sleeve. Insert the synchronizer hub and sleeve. Insert the synchronizer pieces, then install the synchronizer springs.

4. Install the assembled 3-4 speed synchronizer assembly on the mainshaft, with the synchronizer piece fitted into the ring groove in the synchronizer. Install a selected snapring so that the synchronizer hub will have end-play of 0-.003 in.

5. Slide the 2nd speed gear and needle bearing over the mainshaft from the rear end.

6. Install the synchronizer ring.

7. Assemble the 1-2 speed synchronizer hub and sleeve. Insert the synchronizer spring. The synchronizer spring should be installed in the same manner as the 3-4 speed synchronizer spring.

8. Install the assembled 1-2 speed synchronizer assembly on the mainshaft, fitting the synchronizer piece into the groove in the synchronizer.

9. Install the synchronizer ring. Install the 1st speed gear, needle bearing and sleeve.

10. Install the bearing spacer. Check to see if, when the bearing spacer is pressed firmly forward, the 1st and 2nd speed gears have an endplay in excess of 0.001-0.007 in. Check the gear and hub ends for wear.

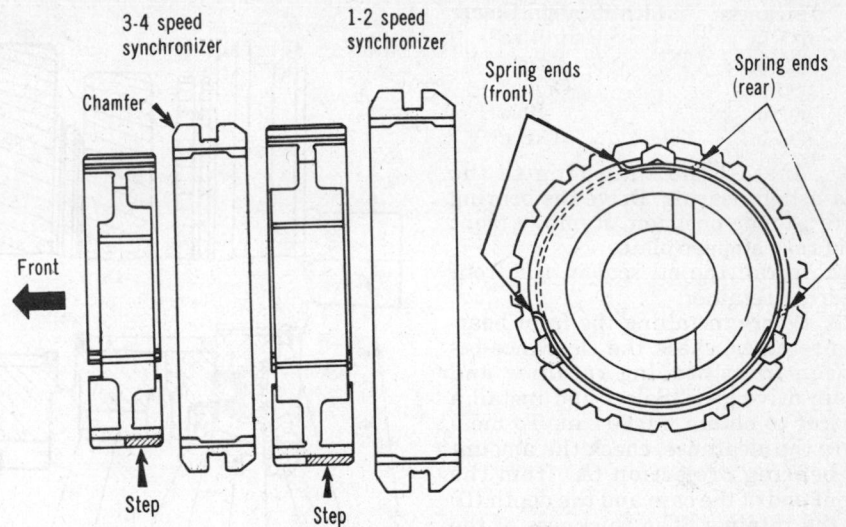

Assembled view of synchronizers

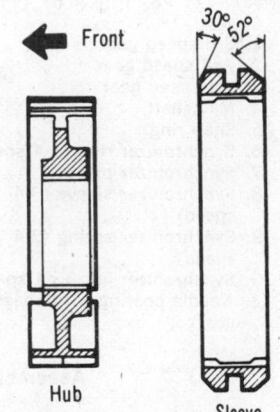

3-4-speed synchronizer

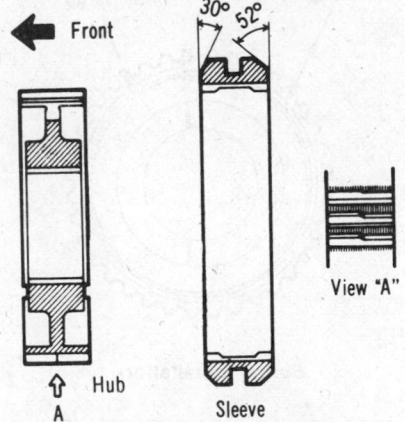

1-2-speed synchronizer

Thickness:	Identification Color:
.085 in.	Blue
.087 in.	None
.090 in.	Brown
.093 in.	White

14. Install the countershaft gear.

15. Insert countershaft gear support special tool into the case to support the countergear.

16. After installing the snap-ring, install the countershaft gear bearing.

17. To install the countershaft gear front bearing, first install the outer race only into the transmission case and then install the needle bearing. The outer race and needle bearing, if assembled before installation, will damage the countershaft at the time of installation. To install the countershaft gear bearing, attach the snapring to the outer race and using an aluminum rod, drive the bearing into place while tapping the circumference of the outer race evenly. Do not attempt to force the outer race into position.

18. Support the rear of the mainshaft.

19. Insert front stopper plate tool between the main drive gear and the synchronizer ring and insert the rear stopper plate tool between the 3rd speed gear and the synchronizer ring, with the stamped tool number on the tools directed to the front of the transmission.

20. To install the main drive gear bearing, first install the snap-ring to the bearing, and then using a bearing installer, drive the bearing into position. Subsequently, install the snapring (small) on the main drive gear. This snap-ring must be selected and installed to obtain 0-.002 in. clearance between the bearing inner race and the snap-ring.

11. Install the mainshaft.

12. Install the synchronizer ring and the needle bearing to the main drive gear, and install the main drive gear.

13. Install the 1-2 speed and 3-4 speed shift forks. Shift the 3-4 speed synchronizer sleeve to 3rd speed side until the 1st speed gear rear bearing spacer is out of the case.

Thickness:	Identification Color:
.087 in.	Dark Blue
.089 in.	Brown
.090 in.	Orange
.092 in.	Blue
.093 in.	Green

21. Install the snap-ring to the mainshaft bearing. Drive the bearing into proper position. Remove front and rear stopper plates.

22. Install the oil seal in the front bearing retainer.

23. Before installing the front bearing retainer, check the clearance between front bearing retainer and main drive gear. Select and install a spacer to obtain 0-0.004 in. To measure the clearance, check the amount of bearing projection (A) from the front end of the case and the depth (B) of the retainer. The thickness of the spacer to be installed can be obtained from the formula (B + .3 (thickness of gasket) - A = Clearance). (0-.004 in.)

24. Install the front bearing retainer in the transmission case.

25. Install the rear retainer.

26. Install the counter reverse gear and the spacer with the relieved side toward the bearing.

27. Install two interlock plungers.

28. Assemble the overdrive-reverse synchronizer.

Thickness:	Identification Color:
.033 in.	Black
.037 in.	None
.040 in.	Red
.044 in.	White
.047 in.	Yellow
.051 in.	Blue
.054 in.	Green

NOTE: The synchronizer spring should be installed in the same manner as the 3-4 speed synchronizer.

29. Install the spacer on the mainshaft from the rear. Install the synchronizer ring, overdrive gear, needle bearing and sleeve to the synchronizer assembly assembled above.

30. Install the mainshaft locknut.

31. Insert the 3-4 speed shift rail into the case from the rear and further into the 1-2 speed and 3-4 speed shift forks.

32. Insert the 1-2 speed shift rail into the case from the rear and further into the shift forks. At the same time, align the counter-overdrive gear with the relieved portion of the shift rail and install both parts simultaneously since they cannot be installed individually.

33. Install the spring pins into the holes. In this case the pin must not project out of the fork, and the slit of the pin must be in the direction of the axis of the shift rail.

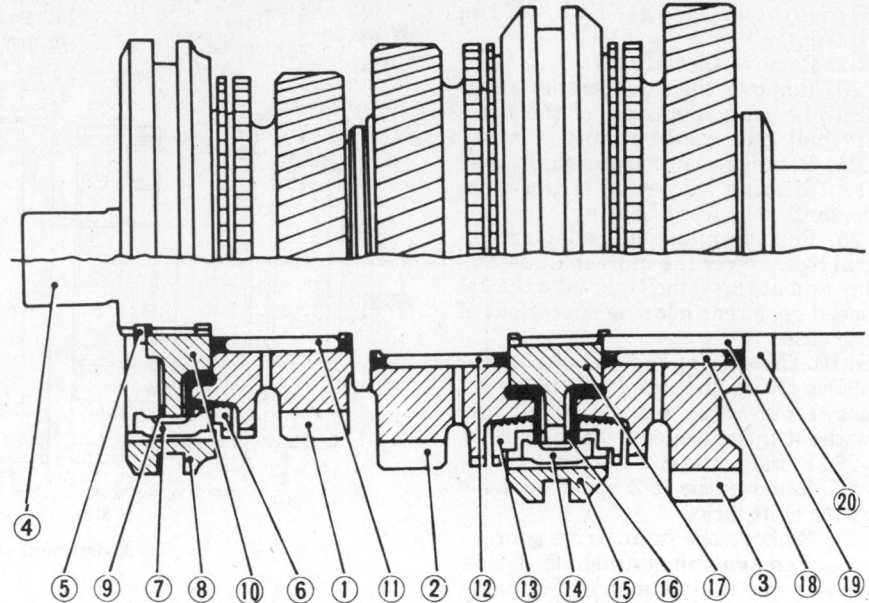

1. 3rd speed gear
2. 2nd speed gear
3. 1st speed gear
4. Mainshaft
5. Snap ring
6. Synchronizer ring (3-4 speed)
7. Synchronizer piece
8. Synchronizer sleeve (3-4 speed)
9. Synchronizer spring (3-4 speed)
10. Synchronizer hub (3-4 speed)
11. Needle bearing (3rd speed gear)
12. Needle bearing (2nd speed gear)
13. Synchronizer ring (1-2 speed)
14. Synchronizer piece
15. Synchronizer sleeve (1-2 speed)
16. Synchronizer spring (1-2 speed)
17. Synchronizer hub (1-2 speed)
18. Needle bearing (1st speed gear)
19. 1st gear bearing sleeve
20. Bearing spacer

Assembled view of mainshaft

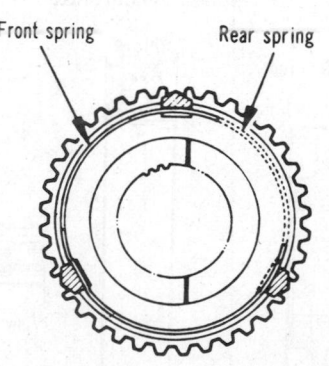

Front spring   Rear spring

Spring installation

Thickness:	Identification Color:
.0591 in.	Red
.0630 in.	White

34. Install the poppet balls and springs. Install the plugs until their heads are flush with the case surface and then apply sealant to them. The springs must be installed with their tapered ends directed inside (on the ball side).

35. Tighten the mainshaft and countershaft gear nuts.

36. Insert the reverse idler shaft into the case. Install the spacer bushing, gear, needle bearing and thrust washer. The thrust washer must be installed with the ground side on the gear side.

37. Install the rear ball bearing on the mainshaft. Install the snap-ring. There should be 0-0.007 in. clearance.

38. Install the speedometer drive gear and snap-ring.

39. Assemble the extension housing.

40. Install the extension housing assembly in the case. When installing the extension housing, tilt the change shifter fully down to the left and install the change lever in the groove provided in the selector. Install the back-up switch.

41. Install neutral return plungers A and B, springs and steel ball, and spring.

42. Install the under cover and gasket.

43. Install the transmission control lever.

TYPE 2

5 Speed Transmission Model KM 132, B, G Chrysler Corp./ Mitsubishi

DISASSEMBLY

1. Remove the clutch release bearing and carrier.
2. Remove the spring pin and the clutch control shaft. Remove the felt, return spring and clutch shift arm.
3. Remove the case cover.
4. Remove the back-up light switch.
5. Remove the extension housing.
6. Remove the speedometer drive gear.
7. Remove the ball bearing from the mainshaft rear end.

8. Loosen three poppet spring plugs, then remove three poppet springs and three balls.
9. Remove the 3-4 and 1-2 speed shift fork spring pins. Pull off each shift rail toward the rear of the transmission case, then remove the shift fork. Remove the interlock plunger.
10. Remove the overdrive and reverse shift forks spring pins, shift rails and forks.
11. Loosen the locknuts (mainshaft and countershaft rear ends).
12. Pull off the counter overdrive gear and the ball bearing at the same time using a puller. Remove the spacer and the counter reverse gear.
13. Remove the overdrive gear and sleeve from the mainshaft. Remove the overtop synchronizer assembly and spacer.
14. Remove the reverse idler gear.
15. Remove the rear bearing retainer.
16. Drive the reverse idler gear shaft from inside the case.
17. Remove the front bearing retainer.

18. With the countergear pressed to the rear, remove the rear bearing snap-ring. Remove the counter rear bearing.
19. Remove the counter front bearing.
20. Remove the countergear from the inside of the case.
21. Remove the main drive pinion from the front of the case. Remove the main drive pinion bearing.
22. Remove the mainshaft bearing snap-ring. Remove the ball bearing.
23. Pull the mainshaft assembly from the case.
24. Disassemble the mainshaft in the following order:
    a. Remove the 1st gear, the 1-2 speed synchronizer and the 2nd speed gear toward the rear of the mainshaft.
    b. Remove the snap-ring from the forward end of the mainshaft. Remove the 3-4 speed synchronizer and the 3rd gear.
25. Disassemble the extension housing.
    a. Remove the lock plate and the speedometer driven gear.

1. Transmission case
2. Main drive pinion
3. Synchronizer assy (3-4 speed)
4. 3rd speed gear
5. 2nd speed gear
6. Synchronizer assy (1-2 speed)
7. 1st speed gear
8. Rear bearing retainer
9. Synchronizer assy (overtop)
10. Overtop gear
11. Control finger

12. Neutral return finger
13. Control shaft
14. Control lever cover
15. Control lever assy
16. Stopper plate
17. Control housing
18. Change shifter
19. Mainshaft
20. Speedometer drive gear
21. Extension housing
22. Counter overtop gear

23. Counter reverse gear
24. Reverse idler gear
25. Reverse idler gear shaft
26. Case cover
27. Counter gear
28. Front bearing retainer
29. Clutch shift arm
30. Release bearing carrier
31. Clutch control shaft
32. Return spring

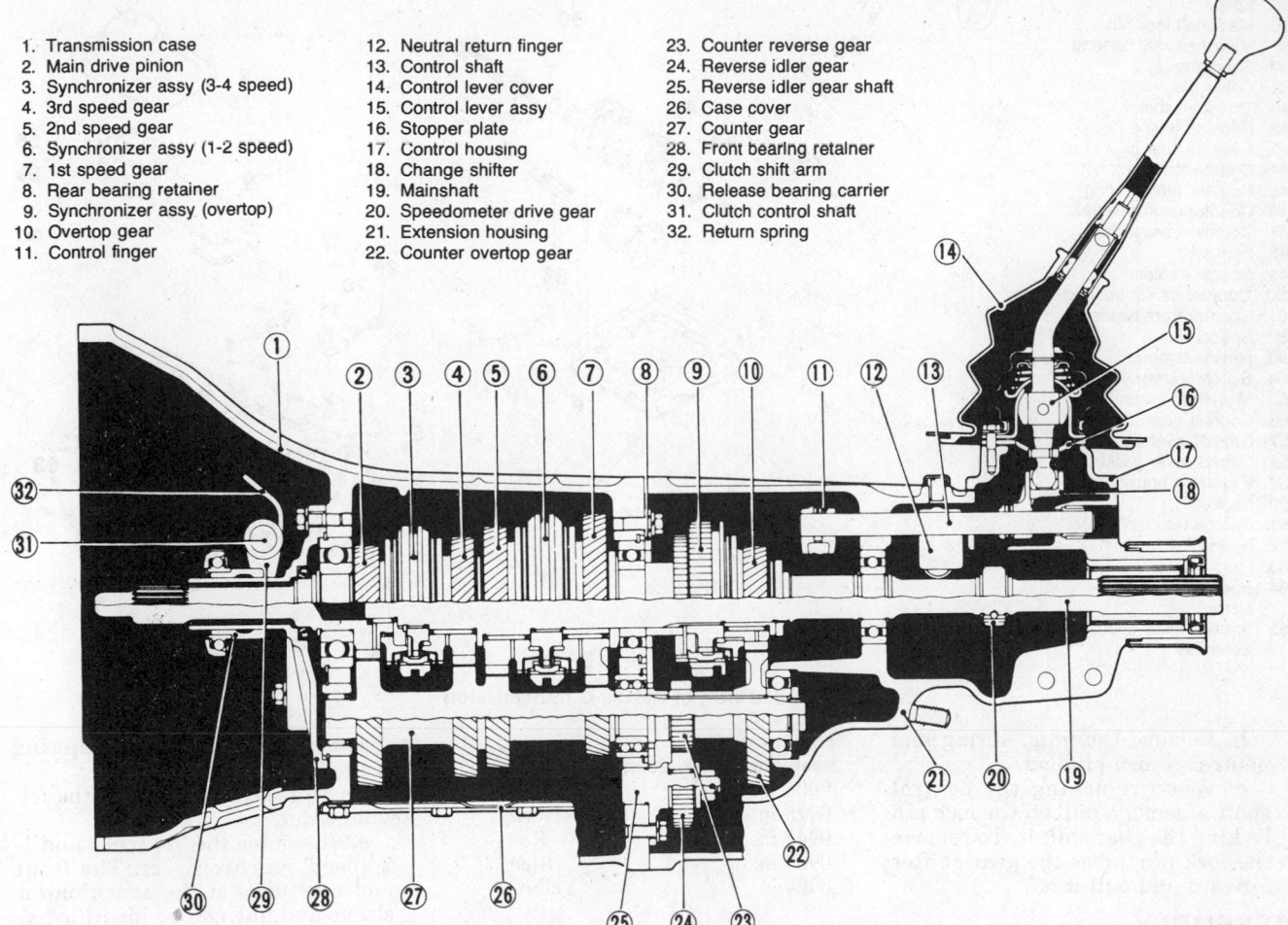

Cross section of 5-speed transmission, model KM 132

1. Clutch release bearing
2. Return clip (2)
3. Clutch release fork
4. Front bearing retainer
5. Front bearing retainer gasket
6. Snap ring
7. Main drive gear assembly
8. Transmission case
9. Spring pin (2)
10. 3-4 speed shift fork
11. 1-2 speed shift fork
12. OD-R shift fork
13. Plug (3)
14. Poppet spring (3)
15. Poppet ball (3)
16. OD-R shift rail
17. 3-4 speed shift rail
18. 1-2 speed shift rail
19. Interlock plunger (2)
20. Mainshaft center bearing
21. Rear bearing retainer
22. Needle bearing
23. Bearing sleeve
24. Reverse gear
25. Synchronizer hub
26. Synchronizer spring (2)
27. Synchronizer key (3)
28. Synchronizer sleeve
29. Synchronizer ring
30. Bearing spacer
31. Needle bearing
32. Overdrive gear
33. Bearing sleeve
34. Steel ball
35. Spacer
36. Mainshaft lock nut
37. Mainshaft rear bearing
38. Snap ring (2)
39. Cotter pin
40. Thrust washer
42. Needle bearing (2)
43. Reverse idler gear shaft
44. Countershaft lock nut
45. Counter rear bearing
46. Counter overdrive gear
47. Counter reverse gear
48. Spacer
49. Spacer - select
50. Counter center bearing
51. Counter front bearing
52. Spacer
53. Needle bearing
54. Synchronizer ring
55. Mainshaft assembly
56. Counter gear
57. Control lever assembly
58. Control lever gasket
59. Extension housing cover
60. Gasket
61. Neutral return plunger "A"
62. Spring
63. Plug
64. Speedometer sleeve clamp
65. Speedometer gear assembly

66. Steel ball
67. Gasket
68. Back-up light switch
69. Plug
70. Spring
71. Neutral return plunger "B"
72. Steel ball
73. Resistance spring
74. Extension housing gasket
75. Extension housing
76. Under cover gasket
77. Under cover
78. Drain plug
79. Release fork boot
80. Clutch release cylinder
81. Oil filler plug

Exploded view of KM132-G transmission

b. Remove the plug, spring and neutral return plunger.

c. When removing the control shaft assembly, pull off the lock pin locking the gear shifter. To remove the lock pin, press the gear shifter forward and pull it off.

ASSEMBLY

1. Install the ball bearing on the

Thickness of Snap-Ring:	Identification Color:
.0906 in.	White
.0925 in.	None
.0945 in.	Red
.0965 in.	Blue
.0984 in.	Yellow

main drive pinion. Install a selective snap-ring so that there will be 0-0.002

in. clearance between the snap-ring and the bearing.

2. Install the mainshaft in the following order.

a. Assemble the 3-4 speed and 1-2 speed synchronizers. The front and rear ends of the synchronizer sleeve and hub can be identified as shown. The synchronizer spring can be installed as shown.

b. Install the needle bearing, the 3rd gear, the synchronizer assembly on to the mainshaft from the front end. Select and install a snapring of proper size so that the 3-4 speed synchronizer hub end-play will be 0-0.003 in.

Thickness of

Snap-Ring:	Identification Color:
.0846 in.	None
.0874 in.	Yellow
.0902 in.	Green
.0929 in.	White

c. Install the needle bearing, the 2nd speed gear, the synchronizer assembly, the bearing sleeve, the needle bearing, the 1st speed gear, and the bearing spacer on the mainshaft from the rear. With the bearing spacer pressed forward, check the 2nd and 1st gear end-play (0.0016-0.0079 in.).

3. Install the mainshaft into the transmission case and drive in the mainshaft center bearing.

4. Install the needle bearing and the synchronizer ring. Install the main drive pinion assembly into the case from the front.

5. Install the countershaft gear into the case. Drive the front bearing into the case.

6. Install the snap-ring on the counter-shaft rear bearing.

7. Install the front bearing retainer. select and install a spacer of proper size so that the clearance will be 0-0.0039 in. Replace the front bearing retainer oil seal.

8. Install the rear bearing retainer.

Thickness of Spacer:

	Identification Color:
.0030 in.	Black
.0366 in.	None
.0402 in.	Red
.0437 in.	White
.0472 in.	Yellow
.0508 in.	Blue
.0543 in.	Green

9. Install the reverse idler gear shaft.

10. Install the needle bearing, the reverse idler gear and the thrust washer. Check the reverse idler gear end-play (.0047-.0110 in.). Install the thrust washer with the ground side toward the gear side.

11. Assemble the overdrive synchronizer.

12. Install the spacer, the stop plate, the overdrive synchronizer assembly, the overdrive gear bearing sleeve, the needle bearing, the synchronizer ring and the overdrive gear in the written order on to the mainshaft from the rear end Check the overdrive gear end-play.

13. Install the spacer, the counter reverse gear, the spacer, the counter overdrive gear and the ball bearing on the countershaft gear from the rear end.

14. Insert the 3-4 and 1-2 speed shift forks into respective synchronizer sleeves. Insert each shift rail from the rear of the spring case. Lock the shift forks and rails with spring pins. Install an interlock plunger between shift rails. The pin should be installed with the slit in the axial direction of the shift rail.

15. Insert the ball and poppet spring into each shift rail. Install the poppet spring with the small end on the ball side.

16. Install the ball bearing on to the rear end of the mainshaft.

17. Install the speedometer drive gear.

18. Install the extension housing. Turn the change shifter fully down to the left. Make sure the forward end of the control finger is snugly fitted in the slot of the shift lug.

19. Install the neutral return plungers and the spring, and resistance spring and ball. Tighten each plug till its top is flush with the boss top surface.

20. Install the speedometer driven gear sleeve into the extension housing and into mesh with the drive gear.

21. Install the back-up light switch. Remember the steel ball.

22. Install the under cover.

23. Insert the clutch control shaft. Install the packing (felt), the return spring and the clutch shift arm. The spring pin should be installed in such a manner that the slip will be at right angles with the axis of the control shaft.

24. Install the transmission control level assembly. Fill the gear shifter area with grease.

25. After reassembly, rotate the drive pinion to see if it rotates smoothly.

KM132-G Transmission

This transmission is an improved model of the KM132-B used in the 1985–88 models, without the intercooler. The major differences from the KM132-B to the KM132-G are as follows:

1. All gears, except the reverse gear, are surface-treated to improve durability.

2. A wider main drive gear is used to provide higher support capability.

3. The transmission case front wall is thicker and the front bearing retainer total length is longer than those used on the KM132-B models.

4. The main shaft center bearing with increased supporting capacity is used, along with an increase in width of the inner race. Both the front and rear spacers of the bearings are not used.

5. The counter overdrive gear spacer is made integral with the gear to reinforce the splined section of the gear.

NOTE: The disassembly, inspection and reassembly of the KM132-G is applicable to the procedures outlined for the KM132 models.

TYPE 3

4 Speed Transmission Models 262/9.10, 9.20, 9.30, 9.35, 9.90 BMW

DISASSEMBLY

1. Remove the console bracket from the rear of the transmission housing.

2. Remove the rear crossmember and the exhaust system bracket.

3. Slide the spring sleeve cover from the selector rod connector and drive the round pin from the coupler. Remove the selector rod connector.

4. Mount the transmission securely and drain the lubricating oil.

5. Remove the front cover retaining bolts and remove the cover with shims.

NOTE: Observe the difference in the length of the bolts and mark them for assembly.

6. Remove the circlip, spacer and support disc from the input shaft.

7. Using a bearing puller tool, remove the front bearing from the input shaft.

8. Using a bearing puller tool, remove the countershaft bearing.

9. Remove the selector lever lockpin cover, the lockpin and spring from the upper front side of the transmission case.

10. Remove the back-up light switch from the left front side of the transmission case.

11. Remove the front transmission case retaining bolts and remove the case from over the gear train.

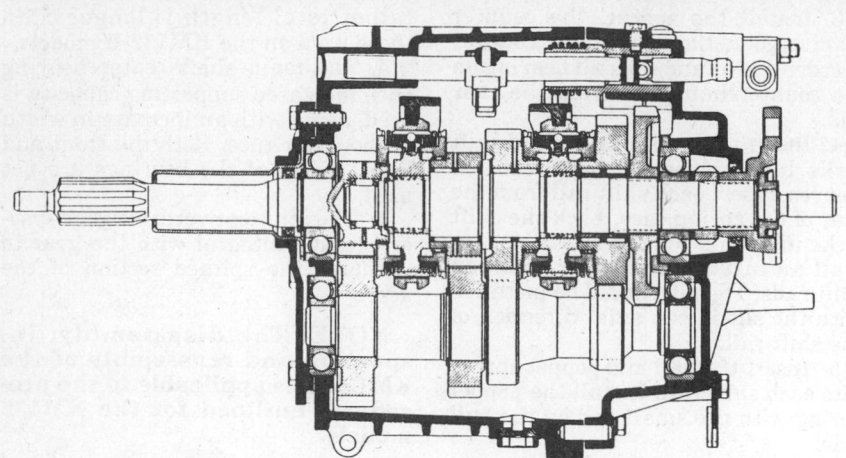

Cross section of 4-speed transmission—262 model (Getrag)

12. Loosen the reverse gear selector lever holding bolt from outside the rear surface of the case, far enough so that the lever can be removed.

13. Using a pin punch, remove the lock-pins from the 3rd-4th and reverse selector rods and forks.

14. Pull the reverse gear selector rod from the rear case. Do not lose the detent balls.

15. Turn the selector shaft so that the 3rd-4th gear selector rod can be pulled from the rear case. Do not lose the detent balls.

16. Install an output flange holding tool or equivalent on the output shaft flange, straighten the retaining nut lock-washer and remove the retaining nut from the shaft.

NOTE: certain transmissions will have a collared nut without a lock washer and will require the use of a thread-lock compound.

17. Remove the rear bearing cover retaining bolts and remove the cover.

NOTE: The speedometer driven gear should have been removed during the transmission R & R procedure. If not, remove it before the rear bearing housing is taken from the case.

18. Heat the rear transmission case to approximately 175°F (80°C). Remove the input shaft, countershaft, reverse gear, 1st-2nd gear selector rod and the selector forks from the case.

NOTE: The use of wet hot towels placed over the case is recommended, rather than the use of openheat. Do not lose the balls and spring from the selector rod detents.

19. Remove the rollers from the selector shaft and remove the shaft from the case.

20. Remove all selector rod sealing covers from the case.

21. Remove the input shaft and its needle bearing cage. Remove the circlip, support disc, synchronizer assembly with the synchronizer (baulk) rings attached, the needle bearing cage and the 3rd gear.

22. Place the output shaft in a press or equivalent tool and remove the 2nd gear, synchronizer assembly with the synchronizer (baulk) rings, 1st gear, support ring, ball bearing, support disc and the speedometer drive gear from the shaft.

——— CAUTION ———

Mark the synchronizer assemblies so that they can be reassembled with their respective gears.

23. The 4th and 3rd gears can be pressed from the countergear assembly. A circlip must be removed before the 3rd gear can be pressed off.

——— CAUTION ———

Note the direction of the gears during the removal.

24. Remove the sliding sleeve from the synchronizer hub. Do not lose the balls, springs and pressure pads from the hub.

25. The seals, gaskets, necessary replacement parts should be renewed in preparation for assembly.

ASSEMBLY

1. Assemble the synchronizer sliding sleeve to the synchronizer hub, halfway, and install the springs, pressure pads and the balls in their positions on the hub. Press the balls in until the sleeve can be slid over the hub completely.

NOTE: The convex face of the pressure pads must face the sliding sleeve.

2. Install the synchronizer (baulk) rings in place on the synchronizer assembly and measure the distance between the ring and the body, in the area of the ring stops. The clearance should not be less than 0.031 inch (0.8mm) for used rings, nor less than 0.039 inch (1.0mm) for new rings.

3. Assemble the countergear assembly by pressing the 3rd gear in place, after heating the gear to approximately 250-300°F (120-150°C). Install the circlip in place on the shaft.

4. Press the 4th gear in place on the shaft after heating the gear to the same temperatures as the 3rd gear.

NOTE: Both the 3rd and 4th gears must be installed with the raised collar on the gear bore, facing the 2nd gear.

5. Install the 2nd speed gear and needle cage on the rear of the output shaft and press into place. Position the 1st/2nd synchronizer assembly in place on the shaft and press into place.

NOTE: Assemble the synchronizer (baulk) rings so that they are reused with the same gears.

6. Install the 1st gear, the needle cage, spacer, reverse gear, support ring, ball bearing, support disc and the speedometer gear in place on the shaft.

7. Install the 3rd gear, needle cage, synchronizer assembly, support disc and circlip in place on the front of the output shaft.

NOTE: Assemble the synchronizer (baulk) rings so that they are reused with the same gears.

8. Install the needle bearing in the bore of the input shaft and install the input shaft onto the front of the output shaft.

The rear bearing shim size must be determined before the transmission is reassembled. The following procedure should be followed:

   a. Measure the case depth to the bearing seat with a depth gauge.

   b. Measure the bearing seat depth of the bearing bracket with a depth gauge.

   c. Measure the bearing outer race thickness in width.

   d. Add the results of the case and bracket together and subtract the thickness of the bearing race from the results to obtain the desired thickness of the shim.

9. Install two guide pins into the rear bearing holder and with the use of both hands, install the output shaft, countershaft and reverse gear assem-

1. Input shaft
2. Needle bearing cage
3. Circlip
4. Support disc
5. Synchronizer ring
6. Hub with sliding sleeve
7. Synchronizer ring
8. Needle bearing cage
9. Gear wheel
10. 2nd gear
11. Needle bearing cage
12. Synchronizer ring
13. Hub with sliding sleeve
14. Synchronizer ring
15. 1st gear
16. Needle bearing cage
17. Spacer
18. Reverse gear
19. Support ring
20. Ball bearing
21. Support disc
22. Speedometer drive gear

Input and mainshaft components

blies into the transmission rear case. Heat the case to 175°F (80°C).

CAUTION

Do not drop the gear assemblies during the installation.

10. Install the remaining bolts into the rear bearing holder and tighten securely. Remove the guide pins.
11. Mount the reverse gear selector lever to the selector rod and secure with the rolled pin.
12. Install the selector rod into the transmission case. Install the rollers on the selector shaft.
13. Place the selector forks on their respective sliding sleeves.

   NOTE: The high selector fork is the 3rd-4th.

14. Install the detent balls as the selector rods are installed.
15. Turn the selector shaft to the reverse position and install the 1st-2nd gear selector shaft.
16. Install the 3rd-4th selector rod. Secure the selector rods to the shifting forks with the rolled pins.
17. Install the shifting rod covers in the case and seal with a sealing compound.
18. Install and secure the selector le-

ver for the reverse gear arm. Install the bolt into the lever and do not cross thread.
19. Install the output shaft flange, the nut and tighten securely. Lock the washer, if so equipped.
20. Install a new gasket and install the transmission front case. Secure the case to the rear case with the retaining bolts and tighten securely.
21. Install the back-up light switch and lockpin and spring.
22. Heat the grooved inner races of the countershaft and input shaft bearings and install them on their respective shafts with a bearing installing tool.

   NOTE: Heat the inner races to approximately 175° (80°C).

CAUTION

Be sure the bearings are seated to the shafts tightly.

23. Install the support disc, spacer and circlip on the input shaft. Be sure the circlip is engaged in its groove on the shaft.
24. To find the proper shims to be used on the front bearings, measure as outlined:
   a. Measure the distance from the

front of the transmission case to the outer surface of the bearing race on the input shaft and record the reading.
   b. Measure the distance from the front of the transmission case to the outer surface of the bearing race on the countershaft. Record the reading.
   c. Attach the gasket to the front bearing housing and measure with a depth gauge, the distance from the surface of the gasket and the inner surface of the front bearing housing seat, for both the input shaft bearing and the countershaft bearing. Record each measurement.
   d. Subtract the measurement reading of the transmission case to bearing results from the results of the depth measurement of the bearing seats in the front bearing housing.
   e. The difference is the size of the shims needed to properly control the end-play of the input and countershaft bearings.

25. Install the shims and retain with a coating of grease, in the front bearing cover. Install the cover on the front case and secure with the retaining bolts.

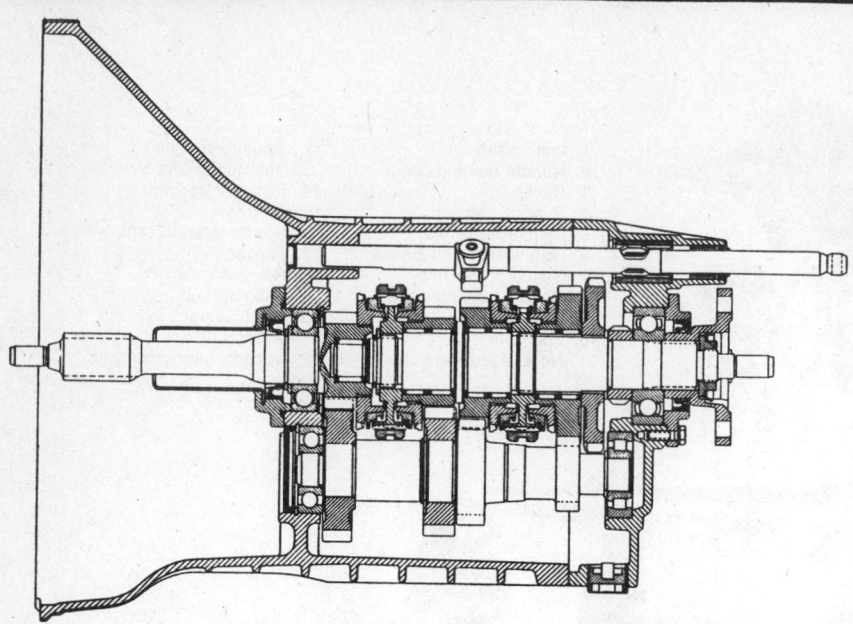

Cross section of 4-speed transmission, model 242/9 (Getrag)

NOTE: Be sure the guide flange is installed with the front cover.

— CAUTION —
Install the bolts in their original position.

26. Install the selector rod connector and install the round pin into the coupler. Slide the spring sleeve cover into its place on the coupler.
27. Install the exhaust system bracket and the rear crossmember to the transmission case.
28. Install the console bracket to the rear of the transmission case.

TYPE 4

4 Speed Transmission Models 242/9, 18, 18.50 BMW

DISASSEMBLY

1. Remove the crossmember and exhaust system bracket from the rear of the transmission.
2. Mount the transmission securely and drain the lubricating oil from the unit. Remove the console from the transmission.
3. Remove the clutch release bearing assembly and release lever from the front of the transmission.
4. Remove the front guide sleeve and retaining bolts. Do not lose the shims.

5. Remove the circlip and shim from the input shaft.
6. Remove the case cover mounting bolts and drive the two dowel pins from the case cover.
7. Using a special case puller or equivalent, remove the case cover from the transmission.

NOTE: The input shaft bearing will remain with the case cover as the cover is removed from the transmission case.

8. Remove the front bearing from the case cover by driving it from the rear to the front. Do not lose the accompanying shim.
9. Remove the lockpin and spring from the case.

NOTE: The lockpin maintains the selector shaft positioning.

10. Move the 3rd/4th selector lever and rod to the third speed position. Drive the fork retaining pin downward very carefully until rod can be pulled out.

— CAUTION —
The fork retaining pin must be driven downward between the teeth of the synchronizer body. The pin should remain in the lower part of the selector fork.

11. Slide the locking sleeve away from the pin of the selector shaft coupler and drive the pin from the coupler.
12. Remove the selector rod by pulling it forward and out of the shifting fork.
13. Move the gear sleeve back to the

neutral position and remove the selector fork.
14. Remove the bushing and the speedometer driven gear.
15. Straighten the bend in the lockplate on the output flange retaining nut. Install a flange holding tool and remove the locknut. Pull the flange from the output shaft.
16. Remove the rear bearing support ring and shims.
17. Using a special bearing puller or equivalent, remove the rear bearing from the transmission cover.

NOTE: A 0.078 in. (2.0mm) metal strip must be placed between the 2nd and 3rd gears to prevent the pressing off of the 2nd gear synchronizer body during the removal of the rear bearing from the shaft and cover.

18. Lift the input and output shaft assemblies slightly and remove the countergear assembly from the end bearing and out of the cover.
19. Pull the selector fork, the reverse gear and the selector rod from the transmission cover. Do not lose the detent balls.
20. Remove the input and output shaft assemblies, align with the 1st/2nd selector rod and fork, from the transmission cover. Do not lose the detent balls.
21. Remove the back-up lamp switch and the end cap for the 1st/2nd selector shaft.
22. Remove the input shaft from the output shaft and remove the 4th speed synchronizer (baulk) ring.
23. Remove the circlip from the front of the output shaft and remove the support disc, synchronizer body assembly, 3rd gear synchronizer (baulk) ring, needle bearing race and the 3rd gear from the shaft.
24. Place the output shaft into a press or equivalent and remove the speedometer drive gear, washer, reverse gear, spacer, needle bearing race, 1st gear, synchronizer (baulk) ring, synchronizer body with the sliding sleeve, synchronizer (baulk) ring, needle bearing race and the 2nd speed gear from the shaft.
25. The 3rd and 4th gears can be pressed from the countershaft gear assembly, along with the roller bearing.
26. The pilot bearing can be removed from the bore of the input shaft.
27. The synchronizer unit can be disasembled by sliding the sleeve off the hub. The pressure pads will drop from the unit as the sleeve is removed.
28. Replace all worn, damaged or broken parts, along with new gaskets and seals.

1. Synchronizer ring
2. Circlip
3. Support disc
4. Hub and sliding sleeve
5. 3rd gear synchronizer ring
6. Needle bearing cage
7. 3rd gear

8. Speedometer drive gear
9. Washer
10. Reverse gear
11. Spacer
12. Needle bearing cage
13. 1st gear

14. Synchronizer ring
15. Hub and sliding sleeve
16. Synchronizer ring
17. Needle bearing cage
18. 2nd gear
19. Output shaft

Output shaft components

ASSEMBLY

1. Install the synchronizer springs onto the hub with the hooked ends of the springs in different pressure pads.

2. Install the pressure pads in place slide the sleeve, with the flat teeth locations, over the pressure pads.

3. If the 3rd and 4th gears have been removed from the countershaft, reinstall or replace the gears back on to the shaft. Heat the gears to 250 to 300°F (120 to 150°C) and install. The high collar on the bore of the 3rd and 4th gears should face the 2nd gear. Install the bearing and race onto the shaft.

4. Place the output shaft in an upright position with the rear of the shaft up. Place the 2nd speed gear and needle bearing assembly onto the shaft. Install the 1st/2nd synchronizer assembly with the two synchronizer (baulk rings onto the shaft, followed by the 1st speed gear, needle bearing, spacer, reverse gear wheel, washer and complete the assembly by pressing the speedometer gear onto the shaft.

NOTE: The end-play of the gear train should be 0.003 in. (0.09mm). Adjust by changing the selective washer between the speedometer gear and the reverse gear.

5. Invert the output shaft and install the 3rd gear onto the shaft. Install the synchronizer assembly less the 4th speed synchronizer (baulk) ring onto the shaft and retain with the support disc and circlip.

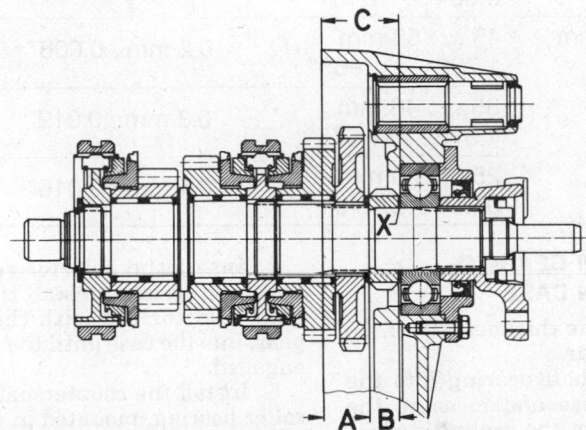

Measurement of extension case and gear assembly to determine shim "X" thickness

Measurements Prior to Transmission Assembly

Washer type shims are used to control the end play of the shafts and gears, while maintaining gear positioning, so that tooth contact is in proper relationship with each other. It is most important to inspect, measure and correct the shim packs to obtain the necessary preloads and clearances.

INPUT SHAFT

1. Install a 0.039 in. (1.0mm) shim and the ball bearing into the case bore.

2. With a depth gauge, measure the distance, A, from the sealing surface of the case to the surface of the bearing race.

3. A numerical figure is electrically engraved on the input shaft and represents column B in the accompanying chart.

4. The thickness of the shim, X, needed on the input shaft can be determined by corresponding the measurements A and B to the chart and locating the proper shim from column X.

COUNTERSHAFT ASSEMBLY

1. Measure the distance, A, from the sealing surface of the case housing to the circlip in the bottom of the housing.

2. Install the countershaft into the transmission case bearing and measure the distance, B, from the top of the large bearing race to the sealing surface of the case, with the gasket installed.

3. Determine the thickness of the shim, C, by subtracting distance B from distance A. The result is shim C.

NOTE: The "C" shims can be used to change tooth engagement.

"A"	"B"	"X"
153.9 mm 6.059"	45 . . . 50 mm 1.772 . . . 1.968"	0.5 mm / 0.020"
	35 . . . 40 mm 1.378 . . . 1.575"	0.6 mm / 0.024"
	25 . . . 30 mm 0.984 . . . 1.181"	0.7 mm / 0.027"
153.8 mm 6.055"	45 . . . 50 mm 1.772 . . . 1.968"	0.4 mm / 0.016"
	35 . . . 40 mm 1.378 . . . 1.575"	0.5 mm / 0.020"
	25 . . . 30 mm 0.984 . . . 1.181"	0.6 mm / 0.024"
153.7 mm 6.051"	45 . . . 50 mm 1.772 . . . 1.968"	0.3 mm / 0.012"
	35 . . . 40 mm 1.378 . . . 1.575"	0.4 mm / 0.016"
	25 . . . 30 mm 0.984 . . . 1.181"	0.5 mm / 0.020"
153.6 mm 6.047"	45 . . . 50 mm 1.722 . . . 1.968"	0.2 mm / 0.008"
	35 . . . 40 mm 1.378 . . . 1.575"	0.3 mm / 0.012"
	25 . . . 30 mm 0.984 . . . 1.181"	0.4 mm / 0.016"

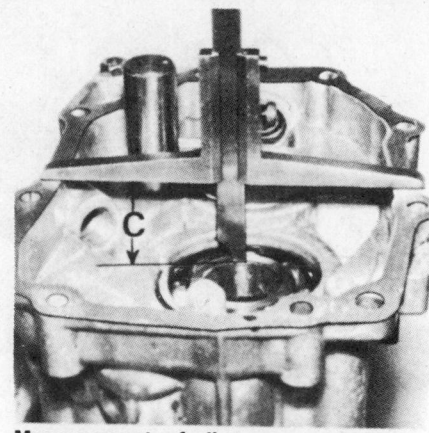

Measurement of distance between extension case edge and ball bearing. "C" equals distance.

Measurement of case edge to ball bearing . . . "A" equals distance.

SPEEDOMETER GEAR-TO-TRANSMISSION CASE

1. Measure the thickness, B, of the speedometer gear.

2. Press the ball bearing into the transmission case and measure the distance, C, from the sealing surface of the case to the race of the bearing, without the gasket installed.

3. The nominal distance, A, is predetermined distance and is used to arrive at the proper sized shim.

4. Subtract distance B from the nominal distance A. Subtract the result of A minus B from distance C, which is the proper sized shim, X, to be used between the speedometer gear and the ball bearing of the case.

5. An example is as follows:

```
Example:   A   22.0mm (0.866 in.)
                nominal distance
         + B   14.8mm (0.582 in.)
           ──────────────────────
               36.8mm (1.488 in.)
           C   37.0mm (1.456 in.)
         −     36.8mm (1.448 in.)
           ──────────────────────
           X   0.2mm (0.008 in.)
```

Transmission Assembly After Basic Measurements

1. Have the transmission case in a secure support.

2. Insert the selector rod detent balls and springs. Install the reverse gear selector rod with the reverse gear, into the case until the 1st lock is engaged.

3. Install the countershaft into the roller bearing, mounted in the case.

4. Install the input shaft on the output shaft and install the assembly into its position on the transmission case.

5. Install the predetermined shim between the speedometer gear and the ball bearing. Install the bearing into the case, but do not seat completely.

6. Using a special bearing installer tool or equivalent, seat the bearing on the output shaft and into the transmission case.

7. Check the tooth engagement of the input, output and countergear assemblies. Tooth engagement can be changed by movement of shims.

8. Install the speedometer bushing and driven gear.

9. Set the transmission assembly in the upright position with the output shaft pointing upward. Measure the distance A, from the case to the ball bearing race.

10. Measure the distance B, from the shoulder height of the sealing cover, to the surface of the gasket on the cover.

11. Subtract distance B from distance A and the result is the thickness of the needed shim between the ball bearing and the sealing cover.

CAUTION

There should be no end-play between the ball bearing race and the sealing cover. Remeasure and remove play with shims.

12. Secure the sealing cover and install the output flange. Install the locknut and washer. Jam the lockplate washer into the groove of the flange.

13. Install the 1st-2nd gear selector rod and fork into place. Insert the locking detent balls and springs. Secure the fork to the rod with the rolled pin.

14. Install the 3rd-4th selector fork into place on the sliding sleeve. Install the main selector rod. Install the lockpin and spring into the tapered bushing. Install the locking detent balls and springs.

15. Install the 3rd-4th gear selector

Location of shim "X" and engraved measurement "B".

rod and secure to the fork with the rolled pin. (Remove pin and reinstall from the top of the fork.)

16. Install the back-up lamp switch and the selector rod cap.

17. Install the gasket on the mating surfaces of the transmission case and housing. Install the predetermined shims on their respective locations and install the transmission housing over the gear assembly.

18. Bolt the housing to the case securely.

NOTE: It may be necessary to heat the transmission area of the input shaft to install the front bearing.

19. Install the shim and bearing onto the input shaft and housing. Install washer and circlip.

20. Install the clutch release guide sleeve and install a shim to eliminate any existing play between the guide and the bearing.

21. Measure the distance between the case and the ball bearing. This distance is A. Measure the distance from the top of the shoulder of the guide sleeve to the mating surface, with the gasket installed. This distance is B.

22. Subtract distance B from distance A and the result is the thickness of shim needed to remove the existing play between the guide and the bearing.

23. Install the selector rod coupler and secure with the pin. Slide the sleeve over the pin location.

24. Install the console onto the transmission case.

25. Fill the unit with the proper level of lubricating oil.

26. Install the clutch release bearing assembly and the operating lever.

27. Install the crossmember and the exhaust system bracket.

TYPE 5

5 Speed Transmission Model 265/6, 265/OD, 260/5, 260/OD, 240 (ZF-S5-16) BMW

DISASSEMBLY

1. Remove the transmission from the vehicle and mount it on a transmission stand.

2. Drain the lubricant and then remove the console.

3. Engage 3rd gear, pull back on the spring sleeve and knock out the dowel pin. Pull off the selector rod.

4. Disconnect the extension bracket and the crossmember (with the rubber mount). Unscrew the back-up light switch.

5. Unscrew the seven mounting bolts and remove the guide flange.

NOTE: Be careful not to lose any shims upon removal of the guide flange.

6. Remove the circlip and slotted washer from around the input shaft.

7. Remove the cover, spring and lockpin.

8. Knock out the guide pin aligning the front case and then unscrew the mounting bolts.

9. Separate the front case from the transmission.

10. Remove the lock plate from the rear case.

11. While holding the output flange with the special tool, remove the collar nut. Pull off the output flange.

12. Swing the selector shaft against its left stop and push forward; this will engage 2nd gear.

13. Unscrew the rear mounting bolts and pull off the rear case.

— CAUTION —

Always make sure that 2nd gear is engaged before removing the rear transmission case.

14. Remove the radial oil seal.

15. Swing down the output shaft and pull 5th gear off the layshaft with a gear puller.

NOTE: The bearing inner race will be removed with the gear.

— CAUTION —

To avoid damage to 3rd gear when removing 5th, make sure that there is always play between 3rd gear and the layshaft. If possible, push up on the output shaft.

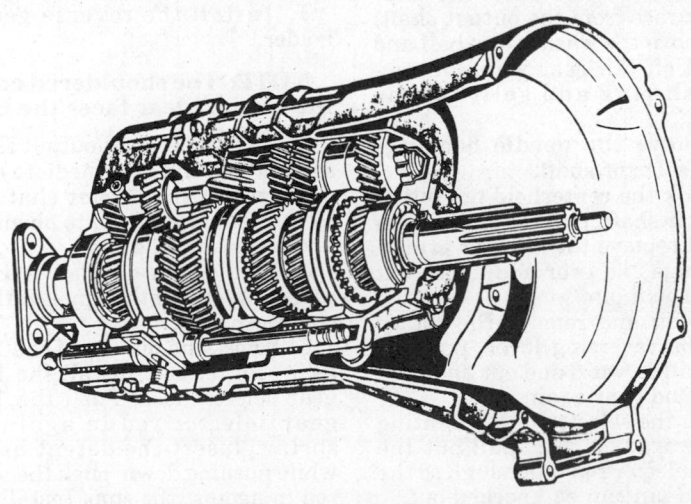

Phantom view of ZE S5-16 ZF synchromesh five speed transmission

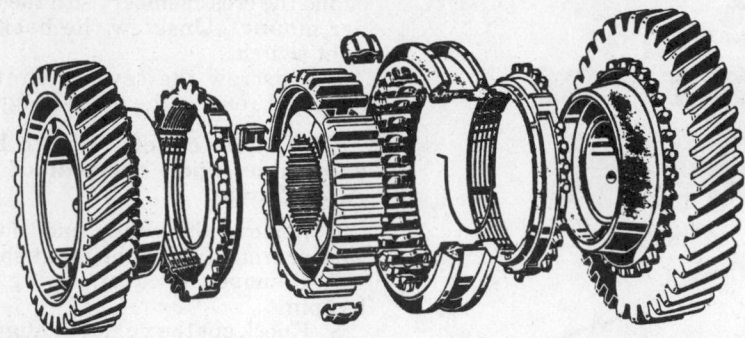

Exploded view of synchronizer assembly, ZF S5-16 five speed transmission

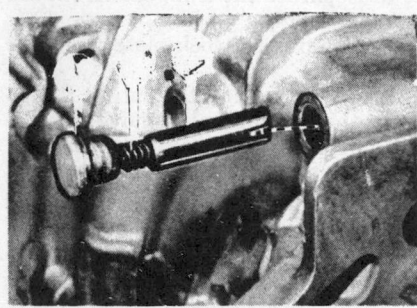

Removing the lockpin

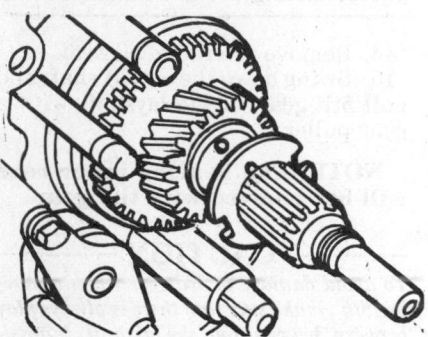

Remove the bearing inner race

16. Using a puller, remove the bearing inner race from the output shaft.

17. Remove the washer and ball and then pull off 5th gear with the synchromesh ring and split needle bearing.

18. Remove the needle bearings from the selector shaft.

19. Knock the centerhold pin out of the selector shaft, pull the shaft backward and remove the selector arm.

20. Engage 2nd gear and knock out the centerhold pin.

21. Pull off and remove the rotary lick on the reversing lever, pull the selector rail forward and out and then take out 2nd gear again.

22. With the selector fork operating sleeve toward the rear, pull out the 5th gear selector rod far enough so the centerhold pin can be knocked out.

23. Pull off the sliding sleeve and the 5th gear selector fork. Pull out the selector rod forward.

24. Pull the guide sleeve and bearing inner race off of the output shaft.

25. Remove the synchromesh ring. Pull off the reverse gear and needle bearing.

26. Engage 3rd gear and then knock out the pin.

NOTE: Knock the pin onto the tooth of 3rd gear until the selector rod can be pulled out forward. Remove the 3rd/4th gear selector rod.

27. Pull the output shaft toward the rear far enough so that the bearing inner race can be pulled off. Remove the shim.

28. Pull the input shaft, output shaft, layshaft and 1st/2nd gear selector rod out of the intermediate case.

29. Disconnect the holder and remove the reverse gear.

30. Unscrew the bolt and thrust washer holding the front end of the reverse gear shaft and remove the shaft.

ASSEMBLY

1. Install the reverse gear and holder.

NOTE: The shouldered collar of the reverse gear faces the holder.

2. Install the input/output shaft assembly into the intermediate case.

3. Install the output shaft shim. Heat the bearing bush to about 175°F and press onto the shaft.

4. Position the needle bearing and reverse gear and then mount the synchromesh ring.

5. Knock the pin out of the 1st/2nd gear selector rod. Install the 1st/2nd gear selector fork. Push the 1st/2nd gear selector rod in against the spring. Insert the detent ball and while pushing down, push the selector rod in against the stop. Install a new centerhold pin (6 x 32mm).

6. Install the 3rd/4th gear selector fork and then repeat Step 5.

7. Insert the guide sleeve in the sliding sleeve so that the tab on the locking lever aligns with the opening in the sliding sleeve. Push the balls in far enough so that the guide sleeve slides into the sliding sleeve.

NOTE: The shouldered end of the sliding sleeve must be opposite the centering pin.

8. Install the guide sleeve so that the centering pin faces 5th gear.

9. Install the 5th/reverse gear selector fork. Insert the locking ball and push the selector rod in against the spring. Insert the detent ball and while pushing down, turn the selector rod while pushing in so that the openings are opposite the detent balls.

10. Push the selector rod in far enough so that a new centerhold pin (6 x 26mm) can be pressed in. Push the rod and guide sleeve in against the stop.

11. Install the reverse lever with the smooth sides facing down.

12. Install the selector rail, push on the rotary lock and then press in a new pin (6 x 26mm).

13. Place a small rod in the centering pin, heat the bearing bush to about 175°F and then press it onto the output shaft.

14. Install the split needle bearing, synchromesh ring and 5th gear.

15. Mount the transmission on a press and lubricate the contact surface on the layshaft with oil. Heat 5th gear to about 300°F, mount it on the layshaft and then press it on.

NOTE: Lift and turn 5th gear until the teeth mesh.

16. Knock the bearing inner race onto the layshaft so that the collar faces the gear.

17. Insert the ball with grease and press on the washer.

18. Heat the ball bearing inner race to about 175°F and then press it onto the output shaft.

NOTE: The opening in the inner race (rotary lock) must engage with the ball in the output shaft. Make a reference line to facilitate installation of the bearing race.

19. Install the selector shaft while pushing on the selector arm with the long arm facing the 3rd/4th gear selector rod. Install a new centerhold pin (6 x 32mm).

NOTE: The stop on the selector shaft must face the selector rail.

20. Hold the four needles on the selector shaft with grease.

Make a reference line to facilitate installation of the bearing race

21. Swing up the output shaft so that 2nd gear is engaged. Slide the 5th/reverse gear selector rod in until the opening is aligned with the end of the 1st/2nd gear selector rod.

22. Clean the sealing surfaces of the rear and intermediate cases thoroughly and then apply Loctite®.

NOTE: The lockpin must move easily and touch bottom.

23. Hold the needles with grease. Position the rear transmission case making sure that the spring of the selector arm engages on the lever.

24. Using an awl, push the lockpin into the opening of the 1st/2nd gear selector rod.

25. Bold down the rear transmission case and then press on the bearing inner race.

26. Install the space over the output shaft and then press in the radial oil seal.

27. Clean the sealing surfaces of the front and intermediate cases, coat with Loctite® and then attach the front case.

28. Install the back-up light switch and the lockpin.

29. Heat the bearing inner race to 175°F, pull out the input shaft and press on the bearing race.

30. Install the slotted washer and circlip on the input shaft.

NOTE: Play between the washer and circlip should be 0-0.0035 in. Adjustment is made with different thickness circlips.

31. Check that the grooved ball bearing play of the input shaft and layshaft to the guide flange is 0.307 in. (input shaft) and 0.169 in. (layshaft).

32. Position the shims and install the guide flange.

33. Installation of the remaining components is in the reverse order of removal.

TYPE 6

5 Speed Transmission Model FS5R90A Datsun

DISASSEMBLY

1. Remove the transmission from the vehicle and attach it to a stand.

2. Drain the oil and then remove the shift lever assembly and damper sleeve.

3. Remove the pin from the offset lever.

4. Unscrew the mounting bolts and seperate the extension housing from the transmission case. The offset lever, detent spring and ball will be removed with it.

NOTE: When removing the extension housing, be careful not to lose the thrust race and funnel.

5. Unscrew the transmission case cover bolts and then tap the cover lightly with a rubber mallet. Slide the cover toward the right side of the case and remove it.

6. Pull the shifter shaft to the rear and remove the striking lever-to-shifter shaft roll pin. Remove the shaft through the rear of the cover.

7. Remove the selector plates from the shift fork assemblies.

8. Remove the back-up light switch.

9. Remove the retainer ring and pivot pin.

10. Remove the funnel, thrust race and the needle thrust bearing.

11. Remove the snap-ring and thrust race from the back of the 5th gear synchronizer hub.

12. Remove the pin from the 5th gear shift fork. Remove the fork, synchronizer and counter gear.

13. Remove the front bearing retainer.

14. Remove the input shaft and main drive gear assembly. Position the flat area of the main drive gear toward the counter gear and remove it through the front of the case.

15. Remove the rear bearing race from the front of the mainshaft and then lift the mainshaft assembly out through the top of the case.

16. Remove the 5th gear shift rail, the reverse fork with 5th and the reverse relay lever and spring.

17. Remove the pin from the reverse idler shaft and then remove the shaft and gear.

18. Remove the snap-ring and spac-er from the rear of the counter gear bearing. Press the gear toward the rear of the case until the bearing is free and then remove it.

CAUTION
When pressing out the bearing, do not let it drop into the case.

19. Remove the counter gear and the front thrust washer. Press the bearing from the case.

NOTE: This bearing should not be removed unless replacement is absolutely necessary.

20. Remove the speedometer gear and drive ball from the main shaft.

21. Press the 3rd/4th gear synchronizer from the mainshaft. Remove 3rd gear.

22. Press 5th gear from the mainshaft.

23. Slip the bearing off of the shaft and then remove the thrust washer.

24. Remove the pin and then press 1st gear from the mainshaft.

25. Remove the snap-ring, thrust washer and 2nd gear.

26. Remove the 1st/2nd gear synchronizer sleeve, inserts and springs.

ASSEMBLY

1. Install the 1st/2nd gear synchronizer sleeve, inserts and springs on the synchronizer hub.

2. Install 2nd gear, its thrust washer and snap-ring. Install 1st gear.

3. Position the thrust washer positioning pin so that it projects 0.12 in. above the bearing surface.

4. Install the thrust washer against 1st gear so that the slot in the washer aligns with the pin.

5. Install the rear bearing and then press 5th gear onto the mainshaft.

6. Install 3rd gear and then press the 3rd/4th gear synchronizer onto the front of the mainshaft.

NOTE: Be sure that the portion of the hub with the extended hose faces forward.

7. Install the speedometer drive, ball, gear and snap-ring.

8. Install the front counter gear bearing:

    a. Apply a small bead of adheasive to the outside diameter of the bearing.

    b. Press the bearing into the case until the edge is flush with the case.

9. Position the counter gear thrust washer into the case so that the tang is aligned with the notch in the case.

NOTE: The washer may be held in position with a light coating of petroleum jelly.

1 Ball bearing
2 Input shaft with 4th gear
3 Rotary lock
4 Needle bearing
5 Synchromesh ring
6 Circlip
7 Washer
8 Pressure piece
9 Ball
10 Spring
11 Guide sleeve
12 Sliding sleeve
13 3rd gear
14 Needle bearing
15 Bearing bush
16 Output shaft
17 Ball
18 2nd gear
19 1st gear
20 Bearing race
21 Roller bearing
22 Shim X
23 Reverse gear
24 Circlip
25 Bearing bush
26 Split needle bearing
27 5th gear
28 Washer
29 Ball bearing
31 Spacer
32 Radial oil seal
33 Output flange
34 Collar nut
35 Lockplate
36 Roller bearing
37 4th gear

38 Circlip
39 3rd gear
40 Layshaft
41 Roller bearing
42 5th gear
43 Roller bearing
44 Bolt
45 Washer

46 Plain washer
47 Thrust washer
48 Needle bearing
49 Reverse gear
50 Bearing pin
51 Bearing bracket

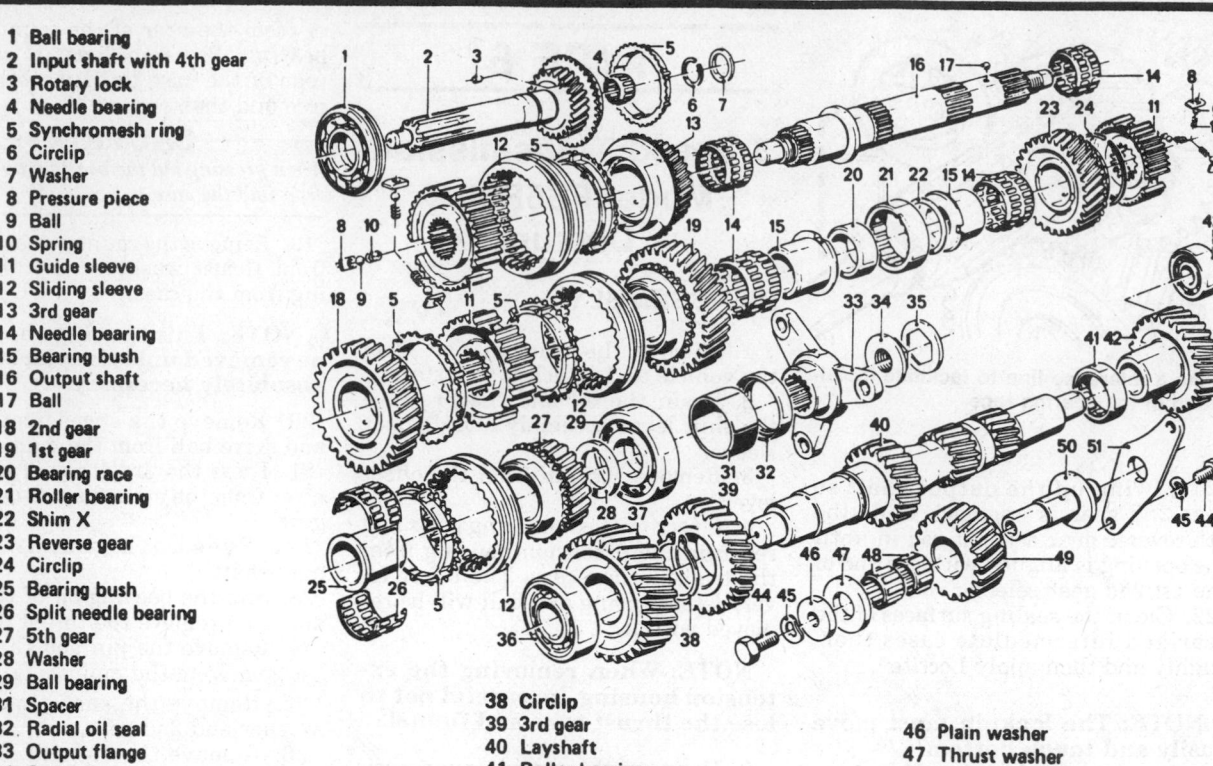

Exploded view of the gear and shaft assembly

10. Install the counter gear into the case and engage its front journal with the front bearing.

11. Install the rear counter gear bearing as follows:

a. Position the spacer at the rear of the counter gear.

b. Install a bearing protector on the counter gear.

c. Install the bearing over the protector and then press it into the case. When properly installed, the bearing race should protrude from the case 0.1228-0.1268 in.

d. Install a spacer and snap-ring behind the bearing.

12. Position the reverse idler gear into the case with the shift fork groove facing the rear. Install the reverse idler shaft, O-ring and retaining pin.

13. Install the reverse fork with 5th gear and reverse relay lever, 5th gear shift rail and the spring.

14. Install the back-up light switch.

15. Place the mainshaft assembly into the case and install the mainshaft rear bearing race.

16. Position the roller bearing into the main drive gear and hold them in position with a light coating of petroleum jelly.

17. Install the input shaft and main drive gear assembly, needle thrust bearing, thrust bearing race and locking ring into the case.

NOTE: Be sure that the flat area of the main drive gear is aligned with the counter gear. Be careful not to dislodge the roller bearings during installation.

18. Remove at least 0.0058 in. from under the front bearing race in the retainer. Install the remaining shims and race into the retainer.

19. Install the front bearing retainer to the case so that the oil collector groove is facing up. Tighten the bolts to 11-20 ft. lbs.

20. Install the 4th gear shift fork, counter gear and synchronizer as a unit. Install the retaining pin with the pin holes in the shift fork and rail in alignment.

21. Install the thrust race and snap-ring to the rear of the 5th gear synchronizer hub.

22. Locate the selector plates on the fork assemblies.

23. Slide the shifter shaft through the hole in the rear of the case cover and then assemble the 1st/2nd gear shift fork, interlock plate, striking lever and the 3rd/4th gear shift fork. Install the shifter shaft roll pin in the striking lever.

24. Apply a continuous bead of seal-ant to the cover-to-case mating surface and then install the cover.

25. Apply sealant to the threads of the two cover alignment dowels and install them. Apply sealant to the remaining bolt threads and tighten them to 6.0-12.8 ft. lbs.

26. Clean the mating surfaces of the case-to-rear extension housing and apply sealant to the mating surface of the case.

27. Using a light coating of petroleum jelly to retain them, locate the needle thrust bearing, race and funnel on the rear of the counter shaft.

28. Place the detent ball, spring and offset lever into position on the guide plate and then connect the extension housing to the case.

29. Align the holes in the shifter shaft and offset lever and then install the retaining pin.

30. Insert the mounting bolts and tighten them to 20-46 ft. lbs.

31. Apply sealant to the shift cover hole in the extension housing. Assemble the damper sleeve into the offset lever and then install the shift lever. Tighten the mounting bolts to 11-20 ft. lbs.

32. Install the drain plug and fill with lubricant.

33. Push the input shaft to the rear and mount a dial indicator so the stem

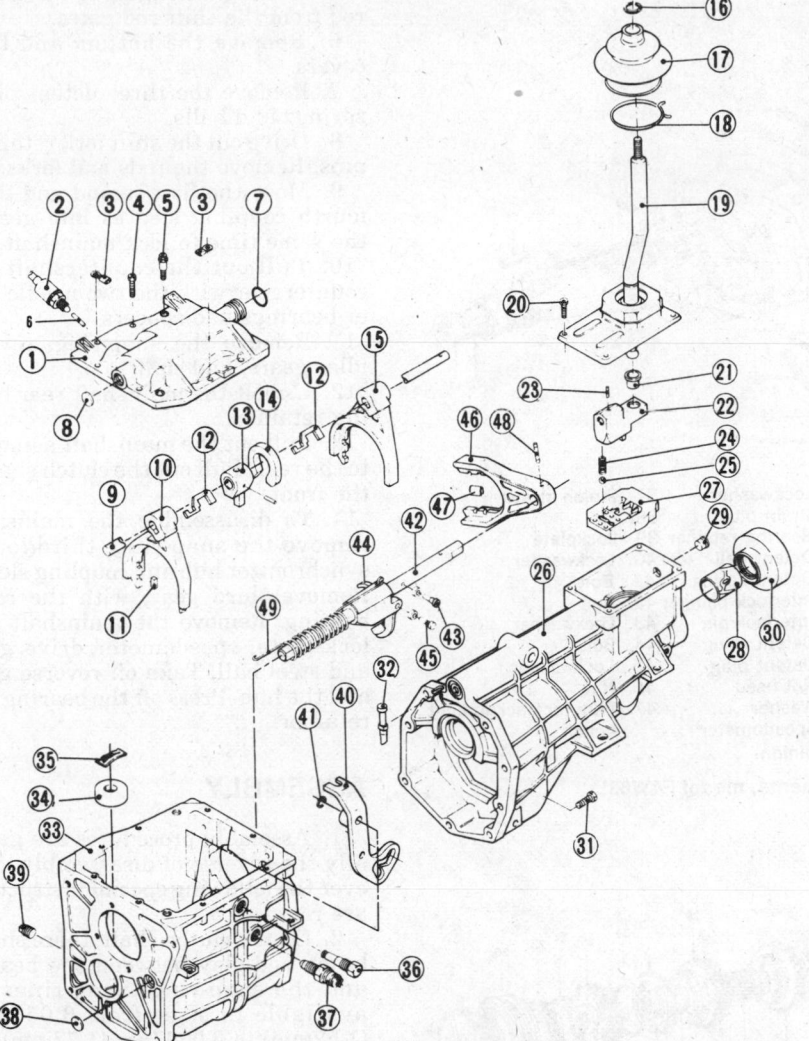

Checking the preload

rests against the front end of the shaft. Zero the indicator.

34. Push the output shaft forward and note the indicator reading. Remove the indicator.

35. Remove the bearing retainer and race. Select the proper thickness shim to provide 0.0051-0.0098 in. preload.

NOTE: To get the desired shim thickness, add the dial indicator reading from Step 34 to the desired preload. The resulting total is the proper shim thickness.

36. Apply sealant to the bearing retainer mating surface and the bolt threads. Install the shims and race into the retainer as in Step 19.

37. Install the transmission into the vehicle.

TYPE 7

4 Speed Transmission Model F4W63L Datsun

DISASSEMBLY

The reverse and reverse idler drive gears are contained in the extension housing of the transmission. On late units, the cast ribbed bottom cover is replaced by a stamped steel cover. Virtually all of these transmissions imported to the U.S. have a modified extension housing incorporating a floorshift mechanism.

1. Drain the transmission.

2. Remove the clutch throw-out lever and release bearing.

3. Remove the clevis pin which connects the striker rod to the shift lever.

4. Remove the speedometer drive pinion assembly.

5. Unbolt and remove the exten-

1 Case cover	26 Extension housing	Not serviced
2 Neutral switch	27 Detent & guide plate	separately
3 Wiring clip	28 Bushing	
4 Hex head bolt	29 Cup plug	
5 Hex head shoulder bolt	30 Oil seal	
6 Pin	31 Hex head flanged bolt	
7 O-ring	32 Breather	
8 Welsh plug	33 Case	
9 Shifter shaft	34 Magnet	
10 3–4 shift fork	35 Clip	
11 Shift fork insert	36 Pivot pin	
12 Selector plate	37 Back-up lamp switch	
13 Control selector arm	38 Welsh plug	
14 Interlock plate	39 Pipe plug	
15 1–2 shift fork	40 5th and reverse relay lever	
16 Boot retainer	41 Retaining ring	
17 Boot	42 5th and reverse shift rail	Not serviced
18 Boot retainer	43 Roller cam and pin	separately
19 Control lever/housing assembly	44 Reverse shift fork	Not serviced
20 Control housing screw	45 Roller cam and pin	separately
21 Damper sleeve	46 5th gear shift fork	
22 Offset lever	47 Insert	
23 Spring-pin	48 Spring-pin	
24 Detent spring	49 Spring	
25 Ball		

Exploded view of transmission assembly

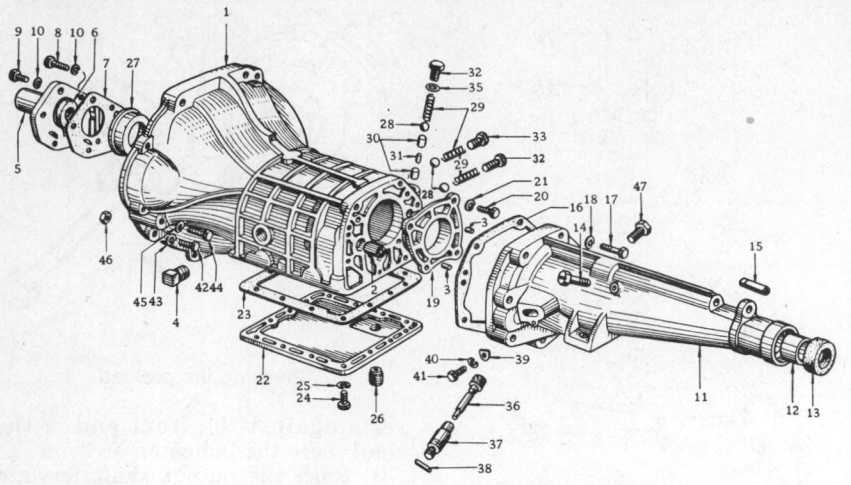

Transmission case components, model F4W63L

1. Case	13. Oil seal	25. Lockwasher	37. Pinion sleeve
2. Needle bearing	14. Breather	26. Drain plug	38. Pin
3. Dowel pin	15. Striker bushing	27. Bearing retainer	39. Lockplate
4. Plug assembly	16. Gasket	28. Detent ball	40. Lockwasher
5. Front cover	17. Bolt	29. Detent spring	41. Bolt
6. Oil seal	18. Lockwasher	30. Interlock plunger	42. Bolt
7. Gasket	19. Bearing retainer	31. Interlock pin	43. Lockwasher
8. Bolt	20. Bolt	32. Detent plug	44. Bolt
9. Bolt	21. Lockwasher	33. Detent plug	45. Lockwasher
10. Lockwasher	22. Bottom cover	34. Not used	46. Nut
11. Extension housing	23. Gasket	35. Washer	47. Plug for backup light switch
12. Bushing	24. Bolt	36. Speedometer pinion	

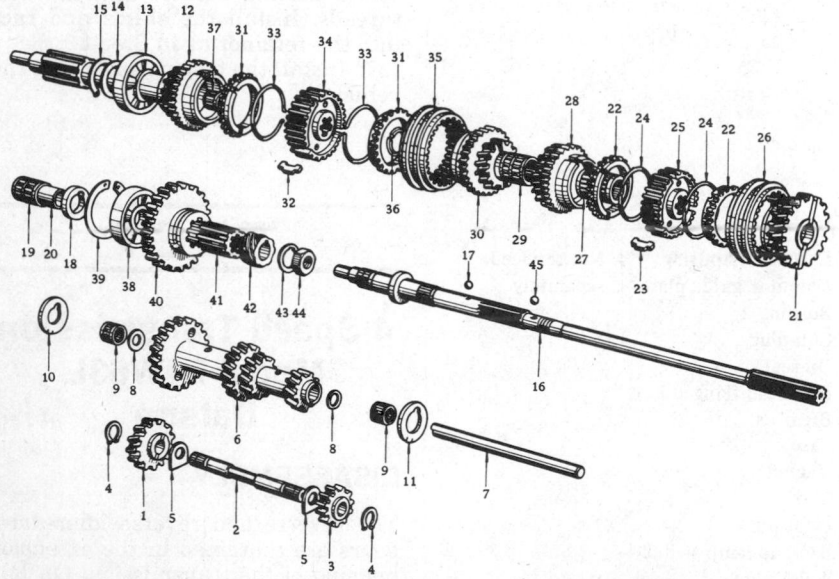

1. Reverse idler gear	15. Snap-ring	30. Third gear
2. Reverse idler shaft	16. Mainshaft	31. Baulk ring
3. Main reverse idler gear	17. 5/32" steel ball	32. Shifting insert
4. Snap-ring	18. Thrust washer	33. Spreader ring
5. Thrust washer	19. Needle bearing	34. Third/fourth synchro hub
6. Countergear	20. First gear bushing	35. Coupling sleeve
7. Countershaft	21. First gear	36. Snap-ring
8. Spacer	22. Baulk ring	37. Pilot bearing
9. Needle bearing	23. Shifting insert	38. Bearing
10. Front countershaft thrust washer	24. Spreader ring	39. Snap-ring
11. Rear countershaft thrust washer	25. First/second synchro hub	40. Reverse gear
12. Main drive gear	26. Coupling sleeve	41. Reverse gear hub
13. Main drive gear bearing	27. Needle bearing	42. Speedometer drive gear
14. Washer	28. Second gear	43. Lockwasher
	29. Needle bearing	44. Nut
		45. Steel ball

Exploded view of gear train components

sion housing, disengaging the striker rod from the shift rod gates.

6. Remove the bottom and front covers.

7. Remove the three detent plugs, springs and balls.

8. Drive out the shift fork retaining pins. Remove the rods and forks.

9. Move the first/second and third/fourth coupling sleeves into gear at the same time to lock mainshaft.

10. Pull out the countershaft and countergear with the two needle roller bearings and spacers.

11. Remove the snap-ring, reverse idler gears, and shaft.

12. Unbolt the mainshaft rear bearing retainer.

13. Pull out the mainshaft assembly to the rear. Pull out the clutch shaft to the front.

14. To disassemble the mainshaft, remove the snap-ring, third/fourth synchronizer hub and coupling sleeve. Remove third gear, with the roller bearing. Remove the mainshaft nut, lock-plate, speedometer drive gear, and steel ball. Take off reverse gear, and the hub. Press off the bearing and retainer.

ASSEMBLY

1. Assembly procedures are generally the reverse of disassembly, however the following special instructions are required.

2. On the clutch shaft, there should be no end-play between the bearing and the snap-ring. Snap-rings are available in sizes from 0.0598 in. (1.52mm) to 0.0697 in. (1.77mm).

3. Some of these transmissions use a servo type synchronizer which utilizes brake bands. To assemble these synchronizers, place each gear on a flat surface. Install the synchronizer ring into the clutch gear. Place the thrust block and anchor block and install the circlip into the groove.

4. Third gear should be adjusted to give an end-play of 0.0020-0.0059 in. Snap-rings for adjustment are available in sizes from 0.0551 in. to 0.0630 in.

5. Install the reverse idler driving gear on the reverse shaft and fasten with a snapring. Install the shaft and gear into case, placing a thrust washer between the gear and case. Place a thrust washer, idler gear, and snapring on the inside end of the shaft. Idler gear end-play should be 0.0039-0.0118 in. Snap-rings are available in sizes from 0.0433 in to 0.0591 in.

6. Countergear end-play should be 0.0020-0.0059 in. Thrust washers for adjustment are available from 0.0945 in. to 0.1024 in.

7. To assemble the shift mecha-

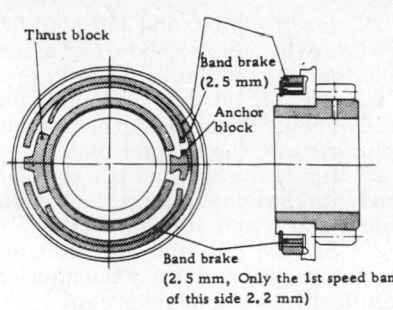

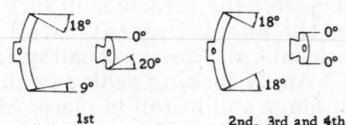

Servo type synchronizer assembly details

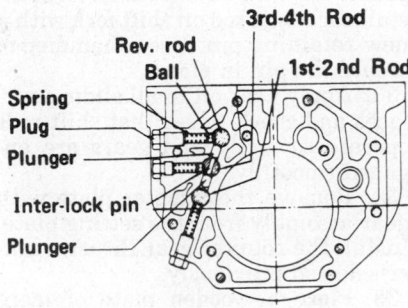

Shift rod interlock details for four speed bottom cover transmission

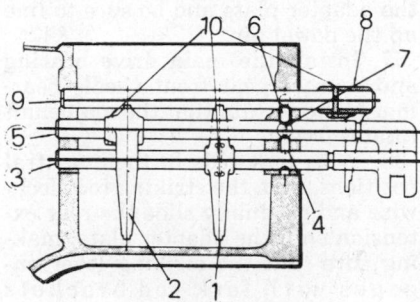

1. First/second shift fork
2. Third/fourth shift fork
3. First/second shift rod
4. Interlock plunger
5. Third/fourth shift rod
6. Interlock plunger
7. Interlock pin
8. Reverse shift fork
9. Reverse shift rod
10. Fork retaining pin

Shift rod and fork details, four speed bottom cover transmission

nism, place the first/second and third/fourth forks onto their sleeves. Insert the first/second shift rod. Install an interlock plunger and then the third/fourth shift rod with the interlock pin. Install the other interlock plunger and then the reverse shift fork and rod. Place a detent ball and spring

into each detent hole. Use sealant on the plug threads.

8. Install the extension housing, engaging the striker rod with the shift rod.

TYPE 8

4 Speed Transmission Model F4W60L Datsun

DISASSEMBLY

1. Drain the transmission oil thoroughly.
2. Remove the dust cover from the transmission case and remove the release bearing and lever.
3. Remove the reverse lamp switch and top detecting switch if equipped.
4. Remove the speedometer pinion assembly.

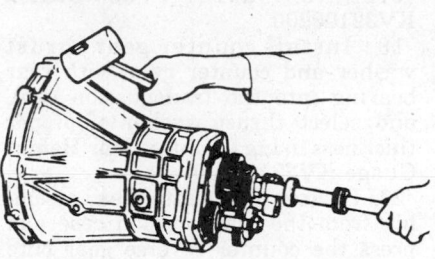

Trans case and adpater plate

5. Remove the nut and stopper pin bolt from the rear end of the rear extension.
6. Remove the return spring plug, return spring, reverse check spring and plunger from the rear extension.
7. Remove the front cover with O'ring and adjusting shim.
8. Remove the main drive bearing snap ring with snap ring pliers.
9. Remove the rear extension housing bolts and turn the striking rod clockwise. Drive the rear extension backward by lightly tapping around it with a rubber malot.
10. Seperate the transmission case from the adapter plate using a rubber malot.
11. Mount the adapter plate assembly into a holding fixture and mount in a vise.
12. Detach the counter gear thrust washer and drive out the retaining pins from each fork rod with a pin punch.
13. Drive out reverse gear shift fork

and reverse idler gear. Remove the three check ball plugs.
14. Drive out the fork rods from the adapter plate by lightly tapping on the front end. Detach the shift forks.

NOTE: **Each gear and shaft can be detached from the adapter plate without removing each fork rod.**

15. Remove the reverse gear snap ring from the rear of the mainshaft using snap ring pliers.

NOTE: **It is necessary to measure end play, before disassembling mainshaft and after reassembling mainshaft.**

16. Remove the bearing retainer attaching screws with an impact driver and remove the bearing retainer.
17. Remove the snap ring from the mainshaft rear bearing.
18. Drive out the mainshaft gear assembly together with the counter gear assembly by lightly tapping the rear while holding the front by hand.
19. Remove the counter gear, main drive gear and mainshaft assembly in that order.
20. Disassemble the mainshaft gear assembly as follows:
    a. Remove the snap ring from the mainshaft front end.
    b. Remove the 3rd. and 4th. synchronizer assembly, bulk rings, 3rd. gear and mainshaft needle bearing toward the front side.
    c. Press out the mainshaft bearing using the proper tool.
    d. Remove the thrust washer, 1st. gear, needle bearing, bushing, 1st. and 2nd. synchronizer assembly, baulk rings, 2nd. gear and needle bearing from mainshaft.
21. Remove the snap ring and spacer. Press out the main drive bearing using proper tools.
22. Remove the snap ring from the rear of the counter gear. Press out the counter reverse gear and the counter gear rear bearing.
23. Remove the spread springs and take out the shifting inserts. Seperate the coupling sleeve from the synchro hub.
24. Remove the reverse idler shaft snap ring from the adapter plate. Draw out the reverse idler shaft by lightly tapping on the end with soft hammer.
25. Remove the lock pin nut and lock pin from the striking lever. Remove the striking lever.
26. Remove the striking rod and striking guide from the rear end of the rear extension.

NOTE: **Do not remove the rear extension bushing from the rear extension.**

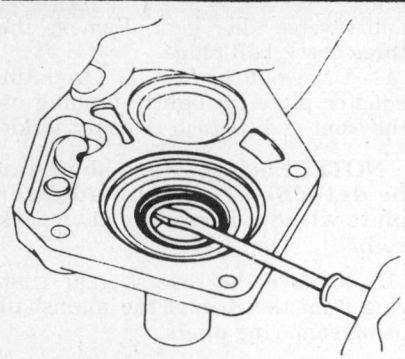

Front cover oil seal

ASSEMBLY

1. Drive new seal into place on the front cover using a press and an Oil Seal Drift.

NOTE: When pressing the oil seal into place, apply a coat of gear oil to the surface adjoining the oil seal.

2. Lubricate the seal lip and main drive shaft with gear oil when installing the front cover.

3. Press the countershaft needle bearing into the transmission case from the outside.

4. Install the withdrawal lever ball pin on the case and tighten the screw.

5. Drive the new seal into place on the rear extension using a press and an Oil Seal Drift.

6. Coat the oil seal lip and bushing with gear oil for initial lubrication. Pack the cavity between the seal lips with recommended multi—purpose grease when installing.

7. Apply grease to O'ring and plunger grooves in striking rod guide. Insert the striking rod with guide through the rear extension.

8. Install the striking lever on the front end of the striking rod. Install the lock pin and nut and tighten it to 6.5–8.7 ft. lbs. (8.8–11.8 Nm).

9. Place the adapter plate and setting plate in a vise with the fork rod hole side up.

10. Install the reverse idler shaft in the adapter plate and secure it with snap rings.

11. Assemble the synchronizer assembly in the following procedure:

a. Place the synchro hub into the coupling sleeve.

b. Fit shifting inserts in three grooves in synchro hub.

c. Insert the protrusion of the spread spring into groove so that the insert is securely attached to the inner side of the coupling sleeve. Install the other spread spring on the opposite side of the synchro hub.

NOTE: Be careful not to hook front and rear ends of the spread spring to the same insert.

12. Assemble the 2nd. gear needle bearing, 2nd. gear, baulk ring, 1st. and 2nd. speed synchronizer assembly, 1st. gear baulk ring, 1st. gear bushing, needle bearing, 1st. gear and thrust washer on the mainshaft.

13. Press the mainshaft bearing onto the mainshaft.

14. Position 3rd. gear needle bearing, 3rd. gear, baulk ring, and 3rd. and 4th. synchronizer assembly on the front side of the mainshaft.

15. Fit a new snap ring in place so that a minimum clearance exists between the end face of the hub and ring.

16. Press the main drive gear bearing onto the shaft using the proper tools.

17. Place the main drive bearing spacer on the bearing and secure the bearing with a new thicker snap ring that will eliminate end play.

18. Press the counter gear rear bearing onto the counter gear using Countershaft Bearing Press Stand KV32100200.

19. Install counter gear thrust washer and counter gear with rear bearing into the transmission case, and select thrust washer of proper thickness using Counter Gear Height Guage KV32100100.

20. Remove the counter gear assembly from the transmission case and press the counter reverse gear onto the assembly. Fit snap ring to groove in rear end of the counter gear.

21. Install the baulk ring on the main drive gear, and combine with the mainshaft to complete the mainshaft assembly.

NOTE: Be sure to install the pilot bearing in place when combining with mainshaft.

22. Combine the mainshaft assembly with the counter gear assembly and place them into the adapter plate simultaneously.

23. Pull the mainshaft assembly into the adapter plate using Mainshaft Puller KV32100400. Install the counter gear assembly together with mainshaft assembly.

24. Install the bearing retainer on the adapter plate and torque the screws to 5.1–7.2 ft. lbs. (6.9–9.8 Nm). Stake each screw at two points with a punch.

25. Install the mainshaft reverse gear and thrust washer on the rear end of the mainshaft and secure it with a new snap ring.

NOTE: Install the thrust washer so that its concave side is on the mainshaft reverse gear.

26. Insert the 1st. and 2nd. shift fork rod into the adapter plate, and assemble the 1st. and 2nd. shift fork.

27. Set the 1st. and 2nd. shift fork rod at neutral and insert the interlock plunger into the adapter plate.

28. Insert the 3rd. and 4th. shift fork rod into the adapter plate, and assemble the 3rd. and 4th. shift fork.

29. Set the 3rd. and 4th. shift fork rod at neutral and insert the interlock plunger into the adapter plate.

30. Insert the reverse shift fork rod into the adapter plate. Install the check balls and the check ball springs.

31. Apply locking sealer to check ball plugs and install in place. Align the notches in the reverse, 3rd. and 4th. and 1st. and 2nd. shift fork rods with check balls.

32. Install the reverse idler gear together with the reverse shift fork. Install each fork rod on shift fork with a new retaining pin. Use a hammer to secure the pin in place.

33. Apply gear oil to all sliding surfaces and check to see that shift rods operate correctly and gears are engaged smoothly.

34. Remove the adapter plate with gear assembly from the setting plate. Install the counter gear thrust washer selected previously.

35. Place a wooden plate of more than 0.59 in. (15mm) thick under transmission case to make it level.

36. Slide the transmission case onto the adapter plate and be sure to line up the dowel pin.

37. Install the main drive bearing and counter gear front needle bearing. Make certain that the mainshaft rotates freely.

38. With fork rods in their neutral positions, turn the striking rod clockwise and gradually slide the rear extension onto the adapter plate, making sure that the striking lever engages with fork rod brackets correctly.

39. Install the through bolts with the washer and tighten to 12–16 ft. lbs. (16–22 Nm).

40. Apply sealant and install the stopper pin bolt into the rear extension and tighten to 3.6–5.8 ft. lbs. (4.9–7.8 Nm).

41. Apply grease to the plunger and install it in the rear extension. Install the reverse check spring and the return spring. Apply sealer to the return spring plug and install it in place 3.6–7.2 ft. lbs. (4.9–9.8 Nm).

42. To select a front cover adjusting shim, using a caliper depth gauge measure from the front end of the transmission case to main drive bearing outer race with front cover adjusting shim in place. Select a shim of thew thickness measured.

43. Install the front cover to transmission case with the adjusting shim and O'ring in place. Tighten the bolt to 7–12 ft. lbs. (10–16 Nm).

44. Install the speedometer pinion assembly and tighten the securing bolt to 2.2–3.6 ft. lbs. (2.9–4.9 Nm).

45. Install the reverse lamp switch and at the same time install the top detecting switch if so equipped. Tighten to 14–25 ft. lbs. (20–34 Nm).

46. Apply a light coat of multi—purpose grease to withdrawal lever, release bearing and bearing sleeve and install them on the transmission case. After connecting them with the holder spring, install the dust cover to the transmission case.

47. Install the control lever and move it through all gears to make sure that they operate smoothly.

48. Install the drain plug coated with sealant and tighten to 18–29 ft. lbs. (25–39 Nm).

TYPE 9

5 Speed Transmission Model FS5W71B and FS5W71C Datsun

These transmissions are similar to the 4 speed transmission, model F4W71B and the overhaul can be accomplished by following the outline for the disassembly and assembly of the model F4W71B transmission.

Servo type synchromesh is used, instead of the Borg-Warner type in the four speed. Shift linkage and interlock arrangements are the same, except the reverse shift rod also operates fifth gear. Most service procedures are identical to those for the four speed unit. Those unique to the five-speed follow.

DISASSEMBLY

To disassemble the synchronizers, remove the circlip, synchronizer ring, thrust block, brake band, and anchor block. Be careful not to mix parts of the different synchronizer assemblies.

ASSEMBLY

1. The synchronizer assemblies for second, third, and fourth are identical. When assembling the first gear synchronizer, be sure to install the 0.0866 in. thick brake band at the bottom.

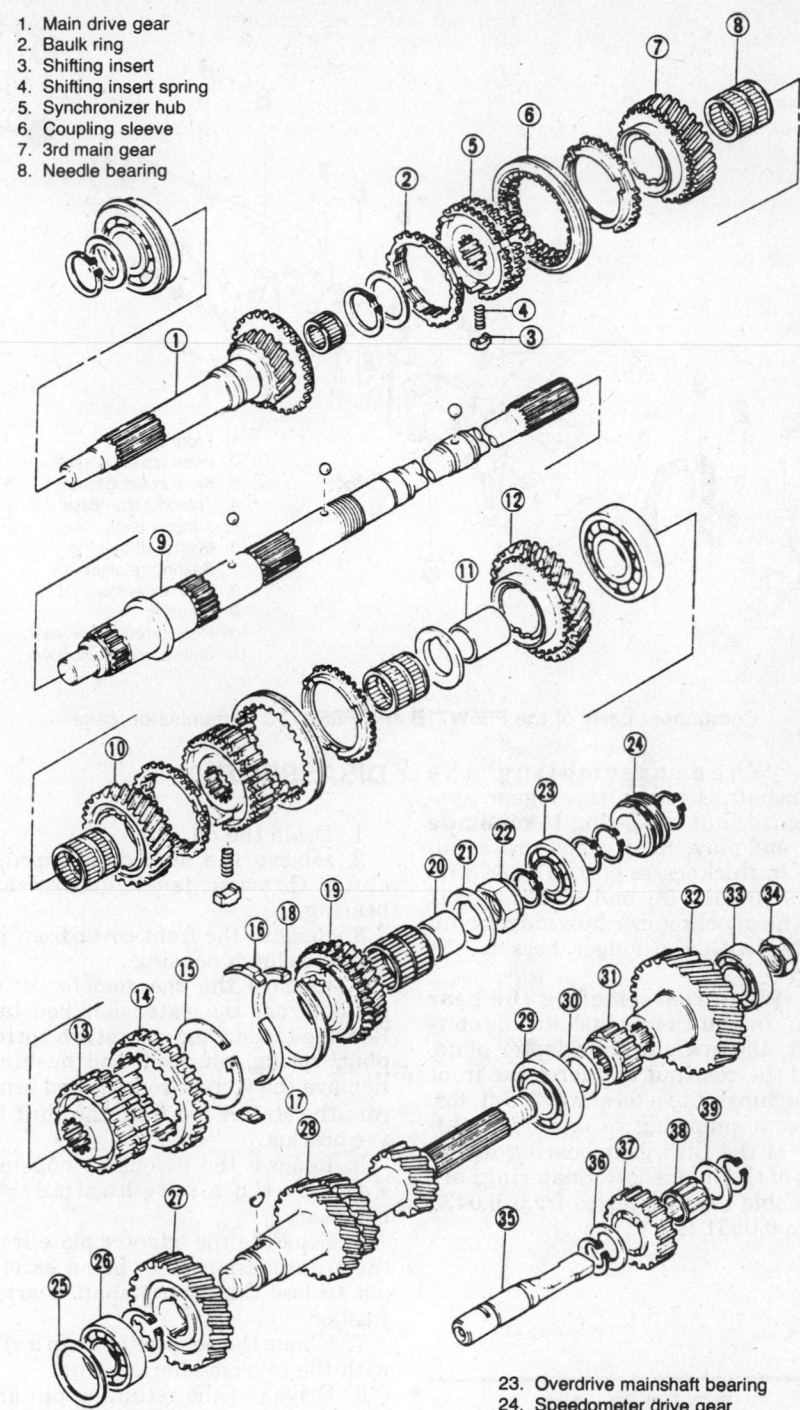

1. Main drive gear
2. Baulk ring
3. Shifting insert
4. Shifting insert spring
5. Synchronizer hub
6. Coupling sleeve
7. 3rd main gear
8. Needle bearing
9. Mainshaft
10. 2nd main gear
11. Bushing
12. 1st main gear
13. OD-reverse synchronizer hub
14. Reverse gear
15. Circlip
16. Thrust block
17. Brake band
18. Synchronizer ring
19. Overdrive main gear
20. Overdrive gear bushing
21. Washer
22. Mainshaft nut
23. Overdrive mainshaft bearing
24. Speedometer drive gear
25. Countershaft front bearing shim
26. Countershaft front bearing
27. Countershaft drive gear
28. Countershaft
29. Countershaft bearing
30. Reverse counter gear spacer
31. Reverse counter gear
32. Overdrive counter gear
33. Countershaft rear bearing
34. Countershaft nut
35. Reverse idler shaft
36. Reverse idler thrust washer
37. Reverse idler gear
38. Reverse idler gear bearing
39. Reverse idler thrust washer

Exploded view of the gear train—FS5W71B and FS5W71C

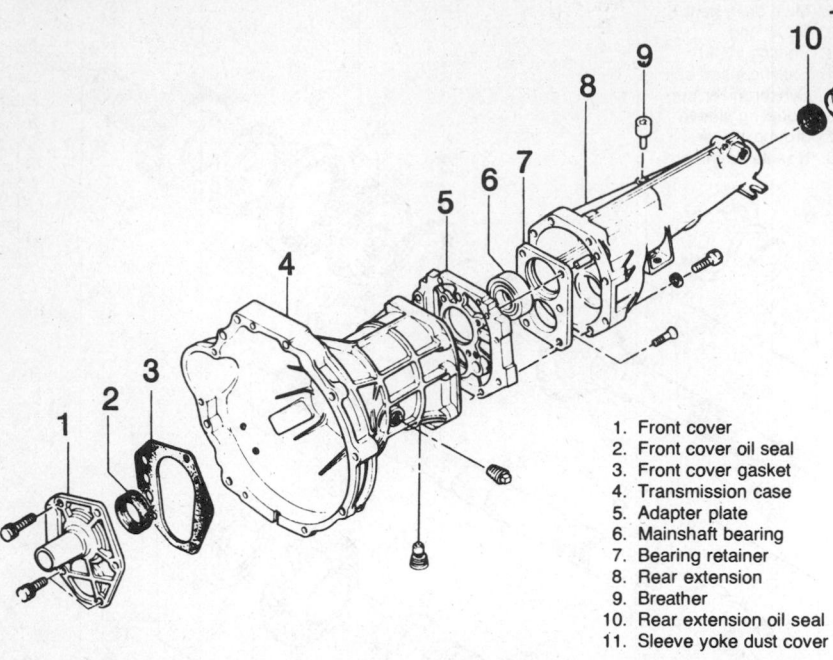

1. Front cover
2. Front cover oil seal
3. Front cover gasket
4. Transmission case
5. Adapter plate
6. Mainshaft bearing
7. Bearing retainer
8. Rear extension
9. Breather
10. Rear extension oil seal
11. Sleeve yoke dust cover

Component parts of the FS5W71B and FS5W71C transmission case

2. When assembling the mainshaft, select a third gear synchronizer hub snap-ring to minimize hub end-play. Snap rings are available in thicknesses of 0.061-0.063 in. 0.0591-0.0610 in. and 0.0571-0.0591 in. The synchronizer hub must be installed with the longer boss to the rear.

3. When reassembling the gear train, install the mainshaft, countershaft, and gears to the adapter plate. Hold the rear nut and force the front nut against it to a torque of 217 ft. lbs. Select a snap-ring to minimize end-play of the fifth gear bearing at the rear of the mainshaft. Snap-rings are available in thicknesses from 0.0433 in. to 0.0551 in.

TYPE 10

4 Speed Transmission Model F4W56A Datsun

This transmission is constructed in two sections: a combined clutch and transmission housing, and an extension housing. There is a cast iron adapter plate between the housings. There are no case cover plates.

DISASSEMBLY

1. Drain the oil.
2. remove the dust cover, spring, clutch throwout lever, and release bearing.
3. Remove the front cover from inside the clutch housing.
4. Remove the speedometer drive pinion from the extension housing. Remove the striker rod return spring plug, spring, plunger, and bushing. Remove the striker rod pin and separate the striker rod from the shift lever bracket.
5. Remove the extension housing. Tap it with a soft hammer, if necessary.
6. Separate the adapter plate from the transmission case, being careful not to lose the countershaft bearing washer.
7. Clamp the adapter plate in a vise with the reverse idler gear up.
8. Drive out the retaining pin and remove the reverse shift fork and reverse idler gear.
9. Remove the mainshaft rear snap-ring, washer, and reverse gear.
10. Drive out the remaining shift fork retaining pins. Remove all three detent plugs, springs, and balls. Remove the forks and shift rods. Be careful not to lose the interlock plungers.
11. Tap the rear of the mainshaft with a soft hammer to separate the mainshaft and countershaft from the adapter plate. Be careful not to drop the shafts. Separate the clutch shaft from the mainshaft.

12. From the front of the mainshaft, remove the needle bearing, synchronizer hub thrust washer, steel locating ball, third/fourth synchronizer, baulk ring, third gear, and needle bearing.
13. Press off the mainshaft bearing to the rear. Remove the thrust washer, first gear, needle bearing, baulk ring, first/second synchronizer, snap-ring and bearing.

ASSEMBLY

1. Press on the countershaft bearings. Install the countershaft assembly to the transmission case and replace the adapter plate temporarily. Countershaft end-play should be 0-0.0079 in. Front bearing shims are available for adjustment in thicknesses from 0.0315 in. to 0.0512 in. Remove the countershaft assembly from the case.
2. Install the coupling sleeve, shifting inserts, and spring on the synchronizer hub. Be careful not to hook the front and rear ends of the spring to the same insert.
3. Install the needle bearing from the rear of the mainshaft. Install second gear, the baulk ring, and synchronizer hub assembly. Align the shifting insert to the baulk ring groove. Install the first gear side needle bearing, baulk ring, and first gear. Install the mainshaft thrust washer and press on the rear bearing.

On the mainshaft front end, replace the needle bearing, third gear, baulk ring, synchronizer hub assembly, steel locating ball, thrust washer, and pilot bearing. Be sure to grease the sliding surface of the steel ball and thrust washer. The dimpled side of the thrust washer must face to the front and the oil grooved side to the rear.

4. Replace the main bearing, washer, and snap-ring onto the clutch shaft. The web side of the washer must face the bearing. Place the baulk ring on the clutch shaft and assemble the clutch shaft to the mainshaft.
5. Align the mainshaft assembly with the countershaft assembly and install them to the adapter plate by lightly tapping on the clutch shaft with a soft hammer.
6. Place the first/second and third/fourth shift forks on the shift rods, being careful that the forks are not reversed. Install all three shift rods and the detent and interlock parts. Apply locking agent to the detent plug threads and screw the plugs in flush. Make sure the shift forks are in their grooves and drive in the remaining pins.

7.Install the mainshaft reverse gear, thrust washer, and snap-ring. Face the web side of the thrust washer to the gear.

8.Replace the reverse idler gear and pin on the reverse shift fork. Check interlock action by attempting to shift two shift rods at once.

9.Install the adapter plate to the transmission case. Make sure to install the countergear front shim selected in Step 1. Use sealant on the joint and seat the plate by tapping with a soft hammer.

10. Align the striker lever and install the extension housing. Use sealant on the joint. Install the bushing, plunger return spring, and plug. Use sealant on the plug threads. Install the striker rod pin and the speedometer drive pinion.

11. Select clutch shaft bearing shim(s) by measuring the amount the bearing outer race is recessed below the machined surface for the front cover. The depth should be 0.1969-0.2028 in. Shims are available for adjustment in thicknesses of 0.0039 in., 0.0079 in., and 0.0197 in.

12. Place the oil seal in the front cover, grease the seal lip, and install the cover and O-ring with the shim(s) selected in Step 11.

13. Replace the clutch release bearing, return spring, and withdrawal lever.

14. Check shifting action. Rotate the clutch shaft slowly in neutral. The rear of the mainshaft should not turn.

TYPE 11

5 Speed Transmission Model FS5W63A, L Datsun

DISASSEMBLY

1. Secure the transmission and drain the lubricant.
2. Remove the dust cover, the clutch release bearing and the operating lever.
3. Remove the electrical switches from the case.
4. Remove the speedometer driven gear assembly.
5. Remove the front main drive gear bearing cover and detach the countershaft front bearing shim.
6. Remove the main drive gear bearing snap-ring from the outer race.

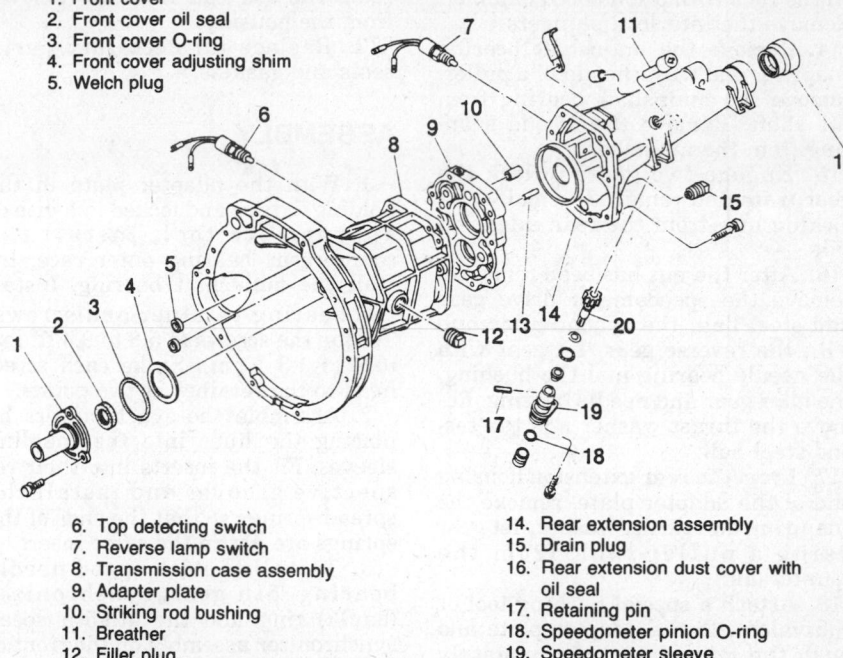

1. Front cover
2. Front cover oil seal
3. Front cover O-ring
4. Front cover adjusting shim
5. Welch plug
6. Top detecting switch
7. Reverse lamp switch
8. Transmission case assembly
9. Adapter plate
10. Striking rod bushing
11. Breather
12. Filler plug
13. Rear extension dowel pin
14. Rear extension assembly
15. Drain plug
16. Rear extension dust cover with oil seal
17. Retaining pin
18. Speedometer pinion O-ring
19. Speedometer sleeve
20. Speedometer pinion

Transmission case components—model F4W56A

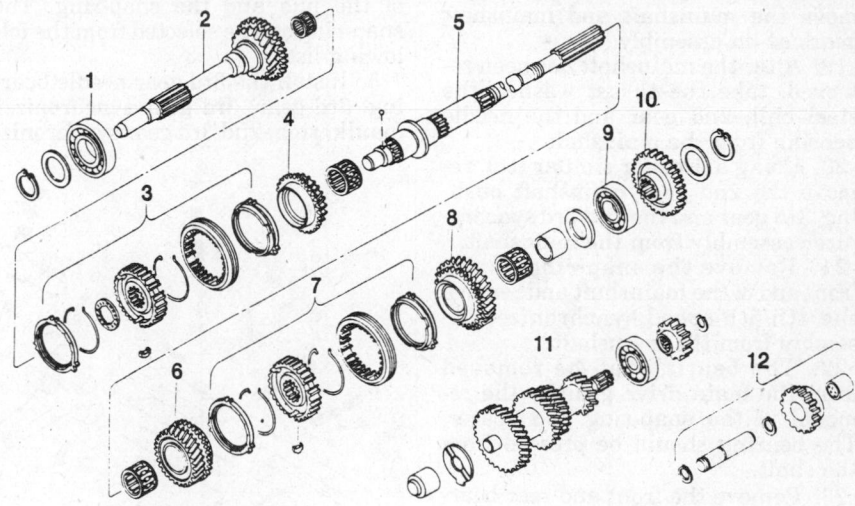

1. Main drive bearing
2. Main drive gear
3. 3rd & top synchronizer
4. 3rd gear, mainshaft
5. Mainshaft
6. 2nd gear, mainshaft
7. 1st & 2nd synchronizer
8. 1st gear, mainshaft
9. Mainshaft bearing
10. Reverse gear, mainshaft
11. Counter gear assembly
12. Idler gear assembly

Exploded view of the gear train components

7. Remove the return spring plug, the return spring and plunger from the rear extension.

8. Remove the rear extension housing retaining bolts and with the use of a puller, remove the housing from the transmission case and adapter plate.

9. Separate the adapter plate from the transmission case by lightly tapping the case from the adapter plate.

10. Mount the adapter plate assembly into a holding fixture, either purchased or fabricated, and mount in a vise or similar tool.

11. Drive the retaining pins from the shifting forks and selector shaft rods with a pin punch.

12. Remove the three selector rod check ball plugs. Remove the check balls and springs.

13. Remove the selector rods from the front to the rear by lightly tapping

on the rods with a soft-faced hammer. Remove the interlock plungers.

14. Remove the mainshaft bearing snapring and with the aid of a puller, remove the mainshaft bearing from the shaft. Remove the second snapring from the mainshaft.

15. Engage two gears to lock the gear train and remove the mainshaft locking nut, from the rear extension side.

16. After the nut has been removed, remove the speedometer drive gear and steel ball, the synchronizer hub with the reverse gear, 1st gear with the needle bearing and the bushing, the idler gear and needle bearing. Remove the thrust washer and the second steel ball.

17. From the rear extension housing end of the adapter plate, remove the snap-ring and thrust washer, 1st gear using a puller tool, from the countershaft.

18. Attach a special pushing tool or equivalent, to the adapter plate and push the mainshaft approximately 0.39 in (10mm) from the adapter plate. Remove the main drive gear and the countergear. Holding the mainshaft gear assembly by hand, remove the mainshaft and mainshaft gears as an assembly.

19. After the mainshaft has been removed, take the thrust washer, the steel ball, 2nd gear and the needle bearing from the mainshaft.

20. Using a press or similar tool, remove the 2nd gear mainshaft bushing, 3rd gear and the 2nd/3rd synchronizer assembly from the mainshaft.

21. Remove the snap-ring on the front end of the mainshaft and remove the 4th/5th speed synchronizer assembly from the mainshaft.

22. The bearing can be removed from the main drive gear by the removal of the snap-ring and spacer. The bearing should be pressed from the shaft.

23. Remove the front and rear bearings from the countergear by using a press or similar tool.

24. To disassemble the synchronizers, remove the spread springs and the shift inserts. Separate the coupling sleeve from the hub.

25. With the adapter plate still in the holding fixture, remove the bearing retainer bolts with an appropriate tool. Remove the bearing from the rear extension side of the adapter plate. The outer race of the counter gear rear bearing can be removed from the adapter plate with the aid of a brass punch.

26. The rear extension housing can be disassembled by the removal of the lock pin from the striking lever and the main selector shift rod (striking rod). The rod can then be removed from the housing.

27. Replace all necessary parts, seals and gaskets.

ASSEMBLY

1. With the adapter plate in the holding fixture and locked in a vise or appropriate tool, install the countergear bearing outer race. Install the mainshaft bearing. Install the bearing retainer and screws. Torque the screws to 5.8 to 9.4 ft. lbs. (0.8 to 1.3 Kgm). Stake each screw head to the retainer at two points.

2. Assemble the synchronizers by placing the hubs into the coupling sleeves. Fit the inserts into their respective grooves and install the spread springs so that the ends of the springs are not in the same insert.

3. Install the 5th speed needle bearing, 5th gear, synchronizer (baulk) ring and the 4th/5th speed synchronizer assembly on the front of the mainshaft.

4. Install a selective snap-ring onto the mainshaft so that the minimum clearance exists between the end face of the hub and the snap-ring. The snap-ring can be selected from the following list:

5. Install the 3rd gear needle bearing, 3rd gear, 3rd gear synchronizer (baulk) ring, 2nd/3rd gear synchroniz-er, fit the 2nd gear bushing to the mainshaft, aling with the mainshaft bearing thrust washer.

6. Install the 2nd speed synchronizer (baulk) ring, needle bearing, 2nd gear, steel ball and the thrust washer.

7. Press the main drive gear bearing on to the main drive gear and install the spacer and secure with a snap-ring that will eliminate end-play between the spacer and the snapring. A selective snap-ring can be selected from the following list.

8. Press the front and rear bearings onto the countergear with appropriate tools.

9. Place the mainshaft assembly into the adapter plate and place the mainshaft nut onto the shaft.

10. Using a puler type tool, move the mainshaft into the adapter plate until the thrust washer to bearing clearance is approximately 0.39 in. (10mm).

11. Install the pilot bearing into the main drive gear bore and install the main drive gear and the synchronizer (baulk) ring onto the main assembly.

12. Assemble the countergear assembly to the mainshaft gear assembly.

13. Continuing the pulling effort, move the mainshaft and countergear assemblies into the adapter plate.

14. Place the 1st countergear on the countergear assembly and press into

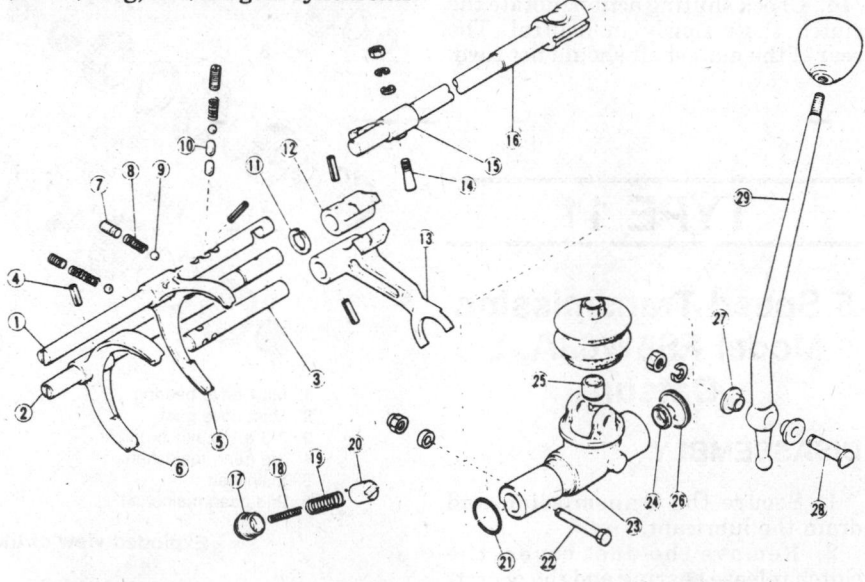

1. 1st & 2nd fork rod	11. Stopper ring	21. O-ring
2. 3rd & top fork rod	12. Shift rod A bracket	22. Stopper pin bolt
3. Reverse fork rod	13. Reverse shift fork	23. Striking guide assembly
4. Retaining pin	14. Lock pin	24. Striking guide oil seal
5. 1st & 2nd shift fork	15. Striking lever	25. Control lever bushing
6. 3rd & top shift fork	16. Striking rod	26. Expansion plug
7. Checking ball plug	17. Return spring plug	27. Control pin bushing
8. Check ball spring	18. Reverse check spring	28. Control arm pin
9. Check ball	19. Return spring	29. Control lever
10. Interlock plunger	20. Plunger	

Exploded view of shift selector rod and fork components

1. Front cover
2. Front cover oil seal
3. Withdrawal lever ball pin
4. Transmission case
5. Breather
6. Reverse lamp switch
7. Top switch (U.S.A. models)
8. Sleeve yoke dust cover
9. Rear extension oil seal
10. Speedometer pinion
11. Speedometer sleeve
12. Rear extension
13. Adapter plate

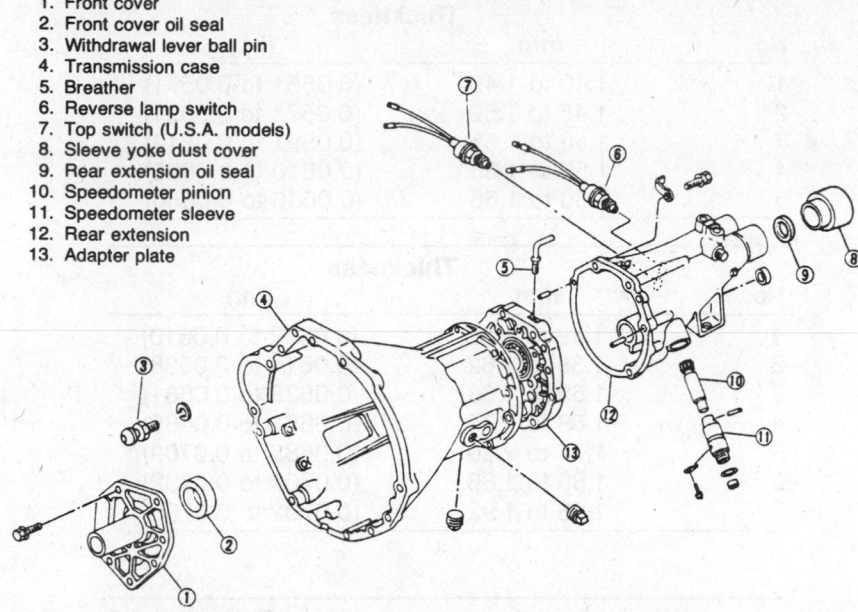

Transmission case components, model FS5W63A

into the adapter plate, position the 1st/reverse fork into its gear position, and slide the selector rod into the fork.

No.	Thickness	
	mm	(in)
1	1.1	(0.043)
2	1.2	(0.047)
3	1.3	(0.051)
4	1.4	(0.055)

20. Place the 1st/reverse selector rod in the neutral position and install the interlock plunger into the adapter plate.

21. Insert the 2nd/3rd selector rod into the adapter plate, position the 2nd/3rd and 4th/5th forks in their respective gear grooves and slide the 2nd/3rd selector rod through the 2nd/3rd and 4th/5th forks.

22. Place the 2nd/3rd selector rod in the neutral position and insert the interlock plunger in the adapter plate.

23. Install the 4th/5th selector rod

position. Install the spacer on the rear of the 1st countergear and secure it with a new snap-ring.

15. Install the steel ball and the thick thrust washer on the end of the mainshaft, install the synchronizer with the reverse gear, 1st gear along with the needle bearing and bushing, the idler gear and the needle bearing.

16. Install the mainshaft nut and tighten it snugly. Lock two gears at the same time to lock the gear train, and tighten the locknut to 101 to 123 ft. lbs. (14 to 17 Kg-m). stake the nut to the groove of the mainshaft with a punch.

17. Check the gear end-play, which should conform to the following specifications:

1st gear
0.27 to 0.37mm
(0.0106 to 0.0146 in.)

2nd gear
0.20 to 0.30mm
(0.0079 to 0.0118 in.)

3rd gear
0.05 to 0.15mm
(0.0020 to 0.0059 in.)

5th gear
0.05 to 0.20mm
(0.0020 to 0.0079 in.)

Reverse idler gear
0.15 to 0.40mm
(0.0059 to 0.0157 in.)

18. Fit a 0.043 in. (1.1mm) thick snap-ring to the front side of the mainshaft end bearing. Install the mainshaft end bearing and fit another snap-ring to the mainshaft on the rear side of the bearing, to eliminate end-play.

19. Place the 1st/reverse selector rod

1. Main drive bearing
2. Main drive gear
3. 4th and 5th synchronizer
4. 5th gear, mainshaft

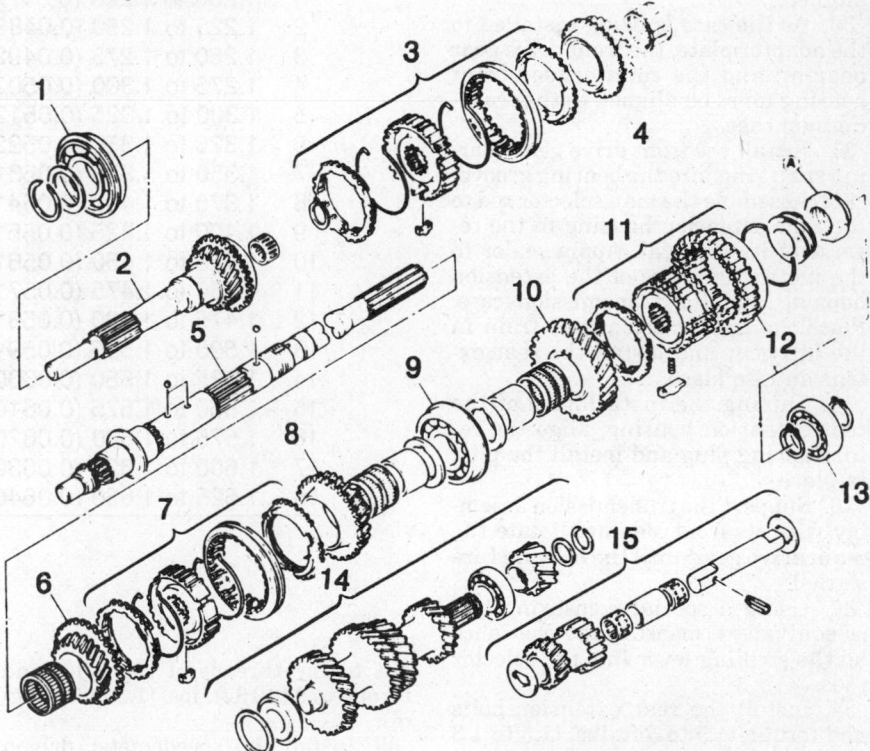

5. Mainshaft
6. 3rd gear, mainshaft
7. 3rd and 2nd synchronizer
8. 2nd gear, mainshaft

9. Mainshaft bearing
10. 1st gear, mainshaft
11. Reverse and 1st synchronizer
12. Reverse gear, mainshaft
13. Mainshaft end bearing
14. Counter gear assembly
15. Idler gear assembly

Exploded view of gear train components

into the adapter plate and through the 4/5th fork.

24. Secure the forks to the selector rods with the retaining pins.

25. Install the check balls and springs in their respective bores of the adapter plate.

26. Apply sealer to the check ball plugs and install the plugs in the adapter plate.

NOTE: The check ball plug for the 1st/reverse selector rod is longer than the other plugs.

27. To insure that the interlock plungers are operating properly, slide the 2nd/3rd selector rod into gear and attempt to move the other selector rods into gear. The gears should not mesh. Continue to check the remaining selector rods.

28. Remove the adapter plate from the holder tool. Apply sealer to the mating surfaces of the transmission case and the adapter plate.

29. Slide the transmission case onto the adapter plate by lightly tapping on the case with a soft hammer until the case and the adapter plate meet. Be sure the dowel pin is properly aligned.

30. As the case is being installed to the adapter plate, the front drive gear bearing and the countergear front bearing must be aligned to the transmission case.

31. Install the front drive gear bearing snap-ring into the bearing groove.

32. Assemble the man selector rod to the rear extension housing in the reverse of its removal. Apply sealer to the mating surfaces of the extension housing and the transmission case. Place the transmission gear train in the 5th gear and install the rear extension into place.

33. During the installation of the rear extension housing, aligo the return spring plug and install the plug in place.

36. Support the transmission assembly with its front side up. Rotate the main drive gear until the bearings are settled.

37. Using a special measuring tool or equivalent, measure the clearance bn the striking lever into the selector rods.

34. Install the rear extension bolts and torque to 9 to 3 ft. lbs. (1.3 to 1.8 Kg-m).

35. Install the plunger into the rear extension. Install the reverse check spring and the return spring. Apply sealer tetween the measuring tool, mounted on the countergear, and the transmission case, using a thickness gauge.

38. When the correct shim is selected, install the front cover. Apply seal-

No.	Thickness mm	(in.)
1	1.40 to 1.45	(0.0551 to 0.0571)
2	1.45 to 1.50	(0.0571 to 0.0591)
3	1.50 to 1.55	(0.0591 to 0.0610)
4	1.55 to 1.60	(0.0610 to 0.0630)
5	1.60 to 1.65	(0.0630 to 0.0650)

No.	Thickness mm	(in.)
1	1.49 to 1.55	(0.0587 to 0.0610)
2	1.56 to 1.62	(0.0614 to 0.0638)
3	1.62 to 1.68	(0.0638 to 0.0661)
4	1.68 to 1.74	(0.0661 to 0.0685)
5	1.74 to 1.80	(0.0685 to 0.0709)
6	1.80 to 1.86	(0.0709 to 0.0732)
7	1.86 to 1.92	(0.0732 to 0.0756)

No.	"H" mm	(in)	Thickness of countershaft front bearing shim mm	(in)
1	1.200 to 1.225	(0.0472 to 0.0482)	1.350	(0.0531)
2	1.225 to 1.250	(0.0482 to 0.0492)	1.375	(0.0541)
3	1.250 to 1.275	(0.0492 to 0.0502)	1.400	(0.0551)
4	1.275 to 1.300	(0.0502 to 0.0512)	1.425	(0.0561)
5	1.300 to 1.325	(0.0512 to 0.0522)	1.450	(0.0571)
6	1.325 to 1.350	(0.0522 to 0.0531)	1.475	(0.0581)
7	1.350 to 1.375	(0.0531 to 0.0541)	1.500	(0.0591)
8	1.375 to 1.400	(0.0541 to 0.0551)	1.525	(0.0600)
9	1.400 to 1.425	(0.0551 to 0.0561)	1.550	(0.0610)
10	1.425 to 1.450	(0.0561 to 0.0571)	1.575	(0.0620)
11	1.450 to 1.475	(0.0571 to 0.0581)	1.600	(0.0630)
12	1.475 to 1.500	(0.0581 to 0.0591)	1.625	(0.0640)
13	1.500 to 1.525	(0.0591 to 0.0600)	1.650	(0.0650)
14	1.525 to 1.550	(0.0600 to 0.0610)	1.675	(0.0659)
15	1.550 to 1.575	(0.0610 to 0.0620)	1.700	(0.0669)
16	1.575 to 1.600	(0.0620 to 0.0630)	1.725	(0.0679)
17	1.600 to 1.625	(0.0630 to 0.0640)	1.750	(0.0689)
18	1.625 to 1.650	(0.0640 to 0.0650)	1.775	(0.0699)

ant to the threads of the bolts and torque to 9 to 13 ft. lbs. (1.3 to 0.8 Kg-m).

39. Install the speedometer driven gear assembly, install the electrical switches that were removed during the disassembly.

40. Install the operating lever, the clutch release bearing and the return spring.

41. Install the dust cover, fill the transmission to the proper level with lubricant.

TYPE 12

4 Speed Transmission Model F4W63L Datsun

DISASSEMBLY

1. Secure the transmission and drain the lubricant.

2. Remove the dust cover from the transmission case.

3. Remove the release bearing and the operating lever. Remove the electrical switches from the case.

4. Remove the speedometer driven gear assembly.

5. Remove the front cover and the bottom cover from the transmission assembly.

6. Position the gearshift into the neutral position and pull out the striking rod (main shift control rod) pin bolt.

7. Remove the rear extension housing retaining bolts and tap the housing with a soft hammer to remove it from the transmission case.

8. Remove the striking rod (main shift control rod).

9. Drive the shifting fork retaining pins from the forks and selector shafts.

10. Remove the three check ball plugs. Do not lose the check balls and springs. Remove the two interlock plungers.

11. Remove the selector rods and shifting forks from the transmission. Keep in their proper order for installation.

12. Lock the gear train by meshing two gears at the same time. Straighten the lock washer and loosen the nut on the mainshaft. Place the gear train back in the neutral position.

13. Use a dummy countershaft tool or equivalent, and push the countershaft from the transmission case, from the rear to the front. Do not drop the needle bearings or thrust washers into the transmission.

14. Remove the counter gear assembly from the case.

15. Remove the snap-ring retaining the reverse idler counter gear in place and remove the shaft from the rear of the case. Do not remove the needle bearing.

16. Remove the mainshaft bearing retainer and bolts. Remove the mainshaft assembly from the rear of the transmission case. Remove the loose synchronizer (baulk) ring from the front of the mainshaft.

17. Remove the pilot bearing located between the main drive gear and the mainshaft.

18. Using a wooden shaft, drive the main drive gear and bearing from the transmission case. Do not allow the gear to drop.

19. The main drive gear bearing can be removed after the retaining snap-ring is removed. A press or bearing puller should be used.

20. Remove the front retaining snap-ring from the mainshaft and remove the 3rd/4th synchronizer assembly, the 3rd gear and mainshaft nee-

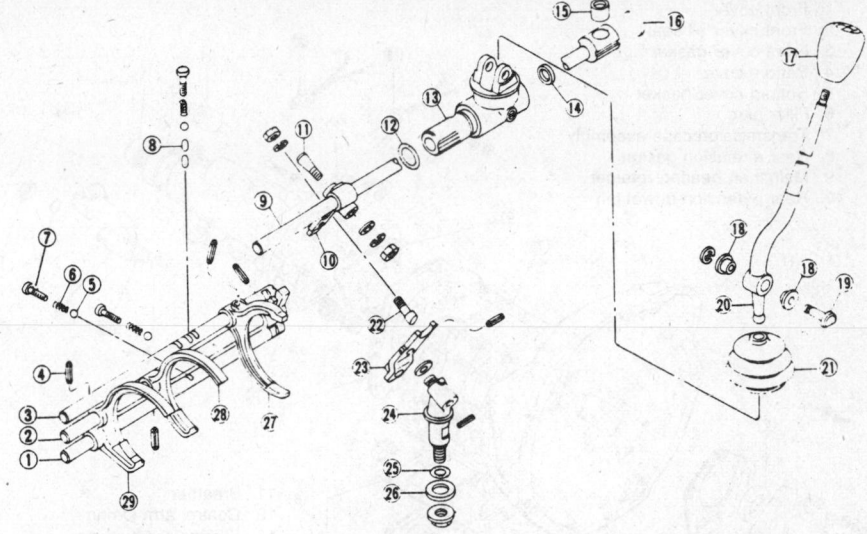

1. 4th and 5th fork rod
2. 2nd and 3rd fork rod
3. 1st and reverse fork rod
4. Retaining pin
5. Checking ball
6. Check ball spring
7. Check ball plug
8. Interlock plunger
9. Striking rod
10. Striking lever
11. Lock pin
12. O-ring
13. Striking guide
14. Striking guide oil seal
15. Control lever bushing
16. Expansion plug
17. Control lever knob
18. Control pin bushing
19. Control arm pin
20. Control lever
21. Control lever boot
22. Striking pin
23. Shift arm
24. Shift arm bracket
25. Arm bracket O-ring
26. Arm bracket plain washer
27. 1st and reverse shift fork
28. 2nd and 3rd shift fork
29. 4th and 5th shift fork

Exploded view of shift selector rod and fork components

dle bearing from the shaft.

21. Remove the locknut from the mainshaft and remove the reverse gear, reverse gear hub and the speedometer drive gear.

NOTE: Do not lose the steel ball locating the speedometer drive gear to the mainshaft.

22. Install a suitable puller or set in a press and remove the 1st speed gear along with the bearing and retainer.

— **CAUTION** —
Do not attach pulling or press tool to the 2nd gear as damage to the 1st gear mainshaft bushing can result. Do not remove the needle bearing with the 1st gear bearing as the needle bearing could be damaged by the second steel ball on the mainshaft.

23. Remove the second steel ball on the mainshaft and install a puller or set in a press and remove the 1st gear bushing, along with the 1st/2nd synchronizer assembly and the 2nd gear.

24. To disassemble the synchronizers, remove the spread springs and take out the shifting inserts. Separate the coupling sleeve from the synchronizer hub.

25. Clean the assemblies, replace the necessary parts and replace the necessary seals and gaskets.

ASSEMBLY

1. Install the synchronizer hub into the coupling sleeve and fit the three shift inserts in their respective grooves.

2. Install the spread springs on each side of the coupling sleeve and hook into the shift inserts.

NOTE: Do not hook the spread spring ends in the same shift insert.

3. Assemble the 2nd gear needle bearing, 2nd gear, 2nd gear synchronizer (baulk) ring and the 1st/2nd speed synchronizer assembly onto the mainshaft.

4. Install the 1st gear bushing onto the mainshaft by using a brass drift. Install the 1st gear synchronizer (baulk) ring, needle bearing, steel ball and the thrust washer onto the mainshaft.

5. Press the mainshaft bearing and the reverse hub onto the mainshaft.

6. Install the 3rd gear needle roller bearing, 3rd synchronizer (baulk) ring, 3rd/4th speed synchronizer assembly onto the mainshaft.

7. Install a new snap-ring onto the mainshaft so that a minimum of clearance exists between the face of the hub and the snap-ring groove.

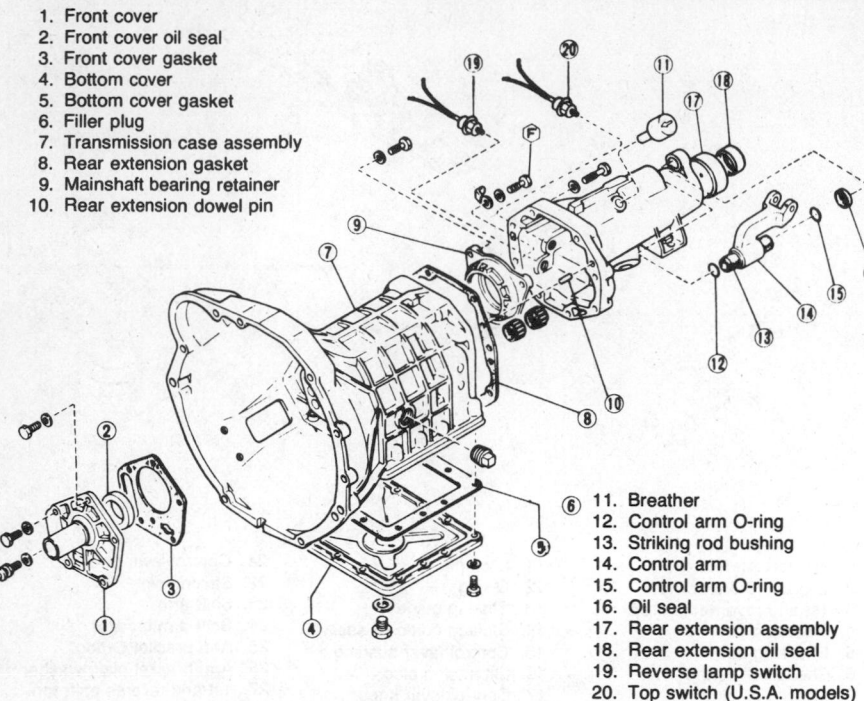

1. Front cover
2. Front cover oil seal
3. Front cover gasket
4. Bottom cover
5. Bottom cover gasket
6. Filler plug
7. Transmission case assembly
8. Rear extension gasket
9. Mainshaft bearing retainer
10. Rear extension dowel pin

11. Breather
12. Control arm O-ring
13. Striking rod bushing
14. Control arm
15. Control arm O-ring
16. Oil seal
17. Rear extension assembly
18. Rear extension oil seal
19. Reverse lamp switch
20. Top switch (U.S.A. models)

Transmission case components, model F4W63L

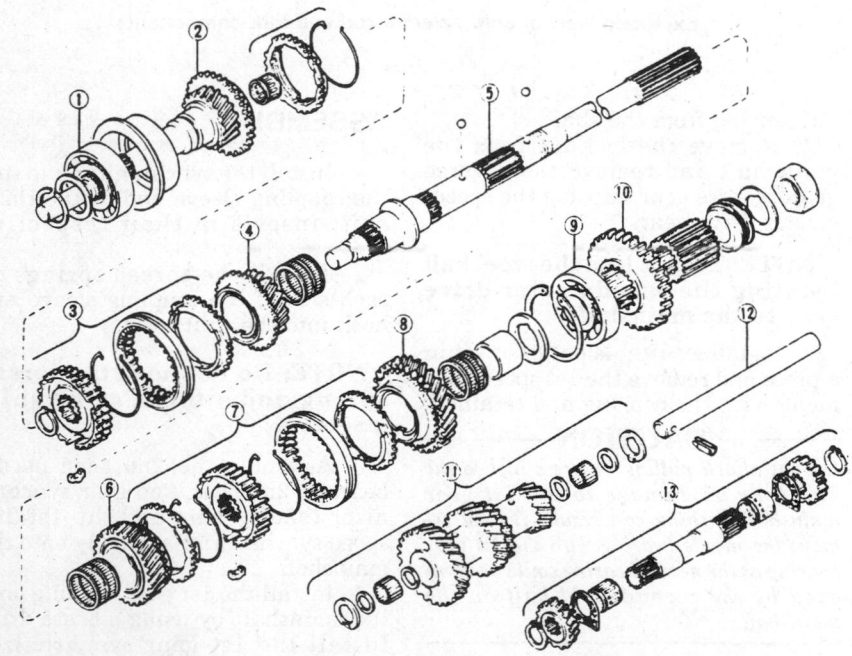

1. Main drive bearing
2. Main drive gear
3. 3rd & 4th synchronizer
4. 3rd gear, mainshaft
5. Mainshaft

6. 2nd gear, mainshaft
7. 1st & 2nd synchronizer
8. 1st gear, mainshaft
9. Mainshaft bearing

10. Reverse gear, mainshaft
11. Counter gear assembly
12. Countershaft
13. Idler gear assembly

Exploded view of gear train components

8. Install the reverse gear, the steel ball, the speedometer gear, lock plate and the nut onto the mainshaft.

9. Install the mainshaft assembly into the rear of the transmission case and install the mainshaft bearing re-tainer plate and bolts. Torque to 5.8 to 7.2 ft. lbs. (7.8 to 9.8 Nm).

10. Install the main drive gear bearing in place, using a press or bearing installer. Install the spacer and the retaining selector snap-ring, so that a minimum of clearance exists between the spacer and the snap-ring.

11. Install the pilot bearing into the bore of the main drive gear assembly into the transmission case front.

12. Install the reverse idler shaft into the transmission case from the rear, with the identification mark facing towards the rear.

13. Assemble the thrust washer and the reverse idler (helical) gear and seat the snap-ring in its groove in the top of the reverse idler shaft.

14. Insert a 0.004 in. (0.1mm) feeler gauge blade between the gear and the thrust washer. With the shaft pushed fully to the rear, install the thrust washer and the spur gear and fit the snap-ring, selected to obtain the proper end-play for the reverse idler gear.

15. The reverse idler gear end-play is 0.0039 to 0.0118 in. (0.10 to 0.30mm).

NOTE: Install the thrust washers so that the grooved sides are facing towards the gears.

16. Install a dummy shaft or equivalent into the countergear and install the inner washers into the gear. Apply grease to the needle bearings and install 21 bearings on each end of the gear. Install the outer washers and the thrust washers in place on the gear assembly. Place the gear assembly into the transmission.

NOTE: If a dummy counter-shaft is used, the shaft should only be as long as the gear assembly and the diameter smaller than the original countershaft.

17. Install the retaining pin in the front of the countershaft and push the shaft into the transmission case, from the front to the rear, engaging the thrust washer, the countergear and forcing the dummy shaft (if used) out through the hole in the back of the case.

18. The rear thrust washer is used to determine the countergear end-play. The end-play is 0.0020 to 0.0059 in. (0.5 to 0.15mm).

19. After the end-play has been determined, locate the countershaft pin in its indent at the front of the transmission case.

20. Mesh two gears so that the transmission gear train is locked. Tighten the mainshaft locknut to 58 to 80 ft. lbs. (8.0 t 11.0 Kg-m). Secure the mainshaft locknut washer by bending over the nut.

21. Install the 1st/2nd selector shift fork and the 3rd/4th shift fork with the grooves of the coupling sleeves.

22. Install the 1st/2nd selector shift rod into the case and through the se-

Thickness		
No.	mm	(in.)
1	1.49 to 1.55	(0.0587 to 0.0610)
2	1.56 to 1.62	(0.0614 to 0.0638)
3	1.62 to 1.68	(0.0638 to 0.0661)
4	1.68 to 1.74	(0.0661 to 0.0685)
5	1.74 to 1.80	(0.0685 to 0.0709)
6	1.80 to 1.86	(0.0709 to 0.0732)
7	1.86 to 1.92	(0.0732 to 0.0756)

Thickness		
No.	mm	(in.)
1	1.15 to 1.25	(0.0453 to 0.0492)
2	1.35 to 1.45	(0.0531 to 0.0571)
3	1.25 to 1.35	(0.0492 to 0.0531)
4	1.45 to 1.55	(0.0571 to 0.0610)
5	1.05 to 1.15	(0.0413 to 0.0453)

Thickness		
No.	mm	(in.)
1	2.35 to 2.40	(0.0925 to 0.0945)
2	2.40 to 2.45	(0.0945 to 0.0965)
3	2.45 to 2.50	(0.0965 to 0.0984)
4	2.50 to 2.55	(0.0984 to 0.1004)
5	2.55 to 2.60	(0.1004 to 0.1024)

Thickness		
No.	mm	(in.)
1	1.40 to 1.45	(0.0551 to 0.0571)
2	1.45 to 1.50	(0.0571 to 0.0591)
3	1.50 to 1.55	(0.0591 to 0.0610)
4	1.55 to 1.60	(0.0610 to 0.0630)
5	1.60 to 1.65	(0.0630 to 0.0650)

lector fork. Install the retaining pin through the fork and rod.

23. Place the 1st/2nd shift fork and gear in the Neutral position. Install the interlock plunger and install the 3rd/4th selector shift rod into the case and the 3rd/4th shift fork. Install the retaining pin in the fork and rod.

24. Place the 3rd/4th selector rod in the Neutral position and install the interlock plunger.

25. Install the reverse shift selector rod through the reverse shift fork and install the retaining pin.

26. Install the check balls and the check ball springs. Install sealer on the plugs and install them into their respective bores.

NOTE: The check ball plug for the 3rd/4th fork and shift rod is shorter than those for the reverse and 1st/2nd fork and shift rods.

--- CAUTION ---
To insure that the interlock plungers are properly installed, slide the 3rd/4th fork selector rod into gear and try to operate the other selector rods. All other gears should not mesh. Operate the other selector rods and check in the same manner.

27. Place all gears in the Neutral position and install the rear extension to the transmission case, using sealer on the mating surfaces.

28. As the rear extension housing is being installed, align the striking lever to the shift rod brackets.

29. Install the front main shaft cover. Apply sealer to the threads of the bolt and torque to 5.8 to 7.2 ft. lbs. (0.8 to 1.0 Kg-m).

30. Install the clutch release bearing and the operating shaft to the front of the case. Install the dust cover.

31. Install the electrical switches that were removed during the disassembly.

32. Install the speedometer driven gear assembly.

33. Install the bottom cover to the case and fill the unit with the proper level of lubricant.

TYPE 13

5 Speed Transmission Model FS5W60A Datsun

DISASSEMBLY

1. Secure the transmission and drain the lubricating oil.

2. Remove the dust cover from the transmission case.

3. Remove the clutch release bearing and withdraw the pivot lever.

4. Remove the electrical switches from the case.

5. Remove the speedometer driven gear assembly.

6. Remove the shift selector stopper pin bolt and nut from the boss of the rear extension housing.

7. Remove the shift selector return spring plug, return spring and plunger from the rear extension.

8. Remove the reverse check sleeves assembly.

9. Remove the front bearing cover, O-ring and front cover adjusting shim.

10. Remove the main bearing snapring from the groove in the bearing outer race.

11. Remove the rear extension retaining bolts and turn the shift selector rod clockwise.

12. Using a special puller, remove the rear extension housing from the output shaft.

13. Separate the transmission case from the adapter plate by tapping evenly around the transmission case.

NOTE: Do not pry the units apart with a prybar. Damage can occur to the mating surfaces.

14. A special type holding tool should be used to hold the adapter plate so that it can be held in a vice or other holding tool. This plate can be purchased or fabricated.

15. Mount the unit in the holding tool and remove the countergear thrust washer.

16. Using a pin punch, remove the retaining pins from the forks and selector rods.

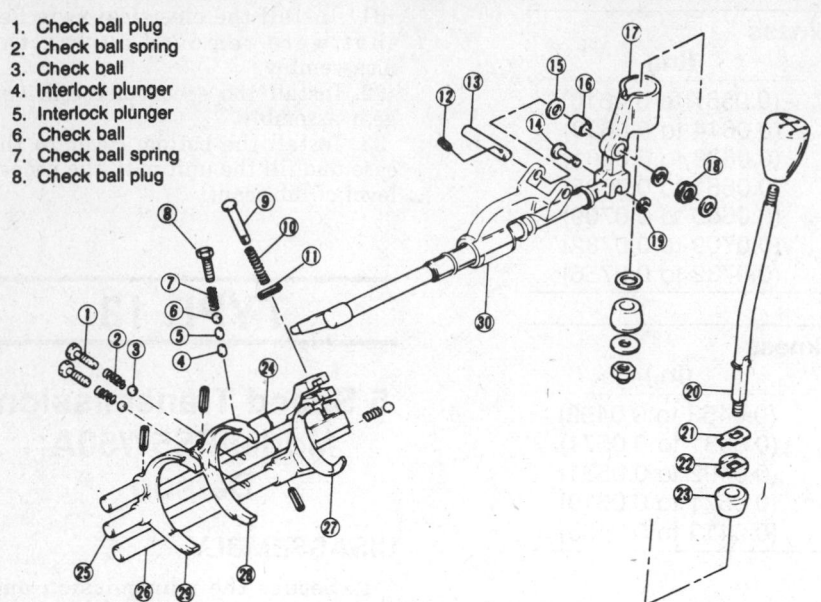

1. Check ball plug
2. Check ball spring
3. Check ball
4. Interlock plunger
5. Interlock plunger
6. Check ball
7. Check ball spring
8. Check ball plug

9. Reverse fork pin
10. Reverse pin return spring
11. Roller pin
12. Retaining pin
13. Control arm pin
14. Striking rod pin
15. Thrust washer

16. Control bushing
17. Control lever bracket
18. Control spring
19. Striking pin C-ring
20. Control lever
21. Control lever upper washer
22. Control lever upper washer

23. Control lever rubber
24. 1st and 2nd fork rod
25. 3rd and 4th fork rod
26. Reverse fork rod
27. Reverse shift fork
28. 1st and 2nd shift fork
29. 3rd and 4th fork rod
30. Control arm

Exploded view of shift selector rod and fork components

17. Remove the check ball plugs (3).
18. Remove the selector rods from the adapter plate and detach the forks from the rods.

———— **CAUTION** ————

Do not lose the check balls, springs and the two interlock plungers.

NOTE: Each gear and shaft can be removed from the adapter plate independently of the other shaft and without the removal of the selector rods and forks.

19. Remove the outer snap-ring of the mainshaft end bearing with a bearing puller. Remove the second bearing snap-ring from the shaft.
20. Engage the 1st and reverse speeds so that the gear train is located in two gears at the same time. Remove the countergear nut after releasing the staking.
21. From the rear extension side of the adapter plate, remove the mainshaft holding snap-ring, C-ring holder, C-ring and the thrust washer.
22. Remove the O.D. main gear with the needle bearings and the O.D. countergear together.
23. Remove the synchronizer (baulk) ring, the coupling sleeve, the O.D. and reverse synchronizer hub snap-ring, the O.D. and reverse synchronizer hub and the reverse gear together with the needle bearing and bushing, and the reverse countergear at one time.
24. Remove the bearing retainer screws from the adapter plate. Remove the bearing retainer.
25. Remove the snap-ring from the mainshaft rear bearing and remove the mainshaft assembly together with the countergear by lightly tapping on the rear shaft while holding the front of the mainshaft and countergear assembly by hand to avoid dropping the assembly.
26. Remove the snap-ring and spacer from the reverse idler shaft and tap the idler shaft outward slightly.
27. Using a pin punch, remove the retaining pin from the reverse idler shaft and remove the shaft. Remove the thrust washers, spacer and reverse idler gear with the needle bearing.
28. Disassemble the mainshaft assembly by removing the snap-ring from the shaft front end. Remove the 3rd/4th synchronizer assembly, synchronizer (baulk) rings, 3rd gear and the mainshaft needle bearing toward the front side.
29. Remove the mainshaft bearing with a puller.
30. Remove the thrust washer and 1st gear, together with the needle bearing and bushing, synchronizer (baulk) rings, coupling sleeve, 1st/2nd synchronizer hub and the 2nd gear with the needle bearing.
31. Remove the snap-ring and spacer from the maindrive gear and remove the bearing with a press or puller.
32. The countershaft rear bearing can be removed with the use of a press.
33. The synchronziers can be disassembled for repairs by removing the spread spring and removing the shifting insert. Separate the coupling sleeve from the synchronizer hub.

ASSEMBLY

1. Replace any bearings, seals or worn parts as required.
2. Install the synchronizer hub into the coupling sleeve and fit the shifting inserts into their respective grooves on the assembly.
3. Install the spread springs to the inserts so that the insert is securely attached to the inner side of the coupling sleeve.

———— **CAUTION** ————

Do not hook the ends of the spread springs to the same insert. The hub and sleeve should operate smoothly when moved by hand.

4. Install the 2nd gear needle bearing, 2nd gear, synchronizer (baulk) ring, 1st/2nd speed synchronizer assembly, 1st gear synchronizer (baulk) ring, 1st gear bushing, needle bearing, 1st gear and thrust washer onto the mainshaft.
5. Press the bearing onto the mainshaft, using a press or bearing installer.
6. Install the 3rd gear needle bearing, 3rd gear, synchronizer (baulk) ring, 3rd/4th synchronizer assembly on the front side of the mainshaft.
7. Install a selective snap-ring on the mainshaft so that a minimum clearance exists between the face of the hub and the ring.

———— **CAUTION** ————

Be sure the snap-ring is fully seated in its groove.

8. Install the main drive gear bearing onto the shaft. Install the main drive bearing spacer on the main drive bearing and secure the bering with a proper sized snap-ring that will eliminate any end-play.
9. Install the countergear thrust washer and countergear into the transmission case and select the countergear thrust washer of proper thickness, by using a straightedge, from the countergear face to the transmission case, allowing for stan-

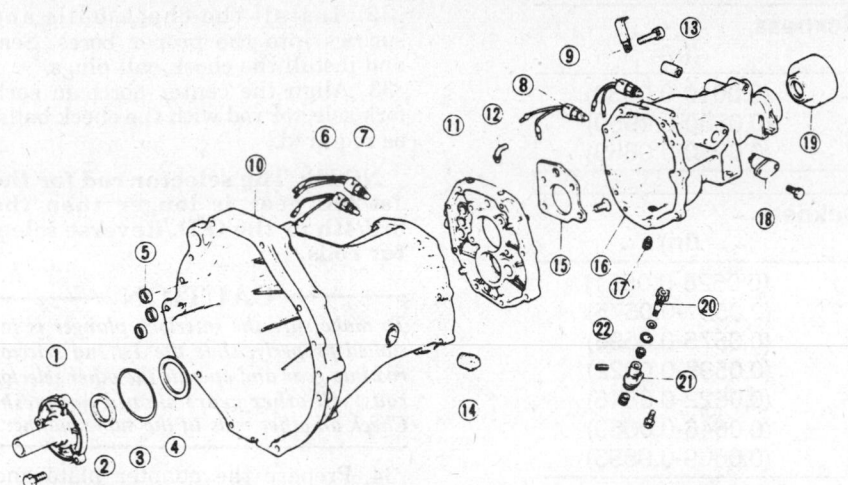

1. Front cover
2. Front cover oil seal
3. Front cover O-ring
4. Front cover adjusting shim
5. Welch plug
6. Top gear switch
7. O.D. gear switch
8. Reverse lamp switch
9. Neutral switch
10. Transmission case assembly
11. Adapter plate
12. Breather
13. Return spring bushing
14. Filler plug
15. Bearing retainer
16. Rear extension assembly
17. Drain plug
18. Reverse check sleeve
19. Rear extension dust cover with oil seal
20. Speedometer pinion
21. Speedometer sleeve
22. Retaining pin

Transmission case components, model FS5W60A

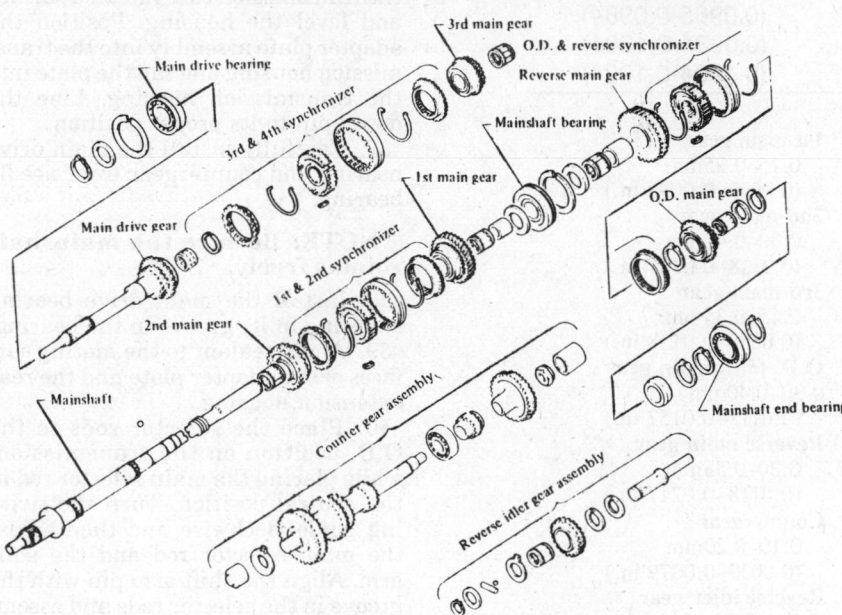

Exploded view of gear train components

dard end-play of 0.0039-0.0079 in. (0.10mm-0.20mm).

10. Remove the countergear from the transmission and keep the thrust washer with the gear.

11. Install the thrust washers, needle bearing, reverse idler gear and inner thrust washer in place on the reverse idler shaft. Install a new retaining pin in the reverse idler shaft.

12. Install the reverse idler shaft into the adapter plate. Position a thrust washer and install a new snapring so that the minimum clearance exists between the adapter plate and the thrust washer.

13. Install a synchronizer (baulk) ring on the main drive gear and place with the mainshaft to complete this portion of the assembly.

NOTE: Install the pilot bearing in place before coupling the main drive gear to the mainshaft.

14.Combine the mainshaft assembly with the ocuntergear assembly and place them into the adapter plate as a unit.

NOTE: Use a puller tool to move the mainshaft into the adapter plate. Carefully hold the gears to avoid dropping them until in position.

—————— **CAUTION** ——————

Be sure the snap-ring grooves on the mainshaft rear bearing clears the adapter plate.

15. Install the rear bearing snapring into its groove. Install the bearing retainer and install the retaining screws. Torque to 5.1-7.2 ft. lbs. (6.9-9.8 Nm).

IMPORTANT: Stake each screw at two points with a center punch.

No.	Thickness	
	mm	(in)
1	1.1	(0.043)
2	1.2	(0.047)

16. Place the thrust washer, reverse gear bushing, needle bearing and the reverse main drive gear on the end of the mainshaft.

17. Install the reverse countergear on the end of the coutnershaft.

18. Install the O.D. and reverse synchronizer assembly and install a new snap-ring so that the minimum amount of clearance exists between the end face of the hub and the snap-ring.

19. Position the synchronizer (baulk) ring, O.D. gear needle bearing and the O.D. Sheet main gear on the end of the mainshaft.

No.	Thickness	
	mm	(in)
1	1.32	(0.0520)
2	1.38	(0.0543)
3	1.46	(0.0575)
4	1.54	(0.0606)
5	1.62	(0.0638)

20. Install the O.D. countergear on the end of the mainshaft.

21. Place the thrust washer in place so that a minimum of clearance exists between the C-holder and the ring. Position the C-ring and the C-ring holder and fit a new mainshaft holder snap-ring.

22. Engage the 1st and reverse gears and tighten the countershaft nut to 36-43 ft. lbs. (49-59 Nm).

23. Stake the countershaft nut to the groove in the countershaft with a punch.

24. Measure the gear end-play. The measurements are as follows:

No.	Thickness mm	(in)
1	1.55-1.60	(0.0610-0.0630)
2	1.60-1.65	(0.0630-0.0650)
3	1.65-1.70	(0.0650-0.0669)

No.	Thickness mm	(in)
1	1.34-1.40	(0.0528-0.0551)
2	1.40-1.46	(0.0551-0.0575)
3	1.46-1.52	(0.0575-0.0598)
4	1.52-1.58	(0.0598-0.0622)
5	1.58-1.64	(0.0622-0.0646)
6	1.64-1.70	(0.0646-0.0669)
7	1.70-1.76	(0.0669-0.0693)

No.	Thickness mm	(in)
1	2.20-2.25	(0.0866-0.0886)
2	2.25-2.30	(0.0886-0.0906)
3	2.30-2.35	(0.0906-0.0925)
4	2.35-2.40	(0.0925-0.0945)
5	2.40-2.45	(0.0945-0.0965)
6	2.45-2.50	(0.0965-0.0984)
7	2.50-2.55	(0.0984-0.1004)
8	2.55-2.60	(0.1004-0.1024)

25. Place a snap-ring to the front of the mainshaft end bearing, Measuring 0.0453 in. (1.15mm).

26. Install the mainshaft end bearing using a bearing installer. Fit a snap-ring to the rear side of the bearing to eliminate any end-play. The available snap-rings are as follows:

No.	Thickness mm	(in.)
1	1.15	(0.0453)
2	1.02	(0.047)

27. Install the O.D. and reverse fork and selector rod into the adapter plate. Place the rod in the neutral position and install the interlock plunger into its bore in the adapter plate.

28. Install the 3rd/4th selector rod into the fork and install a new snapring. Install the selector rod and fork into the adapter plate.

29. Insert the interlock plunger into the adapter plate with the selector rods in the neutral position.

30. Install the 1st/2nd selector rod into the fork and install both into the adapter plate.

31. Secure all the selector rods and forks with new retaining pins.

IMPORTANT: Properly align the groove in the assembled selector rod with the interlock plung-er, during the assembly. Align the shift forks with their respective coupling sleeves before installing.

1st main gear
0.15–0.25mm
(0.0059–0.0098 in.)
2nd main gear
0.30–0.40mm
(0.0118–0.0157 in.)
3rd main gear
0.15–0.35mm
(0.0059–0.0138 in.)
O.D. (5th) main gear
0.30–0.40mm
(0.0118–0.0157 in.)
Reverse main gear
0.30–0.55mm
(0.0118–0.0217 in.)
Countergear
0.10–0.20mm
(0.0039–0.0079 in.)
Reverse idler gear
0–0.20mm
(0–0.0079 in.)

No.	Thickness mm	(in.)
1	7.87	(0.3098)
2	7.94	(0.3126)
3	8.01	(0.3154)
4	8.08	(0.3181)
5	8.15	(0.3209)
6	8.22	(0.3236)

32. Install the check balls and springs into the proper bores. Seal and install the check ball plugs.

33. Align the center notch in each fork selector rod with the check balls, as required.

NOTE: The selector rod for the 1st/2nd gear is longer than the 3rd/4th or the O.D./Reverse selector rods.

————— CAUTION —————

To make sure the interlock plunger is installed properly, slide the 1st/2nd selector rod into gear and operate the other selector rods. All other gears should not mesh. Check all other rods in the same manner.

34. Prepare the adapter plate and transmission case by installing a sealer to the mating surfaces.

35. Apply grease to the sliding surface of the thrust washer for the countergear, that was selected previously. The oil groove should face to the front while the dimpled side should face towards the thrust side.

36. Place the clutch housing end of the transmission case flat on a surface and level the housing. Position the adapter plate assembly into the transmission housing and tap the plate into the transmission housing. Line the dowel pin to its proper position.

37. Carefully install the main drive bearing and countergear front needle bearing.

NOTE: Be sure the mainshaft rotates freely.

38. Install the main drive bearing snapring in its groove in the bearing.

39. Apply sealant to the mating surfaces of the adapter plate and the rear extension housing.

40. Place the selector rods in the O.D. position on the transmission, while placing the main selector rod in the neutral position. Turn the striking guide clockwise and then adjust the main selector rod and the shift arm. Align the shift arm pin with the groove in the selector rods and assemble the rear extension housing to the adapter plate. Install the retaining bolts and torque to 12-16 ft. lbs. (16-22 Nm).

41. Install grease to the plunger and install it into the rear extension. Install the return spring, apply sealer to the returnspring plug and install it.

42. Turn the transmission assembly so that the front is up. Measure the distance from the front end of the transmission case to the main drive bearing outer race with a depth gauge. Select a shim to correspond to the dimension or thickness "A". The front cover adjusting shim can be one of seven shims.

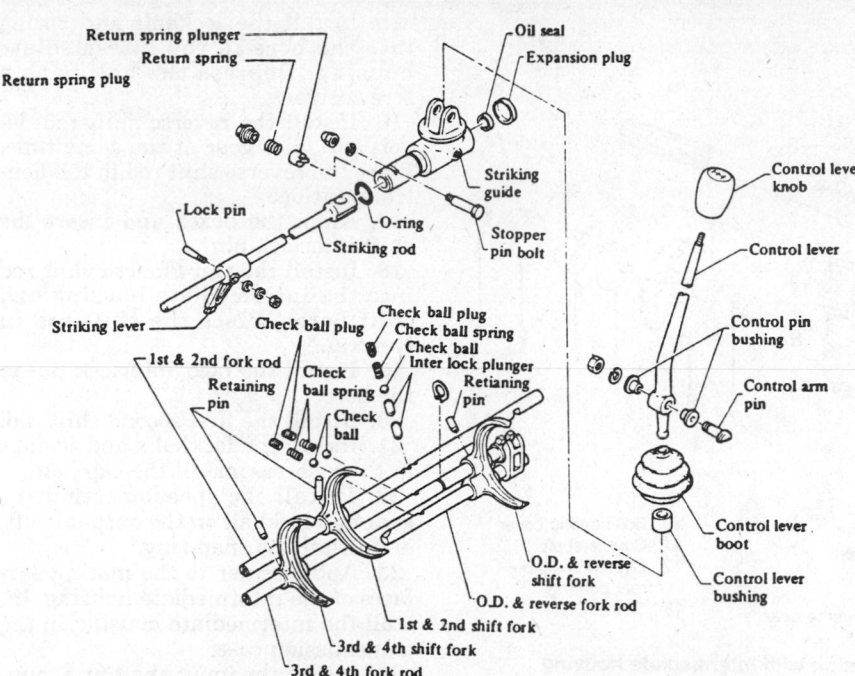

Exploded view of shift selector rod and fork components

No.	"A" mm	(in.)	Adjusting shim mm	(in.)
1	6.05-6.09	(0.2382-0.2398)	0.50	(0.0197)
2	6.10-6.14	(0.2402-0.2417)	0.55	(0.0217)
3	6.15-6.19	(0.2421-0.2437)	0.60	(0.0236)
4	6.20-6.24	(0.2441-0.2457)	0.65	(0.0256)
5	6.25-6.29	(0.2461-0.2476)	0.70	(0.0276)
6	6.30-6.34	(0.2480-0.2496)	0.75	(0.0295)
7	6.35-6.39	(0.2500-0.2516)	0.80	(0.0315)

43. Install the front cover with the adjusting shim and the O-ring in place.

44. Install the speedometer driven gear and install the securing bolt and nut.

45. Install a new O-ring in the groove of the reverse check sleeve and tighten the bolts.

46. Replace the electrical switches that were removed during the disassembly.

47. Install the pivot lever, the release bearing and sleeve. Connect the holding spring and install the dust cover.

TYPE 14

4 and 5 Speed Transmission Mazda

The 4 and 5 speed transmission are basically the same, with an added housing located between the adapter plate and the rear extension housing, to carry the 5th and reverse gears. Added roller bearings are used in the housing to prevent shaft misalignment.

DISASSEMBLY

1. Remove the throw-out bearing return spring, throw-out bearing, and the release fork.

2. Remove the bearing housing.

3. Remove the input shaft and countershaft snap-rings.

4. Remove the floorshift lever retainer, complete with gasket.

5. Unfasten the cap bolt and withdraw the spring, steel ball, select lock pin and spring from the retainer.

6. Remove the extension housing. Turn the control lever as far left as it will go and slide the extension housing off the output shaft.

7. Remove the spring seat and spring from the end of the shift control lever.

8. Loosen the spring cap and withdraw the spring and plunger from their bore.

9. Remove the control rod and boss from the extension housing.

10. Remove the speedometer driven gear. Remove the back-up light switch.

11. Remove the speedometer drive gear.

12. Tap the front ends of the input shaft and countershaft with a plastic hammer, then remove the intermediate housing assembly from the transmission case.

13. Remove the three cap bolts; then withdraw the springs and lockballs.

14. Remove the reverse shift rod, reverse idler gear, and shift lever.

15. Remove the setscrews from all the shift forks and push the shift rods rearward to remove them. Remove the shift forks.

16. Withdraw the reverse shift rod lockball, spring, and interlock pins from the intermediate housing.

17. Remove reverse gear and key from the output shaft.

18. Remove the reverse countergear.

19. Remove the countershaft and output shaft from the intermediate housing.

20. Remove the bearings from the intermediate housing and transmission case.

21. Remove the snap-ring from the output shaft.

22. Slid the third/fourth clutch hub, sleeve, synchronizer ring, and third gear off the output shaft.

23. Remove the thrust washer, first gear, sleeve, synchronizer ring, and second gear from the rear of the output shaft.

ASSEMBLY

1. Install the third/fourth synchronizer clutch hub on the sleeve. Place the three synchronizer keys in the clutch hub key slots. Install the key springs with their open ends 120° apart.

2. Install third gear and the synchronizer ring on the front of the output shaft. Install the third/fourth clutch hub assembly on the output shaft. Be sure that the larger boss faces the front of the shaft.

3. Secure the gear and synchronizer with the snap-ring.

4. Repeat Step 1 for the first/second synchronizer assembly.

5. Position the synchronizer ring on second gear. Slide second gear on the output shaft so that the synchronizer ring faces the rear of the shaft.

6. Install the first/second clutch hub assembly on the output shaft so that its oil grooves face the front of

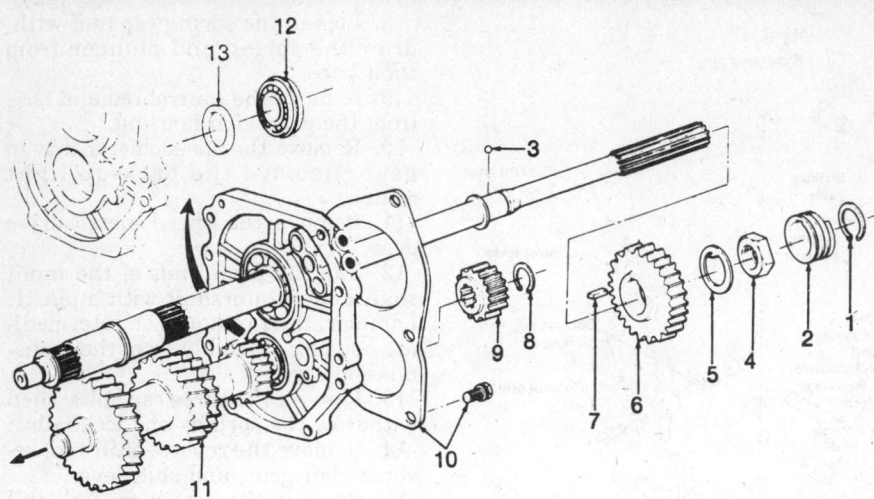

1. Snap-ring
2. Speedometer drive gear
3. Ball
4. Locknut
5. Lock washer
6. Reverse gear
7. Key
8. Snap-ring
9. Counter reverse gear
10. Bolt/bearing cover
11. Countershaft
12. Countershaft rear bearing
13. Shim

Gear train position in 4-speed transmission with intermediate housing

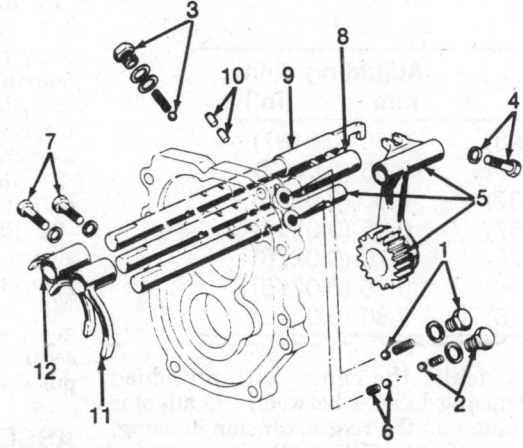

1. Spring cap bolt/packing/spring/locking ball
2. Spring cap bolt/packing/spring/locking ball
3. Spring cap bolt/packing/spring/locking ball
4. Bolt/washer
5. Shift fork (Reverse)/rod/reverse idler gear
6. Spring/locking ball
7. Bolt/washer
8. Shift rod (3rd & 4th)
9. Shift rod (1st & 2nd)
10. Interlock pin
11. Shift fork (3rd & 4th)
12. Shift fork (1st & 2nd)

Exploded view of shift selector rods and forks, 4-speed with intermediate housing

the shaft. Engage the keys in the notches on the second gear synchronizer ring.

7. Slide the first gear sleeve onto the output shaft. Position the synchronizer ring on first gear. Install the first gear on the output shaft so that the synchronizer ring faces frontward. Rotate the first gear as required to engage the notches in the synchronizer ring with the keys in the clutch hub.

8. Slip the thrust washer on the rear of the output shaft. Install the needle bearing on the front of the output shaft.

9. Install the synchronizer ring on fourth gear and install the input shaft on the front of the output shaft.

10. Press the countershaft rear bearing and shim into the intermediate housing, then press the countershaft into the rear bearing.

11. Keep the thrust washer and first gear from falling off the output shaft by supporting the shaft. Install the output shaft on the intermediate housing. Be sure that each output shaft gear engages with its opposite number on the countershaft.

12. Tap the output shaft bearing and shim into the intermediate housing with a plastic hammer. Install the cover.

13. Install reverse gear on the output shaft and secure it with its key.

NOTE: The chamfer on the teeth of both the reverse gear and the reverse countergear should face rearward.

14. Install the reverse countergear.

15. Install the lockball and spring into the bore in the intermediate housing. Depress the ball with a screwdriver.

16. Install the reverse shift rod, lever, and idler gear at the same time. Place the reverse shift rod in the neutral position.

17. Align the boxes and insert the shift interlock pin.

18. Install the third/fourth shift rod into the intermediate housing and shift bores. Place the shift rod in Neutral.

19. Install the next interlock pin in the bore.

20. Install the first/second shift rod.

21. Install the lockballs and springs in their bores. Install the cap bolt.

22. Install the speedometer drive gear and lockball on the output shaft, and install its snap-ring.

23. Apply sealer to the mating surfaces of the intermediate housing. Install the intermediate housing in the transmission case.

24. Install the input shaft and countershaft front bearings in the transmission case.

25. Secure the speedometer driven gear.

26. Install the control rod through the holes in the front of the extension housing.

27. Align the key with the keyway and install the yoke on the end of the control rod. Install the yoke lockbolt.

28. Fit the plunger and spring into the extension housing bore and secure with the spring cap.

29. Turn the control rod all the way to the left and install the extension housing on the intermediate housing.

30. Insert the sprig and select lockpin inside the gearshift retainer. Align the steel ball and spring with the lockpin slot, and secure it with the spring cap.

31. Install the spring and spring seat in the control rod yoke.

32. Install the gearshift lever retainer over its gasket on the extension housing.

33. Lubricate the lip of the front bearing cover oil seal and secure the cover on the transmission case.

34. Check the clearance between the front bearing cover and bearing. It should be less than 0.006 in. If it is not within specifications insert additional adjusting shims. The shims are available in 0.006 in. or 0.012 in. sizes.

35. Install the throwout bearing, return spring and release fork.

5 Speed

The disassembly and assembly of the rear extension housing, selector levers and forks are completed in the same manner as the 4 speed transmission. After this has been done, the added housing can be removed by taking out the retaining bolts. The housing will have to be lightly tapped with a soft-faced hammer. The removal of the housing exposes the 5th/reverse synchronizer assembly, the reverse countergear, the countershaft and mainshaft bearings. The bearings are pulled from the shafts and then the gears can be removed. the assembly is in the reverse of the removal procedure.

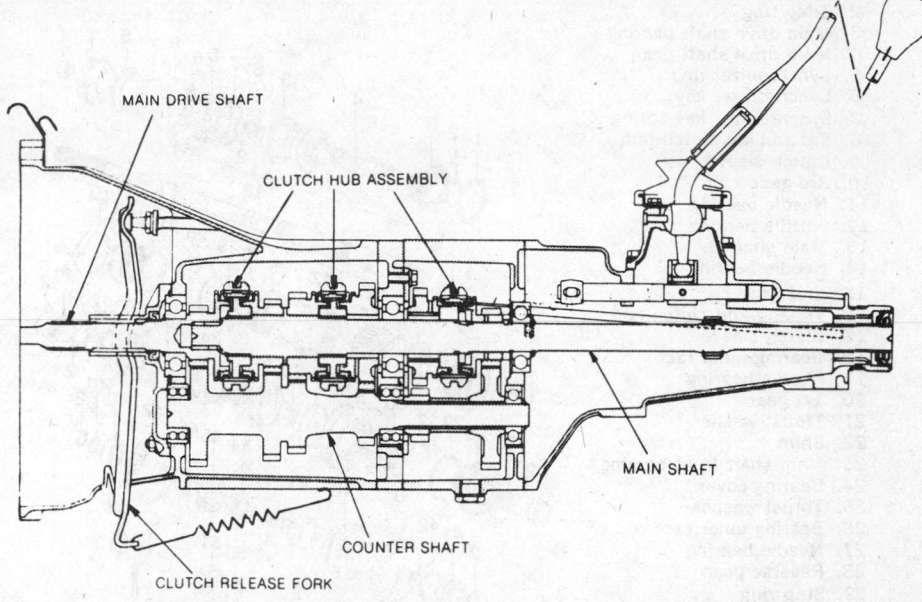

Cross section of 5-speed transmission showing added housing

TYPE 15

5 Speed Transmission

(Mazda)

DISASSEMBLY

1. Pull the release fork outward until the spring clip of the fork releases from the ballpivot.
2. Remove the fork and release bearing.
3. Remove the clutch busing shim and gasket.
4. Remove the gearshift lever retainer and gasket.
5. Remove the spring and steel ball, select lock spindle and spring from the gearshift lever retainer.
6. Remove the extension housing with the control lever end down to the left as far as it will go.
7. Remove the control lever end, key and control rod.
8. Remove the lock plate and speedometer gear.
9. Remove the back-up light switch.
10. Remove the snap-ring and slide the speedometer drive gear from the mainshaft.
11. Remove the bottom cover and gasket.
12. Remove the shift rod ends.
13. Remove the rear bearing housing.
14. Remove the snap-ring and remove the mainshaft rear bearing, thrust washer and race, using Mazda puller No. 49 0839 425C or equivalent.
15. Remove the washer and countershaft rear bearing, using Mazda puller No. 49 0839 425C or equivalent.
16. Remove the counter fifth gear.
17. Remove the intermediate housing.
18. Remove the springs and shift locking balls.

19. Remove the two blind covers and gaskets from the case.
20. Remove the reverse/fifth shift rod, fork and interlock pin.
21. Remove the first/second and third/fourth shift forks, rods and interlock pins.
22. Remove the snap-ring and slide the washer, fifth gear and synchronizer ring from the mainshaft. Also, remove the steel ball and needle bearing.
23. Lock the rotation of the mainshaft with second and reverse.
24. Remove the locknut and slide the reverse/fifth clutch hub and sleeve assembly, synchronizer ring, reverse gear and needle bearing from the mainshaft.
25. Remove the spacer and counter reverse gear from the countershaft.
26. Remove the reverse idler gear, thrust washers and shaft from the transmission case.
27. Remove the bearing rear cover plate.
28. Remove the snap-ring from the front end of the countershaft and install Mazda tool No. 49 0839 445 synchronizer ring holder or its equivalent between the fourth synchronizer ring and the synchromesh gear on the main driveshaft.
29. Remove the countershaft front bearing.
30. Remove the adjusting shim from the countershaft front bearing bore.
31. Remove the countershaft center bearing outer race.
32. With a special puller and attachment, remove the mainshaft front bearing, thrust trasher and inner race

along with the adjusting shim from the mainshaft front bearing bore.
33. Remove the snap-ring, and remove the main driveshaft bearing.
34. Remove the countershaft center bearing inner race with the puller.
35. Separate the input shaft from the mainshaft and remove the input shaft.
36. Remove the synchronizer ring and needle bearing from the input shaft.
37. Remove the mainshaft assembly.
38. Remove the first/second and third/fourth shift forks from the case.
39. Remove the snap-ring and slide the third/fourth clutch hub and sleeve assembly, synchronizer ring and third gear from the mainshaft.
40. Remove the thrust washer, first gear and needle bearing from the rear of the mainshaft.
41. Press out the needle bearing inner race, synchronizer ring, first and second clutch hub, sleeve assembly, synchronizer ring and second gear from the mainshaft.

ASSEMBLY

1. Install the third/fourth clutch hub into the sleeve, place the three keys into the clutch hub slots and install the springs onto the hub.
2. Assemble the first/second and reverse/fifth clutch hub and sleeve as described in Step 1.
3. Install the needle bearing, second gear, synchronizer ring, and first/second clutch assembly on the rear section of the mainshaft.

1. Shim
2. Snap ring
3. Main drive shaft bearing
4. Main drive shaft gear
5. Synchronizer ring
6. Synchronizer key
7. Synchronizer key spring
8. 3rd-and-4th clutch hub
9. Clutch sleeve
10. 3rd gear
11. Needle bearing
12. Needle bearing
13. Main shaft
14. Needle bearing
15. 2nd gear
16. 1st-and-2nd clutch hub
17. Clutch sleeve
18. Bearing inner race
19. Needle bearing
20. 1st gear
21. Thrust washer
22. Shim
23. Main shaft front bearing
24. Bearing cover
25. Thrust washer
26. Bearing inner race
27. Needle bearing
28. Reverse gear
29. Stop ring
30. Rev.-and-5th clutch hub
31. Clutch sleeve
32. Main shaft lock nut
33. Needle bearing
34. 5th gear
35. Thrust washer
36. Lock ball
37. Main shaft rear bearing
38. Thrust washer
39. Lock ball
40. Speedometer drive gear
41. Counter shaft front bearing
42. Shim

43. Counter shaft
44. Counter shaft center bearing
45. Counter reverse gear
46. Spacer
47. Reverse gear
48. Counter shaft rear bearing
49. Thrust washer
50. Thrust washer
51. Reverse idler gear
52. Idler gear shaft
53. Thrust washer

Mazda 5-speed gear train

15. Install the input shaft bearing in the same way.

16. Check the countershaft front bearing end-play in the same way as the mainshaft bearing end-play.

17. Install the front bearing snapring.

18. Press the countershaft center bearing into position.

19. Install the bearing cover plate.

20. Install the reverse idler gearshaft, thrust washers and reverse idler gear.

21. Install the counter reverse gear and spacer on the rear end on the countershaft.

22. Install the thrust washer and press the needle bearing inner race of the reverse gear on the mainshaft.

23. Install the needle bearing, reverse gear, synchronizer ring, reverse/fifth clutch assembly and new mainshaft locknut on the mainshaft.

24. Lock the mainshaft with the second and reverse gears. Tighten the locknut to 95-152 ft. lbs.

25. Install the needle bearing, synchronizer ring and fifth gear on the mainshaft.

26. Install the thrust washer, steel ball and snap-ring on the mainshaft.

27. Check the thrust washer-to-snap-ring clearance. It should be 0.0039-0.0118 in.

28. Install the first/second shift rod through the holes in the case and fork.

29. Install the interlock pin with a special installer and guide.

4. Press on the first gear needle bearing inner race.

5. Install the third gear and synchronizer ring onto the front section of the mainshaft.

6. Install the third/fourth clutch assembly onto the mainshaft.

7. Install the snap-ring on the mainshaft.

8. Install the needle bearing, synchronizer ring, first gear and thrust washer on the mainshaft.

9. Install the mainshaft assembly.

10. Install the needle bearing on the front end of the mainshaft.

11. Install the first/second and third/fourth shift forks in their respective clutch sleeves.

12. Check the mainshaft bearing end-play. Check the depth of the mainshaft bearing bore in the case. Measure the mainshaft bearing height. The difference indicates the required adjusting shim to give a total end-play of less than 0.0039 in.

13. Install the synchronizer ring holder tool between the fourth synchronizer ring and the synchromesh gear on the input shaft.

14. Position the shims and mainshaft bearing in the bore and install with a press.

1. Shift fork
2. Shift fork
3. Shift fork
4. 3rd-and-4th shift rod
5. 1st-and-2nd shift rod
6. Rev.-and-5th shift rod
7. Stop ring
8. Shift rod end
9. Shift rod end
10. Shift rod end
11. Detent ball
12. Detent spring
13. Washer
14. Spring cap bolt
15. Interlock pin

Mazda 5-speed shift rod and forks

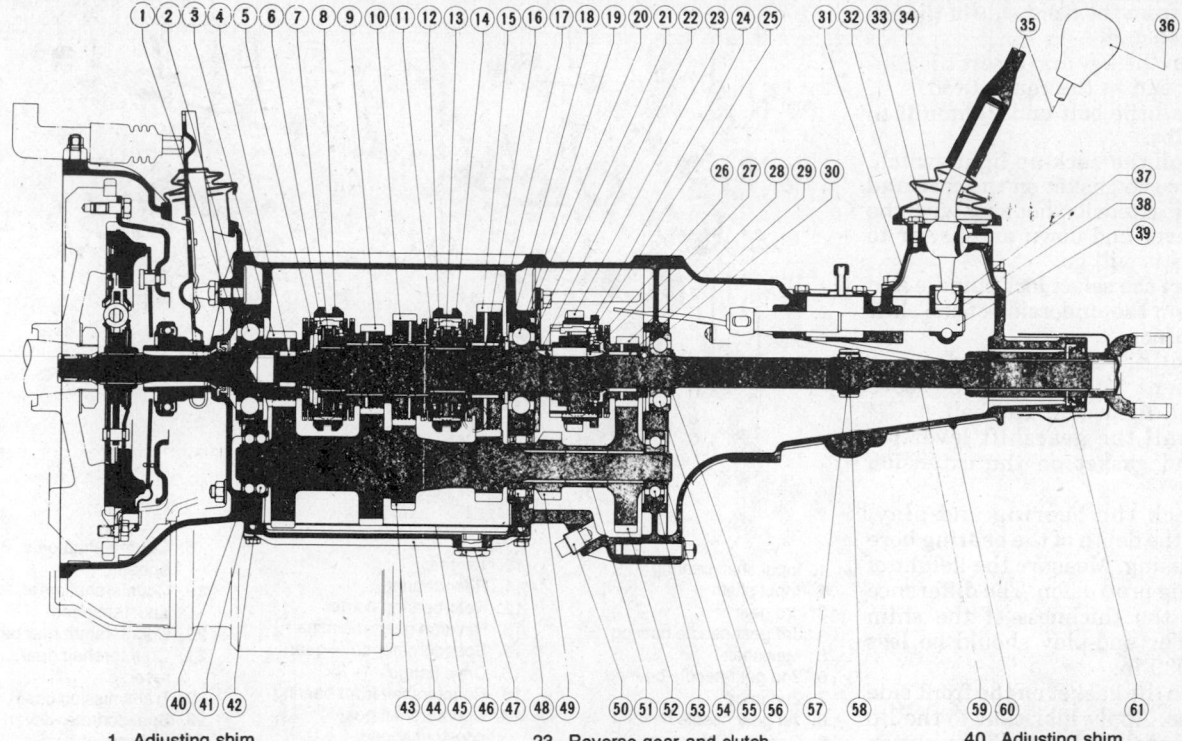

Cross section of Mazda 5-speed transmission

1. Adjusting shim
2. Main driveshaft bearing
3. Main driveshaft gear
4. Needle bearing
5. Synchronizer ring
6. Synchronizer key
7. 3rd-and-4th clutch hub
8. Clutch sleeve
9. 3rd gear
10. 2nd gear
11. Synchronizer ring
12. Synchronizer key
13. 1st-and-2nd clutch hub
14. Clutch sleeve
15. 1st gear
16. Needle bearing
17. Needle bearing inner race
18. Thrust washer
19. Mainshaft front bearing
20. Adjusting shim
21. Bearing cover plate
22. Spacer

23. Reverse gear and clutch sleeve assembly
24. Synchronizer key
25. Synchronizer ring
26. Lock washer
27. Locknut
28. 5th gear
29. Needle bearing
30. Thrust washer
31. Gearshift lever retainer
32. Cover
33. Gasket
34. Boot
35. Gearshift lever
36. Gearshift lever knob
37. Bush
38. Gearshift control lever end
39. Gearshift control lever

40. Adjusting shim
41. Transmission case
42. Countershaft front bearing
43. Countershaft
44. Transmission under cover
45. Gasket
46. Drain plug
47. Gasket
48. Countershaft center bearing
49. Counter reverse gear
50. Drain plug
51. Spacer
52. Counter 5th gear
53. Countershaft rear bearing
54. Thrust washer
55. Mainshaft rear bearing
56. Thrust washer
57. Speedometer drive gear
58. Lock ball
59. Mainshaft
60. Extension housng
61. Mainshaft oil seal

30. Install the third/fourth shift rod through the holes in the case and fork.

31. Align the holes and install the lockbolts of each shift fork and rod.

32. Install the interlock pin as above.

33. Position the reverse/fifth shift fork on the clutch sleeve and install the shift rod.

34. Tighten the lockbolt.

35. Install the three shift locking balls, springs and cap bolts.

36. Place the third/fourth clutch sleeve in third gear.

37. Check the clearance between the synchronizer key and the exposed edge of the synchronizer ring with a feeler gauge. The gap should be 0.026-0.079 in. Adjust by varying thrust washers.

38. Install the two blind covers and gaskets.

39. Install the undercover and gasket.

40. Apply a thin coat of sealer to the mating edges and install the intermediate housing on the transmission case. Align the lockbolt holes of the housing and reverse idler gearshaft, install and tighten the lockbolt.

41. Position the counter fifth gear and bearing to the rear end of the countershaft and install with a press.

42. Install the thrust washer and snap-ring.

43. Check the clearance between the washer and snap-ring. Clearance should be less than 0.0039 in.

44. Install the mainshaft rear bearing.

45. Install the thrust washer and snap-ring.

46. Check the thrust washer-to-snap-ring clearance. Clearance should be less than 0.0059 in.

47. Apply a thin coat of sealing agent to the mating surfaces and install the bearing housing on the intermediate housing.

48. Install the shift rod ends on their respective rods.

49. Install the speedometer drive gear and steel ball on the mainshaft. Secure it with a snap-ring.

50. Install a speedometer driven gear assembly on the extension housing and secure it with the bolt and lock plate.

51. Insert the control rod through

the holes from the front side of the extension housing.

52. Align the key and insert the control lever end in the control rod.

53. Install the bolt and tighten it to 20-30 ft. lbs.

54. Install the back-up light switch.

55. Place the gasket on the case and install the extension housing with the control lever end down and as far to the left as it will go.

56. Insert the select lock spindle and spring from the underside of the shift lever retainer.

57. Install the steel ball and spring in alignment with the spindle groove and install the spring cap bolt.

58. Install the gearshift lever retainer and gasket on the extension housing.

59. Check the bearing end-play. Measure the depth of the bearing bore in the housing. Measure the height of the bearing protrusion. The difference indicates the thickness of the shim needed. The end-play should be less than 0.0039 in.

60. Place the gasket on the front side of the case. Apply lubricant to the lip of the oil seal and install the clutch housing on the case.

61. Install the release bearing and fork on the clutch housing.

1. Input shaft bearing
2. Input shaft
3. 3rd gear
4. 3rd gear needle bearing
5. Mainshaft
6. 2nd gear needle bearing
7. 2nd gear
8. 1st gear needle bearing
9. Reverse slide gear
10. 1st gear
11. Rear bearing
12. Rear bearing holder
13. Reverse gear, mainshaft
14. Speedometer drive gear
15. Drive flange
16. Countershaft front bearing
17. Countershaft gear, constant speed
18. Countershaft gear, 3rd speed
19. Countershaft gear, 2nd and 1st speed
20. Countershaft rear bearing
21. Countershaft gear, reverse
22. Transmission case
23. Speedometer driven gear
24. Side cover

Exploded view of typical Mercedes-Benz 4-speed

TYPE 16

4 and 5 Speed Transmission Mercedes-Benz

DISASSEMBLY AND ASSEMBLY

The G 76/18, G76/18A, G 76/18B, G 76/27 and G 76/27A 4-speed manual transmissions are all very much alike. Overhaul is predominantly given for the G 76/18C since only minor modifications have been made. For disassembly and assembly of the 716 series 5-speed transmission, follow the same procedure as the 4-speed transmissions.

1. Remove the throwout bearing and fork.

2. Remove the clutch housing with the slave cylinder.

3. Remove the reverse shift lever clamp.

4. Remove the reverse shift lever.

5. Remove the side cover.

6. Remove the shift forks.

7. Disassemble the side cover and forks.

8. Unbolt and remove the transmission front cover.

9. Remove the bearing housing.

10. Remove the rear transmission cover.

11. Press out the speedometer drive gear.

12. Remove the tachometer drive seal.

13. Remove the reverse gear from the mainshaft.

14. Remove the reverse sliding gear shaft from the housing while holding the sliding gear.

15. Unlock the nut on the rear of the countershaft.

16. Remove reverse gear from the countershaft.

17. Knock the pin from reverse shifter shaft and move the shaft as far forward as possible.

18. Remove the shift rod from the housing.

19. Unlock the slotted nut.

20. Remove the front countershaft bearing. On G 76/27A transmissions, the bearing is beveled and is removed toward the inside of the case.

21. Remove the rear countershaft bearing.

22. Lift the mainshaft at the rear and pull the input shaft out of the housing.

23. Push the mainshaft completely rearward and remove it at an angle.

24. Remove the countershaft from the housing.

25. Disassemble the mainshaft, if necessary.

26. If necessary, disassemble the countershaft.

27. Assembly is basically the reverse of disassembly. Try to obtain 0 end-play on the main and input shafts.

TYPE 17

4 Speed Transmission Isuzu

DISASSEMBLY

1. Remove the boot, clutch fork and throwout bearing.

2. Remove bearing retainer, gasket and spring washer.

3. Remove the speedometer gear and bushing.

4. Remove the shifter cover and gasket.

5. Remove the back-up switch on California vehicles and both back-up and CRS (Coasting Richer System) switches on all others.

6. Remove the rear extension and gasket.

7. Remove the thrust washers and reverse idler gear.

8. Remove the snap-rings, speedometer drive gear and key from the mainshaft.

9. Remove the spring pin from the reverse shifter fork and reverse gear.

10. Remove the snap-ring from the outer circumference of the clutch gear shaft ball bearing.

11. Remove the center support assembly from the transmission case.

12. Drive out the spring pins from the third and fourth and first and second shift forks.

NOTE: When removing the spring pin, hold a round bar against the end of the shifter rods to prevent damage.

13. Remove the detent spring plate from the center support, then remove the detent springs and balls.

14. Remove the first and second and the third and fourth shifter rods from the center support, then remove the shifter forks.

15. Remove the reverse shifter rod forward as it is fitted with a stopper pin.

NOTE: Be careful not to lose the detent interlock plugs located between the shifter rods in the center support.

16. Move both synchronizers rearward to prevent turning of the mainshaft.

NOTE: It may be necessary to tap the synchronizers with the hammer handle to get them engaged.

17. Remove the locknut and washer from the mainshaft.

18. Remove the nut, washer, countershaft reverse gear and collar from the rear of the countergear.

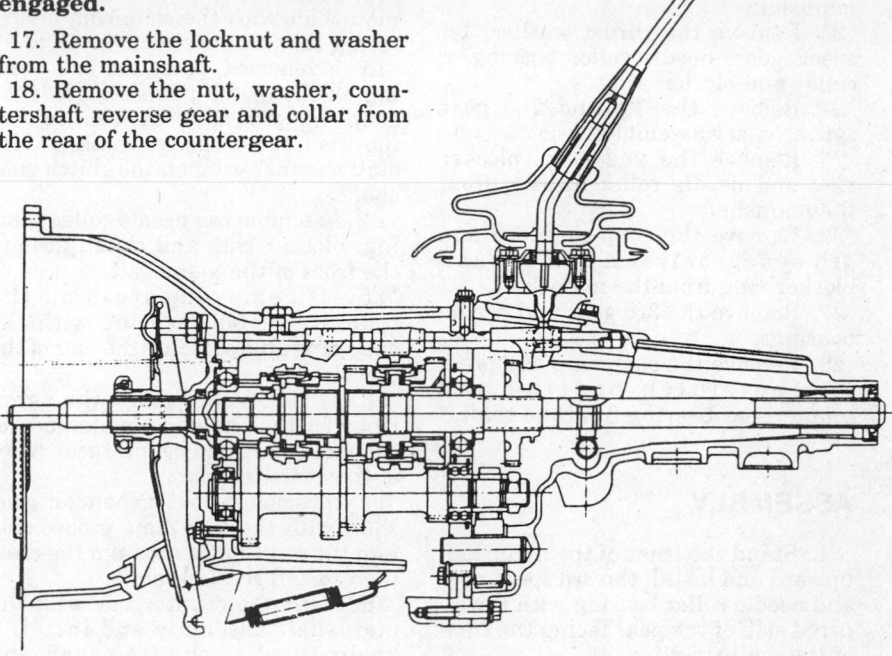

Cross section of the four speed transmission for the Isuzu I-Mark (RWD) vehicles

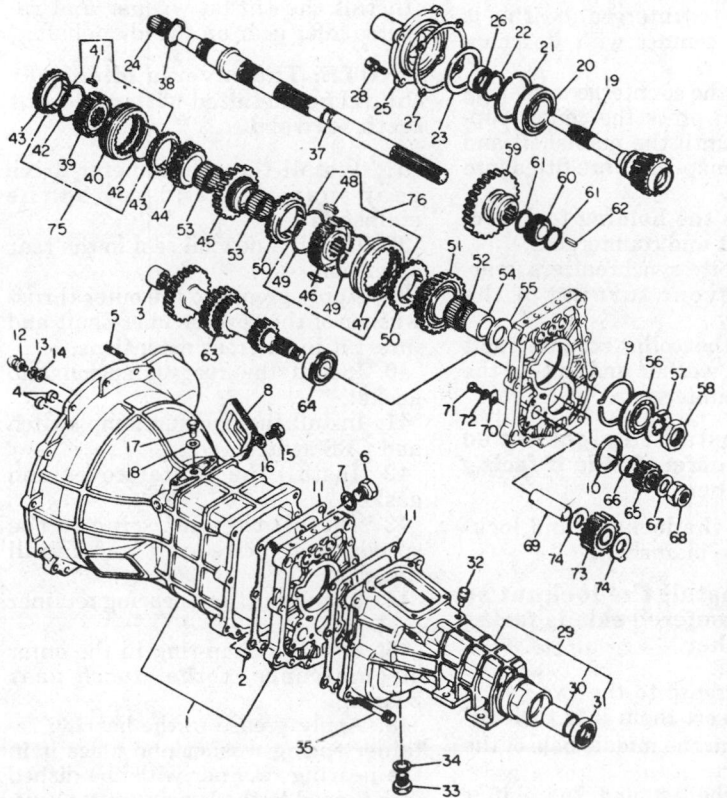

1. Case, w/center support	39. Hub, synchronizer, 3rd-4th
2. Pin, guide	40. Sleeve, synchronizer
3. Bearing, needle	41. Key, synchronizer
4. Plug, shift rod	42. Spring, synchronizer
5. Stud.	43. Ring, blocker
6. Plug, oil filler	44. Gear assy., 3rd
7. O-ring, oil filler	45. Gear assy., 2nd
8. Dust cover, shift fork	46. Hub, synchronizer, 1st-2nd
9. Ring, snap, mainshaft	47. Sleeve, synchronizer
10. Ring, snap counter gear	48. Key, synchronizer
11. Gasket, case and rear cover	49. Spring, synchronizer
12. Ball stud	50. Ring blocker
13. Washer, lock	51. Gear assy., 1st
14. Washer, plain	52. Bearing, needle, 1st
15. Plug, screw	53. Bearing, needle, 2nd
16. Gasket, plug (Calif. spec.)	54. Collar, needle bearing
17. Plug, screw (Calif. spec.)	55. Washer, thrust, 1st
18. Gasket, plug (Calif. spec.)	56. Bearing, mainshaft
19. Shaft, clutch gear	57. Washer, lock, mainshaft
20. Bearing, ball	58. Nut, mainshaft
21. Ring, snap	59. Gear, reverse
22. Ring, snap	60. Gear, speed drive
23. Spring, belleville	61. Ring, snap, drive gear
24. Bearing, needle	62. Key
25. Bearing retainer	63. Gear, counter
26. Seal, oil, bearing retainer	64. Bearing, angular ball
27. Gasket, bearing retainer	65. Gear, counter reverse
28. Bolt	66. Spacer
29. Extension Assy., rear, w/bushing and seal	67. Washer, plain
30. Bushing	68. Nut, self lock
31. Seal, oil, rear extension	69. Shaft, reverse idle
32. Breather assy.	70. Plate, lock
33. Plug, oil drain	71. Bolt, lock
34. O-ring, oil drain	72. Washer, spring
35. Bolt	73. Gear, reverse idle
37. Shaft main	74. Washer, thrust
38. Ring, snap	75. Synchronizer assy., 3rd-4th
	76. Synchronizer assy., 1st-2nd

Isuzu 4-speed manual transmission

19. Remove the center support countergear bearing snap-ring.

20. Remove the center support.

21. Separate the clutch gear, needle bearings and blocker ring from the mainshaft assembly.

22. Press the rear bearing from the mainshaft.

23. Remove the thrust washer, 1st speed gear, needle roller bearing, a collar and blocker ring.

24. Remove the 1st and 2nd gear synchronizer assembly.

25. Remove the 2nd gear, blocker ring and needle roller bearing from the mainshaft.

26. Remove the snap-ring, 3rd and 4th synchronizer assembly and blocker ring from the mainshaft.

27. Remove the 3rd gear and needle bearings.

28. Remove the snap-ring and press off the clutch bearing and countergear bearing from the shaft.

ASSEMBLY

1. Stand the front of the mainshaft upward and install the 3rd speed gear and needle roller bearing with the tapered side of the gear facing the front of the mainshaft.

2. Install a blocker ring with the clutching teeth upward over the synchronizing surface of the 3rd speed gear.

3. If it is necessary to reassemble the synchronizer assembly turn the face of the synchronizer hub with the heavy boss to the face of the sleeve with the light chamfering on the outer rim.

4. Fit the keys into the key groove and position the synchronizer springs into the hole in the side face of the hub.

5. Install the 3rd and 4th synchronizer assembly on the mainshaft with the face of the sleeve with the light chamfer rearward.

6. Turn the rear of the mainshaft upward and install the 2nd speed gear and needle roller bearing on the mainshaft with the tapered surface of the gear facing the rear of the mainshaft.

7. Install a blocker ring with the clutching teeth downward over the synchronizing surface of the 2nd speed gear.

8. Install the 1st and 2nd synchronizer assembly with the chamfer on the sleeve facing the front of the mainshaft.

9. Install a blocker ring with the clutching teeth rearward.

10. Install the collar, needle roller bearing and 1st speed gear on the mainshaft.

NOTE: The tapered side of the gear should be facing the front of the mainshaft.

11. Install the 1st speed gear thrust washer on the mainshaft with the grooved side facing 1st gear.

12. Press the rear bearing on the mainshaft with the snap-ring groove facing the front of the mainshaft.

13. If removed, press the ball bearing on the clutch gearshaft with the snap-ring groove on the bearing facing the front of the transmission. Install the snap-ring on the clutch gear shaft.

14. Assemble the needle roller bearing, blocker ring and clutch gear to the front of the mainshaft.

15. If removed, press on the countergear ball bearing with the snap-ring groove facing the rear of the transmission.

16. If removed, install the snap-rings in the inner circumference of the mainshaft and countergear holes of the center support.

17. If removed, insert the idler gear shaft with the lock plate groove side into the center support from the rear, then install the lock plate.

18. Mesh the countergear with the mainshaft assembly and install a holding tool on the mainshaft and countergear.

19. Install the center support.

20. Press the center support onto the shaft until the countergear bearing is brought into contact with its snap-ring.

21. Expand the countergear bearing snap-ring and press the center support further until the mainshaft and countergear snap-rings are fitted into their grooves.

22. Remove the holding tool from the mainshaft and countergear.

23. Move both synchronizers rearward to prevent turning of the mainshaft.

24. Install the collar, countershaft reverse gear, washer and nut on the rear of the countergear.

NOTE: Install the locknut so that the chamfered side if facing the lockwasher.

25. Install the locknut and lockwasher on the mainshaft.

NOTE: Install the locknut so that the chamfered side is facing the lockwasher.

26. Apply grease to the two detent plugs and insert them into their detent holes from the middle hole of the center support.

27. Install the 1st and 2nd shifter forks and the 3rd and 4th into their grooves in the synchronizer assembly.

28. Install 3rd and 4th shifter rod from the rear of the center support through the middle hole and into the 1st and 2nd, 3rd and 4th shifter forks. Align the spring pin hole in the shifter fork with the hole in the shifter rod.

NOTE: Identify the 3rd and 4th shifter rod by the two detent grooves on the side of the rod.

29. Install the 1st and 2nd shifter rod from the rear of the center support through the 1st and 2nd shifter fork and align the hole in the rod to the hole in the shifter fork.

30. If removed, install the stopper pin in the reverse shifter rod and the front of the center support.

31. Install the two spring pins in the 1st/2nd and 3rd/4th shifter forks.

32. Install the detent balls, spring, gasket and retainer on the center support

33. Install the center support assembly and gasket.

34. Assemble the reverse shifter fork to the reverse gear and install these parts into position from the rear side of the mainshaft, then connect them to the reverse shifter rod.

35. Install the spring pin in the reverse shifter fork.

36. Install the thrust washer and reverse idler gear on the idler shaft.

NOTE: The reverse idler gear should be installed with undercut teeth forward.

37. Install the speedometer drive gear snap-ring and key on the mainshaft.

38. Install a new oil seal in the rear extension.

39. Apply grease to the outer thrust washer of the reverse idler shaft and insert it in the rear extensions.

40. Install the rear extension and gasket.

41. Install the back-up lamp switch and CRS switch.

42. Install the shifter cover and gasket.

43. Install the oil O-ring to the speedometer drive gear and install the gear.

44. Install the front bearing retainer seal.

45. Install a snap-ring in the outer circumfrence of the clutch gear bearing.

46. Apply grease to the bearing retainer spring washer and place it in the bearing retainer with the dished face turned to the bearing outer race.

47. Install the bearing retainer to the front of the transmission case.

NOTE: The shorter bolts are used on countergear front bearing side of the bearing retainer.

48. Install the ball stud to the bearing retainer.

49. Install the boot clutch fork and throwout bearing, then install the retaining spring.

TYPE 18

5 Speed Transmission Isuzu

DISASSEMBLY

1. Drain the gear box of lubrication.

2. Remove the clutch release bearing and yoke assembly from the bell housing. Remove the clutch fork ball stud, if necessary, for removal clearance of the front bearing retainer.

3. Remove the front bearing retainer and Belleville spring.

4. Remove the speedometer driven gear and shift lever quadrant from the extension housing.

NOTE: Remove the Coasting Richer System switch from the quadrant on California models.

5. Remove the back-up lamp switch and the extension housing from the gear box.

6. Remove the snap-rings, speedometer drive gear, key, spacer and bearing from the mainshaft.

7. Remove the snap-ring, thrust washer and lock ball from the fifth gear on the mainshaft.

8. Remove the large snap-ring from the front bearing.

9. Remove the center support plate from the transmission case, with the mainshaft, countergear and drive gear as an assembly.

10. Support the ends of the 1st and 2nd, 3rd and 4th and 5th and reverse shift forks and drive the retaining pins from the forks.

11. Remove the detent spring plate from the center support plate and remove the three springs and balls.

12. Remove the shifter shafts from the center support plate and remove the shift forks and interlock pins.

13. To prevent the turning of the mainshaft and countergear while removing the locking nuts from the gear assembly, engage the synchronizers in 1st and 3rd gears.

14. Remove the nut and washer retaining the countergear and by using a puller, remove the ball bearing and

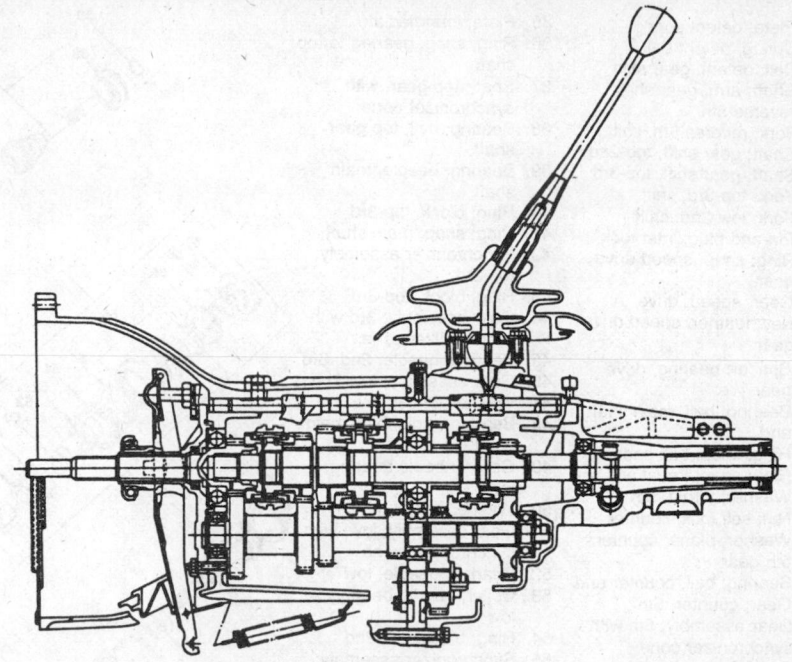

Cross section of the five speed transmission for the Isuzu I-Mark (RWD) vehicles

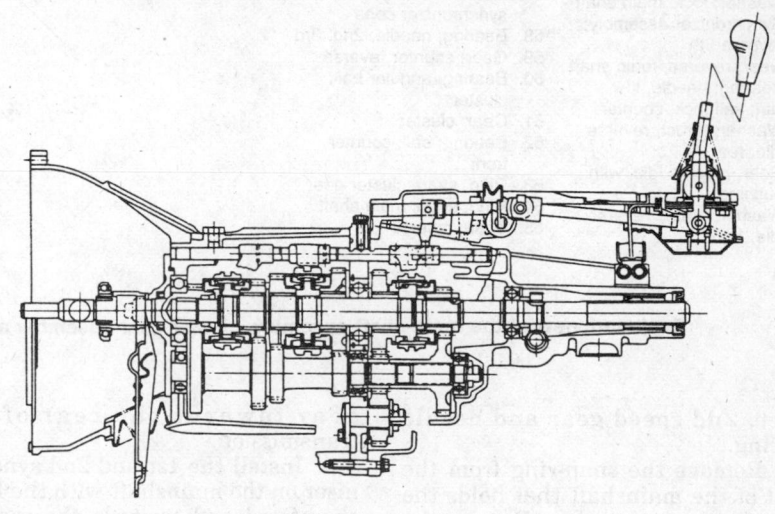

Cross section of the five speed transmission for the Isuzu Impulse vehicles

the fifth gear from the rear of the countershaft.

15. Remove the fifth gear, blocker ring and needle bearing from the mainshaft.

16. Remove the nut from the reverse idler gearshaft and remove the thrust washers and gear from the idler gearshaft.

17. Straighten the mainshaft locking retainer tab and remove the nut and retainer from the mainshaft.

18. Remove the synchronizer assembly, reverse gear, needle bearing, collar and thrust washer.

19. Remove the reverse gear from the countergear and reposition the synchronizers to the neutral position.

20. Expand the countergear bearing snap-ring and move the center support plate by gently tapping on its front.

21. Expand the mainshaft bearing snap-ring and move the mainshaft inward. Remove the mainshaft and countergear.

22. Remove the drive gear, needle bearing and blocker ring from the mainshaft.

23. Remove the rear bearing from the mainshaft with the aid of a puller or press.

24. Remove the thrust washer, 1st speed gear, needle bearings and spacer.

25. Remove the 1st and 2nd synchro-

1. Plate; detent spring
2. Spring; detent ball
3. Ball; detent, gear shift
4. Shaft; arm, gear shift, reverse-5th
5. Fork; reverse-5th, shift
6. Shaft; gear shift, top-2nd
7. Shaft; gear shift, top-3rd
8. Fork; top-3rd, shift
9. Fork; low-2nd, shift
10. Pin and plug; inter lock
11. Ring; snap, speed drive gear
12. Gear; speed, drive
13. Key; feather, speed drive gear
14. Spacer; bearing, drive gear
15. Bearing; ball, main shaft end
16. Ring; snap, ball bearing
17. Ring; snap, thrust washer
18. Washer; thrust, 5th
19. Nut; self lock, counter
20. Washer; plane, counter 5th gear
21. Bearing; ball, counter end
22. Gear; counter, 5th
23. Gear assembly; 5th with synchronizer cone
24. Bearing; needle, 5th
25. Ring; block, 5th
26. Nut; main shaft
27. Washer; lock, main shaft
28. Synchronizer assembly; reverse-5th
29. Gear; reverse, main shaft
30. Bearing; needle, low
31. Nut; self lock, counter
32. Washer; thrust, reverse idle, rear
33. Gear; reverse idle, with bushing
34. Washer; thrust, reverse idle, front
35. Plate; intermediate
36. Ring; snap, bearing to top shaft
37. Shaft; top gear, with synchronizer cone
38. Bearing; ball, top gear shaft
39. Bearing; needle, main shaft
40. Ring; block, top-3rd
41. Ring; snap, main shaft
42. Synchronizer assembly; top-3rd
43. Ring; block, top-3rd
44. Gear assembly; 3rd with synchronizer cone
45. Bearing; needle, 2nd, 3rd
46. Gear assembly; low-2nd
47. Washer; thrust, low
48. Bearing; radial ball, main shaft
49. Coller; needle bearing, low
50. Washer; thrust, low
51. Gear assembly; low, with synchronizer cone
52. Bearing; needle, low
53. Coller; needle bearing, low
54. Ring; block, low-2nd
55. Synchronizer assembly; low-2nd
56. Ring; block, low-2nd
57. Gear assembly; 2nd with synchronizer cone
58. Bearing; needle, 2nd, 3rd
59. Gear; counter reverse
60. Bearing; angular ball, cluster
61. Gear; cluster
62. Bearing; ball, counter front
63. Ring; snap, cluster gear
64. Ring; snap, main shaft
65. Shaft; reverse idle

Exploded view of the main shaft assembly, cluster gear assembly and top gear assembly—Isuzu Impulse

nizer, 2nd speed gear and needle bearing.

26. Remove the snap-ring from the front of the mainshaft that holds the 3rd and 4th synchronizer. Remove the 3rd speed gear and needle bearing.

27. Remove the snap-ring from the drive gearshaft and with the use of a puller or a press, remove the front bearing.

ASSEMBLY

1. Place the coned side of the 3rd speed gear towards the front of the transmission and install it and the needle bearing on the front of the mainshaft.

2. Install the 3rd and 4th synchronizer on the mainshaft with the chamfered end towards the front of the transmission. Retain with a snap-ring.

3. Install the 2nd speed gear and needle bearing on the rear of the mainshaft with the coned end of the gear towards the rear of the transmission.

4. Install the 1st and 2nd synchronizer on the mainshaft with the large chamfered end towards the rear on the transmission.

5. Install the spacer, needle bearings and 1st speed gear on the mainshaft, with the coned end of the gear towards the front of the transmission.

6. Install the first gear thrust washer with the slots towards the gear.

7. Press the rear bearing onto the mainshaft with the snap-ring groove towards the front of the transmission.

8. Install the center support plate snap-rings and reverse idler shaft. Torque bolts to 14 ft. lbs.

9. Install the drive gear on the front of the mainshaft and engage with the countergear to install the center support plate.

10. Install countergear and mainshaft bearings into the center support plate and while expanding the snap-rings, move the bearings into place on the support plate and engage the snap-rings in the bearing grooves.

11. Engage the gears in 1st and 3rd to prevent turning and install the reverse gear on the countergear.

12. Install the thrust washer on the mainshaft with the oil grooves turned towards the reverse gear. Install the collar, needle bearings and reverse gear on the mainshaft.

13. Install the synchronizer assembly so that the face of the clutch hub boss is turned to the reverse gear side.

14. Install the locking retainer and nut on the front of the mainshaft. Torque the nut to 94 ft. lbs. Bend the retainer tab to lock the nut in place.

15. Install the thrust washers and reverse idler gear on the reverse idler shaft and tighten the nut to 80 ft. lbs.

NOTE: Install new self locking nut on countergear.

16. Install the blocker ring, needle bearing and 5th gear on the mainshaft.

17. Install the countergear 5th gear, ball bearing, washer and self-locking nut on the rear of the countergear. Torque the nut to 80 ft. lbs.

NOTE: Install new self-locking nut on countergear.

18. Reposition the synchronizers to the neutral position.

19. Lubricate the interlock pins and install in the center support plate.

20. Place the shift forks on the synchronizer sleeves and install the 3rd and 4th shifter shaft through the center support plate shifter shaft through the center support plate and into the shift fork for 3rd and 4th gear.

21. Install the 1st and 2nd shifter shaft through the center support plate and through the 1st and 2nd shift fork.

22. Install the reverse and 5th shifter shaft through the center support plate and into the reverse and 5th gear fork.

23. Install the three detent balls and springs in the center support plate and retain with the detent plate and gasket. Torque the bolts to 14 ft. lbs.

24. Install the retaining pins in the shifter forks to the shifter shafts while supporting the ends of the shaft with a bar or block of wood.

25. Install the countergear needle bearing in the front of the transmission case.

26. Install a new gasket on the transmission case and install the center support plate assembly into the transmission case.

27. Install the large snap-ring on the front bearing of the mainshaft.

28. Install the lock ball and thrust washer on the mainshaft and retain with a snap-ring.

29. Measure the clearance between the 5th gear and the thrust washer on the mainshaft. The clearance should be 0.010-0.016 in.

30. If the clearance is out of specifications replace the thrust washer with one of the following:

Part Number	Thickness (inches)	(Millimeters)
94025579	0.3014	7.656
94025580	0.3073	7.805
94025581	0.3132	7.955
94025582	0.3191	8.105

31. Install the speedometer drive gear front snap-ring, ball bearing and key onto the mainshaft.

32. Align the groove in the speedometer drive gear with the key on the mainshaft and install the gear. Retain with a snap-ring.

33. Install the rear extension housing with a new gasket on the center support plate. Torque the bolts to 27 ft. lbs.

34. Install the shift lever squadrant with gasket on the extension housing. Torque the bolts to 14 ft. lbs.

35. Install the speedometer driven gear and torque the retaining bolt to 14 ft. lbs.

36. California Models only: Install the CRS switch on the extension housing.

37. Install the Belleview washer with the dished side towards the drive gear bearing and install the bearing retainer and gasket. Torque the bolts to 14 ft. lbs.

NOTE: Seal the tower left bolt with a non-hardening sealer or equivalent.

38. Install the clutch release bearing and yoke assembly on the bell housing.

NOTE: The gearshift lever is installed when the transmission is in the vehicle.

TYPE 19

4 and 5 Speed Transmissions Models K40, K50, K51 Toyota

DISASSEMBLY

1. Secure the transmission and drain the lubricant from the unit.
2. Remove the clutch release bearing, fork, boot and spring.
3. Remove the countershaft cover

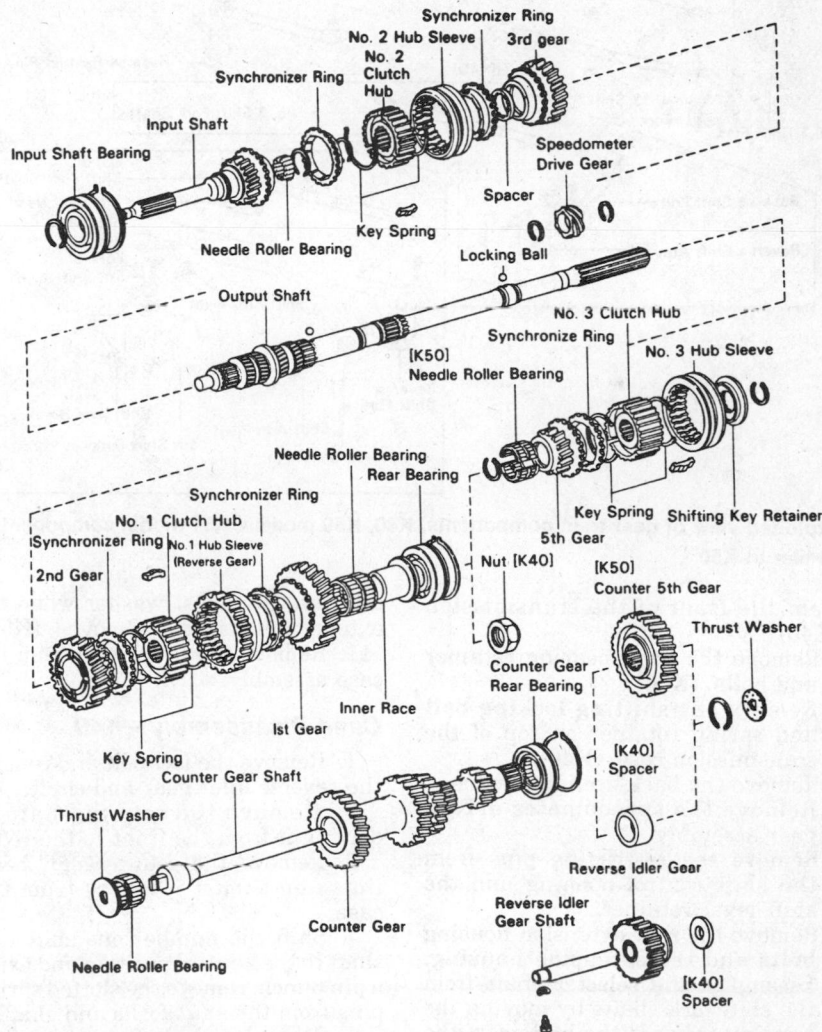

Exploded view of case and shifting mechanisms, K40, K50 models. K51 model components similar to K50

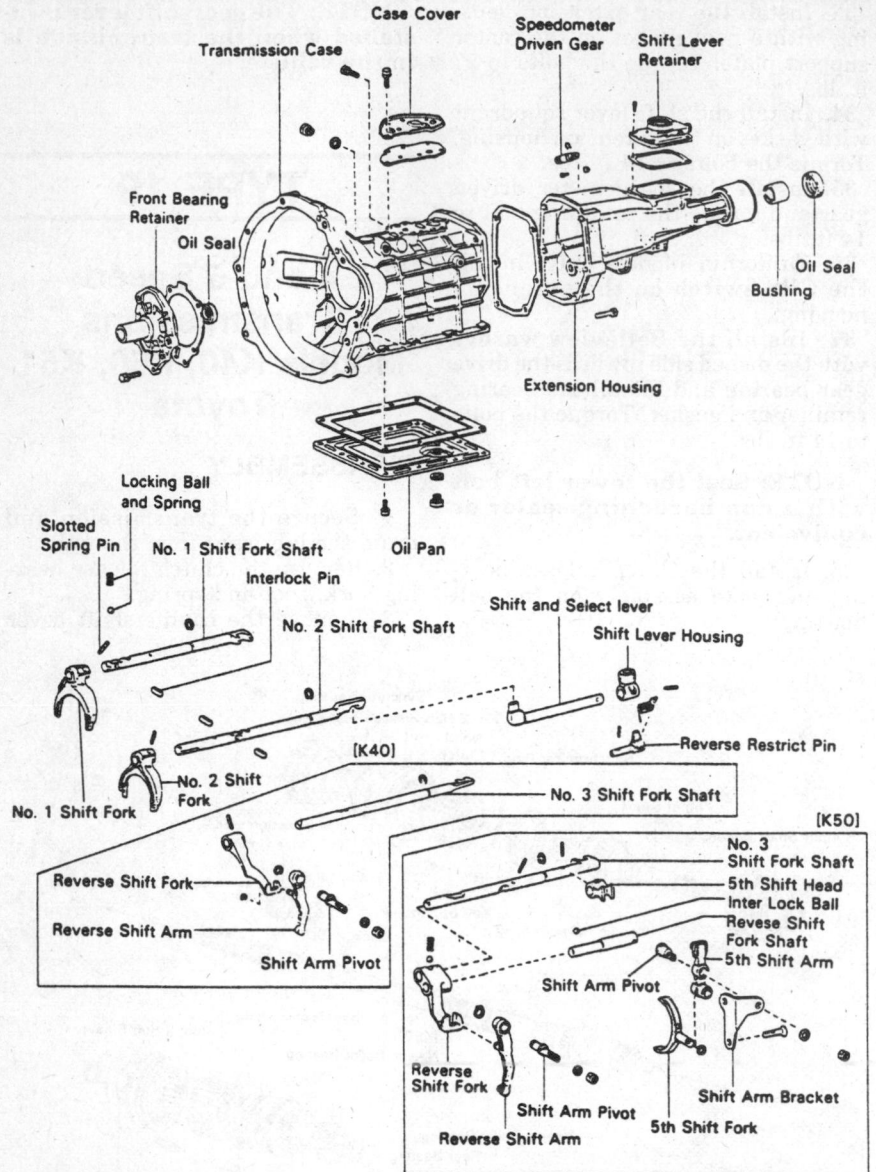

Exploded view of gear train components, K40, K50 models. K51 model components similar to K50

from the front of the transmission (K40)

4. Remove the front bearing retainer and bolts. (K40).

5. Remove the shifting locking ball and spring retainer on top of the transmission case. (K40).

6. Remove the back-up light switch.

7. Remove the speedometer driven gear assembly.

8. Remove the restricting pins from the shift control opening and the shift lever retainer.

9. Remove the rear extension housing bolts and the extension housing. Disengage the selector shaft from the shift fork shafts by moving the housing towards the bottom of the case.

10. Locate and retain the

countergear thrust washer when the extension housing is removed. (K50).

11. Remove the lower pan from the case assembly.

Case Disassembly—K40

1. Remove the lockbolt and remove the reverse idler gear and shaft.

2. Remove the countershaft by driving it from the front to the rear.

3. Remove the countergear, bearings and thrust washers from the case.

4. Shift the number one shift fork shaft to the neutral position and using a pin punch, remove the slotted spring pins from the shift forks and shafts.

5. Set each fork shaft to the neutral position and pull the shaft from the case.

6. Shift the number one clutch hub sleeve into 2nd gear and remove the shift fork from inside the case.

7. Arrange the three interlock pins and slotted spring pins and lay aside for the assembly.

8. Remove the output shaft from the rear of the transmission with the gear intact. Remove the input shaft and bearing.

9. Remove the snap-rings at the speedometer drive gear and remove the gear from the shaft.

10. Release the staked parts of the locknut on the mainshaft and remove the nut from the shaft with a holding tool and special wrench.

11. Remove the rear bearing and housing from the mainshaft.

12. Remove the 1st gear, bushing, needle bearing and locking ball from the shaft.

13. Remove the synchronizer (baulk) ring, 1s/2nd clutch hub and sleeve, synchronizer (baulk) ring and the 2nd speed gear from the shaft.

14. Remove the snap-rings from the front of the shaft and remove the 3rd/4th synchronizer assembly and the 3rd speed gear, with a spacer.

Case Disassembly—K50

1. Remove the snap-rings and speedometer drive gear from the output or mainshaft.

2. Remove the 5th gearshift arm bracket, arm and the number 3 shift fork.

3. Remove the snap-ring and the shifting key retainer from the mainshaft.

4. Remove the number three clutch hub and sleeve, the synchronizer (baulk) ring and the 5th gear with its needle roller bearings.

5. Remove the snap-ring from the countergear and remove the counter 5th gear, the countergear rear bearing and sleeve. The sleeve is retained with a snap-ring.

6. Remove the locking bolt and pull the reverse idler shaft from the case. Remove the reverse idler gear.

7. Remove the countergear, thrust washer and the front bearing from the case as a unit.

8. Remove the locking balls and springs cover from the top of the transmission case. Remove the springs and balls.

9. Using a pin punch, drive the slotted spring pins from the forks and shafts.

10. Place each shaft into the neutral position and remove from the case.

11. Arrange the slotted spring pins, the interlock pins, and locking ball for easier assembly.

12. Shift the number one clutch into

2nd gear and remove the shift fork from inside the case.

13. Remove the input shaft and front bearing retainer from the front of the case.

14. Secure the pilot bearing rollers and the 4th speed synchronizer (baulk) ring.

15. Spread the expanding snap-ring on the rear bearing and remove the output shaft assembly from the front of the transmission case.

16. Disassemble the mainshaft by removing the rear snap-ring and removing the rear bearing, bushing, needle roller bearing and locating ball. Continue by removing the 1st gear, synchronizer (baulk) ring, number one clutch hub, sleeve, synchronizer (baulk) ring and the second gear.

17. Remove the front snap-ring, the number two clutch hub, sleeve, synchronizer (baulk) ring and the second gear.

NOTE: During the disassembly and assembly of the K40 and K50 transmissions, the need to press bearings or gears from and back onto the shafts will exist. Govern the disassembly and assembly procedures accordingly.

INSPECTION

Inspect the gears, shafts, bearings and other internal components and replace or repair the necessary parts. Install new seals and gaskets during the reassembly.

ASSEMBLY

Case Assembly—K40

1. Place the mainshaft in an upright position with the rear of the shaft pointing up. Place the 2nd speed gear and the synchronizer (baulk) ring onto the shaft, followed by the number one clutch hub and sleeve. Ring identification: Narrow insert gap for 1st gear and wide insert gap for 2nd gear.

2. Install the second synchronizer (baulk) ring, the 1st gear, the locking ball, the needle roller bearing and the bushing.

3. Install the rear bearing and housing onto the shaft and retain it with a washer and locknut. Tighten the locknut to a torque of 33-72 ft. lbs. (4.5-10 Kg-m) with the special wrench and the shaft holding tool. Stake the nut to the shaft.

4. Measure the thrust clearance of the 1st and 2nd speed gears:

   1st gear-0.0071-0.0110 in. (0.18-0.28mm)

2nd gear-0.0039-0.0098 in. (0.10-0.25mm)

5. Install the 3rd gear on the front of the shaft. Line up the shifting key inserts with the insert slots in the synchronizer (baulk) ring and install the number two clutch hub and sleeve.

6. Push the number two clutch hub inward as far as it will go and measure the 3rd gear thrust clearance:

   3rd gear-0.0020-0.0079 in. (0.05-0.20mm)

   Limit-0.0018 in. (0.30mm)

7. When the 3rd gear thrust clearance is not within specifications, select a spacer from the following list:

Thickness	
mm	(in.)
4.30–4.35	(0.1693–0.1713)
4.35–4.40	(0.1713–0.1732)
4.40–4.45	(0.1732–0.1752)

8. Select a snap ring that will control the clearance to zero between the snap ring and the clutch hub, from the following list:

Thickness	
mm	(in.)
2.05–2.10	(0.0807–0.0827)
2.10–2.15	(0.0827–0.0846)
2.15–2.20	(0.0846–0.0866)
2.20–2.25	(0.0866–0.0886)
2.25–2.30	(0.0886–0.0906)
2.30–2.35	(0.0906–0.0925)
2.35–2.40	(0.0925–0.0945)
2.40–2.45	(0.0945–0.0965)

9. Install the snap-ring in place on the mainshaft.

10. If not previously done, install the front bearing on the input shaft. Install the needle roller bearings into the bore of the mainshaft and hold in place with grease.

11. Install the input shaft into the transmission case and select a front bearing retainer gasket in the following manner.

   a. If the bearing face extends outside of the case machined surface, use a bearing retainer gasket of 0.020 in. (0.5mm) in thickness.

   b. If the bearing face is below the case machined surface, use a bearing retainer gasket of 0.012 in. (0.3mm) in thickness.

12. Lubricate the front bearing retainer oil seal and install the retainer to the case. Torque the bolts 11-15 ft. lbs. (1.5-2.2 Kg-m).

13. Set the transmission case upright with the input shaft on the bottom. Be sure the needle bearings remain in their proper position in the input shaft bore.

14. Carefully insert the mainshaft assembly into the transmission case and align the shifting key inserts with the slots in the synchronizer (baulk) ring.

15. Align the pin on the rear bearing housing with the groove in the transmission case. Be sure the mainshaft and the input shaft rotate freely.

16. Temporarily, install a holding tool over the rear bearing retainer so that the gear train is held securely. Place the transmission with the bottom up.

17. Shift the synchronizer assembly sleeve into the 2nd speed position. Install the reverse shift fork, the 1st/2nd shift fork and the 3rd/4th shift fork in their respective sleeve grooves.

18. Insert the shift shafts into the transmission case and through their respective shifting forks. Place the center shaft in the neutral position, along with the reverse shifting shaft in the neutral position.

19. Install the 1st-2nd shifting shaft to the point where the shaft dummy hole and the case hole line up.

20. Insert a probe into the case hole and be sure the outer two shaft holes line up and the probe touches the inner shaft.

21. Install the interlock pins and push the inner shaft to the neutral position. Move the center shift shaft to the third speed position. The outer shafts should not move.

22. Align the forks to the holes in the shafts and install the slotted spring pins.

23. Coat the countergear thrust washers with grease and place them on the inner walls of the transmission case. Insert the countershaft from the rear of the case until the shaft end is even with the rear thrust washer.

24. Carefully install the countergear and push the countershaft into the transmission case and the countergear bearings. Measure the thrust clearance and correct by selecting a proper sized thrust washer. The thrust clearance should be 0.0020-0.0098 in. (0.05-0.25mm).

25. Install the reverse idler gear and shaft. An adjustment can be made to prevent the gear from contacting the case surface. A spacer can be installed between the gear and the case. A clearance of 0.039-0.079 in. (1.0-2.0mm) should exist between the teeth of the reverse gear and the teeth

Thickness	
mm	(in.)
1.30–1.35	(0.0512–0.0531)
1.40–1.45	(0.0551–0.0571)
1.50–1.55	(0.0591–0.0610)
1.60–1.65	(0.0630–0.0650)

of the countergear. A pivot screw and locknut are provided on the case to help in the adjustment of the reverse gear clearance.

26. Set the transmission upright with the output shaft in the horizontal position and the pan opening down.

27. Install the three balls and springs into the holes in the case top and install the locking ball and spring cover.

28. Install the countergear shaft cover on the front of the transmission case.

29. Shift the fork shafts and be sure the shifting of the gear sleeves, forks and linkage is proper.

Case Assembly—K50

1. Position the mainshaft with the rear of the shaft pointing upward. Install the 2nd speed gear and the synchronizer (baulk) ring onto the shaft, followed by the number one clutch hub and sleeve. Ring identification: Narrow insert gap for 1st gear and the wide insert gap for the 2nd gear.

2. Install the second synchronizer (baulk) ring, the 1st gear, the locking ball, the needle roller bearing and the bushing.

3. Install the rear bearing and select a selective snap-ring that will allow zero thrust clearance. The snap-ring thicknesses are as follows:

Thickness	
mm	(in.)
2.05–2.10	(0.0807–0.0827)
2.10–2.15	(0.0827–0.0846)
2.15–2.20	(0.0846–0.0866)
2.20–2.25	(0.0866–0.0886)
2.25–2.30	(0.0886–0.0906)
2.30–2.35	(0.0906–0.0925)
2.35–2.40	(0.0925–0.0945)
2.40–2.45	(0.0945–0.0965)
2.45–2.50	(0.0965–0.0984)
2.50–2.55	(0.0984–0.1004)

4. Install the snap-ring on the mainshaft in its groove. Check the thrust clearances of the 1st and 2nd gears. The clearances should be as follows:

1st gear-0.0071-0.0110 in. (0.18-0.28mm)

2nd gear-0.039-0.0098 in. (0.10-0.25mm)

Limit-0.0118 in. (0.30mm)

5. Install the 3rd gear onto the front of the shaft and install the synchronizer hub and sleeve, along with the inner synchronizer (baulk) ring in place on the gear unit.

6. Push inward on the number two clutch hub and measure the 3rd gear

thrust clearance. The clearance should be as follows:

3rd gear—0.09020-0.0079 in (0.05-0.20mm)

Limit—0.0118 in. (0.30)

Install one of the following spacers as required:

Thickness	
mm	(in.)
4.30–4.35	(0.1693–0.1713)
4.35–4.40	(0.1713–0.1732)
4.40–4.45	(0.1732–0.1752)

7. Select a snap-ring of proper thickness to provide zero clearance between the snap-ring and the clutch hub, and install on the shaft. A list of available snap-rings are as follows:

Thickness	
mm	(in.)
2.05–2.10	(0.0807–0.0827)
2.10–2.15	(0.0827–0.0846)
2.15–2.20	(0.0846–0.0866)
2.20–2.25	(0.0866–0.0886)
2.25–2.30	(0.0886–0.0906)
2.30–2.35	(0.0906–0.0925)
2.35–2.40	(0.0925–0.0945)
2.40–2.45	(0.0945–0.0965)

8. Install the mainshaft assembly into the transmission case from the front. Stand the case assembly upright and pull the mainshaft assembly upward, seating the bearing into the case bore, while having the bearing snap-ring expanded in the case. Secure the bearing in the case with the snap-ring.

9. Install the roller bearing and housing on the input shaft, if not previously done. Install the needle bearings in the bore of the input shaft, holding them in place with grease. Place the synchronizer (baulk) ring on the input shaft and install the shaft assembly into the front of the case. Align the shifting key insert slots properly during the installation.

10. Install the front bearing retainer bolts and torque to 11-15 ft. lbs.

11. Shift the transmission gear train into the 2nd gear. Install the shift forks in their respective sleeve grooves.

12. Install the reverse shift shaft and fork. Install the interlock ball (coated with grease) into the hole in the reverse shift fork. Push it into position into the shaft groove.

13. Position the three shafts into their respective bores in the transmission case and position in the neutral mode, having entered the bores of the shifting forks. Move the 1st/2nd speed shaft until the dummy hole on the

shaft is lined up with the case hole. Insert a probe in the hole to be sure the shafts are aligned.

14. Install the grease coated interlock pins and push them into position with a probe. Move the three fork shafts in the neutral position. Shift the number two or center shaft into the 3rd gear position and check that the remaining shafts do not move.

15. Align the pin holes in the shift forks and shift fork shafts and secure with the slotted spring pins.

16. Assemble the countergear and shaft with the thrust washer oil groove facing the countergear side, and install into the transmission case. Install the rear bearing and outer race into position in the case. The outer snap-ring must be expanded during this operation.

17. Install the reverse idler gear and shaft. Have the shift arm engaged with the hub of the reverse idler gear.

18. Install the 5th gear on the countershaft with the stepped side of the gear hub facing the case. Secure the gear to the shaft with a snap-ring of a selected size to provide zero clearance, as taken from the following list:

Thickness	
mm	(in.)
2.25–2.35	(0.0886–0.0925)
2.35–2.45	(0.0925–0.0965)
2.45–2.55	(0.0965–0.1004)

19. Select a countergear thrust washer by installing a thrust washer in place on the countergear and installing the rear extension housing and torquing the retaining bolts 22-32 ft. lbs. (3.0-4.5 Kg-m) and measuring the thrust clearance of the countergear to case.

NOTE: Position the thrust washer with the oil groove facing the 5th gear.

20. The thrust clearance should be 0.0031-0.0157 in. (0.08-0.40mm). Select the proper sized thrust washer from the following list:

Thickness	
mm	(in.)
1.71–1.81	(0.0673–0.0713)
1.83–1.93	(0.0720–0.0760)
1.95–2.05	(0.0768–0.0807)

21. Remove the extension housing and install the proper thrust washer in place on the counter 5th gear.

22. Align the shifting key insert slots and install the 5th gear and the 5th synchronizer assembly onto the output shaft. Tap the output shaft to the front of the transmission and with

Thickness	
mm	(in.)
2.05–2.10	(0.0807–0.0827)
2.10–2.15	(0.0827–0.0846)
2.15–2.20	(0.0846–0.0866)
2.20–2.25	(0.0866–0.0886)
2.25–2.30	(0.0886–0.0906)
2.30–2.35	(0.0906–0.0925)
2.35–2.40	(0.0925–0.0945)
2.40–2.45	(0.0945–0.0965)
2.45–2.50	(0.0965–0.0984)
2.50–2.55	(0.0984–0.1004)
2.55–2.60	(0.1004–0.1024)
2.60–2.65	(0.1024–0.1043)
2.65–2.70	(0.1043–0.1063)
2.70–2.75	(0.1063–0.1083)
2.75–2.80	(0.1083–0.1102)

a snap-ring retainer pressed against the hub, select a snap-ring to provide a thrust clearance of 0-.008-0.012 in. (0.2-0.3mm) between the 5th gear hub and the rear bearing face.

23. Install the snap-ring and re-check the thrust clearance. Push up on the reverse idler gear until the fork shaft is in a position with the groove above the case.

24. Install the 5th gearshift arm bracket in place on the rear of the case and engage the bracket in the reverse shaft fork. Position the fork claw in the hub sleeve groove and the shift arm shaft in the gearshift head 1st groove.

25. Install the three locking balls and springs in the bores of the case. Install the cover and the retaining bolts.

26. Install the inner snap-ring, the speedometer drive gear and the outer snap-ring on the mainshaft. Be sure the locking ball is placed between the gear and the shaft.

27. Adjust the reverse idler gear position so that a clearance of 0.039-0.79 in. (1.0-2.0mm) exists between the gear teeth of the countergear and the reverse idler gear teeth by the adjustment of the pivot bolt and locknut, located on the outside of the case.

28. Adjust the 5th speed synchronizer sleeve position so that the bottom of the sleeve groove is (0.039-0.059 in. (1.0-1.5mm) above the rear face of the counter 5th gear.

K40, K50

1. Install the thrust washer on the counter 5th gear with the oil groove towards the gear side. (K50). Install the rear gaskets.

2. Align the shifting fork shafts in the neutral position and install the rear extension housing. Engage the selector shaft to the shift fork shafts.

Install the housing retaining bolts and torque to 22-32 ft. lbs.

3. Install the shift control restricting pins and torque to the following values:

K40 – Black = 1st and 2nd
White = Reverse
K50 – Black = 1st and 2nd
White = 5th and Reverse
All – 27-31 ft. lbs. (3.7-4.3 Kg-m)

4. Install the speedometer driven gear assembly.

5. Install the back-up light switch.

6. Install the clutch release bearing, fork, boot and spring.

7. Install the bottom cover and gasket. Fill the transmission with lubricant to its proper level.

8. Attach the shift lever and make sure the shifting of the gear train is proper.

TYPE 20

4 and 5 Speed Transmissions Models T40, T41, T50 Toyota

DISASSEMBLY

---- **CAUTION** ----

The clutch housing, split transmission cage, and extension housing are all made of aluminum.

---

1. Drain the oil.

2. Remove the clutch housing, bearing retainer, release bearing, and release fork.

3. Remove the speedometer shaft sleeve and driven gear.

4. Remove the extension housing.

5. Remove the back-up light switch.

6. Separate the case halves. Do not pry apart.

7. Measure gear backlash. The backlash for all gears should be 0.004-0.008 in.

8. Remove the countergear set from the right-hand half of the case.

9. Use a magnet to remove the ball from the second countergear bearing.

10. Withdraw the input and the output shafts as a unit.

11. Use a punch to drive the three slotted spring pins out of the shift forks and shfit fork shafts.

NOTE: The slotted pin cannot always be fully removed from the first/second shift fork; however,

the shift fork can still be withdrawn. Do not try to force the pin out, as damage to the transmission case could result.

12. Remove the case cover and the three detent balls and springs.

13. Remove the shift fork shafts in the following order:
   a. First/second shaft
   b. Pin
   c. Reverse shift fork shaft
   d. Third/fourth shaft
   e. Pin

14. Measure the thrust clearance of the reverse idler gear. The specified clearance is 0.002-0.020 in.

15. Remove the idler shaft. Remove the gear and washer.

16. Measure the thrust clearance of the gears on the open shaft.

17. Disassemble the components of the output shaft . Five-speed transmissions have an extra gearset and related parts.

Replace the front bearing if it is rough or noisy. Use a drift and a press. Remove the snap-ring first.

For bearing installing, replacement snap-rings are available in a range of sizes (0.0925-0.1024 in.) to obtain minimum axial play between the input shaft and the bearing.

ASSEMBLY

1. Assemble the components of the synchronizer hubs, and the output shaft.

2. Install the rear bushing on the output shaft, being careful to install it in the proper direction.

3. Install the ball into the groove of the bushing and slide the bushing over the shaft.

4. Install the needle roller bearing, reverse gear, the ball and the reverse gear synchronizer hub.

5. Install the following items on the output shaft of the four-speed transmission, in the order indicated:
   a. Large-diameter reverse gear spacer
   b. Long spacer
   c. Shims

6. Install the following items on the output shaft of the five-speed transmission in the order indicated:
   a. Ball
   b. Fifth gear synchronizer ring
   c. Fifth gear
   d. Needle roller bearing
   e. Bushing
   f. Rear support ball bearing.

7. Install the shims and the nut on the end of the output shaft.

NOTE: If the original nut is being used, change the number of shims to alter the locking portion of the nut.

4-Speed (T40)   5-Speed (T50)

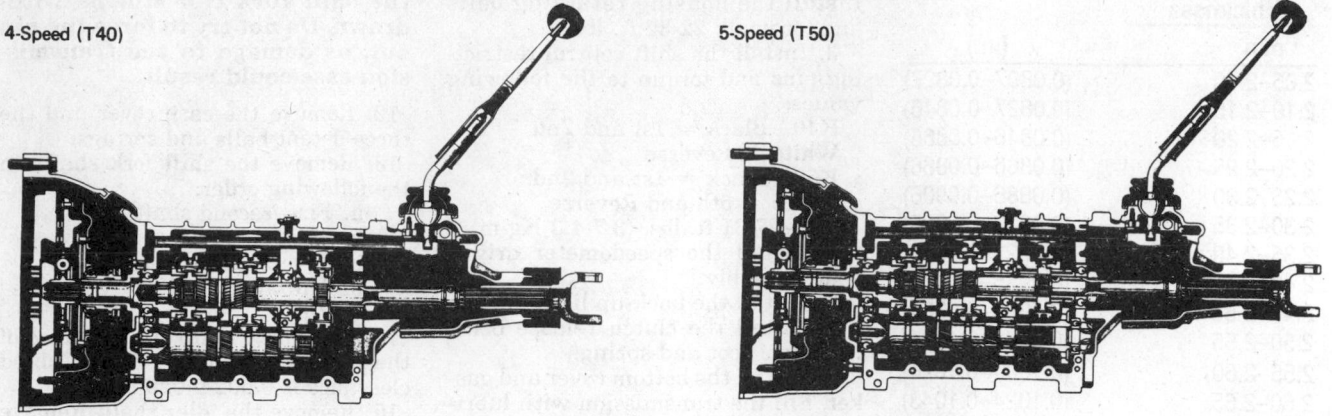

Cross section of models T 40 and T 50 transmissions

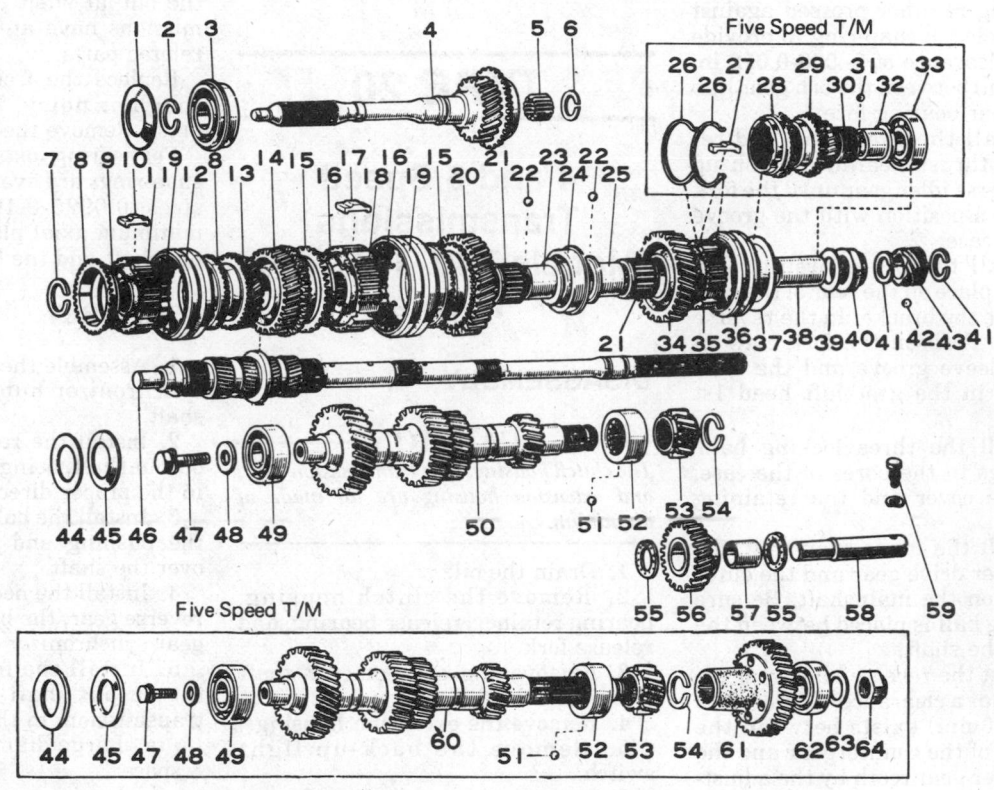

Five Speed T/M

Five Speed T/M

1. Conical spring
2. Shaft snap-ring
3. **Ball bearing**
4. Input shaft
5. Roller
6. Snap-ring
7. Shaft snap-ring
8. Synchronizer ring
9. Shift-key spring
10. Shift-key
11. Clutch hub
12. **Hub sleeve**
13. Third gear assembly
14. Second gear assembly
15. **Synchronizer** ring
16. Shift-key spring
17. **Shift-key**

18. Clutch hub
19. Hub sleeve
20. First gear assembly
21. Needle roller bearing
22. Ball
23. First gear bushing
24. Ball bearing
25. Reverse gear bushing
26. **Shift-key spring***
27. **Shift-key***
28. Synchronizer ring*
29. **Fifth gear assembly***
30. Needle roller bearing*
31. **Ball***
32. Fifth gear bushing*
33. Ball bearing*

34. Reverse gear
35. Clutch hub
36. Hub sleeve
37. Spacer
38. Spacer (long)
39. Shim
40. Nut
41. Shaft snap-ring
42. Ball
43. Speedometer drive gear
44. Shim
45. Conical spring
46. Output shaft
47. Bolt and washer
48. Plate washer
49. Ball bearing
50. Countergear

51. Ball
52. Roller bearing
53. Reverse countergear
54. Snap-ring
55. Thrust washer—reverse idler gear
56. Reverse idler gear
57. Bushing
58. Reverse idler gear shaft
59. Shaft retaining bolt
60. Countergear*
61. Fifth-speed countergear*
62. Ball bearing*
63. Shim*
64. Nut*

* Five-speed transmission only

4 and 5 speed transmission components, T40, T41, T50 models

8. Check the thrust clearance of each gear.

9. Working from the rear of the output shaft, install 3rd gear, synchronizer, spacer, and 3rd/4th synchronizer hub (should face forward).

10. Select a snap-ring to obtain a thrust clearance of less than 0.002 in. for the 3rd/4th synchronizer hub.

11. Assemble the following from the rear of the output shaft:
    a. Snap-ring
    b. Key
    c. Speedometer drive gear
    d. Snap-ring

12. Check thrust clearance of gears.

13. Install the fork and shaft assembly in the transmission case.

14. Insert the straight pins in the grooves on either side of the third/fourth shaft.

15. Assemble the first/second gear shaft and fork.

16. Perform Step 11 for the reverse shift fork shaft.

17. Insert the three detent balls, followed by their springs.

18. Place the cover gasket on the case and install the cover.

19. Use a punch to drive a slotted spring pin into each shift fork to secure it.

20. Assemble the input and output shafts.

21. Install the shift forks into their respective grooves on the input/output shaft assembly.

22. Install the shaft assembly in the right-hand half of the transmission case, so that the snap-ring is positioned firmly against the front surface of the transmission case.

23. Apply grease to the countergear rear bearing lockball. Insert the ball into the hole in the rear bearing outer race.

24. Place the countergear assembly into the right-hand half of the transmission case. Mate the lockball with the hole in the transmission case. Place the bearing snap-ring firmly against the front surface of the transmission case.

25. Install the reverse idler gear.

26. Install the washers, so that their protrusions align with the grooves in the transmission case.

27. Install the shaft into the case and through the gears and washers.

28. Align the grooves in the idler shaft with the hole in the shaft boss. Install the retaining bolt and washer into the boss.

29. Apply a light coating of liquid sealer over the joint surfaces of the transmission case halves.

--- CAUTION ---

Do not apply sealer to the 1/2 in. hole for the back-up light switch.

30. Align the transmission case locating pins with their holes and assemble the halves of the case.

NOTE: There are four different bolt lengths, do not install the wrong bolt in the wrong hole.

31. Insert the ball, spring, and washer in the back-up light switch hole. Screw in the switch assembly.

32. Install the gasket and bolt the extension housing to the rear of the transmission.

33. Install the speedometer shaft sleeve and drive gear.

34. Apply grease to the comical springs. Install one spring over the input shaft bearing and the other over the countershaft bearing. Install the spacer over the countershaft bearing spring, after coating the spacer with grease.

35. Install the gasket and the clutch housing.

TYPE 21

5 Speed Transmissions Models W50, W55, W58 Toyota

DISASSEMBLY

1. Drain the oil.

2. Remove the clutch housing, with the release fork, bearing and hub still attached.

3. Remove the back-up light switch.

4. Remove the gearshift lever retainer.

5. Rotate the shift rod housing counterclockwise (viewed from behind) and then disconnect the rod from the shift fork shafts.

6. Unbolt and remove the extension housing.

7. Drive out the slotted pin and separate the shift rod, housing and spring.

8. Remove the front bearing retainer.

9. Take off both of the front countershaft covers, and the spacer.

10. Remove the snap-rings from the input and countershaft bearings.

11. Remove the intermediate plate.

12. When removing the intermediate plate, leave all the gears and other parts attached.

13. Remove the speedometer driven gear.

NOTE: There are two reverse restrictor pins. The pins are located underneath plugs on the extension housing.

14. Remove the straight screw plugs from the shift forks and withdraw the springs.

15. Drive the slotted spring pins out of each shift fork.

16. Slide the gear shift fork shafts back and remove the forks.

17. Remove the speedometer drive gear snap-ring and remove the drive gear.

18. Remove the output shaft bearing.

19. Remove the countershaft bearing.

20. Remove the fifth and reverse gears from the countershaft.

21. Remove the snap-ring, fifth gear, its synchronizer ring, needle roller bearing, and fifth gear bearing inner race from the output shaft.

22. Remove the reverse gear and clutch hub from the output shaft.

23. Loosen the bolt and remove the reverse idler gear stop from the rear cover. Withdraw the reverse idler shaft from the rear; remove the reverse idler gear and spacer.

24. Remove the output shaft rear

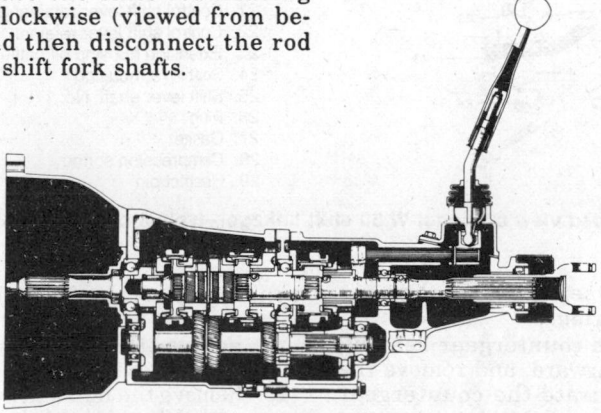

Cross section of model W 50 transmission

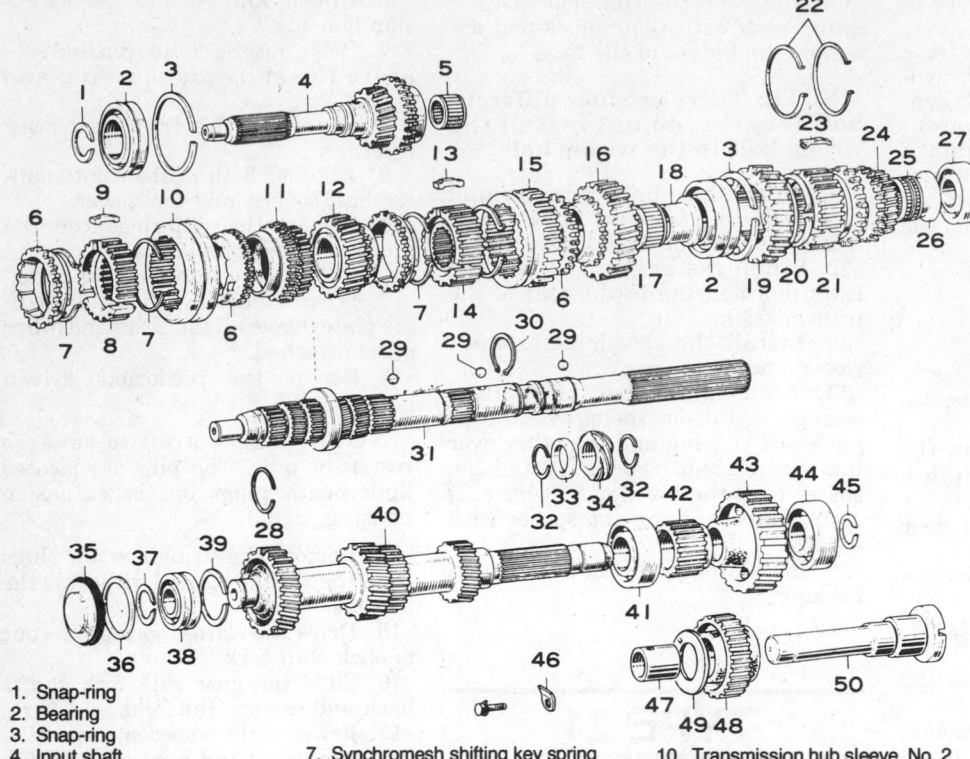

1. Snap-ring
2. Bearing
3. Snap-ring
4. Input shaft
5. Bearing
6. Synchronizer ring, No. 2
7. Synchromesh shifting key spring
8. Transmission clutch hub, No. 2
9. Synchromesh shifting key, No. 2
10. Transmission hub sleeve, No. 2
11. Third gear
12. Second gear sub-assembly

13. Synchromesh shifting key, No. 1
14. Transmission clutch hub, No. 1
15. Reverse gear
16. First gear
17. Bearing
18. First gear bearing inner race
19. Reverse gear
20. Snap-ring
21. Transmission clutch hub, No. 3
22. Synchromesh shifting key spring
23. Synchromesh shifting key, No. 3
24. Fifth gear
25. Bearing
26. Fifth gear bushing
27. Bearing
28. Snap-ring
29. Ball
30. Snap-ring
31. Output shaft
32. Snap-ring
33. Spacer
34. Speedometer drive gear
35. Countershaft cover
36. Spacer
37. Snap-ring
38. Bearing
39. Snap-ring
40. Counter gear
41. Bearing
42. Countershaft reverse gear
43. Countershaft fifth gear
44. Bearing
45. Snap-ring
46. Stopper
47. Bimetal formed bushing
48. Reverse idler gear
49. Reverse idler gear shaft spacer
50. Reverse idler gear shaft

Exploded view of gear train, model W 50 transmission

1. Gear shift fork, No. 2
2. Gear shift fork, No. 1
3. Gear shift fork, No. 3
4. Slotted spring pin
5. Gear shift fork shaft, No. 1
6. Gear shift fork shaft, No. 2
7. Gear shift fork shaft, No. 3
8. Shift interlock pin
9. Ball
10. Compression spring
11. Plug
12. Plug
13. Reverse restrict pin
14. Compression spring
15. Cotter pin
16. Shift lever knob sub-assembly
17. Shift lever
18. Shift and select lever boot
19. Transmission shift lever ball seat
20. Conical spring
21. Control shift lever retainer gasket, No. 2
22. Control shift lever retainer
23. Extension housing oil baffle
24. Shift lever housing
25. Shift lever shaft, No. 1
26. Plug
27. Gasket
28. Compression spring
29. Restrict pin

Exploded view of model W 50 shift linkage—typical of model P-51

30. Remove the following items from the output shaft, in the order listed:
   a. First gear
   b. Roller bearing with inner race
   c. Synchronizer ring
   d. Reverse gear
   e. Clutch hub
   f. Second gear
   g. Synchronizer ring

ASSEMBLY

1. Install the sleeve over the third gear synchronizer hub. Insert the three shift keys into the hub and sleeve keyways install the two hub springs.

2. Assemble the synchronizer ring to third gear, and fit both of them on the output shaft.

3. Insert the third/fourth synchronizer hub on the output shaft, until it contacts the shoulder of the shaft.

4. Select a snap-ring to provide 0.002 in. axial play for the synchronizer hub and fit it onto the shaft. Snap-rings are available in a range of sizes.

5. Measure third gear thrust clearance with a feeler gauge. The clearance should be 0.004-0.010 in. Replace third gear if the clearance exceeds the limit of 0.010 in.

6. Install the synchronizer ring for

bearing retainer. Remove the rear bearing snap-ring.

25. Push the countergear bearing outer race rearward, and remove the bearing. Separate the countergear from the intermediate plate.

26. Separate the input shaft and

synchronizer ring from the output shaft.

27. Remove the output shaft from the intermediate plate.

28. Remove the hub and synchronizer ring, followed by third gear.

29. Press off the rear bearing.

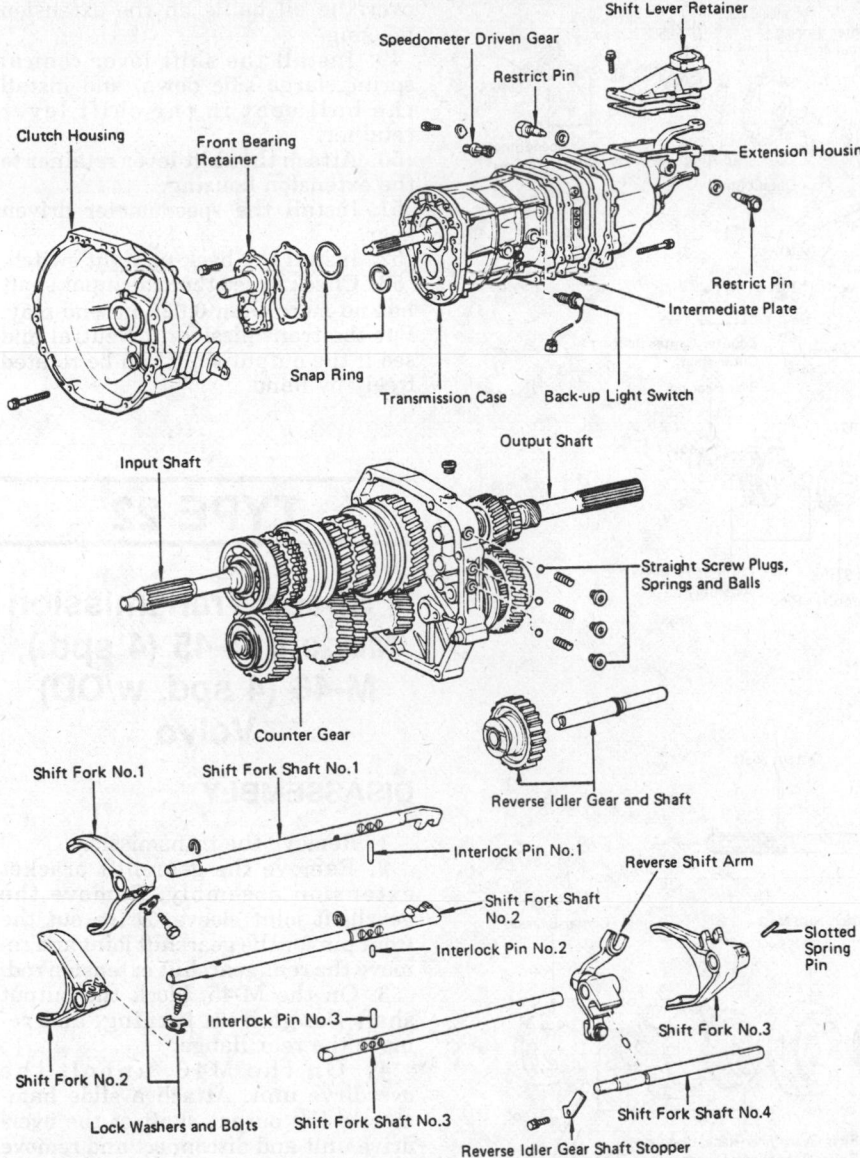

Clutch Housing

Front Bearing Retainer

Speedometer Driven Gear

Shift Lever Retainer

Restrict Pin

Extension Housing

Restrict Pin

Intermediate Plate

Snap Ring

Transmission Case

Back-up Light Switch

Input Shaft

Output Shaft

Straight Screw Plugs, Springs and Balls

Counter Gear

Reverse Idler Gear and Shaft

Shift Fork No.1

Shift Fork Shaft No.1

Interlock Pin No.1

Reverse Shift Arm

Shift Fork Shaft No.2

Interlock Pin No.2

Slotted Spring Pin

Interlock Pin No.3

Shift Fork No.3

Shift Fork No.2

Shift Fork Shaft No.3

Shift Fork Shaft No.4

Lock Washers and Bolts

Reverse Idler Gear Shaft Stopper

Detailed view of the W58 transmission

second gear to the gear and install the asembly on the output shaft.

7. Install the reverse gear over its clutch hub.

8. Install the reverse gear and hub on the output shaft so that they contact the shoulder.

9. Measure second gear thrust clearance; it should be between 0.004-0.010 in. Replace the gear if the clearance is more than 0.010 in.

10. Coat the locking ball with grease. Insert it, and the roller bearing inner race, on the output shaft.

11. Assemble first gear with its synchronizer ring, bearing and bearing inner race. Install them on the output shaft, so that the end of the inner race contacts the clutch hub and the groove on the inner race aligns with the locking ball.

12. Press the rear bearing onto the output shaft.

13. Measure the gear thrust clearance.

NOTE: The thrust clearance of all gears in the W-50 5-speed transmission should be between 0.006-0.010 in.; the thrust clearance limit for all gears is 0.012 in.

14. Use a press to insert the straight pin into the intermediate plate, until it protrudes 1/4-5/16 in. from the cover front side.

15. Install the output shaft on the intermediate plate.

16. Coat the roller bearing with grease and install it over the input shaft.

17. Apply gear oil to the front synchronizer ring on the output shaft.

18. Assemble the output shaft and the input shaft.

19. Install the countergear on the intermediate plate.

20. Install the cylindrical roller bearing into the intermediate plate, and then install the spacer.

21. Assemble the output shaft and countergear, then fit them through the holes in the snap-ring sticks out beyond the intermediate plate. Install the snap-ring sticks out beyond the intermediate plate. Install the snap-ring and then push the shafts back until the snap-ring is flush with the intermediate plate surface.

22. Install the shaft through the reverse sidler gear. Insert the end of the shaft into the end of the intermediate plate.

23. Install the spacer on the idler shaft and secure it with a snap-ring.

24. Lock the reverse idler shaft on the intermediate plate with its stop. Check the reverse idler gear thrust clearance, it should be 0.006-0.010 in.

25. Install the reverse clutch hub on the reverse gear.

26. Install the three shift keys into the hub keyways and secure them with the two springs and a snap-ring.

27. Slide the reverse gear hub over the output shaft until it registers against the inner race of the intermediate plate bearing.

28. Insert the inner race lockball into the output shaft bore, after greasing it so that it can't fall out.

29. Assemble fifth gear, its synchronizer ring, needle roller bearing, and race. Slide the assembly onto the output shaft until the inner bearing face rests against the reverse clutch hub. Be sure that the inner race groove is aligned with the lockball.

30. Secure fifth gear with a snap-ring.

31. Measure fifth gear thrust clearance; it should be 0.004-0.010 in. The thrust clearance limit is 0.012 in.

32. Install the countershaft reverse gear so that it just rests against the bearing inner race. Install the countershaft fifth gear and then install the countershaft bearing with a brass drift.

33. Install a snap-ring on the countershaft; select a snap-ring from one of the four available sizes.

34. Install a snap-ring on the output shaft, and drive its bearing into place with a brass drift. Coat the bearing with grease first.

35. Install the spacer, ball, and speedometer drive gear on the output shaft.

36. Install the three shift forks in their hub sleeve grooves. Install the first and third shift fork shafts and secure them with their interlock pins.

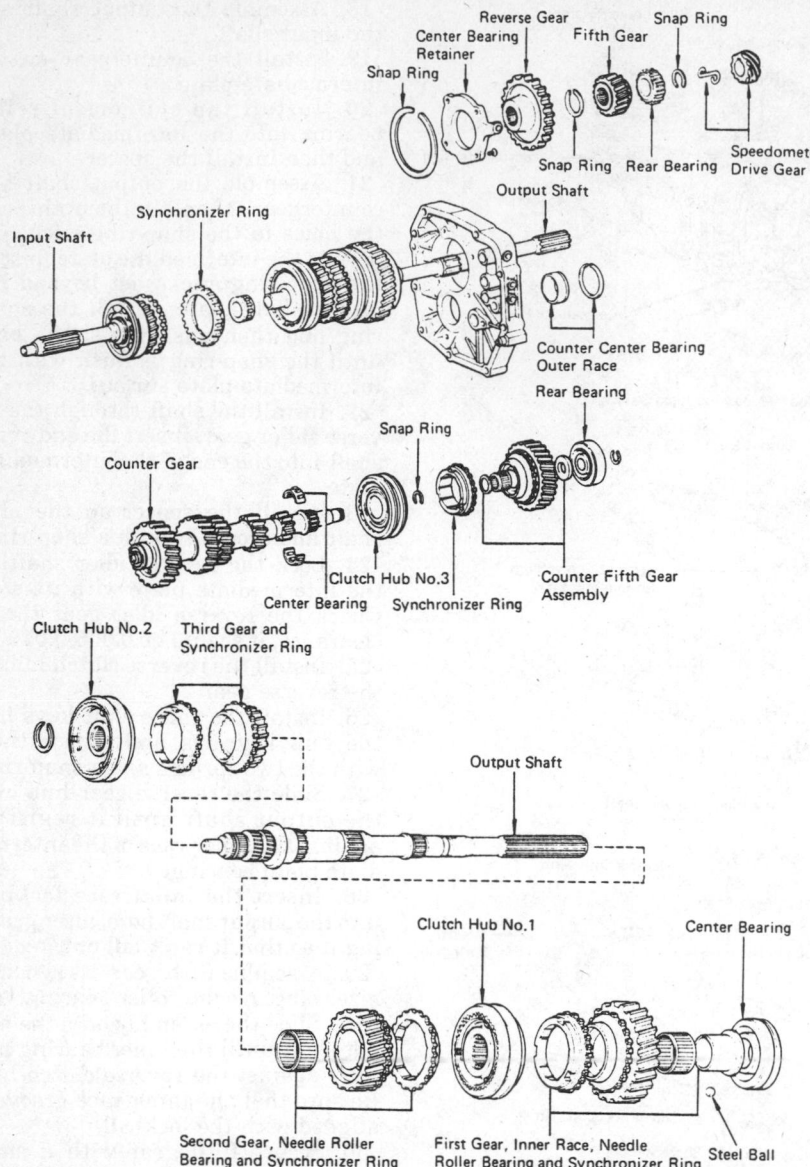

Reverse Gear
Center Bearing
Retainer
Fifth Gear
Snap Ring
Snap Ring
Snap Ring
Snap Ring
Rear Bearing
Speedometer
Drive Gear
Output Shaft
Input Shaft
Synchronizer Ring
Counter Center Bearing
Outer Race
Rear Bearing
Counter Gear
Snap Ring
Clutch Hub No.3
Center Bearing
Synchronizer Ring
Counter Fifth Gear
Assembly
Clutch Hub No.2
Third Gear and
Synchronizer Ring
Output Shaft
Clutch Hub No.1
Center Bearing
Second Gear, Needle Roller
Bearing and Synchronizer Ring
First Gear, Inner Race, Needle
Roller Bearing and Synchronizer Ring
Steel Ball

Exploded view of the gear train—model W55 transmission

Install the second shift fork shaft next.

NOTE: Place each shift fork shaft in Neutral during assembly.

37. Secure the shift fork shafts to the end cover by inserting the lockballs into their bores, followed by the lockball springs.

38. Use a new gasket between the transmission case and the intermediate plate. Side the case into place.

39. Fit snap-rings on the input shaft and countershaft front bearings.

40. Install the shift lever housing on the end of the shifter shaft. Slide the shifter shaft into the extension housing and secure it with a slotted spring pin.

41. Install a new gasket and slide the extension housing into place until there is about and inch of clearance between it and the intermediate plate.

42. Rotate the shift lever housing clockwise (as viewed from the rear) to engage the shifter shaft with the selector lever and the shift fork shaft.

43. Slide the extension housing the rest of the way.

44. Install the spacer and then the countershaft end covers.

45. Align the front bearing retainer gasket with the oil holes. Install the bearing retainer over the gasket.

46. Bolt the clutch housing onto the front of the transmission case.

47. Fit the restrictor pins and springs into their extension housing bores.

48. Install the shift lever retainer over the oil baffle on the extension housing.

49. Install the shift lever conical spring, large side down, and install the ball seat in the shift lever retainer.

50. Attach the shift lever retainer to the extension housing.

51. Install the speedometer driven gear.

52. Install the back-up light switch.

53. Check to see that the input shaft has no more than 0.020 in. end-play. Put the transmission in Neutral and see if the output shaft can be rotated freely by hand.

TYPE 22

4 Speed Transmission Models M-45 (4 spd.), M-46 (4 spd. w/OD) Volvo

DISASSEMBLY

1. Remove the transmission.

2. Remove the gearshift bracket extension assembly. Remove the gearhsift joint sleeve. Drive out the front pin for the gearshift joint and remove the rear gearshift extension rod.

3. On the M-45, block the output shaft flange from turning, and remove the rear flange.

4. On the M46, unbolt the overdirve unit. Attach a slide hammer to the output shaft of the overdrive unit and disconnect and remove the overdrive. Unbolt the intermediate housing.

5. On the M45, remove the speedometer driven gear. Remove the transmission rear cover, noting placement of bearing shims (if so equipped). Remove the speedometer drive gear.

6. Remove the back-up light switch.

7. Remove the top cover and gasket. Use a magnet to remove the spring detent balls.

8. Knock out the lockpins for the shift forks and shift reials.

NOTE: The forward gear shifters should be separated so that the pins do not damage the gears when driven out.

9. Remove the shift rails, shift forks and shifters for all forward speeds.

10. On the M46, remove the snapring and oil pump eccentric for the

overdrive from the output shaft. Remove the eccentric retaining key.

11. Remove the mainshaft (output shaft) bearing inner and outer snap-rings. Before removing the mainshaft bearing, place a metal spacer (guard plate Volvo No. 2985) between the input shaft and the front synchronizer ring to prevent damage to the ring during bearing removal. Remove the mainshaft bearing ring and pull off the bearing. Remove the bearing thrust washer.

12. Remove the flywheel (bell) housing.

13. Remove the snap-ring and spacer rings retaining the input shaft bearing. With the front synchronizer ring protective spacer still in place, pull out the input shaft bearing. Remove the protective plate.

14. Knock the intermediate shaft back and remove the rear outer race for the intermediate shaft. Then, knock the shaft forward and remove the front intermediate shaft outer race.

15. Remove the input shaft.

16. Lift out the 4th gear synchronizer ring.

17. Lift out the mainshaft.

18. Lift out the intermediate shaft.

19. Drive back the reverse gear sliding shaft and remove the gear shift rail, unhook and remove the reverse gear shift fork. Remove the reverse gear shift fork. Remove the reverse gear shift rail.

20. Pull off the intermediate shaft bearing.

21. Remove 1st gear and its synchronizer ring from the mainshaft. Remove the snap-ring for the 1-2 synchronizer hub. Press off the synchronizer hub and gear. Remove the 304 synchronizer hub snap-ring and press off that gear and hub.

22. If the shift mechanism needs repair, unhook the detent plate spring, remove the three retaining bolts, and remove the detent plate. Remove the shift shaft. If necessary, remove the shaft seal at the rear of the cover.

23. If leaking, remove the bell housing seal at the rear of the cover.

24. Push the two synchronizer hubs out of their sleeves and inspect for wear.

ASSEMBLY

1. Install new seals in the bell housing, shift cover and rear cover as required. Install the shifter assembly in the cover. The detent plate is installed with the flat washers between the plate and C-clips.

2. Connect the 3rd and 4th gear synchronizer hubs. The dogs must be positioned in the grounded slots in the

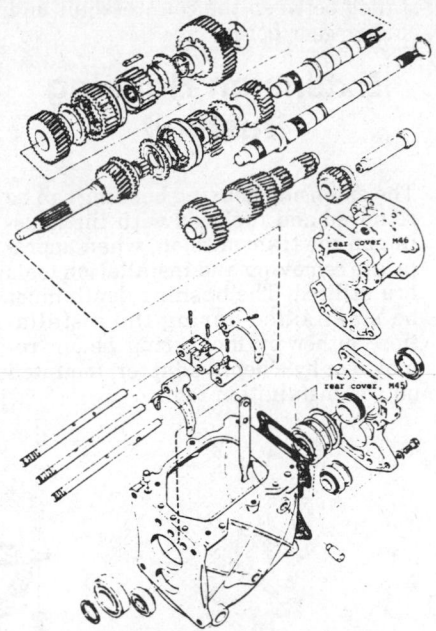

Volvo M45, M46 gear train

hub. The sleeve end with the turned groove must face in the same direction as the hub flat end.

3. Assemble the mainshaft: install the 3rd gear and synchronizer ring, 3rd/4th synchronizer hubs, and snap-ring; install the 2nd gear and synchronizer ring, 1st/2nd synchronizer hubs, and snap-ring; install the 1st gear and synchronizer ring.

4. Press on the two intermediate shaft bearings.

5. Press on the input shaft bearing, and install its snap-ring.

NOTE: Do not install the spacer ring yet.

6. Install the reverse gear shift rail (without lockpin), shift fork and shifter. Install the reverse gear and shaft. Check that the reverse gear shaft aligns flush with the outside of the case. Also, check that the clearance between the reverse gear and shift fork is 0.004-0.08 in. Adjust as necessary by knocking the shift fork pivot in axil with a punch.

7. Lay the intermediate shaft at the bottom of the case. Slip the thrust washer, ball bearing and positioning ring over the output end of the mainshaft. Pres the mainshaft end of the mainshaft. Press the mainshaft bearing into place, taking care not to damage the reverse gear. When the bearing seats properly, the positioning ring will butt against the case.

8. Grease and install the input shaft inner roller bearing.

9. On the M46, install the snap-ring for the mainshaft bearing. Install the Woodrull key, overdrive oil pump eccentric and snap-ring on the mainshaft extension.

10. Position the 4th gear synchronizer ring in its hub.

11. Push the input shaft into the case all the way, so it makes contact with the mainshaft.

12. Lift up the intermediate shaft so that both bearings locate in the case.

13. Pull out the input shaft slightly to install the spacer ring. Then push the input shaft back in so that the spacer rings contact the case.

14. Install the intermediate shaft outer bearing races.

15. Determine the shim thickness required between the bell housing and the input shaft bearing. Measure how much the input shaft bearing protrudes from the case, and measure the depth of the bearing seat in the bell housing. Subtract bell housing seat depth and bell housing gasket thickness (0.25mm) from the input shaft bearing protrusion height, and then subtract from this the allowable clearance (0.01-0.15 and 0.20mm sizes.

16. Install the bell housing.

17. Install the shift forks on the synchronizer hubs (the forks are identical). Install the forward shift rails and shifters (not interchangeable) and secure with the lock pins. Drive in the pins until flush.

18. Determine the shim thickness required between the rear cover and the intermediate shaft outer race, and the shim thickness between the rear cover and the mainshaft bearing. Allowable clearance is 1.98mm for the intermediate shaft outer race, and 0.24mm for the mainshaft bearing. Gasket thickness is 0.25mm. When measuring, turn the transmission case vertical with the input shaft facing down, to take any slack out of the intermediate or mainshafts.

19. On the M45, install the speedometer drive gear.

20. Install the rear cover (or intermediate housing on the M46) with shims and a new gasket.

21. On the M45, install the output shaft flange. Install the speedometer driven gear and new O-ring. Install the gear retainer and bolt.

22. Position the top cover gasket with shifter detent balls and springs. Install the back-up light switch. Check gear operation by inserting a punch through the shift and rotating the mainshaft.

23. On the M46, install the overdrive assembly.

24. Install a new rubber O-ring in the gearshift rod joint. Connect the gearshift rod and drive in the locking pin. Install the cover sleeve.

25. Install the gearshift bracket ex-

tension assembly with the spacers, rubber washers, and flat washers as shown to eliminate vibration. First install the two upper bolts flush with the spacer sleeve, and then the two lower bolts. Then, tighten all four bolts to 15-18 lbs.

26. Fill the transmission with 0.8 qts. (2.4 qts. with overdrive M467) of 80W/90 hypid gear oil. Install the plug(s).

TYPE 23

5-Speed Overdrive Transmission Merkur XR4Ti

DESCRIPTION

This transmission has three forward reduction gear ratios, a one—to—one 4th. gear ratio and an overdrive 5th. gear ratio. These forward ratios are provided through helical—cut, constant mesh gears. Reverse gear is provided through an idler gear that slides along a shaft to engage spur gears on the cluster gear and output shaft. All gears, except the fifth speed gears are contained in the case. The fifth speed gears are located on the back of the case in the extension housing.

Three synchronizers are used to lick the driven gears to the output shaft. Two synchronizers provide first through fourth gears, while the third synchronizer provides fifth gear. The synchronizers are shifted by three forks attached to a common shift rail. A system of interlocks on the shaft prevents the engagement of more than one gear at any one time. The shift rail extends from the shift lever mounted on the extension housing to the front of the case. At the front of the case a spring loaded plunger contacts the shift rail to provide the shift detent. Reverse gear requires an intermediate lever between the shift rail and the sliding gear. The lever is mounted on a pivot pin which is pressed into the left side of the case. A sprig returns the lever to the released position when the transmission is shifted out of reverse.

The input and output shafts are supported in the case on ball bearings to provide durability and quiet operation. The rear of the cluster gear is supported in the case on a roller bearing. The front of the cluster gear is supported on 21 needle bearings installed between the countershaft and cluster gear bore.

Extension Housing Bushing

The extension housing bushing can be removed and replaced with the housing on the transmission, when appropriate removing and installation tools are utilized. The bushing depth must be maintained during the installation, either by measuring before removal or by a depth adapter, mounted on the installation tool.

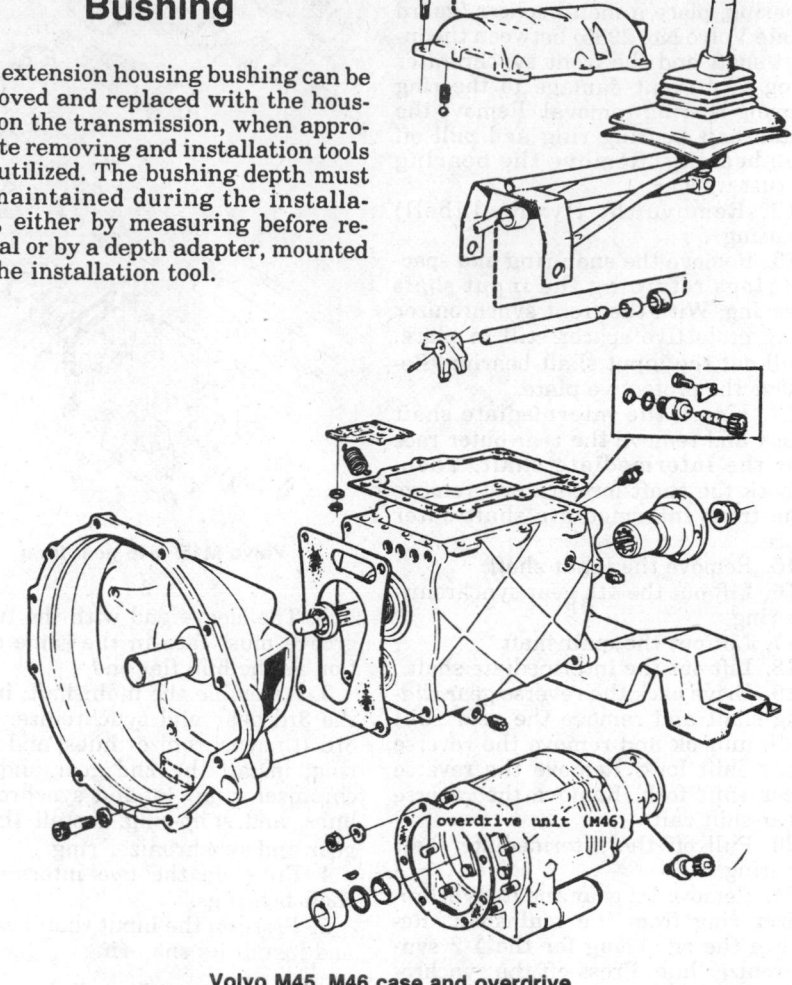

Volvo M45, M46 case and overdrive

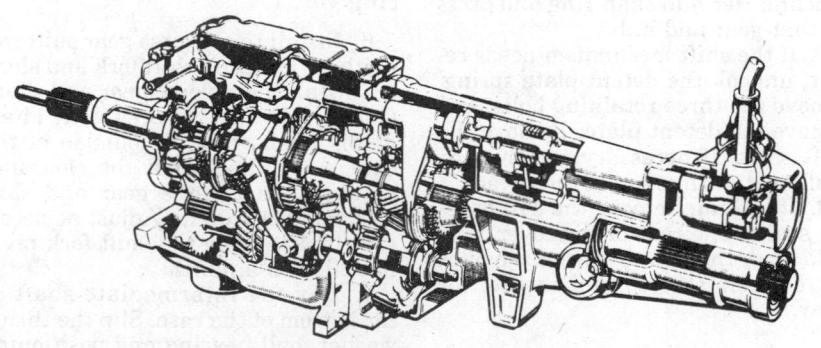

Phantom view of Merkur XR4Ti five speed overdrive transmission

Shift Lever and Boot

REMOVAL

1. Remove the shift knob and the bezel attaching screws at the console. Remove the bezel.

2. If equipped with power windows, raise the bezel, disconnect the wiring connections from the switches and remove the bezel.

3. Remove the shift boot and foam insulator.

4. Remove the screws attaching the

shift lever boot retainer to the floor pan and remove the retainer.

5. Remove the shift lever attaching screws using a No. 40 torx socket and remove the shift lever.

INSTALLATION

1. Install the shift lever and install the retaining screws. Torque to 16-19 ft. lbs. (21-26 Nm).

2. Position the boot retainer and install the attaching screws.

3. Install the shift lever boot and the foam insulator.

4. If equipped with power windows, connect the wiring connectors and position the console bezel.

5. Install the console bezel attaching screws and install the shift lever knob.

Transmission

DISASSEMBLY

1. Remove the clutch release lever and bearing from the flywheel housing.

2. Remove the flywheel housing from the case.

3. If available, mount the transmission in a holding fixture. If not available, secure the case to a work surface in an upright position.

4. Remove the speedometer gear from the extension housing.

5. Remove the back-up light switch and the Neutral safety switches from the extension housing.

6. Remove the case cover retaining bolts, remove the cover with gasket, turn the transmission case over and allow the oil to drain into a suitable container.

7. Remove the shift detent bore plug and using a small magnet, remove the detent spring and detent plunger.

8. Drive the welsh plug from the extension housing, using a brass drift and light hammer.

9. Shift the transmission into reverse gear to gain access to the offset lever roll pin. Remove the pin with the use of an 1/8 inch pin punch.

10. Remove the offset lever and roll pin from the extension housing.

11. Remove the fifth gear interlock plate retaining bolts.

12. Remove the fifth gear interlock plate, detent spring and the detent plunger.

13. Remove the extension housing retaining bolts. Remove the extension housing and gasket.

14. With the use of an 1/8 inch pin punch and hammer, remove the shift rail roll pin.

15. Remove the shift rail and the fifth gear interlock. Pull the shifter

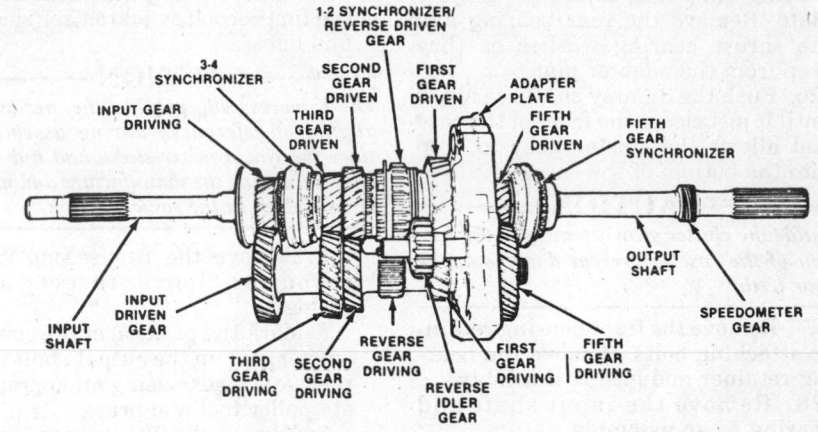

Gear component location

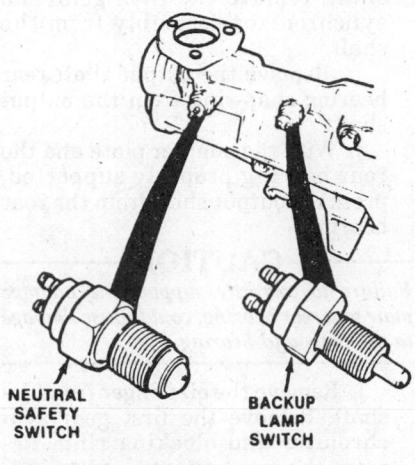

Neutral start safety switch and back-up lamp switch locations

shaft out of the transmission with a twisting motion.

16. Remove the shift interlock for the first/second and third/fourth shift forks. Remove the shift forks.

17. Remove the fifth gear shift fork from the rear of the transmission.

18. Remove the fifth gear synchronizer snap-ring from the output shaft.

19. Slide the fifth gear and the synchronizer assembly rearward until it stops against the speedometer gear.

20. Shift the transmission into first and reverse gears to prevent rotation of the mainshaft and cluster gears. To hold the reverse idler gear in position, install a cover bolt into the transmission case and stretch a rubber band from the reverse lever to the bolt.

NOTE: The cover bolt can be left in place, since it will be needed during the assembly.

21. Partially install a dummy shaft through the front of the case to support the cluster gear during the removal of the fifth gear.

22. Pull the countershaft out of the cluster gear from the rear of the case,

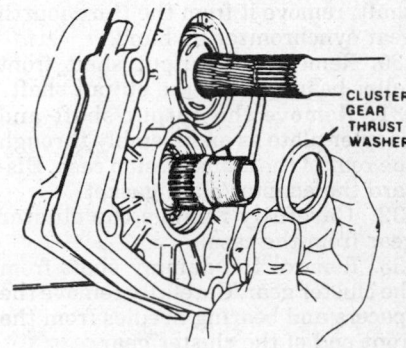

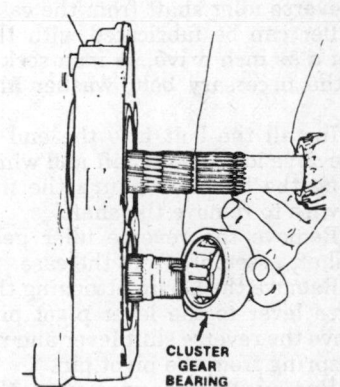

Cluster gear thrust washer and bearing assembly

allowing the dummy shaft to follow the countershaft. Do not allow the dummy shaft to move any further into the case than the point where its end is flush with the front exterior face of the case.

23. Remove the nut staking from the fifth gear retaining nut. Using the proper sized socket, remove the fifth gear attaching nut.

24. Remove the fifth gear with an appropriate puller having puller jaws that will fully engage with the underside of the fifth gear.

25. Remove the cluster gear rear

bearing snap-ring from the adapter plate. Remove the rear bearing and the thrust bearing washer as they drop from the adapter plate.

26. Push the dummy shaft rearward until it just clears the front of the case and allows the cluster gear to drop into the bottom of the case.

CAUTION

Guide the cluster gear assembly to the bottom of the case to prevent damage to the gear teeth.

27. Remove the front bearing retainer attaching bolts. Remove the bearing retainer and gasket assembly.

28. Remove the input shaft and bearing as an assembly.

29. If the fourth gear blocking ring does not come out with the input shaft, remove it from the third/fourth gear synchronizer by hand.

30. Remove the output shaft front roller bearing from the output shaft.

31. Remove the output shaft and adapter plate as an assembly through the rear of the transmission case. Discard the adapter plate gasket.

32. Carefully remove the cluster gear from the case.

33. Remove the dummy shaft from the cluster gear. Carefully remove the spacers and bearing needles from the front end of the cluster gear.

34. A puller tool is needed to remove the reverse idler shaft from the case. A puller can be fabricated with the use of a 3/8 inch drive, 7/8 inch socket and the necessary bolt, washer and nut.

35. Install the bolt into the end of the reverse idler gear shaft and while holding the bolt head, turn the nut clockwise to remove the shaft.

36. Remove the reverse idler gear and shaft assembly from the case.

37. Remove the C-clip attaching the reverse lever to the lever pivot pin. Remove the reverse shift lever and return spring from the pivot pin.

38. Remove the magnet from the case carefully, as the magnet is ceramic and can easily be broken.

39. Disassemble the output shaft assembly in the following manner.

a. Remove the snap-ring from the shaft that is retaining the third/fourth gear synchronizer.

b. Remove the third/fourth synchronizer, third gear belcing ring and the third gear as an assembly.

c. Remove the retaining ring and the thrust washer halves. Remove the second speed gear and the blocking ring.

NOTE: A snap-ring is installed on the second gear to prevent the synchronizer from over-traveling. If necessary, remove the snapring from the gear.

d. Make an alignment mark on the first/second synchronizer sleeve and hub.

CAUTION

These marks will provide the necessary alignment references during assembly, since the synchronizer sleeve and hub are matched during the manufacture and must be assembled in the same position.

e. Remove the first/second synchronizer sleeve, inserts and spring.

f. Mark the position of the speedometer gear on the output shaft and remove the gear using an appropriate puller tool and press.

g. Remove the fifth gear synchronizer snap-ring from the output shaft, remove the fifth gear and synchronizer assembly from the shaft.

h. Remove the output shaft rear bearing snap-ring from the output shaft.

i. With the adapter plate and the rear bearing properly supported, press the output shaft from the rear bearing.

CAUTION

Failure to correctly support the adaptor plate and rear bearing. could cause damage to the plate and bearing.

j. Remove the oil slinger from the shaft. Remove the first gear synchronizer and blocking ring. Remove the synchronizer insert ring.

40. Remove the snap-ring from the adapter plate and remove the rear bearing from the plate, using a press and an appropriate pressing tool.

41. To remove the bearing from the input shaft, remove the snap-ring from the input shaft and the snapring from the outer race of the bearing. Place the bearing in a press platform and press the input shaft from the bearing.

42. To remove the varied seals from the transmission and components, the use of a slide hammer and seal remover jaws are recommended.

43. Before disassembling a synchronizer assembly, make an alignment mark on the mated parts. The parts are matched during assembly at time of manufacture and must be assembled to their original positions.

44. The transmission components can now be inspected for damage, wear, scoring or pitting. Replace the necessary components as required.

ASSEMBLY

Synchronizer

1. Align the reference marks made during the disassembly and slide the

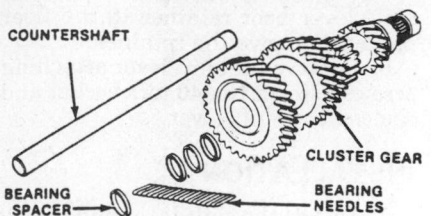

Exploded view of clutch gear components

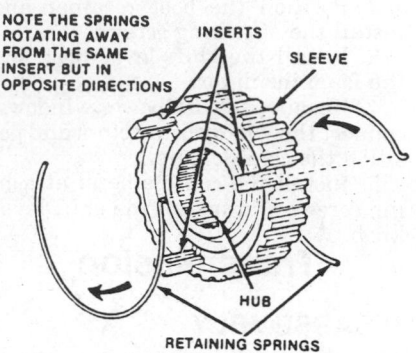

Installation of synchronizer insert retaining spring

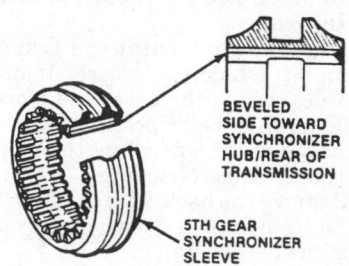

Correct positioning of fifth gear synchronizer

slide of the synchronizer sleeve over the hub.

CAUTION

When assembling the fifth gear synchronizer, be sure the beveled side of the synchronizer sleeve faces the synchronizer hub.

2. Install the inserts and springs. The hooked end of the springs engage the same insert but rotates away from the insert in the opposite directions.

NOTE: When assembling the sleeve and hub, hold both square with each other. Do not force the hub into the sleeve since both are an extremely close fit.

3. Install the insert retainer, gear, blocking ring and hub into the fifth gear synchronizer.

ASSEMBLY

Front Bearing Retainer Seal

1. Using a socket of suitable size,

install a new seal into the bearing retainer.

2. Lubricate the seal lip with appropriate lubrication.

ASSEMBLY

Input Shaft Bearing

1. Install the input shaft bearing using a press and plate. To prevent damage to the synchronizer taper of the bearing bore, place a suitable plate between the press ram and the input shaft.

2. Install the snap-ring on the bearing outer race.

3. Install a new selective snap-ring on the input shaft.

INSTALLATION

Output Shaft Bearing

1. Install the output shaft rear bearing in the adapter plate, using a press and installer tube.

2. Install a new selective snap-ring in the adapter plate bore.

ASSEMBLY

Output Shaft Components

1. Assemble the first/second synchronizer.

NOTE: Be sure the shift fork groove faces the front of the output shaft as viewed in its assembled position when in the transmission.

2. Install the second gear blocking ring and second gear.

3. Install the thrust washer halves and the retaining ring. Be sure the thrust with the tang engages the hole in the output shaft.

4. Install the third gear and the third gear blocking ring. Install the third/fourth synchronizer.

5. Install a new selective fit third/fourth synchronizer snap-ring.

6. Install the first gear blocking ring and the first gear.

7. Install the oil slinger with the oil groove facing first gear.

8. With the use of a front cover aligning tool, Ford part number T57L-4621-B, or equivalent, install the rear bearing and adapter plate assembly.

9. Install the new selective fit rear bearing snap-ring on the output shaft.

10. Install the fifth gear and fifth gear synchronizer assembly.

NOTE: Be sure the synchronizer is assembled with the beveled side of the synchronizer sleeve facing the speedometer gear end of the output shaft.

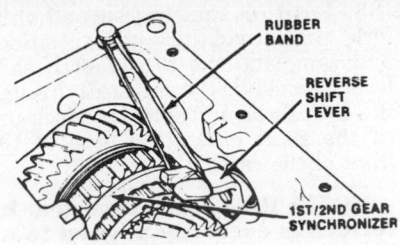

Use of rubber band to hold reverse shift lever

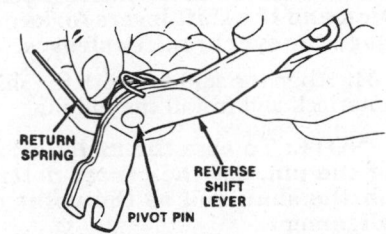

Correct positioning of flat on countershaft

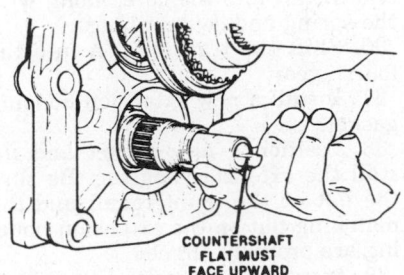

Installation of return spring on reverse shift levers

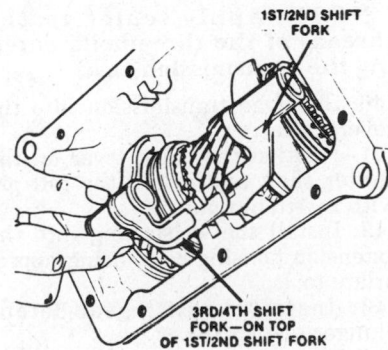

Correct installation of shift forks

11. Install the new selective fit fifth gear snap-ring on the output shaft.

12. Install the speedometer gear with a bearing installer tool or equivalent. Press the gear onto the shaft until it aligns with the mark made during disassembly.

NOTE: The speedometer gear should require a fair amount of force due to the interference fit between the gear and the output shaft. If the gear seems loose on the shaft, replace the gear and/or shaft. If a new output shaft has been installed, press the speed-

ometer gear onto the shaft until the distance from the front face of the gear to the rear face of the fifth gear synchronizer hub measures $4 \frac{27}{32}$–$4 \frac{7}{8}$ inch.

Transmission

ASSEMBLY

1. Install the ceramic magnet into the case.

2. Install the reverse shift lever return spring on the lever.

3. Position the return spring and the reverse shift lever on the pivot pin.

NOTE: Be sure the spring is tensioned to return the lever to the released position and install the C-clip.

4. Position the reverse idler gear in the case with the shoulder facing the rear of the case, and with the gear engaged in the reverse shift lever.

5. Install the reverse idler gear shaft. Tap the shaft into the case with the aid of a plastic tipped hammer.

6. Position the countershaft in the cluster gear and install three bearing spacers in the front end of the cluster gear.

7. Install the needle bearings (21) into the cluster gear. Lubricate them with petroleum jelly to retain them in place.

8. Install the remaining bearing spacers on the cluster gear.

9. Install the cluster gear with the bottom countershaft and lay it on the bottom of the case. Push the countershaft to the front until it supports the front needle bearings. As the front of the cluster gear enters the case, pull the countershaft rearward until the front of the shaft end is flush with the end of the cluster gear.

NOTE: Be sure the bearing spacer does not fall off the end of the countershaft while the cluster gear is being lowered into the case.

10. With a new gasket installed on the adaptor plate, install the output shaft, adapter plate and gasket as an assembly.

11. Coat the input shaft roller bearing with transmission oil and install in the end of the input shaft.

12. Install the fourth gear blocking ring.

13. Install the input shaft.

14. Install a new gasket on the front bearing retainer. Position the bearing retainer. Position the bearing retainer on the case with the groove in the gasket and retainer, facing the bot-

tom of the case to align with the oil drain hole.

15. Install the front bearing retainer attaching bolts and tighten to 7-8 ft. lbs. (9–11 Nm.).

16. Rotate the countershaft until the flat on the rear end of the shaft is facing up in the horizontal position.

———— CAUTION ————

The positioning of the countershaft flat is critical because it must fit into a matching flat in the extensionhousing. If the flat is not correct, the extension housing will not fit correctly.

17. Raise the front of the cluster gear to align the countershaft with the countershaft bore in the case. While holding this alignment, tap the countershaft forward into the case bore.

18. Remove the fifth gear synchronizer snap-ring from the output shaft groove.

19. Slide the synchronizer and snap-ring rearward against the speedometer gear to allow clearance for installation of the fifth gear.

20. Install the cluster gear rear bearing.

21. Install the cluster gear bearing spacer.

22. Install the cluster gear rear bearing snap-ring.

23. Install the fifth gear on the cluster gear using a forcing tool assembly.

24. Position the fifth gear and the fifth gear synchronizer. Install the fifth gear synchronizer snap-ring.

25. If necessary, install a cover bolt into the transmission case, in order to hold the reverse idler gear into position. Using a rubber band, stretch it from the reverse lever to the cover bolt.

26. To prevent rotation of the mainshaft and cluster gear, shift the transmission into first and reverse gears.

27. Install the fifth gear attaching nut and washer.

28. Using a 1-7/16 inch, twelve point socket, tighten the fifth gear attaching nut to 89-111 ft. lbs. (120–150 Nm.).

29. Stake the fifth gear attaching nut, using a staking punch and light hammer.

30. Remove the rubber band and the cover bolt. Shift the transmission out of the first and reverse gears.

31. Install the first/second and third/fourth shift forks. Be sure the third/fourth fork is on top of the first/second fork.

32. Position the fifth gearshift fork and interlock on the fifth gear synchronizer. Slide the shift rail through the interlock and shift fork until it enters the case.

33. Position the first/second shift fork, the second/third shift interlock and cam, and the third/fourth shift fork. Then slide the shift rail through the shift forks and shift interlock until the shaft enters the bore at the front of the case.

NOTE: Be sure the fifth gear interlock is correctly aligned to allow the shift rail to slide through the shifter fork. Be sure the synchronizers are in the neutral position and the shift levers forks engage the synchronizer sleeves.

34. Align the shift rail with the shift interlock and install the roll pin.

NOTE: To ease the installation of the pin, use the center detent on the shaft rail as the point of alignment.

35. Apply sealant to the detent plug and install into the bore, along with the spring and detent plunger.

36. Shift the transmission into the fourth gear.

37. Install a new extension housing gasket.

38. Position a new gasket and install the extension housing. Be sure the flat on the countershaft and the matching flat on the extension housing are properly aligned.

39. Install the extension housing attaching bolts and torque to 33-36 ft. lbs. (40–49 Nm.).

NOTE: Apply sealer to the threads of the three bolts entering the transmission case.

40. Shift the transmission into the reverse gear.

41. Position the offset lever on the shifter shaft and install the roll pin with a 1/8th pin punch.

42. Install the welsh plug into the extension housing bore, using appropriate tools.

43. Install the fifth gear detent plunger and spring.

44. Tighten the lockplate retaining bolts to 16019 ft. lbs. after coating them with a sealant.

45. With the use of a new gasket, install the cover on the transmission case and torque the retaining bolts to 14–15 ft. lbs. (18–20 Nm). Be sure the cover guide engages the shift interlock.

46. Wrap the threads of the back-up light switch and the neutral start switch and the neutral start switch with teflon thread type tape and install into the extension housing.

47. Tighten the switches to 7-10 ft. lbs. (10–14 Nm).

48. Install the flywheel housing and tighten the retaining bolts to 52-67 ft. lbs. (70–90 Nm).

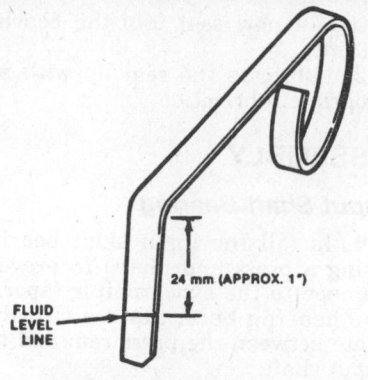

Fabrication of tool to check fluid level in the early transmission models

49. Install the clutch release bearing lever and the bearing assembly.

50. Fill the transmission with lubricant, equal to Ford specification ESD-M-2C175A or equivalent, to its proper level.

51. Install the speedometer driven gear in the extension housing.

NOTE: The transmission lubricant is a semisynthetic oil. When adding oil to the transmission use only lubricant equal to Ford specification ESD-M,-2C175A.

Fluid Level Check

Check the oil level on early production models with the aid of a fabricated dipstick. The oil level will not be in line with the oil filler hole. The oil level will be approximately 1 inch (24mm) below the filler hole. These transmissions can be identified by a yellow paint square on the side of the extension housing. The fill plug location on later production models are lowered to make the bottom of the fill hole even with the lubrication level.

TYPE 24

5 Speed Transmission Model RS5W71C Datsun

DISASSEMBLY

1. Remove the transmission from the vehicle and drain the fluid. Place the transmission on a stand.

2. Remove the rear extension. Remove the front cover and gasket.

3. Remove the shim of the counter-

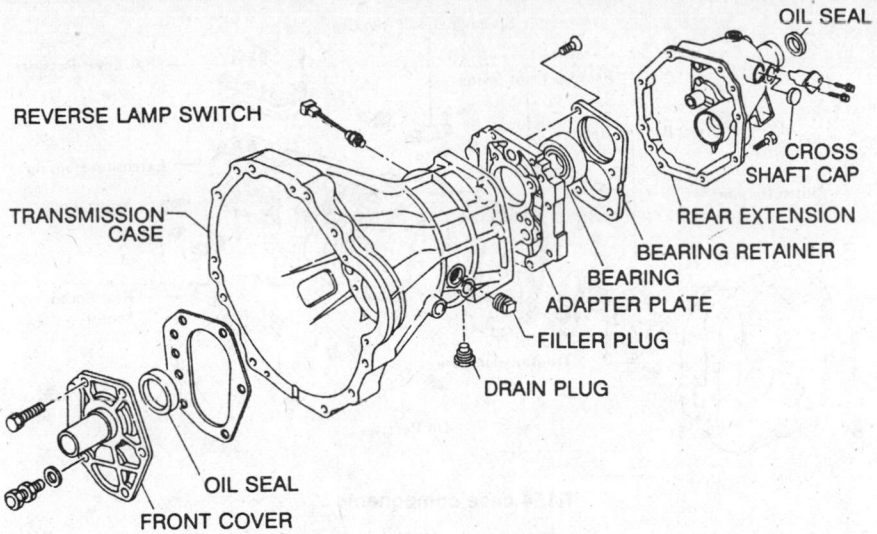

REVERSE LAMP SWITCH

TRANSMISSION CASE

OIL SEAL

CROSS SHAFT CAP

REAR EXTENSION

BEARING RETAINER

BEARING

ADAPTER PLATE

FILLER PLUG

DRAIN PLUG

OIL SEAL

FRONT COVER

RS5W71C case components

shaft front bearing and the snap ring of the main drive gear ball bearing.

4. Seperate the transmission case from the adapter plate. Remove the oil seal from the front cover.

5. Set the adapter plate on a mounting tool and mount it in a vice.

6. Remove the check ball plugs, springs and the check balls. Drive out the retaining pins then drive out the fork rods and remove the interlock balls.

7. Before disassembling the gear components, measure each gear end play. Replace all worn parts.

8. Mesh 2nd. and reverse gear, then draw out the counter front bearing with suitable.

9. Remove the snap ring and then remove the sub–gear bracket, spring and sub–gear.

10. Draw out the counter drive gear with the main drive gear assembly with suitable puller.

11. Disassemble the parts at the rear of the adapter plate as follows:

a. Loosen the counter shaft and mainshaft nuts. The mainshaft nut is a left hand thread.

b. Pull out the overdrive counter gear and bearing with a suitable puller.

c. Draw out the reverse cunter gear and spacer.

d. Remove the snap rings from the reverse idler shaft and draw out the gear, thrust washers and bearing.

e. Remove the snap ring and pull out the overdrive mainshaft bearing.

f. Remove the mainshaft nut.

g. Remove the speedometer drive gear and steel ball. Remove the steel roller and washer.

h. Remove the overdrive main

gear, needle bearing and baulk ring.

i. Remove the overdrive coupling sleeve, shifting inserts and springs.

j. Press out the mainshaft and countergear alternately.

NOTE: Make sure to alternate pressing of mainshaft and counter gear, to avoid the front surface of one contacting the rear surface of the other.

12. Remove the first gear washer and steel ball, then the 1st. main gear and needle bearing.

13. Press out the 2nd. main gear together with the 1st. gear bushing and

1st. and 2nd. synchronizers.

14. Remove the mainshaft front snap ring.

15. Press out the 3rd. main gear and needle bearing together with the 3rd. and 4th. synchronizers.

16. Remove the snap ring and washer and the main drive gear bearing.

17. Inspect all components for wear and other damage. Check the clearance between the gears and baulk rings.

ASSEMBLY

1. Install the mainshaft ball bearing and the counter gear rear bearing in the adapter plate. Install the oil gutter and and bearing retainer on the adapter plate.

2. Insert the reverse shaft then install the bearing retainer. Tighten each serew then stake it at two points.

3. Press in the main drive gear bearing and install the spacer. Select the proper snap ring to minimize the clearance of the groove.

4. Assemble the synchronizers.

5. Assemble the 2nd. main gear, needle bearing and 1st. and 2nd. synchronizer, then press the 1st. gear bushing on the mainshaft.

6. Install the 1st. main gear. Apply grease and install the steel ball and thrust washer.

7. Press the mainshaft assembly to the adapter plate using the proper tool.

8. Press the counter gear into the adapter plate.

9. Install the 3rd. main gear, then press the 3rd. and 4th. synchronizers.

10. Install the thrust washer on the mainshaft and secure it with the front snap ring.

11. Apply gear oil to mainshaft pilot bearing and install it on the mainshaft.

12. Press the counter drive gear with the main drive gear using the proper tool.

13. Install the sub-gear and bracket on the counter drive gear and then select the proper snap ring to minimize the clearance of the groove in the counter gear. Allowable clearance of the groove is 0–0.0071 in. (0–0.18 mm).

14. Remove the snap ring, sub-gear and bracket from the counter gear, then reinstall the assembly with the sub-gear spring. Install the selected counter drive gear snap ring.

15. Press the counter gear front bearing onto the counter gear.

16. Assemble the parts at the rear of the adapter plate as follows:

a. Install the reverse idler gear to the reverse idler shaft with spacers, snap rings and needle bearing.

b. Install the insert retainer and overdrive synchronizer to the mainshaft.

c. Install the overdrive gear bushing using the proper tool.

d. Install the overdrive main gear and needle bearing.

e. Install the spacer, reverse counter gear and overdrive counter gear.

NOTE: The overdrive main gear and the counter gear should be handled as a matched set.

f. Install the washer, roller bearing, steel roller, thrust washer, steel ball and the speedometer drive gear.

g. Tighten the mainshaft lock nut temporarily. Install the counter shaft rear end bearing with the proper tool.

17. Mesh the 2nd. and reverse gears, then tighten the mainshaft lock nut with tool.

18. Tighten the countershaft lock nut. Stake the mainshaft lock nut and the countershaft lock nut with a punch. Check the gear end play.

19. Install the shift rods, interlock

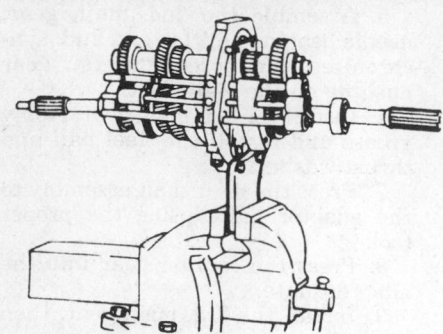

Adapter plate mounting tool

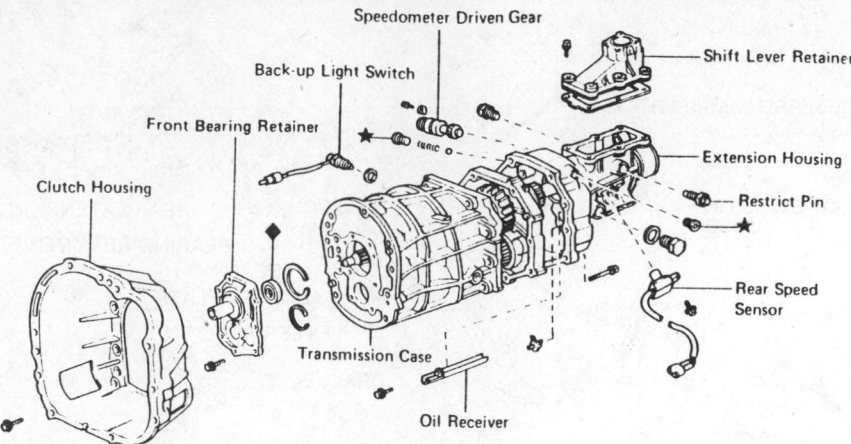

R154 case components

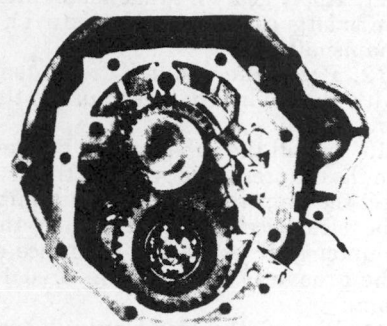

Adapter plate

plunger, interlock balls and check balls.

20. Install the shift forks as follows:
    a. 1st. and 2nd. shift fork.
    b. 3rd. and 4th. shift fork.
    c. Overdrive and reverse shift fork.

21. Apply multi-purpose grease to the front cover oil seal lip, then install it in the case.

22. Apply sealant to the mating surface of the transmission case.

23. Slide the gear assembly onto the adapter plate by lightly tapping with a soft hammer. Apply sealant to the mating surface of the adapter plate.

24. Install the rear extension.

25. Fit the main drive bearing snap ring.

26. Select the counter front bearing shim.

27. Install the gasket and the front cover.

TYPE 25

5 Speed Transmission Model R154 Toyota

DISASSEMBLY

1. Remove the back-up light

switch, speedometer driven gear, shift lever retainer, restrict pins and rear speed sensor.

2. Remove the clutch housing from the transmission case.

3. Using a torx socket wrench, remove the screw plug from the extension housing. Using a magnetic finger, remove the spring and ball.

4. Remove the 10 extension housing bolts and the shift lever housing set bolt. Using a soft hammer, tap the extension housing and remove the shift lever housing and the select lever.

5. Remove the 8 front bearing retainer bolts and tap the retainer to remove it. Remove the two bearing snap rings.

6. Using a brass hammer, carefully tap off the transmission case. Remove the transmission case from the intermediate plate. Remove the magnet from the intermediate plate and mount the plate in a vise.

7. Using a torx socket wrench, remove the 4 straight screw plugs. Using a magnetic finger, remove the 4 springs and balls.

8. Remove the set bolts.

9. Using two screwdrivers and a hammer, remove the three snap rings. Using a pin punch and hammer, drive out the two pins

10. Pull out the No.5 shift fork shaft from the intermediate plate.

11. Remove the No.2 shift fork shaft and shift fork. Using a magnetic finger, remove the interlock pin from the intermediate plate.

12. Remove the No.1 shift fork shaft and shift fork. Remove the interlock pins from the shaft hole and the intermediate plate.

13. Remove the No.3 shift fork shaft and the interlock pin and locking ball from the shaft hole and intermediate plate.

14. Remove the No.4 shaft, the No. 3

fork and the rerverse shift head.

15. Remove the reverse shift arm and bracket.

16. Remove the speedometer drive gear.

17. Remove the output shaft rear bearing and spacer.

18. Measure the counter 5th. gear thrust clearance, standard clearance is 0.0039–0.0138 in. (0.10–0.35mm).

19. Engage the No.5 gear double meshing, loosen the staked parts of the nut and remove the lock nut. Disengage the gear double meshing. Remove the spline piece. Remove the counter 5th. gear with the No.3 hub sleeve.

20. Remove the thrust washer and ball.

21. Remove the four bolts and the rear bearing retainer.

22. Pull the reverse idler gear and shaft toward the rear to remove them.

23. Remove the output shaft, counter gear and input shaft as a unit from the intermediate plate.

24. Remove the counter rear bearing from the intermediate plate. Measure each gear thrust clearance.

25. Remove the fifth gear, center bearing and first gear assembly.

26. Using a press, remove the No.1 hub sleeve, synchronizer and 2nd. gear.

27. Remove the No.2 hub sleeve assembly and 3rd. gear.

ASSEMBLY

1. Insert the No.1 and the No.2 clutch hubs into the hub sleeves.

— **CAUTION** —
Install the key springs positioned so that their end gaps are not in line.

2. Apply gear oil to the shaft and needle roller bearing. Place the synchronizer ring on the gear and align

the ring slots with the shifting keys. Install the needle roller bearing in the 3rd. gear.

3. Using a press, install the 3rd. gear and the No.2 hub sleeve. Install the snap ring and measure the 3rd. gear thrust clearance. Standard clearance is 0.0039–0.0098 in. (0.10–0.25 mm).

4. Install the 2nd. gear and the No.1 hub sleeve.

5. Install the spacer on the output shaft. Assemble the 1st. gear, synchronizer ring and needle roller bearing. Install the assembly on the output shaft with the synchronizer ring slots aligned with the shifting keys.

6. Install the straight pin and the 1st. gear thrust washer.

7. Drive in the output shaft center bearing with the outer race snap ring groove toward the rear.

8. Using a feeler gauge, measure the 1st. and 2nd. gear thrust clearance. Standard clearance is:

    a. 1st. gear 0.0039–0.0177 in. (0.10–0.45 mm).

    b. 2nd. gear 0.0039–0.0098 in. (0.10–0.25 mm).

9. Install the 5th. gear.

10. Install the output shaft into the intermediate plate by pushing on the shaft and tapping on the plate. Install the snap ring.

11. Install the input shaft to the output shaft withe the synchronizer ring slots aligned with the shifting keys.

12. Install the counter gear into the intermediate plate and install the counter rear bearing with a soft hammer.

13. Install the reverse shift arm bracket and torque the bolts to 13 ft. lbs. (18 Nm).

14. Install the reverse idler gear and shaft.

15. Align the rear bearing retainer to the reverse idler shaft groove. Install and torque the bolts to 13 ft. lbs. (18 Nm).

16. Install the shifting keys and the No.3 hub sleeve onto the counter 5th. gear.

17. Install the ball and thrust washer.

18. Install the counter 5th. gear with the No.3 hub sleeve assembly and needle roller bearings.

19. Engage the gear double meshing, install the synchronizer ring on the No.5 spline piece. Align the synchronizer ring slots with the shifting keys. Install a new lock nut on the end of the counter gear and press fit the counter spline piece to the counter gear. Stake the lock nut and disengage the gear double meshing.

20. Measure the counter 5th. gear thrust clearance, standard clearance

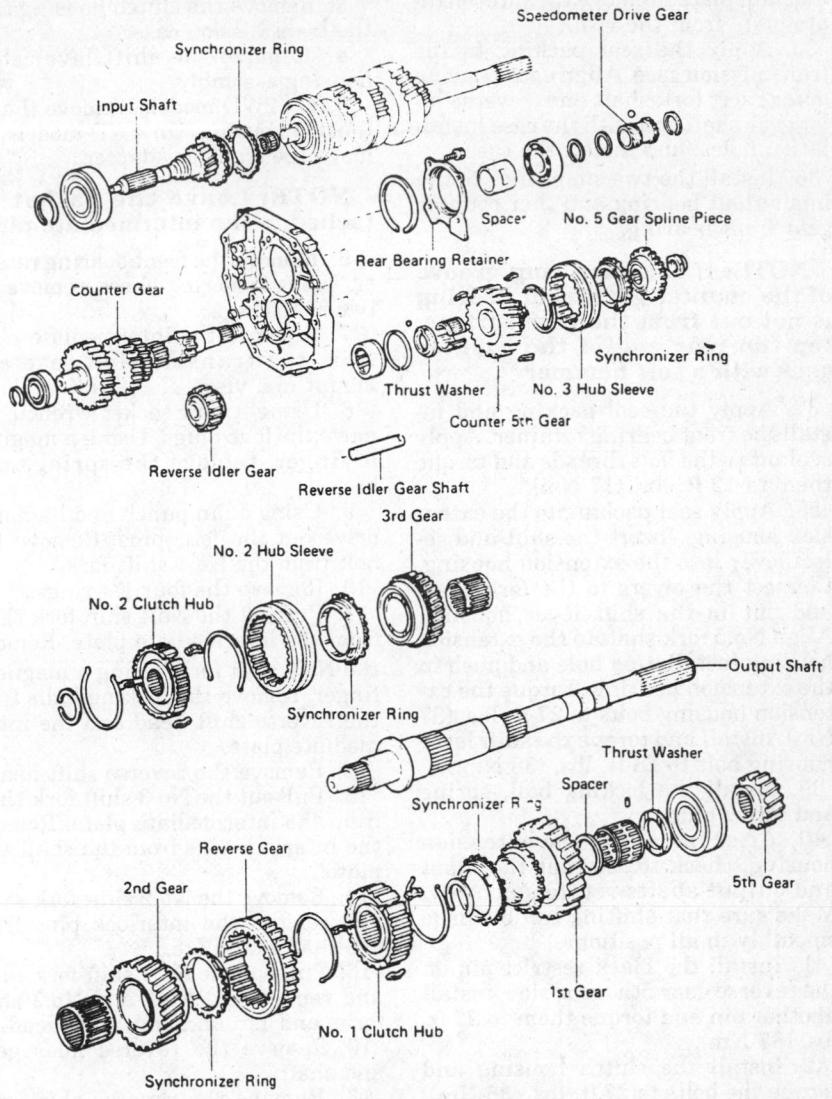

Gear components

is: 0.0039–0.0138 in. (0.010–0.35 mm).

21. Install the spacer. Drive in the output shaft rear bearing and install the select fit snap ring.

23. Install the speedometer drive gear.

24. Align the reverse shift arm shoe to the reverse idler gear groove, and install it to the pivot of the bracket.

25. Place the No.3 shift fork into the groove of the No.3 hub sleeve. Install the No.4 shift fork shaft to the No.3 shift fork, reverse shift head and shift fork through the intermediate plate. Install the locking ball into the reverse shift head.

26. Using a magnetic finger and screwdriver, install the locking ball into the intermediate plate. Install the interlock pin into the shaft hole. Install the No.3 fork shaft to the reverse shift fork and shift head through the intermediate plate.

27. Install the No.1 shift fork shaft and shift fork.

28. Install the No.2 shift fork shaft and shift fork.

29. Install the No.5 fork shaft to the reverse shift head through the intermediate plate.

30. Using a pin punch and hammer, drive in the two slotted spring pins to the reverse shift head and shift and shift fork.

31. Check the interlock by shifting the No.1 fork shaft to the 1st. speed position, N0.2, 3, 4, and 5 fork shafts should not move.

32. Install the snap rings and the three set bolts. Torque the set bolts to 14 ft. lbs. (20 Nm).

33. Install the locking balls, springs and screw plugs. Apply sealant to the plug threads. Using a torx socket wrench, torque the screw plugs to 14 ft. lbs. (19 Nm).

34. Install the magnet to the inter-

mediate plate. Remove the intermediate plate from the vise.

35. Apply the seal packing to the transmission case. Align each bearing outer race, fork shaft end, reverse idler gear shaft end with the case installation holes, and install the case.

36. Install the two snap rings to the input shaft bearing and ther counter gear front bearing.

NOTE: If the snap ring groove of the counter gear front bearing is not out from the case surface, tap the rear end of the counter gear with a soft hammer.

37. Apply the seal packing and install the front bearing retainer. Apply sealant to the bolt threads and torque them to 12 ft. lbs. (17 Nm).

38. Apply seal packing to the extension housing. Insert the shift and select lever into the extension housing. Connect the levers to the fork shaft and put in the shift lever housing. Align No.5 fork shaft to the extension housing installation hole and push in the extension housing. Torque the extension housing bolts to 27 ft. lbs. (37 Nm). Install and torque the shift lever housing bolt to 28 ft. lbs. (38 Nm.).

39. Install the locking ball, spring and screw plug.

40. After installing the extension housing, check to see that the input and output shafts rotate smoothly. Make sure that shifting can be made smoothly to all positions.

41. Install the black restrict pin on the reverse gear/5th. gear side, install another pin and torque them to 27 ft. lbs. (37 Nm).

42. Install the clutch housing and torque the bolts to 27 ft. lbs. (36 Nm).

43. Install the shift lever retainer and torque to 12 ft. lbs. (16 Nm).

44. Install the back—up light switch and torque to 33 ft. lbs. (44 Nm).

45. Install the speedometer driven gear and install the transmission into the vehicle.

TYPE 26

5 Speed Transmission
Model G53
Toyota

DISASSEMBLY

1. Remove the release fork and bearing.

2. Remove the back—up light switch and speedometer driven gear on 2WD models.

3. Remove the clutch housing from the transmission case.

4. Remove the shift lever shaft housing assembly.

5. On 2WD models, remove the extension housing. On 4WD models, remove the transfer adaptor.

NOTE: Leave the gasket attached to the intermediate plate.

6. Remove the front bearing retainer. Using snap ring pliers, remove the two snap rings.

7. Seperate the intermediate plate from the transmission case and mount in a vise.

8. Using a torx socket wrench, remove the four plugs. Using a magnetic finger, remove the springs and balls.

9. Using a pin punch and hammer, drive out the four pins. Remove the bolt from the No.1 shift fork.

10. Remove the four E—rings.

11. Pull out the No.4 shift fork shaft from the intermediate plate. Remove the No.3 shift fork. Using a magnetic finger, remove the locking balls from the reverse shift head and the intermediate plate.

12. Remove the reverse shift head.

13. Pull out the No.3 shift fork shaft from the intermediate plate. Remove the interlock pins from the shaft and plate.

14. Remove the No.2 shift fork shaft and remove the interlock pins from the shaft and plate.

15. Pull out the No.1 shift fork shaft and remove the No.1 and No.2 shift forks and 1st. and 2nd. shift head.

16. Remove the reverse idler gear and shaft.

17. Remove the reverse shift arm from the bracket.

18. Using a feeler gauge, measure the counter 5th. gear thrust clearance. Standard clearance is 0.0039–0.0118 in. (0.10–0.30 mm).

19. Engage the gear double meshing. Using a hammer and chisel, loosen the staked part and remove the lock nut. Disengage the gear double meshing and remove the No.5 gear spline piece, synchronizer ring, needle roller bearings and counter 5th. gear.

20. Remove the spacer. Using a magnetic finger, remove the ball.

21. Remove the reverse shift arm bracket.

22. Remove the four screws with a torx socket wrench and remove the rear bearing retainer and snap ring.

23. Remove the output shaft, counter gear and input shaft as a unit from the intermediate plate. Remove the counter rear bearing from the intermediate plate.

24. On 2WD models remove the speedometer drive gear.

25. Measure the thrust clearance of each gear. Standard clearance is 0.0039–0.0098 in. (0.10–0.25 mm).

26. Remove the 5th. gear, rear bearing, 1st. gear, inner race and needle roller bearing. Remove the locking ball.

27. Using a press, remove the No.1 hub sleeve, synchronizer ring and 2nd. gear.

28. Remove the No.2 hub sleeve assembly and 3rd. gear.

29. Remove the lever lock pin and nut, then the select outer lever, plate washer and lever shaft from the shift lever shaft housing.

30. Remove the lever lock pin and pull out the shift outer lever and boot.

31. Using a pin punch and hammer, drive out the slotted spring pin. Remove the shift and select lever and shaft.

32. Remove the seat and the compression spring.

33. Remove the reverse restrict pin and the compression spring.

ASSEMBLY

1. Install the reverse restrict pin and the compression spring. Using a pin punch and hammer, drive in the slotted spring pin.

2. Install the seat and the compression spring.

3. Install the shift and select lever and shaft to the shift lever shaft housing.

NOTE: One of the spline teeth of the shaft has been eliminated. Be certain to correctly align this portion of the matching portion on the lever during assembly.

4. Install the shift outer lever and boot to the shaft with the lever lock pin and nut. Torque the nut to 9 ft. lbs. (12 Nm).

5. Install the select outer lever, plate washer and lever shaft with the lever lock pin and nut. Torque the nut to 69 in. lbs. (7.8 Nm).

6. Insert the No.1 and No.2 clutch hubs into the hub sleeves.

— **CAUTION** —

Install the key springs positioned so that their end gaps are not in line.

7. Apply gear oil to the shaft and needle roller bearing. Place the synchronizer ring on the gear and align the ring slots with the shifting keys. Install the needle roller bearing in the 3rd. gear and press in the 3rd. gear and the No.2 hub sleeve.

8. Install the snap ring and measure the 3rd. gear thrust clearance. Standard clearance is 0.0039–0.0098 in. (0.10–0.25 mm).

9. Install the 2nd. gear and the No.1 hub sleeve assembly.

10. Install the locking ball in the shaft. Apply gear oil to the needle roller bearing. Assemble the 1st. gear synchronizer ring, needle roller bearing and bearing inner race. Install the assembly on the output shaft with the synchronizer ring slots aligned with the shifting keys. Turn the inner race to align it with the locking ball.

11. Install the output shaft rear bearing with the outer race snap ring groove toward the rear.

NOTE: Hold the 1st. gear inner race with a screwdriver to prevent it from falling.

12. Check the 1st. and 2nd. gear thrust clearance and install the 5th. gear.

13. Install a snap ring that will allow minimum axial play.

14. On 2WD models, install the speedometer drive gear.

15. Install the output shaft into the intermediate plate by pulling on the output shaft and tapping on the intermediate plate.

16. Install the input shaft to the output shaft with the synchronizer ring slots aligned with the shifting keys.

17. Install the counter gear into the intermediate plate and install the counter rear bearing. Install the bearing snap ring.

NOTE: Be sure that the snap ring is flush with the intermediate plate surface.

18. Install the rear bearing retainer. Using a torx socket wrench, torque the screws to 13 ft. lbs. (18 Nm).

19. Install the reverse arm bracket, ball and spacer.

20. Install the counter 5th. gear into the No.3 hub sleeve and install the assembly with needle roller bearings.

21. Engage the gear double meshing. Install the synchronizer ring onto the No.5 gear spline piece. Align the synchronizer ring slots with the shifting keys. Install a new lock nut on the end of the counter gear and press fit the gear spline piece to the counter gear. Torque the lock nut to 87 ft. lbs. (118 Nm) and disengage the gear double meshing.

22. Check the counter 5th. gear thrust clearance. Install the reverse shift arm to the bracket.

23. Install the reverse idler gear on the shaft. Align the reverse shift arm shoe to the reverse idler gear groove and insert the reverse idler gear shaft to the intermediate plate. Install the reverse idler gear shaft stopper and torque the bolt to 13 ft. lbs. (17 Nm).

24. Install the No.1 shift fork shaft, No.1 and No.2 shiftr forks and 1st. and 2nd. shift head.

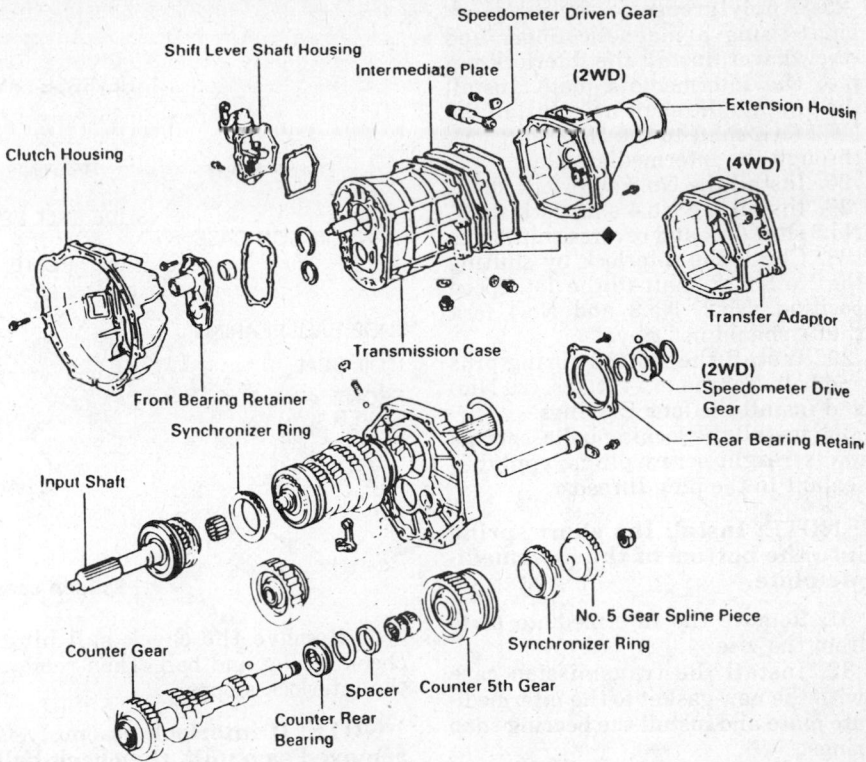

G53 case and adapter plate

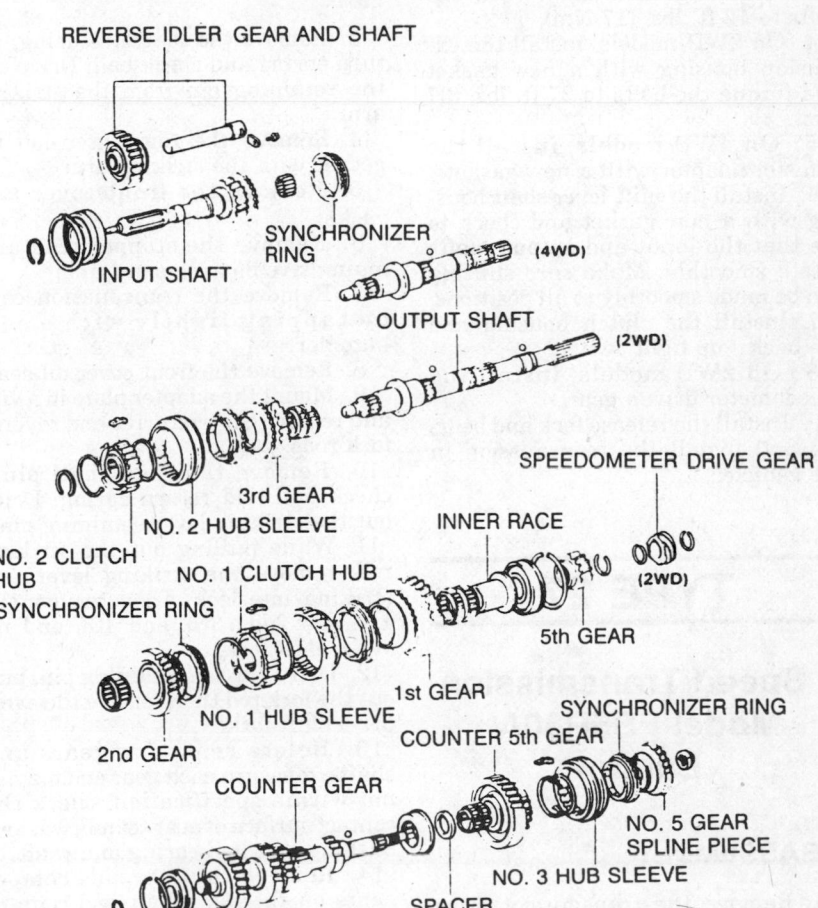

Gear components

25. Apply grease to the interlock pins. Using a magnetic finger and screwdriver, install the interlock pin into the intermediate plate. Install the pin into the shaft hole. Install the No.2 fork shaft to the No.2 shift fork through the intermediate plate.

26. Install the No.3 shift fork shaft.

27. Install the No.4 shift fork shaft, No.3 shift fork and reverse shift head.

28. Check the interlock by shifting the No.1 fork shaft to the 1st. speed position. No.2, No.3 and No.4 fork shafts should not move.

29. Install the slotted spring pins and bolt. Torque to 14 ft. lbs. (20 Nm) and install the four E—rings.

30. Install the locking balls, springs and straight screw plugs, applying sealant to the plug threads.

NOTE: Install the short spring into the bottom of the intermediate plate.

31. Remove the intermediate plate from the vise.

32. Install the transmission case with the new gasket to the intermediate plate and install the bearing snap rings.

33. Install the front bearing retainer with a new gasket and torque the bolts to 12 ft. lbs. (17 Nm).

34. On 2WD models, install the extension housing with a new gasket and torque the bolts to 27 ft. lbs. (37 Nm).

35. On 4WD models, install the transfer adaptor with a new gasket.

36. Install the shift lever shaft housing with a new gasket and check to see that the input and output shafts rotate smoothly. Make sure shifting can be made smoothly to all positions.

37. Install the clutch housing and the back—up light switch.

38. On 2WD models, install the speedometer driven gear.

39. Install the release fork and bearing and install the transmission in the vehicle.

TYPE 27

5 Speed Transmission Model FS5R30A Datsun

DISASSEMBLY

1. Remove the transmission from the vehicle and attach it to a stand. Drain all remaining fluid out.

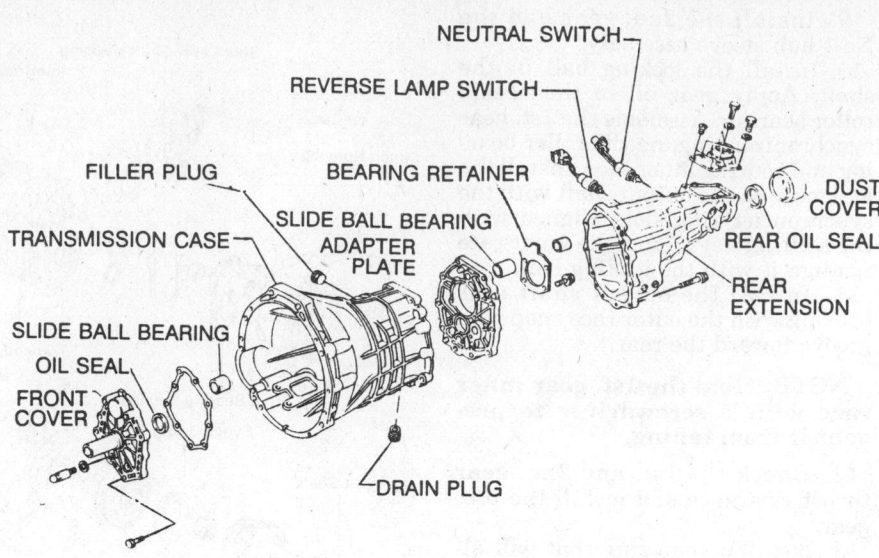

FS5R30A case components

2. Remove the check ball plug, check spring and ball. Then remove the interlock stopper.

NOTE: If interlock assembly is removed as a unit, the check ball can fall into the transmission case.

3. Remove the control housing, return spring and check ball. Drive out the retaining pin from the striking arm.

4. Remove the rear extension together with the striking arm.

5. Remove the front cover and gasket.

6. Remove the stopper ring and main drive bearing snap ring.

7. Remove the transmission case by tapping lightly with a soft hammer.

8. Remove the front cover oil seal.

9. Mount the adapter plate in a vise and remove the overdrive and reverse fork rods.

10. Remove the check ball plug, check ball and return spring. Drive out the striking lever retaining pin.

11. While pulling out the striking rod, remove the striking lever and striking interlock. Then remove the 1st. and 2nd., 3rd. and 4th. and reverse shift fork.

12. Drive out the retaining pin, pull out the fork rod then remove the overdrive shift fork.

13. Before removing gears and shafts, measure each gear end play. If not within specification, check the contact surface of gear to hub, washer, bushing, needle bearing and shaft.

14. Remove the rear side components on the mainshaft and counter gear.

a. Remove the snap ring, speed-

ometer drive gear and steel ball.

b. Remove the reverse coupling sleeve.

c. Remove the mainshaft and counter gear rear snap rings.

d. Using a punch and hammer, remove the C—ring holder and the C—rings from the mainshaft.

e. Pull out the counter gear rear end bearing.

f. Remove the reverse idler gear and thrust washers.

g. Remove the sub gear from the reverse idler gear. Pull out the mainshaft rear bearing.

h. Pull out the reverse main gear together with the mainshaft spacer and reverse synchronizer hub. Then remove the reverse gear needle bearings.

i. Pull out the reverse counter gear.

j. Remove the overdrive coupling sleeve together with the baulk ring, reverse baulk ring and spring inserts.

k. Pull out the reverse gear bushing.

l. Pull out the overdrive counter gear together with the reverse cone.

15. Remove the front side components on the mainshaft.

a. Remove the 1st. gear washer, steel ball and needle bearing. Remove the 1st. main gear.

b. Press out the 2nd. main gear together with the 1st. gear bushing and 1st. and 2nd. synchronizer assembly.

c. Remove the mainshaft front snap ring.

d. Press out the 3rd.main gear together with the 3rd. and 4th. synchronizer assembly and the 3rd. gear needle bearing.

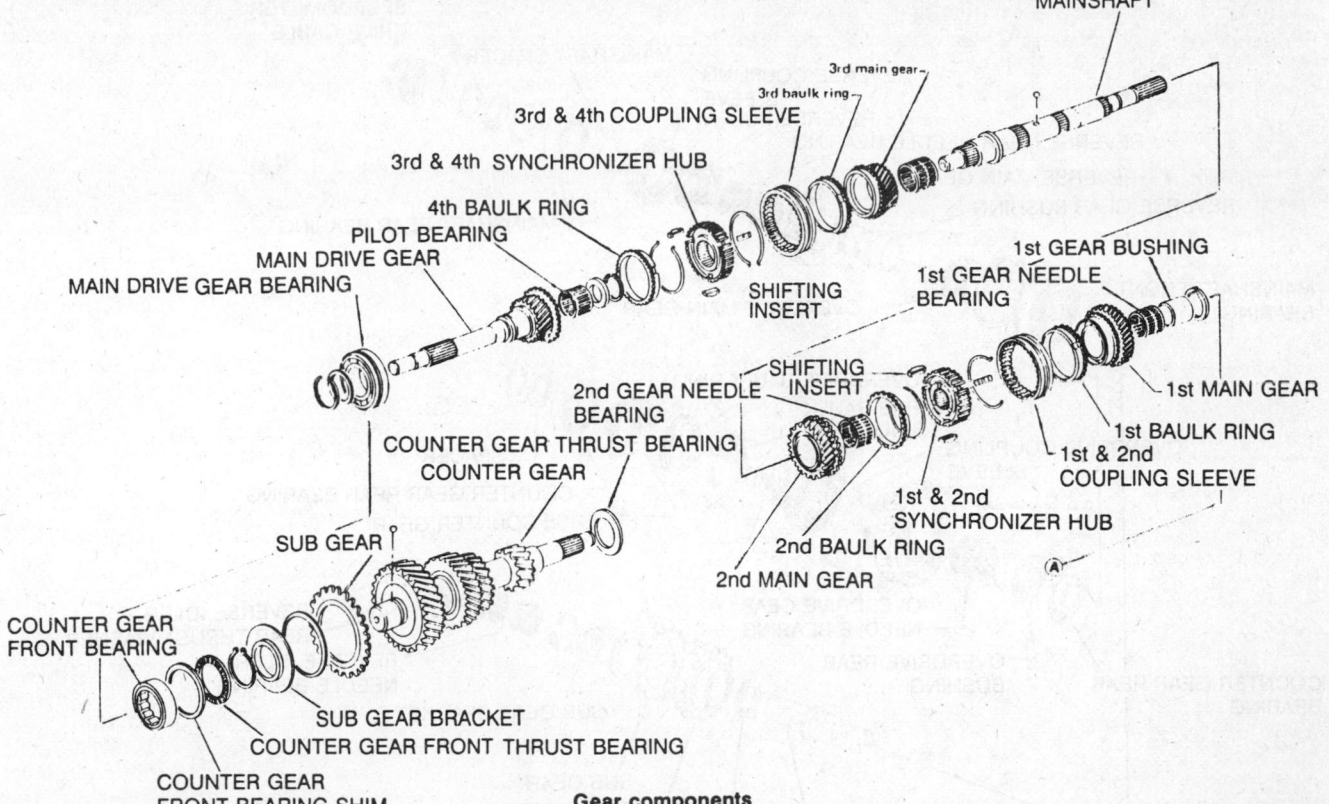

Gear components

16. Remove the front side components on the counter gear.

a. Remove the counter gear rear thrust bearing.

b. Remove the sub gear components.

17. Press out the main drive gear bearing.

18. Remove the bearings from the case components.

ASSEMBLY

1. Install the bearings into the case components.

2. Press in the main drive gear bearing and install the spacer.

3. Select the proper main drive gear snap ring to minimize the clearance of the groove.

NOTE: Allowable clearance of the groove is 0–0.004 in. (0–0.1mm).

4. Install the counter gear rear thrust bearing and the sub gear snap ring.

5. Assemble the 1st. and 2nd. synchronizer and the 3rd. and 4th. synchronizer.

6. Press on the 3rd. and 4th. synchronizer assembly together with the 3rd. main gear and the 3rd. gear needle bearing.

7. Select the proper snap ring to minimize the clearance of the groove.

NOTE: Allowable clearance of the groove is 0–0.004 in. (0–0.1mm).

8. Press on the 1st. and 2nd. synchronizer assembly together with the 2nd. main gear and 2nd. gear needle bearing.

9. Press on the 1st. gear bushing and install the 1st. main gear needle bearing.

10. Apply multi–purpose grease and install the steel ball and the 1st. gear washer.

11. Install the counter gear with the sub gear components, counter gear front and rear thrust bearing on the adapter plate.

12. Remove the counter gear front bearing shim from the transmission case.

13. Place the adapter plate and counter gear assembly in the transmission case and tighten with two bolts.

14. Using a dial indicator on the rear end of the counter gear, move the counter gear up and down to measure deflection. Counter gear end play is 0.0039–0.0098 in. (0.10–0.25 mm).

15. Install the reverse idler gear, needle bearings, thrust washers, and shaft into the rear extension.

16. Place a dial indicator on the front end of the reverse idler shaft. Use a straight edge on the front surface of the rear extension as a stopper

of the reverse idler shaft. Move the shaft up and down to measure the end play. Reverse idler gear end play is 0.0118–0.0209 in. (0.30–0.53 mm). If not within specification replace the rear thrust washer.

17. Install the mainshaft and counter gear on the adapter plate and the main drive gear on the mainshaft.

NOTE: When installing the counter gear into the rear bearing, push up on upper roller of rear bearing with a screwdriver.

18. Install the overdrive gear bushing while pushing on the front of the counter gear and install the overdrive main gear.

19. Install the adapter plate with the gear assembly into the transmission case. Install the overdrive gear needle bearing, counter gear and then the reverse idler shaft.

20. Install the reverse gear bushing and cone. Install the insert springs and reverse baulk ring on the overdrive coupling sleeve. Then install them and the overdrive baulk ring on the overdrive counter gear.

21. Install the reverse counter gear. Install the sub gear on the reverse idler gear.

22. Install the reverse gear needle bearing, main gear, isler gear and thrust washers. Install the reverse hub.

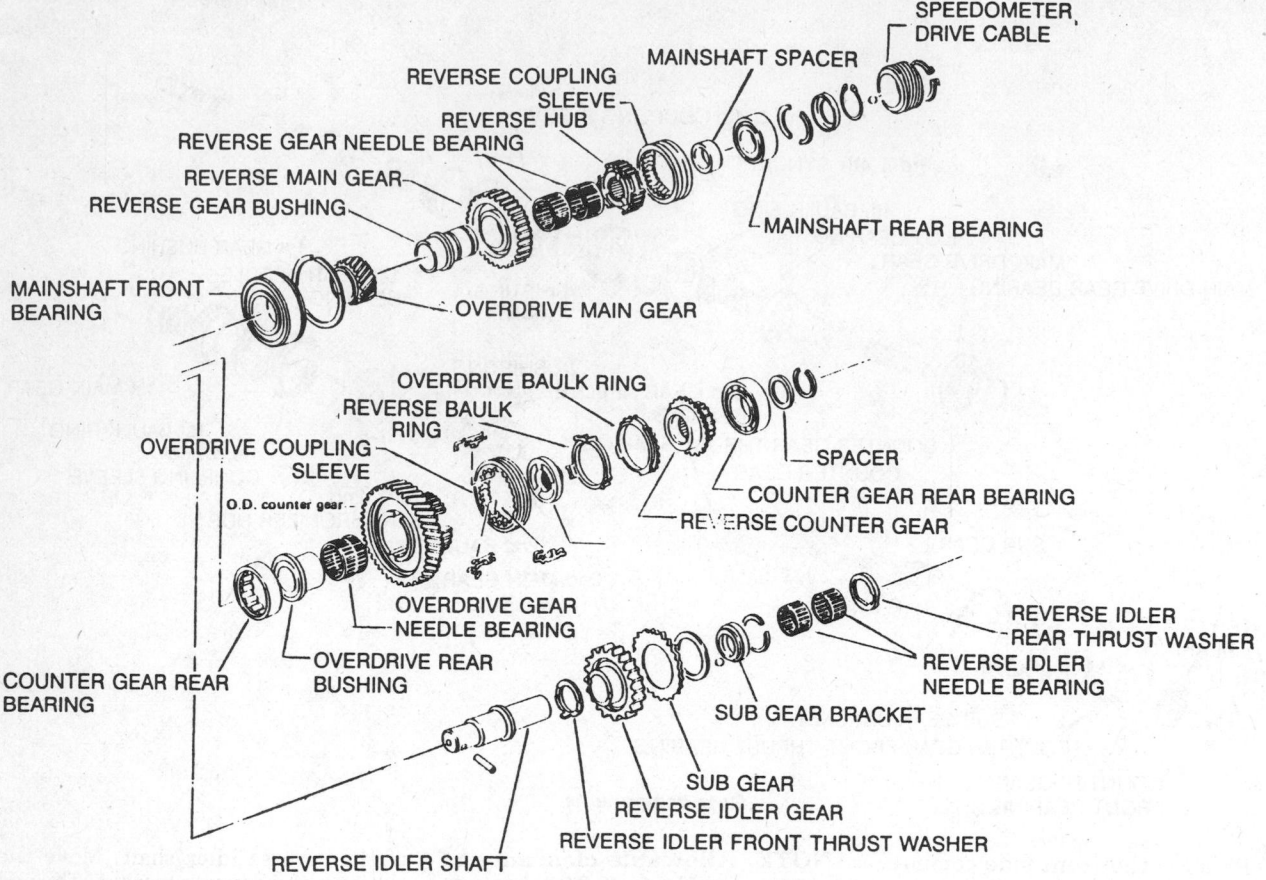

Gear components

23. Install the mainshaft spacer and rear bearing. Install the speedometer drive gear. Install the counter gear rear end bearing.

24. Seperate the adapter plate from the transmission case and mount it in a vice. Select the proper mainshaft C—ring and counter gear rear snap ring to minimize the clearance of the grooves.

25. Install the reverse coupling sleeve.

26. Install the overdrive shift fork rod and fork and retaining pin.

27. Install the 1st. and 2nd., 3rd and 4th. and reverse shift fork onto coupling sleeve.

28. Put the striking rod through the hole of the shift forks, striking lever and interlock. Make sure the striking rod moves smoothly.

29. Apply sealant to the thread of the check ball plug and install it and the return spring in the adapter plate.

30. Apply multi—purpose grease to the oil seal lip and install it in the front cover.

31. Install the selected counter gear front bearing shim onto the transmission case then the gear assembly.

32. Put the check spring and ball into the interlock stopper. Apply multi—purpose grease to the check ball. Install the stopper assembly and then tighten the check ball plug.

33. Install the stopper ring and the main drive bearing snap ring.

34. Install the front cover and gasket. Apply sealant to the thread of the bottom three bolts.

35. Install the rear extension together with the striking arm. Install the return spring and check ball and then install the control housing. Tighten the control housing bolts to specifications.

Manual Transaxle Overhaul 30

MANUAL TRANSAXLE APPLICATION CHART

Make	Vehicle		Transmission		Reference Type No.	Page
	Year	Model	Model	Speeds		
Acura	1987-88	Integra, Legend	C34P	5	31	30-104
Audi	1981-83	4000 4 cyl	014	4	2	30-6
	1981-88	4000 4 cyl	013	5	22	30-73
	1981-88	4000 5 cyl	088	4	1	30-4
	1984-88	4000 Quattro	016	5	24	30-80
	1981-83	5000	088	4	1	30-4
	1981-88	5000	016	5	24	30-80
Chrysler Corp.	1981-83	Colt, Champ	KM160	4	3	30-11
			KM165	4 ①	3	30-11
	1984	Colt exc. Turbo	KM160	4	3	30-11
		Colt Turbo	KM166	4 ①	3	30-11
		Colt Vista	KM166	4 ①	3	30-11
			KM163	5	4	30-15
	1985-86	Colt	KM161	4	3	30-11
		Colt Turbo	KM163	5	4	30-15
		Colt Vista	KM163	5	4	30-15
	1987-88	Colt	KM200	4	30	30-103
		Colt Vista	KM201, 206	4	30	30-103
	1986-88	Colt Vista 4WD	KM182	5	5	30-19
Honda	1980-87	All exc. 4WD	—	4 & 5	8	30-26
	1985-87	4WD	—	5	9	30-28
Hyundai	1986-88	Excel	KM161	4	3	30-11
			KM162	5	4	30-15
Isuzu	1985-88	I-Mark	—	5	26	30-87

MANUAL TRANSAXLE APPLICATION CHART

Make	Vehicle		Transmission		Reference Type No.	Page
	Year	Model	Model	Speeds		
Mazda	1981-88	GLC, 323, 626	—	4 & 5	25	30-85
Mitsubishi	1983	Cordia, Tredia	KM163	5	4	30-15
			KM166	4 ①	3	30-11
	1984	Cordia, Tredia	KM163	5	4	30-15
			KM166	4 ①	3	30-11
	1985-87	Cordia, Tredia	KM163	5	4	30-15
		Mirage	KM161	4	3	30-11
		Miarge Turbo	KM163	5	4	30-15
	1987-88	Mirage	KM200	4	30	30-103
			KM201, 206	5	30	30-103
	1987-88	Galant	KM210	5	30	30-103
Nissan/Datsun	1981	310	F4WF60A	4	6	30-21
			F5WF60A	4	6	30-21
	1982	310	RN4F30A	4	7	30-22
			RS5F30A	5	7	30-22
	1982-83	Sentra	RN4F30A	4	7	30-22
			RN4F30A	5	7	30-22
	1982-86	Stanza	RS5F50A	5	7	30-22
	1987-88	Stanza	RS5F50A	5	27	30-90
		Sentra	RS5F31A	5	7	30-22
	1987-88	Stanza Wagon	RS5F50A	5	27	30-90
	1986-88	Pulsar	RS5F31A	5	7	30-22
	1985-88	Maxima	RS5F50A	5	7	30-22
Porsche	1981-83	911	915/63	5	10	30-32
	1984	911	915/68, 70	5	10	30-32
	1985-88	911	915/73	5	10	30-32
	1986-88	911 Turbo	930/36	4	10	30-32
	1981-82	924	016/9	5	24	30-80
	1981-82	924 Turbo	016 G	5	24	30-80
	1981-82	928	G28.05	5	11	30-35
	1983-84	928S	G28.07, 08	5	11	30-35
	1985-88	928S	G28.11	5	11	30-35
	1983-88	944	016K	5	24	30-80
	1986-88	944 Turbo	016R	5	24	30-80

MANUAL TRANSAXLE APPLICATION CHART

Make	Vehicle		Transmission		Reference Type No.	Page
	Year	Model	Model	Speeds		
SAAB	1981-88	99, 900, 9000	—	4	12	30-38
			—	5	13	30-40
Sterling	1987-88	825S, 825SL	C3P4	5	31	30-104
Subaru	1981-88	All 2WD	—	4	14	30-41
			—	5	15	30-44
	1981-88	All 4WD exc. 1800, XT Coupe	—	4	16	30-45
	1985-88	1800, XT Coupe	—	5	17	30-49
Toyota	1981	Tercel	Z40, Z50	4&5	18	30-58
	1982	Tercel	Z41, 42, 51	5	19	30-61
	1983-84	Tercel 2WD	Z44, 52	5	19	30-61
		Tercel 4WD	Z52F	5	19	30-61
	1985-88	Tercel 2WD	Z45, 46, 53	5	28	30-93
		Tercel 4WD	Z54F	5	28	30-93
	1984	Corolla (FWD)	C51	5	21	30-69
			S41,50	5	20	30-64
	1985	Corolla (FWD)	C51	5	21	30-69
			S50	5	20	30-64
	1986–88	Corolla (FWD)	C51, C52	5	21	30-69
	1983-85	Camry	S41, 50	5	20	30-64
	1986-88	Camry	S51	5	20	30-64
Volkswagen	1981	Dasher	XK	4	2	30-6
	1982-88	Quantum	013, 093	5	22	30-73
	1981-88	Rabbit, Scirocco,	020	4	22	30-73
		Jetta, GTI	020F	5	22	30-73
	1981-88	Vanagon	091	4	23	30-76
			094	5	23	30-76
	1987-88	Fox, Golf, GTI	014	4	22	30-73
			020F	5	22	30-73
Yugo	1986-88	GV	—	4	29	30-101

① (twinstick)

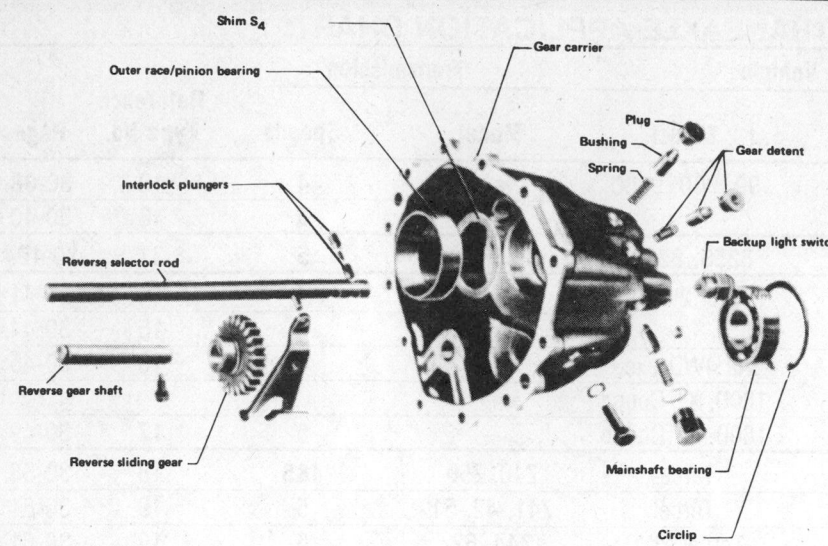

Shim S₄

Outer race/pinion bearing

Interlock plungers

Reverse selector rod

Reverse gear shaft

Reverse sliding gear

Gear carrier

Plug

Bushing

Spring

Gear detent

Backup light switch

Mainshaft bearing

Circlip

Gear carrier housing

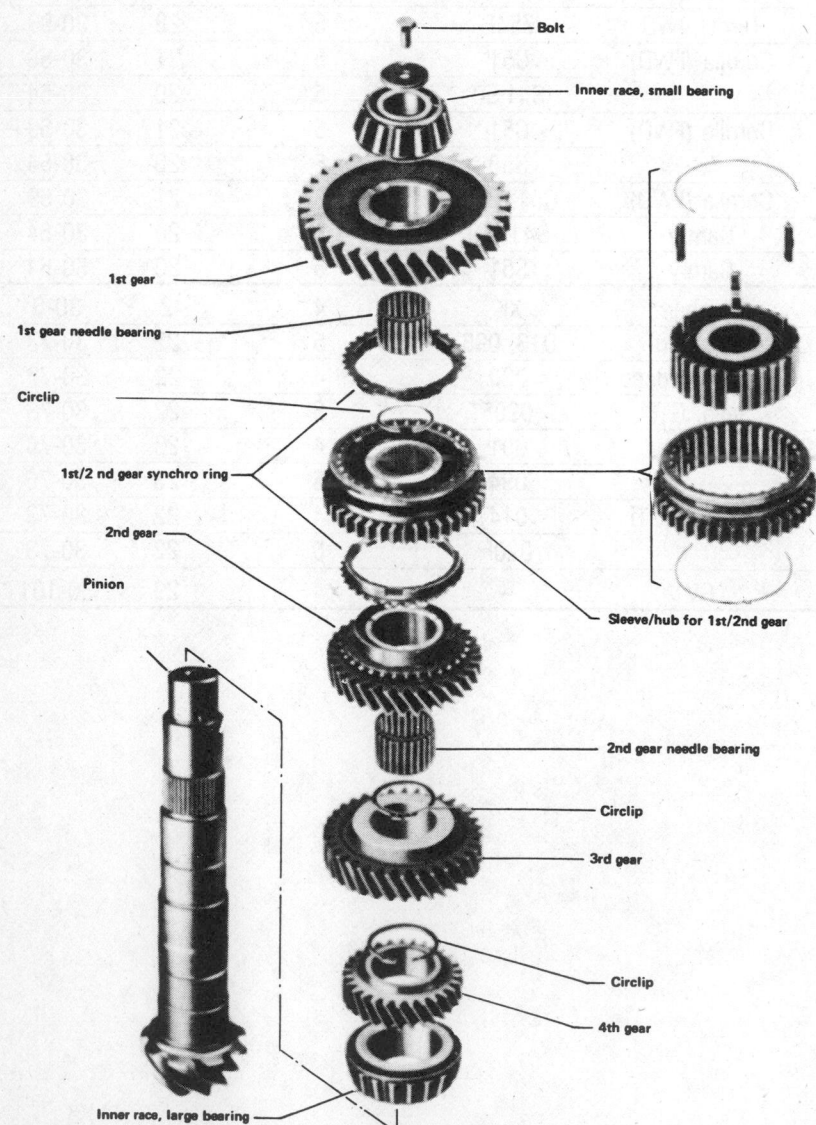

Bolt

Inner race, small bearing

1st gear

1st gear needle bearing

Circlip

1st/2nd gear synchro ring

2nd gear

Pinion

Sleeve/hub for 1st/2nd gear

2nd gear needle bearing

Circlip

3rd gear

Circlip

4th gear

Inner race, large bearing

Pinion shaft assembly

TYPE 1

4 Speed Transaxle Model 088 Audi

DISASSEMBLY

1. Mount the transaxle in a holding fixture.
2. Block the drive flange with a drift and remove the center bolt. Remove both drive flanges.
3. Remove the differential cover and O-ring. Remove the differential.

CAUTION

If the tapered roller bearings on the pinion shaft are to be replaced, it is necessary to measure the pinion position before the transaxle is disassembled. Both pinion shaft bearings must be replaced at the same time with bearings of the same make. The pinion must be set to its original position when the transaxle is assembled.

---

4. Remove the bolts holding the gear carrier to the final drive housing.
5. Remove the dowel pin from the gear carrier.
6. Remove the selector shaft spring and cap. Push the selector shaft into the final drive housing.
7. Separate the gear carrier and the final drive housing.
8. Remove the end cap from the gear carrier. Remove the mainshaft bolt and washer.
9. Remove the shift rod stopscrews, spring, and interlock plungers.
10. Drive the spring pin out of the third/fourth gear shaft fork.
11. Pull the third/fourth gear selector rod out of the gear carrier. The shift fork will stay on the mainshaft.
12. Press the mainshaft out of the bearing. Guide the mainshaft and pinion shaft with the selector rod and fork for first/second gear.
13. Remove the main and pinion shafts together with the selector rod and shift forks. Swing the pinion shaft slightly to clear the reverse sliding gear.
14. Remove the speedometer drive gear.
15. Pry the oil seal from the differential cover.
16. Remove the bearing race from the differential cover. Remove the shim and record the size.
17. Remove the drive flange oil seal.
18. Pull the differential bearing outer race out of the final drive housing. Remove the shim and record the size.
19. Remove the selector shaft and oil seal.

20. Remove the clutch release shaft, bearing springs, and bushings. Remove the clutch bearing guide sleeve.

21. Remove the mainshaft oil seal.

22. Remove the pinion shaft needle bearings from the final drive housing.

23. Remove the mainshaft needle bearings.

24. Remove the reverse gear relay lever and the reverse selector rod.

25. Remove the reverse shaft and gear.

26. Press the synchronizer assembly (with third gear) off the mainshaft. Remove the needle bearings.

27. Remove the pinion shaft bolt.

28. Press the bearing (along with first gear and synchronizer ring) off the pinion shaft. Remove the needle bearings.

29. Remove the circlip from the synchronizer.

30. Press the synchronizer assembly (along with second gear and synchronizer ring) off the pinion shaft. Remove the needle bearings.

31. Remove the third gear circlip and press third gear off the pinion shaft.

32. Remove the circlip from fourth gear and press it off the pinion shaft.

33. Press the large tapered roller bearing off the pinion shaft.

34. Remove the spring pin from the pinion gear shaft in the differential housing and drive the shaft out. Remove the thrust washers and pinion gears.

35. Remove the side gears, threaded washers, and shims. Record the shim size.

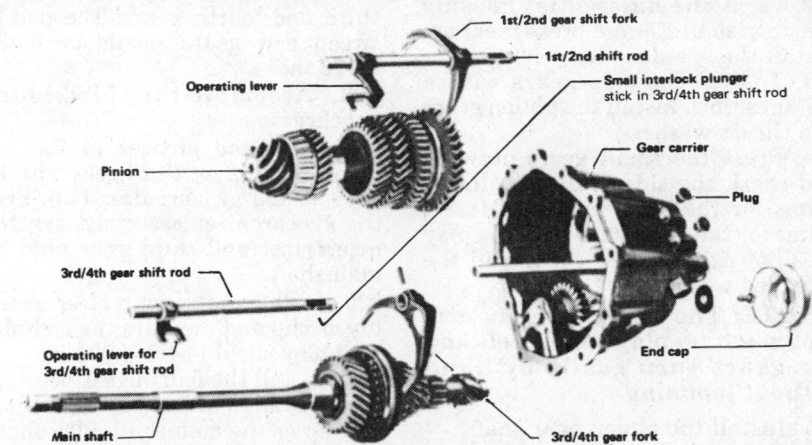

Gear carrier with gear train and selector components

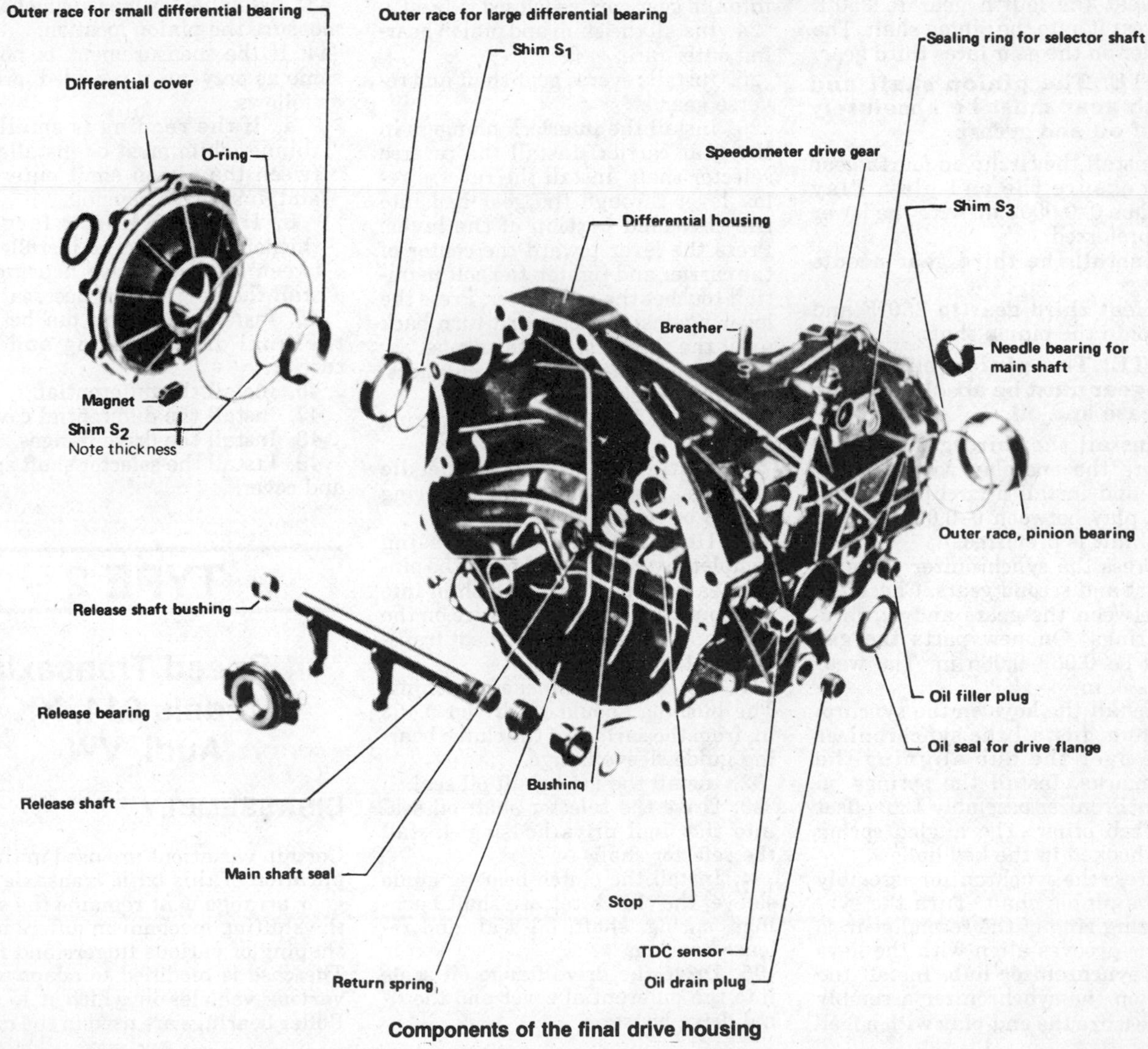

1st/2nd gear shift fork
1st/2nd shift rod
Operating lever
Small interlock plunger stick in 3rd/4th gear shift rod
Pinion
Gear carrier
Plug
3rd/4th gear shift rod
Operating lever for 3rd/4th gear shift rod
End cap
Main shaft
3rd/4th gear fork

Outer race for small differential bearing
Outer race for large differential bearing
Shim S1
Sealing ring for selector shaft
Differential cover
O-ring
Speedometer drive gear
Shim S3
Differential housing
Needle bearing for main shaft
Breather
Magnet
Shim S2
Note thickness
Outer race, pinion bearing
Release shaft bushing
Release bearing
Oil filler plug
Oil seal for drive flange
Release shaft
Main shaft seal
Bushing
Stop
TDC sensor
Oil drain plug
Return spring

Components of the final drive housing

36. Remove the differential bearings and speedometer drive gear.
37. Remove the ring gear.

ASSEMBLY

1. Heat the ring gear to 212°F and install it.
2. Heat the differential housing bearings to 212°F and press them on. Install the speedometer drive gear.
3. Install the side gears with a 0.5mm shims. Install the pinion gears and thrust washers.
4. Press the small gears outward and check the side gear play. Insert shims for the side gear play. Insert shims for the side gears until the play does not exceed 0.003 in. Install the threaded washers.

NOTE: The adjustment is correct when no play can be felt and the gears turn easily by hand without jamming.

5. Install the pinion gear shaft.
6. Press the large tapered roller bearing onto the pinion shaft.
7. Heat the fourth gear to 250°F and press it onto the pinion shaft. The shoulder on the gear faces third gear.

NOTE: The pinion shaft and fourth gear must be absolutely free of oil and grease.

8. Install the circlip on fourth gear and measure the end-play. Play should be 0–0.0007 in. with the lower limit preferred.
9. Install the third gear needle bearings.
10. Heat third gear to 250°F and press onto the pinion shaft.

NOTE: The pinion shaft and third gear must be absolutely free of grease and oil.

11. Install the third gear circlip. Measure the end-play with a feeler gauge and install a circlip that will give a play between 0–0.001 in. The lower limit is preferred.
12. Press the synchronizer rings on the first and second gears. Check the gap between the gears and synchronizer rings. On new parts the gap should be 0.039–0.066 in. The wear limit is 0. in.
13. Install the keys on the synchronizer hug. Install the synchronizer sleeve over the hub aligning the matchmarks. Install the springs on the synchronizer assembly 120° offset from each other. The angled spring end is hooked in the key hollow.
14. Press the synchronizer assembly onto the pinion shaft. Turn the synchronizing ring of the second gear so that the grooves align with the keys in the synchronizer hub. Install the circlip on the synchronizer assembly and measure the end-play with a feel-

er gauge. Play should be 0–0.0007 in. with the lower limit preferred.
15. Press the small tapered roller bearing onto the pinion shaft. Install the washer and bolt.
16. Install the third gear needle bearings.
17. Install the synchronizer rings on third and fourth gears. The gap between new gears should be 0.039–0.066 in.
18. Assemble the third/fourth synchronizer.
19. Align the grooves in the synchronizer ring for third gear with the keys in the synchronizer hub. Press the synchronizer assembly, synchronizer ring, and third gear onto the mainshaft.
20. Install the synchronizer assembly circlip and measure the end-play. End-play should be 0–0.001 in.
21. Install the fourth gear bearings.
22. Install fourth gear and thrust washer on the mainshaft. Play should be 0.007–0.013 in.
23. Drive the mainshaft bearing into the gear carrier (closed side out).
24. Install the shim and pinion bearing outer race.
25. Install reverse gear shaft and reverse gear.
26. Install the interlock plungers in the gear carrier. Install the reverse selector shaft. Install the reverse relay lever through the gear and into the threaded portion of the lever. Press the lever toward the center of the carrier and tighten the bolt in until it touches the relay lever. Press the lever against the bolt and turn back until the thread starts to engage.
27. Install the interlock plungers, bushings, springs and plugs.
28. Install the differential bearing shim and outer race.
29. Install the mainshaft needle bearings. The lettering on the bearing should be toward the drift.
30. Heat the final drive housing completely to 212°F and press the pinion bearing outer race and shim into the housing. Hold the pressure on the race for 1–2 minutes until heat transfer has taken place.
31. Install the mainshaft bushing. The bushing should be driven 0.452 in. from the surface of the clutch bearing guide sleeve flange.
32. Install the mainshaft oil seal.
33. Drive the selector shaft oil seal into the final drive housing. Install the selector shaft.
34. Install the clutch bearing guide sleeve, the clutch release shaft bushings, spring, shaft, oil seal, and release bearing.
35. Drive the drive flange oil seals into the differential cover and the final drive housing.

36. Install the main and pinion shafts along with the shift forks and first/second gear selector rod. These components must be installed as an assembly. Hook the hole in web of third/fourth gear fork over the reverse selector rod.

NOTE: Make sure the interlock plungers engage the shift selector rod.

37. Pull the mainshaft into the bearing with an 8mm bolt. When fully seated, install the mainshaft bolt.
38. Move the selector rods for fitst/second and reverse into neutral.
39. Slide the third/fourth selector rod into the shift fork and gear carrier. Make sure that the interlock plungers engage. Secure the shift fork to the rod with a new spring pin.
40. Install the shift rod stop screws.
41. Press the mainshaft cap and O-ring into the gear carrier. Make sure that the interlock plungers engage. Secure the shift fork to the rod with a new spring pin.
42. Install the gear carrier.
43. Assemble the measuring bar and measure the pinion location.
44. If the measurement is not the same as previously recorded, proceed as follows:
   a. If the reading is smaller, a thinner shim must be installed between the pinion shaft outer race and final drive housing.
   b. If the reading is larger, a thicker shim must be installed between the final drive housing. Install the new shim if necessary.
45. Install the dowel pin between the final drive housing and gear carrier.
46. Install the differential.
47. Install the differential cover.
48. Install the drive flanges.
49. Install the selector shaft spring and cover.

TYPE 2

4 Speed Transaxle Models 014, XK Audi, VW

DISASSEMBLY

Certain variations are used in the application of this basic transaxle. The gear arrangement remains the same, the shifting mechanism differs in the shaping of various fingers and forks. The case is modified to adapt to the various vehicles in which it is used. Roller bearings are used in the majority of applications, while tapered bearings are used in the remainder. Needle cages bearings may be found as split, one piece or with a foldable cage. A pinion nut is used on varied models, while a bolt and washer are used on others.

1. Mount the transaxle in a holding fixture.
2. Separate the shift housing from the transaxle.
3. Mount a dial gauge and zero the gauge with a 3mm preload.

———————— CAUTION ————————

The greatest care must be taken when determining the thickness of the gasket and skim used between the shift housing and the gear carrier. The thickness of these two parts influence the position of the drive pinion. If the bearings for the mainshaft, pinion shaft are replaced, the measurements must be remade and new skim and gasket sizes selected.

4. Measure the distance between the mainshaft bearing and the gear carrier (a). Record this reading. Make sure that the bearing is fully seated.
5. Measure the distance between the pinion bearing and the gear carrier (b). Record the reading. Make sure that the bearing is fully seated.
6. Measure the distance between the end face and the shim contact surface on the gear carrier (c). Record the reading.
7. Determine the shim thickness as follows; add the measurements from Step 4 (a) and 6 (c), then subtract step 5 (b). This will give the shim thickness required.
8. The gasket thickness is determined by the mainshaft bearing projection obtained in Step 4.

NOTE: When replacing the transmission housing, gear carrier, first gear needle bearing or the pinion bearing, the exact location of the pinion must be determined before disassembly. Once the new parts have been installed, it will be necessary to set the pinion to its original position.

9. Block the drive flange and remove the bolt.
10. Remove the final drive cover. Remove the differential assembly.

NOTE: To perform the following operation, it is necessary to have special Volkswagen tools or equivalent.

11. Assemble the tool universal bar. Zero the dial indicator with a 2mm preload.
12. Install the measuring plate tool on the pinion and install the measuring bar in the final drive housing.
13. Install the final drive cover and tighten the retaining nuts to 18 ft. lbs.

14. Move the second centering disc outward with the movable setting ring until the measuring bar can be turned by hand.
15. Turn the measuring bar until the measuring pin extension touches the plate on the pinion. Note the indicator needle at the point of maximum deflection. Record the reading.

NOTE: After parts have been replaced, this setting must be reproduced as closely as possible.

16. Separate the gear carrier from the final drive housing.
17. Drive the spring pin out of the 3rd/4th shift fork in the direction of the pinion.
18. Move the shift fork along the selector shaft and engage 3rd gear. Do not move the shaft.
19. Engage reverse gear. Place the gear carrier in the final drive housing. Loosen the pinion nut. Remove the gear carrier from the final drive housing. Remove the 3rd/4th shift fork.
20. Remove the mainshaft bearing using a suitable bearing puller. Remove the mainshaft.
21. Drive the reverse gear shaft out of the gear carrier.
22. Place the remaining gears in neutral and press the pinion shaft out of the gear carrier along with the 1st/2nd selector shaft and shift fork.
23. Remove the inner shift lever spring from the shift housing, remove the shift lever.
24. Press the transmission rear mount off the shift housing.
25. Pry the inner shift lever oil seal out of the shift housing.
26. Drive the inner shift lever rear bushing out of the shift housing.
27. Press the inner shift lever from bushing out of the shift housing.
28. Pry the mainshaft oil seal out of the final drive housing from the final drive housing.
29. Drive the mainshaft sleeve out of the final drive housing from the gear carrier end.
30. Drive the mainshaft needle bearings out of the final drive housing from the front (flywheel side).
31. Remove the dowel pin from the pinion bearing and drive it out of the final drive housing.
32. Using a slide hammer, pull the clutch release shaft bushing out of the final drive housing.
33. Pull the starter bushing out of the final drive housing.
34. Drive the pinion bearing out of the gear carrier.
35. Remove the pin from the reverse gear selector shaft.
36. Drive the 1st/2nd and 3rd/4th interlock plungers through the gear carrier and remove through the ac-

cess hole in the rear of the gear carrier.
37. Tap the remaining interlock plunger plug out.
38. Remove the circlip from the mainshaft which holds the 4th gear and the synchronizer ring. Remove the parts from the shaft.
39. Remove the circlip retaining the synchronizer hub, synchronizer ring, and third gear from the main shaft.
40. Press the synchronizer hub and third gear off the mainshaft.
41. Press the pinion bearing inner race along with the first gear off the pinion shaft.
42. Press the synchronizer hub for 1st/2nd gear along with second gear off the pinion shaft.
43. Remove the third gear circlip from the pinion shaft.
44. Press the third gear off the pinion shaft.
45. Press the fourth gear off the pinion shaft.

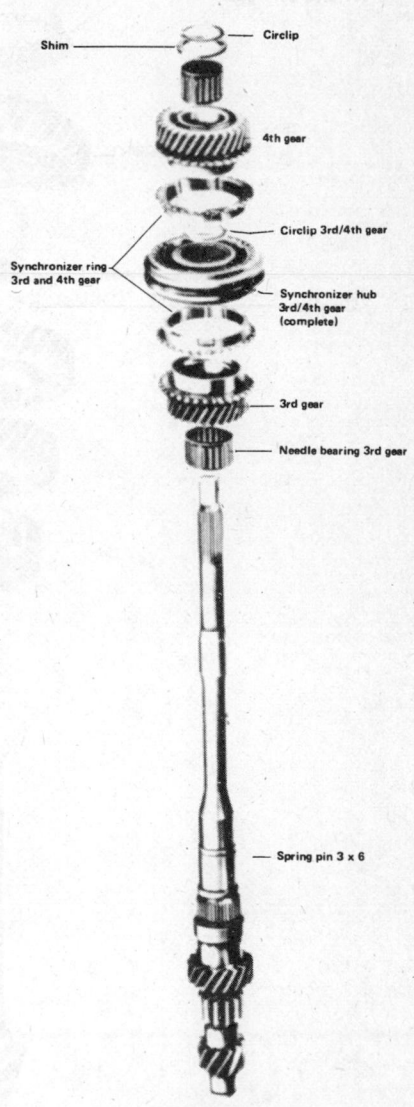

Shim — Circlip
4th gear
Circlip 3rd/4th gear
Synchronizer ring 3rd and 4th gear
Synchronizer hub 3rd/4th gear (complete)
3rd gear
Needle bearing 3rd gear
Spring pin 3 x 6

Mainshaft assembly

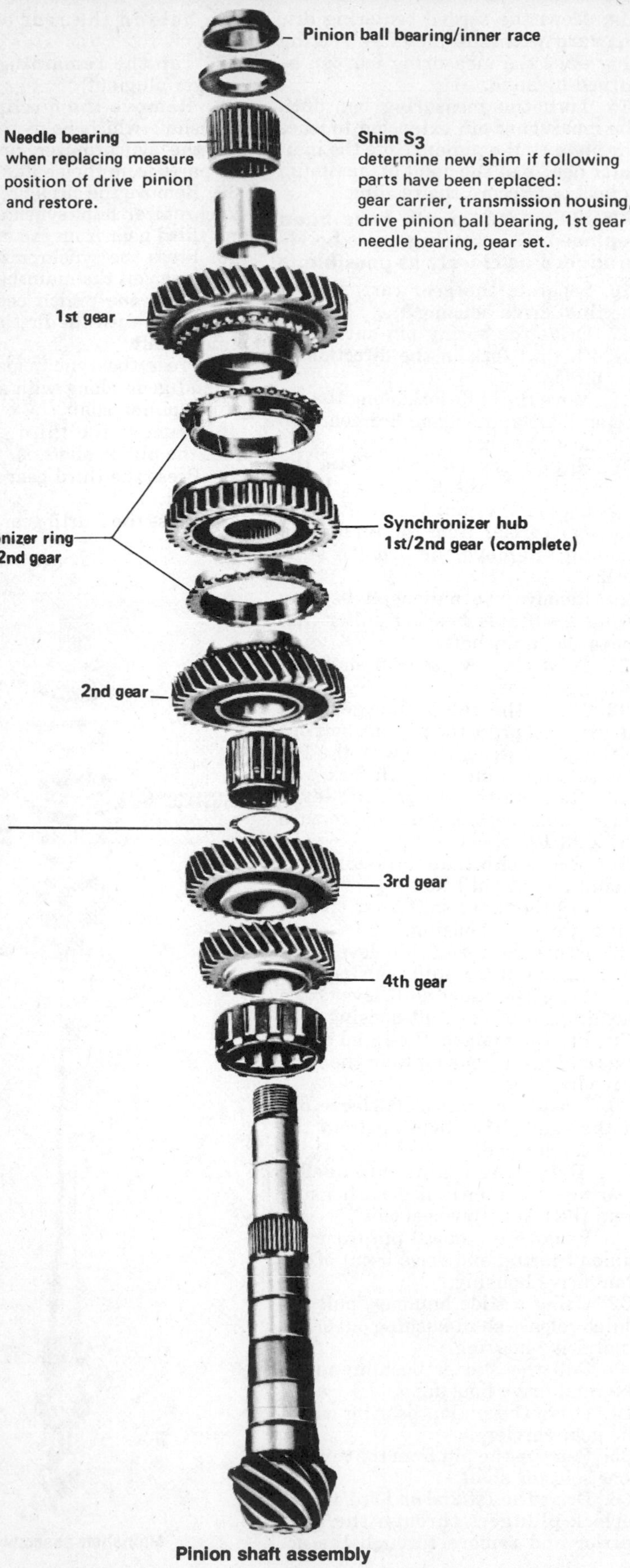

Pinion ball bearing/inner race

Needle bearing when replacing measure position of drive pinion and restore.

Shim S₃ determine new shim if following parts have been replaced: gear carrier, transmission housing, drive pinion ball bearing, 1st gear needle bearing, gear set.

1st gear

Synchronizer ring 1st and 2nd gear

Synchronizer hub 1st/2nd gear (complete)

2nd gear

Circlip

3rd gear

4th gear

Pinion shaft assembly

46. Remove the drive flange oil seal from the final drive housing by prying.
47. Drive the differential outer bearing race and shim out of the final drive cover.
48. Using a suitable puller, remove the differential bearing inner race/cage from the side opposite the ring gear.
49. Pull the bearing from the ring gear side of the differential assembly, along with the speedometer drive gear and bushing.
50. Remove the bolts holding the ring gear to the differential housing and drive the housing and gear apart.
51. Remove the circlip from the pinion gear shaft. Slide the shaft out of the differential housing.
52. Remove the pinion gears, side gears and the drive flange nuts.

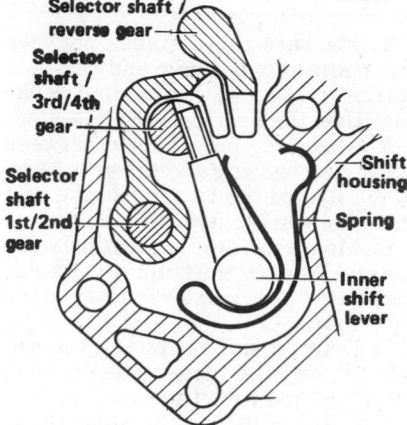

Selector shaft / reverse gear

Selector shaft / 3rd/4th gear

Selector shaft 1st/2nd gear

Shift housing

Spring

Inner shift lever

Spring loaded inner shift lever

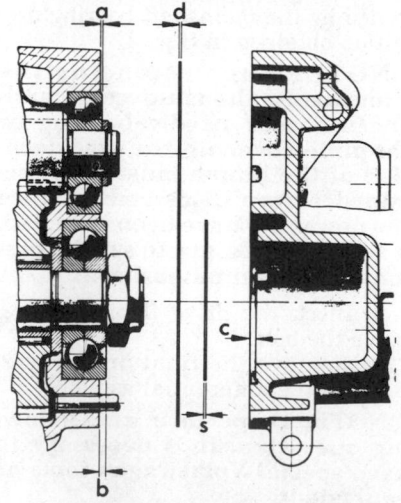

a — between main shaft bearing and gear carrier
b — between pinion bearing and gear carrier
c — between end face of gearshift housing and shim contact in gearshift housing
d — gasket thickness
s — shim thickness

End cover gasket and shim dimensions

ASSEMBLY

1. Insert the side gears and drive flange nuts. Bolt the drive flanges to the side gears.

2. Insert the pinion gears and move the drive flange until the pinion gears are aligned. Install the pinion shaft. Remove the drive flanges.

NOTE: The drive pinion and the ring gears are matched units and can be replaced only as a matched set.

3. Heat the ring gear to approximately 212°F and center on the differential housing with a drift.

4. Install the bearing opposite to the ring gear by heating to 212°F and pressing onto the differential housing.

5. Install the bearing on the ring gear side of the differential housing by heating to 212°F and pressing onto the differential housing.

6. Insert 1.8mm shim onto differential housing and press drive gear bushing on.

7. Insert the shim into the final drive cover and drive the outer bearing race into place and insert the shim in the final drive housing.

8. Drive the right side drive flange oil seal into place in the final drive housing.

9. Press the 4th gear onto the pinion shaft while holding the bearing with the wide shoulder facing the pinion head.

10. Press the third gear onto the pinion shaft.

11. Measure with a feeler gauge the space between the third gear and the pinion shaft. Install a circlip of the correct size.

12. Position the three keys in the slots in the 1st/2nd gear synchronizer hub.

13. Place the synchronizer sleeve over the synchronizer hub and align marks.

14. Install the springs 120° offset with the angled ends engaged in the hollow of a key.

15. Position the shift fork slot and the groove in the synchronizer hub so that they face the first gear and press the synchronizer assembly onto the pinion shaft.

16. Press the synchronizer ring onto the first gear and measure the gap between the parts with a feeler gauge. New parts should be between 0.042–0.066 in. and a used part should be no more than 0.023 in.

17. Install the first gear on the pinion shaft, slide on bearing and shim.

18. Press the inner race onto the pinion shaft.

19. Assemble the 3rd/4th gear synchronizer in the same way as the 1st/2nd synchronizer.

20. Press the synchronizer rings onto the third and fourth gears. Check the gap between the synchronizer rings and the gears. New parts should measure 0.053–0.075 in. and used parts should be no more than 0.023 in.

21. Install needle bearing on mainshaft.

22. Press the synchronizer hub along with the third gear onto the mainshaft. The chamfer on the synchronizer hub inner splines faces third gear.

23. Install the circlip on the mainshaft for the synchronizer assembly.

24. Install the needle bearing.

25. Install the spring pin in the mainshaft and align the pin with the slot in the 4th gear.

26. Install the fourth gear and shim, secure with the circlip.

CAUTION

Before measuring end-play, press the synchronizer and third gear against the circlip located against the synchronizer hub.

27. Measure the end-play between the shim and fourth gear. If the measurement is not between 0.10–0.40mm, remove the circlip and install a shim that will bring the measurement within limits.

28. Install the plunger and spring for the first/second shift selector shaft. Install the interlock plunger (between the 1st/2nd and the 3rd/4th shafts) from the top of the case.

29. Install the plunger and spring for the 3rd/4th selector shaft. Hold down the plunger and install the 3rd/4th shift selector shaft.

30. Install the pin for the reverse gear selector shaft.

31. Install the second interlock plunger from the top of the gear carrier.

32. Install the reverse gear selector shaft. Install the remaining spring and plunger. Install the reverse lever pin in selector shaft.

NOTE: The first/second selector shaft is not installed until the gear train is in place.

33. Install the plugs in the interlock plunger bores.

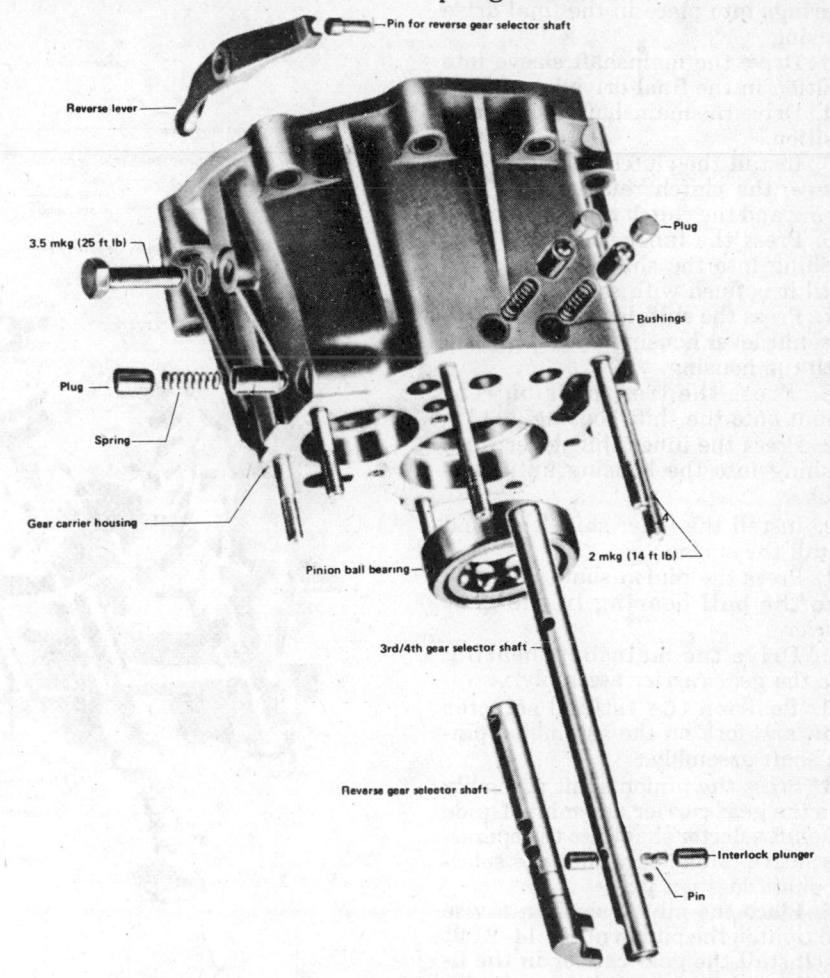

Labels: Pin for reverse gear selector shaft — Reverse lever — 3.5 mkg (25 ft lb) — Plug — Plug — Bushings — Spring — Gear carrier housing — Pinion ball bearing — 2 mkg (14 ft lb) — 3rd/4th gear selector shaft — Reverse gear selector shaft — Interlock plunger — Pin

Gear carrier housing and shift rod interlock components

34. Install the reverse sliding gear. Insert the reverse lever with the shift segment.

35. Install the bolt and washer and press the reverse lever toward the center of the gear carrier.

36. Turn the bolt in until it touches the reverse lever. Press the lever against the bolt and make certain that the threads engage smoothly. Continue until the bolt is seated in the gear carrier. Tighten the bolt to 25 ft. lbs.

37. Check the operation of the reverse selector several times. Make sure that the lever moves easily in all positions. Remove the reverse sliding gear.

38. Press the pinion bearing into the gear carrier.

39. Drive a new starter bushing into the final drive housing.

40. Drive a new clutch release shaft bushing into the final drive housing.

41. Align the pinion bearing outer race with the hole in the final drive housing drive into place. The groove on the side must be toward the gear carrier. Install the dowel pin.

42. Drive the mainshaft needle bearings into place in the final drive housing.

43. Drive the mainshaft sleeve into position in the final drive housing.

44. Drive the mainshaft oil seal into position.

45. Install the clutch bearing guide sleeve, the clutch release shaft and spring and the clutch release bearing.

46. Press the inner shift lever rear bushing into the shift lever housing until it is flush with shoulder.

47. Press the shift lever oil seal into the shift lever housing until it is flush with the housing.

48. Press the transmission rear mount onto the shift housing.

49. Press the inner shift lever front bushing into the housing until it is flush.

50. Install the inner shift lever and install the spring.

51. Press the pinion shaft assembly into the ball bearing in the gear carrier.

52. Drive the mainshaft bearing into the gear carrier assembly.

53. Position the 1st/2nd selector shaft and fork on the assembled pinion shaft assembly.

54. Press the pinion shaft assembly into the gear carrier assembly. Guide the shift selector shaft into the operating sleeve. Make sure that the selector shaft does not jam.

55. Place the pinion shaft in a vise and tighten the pinion nut to 14–21 ft. lbs. Install the gear carrier in the final drive housing and secure with four nuts.

56. Repeat the measurements from Steps 11 thru 15 of disassembly. If the measurements are not the same as previously recorded, proceed as follows:

a. If the second measurement is smaller, a thinner shim must be installed (between the pinion shaft inner bearing race and needle bearing on the pinion shaft).

b. If the measurement is the same or very close to the original reading proceed to the next step.

c. If the measurement is larger, a thicker shim must be installed.

57. Remove the gear carrier from the final drive housing, install new shim if needed.

58. Place the mainshaft assembly in the gear carrier. Install the shim and circlip.

Exploded view of 1st/2nd synchronizer

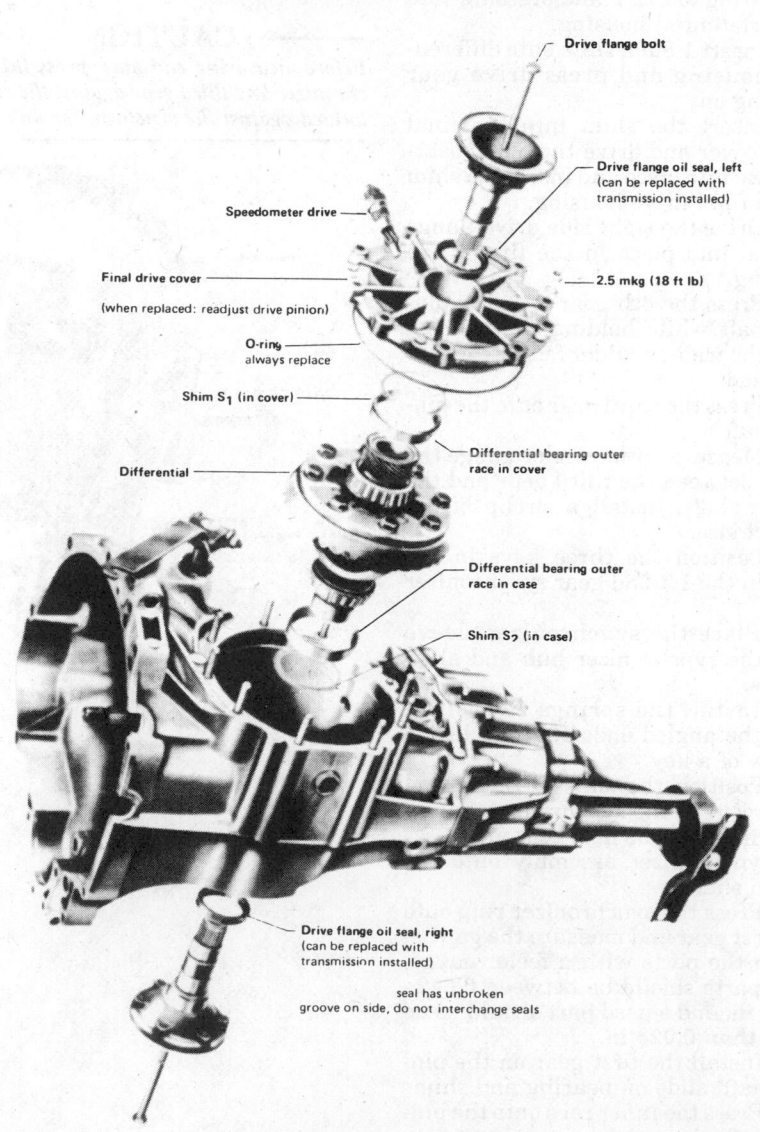

Drive flange bolt

Drive flange oil seal, left
(can be replaced with
transmission installed)

Speedometer drive

Final drive cover
(when replaced: readjust drive pinion)

2.5 mkg (18 ft lb)

O-ring
always replace

Shim S₁ (in cover)

Differential bearing outer
race in cover

Differential

Differential bearing outer
race in case

Shim S₂ (in case)

Drive flange oil seal, right
(can be replaced with
transmission installed)

seal has unbroken
groove on side, do not interchange seals

Components of differential housing

59. Install the 3rd/4th shift fork with the wider shoulder facing toward fourth gear. Secure the shift fork with a new spring pin.

60. Block the gear train and tighten the pinion nut to 72 ft. lbs.

61. Install the first/second gear selector dog.

62. Install the gear carrier assembly on the final drive housing. Install the dowel pins before tightening the nuts or bolts.

63. Install the differential assembly into the final drive housing.

64. Install the final drive cover.

65. Install the drive flanges and block with suitable drift.

66. Repeat the measurements from Steps 3 thru 8 of disassembly. Select the proper shim and gasket to be installed between the gear carrier and shift housing.

67. Install the shift housing on the gear carrier assembly.

TYPE 3

4 Speed Transaxle — Model KM 160, 161
4 Speed Transaxle w/Twin Stick — Model KM 165, 166
Chrysler Corp./ Hyundai/Mitsubishi

DISASSEMBLY OF TRANSAXLE

1. Mount the transaxle securely and drain the lubricating oil.

2. Remove the clutch operating bracket and the transaxle mounting bracket.

3. Remove the backup lamp switch and the steel ball from inside the transaxle case.

4. Remove the rear cover from the transaxle case. Remove the two spacers from the rear of the tapered roller bearings.

5. Remove the transaxle case, exposing the gear train assembly.

6. Locate all the shift rails in the neutral position.

NOTE: The shift rails would be locked if any one of the shift rails are in a position other than neutral.

7. Remove the three poppet plugs and remove the springs and balls (three each).

8. Remove the reverse idler shaft and the reverse idler gear.

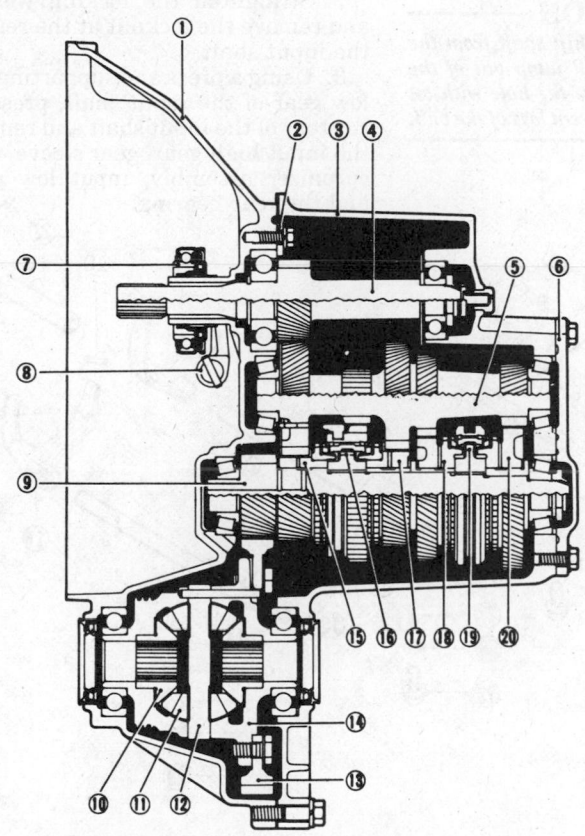

Cross section of model KM 160 transaxle

1. Clutch housing	12. Pinion shaft
2. Bearing retainer	13. Differential drive gear
3. Transaxle	14. Differential case
4. Input shaft	15. 4th speed gear
5. Intermediate gear	16. 3rd and 4th speed
6. Rear cover	synchronizer assembly
7. Clutch release bearing	17. 3rd speed gear
8. Clutch release fork	18. 2nd speed gear
9. Output shaft	19. 1st and 2nd speed
10. Differential side gear	synchronizer assembly
11. Differential pinion	20. 1st speed gear

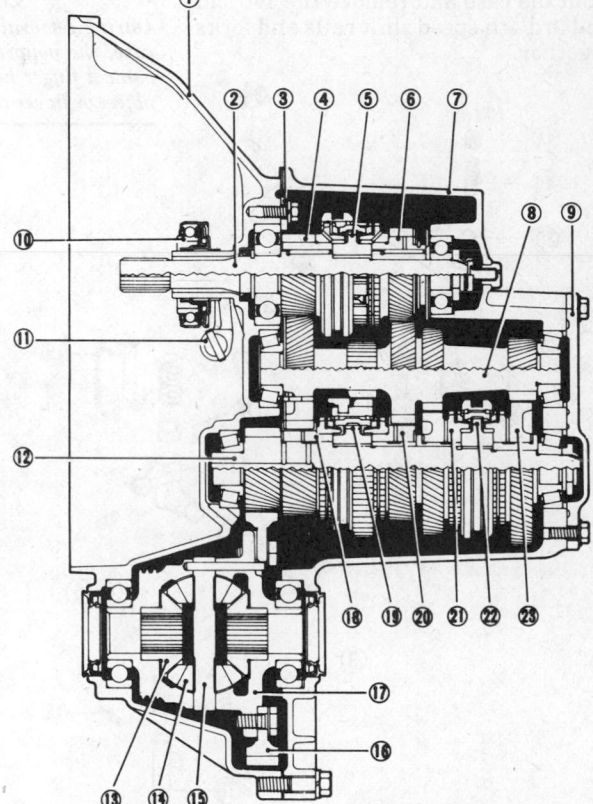

Cross section of model KM 165 transaxle (twin-stick)

1. Clutch housing	14. Differential pinion
2. Input shaft	15. Pinion shaft
3. Bearing retainer	16. Differential drive gear
4. Input low gear	17. Differential case
5. Synchronizer assembly	18. 4th speed gear
6. Input high gear	19. 3rd and 4th speed
7. Transaxle case	synchronizer assembly
8. Intermediate gear	20. 3rd speed gear
9. Rear cover	21. 2nd speed gear
10. Clutch release bearing	22. 1st and 2nd speed
11. Clutch release fork	synchronizer assembly
12. Output shaft	23. 1st speed gear
13. Differential side gear	

NOTE: The reverse idler shaft sometimes will come off with the removal of the transaxle case.

9. Remove the reverse shift lever assembly.

10. Remove the reverse shift rail and the 3rd/4th speed shift rail spacer collar.

11. Using a pin punch and light hammer, remove the spring pins from the 1st/2nd and 3rd/4th speed shift forks.

—————— **CAUTION** ——————

Support the shift forks before attempting to remove the spring plugs.

—————————————————

12. Pull the 1st/2nd speed shift rail upward from the case, sliding the rail through the fork.

NOTE: The 1st/2nd speed shift rail and fork cannot be removed until after Step 13.

13. Pull the 3rd/4th speed shift rail from the case and remove the 1st/2nd and 3rd/4th speed shift rails and forks together.

14. Move the 3rd/4th speed synchronizer into the 4th speed position and remove the output shaft assembly.

15. Remove the differential assembly from the case.

16. KM 165/166 models—Remove the plug, poppet and spring for the two-speed shift rail and fork.

17. Remove the bolts from the input input shaft bearing retainer and remove the input shaft assembly.

18. KM 165/166 models—Remove the shift rail and fork, along with the intermediate shaft assembly, when the input shaft is removed.

19. Remove the shift shaft spring retainer and pull out the spring pin with pliers.

20. Move the shift shaft towards the outside of the case by using a pin punch in the pin hole. Pull the shaft from the case and remove the control finger, two springs, spacer collar poppet spring and ball.

—————— **CAUTION** ——————

During removal of the shift shaft from the case, the poppet ball will jump out of the control finger hole. Close the hole with an object or finger tip to prevent loss of the ball.

21. Put an identifying mark on the tapered roller bearing outer race and remove it from the case.

22. Remove the lock and the speedometer driven gear assembly.

Input Shaft

DISASSEMBLY

KM 160/161

1. Remove the front bearing snapring and using a special puller, remove the front bearing from the input shaft.

2. Straighten the locking washer and remove the locknut at the rear of the input shaft.

3. Using a press or a special puller, remove the rear bearing from the shaft.

KM 165/166

1. Remove the front bearing snapring and remove the front bearing with a special puller.

2. Straighten the locking washer and remove the locknut at the rear of the input shaft.

3. Using a press and supporting the low gear of the input shaft, press on the rear of the input shaft and remove the input high gear, gear sleeve, synchronizer assembly, input low gear and the rear bearing.

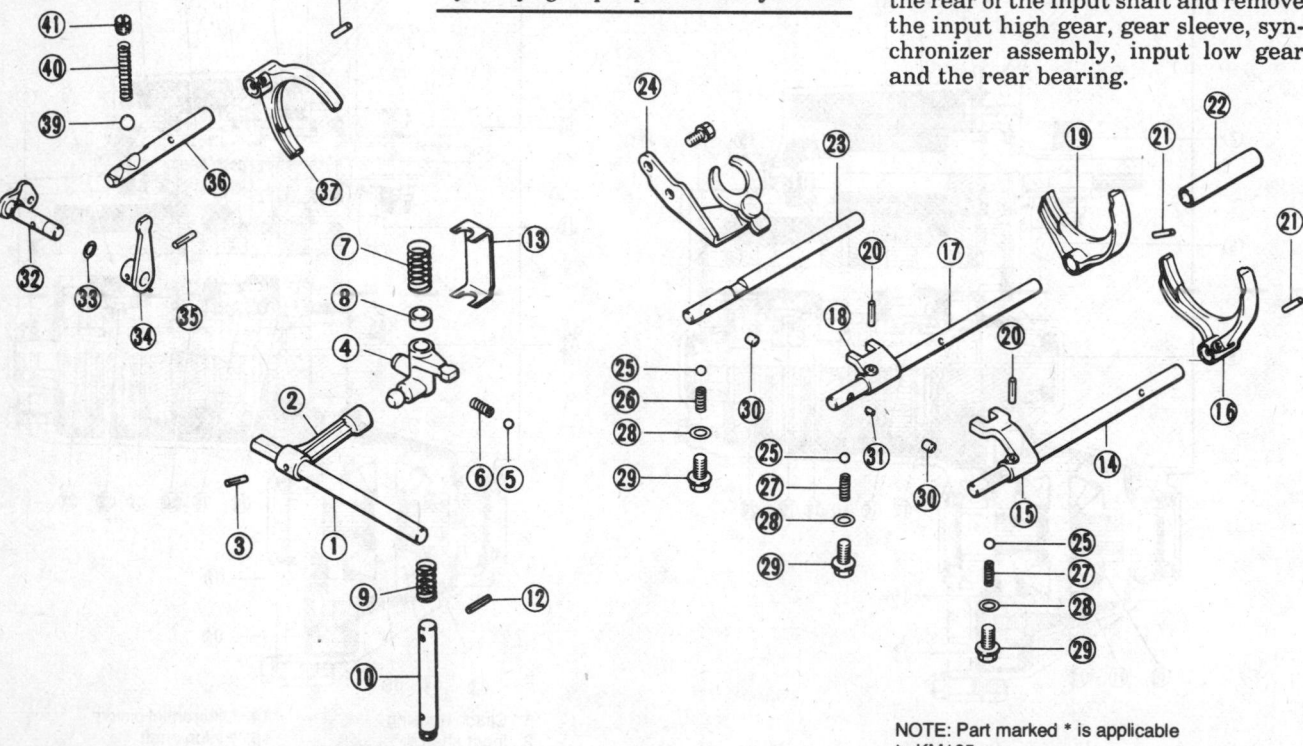

NOTE: Part marked * is applicable to KM165.

1. Control shaft	9. Reverse restrict spring	18. Shift lug	26. Reverse spring
2. Control lug	10. Shift shaft	19. Shift fork	[Length; 16.6 mm (.65 in.)]
3. Lock pin	11. O-ring	20. Lock pin	27. Spring
4. Control finger	12. Spring pin	21. Spring pin	[Length; 18.9 mm (.74 in.)]
5. Steel ball	13. Spring retainer	22. Spacer collar	28. Gasket
6. Spring	14. 1st and 2nd speed shift rail	23. Reverse shift rail	29. Plug
[Length; 18.9 mm (.74 in.)]	15. Shift lug	24. Reverse shift lever	30. Interlock plunger A
7. Neutral return spring	16. Shift fork	assembly	31. Interlock plunger B
8. Spacer collar	17. 3rd and 4th speed shift rail	25. Steel ball	*32. Selector shaft

*33. O-ring
*34. Selector finger
*35. Lock pin
*36. Shift rail
*37. Shift fork
*38. Lock pin
*39. Steel ball
*40. Spring
*41. Plug

Exploded view of shift mechanism

NOTE: To remove the rear bearing only, use a special puller. The input high gear will come off with the rear bearing.

ASSEMBLY
KM 160/161

1. Install the front bearing on the input shaft, using a bearing installer tool.

2. Install the front bearing selective snap-ring into the snap-ring groove.

3. Install a spacer to the rear of the input shaft, with the stepped side towards the rear bearing.

4. Install the rear bearing on the input shaft, using a bearing installer tool.

5. Install the locknut to the end of the input shaft and tighten to 66–79 ft. lbs. (89–107 Nm). Stake the locknut into the notch of the input shaft only. Lock the lock plate, if reused.

———— CAUTION ————
The shaft end will interfere with the breather if it is deformed by staking, resulting in breakage.

KM 165/166

1. Install the front bearing on the input shaft using a bearing installer.

2. Install the front bearing selective snap-ring into the snap-ring groove.

3. Install the synchronizer hub with the .16 inch (4mm) diameter slot in the oil groove, facing the clutch or engine side.

4. The synchronizer sleeve must be installed with the 30° chamfer on the clutch or engine side.

NOTE: The opposite side of the synchronizer sleeve is machined at a 45° angle.

5. Install the synchronizer spring with its stepped part positioned on the synchronizer key. Alternate the stepped parts of the front and rear springs to avoid having the stepped parts on the same key.

6. Install the sub-gear to the input high gear and lubricate the entire surface.

7. Install the cone spring and install a new snap-ring, making sure the inner side of the cone spring is not in the snap-ring groove.

8. Install the input low gear and the needle bearing on the input shaft.

9. Install the synchronizer ring.

10. Using a special installer tool, press-fit the synchronizer assembly onto the input shaft with the synchronizer key correctly aligned with the synchronizer ring keyway.

11. Install the input high gear sleeve with a special installer tool.

The input low gear should rotate smoothly. Install the synchronizer ring, the input high gear and needle bearing.

12. Install the spacer with the stepped side facing the rear bearing side.

13. Install the rear bearing with a special installer tool.

14. Install and tighten the input shaft rear nut to 66–79 ft. lbs. (89–107 Nm.) and stake in place into the notch on the input shaft. Should the lockplate be reused, bend the plate over a shoulder of the locknut.

Output Shaft
DISASSEMBLY

1. Unlock the rear locknut plate and remove the locknut from the shaft.

2. Remove the front and rear tapered bearings from the output shaft, using special bearing puller tools.

3. Using a puller tool, remove the 1st speed gear, gear sleeve, 1st and 2nd speed synchronizer assembly and the 2nd speed gear.

4. Remove the 2nd speed gear sleeve, 3rd speed gear, 3rd speed gear sleeve, 3rd/4th speed synchronizer assembly and the 4th speed gear.

ASSEMBLY

1. Assemble the synchronizers in the following manner.

   a. 3rd/4th synchronizer: Position the sleeve over the hub with the fork groove on the same side as the 0.160 inch (4mm) oil groove on the hub.

   b. 1st/2nd synchronizer: Position the sleeve over the hub with the 30° chamfer on the same side as the 0.160 inch (4mm) oil groove on the hub.

   c. Install the synchronizer springs into the 3rd/4th and 1st/2nd synchronizer unit with the stepped part of the springs on the synchronizer key.

NOTE: Do not have the stepped part of the front and rear springs on the same key. Alternate between keys.

2. Install the 4th speed gear onto the output shaft and install the synchronizer ring.

NOTE: Lubricate the contact surfaces with gear oil.

3. Press the 3rd/4th synchronizer unit to the output shaft with the oil grooves on the hub and the fork groove in the sleeve facing towards the clutch (engine) side. Align the synchronizer ring keyway with the synchronizer ring key. After the in-

stallation, be sure the 4th speed gear rotates freely.

4. Install the 3rd speed gear sleeve pressing into place. Install the 3rd speed gear assembly.

5. Install the 2nd speed gear sleeve by pressing into place. Be sure the 3rd speed gear rotates freely.

6. Install the 2nd speed gear and the 1st/2nd synchronizer ring.

7. Install the 1st/2nd speed synchronizer assembly onto the output shaft by pressing with the proper tools. Be sure the 2nd speed gear rotates freely.

8. Install the 1st/2nd synchronizer ring. Press the 1st/2nd speed synchronizer assembly into place on the output shaft. Be sure the 2nd speed gear rotates freely.

9. Install the 1st/2nd speed synchronizer ring with the keyways properly aligned with the keys.

10. Install 1st gear to the gear sleeve and press the unit onto the output shaft. Be sure the 1st speed gear rotates freely.

11. Install the front and rear tapered bearings on the front and the rear of the shaft.

12. Install the locknut on the rear of the shaft and torque to 66–79 ft. lbs. (89–107 Nm). Lock the locking plate to the nut, if used. Stake the locknut securely to the output shaft.

Intermediate Shaft
DISASSEMBLY

1. Remove the front tapered bearing with a press unit.

2. Remove the sub-gear and the spring assembly.

ASSEMBLY

1. Assemble the sub-gear spring assembly to the intermediate shaft gear with the longer end of the spring fitted to the 0.160 in. (4mm) diameter hole in the sub-gear.

2. Install the sub-gear and insert the remaining end of the sub-gear spring into the smallest hole in the sub-gear, 0.160 in. (4mm).

3. Install the front and rear tapered roller bearings on the shaft with a press tool.

Speedometer Driven Gear

NOTE: The speedometer driven gear assembly cannot be removed without disassembly of the transaxle.

DISASSEMBLY

1. Using a pin punch, remove the spring pin from the sleeve and driven gear shaft.

2. Separate the driven gear from the sleeve and remove the O-rings.

ASSEMBLY

1. Install new O-rings and lubricate the driven gearshaft.
2. Insert the driven gearshaft into the sleeve.
3. Align the sleeve hole with the pin slot in the driven gear.
4. Install the spring pin in such a manner so as not to contact the gearshaft with the slit in the spring pin.

Control Shaft or Control Lug

REMOVAL

1. A centering hole is located on a 16mm boss, on the engine side of the lower part of the clutch housing.
2. Drill through the centering hole with a drill with a diameter of .470 in. (12mm).
3. Remove the lock pin from the control shaft and lug.

INSTALLATION

1. Install the control shaft and lug. Install a new lock pin through the control lug and shaft.
2. Install a 0.470 in. (12mm) cup plug in the drilled hole and seal the plug with a bonding sealant.

Differential

The overhaul of the differential assembly is confined to the replacement of the side bearings, ring gear and the differential and pinion gears. The replacement is done in the conventional manner. Necessary measurements during the assembly are given in the transaxle assembly procedures.

ASSEMBLY OF TRANSAXLE

NOTE: Lubricate all seals and O-rings during the assembly.

1. Prepare the transaxle case for component assembly by replacing all oil seals and case internal small parts that were removed during the disassembly.
2. Install the speedometer driven gear assembly into the clutch housing. Install the locking plate into the groove cut into the sleeve.
3. Model KM 165/166—Install an O-ring onto the selector shaft and lubricate the ring and the bore in the case. Install the shaft into the case and install the selector finger. Install the lock pin so that it is flush on the clutch housing side of the selector finger.
4. Install the poppet spring and steel ball into the control finger and with the use of a special tool, force the poppet ball into its bore. Leave the tool in position.

5. Install a new O-ring onto the shift shaft and install the shaft into the clutch housing and engage the reverse restrict spring and the control finger.
6. Press the shift shaft inward until the special tool, used to hold the poppet ball and spring, is forced out. Recover and lay aside. Install the spacer collar and the neutral return spring and force the shift shaft to its bore in the opposite side of the case opening.
7. Align the spring pin holes and install the spring pins.
8. Install the spring retainer in place over the control finger assembly.
9. Install the differential gear assembly into the clutch housing. Adjust the differential case end-play as follows:

Inch	MM	I.D. Mark
0.0516	1.31	E
0.0551	1.40	None
0.0587	1.49	C
0.0622	1.58	B
0.0657	1.67	A
0.0693	1.76	F

a. Place two pieces of plastic type gauge material, approximately ¾ inch in length, on the differential ball bearing outer race, 180° apart.

b. Install the transaxle case and gasket. Tighten the mounting bolts to 26–30 ft. lbs. (35–41 Nm). Remove the bolts and the transaxle case. Lay the case aside for later installation.

c. Measure the thickness of the plastic type gauge material and select a spacer of the proper thickness to provide the standard end-play. The end-play should range between 0.000–0.0059 in. (0.0–0.15mm).

d. Spacer thicknesses are as follows:

10. Turn the sub-gear in the direction of the embossed arrow to align the .310 in. (8mm) hole in the intermediate gear with that in the sub-gear. Insert a bar or bolt in the holes to maintain alignment.
11. Install the input shaft assembly and the intermediate shaft assembly into the clutch housing as a unit.

NOTE: KM 165/166 models-Install the selector shift rail and fork assembly at the same time.

12. Install the selector shaft poppet ball, poppet spring and plug. Apply sealer to the plug and seat it flush with the housing surface.

13. Install the input shaft bearing retainer and remove the bar or bolt used to retain the alignment of the sub-gear to the intermediate gear.
14. Install the output shaft assembly.
15. Install the interlock plungers into the housing. Reassemble the 1st/2nd and 3rd/4th speed shift rails and forks in the reverse order of removal, into the housing.
16. Align the holes in the shift rail and the shift fork and install the pin. The pin must have its slit on the shift rail center line. Even the spring pin protrusion on both sides.
17. Install the reverse shift rail and install the three poppet balls, springs and plugs.

NOTE: The poppet spring with the white paint I.D. must be installed in the poppet hole of the reverse shift rail. Install the small diameter ends of the springs towards the steel balls.

18. Install the reverse shift lever assembly, the reverse idler gear and shaft and apply lubricant to the gear and shaft.
19. Measure the height of the reverse idler gear. The height from the face of the case to the upper flat of the gear should be 1.4429–1.5374 in. (37.85 ± 1.2mm). If less than specified, replace the reverse shift lever assembly.
20. Apply sealer to the gasket and install onto the clutch housing.
21. Install the selected spacer on the differential side bearing and install the transaxle case. Install the bolts and torque to 26–30 ft. lbs. (35–41 Nm).
22. Install the intermediate and output shaft rear tapered bearing outer races and press them in by hand.
23. Install the oil seal into the axle output shaft case hole, if not previously done.

NOTE: The oil seal hole must be chamfered before the seal is installed into the case, to prevent periphery damage to the seal and subsequent leakage.

24. To select the outer race end spacer, use the following procedure:

a. Seat the outer races properly and measure the depths of the transaxle case to the races, using a depth micrometer.

b. Select a spacer for each race 0.004 in. (0.4mm) thicker than the measured value.

c. Install the spacers in their respective bores and install the rear cover. Torque the bolts to 14–16 ft. lbs. (19–22 Nm).

d. Using the special tool seal installer or equivalent, shift the transaxle to any desired gear, while rotating the input shaft.

NOTE: The input shaft may turn hard and the installation of the clutch plate may be necessary to assist in turning the shaft.

e. Remove the rear cover after setting the transaxle in a position with the rear cover up.

f. Remove the spacers and re-measure the depth as was done in Step a.

Inch	MN	I.D. Mark
.0724	1.84	84
.0736	1.87	87
.0748	1.90	90
.0760	1.93	93
.0772	1.96	96
.0783	1.99	99
.0795	2.02	02
.0807	2.05	05
.0819	2.08	08
.0831	2.11	11
.0843	2.14	14
.0854	2.17	17
.0866	2.20	20
.0878	2.23	23
.0890	2.26	26
.0902	2.29	29
.0913	2.32	32
.0925	2.35	35
.0937	2.38	38
.0949	2.41	41
.0961	2.44	44
.0972	2.47	47
.0984	2.50	50
.0996	2.53	53
.1008	2.56	56
.1020	2.59	59
.1031	2.62	62
.1043	2.65	65
.1055	2.68	68

g. Reselect spacers of proper thicknes so that an end-play of 0.000–0.0020 in. (0.0–0.05mm) exists at the tapered roller bearing outer races.

h. Spacer thicknesses are as follows:

25. Apply sealer to the gasket and reinstall the rear cover. Torque the bolts to 14–16 ft. lbs. (19–22 Nm).

26. Install the back-up lamp switch with washer and steel ball in place.

27. Verify that the transaxle shifts and the internal gear rotate smoothly.

TYPE 4

5 Speed Transaxle Model KM 162, 163

Chrysler Corp./ Hyundai/Mitsubishi

Input, Intermediate Shafts and Select Shift Forks

DISASSEMBLY

1. Remove the transaxle mounting bracket.

2. Remove the two select actuator mounting bolts for 5-speed M/T only or clutch cable bracket for 4 x 2 speed M/T only.

3. Remove the clamp for harness of select switch (5-speed M/T only) and back-up light switch.

4. Remove the back-up light switch and the steel ball.

5. Remove the select switch (5-speed M/T only).

6. Pull the select actuator to remove the rod and shift rail connection from transaxle (5-speed M/T only).

7. Remove the snap-ring and pin, and then remove the select actuator (5-speed M/T only).

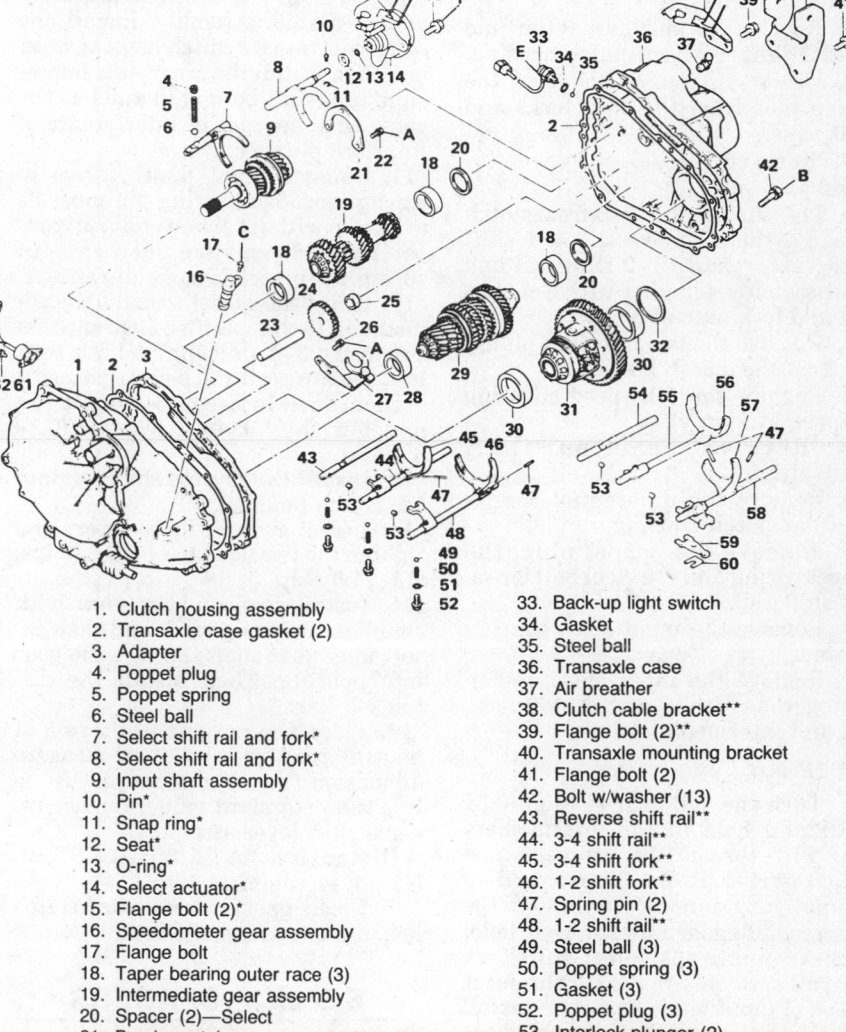

1. Clutch housing assembly
2. Transaxle case gasket (2)
3. Adapter
4. Poppet plug
5. Poppet spring
6. Steel ball
7. Select shift rail and fork*
8. Select shift rail and fork*
9. Input shaft assembly
10. Pin*
11. Snap ring*
12. Seat*
13. O-ring*
14. Select actuator*
15. Flange bolt (2)*
16. Speedometer gear assembly
17. Flange bolt
18. Taper bearing outer race (3)
19. Intermediate gear assembly
20. Spacer (2)—Select
21. Bearing retainer
22. Bolt w/washer (2)
23. Reverse idler gear shaft
24. Reverse idler gear
25. Distance collar
26. Bolt w/washer (2)
27. Reverse shift lever assembly
28. Taper bearing outer race
29. Output shaft assembly
30. Taper bearing outer race (2)
31. Differential assembly
32. Spacer—Select
33. Back-up light switch
34. Gasket
35. Steel ball
36. Transaxle case
37. Air breather
38. Clutch cable bracket**
39. Flange bolt (2)**
40. Transaxle mounting bracket
41. Flange bolt (2)
42. Bolt w/washer (13)
43. Reverse shift rail**
44. 3-4 shift rail**
45. 3-4 shift fork**
46. 1-2 shift fork**
47. Spring pin (2)
48. 1-2 shift rail**
49. Steel ball (3)
50. Poppet spring (3)
51. Gasket (3)
52. Poppet plug (3)
53. Interlock plunger (2)
54. Reverse shift rail*
55. 1-2 shift rail*
56. 1-2 shift fork*
57. 3-4-5 shift fork*
58. 3-4-5 shift rail*
59. 5th speed shift lug*
60. Selector spacer*
61. Select switch*
62. Bolt w/washer (2)*

NOTE: * 5-speed MT/T only
   ** 4 × 2-speed only

Exploded view of KM 163 Transaxle

8. Remove the speedometer gear assembly locking bolt.

9. Pull the speedometer gear assembly from the clutch housing.

10. Remove the transaxle-to-clutch housing tightening bolt.

11. Remove the transaxle case and gasket.

12. Remove the adapter and gasket.

13. Remove the spacer for differential end play adjustment.

14. Remove the three poppet plugs and gasket, and then three poppet springs and steel balls.

15. Pull the reverse idler gear shaft and remove reverse idler gear.

16. Remove the reverse shift lever from clutch housing.

17. Remove the distance collar and reverse shift rail from clutch housing.

18. Use a pin punch to drive the spring pins from the shift forks and shift rails.

19. Remove the select spacer (5-speed M/T only).

20. Pull the 1-2 shift rail from clutch housing, then remove the 3–4 shift rail. Next, remove 1–2 shift rail and fork assembly, together with 3–4 shift rail and fork assembly.

21. Remove the two interlock plungers from the clutch housing.

22. Remove the 5th speed shift lug (5-speed M/T only).

23. Remove the output shaft assembly.

24. Remove the differential assembly from clutch housing.

25. Remove the poppet plug, the poppet spring and the steel ball for select shift rail.

26. Remove the input shaft bearing retainer.

27. Remove the input shaft assembly together with the select shift fork, rail and intermediate shaft.

ASSEMBLY

1. Turn the sub gear to align 0.31 in. (8mm) hole in the intermediate gear with that in the sub gear, and then insert 0.31 in. (8mm) 1.38 in (3.5mm) long dummy pin through the intermediate gear into sub gear hole.

2. Assemble the select shift fork and rail assembly to the synchronizer sleeve of input shaft, and then install these components and intermediate shaft as a unit.

3. Install the front bearing retainer and tighten the three bolts to 11–15.5 ft. lbs. (15–21.5 Nm).

4. Install select shaft poppet ball, poppet spring and plug. Plug must be turned until its end is flush with housing surface. Apply sealant to periphery of plug head.

5. Install the differential assembly to the clutch housing.

6. Install the output shaft assembly.

7. Make sure that the gears are meshed properly, and then remove dummy pin from the sub gear and intermediate gear.

8. Install 5th speed shift lug to pin on the clutch housing. (5-speed M/T only).

― CAUTION ―

Pay attention to the direction of installation. If the shift lug is installed the wrong way, hard shifting may result.

9. Insert the two interlock plungers into the holes in the clutch housing.

10. Install 1–2 shift rail assembly together with 3–4 shift rail assembly or 3–4–5 shift assembly. Install one shift rails into its clutch housing hole, and then install the other. It is impossible to install both shift rails at the same time because of interference of interlock plunger.

11. Using a blunt punch, drive in spring pins. This spring pin must be driven in with its slit on shift rail center line. Make sure both ends of spring pin protrude same distance.

12. Select the spacer to make the adjustment to the specified clearance between the 3–4 shift lug and 5th shift lug. Then install the select spacer.

Clearance between 3–4 shift lug and 5th shift 0.004–0.020 in. (0.1–0.5mm).

13. Install the reverse shift rail into the clutch housing.

14. Install reverse shift lever, and tighten the two bolts to 11–15.5 ft. lbs. (15–21.5 Nm).

15. Install reverse idler gear with chamfered side upward, and then insert idler gear shaft through the gear into housing. Then install the distance collar.

16. Place the reverse shift rail in neutral position, and then measure dimension "A". If dimension "A" is less than standard value, replace reverse shift lever assembly.

Dimension "A" 1.657–1.751 in. (42.08–44.48mm).

17. Clean gasket surfaces of clutch housing and transaxle case.

SELECT SPACERS

Thickness in. (mm)	Ident. mark
.024 (0.6)	G
.035 (0.9)	F
.047 (1.2)	E
.059 (1.5)	D
.071 (1.8)	C
.083 (2.1)	B
.094 (2.4)	A
.106 (2.7)	None

18. Adjust the output shaft, intermediate shaft and differential case end play or preload as follows:

19. Remove the outer races of output shaft and intermediate shaft bearings from transaxle case.

20. Place 2 pieces of solder, about 4 in. (10mm)–long on outer race of transaxle case.

21. Insert outer races to transaxle case. Securely install the outer race so as not to move the solder.

22. Place 2 pieces of solder, about .79 in. (20mm) long, on ball bearing outer race.

23. Place the new transaxle case gasket and the adapter on the clutch housing.

24. Install the new gasket and transaxle case assembly on the clutch housing, and tighten 13 bolts to 26–30 ft. lbs. (35–41 Nm).

25. Remove bolts and remove transaxle case.

26. Measure thickness of crushed solder with micrometer. Select a spacer of proper thickness to ensure standard end play.

Differential case end play 0–.006 in. (0–0.15mm).

SPACERS FOR DIFFERENTIAL

Thickness in. (mm)	Ident. mark
.0516 (1.31)	E
.0551 (1.40)	None
.0587 (1.49)	C
.0622 (1.58)	B
.0657 (1.67)	A
.0693 (1.76)	F

27. Remove both taper bearing outer races from the transaxle case.

― CAUTION ―

Before installing the outer race of bearing to intermediate and output shaft, make sure that it is installed to proper parts. If the outer race is installed to other parts, the end play and preload cannot be adjusted properly.

28. Remove solder pieces from case and measure the thickness of the crushed solder with a micrometer. Select a spacer of proper thickness to ensure standard end play or preload.

Intermediate gear end play 0–.0020 in. (0–0.05mm)

Output shaft preload .0059–.0079 in. (0.15–0.20mm)

29. Install spacers, selected in accordance with step 28, to the transaxle case, and then install taper roller bearing outer races to the transaxle case.

30. Place spacer, selected in accordance with step 26, on the differential

ball bearing outer races to the transaxle case.

31. Apply sealant to both sides of new transaxle case gasket, and then place gasket on the clutch housing. Apply drying sealant to clutch housing side of gasket and apply non-drying sealant to adapter side.

CAUTION

Do not apply drying sealant to both sides of transaxle case gasket.

---

32. Install the adapter.
33. Apply sealant to both sides of new gasket, and then place gasket on the adapter. Apply drying sealant to adapter side of gasket and apply non-drying sealant to case side.
34. Install the transaxle case assembly on the clutch housing and tighten 13 bolts to 35–41 Nm (26–30 ft. lbs).
35. With Special Tool MD998324 or equivalent, attached to control shaft, verify that control shifts smoothly.
36. Install the speedometer gear assembly into the clutch housing and tighten the flange bolt.
37. Connect the select actuator rod to the select shift rail and insert the pin. Then install the snap-ring onto the pin.—5-speed MTX only.
38. Tighten the actuator mounting bolts to the specified torque—5-speed MTX only.
39. When installing the select switch, assure that the transaxle is in Neutral, then align the mating marks. Tighten the bolts securely—5-speed MTX only.
40. Install the steel ball and the back-up light switch.
41. Install the transaxle mounting bracket and clutch cable bracket for 4x2-speed MTX.

Input Shaft

DISASSEMBLY

1. Clamp the input shaft in a vise with lock nut side up (protect input shaft splines from vise jaws).
2. Remove the staking from the locking nut lock with a blunt punch, then remove the locking nut.
3. Remove the front bearing snap-ring with snap-ring pliers.
4. With the front bearing supported, press the input shaft and remove the front bearing.
5. With the input low gear supported on a press base, press the input shaft down to remove rear bearing, oil slinger, gears and synchronizer.

INSPECTION

1. Check the splines for wear or damage; replace if necessary.
2. Check the gears for wear or damage; replace if necessary.

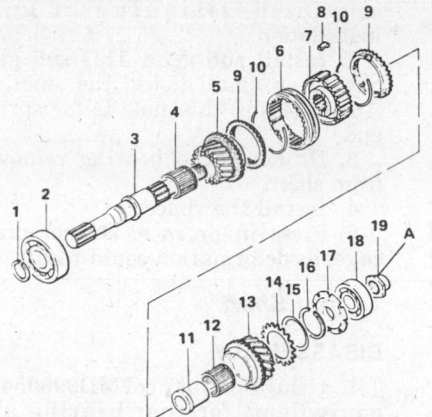

1. Snap ring
2. Front bearing
3. Input shaft
4. Needle bearing
5. Input low gear
6. Synchronizer sleeve
7. Synchronizer hub
8. Synchronizer key (3)
9. Synchronizer ring (2)
10. Synchronizer springs (2)
11. Gear sleeve
12. Needle bearing
13. Input high gear
14. Sub gear
15. Cone spring
16. Snap ring
17. Oil slinger
18. Rear bearing
19. Locking nut

Input shaft components, KM 163 models

RANGE OF SPACERS

Thickness in. (mm)	Identification mark
.0724 (1.84)	84
.0736 (1.87)	87
.0748 (1.90)	90
.0760 (1.93)	93
.0772 (1.96)	96
.0783 (1.99)	99
.0795 (2.02)	02
.0807 (2.05)	05
.0819 (2.08)	08
.0831 (2.11)	11
.0843 (2.14)	14
.0854 (2.17)	17
.0866 (2.20)	20
.0878 (2.23)	23
.0890 (2.26)	26
.0902 (2.29)	29
.0913 (2.32)	32
.0925 (2.35)	35
.0937 (2.38)	38
.0949 (2.41)	41
.0961 (2.44)	44
.0972 (2.47)	47
.0984 (2.50)	50
.0996 (2.53)	53
.1008 (2.56)	56
.1020 (2.59)	59
.1031 (2.62)	62
.1043 (2.65)	65
.1055 (2.68)	68

3. Check the bearings for noise or damage; replace if necessary.

ASSEMBLY

1. Assemble the synchronizer hub and sleeve. Make sure the hub and sleeve slide smoothly.
2. Insert the three synchronizer keys into grooves of hub.

3. Install the two synchronizer springs, and make sure that they are installed in opposite directions.
4. Install sub gear to input high gear. Apply gear oil to entire surface of gear.
5. Install cone spring in direction.
6. Install new snap-ring. When installing, make sure inner side of cone spring is not in snap-ring groove.
7. Insert the needle bearing for input low gear to the input shaft.
8. Install the input low gear onto the input shaft.
9. Install the synchronizer ring onto the cone portion of input low gear.
10. Install the assembled synchronizer to input shaft, and then press synchronizer assembly onto input shaft.
11. Press input high gear sleeve onto the input shaft.
12. Install the needle bearing onto sleeve.
13. Install the synchronizer ring.
14. Install the assembled input high gear onto the needle bearing.
15. Install the oil slinger onto the input shaft.
16. Press rear bearing onto input shaft rear end.
17. Tighten input shaft rear end locking nut to specified torque and stake it. Stake locking nut only at notch of shaft. Shaft rear end deformed by staking will interfere with breather, resulting in breakage.
Tightening torque 66–79 ft. lbs. (89–107 Nm).
18. Install front bearing onto input shaft.
19. Install front bearing snap-ring. There are three types of snap-rings available which differ in thickness. Select the thickest snap-ring which fits in snap-ring groove. When installing snap-ring, be careful not to damage oil seal contacting surface of input shaft. Do not reuse used snap-ring.

Intermediate Gear

DISASSEMBLY

1. Remove taper bearing inner race from intermediate gear.

Intermediate Shaft

REASSEMBLY

1. Install sub gear spring to intermediate shaft gear with longer leg [approximately .28 in. (7mm) fitted in .16 in. (4mm)] diameter hole in gear.

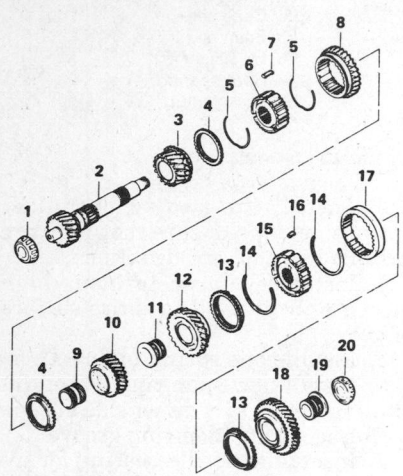

1. Taper roller bearing inner race
2. Output shaft
3. 4th speed gear
4. Synchronizer ring (2)
5. Synchronizer springs (2)
6. 3-4 Synchronizer hub
7. Synchronizer key (3)
8. Synchronizer sleeve
9. Gear sleeve
10. 3rd speed gear
11. Gear sleeve
12. 2nd speed gear
13. Synchronizer ring (2)
14. Synchronizer springs (2)
15. 1-2 Synchronizer hub
16. Synchronizer key (3)
17. 1-2 Synchronizer sleeve
18. 1st speed gear
19. Gear sleeve
20. Taper roller bearing inner race

Output shaft components, KM 163 models

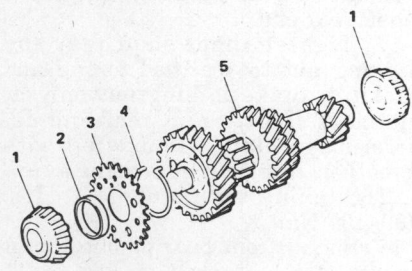

1. Taper roller bearing inner race (2)
2. Spacer
3. Sub gear
4. Spring
5. Intermediate gear

Intermediate gear components, KM 163 models

Two larger [.31 in. (8mm) dia.] holes are for positioning at gear installation.

2. Install sub gear. This sub gear has seven small holes; the smallest .16 in. (4mm) dia. hole is for spring end.

3. Do not reuse bearing removed from shaft.

4. Install the spacer.

5. Press inner race. Do not press cage, as deformation could result.

Output Shaft

DISASSEMBLY

1. Using Special Tool MD998354 or equivalent, for rear bearing and MD998359 or equivalent, for front bearing, remove taper bearing inner race from output shaft.

——— CAUTION ———
When MD998354 is used, it is important that tool is held securely with cylinder.

2. Holding 2nd speed gear, press rear end of shaft with press to remove 1st speed gear, gear sleeve, 1-2 synchronizer assembly and 2nd speed gear.

3. Holding 4th speed gear, press rear end of shaft with press to remove 2nd speed gear sleeve, 3rd speed gear, sleeve, 3-4 synchronizer assembly and 4th speed gear.

4. Special Tool MD998355 or equivalent, should be used to remove the gear according to the following steps.

   a. Holding 3rd speed gear in Special Tool MD998355, remove 2nd speed gear sleeve and 3rd speed gear.

   b. Holding 3-4 synchronizer ring in Gear Puller, remove 3rd speed gear sleeve and 3-04 synchronizer.

——— CAUTION ———
1. Step (a) must be done at first.
2. Step (b) never be done to remove the 3rd gear and 3-4 speed synchronizer at same time.

ASSEMBLY

1. Assemble the synchronizer hub and sleeve. Make sure the hub and sleeve slide smoothly.

2. Insert the three synchronizer keys into grooves of hub.

3. Install the two synchronizer springs, and make sure that they are installed in opposite directions.

4. Install the 4th speed gear onto the output shaft.

5. Install the synchronizer ring onto the cone portion of 4th speed gear.

6. Press 3-4 synchronizer onto output shaft. Make sure that the keyways of synchronizer ring are correct-

ly aligned with synchronizer keys. After installation of synchronizer, make certain that 4th speed gear rotates smoothly.

7. Press gear sleeve for 3rd speed gear onto output shaft.

8. Install the synchronizer ring onto the 3-4 synchronizer.

9. Install the 3rd speed gear onto the outer shaft.

10. Press gear sleeve for 2nd speed gear onto the output shaft.

11. Install the 2nd speed gear onto the outer shaft.

12. Install the synchronizer ring onto the cone portion of 2nd speed gear.

13. Press 1-2 synchronizer onto output shaft. Make sure that keyways of synchronizer rings are correctly aligned with synchronizer keys.

14. Install the synchronizer ring and 1st speed gear.

15. Insert the 1st speed gear sleeve onto the output shaft.

16. Using Special Tool MD998322 or equivalent for rear bearing and MD998318 or equivalent for front bearing, press taper roller bearing onto front and rear ends of output shaft. Be sure to set installer so that it will push only on bearing inner race.

Drive Gear

DISASSEMBLY

1. Remove the drive gear retaining bolts and remove the drive gear from differential case.

2. Remove the taper roller bearing inner race.

3. Drive out the lock pin with a punch inserted in hole "A".

4. Pull out the pinion shaft, and then remove the pinion gears and washers.

5. Remove the side gears and spacers.

ASSEMBLY

1. With spacers installed to back of differential side gears, install gears in differential case. If reusing removed parts, install them in original positions noted during disassembly. If using new differential side gears, install spacers of medium thickness.

2. Install washers to back of pinion gears and install gears in differential case, then insert pinion shaft.

3. Measure backlash between differential side gear and pinion. If specified backlash is not obtained, select spacers of proper size, disassemble and reassemble gears, and then adjust backlash. Backlash of both right and left gears must be equal.

4. Install pinion shaft lock pin. After installation, check to ensure that projection is less than 118 in. (3.mm).

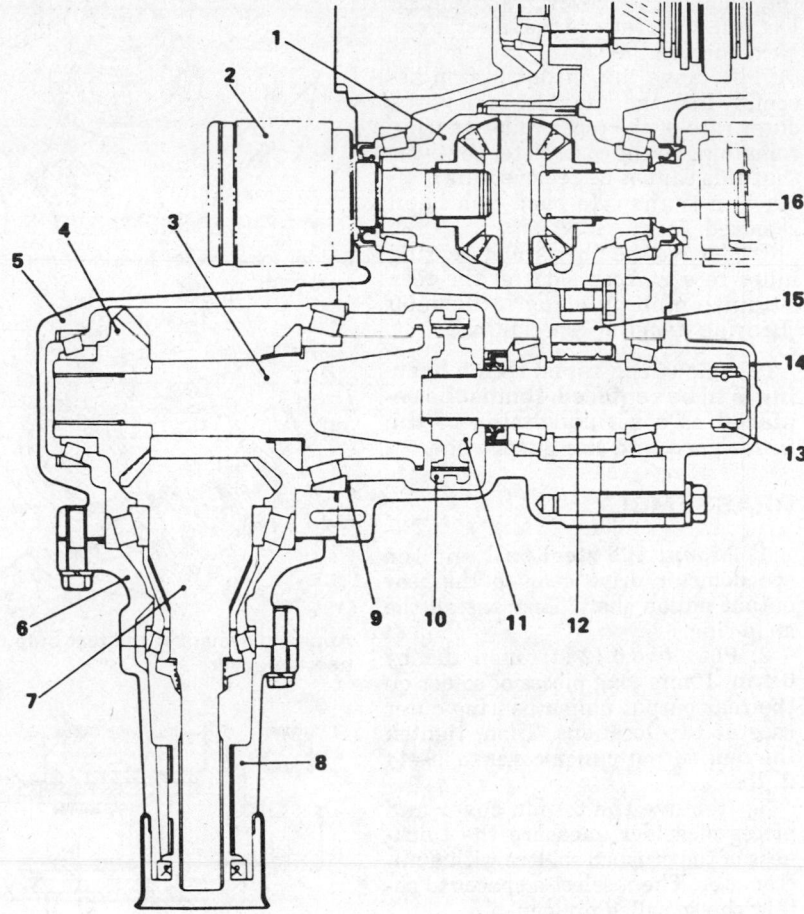

1. Front differential
2. Drive shaft (Left)
3. Rear output clutch shaft
4. Drive bevel gear
5. Transfer case
6. Driven bevel gear case
7. Driven bevel gear
8. Extension housing
9. Spacer (Selected)
10. Clutch sleeve
11. Clutch hub
12. Rear output pinion
13. Speedometer drive shaft
14. Rear output pinion cover
15. Differential drive gear
16. Drive shaft (Right)
17. Spring
18. Shift rail B
19. Select actuator
20. Shift rail A
21. Shift fork
22. Upper cover
23. 4WD switch

CAUTION

1. Lock pin must not be reused.
2. Lock pin not requiring installation load of more than 440 lbs. (1,960 N) must not be used.

5. Press Taper roller bearing inner races onto both ends of differential case. Apply load to inner race when pressing in bearings.
6. Install the drive gear onto the case.
7. Apply a small amount of ATF, and then a generous amount of thread lock cement to the ring gear retaining bolts. Then assemble quickly and tighten bolts to specified torque in sequence.
Tightening torque 94–101 ft. lbs. (128–137 Nm).

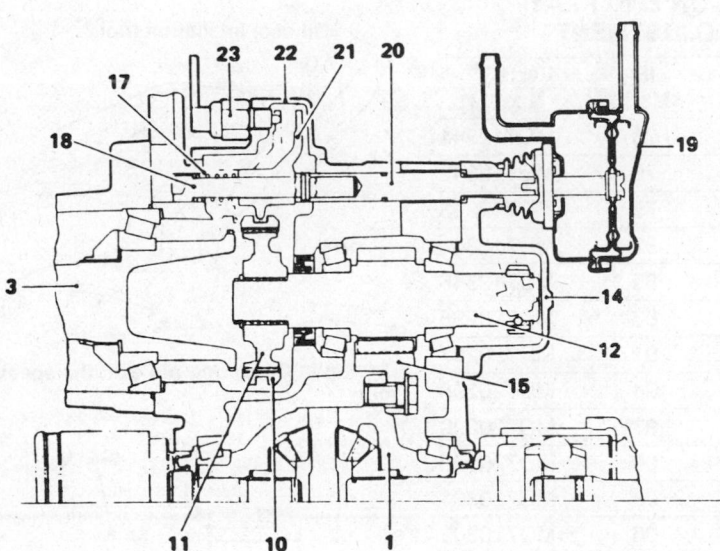

KM182 Transfer case section

TYPE 5

5 Speed Transaxle Model KM182 Chrysler Corp.

NOTE: The KM182 model designation if for the 5-speed transaxle and 4WD transfer case assembly. The transaxle section of this model is the same as the KM163 manual 5-speed, please refer to that section for overhaul procedures of the transaxle. The following procedures apply only to the transfer case section.

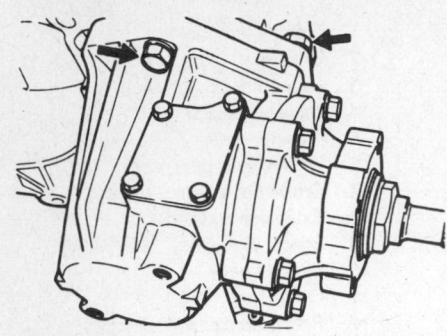

Removing the transfer case from the transaxle

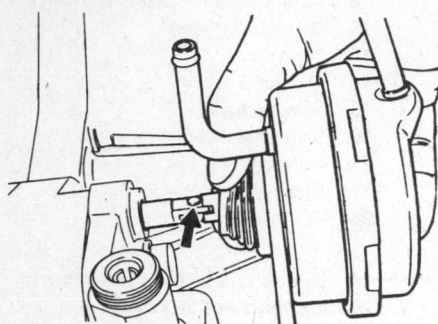

Removing the actuator

DISASSEMBLY

1. Remove the extension housing.
2. Remove the transfer case installation bolt, and then remove the transfer case assembly.
3. Remove the O-ring and spacer.
4. Remove the engage switch from the upper cover.
5. remove the upper cover.
6. Remove the select actuator installation bolt.
7. Pull the select actuator and move the collar toward the actuator, pull out the pin, and then remove the actuator from the shift rail.
8. Remove the speedometer gear assembly.
9. After removing the speedometer gear sleeve attaching bolt, remove the speedometer driven gear assembly from the rear output pinion cover.
10. Remove the rear output pinion cover to remove the spacer.
11. Remove the snap-ring, then, remove the speedometer drive gear and steel ball from the rear output pinion.
12. Using a punch, remove the spring pin of the shift rail for 2WD–4WD switching.
13. Remove the shift rail "A" toward the actuator side.
14. Remove the shift rail "B" toward the transfer case side, and then remove the shift fork.
15. Remove the snap-ring, and then remove the clutch hub and clutch sleeve from the rear output pinion side.

16. Remove the pin that connects the high/low select lever and the select rail, then remove the select lever. Next remove the boot.
17. Remove the output pinion assembly from the case. Also remove the outer race of the taper roller bearing remaining in the case. Note, however, that this cannot be removed until after the transaxle case has been removed.
18. Remove the taper roller bearing inner race at both sides of the rear output pinion by using MB990560 "Bearing Remover" special tool.

NOTE: If the taper roller bearing is to be replaced, it must be replaced as a set consisting of the inner race and the outer race.

REASSEMBLY

1. Mount the steel ball and the speedometer drive gear to the rear output pinion shaft. Then install the snap-ring.
2. Place two 0.12 in. (3mm) dia. by 0.4 in. 10mm long pieces of solder on the rear output pinion bearing outer race at two locations. Then, tighten the rear output pinion cover to 39–44 ft. lbs.
3. Remove the pinion cover and pieces of solder, measure the thickness of the crushed solders with a micrometer. Then, select a spacer to obtain the specified preload.

SPACER FOR REAR OUTPUT PINION END PLAY ADJUSTMENT

Thickness mm (in.)	ID Mark	Parts No.
1.73 (0.068)	73	MD712341
1.76 (0.069)	76	MD712342
1.79 (0.070)	79	MD712343
1.82 (0.072)	82	MD712344
1.85 (0.073)	85	MD712345
1.88 (0.074)	88	MD720296
1.91 (0.075)	91	MD720297
1.94 (0.076)	94	MD720298
1.97 (0.078)	97	MD720299
2.00 (0.079)	00	MD720300
2.03 (0.080)	03	MD720301
2.06 (0.081)	06	MD720302
2.09 (0.082)	09	MD720303
2.12 (0.083)	12	MD720304
2.15 (0.085)	15	MD720305
2.18 (0.086)	18	MD720306
2.21 (0.087)	21	MD720307
2.24 (0.088)	24	MD720308

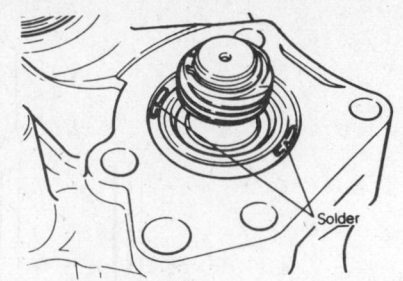

Solder location for bearing preload measurement

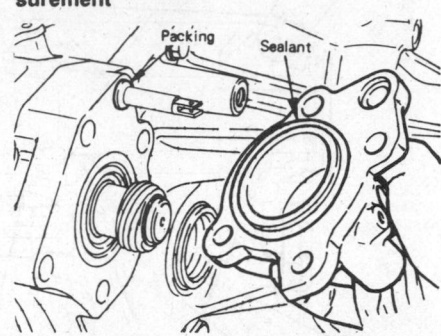

Applying sealant to the rear output shaft bearing cover

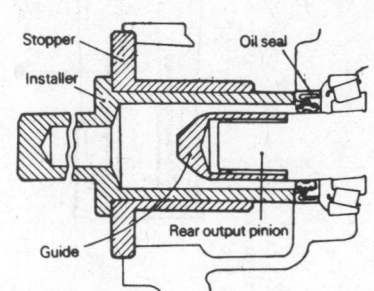

Oil seal installation tool

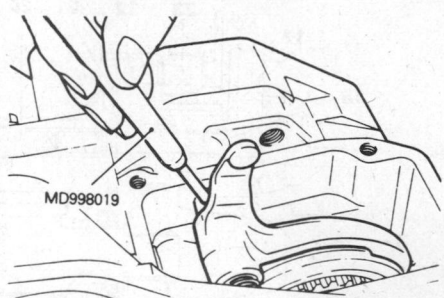

Driving in the spring pin with the special tool

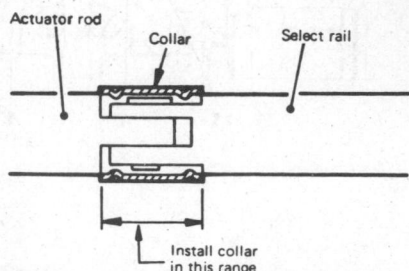

Actuator rod and select rail collar positioning

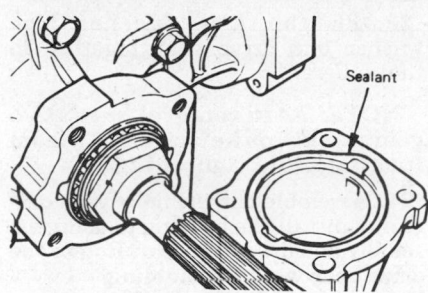

Applying sealant to the extension housing

4. Install the O-ring and packing on the shift rail "A", then install the rail into the transfer case.

5. Apply RTV silicone sealer to the rear output pinion cover gasket surface in the same way as with the transaxle case.

6. Attach the cover and tighten the bolts to 39–44 ft. lbs.

7. Using special tool MD998252 Oil Seal Installer, press the rear output pinion oil seal into the clutch housing using the following procedures:

   a. Insert the guide so that the rear output pinion spline doesn't get scarred.

   b. Using a plastic hammer, evenly tap in the oil seal through the stopper, to the installed tool.

8. Mount the clutch hub and sleeve on the rear output pinion shaft.

9. Install the snap-ring onto the shaft. The snap-ring to be used must be the thickest one which can fit in the snap-ring groove in the shaft.

10. Fit the shift fork in the clutch sleeve and insert the shift rail and spring into the case, then pass the shift rail through the shift fork.

11. With the pinion holes in the shift rail "A" and "B" aligned, drive a new spring pin into the hole using special tool MD998019 Lock Pin Installer. Ensure that the spring pin slit is at the right angle to the rail centerline.

NOTE: Always use a new spring pin.

12. Fit a new collar over the 4WD select actuator rod.

NOTE: Do not reuse the collar.

13. Connect the select actuator rod with shift rail "A" and insert the pin, facing its head upward.

14. Slide the collar to the collar to the position shown in the illustration.

15. Force the 4WD select actuator toward the transaxle case side and tighten the bolts.

16. Clean both surfaces of the clutch housing and the transfer case.

17. Place two 0.12 in. (3mm) dia. by 0.4 in. 10mm long pieces of solder on the clutch housing at two locations.

18. Mount the transfer case assembly and tighten the bolts to 39–44 ft. lbs.

19. Remove the transfer case assembly and measure the thickness of the crushed solders with a micrometer. Then, select a spacer to obtain .0059–.0079 in. (0.15–0.20mm) output clutch shaft end play.

20. Apply RTV silicone sealer to the outer perimeter of the clutch housing shift rail hole. Use only enough sealant to eliminate squeeze-out from shift rail hole when the transfer case is tightened.

21. Install the transfer case with the spacers and O-rings mounted and tighten the 7 bolts to 39–44 ft. lbs.

22. Apply sealant to the upper cover gasket and install it under the clutch housing.

23. Tighten the upper cover attaching 6–7 ft. lbs.

24. Mount the engage switch on the upper cover.

25. Install the oil level gauge.

26. Clean the gasket surfaces of both the transfer case and the extension housing.

27. Apply RTV silicone sealer to the gasket surface of the extension housing.

28. Mount the extension housing on the transfer case and tighten the bolts to 11–15 ft. lbs.

TYPE 6

4 and 5 Speed Transaxle Models F4WF60A, F5WF60A Datsun

DISASSEMBLY

1. Remove the reverse light switch and drain the transmission.

2. Remove the bearing housing and primary gear as a unit.

3. Remove the primary gear cover.

4. Take the bottom cover off the transmission. Put reverse and 1st gears into position (to keep the shaft from turning) and remove the main gear locknut.

5. Remove the primary gear cover.

6. Remove the clutch housing.

7. If necessary, drive out the drive and idler bearing with a puller. Then press the bearing out of the main drive input gear.

8. Remove the differential side flanges.

9. Remove the speedometer pinion gear.

10. Remove the differential case as a unit.

11. Pull the differential side bearings and remove the ring gear mounting bolts.

12. Remove the differential case and withdraw the pinion shaft and remove the side gear and pinion mate.

13. Loosen bolts D1 and D2 and remove the fork lever and bracket. Loosen double nuts E1 and bolts D3 and remove the bearing retainer.

NOTE: Double nuts E1 should be loosened before bolts D3.

14. Remove the reverse idler gear and shaft and drive out the countergear and countershaft guide.

NOTE: The needle bearing on countergear is not a retainer type. When removing the gear, do not allow the bearing to come off.

15. Remove the transmission case service plug. This will allow access to the roll pin on the 1st/2nd shift fork.

Using a punch, drive the roll pins out of the shift forks. Withdraw the fork rods and remove the shift forks.

NOTE: When driving out the roll pin from the 3rd/4th shift fork, shift the rod to 3rd gear before starting. Also be careful of the placement of the interlock plungers.

16. Remove the mainshaft gear assembly and the main drive gear toward the final drive gear side.

NOTE: The locknut is caulked, but you do not have to remove the caulking for loosening.

17. Remove the mainshaft components in this order: 3rd/4th synchronizer, 3rd gear, main gear bushing, main gear spacer, 2nd gear, main gear bushing, 1st/2nd synchronizer, 1st gear, main gear bushing and reverse gear.

NOTE: The 3rd main gear bushing and mainshaft are press fit. Remove the bushing with the main gear spacer and the 2nd main gear with a puller.

18. Press out the bearing from the mainshaft.

19. To disassemble a synchronizer, remove the spread springs and the shifting inserts, then separate the coupling sleeve from the synchro-hub.

ASSEMBLY

Generally, the procedures for assembly are the reverse of removal. However, there are certain steps you must observe.

1. Slide the synchro-hub into the coupling sleeve and fit the shifting inserts into their grooves.

2. Put one spread spring on the lower side of the shifting inserts to hold them to the inner side of the coupling sleeve. Put the other spread spring on the opposite side of the synchro-hub.

NOTE: Make sure the spread springs are opposite each other.

3. Press the ball bearing onto the mainshaft and assemble the reverse gear. Assemble the main gear bushing and 1st gear.

NOTE: Be sure to align the oil hole in the bushing with the one on the mainshaft.

4. Assemble baulk ring synchronizer, main gear bushing, baulk ring, 2nd gear, main gear spacer, main gear bushing, 3rd gear, baulk ring, synchronizer and locknut on the mainshaft.

5. Put the spacers and needles into both sides of the countergear. Be sure to grease the needles before inserting.

6. Insert a countershaft guide into the countergear.

7. Press the differential side bearing into the differential case.

8. Put the pinion mates, side gears, thrust washers and pinion shaft in the case.

9. Select the proper thrust washer to adjust side gear end-play to 0.008 in., then apply oil to the gear teeth and thrust surfaces.

10. Put the ring gear onto the differential case.

11. Press in the differential side flange oil seals after lubricating their lips with grease.

12. Assemble the main drive gear and mainshaft in the transmission case.

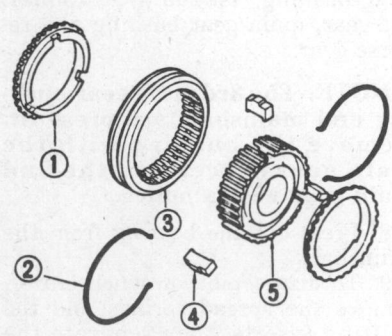

1. Baulk ring
2. Spread spring
3. Coupling sleeve
4. Shifting insert
5. Synchronizer hub

Exploded view of synchronizer unit

13. Put in the 1st/2nd shift fork and the 3rd/4th fork. Make sure they are into their grooves in the coupling sleeves.

14. Slide the 3rd/4th fork rod through the transmission case and the 3rd/4th shift fork. Secure it with a new retaining pin.

15. Assemble the check ball, spring and check ball plug. Before tightening, apply sealer to the plug. Be sure to align the notch in the 3rd/4th rod with the check ball. Place the unit in Neutral. Assemble the 1st/2nd and reverse fork rod similarly.

16. With the countershaft guide in place in the countergear, install the countergear, thrust washers and thrust spring on the transmission case. Insert the countershaft into the countergear and drive out the guide.

NOTE: Pay attention to the direction of thrust washer assembly. Align the cut out portion of the countershaft with the bearing retainer.

17. Assemble the reverse idler shaft, reverse idler gear, bearing retainer, reverse fork and fork bracket with the cutout portion of the reverse idler shaft aligned with the bearing retainer.

18. Before installing the differential case, measure bearing height "H".

If it is 4.720–4.730 in., a shim is not needed.

If it is 4.715–4.719 in., use a 0.0078 shim.

If it is 4.710–4.714 in., use a 0.0118 shim.

19. With the fork rods in Neutral, put the case cover onto the transmission.

NOTE: Make sure the shifter engages with the fork rod brackets correctly. If the resin-coating comes off the bolt threads, the bolt should not be reused.

20. Assemble the differential side flanges.

21. Put the clutch housing on the transmission case and press the bearings onto the primary and main drive input gears. Assemble the sub-gear on the idler gear.

a. Insert both ends of the ring spring into the 0.197 in. hole on the primary idler gear and sub-gear. Install the spacer and press the bearing onto the idler gear.

NOTE: Select a spacer that will insure that the sub-gear end-play is less than 0.004 in.

22. Put the idler gear into the clutch housing and assemble the main drive gear, setting the idler sub-gear by inserting a bar into the hole in the idler gear through the sub-gear.

23. Put the thrust washer, lock washer and drive gear together in that order.

NOTE: As in removal, mesh two gears to keep the mainshaft from turning while tightening.

24. Assemble the primary gear cover and install the bearing housing assembly and drive the gear. Rotate the drive gear while assembling.

25. Assemble the bottom cover, speedometer gear, reverse light switch, drain plug and service hole plug.

5-Speed Transaxle

Most of the procedures described in the 4-speed section apply to the 5-speed, with the following exceptions:

When removing the mainshaft and drive gear, you may have to tap the end of the mainshaft with a hammer.

When assembling the 3rd main gear bushing, make sure the claw is lined up with the main gear spacer and that the thinner spline tooth side of the 2nd/3rd synchro-hub must point towards 3rd gear.

When installing the main gear spacer, make sure that the uneven side is pointed toward 4th gear. The 4th gear bushing is the same as the 4-speed main gear bushing.

TYPE 7

4 and 5 Speed Transaxle Model RN4F30A, RS5F30A and RS5F31A Nissan/Datsun

TRANSMISSION CASE

Disassembly

1. Drain the oil from the transmission case.

2. Remove the mounting bolts, tap the case lightly with a rubber mallet and then lift off the transmission case.

NOTE: When removing the transmission case, tilt it slightly to prevent interference from the 5th gear shift fork.

3. Disconnect the back-up light switch and then remove the oil gutter.

4. Remove the input shaft bearing.

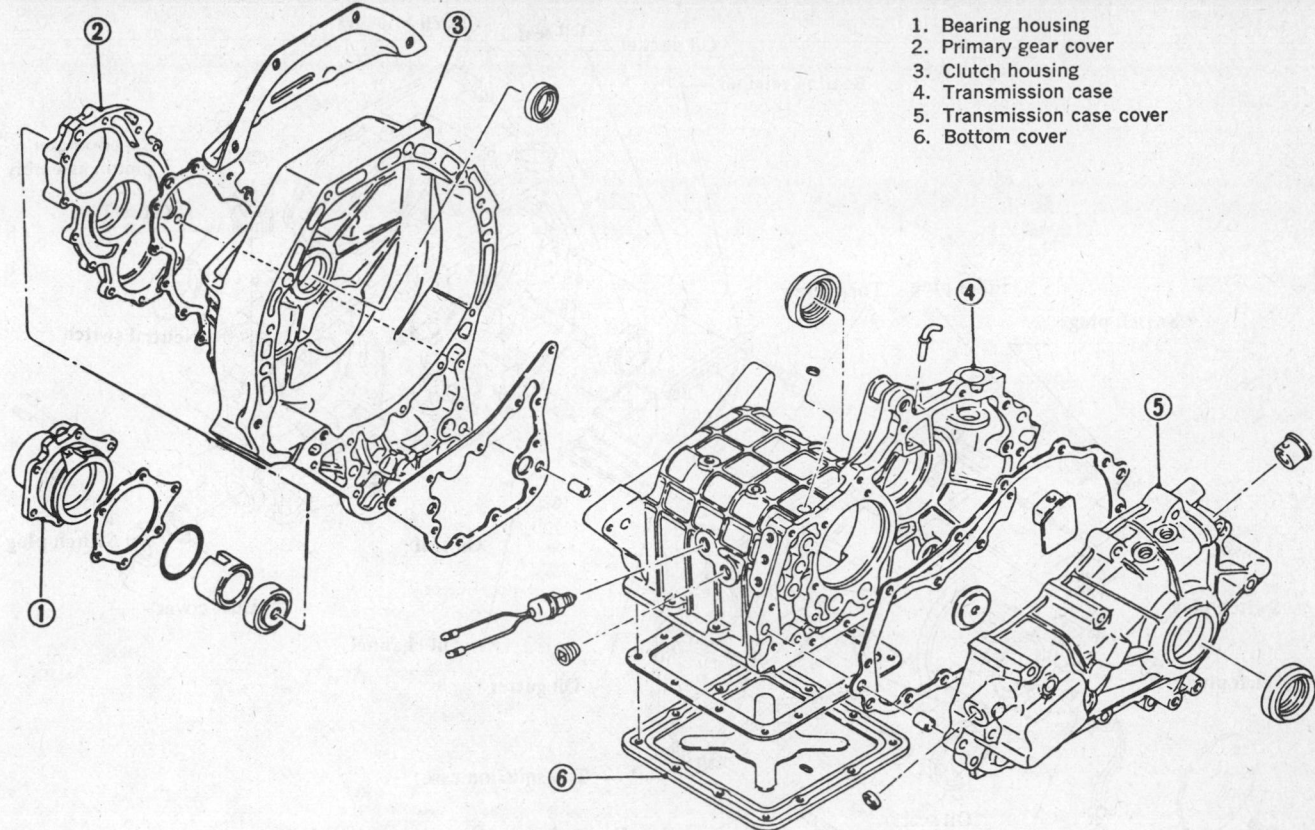

1. Bearing housing
2. Primary gear cover
3. Clutch housing
4. Transmission case
5. Transmission case cover
6. Bottom cover

Transaxle case components

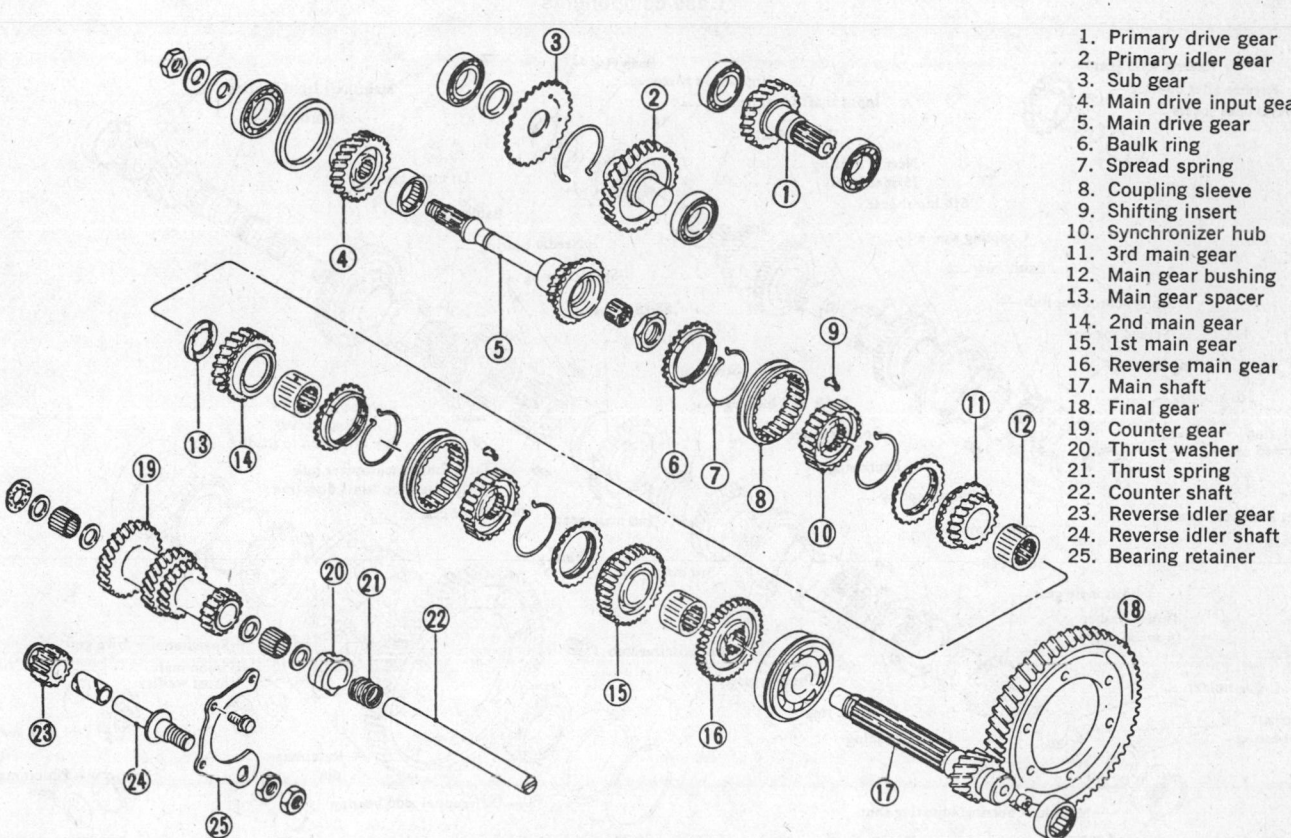

1. Primary drive gear
2. Primary idler gear
3. Sub gear
4. Main drive input gear
5. Main drive gear
6. Baulk ring
7. Spread spring
8. Coupling sleeve
9. Shifting insert
10. Synchronizer hub
11. 3rd main gear
12. Main gear bushing
13. Main gear spacer
14. 2nd main gear
15. 1st main gear
16. Reverse main gear
17. Main shaft
18. Final gear
19. Counter gear
20. Thrust washer
21. Thrust spring
22. Counter shaft
23. Reverse idler gear
24. Reverse idler shaft
25. Bearing retainer

4-speed gear components

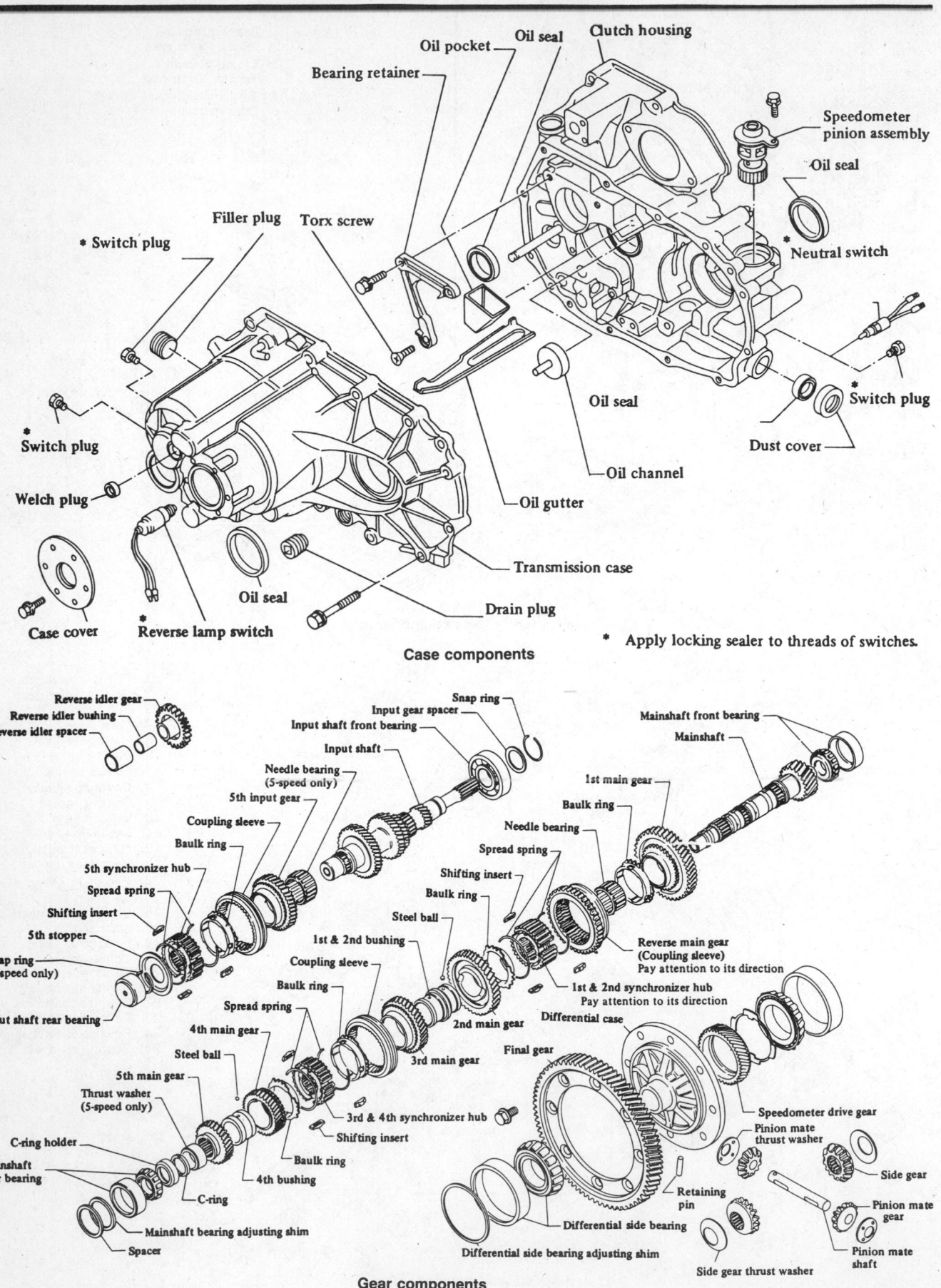

Oil pocket
Oil seal
Clutch housing
Bearing retainer
Speedometer pinion assembly
Oil seal
Filler plug
Torx screw
* Neutral switch
* Switch plug
* Switch plug
Switch plug
Dust cover
Welch plug
Oil seal
Oil channel
Oil gutter
Case cover
Oil seal
Transmission case
* Reverse lamp switch
Drain plug

Case components

* Apply locking sealer to threads of switches.

Reverse idler gear
Snap ring
Mainshaft front bearing
Reverse idler bushing
Input gear spacer
Mainshaft
Reverse idler spacer
Input shaft front bearing
Input shaft
Needle bearing
(5-speed only)
1st main gear
5th input gear
Baulk ring
Coupling sleeve
Needle bearing
Baulk ring
Spread spring
5th synchronizer hub
Shifting insert
Spread spring
Baulk ring
Shifting insert
Steel ball
Reverse main gear
(Coupling sleeve)
Pay attention to its direction
5th stopper
1st & 2nd bushing
Snap ring
(5-speed only)
Coupling sleeve
1st & 2nd synchronizer hub
Pay attention to its direction
Baulk ring
Input shaft rear bearing
Spread spring
2nd main gear
Differential case
4th main gear
3rd main gear
Steel ball
Final gear
5th main gear
Speedometer drive gear
Thrust washer
(5-speed only)
3rd & 4th synchronizer hub
Pinion mate
thrust washer
C-ring holder
Shifting insert
Side gear
Mainshaft
rear bearing
Baulk ring
4th bushing
Retaining
pin
Pinion mate
gear
C-ring
Mainshaft bearing adjusting shim
Differential side bearing
Pinion mate
shaft
Spacer
Differential side bearing adjusting shim
Side gear thrust washer

Gear components

5. Remove the case cover, the mainshaft bearing adjusting shim and the spacer.

6. Remove the mainshaft bearing rear outer race and the differential side bearing outer race.

7. Draw out the reverse idler spacer.

Assembly

1. Press fit the differential side bearing outer race and the mainshaft rear bearing outer race.

2. Instal the input shaft needle bearing. Apply sealant to the welch plug and then install it on the transmission case.

3. Install the oil gutter. Apply sealant to the back-up light switch and install it.

4. If the transmission case has been replaced, adjust the differential side bearing and the mainshaft rotary frictional force by means of shims.

5. Apply an even coating of sealant to the mating surfaces of the transmission case and the clutch housing. Mount the case on the clutch housing and tighten the mounting bolts to 12–15 ft. lbs.

6. Remove the transmission case cover. Clean the mating surfaces and apply sealant to the transmission case.

7. Install the case cover with the convex side facing outward. Tighten the mounting bolts to 4.6–6.1 ft. lbs.

8. Check that the gears move freely and then install the drain plug (with sealant) and fill with lubricant.

CLUTCH HOUSING

Disassembly

1. Drain the oil and then remove the transmission case.

2. Draw out the reverse idler spacer and fork shaft, then remove the 5th/3rd/4th shift fork.

NOTE: Do not lose the shifter caps.

3. Remove the control bracket with the 1st and 2nd gear shift fork.

NOTE: Be careful not to lose the select check ball, spring and the shifter caps (5-speed only).

On Stanza:

4. Remove the mainshaft and final drive assembly. Be sure to pull the mainshaft straight out.

5. Remove the bearing retainer securing bolts.

All other Models:

6. Remove the three screws and detach the bearing retainer. One of the

screws is special torx type and should be removed using a special torx-head allen wrench.

7. Turn the clutch housing so that its side is facing down. Lightly tap the end of the input shaft (on the engine side) with a rubber mallet and then remove the input shaft along with the bearing retainer and reverse idler gear.

NOTE: Don't remove the reverse idler shaft from the clutch housing because these fittings will be loose.

— **CAUTION** —
Do not scratch the oil seal lip with the input shaft spline while removing the shaft.

8. Remove the reverse idler gear and final drive assembly.

9. Remove the oil pocket, shift check ball springs and then the check ball plugs.

10. Drive the retaining pins out of the striking lever. Remove the striking rod, lever and interlock.

a. Select a position where the pin doesn't interfere with the clutch housing when removing it.

b. When removing the striking rod, be careful not to damage the oil seal lip. It may be a good idea to tape the edges of the striking rod when removing it.

1. Primary drive gear
2. Primary idler gear
3. Sub gear
4. Main drive input gear
5. Main drive gear
6. Baulk ring
7. Spread spring
8. Coupling sleeve
9. Shifting insert
10. Synchronizer hub
11. 4th main gear
12. 4th gear bushing

13. Main gear spacer
14. 3rd main gear
15. 2nd main gear
16. Reverse main gear
17. Main shaft
18. Final gear
19. 1st main gear
20. Counter gear
21. 1st-reverse counter gear
22. Reverse idler gear
23. Reverse idler input gear

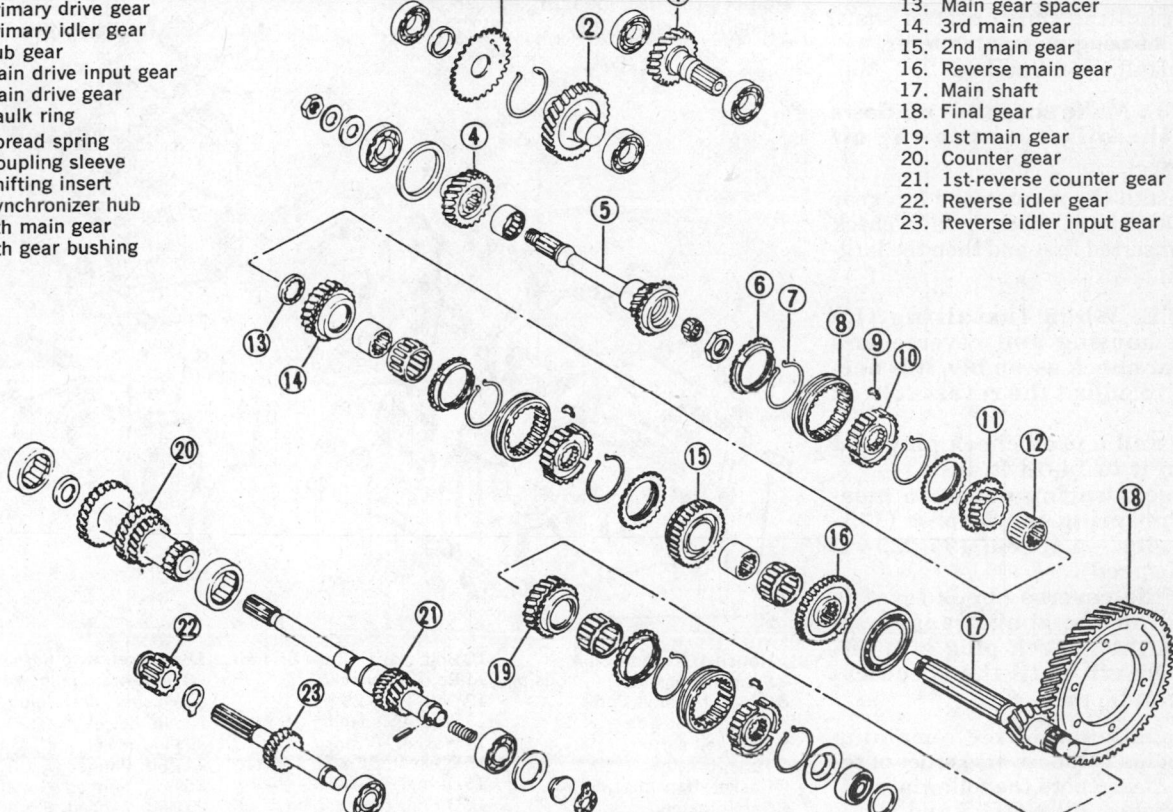

5-speed gear components

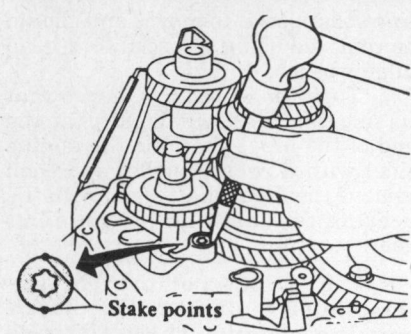

Stake the head of the Torx screw after installation

11. Remove the reverse and 5th gear check plug and then detach the check spring and balls. Remove the reverse and 5th gear check assembly.

12. Remove the clutch control shaft, release bearing and clutch lever.

13. Remove the mainshaft bearing outer race. Remove the differential side baring outer race.

14. Remove the oil channel.

Assembly

1. Install a new oil channel so that the oil groove in the channel faces the oil pocket.

2. Install the mainshaft bearing and differential side bearing outer races.

3. Install the clutch control shaft, release bearing and clutch lever.

4. Install the oil pocket.

NOTE: Make sure that oil flows from the oil pocket to the oil channel.

5. Install the reverse and 5th gear check assembly. The smaller check ball is inserted first and then the larger one.

NOTE: When installing the clutch housing and reverse and 5th gear check assembly, it is necessary to adjust the reverse check force.

a. Install a used check plug and tighten it to 14–18 ft. lbs.

b. Use a spring gauge to measure the spring check force (139–100 in. lbs.– 4 speed; 195–239 in. lbs. – 5 speed).

c. If the reverse check force is not within the above ranges, select another check plug of a different length until the specifications can be met.

6. Installation of the remaining components is the reverse order of removal. Please note the following:

a. Follow all NOTES and CAUTIONS listed under the Disassembly procedures.

b. Apply a locking sealer to the threads of the torx screw and tighten it to 12–15 ft. lbs. Use a punch and stake the head of the screw at two points.

c. Tighten the bearing retainer bolts to 12–15 ft. lbs.

d. Coat the select check ball (5 speed) and shifter caps with grease before installing.

e. Coat the support spring with grease before installing it. This will prevent the spring from falling into the hole for the fork shaft in the clutch housing.

TYPE 8

4 and 5 Speed Transaxle Honda

DISASSEMBLY

1. Remove the transmission end cover. Check the transmission mainshaft and countershaft end-play. End-play should be between 0.002–0.003 in. If the clearance is excessive, inspect the ball bearings after transmission disassembly.

2. Remove the locking tab from the mainshaft locknut. The mainshaft locknut has left hand threads. Place the transmission in gear and place the proper size wrench on the countershaft to keep it from moving. Remove the mainshaft locknut.

3. Remove the mainshaft bearing and the large snap-ring.

4. Loosen the three shift detent lock ball screws. Remove the screws, springs and balls.

5. Remove the transmission case bolts. Lightly tap the case with a hammer and drift and separate the case. Do not pry the case apart with a screwdriver.

6. Remove the reverse idler gear and shaft. Remove the reverse shift fork.

7. Remove the shift selector assembly. If repair to the shift selector is necessary, disassemble as follows:

a. Remove the two screws and retaining plate. Stake the screws when reinstalling.

b. Push the shift arm into the reverse position (towards the large spring). Then release it.

c. The pivot shaft holds a spring loaded detent. Do not lose the detent ball and spring when removing. Remove the pivot shaft.

d. Remove the interlock bar and shift arms.

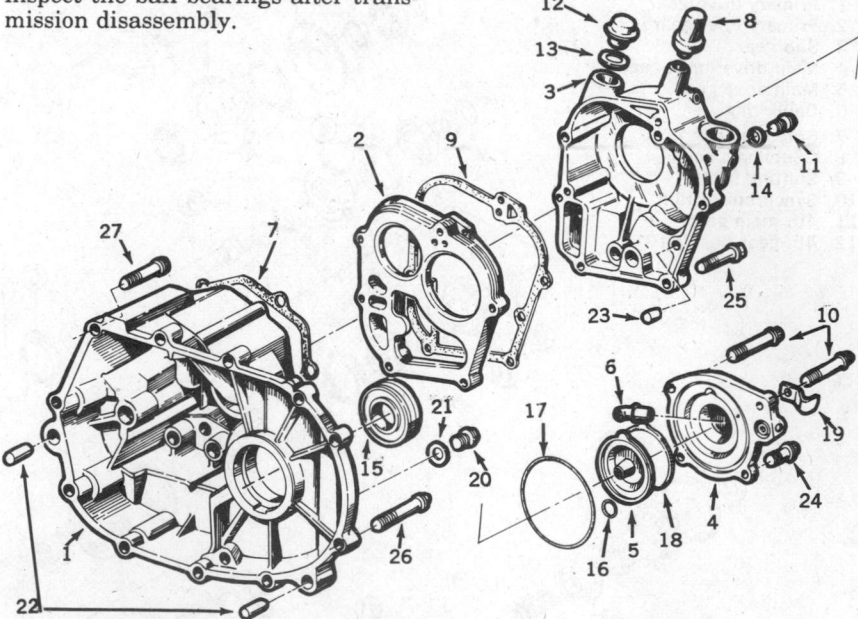

1 Housing, transmission	10 Bolt, flanged, 6 x 85 mm	19 Bracket, wire harness
2 Spacer, transmission housing	11 Bolt, oil check	20 Bolt, drain plug, 14 mm
3 Cover, transmission	12 Bolt, plug 25 mm	21 Washer, drain plug, 14 mm
4 Cover, right side	13 Washer, sealing, 25 mm	22 Pin, dowel, 14 x 20 mm
5 Plate, oil barrier	14 Washer, 8 mm	23 Pin, dowel, 8 x 14 mm
6 Tube, breather	15 Oil seal, 35 x 56 x 9 mm	24 Bolt, flanged, 6 x 20 mm
7 Gasket, transmission housing	16 O-ring, 9.4 x 2.4	25 Bolt, flanged, 6 x 45 mm
8 Cap, breather	17 O-ring, 64.5 x 3	26 Bolt, flanged, 8 x 40 mm
9 Gasket, transmission case	18 O-ring, 42 x 2.4	27 Bolt, flanged, 8 x 45 mm

Exploded view of housing and cover assemblies

e. During reassembly, insert a screwdriver into the reverse side (large spring end) of the arm assembly to hold down the detent ball, while inserting the pivot shaft.

8. Remove the shift fork retaining bolts and pull the shift shafts up until they clear the case. Remove the forks and shafts.

NOTE: When reinstalling the fork retaining bolts turn the shaft so the threaded portion of the hole is facing away from the bolt.

9. Remove the mainshaft and countershaft and at the same time by holding the two shafts and lightly taping the flywheel end of the mainshaft.

10. Remove the shift rod boot, shift rim, lock washer and bolt. Remove the shift rod and shift arm.

NOTE: During installation of the shift arm retaining bolt, turn the shaft so that the threaded portion of the hole is facing away from the bolt.

11. Measure the side clearance of the low gear with a feeler gauge, if the clearance is excessive, replace the thrust plate. Perform the same measurement on the remaining gears, if the clearance is beyond the service limit, replace the bearing race (spacer). See chart for specifications.

12. If the countershaft must be disassembled to adjust the clearances, or replace gears, remove the locknut by installing the shaft in case and holding the differential securely.

NOTE: Place the end lugs of the holder in the case and center the lug in the hole of the differential carrier.

13. Remove the two screws and retaining plate which hold the countershaft bearing. Remove the countershaft bearing with a bearing puller.

14. Clean all component parts thoroughly in the proper solvent.

15. Inspect the surfaces of each gear and blocking ring for roughness or damage. Apply a thin coat of oil to the tapered surfaces of each gear and push them together with a rotating motion. Measure the distance between the ring and gear. Replace all necessary parts. Clearance should be between 0.120–0.139 in.

16. Measure the clearance between the shift forks and synchronizer sleeves. The clearance should be between 0.039–0.018. If clearances are excessive, replace the shift forks, synchronizers or both.

17. Ensure that there are no restrictions in the oil holes on the countershaft. Check the splines for wear.

18. Inspect the condition of the mainshaft and countershaft bearing surfaces. Check run-out, gear tooth and spline condition.

19. Check the condition of all the gears. Check the condition of all bearing surfaces.

20. Inspect the bearing race (spacer) of each gear.

21. Replace all questionable parts.

ASSEMBLY

1. Transmission should be assembled in the reverse order of disassembly. During assembly, note the following points:

2. Check the differential bearing clearance.

3. Apply a thin coat of oil to all parts before they are installed.

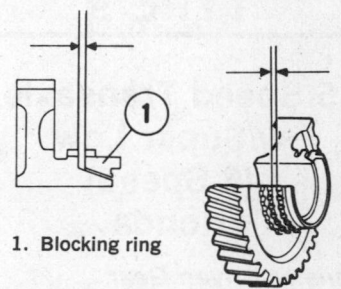

1. Blocking ring

Measuring the clearance between the synchronizer ring and gear hub

1. Needle roller bearing set plate
2. Needle roller bearing
3. Clutch case
4. Reverse gear shaft
5. Reverse idle gear
6. Reverse shift fork
7. Shift selector assembly
8. Countershaft gear assembly
9. Main shaft
10. First/second fork shaft
11. Reverse fork shaft
12. Third/fourth fork shaft
13. Steel ball
14. Ball set spring
15. Drain plug washer
16. Set ball spring screw
17. Ball bearing
18. Needle roller bearing
19. 48 mm snap ring
20. Ball bearing
21. 62 mm snap ring
22. 23 mm lock nut
23. 20 mm lock nut
24. Transmission rear cover
25. Speedometer gear

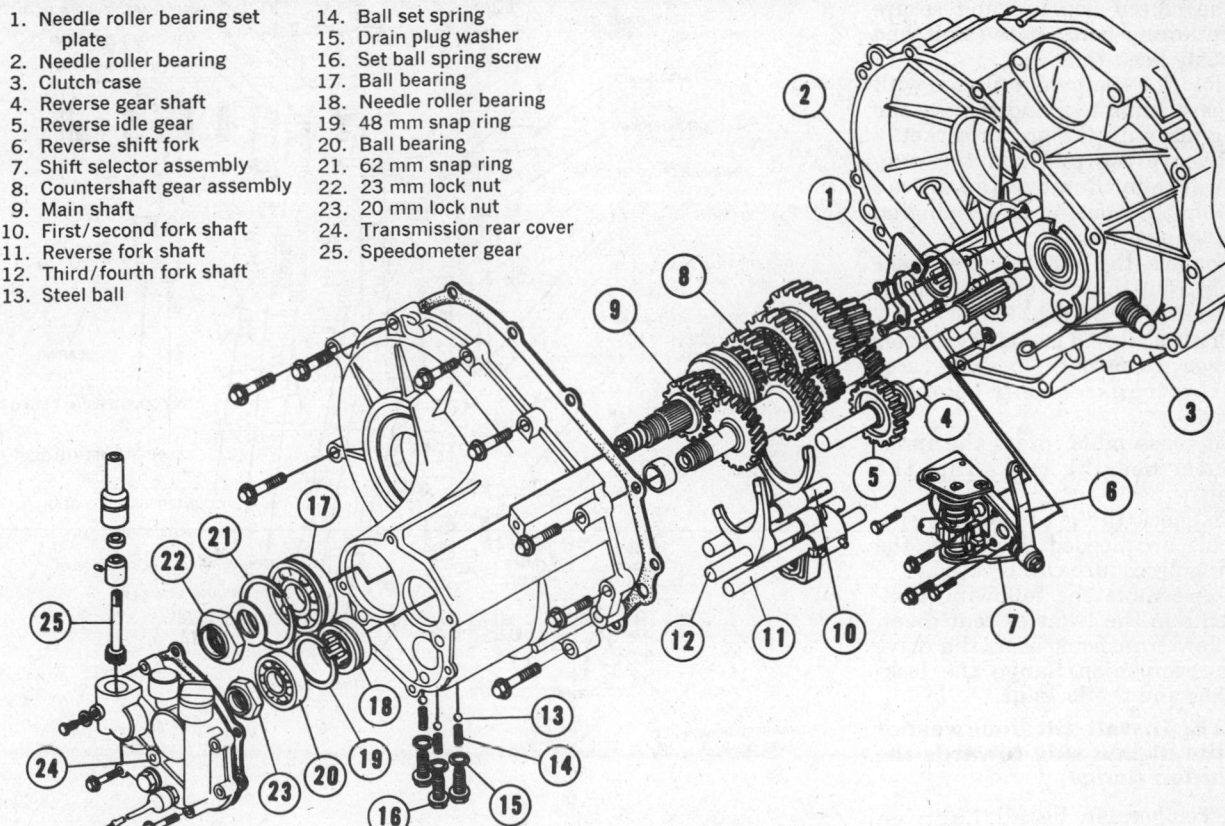

Exploded view of typical Honda manual transmission

4. Be certain that hub and synchronizer teeth match when they are assembled.

5. The mainshaft and countershaft must be installed at the same time. Next, install the third/fourth shift fork and shaft, first/second shift fork and shaft, and then the reverse shaft.

6. When the shift selector assembly is installed, there are two special bolts which must be inserted first. These bolts locate the assembly.

7. Lock the mainshaft and countershaft locknuts with a punch.

8. Make sure that the mainshaft and countershaft turn smoothly and that all gears engage freely. Check and be certain that all bolts are properly torqued.

TYPE 9

5 Speed Transaxle w/Super Low (6 Speed) Honda

Transfer Driven Gear

DISASSEMBLY

1. Slide the driven gear assembly into the clutch housing and secure with retaining bolts, if the unit had previously been removed.

2. Hold the companion flange with a flange holding tool and remove the locking nut with the proper socket.

3. Remove the tool and the companion flange. Remove the driven gear from the housing by tapping on the driven gear shaft.

4. Remove the inner driven gear bearing from the driven gear shaft, using a bearing puller tool.

5. Pry the oil seal from the transfer rear cover. Remove the bearing races from the transfer rear cover as required.

6. To reassemble, press the inner and outer bearing races into the housing.

7. To check the gear preload, special tools are needed. However, the following procedure can be used.

a. Assemble the following components in the transfer rear cover, the new transfer spacer, the drive gear, companion flange the lockwasher and the locknut.

NOTE: Install the lockwasher with the dished side towards the companion flange.

b. Temporarily install the driven gear assembly and the retaining bolts in the transfer case.

c. To measure the preload, tighten the locknut to the specified torque of 87 ft. lbs. (120 Nm), using the flange holder tool and the proper socket and wrench combination.

d. Remove the driven gear assembly from the transfer case and position the assembly in a vise with protective jaws. Measure the preload.

e. Measure the preload by first turning the companion flange several times to assure normal bearing to race contact. Rotate the shaft assembly with the appropriate torque wrench.

f. The preload should be 7.0 to 9.5 inch lbs. (0.8 to 1.1 Nm), replace the transfer spacer with a new one and readjust. Do not attempt to adjust the preload by loosening the locknut.

g. If the preload is less than 7.0 inch lbs. (0.8 Nm), adjust by tightening the locknut a little at a time until the proper preload is achieved.

h. Replace the transfer spacer with a new one if the preload is still outside the specified limits when the locknut is tightened to 166 ft. lbs. (230 Nm).

ASSEMBLY

1. Apply sealant to the clutch case mating surfaces of the transfer case.

NOTE: The transaxle uses no gaskets between the major housing, depending upon sealant to prevent fluid leakages.

2. Install the following pats, the transfer thrust shim, the drive gear, the drive gear thrust shim and the left side cover.

4. Follow the assembly in Step 3 with the assembly of the following parts, the driven gear thrust shim, the driven gear assembly and the driven gear assembly bolts.

5. Measure the total bearing preload by rotating the companion flange several times to assure normal bearing to race contact. Place the selector

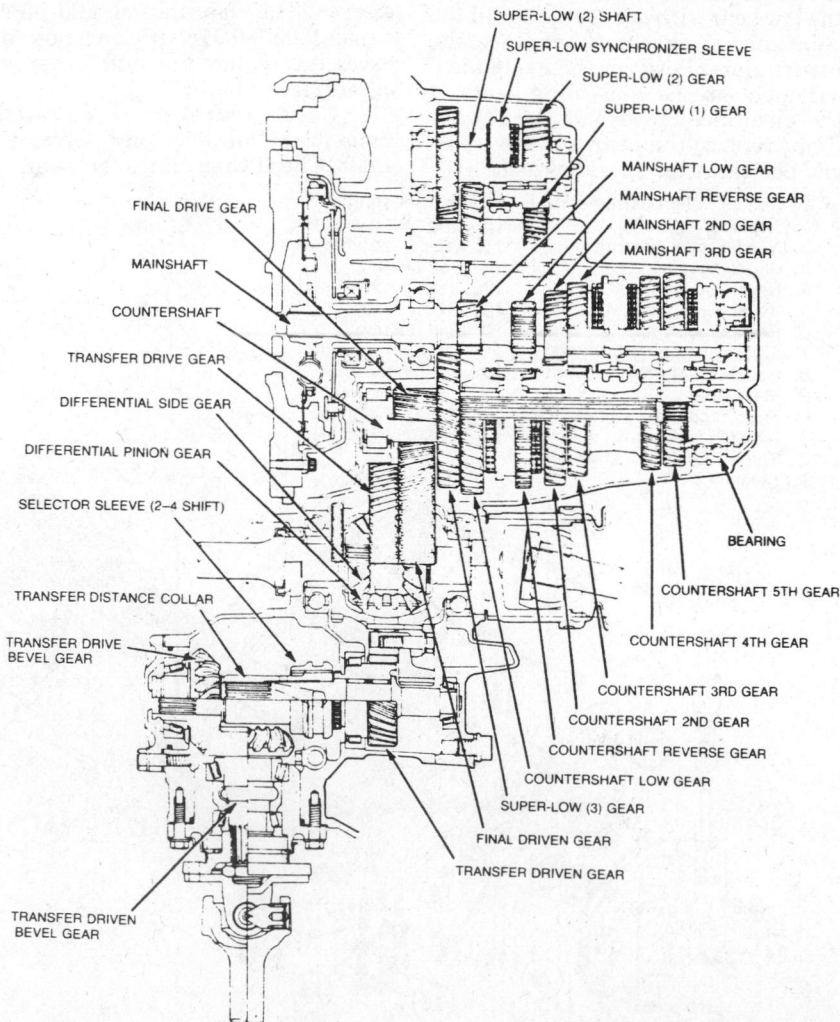

Cross section of Honda 5 speed manual transaxle with Super-Low

lever in the 2WD position and measure the preload with an appropriate torque wrench.

6. The total bearing preload should be 6.1–8.75 inch lbs. (0.7–1.0 Nm). This preload is greater than the preload on the driven gear assembly when tested alone. Example: If the preload of the driven assembly alone was 7.9 inch lbs. (0.9 Nm), the total bearing preload should be between 14–16 inch lbs. (1.6–1.9 Nm).

7. If the preload is outside of the specifications, adjust it by replacing the transfer thrust shim.

a. If the total bearing preload is less than specifications, reduce the size of the transfer thrust shim.

b. If the total bearing preload is more than specifications, increase the size of the transfer thrust shim.

Transfer Driven Gear Assembly

BACKLASH INSPECTION

1. Shift the selector lever to the 2WD position.

2. With the drive shaft disconnected, check the backlash at the companion flange with the use of a dial indicator mounted to the transaxle case.

3. Measure the backlash, turn the companion flange 180° and remeasure. The standard measurement is 0.004–0.006 in. (0.09–0.14mm).

4. If the backlash is out of specifications, the driven gear thrust washer must be changed. Proper tooth contact must be retained after the backlash adjustment has been completed.

5. To check for proper tooth contact, remove the driven gear assembly from the transfer case and paint the driven gear teeth evenly with Prussian Blue or equivalent.

6. Reinstall the driven gear assembly back into the transfer case and tighten the bolts evenly to 20 ft. lbs. (26 Nm).

7. With the selector lever in 2WD, rotate the companion flange one full turn in both directions.

8. Remove the driven gear assembly from the transfer case and note the gear impressions on the gear. The correct tooth contact should be in the center of the tooth face and even between the top of the tooth and the bottom of the tooth.

9. The checking and adjustment of the driven gear assembly must be continued until the proper tooth contact is obtained.

a. If the tooth pattern shows toe contact, use a thicker drive gear thrust shim and increase the thickness of the transfer thrust shim and increase the thickness of the transfer thrust shim and equal amount.

b. If the pattern of the teeth shows heel contact, too much back lash is indicated. To correct this condition, reduce the thickness of the drive gear thrust shim. The thickness of the transfer thrust shim must also be reduced by the amount by which the drive gear thrust washer shim is reduced.

c. The driven gear thrust shim will have to be changed also to compensate for the change in backlash.

d. To correct face contact (contact too near the tooth edge), use a thicker driven gear thrust shim to move the drive gear away from the drive gear. The backlash should remain within limits.

e. To correct flank contact (contact too near the bottom of the tooth), move the driven gear in towards the drive gear by using a thinner shim for the driven gear, while retaining the correct backlash.

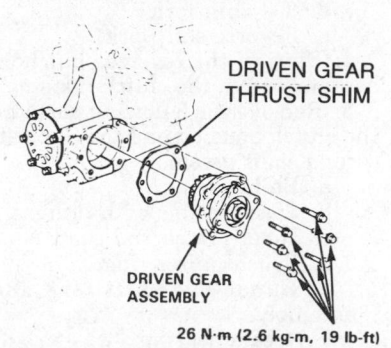

Exploded view of driven gear of transfer case assembly

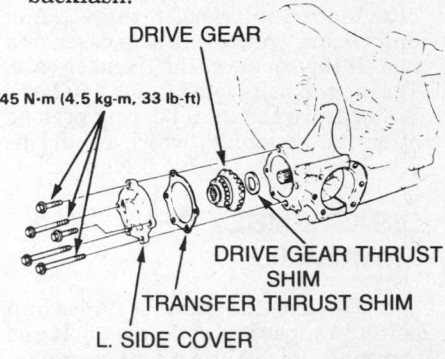

Exploded view of drive gear of transfer case assembly

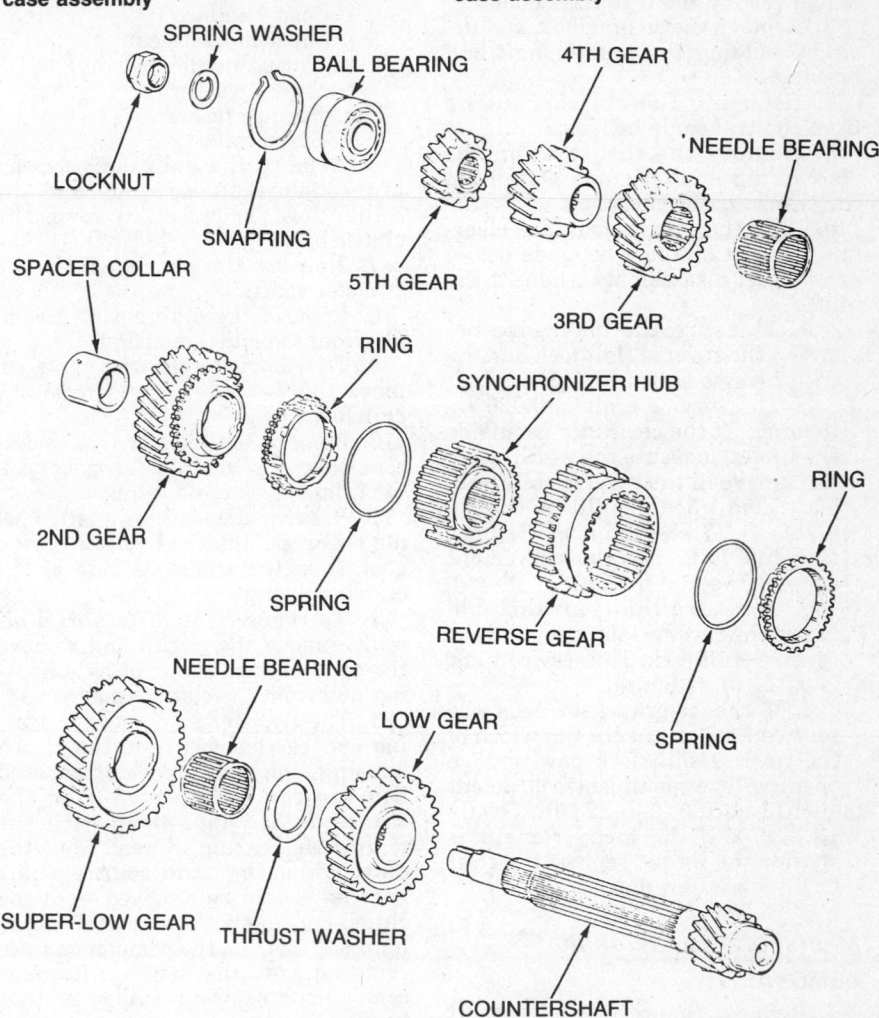

Exploded view of countershaft assembly with Super-Low

10. When the tooth contact and backlash is correct, apply a coating of sealant to the mating surfaces of the clutch and transfer cases. No gaskets are used.

11. Install the thrust shim and the O-ring on the driven gear assembly and install the assembly into the transfer case opening. Torque the bolts to 20 ft. lbs. (26 Nm). Slide the drive gear thrust shim and drive gear onto the transfer shaft.

12. Place the transfer thrust shim and O-ring on the left side cover and install the cover on the transfer case. Torque the bolts to 33 ft. lbs. (45 Nm). Re-measure the total bearing preload after the assembly, which should be 6.1–7.9 inch lbs. (0.7–1.0 Nm).

DISASSEMBLY OF TRANSAXLE

1. Remove the Reverse idle shaft bolt, the super low shift lever bolt and the super low shift set ball screw.

2. Remove the bolts attaching the clutch case to the transaxle housing.

3. Remove the sealing bolt and the circlip holding the countershaft ball bearings.

4. Separate the clutch housing from the transaxle housing.

5. Remove the thrust shim, the dish spring and oil guide plate from the transmission housing.

6. With the cover removed, a clearance inspection must be made before any further disassembly is done to the unit.

   a. Measure the clearance between the reverse shift fork and the fifth/reverse shift piece pin.

   b. The service limit is 0.020 in. (0.5mm). If the clearance is outside the limits, measure the width of the "L" groove in the reverse shift fork. This clearance should be 0.278–0.285 in. (7.05–7.25mm). Replace the shift fork if the measurement exceeds the maximum.

   c. Measure the clearance between the reverse idler gear and the reverse shift fork. The service limit is 0.071 in. (1.8mm).

   d. If the clearance exceeds the service limit, measure the width of the reverse shift fork pawl groove opening. The opening measurement should be 0.512–0.524 in. (13.0–13.3mm). If the measurement is outside the limits, replace the shift fork with a new one.

Mainshaft/Countershaft
REMOVAL

1. Remove the revere idler shaft and reverse idler gear from the clutch housing.

2. Remove the following parts from the reverse shift holder assembly:
   a. 1–2 shift fork shaft.
   b. Super-low shift piece bar.
   c. Super-low shift lever.
   d. Super-low shift piece.
   e. 1–2 shift fork.

3. Remove the following parts from the clutch housing:
   a. Special bolt (6mm).
   b. Lock plate.
   c. Fifth/reverse shift fork shaft.
   d. 3–4 shift fork.
   e. Reverse shift fork.

4. Remove the reverse shift holder assembly from the clutch housing.

5. Remove the following parts from the clutch housing and the Super-low second shaft assembly
   a. Ball bearing.
   b. Spacer collar with flanges.
   c. Super-low second gear.
   d. Synchronizer ring.
   e. Super-low shift fork shaft assembly.
   f. Needle bearing.
   g. Thrust washer.
   h. Super-low/1st shaft.
   i. Spacer collar.
   j. Super-low/1st gear.
   k. Thrust needle bearing.
   l. Thrust washer.
   m. Spring washer.
   n. Space collar.

6. Remove the mainshaft assembly, countershaft assembly and the Super-low second shaft form the clutch housing.

7. Remove the bearing from the transfer shaft.

8. Remove the differential assembly from the clutch housing.

9. To remove the transfer shaft, remove the 2–4 selector rod from the clutch housing.

10. Remove the selector fork, selector sleeve, and the transfer spacer collar from the clutch housing.

11. Remove the selector shaft, needle bearings, and the transfer driven gear from the transaxle side of the clutch housing.

12. To remove the differential oil seal, remove the circlip and remove the oil seal from the transaxle housing and from the clutch case.

13. The transfer shaft needle bearing can be removed from the clutch housing, the transfer shaft tapered bearing can be removed from the transaxle housing, along with the mainshaft bearing/oil seal from the clutch housing. The countershaft bearing should be removed from the clutch housing with the use of a slide hammer tool. As the components are removed from the major units, new components can be installed at that time.

14. Inspect the mainshaft and the countershaft for damage, excessive wear or broken teeth. Examine the splines for wear.

15. Examine the synchronizer units for worn teeth, roughness or wear, scoring galling or cracks.

16. To measure the clearance between the ring and the gear, hold the ring against the gear evenly while measuring the clearance with a feeler gauge. The service limit is 0.016 in. (0.4mm). If necessary, replace the unit.

17. To assemble the mainshaft, install the components in the following order on the mainshaft:
    a. Needle bearing
    b. Third gear
    c. Synchronizer assembly
    d. Fourth gear
    e. Needle bearings
    f. Spacer collar
    g. Needle bearing
    h. Fifth gear
    i. Synchronizer assembly
    j. Ball bearing

18. To measure the clearance of the components of the mainshaft, push down on the bearing race with a socket and measure the clearance between the third and second gears.

    a. The third gear clearance service limit is 0.012 in. (0.3mm). If the measurement is out of specifications, measure the thickness of the third gear, which should have a service limit of 1.272 in. (32.3mm). If this reading is within specifications, replace the synchronizer hub.

    b. Measure the clearance between the fourth gear and the spacer collar, and the fifth gear and the spacer collar. The service limit is 0.012 in. (0.3mm). If the measurement is out of specifications, measure each side of the spacer collar from the inside lip of the spacer lug. Service limit of 1.024 (26.01mm) is allowed.

    c. If the measurement of the spacer collar is within specifications measure the thickness of the fourth and fifth gears. The fourth gear service limit thickness is 1.220 in. (30.8mm), while the fifth gear service limit is 1.193 in. (30.3mm). if the measurements are out of specifications, replace the gears. If the gears are within specifications, but the clearance is still out of specifications, replace the synchronizer hub.

19. To determine the mainshaft shim selection, remove the thrust shim, the dish spring and the oil guide plate from the transmission housing.

20. Install the 3–4 synchronizer hub, spacer collar, fifth synchronizer hub and the ball bearing on the mainshaft. Install the assembly into the transaxle case.

21. Measure the distance between

the end of the transaxle case and the mainshaft.

a. Use a straight edge and vernier caliper.

b. Measure at three locations and average the readings.

22. Measure the distance between the end of the clutch housing and the bearing inner race. Again, average the readings.

23. Calculate the thickness of the shim to be added, as follows

a. Add the measurement recorded in step 21 and step 22.

b. Subtract 0.039 in. (1mm), representing the height of the dish spring after installation, and the remainder is the thickness of the shim needed.

Shim needed would be 1.60mm.

c. When making this measurement, if the inner race protrudes above the clutch housing, measure the height it protrudes and subtract this amount from the measurement. Then subtract the 1.0mm dish spring to compute the shim needed.

Shim needed would be 1/60mm.

d. Thickness of the shims vary from 0.043 in. (1.10mm) to 0.085 in. (2.15mm), available in thickness of 0.002 in. (0.05mm) increments, for a total of 22 different sizes.

24. Check the thrust clearance as outlined in the following steps:

a. Install the dish spring and shim selected in the transaxle housing.

b. Install the mainshaft into the clutch housing.

c. Place the transaxle cover housing over the mainshaft and onto the clutch housing.

d. Tighten the clutch and transaxle retaining bolts.

e. Reach through the 18mm sealing bolt hole and measure the clearance between the dish spring and the thrush shim at its opening.

f. The scale 0.3mm side should fit while the scale side 0.49mm side should not of the special measuring tool, 07998SD9000A or its equivalent.

g. If the clearance is incorrect, the adjusting shims must be changed to correct the specifications.

Countershaft

CLEARANCE INSPECTION

1. Assemble the gears, spacer collars, thrust washers, synchronizer hub and rings to the countershaft, in the following manner:

a. Super-low gear
b. Selective thrust washer
c. Needle bearing
d. Low gear

e. Reverse gear and synchronizer assembly
f. Second gear
g. Spacer collar
h. Needle bearing
i. Third gear
j. Fourth gear
k. Fifth gear
l. Ball bearing
m. Lockwasher and locknut

2. Tighten the countershaft locknut to a torque of 80 ft. lbs. (110 Nm).

NOTE: Place the countershaft assembly in a soft jawed vice before tightening the locknut.

3. Measure and record the clearance between the Super-low gear and thrust washer. The service limit is 0.0007 in. (0.18mm).

4. If the clearance is out of specifications, select the appropriate thrust washer or spacer collar for the correct clearance.

5. Measure the clearance between the second gear and third gears. The service limit is 0.007 in. (0.18mm).

6. If the clearance is out of specifications, select the appropriate thrust washer or collar for the correct clearance.

ASSEMBLY OF TRANSAXLE

1. Install the guide plate, dish spring and mainshaft thrust shim in the transaxle housing.

NOTE: Use the correct thrust shim for the mainshaft for the proper thrust clearance.

2. Install the oil gutter and collect plates in the transaxle housing.

3. Install the transfer shaft assembly and the 2-4 selector rod.

4. Install the differential assembly in the clutch housing.

5. Install the bearing on the transfer shaft.

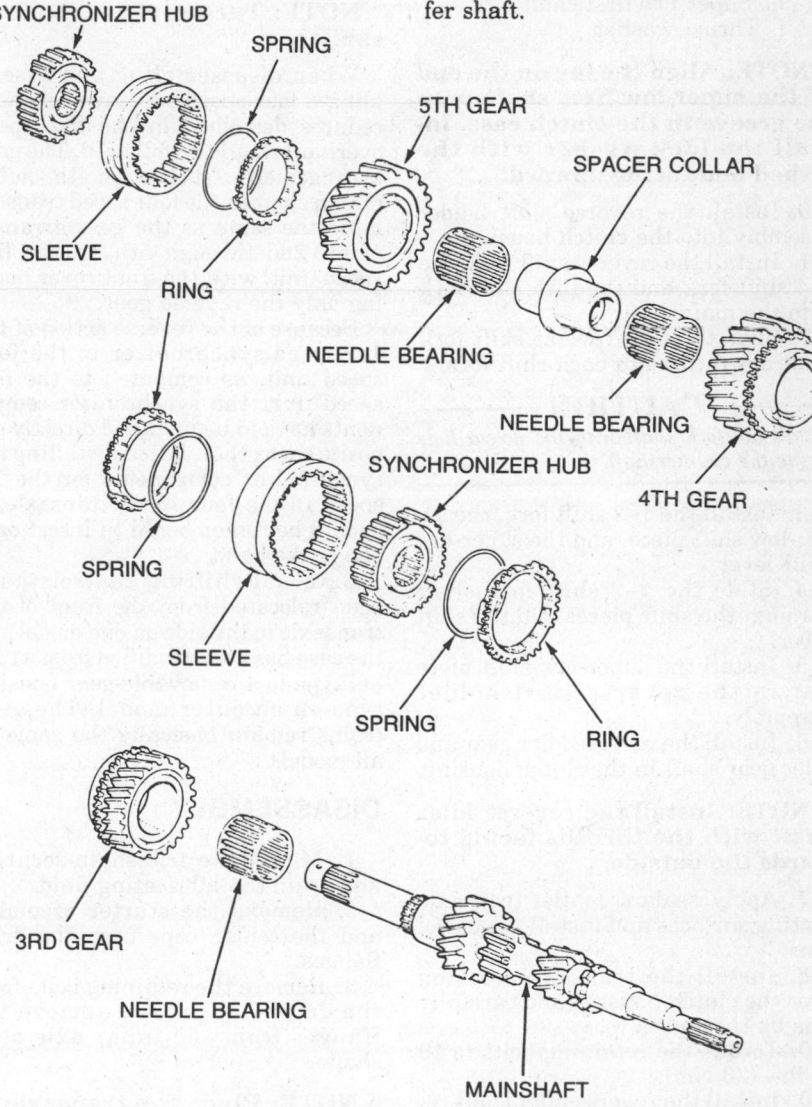

Exploded view of mainshaft assembly

SYNCHRONIZER HUB
SPRING
5TH GEAR
SPACER COLLAR
SLEEVE
RING
NEEDLE BEARING
NEEDLE BEARING
4TH GEAR
SPRING
SYNCHRONIZER HUB
SLEEVE
SPRING
RING
3RD GEAR
NEEDLE BEARING
MAINSHAFT

6. Install the super-low/second shaft, countershaft assembly and the mainshaft assembly in the clutch housing.

7. Install the super-low shift piece and the shift fork on the super-low shift fork shaft.

8. Assemble the super-low shift fork shaft assembly with the following components:
   a. Ball bearing
   b. Flanged spacer collar
   c. Super-low/second gear
   d. Synchronizer hub assembly
   e. Needle bearing

9. Install the following components into the clutch housing:
   a. Spacer collar
   b. Lock washer
   c. Thrust washer
   d. Thrust needle bearing
   e. Super-low/first gear
   f. Needle bearing
   g. Spacer collar
   h. Super-low/first shaft
   i. Thrust washer

NOTE: Align the lug on the end of the super-low/first shaft with the groove in the clutch case. Install the lock washer with the dished end facing upward.

10. Install the reverse shift holder assembly into the clutch housing.

11. Install the reverse shift fork, the 3-4 shift fork and the fifth shift fork onto the mainshaft.

12. Slide the fifth/reverse shift fork shaft down through each shift fork.

——————— CAUTION ———————
Install the fork shaft with the detent hole facing the countershaft.

13. Install the 1-2 shift fork, the super-low shift piece, and the super-low shift lever.

14. Slide the 1-2 shift fork shaft through the shift pieces and the shift lever.

15. Install the super-low shift piece bar in the reverse shift holder assembly.

16. Install the reverse idler gear and idler gear shaft in the clutch housing.

NOTE: Install the reverse idler shaft with the threads facing towards the outside.

17. Apply sealant to the transaxle mating surfaces and install the dowel pins.

18. Install the transaxle housing over the clutch housing and carefully line-up the shafts.

19. Torque the retaining bolts to 19 ft. lbs. (26 Nm).

20. Install the reverse idler shaft retaining bolt and washer. Install the detent ball, spring, washer and super-low shift detent ball screw. Install the super-low shift lever bolt.

21. Install the circlip in the bore of the transaxle housing.

22. Install the oil seal into the transaxle housing and the oil seal in the clutch housing.

23. Fill with oil and install in the vehicle.

——————————————————————

TYPE 10

4 Speed Transaxle Model 930/36
5 Speed Transaxle Model 915/63, 68, 70, 73
Porsche

NOTE: Turbo (930) transaxle similar.

When disassembling and assembling a four speed transaxle, the procedures described in the five speed overhaul should be followed. The gear arrangement, 1st through 4th, on the pinion shaft in the four speed transaxle, is the same as the gear arrangement, 2nd through 5th, in the five speed unit, with the front cover housing only the reverse gear.

Because of the reverse action of the 1st speed synchronizer in the four speed unit, as compared to the five speed unit, the synchronizer components have to be installed directly opposite each other. When installing the synchronizer components for the 1st speed in the four speed transaxle, it should be remembered to insert only one brake band.

External shifting controls have been relocated from the front of the transaxle to the side on one model and the case has been modified from a tunnel type to a removable gear housing type on an outer model. The gear trains remain basically the same in all models.

DISASSEMBLY

1. Mount the transaxle securely and drain the lubricating fluid.

2. Remove the starter assembly and the center caps from the drive flanges.

3. Remove the retaining bolts from the drive flanges and remove the flanges from the inner axle stub shafts.

NOTE: Place the transaxle in gear and block the input shaft to prevent turning.

4. Remove the side cover assembly and withdraw the differential assembly.

5. Remove the crossmember from the front cover, if not previously done, and remove the front cover assembly.

——————— CAUTION ———————
During the front cover removal, the reverse gear components may drop. Prevent from falling to the floor.

——————————————————————

6. Remove the 1st/reverse selector fork retaining screw and remove the gear with the fork.

7. Remove the roll pin from the pinion shaft.

8. Remove the roll pin from the castled nut on the input shaft. Remove the castle nut and the 1st speed gear.

9. Place the transaxle gears in the neutral position and remove the retaining nut from the plate of the inner shift rod guide fork and remove the guide fork.

10. Remove the inner shift rod through the rear access hole. Shift the gears into the 5th speed position with a suitable bar and remove the intermediate plate with the gear clusters.

NOTE: A plastic hammer may be needed to lightly tap the plate loose.

——————— CAUTION ———————
The gear cluster can be installed or removed from the housing only when the transaxle gears are in the 5th speed gear position.

——————————————————————

Intermediate Plate and Gear Cluster
DISASSEMBLY

1. Install the intermediate plate assembly in a vise or similar holder and remove the 1st/reverse hub gear, using two suitable prybars.

2. Remove the gear Number two of the 1st speed, along with the needle bearing cage.

3. Shift the gear assembly into neutral position. Remove the selector shaft detent plug and remove the detent spring.

4. Remove the 1st/reverse selector shaft, along with the detent ball.

NOTE: Mark all selector forks and rails during the disassembly to avoid assembly problems.

5. Remove the 2nd/3rd selector fork retaining screw. Remove the selector shaft, fork and detent.

6. Remove the 4th and 5th selector fork retaining screw. Remove the selector shaft, fork and detent ball.

7. Remove the detent ball, spring and detent.

8. The input and pinion shafts must be pressed from the intermediate plate.

NOTE: To allow the intermediate plate to lay flat on the press, drive the aligning dowels into the plate and remove the throttle linkage.

9. Remove the bearing plate assembly. Heat the intermediate plate to 248°F (120°C) and press the bearings from the plate. Remove the detent bushings as necessary.

ASSEMBLY

1. Install the detent bushings, if removed.

——————— CAUTION ———————

Do not allow the bushings to protrude into the selector shaft bores.

————————————————————

2. Heat the intermediate plate to 248°F (120°C) and press the two bearings into place.
3. Install the bearing brace plate assembly. Torque the retaining bolts to 18 ft. lbs. and lock the bolt heads in place with the lock plates.
4. Insert the input shaft and pinion shaft assemblies into the intermediate plate assembly.
5. Reposition the aligning dowels and the throttle linkage.

Housing Assembly

DISASSEMBLY AND ASSEMBLY

1. Before any attempt is made to install the bearing races, heat the housing to 248°F (120°C).
2. The bearing races can be installed with installer tools and a hammer. Replace the necessary seal or seals.
3. To prevent damages to the housing, install the bearing races squarely in to the housing.

Pinion Shaft

DISASSEMBLY AND ASSEMBLY

1. Remove the retaining bolt with the speedometer gear attached, from the pinion shaft.
2. The gear assemblies are removed by pressing the shaft from the gears.
3. Mark and identify all components so as to maintain proper assembly sequence.

——————— CAUTION ———————

Note the number and thickness of spacers between the roller bearings and thick spacers to avoid recomputing spacer thickness during reassembly.

————————————————————

NOTE: Later transaxles have the thrust washer and spacer replaced with a single, beveled thrust washer.

Input Shaft

DISASSEMBLY AND ASSEMBLY

1. Straighten the locking tabs from the hex nut. Remove the retaining hex nut from the shaft, using the necessary special tools.
2. Press the roller bearing from the shaft, using special tools as necessary.
3. Remove the gears and components from the input shaft.

NOTE: Mark the needle bearing cages to properly install them during the installation procedure.

4. To remove the inner half of the ball bearing race from the stub end of the shaft, drive the race away from its seat with a drift punch or similar tool, and remove with a puller.
5. The reassembly of the shaft and components should be done in the reverse of the removal procedure.

6. The locknut should be torqued to 72–86 ft. lbs. Be sure to secure the nut with the locking tabs of the lock plate edge.

Differential Assembly

The differential assembly is overhauled in the conventional manner. Special measuring tools are needed to measure the preload tooth contact and to determine the thickness of necessary shims and spacers.

TRANSAXLE REASSEMBLY

1. Having the transaxle case overhauled as required and the intermediate plate assembled, place the gears in the 5th speed and prepare to install the assembly into the case.
2. Guide the intermediate plate assembly into the case and lightly tighten at four housing studs.

Correct assembly of 1st speed synchronizer for the 5-speed gear train

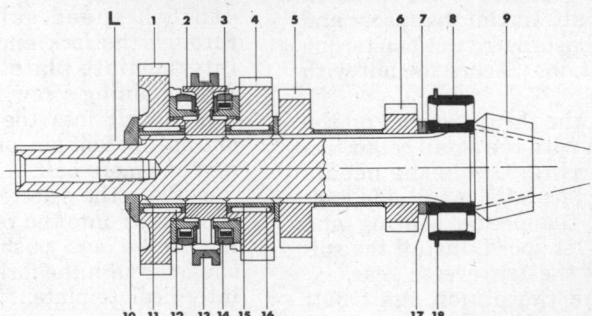

L. Four-point ballbearing	6. Gear II for 4th speed (Fixed)	12. Needle bearing cage (gear speeds 1 thru 4)
1. Gear II for 1st speed (Freewheeling)	7. Spacer	13. Sliding sleeve
2. Spider	8. Roller bearing	14. Synchronizing ring
3. Brake band	9. Pinion shaft	15. Needle bearing inner race
4. Gear II for 2nd speed (Freewheeling)	10. Thrust washer (6.6 mm thickness)	16. Needle bearing cage
5. Gear II for 3rd speed (Fixed)	11. Needle bearing inner race (gear speeds 1 thru 4)	17. Spacers
		18. Retaining ring

Cross section of 4-speed pinion shaft assembly

Location of 1st/reverse sliding gear with selector fork in place—5-speed

Gear train assembled in the intermediate plate—typical

Correct assembly of 1st speed synchronizer for the 4-speed gear train

3. Install gear one of 1st speed on the input shaft. Install the spacer and tighten the castellated nut to a torque of 43 to 47 ft. lbs. Secure the nut with a spiral pin.

4. Install the thrust washer on the pinion shaft with the small collar facing the bearing. Guide the needle bearing in place with a suitable tool.

5. Install the needle bearing and gear two of 1st speed. Install the spider wheel of the 1st/reverse gear.

6. Tighten the pinion shaft bolt (with extension for tachometer) to 80 to 86 ft. lbs. Block the gear train to prevent turning.

7. Remove the intermediate plate assembly from the case assembly. Place the intermediate plate assembly into a holder so that the select shafts can be installed.

8. Install the shafts in the following order:

a. Place the selector sleeve of the 4th/5th speed selector shaft through the fork and through the intermediate plate. Tighten the fork retaining screw.

b. Install into the detent bore, one ball, detent pin, one long spring and one more ball.

c. Place the selector fork of 2nd/3rd speeds onto the respective sliding sleeve and push the selector shaft through the fork and into the intermediate plate.

NOTE: The 4th/5th selector shaft must be in the neutral position and the detent ball pressed down.

d. Tighten the fork retaining screw and move the selector lever to the neutral position. Insert the detent.

e. Install the 1st/reverse selector shaft into the intermediate plate and install the detent ball and short spring. Tighten the fork retaining screw.

f. Slide the selector fork and the sliding gear for the 1st/reverse speed together onto the spider wheel and selector shaft. Install and tighten the fork retaining screw.

NOTE: The sliding sleeves must be adjusted to a position in the exact center in relation to the synchronizer rings when in the neutral position. The forks can be moved by loosening the retaining bolts. A special gauge block is available for this operation, but normally not available to the average repair shop.

g. When the adjustment of the forks are completed, torque the retaining bolts to 18 ft. lbs.

9. Install the inner shift rod into the transaxle housing, after having installed the shift finger onto the shaft and securing it with the retaining pin and cotter pin.

10. Guide the intermediate plate assembly into the transaxle housing with gaskets attached, carefully to avoid damage to the input shaft seal.

NOTE: The gear train assembly must be in the 5th speed position.

11. Shift the gear train into Neutral. Guide the inner shift rod into its proper position at the selector shaft tabs and into the rear rod bore.

12. Install the guide fork of the inner shift rod, using a new gasket and be sure the inner shift rod enters the guide fork.

13. Assemble the front cover and install on the transaxle assembly.

a. Install the bearing cages and the spacer bushings.

b. Install the reverse gear, axial thrust needle bearing and the thrust washer.

c. Install the tachometer elbow unit drive unit into the cover and align the indent for the set screw with the hole in the cover.

d. Install a new gasket and install the front cover. Pull the reverse gear and its axial thrust needle bearing with the thrust washer as far to the end of the shaft as possible to clear the sliding gear of the 1st/reverse speed gear.

NOTE: The machined recess in the thrust washer must align with the outer collar of the pinion shaft bearing.

14. Install the retaining nuts and torque to 15.2 to 16.6 ft. lbs.
15. Install the transaxle support.

TYPE 11

5 Speed Transaxle Model G 2.03, 05, 07, 08, 11 Porsche

DESCRIPTIONS

The Porsche model G28 transaxles have continually been modified through out the series to improve the operation and duribility of the units.

Some of the components have been interchangable during the series and the basic disassembly and assembly remain the same. The following information is to update the procedures for repairs to the units and to prevent attempts to interchange component when the models changes have occurred.

Transaxle G 28/11
1984–88

1. The input shaft and the drive pinion have the same axis and when in fifth gear, both shafts are connected by an operating sleeve and rotate together as a unit.
2. Changes have been made on the transaxle case as well as on the drive pinion bearings, synchronization , gear sets and the shifting. A new synchronization has been added to the reverse gear.
3. The aluminum transmission case is of a single piece designed and is equipped with simple covers in the top and final drive area.
4. Different shifting levers have been used and must not be combined with the older types used with models G28/01 to G28/08.

5. Adjustments must be made to the second and third selector forks and to the fourth and fifth selector forks, which are no longer retained to the shafts with pins. The selector fork for the first and reverse gear is still locked with a retaining pin.
6. The three internal selector rod locking springs have been deleted and the returning forces of the selector rods are determined with two adjustable spring elements, one on each side of the case assembly.

DISASSEMBLY

1. Mount the transaxle assembly securely and drain the lubricating oil.
2. Remove the rear cover and top cover from the transaxle case.
3. remove the right and left axle flange retaining bolts and remove the axle flanges.
4. Remove the right and left side cover retaining bolts and carefully separate the side covers, with shims, from the transaxle case. Carefully remove the differential carrier assembly.
5. Drive the mainshift rod pin from the shift finger with a pin punch or other suitable tool. Remove the lockout spring and pin from the shaft. Remove the shaft from the transaxle case.
6. Remove the shift shaft interlock mechanism by removing the screw plugs, located on the left and right sides of the case, near the front upper sides.
7. Drive the pins from the shift fingers and shift forks with a pin punch or other suitable tool. remove the shafts to the rear of the transaxle case, being careful not to exert undue force. Remove the interlock detents and springs as the shafts are removed. Remove the shift fingers and forks from the case.
8. Remove the input shaft oil seal holder by pulling outward while turning.
9. Remove the countershaft retaining circlip from the transaxle case. From the rear of the case, tap the countershaft forward and out of the case.

NOTE: The pinion shaft bearing plate may have to be loosened.

--- **CAUTION** ---
To avoid damage to the case or gears, hold the countergears from falling into the case with wire as a support.

10. With the use of a special puller to maintain straightness, remove the input shaft from the case.
11. Remove the pinion shaft bearing

retainer plate bolts and remove the pinion shaft assembly by using a puller.
12. Lit the countergear assembly from the case.
13. Using an appropriate driver, remove the reverse idler shaft from the gear and case.
14. Remove the shift shaft oil seals from the case.

Input Shaft
DISASSEMBLY

1. Remove the synchronizer ring, shift band, stop and thrust block from the input shaft.
2. Remove the front ball bearing circlip and press the bearing from the input shaft.
3. With an appropriate puller, remove the two needle bearings and spacer from the input shaft.

ASSEMBLY

1. Install one needle bearing into the input shaft, followed by the spacer and the second needle bearing.
2. Heat the ball bearing assembly to 212°F (100°C) and drive it on to the input shaft. Install the retaining circlip.
3. Install the thrust block, stop, shift band and secure with the synchronizer ring on the input shaft.

Mainshaft
DISASSEMBLY

1. Remove the circlip and shims from the front of the mainshaft. Note the number and thickness of the shims for reassembly.
2. Using a press, remove the gears, bearings and races from the mainshaft, noting the direction of each gear and component for reassembly. Mark the disassembled parts as required. Note the location of all shims for reassembly.
3. Remove the locknut from the mainshaft with the appropriate tools and remove the reverse gear. Press the front tapered bearing and bearing retaining plate from the mainshaft. Press the rear tapered bearing from the mainshaft.

ASSEMBLY

1. Heat the rear tapered bearing to 212°F (100°C) and drive it on to the mainshaft.
2. Place the bearing retaining plate on the mainshaft and heat the front tapered bearing as was done to the rear bearing, and drive the front bearing on to the mainshaft.
3. Install the reverse gear with the small depression on the hub towards the front of the mainshaft. Install the locknut and torque to 109 to 130 ft.

lbs. Stake the locknut collar to the small depression in the reverse gear hub.

4. To properly position the gears on the mainshaft, selective shims must be used in conjunction with the locknut. To obtain the proper specification, the following formula must be used.

Measuring Formula

The design specification is 108.80mm from the rear face of the pinion gear to the front face of the selective shim and should be measured with a sliding caliper or micrometer. To obtain the proper specification without the needed shim, use the formula by substituting the resulting readings, as illustrated by the example

5. Following the disassembly order, replace the gears, spacers, bearings and circlips on the mainshaft.

NOTE: The inner races for the needle bearing have to be heated to 212°F (100°C) before installation on the mainshaft.

Determining Shim Thickness

1. Place the gear train of the mainshaft in a press, under approximately 5 ton, and measure the space between the front circlip and the 4th/5th gear hub.

2. Select a shim with maximum thickness to remove all play between the circlip and the gear hub.

3. Remove the unit from the press, remove the circlip and install the shim. Reinstall the circlip.

Determining Input Shaft Clearance (During Assembly)

1. The clearance between the input shaft and the 4th/5th gear hub can be determined by inserting a feeler gauge between the shaft end and the gear hub. The clearance should be 0.2–0.3mm.

2. Should this clearance not be obtained, the mainshaft will have to be disassembled and the shim thickness at the locknut be rechecked and corrected.

3. Reassemble the mainshaft and recheck the clearance, again under pressure, between the circlip and the 4th/5th gear hub. Correct as required.

4. Recheck the clearance between the input shaft and the 4th/5th gear hub.

Synchronizer Component Identification

1ST GEAR

Synchronizer ring—One groove on face.
Thrust block—Two beveled sides.
Shift band—Uneven shift bands.
Stop—Two straight sides.
Installation note: Short side of shift band must be to the right of the thrust block.

2ND GEAR

Synchronizer ring—Two grooves on the face or a red dot.
Thrust block—Two beveled sides.
Shift band—Even shift bands.
Stop—One straight and one beveled side.
Installation note: Beveled side of stop must be faced to the right as seen from the top view.

3RD GEAR

Synchronizer ring—Two grooves on the face or a red dot.
Thrust block—Two beveled sides.
Shift band—Two separate shift bands.
Stop—Beveled sides.

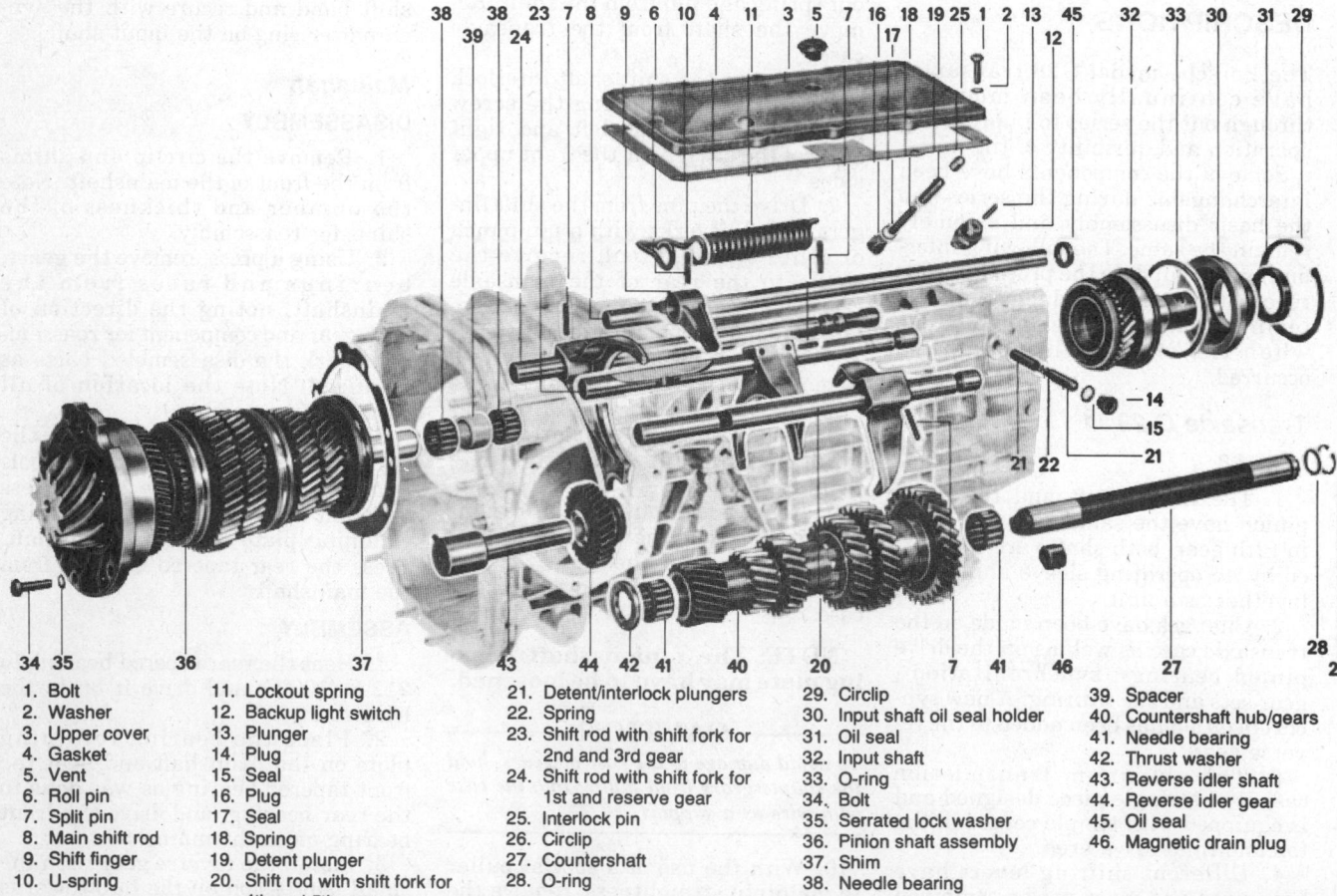

1. Bolt	11. Lockout spring	21. Detent/interlock plungers	29. Circlip	39. Spacer
2. Washer	12. Backup light switch	22. Spring	30. Input shaft oil seal holder	40. Countershaft hub/gears
3. Upper cover	13. Plunger	23. Shift rod with shift fork for 2nd and 3rd gear	31. Oil seal	41. Needle bearing
4. Gasket	14. Plug	24. Shift rod with shift fork for 1st and reverse gear	32. Input shaft	42. Thrust washer
5. Vent	15. Seal	25. Interlock pin	33. O-ring	43. Reverse idler shaft
6. Roll pin	16. Plug	26. Circlip	34. Bolt	44. Reverse idler gear
7. Split pin	17. Seal	27. Countershaft	35. Serrated lock washer	45. Oil seal
8. Main shift rod	18. Spring	28. O-ring	36. Pinion shaft assembly	46. Magnetic drain plug
9. Shift finger	19. Detent plunger		37. Shim	
10. U-spring	20. Shift rod with shift fork for 4th and 5th gear		38. Needle bearing	

Exploded view of shifting mechanism and gear train—928

4TH GEAR

Synchronizer rings—No grooves.
Thrust block—Two beveled sides.
Shift band—Two separate shift bands.
Stop—Beveled sides.

5TH GEAR

Synchronizer ring—No grooves (0.6mm wider).
Thrust block—Two beveled sides.
Shift band—Two separate shift bands.
Stop—Beveled sides.

NOTE: All synchronizers should have an installed diameter of 86.0 ± 0.24mm, measured at the highest point of the ring.

Countershaft

DISASSEMBLY

1. Remove the circlip from the countershaft hub.
2. Press the 3rd, 4th and 5th gears from the countershaft hub.

INSTALLATION

1. Heat the gears to approximately 212°F (100°C) and press them into their proper position.
2. Install the circlip on the countershaft hub.

TRANSMISSION ASSEMBLY

1. Place the assembled countershaft assembly into the transmission case with lift wires attached.
2. Install the mainshaft into the case and install the bolts in the bearing retaining plate to case.
3. Install the input shaft assembly in the front of the transmission case.
4. With the lifting wire, raise the countershaft hub assembly in place and insert the countershaft from the front of the transmission case and towards the rear, engaging the notched portion of the shaft into the slot provided by the installation of the mainshaft bearing retainer plate.

NOTE: The bearing retaining plate may have to be loosened to allow the entry of the countershaft into its position in the rear of the case. Retighten the bearing retaining plate.

5. Check the gear train freeness of rotation and proper clearances.
6. Install the shift rods, forks and finger in their proper locations and install the retaining pins through the forks and fingers to engage the shift rods. Install the necessary detent plungers and springs during the shift rod installation.
7. Install the detent plugs, necessary circlips and the input shaft oil seal holder.
8. Install the mainshaft rod and shift finger. Install the retaining pin into the finger and through the shaft.
9. Install the differential carrier assembly and the side covers with the removed shims.

NOTE: Should the differential need to be adjusted, refer to the individual car section.

10. Install the left and right axle flanges and retain with the retaining bolts.
11. Install the top and rear cover, using new gaskets.
12. Fill the transmission and the differential with hypoid type oil, 90 weight. Each must be filled separately.

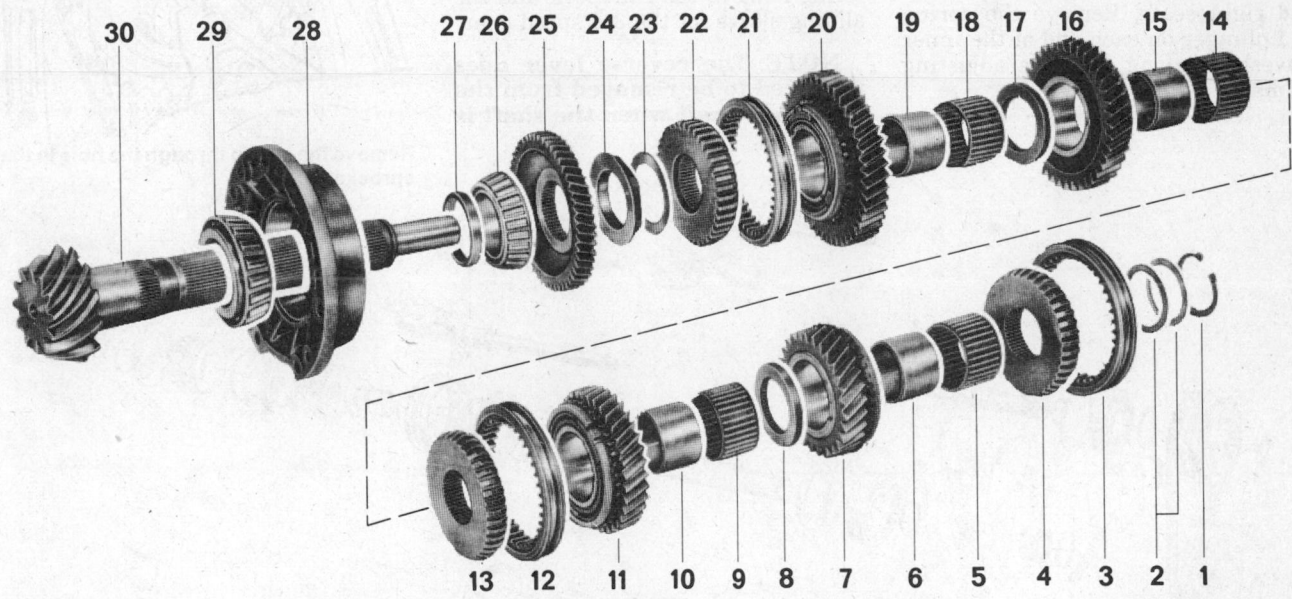

1. Circlip	7. Gear, 4th speed	13. Hub
2. Shim (distance y)	8. Thrust washer	14. Needle bearing
3. Shift sleeve	9. Needle bearing	15. Inner race
4. Hub	10. Inner race	16. Gear, 2nd speed
5. Needle bearing	11. Gear, 3rd speed	17. Thrust washer
6. Inner race	12. Shift sleeve	18. Needle bearing

19. Inner race	26. Tapered roller bearing inner race
20. Gear, 1st speed	27. Shim
21. Shift sleeve	28. Bearing retaining plate
22. Hub	29. Tapered roller bearing inner race
23. Shim (distance x)	30. Pinion shaft
24. Locknut	
25. Reverse gear	

Exploded view of pinion shaft gear assembly—928

TYPE 12

4 Speed Transaxle SAAB

DISASSEMBLY

NOTE: The disassembly and assembly of the transaxle gear train can be accomplished without separating the engine and gearbox. However, the engine flywheel must be removed.

──────── CAUTION ────────

Before the transaxle disassembly is begun, measure the backlash of the differential ring and pinion gears, so that the same backlash is obtained during the reassembly, providing no affected components for the differential are replaced. Upon removal of the differential bearing seats, measure and mark the shims for later installation.

1. Secure the transaxle and drain the lubricating oil. Remove the side and end plates from the case.
2. Remove the differential bearing seat retaining bolts and with the aid of a puller type tool, remove the left and right seats. Remove the spring and plunger on each end of the inner driveshaft, along with the adjusting shims.

NOTE: The inner driveshafts will be removed with the seats as an assembly.

3. Remove the differential assembly from the housing.
4. Remove the lock plate that holds the intermediate and reverse gear shafts in place.
5. Using a special pulling tool or the equivalent, pull the intermediate gear shaft from the housing and allow the intermediate gear set to drop downward.
6. Remove the primary gear housing retaining bolts and separate the primary gear housing from the transaxle housing.
7. With the primary gear housing separated from the transaxle housing, the intermediate gear set can be removed from the transaxle.
8. Remove the transaxle side cover, if not already removed, and take out the spring and ball catch for the gear selector rod.
9. Remove the reverse gear selector shaft retaining screw, turn the gear selector rod so the driver is detached from the reverse gear shift and pull out the shaft.
10. Remove the shift shaft for the 1st/2nd gear, 3rd top gear and shift forks. Remove the shift fork and the sliding sleeve for the 3rd speed gear.

NOTE: The reverse lever does not need to be removed from the gear shift shaft when the shaft is removed.

11. Remove the reverse gear shaft and lift the reverse idler gear from the housing.
12. Remove the needle bearing from the pinion shaft and install a special holding tool or equivalent, as a lock on the reverse gear of the pinion shaft. Remove the pinion nut from the shaft.
13. Remove the gear holding tool and remove the 3rd/4th gear synchronizer hub and 3rd gear.
14. Remove the four pinion shaft bearing housing screws. Install a special pushing tool or equivalent, and remove the pinion shaft from the housing. Remove the gears, sleeves, washers and shims from the housing, noting each component's location.

Pinion Shaft Housing

DISASSEMBLY

1. To remove the pinion shaft from the pinion shaft housing, pinion bear-

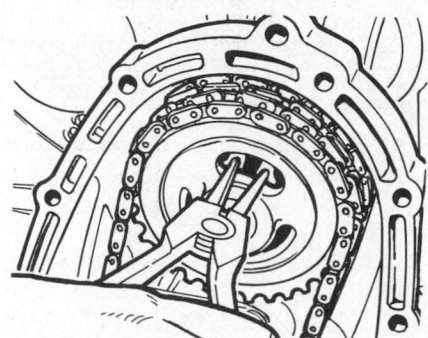

Remove the circlip through the hole in the sprocket

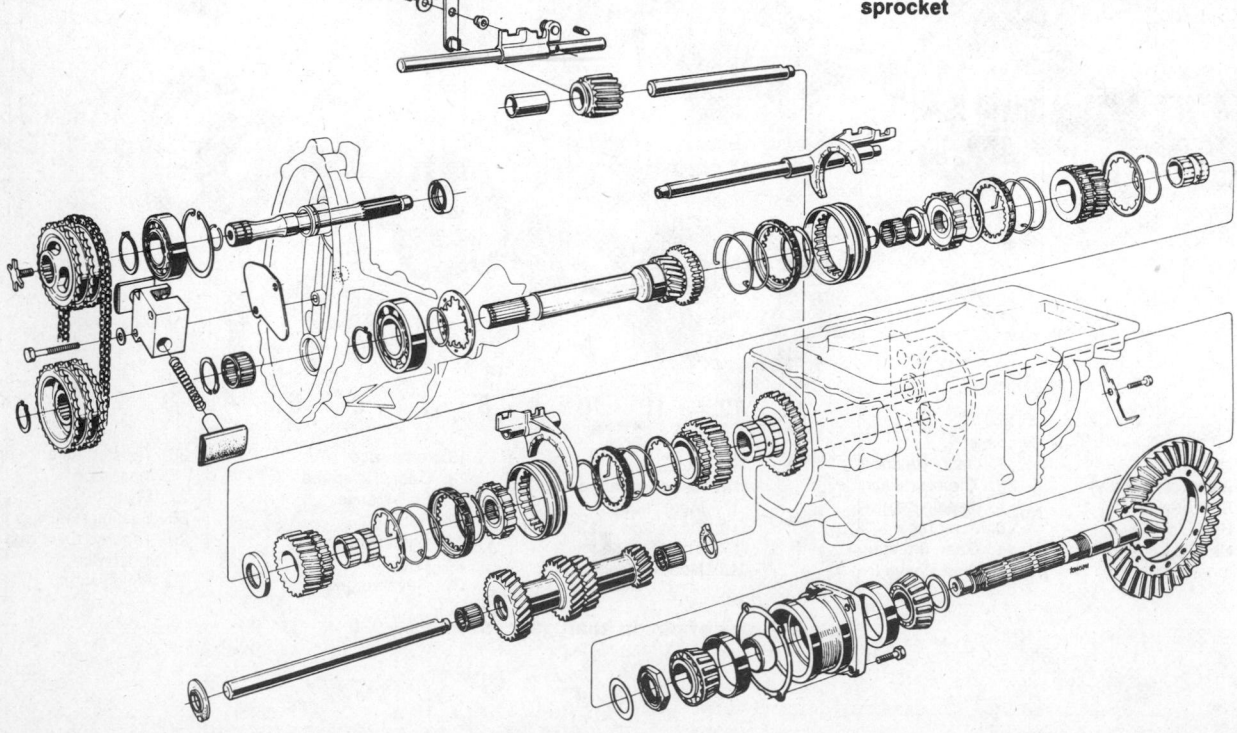

Exploded view of transaxle, chain driven primary gear train

ing nut must be removed. The pinion shaft can then be pressed from the housing and the front bearing removed.

2. Place the pinion shaft and rear bearing in a press and remove the rear bearing from the shaft.

3. Remove the outer races from the pinion shaft housing as required, with a press and the necessary special tools.

ASSEMBLY

1. Install the outer races in the pinion shaft housing and seat firmly.

2. Press the rear bearing onto the pinion shaft. Fit the spacer and bearing housing onto the shaft.

NOTE: The bearings should be lightly oiled before assembly.

3. Place the shaft assembly in a press or equivalent tool, install the front bearing and force it into place on the shaft, while turning the housing until a resistance is felt.

4. Install a "locking" substance on the shaft threads and install the locking nut.

5. Wrap a cord around the pinion housing and attach a pull scale to the cord.

6. Tighten the locking nut until a pull torque of 10–15 lbs. (47–71 N) is attained for new bearings, or a pull torque of 4.2–9.2 lbs. (19–43 N) is reached for bearings having more than 1200 miles (2,000 KM), considered to be used bearings.

7. When the bearing pull torque is correct, lock the pinion nut in place on the shaft with a center punch or drift.

Primary Gear Case

DISASSEMBLY

1. Remove the retaining bolts and separate the cover from the primary gear housing.

2. Remove the chain tensioner assembly.

3. Remove the circlip from the lower gear sprocket and the circlip from the upper gear, through the opening in the gear sprocket.

4. Remove the gear sprockets and the chain at the same time. It may be necessary to apply pressure to the sprockets to remove.

5. Remove the upper gear sprocket circlip and remove the sprocket bearing, if necessary.

6. Remove the four screws and bearing retainer at the input gear to the gearbox.

7. Press the input shaft from the primary gear case.

8. Remove the circlip and press the bearing from the input shaft.

9. Remove the needle bearing

circlip and remove the needle bearing from the primary gear case.

10. Remove the clutch shaft seal.

ASSEMBLY

1. Install a new clutch shaft seal.

2. Install the needle bearing and circlip into the primary gear case.

NOTE: The mark on the needle bearing should be facing out.

3. Install the ball bearing onto the input shaft and fit the circlip on the shaft.

4. Press the input shaft assembly into the primary gear case.

5. Place the bearing retainer onto the primary gear case and apply a sealing compound to the screw threads.

6. Install the bearing, race and circlip into the upper gear sprocket.

NOTE: The chamfer of the circlip must face outward when the gear is installed.

7. Install the chain on the sprocket gears and install onto the splines and stud in the primary gear case. Install the two circlips.

8. Install the chain tensioner with the oil passage at the top and place the backing plate so that its top edge is in line with the top edge of the chain tensioner housing. Apply a thread sealant to the chain tensioner bolts and install.

9. Install the primary gear cover and new gasket.

ASSEMBLY OF TRANSAXLE

1. Install the guide studs into the transaxle housing and install the pinion assembly into the case, with the original shims between the bearing housing and the transaxle housing.

NOTE: Should new components be installed that would change the pinion depth, special tools would have to be used to correct the components to the proper pinion depth setting.

2. Remove the guide studs and install the four retaining bolts into the bearing housing.

NOTE: Any measurement operations and adjustments must be done before the bolts are secured with a "locking" substance.

3. The distance between the connecting surface for the primary gear housing and the pinion shaft nut should be checked before installing the reverse gear on the pinion shaft. The distance should be 7.677–7.681 inches (195.0–1–95.1mm). Adjust a

depth gauge to measurement and measure the clearance with a feeler gauge. Install the necessary shims to close the clearance between the pinion nut and the reverse gear.

NOTE: If the pinion shaft depth was not changed, the original shims can be reused.

4. After the necessary shims have been selected and installed on the pinion shaft, install the reverse gear on the shaft.

NOTE: The gears will have to be driven on the pinion shaft with a sleeve and a plastic tipped hammer.

5. Install the 1st gear on the bearing sleeve of the reverse gear.

6. Install the 1st/2nd synchronizer hub in place on the pinion shaft. Place the 1st/2nd gear shift fork into the sliding sleeve and mount on the synchronizer hub.

7. Install the 2nd gear sleeve and mount the 2nd gear onto the sleeve.

8. Install the spacer and sleeve for the 3rd gear. Install the 3rd gear on the sleeve.

9. Install the 3rd/4th synchronizer hub. Place the 3rd/4th shifting fork into the sliding sleeve of the 3rd/4th gear and install on the synchronizer hub.

10. Lock the reverse gear so that the pinion shaft does not turn. Install and torque the pinion shaft nut to 30–45 ft. lbs. (40 to 60 Nm).

11. Secure the nut to the pinion shaft.

12. Install the pinion shaft needle bearing and its locking ring. Remove the shaft locking tool.

13. Locate the sliding sleeves in the neutral position and install the shift shaft for the 1st, 2nd, 3rd and 4th gear shift forks.

14. Turn the gear selector shaft clockwise to gain clearance to install the reverse gear shift shaft. Install the shaft and lock with the stop screw.

15. Mount the needle bearings into the intermediate gear assembly, using grease to hold them in place. Install the gear set into the bottom of the gear box housing.

16. Have the thrust washer located in the correct position for the intermediate gear assembly, on the primary gear housing. Be sure the connecting tube is fitted to the output shaft of the primary gear.

17. Seal the mating surface of the primary gear housing and mount it to the transaxle case.

NOTE: Do not tighten the primary gear housing screws until the intermediate gear shaft is installed.

18. Insert the intermediate gear shaft into position. Move the intermediate gear assembly in order that the shaft can be installed. Align the thrust washer so the shaft can be installed through it. Tighten the primary gear housing retaining screws.

19. Install the reverse gear and shaft. Be sure the reverse lever is fitted into the groove on the reverse gear. Install the lock plate over the reverse gear and the intermediate gear shaft ends. Secure the screw.

20. Install the spring and lock ball for the gear selector rod and fit the housing cover in place and secure with the retaining bolts.

21. Install the differential assembly into the housing.

22. Using the shims that were removed during the disassembly, install the inner drive shaft assemblies in place on the housing. Measure the differential gear backlash and adjust the measurements obtained before the disassembly.

23. Complete the assembly by installing the cover onto the housing and filling the unit with lubricating oil to the specified level.

Pinion shaft gear assembly.

TYPE 13

---

5 Speed Transaxle SAAB

DISASSEMBLY

1. Follow Steps 1–3 of the 4 speed transaxle procedure. Pay attention to all "NOTES" and "CAUTIONS".

2. Remove the dowel pin in the gear shift fork for 5th gear.

3. Move the gear wheel for reverse into the reverse position and then select 5th gear.

4. Free the shaft (lower sprocket) tab washer from the input shaft and then remove the nut.

5. Remove the chain tensioner.

6. Working through the hole on the upper sprocket, remove the circlip from in front of the sprocket bearing.

7. Remove the sprockets and chains together as one unit.

NOTE: A slide hammer and/or a gear pulley may be necessary to remove the sprocket and chain assembly.

8. Separate the pinion on the input shaft from the gear wheel on the input layshaft by removing the circlip from the groove and sliding the synchromesh sleeve toward the pinion.

9. Remove the locking plate for the layshaft and reverse gear shaft. Using special tools 83 90 049 and 83 90 270, pull out the layshaft gear cluster and then remove the pinion from the input layshaft. The pinion should be removed through the side of the transmission case along with the synchromesh sleeve and thrust washer.

10. Remove the bolts and oil catcher from the input shaft bearing case. Remove the bearing case by means of a side hammer.

11. Slide the gear selector for 5th gear through the full extent of its travel and then remove the selector fork and the synchromesh sleeve.

12. Up to and including gearbox No. 436500, remove the circlip and shims from the 5th gear synchrohub. Also remove the adjacent spacer from the pinion shaft.

13. On models having a gearbox number higher than 436500, remove the reverse gear and shaft. Lock the reverse gearwheel, remove the circlip and then unscrew the nut securing the synchrohub for 5th gear. Retain the hub and spacer.

14. Remove all primary gear case retaining bolts and then drift in the dowel pins so that the case can be separated from the gearbox housing.

NOTE: The 5th gear selector will remain in the housing and can be removed later. File away any burrs around the hole in the shaft so that the aperature in the gear housing will not be damaged upon reassembly.

15. Remove the layshaft and layshaft gear cluster. Save the needle bearings and thrust washer for reuse.

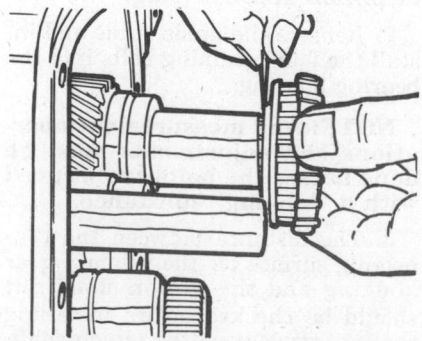

Use shims to remove the play between the synchrohub and sleeve

16. Remove the selector shafts and the selectors. Remove the selectors for 1st and 2nd gears along with their synchromesh units. Remove the reverse selector together with the shaft for 5th and reverse gear.

17. The selector shafts should be removed from the front. The aperature for the taper pin should be filed free of any burrs. The selector, double lockout and the spring can be removed later. Don't lose the selector ball and guide pin.

18. Remove the four bolts for the pinion shaft bearing housing and then press out the shaft. Be sure to keep the gear wheels, sleeves, washers and shims in order.

Pinion Shaft and Housing

For all pinion shaft and housing disassembly and assembly procedures, please refer to the steps in the "4 Speed Transaxle" section.

ASSEMBLY

1. Screw two locating studs in to the transmission case and then shim and position the pinion shaft assembly into the case. Use a rubber mallet and a drift and gently tap the assembly into position. Install the retaining bolts for the bearing housing and tighten them to 15–18.5 ft. lbs.

2. Before installing the reverse gear onto the pinion shaft, check that the distance between the primary gear housing mating surface and the pinion shaft nut is 7.677–7.681 in. If it is not, shims must be replaced between the nut and the reverse gear. Shims are available in thicknesses of 0.018, 0.0157, and 0.0197 in. If the distance is correct, the shims used earlier may be replaced.

3. Using a rubber mallet and a sleeve, install the reverse gear.

4. Install 1st gear on the bearing sleeve of reverse gear.

5. Install the 1st/2nd gear synchromesh hub. Position the 1st/2nd gear shift fork into the 1st/2nd gear synchromesh sleeve and then install it on the hub.

6. Press the 2nd gear sleeve onto the shaft and then install 2nd gear onto the sleeve.

7. Repeat Step 6 for the 3rd gear assembly.

8. Repeat Step 5 for 3rd/4th gear. Fit the bushing for 4th gear onto the shaft and then install the gear over it. Install the ball bearing bushing.

9. If the selector shaft was removed, install it together with the double lockout guide pin.

10. Slide the synchromesh sleeves onto the pinion shaft while in the neutral position and then install the 1st/

2nd gear shift shaft and the 3rd/4th gear shift forks.

11. Install the reverse selector shaft with the selector. Seal the shaft stop bolt with Loctite® and tighten it.

12. Install the 5th gear selector on the reverse selector shaft.

13. Fit the needle bearing into the layshaft gear cluster and then position the whole assembly inside the gearbox housing.

14. Position the layshaft and raise the layshaft gear cluster so that it lines up with the cluster so that it holds the gears in position. The thrust washer can be installed later.

15. Slide the spacer, along with the 5th gear synchrohub and the circlip onto the pinion shaft. Insert shims between the hub and the sleeve so that there is no play between any of the parts on the pinion shaft. After all play has been removed, the spacer, hub and circlip should be removed.

16. Apply sealing compound to the mating surface of the primary gear casing and then bolt the basing to the gearbox housing.

17. Reinstall the spacer and the synchrohub on the pinion shaft.

18. Fit the shims which were used in Step 15 to the hub so that once the circlip is installed there will be no axial play. Install a locking tool (special tool 8790503) on the reverse gear and tighten the nut to 37 ± 7 ft. lbs.

19. Using a drift with a rounded nose, upset the flange of the nut in the groove in the hub.

20. Install the input shaft along with the bearing housing, oil catcher and connecting pipes. Using three guide pins for alignment and the sprocket as a spacer between the adapter and the bearing housing, insert the bearing housing far enough for the shaft to meet the synchromesh sleeve. Use a slide hammer and drive the bearing housing into place.

NOTE: Check the compression of the bearing before installation.

21. Up to and including gearbox No. 437802 (1982 models), install the thrust washer for the constant-mesh gear on the input layshaft. Grease the washer and position it so that the locating tab is in the special recess.

On gearboxes No. 437803 and later (1982 models), install a new bearing without a thrust washer.

22. Install the input layshaft gear along with the sleeve, circlip and bearing rollers. Slide the layshaft back so that the input layshaft gear can be fitted.

23. Push the synchromesh sleeve onto the layshaft and fit the circlip in the groove.

24. Install the layshaft thrust wash-er. Withdraw the layshaft and slide the washer into position. Insert the shaft so that it locks into position.

25. Install the reverse gear wheel and shaft. Adjust the shaft until it locks in position.

NOTE: Make sure that the reverse lever engages the groove in the reverse gear.

26. Slide the locking plate over the shaft ends and install the bolt with Loctite®.

27. Install the primary gear sprockets and chains. Make sure that the hole for the tab washer on the lower sprocket is facing outward.

28. Install the chain tensioner using Loctite® on the mounting bolts.

29. Screw the nut onto the input shaft. Pull reverse and 5th gears at the same time so as to lock the input shaft and then tighten the nut. Using a round drift, knock one of the nut tabs into the recess in the gear wheel.

30. Install the dowel in the gear selector fork for 5th gear.

31. Install the differential.

32. Check and replace the shaft seals in the bearing retaining housings if necessary. Adjust the crownwheel backlash if necessary. Install the two driveshafts and inner joints—make sure that the seals are not damaged. Install the selector ball and spring and then install the gearbox top cover assembly and gasket.

33. Install the final drive unit, cover and gasket. Install the primary gear housing and the chain cover and gaskets.

34. Install the transaxle (if removed) and refill with the proper gear lubricant.

TYPE 14

4 Speed Transaxle Subaru

DISASSEMBLY

1. Disconnect the return springs from the release bearing holder and remove the clutch fork and release bearing holder.

2. Remove the transmission cover.

3. Wind vinyl tape on the spline of the right and left axle drive shafts to prevent the oil seals from being damaged when separating the case.

4. Separate the transmission case by removing the seventeen bolts.

NOTE: The case will separate easily if the two areas around the knock pins are tapped upward with a plastic hammer.

5. Use the shank of a hammer and remove the drive pinion.

6. Remove the transmission mainshaft.

7. Remove the differential.

8. Remove the three shifter rail spring plugs.

9. Remove the shifter forks and rails.

NOTE: When pulling out a rail, keep the other rails placed in Neutral. Pull the rail for the 4th/ 3rd by turning 90°.

10. Remove the one screw on the right and left side of the transmission case and remove the oil seal holder lock plate. Using a special oil seal holder wrench remove the oil seal holder and O-rings.

12. Pull the knock pins out and then pull out the reverse idler gear shaft, reverse idler gear and shifter lever.

13. Disassemble the transmission mainshaft.

   a. Remove the snap-ring.

   b. Press off the ball bearing, main shaft collar, 4th drive gear, synchronizer hub, 4th drive gear bushing and the 3rd drive gear.

NOTE: The 3rd drive gear bushing may be left installed but if replacement is necessary, cut a groove with a grinder and drive it off with a chisel. When the bushing moves a little remove it with a press.

14. Disassemble the drive pinion.

   a. Unscrew the drive pinion locknut.

   b. Remove the ball bearing and the 4th/3rd driven gear with a press then remove the 2nd gear and needle bearing by hand.

   c. Remove the 1st driven gear, needle bearing race, synchronizer hub and needle bearing by using a press.

   d. Remove the needle bearing race, drive pinion spacer and roller bearing by using a press.

15. Disassemble the transmission cover.

   a. Remove the back-up light switch and remove the reverse accent spring, ball and straight pin.

   b. Remove the plug in the upper part of the cover and then remove the reverse accent shaft and reverse return spring.

16. Disassemble the differential assembly.

   a. Remove the right and left snap-rings and then remove the two axle driveshafts.

   b. Remove the ring gear.

   c. Drive out the straight pin toward the ring gear.

   d. Pull out the differential pinion

1. Reverse idle gear complete
2. Reverse idler gear bushing
3. Reverse idler gear shaft
4. Knock pin
5. Reverse shifter rail
6. Shifter fork rail
7. Shifter fork rail 2
8. Shifter rail plunger 2
9. Shifter rail plunger
10. Shifter fork
11. Shifter fork set screw
12. Reverse shifter rail arm
13. Reverse shifter lever complete
14. Shifter fork 2
15. Transmission main shaft collar 2
16. Snap-ring (outer)
17. Ball bearing
18. Transmission main shaft collar
19. Gear set
20. Synchronizer ring
21. 4th drive gear bushing
22. Synchronizer sleeve
23. Synchronizer hub spring
24. Synchronizer hub
25. Synchronizer hub insert
26. Third drive gear bushing
27. Transmission main shaft
28. Needle bearing
29. Oil seal
30. Drive pinion lock nut
31. Drive pinion lock washer
32. Ball bearing
33. Bolt
34. Spring washer
35. Drive pinion shim
36. Second driven gear
37. Synchronizer ring 2
38. Needle bearing
39. Needle bearing inner race
40. Reverse driven gear
41. Synchronizer hub spring 2
42. Synchronizer hub 2
43. Synchronizer hub insert 2
44. Low (1st) driven gear
45. Drive pinion spacer
46. Roller bearing
47. Key

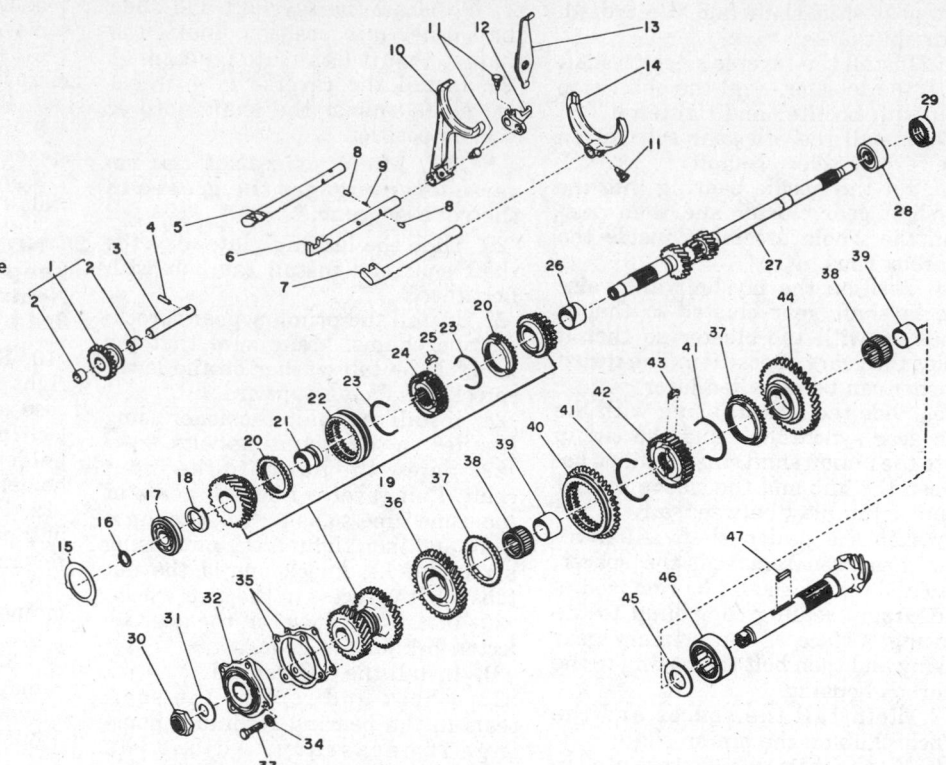

Exploded view of 4-speed transaxle gear assemblies

1. Roller bearing
2. Bolt
3. Crown gear lock washer
4. Differential pinion shaft
5. Differential case
6. Straight pin
7. Axle drive shaft
8. Axle shaft oil seal holder
9. O-ring
10. Oil seal (RH)
11. Pinion & crown gear set (AT)
12. Pinion & crown gear set (4WD)
13-1. Pinion & crown gear set (4-speed)
13-2. Pinion & crown gear set (5-speed)
14. Washer
15. Differential side gear
16. Differential pinion
17. Snap-ring
18. Oil seal (LH)

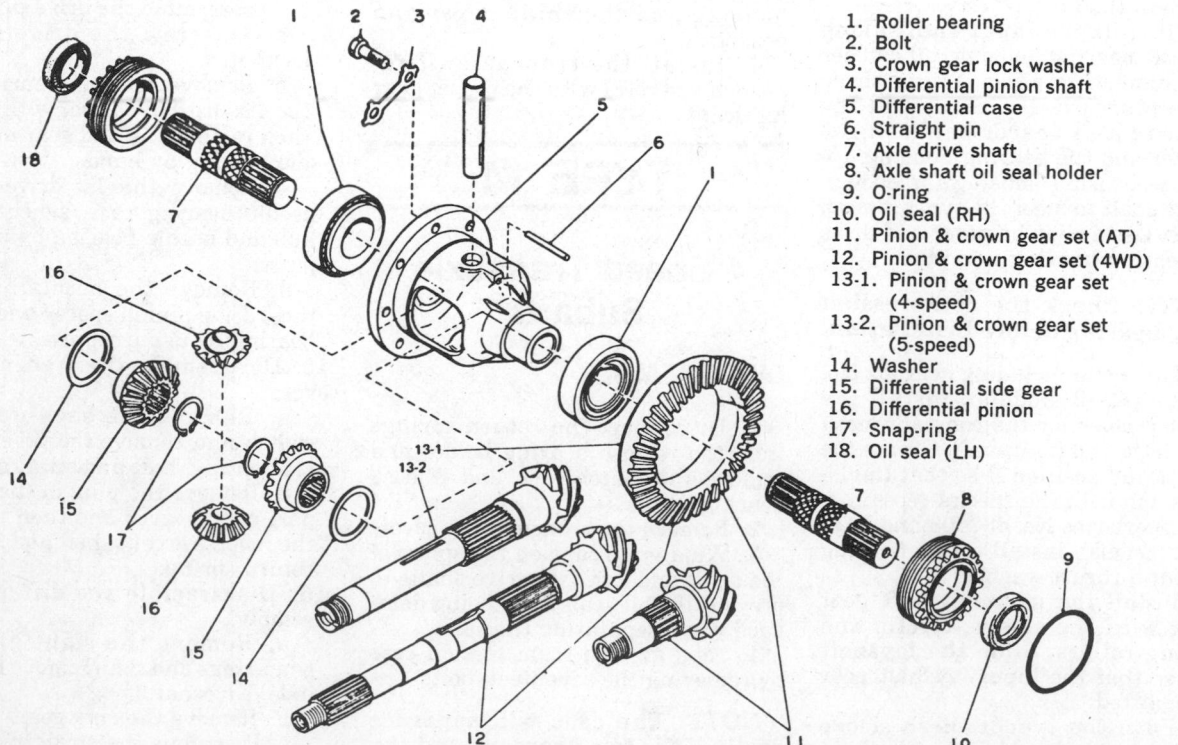

Exploded view of differential assembly and the three pinion gear lengths

shaft and then remove the differential pinion, side gear and washer.

e. Remove the roller bearing by using a puller.

ASSEMBLY

1. Reassemble the transmission mainshaft.

NOTE: Install the hub so that the end of the spline having the narrow tooth width is on the 3rd gear side. The shorter insert is for the 4th/3rd synchronizer and the longer insert is for the 1st/2nd synchronizer.

2. Reassemble the drive pinion.
   a. Install the roller bearing in the drive pinion and press on the spacer.
   b. Install the three synchronizer inserts, reverse driven gear and the two springs on the hub.

NOTE: Install the reverse driven gear so that its toothed side and the side of the synchronizer hub has its lower boss face in the same direction.

   c. Install the needle bearing race with a press.
   d. Install the needle bearing, 1st driven gear, synchronizer rings and hub which was sub-assembled in (c).
   e. Install the needle bearing race with a press.
   f. Install the 2nd driven gear and insert a key into the groove on the drive pinion.
   g. Install the 4th/3rd driven gear with a press.
   h. Install the ball bearings with a press.
   i. Install the drive pinion lockwasher.

NOTE: Stake the locknut in two places.

3. Reassemble the differential.
   a. Install the side and pinion gears on the case and then insert the pinion shaft.
   b. Measure the backlash between the gear and pinion and make adjustment using the proper washers.
   c. Align the differential pinion shaft with the holes on the differential case and drive the straight pin in from the ring gear side. Drive it in until it falls in about 0.039 in. then stake the pin.
   d. Press on the roller bearing on the differential case.
   e. Using new lockwashers, clamp the ring gear on the case.
   f. Install the axle driveshafts and lock it with snap-rings.

g. Measure the clearance between the pinion shaft and the tip of the axle driveshaft. Clearance should be 0–0.00079 in. Make adjustment by selecting the proper snap-ring.

NOTE: The figure of the lower three digits marked on the drive pinion end face is the match number for combining it with the ring gear. The upper figure is for thee shim adjustment. The first three digits on the ring gear indicates a number for combination with the drive pinion. The following digits indicate a value of appropriate backlash.

   h. Adjust the drive pinion shim, place the drive pinion on the transmission case without a shim and tighten the pinion.
   i. Press on the oil seal into the axle shaft oil seal holder.
4. Position the transmission case on the stand and screw the axle shaft oil seal holder into the case using the special wrench.

NOTE: Make sure the holder marked "R" is installed on the right side and holder marked "L" is installed on the left side.

5. Install the outer snap-ring and washer on the speedometer shaft, then install them into the transmission case. Install the speedometer driven gear on the shaft. Install the oil seal.

NOTE: Install the outer snap-ring on the speedometer driveshaft from the driven gear side.

6. Install the reverse shifter lever into the transmission case. Install the reverse idler gear and shaft.
7. Install the reverse shifter rail arm to the end of the reverse shifter lever. Install the reverse shifter rail.
8. Install the shifter fork rail spring, ball and gasket in the case and tighten the shifter rail spring plug.
9. Shifter the reverse shifter rail and select the reverse shifter rail arm so that the clearance between the reverse idler gear and the wall of the case is 0.059–0.079 in.
10. Install the shifter rail plunger into the hold of the case.
11. Winde tape around the splines of the axle driveshafts of the differential assembly to prevent damage to the oil seals.
12. Install the differential on the axle shaft oil seal holder.
13. Install the needle bearing on the transmission mainshaft and install the case.

NOTE: Make sure the knock pin

of the case is fitted into the hole in the needle bearing outer race. To prevent damage to the roller bearing place the open end of the roving plunger on the bearing.

14. Install the shifter fork. Install the shifter rail plunger in the shifter fork rail.
15. Install the shims in the drive pinion selected in Step "k" under reassembling the differential assembly, and then install into the transmission case.
16. When installing the roller bearing outer race knock hole to the knock pin of the case, position the knock hole to the edge of the transmission case and put a mark on top of the outer race. Turn the outer race so that the mark comes to the edge of the transmission case while slightly up the drive pinion, then slightly move the outer race right and left and front and rear until the knock pin fits into the knock hole.
17. Install the shifter rail plunger.
18. Install the shifter fork and shifter fork rail.
19. Install the shifter fork rail spring, ball and gasket into the case.
20. Select the shifter forks so that the synchronizer sleeve and reverse drive gear come to the center of the gears when the mainshaft and drive pinion are placed in the normal position (both the shaft and drive pinion are forced against the forward side without any clearance).
21. Check clearance A at the end of each rail. If dimension A is not within the range of 0.012–0.063 in., replace the rail, fork and set screw so that the proper dimension is obtained.
22. Install the mainshaft oil seal with its end surface A as shown in the illustration.

NOTE: When joining the case from above, be careful not to let the oil seal tilt. Apply liquid gasket to the case surfaces, remove the outer race of the roller bearings and make sure the speedometer gear tooth is meshed.

23. Clamp the clutch cable bracket, and back-up lamp wire clip together.
24. Instal the drive pinion onto the case.
25. Install the outer race of the roller bearing.
26. Check and adjust the backlash of the ring gear and check the adjustment of preload on the roller bearing. Special tools are necessary unless it is done by trial-and-error. Backlash is as specified between 0.0039–0.0059 in.
27. Check the tooth contact of the hypoid gear as follows. To reduce backlash, loosen the holder on the up-

per case side and turn in the holder on the lower case side by the same amount. To increase backlash, loosen the lower and turn in the upper.

28. Remove the lock plate (driveshaft holder). Loosen the driveshaft holder until the O-ring groove appears, install the O-ring into the groove and tighten the holder into position where the holder has been tightened in. Do this on both upper and lower heads.

29. Tighten the lock plate. Remove the protective vinyl tape wound on the axle shafts.

30. Reassemble the transmission cover.

31. Install the transmission cover.

a. Adjust the bearing side clearance 0–0.0118 in. using collar (transmission main shaft). For adjustment, insert collar if required.

b. Install the shifter arm in the cover (and install the cover to the transmission).

c. Adjust the transmission cover by inserting a bar through the hole of the shifter arm and shift the gear into 4th. Move the shifter arm from 4th position to 2nd and reverse position. The arm will move lightly toward 2nd side but heavy to reverse side because of the function of the return spring, and the arm will come into contact with the stopper at the end. To adjust, remove the plug on the cover and change the thickness of the aluminum gasket, so that the light stroke and heavy stroke become the same.

32. Install the clutch release fork and release bearing holder and secure them with return springs.

NOTE: Fill the internal groove of the holder with grease.

TYPE 15

5 Speed Transaxle Subaru

DISASSEMBLY

1. Remove the transmission.
2. Remove the clutch release fork and release bearing holder.
3. Remove the transmission rear cover.
4. Drive out the spring pin on the shifter fork.
5. Shift the gears into first gear, install the mainshaft stopper (special tool), release the staking on the drive pinion locknut and remove the nut.
6. Remove the synchronizer hub and shifter fork together.

7. Remove the 5th driven gear, needle bearing inner race, needle bearing and drive pinion spacer.
8. Remove the three bolts retaining the drive pinion assembly to the case.
9. Separate the left and right sections of the transmission case.
10. Remove the drive pinion assembly mainshaft assembly and differential assembly.
11. Remove the three shifter rail spring plugs.
12. Remove the shifter fork setscrew, shifter fork and shifter fork rail of 3rd/4th and 1st/2nd.

a. To remove the shifter fork rail, position the rest of the rails in neutral.

b. To remove the 3rd and 4th rails, turn them 90 degrees and let the shifter rail plunger fall in the groove of the reverse shifter rail.

13. Take out the lock pin and the reverse idler gear shaft, then remove the reverse idler gear and the reverse shifter lever as a unit.

14. Remove the outer snap-ring and take out the reverse shifter rail arm from the rail then remove the ball and spring.

15. Disassemble the mainshaft.

a. Using the special wrench and holder, remove the locknut and remove the 5th drive gear with a press.

b. Remove the woodruff key.

c. Remove the ball bearing and 4th drive gear using a press.

d. Disassemble the synchronizer hub, third drive gear and 4th drive gear bushing using a press.

e. Remove the outer snap-ring, 1st driven gear washer 1st driven gear spring and 2nd driven gear spring, from the 1st driven gear and 2nd driven gear which were removed from the drive pinion.

16. The procedure for disassembling the main shaft differential gear, shift fork, etc., is the same as the 4 speed transmission disassembly Steps 14–16.

ASSEMBLY

NOTE: Since some assembly procedures are the same as the 4-speed transmission, refer to that section where noted.

1. Reassemble the drive pinion component parts following the procedure in the four speed transmission section until the ball bearing, then install the spacer, needle bearing race, needle bearing, fifth driven gear, synchronizer hub, stopper, lockwasher and nut. Tighten the locknut to 60 ft. lbs.

2. Select a drive pinion shim (see Step 3–4 speed assembly procedures).

3. Put the shifter rail spring and ball in the reverse shifter rail arm. Insert the reverse shifter rail.
4. Install the outer snap-ring.
5. Put the shifter fork rail spring, ball and gasket in the case.
6. Select the reverse shifter lever so that the gap between the reverse idler gear and the case wall becomes 0.06–0.118 in. by shifting the reverse shifter rail.
7. Shift it to the Neutral position, then select the right size washer so that the gap between the case wall becomes 0–0.002 in.
8. Put the shifter rail plunger into the grooves of the case and the reverse shifter rail arm.
9. Install the 1st driven gear spring (subgear) with the outer snap-ring and 1st driven gear washer to the 2nd driven gear.

NOTE: The clearance between the tooth tops of the gear and spring (subgear) is 0.0039–0.0197 in.

10. Reassemble the transmission mainshaft as given in Step 1 under assembly of 4 speed transmission. Then, install a key, 5th drive gear, lock washer and locknut to the mainshaft.
11. Fit the differential assembly into the case.
12. Attach the mainshaft assembly.
13. Insert a shifter rail plunger and install a shifter fork and rail.
14. Install the adjustment shim selected before with the drive pinion assembly and then install them to the case.
15. Insert the shifter rail plunger.
16. Install the shifter fork and shifter rail.
17. Install the shifter fork rail spring and ball in the case.
18. Select the shifter fork so that the synchronizer sleeve comes to the center of the 3rd and 4th drive gears.
19. Select the next shifter fork so that he reverse driven gear comes to the center of the 1st and 2nd driven gears.
20. Apply a liquid gasket to the mating surfaces of the case halves and put them together.
21. Tighten the drive pinion on to the transmission case.
22. Inspect the ring gear backlash and the tooth contact as described under 4 speed transmission assembly Steps 26 and 27.
23. Remove the locknut of the drive pinion assembly to remove the lockwasher, stoppers and hub.
24. Install the hub, fork and rail using the spring pin.
25. Install the synchronizer stoppers and drive pinion lockwasher. Using the mainshaft stopper tool, tighten the pinion locknut to 58 ft. lbs.

NOTE: Shift the gear to 1st position when tightening the drive pinion locknut.

26. Select the last shifter fork so that the clearance between the sleeve and the 5th driven gear becomes 0.008 to 0.020 when the gear is in the 5th position.

27. Stake the drive pinion locknut.

28. Check the clearance between the edges of each rail. If the clearance is not within 0.012–0.063 in., replace the rail, fork and setscrew as ncessary.

29. Select the correct mainshaft collar.

30. Install the rear cover.

TYPE 16

4 Speed Transaxle Subaru with 4/WD

DISASSEMBLY

NOTE: Since some of the overhaul procedures are the same as the 4 speed transmission refer to that section when noted.

1. Remove the transmission.

2. Drive out the straight pin and pull out the shifter fork rail, for, ball and spring.

3. Remove the case assembly.

4. Shift the gear to the 1st position, release the staked part of the nut, then using a main shaft stopper, remove the locknut and take out the rear shaft drive gear from the drive pinion.

5. Remove the case assembly

6. Remove the race, needle bearing collar and washer from the drive pinion.

7. Shift the sleeve into the drive position and using a holder, remove the mainshaft locknut.

8. Remove the ball bearing assembly.

9. Remove the mainshaft spacer, rear shaft driven gear, sleeve, synchronizer hub and rear drive spacer from the rear driveshaft.

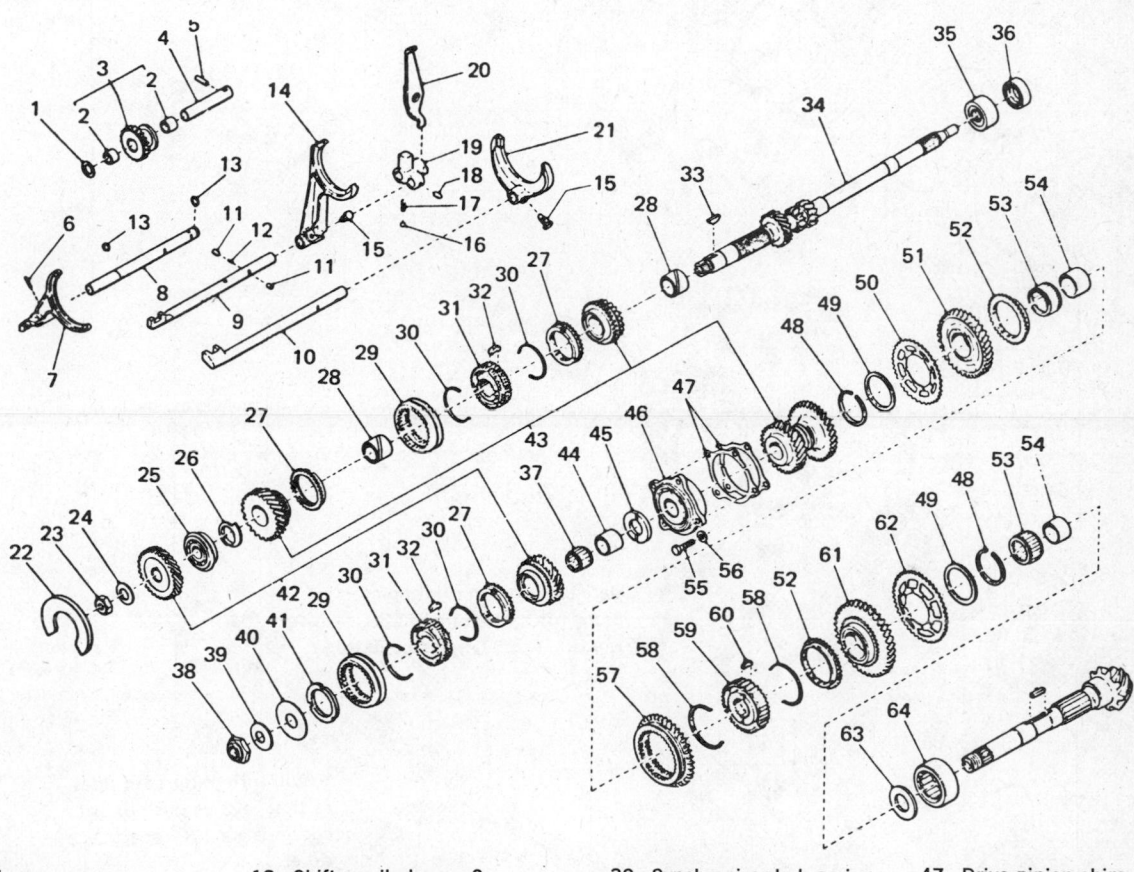

1. Washer	18. Shifter rail plunger 2
2. Reverse idler gear bushing	19. Reverse shifter rail arm
3. Reverse idler gear complete	20. Reverse shifter lever complete
4. Reverse idler gear shaft	21. Shifter fork 2
5. Knock pin	22. Transmission main shaft collar 2
6. Spring pin	23. Transmission main shaft lock nut
7. Shifter fork 3	24. Transmission main shaft lock washer
8. Reverse shifter rail	25. Ball bearing
9. Shifter fork rail	26. Transmission main shaft collar
10. Shifter fork rail 2	27. Synchronizer ring
11. Shifter rail plunger 2	28. 4th drive gear bushing
12. Shifter rail plunger	28. 3rd drive gear bushing
13. Snap ring (outer)	29. Synchronizer sleeve
14. Shifter fork	
15. Shifter fork set screw	
16. Ball	
17. Shifter fork rail spring 2	

30. Synchronizer hub spring	47. Drive pinion shim
31. Synchronizer hub	48. Snap ring
32. Synchronizer hub insert	49. Low (1st) driven gear washer
33. Woodruff key	50. Second driven spring gear
34. Transmission main shaft	51. Second driven gear
35. Needle bearing	52. Synchronizer ring 2
36. Oil seal	53. Needle bearing
37. Needle bearing	54. Needle bearing inner race
38. Drive pinion lock nut	55. Bolt
39. Drive pinion lock washer	56. Spring washer
40. Synchronizer stopper 2	57. Reverse driven gear
41. Synchronizer stopper	58. Synchronizer hub spring 2
42. Fifth gear set	59. Synchronizer hub 2
43. Third and fourth gear set	60. Synchronizer hub insert 2
44. Needle bearing inner race 5	61. Low (1st) driven gear
45. Drive pinion spacer 2	62. Low (1st) driven spring gear
46. Ball bearing	63. Drive pinion spacer
	64. Roller bearing

Exploded view of 5-speed transaxle gear assemblies

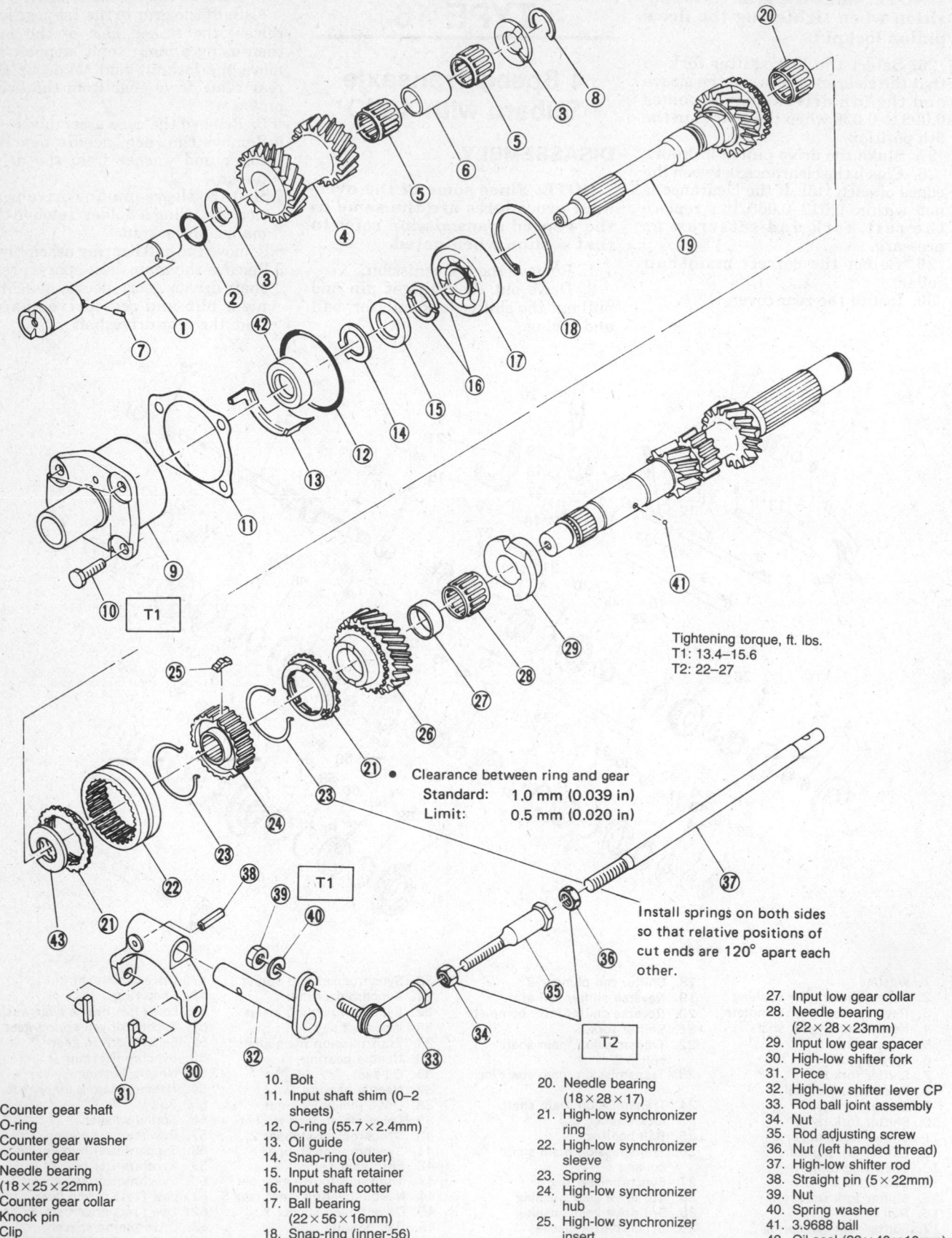

* Selective parts

Tightening torque, ft. lbs.
T1: 13.4–15.6
T2: 22–27

• Clearance between ring and gear
  Standard: 1.0 mm (0.039 in)
  Limit: 0.5 mm (0.020 in)

Install springs on both sides so that relative positions of cut ends are 120° apart each other.

1. Counter gear shaft
2. O-ring
3. Counter gear washer
4. Counter gear
5. Needle bearing (18 × 25 × 22mm)
6. Counter gear collar
7. Knock pin
8. Clip
9. Input shaft holder
10. Bolt
11. Input shaft shim (0–2 sheets)
12. O-ring (55.7 × 2.4mm)
13. Oil guide
14. Snap-ring (outer)
15. Input shaft retainer
16. Input shaft cotter
17. Ball bearing (22 × 56 × 16mm)
18. Snap-ring (inner-56)
19. Input shaft
20. Needle bearing (18 × 28 × 17)
21. High-low synchronizer ring
22. High-low synchronizer sleeve
23. Spring
24. High-low synchronizer hub
25. High-low synchronizer insert
26. Input low gear
27. Input low gear collar
28. Needle bearing (22 × 28 × 23mm)
29. Input low gear spacer
30. High-low shifter fork
31. Piece
32. High-low shifter lever CP
33. Rod ball joint assembly
34. Nut
35. Rod adjusting screw
36. Nut (left handed thread)
37. High-low shifter rod
38. Straight pin (5 × 22mm)
39. Nut
40. Spring washer
41. 3.9688 ball
42. Oil seal (22 × 40 × 10mm)
43. Snap-ring (outer-22)

Auxiliary transmission and High-Low shift linkage—Subaru 4-wheel drive

* Selective parts

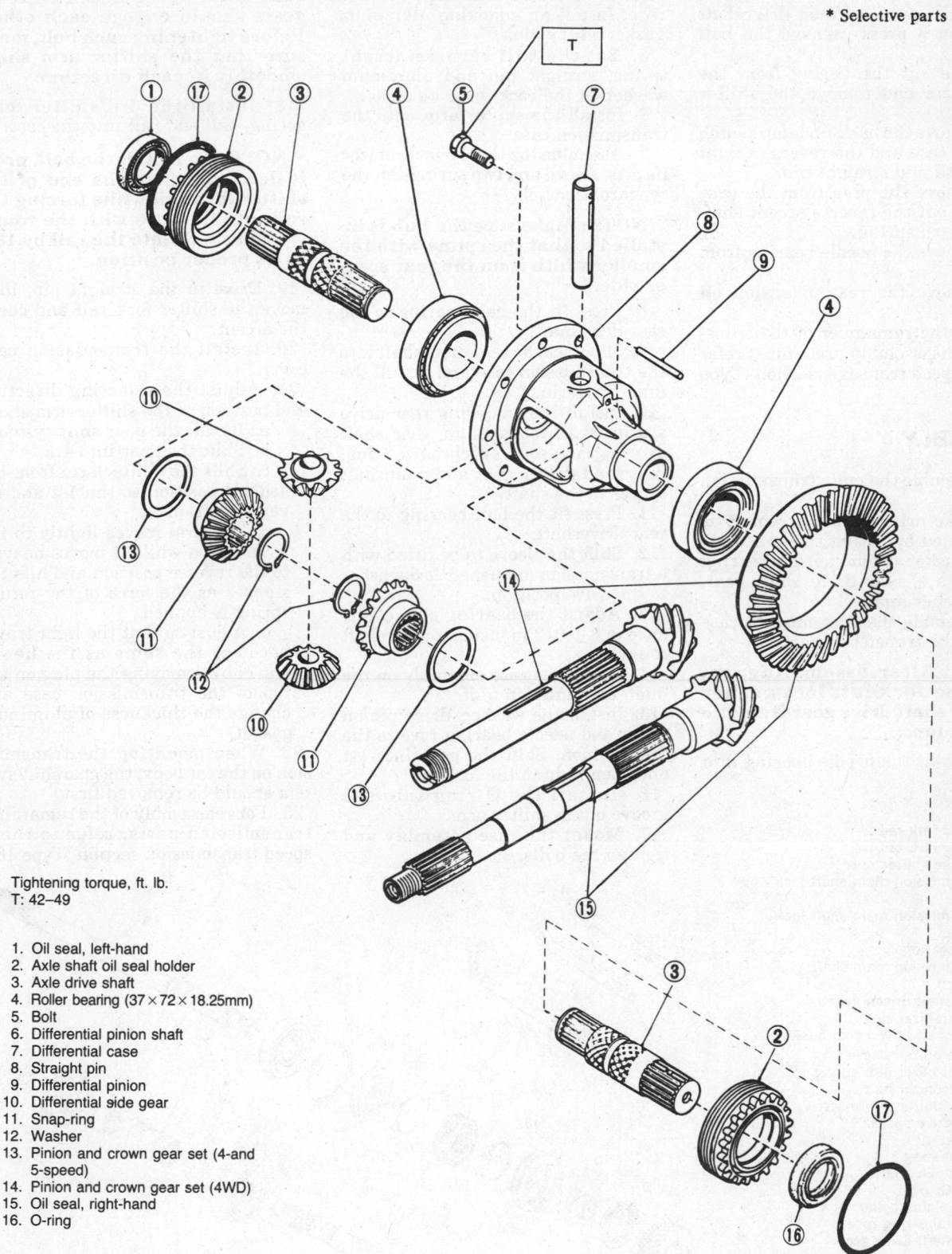

Tightening torque, ft. lb.
T: 42–49

1. Oil seal, left-hand
2. Axle shaft oil seal holder
3. Axle drive shaft
4. Roller bearing (37 × 72 × 18.25mm)
5. Bolt
6. Differential pinion shaft
7. Differential case
8. Straight pin
9. Differential pinion
10. Differential side gear
11. Snap-ring
12. Washer
13. Pinion and crown gear set (4-and 5-speed)
14. Pinion and crown gear set (4WD)
15. Oil seal, right-hand
16. O-ring

Exploded view of the Subaru differential unit

10. Remove the snap-ring from the case.

11. Punch out the rear driveshaft and using a press, remove the ball bearing.

12. Take out the O-ring from the shifter arm and remove the shifter arm.

13. Remove the back-up lamp switch from the case and the reverse accent spring ball and straight pin.

14. Remove the plug from the case and take out the reverse accent shafter and turn spring.

15. Remove the needle bearing from the case.

16. Remove the rear extension oil seal.

17. For the remainder of the transmission disassembly procedures refer to the 4 speed transaxle section (Type 18).

ASSEMBLY

1. Assemble the main transmission unit.

   a. The drive pinion assembly is assembled by fitting the ball bearing, washer collar, needle bearing inner race, rear drive shaft gear, lockwasher and locknut.

2. Assemble the transmission case without the transfer system.

NOTE: After assembling, remove the locknut, lockwasher and rear shaft drive gear from the drive pinion.

3. Press fit the needle bearing into the case.

1. Shifter fork rail 2
2. Shifter fork rail
3. Reverse shifter rail
4. Transmission main shaft lock nut
5. Transmission main shaft lock washer
6. Ball bearing
7. Transmission main shaft collar
8. Rear shaft driven gear
9. Synchronizer ring
10. Rear shaft driven gear bushing
11. Synchronizer sleeve
12. Synchronizer hub spring
13. Synchronizer hub
14. Synchronizer hub insert
15. Rear drive spacer
16. Snap ring
17. Ball bearing
18. Rear drive shaft
19. Washer
20. Drive pinion collar
21. Needle bearing race 5
22. Rear shaft drive gear

4. Insert the reverse return spring and the reverse accent shaft into the case. Install an adjusting aluminum gasket on the plug.

5. Set the ball reverse accent spring, straight pin and aluminum washer on the back-up lamp switch.

6. Install the shifter arm onto the transmission case.

7. Assemble the three synchronizer inserts, sleeve and two springs on the synchronizer hub.

NOTE: Make sure the hub is installed so that the spline with the smaller width is on the rear spacer side.

8. Press fit the ball bearing to the rear driveshaft.

9. Hammer the rear driveshaft into the transmission case and install the inner snap-ring.

10. Install the snap-ring rear drive spacer, synchronizer hub, rear shaft driven gear sleeve, synchronizer ring, rear shaft driven gear and mainshaft spacer to the shaft.

11. Press fit the ball bearing to the rear driveshaft.

12. Shift the sleeve to be fitted with a transmission mainshaft lockwasher to the drive position.

13. Adjust the bearing side clearance to 0–0.012 in. using a mainshaft collar.

14. Mount the case assembly on the main transmission unit.

15. Install the washer, drive pinion collar and needle bearing race to the drive pinion. Shift the gear into 1st and then tighten the locknut.

16. Install the O-ring into the groove of the shifter arm.

17. Mount the case assembly and tighten the bolts.

NOTE: When installing, the rear shift drive and 4th drive gears should engage each other. Before tightening each bolt, make sure that the shifter arm shifts smoothly in each direction.

18. Install the 3rd shifter fork, spring, ball and rail into the case.

NOTE: To install the ball, press it down by using the end of the shifter fork rail while forcing the rail into the case with the round side down. Rotate the rail by 180° to its proper position.

19. Drive in the straight pin, then move the shifter fork rail and check the accent.

20. Install the transmission case cover.

21. Adjust the selecting direction and position of the shifter arm shaft.

   a. Install the gear shift system.
   b. Shift the gear into 4th.
   c. Shift the shifter arm from the 4th/3rd position to the 1st and reverse position.
   d. The arm moves lightly to the 1st position while it moves heavily to the reverse position and hits the stopper as the force of the return spring is applied.
   e. Adjust so that the light travel becomes the same as the heavy travel by removing the plug on the top of the transmission case and change the thickness of aluminum gasket.

22. When mounting the transmission on the car body, the gearshift system should be removed first.

23. For reassembly of the remaining transmission parts, refer to the 4 speed transmission section (Type 18).

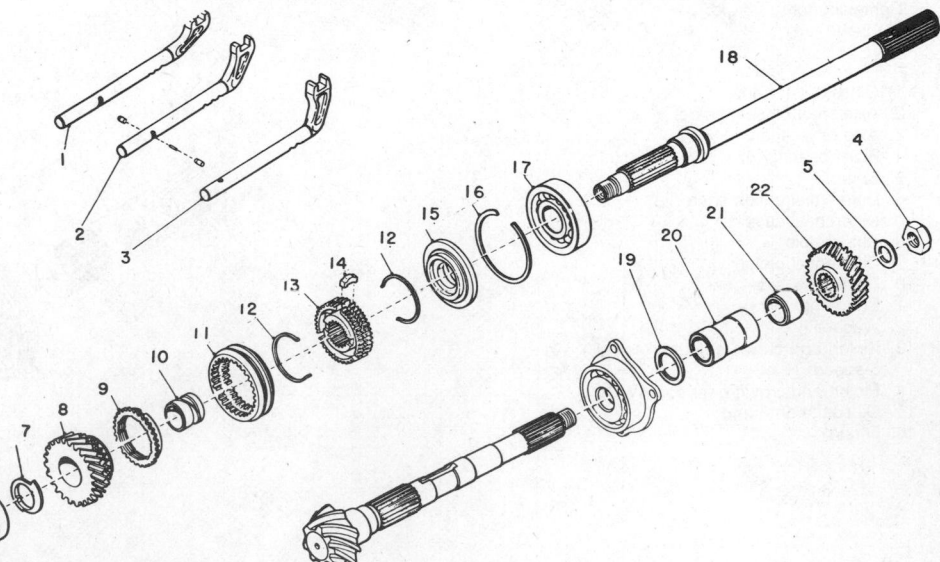

Exploded view of added gears and shafts for the 4 wheel drive unit

TYPE 17

4 Speed Transaxle 2WD
5 Speed Transaxle 2WD & 4WD Subaru

DISASSEMBLY

NOTE: Abbreviations to be used through out the disassembly and assembly steps pertaining to the various transaxles used in the Subaru 1800 models.

D/R — 4WD Dual Range (5x2)
W/R — 4WD Single Range (5x1)
4-spd. — 2WD 4 speed
5-spd. — 2WD 5 speed

1. Place removed transaxle assembly in a secure holder.
2. Remove the clutch release lever and bearing.

NOTE: Do not deform the clutch sleeve clips and release lever retaining springs during the removal.

3. Remove the high-low shifter rod assembly from D/R models.
4. Remove the actuator and cable assembly from the S/R models.
5. Remove the transfer shifter bracket from the S/R models.
6. Remove the transfer cover from both the D/R and the S/R models.
7. Remove the plug from the transfer case, D/R and the S/R models. Remove the spring and ball from the inside.
8. Remove the clip from the transfer shifter rod on the D/R models. Position the shifter rod to the LO position and remove the clip on the rod with an appropriate tool. (4WD models).
9. Remove the transfer shifter rod by setting the transfer shifting rod to the HI position and pull the rod holding the transfer shifter fork straight out on the D/R models.
10. On the D/R models, remove the pin and clip from the interlock rod.
11. Turn the interlock rod 90° and pull straight out.

CAUTION

The transfer shifter fork has a spring and ball within its self, so do not allow them to pop out.

12. On the D/R models, push the high and low fork rod in until it butts up against the other side, move the transfer shifter fork as far as it will

come out of the transfer case, which contains the switch. Remove the fork by pulling it straight up.

CAUTION

Do not drop the ball and spring, plunger and interlock that are contained in the transfer shifter fork.

13. To remove the high-low fork rod on the D/R models, pull the high and low fork rod backward to remove it from the transaxle case. Do not drop the ball and spring.
14. On the S/R models, drive out the retaining pin from the transfer shifter fork.

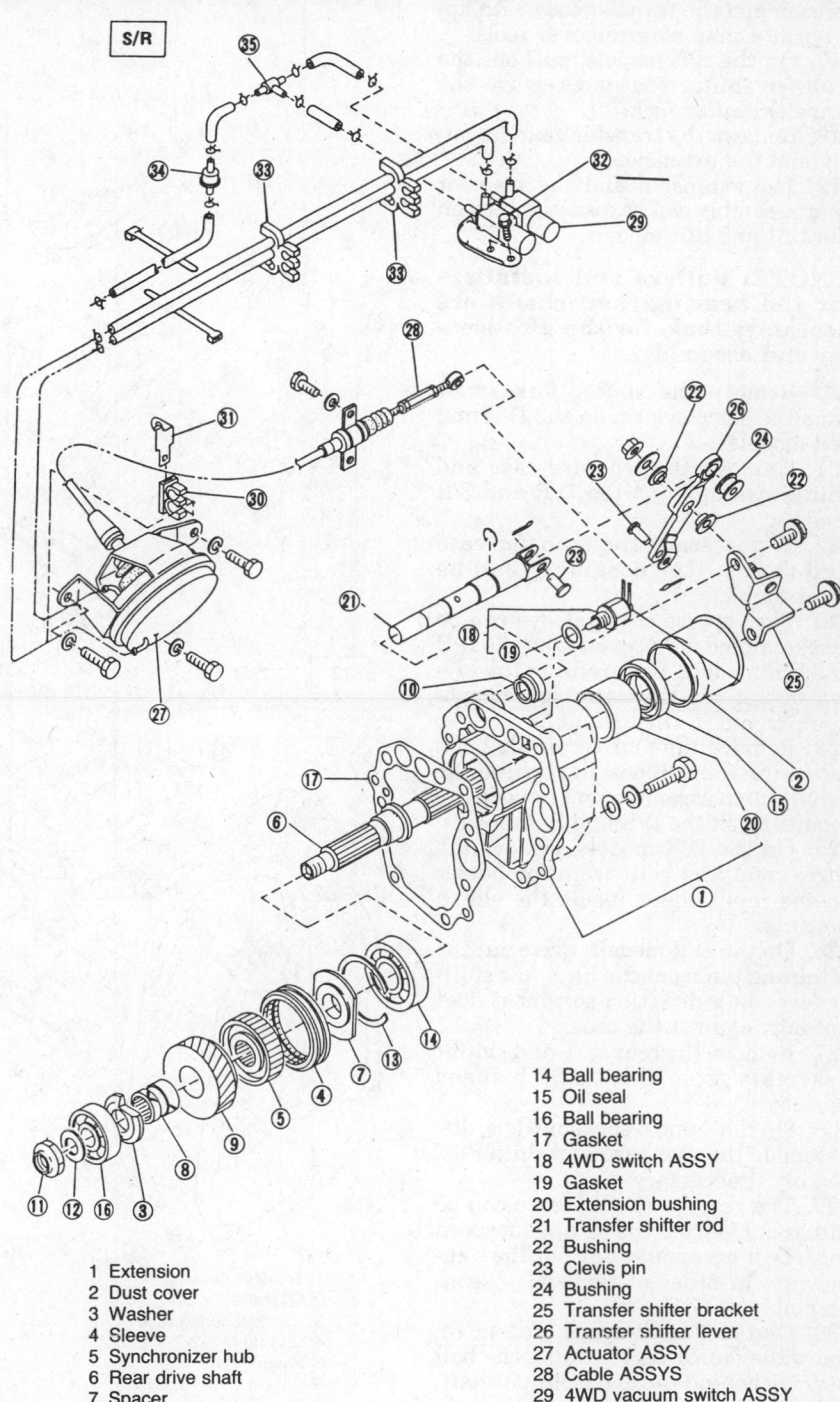

14 Ball bearing
15 Oil seal
16 Ball bearing
17 Gasket
18 4WD switch ASSY
19 Gasket
20 Extension bushing
21 Transfer shifter rod
22 Bushing
23 Clevis pin
24 Bushing
25 Transfer shifter bracket
26 Transfer shifter lever
27 Actuator ASSY
28 Cable ASSYS
29 4WD vacuum switch ASSY
30 Hose support
31 Hose stay
32 Tapping screw
33 Hose support
34 Check valve
35 Connector

1 Extension
2 Dust cover
3 Washer
4 Sleeve
5 Synchronizer hub
6 Rear drive shaft
7 Spacer
8 Bushing
9 Transfer driven gear
10 Oil seal
11 Lock nut
12 Lock washer
13 Snap ring (IN)

Exploded view of extension and transfer control system, 4WD

15. Remove the bolts from the extension housing.

16. On the S/R models, remove the snap-ring from the transfer shifter rod. Separate the extension from the transfer case and remove the snapring installed to the transfer shifter rod through the gap between the extension and the transfer case with appropriate snap-ring remover tools.

17. On the S/R models, pull out the transfer shifter rod and remove the transfer shifter fork.

18. Remove the transfer gear assembly and the extension.

19. The extension and the transfer gear assembly can be disassembled on the D/R and S/R models.

NOTE: Pullers and installers for the bearings and shafts are necessary tools for the disassembly and assembly.

20. Remove the shifter fork screw from the selector arm on the D/R and S/R models.

21. Remove the transfer case and shifter assembly on the D/R and S/R models.

22. If necessary the transfer case and the shifter assembly can be disassembled.

23. The reverse check sleeve can be disassembled, if necessary, on the D/R and S/R models. Be careful in the laying out of the disassembled components to aid in the assembly.

24. Remove the four retaining bolts mounting the ball bearing behind the drive pinion assembly and remove the mounting on the D/R and S/R models.

25. On the D/R models, remove the three retaining bolts from the holder on the input shaft, inside the clutch housing.

26. On the D/R models, drive out the retaining pin from the high-low shifter lever in a direction so that it does not butt against the case.

27. Remove the rear case and shifter assembly from the 4 and 5 speed models.

28. On the 4 and 5 speed models, disassemble the rear case and shifter assembly if necessary.

29. The reverse check sleeve can be disassembled on the 4 and 5 speed models, if necessary. Lay out the components in order of removal to ease assembly.

30. On the 4 and 5 speed models, remove the four bolts retaining the ball bearing behind the drive pinion shaft.

31. Place vinyl tape around the axle drive shafts splines to prevent damage to the oil seals.

32. Separate the transaxle case by removing the seventeen mounting bolts.

33. Remove the drive pinion shaft assembly from the LH case assembly.

34. The drive pinion shaft can now be disassembled.

NOTE: Pullers must be used to remove and install the various components of the drive pinion shaft assembly.

35. On the 4 and 5 speed models, the drive pinion shaft assembly can be disassembled.

NOTE: Bearing remover and installer tools are required during the disassembly and assembly procedures.

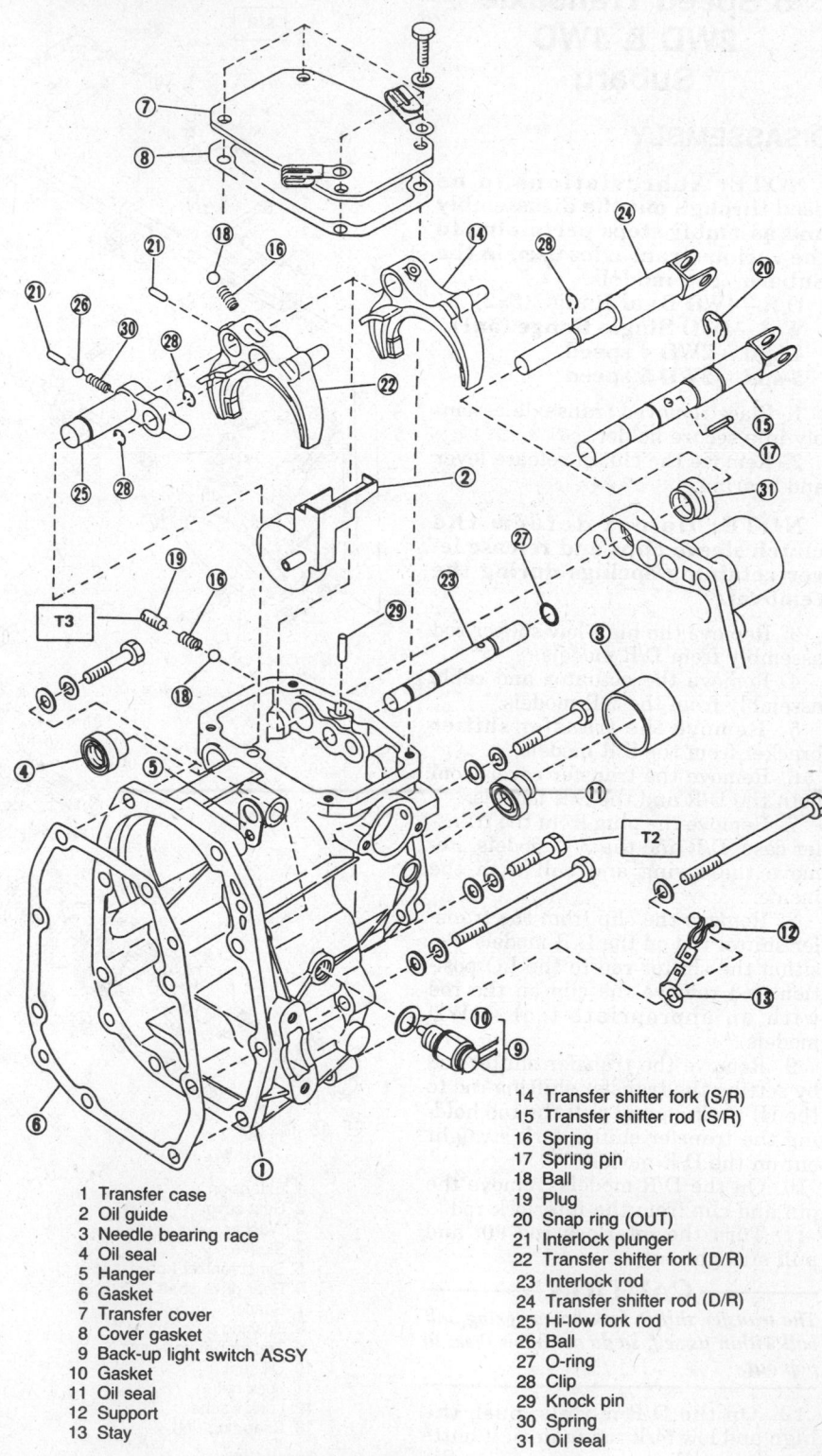

1 Transfer case
2 Oil guide
3 Needle bearing race
4 Oil seal
5 Hanger
6 Gasket
7 Transfer cover
8 Cover gasket
9 Back-up light switch ASSY
10 Gasket
11 Oil seal
12 Support
13 Stay
14 Transfer shifter fork (S/R)
15 Transfer shifter rod (S/R)
16 Spring
17 Spring pin
18 Ball
19 Plug
20 Snap ring (OUT)
21 Interlock plunger
22 Transfer shifter fork (D/R)
23 Interlock rod
24 Transfer shifter rod (D/R)
25 Hi-low fork rod
26 Ball
27 O-ring
28 Clip
29 Knock pin
30 Spring
31 Oil seal

Exploded view of transfer case, 4WD

36. On the D/R models, raise the main shaft slightly and remove the high-low shifter fork together with the high-low shifter shaft.

37. On the D/R models, remove the main shaft assembly and the input shaft assembly from the left hand case.

— **CAUTION** —

Do not drop either of the shaft assemblies, since each are separate of the other.

38. On the D/R models, separate the mainshaft assembly and the input shaft assembly. Be sure the needle bearing is inserted in the input shaft. Do not drop the high and low baulk rings.

39. On the S/R, 4 and 5 speed models, remove the mainshaft from the left case assembly.

40. The main shaft can now be disassembled.

NOTE: Bearing removers and installers, pullers and special wrenches are needed during the disassemble of the mainshafts.

41. The input shaft can be disassembled, using snap-ring pliers and a press.

42. Remove the differential assembly from the transaxle case.

— **CAUTION** —

Do Not confuse the right and left roller bearings and outer races. Keep together and on the correct side.

43. Disassemble the differential assembly for D/R, S/R, 4 and 5 speed models.

NOTE: The axle shafts are retained by snap-rings.

44. The remaining case components can now be removed. Keep in correct order for ease of assembly.

ASSEMBLY

D/R and S/R Models

1. Assemble the 1–2 synchronizer hub by installing the reverse driven gear, the three shifting inserts and the two synchronizer springs.

2. Install the three shifting inserts, the coupling sleeve and the two synchronizer springs.

3. Install the three shifting inserts, the one high-low synchronizer sleeve and the two high-low synchronizer springs on the high-low synchronizer hub (D/R Models).

4. Install the third drive gear, baulk ring and sleeve/hub assembly on the transmission main shaft. Install the fourth needle race on the shaft with an appropriate tool. Install

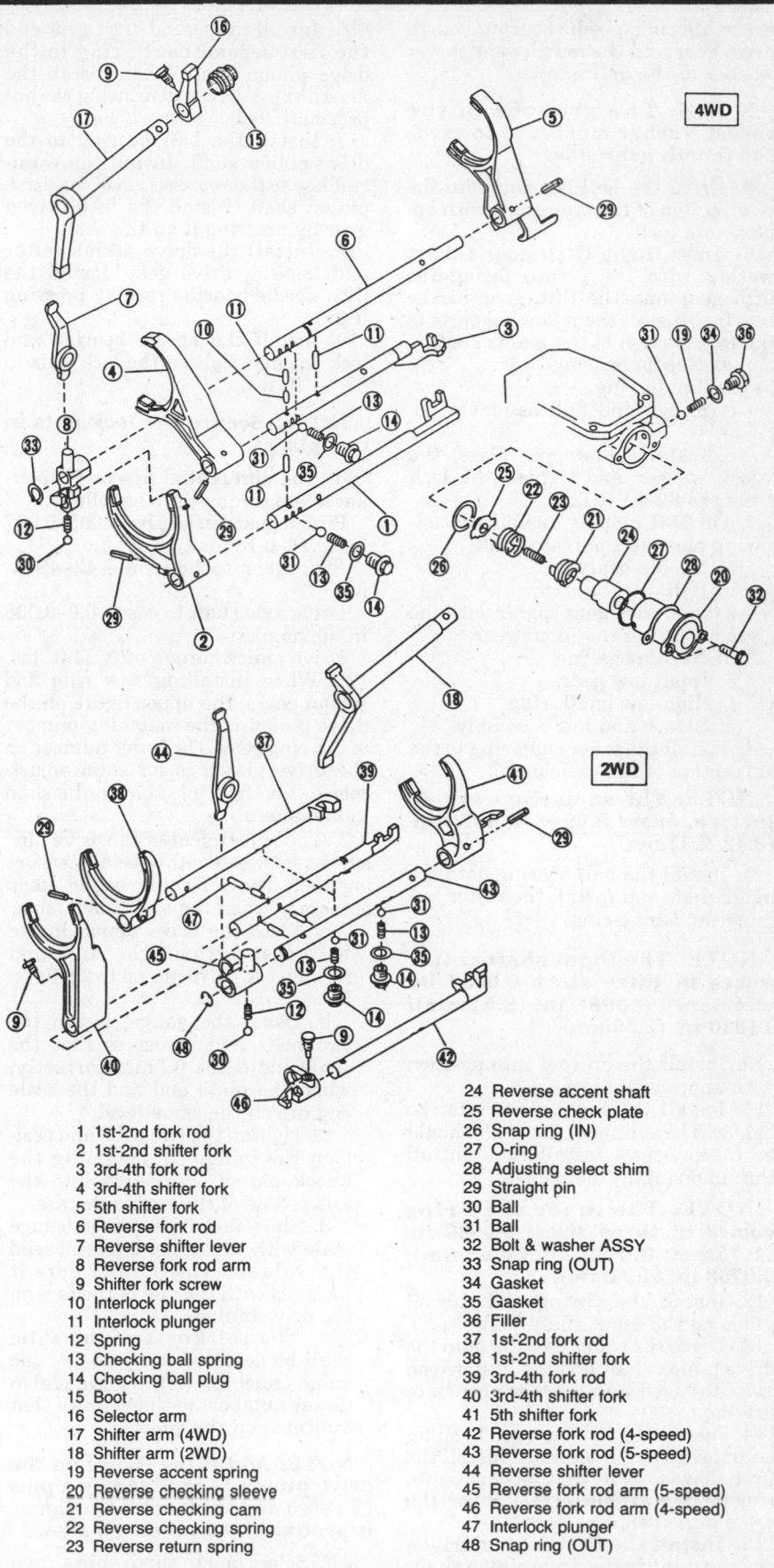

1 1st-2nd fork rod	24 Reverse accent shaft
2 1st-2nd shifter fork	25 Reverse check plate
3 3rd-4th fork rod	26 Snap ring (IN)
4 3rd-4th shifter fork	27 O-ring
5 5th shifter fork	28 Adjusting select shim
6 Reverse fork rod	29 Straight pin
7 Reverse shifter lever	30 Ball
8 Reverse fork rod arm	31 Ball
9 Shifter fork screw	32 Bolt & washer ASSY
10 Interlock plunger	33 Snap ring (OUT)
11 Interlock plunger	34 Gasket
12 Spring	35 Gasket
13 Checking ball spring	36 Filler
14 Checking ball plug	37 1st-2nd fork rod
15 Boot	38 1st-2nd shifter fork
16 Selector arm	39 3rd-4th fork rod
17 Shifter arm (4WD)	40 3rd-4th shifter fork
18 Shifter arm (2WD)	41 5th shifter fork
19 Reverse accent spring	42 Reverse fork rod (4-speed)
20 Reverse checking sleeve	43 Reverse fork rod (5-speed)
21 Reverse checking cam	44 Reverse shifter lever
22 Reverse checking spring	45 Reverse fork rod arm (5-speed)
23 Reverse return spring	46 Reverse fork rod arm (4-speed)
	47 Interlock plunger
	48 Snap ring (OUT)

Exploded view of shifting mechanism, 4WD and 2WD transaxles

the baulk ring, needle bearing, fourth drive gear and the fourth gear thrust washer to the mainshaft.

NOTE: The grooves in the thrust washer must face towards the fourth gear side.

5. Drive the ball bearing onto the rear section of the mainshaft with appropriate tools.

6. Install the fifth gear thrust washer with the groove facing the fifth gear and the fifth gear needle bearing. Install the following parts to the rear section of the mains shaft:
   a. Needle bearing.
   b. Baulk ring.
   c. Sleeve and hub assembly no. two.
   d. Instal the stopper plate, the lock washer and tighten the lock nuts to 82–91 ft. lbs.

7. On D/R models, install the following parts to the main shaft;
   a. Needle bearings.
   b. Ball.
   c. Input low gear spacer with the groove facing the input gear.
   d. Needle bearing.
   e. Input low gear.
   f. High-low baulk ring.
   g. Sleeve and hub assembly.

8. Install the other snap-ring to the rod section of the mainshaft.

NOTE: The snap-rings are selective, from 0.0953–0.0933 in. (2.42–2.37mm).

9. Install the ball bearing onto the input shaft and install the cotter, retainer and snap-ring.

NOTE: The input shaft cotter comes in three sizes: 0.0957 in. (2.43mm); 0.0988 in. (2.51mm); 0.1020 in. (2.59mm).

10. Install the oil seal into position with appropriate tool.

11. Install the input shaft into the holder. The splines of the shaft should be taped before installation. Install the snap-ring in the holder.

NOTE: The inner snap-ring comes in three sizes: 0.0689 in. (1.75mm; 0.0720 in. (1.83mm); 0.0753 in. (1.91mm).

12. Install the O-ring and the oil guide on the input shaft holder.

13. Drive the roller bearing onto the drive pinion shaft and the first driven gear thrust plate with appropriate driving tools.

14. Install the driven gear bushing onto the drive pinion shaft. Install the first driven gear first/second baulk ring and gear/hub assembly to the drive pinion shaft.

15. Install the first/second driven gear bushing to the drive pinion shaft, using appropriate tools.

16. Install the second drive gear and the first/second baulk ring to the drive pinion shaft. Then install the fourth/third driven gear using the appropriate tools.

17. Install the ball bearing to the drive pinion shaft. Install the woodruff key to the rear section of the drive pinion shaft. Install the fifth driven gear by pressing it on the shaft.

18. Install the drive pinion collar and transfer drive gear. Install the fifth needle bearing race by pressing it on.

19. Install the needle bearing and lock washer, tighten the lock nuts to 83–91 ft. lbs.

NOTE: Secure the lock nuts in two places.

20. The differential assembly tolerances are torques, are as follows:
   Pinion gear backlash – 0.005–0.007 in. (0.13–0.18mm).
   Ring gear to housing – 42–49 ft. lbs.
   Drive axle shaft to case – 0.0–0.008 in. (0.2mm).
   Drive pinion torque – 20–24 ft. lbs.

21. When installing new ring and pinion gears, the upper figure on the drive pinion is the matching number of the ring gear. The lower number on the drive pinion is for shim adjustment. If no figure is shown, the shim value is zero.

22. The adjustment of the drive pinion is completed with special measuring tool. The following is the steps necessary when the tool is available.
   a. Place the drive pinion in the R.H. case without the shim and tighten the drive pinion to 20–24 ft. lbs.
   b. Using the gauge, loosen the two bolts and adjust so that the scale indicates 0.5mm correctly, when the plate end and the scale end are on the same level.
   c. Tighten the two bolts and position the gauge by inserting the knock pin of the gauge into the knock hole of the transaxle case.
   d. Slide the drive pinion gauge scale with the finger tips and read the value at the point where it matches with the end of the face on the drive pinion.
   e. The thickness of the shim shall be determined by adding the value indicated on the drive pinion (lower number) to the value of that indicated on the gauge.

NOTE: Add if the figure on the drive pinion is prefixed by a plus (+) sign and subtract if the figure is prefixed by a minus (–) sign.

   f. Select one to three shims from a select group of shims, ranging from 0.0059–0.0197 in. (0.150–0.500mm).

23. Place the main shaft assembly and the input shaft on the main case without a shim.

24. To determine the proper shim, follow the steps outlined:
   a. $D = A - (B + C)$
   A = Main case length 33.58 in (853mm)
   B = Nut shaft length measured from inside the holder lip and the end of the gear portion of the input shaft.
   C = Main shaft assembly length, measured from the inside of the rear holder lip and the inside of the first/second drive gear.
   b. The dimensions desired are as follows:
   D – 2.0846 in (52.95mm) – no shims needed.
   D – 2.0842–2.0650 in. (52.95–52.45mm) – one shim needed.
   D – 2.0646 in (52.44mm) maximum two shims needed.

NOTE: The thickness of the shim is 0.0177–0.0217 in (0.45–0.55mm).

25. Install the oil seals in the differential side retainers using the paper installation tools.

26. Screw in the differential side retainer, without the O-ring, into the left hand case from the bottom, after properly supporting the case.

27. On the D/R models, install the oil seal into the case.

28. Install the outer snap-ring and washer onto the speedometer shaft and fit them into the case. Install the speedometer driven gear and retain it with a snap-ring.

29. On the D/R models, install the O-ring, straight pin at the front on the counter gear shaft. As the counter gear shaft is being installed into the case, install the following components:
   a. The two counter gear washers.
   b. The two needle bearings.
   c. Counter gear collar.
   d. Counter gear.
   e. Straight pin.
   f. The clip.

NOTE: Position the cut-out portion of the countergear shaft to fit the input gear holder, when it is installed.

30. Position the interlock plungers for the 1–2 and 3–4 fork rods and the reverse shifter rod. Install the rods and install the outer snap-ring.

31. Install the reverse idler gear and shaft. Secure it with the straight pin. Be sure to install the reverse idler shaft from the rear side.

32. Position the ball, spring and gasket in the reverse shifter rod hole in

the left case and tighten the checking ball plug. Torque to 14 ft. lbs.

33. Move the reverse shifter rod towards the REV side. Adjust so the clearance between the reverse idler gear and the case wall is 0.236–0.295 in. (6.0–7.5mm), using the reverse shifter lever. If necessary, the reverse shifter lever must be replaced.

34. After installation of a suitable reverse shifter lever, shift into NEUTRAL and adjust the clearance between reverse idler gear and the case wall to 0–0.020 in. (0–0.5mm). Washers are used to correct the clearance.

35. Install the shift levers and rods, using the straight pins to hold them.

36. After the selector rods and forks have been installed, set the main shaft and drive pinion shaft into position so that no clearance is present between the two when moved all the way to the front. Be sure the 1–2, 3–4 and the 5–reverse shifter forks are positioned in the center of their respective synchronizing mechanisms.

37. Clean the mating surfaces, apply liquid gasket material and place the left and right case together.

38. Tighten the 17 bolts with the brackets and clips in their respective positions. Tighten the 8mm bolts to 18 ft. lbs. and the 10mm bolts to 29 ft. lbs.

39. Be sure the bolts are inserted from the bottom and the nuts are on the top. Check to make sure the drive pinion shim and the input shaft holder shim are not caught between the two case halves. Confirm that the counter gear and the speedometer gear teeth are meshed properly and the high-low shifter shaft is inserted properly.

40. Tighten the ball bearing attachment bolts at the drive pinion holder (rear). Torque to 20–24 ft. lbs.

41. D/R models, tighten the three input shaft holder retaining bolts to 13.4–15.6 ft. lbs.

42. Install the upper bearing cup.

43. To adjust the backlash of the hypoid gear and preload adjustment of the roller bearings, proceed with the following steps:

a. With special tools, place the case assembly on its left side and in-

stall a weight tool on the bearing cup.

b. Screw the retainer assembly into the left side case with the special wrench.

c. With a special wrench handle tool on the main shaft, shift the gear box into the fifth gear and turn the shaft several times. Screw the retainer while turning the handle until a slight resistance is felt on the wrench.

d. This is the contact point of the hypoid gear and the drive pinion shaft. Repeat this sequence several times to ensure the contact point.

e. Remove the weight and screw in the retainer without the O-ring on the upper side and stop at a point where slight resistance is felt.

NOTE: At this point, the backlash between the hypoid gear and the pinion shaft is zero.

f. Fit the lock plate. Loosen the retainer on the lower side by 1½ notches on the lock plate and turn the retainer on the upper side of the

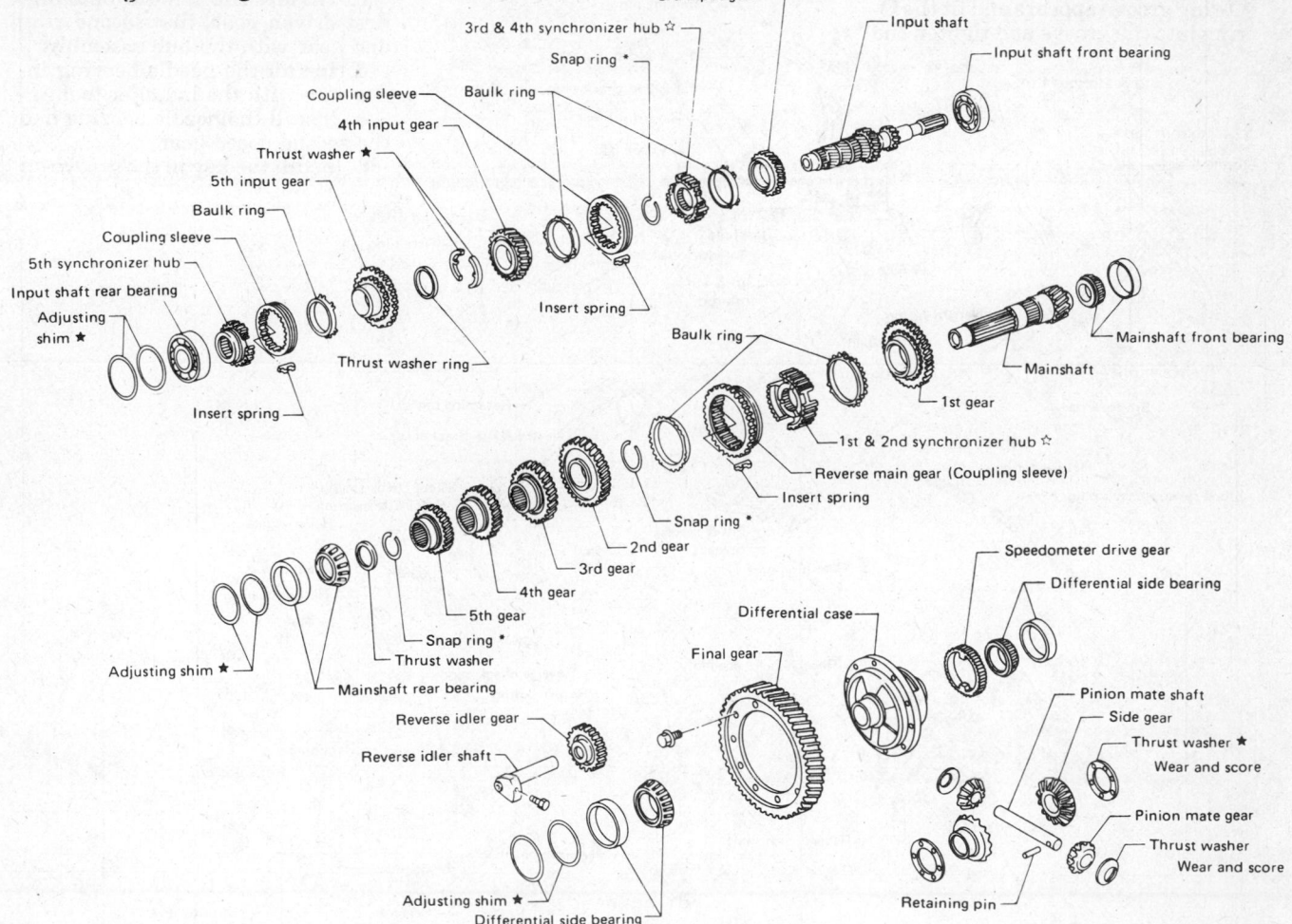

Exploded view of transaxle gear train, Subaru XT Coupe

case by the same amount in order to obtain the backlash.

g. Turn in the retainer on the upper side an additional ½ to 1 notch in order to preload the taper roller bearing.

h. Temporarily tighten both the upper and lower lock plate for later readjustment.

i. Turn the mainshaft several times, tap the retainer lightly with a plastic hammer and repeat this sequence at least a dozen times.

j. With the use of a dial indicator, check the backlash between the hypoid gear and the pinion gear. The backlash should be 0.0039–0.0071 in. (0.10–0.18mm).

k. Check the tooth pattern of the hypoid gear and the pinion shaft gear with red lead, Prussian Blue or equivalent.

l. To increase the backlash, loosen the holder on the lower (L.H.) and turn the holder on the upper side (R.H.) by the same amount.

m. After checking the tooth contact of the gears, remove the lock plate. Loosen the retainer until the O-ring groove appears and fit the O-ring into the groove and tighten the

retainer into the position where the retainer had been tighten to. Install the lock plate and tighten. Torque to 16020 ft. lbs.

n. Complete this operation on both the upper and lower retainers.

44. Install the reverse check sleeve assembly.

45. Install the transfer case and shifter assembly. Secure the case and torque to 18 ft. lbs.

46. Complete the assembly of the transfer case assembly in the reverse of its disassembly.

47. Complete the assembly of the clutch lever and release bearing in the reverse of their removal.

ASSEMBLY

2WD – 4 Speed and 5 Speed Units

1. To assemble the synchronizer hubs and gears, refer to the procedure outlined in the 4WD section.

2. Assemble the mainshaft in the following order:

a. Install the fifth needle bearing race with special tools.

b. Install the third drive gear, ring and sleeve assembly.

c. Install the fifth needle bearing race.

d. Install the ring, fourth drive gear and the fourth drive gear thrust washer.

e. Install the ball bearing with special installing tools.

f. Install the snap-ring. Rings are selective sized.

g. Select the correct snap-ring to provide a clearance of 0.0–0.0020 in.

h. Assemble the woodruff key and then the fifth gear.

i. On the fife speed models, tighten the locknut to 54–62 ft. lbs. After tightening the nut, stake it in place.

3. Assemble the drive pinion assembly in the following manner:

a. Install the roller bearing in the drive pinion and install the first gear thrust plate with special tools.

b. Install the needle bearing inner race.

c. Install the needle bearing, first driven gear, first-second ring and gear with the hub assembly.

d. Install the needle bearing inner race with the installer tool.

e. Install the needle bearing and the second speed gear.

f. Install the key in the groove on

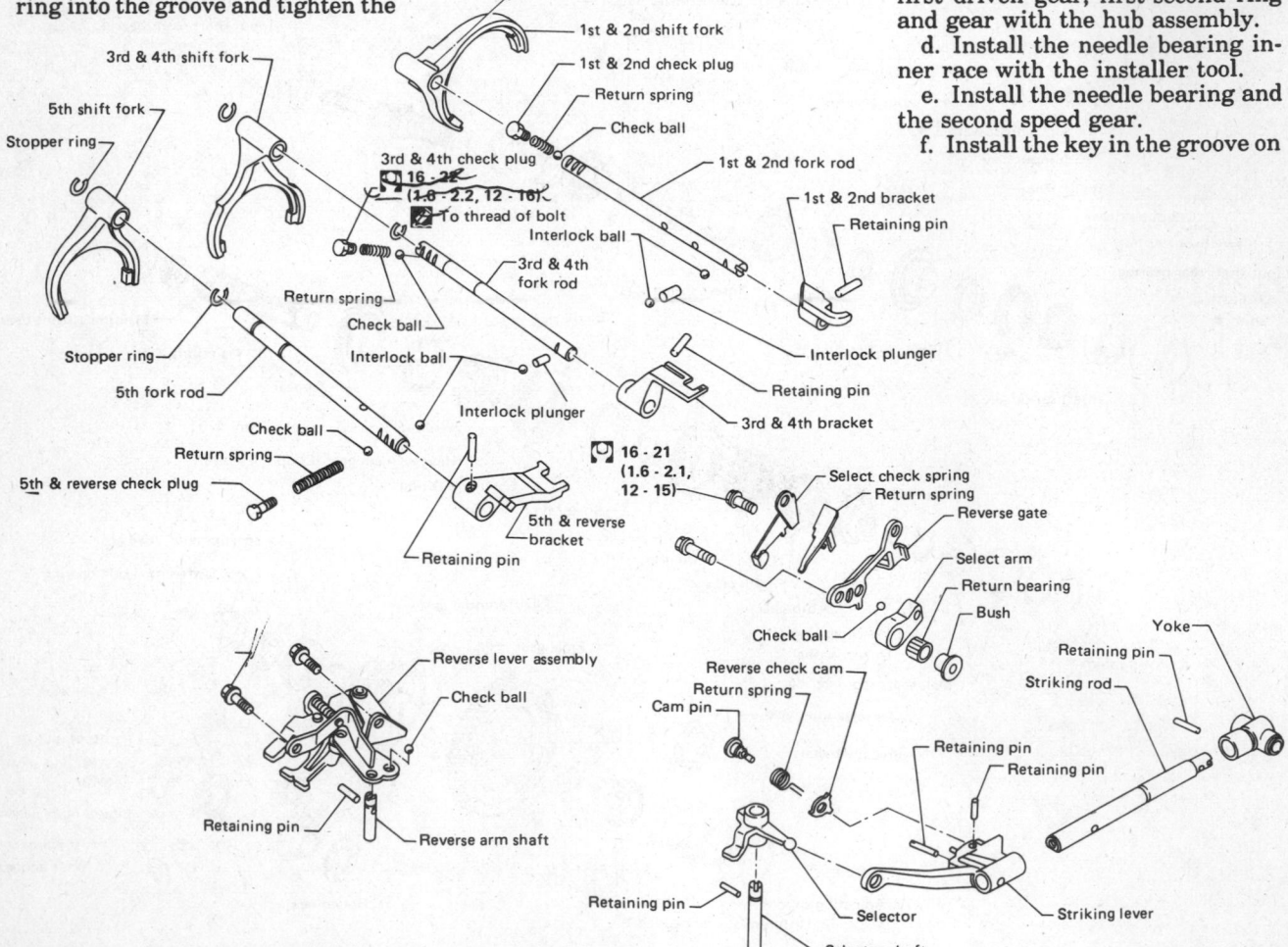

Exploded view of transaxle shift rods and fork assemblies, Subaru XT Coupe

the drive pinion shaft and install the third-fourth driven gear with the installer tool.

g. Install the ball bearing with special installer tools.

h. On the four speed models, install the lock washer and tighten the locknut to a torque of 52–62 ft. lbs.

i. After tightening the locknut to specifications, stake the locknut in two locations.

j. On the five speed models, install the fifth gear thrust washer and install the fifth gear needle bearing inner race.

k. On the five speed models, install the needle bearing, fifth driven gear, rings, sleeve and hub assembly, insert guide, insert stopper plate, lockwasher and locknut.

l. On the five speed models, tighten the locknut and torque to 54–62 ft. lbs.

4. To install the differential assembly, follow these procedure steps:

a. Instal the differential bevel gears and differential pinions with washers into the case and install the pinion shaft.

b. Measure the backlash which should be 0.0051–0.0071 in. between the gears. Adjust with selective washers as required.

c. Install the straight roll pin into place through the case and pinion shaft. Stake the hole portion.

d. Install the bearing cones on the housing using installers.

e. Install the rig gear on the case. Tighten the bolts to 42–49 ft. lbs.

f. Install the axle drive shafts and lock them with snap-rings. The standard clearance of the rings to shaft drive axle is 0–0.0079 in.

g. The marks on the pinion shaft gear and the ring gear are the same for the 4WD assembly. Refer to that portion of the section for procedures. The shim thickness range from 0.0059–0.0197 in.

5. Install the oil seal into the retainer with a seal installer tool.

6. Install the differential side retainer assembly in the same manner as was done for the 4WD unit.

7. After installing the outer snap-ring and washer onto the speedometer shaft, fit them into the case. Install the speedometer shaft, fit them into the case. Install the speedometer driven gear on the shaft and retain it with a snap-ring.

8. To adjust the reverse idler gear position, shift the reverse shifter rod and select reverse shifter rail arm (4 speed) or reverse shifter lever (5 speed) so that the clearance between the reverse idler gear and the case wall is 0.059–0.118 in.

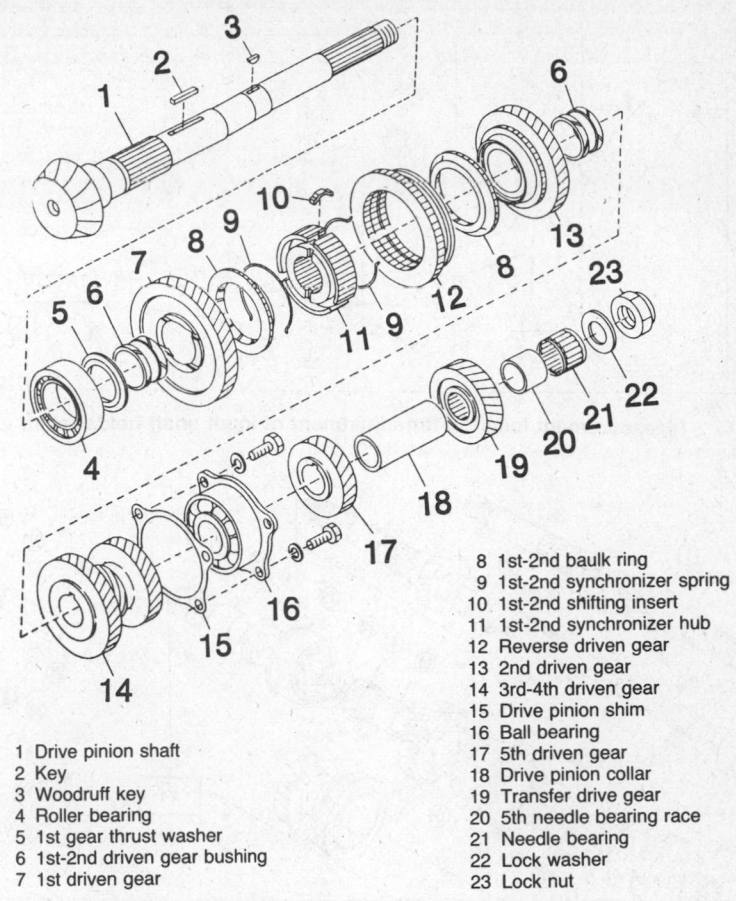

1 Drive pinion shaft
2 Key
3 Woodruff key
4 Roller bearing
5 1st gear thrust washer
6 1st-2nd driven gear bushing
7 1st driven gear
8 1st-2nd baulk ring
9 1st-2nd synchronizer spring
10 1st-2nd shifting insert
11 1st-2nd synchronizer hub
12 Reverse driven gear
13 2nd driven gear
14 3rd-4th driven gear
15 Drive pinion shim
16 Ball bearing
17 5th driven gear
18 Drive pinion collar
19 Transfer drive gear
20 5th needle bearing race
21 Needle bearing
22 Lock washer
23 Lock nut

Exploded view of drive pinion shaft assembly, 4WD

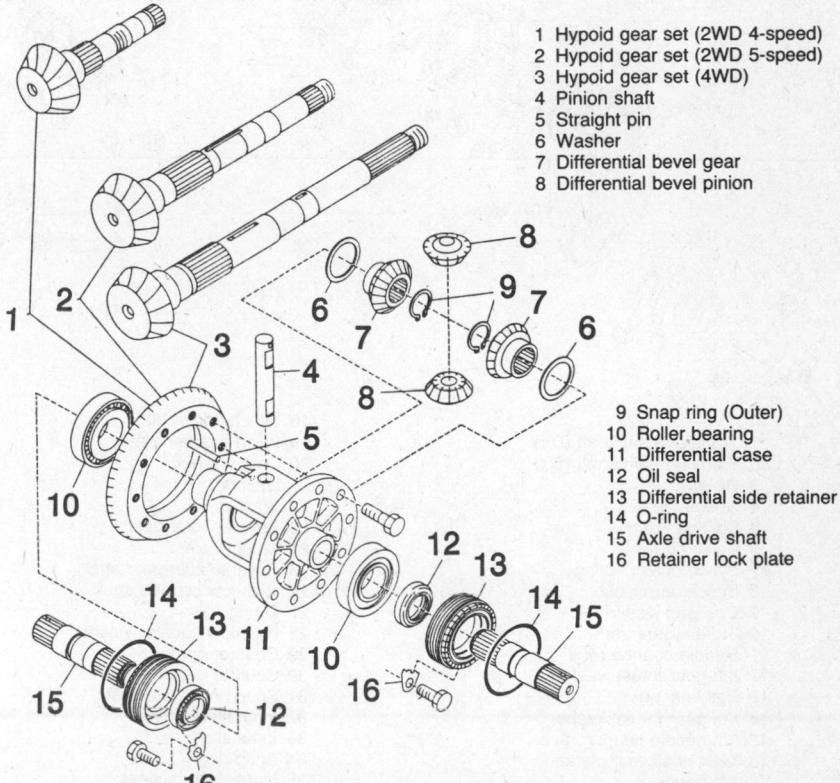

1 Hypoid gear set (2WD 4-speed)
2 Hypoid gear set (2WD 5-speed)
3 Hypoid gear set (4WD)
4 Pinion shaft
5 Straight pin
6 Washer
7 Differential bevel gear
8 Differential bevel pinion
9 Snap ring (Outer)
10 Roller bearing
11 Differential case
12 Oil seal
13 Differential side retainer
14 O-ring
15 Axle drive shaft
16 Retainer lock plate

Exploded view of differential assembly, 4WD and 2WD assemblies

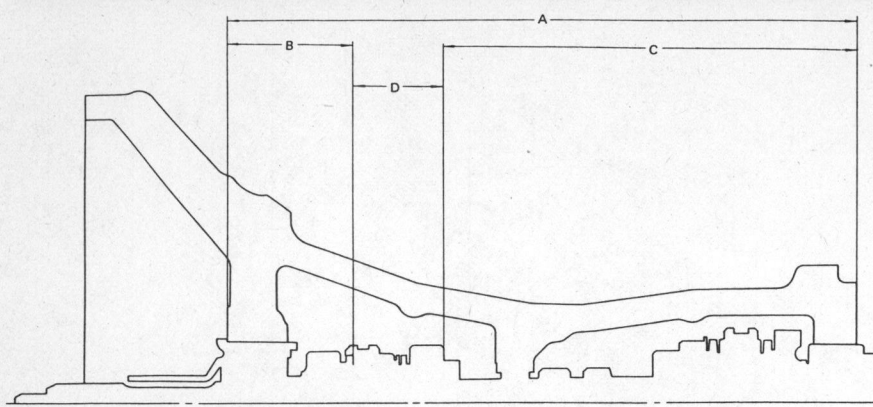

Measurement location for adjustment of input shaft holder shim

9. 5 speed models – After selecting the reverse shifter from a selective group, shift it into NEUTRAL position. Then select a selective washer so that the gap between the washer and the case wall is 0–0.020 in.

10. 4 speed models – Install the reverse shifter rail arm to the end of the reverse shifter lever. Fit the shifter rod and tighten the shifter fork set screw to a torque of 13.4–15.6 ft. lbs.

11. 5 Speed models – Put the reverse shifter arm spring and ball in reverse shifter rail arm. Install the reverse shifter rod into the case and arm with an installer tool and then fit the snapring.

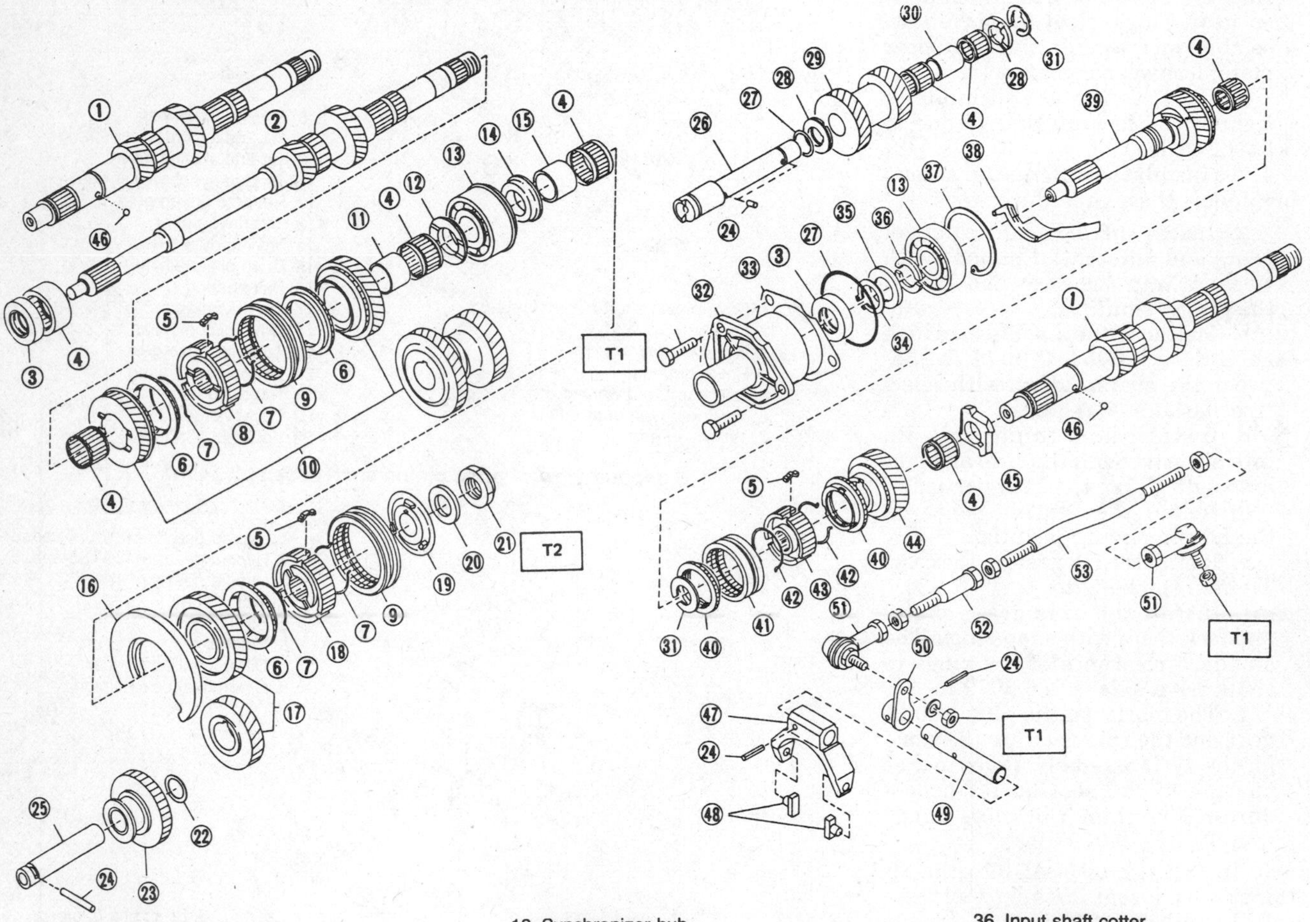

1 Transfer main shaft (D/r)	18 Synchronizer hub	36 Input shaft cotter
2 Transfer main shaft (S/r)	19 Insert stopper plate	37 Snap ring (Inner-62)
3 Oil seal	20 Lock washer	38 Oil guide
4 Needle bearing	21 Lock nut	39 Input shaft
5 Shifting insert	22 Washer	40 High-low baulk ring
6 Baulk ring	23 Reverse idler gear	41 High-low coupling sleeve
7 Synchronizer spring	24 Straight pin	42 High-low synchronizer spring
8 Synchronizer hub	25 Reverse idler gear shaft	43 High-low synchronizer hub
9 Coupling sleeve	26 High-low counter shaft	44 Input low gear
10 3rd-4th gear set	27 O-ring	45 Input low gear spacer
11 Needle bearing race	28 High-low counter washer	46 Ball
12 4th gear thrust washer	29 Counter gear	47 High-low shifter fork
13 Ball bearing	30 Counter gear collar	48 High-low shifter piece
14 5th gear thrust washer	31 Snap ring (Outer-25)	49 High-low shifter shaft
15 5th needle bearing race	32 Input shaft holder	50 High-low shifter lever
*16 Main shaft rear platae	33 Input shaft shim	51 Ball joint rod
17 5th gear set	34 Snap ring (Outer)	52 Rod adjusting screw
	35 Input shaft retainer	53 High-low shifter rod

Exploded view of 4WD mainshaft and High-Low shift linkage on dual range unit

12. Install the reverse idler gear and shaft. Retain it with the retaining pin.

13. For the reverse shifter rail, install the ball, spring and gasket into the case and tighten the plug. (13.4–15.6 ft. lbs.).

14. Install the plungers in the case and on the 5 speed models, install the reverse shifter rod arm.

15. Install the 5th shifter fork on the reverse shifter rod and install the retaining pin.

16. Install the differential assembly.

NOTE: Install tape around the splines of the right and left dirve axles.

17. Install the needle bearing and oil seal on the transaxle mainshaft and install the mainshaft into the case.

18. Install the 3rd–4th shifter fork and 3rd–4th shifter rod with the plunger and tighten the set screw to 13.4–15.6 ft. lbs. torque.

19. Install the ball, spring and gasket into the case and tighten the plug to 13.4–15.6 ft. lbs. torque.

20. Install the drive pinion shaft with the correct sized shims into the case.

21. Install the plunger into the case, along with the 1st–2nd shifter fork and the shifter rod. Secure with the retaining pin.

NOTE: When installing rods, shift the other installed rods into the NEUTRAL position.

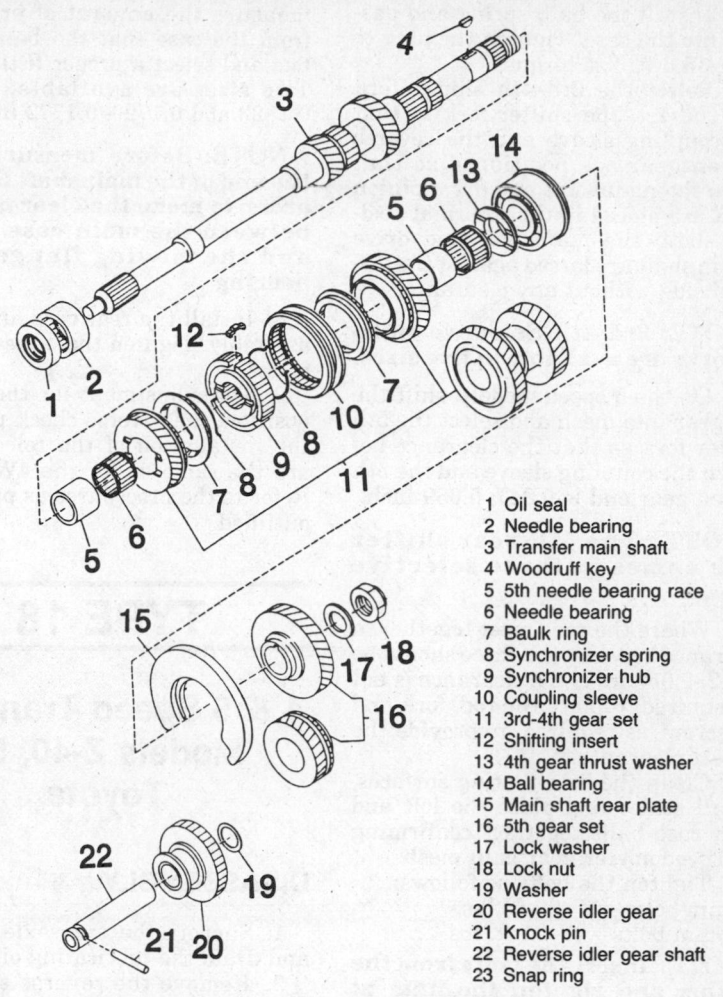

1 Oil seal
2 Needle bearing
3 Transfer main shaft
4 Woodruff key
5 5th needle bearing race
6 Needle bearing
7 Baulk ring
8 Synchronizer spring
9 Synchronizer hub
10 Coupling sleeve
11 3rd-4th gear set
12 Shifting insert
13 4th gear thrust washer
14 Ball bearing
15 Main shaft rear plate
16 5th gear set
17 Lock washer
18 Lock nut
19 Washer
20 Reverse idler gear
21 Knock pin
22 Reverse idler gear shaft
23 Snap ring

Exploded view of 2WD transaxle mainshaft

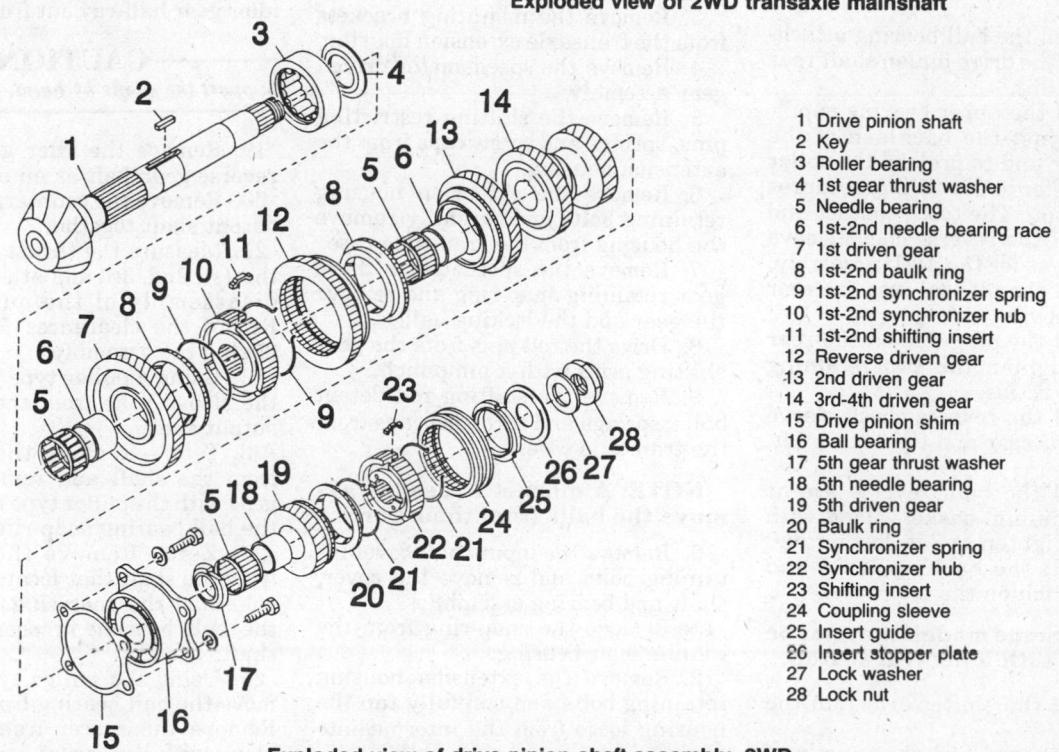

1 Drive pinion shaft
2 Key
3 Roller bearing
4 1st gear thrust washer
5 Needle bearing
6 1st-2nd needle bearing race
7 1st driven gear
8 1st-2nd baulk ring
9 1st-2nd synchronizer spring
10 1st-2nd synchronizer hub
11 1st-2nd shifting insert
12 Reverse driven gear
13 2nd driven gear
14 3rd-4th driven gear
15 Drive pinion shim
16 Ball bearing
17 5th gear thrust washer
18 5th needle bearing
19 5th driven gear
20 Baulk ring
21 Synchronizer spring
22 Synchronizer hub
23 Shifting insert
24 Coupling sleeve
25 Insert guide
26 Insert stopper plate
27 Lock washer
28 Lock nut

Exploded view of drive pinion shaft assembly, 2WD

22. Install the ball, spring and gasket into the case. Tighten the plug to 13.4–15.6 ft. lbs. torque.

23. Select the 3rd–4th shifter fork and the 1st–2nd shifter fork so that the coupling sleeve and the reverse driven gear are positioned so that when the mainshaft and drive pinion shaft are placed in their normal position (both the mainshaft and drive pinion shaft are forced against the forward side without any clearance.

NOTE: 3rd–4th Selective shifter forks are available in five sizes.

24. On the 5 speed models, shift the 5th gear into mesh and select the 5th shifter fork so that the clearance between the coupling sleeve and the 5th driven gear end is 0.047–0.059 inch.

NOTE: The 5th gear shifter fork comes in three selective sizes.

25. Where the rods meet together, a clearance between the three should be 0.012–0.063 in. If the clearance is not as required, replace the rod, fork and set screw, as required, to provide the correct clearance.

26. Clean the case mating surfaces, install sealer and place the left and right case halves together, confirming the speedometer gear is in mesh.

27. Tighten the bolts as follows:
   8mm bolts – 17–20 ft. lbs.
   10mm bolts – 27–31 ft. lbs.

NOTE: Insert the bolts from the bottom and tighten the nuts at the top.

28. Tighten the ball bearing attaching bolts at the drive pinion shaft rear to 20–24 ft. lbs.

29. Install the upper bearing cup.

30. To adjust the backlash of the hypoid gear and to preload the roller bearings, refer to the 4WD procedures of this section. The tooth contact and assembly of the reverse check sleeve is the same as for the 4WD assembly.

31. Install the oil seal into the rear of the case bore.

32. Install the oil guide on the rear case and tighten the two retaining bolts to 4.7 ft. lbs.

33. Install the reverse check sleeve into the rear case and tighten to 7 ft. lbs. torque.

34. Install the ball, reverse accent spring aluminum gasket, along with the filler. Tighten to 7 ft. lbs. torque.

35. Install the back-up lamp and neutral switch on the rear case.

NOTE: Some models may not be equipped with a neutral switch.

36. Install the shifter arm into the rear case.

37. With special tool or equivalent, measure the amount of protrusion from the case that the ball bearing has and select a proper fitting plate. Two sizes are available, 0.1772–0.1823 and 0.1720–0.1772 inches.

NOTE: Before measuring, tap the end of the mainshaft lightly in order to make the clearance zero between the main case surface and the moving flange of the bearing

38. Install the rear case and shifter assembly. Tighten the bolts to 17–20 ft. lbs.

39. The adjustment for the neutral position, the reverse check plate and the installation of the release lever are the same as for the 4WD units. Refer to the procedures as previously outlined.

TYPE 18

4 & 5 Speed Transaxle Models Z-40, 50 Toyota

DISASSEMBLY

1. Support the transaxle securely and drain the lubricating oil.

2. Remove the reverse shift arm pivot and the back-up lamp switch.

3. Remove the mounting brackets from the transaxle extension housing.

4. Remove the speedometer driven gear assembly.

5. Remove the shifting restricting pins, springs and screw caps from the extension housing.

6. Remove the extension housing retaining bolts and carefully remove the housing from the transaxle case.

7. Remove the speedometer drive gear retaining snap-ring and remove the gear and the locking ball.

8. Drive the roll pins from the gear shifting arms with a pin punch.

9. Remove the shifting rod detent balls, springs and threaded caps from the transaxle case.

NOTE: A magnet is used to remove the balls from their bores.

10. Remove the input shaft cover retaining bolts and remove the cover, shaft and bearing assemblies.

11. Remove the snap-ring from the countershaft bearing.

12. Remove the extension housing retaining bolts and carefully tap the housing loose from the intermediate plate.

13. Remove the case from the intermediate plate and remove the reverse shift arm from the pivot shaft.

14. Remove the rolled pins from the gear shift head and the shift forks. Pull the No. 3 shift rod from the intermediate plate. Remove the No. 3 shift fork from the coupling sleeve.

15. Remove the interlock pin and pull the No. 2 shift rod from the intermediate plate. Remove the shift fork from the coupling sleeve.

16. Remove the interlock pin and pull the No. 1 rod from the intermediate plate. Remove the No. 1 shift fork from the coupling sleeve. Remove reverse shift fork.

17. To remove the gear assemblies from the intermediate plate, perform the following procedures as applies to each transaxle:
   a. Z-50 – Measure the 5th gear thrust clearance which should be 0.0059–0.0128 in (0.15–0.325mm), and with a service limit of 0.016 in. (0.4mm). Remove the retaining snap-ring and remove the 5th gear, clutch hub and synchronizer ring with a puller type tool. Remove the roller bearing cage, the spacer and the steel locater ball.
   b. Z-40 – Remove the countergear plate, bolt and lock washer.

18. Remove the output shaft bearing retainer and bolts from the intermediate plate. Remove the two ball bearing snap-rings and with a plastic hammer or equivalent, force the output shaft, the reverse gearshaft and idler gear halfway out from the plate.

--- **CAUTION** ---
Support the shafts by hand.

19. Remove the idler gear and the reverse gearshaft as an assembly.

20. Remove the countergear and the output shaft together.

21. Measure the thrust clearance of the 1st, 2nd, 3rd and 4th gears before disassembly of the output shaft. Record the clearances for reference during the assembly.

22. Using a puller type tool, remove the sleeve yoke from the end of the output shaft.

23. Z-50 – Remove the snap-ring from the shaft and remove the 5th gear with the puller type tool. Remove the ball bearing snap-ring.

24. Z-40 – Remove the snap-ring from the shaft that locates the sleeve yoke and the snap-ring that retains the ball bearing in position on the shaft.

25. Using the puller type tool. Remove the ball bearing from the shaft. Remove the spacer from the shaft, along with the thrust bearing.

CAUTION

Do not drop the thrust bearing.

---

26. Remove the 4th gear and the half needle bearing cages from the shaft.

27. Remove the snap-ring from the shaft and remove the No. 2 clutch hub, synchronizer ring and the 3rd speed gear from the shaft with the puller type tool.

28. Remove the snap-ring from the front of the shaft and remove the bushing needle bearing 1st gear and the synchronizer ring. Using a magnet, remove the locating locking ball from the shaft.

29. Remove the No. 1 clutch hub, synchronizer ring and the second gear from the shaft.

30. Inspect the gears, bearings, case, housing, plate, synchronizers, shafts and the remaining parts of the trans-axle for wear and damage. Replace the necessary parts before the assembly.

ASSEMBLY

1. Begin the assembly by placing the 2nd gear on the output shaft followed by the synchronizer ring and the Number one clutch hub. Install the locking ball in place on the shaft and install the synchronizer ring, the 1st gear, bearing and the bushing. Install the snap-ring of a thickness to obtain a thrust clearance of zero. The following snap-rings are available:

2. Check the thrust clearances of the 1st and 2nd gears. The clearances should be as listed:

1st gears — 0.0059–0.0108 in. (0.15–0.275mm)

Service limit — 0.0118 in (0.30mm)

2nd gears — 0.0059–0.004 in. (0.15–0.25mm)

Service limit — 0.0118 in (0.30mm)

3. Install the No. 2 clutch hub on the shaft and align the shifting keys with the key slots in the synchronizer rings.

SNAP-RING SIZES

Mark	Thickness	
	in.	mm
1	0.0846–0.0866	2.15–2.20
2	0.0866–0.0886	2.20–2.25
3	0.0886–0.0906	2.25–2.30
4	0.0906–0.0925	2.30–2.35
5	0.0925–0.0945	2.35–2.40
6	0.0945–0.0965	2.40–2.45
7	0.0965–0.0984	2.45–2.50
8	0.0984–0.1004	2.50–2.55
9	0.1004–0.1024	2.55–2.60

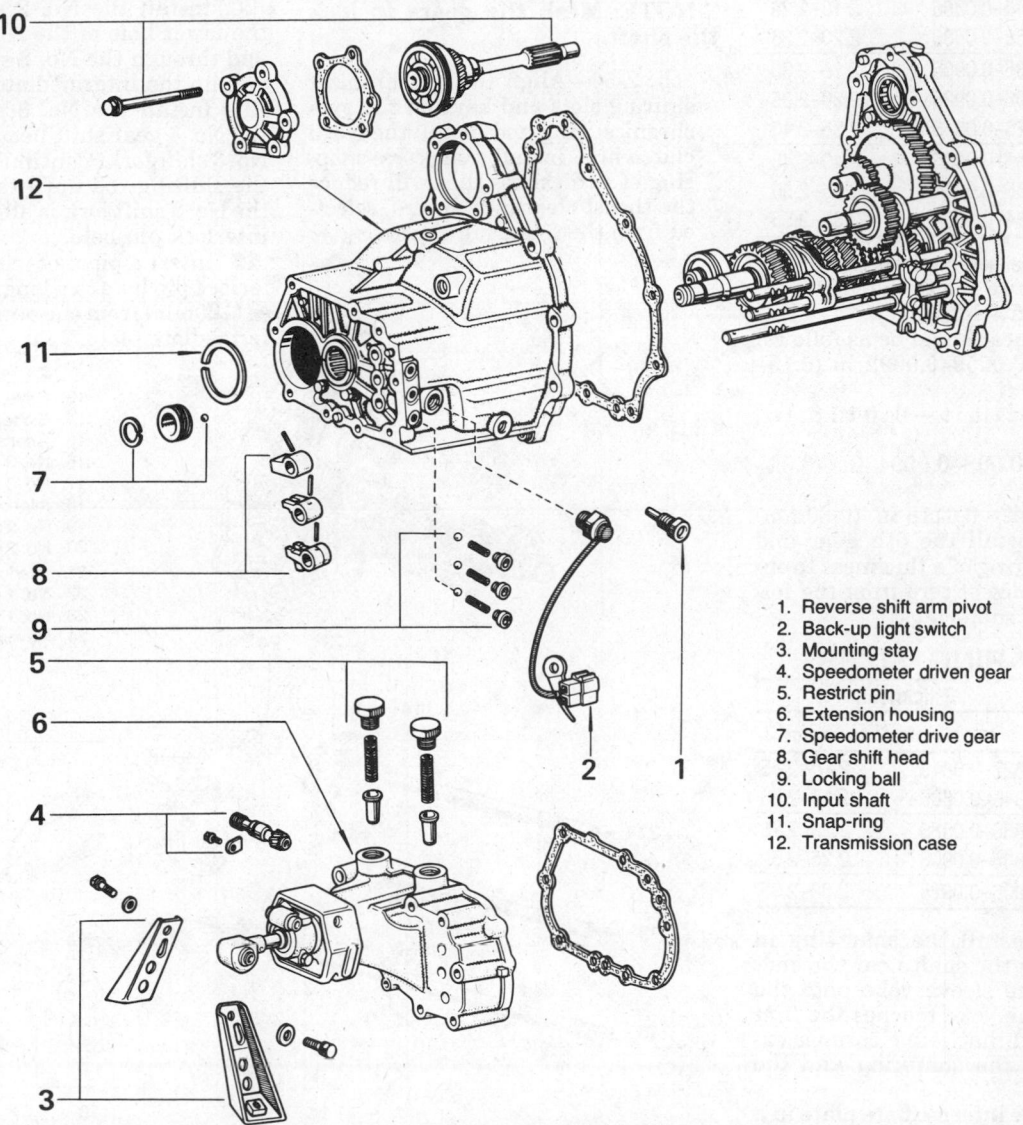

1. Reverse shift arm pivot
2. Back-up light switch
3. Mounting stay
4. Speedometer driven gear
5. Restrict pin
6. Extension housing
7. Speedometer drive gear
8. Gear shift head
9. Locking ball
10. Input shaft
11. Snap-ring
12. Transmission case

Exploded view of transaxle gear housing, cover and intermediate plate

4. Install the widest thrust bearing against the No. 2 clutch hub. Install the half needle bearing cages, synchronizer ring and the 4th speed gear.

5. Install the spacer and the snap-ring to the front side of the 4th gear.

6. Install the smaller thrust washer facing the 4th speed gear.

NOTE: The spacer will have to be pressed onto the shaft.

7. Press the ball bearing onto the shaft with the groove on the bearing facing towards the front.

8. Select a snap-ring of a thickness to obtain a thrust clearance of zero from the following list of available snap-rings:

SNAP-RING SIZES

Mark	Thickness	
	in.	mm
2	0.0827–0.0846	2.10–2.15
3	0.0846–0.0866	2.15–2.20
4	0.0866–0.0886	2.20–2.25
5	0.0886–0.0906	2.25–2.30
6	0.0906–0.0925	2.30–2.35
7	0.0925–0.0945	2.35–2.40
8	0.0945–0.0965	2.40–2.45
9	0.0965–0.0984	2.45–2.50
10	0.0984–0.1004	2.50–2.55

9. With the selected snap-ring installed, measure the thrust clearance of the 3rd and 4th gears.

The clearance should be as follows:
3rd gear – 0.0059–0.0098 in (0.15–0.25mm)

Service limit – 0.0118 in. (0.30mm)

4th gear – 0.008–0.0094 in. (0.02–0.24mm)

Service limit – 0.0118 in. (0.30mm)

10. Z-50 – Install the 5th gear and select a snap-ring of a thickness to obtain a clearance of zero from the following list of snap-rings:

SNAP-RING SIZES

Mark	Thickness	
	in.	mm
2	0.0827–0.0846	2.10–2.15
3	0.0846–0.0866	2.15–2.20
4	0.0866–0.0886	2.20–2.25
5	0.0886–0.0906	2.25–2.30
6	0.0906–0.0925	2.30–2.35

11. Z-40 – Install the snap-ring in the groove on the shaft near the end.

12. Press the sleeve yoke onto the shaft until the yoke touches the first snap-ring and that zero clearance exists between the snap-ring and the shaft groove.

13. Place the intermediate plate in a holder and place the assembled output shaft and the countershaft gear assembly into the intermediate plate, approximately half-way.

14. Align the idler gear with the notched portion of the reverse idler gearshaft. Tap the idler gearshaft bearing approximately half way into the intermediate plate.

NOTE: Be sure the idler gear and the output shaft spacers are not in contact with each other.

15. Tap each gearshaft until the bearings are in the intermediate plate. Install the retaining snap-rings on the bearings.

16. Install the bearing retainer and secure the retaining bolts.

17.
  a. Z-40 – Align the countergear plate with the countershaft protrusion and install the bolt and lockwasher. Torque to 8–11 ft. lbs.

NOTE: Mesh the gears to lock the shaft.

  b. Z-50 – Align the synchronizer shifting slots and keys on the synchronizer ring and install the No. 3 clutch hub. Install a selective snap-ring of a thickness that will reduce the thrust clearance to zero, selected from the following chart:

SNAP-RING SIZES

Thickness	
in.	mm
0.0709–0.0728	1.80–1.85
0.0728–0.0748	1.85–1.90
0.0748–0.0768	1.90–1.95
0.0768–0.0787	1.95–2.00
0.0787–0.0807	2.00–2.05
0.0807–0.0827	2.05–2.10
0.0827–0.0846	2.10–2.15

18. Measure the 5th gear thrust clearance. The clearance should be 0.0059–0.0128 in. (0.5–0.325mm), with a service limit of 0.0157 in. (0.40mm).

19. Fit the shifting forks into their respective coupling sleeves. Insert the number of shift rod into the No. 1 shifting fork, the reverse shift fork and into the intermediate plate bore.

20. Install the No. 2 shift rod into the lower hole of the No. 1 shift fork and through the No. 2 shift fork, and on into the intermediate plate bore.

21. Install the No. 3 shift rod into the No. 4 gear shift head and into the No. 3 shift fork. Continue inward with the shifting rod until the pin hole of the No. 3 shift fork is aligned with the interlock pin hole.

22. Insert a piece of wire into the interlock pin hole to a length of 4.7 inches (120mm) from the outside of the intermediate plate.

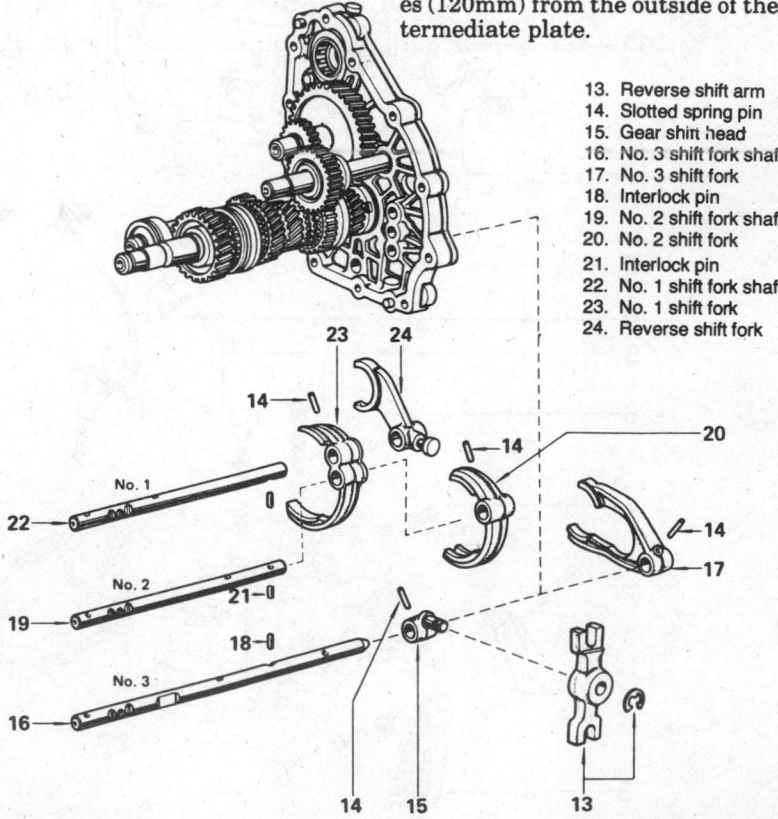

13. Reverse shift arm
14. Slotted spring pin
15. Gear shift head
16. No. 3 shift fork shaft
17. No. 3 shift fork
18. Interlock pin
19. No. 2 shift fork shaft
20. No. 2 shift fork
21. Interlock pin
22. No. 1 shift fork shaft
23. No. 1 shift fork
24. Reverse shift fork

Exploded view of shift mechanism, typical of models Z50 and Z40 transaxles

23. Assemble the interlock pins so that a long pin is inserted first, followed by the small pin and then the same sized pin as the first one, for a total of three. Push the pins inward with a piece of wire and verify that the distance is 3.1 inches (80mm) from the outside of the intermediate plate.

24. In the transaxle of the Z-50, install the number three shaft into the fork controlling the 5th speed synchronizer.

25. Place the shift rods in the neutral position. Move the No. 2 shift rod into the 3rd gear position and the number one and two shafts should not move.

26. Apply sealer to the plug for the interlocks and tighten into place.

27. Align the pin holes in the shift forks and shift fork shafts. Drive the roll pins into place and secure the forks to the shafts.

28. Install the gasket to the intermediate plate and carefully install the case to the plate.

29. Install the countershaft snapring to the ball bearing. Install the detent locking balls and springs. Apply sealer to the detent plugs and install.

30. Install the reverse shift arm pivot bolt through the under side of the reverse shift arm.

31. Install the gear shift heads to the shift rods and instal the roll pins to retain the heads.

32. Install the locating ball, the speedometer drive gear and the snapring.

33. Apply the gasket and sealer to the mating surface of the case and engage the end of the shift lever shaft and the number two shift head, on the extension housing. Install the retaining bolts and secure.

34. Install the restricting pins in their proper positions as follows:
   Green—1st and 2nd gears
   Red—5th and reverse

35. Install the mounting brackets to their marked positions.

36. Fill the transaxle with lubricating oil to its proper level.

37. Be sure the transaxle gear shifts smoothly in all positions.

38. Install the input shaft, gasket and retainer. Secure with the retaining bolts.

39. Install the speedometer driven gear assembly and electrical switch.

TYPE 19

4 & 5 Speed Transaxle Models Z41, 42, 44, 51, 52 and (4x4) 52F Toyota

DISASSEMBLY

1. Support and drain the transaxle.

2. Remove the pivot from the reverse shifter arm. Remove the backup light switch. Remove the 4x4 switch (Z52F only).

3. Remove the speedometer driven gear.

4. Remove the rear mounting stay and then the restrict pins.

5. Remove the retaining bolts and then remove the extension housing from the transmission case (all but Z52F).

6. On the Z52F only:
   a. Remove the transmission case cover, the spring and ball.

NOTE: Use a magnet to remove the ball from its seating.

   b. Remove the straight screw plug and then, using a punch hammer, drive out the pin.
   c. Unscrew the six bolts for the shift lever retainer. Remove the shift lever housing set bolt and lock plate and then remove the housing.
   d. Remove the mounting bolts and then lift off the extension housing.
   e. Remove the straight screw plug for the 4x4 shift fork shaft. Use a magnet to remove the spring and ball. Remove the shift fork shaft along with the hub, hub sleeve and shift fork.
   f. Temporarily re-install the input shaft, cover the tip of the shaft with a cloth and secure the shaft in

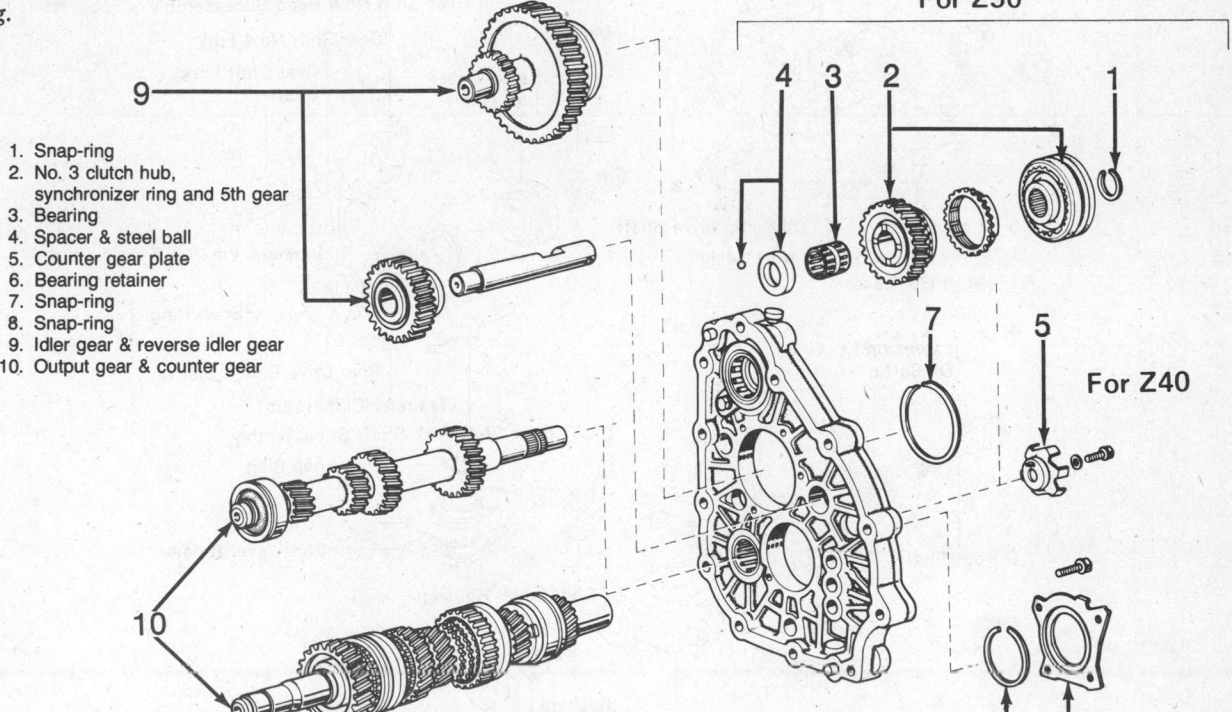

1. Snap-ring
2. No. 3 clutch hub, synchronizer ring and 5th gear
3. Bearing
4. Spacer & steel ball
5. Counter gear plate
6. Bearing retainer
7. Snap-ring
8. Snap-ring
9. Idler gear & reverse idler gear
10. Output gear & counter gear

Exploded view of intermediate plate and gears—model Z40 and Z50 parts illustrated

place with a pair of pliers. Remove the oil pump drive shaft and then the input shaft.

NOTE: The oil pump drive shaft has left-hand threads.

g. Remove the set bolt and lock plate for the No. 4 gear shift shaft. the shift fork. Remove the interlock pins from the shift fork shafts and the intermediate plate.

18. On the Z51, 52 and 52F, use a feeler gauge and measure the counter 5th gear thrust clearance.

Standard clearance: 0.0059–0.0157 in. (0.15–0.325mm)

Maximum clearance: 0.0157 in (0.4mm)

19. On the Z52 and 52F, remove the hole snap-ring and then remove the shifting key retainer.

On the Z51, 52, and 52F, remove the snap-ring with snap-ring pliers. Using a two-armed gear puller, remove the No. 3 clutch hub, the synchronizer ring and the counter 5th gear together as an assembly. Remove the needle roller bearing.

20. Remove the spacer and steel ball (Z51, 52 and 52F). Remove the counter gear plate (Z41, 42 and 44).

21. Remove the bearing retainer and then the two bearing snap-rings.

22. Use a rubber mallet to tap the reverse gear shaft, the idler gear and the output shaft halfway out from the

Using snap-ring pliers, remove the snap-ring from shaft and then remove the No. 4 shift fork along with the No. 4 shift fork shaft. Use a magnet and remove the inter-lock

pin which should still be in its seating.

h. Unscrew the nine transfer case-to-transmission case mounting bolts. Swivel the selector level and remove the tip from the shift head groove and then pull off the transfer case along with the selector lever and the extra low gear.

i. Remove the output shaft and the oil pump gear from the extension housing.

7. Remove the speedometer drive gear.

8. Remove the gear shift head as follows:

a. On all models but the Z52F, use a pin punch and a hammer and drive out the slotted spring pins. Remove the gear shift heads.

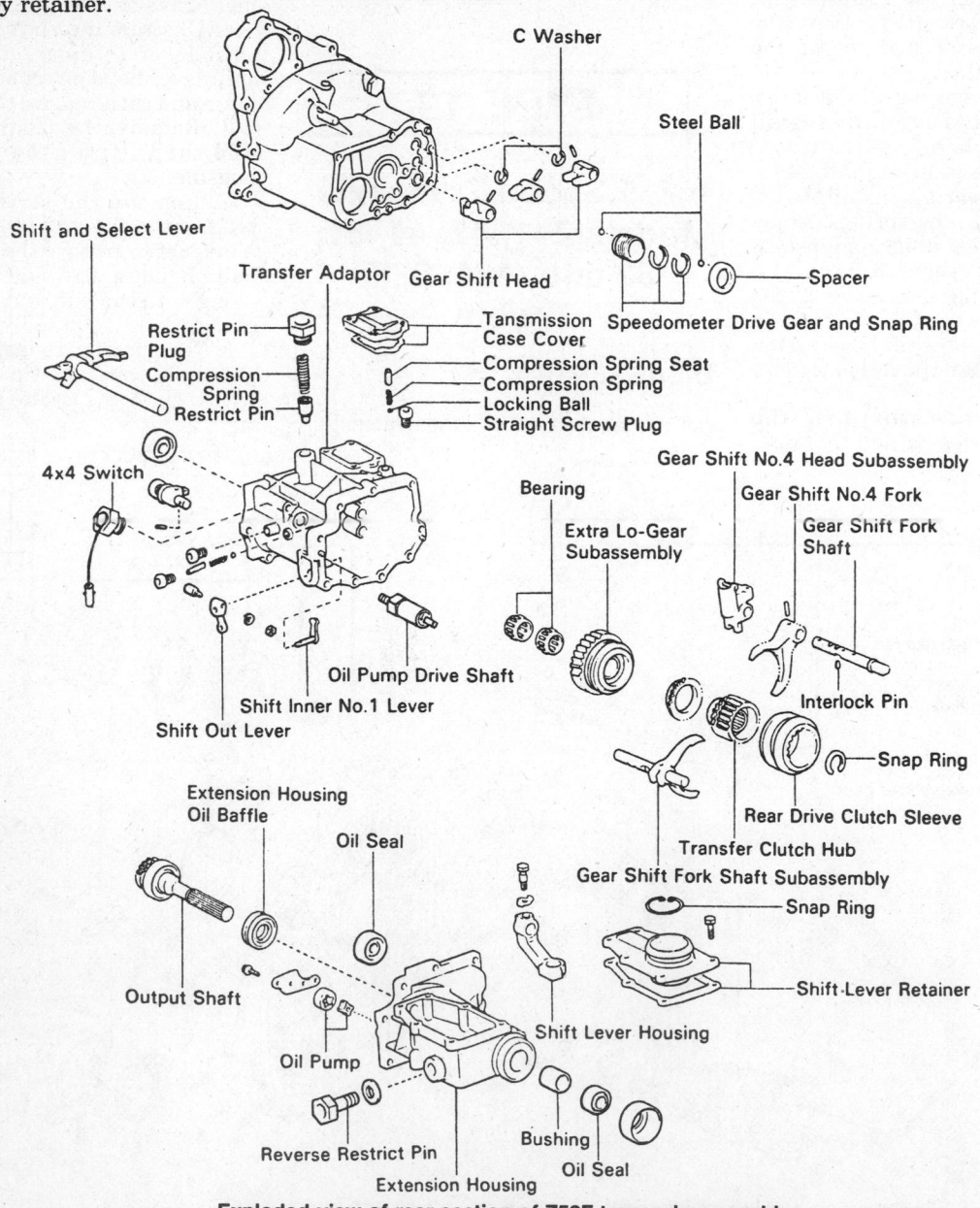

Exploded view of rear section of Z52F transaxle assembly

b. On the Z52F, remove the C washer from the No. 1 and 2 shift fork shafts.

9. Using a special hexagon wrench, remove the straight screw plugs. Using a magnet, lift out the springs and balls.

10. Using snap-ring pliers, remove the bearing snap-ring.

11. Remove the transmission case cover and then pull out the input shaft.

12. Using a rubber mallet, lightly tap on the transmission case protrusion to break the seal between it and the intermediate plate. Remove the case from the intermediate plate.

13. Mount the intermediate plate in a soft-jawed vise.

— CAUTION —

Use the protrusion on the lower part of the intermediate plate to secure it in the vise.

14. On the Z41, 42 and 51, remove the E-ring that retains the reverse shift arm and then remove the arm.

15. On the Z44, 52 and 52F, remove the straight screw plug, spring and ball as detailed previously in this section.

16. Using a pin punch and a hammer, drive out the four slotted spring pins. Remove the gearshift head.

17. Set each shift fork to the neutral position, hold the shift fork, pull out the shift fork shaft and then remove intermediate plate.

— CAUTION —

Support the gear shaft by hand.

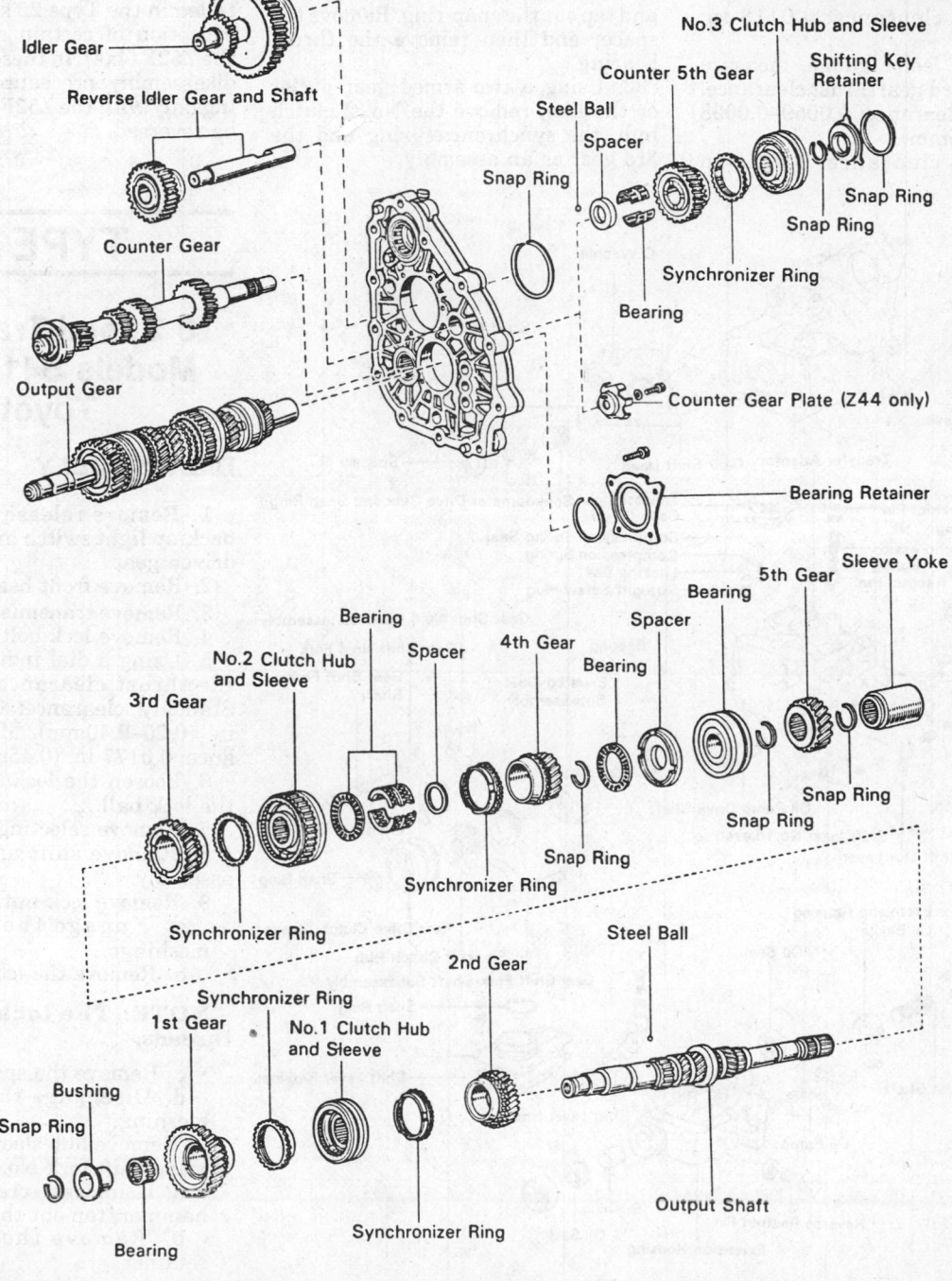

Exploded view of Z44, 52 and 52F transaxle gear assemblies

23. Remove the idler gear and the reverse gear shaft together and then use a rubber mallet to tap out the counter gear and output shaft together.

— **CAUTION** —

Support the gear and shaft by hand.

24. Using a dial indicator, measure the 1st and 4th gear thrust clearance.
  Standard clearance:
  1st gear—0.0059–0.0108 in. (0.140–0.275mm)
  4th gear—0.0008–0.0094 in. (0.02–0.24mm)
  Maximum clearance: 0.0118 in. (0.3mm)
25. Using a feeler gauge, measure the 2nd and 3rd gear thrust clearance.
  Standard clearance: 0.0059–0.0098 in. (0.15–0.25mm)
  Maximum clearance: 0.0118 in (0.3mm)

26. Press out the sleeve yoke. Remove the snap-ring and then press off 5th gear (Z51, 52 and 52F only).
27. Remove the output shaft front bearing snap-ring and then press out the bearing. Press out the spacer and then remove the thrust bearing.
28. Remove 4th gear, the synchronizer ring and the needle roller bearing from the shaft as an assembly.

— **CAUTION** —

Be careful not to drop the needle roller bearing when removing 4th gear.

29. Use two drivers and a hammer and tap out the snap-ring. Remove the spacer and then remove the thrust bearing.
30. Using a two-armed gear puller or the like, remove the No. 2 clutch hub, the synchronizer ring and 3rd gear as an assembly.

31. Remove the snap-ring and then remove 1st gear, the synchronizer ring, the needle roller bearing and the inner race as an assembly from the shaft.
32. Remove the steel ball.
33. Use a two-armed gear puller and remove the No. 1 clutch hub, the synchronizer ring and 2nd gear as an assembly.

ASSEMBLY

Assembly procedures for the Type 23 transaxle are identical to those detailed in the Type 22 section with the exception of certain steps involving the Z52F (4x4). In these instances, the disassembly procedures (those dealing only with the Z52F) should simply be reversed.

TYPE 20

5 Speed Transaxle Models S41, 50, 51 Toyota

DISASSEMBLY

1. Remove release fork, bearing, back-up light switch and speedometer driven gear.
2. Remove front bearing retainer.
3. Remove transmission case cover.
4. Remove lock bolt with washer.
5. Using a dial indicator, measure the thrust clearance (S 50, S 51). Standard clearance: 0.0079–0.00157 in. (0.20–0.40mm). Maximum clearance: 0.0177 in. (0.45mm).
6. Loosen the locknut and remove the lock ball.
7. Remove selecting bellcrank.
8. Remove shift and select lever assembly.
9. Remove lock nut.
  a. Engage the gear double meshing.
  b. Remove the lock nut.

NOTE: The lock nut has LH threads.

  c. Remove the spacer (S41).
  d. Disengage the gear double meshing.
10. Remove hub sleeve No. 3 assembly and shift fork No. 3.
  a. Using two screwdrivers and a hammer, tap out the snap-ring.
  b. Remove the shifting key retainer.
  c. Using three case cover set bolts, tighten the three bolts a little

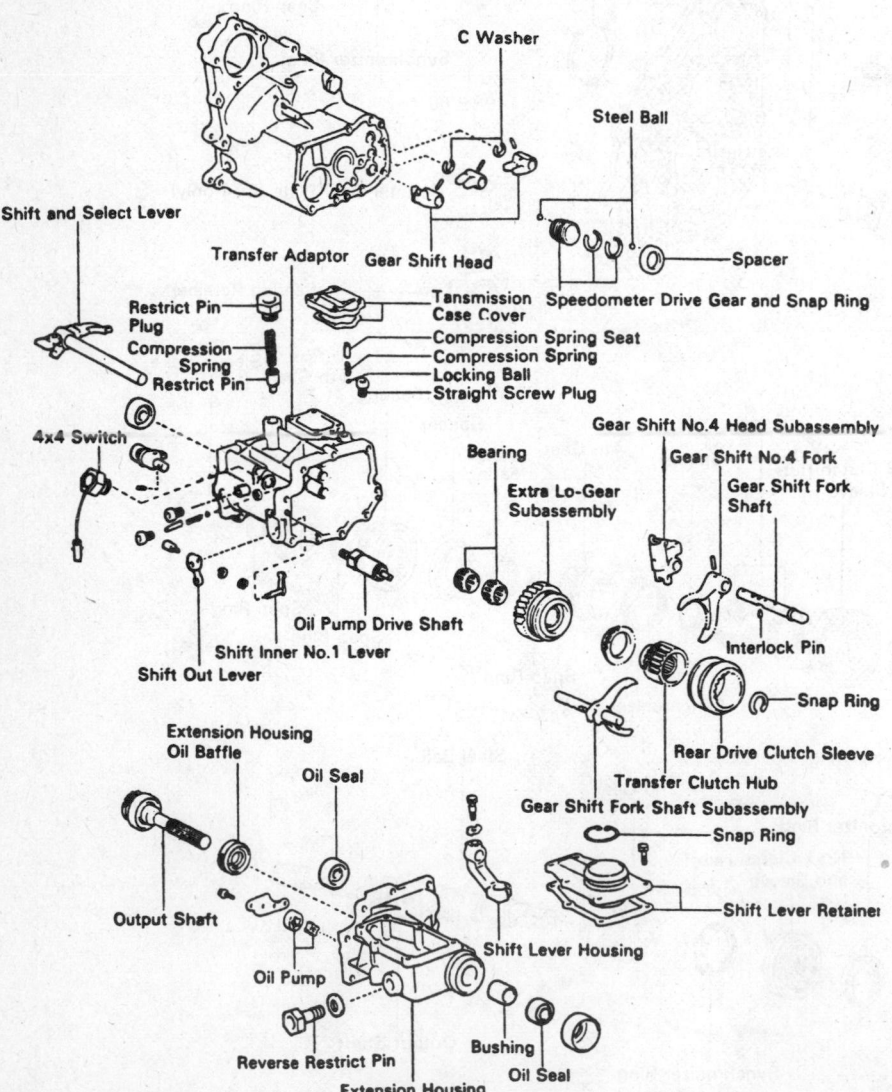

Exploded view of the Z52F (4X4) transfer case and components

Labels on diagram: C Washer · Steel Ball · Spacer · Shift and Select Lever · Transfer Adaptor · Gear Shift Head · Speedometer Drive Gear and Snap Ring · Restrict Pin Plug · Compression Spring · Restrict Pin · Transmission Case Cover · Compression Spring Seat · Compression Spring · Locking Ball · Straight Screw Plug · 4x4 Switch · Bearing · Extra Lo-Gear Subassembly · Gear Shift No.4 Head Subassembly · Gear Shift No.4 Fork · Gear Shift Fork Shaft · Oil Pump Drive Shaft · Shift Inner No.1 Lever · Shift Out Lever · Interlock Pin · Snap Ring · Rear Drive Clutch Sleeve · Transfer Clutch Hub · Extension Housing Oil Baffle · Oil Seal · Gear Shift Fork Shaft Subassembly · Snap Ring · Output Shaft · Oil Pump · Shift Lever Retainer · Shift Lever Housing · Reverse Restrict Pin · Extension Housing · Bushing · Oil Seal

at a time and remove hub sleeve No. 3 and shift fork No. 3.

11. Remove fifth gear, synchronizer ring, needle roller bearing and spacer.

12. Remove fifth driven gear.

13. Remove rear bearing retainer.

14. Remove two bearing snap-rings by using snap-ring pliers.

15. Remove reverse idler gear shaft lock bolt.

16. Remove differential side bearing retainer and shim.

17. To remove transmission case, remove the seventeen bolts and tap off the case with a plastic hammer.

18. Remove reverse shift arm bracket.

   a. Shift fork shaft into reverse.

   b. Remove the two bolts and pull off the bracket.

19. Remove reverse idler gear and shaft by pulling out the shaft.

20. Remove shift fork shaft No. 1, shift head No. 1, shift fork No. 1 and No. 2.

   a. Drive out the slotted spring pin from fork shaft No. 1.

   b. Drive out the slotted spring pin from shift head and fork shaft No. 1.

   c. Pull out fork shaft No. 1 with the shift head and shift forks.

21. Remove reverse shift fork and interlock pin.

22. Remove fork shaft No. 2.

   a. Remove the straight screw plug.

   b. Using a pin punch and hammer, drive out the slotted spring pin.

   c. Pull out the shaft.

23. Remove input and output shaft together from transaxle case.

24. Remove differential assembly.

25. Remove magnet.

26. Measure third and fourth gear thrust clearance.

Using a feeler gauge, measure the thrust clearance.

Standard clearance:

   3rd gear – 0.0039–0.0098 in. (0.10–0.25mm)

   4th gear – 0.0079–0.0177 in (0.20–0.45mm)

Maximum clearance:

   3rd gear – 0.0118 in. (0.30mm)

   4th gear – 0.0197 in. (0.50mm)

27. Remove snap ring from input shaft.

28. Remove radial ball bearing, fourth gear needle roller bearings, synchronizer ring and spacer from input shaft.

   a. Using a press, remove the radial ball bearing and 4th gear.

   b. Remove the needle roller bearings, synchronizer ring and spacer.

29. Remove snap-ring.

30. Remove hub sleeve No. 2 assembly, third gear, synchronizer ring and needle roller bearing.

31. Measure first and second gear thrust clearance by using a feeler gauge.

   1st gear – 0.0039–0.0114 in. (0.10–0.29mm)

   2nd gear – 0.0079–0.0173 in. (0.20–0.33mm).

Maximum clearance:

   1st gear – 0.0138 in. (0.35mm)

   2nd gear – 0.0197 in. (0.50mm)

32. Remove radial ball bearing, fourth driven gear and output gear spacer form output shaft.

   a. Using a press, remove the radial ball bearing and 4th driven gear.

   b. Remove the spacer.

33. Remove third driven gear, second gear, needle roller bearing, spacer and synchronizer ring.

   a. Shift hub sleeve No. 1 into 1st gear.

   b. Using a press, remove the 3d driven gear and 2nd gear.

   c. Remove the needle roller bearing, spacer and synchronizer ring.

34. Remove snap-ring.

35. Remove hub sleeve No. 1 assembly, first gear, synchronizer ring and needle roller bearing.

   a. Using a press, remove hub sleeve No. 1, 1st gear and synchronizer ring.

   b. Remove the needle roller bearing and spacer.

36. Disassemble shift and select lever assembly.

   a. Remove the lever lock pin and nut.

   b. Remove the control shift lever.

   c. Remove the dust boot.

   d. Remove the control shaft cover.

   e. Remove the two E-rings.

   f. Remove the select spring seat No. 2 and spring.

   g. Remove the shift inner lever No. 2.

   h. Using a pin punch and hammer, drive out the slotted spring pin.

   i. Remove the shift fork lock plate, shift inner lever No. 1 select spring seat No. 1 and spring

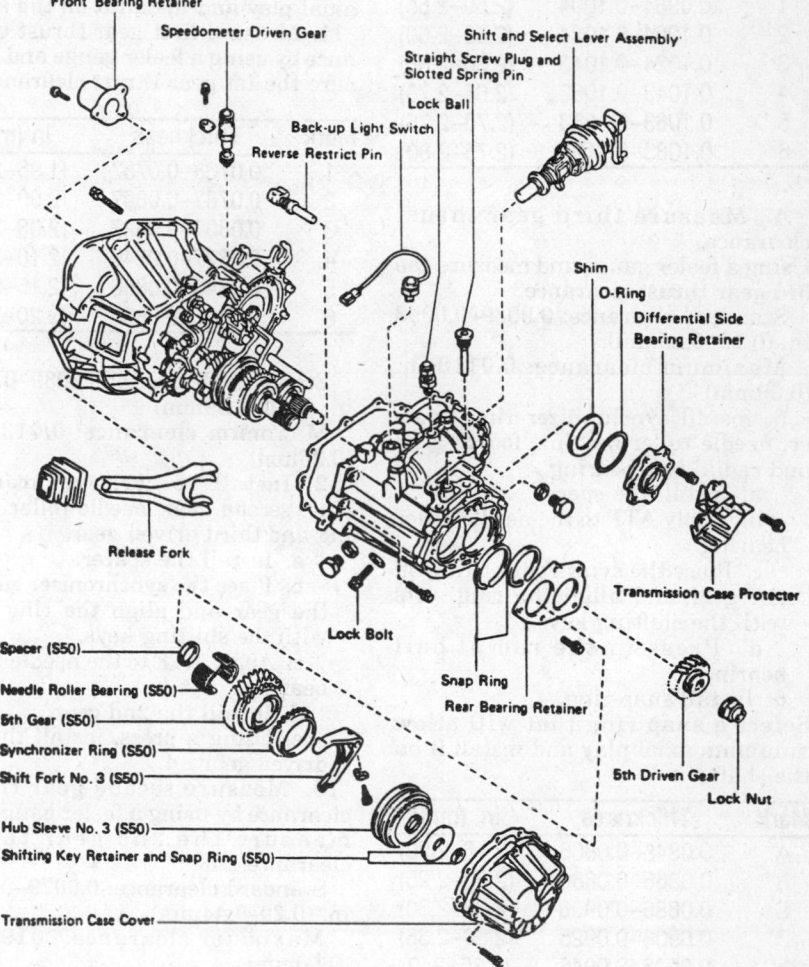

Exploded view of S41 and S50 transaxles

Front Bearing Retainer
Speedometer Driven Gear
Shift and Select Lever Assembly
Straight Screw Plug and Slotted Spring Pin
Lock Ball
Back-up Light Switch
Reverse Restrict Pin
Shim
O-Ring
Differential Side Bearing Retainer
Release Fork
Transmission Case Protecter
Lock Bolt
Snap Ring
Rear Bearing Retainer
Spacer (S50)
Needle Roller Bearing (S50)
5th Gear (S50)
Synchronizer Ring (S50)
Shift Fork No. 3 (S50)
Hub Sleeve No. 3 (S50)
Shifting Key Retainer and Snap Ring (S50)
Transmission Case Cover
5th Driven Gear
Lock Nut

ASSEMBLY

1. Insert clutch hub No. 2 into hub sleeve.

   a. Install the clutch hub and shifting keys to the hub sleeve.

   b. Install the shifting key springs under the shifting keys.

——————— CAUTION ———————

Install the key springs positioned so that their end gaps are not in line.

2. Install third gear, needle roller bearings, synchronizer ring and hub sleeve No. 2 assembly to input shaft.

   a. Apply ATF to the needle roller bearings.

   b. Place the synchronizer ring on the gear and align the ring slots with the shifting keys.

   c. Using a press, install the 3rd gear and hub sleeve No. 2.

3. Install snap-ring

Select a snap-ring that will allow minimum axial play and install it on the shaft.

Mark	Thickness	in. (mm)
1	0.0984–0.1004	(2.50–2.55)
2	0.1004–0.1024	(2.55–2.60)
3	0.1024–0.1043	(2.60–2.65)
4	0.1043–0.1063	(2.65–2.70)
5	0.1063–0.1083	(2.70–2.75)
6	0.1083–0.1102	(2.75–2.80)

4. Measure third gear thrust clearance.

Using a feeler gauge and measure the 3rd gear thrust clearance.

   Standard clearance: 0.0039–0.0098 in. (0.10–0.25mm).

   Maximum clearance: 0.0118 in. (0.30mm).

5. Install synchronizer ring, spacer, needle roller bearing, fourth gear and radial ball bearing.

   a. Install the spacer.

   b. Apply ATF to the needle roller bearing.

   c. Place the synchronizer ring on the gear and align the ring slots with the shifting keys.

   d. Press in the radial ball bearing.

6. Install snap-ring.

Select a snap-ring that will allow minimum axial play and install it on the shaft.

Mark	Thickness	in. (mm)
A	0.0846–0.0866	(2.15–2.20)
B	0.0866–0.0886	(2.20–2.25)
C	0.0886–0.0906	(2.25–2.30)
D	0.0906–0.0925	(2.30–2.35)
E	0.0925–0.0945	(2.35–240)

7. Measure fourth gear thrust clearance by using a feeler gauge and measure the 4th gear thrust clearance.

   Standard clearance: 0.0079–0.0177 in. (0.20–0.45mm)

   Maximum clearance: 0.0197 in. (0.50mm).

8. Insert clutch hub No. 1 into hub sleeve.

   a. Install the clutch hub and shifting keys to the hub sleeve.

   b. Install the shifting key springs under the shifting keys.

——————— CAUTION ———————

Install the key springs positioned so that their end gaps are not in line.

9. Install spacer, first gear, needle roller bearing, synchronizer ring and hub sleeve No. 1 to output shaft.

   a. Apply ATF to the needle roller bearing.

   b. Place the synchronizer ring on the gear and align the ring slots with the shifting keys.

   c. Using a press, install the 1st gear and hub sleeve No. 1.

10. Install snap-ring and select a snap-ring that will allow minimum axial play and install it on the shaft.

11. Measure first gear thrust clearance by using a feeler gauge and measure the 1st gear thrust clearance.

Mark	Thickness	in (mm)
1	0.0768–0.0787	(1.95–2.00)
2	0.0787–0.0807	(2.00–2.05)
3	0.0807–0.0827	(2.05–2.10)
4	0.0827–0.0846	(2.10–2.15)
5	0.0846–0.0866	(2.15–2.20)
6	0.0866–0.0886	(2.20–2.25)

   Standard clearance: 0.0039–0.0114 in. (0.10–0.29mm)

   Maximum clearance: 0.0138 in. (0.35mm)

12. Install spacer, synchronizer ring, second gear, needle roller bearing and third driven gear.

   a. Install the spacer.

   b. Place the synchronizer ring on the gear and align the ring slots with the shifting keys.

   c. Apply ATF to the needle roller bearing.

   d. Install the 2nd gear.

   e. Using a press, install the 3rd driven gear.

13. Measure second gear thrust clearance by using a feeler gauge and measure the 2nd gear thrust clearance.

   Standard clearance: 0.0079–0.0173 in. (0.20–0.44mm).

   Maximum clearance: .0197 in. (0.50mm).

14. Install output gear spacer, fourth driven gear and radial ball bearing.

   a. Install the spacer.

   b. Press in the 4th driven gear and bearing.

15. Install magnet.

16. Adjust differential side bearing preload.

   a. Install the differential to the transaxle case.

   b. Install the transmission case with the used gasket.

   c. Install and torque the case bolts. Torque: 22 ft. lb. (29 Nm).

   d. Install the thinnest shim into the transmission case.

   e. Install the bearing retainer without an O-ring.

   f. Install and torque the retainer bolts. Torque: 13 ft. lb. (18 Nm).

   g. Measure the preload. Preload (starting): 8.7–13.9 in. lb. (1.0–1.6 Nm).

   h. If the preload is not within specification, remove the bearing retainer.

   i. Reselect a adjusting shim.

NOTE: The preload will change about 2.6–3.5 in. lb., 0.3–0.4 Nm) with each shim thickness.

17. Remove bearing retainer, shim and transmission case with gasket.

   a. If the preload is adjusted within specification, remove the bearing retainer, shim and transmission case with gasket.

   b. Be careful not to lose the adjusted shim.

18. Install input and output shaft together.

19. Install fork shaft No. 2.

   a. Insert fork shaft No. 2 to the transaxle case and align the slotted spring pin.

   b. Using a pin punch and hammer drive in the slotted spring pin.

   c. Install the straight screw plug. Torque: 9 ft. lb. (13 Nm).

20. Install reverse shift fork and interlock pin.

   a. Insert interlock pin to the reverse shift fork hole.

   b. Install the reverse shift fork onto fork shaft No. 2.

21. Install reverse shift arm.

   a. Put the reverse shift arm pivot into the reverse shift fork and install the reverse shift arm to the transaxle case.

   b. Shift the reverse shift arm into reverse.

   c. Install and torque the bolts. Torque: 13 ft. lb. (18 Nm).

22. Install reverse idler gear and shaft by aligning the transaxle case slot and slotted spring pin.

23. Install fork shift No. 1, No 2, shift head No. 1 and fork shaft No. 1.

   a. Place shift for No. 1 and No. 2 into the groove of hub sleeve No. 1 and No. 2.

b. Hold shift head No. 1 and insert fork shaft No. 1 into the transaxle case through shift fork No. 1, No. 2, shift head No. 1 and reverse shift fork.

c. Using a pin punch and hammer, drive the slotted spring pin into shift head No. 1 and fork shaft No. 1.

d. Shift fork shaft into reverse.

e. Using a pin punch and hammer, drive the slotted spring pin into fork shaft No. 1.

24. Install transmission case with new gasket.

a. Install and torque the seventeen bolts. Torque: 22 ft. lb. (29 Nm).

25. Install shim and side bearing retainer with O-ring.

a. Install the O-ring on the retainer.

b. Install the shim and retainer.

c. Install and torque the six bolts. Torque: 13 ft. lb. (18 Nm).

26. Install and torque reverse idler gear shaft lock bolt. Torque 18 ft. lb. (25 Nm).

27. Install two bearing snap-rings.

28. Install rear bearing retainer.

a. Install and torque the five bolts. Torque: 13 ft. lb. (18 Nm).

29. Install fifth driven gear (S50).

30. Install spacer, needle roller bearings, fifth gear and synchronizer ring (S50).

a. Install the spacer.

b. Apply ATF to the needle roller bearings.

c. Install the 5th gear with the needle roller bearings and synchronizer ring.

31. Insert clutch hub No. 3 into hub sleeve (S50, S51).

a. Install the clutch hub and shifting keys to the hub sleeve.

b. Install the shifting key springs under the shifting keys.

— CAUTION —

Install the key springs positioned so that their end gaps are not in line.

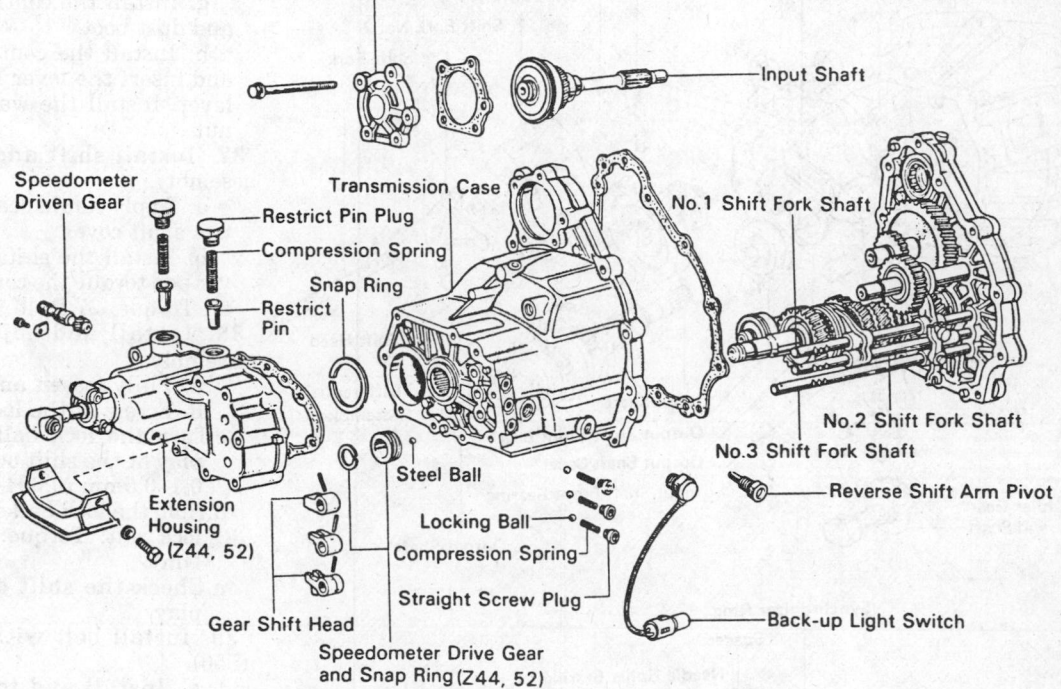

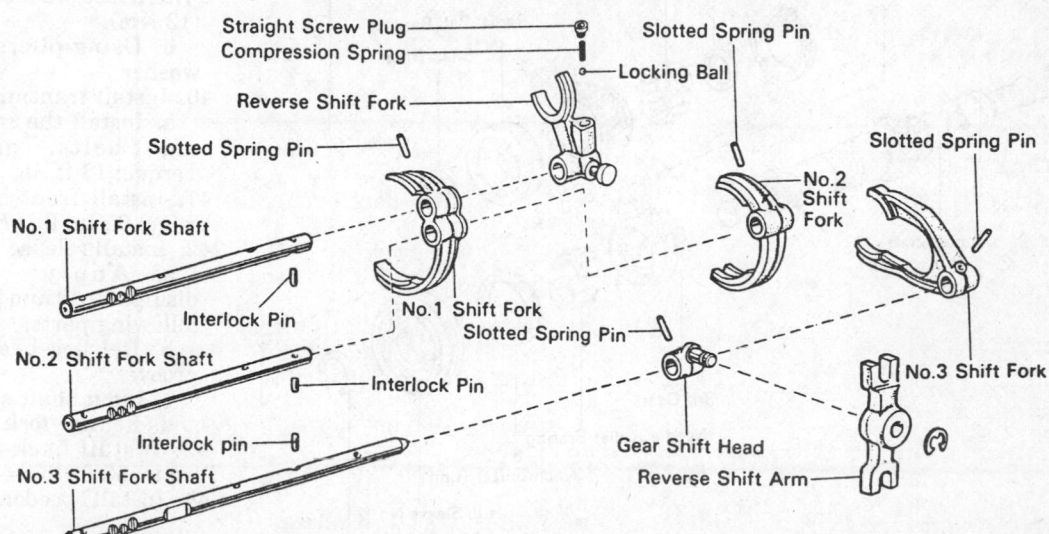

Exploded view of transaxle case and shifting mechanism, Z44, 52 and 52F models

32. Install hub sleeve No. 3 assembly with shift fork No. 3 (S50).

    a. Drive in hub sleeve No. 3 with shift fork No. 3.

—————— CAUTION ——————

Align the synchronizer ring slots with the shifting keys.

33. Measure fifth gear thrust clearance (S50, S51).

    a. Using a dial indicator, measure the thrust clearance.

    Standard clearance: 0.0079–0.0157 in. (0.20–0.40mm).

Maximum clearance: 0.0177 in. (0.45mm).

34. Install shifting key retainer ad snap ring (S50, S51).

    a. Install the retainer.

    b. Select a snap-ring that will allow minimum axial play and install it on the shaft.

35. Install lock nut.

    a. Engage the gear double meshing.

    b. Install the space (S41).

    c. Install and torque the nut. Torque: 90 ft. lb. (123 Nm).

NOTE: The lock nut has LH threads.

    d. Disengage the gear double meshing.

    e. Stake the lock nut.

36. Assemble shift and select lever assembly.

    a. Apply ATF to the shaft.

    b. Install select spring seat No. 1, spring and E-ring.

    c. Install shift inner lever No. 1 with the shift fork lock plate.

    d. Align shift inner lever No. 2 with No. 1 and install it.

    e. Install select spring seat No. 2 spring and E-ring.

    f. Using a pin punch and hammer, drive in the slotted spring pin.

    g. Install the control shaft cover and dust boot.

    h. Install the control shaft lever and insert the lever lock pin to the lever. Install the washer and lock nut.

37. Install shift and select lever assembly.

    a. Apply liquid sealer to the control shaft cover.

    b. Install the shift and select lever and torque the control shaft cover. Torque: 27 ft. lb. (37 Nm).

38. Install and adjust lock ball assembly.

    a. Fully loosen and lock nut.

    b. Screw in the lock ball.

    c. Turn the lock ball to where the play at the shift outer lever tip is 0.1–0.5mm (0.004–0.020 in.).

    d. Hold the lock ball and tighten the lock nut. Torque: 27 ft. lb. (37 Nm).

    e. Check the shift outer level tip play.

39. Install bolt with lock washer (S50).

    a. Install and torque the bolt with a lock washer. Torque: 9 ft. lb. (12 Nm).

    b. Using pliers, stake the lock washer.

40. Install transmission case cover.

    a. Install the case cover and the eight bolts. Torque the bolts. Torque: 13 ft. lb. (18 Nm).

41. Install front bearing retainer. Torque: 65 in. lb. (7.4 Nm).

42. Install release fork and bearing.

    a. Apply molybdenum disulphide litium base grease to the following parts.

    b. Release bearing hub inside groove.

    c. Input shaft spline.

    d. Release fork contact surface.

43. Install back-up light switch. Torque: 33 ft. lb. (44 Nm).

44. Install speedometer driven gear.

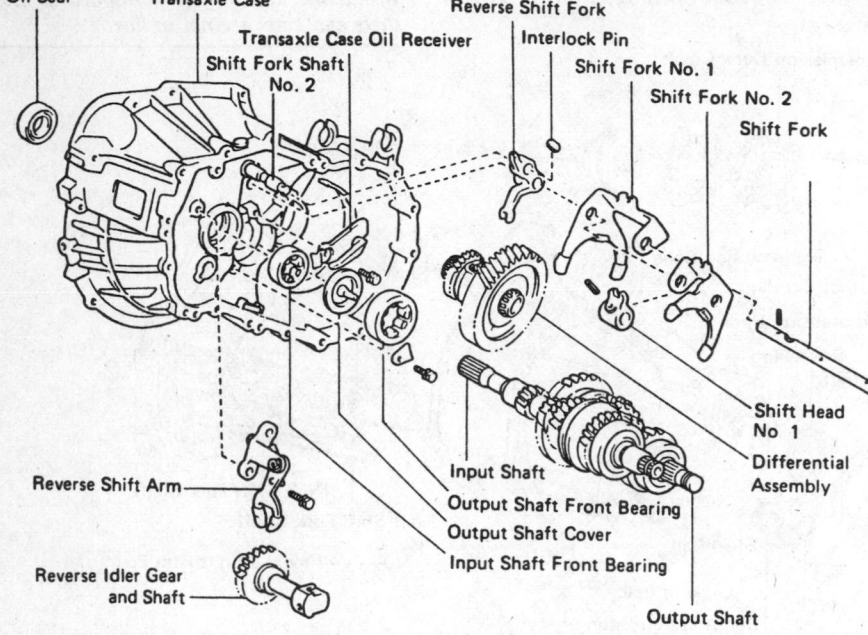

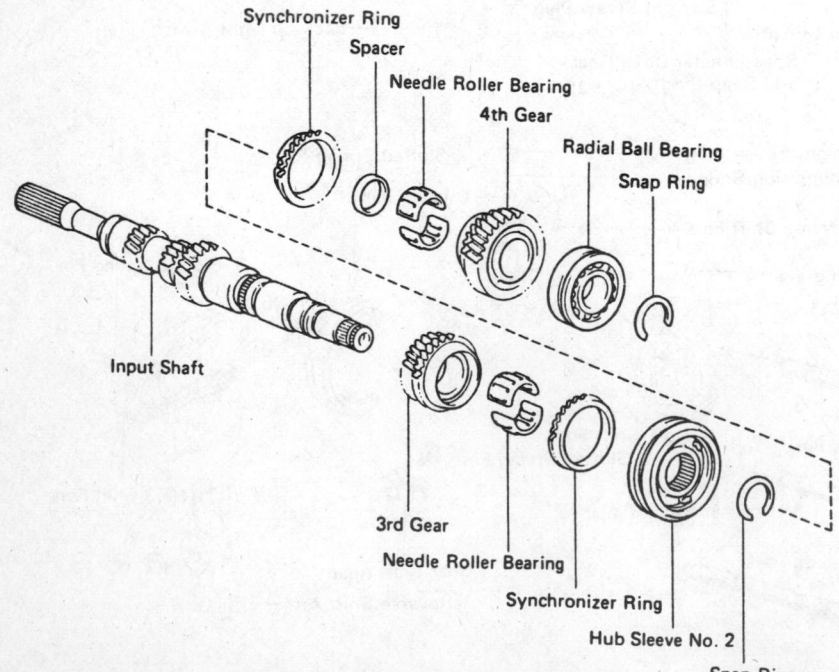

Exploded view of Input shaft assemblies, S 41, S 50, S 51 models

TYPE 21

5 Speed Transaxle Model C51 Toyota

DISASSEMBLY

1. Remove release fork, bearing and speedometer driven gear.
2. Remove back-up light switch.
3. Remove front bearing retainer.

4. Remove transmission case cover.
5. Measure fifth gear thrust clearance. Using a dial indicator, measure the thrust clearance.
   Standard clearance: 0.0039–0.224 in. (0.10–0.57mm).
   Maximum clearance: 0.0256 in. (0.65mm).
6. Remove selecting bellcrank.
7. Remove lock bolt.
8. Remove shift and select lever assembly.
9. Remove lock nut.
   a. Engage the gear double meshing.
   b. Remove the lock nut.
   c. Disengage the gear double meshing.

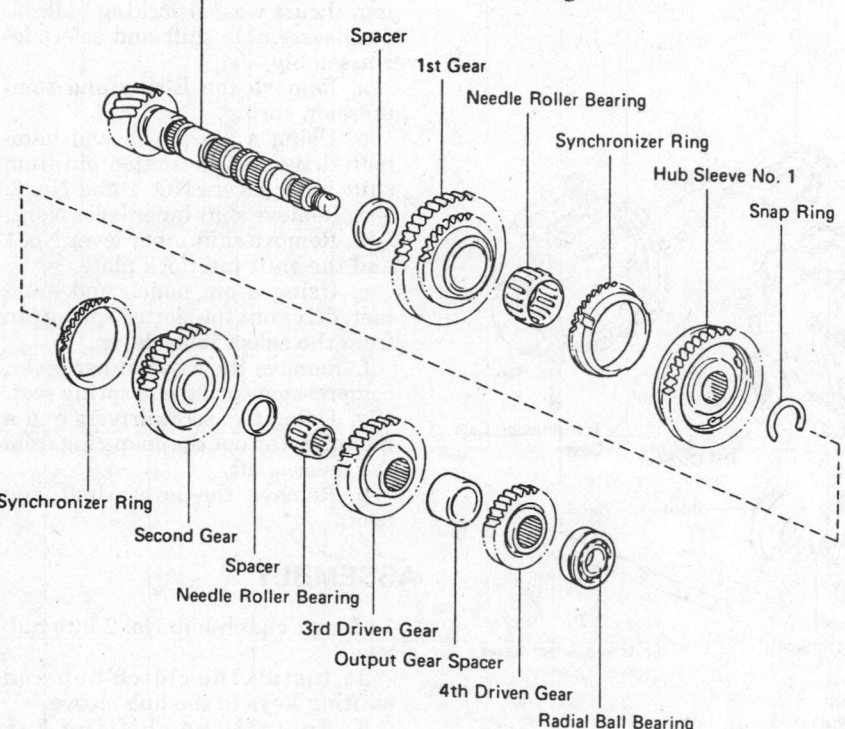

10. Remove hub sleeve No. 3 assembly and shift fork No. 3.
    a. Remove the bolt with the lock washer from shift fork No. 3.
    b. Using two screwdrivers and a hammer, tap out the snap-ring.
    c. Remove the hub sleeve No. 3 assembly and shift fork No. 3.
11. Remove fifth gear, synchronizing ring, needle roller bearing and spacer.
12. Remove fifth driven gear.
13. Remove rear bearing retainer.
14. Remove two bearing snap-rings.
15. Remove reverse idler gear shaft lick bolt.
16. Remove snap-ring from No. 2 shift fork shaft.
17. Remove plug, seat, spring and ball.
    a. Remove the four plugs.
    b. Using a magnetic finger, remove the four springs and balls.
18. Remove transmission case. Remove the sixteen bolts and tap off the case with a plastic hammer.
19. Remove reverse shift arm bracket. Remove the two bolts and pull off the bracket.
20. Remove reverse idler gear and shaft.
21. Remove shift forks and shift fork shaft.
    a. Using two screwdrivers and a hammer, tap out the three snap-rings.
    b. Pry out the lock washers and remove the two balls.
    c. Remove fork shaft No. 2 and shift head.
    d. Using a magnetic finger, remove the two balls.
    e. Remove fork shaft No. 3 and reverse shift fork.
    f. Pull out fork shaft No. 1.
    g. Remove shift forks No. 1 and No. 2.
22. Remove input and output shaft together from transaxle case.
23. Remove differential assembly.
24. Remove magnet and oil receiver.
25. Measure third and fourth gear thrust clearance by using a feeler gauge and measure the thrust clearance.

Standard clearance:
   3rd gear — 0.0039–0.0138 in. (0.10–0.35mm).
   4th gear — 0.0039–0.0217 in. (0.10–0.55mm).
Maximum clearance:
   3rd gear — 0.0157 in. (0.40mm).
   4th gear — 0.0236 in. (0.60mm).
26. Remove snap-ring from input shaft.
27. Remove radial ball bearing, fourth gear, needle roller bearing and synchronizer ring from input shaft.
    a. Using a press, remove the radial ball bearing and 4th gear.

Exploded view of output shaft assembly, S41, S50, and S51 models

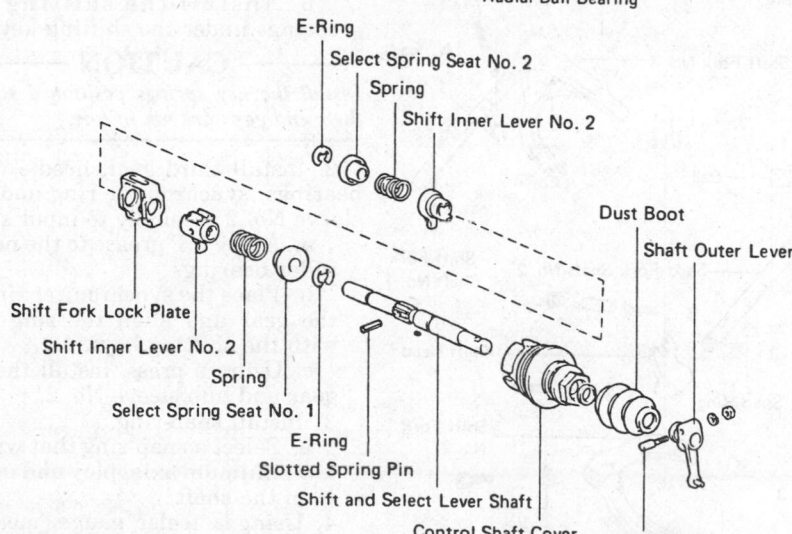

b. Remove the needle roller bearings and synchronizer ring.

28. Remove snap-ring. Using snap-ring pliers.

29. Remove hub; sleeve No. 2 assembly. Third gear, synchronizer ring and needle roller bearing.

a. Using a press, remove hub sleeve No. 2, 3rd gear, synchronizer ring and needle roller bearings.

30. Measure first and second gear thrust clearance by using a feeler gauge and measure the thrust clearance.

Standard clearance:
1st gear – 0.0039–0.0157 in. (0.10–0.40mm).
2nd gear – 0.0039–0.0177 in. (0.10–0.45mm).

Maximum clearance:
1st gear – 0.0177 in. (0.45mm).
2nd gear – 0.0197 in. (0.50mm).

31. Remove radial ball bearing, fourth drive gear and spacer from output shaft.

a. Using a press, remove the radial ball bearing and driven gear.

b. Remove the spacer.

32. Remove third driven gear, second gear needle roller bearing, spacer and synchronizer ring.

a. Shift hub sleeve No. 1 into 1st gear.

b. Using a press, remove the 3rd drive gear and 2nd gear.

c. Remove the needle roller bearing, spacer and synchronizing ring.

d. Remove snap-ring.

34. Remove hub sleeve No. 1 assembly, first gear, synchronizer ring, needle roller bearing, thrust washer and locking ball.

a. Using a press, remove hub sleeve No. 1, 1st gear synchronizer ring.

b. Remove the needle roller bearing, thrust washer locking ball.

35. Disassemble shift and select lever assembly.

a. Remove the E-ring and compression spring.

b. Using a pin punch and hammer, drive out the slotted pin from shift inner levers NO. 1 and No. 2.

c. Remove shift inner lever No. 2.

d. Remove shift inner lever No. 1 and the shift interlock plate.

e. Using a pin punch and hammer, drive out the slotted spring pin from the select inner lever.

f. Remove the select inner lever, compression spring and spring seat.

g. Using two screwdrivers and a hammer, tap out the snap-ring from the lever shaft.

h. Remove the lever shaft and boot.

ASSEMBLY

1. Insert clutch hub No. 2 into hub sleeve.

a. Install the clutch hub and shifting keys to the hub sleeve.

b. Install the shifting key springs under the shifting keys.

—— **CAUTION** ——
Install the key springs positioned so that their end gaps are not in line.

2. Install third gear, needle roller bearings, synchronizer ring and hub sleeve No. 2 assembly to input shaft.

a. Apply MP grease to the needle roller bearings.

b. Place the synchronizer ring on the gear and align the ring slots with the shifting keys.

c. Using a press, install the 3rd gear and hub sleeve No. 2.

3. Install snap-ring.

a. Select a snap-ring that will allow minimum axial play and install it on the shaft.

4. Using a feeler gauge, measure the 3rd gear thrust clearance.
Maximum clearance: 0.0039 in. (0.10mm).

Reverse Restrict Pin

Protector

Transmission Case

Plug

RH Oil Seal

Transmission Case Cover

Shift Interlock Plate

Snap Ring

Boot

Lock Bolt

Spring

Spring

Oil Seal

Shift and Select Lever

Select Spring Seat

Select Inner Lever

Slotted Spring Pin

E-Ring

Shift Inner No. 1 Lever

Shift Fork No. 1

Select No. 2 Seat

Shift Inner No. 2 Lever

Straight Screw Plug

Ball

Reverse Shift Fork

Plug

Seat

Spring

Ball

Shift Fork Shaft No. 2

Shift Fork Shaft No. 1

Shift Head

Shift Fork No. 2

Snap Ring

Shift Fork Shaft No. 3

Shift Fork No. 3

Bolt and Lock Washer

Exploded view of C51 transaxle case and shifting mechanism

Mark	Thickness	in. (mm)
A	0.0902	(2.29)
B	0.0925	(2.35)
C	0.0949	(2.41)
D	0.0972	(2.47)
E	0.0996	(2.53)
F	0.1020	(2.59)

5. Install synchronizer ring, needle roller bearing, fourth gear and radial ball bearing.

a. Apply MP grease to the needle roller bearing.

b. Place the synchronizer ring on the gear and align the ring slots with the shifting keys.

c. Press in the radial ball bearing.

6. Install snap-ring. Select a snap-ring that will allow minimum axial play and install it on the shaft.

7. Using a feeler gauge, measure the 4th gear thrust clearance. Maximum clearance: 0.0039 in. (0.10mm).

8. If input shaft was replaced, drive in slotted spring. If the input shaft was replaced, drive the slotted ring pin in the output shaft to a depth of 0.236 in. (6.0mm).

Mark	Thickness	in. (mm)
0	0.0906	(2.30)
1	0.0929	(2.36)
2	0.0953	(2.42)
3	0.0976	(2.48)
4	0.1000	(2.54)
5	0.1024	(2.60)

9. Insert clutch hub No. 1 into hub sleeve.

a. Install the clutch hub and shifting keys to the hub sleeve.

b. Install the shifting key springs under the shifting keys.

CAUTION

Install the key springs positioned so that their end gaps are not in line.

10. Install thrust washer, first gear, needle roller gearing, synchronizer ring and hub sleeve No. 1 to output shaft.

a. Install the locking ball in the shaft.

b. Fit the thrust washer groove securely over the locking ball when installing the thrust washer on the shaft.

c. Apply MP grease to the needle roller bearing.

d. Place the synchronizer ring on the gear and align the ring slots with the shifting keys.

e. Using a press, install the 1st gear and hub sleeve No. 1.

11. Install a snap-ring that will allow minimum axial play and install it on the shaft.

12. Using a feeder gauge, measure the 1st gear thrust clearance. Maximum clearance: 0.0039 in. (0.10mm).

13. Install spacer, synchronizer ring, second gear, needle roller bearing and third driven gear.

a. Install the spacer.

b. Place the synchronizer ring on the gear and align the ring slots with the shifting keys.

c. Apply MP grease to the needle roller bearing.

d. Install the 2nd gear.

e. Using a press, install the 3rd driven gear.

14. Using a feeler gauge, measure the 2nd gear thrust clearance.

Standard clearance: 0.0039–0.0177 in. (0.10–0.45mm).

Maximum clearance: 0.00197 in. (0.50mm).

15. Install output gear spacer, fourth driven gear and radial ball bearing.

Mark	Thickness	in. (mm)
A	0.0984	(2.50)
B	0.1008	(2.56)
C	0.1031	(2.62)
D	0.1055	(2.68)
E	0.1079	(2.74)
F	0.1102	(2.80)

a. Install the spacer.

b. Press in the 4th driven gear and bearing.

16. Install magnet.

17. Install oil receiver with two bolts.

18. Adjust differential side bearing preload.

a. Install the thinnest shim into the transmission case.

b. Drive in the outer race of the side bearing.

c. Install the differential to the transaxle case.

d. Install the transmission case.

e. Install and torque the case bolts. Torque: 22 ft. lbs. (29 Nm).

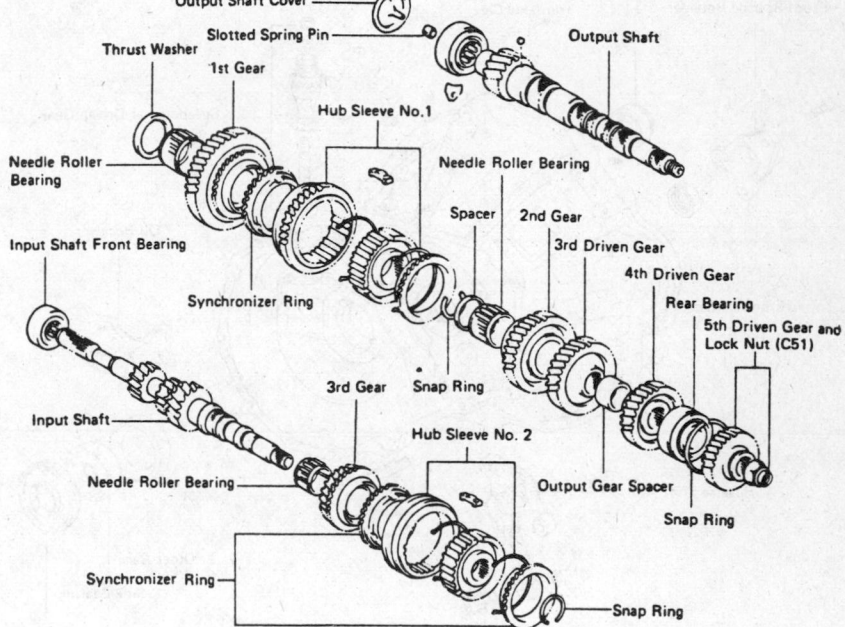

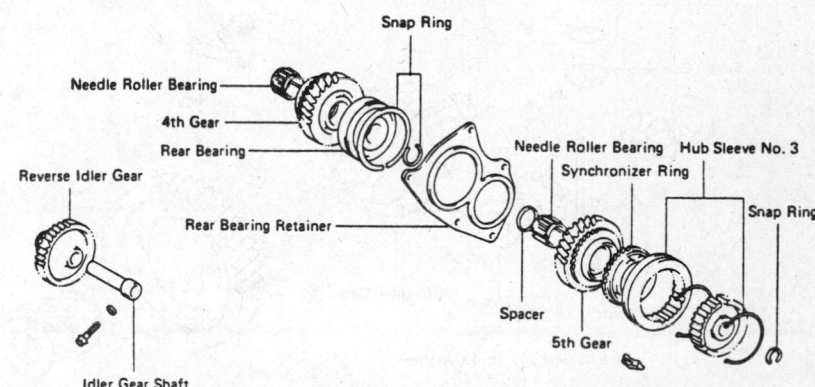

Exploded view of C51 transaxle shaft and gear assemblies

Mark	Thickness	in. (mm)
Q	0.0827	(2.10)
R	0.0846	(2.15)
S	0.0866	(2.20)
T	0.0886	(2.25)
U	0.0906	(2.30)
A	0.0925	(2.35)
B	0.0945	(2.40)
C	0.0965	(2.45)
D	0.0984	(2.50)
E	0.1004	(2.55)
F	0.1024	(2.60)
G	0.1043	(2.65)
H	0.1063	(2.70)
J	0.1083	(2.75)
K	0.1102	(2.80)
L	0.1122	(2.85)
M	0.1142	(2.90)
N	0.1161	(2.95)
P	0.1181	(3.00)

f. Measure the preload.
Preload:
New bearing: 6.9–13.9 inch lbs. (0.5–1.0 Nm).
Reused bearing: 4.3–8.7 inch lbs. (0.5–1.0 Nm).

g. If the preload is not within specifications, remove the transmission case side outer race of the side bearing.

h. Reselect an adjusting shim.

NOTE: The preload will change about 2.6–3.5 in. lb. (0.3–0.4 Nm) with each shim thickness.

19. Remove outer race, shim and transmission case. If the preload is adjusted within specification, remove the outer race, shim and transmission case.

Be careful not to loose the adjusted shim.

20. Install the input and output shafts together.

21. Install shift forks and shift fork shaft.

a. Place shift forks No. 1 and No. 2 into the groove of hub sleeves No. 1 and No. 2.

b. Insert fork shaft No. 1 into the shift fork No. 1 hole.

c. Insert the two interlock balls into the reverse shift fork hole.

d. Install fork shaft No. 3 and reverse shift fork.

e. Install fork shaft No. 2 and shift head.

f. Install the three lock washers and bolts. Torque: 9 ft. lbs. (12 Nm).

g. Using pliers, stake the bolts with lock washers.

h. Install the three snap-rings.

22. Install reverse shift arm.

a. Put the reverse shift fork pivot into the reverse shift arm and install the reverse shift arm to the transaxle case.

b. Install and torque the bolts.

23. Install reverse idler gear and shaft.

24. Install transmission case.

a. Remove any packing material and be careful not to drop oil on the contacting surfaces of the transmission case or transaxle case.

b. Apply seal packing to the transmission case.

NOTE: Install the transmission case as soon as the seal packing is applied.

c. Install and torque the sixteen bolts. Torque: 22 ft. lbs. (29 Nm).

25. Install ball, spring, seat plug.

a. Insert the balls, springs, and seats into the holes.

b. Apply liquid sealer to the plugs.

c. Tighten the four plugs. Torque: 18 ft. lbs. (25 Nm).

26. Install and torque reverse idler gear shaft lock bolt. Torque: 29 ft. lbs. (29 Nm).

27. Install two bearing snap-rings.

28. Install snap-ring to fork shaft No. 2.

29. Install rear bearing retainer. Install and torque the five bolts. Torque: 14 ft. lbs. (19 Nm).

30. Install fifth driven gear.

31. Install spacer, needle roller bearing, fifth gear and synchronizer ring.

32. Insert clutch hub No. 3 into hub sleever.

a. Install the clutch hub and shifting keys to the hub sleeve.

b. Install the shifting key springs under the shifting keys.

— **CAUTION** —

Install the key springs positioned so that their end gaps are not in line.

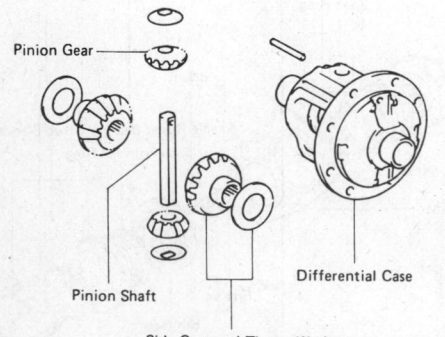
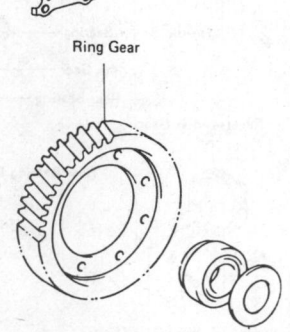

Exploded view of C51 transaxle differential assembly

Front Bearing Retainer
RH Oil Seal
Transaxle Case
Speedometer Driven Gear
Front Oil Seal
Oil Receiver
Reverse Shift Arm
Magnet
Outer Race
Side Bearing
Speedometer Drive Gear
Pinion Gear
Ring Gear
Pinion Shaft
Differential Case
Side Gear and Thrust Washer

33. Install hub sleeve No. 3 assembly with shift fork No. 3. Drive in hub sleever No. 3 with shift fork No. 3.

—————— **CAUTION** ——————

Align the synchronizer ring slots with the shifting keys.

34. Measure fifth gear thrust clearance. Maximum clearance: 0.0039 in. (0.10mm).

35. Install snap-ring. Select a snap-ring that will allow minimum axial play and install it on the shaft.

36. Install lock nut.

Mark	Thickness	in. (mm)
A	0.0886	(2.25)
B	0.0909	(2.31)
C	0.0933	(2.37)
D	0.0957	(2.43)
E	0.0980	(2.49)
F	0.1004	(2.55)
G	0.1028	(2.61)

a. Engage the gear double meshing.

b. Install and torque the nut. Torque: 87 ft. lbs. (118 Nm).

c. Disengage the gear double meshing.

d. Stake the lock nut.

37. Install bolt with lock washer.

a. Install and torque the bolt with a lock washer. Torque: 9 ft. lbs. (12 Nm).

b. Using pliers, stake the lock washer.

38. Assemble shift and select lever assembly.

a. Apply MP grease to the shaft.

b. Install the boot and shaft to the control shaft cover.

NOTE: Make sure to install the boot in correct direction. Position the air bleed of the boot downward.

c. Install the snap-ring and spring seat.

d. Install the compression spring and select inner lever.

e. Using a pin punch and hammer, drive in the slotted spring pin.

f. Align the interlock plate with shift inner lever No. 1 and install it.

g. Install shift inner lever No. 2.

h. Using a pin punch and hammer, drive in the slotted spring pin.

i. Install the compression spring, seat E-ring.

39. Install shift and select lever assembly.

a. Place the gasket in position on the control shaft cover.

b. Install the shift and select lever, and torque the bolts. Torque: 14 ft. lbs. (20 Nm).

c. Install the bellcrank to the transmission case.

40. Install lock bolt. Torque: 22 ft. lbs. (29 Nm).

41. Install transmission case cover. Install the case cover and the eight bolts. Torque the bolts. Torque: 13 ft. lbs. (18 Nm).

42. Install front bearing retianer. Torque: 8 ft. lbs. (11 Nm).

43. Install release fork and bearing.

a. Apply molybdenum disulphide litium base grease to the following parts:

b. Release bearing hub inside groove.

c. Input shaft spine.

d. Release fork contact surface.

44. Install back-up light switch. Torque: 30 ft. lbs. (40 Nm).

TYPE 22

4 and 5 Speed Transaxle Models 013, 093 Audi Models 013, 020 Volkswagen

DISASSEMBLY

1. Mount the transaxle assembly in a holding fixture.

2. Remove the end cover and gasket.

3. Remove the circlips from the clutch release shaft. Slide the shaft out of the gear carrier and remove the clutch lever and return spring.

4. Remove the clutch release bearing and clutch pushrod.

5. Mount a bar with a locknut and spacer across the final drive housing to support the mainshaft.

6. Remove the selector shaft cover. Remove the interlock plunger springs, and the selector shaft.

7. Remove the circlip from the gear carrier side drive flange. Install the special tool with two bolts on the drive flange. Remove the drive flange.

8. Remove the plastic caps covering the clamping screws. Remove the clamping screw nuts.

9. Remove the reverse shaft retaining bolt.

10. Mount the special tool on the gear carrier assembly and lift the gear carrier off the final drive assembly while threading the special tool bolt in.

11. Drive the drive flange oil seal out of the gear carrier housing.

12. Pry the clutch operatng shaft oil seal out of the carrier housing.

13. Pull the pinion shaft needle bearing out of the gear carrier.

14. Remove the shift fork assembly and the mainshaft from the final drive housing.

15. Remove the remaining drive flange as outlined in Step 7.

16. Remove the needle bearing stop and the first circlip from the pinion shaft. Lift fourth gear off the shaft.

17. Remove the second circlip from the pinion shaft. Lift third gear, second gear, second gear inner race and the needle bearing off the shaft.

18. Remove the verse shaft and gear.

19. Using a gear puller, remove the synchronizer hub and first/second gear from the pinion shaft.

20. Remove the pinion bearing cover and outer bearing race. Remove the pinion shaft.

21. Remove the differential assembly.

22. Pry the mainshaft oil sealout of the final drive housing.

23. Drive the drive flange oil seal out of the final drive housing.

24. Pull the starter bushing out of the final drive housing.

25. Pull the pinion outer bearing race out of the final drive housing.

26. Drive the differential outer bearing race out of the final drive housing.

27. Pull the mainshaft needle bearing out of the final drive housing.

28. Remove the two circlips from the shift fork shaft and slide the components off the shaft.

29. remove the first circlip from the mainshaft and discard. Press the bearing off the shaft.

30. Mount the separator assembly on fourth gear and press the gear off the mainshaft. Remove the needle bearings.

31. Remove the second circlip from the mainshaft and discard. Press third gear and the synchronizer assembly off the shaft. Remove the needle bearings.

32. Slide a ⅜ in. rod in the mainshaft and drive the clutch pushrod out.

33. Press the two tapered roller bearings off the pinion shaft.

34. Remove the clrclips from the differential pinion shaft and drive out.

35. Remove the circlips from the drive flange shafts. Remove the side gears and thrust washers.

37. Press the tapered roller bearing off the housing side of the differential.

38. Remove the tapered roller bearing from the ring gear side of the differential.

39. Remove the ring gear.

ASSEMBLY

NOTE: The ring gear and pin-

ion shaft can be replaced only as a matched set.

1. Heat the pinion shaft small tapered bearing to 212°F and press it onto the shaft.

2. Heat the pinion shaft large tapered bearing to 212°F and press onto the shaft.

3. Place a 0.75mm shim in the pinion bore in the final drive housing and press the small bearing outer position.

4. Install the pinion shaft and cover.

5. Assemble the pinion adjustment fixture tools. Place the end plate on the pinion shaft. Attach the dial indicator and zero with a 1mm preload.

--------- CAUTION ---------

Do not turn the pinion shaft while measuring because the bearings will settle and give an incorrect reading.

6. Move the pinion shaft up and down and note the reading.

7. Specified bearing preload is obtained by adding the constant figure of 0.20mm to the measured reading and the shim thickness (0.75mm).

8. Remove the pinion shaft cover and the pinion shaft. Pull the pinion shaft cover and the pinion shaft. Pull the pinion shaft small bearing outer race of the final drive housing.

9. Install the correct shim and press the pinion shaft small bearing outer race into the final drive housing.

NOTE: If new bearings have been installed on the pinion shaft, check the pinion shaft turning torque. Reading should be 4.4–13.1 inch lbs.

10. Install the side gears and thrust washers in the differential housing.

11. Install the pinion gears and thrust washers. Drive the pinion shaft into the differential housing.

12. Install centering pins on the differential housing. Heat the ring gear to 212°F and press onto the differential housing.

13. Heat the housing side differential bearing to 212°F and press the bearing into place.

14. Heat the ring gear side bearing to 212°F and press the bearing into place.

NOTE: If new bearings have been installed, the differential must be adjusted.

15. Slide the drive flange shafts into the side gears. Determine the thickness of the circlip by pressing the drive flange shaft against the pinion gearshaft, while pressing the side gears against the housing. Insert the

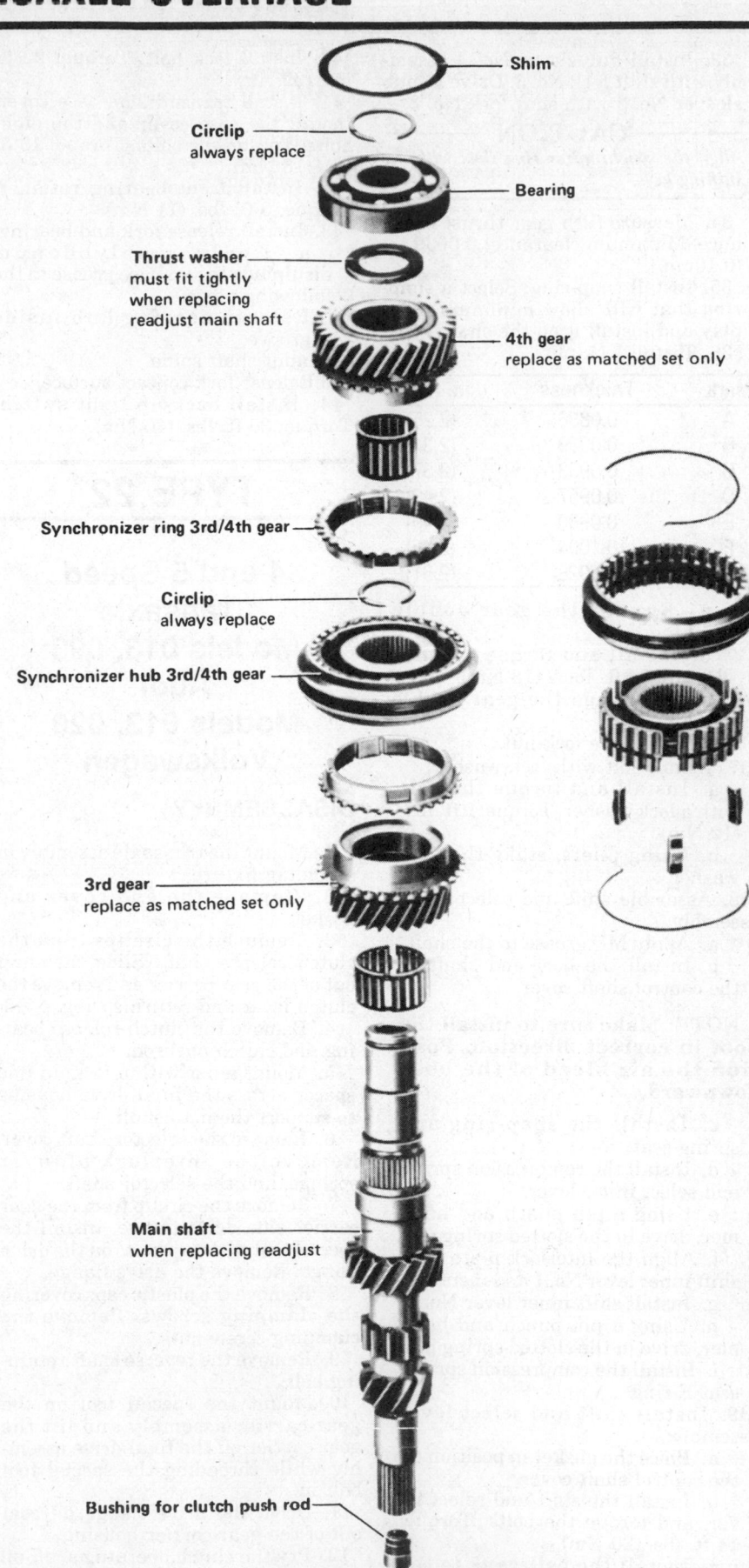

Shim

Circlip
always replace

Bearing

Thrust washer
must fit tightly
when replacing
readjust main shaft

4th gear
replace as matched set only

Synchronizer ring 3rd/4th gear

Circlip
always replace

Synchronizer hub 3rd/4th gear

3rd gear
replace as matched set only

Main shaft
when replacing readjust

Bushing for clutch push rod

Exploded view of mainshaft assembly

thickest possible circlip. The circlip should not be jammed sideways.

———— CAUTION ————

The differential inner and outer bearing races are matched to their bearings and cannot be interchanged.

16. If new differential bearings have been installed, proceed as follows:

   a. Install the race in the final drive housing with a 1mm shim.

   b. Install the race in the gear carrier without a shim.

   c. Place the differential assembly in the final drive housing. Install the gear carrier on the final drive housing, with the gasket.

   d. Install the dial indicator fixture on the gear carrier tool and place the end plate on the drive flange. Install the dial indicator with a 1mm preload.

———— CAUTION ————

Do not turn the differential when making the measurements because the bearings will settle and give incorrect readings.

   e. Move the differential up and down and note the reading.

   f. The correct bearing preload is determined by adding a constant figure or .40mm to the measured reading.

   g. Remove the gear carrier from the final drive housing.

   h. Pull the bearing race out of the gear carrier housing with a suitable extractor.

   i. Install the shims in the gear carrier starting with the thickest. Install the bearing race.

17. With the differential in the final drive housing, install the pinion shaft and tighten the nuts on the cover plate to 14 ft. lbs.

NOTE: Synchronizers can be replaced only as a matched unit.

18. Position the keys in the slots in the synchronizer hub. Place the synchronizer sleeve over the hub and align the marks. Install the springs 120° offset with the angled ends engaged in the hollow of a key.

19. Press the synchronizer rings onto the first and second gears. Check the gap between the ring and gear with a feeler gauge. The gap on new parts should be between 0.042–0.066 in. and no less than 0.019 in. on used parts.

20. Install the thrust washer and needle bearing for first gear on the pinion shaft. The recess in the thrust washers faces the roller bearing.

21. Align the grooves in the first gear synchronizer ring with the synchronizer shift keys. Position the shift fork slot in the operating sleeve to-

ward second gear. The groove on the synchronizer hub should face toward first gear.

22. Heat the first gear and synchronizer as an assembly to 250°F and press onto the pinion shaft.

23. Drive the second gear needle bearing race onto the pinion shaft.

24. Install the second gear needle bearings and second gear.

25. Install third gear on the pinion shaft with the collar facing toward

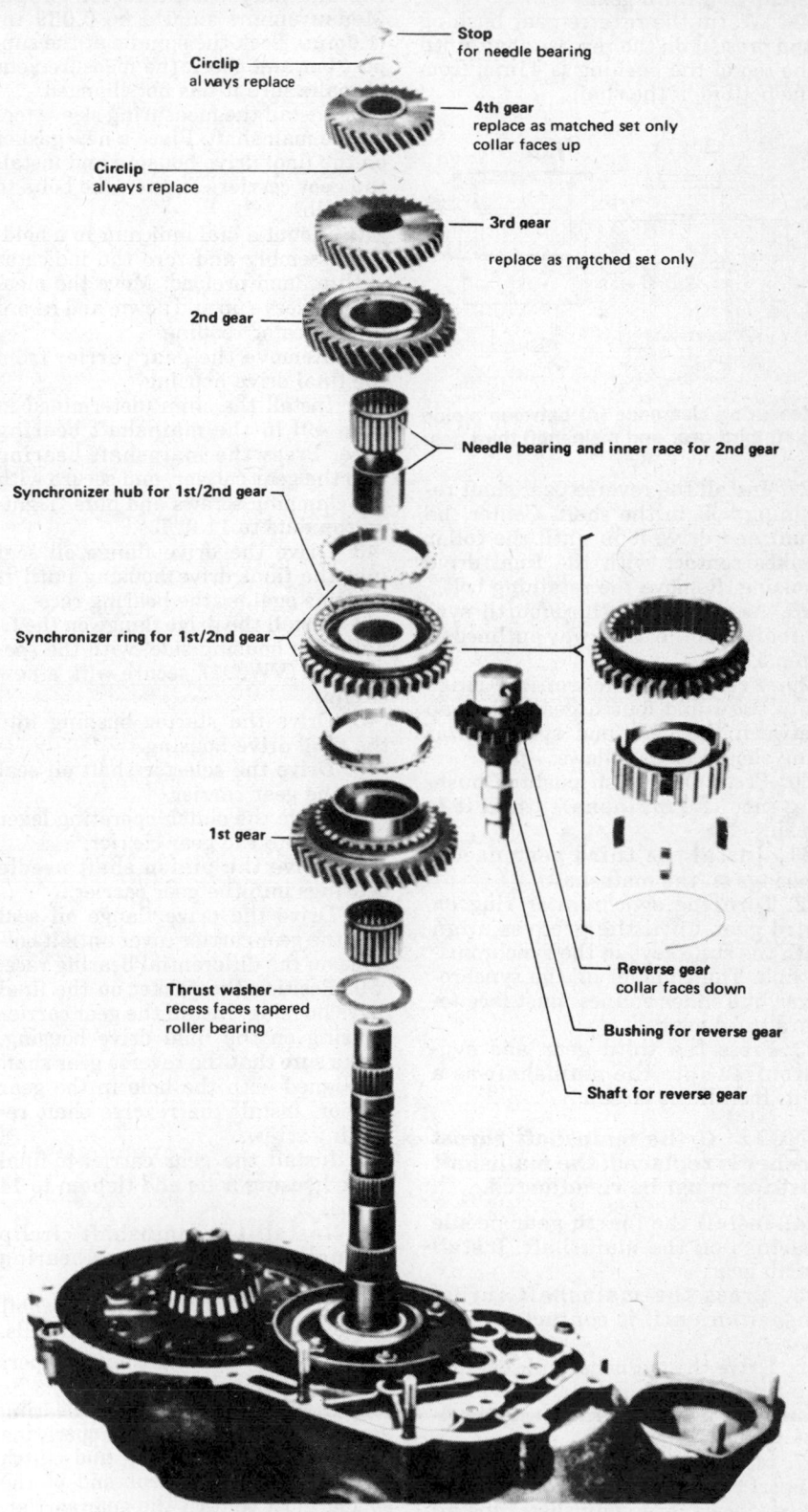

Exploded view of pinion shaft gear assembly

Labels:
- Stop for needle bearing
- Circlip always replace
- 4th gear replace as matched set only collar faces up
- Circlip always replace
- 3rd gear replace as matched set only
- 2nd gear
- Needle bearing and inner race for 2nd gear
- Synchronizer hub for 1st/2nd gear
- Synchronizer ring for 1st/2nd gear
- 1st gear
- Thrust washer recess faces tapered roller bearing
- Reverse gear collar faces down
- Bushing for reverse gear
- Shaft for reverse gear

second gear. Secure third gear with the collar facing toward second gear. Secure third gear with the selective circlip which will give an axial play between 0.00–0.20mm. Measure the play with a feeler gauge between the circlip and third gear.

26. Warm the reverse gear bushing and press it on the reverse shaft until the top of the bushing is 41mm from the bottom of the shaft.

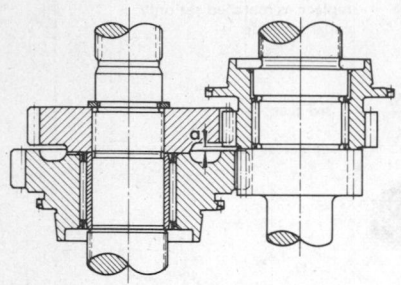

Measuring clearance (A) between pinion shaft third gear and mainshaft third gear

27. Install the reverse gear shaft retaining bolt in the shaft. Center the shaft and drive it in until the collar makes contact with the final drive housing. Remove the retaining bolt.

28. Assemble the third/fourth synchronizer in the same way outlined in Step 57.

29. Press the synchronizer rings onto third and fourth gear. The gap between the gear and synchronizer ring should be as follows:

30. Press the clutch pushrod bushing into the mainshaft until it is flush.

31. Instal the third gear needle bearings on the mainshaft.

32. Turn the synchronizer ring on third gear until the grooves align with the shift keys in the synchronizer hub. The chamfer on the synchronizer hub inner splines must face toward third gear.

33. Press the third gear and synchronizer onto the mainshaft as a unit. Install the circlip.

NOTE: If the mainshaft thrust washer is replaced, the mainshaft position must be re-adjusted.

34. Install the fourth gear needle bearings on the mainshaft. Install fourth gear.

35. Press the mainshaft thrust washer on until it contacts fourth gear.

36. Drive the mainshaft oil seal into the final drive housing. Drive the mainshaft needle bearings into the final drive housing.

37. Make sure that the mainshaft support bar, locknut and spacer are in place. Insert the mainshaft. Install the shift fork assembly and secure

with the circlips. Make sure that the gears are in Neutral.

38. Lift the shaft with the spindle until the play between second gear on the pinion shaft and third gear on the mainshaft can be checked. Measure the end-play with a feeler gauge. Measurement should be 0.039 in. (1.0mm). Lock the spindle at the support bar and check the measurement to make sure it has not changed.

39. Install the measuring sleeve tool on the mainshaft. Place a new gasket on the final drive housing and install the gear carrier. Tighten the bolts to 14 ft. lbs.

40. Mount a dial indicator in a holding assembly and zero the indicator with a 3mm preload. Move the measuring sleeve up and down, and record the indicator reading.

41. Remove the gear carrier from the final drive housing.

42. Install the shim (determined in Step 40) in the mainshaft bearing bore. Press the mainshaft bearing into the gear carrier, and secure with the clamping screws and nuts. Tighten the nuts to 11 ft. lbs.

43. Drive the drive flange oil seal into the final drive housing until it bottoms against the bearing race.

44. Install the drive flange on the final drive housing side, with the special tool (VW391), secure with a new circlip.

45. Drive the starter bushing into the final drive housing.

46. Drive the selector shaft oil seal into the gear carrier.

47. Drive the clutch operating lever oil seal into the gear carrier.

48. Drive the pinion shaft needle bearings into the gear carrier.

49. Drive the drive flange oil seal into the gear carrier cover until it bottoms on the differential bearing race.

50. Position the gasket on the final drive housing. Install the gear carrier housing on the final drive housing. Make sure that the reverse gear shaft is aligned with the hole in the gear carrier, install the reverse shaft retaining screw.

51. Install the gear carrier-to-final drive housing bolts and tighten to 14 ft. lbs.

52. Install the mainshaft circlip through the clutch release bearing opening in the gear carrier.

53. Install the remaining driveshaft flange and circlip using special tools.

54. Remove the mainshaft support bar. Insert the clutch pushrod.

55. Insert the clutch release bearing assembly. Insert the clutch operating lever through the spring and clutch bearing lever. The bent end of the spring must contact the gear carrier. The center part of the spring is

hooked over the end of the clutch bearing lever. Install the two circlips. Install the gasket and cover.

56. Insert the selector shaft and springs into the select or opening in the gear carrier assembly. Lubricate the selector with a multipurpose grease before assembly. Install the selector shaft cover.

57. Install the interlock plunger assembly in the gear carrier assembly. Adjust the interlock plunger as follows:

   a. Turn the slotted screw (interlock plunger) in until the nut starts to move out (bottoms).

   b. Back the slotted screw out ¼ turn.

   c. Install the plastic cap.

58. Install the plastic caps over the bearing clamping screws.

TYPE 23

4 Speed Transaxle Model 091 and 094 Volkswagen

NOTE: Many special tools are required in the overhaul procedures of these transaxles. Use only recommended or equivalent tools to prevent personal injury or damage to the units.

DISASSEMBLY

1. Mount the transaxle securely and drain the lubricating oil form the unit.

2. Pry the caps from the center on the left and right drive flanges and remove the circlips from the stub axles. Using a puller, remove the drive flanges.

3. Mark the positions of the differential adjusting rings and measure the distance or depth to which the rings are screwed into the transaxle case. Record the readings for the assembly references.

4. Loosen the left differential adjusting ring to relieve the tension within the transaxle housing and remove the clutch housing assembly. Remove the rear driveshaft by unscrewing the shaft from the front drive or mainshaft. Remove the reverse gear.

5. Remove the left and right differential adjusting rings and lift the differential assembly from the case.

6. Remove the pinion gear assembly retaining ring form the differential side of the transaxle case.

NOTE: The retaining ring is peened, so that extra effort must be used to remove the ring.

7. Remove the gear shift housing from the gear carrier housing carefully to avoid damaging the housing mating surfaces.

8. Remove the gear carrier housing from the transaxle case and press the gear train from the transaxle case.

NOTE: Locate the shims from between the tapered roller bearing and the transaxle case for reuse during the reassembly.

9. The pinion and mainshaft must be pressed from the gear carrier housing.

——— **CAUTION** ———

Remove the circlips before attempting any press work.

Mainshaft (Driveshaft)

DISASSEMBLY

1. Remove the 4th speed gear and roller bearing.

2. Remove the circlip and press the 3rd/4th synchronizer hub from the shaft. Remove the lower circlip.

3. Remove the 3rd speed gear and the caged needle bearing from the shaft.

ASSEMBLY

1. Install the caged needle bearing on the shaft and install the 3rd speed gear. Install the circlip.

2. Install the sleeve and hub for the 3rd and 4th gears. Install the second circlip.

NOTE: The identify groove on the synchronizer ring should be towards the 4th speed gear.

3. Install the roller bearing and the 4th speed gear assembly.

Pinion Shaft

DISASSEMBLY

1. Remove the upper circlip by applying pressure against the 4th speed gear to compress the spacer spring. Remove the pressure cautiously to avoid personal injury.

2. Remove the second circlip, the 3rd speed gear and the 2nd speed gear with needle bearing.

3. Remove the third circlip and remove the 1st/2nd speed gear assembly.

4. Remove the anti-rotation ring from the synchronizer hub with a punch.

5. Unscrew the inner race from the pinion shaft with a special tool. Press the tapered bearing assembly from the pinion shaft.

ASSEMBLY

NOTE: Should the pinion shaft or the tapered bearing be replaced, the pinion depth should be checked before total assembly is completed. Special tools are needed for the measurements.

1. Heat the tapered bearing assembly to 212°F (100°C) and press into position on the pinion shaft.

2. Oil the bearing with hypoid oil and install the pinion and bearing assembly into the transaxle case. Install the retaining ring and torque to 159 ft. lbs.

3. Install an inch-pound torque wrench or equivalent on to the end of the pinion shaft and turn the shaft in both directions approximately 15 to 20 turns and read the turning torque. The torque should be between 2.7 to 18.2 in. lbs. for new bearings and 2.7 to 6.1 in. lbs. for used bearings or for bearings that have been run at least 30 miles (50 km).

4. Remove the tapered bearing assembly and pinion shaft from the case and continue the assembly.

5. Install the inner race and torque to 144 ft. lbs. Peen locking shoulder into gear spline.

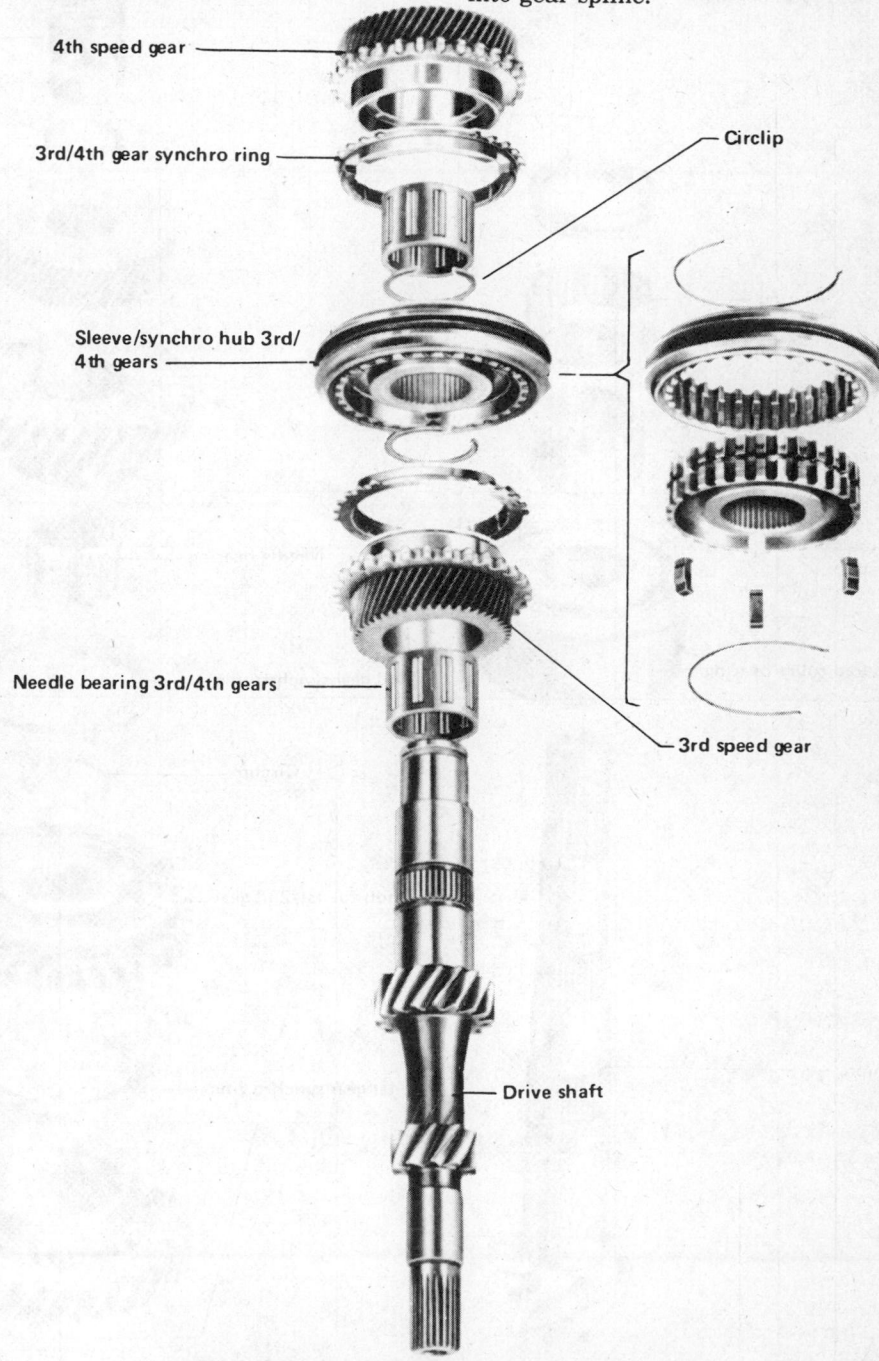

4th speed gear

3rd/4th gear synchro ring

Circlip

Sleeve/synchro hub 3rd/4th gears

Needle bearing 3rd/4th gears

3rd speed gear

Drive shaft

Exploded view of driveshaft (mainshaft) assembly

6. Install the inner race of the 1st gear needle bearing and a new anti-rotation ring.

7. Install the 1st speed gear, the sleeve and hub for the 1st/2nd gear. Install the retaining circlip.

8. Install the 2nd speed gear needle bearing, the 2nd speed gear and the 3rd speed gear on the shaft and retain with a circlip. Measure the play between the circlip and the 3rd speed gear. The clearance should be 0.002 to 0.008 in (0.5 to 0.20mm).

9. Install the spacer spring and the 4th speed gear on the shaft. Safely depress the gear and spring and install the end circlip.

Gear Carrier Housing
DISASSEMBLY AND ASSEMBLY

1. The mainshaft bearing and pinion shaft bearings are pressed both in and out.

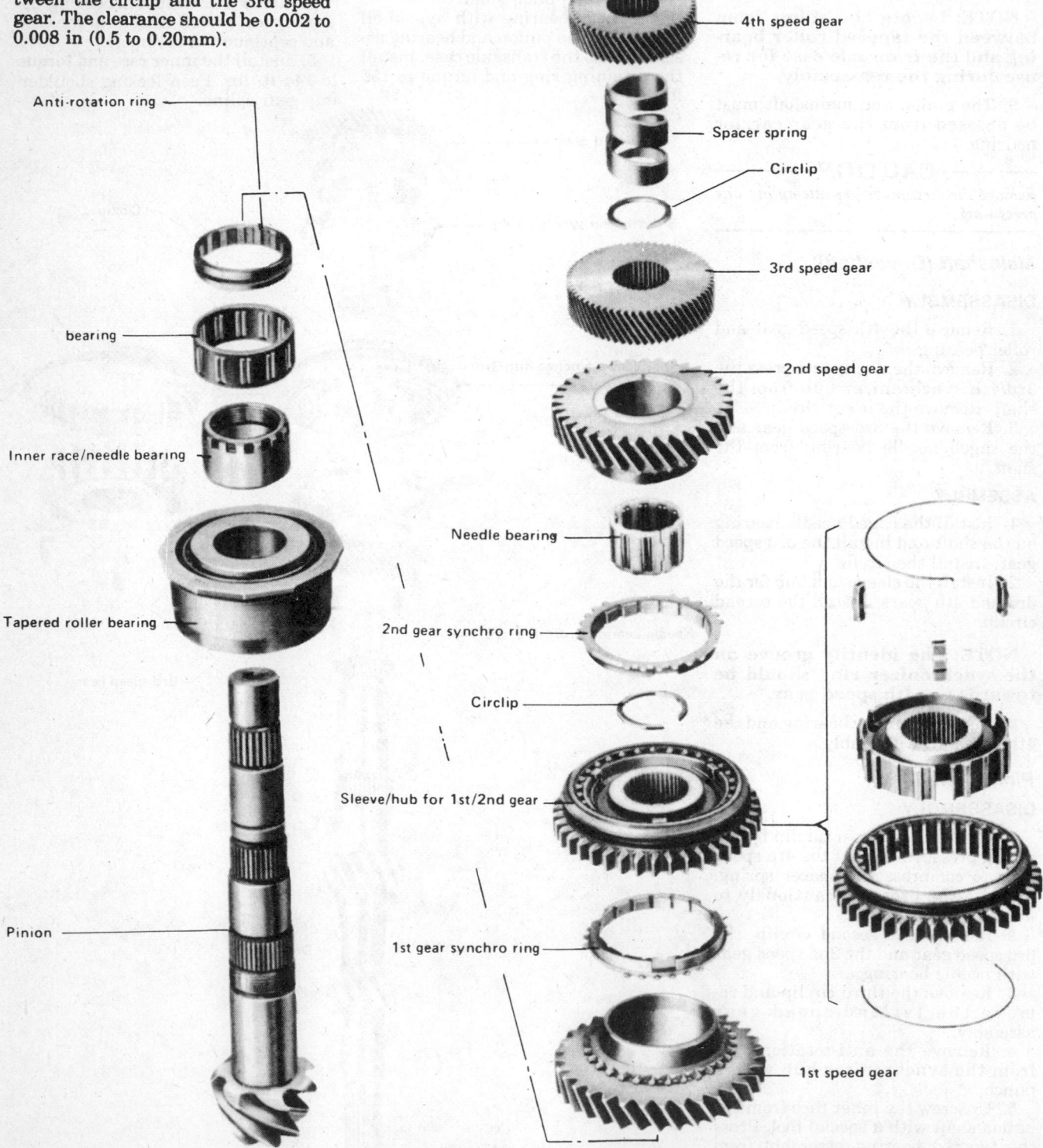

Exploded view of pinion shaft assembly

Labels:
- Anti-rotation ring
- bearing
- Inner race/needle bearing
- Tapered roller bearing
- Pinion
- Circlip
- 4th speed gear
- Spacer spring
- Circlip
- 3rd speed gear
- 2nd speed gear
- Needle bearing
- 2nd gear synchro ring
- Circlip
- Sleeve/hub for 1st/2nd gear
- 1st gear synchro ring
- 1st speed gear

2. The detent springs and interlock pins must be removed before the shift rods can be removed.

3. The bracket for the intermediate shift lever is removable by removing attaching bolts.

4. The relay rod, rocker lever, relay shaft bracket and small components are removable. Note the location and direction of the individual parts for ease of reassembly.

Synchronizer Rings

MARKINGS ON RINGS

1. 1st gear ring has no notch on the outer surface, is made of brass and the friction surface is treated with molybdenum.

2. The 2nd, 3rd and 4th gear rings have three notches on the outer surface or three depressions on the end face of the rings.

3. The 2nd gear ring is made of brass and has the friction surface coated with molybdenum.

4. The 3rd gear ring is steel and the friction surface is treated with molybdenum.

5. The 4th gear ring is made of brass and has no special coating.

6. The clearance between the ring and gear cone while under pressure is:

1st gear — 0.040–0.064 inch (1.0–1.6mm).

3rd and 4th gear — 0.040–0.066 inch (1.0–1.7mm).

7. The sleeves and the hubs are not matched and may be replaced separately. They must slide smoothly and have minimum backlash.

Reverse Drive Gear and Shaft

The reverse gear and shaft assemblies are removed and installed as a unit. The disassembly can be accomplished with the gear and shaft assemblies out of the case.

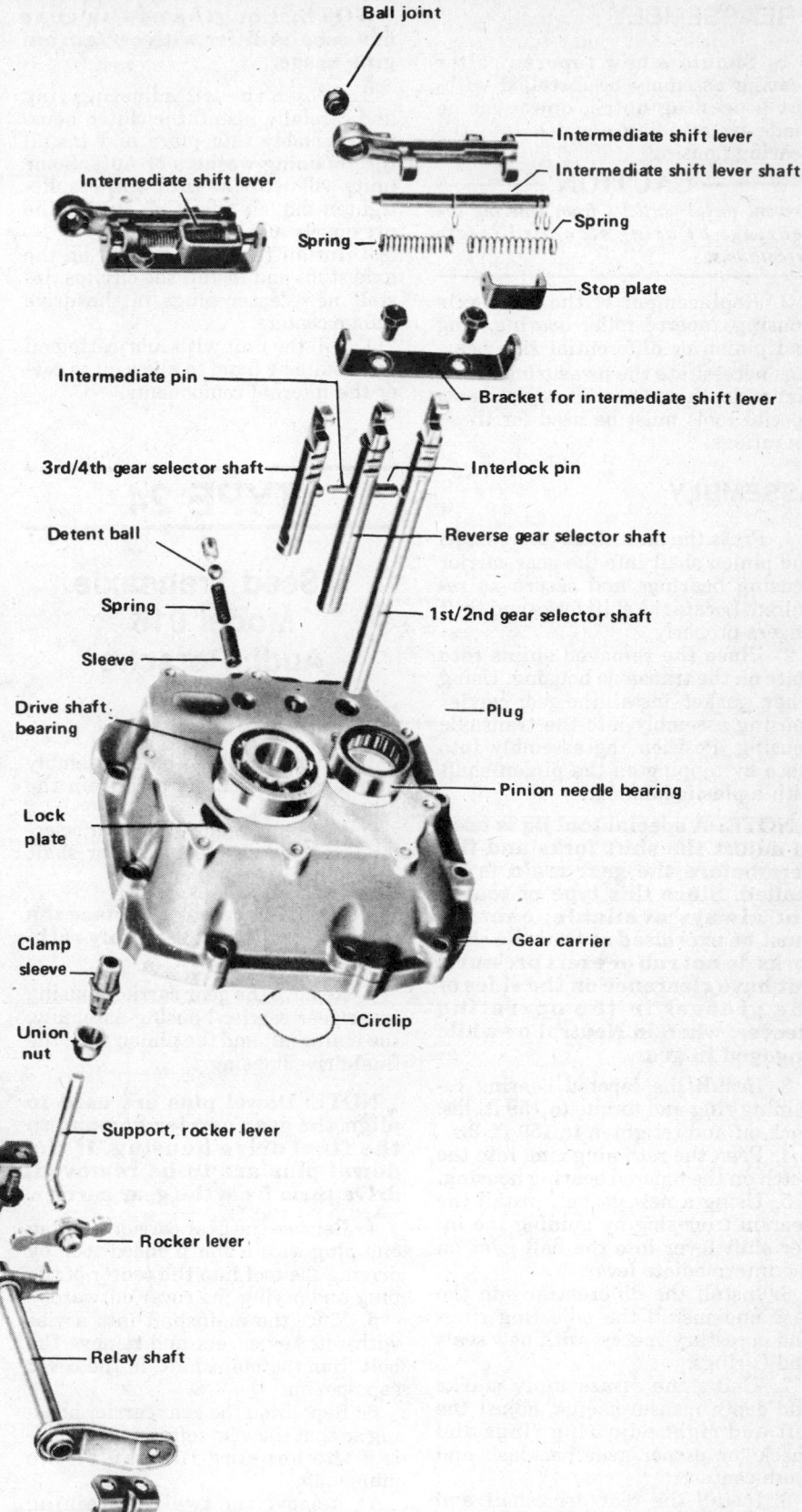

Exploded view of gear carrier housing and shift mechanism

PREASSEMBLY

1. Should a new tapered roller bearing assembly be installed without a peening notch, one must be made by grinding a notch into the bearing housing.

—— CAUTION ——

Prevent metal particles from entering the bearings by using standard safety precautions.

2. Replacement of the transaxle housing, tapered roller bearing, ring and pinion or differential side bearings necessitate the measuring of the pinion depth and carrier adjustment. Special tools must be used for these operations.

ASSEMBLY

1. Press the mainshaft (driveshaft) and pinion shaft into the gear carrier housing bearings and secure as required. Locate the shift forks and shift fingers properly.
2. Place the removed shims into place on the transaxle housing. Using a new gasket, install the gear carrier housing assembly into the transaxle housing. Position the assembly into place by tapping on the pinion shaft with a plastic hammer.

NOTE: A special tool jig is used to adjust the shift forks and fingers before the gear train is installed. Since this type of tool is not always available, caution must be exercised so that the shift forks do not rub or exert pressure, but have clearance on the sides of the grooves in the operating sleeves, when in Neutral or while engaged in gear.

3. Install the tapered bearing retaining ring and torque to 159 ft. lbs. back off and retighten to 159 ft. lbs.
4. Peen the retaining ring into the notch on the tapered bearing housing.
5. Using a new gasket, install the gearshift housing by guiding the inner shift lever into the ball joint on the intermediate lever.
6. Install the differential into the case and install the adjusting rings and necessary spacers with new seals and O-rings.
7. Using the disassembly marks and depth measurements, adjust the left and right adjusting rings and check for proper gear backlash and tooth contact.
8. Install the rear driveshaft and the reverse gear. Tighten the rear driveshaft stud into the forward driveshaft (mainshaft) snugly and back off one spline. Install the reverse drive gear.

NOTE: Lengths of the rear driveshafts differ with certain engine usage.

9. Loosen the left adjusting ring and carefully install the clutch housing assembly into place and install the retaining washers or nuts. Some units will use bolts with washers. Retighten the left adjusting ring to the previously marked position.
10. Install the drive flanges on the axle stubs and install the circlips. Install new center plugs in the drive flange centers.
11. Fill the unit with lubricating oil and rotate by hand to allow oil to cover the internal components.

TYPE 24

5 Seed Transaxle
Model 016
Audi, Porsche

DISASSEMBLY

1. Mount the transaxle assembly into a holder securely and drain the lubricating oil.
2. Mark and remove the gear selector lever and the gear selector shaft assembly.

NOTE: If necessary, replace the gear selector shaft assembly rather than repairing it.

3. Remove the gear carrier housing cover/gear carrier housing assembly, the mainshaft and the pinion from the final drive housing.

NOTE: Dowel pins are used to align the gear carrier housing to the final drive housing. If the dowel pins are to be removed, drive them from the gear carrier.

4. Remove the gear carrier housing end plug with a sharp ended tool, by driving the tool into the center of the plug and prying the cover outward.
5. Place the mainshaft into a vise with soft jaw covers and remove the bolt from the mainshaft, in the cover cap opening.
6. Reposition the gear carrier housing so that the vise soft jaws are holding the housing instead of the mainshaft.
7. Remove the twelve retaining bolts from the gear carrier housing cover and separate the cover from the gear housing.
8. Remove the mainshaft bearing inner race form gear carrier housing.

9. Remove the 5th gear clutch hub and mainshaft bearing inner race from the cover end of the mainshaft.
10. Remove the 5th gear synchronizer ring.
11. Drive the 5th gear shift fork roll pin from the fork with a pin punch.

—— CAUTION ——

Support the selector rod and fork to avoid damage to the gear carrier housing.

12. Remove the circlip, the 5th speed gear with the synchronizer hub, needle bearing and the 5th speed gear shift fork.

NOTE: The 5th/reverse gear selector rod will remain in the gear carrier housing.

13. Remove the selector rod stop screws from the outside of the gear carrier housing.
14. Reposition the gear carrier housing assembly in the jaws of the vise, with the soft jaw covers, and clamp the 4th speed gear in the vise.
15. Remove the bolt from the pinion shaft and remove the 5th gear and the adjustment shim.
16. Reposition the gear carrier housing in the soft jawed vise and drive the 1st/2nd gear selector fork roll pin from the fork.

—— CAUTION ——

Support the selector rod and fork to avoid damage to the gear carrier housing.

17. Remove the 3rd/4th gear selector fork roll pin.

—— CAUTION ——

Support the selector rod and fork to avoid damage to the gear carrier housing.

18. Remove the 3rd/4th selector rod from the gear carrier housing. The shifting fork should remain in the synchronizer hub.

NOTE: Do not lose the indent or interlock pin.

19. Remove the relay lever bolt from the reverse gear relay lever.
20. Pull the pinion and mainshaft partially form the gear carrier housing and remove the mainshaft with the 3rd/4th gear shift fork on the synchronizer hub.
21. Pull the pinion from the housing, far enough so that the selector rod and shift fork of the 1st/2nd gears can be removed, after the reverse gear spring clip on the pinion side is unhooked and turned.
22. Remove the pinion from the housing.
23. Inspect the transaxle components, replace all seals and gaskets, gears that are damaged or worn, and bearings, both needle and ball.

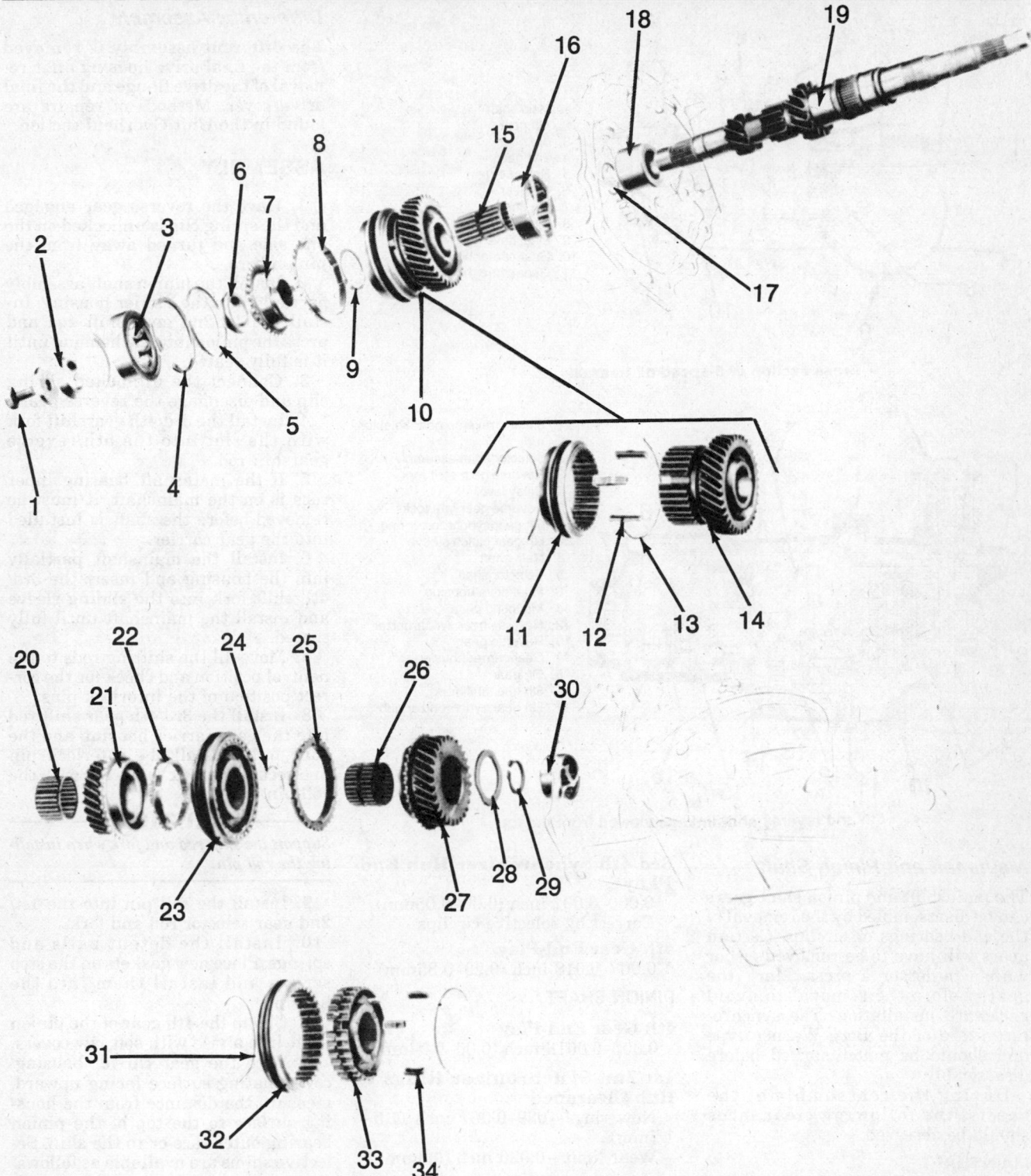

1. Bolt
2. Main shaft bearing outer race
3. Main shaft bearing
4. Circlip
5. Baffle plate
6. Main shaft bearing inner race
7. 5th gear clutch hub
8. 5th gear synchronizer ring
9. Circlip
10. 5th gear with synchronizer hub and sleeve
11. Sleeve
12. Hollow key
13. Spring
14. 5th gear with synchronizer hub
15. 5th gear needle bearing
16. Main shaft bearing
17. Circlip
18. Mainshaft bearing inner race
19. Mainshaft
20. 3rd gear needle bearing
21. 3rd gear
22. 3rd gear synchronizer ring
23. 3rd & 4th gear synchronizer hub
24. Circlip
25. 4th gear synchronizer ring
26. 4th gear needle bearing
27. 4th gear
28. 4th gear thrust washer
29. Circlip
30. Main shaft needle bearing
31. Spring
32. Sleeve
33. Hub
34. Hollow key

Exploded view of mainshaft assembly

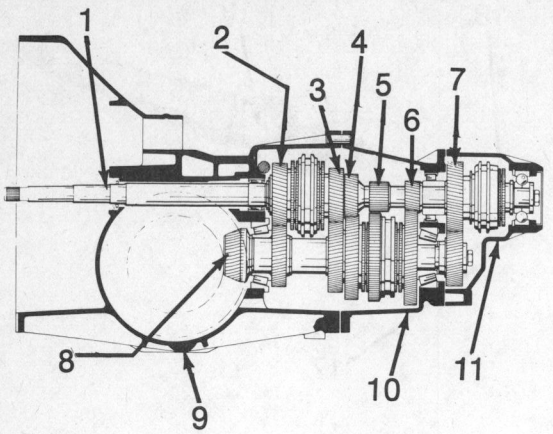

1. Main shaft
2. 4th gear
3. 3rd gear
4. 2nd gear
5. Reverse gear
6. 1st gear
7. 5th gear
8. Pinion
9. Final drive housing
10. Gear carrier housing
11. Gear carrier housing cover

Cross section of 5-speed oil transaxle

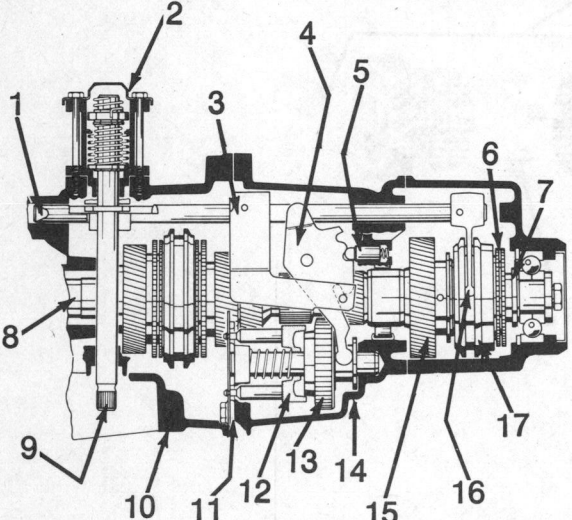

1. 5th and reverse gear selector rod
2. Selector shaft assembly
3. Reverse gear shift fork
4. Relay lever
5. Reverse gear interlock
6. 5th gear synchronizer ring
7. 5th gear clutch sleeve
8. Main shaft
9. Selector shaft
10. Final drive housing
11. Mounting plate
12. Reverse gear synchronizer
13. Reverse gear
14. Gear carrier housing
15. 5th gear
16. 5th gear shift fork
17. 5th gear synchronizer hub

5th and reverse shift linkage viewed from the top

Mainshaft and Pinion Shaft

The mainshaft and pinion shaft gears can be disassembled by the removal of the end bearings or circlips. Certain gears will have to be removed either with a puller or a press. Mark the gears before the removal to avoid backward installation. The synchronizers are of the Borg Warner type and should be matchmarked before disassembly.

During the reassembly of the shafts, the following clearances should be observed.

MAINSHAFT

3rd/4th Synchronizer Rings-to-Hub Clearance

New rings—0.039–0.067 inch (1.0–1.7mm).
Wear limit—0.20 inch (0.5mm)

5th Gear Synchronizer Ring to Hub Clearance

New ring—0.039–0.075 inch (1.0–1.9mm).
Wear limit—0.020 inch (0.5mm)

3rd/4th Synchronizer Hub End-PLay

0.000–0.002 inch (0.00–0.05mm)
Correct by selective circlips

4th Gear End-Play

0.008–0.018 inch (0.20–0.35mm)

PINION SHAFT

4th Gear End-Play

0.000–0.0016 inch (0.00–0.04mm)

1st/2nd Synchronizer Rings to Hub Clearance

New rings—039–0.067 inch (1.0–1.7mm).
Wear limit—0.020 inch (0.5mm).

1st/2nd Synchronizer Hub End-Play

0.00–0.0016 inch (0.00–0.04mm)
Correct by selective circlip.

Reverse Gear Synchronizer Clearance

New ring—0.029–0.090 inch (0.75–2.3mm)
Wear limit—0.007 inch (0.2mm).

Differential Assembly

The different assembly is removed from the final drive housing after removal of the drive flange and the final drive cover. Methods of repairs are found in the Unit Overhaul section.

ASSEMBLY

1. Have the reverse gear engaged and the spring clip is unhooked on the one side and turned away from the pinion bore.

2. Install the pinion shaft assembly partially into the carrier housing. Install the 1st/2nd gear shift rod and press the pinion into the housing until it is fully seated.

3. Connect the unhooked spring clip and disengage the reverse gear.

4. Install the 3rd/4th gearshift fork with the slot into the 5th/reverse gearshift rod.

5. If the mainshaft bearing inner race is on the mainshaft, it must be removed before the shaft is installed into the gear carrier.

6. Install the mainshaft partially into the housing and insert the 3rd/4th shift fork into the sliding sleeve and install the mainshaft until fully seated.

7. Move all the shifting rods to the neutral position and check for the correct position of the interlock pins.

8. Install the 3rd/4th gear shift rod into the gear carrier housing and the shift fork. Install the interlock pin and secure the fork to the rod with the roll pin.

— **CAUTION** —

Support the shift rod and fork when installing the roll pin.

9. Install the roll pin into the 1st/2nd gear selector rod and fork.

10. Install the detent balls and springs. Place new gaskets on the stop screws and install them into the housing.

11. Clamp the 4th gear of the pinion shaft into a vise with soft jaw covers.

12. With the gear carrier housing/cover mating surface facing upward, measure the distance from the housing surface to the top of the pinion bearing outer race or to the shin. Selective shims are available as follows.

Depth (mm)	Shim Thickness (mm)
8.35–8.64	1.1
8.65–8.94	1.4
8.95–9.24	1.7
9.25–9.54	2.0
9.55–9.84	2.3

NOTE: Measurements are in mm. Convert to inches required.

13. Heat the 5th gear to 250°F (120°C) and drive on the pinion shaft until seated on the selected shim.

NOTE: Be sure the collar of the gear faces the pinion head.

14. Install the washer and bolt and torque to 36 ft. lbs. (50 Nm).

15. Heat the main bearing inner race to 250°F (120°C) and drive on the mainshaft. Select a circlip of proper thickness to fit tightly in the groove on the mainshaft.

16. Install the 5th gear with synchronizer hub, needle bearing and shift rod. Support the shift rod and install the roll pin.

17. Install the retaining circlip and install the 5th gear synchronizer ring.

18. Heat the 5th gear clutch hub to 250°F (120°C) and drive on the mainshaft. Drive on the mainshaft inner bearing race with a driving sleeve type tool.

19. Install the dowel pins and a new gasket to the mating surface.

20. Carefully install the gear carrier

housing cover, and drive the second mainshaft inner bearing race onto the shaft.

21. Install the washer and bolt onto the mainshaft and tighten to 36 ft. lbs. (50 Nm).

22. Install the cover retaining bolts and tighten to 18 ft. lbs. (25 Nm).

23. Install a new cover cap into the end of the gear carrier housing cover.

24. Assemble the gear carrier housing/cover assembly to the final drive housing and install the retaining bolts. Tighten to 18 ft. lbs. (25 Nm).

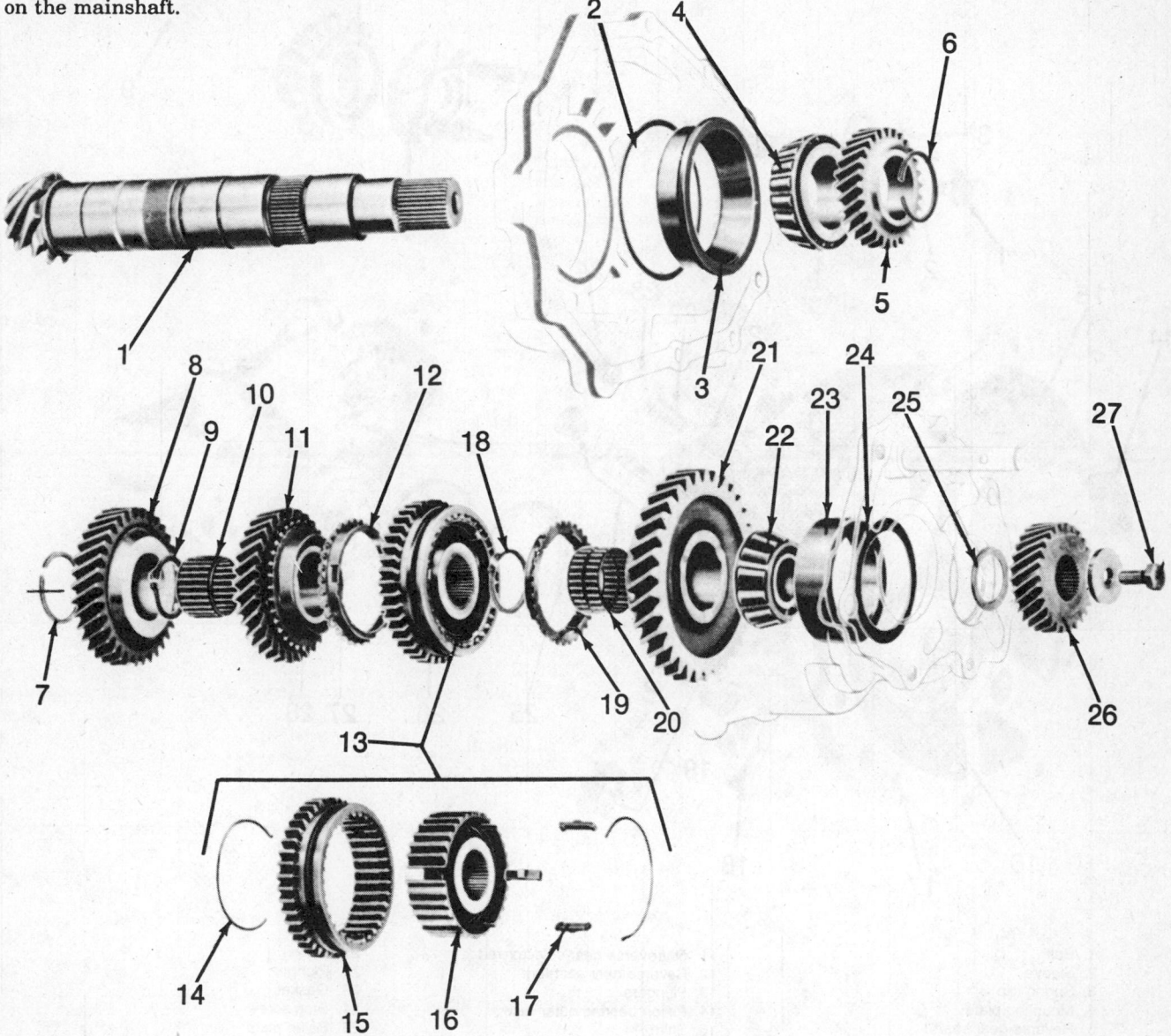

Exploded view of pinion shaft assembly

1. Pinion
2. Shim
3. Pinion bearing outer race
4. Pinion bearing
5. 4th gear
6. Circlip
7. Circlip
8. 3rd gear
9. Circlip
10. 2nd gear needle bearing
11. 2nd gear
12. 2nd gear synchronizer ring
13. Synchronizer sleeve/hub for 1st and 2nd gears
14. Spring
15. Synchronizer sleeve
16. Synchronizer hub
17. Hollow keys
18. Circlip
19. 1st gear synchronizer ring
20. 1st gear needle bearing
21. 1st gear
22. Pinion bearing
23. Pinion bearing outer race
24. Shim
25. Shim for 5th gear
26. 5th gear
27. Bolt

25. Install the selector shaft housing into the final drive housing and retain with the retaining bolts. Tighten to 7 ft. lbs. (10 Nm).

26. Install the selector shaft lever flush with the toothed end of the selector shaft. Tighten the clamping bolt.

27. Fill the unit to its proper level with lubricating oil and check for proper shifting on the internal gears.

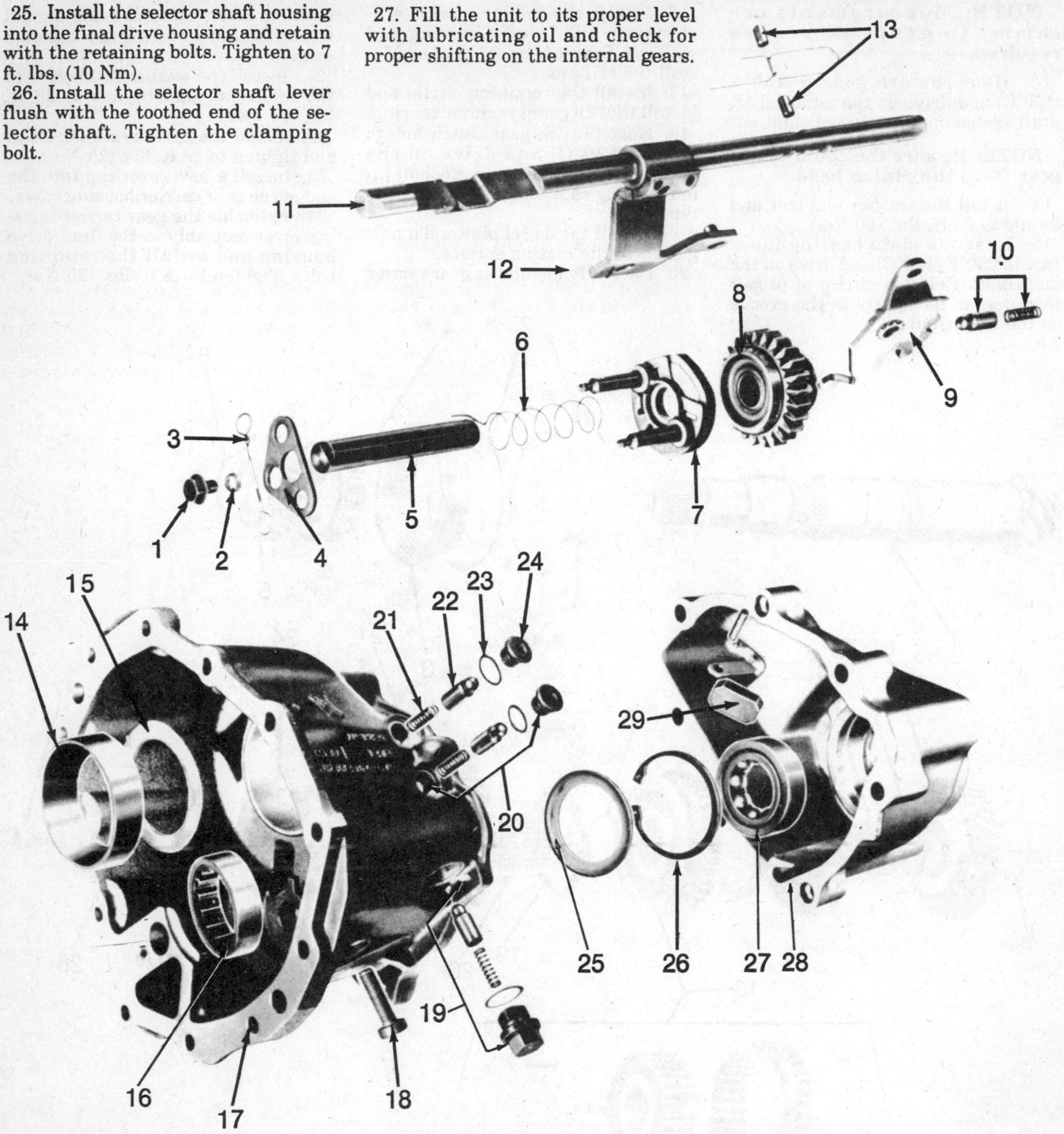

1. Bolt
2. Sleeve
3. Spring clip
4. Mounting plate
5. Reverse gear shaft
6. Spring
7. Reverse gear synchronizer
8. Reverse gear
9. Reverse gear relay lever
10. Reverse gear interlock plunger

11. 5th/reverse gear selector rod
12. Reverse gear shift fork
13. Plungers
14. Pinion bearing outer race
15. Shim
16. Main shaft bearing
17. Gear carrier housing
18. Relay lever bolt
19. 5th gear interlock mechanism
20. 1st to 4th gear interlock mechanism

21. Spring
22. Plunger
23. Gasket
24. Stop screw
25. Baffle plate
26. Circlip
27. Mainshaft bearing
28. Gear carrier housing cover
29. Magnet

Exploded view of gear carrier housing and cover components

TYPE 25

4 and 5 Speed Transaxle Mazda

DISASSEMBLY AND ASSEMBLY

NOTE: The procedures described are for both the four speed and the five speed transaxle. The five speed unit has a rear cover which easily distinguishes it from the other unit.

Disassembly (Fifth Gear)

1. Remove the rear cover. Remove the roll pin that secures the fifth gear shift fork to the selector shaft. Shift the transaxle unit into either first or second gear.

NOTE: Do not shift into fourth gear as by doing this you may cause damage to the gears.

2. Move the fifth gear clutch sleeve, to engage fifth gear and double lock the transmission.

3. Straighten the tab of the locknut on both the primary and secondary shafts. Remove the locknuts from the shafts.

4. Pull the fifth gear clutch hub assembly out along with the fifth fork.

NOTE: Remove the fork to gain access to the primary shaft locknut.

5. Reinstall the fifth gear clutch hub and move the sleeve to the fifth gear position in order t lock the transmission.

6. Remove the primary shaft locknut and remove the fifth gear from the transmission case.

Assembly (Fifth Gear)

1. Install the fifth gear on the primary shaft. Be sure that the marked boss is facing toward the locknut. Install the bush and the fifth gear on the secondary shaft.

2. Install the synchronizer ring and clutch hub and the selector fork. Do not install the shift fork pin.

NOTE: The stop washer or plate for the clutch hub must be installed between the locknut and clutch hub to prevent overtravel of the clutch when shifting into reverse gear to prevent the synchronizer keys from falling out.

3. Install the locknuts on both shafts and tighten them slightly.

4. Shift into first or second gear only, using the control rod. Shift into fifth gear to double lock the transmission.

5. Tighten the primary shaft locknut and lock the hub.

NOTE: Do not tighten the secondary shaft locknut until the selector fork is installed. Remove the locknut and clutch hub from the secondary gear shaft and reassemble it with the selector fork. Do not insert the drive pin at this time.

6. Move the fifth gear selector clutch to engage the fifth gear in order to lock the transmission.

7. Shift the unit into either first or second gear.

8. Install the roll pin securing the fifth gear shift fork to the selector shaft. Install the cover.

Primary Shaft

The Mazda manual transaxle uses two types of primary shafts, one for the four speed transaxle and one for the five speed transaxle. Both shafts are made as a cluster with reverse, first, second, third and fourth gears integral. The fifth gear (when equipped) is splined into the end of the shaft, thus distinguishing between the four and five speed unit.

Secondary Shaft

The secondary shaft assembly consists of the secondary shaft, gears, clutch hub and sleeve assemblies, synchro rings and bearings. The secondary shaft is manufactured integrally with the final drive gear.

There are three different types of secondary shafts used in the four speed transaxle and two different types used in the five speed transaxle. All of these shafts vary by the number of gear teeth on the final drive gears.

NOTE: The combination of the final drive gear on the secondary shaft and ring gear are identified by the groove provided in the construction of each individual gear.

DISASSEMBLY AND ASSEMBLY (SECONDARY GEARS)

1. Install a suitable bearing puller in the grooves between the gear and the gear spline of fourth gear. Remove the bearing and the fourth gear from the assembly.

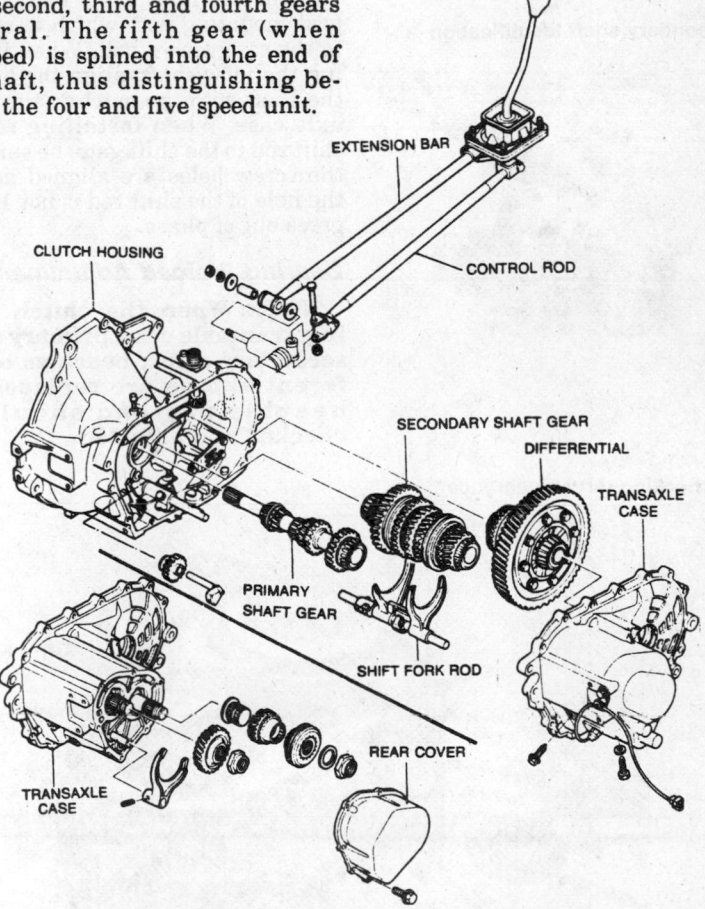

Mazda GLC manual transaxle—exploded view

2. Remove the snap-ring on the third and fourth clutch hub. Slide out the clutch hub and the sleeve assembly.

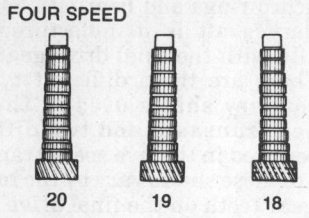

FOUR SPEED

20   19   18

FIVE SPEED

20   19

DIFFERENTIAL RING GEAR

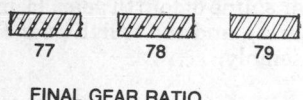

77   78   79

FINAL GEAR RATIO

3.850   4.105   4.388

Secondary shaft identification

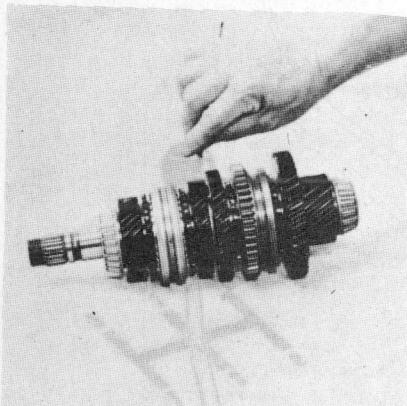

Checking thrust clearance

3. Remove the third gear, the thrust washer and the second gear.

4. Remove the snap-ring, and slide out the clutch hub and reverse gear assembly and first gear.

5. Install the bearing remover tool under the rollers and press out the shaft.

6. Assembly is the reverse of disassembly.

Synchronizer Rings

Bridge type synchronizer rings are used in the Mazda transaxle. There are three different synchronizer rings; one for second, third and fourth speed, another for first and third speed and one for fifth speed if the vehicle is so equipped. The first speed synchro ring can be identified from the other two because it has less teeth.

Thrust Clearance

The thrust clearance of each gear is checked by using a feeler gauge. The specification for thrust clearance is .020 in (.5mm).

Reverse Idler Shaft and Shift Rod

The reverse idler shaft has an integral mounting post which is secured to the case with a bolt. When installing the idler shaft, align the holes of the shaft with the notch in the transaxle case. When installing reverse shift rod to the shift gate, be sure that the screw holes are aligned ad that the hole of the shift rod is not 180 degrees out of phase.

Bearing Preload Adjustment

NOTE: When the clutch housing, transaxle case, primary shaft, secondary shaft, bearings or differential case are replaced the bearing preload should be checked and adjusted.

1. Remove the oil seal and the differential bearing outer race. Adjust the shim from the transaxle case.

2. Remove the bearing outer races from the primary and secondary shafts. Adjust the shims from the transaxle case and the clutch housing.

3. Reinstall the outer races to the transaxle case.

4. Install the outer races to (removed in Step 2) to their respective selectors. Install the selectors, primary shaft assembly and the secondary shaft assembly to the clutch housing.

5. Install the transaxle case and place the ten collars between the transaxle case and the clutch housing.

NOTE: The collars should be positioned as shown in the illustration.

6. To properly settle each bearing, using the tool turn the selector in a direction where the gap is widened until it cannot be turned by hand. Then turn the selector in the opposite direction until the gap is eliminated. Manually turn the selector to a direction where the gap becomes wider until the selector cannot be turned.

NOTE: Make sure that the shaft turns smoothly.

7. Measure the gap of the selector with a feeler gauge.

NOTE: This measurement should be taken at several places along the circumference of the selector.

8. Take the maximum reading and determine the shim to be used as follows.

9. For the primary shaft bearing, first subtract 1.00mm (thickness of the diaphram spring) from the gap (determined in Step 7).

(Example) Measurement 1.39mm minus 1.00mm equals .39mm, select the next larger and close shim which would be .40mm.

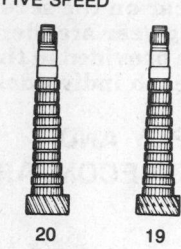

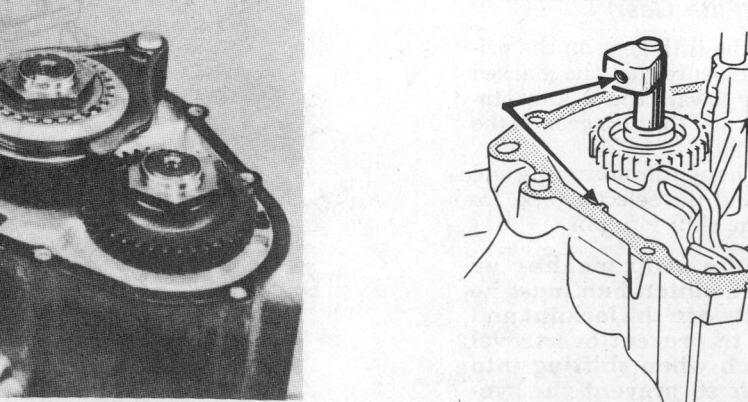

Checking thrust clearance—fifth gear   **Reverse idler shaft alignment**

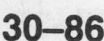

NOTE: Do not use more than two shims.

10. For the secondary shaft bearing, select a shim which has a thickness that is larger and closer to the gap (determined in Step 7).

(Example) Measurement .42mm, select the next larger and closer shim which would be .45mm.

NOTE: Do not use more than two shims to accomplish this task.

11. For the differential bearing, set the preload adapters (tool #49-00180-510A and #49-FT01-515 or equivalent) to the pinion shaft through the hole for the driveshaft of the transaxle case. Hook a spring scale to the adapter and check the bearing preload.

NOTE: While checking the preload, turn the selector until the reading of the spring scale becomes 1.1-1.5 lb.

12. Then measure the gap of the selector on the differential using a feeler gauge.

NOTE: This measurement should be taken in several places along the circumference of the selector.

13. Select a shim that has a thickness larger and closer to the maximum reading that was taken in the previous step.

(Example) Measurement .54mm, select the next larger and closer shim which would be .60mm.

NOTE: Do not use more than three shims to accomplish this task.

14. Remove the shim selectors and each bearing outer race. Instal the shims selected in previous steps between the transaxle case and bearing outer race.

15. A diaphram spring is used to keep the bearing preload as specified and also to maintain low level gear noise. So when installing the diaphram spring, be sure it is in the proper direction.

16. When installing the oil funnel on the clutch housing, be sure that it is in the proper position.

17. After assembly the treansaxle, recheck the preloads of the differential bearing and the primary shaft bearing.

18. The differential bearing preload should be .3-6.6 in. lbs., and the reading on the spring scale should be .07-1.7 lb.

19. The primary shaft preload should be 1.7-3.5 in. lbs., and the reading on the spring scale should be .4-.9 lb.

Differential

The final gear is helical cut with the same tooth design as that used in the transmission. No adjustments are required.

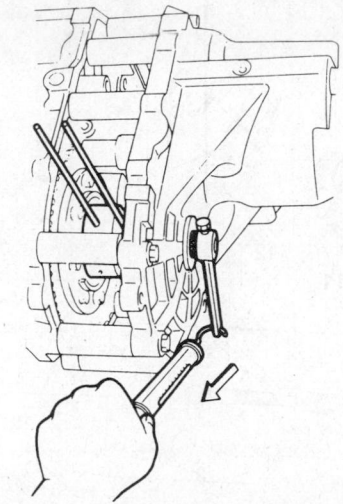

Checking differential bearing preload

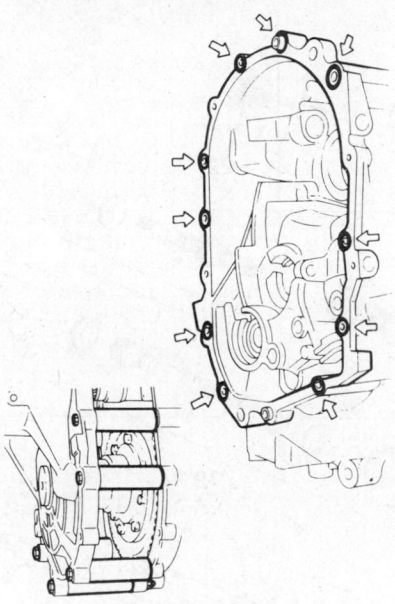

Collar positioning

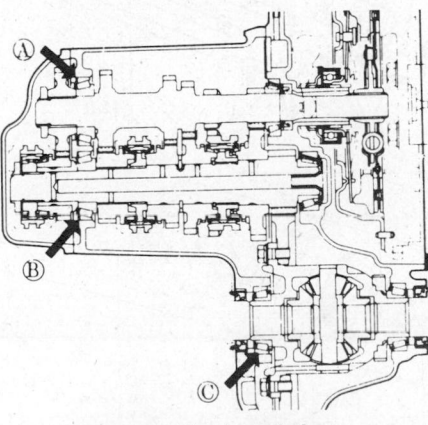

Selected shim installation

There are three different ring gears in numbers of gear teeth on the manual transaxle. They are indicated by the marks (grooves) provided on the gear outer surface.

The backlash between the differential side gear and pinion gear is adjusted by the thrust washer installed behind the side gear teeth. There are three different thicknesses of thrust washers available.

When checking the backlash, insert both driveshafts into the side gears.

TYPE 26

5 Speed Transaxle
Isuzu

DISASSEMBLY

1. Mount the transaxle assembly securely on a transmission stand and drain the lubricating oil.
2. Remove the rear cover and the quadrant box assembly.
3. Disconnect the wire connectors from the two switches, then remove the two switches and the pins beneath them.
4. Remove the retaining nut, sleeve and hub.
5. Shift the transaxle into 5th gear and remove the retaining nut.
6. Using a gear puller, special tool No. J-35274 or equivalent, remove the 5th input gear.
7. Remove the bearing retainer from the transaxle using a Torx bit No. 45, Special tool No. J-29843-8.
8. Remove the needle bearing collar and thrust washer using a gear puller, special tool No. J-22888-30 "Puller Leg", and J-22888 "Puller Body".
9. Remove the idler shaft bolt and gasket.
10. Disassemble the transaxle case.
11. Remove the reverse; detent plug and, spring and ball.
12. Remove the 5th/reverse shift rod and fork assembly using the following procedure: Lift the 5th gear shaft. With the detent aligned facing the same way, remove the 5th and reverse shafts at the same time.
13. Remove the 1st/2nd, 3rd/4th shift fork, slide the 1-2 shaft upward to clear the housing and remove the fork and shaft from the case.
14. Remove the interlock pin.
15. Remove the idler gear, shaft and pin.
16. Remove the input shaft assembly, then the output shaft assembly.

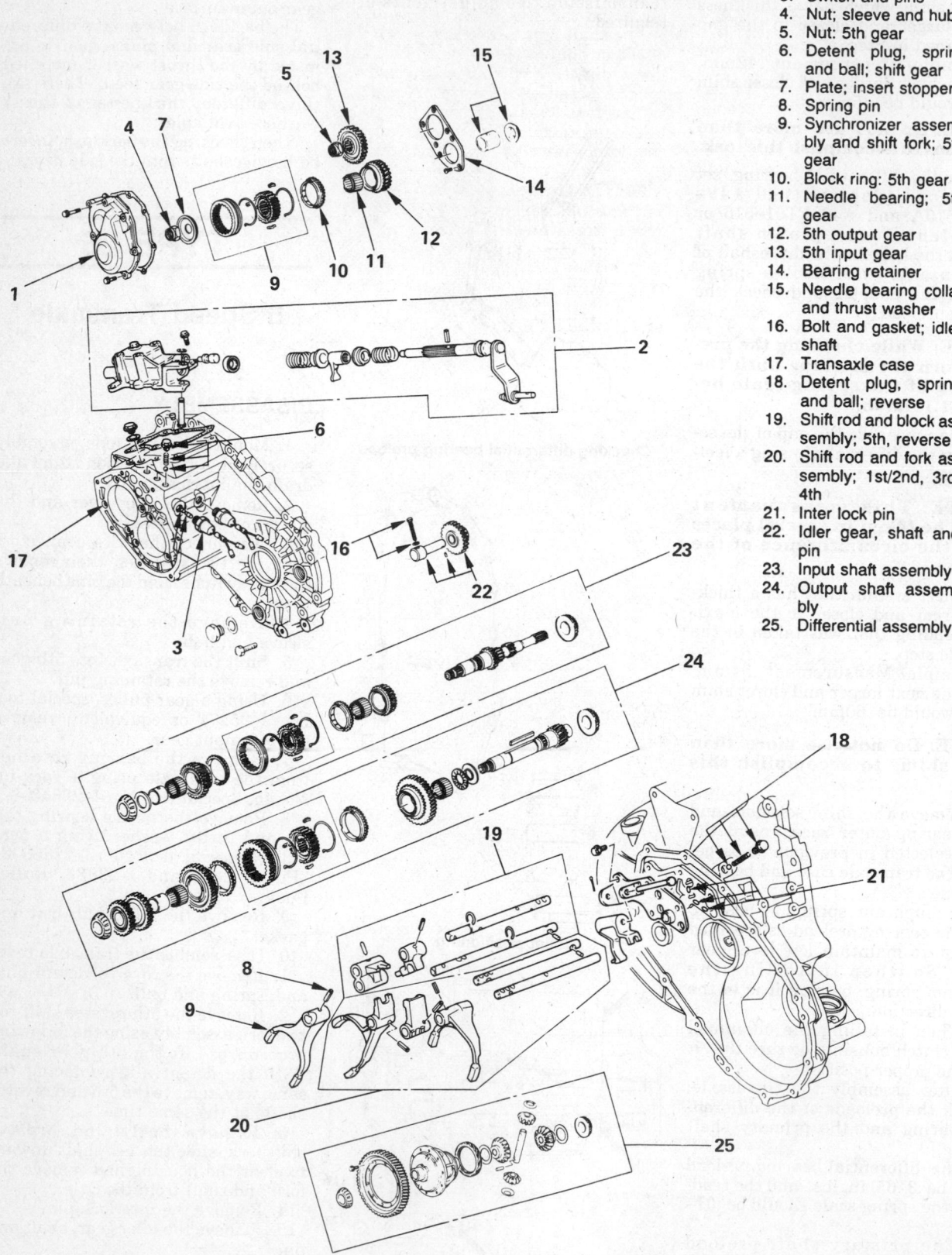

1. Rear cover
2. Quadrant box assembly
3. Switch and pins
4. Nut; sleeve and hub
5. Nut: 5th gear
6. Detent plug, spring and ball; shift gear
7. Plate; insert stopper
8. Spring pin
9. Synchronizer assembly and shift fork; 5th gear
10. Block ring: 5th gear
11. Needle bearing; 5th gear
12. 5th output gear
13. 5th input gear
14. Bearing retainer
15. Needle bearing collar and thrust washer
16. Bolt and gasket; idler shaft
17. Transaxle case
18. Detent plug, spring and ball; reverse
19. Shift rod and block assembly; 5th, reverse
20. Shift rod and fork assembly; 1st/2nd, 3rd/4th
21. Inter lock pin
22. Idler gear, shaft and pin
23. Input shaft assembly
24. Output shaft assembly
25. Differential assembly

I-Mark 5 speed manual transaxle—exploded view

17. Remove the differential assembly.

Input Shaft

DISASSEMBLY

1. Remove the input shaft front bearing by placing the input shaft in a press and pressing off the front bearing using the bearing removal special tool No. J–22912–01 or equivalent.

2. Remove all the input shaft components in the order shown in the illustration with a press and the special tool mentioned in Step 1.

ASSEMBLY

NOTE: Coat all components with clean engine oil during assembly.

1. Take the input shaft and install the 3rd and 4th needle bearing, 3rd gear, and the 3rd and 4th block ring.

2. Press the 3rd/4th collar, 4th gear, and the synchronizer assembly on the shaft using special tool No. J–33374 or equivalent. Note the installation direction when assembling the syncros assembly. The insert spring set positons should differ for right or left. The ends of the insert spring should not interfere with the hub.

NOTE: Do not twist the inserts in the block ring opening portions when pressing in.

3. Install the 3rd and 4th blocking ring, needle bearing, and 4th gear.

4. Install the 4th gear thrust washer with the inset towards 4th gear.

5. Using a press and special tool No. J–33374 or equivalent, install the input shaft front and rear bearings.

Output Shaft

DISASSEMBLY

1. Remove the input shaft front bearing by placing the input shaft in a press and pressing off the front bearing using a suitable short bar and special tool No. J–22227 or equivalent.

2. Remove the output shaft rear bearing and 3rd/4th gear together using special tool No. J–2291–01 and a press.

3. Remove the Output shaft key, 1st and 2nd needle bearing, 2nd gear, and the 1st and 2nd blocking ring.

4. Remove 1st gear, 1st gear blocking ring, 1st/2nd synchronizer assembly, 1st/2nd collar and 2nd gear using a hydraulic press.

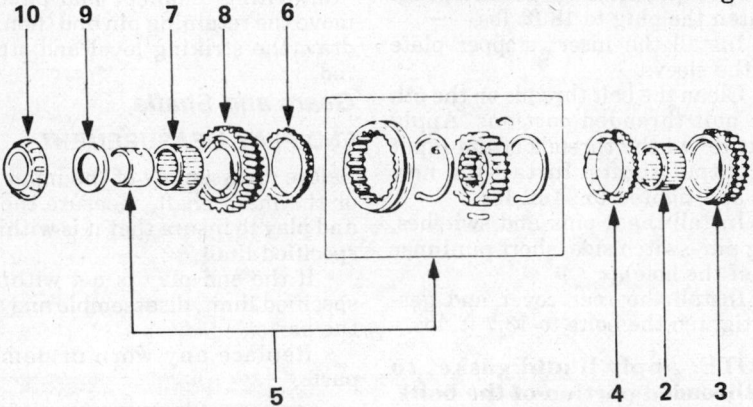
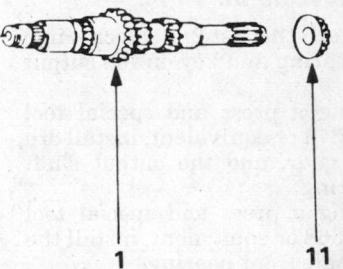

Reassembly steps

1. Input shaft
2. Needle bearing; 3rd and 4th
3. 3rd gear
4. Block ring; 3rd and 4th
5. Synchronizer assembly; 3rd/4th, collar; 4th gear
6. Blocking; 3rd and 4th
7. Needle bearing: 3rd and 4th
8. 4th gear
9. Thrust washer; 4th gear
10. Input shaft rear bearing
11. Input shaft front bearing

Input shaft assembly

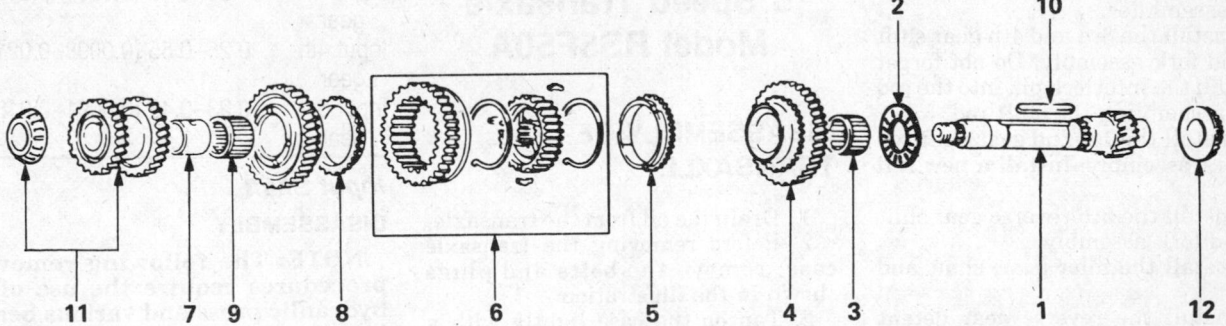

Reassembly steps

1. Output shaft
2. Thrust bearing
3. Needle bearing; 1st and 2nd
4. 1st gear
5. Block ring; 1st and 2nd
6. Synchronizer assembly; 1st/2nd
7. Collar; 2nd
8. Block ring: 1st and 2nd
9. Needle bearing
10. Key
11. 3rd and 4th gear, output shaft rear bearing
12. Output shaft front bearing

Output shaft assembly

5. Remove the 1st and 2nd needle bearing, then remove the thrust bearing.

ASSEMBLY

NOTE: Coat all components with clean engine oil during assembly.

1. Take the output shaft and install the thrust bearing, 1st and 2nd needle bearing, and 1st gear.
2. Install the 1st/2nd block ring.
3. Press the 1st/2nd collar, 2nd gear, and the synchronizer assembly on the shaft using special tool No. J–8853–01 or equivalent. Note the installation direction when assembling the synchronizer assembly. The insert spring set position should differ for right or left. The ends of the insert spring should not interfere with the hub.

NOTE: Do not twist the inserts in the block ring opening portions when pressing in.

4. Install the 1st/2nd block ring, needle bearing and key on the output shaft.
5. Using a press and special tool No. J–33374 or equivalent, install 3rd and 4th gear, and the output shaft rear bearing.
6. Using a press and special tool No. J–33368 or equivalent, install the output shaft front bearing.

ASSEMBLY OF TRANSAXLE

1. Install the clutch and differential housing.
2. Apply grease to the three interlock pins and place the pins onto the positions shown in the illustration.
3. Install the differential assembly.
4. Install the input and output shaft assemblies.
5. Install the 3rd and 4th gear shift rod and fork assembly. Do not forget to install the interlock pin into the rod when assembling the shift rod.
6. Install the 1st/2nd gear shift rod and fork assembly. Install a new roll pin.
7. Install the 5th/reverse gear shift rod and fork assembly.
8. Install the idler gear, shaft and pin.
9. Install the reverse gear detent plug, spring and ball.
10. Clean the mating surfaces of the clutch housing and transaxle case. Apply Locktite® primer N or equivalent to the mating surface of the clutch housing. After drying, apply the liquid gasket to the mating surface of the clutch housing. Then tighten the case bolts in a diagonal sequence to 27 ft. lbs.

11. Install the idler shaft bolt and gasket and tighten to 27 ft. lbs.
12. Install the needle bearing collar and thrust washer together using a hammer and special tool No. J33374.
13. Install the 5th gear needle bearing.
14. Install the 5th gear, input and output gears.
15. Install the 5th gear block ring.
16. Install the 5th gear synchronizer assembly while noting the hub and sleeve direction. Drive in the new roll pin after installation.

NOTE: The insert set positions should differ for both sides. The ends of the insert spring should not interfere with the hub.

17. Install the 1st/2nd, 3rd/4th and 5th spring ball and detent plug. Tighten the plug to 18 ft. lbs.
18. Install the insert stopper plate and the sleeve.
19. Clean the bolt threads on the 5th gear bolt threaded portions. Apply Locktite® to the threads of the input and output shafts. Install the new nuts and tighten to 94 ft. lbs.
20. Install the 2 pins and switches, (long pin–switch side, short pin-inner side of the hole).
21. Install the rear cover and gasket, tighten the bolts to 13.7 ft. lbs.

NOTE: Apply liquid gasket to the threaded portion of the bolts.

22. Install the quadrant box assembly and tighten the bolts to 13.7 ft. lbs.

TYPE 27

5 Speed Transaxle Model RS5F50A

DISASSEMBLY OF TRANSAXLE

1. Drain the oil from the transaxle.
2. Before removing the transaxle case, remove the bolts and plugs shown in the illustration.
3. Tap on the case lightly with a rubber mallet and then lift off the transaxle case.
4. With a rubber mallet, remove the position switch from the case.
5. Mesh the 4th gear, and then remove the reverse idler gear.
6. Remove the reverse arm shaft and the reverse level assembly.
7. Remove the 5th and reverse check plug, spring and ball.

8. Remove the stopper rings and retaining pins from the 5th/reverse and 3rd/4th fork rods.
9. Remove the 5th/reverse and 3rd/4th fork rods. Then remove the forks and brackets.
10. Remove both the input and mainshafts with the 1st/2nd fork and fork rod as a set.
11. Remove the final drive assembly.
12. Remove the reverse check assembly.
13. With a hammer and punch, remove the retaining pin and detach the selector.
14. To make it easier to remove the retaining pin which hods the striking lever to the striking rod, remove the drain plug.
15. With a hammer and punch remove the retaining pin and then withdraw the striking level and striking rod.

Gears and Shafts

END PLAY MEASUREMENT

Before disassembly of the input shaft or the main shaft, measure the gear and play to insure that it is within the specified limit.
• If the end play is not within the specified limit, disassemble and check the parts.
• Replace any worn or damaged parts.

STANDARD END PLAY

Position	mm (in)
Main 1st gear	0.23–0.43 (0.0091–0.0169)
Main 2nd gear	0.23–0.58 (0.0091–0.0228)
Input 3rd gear	0.23–0.43 (0.0091–0.0169)
Input 4th gear	0.25–0.55 (0.0098–0.0217)
Input 5th gear	0.23–0.48 (0.0091–0.0189)

Input Shaft

DISASSEMBLY

NOTE: The following removal procedures require the use of a hydraulic press and various bearing adapter.

1. Using a press and bearing adapter, remove the input shaft rear bearing.
2. Using a press and bearing adapter, remove the 5th gear synchronizer and the 5th input gear.
3. Remove the thrust washer ring, thrust washers and the 4th input gear.

4. Remove the snap-ring, and then using a press and bearing adapter, remove the 3rd/4th synchronizer and the 3rd input gear.

5. Press off the input shaft front bearing.

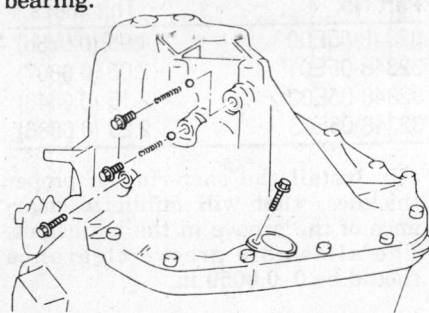

Remove these bolts before removing the case

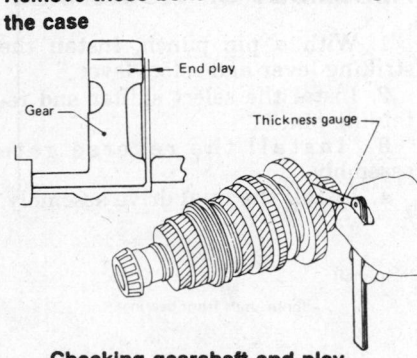

Checking gearshaft end play

ASSEMBLY

1. Place the inserts in the three grooves on the coupling sleeve of the 3rd/4th synchronizer and the 5th synchronizer.

2. Lubricate the 3rd input gear inner surface with gear oil, then install the 3rd input gear and 3rd baulk ring.

3. Press the 3rd/4th synchronizer hub together, pay attention to its direction shown in the illustration.

4. Install the snap-ring of the proper thickness that will minimize the clearance of the groove in the input shaft. The allowable groove clearance should be 0–0.0039 in.

5. Lubricate the 4th input gear with gear oil, then install the 4th input gear, thrust washers and thrust washer ring. The thrust washers should be selected to minimize clearance of the groove in the input shaft. The allowable groove clearance should be 0–0.0024 in.

6. Lubricate the inner surface of 5th gear with gear oil, then install 5th gear.

7. Press on the 5th gear synchronizer.

8. Install the input shaft front and rear bearing.

9. Measure the gear end play. Refer to the previous section "End Play Measurement".

3rd & 4th SYNCHRONIZER HUB SNAP RING

Part No.	Thickness mm(in.) Thickness
32269-03E00	2.00 (0.0787)
32269-03E01	2.05 (0.0807)
32269-03E02	2.10 (0.0827)
32269-03E03	1.95 (0.0768)

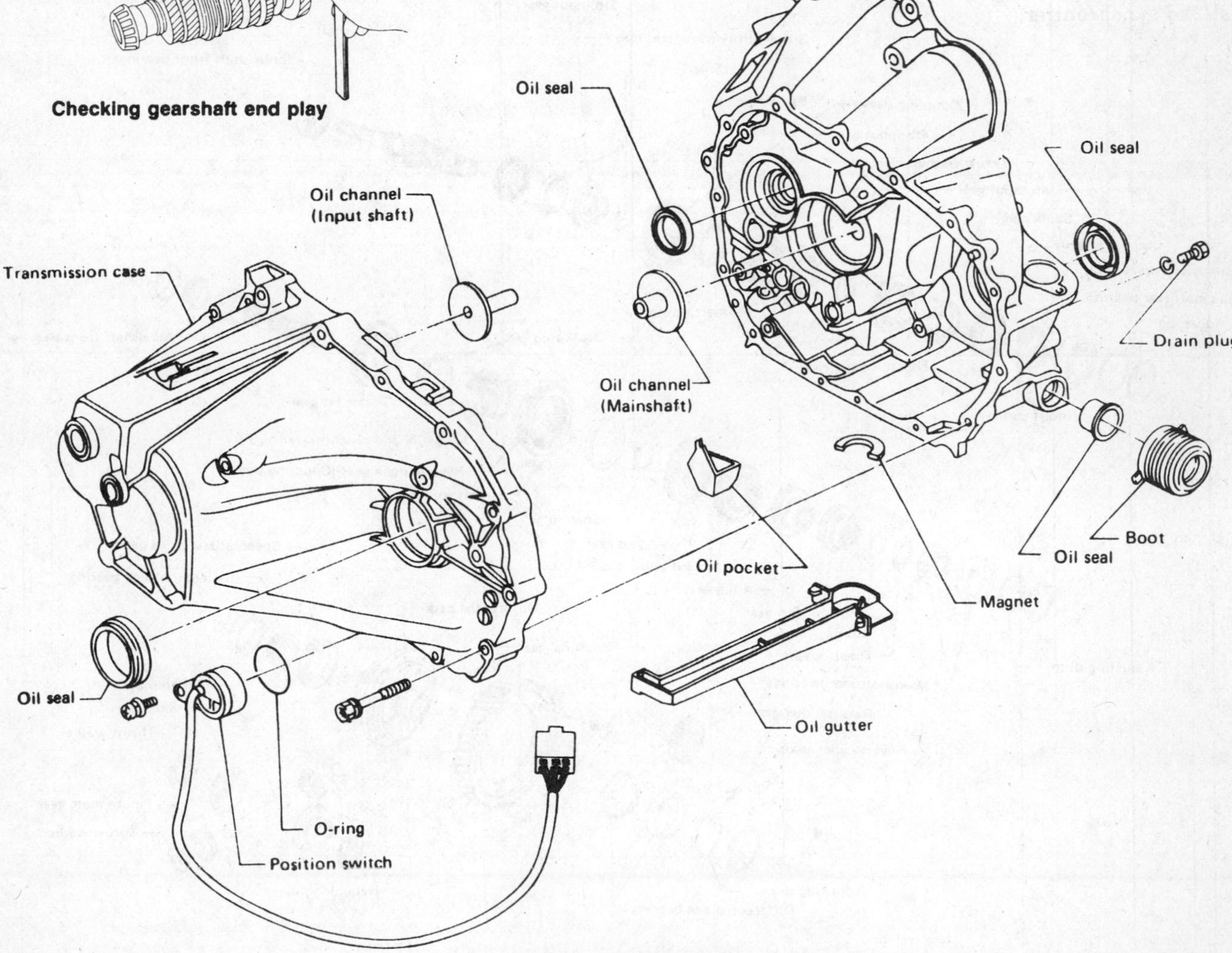

Case components – RS5F50A transaxle

Mainshaft

DISASSEMBLY

NOTE: The following removal procedures require the use of a hydraulic press and various bearing adapters.

1. Using a press and bearing adapter, remove the mainshaft rear bearing.

2. Remove the thrust washer and snap-ring.

3. Using a press and bearing adapter, remove the 5th and 4th main gears.

4. Using a press and bearing adapter, remove the 3rd and the 2nd main gears.

5. Remove the snap-ring, and then using a press and bearing adapter, remove the 1st/2nd synchronizer and the 1st main gear.

6. Press off the mainshaft front bearing.

ASSEMBLY

1. Place the inserts in the three grooves on the coupling sleeve of the 1st/2nd synchronizer.

2. Lubricate the 1st gear inner surface with gear oil, then install the 1st gear and 1st baulk ring.

3. Press the 1st/2nd synchronizer hub together, pay attention to its direction shown in the illustration.

4. Install the coupling sleeve with three inserts and the 2nd gear baulk ring.

5. Install the snap-ring of the proper thickness that will minimize the clearance of the groove in the mainshaft. The allowable groove clearance should be 0–0.0039 in.

1st & 2nd SYNCHRONIZER HUB SNAP RING

mm (in.)

Part No.	Thickness
32269-03E00	2.00 (0.0787)
32269-03E01	2.05 (0.0807)
32269-03E02	2.10 (0.0827)
32269-03E03	1.95 (0.0768)

6. Lubricate the 2nd gear with gear oil, then install the 2nd gear.

7. Press on 3rd gear.

8. Press on 4th gear.

9. Press on 5th gear.

5TH GEAR SNAP RING

mm (in.)

Part No.	Thickness
32348-05E00	1.95 (0.0768)
32348-05E01	2.05 (0.0807)
32348-05E02	2.15 (0.0846)
32348-05E03	2.25 (0.0886)

10. Install the snap-ring of proper thickness that will minimize clearance of the groove in the mainshaft. The allowable groove clearance should be 0–0.0059 in.

ASSEMBLY OF TRANSAXLE

1. With a pin punch, install the striking lever and select lever.

2. Instal the select shifter and retaining pin.

3. Install the reverse gate assembly.

4. Install the final drive assembly.

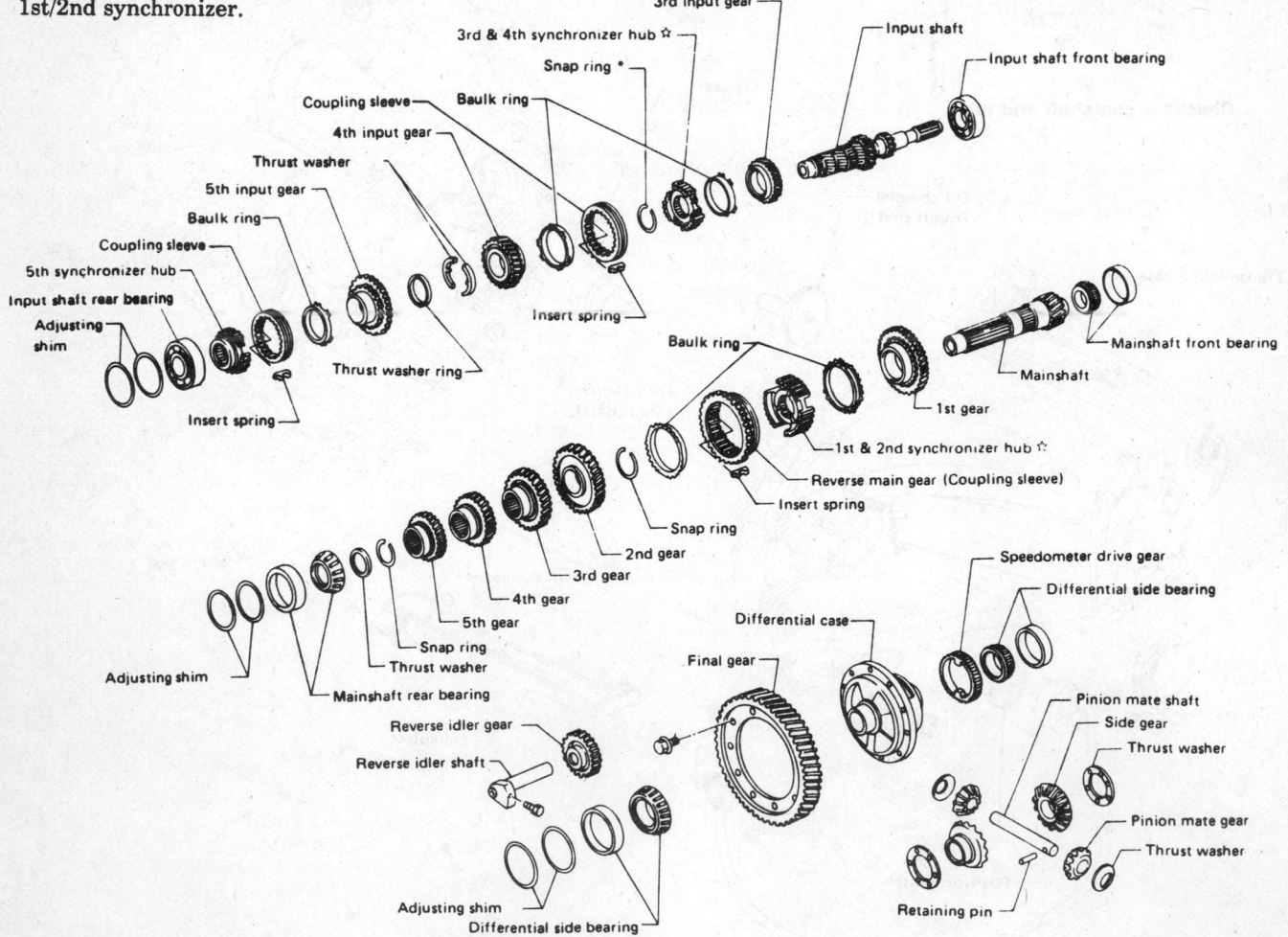

Gear components – RS5F50A transaxle

5. Install the input shaft and the mainshaft with the 1st and 2nd shift fork assembly.

NOTE: Be careful not to damage the input shaft oil seal during installation.

6. Install the interlock balls and plunger.

7. Install the 3rd/4th shift fork and bracket, then install the 3rd/4th shift rod, circular clip and retaining pin.

8. Install the interlock balls.

9. Install the 5th shift fork and bracket, then install the shift rod, circular clip and retaining pin.

10. Install the 5th reverse check plug, spring and ball.

11. Install the reverse lever assembly.

12. Install the reverse arm shaft and retaining pin.

13. Mesh 4th gear. Then install the reverse idler gear and shaft, paying attention to the direction of the tapped hole shown in the illustration.

14. Place the "U" shaped magnet on the clutch housing.

NOTE: To aid in the installation of the transaxle case, place the shift selector in the 1st/2nd shift bracket or between the 1st/2nd bracket and the 3rd/4th bracket.

15. Apply sealant to the mating surface of the transmission case and install it.

16. Install the position switch.

17. Apply sealant to the threads of the check plugs. Install the balls, springs and plugs.

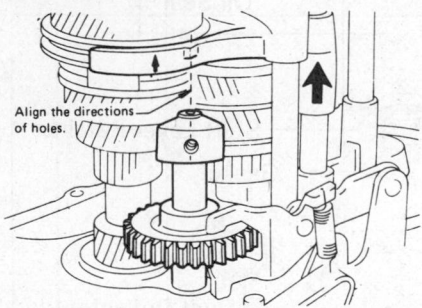

Align the directions of holes.

Instalation of the reverse idler gear shaft

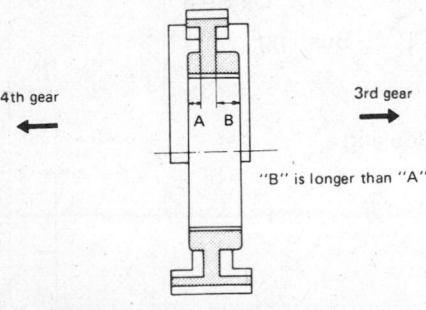

4th gear   3rd gear

"B" is longer than "A".

3rd/4th synchronizer hub assembly

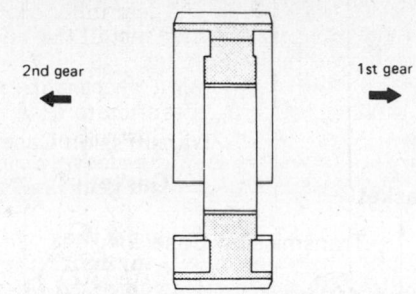

2nd gear   1st gear

1st/2nd synchronizer hub assembly

18. After assembly, check that you can shift into each gear smoothly.

TYPE 28

5 Speed Transaxle Models Z45, 46, 53 and (4x4) 54F Toyota

DISASSEMBLY OF TRANSAXLE

1. Support and drain the transaxle.

2. Remove the speedometer driven gear.

3. Remove the back-up light switch. Remove the 4WD indicator switch and the extra low gear indicator switch (Z54F only).

4. Remove the extension housing (Z45, 56, 53 only) as follows:

   a. Remove the two plug, spring and the reverse restrict pin.

   b. Tap on the extension housing using a plastic faced hammer.

   c. Turn the select lever and disconnect the tip from the shift head groove.

   d. If necessary, remove the shifting rod end and remove the select lever from the extension housing.

5. Remove the extension housing (Z54F) as follows:

   a. Remove the reverse restrict pin.

   b. Remove the six bolts, shift lever retainer and gasket.

   c. Unstake the lockwasher of the select housing mounting bolt.

   d. Remove the select lever housing mounting bolt.

   e. Remove the nine bolts, extension housing, select lever housing and gasket.

6. Remove the transfer output shaft and oil pump rotors (Z54F only). Remove the three bolts, oil pump cover. Then remove the oil pump rotors,

transfer output shaft, and the oil baffle.

7. Remove the transfer shift fork (Z54F) as follows:

   a. Using special tool No. 09313–30021 or equivalent, remove the screw plug.

   b. Using a magnetic finger, remove the spring seat, spring and the detent ball.

   c. Pull out the shift fork, shift shaft and hub sleeve together as an assembly.

   d. Remove the No. 4 synchronizer ring.

   e. If necessary, disassemble the shift fork and the shift fork shaft.

8. Remove the oil pump drive shaft (Z54F) as follows:

   a. Cover the tip of the input shaft with a shop cloth to protect it.

   b. Take a pair of pliers and remove the oil pump drive shaft.

9. Remove the transfer clutch hub (Z54F) as follows:

   a. Using snap-ring pliers, remove the snap-ring.

   b. Remove the clutch hub and No. 4 synchronizer ring.

10. Remove the No. 4 shift fork shaft and No. 4 shift head (Z54F) as follows:

   a. Remove the four bolts, transfer case cover and gasket.

   b. Remove the spring and seat.

   c. Using a magnetic finger remove the detent ball.

   d. Unstake the lock plate of the No. 4 shift head mount bolt.

   e. Remove the No. 4 shift head mounting bolt.

   f. Using the special tool No. 09313–30021, remove the screw plug.

   g. Using a pin punch and hammer, tap out the slotted spring pin.

   h. Pull out the No. 4 shift fork and remove the No. 4 shift head.

   i. Using a magnetic finger, remove the interlock pin.

11. Remove the transfer adapter (Z54F) as follows:

NOTE: The oil pump drive shaft has left-hand threads.

   a. Remove the plug, spring and reverse restrict pin.

   b. Remove the nine case bolts.

   c. Using a soft-faced hammer, tap the transfer adapter.

   d. Turn the select lever and disconnect the tip from the shift head groove. Remove the transfer adapter, select lever No. 4 shift fork and the extra low gear assembly.

12. Check the extra low gear thrust clearance (Z54F) as follows:

   a. Install the needle roller bearing, extra low gear, transfer clutch hub with the snap-ring.

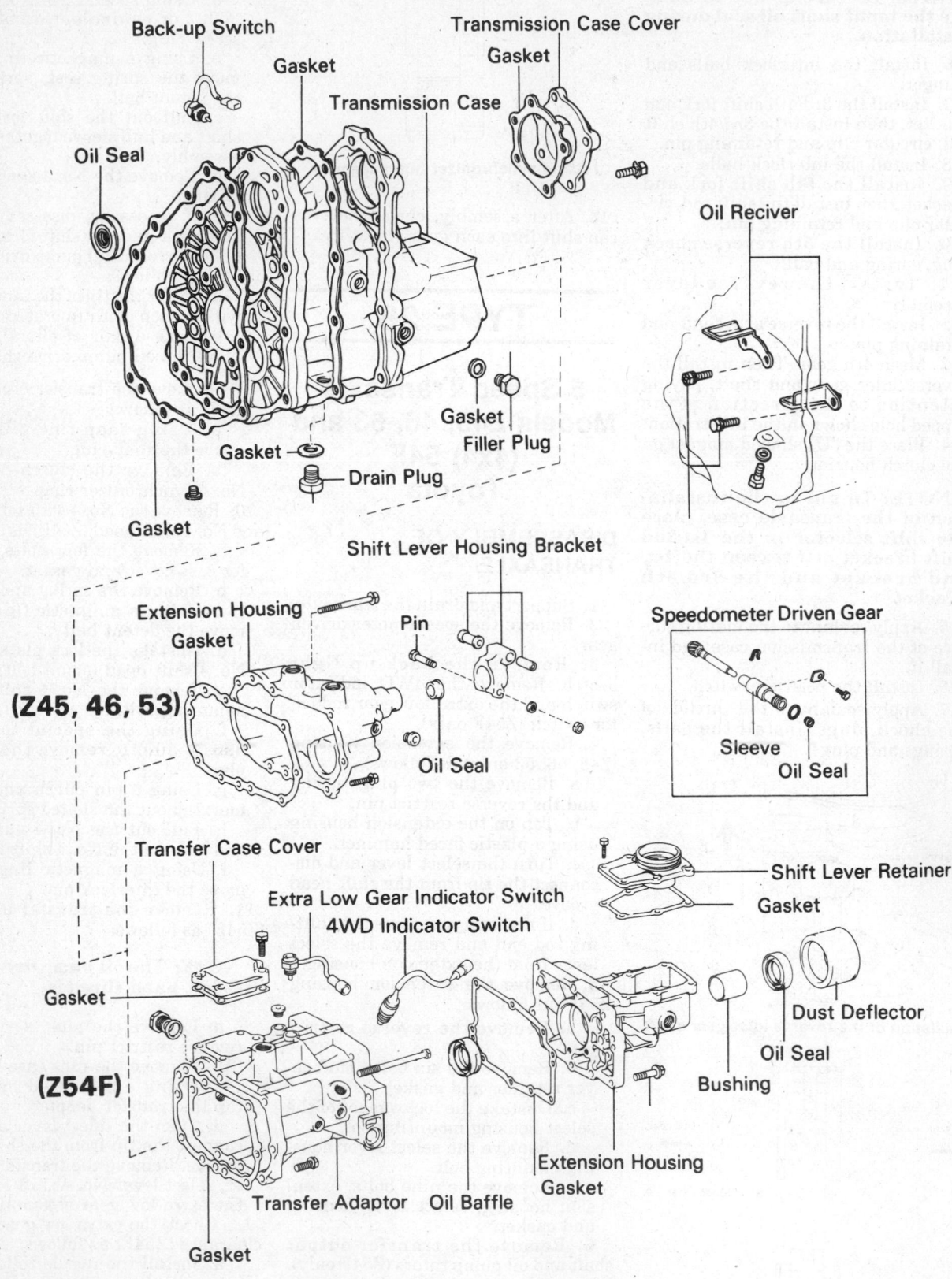

Back-up Switch

Gasket

Transmission Case Cover

Gasket

Transmission Case

Oil Seal

Oil Reciver

Gasket

Gasket
Filler Plug

Gasket

Drain Plug

Gasket

Shift Lever Housing Bracket

Extension Housing
Gasket

Pin

Oil Seal

(Z45, 46, 53)

Speedometer Driven Gear

Sleeve

Oil Seal

Transfer Case Cover

Extra Low Gear Indicator Switch
4WD Indicator Switch

Shift Lever Retainer

Gasket

Gasket

Dust Deflector

Oil Seal

Bushing

(Z54F)

Extension Housing
Gasket

Transfer Adaptor   Oil Baffle

Gasket

Exploded view of transaxle assembly

Z45, 46, 53, 54F

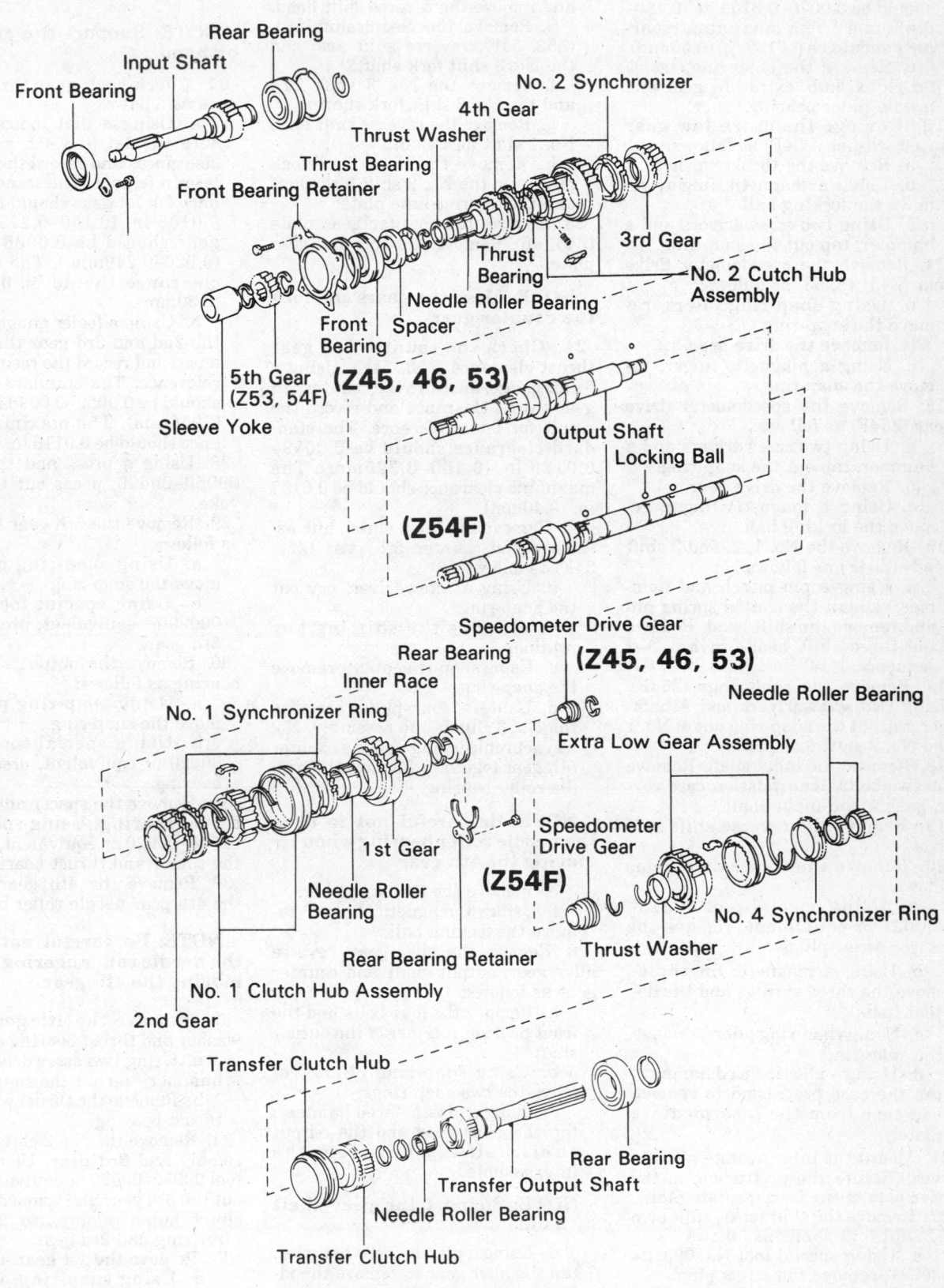

Exploded view of gear components

b. Using a feeler gauge, measure the extra low gear thrust clearance, and record the result for late reference. The standard clearance should be 0.0070–0.0169 in. (0.180–0.430mm). The maximum clearance should be 0.0197 in. (0.50mm).

c. Remove the snap-ring, transfer clutch hub, extra low gear and needle roller bearing.

13. Remove the extra low gear thrust washer (Z54F) as follows:

a. Remove the thrust washer.

b. Using a magnetic finger, remove the locking ball.

c. Using two screwdrivers and a hammer, tap out the snap-ring.

14. Remove the speedometer drive gear (Z45, 46, 53) as follows:

a. Using snap-ring pliers, remove the snap-ring.

b. Remove the drive gear.

c. Using a magnetic finger, remove the snap-ring.

15. Remove the speedometer drive gear (Z54F) as follows:

a. Using two screwdrivers and a hammer, tap out the snap-ring.

b. Remove the drive gear.

c. Using a magnetic finger, remove the locking ball.

16. Remove the No. 1, 2, and 3 shift heads (Z54F) as follows:

a. Using a pin punch and hammer, tap out the slotted spring pin and remove the shift head. Remove the three shift heads in a 1–3–2 sequence.

17. Remove the snap-rings (Z54F). Using two screwdrivers and a hammer, tap out the snap-ring out of No. 1 and No. 2 shift fork shafts.

18. Remove the input shaft. Remove the two bolts, transmission case cover, gasket and input shaft.

19. Remove the reverse shift arm pivot.

20. Remove the transaxle case as follows:

a. Using special tool 09313–30021 or equivalent, remove the three screw plugs.

b. Using a magnetic finger, remove the three springs and the detent balls.

c. Using snap-ring pliers, remove the snap-ring.

d. Using a plastic-faced hammer, tap the case protrusion to remove the case from the intermediate plate.

21. Mount the intermediate plate in a vise. Secure the protrusion on the lower part of the intermediate plate.

22. Remove the shift forks, shift arm and shift fork shafts as follows:

a. Using special tool No. 09313–30021, remove the screw plug.

b. Using a magnetic finger, remove the spring and the detent ball.

c. Remove the shift fork mount bolts.

d. Using a pin punch and hammer, tap out the slotted spring pin and remove the reverse shift head.

e. Remove the No. 3 shift fork (Z53, 54F), reverse shift arm and the No. 3 shift fork shaft.

f. Remove the No. 2 shift fork and the No. 2 shift fork shaft.

g. Remove the reverse shift fork, No. 1 shift fork shaft.

h. Remove the three interlock pins from the No. 2 shift fork shaft and the intermediate plate.

23. Remove the counter gear plate (Z45, 46). Remove the bolt and gear plate.

NOTE: Mesh the gears and lock the counter gear.

24. Check the counter 5th gear thrust clearance (Z53, 54F). Using a feeler gauge, measure the counter 5th gear thrust clearance and record the result for later reference. The standard clearance should be 0.0059–0.0128 in. (0.150–0.325mm). The maximum clearance should be 0.0157 in. (0.40mm).

25. Remove the No. 3 clutch hub assembly and counter 5th gear (Z53, 54F) as follows:

a. Using a screwdriver, pry out the snap-ring.

b. Remove the shifting key retainer.

c. Using snap-ring pliers, remove the snap-ring.

d. Using a gear puller, remove the No. 3 clutch hub assembly, No. 3 synchronizer ring and the counter 5th gear together. Remove the needle roller bearing.

NOTE: Be careful not to drop the needle roller bearing when removing the 5th gear.

e. Remove the thrust washer.

f. Using a magnetic finger, remove the locking ball.

26. Remove the idler gear, reverse idler gear, output shaft and counter gear as follows:

a. Remove the four bolts and the front bearing retainer of the output shaft.

b. Using snap-ring pliers, remove the two snap-rings.

c. Using a plastic-faced hammer, tap the idler gear and the output shaft halfway out from the intermediate.

NOTE: Support the gear shaft by hand.

d. Using a plastic-faced hammer, tap the idler gear to remove the idler gear, reverse idler gear and reverse idler gear shaft together.

e. Using a plastic-faced hammer, tap the output shaft to remove the output shaft and counter gear together.

NOTE: Support the gear shaft by hand.

27. Check each gear thrust clearance as follows:

a. Using a dial indicator, measure the 1st and 4th gear thrust clearances and record the result for later reference. The standard clearance for 1st gear should be 0.0059–0.0108 in. (0.150–0.275mm), 4th gear should be 0.0008–0.094 in (0.020–0.249mm.). The maximum clearance should be 0.0118 in. (0.30mm).

b. Using a feeler gauge, measure the 2nd and 3rd gear thrust clearances and record the result for later reference. The standard clearance should be 0.0059–0.0098 in. (0.150–0.250mm). The maximum clearance should be 0.0118 in. (0.30mm).

28. Using a press and special tool 09950–00020, press out the sleeve yoke.

29. Remove the 5th gear (Z53, 54F) as follows:

a. Using snap-ring pliers, remove the snap-ring.

b. Using special tool 09950–00020 or equivalent, press out the 5th gear.

30. Remove the output shaft front bearing as follows:

a. Using snap-ring pliers, remove the snap-ring.

b. Using special tool 09950–00020 or equivalent, press out the bearing.

31. Remove the spacer and 4th gear thrust bearing. Using special tool 09950–00020 or equivalent, press out the spacer and thrust bearing.

32. Remove the 4th gear. Remove the 4th gear needle roller bearing.

NOTE: Be careful not to drop the needle roller bearing when removing the 4th gear.

33. Remove the 4th gear thrust washer and thrust bearing as follows:

a. Using two screwdrivers and a hammer, tap out the snap-ring.

b. Remove the thrust washer and thrust bearing.

34. Remove the No. 2 clutch hub assembly and 3rd gear. Using special tool 09950–00020 or equivalent, press out the 3rd gear and remove the No. 2 clutch hub assembly, No. 2 synchronizer ring and 3rd gear.

35. Remove the 1st gear as follows:

a. Using snap-ring pliers, remove the snap-ring.

b. Remove the 1st gear, inner

race, needle roller bearing and No. 1 synchronizer ring.

c. Using a magnetic finger, remove the locking ball.

36. Remove the No. 1 clutch hub assembly and 2nd gear. Using special tool 09950–00020 or equivalent, press out the 2nd gear and remove the No. 1 clutch hub assembly, No. 1 synchronizer ring and 2nd gear.

ASSEMBLY OF TRANSAXLE

1. Install the 2nd gear as follows:
a. Apply gear oil to the output shaft.
b. Slide the 2nd gear and the No. 1 synchronizer ring onto the output shaft.

2. Assemble the No. 1 clutch hub and hub sleeve as follows:
a. Install the clutch hub and shifting keys to the hub sleeve.
b. Install the shifting key springs under the shifting keys.

NOTE: Install the key springs positioned so that their end gaps are not in line.

3. Install the No. 1 clutch hub assembly using special tool No. 09515–30010 and a press, align the synchronizer ring slots with the shifting keys and press in the clutch hub.

4. Assemble the 1st gear, needle roller bearing and inner race. Apply gear oil to the bearing.

5. Install the 1st gear assembly as follows:
a. Install the locking ball in the shaft.
b. Slide the No. 1 synchronizer ring and 1st gear on the output shaft with the synchronizer ring slots aligned with the shifting keys, turn the inner race to align it with the locking ball.
c. Select a snap-ring that will allow minimum axial play and install it on the shaft.

Snap ring thickness mm (in.)
2.15–2.20 (0.0846–0.0866)
2.20–2.25 (0.0866–0.0886)
2.25–2.30 (0.0886–0.0906)
2.30–2.35 (0.0906–0.0925)
2.35–2.40 (0.0925–0.0945)
2.40–2.45 (0.0945–0.0965)
2.45–2.50 (0.0965–0.0984)
2.50–2.55 (0.0984–0.1004)
2.55–2.60 (0.1004–0.1024)

6. Check the 2nd gear thrust clearance. Using a feeler gauge, measure the 2nd gear thrust clearance. The standard clearance should be 0.0059–0.0098 in. (0.150–0.250mm). The maximum clearance should be 0.0118 in. (0.30mm).

7. Check the first gear thrust clearance. Using a dial indicator, measure the 1st gear thrust clearance. The standard clearance should be 0.0059–0.0108 in. (0.150–0.275mm). The maximum clearance should be 0.0118 in. (0.30mm).

8. Install the 3rd gear as follows:
a. Apply gear oil to the output shaft.
b. Slide the 3rd gear and No. 2 synchronizer ring onto the output shaft.

9. Assemble the No. 2 clutch hub and hub sleeve as follows:
a. Install the key springs and shifting keys to the clutch hub.
b. Install the clutch hub to the hub sleeve.

10. Install the No. 2 clutch hub assembly. Using special tool No. 09515–30010 or equivalent and a press, align the synchronizer ring slots with the shifting keys and press in the clutch hub.

11. Install the 4th gear as follows:
a. Apply gear oil to the output shaft.
b. Slide the large thrust bearing onto the output shaft.
c. Slide the No. 2 synchronizer ring, needle roller bearing and 5th gear onto the output shaft. Align the synchronizer ring slots with the shifting keys.
d. Slide the thrust washer onto the output shaft.
e. Using a plastic-faced hammer, tap in the snap-ring.

12. Install the 4th gear small thrust bearing and spacer as follows:
a. Stick the thrust bearing onto the spacer with MP grease.
b. Using special tool No. 09612–22011 or equivalent and a press, press in the spacer.

13. Install the output shaft front bearing as follows:
a. Using special tool No. 09612–22011 or equivalent and a press, press in the bearing.
b. Select a snap-ring that will allow minimum axial play and install it on the shaft.

Snap ring thickness mm (in.)
2.10–2.15 (0.0827–0.0846)
2.15–2.20 (0.0846–0.0866)
2.20–2.25 (0.0866–0.0886)
2.25–2.30 (0.0886–0.0906)
2.30–2.35 (0.0906–0.0925)
2.35–2.40 (0.0925–0.0945)
2.40–2.45 (0.0945–0.0965)
2.45–2.50 (0.0965–0.0984)
2.50–2.55 (0.0984–0.1004)

14. Check the 3rd gear thrust clearance. Using a feeler gauge, measure the 3rd gear thrust clearance. The standard clearance should be 0.0059–0.0098 in. (0.150–0.250mm). The maximum clearance should be 0.0118 in. (0.30mm).

15. Check the 4th gear thrust clearance. Using a dial indicator, measure the 4th gear thrust clearance. The standard clearance should be 0.0008–0.0094 in. (0.020–0.024mm). The maximum clearance should be 0.0118 in. (0.30mm).

16. Install the 5th gear (Z53, 54F) as follows:
a. Using special tool No. 09612–22011 or equivalent and a press, press in the 5th gear.
b. Select a snap-ring that will allow minimum axial play and install the snap-ring (Z45, 46).

Snap ring thickness mm (in.)
2.10–2.15 (0.0827–0.0846)
2.15–2.20 (0.0846–0.0866)
2.20–2.25 (0.0866–0.0886)
2.25–2.30 (0.0886–0.0906)
2.30–2.35 (0.0906–0.0925)
2.35–2.40 (0.0925–0.0945)

17. Install the sleeve yoke. Using a press, press in the sleeve yoke.

18. Mount the intermediate plate in a vise. Secure the protrusion on the lower part of the intermediate plate.

19. Install the output shaft, counter gear, idler gear and reverse idler gear as follows:
a. Using a plastic-faced hammer, tap in the output shaft and counter gear together about halfway.
b. Align the idler gear with the notched portion of the reverse idler gear shaft.
c. Using a plastic-faced hammer, tap in the idler gear shaft bearing about halfway.

NOTE: Insure that the idler gear and output shaft spacer do not contact each other.

d. Using a plastic-faced hammer, tap each gear shaft until the bearing is in as far as it will go.
e. Using snap-ring pliers, install the two snap-rings.
f. Install the output shaft front bearing retainer with the four nuts. Torque the nuts to 19 ft. lbs.

20. Install the counter gear plate (Z45, 46) as follows:
a. Align the plate protrusion with the shaft control.
b. Install the gear plate with the bolt. Torque the bolt to 9 ft. lbs.

NOTE: Mesh the gears and lock the counter gear.

21. Install the counter 5th gear (Z53, 54F) as follows:

a. Apply gear oil to the shaft of the counter gear.

b. Install the locking ball in the shaft.

c. Slide the thrust washer onto the output shaft. Align the locking ball groove of the thrust washer with the locking ball.

d. Slide the needle roller bearing, counter 5th gear and No. 3 synchronizer ring.

22. Assemble the No. 3 clutch hub and hub sleeve (Z53, 54F) as follows:

a. Install the clutch hub and shifting keys to the hub sleeve.

b. Install the shifting key springs under the shifting keys.

NOTE: Install the key springs positioned so that their end gaps are not in line.

23. Install the No. 3 clutch hub assembly (Z53, 54F) as follows:

a. Using special tool No. 09612–22010 or equivalent and a press, align the synchronizer ring slots with the shifting keys and press in the clutch hub.

b. Select a snap-ring that will allow minimum axial play and install it on the shaft.

24. Check the counter 5th gear thrust clearance (Z53, 54F). Using a feeler gauge, measure the 5th gear thrust clearance. The standard clearance should be 0.0059–0.0128 in. (0.150–0.325mm). The maximum clearance should be 0.0157 in. (0.40mm).

25. Install the shifting key retainer for 5th gear (Z53, 54F) as follows:

a. Align the claws of the key retainer with the key groove of the clutch hub.

b. Install the key retainer with the snap-ring.

Snap ring thickness

1.80–1.85 (0.0709–0.0728)
1.85–1.90 (0.0728–0.0748)
1.90–1.95 (0.0748–0.0768)
1.95–2.00 (0.0768–0.0787)
2.00–2.05 (0.0787–0.0807)
2.05–2.10 (0.0807–0.0827)
2.10–2.15 (0.0827–0.0846)

26. Install the shift forks, shift arm and shift fork shafts as follows:

a. Assemble the reverse shift arm and shift head with the E-ring.

b. Install the No. 1 shift fork, reverse shift fork and No. 1 shift fork shaft.

(1.) Align the No. 1 shift fork, reverse shift fork and No. 1 shift fork shaft.

(2.) Align the reverse shift fork with the reverse gear groove.

c. Install the No. 2 shift fork and No. 2 shift fork shaft. Align the No. 2 shift fork with the No. 2 hub sleeve groove.

d. Using special tool No. 093133–30021, remove the screw plug (for interlock pin).

e. Align the interlock pin groove of the No. 1 shift fork shaft with the interlock pin hole of the No. 2 shift fork shaft.

(1.) Place the No. 1 and No. 2 hub sleeve in the Neutral position.

(2.) Align the mount bolt holes of the No. 1 shift fork and No. 1 shift fork shaft.

(3.) Align the mount bolt holes of the No. 2 shift fork and No. 1 shift fork shaft.

f. Install the three interlock pins. Coat MP grease to the interlock pin.

g. Install the reverse shift arm, No. 3 shift fork (Z53, 54F) and No. 3 shift fork shaft.

(1.) Connect the reverse shift arm and reverse shift fork.

(2.) Align the No. 3 shift fork with the No. 3 hub sleeve groove (Z53–54F).

h. Apply MP grease on the threads and under the screw plug head.

i. Using special tool No. 09313–30021, install and torque the screw plug to 16 ft. lbs.

j. Align the pin holes of the reverse shift fork shaft.

k. Using a pin punch and hammer, tap in the slotted spring pin until it is flush with the shift fork.

l. Install and torque the shift fork mount bolts to 13 ft. lbs.

m. Install the detent ball and spring into the reverse shift fork hole.

n. Using special tool No. 09313–30021 or equivalent, install and torque the screw plug to 16 ft. lbs.

27. Dismount the intermediate plate from the vise.

28. Install the transmission case as follows:

a. Place a new gasket in position on the intermediate plate.

b. Assemble the transmission case and intermediate plate.

c. Using snap-ring pliers, install the snap-ring.

d. Install the detent ball and spring into each hole.

e. Apply liquid sealer on the threads under the screw plug heads.

f. Using special tool No. 09313–30021SST, install and torque the three screw plugs to 16 ft. lbs.

29. Install the reverse shift arm pivot as follows:

a. Install a new gasket to the shift arm pivot.

b. Insert the shift arm pivot through the reverse shift arm.

c. Torque the shift arm pivot to 22 ft. lbs.

30. Install the snap-rings (Z54F). Using a plastic-faced hammer, tap the snap-ring on the No. 1 and No. 2 shift fork shafts.

31. Install the shift heads (No. 1, No. 2 AND No. 3) as follows:

a. Slide the shift head onto each shift fork shaft.

b. Align the pin holes of the shift head and shift fork shaft.

c. Using a pin punch and hammer, tap in the slotted spring pin until it is flush with the shift fork. Install the three slotted spring pins.

32. Install the speedometer drive gear (Z45, 46, 53) as follows:

a. Install the locking ball in the output shaft.

b. Slide the drive gear onto the shaft. Align the locking ball groove of the drive gear with the locking ball.

c. Using snap-ring pliers, install the snap-ring.

33. Install the speedometer drive gear as (Z54F) as follows:

a. Install the locking ball in the output shaft.

b. Slide the drive gear onto the output shaft. Align the locking ball groove of the drive gear with the locking ball.

c. Using a plastic-faced hammer, tap in the snap-ring.

34. Install the thrust washer of extra low gear (Z54F) as follows:

a. Using a plastic-faced hammer, tap in the snap-ring.

b. Install the locking ball in the output shaft.

c. Slide the thrust washer on the output shaft. Align the locking ball groove of the thrust washer with the locking ball.

35. Check the extra low gear thrust clearance (Z54F) as follows:

a. Install the needle roller bearings, extra low gear and transfer clutch hub with the snap-ring.

b. Using a feeler gauge, measure the extra low gear thrust clearance. The standard clearance should be 0.0070–0.0169 in. (0.180–0.430mm). The maximum clearance should be 0.0197 in. (0.50mm).

c. Remove the snap-ring, transfer clutch hub, extra low gear and needle roller bearing.

36. Assemble the extra low gear and No. 4 hub sleeve (Z54F) as follows:

a. Install the extra low gear shifting keys to the hub sleeve.

b. Install the shifting key springs under the shifting keys.

Z45, 46, 53, 54F

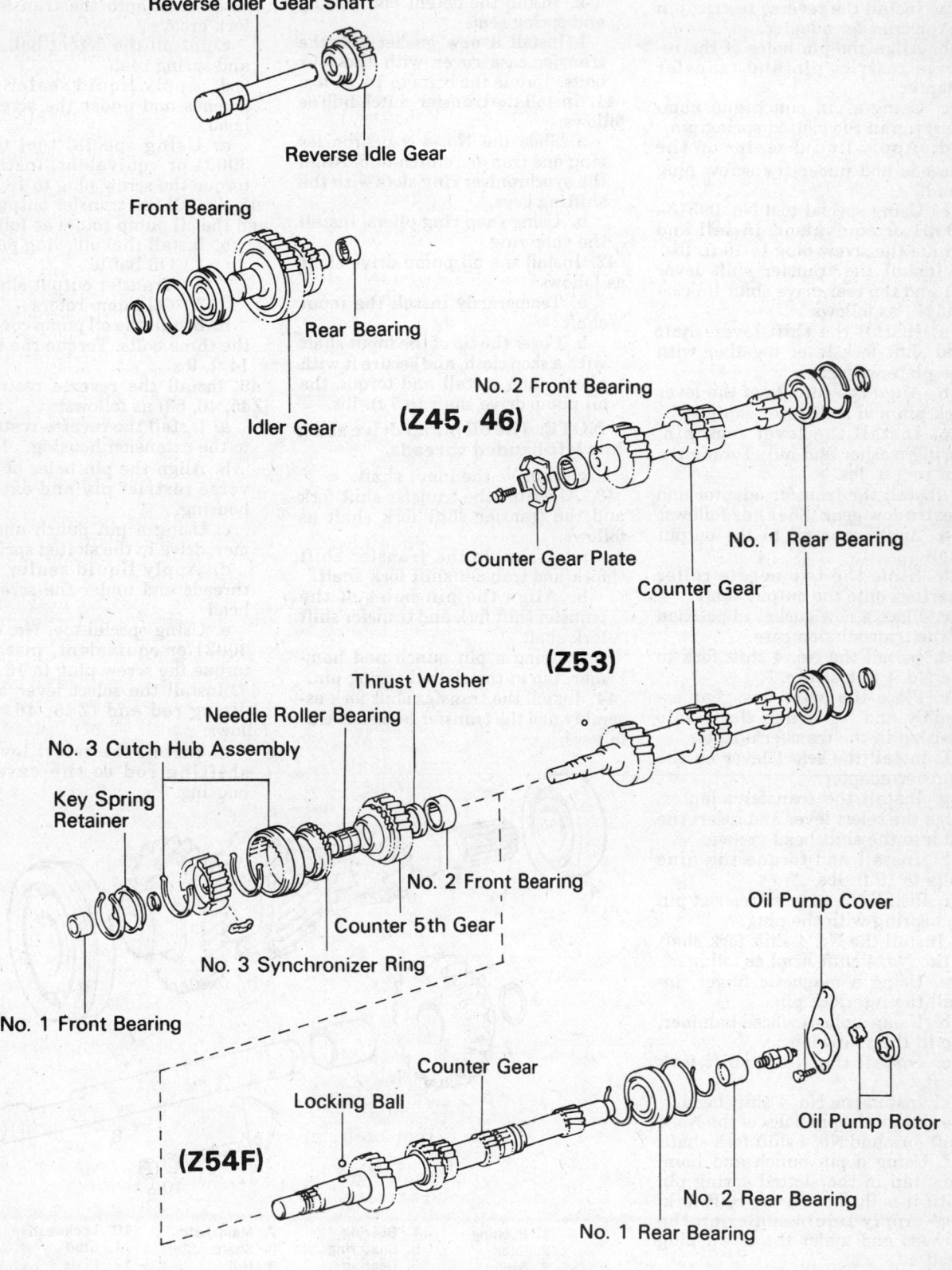

- Reverse Idler Gear Shaft
- Reverse Idle Gear
- Front Bearing
- Rear Bearing
- Idler Gear
- No. 2 Front Bearing

(Z45, 46)

- Counter Gear Plate
- No. 1 Rear Bearing
- Counter Gear

(Z53)

- Thrust Washer
- Needle Roller Bearing
- No. 3 Cutch Hub Assembly
- Key Spring Retainer
- No. 2 Front Bearing
- Counter 5th Gear
- No. 3 Synchronizer Ring
- No. 1 Front Bearing
- Oil Pump Cover
- Oil Pump Rotor

- Counter Gear
- Locking Ball
- No. 2 Rear Bearing
- No. 1 Rear Bearing

(Z54F)

Exploded view of gear components

NOTE: Install the key springs positioned so that their end gaps are not in line.

37. Install the reverse restrict pin (Z54F) as follows:

a. Install the reverse restrict pin to the transfer adaptor.

b. Align the pin holes of the reverse restrict pin and transfer adapter.

c. Using a pin punch and hammer, tap in the slotted spring pin.

d. Apply liquid sealer on the threads and under the screw plug head.

e. Using special tool No. 09313–30021 or equivalent, install and torque the screw plug to 16 ft. lbs.

38. Install the transfer shift lever shaft and the rear drive shaft link lever (54F) as follows:

a. Install the shift lever shaft and shift fork lever together with the plate washer.

b. Align the cutouts of the lever lock pin and shift lever shaft.

c. Install the lever lock pin, spring washer and nut. Torque the nut to 9 ft. lbs.

39. Install the transfer adaptor and the extra low gear (Z54F) as follows:

a. Apply gear oil to the output shaft.

b. Slide the two needle roller bearings onto the output shaft.

c. Place a new gasket in position of the transmission case.

d. Install the No. 4 shift fork to the No. 4 hub sleeve.

e. Place the extra low gear assembly and No. 4 hub sleeve into position in the transfer adaptor.

f. Install the select lever on the transfer adapter.

g. Install the transfer adapter. Turn the select lever and insert the tip into the shift head groove.

h. Install and torque the nine bolts to 19 ft. lbs.

i. Install the reverse restrict pin and spring with the plug.

40. Install the No. 4 shift fork shaft and the No. 4 shift head as follows:

a. Using a magnetic finger, install the interlock pin.

b. Using a plastic-faced hammer, tap in the snap-ring.

c. Install the No. 4 shift fork shaft.

d. Install the No. 4 shift head.

e. Align the pin holes of the No. 4 shift fork and No. 4 shift fork shaft.

f. Using a pin punch and hammer, tap in the slotted spring pin until it is flush with the shift fork.

g. Apply liquid sealer on the threads and under the screw plug head.

h. Using special tool No. 09313–30021 or equivalent, install and torque the screw plug to 18 ft. lbs.

i. Install the No. 4 shift fork mount bolt together with a new lock plate.

j. Stake the lock plate.

k. Install the detent ball, spring and spring seat.

l. Install a new gasket and the transfer case cover with the four bolts. Torque the bolts to 14. ft. lbs.

41. Install the transfer clutch hub as follows:

a. Slide the No. 4 synchronizer ring and transfer clutch hub. Align the synchronizer ring slots with the shifting keys.

b. Using snap-ring pliers, install the snap-ring.

42. Install the oil pump drive shaft as follows:

a. Temporarily install the input shaft.

b. Cover the tip of the input shaft with a shop cloth, and secure it with pliers, then install and torque the oil pump drive shaft to 9 ft. lbs.

NOTE: The oil pump drive shaft has left-handed threads.

c. Remove the input shaft.

43. Assemble the transfer shift fork and the transfer shift fork shaft as follows:

a. Assemble the transfer shift fork and transfer shift fork shaft.

b. Align the pin holes of the transfer shift fork and transfer shift fork shaft.

c. Using a pin punch and hammer, tap in the slotted spring pin.

44. Install the transfer shift fork assembly and the transfer hub sleeve as follows:

a. Place the transfer shift fork on the transfer hub sleeve.

b. Install the transfer shift fork assembly and transfer hub sleeve together. Connect the transfer shift lever shaft into the transfer shift fork groove.

c. Install the detent ball, spring and spring seat.

d. Apply liquid sealer on the threads and under the screw plug head.

e. Using special tool 09313–30021 or equivalent, install and torque the screw plug to 18 ft. lbs.

45. Install the transfer output shaft and the oil pump rotors as follows:

a. Install the following parts:
(1.) Oil baffle
(2.) Transfer output shaft
(3.) Oil pump rotors

b. Install the oil pump cover with the three bolts. Torque the bolts to 14 ft. lbs.

46. Install the reverse restrict pin (Z45, 46, 53) as follows:

a. Install the reverse restrict pin to the extension housing.

b. Align the pin holes of the reverse restrict pin and extension housing.

c. Using a pin punch and hammer, drive in the slotted spring pin.

d. Apply liquid sealer on the threads and under the screw plug head.

e. Using special tool No. 09313–30021 or equivalent, install and torque the screw plug to 16 ft. lbs.

47. Install the select lever and the shifting rod end (Z45, 46, 53) as follows:

a. Install the select lever and shifting rod to the extension housing.

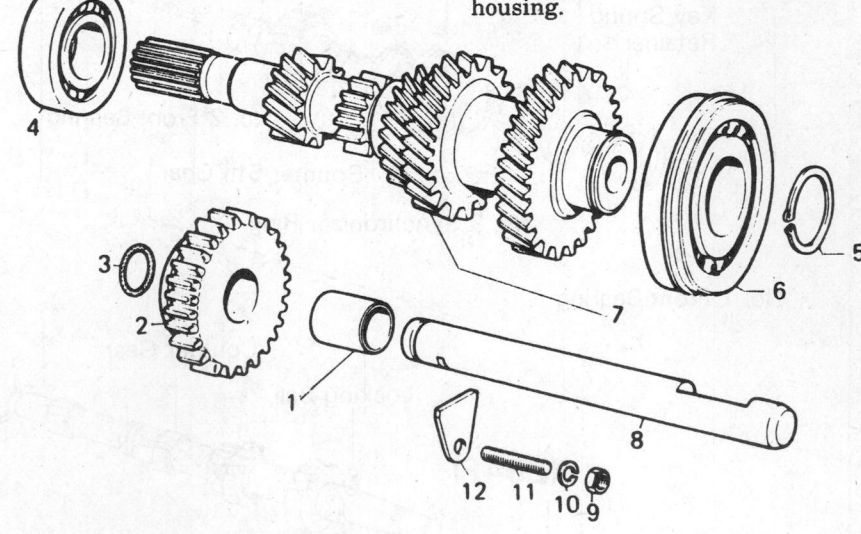

1. Bushing	4. Bearing	7. Mainshaft	10. Lockwasher
2. Gear	5. Snap ring	8. Shaft	11. Stud
3. Seal	6. Bearing	9. Nut	12. Plate

Mainshaft and reverse idler gear

b. Align the cutouts of the lever lock pin and select level.

c. Install the level lock pin, spring washer and nut. Torque the nut to 14 ft. lbs.

48. Install the extension housing (Z45, 46, 53) as follows:

a. Place a new gasket in position on the transmission case.

b. Install the extension housing. Turn the tip into the shift head groove.

c. Install and torque the nine bolts to 19 ft. lbs.

d. Install two reverse restrict pins, spring and plugs. Torque the plugs to 30 ft. lbs.

49. Install the extension housing (Z54F) as follows:

a. Place a new gasket in position on the transfer adaptor.

b. Install the extension housing and select lever housing together.

c. Install and torque the nine bolts to 19 ft. lbs.

d. Install the mount bolt of the select lever housing together with a new lock plate. Torque the bolt to 25 ft. lbs.

e. Stake the lock plate.

f. Install a new gasket and the shift lever retainer with the six

bolts. Torque the bolts to 14 ft. lbs.

g. Install a new gasket and reverse restrict pin. Torque the restrict pin to 30 ft. lbs.

50. Install the following switches:

a. Back-up light switch (brass color).

b. 4WD indicator switch (chrome color) (Z54F only).

c. Extra low gear (EL) indicator switch (Z54F only).

51. Install the speedometer drive gear.

52. Install the mounting insulator.

TYPE 29

4 Speed Transaxle Yugo

DISASSEMBLY

1. Remove the drain plug and drain the lubricant from the transmission/differential.

2. Remove the screws securing the oil boots and remove the axle shafts together wit the oil boots.

3. Remove the nuts retaining the cover and remove the cover and gasket.

4. Remove the snap-ring from the mainshaft bearing.

5. Compress the spring washer in the countershaft and remove the snap-ring from the countershaft.

6. Remove the detent ball spring cover and gasket for the shift control rods. Remove the three ball springs and balls.

7. Remove the two ball bearings from the mainshaft and countershaft.

8. Remove the nuts attaching the transmission housing to the main case and lift the case off the studs.

9. Remove the screws retaining the gearshift forks and dogs to the rods. Remove the rods, forks, and dogs from their seats in the housing.

10. Remove the gear selector and engagement lever support.

11. Remove the gasket between the maincase and the housing.

12. Remove the nut securing the reverse gearshaft retaining plate and remove the plate and the reverse gearshaft.

13. Install the bearing (?) ...[illegible] into the camshaft case, and ...[illegible] transmission case. ...[illegible] tip of the cover bearing race for the differential to ...[illegible] into the case.

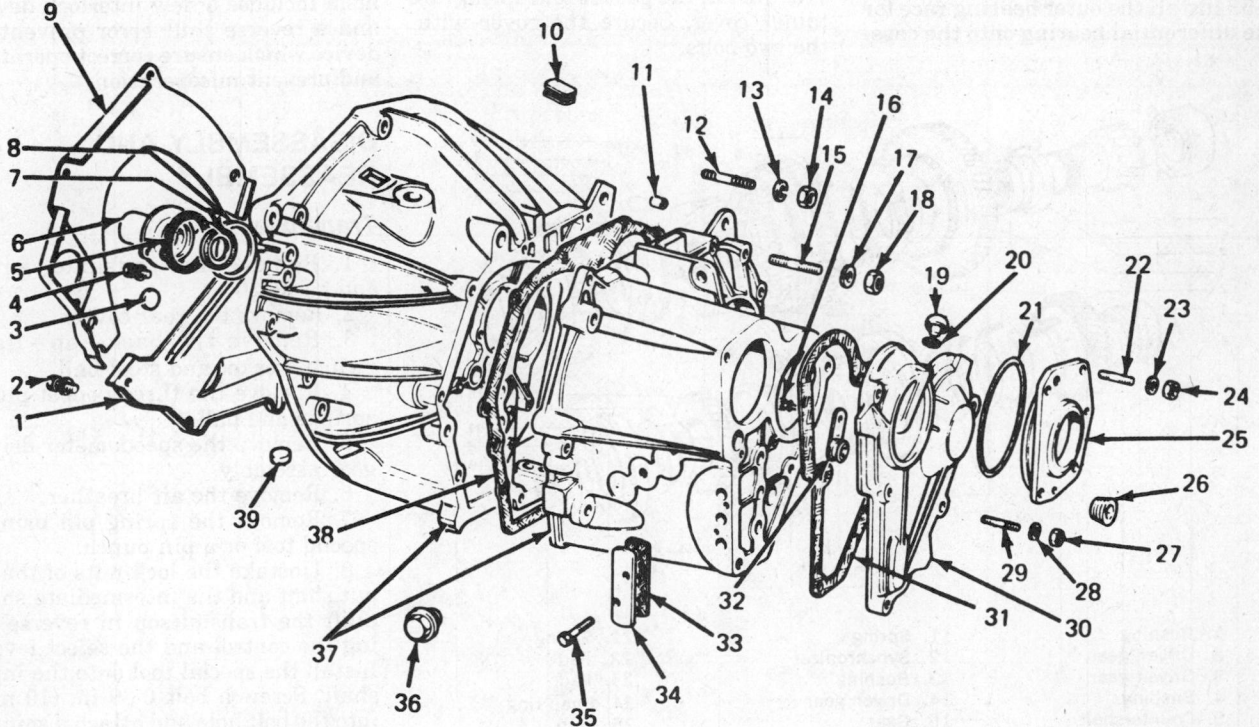

1. Cover	6. Cover	11. Dowel	16. Bolt and washer	21. Seal	26. Plug	31. Gasket	36. Plug
2. Bolt and washer	7. Seal	12. Stud	17. Lockwasher	22. Stud	27. Nut	32. Magnet	37. Case
3. Plug	8. Plug	13. Lockwasher	18. Nut	23. Lockwasher	28. Lockwasher	33. Gasket	38. Gasket
4. Bolt and washer	9. Cover	14. Nut	19. Vent	24. Nut	29. Stud	34. Cover	39. Plug
5. Gasket	10. Plug	15. Stud	20. Gasket	25. Flange	30. Cover	35. Bolt	

Transaxle case assembly

13. Remove the mainshaft and countershaft assemblies together with the differential assembly.

14. Remove the screw retaining the shift lever and remove the gear shift control rod.

ASSEMBLY

1. Clean all of the parts with solvent and check the maincase, housing and cover for cracks and wear or damage to the bearing seats. Check all of the seals for deterioration or wear. Check all shafts for chipping or excessive wear. Check the splines for wear or damage.

Check and make sure that the sliding sleeve hubs for the engagement of first/second and third/fourth gears are not nicked. Check the sleeve sliding surface.

Check the synchronizer rings for signs of deterioration on the inside surface and on the teeth that mesh with the sliding sleeves. The rings must not be loose in their gear seat.

If splined parts do not slide easily and smoothly, remove the cause with a very fine file or replace the defective parts.

2. Install the bearing for the countershaft into the clutch cover end for the transmission case.

3. Install the outer bearing race for the differential bearing onto the case.

4. Install the gear shift control rod in the housing with the spring, gasket, cover, and boot. Next install the control lever.

5. Install the differential assembly in the housing.

6. Install the countershaft assembly in the housing.

7. Install the mainshaft assembly in the housing.

8. Install the reverse gearshaft with its gasket in the housing. Secure the reverse gearshaft assembly with the plate and nut.

9. Install the gasket onto the housing mating surface.

10. Make sure that the gear selector and engagement lever is sealed on the control lever attached to the gear control rod. Install the support for the selector and engagement lever on the housing. Secure the support with the nut.

11. Install the rod detent rollers in their seats on the support.

12. Install the gear selector rods, forks, and dogs.

13. Install the transmission case on the housing.

14. Secure the two halves of the transmission case together with the washers and nuts.

15. Install the three detent balls and springs in the transmission case.

16. Install the gasket and spring retainer cover. Secure the cover with the two bolts.

17. Install the bearing on the countershaft. Install the two spring washers and snap-ring on the countershaft. Install the snap-ring on the mainshaft.

18. Install the gasket and cover on the transmission.

19. Set the differential bearing.

20. Install the clutch release fork lever and sliding sleeve.

TYPE 30

4 Speed Transaxle Model KM 200 Chrysler Corp./ Mitsubishi

KM 201, KM 206 and KM 210 are five speed models basically the same as the four speed model KM 200. All three transaxles have a large diameter, large capacity synchronizer which, combined with improved shift control mechanism, reduces shift operation force and gives comfortable shift feeling. The shift control mechanism includes a new interlock device and a reverse shift error prevention device which ensure correct operation and prevent misoperation.

DISASSEMBLY AND REASSEMBLY

Transaxle

1. Remove the transaxle switch and gasket.

2. Remove the rear cover.

3. Remove the back—up—light switch, gasket and steel ball.

4. Remove the three poppet plugs, springs and balls.

5. Remove the speedometer driven gear assembly.

6. Remove the air breather.

7. Remove the spring pin using a special tool or a pin punch.

8. Unstake the lock nuts of the input shaft and the intermediate shaft. Shift the transmisson in reverse using the control and the select levers. Install the special tool onto the input shaft. Screw a bolt 0.39 in. (10 mm) into the bolt hole and attach a spinner handle to the special tool. Remove the lock nut using the bolt as a spinner handle stopper.

9. Remove the 5th. speed synchronizer assembly and shift fork.

10. Remove the synchronizer ring and the 5th. speed gear.

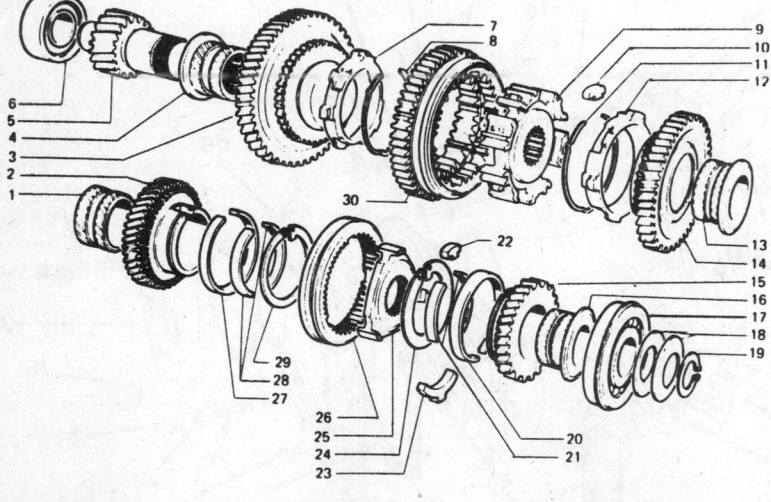

1. Bushing	11. Spring	21. Spring
2. Driven gear	12. Synchronizer	22. Pad
3. Driven gear	13. Bushing	23. Pad
4. Bushing	14. Driven gear	24. Snap ring
5. Countershaft	15. Gear	25. Hub
6. Bearing	16. Bushing	26. Sleeve
7. Synchronizer	17. Bearing	27. Synchronizer
8. Spring	18. Spring washer	28. Spring
9. Hub	19. Snap ring	29. Snap ring
10. Pad	20. Synchronizer	30. Sleeve

Drive gear assembly on countershaft

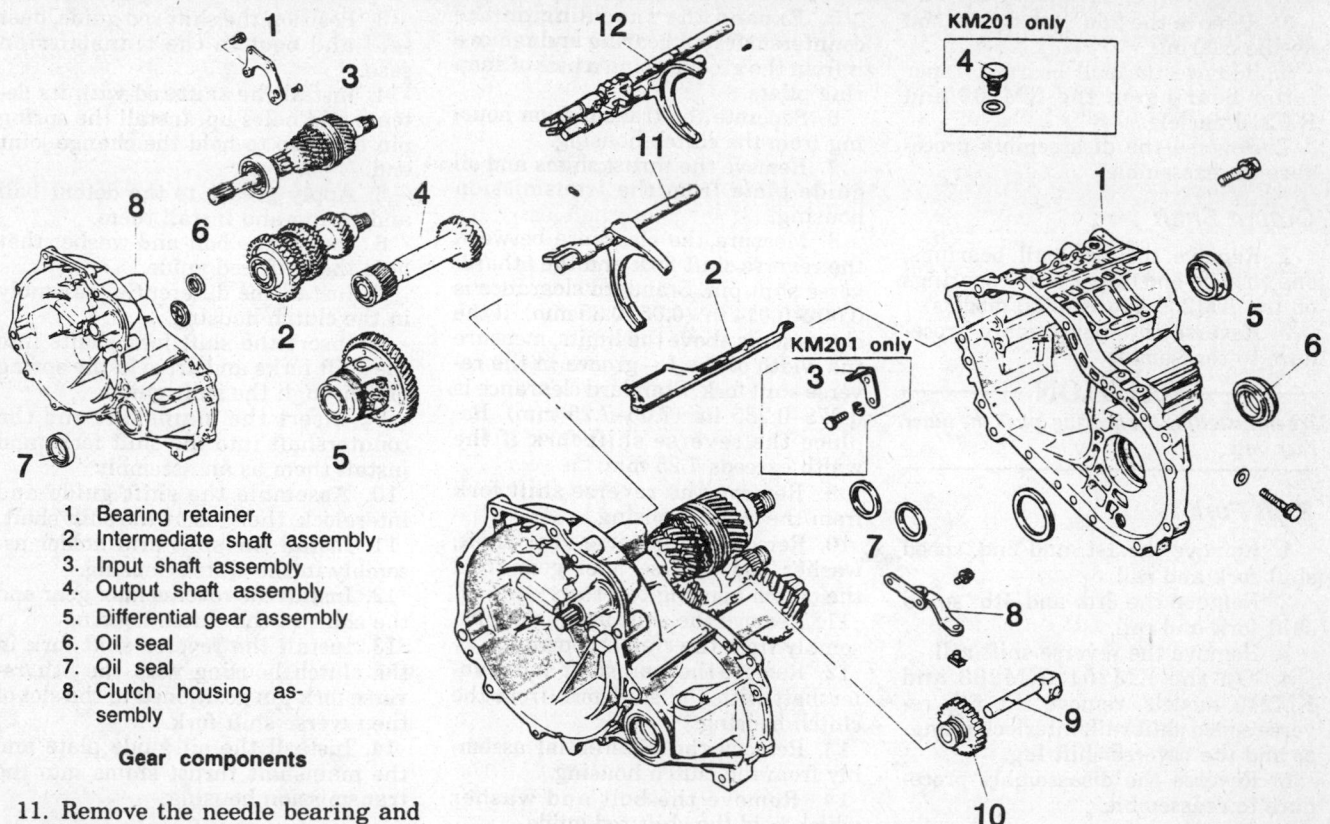

1. Bearing retainer
2. Intermediate shaft assembly
3. Input shaft assembly
4. Output shaft assembly
5. Differential gear assembly
6. Oil seal
7. Oil seal
8. Clutch housing assembly

Gear components

11. Remove the needle bearing and the bearing sleeve.

12. Remove the dished washer, roller bearing and the 5th. speed intermediate gear.

13. Reverse the idler gear shaft bolt and remove the bolt and gasket.

14. Seperate the transmission case from the clutch housing assembly.

15. Remove the oil guide from the transmission case assembly.

16. On the KM201 model, remove the bolt, spring washer and stopper bracket. Remove the restrict ball assembly and gasket.

17. Remove the outer ring and oil seal from the transmission case.

18. Remove the three spacers. Remove the shift lever assembly and the lever shoe.

19. Remove the reverse idler gear and shaft.

20. Using the special tool or a pin punch, remove the spring pins.

21. Shift the 1st. and 2nd. speed shift fork to the 2nd. speed. Shift the 3rd. and 4th. fork to the 4th. speed and remove the shift rail assembly.

22. Remove the bearing retainer. Lift up the input shaft assembly and remove the intermediate gear assembly.

23. Remove the input shaft, output shaft and the differential gear assembly.

24. Remove the oil guide and the two oil seals from the clutch housing.

25. Reverse the disassembly procedure to reassemble.

1. Transmission case
2. Oil guide
3. Stopper bracket
4. Restrict ball assembly
5. Outer ring
6. Oil seal
7. Spacer
8. Reverse shift lever assembly
9. Reverse idler gear shaft
10. Reverse idler gear
11. Shift rail assembly
12. Shift rail assembly

Transaxle Assembly

— **CAUTION** —

Use NEW seals and spring pins where required.

Input Shaft

1. Remove the snap ring and the front bearing, using the proper tool.

2. Remove the rear bearing, spacer and the 4th. speed gear.

3. Remove the needle bearing and sleeve.

4. Remove the synchronizer ring and spring.

5. Remove the 3rd. and 4th. speed synchronizer sleeve, key and hub. Remove the synchronizer ring.

6. Remove the 3rd. speed gear and the needle bearing.

7. Reverse the disassembly procedure to reassemble.

— **CAUTION** —

When installing the synchronizer springs, make sure that the front and rear ones are not faced in the same direction.

NOTE: When installing the synchronizer assembly, seat the three keys correctly in respective grooves of the ring. After installation of the synchronizer assembly, check that the 3rd. speed gear rotates smoothly.

Intermediate Gear

1. Remove the snap ring, ball bearing (taper roller bearing on the KM206 and KM210 models) and the bearing sleeve.

— **CAUTION** —

Do not reuse the bearing removed from the shaft. Replace the inner and outer races of the taper roller bearing as a set.

2. Remove the 1st. speed gear and needle bearing.

3. Remove the synchronizer ring and spring.

4. Remove the 1st. and 2nd. speed synchronizer sleeve, key and hub. Remove the synchronizer ring.

5. Remove the 2nd. speed gear and needle bearing.

6. Remove the ball bearing (taper roller bearing on the KM206 and KM210 models).

7. Reverse the disassembly procedure to reassemble.

Output Shaft

1. Remove the two ball bearings, one on each end (taper roller bearings on the KM206 and KM210 models).

2. Reverse the disassembly procedure to reassemble.

———— CAUTION ————

When Installing the bearing, push the inner race only.

Shift Fork

1. Remove the 1st. and 2nd. speed shift fork and rail.

2. Remove the 3rd. and 4th. speed shift fork and rail.

3. Remove the reverse shift rail.

4. On the KM201, KM206 and KM210 models, remove the 5th./reverse speed shift rail, interlock plunger and the reverse shift lug.

5. Reverse the disassembly procedure to reassemble.

TYPE 31

5 Speed Transaxle Model C34P Acura/Sterling

DISASSEMBLY

1. Remove the back—up light switch.

2. Remove the ball spring setting screw and washer. Remove the spring and detent ball from the transmission housing with a magnet.

3. Remove the reverse idler shaft bolt and the 8mm bolt from the transmission housing.

4. Remove the 10mm bolts attaching the transmission housing to the clutch housing. Remove the 32mm sealing bolt.

5. Expand the snap ring on the countershaft ball bearing and remove it from the groove using a pair of snap ring pliers.

6. Seperate the transmission housing from the clutch housing.

7. Remove the thrust shims and oil guide plate from the transmission housing.

8. Measure the clearance between the reverse shift fork and the 5th./reverse shift pin. Standard clearance is 0.002–0.014 in. (0.05–0.35 mm). If the clearance is above the limits, measure the width of the L—groove in the reverse shift fork. Standard clearance is 0.278–0.285 in. (7.05–7.25 mm). Replace the reverse shift fork if the width exceeds 7.25 mm.

9. Remove the reverse shift fork from the clutch housing.

10. Remove the reverse idler shaft, washer and reverse idler gear from the clutch housing together.

11. Remove the shift arm holder assembly from the clutch housing.

12. Remove the mainshaft and countershaft with the shift fork from the clutch housing.

13. Remove the differential assembly from the clutch housing.

14. Remove the bolt and washer which hold the shift rod guide.

15. Remove the detent ball and spring from the clutch housing.

16. Remove the shift rod and boot from the clutch housing.

17. Remove the spring pin, clip and shift joint end from the shift rod.

18. Remove the shift fork shaft by removing the spring pin from the 5th./reverse shift guide.

19. Remove the two bolts and the retaining plate from the clutch housing. Remove the magnetic plate.

20. Remove the needle bearing with a bearing puller.

ASSEMBLY

1. Position the oil guide plate and new needle bearing (holes facing up) in the bore of the clutch housing. Drive in the bearing using the proper tool and install the retaining plate.

2. Remove the mainshaft oil seal from the clutch side of the clutch housing. Drive the new seal in from the transmission side of the housing.

3. Position the shift rod guide, dust seal and boot in the transmission case.

4. Install the shift rod with its detents and holes up. Install the spring pin and clip to hold the change joint end.

5. Apply grease to the detent ball and spring and install them.

6. Install the bolt and washer that hold the shift rod guide.

7. Install the differential assembly in the clutch housing.

8. Insert the shift fork shafts into the shift forks and drive in the spring pin through the shift guide.

9. Insert the mainshaft and the countershaft into the shift forks and install them as an assembly.

10. Assemble the shift guide and interelock, then insert the shift shaft.

11. Install the shift arm holder assembly in the clutch housing.

12. Install the reverse idler gear and the shaft in the clutch housing.

13. Install the reverse shift fork in the clutch housing with the 5th./reverse fork pin positioned in the slot of the reverse shift fork.

14. Instasll the oil guide plate and the mainshaft thrust shims into the transmission housing.

NOTE: If installing two shims, mstagger the end gaps 180 degrees apart.

15. Apply sealant to the mating surfaces of transmission housing and the clutch housing.

16. Install the dowl pins on the clutch housing and mount the transmission housing to it. Install the snap ring to the countershaft ball bearing. Torque the bolts to 33 ft. lbs. (45 Nm).

17. Install the 32 mm sealing bolt.

18. Install the reverse idler shaft bolt and hook.

19. Install the back—up light switch.

20. Install the steel ball 0.375 in. (9.5 mm), spring, new washer and setting screw.

NOTE: Be sure to install the 9.5mm steel ball. It is different in size from the shift rod steel ball. 21.

Install the transmission in the vehicle, refill with fluid and adjust the clutch pedal free play.

Strut Overhaul 31

STRUT SERVICE AND REPAIR

MacPherson struts are appearing on the front (and rear) wheels of more and more cars. The strut design takes up less room in the engine compartment, compared to a conventional upper and lower arm with shock absorber arrangement. The trend toward smaller, lighter and more efficient vehicles mandates the use of a strut suspension to permit more room for engine accessories and front wheel drive components.

Strut Suspension Design

In a conventional front suspension, the wheel is attached to a spindle, which is in turn connected to upper and lower control arms through upper and lower ball joints. A coil spring between the control arms (sometimes on top of the upper arm) supports the weight of the vehicle and a shock absorber controls rebound and dampens oscillations.

In a MacPherson strut type suspension, the strut performs a shock dampening function like a shock absorber, but unlike a conventional shock absorber the strut is a structural part of the vehicle's suspension.

The strut assembly usually contains a spring seat to retain the coil spring that supports the vehicle's weight. The shock absorber is built into the body of the strut housing. The strut is normally attached at the bottom to the lower control arm and at

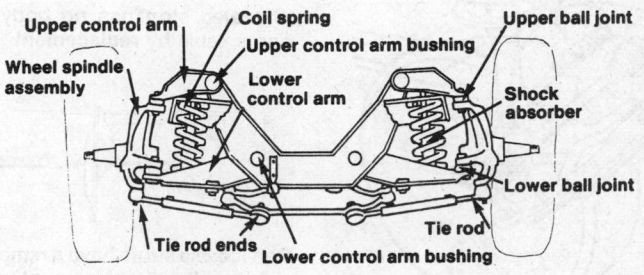

Conventional upper and lower arm suspension

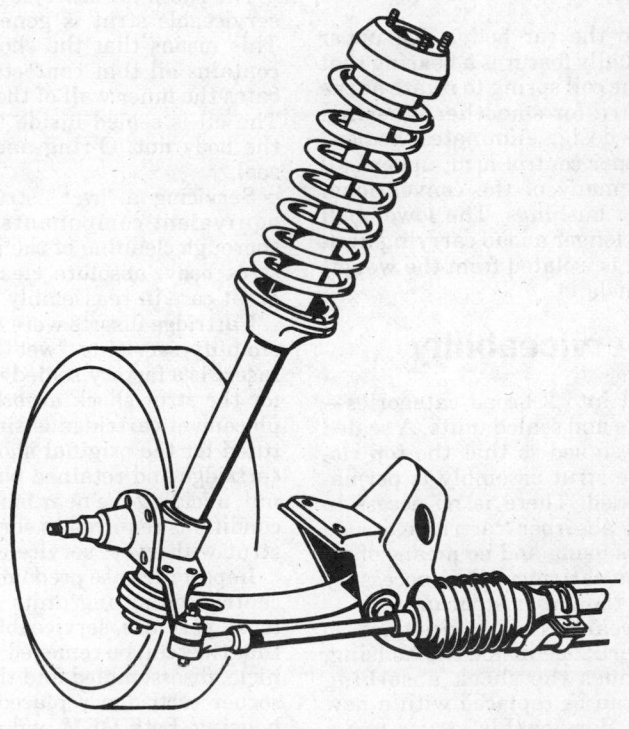

Strut with concentric coil spring (rear wheel drive)

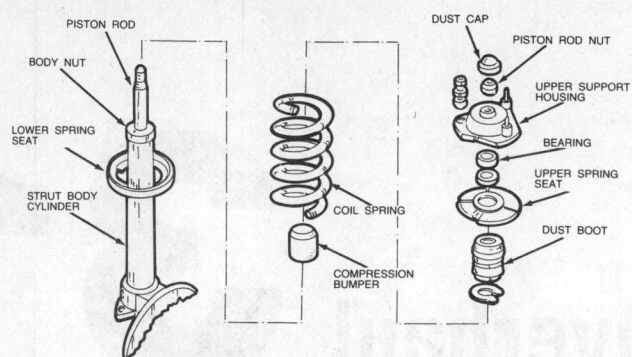

Exploded view of a typical strut

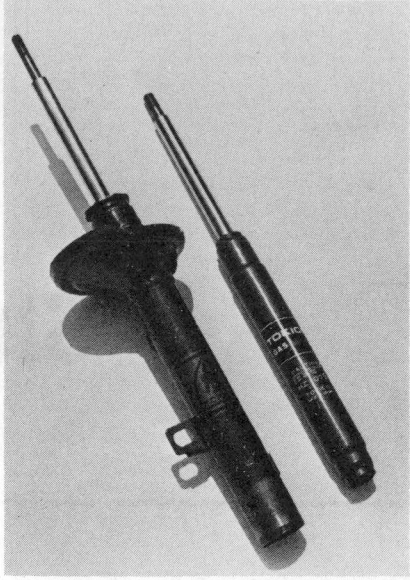

A replacement sealed strut on the left, compared to a replacement strut cartridge used on serviceable type struts on the right

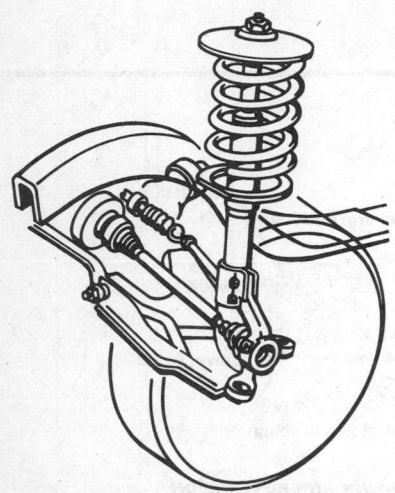

Strut with concentric coil spring (front wheel drive)

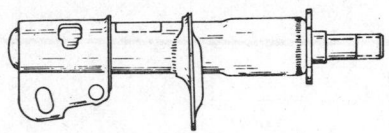

A sealed strut has no body nut and is serviceable by replacement

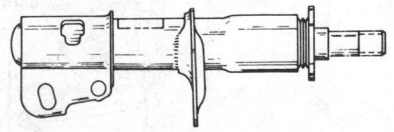

Serviceable struts have a removeable body nut to allow replacement of the strut cartridge

the top to the car body. The upper mount usually features a bearing that permits the coil spring to rotate as the wheels turn for smoother steering. The entire design eliminates the need for the upper control arm, upper ball joint and many of the conventional suspension bushings. The lower ball joint is no longer a load carrying unit, because it is isolated from the weight of the vehicle.

Serviceability

Struts fall into 2 broad categories — serviceable and sealed units. A sealed strut is designed so that the top closure of the strut assembly is permanently sealed. There is no access to the shock absorber cartridge inside the strut housing and no means of replacing the cartridge. It is necessary to replace the entire strut unit.

A serviceable strut is designed so that the cartridge inside the housing, that provides the shock absorbing function, can be replaced with a new cartridge. Serviceable struts use a threaded body nut in place of a sealed cap to retain the cartridge.

The shock absorber device inside a serviceable strut is generally "wet." This means that the shock absorber contains oil that contacts and lubricates the inner wall of the strut body. The oil is sealed inside the strut by the body nut, O-ring and piston rod seal.

Servicing a "wet" strut with the equivalent components involves a thorough cleaning of the inside of the strut body, absolute cleanliness and great care in reassembly.

Cartridge inserts were developed to simplify servicing "wet" struts. The insert is a factory sealed replacement for the strut shock absorber. The replacement cartridge is simply substituted for the original shock absorber cartridge and retained with the body nut, avoiding the near laboratory-like conditions required to service a "wet" strut with "wet" service components.

Import cars use predominantly concentric coil spring units and, for the most part are serviceable, meaning that they can be removed from the vehicle, disassembled and the shock absorber cartridge replaced in the old housing. Both OEM and aftermarket replacement cartriges can be used in these struts if they are serviceable.

Exceptions to the serviceable struts include some of the later model import cars, but even on these cars OEM struts can be replaced with aftermarket sealed strut assemblies.

WHEEL ALIGNMENT

It is not always necessary to re-align the wheels after struts are serviced. If care is taken matchmarking affected components and in reassembling, alignment may be unaffected. However, if wheels were not in proper alignment prior to service, or if the entire strut assembly was replaced, a wheel alignment check should be made. Generally, only camber is adjustable, and then only within a narrow range.

Do not attempt to bend components to correct wheel alignment.

Since the majority of OEM struts are serviced by replacement, most manufacturers recommend wheel alignment following strut replacement.

On most serviceable import struts, the position of the upper bearing plate or lower mount can be matchmarked and wheel alignment will be maintained during reassembly.

Tools

Without the right tools, a strut job will take longer than necessary and can be dangerous.

A normal selection of hand tools such as open end and box wrenches, sockets, pliers, screwdrivers and hammers are necessary to work on struts.

Extensions and universal joints will help reach tight spots. Be sure to have both metric and inch-sized wrenches on hand.

In addition to the normal handtools, some sort of spanner is necessary to remove the body nut on serviceable struts. Sometimes a pipe wrench can be used successfully. Also a strut vise should be used to avoid damage to the strut housing during the overhaul procedure.

Strut and cartridge replacement requires a spring compressor.

Makeshift tools for compressing coil springs—threaded rod, chains, wire or other methods—should never be used. The coil spring is under tremendous compression and can fly off causing personal injury and damage to equipment. Use only a good quality spring compressor such as described below.

Economy, or manual, spring compressors are the least expensive but more time consuming to use. Angle hooks grasp the spring coils and must be compressed with a wrench. For those who service struts infrequently, this is probably the wisest investment for purchase.

CAUTION

When using an "economy type" spring compressor be certain to install J-Bolts or U-Bolts around the coil spring-to-the-tool. This is to prevent the tool from slipping off the spring and causing personal injury.

Other manual spring compressors (jaws type) are faster to operate, have a more positive gripping action and can be used on or off the car. These types are probably not cost effective for the do-it-yourselfer, but can be rented from auto supply stores for single-time use. These are also safer to use than the "economy type" spring compressors.

This type of spanner wrench comes with adapter inserts for various applications of body nuts. A torque wrench can be used with this spanner for tightening the strut body nut

MAINTAINING WHEEL ALIGNMENT

The location and method of adjusting wheel alignment determines the components that must be match-marked to maintain wheel alignment. There are 4 basic methods of adjusting wheel alignment. Almost all cars use one of these or a slight variation.

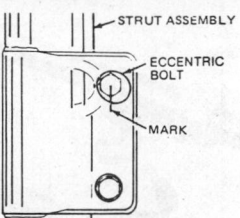

Mark the eccentric (camber adjusting bolt) relative to the clevis mounting bracket.

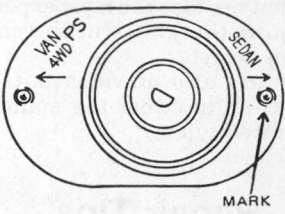

Mark the mounting stud that faces the front of the vehicle. This type of bracket is reversible for varying applications.

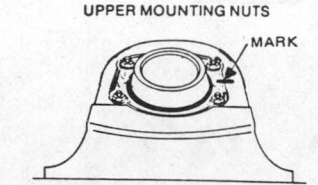

Mark the upper support housing relative to the inner fender before removing the strut from the upper mount.

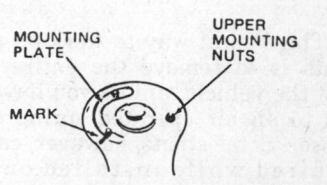

Mark the location of the mounting plate relative to the location on the inner fender.

A simple spanner wrench designed for use with body nuts equipped with recessed lugs. A pipe wrench is a frequent substitute

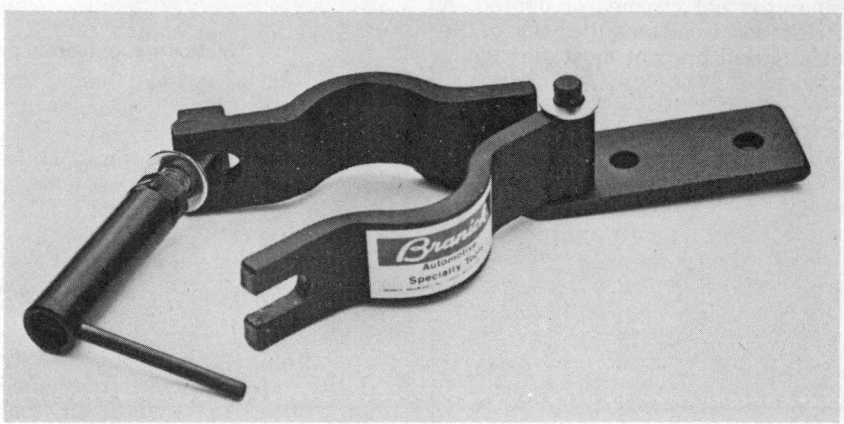

A strut vise should be used to prevent damage to the strut housing during overhaul. It may be placed in a bench vise or mounted to a workbench

For high volume work, compressors that are pneumatically or hydraulically operated are best. Air operated compressors are suitable for all types of struts (through use of adaptors), are lightweight and can be used on or off the vehicle. Bench mounted hydraulically operated units are probably the safest, but are also the most expensive and require that the strut be removed from the vehicle.

There are also universal kits that fit all struts in either the manual or air operated types.

Repair Tips

• Make sure you have all the tools you'll need. NEVER IMPROVISE A SPRING COMPRESSOR.

• Normally both front struts should be repaired or replaced at the same time.

• The easiest way to work on most struts is to remove the entire unit from the vehicle, unless you have access to an air operated spring compressor. Some struts, however, can be repaired while installed on the vehicle.

• Always read the instructions packaged with any replacement parts. In particular, note whether the body nut is supplied new or re-used.

• Mark the position(s) of any bearing plate nuts or cam bolts to assure proper alignment after installation.

• Be sure to protect the rubber boot on the drive axle of front wheel drive cars.

• If necessary to remove the brake caliper, do not let the caliper hang by the brake hose. Suspend the caliper from a wire hook or rope.

• Be careful in clamping a strut in a vise. Special strut vises are available to hold struts, but are not absolutely necessary if care is used to be sure the housing is not crushed or dented. A block of soft wood on either side of the housing will prevent most damage.

• Use a spring compressor to relieve tension from the spring. Be sure to clean and lubricate the screw threads, particularly on hand operated (manual) spring compressors.

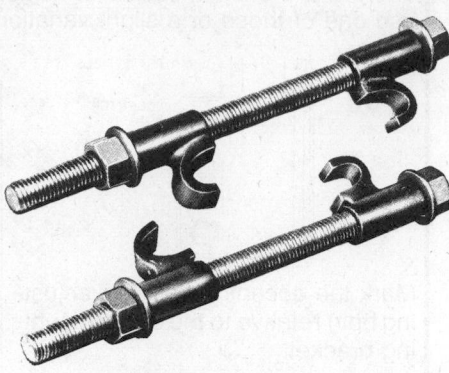

An economical manual spring compressor

"Jaws" type spring compressor

Stationary, universal pneumatic spring compressor

Some springs have a special coating that should not be scuffed.

• If you are replacing the strut cartridge, clean the inside of the strut housing and the body nut threads before replacing the oil and installing a new cartridge.

• Be sure to use OEM quality fasteners any time a fastener is replaced.

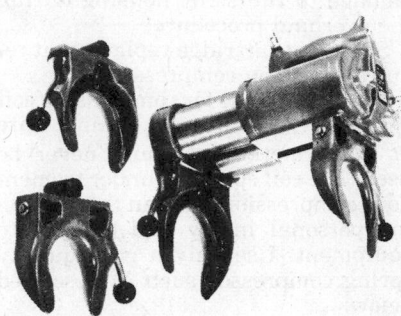

Lightweight, air operated, portable spring compressor can be used on or off the vehicle. Extra shoes are available to handle all strut applications

Mark the position of the attachments that control wheel alignment. See Maintaining Wheel Alignment earlier in this section

STRUT OVERHAUL

Following is a typical overhaul procedure of a serviceable MacPherson strut, after having removed the strut from the vehicle. The vehicle should be firmly and safely supported on jackstands. If it is necessary, to separate the brake line from the strut for strut removal, the brakes will have to be bled after reinstallation. Examine the strut assembly for damage, dented strut body, spring seat, broken or missing strut mounting parts. Any of these will require replacement of the complete assembly. Also inspect other suspension components for wear or damage. See the manufacturer's car section for specific MacPherson strut removal and installation procedures.

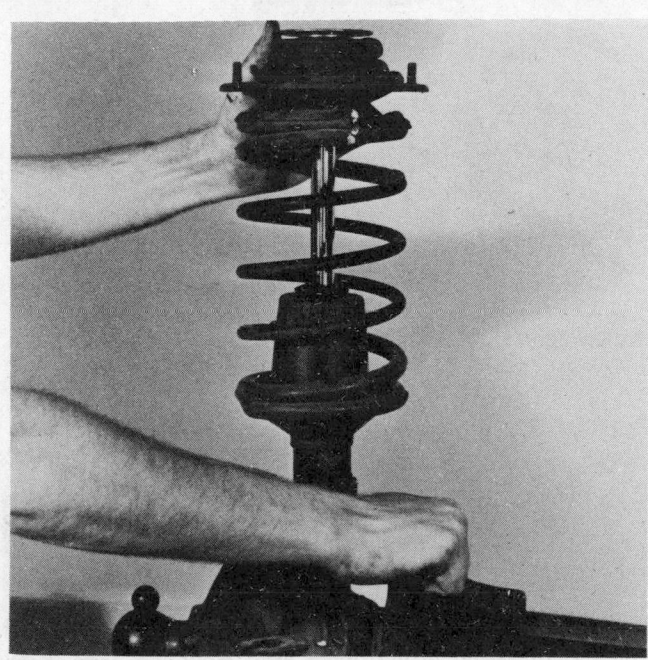

Step 1. **To make service easier, clamp the strut in a strut vise. The strut vise is designed to clamp the strut tight without damage to the strut cylinder. It is very handy for strut work and can be used in a bench vise or mounted to a workbench**

Step 3. **Position the spring compressor on the spring. Turn the load screw to open or close the compressor until the maximum number of spring coils can be engaged**

Step 2. **Matchmark the upper end of the coil spring and bearing plate to avoid confusion during reassembly**

Step 4. **Tighten the load screw until the coil spring is loose from the spring seat. There is no need to compress the spring further than this point**

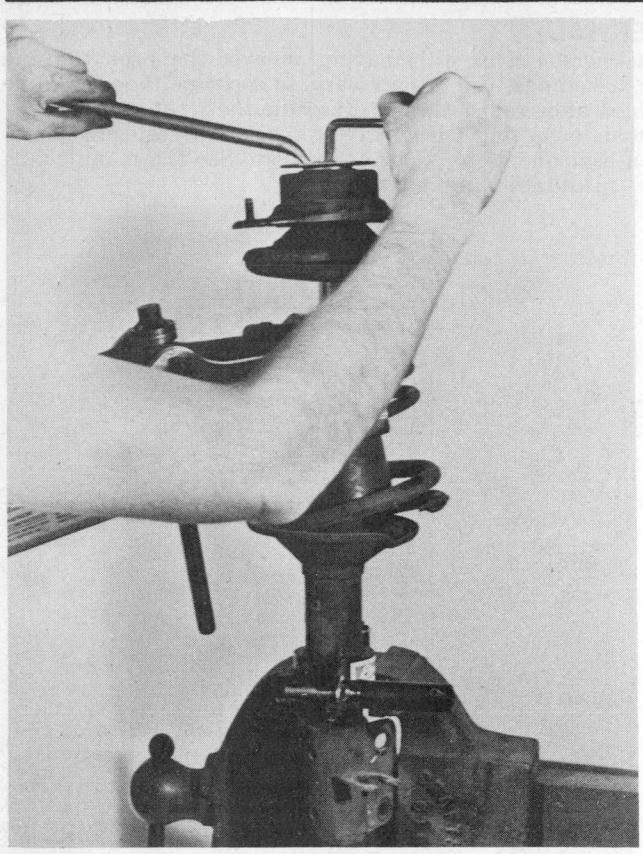

Step 5. Using an offset wrench and an Allen wrench, loosen the piston rod nut

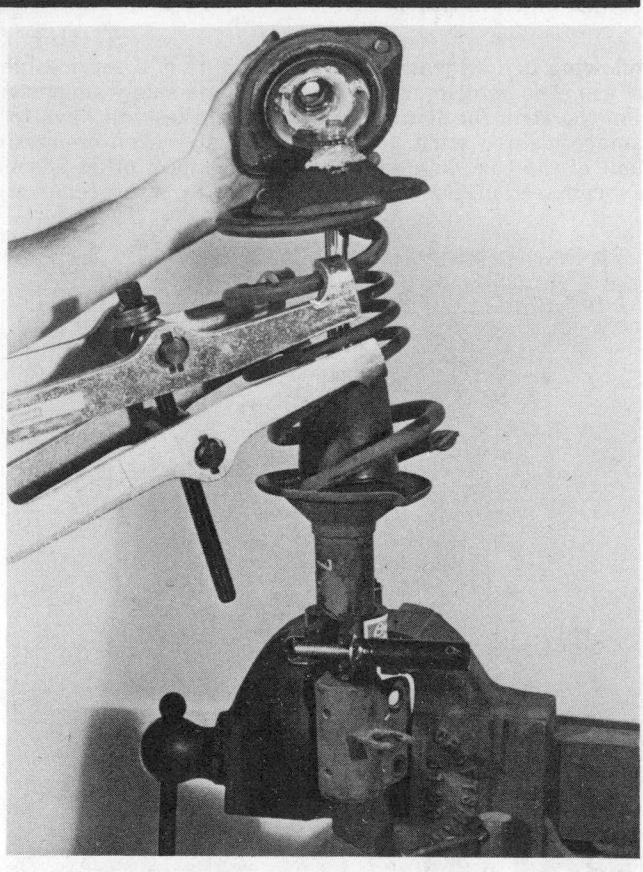

Step 7. Disassemble the upper strut mounting parts. Keep the mounting parts in order of their removal. They'll be reassembled in reverse order

Step 6. Remove the piston rod nut from the strut piston rod

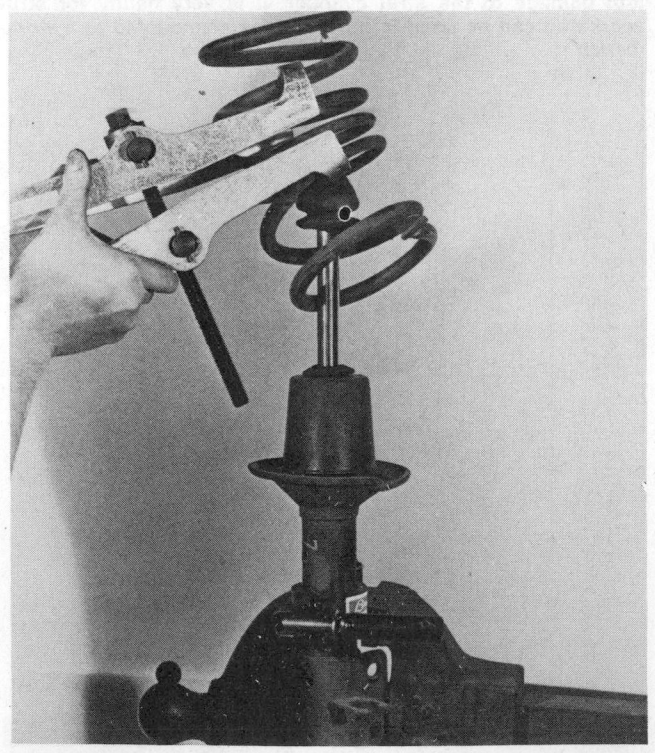

Step 8. Remove the coil spring and compressor from the strut. There is no need to remove the compressor from the coil spring

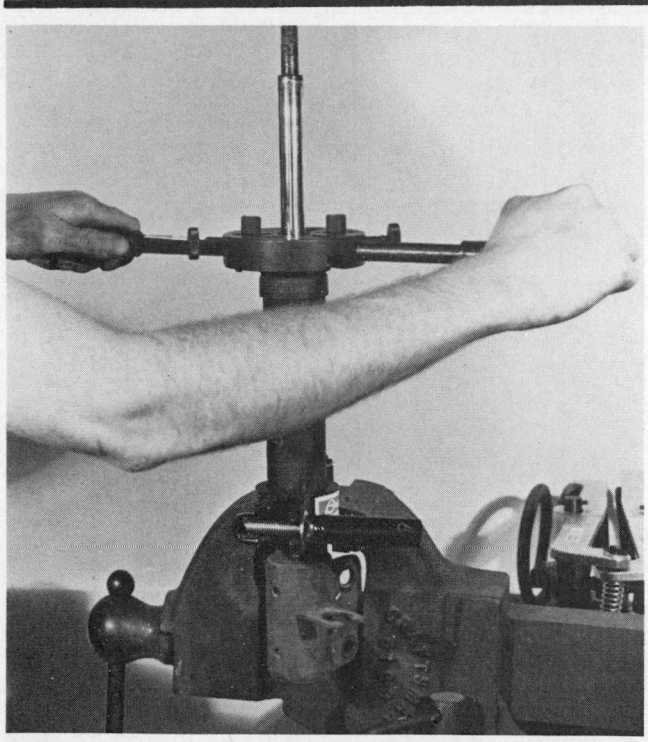

Step 9. **Use a spanner wrench or a pipe wrench to loosen the body nut**

Step 10. **Remove the body nut and discard if a new body nut came with the replacement cartridge. If not, save the body nut**

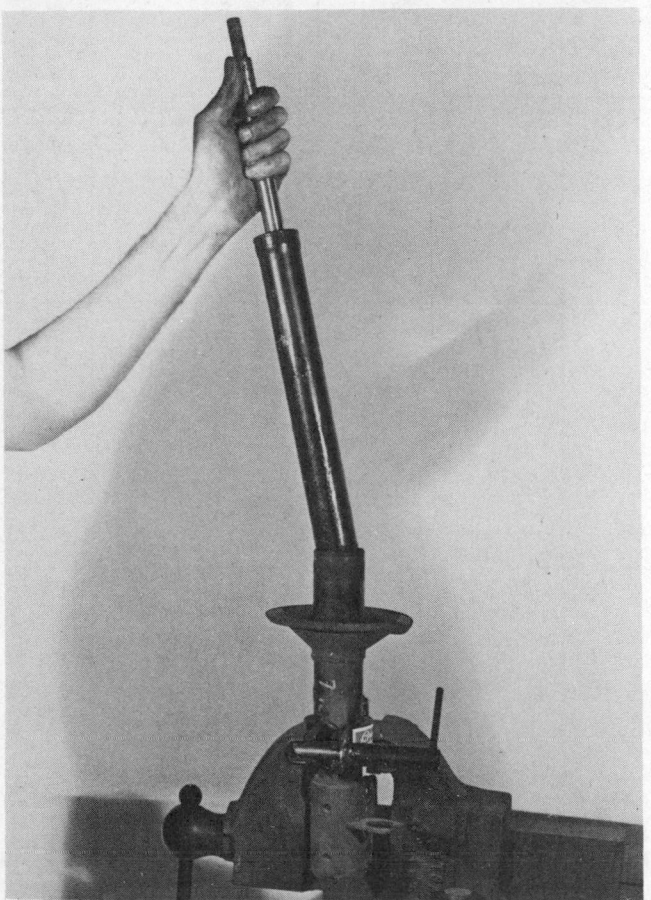

Step 11. **Grasp the piston rod and pull the cartridge out of the housing. Remove it slowly to avoid splashing oil. Be sure all pieces are removed from the housing**

Step 12. **Pour all of the strut fluid into a suitable container, clean the inside of the strut cylinder, and inspect the cylinder for dents and to insure that all loose parts have been remove from inside the strut body**

Step 13. **Refill the strut housing with approximately one once of the original oil or fresh oil. The oil helps dissipate internal cartridge heat during operation and results in a much cooler running, longer lasting unit. Do not overfill with oil—otherwise the oil may leak at the body nut after it expands when heated**

Step 14. **Insert the new replacement strut cartridge into the strut body**

Step 15. **Insert any special bushings which should be included with the replacement cartridge**

Step 16. **Place the body nut on the strut housing and start it by hand. Be sure not to cross-thread it**

Step 17. **Tighten the body nut cap securely**

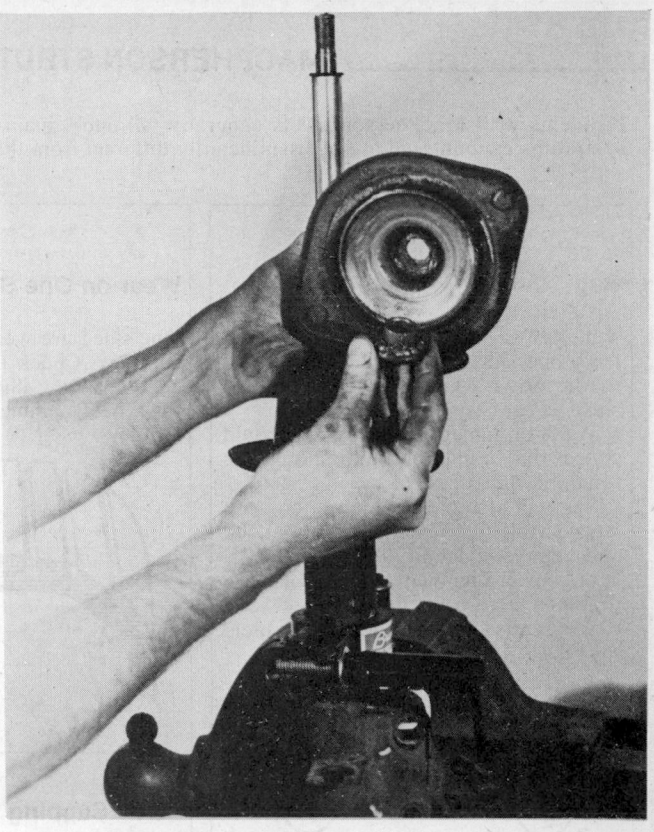

Step 19. **Repack the upper strut bearing with grease. Replace if excessive play is apparent**

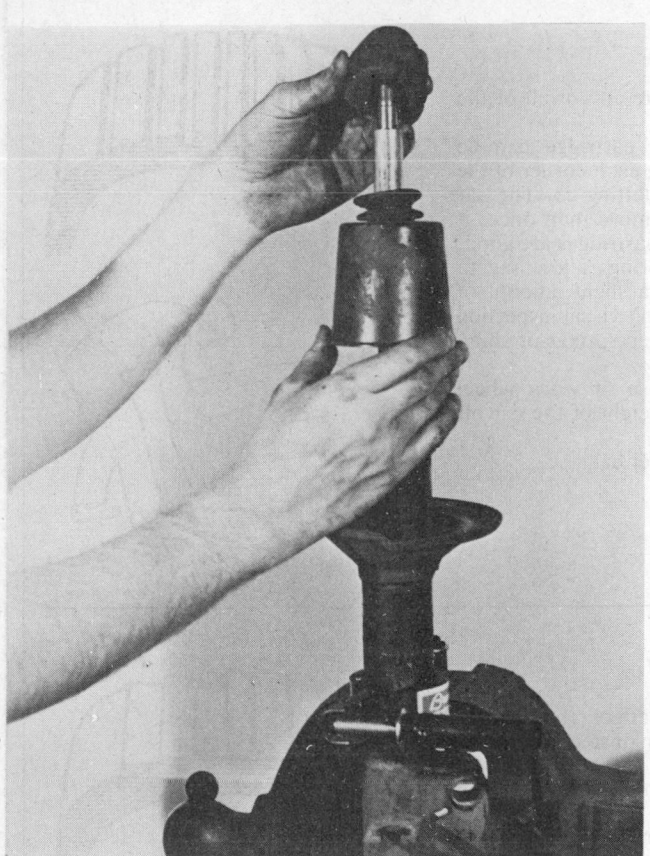

Step 18. **Inspect the upper strut mounting parts prior to reassembly. Replace any damaged components**

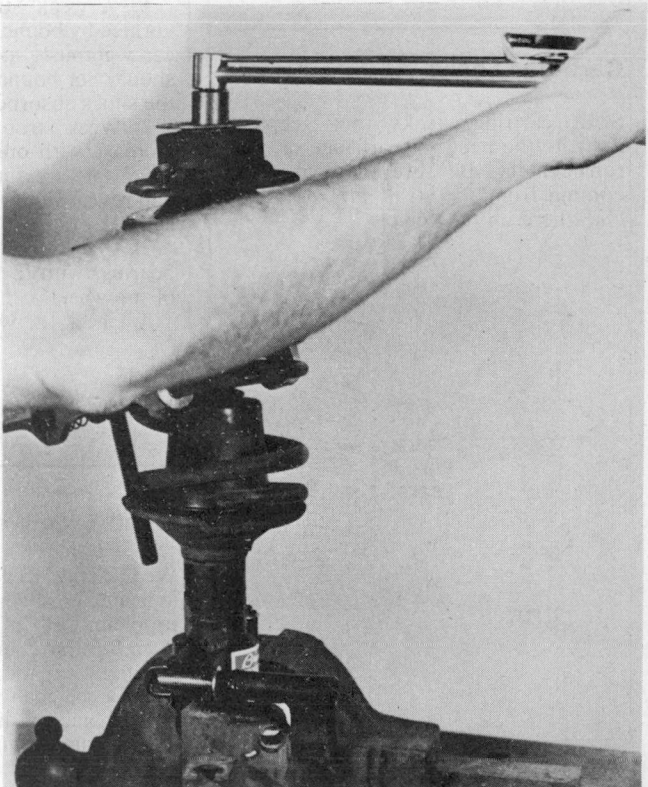

Step 20. **Re-assemble the coil spring and upper mounting parts in reverse order. Tighten the piston rod nut to specification and remove the spring compressor. Install the strut in the vehicle. See the car section for details**

--- **MACPHERSON STRUT PROBLEM DIAGNOSIS** ---

Problems with MacPherson struts generally fall into 3 main categories: suspension, tire wear and steering. In general, the symptoms encountered are not significantly different from those encountered on conventional suspensions.

Suspension

Sag

Vehicle "sag" is a visible tilt of the car from one side to the other or one end to the other while parked on a level surface.

Weak or damaged strut springs could cause this condition and should be repaired immediately.

Sag will also cause steering and tire wear problems to be more pronounced and vehicle instability on rough roads. Front wheel alignment will not solve the problem.

Weak strut springs increase vehicle sag. See "Tire Cupping".

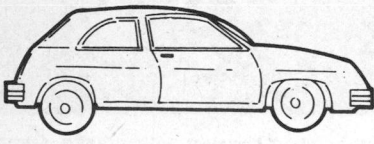

Cartridge Leaks

Strut cartridge leaks (not seepage) indicate the need for cartridge or strut replacement. Be sure the leakage is coming from the strut, and not from elsewhere on the vehicle.

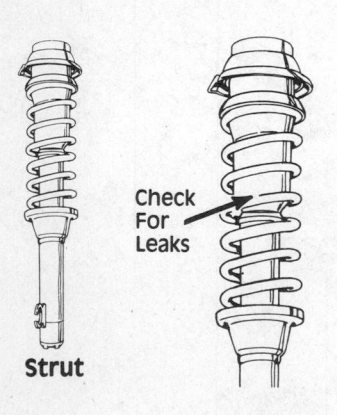

Check For Leaks

Strut

Abnormal Tire Wear

Wear on One Side

One sided tire wear indicates incorrect camber. Check the causes in the accompanying illustration and be sure the wheel alignment is correct.

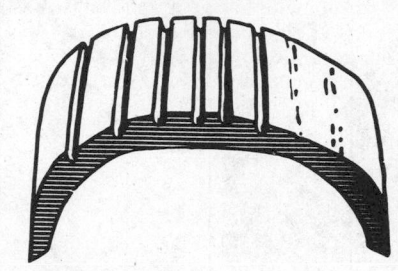

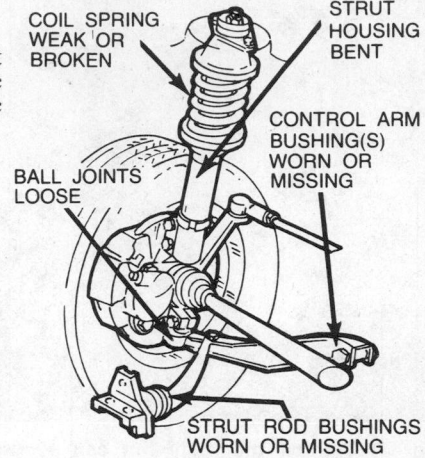

COIL SPRING WEAK OR BROKEN

STRUT HOUSING BENT

CONTROL ARM BUSHING(S) WORN OR MISSING

BALL JOINTS LOOSE

STRUT ROD BUSHINGS WORN OR MISSING

Tire "Cupping"

Cupped tires indicate any or all of the following problems.

1. A weak strut cartridge can be verified by bouncing each corner of the car vigorously and letting go. The car should not bounce more than once, if the shock absorber cartridges are good.

2. Weak strut springs allow sag to increase with only a slight amount of downward pressure. A visual inspection will reveal any broken springs or shiny spots.

3. Check for loose or worn wheel bearings with the weight of the car off of the wheel.

4. Check the wheel balance.

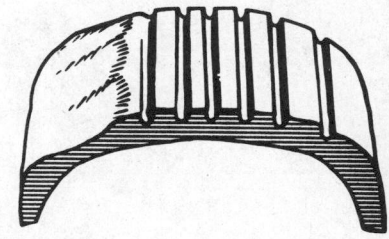

Tread Edge Wear

Wear along tread edges (feathering) indicates a suspension or steering system problem.

1. Strut rod bushings are worn or missing.

2. Tie rod end wear can be determined by grabbing the tie rod end firmly and forcing it up, down or sideways to check for lost motion.

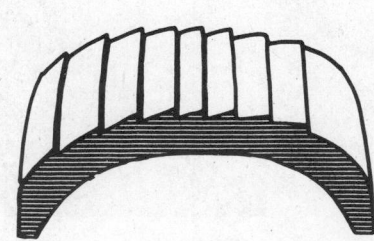

MACPHERSON STRUT PROBLEM DIAGNOSIS

Problems with MacPherson struts generally fall into 3 main categories: suspension, tire wear and steering. In general, the symptoms encountered are not significantly different from those encountered on conventional suspensions.

Steering

Tires

Both front tires should match and both rear tires should match. Be sure air pressure is correct.

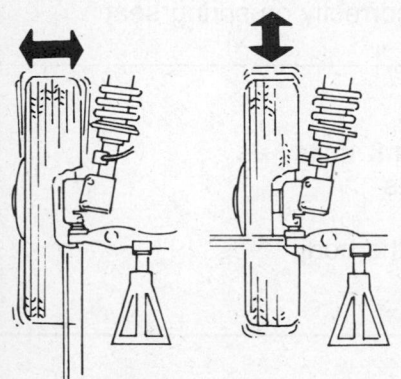

Strut Rod Bushings

Grasp the strut rod and shake it. Any noticeable play indicates excessive wear and need for parts replacement.

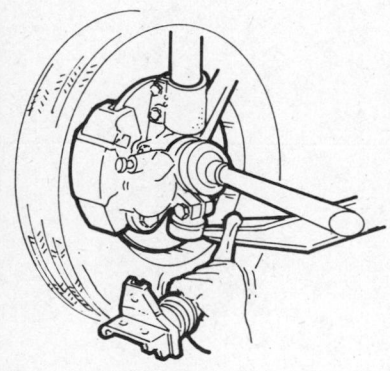

Ball Joints

Support the car under the frame or crossmember so that the jack does not interfere with the control arm. Rock the tire in and out and up and down. Excessive movement means that both ball joints should be replaced.

Struts with lower weight-carrying ball joints should be supported at the outer edge of the lower control arm. These vehicles usually have wear indicating ball joints that can be checked visually.

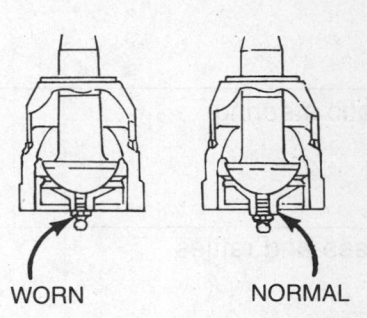

WORN   NORMAL

Stabilizer Bar Bushings

Check for worn bushings or lost motion with the vehicle level and the weight evenly distributed on all wheels.

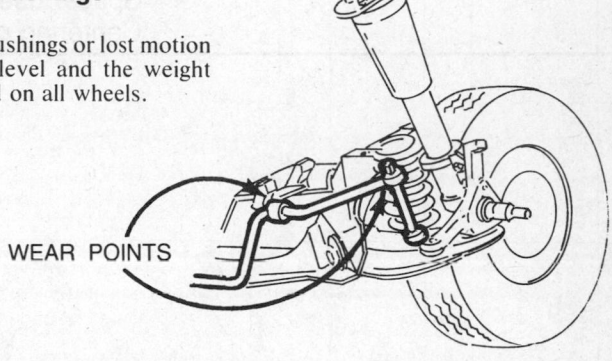

WEAR POINTS

Control Arm Bushings

Support the car under the frame or body and remove the weight from the wheel and control arm. Check for free-play in the bushings at the pivot point, using a pry bar.

NOTE: Some control arm bushings are serviceable only by replacing the entire arm.

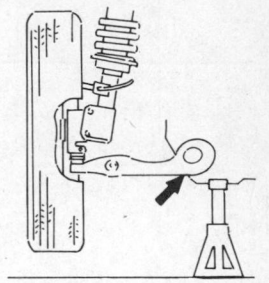

Strut Assembly

Check the strut assembly for cracks or dents in the housing. Look for worn, bent or loose piston rods or dents that will inhibit piston rod movement.

Steering Gear

Check for worn steering gear or loose or worn mounting bolts and bushings.

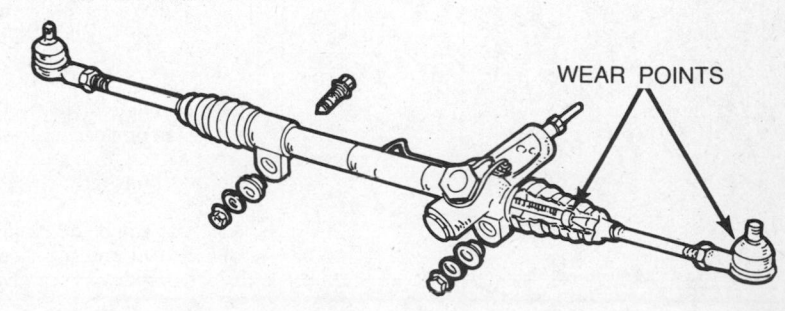

WEAR POINTS

ROAD TEST TROUBLESHOOTING

Following are possible solutions to common potential problems which might be noticed during the road test after strut service is completed. Many are not exclusively strut service related.

Problem	Correction

Brake pedal low or soft	Bleed brakes
	Check for leaks
	    Brake lines
	    Wheel cylinder
	    Caliper piston seal

Erratic steering	Check upper support housing components for proper assembly Check spring assembly right side up Check for spring helix riding correctly on spring seat Check wheel alignment

Noises and rattles	Check torques
	    Piston rod nut
	    Upper support housing nuts & bolts
	    Lower mounting nuts & bolts
	    Body nut
	Check cartridge assembly in the body
	    Spacer used
	    Centering collar used

BRAKE SYSTEM

Understanding the Brakes

HYDRAULIC SYSTEM

Basic Operating Principles

Hydraulic systems are used to actuate the brakes of all modern automobiles. The system transports the power required to force the frictional surfaces of the braking system together from the pedal to the individual brake units at each wheel. A hydraulic system is used for two reasons. First, fluid under pressure can be carried to all parts of an automobile by small hoses — some of which are flexible — without taking up significant amount of room or posing routing problems. Second, a great mechanical advantage can be given to the brake pedal end of the system, and the foot pressure required to actuate the brakes can be reduced by making the surface area of the master cylinder pistons smaller than that of any of the pistons in the wheel cylinders or calipers.

The master cylinder consists of a fluid reservoir and a double cylinder and piston assembly. Double type master cylinders are designed to separate two two-wheel braking systems hydraulically in case of a leak. The standard approach has been to utilize two separate two-wheel circuits; one for the front wheels and another for the rear wheels.

Most newer models now use a diagonally split system; i.e. one front wheel and the opposite rear wheel make up one braking circuit, while the remaining circuit consists of the other front wheel and its opposite side rear wheel.

Steel lines carry the brake fluid to a point on the vehicle's frame near each of the vehicle's wheels. The fluid is then carried to the wheel cylinders and/or calipers by flexible tubes in order to allow for suspension and steering movements.

The hydraulic system operates as follows: When at rest, the entire system, from the piston(s) in the master cylinder to those in the wheel cylinders or calipers, is full of brake fluid. Upon application of the brake pedal, fluid trapped in front of the master cylinder piston(s) is forced through the lines to the slave cylinders (wheel cylinders or calipers). Here, it forces the pistons outward, in the case of drum brakes, and inward toward the disc, in the case of disc brakes. The motion of the pistons is opposed by return springs mounted outside the cylinders in the drum brakes, and by internal springs or seals, in disc brakes.

Upon release of the brake pedal, a spring located inside the master cylinder immediately returns the master cylinder pistons to the normal position. The pistons contain check valves and the master cylinder has compensating ports drilled into it. These are uncovered as the pistons reach their normal position. The piston check valves allow fluid to flow toward the wheel cylinders or calipers as the pistons withdraw. Then, as the return springs force the shoes into the released position, the excess fluid flows back to the reservoir through the compensating ports. It is during the time the pedal is in the released position that any fluid that has leaked out of the system will be replaced through the compensating ports.

Dual circuit master cylinders employ two pistons, located one behind the other, in the same cylinder. The primary piston is actuated directly by mechanical linkage from the brake pedal. The secondary piston is actuated by fluid trapped between the two pistons. If a leak develops in the front of the secondary piston, it moves forward until it bottoms against the front of the master cylinder, and the fluid trapped between the pistons will operate one side of the split system. If the other side of the system develops a leak, the primary piston will move forward until direct contact with the secondary piston takes place, and it will force the secondary piston to actuate the other side of the split system. In either case, the brake pedal moves farther when the brakes are applied, and less braking power is available.

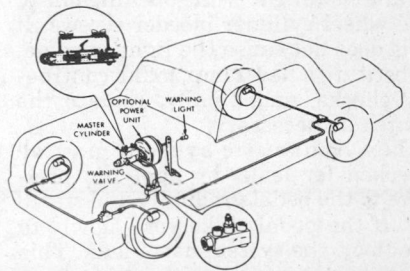

Dual braking system—front-to-rear split

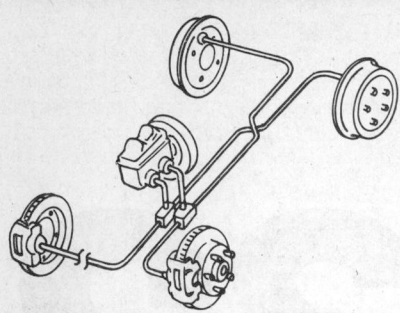

Dual braking system—diagonally split

All dual-circuit systems use a distributor switch to warn the driver when only half of the braking system is operational. This switch is located in a valve body which is mounted on the firewall, or the frame below the master cylinder. A hydraulic piston receives pressure from both circuits, each circuit's pressure being applied to one end of the piston. When the pressures are in balance, the piston remains stationary. When one circuit has a leak, however, the greater pressure in that circuit during application of the brakes will push the piston to one side, closing the distributor switch and activating the brake warning light.

In disc brake systems, this valve body also contains a metering valve and, in some cases, a proportioning valve (or valves). The metering valve keeps pressure from traveling to the disc brakes on the front wheels until the brake shoes or pads on the rear wheels have contacted the drums or rotors, ensuring that the front brakes will never be used alone. The proportioning valve throttles the pressure to the rear brakes so as to avoid rear wheel lock-up during very hard braking.

These valves may be tested by removing the lines to the front and rear brake systems and installing special brake pressure testing gauges. Front and rear system pressures are then compared as the pedal is gradually depressed. Specifications vary with the manufacturer and design of the brake system.

Brake system warning lights may be tested by depressing the brake pedal and holding it while opening one of the wheel cylinder bleeder screws. If this does not cause the light to go on, substitute a new lamp, make continuity checks, and, finally, replace the switch as necessary.

The hydraulic system may be checked for leaks by applying pressure to the pedal gradually and steadily. If the pedal sinks very slowly to the floor, the system has a leak. This is not to be confused with a springy or spongy feel due to the compression of air within the lines. If the system leaks, there will be a gradual change in the position of the pedal with a constant pressure.

Check for leaks along all lines and at wheel cylinders. If no external leaks are apparent, the problem is inside the master cylinder.

DISC BRAKES

Basic Operating Principles

Instead of the traditional expanding brakes that press outward against a circular drum, disc brakes systems utilize a cast iron disc with brake pads positioned on either side of it. Braking effect is achieved in a manner similar to the way you would squeeze a spinning phonograph record between your

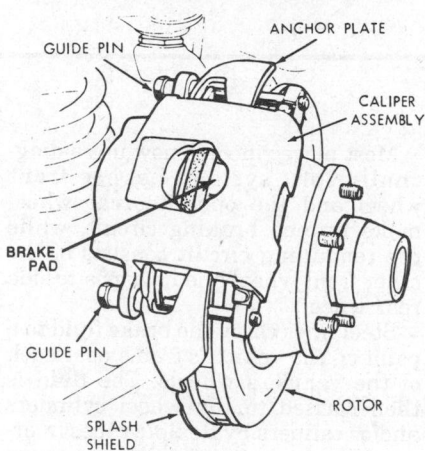

Typical disc brake assembly

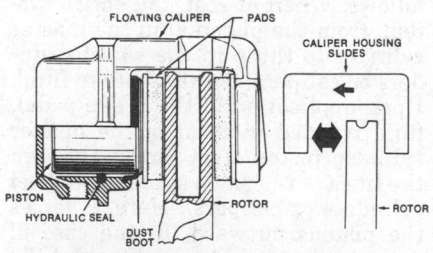

Typical floating caliper disc brake (sliding caliper similar)

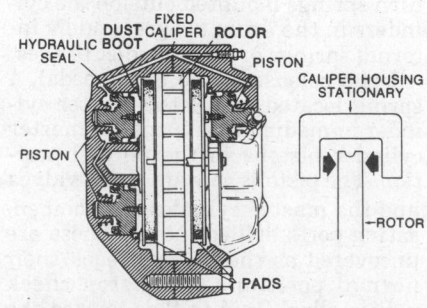

Typical fixed caliper disc brake (four piston shown)

fingers. The disc (rotor) is a one-piece casting which may be equipped with cooling fins between the two braking surfaces. The fins (if equipped) enable air to circulate between the braking surfaces making them less sensitive to heat buildup and more resistant to fade. Dirt and water do not affect braking action since contaminants are thrown off by the centrifugal action of the rotor or scraped off by the pads. Also, the equal clamping action of the two brake pads tends to ensure uniform, straightline stops. All disc brakes are inherently self-adjusting.

There are three general types of disc brake:

1. A fixed caliper, two or four-piston type.
2. A floating caliper, single piston or double piston back-to-back type.
3. A sliding caliper, single piston or double piston back-to-back type.

The fixed caliper design uses one or two pistons mounted on either side of the rotor (in each side of the caliper). The caliper is mounted rigidly and does not move.

The sliding and floating designs are quite similar. In fact, these two types are often lumped together. In both designs, the pad on the inside of the rotor is moved into contact with the rotor by hydraulic force. The caliper, which is not held in a fixed position, moves slightly, bringing the outside pad into contact with the rotor. There are various methods of attaching floating calipers. Some pivot at the bottom or top, and some slide on mounting bolts. In any event, the end result is the same.

DRUM BRAKES

Basic Operating Principles

Drum brakes employ two brakes shoes mounted on a stationary backing plate. These shoes are positioned inside a circular cast iron (or aluminum) drum which rotates with the wheel assembly. The shoes are held in place by springs; this allows them to slide toward the drums (when they are applied) while keeping the lining and drums in alignment. The shoes are actuated by a wheel cylinder which is mounted at the top of the backing plate. When the brakes are applied, hydraulic pressure forces the wheel cylinder's two actuating links outward. Since these links bear directly against the top of the brake shoes, the tops of the shoes are then forced outward against the inner side of the drum. This action forces the bottom of the two shoes to contact the brake drum by rotating the entire assembly slightly (known as servo action). When pressure within the wheel cylinder is relaxed, return springs pull the shoes back away from the drum.

Most modern drum brakes are designed to self-adjust themselves during application when the vehicle is moving in reverse. This motion causes both shoes to rotate very slightly with the drum, rocking an adjusting lever, thereby causing rotation of the adjusting screw by means of a star wheel.

POWER BRAKE BOOSTERS

Power brakes operate just as standard brake systems except in the actuation of the master cylinder pistons. A vacuum diaphragm is located on the front of the master cylinder and assists the drive in applying the brakes, reducing both the effort and travel he must put into moving the brake pedal.

The vacuum diaphragm housing is connected to the intake manifold by a vacuum hose. A check valve is placed at the point where the hose enters the diaphragm housing, so that during periods of low manifold vacuum, brake assist vacuum will not be lost.

Depressing the brake pedal closes off the vacuum source and allows atmospheric pressure to enter on one side of the diaphragm. This causes the master cylinder pistons to move and apply the brakes. When the brake pedal is released, vacuum is applied to both sides of the diaphragm, and return springs return the diaphragm and master cylinder pistons to the released position. If the vacuum fails, the brake pedal rod will butt against the end of the master cylinder actuating rod, and direct mechanical application will occur as the pedal is depressed.

HYDRAULIC CYLINDERS AND VALVES

Master Cylinders

The master cylinder is a type of hydraulic pump that is operated by a push rod attached to the brake pedal or by a push rod that is part of the power brake booster. The cylinder provides a means of converting mechanical force into hydraulic pressure.

DUAL MASTER CYLINDER

In this type there are two separate hydraulic pressure systems. One of the hydraulic systems may be connected to the front brakes, and the other to the rear brakes, or the system may connect diagonal wheels. If one system fails, the other system remains operational, thus providing an additional safety measure. There are two distinct fluid reservoirs and each has a vent and replenishing port that leads into the cylinder bore. These ports have been called compensating and inlet ports or bypass ports, and the terms have been used inconsistently causing confusion. The terms "vents" and "replenishing ports" are now standardized S.A.E. terms. An airtight seal for the reservoir is provided in the form of a rubber diaphragm, which is held in place by a metal cover. A bail type retainer or a

bolt usually holds the cover on the reservoirs. The cover is vented to permit atmospheric pressure to enter above the diaphragm. The diaphragm prevents moisture and debris from contaminating the fluid. The cylinder

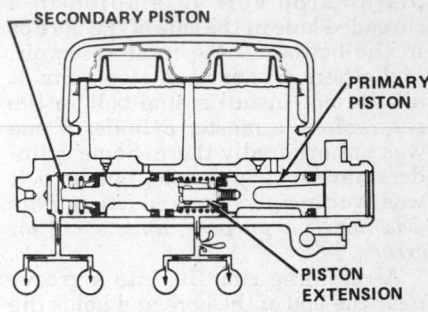

Primary system failure

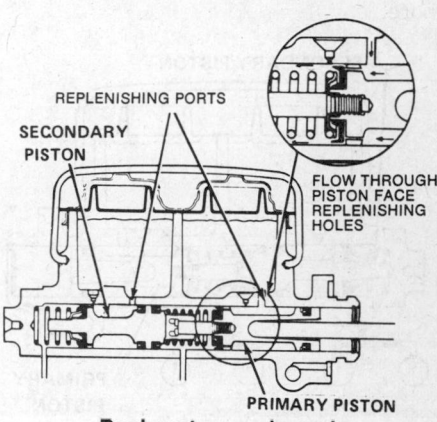

Dual system—released

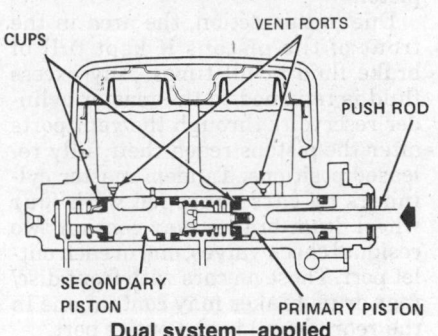

Dual system—applied

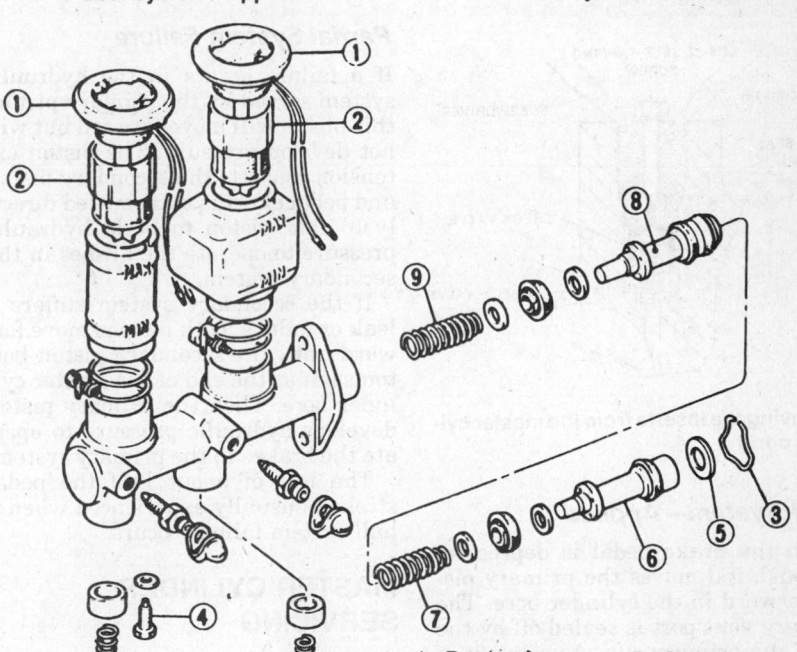

1. Reservoir cap
2. Strainer
3. Stopper ring
4. Stopper screw
5. Stopper
6. Primary piston
7. Spring
8. Secondary piston
9. Spring
10. Plug
11. Check valve

Exploded view of a dual system master cylinder

bore contains the return springs, two pistons, and the seals. The piston stop bolt (if present) may be assembled in a thread hole in the bottom of the cylinder.

Some master cylinders have the piston stop bolt assembled in a threaded hole in the side of the bore or in the bottom of the front reservoir, and others do not have stop bolts at all. Do not install a stop bolt in the reservoir of a master cylinder if one was not originally there. Some cylinders have a tapped hole, but no bolt was ever installed in production. *This was done on purpose, and is not an error.*

A retaining ring fits into a groove near the end of the bore and holds the piston assemblies in the cylinder bore.

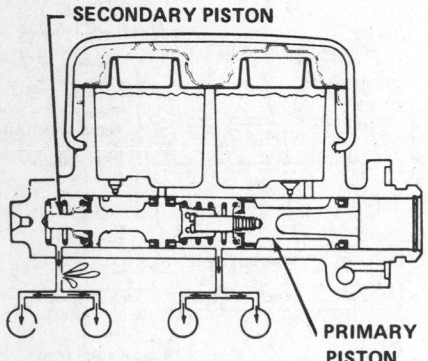

SECONDARY PISTON

PRIMARY PISTON

Secondary system failure

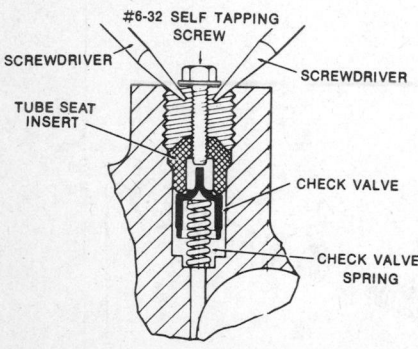

#6-32 SELF TAPPING SCREW

SCREWDRIVER

SCREWDRIVER

TUBE SEAT INSERT

CHECK VALVE

CHECK VALVE SPRING

Removing the inserts from the master cylinder ports

Dual System—Applied

When the brake pedal is depressed, the push rod moves the primary piston forward in the cylinder bore. The primary vent port is sealed off by the lip of the primary cup. As a result, a solid column of fluid is created between the primary and secondary pistons.

With the help of the primary piston return spring, this column moves the secondary piston forward in the cylinder bore. This closes the secondary vent port. When both ports are closed, any further movement of the pushrod and pistons serves to increase the hydraulic pressure in the area ahead of each piston. This pressure is then transmitted through the two hydraulic brake systems to the brakes at each wheel.

Dual System—Released

When the brake pedal is released, the piston return springs move both pistons to their normal released positions. The piston may move faster than the fluid can return from the wheel cylinders, creating a low pressure ahead of the piston.

To allow rapid pedal return, this low pressure must be relieved. Fluid flows from the reservoir through the replenishing port. It then flows around the outside of the piston and cup lips to the area ahead of the piston.

Due to this action, the area in the front of the pistons if kept full of brake fluid at all times. Any excess fluid is returned to the master cylinder reservoirs through the vent ports after the pistons reach their fully released positions. Tandem master cylinders on cars equipped with four wheel drum brakes may contain two residual check valves, one in each outlet port. Those on cars with front disc/rear drum brakes may contain one in the rear (drum) brake outlet port.

Partial System Failure

If a failure occurs in the hydraulic system served by the primary piston, this piston will move forward but will not develop pressure. The piston extension contacts the secondary piston and pedal effort is transmitted directly to that piston to build hydraulic pressure to operate the brakes in the secondary system.

If the secondary system suffers a leak or failure, both pistons move forward until the secondary piston bottoms out at the end of the master cylinder bore. Then the primary piston develops hydraulic pressure to operate the brakes in the primary system.

The loss of about half the pedal stroke is usually experienced when a half system failure occurs.

MASTER CYLINDER SERVICING

Just like any other brakes parts, master cylinders require periodic service. The usual reason for a master cylinder failure is that the cups don't seal anymore. Fluid leaks past cups internally, and sometimes shows up s an external leak as well. A common symptom is a "spongy" brake pedal that goes all the way to the floor when all other brake components are in good shape. The rubber parts wear with usage or may deteriorate with age or fluid contamination. Corrosion or deposits formed in the bore due to moisture or dirt in the hydraulic system may result in wear of the cylinder bore or the parts therein. Also, the fluid levels in the reservoirs should be checked periodically. Whenever needed, clean brake fluid should be added to maintain the fluid level $1/4-1/2$ in. (6–13mm) from the top of the reservoir.

Removal and Disassembly

1. Clean the area around the master cylinder to prevent dirt and grease from contaminating the cylinder or the hydraulic lines. Disconnect the tubes, remove nuts or bolts that secure the master cylinder to the firewall or power brake, and remove the master cylinder from the car (for further details, refer to appropriate car section).

On cars with manual brakes, the push rod must be disconnected from the brake pedal before removing the master cylinder from the car.

2. Remove the reservoir cover, and drain the brake fluid from the reservoir. Then remove the piston stop bolt, if present, from the master cylinder. Remove the boot and snap ring, then slide the primary piston assembly out of the master cylinder. Next, remove the secondary piston assembly by tapping the master cylinder, or by using needle nose pliers to pull it from its bore, or by carefully using compressed air. Disassemble the secondary piston assembly.

3. Clamp the master cylinder in a vise with the outlet ports facing up. Test for the presence of a check valve by probing with wire through the hole in the tube seats. Replace tube seat(s) and check valve(s) only if a check valve is present and supplied in the rebuild kit. Remove the tube seat inserts, if required, by partially threading a self-tapping screw into each tube seat and using two screwdrivers to pry each seat out of the master cylinder. Remove the residual check valve and the spring from the outlet(s) (if present).

Plastic Reservoir Cleaning and Removal

Plastic reservoirs need to be removed only for the following reasons:

a. Reservoir is damaged or the rubber grommet(s) between the reservoir and bore is leaking.

b. Removal of the stop pin from

Chrysler style plastic reservoir master cylinders to allow for the removal of pistons. Pin is located underneath front reservoir nipple.

The reservoir should be removed by first clamping the master cylinder flange in a vise. Next remove the reservoir. Grasp the reservoir base on one end and pull away from the body. Some must be removed by prying between the reservoir and casting with a pry bar. Grommets can be reused if they are in good condition. Whether or not the reservoir is removed, it and the covers or caps should be thoroughly cleaned.

Cleaning and Inspection

Thoroughly clean the master cylinder and any other parts to be reused in clean alcohol. DO NOT USE PETROLEUM PRODUCTS FOR CLEANING. If the bore is not badly scored, rusted or corroded, it is possible to rebuild the master cylinder in some cases. A slight bit of honing is permissible to clean cups are facing.

—————— CAUTION ——————
Aluminum cylinder bores cannot be honed. The cylinder MUST be replaced if the bore is scored.

Lubricate all new rubber parts with brake fluid or brake system assembly lubricant.

CAST IRON BORE CLEAN-UP

Crocus cloth or an approved cylinder hone should be used to remove lightly pitted, scored, or corroded areas from the bore.

—————— CAUTION ——————
If an aluminum master cylinder has pits or scratches in the bore, it must be replaced.

Brake fluid can be used as a lubricant while honing lightly. The master cylinder should be replaced if it cannot be cleaned up readily. After using the crocus cloth or a hone, the master cylinder should be throughly washed in clean alcohol or brake fluid to remove all dust and grit. If alcohol is used, dry parts throughly before reinstalling.

—————— CAUTION ——————
Other solvents should not be used.

Then the clearance between the bore wall and the piston (primary piston of a dual system master cylinder) should be checked. If a narrow ($^1/_8$–$^1/_4$ in. wide) 0.006 in. (0.15mm) feeler gauge can be inserted between the wall and a new piston, the clearance is excessive, and the master cylinder should be replaced. The maximum clearance allowed for units containing pistons without replenishing holes is 0.009 in. (0.23mm).

ALUMINUM BORE CLEAN-UP

Inspect the bore for scoring, corrosion and pitting. If the bore is scored or badly pitted and corroded the assembly should be replaced. *Under no conditions should the bore be cleaned with an abrasive material.* This will remove the wear and corrosion resistant anodized surface. Clean the bore with a clean piece of cloth around a wooden dowel and wash thoroughly with alcohol. Do not confuse bore discoloration or staining with corrosion.

Reassembly and Installation

1. Carefully install the new cups or seals in the same positions and in reverse order of removal.
2. Use brake fluid or assembly fluid very generously to keep from damaging the seals.
3. Placing the small end of the pressure spring into the secondary piston retainer, slide the assembly into the cylinder bore, taking care not to nick or gouge any rubber part.
4. Place the spring retainer of the primary piston assembly over the secondary piston shoulder and push both assemblies into the bore.
5. Install and tighten the piston retaining screw and gasket, while holding the pistons in their seated positions. At the same time, reinstall any piston snap rings.
6. Install the residual check valve and spring in the proper master cylinder outlet (or both outlets, if originally present). If the tube seat inserts were removed, install new seats in both fluid outlets making sure that they are securely seated.

Bleeding and Checking

1. Bleed the hydraulic system as described later in this section.

NOTE: Be sure to bench bleed a rebuilt or new master cylinder before installation.

2. Check master cylinder vent port clearance by watching for a spurt of brake fluid in both reservoir vent holes when the brake pedal is slightly depressed, indicating proper port clearance.

Master Cylinder Push Rod Adjustment

After assembly of the master cylinder to the power section, the piston cup in the hydraulic cylinder should just clear the compensating port hole when the brake pedal is fully released. If the push rod is too long, it will hold the piston over the port.

A push rod that is too short, will give too much loose travel (excessive pedal play).

Apply the brakes and release the pedal all the way observing brake fluid flow back into the master cylinder.

A full flow indicates the piston is coming back far enough to release the fluid.

A slow return of fluid indicates the piston is not coming back far enough to clear the ports. The push rod adjustment is too tight, and should be shortened.

Wheel Cylinders

DRUM BRAKE WHEEL CYLINDER

The wheel cylinder performs in response to the master cylinder. It receives fluid from the hydraulic hose through its inlet port. As the pressure increases, the wheel cylinder cups and pistons are forced apart. As a result, the hydraulic pressure is converted into mechanical force acting on the brake shoes. The wheel cylinder size may vary from front to rear. The variation in wheel cylinder size (diameter) is one of the factors controlling the distribution of braking force in a vehicle.

WHEEL CYLINDER OPERATION

The space between the caps in the cylinder bore must remain filled with fluid at all times. After depressing the

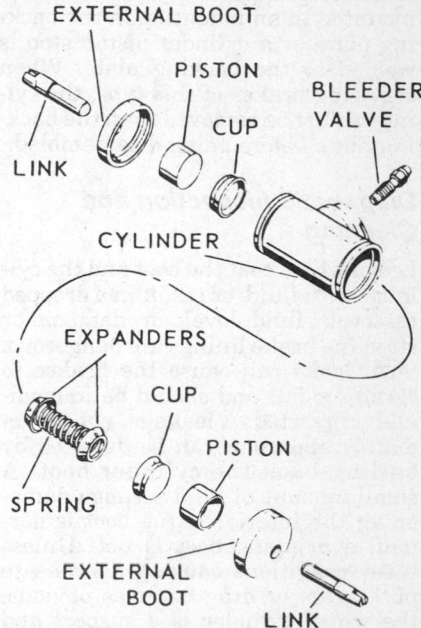

Typical wheel cylinder components

brake pedal, additional brake fluid is forced into the cylinder bore. As a result of this, cups and pistons move outward in the cylinder bore pushing the shoe links an the brake shoes outward to contact the drum and apply the brakes.

On some designs, the end of the shoe web bears directly against the pistons and therefore, shoe links are not used.

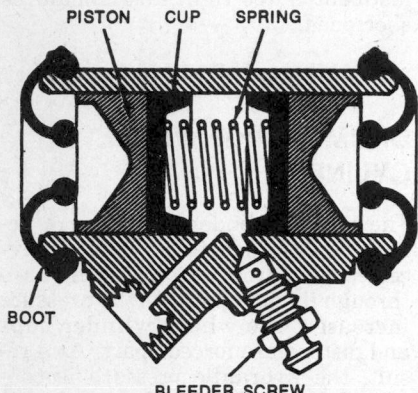

Double piston wheel cylinder

SERVICE PROCEDURES

Wheel cylinders may need reconditioning or replacement whenever the brake shoes are replaced or when required to correct a leak condition. On many designs, the wheel cylinders can be disassembled without removing them from the backing plate. On some designs, however, the cylinder is mounted in an indention in the backing plate or a cylinder piston stop is welded to the backing plate. When servicing brakes of this type, the cylinder must be removed from the backing plate before being disassembled.

Diagnostic Inspection and Cleaning

Leaks which coat the boot and the cylinder with fluid, or result in a dropped reservoir fluid level, or dampen or stain the brake linings are dangerous. Such leaks can cause the brakes to "grab" or fail and should be immediately corrected. A leakage, not immediately apparent, can be detected by pulling back the cylinder boot. A small amount of fluid seepage dampening the interior of the boot is normal; a dripping boot is not. Unless other conditions causing a brake to pull, grab, or drag becomes obvious, the wheel cylinder is a suspect and should be included in general reconditioning.

Cylinder binding may be caused by rust, deposits, grime, or swollen cups due to fluid contamination, or by a cup wedged into an excessive piston clearance. If the clearance between the pistons and the bore wall exceeds allowable values, a condition called "heel drag" may exist. It can result in rapid cup wear and can cause the pistons to retract very slowly when the brakes are released.

A typical example of a scored, pitted, or corroded cylinder bore is shown in the accompanying illustration. A ring of hard, crystal-like substance is sometimes noticed in the cylinder bore where the piston stops after the brakes are released.

Light roughness or deposits can be removed with crocus cloth or an approved cylinder hone. While honing lightly, brake fluid can be used as a lubricant. If the bore cannot be cleaned up readily, the cylinder must be replaced.

NOTE: Aluminum wheel cylinders must not be honed.

——— CAUTION ———
Hydraulic system parts should not be allowed to come in contact with oil or grease, neither should those be handled with greasy hands. Even a trace of petroleum based product is sufficient to cause damage to the rubber parts.

Reconditioning Wheel Cylinders

It is common practice to recondition a wheel cylinder without dismounting it, however some brakes are equipped with external piston stops which prevent disassembly unless the cylinder is removed. In order to dismount, remove the shoe springs and spread the shoes apart, disconnect the brake line, remove the mounting bolts or retaining clips, and pull the cylinder free.

Pull the protective dust boots off the cylinder. Internal parts should slide out, or be picked out easily. Parts can be driven out with a wooden dowel, or blown out at low pressure by applying compressed air to the fluid inlet port. Parts which cannot be removed easily indicate they are damaged beyond repair and the cylinder should be replaced.

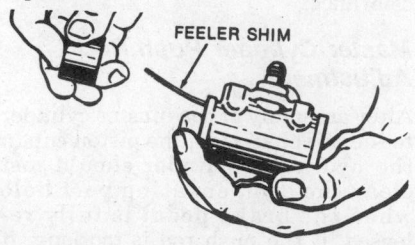

Checking the maximum piston clearance

Clean the cylinder and the parts in alcohol and/or brake fluid (do NOT use gasoline or other petroleum based products). Use only lint-free wiping cloths. Crocus cloth can be used to clean minute scratches, signs of rust, corrosion or discoloration from the cylinder bore and pistons. Slide the cloth in a circular rather than a lengthwise motion. A clean-up hone may be used. After a cylinder has been honed, inspect it for excessive piston clearance and remove any burrs formed on the edge of fluid intake or bleeder screw ports.

——— CAUTION ———
Do not rebuild aluminum cylinders.

To check the maximum piston clearance, place a $1/4$ in. (6mm) wide strip of feeler shim lengthwise in the cylinder bore.

If the piston an be inserted with the shim in place, the cylinder is oversize, and should be discarded. Depending upon the cylinder bore diameter, the shim (or the feeler gauge) thickness can vary as follows:

Cylinder Bore	Shim
¾ in.–1³⁄₁₆ in. (19–30mm)	.006″ (.15mm)
1¼ in.–1⁷⁄₁₆ in. (32–37mm)	.007 in. (.18mm)
1½ in. up (38mm)	.008 in. (.2mm)

Assemble the cylinder with the internal parts, making sure that the cylinder wall is wet with brake fluid. Insert the cups and pistons from each end of a double-end cylinder; do not slide them through the cylinder. Cup lips should always face inward.

Hydraulic Control Valves

PRESSURE DIFFERENTIAL VALVE

The pressure differential valve activates a dash panel warning light if pressure loss in the brake system occurs. If pressure loss occurs in one half of the split system, the other system's normal pressure causes the piston in the switch to compress a spring until it touches an electrical contact. This causes the warning lamp on the dash panel to light, thus warning the driver of possible brake failure.

On some cars the spring balance piston automatically recenters as the brake pedal is released, warning the driver only upon brake application.

On other cars, the remains on until manually cancelled.

Valves may be located separately or as part of a combination valve. On certain front wheel drive cars, the valve and switch are usually incorporated into the master cylinder.

Re-Setting Valves

On some cars, the valve piston(s) remain off center after failure, until necessary repairs are made. The valve will automatically reset itself (after repairs) when pressure is equal on both sides of the system.

If the light does not go out, bleed the brake system that is opposite the failed system. If the front brakes failed, bleed the rear brakes, this should force the light control piston toward center.

If this fails, remove the terminal switch. If brake fluid is present in the electrical area, the seals are gone, replace the complete valve assembly.

METERING VALVE

The metering valve's function is to improve braking balance between the front and rear brakes, especially during light brake application.

The metering valve prevents application of the front disc brakes until the rear brakes overcome the return spring pressure. Thus, when the front disc pads contact the rotor, the rear shoes will contact the brake drum at the same time.

Inspect the metering valve each time the brakes are serviced. A slight amount of moisture inside the boot does not indicate a defective valve, however, fluid leakage indicates a damaged or worn valve. If fluid leakage is present, the valve must be replaced.

The metering valve can be checked very simply. With the car stopped, gently apply the brakes. At about an inch of travel, a very small change in pedal effort (like a small bump) will be felt if the valve is operating properly. Metering valves are not serviceable, and must be replaced if defective.

PROPORTIONING VALVE

The proportioning (pressure control) valve is used, on some cars, to reduce the hydraulic pressure to the rear wheels to prevent skid during heavy brake application and to provide better brake balance. It is usually mounted in line to the rear wheels.

Whenever the brakes are serviced, the valve should be inspected for leakage. Premature rear brake application during light braking can mean a bad proportioning valve. Repair is by replacement of the valve. Make sure the valve port marked "R" is connected toward the rear wheels.

On some front wheel drive cars, the proportioning valve(s) is (are) screwed into the master cylinder. Since these cars usually have a diagonally split brake system, two valves are required. One rear brake line screws into each valve. The early type valves were steel, an occasional "clunking" noise was encountered on some early models, but does not affect brake efficiency. Replacement valves are now made of aluminum. Never mix an aluminum valve with a steel valves, always use two aluminum valves.

COMBINATION VALVE

The combination valve may perform two or three functions. They are; metering, proportioning and brake failure warning.

Variations of the two-way combination valve are; proportioning and brake failure warning or metering and brake failure warning.

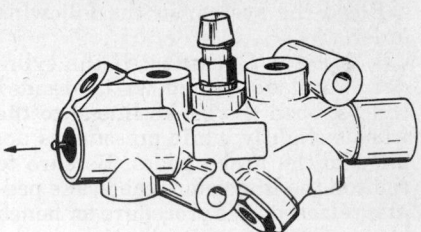

3—way combination valve

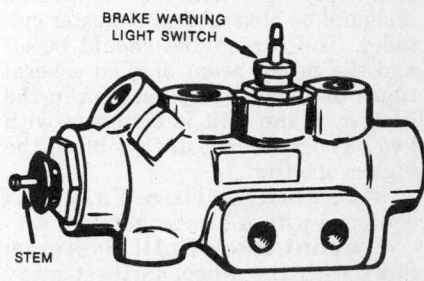

Two—way combination valve (metering and brake warning light switch)

A three-way combination valve directs brake fluid to the appropriate wheel, performs necessary valving and contains a brake failure warning.

The combination valve is usually mounted under the hood close to the master cylinder, where the brake lines can be easily connected and routed to the front or rear wheels.

The combination valve is nonserviceable and must be replaced if malfunctioning.

Brake Bleeding

The hydraulic brake system must be free of air to operate properly. Air can enter the system when hydraulic parts are disconnected for servicing or replacement, or when the fluid level in the master cylinder reservoir(s) is very low. Air in the system will give the brake pedal a spongy feeling upon application.

The quickest and easiest of the two ways for system bleeding is the pressure method, but special equipment is needed to externally pressurize the hydraulic system. The other, more commonly used method of brake bleeding is done manually.

BLEEDING SEQUENCE

Bleeding may be required at only one or two wheels or at the master cylinder, depending upon what point the system was opened to air. If after bleeding the cylinder/caliper that was rebuilt or replaced, the pedal still has a spongy feeling upon application, it will be necessary to bleed the entire system.

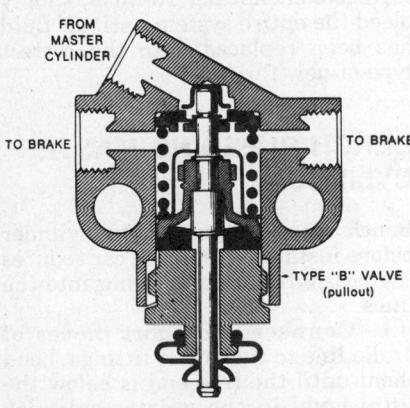

Typical pressure metering valve

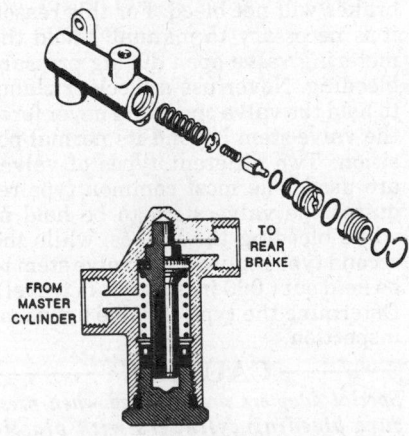

Typical proportioning valve

Bleed the system in the following order:

1. **Master Cylinder:** If the cylinder is not equipped with bleeder screws, open the brake line(s) to the wheels slightly while pressure is applied to the brake pedal. Be sure to tighten the line before the brake pedal is released. The procedure for bench bleeding the master cylinder is in the following section.

2. **Power Brake Booster:** If the unit is equipped with bleeder screws, it should be bled after the master cylinder. The car engine should be off and the brake pedal applied several times to exhaust any vacuum in the booster. If the unit is equipped with two bleeder screws, always bleed the higher one first.

3. **Combination Valve:** If equipped with a bleeder screw.

4. **Front/Back Split Systems:** Start with the wheel farthest away from the master cylinder, usually the right rear wheel. Bleed the other rear wheel, right front and then left front.

NOTE: If you are unsuccessful in bleeding the front wheels, it may be necessary to deactivate the metering valve. This is accomplished by either pushing in, or pulling out a button or stem on the valve. The valve may be held by hand, with a special tool or taped, it should remain deactivated while the front brakes are bled.

5. **Diagonally Split System:** Start with the right rear then the left front. The left rear then the right front.

6. **Rear Disc Brakes:** If the car is equipped with rear disc brakes and the calipers have two bleeder screws, bleed the inner first and then the outer.

— **CAUTION** —
Do not allow brake fluid to spill on the car's finish, it will remove the paint. Flush the area with water.

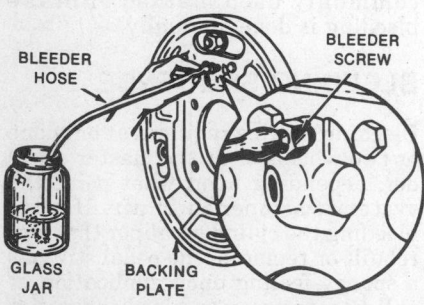

Manual bleeding drum brakes

MANUAL BLEEDING

1. Clean the bleeder screw at each wheel.
2. Start with the wheel farthest from the master cylinder (right rear).
3. Attach a small rubber hose to the bleeder screw and place the end in a clear container of brake fluid.
4. Fill the master cylinder with brake fluid (check often during bleeding). Have an assistant slowly pump up the brake pedal and hold pressure.
5. Open the bleed screw about one-quarter turn, press the brake pedal to the floor, close the bleed screw and slowly release the pedal. Continue until no more air bubbles are forced from the cylinder on application of the brake pedal.
6. Repeat the procedure on all remaining wheel cylinders and calipers.

Master cylinders equipped with bleed screws may be bled independently. When bleeding the Bendix-type dual master cylinder it is necessary to solidly cap one reservoir section while bleeding the other to prevent pressure loss through the cap vent hole.

NOTE: The disc should be rotated to make sure that the piston has returned to the unapplied position when bleeding is completed and the bleed screw closed.

— **CAUTION** —
The bleeder valve at the wheel cylinder must be closed at the end of each stroke, and before the brake pedal is released, to ensure that no air can enter the system. It is also important that the pedal must be returned to the full up position so the piston in the master cylinder moves back enough to clear the bypass outlets.

PRESSURE BLEEDING DISC BRAKES

Pressure bleeding disc brakes will close the metering valve and the front brakes will not bleed. For this reason it is necessary to manually hold the metering valve open during pressure bleeding. Never use a block or clamp to hold the valve open, and never force the valve stem beyond its normal position. Two different types of valves are used. The most common type requires the valve stem to be held in while bleeding the brakes, while the second type requires the valve stem to be held out (.060 in. minimum travel). Determine the type of valve by visual inspection.

— **CAUTION** —
Special adapters are required when pressure bleeding cylinders with plastic reservoirs.

Pressure bleeding equipment should be diaphragm type; placing a diaphragm between the pressurized air supply and the brake fluid. This prevents moisture and other contaminants from entering the hydraulic system.

NOTE: Front disc/rear drum equipped vehicles use a metering valve which closes off pressure to the front brakes under certain conditions. These systems contain manual release actuators which must be engaged to pressure bleed the front brakes.

1. Connect the tank hydraulic hose and adapter to the master cylinder.
2. Close the hydraulic valve on the bleeder equipment.
3. Apply air pressure to the bleeder equipment.

— **CAUTION** —
Follow the equipment manufacturer's recommendations for correct air pressure.

4. Open the valve to bleed air out of the pressure hose to the master cylinder.

NOTE: Never bleed this system using the secondary piston stopscrew on the bottom of many master cylinders.

5. Open the hydraulic valve and bleed each wheel cylinder and caliper. Bleed the rear brake system first when bleeding both front and rear systems.

FLUSHING HYDRAULIC BRAKE SYSTEMS

Hydraulic brake systems must be totally flushed if the fluid becomes contaminated with water, dirt or other corrosive chemicals. To flush, simply bleed the entire system until *all* fluid has been replaced with the correct type of new fluid.

BENCH BLEEDING MASTER CYLINDER

Bench bleeding the master cylinder before installing it on the car reduces the possibility of air getting into the lines.

1. Connect two short pieces of brake line to the outlet fittings, bend them until the free end is below the fluid level in the master cylinder reservoir(s).

2. Fill the reservoirs with fresh brake fluid. Pump the piston until no more air bubbles appear in the reservoir(s).

3. Disconnect the two short lines, refill the master cylinder and securely install the cylinder cap(s).

4. Install the master cylinder on the car. Attach the lines but do not completely tighten them. Force any air that may have been trapped in the connection by slowly depressing the brake pedal. Tighten the lines before releasing the brake pedal.

POWER BRAKES

Vacuum Operated Booster

Power brakes operate just as standard brake systems except in the actuation of the master cylinder pistons. A vacuum diaphragm is located on the front of the master cylinder and assists the driver in applying the brakes, reducing both the effort and travel he must put into moving the brake pedal.

The vacuum diaphragm housing is connected to the intake manifold by a vacuum hose. A check valve is placed at the point where the hose enters the diaphragm housing, so that during periods of low manifold vacuum brake assist vacuum will not be lost.

Depressing the brake pedal closes off the vacuum source and allows atmospheric pressure to enter on one side of the diaphragm. This causes the master cylinder pistons to move and apply the brakes. When the brake pedal is released, vacuum is applied to both sides of the diaphragm, and return springs return the diaphragm and master cylinder pistons to the released position. If the vacuum fails, the brake pedal rod will butt against the end of the master cylinder actuating rod, and direct mechanical application will occur as the pedal is depressed.

The hydraulic and mechanical problems that apply to conventional brake systems also apply to power brakes, and should be checked for if the tests and chart below do not reveal the problem.

Tests for a system vacuum leak as described below:

1. Operate the engine at idle with the transmission in Neutral without touching the brake pedal for at least one minute.

2. Turn off the engine and wait one minute.

3. Test for the presence of assist vacuum by depressing the brake pedal and releasing it several times. Light application will produce less and less pedal travel, if vacuum was present. If there is no vacuum, air is leaking into the system somewhere. Test for system operation as follows:

1. Pump the brake pedal (with engine off) until the supply vacuum is totally gone.

2. Put a light, steady pressure on the pedal.

3. Start the engine, and operate it at idle with the transmission in Neutral. If the system is operating, the brake pedal should fall toward the floor if constant pressure is maintained on the pedal.

Power brake systems may be tested for hydraulic leaks just as ordinary systems are tested, except that the engine should be idling with the transmission in Neutral throughout the test.

POWER BRAKE BOOSTER TROUBLESHOOTING CHART

The following items are in addition to those listed in the General Troubleshooting Section. Check those items first.

Hard Pedal

1. Faulty vacuum check valve.
2. Vacuum hose kinked, collapsed, plugged, leaky, or improperly connected.
3. Internal leak in unit.
4. Damaged vacuum cylinder.
5. Damaged valve plunger.
6. Broken or faulty springs.
7. Broken plunger stem.

Grabbing Brakes

1. Damaged vacuum cylinder.
2. Faulty vacuum check valve.
3. Vacuum hose leaky or improperly connected.
4. Broken plunger stem.

Pedal Goes to Floor

Generally, when this problem occurs, it is not caused by the power brake booster. In rare cases, a broken plunger stem may be at fault.

Overhaul

Most power brake boosters are serviced by replacement only. In many cases, repair parts are not available. A good many special tools are required for rebuilding these units. For these reasons, it would be most practical to replace a failed booster with a new or remanufactured unit.

ANTI-LOCK BRAKING SYSTEM (ABS)

OPERATION

The Anti-Lock Braking System (ABS) is essentially a brake system enhancement. The purpose of ABS is to increase the driver's control over a vehicle during braking-especially steering control. When a vehicle equipped with a conventional brake system must brake suddenly, one or more wheels may lock up offering little or no steering control to avoid hazards. ABS is designed to prevent braked wheels from locking. The advantages of the system are considerable. For instance, during a high-speed stop while entering a curve, ABS is designed to allow the driver to steer through the curve while decelerating. Additionally, ABS is designed to enhance the braking action of each front wheel independently and the two rear wheels independent of the front wheels. This allows controlled braking even if one or more wheels encounters a slippery surface. In this situation, ABS will automatically sense the initial loss of adhesion in any one wheel and reduce or prevent further hydraulic pressure on that wheel's brake caliper, or if the rear wheels-both calipers until adhesion is regained.

COMPONENTS

ABS is essentially the familiar split circuit hydraulic four wheel disc brake system in which a sophisticated electronic and mechanical override system has been carefully mated. Three or four wheel speed sensors (depending on vehicle system design), an electronic control unit and a hydraulic unit that incorporates solenoid operated brakes line valves are the major components of the system. The sensors monitor the rotation speed of the wheels and provide data about wheel acceleration and deceleration over very small intervals of time. The signals from the sensors are transmitted to the control unit. The control unit monitors the signals and compares them to a contained program. If one of the sensors suddenly shows a deceleration rate that exceeds the threshold values of the programmed system-(indicating that a wheel is about to lock and skid)-the computer activates the hydraulic control unit to maintain the optimum brake pressure in that wheel, or both rear wheels to prevent lock-up. If, for any reason, the ABS should malfunction the brakes will operate as a normal system without ABS and a warning light will go on indicating service is required.

SERVICING DISC BRAKES

Disc Brake Caliper

An integral part of the caliper, the caliper bore(s) contains the piston(s) that direct thrust against the brake pads supported within the caliper. Since all braking forces (pad application force) are applied on each side of the rotor with no self energization, the cylinder and piston are large in comparison to a drum brake wheel cylinder.

Fixed-Type

A fixed type caliper is mounted solidly to the spindle bracket.

Pistons are located on both sides of the rotor, in inboard and outboard caliper halves. Fluid passes between caliper halves through an external crossover tube or through internal passages. A bleeder screw is located in the inboard caliper half. A dust boot protecting each cylinder fits in a circumferential groove on the piston.

Floating or Sliding-Type

Floating or sliding calipers are free to move in a fixed bracket or support.

The piston(s) is located only on the inboard side of the caliper housing, which straddles the rotor. The cylinder piston(s) applies the inboard brake shoe directly, and simultaneously hydraulic pressure slide the caliper in a clamping action which forces the caliper to apply the outboard brake shoe.

The actual applying movement is small. The unit merely grips during application, relaxes upon release, and the shoes do not retract an appreciable distance from the rotor. The fluid inlet port and the bleeder screw are located on the inboard side of the caliper. A dust boot is fitted into a circumferential groove on the piston and into a recess at or near the outer end of the cylinder bore.

A scratched piston, nicked seal, or a sludge or varnish deposit which limits the sealing edge away from the piston will cause a fluid leak. A serious leak could develop if calipers are not reconditioned when new pads are installed. Then dust and road grime, gradually accumulating behind the dust boot, could be carried into the seal when the piston is shoved inward to accomodate new thick linings. Old seals may have taken a "set", thus preventing proper seating in the retainer groove and on the piston. Therefore, when reconditioning calipers, new seals should be installed.

OVERHAUL PROCEDURES

Before servicing, siphon or syringe about $^2/_3$ of the fluid from the master cylinder reservoir; do not, however, lower the fluid level below the cylinder intake port.

1. To prevent a gravity loss of fluid, plug the brake line after disconnecting it from the caliper.
2. To overhaul, remove the caliper from the vehicle, allow the unit to drain, and remove the brake shoes.
3. For benchwork, clamp the caliper housing in a soft jawed vice.
4. On fixed-caliper types, remove the bridge bolts and separate the caliper into halves. Remove the sealing O-rings at crossover points, if the unit has internal fluid passages across the halves.
5. Whenever required, use special tools to remove pistons, dust boots, and seals. If compressed air is used, apply it gradually, gently ease the pistons from the cylinders, and trap

them in a clean cloth; do not allow them to pop out. *Take care to avoid pinching hands or fingers.*

6. While removing stroking type seals and boots, work the lip of the boot from the groove in the caliper. After the boot is free, pull the piston, and strip the seal and boot from the piston.
7. While removing fixed position (rectangular ring) seals and boots, pull the piston through the boot. *Do not use a metal tool which would scratch the piston.* Use a small pointed wooden or plastic tool to lift the boots and seals from the grooves in the cylinder bore.

Cleaning, Inspection, and Installation

Use only alcohol and/or brake fluid and a lint free wiping cloth to clean the caliper and parts.

--- CAUTION ---
Other solvents should not be used. Blow out passages with compressed air. Always wear eye protection when using compressed air or cleaning calipers.

1. To correct minor imperfections in the cylinder bore, polish with a fine grade crocus cloth working in a circular rather than a lengthwise motion. Do not use any form of abrasive on a plated piston. Discard a piston which is pitted or has signs of plating wear.
2. Inspect the new seal. It should lie flat and be round. If it had suffered a distorted "set" during its shelf life, do not use it. Lubricate the cylinder wall and parts with brake fluid.
3. While installing the stroking type seals and boots, stretch the boot and seal over the piston and seat then in position.
4. Use special alignment tools for inserting lip culp seals.
5. Install the fixed position (rectangular ring) seals and be sure the ring does not twist or roll into the groove.
6. Where the boot lip is retained inside the cylinder bore, the following method works as well:
   a. Lubricate the bottom inside edge of the piston and brake seal in the caliper with brake fluid.
   b. Pull the boot over the bottom end of the piston so that the boot is positioned on the bottom of the piston with the lip about $^1/_4$ inch up from bottom end.
   c. Hold the piston suspended over bore.
   d. Insert the back boot lip into the groove in the caliper.
   e. Tuck the sides of the boot into the groove and work forward until only one bulge remains.
   f. Tuck the final bulge into the front of the groove.

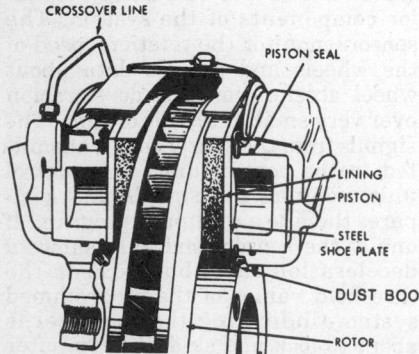

Fixed caliper disc brake

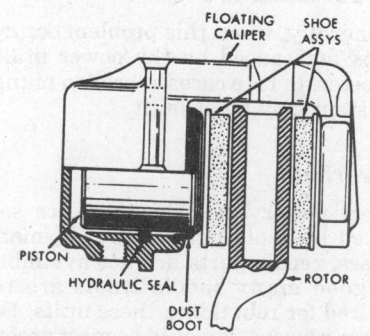

Floating caliper disc brake (sliding caliper similar)

g. Push the piston carefully through the seal and boot to the bottom of the bore. The inside of the boot should slide on the piston and come to rest in the boot groove.

If the boot lip is retained outside the cylinder bore, first stretch the boot over the piston and seat it in its groove, then press the piston through the seal.

Fully depress the piston. You'll need 50–100 pounds of force to fasten the boot lip in place. On some designs, it is necessary to use a wooden drift or a special tool to seat the metal boot in the caliper counterbore below the face of the caliper.

Installing Fixed Caliper Bridge Bolts

If the caliper contains internal fluid crossover passages, be sure to install the new O-ring seals at the joints.

Install high tensile strength bridge bolts on the mated caliper halves.

Never replace the bridge bolts with ordinary standard hardware bolts; order the bolts by part numbers only. Tighten the bridge bolts, using a specified torque wrench as follows specified by the manufacturer.

OVERHAUL NOTES

Field reports indicate that two factors determine whether to replace or rebuild calipers:

1. Can the piston or pistons be moved?

2. Will the bleed screw break off when removal is attempted? (Rebuilders will not accept a caliper with a broken bleed screw.) Since there is no way to predict how a bleed screw will react, follow this procedure to attempt removal.

1. Insert a drill shank into the bleed screw hole (snug fit).

2. Tap the screw on all sides.

3. With a six point wrench apply pressure gently while working the drill up and down slightly.

4. If the drill starts to bind, the screw is beginning to collapse and cannot be removed intact.

Heating the caliper is another successful, but time consuming, bleed screw removal technique.

1. Remove the caliper from the car.

2. Heat the caliper.

3. Shrink the bleed screw by applying dry ice, and attempt removal.

BLEEDER SCREW REPLACEMENT

1. Using the existing hole in the bleeder screw for a pilot, drill $1/4$ in. hole completely through the existing bleeder.

2. Increase the hole to $7/16$ in.

3. Tap hole using a ¼ in. (18-National pipe tab) ½ in. deep-(full thread.)

4. Install bleeder repair kit.

5. Test for leaks and full brake pedal pressure.

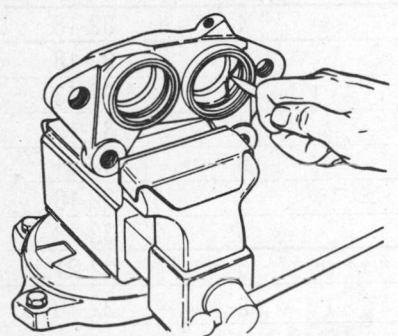

Removing a fixed position rectangular ring seal

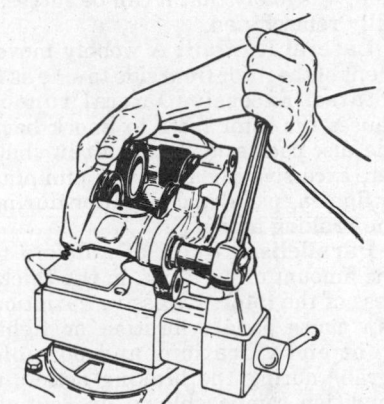

Removing the fixed caliper bridge bolts

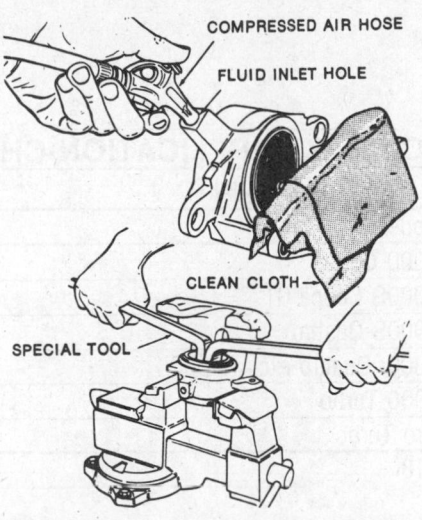

COMPRESSED AIR HOSE

FLUID INLET HOLE

CLEAN CLOTH

SPECIAL TOOL

Removing a hollow-end piston with compressed air (top) or the special tool (bottom)

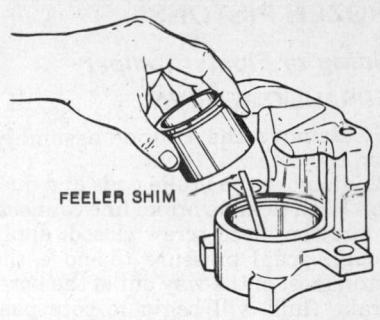

FEELER SHIM

Checking maximum piston clearance

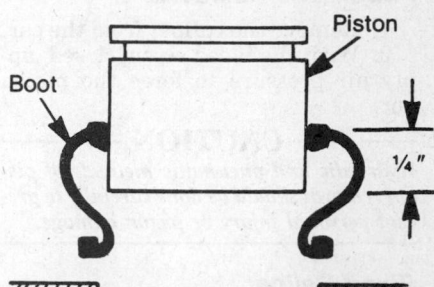

Piston

Boot

¼"

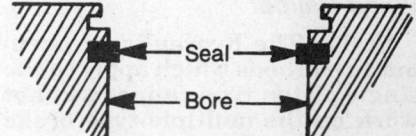

Seal

Bore

Typical boot installation

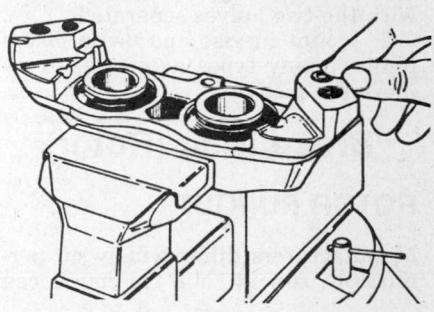

Replacing the O-rings in the internal cross-over passages

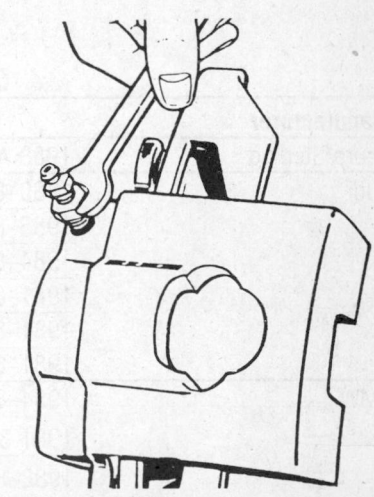

Replacing a disc brake bleeder screw

FROZEN PISTONS

Sliding or Floater Caliper

HYDRAULIC REMOVAL

1. Remove the caliper assembly from the rotor.
2. Remove the brake pads and dust seal. With flexible brake line connected and the bleed screw closed, apply enough pedal pressure to move the piston most of the way out of the bore. (Brake fluid will begin to ooze past the piston inner seal.)

PNEUMATIC REMOVAL

1. Remove the caliper from the car.
2. With the bleed screw closed, apply air pressure to force the piston out.

——— CAUTION ———
Hydraulic and pneumatic methods of piston removal should be done carefully to prevent personal injury or piston damage.

Fixed Caliper

NOTE: **The hydraulic or pneumatic methods which apply to the single piston type caliper will not work on the multiple type brake caliper.**

1. Remove the caliper from the car with the two halves separated.
2. Mount in vise and use a piston puller (many types available) to remove the pistons.

Brake Disc (Rotor)

ROTOR RUNOUT

Manufacturers differ widely on permissible runout, but too much can sometimes be felt as a pulsation at the brake pedal. A wobble pump effect is created when a rotor is not perfectly smooth and the pad hits the high spots forcing fluid back into the master cylinder. This alternating pressure causes a pulsating feeling which can be felt at the pedal when the brakes are applied. This excessive runout also causes the brakes to be out of adjustment because disc brakes are self-adjusting; they are designed so that the pads drag on the rotor at all times and therefore automatically compensate for wear.

To check the actual runout of the rotor, first tighten the wheel spindle nut to a snug bearing adjustment, end-play removed. Fasten a dial indicator on the suspension at a convenient place so that the the indicator stylus contacts the rotor face approximately one inch from its outer edge. Set the dial at zero. Check the total indicator reading while turning the rotor one full revolution. If the rotor is warped beyond the runout specification, it is likely that it can be successfully remachined.

Lateral Runout: A wobbly movement of the rotor from side to side as it rotates. Excessive lateral runout causes the rotor faces to knock back the disc pads and can result in chatter, excessive pedal travel, pumping or fighting pedal and vibration during the braking action.

Parallelism (lack of): Refers to the amount of variation in the thickness of the rotor. Excessive variation can cause pedal vibration or fight, front end vibrations and possible "grab" during the braking action; a condition comparable to an "out-of-round brake drum". Check parallelism with a micrometer . "Mike" the thickness at eight or more equally spaced points, equally distant from the outer edge of the rotor, preferably at mid-points of the braking surface. Parallelism is then the amount of variation between maximum and minimum measurements.

Surface or Micro-inch finish, flatness, smoothness: Different from parallelism, these terms refer to the degree of perfection of the flat surface on each side of the rotor; that is, the minute hills, valleys and swirls inherent in machining the surface. In a visual inspection, the remachined surface should have a fine ground polish with, at most, only a faint trace of nondirectional swirls.

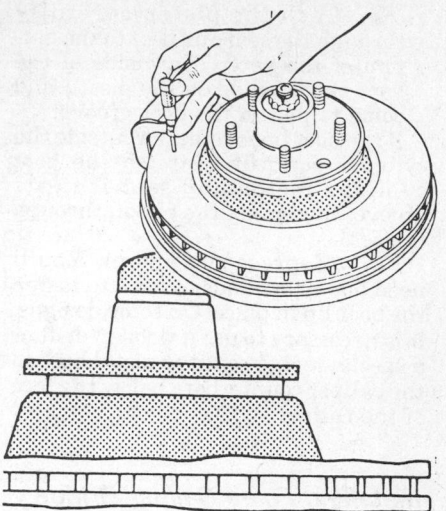

Parallelism

DISC BRAKE APPLICATION CHART

Manufacturer	Year & Model		Type No.	Page
Acura/Sterling	1988 All Models		4	32-18
Audi	1980–84 4000 Coupe		4	32-18
	1985–88 4000S Coupe GT		4	32-18
	1984–88 4000S Quattro		4	32-18
	1981–88 5000, Quattro exc. Turbo		6	32-21
	1981–88 5000 Turbo		4	32-18
	1981–Quattro Turbo		4	32-18
BMW	1984–88 318i		6	32-21
	1981 320i		2	32-16
	1982–83 320i	ATE System	2	32-16
		Girling System	4	32-18

DISC BRAKE APPLICATION CHART

Manufacturer	Year & Model		Type No.	Page
BMW	1982–88 320e		4	32-18
	1982–88 528e		4	32-18
	1983–88, 533i, 535i, 633CSi, 635CSi		4	32-18
	1982 633CSi, 733i		2	32-16
Chrysler Corp.	1981–82 Champ		3	32-18
	1982–88 Colt exc. Turbo		3	32-18
	1984–88 Colt Turbo		4	32-18
	1981 Challenger, Sapporo	Front	5	32-21
		Rear	9	32-24
	1984 Conquest	Front	4	32-18
		Rear	9	32-24
	1984–88 Vista		4	32-18
Honda	1981 Accord		4	32-18
	1982–88 Accord		4	32-18
	1981–83 Civic Wagon		5	32-21
	1984–86 Civic Wagon		5	32-21
	1981–88 Civic		4	32-18
	1981–88 Civic		4	32-18
	1984–88 CRX		4	32-18
	1982–88 Prelude		4	32-18
Hyundai	Excel		4	32-18
Isuzu	1981–84 I-Mark		2	32-16
	1985–88 I-Mark		4	32-18
	1983–88 Impulse		4	32-18
Mazda	1981–84 GLC		5	32-21
	1985 GLC		4	32-18
	1986–88 323		4	32-18
	1982 626		4	32-18
	1981–85 RX7		4	32-18
	1986–88 RX7	Front	2	32-16
		Rear	4	32-18
Mercedes–Benz	1981–88 All Models		2	32-16
Mitsubishi	1983 Cordia, Tredia		1	32-16
	1984–88 Cordia, Tredia		4	32-18
	1985–88 Galant	Front	4	32-18
		Rear	9	32-24
	1985–88 Mirage		4	32-18
	1983–88 Starion	Front	4	32-18
		Rear	9	32-24
	1988 Precis		4	32-18

DISC BRAKE APPLICATION CHART

Manufacturer	Year & Model		Type No.	Page
Nissan/Datsun	1981 200 SX	Front	7	32-22
		Rear	10	32-25
	1982–88 200 SX	Front	7	32-22
		Rear	10	32-25
	1981–82 210		7	32-22
	1981 280 ZX	Front	7	32-22
		Rear	10	32-25
	1982–88 300 ZX		4	32-18
	1981–82 310		7	32-22
	1981 510		7	32-22
	1981 810		4	32-18
	1982–88 Maxima		4	32-18
	1983–88 Pulsar, Sentra		4	32-18
	1982–88 Stanza		4	32-18
Porsche	1981–88 911		2	32-16
	1981–88 924, 928, 944		6	32-21
Renault	1983–88 Alliance, Encore		4	32-18
	1981–85 Fuego		8	32-23
	1981–84 Le Car		5	32-21
	1981–83 18i		8	32-23
	1984–86 18i Sportwagon		4	32-18
	1987–88 Medallion		4	32-18
	1987–88 GTA		4	32-18
SAAB	1981–88 900, 9000	Front	7	32-22
		Rear	2	32-16
Subaru	All except Justy	Front	9	32-24
		Rear	4	32-18
	1987–88 Justy		4	32-18

DISC BRAKE APPLICATION CHART

Manufacturer	Year & Model		Type No.	Page
Toyota	1983–88 Camry		4	32-18
	1981 Celica		5	32-21
	1982–88 Celica		4	32-18
	1982–83 Corolla		3	32-18
	1984–88 Corolla exc. Coupe, FX16		4	32-18
	1984–85 Coupe		4	32-18
	1981–82 Corona		2	32-16
	1981–88 Cressida	Front	4	32-18
		Rear	3	32-18
		Rear (1985)	4	32-18
	1987–88 FX16		4	32-18
	1985–88 MR2		4	32-18
	1981–84 Starlet		4	32-18
	1981 Supra		5	32-21
	1982–88 Supra		4	32-18
	1981 Tercel		4	32-18
	1984–88 Van		4	32-18
Volkswagen	1981–84 All w/KH calipers	Before 2/84	1	32-16
		After 2/84	4	32-18
	1981 w/Girling calipers		7	32-22
	1985–88 All exc. Fox		4	32-18
	1987–88 Fox		1	32-16
	1981–88 Vanagon		2	32-16
Volvo	1981–88 240, 260		2	32-16
	1981–88 740, 760		2	32-16
	1987–88 780	Front	4	32-18
		Rear	2	32-16
Yugo	1986–88 GV, GVL, GVX		5	32-21

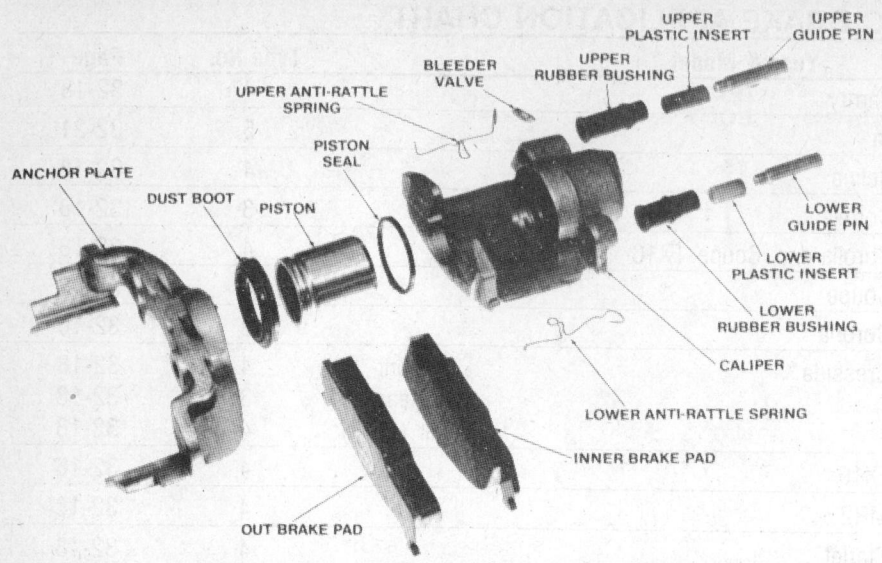

Exploded view of a Kelsey–Hayes floating caliper

10. Install the anti-rattle springs between the anchor plate and brake pad ears. The loops on the springs should be positioned inboard.

11. Fill the reservoir with brake fluid and pump the brake pedal several times to set the piston. It should not be necessary to bleed the system; however, if a firm pedal cannot be obtained, the system must be bled (see "Bleeding the Brakes" in this section).

12. Install the wheel and lower the vehicle.

TYPE 2

ATE, Girling, Sumitomo, Teves, etc. Fixed Caliper

These units are either two or four piston, two-piece calipers that are fixed directly to the steering knuckle or spindle.

Brake pads may be changed without removing the caliper on all of these models. There may be some differences in retainers or anti-rattle springs from the illustrations, but all versions are basically the same. Before removing any parts, carefully note the position of any springs, retainers or clips. Change pads on one wheel at a time and use the other as a reference.

All pads on all models are held in position by either retaining pins or retainer plates. The retainer plates are bolted to the caliper housing and need only be loosened and rotated out of the way for pad removal.

PAD REPLACEMENT

1. Raise the front (or rear) of the vehicle and support it with jackstands. Remove the wheel.

2. Siphon a sufficient quantity of brake fluid from the master cylinder reservoir to prevent the brake fluid from overflowing the master cylinder when removing or installing new pads. This is necessary as the pistons must be forced into the cylinder bore to provide sufficient clearance to remove the pads.

3. Some models may use a cover plate over the access hole for the pads, if so, remove it. Disconnect the brake pad lining wear indicator wire on models so equipped.

4. Carefully clean the exterior of the caliper with a wire brush and note the position of any dampening shims or anti-rattle springs.

TYPE 1

Kelsey-Hayes Floating Caliper

This unit is a single piston, one-piece caliper which floats on two guide pins screwed into the adapter (anchor plate). The adaptor, in turn, is held to the steering knuckle with two bolts. As the brake pads wear, the caliper floats along the adaptor and guide pins during braking.

PAD REPLACEMENT

1. Raise the front of the vehicle and support it with jackstands. Remove the wheel.

2. Siphon some brake fluid from the master cylinder reservoir to prevent its overflowing when the piston is retracted into the cylinder bore.

3. Disconnect the brake pad warning indicator if so equipped.

4. Remove the anti-rattle springs.

5. Remove the guide pine that attach the caliper to the anchor plate.

6. Lift off the caliper and position it out of the way with some wire-you need not remove the brake lines.

— CAUTION —

Never allow the caliper to hang by its brake lines.

7. Slide the outer pad out of the anchor plate. Slide the rotor of the hub and remove the inner pad. Check the rotor as detailed in the appropriate section. Check the caliper for fluid

Kelsey–Hayes floating caliper disc brake assembly

leaks or cracked boots. If any damage is found, the caliper will require overhauling or replacement.

8. Carefully clean the anchor plate with a wire brush or some other abrasive material. Install the inner pad, rotor and outer pad, new brake pads into position on the anchor plate. The inner pad usually has chamfered edges.

NOTE: When replacing brake pads, always replace both pads on both sides of the vehicle. Mixed pads will cause uneven braking.

9. Slowly and carefully push the piston into its bore until it's bottomed and then position the caliper onto the anchor plate. Install the guide pins by pushing them carefully into the bushings and threading them into the adapter.

NOTE: The upper guide pin is usually longer than the lower one.

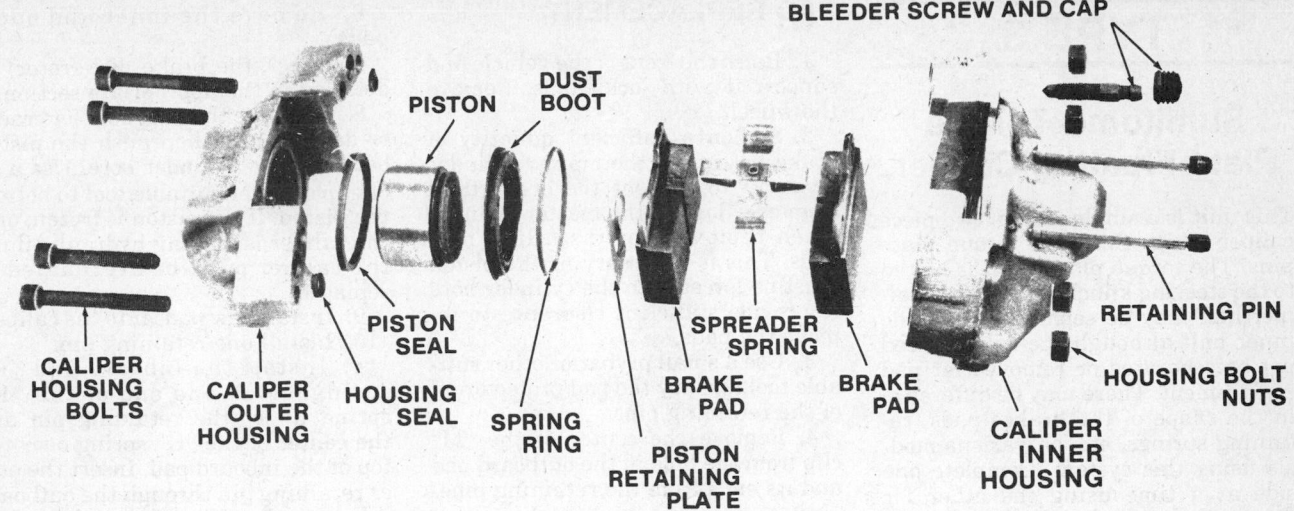

Exploded view of a two–piston fixed caliper

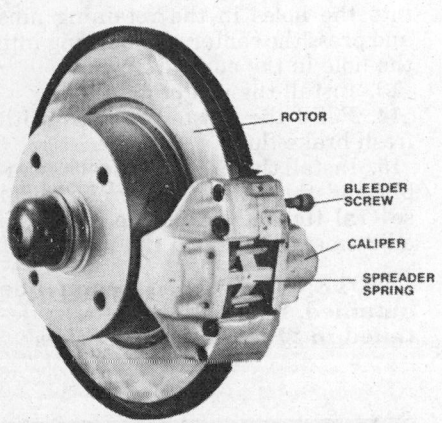

Typical fixed caliper disc brake assembly

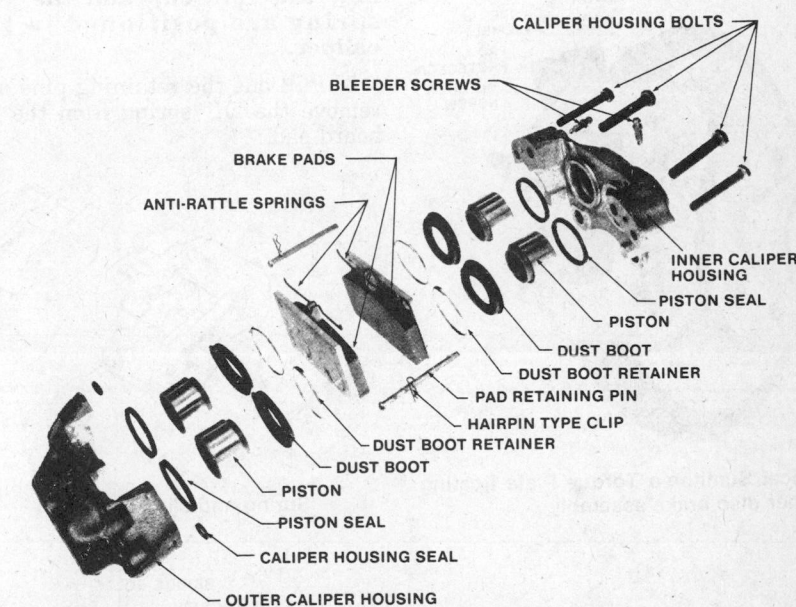

Exploded view of a four–piston fixed caliper

5. Remove the pad retaining pins and any retaining clips holding them. Remove the anti-rattle springs if so equipped. Some pads may be held in position by a plate with a retaining bolt. If so, loosen the bolt and swing the plate away. Lift out the spreader spring if so equipped.

NOTE: It is a good idea to remove one retaining spring or plate and then remove the anti-rattle spring or spreader spring. Remove the second retaining pin or plate last.

6. Force the old pads away from the rotor for easy withdrawl and remove the pads from the caliper.

7. If so equipped, remove the lower anti-rattle springs and dampening shims using needlenose pliers.

8. Check the brake disc (rotor) as detailed in the appropriate section.

9. Examine the dust boot for cracks or damage and push the pistons back into the cylinder bores. If the pistons are frozen or if the caliper is leaking hydraulic fluid, it must be overhauled.

10. Install the anti-rattle spring or dampening shims and slip the new pads into the caliper. If dampening shims are used, be sure that the directional arrow on the shims face the forward rotation of the rotor.

11. Install one pad retaining pin and hairpin clip. Position the anti-rattle springs and/or spreader spring and

then install the other pad retaining pin and clip.

12. Refill the master cylinder to the correct level with the proper brake fluid.

13. Replace the wheel and lower the vehicle. Pump the brake pedal several times to bring the pads into correct adjustment. Road test the vehicle.

NOTE: If a firm pedal cannot be obtained, the system will require bleeding (see "Bleeding the Brakes" in this section).

32 BRAKES

TYPE 3

Sumitomo Torque Plate Floating Caliper

This unit is a single piston, two-piece caliper which floats on torque plate pins. The torque plate itself is bolted to the steering knuckle. The outer caliper half may be separated from the inner half although the caliper need not be separated or removed for pad replacement. There may be difference in the shape of the brakes pads, retaining springs, etc. on various models using this system. Complete one side at a time using the other for reference.

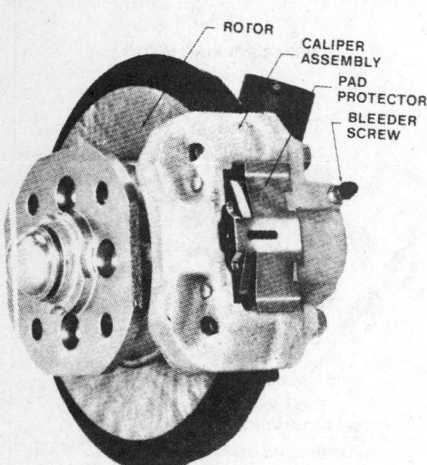

Typical Sumitomo Torque Plate floating caliper disc brake assembly

PAD REPLACEMENT

1. Raise the front of the vehicle and support it with jackstands. Remove the wheel.

2. Siphon a sufficient quantity of brake fluid from the master cylinder reservoir to prevent the brake fluid from overflowing the master cylinder when removing or installing new pads. This is necessary as the piston must be forced into the cylinder bore to provide sufficient clearance to remove the pads.

3. Use a small prybar or other suitable tool and pry the pad protector off of the retaining pins.

4. Remove the center of the "M" clip from the hole in the outboard pad and its ends from the retaining pins.

NOTE: To facilitate the reassembly operation later on, note how the "M" clip and the "K" spring are positioned in the caliper.

5. Pull out the retaining pins and remove the "K" spring from the inboard pad.

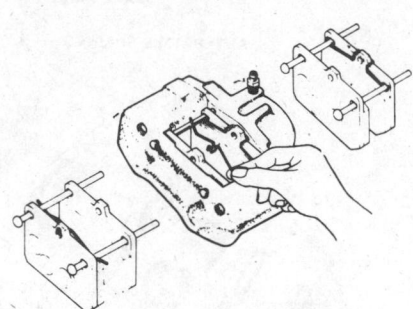

Spring and clip installation

6. Remove the inner and outer pads.

7. Check the brake disc (rotor) as detailed in the appropriate section.

8. Examine the dust boot for cracks or damage and then push the piston back into the cylinder bore. Use a C-clamp or other suitable tool to bottom the piston. If the piston is frozen, or if the caliper is leaking hydraulic fluid, the caliper must be overhauled or replaced.

9. Install new pads into the caliper.

10. Install one retaining pin.

11. Install the inboard pad "K" spring. Hook one end of the "K" spring under the retaining pin and the center of the "K" spring over the top of the inboard pad. Insert the other retaining pin through the outboard pad, over the "K" spring and through the inboard pad.

12. Insert the ends of the "M" clip into the holes in the retaining pins and press the center of the spring into the hole in the outboard pad.

13. Install the pad protector.

14. Refill the master cylinder with fresh brake fluid.

15. Install the tire and wheel assembly and then pump the brake pedal several times to bring the pads into adjustment. Road test the vehicle.

NOTE: If a firm pedal cannot be obtained, bleed the system as detailed in "Bleeding the Brakes".

TYPE 4

ATE, Girling, etc. Floating Caliper

Although similar in many respects to a sliding caliper, this single piston unit floats on guide pins and bushings which are threaded into a mounting bracket. The mounting bracket is bolted to the steering knuckle.

Variations in pad retainers, shims, anti-rattle and retaining springs will be encountered but the service procedures are all basically the same. Note the position of all springs, clips or shims when removing the pads. Work on one side at a time and use the other for a reference.

PAD REPLACEMENT

1. Raise and support the front (or rear) of the vehicle on jackstands. Remove the wheel.

2. Siphon a sufficient quantity of brake fluid from the master cylinder

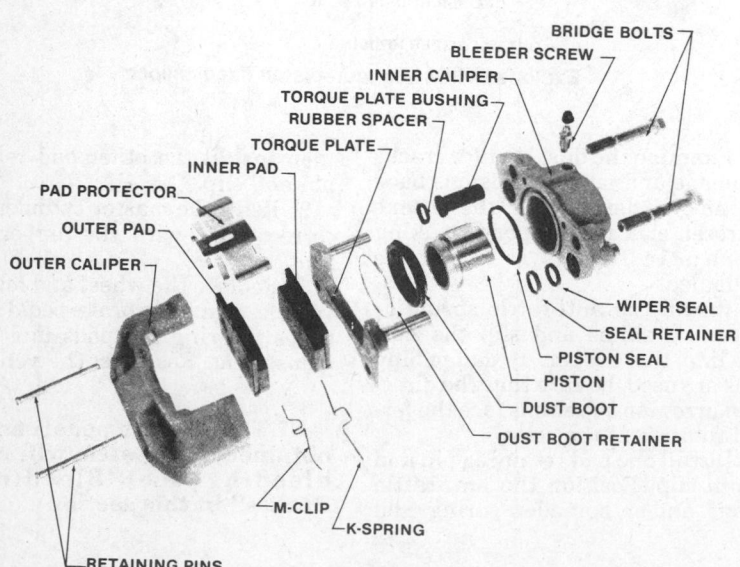

Exploded view of a Sumitomo Torque Plate floating caliper

reservoir to prevent the brake fluid from overflowing the master cylinder when removing or installing new pads. This is necessary as the piston must be forced into the cylinder bore to provide sufficient clearance to remove the pads.

3. Grasp the caliper from behind and pull it toward you. This will push the piston back into the cylinder bore.

4. Disconnect the brake pad lining wear indicator if so equipped. Remove any anti-rattle springs or clips if so equipped.

NOTE: Depending on the model and year of the particular caliper, you may not have to remove it entirely to get at the brake pads. If

the caliper is the "swing" type, remove the upper or lower guide bolt, pivot the caliper on the other loosened bolt and swing it upward exposing the brake pads. If this method is employed, skip to Step 7.

5. Remove the caliper guide pins.
6. Remove the caliper from the rotor by slowly sliding it out and away from the rotor. Position the caliper out of the way and support it with wire so that it doesn't hang by the brake line.
7. Slide the inboard pad out of the adapter.
8. Remove the inboard pad. Remove any shims or shields behind the pads and note their positions.
9. Install the anti-rattle hardware and then the pads (in their proper positions!).

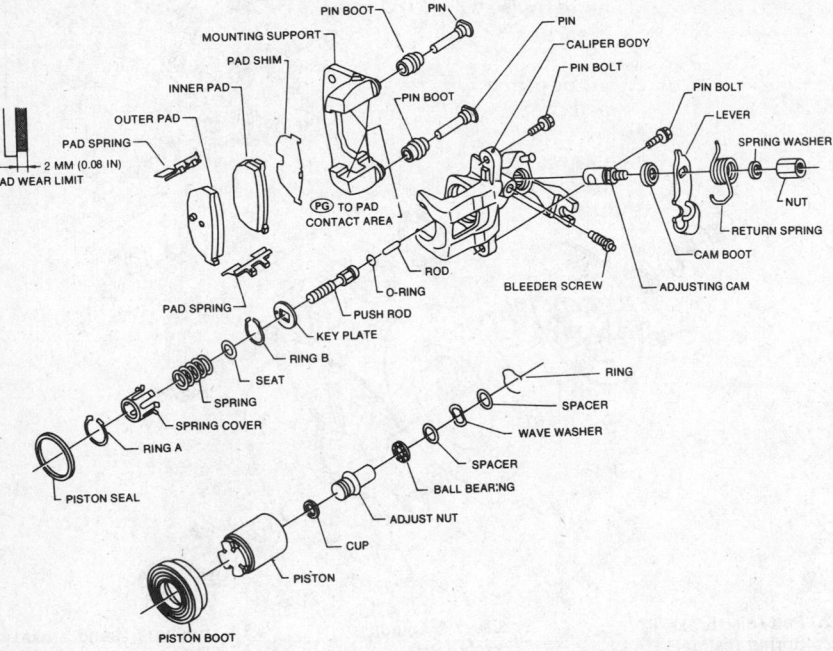

Exploded view of a Type 4 floating caliper with parking brake (Datsun shown, others similar)

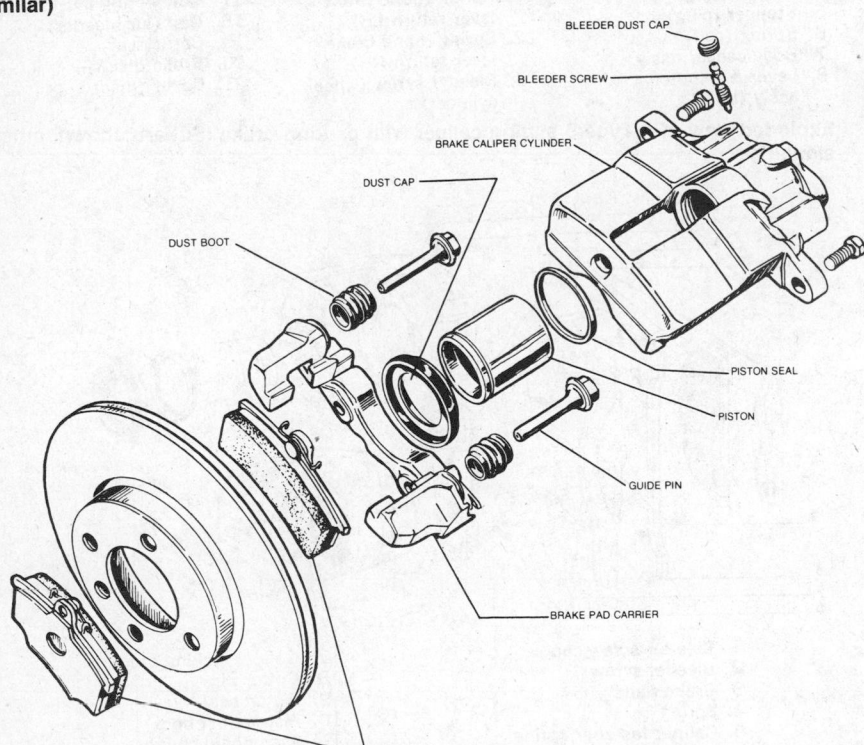

Exploded view of a typical Type 4 floating caliper

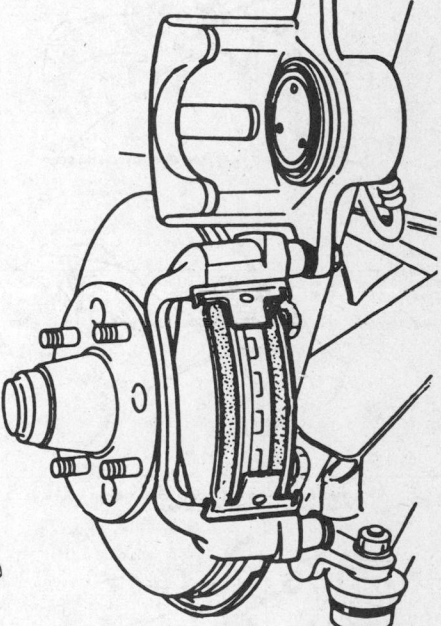

On some models, the caliper cylinder may be pivoted upwards to remove the pads

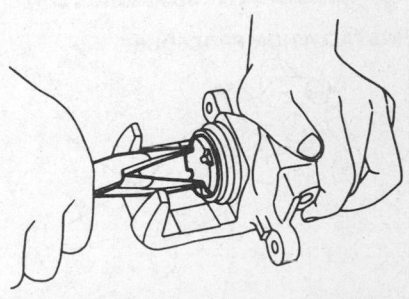

Using needle-nosed pliers to turn the piston before pushing it into the cylinder bore

10. If equipped with the parking brake, use a suitable tool/allen wrench to rotate the caliper piston back into the caliper bore. If not equipped with the parking brake, use a C-clamp to push the caliper piston into the bore.

11. Install any pad shims or heat shields.

12. Reposition the caliper and install the guide pins.

NOTE: If the caliper is the "swing" type, you need only pivot it back into position and install the lower guide pin. On 280ZX front calipers, insert a lever into the opening in the cylinder body as shown in the accompanying illustration and push the piston in by catching the torque member.

REMOVAL PROCEDURE

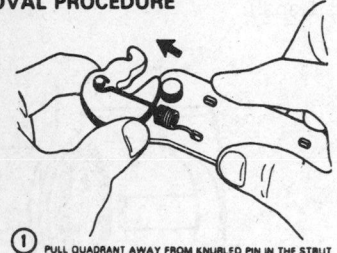

① PULL QUADRANT AWAY FROM KNURLED PIN IN THE STRUT

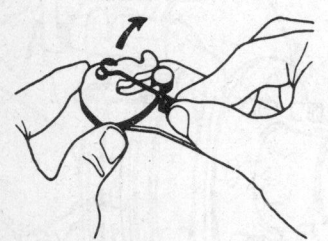

② REMOVE THE SPRING AND SLIDE QUADRANT OUT OF STRUT — BE CAREFUL NOT TO OVERSTRESS SPRING.

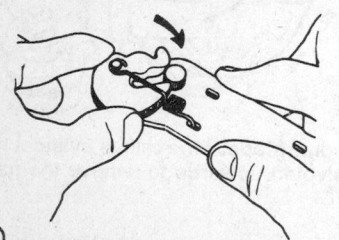

② ROTATE QUADRANT UNTIL TEETH ARE NO LONGER MESHED WITH PIN.

INSTALLATION PROCEDURE

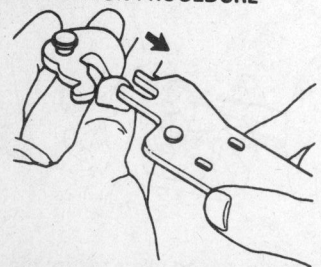

INSTALL ADJUSTER QUADRANT PIN INTO SLOT IN STRUT. TURN ASSEMBLY OVER AND INSTALL SPRING.

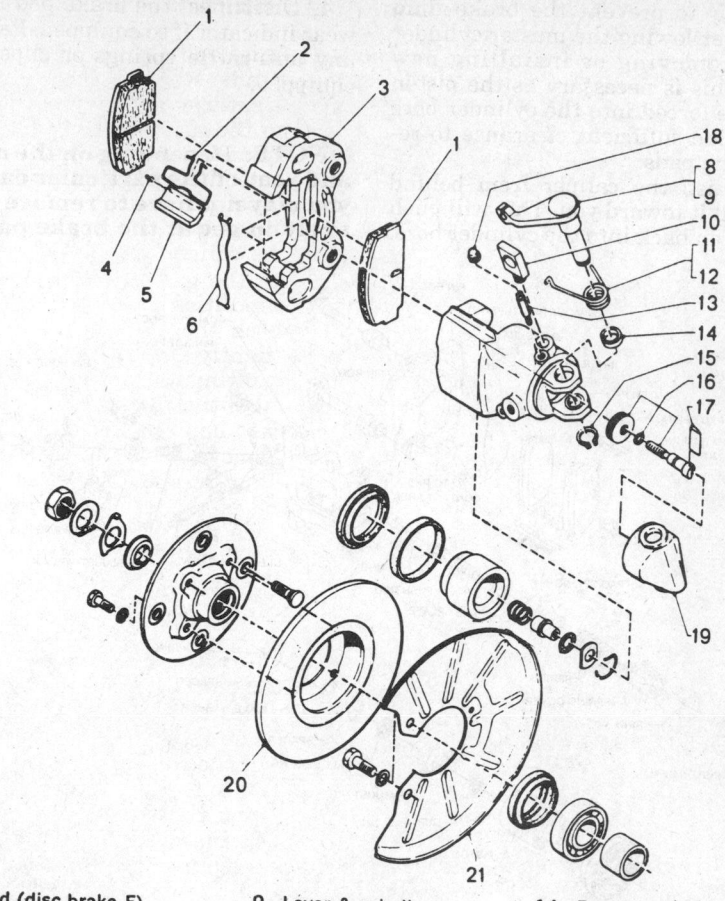

1. Pad (disc brake F)
2. Spring (caliper)
3. Bracket (mounting)
4. Pin (caliper)
5. Stopper (plug)
6. Spring (pad)
7. Body caliper ass'y
8. Lever & spindle ass'y (LH)
9. Lever & spindle ass'y (RH)
10. Bracket (hand brake)
11. Spring (hand brake lever return LH)
12. Spring (hand brake lever return RH)
13. Bleeder screw (wheel cylinder)
14. Bushing (hand brake)
15. Retaining spring
16. Spindle ass'y
17. Connecting link
18. Cap (air bleeder)
19. Cap (lever)
20. Brake disc (F)
21. Cover (disc)

Exploded view of a Type 5 sliding caliper with parking brake (Subaru shown, others similar)

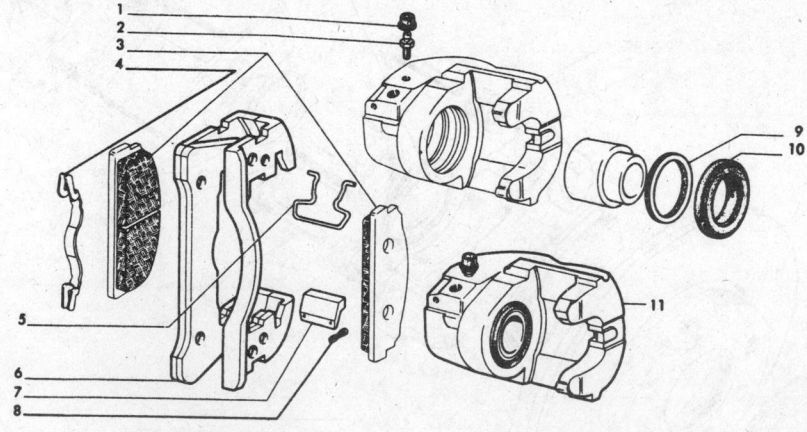

1. Bleeder screw cap
2. Bleeder screw
3. Brake pads
4. Spring
5. Caliper fastener spring
6. Caliper support bracket
7. Caliper locking block
8. Cotter pin
9. Piston seal
10. Piston dust boot
11. Assembled caliper

Exploded view of a Type 5 sliding caliper

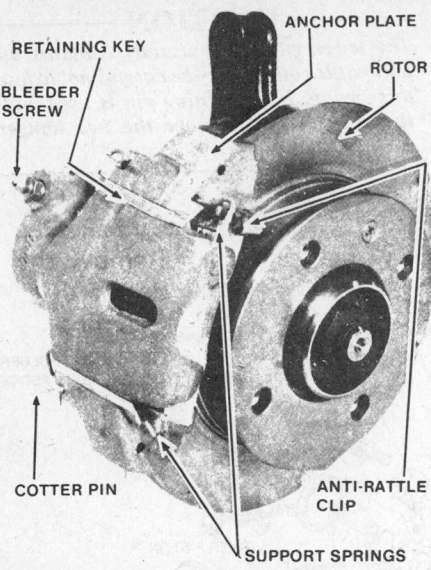

Typical sliding caliper disc brake assembly

13. Refill the master cylinder with fresh brake fluid.

14. Install the tire and wheel assembly and then pump the brake pedal several times to bring the pads into adjustment. Road test the vehicle.

NOTE: After installing new pads on models where caliper is mounted as a rear disc brake depress the pedal firmly (about 40 times—engine off) to set proper adjustment. Check the parking brake operation, adjust the cable if necessary.

NOTE: If a firm pedal cannot be obtained, bleed the system as detailed in "Bleeding the Brakes".

TYPE 5

Akebono, Girling, etc. Sliding Caliper

A single piston sliding caliper system. The caliper is held to a mounting plate or adapter by guide or keys. Support plates are used under the pads to prevent rattling. Variations occur depending on model, however, servicing is similar. Work on one side at a time using the other for reference.

NOTE: If the caliper is equipped with the parking brake system, refer to TYPE 7 for procedure.

PAD REPLACEMENT

1. Raise and support the vehicle on jackstands. Remove the wheel. Remove a sufficient amount of brake fluid from the master cylinder to allow for expansion when fluid is forced back into the master cylinder when the caliper pistons are retracted.

2. Remove the clips or pins that retain the caliper guide(s) in position. Tap out the guide(s) or key(s). Make note of position for reinstallation.

3. Rock the caliper to retach the pads slightly and lift the caliper from the mounting bracket. Secure the caliper out of the way, do not permit the caliper to hang by the brake hose.

4. Remove the brake pads from the mounting bracket. Take note of the position of the pad support springs. They are not interchangeable and must be installed correctly.

5. Push the caliper piston back into the caliper bore with a suitable C-clamp.

6. Clean the metal contact points on the mounting bracket and caliper. Place the brake pads and support springs on the mounting bracket and reinstall the caliper.

7. Apply the brakes several times to position the pads. Fill the master cylinder and check for a firm pedal. Bleed the brake system if necessary.

TYPE 6

ATE, etc. Sliding Yoke Caliper

This unit may have one piston, or two in a single cylinder. It has a fixed mounting frame which is bolted to the steering knuckle. The pads are retained in the fixed frame. A floating frame, or yoke, slides on the fixed frame. The cylinder attaches to this yoke, creating a caliper. Braking pressure forces the piston against the inner pad. The reaction causes the yoke to move in the opposite direction, applying pressure to the outer pad. The yoke does not have to be removed to replace the pads.

PAD REPLACEMENT

1. Raise the front (or rear) of the vehicle and support it with jackstands. Remove the wheel.

2. Siphon a sufficient quantity of brake fluid from the master cylinder reservoir to prevent the brake fluid from overflowing the master cylinder

when removing or installing new pads. This is necessary as the piston must be forced into the cylinder bore to provide sufficient clearance to remove the pads.

3. Disconnect the wire connector leading to the brake pad wear indicator.

4. Remove the brake pad retaining clips on the inside of the caliper and then drive out the retaining pins. Don't lose the pad positioner (spreader) that is held down by the pins.

5. Pry out the inner brake pad with a suitable tool inserted. Through the brake pad retaining pin holes.

6. The outer pads are secured by a notch at the top of the pad. Grasp the caliper assembly from the inside and pull it toward yourself. Remove the pad in the same manner as the inner and detach the wear indicator.

7. Check the brake disc (rotor) as detailed in the appropriate section.

8. Inspect the caliper and piston assembly for breaks, cracks or other damage. Overhaul or replace the caliper as necessary.

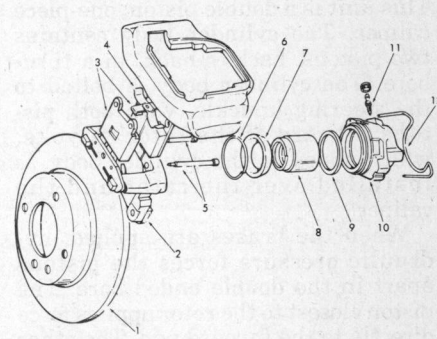

1. Brake disc
2. Caliper mounting frame
3. Pads
4. Cross spring
5. Retaining pins
6. Clamp ring
7. Boot
8. Piston
9. Seal
10. Cylinder
11. Bleeder nipple
12. Guide spring

Exploded view of an ATE sliding yoke caliper

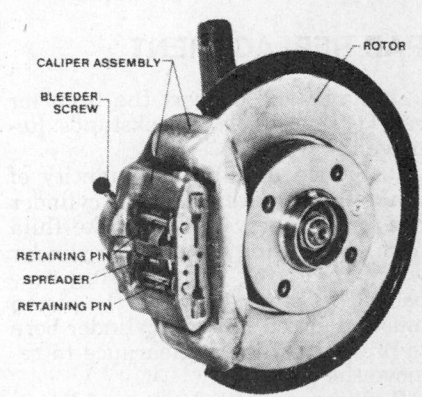

Typical ATE sliding yoke disc brake assembly

9. Use a C-clamp and press the piston back into the cylinder bore. If the caliper is equipped with a piston retaining plate, piston rotation may be necessary for proper plate location.

10. Install the wear indicator on the outer pad and then install both pads.

11. Installation of the remaining components is the reverse order of removal.

12. Top off the master cylinder with fresh brake fluid.

13. Pump the brake pedal several times to bring the pads into adjustment. Road test the vehicle. If a firm pedal cannot be obtained, bleed the brakes as detailed in "Bleeding the Brakes".

TYPE 7

Girling/Annette Sliding Yoke Caliper

This unit is a double piston, one-piece caliper. The cylinder body contains two pistons, back-to-back, in a thrubore. The cylinder body is bolted to the steering knuckle, with both pistons inboard of the rotor. A yoke, which slides on the cylinder body, is installed over the rotor and the caliper.

When the brakes are applied, hydraulic pressure forces the pistons apart in the double ended bore. The piston closest to the rotor applies force directly to the inboard pad. The other piston applies force to the yoke, which transmits the force to the outer pad, creating a friction force on each side of the rotor.

One variation has a yoke that floats on guide pins screwed into the cylinder body.

The yokes do not have to be removed to replace the brake pads.

PAD REPLACEMENT

1. Raise and support the front (or rear) of the vehicle on jackstands. Remove the wheel.

2. Siphon a sufficient quantity of brake fluid from the master cylinder reservoir to prevent the brake fluid from overflowing the master cylinder when removing or installing new pads. This is necessary as the piston must be forced into the cylinder bore to provide sufficient clearance to remove the pads.

3. Disconnect the brake pad lining wear indicator if so equipped.

4. Remove the dust cover and/or anti-rattle (damper) clip if so equipped.

5. Lift off the wire clip(s) which hold the guide pins or retaining pin in place.

6. Remove the upper guide pin and the two hanger springs. Carefully tap out the lower guide pin.

CAUTION

The lower guide pin usually contains an anti-rattle coil spring--be careful not to lose this spring. If a retaining pin is used, pull the pin out and remove the two hanger springs.

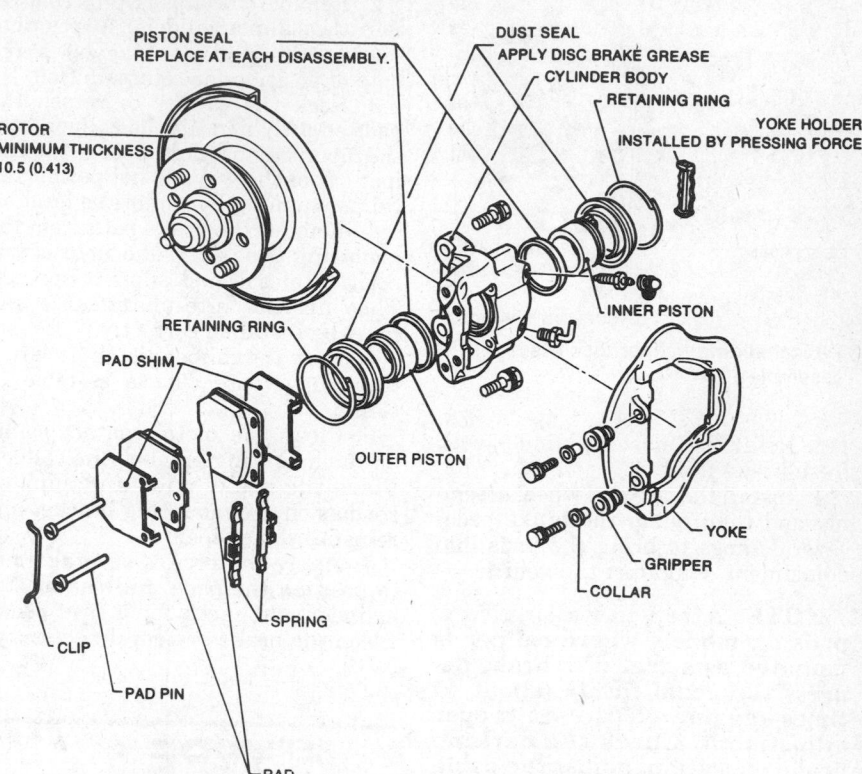

Exploded view of a Type 7 sliding yoke caliper

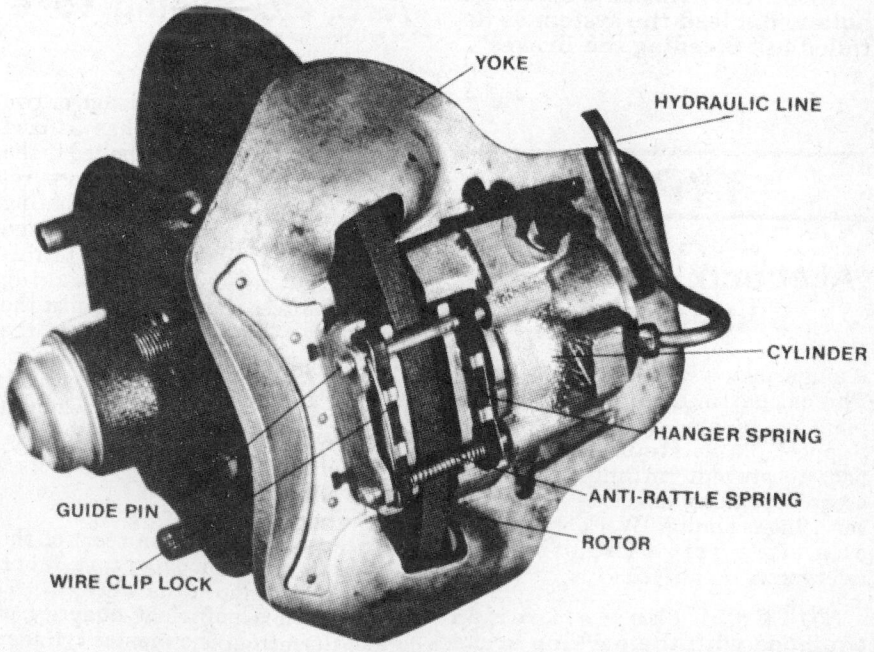

Typical Type 7 sliding yoke caliper disc brake assembly

7. Slide the yoke outward and remove the outer brake pad and the anti-noise shim (if so equipped).

8. Slide the yoke inward and remove the inner pad and anti-rattle shim.

9. Check the rotor as detailed in the appropriate section.

10. Inspect the caliper and piston assembly for breaks, cracks or other damage. Overhaul or replace the caliper as necessary.

11. Push the piston next to the rotor back into the cylinder bore until the end of the piston is flush with the boot retaining ring.

----- CAUTION -----

If the piston is pushed further than this, the seal will be damaged and the caliper assembly will have to be overhauled.

12. Retract the piston farthest from the rotor by pulling the yoke toward the outside of the vehicle.

13. Install the outboard pad. Anti-noise shims (of so equipped) must be located on the plate side of the pad with the triangular cutout pointing toward the top of the caliper.

14. Install the inboard pad with the shims (if so equipped) in the correct position.

15. Replace the lower guide pin and the anti-rattle coil spring.

16. Hook the hanger springs under the pin and over the brake pads.

17. Install the upper guide pin over the ends of the hanger springs.

NOTE: If a single two-sided retaining pin is used, install the pin and then install the hanger springs as in Steps 16–17.

18. Insert the wire clip locks into the holes in the guide pins or retaining pin.

19. Refill the master cylinder with fresh brake fluid.

20. Install the tire and wheel assembly. Pump the brake pedal several times to bring the pads into adjustment. Road test the vehicle. If a firm pedal cannot be obtained, refer to "Bleeding the Brakes".

TYPE 8

Bendix Floating Caliper

This is a single piston unit that floats on guide pins and bellows bushings which are threaded into the mounting bracket. The mounting bracket is

1. Yoke	20. Spring cover
2. Yoke spring	21. Spring
3. Clip	22. Spring seat
4. Pad pin	23. Snap ring C
5. Anti-squeal spring	24. Key plate
6. Pad	25. Push rod
7. Retaining ring	26. O-ring
8. Dust seal	27. Strut
9. Outer piston	28. Inner piston
10. Oil seal	29. Cam
11. Adjusting nut	30. Toggle lever
12. Bearing	31. Spring
13. Spacer	32. Washer
14. Wave washer	33. Nut
15. Snap ring B	
16. Piston seal	
17. Cylinder body	
18. Retainer	
19. Snap ring A	

Exploded view of a Type 7 sliding yoke caliper with parking brake

bolted to the stub axle carrier. This caliper is unique in that it is mounted on the leading edge of the brake disc, where most are mounted on the trailing edge.

The caliper does not have to be removed when replacing the brake pads.

PAD REPLACEMENT

1. Raise and support the front of the vehicle on jackstands. Remove the wheel.

2. Siphon a sufficient quantity of brake fluid from the master cylinder reservoir to prevent the brake fluid from overflowing the master cylinder when removing or installing new pads. This is necessary as the piston must be forced into the cylinder bore to provide sufficient clearance to remove the pads.

3. Grasp the cylinder from behind and carefully pull it toward you. This will push the piston back into the cylinder bore.

4. Disconnect the brake pad lining wear indicator wires. Remove the anti-rattle springs.

5. Remove the retaining key clip on the upper side of the caliper. Remove the retaining key.

6. Lift out the brake pads.

7. Inspect the brake disc (rotor) as detailed in the appropriate section.

8. Inspect the caliper and piston assembly for breaks, cracks or other damage. Overhaul or replace the caliper as necessary.

9. Push the piston all the way back

into its bore (a C-clamp may be necessary for this operation).

10. Slide the new pads into their original position.

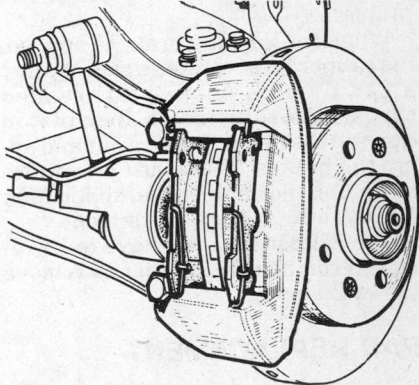

Typical Bendix floating caliper disc brake assembly

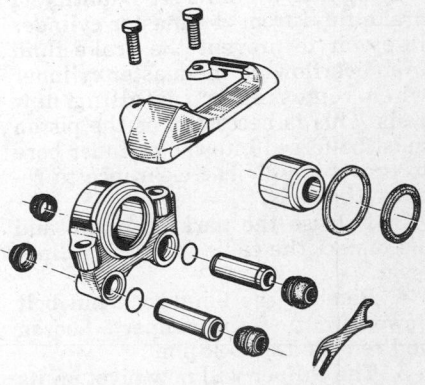

Exploded view of the Bendix floating caliper

11. Slide the retaining key into position and replace the clip.

12. Reinstall the anti-rattle springs and the wear indicator.

13. Refill the master cylinder with fresh brake fluid.

14. Install the tire and wheel assembly and then pump the brakes several times to bring the pads into adjustment. Road test the vehicle.

NOTE: Is a firm pedal cannot be obtained, bleed the system as detailed in "Bleeding the Brakes".

6. Remove the pads. Note the positions of the pad shims and the inner and outer pad clips.

7. Inspect the brake disc (rotor) as detailed in the appropriate section.

8. Inspect the caliper and piston assembly for breaks, cracks or other damage. Overhaul or replace the caliper if necessary.

9. Turn the caliper piston clockwise into the cylinder bore and align the notches. Make sure the boot is not twisted or pinched.

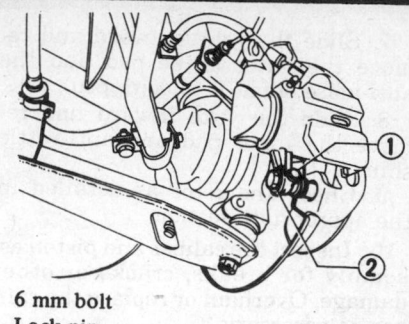

6 mm bolt
Lock pin

Removing the lock pin

TYPE 9

Akebono Floating Caliper W/Parking Brake

This is a single piston unit that floats on guide pins and bushings which are threaded into a mounting bracket. The mounting bracket is bolted to the steering knuckle. This unit also incorporates a parking brake into the caliper.

When the parking brake is applied, the caliper lever rotates a cam against a pawl which pushes a threaded thrust screw in the caliper piston causing the piston to move out and apply the brakes. The thrust screw also moves on normal brake application maintaining correct adjustment.

The caliper does not have to be removed completely in order to remove the brake pads.

PAD REPLACEMENT

1. Raise and support the front of the vehicle on jackstands. Remove the wheel.

2. Siphon a sufficient quantity of brake fluid from the master cylinder reservoir to prevent the brake fluid from overflowing the master cylinder when removing or installing new pads. This is necessary as the piston must be forced into the cylinder bore to provide sufficient clearance to remove the pads.

3. Release the parking brake and disconnect the cable from the caliper lever.

4. Remove the 6mm lock pin bolt (lower front of the caliper). Loosen and remove the lock pin.

5. The caliper will now pivot on its support, swing it up and out of the way.

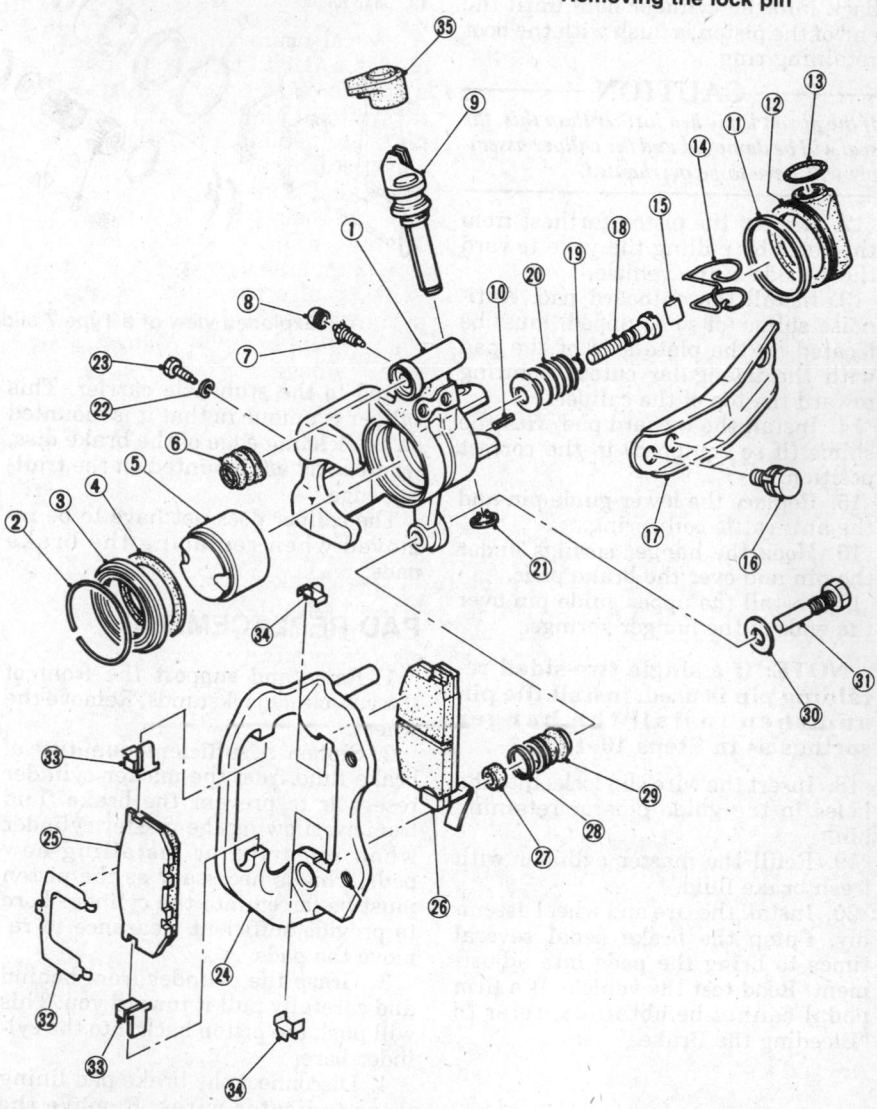

1	Caliper body	13	Gutter spring	25	Outer pad
2	Boot ring	14	Return spring	26	Inner pad
3	Piston boot	15	Connecting link	27	Rubber bushing
4	Piston seal	16	Bolt assembly	28	Retainer
5	Piston	17	Bracket	29	Lock pin boot
6	Guide pin boot	18	Spindle	30	Cone spring
7	Air bleeder screw	19	O-ring	31	Lock pin
8	Air bleeder cap	20	Cone spring	32	Shim
9	Lever & spindle	21	Snap ring	33	Outer pad clip
10	Spring pin	22	Spring washer	34	Inner pad clip
11	Cap ring	23	Bolt	35	Lever cap (upper)
12	Lever cap	24	Support		

Exploded view of the Type 9 floating caliper

NOTE: Do not force the piston into the cylinder bore. The piston is mounted on a threaded spindle which will bend under pressure.

10. Insert the new pads making sure that all shims and clips are in their original positions.

11. Swing the caliper down into position and install the lock pin and the 6mm bolt.

12. Reconnect the parking brake.

13. Refill the master cylinder with fresh brake fluid.

14. Install the tire and wheel assembly and then pump the brake pedal several times to bring the pads into adjustment. Road test the vehicle.

NOTE: If a firm pedal cannot be obtained, bleed the system as detailed in "Bleeding the Brakes".

TYPE 10

Sumitomo, etc. Sliding Yoke Caliper W/ Integral Parking Brake

A single cylinder, dual piston caliper similar to the Girling sliding yoke caliper featuring an integral parking brake mechanism. Work on one side at a time using the other side as reference.

PAD REPLACEMENT

1. Raise and support the vehicle on jackstands. Remove the wheel.

2. Remove a sufficient amount of brake fluid from the master cylinder to allow for level expansion when the caliper pistons are retracted.

3. Release the parking brake and disconnect the cable from the caliper lever.

4. Unbolt and remove the caliper. Do not permit the caliper to be suspended by the brake hose or damage to the hose may occur.

5. Remove the pads making note of the location of the various springs, clips and pins.

6. Open the bleeder valve slightly to relieve pressure to the pistons an screw the outboard piston clockwise into the bore. Take care not to allow the inboard piston to come out of its bore.

7. Install the brake pads. Rotate the inboard piston so that the tab on the pad will align with the slot in the piston.

8. Install the caliper. Connect the parking brake cable. Bleed the system filling the master cylinder as necessary to maintain the proper level.

9. Install the wheel and lower the vehicle. Check the operation of the parking brake and test drive.

SERVICING DRUM BRAKES

A typical drum brake assembly includes a backing or support plate, with one or two wheel cylinders attached to it. Mounted on the backing plate are two lined brake shoes with shoe return springs and hold-down parts, and a means of adjusting the shoes to compensate for lining wear. A brake drum encloses these parts. The drum brakes on the rear of most vehicles also normally include the parts required for parking brakes. All of the drum brakes used on modern vehicles have these components but there is a variety of configurations for each.

Drum brakes are designed to be either "servo" or "non-servo" acting.

Servo Type Brakes

In these brakes the shoes are assembled to form a compound, "primary" and "secondary" shoe unit joined at one end by an adjustable floating link.

The drag of a normal (forward) drum rotation causes the primary shoe to leave its anchor and holds the secondary shoe anchored.

All of the forces applying and anchoring the primary shoe are transmitted through the shoe link, in a servo action, and also apply the secondary shoe, thus compounding its braking effect. When the drum is rotated backward, this compounding action of the shoes is reversed. When equipped with a double-end wheel cylinder (two opposed pistons), brake effectiveness can be substantially the same with either forward or reverse movement of the vehicle. With a single-end wheel cylinder (one piston), the brake is energized in only one direction. Since the secondary shoe performs more of the work in forward movement, it shows more lining wear. A longer or thicker lining is often used to offset this wear.

Non-Servo Type Brakes

In these brakes each shoe is separately anchored and their action is not compounded. On single cylinder brakes a "forward" or "leading" shoe is self-energized by the usual (forward) drum rotation while a "reverse" or "trailing" shoe is de-energized. When the drum is rotated backward, this action reverses, thus energizing the reverse shoe and de-energizing the forward shoe. The lining wear is

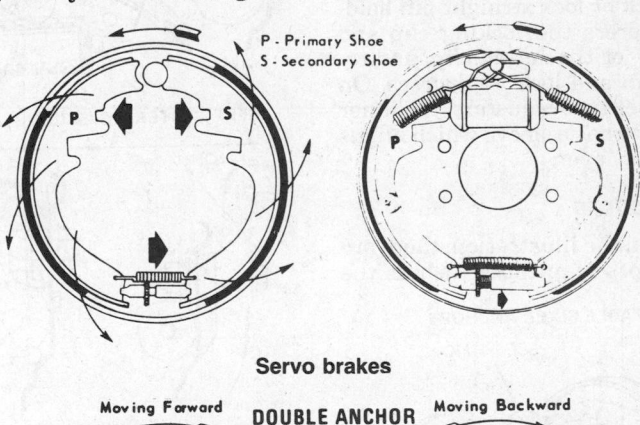

P - Primary Shoe
S - Secondary Shoe

Servo brakes

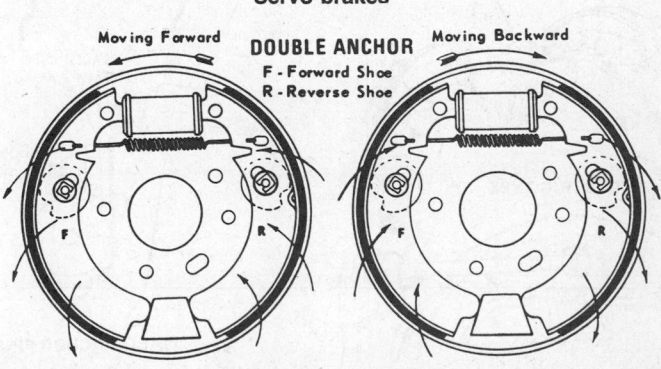

Moving Forward   Moving Backward

DOUBLE ANCHOR
F - Forward Shoe
R - Reverse Shoe

Non–servo brakes

unbalanced because the shoe perform different amounts of work; the wear is more rapid on the forward acting shoe during a forward stop.

Large two cylinder non-servo brakes, found on certain models, make use of two double-end wheel cylinders which enable the shoes to be anchored or actuated at either end. This arrangement is non-directional in effectiveness. With two-cylinder brakes, lining wear is balanced on both sides.

MECHANICAL COMPONENTS

To be sure of restoring the brake components correctly after servicing, closely observe the arrangement of shoe hook-up parts as the brake is disassembled. These arrangements may vary on different models. Usually the brake shoes are held in a sliding fit by spring tensions, at rest upon their anchor by the return springs, and against support pads by spring or clip type hold-downs. Opposite the anchor, a star wheel adjuster links the shoe webs and provides a threaded adjustment which permits the shoes to be expanded or contracted. Some rear brakes have adjustable links. The shoes are held against the adjuster by a spring.

Shoe Hold-Downs

Various shoe hold-downs are shown in the illustration.

To unlock or lock straight pin hold-downs, depress the locking cup and coil spring, or the spring clip, and rotate the pin and lock 90 degrees. On certain lever type adjusters, the inner (bottom) cup has a sleeve which aligns the adjuster lever.

Shoe Anchors

As shown in the illustration, there are various types of anchors such as the

fixed non-adjustable type, or self-centering shoe sliding type, or, on some earlier models, adjustable fixed type providing either an eccentric or a slotted adjustment.

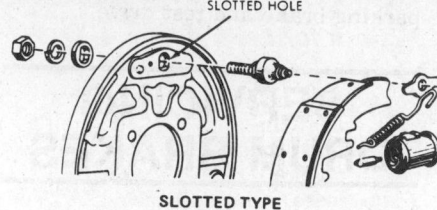

SLOTTED HOLE

SLOTTED TYPE

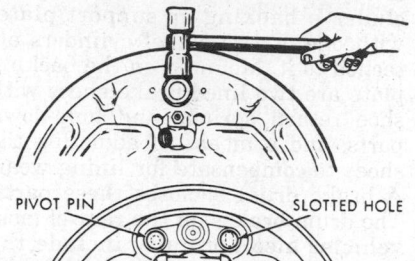

PIVOT PIN — SLOTTED HOLE

PIVOTED SLOTTED TYPE

Anchor adjustment—slotted type

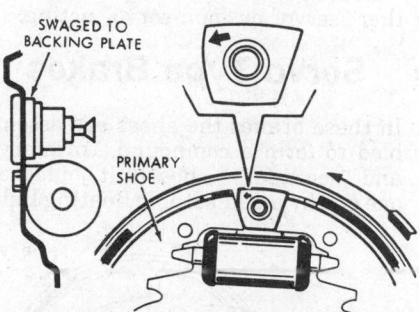

SWAGED TO BACKING PLATE

PRIMARY SHOE

SELF-CENTERING (SLIDING) ANCHOR.

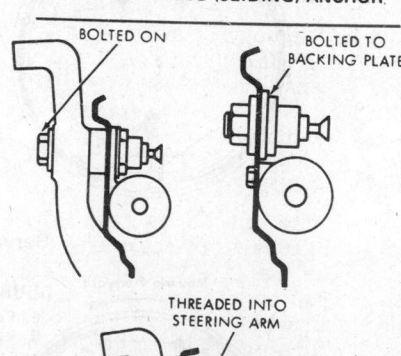

BOLTED ON

BOLTED TO BACKING PLATE

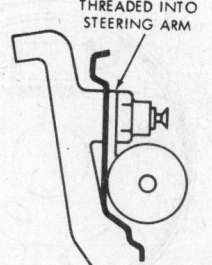

THREADED INTO STEERING ARM

FIXED ANCHOR PINS

Different types of shoe anchors

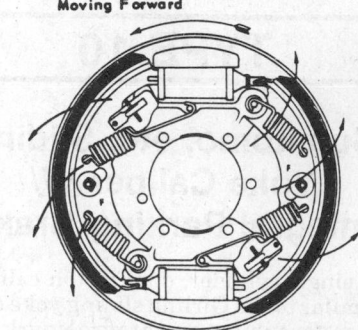

ADJUSTER HOLE

ADJUSTER LEVER PUSH BACK 1/16" MAX. (1.5 mm)

MOVE HANDLE UPWARD TO RETRACT BRAKE SHOES DOWNWARD TO EXPAND

Some drums can be removed by backing off the self-adjuster

NON-DIRECTIONAL ACTING

Moving Forward

Moving Backward

Two cylinder, non-servo brake

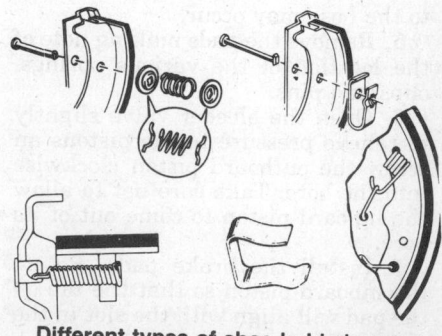

Different types of shoe hold-downs

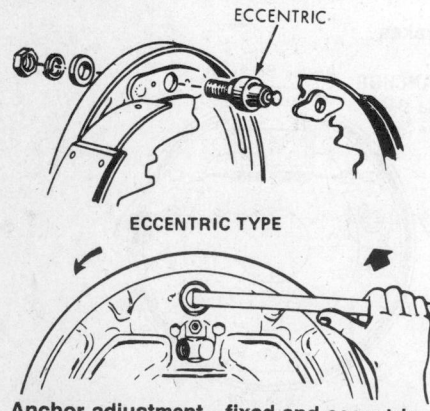

ADJUSTABLE FIXED ANCHORS

ECCENTRIC

ECCENTRIC TYPE

Anchor adjustment—fixed and eccentric

On adjustable anchors, when necessary to re-center the shoes in he drum or drum gauge, loosen the locknut enough to permit the anchor to slip out, but not so much that it can tilt.

On eccentric type anchors, tighten the star wheel to heavy brake drag. Rotate the eccentric anchor in the direction which frees the brake until drag cannot be relieved. Tighten the anchor nut. Back off the star wheel to a normal manual adjustment.

On the slotted type anchor, tighten the star wheel to heavy drag. Tap the support plate until the anchor slips and frees the brake. Repeat this sequence until drag cannot be relieved. Tighten the locknut to the proper torque. Back off the star wheel to a normal manual adjustment.

Brake Shoes

In the same brake sizes, there can be differences in web thickness, shape of web cut-outs and positions of any reinforcements. Some vehicles require shoes made of higher tensile strength steels. Higher strength shoes usually are coded with a letter symbol stamped on the shoe web. Shoes with extra web holes or table nibs or tabs which do not cause interference generally are considered interchangeable with other shoes.

Stops

An eccentric stop under the primary or secondary shoe web on tilted front brakes prevents the shoes from bumping against the drum. Before adjusting the star wheel, loosen the locknut on the support plate and rotate the eccentric in the forward direction until the shoe drags. Back-off until drag is relieved and tighten the locknut.

PISTON STOPS

If the brake is equipped with piston stops, the wheel cylinder must be dismounted for reconditioning.

BASIC SERVICE

—————— CAUTION ——————

Do not blow the brake dust out of the drums with compressed air or lung power; always use a damp cloth and wipe it out. Brake linings contain asbestos, a known cancer causing substance. Dispose of the cloth after use.

NOTE: Never work on a car supported only on a jack. Use a hydraulic lift or jack stands to support the vehicle while working.

Raising both front or rear wheels at once and supporting them on jack stands also allows comparison of the brake being serviced to the brake on the opposite side.

Check for Leaks

Press the brake pedal to ensure that there are no leaks in the hydraulic system. If the pedal does not remain hard, and drops to the floor, it is an indication of a leak in the master cylinder, hoses, wheel cylinders, or disc brake calipers. When performing this test, the engine should be running if the car is equipped with power brakes. With power brakes it is normal for the pedal to drop slightly when the engine starts. If it continues to drop, start looking for a leak.

Drum Removal

Safely support the car and release the parking brake if working on the rear axle. Remove the lug nuts, the wheel/tire assembly and then pull off the drums. If the brake shoes have expanded too tightly against the drum, or have cut into the friction surface of the brake drum, the drums may be too tight for removal. In such a case, adjust the shoes inward before the brake drum is removed. On cars with self-adjusting mechanisms, reach through the adjusting slot with a very small prybar (or similar tool) and carefully push the self-adjusting lever away from the star wheel by a maximum of $\frac{1}{16}$ in. (1.5mm). While holding the lever back, insert a brake adjusting tool into the slot and turn the star wheel in the proper direction until the brake drum can be removed. On cars with manual adjusting mechanisms, try lightly tapping the drum with a rubber mallet. If this does not work, simply reverse the manual adjustment procedures given later in this section until the drum can be removed.

Drum Inspection

Check the drums fro any cracks, scores, grooves, or an out-of-round condition. Replace of cracked. Slight scores can be removed with fine emery cloth while extensive scoring requires turning the drum on a lathe.

If the friction surface of the brake drum appears scored or otherwise damaged beyond repair, it will require reconditioning. After machining, the drum diameter must not exceed the diameter cast on the drum or 0.060 in. (1.5mm) over the original nominal diameter. Carefully look for signs of grease or oil at the center of the assembly. If any leak is noticed, the seal should be replaced.

Rebuild the Cylinders

It is *always* a good idea to rebuild or replace the wheel cylinders when relining the brakes. This will help assure a proper operating brake system.

Remove Brake Shoes

It is convenient to disassemble one wheel at a time so the opposite side serves as a reference. Carefully note the colors and locations of different springs and parts. This is necessary to distinguish different springs that appear to be the same but have different tensions. If there are extra unused holes close to the ones in which the springs are located, use a dab of paint or other marking on the new shoes to identify the holes to be used. Replace any discolored springs and other parts

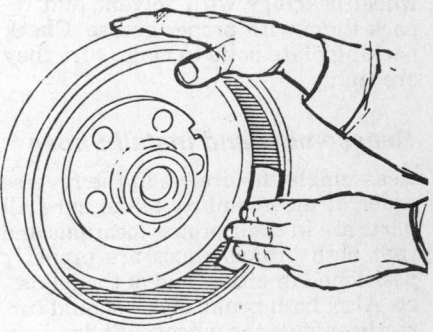

Sanding the drum

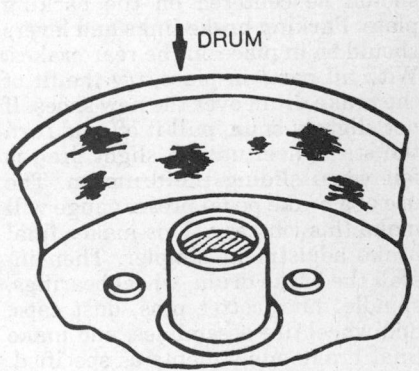

Hard or chill spots

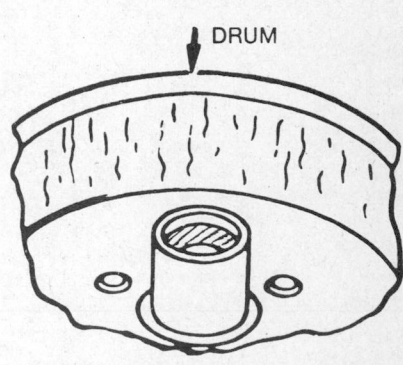

Heat checks

found corroded or distorted. Use special tools whenever necessary. Examine the springs for signs of stretching or other defects and replace if their condition is at all questionable. Examine the flexible brake hoses and replace any that show signs of cracking or other damage.

Clean and Lubricate Shoes

With all the brake parts off, clean the backing plate with a damp cloth to avoid raising any asbestos dust, and dispose of the rag after use. Clean any rust with a wire brush. File smooth any ridges or rough edges on the contact points on the backing plate, and lubricate with approved brake lubricant. Clean and lightly lubricate the adjuster threads, and screw the adjuster all the way together to facilitate reassembly later on. Wash the wheel bearings with solvent and repack them with proper grease. Check backing plate bolts to make sure they are tight.

Reassemble and Install Shoes

Reassemble the brakes in the reverse order of disassembly. Make sure all parts are in their proper locations and that both brakes shoes are properly positioned in either end of the adjuster. Also, both brake shoes should correctly engage the wheel cylinder push rods and parking brake links, and should be centered on the backing plate. Parking brake links and levers should be in place on the rear brakes. With all parts in place, try the fit of the brake drum over the new shoes. If not slightly snug, pull it off and turn the star wheel until a slight drag is felt when sliding the drum on. The use of a brake pedal preset gauge will make this job easy. This makes final brake adjustment simpler. Then install the brake drum, wheel bearings, spindle nuts, cotter pins, dust caps, and wheel/tire assemblies, and make final brake adjustments as specified. Torque the spindle and lug nuts to specifications.

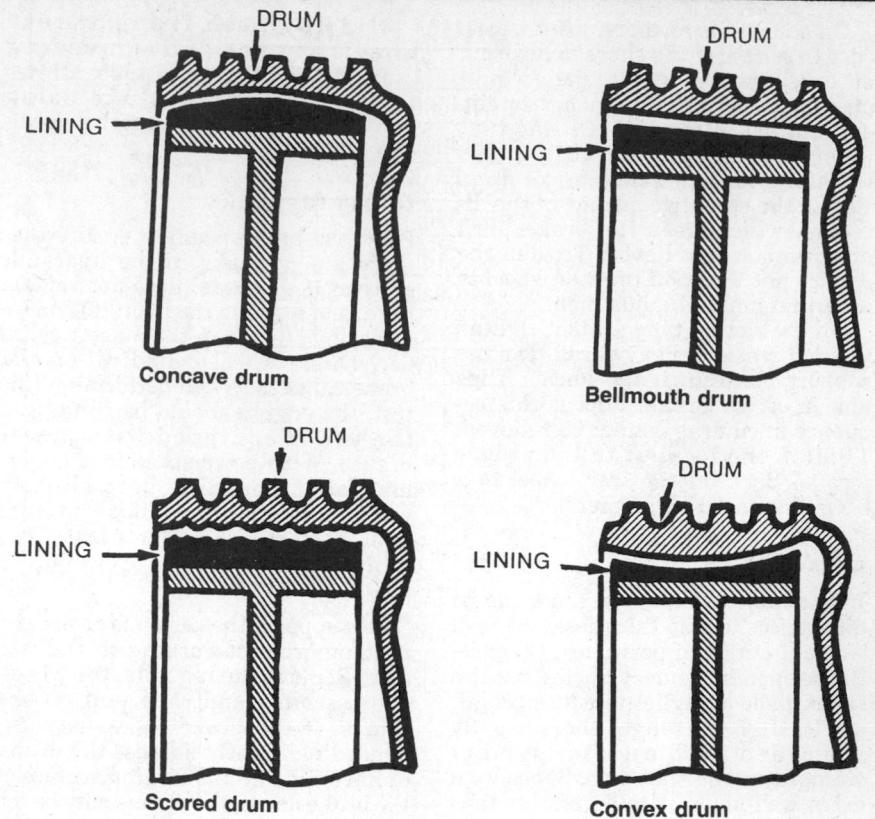

Concave drum

Bellmouth drum

Scored drum

Convex drum

CHILTON TIPS

The primary brake shoe is the one toward the front of the car, and its lining is usually shorter than that on the secondary (rearward) shoe.

Self-adjusting mechanisms are usually mounted on the secondary shoe.

Bleed and Road-Test

Bleed the brakes to make sure of a high, hard brake pedal, and road-test the car. Most self-adjusting mechanisms are activated only during the rearward motion of the car. So, whenever servicing self-adjusting brakes, make sure that the road test included enough stops, traveling in reverse, to allow the self-adjusters to perform the proper match-up of all wheels. Or, operate the parking brake several times if that activates the automatic adjuster.

The star wheel part of an adjuster usually (but not always) goes toward the rear of the car.

Different colors springs belong in different locations.

Self-adjusters and related parts are not interchangeable from one side of a car to the other since the direction of adjuster rotation varies from one side of a car to the other. Most adjusters on one side of a car have right hand threads, and the adjusters on the other side have left hand threads.

Never press the brake pedal when one or more brakes drums are off, or a wheel cylinder will pop apart.

DRUM BRAKE APPLICATION CHART

Manufacturer	Year & Model	Type No.	Page
Audi	1981-84 4000	12	32-39
	1981-88 4000S, Coupe, GT	12	32-39
	1981-88 5000	12	32-39
BMW	1981-83 320i	5	32-32
	1984-85 318i	10	32-37
Chrylser Corp.	1981-84 Challenger, Sapporo, Colt (RWD)	9	32-36
	1981-88 Colt, Champ (FWD)	14	32-40
Honda	1981-88 Civic, CRX	11	32-39
	1981 Accord	8	32-35
	1982-88 Accord	3	32-31
	1981-82 Prelude	11	32-39
	1983 Prelude	3	32-31
Hyundai	1986-88 Excel	14	32-40
Isuzu	1981-88 I-Mark	9	32-36
Mazda	1981-83 RX7	13	32-40
	1981-88 GLC, 323	15	32-41
	1982 626	13	32-40
	1983-88 626	11	32-39
Merkur	1985-88 XR4Ti	2	32-30
Mitsubishi	1983-88 Cordia, Tredia	9	32-36
	1985-88 Galant	8	32-35
	1985-88 Mirage	14	32-40
	1987-88 Van/Wagon	9	32-36
Nissan/Datsun	1982-88 All exc. Sentra, Pulsar	14	32-40
	1982 Sentra, Pulsar	14	32-40
Porsche	1981-82 924	1	32-30
Renault	1981-86 18i, Fuego, Sportwagon	9	32-36
	1982-88 Alliance, Encore, GTA	3	32-31
	1981-83 LeCar	5	32-32
Subaru	1981-84 All Models exc. Justy	8	32-35
	1987-88 Justy	11	32-39
Toyota	1981-88 All exc. Celica/Supra	3, 4, 5, 6, 14	32-31 32-33
	1981 Celica/Supra	3	32-31
Volkswagon	1981-88 Vanagon	1	32-30
	1981-88 Rabbit, Scirocco, Jetta, Quantum, Golf, Fox	10, 12	32-37
Yugo	1987-88 All Models	16	32-42

TYPE 1

Lockheed Non-Servo — Manual Adjuster

This brake consists of non-servo forward and reverse shoes with double-end type wheel cylinder. The shoes anchor upon the slotted adjusting screws which permit them a sliding self centering action. Brakes are mounted with the cylinder at the top and the adjuster at the bottom.

Front wheel brake   Rear wheel brake

Typical Lockhead non-servo drum brake assembly (left—front brakes; right—rear brakes)

FRONT
1. Adjusting screw
2. Anchor block
3. Front return spring
4. Adjusting nut
5. Guide spring with cup and pin
6. Cylinder
7. Rear return spring
8. Back plate
9. Brake shoe with lining

REAR
1. Cylinder
2. Brake shoe with lining
3. Upper return spring
4. Spring with cup and pin
5. Lower return spring
6. Adjusting screw
7. Back plate
8. Connecting link
9. Lever
10. Brake cable
11. Adjusting nut
12. Anchor block

REMOVAL & INSTALLATION

1. Raise the front/rear of the vehicle and support it with jackstands. Remove the tire and wheel.
2. Remove the drums (some vehicles may require special pullers).
3. Detach both retracting springs.
4. Remove both hold-down springs and lift the brake shoes from the backing plate. On the rear wheels, unhook the parking brake cable from the parking brake lever before shoe removal.
5. Clean and lubricate the backing plate as detailed earlier.

6. Check the wheel cylinder for frozen pistons or fluid leaks. If any are found, rebuild or replace the cylinder. Disassemble the adjusters and clean and lubricate them.
7. Install the parking brake lever on a new reverse shoe (only on rear wheel brakes).
8. Place new brake shoes on the backing plate and attach the hold-down springs.

NOTE: Slots in the adjusting screws must be slanted toward the center of the assembly.

The ends of the shoes should engage the wheel cylinder piston slots, and the adjuster slots. If the adjuster screw ends have a slot with a bevel on one side, make sure the bevel lines up with the bevel on the shoe web.

The end of the shoe with a slot for the parking strut should be installed near the wheel cylinder.

9. For rear wheels, hook the parking brake lever on the parking brake cable and then install the parking brake strut.
10. Install the heavier retracting spring between the toe or cylinder ends of the brake shoes.
11. Attach the lighter retracting spring to the heel or anchor ends of the shoes.
12. Replace the drums, bleed and adjust the assembly and road test the car.

ADJUSTMENT

Insert an adjusting spoon or a small screwdriver through the adjusting hole in the backing plate and expand the shoe assembly by revolving the notched adjusting wheel in a clockwise direction when facing the end of the wheel cylinder. Adjust the shoe until a heavy drag is felt when turning the wheel and drum; then, back off the adjustment until the wheel spins freely. Adjust one shoe at a time and repeat this procedure at all brakes shoes.

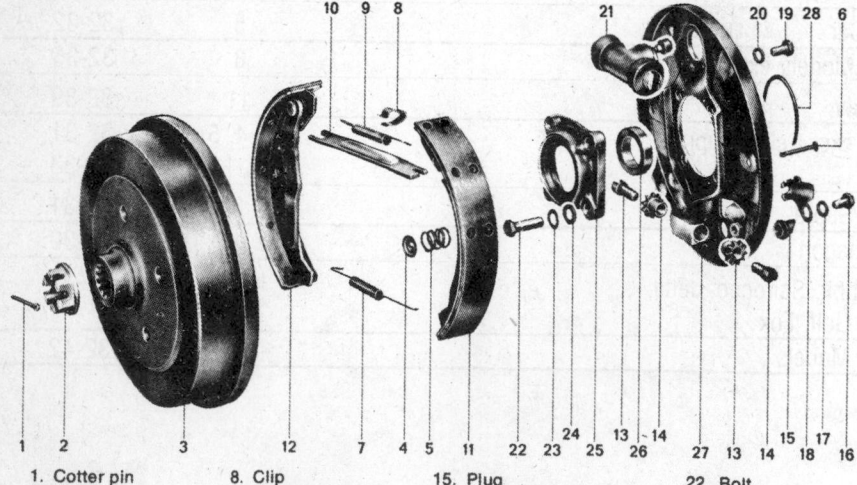

1. Cotter pin
2. Castle nut
3. Brake drum
4. Spring retainer
5. Spring
6. Pin
7. Return spring
8. Clip
9. Return spring
10. Pressure rod
11. Brake shoe
12. Brake lever
13. Adjusting screw
14. Adjusting nut
15. Plug
16. Bolt
17. Lockwasher
18. Holder
19. Bolt
20. Lockwasher
21. Wheel brake cylinder
22. Bolt
23. Washer
24. Plain washer
25. Cover
26. Spacer
27. Brake carrier
28. Seal

Exploded view of a Type 1 drum brake

TYPE 2

Fixed Anchoring — Self-Adjusting

REMOVAL & INSTALLATION

1. Raise and support the rear of the vehicle on jackstands. Remove the wheel and brake drum.

2. Remove the hold-down pins and springs by pushing down on and rotating the outer washer 90 degrees. It may be necessary to hold the back of the pin (behind the backing plate) while pressing down and turning the washer.

3. After the hold-down pins and springs have been removed from both brake shoes, remove both shoes and the adjuster assembly by lifting up and away from the bottom anchor plate and shoe guide. Take care not to damage the wheel cylinder boots when removing the shoes from the wheel cylinder.

4. Remove the parking brake cable from the brake lever to allow the removal of the shoes and adjuster assembly.

5. Remove the lower shoe to shoe spring by rotating the leading brake shoe to release the spring tension. Do not pry the spring from the shoe.

6. Remove the adjuster strut from the trailing shoe by pulling the strut away from the shoe and twisting it downward toward yourself until the spring tension is released. Remove the spring from the slot.

7. Remove the parking brake lever from the shoe by disconnecting the horseshoe clip and spring washer and pulling the lever from the shoe.

8. If for any reason the adjuster assembly must be taken apart, do the following: pull the adjuster quadrant (U-shaped lever) away from the knurled pin on the adjuster strut by rotating the quadrant in either direction until the teeth are no longer engaged with the pin. Remove the spring and slide the quadrant out of the slot on the end of the adjuster strut. Do not put too much stress on the spring during disassembly.

9. Clean the brake backing (mounting) plate with a soft paint brush or vacuum cleaner.

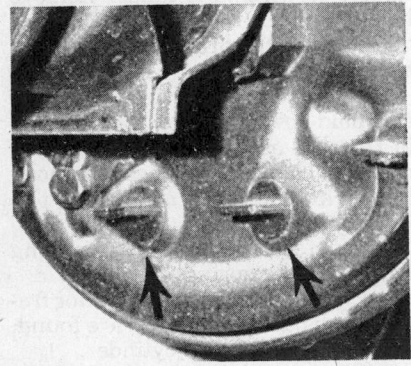

Rear drum brake shoe adjusters are found behind the two lower rubber plugs on the backing plate. The two higher plugs (if so equipped) are removed to check brake shoe wear

---
— **CAUTION** —

Never inhale the dust from the brake linings. Asbestos dust when inhaled can be injurious to your health. Use a vacuum cleaner. Do not blow off the dust with air pressure.

---

10. Apply a thin film of high temperature grease at the points on the backing plate where the brake shoes make contact.

11. Apply a thin film of multi-purpose grease to the adjuster strut at the point between the quadrant and the strut.

12. If the adjuster has been disassembled; install the quadrant mounting pin into the slot on the adjuster strut and install the adjuster spring.

13. Assemble the parking brake lever to the trailing shoe. Install the spring washer and a new horseshoe clip, squeeze the clip with pliers until the lever is secured on the shoe.

14. Install the adjuster strut attaching spring on to the trailing shoe. Attach the adjusting strut by fastening the spring in the slot and pivoting the strut into position. This will tension the spring. Make sure the end of the spring where the hook is parallel to the center line of the spring coils is hooked into the web of the brake shoe. The installed spring should be flat against the web and parallel to the adjuster strut.

15. Install the shoe to shoe spring with the longest hook attached to the trailing shoe.

16. Install the leading shoe to adjuster strut spring by installing the spring to both parts and pivoting the leading shoe over the quadrant and into position, this will tension the spring.

17. Place the shoes and adjuster assembly onto the backing plate. Spread the shoes slightly and position them into the wheel cylinder piston inserts and anchor plate. Take care not to damage the wheel cylinder boots.

18. Attach the parking brake cable to the parking brake lever.

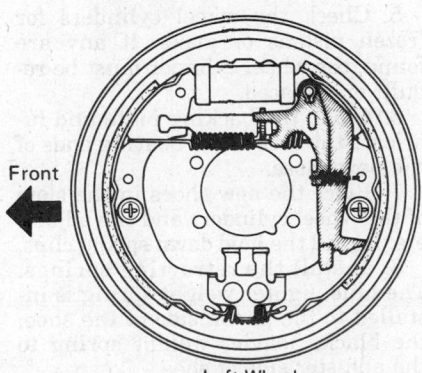

Front ←

Typical Type 3 drum brake assembly

Left Wheel

---

19. Install the hold-down pins, springs and washers.

20. Install the remaining components in the reverse order of removal.

ADJUSTMENT

1. Remove the brake drum.

2. Pivot the adjuster quadrant until the third or fourth notch from the outer end meshes with the knurled pin on the adjuster strut.

3. Reinstall the brake drum.

TYPE 3

Non-Servo—Semi-Automatic Adjuster

This brake consists of non-servo forward and reverse shoes with a double-ended type wheel cylinder. The brake shoes are adjusted automatically whenever the parking brake is applied.

REMOVAL & INSTALLATION

1. Raise the rear of the vehicle and support it with jackstands. Remove the tire and the wheel.

2. Remove the brake drum. Tap the drum lightly with a mallet in order to free it. If the drum cannot be removed easily, insert a screwdriver into the hole in the backing plate and hold the automatic adjuster lever away from the adjusting bolt. Using another screwdriver, relieve the brake shoe tension by turning the adjusting bolt clockwise. If the drum will still not come off, use a puller; but first make sure that the parking brake is released.

— **CAUTION** —

Do not depress the brake pedal once the brake drum has been removed.

---

3. Unhook the shoe tension springs from the shoes with the aid of a brake spring removing tool.

4. Remove the brake shoe securing springs.

5. Disconnect the parking brake cable at the parking brake shoe lever.

6. Withdraw the shoes, complete with the parking brake shoe lever.

7. Unfasten the C-clip and remove the adjuster assembly from the shoes.

8. Inspect the shoe for wear and scoring.

9. Check the wheel cylinder for frozen pistons or fluid leaks.

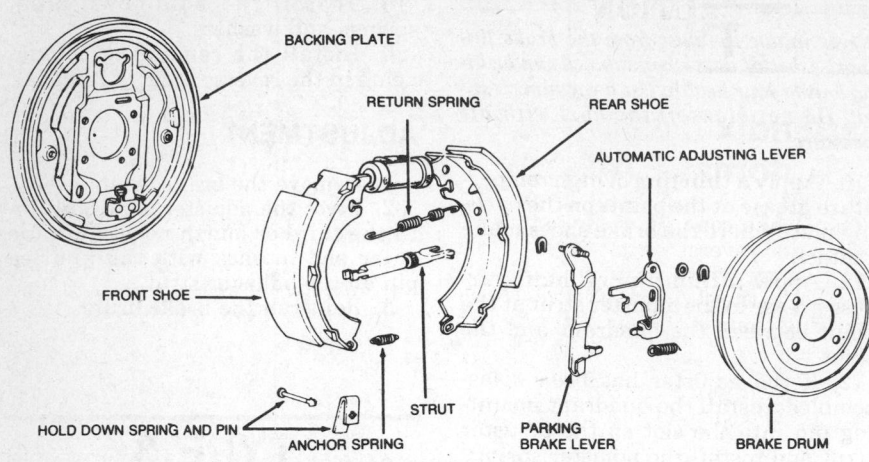

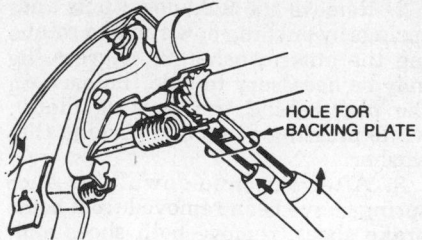

Backing off the brake shoes to remove
the brake drum—Type 3

BACKING PLATE

RETURN SPRING

REAR SHOE

AUTOMATIC ADJUSTING LEVER

FRONT SHOE

HOLD DOWN SPRING AND PIN

ANCHOR SPRING

STRUT

PARKING
BRAKE LEVER

BRAKE DRUM

Exploded view of a Type 3 drum brake

HOLE FOR
BACKING PLATE

10. Clean and inspect all parts. Lubricate the backing plate bosses and anchor plate.

11. Check the tension springs to see if they are weak, distorted or rusted.

12. Inspect the teeth on the automatic adjuster wheel for chipping or other damage.

Installation is performed in the following order:

NOTE: Grease the point of the shoe which slides against the backing plate. Do not get grease on the linings.

1. Attach the parking brake shoe lever and the automatic adjuster lever to the rear side of the shoe.

2. Fasten the parking brake cable to the lever on the brake shoe.

3. Install the automatic adjuster and fit the tension spring on the adjuster lever.

4. Install the securing spring on the *rear* shoe and then install the securing spring on the *front* shoe.

NOTE: The tension spring should be installed on the anchor, before performing Step 4.

5. Hook one end of the tension spring over the rear shoe with the tool used during removal; hook the other end over the front shoe.

——— **CAUTION** ———

Be sure that the wheel cylinder boots are not being pinched in the ends of the shoes.

6. Test the automatic adjuster by operating the parking brake shoe lever.

7. Install the drum and adjust the brakes.

ADJUSTMENT

These brakes are equipped with automatic actuated by the parking brake mechanism. No periodic adjustment

of the drum brakes is necessary if this mechanism is working properly. If the brake shoe to drum clearance is incorrect, and applying and releasing the parking brake a few times does not adjust it properly, the parts will have to be disassembled for repair.

TYPE 4

Non-Servo —
Manual Adjuster

This brake is a non-servo unit two single-piston wheel cylinders that act upon an individual shoe.

REMOVAL & INSTALLATION

1. Raise the rear of the vehicle and support it with jackstands. Remove the tire and wheel.

2. Remove the brake drum as previously detailed.

3. Remove the retracting springs and hold down spring clips.

4. Lift the shoes off of the backing plate.

5. Check the wheel cylinders for frozen pistons or leaks. If any are found, the wheel cylinder must be rebuilt or replaced.

6. Clean the backing plate and lubricate the bosses and bearing ends of the new shoes.

7. Place the new shoes in the slots of the wheel cylinders and the adjusters. Install the hold down spring clips.

8. Install the retracting springs. The blue, lighter weight spring is installed to the piston side of the shoe; the black, heavier weight spring to the adjuster side of shoe.

9. The shoes must slide freely in the slots.

10. Replace the drum and wheel; bleed and adjust the brake.

11. Road test the car.

ADJUSTMENT

Adjust each shoe individually by rotating the notched adjuster (backing plate side) until a heavy drag is felt when turning the wheel and drum in a forward direction. Back off the adjuster until the wheel spins freely.

TYPE 5

Bendix Non-Servo,
Self-Centering —
Manual Adjuster

This brake consists of non-servo forward and reverse shoes with a double-ended type wheel cylinder. The brake shoes are self-centering by means of an anchor block and two adjusting cams.

REMOVAL & INSTALLATION

1. Raise the rear of the vehicle an support it with jackstands. Remove the tire and the wheel.

2. Remove the brake drums as previously detailed.

3. Remove the retracting spring (and hold-down springs, if used) and lift the shoe assembly from the backing plate. On the rear wheels, unhook the parking brake cable from the parking brake lever.

4. Separate the shoes by removing the connecting spring.

5. Check the wheel cylinder for frozen pistons or leaks. If any are found, rebuild or replace the cylinder.

6. Clean and lubricate the backing plate bosses and hold-down clips.

7. Install the parking brake lever on the new reverse shoe.

8. Attach the connecting springs to the heel ends of the shoes.

9. Mount the shoes on the backing plate. For the rear wheels, hook the parking brake lever on the parking brake cable and install the parking brake strut.

10. Attach the retracting springs to the toe ends of the shoes.

11. Replace the drums. Center the shoes in the drums by depressing the pedal.

12. Bleed and adjust the brakes.

13. Road test the car.

ADJUSTMENT

Because of the self-centering feature of this brake, only minor adjustments to compensate for lining wear are necessary.

1. Jack up the car and support it with jackstands.

2. See that the parking brake lever is in the fully released position. Check the rear brake shoes to make certain they have not been moved away from the adjusting cams (partially applied) by improper adjustment of the cable (or cables) or by a sticking cable. If the shoes are not resting against the adjusting cams, back off or disconnect the parking brake cable.

3. Expand the brake shoes by turning the adjusting cams. If the adjusting cams have locks, loosen the lock nut. Spin the wheel, while turning the adjusting cam in the proper direction, until a heavy drag is reached and then back the cam off gradually in the opposite direction until the wheel spins freely. When adjusting the forward shoe, spin the wheel in the forward direction. When adjusting the reverse shoe, spin the wheel in the reverse direction.

4. Apply the brake pedal firmly a few times and check all wheels to be sure that they spin freely. If a brake drag is noticed at this point, readjust the brake in accordance with Step 3.

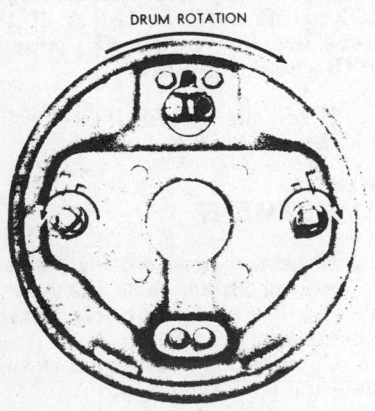

Adjustment of the Type 5 brake shoes is made by means of adjusting cams found on the backing plate

TYPE 6

Bendix Non-Servo — Automatic Adjuster

This brake consists of non-servo forward and reverse shoes with a double-ended type wheel cylinder. The shoes anchor to the slotted anchor plate permitting them a sliding self-centering action.

Typical Type 4 drum brake assembly

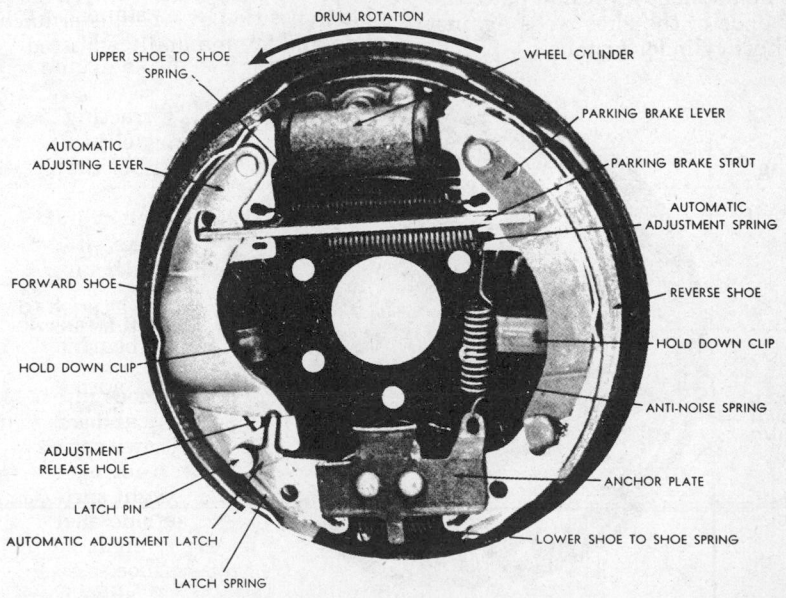

Typical Type 6 drum brake assembly

REMOVAL & INSTALLATION

1. Raise the rear of the vehicle and support it with jackstands. Remove the tire and the wheel.

2. Before removing the brake drum, remove the rubber grommet from the adjustment release hole in the backing plate. Insert a small prybar and push down on the adjustment latch. This will allow the shoes to retract and will eliminate possible interference between the brake shoes and brake drum.

3. Remove the brake drum and disengage the automatic adjuster spring from the strut and the reverse shoe. Remove the anti-noise spring.

4. Remove the upper shoe-to-shoe spring.

5. Remove the strut and disengage the shoes from the hold-down springs. Check the springs for cracks or fatigue.

6. Unhook the lower shoe-to-shoe spring. Remove the spring and forward shoe assembly.

7. Disconnect the parking brake cable and remove the parking brake lever from the reverse shoe.

8. Remove the adjusting latch and the automatic adjusting lever from the forward shoe. Check for worn or damaged teeth.

To install:

1. Clean and inspect all parts. Replace if necessary.

2. Lubricate the shoe guide pads on the backing plate and the curved edges of the anchor plate.

3. Lubricate the latch pin (long pin) and attach the latch to the outer surface of the forward shoe web.

4. Lubricate the adjustment lever pin (short pin) and attach the adjustment lever to the web of the forward shoe.

5. Lubricate the parking brake lever pin and attach the parking brake lever to the web of the reverse shoe. The reverse shoe has a short lining.

6. Attach the parking brake cable.

7. Attach the lower shoe-to-shoe spring to the forward and reverse shoes.

8. Place the forward and reverse shoes in position on the backing plate and install the parking brake strut. Engage the tab on the strut in the slot of the adjustment lever and place the upper ends of the shoe webs against the wheel cylinder pistons.

9. Install the upper shoe-to-shoe spring.

10. Install the automatic adjustment spring. The spring must hold the strut tight against the parking brake lever.

11. Lubricate the inner surfaces of the shoe hold-down springs and install the springs over the shoe webs.

12. Install the latch spring over the latch pivot pin. With the adjustment lever against the shoe rim, hook the spring over the latch.

13. Attach the anti-noise spring between the anchor plate and reverse shoe.

14. Install the drum and wheel. Bleed the system if necessary and then road test the vehicle.

ADJUSTMENT

An initial adjustment can be made after the brake drum has been removed and replaced applying by applying the handbrake several times. Aside from this initial adjustment, the brakes are self-adjusting and no further adjustment should ever be required.

TYPE 7

Non-Servo— Manual Adjuster

This brake consists of non-servo forward and reverse shoes with a double-ended wheel cylinder. The shoes are held in position by an adjuster/anchor plate and are manually adjusted.

REMOVAL & INSTALLATION

1. Raise the rear of the vehicle and support it with jackstands. Remove the tire and wheel assembly.

2. Remove the brake drum. If it is necessary to retract the shoes in order to remove a worn drum, remove the dust cover and back off on the adjusting bolt located on the inboard side of the backing plate.

3. Remove the upper and lower shoe-to-shoe return springs.

4. Remove the brake shoe hold-down springs and lift the shoes from the backing plate.

5. Check the wheel cylinder for frozen pistons or fluid leaks. If any are found, rebuild or replace the wheel cylinder.

6. Clean and inspect all parts. Lubricate the backing plate bosses and the adjuster assembly.

7. Apply a thin coat of grease to the adjuster.

8. Back off all adjustment on the adjusting bolt located behind the backing plate.

9. Mount the new shoes to the backing plate and install the brake shoe hold-down springs. Be sure that the webs of the shoes are properly engaged in the parking brake mechanism, adjuster assembly and wheel cylinder.

10. Install the upper and lower shoe-to-shoe return springs.

NOTE: The upper and lower shoe-to-shoe return springs are not interchangeable and must installed in the proper direction. Use the other wheel for reference if necessary when installing these springs.

11. Install the drum and then install the wheel and tire assembly.

NOTE: The drum may not fit if the adjustment bolt has not been backed off sufficiently or if the shoes are not centered properly on the backing plate.

12. Bleed the system if necessary and then road test the vehicle.

ADJUSTMENT

1. Block the front wheels, release the parking brake, raise the rear of the vehicle and support it with jackstands.

2. Depress the brake pedal several times and then release it.

3. Locate the adjuster on the inboard side of the brake backing plate and turn it clockwise until the wheel will no longer spin.

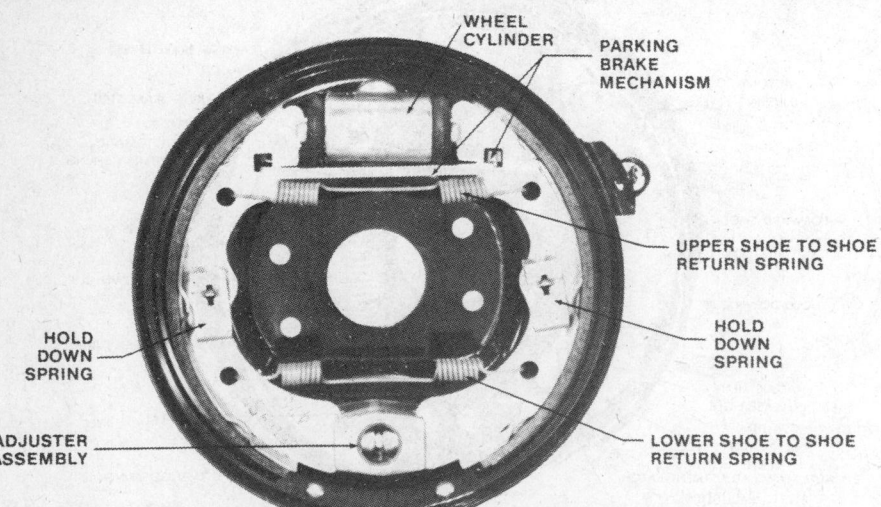

WHEEL CYLINDER
PARKING BRAKE MECHANISM
UPPER SHOE TO SHOE RETURN SPRING
HOLD DOWN SPRING
HOLD DOWN SPRING
ADJUSTER ASSEMBLY
LOWER SHOE TO SHOE RETURN SPRING

Typical Type 7 drum brake assembly

4. Back off the adjuster (counter-clockwise) approximately two (2) turns or until the wheel just begins to turn freely.

TYPE 8

Non-Servo — Automatic Adjuster

This brake consists of non-servo forward and reverse shoes with a double-ended wheel cylinder. The shoe are held in position by an anchor plate and are automatically adjusted.

REMOVAL & INSTALLATION

1. Raise the rear of the vehicle and support it with jackstands. Remove the tire and wheel assembly.
2. Remove the drum. If it is necessary to retract the shoes in order to remove a worn drum, insert a small prybar through the hole in the backing plate and press down on the adjusting latch.
3. Remove the brake shoe hold-down springs.
4. Remove the upper strut-to-shoe spring and the upper shoe-to-shoe return spring.
5. Remove the reverse shoe along with the lower shoe-to-shoe return spring.
6. Holding the adjusting latch on the forward shoe downward, pull the adjusting lever toward the center of the brake and then remove the leading shoe assembly.
7. Check the wheel cylinder for frozen pistons or leaks. If any are found, rebuild or replace the cylinder.

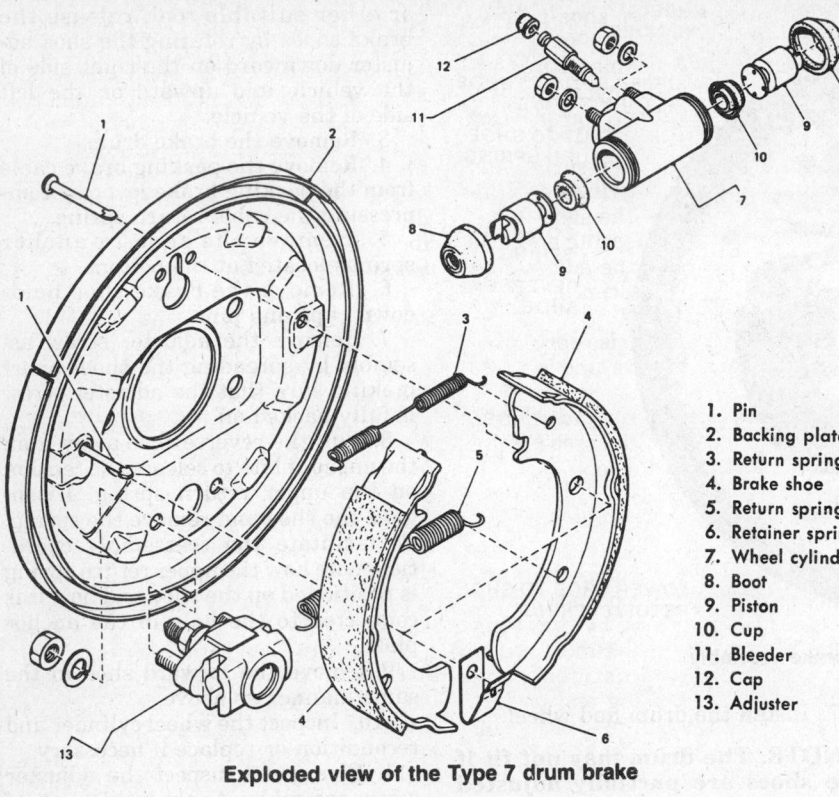

1. Pin
2. Backing plate
3. Return spring
4. Brake shoe
5. Return spring
6. Retainer spring
7. Wheel cylinder
8. Boot
9. Piston
10. Cup
11. Bleeder
12. Cap
13. Adjuster

Exploded view of the Type 7 drum brake

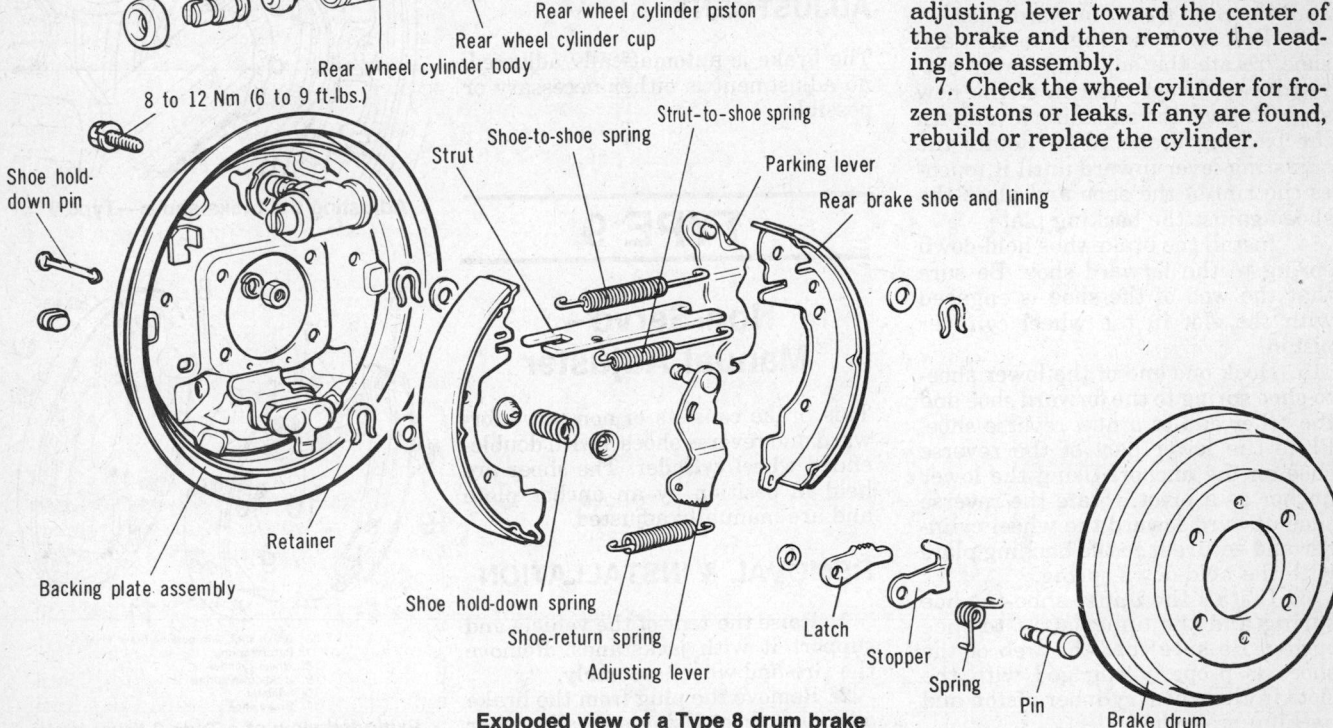

Bleeder screw cap

Bleeder screw (right rear wheel cylinder only)
7 to 9 Nm (5 to 7 ft-lbs.)

Rear wheel cylinder boot
Rear wheel cylinder piston
Rear wheel cylinder cup
Rear wheel cylinder body

8 to 12 Nm (6 to 9 ft-lbs.)

Shoe hold-down pin

Strut
Shoe-to-shoe spring
Strut-to-shoe spring
Parking lever
Rear brake shoe and lining

Backing plate assembly

Retainer

Shoe hold-down spring
Shoe-return spring
Adjusting lever

Latch
Stopper
Spring
Pin
Brake drum

Exploded view of a Type 8 drum brake

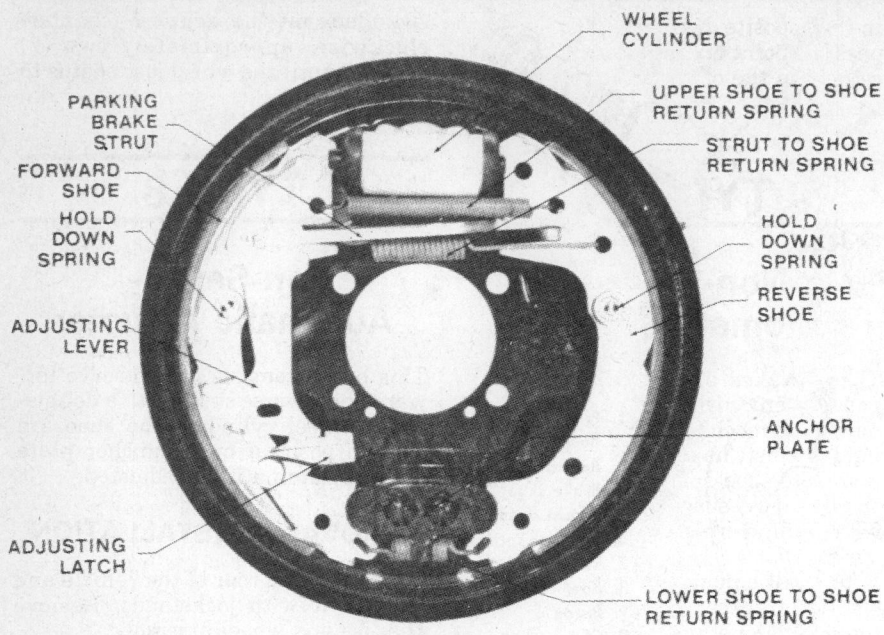

PARKING BRAKE STRUT
FORWARD SHOE
HOLD DOWN SPRING
ADJUSTING LEVER
ADJUSTING LATCH
WHEEL CYLINDER
UPPER SHOE TO SHOE RETURN SPRING
STRUT TO SHOE RETURN SPRING
HOLD DOWN SPRING
REVERSE SHOE
ANCHOR PLATE
LOWER SHOE TO SHOE RETURN SPRING

Typical Type 8 drum brake assembly

8. Inspect old springs. If old springs are damaged or have been overheated, they should be replaced. Indications of overheated springs are paint discoloration and distortion.

9. Inspect the drum and recondition or replace if necessary.

10. Check the adjusting lever and adjusting latch for wear or damage. Replace the damaged parts.

11. Clean and lubricate the backing plate bosses.

12. Remove the adjusting lever and latch from the forward shoe and install them on a new forward shoe.

13. Before mounting the forward shoe, rotate the adjusting lever outward away from the rim of the new shoe. Engage the adjusting lever with the parking brake strut. Rotate the adjusting lever inward until it touches the rim of the shoe and place the shoe against the backing plate.

14. Install the brake shoe hold-down spring to the forward shoe. Be sure that the web of the shoe is engaged with the slot in the wheel cylinder piston.

15. Hook one end of the lower shoe-to-shoe spring to the forward shoe and the other end to a new reverse shoe. Place the lower part of the reverse shoe on the anchor. Using the lower anchor as a pivot, rotate the reverse shoe upward toward the wheel cylinder and secure it to the backing plate with the hold-down spring.

16. Install the upper shoe-to-shoe spring and the upper strut-to-shoe spring. Be sure that the web of the shoes is properly engaged with the slots in the wheel cylinder piston and parking brake lever.

17. Install the drum and wheel.

NOTE: The drum may not fit if the shoes are partially adjusted outward of if they are not centered properly on the backing plate.

18. Apply the brake pedal a few times to bring the brake shoes into adjustment.

19. Bleed the system and road test the vehicle.

ADJUSTMENT

The brake is automatically adjusted; no adjustment is either necessary or possible.

TYPE 9

Non-Servo— Manual Adjuster

This brake consists of non-servo forward and reverse shoes a with double-ended wheel cylinder. The shoes are held in position by an anchor plate and are manually adjusted.

REMOVAL & INSTALLATION

1. Raise the rear of the vehicle and support it with jackstands. Remove the tire and wheel assembly.

2. Remove the plug from the brake adjusting hole. Using a small prybar

or other suitable tool, release the brake shoes by rotating the shoe adjuster downward on the right side of the vehicle and upward on the left side of the vehicle.

3. Remove the brake drum.

4. Remove the parking brake cable from the parking brake lever by compressing the cable return spring.

5. Remove the shoe-to-anchor springs located at the bottom.

6. Remove the brake shoe hold-down clips and pins.

7. Remove the adjuster screw assembly by spreading the shoes apart making sure that the adjuster screw is fully backed off.

8. Pull the reverse shoe away from the anchor plate to release the tension on the upper return spring. Disengage the shoe and remove the spring. To facilitate the reassembly operation, note how the upper return spring is positioned on the shoe and how it is connected to the hole in the anchor plate.

9. Remove the forward shoe in the same manner as above.

10. Inspect the wheel cylinder and recondition or replace if necessary.

11. Clean and inspect the adjuster screw assembly. Apply a thin coat of lubricant to the adjuster threads.

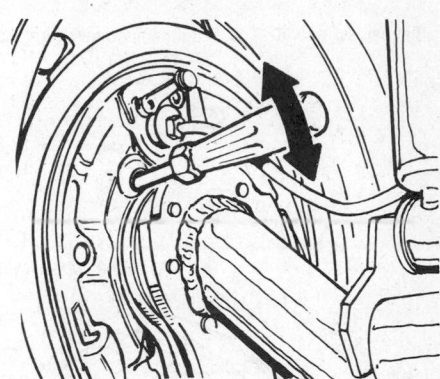

Adjusting the brake shoes—Type 9

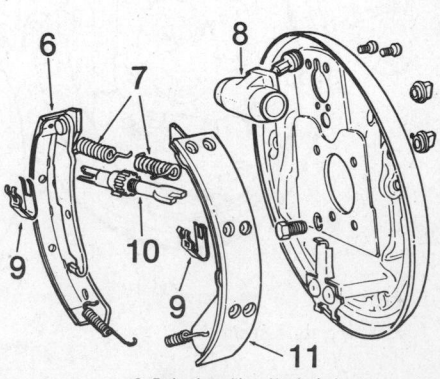

6. Brake shoe with parking brake lever
7. Return spring
8. Wheel cylinder
9. Hold-down spring
10. Adjuster
11. Brake shoe

Exploded view of a Type 9 drum brake

12. Inspect the old springs. If old springs are damaged or have been overheated, they should be replaced. Indications of overheating are paint discoloration or distortion.

13. Lubricate the bosses on the anchor plate which make contact with the brake shoe tabs.

To install:

1. Remove the parking brake lever and attach the parking brake lever to the web of a new reverse shoe.

2. Position the upper return spring on the forward shoe and hook the other end of the spring into the hole in the backing plate.

3. Rotate the shoe outward with the upper part of the shoe against the wheel cylinder piston and insert the bottom part of the shoe under the anchor plate.

4. Repeat the above procedure for the reverse shoe.

5. With the adjuster screw fully retracted, position the straight forked end of the adjuster screw assembly on the parking brake lever. Make sure that the spring lock on the adjuster screw is on the outside and away from the adjusting hole.

6. Rotate the bottom of the forward shoe off the anchor plate and insert the curved fork end of the adjuster screw assembly into the web of the forward shoe.

NOTE: Make sure that the curved portion of the forked end is facing downward and that the spring lock is on the outside and away from the adjusting hole.

7. Insert the pins for the hold-down clips through the backing plate and web of the shoes. Install the hold-down clips.

8. Install the shoe-to-anchor springs.

9. Compress the brake cable return spring and attach the cable to the bottom of the parking brake lever.

10. Install the brake drum.

11. Install the wheel and tire assembly.

12. Adjust the brakes.

13. Bleed the system and road test the car.

ADJUSTMENT

Adjust the brakes through the adjusting hole located in the backing plate. Adjustment is made manually by spreading the adjuster screw assembly which is located directly under the wheel cylinder. Insert a small prybar or other suitable tool through the hole in the backing plate and rotate the adjuster wheel clockwise until the brakes drag as you turn the wheel in a forward direction. Turn the adjuster

in the opposite direction until you just pass the point of drag. Repeat the procedure on the other wheel.

TYPE 10

Non-Servo – Automatic Adjuster

These brakes are a leading-trailing shoe design with a ratchet type self-adjusting mechanism. The shoes are held against the anchors at the top by a shoe-to-shoe spring. At the bottom the shoe webs are held against the wheel cylinder piston ends by a return spring.

The self-adjusting mechanism consists of a spacer strut and a pair of toothed ratchets attached to the primary brake shoe. The parking brake actuating lever is pivoted on the spacer strut.

The self-adjusting mechanism automatically senses the correct lining to drum clearance. As the linings wear, the clearance is adjusted by increasing the effective length of the spacer strut. This strut has projections to engage the inner edge of the secondary shoe via the handbrake lever and the inner edge of the large ratchet on the primary shoe. As wear on the linings increases, the movement of the shoes to bring them in contact with the drums becomes greater than the gap. The spacer strut, bearing on the shoe web, is moved together with the secondary shoe to close the gap. Further movement causes the large ratchet, behind the primary shoe, to rotate in-

wards against the spring-loaded small ratchet, and the serrations on the mating edges maintain this new setting until further wear on the shoes results in another readjustment. On releasing brake pedal pressure, the return springs cause the shoes to move into contact with the shoulders of the spacer strut/handbrake actuating lever, thus restoring the clearance between the linings and the drum proportionate to the gap shown.

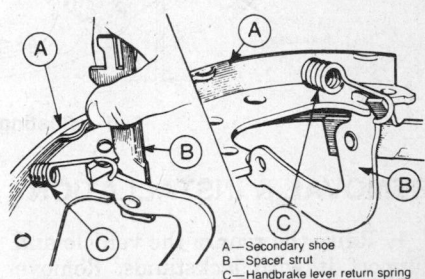

Assembling the secondary shoe components

A—Secondary shoe
B—Spacer strut
C—Handbrake lever return spring

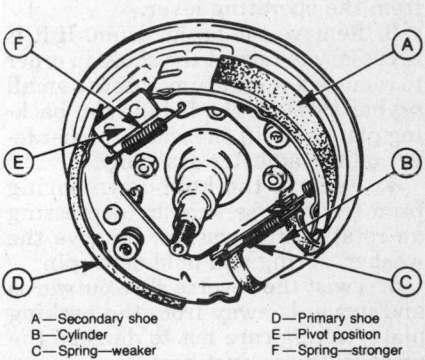

Typical Type 10 drum brake assembly

A—Secondary shoe   D—Primary shoe
B—Cylinder   E—Pivot position
C—Spring—weaker   F—Spring—stronger

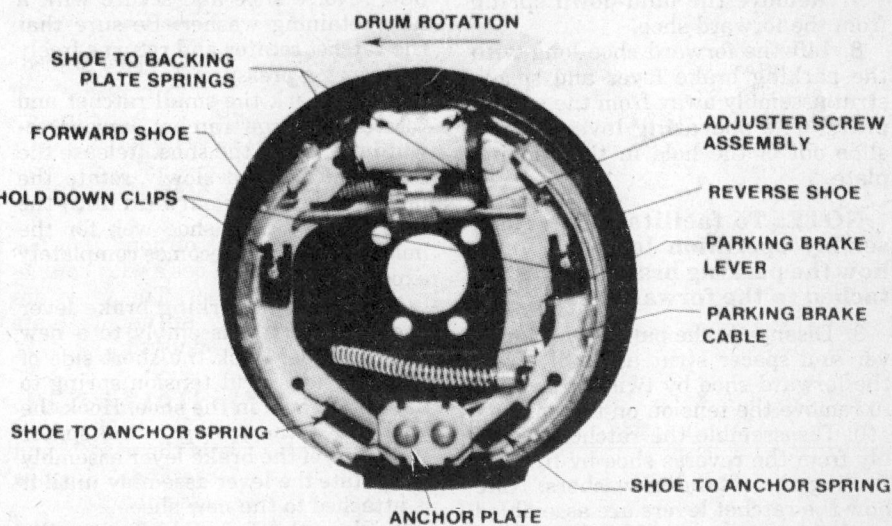

DRUM ROTATION

SHOE TO BACKING PLATE SPRINGS

FORWARD SHOE

HOLD DOWN CLIPS

ADJUSTER SCREW ASSEMBLY

REVERSE SHOE

PARKING BRAKE LEVER

PARKING BRAKE CABLE

SHOE TO ANCHOR SPRING

SHOE TO ANCHOR SPRING

ANCHOR PLATE

Typical Type 9 drum brake assembly

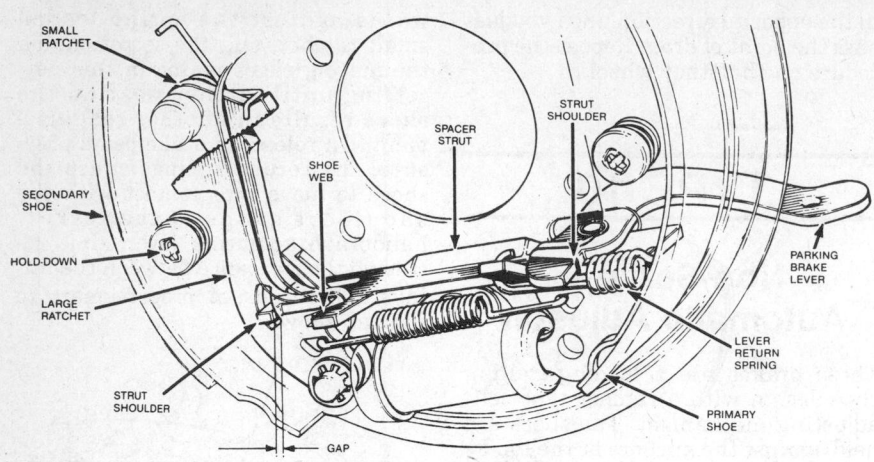

SMALL RATCHET

SECONDARY SHOE

HOLD-DOWN

LARGE RATCHET

STRUT SHOULDER

GAP

SHOE WEB

SPACER STRUT

STRUT SHOULDER

PARKING BRAKE LEVER

LEVER RETURN SPRING

PRIMARY SHOE

Self–adjusting mechanism

REMOVAL & INSTALLATION

1. Raise the rear of the vehicle and support it with jackstands. Remove the wheel and tire assembly.

2. Disconnect the brake cable from the operating lever at the back of the backing plate. Remove the dust boot from the operating lever.

3. Remove the brake drum. If it is necessary to retract the shoes in order to remove a worn drum, insert a small prybar through the hole in the backing plate and lift the small ratchet lever on the adjuster assembly.

4. Remove the hold-down spring from the reverse shoe by depressing an rotating the washer. Remove the washer, spring and hold-down pin.

5. Twist the reverse shoe outwards and upwards away from the backing plate, taking care not to damage the wheel cylinder dust boot.

6. Unfasten the upper and lower shoe-to-shoe return springs and remove the shoe and springs.

7. Remove the hold-down spring from the forward shoe.

8. Lift the forward shoe long with the parking brake lever and spacer strut assembly away from the anchor plate. The operating lever should slide out of the hole in the backing plate.

NOTE: To facilitate the reassembly operation later on, note how the parking brake lever is attached to the forward shoe.

9. Disengage the parking brake lever and spacer strut assembly from the forward shoe by twisting inward to remove the tension on the spring.

10. Disassemble the ratchet assembly from the reverse shoe by first removing the retaining washers. Note how the ratchet levers are assembled so that you can put them back on a new shoe in the same way.

11. Rotate the large ratchet lever outward from under the tension spring and remove the ratchet lever from the shoe.

12. Remove the pressure spring and the small ratchet lever.

13. Check the wheel cylinder for frozen pistons or leaks. If any are found, rebuild or replace the wheel cylinder.

14. Inspect the old springs. If the old springs are damaged or have been overheated, they should be replaced. Indications of overheating are paint discoloration and distortion.

15. Inspect the drum and recondition or replace if necessary.

16. Check the adjusting lever and adjusting latch for wear or damage. Replace the damaged parts.

17. Clean and lubricate the backing plate bosses.

18. Install the large ratchet on a new reverse shoe and secure it with a new retaining washer.

19. Install the small ratchet and pressure spring on the pivot of the new reverse shoe and secure with a new retaining washer. Be sure that the ratchet rotates and returns freely with spring pressure.

20. Pull back the small ratchet and rotate the large ratchet inward toward the rim of the shoe. Release the small ratchet and slowly rotate the large ratchet lever outward until the hole in the brake shoe web for the hold-down spring becomes completely exposed.

21. Attach the parking brake lever and spacer strut assembly to a new forward shoe. Hook the short side of the lever and strut tension spring to the slotted hole in the shoe. Hook the long end of the spring to the spacer strut part of the brake lever assembly and rotate the lever assembly until it is attached to the new shoe.

22. Place the forward shoe on the backing plate by inserting the operating lever through the hole in the backing plate. Insert the forked end of the spacer strut into the slotted carrier plate. Rest the upper part of the shoe against the anchor plate and the lower part against the wheel cylinder piston.

23. Insert the hold-down pin through the backing plate and web of the shoe. Install the hold-down spring and washer.

24. Before mounting the reverse shoe, note the slot in the long ratchet lever. The spacer strut must be engaged in the slotted hole in the long ratchet lever when the shoe is mounted to the backing plate.

25. Hook the stronger (thicker) shoe-to-shoe spring through the hole at the top of the already installed forward shoe.

26. Hook the reverse shoe to the other end of the shoe spring. Place the upper part of the shoe against the anchor plate and using the anchor plate as a pivot, rotate the bottom part of the shoe outward. Position the lower part of the shoe against the wheel cylinder piston making sure that the spacer strut is engaged in the hole in the ratchet lever.

27. Insert the hold-down pin through the backing plate. Install the hold-down spring and washer.

28. Install the lower shoe-to-shoe spring (the weaker of the two springs) using a pair of pliers or other suitable tool.

29. Before installing the brake drum, lift the small ratchet lever upwards against the spring. This will allow the long ratchet lever to rotate inward toward the rim of the shoe and provide the clearance needed to install the drum.

30. Replace the dust boot over the operating lever behind the backing plate.

31. Reconnect the brake cable to the operating lever.

32. Install the brake drum and wheel.

Press the proportioning valve lever in the direction of the rear axle (Audi shown)

NOTE: **The drum may not fit if the shoes are partially adjusted outward of if they are not centered properly on the backing plate.**

33. Apply the brake pedal a few times to bring the brake shoe into adjustment.

34. Bleed the system and road test the vehicle.

TYPE 11

Non-Servo— Automatic Adjuster

This brake consists of non-servo forward and reverse shoes with a double-ended wheel cylinder. The shoes are mounted by means of hold-down springs and an anchor plate. Adjustment is performed automatically.

REMOVAL & INSTALLATION

1. Raise the rear of the vehicle and support it with jackstands. Remove the tire and wheel assembly.

2. Remove the brake drum.

NOTE: **If it is necessary to retract the shoes in order to remove a worn drum, insert a small prybar through the one of the stud holes in the brake drum. Retract the adjuster wedge upward by pressing down on the prybar.**

3. Remove the adjusting wedge spring.

4. Remove the upper and lower return springs.

5. Remove the hold-down springs.

6. Lift the shoes from the backing plate and disconnect the parking brake cable from the lever.

7. Disconnect the rear shoe from the push bar.

8. Clamp the push bar in a vise and remove the tensioning spring and adjusting wedge.

9. Check the wheel cylinder for frozen pistons or leaks. If any are found, rebuild or replace the wheel cylinder.

10. Inspect old springs. If old springs are damaged or have been overheated, they should be replaced. Indications of overheated springs are paint discoloration and distortion.

11. Inspect the brake drum and recondition or replace if necessary.

12. Clean and lubricate all contact points on the backing plate.

13. Attach the push bar and tensioning spring to the new front shoe.

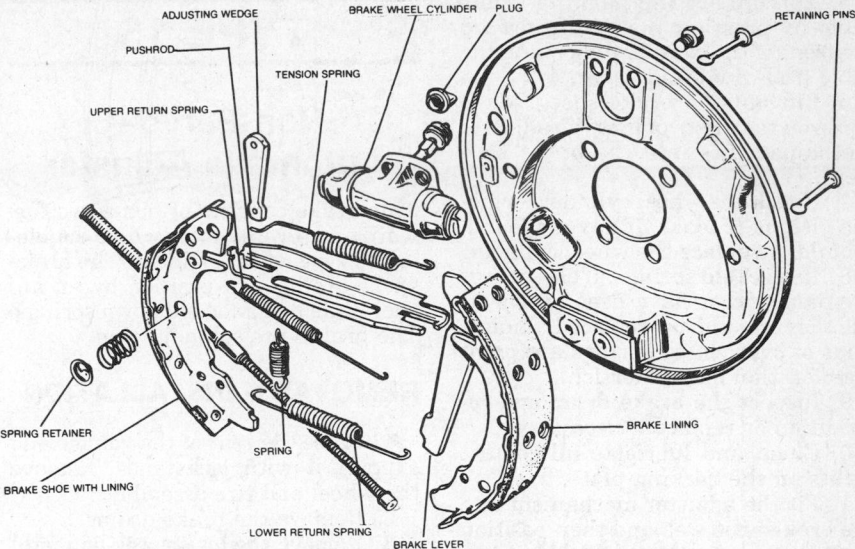

Exploded view of the Type 11 drum brake assembly

14. Insert the adjusting wedge so that its lug is pointing toward the backing plate.

15. Remove the parking brake lever from the old rear shoe and attach it onto the new rear brake shoe.

16. Install the push bar onto the rear brake shoe and parking brake lever assembly.

17. Connect the parking brake cable to the lever and place the whole assembly onto the backing plate.

18. Install the hold-down springs.

19. Install the upper and lower return springs.

20. Install the adjusting wedge spring.

21. Center the brakes shoe on the backing plate making sure that the adjusting wedge is fully released before installing the drum.

22. Install the drum and wheel assembly and torque the wheel lugs to the manufacturer's specifications.

23. Apply the brake pedal several times to bring the brake shoes into adjustment.

24. Bleed the system and road test the vehicle.

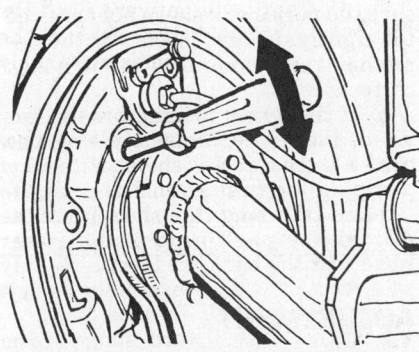

Adjusting the brake shoes—Type 12

ADJUSTMENT

This brake adjusts itself automatically; aside from the initial adjustments given in the previous section, no adjustments are either necessary or possible.

TYPE 12

Non-Servo— Manual Adjuster

This brake consists of non-servo forward and reverse shoes with a double-ended wheel cylinder. The brake shoes are retained in position by an anchor plate and retaining springs.

REMOVAL & INSTALLATION

1. Raise the rear of the car and support it with jackstands.

2. Remove the wheels an then remove the brake drum.

NOTE: **If the drum does not come off easily, the brakes will have to be backed off. First, push the lever on the proportioning valve toward the rear axle to relieve residual brake pressure. Next remove the plug on he backing plate and turn the adjusting wheel to back off the brake shoes.**

3. Use brake pliers to remove the upper and lower return springs.

4. Turn and remove the washers to release the brake shoe retaining springs.

5. Disconnect the parking brake cable by pressing the spring toward the front of the car and unhooking the cable from the brake lever.

6. Lift out the brake shoes. Make sure you take note of how the adjuster mechanism fits into the brake shoe web.

7. Check the wheel cylinder for frozen pistons or leaks. If any are found, rebuild or replace the wheel cylinder.

8. Inspect old springs. If old springs are damaged or have been overheated, they should be replaced. Indications of overheated springs are paint discoloration and distortion.

9. Inspect the brake drum and recondition or replace if necessary.

10. Clean and lubricate all contact points on the backing plate.

11. Fit the adjuster mechanism into the brake shoe web and then position the shoes onto the brake backing plate.

12. Push the retaining pin springs in and turn the washers onto the retaining pins.

13. Squeeze the spring and hook the parking brake cable to the parking brake lever.

14. Install the upper and lower retaining springs.

15. Install the brake drums and wheels and then lower the the vehicle.

16. Bleed (if necessary) and adjust the brakes. Road test the vehicle.

ADJUSTMENT

1. Press the lever of the proportioning valve in the direction of the rear axle to relieve the residual brake pressure.

2. Remove the rubber plug from the brake backing plate.

3. Insert a small prybar into the hole and turn the adjusting wheel until the brake linings are just touching the drum.

4. Back off the adjusting wheel 6–8 teeth and replace the rubber plug.

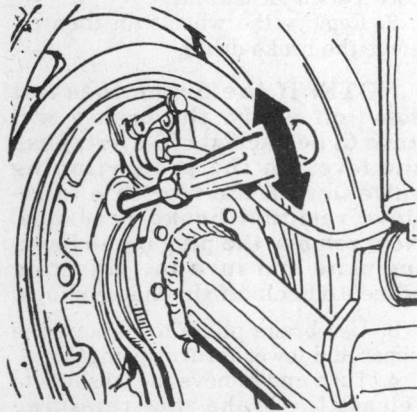

Adjusting the brake shoes—Type 13

TYPE 13

Non-Servo— Automatic Adjuster

This brake consists of non-servo forward and reverse shoes with a double-ended type wheel cylinder. The brake shoes are held in position by an anchor plate and two hold-down springs. The brakes are self-adjusting.

REMOVAL & INSTALLATION

1. Raise the rear of the vehicle and support it with jackstands. Remove the wheel and tire assembly.

2. Remove the brake drums.

3. Remove the lower pressed metal spring clip, the shoe return spring (the large one piece spring between the two shoes), and the two shoe hold-down springs.

4. Remove the shoes and adjuster as an assembly. Disconnect the parking brake cable from the lever, remove the spring between the shoes and the lever from the rear (trailing) shoe. Disconnect the adjuster retaining spring and remove the adjuster, turn the star wheel into the adjuster body after cleaning and lubricating the threads.

5. The wheel cylinder may be removed for service or replacement, if necessary.

6. Clean the backing plate with a wire brush. Install the wheel cylinder if it was removed. Lubricate all contact points on the backing plate, anchor plate, wheel cylinder-to-shoe contact and parking brake strut joints and contacts. Installation of the brake shoes, from this point, is the reverse of removal after the lever has been transferred to the new rear (trailing) shoe.

7. Pre-adjustment of the brake shoe can be made by turning the adjuster star wheel out until the drum will just slide on over the brake shoes. Before installing the drum, make sure the parking brake is not adjusted too tightly, if it is, loosen, or the adjustment of the rear brakes will not be correct.

8. If the wheel cylinders were serviced, bleed the brake system. The brake shoes are then adjusted by pumping the brake pedal and applying and releasing the parking brake. Adjust the parking brake stroke. Road test the car.

ADJUSTMENT

The brakes are self-adjusting. Aside from the initial adjustments given in the "Removal and Installation" section, no adjustments are either necessary or possible.

TYPE 14

Non-Servo— Automatic Adjuster

This brakes consists of non-servo forward and reverse shoes with a double-ended type wheel cylinder. The shoes are held in position by an anchor plate and anti-rattle springs. The wheel cylinder is located at the top or bottom of the brake backing plate depending upon the particular application. These brakes are self-adjusting.

REMOVAL & INSTALLATION

1. Raise the rear of the vehicle and support it with jackstands. Remove the tire and wheel assembly.

2. Engage the parking brake. Pull the pin out and then remove the stopper from the toggle lever. Release the parking brake.

3. Remove the brake drum.

NOTE: If the brake drum cannot be easily removed, install two (2) bolts (8mm) in the holes and drive it out.

4. Remove the return springs.

5. Push the anti-rattle spring retainers in and turn them so they can be removed from the pins.

6. Remove the brake shoes.

7. Clean the brake backing plate and check the wheel cylinder for leaks or other damage; replace as necessary.

8. Hook the return springs into the new shoes. The springs should be between the shoes and the backing plate. The longer return spring must be adjacent to the wheel cylinder. A very thin film of grease may be applied to the pivot points at the ends of the brake shoes. Grease the shoe locating buttons on the backing plate, also. Be careful not to get grease on the linings or the drums.

9. Place one shoe in the adjuster and piston slots, and pry the other shoe into position.

10. Press and turn the anti-rattle spring retainers onto the pins.

11. Replace the drums and wheels. Adjust the brakes. Bleed the hydraulic system if the brake lines were disconnected.

REMOVAL & INSTALLATION

1. Raise the rear of the vehicle and support it with jackstands. Remove the tire and wheel assembly.

2. Engage the parking brake. Pull the pin out and then remove the stopper from the toggle lever. Release the parking brake.

3. Remove the brake drum.

NOTE: If the brake drum cannot be easily removed, install two (2) bolts (8mm) in the holes and rive it out.

4. Remove the return springs.

5. Push the anti-rattle spring retainers in and turn them so they can be removed from the pins.

6. Remove the brake shoes.

7. Clean the brake backing plate and check the wheel cylinder for leaks or other damage; replace if necessary.

8. Hook the return springs into the new shoes. The springs should be between the shoes and the backing plate. The longer return spring must be adjacent to the wheel cylinder. A very thin film of grease my be applied to the pivot points at the ends of the brake shoes. Grease the shoe locating buttons on the backing plate, also. Be careful not to get grease on the linings or drums.

9. Place one shoe on the adjuster and piston slots, and pry the other shoe onto position.

10. Press and turn the anti-rattle spring retainers onto the pins.

11. Replace the drums and wheels. Adjust the brakes. Bleed the hydraulic system if the brake lines were disconnected.

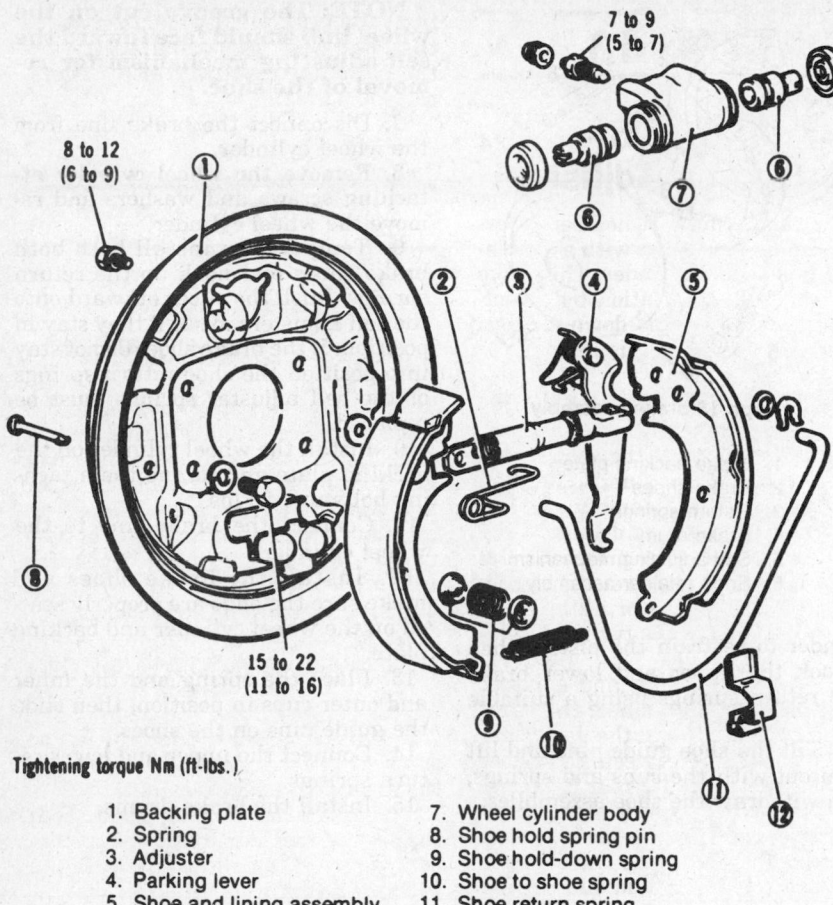

Tightening torque Nm (ft-lbs.)

1. Backing plate
2. Spring
3. Adjuster
4. Parking lever
5. Shoe and lining assembly
6. Piston
7. Wheel cylinder body
8. Shoe hold spring pin
9. Shoe hold-down spring
10. Shoe to shoe spring
11. Shoe return spring
12. Clip spring

Exploded view of the Type 14 drum brake

12. Reconnect the handbrake, making sure that it does not cause the shoes to drag when it is released.

ADJUSTMENT

These brakes adjust themselves automatically with each application of the brake pedal or the parking brake; other than this, no adjustments are either necessary or possible.

TYPE 15

Non-Servo— Automatic Adjuster

This brake consists of non-servo forward and reverse shoes with a double-ended type wheel cylinder. The shoes are held in position by an anchor plate and anti-rattle springs. The wheel cylinder is located at the top or bottom of the brake backing plate depending upon the particular application. These brakes are self-adjusting.

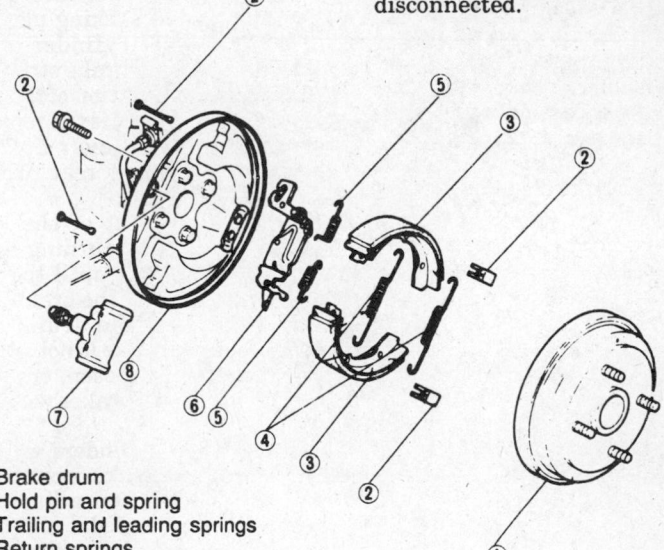

1. Brake drum
2. Hold pin and spring
3. Trailing and leading springs
4. Return springs
5. Anti-rattle springs
6. Adjuster
7. Wheel cylinder assembly
8. Backing plate

Type 15 brake assembly

12. Reconnect the handbrake, making sure that it does not cause the shoes to drag when it is released.

ADJUSTMENT

These brakes adjust themselves automatically with each application of the brake pedal or the parking brake; other than this, no adjustments are either necessary or possible.

TYPE 16

Non-Servo – Automatic Adjuster

REMOVAL & INSTALLATION

1. Jack up the rear of the car and support it safely.
2. Remove the wheels and brake drums.
3. Plug the outlet ports in the brake fluid reservoir.
4. Install suitable tool (Yugo recommends tool A 72257) to the wheel

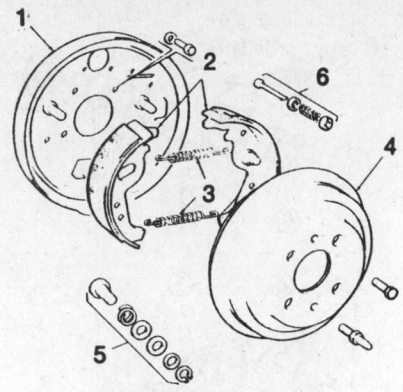

Type 16 brake assembly

1. Brake backing plate
2. Brake shoes
3. Return springs
4. Brake drum
5. Self adjusting mechanism
6. Shoe retainer assembly

cylinder to restrain the piston, then unhook the upper and lower brake shoe return springs using a suitable tool.

5. Tilt the shoe guide pins and lift them out with the cups and springs, then withdraw the shoe assemblies.

NOTE: The groove cut on the wheel hub should face toward the self-adjusting mechanism for removal of the shoe.

7. Disconnect the brake line from the wheel cylinder.
8. Remove the wheel cylinder attaching screws and washers and remove the wheel cylinder.
9. Temporarily install both both brake shoes and hook up the return springs. Push the shoes outward onto the self adjusters to see if they stay in position. If the brake shoes do not stay into position the shoe return springs or the self adjuster springs must be replaced.
10. Install the wheel cylinder on the backing plate and torque the attaching bolts to 7 ft. lbs.
11. Connect the brake line to the wheel cylinder.
12. Install the brake shoes and make sure the ends are properly seated on the wheel cylinder and backing plate.
13. Place the spring and the inner and outer cups in position, then slide the guide pins on the shoes.
14. Connect the upper and lower return springs.
15. Install the brake drums.